P9-DDP-243

WEBSTER'S NEW WORLD®

COLLEGE DICTIONARY

FIFTH EDITION

WEBSTER'S NEW WORLD®

COLLEGE DICTIONARY

FIFTH EDITION

HOUGHTON MIFFLIN HARCOURT

BOSTON NEW YORK

Words are included in this dictionary on the basis of their usage. Words that are known to have current trademark registrations are shown with an initial capital and are also identified as trademarks. No investigation has been made of common-law trademark rights in any word, because such investigation is impracticable. The inclusion of any word in this dictionary is not, however, an expression of the publisher's opinion as to whether or not it is subject to proprietary rights. Indeed, no definition in this dictionary is to be regarded as affecting the validity of any trademark.

ISBN: 978-0-544-59822-5 (hardcover)
ISBN: 978-0-544-16553-3 (hardcover with CD-ROM)

Visit our website: hmhco.com

Library of Congress Cataloging-in-Publication Data
Webster's New world college dictionary / Editors of Webster's New World
College Dictionaries.—Fifth Edition.
pages cm
ISBN 978-0-544-16606-6 (hardback)—ISBN 978-0-544-16553-3 (hardcover with cd-rom)
1. English language—Dictionaries. I. Title: New world college dictionary.
II. Title: World college dictionary.
PE1628.W5629 2014
423—dc23
2014004003

Manufactured in the United States of America
2 3 4 5 6 7 8 9 - DOC - 22 21 20 19 18 17 16
4500612455

CONTENTS

EDITORIAL AND PRODUCTION STAFF

PUBLISHER
Bruce Nichols

SENIOR EDITORS
Andrew N. Sparks
Jonathan L. Goldman
Donald Stewart

EDITORS
James E. Naso
Katherine Soltis
Stephen P. Teresi
Laura Borovac Walker
Jennifer Wellman Wason

PROOFREADERS
Peter Chipman
Emily A. Neeves
Louise E. Robbins

CITATION READERS
Batya Jundef
Joan Komic

PRINCIPAL ARTIST
Anita S. Rogoff

SUPPLEMENTAL CARTOGRAPHY
Ortelius Design, Inc.

MANAGING EDITOR
Steve Kleinedler

PRODUCTION SUPERVISOR
Margaret Anne Miles

PRODUCTION COORDINATOR
Cynthia Sadonick

DATABASE PRODUCTION COORDINATOR
Christopher Granniss

DATA PROCESSING
Betty Dziedzic Thompson

BOOK DESIGNER
David Futato

PRINT PRODUCTION DIRECTOR
Donna Baxter McCarthy

PRINT PRODUCTION
LEAD COORDINATOR
Diane Varone

FOREWORD

In 1941, the World Publishing Company, founded in the early 1900s in Cleveland, Ohio, hired a staff of scholars to create a new dictionary. Determined to break with the conservatism that characterized many reference books of the time, this team of lexicographers set out to produce a mid-20th-century dictionary that would accurately reflect the era and its language. Led by chief editors David B. Guralnik and Joseph H. Friend, their goal was to create a completely new kind of dictionary built on a foundation of contemporary linguistics, psychology, and allied sciences.

Unlike other leading dictionaries of that time, which were stiffly formal and authoritarian, this new work was to be a more friendly, open guide that showed how language is actually used. The editors sought to record the relaxed pronunciations used in ordinary conversation rather than those used in more formal speech, as traditionally recorded in other dictionaries. They also established an easily understood phonemic system for transcribing pronunciations, and they expanded the etymologies to include Indo-European bases and the cognate relationships of words within the language. The most important innovation, however, was in the style of the definitions, which used 20th-century language in a manner that conveyed meaning with sureness, clarity, and ease.

Webster's New World Dictionary of the American Language was ultimately published in September 1951 in a two-volume encyclopedic edition. A single-volume college edition followed in 1953. Reviews of the work were enthusiastic in their praise. The December 1951 issue of *Library Journal* hailed the work as a "dictionary that marks a great advance in American lexicography."

In 1970, a completely revised Second College Edition was published. It was the first dictionary to identify Americanisms—those terms and usages that first appeared in the United States or that were coined by Americans. It was also the first to give etymologies of American place names.

The value of the dictionary's editorial innovations did not go unnoticed. In 1970, the dictionary was chosen by the American Printing House for the Blind, in conjunction with the Library of Congress, as the first dictionary of its scope to be embossed in Braille in its entirety; the resulting work took up seventy-two large volumes. In 1975, the *New York Times* announced it was replacing the dictionary it had used for decades with the Second College Edition of *Webster's New World Dictionary* as its first reference and as the basis for its forthcoming *Manual of Style and Usage*. The next year, both The Associated Press and United Press International adopted the dictionary and based their style manuals on it as well. They cited the frequency and thoroughness of updates, the reliability of the information, and the clarity of the definitions as reasons for choosing the work. Subsequently, most leading U.S. newspapers selected *Webster's New World Dictionary* as their dictionary of first choice.

The Third College Edition was launched in 1988, and the Fourth College Edition in 1999. By 2013, sixty-two years after the original dictionary was published, about one hundred million Webster's New World dictionaries, in various editions, had been printed.

The present work, the Fifth College Edition, retains the many acclaimed virtues of the Webster's New World tradition while bolstering the coverage of the rapidly growing lexicon of contemporary English.

As society changes, adapting to technological innovation and cultural shifts, language changes along with it. New words are coined, existing words take on new meanings, pronunciations change, words shift in tone—all part of the continuing process by which a language remains vigorous and useful. The editorial staff of Webster's New World, having a combined two hundred years of lexicographic experience, conducts a wide-reaching program of language monitoring to document such change. Their research has served as the foundation for this latest full-scale, authoritative revision of the dictionary.

The results of these efforts to keep the dictionary current can be seen in the thousands of new words and meanings added in this edition. These additions help document the continuing evolution of American English and reflect the subtle interplay between language and culture. They range across a variety of fields: from the technical terminology ushered in by the digital revolution, to the jargon of professional sports; from the specialized terms that have accompanied America's continuing preoccupation with cooking and dining, to slang terms that appear to have achieved permanence. Although coverage of new terms is the most obvious aspect of any new edition of a dictionary, other changes have resulted from a thorough editorial review of the preceding edition. These include changes in spelling and pronunciation, which are no less fluid than the lexicon itself.

For all its many changes, however, this new edition preserves those characteristics for which Webster's New World dictionaries are justly famous: the clarity of definitions; the open, uncramped style; the easily grasped pronunciations; the single alphabetical listing of all entries, including biographical and geographical entries, foreign terms, and abbreviations; and an overall user-friendliness.

All Webster's New World dictionaries strive to remain faithful to the principles and standards first set forth more than sixty years ago by David B. Guralnik. Mr. Guralnik's work represents a landmark contribution to American lexicography. We offer this edition in the hope that it will serve the modern reader as well as previous editions have—as an indispensable reference work covering the English language today. We regard it as a scholarly account of the past and as an inviting gateway to the future.

The Editorial Staff of
Webster's New World College Dictionary

ABBREVIATIONS AND SYMBOLS USED IN THIS DICTIONARY

abbrev.	abbreviation, abbreviated
abl.	ablative
acc.	accusative
adj.	adjective
adv.	adverb
Aeron.	Aeronautics
Afr	African
Afrik	Afrikaans
Agric.	Agriculture
Alb	Albanian
alt.	alternative
Am	American
AmFr	American French
AmInd	Amerindian
AmSp	American Spanish
Anat.	Anatomy
Anglo-Fr	Anglo-French
Anglo-Ind	Anglo-Indian
Anglo-Ir	Anglo-Irish
Anglo-L	Anglo-Latin
Anglo-Norm	Anglo-Norman
ANT.	Antonym(s)
Anthrop.	Anthropology
Ar	Arabic
Aram	Aramaic
Archaeol.	Archaeology
Archit.	Architecture
Arith.	Arithmetic
Arm	Armenian
art.	article (grammar)
assoc.	associated, association
Assyr	Assyrian
Astrol.	Astrology
Astron.	Astronomy
at. no.	atomic number
aug.	augmentative
Austral	Australian
b.	born
Bab	Babylonian
back-form.	back-formation
Beng	Bengali
Biochem.	Biochemistry
Biol.	Biology
Bot.	Botany
BrazPort	Brazilian Portuguese
Bret	Breton
Brit	British
Bulg	Bulgarian
C	Celsius
c.	century, centuries
c.	circa
cap.	capital city
caus.	causative
cc	cubic centimeter(s)
Cdn	Canadian
CdnFr	Canadian French
Celt	Celtic
cent.	century, centuries
cf.	compare
Ch.	Church
Chem.	Chemistry
Chin	Chinese
Chron.	Chronicles (Bible)
Class.	Classical
cm	centimeter(s)
Col.	Colossians
comb.	combination, combining
comp.	compound
compar.	comparative
Comput.	Computer Science
conj.	conjunction
Cor.	Corinthians
cu	cubic
Dan	Danish
Dan.	Daniel (Bible)
dat.	dative
deriv.	derived, derivative
Deut.	Deuteronomy
dial.	dialect, dialectal
dim.	diminutive
Du	Dutch
dupl.	duplicated, duplication
E	eastern; English (in etym. and pronun.)
EC	east central
Eccles.	Ecclesiastical
Ecol.	Ecology
Econ.	Economics
Educ.	Education
EFris	East Frisian
e.g.	for example
Egypt	Egyptian
Elec.	Electricity
Eng.	English
Eph.	Ephesians
equiv.	equivalent
Esk	Eskimo
esp.	especially
est.	estimated
etc.	and the like
Etr	Etruscan
etym.	etymology
Ex.	example; Exodus
Ezek.	Ezekiel
F	Fahrenheit
fem.	feminine
fig.	figurative, figuratively
Finn	Finnish
Fl	Flemish
fl	fluid
fl.	flourished; lived (of people)
fol.	following entry
Fr	French
Frank	Frankish
freq.	frequentative
Fris	Frisian
ft	foot, feet
fut.	future
g	gram(s)
Gael	Gaelic
Gal.	Galatians
gal	gallon(s)
Gaul	Gaulish
Gen.	Genesis
gen.	genitive
Geog.	Geography
Geol.	Geology
Geom.	Geometry
Ger	German
ger.	gerund, gerundive
GeV	billion electron volts
Gmc	Germanic
Goth	Gothic
gov.	governor
Gr	Classical Greek
Gram.	Grammar
Gr(Ec)	Ecclesiastical Greek
Gym.	Gymnastics
Hab.	Habakkuk
Hag.	Haggai
Haw	Hawaiian
Heb	Classical Hebrew (language)
Heb.	Hebrews (Bible)
Heb-Aram	Hebrew-Aramaic
Hort.	Horticulture
Hos.	Hosea
Hung	Hungarian
Hz	hertz
Ice	Icelandic
IE	Indo-European
i.e.	that is
imper.	imperative
imperf.	imperfect
in	inch(es)
incl.	including
Ind	Indian; Indic (in etym.)
indic.	indicative
inf.	infinitive
infl.	influenced, influence
intens.	intensive
interj.	interjection
Ir	Irish
Iran	Iranian
irreg.	irregular
Isa.	Isaiah
It	Italian
Jer.	Jeremiah
Josh.	Joshua
Jpn	Japanese
Judg.	Judges (Bible)
K	Kelvin
kg	kilogram(s)
KJV	King James Version
km	kilometer(s)
km^2	square kilometer(s)
Kor	Korean
kPa	kilopascal(s)
l	liter(s)
L	Classical Latin
Lam.	Lamentations

lb	pound(s)
lb/in^2	pound(s) per square inch
L(Ec)	Ecclesiastical Latin
Lev.	Leviticus
LGr	Late Greek
LGr(Ec)	Ecclesiastical Late Greek
Linguis.	Linguistics
lit.	literally
Lith	Lithuanian
LL	Late Latin
LL(Ec)	Ecclesiastical Late Latin
LME	Late Middle English
LowG	Low German
lt. gov.	lieutenant governor
LWS	Late West Saxon
LXX	Septuagint
m	meter(s)
Macc.	Maccabees
Mal.	Malachi
masc.	masculine
Math.	Mathematics
Matt.	Matthew (Bible)
MDu	Middle Dutch
ME	Middle English
Mech.	Mechanics
Med.	Medicine
met.	metropolitan
Meteorol.	Meteorology
MeV	million electron volts
Mex	Mexican
MexSp	Mexican Spanish
MFl	Middle Flemish
MFr	Middle French
MGr	Medieval Greek
MHeb	Medieval Hebrew
MHG	Middle High German
mi	mile(s)
Mic.	Micah
Microbiol.	Microbiology
Mil.	Military
MIr	Middle Irish
mistransl.	mistranslation
ml	milliliter(s)
ML	Medieval Latin
ML(Ec)	Ecclesiastical Medieval Latin
MLowG	Middle Low German
mm	millimeter(s)
ModE	Modern English
ModGr	Modern Greek
ModHeb	Modern Hebrew
ModL	Modern Latin
Mpa	megapascal(s)
mph	mile(s) per hour
MScot	Middle Scottish
Mt.	Mount
mya	million years ago
Myth.	Mythology
N	northern
n.	noun
Nah.	Nahum
NAmFr	North American French
Naut.	nautical usage
NC	north central
NE	northeastern
Neh.	Nehemiah
Netherl	Netherlandic
neut.	neuter
NGmc	North Germanic
NM/h	nautical mile(s) per hour
nom.	nominative
Norm	Norman
NormFr	Norman French
Norw	Norwegian
N.T.	New Testament
Num.	Numbers (Bible)
NW	northwestern
N.Z.	New Zealand
Ob.	Obadiah
obj.	object, objective
obs.	obsolete
occas.	occasionally
OCelt	Old Celtic
ODan	Old Danish
ODu	Old Dutch
OE	Old English
OFr	Old French
OFris	Old Frisian
OHG	Old High German
OIce	Old Icelandic
OInd	Old Indic
OIr	Old Irish
OIt	Old Italian
OL	Old Latin
OLowFranc	Old Low Franconian
OLowG	Old Low German
ON	Old Norse
OPers	Old Persian
OProv	Old Provençal
OPrus	Old Prussian
orig.	origin, original(ly)
OS	Old Saxon
Osco-Umb	Osco-Umbrian
OSlav	Old Church Slavonic
OSp	Old Spanish
OSw	Old Swedish
O.T.	Old Testament
OWelsh	Old Welsh
oz	ounce(s)
Pa	pascal(s)
PaGer	Pennsylvania German
part.	participle, participial
pass.	passive voice
perf.	perfect tense
pers.	person; personal (grammar)
Pers	Persian
Pet.	Peter (Bible)
PGmc	Proto-Germanic
Phil.	Philippians
Philem.	Philemon
Philos.	Philosophy
Phoen	Phoenician
Phonet.	Phonetics
Photog.	Photography
phr.	phrase
Physiol.	Physiology
PidE	Pidgin English
pl.	plural
pl.n.	plural noun
Poet.	Poetic
Pol	Polish
pop.	population
Port	Portuguese
poss.	possessive
pp.	past participle
prec.	preceding entry
prep.	preposition
pres.	present tense
Pres.	President
pret.	preterit
priv.	privative
prob.	probably
pron.	pronoun
pronun.	pronunciation
Prov	Provençal
Prov.	Proverbs (Bible)
prp.	present participle
Prus	Prussian
Ps.	Psalms
pseud.	pseudonym
Psychol.	Psychology
pt	pint(s)
pt.	past tense
qt	quart(s)
R.C.Ch.	Roman Catholic Church
redupl.	reduplicated, reduplication
ref.	reference; refer
refl.	reflexive
Rev.	Revelation
Rom.	Romans (Bible); Roman
RSV	Revised Standard Version
Russ	Russian
S	southern
Sam.	Samuel (Bible)
SAmSp	South American Spanish
Sans	Sanskrit
SC	south central
Scand	Scandinavian
Scot	Scottish, Scots
SE	southeastern
Sem	Semitic
Serb	Serbian
sing.	singular
sing.n.	singular noun
SinoJpn	Sino-Japanese
Slav	Slavic, Slavonic
S. of Sol.	Song of Solomon
Sp	Spanish
sp.	spelling, spelled
specif.	specifically
sq	square
subj.	subject; subjective
subjunc.	subjunctive
superl.	superlative
SW	southwestern
Swed	Swedish
SYN.	Synonymy
TalmudHeb	Talmudic Hebrew
Theol.	Theology
Thess.	Thessalonians
Tim.	Timothy (Bible)
Tit.	Titus (Bible)
transl.	translated, translation
Turk	Turkish
TV	television
ult.	ultimately
UN	United Nations
uncert.	uncertain
U.S.	United States
U.S.S.R.	Union of Soviet Socialist Republics
v.	verb
var.	variant; variety
v.aux.	auxiliary verb
Vet.Med.	Veterinary Medicine
vi.	intransitive verb
VL	Vulgar Latin
voc.	vocative
vt.	transitive verb
Vulg.	Vulgate
W	western
WAfr	West African
WC	west central
WFris	West Frisian
WGmc	West Germanic
WInd	West Indian
WS	West Saxon
WWI	World War I
WWII	World War II
yd	yard(s)
Zech.	Zechariah
Zeph.	Zephaniah
Zool.	Zoology

SYMBOLS

☆	Americanism
*	an unverified form
+	plus
°	degree
<	derived from (in etymologies)
>	related to (in etymologies)
?	uncertain or unknown; perhaps
&	and
➥	Usage Note

GUIDE TO THE DICTIONARY

This dictionary presents information about words in the form of a paragraph for each word. The Guide to the Dictionary that follows explains the elements of such a paragraph. The sample paragraphs below have the most important of these elements identified by labels that contain references to parts of the Guide. In the remainder of the Guide, the user can also find explanations of other important elements.

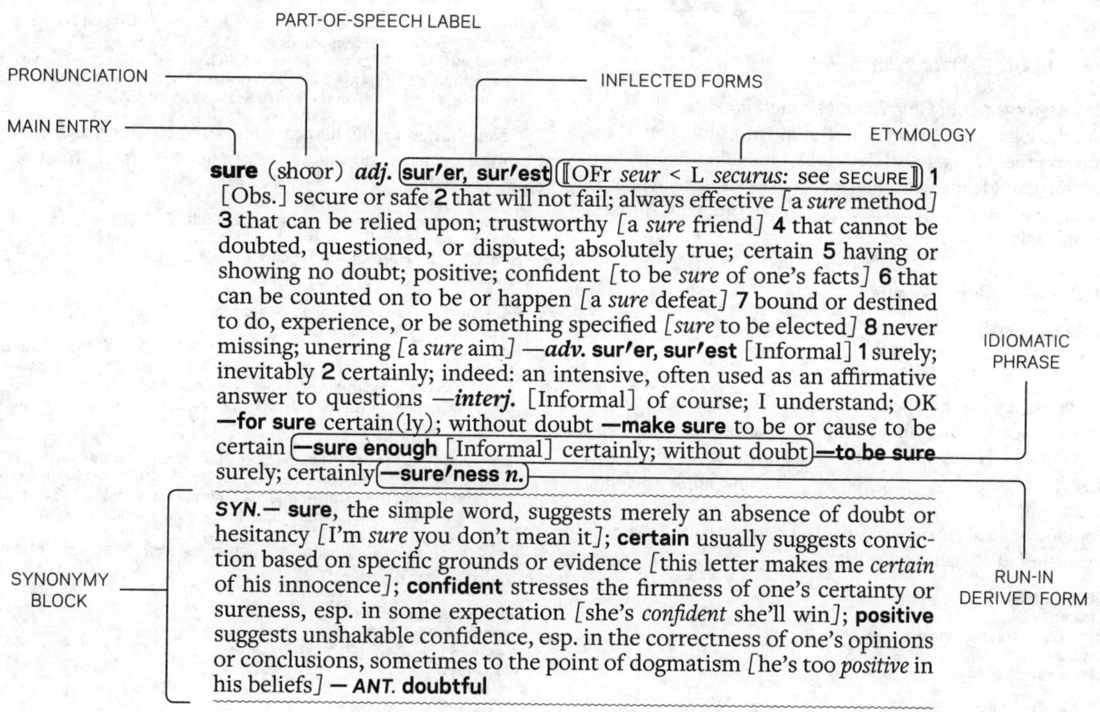
PART-OF-SPEECH LABEL
PRONUNCIATION
INFLECTED FORMS
MAIN ENTRY
ETYMOLOGY
IDIOMATIC PHRASE
SYNONYMY BLOCK
RUN-IN DERIVED FORM
sure (shoor) *adj.* **sur′er, sur′est** ⟦OFr *seur* < L *securus:* see SECURE⟧ **1** [Obs.] secure or safe **2** that will not fail; always effective [a *sure* method] **3** that can be relied upon; trustworthy [a *sure* friend] **4** that cannot be doubted, questioned, or disputed; absolutely true; certain **5** having or showing no doubt; positive; confident [to be *sure* of one's facts] **6** that can be counted on to be or happen [a *sure* defeat] **7** bound or destined to do, experience, or be something specified [*sure* to be elected] **8** never missing; unerring [a *sure* aim] ***—adv.*** **sur′er, sur′est** [Informal] **1** surely; inevitably **2** certainly; indeed: an intensive, often used as an affirmative answer to questions ***—interj.*** [Informal] of course; I understand; OK **—for sure** certain(ly); without doubt **—make sure** to be or cause to be certain **—sure enough** [Informal] certainly; without doubt **—to be sure** surely; certainly **—sure′ness** ***n.***
SYN.— **sure**, the simple word, suggests merely an absence of doubt or hesitancy [I'm *sure* you don't mean it]; **certain** usually suggests conviction based on specific grounds or evidence [this letter makes me *certain* of his innocence]; **confident** stresses the firmness of one's certainty or sureness, esp. in some expectation [she's *confident* she'll win]; **positive** suggests unshakable confidence, esp. in the correctness of one's opinions or conclusions, sometimes to the point of dogmatism [he's too *positive* in his beliefs] — ***ANT.*** **doubtful**

CONTENTS

I. GUIDE WORDS

Two guide words appear at the top of each page showing the alphabetical range of the entries on that page.

The first main entry word and the last main entry word on a page serve as the guide words for that page.

allure • alpaca 40

II. THE MAIN ENTRY WORD

A. *Arrangement of entries in this dictionary*

This dictionary lists all main entries in strict alphabetical order and sets them in large boldface type, extending slightly into the left margin. Main entries include single words, hyphenated and unhyphenated compounds, proper names, prefixes, suffixes, and abbreviations.

black
Black (blak), **Hugo (La Fayette)**
☆**black alder**
black-and-blue
blackberry
bldg *abbrev.*

Some entries are alphabetized in special ways.

This dictionary lists BIOGRAPHICAL ENTRIES (people) and GEOGRAPHICAL ENTRIES (places) in alphabetical order in the A-Z main section. There are some special rules that apply to them, however.

For biographical entries, only the last name is used in arranging the names in alphabetical order.

Stoke-on-Trent
stoker
Stokes, Sir **George Gabriel**
☆**stokesia**
Stokowski, **Leopold**

If there are two or more persons with the same family name, this dictionary lists them in a single entry block in alphabetical order by first names.

Williams (...) **1 Hank** (...) (born *Hiram Williams*) 1923-53; U.S. country music singer & composer **2 Ralph Vaughan** *see* VAUGHAN WILLIAMS **3 Roger** 1603?-83; Eng. clergyman & colonist in America: founder of R.I. **4 Tennessee** (born *Thomas Lanier Williams*) 1914-83; U.S. playwright **5 William Carlos** (...) 1883-1963; U.S. poet & writer

Johnson (...) **1 Andrew** 1808-75; 17th president of the U.S. (1865-69) **2 James Weldon** (...) 1871-1938; U.S. writer & diplomat **3 Lyndon Baines** (...) 1908-73; 36th president of the U.S. (1963-69) **4 Philip Cortelyou** (...) 1906-2005; U.S. architect **5 Robert (Leroy)** 1911-38; U.S. blues guitarist, singer, & composer **6 Samuel** 1709-84; Eng. lexicographer, writer, & critic: known as *Dr. Johnson*

Names in parentheses are disregarded when alphabetizing.

Joliot-Curie (...) **1 (Jean) Frédéric** (...) ... **2 Irène** (...) ...

Biographical and geographical names are in separate entry blocks.

Cleveland[1] (...), **(Stephen) Grover** (...) 1837-1908; 22d and 24th president of the U.S. (1885-89; 1893-97)
Cleveland[2] (...) **1** ⟦after Moses *Cleaveland* (1754-1806), surveyor of the WESTERN RESERVE⟧ city and port in NE Ohio, on Lake Erie **2** county in N England, on the North Sea: 231 sq mi (597 sq km)

Given names, family names, names in mythology, and names of biblical persons and places are entered separately from biographical entries.

Simon[1] (...) *n.* ⟦...⟧ **1** a masculine name: dim. *Si* **2** *Bible a)* one of the twelve Apostles, called *Peter* or **Simon Peter**: see PETER[1] *b)* ...
Simon[2] (...) **1 Herbert A(lexander)** 1916-2001; U.S. social scientist & economist

Bonaparte[1] (...) *n.* name of a Corsican family of Italian origin to which belonged Napoleon I and his four brothers
Bonaparte[2] (...) **1 Jérôme** ... **2 Joseph** ... **3 Louis** 1778-1846; king of Holland (1806-10): father of Louis Napoleon **4 Lucien** ... **5 Napoleon** (...) 1769-1821; Fr. military leader & emperor of France (1804-15), born in Corsica: in full *Napoleon I* See also NAPOLEON II, LOUIS NAPOLEON

Rothschild[1] (...) *n.* name of a family of European bankers
Rothschild[2] (...) **1 Meyer An·selm** (...) 1743-1812; Ger. founder of the banking house of Rothschild: also **Meyer Am·schel** (...) **2 Nathan Meyer** 1777-1836; Eng. banker, born in Germany: son of Meyer Anselm

This dictionary lists names beginning with **Mac** and **Mc** in strict alphabetical order.

MacDowell (...), **Edward**
macebearer
Macleod (...), **J(ohn) J(ames) R(ickard)**
makefast
☆**maser**
McCullers (...), **Carson**

Strict alphabetical order for **Saint** and **St.** is followed when they appear as part of proper names other than the names of canonized persons.

Saint Bernard ... any of a breed of very large, ... dog ...
Sainte-Beuve (...), **Charles Augustin** (...) 1804–69; Fr. literary critic ...
Saint-Exupéry (...), **Antoine de** (...) 1900–44; Fr. aviator & writer
squint (...) *vi.* ...
St. Bernard 1 *var. of* SAINT BERNARD (dog) ...
St-Denis (...) capital of Réunion Island
steel (...) *n.* ...
St. Helens (...), **Mount** ⟦...⟧ volcanic mountain ...

The listing of canonized persons is in alphabetical order by their given names, which appear in boldface. The designation "Saint" follows in lightface type, either directly after a comma or at the beginning of a numbered sense within a proper-name block.

Augustine[2] (...) 1 Saint ... early Christian church father, ...
St. Augustine (...) ⟦...⟧ seaport in NE Fla.; ...

B. *Some special kinds of main entries*

The BIOGRAPHICAL ENTRY

This dictionary lists biographical entries under the name by which the people are best known. Nicknames or birth names may be given elsewhere in the entry block.

Ellington (...), **Duke** (born *Edward Kennedy Ellington*) ...
Parker (...) **1 Charlie** (...) (born *Charles Christopher Parker, Jr.*) ...
Holiday (...), **Billie** (born *Eleonora Fagan Holiday*) ...: also called *Lady Day*
Teresa[2] (...) 1 Mother (born *Agnes Gonxha Bojaxhiu*) ...
Dumas (...) **1 Alexandre** ...: called *Dumas père* **2 Alexandre** ...: called *Dumas fils*: son of *Dumas père*

The entry may also include titles.

Gielgud (...), Sir (**Arthur**) **John** ...
Spark (...), Dame **Muriel** (**Sarah**) (born *Muriel Sarah Camberg*) ...

The entry typically includes birth and death dates, terms of office, dates of reign, etc. When a date is uncertain a question mark is used.

Sinatra (...), **Frank** ... 1915–98
John Paul 1 John Paul I (...) 1912–78; pope (1978) **2 John Paul II** (...) 1920–2005; pope (1978–2005)
Aelfric (...) A.D. 955?–1020?; Eng. abbot and writer: ...

The GEOGRAPHICAL ENTRY

Generally, U.S. cities with census populations of 100,000 and over are entered. Cities or towns with fewer people but of some historical note are also entered.

Gettysburg (...) ... town in S Pa.: site of a crucial battle (July, 1863) of the Civil War and of a famous address by Abraham Lincoln dedicating a National Cemetery

World cities with a large population or of historical note are entered.

Karachi (...) capital of Sind province, Pakistan, on the Arabian Sea: former (1947–59) capital of Pakistan
Anzio (...) port on the W coast of Italy, south of Rome: site of Allied beachhead (Jan., 1944) in the invasion of Italy in WWII

Many other geographical units are entered, such as regions, territories, U.S. states, and Canadian provinces.

Dasht-e-Lut (...) vast desert region of central and SE Iran, extending southward from the Dasht-e-Kavir
Donets Basin major industrial and coal-producing region in the lower valley of the Donets River
British Indian Ocean Territory British territory in the Indian Ocean, between Sri Lanka & Mauritius, consisting of the Chagos Archipelago: 23 sq mi (60 sq km)
Maryland (...) ⟦...⟧ state of the E U.S., on the Atlantic: one of the 13 original states: 9,774 sq mi (25,314 sq km); cap. Annapolis: abbrev. *MD* or *Md*

The TRADEMARK AND SERVICE MARK

This dictionary lists trademarks and service marks in alphabetical order in the A-Z main section.

astrosphere (...) *n.* ...
AstroTurf (...) *trademark for* ...
astute (...) *adj.* ...

Within an entry the trademark or service mark is given first, and a generic noun or verb sense related to it may follow.

☆**Kleenex** (...) ⟦...⟧ *trademark for* soft tissue paper used as a handkerchief, etc. —*n.* [*occas.* **k-**] a piece of such paper
Welcome Wagon *service mark for* a welcoming service that provides information about a community to new residents — [*occas.* **w- w-**] **1** any such service ...

The dictionary also lists some abbreviations as trademarks or service marks.

ACT *trademark* American College Test
PX *service mark* Post Exchange

The ABBREVIATION

In this dictionary most abbreviation main entries appear without periods. The developing practice of most publications and institutions has been to eliminate periods in many contexts. This dictionary follows that practice. However, since writers and publishers continue to use periods for certain abbreviations, the user should not feel prohibited from doing so as well.

There are exceptions, as in the abbreviations of some Latin phrases and academic degrees.

ad loc. *abbrev.* ⟦L *ad locum*⟧ at or to the place
HH.D. or **HHD** *abbrev.* Doctor of Humanities

The dictionary user can assume that some abbreviations will continue to have periods, others will have periods for certain meanings, and many will never have periods in general use.

C. *Alternative spellings and variant forms*

This dictionary lists ALTERNATIVE SPELLINGS in various ways, usually depending on how often they appear in use:

1. as joint main entries: this implies that both spellings occur equally, or almost equally, often and that neither one is "more correct" or to be preferred.

ax[1] or **axe**
the·a·ter or **the·a·tre**

2. at the end of an entry block, part of speech, or individual meaning, in small boldface: this treatment is used when the alternative spelling occurs less often than the main entry spelling or when it has a particular quality that needs mentioning, such as being British, dialectal, poetic, or rare.

la·sa·gna ... Also sp. **la·sa′gne**
pro·logue ... Also sp. **pro′log′**
mis·de·mean·or ... Brit. sp. **mis′de·mean′our**

This dictionary also lists VARIANT FORMS at the end of the entry block, part of speech, or individual meaning. This implies that the variant occurs less often than the main entry or has a special quality, as in being British, dialectal, poetic, or rare.

con·cur·rence ... Also **con·cur′ren·cy**
COBOL ... : also written **Cobol**
cab·driv·er ... : also [Informal] **cab′by**
ty·phoid ... : in full **typhoid fever**

This dictionary lists alternative spellings and variant forms that belong to particular parts of speech at the end of the final meaning of that particular part of speech. Similarly, it lists forms belonging to a particular meaning at the end of that meaning.

bo·tan·i·cal *adj.* ... **1** ... **2** ... **3** ... Also **bo·tan′ic** —*n.* ...
☆**Pull·man** ... **1** ... : also **Pullman car** **2** ... : also **pullman case**

The dictionary lists as separate main entries alternative spellings and variant forms that are alphabetically distant from the spelling that is more commonly used.

Such entries have a definition [in small capital letters] that is simply a cross-reference to the main spelling or form.

cen·tre (...) *n., vt., vi.* (...) *Brit. sp. of* CENTER

In some cases, the alternative spellings may involve diacritics, hyphens, or the like.

chaî·né (...) *n.* ... : also written **chainé**

D. Cross-references

Some entries consist simply of a cross-reference to another entry having the same meaning, with the cross-reference shown in small capitals.

curb roof 1 MANSARD (ROOF) 2 GAMBREL ROOF

Sometimes a definition includes a term in small capitals. This shows that additional information that may be useful in understanding the definition is at the main entry for the term.

beam·y (...) *adj.* ... 3 *Naut.* having a broad BEAM (*n.* I, 8)

A "*see*" followed by small capitals tells the user that a particular word is defined or explained within the definition of another word.

I·a·go (...) *n. see* OTHELLO

E. Homographs

Homographs are main entries that have the same spelling but are different in meaning and origin, as **bat** (a club), **bat** (the animal), and **bat** (to wink).

This dictionary enters homographs in separate blocks and marks them with superscript numbers immediately following the boldface spellings.

bat¹ (...) *n.* ...
bat² (...) *n.* ...
bat³ (...) *vt.* ...

When a part of an etymology, definition, etc. refers to a homograph, the cross-reference includes the superscript of that homograph.

floc (...) *n.* ... 2 FLOCK² (senses 1, 2, & 3)

In this dictionary main entries having the same spelling, including proper nouns (including biographical or geographical entries) and abbreviations, are homographs and thus do have superscripts.

Main entries that differ from others with the same spelling merely by having markings such as accents or hyphens or by being italicized or capitalized are not homographs and thus do not have superscripts.

do·ré (...) *adj.* ...
Do·ré (...), (**Paul**) **Gus·tave** ...

F. Americanisms

Words and phrases that had their first use in the United States or that were coined by Americans are Americanisms. Meanings of previously existing words or phrases that had their first use in this country are also Americanisms.

This dictionary indicates Americanisms with an open star (☆).

If the star comes before the entry word, the word itself came into the language as an Americanism.

☆**chow·der** (...) *n.* ...

If the star comes before a particular part of speech, that part of speech came into the language as an Americanism.

dai·ly (...) *adj.* ... —☆*n.* ...

If the star comes before a single definition or subsense of a definition, only that definition or subsense is an Americanism.

hum·mer (...) *n.* 1 ... ☆2 ... ☆3 ...

G. Foreign terms

The English language contains many words and phrases borrowed from other languages. Some of these words and phrases have become a standard part of the English language, while others keep their foreignness for many readers and speakers of English.

Words that are now part of the English language appear as entry words in boldface roman type.

☆**me·sa** (...) *n.* ⟦Sp < L *mensa*, a table: see MENSAL⟧ a small, high plateau or flat tableland with steep sides, esp. in the SW U.S.

Words that are still thought of as being foreign to some degree appear as entry words in boldface italic type. This is a signal to the reader to print these words and phrases in italics or to underline them in handwriting.

bon·jour ... *interj., n.* ⟦Fr⟧ good day; good morning

Most entry words in italics give the actual foreign spelling, if the original language uses the Roman alphabet. In some cases, however, the entry word in italics represents the most common spelling in use in English. In many such cases, the original spelling or transliteration is in the etymology.

bom·bé (...) *adj.* ⟦Fr < *bombe*, bomb (because of the shape)⟧ ...
mo·shav (...) *n.*, *pl.* **mo·sha·vim** (...) ⟦ModHeb *mōshābh* < Heb, a dwelling⟧ ...

The entry words for commonly used abbreviations of non-English terms are not in boldface italic type. Their etymologies show the language of origin and the full, unabbreviated form of the term.

i.e. *abbrev.* ⟦L *id est*⟧ that is (to say)

H. Prefixes, suffixes, and combining forms

The very full coverage of affixes (prefixes, suffixes, and combining forms) makes it possible for a dictionary user to understand and pronounce many words that are not entered in the dictionary. The user can form these words by combining affixes with words that are already entered.

This dictionary enters prefixes, and combining forms used at the beginning of words, with a hyphen at the end.

car·di·o- (...) ... *combining form* of the heart ...

This dictionary enters suffixes, and combining forms used at the end of words, with a hyphen at the beginning.

-ness (...) ... *suffix* state, quality, or instance of being ...

This dictionary enters infixes (forms which appear in the middle of words) with a hyphen at the beginning and at the end.

-i- (...) *infix* forming compound words: a connective vowel originally used for combining Latin elements only, but now used freely

I. Word division

Dividing words at the end of a line is more complicated than it used to be. Today computer programs sometimes divide words in ways that would not have been acceptable at one time. However, there are some general rules still in effect for most writing.

1. Do not divide words having four letters or fewer; thus, avoid:

a-go
on-ly
tri-o

2. Do not divide a word so as to leave only one letter at the end of a line; thus, avoid:

a-bout
e-lect
i-tinerary

3. Do not divide a word so as to carry only one letter over to the following line; thus, avoid:

anemi-a
radi-o
savor-y

In this dictionary, a CENTER DOT (·) indicates a syllable break for all boldface entry words, including main entries, inflected forms (truncated and not truncated), and run-in derived forms.

The center dot appears between syllables; thus:

an·noy
cer·e·mo·ni·al
hy·po·thal·a·mus

However, as you can see from the above, not every syllable break is a judicious place to break a word when typing or writing.

III. PARTS OF SPEECH

A. *Part-of-speech labels*

This dictionary provides part-of-speech labels for most main entry words that are solid or hyphenated forms. It does not give part-of-speech labels for open compounds or for prefixes, suffixes, combining forms, abbreviations, trademarks and service marks, and biographical and geographical entries.

You will find the following labels for the parts of speech traditionally used to classify words in English grammar. They appear in boldface italic type and typically follow the pronunciations.

n.	noun
v.	verb
vt.	transitive verb
vi.	intransitive verb
adj.	adjective
adv.	adverb
prep.	preposition
conj.	conjunction
pron.	pronoun
interj.	interjection

This dictionary also uses the following labels:

pl.n.	plural noun
sing.n.	singular noun
v.aux.	auxiliary verb
v.impersonal	impersonal verb
definite article	
indefinite article	
possessive pronominal adj.	

When an entry word has more than one part of speech, long dashes introduce each different part of speech in the entry block.

square (...) ***n.*** ⟦...⟧ ... ***—vt.*** ... ***—vi.*** ... ***—adj.*** ... ***—adv.*** ...

Sometimes an entry will have two or more parts of speech, separated by commas, and a definition or cross-reference understood to apply to all of them.

draught (...) ***n., vt., adj.*** *now chiefly Brit. sp. of* DRAFT
☆**max**[1] (...) [Slang] ***n., adj.*** MAXIMUM ***—vi.*** ...
whole-hog (...) ***adj., adv.*** ☆[Slang] without restraint or reservation; complete(ly)

In some long and complicated entries Roman numerals (**I**, **II**, etc.) are used to separate groupings of related definitions into smaller sections.

go[1] (gō) ***vi.*** **went, gone, go′ing** (...) **I.** *indicating motion without reference to destination or point of departure* **1** to move along; travel; proceed [to *go* 90 miles an hour] **2** ... **II.** *indicating motion from a point of departure* **1** to move off; leave; depart **2** ... **III.** *indicating motion toward a place, point, etc.* **1** to move toward a place or person or in a certain direction [to *go* to the back of the room] **2** ...

B. *Some unusual uses of regular parts of speech*

It is theoretically possible to use almost any word as whatever part of speech is required. Most such uses would be for only a single occasion and would not be entered in this dictionary. There are, however, two fairly common uses that are often entered:

1. Almost any transitive verb can be used as an intransitive verb, with the object understood. For example, "he defined the word" (transitive use); "try to define carefully before proceeding with your argument" (intransitive use).

2. Nouns can be used attributively, as adjectives (e.g., a *cloth* cover; a *family* affair).

IV. INFLECTED FORMS

Inflection is the way some words change form so as to serve particular grammatical functions. The resulting forms are called "inflected forms" or "inflections."

This dictionary usually shows only those inflected forms that are irregular or that present specific difficulties. Regular inflected forms typically are not shown.

Inflected forms are entered in boldface type just after the part-of-speech label. Most of them are truncated or shortened. Syllabification, stress marking, and pronunciation are also indicated when necessary.

This dictionary gives three types of inflected forms: plurals of nouns, principal parts of verbs, and comparative and superlative forms of adjectives and adverbs.

A. *Showing plurals*

This dictionary does not show plurals that are:

1. formed regularly by adding *-s* to the singular (*cats*)

2. formed regularly by adding *-es* to a singular that ends with *s, x, z,* or *sh* (*boxes, bushes*)

3. formed regularly by adding *-es* to a singular that ends with *ch* when the *ch* is pronounced (ch) (*churches*) or by adding *-s* when *ch* is pronounced (k) (*stomach*)

This dictionary does show plurals when:

1. a final *y* in the singular is replaced by *i* in the plural

cit·y (...) ***n.,*** *pl.* **cit′ies**

2. the singular ends in *o*

bo·le·ro (...) ***n.,*** *pl.* **-ros**
ve·to (...) ***n.,*** *pl.* **-toes**

3. the plural is irregular or presents a special problem

tooth (...) ***n.,*** *pl.* **teeth**
son-in-law (...) ***n.,*** *pl.* **sons′-in-law′**

4. there are variant plural forms

a·moe·ba (...) ***n.,*** *pl.* **-bas** or **-bae**
die[2] (...) ***n.,*** *pl.* for 1 & 2, **dice**; for 3 & 4, **dies**

This dictionary also enters, as main entries, plurals that are alphabetically distant from their singular forms.

lice (...) ***n.,*** *pl. of* LOUSE

B. *Showing the principal parts of verbs*

This dictionary often enters infinitives with some of their inflected forms. In English, the infinitive is usually the first-person, present-tense form of the verb ("go," as in "I go"; "run," as in "We run"). The inflected forms shown in this dictionary are the principal parts of the English verb: past tense, past participle, and present participle.

If only two principal parts are shown, as at **love**, the first is both the past tense and the past participle (**loved**) and the second is the present participle (**loving**). If three principal parts are shown, as at **go**, the first is the past tense (**went**), the second is the past participle (**gone**), and the third is the present participle (**going**).

This dictionary does not show principal parts when:

1. the past tense and past participle are formed by simply adding *-ed* to the infinitive, with no other change being made. At the entries **search**, **talk**, and **wait**, the principal parts **searched**, **talked**, and **waited** are not shown.

2. the present participle is formed by simply adding *-ing* to the infinitive, with no other change being made. At **search**, **talk**, and **wait**, the principal parts **searching**, **talking**, and **waiting** are not given.

This dictionary does show principal parts when there is a change other than, or in addition to, the simple appending of *-ed* or *-ing* to the infinitive, as when:

1. the final consonant is doubled before adding *-ed* or *-ing*

ship ... *vt.* **shipped, ship′ping**

2. the final *-e* is dropped in forming the present participle

love ... *vt.* **loved, lov′ing**

3. the final *-y* is replaced by *-ie* in forming the past tense or past participle

rea·dy ... *vt.* **read′ied, read′ying**

4. one or more of the parts are significantly different in form from the infinitive

go[1] (...) *vi.* **went, gone, go′ing**

5. one or more of the parts have variant forms

trav·el (...) *vt.* **-eled** or **-elled, -el·ing** or **-el·ling**

Some principal parts are entered separately:

1. principal parts that are alphabetically distant from their infinitive forms

gone (...) *vi., vt. pp. of* GO[1]

2. some verb inflections that are not shown with their infinitive forms, as present tense inflections formed by adding *-s* or *-es* to the infinitive: the precise grammatical relationship of such inflections is indicated

goes (...) *vi., vt. 3d pers. sing., pres. indic., of* GO[1]

C. *Showing comparatives and superlatives of adjectives and adverbs*

This dictionary does not show comparatives and superlatives formed by the simple addition of *-er* or *-est* to the base form or by the addition of *more* or *most*. For example, at **tall** the comparative form **taller** and the superlative form **tallest** are not given.

This dictionary does show comparative and superlative forms when there is a change other than, or in addition to, the simple appending of *-er* or *-est* to the base form, as when:

1. the final *-e* is dropped and *-er* and *-est* are added

rare[1] (...) *adj.* **rar′er, rar′est**

2. the final *y* of the base form is replaced with *i*

hap·py (...) *adj.* **-pi·er, -pi·est**

3. the comparative or superlative forms are significantly different from the base form.

good (...) *adj.* **bet′ter, best**
well[2] (...) *adv.* **bet′ter, best**

Comparatives and superlatives that are alphabetically distant from the base form are also entered separately.

best (...) *adj.* ... 1 *superl. of* GOOD ... —*adv.* 1 *superl. of* WELL[2]

D. *Other types of inflected forms*

Some inflected forms that are variants of the modern or common form may be entered, such as those that are informal, archaic, dialectal, or British.

Some variant inflected forms are shown within the entry block for the more modern or common form.

sneak (...) *vi.* **sneaked** or ☆**snuck, sneak′ing**

Other variant inflected forms, if alphabetically distant, are shown as main entries with cross-references to their more modern or common forms.

spake (...) *vi., vt. archaic pt. of* SPEAK

V. THE ETYMOLOGY

Etymologies give a capsulized history of the derivation of a word and have long been a strong feature of this dictionary. A better understanding of the current usage of a word often can come from a fuller knowledge of that word's history. A better understanding of how language works can come from knowing how words are related to other English words and to words in other Indo-European languages.

This dictionary shows how words are related to one another and shows, where possible, the line of ancestry back to the Indo-European base, either directly or through cross-references.

A. *How etymologies are organized*

Etymologies appear inside double brackets and before definitions.

Special symbols are used in etymologies:

*	an unverified form
<	derived from
>	related to
?	uncertain or unknown; perhaps

Abbreviations for language labels used in etymologies appear on pages ix and x.

B. *A typical etymology*

The following entry for **fish** shows the form and content of a typical etymology:

fish (...) *n.* ... ⟦ME < OE *fisc*, akin to Ger. *fisch*, Du *visch* < IE base **pisk-* > L *piscis*⟧

Italicized words within etymologies are generally either words in the entry word's line of ancestry (*fisc*, **pisk-* in the above example) or words otherwise related to it (*fisch*, *visch*, and *piscis*).

The first part of this etymology has to do with the history of the word in the English language. In Middle English (ME) the word had the same form and meaning as in Modern English. This form comes from the Old English (OE) word *fisc*.

The words "akin to" (following *fisc*) introduce related words having the same meaning but coming from other Germanic languages, German *fisch* and Dutch *visch*.

The next part takes the word back to the Indo-European base (**pisk-*). The asterisk (*) indicates that the form is hypothetical, since no written record of Indo-European exists.

The final part is a Latin word (*piscis*) meaning "fish," which is related to the English word but is not in the direct line of its ancestry.

C. *Other ways of showing etymologies*

Some words have etymologies that are made up of the individual parts of the word shown as cross-references (appearing in small capitals). Each of these parts has a separate entry, together with its own etymology, elsewhere in the dictionary.

car·bo·hy·drate (...) ***n.*** ⟦CARBO- + HYDRATE⟧
☆**con·trail** (...) ***n.*** ⟦CON(DENSATION) + TRAIL⟧

In the etymology for **contrail** above, parentheses set off the part of the word "condensation" that was dropped in forming the entry word. It is always the entire word, however, that will be found in the dictionary.

Some words have more than one etymology. An individual part of speech or a particular sense might have its own etymology in double brackets.

dis·ease (...) ***n.*** ⟦ME *disese*, inconvenience, trouble, sickness < OFr *desaise*, discomfort < *des-*, DIS- + *aise*, EASE⟧ **1** ... **2** ... **—*vt.*** ... ⟦ME *disesen* < OFr *desaaisier* < the n.⟧ to cause disease in; ...
trail·er (...) ***n.*** **1** a person, animal, or thing that trails another ☆**2** ... ☆**4** *Film a)* ⟦so called because originally attached to the end of a reel of film⟧ an advertisement for a feature film, typically consisting of brief portions of scenes from that film *b)* a blank length of film at the end of a reel **—*vt.*** ...

Some etymologies are given as additional information after the definition. This method is usually used when the information gives a better understanding of the definition or connects the definition with another meaning of the word.

dog days the hot, uncomfortable days in July and August: so called because during that period the Dog Star (Sirius) rises and sets with the sun
dig·it (...) ***n.*** ⟦ME < L *digitus*, a finger, toe, inch < ...⟧ **1** a finger or toe **2** ... **3** any numeral from 0 to 9: so called because originally counted on the fingers

Many words lack etymologies because the parts making up the word are obvious to the user (**undoubted**) or because the definition that follows clearly explains the sources of the word (**bluebottle**).

un·doubt·ed (...) ***adj.*** not doubted, called in question, or disputed; certain
blue·bot·tle (...) ***n.*** **1** any of various plants with blue, bottle-shaped flowers, ...

A question mark (?) either indicates that it is impossible to determine some part of the etymology or marks a reasonable guess or hypothesis about it.

box[2] (...) ***n.*** ⟦ME < ?⟧
mel·a·mine (...) ***n.*** ⟦Ger *melamin* < *melam*, an ammonium thiocyanate distillate < *mel* < ? + *am(monium)*, AMMONIUM + *-in*, -INE[3]⟧
fuzz (...) ***n.*** ⟦< ? Du *voos*, spongy, or back-form. < fol.⟧

VI. DEFINITIONS

A. *The arrangement of meanings*

In general this dictionary arranges the meanings in historical order.

chat[1] (...) ***vi.*** ... ⟦...⟧ **1** to talk or converse in a light, easy, informal manner **2** *Comput.* to hold a real-time electronic conversation by exchanging typed messages ... **—*n.*** **1** small talk; chitchat [a letter filled with *chat* about books] **2** an easy, informal talk or conversation **3** *Comput.* the act or instance of chatting: see CHAT[1] (*vi.* 2) **4** any of various passerine birds with a chattering call ☆**5** any of several songbirds of various families characterized by a chattering song; esp., a yellow-breasted wood warbler (*Icteria virens*) of North America ...
glob·al (...) ***adj.*** **1** round like a ball; globe-shaped **2** of, relating to, or including the whole earth; worldwide **3** complete or comprehensive **4** being or having to do with a business, operation, system, etc. carried on or extending throughout all or much of the world [a *global* company, *global* communications] **5** *Comput.* pertaining to or including an entire file, database, etc. ...
serv·er (...) ***n.*** **1** a person who serves, as a waiter, a player who serves the ball, or an assistant to the celebrant at Mass **2** a thing used in serving, as a tray, cart, etc. **3** *Comput.* within a NETWORK (sense 3*a*), a computer that provides other computers access to shared peripherals, programs, or databases

The order actually starts with the etymology. It may include meanings of a word before modern English times or in the language or languages from which the main entry word derives, such as Latin or Middle French or modern Japanese.

ben·e·fit (...) ***n.*** ⟦ME *benefet* < OFr *bienfait*, a kindness < L *benefactum*, meritorious act < *benefacere*: see BENEFACTION⟧

Next in order may come the original modern English meanings which are now often archaic or obsolete.

1 [Archaic] a kindly, charitable act; benefaction

Finally, the entry contains the most recent meanings still in use. The most common present-day meaning of a word may therefore appear near the end of an entry.

2 *a)* gain or advantage [tax legislation for the *benefit* of the rich] *b)* a favorable or beneficial circumstance, condition, or result [several *benefits* to good nutrition] **3** FRINGE BENEFIT **4** [*often pl.*] payments made by an insurance company, public agency, welfare society, etc. as during sickness, retirement, unemployment, etc. or for death **5** any public performance, bazaar, dance, etc. the proceeds of which are to help a certain person, group, or cause ...

In longer entries it is sometimes more useful to put meanings together in related groups rather than in a strict historical order.

The order of the senses in any given entry should not always be taken as strictly chronological. The exact historical development of the different meanings of a word is often unclear. Several different meanings may have developed at the same time.

B. *How meanings are numbered and grouped together*

Multiple definitions under a part of speech are numbered in order, using boldface numerals. Numbering starts over for each new part of speech and for each idiomatic phrase.

If a primary sense of a word requires subdivision into several closely related meanings, such meanings are indicated by italicized letters following the numbered sense.

cir·cuit (...) ***n.*** ⟦...⟧ **1** ... **2** ... **3** ... **4** *a)* the regular journey of a person performing certain duties, as of an itinerant preacher or a judge holding court at designated places *b)* the district periodically traveled through in the performance of such duties *c)* the route traveled ☆**5** ... **6** *a)* a number of associated theaters at which plays, movies, etc. are shown in turn *b)* a group of nightclubs, resorts, etc. at which entertainers appear in turn ☆*c)* a sequence of contests or matches held at various places, in which a particular group of athletes compete; also, an association or league of athletic teams [the professional bowlers' *circuit*] ...

The abbreviations *esp.* (especially) and *specif.* (specifically) often follow an introductory general definition and introduce one or more related particular meanings.

Use of *esp.* suggests that a particular meaning is more frequently encountered than the general meaning.

coun·ty (...) ***n.***, ***pl.*** **-ties** ⟦...⟧ **1** a small administrative district of a country; esp., ☆*a)* the largest local administrative subdivision of most states of the U.S. *b)* any of the chief administrative districts into which England, Wales, Northern Ireland, and Ireland are divided *c)* an administrative district in certain Canadian provinces *d)* an electoral district in rural New Zealand **2** ...

The use of *specif.* suggests that the particular meaning is less frequently encountered than, or as frequently encountered as, the general meaning.

tar·get (...) *n.* ⟦...⟧ **1** [Historical] a small shield, esp. a round one **2** *a)* a round, flat board, straw coil, etc., often one marked with concentric circles, set up to be aimed at, as in archery or rifle practice *b)* any object that is shot at, thrown at, etc. **3** ... **4** ... **5** ... **6** ... **7** something resembling a target in shape or use; specif., ☆*a)* the sliding sight on a surveyor's leveling rod ☆*b)* a disk-shaped signal on a railroad switch *c)* a metallic insert, usually of tungsten or molybdenum, in the anode of an X-ray tube, upon which the stream of cathode rays impinges and from which X-rays emanate *d)* a surface, object, etc. subjected to irradiation or to bombardment as by nuclear particles *—vt.* ...

If a basic word has a large number of meanings that can conveniently be grouped together under a few major headings, this has been done. The sections, indicated by Roman numerals, are then further subdivided into individual numbered meanings.

time (...) *n.* ⟦...⟧ **I.** *duration; continuance* **1** ... **2** ... **3** ... **II.** *a period or interval* **1** ... **2** ... **3** ... **4** ... **III.** *a point in duration; moment; instant; occasion* **1** ... **2** ... **3** ...

C. *Capitalization*

If a main-entry word is capitalized in all its meanings, the entry word itself is printed with a capital letter.

A·mer·i·ca (...) ⟦...⟧ **1** North America, South America, and the West Indies, considered together: also **the Americas** **2** North America ☆**3** the United States of America

If a capitalized main-entry word has a meaning or meanings that are uncapitalized, they are marked with the corresponding small-boldface, lowercase letter followed by a short dash and enclosed in brackets.

Sat·su·ma (...) *n.* ⟦...⟧ **1** a variety of Japanese pottery ☆**2** [**s-**] a small, loose-skinned variety of orange, grown in Florida and Alabama

If a lowercase main-entry word has a meaning or meanings that are capitalized, they are marked with the corresponding small-boldface, uppercase letter followed by a short dash and enclosed in brackets.

fed·er·al (...) *adj.* ⟦...⟧ **1** of or formed by a compact; specif., designating or of a union of states, groups, etc. in which each member agrees to subordinate its governmental power to that of the central authority in certain specified common affairs **2** ... ☆**3** [**F-**] of or supporting the Federalist Party or its principle of strong centralized government ☆**4** [**F-**] of or pertaining to the style in architecture and furniture based on classical Roman models that flourished in the U.S. from 1780 into the 1830s ... *—n.* ☆**1** [**F-**] a Federalist ☆**2** ...

In usage notes regarding capitalization, a self-explanatory qualifying term such as "usually," "often," "sometimes," "also," or "occas." in italics may be added.

Eng·lish (...) *adj.* ⟦...⟧ ... *—n.* **1** ... **2** the English language of a specific period or place: see AMERICAN ENGLISH, BRITISH ENGLISH, CANADIAN ENGLISH, OLD ENGLISH, MIDDLE ENGLISH, MODERN ENGLISH **3** ... ☆**6** [*sometimes* **e-**] *Billiards, Bowling, etc.* a spinning motion given to a ball, as by striking it on one side **7** ... *—vt.* **1** to translate into English **2** ... ☆**3** [*sometimes* **e-**] *Billiards, Bowling, etc.* to give English to (a ball) ...

D. *Showing the plural form of a noun*

In a singular noun entry, the designation "[*pl.*]" (or "[*often pl.*]," "[*usually pl.*]," etc.) before a definition indicates that it is (or *often, usually*, etc. is) the plural form of the entry word that has the meaning given in the definition.

rush[1] (...) ... *n.* ... **8** [*usually pl.*] *Film* a first print made shortly after the filming of a scene or scenes, for inspection by the director
day (...) *n.* ⟦...⟧ ... **4** [*also pl.*] a period or time; era; age [the best writer of her *day*, in *days* of old]

If such a plural meaning is used as a singular with a singular verb, the additional note "*with sing. v.*" is added inside the brackets.

bone (...) *n.* ⟦...⟧ ... **7** *a)* [*pl.*] flat sticks used as clappers in minstrel shows ☆*b)* [*pl., with sing. v.*] an end man in a minstrel show **8** BONE WHITE ...

The note "*usually used in pl.*" at the end of a singular noun definition indicates that, although the entry word is sometimes used in the singular with the meaning shown in the definition, it is usually used in the plural with that meaning pluralized.

ex·trem·i·ty (...) *n., pl.* **-ties** ⟦...⟧ ... **5** an extreme measure; severe or strong action: *usually used in pl.*
hand·cuff (...) *n.* either of a pair of connected metal rings that can be locked about the wrists, as in restraining a prisoner: *usually used in pl.* ...

If a noun has one or more meanings that apply only to the plural form, the plural form becomes a main entry with the label "*pl.n.*"

goods (...) *pl.n.* **1** movable personal property **2** merchandise; wares **3** fabric; cloth ...

If a noun has a plural form but the meanings are singular, then a "*n.*" label is used.

pho·net·ics (...) *n.* ⟦...⟧ **1** the study of speech sounds, their production and combination, and their representation by written symbols **2** the description and analysis of the sounds of a particular language [the *phonetics* of English]

If a noun has some meanings that take a plural verb and others that take a singular verb, then both a "*pl.n.*" and a "*n.*" label are used in the same entry.

phys·ics (...) *n.* ⟦...⟧ ... **2** *a)* the science dealing with the properties, changes, interactions, etc. of matter and energy in which energy is considered to be continuous ... *b)* a specific system of physics **3** a book or treatise on any of these *—pl.n.* physical properties or processes [the *physics* of flight]

E. *A verb with an accompanying preposition*

In many instances a specific preposition or prepositions follow a particular verb in general use. This dictionary indicates such a condition either by including the preposition in the definition, italicized and usually enclosed in parentheses, or by adding a note after the definition, pointing out the particular prepositions associated with that definition of the verb.

glance[1] (...) *vi.* ... ⟦...⟧ **1** to strike a surface obliquely and go off at an angle: usually with *off* **2** to make an indirect or passing reference: with *over, at*, etc.
leap·frog (...) ... *—vi.* ... **1** to jump in or as if in leapfrog; skip (*over*)
top·ple (...) *vi.* ... **1** to fall (*over*) because or as if top-heavy

This dictionary enters verbal phrases consisting of a verb and an adverb as IDIOMATIC PHRASES under the key verb.

make[1] (...) *vt.* ... **—make out** **1** to see or hear with some difficulty but clearly enough to understand **2** to understand **3** to write out **4** to fill out (as a blank form) ... **—make over** **1** to change; renovate **2** to transfer the ownership of by or as by signing a legal document

F. *Objects of transitive verbs*

In definitions of transitive verbs the specific or generalized objects of the verb, if they are shown, are enclosed in parentheses, since such objects are not part of the definition. A typical object also can be shown in an example.

lace (...) *n.* ⟦...⟧ ... *—vt.* ... **1** to draw the ends of (a garment, shoe, etc.) together and fasten with a lace
mix (...) *vt.* ⟦...⟧ **1** ... **2** to make by putting ingredients together [to *mix* a cocktail]

If a definition is both transitive and intransitive, the object of the transitive verb may be shown in parentheses. To understand the meaning as an intransitive verb, ignore the parentheses and include the object as part of the definition.

copy (...) ... *—vt., vi.* ... 1 to make a copy or copies of (a piece of writing, a computer file, etc.); reproduce; transcribe 2 to make or do something in imitation of (some thing or person); imitate 3 to hear and understand: used as in radio communication 4 [Informal] to provide (someone) with a copy of a specified document, text, etc. *[copy* all staff members with the annual report*]*

G. *Showing additional information and notes*

If a note or comment supplementing or further explaining the definition applies to a single meaning, it is preceded by a colon. If the note applies only to a submeaning, then it is enclosed in parentheses.

e·lect (...) ⟦...⟧ *adj.* ... 2 elected but not yet installed in office: usually used in comb. *[*the mayor-*elect]*
di·ur·nal (...) *adj.* ⟦...⟧ ... 2 of, done, or happening in the daytime: opposed to NOCTURNAL 3 *a)* *Bot.* opening in the daytime and closing at night (said of a flower) *b)* *Zool.* active in the daytime

If the note or comment applies to the whole part of speech, to more than one meaning of a part of speech, or to the entry word itself, it begins with a capital letter and no colon introduces it.

☆**amp**[1] (...) *n. short for:* 1 AMPERE 2 AMPLIFIER *—vt.* [Slang] 1 to increase, augment, enhance, or intensify 2 to excite or arouse Usually with *up*

Often such notes are preceded by the symbol ➥

he[1] (...) *pron.* ... ⟦...⟧ 1 the man, boy, or male animal (or, sometimes, the thing regarded as male) previously mentioned: ... 2 the person; the one; anyone *[he* who laughs last laughs best*]* 3 the person just mentioned: used following such antecedents as *everyone, somebody*, or *no one [*everyone ran just as fast as *he* could*]* ➥ Senses 2 & 3, although used traditionally without distinction as to gender, are now often objected to by many as carrying a masculine implication

Some explanatory notes consist of a series of related items, as in geographical and chemical definitions. Such notes are preceded by a colon and the semicolon is used to separate individual items. Some entries have more than one note, each one introduced by a colon.

ox·y·gen (...) *n.* ⟦...⟧ a colorless, odorless, tasteless, gaseous chemical element that occurs free in the atmosphere, forming one fifth of its volume, and in combination in water, sandstone, limestone, etc.: it is very active, combines with nearly all other elements, is the most common element in the earth's crust, and is essential to life processes and to combustion: symbol, O; at. no. 8: see the periodic table of elements in the Reference Supplement ...
O·hi·o (...) ... 2 ⟦...⟧ Midwestern state of the NC U.S.: admitted 1803; 40,952 sq mi (106,065 sq km); cap. Columbus: abbrev. *OH* or *O*

H. *Illustrative examples*

Examples of usage are enclosed in lightface, slanted italic brackets, with the word that is being illustrated set in italics. These brief illustrative examples, which show how the word is actually used in a phrase or sentence, are helpful in clarifying meaning, separating out individual uses from a large group of meanings for a basic word, showing level of usage or special connotation, and supplying additional information.

hip[3] (...) *interj.* used in cheers *[hip, hip,* hurray!*]*
par·ty (...) *n.* ... ⟦...⟧ ... 2 any group of persons acting together; specif., *a)* a group sent out on a task or mission *[*a surveying *party] b)* a group meeting together socially to accomplish a task *[*a quilting *party]* ... 3 a gathering for social entertainment, or the entertainment itself, often of a specific nature *[*a birthday *party*, cocktail *party]*
chance (...) *n.* ⟦...⟧ ... 6 *[often pl.]* a possibility or probability *[*there is little *chance* of success; what are their *chances* of winning?*]*
raise (...) *vt.* ... ⟦...⟧ ... 6 to improve the position, rank, or situation of *[*to *raise* oneself from poverty*]* ... 8 to cause to come about; provoke; inspire *[*the joke *raised* a laugh*]*

Some words used in special fields, such as mathematics, need examples that give a concrete illustration of what the definition of the word describes. Such examples are introduced by the abbreviation "Ex.:" and are enclosed in parentheses.

pal·in·drome (...) *n.* ⟦...⟧ a word, phrase, or sentence that reads the same backward or forward (Ex.: madam)
binomial theorem the general formula for the expansion of any binomial when raised to a power that is a positive whole number; ... (Ex.: $(a + b)^2 = a^2 + 2ab + b^2$)

I. *Internal entry words*

Entry words occasionally occur within definitions in small boldface type. In such cases, the meaning of the inserted entry word can be determined from the context of the definition.

ci·der (...) *n.* ⟦...⟧ the juice pressed from apples or, formerly, other fruits, used as a beverage or for making vinegar: **hard cider** is fermented and **sweet cider** is not
e·lix·ir (...) *n.* ⟦...⟧ 1 a substance sought by medieval alchemists because it was thought to have the power to change base metals into gold or (in full **elixir of life**) to prolong life indefinitely

J. *Cross-references*

Cross-references to other entries, illustrations, etc. are shown in small capitals.

pulp (...) *n.* ⟦...⟧ ... ☆7 a magazine printed on rough, inferior paper stock made from wood pulp and traditionally characterized by sensational stories of love, crime, etc.: distinguished from SLICK (*n.* 3)
ex·tro·vert (...) *n.* ⟦...⟧ 1 *Psychol.* someone characterized by EXTROVERSION (sense 2) 2 someone characterized by a tendency to be outgoing and socially active Opposed to INTROVERT
de·duc·tion (...) *n.* ⟦...⟧ ... 3 *Logic* the act or process of deducing; reasoning from the general to the specific, or from premises to a logically valid conclusion; also, a conclusion reached by such reasoning: distinguished from INDUCTION
☆**ma·jor·ette** (...) *n. short for* DRUM MAJORETTE
I·a·go (...) *n. see* OTHELLO
den·tin (...) *n.* ⟦< L *dens*, tooth + -INE[3]⟧ the hard, dense, calcareous tissue forming the body of a tooth, under the enamel and surrounding the pulp canal: *see* TOOTH, illus.: ...

Many cross-references are also made to the charts and tables in the back of the book.

baht ... : see the table of monetary units in the Reference Supplement
cal·ci·um ... : see the periodic table of elements in the Reference Supplement
Ju·ras·sic ... : see the geologic time chart in the Reference Supplement
metric system ... : see the table of weights and measures in the Reference Supplement
A·dar ... : see the Jewish calendar in the Reference Supplement
gale[1] ... (see the Beaufort scale in the Reference Supplement)

VII. USAGE LABELS AND NOTES

People use language in different ways depending on, for example, where they grew up, how old they are, how much education they have, and what kind of work they do. Also, each person uses language differently from hour to hour and from day to day, depending on the situation in which that person uses the words or the purpose for which they are used.

The language a scientist uses in writing a report is probably quite different from that which he or she uses in writing a thank-you letter to a friend. What is good usage in a formal literary essay would sound rather stiff and inappropriate in a lunch-table conversation.

A usage label shows that a word or meaning is normally used only in a certain kind of situation, that it is no longer used at all, or that its use is limited in some other way. All usage labels appear within brackets.

A. *Location of usage labels*

If a usage label applies to a single meaning, it appears directly after the number or letter (for a subsense) that introduces the meaning.

dan·dy (...) *n.* ... 1 ... 2 ... 3 [Informal] something very good or first-rate —*adj.* ... 1 [Rare] of or for a dandy; foppish ☆2 [Informal] very good; first-rate ...

If a label applies to all of the meanings for a whole part of speech, it appears just after the part-of-speech abbreviation.

☆**left·y** (...) *n.* ... [Slang] 1 a left-handed person 2 LEFTIST

If the label applies to the whole entry, it appears before the first part-of-speech abbreviation.

☆**stash** (...) [Informal] *vt.* ... —*n.* 1 ... 2 ...

B. *Usage labels common to this dictionary*

Informal: The word or meaning is widely used in everyday talk, personal letters, etc., but not in formal speaking or writing.

Slang: The word or meaning is not generally considered standard usage but is used, even by the best speakers and writers, in very informal situations or for creating special effects. People belonging to a certain group, such as teenagers or jazz musicians, often use a particular group of slang terms.

Old Informal, Old Slang: The word or meaning was informal or slang when actively used in the not-so-distant past and is no longer used much today.

Obs.: The word or meaning is no longer used at all, although it may be found in very old writings.

Archaic: The word or meaning is not used in ordinary speech or writing today, but still may be found in certain special situations such as some religious readings, in highly formal writing, and in older books.

Old-fashioned: The word or meaning is not yet archaic, but does have an old-fashioned flavor and is most often used by older people for something that younger people may have another term for.

Rare: The word or meaning has never been used much.

Now Rare: The word or meaning is not used much today, but was common once.

Historical: The word or meaning refers to something, such as an object or institution, that no longer exists and for which there is not a more modern equivalent term.

Old Poet.: The word or meaning was often used in the past, especially in poetry, but today is used only in certain kinds of traditional or somewhat old-fashioned verse.

Literary: The word or meaning is regarded as having an elevated, polished, highly formal quality. Unlike a word or meaning labeled *Old Poet.*, it is not thought to be about to pass out of use.

Dial.: The word or meaning is used commonly only in certan geographical areas. When a word or meaning is used chiefly or only in some specific area of the U.S., a more specific label, such as *South, Northeast*, or *Southwest*, is used.

Brit.: The word or meaning is used chiefly in Great Britain and also, usually, in the other English-speaking regions of the world outside the U.S.

Cdn. (or *Irish, Austral.*, etc.): The word or meaning is used chiefly in Canada (or Ireland, Australia, etc.).

Vulgar: The word or meaning is regarded by many people as being indecent or extremely coarse and hence unsuitable for use in many social situations.

C. *Other ways of showing usage information*

Often this dictionary supplies information about usage in a short note after a definition or entry. Such a note might indicate that a word or meaning is used to insult or belittle the members of some group or is often used in an ironic or humorous way.

speech·i·fy (...) *vi.* ... to make a speech: used humorously or contemptuously

A note also might indicate that there may be some objection to a common usage.

in·fer (...) *vt.* ... 3 to indicate indirectly; imply: in this sense, still regarded as a loose usage by many

This dictionary also contains a number of longer usage notes in the form of separate paragraphs placed at the end of entries and introduced by the word ***USAGE***.

can[1] (...) *v.aux.* ...
USAGE—traditional grammar makes a clear distinction between **can** (for ability) and **may** (for permission), the classic example being the retort, "Yes, you *can* go, but you *may* not"; in everyday speech and writing, however, **can** is generally accepted for both meanings, with **may** being used only when the notion of permission is important to the sense of an utterance and there is a possibility of ambiguity

VIII. FIELD LABELS

This dictionary uses a variety of italicized labels for technical or highly specialized meanings. When there are a number of labeled senses, those with field labels are generally placed after those with bracketed labels.

pouch (...) *n.* ⟦...⟧ 1 a small bag or sack for carrying something, as in one's pocket *[a leather tobacco pouch]* ☆2 a mailbag, specif. one whose opening can be locked, as for sending diplomatic dispatches 3 [Scot.] a pocket (in clothing) 4 [Archaic] a purse 5 *Anat.* any pouchlike cavity or part 6 *Zool. a)* MARSUPIUM (sense 1) *b)* a baglike part, as of a pelican's bill or a gopher's cheeks, used to carry food

Several such labeled meanings within a single entry block are usually grouped together at the end of a part of speech, arranged alphabetically by label.

run (...) *vi.* ... —*vt.* ... 23 *Billiards* ... 24 *Bridge* ... 25 *Comput.* ... 26 *Golf* ... —*n.* ... ☆21 *Baseball* ... 22 *Billiards* ... 23 *Cricket* ... 26 *Music* ... 27 *Naut.* ...

IX. BIOLOGICAL NAMES

Biologists assign a unique Modern Latin or Latinized name to every type of organism, as an animal or plant, every bacterium, etc. The scientific name is not generally a main entry in this dictionary, but it does appear typically in the definition (within parentheses) of the organism's common name, conforming to the standard international rules of taxonomy for typeface and capitalization. For example, the biological scientific name for the domestic dog is *Canis familiaris*. This two-word, or binomial, name fits into the standard classification system as shown below:

kingdom	Animalia	animal
phylum	Chordata	chordate
subphylum	Vertebrata	vertebrate
class	Mammalia	mammal
order	Carnivora	carnivore
family	Canidae	canine
genus + species	*Canis familiaris*	dog

This dictionary makes it easy to trace the taxonomic lineage of any animal, plant, etc. by simply linking the biological scientific names in related entries. For example, the entry for *dog* links to *canine*, which links to the entry for *carnivore*, and so on. By continuing to follow these links, *dog* to *canine* to *carnivore* to *mammal* to *vertebrate* to *chordate* to *animal*, the complete taxonomic profile takes shape.

dog (...) *n.* ... 1 *a*) any of a large and varied group of domesticated canines (*Canis familiaris*) often kept as a house pet or used for hunting, guarding people or property, etc.
ca·nine (...) *adj.* ... 2 of the family (Canidae) of carnivores that includes dogs, wolves, jackals, and foxes
car·ni·vore (...) *n.* ... 1 any of an order (Carnivora) of fanged, flesh-eating mammals, including the dog, bear, cat, and seal
mam·mal (...) *n.* ... any of a large class (Mammalia) of warm blooded, usually hairy vertebrates whose offspring are fed with milk secreted by the female mammary glands
ver·te·brate (...) ... *—n.* any of a large subphylum (Vertebrata) of chordate animals, including all mammals, fishes, birds, reptiles, and amphibians, characterized by a brain enclosed in a cranium and a segmented spinal column
chor·date (...) *n.* ... any of a phylum (Chordata) of animals having at some stage of development a notochord, gill slits, and a dorsal tubular nerve cord: the phylum includes the vertebrates, tunicates, and lancelets
an·i·mal (...) *n.* ... 1 any of a kingdom (Animalia) of eukaryotes generally characterized by a multicellular body, the ability to move quickly and obtain food, specialized sense organs, and sexual reproduction

Organisms that are subspecies have three-word, or *trinomial*, names.

red grouse a reddish-brown ptarmigan (*Lagopus lagopus scotica*) of the British Isles that does not turn white in winter

Plants that are cultivated varieties also have trinomial names but include an abbreviation for "variety" in roman type.

broc·co·li (...) *n.* ⟦...⟧ 1 a plant (*Brassica oleracea* var. *italica*) of the crucifer family, related to the cauliflower ...

A genus name is abbreviated when it is used more than once in a definition.

lap·wing (...) *n.* ... any of a genus (*Vanellus*) of black-and-white plovers; esp., an Old World crested species (*V. vanellus*) with broad, rounded wings, noted for spectacular aerial displays

X. IDIOMATIC PHRASES

An idiomatic phrase is a phrase that has a meaning that is different from the combination of the usual or literal meanings of the individual words that make up that phrase.

A. *Placement of idiomatic phrases within the entry block*

Idiomatic phrases are listed under the key word of the phrase. The key word is generally the most distinctive or important word of the phrase.

through the mill is listed under **mill**
hard and fast is listed under **hard**
call names is listed under **name**

Idiomatic phrases are located at or near the end of the entry block, after the definitions of all the parts of speech. A long dash comes before each idiomatic phrase. Phrases are entered in alphabetical order.

busi·ness (...) *n.* ⟦...⟧ 1 one's work, occupation, or profession 2 ... *—adj.* 1 of or for business 2 ... **—do business with** ... **—☆give** (or **get**) **the business** ... **—mean business** ...

B. *Alternative forms of idiomatic phrases*

Various uses of parentheses indicate alternative forms of idiomatic phrases.

In the phrase **(at) full tilt** under the entry for **tilt**, the parentheses indicate that the two-word phrase **full tilt** and the longer phrase **at full tilt** have the same meaning, "at full speed."

tilt[1] (...) ... **—(at) full tilt** at full speed or with the greatest force or energy

In the phrase **lay** (or **set** or **clap**) **eyes on** under the entry for **eye**, the parentheses indicate that **lay eyes on**, **set eyes on**, and **clap eyes on** all have the same meaning.

eye (...) *n.* ... **—lay** (or **set** or **clap**) **eyes on** to see; look at

In the phrase **break** (or **keep**) **faith** under the entry for **faith**, there are parentheses both in the idiomatic phrase and in the definitions of that phrase.

faith (...) *n.* ... **—break** (or **keep**) **faith** 1 to be disloyal (or loyal) to one's beliefs, principles, etc. ...

This arrangement indicates that **break faith** and **keep faith** have different meanings. In order to understand the meaning of the alternative phrase **keep faith**, the dictionary user must substitute the alternative parenthetical word "loyal" for "disloyal" when reading the definition.

XI. RUN-IN DERIVED FORMS

It is possible in English to create an almost infinite number of derived forms simply by adding certain prefixes or suffixes to the base word.

This dictionary includes as run-in entries in boldface type only those derived words one might reasonably expect to encounter in literature or ordinary usage. Such an entry is included when its meaning can be readily understood from the meaning of the base word plus the meaning of the suffix.

great ... **—great′ly** *adv.* **—great′ness** *n.*
live·ly ... **—live′li·ness** *n.*
new ... **—new′ness** *n.*

Here, one must combine the meaning of the base word (**great**, **lively**, or **new**) and the meaning of the suffix **-ness** (which is found as a separate entry in this dictionary and means "state, quality, or instance of being").

Many words formed with common suffixes such as *-able*, *-er*, *-less*, *-like*, *-ly*, *-tion*, etc. are similarly run in at the end of the entry for the base word from which they are derived.

All run-in derived forms are syllabified and either accented to show stress in pronunciation or, where necessary, pronounced in full or in part. A dash precedes each run-in derived form.

im·ag·ism (...) *n.* ... **—im′ag·ist** *n., adj.* **—im′ag·is′tic** *adj.*

If two synonymous run-in derived forms share a part-of-speech label, the more frequently used form appears first and the part-of-speech label is given after the first form.

change·a·ble (...) *adj.* ... **—change′a·bil′i·ty** *n.*, **change′a·ble·ness**

When a derived word has a meaning or meanings different from those which can be deduced from the sum of its parts, it has been entered separately, pronounced, and fully defined (e.g., **producer**).

XII. THE SYNONYMY

Synonyms are words that are closely related in meaning. However it is unwise to substitute one synonym for another automatically or unthinkingly. There are small, often subtle differences between synonyms. A person who wants to write and speak clearly and precisely must understand these differences.

A. *Parts of a synonymy*

This dictionary includes many short, offset paragraphs containing a list of synonyms together with explanations pointing out the differences between them. Such a paragraph is called a synonymy.

laugh (...) *vi.* ⟦...⟧ **1** to make the explosive sounds of the voice, and the characteristic movements of the features and body, that express mirth, amusement, ridicule, etc. ... —*n.* **1** the act or sound of laughing ...

SYN.—**laugh** is the general word for the sounds or exhalation made in expressing mirth, amusement, etc.; **chuckle** implies soft laughter in low tones, expressive of mild amusement or inward satisfaction; **giggle** and **titter** both refer to a half-suppressed laugh consisting of a series of rapid, high-pitched sounds, suggesting embarrassment, silliness, etc., but **titter** is also used of a laugh of mild amusement suppressed in affected politeness; **snicker** is used of a sly, half-suppressed laugh, as at another's discomfiture or a bawdy story; **guffaw** refers to loud, coarse laughter

The abbreviation **SYN.** introduces each synonymy.

In each synonymy there is a word considered to be the most basic or inclusive. The synonymy builds on that word and is located within the entry for that word.

B. *Cross-references to a synonymy*

Generally, each synonym in the synonymy paragraph has its own main entry in this dictionary. At each of these main entries there is a cross-reference to the synonymy. For example, at the end of the entry for **guffaw**, there is a note:

—**SYN.** LAUGH

Sometimes the basic word in one synonymy also appears, with a different meaning, in another synonymy. When this occurs a cross-reference is placed at the end of the first synonymy rather than in the entry block of the basic word that precedes it.

For example, at the end of the synonymy at **acute**, there is a note "See also **sharp**." This note refers the user to the synonymy at **sharp**, where another meaning of **acute** is compared to related synonyms.

The abbreviation ***ANT.*** at the end of a synonymy introduces antonyms listed in boldface. At the end of the synonymy at **cruel**, there is a note **—*ANT.* humane, kind** indicating that "humane" and "kind" are antonyms of "cruel" and that additional antonyms may be found at the entries for **humane** and **kind**.

XIII. THE REFERENCE SUPPLEMENT

The Reference Supplement in the back of the dictionary contains additional useful information. Much of the information there is statistical or technical data presented in tables or charts.

These tables and charts supply such information as the atomic weights of chemical elements, standard weights and measures and their metric equivalents, the dates of geologic time periods, and major calendar systems.

For a complete listing of the types of information available in the Reference Supplement see the Contents page in the front of the book.

Many entries in the dictionary contain cross-references to the information in the Reference Supplement.

bo·ron (...) *n.* ⟦...⟧ a nonmetallic chemical element ...: symbol, B; at. no. 5: see the periodic table of elements in the Reference Supplement
Ju·ras·sic (...) *adj.* ... **—the Jurassic** the Jurassic Period or its rocks: see the geologic time chart in the Reference Supplement

GUIDE TO PRONUNCIATION

This dictionary shows pronunciations of words as they are spoken carefully and individually. It does not give pronunciations of words in running speech, where much variation occurs.

The pronunciations in this dictionary reflect spoken American English in the variety most widely used throughout the United States. Regional and local American English pronunciations are included as well as British English and foreign pronunciations wherever necessary or appropriate.

The International Phonetic Alphabet (IPA), a highly specialized and complex system of phonetic symbols employed by linguists, has not been used in this book. Instead, the pronunciation symbols in *Webster's New World* dictionaries are of the type that have been in American dictionaries for many years.

I. GENERAL STYLE

Pronunciations are given inside parentheses, immediately after a boldface entry.

mil·len·ni·um (mi len′ē əm) ...

Pronunciations are divided into syllables to help the dictionary user. Syllable division is based on phonetic principles and does not necessarily correspond to how words are divided (see GUIDE TO THE DICTIONARY II, *I: Word division*).

Pronunciations are not supplied for most open compounds.

natural childbirth childbirth involving ...

The entry **natural childbirth** does not have a pronunciation, since the words that make it up, **natural** and **childbirth**, are already pronounced at their own entries. Pronunciations are shown for words in open compounds when they are not supplied elsewhere.

non·stri·at·ed muscle (nän′strī′āt′id) SMOOTH MUSCLE

Occasionally, pronunciations are shown for open compounds because they have stress patterns that are not typical.

More than one pronunciation may be shown. Each variant pronunciation may be thought of as being widely used in American speech unless a note adds qualifications. These notes, such as *occas.*, *chiefly Brit*, and *now rare*, indicate that a particular variant pronunciation does not occur regularly in American English.

This dictionary often abbreviates pronunciations so that only the changed part of a particular pronunciation is shown.

Hyphens are used to indicate which part of the pronunciation is unchanged.

A hyphen before a shortened pronunciation indicates that the change occurs in the last part of the word.

ben·e·fi·ci·ar·y (ben′ə fish′ē er′ ē, -fish′ər ē)

A hyphen after a shortened pronunciation indicates that the change occurs in the first part of the word.

ec·o·nom·ic (ek′ə näm′ik, ē′kə-)

Hyphens before and after a shortened pronunciation indicate that the change occurs within the word.

ri·bo·nu·cle·ase (rī′bō no͞o′klē ās′, -nyo͞o′-)

Various methods of shortening may be used within a single pronunciation.

re·du·pli·cate (ri do͞o′plə kāt′, -dyo͞o′-; *for adj. & n., usually,* -kit)

Shortened pronunciations are also shown for inflected forms and run-in derived forms. This kind of shortening requires the user to look back to the pronunciation of a main entry at which a full pronunciation is shown.

a·lum·nus (ə lum′nəs) *n., pl.* **-ni** (-nī′)
fru·gal (fro͞o′gəl) *adj.* 1 ... 2 ... —**fru·gal′i·ty** (-gal′ə tē)

Shortened pronunciations are shown for a series of main entries in which all the entries share a common element. Full pronunciation is given at the first entry in the sequence.

fire·arm (fīr′ärm′)
fire·ball (-bôl′)
fire·ball·er (-bôl′ər)
☆**fire·base** (-bās′)

II. STRESS MARKS

Individual syllables are spoken with varying amounts of force. Stress marks are used to indicate the relative force with which a given syllable is spoken.

A heavy mark [′], called a PRIMARY STRESS, is placed after the syllable spoken with the most force. A light mark [′], called a SECONDARY STRESS, is placed after a syllable spoken with less force.

Syllables receiving little or no force, called UNSTRESSED SYLLABLES, are shown with no markings.

dic·tion·ar·y (dik′shə ner′ē)

In the example above, the first syllable receives the greatest, or primary, stress; the third syllable receives slightly less, or secondary, stress; and the second and fourth syllables are unstressed.

III. PRONUNCIATION SYMBOLS USED

The best way to learn how to read the pronunciations is by looking at the PRONUNCIATION KEY shown below.

The Pronunciation Key lists the pronunciation symbols used in this dictionary along with several KEY WORDS. Key words are short, familiar words that illustrate each of the various sounds represented by the symbols.

Note that most of the pronunciation symbols are letters of the alphabet. These symbols represent the usual sounds associated with these letters. Thus, the symbol [b] represents the sound of *b* in *bed*, [d] the sound of *d* in *dog*, [k] the sound of *k* in *kiss* or of *c* in *cot*, etc.

A. *Pronunciation Key for American English sounds*

Symbol	Key Word	IPA Symbol
Vowel Sounds		
a	at, cap, parrot	æ
ā	ape, play, sail	eɪ
ä	cot, father, heart	ɑ
e	ten, wealth, merry	ɛ
ē	even, feet, money	i
i	is, stick, mirror	ɪ
ī	ice, high, sky	aɪ
ō	go, open, tone	oʊ
ô	all, law, horn	ɔ
o͝o	could, look, pull	ʊ
yo͝o	cure, furious, globule, your	jʊ
o͞o	boot, crew, tune	u
yo͞o	cute, few, use	ju
oi	boy, oil, royal	ɔɪ
ou	cow, out, sour	aʊ
u	mud, ton, blood, trouble	ʌ
ʉr	her, sir, word	ɝ
ə	ago, agent, collect, focus	ə
Consonant Sounds		
b	bed, table, rob	b
d	dog, middle, sad	d
f	for, phone, cough	f
g	get, wiggle, dog	g
h	hat, hope, ahead	h
hw	which, white	hw
j	joy, badge, agent	dʒ
k	kill, cat, quiet	k
l	let, yellow, ball	l
′l	cattle, paddle	l̩
m	meet, number, time	m
n	net, candle, ton	n
′n	sudden, sweeten	n̩
p	put, sample, escape	p
r	red, wrong, born	ɹ
s	sit, castle, office	s
t	top, letter, cat	t
v	voice, every, love	v
w	wet, always, quart	w
y	yes, canyon, onion	j
z	zoo, misery, rise	z
ch	chew, nature, punch	tʃ
sh	shell, machine, bush	ʃ
th	thin, nothing, truth	θ
th	then, other, bathe	ð
zh	beige, measure, seizure	ʒ
ŋ	ring, anger, drink	ŋ

B. *Explanation of certain English sounds*

ŋ represents the sound of *ng* in *long* and *sing*, and of *n* in *drink* and *sunk*.

th and *th* the first symbol represents the sound of *th* in *thin* and *ether*; the second in *then* and *other*. The first sound is unvoiced, or made without vibrating the vocal cords. The second, a voiced sound, is made with vibration of the vocal cords.

w represents a sound that has characteristics of both a consonant and a vowel. It is the initial consonant sound in the words *wet* and *wait*. It is also the sound represented by the vowel *u* in words such as *quick* (kwik) and *Kuala Lumpur* (kwä′lə lo͝om po͝or′). The sound is voiced.

hw Many American speakers do not make a distinction between *witch* and *which*, pronouncing both (wich). A large number of speakers do make a distinction, pronouncing the latter word (hwich). The sound of [hw] is spoken with a slightly increased outflow of breath, such as occurs when saying [h]. Both [w] and [hw] are shown wherever this variation occurs.

y Like [w], this symbol represents a sound that has characteristics of both a consonant and a vowel. It is the initial consonant sound in the words *yet* and *you*. It represents a vowel sound in words such as *canyon* (kan′yən) and *onion* (un′yən). The symbol is also combined with the vowel symbols [ŏŏ] and [ōō] in order to represent the vowel sound in words such as *pure* (pyŏŏr) and *cute* (kyōōt).

ʉ represents the sound of *u* in *fur*, *o* in *word*, and *i* in *third*. This sound is nearly always followed by [r] in American English. The vowel occurs without a following [r] in certain foreign pronunciations.

ə the schwa represents the sound of *a* in *ago*, *e* in *agent* and *murder*, *o* in *collect*, and *u* in *focus*. The sound is often indistinct and occurs only in unstressed syllables.

ʼ the apostrophe represents a schwa-like sound so shortened that it may seem to be hardly present at all. The consonant that follows the apostrophe, usually *l* or *n*, is sometimes called a syllabic consonant because it appears to form a syllable having no vowel sound. Syllables made up of or containing a syllabic consonant are always unstressed. The apostrophe is used in the pronunciation of words like *cattle* (kat′ʼl) and *sudden* (sud′ʼn).

C. Pronunciation Key for foreign sounds

ȧ used in French pronunciations. It represents a sound in between [a], as in *cat*, and [ä], as in *cot*. The arching of the tongue to form this vowel occurs at a point between the front and back of the mouth.

ë used in French pronunciations. The sound is made by rounding the lips as though to say *oh* while pronouncing the sound [e], as in *get*.

ö used chiefly in French and German pronunciations. The sound is made by rounding the lips as though to say *oh* while pronouncing the sound [ā], as in *ate*.

ô represents a range of sounds between [ô] and [u] from a variety of languages, including French, German, Spanish, and Italian. The sound may be approximated by rounding the lips loosely as for [ô] and pronouncing [u], as in *cut*.

ü represents variously the vowel sound in the French word *duc* and the German word *grün*. Make the sound by rounding the lips as for saying [ô] and pronouncing [ē].

kh represents variously the final consonant sound of the German *doch* and the Scots English *loch*. Make the sound by saying [k] while allowing the breath to escape in a stream, as in saying [h].

H represents the consonant sound of the German word *ich*. Make the sound by pronouncing [sh] while keeping the tip of the tongue pointed downward.

n indicates that the vowel sound preceding it is voiced with air expelled through both the mouth cavity and nasal passage. It is a nasalized vowel. Note that this symbol does not represent the sound of the consonant [n]. For example, the sound occurs in the pronunciations of French words, such as *bonjour* (bōn zhōōr′).

r represents the sound of *r* as it occurs in a variety of languages. The sound is sometimes made with a vibrating, or trilling, of the tip of the tongue, as in Italian and Russian, or with a trilling of the uvula, as in French and German.

ʼ the apostrophe has two functions in the pronunciation of French words. It is used to indicate that a final consonant *l*, as in *fille* (fē′yʼ), or *r*, as in *lettre* (le′trʼ), is spoken with a short, voiceless sound. In the case of *fille*, the [l] is so shortened as to be more like a voiceless [y]. The apostrophe is also used to indicate that a letter *e* is silent or nearly so, as in *dirigisme* (dē rē zhēs′mʼ) or *table* (tȧ′blʼ). In running French speech, certain of these "silent" letters may be given fuller sounding. Note that in the case of *table*, unlike that of *fille*, the consonant *l* is voiced.

yʼ used in the pronunciations of certain Russian words, such as *Sevastopol* (se′väs tô′pəl yʼ). The symbol indicates that the final consonant of the word is pronounced with the blade of the tongue (the flat part just behind the tip) raised toward the hard palate. It is a palatalized sound. The sound is made by pronouncing an unvoiced [y] immediately after pronouncing the consonant.

IV. FOREIGN PRONUNCIATIONS

Foreign pronunciations should be thought of as approximations. Each language has its own particular ways of making speech sounds. In addition, each language has its own dialects. The French spoken in Paris differs from that spoken in Montreal. The Spanish of Madrid is not the Spanish of Mexico City. The Italian spoken in Milan will differ in significant ways from the Italian spoken in Naples.

Foreign words used in speech and writing often work their way into a language over time. This process is called assimilation. Assimiliation, unfortunately, does not operate on a timetable. Some foreign words turn up in English speech and writing for decades and always remain essentially foreign. Other foreign words become assimilated in a relatively short time. It might seem obvious to suggest that a French culinary term might have a far shorter pathway to assimilation into English than a French philosophical term. Yet, certain French philosophical terms have entered the English language while many French culinary terms have not. The editors of this dictionary have attempted to judge the degree of assimilation of foreign entries as accurately as possible, given the difficulties involved. See also the Pronunciation Key for foreign sounds (above).

V. BRITISH PRONUNCIATIONS

British pronunciations are sometimes shown in addition to those of American English. These British pronunciations are based upon the educated form of British English known as Received Pronunciation (RP), the form traditionally used by most newsreaders at the BBC.

The British pronunciation shows the main ways in which the British form differs from the American. Certain subtle differences in vowel quality are not shown. The British practice of eliminating or reducing the sound of *r*, as at the ends of syllables, is also not shown.

A

a[1] or **A** (ā) ***n., pl.*** **a's, A's** **1** the first letter of the English alphabet: from the Greek *alpha*, a borrowing from the Phoenician **2** any of the speech sounds that this letter represents, as, in English, the vowel (a) of *hat*, (ä) of *father*, (ā) of *bake*, or (ô) of *call* **3** a type or impression for *a* or A **4** the first in a sequence or group **5** an object shaped like A —***adj.*** **1** of *a* or A **2** first in a sequence or group **3** shaped like A —**from A to Z** from beginning to end; completely; exhaustively

a[2] (ə; *stressed*, ā) ***adj., indefinite article*** ⟦form of *an* before consonants: see AN[1], *adj.*⟧ **1** one; one sort of [we planted *a* tree] **2** each; any one [*a* gun is dangerous]: *a* connotes a thing not previously noted or recognized, in contrast with *the*, which connotes a thing previously noted or recognized —***prep.*** ⟦< OE *an, on*, in, on, at⟧ to each; in each; for each; per [once *a* day] ***USAGE***—Before words beginning with a consonant sound or a sounded *h*, *a* is used [*a* child, *a* home, *a* uniform, *a* eunuch]; before words beginning with a vowel sound or a silent *h*, *an* is used [*an* ultimatum, *an* honor]. See also AN[1]

a[3] or **a'** (ô, ä) ***adj.*** [Scot.] all

a[4] *abbrev.* **1** about **2** absent **3** *Physics* acceleration **4** active **5** adjective **6** adult **7** alto **8** ⟦L *ante meridiem*⟧ AM[2] [7:00 *a*] **9** anonymous **10** answer **11** are (unit of area) **12** atto-

A[1] (ā) ***n.*** **1** a blood type: see ABO SYSTEM ☆**2** *Educ.* a grade indicating excellence [an A in history] **3** *Music* *a)* the sixth tone or note in the ascending scale of C major *b)* a key, string, etc. producing this tone *c)* the scale having this tone as the keynote —***adj.*** first-class; A 1: see A ONE

A[2] *abbrev.* **1** *Physics* absolute **2** adenine **3** America(n) **4** ampere **5** analog **6** angstrom: also **Å** **7** anode **8** answer **9** April **10** [Archaic] *Chem.* argon **11** *Baseball, Basketball, Hockey* assist(s) **12** attendance **13** August

a-[1] (ə) ⟦weakened form of OE *an, on*, in, ON⟧ *prefix* **1** in, into, on, at, to [*ashore, abed*] **2** in the act or state of [*asleep, a*-crying, *a*-wishing]

a-[2] (ə; *for 3* ā) *prefix* **1** ⟦OE *a-*, out of, up⟧ up, out: now generally used as an intensive [*awake, arise*] **2** ⟦OE *of-, af-*⟧ off, of [*akin*] **3** ⟦Gr *a-, an-*, not⟧ not, without: it becomes *an-* before a vowel [*amoral, atypical*] **4** AB-: used before *m, p*, or *v* [*avert*] **5** AD-: used before *sc, sp*, or *st* [*ascribe*]

☆**a·a** (ä'ä') ***n.*** ⟦Haw *'a'ā*⟧ a type of basaltic rock, usually dark-colored with a jagged surface, formed in large sheets from slow-moving lava: cf. PAHOEHOE

AA *abbrev.* **1** *trademark* Alcoholics Anonymous **2** antiaircraft **3** Associate in (or of) Arts

AAA (trip'əl ā') *trademark* American Automobile Association

AAAL *abbrev.* American Academy of Arts and Letters

AAAS *abbrev.* American Association for the Advancement of Science

Aa·chen (ä'kən; *Ger* ä'khən) city in North Rhine-Westphalia, W Germany, on the Belgian border: Fr. name AIX-LA-CHAPELLE

AADHD *abbrev.* adult attention deficit hyperactivity disorder

aah (ä) ***interj.*** used to express surprise, delight, etc. —***vi.*** to exclaim with surprise, delight, etc. [they oohed and *aahed* at the baby]

Aal·borg (ôl'bôrg', -bôr') *alt. sp. of* ÅLBORG

Aal·to (äl'tô'), **(Hugo) Al·var (Henrik)** (äl'vär') 1898-1976; Finn. architect & furniture designer

AAM *abbrev.* air-to-air missile

A & R *abbrev.* Artist(s) and Repertoire: with reference to those officials of commercial recording companies who select the performers and supervise the production of recordings

Aar (är) *var. of* AARE

aard·vark (ärd'värk') ***n.*** ⟦obs. Afrik, earth pig < Du *aarde*, EARTH + *vark*, pig: for IE base see FARROW[1]⟧ a large, burrowing, nocturnal S African mammal (*Orycteropus afer*, order Tubulidentata) that feeds on ants and termites: it is squat and heavy with a long, sticky tongue and a long head ending in a round, piglike snout

aard·wolf (ärd'woolf') ***n., pl.*** **-wolves'** (-woolvz') ⟦Afrik, earth wolf⟧ a nocturnal S African carnivore (*Proteles cristatus*) of the same family as the hyena, that feeds chiefly on termites and insect larvae

Aa·re (ä'rə) river in central and N Switzerland, flowing into the Rhine: *c.* 180 mi (290 km)

Aar·gau (är'gou') canton of N Switzerland: 542 sq mi (1,404 sq km)

aargh (är: *conventionalized pronun.*) ***interj.*** ⟦echoic⟧ used to express disgust, nausea, or any other forceful negative reaction: also sp. **aarrgh** or **aarrghh**

Aar·hus (ôr'hoos') *alt. sp. of* ÅRHUS

Aar·on (er'ən, ar'-) ***n.*** ⟦LL < Gr *Aarōn* < Heb *aharon*, lit., the exalted one⟧ **1** a masculine name **2** *Bible* the older brother of Moses and first high priest of the Hebrews: Ex. 4, 40:13-16

Aa·ron·ic (er än'ik, ar-) ***adj.*** **1** of or characteristic of Aaron **2** Levitical ☆**3** *Mormon Ch.* designating or of the second, and lesser, order of priests: cf. MELCHIZEDEK

AARP (*often* ärp) *abbrev.* American Association of Retired Persons

AAU *abbrev.* Amateur Athletic Union

AAUP *abbrev.* American Association of University Professors

AAUW *abbrev.* American Association of University Women

ab (ab) ***adj.*** ⟦< the n., sing. of ABS[1]⟧ of or having to do with the abdominal muscles [a tough *ab* workout]

Ab (äb; *Heb* äv) ***n.*** ⟦Heb⟧ the eleventh month of the Jewish year: see the Jewish calendar in the Reference Supplement

AB[1] (ā'bē') ***n.*** a blood type: see ABO SYSTEM

AB[2] *abbrev.* **1** airman basic **2** Alberta (Canada) **3** *Baseball* (times) at bat: also **ab** **4** ⟦ModL *Artium Baccalaureus*⟧ Bachelor of Arts: also **A.B.**

ab- (ab, əb) ⟦L⟧ *prefix* away, from, from off, down [*abdicate*]: it becomes *a-* before *m, p*, or *v* and often *abs-* before *c* or *t*

a·ba (ä'bə, ə bä') ***n.*** ⟦Ar *'abā'*, cloak-like woolen wrap⟧ **1** a coarse fabric of wool or hair fiber with a felted finish **2** a loose, sleeveless robe worn by Arabs

ABA *abbrev.* **1** American Bar Association **2** American Booksellers Association

ab·a·cá (ab'ə kä', ä'bə-) ***n.*** ⟦Tagalog⟧ MANILA HEMP

a·back (ə bak') ***adv.*** ⟦OE *on bæc*, at or on the back⟧ **1** [Archaic] backward; back **2** *Naut.* backward against the mast, as the sails of a square-rigged vessel in a wind from straight ahead —**taken aback** **1** *Naut.* in an unmanageable condition, as because of a sudden shift of wind to the opposite side of the sails **2** startled and confused

ab·a·cus (ab'ə kəs; *occas.* ə bak'əs) ***n., pl.*** **ab'a·cus·es** or **ab'a·ci'** (-sī') ⟦L < Gr *abax* (gen. *abakos*), counting board, slab⟧ **1** a frame with beads or balls that can be slid on wires or in slots, for doing or teaching arithmetic **2** *Archit.* a slab forming the uppermost part of the capital of a column

abacus

A·ba·dán (ä'bə dän', ab'ə dan') **1** island in the Shatt-al-Arab, SW Iran: 42 mi (68 km) long **2** city on this island: an oil-refining center

A·bad·don (ə bad''n) ***n.*** ⟦Heb, destruction, abyss⟧ *Bible* **1** the place of the dead; nether world: Job 26:6 **2** in *Revelation*, the angel of the abyss; Apollyon: Rev. 9:11

a·baft (ə baft') ***adv.*** ⟦ME *o baft* < OE *on*, ON + *bæftan* < *be*, BY + *æftan*, AFT[1]⟧ at or toward the stern or rear of a ship; aft —***prep.*** *Naut.* to the rear of; behind [located just *abaft* the bridge]

☆**ab·a·lo·ne** (ab'ə lō'nē) ***n.*** ⟦Calif. MexSp *aulón* < Costanoan (a Penutian language) *aulun*⟧ any of a family (Haliotidae) of edible gastropod sea mollusks with an oval, somewhat spiral shell perforated near the edge and lined with mother-of-pearl

a·ban·don (ə ban'dən) ***vt.*** ⟦ME *abandonen* < OFr *abandoner* < *mettre a bandon*, to put under (someone else's) ban, relinquish: see BAN[1]⟧ **1** to give up (something) completely or forever [to *abandon* all hope] **2** to leave, as in danger or out of necessity; forsake; desert **3** to yield (oneself) completely, as to a feeling, desire, etc. —***n.*** unrestrained freedom of action or emotion; surrender to one's impulses [to shout in wild *abandon*] —**a·ban'don·ment** ***n.***

SYN.—**abandon** implies leaving a person or thing, either as a final, necessary measure [to *abandon* a drought area] or as a complete rejection of one's responsibilities, claims, etc. [she *abandoned* her child]; **desert** emphasizes leaving in willful violation, as of one's obligation or oath [the soldier *deserted* his post]; **forsake** stresses renouncing a person or thing formerly dear to one [to *forsake* one's friends or ideals]; **quit**, basically implying to leave or give up, is now commonly used to mean stop [she *quit* her job] See also **relinquish** —***ANT.*** **reclaim**

a·ban·doned (ə ban'dənd) ***adj.*** **1** given up; forsaken; deserted **2** shamefully wicked; immoral **3** unrestrained

à bas (ä bä') ⟦Fr⟧ down with: an expression of disapproval: opposed to VIVE

a·base (ə bās') ***vt.*** **a·based', a·bas'ing** ⟦ME *abessen* < OFr *abaissier* < ML *abassare*, to lower, bring down < L *ad-* (see A-[2]) + VL *bassus*, low⟧ **1** to humble or humiliate [he *abased* himself before the king] **2** [Archaic] to lower; cast down —**SYN.** DEGRADE —**a·base′ment** *n.*

a·bash (ə bash′) *vt.* ⟦ME *abaishen* < OFr *esbahir*, to astonish < *es-*, intens. (< L *ex-*) + stem of *baer*, to gape: see BAY[2]⟧ to make embarrassed and ill at ease; make self-conscious; disconcert —**SYN.** EMBARRASS —**a·bash′ed·ly** (-əd lē) *adv.* —**a·bash′ment** *n.*

a·bate (ə bāt′) *vt.* **a·bat′ed, a·bat′ing** ⟦ME *abaten* < OFr *abattre*, to beat down: see A-[2] & BATTER[1]⟧ **1** to make less in amount, degree, force, etc. **2** to deduct **3** *Law* to put a stop to (a suit or action), end (a nuisance), etc.; terminate —*vi.* to become less in amount, degree, force, etc.; diminish —**SYN.** WANE —**a·bat′a·ble** *adj.* —**a·bat′er** *n.*, *Law* **a·ba′tor** (-ər, -ôr)

a·bate·ment (-mənt) *n.* ⟦OFr: see prec.⟧ **1** a lessening or reduction **2** an amount deducted; extent of a reduction **3** *Law* the termination of a suit, quashing of a nuisance, etc.

ab·a·tis or **ab·at·tis** (ab′ə tis, -tē′) *n., pl.* **ab′a·tis** or **ab′at·tis** (-tis, -tēz′) ⟦Fr < OFr *abateïs* < *abattre*: see ABATE⟧ a barricade of felled trees, with branches pointed toward the enemy: now often reinforced with barbed wire

ab·at·toir (ab′ə twär′, ab′ə twär′) *n.* ⟦Fr < *abattre*: see ABATE⟧ a slaughterhouse

ab·ax·i·al (ab ak′sē əl) *adj.* ⟦AB- + AXIAL⟧ away from or facing away from the axis [the *abaxial* surface of a leaf]

a·bay·a (ə bī′ə) *n.* ⟦Ar *ʿabāya*⟧ a long, loose, often black, robelike outer garment worn outside the home by women in some Muslim countries

ab·ba[1] (ab′ə, ä′bə) *n.* ⟦ME < LL(Ec) < Aram⟧ **1** father: title of a bishop in the Syrian, Coptic, and Ethiopian Christian churches **2** [**A-**] *Bible* God: Mark 14:36

ab·ba[2] (ä′bə, ə bä′) *n.* ABA (sense 2)

ab·ba·cy (ab′ə sē) *n., pl.* **-cies** ⟦ME < LL(Ec) *abbatia* < *abbas*, ABBOT⟧ an abbot's position, jurisdiction, or term of office

Ab·bas·sid (ə bas′id, ab′ə sid′) *n.* a member of the dynasty of caliphs that ruled Baghdad (A.D. 750-1258) and claimed descent from Muhammad's uncle, Abbas —*adj.* of this dynasty

ab·ba·tial (ə bā′shəl) *adj.* ⟦Fr < ML *abbatialis* < LL(Ec) *abbatia*, ABBACY⟧ of an abbot, abbess, or abbey

ab·bé (a′bā; *Fr* à bā′) *n.* ⟦Fr < LL(Ec) *abbas* < LGr(Ec), ABBOT⟧ **1** a French title of respect, given to a priest, minister, etc. **2** a priest, minister, etc. addressed with this title

ab·bess (ab′əs) *n.* ⟦ME *abbes* < OFr *abesse* < LL(Ec) *abbatissa*, fem. of *abbas*, ABBOT⟧ a woman who is head of an abbey of nuns

Ab·be·vil·li·an (ab′ə vil′ē ən, ab vil′-; -vil′yən) *adj.* ⟦after *Abbeville*, town in N France⟧ designating or of a Lower Paleolithic culture characterized by stone hand axes

ab·bey (ab′ē) *n.* ⟦ME *abbeie* < OFr *abaie* < LL(Ec) *abbatia*, ABBACY⟧ **1** a monastery headed by an abbot, or a convent of nuns headed by an abbess **2** the monks or nuns in such a place, collectively **3** a church or building belonging to an abbey —**SYN.** CLOISTER

ab·bot (ab′ət) *n.* ⟦OE *abbod* < LL(Ec) *abbas* < LGr(Ec) < Aram *abbā*, father⟧ a man who is head of an abbey of monks

Ab·bot (ab′ət), **Charles Gree·ley** (grē′lē) 1872-1973; U.S. astrophysicist

Ab·bots·ford (ab′əts fərd) **1** estate (1812-32) of Sir Walter Scott, on the Tweed in SE Scotland **2** ⟦prob. both after H. B. *Abbott* (1829-1915), Cdn railway engineer & official, and after the Scottish estate⟧ city in SW British Columbia, Canada

abbr or **abbrev** *abbrev.* **1** abbreviated **2** abbreviation

ab·bre·vi·ate (ə brē′vē āt′) *vt.* **-at′ed, -at′ing** ⟦< LL *abbreviatus*, pp. of *abbreviare* < L *ad-*, to + *breviare* < *brevis*, BRIEF⟧ **1** to make shorter **2** to shorten (a word or phrase) by leaving out letters or, sometimes, by substituting letters, numerals, symbols, etc. —**SYN.** SHORTEN —**ab·bre′vi·a′tor** *n.*

ab·bre·vi·a·tion (ə brē′vē ā′shən) *n.* ⟦ME < MFr *abréviation* < LL *abbreviatio*: see prec.⟧ **1** a making shorter **2** the fact or state of being made shorter **3** a shortened form of a word or phrase, as *N.Y.* for *New York*, *Mr.* for *Mister*, *lb* for *pound*, *ctn* for *cotangent*

ABC[1] (ā′bē′sē′) *n., pl.* **ABC's** [*usually pl.*] **1** the alphabet **2** the basic or simplest elements (of a subject); rudiments

ABC[2] *abbrev.* **1** American Bowling Congress **2** *service mark* American Broadcasting Company

ab·cou·lomb (ab ko͞o′läm, -lōm) *n.* ⟦AB(SOLUTE) + COULOMB⟧ the basic unit of electric charge in the CGS system, equal to ten coulombs: abbrev. *aC*

ABC soil a vertical section of soil made up of three distinct layers: the top layer (*A-horizon*) is mostly humus, the middle layer (*B-horizon*) is of clay and oxidized material, and the bottom layer (*C-horizon*) consists of loose rock and other mineral materials

ABD *abbrev.* all but dissertation: used informally of one with all PhD requirements completed except the dissertation

Ab·di·as (ab dī′əs) *n. Douay Bible name for* OBADIAH

ab·di·cate (ab′di kāt′) *vt., vi.* **-cat′ed, -cat′ing** ⟦< L *abdicatus*, pp. of *abdicare*, to deny, renounce < *ab-*, off + *dicare*, to proclaim, akin to *dicere*, to say: see DICTION⟧ **1** to give up formally (a high office, throne, authority, etc.) **2** to surrender or repudiate (a right, responsibility, etc.) —**ab′di·ca′tion** *n.* —**ab′di·ca′tor** *n.*

ab·do·men (ab′də mən; ab dō′mən, əb-) *n.* ⟦L⟧ **1** in vertebrates *a)* the part of the body cavity from the thorax to the pelvic girdle, containing the digestive organs, etc.; belly: in mammals, the diaphragm separates this from the thorax *b)* the region of the trunk between the chest and pelvis **2** in arthropods, the posterior body segment containing the reproductive organs, etc.

ab·dom·i·nal (ab däm′ə nəl, əb-) *adj.* ⟦ModL *abdominalis* < L *abdomen*⟧ of, in, on, or for the abdomen

ab·du·cent (ab do͞o′sənt, -dyo͞o′-; əb-) *adj.* ⟦L *abducens*, prp. of *abducere*, ABDUCT⟧ *Physiol.* that abducts

ab·duct (ab dukt′, əb-) *vt.* ⟦< L *abductus*, pp. of *abducere*, to lead away < *ab-*, away + *ducere*, to lead: see DUCT⟧ **1** to take (a person) away unlawfully and by force or fraud; kidnap **2** *Physiol.* to pull (a part of the body) away from the median axis: said of a muscle: opposed to ADDUCT —**ab·duc′tor** *n.*

ab·duc·tion (ab duk′shən, əb-) *n.* ⟦LL *abductio*: see prec.⟧ **1** an abducting or being abducted **2** *Law* the carrying off of a person by force or fraud; esp., the kidnapping of a woman for marriage, prostitution, etc. **3** *Physiol.* *a)* an abducting of a part of the body *b)* the changed position resulting from this

Abd·ul-A·ziz (äb′do͝ol ä zēz′) 1830-76; sultan of Turkey (1861-76)

Abd·ul-Ha·mid II (-hä mēd′) 1842-1918; sultan of Turkey (1876-1909)

Abd·ul-Me·djid or **Abd·ul-Me·jid** (-me jēd′) 1823-61; sultan of Turkey (1839-61)

a·beam (ə bēm′) *adv., adj.* ⟦A-[1] + BEAM⟧ **1** at right angles to a ship's length or keel **2** abreast (*of*) the middle of a ship's side

a·be·ce·dar·i·an (ā′bē sē der′ē ən) *n.* ⟦ML *abecedarius* < *A, B, C, D*⟧ **1** a person learning the alphabet; beginning student **2** any beginner or novice —*adj.* **1** of the alphabet **2** elementary

a·bed (ə bed′) *adv., adj.* ⟦ME *abedde* < OE *on bedde*: see A-[1] & BED⟧ in bed; on a bed

A·bed·ne·go (ə bed′nə gō′) *n.* ⟦Aram *aved nego*, prob., lit., servant of Nego⟧ *Bible* one of the three captives who came out of the fiery furnace unharmed: Dan. 3:12-27

A·bel (ā′bəl) *n.* ⟦L < Gr *Abel* < ? Heb *hevel*, lit., breath⟧ **1** a masculine name **2** *Bible* the second son of Adam and Eve, killed by his brother Cain: Gen. 4

A·bé·lard (à bā lȧr′), **Pierre** (pyer) 1079-1142; Fr. philosopher, teacher, & theologian: see also HÉLOÏSE: Eng. name **Peter Ab·e·lard** (ab′ə lärd′)

a·bele (ə bēl′; ā′bēl′, -bəl) *n.* ⟦Du *abeel* < OFr *abel*, *aubel* < ML *albellus*, dim. of L *albus*, white⟧ WHITE POPLAR (sense 1)

a·be·li·a (ə bēl′yə, ə bē′lē ə) *n.* ⟦after C. *Abel* (1780–1826), Brit botanist⟧ any of a genus (*Abelia*) of evergreen or deciduous ornamental shrubs of the honeysuckle family with clusters of fragrant, white, pink, or purple flowers

A·be·li·an group (ə bē′lē ən, -bēl′yən) ⟦after Niels H. *Abel* (1802-29), Norw mathematician⟧ *Math.* a commutative group

Ab·e·na·ki (ab′ə nak′ē, -nä′kē) *n.* ⟦NAmFr *Abénaki* < E Abenaki *wapánahki*, lit., easterner⟧ **1** *pl.* **-ki** a member of a group of E Algonquian peoples living mainly in Maine and S Quebec **2** *a)* any of the languages spoken by these peoples, esp. **Eastern Abenaki** or **Western Abenaki** *b)* these languages as a group

Ab·er·deen (ab′ər dēn′; *for 3*, ab′ər dēn′) **1** administrative division of E Scotland: formerly a county **2** fishing port in E Scotland, on the North Sea **3** town in NW Md.: site of Aberdeen Proving Ground of the U.S. Army —**Ab′er·do′ni·an** (-dō′nē ən) *adj., n.*

Aberdeen Angus ⟦after prec. + ANGUS[1]⟧ any of a breed of black, hornless cattle, originally from Scotland, raised for beef

Ab·er·nath·y (ab′ər nath′ē), **Ralph David** 1926-90; U.S. clergyman & civil rights leader

ab·er·rant (ab′ər ənt, ə ber′ənt) *adj.* ⟦< L *aberrans*, prp. of *aberrare*, to go astray < *ab-*, from + *errare*, to wander: see ERR⟧ **1** turning away from what is right, true, etc. **2** deviating from what is normal or typical —*n.* an aberrant person or thing —**ab·er′rance** (-əns) *n.*, **ab·er′ran·cy** (-ən sē)

ab·er·ra·tion (ab′ər ā′shən) *n.* ⟦L *abberatio* < *aberrare*: see prec.⟧ **1** a departure from what is right, true, correct, etc. **2** a deviation from the normal or the typical **3** mental disorder or lapse **4** *Astron.* a small, periodic apparent change in the observed position of a celestial object, caused by the constantly changing position of the earth and the finite speed of the object's light **5** *Optics* *a)* the failure of light rays from one point to converge at a single focus *b)* a fault in a lens or mirror causing such failure: see CHROMATIC ABERRATION, SPHERICAL ABERRATION —**ab′er·ra′tion·al** *adj.*

a·bet (ə bet′) *vt.* **a·bet′ted, a·bet′ting** ⟦ME *abetten* < OFr *abeter*, to incite < *a-*, to + *beter*, to bait < ON *beita*: see BAIT⟧ to incite, sanction, or help, esp. in wrongdoing —**a·bet′ment** *n.* —**a·bet′tor** *n.*, **a·bet′ter**

a·bey·ance (ə bā′əns) *n.* ⟦Anglo-Fr *abeiance* < OFr *abeance*, expectation < *a-*, to, at + *bayer*, to gape, wait expectantly: see BAY[2]⟧ **1** temporary suspension, as of an activity or function **2** *Law* a state of not having been determined or settled, as of lands the present ownership of which has not been established

ab·hor (ab hôr′, əb-) *vt.* **-horred′, -hor′ring** ⟦ME *abhorren* < L *abhorrere* < *ab-*, away, from + *horrere*, to shudder: see HORRID⟧ to shrink from in disgust, hatred, etc.; detest —**SYN.** HATE —**ab·hor′rer** *n.*

ab·hor·rence (-hôr′əns, -här′-) *n.* **1** an abhorring; loathing; detestation **2** something abhorred; something repugnant —**SYN.** AVERSION

ab·hor·rent (-ənt) *adj.* ⟦L *abhorrens*, prp. of *abhorrere*, ABHOR⟧ **1** causing disgust, hatred, etc.; detestable [an *abhorrent* crime] **2** feeling abhorrence **3** opposed or contrary (*to*) [*abhorrent* to his principles] —**SYN.** HATEFUL —**ab·hor′rent·ly** *adv.*

a·bide (ə bīd′) *vi.* **a·bid′ed** or [Now Rare] **a·bode** (ə bōd′), **a·bid′ing** ⟦ME *abiden* < OE *ābīdan* < *ā-*, intens. + *bīdan*, BIDE⟧ **1** to stand fast; remain; go on being **2** [Archaic] to stay; reside (*in* or *at*) —*vt.* **1** to await **2** to submit to; put up with —**SYN.** CONTINUE, STAY[3] —**abide by 1** to live up to (a promise, agreement, etc.) **2** to submit to and carry out (a rule, decision, etc.) —**a·bid′ance** *n.* —**a·bid′er** *n.*

a·bid·ing (ə bīd′iŋ) ***adj.*** continuing without change; enduring; lasting

Ab·i·djan (ab′ə jän′) seaport in the Ivory Coast, on the Gulf of Guinea: former capital (until 1983)

à bien·tôt (à byan tō′) ⟦Fr < *à*, to + *bientôt*, soon⟧ goodbye; I'll see you soon

Ab·i·gail (ab′ə gāl′) ***n.*** **1** ⟦Heb *avigayil*, lit., father is rejoicing⟧ a feminine name: dim. *Abby, Gail* **2** ⟦< *Abigail*, name of a maid in *The Scornful Lady* by Beaumont and Fletcher (*c.* 1613)⟧ [**a-**] a lady's maid

Ab·i·lene (ab′ə lēn′) ⟦ult. < Luke 3:1 < ?⟧ city in central Tex.

a·bil·i·ty (ə bil′ə tē) ***n.***, *pl.* **-ties** ⟦ME *abilite* < MFr *habilité* < L *habilitas* < *habilis*: see ABLE⟧ **1** a being able; power to do (something physical or mental) **2** skill, expertness, or talent

-a·bil·i·ty (ə bil′ə tē) ⟦L *-abilitas*: see -ABLE & -ITY⟧ *suffix forming nouns* a (specified) ability, capacity, or tendency

ab i·ni·ti·o (ab′ i nish′ē ō′, -nish′ō; äb′-) ⟦L⟧ from the beginning

ab in·tra (ab in′trə, äb-) ⟦L⟧ from within

a·bi·o·gen·e·sis (ā′bī′ō jen′ə sis, ab′ē ō-) ***n.*** ⟦ModL < Gr *abios*, lifeless (< *a-*, not + *bios*, life: see BIO-) + -GENESIS⟧ SPONTANEOUS GENERATION —**a′bi′o·ge·net′ic** *adj.* —**a′bi′o·ge·net′i·cal·ly** *adv.*

a·bi·og·e·nist (ā′bī äj′ə nist, ab′ē ä′-) ***n.*** a person who believes in abiogenesis

a·bi·ot·ic (ā′bī ät′ik) ***adj.*** ⟦A-[2] (sense 3) + BIOTIC⟧ of nonliving substances or environmental factors

ab·ject (ab′jekt′, ab jekt′) ***adj.*** ⟦ME < L *abjectus*, pp. of *abjicere*, to throw away < *ab-*, from + *jacere*, to throw: see JET[1]⟧ **1** of the lowest degree; miserable; wretched [*abject* poverty] **2** lacking self-respect; degraded [an *abject* coward] —***SYN.*** BASE[2] —**ab′ject′ly** *adv.* —**ab′ject′ness** *n.*

ab·jec·tion (-jek′shən) ***n.*** **1** an abject state or condition **2** *Bot.* the projection of spores from a sporophore

ab·jure (ab joor′, əb-) ***vt.*** **-jured′**, **-jur′ing** ⟦ME *abjuren* < L *abjurare* < *ab-*, from, away + *jurare*, to swear: see JURY[1]⟧ **1** to give up (rights, allegiance, etc.) under oath; renounce **2** to give up (opinions) publicly; recant —**ab′ju·ra·tion** (ab′jə rā′shən) *n.* —**ab·jur·a·to′ry** (ab joor′ə tôr′ē) *adj.* —**ab·jur′er** *n.*

Ab·kha·zi·a (äb kä′zē ə) autonomous region in NW Georgia, on the Black Sea: cap. Sukhumi

abl *abbrev.* ablative

ab·lac·ta·tion (ab′lak tā′shən) ***n.*** ⟦LL *ablactatio* < L *ablactare*, to wean < *ab-*, from + *lac*, milk: see LACTO-⟧ the act or process of weaning

ab·late (ab lāt′) ***vt.*** **-lat′ed**, **-lat′ing** ⟦back-form. < *ablation* < LL(Ec) *ablatio*, a taking away < L *ablatus*: see fol. ⟧ **1** to remove, as by surgery **2** to wear away, melt, or vaporize (surface material) by entering into or passing through the atmosphere at supersonic speed: see HEAT SHIELD **3** *Geol.* to wear away, as by erosion —*vi.* to undergo ablation —**ab·la′tion** *n.*

ab·la·tive (ab′lə tiv; *for adj. 2*, ab lāt′iv) ***adj.*** ⟦ME < L *ablativus* < *ablatus*, pp. of *auferre* < *ab-*, away + *ferre*, to BEAR[1]⟧ **1** *Gram.* designating, of, or in a case expressing removal, deprivation, direction away from, source, cause, or agency **2** that ablates, as the protective coating material on the nose cone of a space missile —*n. Gram.* **1** the ablative case: this case is expressed by inflection in languages such as Latin, Sanskrit, and Hungarian **2** a word or phrase in this case

ablative absolute *Gram.* in Latin, a grammatically independent phrase containing a noun in the ablative case and a participle, pronoun, or second noun also in the ablative case, used to express time, cause, or circumstance

ab·laut (ab′lout′, äb′-; *Ger* äp′lout′) ***n.*** ⟦Ger < *ab-*, off, from + *laut*, sound: see LOUD⟧ patterned change of base vowels in forms of a word or in related words to show changes in tense, meaning, etc., as in the Indo-European languages (Ex.: dr*i*nk, dr*a*nk, dr*u*nk)

a·blaze (ə blāz′) ***adj.*** ⟦A-[1] + BLAZE[1]⟧ **1** on fire; burning brightly **2** blazing; flaming **3** greatly excited; eager

a·ble (ā′bəl) ***adj.*** **a′bler** (-blər), **a′blest** (-bləst) ⟦ME < OFr *hable*, *habile* < L *habilis*, easily handled, apt < *habere*, to have, hold: see HABIT⟧ **1** having enough power, skill, etc. to do something [*able* to read] **2** having much power of mind; skilled; talented [an *able* teacher] **3** *Law* legally qualified, authorized, or competent to do a specified act

SYN.—**able** implies having power or ability to do something [*able* to make payments] but sometimes suggests superior power or skill [an *able* orator]; **capable** usually implies the mere meeting of ordinary requirements [a *capable* machinist]; **competent** and **qualified** both imply the possession of the requisite qualifications for the specified work, situation, etc., but **qualified** stresses compliance with specified requirements [a *competent* critic of modern art, a *qualified* voter] —***ANT.*** **inept**

-a·ble (ə bəl) ⟦ME < OFr < L *-abilis*⟧ *suffix forming adjectives* **1** that can or will [*perishable*] **2** capable of being ___ed [*manageable*] **3** worthy of being ___ed [*lovable*] **4** having qualities of [*comfortable*] **5** tending or inclined to [*peaceable*] See also -BLE, -IBLE

a·ble-bod·ied (ā′bəl bäd′ēd) ***adj.*** healthy and strong

able-bodied seaman a trained merchant seaman, more highly skilled than, and ranking above, an ordinary seaman: also **able seaman**

a·bloom (ə bloom′) ***adj.*** ⟦A-[1] + BLOOM[1]⟧ in bloom; in flower

ab·lu·ent (ab′loo ənt) ***adj.*** ⟦L *abluens*, prp. of *abluere*: see fol. ⟧ that makes clean —*n.* any substance used for cleaning

ab·lu·tion (ab loo′shən, əb-) ***n.*** ⟦ME *ablucioun* < L *ablutio* < *abluere* < *ab-*, off + *luere*, var. of *lavere*, to LAVE⟧ **1** [*usually pl.*] a washing of the body, esp. as a religious ceremony **2** the liquid used for such washing —**ab·lu′tion·ar′y** *adj.*

a·bly (ā′blē) ***adv.*** in an able manner; skillfully

-a·bly (ə blē) *suffix forming adverbs* in a way indicating a (specified) ability, tendency, etc.

ABM *abbrev.* antiballistic missile

☆**Ab·na·ki** (ab nak′ē, -nä′kē) ***n.*** *var. of* ABENAKI

ab·ne·gate (ab′nə gāt′) ***vt.*** **-gat′ed**, **-gat′ing** ⟦< L *abnegatus*, pp. of *abnegare* < *ab-*, away, from + *negare*, to deny: see NEGATION⟧ to give up (rights, claims, etc.); renounce —**ab′ne·ga′tor** *n.*

ab·ne·ga·tion (ab′nə gā′shən) ***n.*** ⟦ME *abnegacioun* < LL *abnegatio*: see prec. ⟧ a giving up of rights, etc.; self-denial; renunciation

Ab·ner (ab′nər) ***n.*** ⟦L < Heb *avner*, lit., the father is a light⟧ a masculine name

ab·nor·mal (ab nôr′məl, əb-) ***adj.*** ⟦earlier *anormal* < Fr *anormal*, *anomal* < LL *anomalus* < Gr *anōmalos* (see ANOMALOUS) infl. by L *abnormis* < *ab-*, from + *norma*, NORM⟧ not normal; not average; not typical; not usual; irregular, esp. to a considerable degree —***SYN.*** IRREGULAR —**ab·nor′mal·ly** *adv.* —**ab·nor′mal·ism′** *n.*

ab·nor·mal·i·ty (ab′nôr mal′ə tē) ***n.*** **1** the quality or condition of being abnormal **2** *pl.* **-ties** an abnormal thing; malformation

abnormal psychology the branch of psychology dealing with mental disorders or maladaptive behavior and the study of INTELLECTUAL DISABILITY, hypnosis, dreams, etc.

ab·nor·mi·ty (ab nôr′mə tē) ***n.***, *pl.* **-ties** ⟦< L *abnormis* (see ABNORMAL) + -ITY⟧ [Rare] abnormality or monstrosity

ab·o (ab′ō) ***n.***, *pl.* **-os** [Austral. Slang] *short for* ABORIGINE (sense 1*b*): an offensive term

Å·bo (ō′boo) *Swed. name for* TURKU

a·board (ə bôrd′) ***adv.*** ⟦ME *abord* < OFr *a bord*: see BOARD⟧ **1** on board; on, in, or into a ship, airplane, etc. **2** *Naut.* alongside [the sailboat passed our ship close *aboard*] **3** as a participant, partner, employee, etc.: usually in the phrases **come aboard** and **welcome aboard** —***prep.*** on board of; on; in —☆**all aboard!** **1** get on! get in!: a warning to passengers that the train, car, airplane, etc. will start soon **2** everyone (is) aboard!: a signal to the driver or pilot that the trip may begin

a·bode[1] (ə bōd′) ***n.*** ⟦ME *abad*, *abood* < pp. of *abiden*, ABIDE⟧ a place where one lives or stays; home; residence

a·bode[2] (ə bōd′) ***vi.***, ***vt.*** *now rare pt. & pp. of* ABIDE

a·bol·ish (ə bäl′ish) ***vt.*** ⟦ME *abolisshen* < OFr *aboliss-*, extended stem of *abolir* < L *abolescere*, to decay little by little, inceptive of *abolere*, to retard, destroy: formed, with *ab-*, from, to contrast with *adolere*, to increase, grow⟧ to do away with completely; put an end to; esp., to make (a law, etc.) null and void —**a·bol′ish·er** *n.* —**a·bol′ish·ment** *n.*

SYN.—**abolish** denotes a complete doing away with something, as a practice, institution, or condition [to *abolish* slavery, bias, etc.]; **annul** and **abrogate** stress a canceling by authority or formal action [the marriage was *annulled*; the law *abrogated* certain privileges]; **rescind**, **revoke**, and **repeal** all describe the setting aside of laws, orders, etc. [to *rescind* an order, *revoke* a charter, *repeal* a law] —***ANT.*** **establish**

ab·o·li·tion (ab′ə lish′ən) ***n.*** ⟦Fr or L⟧ **1** an abolishing or being abolished **2** [*occas.* **A-**] the abolishing of slavery in the U.S. —**ab′o·li′tion·ar′y** *adj.*

ab·o·li·tion·ist (-ist) ***n.*** **1** a person in favor of abolishing some law, custom, etc. **2** [*occas.* **A-**] one who favored the abolition of slavery in the U.S. —**ab′o·li′tion·ism′** *n.*

ab·o·ma·sum (ab′ə mā′səm) ***n.***, *pl.* **-ma′sa** (-sə) ⟦ModL < AB- + OMASUM⟧ the fourth, or digesting, chamber of the stomach of a cud-chewing animal, as the cow

☆**A-bomb** (ā′bäm′) ***n.*** ATOMIC BOMB —***vt.*** to attack or destroy with an atomic bomb

a·bom·i·na·ble (ə bäm′ə nə bəl) ***adj.*** ⟦ME *abhominable* (sp. infl. by folk etym. deriv. < L *ab homine*, away from man, inhuman) < OFr *abominable* < L *abominabilis* < *abominari*: see ABOMINATE⟧ **1** nasty and disgusting; vile; loathsome **2** highly unpleasant; disagreeable; very bad [*abominable* taste] —***SYN.*** HATEFUL —**a·bom′i·na·bly** *adv.*

Abominable Snowman ⟦prob. mistransl. of a Tibetan phr., itself possibly transcribed faultily⟧ *Folklore* a large, hairy, manlike animal living in the Himalayas: also called *yeti*

a·bom·i·nate (ə bäm′ə nāt′) ***vt.*** **-nat′ed**, **-nat′ing** ⟦< L *abominatus*, pp. of *abominari*, to regard as an ill omen: see AB- & OMEN⟧ **1** to feel hatred and disgust for; loathe **2** to dislike very much —**a·bom′i·na′tor** *n.*

a·bom·i·na·tion (ə bäm′ə nā′shən) ***n.*** **1** an abominating; great hatred and disgust; loathing **2** anything hateful and disgusting

à bon mar·ché (à bōn màr shā′) ⟦Fr⟧ at a good bargain; cheap

ab·o·rig·i·nal (ab′ə rij′ə nəl) ***adj.*** ⟦< fol. + -AL⟧ **1** existing (in a place) from the beginning or from earliest days; first; indigenous **2** *a)* of or characteristic of aborigines *b)* [**A-**] of or characteristic of the Aborigines of Australia —*n.* **1** an aboriginal animal, plant, or person **2** [**A-**] ABORIGINE (sense 1*b*) —***SYN.*** NATIVE —**ab′o·rig′i·nal·ly** *adv.*

ab·o·rig·i·ne (ab′ə rij′ə nē′) ***n.***, *pl.* **-nes′** ⟦L, first inhabitant < *ab-*, from + *origine*, ORIGIN⟧ **1** *a)* any of the first or earliest known inhabitants of a certain region; native *b)* [**A-**] a member of the aboriginal people of Australia **2** [*pl.*] the native animals or plants of a certain region

a·born·ing (ə bôr′niŋ) ***adv.*** while being born or created [the plan died *aborning*]

a·bort (ə bôrt′) ***vi.*** ⟦L *abortare* < *abortus*, pp. of *aboriri*, to miscarry, pass away, orig., to set (as the sun) < *ab-*, from + *oriri*, to arise: see ORIENT⟧ **1**

to give birth before the embryo or fetus is viable; have a miscarriage **2** to fail to be completed **3** *Biol.* to fail to develop; stay rudimentary —*vt.* **1** *a)* to end (a pregnancy) prematurely *b)* to cause (an embryo or fetus) to be expelled so as to end its life *c)* to cause to have an abortion **2** to check (a disease) before fully developed ☆**3** to cut short (an action or operation of an aircraft, spacecraft, etc.), as because of some failure in the equipment —*n.* a premature termination of a flight, mission, etc.

a·bor·ti·cide (ə bôrt′ə sīd′) *n.* ⟦ABORTI(ON) + -CIDE⟧ **1** destruction of the embryo or fetus in the womb **2** an abortifacient

a·bor·ti·fa·cient (ə bôrt′ə fā′shənt) *adj.* ⟦< fol. + -FACIENT⟧ causing abortion —*n.* a drug or agent that causes abortion

a·bor·tion (ə bôr′shən) *n.* ⟦L *abortio*: see ABORT⟧ **1** *a)* any spontaneous expulsion of an embryo or a fetus before it is sufficiently developed to survive; miscarriage *b)* any deliberate procedure that removes, or induces the expulsion of, a dead embryo or fetus or a living embryo or fetus with the purpose of causing its death **2** an aborted embryo or fetus **3** anything immature and incomplete or unsuccessful, as a deformed creature, a badly developed plan, etc. **4** *Biol.* *a)* arrest of development *b)* an organ whose development has been arrested

☆**a·bor·tion·ist** (-ist) *n.* a person who performs an abortion, esp. illegally

a·bor·tive (ə bôrt′iv) *adj.* ⟦ME *abortif* < L *abortivus*: see ABORT⟧ **1** coming to nothing; unsuccessful; fruitless **2** *Biol.* arrested in development; rudimentary **3** *Med.* *a)* causing abortion *b)* halting a disease process **4** [Obs.] born prematurely —*SYN.* FUTILE

a·bor·tus (ə bôrt′əs) *n., pl.* **-tus·es** ⟦< L *abortus*, miscarried: see ABORT⟧ an aborted fetus

ABO system a system of antigens found on human red blood cells, together with the corresponding antibodies of these antigens: inherited antigens determine major blood types (A, B, AB, O), which help determine compatibility for blood transfusions

a·bou·li·a (ə bo͞o′lē ə, -byo͞o′-) *n. alt. sp. of* ABULIA

a·bound (ə bound′) *vi.* ⟦ME *abounden* < OFr *abonder* < L *abundare*, to overflow < *ab-*, away + *undare*, to rise in waves < *unda*, a wave: see WATER⟧ **1** to be plentiful; exist in large numbers or amounts [tropical plants *abound* in the jungle] **2** to have plenty; be filled; be wealthy (*in*) or teem (*with*) [a land that *abounds* in grain, woods that *abound* with game]

a·bout (ə bout′) *adv.* ⟦ME *aboute(n)* < OE *onbūtan*, around < *on*, ON + *be*, BY + *ūtan*, outside < *ūt*, OUT: all senses develop from the sense of "around"⟧ **1** on every side; all around [look *about*] **2** here and there; in all directions [travel *about*] **3** in circumference; around the outside [ten miles *about*] **4** near [standing somewhere *about*] **5** in the opposite direction; to a reversed position [turn it *about*] **6** in succession or rotation [play fair—turn and turn *about*] **7** approximately: used with numbers, measurements, quantities, etc. [*about* four years old, *about* room temperature] **8** [Informal] all but; almost; nearly: used with words expressing qualities or degree [*about* ready, *about* the nicest man we've met] —*adj.* **1** astir; on the move [he is up and *about* again] **2** in the vicinity; prevalent [typhoid is *about*] **3** *a)* ready; likely immediately (followed by an infinitive) [I was *about* to speak] *b)* willing or inclined (used with *not* and an infinitive) [I'm not *about* to exercise regularly] ➥Used only in the predicate —*prep.* **1** around; on all sides of **2** here and there in; everywhere in [rambling *about* the town] **3** near to in time or space [born *about* 1960, keeping my keys *about* me] **4** concerned with; attending to [go *about* your business] **5** on the subject of; concerning [a book *about* ships] **6** in connection with; pertaining to [the most interesting thing *about* her] —**be what something is all about** [Informal] to be the true purpose of or reason for something

☆**a·bout-face** (ə bout′fās′) *n.* **1** a sharp turn to the opposite direction, esp. in response to a military command **2** a sharp change in attitude or opinion —*vi.* **-faced′**, **-fac′ing** to turn or face in the opposite direction

a·bove (ə buv′) *adv.* ⟦ME *above(n)* < OE *abūfan*, *onbūfan*, overhead, above < *on-*, intens. + *bufan* < *be*, BY + *ufan*, over, on high⟧ **1** in, at, or to a higher place; overhead; up **2** in or to heaven **3** at a previous place (in a piece of writing): often used in hyphenated compounds [*above*-mentioned] **4** higher in power, status, etc. —*prep.* **1** higher than; over; on top of **2** beyond; past [the road *above* the village] **3** at a point upstream of **4** superior to; better than [*above* the average] **5** *a)* too honorable to engage in [she was not *above* cheating] *b)* too proud, important, etc. to engage in [he was *above* helping with the dishes] **6** in excess of; more than [*above* fifty dollars] —*adj.* placed, found, mentioned, etc. above or earlier [as stated in the *above* rules] —*n.* something or someone listed or mentioned above —**above all** most of all; mainly

a·bove·board (-bôrd′, -bōrd′) *adv., adj.* ⟦prec. + BOARD (table): orig. a card player's term for cards in plain view⟧ without dishonesty or concealment [be open and *aboveboard* with me]

a·bove·ground (-ground′, -ground′) *adj.* **1** occurring, situated, etc. above or on the surface of the earth **2** not secret or hidden; free, open, etc. —*adv.* **1** above or on the surface of the earth **2** not secretly; openly, etc. Also **a·bove′-ground′**

a·bove-men·tioned (-men′shənd, -chənd) *adj.* mentioned above or earlier

ab o·vo (ab ō′vō, äb-) ⟦L, from the egg⟧ from the beginning

Abp *abbrev.* Archbishop

abr *abbrev.* **1** abridged **2** abridgment

ab·ra·ca·dab·ra (ab′rə kə dab′rə) *n.* ⟦LL, prob. of Balkan orig., but assumed to be < LGr *Abraxas*, cabalistic name of the almighty God⟧ **1** a word supposed to have magic powers, and hence used in incantations, on amulets, etc. **2** a magic spell or formula **3** foolish or meaningless talk; gibberish —*interj.* used, as by a magician, to signify, or seemingly command, a sudden change or occurrence

☆**a·brad·ant** (ə brād′nt) *adj.* abrading —*n.* an abrasive

a·brade (ə brād′) *vt., vi.* **a·brad′ed**, **a·brad′ing** ⟦L *abradere* < *ab-*, away + *radere*, to scrape: see RAT⟧ to scrape or rub off; wear away by scraping or rubbing —**a·brad′er** *n.*

A·bra·ham[1] (ā′brə ham′) *n.* ⟦Heb *avraham*, lit., father of many: the orig. form, *avram*, means "father is exalted": see Gen. 17:5⟧ **1** a masculine name: dim. *Abe* **2** *Bible* the first patriarch and ancestor of the Hebrews: Gen. 12-25 —**in Abraham's bosom 1** at rest with one's dead ancestors **2** in a state of heavenly bliss, peace, etc.

A·bra·ham[2] (ā′brə ham′), **Plains of** plateau in the city of Quebec, on the St. Lawrence: site of a battle (1759) in which the British under Wolfe defeated the French under Montcalm, leading to British control of Canada

A·bra·ham·ic (ā′brə ham′ik) *adj.* ⟦after ABRAHAM[1], earliest Hebrew patriarch, revered also by Christians and Muslims⟧ of or having to do with Judaism, Christianity, and Islam regarded as having a relationship based on certain shared beliefs

A·bram (ā′brəm) *n. var. of* ABRAHAM[1]

a·bran·chi·ate (ā braŋ′kē it, -āt′) *adj.* ⟦< Gr *a-*, not + *branchia*, gills + -ATE[1]⟧ without gills —*n.* an animal without gills Also **a·bran′chi·al** (-əl)

a·bra·sion (ə brā′zhən) *n.* ⟦LL *abrasio* < L *abradere*, ABRADE⟧ **1** a scraping or rubbing off, as of skin **2** a wearing away by rubbing or scraping, as of rock by wind, water, etc. **3** an abraded spot or area

a·bra·sive (ə brā′siv, -ziv) *adj.* ⟦< L *abrasus*, pp. of *abradere*, ABRADE + -IVE⟧ **1** causing abrasion **2** tending to provoke anger, ill will, etc.; aggressively annoying; irritating —*n.* something that is used for grinding, polishing, etc., as sandpaper or emery

a·bra·zo (ä brä′thō, -sō) *n., pl.* **-zos** (-thōs, -sōs) ⟦Sp⟧ an embrace or hug, esp. in greeting a person

ab·re·ac·tion (ab′rē ak′shən) *n.* ⟦AB- + REACTION, transl. of Ger *abreagierung*⟧ *Psychoanalysis* the release of emotions as the result of recalling or reliving a traumatic, repressed experience with which they are associated: cf. CATHARSIS —**ab′re·act′** *vt.* —**ab′re·ac′tive** *adj.*

a·breast (ə brest′) *adv., adj.* ⟦A-[1] + BREAST⟧ **1** side by side, as in going or facing forward: often with *of* or *with* **2** informed (*of*) or conversant (*with*) recent developments

a·bridge (ə brij′) *vt.* **a·bridged′**, **a·bridg′ing** ⟦ME *abregen* < OFr *abregier* < LL *abbreviare*, ABBREVIATE⟧ **1** to reduce in scope, extent, etc.; shorten **2** to shorten (a piece of writing) while preserving its substance; condense **3** to lessen or curtail (rights, authority, etc.) **4** [Rare] to deprive (a person) *of* rights, privileges, etc. —*SYN.* SHORTEN —**a·bridg′a·ble** *adj.*, **a·bridge′a·ble** —**a·bridg′er** *n.*

a·bridg·ment or **a·bridge·ment** (ə brij′mənt) *n.* ⟦ME *abregement* < OFr < *abregier*: see prec.⟧ **1** an abridging or being abridged **2** a curtailment, as of rights **3** an abridged form, as of a book

SYN.—**abridgment** describes a work condensed from a larger work by omitting the less important parts, but keeping the main contents more or less unaltered; an **abstract** is a short statement of the basic contents of a book, court record, etc. often used as an index to the original material; **brief** and **summary** both imply a statement of the main points of the matter under consideration [the *brief* of a legal argument], **summary**, especially, connoting a recapitulating statement; a **synopsis** is a condensed, orderly treatment, as of the plot of a novel, that permits a quick general view of the whole; a **digest** is a concise, systematic treatment, generally more comprehensive in scope than a synopsis, and, in the case of technical material, often arranged under titles for quick reference; an **epitome** is a statement of the essence of a subject in the shortest possible form —*ANT.* **expansion**

a·broach (ə brōch′) *adv., adj.* ⟦ME *abroche* < *a-*, on + *broche*, skewer, spit: see BROACH⟧ **1** opened so that the liquid contents can come out; broached **2** in motion; astir

a·broad (ə brôd′) *adv.* ⟦ME *abrode* < *on brod*: see ON & BROAD⟧ **1** broadly; far and wide **2** in circulation; current [a report is *abroad* that he has won] **3** outside one's house; outdoors [to stroll *abroad*] **4** outside one's own country; to or in foreign countries; specif., to or in another continent; overseas **5** wide of the mark; in error —**from abroad** from a foreign land or lands, specif. a land or lands overseas

ab·ro·gate (ab′rə gāt′) *vt.* **-gat′ed**, **-gat′ing** ⟦< L *abrogatus*, pp. of *abrogare*, to repeal < *ab-*, away + *rogare*, to ask: see ROGATION⟧ to cancel or repeal by authority; annul —*SYN.* ABOLISH —**ab′ro·ga·ble** (-gə bəl) *adj.* —**ab′ro·ga′tion** (-gā′shən) *n.* —**ab′ro·ga′tive** *adj.* —**ab′ro·ga′tor** *n.*

a·brupt (ə brupt′) *adj.* ⟦L *abruptus*, pp. of *abrumpere*, to break off < *ab-*, off + *rumpere*, to break: see RUPTURE⟧ **1** coming, happening, or ending suddenly; sudden; unexpected **2** curt or gruff in behavior or speech; brusque **3** very steep: said as of a precipice **4** jumping from topic to topic without proper transitions; jerky and disconnected **5** *Geol.* having sudden variations in composition, form, etc.: said esp. of adjacent rock formations —*SYN.* STEEP[1], SUDDEN —**a·brupt′ly** *adv.* —**a·brupt′ness** *n.*

ab·rup·tion (ab rup′shən, əb-) *n.* ⟦L *abruptio*: see prec.⟧ a sudden breaking away (of parts of a mass or, esp., of the placenta from the uterus)

A·bruz·zi (ä bro͞o′tsē) region of central Italy, on the Adriatic: 4,168 sq mi (10,795 sq km)

abs[1] (abz) *pl.n.* [Slang] abdominal muscles

abs[2] *abbrev.* absolute (temperature)

ABS[1] (ā′bē′es′) ***n.*** acrylonitrile butadiene styrene, a hard, tough, lightweight plastic used for automobile parts, countertops, etc.: in full **ABS resin**

ABS[2] (ā′bē′es′) *abbrev.* anti-lock braking (or brake) system

abs- (abs, əbs) *prefix* AB-: used before *c* or *t* [*abstract*]

Ab·sa·lom (ab′sə ləm, -läm′) ***n.*** ⟦L < Heb *avshalom*, lit., the father is peace⟧ *Bible* David's favorite son, killed after rebelling against his father: 2 Sam. 18

ab·scess (ab′ses′) ***n.*** ⟦L *abscessus* < *abscedere*, to go from < *ab(s)-*, from + *cedere*, to go: from the notion that humors go from the body into the swelling⟧ a swollen, inflamed area in bodily tissues, in which pus gathers —***vi.*** to form an abscess —**ab′scessed′** ***adj.***

ab·scise (ab sīz′) ***vi., vt.*** **-scised′, -scis′ing** ⟦< L *abscisus*, pp. of *abscidere*, to cut off < *abs-*, var. of *ab-*, AB- + *caedere*, to cut: see -CIDE⟧ to separate by abscission

ab·scis·ic acid (ab sis′ik, -siz′-) an organic acid, $C_{15}H_{20}O_4$, which acts as a growth regulator causing dormancy and abscission of leaves and fruit: sometimes called **ab·scis·in** (ab sis′in, -siz′-)

ab·scis·sa (ab sis′ə, əb-) ***n.***, *pl.* **-sas** or **-sae** (-ē) ⟦L *abscissa (linea)*, (a line) cut off, fem. of *abscissus*, pp. of *abscindere*, to cut off < *ab-*, from, off + *scindere*, to cut < IE **skei-*: for base see SAW[2]⟧ *Math.* the horizontal Cartesian coordinate on a plane, measured from the y-axis along a line parallel with the x-axis to point P

ab·scis·sion (ab sizh′ən) ***n.*** ⟦ME *abscisioun* < L *abscissio*: see prec. ⟧ **1** a cutting off, as by surgery **2** the normal separation of fruit, leaves, etc. from plants by the development of a thin layer of pithy cells at the base of their stems

ab·scond (ab skänd′, əb-) ***vi.*** ⟦L *abscondere* < *ab(s)-*, from, away + *condere*, to hide: see RECONDITE⟧ to go away hastily and secretly; run away and hide, esp. in order to escape the law —**ab·scond′er** ***n.***

ab·seil (äp′zīl′, -sīl′; äb′-) ***vi.*** ⟦Ger *abseilen* < *ab*, down + *seil*, a rope⟧ to descend by rappelling —***n.*** such a descent

ab·sence (ab′səns) ***n.*** ⟦ME < OFr < L *absentia*: see fol. ⟧ **1** the condition of being absent, or away **2** the time of being away **3** the fact of being without; lack [in the *absence* of evidence] **4** inattentiveness

ab·sent (ab′sənt; *for v.*, ab sent′, əb-) ***adj.*** ⟦ME < OFr < L *absens*, prp. of *abesse* < *ab-*, away + *esse*, to be: see IS[1]⟧ **1** not present; away **2** not existing; lacking **3** not attentive; absorbed in thought —***vt.*** to keep (oneself) away [to *absent* oneself from classes] —☆***prep.*** in the absence of; lacking [*absent* her testimony, our case is weak]

ab·sen·tee (ab′sən tē′) ***n.*** a person who is absent, as from work, school, etc. —***adj.*** designating or of a landlord or owner whose personal residence is distant from any other property owned, esp. from such property rented to another

☆**absentee ballot** a preelection ballot to be marked and delivered to a board of elections by a person (**absentee voter**) unable to be at the polls at election time

ab·sen·tee·ism (ab′sən tē′iz′əm) ***n.*** absence from work, school, etc., esp. when deliberate or habitual

ab·sen·te re·o (ab sen′tē rē′ō, äb sen′tā rā′ō) ⟦L⟧ in the absence of the defendant

ab·sent·ly (ab′sənt lē) ***adv.*** in an absent or preoccupied manner; inattentively

ab·sent-mind·ed or **ab·sent·mind·ed** (ab′sənt mīn′did, -mīn′-) ***adj.*** **1** so dreamy or lost in thought as not to pay attention to what one is doing or what is going on around one **2** habitually forgetful —**ab′sent-mind′ed·ly** ***adv.*** —**ab′sent-mind′ed·ness** ***n.***

SYN.—**absent-minded** suggests an aimless wandering of the mind away from the immediate situation, often implying a habitual tendency of this kind [the *absent-minded* professor]; **abstracted** suggests a withdrawal of the mind from the immediate present and a serious concern with some other subject; **preoccupied** implies that the attention cannot be readily turned to something new because of its concern with a present matter; **distrait** suggests inability to concentrate, often emphasizing such a condition as a mood; **distraught** implies a similar inability to concentrate, specifically because of worry, grief, etc.; **inattentive** implies a failure to pay attention, emphasizing such behavior as a lack of discipline

absent without leave *Mil.* absent from duty without official permission but with no intention of deserting: abbrev. *AWOL*

ab·sinthe or **ab·sinth** (ab′sinth′) ***n.*** ⟦ME < OFr < L *absinthium* < Gr *apsinthion*⟧ **1** wormwood (*Artemisia absinthium*) or its essence **2** *a)* a green, bitter, toxic liqueur made with wormwood oil and anise: now illegal in most countries *b)* a similar drink, as anis or pastis, made with a wormwood substitute

ab·sit o·men (ab′sit ō′men′, äb′-) ⟦L⟧ may there be no (ill) omen (in it)

ab·so·lute (ab′sə lo͞ot′, ab′sə lo͞ot′) ***adj.*** ⟦ME *absolut* < L *absolutus*, pp. of *absolvere*, to loosen from: see ABSOLVE⟧ **1** perfect; complete; whole [*absolute* silence] **2** not mixed; pure [*absolute* alcohol] **3** not limited by a constitution, parliament, etc.; unrestricted [an *absolute* ruler] **4** positive; definite [an *absolute* certainty] **5** not doubted; actual; real [an *absolute* truth] **6** not dependent on, or without reference to, anything else; not relative **7** *Gram.* *a)* forming part of a sentence, but not in the usual relations of syntax (in the sentence "The weather being good, they went," *the weather being good* is an *absolute* construction) *b)* used without an explicit object (said of a verb usually transitive, such as *steal* in the sentence "Thieves steal.") *c)* used alone, with the noun understood (said of a pronoun or an adjective, such as *ours* and *brave* in the sentence "Ours are the brave.") **8** *Law* without condition or encumbrance [*absolute* ownership] **9** *Physics* of the absolute temperature scale —***n.*** something that is absolute —**the Absolute** *Philos.* ultimate reality regarded as uncaused, unmodified, unified and complete, timeless, etc. —**ab′so·lute′ness** ***n.***

absolute altitude the altitude of an aircraft over the surface of the land or water below

absolute ceiling the maximum altitude above sea level at which a given aircraft can maintain normal horizontal flight

absolute humidity the mass of water vapor in a specified volume of air, usually measured in grams per cubic meter: cf. RELATIVE HUMIDITY

ab·so·lute·ly (ab′sə lo͞ot′lē, ab′sə lo͞ot′lē) ***adv.*** completely or unconditionally —***interj.*** yes: used for emphasis

absolute magnitude the apparent magnitude a star would have at a distance of ten parsecs from the observer

absolute music music that does not seek to suggest a story, scene, etc. but is concerned purely with tone, structure, etc.: distinguished from PROGRAM MUSIC

absolute pitch **1** the pitch of a tone as determined by its rate of vibration **2** the ability to identify the pitch of any tone heard, or to sing a given tone, without hearing a known pitch beforehand

absolute temperature temperature measured from absolute zero on the Kelvin scale or on the Rankine scale

absolute value **1** the magnitude of a real number, disregarding its positive or negative sign [the *absolute value* of −4 or +4, written |−4| or |+4|, is 4] **2** the magnitude of a complex number; modulus

absolute zero the temperature at which matter has no heat and its molecules are completely still; theoretically, the lowest possible temperature: equal to about −273.16°C or about −459.69°F or 0°K

ab·so·lu·tion (ab′sə lo͞o′shən) ***n.*** ⟦ME *absolucium* < OFr *absolution* < L *absolutio* < *absolvere*: see ABSOLVE⟧ **1** a formal freeing (*from* guilt or obligation); forgiveness **2** *a)* remission (*of* sin or penalty for it); specif., in some churches, remission given by a priest in the sacrament of penance *b)* the statement of such remission

ab·so·lut·ism (ab′sə lo͞o tiz′əm) ***n.*** **1** the doctrine or system of government under which the ruler has unlimited powers; despotism **2** the quality of being absolute **3** *Philos.* any doctrine involving the existence of some metaphysical or axiological principle that is absolute, or not relative —**ab′so·lut′ist** (-lo͞ot′ist) ***n., adj.*** —**ab′so·lu·tis′tic** (-lo͞o tis′tik) ***adj.***

ab·so·lut·ive (ab′sə lo͞ot′iv) ***adj.*** *Gram.* designating, of, or in the case that is shared by the direct object of a transitive verb and the subject of an intransitive verb in an ergative language

ab·so·lut·ize (ab′sə lo͞o tīz′) ***vt.*** **-ized′, -iz′ing** to make absolute; make into an absolute

ab·solve (ab zälv′, -sälv′, -zôlv′, -sôlv′; əb-) ***vt.*** **-solved′, -solv′ing** ⟦ME *absolven* < L *absolvere*, to loosen from < *ab-*, from + *solvere*: see SOLVE⟧ **1** to pronounce free from guilt or blame; acquit **2** *a)* to give religious absolution to *b)* to remit (a sin) **3** to free (*from* a duty, promise, etc.) —**ab·sol′vent** ***adj., n.*** —**ab·solv′er** ***n.***

SYN.—**absolve** implies a setting free from responsibilities or obligation [*absolved* from her promise] or from the penalties for their violation; **acquit** means to release from a specific charge by a judicial decision, usually for lack of evidence; to **exonerate** is to relieve of the blame for a wrongdoing; to **pardon** is to release from punishment for an offense [the prisoner was *pardoned* by the governor]; **forgive** implies giving up all claim that an offense be punished as well as any resentment or vengeful feelings; to **vindicate** is to clear (a person or thing under attack) through evidence of the unfairness of the charge, criticism, etc. —*ANT.* **blame**

ab·sorb (ab sôrb′, -zôrb′; əb-) ***vt.*** ⟦L *absorbere* < *ab-*, from + *sorbere*, to suck in: see SLURP⟧ **1** to suck up [blotting paper *absorbs* ink] **2** to take up the full attention or energy of; engross **3** to take in and incorporate; assimilate **4** to assume the burden of (costs or expenses) **5** to take in (a shock or jolt) with little or no recoil or reaction **6** to take in and not reflect (light, sound, etc.) —**ab·sorb′a·bil′i·ty** ***n.*** —**ab·sorb′a·ble** ***adj.*** —**ab·sorb′er** ***n.***

ab·sorbed (-sôrbd′, -zôrbd′) ***adj.*** **1** taken in, sucked up, assimilated, etc. **2** greatly interested; wholly occupied [*absorbed* in reading]

ab·sorb·ent (ab sôr′bənt, -zôr′-; əb-) ***adj.*** ⟦L *absorbens*, prp. of *absorbere*: see ABSORB⟧ capable of absorbing moisture, light rays, etc. —***n.*** a thing or substance that absorbs —**ab·sorb′en·cy** ***n.***

☆**absorbent cotton** raw cotton made absorbent by the removal of its wax: used for surgical dressings, etc.

ab·sorb·ing (ab sôr′biŋ, -zôr′-; əb-) ***adj.*** very interesting; engrossing [an *absorbing* tale] —**ab·sorb′ing·ly** ***adv.***

ab·sorp·ti·om·e·try (ab sôrp′shē äm′ə trē, -zôrp′-) ***n.*** ⟦fol. + -METRY⟧ measurement of the amount of electromagnetic radiation absorbed by something being tested or analyzed: radiologists often use this to determine bone density

ab·sorp·tion (ab sôrp′shən, -zôrp′-; əb-) ***n.*** ⟦L *absorptio* < *absorbere*: see ABSORB⟧ **1** an absorbing or being absorbed **2** the fact or state of being much interested or engrossed **3** *Biol.* the passing of nutrient material, medication, etc. into or through tissues, as the intestinal walls, the blood, etc. **4** *Physics* *a)* a taking in and not reflecting, as of radiant energy *b)* partial loss in energy of light, radio waves, etc. passing through a medium —**ab·sorp′tive** (-tiv) ***adj.***

absorption spectrum a spectrum with a pattern of dark bands or lines created when light passes through a gas or liquid into a spectroscope: the chemical elements of the gas or liquid absorb specific wavelengths of light creating a unique pattern which can be used to analyze the gas or liquid chemically

ab·stain (ab stān′, əb-) *vi.* ⟦ME *absteinen* < OFr *abstenir* < L *abstinere,* to hold back < *ab(s)-,* from + *tenere,* to hold: see TENANT⟧ to hold oneself back; voluntarily do without; refrain *(from)* [to *abstain* from smoking] —***SYN.*** REFRAIN[1] —**ab·stain′er** *n.*

ab·ste·mi·ous (ab stē′mē əs, əb-) *adj.* ⟦L *abstemius,* abstaining from alcoholic liquor < *ab(s)-,* from + root of *temetum,* strong drink⟧ **1** moderate, esp. in eating and drinking; temperate **2** characterized by abstinence

ab·sten·tion (ab sten′shən, əb-) *n.* ⟦L *abstentio* < *abstinere,* ABSTAIN⟧ the act or an instance of abstaining —**ab·sten′tious** *adj.*

ab·sterge (ab sturj′) *vt.* **-sterged′, -sterg′ing** ⟦L *abstergere* < *ab(s)-,* away + *tergere,* to wipe: see DETERGE⟧ [Archaic] **1** to wipe away; clean **2** to purge —**ab·ster′gent** *adj., n.* —**ab·ster·sion** (ab stur′shən) *n.*

ab·sti·nence (ab′stə nəns) *n.* ⟦ME < OFr < L *abstinentia* < prp. of *abstinere*: see ABSTAIN⟧ **1** the act of voluntarily doing without some or all food, drink, or other pleasures; specif., *a)* abstention from alcoholic beverages *b)* abstention from sexual intercourse **2** *R.C.Ch.* abstention from flesh meat on certain designated days —**ab′sti·nent** *adj.* —**ab′sti·nent·ly** *adv.*

ab·stract (*for adj.,* ab strakt′, ab′strakt′; *for n. 1 & vt. 4,* ab′strakt′; *for n. 2,* ab′strakt′, ab strakt′; *for vt. 1, 2, & 3,* ab strakt′) *adj.* ⟦< L *abstractus,* pp. of *abstrahere,* to draw from, separate < *ab(s)-,* from + *trahere,* to DRAW⟧ **1** thought of apart from any particular instances or material objects; not concrete **2** expressing a quality thought of apart from any particular or material object [beauty is an *abstract* word] **3** not easy to understand because of being extremely complex, remote from concrete reality, etc.; abstruse **4** theoretical; not practical or applied **5** designating or of art abstracted from reality, in which designs or forms may be definite and geometric or fluid and amorphous: a generic term that encompasses various nonrealistic contemporary schools —*n.* **1** a brief statement of the essential content of a book, article, speech, court record, etc.; summary **2** an abstract thing, condition, idea, etc. —*vt.* **1** to take away; remove **2** to take dishonestly; steal **3** to think of (a quality) apart from any particular instance or material object that has it; also, to form (a general idea) from particular instances **4** to summarize; make an abstract of —***SYN.*** ABRIDGMENT —**in the abstract** in theory as apart from practice —**ab·stract′er** *n.* —**ab·stract′ly** *adv.* —**ab·stract′ness** *n.*

ab·stract·ed (ab strak′tid) *adj.* **1** removed or separated *(from* something) **2** withdrawn in mind; absent-minded —***SYN.*** ABSENT-MINDED —**ab·stract′ed·ly** *adv.* —**ab·stract′ed·ness** *n.*

☆**abstract expressionism** a post-WWII movement in painting characterized by emphasis on the artist's spontaneous and self-expressive application of paint in creating a nonrepresentational composition

ab·strac·tion (ab strak′shən) *n.* ⟦ME *abstraccioun* < LL *abstractio*: see ABSTRACT⟧ **1** an abstracting or being abstracted; removal **2** formation of an idea, as of a quality or property of a thing, in such a way as to apprehend that quality or property apart from any particular instances of it in the material world **3** an idea so formed, or a word or term for it ["honesty" and "whiteness" are *abstractions*] **4** an unrealistic or impractical notion **5** mental withdrawal; absent-mindedness **6** an abstract quality **7** a picture, statue, etc. that is wholly or partly abstract

ab·strac·tion·ism (-iz′əm) *n.* the theory and practice of the abstract, esp. in art —**ab·strac′tion·ist** *adj., n.*

ab·strac·tive (ab strak′tiv) *adj.* **1** that abstracts or can abstract **2** of or having to do with abstraction —**ab·strac′tive·ly** *adv.*

abstract of title a brief history of the ownership of a piece of real estate, from the original grant through the present holder, including a statement of liens to which it may be subject

ab·strict (ab strikt′) *vt., vi.* to undergo, or produce by, abstriction

ab·stric·tion (ab strik′shən) *n.* ⟦< L *ab-,* from + *strictio,* a binding < *strictus,* pp. of *stringere*: see STRINGENT⟧ *Bot.* any natural separation of a spore from its sporophore

ab·struse (ab stro͞os′, əb-) *adj.* ⟦L *abstrusus,* pp. of *abstrudere,* to thrust away < *ab(s)-,* away + *trudere,* to THRUST⟧ hard to understand because of being extremely complex, intellectually demanding, highly abstract, etc.; deep; recondite —**ab·struse′ly** *adv.* —**ab·struse′ness** *n.* —**ab·stru′si·ty** *n., pl.* **-ties**

ab·surd (ab surd′, -zurd′; əb-) *adj.* ⟦Fr *absurde* < L *absurdus,* not to be heard of < *ab-,* intens. + *surdus,* dull, deaf, insensible⟧ so clearly untrue or unreasonable as to be laughable or ridiculous —**ab·surd′ly** *adv.* —**ab·surd′ness** *n.*

SYN.—**absurd** means laughably inconsistent with what is judged as true or reasonable [an *absurd* hypothesis]; **ludicrous** is applied to what is laughable from incongruity or exaggeration [a *ludicrous* facial expression]; **preposterous** is used to describe anything flagrantly absurd or ludicrous; **foolish** describes that which shows lack of good judgment or of common sense [don't take *foolish* chances]; **silly** and **ridiculous** apply to whatever excites amusement or contempt by reason of its extreme foolishness, **silly** often indicating an utterly nonsensical quality —***ANT.*** **sensible, logical**

ab·surd·ist (ab sur′dist, -zur′-; əb-) *adj.* **1** designating or holding the belief that human existence is absurd, irrational, meaningless, etc. **2** of, relating to, or associated with the theater of the absurd —*n.* an absurdist thinker, writer, etc. —**ab·surd′ism′** *n.*

ab·surd·i·ty (ab sur′də tē, -zur′-; əb-) *n.* **1** the quality or state of being absurd; nonsense **2** *pl.* **-ties** an absurd idea or thing

A·bu al-Qā·sim (ä bo͞o′ äl kä′sim) (L. name *Albucasis*) A.D. 936?-1013?; Arab surgeon & medical encyclopedist, in Spain: also **A·bul Ka·sim** (ä bo͝ol′ kä′sim)

A·bu-Bakr (ä bo͞o′ bä′kər) A.D. 573-634; successor of Muhammad & 1st caliph of Islam (A.D. 632-634): father of Aisha: also **A·bu-Bekr** (ä bo͞o′ bek′ ər)

A·bu Dha·bi (ä′bo͞o dä′bē) **1** largest emirate of the United Arab Emirates: *c.* 26,000 sq mi (67,340 sq km) **2** its chief city, on the Persian Gulf: capital of United Arab Emirates

A·bu·ja (ə bo͞o′jə) capital of Nigeria, in the central part

A·bu·kir (ä′bo͞o kir′) bay at the mouth of the Nile, near Alexandria, Egypt: site of the British victory (1798) under Nelson over the French: also sp. **A·bu Qir**

a·bu·li·a (ə bo͞o′lē ə, -byo͞o′-) *n.* ⟦ModL < Gr *aboulia,* indecision < *a-,* without + *boulē,* will, determination⟧ *Psychol.* loss of the ability to exercise willpower and make decisions —**a·bu′lic** (-lik) *adj.*

a·bun·dance (ə bun′dəns) *n.* ⟦ME *aboundaunce* < OFr *abondaunce* < L *abundantia* < prp. of *abundare*: see ABOUND⟧ **1** a great supply; more than sufficient quantity **2** great plenty; wealth

a·bun·dant (ə bun′dənt) *adj.* ⟦ME *aboundaunt* < OFr *abondaunt* < L prp. of *abundare*: see ABOUND⟧ **1** very plentiful; more than sufficient; ample **2** well-supplied; rich *(in* something) [woods *abundant* in game] —***SYN.*** PLENTIFUL —**a·bun′dant·ly** *adv.*

a·buse (ə byo͞oz′; *for n.,* ə byo͞os′) *vt.* **a·bused′, a·bus′ing** ⟦ME *abusen* < OFr *abuser* < L *abusus,* pp. of *abuti,* misuse < *ab-,* away, from + *uti,* to use⟧ **1** to use wrongly; misuse [to *abuse* a privilege] **2** *a)* to hurt by treating badly; mistreat *b)* to inflict physical, sexual, or psychological harm upon **3** to use insulting, coarse, or bad language about or to; revile —*n.* **1** wrong, bad, or excessive use **2** mistreatment, esp. by the infliction of physical, sexual, or psychological harm; injury **3** a bad, unjust, or corrupt custom or practice **4** insulting or coarse language **5** [Obs.] deception —***SYN.*** WRONG —**a·bus·er** (ə byo͞o′zər) *n.* —**a·bus′a·ble** *adj.*

A·bu Sim·bel (ä′bo͞o sim′bəl) village in S Egypt, on the Nile: site of two temples, built (13th cent. B.C.) for Ramses II

a·bu·sive (ə byo͞o′siv; *also,* -ziv) *adj.* ⟦Fr *abusif* < L *abusivus* < *abusus*: see ABUSE⟧ **1** involving or characterized by abuse or misuse; abusing; mistreating **2** coarse and insulting in language; scurrilous; harshly scolding —**a·bu′sive·ly** *adv.* —**a·bu′sive·ness** *n.*

a·but (ə but′) *vi.* **a·but′ted, a·but′ting** ⟦ME *aboutien* < OFr *abouter,* to join end to end < *a-,* to + *bout,* end⟧ to end *(on)* or lean *(upon)* at one end; border *(on)*; terminate *(against)* —*vt.* to end at; border upon

a·bu·ti·lon (ə byo͞ot′'l än′) *n.* ⟦ModL < Ar *aubūṭīlūn*⟧ any of a number of related plants or shrubs (genus *Abutilon*) of the mallow family, with showy flowers of white, yellow, or red

a·but·ment (ə but′mənt) *n.* **1** the act or an instance of abutting **2** something that abuts or borders upon something else **3** the point of contact between a support and the thing supported **4** *a)* that part of a support which carries the weight of an arch and resists its pressure *b)* the supporting structure at either end of a bridge

abutment

a·but·tals (ə but′'lz) *pl.n.* abutting parts of land; boundaries

☆**a·but·ter** (ə but′ər) *n.* the owner of abutting land

A·bu Za·by (*or* **Za·bi**) (ä′bo͞o zä′bē) *Ar. name for* ABU DHABI

a·buzz (ə buz′) *adj.* **1** filled with buzzing **2** full of activity, talk, etc.

a·by or **a·bye** (ə bī′) *vt. pt. & pp.* **a·bought′** (-bôt′) ⟦ME *abien* < OE *abycgan* < *a-,* for *bycgan,* BUY⟧ [Archaic] to pay the penalty for

A·by·dos (ə bī′däs′) **1** ancient city in Asia Minor, on the Hellespont **2** ancient city in central Egypt, near the Nile, north of Thebes

Ab·y·la (ab′ə lə) *ancient name for* a mountain at Ceuta, N Africa: see PILLARS OF HERCULES

a·bysm (ə biz′əm) *n.* ⟦OFr *abisme* < ML *abysmus,* altered after suffix *-ismus* (see -ISM) < L *abyssus*: see ABYSS⟧ [Old Poet.] an abyss

a·bys·mal (ə biz′məl) *adj.* ⟦prec. + -AL⟧ **1** of or like an abyss; bottomless; unfathomable **2** wretched to the point of despair; immeasurably bad [*abysmal* poverty] —**a·bys′mal·ly** *adv.*

a·byss (ə bis′) *n.* ⟦L *abyssus* < Gr *abyssos* < *a-,* without + *byssos,* bottom⟧ **1** a deep fissure in the earth; bottomless gulf; chasm **2** anything too deep for measurement; profound depth [*abyss* of shame, of time, etc.] **3** the ocean depths **4** *Theol.* the primeval void or chaos before the Creation

a·bys·sal (ə bis′əl) *adj.* **1** of or having to do with an abyss **2** designating or of the ecological zone **(abyssal zone)** along the deep ocean floor between the bathyal and hadal zones

Ab·ys·sin·i·a (ab′ə sin′ē ə) *former name for* ETHIOPIA

Ab·ys·sin·i·an (ab′ə sin′ē ən) *n.* **1** ETHIOPIAN **2** any of a breed of short-haired domestic cat with a rounded, wedge-shaped head and ruddy brown, reddish, or grayish-blue coat, originating in Egypt or Ethiopia (Abyssinia) —*adj.* ETHIOPIAN (*adj.* 1)

ac *abbrev.* **1** account **2** acre(s)

aC *abbrev.* abcoulomb(s)

AC *abbrev.* **1** air conditioning **2** alternating current **3** Athletic Club **4** ⟦L *Ante Christum*⟧ before Christ: used with dates **5** ⟦L *ante cibum*⟧ *Pharmacy* before meals Also, for senses 1, 2, & 5, **ac**

Ac[1] *abbrev. Bible* Acts

Ac[2] *Chem. symbol for* actinium

ac- (ak, ək, ik) *prefix* AD-: used before *c* or *q*

-ac (ak, ək) ⟦Fr *-aque* < L *-acus* < Gr *-akos* (or directly < any of these)⟧ *suffix forming adjectives* **1** characteristic of *[elegiac, demoniac]* **2** of, relating to *[cardiac, coeliac]* **3** affected by or having *[maniac]* The resulting adjectives are sometimes used as nouns

A/C *abbrev.* **1** *Bookkeeping* account **2** *Bookkeeping* account current **3** air conditioning Also, for 1 & 2, **a/c**

a.c. *abbrev.* ⟦L *ante cibum*⟧ *Pharmacy* before meals

a·ca·cia (ə kā′shə) *n.* ⟦ME < OFr *acacie* < L *acacia* < Gr *akakia*, shittah tree, thorny tree; prob. < *akē*, a point, thorn < IE base **ak*-: see ACID⟧ **1** *a)* any of several trees, shrubs, or other plants (genus *Acacia*) of the mimosa family, with clusters of yellow or white flowers: many are cultivated as ornamentals, and some yield gum arabic, dyes, or perfumes *b)* the flower **2** GUM ARABIC **3** LOCUST (sense 3*a*): also called **false acacia**

acad *abbrev.* **1** academic **2** [*also* **A-**] academy

Ac·a·deme (ak′ə dēm′, ak′ə dēm′) *n.* ⟦< Gr *akadēmeia*, the grove of *Akadēmos*, figure in ancient Greek legend⟧ **1** THE ACADEMY (sense 1) (see phrase under ACADEMY) **2** [*often* **a-**] the academic world

ac·a·de·mi·a (ak′ə dē′mē ə, -dā′-) *n.* ⟦L: see ACADEMY⟧ the academic world; academe

ac·a·dem·ic (ak′ə dem′ik) *adj.* ⟦L *academicus* < *academia*: see ACADEMY⟧ **1** of colleges, universities, etc.; scholastic; scholarly **2** having to do with general or liberal rather than technical or vocational education **3** of or belonging to an academy of scholars, artists, etc. **4** following fixed rules or conventions; pedantic or formalistic *[an academic style of painting]* **5** merely theoretical; having no direct practical application *[an academic question]* Also **ac′a·dem′i·cal** (-i kəl) —*n.* a teacher or scholar at a college or university

ac·a·dem·i·cal·ly (-i kəl ē) *adv.* **1** in relation to an academy **2** in an academic manner; pedantically **3** from an academic point of view

ac·a·dem·i·cals (ak′ə dem′i kəlz) *pl.n.* traditional academic clothing; cap and gown

☆**academic freedom** freedom of a teacher or student to hold and express views without fear of arbitrary interference by officials

a·cad·e·mi·cian (ə kad′ə mish′ən, ak′ə də-) *n.* ⟦Fr *académicien*⟧ **1** a member of an ACADEMY (sense 3) **2** an artist, writer, etc. who follows certain academic rules or conventions

ac·a·dem·i·cism (ak′ə dem′ə siz′əm) *n.* the quality of being academic; esp., formal or pedantic quality, spirit, etc.: also **a·cad·e·mism** (ə kad′ə miz′əm)

a·cad·e·my (ə kad′ə mē) *n., pl.* **-mies** ⟦Fr *académie* < L *academia* < Gr *akadēmeia*: see ACADEME⟧ **1** a private secondary or high school **2** a school offering instruction in a special field *[a music academy]* **3** an association of scholars, writers, artists, etc., for advancing literature, art, or science —**the Academy 1** the public park near Athens where Plato taught and founded a school for the study of philosophy **2** this school **3** Plato's followers or their philosophy **4** the academic world

☆**Academy Award** *trademark for* any of the annual awards for artistic and technical achievement given by the Academy of Motion Picture Arts and Sciences: see OSCAR[2]

A·ca·di·a (ə kā′dē ə) ⟦Fr *Acadia*, prob. < *Archadia*, name given by VERRAZANO (1524), after *Arcadia*, place of rural peace⟧ region & former French colony (1604-1713) on the NE coast of North America, including what are now the Canadian provinces of Nova Scotia, New Brunswick, and Prince Edward Island, plus parts of Quebec and parts of Maine —**A·ca′di·an** *adj., n.*

☆**Acadian flycatcher** a small, greenish tyrant flycatcher (*Empidonax virescens*) found in deciduous forests of E North America

☆**Acadian owl** SAW-WHET OWL

ac·a·jou (ak′ə zho͞o′) *n.* ⟦Fr, CASHEW⟧ **1** any of several tropical trees yielding fine cabinet wood, including the mahogany **2** the cashew

ac·a·leph (ak′ə lef′) *n.* ⟦< Gr *akalēphē*, a nettle⟧ [Obs.] any of several invertebrate animals, as jellyfish, that swim or float about in the open sea; coelenterate or ctenophore (former class Acalephes, phylum Zoophyta): also **ac′a·lephe′** (-lēf′)

a·can·thine (ə kan′thin, -thīn′, -thēn′) *adj.* of or resembling an acanthus or its leaves

a·can·tho- (ə kan′thō, -thə) ⟦< Gr *akantha*, thorn < *akē*, a point < IE base **ak*-: see ACID⟧ *combining form* thorn *[acanthocephalan]*: also, before a vowel, **a·canth-** (ə kanth′)

a·can·tho·ceph·a·lan (ə kan′thō sef′ə lən, -thə-) *n.* ⟦< ModL < prec. + CEPHAL- + -AN⟧ any of a phylum (Acanthocephala) of intestinal worms, lacking a digestive tract and having a proboscis bearing rows of thornlike hooks

a·can·thoid (ə kan′thoid′) *adj.* spiny; spine-shaped: also **a·can′thous** (-thəs)

ac·an·thop·ter·yg·i·an (ak′ən thäp′tə rij′ē ən) *n.* ⟦< ACANTHO- + Gr *pteryg-ion*, a fin: see PTERO-⟧ any of the percoid fishes, as the basses or perches

a·can·thus (ə kan′thəs) *n., pl.* **-thus·es** or **-thi′** (-thī′, -thē′) ⟦ModL < L < Gr *akanthos*: see ACANTHO-⟧ **1** any of a genus (*Acanthus*) of thistlelike plants of the acanthus family with lobed, often spiny leaves and long spikes of white or colored flowers, found in the Mediterranean region **2** *Archit.* a motif or conventional representation of the leaf of this plant, used esp. on the capitals of Corinthian columns —*adj.* designating a family (Acanthaceae, order Scrophulariales) of dicotyledonous plants, including bear's-breech

a cap·pel·la (ä′ kə pel′ə) ⟦It, in chapel style < L *ad*, to, according to + ML *capella*, CHAPEL⟧ without instrumental accompaniment: said of choral singing and of unaccompanied vocalists or vocal groups in popular music: also sp. **a ca·pel′la**

a ca·pric·cio (ä′ kə prē′chō) ⟦It < *a*, at + *capriccio*: see CAPRICE⟧ *Musical Direction* at (one's) pleasure; at whatever tempo and with whatever expression the performer likes

A·ca·pul·co (ä′kə po͞ol′kō, ak′ə-) city in S Mexico, on the Pacific: winter resort: in full **Acapulco de Juá·rez** (dā hwär′ez′, -wär′-; -əs)

ac·a·ri·a·sis (ak′ə rī′ə sis) *n.* ⟦ModL: see fol. & -ASIS⟧ an infestation with acarids, or the resulting skin disease

ac·a·rid (ak′ə rid′) *n.* ⟦< Gr *akari*, mite < *akarēs*, tiny, lit., too short to cut < *a-*, not + *keirein*, to cut, akin to SHEAR⟧ any of a subclass (Acari) of small arachnids, including the ticks and mites, which are parasites and agricultural pests

A·ca·ri·gua (ä′kə rig′wə) city in NW Venezuela

Ac·ar·na·ni·a (ak′ər nā′nē ə) region on the W coast of ancient Greece

ac·a·roid (ak′ə roid′) *adj.* of or like an acarid

acaroid resin an alcohol-soluble gum resin taken from various grass trees, used in varnishes, inks, etc.: it is unique among natural resins because it forms a hard, insoluble, chemical-resistant film when heated

ac·a·rol·o·gy (ak′ə räl′ə jē) *n.* ⟦see ACARID & -LOGY⟧ the scientific study of mites and ticks —**ac′a·rol′o·gist** *n.*

a·car·pel·ous or **a·car·pel·lous** (ā kär′pə ləs) *adj.* ⟦A-[2] + CARPEL + -OUS⟧ *Bot.* without carpels

a·car·pous (ā kär′pəs) *adj.* ⟦Gr *akarpos* < *a-*, without + *karpos*, fruit: see CARPEL⟧ bearing no fruit; sterile

a·cat·a·lec·tic (ā′kat′ə lek′tik) *adj.* ⟦LL *acatalecticus* < Gr *akatalēktos*, incessant < *a-*, without + *katalēgein*: see CATALECTIC⟧ *Prosody* having the full number of syllables, esp. in the last foot —*n.* an acatalectic line of verse

a·cau·dal (ā kôd′'l) *adj.* ⟦A-[2] + CAUDAL⟧ having no tail: also **a·cau·date** (ā kô′dāt′)

a·cau·les·cent (ā′kô les′'nt) *adj.* ⟦A-[2] + CAULESCENT⟧ *Bot.* having no stem or only a very short stem: also **a·cau·lous** (ā kô′ləs) —**a′cau·les′cence** *n.*

acc *abbrev.* **1** accompaniment **2** account **3** accusative

Ac·cad (ak′ad′, äk′äd′) *alt. sp. of* AKKAD —**Ac·ca·di·an** (ə kā′dē ən) *adj., n.*

ac·cede (ak sēd′) *vi.* **-ced′ed, -ced′ing** ⟦L *accedere* < *ad-*, to + *cedere*, to go: see CEDE⟧ **1** to enter upon the duties (of an office); attain (*to*) **2** to give assent; give in; agree (*to*) **3** to become a party (*to* a treaty) between nations —*SYN.* CONSENT —**ac·ced′ence** *n.* —**ac·ced′er** *n.*

ac·cel·er·an·do (ä chel′ə rän′dō′) *adj., adv.* ⟦It, prp. of *accelerare* < L: see ACCELERATE⟧ [*also in italics*] *Musical Direction* with gradually quickening tempo

ac·cel·er·ant (ak sel′ər ənt, ək-) *adj.* ⟦L *accelerans*, prp. of *accelerare*: see fol.⟧ accelerating —*n.* **1** something that increases the speed of a process **2** *Chem. former term for* CATALYST

ac·cel·er·ate (ak sel′ər āt′, -ə rāt′; ək-) *vt.* **-at′ed, -at′ing** ⟦< L *acceleratus*, pp. of *accelerare* < *ad-*, to + *celerare*, to hasten < *celer*, swift < IE base **kel-*, to drive > OE *haldan*, HOLD[1]⟧ **1** to increase the speed of **2** to cause to develop or progress more quickly **3** *Physics* to cause a change in the velocity of (a moving body) **4** to cause to happen sooner —*vi.* to go, progress, or develop faster

ac·cel·er·a·tion (ak sel′ər ā′shən, -ə rā′-; ək-) *n.* **1** an accelerating or being accelerated **2** the rate of change in the velocity of a moving body: abbrev. *a*

acceleration of gravity the gravitational acceleration of a freely falling object, expressed in terms of the rate of increase of velocity per second: on earth 980.665 cm (32.17 ft) per second per second is the standard: abbrev. *g*

ac·cel·er·a·tive (ak sel′ər āt′iv, -ə rāt′-; -sel′ər ət iv; ək-) *adj.* of, causing, or increasing acceleration

ac·cel·er·a·tor (ak sel′ər āt′ər, -ə rāt′-; ək-) *n.* **1** a person or thing that accelerates or increases the speed of something; specif., *a)* a device, such as the foot throttle of an automobile, for increasing the speed of a machine *b)* a nerve or muscle that speeds up a body function **2** *Chem.* a substance that speeds up a reaction **3** *Nuclear Physics* a betatron, cyclotron, synchrotron, linear accelerator, or similar apparatus that accelerates charged particles to high energies: accelerators are used for experimental purposes **4** *Photog.* a chemical that speeds up developing

☆**ac·cel·er·om·e·ter** (ak sel′ər äm′ət ər, -ə räm′-; ək-) *n.* ⟦ACCELER(ATE) + -O- + -METER⟧ a mechanical or electromechanical instrument for measuring acceleration, as of an aircraft, or for detecting vibrations, as in machinery

ac·cent (ak′sent′; *chiefly Brit*, -sənt; *for v.*, ak′sent′, ak sent′) *n.* ⟦Fr < L *accentus* < *ad-*, to + *cantus*, pp. of *canere*, to sing: a L rendering of Gr *prosōidia* (see PROSODY), orig. referring to the pitch scheme of Gr verse⟧ **1** the emphasis (by stress, pitch, or both) given to a particular syllable or word when it is spoken **2** a mark used in writing or printing to show the placing and kind of this emphasis, as in the primary (′) and secondary (′) accenting of English (*ac·cel′er·a′tor, ac′a·dem′i·cal·ly*, etc.) **3** a mark used to distinguish between various sounds represented by the same letter *[in French there are acute (´), grave (`), and circumflex (^) accents]* **4** the pitch contour of a phrase **5** *a)* a distinguishing regional or national manner of pronunciation [Irish *accent*, Southern *accent*] *b)* a manner of articulating the sounds of another language that is influenced by the phonology of one's native language [speaking Russian with a heavy Midwestern American *accent*] **6** [*often pl.*] a voice modulation expressive of an emotion [*accents* of love] **7** [*pl.*] [Old Poet.] speech; words; utterance [in *accents* mild] **8** a distinguishing style of expression **9** a striking or prominent feature of any artistic composition [the classical *accent* of a pillar] **10** an object or detail that lends emphasis, as by contrast with that which surrounds it **11** special emphasis or attention [to put the *accent* on highway construction] **12** a mark used with a number or letter, as in mathematics to indicate a variable (a′), or in measurement of length (10′ 5″, ten feet five inches) or of time (3′ 16″, three minutes sixteen seconds) **13** *Music a)* emphasis or stress on a note or chord *b)* a mark or sign showing this **14** *Music, Prosody* rhythmic stress or beat —*vt.* **1** to pronounce (a syllable, word, or phrase) with special stress **2** to mark with an accent **3** to emphasize

ac·cen·tu·al (ak sen′cho͞o əl, ək-) *adj.* ⟦< L *accentus* (see prec.) + -AL⟧ **1** of or having to do with accent **2** having rhythm based on stress rather than on the number of syllables or length of sounds, as some poetry —**ac·cen′tu·al·ly** *adv.*

ac·cen·tu·ate (ak sen′cho͞o āt′, ək-) *vt.* **-at′ed, -at′ing** ⟦< ML *accentuatus*, pp. of *accentuare* < L *accentus*, ACCENT⟧ **1** to pronounce or mark with an accent or stress **2** to emphasize; heighten the effect of —**ac·cen′tu·a′tion** *n.*

ac·cept (ak sept′, ək-) *vt.* ⟦ME *accepten* < OFr *accepter* < L *acceptare* < pp. stem of *accipere* < *ad-*, to + *capere*, to take: see HAVE⟧ **1** to take (what is offered or given); receive, esp. willingly **2** to receive favorably; approve [to *accept* a theory] **3** to submit to; be resigned to [he had to *accept* defeat] **4** to believe in **5** to understand as having a certain meaning **6** to respond to in the affirmative [to *accept* an invitation] **7** to admit as a student, member, etc. **8** to agree to take the responsibilities of (a job, office, etc.) **9** to receive (a committee report) as satisfactory according to parliamentary procedure **10** *Business* to agree, as by a signed promise, to pay **11** *Law* to receive with intent to retain and adopt —*vi.* to accept something offered —*SYN.* RECEIVE —**ac·cept′er** *n.*

ac·cept·a·ble (ak sep′tə bəl, ək-) *adj.* **1** worth accepting; satisfactory or, sometimes, merely adequate **2** tolerable; bearable —**ac·cept′a·bil′i·ty** *n.*, **ac·cept′a·ble·ness** —**ac·cept′a·bly** *adv.*

ac·cept·ance (ak sep′təns, ək-) *n.* **1** an accepting or being accepted **2** approving reception; approval; acceptability **3** belief in; assent **4** a draft or bill of exchange that has been accepted for payment: cf. BANKER'S ACCEPTANCE, TRADE ACCEPTANCE **5** *Law* an express or implied act by which one accepts an obligation, offer, contract, etc. together with all its legal consequences

ac·cept·ant (-tənt) *adj.* readily accepting; receptive

ac·cep·ta·tion (ak′sep tā′shən) *n.* ⟦LL *acceptatio*: see ACCEPT⟧ **1** the generally accepted meaning (of a word or expression) **2** [Archaic] acceptance

ac·cept·ed (ak sep′tid, ək-) *adj.* generally regarded as true, valid, proper, etc.; conventional; approved

ac·cep·tor (ak sep′tər, ək-) *n.* ⟦L⟧ **1** one who accepts; specif., a person who signs a promise to pay a draft or bill of exchange **2** *Chem.* an atom that receives a pair of electrons from another atom to form a covalent bond with it **3** *Electronics* an impurity, as gallium or boron, added to a semiconductor crystal to make a p-type semiconductor

ac·cess (ak′ses′) *n.* ⟦ME & OFr *acces* < L *accessus*, pp. of *accedere*, ACCEDE⟧ **1** the act of coming toward or near to; approach **2** a way or means of approaching, getting, using, etc. **3** the right to enter, approach, or use; admittance **4** increase or growth **5** an outburst; paroxysm [an *access* of anger] —*vt.* to gain or have access to; esp., to retrieve data from, or add data to, a database [branch officials can *access* the central database]

ac·ces·sa·ry (ak ses′ər ē, ək-) *adj., n., pl.* **-ries** ACCESSORY

ac·ces·si·ble (ak ses′ə bəl, ək-) *adj.* ⟦Fr < LL(Ec) *accessibilis* < L *accessus*, ACCESS⟧ **1** that can be approached or entered **2** easy to approach or enter **3** that can be gotten; obtainable **4** open to the influence of: with *to* [*accessible* to pity] **5** able to be readily understood or generally appreciated [an *accessible* modern poet] —**ac·ces′si·bil′i·ty** *n.* —**ac·ces′si·bly** *adv.*

ac·ces·sion (ak sesh′ən, ək-) *n.* ⟦Fr < L *accessio* < *accessus*, ACCESS⟧ **1** the act of coming to or attaining (a throne, power, etc.) [the *accession* of a new king] **2** assent; agreement **3** *a)* increase by addition *b)* an item added, as to a library or museum **4** an outburst; paroxysm; access **5** *Law a)* addition to property by improvements or natural growth *b)* the owner's right to the increase in value due to such additions —☆*vt.* to record (a book, etc.) as a new accession —**ac·ces′sion·al** *adj.*

ac·ces·so·ri·al (ak′se sôr′ē əl) *adj.* ⟦< ML *accessorius* (see ACCESSORY) + -AL⟧ of or like an accessory; supplementary

☆**ac·ces·so·rize** (ak ses′ə rīz′, ək-) *vt.* **-rized′, -riz′ing** to equip, decorate, supplement, etc. with accessories

ac·ces·so·ry (ak ses′ər ē, ək-; *also* ə ses′-) *adj.* ⟦ML *accessorius* < L *accessus*, pp. of *accedere*, ACCEDE⟧ **1** extra; additional; helping in a secondary or subordinate way **2** *Geol.* occurring in minor amounts in a specified rock; nonessential [*accessory* minerals are disregarded in classifying rocks] **3** *Law* acting as an accessory; helping in an unlawful act —*n., pl.* **-ries** ⟦ME *accessorie* < ML: see the *adj.*⟧ **1** something extra; thing added to help in a secondary way; specif., *a)* an article worn or carried to complete one's outfit, as a purse or gloves *b)* a piece of optional equipment for convenience, comfort, appearance, etc. [the *accessories* of an automobile] **2** *Law* a person who, though absent, helps another to break or escape the law; accomplice —**accessory before (or after) the fact** a person who, though absent at the commission of a felony, aids or abets the accused before (or after) its commission

accessory fruit a fruit having enlarged accessory structures in addition to those formed from the ovary, as the strawberry, in which the fleshy tissue is the enlarged receptacle and the true fruits are the small, dry achenes borne on its surface: see FALSE FRUIT

☆**access time** the length of time required by a computer to retrieve or store data

ac·ciac·ca·tu·ra (ə chä′kə to͝or′ə; *It*, ät chäk′kä to͞o′rä′) *n., pl.* **-tu′re′** (-to͞o′rä′) or Eng. **-tu′ras** (-to͝or′əz) ⟦It < *acciaccare*, to crush < *accia*, ax < L *ascia*: see AX[1]⟧ in keyboard music of the Baroque period, a short grace note sounded together with the principal note or chord, but quickly released

ac·ci·dence (ak′sə dəns) *n.* ⟦ME *accidens*, inflection < L *accidentia*, that which happens < *accidens*: see fol. ⟧ **1** the part of grammar that deals with the inflection of words **2** the elementary or first parts of a subject; rudiments

ac·ci·dent (ak′sə dənt) *n.* ⟦ME < OFr < L *accidens*, prp. of *accidere*, to fall upon, happen < *ad-*, to + *cadere*, to fall: see CASE[1]⟧ **1** a happening that is not expected, foreseen, or intended **2** an unpleasant and unintended happening, sometimes resulting from negligence, that results in injury, loss, damage, etc. **3** *a)* a collision involving a motor vehicle *b)* the wreckage, etc. at the scene of such a collision [watch out for the *accident* on the freeway overpass] **4** fortune; chance [to meet by *accident*] **5** an attribute or quality that is not essential **6** *Geog., Geol.* an irregular formation **7** *Law* an unforeseen event that occurs without anyone's fault or negligence

ac·ci·den·tal (ak′sə dent′'l) *adj.* ⟦ME < LL *accidentalis*: see prec. ⟧ **1** happening by chance; fortuitous **2** belonging but not essential; attributive; incidental **3** *Music* of an accidental —*n.* **1** a nonessential quality or feature **2** *Music a)* a sign, as a sharp, flat, or natural, placed before a note to show a change of pitch from that indicated by the key signature *b)* the tone indicated by such a sign —**ac′ci·den′tal·ly** *adv.*

SYN.—**accidental** describes that which occurs by chance [an *accidental* encounter] or outside the normal course of events [an *accidental* attribute]; **fortuitous**, which frequently suggests a complete absence of cause, now usually refers to chance events of a fortunate nature; **casual** describes the unpremeditated, random, informal, or irregular quality of something [a *casual* visit, remark, dress, etc.]; **incidental** emphasizes the nonessential or secondary nature of something [an *incidental* consideration]; **adventitious** refers to that which is added extrinsically and connotes a lack of essential connection

☆**accident insurance** insurance against injury due to accident

ac·ci·dent-prone (ak′sə dənt prōn′) *adj.* having an apparent tendency or inclination to become involved in accidents —**ac′ci·dent-prone′ness** *n.*

ac·ci·die (ak′sə dē′) *n.* ACEDIA: also **ac·cid·i·a** (ak sid′ē ə)

ac·cip·i·ter (ak sip′ət ər) *n.* ⟦L < **acupeter*, swift-winged < IE **aku-*, swift, prob. < base **ak-* (see ACID) + **peter-*, wing: see FEATHER⟧ any of a genus (*Accipiter*) of small to medium-sized hawks with short, rounded wings and a long tail, as Cooper's hawk

ac·cip·i·trine (ak sip′ə trin′) *adj.* of or relating to a family (Accipitridae) of diurnal birds of prey, including hawks, eagles, and kites

ac·claim (ə klām′) *vt.* ⟦L *acclamare* < *ad-*, to + *clamare*, to cry out: see CLAMOR⟧ **1** to greet with loud applause or approval **2** to announce with much applause or praise; hail [they *acclaimed* him president] —*vi.* to shout approval —*n.* loud applause or strong approval —*SYN.* PRAISE —**ac·claim′er** *n.*

ac·cla·ma·tion (ak′lə mā′shən) *n.* **1** an acclaiming or being acclaimed **2** loud applause or strong approval **3** a vote by voice; esp., an enthusiastic approving vote without an actual count [elected by *acclamation*] —**ac·clam·a·to·ry** (ə klam′ə tôr′ē) *adj.*

ac·cli·mate (ak′lə māt′, ə klī′mət) *vt., vi.* **-mat′ed, -mat′ing** ⟦Fr *acclimater*: see AD- & CLIMATE⟧ to accustom or become accustomed to a different climate, environment, or circumstances, as by physiological or psychological changes —**ac′cli·ma′tion** *n.*

ac·cli·ma·tize (ə klī′mə tīz′) *vt., vi.* **-tized′, -tiz′ing** ACCLIMATE —**ac·cli′ma·ti·za′tion** *n.*

ac·cliv·i·ty (ə kliv′ə tē) *n., pl.* **-ties** ⟦L *acclivitas* < *acclivis*, uphill < *ad-*, up + *clivus*, hill < IE base **klei-*, to incline: see LEAN[1]⟧ an upward slope of ground: opposed to DECLIVITY

ac·co·lade (ak′ə lād′, ak′ə lād′) *n.* ⟦Fr < Prov *acolada* < VL **accolare*, to embrace < L *ad*, to + *collum*, neck: see WHEEL⟧ **1** an embrace formerly used in conferring knighthood **2** a touch on the shoulder with the flat side of a sword, now used in conferring knighthood **3** *a)* anything done or given as a sign of great respect, approval, appreciation, etc. *b)* [*usually pl.*] words of praise **4** *Music* BRACE[1] (sense 5*b*)

ac·com·mo·date (ə käm′ə dāt′) *vt.* **-dat′ed, -dat′ing** ⟦< L *accommodatus*, pp. of *accommodare* < *ad-*, to + *commodare*, to fit < *commodus*: see COMMODE⟧ **1** to make fit; adjust; adapt [to *accommodate* oneself to changes] **2** to reconcile (differences) **3** to provide (someone) *with* something needed or desired **4** to do a service or favor for **5** to have space for [a table to *accommodate* six diners] **6** to provide lodging for —*vi.* to become adjusted, as the lens of the eye in focusing on objects at various distances —*SYN.* ADAPT, CONTAIN —**ac·com′mo·dat′ive** *adj.* —**ac·com′mo·da′tor** *n.*

ac·com·mo·dat·ing (-dāt′iŋ) *adj.* willing to please; ready to help; obliging —**ac·com′mo·dat′ing·ly** *adv.*

ac·com·mo·da·tion (ə käm′ə dā′shən) *n.* **1** an accommodating or being accommodated; adaptation (*to* a purpose); adjustment **2** reconciliation of differences **3** willingness to do favors or services **4** a help or convenience **5** [*pl.*] lodgings, sometimes, specif., with board included **6** [*pl.*] traveling space, as in a railroad train or airplane; seat, berth, etc. **7** the automatic adjustment of the eye, esp. the lens and pupil, for focusing on objects at various distances **8** the act of making or endorsing an accommodation paper

ac·com·mo·da·tion·ist (-ist) ***n.*** a person who seeks to promote adaptation to or compromise with an opposing point of view

accommodation ladder a portable set of steps held in place temporarily along a ship's side for access to or from a small boat or pier

accommodation paper (*or* **bill** *or* **note)** a bill of exchange cosigned by one party as maker, acceptor, or endorser without requiring collateral or a fee, in order to lend his or her credit reputation to the second party

☆**accommodation train** a railroad train that stops at all or nearly all stations

ac·com·pa·ni·ment (ə kum′pə nə mənt, -nē-; *often,* ə kump′nə-, -nē-) ***n.*** **1** anything that accompanies something else; thing added, usually for order or symmetry **2** *Music* a part, usually instrumental, performed together with the main part for richer effect [the piano *accompaniment* to a song]

ac·com·pa·nist (ə kum′pə nist; *often,* ə kump′nist) ***n.*** a person who plays or sings an accompaniment: also **ac·com′pa·ny·ist** (-nē ist)

ac·com·pa·ny (ə kum′pə nē; *often,* ə kump′nē) ***vt.*** **-nied, -ny·ing** ⟦MFr *acompaignier* < *ac-*, AD- + OFr *compagnon*: see COMPANION[1]⟧ **1** to go or be together with; attend **2** to send (*with*); add to; supplement [to *accompany* words with acts] **3** to play or sing a musical accompaniment for or to —***vi.*** to perform a musical accompaniment

SYN.—accompany means to go or be together with as a companion, associate, attribute, etc., and usually connotes equality of relationship [he *accompanied* her to the theater]; **attend** implies presence either in a subordinate position or to render services, etc. [Dr. Jones *attended* the patient]; **escort** and **convoy** are both applied to the accompanying, as by an armed guard, of persons or things needing protection (**convoy**, esp. in the case of sea travel and **escort**, in the case of land travel); **escort** also implies an accompanying as a mark of honor or an act of courtesy; **chaperone** implies accompaniment, for reasons of propriety, of young unmarried people by an older or married person

ac·com·plice (ə käm′plis) ***n.*** ⟦< ME *a complice* (the article *a* is merged, infl. by *accomplish*) < OFr *complice* < LL *complex*: see COMPLICE⟧ a person who knowingly participates with another in an unlawful act; partner in crime —***SYN.*** ASSOCIATE

ac·com·plish (ə käm′plish; *also,* -kum′-) ***vt.*** ⟦ME *accomplisshen* < OFr *accompliss-*, extended stem of *acomplir* < VL **adcomplere* < L *ad-*, intens. + *complere*: see COMPLETE⟧ **1** to do; succeed in doing; complete (a task, time, or distance) **2** to make complete; perfect —***SYN.*** PERFORM, REACH —**ac·com′plish·a·ble** ***adj.***

ac·com·plished (-plisht) ***adj.*** **1** done; done successfully; completed **2** skilled; proficient [an *accomplished* pianist] **3** having social poise; polished

ac·com·plish·ment (ə käm′plish mənt; *also,* -kum′-) ***n.*** **1** an accomplishing or being accomplished; completion **2** something accomplished or done successfully; work completed; achievement **3** a social art or skill: *usually used in pl.*

ac·cord (ə kôrd′) ***vt.*** ⟦ME *acorden* < OFr *acorder* < VL **accordare* < L *ad-*, to + *cor* (gen. *cordis*), HEART⟧ **1** to make agree or harmonize; reconcile **2** to grant or concede; bestow —***vi.*** to be in agreement or harmony (*with*) —***n.*** **1** mutual agreement; harmony **2** an informal agreement, as between countries **3** harmony of sound, color, etc. **4** [Obs.] consent; permission —***SYN.*** AGREE —**of one's own accord** willingly, without being asked —**with one accord** all agreeing; with no one dissenting

ac·cord·ance (ə kôr′dəns) ***n.*** ⟦ME < OFr *acordance* < *acordant*: see fol.⟧ **1** agreement; harmony; conformity [in *accordance* with the plans] **2** the act of granting

ac·cord·ant (ə kôr′dənt) ***adj.*** ⟦ME < OFr *acordant*, prp. of *acorder*: see ACCORD⟧ in agreement or harmony (*with* or *to*) —**ac·cord′ant·ly** ***adv.***

ac·cord·ing (ə kôr′diŋ) ***adj.*** agreeing; in harmony —**according as** **1** to the degree that; in proportion as **2** depending on whether; if —**according to** **1** in agreement with **2** in the order of [arranged *according to* size] **3** as stated in or reported by

ac·cord·ing·ly (-lē) ***adv.*** **1** in a way that is fitting and proper; correspondingly **2** therefore

ac·cor·di·on (ə kôr′dē ən) ***n.*** ⟦Ger *akkordion* < *akkord*, harmony (prob. < It *accordare*, to be in tune: see ACCORD) + *-ion* as in ORCHESTRION⟧ a musical instrument with keys, metal reeds, and a bellows: it is played by alternately pulling out and pressing together the bellows to force air through the reeds, which are opened by fingering the keys —***adj.*** having folds, or folding, like the bellows of an accordion [*accordion* pleats] —**ac·cor′di·on·ist** ***n.***

accordion

ac·cost (ə kôst′, -käst′) ***vt.*** ⟦Fr *accoster* < It *accostare*, to bring side by side < VL **accostare* < L *ad-*, to + *costa*, rib, side⟧ **1** to approach and speak to; greet first, before being greeted, esp. in an intrusive way **2** to solicit for sexual purposes: said of a prostitute, etc.

ac·couche·ment (ə ko͞osh′mənt; *Fr* à ko͞osh män′) ***n.*** ⟦Fr < *accoucher*, put to bed, give birth < OFr *acoucher*, lie down < L *ad-*, to + *collocare*: see COUCH⟧ [*also in italics*] confinement for giving birth to a child; childbirth

ac·cou·cheur (a′ko͞o shʉr′) ***n.*** ⟦Fr: see prec.⟧ OBSTETRICIAN

ac·cou·cheuse (a′ko͞o shʉz′) ***n.*** ⟦Fr, fem. of prec.⟧ MIDWIFE

ac·count (ə kount′) ***vt.*** ⟦ME *acounten* < OFr *aconter* < *a-*, to + *conter*, to tell < *compter* < L *computare*: see COMPUTE⟧ to consider or judge to be; deem; value —***vi.*** **1** to furnish a reckoning (*to* someone) of money received and paid out **2** to make satisfactory amends (*for*) [he will *account* for his crime] **3** to give satisfactory reasons or an explanation (*for*) [can he *account* for his actions?] **4** to know or provide the whereabouts or fate of: with *for* [to *account* for all members of the platoon] **5** to be the cause, agent, or source of: with *for* **6** to do away with as by killing: with *for* [he *accounted* for five of the enemy] —***n.*** **1** a counting; calculation **2** [*often pl.*] a record of the financial data pertaining to a specific asset, liability, income item, expense item, or net-worth item **3** BANK ACCOUNT **4** *a)* a record of the financial transactions relating to a specific person, property, business, etc. *b)* a customer or client, esp. one with whom there is a regular or formal business relationship *c)* such a relationship, as that between a brokerage or advertising agency and each of its clients **5** worth; importance [a thing of small *account*] **6** an explanation **7** a report; description; story —**call to account** **1** to demand an explanation of **2** to reprimand —**give a good account of oneself** to acquit oneself creditably —**on account** **1** on a charge account; on the installment plan **2** as partial payment —**on someone's account** for someone's sake —**on account of** **1** because of **2** for (someone's) sake —**on no account** not under any circumstances —**take account of** **1** to take into consideration; allow for **2** to take notice of; note —**take into account** to take into consideration —**turn to account** to get use or profit from

ac·count·a·ble (ə kount′ə bəl) ***adj.*** **1** obliged to account for one's acts; responsible **2** capable of being accounted for; explainable —***SYN.*** RESPONSIBLE —**ac·count′a·bil′i·ty** ***n.***, **ac·count′a·ble·ness** —**ac·count′a·bly** ***adv.***

ac·count·an·cy (ə kount′'n sē) ***n.*** the keeping or inspecting of commercial accounts; work of an accountant

ac·count·ant (ə kount′'nt) ***n.*** a person whose work is to inspect, keep, or adjust accounts: see CERTIFIED PUBLIC ACCOUNTANT

account book a book in which business accounts are set down

account current a record of business transactions that shows the total amount of money owed as of the date of the summarizing statement

account executive an executive in an advertising agency, stockbrokerage, etc. who handles the accounts of, and maintains direct contact with, one or more established clients and seeks new clients

ac·count·ing (ə kount′iŋ) ***n.*** **1** the principles or practice of systematically recording, presenting, and interpreting financial accounts **2** a statement of debits and credits **3** a settling or balancing of accounts

account payable *pl.* **accounts payable** the amount owed by a business to a creditor, usually for goods or services

account receivable *pl.* **accounts receivable** the amount owed to a business by a debtor, usually for goods or services

ac·cou·ple·ment (ə kup′əl mənt) ***n.*** ⟦Fr < *accoupler*, to couple up < OFr *acoupler* < ML *accopulare* < L *ad-*, to + *copulare*, to COUPLE⟧ **1** *Archit.* the placing of columns in pairs close together **2** *Carpentry* a brace or tie of timber

ac·cou·ter or **ac·cou·tre** (ə ko͞ot′ər) ***vt.*** **-tered** or **-tred, -ter·ing** or **-tring** (ə ko͞ot′ər iŋ, -ko͞o′triŋ) ⟦Fr *accoutrer*, earlier *accoustrer*; prob. < *à-*, to + OFr *costure* < VL **consutura*, seam, sewing < L *consuere*, to sew < *con-*, together + *suere*, SEW⟧ to outfit; equip, esp. for military service

ac·cou·ter·ment or **ac·cou·tre·ment** (ə ko͞ot′ər mənt, -ko͞o′trə-) ***n.*** **1** an accoutering or being accoutered **2** [*pl.*] *a)* personal outfit; clothes; apparel *b)* furnishings; trappings; equipment; specif., a soldier's equipment except clothes and weapons

Ac·cra (ə krä′) capital of Ghana: seaport on the Gulf of Guinea

ac·cred·it (ə kred′it) ***vt.*** ⟦Fr *accréditer*, to give credit or authority < *à*, to + *crédit*, CREDIT⟧ **1** to bring into credit or favor **2** to authorize; give credentials to [an *accredited* representative] **3** to certify as meeting certain set standards [colleges may be *accredited* by regional associations] **4** to attribute; credit [an action *accredited* to him] —***SYN.*** AUTHORIZE —**ac·cred′i·ta′tion** ***n.***

ac·crete (ə krēt′) ***vi.*** **-cret′ed, -cret′ing** ⟦< L *accretus*, pp. of *accrescere*: see fol.⟧ **1** to grow by being added to **2** to grow together; adhere —***vt.*** to cause to adhere or unite (*to*) —***adj.*** *Bot.* grown together

ac·cre·tion (ə krē′shən) ***n.*** ⟦L *accretio* < *accrescere*, to increase < *ad-*, to + *crescere*, to grow: see CRESCENT⟧ **1** growth in size, esp. by addition or accumulation **2** a growing together of parts normally separate **3** accumulated matter [the *accretion* of earth on the shore] **4** a part added separately; addition **5** a whole resulting from such growth or accumulation **6** *Law* the addition of soil to land by gradual, natural deposits —**ac·cre′tive** (-krēt′iv) ***adj.***

ac·cru·al (ə kro͞o′əl) ***n.*** **1** the act or process of accruing **2** the amount that accrues Also **ac·crue·ment** (ə kro͞o′mənt)

ac·crue (ə kro͞o′) ***vi.*** **-crued′, -cru′ing** ⟦ME *acreuen* < OFr *acreu*, pp. of *acroistre*, increase < L *accrescere*: see ACCRETION⟧ **1** to come as a natural growth, advantage, or right (*to*) **2** to be added periodically as an increase: said esp. of interest on money —***vt.*** to accumulate periodically as an increase [savings accounts *accrue* interest]

acct *abbrev.* **1** account **2** accountant

☆**ac·cul·tur·ate** (ə kul′chər āt′) *vi., vt.* **-at′ed, -at′ing** ⟦back-form. < fol.⟧ to undergo, or alter by, acculturation

☆**ac·cul·tur·a·tion** (ə kul′chər ā′shən) *n.* ⟦AC- + CULTUR(E) + -ATION⟧ *Sociology* **1** the process of conditioning a child to the patterns or customs of a culture **2** the process of becoming adapted to a new or different culture with more or less advanced patterns **3** the mutual influence of different cultures in close contact —**ac·cul′tur·a′tive** *adj.*

ac·cum·bent (ə kum′bənt) *adj.* ⟦L *accumbens*, prp. of *accumbere* < *ad-*, to + *cubare*, to recline⟧ **1** lying down **2** *Bot.* lying against some other part: said esp. of certain cotyledons —**ac·cum′ben·cy** *n.*

ac·cu·mu·late (ə kyōōm′yōō lāt′, -yə-) *vt., vi.* **-lat′ed, -lat′ing** ⟦< L *accumulatus*, pp. of *accumulare* < *ad-*, to + *cumulare*, to heap: see CUMULUS⟧ to pile up, collect, or gather together, esp. over a period of time —**ac·cu′mu·la·ble** (-lə bəl) *adj.*

ac·cu·mu·la·tion (ə kyōōm′yōō lā′shən, -yə-) *n.* **1** an accumulating or being accumulated; collection **2** accumulated or collected material; heap **3** the addition to capital of interest or profits

ac·cu·mu·la·tive (ə kyōōm′yōō lāt′iv, -lət iv; -yə-) *adj.* **1** resulting from accumulation; cumulative **2** tending to accumulate **3** acquisitive —**ac·cu′mu·la′tive·ly** *adv.*

ac·cu·mu·la·tor (ə kyōōm′yōō lāt′ər, -yə-) *n.* **1** a person or thing that accumulates **2** *a)* an apparatus that collects and stores energy *b)* [Brit.] STORAGE BATTERY **3** a type of shock absorber **4** a device or circuit unit performing one or more of the operations of storage, arithmetic, and logic, as in a computer, cash register, etc.

ac·cu·ra·cy (ak′yə rə sē) *n.* the quality or state of being accurate or exact; precision; exactness

ac·cu·rate (ak′yə rət) *adj.* ⟦L *accuratus*, pp. of *accurare* < *ad-*, to + *curare*, to take care < *cura*, care: see CURE⟧ **1** careful and exact **2** free from mistakes or errors; precise **3** adhering closely to a standard [an *accurate* thermometer] —*SYN.* CORRECT —**ac′cu·rate·ly** *adv.* —**ac′cu·rate·ness** *n.*

ac·curs·ed (ə kʉrs′id, -kʉrst′) *adj.* ⟦ME *acursed*, pp. of *acursen*, pronounce a curse upon, excommunicate < *a-*, intens. + *cursien*: see CURSE⟧ **1** under a curse; ill-fated **2** deserving to be cursed; damnable; abominable Also **ac·curst** (ə kʉrst′) —**ac·curs′ed·ly** *adv.* —**ac·curs′ed·ness** *n.*

accus *abbrev.* accusative

ac·cus·al (ə kyōō′zəl) *n.* ACCUSATION

ac·cu·sa·tion (ak′yōō zā′shən, -yə-) *n.* **1** an accusing or being accused **2** the crime or wrong of which a person is accused

ac·cu·sa·ti·val (ə kyōō′zə tī′vəl) *adj.* of the accusative case

ac·cu·sa·tive (ə kyōō′zə tiv) *adj.* ⟦ME *acusatif* < L *accusativus* < *accusare*, ACCUSE: L mistransl. (by PRISCIAN) of Gr grammatical term correctly rendered *causativus*, causative: the goal or end point of an action was orig. considered to be its cause⟧ **1** *Gram.* designating, of, or in the case of the direct object of a finite verb: also sometimes used of the objective case in English **2** accusatory —*n.* **1** the accusative case **2** a word in this case —**ac·cu′sa·tive·ly** *adv.*

ac·cu·sa·to·ri·al (ə kyōō′zə tôr′ē əl) *adj.* ⟦L *accusatorius*: see ACCUSE⟧ of, or in the manner of, an accuser

ac·cu·sa·to·ry (ə kyōō′zə tôr′ē) *adj.* making or containing an accusation; accusing

ac·cuse (ə kyōōz′) *vt.* **-cused′, -cus′ing** ⟦ME *acusen* < OFr *acuser* < L *accusare*, to call to account < *ad-*, to + *causa*, CAUSE⟧ **1** to find at fault; blame **2** to bring formal charges against (*of* doing wrong, breaking the law, etc.) —**the accused** *Law* the person or persons formally charged with commission of a crime —**ac·cus′er** *n.* —**ac·cus′ing·ly** *adv.*

SYN.—accuse means to find fault for offenses of varying gravity [to *accuse* someone of murder, carelessness, etc.]; to **charge** is to make an accusation of a legal or formal nature [the police *charged* her with jaywalking]; **indict** describes the action of a grand jury and means to find a case against a person and order the person to be brought to trial; **arraign** means to call a person before a court to be informed of pending charges; **impeach** means to charge a public official with misconduct in office, but in nonlegal usage means to challenge a person's motives, etc.

ac·cus·tom (ə kus′təm) *vt.* ⟦ME *accustomen* < OFr *acostumer* < *a-*, to + *costume*: see CUSTOM⟧ to make familiar by custom, habit, or use; habituate (*to*)

ac·cus·tomed (ə kus′təmd) *adj.* **1** customary; usual; characteristic [he spoke with *accustomed* ease] **2** used (*to*); habituated (*to*) [*accustomed* to obeying orders] —*SYN.* USUAL

AC/DC or **A.C./D.C.** (ā′sē′dē′sē′) *adj.* ⟦by analogy with devices using either alternating or direct current⟧ [Slang] BISEXUAL (*adj.* 3)

ace (ās) *n.* ⟦ME *as, aas* < L *as*, unit, unity, AS[2]⟧ **1** a playing card, domino, etc. marked with one large, centered pip **2** *Handball, Racket Sports a)* a score made by a serve that one's opponent fails to touch *b)* such a serve **3** *Golf* the act of hitting the ball so that it goes into the hole on the drive; hole in one **4** a combat pilot who has destroyed at least five enemy planes **5** an expert in any activity —*adj.* [Informal] first-rate; expert [an *ace* salesman] —*vt.* **aced, ac′ing 1** to score an ace against, as in tennis **2** to make an ace on (a particular hole) in golf **3** [Slang] to defeat completely; get the best of: often with *out* ☆**4** [Informal] to do very well, esp., by earning a grade of A, in, on, etc. [she *aced* the course] —**within an ace of** on the verge of; very close to

ACE *abbrev.* American Council on Education

-a·ce·a (ā′shē ə, ā′shə; ā′sē ə) ⟦L, neut. pl. of *-aceus*⟧ *suffix Zool.* the scientific name of a (specified) class or order

-a·ce·ae (ā′sē ē′) ⟦L, fem. pl. of *-aceus*⟧ *suffix Bot.* the scientific name of a (specified) family

Ace bandage (ās) ⟦< *Ace*, a trademark for such a bandage⟧ an elasticized cloth bandage wrapped around an ankle, knee, etc. to provide firm support, as for a strain or sprain

a·ce·di·a (ə sē′dē ə) *n.* ⟦LL < Gr *akēdia* < *a-*, not + *kēdos*, care: see HATE⟧ spiritual sloth or apathy

☆**ace-high** (ās′hī′) *adj.* ⟦orig. a poker term for a hand containing an ace, esp. as completing a straight⟧ [Informal] esteemed; respected

ACE inhibitor (ā′sē′ē′, ās) ⟦*a*(*ngiotensin-*)*c*(*onverting*) *e*(*nzyme*)⟧ any of a class of drugs, including captopril, that inhibit or block the action of an enzyme (**ACE**) that produces the powerful vasoconstrictor angiotensin, used to treat high blood pressure, heart failure, diabetic kidney disease, etc.

☆**ace in the hole 1** *Stud Poker* an ace dealt and kept face down until the deal is over **2** [Slang] any advantage held in reserve until needed

A·cel·da·ma (ə sel′də mə) *n.* ⟦L < Gr *Akeldama* < Aram *chakal-dema*, field of blood⟧ **1** *Bible* the field near Jerusalem bought with the money given Judas for betraying Jesus: Acts 1:19; Matt. 27:8 **2** a place of bloodshed

-a·ceous (ā′shəs) ⟦L *-aceus*⟧ *suffix forming adjectives* of the nature of, like, belonging to, producing, or characterized by [*herbaceous*]: corresponds to -ACEA, -ACEAE

a·ceph·a·lous (ā sef′ə ləs) *adj.* ⟦LL *acephalus* < Gr *akephalos* < *a-*, without + *kephalē*, head: see CEPHALIC⟧ **1** *Zool.* having no part of the body differentiated as the head **2** having no leader

ac·e·pro·ma·zine (as′ə prō′mə zēn′, -prăm′ə-; -zin) *n.* an orange-colored oil, $C_{19}H_{22}N_2OS$, used as a tranquilizer, esp. to immobilize large animals, and to relieve nausea: also called *acetyl promazine*

☆**a·ce·qui·a** (ə sā′kē ə) *n.* ⟦Sp < Ar *as-sāqiya* < *al-sāqiya*, fem. prp. of *saqā*, to give to drink, irrigate⟧ in the Southwest, an irrigation canal

ac·er·ate (as′ər āt′, -ər it) *adj.* ⟦L *aceratus*, needlelike < *acus*: see ACEROSE[1]⟧ *Biol.* needle-shaped

a·cerb (ə sʉrb′) *adj. var. of* ACERBIC

ac·er·bate (as′ər bāt′) *vt.* **-bat′ed, -bat′ing** ⟦< L *acerbatus*, pp. of *acerbare*, to make harsh or bitter⟧ **1** to make sour or bitter **2** to irritate; vex

a·cer·bic (ə sʉr′bik) *adj.* ⟦Fr *acerbe* < L *acerbus*: see fol.⟧ **1** sour in taste **2** sharp, bitter, or harsh in temper, language, etc.

a·cer·bi·ty (-bə tē) *n.* ⟦Fr *acerbité* < L *acerbitas* < *acerbus*, bitter < IE base **ak̂-*: see ACID⟧ **1** a sour, astringent quality **2** sharpness, bitterness, or harshness of temper, words, etc.

ac·er·ose[1] (as′ər ōs′) *adj.* ⟦< L *acus* (gen. *aceris*), a needle < IE base **ak̂-* (see ACID); form infl. by fol.⟧ *Bot.* shaped like a needle; having a sharp, stiff point

ac·er·ose[2] (as′ər ōs′) *adj.* ⟦L *acerosus*, full of chaff < *acus* (gen. *aceris*): see EAR[2]⟧ **1** like chaff **2** mixed with chaff

a·cer·vate (ə sʉr′vit, -vāt′) *adj.* ⟦L *acervatus*, pp. of *acervare*, to heap up < *acervus*, a heap⟧ *Biol.* growing in tight clusters or heaps

a·cet- (ə sēt′, -set′; as′et, -it, -ət) *combining form* ACETO-: used before a vowel [*acetanilide*]

ac·e·tab·u·lum (as′i tab′yōō ləm, -yə-) *n., pl.* **-la** (-lə) or **-lums** ⟦L, orig., vinegar cup < *acetum* (see ACETO-) + *-abulum*, dim. of *-abrum*, receptacle⟧ **1** *Anat.* the cup-shaped socket of the hipbone, into which the head of the thighbone fits **2** *Zool. a)* any suction disc of flukes, leeches, cephalopods, etc. *b)* the cavity into which an insect's leg fits —**ac′e·tab′u·lar** (-lər) *adj.*

ac·e·tal (as′i tal′) *n.* ⟦ACET(O)- + -AL⟧ any of a class of organic compounds; esp., $CH_3CH(OC_2H_5)_2$, a colorless, slightly soluble, volatile liquid formed by the partial oxidation of ethyl alcohol: used as a solvent, in organic synthesis, and sometimes as a hypnotic

ac·et·al·de·hyde (as′et al′də hīd′) *n.* ⟦contr. < *acetic aldehyde*⟧ a colorless, soluble, flammable, liquid aldehyde, CH_3CHO, formed by the oxidation of ethylene: used as a solvent and as a raw material in making many organic compounds

ac·et·am·ide (as′et am′īd, -id; ə set′ə mīd, -mid) *n.* ⟦ACET(O)- + AMIDE⟧ colorless, soluble, organic crystals, CH_3CONH_2, the amide of acetic acid: used as a solvent, in lacquers and explosives, and in making organic compounds

ac·e·ta·min·o·phen (ə sēt′ə min′ə fən, as′ə tə-) *n.* ⟦ACET(O)- + AMINO- + PHEN(OL)⟧ a white, crystalline powder, $CH_3CONHC_6H_4OH$, used for reducing fever and relieving pain

ac·et·an·i·lide (as′ət an′ə līd′) *n.* ⟦ACET(O)- + ANIL(INE) + -IDE⟧ a white, crystalline organic substance, $C_6H_5NHCOCH_3$, produced by the action of acetic acid on aniline: it is used as a drug to lessen pain and fever, in making dyes, etc.

ac·e·tate (as′i tāt′) *n.* ⟦ACET(IC) + -ATE[2]⟧ **1** *a)* a salt of acetic acid containing the monovalent, negative radical CH_3COO *b)* an uncharged ester of this acid **2** CELLULOSE ACETATE **3** an article or material made with an acetate or with cellulose acetate

ac·e·tat·ed (-id) *adj.* treated with acetic acid

a·ce·tic (ə sēt′ik, -set′-) *adj.* ⟦Fr *acétique* < L *acetum*: see ACETO- & -IC⟧ of, like, containing, or producing acetic acid or vinegar

acetic acid a sour, colorless, liquid organic acid, CH_3COOH, having a sharp odor: it is contained in vinegar (3 to 8%) and is used with alcohols to produce esters, esp. cellulose acetate

acetic anhydride a combustible, colorless liquid, $(CH_3CO)_2O$, that decomposes in water to form acetic acid: used in plastics and organic synthesis

a·cet·i·fy (ə set′ə fī′, -sēt′-) *vt., vi.* **-fied′, -fy′ing** to change into vinegar or acetic acid —**a·cet′i·fi·ca′tion** *n.*

ac·e·tim·e·ter (as′ə tim′ət ər) *n.* ACETOMETER

ac·e·tin (as′ə tin′) ***n.*** ⟦ACETO- + -IN[1]⟧ a thick, colorless liquid, $C_3H_5(OH)_2OOCCH_3$, soluble in water: it is used in making explosives and as a solvent

ac·e·to- (ə sēt′ō, as′i tō′) ⟦< L *acetum*, vinegar < pp. of *acere*, to turn sour < IE base *ak̑-: see ACID⟧ *combining form* of or related to acetic acid or acetyl [*acetophenetidin*]

ac·e·tom·e·ter (as′i täm′ət ər) ***n.*** an instrument used to find the amount of acetic acid present in vinegar or another solution: also called *acetimeter*

ac·e·tone (as′i tōn′) ***n.*** ⟦ACET(O)- + -ONE⟧ a colorless, flammable, volatile liquid, CH_3COCH_3, used in organic synthesis and as a solvent, esp. in making rayon: it is found in small amounts in normal urine but in greater amounts in diabetic urine —**ac′e·ton′ic** (-tän′ik) ***adj.***

acetone body KETONE BODY

a·ce·to·phe·net·i·din (ə sēt′ō fə net′ə din, as′i tō′-) ***n.*** ⟦ACETO- + PHENETI-DIN(E)⟧ PHENACETIN

ac·e·tous (as′i təs, ə sēt′əs) ***adj.*** ⟦< LL *acetosus*, sour: see ACETO- & -OUS⟧ of, producing, or like vinegar; sour: also **ac′e·tose′** (-tōs′)

a·ce·tum (ə sēt′əm) ***n.*** ⟦L: see ACETO-⟧ *Pharmacy* vinegar or a solution of a drug in dilute acetic acid

a·ce·tyl (ə sēt′'l; as′ə til′, -təl, -tēl′) ***n.*** ⟦ACET(IC) + -YL⟧ the radical CH_3CO, derived from acetic acid: found only in compounds —**ac·e·tyl·ic** (as′ə til′ ik) ***adj.***

a·cet·y·late (ə set′'l āt′, -sēt′-) ***vt.*** **-lat′ed, -lat′ing** to combine an acetyl radical with (an organic compound) —**a·cet′y·la′tion** ***n.***

ac·e·tyl·cho·line (as′i til′kō′lēn) ***n.*** ⟦ACETYL + CHOLINE⟧ the acetic acid ester of choline, $(CH_3)_3N(OH)CH_2CH_2OCOCH_3$, found in many bodily tissues, esp. at neuromuscular junctions, acting as a nerve impulse transmitter: its chloride or bromide is used in medicine for various disorders

a·cet·y·lene (ə set′'l ēn′) ***n.*** ⟦ACETYL + -ENE⟧ a colorless, poisonous, highly flammable gaseous hydrocarbon, $HC⋮CH$, produced by the reaction of water and calcium carbide: used in organic compound synthesis, for lighting, and with oxygen in welding: the simplest alkyne

acetylene series a group of similar hydrocarbons: see ALKYNE

acetyl pro·ma·zine (prō′mə zēn′, präm′ə-; -zin) ACEPROMAZINE

a·ce·tyl·sal·i·cyl·ic acid (ə sēt′'l sal′ə sil′ik, as′ə til-) ASPIRIN

ace·y-deuce·y (ā′sē do͞o′sē) ***n.*** ⟦< ACE + DEUCE[1]⟧ a variation of the game of backgammon, in which the throw of a 1 and a 2 has special value: also sp. **acey-deucy**

ach (äkh) ***interj.*** ⟦Ger, also some Celtic languages⟧ [*also in roman type*] used to express variously complaint, surprise, sympathy, worry, etc.

ACH *abbrev. Banking* Automated Clearing House

A·chae·a (ə kē′ə) ancient region in the N Peloponnesus: also **A·chai·a** (ə kā′ə, -kī′-)

A·chae·an (ə kē′ən) ***adj.*** **1** of Achaea or its people or culture **2** loosely, Greek —***n.*** **1** a person born or living in Achaea **2** loosely, a Greek

A·cha·tes (ə kāt′ēz′) ***n.*** in Virgil's *Aeneid*, a loyal companion of Aeneas

ache (āk) ***vi.*** **ached, ach′ing** ⟦orig. *ake* < ME *aken* < OE *acan*, akin to LowG *äken*, to smart & MDu *akel*, sorrow, shame < IE base **agos*-, fault, guilt, sin: sp. *ache* through confusion with the n.⟧ **1** to have or give dull, steady pain **2** to feel sympathy, pity, etc. (*for*) **3** to yearn or long: with *for* or an infinitive —***n.*** ⟦ME < OE *ece, æce* < the v.⟧ a dull, continuous pain —**ach′ing·ly** ***adv.***

A·che·be (ä chā′bā), **Chin·ua** (chin′yo͞o wä′) (born *Albert Chinualumgu Achebe*) 1930-2013; Nigerian critic & writer

a·chene (ā kēn′, ə-) ***n.*** ⟦ModL *achenium* < Gr *a*-, not + *chainein*, to gape: see YAWN⟧ any small, dry, indehiscent fruit, as the strawberry, with one seed which is attached to the ovary wall at only one point: see CARYOPSIS

A·cher·nar (ā′kər när′) ***n.*** ⟦Ar *'akhīr nahr* < *'akhīr*, the end, final + *nahr*, river: the Ar name of the constellation itself is *nahr 'urdunn*, lit., river Jordan⟧ the brightest star in the constellation Eridanus: magnitude, 0.45

Ach·er·on (ak′ər än′) ***n.*** ⟦L < Gr; assoc. with *achos*, pain, hence "river of woe"⟧ **1** *Class. Myth.* a river in Hades: often identified as the river across which Charon ferries the dead: cf. STYX **2** Hades; infernal regions

A·cheu·le·an or **A·cheu·li·an** (ə sho͞o′lē ən) ***adj.*** ⟦Fr *acheuléen*, after *St. Acheul*, France, where remains were found⟧ designating or of a Lower Paleolithic culture characterized by skillfully made bifacial flint hand axes

à che·val (àsh vȧl′) ⟦Fr⟧ **1** on horseback; astraddle **2** straddling (an issue)

a·chieve (ə chēv′) ***vt.*** **a·chieved′, a·chiev′ing** ⟦ME *acheven* < OFr *achever*, to finish < *a*-, to + *chief*, head: see CHIEF⟧ **1** to do; succeed in doing; accomplish **2** to get or reach by exertion; attain; gain [to *achieve* one's goals] —***vi.*** to bring about a desired result; succeed —***SYN.*** PERFORM, REACH —**a·chiev′a·ble** ***adj.*** —**a·chiev′er** ***n.***

a·chieve·ment (-mənt) ***n.*** **1** the act of achieving **2** a thing achieved, esp. by skill, work, courage, etc.; feat **3** COAT OF ARMS

☆**achievement test** a test, often in a standardized format, for measuring a student's mastery of a given subject or skill

ach·il·le·a (ak′ə lē′ə, ə kil′ē ə) ***n.*** ⟦ModL < L, a medicinal plant said to have been used by *Achilles*⟧ YARROW

A·chil·les (ə kil′ēz′) ***n.*** ⟦L < Gr *Achilleus*⟧ *Gr. Myth.* Greek warrior and leader in the Trojan War who kills Hector and is killed by Paris with an arrow that strikes his only vulnerable spot, his heel: he is the hero of Homer's *Iliad*

Achilles' heel (one's) vulnerable or susceptible spot

Achilles tendon the tendon connecting the back of the heel to the muscles of the calf: also written **Achilles' tendon**

a·chi·o·te (ä′chē ō′tē, -tā′) ***n.*** ⟦AmSp < Nahuatl *achiotl*⟧ **1** the reddish-brown seed of the tree that is the source of annatto, ground to make a reddish spice used esp. in Puerto Rican cooking **2** this spice

A·chit·o·phel (ə kit′ə fel′) ***n.*** AHITHOPHEL

ach·la·myd·e·ous (ak′lə mid′ē əs) ***adj.*** ⟦< A-[2] + Gr *chlamys* (gen. *chlamydos*), a cloak, coat + -EOUS⟧ *Bot.* having neither sepals nor petals; without a perianth

a·chlor·hy·dri·a (ā′klôr hī′drē ə) ***n.*** ⟦ModL: see A-[2] & CHLOR- & HYDRO- & -IA⟧ a stomach disorder in which the stomach fails to secrete hydrochloric acid —**a′chlor·hy′dric** (-hī′drik) ***adj.***

a·chon·drite (ā kän′drīt′) ***n.*** ⟦A-[2] + CHONDRITE⟧ the type of stony meteorite that contains no chondrules —**a′chon·drit′ic** (-drit′ik) ***adj.***

a·chon·dro·pla·sia (ə kän′drə plā′zhə, -zhē ə) ***n.*** ⟦ModL: see A-[2] & CHONDRO- & -PLASIA⟧ a congenital disorder of bone formation that results in deformities and dwarfing of the skeleton —**a·chon′dro·plas′tic** (-plas′tik) ***adj.***

a·choo (ä cho͞o′) ***interj.*** ⟦echoic⟧ used to suggest or imitate the sound of a sneeze

ach·ro·mat·ic (ak′rə mat′ik, ā′krə-) ***adj.*** ⟦Gr *achrōmatos* < *a*-, without + *chrōma*, color (see CHROME) + -IC⟧ **1** colorless; specif., designating or of the group of colors comprising black, white, and gray: opposed to CHROMATIC (***adj.*** 2): see also COLOR (***n.*** 3-4) **2** refracting white light without breaking it up into its component colors **3** forming visual images whose outline is free from prismatic colors [an *achromatic* lens] **4** *Biol.* *a)* staining poorly with the usual stains *b)* made of achromatin **5** *Music* without accidentals; diatonic [an *achromatic* scale] —**ach′ro·mat′i·cal·ly** ***adv.***

a·chro·ma·tin (ā krō′mə tin) ***n.*** ⟦A-[2] + CHROMATIN⟧ *Biol.* that material of the cell nucleus not easily colored by the usual stains, including the nuclear membrane, linin, and karyolymph

a·chro·ma·tism (-tiz′əm) ***n.*** the condition or quality of being achromatic; lack of color: also **a·chro′ma·tic′i·ty** (-tis′ə tē)

a·chro·ma·tize (-tīz′) ***vt.*** **-tized′, -tiz′ing** to make achromatic; rid of color

a·chro·ma·tous (-təs) ***adj.*** ⟦Gr *achrōmatos*: see ACHROMATIC⟧ without color, or without enough color

a·chro·mic (ā krō′mik) ***adj.*** ⟦< Gr *achrōmos* < *a*-, not + *chrōma*, color (see CHROME) + -IC⟧ without color: also **a·chro′mous** (-məs)

☆**A·chro·my·cin** (ā′krō mī′sin, -krə-) ***n.*** ⟦former trademark < *achro-* (< Gr *achrōmos*, see prec.) + MYC- + -IN[1]⟧ TETRACYCLINE

ach·tung (äkh′to͝oŋ) ***interj.*** ⟦Ger, lit., attention⟧ [*also in roman type*] (pay) attention

ach·y (āk′ē) ***adj.*** **ach′i·er, ach′i·est** having an ache, or dull, steady pain —**ach′i·ness** ***n.***

a·ci·clo·vir (ā sī′klō vir′, -klə-) ***n.*** *alt. sp. of* ACYCLOVIR

a·cic·u·la (ə sik′yo͞o lə, -yə-) ***n.***, *pl.* **-lae′** (-lē′) ⟦ModL < LL, dim. of L *acus*: see ACEROSE[1]⟧ *Biol., Geol.* a needlelike spine, prickle, particle, or crystal; esp., an ice crystal —**a·cic′u·lar** (-lər) ***adj.***

a·cic·u·late (-lit, -lāt′) ***adj.*** **1** having aciculae **2** having marks like scratches made by a needle Also **a·cic′u·lat′ed**

a·cic·u·lum (-ləm) ***n.***, *pl.* **-lums** or **-la** (-lə) ⟦ModL < *acicula*⟧ *Zool.* a bristle-like part; seta

ac·id (as′id) ***adj.*** ⟦L *acidus*, sour < IE base *ak̑-, sharp, pointed > EAR[2]⟧ **1** sharp and biting to the taste; sour; tart **2** sharp or sarcastic in temperament or speech **3** that is, or has the properties of, an acid **4** having too heavy a concentration of acid **5** ⟦because such colors often have a sharp, piercing quality or effect⟧ designating or of color that is vivid or luminous [*acid* green] —***n.*** **1** a sour substance [use vinegar or another *acid* in the marinade to tenderize the meat before grilling] **2** [Slang] LSD **3** *Chem.* any compound that can react with a base to form a salt, the hydrogen of the acid being replaced by a positive ion; in modern theory, any substance that produces a positive ion and accepts electrons from a base to form covalent bonds: in water solution an acid tastes sour, turns blue litmus paper red, and, in the dissociation theory, produces free hydrogen ions: see PH —***SYN.*** SOUR —**ac′id·ly** ***adv.*** —**ac′id·ness** ***n.***

ac·i·dan·the·ra (as′ə dan′thər ə) ***n.*** ⟦ModL < Gr *akis* (gen. *akidis*), a pointed object < IE base *ak̑- (see prec.) + ModL *anthera*, ANTHER⟧ any of several bulbous African plants (genus *Acidanthera*) of the iris family, with cream-colored, long-tubed blossoms: they are often grown as potted ornamental plants

ac·i·de·mi·a (as′ə dē′mē ə) ***n.*** ⟦ACID + -EMIA⟧ abnormally low pH of the blood

ac·id-fast (as′id fast′) ***adj.*** that does not readily lose its color when exposed to acids after being stained: said esp. of certain bacteria and tissues

ac·id-form·ing (-fôr′miŋ) ***adj.*** **1** forming an acid in chemical reaction; acidic **2** yielding a large acid residue in metabolism

ac·id·head (-hed′) ***n.*** ⟦ACID (***n.*** 2) + HEAD (***n.*** 22*a*)⟧ [Slang] a habitual user of LSD

a·cid·ic (ə sid′ik) ***adj.*** **1** ACID-FORMING **2** acid **3** *Geol.* designating or of igneous rocks with more than 66% silica

a·cid·i·fy (ə sid′ə fī′) ***vt., vi.*** **-fied′, -fy′ing** **1** to make or become sour or acid **2** to change into an acid —**a·cid′i·fi′a·ble** ***adj.*** —**a·cid′i·fi·ca′tion** ***n.*** —**a·cid′i·fi′er** ***n.***

ac·i·dim·e·ter (as′ə dim′ət ər) ***n.*** an instrument used to find the amount or strength of acid present in a solution —**a·cid·i·met·ric** (ə sid′ə me′trik) ***adj.*** —**ac′i·dim′e·try** (-ə trē) ***n.***

a·cid·i·ty (ə sid′ə tē) ***n.***, *pl.* **-ties** ⟦Fr *acidité* < L *aciditas* < *acidus*: see ACID⟧ **1** acid quality or condition; sourness **2** the degree of this **3** hyperacidity

acid number a number indicating the amount of free acid present in a substance, equal to the number of milligrams of potassium hydroxide needed to neutralize the free fatty acids present in one gram of fat or oil: also called **acid value**

a·cid·o·phil (ə sid′ə fil) ***n.*** ⟦ACID + -O- + -PHIL⟧ **1** a cell, substance, or tissue easily stained by acid dyes, as any of the alpha cells in the anterior pituitary **2** an organism that has an affinity for and grows well in an acid environment: also **a·cid′o·phile′** (-fīl′) —**ac·i·do·phil·ic** (as′ə dō′fil′ik) ***adj.***

ac·i·doph·i·lus milk (as′ə däf′ə ləs) milk with bacteria (*Lactobacillus acidophilus*) added that is used to modify intestinal bacteria

ac·i·do·sis (as′ə dō′sis) ***n., pl.*** **-ses′** (-sēz′) ⟦ModL: see ACID & -OSIS⟧ an abnormal condition in the body, often due to faulty metabolism in which excessive acid, or a loss of alkali, lowers the pH of the blood and tissue: cf. ALKALOSIS —**ac′i·dot′ic** (-dät′ik) ***adj.***

acid rain rain or other precipitation with a high concentration of acids produced by sulfur dioxide, nitrogen dioxide, and other such gases that result from the combustion of fossil fuels: it has a destructive effect on plant and aquatic life, buildings, etc.

acid reflux reflux of stomach acid, etc. into the esophagus, resulting in heartburn and, when chronic, often leading to erosion or ulceration of the esophageal lining

☆**acid rock** ⟦ACID (*n.* 2) + ROCK[2] (*n.* 3b)⟧ a form of rock music of the late 1960s and early 1970s intended to simulate or enhance a hallucinogenic experience and characterized by mystical or surrealistic lyrics, loud or distorted sounds, modal harmonies, etc.

acid test ⟦orig. a *test* of gold by *acid*⟧ a crucial, final test that proves the value or quality of something

a·cid·u·late (ə sij′o͞o lāt′) ***vt.*** ⟦< L *acidulus* (see fol.) + -ATE[1]⟧ **-lat′ed, -lat′ing** to make somewhat acid or sour —**a·cid′u·la′tion** ***n.***

a·cid·u·lous (-ləs) ***adj.*** ⟦L *acidulus*, dim. of *acidus*: see ACID⟧ **1** somewhat acid or sour **2** somewhat sarcastic Also **a·cid′u·lent** (-lənt) —***SYN.*** SOUR

ac·i·er·ate (as′ē ər āt′) ***vt.*** **-at′ed, -at′ing** ⟦Fr *acier*, steel < LL *aciarium* < L *acies*, sharpness < *acer*, sharp < IE base **ak̂-* (see ACID) + -ATE[1]⟧ to change into steel

ac·i·form (as′ə fôrm′) ***adj.*** ⟦< L *acus*, needle (see ACEROSE[1]) + -FORM⟧ needle-shaped; sharp

ac·i·nac·i·form (as′ə nas′ə fôrm′) ***adj.*** ⟦< L *acinaces*, short sword < Gr *akinakēs*, of Pers orig. + -FORM⟧ *Bot.* shaped like a scimitar

a·cin·i·form (ə sin′ə fôrm′) ***adj.*** ⟦< L *acinus*, grape + -FORM⟧ formed like a cluster of grapes

ac·i·nus (as′i nəs) ***n., pl.*** **-ni′** (-nī′) ⟦ModL: see prec. ⟧ *Anat.* one of the small sacs of a compound or racemose gland —**ac′i·nous** (-nəs) ***adj.***, **ac′i·nose′** (-nōs′)

-a·cious (ā′shəs) ⟦< L *-ax* (gen. *-acis*) + -OUS⟧ *suffix forming adjectives* characterized by, inclined to, full of [*tenacious, fallacious*]

-ac·i·ty (as′ə tē) ⟦Fr *-acité* < L *-acitas*⟧ *suffix forming nouns* a (specified) characteristic, quality, or tendency

ack-ack (ak′ak′) ***n.*** ⟦echoic; prob. expansion of abbrev. *A.A.*, antiaircraft artillery⟧ [Slang] an antiaircraft gun or its fire

ack·ee (ak′ē, a kē′) ***n.*** ⟦< ?⟧ **1** a W African tree (*Blighia sapida*) of the soapberry family, widely grown in the tropics **2** its fruit, poisonous if not ripe, and containing large, black seeds with fleshy, white arils **3** a dish made by cooking these arils: often combined with salted cod, as in Jamaica

ac·knowl·edge (ak näl′ij, ək-) ***vt.*** **-edged, -edg·ing** ⟦earlier *aknowledge* < ME *knowlechen* < *knowleche* (see KNOWLEDGE): infl. by ME *aknowen* < OE *oncnawan*, to understand, know, with Latinized prefix⟧ **1** to admit to be true or as stated; confess **2** to recognize the authority or claims of **3** to recognize and answer (a greeting or greeter, an introduction, etc.) **4** to express thanks for **5** to state that one has received (a letter, gift, favor, payment, etc.) **6** *Law* to admit or affirm as genuine; certify in legal form [*to acknowledge* a deed] —**ac·knowl′edge·a·ble** ***adj.***

SYN.—acknowledge implies the reluctant disclosure of something one might have kept secret [he *acknowledged* the child as his]; **admit** describes assent that has been elicited by persuasion and implies a conceding of a fact, etc. [I'll *admit* you're right]; **own** denotes an informal acknowledgment of something in connection with oneself [to *own* to a liking for turnips]; **avow** implies an open, emphatic declaration, often as an act of affirmation; **confess** is applied to a formal acknowledgment of a sin, crime, etc., but in a weakened sense is used interchangeably with **admit** in making simple declarations [I'll *confess* I don't like him] —***ANT.*** **deny**

ac·knowl·edged (-ijd) ***adj.*** commonly recognized or accepted [the *acknowledged* leader of the group]

ac·knowl·edg·ment or **ac·knowl·edge·ment** (-mənt) ***n.*** **1** an acknowledging or being acknowledged; admission; avowal **2** something done or given in acknowledging, as an expression of thanks **3** recognition of the authority or claims of **4** a legal avowal or certificate

ACL *abbrev.* anterior cruciate ligament (of the knee)

a·clin·ic line (ā klin′ik) ⟦Gr *aklinēs* < *a-*, not + *klinein*, to incline (see LEAN[1]) + -IC⟧ MAGNETIC EQUATOR

ACLU *trademark* American Civil Liberties Union

ac·me (ak′mē) ***n.*** ⟦Gr *akmē*, a point, top, age of maturity < IE base **ak̂-*: see ACID⟧ the highest point; point of culmination; peak —***SYN.*** SUMMIT

ac·ne (ak′nē) ***n.*** ⟦ModL < Gr *aknas*, misreading of *akmas*, acc. pl. of *akmē*, facial eruption, point: see prec. ⟧ a common, chronic skin disease, esp. among adolescents and young adults, characterized by inflammation of the sebaceous apparatus, usually causing pimples on the face, back, and chest —**ac′ned** ***adj.***

ac·node (ak′nōd′) ***n.*** ⟦< L *acus* (see ACEROSE[1]) + NODE⟧ *Math.* an isolated point on the graph of an equation

a·cock (ə käk′) ***adv., adj.*** in a cocked or tilted position

ac·o·lyte (ak′ə līt′) ***n.*** ⟦ME *acolit* < ML *acolytus* < Gr *akolouthos*, follower < *a-*, copulative + *keleuthos*, a way⟧ **1** in some Christian churches *a)* one of the MINOR ORDERS, the special function of which is to serve at the Eucharist *b)* any person upon whom this order has been conferred *c)* any person who serves at the Eucharist *d)* SERVER; ALTAR BOY; ALTAR GIRL **2** an attendant; follower; helper

A·con·ca·gua (ä kôn kä′gwə) mountain of the Andes in W Argentina: 22,835 ft (6,960 m): highest peak in the Western Hemisphere

ac·o·nite (ak′ə nīt′) ***n.*** ⟦ModL *aconitum* < L < Gr *akoniton*⟧ **1** any of a genus (*Aconitum*) of poisonous plants of the buttercup family, with blue, purple, or yellow hoodlike flowers; monkshood; wolfsbane **2** a rapidly acting poisonous drug usually made from the dried roots of a European monkshood (*Aconitum napellus*) and formerly used as a cardiac and respiratory sedative: also **ac′o·ni′tum** (-nīt′əm)

a·corn (ā′kôrn′) ***n.*** ⟦ME *akorn* < OE *æcern*, nut, mast of trees; akin to Goth *akran*, ON *akarn* < IE base **əg-*, to grow, fruit: form infl. by assoc. with OE *ac*, oak + *corn*, grain⟧ the fruit of the oak tree; an oak nut

acorn barnacle any of a genus (*Balanus*) of stalkless barnacles that resemble acorns

☆**acorn squash** a kind of winter squash, acorn-shaped with ridged, dark-green skin and sweet, yellow flesh

☆**acorn tube** *Electronics* a small vacuum tube shaped like an acorn

a·cot·y·le·don (ā′kät′ə lēd′'n) ***n.*** any plant lacking seed leaves (cotyledons), as dodder

a·cous·tic (ə ko͞os′tik) ***adj.*** ⟦Fr *acoustique* < Gr *akoustikos*, of or for hearing < *akouein*, to hear < *a-* (< ?) + IE base **keu-*, to heed, HEAR⟧ **1** having to do with hearing or with sound as it is heard **2** of acoustics **3** *a)* designating a musical instrument, usually a string instrument, whose sounds are not generated electronically *b)* employing such an instrument or instruments

a·cous·ti·cal (-ti kəl) ***adj.*** acoustic; specif., having to do with the control of sound [*acoustical* tile absorbs sounds]

a·cous·ti·cal·ly (-tik lē) ***adv.*** with reference to acoustics; from the standpoint of acoustics

ac·ous·ti·cian (a′ko͞os tish′ən) ***n.*** an expert in acoustics

a·cous·tics (ə ko͞os′tiks) ***pl.n.*** the qualities of a room, theater, etc. that have to do with how clearly sounds can be heard or transmitted in it —***n.*** the branch of physics dealing with sound, esp. with its transmission

a·cous·to·op·tics (ə ko͞os′tō äp′tiks) ***n.*** the branch of physics dealing with the relationships between acoustics and light —**a·cous′to·op′tic** ***adj.***, **a·cous′to·op′ti·cal**

à cou·vert (à ko͞o ver′) ⟦Fr⟧ under cover; secure

ACP *abbrev.* American College of Physicians

ac·quaint (ə kwānt′) ***vt.*** ⟦ME *aqueinten* < OFr *acointier* < ML *adcognitare* < L *ad-*, to + *cognitus*, pp. of *cognoscere*, to know thoroughly < *con-*, with *gnoscere*, KNOW⟧ **1** to let (someone) know; give knowledge to; make (someone) aware; inform: followed by *with* [to *acquaint* oneself with the facts] **2** to cause to know personally; make (someone) familiar *with* someone or something [are you *acquainted* with my brother?] —***SYN.*** NOTIFY

ac·quaint·ance (ə kwānt′'ns) ***n.*** **1** knowledge (of something) gotten from personal experience or study of it [an intimate *acquaintance* with the plays of Jonson] **2** the state or relation of being acquainted (*with* someone) **3** a person or persons whom one knows, but not intimately —**make someone's acquaintance** to become an acquaintance of someone —**ac·quaint′ance·ship′** ***n.***

acquaintance rape DATE RAPE

ac·qui·esce (ak′wē es′) ***vi.*** **-esced′, -esc′ing** ⟦Fr *acquiescer*, to yield to < L *acquiescere* < *ad-*, to + *quiescere*: see QUIET⟧ to agree or consent quietly without protest, but without enthusiasm: often with *in* [to *acquiesce* in a decision] —***SYN.*** CONSENT

ac·qui·es·cence (ak′wē es′əns) ***n.*** the act of acquiescing; agreement or consent without protest

ac·qui·es·cent (-es′ənt) ***adj.*** acquiescing; agreeing or consenting without protest —**ac′qui·es′cent·ly** ***adv.***

ac·quire (ə kwīr′) ***vt.*** **-quired′, -quir′ing** ⟦L *acquirere* < *ad-*, to + *quaerere*, to seek⟧ **1** to get or gain by one's own efforts or actions [to *acquire* an education] **2** to come to have as one's own; get possession of [to *acquire* certain traits] —***SYN.*** GET —**ac·quir′a·ble** ***adj.***

acquired character *Biol.* a modification of structure or function caused by environmental factors: now generally regarded as not inheritable: also **acquired characteristic**

acquired immune deficiency syndrome AIDS: also **acquired immunodeficiency syndrome**

acquired taste something that one comes to like or appreciate over a period of time

ac·quire·ment (ə kwīr′mənt) ***n.*** **1** an acquiring or being acquired **2** something acquired, as a skill or ability gained by learning

ac·qui·si·tion (ak′wə zish′ən) ***n.*** ⟦L *acquisitio* < pp. of *acquirere*, ACQUIRE⟧ **1** an acquiring or being acquired **2** something or someone acquired or added

ac·quis·i·tive (ə kwiz′ə tiv) ***adj.*** ⟦LL *acquisitivus* < pp. of L *acquirere*: see ACQUIRE⟧ eager to acquire; good at getting and holding wealth, etc.; grasping —***SYN.*** GREEDY —**ac·quis′i·tive·ly** ***adv.*** —**ac·quis′i·tive·ness** ***n.***

ac·quit (ə kwit′) ***vt.*** **-quit′ted, -quit′ting** ⟦ME *aquiten* < OFr *aquiter*, to free < ML *acquitare*, to settle a claim < L *ad-*, to + *quietare*: see QUIET⟧ **1**

to release from a duty, obligation, etc. **2** to clear (a person) of a charge, as by declaring him or her not guilty; exonerate **3** to bear or conduct (oneself); behave **4** [Archaic] to pay (a debt or claim) —**SYN.** ABSOLVE, BEHAVE —**ac·quit′ter** *n.*

ac·quit·tal (ə kwit′'l) *n.* ⟦ME *aquital* < Anglo-Fr *aquitaille*: see prec. ⟧ **1** an acquitting; discharge (of duty, obligation, etc.) **2** *Law* a setting free or being set free by judgment of the court

ac·quit·tance (ə kwit′'ns) *n.* ⟦ME *aquitaunce* < OFr *aquitance*: see ACQUIT & -ANCE⟧ **1** a settlement of, or release from, debt or liability **2** a record of this; receipt

a·cre (ā′kər) *n.* ⟦ME < OE *æcer*, field (akin to Goth *akrs*, Ger *acker*, L *ager*) < IE **aĝros* (> Gr *agros*), field, lit., place to which cattle are driven < base **aĝ-*: see ACT¹⟧ **1** a unit of land area in the FPS system, equal to 4,840 square yards or 160 square rods (0.4047 hectare or 4,046.8564 square meters): abbrev. *ac* **2** [*pl.*] specific holdings in land; lands **3** [*pl.*] [Informal] a large quantity **4** [Obs.] field: see GOD'S ACRE

A·cre¹ (ä′kər, ā′-) AKKO

A·cre² (ä′krə) state of westernmost Brazil: 58,915 sq mi (152,589 sq km); cap. Rio Branco

a·cre·age (ā′kər ij, ā′krij) *n.* ⟦ACRE + -AGE⟧ the number of acres in a piece of land; acres collectively

☆**a·cre-foot** (ā′kər foot′) *n.* the quantity of irrigation water (43,560 cubic feet or *c.* 325,851 U.S. gallons) that would cover one acre to a depth of one foot

☆**a·cre-inch** (-inch′) *n.* one twelfth of an acre-foot, or 3,630 cubic feet (*c.* 27,154 U.S. gallons)

ac·rid (ak′rid) *adj.* ⟦< L *acris*, fem. of *acer*, sharp < IE base **ak̑-* (see ACID): form infl. by ACID⟧ **1** sharp, bitter, stinging, or irritating to the taste or smell **2** bitter or sarcastic in speech, etc. —**a·crid·i·ty** (ə krid′ə tē) *n.*, **ac′rid·ness** —**ac′rid·ly** *adv.*

ac·ri·dine (ak′rə dēn′, -din) *n.* ⟦prec. + -INE³⟧ a colorless, crystalline, cyclic compound, $C_{13}H_9N$, found in coal tar: used to make dyes, of which some are used as antiseptics

ac·ri·fla·vine (ak′rə flā′vēn′, -vin) *n.* ⟦< prec. + FLAVINE⟧ a deep-orange, odorless powder, $C_{14}H_{14}N_3Cl$, prepared from acridine: used as a dye reagent and, esp. formerly, as an antiseptic

Ac·ri·lan (ak′ri lan′) ⟦< ACR(YLIC) + -I- + L *lana*, WOOL⟧ *trademark for* a synthetic acrylic fiber

ac·ri·mo·ni·ous (ak′ri mō′nē əs) *adj.* ⟦ML *acrimoniosus*: see fol. ⟧ bitter and caustic in temper, manner, or speech —**ac′ri·mo′ni·ous·ly** *adv.* —**ac′ri·mo′ni·ous·ness** *n.*

ac·ri·mo·ny (ak′ri mō′nē) *n.* ⟦L *acrimonia*, sharpness < *acer*, sharp < IE base **ak̑-*: see ACID⟧ bitterness or harshness of temper, manner, or speech; asperity

a·crit·i·cal (ā krit′i kəl) *adj.* **1** not critical; having no tendency to criticism or critical judgment **2** *Med.* showing no signs of a crisis

ac·ro- (ak′rō, ak′rə) ⟦< Gr *akros*, at the point, end, or top < IE base **ak̑-*: see ACID⟧ *combining form* **1** pointed *[acrocephaly]* **2** highest, topmost, at the extremities *[acrospire]*

ac·ro·bat (ak′rə bat′) *n.* ⟦Fr *acrobate* < Gr *akrobatos*, walking on tiptoe < *akros* (see prec.) + *bainein*, to walk, go⟧ an expert performer of tricks in tumbling or on the trapeze, tightrope, etc.; skilled gymnast —**ac′ro·bat′ic** *adj.* —**ac′ro·bat′i·cal·ly** *adv.*

ac·ro·bat·ics (ak′rə bat′iks) *pl.n.* [*also with sing. v.*] **1** the art, skill, or tricks of an acrobat **2** any difficult or intricate tricks requiring great skill or agility *[mental acrobatics]*

ac·ro·car·pous (ak′rō kär′pəs) *adj.* ⟦ACRO- + -CARPOUS⟧ bearing fruit at the end of the stalk, as some mosses

ac·ro·ceph·a·ly (ak′rō sef′ə lē) *n.* ⟦< ACRO- + Gr *kephalē*, head: see CEPHALIC⟧ OXYCEPHALY —**ac′ro·ce·phal′ic** (-sə fal′ik) *adj.*, **ac′ro·ceph′a·lous** (-sef′ə ləs)

ac·ro·gen (ak′rə jən) *n.* ⟦ACRO- + -GEN⟧ a plant, such as a fern or moss, having a perennial stem with the growing point at the tip —**a·crog·e·nous** (ə kräj′ə nəs) *adj.*, **ac′ro·gen′ic** (-jen′ik) —**a·crog′e·nous·ly** *adv.*

a·cro·le·in (ə krō′lē in) *n.* ⟦ACR(ID) + L *olere*, to smell + -IN¹⟧ a yellowish or colorless, acrid liquid, CH_2:CHCHO, whose fumes irritate the eyes: it is formed by the decomposition of glycerol and is used in organic synthesis and in plastics, poison gas, etc.

ac·ro·lith (ak′rō lith′) *n.* ⟦L *acrolithus* < Gr *akrolithos* < *akros* (see ACRO-) + *lithos*, stone⟧ in early Greek sculpture, a statue with stone head, hands, and feet, and a wooden trunk

ac·ro·meg·a·ly (ak′rō meg′ə lē) *n.* ⟦Fr *acromégalie*: see ACRO- & MEGALO-⟧ a disease in which there is enlargement of the bones of the head, hands, and feet, resulting from an overproduction of growth hormone that is caused, usually, by a tumor in the pituitary —**ac′ro·me·gal′ic** (-mə gal′ik) *adj.*

a·cro·mi·on (ə krō′mē ən) *n.* ⟦Gr *akrōmion* < *akrōmia*, point of the shoulder < *akros* (see ACRO-) + *ōmos*, the shoulder⟧ the outer upper point of the shoulder blade, or scapula

a·cron·i·cal or **a·cron·y·cal** (ə krän′i kəl) *adj.* ⟦Gr *akronychos*, at sunset < *akros* (see ACRO-) + *nyx*, NIGHT⟧ *Astron.* happening at sunset, as the rising of a star

☆**ac·ro·nym** (ak′rə nim′) *n.* ⟦ACR(O)- + -ONYM⟧ a word formed from the first (or first few) letters of a series of words, as *radar*, from *ra*dio *d*etecting *a*nd *r*anging —**ac′ro·nym′ic** *adj.*

a·crop·e·tal (ə kräp′ə təl) *adj.* ⟦ACRO- + -PETAL⟧ developing or moving from the base of the stem toward the apex: used to describe the development of tissues or movement of hormones in plants: opposed to BASIPETAL —**a·crop′e·tal·ly** *adv.*

ac·ro·pho·bi·a (ak′rə fō′bē ə) *n.* ⟦ACRO- + PHOBIA⟧ an abnormal fear of being in high places —**ac′ro·phobe′** *n.* —**ac′ro·pho′bic** *adj.*

a·crop·o·lis (ə kräp′ə lis) *n.* ⟦Gr *akropolis* < *akros* (see ACRO-) + *polis*, city⟧ the fortified upper part of an ancient Greek city

Acrop·o·lis (ə kräp′ə lis) the fortified upper part of Athens, on which the Parthenon was built

ac·ro·some (ak′rə sōm′) *n.* a thin sac usually at the head of a sperm cell containing enzymes which dissolve the protective layers of an egg cell —**ac′ro·so′mal** *adj.*

ac·ro·spire (ak′rō spīr′) *n.* ⟦altered as if < ACRO- + SPIRE¹ < Eng dial. *akerspire* < OE *æhher* (Northumbrian dial.), *ēar*, EAR² + *spīr*, SPIRE²⟧ *Bot.* the spiral primary bud of germinating grain

a·cross (ə krôs′, ə kräs′) *adv.* ⟦ME *acros* < *a-*, on, in + *cros*, cross, after Anglo-Fr *an croix*⟧ **1** so as to cross; crosswise **2** from one side to the other **3** on or to the other side —*prep.* **1** from one side to the other of, or so as to cross **2** on or to the other side of; over; through **3** *see* COME ACROSS (phrase under COME) and RUN ACROSS (phrase under RUN)

☆**a·cross-the-board** (-*th*ə bôrd′) *adj.* **1** *Horse Racing* combining win, place, and show, as a bet **2** including or affecting all classes or groups Also written **across the board**

a·cros·tic (ə krôs′tik, -kräs′-) *n.* ⟦Gr *akrostichos* < *akros* (see ACRO-) + *stichos*, line of verse⟧ a verse or arrangement of words in which certain letters in each line, such as the first or last, when taken in order spell out a word, motto, etc. —*adj.* of or like an acrostic: also **a·cros′ti·cal** —**a·cros′ti·cal·ly** *adv.*

a·cryl·a·mide (ə kril′ə mīd′) *n.* ⟦ACRYL(IC) + AMIDE⟧ a toxic, colorless, crystalline amide, H_2C:CHCONH$_2$, derived from acrylonitrile: it polymerizes readily and is used in making textile fibers, dyes, paper, etc.

ac·ry·late (ak′rə lāt′) *n.* ⟦< fol. + -ATE²⟧ **1** a salt of acrylic acid containing the radical $C_3H_3O_2$ and used as a monomer to form various acrylic polymers **2** ACRYLIC RESIN

a·cryl·ic (ə kril′ik) *adj.* ⟦ACR(OLEIN) + -YL + -IC⟧ **1** of or pertaining to acrylic acid or products made of it **2** designating or of a series of olefin acids with the general formula $C_nH_{2n-2}O_2$ **3** designating or of an acrylic resin product (paint, fiber, plastic, adhesive, etc.) —*n. short for:* **1** ACRYLIC PAINTING **2** ACRYLIC FIBER

acrylic acid a colorless, pungent, liquid acid, H_2C:CHCOOH, that is readily polymerized to form acrylic resins

acrylic color a color or paint made by mixing pigments in a solution of acrylic resin: also **acrylic paint**

acrylic fiber any of a group of synthetic polymeric fibers composed at least 85 percent by weight of acrylonitrile units and made into fabrics

acrylic painting a painting done with pigments in a solution of an acrylic resin: it dries quickly with a brilliance and depth comparable to those of both watercolor and oil paints

acrylic resin any of a group of transparent, thermoplastic polymeric resins derived from acrylic acid, methacrylic acid, or their esters, or from acrylonitrile: used in making molded plastics, paints, textile fibers, etc.

ac·ry·lo·ni·trile (ak′rə lō nī′tril) *n.* ⟦< ACRYL(IC) + -O- + NITRILE⟧ a colorless, liquid monomer, H_2C:CHCN, boiling at 78°C, that is polymerized to form acrylic resins for acrylic fibers, synthetic rubber, and soil conditioners: a known carcinogen

ACS *abbrev.* **1** American Cancer Society **2** American Chemical Society **3** American College of Surgeons **4** Association of Caribbean States

ACSW *abbrev.* Academy of Certified Social Workers

act¹ (akt) *n.* ⟦ME < OFr *acte* < L *actus*, a doing or moving, *actum*, thing done, pp. of *agere*, to do < IE base **aĝ-*, to drive, do > Gr *agein*, to lead⟧ **1** a thing done; deed **2** an action; doing *[caught in the act of stealing]* **3** a decision (of a court, legislature, etc.); law; decree **4** a document formally stating what has been done, made into law, etc. **5** one of the main divisions of a drama or opera **6** any of the separate performances on a variety program **7** a show of feeling or behavior that is not sincere and is put on just for effect —*vt.* ⟦ME *acten* < L *actus*: see the *n.*⟧ **1** to play the part of **2** to perform in (a play) **3** to behave in a way suitable for *[don't act the child]* —*vi.* **1** to perform in a play, film, etc.; play a role **2** to behave as though playing a role **3** to be suited to performance: said of a play or a role **4** to behave; comport oneself *[act like a lady]* **5** to do something *[we must act now to forestall disaster]* **6** to serve or function *[the fence acts as a barrier]* **7** to serve as spokesman or substitute (*for*) *[he's acting for the committee]* **8** to have an effect *[acids act on metal]* **9** to appear to be *[he acted very angry]* —**act out** *Psychiatry* to behave in a way that unconsciously expresses (feelings that were repressed in an earlier situation) —☆**act up** [Informal] **1** to be playful **2** to misbehave **3** to become inflamed, painful, etc. —☆**clean up one's act** [Informal] to reform one's conduct, improve one's practices, etc. —☆**get one's act together** [Informal] to organize one's ideas, procedures, etc. so as to function more effectively

act² *abbrev.* active

ACT *trademark* American College Test

act·a·ble (ak′tə bəl) *adj.* that can be acted: said of a play, a role, etc. —**act′a·bil′i·ty** (-bil′ə tē) *n.*

Ac·tae·on (ak tē′ən) *n.* ⟦L < Gr *Aktaiōn*⟧ *Gr. Myth.* a hunter who makes Artemis angry by watching her bathe: she changes him into a stag, and his dogs tear him to pieces

Ac·ta Sanc·to·rum (äk′tə säŋk tôr′əm) ⟦L⟧ *R.C.Ch.* a collection of lives of the saints edited by Jesuit scholars and first published in Antwerp in 1643

ac·te gra·tuit (åk tə grå twē′) *pl.* **ac·tes gra·tuits** (åk tə grå twē′) ⟦Fr, lit., gratuitous act: term introduced in fiction (1914) by A. GIDE⟧ an action taken on impulse without apparent cause or justification

actg *abbrev.* acting

☆**ACTH** (ā′sē′tē′āch′) *n.* ⟦A(DRENO)C(ORTICO)T(ROPIC) H(ORMONE)⟧ a polypeptide hormone of the anterior part of the pituitary gland that stimulates hormone production of the adrenal cortex

ac·tin (ak′tin) *n.* ⟦< L *actus* (see ACT[1]) + -IN[1]⟧ a protein in muscles: see ACTOMYOSIN

ac·tin- (ak′tin) *combining form* ACTINO-: used before a vowel [*actinal*]

ac·ti·nal (ak′ti nəl, ak tī′nəl) *adj.* ⟦ACTIN(O)- + -AL⟧ of the oral region of a radiate animal, from which the rays or tentacles grow

act·ing (ak′tiŋ) *adj.* **1** adapted for performance on a stage [*an acting* version of a play] **2** that acts; functioning **3** temporarily taking over the duties (of a specified position) [the *acting* chairman] —*n.* the act, art, or occupation of performing in plays, movies, etc. —**SYN.** TEMPORARY

ac·tin·i·a (ak tin′ē ə) *n., pl.* **-i·ae′** (-ē ē′) or **-i·as** ⟦ModL < Gr *aktis* (gen. *aktinos*), a ray⟧ any of a genus (*Actinia*) of sea anemones —**ac·tin′i·an** *adj., n.*

ac·tin·ic (ak tin′ik) *adj.* having to do with actinism —**ac·tin′i·cal·ly** *adv.*

actinic rays light rays, esp. the violet and ultraviolet parts of the spectrum, that produce chemical changes, as in photography

ac·ti·nide (ak′tə nīd′) *n.* ⟦< ACTIN(IUM) + -IDE⟧ any of the elements in the series (**actinide series**) of radioactive, metallic chemical elements from element 89 (actinium) through element 103 (lawrencium): actinides resemble lanthanides in electronic structure: see the periodic table of elements in the Reference Supplement

ac·tin·i·form (ak tin′ə fôrm′) *adj.* ⟦ACTIN(O)- + -I- + -FORM⟧ *Zool.* having radial form; rayed

ac·tin·ism (ak′tin iz′əm) *n.* ⟦ACTIN- + -ISM⟧ that property of ultraviolet light, X-rays, or other radiations, by which chemical changes are produced

ac·tin·i·um (ak tin′ē əm) *n.* ⟦ModL < ACTINO- + -IUM⟧ a white, radioactive, metallic chemical element, the first member of the actinide series, found in pitchblende and other minerals or formed in reactors by the neutron irradiation of radium: symbol, Ac; at. no. 89: see the periodic table of elements in the Reference Supplement

actinium series natural radioactive decay series starting with uranium-235 and ending with lead-207

ac·ti·no- (ak′tə nō′, ak tin′ə) ⟦< Gr *aktis* (gen. *aktinos*), ray⟧ *combining form* **1** of actinism or actinic rays [*actinometer*] **2** *Biol.* of radiated structure [*actinomycete*]

ac·tin·o·graph (ak tin′ə graf′) *n.* a recording actinometer

ac·ti·noid (ak′tə noid′) *adj.* having a radial form, as a sea anemone —*n.* *Chem.* ACTINIDE

ac·tin·o·lite (ak tin′ə līt′) *n.* a dark-colored, often greenish amphibole, $Ca_2(Mg, Fe)_5(Si_8O_{22})(OH)_2$, commonly found in schists and marbles

ac·ti·nol·o·gy (ak′tə näl′ə jē) *n.* the science of light rays and their chemical effects

ac·ti·nom·e·ter (ak′tə näm′ət ər) *n.* **1** *Physics* an instrument for measuring the intensity of the sun's rays, or the actinic effect of light rays **2** *Photog.* EXPOSURE METER —**ac′ti·no′met′ric** (-nō′me′trik) *adj.* —**ac′ti·nom′e·try** (-näm′ə trē) *n.*

ac·ti·no·mor·phic (ak′tə nō′môr′fik) *adj. Biol.* having radial symmetry, as a flower or a starfish: also **ac′ti·no·mor′phous** (-fəs)

ac·ti·no·my·cete (ak′tə nō′mī′sēt′, -mī sēt′) *n.* ⟦< ModL < ACTINO- + -MYCETE⟧ any of various bacteria (order Actinomycetales) with a branching, filamentous structure; esp., any of a family (Actinomycetaceae) of Gram-positive bacteria that are pathogenic to humans and animals —**ac′ti·no·my·ce′tous** (-sēt′əs) *adj.*

☆**ac·ti·no·my·cin** (-mī′sin) *n.* ⟦< prec. + -IN[1]⟧ any of various antibiotic polypeptides derived from streptomyces soil bacteria: active against certain bacteria and fungi and some neoplasms

ac·ti·no·my·co·sis (-mī kō′sis) *n.* an infection caused by certain actinomycetes, that may result in bony degeneration of the jaws, and abscesses in the lungs, intestines, etc. of humans and other mammals

ac·ti·non (ak′tə nän′) *n.* ⟦ModL < ACTINIUM + -ON⟧ a gaseous radioisotope of radon, formed by disintegration of actinium: at. no. 86; half-life of 3.92 seconds

ac·ti·no·u·ra·ni·um (ak′tə nō′yoo rā′nē əm) *n.* ⟦< ACTINIUM + URANIUM⟧ the uranium isotope of mass number 235: begins the actinium series

ac·ti·no·zo·an (-zō′ən) *n.* ⟦< ModL *Actinozoa* (see ACTINO- & -ZOA) + -AN⟧ ANTHOZOAN

ac·tion (ak′shən) *n.* ⟦ME *accion* < OFr *action* < L *actio* < pp. of *agere*: see ACT[1]⟧ **1** the doing of something; state of being in motion or of working **2** an act or thing done **3** [*pl.*] behavior; habitual conduct **4** habitual activity characterized by energy and boldness [a man of *action*] **5** the effect produced by something [the *action* of a drug] **6** the way of moving, working, etc., as of a machine, an organ of the body, etc. **7** the moving parts or mechanism, as of a gun, piano, etc. **8** *a)* the sequence of happenings in a story or play; plot *b)* any of such happenings *c)* such happenings when exciting **9** a legal proceeding by which one seeks to have a wrong put right; lawsuit **10** *a)* a military encounter *b)* military combat in general **11** the appearance of animation in a painting, sculpture, etc. **12** [Slang] activity or excitement, specif., *a)* gambling activity *b)* sexual activity —*adj.* designating or of a type of film characterized by a fast-paced plot, a series of suspenseful confrontations, violent fight and chase scenes, etc. —**SYN.** BATTLE[1] —**bring action** to start a lawsuit —**see action** to participate in military combat —**take action** **1** to become active **2** to start a lawsuit

☆**ACTION** (ak′shən) *n.* a federal agency established in 1971 to supervise all U.S. government programs and agencies for volunteers, as the Peace Corps, VISTA, etc.

ac·tion·a·ble (-ə bəl) *adj. Law* that gives cause for an action or lawsuit

ac·tion·er (-ər) *n.* [Informal] an action film

action figure a plastic, doll-like toy with movable limbs, typically made in the likeness of a superhero, movie character, or celebrity

☆**action painting** a form of abstract expressionism in which such methods as the spattering or dripping of paint are used to create bold, fluid, apparently random compositions

Ac·ti·um (ak′tē əm, -shē əm) cape on the NW coast of Acarnania (in ancient Greece): the forces of Mark Antony and Cleopatra were defeated by those of Octavian in a naval battle near Actium (31 B.C.)

ac·ti·vate (ak′tə vāt′) *vt.* **-vat′ed, -vat′ing** **1** to make active; cause to engage in activity **2** to put (an inactive military unit) on an active status by assigning personnel, equipment, etc. to it **3** to make radioactive **4** to make capable of reacting or of accelerating a chemical reaction **5** to treat (sewage) with air so that aerobes will become active in it, thus purifying it —**ac′ti·va′tion** *n.*

activated carbon a form of highly porous carbon that can easily adsorb gases, vapors, and colloidal particles: it is made by destructive distillation of wood, peat, etc., followed by heating the resultant product to high temperatures with steam or carbon dioxide: also called **activated charcoal** or **active carbon**

ac·ti·va·tor (ak′tə vāt′ər) *n.* **1** a thing or person that activates **2** *Chem.* a substance used to induce or accelerate a chemical reaction

ac·tive (ak′tiv) *adj.* ⟦ME & OFr *actif* < L *activus* < *actus*, pp. of *agere*: see ACT[1]⟧ **1** that is acting, functioning, working, moving, etc. **2** capable of acting, functioning, etc. **3** causing action, motion, or change **4** characterized by much action or motion; lively, busy, agile, quick, etc. [an *active* mind, an *active* boy] **5** actual, not just nominal; participating [an *active* interest, to play an *active* role] **6** necessitating action or work **7** *a)* currently in operation, in effect, in progress, etc. [an *active* law, an *active* disease] *b)* in eruption [an *active* volcano] **8** requiring or using electric power to function [*active* speakers] **9** *Gram.* *a)* denoting the voice or form of a verb whose subject is the performer, or agent, of the action of the verb (opposed to PASSIVE) *b)* in or of the active voice *c)* showing action rather than state of being (said of verbs like *throw* and *walk*) —*n.* **1** an active member of an organization **2** *Gram.* *a)* the active voice *b)* a verb in this voice —**ac′tive·ly** *adv.* —**ac′tive·ness** *n.*

SYN.—**active** implies a state of motion, operation, etc. ranging from cases of normal functioning to instances of quickened activity [he's still *active* at eighty; an *active* market]; **energetic** suggests a concentrated exertion of energy or effort [an *energetic* workout]; **vigorous** implies forcefulness, robustness, and strength as an inherent quality [a *vigorous* plant]; **strenuous** is applied to things that make trying demands on one's strength, energy, etc. [a *strenuous* trip]; **brisk** implies liveliness and vigor of motion [a *brisk* walk]

☆**active duty** (*or* **service**) full-time service, esp. in the armed forces

active immunity immunity (to a disease) due to the production of antibodies by the body: see PASSIVE IMMUNITY

ac·tive-ma·trix (ak′tiv mā′triks) *adj.* ⟦in ref. to the collective effect of the activity of the individual transistors⟧ designating, of, or having to do with a type of very thin, high-quality LCD video screen consisting of a grid of thousands of tiny transistors that light up individually, usually in various colors that are controlled by the level of current in each transistor

active transport the passage of ions or molecules from one side of a cell membrane to another in opposition to inhibiting conditions, as osmotic equilibrium, by means of energy released in cell metabolism

ac·tive·wear (ak′tiv wer′) *n.* clothing designed for wear while engaging in recreation or other informal activity; sportswear: also written **active wear**

ac·tiv·ism (ak′tə viz′əm) *n.* the doctrine or policy of taking positive, direct action to achieve an end, esp. a political or social end —**ac′tiv·ist** *adj., n.*

ac·tiv·i·ty (ak tiv′ə tē) *n., pl.* **-ties** **1** the quality or state of being active; action **2** energetic action; liveliness; alertness **3** a normal function of the body or mind **4** an active force **5** any specific action or pursuit [recreational *activities*] **6** *Chem.* *a)* the ability to react with other chemicals *b)* a thermodynamic quantity which represents the effective concentration of a substance in a reacting chemical system *c)* *short for* OPTICAL ACTIVITY

activity series *Chem.* a table of metals, listed in the order of their ability to replace other metals while in solution

ac·tiv·ize (ak′tə vīz′) *vt.* **-ized′, -iz′ing** to activate

act of God *Law* an occurrence, esp. a disaster, that is due entirely to the forces of nature and that could not reasonably have been prevented

ac·to·my·o·sin (ak′tō mī′ə sin′) *n.* a complex of two proteins (actin and myosin) in muscle tissue, interacting with ATP to bring about muscular contraction

Ac·ton (ak′tən), 1st Baron (*John Emerick Edward Dalberg-Acton*) 1834-1902; Eng. historian: known as *Lord Acton*

ac·tor (ak′tər) *n.* ⟦ME *actour*, a doer, steward, plaintiff < L *actor*, a doer, advocate < *actus*: see ACT[1]⟧ **1** a person who does something or participates in something **2** a person, often, specif., a man, who acts in plays, movies, etc.

ac·tress (ak′tris) *n.* ⟦see -ESS⟧ a woman or girl who acts in plays, movies, etc.

ac·tress·y (ak′trə sē) ***adj.*** of or like an actress; esp., affected, stagy, or overly dramatic

Acts (akts) ***n.*** a book of the New Testament, ascribed to Luke: abbrev. *Ac*: full title **The Acts of the Apostles**

ac·tu·al (ak′cho͞o əl, -sho͞o-; *often,* -chəl, -shəl) ***adj.*** ⟦ME < LL *actualis,* active, practical < L *actus:* see ACT[1]⟧ **1** existing in reality or in fact; not merely possible, but real; as it really is [the *actual* cost of the dam] **2** existing at present or at the time —***SYN.*** TRUE

ac·tu·al·i·ty (ak′cho͞o al′ə tē, -sho͞o-) ***n.*** **1** the state of being actual; reality **2** *pl.* **-ties** an actual thing or condition; fact

ac·tu·al·ize (ak′cho͞o əl īz′, -sho͞o-) ***vt.*** **-ized′, -iz′ing** to make actual or real; realize in action —***vi.*** to become actual, real, fully developed, etc. —**ac′tu·al·i·za′tion** ***n.***

ac·tu·al·ly (ak′cho͞o əl ē, -sho͞o-; *often,* -chə lē, -shə-) ***adv.*** as a matter of actual fact; really

actual sin *Theol.* any sin knowingly committed by an individual: distinguished from ORIGINAL SIN

ac·tu·ar·i·al (ak′cho͞o er′ē əl) ***adj.*** **1** of actuaries or their work **2** calculated by actuaries —**ac′tu·ar′i·al·ly** ***adv.***

ac·tu·ar·y (ak′cho͞o er′ē) ***n., pl.*** **-ies** ⟦L *actuarius,* clerk < *actus:* see ACT[1]⟧ a person whose work is to calculate statistically risks, premiums, life expectancies, etc. for insurance

ac·tu·ate (ak′cho͞o āt′) ***vt.*** **-at′ed, -at′ing** ⟦< ML *actuatus,* pp. of *actuare* < L *actus:* see ACT[1]⟧ **1** to put into action or motion **2** to cause to take action [what motives *actuated* him?] —**ac′tu·a′tion** ***n.*** —**ac′tu·a′tor** ***n.***

ac·u·ate (ak′yo͞o it, -āt′) ***adj.*** ⟦< L *acus,* needle (see ACEROSE[1]) + -ATE[1]⟧ having a sharp point

A·cuff (ā′kuf′), **Roy** 1903-92; U.S. composer & country music singer

a·cu·i·ty (ə kyo͞o′ə tē) ***n.*** ⟦Fr *acuité* < ML *acuitas* < L *acus,* needle: see ACEROSE[1]⟧ acuteness; keenness, as of thought or vision

a·cu·le·ate (ə kyo͞o′lē it, -āt′) ***adj.*** ⟦L *aculeatus*⟧ having an aculeus or aculei

a·cu·le·us (ə kyo͞o′lē əs) ***n., pl.*** **-le·i′** (-ī′) ⟦L, dim. of *acus,* needle: see ACEROSE[1]⟧ **1** *Bot.* a prickle **2** *Zool.* a sting

a·cu·men (ə kyo͞o′mən, ak′yə mən) ***n.*** ⟦L, a point, sting, mental acuteness < *acuere,* to sharpen < IE base **ak̑-*: see ACID⟧ keenness and quickness in understanding and dealing with a situation; shrewdness

a·cu·mi·nate (ə kyo͞o′mə nit; *for v.,* -nāt′) ***adj.*** ⟦L *acuminatus,* pp. of *acuminare,* to sharpen < *acumen:* see prec. ⟧ pointed; tapering to a point [an *acuminate* leaf] —***vt.*** **-nat′ed, -nat′ing** to make sharp or pointed —**a·cu′mi·na′tion** ***n.***

ac·u·pres·sure (ak′yo͞o presh′ər, -yə-) ***n.*** ⟦fol. + PRESSURE⟧ **1** a practice analogous to acupuncture but involving the application of manual pressure to parts of the body rather than the insertion of needles **2** *Med.* a procedure of placing needles in the tissue adjacent to a seriously bleeding vessel to compress the vessel and stop the bleeding

ac·u·punc·ture (ak′yo͞o puŋk′chər, -yə-) ***n.*** ⟦< L *acus,* needle (see ACEROSE[1]) + PUNCTURE⟧ the ancient practice, esp. as carried on by the Chinese, of piercing parts of the body with needles in seeking to treat disease or relieve pain —**ac′u·punc′tur·ist** ***n.***

a·cute (ə kyo͞ot′) ***adj.*** ⟦L *acutus,* pp. of *acuere,* sharpen: see ACUMEN⟧ **1** having a sharp point **2** keen or quick of mind; shrewd **3** sensitive to impressions [*acute* hearing] **4** severe and sharp, as pain, jealousy, etc. **5** severe but of short duration; not chronic: said of some diseases **6** very serious; critical; crucial [an *acute* shortage of workers] **7** shrill; high in pitch **8** of less than 90 degrees [an *acute* angle] **9** INTENSIVE (sense 3) —**a·cute′ly** ***adv.*** —**a·cute′ness** ***n.***

SYN.—**acute** suggests severe intensification of an event, condition, etc. that is sharply approaching a climax [an *acute* shortage]; **critical** is applied to a turning point which will decisively determine an outcome [the *critical* battle of a war]; **crucial** comes into contrast with **critical** where a trial determining a line of action rather than a decisive turning point is involved [a *crucial* debate on foreign policy] See also **sharp**

acute accent a mark (´) used to indicate *a)* the quality or length of a vowel, as in French *idée b)* primary stress, as in Spanish *olé c)* any stress on a spoken sound or syllable, as in the scanning of verse

ACV *abbrev.* ⟦*a(ir-)c(ushion) v(ehicle)*⟧ HOVERCRAFT

-a·cy (ə sē) ⟦variously < Fr *-atie* < L *-acia, -atia* < Gr *-ateia*⟧ *suffix forming nouns* quality, condition, position, etc. [*supremacy*]

a·cy·clic (ā sīk′lik) ***adj.*** **1** not cyclic; not in cycles **2** *Chem.* having the structure of an open chain

a·cy·clo·vir (ā sī′klō vir′, -klə-) ***n.*** ⟦prec. + -O- + (ANTI)VIR(AL)⟧ a synthetic, white, crystalline powder, $C_8H_{11}O_3N_5$, used as a drug to treat infections caused by various types of herpesviruses

ac·yl (as′il) ***n.*** ⟦AC(ID) + -YL⟧ *Chem.* a radical, RCO, derived from an organic acid by the removal of the OH group

a·cyl·o·in (ə sil′ō in) ***n.*** ⟦prec. + (BENZ)OIN⟧ any of a group of ketones with the general formula RCH(OH)COR; esp., benzoin

ad[1] (ad) [Informal] ***n.*** an advertisement —***adj.*** of or having to do with advertising [an *ad* agency]

ad[2] (ad) ***n.*** *Tennis short for* ADVANTAGE (sense 4) —**ad in** server's advantage —**ad out** receiver's advantage

ad[3] (ad) ***prep.*** ⟦L⟧ *Pharmacy* up to; so as to make

AD or **A.D.** *abbrev.* **1** *Mil.* active duty **2** ⟦L *Anno Domini,* in the year of the Lord⟧ of the Christian era: used with dates

ad- (ad, əd, id) ⟦L *ad-,* to, at, toward; akin to AT[1]⟧ *prefix* motion toward, addition to, nearness to [*adsorb, adjoin, adrenal*] In words of Latin origin it becomes *ac-* before *c* or *q*; *af-* before *f*; *ag-* before *g*; *al-* before *l*; *an-* before *n*; *ap-* before *p*; *ar-* before *r*; *as-* before *s*; *at-* before *t*; and *a-* before *sc, sp,* or *st*: many apparent English instances of this prefix are Latinizations, often erroneous, of French or even of English words See ADVANCE, ADMIRAL, ACCURSED, ACKNOWLEDGE

-ad[1] (ad, əd, id) ⟦Gr *-as, -ad-*⟧ *suffix forming nouns* **1** the name of any of certain collective numerals [*dyad*] **2** the title of any of certain poems [*Iliad*] **3** any of certain plants [*cycad*]

-ad[2] (ad) ⟦L *ad,* toward⟧ *suffix forming adverbs* toward, in the direction of [*caudad, cephalad*]

A·da (ā′də) ***n.*** **1** ⟦Heb *ada,* beauty⟧ a feminine name: also **A·dah** **2** ⟦after Augusta *Ada* Byron (1815-52), daughter of Lord BYRON[2], for her pioneering work on early mechanical computing devices⟧ a modular computer language employing English words

ADA (ā′də) *abbrev.* **1** American Dental Association **2** Americans for Democratic Action **3** Americans with Disabilities Act

ad ab·sur·dum (ad′ ab surd′əm, äd′ äb-) ⟦L⟧ to the point of absurdity; to a ridiculous extreme

a·dac·ty·lous (ā dak′tə ləs) ***adj.*** ⟦A-[2] + DACTYL + -OUS⟧ lacking fingers or toes from birth

ad·age (ad′ij) ***n.*** ⟦Fr < L *adagium, adagio* < *ad-,* to + *aio,* I say < **agyo* < IE base **ēg̑-,* speak, say⟧ an old saying that has been popularly accepted as a truth —***SYN.*** SAYING

a·da·gio (ə dä′jō, -zhō; -jē ō′, -zhē ō′) [*also in italics*] *Music* ***adj., adv.*** ⟦It *ad agio,* lit., at ease⟧ (in a) slow and leisurely (manner): often used as a musical direction —***n., pl.*** **-gios** **1** an adagio movement or passage **2** a slow ballet dance, esp. the main section of a pas de deux, requiring skillful partnering and balancing

Ad·am[1] (ad′əm) ***adj.*** ⟦after Robert and James *Adam,* 18th-c. Brit architects, its originators⟧ relating to a style of English furniture and architecture characterized by straight lines and ornamental motifs of garlands, medallions, etc.

Ad·am[2] (ad′əm) ***n.*** ⟦Heb < *adam,* a human being⟧ **1** a masculine name **2** *Bible* the first man: Gen. 1-5 —**not know someone from Adam** not know someone at all —**the old Adam** the supposed human tendency to sin —**A·dam·ic** (ə dam′ik, ad′əm ik) ***adj.,*** **A·dam′i·cal**

Ad·am-and-Eve (ad′əm ən ēv′) ***n.*** PUTTYROOT

ad·a·mant (ad′ə mənt, -mant′) ***n.*** ⟦ME & OFr < L *adamas* (gen. *adamantis*), the hardest metal < Gr *adamas* (gen. *adamantos*) < *a-,* not + *daman,* to subdue: see TAME⟧ **1** in ancient times, a hard stone or substance that was supposedly unbreakable **2** [Old Poet.] unbreakable hardness —***adj.*** **1** too hard to be broken **2** not giving in or relenting; unyielding —***SYN.*** INFLEXIBLE —**ad′a·mant·ly** ***adv.***

ad·a·man·tine (ad′ə man′tin; *also,* -tēn′, -tīn′) ***adj.*** ⟦ME < L *adamantinus,* hard as steel < Gr *adamantinos*⟧ **1** of or like adamant; very hard, as dental enamel; unbreakable **2** unyielding; firm

Ad·am·ite (ad′əm īt′) ***n.*** **1** a human being; person thought of as descended from Adam **2** a person who goes naked in imitation of Adam, as did members of some early religious sects —**Ad′am·it′ic** (-it′ik) ***adj.***

Ad·ams[1] (ad′əmz) **1 Abigail** (born *Abigail Smith*) 1744-1818: wife of John Adams **2 An·sel** (an′səl) 1902-84; U.S. photographer **3 Charles Francis** 1807-86; U.S. statesman: son of John Quincy **4 Henry (Brooks)** 1838-1918; U.S. historian & writer: son of Charles Francis **5 John** 1735-1826; 2d president of the U.S. (1797-1801) **6 John Quin·cy** (kwin′zē, -sē) 1767-1848; 6th president of the U.S. (1825-29): son of John & Abigail **7 Samuel** 1722-1803; Am. statesman & Revolutionary leader

Ad·ams[2] (ad′əmz), **Mount** **1** ⟦after John ADAMS[1]⟧ mountain of the Cascade Range, S Wash.: 12,307 ft (3,751 m) **2** ⟦after John ADAMS[1]⟧ peak of the White Mountains, N.H.: 5,798 ft (1,767 m)

Adam's apple the projection formed in the front of the throat by the thyroid cartilage: seen chiefly in men

ad·ams·ite (ad′əmz īt′) ***n.*** a yellow, odorless, crystalline compound, $C_6H_4(AsCl)(NH)C_6H_4$, developed for use, in a vaporous form, in chemical warfare

☆**Adam's needle** any of several species (esp. *Yucca filamentosa*) of the yucca plant

A·da·na (ä′də nä′) city in S Turkey

A·da·pa·za·ri (äd′ə pä′zə rē′) city in NW Turkey

a·dapt (ə dapt′) ***vt.*** ⟦Fr *adapter* < L *adaptare* < *ad-,* to + *aptare,* to fit: see APT[1]⟧ **1** to make fit or suitable by changing or adjusting **2** to adjust (oneself) to new or changed circumstances —***vi.*** to adjust oneself

SYN.—**adapt** implies a modifying so as to suit new conditions and suggests flexibility [to *adapt* oneself to a new environment]; **adjust** describes the bringing of things into proper relation through the use of skill or judgment [to *adjust* brakes, to *adjust* differences]; **accommodate** implies a subordinating of one thing to the needs of another and suggests concession or compromise [he *accommodated* his walk to the halting steps of his friend]; **conform** means to bring or act in harmony with some standard pattern, principle, etc. [to *conform* to specifications]

a·dapt·a·ble (ə dap′tə bəl) ***adj.*** **1** that can be adapted or made suitable **2** able to adjust oneself to new or changed circumstances —**a·dapt′a·bil′i·ty** (-bil′ə tē) ***n.***

ad·ap·ta·tion (ad′əp tā′shən) *n.* ⟦Fr < ML *adaptatio*: see ADAPT⟧ **1** an adapting or being adapted **2** a thing resulting from adapting [this play is an *adaptation* of a novel] **3** a change in structure, function, or form that improves the chance of survival for an animal or plant within a given environment **4** the natural reactions of a sense organ to variations in the degree of stimulation **5** *Sociology* a gradual change in behavior to conform to the prevailing cultural patterns —**ad′ap·ta′tion·al** *adj.*

a·dapt·er or **a·dap·tor** (ə dap′tər) *n.* **1** a person or thing that adapts **2** a contrivance for adapting apparatus to new uses **3** a connecting device for parts that would not otherwise fit together

a·dap·tion (ə dap′shən) *n.* ADAPTATION

a·dap·tive (-tiv) *adj.* **1** showing adaptation **2** able to adapt —**a·dap′tive·ly** *adv.*

adaptive radiation ⟦see RADIATE, *vi.* 3⟧ *Biol.* the dispersal of, and adaptation to new environments by, a line of animals or plants, resulting in the evolution of divergent forms, often new species, specialized for surviving in the new habitats

A·dar (ä där′) *n.* ⟦Heb⟧ the sixth month of the Jewish year: see the Jewish calendar in the Reference Supplement

Adar She·ni (shā′nē) ⟦Heb, lit., second Adar⟧ an extra month of the Jewish year, occurring about once every three years between Adar and Nisan: see the Jewish calendar in the Reference Supplement

ad as·tra per as·pe·ra (äd′ äs′trə pər äs′pər ə) ⟦L⟧ to the stars through difficulties

ad·ax·i·al (ad ak′sē əl) *adj. Bot.* designating or on the side toward the axis or stem

ADC *abbrev.* **1** aide-de-camp **2** Aid to Dependent Children

add[1] (ad) *vt.* ⟦ME *adden* < L *addere*, to add < *ad-*, to + *dare*, to give⟧ **1** to join or unite (something) *to* something else so as to increase the quantity, number, size, etc. or change the total effect [to *add* a wing to the building, to *add* seasoning to the sauce] **2** to state further **3** to combine (numbers) into a sum; calculate the total of —*vi.* **1** to cause an increase; be an addition (*to*) [this *adds* to my pleasure] **2** to find a sum by doing arithmetic —**add up 1** to calculate the total of **2** to equal the expected sum [these figures don't *add up*] **3** to seem reasonable [his excuse just doesn't *add up*] —**add up to 1** to reach a total of **2** to mean; signify —**add′a·ble** *adj.*, **add′i·ble**

add[2] *abbrev.* ⟦L *adde*⟧ *Pharmacy* let there be added; add

ADD *abbrev.* **1** American Dialect Dictionary **2** attention deficit (hyperactivity) disorder

Ad·ams (ad′əmz) **1 Charles (Samuel)** 1912-88; U.S. cartoonist **2 Jane** 1860-1935; U.S. social worker & writer: founder of Hull House in Chicago

ad·dax (ad′aks′) *n., pl.* **-dax′es** or **-dax′** ⟦L < ?; mentioned by Pliny as being an African word⟧ a large, whitish antelope (*Addax nasomaculatus*) of the Sahara, with long, twisted horns

ad·dend (ad′end′, ə dend′) *n.* ⟦< fol. ⟧ *Math.* a number or quantity to be added to another

ad·den·dum (ə den′dəm) *n., pl.* **-den′da** (-də) ⟦L, ger. of *addere*, ADD[1]⟧ **1** a thing added or to be added **2** an appendix or supplement to a book, etc. **3** the part of a gear tooth that projects beyond the pitch circle, or the distance that it projects

add·er[1] (ad′ər) *n.* **1** one who adds ☆**2** an adding machine **3** a computer circuit that performs addition

ad·der[2] (ad′ər) *n.* ⟦ME < *nadder* (by faulty separation of *a nadder*) < OE *nædre* < IE base *nətr, *nētr > L *natrix*, watersnake⟧ **1** a small, poisonous snake of Europe; common viper (*Vipera berus*) **2** any of various other snakes, as the poisonous puff adder of Africa or the harmless milk snake of North America

☆**ad·der's-mouth** (ad′ərz mouth′) *n.* any of a number of related orchids (genus *Malaxis*) with greenish flowers

ad·der's-tongue (ad′ərz tuŋ′) *n.* ☆**1** DOGTOOTH VIOLET **2** any of a genus (*Ophioglossum*, family Ophioglossaceae) of ferns with a narrow spike somewhat resembling a snake's tongue

ad·dict (ə dikt′; *for n.*, ad′ikt) *vt.* ⟦< obs. sense, to give (oneself) up to some strong habit, back-form. < fol. ⟧ to cause (someone) to become an addict —*n.* **1** a person physically or psychologically dependent on some habit, esp. on the use of a narcotic drug **2** an ardent supporter; devotee [a baseball *addict*]

ad·dict·ed (ə dik′tid) *adj.* ⟦< obs. adj. *addict*, bound or devoted (to someone) < L *addictus*, pp. of *addicere*, to assent to, assign < *ad-*, to + *dicere*, to say: see DICTION⟧ **1** having a physical or psychological dependence on some habit, esp. on the use of a narcotic drug **2** ardently supportive or devoted to some activity or thing Often with *to*

ad·dic·tion (-shən) *n.* the condition of being addicted (*to* a habit) or of being an addict; specif., the habitual use of narcotic drugs

ad·dic·tive (-tiv) *adj.* relating to or causing addiction

☆**adding machine** a machine that automatically performs addition (and often subtraction, division, etc.) when certain keys are pressed

Ad·dis A·ba·ba (ad′is ab′ə bə, -ä′bə bə) capital of Ethiopia, in the central part

Ad·di·son (ad′i sən), **Joseph** 1672-1719; Eng. essayist & poet

Ad·di·son's disease (ad′i sənz) ⟦after T. *Addison* (1793-1860), Eng physician who identified it⟧ a disease caused by failure of the adrenal glands: it is characterized by anemia, weakness, low blood pressure, and brownish discoloration of the skin

ad·di·tion (ə dish′ən) *n.* ⟦ME *addicion* < OFr *addition* < L *additio* < *addere*: see ADD[1]⟧ **1** an adding of two or more numbers to get a number called the sum **2** a joining of a thing to another thing **3** a thing or part added; increase; specif., a room or rooms added to a building **4** *Law* an identifying title or mark of status after a person's name (Ex.: John Smith, Esq.) —**in addition (to)** besides; as well (as)

ad·di·tion·al (-əl) *adj.* added; more; extra —**ad·di′tion·al·ly** *adv.*

ad·di·tive (ad′ə tiv) *adj.* ⟦LL *additivus*: see ADD[1]⟧ **1** showing or relating to addition **2** to be added —*n.* a substance added to another in small quantities to produce a desired effect, as a preservative added to food or an antiknock added to gasoline

additive inverse the number that must be added to a number to equal zero [−5 is the *additive inverse* of 5]

ad·dle (ad′'l) *adj.* ⟦ME *adel* in *adel-eye*, addle-egg, transl. of L *ovum urinae*, egg of urine, confused form of *ovum urinum* (a rendering of Gr *ourion ōon*, wind-egg) < OE *adela*; akin to MLowG *adele*, mud⟧ **1** rotten: said of an egg **2** muddled; confused: now usually in compounds [*addlebrained*] — *vi., vt.* **-dled, -dling 1** to make or become rotten **2** to make or become muddled or confused

ad·dle·brained (-brānd′) *adj.* having an addle brain; muddled; stupid: also **ad′dle·head′ed** (-hed′id) or **ad′dle·pat′ed** (-pāt′id)

☆**add-on** (ad′än′) *n.* something, as an option or accessory, that can be added to enhance the performance, appearance, etc. of something; specif., a piece of hardware or software designed to enhance a computer setup, application, etc.

ad·dress (ə dres′; *for n. 2, 3, & 7, also* a′dres′) *vt.* ⟦ME *adressen*, to guide, direct < OFr *adresser* < *a-*, to + *dresser* < VL **directiare*, to direct < L *dirigere*: see DIRECT⟧ **1** to direct (spoken or written words) *to* someone **2** to speak to or write to [to *address* an audience]: sometimes used reflexively [he *addressed* himself to both of us] **3** to write the destination on (a letter or parcel) **4** to use a proper form in speaking to [*address* the judge as "Your Honor"] **5** to apply (oneself) or direct (one's energies) *to* something **6** to deal or cope with; handle (problems, issues, etc.) **7** *a)* to take a stance beside and prepare to hit (a golf ball) *b)* to take a stance before (a target in archery) **8** *Comput.* to store (data) in, or retrieve it from, a specific location in memory **9** [Obs.] to make ready; prepare —*n.* **1** a written or spoken speech, esp. a formal one **2** the place to which mail, etc. can be sent to someone; place where someone lives or works **3** the writing on an envelope, parcel, etc. showing its destination **4** skill and tact in handling situations **5** conversational manner **6** [*pl.*] attentions paid in courting or wooing **7** *Comput. a)* a number or other code identifying the specific location of stored data in memory or a storage device *b)* a string of keyboard characters serving as an assigned name or designation, as for a network mailbox, a website, etc. —*SYN.* SPEECH —**ad·dress′er** *n.*, **ad·dres′sor**

ad·dress·a·ble (ə dres′ə bəl) *adj.* **1** that can be addressed **2** designating or of a cable-TV system in which individual programs can be sent only to those customers who agree to pay for them —**ad·dress′a·bil′i·ty** *n.*

☆**ad·dress·ee** (a′dres ē′, ə dres′ē′) *n.* the person to whom mail, etc. is addressed

☆**Ad·dres·so·graph** (ə dres′ə graf′) *trademark for* a machine that automatically prints addresses on letters, etc. from prepared stencils —*n.* such a machine

ad·duce (ə do͞os′, -dyo͞os′) *vt.* **-duced′, -duc′ing** ⟦L *adducere*, to lead or bring to < *ad-*, to + *ducere*: see DUCT⟧ to give as a reason or proof; cite as an example —**ad·duc′er** *n.* —**ad·duc′i·ble** *adj.*, **ad·duce′a·ble**

ad·du·cent (a do͞os′ənt, ə-; -dyo͞os′-) *adj.* ⟦L *adducens*, prp. of *adducere*: see prec.⟧ *Physiol.* that adducts

ad·duct (a dukt′, ə-) *vt.* ⟦< L *adductus*, pp. of *adducere*: see ADDUCE⟧ *Physiol.* to pull (a part of the body) toward the median axis: said of a muscle: opposed to ABDUCT —**ad·duc′tive** (-duk′tiv) *adj.* —**ad·duc′tor** *n.*

ad·duc·tion (a duk′shən, ə-) *n.* ⟦ME *adduccioun* < ML *adductio* < L *adductus*, pp. of *adducere*: see ADDUCE⟧ **1** an adducing or citing **2** *Physiol. a)* an adducting of a part of the body *b)* the changed position resulting from this

Ade (ād), **George** 1866-1944; U.S. humorist

-ade (ād, äd) ⟦Fr *-ade*; Prov, Port, or Sp *-ada*; It *-ata*; all ult. < L *-ata*, fem. ending of pp. of verbs of the first conjugation⟧ *suffix* **1** the act of ___ing [*blockade*] **2** result or product [*arcade*] **3** participant(s) in an action [*brigade*] **4** ⟦after LEMONADE⟧ drink made from the juice of [*limeade*]

Ad·e·la (ad′'l ə, ə del′ə) *n.* a feminine name: dim. *Della*; var. *Adelia*; Fr. *Adèle*: see ADELAIDE[1]

Ad·e·laide[1] (ad′ə lād′) *n.* ⟦Fr *Adélaïde* < Ger *Adelheid* < OHG *Adalheidis*, *Adalheit*, lit., nobility < *adal*, nobility + *-heit*, noun suffix akin to E -HOOD⟧ a feminine name: dim. *Addie*; var. *Adeline, Adela*

Ad·e·laide[2] (ad′ə lād′) capital of South Australia: port on the SE coast of the state

Ad·el·bert (ad′'l burt′, ə del′bərt) *n.* a masculine name: see ALBERT[1]

A·dele (ə del′) *n.* ⟦Fr *Adèle*⟧ a feminine name: see ADELA

A·dé·lie Coast (ad′ə lē′; *Fr* à dā lē′) region in Antarctica, south of Australia, claimed by France: 166,800 sq mi (432,010 sq km): also **Adélie Land**, Fr. name **Terre A·dé·lie** (ter à dā lē′)

Ad·e·line (ad′ə lin′, -lēn′) *n.* a feminine name: var. *Adelina, Aline*: see ADELAIDE[1]

a·demp·tion (ə demp′shən) *n.* ⟦< L *ademptio*, a taking away < *adimere*, take away < *ad-*, to + *emere*, take, buy: see REDEEM⟧ *Law* the extinction of a legacy by, or inferred from, an act of the testator before death, as by the disposal of the bequeathed property

A·den (äd′'n, ād′'n) **1** former British colony & protectorate in SW Arabia, on the Gulf of Aden: now part of the Republic of Yemen **2** seaport in this region: capital of the former People's Democratic Republic of Yemen **3** **Gulf of** gulf of the Arabian Sea, between the S coast of Arabia and Somalia in E Africa

ad·en- (ad′'n) *combining form* ADENO-: used before a vowel [*adenitis*]

A·de·nau·er (ad′'n our; *Ger* ä′dən ou′ər), **Kon·rad** (kän′rad′; *Ger* kôn′rät′) 1876-1967; Ger. statesman: chancellor of the Federal Republic of Germany (1949-63)

ad·e·nine (ad′ə nēn′, -nin′) ***n.*** ⟦ADEN(O)- + -INE[3]⟧ a white, crystalline purine base, $C_5H_5N_5$, contained in the DNA, RNA, and ADP of all tissue: it links with thymine in the DNA structure

ad·e·ni·tis (ad′'n īt′is) ***n.*** ⟦fol. + -ITIS⟧ glandular inflammation

ad·e·no- (ad′'n ō′) ⟦< Gr *adēn*, gland: see INGUINAL⟧ *combining form* gland or glands [*adenoma*]

ad·e·no·car·ci·no·ma (-kär′sə nō′mə) ***n.*** ⟦prec. + CARCINOMA⟧ a malignant tumor of glandular origin or with a glandlike cell arrangement

ad·e·no·hy·poph·y·sis (-hī päf′ə sis) ***n., pl.*** **-ses′** (-sēz′) the anterior lobe of the pituitary gland: it secretes such hormones as ACTH and luteinizing hormone: cf. NEUROHYPOPHYSIS —**ad′e·no·hy′po·phys′e·al** ***adj.***, **ad′e·no·hy′po·phys′i·al** (-hī′pō fiz′ē əl)

ad·e·noid (ad′'n oid′, ad′noid′) ***adj.*** ⟦ADEN(O)- + -OID⟧ **1** glandlike or glandular **2** of or like lymphoid tissue

ad·e·noi·dal (ad′'n oid′'l, ad noid′'l) ***adj.*** **1** adenoid **2** having adenoids **3** having the characteristic difficult breathing or nasal tone that results from enlarged adenoids

ad·e·noid·ec·to·my (ad′'n oid′ek′tə mē, ad′noi dek′-) ***n., pl.*** **-mies** ⟦fol. + -ECTOMY⟧ the surgical removal of the adenoids

ad·e·noids (ad′'n oidz′, ad′noidz′) ***pl.n.*** growths of lymphoid tissue in the upper part of the throat, behind the nose: they can swell up, esp. during childhood, obstruct breathing and speaking, and cause chronic ear infections

ad·e·no·ma (ad′'n ō′mə) ***n.*** ⟦ADEN(O)- + -OMA⟧ a benign tumor of glandular origin or with a glandlike cell arrangement —**ad·e·nom·a·tous** (ad′'n äm′ə təs) ***adj.***

a·den·o·sine (ə den′ə sēn′, -sin) ***n.*** ⟦arbitrary blend of ADENINE & RIBOSE⟧ a white, odorless, crystalline powder, $C_5H_4N_5 \cdot C_5H_9O_4$, obtained from the hydrolysis of yeast nucleic acid: it is a nucleoside consisting of adenine and ribose: see also ADP[1], AMP, ATP

adenosine di·phos·phate (dī fäs′fāt′) ADP[1]

adenosine mon·o·phos·phate (män′ō fäs′fāt′) AMP

adenosine tri·phos·phate (trī fäs′fāt′) ATP

ad·e·no·sis (ad′'n ō′sis) ***n., pl.*** **-ses′** (-sēz′) ⟦ADEN(O)- + -OSIS⟧ any disease of glands; esp., the abnormal development of glandular tissue

ad·e·no·vi·rus (ad′'n ō vī′rəs) ***n.*** ⟦ADENO- + VIRUS⟧ any of a family (Adenoviridae) of DNA viruses that infect chiefly the respiratory tract in birds and mammals, including humans

ad·e·nyl·ic acid (ad′'n il′ik) AMP

a·dept (ə dept′; *also, and for n. always* ad′ept′) ***adj.*** ⟦L *adeptus*, pp. of *adipisci*, to arrive at < *ad-*, to + *apisci*, to pursue, attain: used in ML of alchemists claiming to have arrived at the philosopher's stone⟧ highly skilled; expert —***n.*** **ad′ept′**a person who is highly skilled in some field of knowledge or work; expert —**a·dept′ly** ***adv.*** —**a·dept′ness** ***n.***

ad·e·qua·cy (ad′i kwə sē) ***n.*** the quality or state of being adequate

ad·e·quate (ad′i kwət) ***adj.*** ⟦L *adaequatus*, pp. of *adaequare* < *ad-*, to + *aequare*, to make equal < *aequus*, level, equal⟧ **1** enough or good enough for what is required or needed; sufficient; suitable **2** barely satisfactory; acceptable but not remarkable —***SYN.*** SUFFICIENT —**ad′e·quate·ly** ***adv.*** —**ad′e·quate·ness** ***n.***

à deux (ȧ dö′) ⟦Fr⟧ **1** of or for two **2** intimate(ly)

ad ex·tre·mum (ad′ eks trē′məm, äd′-) ⟦L, at the extreme⟧ **1** to or at the very end **2** at last; finally

ad fin. *abbrev.* ⟦L *ad finem*⟧ to the end; at the end

ADHD *abbrev.* attention deficit hyperactivity disorder

ad·here (ad hir′, əd-) ***vi.*** **-hered′, -her′ing** ⟦L *adhaerere* < *ad-*, to + *haerere*, to stick⟧ **1** to stick fast; stay attached **2** to stay firm in supporting or approving [to *adhere* to a leader, to *adhere* to a plan] —***SYN.*** STICK —**ad·her′er** ***n.***

ad·her·ence (ad hir′əns, əd-) ***n.*** the act of adhering; specif., attachment (*to* a person, cause, etc.); devotion and support

ad·her·ent (ad hir′ənt, əd-) ***adj.*** ⟦Fr < L *adhaerens*, prp. of *adhaerere*: see ADHERE⟧ **1** sticking fast; attached **2** *Bot.* grown together; adnate —***n.*** a supporter or follower (*of* a person, cause, etc.) —***SYN.*** FOLLOWER

ad·he·sion (ad hē′zhən, əd-) ***n.*** ⟦Fr < L *adhaesio* < pp. of *adhaerere*: see ADHERE⟧ **1** the act of sticking (*to* something) or the state of being stuck together **2** devoted attachment; adherence **3** a thing that adheres **4** *Med.* *a)* the joining together, by fibrous tissue, of body parts or tissues that are normally separate: it typically results from inflammation *b)* a band of fibrous tissue abnormally joining body parts or tissues **5** *Physics* the force that holds together the molecules of unlike substances whose surfaces are in contact: distinguished from COHESION

ad·he·sive (ad hē′siv, -ziv; əd-) ***adj.*** ⟦Fr *adhésif* < L *adhaesus*, pp. of *adhaerere*: see ADHERE⟧ **1** sticking and not coming loose; clinging **2** made so as to adhere —***n.*** **1** an adhesive substance, as glue **2** *Philately* an adhesive postage stamp —**ad·he′sive·ly** ***adv.*** —**ad·he′sive·ness** ***n.***

adhesive tape tape with a sticky substance on usually one side, variously used, as for holding bandages in place

ad·hib·it (ad hib′it) ***vt.*** ⟦< L *adhibitus*, pp. of *adhibere*, to summon < *ad-*, to + *habere*, to have⟧ [Rare] **1** to let in; admit **2** to affix **3** to administer, as a remedy —**ad′hi·bi·tion** (ad′hə bish′ən) ***n.***

ad hoc (ad häk′, -hōk′) ⟦L, to this⟧ for a special case only, without general application [an *ad hoc* committee]

ad ho·mi·nem (ad häm′ə nem′) ⟦L, lit., to the person⟧ **1** appealing to prejudice and emotion rather than to reason **2** attacking the character, motives, etc. of an opponent rather than debating the issue on logical grounds

ad·i·a·bat·ic (ad′ē ə bat′ik, ad′ī ə-) ***adj.*** ⟦< Gr *adiabatos*, not to be passed < *a-*, not + *dia*, through + *bainein*, to go: see COME⟧ *Physics* of a process that occurs without loss or gain of heat —**ad′i·a·bat′i·cal·ly** ***adv.***

ad·i·aph·o·rous (ad′ē af′ə rəs, ad′ī af′-) ***adj.*** ⟦Gr *adiaphoros* < *a-*, not + *diaphoros*, different < *diapherein*, to differ < *dia-*, through + *pherein*, to BEAR[1]⟧ **1** morally neutral or indifferent **2** *Med.* neither harmful nor helpful

a·dieu (ə dyo͞o′, -do͞o′; *Fr* ȧ dyö′) ***interj., n., pl.*** **a·dieus′** or **a·dieux** (ə dyo͞o′, -do͞o′; *Fr* ȧ dyö′) ⟦ME < OFr *a dieu*, to God (I commend you) < L *ad*, to + *Deum*, acc. of *Deus*, God; current use chiefly from modern Fr⟧ goodbye; farewell

A·di·ge (ä′dē jā′) river in N Italy, flowing south & east into the Gulf of Venice: *c.* 250 mi (402 km)

ad in·fi·ni·tum (ad in′fə nīt′əm, äd-) ⟦L, to infinity⟧ endlessly; forever; without limit: abbrev. **ad inf.**

ad i·ni·ti·um (ad′ i nish′ē əm, -nish′əm; äd′-) ⟦L⟧ at or to the beginning: abbrev. **ad init.**

ad in·te·rim (ad in′tər im) ⟦L⟧ **1** in the meantime; temporarily **2** temporary: abbrev. **ad int.**

☆**a·di·os** (a′dē ōs′, ä′-; *Sp* ä dyôs′) ***interj.*** ⟦Sp *adiós* < L *ad* + *Deum*: see ADIEU⟧ goodbye; farewell

ad·i·po·cere (ad′ə pō sir′, -pə-) ***n.*** ⟦Fr *adipocire* < L *adeps* (see fol.) + *cera*, wax⟧ a fatty or waxy substance produced in decomposing dead bodies exposed to moisture

ad·i·pose (ad′ə pōs′) ***adj.*** ⟦ModL *adiposus* < L *adeps* (gen. *adipis*), fat; ult. < Gr *aleipha*, fat; akin to *lipos*: see LIPO-⟧ of, like, or containing animal fat; fatty —***n.*** fat in the connective tissue of an animal's body

ad·i·pos·i·ty (ad′ə päs′ə tē) ***n.*** **1** the state of being fat; obesity **2** a tendency to become obese

Adirondack chair ⟦after fol., where it was developed (early 1900s)⟧ an outdoor chair made of wide, wooden slats and having a slanted back, a low, slanted seat, and wide, flat armrests

Ad·i·ron·dack Mountains (ad′ə rän′dak′) mountain range in NE New York: highest peak, Mt. Marcy: also **Adirondacks**

ad·it (ad′it) ***n.*** ⟦L *aditus*, pp. of *adire*, to approach < *ad-*, to + *ire*, to go: see EXIT⟧ an approach or entrance; specif., an almost horizontal passageway into a mine

adj *abbrev.* **1** adjective **2** adjourned **3** adjustment

Adj *abbrev.* Adjutant

ad·ja·cen·cy (ə jā′sən sē) ***n.*** **1** the quality or state of being adjacent; nearness **2** *pl.* **-cies** an adjacent thing

ad·ja·cent (ə jā′sənt) ***adj.*** ⟦L *adjacens*, prp. of *adjacere*, to lie near < *ad-*, to + *jacere*, to lie, throw: see JET[1]⟧ near or close (*to* something); adjoining —**ad·ja′cent·ly** ***adv.***

SYN.—**adjacent** things may or may not be in actual contact with each other, but they are not separated by things of the same kind [*adjacent* angles, *adjacent* farmhouses]; that which is **adjoining** something else touches it at some point or along a line [*adjoining* rooms]; things are **contiguous** when they touch along the whole or most of one side [*contiguous* farms]; **tangent** implies contact at a single, nonintersecting point with a curved line or surface [a line *tangent* to a circle]; **neighboring** things lie near to each other [*neighboring* villages]

adjacent angles two angles having the same vertex and a side in common

ad·jec·ti·val (aj′ik tī′vəl) ***adj.*** **1** of an adjective **2** having the nature or function of an adjective **3** adjective-forming [an *adjectival* suffix] —***n.*** *Linguis.* a word or word group that occurs in functions typical of adjectives —**ad′jec·ti′val·ly** ***adv.***

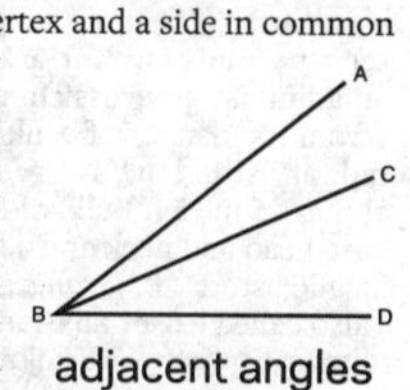

A
C
B
D

adjacent angles
(angles ABC and CBD)

ad·jec·tive (aj′ik tiv) ***n.*** ⟦ME & OFr *adjectif* < L *adjectivus*, that is added < *adjectus*, pp. of *adjicere*, to add to < *ad-*, to + *jacere*, to throw: see JET[1]⟧ any of a class of words used to modify a noun or other substantive, by describing qualities of the entity denoted, stating its limits or quantity, or distinguishing it from others (Ex.: *good, every, Aegean*) —***adj.*** **1** of an adjective **2** having the nature or function of an adjective **3** dependent or subordinate **4** *Law* of or relating to practice and procedure; procedural —**ad′jec·tive·ly** ***adv.***

Adj Gen *abbrev.* Adjutant General

ad·join (ə join′) ***vt.*** ⟦ME *ajoinen* < OFr *ajoindre* < L *adjungere* < *ad-*, to (see AD-) + *jungere*: see JOIN⟧ **1** to be next to; be contiguous to **2** to unite or annex (*to* a person or thing) —***vi.*** to be next to each other; be in contact

ad·join·ing (-iŋ) ***adj.*** touching at some point or along a line; contiguous —***SYN.*** ADJACENT

ad·journ (ə jurn′) ***vt.*** ⟦ME *ajournen* < OFr *ajourner* < *a jorn*, at the (specified) day < *a*, at + *jorn*, day < L *diurnum*, by day < *diurnus*, daily < *dies*, day: see DEITY⟧ to put off or suspend until a future time [to *adjourn* a meeting] —***vi.*** **1** to close a session or meeting for a time [Congress *adjourned* for the summer] **2** [Informal] to move from a place of meeting (*to* another place) [let's *adjourn* to the patio]

SYN.—adjourn is applied to the action as of a deliberative body in bringing a session to a close, with the intention of resuming at a later date; **prorogue** applies to the formal dismissal of a parliament by the crown, subject to reassembly; to **dissolve** an assembly is to terminate it as constituted, so that an election must be held to reconstitute it; **postpone** implies the intentional delaying of an action until a later time; **suspend** denotes the breaking off of proceedings, privileges, etc. for a time, sometimes for such an indefinite time as to suggest cancellation [to *suspend* a sentence]

ad·journ·ment (-mənt) *n.* **1** an adjourning or being adjourned **2** the time of being adjourned

ad·judge (ə juj′) *vt.* **-judged′, -judg′ing** ⟦ME *ajugen* < OFr *ajugier* < L *adjudicare* < *ad-*, to + *judicare*, to judge, decide < *judex*, JUDGE⟧ **1** to judge or decide by law **2** to declare or order by law **3** to give or award (costs, etc.) by law **4** [Rare] to regard; deem

ad·ju·di·cate (ə jo͞o′di kāt′) *vt.* **-cat′ed, -cat′ing** ⟦< L *adjudicatus*, pp. of *adjudicare*: see prec. ⟧ to hear and decide (a case); adjudge *—vi.* to serve as a judge (*in* or *on* a dispute or problem) *—***ad·ju′di·ca′tor** *n.* *—***ad·ju′di·ca·to′ry** (-kə tôr′ē) *adj.*

ad·ju·di·ca·tion (ə jo͞o′di kā′shən) *n.* **1** the act of adjudicating **2** *Law a)* a judge's decision *b)* a decree in bankruptcy determining the status of the bankrupt *—***ad·ju′di·ca′tive** (-kāt′iv, -kə tiv) *adj.*

ad·junct (a′juŋkt′) *n.* ⟦< L *adjunctus*, pp. of *adjungere*, ADJOIN⟧ **1** a thing added to something else, but secondary or not essential to it **2** *a)* a person connected with another as a helper or subordinate associate *b)* an adjunct teacher, professor, etc. **3** *Gram.* a word or phrase that qualifies or modifies another word or other words *—adj.* connected or attached in a secondary or subordinate way, or in a temporary or part-time position *—***ad′junct·ly** *adv.*

ad·junc·tive (ə juŋk′tiv) *adj.* ⟦LL *adjunctivus*⟧ that constitutes an adjunct *—***ad·junc′tive·ly** *adv.*

ad·ju·ra·tion (aj′oo rā′shən) *n.* ⟦L *adjuratio*, a swearing to < pp. of *adjurare*, fol. ⟧ **1** a solemn charge or command **2** an earnest entreaty

ad·jure (ə joor′) *vt.* **-jured′, -jur′ing** ⟦ME *adjuren* < L *adjurare* < *ad-*, to + *jurare*: see JURY[1]⟧ **1** to command or charge solemnly, often under oath or penalty **2** to entreat solemnly; appeal to earnestly *—***ad·jur′a·to′ry** (-ə tôr′ē) *adj.* *—***ad·jur′er** *n.*, **ad·ju′ror**

ad·just (ə just′) *vt.* ⟦ME *ajusten* < OFr *ajoster*, to join < *a-*, to + *joster* (see JOUST); infl. by OFr *juste* < L *justus*, JUST[1]⟧ **1** to change so as to fit, conform, make suitable, etc. **2** to make accurate by regulating [to *adjust* a watch] **3** to settle or arrange rightly [to *adjust* accounts] **4** to resolve or bring into accord [to *adjust* differences] **5** to decide how much is to be paid in settling (an insurance claim) **6** *Mil.* to correct (the gun sight, one's aim, etc.) in firing *—vi.* to come into conformity, as with one's surroundings; become suited, as to one's associates, circumstances, etc. **—SYN.** ADAPT *—***ad·just′a·ble** *adj.* *—***ad·just′er** *n.*, **ad·jus′tor**

ad·just·a·ble-rate (ə just′ə bəl rāt′) *adj.* designating or of a debt obligation, esp. a mortgage on real property, having terms which allow the interest rate to change over time

ad·jus·tive (ə jus′tiv) *adj.* having to do with adjustment

ad·just·ment (ə just′mənt) *n.* **1** an adjusting or being adjusted **2** a means or device by which parts are adjusted to one another [the *adjustment* on a micrometer] **3** the settlement of how much is to be paid in cases of loss or claim, as by insurance **4** a lowering of price, as of damaged or soiled goods

ad·ju·tan·cy (aj′ə tən sē) *n., pl.* **-cies** the rank or office of a military adjutant

ad·ju·tant (aj′ə tənt) *n.* ⟦< L *adjutans*, prp. of *adjutare*: see AID⟧ **1** an assistant **2** *Mil.* a staff officer who serves as an administrative assistant to the commanding officer **3** ⟦from its manner of walking, thought of as resembling a military strut⟧ *a)* a very large stork (*Leptoptilos dubius*) about 1.5 m (5 ft) tall, of India and Southeast Asia, with a bare head and neck and a large, thick bill *b)* a similar but smaller stork (*L. javanicus*) found in the same countries (also called **lesser adjutant**): see MARABOU

adjutant general *pl.* **adjutants general** **1** an officer in an army who is chief administrative assistant of the commanding officer of a corps or division **2** [**A- G-**] *a) U.S. Army* the chief administrative officer, having the rank of major general, in charge of the department that handles personnel records *b)* the administrative officer of the National Guard in each state

adjutant stork

ad·ju·vant (aj′ə vənt) *adj.* ⟦L *adjuvans*, prp. of *adjuvare*: see AID⟧ that helps or aids; auxiliary *—n.* **1** a person or thing that helps **2** a substance added to a drug to aid its action, specif. in increasing immune response

ADL *abbrev.* Anti-Defamation League (of B'nai B'rith)

Ad·ler (ad′lər; *for 1, Ger* äd′lər) **1 Alfred** 1870-1937; Austrian psychiatrist & psychologist **2 Felix** 1851-1933; U.S. educator & social reformer: founder of the Ethical Culture Movement

☆**ad-lib** (ad′lib′) [Informal] *vt., vi.* **-libbed′, -lib′bing** ⟦< AD LIBITUM⟧ to improvise (words, gestures, etc. not in a prepared speech, script, etc.); extemporize *—n.* the act of ad-libbing or an ad-libbed remark: also **ad lib** *—adj.* spoken or done extemporaneously *—adv.* extemporaneously: also **ad lib**

ad lib. *abbrev.* **1** *ad libitum* **2** *Pharmacy* as needed

ad lib·i·tum (ad lib′i təm) ⟦ML < L *ad*, at + *libitum* < *libet*, it pleases: see LOVE⟧ *Musical Direction* at (one's) pleasure; as one pleases: used to indicate that the marked section may be altered in tempo, ornamented, omitted, improvised, etc.

ad li·tem (ad lī′təm) ⟦L, for the suit⟧ designating a person appointed by a court to represent a minor or an incompetent adult in a lawsuit [guardian *ad litem*]

ad lit·te·ram (ad lit′ər am′, äd-) ⟦L⟧ to the letter; exactly

ad loc. *abbrev.* ⟦L *ad locum*⟧ at or to the place

adm or **admin** *abbrev.* **1** administration **2** administrative

Adm *abbrev.* Admiral

☆**ad·man** (ad′man′) *n., pl.* **-men′** (-men′) a man whose work or business is advertising: also **ad man**

ad·mass (ad′mas′) *adj.* ⟦AD[1] + MASS⟧ [Chiefly Brit.] designating or of contemporary culture thought of as dominated by the materialistic values of advertising, the mass media, etc.

ad·meas·ure (ad mezh′ər) *vt.* **-ured, -ur·ing** ⟦ME *amesuren* < OFr *admesurer* < ML *admensurare*: see AD- & MEASURE⟧ to measure out shares of; apportion

ad·meas·ure·ment (-mənt) *n.* **1** the act of admeasuring **2** size

Ad·me·tus (ad mēt′əs) *n.* ⟦L < Gr *Admētos*, lit., wild, unbroken⟧ *Gr. Myth.* a king of Thessaly, husband of Alcestis

admin *abbrev.* administration

ad·min·is·ter (ad min′is tər, əd-) *vt.* ⟦ME *aministren* < OFr *aministrer* < L *administrare* < *ad-*, to + *ministrare*, to serve⟧ **1** to manage or direct (the affairs of a government, institution, etc.) **2** to give out or dispense, as punishment or justice **3** to give or apply (medicine, etc.) **4** to direct the taking of (an oath, pledge, test, etc.) **5** *Law* to act as executor or administrator of (an estate) *—vi.* **1** to act as manager or administrator **2** to furnish help or be of service [*administer* to an invalid's needs] **—SYN.** GOVERN *—***ad·min′is·tra·ble** (-is trə bəl) *adj.* *—***ad·min′is·trant** (-is trənt) *n., adj.*

ad·min·is·trate (ad min′is trāt′, əd-) *vt.* **-trat′ed, -trat′ing** to manage or direct; administer

ad·min·is·tra·tion (ad min′is trā′shən, əd-) *n.* ⟦ME *administracioun* < OFr *administration* < L *administratio* < pp. of *administrare*, ADMINISTER⟧ **1** the act of administering; management; specif., the management of governmental or institutional affairs **2** *a)* administrators collectively *b)* [*often* **A-**] the officials in the executive branch of a government and their policies and principles **3** their term of office **4** the administering (*of* punishment, medicine, a sacrament, an oath, etc.) **5** *Law* the management and settling (*of* an estate) by an administrator or executor

ad·min·is·tra·tive (ad min′is trāt′iv, -min′is trə tiv; əd-) *adj.* of or connected with administration; executive *—***ad·min′is·tra′tive·ly** *adv.*

administrative assistant an assistant having managerial responsibilities

ad·min·is·tra·tor (ad min′is trāt′ər, əd-) *n.* **1** a person who administers **2** an executive or official of a business, institution, etc. **3** *Law* a person appointed by a court to settle an estate: cf. EXECUTOR

ad·min·is·tra·trix (-trā′triks′) *n., pl.* **-tri·ces′** (-trə sēz′) or **-trix′es** [Now Rare] *Law* a woman administrator

ad·mi·ra·ble (ad′mə rə bəl) *adj.* ⟦ME < L *admirabilis* < *admirari*: see ADMIRE⟧ inspiring or deserving admiration or praise; excellent; splendid *—***ad′mi·ra·bil′i·ty** (-bil′ə tē) *n.*, **ad′mi·ra·ble·ness** *—***ad′mi·ra·bly** *adv.*

ad·mi·ral (ad′mə rəl) *n.* ⟦ME *admirail, amirail* < OFr *admiral, amiral* < Ar *ʾamīr al-ʿālī* < *ʾamīr*, leader + *ʿālī*, high; sp. infl. by prec. ⟧ **1** the commanding officer of a navy or fleet **2** *U.S. Navy a)* an officer of the highest rank, ranking just above a vice admiral and having the insignia of four stars (see FLEET ADMIRAL) *b)* generally, any of the officers ranking above a captain, with *admiral* as part of the title of their rank **3** [Archaic] a vessel carrying the admiral; flagship **4** any of various large, colorful butterflies (genera *Limenitis* and *Vanessa*) with unusually small forelegs *—***ad′mi·ral·ship′** *n.*

ad·mi·ral·ty (ad′mə rəl tē) *n., pl.* **-ties** ⟦ME *admiralte* < OFr *admiralté*⟧ **1** the rank, position, or authority of an admiral **2** *a)* [*often* **A-**] the governmental department or officials in charge of naval affairs, as in England *b)* maritime law or court

Admiralty Islands group of small islands in the Bismarck Archipelago, in Papua New Guinea: *c.* 800 sq mi (2,072 sq km): also **Admiralties**

ad·mi·ra·tion (ad′mə rā′shən) *n.* ⟦ME *admiracion* < L *admiratio* < *admirari*: see fol. ⟧ **1** the act of admiring **2** the sense of wonder, delight, and pleased approval inspired by anything fine, skillful, beautiful, etc. **3** a thing or person inspiring such feelings **4** [Archaic] the act of wondering

ad·mire (ad mīr′, əd-) *vt.* **-mired′, -mir′ing** ⟦OFr *admirer* < L *admirari* < *ad-*, at + *mirari*, to wonder: see MIRACLE⟧ **1** to regard with wonder, delight, and pleased approval **2** to have high regard for ☆**3** [Dial.] to like or wish: with an infinitive object [I'd *admire* to go along] **4** [Archaic] to marvel at **—SYN.** REGARD *—***ad·mir′er** *n.* *—***ad·mir′ing·ly** *adv.*

ad·mis·si·ble (ad mis′ə bəl, əd-) *adj.* ⟦Fr < ML *admissibilis* < L *admissus*, pp. of *admittere*, ADMIT⟧ **1** that can be properly accepted or allowed [*admissible* evidence] **2** that ought to be admitted *—***ad·mis′si·bil′i·ty** (-bil′ə tē) *n.* *—***ad·mis′si·bly** *adv.*

ad·mis·sion (ad mish′ən, əd-) *n.* ⟦ME < L *admissio* < *admissus*, pp. of *admittere*, ADMIT⟧ **1** an admitting or being admitted; entrance **2** the right to enter; access **3** a fee paid for the right to enter; entrance fee **4** a conceding, or granting of the truth, of something **5** an acknowledging of, or confessing to, some crime, fault, etc. **6** a thing conceded, acknowledged, or confessed —**ad·mis′sive** (-mis′iv) ***adj.***

Admission Day any of several legal holidays celebrated individually by certain states, commemorating their admission into the Union

ad·mit (ad mit′, əd-) ***vt.* -mit′ted, -mit′ting** ⟦ME *admitten* < L *admittere* < *ad-*, to + *mittere*, to send: see MISSION⟧ **1** to permit to enter or use; let in **2** to entitle to enter [this ticket *admits* two] **3** to allow; leave room for **4** to have room for; hold [the hall *admits* 2,500 people] **5** to concede or grant **6** to acknowledge or confess **7** to permit to practice certain functions [he was *admitted* to the bar] —***vi.*** **1** to give entrance (*to* a place) **2** to allow or warrant: with *of* **3** to confess or own (*to*) —***SYN.*** ACKNOWLEDGE, RECEIVE

ad·mit·tance (ad mit′'ns, əd-) ***n.*** **1** an admitting or being admitted **2** permission or right to enter **3** *Elec.* the ratio of effective current to effective voltage in a circuit carrying an alternating current; the reciprocal of impedance, measured in siemens and consisting of conductance and susceptance: symbol, Y

ad·mit·ted·ly (ad mit′id lē, əd-) ***adv.*** **1** by admission or acknowledgment; confessedly [I am *admittedly* afraid of the dark] **2** by general agreement, or consensus [Julius Caesar was *admittedly* a great general]

ad·mix (ad miks′) ***vt., vi.*** ⟦back-form., by analogy with MIX < *admixt*, mixed with < L *admixtus*: see fol.⟧ to mix (a thing) in; mix with something

ad·mix·ture (ad miks′chər) ***n.*** ⟦< L *admixtus*, pp. of *admiscere* < *ad-*, to + *miscere*, to MIX + -URE⟧ **1** a mixture **2** a thing or ingredient added in mixing

admn *abbrev.* administration

ad·mon·ish (ad män′ish, əd-) ***vt.*** ⟦ME *amonesten* < OFr *amonester* < ML **admonestare*, ult. < L *admonere* < *ad-*, to + *monere*, to warn⟧ **1** to caution against specific faults; warn **2** to reprove mildly **3** to urge or exhort **4** to inform or remind, by way of a warning —***SYN.*** ADVISE —**ad·mon′ish·ing·ly** ***adv.*** —**ad·mon′ish·ment** ***n.***

ad·mo·ni·tion (ad′mə nish′ən) ***n.*** ⟦ME *amoniciоun* < OFr *amonition, admonition* < L *admonitio* < *admonere*: see prec.⟧ **1** an admonishing, or warning to correct some fault **2** a mild rebuke; reprimand

ad·mon·i·tor (ad män′it ər, əd-) ***n.*** ⟦L < *admonere*: see ADMONISH⟧ a person who admonishes

ad·mon·i·to·ry (-i tôr′ē) ***adj.*** admonishing; warning

ad·nate (ad′nāt′) ***adj.*** ⟦< L *adnatus*, pp. of *adnasci*, to be born < *ad-*, to + *nasci*: see GENUS⟧ *Biol.* congenitally joined together: said of unlike parts —**ad·na′tion** ***n.***

ad nau·se·am (ad nô′zē əm, äd-; -sē-) ⟦L, to nausea⟧ to the point of disgust; to a sickening extreme

ad·nex·a (ad nek′sə) ***pl.n.*** ⟦ModL < L, neut. pl. of *adnexus* < *adnectere*: see ANNEX⟧ *Anat.* accessory parts or appendages of an organ [the ovaries are *adnexa* of the uterus] —**ad·nex′al** ***adj.***

a·do (ə do͞o′) ***n.*** ⟦ME *ado* < northern Eng dial. inf. *at do*, to do⟧ fuss; trouble; excitement

☆**a·do·be** (ə dō′bē) ***n.*** ⟦Sp < Ar *aṭ-ṭūba*, the brick < *al*, the + Coptic *tōbe*, brick⟧ **1** unburnt, sun-dried brick **2** the clay of which such brick is made **3** a building made of adobe, esp. in the Southwest

a·do·bo (ə dō′bō) ***n.*** ⟦Sp, sauce for marinating or preserving meat⟧ a Philippine dish consisting of pork or chicken marinated in vinegar, garlic, soy sauce, etc., simmered, and then fried

ad·o·les·cence (ad′ə les′əns) ***n.*** ⟦ME & OFr < L *adolescentia* < *adolescens*: see fol.⟧ **1** the state or quality of being adolescent **2** the time of life between puberty and maturity; youth

ad·o·les·cent (ad′ə les′ənt) ***adj.*** ⟦Fr < L *adolescens*, prp. of *adolescere*, to come to maturity, be kindled, burn < **adalescere* < *ad-*, to + *alescere*, to increase, grow up < *alere*, to feed, sustain; akin to OE *ald* (see OLD), Goth *alan*, to grow⟧ **1** developing from childhood to maturity; growing up **2** of or characteristic of adolescence; youthful, exuberant, immature, unsettled, etc. —***n.*** a boy or a girl from puberty to adulthood; teenage person —***SYN.*** YOUNG

Ad·olph (ad′ôlf′, ā′dôlf′) ***n.*** ⟦L *Adolphus* < OHG *Adolf, Adulf*, lit., noble wolf < *adal*, nobility + *wolf*, WOLF⟧ a masculine name: equiv. L. *Adolphus*, Fr. *Adolphe*, Ger. *Adolf*

Ad·o·na·i (äd′ə nī′, -noi′; ad′-) ***n.*** ⟦Heb, my Lord < NW Sem *Adōn, Adun*, lord; ? akin to Ar *ʾidhn*, command⟧ God; Lord: used in Hebrew reading as a substitute for the "ineffable name" JHVH: see JEHOVAH

A·don·is (ə dän′is, -dōn′-) ***n.*** ⟦L < Gr *Adōnis*⟧ **1** *Gr. Myth.* a handsome young man loved by Aphrodite: he is killed by a wild boar **2** any very handsome young man —**A·don′ic** (-dän′ik) ***adj.***

a·dopt (ə däpt′) ***vt.*** ⟦L *adoptare* < *ad-*, to + *optare*, to choose⟧ **1** to choose and bring into a certain relationship; specif., *a)* to take into one's family by legal process and raise as one's own child *b)* to take possession of as a pet **2** to take up and use (an idea, a practice, etc.) as one's own **3** to choose and follow (a course) **4** to vote to accept (a committee report, motion, etc.) **5** to select as a required textbook —***vi.*** to take a child into one's family legally and raise as one's own —**a·dopt′a·ble** ***adj.*** —**a·dopt′ee′** ***n.*** —**a·dopt′er** ***n.*** —**a·dop′tion** ***n.***

a·dop·tive (ə däp′tiv) ***adj.*** ⟦L *adoptivus*⟧ **1** having to do with adoption **2** having become so by the act of adoption [*adoptive* parents] —**a·dop′tive·ly** ***adv.***

a·dor·a·ble (ə dôr′ə bəl) ***adj.*** ⟦Fr < L *adorabilis*⟧ **1** [Now Rare] worthy of adoration or love **2** [Informal] delightful; charming —**a·dor′a·bil′i·ty** ***n.***, **a·dor′a·ble·ness** —**a·dor′a·bly** ***adv.***

ad·o·ra·tion (ad′ə rā′shən) ***n.*** ⟦Fr < L *adoratio*⟧ **1** a worshiping or paying homage, as to a divinity **2** great love, devotion, and respect

a·dore (ə dôr′) ***vt.* a·dored′, a·dor′ing** ⟦ME *adouren* < OFr *adourer* < L *adorare*, to worship < *ad-*, to + *orare*, to speak: see ORATION⟧ **1** to worship as divine **2** to love greatly or honor highly; idolize **3** [Informal] to like very much —***SYN.*** REVERE[1] —**a·dor′er** ***n.*** —**a·dor′ing·ly** ***adv.***

a·dorn (ə dôrn′) ***vt.*** ⟦ME *adornen* (altered after L) < OFr *aourner* < L *adornare* < *ad-*, to + *ornare*, to fit out: see ORNAMENT⟧ **1** to be an ornament to; add beauty, splendor, or distinction to **2** to put decorations on; ornament

SYN.—**adorn** is used of that which adds to the beauty of something by gracing it with its own beauty [roses *adorned* her hair]; **decorate** implies the addition of something to render attractive what would otherwise be plain or bare [to *decorate* a wall with pictures]; **ornament** is used with reference to accessories which enhance the appearance [a crown *ornamented* with jewels]; **embellish** suggests the addition of something highly ornamental or ostentatious for effect; to **beautify** is to lend beauty to, or heighten the beauty of; **bedeck** emphasizes the addition of showy things [*bedecked* with jewelry]

a·dorn·ment (ə dôrn′mənt) ***n.*** **1** an adorning or being adorned **2** a decoration or ornament

A·dor·no (ə dôr′nō), **Theodore W(iesengrund)** 1903-69; Ger. philosopher & music critic

A·do·wa (äd′ə wə, ad′-) *var. of* ADWA

a·down (ə doun′) ***adv., prep.*** ⟦ME *adoun* < OE *adun*: see DOWN[1]⟧ [Now Rare] down

ADP[1] (ā′dē′pē′) ***n.*** ⟦*a(denosine) d(i)p(hosphate)*⟧ *Biochem.* a nucleotide, $C_{10}H_{15}N_5O_{10}P_2$, present in, and vital to the energy processes of, all living cells: during biological oxidations energy is stored in the ATP molecule as ADP is converted to ATP, which later converts back to ADP, releasing the energy needed for muscular contractions, photosynthesis, bioluminescence, biosynthesis, etc.

ADP[2] *abbrev.* automatic data processing

ADR (ā′dē′är′) ***n.***, *pl.* **ADRs** AMERICAN DEPOSITARY RECEIPT

A·dras·tus (ə dras′təs) ***n.*** *Gr. Myth.* a king of Argos who leads the SEVEN AGAINST THEBES

ad rem (ad′ rem′, äd′-) ⟦L, to (the) thing⟧ (in a manner) dealing directly with the matter at hand; relevant(ly)

a·dre·nal (ə drē′nəl) ***adj.*** ⟦AD- + RENAL⟧ **1** near the kidneys **2** of or from the adrenal glands —***n.*** an adrenal gland

adrenal gland either of a pair of endocrine organs lying immediately above the kidney, consisting of an inner medulla which produces epinephrine and norepinephrine and an outer cortex which produces a variety of steroidal hormones

☆**A·dren·a·lin** (ə dren′ə lin) ⟦ADRENAL + -IN[1]: so named (1901) by J. Takamine, U.S. chemist who first isolated it⟧ *trademark for* EPINEPHRINE —***n.*** [**a-**] *nontechnical name for* EPINEPHRINE: often used fig.: usually **a·dren′a·line** (-lin, -lēn′)

ad·re·ner·gic (ad′rə nur′jik) ***adj.*** ⟦< fol. + Gr *erg(on)*, WORK + -IC⟧ **1** releasing epinephrine or a similar substance [the *adrenergic* nerves of the sympathetic nervous system] **2** like epinephrine in chemical activity [an *adrenergic* drug]

a·dre·no- (ə drē′nō) *combining form* **1** adrenal glands [*adrenocortical*] **2** epinephrine [*adrenergic*] Also, before a vowel, **adren-**

a·dre·no·chrome (ə drē′nō krōm′) ***n.*** a red biochemical, $C_9H_9NO_3$, oxidized from epinephrine and having a hemostatic effect

a·dre·no·cor·ti·cal (-kôr′ti kəl) ***adj.*** of, or produced in, the cortex of the adrenal glands

a·dre·no·cor·ti·co·ster·oid (-kôr′tə kō stir′oid, -ster′-) ***n.*** CORTICOSTEROID

a·dre·no·cor·ti·co·trop·ic (-kôr′ti kō′träp′ik) ***adj.*** ⟦ADRENO- + CORTICO- + -TROPIC⟧ that can stimulate the cortex of the adrenal glands: erroneously **a·dre′no·cor′ti·co′troph′ic** (-träf′ik)

adrenocorticotropic hormone ACTH

A·dri·a·my·cin (ā′drē ə mī′sin) *trademark for* a powerful antibiotic, $C_{27}H_{30}ClNO_{11}$, used intravenously to destroy cancerous tumors despite its potential serious side effects

A·dri·an[1] (ā′drē ən) ***n.*** ⟦L *Adrianus, Hadrianus* < *Adria, Hadria*, name of two Italian cities⟧ a masculine name: fem. *Adrienne*

A·dri·an[2] (ā′drē ən) **1 Adrian IV** (born *Nicholas Breakspear*) 1100?-59; pope (1154-59): the only Eng. pope **2 E(dgar) D(ouglas)** 1st Baron Adrian of Cambridge 1889-1977; Eng. neurophysiologist

A·dri·an·o·ple (ā′drē ə nō′pəl) *former name for* EDIRNE

A·dri·an·op·o·lis (-näp′ə lis) *ancient name for* EDIRNE

A·dri·at·ic (Sea) (ā′drē at′ik) arm of the Mediterranean, between Italy and the Balkan Peninsula

A·dri·enne (ā′drē en′) ***n.*** ⟦fem. of ADRIAN[1], via Fr⟧ a feminine name: see ADRIAN[1]

a·drift (ə drift′) ***adv., adj.*** **1** floating freely without being steered; not anchored; drifting **2** without any particular aim or purpose

a·droit (ə droit′) ***adj.*** ⟦Fr < *à*, to + *droit*, right < L *directus*, pp. of *dirigere*, DIRECT⟧ skillful in a physical or mental way; clever; expert [his *adroit* handling of an awkward situation] —***SYN.*** DEXTEROUS —**a·droit′ly** ***adv.*** —**a·droit′ness** ***n.***

ad·sci·ti·tious (ad′si tish′əs) ***adj.*** ⟦< L *adscitus*, pp. of *adsciscere*, to receive with knowledge, approve < *ad-*, to + *sciscere*, to seek to know < *scire*, to know: see SCIENCE⟧ added from an external source; supplemental

ad·script (ad′skript′) ***adj.*** ⟦L *adscriptus*, pp. of *adscribere* < *ad-*, to + *scribere*, to write⟧ written after

ad·scrip·tion (ad skrip′shən) ***n.*** ASCRIPTION

ADSL *abbrev.* asymmetric digital subscriber line

ad·sorb (ad sôrb′, -zôrb′) *vt.* ⟦< AD- + L *sorbere*: see ABSORB⟧ to collect (a gas, liquid, or dissolved substance) in condensed form on a surface —**ad·sorb′a·ble** *adj.*

ad·sorb·ate (ad sôr′bit, -zôr′-; -bāt′) *n.* a gas, liquid, etc. taken up by adsorption

ad·sorb·ent (ad sôr′bənt, -zôr′-) *adj.* that is capable of adsorbing —*n.* a thing or substance that adsorbs

ad·sorp·tion (ad sôrp′shən, -zôrp′-) *n.* ⟦< ADSORB, by analogy with ABSORPTION⟧ an adsorbing or being adsorbed; adhesion of the molecules of a gas, liquid, or dissolved substance to a surface —**ad·sorp′tive** *adj.*

ad·su·ki bean (ad so͞o′kē, -zo͞o′-) ADZUKI BEAN

ad·u·lar·i·a (a′jo͞o ler′ē ə, -jə-) *n.* ⟦It < Fr *adulaire*, after *Adula*, a group of mountains in Switzerland + *-aire*, -ARY⟧ a transparent or translucent variety of orthoclase

ad·u·late (a′jo͞o lāt′, -jə-) *vt.* **-lat′ed, -lat′ing** ⟦< L *adulatus*, pp. of *adulari*, to fawn upon, orig., to wag the tail < *ad-*, to + **ūlos*, tail < IE **ūlo* < base **wel-* > WALK: cf. WHEEDLE⟧ **1** to praise too highly or flatter servilely **2** to admire intensely or excessively —**ad′u·la′tion** *n.* —**ad′u·la′tor** *n.* —**ad′u·la·to′ry** (-lə tôr′ē) *adj.*

a·dult (ə dult′, ad′ult′) *adj.* ⟦L *adultus*, pp. of *adolescere*: see ADOLESCENT⟧ **1** mature in age, size, strength, etc.; grown-up **2** of or for adult persons [an *adult* novel] **3** containing or providing sexually explicit or, esp., pornographic material [*adult* movies] —*n.* **1** a man or woman who is fully mature; grown-up **2** an animal or plant that is fully developed **3** a person who has reached the age of majority, now generally 18 years —*SYN.* RIPE —**a·dult′hood′** *n.* —**a·dult′ness** *n.*

adult education CONTINUING EDUCATION

a·dul·ter·ant (ə dul′tər ənt) *n.* a substance that adulterates —*adj.* adulterating; making inferior or impure

a·dul·ter·ate (ə dul′tər āt′; *for adj.*, -tər it) *vt.* **-at′ed, -at′ing** ⟦< L *adulteratus*, pp. of *adulterare*, to falsify < *adulter*, an adulterer, counterfeiter < *ad-*, to + *alter*, other, another⟧ to make inferior, impure, not genuine, etc. by adding a harmful, less valuable, or prohibited substance —*adj.* **1** guilty of adultery; adulterous **2** adulterated; not genuine —**a·dul′ter·a′tor** *n.*

a·dul·ter·at·ed (-āt′id) *adj.* **1** made inferior, impure, etc. by adulterating **2** that does not conform to legal standards of purity, processing, labeling, etc.

a·dul·ter·a·tion (ə dul′tər ā′shən) *n.* **1** an adulterating or being adulterated **2** an adulterated substance, commodity, etc.

a·dul·ter·er (ə dul′tər ər) *n.* ⟦altered, after L *adulterare*, from ME *avowterer, avouter* < OFr *avoutre* < *avoutrer*, to commit adultery < L *adulterare*: see ADULTERATE⟧ a person (esp. a man) guilty of adultery

a·dul·ter·ess (ə dul′tər is, ə dul′tris) *n.* a woman guilty of adultery

a·dul·ter·ine (ə dul′tər in, -tər īn′) *adj.* ⟦L *adulterinus* < *adulter*: see ADULTERATE⟧ **1** of adultery **2** due to adulteration

a·dul·ter·ous (ə dul′tər əs, -dul′trəs) *adj.* relating to, characterized by, or guilty of, adultery —**a·dul′ter·ous·ly** *adv.*

a·dul·ter·y (ə dul′tər ē, -dul′trē) *n., pl.* **-ter·ies** ⟦L *adulterium* < *adulter*: see ADULTERATE⟧ voluntary sexual intercourse between a married man and a woman not his wife, or between a married woman and a man not her husband: see also FORNICATION

ad·um·bral (ad um′brəl) *adj.* ⟦see fol.⟧ in shadow; shady

ad·um·brate (ad um′brāt′, ad′əm brāt′) *vt.* **-brat′ed, -brat′ing** ⟦< L *adumbratus*, pp. of *adumbrari*, to shade < *ad-*, to + *umbra*, SHADE⟧ **1** to outline in a shadowy way; sketch **2** to suggest beforehand; foreshadow in a vague way **3** to obscure; overshadow —**ad′um·bra′tion** (-brā′shən) *n.* —**ad·um′bra·tive** (-brə tiv) *adj.*

ad·un·cate (ad uŋ′kāt′, -kit; ə duŋ′-) *adj.* ⟦L *aduncus* < *ad-*, to + *uncus*, hooked, a hook < IE base **ang-*, **ank-*: see ANGLE[1]⟧ curved or hooked, as a parrot's beak

a·dust (ə dust′) *adj.* ⟦L *adustus*, pp. of *adurere*, to burn up < *ad-*, to + *urere*, to burn: see EMBER[1]⟧ [Archaic] **1** scorched; burned **2** parched **3** sunburned **4** sallow and melancholy

A·du·wa (äd′ə wə, ad′-) *var. of* ADWA

adv *abbrev.* **1** ad valorem **2** advance **3** adverb **4** advertisement **5** advisory **6** ⟦L *adversus*⟧ against

ad va·lo·rem (ad′ və lôr′əm) ⟦L⟧ in proportion to the value: a phrase applied to certain duties and taxes levied on goods, property, etc. as a percentage of their value: abbrev. **ad val.**

ad·vance (ad vans′, əd-) *vt.* **-vanced′, -vanc′ing** ⟦ME *avancen* < OFr *avancer*, to forward < VL **abantiare* < L *ab-*, from + *ante*, before: sp. *ad-* by assoc. with L *ad*, to, forward⟧ **1** to bring forward; move forward [to *advance* a chessman] **2** to raise in rank, importance, etc.; promote **3** to help or hasten the success or completion of; further [to *advance* a project] **4** to put forward; propose **5** to bring closer to the present; specif., *a)* to cause (a future event) to happen earlier *b)* to assign a later date to (a past event) **6** to raise the rate of; increase [to *advance* prices] **7** to pay (money) before due **8** to lend —*vi.* **1** to go forward; move ahead **2** to make progress; improve; develop **3** to rise in rank, importance, etc. **4** to rise in price or cost; increase —*n.* **1** a moving forward **2** an improvement; progress [new *advances* in science] **3** a rise in value or cost **4** [*pl.*] approaches to get favor, become acquainted, etc.; overtures (*to* someone) **5** a payment made before due, as of wages **6** a loan —*adj.* **1** in front [*advance* guard] **2** beforehand; ahead of time [*advance* information] —**in advance 1** in front **2** before due; ahead of time —**ad·vanc′er** *n.*

SYN.—**advance** is used to describe assistance in hastening the course of anything or in moving toward an objective; to **promote** is to help in the establishment, development, or success of something [to *promote* good will]; **forward** emphasizes the idea of action as an impetus [concessions were made to *forward* the pact]; **further** emphasizes assistance in bringing a desired goal closer [to *further* a cause] —*ANT.* **retard, check**

ad·vanced (ad vanst′, əd-) *adj.* **1** moved forward; in front [an *advanced* military post] **2** far on in time or in a course of action or events [despite his *advanced* age, at an *advanced* stage in the trial] **3** *a)* ahead or beyond others in progress, complexity, etc. [*advanced* studies] *b)* ahead of the times [her *advanced* views on education] —*SYN.* LIBERAL

☆**advanced credit (***or* **standing)** credit toward a degree allowed to a student by a college for courses taken elsewhere or for high scores on preliminary examinations

advance guard a detachment of troops sent ahead to reconnoiter and protect the line of march

☆**advance man** a person hired to travel in advance of a theatrical company, political candidate, etc. to arrange for publicity, schedule appearances, etc.

ad·vance·ment (ad vans′mənt, əd-) *n.* **1** an advancing or being advanced **2** promotion, as to a higher rank **3** progress or improvement; furtherance **4** *Law* money or property given as an advance share in the estate of a person who later dies without making a will: it is deducted from the total share of the recipient in the intestate's estate

ad·van·tage (ad vant′ij, əd-) *n.* ⟦ME *avantage, avauntage* < OFr *avantage* < *avant*, before < L *ab-* + *ante*: see ADVANCE⟧ **1** a more favorable position; superiority: often with *of* or *over* **2** a favorable or beneficial circumstance, event, etc. **3** gain or benefit **4** *Tennis* the first point scored after deuce —*vt.* **-taged, -tag·ing** to give an advantage to; be a benefit or aid to —**have the advantage of** to have an advantage over —**take advantage of 1** to make use of for one's own benefit **2** to impose upon in a selfish way —**to advantage** so as to result in a good effect

ad·van·taged (-ijd) *adj.* characterized by certain, esp. socioeconomic, advantages [*advantaged* students within a school district]

ad·van·ta·geous (ad′van tā′jəs, -vən-) *adj.* resulting in advantage; favorable; profitable —**ad′van·ta′geous·ly** *adv.*

ad·vec·tion (ad vek′shən) *n.* ⟦AD- + (CON)VECTION⟧ the transference of heat by horizontal currents of air —**ad·vec′tive** (-tiv) *adj.*

Ad·vent (ad′vent′) *n.* ⟦ME & OFr *avent* < ML *adventus* < pp. of L *advenire*, to come < *ad-*, to + *venire*, COME⟧ **1** the period including the four Sundays just before Christmas **2** *Theol.* *a)* the birth of Christ *b)* SECOND COMING **3** [**a-**] a coming or arrival

☆**Ad·vent·ism** (ad′vən tiz′əm) *n.* the belief that the Second Coming of Christ will occur soon

☆**Ad·vent·ist** (ad′vən tist, ad vent′ist) *n.* a member of a Christian sect based on Adventism —*adj.* of Adventism or Adventists

ad·ven·ti·ti·a (ad′ven tish′ə, -tish′ē ə; -vən-) *n.* ⟦ModL < L, for *adventicia*, neut. pl. of *adventicius*: see fol.⟧ the outer covering of an organ, as of an artery: it is made up chiefly of connective tissue

ad·ven·ti·tious (ad′ven tish′əs, -vən-) *adj.* ⟦L *adventicius*, coming from abroad: see ADVENT⟧ **1** added from outside; not inherent; accidental **2** occurring in unusual or abnormal places [*adventitious* roots growing on a stem] —*SYN.* ACCIDENTAL —**ad′ven·ti′tious·ly** *adv.* —**ad′ven·ti′tious·ness** *n.*

ad·ven·tive (ad ven′tiv) *adj.* ⟦L *adventus* (see ADVENT) + -IVE⟧ not native to the environment; rarely or imperfectly naturalized —*n.* an adventive plant or animal

Advent Sunday the first Sunday in Advent

ad·ven·ture (ad ven′chər, əd-) *n.* ⟦ME *aventure* < OFr < VL **adventura*, lit., a happening < L *advenire*: see ADVENT⟧ **1** the encountering of danger **2** a daring, hazardous undertaking **3** an unusual, stirring experience, often of a romantic nature **4** a venture or speculation in business or finance **5** a liking for danger, excitement, etc. [a man full of *adventure*] —*vt.* **-tured, -tur·ing** [Archaic] **1** to put in danger; risk; venture **2** to be bold about; dare —*vi.* **1** to engage in daring undertakings **2** to take a risk

ad·ven·tur·er (ad ven′chər ər, əd-) *n.* **1** a person who has or likes to have adventures **2** SOLDIER OF FORTUNE (sense 1) **3** a financial speculator **4** a person who seeks to become rich, powerful, etc. by dubious schemes

ad·ven·ture·some (ad ven′chər səm, əd-) *adj.* willing to take risks; adventurous

ad·ven·tur·ess (ad ven′chər is, əd-) *n.* a woman adventurer, specif. one who seeks to become rich and socially accepted by exploiting her charms, by scheming, etc.

ad·ven·tur·ism (ad ven′chər iz′əm, əd-) *n.* actions or tactics, esp. in politics or international relations, that are regarded as recklessly daring and involving the risk of serious consequences —**ad·ven′tur·ist** *n., adj.* —**ad·ven′tur·is′tic** *adj.*

ad·ven·tur·ous (ad ven′chər əs, əd-) *adj.* ⟦ME *aventurous* < OFr *aventuros* < *aventure*, ADVENTURE⟧ **1** fond of adventure; willing to take chances; daring **2** full of danger; risky —**ad·ven′tur·ous·ly** *adv.* —**ad·ven′tur·ous·ness** *n.*

ad·verb (ad′vurb′) *n.* ⟦ME *adverbe* < L *adverbium* < *ad-*, to + *verbum*, a word⟧ any of a class of words used generally to modify a verb, an adjective, another adverb, a phrase, or a clause, by expressing time, place, manner, degree, cause, etc.: English adverbs often end in *-ly* (Ex.: *fast, carefully, then*)

ad·ver·bi·al (ad vʉr′bē əl, əd-) ***adj.*** **1** of an adverb **2** having the nature or function of an adverb **3** used to form an adverb [an *adverbial* suffix] ***—n.*** *Linguis.* a word or word group that occurs in grammatical functions typical of adverbs (Ex.: the man ate lobster *with delight*; the man ordered lobster *when he had money*) **—ad·ver′bi·al·ly** ***adv.***

ad ver·bum (ad vʉr′bəm, äd-; -wer′-) ⟦L, to a word⟧ word for word; verbatim

ad·ver·sar·i·al (ad′vər ser′ē əl) ***adj.*** **1** of or characterized by opposition, disagreement, hostility, etc., as between adversaries **2** ADVERSARY

ad·ver·sar·y (ad′vər ser′ē) ***n., pl.*** **-sar′ies** ⟦ME < OFr *adversarie* < L *adversarius* < *adversus*, ADVERSE⟧ a person who opposes or fights against another; opponent; enemy ***—adj.*** of or characterized by opposing parties, as the plaintiff and defendant in a lawsuit **—*SYN.*** OPPONENT **—the Adversary** Satan

ad·ver·sa·tive (ad vʉr′sə tiv, əd-) ***adj.*** ⟦LL *adversativus* < L *adversatus*, pp. of *adversari*, to be opposed to < *adversus*, fol. ⟧ *Gram.* expressing opposition or antithesis, as the words *but, yet, however* ***—n.*** an adversative word

ad·verse (ad vʉrs′, əd-; ad′vʉrs′) ***adj.*** ⟦ME < OFr *avers, advers* < L *adversus*, turned opposite to, pp. of *advertere*, ADVERT[1]⟧ **1** moving or working in an opposite or contrary direction; opposed [*adverse* river currents] **2** unfavorable; harmful [the *adverse* effects of a drought] **3** opposite in position **4** *Bot.* turned toward the stem **—ad·verse′ly** ***adv.***

ad·ver·si·ty (ad vʉr′sə tē, əd-) ***n.*** ⟦ME < OFr *adversité, aversite* < L *adversitas* < *adversus*, prec. ⟧ **1** a state of wretchedness or misfortune; poverty and trouble **2** *pl.* **-ties** an instance of misfortune; calamity

ad·vert[1] (ad vʉrt′, əd-) ***vi.*** ⟦ME *adverten* < OFr *avertir* < L *advertere* < *ad-*, to + *vertere*, to turn: see VERSE⟧ to call attention or turn one's attention (*to*); refer or allude

ad·vert[2] (ad′vʉrt′) ***n.*** [Informal, Chiefly Brit.] *short for* ADVERTISEMENT

ad·vert·ent (ad vʉrt′'nt, əd-) ***adj.*** ⟦L *advertens*, prp. of *advertere*, ADVERT[1]⟧ [Archaic] paying attention; heedful **—ad·vert′ence** ***n.***

ad·ver·tise (ad′vər tīz′) ***vt.*** **-tised′, -tis′ing** ⟦ME *advertisen* < OFr *a(d) vertiss-*, extended stem of *advertir*, to warn, call attention to < L *advertere*, ADVERT[1]⟧ **1** to tell about or praise (a product, service, etc.) publicly, as through newspapers, handbills, radio, television, etc., so as to make people want to buy it **2** to make known; give notice of ***—vi.*** **1** to call the public's attention to things for sale or rent, help wanted, etc., as by printed or broadcast notices; sponsor advertisements **2** to ask (*for*) publicly by printed notice, etc. [*advertise* for a babysitter] **—ad′ver·tis′er** ***n.***

ad·ver·tise·ment (ad′vər tīz′mənt; əd vʉr′tiz mənt, -tis-) ***n.*** **1** the act of advertising **2** a public notice or announcement, usually paid for, as of things for sale, needs, etc.

ad·ver·tis·ing (ad′vər tīz′iŋ) ***n.*** **1** printed or broadcast matter that advertises; advertisements collectively **2** the business or occupation of preparing and issuing advertisements

ad·ver·to·ri·al (ad′vər tôr′ē əl) ***n.*** an advertisement, as in a magazine, produced so as to resemble an article or editorial

ad·vice (ad vīs′, əd-) ***n.*** ⟦ME *avis* < OFr < ML *advisum* < *advisus*, pp. of *advidere* < L *ad-*, at + *videre*, to look⟧ **1** opinion given as to what to do or how to handle a situation; counsel **2** [*usually pl.*] information or report [diplomatic *advices*] **3** LETTER OF ADVICE

ad·vis·a·ble (ad vīz′ə bəl, əd-) ***adj.*** suitable for offering as advice; that can be recommended; wise; sensible **—ad·vis′a·bil′i·ty** ***n.,*** **ad·vis′a·ble·ness** **—ad·vis′a·bly** ***adv.***

ad·vise (ad vīz′, əd-) ***vt.*** **-vised′, -vis′ing** ⟦ME *avisen*, orig., to consider < OFr *aviser* < ML *advisare* < *advisum*: see ADVICE⟧ **1** to give advice or an opinion to; counsel **2** to offer as advice; recommend **3** to notify; inform [he was *advised* of the facts] ***—vi.*** **1** to discuss something and get advice; consult (*with* a person) **2** to give advice **—ad·vis·ee** (ad′vī zē′, ad vī′-) ***n.*** **—ad·vi′sor** ***n.,*** **ad·vis′er**

***SYN.*—advise** means simply to recommend a course of action and implies that the giver of the advice has knowledge or experience; **counsel** implies serious deliberation of weighty matters; **admonish** suggests earnest, gently reproving advice concerning a fault, error, etc., given by someone fitted to do so by age or position; to **caution** or **warn** is to give advice that puts one on guard against possible danger, failure, etc.; **warn** is used especially when a serious danger is involved

ad·vised (ad vīzd′, əd-) ***adj.*** showing or resulting from thought or advice: now chiefly in WELL-ADVISED, ILL-ADVISED

ad·vis·ed·ly (-vīz′id lē) ***adv.*** with due consideration; deliberately

ad·vise·ment (ad vīz′mənt, əd-) ***n.*** ⟦ME & OFr *avisement* < *aviser*, ADVISE⟧ careful consideration **—take under advisement** to consider carefully

ad·vi·so·ry (ad vī′zə rē, əd-) ***adj.*** **1** advising or given the power to advise **2** relating to, or containing, advice ***—n., pl.*** **-ries** a report or warning, esp. one issued by the National Weather Service about weather conditions

ad·vo·ca·cy (ad′və kə sē) ***n.*** ⟦ME & OFr *advocacie* < ML *advocatia* < L *advocatus*: see fol. ⟧ the act of advocating, or speaking or writing in support (*of* something)

ad·vo·cate (ad′və kit; *for v.*, -kāt′) ***n.*** ⟦ME *advocat, avocat* < L *advocatus*, a counselor < *advocare*, to summon (for aid) < *ad-*, to + *vocare*, to call⟧ **1** a person who pleads another's cause; specif., a lawyer **2** a person who speaks or writes in support of something [an *advocate* of lower taxes] ***—vt.*** **-cat′ed, -cat′ing** ⟦< the *n.*⟧ to speak or write in support of; be in favor of **—*SYN.*** SUPPORT **—ad′vo·ca′tor** ***n.***

ad·vo·ca·tion (ad′və kā′shən) ***n.*** ⟦L *advocatio*⟧ **1** [Obs.] advocacy **2** *Scot. Law* the transfer by a superior court to itself of an action pending in an inferior court

ad·voc·a·to·ry (ad väk′ə tôr′ē, ad′və kə-) ***adj.*** **1** of an advocate **2** of advocacy; advocating

ad·vo·ca·tus di·a·bo·li (äd′vō kä′to͞os dē ä′bō lē′, ad′və kāt′əs dī ab′ə lī′) ⟦L⟧ DEVIL'S ADVOCATE

ad·vow·son (ad vou′zən) ***n.*** ⟦ME *avoueson* < OFr < L *advocatio*, a summoning, calling to: see ADVOCATE⟧ *Eng. Law* the right to name the holder of a church benefice

advt. *abbrev.* advertisement

Ad·wa (äd′wə) town in N Ethiopia: site of Menelik II's defeat of the Italians (1896), which led to recognition of Ethiopian independence

a·dy·na·mi·a (ā′dī nā′mē ə, ad′i nā′-) ***n.*** ⟦ModL < Gr < *a-*, without + *dynamis*, power⟧ *Med.* lack of vital force as a result of illness; debility **—a′dy·nam′ic** (-nam′ik) ***adj.***

ad·y·tum (ad′i təm) ***n., pl.*** **ad′y·ta** (-tə) ⟦L < Gr *adyton*, neut. of *adytos*, not to be entered < *a-*, not + *dyein*, to enter⟧ **1** the innermost room or shrine in certain old temples, to be entered only by priests **2** a sanctum

adz or **adze** (adz) ***n.*** ⟦ME *adis, adse* < OE *adesa*, adz, ax⟧ an axlike tool for trimming and smoothing wood, etc., with a curved blade at right angles to the handle

adz

ad·zu·ki bean (ad zo͞o′kē, -so͞o′-) ⟦Jpn *azuki*⟧ **1** a bushy bean plant (*Vigna angularis*) of China and Japan, with black or white pods **2** its small, reddish bean

ae (ā) ***adj.*** ⟦< OE *an*: see ONE⟧ [Scot.] one

æ (ē, i, e) ***n.*** ⟦L *aetatis*⟧ **1** a ligature used to represent a diphthong in some Latin words, equivalent to *ai* in Greek, usually written *æ* or replaced by *e* in modern spelling of derived English words, as in *demon (daemon), ether (aether)*, etc. and pronounced (ē, i, *or* e) **2** an Old English ligature representing a low front unrounded vowel like that in Modern English *hat*: see ASH[2] (*n.* 3) **3** a character in the International Phonetic Alphabet and some other transcription systems, representing this low front unrounded vowel

AE *abbrev.* American English

Æ or **A.E.** *see* RUSSELL[2], George William

Ae·a·cus (ē′ə kəs) ***n.*** ⟦L < Gr *Aiakos*⟧ *Gr. Myth.* a king of Aegina who, after he dies, becomes one of the three judges of the dead in the lower world, with Minos and Rhadamanthus

AEC *abbrev.* Atomic Energy Commission (1946-75)

ae·cid·i·um (ē sid′ē əm) ***n., pl.*** **-cid′i·a** (-sid′ē ə) ⟦ModL, dim. < Gr *aikia*, harm, injury⟧ an aecium **—ae·cid′i·al** ***adj.***

ae·ci·o·spore (ē′shē ō spôr′, ē′sē-) ***n.*** ⟦< AECIUM + SPORE⟧ a spore that develops within an aecium

ae·ci·o·stage (-stāj′) ***n.*** ⟦< fol. + STAGE⟧ the period in their life cycle during which certain rust fungi produce aecia

ae·ci·um (ē′shē əm, ē′sē-) ***n., pl.*** **-ci·a** (-ə) ⟦ModL < Gr *aikia*, injury⟧ a cuplike spore fruit produced in spring by certain rust fungi **—ae′ci·al** ***adj.***

AED *abbrev.* automated external defibrillator

a·ë·des (ā ē′dēz′) ***n., pl.*** **a·ë′des′** ⟦ModL < Gr *aēdēs*, unpleasant < *a-*, not + *hēdys*, SWEET⟧ any of a large genus (*Aëdes*) of mosquitoes, esp. a mosquito (*A. aegypti*) that carries the viruses that cause yellow fever and dengue

ae·dile (ē′dīl′) ***n.*** ⟦L *aedilis* < *aedes*, building: see EDIFY⟧ in ancient Rome, an official in charge of buildings, roads, sanitation, public games, etc.

AEF *abbrev.* American Expeditionary Force (or Forces)

Ae·ge·an (ē jē′ən, i jē′-) ***adj.*** **1** in or of the Aegean Sea **2** designating or of the culture of the Bronze Age people who lived in the Aegean Islands and nearby regions

Aegean Islands the islands in the Aegean Sea; specif., Lesbos, Samos, Khíos, the Cyclades, and the Dodecanese

Aegean Sea arm of the Mediterranean, between Greece & Turkey

Ae·ge·us (ē′jē əs) ***n.*** ⟦L < Gr *Aigeus*⟧ *Gr. Myth.* a king of Athens who drowns himself when he thinks his son Theseus is dead

Ae·gi·na (ē jī′nə) island off the SE coast of Greece: 32 sq mi (83 sq km)

Ae·gir (a′gir′; ē′jir′, ā′-) ***n.*** ⟦ON⟧ *Norse Myth.* the god of the sea

ae·gis (ē′jis) ***n.*** ⟦L < Gr *aigis*, shield of Zeus, goatskin < ? *aix* (gen. *aigos*), goat, hence ? orig. the short goatskin cloak of Zeus⟧ **1** *Gr. Myth.* a shield borne by Zeus and, later, by his daughter Athena and occasionally by Apollo **2** a protection **3** sponsorship; auspices

Ae·gis·thus (ē jis′thəs) ***n.*** ⟦L < Gr *Aigisthos*⟧ *Gr. Myth.* the son of Thyestes and lover of Clytemnestra: he helps her to kill her husband, Agamemnon

Ae·gos·pot·a·mi (ē′gäs′pät′ə mī′) small river in ancient Thrace, flowing into the Hellespont: at its mouth, the Spartan fleet under Lysander defeated the Athenian fleet (405 B.C.), ending the Peloponnesian War: also **Ae′gos′pot′a·mos** (-məs)

Ae·gyp·tus (ē jip′təs) ***n.*** *Gr. Myth.* a king of Egypt whose fifty sons marry the fifty daughters of his brother Danaus: see DANAIDES

Ael·fric (al′frik) A.D. 955?-1020?; Eng. abbot & writer

-ae·mi·a (ē′mē ə, ēm′yə) *combining form* -EMIA

Ae·ne·as (i nē′əs) ***n.*** ⟦L < Gr *Aineias*⟧ *Class. Myth.* a Trojan, son of Anchises and Venus, and hero of Virgil's *Aeneid*: escaping from ruined Troy, Aeneas wanders for years before coming to Latium: he is the traditional forefather of the ancient Romans

Ae·ne·id (ē nē′id, i nē′-) ***n.*** a Latin epic poem by Virgil, about Aeneas and his adventures

Ae·o·li·a (ē ō′lē ə) *var. of* AEOLIS

Ae·o·li·an (ē ō′lē ən, -ōl′yən) *adj.* 1 of Aeolis or its people, language, or culture 2 of Aeolus 3 [*often* a-] of the wind: see also EOLIAN (sense 2) —*n.* 1 a person born or living in Aeolis; a member of any of the Greek tribes that settled in ancient Thessaly, Boeotia, Lesbos, and Asia Minor 2 *var. of* AEOLIC
aeolian harp a box with an opening in it across which gut strings of varying thickness are stretched, tuned in unison: when air blows over them, the strings produce varying harmonies
Ae·ol·ic (ē äl′ik) *n.* a dialect or group of dialects of ancient Greek spoken chiefly in Aeolis, Boeotia, and Thessaly —*adj. var. of* AEOLIAN (*adj.* 1)
Ae·o·lis (ē′ə lis) ancient region on the NW coast of Asia Minor, consisting of a group of cities settled by the Aeolians
ae·o·lo·trop·ic (ē′ə lō′träp′ik) *adj.* ⟦< Gr *aiolos*, varying + -TROPIC⟧ ANISOTROPIC
Ae·o·lus (ē′ə ləs) *n.* ⟦L < Gr *Aiolos*⟧ *Gr. Myth.* 1 the god of the winds 2 a king of Thessaly, the legendary forefather of the Aeolians
ae·on (ē′ən, ē′än′) *n.* EON
ae·o·ni·an (ē ō′nē ən) *adj.* ⟦Gr *aiōnios*: see EON⟧ lasting for eons; eternal
ae·py·or·nis (ē′pē ôr′nis) *n.* ⟦ModL < Gr *aipys*, high, steep + *ornis*, bird: see ORNITHO-⟧ any of a genus (*Aepyornis*) of very large, extinct, flightless birds of Madagascar
ae·quor·in (ē kwôr′in) *n.* ⟦< *Aequorea*, genus name of jellyfish + -IN[1]⟧ a bioluminescent protein extracted from certain jellyfish that emits light when in contact with calcium or strontium ions: used in research to detect and locate calcium
a·er- (er, ar, ā′ər) *combining form* AERO-: used before a vowel [*aerate*]
a·er·ate (er′āt′, ā′ər āt′) *vt.* **-at′ed, -at′ing** ⟦AER(O)- + -ATE[1]⟧ 1 to expose to air, or cause air to circulate through 2 to supply oxygen to (the blood) by the process of respiration 3 to charge (liquid) with gas, as in making soda water —**a·er·a′tion** *n.*
a·er·a·tor (-ər) *n.* a person or thing that aerates; specif., a device for aerating a liquid, or a fumigating device
aer·i- (er′ē, ar′-, ā′ər ē; -i; -ə) *combining form* AERO-
aer·i·al (er′ē əl; *for adj., also* ā ir′ē əl) *adj.* ⟦< L *aerius* < *aer* (see AIR) + -AL⟧ 1 of, in, or by the air 2 like air; light as air 3 not substantial; unreal; imaginary 4 high up; lofty 5 of, for, from, or by means of aircraft or flying [an *aerial* photograph] 6 *Bot.* growing in the air instead of in soil or water —*n.* 1 ANTENNA (sense 2) 2 *Gym.* a running somersault performed without the use of hands —**aer′i·al·ly** *adv.*
aer·i·al·ist (er′ē əl ist) *n.* an acrobat who performs on a trapeze, high wire, etc.
aerial ladder a ladder that can be extended for reaching high places, esp. one mounted on a fire engine
a·er·ie (ā′ər ē, ē′rē, er′ē, ir′ē) *n.* ⟦ME *eire, aire* < OFr *aire* < ML *aeria*, area, prob. ult. < L *ager*, field (see ACRE), but sp. & meaning infl. by L *aer*, air & ME *ei*, egg⟧ 1 the nest of an eagle or other bird of prey that builds in a high place 2 a house or stronghold on a high place 3 [Obs.] the young of an eagle, hawk, etc., in the nest
aer·o (er′ō) *adj.* of or for aeronautics or aircraft
aero. *abbrev.* 1 aeronautic 2 aeronautical 3 aeronautics
aer·o- (er′ō) ⟦< Gr *aēr*, air⟧ *combining form* 1 air [*aerolite*] 2 aircraft or flying [*aerobatics*] 3 gas, gases [*aerodynamics*]
aer·o·bac·ter (er′ō bak′tər) *n.* ⟦ModL: see prec. & BACTERIA⟧ any bacterium of a former genus (*Aerobacter*) normally found in the intestine: now in either of two genera (*Enterobacter* or *Klebsiella*)
aer·o·bal·lis·tics (er′ō bə lis′tiks) *n.* the ballistics of projectiles dropped or launched from aircraft
aer·o·bat·ics (er′ə bat′iks) *pl.n.* ⟦AERO- + (ACRO)BATICS⟧ spectacular feats done with an airplane, as loops or rolls —*n.* the art of performing such feats; stunt flying —**aer′o·bat′ic** *adj.*
aer·obe (er′ōb′) *n.* ⟦< AERO- + Gr *bios*, life⟧ a microorganism that can live and grow only where free oxygen is present
aer·o·bic (er ō′bik) *adj.* 1 able to live, grow, or take place only where free oxygen is present 2 of or produced by aerobes 3 designating or involving exercise, such as running or swimming, that conditions the heart and lungs by increasing the efficiency of oxygen intake by the body
aer·o·bi·cize (er ō′bə sīz′) *vi., vt.* **-cized′, -ciz′ing** to engage in or improve the physical condition of with aerobics —**aer·o′bi·cized′** *adj.* —**aer·o′bi·ciz′er** *n.*
☆**aer·o·bics** (er ō′biks) *pl.n.* ⟦< *Aerobics*, book (1968) by K. H. Cooper, U.S. physician: see AEROBIC & -ICS⟧ aerobic exercises —*n.* [*with sing. or pl. v.*] a system or method of improving one's physical condition by means of such exercises
aer·o·bi·ol·o·gy (er′ō bī äl′ə jē) *n.* the study of microbes, pollutants, etc. that travel through the air —**aer′o·bi′o·log′i·cal** *adj.* —**aer′o·bi·ol′o·gist** *n.*
aer·o·bi·um (er ō′bē əm) *n., pl.* **-bi·a** (-bē ə) ⟦ModL: see AEROBE⟧ an aerobe
aer·o·do·net·ics (er′ō dō net′iks, er′ə-) *n.* ⟦< Gr *aerodonētos*, soaring, air-tossed (< *aēr*, air + *donein*, to shake) + -ICS⟧ the science of soaring in a glider
aer·o·drome (er′ə drōm′) *n.* [Brit.] an airport, esp. a small one
aer·o·dy·nam·ics (er′ō dī nam′iks) *n.* the branch of aeromechanics that deals with the forces (resistance, pressure, etc.) exerted by air or other gases in motion —*pl.n.* the characteristics of the outer body of a vehicle, aircraft, etc., that affect the efficiency with which it moves through the air —**aer′o·dy·nam′ic** *adj.* —**aer′o·dy·nam′i·cal·ly** *adv.* —**aer′o·dy·nam′i·cist** (-ə sist) *n.*
aer·o·dyne (er′ə dīn′) *n.* ⟦AERO- + *-dyne* < Gr *dynamis*, power: see DYNAMIC⟧ any aircraft that is heavier than air and derives its lift chiefly from aerodynamic forces
aer·o·e·las·tic (er′ō ē las′tik, -i las′-) *adj.* of or relating to the elastic properties of structures that are subject to aerodynamic pressures —**aer·o·e·las·tic·i·ty** (er′ō ē′las tis′ə tē, er′ō i las′-) *n.*
aer·o·em·bo·lism (er′ō em′bə liz′əm) *n.* ⟦AERO- + EMBOLISM⟧ an embolism of air bubbles often caused by surgery, induced abortion, or decompression sickness
aer·o·gel (er′ō jel′) *n.* ⟦AERO- + GEL⟧ a substance formed by the suspension of small bubbles of gas in a liquid or solid: the reversal of an aerosol —*adj.* designating or of a small container in which gas under pressure is used to aerate and dispense foam through a valve
aer·o·gramme (er′ə gram′) *n.* ⟦< Fr *aérogramme*: see AERO- & -GRAM⟧ a lightweight letter form with imprinted stamp and gummed flaps, used for airmail correspondence to other countries; air letter: also **aer′o·gram′**
aer·og·ra·phy (er äg′rə fē) *n.* METEOROLOGY: term used esp. in the U.S. Navy —**aer·og′ra·pher** *n.*
aer·o·lite (er′ō līt′) *n.* ⟦AERO- + -LITE⟧ [Archaic] a stony meteorite —**aer′o·lit′ic** (-lit′ik) *adj.*
aer·ol·o·gy (er äl′ə jē) *n.* the branch of meteorology concerned with the study of air, esp. in the upper atmosphere —**aer·o·log·ic** (er′ō läj′ik) *adj.* —**aer·ol′o·gist** (-ə jist) *n.*
aer·o·me·chan·ics (er′ō mə kan′iks) *n.* the branch of mechanics that deals with air or other gases in motion or equilibrium: it includes aerodynamics and aerostatics —**aer′o·me·chan′ic** *adj.*
aer·o·med·i·cine (er′ō med′i sən) *n.* a branch of medicine concerned with the diseases and disorders that are incident to flight in the earth's atmosphere: cf. SPACE MEDICINE —**aer′o·med′i·cal** *adj.*
aer·o·me·te·or·o·graph (er′ō mēt′ē ôr′ə graf′) *n.* a meteorograph used in an aircraft or balloon
aer·om·e·ter (er äm′ət ər) *n.* an instrument for measuring the weight and density of air or other gases —**aer·o·met·ric** (er′ō me′trik) *adj.* —**aer·om′e·try** (-ə trē) *n.*
aer·o·naut (er′ə nôt′, -nät′) *n.* ⟦Fr *aéronaute* < Gr *aēr*, air + *nautēs*, sailor⟧ the pilot of a balloon or airship: now chiefly historical
aer·o·nau·ti·cal (er′ə nôt′i kəl, -nät′-) *adj.* of or concerning aeronautics: also **aer′o·nau′tic** —**aer′o·nau′ti·cal·ly** *adv.*
aeronautical chart a topographic map of an area of the earth's surface, designed as an aid to aircraft navigation
aer·o·nau·tics (er′ə nôt′iks, -nät′-) *n.* the science, art, or work of designing, making, and operating aircraft
aer·o·neu·ro·sis (er′ō no͞o rō′sis, -nyo͞o-) *n.* a nervous disorder of airplane pilots supposedly caused by the tension of excessive flying and characterized by abdominal pains, digestive disturbances, etc.
aer·on·o·my (er än′ə mē) *n.* ⟦AERO- + -NOMY⟧ the science dealing with the physics and chemistry of the upper atmosphere
aer·o·pause (er′ō pôz′, er′ə-) *n.* ⟦AERO- + PAUSE⟧ a region at the upper level of the earth's atmosphere, regarded as the boundary between the atmosphere and outer space
aer·o·pha·gi·a (er′ə fā′jē ə, -fā′jə) *n.* an abnormal, spasmodic swallowing of air: often a symptom of hysteria
aer·o·pho·bi·a (er′ə fō′bē ə) *n.* an abnormal fear of air, esp. of drafts
aer·o·phore (er′ə fôr′) *n.* ⟦AERO- + -PHORE⟧ 1 a device for supplying air to the lungs in case of oxygen shortage 2 an apparatus that cleans air to be breathed again, used as by firefighters
aer·o·plane (er′ə plān′) *n.* ⟦Fr *aéroplane* < *aéro-*, AERO- + base of *planer*, to soar: see PLANE[4]⟧ *Brit. var. of* AIRPLANE
aer·o·pulse (er′ō puls′) *n.* PULSEJET (ENGINE)
aer·o·sat (er′ō sat′) *n.* ⟦AERO(NAUTICAL) + SAT(ELLITE)⟧ any satellite for use in air-traffic control and maritime navigation
aer·o·scope (er′ə skōp′) *n.* an apparatus for gathering bacteria, dust, etc. from the air, for microscopic examination
aer·o·sol (er′ə sôl′, -säl′) *n.* ⟦AERO- + SOL[3]⟧ a suspension of colloidal particles in a gas —*adj.* 1 designating or of a small container in which gas under pressure is used to aerate and dispense a liquid spray through a valve 2 dispensed by such a container [an *aerosol* insecticide, paint, medication]
aer·o·sol·ized (er′ə sôl′īzd′, -säl′-) *adj.* suspended in vapor, a spray, etc.
☆**aer·o·space** (er′ō spās′) *n.* ⟦altered < *air/space* < AIR + SPACE⟧ the earth's atmosphere and the space outside it, considered as one continuous field —*adj.* of aerospace, or of spacecraft or missiles designed for flight in aerospace
aerospace medicine AVIATION MEDICINE
aer·o·sphere (er′ō sfir′) *n.* the atmosphere surrounding the earth
aer·o·stat (er′ō stat′) *n.* ⟦Fr *aérostat*: see AERO- & -STAT⟧ an airship, balloon, or other aircraft that is lifted and sustained by means of one or more containers filled with a gas lighter than air
aer·o·stat·ics (er′ō stat′iks) *n.* ⟦AERO- + STATICS⟧ the branch of aeromechanics that deals with the equilibrium of air or other gases, and with the equilibrium of solid bodies, such as aerostats, floating in air or other gases —**aer′o·stat′ic** *adj.*
aer·o·sta·tion (er′ō stā′shən) *n.* ⟦Fr *aérostation* < *aérostat*, AEROSTAT⟧ the art or science of operating aerostats
aer·o·ther·a·peu·tics (er′ō ther′ə pyo͞ot′iks) *n.* the treatment of disease by the use of air, esp. by exposing patients to changes in atmospheric pressure: also **aer′o·ther′a·py** (-ther′ə pē)

aer·o·ther·mo·dy·nam·ics (er′ō thur′mō dī nam′iks) ***n.*** the study of the relationship of heat and mechanical energy in gases, esp. air —**aer′o·ther′mo·dy·nam′ic** ***adj.***

ae·ru·gi·nous (ē rōō′ji nəs, i-) ***adj.*** ⟦L *aeruginosus* < *aerugo* < *aes*, copper: see ORE⟧ bluish-green, like copper rust

a·er·y[1] (er′ē, ā′er ē) ***adj.*** ⟦L *aerius* < *aer*, AIR⟧ [Old Poet.] airy; unsubstantial; visionary

a·er·y[2] (ā′ər ē, ē′rē, er′ē, ir′ē) ***n.***, *pl.* **a·er′ies** *alt. sp. of* AERIE

Aes·chi·nes (es′ki nēz′) 389-314 B.C.; Athenian orator

Aes·chy·lus (es′ki ləs) 525?-456 B.C.; Gr. writer of tragedies —**Aes·chy·le·an** (es′ki lē′ən) ***adj.***

Aes·cu·la·pi·an (es′kyōō lā′pē ən) ***adj.*** **1** of Aesculapius **2** medical

Aes·cu·la·pi·us (es′kyōō lā′pē əs) ***n.*** ⟦L < Gr *Asklēpios*⟧ *Rom. Myth.* the god of medicine and of healing, son of Apollo: identified with the Greek Asclepius

Ae·sir (a′sir′, ē′-, ā′-) ***pl.n.*** ⟦ON, pl. of *ass*, a god, akin to OE *os*: see OSCAR[1]⟧ *Norse Myth.* the principal gods and goddesses, including Odin, Thor, Balder, Loki, Frigg, and Tyr

Ae·sop (ē′səp, ē′säp′) real or legendary Gr. author of fables: supposed to have lived 6th cent. B.C.

Ae·so·pi·an (ē sō′pē ən, ē säp′ē ən) ***adj.*** **1** of Aesop or characteristic of his fables **2** concealing real purposes or intentions; dissembling [*Aesopian* language] Also **Ae·sop·ic** (ē säp′ik)

aes·the·si·a (es thē′zhə, -zhē ə, -zē ə) ***n.*** *alt. sp. of* ESTHESIA

aes·thete (es′thēt′) ***n.*** ⟦Gr *aisthētēs*, a person who perceives: see fol. ⟧ **1** a person highly sensitive to art and beauty **2** a person who artificially cultivates artistic sensitivity or makes a cult of art and beauty

SYN.—aesthete, although applied to one highly sensitive to art and beauty, is often used derogatorily to connote effeteness or decadence; **dilettante** refers to one who appreciates art as distinguished from one who creates it, but is used disparagingly of one who dabbles superficially in the arts; a **connoisseur** is one who has expert knowledge or a keen discrimination in matters of art and, by extension, in any matters of taste [a *connoisseur* of fine foods]; **virtuoso**, in this comparison, denotes a collector or connoisseur of art objects, and is sometimes used derogatorily to suggest faddishness

aes·thet·ic (es thet′ik) ***adj.*** ⟦Gr *aisthētikos*, sensitive < *aisthanesthai*, to perceive < IE base **awis-* > L *audire*, to hear⟧ **1** of or in relation to aesthetics **2** of beauty **3** sensitive to art and beauty; showing good taste; artistic Also **aes·thet′i·cal** —***n.*** an aesthetic theory or viewpoint

aes·thet·i·cal·ly (es thet′i kəl ē, -i klē) ***adv.*** **1** in an aesthetic manner **2** from the point of view of aesthetics

aes·the·ti·cian (es′thə tish′ən) ***n.*** **1** a student of, or expert in, aesthetics **2** a beautician; cosmetologist

aes·thet·i·cism (es thet′i siz′əm) ***n.*** **1** the doctrine that aesthetic principles underlie all human values **2** *a)* sensitivity to art and beauty *b)* the artificial cultivation of artistic sensitivity

aes·thet·i·cize (es thet′i sīz′) ***vt.*** **-cized′**, **-ciz′ing** to make a subject of aesthetic consideration; view or judge with regard to an aesthetic —**aes·thet′i·ci·za′tion** ***n.***

aes·thet·ics (es thet′iks) ***n.*** ⟦< AESTHETIC⟧ the study or theory of beauty and of the psychological responses to it; specif., the branch of philosophy dealing with art, its creative sources, its forms, and its effects

aes·ti·val (es′tə vəl, es tī′vəl) ***adj.*** *alt. sp. of* ESTIVAL

aes·ti·vate (es′tə vāt′) ***vi.*** **-vat′ed**, **-vat′ing** *alt. sp. of* ESTIVATE

aes·ti·va·tion (es′tə vā′shən) ***n.*** *alt. sp. of* ESTIVATION

aet or **aetat** *abbrev.* ⟦L *aetatis*, gen. of *aetas*, life, AGE⟧ aged (a specified number of years); at the age of

Aeth·el·stan (ath′əl stan′) *alt. sp. of* ATHELSTAN

ae·ther (ē′thər) ***n.*** *former sp. of* ETHER

ae·the·re·al (ē thir′ē əl, i-) ***adj.*** *alt. sp. of* ETHEREAL

ae·ti·ol·o·gy (ēt′ē äl′ə jē) ***n.*** *alt. sp. of* ETIOLOGY

Aet·na (et′nə), **Mount** *alt. sp. of* ETNA, Mount

Ae·to·li·a (ē tō′lē ə) region of ancient Greece, on the Gulf of Corinth —**Ae·to′li·an** ***adj., n.***

AF *abbrev.* **1** Air Force **2** audio-frequency: also **af**

af- (af, əf, if) *prefix* AD-: used before *f*

AFAM or **AF & AM** *abbrev.* Ancient Free and Accepted Masons

a·far (ə fär′) ***adv.*** ⟦ME *a ferr* < *a*, on + *feor*, far⟧ [Archaic] at or to a great distance —***n.*** a great distance: archaic except in the literary phrase **from afar**, from a great distance

AFB *abbrev.* Air Force Base

AFC[1] *service mark* American Football Conference

AFC[2] *abbrev.* automatic frequency control

AFDC *abbrev.* Aid to Families with Dependent Children

a·feard or **a·feared** (ə fird′) ***adj.*** ⟦orig. pp. of ME *aferen*, to frighten < OE *afaeran* < *a-*, intens. < *færan*, to frighten < *fær*, FEAR⟧ [Now Chiefly Dial.] frightened; afraid

a·fe·brile (ā fē′brəl, -brīl′; -fe′brəl) ***adj.*** having no fever

af·fa·ble (af′ə bəl) ***adj.*** ⟦ME *affabyl* < L *affabilis* < *ad-*, to + *fari*, to speak: see FAME⟧ **1** pleasant and easy to approach or talk to; friendly **2** gentle and kindly [an *affable* smile] **—SYN.** AMIABLE —**af′fa·bil′i·ty** (-bil ə tē) ***n.*** —**af′fa·bly** ***adv.***

af·fair (ə fer′) ***n.*** ⟦ME *afere* < OFr *afaire* < *a faire*, to do < L *ad-*, to + *facere*, DO[1]⟧ **1** a thing to be done; business **2** [*pl.*] matters of business or concern **3** any matter, occurrence, or thing **4** a social function or gathering **5** an event that becomes a matter of public controversy **6** ⟦< LOVE AFFAIR⟧ an amorous relationship between two people not married to each other, esp. when at least one person is married to or involved with someone else

af·faire (ə fer′) ***n.*** ⟦Fr⟧ AFFAIR (senses 5 & 6)

af·faire d'a·mour (á fer dá mōōr′) ⟦Fr⟧ a love affair

af·faire de coeur (-də kër′) ⟦Fr, lit., affair of the heart⟧ a love affair

af·faire d'hon·neur (-dô nër′) ⟦Fr, lit., affair of honor⟧ a duel

af·fect[1] (ə fekt′; *for n.* 2, af′ekt′) ***vt.*** ⟦ME *affecten* < L *affectare*, to strive after < *affectus*, pp. of *afficere*, to influence, attack < *ad-*, to + *facere*, DO[1]⟧ **1** to have an effect on; influence; produce a change in [bright light *affects* the eyes] **2** to move or stir the emotions of [his death *affected* us deeply] —***n.*** **1** [Obs.] a disposition or tendency **2** ⟦Ger *affekt* < L *affectus*, state of mind or body: see the *vt.*⟧ *Psychol.* *a)* an emotion or feeling attached to an idea, object, etc. *b)* in general, emotion or emotional response —**af·fect′a·ble** ***adj.***

SYN.—affect implies the producing of an effect strong enough to evoke a reaction; to **influence** is to affect in such a way as to produce a change in action, thought, nature, or behavior [to *influence* legislation]; **impress** is used of that which produces a deep or lasting effect on the mind; **touch** and the stronger **move**, as considered here, are both applied to the arousing of emotion, sympathy, etc., but **move** also denotes an influencing so as to effect a change; **sway** emphasizes an influencing intended to turn a person from a given course [threats will not *sway* us]

af·fect[2] (a fekt′, ə-) ***vt.*** ⟦ME *affecten* < OFr *affecter* < L *affectare*, prec.⟧ **1** to like to have, use, wear, be in, etc. [she *affects* plaid coats] **2** to make a pretense of being, having, feeling, liking, etc.; feign [to *affect* indifference] **3** [Archaic] to aim at; seek **—SYN.** ASSUME —**af·fect′a·ble** ***adj.***

af·fec·ta·tion (af′ek tā′shən, -ik-) ***n.*** ⟦L *affectatio* < pp. of *affectare*, prec.⟧ **1** an affecting or pretending to like, have, etc.; show or pretense **2** artificial behavior meant to impress others; mannerism for effect **—SYN.** POSE[1]

af·fect·ed[1] (ə fekt′id) ***adj.*** ⟦pp. of AFFECT[1]⟧ **1** influenced; acted upon **2** emotionally moved or touched

af·fect·ed[2] (a fekt′id, ə-) ***adj.*** ⟦pp. of AFFECT[2]⟧ **1** assumed for effect; artificial **2** behaving in an artificial way to impress people; full of affectation —**af·fect′ed·ly** ***adv.***

af·fect·ing (ə fekt′iŋ) ***adj.*** emotionally touching; evoking pity, sympathy, etc. **—SYN.** MOVING

af·fec·tion (ə fek′shən) ***n.*** ⟦ME *affeccium* < OFr *affection* < L *affectio*, a state of feeling < pp. of *afficere*: see AFFECT[1]⟧ **1** a mental or emotional state or tendency; disposition or feeling **2** [*often pl.*] fond or tender feeling; warm liking **3** an affecting or being affected **4** [Archaic] a disease; ailment **5** [Archaic] an attribute or property of a thing **—SYN.** LOVE —**af·fec′tion·al** ***adj.***

af·fec·tion·ate (ə fek′shən it) ***adj.*** ⟦altered after -ATE[1] < Fr *affectionné*⟧ **1** full of affection; tender and loving **2** [Obs.] mentally disposed; inclined —**af·fec′tion·ate·ly** ***adv.***

af·fec·tive (a fek′tiv, ə-) ***adj.*** ⟦Fr *affectif* < ML *affectivus* < L *affectus*: see AFFECT[1]⟧ of, or arising from, affects, or feelings; emotional —**af·fec′tive·ly** ***adv.*** —**af·fec·tiv·i·ty** (af′ek tiv′ə tē, -ik-) ***n.***

af·fect·less (af′ekt′lis; af′ekt lis, -ikt-) ***adj.*** lacking emotion, feeling, passion, etc. —**af′fect′less·ly** ***adv.*** —**af′fect′less·ness** ***n.***

af·fen·pin·scher (äf′ən pin′shər, af′-; -chər) ***n.*** ⟦Ger, lit., monkey terrier < *affe* (see APE) + *pinscher*: see DOBERMAN PINSCHER⟧ any of a breed of small dogs, with a stiff, wiry coat of black, red, or gray and facial features that resemble those of a monkey

af·fer·ent (af′ər ənt) ***adj.*** ⟦< L *afferens*, prp. of *afferre* < *ad-*, to + *ferre*, to BEAR[1]⟧ *Physiol.* bringing inward to a central part; specif., designating nerves that transmit impulses to the central nervous system, as to the brain: opposed to EFFERENT —***n.*** an afferent nerve, duct, etc.

af·fi·ance (ə fī′əns) ***n.*** ⟦ME *affiaunce* < OFr *afiance* < *afier*, to trust in < ML *affidare* < *ad-*, to + *fidare*, to trust < L *fidere*: see FIDELITY⟧ **1** [Archaic] trust or faith **2** a plighting of faith; promise of marriage; betrothal —***vt.*** **-anced**, **-anc·ing** to pledge, esp. in marriage; betroth

☆**af·fi·ant** (ə fī′ənt) ***n.*** ⟦< prp. of OFr *afier*: see prec. ⟧ *Law* a person who makes an affidavit; deponent

af·fi·da·vit (af′ə dā′vit; *occas.*, -vid′) ***n.*** ⟦ML, he has made oath; perf. tense of *affidare*: see AFFIANCE⟧ *Law* a written statement given voluntarily and sworn to before a person authorized to administer oaths

af·fil·i·ate (ə fil′ē āt′; *for n., usually*, -it) ***vt.*** **-at′ed**, **-at′ing** ⟦< ML *affiliatus*, pp. of *affiliare*, to adopt as a son < L *ad-*, to + *filius*, son⟧ **1** to take in as a member or branch **2** to connect or associate (oneself) *with* an organization, movement, etc. **3** to trace the origins or source of; specif., to determine legally the paternity of —***vi.*** to associate oneself; join —***n.*** an affiliated individual or organization; member **—SYN.** RELATED

af·fil·i·a·tion (ə fil′ē ā′shən) ***n.*** an affiliating or being affiliated; connection, as with an organization, club, etc.

af·fine[1] (ə fīn′, a-) ***n.*** ⟦Fr *affin* < OFr *afin* < L *affinis*: see AFFINITY⟧ a person related by marriage —**af·fi′nal** ***adj.***

af·fine[2] (ə fīn′, a-) ***adj.*** ⟦ModL *affinis* < L: see AFFINITY⟧ *Math.* of or having to do with projecting or mapping a geometric figure on a second plane or surface so that the new image retains the original parallel straight lines while being shifted, stretched, etc.

af·fined (ə fīnd′, a-) ***adj.*** ⟦< Fr *affiné*, related: see fol.⟧ **1** joined or connected in some way; related **2** [Obs.] under obligation; bound

af·fin·i·ty (ə fin′i tē, a-) ***n.***, *pl.* **-ties** ⟦ME *affinite* < OFr *afinite* < L *affinitas* < *affinis*, adjacent, related by marriage, sharing < *ad-*, to + *finis*, a border⟧ **1** relationship by marriage: distinguished from CONSANGUINITY **2** close relationship; connection **3** similarity of structure, as of species or languages, implying common origin; family resemblance **4** a natural liking or sympathy; esp., a mutual attraction between a man and a woman **5** a person of the opposite sex who especially attracts one **6** the attractive force, of varying strength for various elements, molecules, etc., that causes the atoms of certain elements to combine and stay combined —**af·fin′i·tive** ***adj.***

affinity card a customized credit card offered as part of a special marketing arrangement, as to customers of a retail chain or members of the alumni association of a university

af·firm (ə furm′) ***vt.*** ⟦ME *affermen* < OFr *affermer* < L *affirmare*, to present as fixed < *ad-*, to + *firmare*, to make firm < *firmus*: see FIRM[1]⟧ **1** to say positively; declare firmly; assert to be true: opposed to DENY **2** to make valid; confirm; uphold; ratify (a law, decision, or judgment) —***vi.*** *Law* to declare solemnly, but not under oath; make affirmation —***SYN.*** ASSERT —**af·firm′a·ble** ***adj.*** —**af·firm′er** ***n.***, *Law* **af·firm′ant**

af·firm·ance (ə fur′məns) ***n.*** ⟦ME *affermance* < OFr < L *affirmans*, prp. of *affirmare*, prec. ⟧ **1** an affirming or declaring **2** a confirming **3** *Law* an upholding by a higher court of a lower court's judgment or order

af·fir·ma·tion (af′ər mā′shən) ***n.*** ⟦L *affirmatio*⟧ **1** the act of affirming **2** something affirmed; positive declaration; assertion **3** *Law* a solemn declaration, but not under oath: permitted to one who has conscientious objections to taking oaths

af·firm·a·tive (ə fur′mə tiv) ***adj.*** ⟦ME *affirmatif* < L *affirmativus* < *affirmare*, AFFIRM⟧ **1** saying that something stated is true; answering "yes" [*an affirmative reply*] **2** *a)* bold or confident in asserting [*affirmative people*] *b)* optimistic or hopeful; not negative or cynical **3** *Logic* affirming something about a subject [*"all men are mortal" is an affirmative proposition*] — ***adv., interj.*** yes: so used in radio communication —***n.*** **1** a word or expression indicating assent or agreement (Ex.: *yes, aye*) **2** an affirmative statement **3** the point of view that upholds the proposition being debated —**in the affirmative** **1** in assent or agreement with a plan, suggestion, etc. **2** with an affirmative answer; saying "yes" —**af·firm′a·tive·ly** ***adv.***

☆**affirmative action** a policy or program for correcting the effects of discrimination in the employment or education of members of certain groups, as women, blacks, etc.

af·fix (ə fiks′, a-; *for n.*, af′iks) ***vt.*** ⟦< L *affixus*, pp. of *affigere*, to fasten to < *ad-*, to + *figere*, FIX⟧ **1** to fasten; attach [*to affix a label to a bottle*] **2** to add at the end; append —***n.*** ⟦Fr *affixe* < L *affixus*: see the ***vt.***⟧ **1** a thing affixed **2** *Linguis.* a prefix, suffix, or infix —**af·fix·al** (af′ik səl) ***adj.***

af·fix·a·tion (af′ik sā′shən) ***n.*** **1** affixture **2** *Linguis.* the process of adding affixes to roots or bases in order to vary function, modify meaning, etc.: distinguished from COMPOSITION

af·fix·ture (ə fiks′chər, a-) ***n.*** an affixing or being affixed

af·fla·tus (ə flāt′əs, a-) ***n.*** ⟦L < pp. of *afflare*, to blow on < *ad-*, to + *flare*, to blow < IE base **bhel-*: see BLADDER⟧ inspiration or powerful impulse, as of an artist or poet

af·flict (ə flikt′) ***vt.*** ⟦< L *afflictare*, to injure, vex < *afflictus*, pp. of *affligere*, to strike down < *ad-*, to + *fligere*: see INFLICT⟧ **1** to cause pain or suffering to; distress very much **2** [Obs.] to overthrow

af·flic·tion (ə flik′shən) ***n.*** ⟦ME *affliccion* < OFr *affliction* < L *afflictio*⟧ **1** an afflicted condition; pain; suffering **2** anything causing pain or distress; calamity

SYN.—**affliction** implies pain, suffering, or distress imposed by illness, loss, misfortune, etc.; **trial** suggests suffering that tries one's endurance, but in a weaker sense refers to annoyance that tries one's patience; **tribulation** describes severe affliction continuing over a long and trying period; **misfortune** is applied to a circumstance or event involving adverse fortune and to the suffering or distress occasioned by it

af·flic·tive (ə flik′tiv) ***adj.*** ⟦ML *afflictivus*: see AFFLICT⟧ causing pain or misery —**af·flic′tive·ly** ***adv.***

af·flu·ence (af′lo͞o əns; *occas.*, a flo͞o′-, ə-) ***n.*** ⟦< L *affluentia* < *affluere*, to flow to < *ad-*, to + *fluere*, to flow⟧ **1** a flowing toward; influx **2** [Now Rare] great plenty; abundance **3** an abundance of riches; wealth; opulence Also **af′flu·en·cy** (-ən sē)

af·flu·ent (-ənt) ***adj.*** ⟦ME < L *affluens*, prp. of *affluere*: see prec.⟧ **1** [Archaic] flowing freely **2** [Now Rare] plentiful; abundant **3** wealthy; prosperous; rich [*the affluent society*] —***n.*** **1** a tributary stream: opposed to EFFLUENT (***n.*** specif. *a*) **2** an affluent person —***SYN.*** RICH —**af′flu·ent·ly** ***adv.***

af·flux (a′fluks′) ***n.*** ⟦L *affluxus* < pp. of *affluere*: see AFFLUENCE⟧ a sudden flow toward a point, as of blood to an organ

af·fo·ga·to (äf′ə gät′ō, af′-) ***n.***, *pl.* **-tos** ⟦It, lit., drowned⟧ a beverage or dessert consisting of a scoop of ice cream with hot espresso poured over it

af·ford (ə fôrd′) ***vt.*** ⟦ME *aforthen* < OE *geforthian*, to advance < *forthian*, to further⟧ **1** to have enough or the means for; bear the cost of without serious inconvenience: used with *can* or *be able* [*I'm not able to afford a car; can you afford the time?*] **2** to manage (*to* do something) without risking serious consequences: used with *can* [*I can afford to speak frankly*] **3** to give; furnish [*music affords her pleasure*] —**af·ford′a·bil′i·ty** ***n.*** —**af·ford′a·ble** ***adj.***

af·for·est (ə fôr′ist) ***vt.*** ⟦ML *afforestare*: see AD- & FOREST⟧ to turn (land) into forest; plant many trees on —**af·for′est·a·ble** ***adj.*** —**af·for′est·a′tion** (-əs tā′shən) ***n.***

af·fran·chise (ə fran′chīz′) ***vt.*** **-chised′**, **-chis′ing** ⟦< extended stem of Fr *affranchir* < OFr *afranchir* < *a*, to + *franchir*: see FRANCHISE⟧ to make free; enfranchise

af·fray (ə frā′, a-) ***n.*** ⟦ME *affrai*, an attack, alarm < OFr *esfrei* < *esfrëer*, to frighten < ML **exfridare* < L *ex*, out of + Gmc base *frith-*, peace⟧ a noisy brawl or quarrel; public fight or riot; breach of the peace —***vt.*** ⟦ME *affraien* < OFr *esfraer*⟧ [Archaic] to frighten

af·fri·cate (af′ri kit) ***n.*** ⟦L *affricatus*, pp. of *affricare*, to rub against < *ad-*, to + *fricare*, to rub: see FRIABLE⟧ *Phonet.* a complex sound articulated by the slow release of a stop consonant followed immediately by a fricative at the same place of articulation in the mouth: the English affricates are the voiceless (ch) as in *batch* (IPA [tʃ]) and the voiced (j) as in *badge* (IPA [dʒ]) —**af·fric·a·tive** (ə frik′ə tiv) ***adj., n.***

af·fri·ca·tion (af′ri kā′shən) ***n.*** *Phonet.* the changing of a stop into an affricate

af·fright (ə frīt′) ***vt.*** ⟦ME *afrighten* < OE *afyrhtan*: see FRIGHT⟧ [Archaic] to frighten; terrify —***n.*** [Archaic] great fright or terror, or a cause of terror

af·front (ə frunt′) ***vt.*** ⟦ME *afronten* < OFr *afronter*, to encounter face to face < ML **affrontare* < *ad-*, to + *frons*, forehead⟧ **1** to insult openly or purposely; offend; slight **2** to confront defiantly **3** [Archaic] to come before; meet; face —***n.*** an open or intentional insult; slight to one's dignity —***SYN.*** OFFEND

af·fu·sion (ə fyo͞o′zhən, a-) ***n.*** ⟦ML *affusio* < L *affusus*, pp. of *affundere* < *ad-*, to + *fundere*, to pour: see FOUND[3]⟧ a pouring on, as of water in baptism

Afg or **Afghan** *abbrev.* Afghanistan

Af·ghan (af′gan′, -gən) ***n.*** **1** a person born or living in Afghanistan **2** *former term for* PASHTO **3** any of a breed of swift hunting hound, originally from the Near East, with silky hair and a long, narrow head **4** [**a-**] a soft blanket or shawl, crocheted or knitted, esp. in a geometric design —***adj.*** of Afghanistan, its people, or their language or culture

af·ghan·i (af gan′ē) ***n.***, *pl.* **-is** ⟦Pashto, lit., Afghan⟧ the basic monetary unit of Afghanistan: see the table of monetary units in the Reference Supplement

Af·ghan·i·stan (af gan′i stan′) country in SC Asia, between Iran and Pakistan: 250,001 sq mi (647,500 sq km); cap. Kabul

a·fi·cio·na·da (ə fish′ə nä′dä) ***n.*** a woman aficionado

a·fi·cio·na·do (ə fish′ə nä′dō, -fē′shə-; ə fis′ē ə-, -fē′sē ə-) ***n.***, *pl.* **-dos** ⟦Sp, pp. of *aficionar* < ML **affectionare*, to like, be devoted to < L *affectio*: see AFFECTION⟧ a person who is highly knowledgeable, enthusiastic, and supportive of some sport, art, etc.

a·field (ə fēld′) ***adv.*** **1** in, on, or to the field **2** away (from home) **3** off the right path; astray

a·fire (ə fīr′) ***adv., adj.*** **1** on fire; burning **2** greatly excited

a·flame (ə flām′) ***adv., adj.*** **1** in flames; burning **2** glowing [*aflame with color*] **3** greatly excited

af·la·tox·in (af′lə täks′in) ***n.*** ⟦< ModL *A(spergillus) fla(vus)*, species name of the fungus + TOXIN⟧ any of several toxic or carcinogenic substances produced by a fungus (esp. *Aspergillus flavus*) found on peanuts, corn, etc.

AFL-CIO *abbrev.* American Federation of Labor and Congress of Industrial Organizations: a labor organization formed by merger in 1955

a·float (ə flōt′) ***adj., adv.*** **1** floating freely; not grounded; esp., floating on the surface; not sinking **2** on board ship; at sea **3** flooded [*the lower deck is afloat*] **4** drifting about **5** in circulation; current [*rumors are afloat*] **6** free of trouble, debt, etc., esp. with effort [*he kept the business afloat*]

a·flut·ter (ə flut′ər) ***adv., adj.*** in a flutter

a·foot (ə fo͝ot′) ***adv.*** **1** on foot; walking **2** in motion or operation; in progress; astir

a·fore (ə fôr′) ***adv., prep., conj.*** ⟦ME *afore, aforn* < OE *onforan*, before: see A-[1] & FORE⟧ [Now Dial.] before

a·fore- (ə fôr′) *combining form* before [*aforementioned*]

a·fore·men·tioned (ə fôr′men′shənd, -chənd) ***adj.*** mentioned before or previously

a·fore·said (-sed′) ***adj.*** spoken of before; mentioned previously

a·fore·thought (-thôt′) ***adj.*** thought out beforehand; premeditated

a·fore·time (-tīm′) ***adv.*** [Archaic] in times now past; formerly

a for·ti·o·ri (ā′ fôr′shē ôr′ī′) ⟦L, lit., for a stronger (reason)⟧ all the more: said of a conclusion that follows with even greater logical necessity than another already accepted in the argument

☆**a·foul** (ə foul′) ***adv., adj.*** in a collision or a tangle —**run** (or **fall**) **afoul of** **1** to collide with or become entangled with **2** to get into conflict or trouble with

Afr *abbrev.* **1** Africa **2** African

a·fraid (ə frād′) ***adj.*** ⟦ME *affraied*, pp. of *affraien*, AFFRAY⟧ feeling fear; frightened; apprehensive: followed by *of, that*, or an infinitive: often used informally to indicate regret [*I'm afraid I can't go*]

SYN.—**afraid** is applied to a general feeling of fear or disquiet and is the broadest in application of all the words considered here [*to be afraid of the dark, to be afraid to die*]; **frightened** implies a sudden, usually temporary seizure of fear [*the child was frightened by the dog*]; **timid** implies a lack of courage or self-confidence and suggests overcautiousness or shyness [*too timid to ask for an explanation*]; **timorous** and **fearful** suggest a feeling of disquiet and a tendency to worry rather than an alarming fear [*fearful of making an error*]; **terrified** implies intense, overwhelming fear [*he stood terrified as the tiger charged*] —***ANT.*** **brave, bold**

☆**A-frame** (ā′frām′) ***adj.*** designating or of a structural framework, as of a house, with steeply angled sides meeting at the top like the sides of the letter A —***n.*** a structure with such a framework

af·reet (af′rēt′, ə frēt′) ***n.*** ⟦Ar *ʿifrīt*⟧ *Arabian Myth.* a strong, evil demon or jinni

a·fresh (ə fresh′) *adv.* again; anew

Af·ri·ca (af′ri kə) ⟦L < *Africa (terra)*, African (land), fem. of *Africus* < *Afer*, an African⟧ second largest continent, situated in the Eastern Hemisphere, south of Europe: *c.* 11,608,000 sq mi (30,065,000 sq km)

Af·ri·can (af′ri kən) *adj.* of Africa, esp. sub-Saharan Africa, or its peoples, languages, or cultures —*n.* **1** a member of an indigenous ethnic group of Africa, esp. sub-Saharan Africa **2** a person born or living in Africa

Af·ri·can-A·mer·i·can (-ə mer′i kən) *n.* an AMERICAN (*n.* 1*b*) having ancestors from sub-Saharan Africa; black American —*adj.* of African-Americans or their culture; black Also written **African American**

African elephant *see* ELEPHANT

Af·ri·can·ism (-iz′əm) *n.* **1** an African custom, characteristic, or belief **2** a word, phrase, grammatical construction, or other feature originating in or peculiar to an African language **3** devotion to African customs, traditions, etc.; specif., advocacy of independence for African states or of Pan-Africanism

Af·ri·can·ist (-ist) *n.* **1** a specialist in the study of African languages, cultures, etc. **2** an advocate of Africanism —*adj.* of Africanism

☆**Af·ri·can·ize** (-īz′) *vt.* **-ized′**, **-iz′ing** **1** to staff with native black Africans [to *Africanize* the Nigerian civil service] **2** to give an African outlook, character, etc. to —**Af′ri·can·i·za′tion** *n.*

Africanized bee (*or* **honeybee)** a hybrid of African and European honeybees, developed in Brazil and known for its disease resistance and superior honey production: also called *killer bee*

African lily an African plant (*Agapanthus africanus*) of the lily family with blue or white, funnel-shaped flowers

African sleeping sickness SLEEPING SICKNESS (sense 1)

African violet any of several tropical African plants (genus *Saintpaulia*) of the gesneria family with violet, white, or pinkish flowers and hairy, dark-green leaves, often grown as houseplants

Af·ri·kaans (af′ri käns′, -känz′) *n.* ⟦Afrik < *Afrika*, Africa⟧ an official language of South Africa, developed from 17th-cent. Dutch

Af·ri·kan·der (af′ri kan′dər) *n.* ⟦Afrik < Du *Afrikaner*, with inserted *d*, by analogy with *Hollander*, HOLLANDER⟧ **1** [Archaic] AFRIKANER **2** a breed of cattle with a hump, developed in South Africa from a hairy indigenous breed **3** a hardy breed of sheep developed in South Africa from an indigenous breed

Af·ri·ka·ner (af′ri kän′ər) *n.* ⟦Du⟧ a white South African, esp. one of Dutch ancestry, whose native language is Afrikaans

af·rit (af′rēt′, ə frēt′) *n. alt. sp. of* AFREET

☆**Af·ro** (af′rō′) *adj.* ⟦see fol.⟧ designating or of a full, bushy hair style, as worn by some blacks —*n., pl.* **-ros′** an Afro hair style

Afro- (af′rō) ⟦< L *Afer*, an African⟧ *combining form* African, African and [*Afro*-American]: also, before a vowel, **Afr-**

☆**Af·ro-A·mer·i·can** (af′rō ə mer′i kən) *n., adj.* AFRICAN-AMERICAN

Af·ro-A·sian (af′rō ā′zhən) *adj.* of Africa and Asia jointly

Af·ro·a·si·at·ic or **Af·ro-A·si·at·ic** (af′rō ā′zhē at′ik) *adj.* designating or of a family of African and Asian languages generally divided into the branches Berber, Cushitic, Semitic, Chadic, and ancient Egyptian

Af·ro·cen·tric (af′rō sen′trik) *adj.* ⟦AFRO- + -CENTRIC⟧ centered on, emphasizing, or showing the influence of African or, sometimes, African-American history and culture [an *Afrocentric* curriculum]

AFSCME (afs′mē) *abbrev.* American Federation of State, County, and Municipal Employees

aft[1] (aft) *adv.* ⟦ME *afte* < OE *æftan* (akin to Goth *aftana*, from behind < *afta*, behind, farthest back) < IE base **af-*, off, away⟧ at, near, or toward the stern of a ship or the rear of an aircraft [Smith is stationed *aft* during all emergency drills] —**aft of** to the rear of; behind [located *aft of* the rudderpost]

aft[2] *abbrev.* afternoon

AFT *abbrev.* American Federation of Teachers

af·ter (af′tər, äf′-) *adv.* ⟦ME < OE *æfter* (akin to OHG *aftar* & MHG *after*) < *of*, off + *-ter*, old compar. suffix⟧ **1** behind in place **2** behind in time; later; next —*prep.* **1** behind in place; in back of **2** *a)* behind in time; later than [*after* lunch] *b)* following [year *after* year] **3** *a)* in search of *b)* pursuing, hounding, urging, etc. [they are *after* me for a donation] **4** as a result of; on account of [*after* what has happened, he won't go] **5** in spite of [*after* all we had done, he was still ungrateful] **6** following next to in order, rank, or importance **7** in accordance with; in the manner of; patterned on the model of [a novel *after* Hemingway's style] **8** for; in honor of [a child named *after* Lincoln] **9** concerning; about [she asked *after* you] —*conj.* following the time when; later than —*adj.* **1** next; later **2** nearer the rear (esp. of a ship or aircraft)

af·ter- (af′tər, äf′-) *combining form* coming behind or later [*aftercare*]

af·ter·birth (af′tər burth′) *n.* the placenta and fetal membranes expelled from the uterus after the birth

af·ter·brain (-brān′) *n.* METENCEPHALON (sense 1)

af·ter·burn·er (-burn′ər) *n.* **1** a device within the tailpipe of some jet engines for burning extra fuel to produce additional thrust **2** an auxiliary device, as on internal-combustion engines and incinerators, for burning undesirable exhaust gases produced during the original combustion

af·ter·care (-ker′) *n.* care or treatment of a patient recovering from an illness, operation, etc.

af·ter·clap (-klap′) *n.* an unexpected aftereffect

af·ter·damp (-damp′) *n.* an asphyxiating mixture of gases remaining in a mine after a fire or an explosion of firedamp, usually consisting mostly of nitrogen and carbon dioxide

af·ter·deck (-dek′) *n.* the part of a ship's deck between the midships section and the stern

af·ter·ef·fect (-ə fekt′) *n.* an effect coming later, or as a secondary result

af·ter·glow (-glō′) *n.* **1** the glow remaining after a light has gone, as after sunset **2** the pleasant feeling one has after an enjoyable experience

af·ter-hours (-ourz′, -ourz′) *adj.* **1** occurring, active, etc. after the regular time, esp. after business hours **2** open after the usual or legal closing time [an *after-hours* bar]

af·ter·im·age (-im′ij) *n. Psychol.* an image or sensation that remains or returns after the external stimulus has been withdrawn

af·ter·life (-līf′) *n.* **1** a life after death **2** the part of one's life after a previous part; one's later years

af·ter·mar·ket (-mär′kit) *n.* the market in replacement or repair parts, additional equipment, etc. for some manufactured product, esp. for automobiles

af·ter·math (-math′) *n.* ⟦AFTER + obs. *math*, cutting of grass < OE *mæth* < *māwan*, to mow, with *-th* suffix⟧ **1** a second crop, as of grass, that grows after an earlier mowing **2** a consequence of, or a state of affairs resulting from, something, esp. something destructive or unpleasant

af·ter·most (-mōst′) *adj.* ⟦altered, infl. by MOST < ME *aftemeste* < OE *æftemest*, superl. of *æfter*, AFTER⟧ nearest to the stern

af·ter·noon (af′tər no͞on′; *for adj., often* af′tər no͞on′) *n.* **1** the time of day from noon to evening **2** any period of beginning decline —*adj.* of, in, or for the afternoon

af·ter·noons (-no͞onz′) *adv.* during every afternoon or most afternoons

af·ter·pains (-pānz′) *pl.n.* pains from contractions of the uterus following childbirth

af·ter·piece (-pēs′) *n.* a short sketch presented after a longer dramatic production

☆**af·ter-shave** (-shāv′) *n.* a lotion, usually astringent and perfumed, applied to the face after shaving —*adj.* designating or of such a lotion Also **af′ter·shave′**

af·ter·shock (-shäk′) *n.* a minor earthquake, usually one of a series, that follows a larger earthquake and originates at or near the same place

af·ter·taste (-tāst′) *n.* **1** a taste lingering in the mouth after eating, drinking, or smoking **2** the feeling remaining after an experience

af·ter-tax (-taks′) *adj.* occurring or remaining after the calculation or payment of taxes [*after-tax* earnings]

af·ter·thought (-thôt′) *n.* **1** an idea, explanation, part, etc. coming or added later **2** a thought coming too late, after the occasion for which it was apt

af·ter·time (-tīm′) *n.* the time to come; future

af·ter·ward (-wərd) *adv.* ⟦OE *æfterweard*: see AFTER & -WARD⟧ at a later time; subsequently: also **af′ter·wards**

af·ter·word (-wurd′) *n.* an epilogue, often one consisting of a critical or interpretive commentary by someone other than the author

af·ter·world (-wurld′) *n.* a world after this one; world supposedly existing after death

AFTRA (af′trə) *abbrev.* American Federation of Television and Radio Artists

ag (ag) *adj.* of or having to do with agriculture [*ag* production] —*n. short for* AGRICULTURE Often written **Ag**

AG *abbrev.* **1** Adjutant General **2** Attorney General

Ag[1] *abbrev. Immunology* antigen

Ag[2] ⟦L *argentum*⟧ *Chem. symbol for* silver

ag- (ag, əg) *prefix* AD-: used before *g*

a·ga (ä′gə) *n.* ⟦Turk *ağa*, elder, senior, master⟧ in some Muslim countries, a title of respect for important officials

A·ga·dir (ä′gə dir′, ag′ə-) seaport in SW Morocco, on the Atlantic

a·gain (ə gen′; *also, esp. Cdn & Brit*, -gān′) *adv.* ⟦ME *agen*, *ayein* < OE *ongegn*, *ongean* < *on-*, up to, toward + *gegn*, direct: orig. separable prefix meaning "directly up to," hence, "facing, opposite"⟧ **1** [Rare] back in response; in return [answer *again*] **2** back into a former position or condition [he is well *again*] **3** once more; anew [try *again*] **4** besides; further [*again*, we should note] **5** on the other hand; from the contrary standpoint [he may, and then *again* he may not] **6** [Obs.] in the opposite direction; back —**again and again** often; repeatedly —**as much again** twice as much

a·gainst (ə genst′; *also, esp. Cdn & Brit*, -gānst′) *prep.* ⟦ME *ayeynst*, opposite to, facing < OE *ongegn*, *ongean* (see prec.), with adv. gen. *-es* + unhistoric *-t*⟧ **1** *a)* in opposition to or competition with [a fight *against* evil] *b)* contrary to [*against* one's will] **2** toward so as to press on or strike [push *against* the door; throw the ball *against* the wall] **3** in contact with [a ladder leaned *against* the barn] **4** opposite to the course or direction of [driving *against* the traffic] **5** *a)* in contrast with [green *against* the gold] *b)* in comparison with [items checked *against* a list] **6** in preparation for; for the possibility of [we provided *against* a poor crop] **7** as a debit or charge on [a bill entered *against* our account] **8** [Now Dial.] next to; adjoining [the house *against* the church] —*conj.* [Archaic] by the time that; before —**over against** **1** opposite to **2** as compared with

A·ga Khan IV (ä′gə kän′) (*Karim al Hussaini Shah*) 1936- ; spiritual leader of the Ismailian sect of Muslims (1957-)

a·ga·ma (ə gä′mə) *n.* ⟦ModL < Sp; ? of WInd orig.: cf. Carib *mami*, lizard⟧ any of a family (Agamidae, esp. genus *Agama*) of Old World lizards, some of which can change color

Ag·a·mem·non (ag′ə mem′nän′, -nən) *n.* ⟦Gr⟧ *Gr. Myth.* king of Mycenae, brother of Menelaus, and commander in chief of the Greek army in the Trojan War: killed by his wife Clytemnestra

ag·a·mete (ag′ə mēt′) ***n.*** ⟦ModL *agameta*: see A-[2] & GAMETE⟧ any asexual reproductive cell that develops directly into an adult without fertilization, as in certain protozoans

a·gam·ic (ə gam′ik) ***adj.*** ⟦Gr *agamos*, not married < *a-*, not + *gamos*, marriage: see GAMO-⟧ *Biol.* **1** asexual; having no sexual union **2** able to develop without fertilization by the male; parthenogenetic

ag·a·mo·gen·e·sis (ag′ə mō′jen′ə sis) ***n.*** ⟦ModL < Gr *agamos* (see prec.) + -GENESIS⟧ *Biol.* asexual reproduction as by fission, budding, parthenogenesis, etc.

ag·a·mous (ag′ə məs) ***adj.*** ⟦Gr *agamos*, AGAMIC⟧ AGAMIC

A·ga·na (ə gä′nyə) *var. of* HAGATNA: also sp. **Agaña**

ag·a·pan·thus (ag′ə pan′thəs) ***n.*** ⟦ModL < LGr *agapē*, AGAPE[2] + Gr *anthos*, a flower⟧ AFRICAN LILY

a·gape[1] (ə gāp′) ***adv., adj.*** ⟦A-[1] + GAPE⟧ wide open, as in surprise or wonder; gaping [staring at the sight with mouth *agape*]

ag·a·pe[2] (ag′ə pē′, ä′gə pā′, ə gä′pā′, ä gä′-) ***n.*** ⟦LL(Ec) < LGr *agapē* < Gr *agapan*, to greet with affection, love⟧ **1** a meal that early Christians ate together: see LOVE FEAST **2** *Christian Theol.* *a)* God's love for humanity *b)* spontaneous, altruistic love

a·gar (ä′gər, ā′-; -gär′) ***n.*** ⟦Malay⟧ **1** a gelatinous product made from seaweed and used as a base for bacterial cultures, as a laxative, in jellied and preserved foods, in electrophoresis, etc. **2** a base containing agar Also **a′gar-a′gar**

ag·a·ric (ə gar′ik, ag′ə rik′) ***n.*** ⟦L *agaricum*, larch fungus < Gr *agaricon*, tree fungus, after *Agaria*, a Sarmatian town⟧ any of an order (Agaricales) of basidiomycetous fungi; esp., any of a family (Agaricaceae) of gill fungi, including many common, edible mushrooms

Ag·as·siz (ag′ə sē) **1 Alexander** 1835-1910; U.S. zoologist, geologist, & oceanographer, born in Switzerland: son of (Jean) Louis **2 (Jean) Louis (Rodolphe)** 1807-73; U.S. zoologist & geologist, born in Switzerland

ag·ate (ag′it) ***n.*** ⟦ME *agaten* < OFr *agate* < ML < L *achates* < Gr *achatēs* < ?⟧ **1** a hard semiprecious stone, a variety of chalcedony, with striped or clouded coloring **2** any of various tools having agate parts, as a burnishing instrument with a tip of agate **3** a little ball made of this stone or of glass, used in playing marbles **4** a former small size of printing type, 5½ points

☆**agate line** a unit of measurement for classified advertising space, one column wide and 1⁄14 inch deep

ag·ate·ware (ag′it wer′) ***n.*** **1** pots and pans enameled to look like agate **2** pottery made to look like agate

Ag·a·tha (ag′ə thə) ***n.*** ⟦L < Gr *Agathē*, lit., good, fem. of *agathos*, good⟧ a feminine name

a·ga·ve (ə gä′vē) ***n.*** ⟦ModL < Gr *Agauē*, a proper name, lit., illustrious, fem. of *agauos*, famous⟧ any of several plants (genus *Agave*) of the agave family, as the century plant: some agaves yield a fiber used for rope —***adj.*** designating a family (Agavaceae) of monocotyledonous desert plants (order Liliales)

a·gaze (ə gāz′) ***adv., adj.*** in the act of gazing

agcy *abbrev.* agency

age (āj) ***n.*** ⟦ME < OFr *aäge* < ML **aetaticum* < L *aetas*, contr. < *aevitas*, akin to *aevum*, age, eternity < IE base **aiw-* > AYE[1]⟧ **1** the time that a person or a thing has existed since birth or beginning **2** *a)* a stage of life [she is at the awkward *age*] *b)* a point in life at which a person becomes qualified or able to receive or assume a right, responsibility, etc. [drinking *age*, *age* of reason] **3** the condition of being old; old age [wearied with *age*] **4** a generation **5** *a)* any interval of geologic time; specif., a subdivision of an epoch corresponding to the rock strata of a STAGE (*n.* 13) *b)* any prehistoric cultural period in human development [the Stone *Age*] *c)* a period characterized by some person or by some outstanding feature or influence [the Elizabethan *Age*, the Space *Age*] **6** [*often pl.*] [Informal] a long time —***vi.* aged, ag′ing** or [Chiefly Brit.] **age′ing 1** to grow old or show signs of growing old **2** to ripen or become mature —***vt.* 1** to make, or make seem, old or mature **2** to cause to ripen or become mature over a period of time under fixed conditions [to *age* cheese] —**of age** having reached the age when one has full legal rights: see also COME OF AGE under COME

-age (ij, əj) ⟦OFr < LL *-aticum*, belonging to, related to⟧ *suffix* **1** act, condition, or result of [*marriage, cleavage, usage*] **2** amount or number of [*acreage*] **3** cost of [*postage*] **4** place of [*steerage*] **5** collection of [*peerage, rootage*] **6** home of [*hermitage*] The suffix appears in many words borrowed directly from French into Middle English [*savage, voyage*]

a·ged (ā′jid; *for 3 & 4* ājd) ***adj.*** **1** old; grown old **2** characteristic of old age **3** brought to a desired state of aging **4** of the age of [a boy, *aged* ten years] —**the aged** (ā′jid) old people collectively

A·gee (ā′jē′), **James** 1909-55; U.S. writer

age·ism (āj′iz′əm) ***n.*** ⟦AGE + (RAC)ISM⟧ discrimination against people on the basis of age; specif., discrimination against, and prejudicial stereotyping of, older people: also sp. **ag′ism′** —**age′ist *adj., n.***

age·less (āj′lis) ***adj.*** **1** seemingly not growing older **2** eternal —**age′less·ly *adv.***

age·long (-lôŋ′) ***adj.*** lasting a very long time

age-mate (āj′māt′) ***n.*** a person or animal of the same age, or nearly the same age, as another

a·gen·bite of in·wit (ə gen′bīt′ uv in′wit′) ⟦ME *ayenbite of inwyt*, transl. of L *remorsus*, REMORSE + ME *inwyt, inwit*, conscience, intellect: phrase revived by James Joyce (1922) in *Ulysses*⟧ remorse of conscience

a·gen·cy (ā′jən sē) ***n., pl.* -cies** ⟦ML *agentia* < prp. of L *agere*, ACT[1]⟧ **1** active force; action; power **2** that by which something is done; means; instrumentality **3** the business of any person, firm, etc. empowered to act for another **4** the business office or district of such a person, firm, etc. **5** an administrative division of government with specific functions **6** an organization that offers a particular kind of assistance [a social *agency*]

☆**agency shop 1** a contract arrangement between an employer and the union representing the majority of employees, which requires those who do not wish to be members to pay the union a fee equivalent to union dues **2** a factory, store, etc. in which this arrangement is in effect

a·gen·da (ə jen′də) ***n., pl.* -das** ⟦L, neut. pl. of *agendum*, ger. of *agere*, ACT[1]⟧ **1** program of things to be done; specif., a list of things to be dealt with at a meeting **2** an objective or set of objectives, esp. one that is not pursued openly [a committeeman with his own personal *agenda*]

a·gen·dum (-dəm) ***n., pl.* -da** (-də) or **-dums** AGENDA

a·gen·e·sis (ā jen′ə sis) ***n.*** ⟦A-[2] + -GENESIS⟧ congenital absence of an organ or other part of the body

a·gent (ā′jənt) ***n.*** ⟦L *agens* (gen. *agentis*), prp. of *agere*, ACT[1]⟧ **1** a person or thing that performs an action or brings about a certain result, or that is able to do so **2** an active force or substance producing an effect [a chemical *agent*] **3** a person, firm, etc. empowered to act for another ☆**4** a representative of a government agency [revenue *agent*] ☆**5** [Informal] a traveling salesperson **6** *Gram.* the word or words designating the person or thing that performs the action of the verb in a sentence — ***vi., vt.*** to act or work as an agent (on)

SYN.—an **agent** is, generally, a person or thing that acts or is capable of acting, or, in this comparison, one who or that which acts, or is empowered to act, for another [the company's *agent*]; **factor** now usually denotes an agent for the sale of goods; a **deputy** is a public official to whom certain authority has been delegated by superiors; **proxy** implies the delegation of power to substitute for another in some formal or ceremonial detail [some stockholders vote by *proxy*]

a·gen·tive (ā′jən tiv) ***adj.*** ⟦prec. + -IVE, modeled on GENITIVE⟧ *Gram.* of or producing a grammatical form that denotes the doer of a given action or the means of bringing about a given result —***n.*** an agentive form or affix, as the suffix -ER in *roller* —**a′gen·ti′val** (-tī′vəl) ***adj.***

☆**Agent Orange** ⟦military code name, from the identifying color used on its containers⟧ a highly toxic herbicide sprayed as a defoliant in chemical warfare

a·gent pro·vo·ca·teur (á zhän′ prô vô kȧ tër′) *pl.* **a·gents pro·vo·ca·teurs** (á zhän′ prô vô kȧ tër′) ⟦Fr < *agent*, an agent + *provocateur*, provoking, provocative⟧ **1** a person hired to join a labor union, political party, etc. in order to incite its members to actions that will make them or their organization liable to penalty **2** a secret agent of a foreign nation, esp. one who incites citizens to rebellion, illegal acts, etc.

age of consent *Law* **1** the age at which a person may marry without parental approval **2** the age at which a person is considered legally competent to consent to sexual intercourse

Age of Reason 1 a period of European history in the 18th cent. noted for belief in the ability of reason to discover truth, shape society, etc.: see THE ENLIGHTENMENT **2** [**a- of r-**] the age at which a child is presumed to know right from wrong and be capable of responsible action

age-old (āj′ōld′) ***adj.*** ages old; centuries old; ancient

ag·er·a·tum (aj′ər āt′əm) ***n.*** ⟦ModL < Gr *agēraton*, a kind of plant < *agēratos*, not growing old < *a-*, not + *gēras*, old age⟧ any of several plants (genus *Ageratum*) of the composite family with small, thick heads of usually bluish flowers: widely used as border plants in gardens

A·ges·i·la·us (II) (ə jes′i lā′əs) 442?-360? B.C.; king of Sparta during the decline of its supremacy in ancient Greece

age spot a permanent, brownish spot or patch on the skin, caused by exposure to the sun as over many years

Ag·ga·da or **Ag·ga·dah** (ä′gä dä′, ä gä′dä) ***n., pl.* Ag·ga·dot** (ä′gä dōt′) **1** [*often* **a-**] in the Talmud and midrash, the anecdotes, parables, legends, philosophy, etc. that explain or illustrate points of law: see also HALAKHA **2** the parts of the Talmud and midrash that contain such narratives

Ag·ge·us (a jē′əs) ***n.*** *Douay Bible name for* HAGGAI

☆**ag·gie**[1] (ag′ē) ***n.*** AGATE (sense 3)

☆**ag·gie**[2] (ag′ē) [*also* **A-**] ***n.*** ⟦< AG(RICULTURAL) + -IE⟧ **1** an agricultural school or college **2** a student at, or a graduate of, an agricultural school or college —***adj.*** of an agricultural school or college

ag·gior·na·men·to (ə jôr′nə men′tō) ***n.*** ⟦It < *aggiornare*, to bring up to date, modernize < *a*, to + *giorno*, day⟧ an updating or revitalization, specif. of an organization, in recognition of contemporary conditions

ag·glom·er·ate (ə gläm′ər āt′; *for adj. & n.*, -ər it) ***vt., vi.* -at′ed, -at′ing** ⟦< L *agglomeratus*, pp. of *agglomerare* < *ad-*, to + *glomerare*, to form into a ball < IE base **glem-*, var. of **gel-*, form a ball, sphere, hence akin to CLIMB, CLENCH⟧ to gather into a cluster, mass, or ball —***adj.*** gathered into a mass or ball; clustered —***n.*** **1** a jumbled heap, mass, etc. **2** *Geol.* a mass of fragments of volcanic rock fused by heat —**ag·glom′er·a′tive** (-āt′iv, -ə tiv) ***adj.***

ag·glom·er·a·tion (ə gläm′ər ā′shən) ***n.*** **1** an agglomerating or being agglomerated **2** a jumbled heap, mass, etc.

ag·glu·ti·nant (ə glo͞ot′'n ənt) ***adj.*** ⟦L *agglutinans*, prp. of *agglutinare*: see fol.⟧ sticking together; adhesive

ag·glu·ti·nate (ə glo͞ot′'n it; *for v.*, -āt′) ***adj.*** ⟦L *agglutinatus*, pp. of *agglutinare*, to cement to < *ad-*, to + *glutinare* < *gluten*, glue < IE base **glei-*: see CLAY⟧ **1** stuck together, as with glue **2** *Linguis.* forming words by agglutition — *vt., vi.* **-nat′ed, -nat′ing 1** to stick together, as with glue; join by adhesion **2** *Linguis.* to form (words) by agglutination **3** *Bacteriology, Med.* to clump, as microorganisms, blood cells, etc.

ag·glu·ti·na·tion (ə glo͞ot′'n ā′shən) *n.* **1** an agglutinating or being agglutinated **2** a mass of agglutinated parts **3** *Linguis.* in some languages, the systematic combining of morphemes into words without marked change of form or loss of meaning: distinguished from FUSION (sense 5*a*) **4** *Bacteriology, Med.* the clumping together of microorganisms, blood cells, etc. suspended in fluid

ag·glu·ti·na·tive (ə glo͞ot′'n āt′iv) *adj.* **1** tending to agglutinate **2** *Linguis.* characterized by agglutination

ag·glu·ti·nin (ə glo͞ot′'n in′) *n.* a substance, esp. an antibody, causing agglutination of bacteria, blood cells, antigens, etc.

ag·glu·tin·o·gen (ag′lo͞o tin′ə jən) *n.* any antigen which stimulates the production of agglutinins —**ag′glu·tin′o·gen′ic** (-jen′ik) *adj.*

ag·grade (ə grād′) *vt.* **-grad′ed, -grad′ing** ⟦AG- (var. of AD-) + GRADE⟧ to build up the level or slope of (a riverbed, valley, etc.) by the deposit of sediment —**ag·gra·da·tion** (ag′rə dā′shən) *n.*

ag·gran·dize (ə gran′dīz′; *also,* ag′rən-) *vt.* **-dized′, -diz′ing** ⟦< extended stem of Fr *agrandir,* to augment < *a-,* to + *grandir,* to increase < L *grandire* < *grandis,* great⟧ **1** to make greater, more powerful, richer, etc.: often used reflexively **2** to make seem greater or more exalted —**ag·gran·dize·ment** (ə gran′diz mənt; *also,* ag′rən dīz′-) *n.* —**ag·gran′diz′er** *n.*

ag·gra·vate (ag′rə vāt′) *vt.* **-vat′ed, -vat′ing** ⟦< L *aggravatus,* pp. of *aggravare,* to make heavier < *ad-,* to + *gravis,* heavy: see GRAVE[1]⟧ **1** to make worse; make more burdensome, troublesome, etc. **2** to exasperate; annoy; vex: a longtime usage, although it is objected to by some —*SYN.* INTENSIFY

ag·gra·vat·ed (-id) *adj. Law* designating an especially grave form of a specified offense [*aggravated* robbery]

ag·gra·va·tion (ag′rə vā′shən) *n.* **1** the act of aggravating, or making worse, or the condition of being aggravated **2** a thing or circumstance that aggravates, or makes worse **3** exasperation; annoyance: a longtime usage, although it is objected to by some

ag·gre·gate (ag′rə git; *for v.,* -gāt′) *adj.* ⟦L *aggregatus,* pp. of *aggregare,* to lead to a flock, add to < *ad-,* to + *gregare,* to herd < *grex* (gen. *gregis*), a herd⟧ **1** gathered into, or considered as, a whole; total [the *aggregate* number of unemployed] **2** *Bot. a)* massed into a dense head or cluster, as a flower *b)* formed of closely clustered carpels, as the raspberry **3** *Geol.* made up of a mixture of mineral fragments, crystals, or similar materials [an *aggregate* rock] —*n.* **1** a group or mass of distinct things gathered into, or considered as, a total or whole **2** the sand or pebbles added to cement in making concrete or mortar **3** an aggregate rock —*vt.* **-gat′ed, -gat′ing 1** to gather into a whole or mass **2** to amount to; total —*SYN.* SUM[1] —**in the aggregate** taken all together —**ag′gre·gate·ly** *adv.*

ag·gre·ga·tion (ag′rə gā′shən) *n.* **1** an aggregating or being aggregated **2** a group or mass of distinct things or individuals

ag·gre·ga·tive (ag′rə gāt′iv) *adj.* **1** aggregating or tending to aggregate **2** taken collectively or as a whole

ag·gress (ə gres′) *vi.* ⟦< L *aggressus,* pp. of *aggredi,* to attack, go to < *ad-,* to + *gradi,* to step⟧ to start a quarrel or be the first to attack

ag·gres·sion (ə gresh′ən) *n.* ⟦Fr < L *aggressio:* see prec. ⟧ **1** an unprovoked attack or warlike act; specif., the use of armed force by a state in violation of its international obligations **2** the practice or habit of being aggressive or quarrelsome **3** *Psychiatry* forceful, attacking behavior, either constructively self-assertive and self-protective or destructively hostile to others or to oneself

ag·gres·sive (ə gres′iv) *adj.* **1** aggressing or inclined to aggress; starting fights or quarrels **2** ready or willing to engage issue or engage in direct action; militant **3** full of enterprise and initiative; bold and active; pushing **4** *Psychiatry* of or involving aggression —**ag·gres′sive·ly** *adv.* —**ag·gres′sive·ness** *n.* —**ag·gres·siv·i·ty** (ag′res iv′ə tē, ə gres′-) *n.*

SYN.—**aggressive** implies a bold and energetic pursuit of one's ends, connoting, in derogatory usage, a ruthless desire to dominate and, in a favorable sense, enterprise or initiative; **militant** implies a vigorous, unrelenting espousal of a cause, movement, etc. and rarely suggests the furthering of one's own ends; **assertive** emphasizes self-confidence and a persistent determination to express oneself or one's opinions; **pushing** is applied derogatorily to a forwardness of personality that manifests itself in officiousness or rudeness

ag·gres·sor (ə gres′ər) *n.* ⟦LL⟧ a person, nation, etc. that is guilty of aggression, or makes an unprovoked attack

ag·grieve (ə grēv′) *vt.* **-grieved′, -griev′ing** ⟦ME *agreven* < OFr *agrever,* to aggravate < L *aggravare,* AGGRAVATE⟧ **1** to cause grief or injury to; offend **2** to injure in one's legal rights —*SYN.* WRONG

ag·grieved (ə grēvd′) *adj.* **1** having a grievance; wronged **2** injured in one's legal rights —**ag·griev′ed·ly** (-grēv′id lē) *adv.*

ag·gro (ag′rō) *n.* ⟦< AGGR(ESSION) or AGGR(AVATION) + -O⟧ [Brit. Slang] **1** aggressive feelings or aggravation **2** aggressive activity, as in a fight

a·gha (ä′gə) *n. alt. sp. of* AGA

a·ghast (ə gast′, -gäst′) *adj.* ⟦ME *agast,* pp. of *agasten,* to terrify < *a-,* intens. + *gasten* < OE *gaestan,* to terrify < *gast,* GHOST⟧ feeling great horror or dismay; terrified; horrified

ag·ile (aj′əl, -īl′) *adj.* ⟦Fr < L *agilis* < *agere,* ACT[1]⟧ **1** quick and easy of movement; deft and active **2** keen and lively [an *agile* wit] —**ag′ile·ly** *adv.* —**a·gil·i·ty** (ə jil′ə tē) *n.*

SYN.—**agile** and **nimble** both imply rapidity and lightness of movement, **agile** emphasizing dexterity in the use of the limbs and **nimble**, deftness in the performance of some act; **quick** implies rapidity and promptness, seldom indicating, out of context, the degree of skillfulness; **spry** suggests nimbleness or alacrity, esp. as displayed by vigorous elderly people; **sprightly** implies animation or vivacity and suggests lightheartedness —*ANT.* **torpid, sluggish, lethargic**

a·gin (ə gin′) *prep.* [Dial.] AGAINST

A·gin·court (aj′in kôrt′; *Fr* à zhan ko͞or′) village in N France, near Calais: site of a battle (1415) won by England in the Hundred Years' War with France

ag·i·o (aj′ē ō′) *n., pl.* **-os′** ⟦Fr < It *aggio;* ult. < LL *adjectum,* something added < L *adjectus:* see ADJECTIVE⟧ a fee paid to exchange one kind of money for another or to exchange depreciated money for money of full value

agit *abbrev.* ⟦L *agita*⟧ *Pharmacy* shake or stir

ag·i·ta (aj′i tə) *n.* ⟦< It, prob. dial.; orig., lit., acid indigestion, heartburn⟧ anxiety; agitation

ag·i·tate (aj′i tāt′) *vt.* **-tat′ed, -tat′ing** ⟦< L *agitatus,* pp. of *agitare,* to put in motion < *agere,* ACT[1]⟧ **1** *a)* to move violently *b)* to stir up or shake up **2** to excite or disturb the feelings of **3** to keep discussing so as to stir up interest in and support for —*vi.* to stir up interest and support through speeches and writing so as to produce changes [to *agitate* for better working conditions] —*SYN.* DISTURB

ag·i·tat·ed (-id) *adj.* shaken; perturbed; excited —**ag′i·tat′ed·ly** *adv.*

ag·i·ta·tion (aj′ə tā′shən) *n.* ⟦Fr < L *agitatio*⟧ **1** an agitating or being agitated; violent motion or stirring **2** emotional disturbance or excitement **3** discussion meant to stir up people and produce changes —**ag·i·ta′tion·al** *adj.*

a·gi·ta·to (ä′jē tä′tō) *adj., adv.* ⟦It < L *agitatus:* see AGITATE⟧ *Musical Direction* fast and with excitement

ag·i·ta·tor (aj′i tāt′ər) *n.* **1** a person who tries to stir up people in support of a cause: often used in an unfavorable sense **2** an apparatus for shaking or stirring, as in a washing machine

ag·it·prop (aj′it präp′) *adj.* ⟦Russ < *agitacija,* agitation (< Fr: see AGITATION) + *propaganda,* PROPAGANDA⟧ of or for agitating and propagandizing: a term originally used in the Communist movement, esp. of certain plays, leaflets, etc. —*n.* any agitprop activity or agency

A·gla·ia (ə glā′ə, ə glī′ə) *n.* ⟦L < Gr *Aglaia,* lit., brightness⟧ *Gr. Myth.* Brilliance, one of the three Graces

a·gleam (ə glēm′) *adj.* ⟦orig. an adv.: see A-[1] (sense 2) & GLEAM⟧ gleaming: used only in the predicate

ag·let (ag′lit) *n.* ⟦ME < OFr *aguillette,* dim. of *aiguille* < L *acula,* dim. of *acus,* a needle: see ACEROSE[1]⟧ the metal tip at the end of a cord or lace

a·gley (ə glā′, -glē′) *adv.* ⟦A-[1] + *gley,* squint⟧ [Chiefly Scot.] awry

a·glit·ter (ə glit′ər) *adv., adj.* glittering

a·glow (ə glō′) *adv., adj.* in a glow (of color or emotion)

ag·nail (ag′nāl′) *n.* ⟦ME *angnail* < OE *angnægl,* a corn (on the toe or foot) < *ange,* pain (akin to ANGER) + *nægl,* nail (metal): orig. in reference to the nail-head appearance of the excrescence⟧ **1** a sore or swelling around a fingernail or toenail **2** a hangnail

ag·nate (ag′nāt′) *n.* ⟦L *agnatus* < pp. of *agnasci,* to be born in addition to < *ad-,* to + *nasci,* to be born: see GENUS⟧ a relative through male descent or on the father's side —*adj.* **1** related through male descent or on the father's side **2** akin —**ag·nat·ic** (ag nat′ik) *adj.* —**ag·na′tion** (-nā′shən) *n.*

Ag·nes[1] (ag′nis) *n.* ⟦Fr *Agnès* < L *Agnes, Hagnes* < Gr *hagnē,* fem. of *hagnos,* chaste⟧ a feminine name: dim. *Aggie;* equiv. Sp. *Inez*

Ag·nes[2] (ag′nis), Saint (died A.D. 304); Rom. virgin martyr: her day is Jan. 21: see also SAINT AGNES'S EVE

a·gno·lot·ti (an′yə lä′tē, än′yə lô′tē) *n.* ⟦It⟧ pasta resembling small, crescent-shaped ravioli, filled with meat, spinach, cheese, etc.

ag·no·men (ag nō′mən) *n., pl.* **ag·nom′i·na** (-näm′i nə) ⟦L < *ad-,* to + *nomen,* NAME⟧ **1** in ancient Rome, a name added to the cognomen, esp. as an epithet honoring some achievement **2** a nickname

ag·no·si·a (ag nō′sē ə, -zē-; -nä′-) *n.* ⟦ModL < Gr *a-,* not + *gnōsis,* knowledge + -IA⟧ impairment of the ability to recognize familiar objects, sounds, etc., often as the result of a brain lesion

ag·nos·tic (ag näs′tik) *n.* ⟦coined (1870) by Thomas Henry HUXLEY < A-[2] + GNOSTIC⟧ a person who believes that the human mind cannot know whether there is a God or an ultimate cause, or anything beyond material phenomena —*adj.* **1** of or characteristic of an agnostic or agnosticism **2** not committed to a particular view, concept, method, etc.; neutral [*agnostic* on nuclear energy] —*SYN.* ATHEIST —**ag·nos′ti·cal·ly** *adv.*

ag·nos·ti·cism (-tə siz′əm) *n.* the doctrine of agnostics: distinguished from ATHEISM

Ag·nus De·i (äg′no͞os dā′ē′, ag′nəs-, än′yo͞os′-; -dē′ī′) ⟦L, Lamb of God⟧ **1** a representation of Christ as a lamb, often holding a cross or flag **2** *R.C.Ch. a)* a little wax disk with a lamb pictured on it, blessed by the pope *b)* a prayer in the Latin Mass, beginning *Agnus Dei c)* music for this

a·go (ə gō′) *adj.* ⟦ME *agon,* pp. of *agon,* to depart < OE *agan,* to pass away < *a-,* away + *gan:* see GO[1]⟧ gone by; past; before now: used following the noun [years *ago*] —*adv.* in the past [long *ago*]

a·gog (ə gäg′) *adv., adj.* ⟦ME *agogge* < OFr *en gogues* < *en,* in + *gogue,* joke, joyfulness⟧ in a state of eager anticipation, excitement, or interest

à go-go or **a go-go** (ə gō′gō′) GO-GO (*adj.* 1)

-a·gogue (ə gäg′, -gôg′) ⟦< Gr *agōgos,* leading < *agein,* to lead: see ACT[1]⟧

combining form a substance that induces the secretion of [*galactagogue*]: also **-a·gog′**

ag·on (ag′ōn′, -än′) ***n.***, *pl.* **ag′ons′** or **a·go·nes** (ə gō′nēz′) ⟦Gr *agōn*, assembly, contest < *agein*, to lead: see ACT[1]⟧ **1** any of various competitions (athletic, literary, etc.) for prizes at ancient Greek games **2** the conflict of characters, as in classical Greek drama

ag·o·nal (ag′ə nəl) ***adj.*** of or connected with death pangs

a·gone (ə gôn′) ***adj., adv.*** ⟦ME *agon*, AGO⟧ [Archaic] ago; past

a·gon·ic (ə gän′ik, ā-) ***adj.*** ⟦< Gr *agōnos* < *a-*, without + *gōnia*, an angle⟧ forming no angle

agonic line an imaginary line on the earth's surface along which true north and magnetic north are identical: at any point along this line, the declination of a compass needle equals zero

ag·o·nist (ag′ə nist′) ***n.*** ⟦back-form. < ANTAGONIST⟧ **1** one who takes part in a struggle, as a main character in a drama **2** a muscle whose contraction is counteracted by the movement of another muscle (called the *antagonist*) **3** a substance in the body, or a drug, that acts as a stimulant by binding to a receptor cell, causing a response that may be counteracted by another substance or drug (called the *antagonist*)

ag·o·nis·tes (ag′ə nis′tēz′) ***adj.*** ⟦Gr *agōnistēs* < *agōnizesthai*, to contend < *agōn*, AGON⟧ designating a person engaged in a struggle: used after the word modified

ag·o·nis·tic (ag′ə nis′tik) ***adj.*** ⟦Gr *agōnistikos*, fit for contest < *agōn*, AGON⟧ **1** of ancient Greek athletic contests **2** combative **3** strained for effect Also **ag′o·nis′ti·cal** —**ag′o·nis′ti·cal·ly** ***adv.***

ag·o·nize (ag′ə nīz′) ***vi.*** **-nized′**, **-niz′ing** ⟦LL *agonizare* < Gr *agōnizesthai*, to contend for a prize < *agōn*, AGON⟧ **1** to make convulsive efforts; struggle **2** to be in agony or great pain; feel anguish —***vt.*** to cause great pain to; torture —**ag′o·niz′ing** ***adj.*** —**ag′o·niz′ing·ly** ***adv.***

ag·o·ny (ag′ə nē) ***n.***, *pl.* **-nies** ⟦ME *agonie* < L *agonia* < Gr *agōnia*, a contest for victory < *agōn*, AGON⟧ **1** very great mental or physical pain **2** death pangs **3** a convulsive struggle **4** a sudden, strong outburst (*of* emotion) [an *agony* of joy] —**SYN.** DISTRESS

agony aunt [Brit. Informal] a person, esp. a woman, who replies to the letters of readers in a newspaper or magazine column (**agony column**) giving advice, consolation, etc.

ag·o·ra[1] (ag′ə rə; *now often* ə gôr′ə) ***n.***, *pl.* **-rae′** (-rē′) or **-ras** (-rəz) ⟦Gr < *ageirein*, to assemble < IE base *ger-: see GREGARIOUS⟧ in ancient Greece, an assembly or assembly place, esp. a marketplace

a·go·ra[2] (ä′gō rä′) ***n.***, *pl.* **-rot′** (-rōt′) ⟦ModHeb < Heb *agora*, a unit of weight⟧ a monetary unit of Israel, equal to $\frac{1}{100}$ of a shekel

ag·o·ra·pho·bi·a (ag′ər ə fō′bē ə; *now often* ə gôr′ə-) ***n.*** ⟦AGORA[1] + -PHOBIA⟧ an abnormal fear of being in open or public places —**ag′o·ra·phobe′** ***n.*** —**ag′o·ra·pho′bic** ***adj., n.***

a·gou·ti (ə go͞ot′ē) ***n.***, *pl.* **-tis** ⟦Fr (? via Sp *agutí*) < Tupí-Guaraní *akutí*⟧ a rabbit-sized, nocturnal rodent (family Dasyproctidae) with grizzled fur, found in tropical America: also sp. **a·gou′ty**, *pl.* **-ties**

agr *abbrev.* **1** agricultural **2** agriculture

A·gra (ä′grə) **1** city on the Jumna River, in Uttar Pradesh, India: site of the Taj Mahal **2** former province of India: now part of Uttar Pradesh

a·graffe or **a·grafe** (ə graf′) ***n.*** ⟦Fr *agrafe* < *agrafer*, to hook < OFr *agraper*, to fasten < *grapon*, hook < Frank **krappo* (see GRAPE); form infl. by OFr *grafe*, pointed tool < L *graphium*, stylus < Gr *grapheion*, a chisel⟧ **1** a hook and loop, used to fasten armor or clothing **2** a metal bracket used in building to hold stones together

a·gran·u·lo·cy·to·sis (ā gran′yo͞o lō′sī tō′sis) ***n.*** ⟦A-[2] + GRANULOCYT(E) + -OSIS⟧ a disorder characterized by a significant decrease of granulocytes in the blood and often resulting in high fever, weakness, and ulceration of the mucous membranes

ag·ra·pha (ag′rə fə) ***pl.n.*** ⟦Gr, neut. pl. of *agraphos*, unwritten: see A-[2] & GRAPHIC⟧ sayings ascribed to Jesus but not found in the Gospels

a·graph·i·a (ā graf′ē ə) ***n.*** ⟦ModL < Gr *a-*, without + *graphein*, to write: see GRAPHIC⟧ the partial or total loss of the ability to write —**a·graph′ic** ***adj.***

a·grar·i·an (ə grer′ē ən) ***adj.*** ⟦< L *agrarius* < *ager*, a field: see ACRE⟧ **1** relating to land or to the ownership or division of land **2** of agriculture or farmers generally **3** promoting land reform or the interests of farmers —***n.*** a person who advocates agrarian reform, esp. a more equitable division of land —**a·grar′i·an·ism′** (-iz′əm) ***n.***

a·gree (ə grē′) ***vi.*** **-greed′**, **-gree′ing** ⟦ME *agreen* < OFr *agreer*, to receive kindly < *a gré*, favorably < *a* (L *ad*), to + *gré*, good will < L *gratus*, pleasing: see GRACE⟧ **1** to consent or accede (*to*); say "yes" **2** to be in harmony or accord [their versions *agree*] **3** to be of the same opinion; concur (*with*) **4** to arrive at a satisfactory understanding (*on* or *about* prices, terms, etc.) **5** to be suitable, healthful, etc.: followed by *with* [this climate does not *agree* with him] **6** *Gram.* to be inflected so as to correspond in number, person, case, or gender —***vt.*** **1** to grant or acknowledge [they *agreed* to stop fighting] **2** [Chiefly Brit.] to arrive at an understanding or come to an arrangement on or about [to *agree* a price for the car, to *agree* terms of the truce]

SYN.—**agree** implies a being or going together without conflict and is the general term used in expressing an absence of inconsistencies, inequalities, etc.; **conform** emphasizes agreement in form or basic character; **accord** emphasizes fitness for each other of things that are being considered together; **harmonize** implies a combination or association of different things in a proportionate or pleasing arrangement [*harmonizing* colors]; **correspond** is applied to that which matches, complements, or is analogous to something else [their Foreign Office *corresponds* to our State Department]; **coincide** stresses the identical character of the things considered [their needs *coincide*]; **tally** is applied to a thing that corresponds to another as a counterpart or duplicate See also **consent** —**ANT. differ**

a·gree·a·ble (-ə bəl) ***adj.*** ⟦ME & OFr *agreable* < *agreer*, prec. ⟧ **1** pleasing or pleasant [an *agreeable* melody] **2** willing or ready to consent **3** conformable or in accord **4** that can be approved; acceptable [a contract *agreeable* to both parties] —**SYN.** PLEASANT —**a·gree′a·bil′i·ty** (-ə bil′ə tē) ***n.***, **a·gree′a·ble·ness** —**a·gree′a·bly** ***adv.***

a·greed (ə grēd′) ***adj.*** settled or determined by mutual consent [pay the *agreed* price]

a·gree·ment (ə grē′mənt) ***n.*** **1** the act or fact of agreeing, or of being in harmony or accord **2** an understanding or arrangement between two or more people, countries, etc. **3** a contract **4** *Gram.* correspondence, as between subject and verb, in number, person, etc.

a·gres·tic (ə gres′tik) ***adj.*** ⟦< L *agrestis*, rural < *ager*, field: see ACRE⟧ **1** rural; rustic **2** crude; uncouth

ag·ri- (ag′ri, -rə) *combining form* agriculture, esp. in relation to technology or business [*agrichemicals*]: also **ag′ro-** (-rō, -rə)

☆**ag·ri·busi·ness** (ag′rə biz′nis) ***n.*** ⟦AGRI(CULTURE) + BUSINESS⟧ farming and the businesses associated with farming, as the processing of farm products or the manufacturing of farm equipment

agric *abbrev.* **1** agricultural **2** agriculture

A·gric·o·la (ə grik′ə lə) **1 (Gnaeus Julius)** A.D. 40-93; Rom. general: governor of Britain (A.D. 78?-85?) **2 Geor·gi·us** (jôr′jē əs) (L. name of *Georg Bauer*) 1490-1555; Ger. scholar who made the first scientific classification of minerals: called the *Father of Mineralogy*

ag·ri·cul·ture (ag′ri kul′chər) ***n.*** ⟦Fr < L *agricultura* < *ager*, a field (see ACRE) + *cultura*, cultivation⟧ the science and art of farming; work or business of cultivating the soil, producing crops, and raising livestock —**ag′ri·cul′tur·al** ***adj.*** —**ag′ri·cul′tur·al·ly** ***adv.***

ag·ri·cul·tur·ist (ag′ri kul′chər ist) ***n.*** **1** an agricultural expert **2** a farmer Also **ag′ri·cul′tur·al·ist** (-chər əl ist)

Ag·ri·gen·to (ä′grē jen′tō) city in S Sicily: site of ancient Greek and Roman ruins: ancient Latin name **Ag·ri·gen·tum** (ag′rə jen′təm)

ag·ri·mo·ny (ag′rə mō′nē) ***n.***, *pl.* **-nies** ⟦ME < OE *agrimonia* & OFr *aigremoine*, both < L *agrimonia*, altered after *ager*, field (see ACRE) < *argemonia* < Gr *argemōnē*⟧ **1** any plant of a genus (*Agrimonia*) in the rose family, typically having little yellow flowers on spiky stalks and bearing burlike fruits **2** HEMP AGRIMONY

ag·ri·ol·o·gy (ag′rē äl′ə jē) ***n.*** ⟦< Gr *agrios*, wild < *agros*, field (see ACRE) + -LOGY⟧ the study of the customs of nonliterate peoples whose culture is marked by a simple technology

A·grip·pa (ə grip′ə) **1 (Marcus Vipsanius)** 63?-12 B.C.; Rom. military leader & statesman: commander of Octavian's fleet at ACTIUM **2** *see* HEROD AGRIPPA I

Ag·rip·pi·na (II) (a′gri pī′nə, -pē′-), **(Julia)** A.D. 15?-59; mother of Nero: called *Agrippina the Younger*

ag·ro- (ag′rō) ⟦Gr < *agros*, a field: see ACRE⟧ *combining form* **1** field, earth, soil **2** AGRI-

ag·ro·bi·ol·o·gy (ag′rō bī äl′ə jē) ***n.*** the science of plant growth and nutrition as applied to improvement of crops and control of soil —**ag′ro·bi·o·log′ic** (-bī′ə läj′ik) ***adj.***, **ag′ro·bi′o·log′i·cal** —**ag′ro·bi′o·log′i·cal·ly** ***adv.***

ag·ro·chem·i·cal (ag′rō kem′i kəl) ***n.*** **1** a chemical used to improve the quality and quantity of farm products **2** a chemical derived from agricultural products, as furfural

a·grol·o·gy (ə gräl′ə jē) ***n.*** the science of agricultural production —**a·grol′o·gist** ***n.***

ag·ro·nom·ics (ag′rə näm′iks) ***n.*** AGRONOMY

a·gron·o·my (ə grän′ə mē) ***n.*** ⟦Fr *agronomie* < OFr *agronome*, agriculturist < Gr *agronomos*, overseer of the public lands < *agros* (see ACRE) + *-nomos* (see -NOMY)⟧ the science and economics of crop production; management of farm land —**ag·ro·nom·ic** (ag′rə näm′ik) ***adj.***, **ag′ro·nom′i·cal** —**a·gron′o·mist** ***n.***

ag·ros·tol·o·gy (ag′rəs täl′ə jē) ***n.*** ⟦< L *agrostis* < Gr *agrōstis*, kind of grass < *agros*, a field (see ACRE) + -LOGY⟧ the branch of botany dealing with grasses

a·ground (ə ground′) ***adv., adj.*** on or onto the shore, the bottom, a reef, etc. [the ship ran *aground*]

agt *abbrev.* agent

☆**a·guar·dien·te** (ä′gwär dyen′tā) ***n.*** ⟦Sp, lit., fiery water < *agua* (< L *aqua*, water) + *ardiente*, burning (< L *ardens*: see ARDENT)⟧ any of various common alcoholic liquors of Spain, Latin America, etc.

A·guas·ca·lien·tes (ä′gwäs kä lyen′tās) **1** small, inland state of central Mexico: 2,158 sq mi (5,589 sq km) **2** its capital

a·gue (ā′gyo͞o′) ***n.*** ⟦ME < OFr *ague* < ML (*febris*) *acuta*, violent (fever): see ACUTE⟧ **1** a fever, usually malarial, marked by regularly recurring chills **2** a chill; fit of shivering —**a·gu·ish** (ā′gyo͞o ish) ***adj.***

☆**a·gue·weed** (ā′gyo͞o wēd′) ***n.*** **1** a variety (*Gentiana quinquefolia*) of gentian **2** BONESET

A·gul·has (ə gul′əs), **Cape** southernmost point of Africa, in Western Cape province, South Africa

Agulhas current a fast, warm ocean current flowing southwest along the SE coast of Africa

ah (ä, ô, ôn, an, än) ***interj.*** ⟦natural exclamation similar to Fr & L *ah*, Gr *a*, ON *æ*, OHG *a*, Sans *ā*⟧ used to express variously surprise, delight, regret, disgust, pain, etc.

Ah *abbrev.* ampere-hour: also **Amp-hr, A h, A-h, A-hr,** or **a-hr**

AH or **A.H.** *abbrev.* ⟦L *Anno Hegirae,* in the year of the hegira⟧ of the Muslim era: used with dates: see HEGIRA (sense 1)

a·ha (ä hä′, ə hä′) ***interj.*** used to express triumph, surprise, pleasure, satisfaction, etc., often mixed with irony or mockery

AHA (ā′āch′ā′) ***n.*** ⟦A(LPHA) H(YDROXY) A(CID)⟧ any of a group of natural or synthetic alpha hydroxy acids, including lactic acid and glycolic acid, found in fruit, sour milk, sugar cane, etc. and used in making cleansing creams and lotions that exfoliate the skin

A·hab (ā′hab′) ***n.*** ⟦Heb *ach'av,* lit., father's brother⟧ *Bible* a wicked king of Israel of the 9th cent. B.C.: husband of Jezebel: 1 Kings 16:29-22:40

A·has·u·e·rus (ə haz′yo͞o ir′əs, -has′-) ***n.*** ⟦Heb < OPers *Xxayaršan*⟧ *Bible* either of two kings of the Medes and Persians, esp. the one (often identified as Xerxes I) who was married to Esther: Esth. 1; Ezra 4:6

à haute voix (ȧ ōt vwȧ′) ⟦Fr, lit., in high voice⟧ aloud

a·head (ə hed′) ***adv., adj.*** **1** in or to the front **2** forward; onward **3** *a)* toward the future; in advance [set your clock *ahead* one hour] *b)* at or to an earlier time [let's move the meeting *ahead* one week] **4** winning or leading **5** having something as a profit or advantage —**ahead of** in advance of; before —**get ahead** to advance socially, financially, etc. —**get ahead of** to outdo or excel

a·hem (*a coughing or throat-clearing sound, conventionalized* ə hem′) ***interj.*** ⟦echoic⟧ used to get someone's attention, give a warning, fill a pause, etc.

a·him·sa (ə him′sä′) ***n.*** ⟦Sans *ahimsā,* non-injury < *a-,* not + *himsā,* injury < IE **gheis-,* to wound < base **ĝhei-,* to hurl, projectile > GOAD⟧ *Buddhism, Jainism, etc.* the doctrine that all life is one and sacred, resulting in the principle of nonviolence toward all living creatures

a·his·tor·ic (ā′his tôr′ik) ***adj.*** not related to or concerned with documented history: also **a′his·tor′i·cal**

A·hith·o·phel (ə hith′ə fel′) ***n.*** ⟦Heb *achitofel,* lit., brother is foolishness⟧ *Bible* a counselor of David and associate of Absalom in rebellion against David: 2 Sam. 15-17

a·hi (tuna) (ä′hē′) ⟦Haw⟧ YELLOWFIN (TUNA)

Ah·med·a·bad or **Ah·mad·a·bad** (ä′məd ə bäd′) city in central Gujarat, W India

a·hold (ə hōld′) ***n.*** [Informal] a hold —**get ahold of** GET (A) HOLD OF: see HOLD[1]

-a·hol·ic (ə hôl′ik, -häl′-) ⟦*-a-* + (ALCO)HOLIC⟧ *combining form* one who exhibits an obsessive need for or interest in (something specified): frequently in nonce constructions [*foodaholic, spendaholic*]

A-ho·ri·zon (ā′hə rī′zən) ***n.*** the uppermost soil zone, containing humus: see ABC SOIL

a·hoy (ə hoi′) ***interj.*** ⟦A(H) + HOY[2]⟧ *Naut.* used to hail a ship [ship *ahoy!*]

Ah·ri·man (ä′ri mən) ***n.*** ⟦MPers *Ahrīman,* prob. < Avestan *aṅra mainyu,* the evil (lit., hostile) spirit⟧ in Zoroastrianism, the spirit of evil: see ORMAZD

A·hu·ra Maz·da (ä′ho͝o rə maz′də) ORMAZD

Ah·vaz (ä väz′) city in SW Iran: also **Ah·waz** (ä wäz′)

Ah·ve·nan·maa (ä′ve nän mä′) group of Finn. islands at the entrance to the Gulf of Bothnia: 590 sq mi (1,528 sq km)

ai[1] (ī) ***interj.*** ⟦echoic of natural cry⟧ used to express sorrow, pity, pain, etc.

a·i[2] (ä′ē′) ***n., pl.*** **a′is′** (-ēz′) ⟦Tupí *ai, hai* < the animal's cry⟧ a South American sloth (*Bradypus tridactylus*) with a greenish coat: the color is caused by algae that live on its hair

AI *abbrev.* artificial intelligence

AIA *abbrev.* American Institute of Architects

aid (ād) ***vt., vi.*** ⟦ME *aiden* < OFr *aider* < L *adjutare,* freq. of *adjuvare,* to help < *ad-,* to + *juvare,* to help⟧ to give help or relief (to); assist —***n.*** ⟦ME & OFr *aide* < the v.⟧ **1** help or assistance; esp., financial help **2** a helper; assistant **3** a helpful device [visual *aids*] **4** *alt. sp. of* AIDE (sense 2) **5** *Eng. History a)* a payment in money made by a vassal to his lord *b)* a subsidy granted to the king for a special purpose —***SYN.*** HELP

AID *abbrev.* Agency for International Development

aide (ād′) ***n.*** ⟦Fr: see AID⟧ **1** an assistant **2** an aide-de-camp

aide-de-camp or **aid-de-camp** (ād′də kamp′) ***n., pl.*** **aides′-de-camp′** or **aids′-de-camp′** ⟦Fr, lit., camp assistant⟧ an officer in the army, navy, etc. serving as assistant to a superior

aide-mé·moire (ād′mem wär′; *Fr* ed mā mwȧr′) ***n.*** ⟦Fr, lit., memory aid < *aider,* to help + *mémoire,* memory⟧ a memorandum of a discussion, proposed agreement, etc.

aid·man (ād′man′) ***n., pl.*** **-men′** (-men′) *Mil.* an enlisted person in a medical corps attached to a combat unit

AIDS (ādz) ***n.*** ⟦A(CQUIRED) I(MMUNE) D(EFICIENCY) S(YNDROME)⟧ a condition in which an acquired deficiency of certain leukocytes, esp. T cells, results in a variety of infections, some forms of cancer, and the degeneration of the nervous system: caused by an HIV virus which infects T cells and is transmitted via bodily fluids, esp. sexual secretions and blood

AIDS-re·lat·ed complex (ādz′ ri lāt′id) a condition that may develop into AIDS, characterized by the enlargement of the lymph nodes

☆**aid station** *Mil.* a medical station in a forward area where the sick and wounded are given emergency treatment

ai·grette or **ai·gret** (ā gret′, ā′gret′) ***n.*** ⟦see EGRET⟧ **1** a bunch of the long, white, showy plumes of the egret, once worn for ornament on a hat or in the hair **2** any ornament like this

ai·guille (ā gwēl′, ā′gwēl′) ***n.*** ⟦Fr: see AGLET⟧ **1** a peak of rock shaped like a needle **2** an instrument for drilling holes in rock or masonry

ai·guil·lette (ā′gwi let′) ***n.*** ⟦Fr: see AGLET⟧ a gilt cord hung in loops from the shoulder of certain military uniforms

Ai·ken (ā′kən), **Conrad (Potter)** 1889-1973; U.S. poet & fiction writer

ai·ki·do (ī kē′dō, ī′kē dō′) ***n.*** ⟦Jpn *aikidoo,* lit., the art of matching (the opponent's) spirit < *ai,* a fitting (< *au,* to fit, suit) + SinoJpn *ki,* spirit, soul + SinoJpn *doo,* way, art⟧ a Japanese system of self-defense in which various holds and circular movements are used to exploit to one's own advantage an opponent's strength and weight

ail (āl) ***vt.*** ⟦ME *eilen* < OE *eglian,* to afflict with dread, trouble < *egle,* harmful; akin to Goth *agls,* infamous, ON *agi* > AWE⟧ to be the cause of pain or distress to; trouble —***vi.*** to be in poor health, esp. over a period of time

ai·lan·thus (ā lan′thəs) ***n., pl.*** **-thus·es** ⟦ModL, altered (by assoc. with Gr *anthos,* flower) < *ai lanit,* lit., tree of heaven, the name in a language of Moluccas, Indonesia⟧ any tree or shrub of a genus (*Ailanthus*) of the quassia family, having pointed leaflets, fine-grained wood, and clusters of small, greenish flowers with an unpleasant odor: see TREE OF HEAVEN —**ai·lan′thic** ***adj.***

ailanthus moth a large moth (*Philosamia cynthia*) native to E Asia and now established in the E U.S., whose larvae (**ailanthus silkworms**) feed on ailanthus leaves and produce an inferior silk in making their cocoons

Ai·leen (ī lēn′, ā-) ***n.*** a feminine name: see EILEEN

ai·le·ron (ā′lə rän′) ***n.*** ⟦Fr < OFr *aleron,* wingtip < *aile,* wing < L *ala,* wing, armpit < **agsla* < IE **aks-*: see AXIS[1]⟧ a pilot-controlled airfoil attached to, in, or near the trailing edge of an airplane wing, for controlling the rolling movements of the airplane

Ai·ley (ā′lē), **Alvin, Jr.** 1931-89; U.S. dancer & choreographer

ail·ing (āl′iŋ) ***adj.*** in poor health; sickly —***SYN.*** SICK[1]

ail·ment (āl′mənt) ***n.*** any bodily or mental disorder; illness, esp. a mild, chronic one —***SYN.*** DISEASE

ai·lu·ro·phile (ā lo͝or′ə fīl′, ī-) ***n.*** ⟦< Gr *ailouros,* cat + -PHILE⟧ a person who is strongly attracted to or devoted to cats

ai·lu·ro·pho·bi·a (ā lo͝or′ə fō′bē ə, ī-) ***n.*** ⟦ModL < Gr *ailouros,* cat + -PHOBIA⟧ an abnormal fear of cats —**ai·lu′ro·phobe′** (-fōb′) ***n.***

aim (ām) ***vi., vt.*** ⟦ME *aimen* < OFr *esmer* (< L *aestimare*: see ESTIMATE) & *aesmer* < ML *adaestimare* < L *ad-,* to + *aestimare*⟧ **1** to point (a weapon) or direct (a blow, remark, etc.) so as to hit **2** to direct (one's efforts) [we *aimed* at full victory] **3** to try or intend (*to* do or be something) **4** [Obs.] to guess or conjecture —***n.*** **1** the act of aiming **2** *a)* the ability to hit a target *b)* a weapon's accuracy [the *aim* is accurate up to 100 feet] **3** the object to be attained; intention or purpose **4** [Obs.] a guess or conjecture —***SYN.*** INTENTION —**take aim** **1** to point a weapon, as by viewing along a sight at a target **2** to direct a missile, blow, etc.

aim·less (-lis) ***adj.*** having no aim or purpose —**aim′less·ly** ***adv.*** —**aim′less·ness** ***n.***

ain (ān) ***adj.*** [Scot.] own

ain't (ānt) ⟦early assimilation, with lengthened and raised vowel, of *amn't,* contr. of *am not*; later confused with *a'nt (are not), i'nt (is not), ha'nt (has not, have not)*⟧ *contraction* **1** [Informal] am not **2** *a)* is not or are not *b)* has not or have not: a dialectal or nonstandard usage [you *ain't* seen nothing yet!]

USAGE—Although *ain't* is widely used informally by educated speakers, many people still frown on its use in formal contexts. *Ain't* once was standard for *am not,* and a small number of educated speakers still prefer it to *amn't* or *aren't* in questions [I'm right, *ain't* I?] See also AMN'T, AN'T

Ain·tab (īn täb′) *former name for* GAZIANTEP

Ai·nu (ī′no͞o′) ***n.*** ⟦Ainu, lit., human being (as opposed to a god)⟧ **1** *pl.* **-nus′** or **-nu′** a member of an indigenous people of Japan, now living mainly on Hokkaido and also on Sakhalin Island **2** the language of this people —***adj.*** of the Ainus or their language or culture

ai·o·li or **aï·o·li** (ī ō′lē, ā ō′-) ***n.*** ⟦Fr *ailloli, aïoli* < Prov *aioli* < *ai,* garlic (< L *allium*) + *oli,* oil < L *oleum*⟧ a mayonnaise-type sauce with a base of crushed raw garlic

air (er, ar) ***n.*** ⟦ME < OFr < L *aer* < Gr *aēr,* air, mist⟧ **1** the elastic, invisible mixture of gases (chiefly nitrogen and oxygen, as well as hydrogen, carbon dioxide, argon, neon, helium, etc.) that surrounds the earth; atmosphere **2** space above the earth; sky **3** *a)* a movement of air; breeze; wind *b)* cool, refreshing air; fresh air **4** COMPRESSED AIR **5** an outward appearance; general impression or feeling given by something [an *air* of luxury fills the room] **6** a pervading or surrounding influence or condition; general mood or social environment [controversy troubling the *air* at the convention; an apology designed to clear the *air*] **7** a person's bearing, manner, or appearance **8** [*pl.*] affected, superior manners and graces **9** public expression or publicity [give *air* to your opinions] **10** transportation or travel by aircraft [to go by *air*] **11** the medium through which radio signals are transmitted **12** AIR CONDITIONING **13** *Music a)* a song or tune *b)* the main melody in a harmonized composition, usually the soprano or treble part —***adj.*** of or by aircraft, air forces, etc. [*air* power, *air* safety] —***vt.*** **1** to let air into or through; put where air can dry, cool, freshen, etc. **2** to make known publicly; publicize **3** to broadcast on radio or television —***vi.*** **1** to become aired, dried, cooled, etc. **2** to be broadcast on radio or television —***SYN.*** MELODY, POSE[1] —☆**give (or get) the air** [Slang] to reject (or be rejected) as a lover —**in the air** **1** current or prevalent **2** not decided; not settled; still imaginary —**on (or off) the air** *Radio, TV* that is (or is not) broadcasting or being broadcast —**take the air** to go outdoors, as for fresh air —**up in the air** **1** not settled; not decided **2** [Informal] angry; highly excited, agitated, etc. —**walk (or float) on air** to feel very happy, lively, or exalted

A·ïr (ä′ir′, ə ir′) mountainous region of the S Sahara, in NC Niger: *c.* 30,000 sq mi (77,700 sq km)

air alert 1 a state of readiness by air force units, in which aircraft are put into the air for immediate response to orders 2 the signal for getting into such an alert 3 an alerting, as of civilians, against an air attack

☆**air bag** a bag of nylon, plastic, etc. in a passenger restraint system that inflates instantly within an automobile at the impact of a collision, to protect riders from being thrown forward or to the side: often written **air′bag′**

air ball *Basketball* a shot that misses the basket, basket rim, and backboard

air base an air force establishment for the operation, maintenance, and supply of aircraft and air organizations

air bladder a sac with air or gas in it, found in most fishes and in other animals and some plants: also **air cell**

air·boat (er′bōt′) ***n.*** ☆a light, flat-bottomed boat driven by a propeller revolving in the air

air·borne (-bôrn′) ***adj.*** 1 carried by or through the air [*airborne* bacteria, *airborne* troops] 2 supported only by aerodynamic forces; aloft or flying

☆**air brake** 1 a brake operated by the action of compressed air on a piston 2 popularly, SPEED BRAKE

☆**air·bra·sive** (er′brās′iv) ***n.*** a method of removing deposits from the teeth, or rarely, of preparing teeth for filling, by wearing down the surface with an abrasive substance blown by a jet of air

☆**air·brush** (-brush′) ***n.*** a kind of atomizer operated by compressed air and used for spraying on paint or other liquid: also **air brush** —***vt.*** to paint or modify with or as with an airbrush, esp. in order to hide flaws or improve the appearance of a photograph, film, etc.

air·burst (-burst′) ***n.*** an explosion of a bomb, artillery shell, etc. in the air

air·bus (er′bus′) ***n.*** ⟦AIR(PLANE) + BUS⟧ an airplane designed for mass transportation of passengers; esp., an extremely large, short-range airplane of this kind

air chamber a cavity or compartment full of air, esp. one used in hydraulics to equalize the flow of a fluid

☆**air·check** (er′chek′) ***n.*** a recording, esp. of music, made from a radio broadcast

air cock a small tap or valve for controlling the entrance or escape of air from a pipe, chamber, etc.

☆**air command** 1 a major organizational unit in an air force 2 *U.S. Air Force* the largest unit, usually composed of two or more air forces

☆**air-con·di·tion** (er′kən dish′ən) ***vt.*** to provide with air conditioning —**air′-con·di′tioned *adj.***

☆**air conditioner** a device for air conditioning

☆**air conditioning** a method of filtering air and keeping its humidity and temperature at desired levels, as in buildings and vehicles, esp. so as to cool the air and lower its humidity in warm weather

air controller a military person assigned to monitor, manage, etc. aircraft within a specified region

air-cool (er′ko͞ol′) ***vt.*** to cool by passing air over, into, or through

air-cooled (er′ko͞old′) ***adj.*** 1 cooled by having air passed over, into, or through it [an *air-cooled* engine] 2 air-conditioned

air corridor an air route for aircraft, esp. one established by international agreement

air cover 1 protection given by aircraft to land, sea, or air forces 2 the aircraft giving such protection

air·craft (er′kraft′) ***n.***, *pl.* **-craft′** any structure or machine designed to travel through the air, whether heavier or lighter than air; airplane, airship, balloon, helicopter, etc.

aircraft carrier a warship that carries airplanes, serves as their base and servicing station, and has a large, flat deck for taking off and landing

air·crew (er′kro͞o′) ***n.*** the crew of an aircraft in flight; flight crew

air curtain (*or* door) a downward draft of air at an open doorway for maintaining even temperatures within a building

air cushion 1 a cushion inflated with air 2 *Mech.* a device for lessening shock by means of the elasticity of compressed air

air-cush·ion vehicle (er′ko͝osh′ən) a vehicle that travels just above the surface of land or water on a cushion of air provided by a downward jet from its engines, propellers, etc.

air cylinder an air-filled cylinder, esp. one fitted with a piston for absorbing the recoil of a gun

air·date (er′dāt′) ***n.*** the date scheduled for a radio or television broadcast

☆**air division** *U.S. Air Force* an organizational unit smaller than an air force, usually composed of a headquarters and two or more wings

☆**air·drome** (er′drōm′) ***n.*** ⟦AIR + -DROME⟧ 1 the physical facilities of an air base, excluding personnel 2 an airport; aerodrome

air·drop (-dräp′) ***n.*** the dropping of troops or supplies, as by parachute into a combat area, from an aircraft in flight —***vt.*** **-dropped′**, **-drop′ping** to drop (troops or supplies), as by parachute, from an aircraft

air-dry (er′drī′) ***vt.*** **-dried′**, **-dry′ing** to dry by exposing to the air —***adj.*** so dry as to give off no further moisture upon exposure to the air

Aire·dale (er′dāl′) ***n.*** ⟦after *Airedale*, valley of the River *Aire* in England⟧ any of a breed of large terrier having a dense, wiry, tan coat with black markings

air·fare (er′fer′) ***n.*** the fare for transportation on a commercial airplane

air·field (er′fēld′) ***n.*** a field where aircraft can take off and land; specif., the landing field of an airport, usually a military field

air·flow (-flō′) ***n.*** a flow of air; specif., the flow of air around a moving automobile, aircraft, etc. —***adj.*** 1 allowing free flow of air 2 streamlined

☆**air·foil** (-foil′) ***n.*** 1 a part with a flat or curved surface, as a wing, rudder, etc., specifically designed to keep an aircraft up or control its movements by reacting to the air through which it moves 2 a similar winglike surface designed to improve stability for high-speed cars and boats; spoiler

air force 1 the aviation branch of the armed forces of a country 2 *a)* an organizational unit of an aviation force *b)* in the U.S. Air Force, a unit lower than an air command, usually made up of several air divisions

☆**Air Force Cross** a U.S. Air Force decoration awarded for extraordinary heroism in action

☆**Air Force One** the aircraft in which the President of the U.S. is flying; esp., the full-sized, specially equipped jet airplane normally used

air·frame (-frām′) ***n.*** the structural framework and covering of an airplane, rocket, etc., not including the engine and its related parts

air·freight (er′frāt′) ***n.*** 1 a method or service for transporting cargo by air 2 the cost for such transportation 3 the cargo transported —***vt.*** to transport as or send by airfreight

air gas dry air charged with vapor from petroleum or some other hydrocarbon, used for lighting or heating

air·glow (-glō′) ***n.*** the steady, faint glow, usually seen in the night sky, caused by molecules and atoms in the upper atmosphere that slowly release photochemical energy: visible only over middle and low latitudes

air guitar an imaginary guitar, usually, specif., an electric guitar, that a person pretends to play by imitating and, often, exaggerating the gestures and movements made by actual guitarists, typically rock guitarists

air gun 1 a gun operated by means of compressed air 2 a gunlike device used for spraying paint, insecticide, etc. by means of compressed air

air·head[1] (-hed′) ***n.*** ⟦AIR + (BEACH)HEAD⟧ an area seized in warfare, esp. by an airborne assault, and held to ensure the continuous bringing in of troops and materiel by air

☆**air·head**[2] (-hed′) ***n.*** [Slang] a frivolous, silly, and ignorant person

air hole 1 a hole that permits passage of air 2 an unfrozen or open place in ice covering a body of water 3 AIR POCKET

air·i·ly (er′ə lē) ***adv.*** in an airy, or lighthearted, manner; jauntily; breezily

air·i·ness (-ē nis) ***n.*** 1 the quality or state of being airy, or full of fresh air 2 lightheartedness; jauntiness

air·ing (-iŋ) ***n.*** 1 exposure to the air for drying, freshening, etc. 2 exposure to public knowledge [to give a scandal an *airing*] 3 a walk or ride outdoors

air jacket a compartment filled with air, surrounding some part of a machine, esp. for checking heat transmission

air kiss the act or an instance of simulating a kiss, as when two people nearly touch their cheeks together while puckering up or smacking their lips into the air: often seen as insincere, pretentious, etc. —**air′-kiss′ *vt.*, *vi.* -kissed′**, **-kiss′ing**

air lane a route for travel by air; airway

air·less (-lis) ***adj.*** 1 without air or without fresh air 2 without wind or breeze

air letter 1 an airmail letter 2 AEROGRAMME

air·lift (-lift′) ***n.*** a system of transporting troops, supplies, etc. by aircraft, as when ground routes are blocked —***vt.*** to transport by airlift

☆**air·line** (-līn′) ***n.*** 1 the shortest distance between two points on the earth's surface; great-circle route between two places; beeline: also **air line** 2 a system or company for moving freight and passengers by aircraft 3 a route for travel by air —***adj.*** of or on an airline [*airline* personnel]

air·lin·er (-līn′ər) ***n.*** a large airline-operated aircraft for carrying passengers or freight

air lock 1 an airtight compartment, with adjustable air pressure, between places that do not have the same air pressure, as between the working compartment of a caisson and the outside 2 a blockage, as in a water pipe, caused by trapped air

air·mail (-māl′) ***n.*** 1 mail transported by air; esp., in the U.S., mail going overseas by air 2 a system for transporting mail by air [send it by *airmail*] Also **air mail** —***adj.*** of or used for mail sent by air [an *airmail* stamp] —***vt.*** to send (mail) by air —***adv.*** by airmail [send the letter *airmail*]

air·man (-mən) ***n.***, *pl.* **-men** (-mən) 1 an aviator 2 *U.S. Air Force* an enlisted person of one of the lowest ranks, below sergeant 3 *U.S. Navy* an enlisted person ranking below a petty officer third class, whose general duties are concerned with aircraft

airman first class *U.S. Air Force* an enlisted person ranking above an airman and below a sergeant

air mass *Meteorol.* a huge, uniform body of air having the properties of its place of origin: see POLAR CONTINENTAL, POLAR MARITIME, TROPICAL CONTINENTAL, TROPICAL MARITIME

air mattress an inflatable mattress or pad, as of plastic or rubber, used for camping, as an extra bed, etc.

☆**Air Medal** a U.S. military decoration awarded for meritorious achievement during participation in aerial operations

air mile NAUTICAL MILE

air-mind·ed (er′mīn′did) ***adj.*** interested in or promoting aviation, aircraft, air power, etc.

☆**air·mo·bile** (er′mō′bəl) ***adj.*** *Mil.* designating ground troops that are moved about by aircraft for engaging in ground combat

air piracy the hijacking of an aircraft; skyjacking —**air pirate**

air·plane (er′plān′) ***n.*** ⟦altered, infl. by AIR, from earlier AEROPLANE⟧ a fixed-wing aircraft, heavier than air, that is kept aloft by the aerodynamic forces of air as it is driven forward by a screw propeller or by other means, as jet propulsion

airplane cloth 1 a strong, plain-weave cloth of linen or cotton, originally used for airplane wings 2 a similar cotton cloth used for shirts, etc.

☆**air plant** an epiphyte
☆**air·play** (er′plā′) ***n.*** the playing of a recording over radio or TV
air pocket a downdraft or, sometimes, an updraft that can cause an aircraft to change altitude suddenly
air police members of an air force assigned to carry on police duties
air·port (-pôrt′) ***n.*** a place where aircraft can land and take off, usually equipped with hangars, facilities for refueling and repair, accommodations for passengers, etc.
air power a nation's total capacity for carrying on warfare from the air
air pressure the pressure of atmospheric or compressed air
air·proof (-proof′) ***adj.*** not penetrable by air —***vt.*** to make airproof
air pump a machine for removing or compressing air or for forcing it through something
air raid an attack by aircraft, esp. bombers, against a surface target, as a city
☆**air rifle** a rifle operated by compressed air, that shoots BB's, etc.
air rights rights to the airspace above a building or lot, regarded as the real property of the one who owns the building or lot
air sac any of the air-filled cavities in a bird's body, having connections to the lungs
air·scape (-skāp′) ***n.*** ⟦AIR + -SCAPE⟧ a view of the earth from a high position, as from an aircraft
air scoop a device on an aircraft, for taking in air during flight, as to supply a carburetor, for ventilation, etc.
air·screw (-skroo′) ***n.*** [Brit.] an airplane propeller
air shaft **1** a passage through which fresh air can enter a tunnel, mine, etc. **2** AIR WELL
air·shed (-shed′) ***n.*** ⟦AIR + (WATER)SHED⟧ **1** a region sharing a common flow of air, which may become uniformly polluted and stagnant **2** the air of this region
air·ship (-ship′) ***n.*** any self-propelled, LIGHTER-THAN-AIR aircraft that can be steered; dirigible
air·shot (-shät′) ***n.*** AIRCHECK
air·sick (-sik′) ***adj.*** sick or nauseated from traveling in an aircraft —**air′sick′ness** ***n.***
air·space (-spās′) ***n.*** **1** space for maneuvering an aircraft flying in formation **2** the space extending upward above an area of the earth's surface; specif., the space above a nation over which it can claim jurisdiction **3** the space above private land needed for its quiet enjoyment
air·speed (-spēd′) ***n.*** the speed of an aircraft relative to the air through which it moves rather than to the ground: airspeed equals groundspeed if in still air
air-sprayed (-sprād′) ***adj.*** sprayed by means of compressed air
air spring AIR CUSHION (sense 2)
air·stream (-strēm′) ***n.*** a stream of air; esp., the relative stream of air existing around an aircraft in flight or passing through its jets
air·strike (-strīk′) ***n.*** an attack made by aircraft
air·strip (-strip′) ***n.*** a hard-surfaced area, as at an airhead, adapted for use as a temporary airplane runway
☆**air taxi** a small or medium-sized commercial airplane that carries passengers, and often mail, to places not regularly served by scheduled airlines
air·tight (er′tīt′) ***adj.*** **1** too tight for air or gas to enter or escape **2** having no flaws or weaknesses [an *airtight* alibi] **3** giving no opening for attack; invulnerable [an *airtight* defense]
air·time (er′tīm′) ***n.*** ⟦see AIRDATE⟧ **1** *Radio, TV* the period of time during which a program, part of a program, commercial, etc. may be broadcast: also **air time** **2** the time during which a cell phone is being used: a fee is often charged for this
air-to-air (er′too er′) ***adj.*** launched from an aircraft and directed at a target in the air [*air-to-air* missiles]
air-to-sur·face (-sur′fis) ***adj.*** launched from an aircraft and directed at a land target [*air-to-surface* weapons]: also **air′-to-ground′**
air traffic control a coordinated system designed to manage air traffic safely around airports, along flight routes, etc. —**air′-traf′fic controller**
air valve a valve by which the entrance or escape of air can be regulated
air vesicle *Bot.* a space filled with air, found in many floating water plants
air·waves (er′wāvz′) ***pl.n.*** the medium through which radio signals are transmitted
air·way (-wā′) ***n.*** **1** AIR SHAFT (sense 1) **2** a specific route for air traffic, provided with navigational aids; air lane **3** [*pl.*] airwaves **4** *Med.* *a)* a respiratory passageway *b)* a device used to bring air to the lungs during anesthesia
☆**air well** an open shaft passing through the floors of a building for ventilation
air·wor·thy (-wur′thē) ***adj.*** fit and safe for flying: said of aircraft —**air′wor′thi·ness** ***n.***
air·y (er′ē) ***adj.*** **air′i·er, air′i·est** **1** in the air; high up **2** of air **3** open to the air; breezy **4** unsubstantial as air; visionary **5** light as air; delicate; graceful **6** lighthearted; vivacious **7** affectedly nonchalant; grand
air·y-fair·y (-fer′ē) ***adj.*** [Chiefly Brit.] **1** ⟦redupl.⟧ *a)* fairylike; graceful; delicate *b)* affected, mannered, etc. **2** ⟦as used to connote insubstantiality⟧ not realistic; impractical; visionary
A·i·sha (ä′ē shä′) A.D. 614?-678; Muhammad's favorite wife; daughter of Abu-Bakr
aisle (īl) ***n.*** ⟦ME *ile* < OFr *aile,* wing, section of a building (see AILERON); E -*s*- through confusion with ISLE⟧ **1** a part of a church alongside the nave, choir, or transept, set off by a row of columns or piers **2** a passageway between sections of seats in a theater, rows of merchandise in a store, etc. **3** a narrow passageway, as between rows of trees **4** ⟦in ref. to the *aisle* dividing the seats of the two parties in each house of the U.S. Congress⟧ the political divide between Democrats and Republicans: used with *the* —**roll in the aisles** to respond with boisterous hilarity: said as of a theatrical audience —**walk down the aisle** ⟦in ref. to the center *aisle* of a church⟧ to marry; get married —**aisled** ***adj.***
Aisne (en) river in N France, flowing into the Oise: 175 mi (282 km)
aitch (āch) ***n.*** ⟦ME & OFr *ache* < LL **accha,* **aha;* comb. of primary vowel (ä) with consonantal symbols intended to exemplify the former quality of the sound⟧ the letter H —***adj.*** shaped like H
aitch·bone (āch′bōn′) ***n.*** ⟦by faulty separation of ME *a nache bone* < OFr *nache,* buttock < VL **natica,* dim. < L *natis,* buttock⟧ **1** the rump bone **2** a cut of beef around the rump bone
Aix-en-Pro·vence (eks än prô väns′) city in SE France, near Marseille: also called **Aix** (eks)
Aix-la-Cha·pelle (eks lȧ shȧ pel′) *Fr. name for* AACHEN
Ai·yi·na (e′yē nä) *Gr. name for* AEGINA
A·jac·cio (ä yät′chō) seaport & chief city of Corsica, on the W coast; birthplace of Napoleon
a·jar[1] (ə jär′) ***adv., adj.*** ⟦ME *on char, a-char* < OE *cier,* a turn: see CHORE⟧ slightly open [the door stood *ajar*]
a·jar[2] (ə jär′) ***adv., adj.*** ⟦A-[1] + JAR[1]⟧ not in harmony
A·jax (ā′jaks′) ***n.*** ⟦L < Gr *Aias*⟧ *Gr. Myth.* **1** a strong, brave Greek warrior in the Trojan War who kills himself when Achilles' armor is given to Odysseus: called **Ajax Tel·a·mon** (tel′ə män′) **2** one of the swiftest runners among the Greek warriors in the Trojan War: called **Ajax the Less**
Aj·mer (uj mir′) city in NW India
aj·u·ga (aj′oo gə) ***n.*** BUGLE[3]
AK *abbrev.* Alaska
aka (ā′kā′ā′) *abbrev.* also known as: used before an alias, as in police records [George Desmond *aka* George Destry]: also **a.k.a., a k a, AKA**
A·kan (ä′kän′) ***n.*** **1** *pl.* **A′kan′** or **A′kans′** a member of any of a group of peoples living mainly in Ghana and parts of the Ivory Coast, including the Ashanti of Ghana **2** the Kwa language of these peoples —***adj.*** of the Akan or their language or culture
Ak·bar (ak′bär′) 1542-1605; Mogul emperor of Hindustan (1556-1605): called *the Great*
AKC *abbrev.* American Kennel Club
ak·ee (ak′ē, a kē′) ***n.*** *alt. sp. of* ACKEE
a·kene (ā kēn′, ə-) ***n.*** *Bot. alt. sp. of* ACHENE
AK-47 (ā′kā′fôrt′ē sev′ən) ***n.*** ⟦Russ *a(vtomat) K(alašnikova 19)47,* Kalashnikov automatic rifle of 1947: see KALASHNIKOV⟧ an automatic or semiautomatic assault rifle that is gas-operated and clip-fed: cf. KALASHNIKOV
A·kha·ï·a (ä′kä ē′ä; ə kā′ə, -kī′ə) department of modern Greece, corresponding approximately to ancient Achaea
A·khe·na·ten or **A·khe·na·ton** (ä′ke nät′'n) *var. of* IKHNATON
Akh·ma·to·va (uk mät′ə və, äk′mə tō′və), **An·na** (än′ə) (pseud. of *Anna Andreyevna Gorenko*) 1889-1966; Russ. poet
A·ki·hi·to (ä′kē hē′tō) 1933- ; emperor of Japan (1989-)
a·kim·bo (ə kim′bō) ***adv., adj.*** ⟦ME *in kenebowe,* lit., in keen bow, i.e., in a sharp curve; a folk etym. from ON *keng-boginn,* bow-bent < *keng,* bent + *bogi,* a bow⟧ with hands on hips and elbows bent outward [with arms *akimbo*]

arms akimbo

a·kin (ə kin′) ***adj.*** **1** of one kin; related through a common ancestor **2** having similar qualities; similar
A·ki·ta[1] (ə kēt′ə, ä-) ***n.*** ⟦after *Akita* prefecture, Japan, where orig. bred⟧ any of a breed of large, powerful dog with a thick coat, erect ears, and a bushy, curled tail
A·ki·ta[2] (ə kēt′ə, ä-) city in N Honshu, Japan, on the Sea of Japan
Ak·kad (ak′ad′, äk′äd′) **1** ancient region in N Babylonia (fl. *c.* 2300-2100 B.C.) **2** its chief city, for a time the capital of Babylonia
Ak·ka·di·an (ə kā′dē ən, -kä′-) ***adj.*** of ancient Akkad or its people, language, or culture —***n.*** **1** an extinct Semitic language of the Mesopotamian region, constituting the eastern branch of the Semitic language subfamily **2** a person born or living in ancient Akkad
Ak·ko (ä kō′) city in NW Israel, on the Mediterranean
Ak·mo·la (äk′mō lä′, äk mō′lä) *former name for* ASTANA
Ak·ron (ak′rən) ⟦< Gr *akron,* highest point: because of the city's location between two rivers⟧ city in N Ohio
Ak·sum (äk′soom′) town in N Ethiopia: capital of an ancient kingdom that controlled the surrounding region
Ak·tyu·binsk (äk tyoo′binsk) city in W Kazakhstan
ak·va·vit (äk′və vēt′, ak′-) ***n.*** ⟦Dan: see AQUA VITAE⟧ AQUAVIT
Al *Chem. symbol for* aluminum
AL *abbrev.* **1** Alabama **2** American League **3** American Legion
-al (əl, ′l) ⟦Fr *-al, -el* < L *-alis*⟧ *suffix* **1** *forming adjectives* of, like, or suitable for [*peroneal, hysterical, theatrical*] **2** ⟦ME *-aile* < OFr *-alle* < L *-alia,* neut. pl. of *-alis*⟧ *forming nouns* the act or process of ___ing [*rehearsal, reversal*] **3** ⟦< AL(DEHYDE)⟧ *Chem. forming nouns* *a)* an aldehyde [*furfural*] *b)* a barbiturate [*barbital*]

al-[1] (al) ⟦< Ar *al*⟧ *prefix* the: used in words of Arabic origin [*algebra, alchemy, al*-Mansur]
al-[2] (al, əl) *prefix* AD-: used before *l*
a·la (ā′lə) ***n.***, *pl.* **a′lae′** (-lē′) ⟦L, a wing: see AILERON⟧ **1** *Zool.* a wing **2** a winglike structure, as a lobe of the ear or a side petal of a butterfly-shaped corolla
Ala *abbrev.* Alabama
ALA *abbrev.* American Library Association
à la or **a la** (ä′lə, -lä; al′ə) ⟦Fr *à la* < *à la mode*, in the manner⟧ in the manner or style of [a performance *à la* Charlie Chaplin]
Al·a·bam·a (al′ə bam′ə) ⟦< Fr *Alibamon* < name of a people speaking a Muskogean language⟧ **1** Southern state of the SE U.S., on the Gulf of Mexico: admitted 1819: 50,744 sq mi (131,426 sq km); cap. Montgomery: abbrev. *AL* or *Ala* **2** river flowing through central and SW Ala., joining the Tombigbee to form the Mobile river: 315 mi (607 km)
Al·a·bam·i·an (-ē ən) *adj.* of Alabama: usually used in the predicate —*n.* a person born or living in Alabama Also **Al′a·bam′an**
al·a·bas·ter (al′ə bas′tər) ***n.*** ⟦ME < OFr *alabastre* < L *alabaster* < Gr *alabastros*, earlier *alabastos*, vase for perfumes (often made of alabaster), prob. < Egypt *'*a-labaste*, vessel of (the goddess) Bast⟧ **1** a translucent, whitish, fine-grained variety of gypsum, used for statues, vases, etc. **2** a variety of calcite found esp. in stalactites and stalagmites: it is sometimes streaked or mottled like marble —*adj.* of or like alabaster; esp., smooth and white: also **al′a·bas′trine** (-trin)
a la carte (ä′lə kärt′, al′ə-) ⟦Fr *à la carte*, lit., by the bill of fare⟧ with a separate price for each item on the menu: distinguished from TABLE D'HÔTE
a·lack (ə lak′) ***interj.*** ⟦A(H) + LACK⟧ [Archaic] used to express regret, surprise, dismay, etc.
a·lack·a·day (ə lak′ə dā′) ***interj.*** ⟦for earlier *alack the day*, woe to the day⟧ [Archaic] ALACK
a·lac·ri·ty (ə lak′rə tē) ***n.*** ⟦ME & OFr *alacrite* < L *alacritas*, liveliness < *alacer*, lively⟧ eager willingness or readiness, often manifested by quick, lively action —**a·lac′ri·tous** ***adj.***
A·la Dag or **A·la·dagh** (ä′lä dä′, -däk′) mountain of the Taurus range, S Turkey: *c.* 12,000 ft (3,658 m)
A·lad·din (ə lad′'n) ***n.*** ⟦Ar *A'l-ad-dīn*, lit., height of faith < *a'lā*, height + *al*, the + *dīn*, faith⟧ a boy in *The Arabian Nights* who finds a magic lamp and a magic ring, with which he can call up a jinni to do his bidding
à la fran·çaise (à lä frän sez′) ⟦Fr⟧ in the French manner
A·la·gez (u′lə gyôs′) ARAGATS
A·la·go·as (ä lə gō′əs) state of NE Brazil, on the Atlantic: 10,785 sq mi (27,933 sq km); cap. Maceió
à la grecque (ä′lə grek′; *Fr* à lȧ grek′) ⟦Fr⟧ in the Greek manner; specif., cooked in wine, olive oil, lemon juice, herbs, and spices, and usually served cold
A·lai Mountains (ä lī′) mountain range in S Kyrgyzstan: highest peak, *c.* 19,500 ft (5,944 m)
☆**à la king** (ä′lə kiŋ′) ⟦lit., in kingly style⟧ diced and served in a cream sauce containing mushrooms, pimentos, and green peppers
al·a·me·da (al′ə mē′də, -mā′-) ***n.*** ⟦Sp < *álamo*, poplar tree⟧ in the Southwest, a walk shaded as by alamos
Al·a·mine (al′ə mēn′) ⟦AL(UMINUM) + AMINE⟧ *trademark for* a straight-chain or branched-chain fatty amine of high molecular weight, or a mixture of such amines: these amines are used as corrosion inhibitors, emulsifiers, etc.
☆**al·a·mo** (al′ə mō′) ***n.***, *pl.* **-mos′** ⟦Sp *álamo*, poplar tree⟧ [Southwest] a poplar tree; esp., a cottonwood
Al·a·mo (al′ə mō′) ⟦Sp: see prec. ⟧ Franciscan mission at San Antonio, Tex.: scene of a siege and massacre of Texans by Mexican troops (1836)
a la mode (al′ə mōd′, ä′lə-) ***adv., adj.*** ⟦Fr *à la mode*⟧ **1** in fashion; stylish ☆**2** served with ice cream [pie *a la mode*] Also **à la mode** or **a′la·mode′**
A·la·mo·gor·do (al′ə mə gôr′dō) ⟦Sp < *álamo* (see ALAMO) + *gordo*, big⟧ city in S N.Mex.: site of testing range where first atomic bomb was exploded (July, 1945)
Al·an (al′ən) ***n.*** ⟦ML *Alanus*, of Bret orig.⟧ a masculine name: dim. *Al*; var. *Allan, Allen*
Å·land (ō′länd′, -lənd; ä′-) *Swed. name for* AHVENANMAA
à l'an·glaise (à län glez′) ⟦Fr⟧ in the English manner
al·a·nine (al′ə nēn′) ***n.*** ⟦Ger *alanin* < *al(dehyd)*, ALDEHYDE + *-an-* (arbitrary insert) + *-in*, -INE[3]⟧ a naturally occurring nonessential amino acid, $CH_3CH(NH_2)COOH$: it is a colorless crystal, soluble in water, and is used in biochemical research: see AMINO ACID
a la plan·cha (ä′ lə plän′chə) ⟦Sp, lit., on the plate⟧ (grilled) on a metal plate, esp. in Spanish cooking
a·lar (ā′lər) ***adj.*** ⟦L *alaris* < *ala*, a wing: see AILERON⟧ **1** of or like a wing **2** having wings
A·lar·cón (ä′lär kōn′), **Pe·dro An·to·nio de** (pe′thrô än tô′nyô de) 1833-91; Sp. writer
Al·a·ric (al′ə rik) **1** A.D. 370-410; king of the Visigoths (395?-410): captured Rome (410) **2 Alaric II** died A.D. 507; king of the Visigoths (484?-507): issued a code of laws
a·larm (ə lärm′) ***n.*** ⟦ME *alarme* < OFr < It *all'arme*, to arms⟧ **1** [Archaic] a sudden call to arms **2** a signal, sound, cry, etc. that is a warning of danger **3** a mechanism designed to warn of danger or trespassing [a burglar *alarm*] **4** the bell, buzzer, etc. of an alarm clock **5** fear caused by a sudden awareness of danger —***vt.*** **1** to warn of approaching danger **2** to make suddenly afraid or anxious; frighten —***SYN.*** FEAR, FRIGHTEN
alarm clock a clock that can be set to ring, buzz, or flash a light at any particular time, as to awaken a person
a·larm·ing (-iŋ) ***adj.*** that alarms, or makes suddenly afraid or anxious; frightening —**a·larm′ing·ly** ***adv.***
a·larm·ist (-ist) ***n.*** a person who habitually spreads alarming rumors, exaggerated reports of danger, etc. —***adj.*** of or like an alarmist —**a·larm′ism′** ***n.***
a·lar·um (ə ler′əm, -lär′-) ***n.*** [Archaic] ALARM (esp. sense 1) —**alarums and excursions** **1** [Archaic] a stage direction, esp. in Elizabethan drama, for a scene depicting a battle: see EXCURSION (*n.* 1) **2** any noisy, confused situation
a·la·ry (ā′lə rē, al′ə rē) ***adj.*** ⟦L *alarius* < *ala*, a wing: see AILERON⟧ of or shaped like a wing; alar
a·las (ə las′) ***interj.*** ⟦ME < OFr *a las, helas* < *a-, he-*, AH + *las*, wretched < L *lassus*, weary⟧ used to express sorrow, pity, regret, or worry
Alas *abbrev.* Alaska
A·las·ka (ə las′kə) ⟦prob. via Russ *Aliaska* < Aleut *Alaxsxax̂*, name of the Alaska Peninsula⟧ **1** state of the U.S. in NW North America, separated from Asia by the Bering Strait: land bought from Russia in 1867: admitted 1959: 571,951 sq mi (1,481,348 sq km); cap. Juneau: abbrev. *AK* or *Alas* **2 Gulf of** inlet of the Pacific in the S coast of Alaska between the Alaska Peninsula and the Alexander Archipelago
Alaska Highway highway between Dawson Creek, British Columbia, & Fairbanks, Alas.: 1,523 mi (2,451 km)
A·las·kan (ə las′kən) ***adj.*** of Alaska —***n.*** a person born or living in Alaska
☆**Alaskan malamute** any of a breed of large, strong dog with a thick coat of gray or black-and-white and a bushy tail: it was developed as a sled dog by the Alaskan Eskimos
Alaska Peninsula peninsula extending southwestward from the mainland of Alas.
Alaska Range mountain range in SC Alas.: highest peak, Denali
☆**Alaska Standard Time** a standard time used in the zone which includes all of Alas. except the W Aleutian Islands, corresponding to the mean solar time of the 135th meridian west of Greenwich, England: it is nine hours behind Greenwich time
a·late (ā′lāt′) ***adj.*** ⟦L *alatus* < *ala*, a wing: see AILERON⟧ having wings or winglike attachments: also **a′lat′ed** —***n.*** the winged form of insect species, as ants or termites, having both winged and wingless forms
alb (alb) ***n.*** ⟦ME *albe* (< OE *albe* < ML *alba*), *aube* < OFr *aube* < ML *alba* (vestis), white (cloak), fem. of L *albus*, white: see ELF⟧ a loose, sleeved, full-length, gownlike white linen vestment secured at the waist by a cincture and worn with other vestments as by the celebrant of Mass

alb

Alb *abbrev.* **1** Albania **2** Albanian
al·ba (äl′bə) ***n.*** ⟦Prov, dawn < ML < L *albus*, white⟧ the stylized dawn love song of Provençal troubadour literature: cf. AUBADE
Al·ba (äl′bä), Duke of *var. of* Duke of ALVA
Al·ba·ce·te (äl′bä sā′tā) city in Murcia, SE Spain
al·ba·core (al′bə kôr′) ***n.***, *pl.* **-cores′** or **-core′** ⟦Port *albacora* < Ar *al*, the + *bakāra*, pl. of *buko*, young camel⟧ a tuna (*Thunnus alalunga*) with unusually long pectoral fins, important as a game and food fish in all warm seas; loosely, other similar scombroid fishes
Al·ba Lon·ga (al′bə lôŋ′gə) city in ancient Latium, near where Rome is today: legendary birthplace of Romulus and Remus
Al·ban[1] (al′bən, ôl′-) ***n.*** ⟦L *Albanus*, after *Alba*, name of several Italian cities⟧ a masculine name
Al·ban[2] (al′bən, ôl′-), Saint (died A.D. 304?); Brit. martyr: his day is June 22
Al·ba·ni·a (al bā′nē ə, -bān′yə) country in the W Balkan Peninsula, on the Adriatic: 11,100 sq mi (28,748 sq km); cap. Tirana
Al·ba·ni·an (-bā′nē ən, -bān′yən) ***adj.*** of Albania or its people, language, or culture —***n.*** **1** a person born or living in Albania **2** the language spoken in Albania, constituting a branch of the Indo-European family of languages
Al·ba·ny (ôl′bə nē) ⟦after the Duke of York and *Albany*, later JAMES II⟧ capital of N.Y., on the Hudson
al·ba·tross (al′bə trôs′, -träs′) ***n.***, *pl.* **-tross′es** or **-tross′** ⟦altered, prob. infl. by L *albus*, white < Sp *alcatraz*, lit., pelican < Port, pelican, orig., bucket < Ar *al qādūs*, waterwheel basket, scoop < Gr *kados*, cask, jar; prob. < Heb *kad*, water jug: so named from the former belief that the birds carried water in their beaks⟧ **1** any of a family (Diomedeidae) of large, web-footed tubenose birds found chiefly in the South Seas: they have long, narrow wings and a long, hooked beak **2** ⟦from use of the bird as a symbol of guilt in "The Rime of the Ancient Mariner," poem (1798) by COLERIDGE⟧ a burden or source of distress, esp. one that impairs effective action: often in the phrase **an albatross around one's neck**

Laysan albatross

al·be·do (al bē′dō) ***n.***, *pl.* **-dos** or **-does** ⟦LL(Ec), whiteness < L *albus*, white: see ELF⟧ **1** *Astron.* the reflecting power of a planet, satellite, or asteroid, expressed as a ratio of reflected light to the total amount falling on the surface **2** *Physics* the degree to which a surface reflects subnuclear particles, esp. neutrons, that strike it: expressed as the ratio of the number of particles that leave the surface in any direction to the number that strike it

al·be·it (ôl bē′it) *conj.* ⟦ME *al be it,* al(though) it be⟧ although; even though

Al·be·marle Sound (al′bə märl′) ⟦after William Keppel, 2d Earl of *Albemarle,* gov. of colony of Virginia (1737-54)⟧ arm of the Atlantic extending into NE N.C.: *c.* 60 mi (97 km) long

Al·bé·niz (äl bā′nēs, -nēth), **I·sa·ac (Manuel Francisco)** (ē′sä äk′) 1860-1909; Sp. composer & pianist

Al·ber·ich (äl′ber iH) *n.* ⟦Ger < MHG *alb,* ELF + *rich* (OHG *rihhi*), leader, king, realm⟧ *Gmc. Legend* the king of the dwarfs and leader of the Nibelungs

Al·bers (al′bərz, äl′bərs), **Jo·sef** (yō′zef′) 1888-1976; U.S. painter, born in Germany

Al·bert[1] (al′bərt) *n.* ⟦Fr < OHG *Adalbrecht,* lit., bright through nobility < *adal,* nobility + *beraht,* bright⟧ a masculine name: dim. *Al, Bert*; var. *Adelbert, Elbert*; fem. *Alberta, Albertine*

Al·bert[2] (al′bərt) **1** Prince (*Albert of Saxe-Coburg-Gotha*) 1819-61; husband (Prince Consort) of Queen Victoria of England (1840-61) **2 Albert I** 1875-1934; king of Belgium (1909-34)

Al·bert[3] (al′bərt), **Lake** lake in EC Africa, on the border of the Democratic Republic of the Congo & Uganda: 2,064 sq mi (5,346 sq km)

Al·ber·ta[1] (al bʉrt′ə) *n.* ⟦fem. of ALBERT[1]⟧ a feminine name: var. *Albertine*

Al·ber·ta[2] (al bʉrt′ə) ⟦after Princess Louise Caroline *Alberta*: see LOUISE[2]⟧ province of SW Canada: 247,123 sq mi (640,045 sq km); cap. Edmonton: abbrev. *AB* or *Alta* —**Al·ber′tan** *adj., n.*

Alberta clipper ⟦< prec. + CLIPPER (sense 3*a*)⟧ a severe storm, often with snowfall, originating in W Canada and typically moving east and southeast across the U.S. Midwest

Albert Canal ship canal in Belgium, from Liège to Antwerp: 81 mi (131 km)

Al·ber·ti (äl ber′tē), **Le·on Bat·tis·ta** (le ôn′ bät tēs′tä) 1404-72; It. architect & painter

al·bert·ite (al′bər tīt′) *n.* ⟦after *Albert* county, New Brunswick, where found⟧ a shiny, brittle, usually black variety of asphalt that burns easily with a bright, smoky flame

Albert Memorial monument to Prince Albert of England in Kensington Gardens, London: 175 ft (53 m) high

Albert Ny·an·za (nī an′zə, nē-) Lake ALBERT[3]

Al·ber·tus Mag·nus (al bʉrt′əs mag′nəs), Saint (*Count von Bollstädt*) 1200?-80; Ger. scholastic philosopher: teacher of Thomas Aquinas

al·bes·cent (al bes′ənt) *adj.* ⟦L *albescens,* prp. of *albescere,* to become white < *albus,* white: see ELF⟧ turning white —**al·bes′cence** (-əns) *n.*

Al·bi·gen·ses (al′bə jen′sēz′) *pl.n.* ⟦ML, after *Albi,* town in S France⟧ a religious sect that flourished in the south of France *c.* A.D. 1020-1250 and was finally suppressed for heresy —**Al′bi·gen′si·an** (-sē ən) *adj., n.*

al·bi·nism (al′bə niz′əm) *n.* the condition of being an albino —**al·bin·ic** (al bin′ik) *adj.*

al·bi·no (al bī′nō, -bē′-) *n., pl.* **-nos** ⟦Port, lit., whitish < *albo* < L *albus,* white: see ELF⟧ **1** a person whose skin, hair, and eyes lack normal coloration because of genetic factors: albinos have a white skin, whitish hair, and pink eyes **2** any animal or plant abnormally lacking in color —*adj.* designating or of such a person, animal, or plant [*an albino monkey*]

Al·bi·on (al′bē ən) ⟦L < Celt **Albio,* gen. **Albionus* (> Ir *Alba,* gen. *Albann,* name for Scotland); understood as if < L *albus,* white (see ELF) because the cliffs of S England are white, but thought by some scholars to be of non-IE orig. (see ALPS)⟧ *old poet. name for* ENGLAND

al·bite (al′bīt′) *n.* ⟦< L *albus,* white + -ITE[1]⟧ a usually milky white variety of plagioclase, $NaAlSi_3O_8$, found in various plutonic rocks, esp. granite and syenite, often with twin crystals

Al·bo·in (al′boin′, -bō in′) died A.D. 572; king of the Lombards (565?-572): conqueror of N Italy

Ål·borg (ôl′bôr′) seaport in N Jutland, Denmark

Al·bu·ca·sis (al′byoo kā′sis) *Latin name for* ABU AL-QĀSIM

al·bu·gin·e·ous (al′byo͞o jin′ē əs) *adj.* ⟦ML *albugineus* < L *albugo,* white spot < *albus,* white: see ELF⟧ of or resembling a tough white layer of fibrous bodily tissue, as the white of the eye

al·bum (al′bəm) *n.* ⟦L, neut. of *albus,* white: see ELF⟧ **1** a bound or loose-leaf book with blank pages for mounting pictures, stamps, etc., or for collecting autographs **2** *a)* a booklike holder for phonograph records played at 78 revolutions per minute *b)* a set of records in such a holder **3** one or more LPs, compact discs, tape recordings, etc. packaged in a holder and containing a group of related works or a single long work, as of music or drama **4** an anthology, picture book, or the like

al·bu·men (al byo͞o′mən) *n.* ⟦L < *albus,* white: see ELF⟧ **1** the white of an egg **2** the nutritive protein substance in seeds and around the egg yolk of higher animals **3** ALBUMIN

al·bu·men·ize (-īz′) *vt.* **-ized′, -iz′ing** to cover or treat with albumen or an albuminous solution

al·bu·min (al byo͞o′min) *n.* ⟦ALBUM(EN) + -IN[1]⟧ any of a group of water-soluble proteins found in milk, egg, muscle, blood, and in many vegetable tissues and fluids: albumins are coagulated by heat and are hydrolyzed to a number of amino acids: see GLOBULIN

al·bu·mi·nate (al byo͞o′mə nāt′) *n.* a compound of an albumin with an acid or base

al·bu·mi·noid (-noid′) *adj.* resembling albumin —*n.* **1** an albumin-like protein **2** a scleroprotein

al·bu·mi·nous (-nəs) *adj.* of, like, or containing albumin or albumen

al·bu·mi·nu·ri·a (al byo͞o′mə nyoor′ē ə, -noor′-) *n.* the presence of albumin in the urine, which may indicate kidney disease

al·bu·mose (al′byo͞o mōs′) *n.* any of a class of chemical compounds derived from albumins by the action of certain enzymes, as in digestion

Al·bu·quer·que[1] (äl′bo͞o ker′kə), **Af·fon·so de** (ə fōn′so͞o də) 1453-1515; Port. navigator: established Port. colonies in the East

Al·bu·quer·que[2] (al′bə kʉr′kē) ⟦after the Duke of *Alburquerque,* viceroy (1702-11) of New Spain: altered prob. by confusion with prec.⟧ city in central N.Mex.

al·bur·num (al bʉr′nəm) *n.* ⟦L, neut. of *alburnus,* whitish < *albus,* white: see ELF⟧ SAPWOOD

al·bu·ter·ol (al byo͞ot′ər ôl′, -ōl′) *n.* ⟦prob. by alteration & transposition of elements of the chemical name⟧ a white, crystalline powder, $C_{13}H_{21}NO_3$, used as an inhaled bronchodilator in treating bronchospasms caused by asthma, emphysema, etc.: also used in syrup or tablet form (**albuterol sulfate,** $(C_{13}H_{21}NO_3)_2{\cdot}H_2SO_4$)

alc. *abbrev.* alcohol

Al·cae·us (al sē′əs) fl. 600 B.C.; Gr. lyric poet

Al·ca·ic (al kā′ik) *adj.* of Alcaeus or in the form of his verse —*n.* [*usually pl.*] verse by Alcaeus or in his metrical patterns, consisting of four-stanza odes, with four lines to a stanza

al·cai·de or **al·cay·de** (al kī′dē, -kād′; *Sp* äl kä′ē the) *n.* ⟦Sp < Ar *al-qā'id,* the leader < *qāda,* to lead⟧ a commander or governor of a fortress in Spain, Portugal, or their possessions

Al·ca·lá de He·na·res (äl′kä lä′ de e nä′res) city in central Spain, near Madrid

☆**al·cal·de** (al kal′dē; *Sp* äl käl′de) *n.* ⟦Sp < Ar *al qāḍī,* the judge < *qaḍā,* to judge⟧ the mayor of a Spanish or Spanish-American town, with certain judicial powers

Al·can Highway (al′kan′) ⟦AL(ASKA) + CAN(ADA)⟧ ALASKA HIGHWAY

Al·ca·traz (al′kə traz′) ⟦after Sp *Isla de Alcatraces,* Island of Pelicans⟧ small island in San Francisco Bay: site of a federal prison (1934-63)

al·ca·zar (al′kə zär′, al kaz′ər; *Sp* äl kä′thär′) *n.* ⟦Sp *alcázar* < Ar *al qaṣr,* the castle < ? L *castellum*⟧ **1** a palace or fortress of the Moors in Spain **2** [A-] such a palace in Seville, later used by the Spanish kings

Al·ces·tis (al ses′tis) *n.* ⟦L < Gr *Alkēstis*⟧ *Gr. Myth.* the wife of Admetus, king of Thessaly: she offers her life to save that of her husband, but is rescued from Hades by Hercules

al·che·mist (al′kə mist) *n.* a practitioner of alchemy —**al′che·mis′tic** *adj.,* **al′che·mis′ti·cal**

al·che·mize (-mīz′) *vt.* **-mized′, -miz′ing** to transmute by or as by alchemy

al·che·my (al′kə mē) *n.* ⟦ME *alchymie* < OFr *alchimie* < ML *alchemia* < Ar *al-kīmiyā'* < Gr *chēmeia* < ? *Chēmia,* old name for Egypt < Egyptian *kmt,* lit., black (land); infl. by folk-etym. assoc. with Gr *cheein,* to pour: see FOUND[3]⟧ **1** an early form of chemistry, with philosophic and magical associations, studied in the Middle Ages: its chief aims were to change base metals into gold and to discover the elixir of perpetual youth **2** a power or process of changing one thing into another; esp., a seemingly miraculous power or process of changing a thing into something better —**al·chem·ic** (al kem′ik) *adj.,* **al·chem′i·cal** —**al·chem′i·cal·ly** *adv.*

Al·ci·bi·a·des (al′sə bī′ə dēz′) 450-404 B.C.; Athenian politician & general in the Peloponnesian War

Al·ci·des (al sī′dēz′) *n.* ⟦L < Gr *Alkeidēs*⟧ HERCULES

al·ci·dine (al′sə dīn′, -din) *adj.* ⟦ModL *alcidinus* < ON *alka,* AUK⟧ belonging to a family (Alcidae) of diving shorebirds that have a stocky body, short tail and wings, and webbed feet, as the puffins and murres —**al′cid** (-sid) *n.*

Al·cin·o·üs (al sin′ō əs) *n. Gr. Myth.* father of NAUSICAÄ

ALCM *abbrev.* air-launched cruise missile

Alc·me·ne (alk mē′nē) *n.* ⟦L < Gr *Alkmēnē*⟧ *Gr. Myth.* the mother of Hercules by Zeus, who seduces her in the likeness of her husband, Amphitryon

al·co·hol (al′kə hôl′, -häl′) *n.* ⟦ML, term used by PARACELSUS for fine powder, distilled spirit < Ar *alkuḥl,* antimony powder, collyrium < *al,* the + *kuḥl,* KOHL⟧ **1** a colorless, volatile, pungent liquid, C_2H_5OH: it can be burned as fuel (10-15% of gasohol), is used in industry and medicine, and is the intoxicating element of whiskey, wine, beer, and other fermented or distilled liquors: classed as a depressant drug: also called **ethyl alcohol** **2** any intoxicating liquor with this liquid in it **3** the drinking of such liquors [*alcohol was his downfall*] **4** a class of organic compounds, including ethyl or methyl (wood) alcohol, that contain one or more hydroxyl groups (OH) and form esters in reactions with acids

al·co·hol·ic (al′kə hôl′ik, -häl′-) *adj.* **1** of or containing alcohol **2** caused by alcohol or liquor containing it **3** suffering from alcoholism —*n.* a person who has chronic alcoholism or who habitually drinks alcoholic liquor to excess —**al′co·hol′i·cal·ly** *adv.*

☆**Alcoholics Anonymous** *trademark for* an organization of alcoholics and recovering alcoholics who seek, through mutual counseling, to avoid lapses into drinking

al·co·hol·ism (al′kə hôl′iz′əm, -häl′-) *n.* **1** the habitual or compulsive consumption of alcoholic liquor to excess **2** a chronic diseased condition marked by psychological and nutritional disorders, caused by the compulsive consumption of and dependence on alcoholic liquor

al·co·hol·ize (-īz′) *vt.* **-ized′, -iz′ing** **1** to saturate or treat with alcohol **2** to convert into alcohol

al·co·hol·om·e·ter (al′kə hôl′äm′ət ər, -häl′-) *n.* an instrument, usually a hydrometer, for determining the percentage of alcohol in a liquid

Al·co·ran (al′kō rän′, -ran′) ***n.*** ⟦ME & OFr *alcoran* < Ar *al qur'ān*: see KORAN⟧ [Archaic] the Koran

Al·cor·cón (äl′kôr kôn′) city in central Spain, near Madrid

Al·cott (ôl′kət, al′-; -kät′) **1 (Amos) Bron·son** (brän′sən) 1799-1888; U.S. philosopher and educational reformer **2 Louisa May** 1832-88; U.S. novelist: daughter of (Amos) Bronson

al·cove (al′kōv′) ***n.*** ⟦Fr < Sp *alcoba* < Ar *al-qubba* < *al*, the + *qubba*, arch, vault, dome⟧ **1** a recessed section of a room, as a breakfast nook **2** a secluded bower in a garden; summerhouse

Al·cuin (al′kwin) A.D. 735?-804; Eng. theologian & writer: advisor in the court of Charlemagne

Al·cy·o·ne (al sī′ə nē′) ***n.*** ⟦L < Gr *Alkyonē*, daughter of Aeolus⟧ the brightest star in the Pleiades in the constellation Taurus: magnitude, 2.96

Ald or **Aldm** *abbrev.* Alderman

Al·dan (äl dän′) river in EC Russia, flowing north and east into the Lena River: *c.* 1,700 mi (2,736 km)

Al·deb·a·ran (al deb′ə rən) ***n.*** ⟦Ar *al-dabarān* < *al*, the + *dabarān*, following < *dubara*, to follow: so called because it follows the Pleiades⟧ a giant, orange, binary, variable star, the brightest star in the constellation Taurus: magnitude, 0.87

al·de·hyde (al′də hīd′) ***n.*** ⟦< AL(COHOL) + ModL *dehyd(rogenatum)* < L *de*, without + HYD(ROGEN)⟧ any of a class of organic compounds containing the CHO group, including formaldehyde and acetaldehyde —**al′de·hy′dic** (-hī′dik) ***adj.***

Al·den (ôl′dən), **John** 1599?-1687; Pilgrim settler in Plymouth Colony: character in Longfellow's poem "The Courtship of Miles Standish"

al den·te (äl den′tā, al-) ⟦It, lit., to the tooth⟧ cooked until firm to the bite; chewy: said esp. of pasta

al·der (ôl′dər) ***n.*** ⟦ME *alder, aller* < OE *alor, aler* < IE base **el-*: see ELM⟧ any of a small group of rapidly growing trees and shrubs (genus *Alnus*) of the birch family, having toothed leaves and catkins, and growing in cool, moist soil in temperate and cold climates: the bark is used in dyeing and tanning, the wood is used for bridges and piles because it resists underwater rot, and the roots, which contain nitrogen-fixing organisms, help colonize raw soil

al·der·fly (ôl′dər flī′) ***n.*** ⟦prec. + FLY[2]: prob. so called because they inhabit alders growing near water⟧ any of a family (Sialidae) of weak-flying neuropteran insects found near running water and having aquatic larvae that are often used as fishing bait

al·der·man (ôl′dər mən) ***n.***, *pl.* **-men** (-mən) ⟦ME < OE *ealdorman*, chief, prince < *eald*, OLD + *man*, MAN⟧ **1** in some U.S. cities, a member of the municipal council, usually representing a certain district or ward **2** in England and Wales before 1974, a senior member of a local council **3** *Anglo-Saxon History* the chief officer in a shire; ealdorman —**al′der·man·cy** (-sē) ***n.*** —**al′der·man′ic** (-man′ik) ***adj.***

Al·der·ney[1] (ôl′dər nē) ***n.***, *pl.* **-neys** any of a breed of small dairy cattle originally from ALDERNEY[2]

Al·der·ney[2] (ôl′dər nē) northernmost of the Channel Islands: 3 sq mi (8 sq km)

Al·dine (ôl′dīn′, -dēn′; al′-) ***adj.*** ⟦*Ald(us)* + -INE[1]⟧ from the press of Aldus MANUTIUS and his family, who published fine editions of the classics (*c.* 1494-1597) at Venice and Rome —***n.*** an Aldine book, edition, or type

al·dol (al′dôl′, -dōl′) ***n.*** ⟦Fr < *ald(éhyde)*, ALDEHYDE + *-ol*, -OL[2]⟧ a clear, colorless, syrupy liquid, $CH_3CHOHCH_2CHO$, obtained by condensation of acetaldehyde: used as a solvent, in organic synthesis, and as a hypnotic and sedative

al·dose (al′dōs′) ***n.*** ⟦ALD(EHYDE) + -OSE[2]⟧ *Chem.* any sugar containing the aldehyde group, CHO

al·dos·te·rone (al däs′tə rōn′; al′dō stir′ōn′, -ster′-) ***n.*** ⟦< ALD(EHYDE) + STER(OL) + -ONE⟧ a steroidal hormone, $C_{21}H_{28}O_5$, produced synthetically and by the adrenal cortex glands: the chief regulator of sodium, potassium, and chloride metabolism, thus controlling the body's water and electrolyte balances

al·dos·te·ron·ism (al däs′tə rō niz′əm; al′dō stir′ə niz′əm, -ster′-) ***n.*** the condition arising from too great a secretion of aldosterone, resulting in hypertension and excessive excretion of potassium with fatigue and muscle weakness

☆**al·drin** (ôl′drin, al′-) ***n.*** ⟦Ger, after Kurt *Alder*, 20th-c. Ger chemist⟧ an insecticide containing a naphthalene derivative, $C_{12}H_8Cl_6$, especially effective against insects resistant to DDT: a suspected carcinogen banned by EPA for agricultural uses

Al·drin (ôl′drin), **Edwin Eugene, Jr.** 1930- ; U.S. astronaut: 2d man on the moon: called *Buzz Aldrin*

ale (āl) ***n.*** ⟦ME < OE *ealu, ealo* < IE base **alu(t)-*, bitter, beer, alum⟧ a fermented drink made from malt, hops, and yeast, like beer, but by rapid fermentation at a relatively high temperature

a·le·a·to·ric (ā′lē ə tôr′ik) ***adj.*** designating or of music that involves chance or unpredictability in composition or performance or both

a·le·a·to·ry (ā′lē ə tôr′ē) ***adj.*** ⟦L *aleatorius*, of gambling < *aleator*, gambler < *alea*, chance, a dice game⟧ **1** of or depending on chance, luck, or contingency **2** ALEATORIC

A·lec·to (ə lek′tō) ***n.*** ⟦L < Gr *Alēktō*⟧ *Class. Myth.* one of the three Furies

a·lee (ə lē′) ***adv., adj.*** *Naut.* on or toward the lee side of a ship; leeward

al·e·gar (al′ə gər, ā′lə-) ***n.*** ⟦ME *alegre* < *ale* (see ALE) + *egre*, sour < OFr *aigre*: see VINEGAR⟧ a vinegar resulting from the fermentation of ale; sour ale

ale·house (āl′hous′) ***n.*** a place where ale is sold and served; saloon; tavern

A·lei·chem (ə lā′kəm), **Sho·lom** (shô′ləm) (pseud. of *Solomon Rabinowitz*) 1859-1916; Russ. writer (also in the U.S.) of humorous stories, drama, etc. in Yiddish

A·le·mán (ä′le män′), **Ma·te·o** (mä tā′ō) 1547-1614?; Sp. novelist

Al·e·man·ni (al′ə man′ī′) ***pl.n.*** ⟦ML, pl. of *Alemannus* < OHG *aleman*, a German⟧ the Germanic tribes that invaded and settled in Alsace and parts of Switzerland in the early 5th cent. A.D.: they were conquered by Clovis in A.D. 496

Al·e·man·nic (-man′ik) ***n.*** the group of German dialects spoken in SW Germany and in Alsace and Switzerland —***adj.*** of the Alemanni or their language or culture

Alembert, Jean le Rond d′ *see* D'ALEMBERT

a·lem·bic (ə lem′bik) ***n.*** ⟦ME & OFr *alambic* < ML *alambicus* < Ar *al-anbīq* < *al*, the + *anbīq*, distilling flask < Gr *ambix*, a cup⟧ **1** an apparatus of glass or metal, like a retort, formerly used for distilling **2** anything that refines or purifies

A·len·çon (ə len′sän′, -sən; *Fr* å län sōn′) ***n.*** ⟦after *Alençon*, town in NW France, where orig. made⟧ a needlepoint lace with a solid design on a net background

a·leph (ä′lef′, ä′lif′) ***n.*** ⟦Heb *alef*, lit., ox, leader⟧ the first letter of the Hebrew alphabet (א)

a·leph-null (-nul′) ***n.*** *Math.* in the theory of sets, the smallest infinite cardinal number; the cardinal number of the set of all positive integers: symbol, $\aleph_0$: also called **a′leph′-ze′ro** (-zir′ō)

A·lep·po (ə lep′ō) city in NW Syria: also **A·lep** (ä lep′)

a·lert (ə lurt′) ***adj.*** ⟦Fr *alerte*, earlier *à l'erte* < It *all' erta*, on the watch < *alla*, at the + *erta*, a lookout, high (point) < VL **ergere*, for L *erigere*, to ERECT⟧ **1** watchful and ready, as in facing danger **2** quick in thought or action; active; nimble —***n.*** **1** a warning signal as of an expected air raid; alarm **2** the period during which such a warning is in effect **3** a notice or reminder about some pressing matter or important information [an *alert* to drivers about a detour] —***vt.*** **1** to warn to be ready or watchful [the troops were *alerted*] **2** to inform or make aware of [we *alerted* them to their duties] —**SYN.** INTELLIGENT, WATCHFUL —**on the alert** watchful; vigilant —**a·lert′ly** ***adv.*** —**a·lert′ness** ***n.***

-a·les (ā′lēz′) ⟦L, pl. of *-alis*⟧ *suffix Bot.* forming the scientific names of orders of plants

al·eu·rone (al′yoo rōn′, ə loo′-) ***n.*** ⟦Ger *aleuron* < Gr, wheat meal, flour < *aleein*, to grind < IE base **al-* > Arm *alauri*, a mill⟧ finely granulated protein present in seeds generally and forming the outer layer of cereal seeds —**al′eu·ron′ic** (-rän′ik) ***adj.***

Al·e·ut (al′ē oot′, al′yoot′, ə loot′) ***n.*** ⟦Russ < ? Chukchi *aliuit*, islanders⟧ **1** *pl.* **Al′e·uts′** or **Al′e·ut′** a member of an indigenous people of the Aleutian Islands and parts of mainland Alaska **2** the language of this people, related to Eskimo —***adj.*** of the Aleuts or their language or culture

A·leu·tian (ə loo′shən) ***adj.*** **1** of the Aleutian Islands **2** of the Aleuts or their language or culture —***n.*** ALEUT

Aleutian Islands chain of islands extending *c.* 1,200 mi (1,931 km) southwest from the tip of the Alaska Peninsula: constituting, with the W half of the Alaska Peninsula, a district of Alas.: 15,501 sq mi (40,147 sq km): also **Aleutians**

A level **1** the second, or advanced, level of British secondary-school examinations, taken usually two years after the first **2** a pass on any examination at this level See O LEVEL Also **A′-lev′el**

ale·wife (āl′wīf′) ***n.***, *pl.* **-wives′** (-wīvz′) **1** a woman who keeps an alehouse ☆**2** ⟦< ?⟧ a NW Atlantic clupeid fish (*Alosa pseudoharengus*) that swims up rivers to spawn in the spring: used for food and in fertilizers

Al·ex·an·der[1] (al′ig zan′dər) ***n.*** ⟦L < Gr *Alexandros*, lit., defender of men < *alexein*, to defend + *anēr* (gen. *andros*), man⟧ **1** a masculine name: dim. *Alec, Alex, Sandy*; equiv. Fr. *Alexandre*, It. *Alessandro*, Russ. *Aleksandr*, Scot. *Alistair*, Sp. *Alejandro*; fem. *Alexandra, Alexandrina* ☆**2** a cocktail made of gin, brandy, or rum, with crème de cacao and sweet cream

Al·ex·an·der[2] (al′ig zan′dər) **1 Alexander I** 1777-1825; czar of Russia (1801-25); grandson of Catherine the Great **2 Alexander I** 1876-1903; king of Serbia (1889-1903): assassinated **3 Alexander I** 1888-1934; king of Yugoslavia (1921-34): assassinated **4 Alexander II** 1818-81; czar of Russia (1855-81): emancipated the serfs: assassinated: son of Nicholas I **5 Alexander III** (born *Orlando Bandinelli*) died 1181; pope (1159-81) **6 Alexander III** 1845-94; czar of Russia (1881-94): son of Alexander II **7 Alexander VI** (born *Rodrigo de Borja y Doms*) 1431-1503; pope (1492-1503): father of Cesare & Lucrezia Borgia **8 Sir Harold R(upert) L(eofric) G(eorge)** 1st Viscount Alexander of Tunis 1891-1969; Brit. general & statesman: governor-general of Canada (1946-52)

Alexander Archipelago ⟦after ALEXANDER II, czar at the time Alas. was sold to the U.S.⟧ group of *c.* 1,100 islands in Alas., off the SE coast

Alexander Island ⟦after ALEXANDER I of Russia⟧ island of Antarctica, just west of the base of the Antarctic Peninsula, in the British Antarctic Territory: *c.* 16,700 sq mi (43,253 sq km)

Alexander Nev·sky (nef′skē) ⟦< Russ *nevskij*, of the NEVA, site of a decisive battle (1240) in which he defeated Swed forces⟧ 1220?-63; Russ. military hero, statesman, & saint

Alexander Se·ve·rus (si vir′əs) A.D. 208?-235; Rom. emperor (A.D. 222-235)

Alexander the Great 356-323 B.C.; king of Macedonia (336-323): military conqueror who helped spread Greek culture from Asia Minor & Egypt to India: also **Alexander III**

Al·ex·an·dra (al′ig zan′drə) ***n.*** ⟦fem. of ALEXANDER[1]⟧ a feminine name: dim. *Sandra, Sandy*; var. *Alexandrina*

Al·ex·an·dret·ta (al′ig zan dret′ə) *former name for* ISKENDERUN

Al·ex·an·dri·a (al′ig zan′drē ə) **1** seaport in Egypt, on the Mediterranean at the W end of the Nile delta: founded by Alexander the Great and, later, a center of Hellenistic culture **2** ⟦after the seaport, but with allusion to the *Alexander* family, owners of the town site⟧ city in NE Va., on the Potomac, near Washington, D.C.

Al·ex·an·dri·an (-ən) ***adj.*** **1** of Alexander the Great or his rule **2** of Alexandria, Egypt, or the Hellenistic or late Hellenic culture that flourished there

al·ex·an·drine (al′ig zan′drin, -drēn′) ***n.*** ⟦Fr *alexandrin*: so called from being used in OFr poems on ALEXANDER (THE GREAT)⟧ [*occas.* **A-**] *Prosody* an iambic line having normally six feet; iambic hexameter —***adj.*** of an alexandrine

al·ex·an·drite (al′ig zan′drīt′) ***n.*** ⟦after ALEXANDER II⟧ a variety of chrysoberyl that appears dark green in daylight and deep red under artificial light: it is used in jewelry

A·lex·an·drou·po·lis (ä′lek sän dro͞o′pə lis) seaport in NE Greece, on the Aegean, near the Turkish border

a·lex·i·a (ə lek′sē ə, ā-) ***n.*** ⟦ModL < Gr *a-*, without + *lexis*, word, speech < *legein*, to speak: see LOGIC⟧ a loss of the ability to read, caused by lesions of the brain; word blindness

a·lex·i·phar·mac (ə lek′si fär′mək) ***n.*** ⟦< Gr *alexipharmakon* < *alexein*, to avert + *pharmakon*, a drug, poison⟧ an antidote: also **a·lex′i·phar′mic** (-mik)

A·lex·is[1] (ə lek′sis) ***n.*** ⟦Gr, lit., help < *alexein*, to defend⟧ a masculine and feminine name

A·lex·is[2] (ə lek′sis) 1629-76; czar of Russia (1645-76): father of Peter the Great

A·lex·i·us I (ə lek′sē əs) (*Alexius Comnenus*) 1048-1118; emperor of the Byzantine Empire (1081-1118)

al·fal·fa (al fal′fə) ***n.*** ⟦Sp < Ar *al-fisfiṣa*, fodder in its freshest state⟧ a deep-rooted perennial plant (*Medicago sativa*) of the pea family, with small divided leaves, purple cloverlike flowers, and spiral pods, used extensively for fodder and pasture and as a cover crop

Al·fie·ri (äl fyer′ē), Count **Vit·to·ri·o** (vi tôr′ē ō′) 1749-1803; It. dramatist & poet

☆**al·fil·a·ri·a** or **al·fil·e·ri·a** (al fil′ə rē′ə) ***n.*** ⟦AmSp *alfilerillo* < Sp *alfiler*, a pin < Ar *al-khilāl*, thorn⟧ a European common weed (*Erodium cicutarium*) of the geranium family, which is now utilized as fodder in the SW U.S.

al fi·ne (äl fē′nā) ⟦It⟧ *Musical Direction* to the end: a note to the performer to continue to the end of a repeated section

Al·fon·so XIII (al fän′zō, -sō; *Sp* äl fôn′sô) 1886-1941; king of Spain (1886-1931); deposed

☆**al·for·ja** (al fôr′hə) ***n.*** ⟦Sp < Ar *al-khurj*, saddlebag, portmanteau⟧ a leather or canvas saddlebag used in the W U.S.

Al·fred (al′frəd) ***n.*** ⟦OE *Ælfred*, lit., elf-counsel, hence, wise counselor < *ælf*, ELF + *ræd*, counsel⟧ a masculine name: dim. *Al, Alf, Alfie, Fred*; fem. *Alfreda*

Al·fre·da (al frēd′ə) ***n.*** a feminine name: see ALFRED

Al·fre·do (al frā′dō, äl-) ***adj.*** ⟦after *Alfredo* di Lelio, restaurateur in Rome who created the original version, without cream (early 1900s)⟧ [*occas.* **a-**] coated with a mixture of butter, cream, and grated Parmesan cheese, or now, often, with a white cheese sauce somewhat like this [*fettuccine Alfredo*]

Alfred the Great A.D. 849-899; king of Wessex (871-899): put an end to Dan. conquests in England: promoted Eng. culture

al·fres·co (al fres′kō, äl-) ***adv.*** ⟦It < *al* (< *a* + *il*), in the + *fresco*, cool: see FRESCO⟧ in the open air; outdoors —***adj.*** outdoor Also **al fresco**

Alf·vén wave (äl vān′) ⟦after H. *Alfvén* (1908–95), Swed physicist⟧ a wave traveling in a plasma in the direction of a magnetic field

Alg *abbrev.* Algeria

alg- (alg) *combining form* ALGO-: used before a vowel

al·gae (al′jē′) ***pl.n.**, sing.* **al′ga** (-gə) ⟦pl. of L *alga*, seaweed < IE base **el-*, **ol-*, to be moldy, putrid > Swed *ul*, rancid, Du *uilig*, rotten⟧ any of several divisions of simple photosynthetic organisms, esp. certain thallophytes, variously one-celled, colonial, or filamentous, containing chlorophyll and other pigments (esp. red and brown), and having no true root, stem, or leaf: algae are found in water or damp places, and include seaweeds and pond scum —**al′gal** (-gəl) ***adj.***

al·gar·ro·ba or **al·ga·ro·ba** (al′gə rō′bə) ***n.*** ⟦Sp < Ar *al-kharrūba* < *al*, the + *kharrūba*, CAROB⟧ **1** the carob tree or its pods ☆**2** the mesquite tree or its pods

al·ge- (al′jē) *combining form* ALGO-

al·ge·bra (al′jə brə) ***n.*** ⟦ME < ML < Ar *al-jabr*, the reunion of broken parts < *al*, the + *jabara*, to reunite⟧ **1** a mathematical system using symbols, esp. letters, to generalize certain arithmetic operations and relationships (Ex.: $x + y = x^2$ represents a unique relationship between x and y, and has an infinite number of examples, as $3 + 6 = 9$) **2** any of various symbolic mathematical systems having formal rules of operation, defined relationships, finite processes, etc. [*Boolean algebra*] **3** a textbook or treatise dealing with algebra —**al′ge·bra′ist** (-brā′ist) ***n.***

al·ge·bra·ic (al′jə brā′ik) ***adj.*** **1** of, used in, or characteristic of algebra **2** of a number, etc. expressible by algebraic operations: opposed to TRANSCENDENTAL Also **al′ge·bra′i·cal** —**al′ge·bra′i·cal·ly** ***adv.***

algebraic number a root of a polynomial equation with coefficients that are rational numbers

Al·ge·cir·as (al′ji sir′əs, -sī rəs; *Sp* äl′he thē′räs′) seaport in S Spain, on the Strait of Gibraltar

Al·ger (al′jər), **Horatio** 1832-99; U.S. writer of boys' stories: his books typically deal with rags-to-riches stories of young boys advancing from poverty to wealth and acclaim

Al·ge·ri·a (al jir′ē ə) country in N Africa, on the Mediterranean: 919,595 sq mi (2,381,740 sq km); cap. Algiers —**Al·ge′ri·an** ***adj.**, **n.***

Al·ge·rine (al′jə rēn′) ***adj.*** Algerian —***n.*** **1** a person born in Algeria, esp. one of Berber, Arab, or Moorish descent **2** [**a-**] a soft woolen cloth with bright-colored stripes

Al·ger·non (al′jər nən, -nän′) ***n.*** ⟦apparently < OFr *al grenon*, with a mustache⟧ a masculine name: dim. *Algie, Algy*

al·ge·si- (al jē′zē, -sē) ⟦< Gr *algēsis*, sense of pain⟧ *combining form* ALGO-

-al·gi·a (al′jə, -jē ə) ⟦< Gr *algos*, pain < *algein*, to feel pain⟧ *combining form forming nouns* pain [*neuralgia*]

☆**al·gi·cide** (al′jə sīd′) ***n.*** ⟦< ALG(AE) + -I- + -CIDE⟧ a substance used to prevent or get rid of algae, esp. green scum in a swimming pool: usually copper sulfate: also **al′gae·cide′**

al·gid (al′jid) ***adj.*** ⟦Fr *algide* < L *algidus*, cold < *algere*, to be cold < IE **algh-*, frost, cold⟧ cold; chilly —**al·gid·i·ty** (al jid′ə tē) ***n.***

Al·giers (al jirz′) seaport & capital of Algeria, on the Mediterranean: a base of Barbary pirates until its capture by the French in 1830

al·gin (al′jin) ***n.*** ⟦< ALG(AE) + -IN[1]⟧ **1** ALGINIC ACID **2** a colloidal polysaccharide derived from alginic acid and used as a stabilizer and emulsifier, esp. in ice cream

al·gi·nate (al′jə nāt′) ***n.*** a salt of alginic acid

al·gin·ic acid (al jin′ik) ⟦ALGIN + -IC⟧ a gelatinous material, $(C_6H_8O)_n$, extracted from brown seaweed or kelp: used in jellies, plastics, dentistry, etc.

al·go- (al′gō, -gə) *combining form* ⟦< Gr *algos*, pain⟧ pain [*algometer*]: also **al·gi·o-** (al′jē ō)

al·goid (al′goid′) ***adj.*** ⟦ALG(AE) + -OID⟧ like algae

AL·GOL or **Al·gol** (al′gäl′, -gôl) ***n.*** ⟦*algo(rithmic) l(anguage)*⟧ a computer language employing algebraic symbols, used internationally for scientific computations

Al·gol (al′gäl′) ***n.*** ⟦Ar *al ghūl*, lit., the ghoul: so named because it marks the head of Medusa, held by Perseus, in ancient diagrams of the constellation⟧ a binary, variable star in the constellation Perseus: magnitude 2.09: the fainter star regularly eclipses its brighter companion

al·go·lag·ni·a (al′gō lag′nē ə, -gə-) ***n.*** ⟦ModL < ALGO- + Gr *lagneia*, lust⟧ abnormal sexual pleasure derived from inflicting or suffering pain; sadism or masochism —**al′go·lag′ni·ac** ***n.**,* **al′go·lag′nist** —**al′go·lag′nic** ***adj.***

al·gol·o·gy (al gäl′ə jē) ***n.*** ⟦< ALG(AE) + -LOGY⟧ the branch of botany that deals with algae; phycology —**al·go·log·i·cal** (al′gō läj′i kəl, -gə-) ***adj.*** —**al·gol′o·gist** ***n.***

al·gom·e·ter (al gäm′ət ər) ***n.*** ⟦ALGO- + -METER⟧ a device for measuring the intensity of pain caused by pressure —**al·go·met·ric** (al′gō me′trik, -gə-) ***adj.**,* **al′go·met′ri·cal** —**al·gom′e·try** ***n.***

Al·gon·ki·an (al gäŋ′kē ən, -gän′-) ***adj.**, **n.*** **1** *var. of* ALGONQUIAN **2** [*sometimes* **a-**] *Geol.* PROTEROZOIC

Al·gon·kin (-kin) ***n.*** *var. of* ALGONQUIN

Al·gon·qui·an (-kē ən, -kwē ən) ***adj.*** ⟦< fol.: coined (1891) by J. W. Powell⟧ designating or of a widespread family of over twenty languages spoken by North American Indian peoples, including the Arapaho, Cheyenne, Blackfoot, Ojibwa, Fox, Shawnee, Abenaki, and Delaware —***n.*** **1** this family of languages **2** a member of a people speaking any of these languages

Al·gon·quin (-kin, -kwin) ***n.*** ⟦Fr, earlier *Algoumequin* < ? an Algonquian place or group name⟧ **1** a member of an Algonquian people living near the Ottawa River, Canada **2** a dialect of Ojibwa spoken by this people **3** *archaic var. of* ALGONQUIAN —***adj.*** of the Algonquins or their language or culture

al·go·pho·bi·a (al′gō fō′bē ə, -gə-) ***n.*** ⟦ALGO- + -PHOBIA⟧ an abnormal fear of pain

al·go·rism (al′gə riz′əm) ***n.*** ⟦ME & OFr *algorisme* < ML *algorismus*, after Ar *al-Khwārazmī*, lit., person born in Khwārazm (Khiva), mathematician of the 9th c. A.D.⟧ **1** the Arabic system of numerals; decimal system of counting **2** the act or skill of computing with any kind of numerals **3** ALGORITHM

al·go·rithm (al′gə rith′əm) ***n.*** ⟦altered (after ARITHMETIC) < prec. ⟧ **1** *Math. a)* any systematic method of solving a certain kind of problem *b)* the repetitive calculations used in finding the greatest common divisor of two numbers (called in full **Euclidean algorithm**) **2** *Comput.* a predetermined set of instructions for solving a specific problem in a limited number of steps —**al′go·rith′mic** ***adj.***

al·gum (al′gum′) ***n.*** ⟦Heb *algūm*⟧ a tree mentioned in the Bible: 2 Chron. 2:8

Al·ham·bra (al ham′brə, -häm′-) ***n.*** ⟦Sp < Ar *al ḥamrā'*, lit., the red (house): fem. form of adj. *aḥmar*, red⟧ citadel of the Moorish kings near Granada, Spain, built during the 13th and 14th cent.

Al·ham·bresque (al′ham bresk′) ***adj.*** like the Alhambra, especially in richness of ornamentation

A·li (ä′lē, ä lē′) **1** A.D. 600?-661; 4th caliph of Islam (656-661), considered the 1st caliph by the Shiites (see SHIITE): son-in-law of Muhammad **2 Mehemet** *see* MEHEMET ALI **3 Mu·ham·mad** (mə häm′əd) (born *Cassius Marcellus Clay*) 1942-2016; U.S. boxer

a·li·as (ā′lē əs, āl′yəs) ***n.**, pl.* **a′li·as·es** ⟦L, at another time < *alius*, other: see ELSE⟧ an assumed name; another name —***adv.*** otherwise named [*Bell alias Jones*] —***SYN.*** PSEUDONYM

A·li Ba·ba (ä′lē bä′bə, al′ē bab′ə) in *The Arabian Nights*, a poor woodcutter who accidentally discovers the treasure of a band of forty thieves in a cave: he makes the door of the cave open by saying "Open sesame!"

al·i·bi (al′ə bī′) *n., pl.* **-bis′** ⟦L, contr. < *alius ibi*, elsewhere⟧ **1** *Law* the defensive plea or fact that an accused person was elsewhere than at the scene of the crime with which the person is charged **2** [Informal] an excuse —☆*vi., vt.* **-bied′, -bi′ing** [Informal] to offer an excuse (for)

A·li·can·te (ä′lē kän′te; *E* al′ə kan′tē) seaport in SE Spain, on the Mediterranean

Al·ice (al′is) *n.* ⟦ME *Alys, Aeleis* < OFr *Aliz, Aaliz* < *Adaliz* < OHG *Adalheidis*: see ADELAIDE[1]⟧ a feminine name: dim. *Elsie*; var. *Alicia*

A·li·ci·a (ə lish′ə, -lē′shə; -lish′ē ə, -lē′shē ə) *n.* a feminine name: see ALICE

al·i·cy·clic (al′i sīk′lik) *adj.* ⟦ALI(PHATIC) + CYCLIC: used to translate Ger *alizyklisch*, of similar formation⟧ *Chem.* of or relating to certain cyclic compounds with carbon atoms in any type of closed chain (excluding the benzene ring), but with properties similar to aliphatic compounds: see also AROMATIC (sense 2)

al·i·dade (al′i dād′) *n.* ⟦Fr < Sp *alidada* < Ar *al ʿiḍāda*, two sides or sideposts < *ʿaḍud*, upper arm⟧ **1** a part of an optical or surveying instrument, consisting of the vernier, indicator, etc. **2** a surveying instrument consisting of a telescope mounted on a rule, used in topography Also **al′i·dad′** (-dad′)

al·ien (āl′yən, āl′ē ən) *adj.* ⟦ME & OFr < L *alienus* < *alius*, other: see ELSE⟧ **1** belonging to another country or people; foreign **2** strange; not natural [*cruel words alien to his lips*] **3** opposed or repugnant [*beliefs alien to one's religion*] **4** of aliens —*n.* **1** a foreigner **2** a foreign-born resident in a country who has not become a naturalized citizen **3** an outsider **4** in science fiction, a being in or from outer space and not native to the Earth; extraterrestrial —*vt.* ⟦ME *alienen* < OFr *aliener* < L *alienare*⟧ to transfer (land, property, etc.)

SYN.—alien is applied to a resident who bears political allegiance to another country; **foreigner**, to a visitor or resident from another country, esp. one with a different language, cultural pattern, etc.; **stranger**, to a person from another region who is unacquainted with local people, customs, etc.; **immigrant**, to a person who comes to another country to settle; **émigré**, to a citizen of one country who has left it to take political refuge in another See also **extrinsic** —*ANT.* **citizen, subject, national**

al·ien·a·ble (-ə bəl) *adj.* capable of being alienated or transferred to a new owner —**al′ien·a·bil′i·ty** (-ə bil′ə tē) *n.*

al·ien·age (āl′yən ij′, āl′ē ən-) *n.* the legal status of an alien

al·ien·ate (āl′yən āt′, āl′ē ən-) *vt.* **-at′ed, -at′ing** ⟦< L *alienatus*, pp. of *alienare* < *alius*, other: see ELSE⟧ **1** to transfer the ownership of (property) to another **2** to make unfriendly; estrange [*his behavior alienated his friends*] **3** to cause to be withdrawn or detached, as from one's society **4** to cause a transference of (affection) —**al′ien·a′tor** *n.*

al·ien·a·tion (āl′yən ā′shən, āl′ē ən-) *n.* ⟦ME & OFr < L *alienatio*, separation, aversion, aberration (of the mind): see prec.⟧ **1** an alienating or being alienated; specif., estrangement or detachment **2** mental derangement; insanity

alienation effect ⟦transl. of Ger *Verfremdungseffekt*, as used by B. BRECHT⟧ *Theater* an effect meant to produce a detached, unemotional response to a play by an audience and achieved by the use of techniques (as having the actors read their parts from a script) that emphasize the unreal nature of a performance

al·ien·ee (āl′yən ē′, āl′ē ən ē′) *n.* ⟦ALIEN, *v.* + -EE[1]⟧ a person to whom property is transferred or conveyed

al·ien·ism (āl′yən iz′əm, āl′ē ən iz′əm) *n.* **1** alienage **2** *former name for* PSYCHIATRY

al·ien·ist (-ist) *n.* ⟦Fr *aliéniste* < L *alienatio*: see ALIENATION⟧ *former term for* PSYCHIATRIST, esp. one who testifies in a court of law

al·ien·or (-ôr′, -ər) *n.* ⟦Anglo-Fr < OFr *aliener*: see ALIEN, *vt.* & -OR⟧ a person from whom property is transferred or conveyed

a·lif (ä′lif) *n.* ⟦Ar, akin to Heb *alef*: see ALEPH⟧ the first letter of the Arabic alphabet (ا)

a·li·form (ā′li fôrm′, al′i-) *adj.* ⟦< L *ala* (see AILERON) + -FORM⟧ shaped like a wing; alar

A·li·garh (al′i gär′, ä′li gur′) city in W Uttar Pradesh, N India

a·light[1] (ə līt′) *vi.* **a·light′ed** or **a·lit′, a·light′ing** ⟦ME *alighten* < OE *ālīhtan* < *a-*, out, off + *līhtan*, to dismount, render light < *līht*: see LIGHT[2] (to dismount)⟧ **1** to get down or off; dismount **2** to come down after flight; descend and settle **3** [Rare] to come (*on* or *upon*) accidentally

a·light[2] (ə līt′) *adj.* ⟦ME *aliht*, pp. of *alihten* < OE *alihtan*, to light up⟧ **1** lighted; burning **2** lighted up

a·lign (ə līn′) *vt.* ⟦Fr *aligner* < *a-*, to + *ligner* < *ligne*, LINE[1]⟧ **1** to bring into a straight line; adjust by line **2** to bring (parts or components, as the wheels of a car) into proper coordination **3** to bring into agreement, close cooperation, etc. [*he aligned himself with the liberals*] —*vi.* to come or fall into line; line up

a·lign·ment (-mənt) *n.* **1** an aligning or being aligned; esp., *a)* arrangement in a straight line *b)* a condition of close cooperation [*a new alignment of European nations*] **2** a line or lines formed by aligning **3** *Engineering* a ground plan, as of a fieldwork, railroad, etc.

a·like (ə līk′) *adj.* ⟦ME *olike* < OE *gelic, onlike* & ON *(g)likr, alikr* < PGmc **galik-* < **ga-* (< IE **ge-*, perfective prefix) + **lik-*: see LIKE[1]⟧ like one another; showing resemblance; similar: usually used in the predicate —*adv.* **1** in the same manner; similarly **2** to the same degree; equally —**a·like′ness** *n.*

al·i·ment (al′ə mənt; *for v.* al′ə ment′) *n.* ⟦L *alimentum* < *alere*, to nourish: see OLD⟧ **1** anything that nourishes; food **2** means of support; necessity —*vt.* to supply with aliment; nourish —**al′i·men′tal** (-ment′′l) *adj.*

al·i·men·ta·ry (al′ə men′tə rē, -men′trē) *adj.* ⟦L *alimentarius*: see prec.⟧ **1** connected with food or nutrition **2** nourishing **3** furnishing support or sustenance

alimentary canal (*or* **tract**) the passage in the body through which food passes and in which it is digested, extending from the mouth through the esophagus, stomach, and intestines to the anus

al·i·men·ta·tion (al′ə men tā′shən) *n.* ⟦Fr < ML *alimentatio* < L *alimentum*: see ALIMENT⟧ **1** a nourishing or being nourished **2** nourishment; nutrition **3** support; sustenance —**al′i·men′ta·tive** (-men′tə tiv) *adj.*

al·i·mo·ny (al′ə mō′nē) *n.* ⟦L *alimonia*, food, support < *alere*, to nourish: see OLD⟧ **1** [Obs.] supply of the means of living; maintenance **2** an allowance that a court orders paid to a person by that person's spouse or former spouse after a legal separation or divorce or while legal action on this is pending

a·line (ə līn′) *vt., vi.* **a·lined′, a·lin′ing** ALIGN —**a·line′ment** *n.*

A-line (ā′līn′) *adj.* ⟦because the garment's shape is somewhat like an A⟧ fitting close at the top and flaring at the bottom: said of a woman's dress, coat, skirt, etc.

Al·i·oth (al′ē äth′) *n.* ⟦Ar *alya(t)*, lit., fat of the tail of a sheep⟧ a binary, variable star, the brightest star in the constellation Ursa Major and in the handle of the Big Dipper: magnitude, 1.76

A·li Pa·sha (ä′lē pä shä′) 1741-1822; Turk. governor of Albania & part of Greece, including Janina: deposed & assassinated: called the *Lion of Janina*

al·i·ped (al′ə ped′) *adj.* ⟦L *alipes* < *ala*, wing (see AILERON) + *pes* (gen. *pedis*), FOOT⟧ having a winglike membrane connecting the toes of the feet —*n.* an aliped creature

al·i·phat·ic (al′ə fat′ik) *adj.* ⟦< Gr *aleiphar* (gen. *aleiphatos*), fat, oil + -IC⟧ **1** pertaining to a fat or oil **2** of or relating to a major group of organic compounds, structured in open chains, including alkanes (paraffins), alkenes (olefins), and alkynes (acetylenes): see CYCLIC

al·i·quant (al′i kwənt, -kwänt′) *adj.* ⟦Fr *aliquante* < L *aliquantus*, some, moderate < *alius*, other + *quantus*, how large, how much⟧ *Math.* designating a part of a number that does not divide the number evenly but leaves a remainder [*8 is an aliquant part of 25*]: cf. ALIQUOT

al·i·quot (al′i kwət, -kwät′) *adj.* ⟦Fr *aliquote*, prob. via ML *aliquota* (fem.) < L *aliquot*, some, several < *alius*, other + *quot*, how many⟧ **1** designating or of a portion, part, or sample of a chemical, medicine, etc. **2** *Math.* designating a part of a number that divides the number evenly and leaves no remainder [*8 is an aliquot part of 24*]: cf. ALIQUANT —*n.* an aliquot part

Al Is·kan·da·ri·yah (äl′ is kän′də rē′yä′) *Ar. name for* ALEXANDRIA, Egypt

Al·i·son (al′i sən) *n.* ⟦ME *Alisoun* < OFr *Aliz* (see ALICE) + *-on*, suffix of uncert. meaning⟧ a feminine name: var. *Allison*

A-list (ā′list′) *n.* ⟦see A[1] (*adj.* 2), A ONE⟧ a list of important or prominent persons, as of those regarded as highly desirable guests at upper-class social or cultural events

Al·i·stair (al′i ster′) *n.* ⟦< ALEXANDER[1]⟧ a masculine name

a·lit (ə lit′) *vi. alt. pt. & pp. of* ALIGHT[1]

A·li·to (ə lēt′ō), **Samuel (Anthony, Jr.)** 1950- ; associate justice, U.S. Supreme Court (2006-)

a·li·un·de (ā′lē un′dē) *adv., adj.* ⟦L, lit., from another place⟧ *Law* from some other source [*evidence clarifying a document but not deriving from the document itself is evidence aliunde*]

a·live (ə līv′) *adj.* ⟦ME *alyfe, on live* < OE *on līfe; on*, in + *līfe*, dat. of *līf*, LIFE⟧ **1** having life; living **2** in existence, operation, etc.; unextinguished [*to keep old memories alive*] **3** lively; alert —*SYN.* LIVING —**alive to** fully aware of; perceiving [*alive to the risks involved*] —**alive with** teeming with; full of (living or moving things) [*a garden alive with bees*]

USAGE—Usually used in the predicate, *alive* is also used interjectionally in such phrases as *man alive!* and *sakes alive!*

a·li·yah or **a·li·ya** (ä′lē yä′) *n.* ⟦ModHeb *aliyah* < Heb, lit., a going up, ascent⟧ **1** the act or process of Jews moving to Israel, as to fulfill Zionist ideals or religious duty: often in the phrase **make aliyah**, to engage in this act or process **2** the honor of being called on to read the Torah in a Jewish religious service

a·liz·a·rin (ə liz′ə rin) *n.* ⟦Ger < Fr & Sp *alizari*, dried madder root < Ar *al-ʿuṣāra*, the juice < *ʿaṣara*, to press⟧ a reddish-yellow crystalline compound, $C_6H_4(CO)_2C_6H_2(OH)_2$, produced by oxidizing anthracene and used in dyeing wool, cotton, and silk and in the manufacture of dyestuffs: it was originally made from madder: sometimes called **a·liz′a·rine** (-rin, -rēn)

al·ka·hest (al′kə hest′) *n.* ⟦Fr < ML *alchahest*: apparently coined by PARACELSUS⟧ the hypothetical universal solvent sought by the alchemists

al·ka·les·cence (al′kə les′əns) *n.* ⟦ALKAL(INE) + -ESCENCE⟧ the quality of being alkaline or somewhat alkaline: also **al′ka·les′cen·cy** (-ən sē) —**al′ka·les′cent** *adj.*

al·ka·li (al′kə lī′) *n., pl.* **-lies′** or **-lis′** ⟦ME *alkaly* < Ar *al-qali*, for *al-qily*, the ashes (of saltwort) < *qalā*, to roast in a pan⟧ **1** any base or hydroxide, as soda, potash, etc. that is soluble in water and gives a high concentration of hydroxyl ions in solution; specif., any of the hydroxides and carbonates of the alkali metals **2** any soluble substance, as a mineral salt or mixture of salts, that can neutralize acids, has a pH greater than 7.0, and turns litmus blue: strong alkalies are caustic

al·kal·ic (al kal′ik) ***adj.*** *Geol.* designating or of igneous rocks having an unusually large amount of alkali metals, esp. sodium and potassium

☆**alkali flat** a nearly level plain that is covered with a hard, dry mixture of alkaline salts and sediment, formed in an arid region by the complete evaporation of a shallow lake or basin

alkali metal *Chem.* any of the six highly reactive metals in group IA of the periodic table including, in increasing order of reactivity, lithium, sodium, potassium, rubidium, cesium, and francium: see the periodic table of elements in the Reference Supplement

al·ka·lim·e·ter (al′kə lim′ət ər) ***n.*** an instrument for measuring the amount of alkali in a substance or solution

al·ka·line (al′kə lin, -līn′) ***adj.*** **1** of, like, or having the properties of an alkali **2** having a pH more than 7 **3** containing an alkali —**al′ka·lin′i·ty** (-lin′ə tē) ***n.***

al·ka·line-earth metal (-ʉrth′) any of the six highly reactive chemical elements in group IIA of the periodic table including, in order of increasing reactivity, beryllium, magnesium, calcium, strontium, barium, and radium: an oxide of any of these metals is called an **alkaline earth**: see the periodic table of elements in the Reference Supplement

al·ka·lin·ize (al′kə lin īz′) ***vt.*** **-ized′, -iz′ing** ALKALIZE —**al′ka·lin′i·za′tion** ***n.***

al·ka·lize (al′kə līz′) ***vt.*** **-lized′, -liz′ing** ⟦ALKAL(INE) + -IZE⟧ to make alkaline —**al′ka·li·za′tion** ***n.***

al·ka·loid (al′kə loid′) ***n.*** ⟦ALKAL(I) + -OID⟧ any of a number of heterocyclic, colorless, crystalline, bitter organic substances, such as caffeine, morphine, quinine, and strychnine, having alkaline properties and containing nitrogen: they are found in plants and, sometimes, animals, and are used as drugs and stimulants, but can have a strong toxic effect on the human or animal system —**al′ka·loid′al** ***adj.***

al·ka·lo·sis (al′kə lō′sis) ***n., pl.*** **-ses′** (-sēz′) ⟦ALKAL(I) + -OSIS⟧ an abnormal condition in the body, often due to faulty metabolism, in which excessive alkali, or a loss of acid, raises the pH of the blood and tissue: cf. ACIDOSIS —**al′ka·lot′ic** (-lät′ik) ***adj.***

al·kane (al′kān′) ***n.*** ⟦ALK(YL) + (METH)ANE⟧ any of a series of saturated hydrocarbons with open chains, having the formula C_nH_{2n+2} : these compounds are sometimes said to be in the methane or paraffin series

al·ka·net (al′kə net′) ***n.*** ⟦ME *alknet* < Sp *alcaneta,* dim. of *alcana* < Ar *al-ḥinnā',* the henna⟧ **1** *a)* a perennial plant (*Alkanna tinctoria*) of the borage family, found in SE Europe and Asia Minor *b)* the root of this plant, which yields a red dye *c)* the dark-red coloring matter, $C_{16}H_{16}O_5$, present in this root **2** any of several other plants (genus *Anchusa*) of the borage family, grown for their red dyes or as garden plants **3** GROMWELL

al·kene (al′kēn′) ***n.*** ⟦ALK(YL) + -ENE⟧ any of a series of unsaturated open-chain hydrocarbons containing a double bond and having the general formula C_nH_{2n} : these compounds are sometimes said to be in the ethylene or olefin series

Al·ko·ran (al′kō rän′, -ran′) ***n.*** [Archaic] the Koran

al·ky (al′kē) ***n., pl.*** **-kies** ⟦< ALC(OHOLIC) + -Y[1]⟧ [Slang] an alcoholic: also sp. **al′kie**

al·kyd (al′kid′) ***n.*** ⟦fol. + (ACI)D⟧ any of several synthetic resins made by heating together a polybasic acid, such as phthalic or maleic acid, and a polyhydric alcohol, such as glycerin or a glycol: these resins are used in paints, varnishes, and lacquers: also **alkyd resin**

al·kyl (al′kil′) ***n.*** ⟦ALK(ALI) + -YL⟧ a noncyclic saturated hydrocarbon radical with the general formula C_nH_{2n-1} : also **alkyl radical** —**al·kyl′ic** ***adj.***

al·kyl·a·tion (al′kə lā′shən) ***n.*** the introduction of the alkyl group into hydrocarbons, esp. in petroleum-refining processes for producing high-octane hydrocarbons —**al′kyl·ate′** (-lāt′) ***n., vt.*** **-at′ed, -at′ing**

al·kyne or **al·kine** (al′kīn′) ***n.*** ⟦ALKY(L) + -(I)NE⟧ any of a series of unsaturated open-chain hydrocarbons containing a triple bond and having the general formula C_nH_{2n-2} : these compounds are sometimes said to be in the acetylene series

all (ôl) ***adj.*** ⟦ME *al, all* < OE *eal* < IE **al-no-s* < base **al-, *ol-,* beyond, exceeding > L *ultra*⟧ **1** the whole extent or quantity of [*all* New England, *all* the gold] **2** the entire number of [*all* the men went] **3** every one of [*all* men must eat] **4** the greatest possible; as much as possible [said in *all* sincerity] **5** any; any whatever [true beyond *all* question] **6** alone; only [life is not *all* pleasure] **7** seeming to be nothing but [he was *all* arms and legs] ☆**8** [Dial.] completely used up, consumed, over with, etc. [the bread is *all*] —***pron.*** **1** [*with pl. v.*] everyone [*all* must die] **2** [*with pl. v.*] every one [*all* of us are here; *all* of the pencils are sharpened] **3** everything; the whole thing, matter, situation, etc. [*all* is over between them] **4** every part or bit [*all* of it is gone] —***n.*** **1** one's whole property, effort, etc. [gave his *all*] **2** a totality; whole —***adv.*** **1** wholly; entirely; altogether; quite [*all* worn out, riding *all* through the night] **2** apiece [a score of thirty *all*] —**after all** nevertheless; in spite of everything —**all but 1** all except **2** nearly; almost —**all in** ☆**1** [Informal] very tired; fatigued **2** *a) Poker* having put all one's money in the pot *b)* [Slang] having a personal dedication or commitment to a particular cause or endeavor —**all in all 1** considering everything **2** as a whole **3** everything —**all out** completely; wholeheartedly —**all over 1** ended **2** everywhere; in or on every part of; throughout **3** [Informal] as one characteristically is [that's Mary *all over*] —**all the** as much of (something) as [that's *all the* help you'll get] —**all the better** (or **worse**) so much the better (or worse) —**all the farther** (or **closer,** etc.) [Informal or Dial.] as far (close, etc.) as —**all the same 1** nevertheless **2** of no importance —**and all** [Informal] et cetera (etc.) —☆**as** (or **like**) **all get-out** [Informal] to a considerable degree; greatly [angry *as all get-out*] —**at all 1** in the least; to the slightest degree **2** in any way **3** under any considerations —**for all** in spite of; despite —**in all** altogether; all being counted

all- (ôl) *combining form* **1** wholly, entirely, or exclusively [*all*-American] **2** for every [*all*-purpose] **3** of everything or every part [*all*-inclusive] **4** lasting throughout (a specified period) [*all*-night] **5** ⟦ALL-(AMERICAN)⟧ *Sports* selected as the best of (a specified category) [*all*-league, *all*-conference, *all*-pro]

al·la bre·ve (ä′lä brā′vā) ⟦It, according to the BREVE (***n.*** 3), as it was used in medieval musical notation to indicate a half or a third of the value of the longest note⟧ [*also in italics*] *Music* **1** in 2/2 time: often used as a musical direction **2** 2/2 time, in which the half note receives the beat; cut time

Al·lah (ä′lä′, -lə; al′ə; ä lä′) ***n.*** ⟦Ar *Allāh* < *al,* the + *ilāh,* god, akin to Heb *eloah,* God⟧ *Islam* God

Al·la·ha·bad (al′ə hä bäd′) city in N India, in S Uttar Pradesh, at the juncture of the Jumna and Ganges rivers

☆**all-A·mer·i·can** (ôl′ə mer′i kən) ***adj.*** **1** made up entirely of Americans or American parts **2** representative of the U.S. as a whole, or chosen as the best in the U.S. **3** of all the Americas —***n.*** **1** a hypothetical football team or other team made up of college players voted the best of the year in the U.S. **2** a player chosen for such a team

Al·lan (al′ən) ***n.*** a masculine name: see ALAN

al·lan·to·ic (al′ən tō′ik) ***adj.*** **1** of or in the allantois **2** having an allantois

al·lan·toid (ə lan′toid′) ***adj.*** ⟦Gr *allantoeidēs:* see fol.⟧ of or like the allantois; sausage-shaped

al·lan·to·is (ə lan′tō is) ***n., pl.*** **al·lan·to·i·des** (al′ən tō′ə dēz′) ⟦ModL < Gr *allantoeidēs,* sausage-shaped < *allas,* sausage (prob. < dial. *allē,* garlic, via Oscan **allo* < L *alium, allium*) + *-eidēs,* -OID⟧ a membranous pouch with a rich blood supply in the embryos of birds, reptiles, and mammals: it is an organ of respiration and excretion for embryonic birds and reptiles: in mammals it helps form the placenta

al·lar·gan·do (äl′lär gän′dō) ***adj., adv.*** ⟦It < prp. of *allargare,* to broaden⟧ *Musical Direction* gradually slower and with more power

☆**all-a·round** (ôl′ə round′) ***adj.*** having many abilities, talents, or uses; not specialized; versatile —***adv.*** considering everything; all in all

al·lay (a lā′, ə-) ***vt.*** **-layed′, -lay′ing** ⟦ME *alaien, alleggen,* with confusion of form and meaning of OE *alecgan* (< *a-,* down + *lecgan,* to lay) & OFr *alegier* (< LL *alleviare:* see ALLEVIATE)⟧ **1** to put (fears, etc.) to rest; quiet; calm **2** to lessen, relieve, or alleviate (pain, grief, etc.) —***SYN.*** RELIEVE —**al·lay′er** ***n.***

all-clear (ôl′klir′) ***n.*** a siren blast or other signal that an air raid or practice alert is over

al·lée (ä lā′, a-; *Fr* à-) ***n.*** ⟦Fr < OFr *alee:* see ALLEY[1]⟧ [*also in italics*] a walk or passage, esp. one between two rows of evenly planted trees

al·le·ga·tion (al′ə gā′shən) ***n.*** ⟦ME *allegacioun* < OFr *allegation* < L *allegatio* < *allegare:* see fol.⟧ **1** the act of alleging **2** something alleged; assertion **3** an assertion made without proof **4** *Law* an assertion, made in a pleading, that its maker proposes to support with evidence

al·lege (ə lej′) ***vt.*** **-leged′, -leg′ing** ⟦ME *aleggen,* to produce as evidence; form < OFr *esligier* < VL **exlitigare* < L *ex-,* out of + *litigare* (see LITIGATE); meaning infl. by OFr *alleguer,* declare on oath < L *allegare,* to send, mention, adduce < *ad-,* to + *legare,* to send: see LEGATE⟧ **1** to assert positively, or declare; affirm; esp., to assert without proof **2** to offer as a plea, excuse, etc. [in his defense he *alleged* temporary insanity] **3** [Archaic] to cite as an authority (*for* or *against*) —**al·lege′a·ble** ***adj.***

al·leged (ə lejd′, ə lej′id) ***adj.*** **1** so declared, but without proof or legal conviction [the *alleged* assassin] **2** called by this term, but perhaps improperly so; so-called [his *alleged* friends] —**al·leg′ed·ly** ***adv.***

Al·le·ghe·ny (al′ə gā′nē) ⟦prob. < an Algonquian (? Delaware) name⟧ river in W Pennsylvania, joining the Monongahela at Pittsburgh to form the Ohio: 325 mi (523 km)

Allegheny Mountains mountain range of the Appalachian system, in Pa., Md., W.Va., and Va.: highest peaks, over 4,800 ft (1,463 m): also **Al′le·ghe′nies**

al·le·giance (ə lē′jəns) ***n.*** ⟦ME *alligeaunce,* altered (after *allegeaunce,* a formal declaration < *aleggen,* ALLEGE) < OFr *ligeance* < *lige, liege* (see LIEGE); sense affected by assoc. with L *ligare,* to bind⟧ **1** the duty that was owed by a vassal to his feudal lord **2** the obligation of support and loyalty to one's ruler, government, or country **3** loyalty or devotion, as to a cause, person, etc. —**al·le′giant** (-jənt) ***adj., n.***

SYN.—**allegiance** refers to the duty of a citizen to the government or a similarly felt obligation to support a cause or leader; **fidelity** implies strict adherence to an obligation or trust; **loyalty** suggests a steadfast devotion of an unquestioning kind that one may feel for one's family, friends, or country; **fealty,** now chiefly a literary word, suggests faithfulness that one has sworn to uphold; **homage** implies respect, or honor rendered to a person because of rank or achievement —***ANT.*** **faithlessness, disaffection**

al·le·gor·i·cal (al′ə gôr′i kəl, -gär′-) ***adj.*** **1** of or characteristic of allegory **2** that is or contains an allegory Also **al′le·gor′ic** —**al′le·gor′i·cal·ly** ***adv.***

al·le·go·rist (al′ə gôr′ist, -gər ist) ***n.*** a person who writes allegories —**al′le·go·ris′tic** (-gə ris′tik) ***adj.***

al·le·go·rize (al′ə gə rīz′, -gô rīz′) ***vt.*** **-rized′, -riz′ing** ⟦OFr *allegoriser* < LL *allegorizare:* see fol. & -IZE⟧ **1** to make into or treat as an allegory **2** to interpret in an allegorical sense —***vi.*** to make or use allegories —**al·le·gor·i·za·tion** (al′ə gôr′i zā′shən) ***n.***

al·le·go·ry (al′ə gôr′ē) ***n., pl.*** **-ries** ⟦ME *allegorie* < L *allegoria* < Gr *allēgoria,* description of one thing under the image of another < *állos*, other (see ELSE) + *agoreuein*, to speak in assembly < *agora*, AGORA[1]⟧ **1** a story in which people, things, and happenings have a hidden or symbolic meaning: allegories are used for teaching or explaining ideas, moral principles, etc. **2** the presenting of ideas by means of such stories **3** any symbol or emblem

al·le·gret·to (al′ə gret′ō, ä′lə-) [*also in italics*] *Music adj., adv.* ⟦It, dim. of *allegro*: see fol. ⟧ moderately fast; faster than andante but slower than allegro: often used as a musical direction —*n., pl.* **-tos** an allegretto movement or passage

al·le·gro (ə le′grō′, -lā′-) [*also in italics*] *Music adj., adv.* ⟦It, lit., merry, cheerful < L *alacer*, brisk, sprightly, cheerful⟧ fast; faster than allegretto but not so fast as presto: often used as a musical direction —*n., pl.* **-gros′** an allegro movement or passage

al·lele (ə lēl′) *n.* ⟦Ger *allel* < Gr *allēlōn*, of one another⟧ either of a pair of genes located at the same position on both members of a pair of chromosomes and conveying characters that are inherited in accordance with Mendelian law —**al·lel·ic** (ə lēl′ik, -lel′-) *adj.* —**al·lel′ism′** (-lēl′iz′əm, -lel′-) *n.*

al·lel·o·morph (ə lēl′ō môrf′, ə lel′ō-) *n.* ⟦< prec. + -O- + -MORPH⟧ ALLELE —**al·lel′o·mor′phic** *adj.*

al·lel·op·a·thy (al′əl äp′ə thē, al′ēl-) *n.* ⟦< Gr *allēlōn*, of one another + -O- + -PATHY⟧ the repression or destruction of plants from the effect of certain toxic chemical substances produced and released by other, nearby plants —**al·lel·o·path·ic** (ə lēl′ō path′ik, -lel′-) *adj.*

al·le·lu·ia (al′ə lo͞o′yə, ä′lə-; ä′lä lo͞o′yä′) *interj., n.* ⟦LL(Ec) < Gr *allēlouia* < Heb *haleluya*, HALLELUJAH⟧ HALLELUJAH

al·le·mande (al′ə mand′, -mänd′) *n.* ⟦Fr < *allemand*, German < OFr *aleman* < ML *Alemannus*: see ALEMANNI⟧ **1** a German dance of the 16th century in moderate duple time **2** a stylized instrumental composition evolved from this dance and often used as the first movement of a Baroque suite **3** a figure in a square dance in which two dancers join right or left hands and make a turn

Al·len[1] (al′ən) *n.* a masculine name: see ALAN

Al·len[2] (al′ən), **Ethan** 1738-89; Am. Revolutionary soldier who led the Green Mountain Boys in the capture of Fort Ticonderoga

Al·len·by (al′ən bē), **Edmund Henry Hyn·man** (hin′mən) 1st Viscount Allenby 1861-1936; Brit. army officer: commander of Brit. expeditionary forces in Egypt (1917-18)

Al·len·town (al′ən toun′) ⟦after William *Allen*, the founder⟧ city in E Pa., on the Lehigh River

Allen wrench ⟦after the *Allen* Manufacturing Company of Hartford, Conn., no longer in existence⟧ [*often* **a- w-**] a thin, L-shaped wrench with a hexagonal head at both ends, designed to fit the sockets of certain screws and bolts

☆**al·ler·gen** (al′ər jən, -jen′) *n.* ⟦Ger < *allergie*, ALLERGY + *-gen*, -GEN⟧ a substance inducing an allergic state or reaction —**al′ler·gen′ic** (-jen′ik) *adj.*

☆**al·ler·gic** (ə lur′jik) *adj.* **1** of or caused by allergy **2** having an allergy **3** [Informal] averse or disinclined (*to*) [*allergic* to work]

☆**al·ler·gist** (al′ər jist) *n.* a doctor who specializes in treating allergies

☆**al·ler·gy** (al′ər jē) *n., pl.* **-gies** ⟦Ger *allergie* < Gr *allos*, other (see ELSE) + *-ergeia*, as in *energeia* (see ENERGY)⟧ **1** a hypersensitivity to a specific substance (such as a food, pollen, dust, etc.) or condition (as heat or cold) which in similar amounts or degrees is harmless to most people: it is manifested in a physiological disorder **2** a strong aversion

☆**al·le·thrin** (al′ə thrin′) *n.* ⟦< *all(ene)* (< *allylene* < ALLYL + -ENE) + (PYR)ETHR(UM) + -IN[1]⟧ a thick, pale-yellow, synthetic liquid insecticide, $C_{19}H_{26}O_3$, similar in structure to pyrethrin

al·le·vi·ate (ə lē′vē āt′) *vt.* **-at′ed, -at′ing** ⟦ME *alleviaten* < LL *alleviatus*, pp. of *alleviare*, for L *allevare* < *ad-*, to + *levis*, LIGHT[2]⟧ **1** to make less hard to bear; lighten or relieve (pain, suffering, etc.) **2** to reduce or decrease [to *alleviate* poverty] —*SYN.* RELIEVE —**al·le′vi·a′tor** *n.* —**al·le′vi·a′tive** *adj.*, **al·le′vi·a·to′ry** (-ə tôr′ē)

al·le·vi·a·tion (ə lē′vē ā′shən) *n.* **1** an alleviating or being alleviated **2** a thing that alleviates

al·ley[1] (al′ē) *n., pl.* **-leys** ⟦ME *aly* < OFr *alee* < *aler* (Fr *aller*), to go < ML *alare*, contr. < L *ambulare*, to walk: see AMBLE⟧ **1** a lane in a garden or park, bordered by trees or shrubs **2** a narrow street or walk, specif., a lane behind or alongside a row of buildings or between two rows of buildings that face on adjacent streets **3** *Baseball* the part of the outfield between center field and either left field or right field: also **power alley** **4** *Bowling* LANE[1] (senses 6*a* & *b*) **5** *Tennis* either of the narrow lanes, on opposite sides of the court, that extend the singles area for playing doubles —☆**up (or down) someone's alley** [Slang] suited to someone's tastes or abilities

al·ley[2] (al′ē) *n., pl.* **-leys** ⟦< ALABASTER, formerly used for marbles⟧ a fine marble used as the shooter in playing marbles

☆**alley cat** a homeless, mongrel cat

al·ley-oop (al′ē o͞op′) *interj.* ⟦< Fr *allez* (imper. of *aller*, to go), used as interj. of encouragement, surprise, exhortation + *oop* < ?⟧ used as an exclamation accompanying the act of lifting, rising, etc. —*n. Basketball* a high, lobbed pass to a teammate near the basket who attempts to make a slam-dunk or to tip the ball in

☆**al·ley·way** (al′ē wā′) *n.* **1** an alley between buildings **2** any narrow passageway

all-fired (ôl′fīrd′) [Slang] *adj.* ⟦altered < *hell-fired*⟧ extreme; complete —*adv.* extremely; completely

All Fools' Day APRIL FOOLS' DAY

all fours any of several card games in which four points may be scored during the play of a hand, for winning the high trump, low trump, and jack of trumps, and for "game" (the largest high-card count): see also phrase ON ALL FOURS (at FOUR)

all hail [Archaic] all health: a greeting

All·hal·lows (ôl′hal′ōz′) *n.* ⟦ME *alhalwes* < OE *ealra halgena (dæg)*: see ALL & HALLOW[1]⟧ [Archaic] ALL SAINTS' DAY: also called **All′hal′low·mas** (-hal′ō məs)

All·hal·low·tide (-hal′ō tīd′) *n.* ⟦ME *alle halwen tid*: see prec. & TIDE[1]⟧ [Archaic] the time or season of Allhallows

all·heal (ôl′hēl′) *n.* any of various plants, as selfheal or valerian, thought to have medicinal properties

al·li·a·ceous (al′ē ā′shəs) *adj.* ⟦< L *allium*, garlic + -ACEOUS⟧ **1** of a group of strong-smelling bulb plants of the lily family, including the onion, garlic, etc. **2** having the smell or taste of onions or garlic

al·li·ance (ə lī′əns) *n.* ⟦ME *aliaunce* < OFr *aleiance* < *alier*: see ALLY⟧ **1** an allying or being allied; specif., a union or joining, as of families by marriage **2** a close association for a common objective, as of nations, political parties, etc. **3** the agreement made for such an association **4** the countries, groups, etc. forming such a connection **5** similarity or relationship in characteristics, structure, etc.; affinity

SYN.—**alliance** refers to any association entered into for mutual benefit; **league**, often interchangeable with **alliance**, stresses formality of organization and definiteness of purpose; **coalition** implies a temporary alliance of opposing parties, etc., as in times of emergency; **confederacy** and **confederation** in political usage refer to a combination of independent states for the joint exercise of certain governmental functions, as defense or customs; **union** implies a close, permanent alliance and suggests complete unity of purpose and interest

al·li·cin (al′ə sin′) *n.* ⟦< *alliin*, an amino acid found in garlic oil (< L *allium*, garlic + -IN[1]) + -(I)C + -IN[1]⟧ an unstable, yellowish, oily liquid, $C_6H_{10}OS_2$, extracted from garlic and used as an antibacterial substance in science and industry

al·lied (ə līd′; *also, esp. for 3*, al′īd′) *adj.* ⟦see ALLY⟧ **1** united by kinship, treaty, agreement, etc. **2** closely related [Danish and Swedish are *allied* languages] **3** [**A-**] of the Allies —*SYN.* RELATED

Al·lier (āl yā′) river in central France, flowing northward into the Loire: *c.* 250 mi (402 km)

Al·lies (al′īz′, ə līz′) *pl.n.* **1** in WWI, the nations allied by treaty against Germany and the other Central Powers; orig., Great Britain, France, and Russia, later joined by the U.S., Italy, Japan, etc. **2** in WWII, the nations associated against the Axis, esp. Great Britain, the Soviet Union, and the U.S.: see UNITED NATIONS

al·li·ga·tor (al′ə gāt′ər) *n., pl.* **-tors** or **-tor** ⟦Sp *el lagarto* < *el*, the + L *lacerta, lacertus*: see LIZARD⟧ **1** any of a genus (*Alligator*) of large crocodilian reptiles found in tropical rivers and marshes of the U.S. and China: its snout is shorter and blunter than the crocodile's, and its teeth do not protrude outside its closed mouth **2** a scaly leather made from an alligator's hide ☆**3** a machine, tool, etc. with a strong, movable, often toothed jaw

alligator clip a spring-loaded fastening device having jaws with a sawlike edge that resemble those of an alligator, used as to make a temporary electrical connection

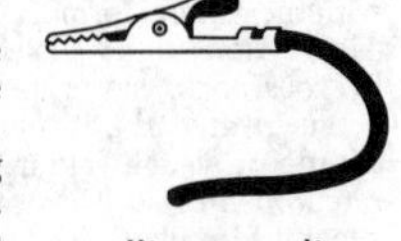

alligator clip

alligator pear ⟦altered (? by folk etym. because of the appearance of the skin) < *avogato*: see AVOCADO⟧ AVOCADO

☆**alligator snapper** a large, freshwater snapping turtle (*Macroclemys temminckii*) of the SE U.S. and the Mississippi Valley, found chiefly in rivers and bayous: it may weigh up to 100 kg (220 lb)

all-im·por·tant (ôl′im pôrt′'nt) *adj.* highly important; necessary; essential

all-in·clu·sive (-in klo͞os′iv) *adj.* including everything; comprehensive

al·lit·er·ate (ə lit′ər āt′) *vi.* **-at′ed, -at′ing** ⟦back-form. < fol. ⟧ **1** to constitute or show alliteration **2** to use alliteration —*vt.* to cause to show alliteration

al·lit·er·a·tion (ə lit′ər ā′shən) *n.* ⟦ML *alliteratio* < L *ad-*, to + *littera*, LETTER[1]⟧ repetition of an initial sound, usually of a consonant or cluster, in two or more words of a phrase, line of poetry, etc. (Ex.: "What a *t*ale of *t*error now their *t*urbulency *t*ells!")

al·lit·er·a·tive (ə lit′ər āt′iv, -ər ə tiv′) *adj.* of, showing, or using alliteration —**al·lit′er·a′tive·ly** *adv.*

al·li·um (al′ē əm) *n.* ⟦ModL < L, garlic⟧ any strong-smelling bulb plant of a genus (*Allium*) of the lily family, as the onion, garlic, leek, etc.

all-night·er (ôl′nīt′ər) *n.* [Informal] something that lasts through the night, as a work or study session or a party

al·lo- (al′ō, al′ə) ⟦< Gr *allos*, other: see ELSE⟧ *combining form* variation, departure from the normal, reversal [*allonym, allomorph*]

al·lo·cate (al′ō kāt′, al′ə-) *vt.* **-cat′ed, -cat′ing** ⟦< ML *allocatus*, pp. of *allocare* < L *ad-*, to + *locare*, to place < *locus*: see LOCUS⟧ **1** to set apart for a specific purpose [to *allocate* funds for housing] **2** to distribute in shares or according to a plan; allot **3** to fix the location of; locate —*SYN.* ALLOT —**al·lo·ca·ble** (al′ə kə bəl) *adj.*, **al′lo·cat′a·ble**

al·lo·ca·tion (al′ō kā′shən, al′ə-) *n.* **1** an allocating or being allocated **2** a thing or amount allocated

al·loch·tho·nous (ə läk′thə nəs) ***adj.*** ⟦ALLO- + (AUTO)CHTHON + -OUS⟧ originating elsewhere; not native to a place

al·lo·cu·tion (al′ō kyōō′shən, al′ə-) ***n.*** ⟦L *allocutio* < *alloqui*, to speak to < *ad-*, to + *loqui*, to speak⟧ a formal address, esp. one warning or advising with authority

al·lod (al′äd′) ***n.*** ALLODIUM

al·lo·di·al (ə lō′dē əl) ***adj.*** of an allodium; freehold

al·lo·di·um (ə lō′dē əm) ***n.*** ⟦ML < Frank **alod*, full and free possession < *all*, all + **ōd*, akin to OE *ead*, wealth < IE **audh-* < base **(a)wē-*, to weave > WEED[2]⟧ *Law* land owned independently, free of any superior claim, and without any rent, payment in service, etc.; a freehold estate: opposed to FEUD[2]

al·log·a·my (ə läg′ə mē) ***n.*** ⟦ALLO- + -GAMY⟧ the process of cross-fertilizing; cross-fertilization —**al·log′a·mous** (-məs) ***adj.***

al·lo·ge·ne·ic (al′ō jə nē′ik, al′ə-) ***adj.*** ⟦< ALLO- + Gr *genos*, race, kind (see GENUS) + -IC⟧ designating or of tissue, an organ, etc. from a genetically different individual of the same species: said of tissue, etc. used in an allograft: cf. SYNGENEIC: also **al′lo·gen′ic** (-jen′ik) —**al′lo·ge·ne′i·cal·ly** ***adv.***

al·lo·graft (al′ō graft′, al′ə-) ***n.*** a graft of tissue or an organ taken from an individual of the same species as the recipient but with different hereditary factors; homograft: see AUTOGRAFT, XENOGRAFT

al·lo·graph (al′ō graf′, al′ə-) ***n.*** ⟦ALLO- + -GRAPH⟧ *Linguis.* **1** any of the ways a unit of a writing system, as the letter of an alphabet, is formed or shaped **2** any of the units or combinations of units that can represent a single phoneme, morpheme, syllable, etc.

al·lom·er·ism (ə läm′ər iz′əm) ***n.*** ⟦< ALLO- + Gr *meros*, part (see MERIT) + -ISM⟧ variation in chemical composition without change in crystalline form —**al·lom′er·ous** (-əs) ***adj.***

al·lom·e·try (ə läm′ə trē) ***n.*** ⟦ALLO- + -METRY⟧ the study and measurement of the relative growth of a part of an organism in comparison with the whole

al·lo·morph (al′ō môrf′, al′ə-) ***n.*** ⟦ALLO- + -MORPH⟧ **1** *Mineralogy a)* any of the crystalline forms of a substance existing in more than one such form *b)* PARAMORPH **2** *Linguis.* any of the variant forms of a morpheme as conditioned by position or adjoining sounds —**al′lo·mor′phic** ***adj.*** —**al′lo·mor′phism′** ***n.***

al·lo·path (al′ō path′, al′ə-) ***n.*** a person who practices or advocates allopathy: also **al·lop·a·thist** (ə läp′ə thist′)

al·lop·a·thy (ə läp′ə thē) ***n.*** ⟦Ger *allopathie* (see ALLO- & -PATHY), after Gr *allopatheia*, subjection to external influences⟧ treatment of disease by remedies that produce effects different from or opposite to those produced by the disease: loosely applied to the general practice of medicine today, but in strict usage opposed to HOMEOPATHY —**al·lo·path·ic** (al′ō path′ik, al′ə-) ***adj.*** —**al′lo·path′i·cal·ly** ***adv.***

al·lo·pat·ric (al′ō pa′trik, al′ə-) ***adj.*** ⟦< ALLO- + Gr *patra*, native village (< *patēr*, FATHER) + -IC⟧ *Biol.* of or pertaining to species of organisms occurring in different but often adjacent areas —**al′lo·pat′ri·cal·ly** ***adv.*** —**al·lop·a·try** (ə läp′ə trē) ***n.***

al·lo·phane (al′ō fān′, al′ə-) ***n.*** ⟦ALLO- + -PHANE, as in Gr *allophanēs*, appearing otherwise: so named because it changes appearance under the blowpipe⟧ a soft clay mineral, a translucent, hydrous silicate of aluminum, of varying composition and color, typically occurring as incrustations in chalk and sandstone

al·lo·phone (al′ō fōn′, al′ə-) ***n.*** ⟦ALLO- + PHONE[1]⟧ *Linguis.* any of the variant forms of a phoneme as conditioned by position or adjoining sounds [the relatively short (a) of *mat* and the relatively long (a) of *mad* are *allophones*] —**al′lo·phon′ic** (-fän′ik) ***adj.***

al·lo·plasm (al′ō plaz′əm, al′ə-) ***n.*** ⟦ALLO- + -PLASM⟧ *Biol.* **1** the special form of protoplasm from which cilia, flagella, etc. develop **2** METAPLASM (sense 1) —**al′lo·plas′mic** (-plaz′mik) ***adj.***, **al′lo·plas·mat′ic** (-plaz mat′ik)

al·lo·pol·y·ploi·dy (al′ō päl′ə ploi′dē, al′ə-) ***n.*** ⟦ALLO- + POLYPLOID + -Y[3]⟧ the state of having two or more sets of chromosomes derived from parents of different species or widely differing strains —**al′lo·pol′y·ploid′** ***n.***, ***adj.***

al·lo·pu·ri·nol (al′ō pyoor′ə nôl′, -nōl′; al′ə-) ***n.*** a white, powdery drug that is an isomer of hypoxanthine and inhibits the production of uric acid: used to treat gout

☆**al·lo·sau·rus** (al′ō sôr′əs, al′ə-) ***n.*** ⟦ModL: see ALLO- & -SAUR⟧ any of a genus (*Allosaurus*) of huge, carnivorous saurischian dinosaurs of the Jurassic and Cretaceous periods: also **al′lo·saur′**

al·lo·ster·ic (al′ō ster′ik, -stir′-; al′ə-) ***adj.*** of or having to do with a protein with a structure that is altered reversibly by a small molecule so that its original function is modified

al·lot (ə lät′) ***vt.*** **-lot′ted, -lot′ting** ⟦OFr *aloter* < *a-*, to + *loter*, to divide by lot or into lots < *lot*, lot, of Gmc orig.: see LOT⟧ **1** to distribute by lot or in arbitrary shares; apportion **2** to give or assign as one's share [each speaker is *allotted* five minutes]

SYN.—**allot** and **assign** both imply the giving of a share or portion with no indication of uniform distribution, **assign** having the extra connotation of authoritativeness [I was *assigned* the task of *allotting* the seats]; **apportion** connotes the just, proportionate, often uniform distribution of a fixed number of portions; **allocate** usually implies the allowance of a fixed amount for a specific purpose [to *allocate* $50 for books]

al·lot·ment (ə lät′mənt) ***n.*** **1** an allotting or being allotted **2** a thing allotted; portion; share **3** [Brit.] a small plot of public land rented to an individual for growing vegetables or flowers **4** *Mil.* a portion of one's pay regularly deducted, as for one's dependents, insurance premiums, etc.

al·lo·trope (al′ō trōp′, al′ə-) ***n.*** an allotropic form

al·lo·trop·ic (al′ō träp′ik, al′ə-) ***adj.*** of or characterized by allotropy: also **al′lo·trop′i·cal** —**al′lo·trop′i·cal·ly** ***adv.***

al·lot·ro·py (ə lä′trə pē) ***n.*** ⟦< Gr *allotropos*, of or in another manner < *allos*, other + *tropos*, way, turn: see TROPE⟧ the property that certain chemical elements and compounds have of existing in two or more different forms, as carbon in the form of charcoal, diamond, lampblack, etc.: also **al·lot′ro·pism′**

all′ot·ta·va (äl′ô tä′vä) ***adj.***, ***adv.*** ⟦It, according to the octave⟧ *Musical Direction* to be played an octave higher, or, sometimes, an octave lower, than the notes in the score

al·lot·tee (ə lät′ē′) ***n.*** a person to whom something is allotted

al·lo·type (al′ō tīp′, al′ə-) ***n.*** **1** *Immunology* a genetic variant, esp. an antibody that acts as an antigen when introduced into the bodies of most other individuals of the same species **2** *Taxonomy* an animal or plant specimen that shows physical characteristics, usually sexual ones, not shown in the holotype —**al′lo·typ′ic** (-tip′ik) ***adj.***

all-out (ôl′out′) ***adj.*** complete or wholehearted [an *all-out* effort]

all·o·ver (ôl′ō′vər) ***adj.*** **1** over the whole surface **2** with the pattern repeated over the whole surface [*allover* embroidery] —***n.*** cloth, etc. with such a pattern

al·low (ə lou′) ***vt.*** ⟦ME *alowen* < OFr *alouer* < ML *allocare*, ALLOCATE; assoc. with OFr *alouer* < L *allaudare*, to extol < *ad-*, to + *laudare*, to praise⟧ **1** to let do, happen, etc.; permit; let [we weren't *allowed* to go] **2** to let have [she *allowed* herself no sweets] **3** to let enter or stay [dogs are not *allowed*] **4** to admit (a claim or the like); acknowledge as true or valid **5** to provide or allot (a certain amount, period of time, etc.) for a purpose [*allow* an inch for shrinkage] **6** [Dial.] *a)* to think; give as one's opinion *b)* to intend —***SYN.*** LET[1] —**allow for** to make allowance, provision, etc. for; keep in mind [*allow for* the difference in their ages] —**allow of** to be subject to; admit of

al·low·a·ble (ə lou′ə bəl) ***adj.*** that can be allowed; permissible —**al·low′a·bly** ***adv.***

al·low·ance (ə lou′əns) ***n.*** **1** the act of allowing, permitting, admitting, etc. [the *allowance* of a claim] **2** something allowed as a share; specif., an amount of money, food, etc. given regularly to a child, dependent, etc. or to military personnel for a specific purpose [travel *allowance*] **3** a reduction in the price of something in consideration of a large order or of turning in a used article, etc. **4** the amount by which something is allowed to be more or less than stated, as to compensate for the weight of the container, inaccuracy of machining, etc. —***vt.*** **-anced, -anc·ing** **1** to put on an allowance or a ration **2** to apportion economically —***adj.*** designating a horse race in which the weight each horse must carry is set by a formula tied to the horse's past performance and earnings —**make allowance (**or **allowances)** to take circumstances, limitations, etc. into consideration —**make allowance (**or **allowances) for** **1** to forgive or excuse because of mitigating factors **2** to leave room, time, etc. for; allow for

al·low·ed·ly (ə lou′id lē) ***adv.*** by allowance or admission; admittedly

al·loy (al′oi; *also, and for v. usually,* ə loi′, a-) ***n.*** ⟦ME *alai* < Anglo-Fr *alei* (OFr *aloi*) < *aleier*: see the ***vt.***⟧ **1** the relative purity of gold or silver; fineness **2** a substance that is a mixture, as by fusion, of two or more metals, or of a metal and something else **3** *a)* [Archaic] a less valuable metal mixed with a more valuable one, often to give hardness *b)* something that lowers the value or quality of another thing when mixed with it —***vt.*** ⟦Fr *aloyer* < OFr *aloier, aleier* < L *alligare* < *ad-*, to + *ligare*, to bind: see LIGATURE⟧ **1** to make (a metal) less pure by mixing with a less valuable metal **2** to mix (metals) to form an alloy **3** to debase by mixing with something inferior

all-pur·pose (ôl′pur′pəs) ***adj.*** for every pertinent purpose; useful in many ways

all right **1** satisfactory; adequate **2** in satisfactory or acceptable condition **3** correct **4** yes; very well: used in reply to a question or merely to preface or resume one's remarks **5** [Informal] certainly [he's the one who did it, *all right*]

all-right (ôl′rīt′) ***adj.*** [Slang] honest, honorable, good, excellent, etc.: used before the noun it modifies

all-round (ôl′round′) ***adj.***, ***adv.*** *var. of* ALL-AROUND

all-round·er (ôl′roun′dər) ***n.*** [Brit.] a person who is skilled in many different areas, esp. in all aspects of a sport, as cricket

☆**alls** (ôlz) ***pron.*** [Dial.] all; all that [*alls* I know is what he told me]

All Saints' Day an annual church festival (Nov. 1) in honor of all the saints

all·seed (ôl′sēd′) ***n.*** any of various plants producing many seeds, as knotgrass or goosefoot

all·sorts (ôl′sôrts) ***pl.n.*** [Brit.] assorted small candies, usually flavored with licorice

All Souls' Day in certain Christian churches, a day (usually Nov. 2) of services and prayer for the dead

all·spice (ôl′spīs′) ***n.*** **1** a West Indian tree (*Pimenta dioica*) of the myrtle family **2** its berry **3** the spice made from this berry: so named because its flavor seems to combine the tastes of several spices

☆**all-star** (ôl′stär′) ***adj.*** **1** made up entirely of outstanding or star performers **2** of or characteristic of all-stars or an all-star event —***n.*** a member of an all-star team or group

all-time (ôl′tīm′) ***adj.*** unsurpassed up to the present time [an *all-time* record]

al·lude (ə lōōd′, a-) ***vi.*** **-lud′ed, -lud′ing** ⟦L *alludere*, to joke, jest < *ad-*, to + *ludere*, to play: see LUDICROUS⟧ to refer in a casual or indirect way (*to*) —***SYN.*** REFER

al·lure (ə loor′, a-) *vt., vi.* **-lured′**, **-lur′ing** ⟦ME *aluren* < OFr *alurer* < *a-*, to + *loirer*, to lure (see LURE); assoc. with Fr *allure*, gait, way of walking, love affair < *aller* (see ALLEY[1])⟧ to tempt with something desirable; attract; entice; fascinate —*n.* the power to entice or attract; fascination —**SYN.** ATTRACT —**al·lure′ment** *n.*

al·lur·ing (ə loor′iŋ, a-) *adj.* tempting strongly; highly attractive; charming —**al·lur′ing·ly** *adv.*

al·lu·sion (ə lo͞o′zhən, a-) *n.* ⟦LL *allusio*, a playing with < *allusus*, pp. of *alludere*: see ALLUDE⟧ **1** the act of alluding **2** an indirect reference; casual mention

al·lu·sive (ə lo͞o′siv, a-) *adj.* **1** containing an allusion **2** using allusion; full of allusions —**al·lu′sive·ly** *adv.* —**al·lu′sive·ness** *n.*

al·lu·vi·al (ə lo͞o′vē əl, a-) *adj.* ⟦< L *alluvius* (see ALLUVION) + -AL⟧ of, found in, or made up of, alluvium —*n.* ALLUVIUM

☆**alluvial cone** a steep, narrow, cone-shaped alluvial fan formed where a swift stream suddenly slows down, as where an upland stream emerges abruptly into a level plain

alluvial fan a gradually sloping mass of alluvium that widens out like a fan from the place where a stream begins to slow down

al·lu·vi·on (ə lo͞o′vē ən, a-) *n.* ⟦Fr < L *alluvio*, an overflowing < *alluere* < *ad-*, to + *luere*, var. of *lavare*, to LAVE⟧ **1** *a)* the washing of water against a shore or bank *b)* an overflowing; flood *c)* ALLUVIUM: these senses are no longer used in geology **2** *Law* a gradual addition to land along a river, lake, etc., as through the deposit of sedimentary material

al·lu·vi·um (ə lo͞o′vē əm, a-) *n., pl.* **-vi·ums** or **-vi·a** (-vē ə) ⟦L, neut. of *alluvius*: see prec.⟧ sand, clay, silt, etc. gradually deposited by moving water, as along a riverbed or the shore of a lake —**SYN.** WASH

all-wheel drive (ôl′hwēl′, -wēl′) an automotive power-delivery system capable of providing driving power to all four wheels simultaneously

al·ly (ə lī′, a-; *also, and for n. usually*, al′ī) *vt.* **-lied′**, **-ly′ing** ⟦ME *alien* < OFr *alier* < L *alligare* < *ad-*, to + *ligare*, to bind: see LIGATURE⟧ **1** to unite or associate for a specific purpose, as families by marriage, nations by treaty, or companies by agreement: generally used reflexively or in the passive **2** to relate by similarity of structure, certain qualities, etc.: usually in the passive [the onion is *allied* to the lily] —*vi.* to become allied —*n., pl.* **-lies** **1** a country, person, or group joined with another or others for a common purpose: see also ALLIES **2** a plant, animal, or thing closely related in structure, etc. to another **3** an associate; helper; auxiliary —**SYN.** ASSOCIATE

al·lyl (al′il) *n.* ⟦ALL(IUM) + -YL⟧ *Chem.* the radical $H_2C{:}CHCH_2$ —**al·lyl·ic** (ə lil′ik, a-) *adj.*

allyl alcohol a poisonous, colorless liquid, $H_2C{:}CHCH_2OH$, with a pungent odor, used in resins, plasticizers, herbicides, etc.

allyl resin any of several thermosetting vinyl resins, derived from esters of allyl alcohol and dibasic acids, that are highly resistant to chemicals, moisture, abrasion, and heat, and are used as laminating adhesives, in varnishes, etc.

allyl thiourea THIOSINAMINE

Al·ma (al′mə) *n.* ⟦L, fem. of *almus*, nourishing, bountiful⟧ a feminine name

Al·ma-A·ta (äl′mə ä tä′) *former name for* ALMATY

Al·ma·gest (al′mə jest′) *n.* ⟦ME < OFr *almageste* < Ar *al majisṭī* < *al*, the + Gr *megistē (syntaxis)*, greatest (work)⟧ **1** a vast work on astronomy and mathematics compiled by Ptolemy *c.* A.D. 140 **2** [**a-**] any of several medieval works like this, variously on astrology, alchemy, etc.

al·ma ma·ter (al′mə mät′ər, äl′-; māt′-) ⟦L, fostering mother⟧ **1** the college or school that one attended **2** its official anthem, or hymn

al·ma·nac (ôl′mə nak′, al′-) *n.* ⟦ME *almenak* < ML *almanachus* < LGr *almenichiaka*, calendar, ? of Coptic orig.⟧ **1** a yearly calendar of days, weeks, and months, with astronomical data, weather forecasts, etc. **2** a book published annually, containing information, usually statistical, on many subjects Also sp. [Archaic] **al′ma·nack′**

al·man·dine (al′mən dēn′, -din′) *n.* ⟦ML *alamandina* < LL *Alabandina (gemma)*, (stone) from *Alabanda*, city in the interior of CARIA⟧ a purplish-red variety of garnet, $Fe_3Al_2(SiO_4)_3$, used as an inexpensive gem and an abrasive: sometimes called **al′man·dite′** (-dīt′)

Al·ma-Tad·e·ma (al′mə tad′i mə), Sir **Lawrence** 1836-1912; Eng. painter, born in the Netherlands

Al·ma·ty (äl′mə tē′, al′-) city in SE Kazakhstan: former capital

Al·me·rí·a (äl′mə rē′ə) seaport in SE Spain, on the Mediterranean

al·might·y (ôl mīt′ē) *adj.* ⟦ME *almihtig* < OE *ealmihtig* < *eal*, ALL + *mihtig*, MIGHTY⟧ **1** having unlimited power; all-powerful **2** [Informal] great; extreme [an *almighty* nuisance] —*adv.* [Slang] extremely —**the Almighty** God —☆**the almighty dollar** ⟦coined (1836) by IRVING[2]⟧ [Informal] money regarded figuratively as a god, or source of great power —**al·might′i·ly** *adv.* —**al·might′i·ness** *n.*

al·mond (ä′mənd; *also* am′ənd & al′mənd, ôl′-) *n.* ⟦ME *almande* < OFr *alemande, amande* < ML *amandola* < L *amygdala* < Gr *amygdalē*⟧ **1** *a)* the edible, nutlike kernel of the small, dry, peachlike fruit of a prunus tree (*Prunus dulcis*) that grows in warm regions *b)* the tree itself **2** anything shaped like an almond, oval and pointed at one or both ends **3** the light-tan color of the almond shell —*adj.* **1** made of almonds **2** having the flavor, shape, or color of an almond

al·mon·er (al′mən ər, ä′mən-) *n.* ⟦ME *almoiner* < OFr *almosnier* < *almosne*, act of mercy < LL(Ec) **alemosyna* < *eleemosyna*: see ALMS⟧ a distributor of alms, as for a church, royal family, etc.

al·most (ôl′mōst′, ôl mōst′) *adv.* ⟦OE *eallmæst*: see ALL & MOST⟧ very nearly but not completely; all but

alms (ämz, älmz) *n., pl.* **alms** ⟦ME *almesse* < OE *ælmesse* < LL(Ec) *eleemosyna* < Gr *eleēmosynē*, pity, mercy (in LXX & N.T., charity, alms) < *eleēmōn*, merciful < *eleos*, mercy, orig., woe, prob. < IE echoic base **el-* > Norw dial. *jalm*, noise⟧ **1** money, food, clothes, etc. given to poor people **2** [Obs.] a deed of mercy —**alms′giv′er** *n.* —**alms′giv′ing** *n.*

alms·house (-hous′) *n.* **1** [Archaic] a home for people too poor to support themselves; poorhouse **2** [Brit.] a privately endowed home for the disabled or aged poor

alms·man (-mən) *n., pl.* **-men** (-mən) [Now Rare] a person, esp. a man, supported by alms

al·ni·co (al′ni kō′) *n.* ⟦AL(UMINUM) + NI(CKEL) + CO(BALT)⟧ any of various alloys of iron containing cobalt, nickel, aluminum, and occasionally copper, titanium, or niobium: used in making strong permanent magnets

Al-O·beid or **al-O·beid** (al′ō bād′) *var. of* EL OBEID

a·lo·di·um (ə lō′dē əm) *n. alt. sp. of* ALLODIUM

al·oe (al′ō′; *for 1* al′ō ē′, al′ō′) *n., pl.* **-oes′** ⟦ME < L < Gr *aloē* < ? Heb *ahalim*, pl. of *ahal*, aloe wood < Sans *agaru*⟧ **1** any of a large genus (*Aloe*) of plants of the lily family, native to Africa, with fleshy leaves that are spiny along the edge and with drooping clusters of tubular, red or yellow flowers **2** [*pl., with sing. v.*] a bitter, laxative drug made from the juice of certain aloe leaves **3** [*pl., with sing. v.*] the aromatic heartwood of several trees of a genus (*Aquilaria*) of the mezereum family, native to the East Indies and Southeast Asia —**al′o·et′ic** (-et′ik) *adj.*

aloe ve·ra (vir′ə, ver′ə) ⟦ModL, name of species < L *aloe* (see prec.) + *vera*, true, fem. of *verus*: see VERY⟧ **1** an aloe (*Aloe vera*) often kept as a houseplant: its juice is thought to heal cuts and burns **2** this plant's juice, often added to cosmetics, ointments, etc.

a·loft (ə lôft′) *adv.* ⟦ME < *o*, *on*, ON + *loft* < ON *lopt*: see LOFT⟧ **1** far above the ground **2** in the air; flying **3** high above the deck of a ship; in the rigging or on a mast

☆**a·lo·ha** (ä lō′hä, -hä′; ə lō′ə) *n., interj.* ⟦Haw, lit., love < Proto-Polynesian **'alo'ofa*⟧ **1** hello **2** goodbye

aloha shirt [Informal] HAWAIIAN SHIRT

al·o·in (al′ō in′) *n.* a bitter, crystalline cathartic prepared from the aloe

a·lone (ə lōn′) *adj., adv.* ⟦ME < *al*, ALL + *one*, ONE⟧ **1** apart from anything or anyone else [the hut stood *alone* on the prairie] **2** without involving any other person [to walk *alone*] **3** without anything further; with nothing more; only [the carton *alone* weighs two pounds] **4** without equal or peer [to stand *alone* as an example of courage] ➥As an adjective, *alone* generally follows the word it modifies —**let alone** **1** to refrain from bothering or interfering with: also **leave alone** **2** not to speak of [we hadn't a dime, *let alone* a dollar] — **let** (or **leave**) **well enough alone** to be content with things as they are and not try to improve them: also [Brit.] **let** (or **leave**) **well alone**

SYN.—**alone**, unqualified, denotes the simple fact of being by oneself or itself; **solitary** conveys the same sense but suggests more strongly the lack of companionship or association [a *solitary* tree in the meadow]; **lonely**, and the more poetic **lone**, convey a heightened sense of solitude and gloom [the *lonely* sentinel walks his post]; **lonesome** suggests a longing or yearning for companionship, often for a particular person [the child is *lonesome* for her mother] —**ANT. accompanied**

a·long (ə lôŋ′) *prep.* ⟦ME < OE *andlang*, along, by the side of < *and-*, over against + *-lang*, in length: see LONG[1]⟧ **1** on or beside the length of; over or throughout the length of [we hiked *along* the trail; *along* the driveway there is a hedge] **2** in the course of [*along* the way] **3** in conformity with [to think *along* certain lines] —*adv.* **1** in a line; lengthwise **2** progressively forward or onward [he walked *along* by himself] **3** as a companion [come *along* with us] **4** with one [she took her camera *along*] ☆**5** on its way; advanced [the program was well *along* when he arrived] ☆**6** [Informal] approaching [*along* toward evening] —**all along** all the time; from the very beginning —**along with** **1** together with **2** in addition to —☆**be along** [Informal] to come or arrive [*I'll be along later*] —**get along** **1** to go forward **2** to survive; manage [to *get along* on a small salary] **3** to be compatible or on friendly terms **4** [Informal] to go away

a·long·shore (ə lôŋ′shôr′) *adv.* along the shore; near or beside the shore

a·long·side (-sīd′) *adv.* at or by the side; side by side —*prep.* at the side of; side by side with —**alongside of** at the side of; beside; adjoining

a·loof (ə lo͞of′) *adv.* ⟦*a-*, A-[1] + *loof* < Du *loef*, LUFF⟧ at a distance but in view; apart —*adj.* **1** at a distance; removed **2** distant in sympathy, interest, etc.; reserved and cool [her manner was *aloof*] —**a·loof′ly** *adv.* —**a·loof′ness** *n.*

al·o·pe·ci·a (al′ə pēsh′ə, -pē′shē ə) *n.* ⟦L, baldness, fox mange < Gr *alōpekia* < *alōpēx*, a fox⟧ loss of hair, esp. on the head; baldness

a·lors (à lôr′) *interj.* ⟦Fr⟧ well then! so!: a generalized exclamation

A·lost (à lôst′) *Fr. name for* AALST

a·lot (ə lät′) *n., adv. slang var. of* A LOT (see the phrase at LOT)

a·loud (ə loud′) *adv.* **1** loudly [to cry *aloud*] **2** in an audible voice; not silently [read the letter *aloud*]

a·low (ə lō′) *adv.* ⟦ME *aloue* < *on*, ON + *loue* < *lah*, LOW[1]⟧ *Naut.* BELOW (sense 5)

Al·o·y·si·us (al′ō ish′əs, -ē əs) *n.* ⟦ML *Aloisius*; prob. < OFr *Loeis*: see LOUIS[1]⟧ a masculine name

alp (alp) *n.* ⟦< L *Alpes*, the ALPS⟧ a high mountain, esp. in Switzerland: see ALPS

al·pac·a (al pak′ə) *n., pl.* **-pac′as** or **-pac′a** ⟦Sp < Aymara *allpaca*⟧ **1** a domesticated South American llama (*Lama glama pacos*) with valuable, long, silky, brown or black wool **2** its wool **3** a thin cloth woven from this wool, often mixed with other fibers **4** a glossy, generally black cloth of cotton or rayon, used for linings, suits, etc.

al·pen·glow (al′pən glō′) *n.* ⟦partial transl. of Ger *alpenglühen* < *alpen*, of the ALPS + *glühen*, GLOW⟧ a reddish glow seen on mountain tops before sunrise or after sunset

al·pen·stock (-stäk′) *n.* ⟦Ger, Alpine staff⟧ a strong iron-pointed staff used by mountain climbers

al·pes·trine (al pes′trin) *adj.* ⟦ML *alpestris* < L *Alpes*: see ALPS⟧ **1** of the Alps or any mountainous region **2** *Bot.* growing in the elevated region closest to the timberline: see also SUBALPINE (sense 2)

al·pha (al′fə) *n.* ⟦Gr < NW Sem: cf. Heb *alef*, ALEPH⟧ **1** the first letter of the Greek alphabet (Α, α) **2** the beginning of anything **3** [**A-**] *Astron.* the name assigned to the brightest star in each constellation: followed by the constellation's name in the genitive case, as *Alpha Centauri* —*adj.* **1** designating or of the socially dominant member of a group, esp. of a group of animals [the *alpha* male] **2** *Chem.* designating the first of two or more positions in which the substituting atom or radical appears relative to some particular carbon atom in an organic compound: usually written α-: the other positions, in order, are beta (β-), gamma (γ-), delta (δ-), etc. See BETA

al·pha-ad·re·ner·gic (al′fə ad′rə nʉr′jik) *adj.* of or having to do with an alpha receptor

alpha and omega **1** the first and last letters of the Greek alphabet **2** the beginning and the end: cf. Rev. 1:8

Al·pha Aq·ui·lae (al′fə ak′wi lē′) *Astron.* ALTAIR

Alpha Au·ri·gae (ô rī′jē) *Astron.* CAPELLA

al·pha·bet (al′fə bet′) *n.* ⟦LL(Ec) *alphabetum* < LGr *alphabētos* < Gr *alpha* + *bēta*, the first two letters of the Greek alphabet⟧ **1** the letters of a language, arranged in a traditional order **2** a system of characters, signs, or symbols used to indicate letters or speech sounds **3** the first elements or principles, as of a branch of knowledge

al·pha·bet·i·cal (al′fə bet′i kəl) *adj.* **1** of or using an alphabet **2** arranged in the regular order of the alphabet Also **al′pha·bet′ic** —**al′pha·bet′i·cal·ly** *adv.*

al·pha·bet·ize (al′fə bə tīz′) *vt.* **-ized′**, **-iz′ing** **1** to arrange in alphabetical order **2** to express by or provide with an alphabet —**al′pha·bet′i·za′tion** (-bet′i zā′shən) *n.* —**al′pha·bet·iz′er** *n.*

alphabet soup **1** a soup containing pasta in the shape of letters **2** ⟦in ref. to a proliferation of agency acronyms and abbreviations⟧ a jumble, as of government bureaucracies

alpha blocker any of a class of drugs used to dilate the blood vessels by blocking the nerve impulses that normally excite the alpha receptors

Al·pha Bo·ö·tis (al′fə bō ō′tis) *Astron.* ARCTURUS

Alpha Ca·nis Ma·jo·ris (kā′nis mə jôr′is) *Astron.* SIRIUS

Alpha Canis Mi·no·ris (mə nôr′əs) *Astron.* PROCYON

Alpha Ca·ri·nae (kə rī′nē) *Astron.* CANOPUS[1]

alpha cells **1** cells in the anterior pituitary that contain acidophil granules **2** cells in the pancreas that produce glucagon

Alpha Cen·tau·ri (sen tô′rī′) a binary star, the brightest star in the constellation Centaurus: magnitude, −0.01: it is the nearest of the stars that are visible to the naked eye, except for the sun

Alpha Cyg·ni (sig′ni′) *Astron.* DENEB

Alpha E·rid·a·ni (ē rid′ə nī′) *Astron.* ACHERNAR

al·pha-fe·to·pro·tein (al′fə fēt′ō prō′tēn′, -tē in) *n.* ⟦ALPHA + FETO- (var. of FETI-) + PROTEIN⟧ a protein in the blood of a normal fetus, occasionally reappearing in an adult, where its presence indicates the possibility of disease or, in a pregnant woman, of fetal malformations

Alpha Gem·i·no·rum (jem′ə nôr′əm) ⟦< L *geminorum*, gen. of *gemini*: see GEMINI⟧ *Astron.* CASTOR

alpha hydroxy acid *see* AHA

alpha iron a soft, crystalline, allotropic form of iron stable below 912°C: it changes from being magnetic to being paramagnetic at 768°C

Alpha Le·o·nis (lē ō′nis) *Astron.* REGULUS[1]

Alpha Ly·rae (lī′rē) *Astron.* VEGA[1]

al·pha·nu·mer·ic (al′fə no͞o mer′ik, -nyo͞o-) *adj.* ⟦ALPHA(BET) + NUMERIC(AL)⟧ having or using both alphabetical and numerical symbols

Alpha O·ri·o·nis (ō rī′ō nis) *Astron.* BETELGEUSE

alpha particle a positively charged particle given off by certain radioactive substances: it consists of two protons and two neutrons (a helium nucleus), and is converted into an atom of helium by the acquisition of two electrons

Alpha Pis·cis Aus·tri·ni (pis′is ôs trī′nī′, pī′sis-) *Astron.* FOMALHAUT

alpha ray a stream of alpha particles, less penetrating than a beta ray

alpha receptor a receptor, found on the surface of some cells of the sympathetic nervous system, that is stimulated by adrenergic substances resulting in constriction of blood vessels and contraction of most smooth muscle: cf. BETA RECEPTOR

Alpha Scor·pi·i (skôr′pē ī′) *Astron.* ANTARES

Alpha Tau·ri (tô′rī′) *Astron.* ALDEBARAN

Alpha Ur·sae Mi·no·ris (ʉr′sē mə nôr′is) *Astron.* POLARIS

Alpha Vir·gi·nis (vʉr′jē nis, vir′-) ⟦see VIRGIN⟧ *Astron.* SPICA

alpha wave any of the electrical waves from the parietal and occipital regions of the brain, having frequencies from 8 to 13 hertz: a sign of relaxation, since they indicate a lack of sensory stimulation in a conscious person: also **alpha rhythm**

Al·phe·us (al fē′əs) *n.* ⟦L < Gr *Alpheios*⟧ *Gr. Myth.* a river god who pursues the nymph Arethusa until she is changed into a stream by Artemis

Al·phon·so (al fän′zō, -sō) *n.* ⟦Sp *Alfonso* < Gmc **Athalfuns* < **athal*; akin to OHG *adal*, nobility + *funs*, ready⟧ a masculine name

alp·horn (alp′hôrn′) *n.* ⟦Ger *alpenhorn* < *Alpen*, Alps (gen. pl.) + *horn*, HORN⟧ a curved, wooden, powerful-sounding horn, from five to twelve or more feet long, used by Swiss Alpine herdsmen for signaling: it is sometimes used in orchestral scores: also **al·pen·horn** (al′pən hôrn′)

Swiss alphorn

al·pho·sis (al fō′sis) *n.* ⟦ModL < Gr *alphos*, dull-white leprosy; akin to L *albus*, white: see ELF⟧ LEUKODERMA

Al·pine (al′pīn′, -pin) *adj.* ⟦L *alpinus* < *Alpes*, the ALPS⟧ **1** of the Alps or the peoples living in the region of the Alps **2** [**a-**] *a)* of or like high mountains *b)* growing in high altitudes above the timberline **3** [*sometimes* **a-**] designating or having to do with downhill or slalom skiing: cf. NORDIC **4** designating or of a physical type of the Caucasoid peoples exemplified by the broad-headed, brown-haired, medium-statured people of the Alps: see also MEDITERRANEAN[1], NORDIC

al·pin·ist (al′pin ist) *n.* ⟦Fr *alpiniste*⟧ [*also* **A-**] a mountain climber

Alps (alps) ⟦L *Alpes*, high mountains; prob. < a non-IE root **alb*-, mountain: thought by some scholars to be also the origin of ALBION⟧ mountain system in SC Europe extending from S France through Switzerland, Italy, SW Germany, Austria, Slovenia, Croatia, and Bosnia and Herzegovina into Serbia, Kosovo, and Montenegro: highest peak, Mont Blanc

Al Qae·da (al kā′də, äl kī′də) ⟦Ar, lit., the base, the foundation⟧ a radical Islamic organization operating through an international network of secret cells: it claims to be engaged in a jihad and has been responsible for many acts of terrorism: also written **al-Qaeda** or **al-Qaida**

al·read·y (ôl red′ē) *adv.* **1** by or before the given or implied time **2** even now or even then [*already* two days late]

USAGE—Also used informally after a phr. to express impatience [that's enough *already!*]

al·right (ôl rīt′) *adj., adv., interj. disputed sp. of* ALL RIGHT

ALS *abbrev.* amyotrophic lateral sclerosis

Al·sace (al sās′, -sas′; al′sas′; *Fr* ȧl zȧs′) **1** historical region of NE France **2** metropolitan region of NE France: 3,196 sq mi (8,280 sq km); chief city, Strasbourg

Al·sace-Lor·raine (-lô rān′; *Fr*, -lô ren′) region in NE France consisting of the former provinces of Alsace and Lorraine: under German control, 1871-1919 and 1940-44: restored to France, 1945

Al·sa·tian (al sā′shən) *adj.* ⟦after *Alsatia*, older name for Alsace < ML *Alisatia*⟧ of Alsace or its people, language, or culture —*n.* **1** a person born or living in Alsace **2** the variety of German spoken in Alsace, France **3** *Brit. name for* GERMAN SHEPHERD

al·sike (al′sik′, -sīk′) *n.* ⟦after *Alsike*, town in Sweden⟧ a European clover (*Trifolium hybridum*) with white or pinkish flowers, grown for fodder: also **alsike clover**

al·so (ôl′sō) *adv.* ⟦ME *al so, al swo* < OE *eallswa* < *eall*, ALL + *swa*, SO[1]⟧ in addition; likewise; too; besides: sometimes used as a conjunctive adverb

☆**al·so-ran** (-ran′) *n.* **1** a horse that fails to finish first, second, or third in a race **2** [Informal] any loser in any competition

alt[1] (alt) *adj.* ⟦It *alto* < L *altus*, high: see ALTITUDE⟧ *Music* high in pitch —*n.* **1** the first octave above the treble staff **2** a tone in this octave

alt[2] *abbrev.* **1** alteration **2** alternate **3** alternative **4** alternator **5** altitude **6** alto

Alta *abbrev.* Alberta (Canada)

Al·ta·ic (al tā′ik) *adj.* **1** of the Altai Mountains or the peoples living there **2** designating or of a group of language families including Turkic, Mongolian, and Tungusic —*n.* this group of language families

Al·tai (*or* Al·tay) Mountains (al′tī′, al tī′) mountain system of central Asia, extending from E Kazakhstan & SC Russia into NW China and W Mongolia: highest peak, *c.* 15,000 ft (4,572 m)

Al·ta·ir (al tā′ir) *n.* ⟦Ar *al-ṭā′ir*, the bird < *ṭara*, to fly⟧ the brightest star in the constellation Aquila: magnitude, 0.76: see also SUMMER TRIANGLE

Al·ta·mi·ra (äl′tä mē′rä) complex of caves in N Spain, near Santander, containing Paleolithic drawings

al·tar (ôl′tər) *n.* ⟦ME *alter* < OE *altare* & OFr *alter*; both < L *altare*, high altar < *altus*, high: see ALTITUDE⟧ **1** a place, esp. a raised platform, where sacrifices or offerings are made to a god, an ancestor, etc. **2** a table, stand, etc. used for sacred purposes in a place of worship, as the Communion table in Christian churches —**lead to the altar** to marry

altar boy a boy or man who acts as a server, esp. at Mass, but who has not been officially appointed or delegated to the ministry of acolyte

altar girl a girl who acts as a server, esp. at Mass

al·tar·piece (-pēs′) *n.* an ornamental carving, painting, etc. above and behind an altar

altar rail in some churches, a railing separating the altar area from the rest of the chancel

alt·az·i·muth (alt′az′ə məth) *n.* ⟦ALT(ITUDE) + AZIMUTH⟧ an instrument or a telescope mounting that moves on a horizontal and a vertical axis, used to measure the altitude and azimuth of a star, planet, etc.

Alt·dorf (ält′dôrf′) town in Switzerland near Lake Lucerne: scene of legendary exploits of William Tell

al·ter (ôl′tər) *vt.* ⟦ME *alteren* < ML *alterare* < L *alter,* other < IE **al-* (see ELSE) + *-tero-,* compar. suffix⟧ **1** to make different in details but not in substance; modify **2** to resew parts of (a garment) for a better fit ☆**3** to castrate or spay —*vi.* to become different; change; vary —**SYN.** CHANGE —**al′ter·a·ble** *adj.*

al·ter·a·tion (ôl′tər ā′shən) *n.* **1** an altering or being altered **2** the result of this; change

al·ter·a·tive (ôl′tər āt′iv, -tər ə tiv) *adj.* ⟦ME & OFr *alteratif* < ML *alterativus:* see ALTER⟧ causing or tending to cause alteration

al·ter·cate (ôl′tər kāt′) *vi.* **-cat′ed, -cat′ing** ⟦< L *altercatus,* pp. of *altercari,* to dispute < *alter,* other: see ALTER⟧ to argue angrily; quarrel

al·ter·ca·tion (ôl′tər kā′shən) *n.* ⟦L *altercatio*⟧ an angry or heated argument —**SYN.** QUARREL²

al·ter ego (ôl′tər) ⟦L, lit., other I⟧ **1** another aspect of oneself **2** a very close friend or constant companion

al·ter i·dem (ôl′tər ē′dəm, -ī′dem′) ⟦L⟧ another of the same kind; second self

al·ter·i·ty (ôl ter′ə tē) *n.* ⟦< Fr *altérité* or LL *alteritas* < L *alter,* other: see ALTER⟧ the quality or condition of being other or different; otherness

al·ter·nant (ôl′tər nənt, al′-) *adj.* alternating —*n. Linguis.* any of the variant forms of an alternation, as an allophone or allomorph

al·ter·nate (ôl′tər nit, al′-; *for v.* ôl′tər nāt′, al′-) *adj.* ⟦L *alternatus,* pp. of *alternare,* to do by turns < *alternus,* one after the other < *alter,* other: see ALTER⟧ **1** occurring by turns; succeeding each other; one and then the other [*alternate* stripes of blue and white] **2** every other; every second [to report on *alternate* Tuesdays] **3** being one of two or more choices; alternative **4** *Bot. a)* growing along the stem singly at different intervals, first on one side then the other, etc. *b)* placed at intervals between other parts, as in a flower —*n.* a person standing by to take the place of another if necessary; substitute —*vt.* **-nat′ed, -nat′ing 1** to do or use by turns **2** to make happen or arrange by turns —*vi.* **1** to act, happen, etc. by turns; follow successively [good times *alternate* with bad] **2** to take turns **3** to exchange places, etc. regularly **4** *Elec.* to reverse direction periodically: said of a current —**SYN.** INTERMITTENT —**al′ter·nate·ly** *adv.*

alternate angles *Geom.* a pair of nonadjacent angles, one on each side of a transversal, that are both interior or both exterior: these paired angles are equal if the lines cut by the transversal are parallel

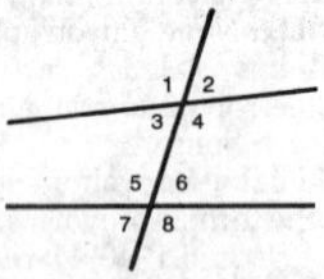

alternating current an electric current that reverses its direction periodically: abbrev. *AC:* cf. DIRECT CURRENT

al·ter·na·tion (ôl′tər nā′shən, al′-) *n.* **1** the act of alternating; occurrence, position, etc. of things by turns **2** *Linguis.* the occurrence of a variant of a morpheme or phoneme

alternation of generations the regular alternation of two distinct body forms in the life cycle of a plant or animal, usually an alternation between a form that reproduces sexually and one that reproduces asexually

alternate angles
3 & 6, 4 & 5 are pairs of alternate interior angles; 1 & 8, 2 & 7, of alternate exterior angles

al·ter·na·tive (ôl tʉr′nə tiv, al-) *adj.* ⟦ML *alternativus:* see ALTERNATE⟧ **1** providing or being a choice between two or among more than two things [*alternative* routes] **2** designating or of an institution, enterprise, etc. that appeals to unconventional or nontraditional interests [an *alternative* school] —*n.* **1** a choice between two or among more than two things **2** either or one of the things to be chosen **3** something remaining to be chosen [is there an *alternative* to going?] —**SYN.** CHOICE —**al·ter′na·tive·ly** *adv.*

alternative rock a broad category of popular rock music typically regarded as somewhat out of the mainstream and variously including elements of punk rock, heavy metal, folk music, etc.: also **alternative music**

al·ter·na·tor (ôl′tər nāt′ər, al′-) *n.* an electric generator or dynamo producing alternating current

al·the·a or **al·thae·a** (al thē′ə) *n.* ⟦ModL *Althaea* < L < Gr *althaia,* wild mallows; formerly used medicinally: see fol.⟧ **1** any plant of a genus (*Althaea*) of the mallow family, esp. the hollyhock, typically with tall spikes of showy flowers **2** ROSE OF SHARON (sense 1)

Al·the·a (al thē′ə) *n.* ⟦L *Althaea* < Gr *Althaia,* lit., healer < *althainein,* to heal: for IE base see OLD⟧ a feminine name

alt·horn (alt′hôrn′) *n.* ⟦Ger < *alt,* ALTO + *horn,* HORN⟧ any of a number of alto or tenor brass instruments, esp. the alto saxhorn: also **alto horn**

al·though (ôl *thō*′) *conj.* ⟦ME < *all, al,* even + THOUGH⟧ in spite of the fact that; granting that; though: now sometimes spelled **al·tho′**

al·ti- (al′tə, -ti) *combining form* ALTO- [*altimeter*]

al·ti·graph (al′tə graf′) *n.* ⟦prec. + -GRAPH⟧ an altimeter that records altitude automatically on a chart

al·tim·e·ter (al tim′ət ər; *also* al′tə mēt′ər) *n.* ⟦ALTI- + -METER⟧ an instrument for measuring height above a given reference level, as the sea or ground: in aircraft it is either an aneroid barometer with a dial marked in feet or meters or an instrument using radar

al·tim·e·try (al tim′ə trē) *n.* ⟦< prec.⟧ the science or practice of measuring altitudes, as with an altimeter

al·ti·pla·no (al′ti plä′nō, äl′-) *n.* ⟦AmSp < Sp *alti-* (< L *altus,* high) + *plano,* a plain < VL < L *planus,* PLANE³⟧ a high plateau, esp. in the Bolivian or Peruvian Andes

al·ti·tude (al′tə to͞od′, -tyo͞od′) *n.* ⟦L *altitudo* < *altus,* high, orig. pp. of *alere,* to nourish, cause to grow: see OLD⟧ **1** height; esp., the height of a thing above the earth's surface or above sea level **2** a high place or region: *usually used in pl.* **3** a high level, rank, etc. **4** *Astron.* the angular height of a planet, star, etc. above the horizon **5** *Geom. a)* the perpendicular distance from the designated base of a figure to its highest point or to the side parallel to the base *b)* any line segment representing such a distance —**SYN.** HEIGHT —**al′ti·tu′di·nal** (-′n əl) *adj.*

al·to (al′tō) *n., pl.* **-tos** ⟦It < L *altus,* high: see prec. ⟧ **1** the range of the lowest adult female voice or the highest adult male voice; specif., *a)* CONTRALTO *b)* COUNTERTENOR **2** *a)* a voice or singer with such a range *b)* an instrument with a similar range within its family, as an alto saxophone *c)* a part for such a voice or instrument **3** in four-part harmony, the second highest part —*adj.* of, for, or having the range of an alto

al·to- (al′tō) ⟦< L *altus,* high⟧ *combining form* high [*altostratus*]

alto clef a C clef on the third line of a staff: used in notation, esp. for the viola

al·to·cu·mu·lus (al′tō kyo͞o′myo͞o ləs, -myə-) *n.* ⟦ALTO- + CUMULUS⟧ the type of white or gray cloud that resembles a sharply defined, wavy patch, found at intermediate altitudes and consisting of small water droplets: see CLOUD

al·to·geth·er (ôl′to͞o *geth*′ər, ôl′to͞o *geth*′ər; -tə-) *adv.* ⟦ME *altogedere:* see ALL & TOGETHER⟧ **1** wholly; completely [not *altogether* wrong] **2** in all; all being counted [he wrote six books *altogether*] **3** everything being considered; on the whole [*altogether* a great success] Distinguished from **all together** —**in the altogether** [Informal] nude

☆**al·to·ist** (al′tō ist) *n. Jazz* a person who plays the alto saxophone

al·to-re·lie·vo (al′tō ri lē′vō, äl′-) *n., pl.* **-vos** ⟦< It *alto,* high + *rilievo,* relief; sp. infl. by RELIEF⟧ HIGH RELIEF

al·to-ri·lie·vo (äl′tô rē lye′vô) *n., pl.* ***al·to-ri·lie·vi*** (äl′tô rē lye′vē) or Eng. **al·to-ri·lie·vos** (al′tō ri lē′vōz, äl′-) ⟦It⟧ ALTO-RELIEVO

al·to·stra·tus (al′tō strāt′əs, -strat′-) *n.* ⟦ALTO- + STRATUS⟧ the type of gray or bluish cloud found at intermediate altitudes and consisting of a thick, dense, extensive layer of ice crystals and water droplets: may cause light precipitation: see CLOUD

al·tri·cial (al trish′əl) *adj.* ⟦ModL *altricialis* < L *altrix,* a nurse, fem. of *altor,* one who nourishes < *alere,* to feed: see OLD⟧ *Ornithology* designating or of birds whose newly hatched young are helpless and hence confined to the nest for some time; nidicolous: opposed to PRECOCIAL

al·tru·ism (al′tro͞o iz′əm) *n.* ⟦Fr *altruisme* < It *altrui* or Fr *autrui,* of or to others < L *alter,* another: see ALTER⟧ **1** unselfish concern for the welfare of others; selflessness **2** *Ethics* the doctrine that the general welfare of society is the proper goal of an individual's actions: opposed to EGOISM —**al′tru·ist** *n.*

al·tru·is·tic (al′tro͞o is′tik) *adj.* of or motivated by altruism; unselfish —**SYN.** PHILANTHROPIC —**al′tru·is′ti·cal·ly** *adv.*

ALU (ā′el′yo͞o′) *n.* ⟦*a*(*rithmetic-*)*l*(*ogic*) *u*(*nit*)⟧ the portion of a computer's central processing unit that performs arithmetic and logical operations

Al-U·bay·yid (al′o͞o bā′id) *var. of* EL OBEID

al·u·del (al′yo͞o del′) *n.* ⟦OFr < Sp < Ar *al uthāl,* lit., the vessels⟧ *Chem.* a pear-shaped vessel open at both ends so that several such vessels may be fitted into one another to form a series: used in the sublimation of iodine, in condensing mercury vapor, etc.

al·u·la (al′yo͞o lə) *n., pl.* **-lae′** (-lē′) ⟦ModL, dim of *ala,* wing: see AILERON⟧ *Ornithology* the terminal part of a bird's wing corresponding to the thumb, consisting of two or more quills; bastard wing

al·um¹ (al′əm) *n.* ⟦ME & OFr < L *alumen,* alum: for IE base see ALE⟧ **1** a double sulfate of a monovalent metal or radical (as sodium, potassium, or ammonium) with a trivalent metal (as aluminum, iron, or chromium): it is used as an astringent, as an emetic, and in the manufacture of baking powders, dyes, and paper: the most common form is potash alum (potassium aluminum sulfate), $KAl(SO_4)_2{\cdot}12H_2O$ **2** aluminum sulfate: an erroneous use

☆**a·lum²** (ə lum′) *n.* [Informal] an alumnus or alumna

a·lu·mi·na (ə lo͞o′mə nə) *n.* ⟦ModL < L *alumen* (gen. *aluminis*), ALUM¹⟧ an oxide of aluminum, Al_2O_3, present in bauxite and clay and found as different forms of corundum, including emery, sapphires, and rubies

a·lu·mi·nate (ə lo͞o′mə nāt, -nət) *n.* a salt of aluminum hydroxide reacting as an acid in an alkaline solution

a·lu·mi·ni·fer·ous (ə lo͞o′mə nif′ər əs) *adj.* yielding or containing alumina or alum

al·u·min·i·um (al′yo͞o min′ē əm) *n.* [Brit.] *var. of* ALUMINUM

a·lu·mi·nize (ə lo͞o′mə nīz′) *vt.* **-nized′, -niz′ing** to coat or treat with aluminum

a·lu·mi·no·ther·my (ə lo͞o′mə nō thʉr′mē) *n.* ⟦< ALUMINUM + Gr *thermē,* heat⟧ a metallurgical process in which aluminum reduces another metal from its oxide, simultaneously releasing great heat

a·lu·mi·nous (ə lo͞o′mə nəs) *adj.* ⟦L *aluminosus*⟧ of or containing alum, alumina, or aluminum

a·lu·mi·num (ə lo͞o′mə nəm) *n.* ⟦ModL < L *alumen:* see ALUMINA⟧ a silvery, lightweight, easily worked, metallic chemical element that resists corrosion and is found abundantly, but only in combination: symbol, Al; at. no. 13: see the periodic table of elements in the Reference Supplement —*adj.* of, containing, or made of aluminum

aluminum hydroxide a white powder, $Al(OH)_3$, obtained from bauxite and used to make glass, paper, etc. and in antacids

aluminum oxide ALUMINA

aluminum sulfate a white crystalline salt, $Al_2(SO_4)_3$, made by treating bauxite or clay with sulfuric acid: it is used in sizing paper, purifying water, fixing dyes, tanning, etc.

☆**a·lum·na** (ə lum′nə) *n., pl.* **-nae** (-nē) ⟦L, fem. of fol. ⟧ a girl or woman alumnus

a·lum·nus (ə lum′nəs) *n., pl.* **-ni′** (-nī′) ⟦L, a pupil, foster son < *alere*, to nourish: see OLD⟧ ☆**1** a person who has attended or is a graduate of a particular school, college, etc.: *alumnus* is still often used just of males, with *alumna* as the corresponding feminine term **2** anyone formerly trained, employed, etc. by a particular organization or institution

☆**al·um·root** (al′əm ro͞ot′) *n.* any of several North American plants of a genus (*Heuchera*) of the saxifrage family, with tiny, bell-shaped flowers and an astringent root; esp., coral bells

A·lun·dum (ə lun′dəm) ⟦AL(UMINA) + (COR)UNDUM⟧ *trademark for* a variety of high-temperature products made from alumina and used in laboratory ware, furnaces, insulators, abrasives, etc.

al·u·nite (al′yo͞o nīt′, -yə-) *n.* ⟦Fr < *alun* < L *alumen*, ALUM[1]⟧ a semihard, hydrous mineral, $KAl_3(SO_4)_2(OH)_6$, used to produce alum

Al·va (al′və; *Sp* äl′vä′), Duke of (*Fernando Álvarez de Toledo*) 1508-82; Sp. general who suppressed a revolt in the Low Countries

Al·vah or **Al·va** (al′və) *n.* ⟦Heb *alva, alvan*; often assoc. with L *albus*, white⟧ a masculine name: var. **Al′van** (-vən)

Al·va·ra·do (äl′və rä′dō), **Pe·dro de** (pe′drō dā) 1495-1541; Sp. general with Cortés in the conquest of Mexico

al·ve·o·lar (al vē′ə lər) *adj.* **1** of or like an alveolus or the alveoli; socketlike **2** *Anat. a)* relating to the part of the jaws containing the sockets of the teeth *b)* designating the ridge of the gums behind the upper front teeth *c)* relating to the air pockets in the lungs **3** *Phonet.* articulated with the tongue touching or near the alveolar ridge: said as of (t), (d), and (s) —*n.* an alveolar sound

al·ve·o·late (al vē′ə lit) *adj.* ⟦L *alveolatus*, hollowed out < *alveolus*, fol. ⟧ honeycombed; full of small cavities: also **al·ve′o·lat′ed** (-lāt′id) —**al·ve′o·la′tion** *n.*

al·ve·o·lus (al vē′ə ləs) *n., pl.* **-li′** (-lī′, -lē′) ⟦L, dim. of *alveus*, a hollow, cavity < *alvus*, the belly, womb < IE base **au-lo-s* > Gr *aulos*, flute, Lith *aulȳs*, beehive⟧ **1** *Anat., Zool.* a small cavity or hollow, as a cell of a honeycomb, air cell of a lung, tooth socket, etc. **2** [*usually pl.*] the alveolar ridge; teethridge

Al·vin (al′vin, -vən) *n.* ⟦Ger *Alwin*, lit., noble friend < OHG *adal*, nobility + *wini*, friend⟧ a masculine name

al·vine (al′vin, -vīn′) *adj.* ⟦< L *alvus*, belly: see ALVEOLUS⟧ of the abdomen or intestines

al·way (ôl′wā) *adv.* [Archaic] always

al·ways (ôl′wāz, ô′wāz) *adv.* ⟦ME, adv. gen. of *alwei, alway* < OE *ealne weg*: see ALL & WAY⟧ **1** at all times; on all occasions; invariably [*always* be courteous] **2** all the time; continuously; forever [*always* present in the atmosphere] **3** at any time; whenever one wishes [you can *always* leave if the show gets boring] **4** in every instance; with no exception [Labor Day is *always* the first Monday of September]

al·yce clover (al′is) ⟦prob. < ModL *Alysicarpus* < Gr *halysis*, chain + *karpos*, fruit⟧ a tropical perennial clover (*Alysicarpus vaginalis*) sometimes used as a cover crop and for fodder

a·lys·sum (ə lis′əm) *n.* ⟦ModL < Gr *alysson*, madwort < *alyssos*, curing madness < *a-*, without + *lyssa*, madness, rage; ? orig., with shining eyes (see LIGHT[1]): cf. LYNX⟧ **1** any of a genus (*Alyssum*) of crucifers with white or yellow flowers and grayish leaves **2** SWEET ALYSSUM

Alz·hei·mer's (disease) (älts′hī′mərz) ⟦after A. *Alzheimer* (1864-1915), Ger physician who first described it⟧ a progressive, irreversible disease characterized by degeneration of the brain cells and commonly leading to severe dementia

am (am) *vi.* ⟦OE *eom, am* < IE **esmi* < base **es-*, BE + **-mi*, suffix of 1st pers. sing.: see BE⟧ *1st pers. sing., pres. indic., of* BE

Am[1] *abbrev.* **1** America **2** American **3** *Bible* Amos

Am[2] *Chem. symbol for* americium

AM[1] (ā′em′) *n.* amplitude-modulation broadcasting or sound transmission, characterized by the capability of transmitting over long distances and by a moderate to high level of noise and static: cf. FM[2]

AM[2] *abbrev.* **1** amplitude modulation **2** ⟦L *ante meridiem*⟧ before noon: used to designate the time from midnight to noon: also **A.M.**, **a.m.**, or **am** **3** ⟦L *Artium Magister*⟧ Master of Arts: also **A.M.**

AMA *abbrev.* American Medical Association

Am·a·dis of Gaul (am′ə dis′) ⟦Sp *Amadís*, lit., love of God⟧ the title character of a medieval prose romance in Spanish

A·ma·do (ə mä′do͞o), **Jor·ge** (zhôr′zhə) 1912-2001; Brazilian writer

A·ma·ga·sa·ki (ä′mə gə sä′kē) city on the S coast of Honshu, Japan, near Osaka

a·mah (ä′mə) *n.* ⟦Anglo-Ind < Port *ama*⟧ in some countries in Asia, a woman servant, esp. one who serves as a baby's nurse

a·main (ə mān′) *adv.* ⟦A-[1], on + MAIN⟧ **1** [Archaic] forcefully; vigorously **2** at or with great speed **3** hastily; suddenly **4** greatly

Am·a·lek (am′ə lek′) *n. Bible* **1** a grandson of Esau: Gen. 36:9-12 **2** the descendants of Amalek, collectively: Ex. 17:8-16 —**Am·a·lek·ite** (am′ə lek′ īt′, am′ə lek′-; ə mal′ə kīt′) *n.*

a·mal·gam (ə mal′gəm) *n.* ⟦ME < ML *amalgama*, prob. via Ar < Gr *malagma*, an emollient < *malassein*, to soften: for IE base see MILL[1]⟧ **1** any alloy of mercury with another metal or other metals [silver *amalgam* is used as a dental filling] **2** a combination or mixture; blend

a·mal·gam·a·ble (ə mal′gə mə bəl) *adj.* that can be amalgamated

a·mal·ga·mate (ə mal′gə māt′) *vt., vi.* **-mat′ed, -mat′ing** **1** to combine in an amalgam **2** to join together into one; unite; combine —**a·mal′ga·mat′ive** *adj.*

a·mal·ga·ma·tion (ə mal′gə mā′shən) *n.* **1** an amalgamating or being amalgamated **2** the result of amalgamating; mixture, blend, merger, etc. **3** *Metallurgy* the extraction of a precious metal from its ore by alloying it with mercury

a·mal·ga·ma·tor (ə mal′gə māt′ər) *n.* **1** a person or thing that amalgamates **2** a machine for the amalgamation of silver, etc. from its ore

Am·al·thae·a or **Am·al·the·a** (am′əl thē′ə) *n.* ⟦L < Gr *Amaltheia*⟧ *Class. Myth.* the goat that nurses Zeus (Jupiter): one of its horns is called the CORNUCOPIA

A·man·a Church Society (ə man′ə) ⟦< Heb *amana*, true, faithful, name for ANTI-LEBANON range in S. of Sol. 4:8⟧ a Christian community in Iowa governed by elders, with no ordained clergy: founded in Germany in 1714, in America since 1843

A·man·da (ə man′də) *n.* ⟦L, lit., worthy to be loved < the gerund stem of *amare*, to love⟧ a feminine name: dim. *Mandy*

a·man·dine (ä′mən dēn′, am′ən-) *adj.* ⟦Fr < *amande* (see ALMOND) + *-ine*, -INE[1]⟧ prepared or garnished with almonds [trout *amandine*]

am·a·ni·ta (am′ə nēt′ə) *n.* ⟦ModL < Gr *amanitai*, pl., a kind of fungus⟧ any of a genus (*Amanita*) of mushrooms (order Agaricales), with white spores and, usually, white gills, some of which, as the death cap and the fly agaric, are very poisonous

a·man·ta·dine hydrochloride (ə man′tə dēn′, -din′) ⟦< *amantadine* < *adamant(ane)*, an organic compound (< Fr) + (AM)INE: see ADAMANT⟧ a white, crystalline drug, $C_{10}H_{17}N \cdot HCl$, used to prevent and treat certain forms of influenza and to treat parkinsonism: also called **amantadine** *n.*

a·man·u·en·sis (ə man′yo͞o en′sis) *n., pl.* **-ses′** (-sēz′) ⟦L < *a-* (*ab*), from + *manu*, abl. of *manus*, a hand (see MANUAL) + *-ensis*, relating to⟧ an assistant who takes dictation or copies something already written; secretary: now a somewhat jocular usage

A·ma·pá (ä′mə pä′) state of N Brazil, on the Atlantic: 54,965 sq mi (142,359 sq km); cap. Macapá

am·a·ranth (am′ə ranth′) *n.* ⟦< ModL < L *amarantus* < Gr *amarantos*, unfading < *a-*, not + *marainein*, to die away: for IE base see MORTAL⟧ **1** any of a genus (*Amaranthus*) of plants of the amaranth family: some species, as the love-lies-bleeding, have colorful leaves and showy, tassel-like flower heads, and other species, as pigweed or tumbleweed, are weeds **2** [Old Poet.] an imaginary flower that never fades or dies **3** a dark purplish red —*adj.* designating a family (Amaranthaceae) of dicotyledonous plants (order Caryophyllales), including the cockscombs

am·a·ran·thine (am′ə ran′thin, -thēn′, -thīn′) *adj.* **1** of or like the amaranth **2** unfading or undying **3** dark purplish-red

am·a·relle (am′ə rel′) *n.* ⟦Ger < ML *amarellum*, dim. < L *amarus*, sour, bitter < IE **amros* < base **om-*, bitter > Sans *amlá-*, sour, Du *amper*, sharp, raw⟧ any of several varieties of sour cherry with colorless juice

a·ma·ret·to (am′ə ret′ō, ä′mə-) *n.* ⟦It, lit., rather bitter < *amaro* (< L *amarus*), bitter⟧ **1** [*also* **A-**] a liqueur with an almond flavor **2** *pl.* **-ti** (-ē) a macaroon made of ground almonds and often containing a bitter flavoring: also **amaretto (or amaretti) cookie**

Am·a·ril·lo (am′ə ril′ō) ⟦Sp, yellow: prob. from color of banks of a nearby stream⟧ city in NW Tex.

am·a·ryl·lis (am′ə ril′is) *n.* ⟦< L & Gr *Amaryllis*, a shepherdess's name in poems by Virgil and Theocritus⟧ any of several plants (esp. genus *Hippeastrum*) of the lily family bearing several white, purple, pink, or red flowers on a leafless stem, including the belladonna lily

a·mass (ə mas′) *vt.* ⟦Fr *amasser* < ML *amassare* < *a-*, to + VL *massare*, to form a lump < L *massa*, a lump, MASS⟧ **1** to pile up; collect together **2** to accumulate (esp. wealth) —**a·mass′er** *n.* —**a·mass′ment** *n.*

am·a·teur (am′ə chər, -cho͝or′; -ə tʉr′, -ə tər) *n.* ⟦Fr < L *amator*, lover < pp. of *amare*, to love⟧ **1** a person who engages in some art, science, sport, etc. for the pleasure of it rather than for money; a nonprofessional; specif., an athlete who is variously forbidden by rule to profit from athletic activity **2** a person who does something without professional skill **3** a person who is somewhat unskillful —*adj.* **1** of or done by an amateur or amateurs **2** being an amateur or made up of amateurs **3** amateurish

SYN.*—amateur** refers to one who does something for the pleasure of it rather than for pay and often implies a relative lack of skill; a **dilettante** is an amateur in the arts, but the word is also applied disparagingly to a superficial dabbler in the arts; **novice** and **neophyte** refer to one who is a beginner, hence inexperienced, in some activity, **neophyte** carrying additional connotations of youthful enthusiasm; **tyro** refers to an inexperienced but self-assertive beginner and generally connotes incompetence —ANT.*** **professional, expert**

am·a·teur·ish (am′ə cho͝or′ish, am′ə tʉr′-) *adj.* like an amateur; inexpert; unskillful —**am′a·teur′ish·ly** *adv.* —**am′a·teur′ish·ness** *n.*

am·a·teur·ism (am′ə chər iz′əm, -tər-) *n.* **1** an amateurish method or quality **2** the nonprofessional status of an amateur

A·ma·ti[1] (ä mä′tē; *E* ə mät′ē) *n.* a violin made by the Amati family

A·ma·ti[2] (ä mä′tē; *E* ə mät′ē), **Ni·co·lò** (nē′kô lô′) 1596-1684; It. violin-maker: member of a family of violin-makers of Cremona, Italy (fl. 16th-17th cent.); teacher of Guarneri & Stradivari

am·a·tive (am′ə tiv) *adj.* ⟦< ML *amatīvus*, lovable < pp. of L *amare*, to love⟧

of or inclined to love, esp. sexual love —**am′a·tive·ly** *adv.* —**am′a·tive·ness** *n.*

am·a·tol (am′ə tôl′, -täl′, -tōl′) *n.* ⟦< AM(MONIUM) + TOL(UENE)⟧ a powerful explosive made up of ammonium nitrate and trinitrotoluene (TNT)

am·a·to·ry (am′ə tôr′ē) *adj.* ⟦L *amatorius* < *amator*, lover: see AMATEUR⟧ of, causing, or showing love, esp. sexual love

am·au·ro·sis (am′ô rō′sis) *n.* ⟦ModL < Gr *amaurōsis* < *amauros*, dark⟧ partial or total blindness —**am′au·rot′ic** (-rät′ik) *adj.*

a·maze (ə māz′) *vt.* **a·mazed′**, **a·maz′ing** ⟦ME (only in pp. *amased*) < OE *āmasian*: < *ā-*, A-[2] + base akin to Norw *masast*, to fall asleep, Swed *mos*, sluggish, sleepy⟧ **1** to fill with great surprise or sudden wonder; astonish **2** [Obs.] to bewilder —*n.* [Old Poet.] amazement —**SYN.** SURPRISE —**a·maz′ed·ly** (-id lē) *adv.* —**a·maz′ing** *adj.* —**a·maz′ing·ly** *adv.*

a·maze·ment (ə māz′mənt) *n.* **1** an amazed condition; great wonder; astonishment **2** [Obs.] bewilderment

Am·a·zon[1] (am′ə zän′, -zən) *n.* ⟦L < Gr *Amazōn*, of unknown orig., but deriv. by folk etym. < *a-*, without + *mazos*, breast, hence the story that the Amazons cut off one breast to facilitate archery⟧ **1** *Gr. Myth.* any of a race of female warriors supposed to have lived in Scythia, near the Black Sea **2** [**a-**] a tall, strong, aggressive woman **3** a small, greenish parrot (genus *Amazona*) of Central and South America, often kept as a pet **4** any of a genus (*Polyergus*) of ants that makes slaves of other ants: also **Amazon ant**

Am·a·zon[2] (am′ə zän′, -zən) ⟦so named by Spaniards, who believed its shores inhabited by female warriors: see prec.⟧ river in South America, flowing from the Andes in Peru across N Brazil into the Atlantic: *c.* 4,000 mi (6,437 km)

A·ma·zo·nas (ä′mə zō′nəs) state of NW Brazil: 605,408 sq mi (1,568,000 sq km); cap. Manaus

Am·a·zo·ni·a (am′ə zō′nē ə) basin of the Amazon River in N South America

Am·a·zo·ni·an (am′ə zō′nē ən) *adj.* **1** of, like, or characteristic of an Amazon **2** [*often* **a-**] of an amazon; tall, strong, aggressive, etc.: said of a woman **3** of the Amazon River or the country around it

am·a·zon·ite (am′ə zən īt′) *n.* ⟦after the AMAZON[2] River⟧ a green microcline, often cut and polished as a gem: also **Amazon stone**

Amb *abbrev.* Ambassador

am·bage (am′bij) *n.*, *pl.* **-bag·es′** (-bi jiz′; am bā′jēz′) ⟦< ME *ambages* (taken as pl.), intentional ambiguity < MFr < L < *amb-*, around + *agere*, to go⟧ [Archaic] **1** a winding pathway: *usually used in pl.* **2** [*pl.*] roundabout, indirect ways of talking or doing things —**am·ba′gious** (-bā′jəs) *adj.*

am·ba·ry or **am·ba·ri** (am bä′rē) *n.* ⟦Hindi *ambārī*⟧ KENAF

am·bas·sa·dor (am bas′ə dər, -dôr′) *n.* ⟦ME *ambassatour* < MFr *ambassateur* < OIt *ambasciatore* < Prov *ambaissador* < **ambaissa*, mission, task < Goth *andbahti*, office, service < Celt **amb(i)actos*, a messenger, servant (> L *ambactus*, a vassal) < IE **ambhi-*, about (see AMBI-) + base **aĝ-*, to do (see ACT[1])⟧ **1** the highest-ranking diplomatic representative appointed by one country or government to represent it in another **2** a special representative: an **ambassador-at-large** is one accredited to no particular country; an **ambassador extraordinary** is one on a special diplomatic mission; an **ambassador plenipotentiary** is one having the power to make treaties **3** an official agent with a special mission **4** an unofficial representative or messenger [an *ambassador* of goodwill] —**am·bas′sa·do′ri·al** (-dôr′ē əl) *adj.* —**am·bas′sa·dor·ship′** *n.*

am·bas·sa·dress (am bas′ə dris) *n.* [Now Rare] **1** a woman ambassador **2** the wife of an ambassador See -ESS

Am·ba·to (äm bät′ō) city in central Ecuador

am·ber (am′bər) *n.* ⟦ME *aumbre*, amber, ambergris < OFr *ambre* < Ar ʿ*anbar*, ambergris⟧ **1** a yellow or brownish-yellow translucent fossil resin found as along seacoasts and used in jewelry, pipestems, etc.: it is hard, easily polished, and quickly charged with static electricity when rubbed **2** the color of amber —*adj.* **1** like or made of amber **2** having the color of amber

☆**Amber Alert** ⟦after *Amber* Hagerman (1986-96), child abducted and murdered⟧ a warning to be on the lookout for a missing child, sent out by the police over an emergency system that uses radio and TV broadcasts, roadside electronic displays, etc.

am·ber·gris (-grēs′, -gris′) *n.* ⟦ME *ambregris* < OFr *ambre gris* < *ambre* (see AMBER) + *gris* < Frank **grīs*, akin to MHG, OS, Du *gris*, gray⟧ a grayish, waxy substance from the intestines of sperm whales, often found floating in tropical seas: used in some perfumes

☆**am·ber·jack** (am′bər jak′) *n.*, *pl.* **-jacks′** or **-jack′** ⟦AMBER + JACK (fish): from its color⟧ any of several large food and game yellowtail fishes (genus *Seriola*) found in the warm waters of all oceans

Am·ber·lite (am′bər līt′) ⟦AMBER + -LITE⟧ *trademark for* various insoluble cross-linked polymers used in water-treatment processes and in pharmacy

am·ber·oid (am′bər oid′) *n.* a material made to resemble amber, formed of small pieces of amber or some other resin pressed together under high temperature

am·bi- (am′bə, -bi) ⟦L, akin to Gr *amphi* < IE base **ambhi-*, **ambho(u)-*, around > BOTH⟧ *combining form* both [*ambidextrous*]

am·bi·dex·trous (am′bə deks′trəs) *adj.* ⟦< earlier *ambidexter* + -OUS⟧ **1** able to use both hands with equal ease **2** very skillful or versatile **3** deceitful; double-dealing —**am′bi·dex·ter′i·ty** (-deks ter′ə tē) *n.* —**am′bi·dex′trous·ly** *adv.*

am·bi·ence (am′bē əns, äm′bē äns′) *n.* ⟦Fr: see fol.⟧ a particular setting or its distinctive atmosphere [the festive *ambience* of a wedding reception]: also sp. **am′bi·ance**

am·bi·ent (am′bē ənt) *adj.* ⟦L *ambiens*, prp. of *ambire*, to go around < *ambi*, around + *ire*, to go: see EXIT⟧ surrounding; on all sides, specif., *a)* not originating from a single source [a room's *ambient* lighting from several windows] *b)* having to do with the conditions in the immediate environment, esp. conditions outdoors [*ambient* air temperature]

am·bi·gu·i·ty (am′bə gyōō′ə tē) *n.* ⟦ME *ambiguite* < L *ambiguitas*⟧ **1** the quality or state of being ambiguous **2** *pl.* **-ties** an ambiguous word, statement, etc.

am·big·u·ous (am big′yōō əs) *adj.* ⟦L *ambiguus* < *ambigere*, to wander < *ambi-*, about, around + *agere*, to do, ACT[1]⟧ **1** having two or more possible meanings **2** not clear; indefinite; vague —**SYN.** OBSCURE —**am·big′u·ous·ly** *adv.* —**am·big′u·ous·ness** *n.*

am·bi·sex·u·al (am′bə sek′shōō əl) *adj.* BISEXUAL (*adj.* 3) —*n.* an ambisexual person —**am′bi·sex′u·al′i·ty** (-sek′shōō al′ə tē) *n.*

am·bit (am′bit) *n.* ⟦L *ambitus*, a going about, revolution < pp. of *ambire*: see AMBIENT⟧ **1** a circuit or circumference **2** the limits or scope; bounds

am·bi·tion (am bish′ən) *n.* ⟦ME < OFr < L *ambitio*, a going around (to solicit votes) < pp. of *ambire*: see AMBIENT⟧ **1** a strong desire to gain a particular objective; specif., the drive to succeed, or to gain fame, power, wealth, etc. **2** the objective strongly desired —*vt.* [Rare] to be ambitious for

am·bi·tious (am bish′əs) *adj.* ⟦ME *ambicious* < L *ambitiosus*, seeking favor < *ambitio*: see prec.⟧ **1** full of or showing ambition **2** greatly desirous (*of* something); eager for **3** demanding great effort, skill, enterprise, etc. [an *ambitious* undertaking] —**am·bi′tious·ly** *adv.*

SYN.—ambitious implies a striving for advancement, wealth, fame, etc., and is used with both favorable and unfavorable connotations; **aspiring** suggests a striving to reach some lofty end regarded as somewhat beyond one's normal expectations [an *aspiring* young poet]; **enterprising** implies an energetic readiness to take risks or undertake new projects in order to succeed; **emulous** suggests ambition characterized by a competitive desire to equal or surpass another

am·biv·a·lence (am biv′ə ləns) *n.* ⟦< Ger *ambivalenz*, after *äquivalenz*, equivalence⟧ simultaneous conflicting feelings toward a person or thing, as love and hate: also [Chiefly Brit.] **am·biv′a·len·cy** —**am·biv′a·lent** *adj.* —**am·biv′a·lent·ly** *adv.*

am·bi·ver·sion (am′bi vʉr′zhən, -shən) *n.* ⟦AMBI- + (INTRO)VERSION⟧ *Psychol.* a condition or character trait that includes elements of both introversion and extroversion —**am′bi·vert′** (-vʉrt′) *n.*

am·ble (am′bəl) *vi.* **-bled**, **-bling** ⟦ME *amblen* < OFr *ambler* < L *ambulare*, to walk < *ambi-*, AMBI- + IE base **al-*, wander⟧ **1** to move at a smooth, easy gait by raising first both legs on one side, then both on the other: said of a horse, etc. **2** to go easily and unhurriedly; walk in a leisurely manner —*n.* **1** a horse's ambling gait **2** a leisurely walking pace —**am′bler** (-blər) *n.*

am·blyg·o·nite (am blig′ə nīt′) *n.* ⟦Ger *amblygonit* < Gr *amblygōnios*, obtuse-angled < *amblys*, dull + *gōnia*, an angle (see KNEE) + *-it*, -ITE[1]⟧ a usually greenish or whitish crystalline mineral, $(Li,Na)Al(PO_4)(F,OH)$: it is an ore of lithium and is found in pegmatite

am·bly·o·pi·a (am′blē ō′pē ə) *n.* ⟦ModL < Gr *amblys*, dull + -OPIA⟧ a loss in sharpness of vision, esp. when not traceable to any intrinsic eye disease —**am′bly·o′pic** (-äp′ik, -ō′pik) *adj.*

am·bo (am′bō′) *n.*, *pl.* **am′bos′** or **am·bo·nes** (am bō′nēz′) ⟦ML, pulpit or lectern < LGr *ambōn*, pulpit < Gr, rim, crest⟧ a pulpit or raised reading stand in early Christian churches

am·bo·cep·tor (am′bō sep′tər, -bə-) *n.* ⟦L *ambo*, both + (RE)CEPTOR⟧ *Immunology* an antibody able to damage or destroy a microorganism or other cell by connecting complement to it

Am·boi·na (am boi′nə) AMBON

Am·boise (än bwäz′) town in WC France, on the Loire, near Tours: site of a royal residence (1483-1560)

Am·bon (am′bän′) **1** one of the Molucca Islands, southwest of Ceram, in Indonesia: 314 sq mi (813 sq km) **2** seaport on this island

Am·boy·na wood (am boi′nə) the mottled, curled wood of an Asian, leguminous tree (*Pterocarpus indicus*), used in making furniture: also sp. **Am·boi′na wood**

am·broid (am′broid′) *n.* AMBEROID

Am·brose[1] (am′brōz′) *n.* ⟦L *Ambrosius* < Gr *ambrosios*: see AMBROSIA⟧ a masculine name

Am·brose[2] (am′brōz′), Saint (A.D. 340?-397); bishop of Milan: his day is Dec. 7 —**Am·bro·si·an** (am brō′zhən; -zhē ən, -zē ən) *adj.*

am·bro·si·a (am brō′zhə; -zhē ə, -zē ə) *n.* ⟦L < Gr < *ambrotos*, immortal < *a-*, not + *brotos*, mortal < **mrotos* < IE **mr̥-to*, dead: for base see MORTAL⟧ **1** *Class. Myth.* the food of the gods **2** anything that tastes or smells delicious **3** RAGWEED

am·bro·si·al (am brō′zhəl; -zhē əl, -zē əl) *adj.* **1** of or fit for the gods; divine **2** like ambrosia; delicious; fragrant Also **am·bro′sian** (-zhən)

☆**am·bro·type** (am′brō tīp′, -brə-) *n.* ⟦< Gr *ambrotos*, immortal (see AMBROSIA) + -TYPE⟧ an early kind of photograph, consisting of a glass negative backed by a dark surface so as to appear positive

am·bry (am′brē) *n.*, *pl.* **-bries** ⟦ME *almerie* < OFr *armarie* < L *armarium*, chest for tools or arms < *arma*, weapons⟧ [Archaic] a cupboard, locker, or pantry

am·bu·la·crum (am′byōō lā′krəm, -byə-) *n.*, *pl.* **-cra** (-krə) ⟦ModL < L, tree-lined walk < *ambulare*: see AMBLE⟧ *Zool.* in echinoderms, that surface area containing a radiating series of perforated plates through which the tube feet extend —**am′bu·la′cral** *adj.*

am·bu·lance (am′byə ləns, -byoo͞-) ***n.*** ⟦Fr < (*hôpital*) *ambulant* < prp. of L *ambulare*: see AMBLE⟧ **1** [Obs.] a mobile field hospital **2** a specially equipped automobile or other vehicle for carrying an ill or injured person, as to a hospital for medical treatment

☆**am·bu·lance-chas·er** (-chās′ər) ***n.*** [Informal] a lawyer who tries to gain clients by encouraging accident victims to sue for damages

am·bu·lant (am′byoo͞ lənt, -byə-) ***adj.*** ⟦< L *ambulans*, prp. of *ambulare*, to walk⟧ moving about; walking

am·bu·late (am′byoo͞ lāt′, -byə-) ***vi.*** **-lat′ed, -lat′ing** ⟦< L *ambulatus*, pp. of *ambulare*: see AMBLE⟧ to move about; walk —**am′bu·la′tion** ***n.***

am·bu·la·to·ry (am′byoo͞ lə tôr′ē, -byə-) ***adj.*** ⟦L *ambulatorius* < *ambulare*: see AMBLE⟧ **1** of or for walking **2** able to walk and not confined to bed [an *ambulatory* patient] **3** moving from one place to another; movable **4** *Law* that can be changed or revoked [an *ambulatory* will] —***n.***, ***pl.*** **-ries** any covered or sheltered place for walking, as in a cloister —***SYN.*** ITINERANT

am·bus·cade (am′bəs kād′; *also, esp. for n.*, am′bəs kād′) ***n.***, ***vt.***, ***vi.*** **-cad′ed, -cad′ing** ⟦Fr *embuscade* < *embusquer*, to ambush, altered (after It *imboscare*) < OFr *embuschier*: see fol. ⟧ AMBUSH —**am′bus·cad′er** ***n.***

am·bush (am′boosh′) ***n.*** ⟦OFr *embusche* < *embuschier*: see the ***vt.***, ***vi.***⟧ **1** a deployment of persons in hiding to make a surprise attack **2** *a)* the persons in hiding *b)* their place of hiding **3** the act of so lying in wait to attack **4** a surprise attack made by persons waiting in ambush —***vt.***, ***vi.*** ⟦ME *embusshen* < OFr *embuschier*, to lay an ambush < ML **imboscare* < *in-*, IN-[1] + *boscus*, woods < Frank *busk*, akin to BUSH[1]⟧ **1** to hide in ambush **2** to attack from ambush —**am′bush′ment** ***n.***

AMD *abbrev.* age-related macular degeneration

AME *abbrev.* African Methodist Episcopal (church)

a·me·ba (ə mē′bə) ***n.***, ***pl.*** **-bas** or **-bae** (-bē) *alt. sp. of* AMOEBA —**a·me′bic** (-bik) ***adj.***, **a·me′boid′** (-boid′), or **a·me′ban** (-bən)

USAGE—although the spelling *ameba* is now standard in scientific usage, both for the word itself and in compounds (such as disease names), the spelling *amoeba* is still common in general usage

am·e·bi·a·sis (am′i bī′ə sis) ***n.*** ⟦ModL *amoebiasis*: see AMOEBA & -IASIS⟧ infestation with amoebas, esp. with a protozoan (*Entamoeba histolytica*) parasitic in the intestines or liver

amebic dysentery a form of dysentery caused by an amoeba (*Entamoeba histolytica*)

a·me·bo·cyte (ə mē′bō sīt′, -bə-) ***n.*** any cell capable of moving like an amoeba, esp. one that floats freely in the blood or other bodily fluids, such as a white blood corpuscle

a·meer (ə mir′) ***n.*** *var. of* EMIR (sense 1)

A·mel·i·a (ə mēl′yə, -mēl′ē ə) ***n.*** ⟦of Gmc orig.; lit., prob. diligent < base of *amal*, work⟧ a feminine name

a·mel·io·rant (ə mēl′yə rənt) ***n.*** a thing that ameliorates

a·mel·io·rate (ə mēl′yə rāt′) ***vt.***, ***vi.*** **-rat′ed, -rat′ing** ⟦< Fr *améliorer* < OFr *ameillorer* < *a-*, to + *meillor* < L *melior*, better⟧ to make or become better; improve —***SYN.*** IMPROVE —**a·mel′io·ra·ble** (-yə rə bəl) ***adj.*** —**a·mel′io·ra′tion** (-yə rā′shən) ***n.*** —**a·mel′io·ra′tive** (-yə rāt′iv, -yə rə tiv) ***adj.*** —**a·mel′io·rat′or** (-yə rāt′ər) ***n.***

a·men (ā′men′, ä′-) ***interj.*** ⟦OE < LL(Ec) < Gr *amēn* < Heb *amen*, truly, certainly⟧ may it be so; so it is: used after a prayer or to express approval —***adv.*** [Archaic] verily —***n.*** an instance of speaking or writing "amen"

A·men (ä′mən) ***n.*** AMON

a·me·na·ble (ə mē′nə bəl, -men′ə-) ***adj.*** ⟦Anglo-Fr < OFr *amener*, to bring about, lead in < *a-*, to + *mener*, to lead < L *minare*, to drive (animals) < *minari*, to threaten: see MENACE⟧ **1** responsible or answerable **2** open to persuasion; agreeable or responsive —***SYN.*** OBEDIENT —**amenable to 1** able to be controlled or affected by [an illness *amenable to* treatment] **2** readily influenced or persuaded by [*amenable to* suggestion] **3** that can be tested by [*amenable to* the laws of physics] —**a·me′na·bil′i·ty** (-bil′ə tē) ***n.*** —**a·me′na·bly** ***adv.***

amen corner ☆in some rural Protestant churches, the seats to the minister's right, once occupied by those leading the responsive amens

a·mend (ə mend′) ***vt.*** ⟦ME *amenden* < OFr *amender* < L *emendare*, to correct: see EMEND⟧ **1** to make better; improve **2** to remove the faults of; correct; emend **3** to change or revise (a legislative bill, law, constitution, etc.) —***vi.*** to improve one's conduct —**a·mend′a·ble** ***adj.*** —**a·mend′er** ***n.***

☆**a·mend·a·to·ry** (ə men′də tôr′ē) ***adj.*** tending or serving to amend; corrective

a·mend·ment (ə mend′mənt) ***n.*** ⟦ME < OFr *amendement* < *amender*, AMEND⟧ **1** a change for the better; improvement **2** a correction of errors, faults, etc. **3** *a)* a revision or addition proposed or made in a bill, law, constitution, etc. *b)* the process of making such changes

a·mends (ə mendz′) ***pl.n.*** ⟦ME < OFr, pl. of *amende*, a fine: see AMEND⟧ [*sometimes with sing. v.*] something given or done to make up for injury, loss, etc. that one has caused [to make *amends* for rudeness]

A·men·ho·tep[1] (ä′mən hō′tep′) ***n.*** name of four kings of Egypt who ruled during the 16th, 15th, & 14th cent. B.C.: also **A·men·o·phis** (ä′mən ō′fis)

A·men·ho·tep[2] (ä′mən hō′tep′) **1 Amenhotep III** fl. 14th cent. B.C.; Egypt. king (reigned 1411?-1375?) **2 Amenhotep IV** IKHNATON

a·men·i·ty (ə men′ə tē; *also*, -mēn′-) ***n.***, ***pl.*** **-ties** ⟦ME & OFr *amenite* < L *amoenitas* < *amoenus*, pleasant; akin to *amare*, to love⟧ **1** pleasant quality; attractiveness **2** *a)* an attractive or desirable feature, as of a particular climate or piece of real estate *b)* anything that adds to a person's comfort; convenience: *often used in pl.* **3** [*pl.*] the courteous acts and pleasant manners of polite social behavior

a·men·or·rhe·a or **a·men·or·rhoe·a** (ā men′ə rē′ə) ***n.*** ⟦ModL < Gr *a-*, not + *mēn*, month + -RRHEA⟧ abnormal absence or suppression of menstruation

A·men-Ra (ä′mən rä′) ***n.*** AMON

am·ent[1] (am′ənt, ā′mənt) ***n.*** ⟦< L *amentum*, thong, strap⟧ CATKIN

a·ment[2] (ā′ment′, -mənt) ***n.*** ⟦back-form. < AMENTIA⟧ a person with severe INTELLECTUAL DISABILITY

am·en·ta·ceous (am′ən tā′shəs) ***adj.*** ⟦AMENT[1] + -ACEOUS⟧ *Bot.* **1** of or like an ament or aments **2** amentiferous

a·men·tia (ā men′shə, ə-) ***n.*** ⟦L, madness < *amens*, senseless < *a-* (*ab*), away, from + *mens*, MIND⟧ a type of severe INTELLECTUAL DISABILITY characterized by subnormal development of intellectual capacity

am·en·tif·er·ous (am′ən tif′ər əs) ***adj.*** ⟦< AMENT[1] + -FEROUS⟧ *Bot.* bearing aments

Amer *abbrev.* American

Am·er·a·sian (am′ər ā′zhən) ***n.*** ⟦AMER(ICAN) + ASIAN⟧ a person of both American and Asian descent, esp. the child of a U.S. serviceman and an Asian woman —***adj.*** **1** both American and Asian [an *Amerasian* child] **2** of or for Amerasians

a·merce (ə murs′) ***vt.*** **a·merced′, a·merc′ing** ⟦ME *amercen* < Anglo-Fr *amercier* < OFr *a merci*, at the mercy of⟧ **1** to punish by imposing an arbitrarily determined fine **2** to punish generally —**a·merce′ment** ***n.***

A·mer·i- (ə mer′i, -mer′ə) *combining form* American, American and

A·mer·i·ca (ə mer′i kə) ⟦ModL, name assoc. (1507) by Martin Waldseemüller (1470?-1522?), Ger cosmographer, with *Americus* Vespucius, Latinized form of Amerigo VESPUCCI, but < ? Sp *Amerrique*, name of a mountain range in Nicaragua, used by early explorers for the newly discovered lands < ? AmInd⟧ **1** North America, South America, and the West Indies, considered together: also **the Americas 2** North America **3** ☆the United States of America

A·mer·i·can (ə mer′i kən) ***adj.*** **1** of or in America ☆**2** of, in, or characteristic of the U.S. or its people or culture [the *American* language] —***n.*** **1** a person born or living in North or South America; specif., *a)* [Obs.] an American Indian *b)* a citizen of the U.S. ☆**2** the English language as spoken and written in the U.S.

☆**A·mer·i·can·a** (ə mer′i kan′ə, -kä′nə) ***pl.n.*** ⟦AMERIC(A) + -ANA⟧ books, papers, objects, facts, etc. having to do with the U.S., its people, and its history

☆**American aloe** CENTURY PLANT

☆**American Beauty** a variety of hybrid, perennial red rose

☆**American chameleon** ANOLE: lizards of this type (family Iguanidae) are incorrectly called "chameleons": see CHAMELEON

☆**American cheese** a process cheese, yellow to orange in color and usually made from Cheddar cheese, popular in the U.S.

American Depositary Receipt a receipt representing foreign shares of stock held on deposit in an American bank: receipts are denominated in U.S. dollars and traded on American exchanges: also *ADR*

☆**American dialects** regional or social varieties of spoken American English identified by differences in grammar, vocabulary, and pronunciation: principal dialect areas are now generally distinguished as Northern, Midland, and Southern

☆**American dream** [*often* **A- D-**] the U.S. ideal according to which equality of opportunity permits any American to aspire to high attainment and material success

American eagle the bald eagle of North America, shown on the coat of arms of the U.S.

American English the English language as spoken and written in the U.S. and as distinguished esp. from BRITISH ENGLISH; American

American Federation of Labor a federation of labor unions of the U.S. and Canada, founded in 1886: merged with the Congress of Industrial Organizations in 1955

American Indian a member of any of the indigenous peoples of the Americas, esp. of North America south of the Arctic; Amerindian: originally named *Indian* by early explorers of the New World, who believed they had reached India

☆**A·mer·i·can·ism** (ə mer′i kən iz′əm) ***n.*** **1** a custom, characteristic, or belief of or originating in the U.S. **2** a word, phrase, grammatical construction, or other feature originating in or peculiar to American English **3** devotion or loyalty to the U.S., or to its traditions, customs, institutions, etc.

A·mer·i·can·ist (-ist) ***n.*** **1** a student of American history, culture, etc. **2** an anthropologist specializing in the study of American Indians and their cultures

☆**American ivy** VIRGINIA CREEPER

☆**A·mer·i·can·ize** (ə mer′i kən īz′) ***vt.***, ***vi.*** **-ized′, -iz′ing** to make or become American in character, manners, methods, ideals, etc.; assimilate to U.S. customs, speech, etc. —**A·mer′i·can·i·za′tion** (-ə zā′shən) ***n.***

American kestrel a small American falcon (*Falco sparverius*) with a reddish-brown back and tail; sparrow hawk

American Legion an organization of veterans of the armed forces of the U.S., founded in 1919

☆**American plan** a system of hotel operation in which the rate charged to guests covers room, service, and meals: distinguished from EUROPEAN PLAN

American Revolution 1 a sequence of actions by American colonists from 1763 to 1775 protesting British domination and culminating in the Revolutionary War **2** the Revolutionary War (1775-83), fought by the American colonies to gain independence from Great Britain

American Samoa island group consisting of seven islands in the South Pacific, north of Tonga: an unincorporated territory of the U.S.: 77 sq mi (199 sq km); cap. Pago Pago on Tutuila Island: abbrev. *AS*

American Sign Language a language consisting of manual signs and gestures, used as by deaf people in North America

American Standard Version a revision of the King James Version of the Bible, published in 1901: issued by members of the American committee who had helped produce the Revised Version (1881, 1885) in England

American water spaniel any of a breed of spaniel with a curly, reddish or dark-brown coat, used as a retriever, esp. of waterfowl

☆**American wigeon** a common North American duck (*Anas americana*), the male of which has a white crown and brownish breast

American wirehair any of a breed of domestic cat similar to the American shorthair (see SHORTHAIR), but with a dense, wiry coat

☆**am·er·ic·i·um** (am′ər ish′ē əm, -is′-) *n.* ⟦ModL, after AMERIC(A) + -IUM: so named by G. T. SEABORG, one of its discoverers, by analogy with EUROPIUM, the corresponding rare earth⟧ a radioactive, metallic chemical element, one of the actinides, produced by the beta decay of an isotope of plutonium: symbol, Am; at. no. 95: see the periodic table of elements in the Reference Supplement

☆**A·mer·i·ka** (ə mer′i kə) ⟦Ger, America⟧ AMERICA (the country): spelling used to suggest that U.S. society is variously fascist, repressive, racist, etc.

Amer. Ind. *abbrev.* American Indian

☆**Am·er·in·di·an** (am′ər in′dē ən) *n., adj.* ⟦AMER(ICAN) + INDIAN: coined by J. W. Powell (1834-92), U.S. ethnologist⟧ AMERICAN INDIAN —**Am′er·ind′** (-ind′) *n., adj.*

A·mers·foort (ä′mərs fôrt′) city in central Netherlands

☆**Am·es·lan** (am′is lan′) *n.* ⟦AME(RICAN) (S)IGN LAN(GUAGE)⟧ AMERICAN SIGN LANGUAGE

☆**Ames Test** (āmz) ⟦after B. *Ames* (b. 1928), U.S. biochemist who developed it⟧ a laboratory test for the carcinogenic potential of a substance, in which bacteria are exposed to the substance to determine whether it will cause mutations

am·e·thyst (am′ə thist) *n.* ⟦ME *ametist* < OFr *ametiste* < L *amethystus* < Gr *amethystos*, not drunk (the Greeks believed that the amethyst prevented intoxication) < *a-*, not + *methystos*, drunk < *methyein*, to be drunk < *methy*, strong drink < IE **medhu-*, honey, MEAD[1]⟧ **1** a purple or violet variety of quartz, used in jewelry **2** popularly, a purple variety of corundum, used in jewelry **3** purple or violet —**am′e·thys′tine** (-this′tin, -tēn′) *adj.*

am·e·tro·pi·a (am′i trō′pē ə) *n.* ⟦ModL < Gr *ametros*, disproportionate (< *a-*, not + *metron*, measure: see METER[1]) + -OPIA⟧ any condition of imperfect refraction of the eye, as nearsightedness, farsightedness, or astigmatism —**am′e·trop′ic** (-träp′ik, -trō′-) *adj.*

☆**Am·ex** (am′eks′) *n. informal name for* the American Stock Exchange

AMG *abbrev.* Allied Military Government

Am·ha·ra (äm hä′rə) former province of NW Ethiopia

Am·har·ic (am har′ik, äm här′-) *n.* the official language of Ethiopia, in the Ethiopic subfamily of the Semitic family of languages

Am·herst (am′ərst), Baron **Jeffrey** 1717-97; Eng. general: led Brit. forces that won control of Canada

a·mi (à mē′) *n., pl.* **a·mis′** (-mē′) ⟦Fr⟧ a (male) friend

a·mi·a·ble (ā′mē ə bəl) *adj.* ⟦ME < OFr < LL *amicabilis*, friendly < L *amicus*, friend: confused with OFr *amable*, lovable < L *amabilis*, worthy of love; both from L *amare*, to love⟧ **1** having a pleasant and friendly disposition; good-natured **2** [Obs.] lovely or lovable —**a′mi·a·bil′i·ty** (-bil′ə tē) *n.* —**a′mi·a·bly** *adv.*

SYN.—**amiable** and **affable** suggest qualities of friendliness, easy temper, etc. that make one likable, **affable** also implying a readiness to be approached, to converse, etc.; a **good-natured** person is one who is disposed to like as well as be liked and is sometimes easily imposed on; **obliging** implies a ready, often cheerful, desire to be helpful [the *obliging* clerk took my order]; **genial** suggests good cheer and sociability [our *genial* host]; **cordial** suggests graciousness and warmth [a *cordial* greeting] —*ANT.* **surly, ill-natured**

am·i·an·thus (am′ē an′thəs) *n.* ⟦altered, infl. by ANTHO- < L *amiantus*, asbestos < Gr *amiantos (lithos)*, lit., unspotted (stone) < *a-*, not + *miainein*, to stain or spot⟧ a kind of asbestos with long, silky fibers

am·i·ca·ble (am′i kə bəl) *adj.* ⟦LL *amicabilis*: see AMIABLE⟧ friendly in feeling; showing good will; peaceable [an *amicable* discussion] —**am′i·ca·bil′i·ty** (-bil′ə tē) *n.* —**am′i·ca·bly** *adv.*

am·ice[1] (am′is) *n.* ⟦ME < OFr *amit* < L *amictus*, a scarf, cloak, thing thrown around the body < pp. of *amicire*, to clothe < *am(bi)-*, around + *-icire* < *jacere*, to throw (see JET[1]); confused with OFr *aumusse*: see fol.⟧ an oblong white linen cloth worn about the neck and shoulders by a priest at Mass

am·ice[2] (am′is) *n.* ⟦altered (after prec.) < OFr *aumusse* < ML *almucia* < Ar *al*, the + *mustaḳa*, fur cloak with long sleeves < Pehlevi *mustak*, fur coat⟧ a fur-lined hood or hooded cape, formerly worn by the clergy

a·mi·cus (ə mē′kəs, -mī′-) *n., pl.* **-ci** (-kē, -sē) *short for* AMICUS CURIAE —*adj.* of or by an amicus curiae [an *amicus* brief]

amicus cu·ri·ae (kyoor′ē ē′) ⟦L, lit., friend of the court⟧ *Law* a person who offers, or is called in, to advise a court on some legal matter

a·mid (ə mid′) *prep.* ⟦ME *amidde* < *on middan* < *on*, at + *middan*, middle⟧ in the middle of; among

am·ide (am′īd′, -id) *n.* ⟦AM(MONIA) + -IDE⟧ **1** any of a group of organic compounds containing the $CO{\cdot}NH_2$ radical (e.g., acetamide) or an acid radical in place of one hydrogen atom of an ammonia molecule (e.g., sulfanilamide) **2** any of the ammono bases in which one hydrogen atom of the ammonia molecule is replaced by a metal (e.g., sodium amide, $NaNH_2$) —**a·mid·ic** (ə mid′ik) *adj.*

am·i·din (am′ə din) *n.* ⟦Fr *amid(on)* < L *amylum*, starch (see AMYLUM) + -IN[1]⟧ *Chem.* a transparent, water-soluble substance made by heating starch in water; soluble starch

am·i·dine (am′ə dēn′, -din) *n.* ⟦AMID(E) + -INE[3]⟧ any nitrogen base having the general formula $RC(:NH)NH_2$: these bases are crystalline solids soluble in alcohol and ether

a·mi·do (ə mē′dō, am′i dō′) *adj.* of an amide or amides

a·mi·do- (ə mē′dō, -də; -mid′ō, -ə; am′i dō′, am′ə-) ⟦< AMIDE⟧ *combining form* having one hydrogen atom in the ammonia molecule replaced by an acid radical [*amidol*]: also **amid-**

a·mi·do·gen (ə mē′də jən, ə mid′ə-) *n.* ⟦prec. + -GEN⟧ the hypothetical radical NH_2

am·i·dol (am′ə dōl′, -dôl′, -däl′) *n.* ⟦Ger, orig. trademark < *amido-*, AMIDO- + *phenol*, PHENOL⟧ a colorless crystalline compound, $C_6H_3(NH_2)_2OH{\cdot}2HCl$, used as a developer in photography

☆**am·i·done** (am′ə dōn′) *n.* ⟦Ger *amidon* < *(dimethyl)ami(no-)d(iphenylheptan)one*⟧ METHADONE

a·mid·ships (ə mid′ships′) *adv., adj.* in or toward the middle of a ship; esp., halfway between bow and stern

a·midst (ə midst′) *prep.* ⟦AMID + ME adv. gen. *-s* + unhistoric *-t*⟧ AMID

a·mie (à mē′) *n., pl.* **a·mies′** (-mē′) ⟦Fr, fem. of AMI⟧ a female friend

Am·i·ens (à myan′; E am′ē ənz) city in N France, on the Somme River

☆**a·mi·go** (ə mē′gō) *n., pl.* **-gos** ⟦Sp < L *amicus*: see AMIABLE⟧ a friend

A·min·di·vi Islands (ä′min də vē′) group of islands in the Arabian Sea, off the SW coast of India: the N part of Lakshadweep territory

a·mine (ə mēn′; am′ēn′, -in) *n.* ⟦AM(MONIA) + -INE[3]⟧ *Chem.* a derivative of ammonia in which hydrogen atoms have been replaced by nonacidic radicals containing hydrogen and carbon atoms (e.g., methylamine, CH_3NH_2) —**a·min′ic** (-min′ik, -mē′nik) *adj.*

a·mi·no (ə mē′nō, am′i nō′) *adj.* of or containing the NH_2 radical in combination with certain nonacidic organic radicals

a·mi·no- (ə mē′nō, am′i nō′) ⟦< AMINE⟧ *combining form* having one hydrogen atom in the ammonia molecule replaced by an alkyl or other nonacidic radical [*aminobenzoic* acid]

amino acid **1** any of a large group of organic acids containing a carboxyl group, COOH, and an amino group, NH_2 **2** any of the amino acids, usually about 20, that link together into polypeptide chains to form proteins that are necessary for all life: in general, they are water-soluble, crystalline, amphoteric electrolytes having mirror-image isomeric forms with right and left optical activity: ten of these (**essential amino acids**) cannot be synthesized by the human body and must be consumed

a·mi·no·ben·zo·ic acid (ə mē′nō ben zō′ik, am′i nō′-) any of several crystalline substances with the same formula, $NH_2C_6H_4COOH$, used in the manufacture of dyes, drugs, suntan lotions, etc.: see also PARA-AMINOBENZOIC ACID

a·mi·no·phe·nol (-fē′nōl, -nôl′, -näl′) *n.* any of several white or light-red crystalline compounds, $NH_2C_6H_4OH$ (esp. *para*-aminophenol), used in making dyes and as a photographic developer

a·mi·no·py·rine (-pī′rēn′, -rin) *n.* ⟦*(dimethyl)amino-* + (ANTI)PYRINE⟧ a colorless, crystalline powder, $C_{13}H_{17}N_3O$, sometimes used to reduce fever or pain: may cause agranulocytosis

amino resin a thermosetting resinous product made by condensation of a compound containing an amine (e.g., melamine or urea) with an aldehyde (e.g., formaldehyde): is used in making permanent-press fabrics and other products: also called **amino plastic** or **a·mi′no·plast′** (-plast′)

a·mi·no·tri·a·zole (-trī′ə zōl′) *n.* ⟦AMINO- + TRIAZOLE⟧ a white, crystalline, soluble powder, $NHNC(NH_2)NCH$, used for killing weeds or other undesired vegetation: a carcinogen

a·mir (ə mir′) *n.* ⟦Ar *amīr*⟧ *var. of* EMIR (sense 1)

A·mis (ā′mis), **Kings·ley** (kinz′lē) 1922-95; Brit. writer

☆**Am·ish** (äm′ish, am′-, ām′-) *pl.n.* ⟦after Jacob *Ammann* (or *Amen*), the founder⟧ the members of a Christian sect that separated from the Mennonites in the 17th cent.: in the U.S. since the 18th cent., the Amish favor plain dress and plain living, with little reliance on modern conveniences, in a chiefly agrarian society —*adj.* designating or of this sect

a·miss (ə mis′) *adv.* ⟦ME *amis, on-mis*: see A-[1] & MISS[1]⟧ in a wrong way; astray, wrongly, faultily, improperly, etc. —*adj.* wrong, faulty, improper, etc.: used only in the predicate

a·mi·to·sis (ā′mī tō′sis, am′i-) *n.* ⟦A-[2] + MITOSIS⟧ *Biol.* cell division in which the nucleus and cytoplasm divide by simple constriction and without halving of chromosomes; direct cell division: opposed to MITOSIS —**a′mi·tot′ic** (-tät′ik) *adj.* —**a′mi·tot′i·cal·ly** *adv.*

am·i·trip·ty·line (am′ə trip′tə lēn′) *n.* ⟦AMI(NE) + TRI- + *(he)ptyl*, a radical derived from heptane + -INE[3]⟧ a white, crystalline drug, $C_{20}H_{23}N{\cdot}HCl$, taken orally, used to treat depression, neuropathic pain, migraine, etc.: in full **amitriptyline hydrochloride**

am·i·trole (am′ə trōl′) *n.* ⟦AMI(NO)- + TR(IAZ)OL(E)⟧ AMINOTRIAZOLE

am·i·ty (am′ə tē) *n., pl.* **-ties** ⟦ME *amite* < OFr *amistie* < VL **amicitas* < L *amicus*, friend < *amare*, to love⟧ friendly, peaceful relations, as between nations; friendship

Am·man (ä′män′, ä män′) capital of Jordan, in the NW part: it is the Biblical city *Rabbah*

am·me·ter (am′mēt′ər) *n.* ⟦AM(PERE) + -METER⟧ an instrument for measuring the strength of an electric current in terms of amperes

am·mine (am′ēn, -in; a mēn′) ***n.*** ⟦AMM(ONIA) + -INE[3]⟧ *Chem.* **1** a molecule of ammonia (NH_3) bonded directly to a metal in certain complex compounds: cf. AMINE **2** any compound containing this molecule

am·mi·no- (a mē′nō, am′i nō′) *combining form* containing one or more ammines

am·mo (am′ō) ***n.*** [Slang] ammunition

Am·mon[1] (am′ən, ä′mən) ***n.*** ⟦L < Gr *Ammōn* < Egypt *Åmen*⟧ *Gr. & Latin name for* AMON

Am·mon[2] (am′ən) ***n.*** ⟦Heb *amon*, lit., prob., populous⟧ *Bible* a son of Lot: Gen. 19:38

Am·mon[3] (am′ən) an ancient kingdom east of the Dead Sea —**Am′mon·ite′** (-ə nīt′) ***adj., n.***

am·mo·ni·a (ə mōn′yə; *occas.*, -mō′nē ə) ***n.*** ⟦(SAL) AMMONIA(C)⟧ **1** a colorless, pungent gas, NH_3: its compounds are used as fertilizers, in medicine, etc. **2** a 10% water solution of this gas: in full **ammonia water**

am·mo·ni·ac (ə mō′nē ak′) ***n.*** ⟦ME *ammoniak* < ML *armoniac* < L *ammoniacum* < Gr *ammōniakon*, gum resin: orig., prob. from its occurrence in plants growing near the temple of Jupiter AMMON[1] in Egypt⟧ a pungent gum resin obtained from the stems of certain plants (esp. *Dorema ammoniacum*) of the umbel family, found in Iran, S Siberia, and N India: used in perfumes, adhesives, and porcelain cements, and formerly in medicine

am·mo·ni·a·cal (am′ə nī′ə kəl) ***adj.*** of, like, or containing ammonia

am·mo·ni·ate (ə mō′nē āt′; *for n.*, -it, -āt′) ***vt.*** **-at′ed, -at′ing** to mix or combine with ammonia —***n.*** any of several compounds containing ammonia —**am·mo′ni·a′tion *n.***

am·mon·ic (ə män′ik, -mō′nik) ***adj.*** of or from ammonia or ammonium

☆**am·mon·i·fi·ca·tion** (ə män′ə fi kā′shən, -mō′nə -) ***n.*** **1** infusion with ammonia or ammonium compounds **2** the production of ammonia by bacterial action in the decay of nitrogenous organic matter

☆**am·mon·i·fy** (ə män′ə fī′, -mō′nə-) ***vi., vt.*** **-fied′, -fy′ing** to undergo or cause to undergo ammonification

am·mo·nite (am′ə nīt′) ***n.*** ⟦ModL *ammonites* < L (*cornu*) *Ammonis*, (horn) of Ammon < Jupiter AMMON[1], whose statues were represented with ram's horns⟧ any of the flat, usually coiled fossil shells of an extinct order (Ammonoidea) of cephalopod mollusks dominant in the Mesozoic era —**am′mo·nit′ic** (-nit′ik) ***adj.***

am·mo·ni·um (ə mō′nē əm) ***n.*** ⟦ModL, coined by BERZELIUS < AMMONIA + -IUM⟧ the monovalent radical NH_4, present in salts produced by the reaction of ammonia with an acid: its compounds are like those of the alkali metals

ammonium chloride a white crystalline compound, NH_4Cl, produced by the reaction of ammonia with hydrochloric acid: it is used in medicine to correct alkalosis, and also in dry cells, fertilizers, dyes, etc.; sal ammoniac

ammonium hydroxide a weak, colorless base, NH_4OH, formed by dissolving ammonia in water

ammonium nitrate a colorless, crystalline salt, NH_4NO_3, used in some explosives, as a fertilizer, and in rocket fuel

ammonium sulfate an ammonium salt, $(NH_4)_2SO_4$, made chiefly from synthetic ammonia and used in making fertilizers, in treating water, etc.

am·mo·no (am′ə nō′) ***adj.*** **1** of or containing ammonia **2** derived from ammonia: used to describe compounds bearing the same relation to ammonia as certain other compounds bear to water [sodium amide, $NaNH_2$, is an *ammono* base corresponding to sodium hydroxide, $NaOH$]

am·mo·no- (am′ə nō′) ⟦< AMMONIA⟧ *combining form* ammonia [*ammonotelic*]

am·mo·no·tel·ic (am′ə nō tel′ik) ***adj.*** ⟦prec. + TELIC⟧ excreting ammonia as the main nitrogenous waste: characteristic of freshwater fishes and many aquatic invertebrates

am·mu·ni·tion (am′yoo nish′ən, -yə-) ***n.*** ⟦Fr *amunition*, by faulty separation of *la munition*: see MUNITIONS⟧ **1** [Obs.] any military supplies **2** anything hurled by a weapon or exploded as a weapon, as bullets, gunpowder, shot, shells, bombs, grenades, rockets, etc. **3** any means of attack or defense [the facts provided him with *ammunition* for his argument]

Amn *abbrev. U.S. Air Force* airman

am·ne·sia (am nē′zhə) ***n.*** ⟦ModL < Gr *amnēsia*, forgetfulness < *a-*, not + *mnasthai*, to remember < IE base **men-*, **mnā-*, to think, be alert > MAN, L *mens*, MIND⟧ partial or total loss of memory caused as by brain injury or by shock —**am·ne′si·ac′** (-zhē ak′) ***adj., n.***, **am·ne′sic** (-zik, -sik) —**am·nes′tic** (-nes′tik) ***adj.***

am·nes·ty (am′nəs tē) ***n.***, *pl.* **-ties** ⟦Fr *amnestie* < L *amnestia* < Gr *amnēstia*, a forgetting: see prec.⟧ **1** a pardon, esp. for political offenses against a government **2** [Archaic] a deliberate overlooking, as of an offense —***vt.*** **-tied, -ty·ing** to grant amnesty to

am·ni·o·cen·te·sis (am′nē ō′sen tē′sis) ***n.*** ⟦ModL < fol. + Gr *kentēsis*, a pricking⟧ the surgical procedure of inserting a hollow needle through the abdominal wall into the uterus of a pregnant woman and extracting amniotic fluid, which may be analyzed to determine the sex of the developing fetus or the presence of disease, genetic defects, etc.

am·ni·on (am′nē ən, -än′) ***n.***, *pl.* **-ni·ons** or **-ni·a** (-ə) ⟦Gr, dim. of *amnos*, lamb < IE **agwhnos* > YEAN, L *agnus*⟧ **1** the innermost membrane of the sac enclosing the embryo of a mammal, reptile, or bird: it is filled with a watery fluid (**amniotic fluid**) **2** a similar membrane of certain invertebrates, esp. insects —**am′ni·ot′ic** (-ät′ik) ***adj.***, **am′ni·on′ic** (-än′ik)

am·n't (am′ənt, ant) *contraction* [Informal] am not: see also AIN'T, AN'T

am·o·bar·bi·tal (am′ō bär′bə tôl′, -tal′) ***n.*** ⟦AM(YL)O- + BARBITAL⟧ a colorless crystalline compound, $C_{11}H_{18}N_2O_3$, used as a sedative and hypnotic

am·o·di·a·quin (-dī′ə kwin′) ***n.*** ⟦*am(in)o-di(hydrochloride)* + *-a-* + *quin(oline)*⟧ a compound, $C_{20}H_{22}ClN_3O$, whose hydrochloride form is used in treating malaria: also **am′o·di′a·quine′** (-kwin′, -kwēn′)

a·moe·ba (ə mē′bə) ***n.***, *pl.* **-bas** or **-bae** (-bē) ⟦ModL < Gr *amoibē*, change < *ameibein*, to change⟧ **1** a one-celled, microscopic organism belonging to any of several families of rhizopods that move and feed using pseudopodia and reproduce by fission; esp., any of a genus (*Amoeba*) found in soil or water or a parasitic genus (*Entamoeba*) found in higher animals and humans **2** something indefinite in shape or perpetually changing, like an amoeba See usage note at AMEBA —**a·moe′bic** (-bik) ***adj.***, **a·moe′boid′** (-boid′), or **a·moe′ban** (-bən)

am·oe·bi·a·sis (am′i bī′ə sis) ***n.*** *alt. sp. of* AMEBIASIS

amoebic dysentery *alt. sp. of* AMEBIC DYSENTERY

a·moe·bo·cyte (ə mē′bō sīt′) ***n.*** ⟦< AMOEBA + -CYTE⟧ *alt. sp. of* AMEBOCYTE

a·mok (ə muk′, -mäk′) ***adj., adv.*** ⟦< Malay *amuk*, attacking furiously, ult. < Old Javanese⟧ *used only in the phrase* **run** (or **go**) **amok** **1** to rush about in a frenzy to kill **2** to lose control of oneself and behave outrageously or violently **3** to become wild or undisciplined

☆**a·mo·le** (ə mō′lā) ***n.*** ⟦MexSp < Nahuatl *a:molli*, lit., soap-root⟧ **1** the root of any of various plants of the SW U.S. and Mexico, used as a substitute for soap **2** any of these plants, esp. the soap plant

A·mon (ä′mən) ***n.*** ⟦Egypt *ymn Amūn*; ? akin to *ymn*, to hide⟧ *Egypt. Myth.* originally, a local god of fertility and life in Egyptian Thebes: later associated with Ra (Re) as the chief deity of Egypt (AMON-RE): identified by the Greeks (and Romans) with Zeus (and Jupiter): also sp. **A′mun**

a·mong (ə muŋ′) ***prep.*** ⟦ME < OE *on gemang*, in the company (of) < *on*, in + *gemang*, a mingling, crowd < *gemengan*, MINGLE⟧ **1** in the company of; surrounded by; included with a group of [you are *among* friends] **2** from place to place in [he passed *among* the crowd] **3** in the number or class of [included *among* his supporters] **4** by or with many of [a book popular *among* executives] **5** as compared with [one *among* thousands] **6** with a portion for each of [the estate was divided *among* the relatives] **7** by the reciprocal action of [don't quarrel *among* yourselves] **8** *a)* by the concerted action of *b)* in the joint possession of

a·mongst (ə muŋst′) ***prep.*** ⟦prec. + adv. gen. *-s* + unhistoric *-t*⟧ *chiefly Brit. var. of* AMONG

A·mon-Re (ä′mən rā′) ***n.*** ⟦Egypt *ymn-r′* < *Amun* + *r′*, sun⟧ *Egypt. Myth.* the chief deity, a composite of the gods AMON and Ra (Re): also **A′mon-Ra′** (-rä′)

a·mon·til·la·do (ə män′tə lä′dō) ***n.*** ⟦< Sp, after *Montilla*, town in Spain + *-ado*, -ATE[2]⟧ a pale, relatively dry sherry

a·mor·al (ā môr′əl) ***adj.*** **1** not to be judged by criteria of morality; neither moral nor immoral **2** without moral sense or principles; incapable of distinguishing between right and wrong —**a·mo·ral·i·ty** (ā′mə ral′ə tē) ***n.*** —**a·mor′al·ly *adv.***

am·o·ret·to (am′ə ret′ō) ***n.***, *pl.* **-ret′ti** (-ret′ē) ⟦It, dim. of *amore* < L *amor*, love⟧ an infant cupid, as in Italian art of the 16th cent.

am·o·rist (am′ə rist) ***n.*** ⟦L *amor*, love + -IST[1]⟧ a person much occupied with love and lovemaking

Am·o·rite (am′ə rīt′) ***n.*** ⟦Heb *emori*⟧ a member of an ancient Semitic people of *c.* 2000 B.C.: in the Bible, regarded as descended from Canaan, son of Ham: Gen. 10:16

am·o·rous (am′ə rəs) ***adj.*** ⟦ME < OFr *amoureus* < LL *amorosus*, loving < L *amor*, love < *amare*, to love⟧ **1** full of love or fond of making love **2** in love; enamored or fond (*of*) **3** full of or showing love or sexual desire [*amorous* words] **4** of sexual love or lovemaking —**am′o·rous·ly *adv.*** —**am′o·rous·ness *n.***

a·mor pa·tri·ae (ä′môr′ pä′trē ä′, -trē′ī′) ⟦L⟧ love of one's country; patriotism

a·mor·phous (ə môr′fəs) ***adj.*** ⟦ModL *amorphus* < Gr *amorphos* < *a-*, without + *morphē*, form⟧ **1** without definite form; shapeless **2** of no definite type; anomalous **3** unorganized; vague **4** *Biol.* without definite or specialized structure, as some lower forms of life **5** *Chem., Mineralogy* not crystalline —**a·mor′phism′** (-fiz′əm) ***n.*** —**a·mor′phous·ly *adv.*** —**a·mor′phous·ness *n.***

am·or·tise (am′ər tīz′, ə môr′-) ***vt.*** **-tised′, -tis′ing** *chiefly Brit. sp. of* AMORTIZE

am·or·ti·za·tion (am′ər ti zā′shən, ə môr′tə-) ***n.*** **1** an amortizing or being amortized **2** money put aside for amortizing a debt, etc.: also **a·mor·tize·ment** (ə môr′tiz mənt)

am·or·tize (am′ər tīz′, ə môr′-) ***vt.*** **-tized′, -tiz′ing** ⟦ME *amortisen* < extended stem of OFr *amortir*, to extinguish, sell in mortmain (< ML *amortire*); or < ML *amortizare*; both ML forms < L *ad*, to + *mors*, death: see MORTAL⟧ **1** to put money aside at intervals, as in a sinking fund, for gradual payment of (a debt, etc.) either at or before maturity **2** *Accounting* to write off (expenditures) by prorating over a fixed period **3** *Law* to reduce, transfer, or sell (property) in mortmain —**am′or·tiz′a·ble *adj.***

a·mor vin·cit om·ni·a (ä′môr′ vin′chit ôm′nē ä′; -vin′sit-, -viŋk′it-) ⟦L⟧ love conquers everything

A·mos (ā′məs) ***n.*** ⟦Heb *amos*, lit., borne (by God?)⟧ **1** a masculine name **2** *Bible* *a)* a Hebrew prophet of the 8th cent. B.C. *b)* the book containing his prophecies (abbrev. *Am.*)

a·mount (ə mount′) ***vi.*** ⟦ME *amounten*, to ascend < OFr *amonter* < *amont*, upward < *a-* (L *ad*), to + *mont* < L *montem*, acc. sing. of *mons*, MOUNTAIN⟧ **1** to add up (*to*); equal in total [the bill *amounts* to $4.50] **2** to be equal (*to*) in meaning, value, or effect [her failure to reply *amounts* to a refusal]

—*n.* 1 the sum of two or more quantities; total 2 the whole meaning, value, or effect 3 a quantity [a fair *amount* of resistance] —**SYN.** SUM[1]
a·mour (a mo͝or′, ä-, ə-) *n.* ⟦Fr < Prov *amor* < L, love⟧ a love affair, esp. of an illicit or secret nature
a·mour fou (á mo͞or fo͞o′) ⟦Fr, lit., insane love⟧ obsessive love or infatuation
a·mour-pro·pre (á mo͞or prô′pr′) *n.* ⟦Fr < *amour*, love (see AMOUR) + *propre*, own, one's own⟧ self-esteem
a·mox·i·cil·lin (ə mäk′sē sil′in) *n.* ⟦AM(INO)- + OX(Y)-[1] + (PEN)ICILLIN⟧ a synthetic antibiotic, $C_{16}H_{19}N_3O_5S$, derived from ampicillin, used orally in treating various bacterial diseases
A·moy (ä moi′) *former name for* XIAMEN
☆**amp**[1] (amp) *n. short for:* 1 AMPERE 2 AMPLIFIER —*vt.* [Slang] 1 to increase, augment, enhance, or intensify 2 to excite or arouse Usually with *up*
amp[2] *abbrev.* 1 amperage 2 ampere(s)
AMP (ā′em′pē′) *n.* ⟦*a(denosine) m(ono)p(hosphate)*⟧ a crystalline nucleotide, $C_{10}H_{14}N_5O_7P$, present in, and vital to the energy processes of, all living cells: also a major regulator of a cell's biochemical activity
am·pe·lop·sis (am′pə läp′sis) *n.* ⟦ModL < Gr *ampelos*, vine + -OPSIS⟧ a climbing vine or shrub of a genus (*Ampelopsis*) in the grape family, widely grown as ornamentals
am·per·age (am′pər ij, am pir′-) *n.* the strength of an electric current, measured in amperes
am·pere (am′pir′) *n.* ⟦after fol.⟧ the basic unit of electric current intensity, equal, in the MKS system, to a rate of flow of charge in a conductor or conducting medium of one coulomb per second and, in the SI system, to a constant current that, if maintained in two straight parallel conductors of infinite length and negligible circular cross section placed one meter apart in a vacuum, would produce between these conductors a force equal to $2{\times}10^{-7}$ newton per meter of length: abbrev. *A* or *amp*: cf. OHM
Am·père (än per′), **An·dré Ma·rie** (än drā mȧ rē′) 1775-1836; Fr. physicist & mathematician
am·pere-hour (am′pir our′) *n.* a standard unit for measuring the quantity of electricity, equal to the flow of a current of one ampere for one hour, or to an elapsed current drain of 3,600 coulombs
am·pere-turn (am′pir turn′) *n.* the basic unit of magnetomotive force in the SI system, equal to the force produced by a current of one ampere flowing around one turn of a wire coil (1.257 gilberts): symbol, NI
am·per·sand (am′pər sand′) *n.* ⟦< *and per se and*, lit., (the sign) & by itself (is) *and*⟧ a sign (& or &) meaning *and*: it represents the Latin word *et* (and)
☆**am·phet·a·mine** (am fet′ə mēn′, -min) *n.* ⟦*a(lpha-)m(ethyl-beta-)ph(enyl-)et(hyl-)amine*⟧ 1 a colorless, liquid drug, $C_6H_5CH_2CH(NH_2)CH_3$, that acts as a stimulant of the central nervous system and is used, usually in its crystalline sulfate or phosphate form, as a medicine to treat narcolepsy, depression, obesity, and Parkinson's disease: often used nonmedically for its stimulant effect, it is potentially habit forming 2 any closely related drug, as Dexedrine
am·phi- (am′fi, -fē, -fə) ⟦< Gr *amphi*, around: see AMBI-⟧ *combining form* 1 on both sides or on both ends [*amphistylar*] 2 around or about 3 of both kinds [*amphibious*]
am·phi·ar·thro·sis (am′fē är thrō′sis) *n.* ⟦ModL < prec. + Gr *arthrōsis*, a jointing < *arthron*, a joint: see ARTHRO-⟧ *Anat.* a form of jointing in which cartilage connects the bones and allows only slight motion
am·phi·as·ter (am′fē as′tər) *n.* ⟦AMPHI- + -ASTER[1]⟧ in mitosis, the long spindle with asters at either end that forms during the prophase, or first stage
am·phib·i·an (am fib′ē ən) *n.* ⟦< ModL *Amphibia* < Gr *amphibia*, neut. pl. of *amphibios*: see AMPHIBIOUS⟧ 1 any of a class (Amphibia) of coldblooded, scaleless vertebrates, consisting of frogs, toads, newts, salamanders, and caecilians, that usually begin life in the water as tadpoles with gills and later develop lungs 2 any amphibious animal or plant 3 any aircraft that can take off from and come down on either land or water 4 a tank or other vehicle that can travel on either land or water —*adj.* 1 of amphibians 2 AMPHIBIOUS
am·phi·bi·ot·ic (am′fi bī ät′ik) *adj.* ⟦< Gr *amphibios* (see fol.) + -IC⟧ *Zool.* that lives in water in one stage of development and on land in another
am·phib·i·ous (am fib′ē əs) *adj.* ⟦Gr *amphibios*, living a double life < *amphi-*, AMPHI- + *bios*, life: see BIO-⟧ 1 that can live both on land and in water 2 that can operate or travel on both land and water 3 designating, of, or for a military operation involving the landing of assault troops on a shore from seaborne transports 4 having two natures or qualities; of a mixed nature —**am·phib′i·ous·ly** *adv.*
am·phi·bole (am′fə bōl′) *n.* ⟦Fr < LL *amphibolus*, ambiguous < Gr *amphibolos* < *amphiballein*, to throw around, doubt < *amphi-*, AMPHI- + *ballein*, to throw: see BALL[2]⟧ any of a group of rock-forming minerals, as hornblende or actinolite, composed largely of silica, calcium, iron, and magnesium: they are common constituents of igneous and metamorphic rocks
am·phib·o·lite (am fib′ə līt′) *n.* ⟦prec. + -ITE[1]⟧ a metamorphic rock consisting largely of amphibole and plagioclase
am·phi·bol·o·gy (am′fə bäl′ə jē) *n., pl.* **-gies** ⟦ME *amphibologie* < LL *amphibologia* (altered after words ending in *-logia*, -LOGY) < L *amphibolia* < Gr, ambiguity < *amphiballein*: see AMPHIBOLE⟧ 1 double or doubtful meaning; ambiguity, esp. from uncertain grammatical construction 2 an ambiguous phrase, proposition, etc. Also **am·phib·o·ly** (am fib′ə lē), *pl.* **-lies** —**am′phi·bol′ic** (-bäl′ik) *adj.*, **am·phib′o·lous** (-ə ləs)
am·phi·brach (am′fə brak′) *n.* ⟦L *amphibrachys* < Gr, lit., short before and after < *amphi-*, AMPHI- + *brachys*, short: see MERRY⟧ a metrical foot consisting, in Greek and Latin verse, of one long syllable between two short ones, or, in English verse, of one accented syllable between two unaccented ones (Ex.: | ĕxplósiŏn |)
am·phi·chro·ic (am′fi krō′ik) *adj.* ⟦< AMPHI- + Gr *chroma*, color (see CHROME) + -IC⟧ *Chem.* exhibiting either of two colors under varying conditions, as litmus
am·phi·coe·lous (am′fi sē′ləs) *adj.* ⟦Gr *amphikoilos* < *amphi-*, AMPHI- + *koilos*, hollow: see CAVE⟧ concave on both sides, as the vertebrae of certain fishes
am·phic·ty·on (am fik′tē än′, -ən) *n.* ⟦< L (pl.) *Amphictyones* < Gr *Amphiktyones* < *amphiktiones*, those that dwelt around, nearest neighbors⟧ a delegate to the council or assembly of an amphictyony
am·phic·ty·o·ny (-ə nē′) *n., pl.* **-nies** ⟦Gr *amphiktyonia*: see prec. ⟧ in ancient Greece, a confederation of states established around a religious center, as at Delphi —**am·phic′ty·on′ic** (-än′ik) *adj.*
am·phi·go·ry (am′fə gôr′ē) *n., pl.* **-ries** ⟦Fr *amphigouri* < ?⟧ a piece of nonsense writing, as in burlesque
am·phim·a·cer (am fim′ə sər) *n.* ⟦< L *amphimacrus* < Gr *amphimakros*, lit., long at both ends < *amphi-*, AMPHI- + *makros*, long: see MACRO-⟧ a metrical foot consisting, in Greek and Latin verse, of one short syllable between two long ones, or, in English verse, of one unaccented syllable between two accented ones (Ex.: | hésĭtáte |)
am·phi·mix·is (am′fə mik′sis) *n.* ⟦ModL < AMPHI- + Gr *mixis*, a mixing: see MIX⟧ *Biol.* 1 the uniting of male and female germ cells from two individuals in reproduction 2 crossbreeding
Am·phi·on (am fī′ən) *n.* ⟦L < Gr *Amphiōn*⟧ *Gr. Myth.* a son of Zeus and Antiope: he builds a wall around Thebes by charming the stones into place with a lyre
am·phi·ox·us (am′fē äk′səs) *n.* ⟦< AMPHI- + Gr *oxys*, sharp⟧ CEPHALOCHORDATE
am·phi·pod (am′fə päd′) *n.* ⟦< ModL < AMPHI- + -POD⟧ any of an order (Amphipoda) of malacostracan crustaceans with a vertically thin body and one set of legs for jumping or walking and another set for swimming, as the sand hopper
am·phi·pro·style (am′fə prō′stīl′, am fip′rə stīl′) *adj.* ⟦L *amphiprostylos* < Gr: see AMPHI- & PROSTYLE⟧ *Archit.* having columns at the front and back, but none along the sides —*n.* an amphiprostyle building
am·phis·bae·na (am′fis bē′nə) *n.* ⟦ME *amphibena* < L *amphisbaena* < Gr *amphisbaina* < *amphis*, on both sides (see AMPHI-) + *bainein*, to go: see COME⟧ *Class. Myth.* a serpent with a head at each end of its body
am·phis·bae·ni·an (am′fis bē′nē ən) *n.* ⟦< ModL: see prec.⟧ any of a legless, burrowing suborder (Amphisbaenia) of tropical reptiles (order Squamata) with a head and tail that look very much alike; worm lizard
am·phi·sty·lar (am′fə stī′lər) *adj.* ⟦< AMPHI- + Gr *stylos*, pillar (see STYLITE) + -AR⟧ *Archit.* having columns at both front and back or on both sides
am·phi·the·a·ter or **am·phi·the·a·tre** (am′fə thē′ə tər) *n.* ⟦L *amphitheatrum* < Gr *amphitheatron*: see AMPHI- & THEATER⟧ 1 a round or oval building with an open space (arena) surrounded by rising rows of seats 2 a scene of conflict, competition, etc.; arena 3 a sloping gallery in a theater 4 a lecture hall with a sloping gallery, esp. one for observing surgical procedures in a medical school or hospital 5 a level place surrounded by rising ground —**am′phi·the·at′ric** (-thē a′trik) *adj.*, **am′phi·the·at′ri·cal**
am·phi·the·ci·um (am′fi thē′shē əm, -sē-) *n., pl.* **-ci·a** (-shē ə, -sē ə) ⟦ModL < AMPHI- + Gr *thēkion*, dim. of *thēkē*, a case: see THECA⟧ *Bot.* the outer layer of cells in the spore case of a bryophyte
Am·phi·tri·te (am′fi trīt′ē) *n.* ⟦L < Gr *Amphitritē*⟧ *Gr. Myth.* one of the Nereids, the goddess of the sea and wife of Poseidon
am·phi·tro·pous (am fi′trə pəs) *adj.* ⟦AMPHI- + -TROPOUS⟧ having a flower ovule with an inverted structure, with the stalk attachment near the middle of the ovule and the opening near the bottom
Am·phi·try·on (am fi′trē ən, -än′) *n.* ⟦L < Gr *Amphitryōn*⟧ *Gr. Myth.* a king of Thebes and the husband of ALCMENE
am·pho·ra (am′fə rə) *n., pl.* **-rae′** (-rē′) or **-ras** ⟦L < Gr *amphoreus*, a jar with two handles, contr. < *amphiphoreus* < *amphi-* (see AMPHI-) + *phoreus*, bearer < *pherein*, BEAR[1]⟧ a tall jar with a narrow neck and base and two handles, used by the ancient Greeks and Romans

amphora

am·pho·ter·ic (am′fə ter′ik) *adj.* ⟦< Gr *amphoteros*, compar. of *amphō*, both; var. of *amphi-*, AMPHI-⟧ *Chem.* having both acid and basic properties
am·pho·ter·i·cin B (am′fə ter′ə sin) ⟦prec. + -IN[1]⟧ an antibiotic compound, $C_{46}H_{73}NO_{20}$, used in treating certain diseases caused by parasitic fungi, such as systemic candidiasis
amp-hr *abbrev.* ampere-hour
am·pi·cil·lin (am′pə sil′in) *n.* ⟦AM(INO)- + P(EN)ICILLIN⟧ a synthetic antibiotic, $C_{16}H_{19}N_3O_4S$, derived from penicillin, having resistance to acids so that it can be taken orally to fight a wide range of bacterial infections
am·ple (am′pəl) *adj.* **-pler** (-plər), **-plest** (-pləst) ⟦ME & OFr < L *amplus*, prob. < *amlos < IE base *am-, to contain⟧ 1 large in size, extent, scope, etc.; spacious; roomy 2 more than enough; abundant 3 enough to fulfill the needs or purpose; adequate —**SYN.** PLENTIFUL —**am′ple·ness** *n.*

am·plex·i·caul (am pleks′i kôl′) ***adj.*** ⟦< L *amplexus*, pp. of *amplectari*, to twine around (< *am-*, for *ambi-*, AMBI- + *plectere*, to braid: see FLAX) + *caulis*, stem: see HOLE⟧ *Bot.* clasping or enveloping the stem, as the leaves of corn or teasels

am·plex·us (am plek′səs) ***n.***, *pl.* **-plex′us** ⟦ModL < L, embrace: see prec.⟧ the mating clasp of the male frog or toad: he clings to the back of the female and fertilizes her eggs as she ejects them into the water

☆**am·pli·dyne** (am′plə dīn′) ***n.*** ⟦AMPLI(FIER) + DYNE⟧ an amplifier that uses direct current and a rotating armature to generate a highly amplified output voltage that is sensitive to small changes in input voltage, used extensively to control servomotors

am·pli·fi·ca·tion (am′plə fi kā′shən) ***n.*** **1** an amplifying or being amplified **2** matter, details, etc. added to amplify a statement, report, etc. **3** a statement, etc. with something added

am·pli·fi·er (am′plə fī′ər) ***n.*** **1** a person or thing that amplifies **2** *Electronics* a device that increases the strength of a weak electrical signal without changing the other characteristics of the signal, specif., any of various devices for amplifying sound

am·pli·fy (am′plə fī′) ***vt.*** **-fied′**, **-fy′ing** ⟦ME *amplifien* < OFr *amplifier* < L *amplificare* < *amplus* (see AMPLE) + *facere*, DO[1]⟧ **1** to make larger or stronger; increase or extend (power, authority, etc.) **2** to develop more fully, as with details, examples, statistics, etc. [to *amplify* a point in a debate] **3** [Rare] to exaggerate **4** *Electronics* to increase the strength of (an electrical signal) by means of an amplifier —***vi.*** to speak or write at length; expatiate

am·pli·tude (-to͞od′, -tyo͞od′) ***n.*** ⟦L *amplitudo* < *amplus*: see AMPLE⟧ **1** the quality of being ample or the amount or degree to which a thing extends **2** an amount that is more than enough; abundance; fullness **3** scope or breadth, as of mind **4** the angular distance of a star from the true east or west point of the horizon, at the moment of its rising or setting **5** the extreme range of a fluctuating quantity, as an alternating current or the swing of a pendulum, generally measured from the average or mean to the extreme

amplitude modulation **1** the variation of the amplitude of a carrier wave in accordance with the signal being broadcast **2** a broadcasting system that uses this Abbrev. *AM* Cf. FREQUENCY MODULATION

am·ply (am′plē) ***adv.*** to an ample degree; liberally; fully

am·pul (am′po͝ol′, -pul′) ***n.*** ⟦< Fr < L *ampulla*, fol.⟧ a sealed glass or plastic container for one dose of a sterile medicine to be injected parenterally: also **am′pule′** (-pyo͞ol′) or **am′poule′** (-po͞ol′)

am·pul·la (am pul′ə, -po͝ol′-) ***n.***, *pl.* **-pul′lae** (-ē) ⟦ME *ampulle* < OE *ampulla* or OFr *ampoule*, both forms < L *ampulla*, dim. of *ampora*, for *amphora*, AMPHORA⟧ **1** a nearly round bottle with two handles, used by the ancient Greeks and Romans **2** *Anat.* a sac or dilated part of a tube or canal, as of a milk duct in a mammary gland —**am·pul′lar** (-ər) ***adj.***

am·pul·la·ceous (am′pə lā′shəs) ***adj.*** ⟦L *ampullaceus*⟧ shaped like an ampulla or a bladder

am·pu·tate (am′pyo͞o tāt′, -pyə-) ***vt., vi.*** **-tat′ed**, **-tat′ing** ⟦< L *amputatus*, pp. of *amputare* < *am-*, for *ambi-*, AMBI- + *putare*, to trim, prune < IE **putos*, part. form of base **peu-*, to strike > PAVE⟧ to cut off (an arm, leg, etc.), esp. by surgery —**am′pu·ta′tion** ***n.*** —**am′pu·ta′tor** ***n.***

am·pu·tee (am′pyo͞o tē′, -pyə-) ***n.*** ⟦prec. + -EE[1]⟧ a person who has had a limb or limbs amputated

Am·ra·va·ti (äm räv′ə tē′, um-) city in N Maharashtra, W India

am·ri·ta (äm rēt′ə, um-) ***n.*** ⟦< Sans *amṛta*, deathless, hence drink that makes immortal < IE base **mer-*: see AMBROSIA⟧ *Hindu Myth.* the ambrosial drink or food granting immortality

Am·rit·sar (äm rit′sər, um-) city in W Punjab, NW India

AMSLAN *abbrev.* AMERICAN SIGN LANGUAGE

Am·ster·dam (am′stər dam′) constitutional capital of the Netherlands: seaport on an inlet of the IJsselmeer & a ship canal to the North Sea: see also HAGUE, The

amt *abbrev.* amount

☆**am·trac** (am′trak′) ***n.*** ⟦AM(PHIBIOUS) + TRAC(TOR)⟧ a small amphibious vehicle with tractor treads, used in sea-to-shore operations in WWII

☆**Am·trak** (am′trak′) ⟦*Am(erican) tr(avel) (tr)a(c)k*⟧ *service mark for* a U.S. passenger railroad system, partly owned and subsidized by the federal government

amu or **AMU** *abbrev.* atomic mass unit

a·muck (ə muk′) ***n.*** *alt. sp. of* AMOK

A·mu Dar·ya (ä mo͞o′ där′yä) river in central Asia rising in the Pamir Mountains & flowing west & northwest into the Aral Sea: *c.* 1,600 mi (2,575 km)

am·u·let (am′yə lit) ***n.*** ⟦Fr *amulette* < L *amuletum*⟧ an object worn on the body because it is believed to have magical power to protect against injury or evil; a charm; talisman

A·mund·sen (ä′mo͝on sən), **Ro·ald** (rō′äl) 1872-1928; Norw. explorer: first person to reach the South Pole (1911)

Amundsen Sea part of the Pacific Ocean bordering on Antarctica, east of the Ross Sea

A·mur (ä mo͝or′) river in NE Asia, flowing along the Russia-China border across E Siberia into Tatar Strait: *c.* 1,800 mi (2,897 km); with principal headstreams, 2,744 mi (4,416 km)

a·muse (ə myo͞oz′) ***vt.*** **a·mused′**, **a·mus′ing** ⟦Fr *amuser* < *à*, at + OFr *muser*, to stare fixedly, MUSE⟧ **1** to keep pleasantly or enjoyably occupied or interested; entertain [we *amused* ourselves with games] **2** to make laugh, smile, etc. by being comical or humorous **3** [Obs.] to engage the attention of so as to deceive; delude; bemuse —**a·mus′a·ble** ***adj.*** —**a·mus′er** ***n.*** —**a·mus′ed·ly** ***adv.***

SYN.—**amuse** suggests the agreeable occupation of the mind, esp. by something that appeals to the sense of humor [the monkey's antics *amused* him]; to **divert** is to take the attention from serious thought or worry to something merry or light; **entertain** implies planned amusement or diversion, often with some intellectual appeal [another guest *entertained* us with folk songs]; **beguile** suggests the occupation of time with an agreeable activity, largely to dispel boredom or tedium —*ANT.* **bore**

a·muse-bouche (ä mo͞oz bo͞osh′; *Fr* å müz-) ***n.***, *pl.* **a·muse-bouches′** (-bo͞osh′) ⟦Fr < *amuser*, to amuse + *bouche*, mouth⟧ [*also in italics*] a small, savory portion of food served before a meal, typically without charge at restaurants

a·muse·ment (ə myo͞oz′mənt) ***n.*** **1** the condition of being amused **2** something that amuses or entertains; entertainment

☆**amusement park** an outdoor area for entertainment, with a merry-go-round, roller coaster, etc., refreshment booths, and the like

amusement tax a tax on various forms of entertainment, paid on admissions to theaters, etc.

a·mu·si·a (ā′myo͞o′zē ə) ***n.*** ⟦ModL < Gr *amousos*, unmusical < *a-*, without + *mousa*, MUSIC⟧ *Psychol.* a disorder characterized by inability to recognize or reproduce musical sounds

a·mus·ing (ə myo͞o′ziŋ) ***adj.*** **1** entertaining; diverting **2** causing laughter or mirth —*SYN.* FUNNY —**a·mus′ing·ly** ***adv.***

a·mu·sive (-ziv, -siv) ***adj.*** amusing or tending to amuse

☆**AMVETS** (am′vets′) *abbrev.* American Veterans of World War II, Korea, and Vietnam

A·my (ā′mē) ***n.*** ⟦ME *Amye* < OFr *Amée*, lit., beloved < fem. pp. of *aimer* to love < L *amare*⟧ a feminine name

a·myg·da·la (ə mig′də lə) ***n.***, *pl.* **-lae′** (-lē′) ⟦ME *amigdale* < L *amygdala*, ALMOND⟧ *Anat.* an almond-shaped structure; esp., a small, round mass of gray matter in the front part of the temporal lobe of the brain

a·myg·da·lin (ə mig′də lin′, -lən) ***n.*** ⟦prec. + -IN[1]⟧ a crystalline glycoside, $C_{20}H_{27}NO_{11}$, present in bitter almonds: it is used as a flavoring agent and is a source of laetrile

a·myg·da·loid (ə mig′də loid′) ***n.*** ⟦AMYGDAL(A) + -OID⟧ igneous rock containing amygdules —***adj.*** **1** almond-shaped **2** of or like amygdaloid; containing amygdules

a·myg·da·loi·dal (ə mig′də loid′'l) ***adj.*** AMYGDALOID

a·myg·dule (ə mig′do͞ol′, -dyo͞ol′) ***n.*** ⟦< L *amygdala*, ALMOND: from the typical shape⟧ a small gas pocket, usually found in volcanic rock, partly or completely filled with a mineral, esp. a zeolite, calcite, or quartz: sometimes called **a·myg·dale** (ə mig′dāl′)

am·yl (am′il) ***n.*** ⟦AM(YLUM) + -YL⟧ any of various isomeric forms of the radical C_5H_{11} —**a·myl·ic** (ə mil′ik) ***adj.***

am·yl- (am′il) *combining form* AMYLO-: used before a vowel

am·y·la·ceous (am′ə lā′shəs) ***adj.*** of or like starch

amyl acetate BANANA OIL

amyl alcohol a colorless, sharp-smelling alcohol, $C_5H_{11}OH$, obtained by the fermentation of starchy substances and also present in fusel oil: it has several isomeric forms

am·yl·ase (am′ə lās′) ***n.*** ⟦AMYL(O)- + -ASE⟧ an enzyme that helps change starch into sugar: it is found in saliva, pancreatic juice, etc.: see also DIASTASE, AMYLOPSIN

am·yl·ene (am′ə lēn′) ***n.*** any of several liquid isomeric hydrocarbons having the formula C_5H_{10}; pentene

amyl nitrite a volatile liquid, $C_5H_{11}NO_2$, that is inhaled to dilate blood vessels, esp. in angina pectoris

am·y·lo- (am′ə lō′) ⟦< AMYLUM⟧ *combining form* **1** starch [*amylogen*] **2** amyl

a·myl·o·gen (ə mil′ə jən) ***n.*** the water-soluble part of the starch granule: also called AMYLOSE (sense 1)

am·y·loid (am′ə loid′) ***n.*** **1** a starchy food or substance **2** a nearly transparent, waxy deposit resulting from degeneration of bodily tissues: a complex protein

am·y·loi·do·sis (am′ə loi dō′sis) ***n.***, *pl.* **-ses′** (-sēz′) a disorder in which an amyloid deposit accumulates in tissue or organs

am·y·lol·y·sis (am′ə läl′ə sis) ***n.*** the changing of starch into soluble substances by the action of enzymes or by hydrolysis with dilute acids —**am′y·lo·lyt′ic** (-lō lit′ik) ***adj.***

am·y·lo·pec·tin (am′ə lō pek′tin) ***n.*** a nearly insoluble substance derived from the outer part of starch granules: it is a polymer of glucose: see also AMYLOSE (sense 1)

am·y·lop·sin (am′ə läp′sin) ***n.*** ⟦AMYLO- + (TRY)PSIN⟧ amylase produced in the pancreas

am·y·lose (am′ə lōs′) ***n.*** **1** the inner, water-soluble content of starch **2** any of a group of complex carbohydrates of the general formula $(C_6H_{10}O_5)_n$, as cellulose or starch, which are converted by hydrolysis into two or more simple sugars

am·y·lum (am′ə ləm) ***n.*** ⟦L < Gr *amylon*, starch, short for *amylon (aleuron)*, (meal) not ground at the mill < *a-*, not + *mylē*, MILL[1]⟧ *Chem. technical name for* STARCH

a·my·o·to·ni·a (ā mī′ō tō′nē ə) ***n.*** ⟦ModL < A-[2] (not) + MYOTONIA⟧ a condition in which the muscle tissues lack normal vigor and tension; lack of muscle tone

a·my·o·troph·ic lateral sclerosis (ā′mī′ō träf′ik, -trō′fik) ⟦< ModL *amyotrophia*, muscular atrophy < Gr *a-*, not + *myos* (see MYO-) + *-trophia*, -TROPHY

+ -IC] a degenerative disease of the nerve cells that control muscular movement; Lou Gehrig's disease

☆**Am·y·tal** (am′ə tôl′) *trademark for* AMOBARBITAL

an[1] (an; *unstressed,* ən, ′n) ***adj., indefinite article*** ⟦weakened var. of ONE < OE *an,* the numeral one; the older and fuller form of A[2]⟧ **1** one; one sort of [to bake *an* apple pie] **2** any one [pick *an* apple from the tree] The chief grammatical function of *an* (or *a*) is to connote a thing not previously noted or recognized, while *the* connotes a thing previously noted or recognized —***prep.*** to each; in each; for each; per [two *an* hour]

USAGE—*An* is now used before all words beginning with a vowel sound or a silent *h* [*an* ox, *an* honor, *an* F in chemistry class]; older British usage favored *an* before the sound (yo͞o) [*an* union], but this is now nearly obsolete; some people continue the practice of using *an* before *h* in an unstressed initial syllable in certain words, whether or not they actually pronounce the *h* [*an* historian] See also A[2]

an[2] or **an′** (an) ***conj.*** ⟦ME < *and,* AND⟧ **1** and: an informal spelling **2** [Archaic] if

an. *abbrev.* ⟦L *anno*⟧ in the year

an-[1] (an) *prefix* A-[2] (sense 3): used before a vowel

an-[2] (an, ən) *prefix* AD-: used before *n*

-an (ən, in, ′n) ⟦Fr *-ain, -en* < L *-anus,* of, belonging to; also directly < L⟧ *suffix forming adjectives and nouns* **1** (one) belonging to or having some relation to [*diocesan*] **2** (one) born in or living in [*Mexican*] **3** (one) believing in or following [*Lutheran*] **4** -ICIAN: used to form nouns only

an·a[1] (an′ə) ***adv.*** ⟦Gr *ana,* apiece, of each⟧ of each (ingredient referred to): used in doctors' prescriptions

a·na[2] (ā′nə, ä′-; an′ə) ***n.*** ⟦< -ANA⟧ a collection of anecdotes, reminiscences, etc., esp. by or about a particular person

ANA *abbrev.* American Nurses' Association

an·a- (an′ə) ⟦L < Gr *ana,* up, on, again, apiece⟧ *prefix* **1** up, upward [*anadromous*] **2** back, backward [*anagram*] **3** again [*Anabaptist*] **4** throughout [*analysis*] **5** according to, similar to [*analogy*]

-a·na (an′ə, ä′nə, ā′nə) ⟦neut. pl. of L *-anus*⟧ *suffix forming nouns* sayings, writings, anecdotes, facts, or objects of [*Americana*]

an·a·bae·na (an′ə bē′nə) ***n.*** ⟦ModL < Gr *anabainein:* see ANABASIS⟧ **1** a freshwater blue-green alga (genus *Anabaena*), often growing in reservoirs, that may make the water taste or smell fishy **2** a mass of such algae

An·a·bap·tist (an′ə bap′tist) ***n.*** ⟦ModL *anabaptista* < LL(Ec) *anabaptismus* < Gr(Ec) *anabaptismos,* second baptism < *anabaptizein* < *ana-,* again + *baptizein,* BAPTIZE⟧ a member of a radical 16th-cent. sect of the Reformation originating in Switzerland, often persecuted because they opposed the taking of oaths, infant baptism, military service, and the holding of public office —***adj.*** of this sect —**An′a·bap′tism′** ***n.***

an·a·bas (an′ə bas′) ***n.*** ⟦ModL < Gr < *anabainein* (see fol.): so named from its habit of climbing⟧ any of a genus (*Anabas*) of freshwater gouramies (family Anabantidae), of Africa and Southeast Asia, that can live for a long time out of water, as the climbing perch

A·nab·a·sis (ə nab′ə sis) ***n.*** ⟦Gr < *anabainein,* to go up < *ana-,* up + *bainein,* to go: see COME⟧ **1** the unsuccessful military expedition (401-400 B.C.) of Cyrus the Younger to overthrow Artaxerxes II **2** a book about this by Xenophon **3** *pl.* **-ses′** (-sēz′) [**a-**] any large military expedition

an·a·bat·ic (an′ə bat′ik) ***adj.*** ⟦< Gr *anabatikos:* see prec.⟧ moving upward: said of air currents or winds

an·a·bi·o·sis (an′ə bī ō′sis) ***n.*** ⟦ModL < Gr < *anabioein,* to come to life again < *ana-,* again + *bioein,* to live < *bios:* see BIO-⟧ a state of suspended animation, esp. of desiccated tardigrades —**an′a·bi·ot′ic** (-ät′ik) ***adj.***

anabolic steroid any of a group of synthetic steroid hormones that promote the growth of tissue, especially muscle tissue, and have been misused by athletes to increase muscle size and strength

a·nab·o·lism (ə nab′ə liz′əm) ***n.*** ⟦< Gr *anabolē,* a rising up < *ana-,* up + *bolē,* a stroke < *ballein,* to throw (see BALL[2]) + -ISM⟧ the process in a plant or animal by which food is changed into living tissue; constructive metabolism: opposed to CATABOLISM —**an′a·bol·ic** (an′ə bäl′ik) ***adj.***

an·a·branch (an′ə branch′) ***n.*** ⟦< *ana(stomosing) branch:* see ANASTOMOSE⟧ **1** a river branch that reenters the main stream **2** a river branch that becomes absorbed by sandy ground

a·nach·ro·nism (ə nak′rə niz′əm) ***n.*** ⟦MGr *anachronismos* < *anachronizein,* to refer to a wrong time < Gr *ana-,* against + *chronos,* time⟧ **1** the representation of something as existing or occurring at other than its proper time, esp. earlier **2** anything that is or seems to be out of its proper time in history —**a·nach′ro·nis′tic** ***adj.,*** **a·nach′ro·nous** (-nəs) —**a·nach′ro·nis′ti·cal·ly** ***adv.***

an·a·clas·tic (an′ə klas′tik) ***adj.*** ⟦Gr *anaklastos,* reflected < *anaklan* < *ana-,* back + *klan,* to break (see CLASTIC) + -IC⟧ *Optics* of, caused by, or causing refraction

an·a·clit·ic (an′ə klit′ik) ***adj.*** ⟦< Gr *anaklitos,* for reclining < *anaklinein,* to lean upon < *ana-,* on + *klinein,* to LEAN[1]⟧ *Psychoanalysis* having the libido dependent upon another instinct

an·a·co·lu·thon (an′ə kə lo͞o′thän′) ***n., pl.*** **-tha** (-thə) or **-thons′** ⟦LGr *anakolouthon* < Gr, neut. of *anakolouthos,* inconsequent < *an-,* not + *akolouthos,* following: see ACOLYTE⟧ **1** a change from one grammatical construction to another within the same sentence, sometimes as a rhetorical device **2** a sentence in which this occurs (Ex.: "A man, young lady! lady, such a man as all the world— why, he's a man of wax!") —**an′a·co·lu′thic** (-thik) ***adj.***

an·a·con·da (an′ə kän′də) ***n.*** ⟦earlier *anacandaia* < Sinhalese *henacandāya,* lit., lightning-stem, a snake of Sri Lanka: name later transferred to this South American boa⟧ a very long, heavy South American boa (*Eunectes murinus*) that lives in trees and water

A·nac·re·on (ə nak′rē ən, -rē än′) 6th cent. B.C.; Gr. lyric poet

A·nac·re·on·tic (ə nak′rē än′tik) ***adj.*** [*sometimes* **a-**] of or like the poetry of Anacreon, as in praising love and conviviality —***n.*** an Anacreontic poem or verse

an·a·cru·sis (an′ə kro͞o′sis) ***n.*** ⟦ModL < Gr *anakrousis* < *anakrouein,* to push back < *ana-,* back + *krouein,* to strike: see RUE[1]⟧ **1** one or more additional, unaccented syllables at the beginning of a line of verse, preceding the regular meter **2** *Music* UPBEAT

☆**an·a·dam·a bread** (an′ə dam′ə) ⟦< ?⟧ a kneaded yeast bread containing cornmeal and, usually, molasses

an·a·dem (an′ə dem′) ***n.*** ⟦L *anadema* < Gr *anadēma* < *anadein,* to bind up, wreathe < *ana-,* up + *dein,* to bind: see DIADEM⟧ [Old Poet.] a wreath or garland for the head

an·a·di·plo·sis (an′ə di plō′sis) ***n.*** ⟦L < Gr *anadiplōsis* < *anadiploun,* to double < *ana-,* up, again + *diploos,* DOUBLE⟧ repetition of the last word or words of one clause or line of verse, at the beginning of the next (Ex.: "He gave his life; his life was all he could give.")

a·nad·ro·mous (ə na′drə məs) ***adj.*** ⟦Gr *anadromos* < *ana-,* upward + *dromos,* a running < *dramein,* to run: see DROMEDARY⟧ going from salt water to fresh water or up rivers to spawn: said of salmon, shad, etc.: cf. CATADROMOUS

A·na·dyr or **A·na·dir** (ä′nä dir′) river in NE Siberia, flowing south & east into the Bering Sea: *c.* 700 mi (1,127 km)

Anadyr Range *former name for* CHUKOT RANGE

a·nae·mi·a (ə nē′mē ə) ***n.*** *alt. sp. of* ANEMIA

an·aer·obe (an′ər ōb′, an er′-) ***n.*** ⟦< ModL *anaerobium:* see AN-[1] & AEROBE⟧ a microorganism that can live and grow where there is no free oxygen: it may not be able to grow if any oxygen is present

an·aer·o·bic (an′ər ō′bik) ***adj.*** **1** of or produced by anaerobes **2** able to live and grow where there is no air or free oxygen, as certain bacteria **3** designating or of exercise, as weight lifting, that increases strength, promotes weight loss, etc., but does not increase cardiovascular efficiency

an·aer·o·bi·um (-bē əm) ***n., pl.*** **-bi·a** (-bē ə) ANAEROBE

an·aes·the·sia (an′əs thē′zhə) ***n.*** ANESTHESIA —**an′aes·thet′ic** (-thet′ik) ***adj., n.*** —**an·aes·the·tist** (ə nes′thə tist) ***n.*** —**an·aes′the·tize′** ***vt.*** **-tized′, -tiz′ing**

an·a·glyph (an′ə glif′) ***n.*** ⟦Gr *anaglyphē* < *ana-,* up + *glyphein,* to carve out: see CLEAVE[1]⟧ **1** an ornament, as a cameo, carved in low relief **2** a photograph made up of two slightly different views, in complementary colors, of the same subject: when looked at through a pair of corresponding color filters, the picture seems three-dimensional

an·a·go·ge or **an·a·go·gy** (an′ə gō′jē) ***n.*** ⟦ME *anagogie* < ML *anagogia* < Gr *anagōgē,* a leading up < *ana-,* up + *agein,* to lead: see ACT[1]⟧ mystical interpretation, as of the Scriptures, intended to reveal a hidden, spiritual meaning —**an′a·gog′ic** (-gäj′ik) ***adj.,*** **an′a·gog′i·cal** —**an′a·gog′i·cal·ly** ***adv.***

an·a·gram (an′ə gram′) ***n.*** ⟦Fr *anagramme* < Gr *ana-,* back + *gramma,* letter (see GRAM[1]), modeled on Gr *anagrammatizein,* to write the letters of a name backwards⟧ **1** a word or phrase made from another by rearranging its letters (Ex.: *now* → *won, dread* → *adder*) **2** [*pl., with sing. v.*] a game whose object is to make words by arranging letters from a common pool or by forming anagrams from other words —**an′a·gram·mat′ic** (-grə mat′ik) ***adj.,*** **an′a·gram·mat′i·cal** —**an′a·gram·mat′i·cal·ly** ***adv.***

an·a·gram·ma·tize (an′ə gram′ə tīz′) ***vt.*** **-tized′, -tiz′ing** to make an anagram of

An·a·heim (an′ə hīm′) ⟦after the Santa *Ana* River (after ANNE[1], the mother of the Virgin Mary) + Ger *heim,* HOME⟧ city in SW Calif.

a·nal[1] (ā′nəl) ***adj.*** ⟦ModL *analis* < *anus,* ANUS⟧ **1** of or near the anus **2** *Psychoanalysis* ***a)*** designating or of the second stage of psychosexual development, in which interest centers in excretory functions ***b)*** designating or of such traits in the adult as orderliness, stinginess, and obstinacy, regarded as unconscious psychic residues of that stage: cf. ORAL **3** [Informal] excessively or obsessively orderly, stingy, stubborn, etc. —**a′nal·ly** ***adv.***

anal[2] *abbrev.* **1** analogy **2** analysis **3** analytic

a·nal·cime (ə nal′sīm′, -sēm′) ***n.*** ⟦< Gr *an-,* not + *alkoimos,* strong: so named from its weak electricity when rubbed⟧ a hard, colorless or white zeolite, $NaAlSi_2O_6 \cdot H_2O$, commonly found in basalts: sometimes called **a·nal′cite′** (-sīt′)

an·a·lects (an′ə lekts′) ***pl.n.*** ⟦L *analecta* < Gr *analekta* < *analegein,* to collect < *ana-,* up + *legein,* to gather⟧ collected literary excerpts or passages: also **an·a·lec·ta** (an′ə lek′tə) —**the Analects** a collection of Confucius' teachings

an·a·lem·ma (an′ə lem′ə) ***n.*** ⟦L, a sundial showing latitude and meridian < Gr *analēmma,* a support, substructure < *analambanein:* see fol.⟧ a curve in the form of an elongated 8 marked with a scale, drawn on a globe of the earth to show the sun's declination and the equation of time for any day of the year: formed by plotting the sun's actual daily position at noon (mean solar time) for a year

an·a·lep·tic (an′ə lep′tik) ***adj.*** ⟦Gr *analēptikos,* restorative < *analambanein,* to recover < *ana-,* up + *lambanein,* to take: see LEMMA[1]⟧ *Med.* restorative; esp., stimulating the nervous system and counteracting drowsiness or the effects of sedatives —***n.*** an analeptic drug

an·al·ge·si·a (an′əl jē′zē ə, -sē ə) ***n.*** ⟦ModL < Gr *analgēsia* < *an-,* without + *algēsia,* pain < *algos,* pain⟧ a fully conscious state in which a person does not feel painful stimuli

an·al·ge·sic (-zik, -sik) *adj.* of or causing analgesia —*n.* any drug, as aspirin, that is taken to relieve pain

an·a·log (an′ə lôg′, -läg′) *adj.* 1 of a system of measurement in which a continuously varying value, as sound, temperature, etc., corresponds proportionally to another value, esp. a voltage 2 of or by means of an analog computer 3 of or having to do with transmission of a signal that varies continuously and analogously with the waveform of the voice or other source [*analog* TVs, telephones, and recordings] 4 using hands, dials, etc. to show numerical amounts, as on a clock: cf. DIGITAL (sense 5) —*n. alt. sp. of* ANALOGUE

☆**analog computer** a computer for processing data represented by a continuous physical variable, as electric current: cf. DIGITAL COMPUTER

an·a·log·i·cal (an′ə läj′i kəl) *adj.* of, expressing, or based upon analogy: also **an′a·log′ic** —**an′a·log′i·cal·ly** *adv.*

a·nal·o·gize (ə nal′ə jīz′) *vi.* **-gized′**, **-giz′ing** to use, or reason by, analogy —*vt.* to explain or liken by analogy

a·nal·o·gous (ə nal′ə gəs) *adj.* ⟦L *analogus* < Gr *analogos*: see ANALOGY⟧ 1 similar or comparable in certain respects 2 *Biol.* similar in function but not in origin and structure —**a·nal′o·gous·ly** *adv.*

an·a·logue (an′ə lôg′, -läg′) *n.* ⟦Fr *analogue* < L *analogus*: see fol.⟧ a thing or part that is analogous

a·nal·o·gy (ə nal′ə jē) *n., pl.* **-gies** ⟦ME & OFr *analogie* < L *analogia* < Gr, proportion < *analogos*, in due ratio < *ana-*, according to + *logos*, word, reckoning: see LOGIC⟧ 1 similarity in some respects between things otherwise unlike; partial resemblance 2 the likening of one thing to another on the basis of some similarity between the two 3 *Biol.* similarity in function between parts dissimilar in origin and structure, as the wing of a bird and that of an insect: cf. HOMOLOGY 4 *Linguis.* the process by which words, constructions, or pronunciations conform to the pattern of other, often unrelated, ones ["energize" is formed from "energy" by *analogy* with "apologize" from "apology"; Old English "handa" became "hands" on *analogy* with other plurals in *-s*] 5 *Logic* an inference from certain admitted resemblances between two or more things to a probable further similarity between them —*SYN.* LIKENESS

an·al·pha·bet·ic (an′al′fə bet′ik) *adj., n.* ⟦< Gr *analphabētos*, not knowing the alphabet (see AN-[1] & ALPHABET) + -IC⟧ illiterate

a·nal-re·ten·tive (ā′nəl ri ten′tiv) *adj.* ANAL[1] (senses 2 & 3) —*n.* a person regarded as being excessively or obsessively orderly, stingy, stubborn, etc.

a·nal·y·sand (ə nal′ə sand′) *n. Psychoanalysis* a person who is undergoing psychoanalysis

an·a·lyse (an′ə līz′) *vt.* **-lysed′**, **-lys′ing** *Brit. sp. of* ANALYZE

a·nal·y·sis (ə nal′ə sis) *n., pl.* **-ses′** (-sēz′) ⟦ML < Gr, a dissolving < *ana-*, up, throughout + *lysis*, a loosing < *lyein*, to loose: see LOSE⟧ 1 *a)* a separating or breaking up of any whole into its parts, esp. with an examination of these parts to find out their nature, proportion, function, interrelationship, etc. *b)* any detailed examination 2 a statement of the results of this process 3 PSYCHOANALYSIS 4 *Linguis.* the use of word order and uninflected function words rather than inflection to express syntactic relationships 5 *Math.* a branch of mathematics, including calculus, that deals with functions and limits and their generalizations 6 SYSTEMS ANALYSIS —**in the last (or final) analysis** after all factors have been considered

an·a·lyst (an′ə list) *n.* ⟦Fr *analyste*⟧ 1 a person who analyzes [a news *analyst*] 2 a psychoanalyst 3 a systems analyst

an·a·lyt·ic (an′ə lit′ik) *adj.* ⟦ML *analyticus* < Gr *analytikos* < *analytos*, soluble: see ANALYSIS⟧ 1 of analysis or analytics 2 that separates into constituent parts 3 skilled in or using analysis [an *analytic* mind] 4 *Linguis.* expressing syntactic relationships by the use of uninflected function words instead of inflections (Ex.: in English, *more often* instead of *oftener*) 5 *Logic* necessarily true by virtue of the meaning of its component terms alone, without reference to external fact, and with its denial resulting in self-contradiction; tautologous [an *analytic* proposition]: opposed to SYNTHETIC

an·a·lyt·i·cal (-i kəl) *adj.* 1 ANALYTIC 2 of or having to do with ANALYTICAL CHEMISTRY —**an′a·lyt′i·cal·ly** *adv.*

analytical chemistry a branch of chemistry that deals with the identification of compounds and mixtures (qualitative analysis) or the determination of the proportions of the constituents (quantitative analysis): techniques commonly used are titration, precipitation, spectroscopy, chromatography, etc.

analytic geometry the branch of geometry in which a coordinate graphing system makes visible, using points, lines, and curves, the numerical relationships of algebraic equations: also called **coordinate geometry** or **Cartesian geometry**

analytic philosophy a 20th-cent. philosophic movement characterized by its method of analyzing concepts and statements in the light of common experience and ordinary language so as to eliminate confusions of thought and resolve many traditional philosophical problems: also **analytical philosophy**

analytic psychology the system of psychology developed by C. G. Jung as a variant of psychoanalysis

an·a·lyt·ics (an′ə lit′iks) *n.* the part of logic having to do with analyzing

an·a·lyze (an′ə līz′) *vt.* **-lyzed′**, **-lyz′ing** ⟦Fr *analyser* < *analyse*, ANALYSIS⟧ 1 to separate (a thing, idea, etc.) into its parts so as to find out their nature, proportion, function, interrelationship, etc. 2 to examine in detail so as to determine the nature or tendencies of 3 to psychoanalyze 4 *Chem.* to examine (compounds or mixtures) by ANALYTICAL CHEMISTRY 5 *Gram.* to resolve (a sentence) into its grammatical elements —**an′a·lyz′a·ble** *adj.* —**an′a·lyz′er** *n.*

an·am·ne·sis (an′am nē′sis) *n.* ⟦Gr *anamnēsis* < *anamimnēskein* < *ana-*, again + *mimnēskein*, to call to mind; akin to *mnasthai*: see AMNESIA⟧ 1 a recollecting of past events 2 *Med.* the case history of a patient —**an′am·nes′tic** (-nes′tik) *adj.*

an·a·mor·phic (an′ə môr′fik) *adj.* of or having to do with anamorphosis or anamorphism

an·a·mor·phism (an′ə môr′fiz′əm) *n.* ⟦ANA- + -MORPH + -ISM⟧ ☆*Geol.* intense metamorphism deep within the earth, producing very dense, highly complex minerals

an·a·mor·pho·scope (an′ə môr′fə skōp′) *n.* ⟦fol. + -SCOPE⟧ a special lens or mirror for making images normal again after distortion by anamorphosis

an·a·mor·pho·sis (an′ə môr′fə sis, -môr fō′sis) *n., pl.* **-ses′** (-sēz′) ⟦Gr *anamorphōsis*, a forming anew < *ana-*, again + *morphoun*, to form⟧ 1 a technique of perspective to produce a distorted image that will look normal when viewed from a particular angle or with a special mirror 2 *Biol.* a gradual change of form by evolution

An·a·ni·as (an′ə nī′əs) *n.* ⟦Gr⟧ *Bible* a man who fell dead when Peter rebuked him for withholding from the apostles a part of the proceeds from a sale of his land: Acts 5:1-10

an·a·pest or **an·a·paest** (an′ə pest′) *n.* ⟦L *anapaestus* < Gr *anapaistos* < *ana-*, back + *paiein*, to strike: so called from reversing the dactyl⟧ 1 a metrical foot consisting, in Greek and Latin verse, of two short syllables followed by a long one, or, as in English, of two unaccented syllables followed by an accented one 2 a line of verse made up of such feet (Ex.: "Ănd thĕ shéen | ŏf thĕir spéars | wăs lĭke stárs | ŏn thĕ séa") —**an′a·pes′tic** *adj., n.*, **an′a·paes′tic**

an·a·phase (an′ə fāz′) *n.* ⟦ANA- + PHASE[1]⟧ *Biol.* the stage in mitosis, after the metaphase and before the telophase, in which the divided chromosomes move apart toward the poles of the spindle

a·naph·o·ra (ə naf′ə rə) *n.* ⟦L < Gr < *ana-*, up, back + *pherein*, to BEAR[1]⟧ repetition of a word or phrase at the beginning of successive clauses, lines of verse, etc.

an·aph·ro·dis·i·ac (an af′rō diz′ē ak′) *adj.* ⟦AN-[1] + APHRODISIAC⟧ that lessens sexual desire —*n.* a drug, etc. that lessens sexual desire

an·a·phy·lax·is (an′ə fə lak′sis) *n.* ⟦ModL < Gr *ana-*, intens. + *phylaxis*, a guarding < *phylassein*, to guard⟧ a condition of hypersensitivity to proteins or other substances, requiring previous exposure to the allergenic substance and resulting in shock or other physical reactions —**an′a·phy·lac′tic** (-lak′tik) *adj.*

an·a·plas·tic (an′ə plas′tik) *adj.* ⟦ANA-, backward + Gr *plastikos*: see PLASTIC⟧ *Med.* characterized by a reversion to a more primitive, imperfectly developed form: said of cells, esp. when cancerous

an·ap·tyx·is (an′ap tiks′is) *n., pl.* **-tyx′es′** (-ēz′) ⟦ModL < Gr, an opening, gaping < fut. stem of *anaptyssein*, to unfold, open < *ana-*, up + *ptyssein*, to fold⟧ epenthesis of a vowel —**an′ap·tyc′tic** (-tik′tik) *adj.*

A·na·pur·na (an′ə pʊʊr′nə, ä′nə-; -pur′-) *alt. sp. of* ANNAPURNA

an·arch (an′ärk′) *n.* ⟦< Gr *anarchos*, without a leader < *an-*, without + *archos*, leader: see -ARCH⟧ [Now Rare] an anarchist

an·ar·chic (an är′kik) *adj.* 1 of, like, or involving anarchy 2 advocating anarchy 3 tending to bring about anarchy; lawless Also **an·ar′chi·cal** —**an·ar′chi·cal·ly** *adv.*

an·ar·chism (an′ər kiz′əm, -är-) *n.* ⟦ANARCH(Y) + -ISM⟧ 1 the theory that all forms of government interfere unjustly with individual liberty and should be replaced by the voluntary association of cooperative groups 2 resistance, sometimes by terrorism, to organized government

an·ar·chist (an′ər kist′, -är′kist) *n.* 1 a person who believes in or advocates anarchism 2 a person who promotes anarchy, as by flouting or ignoring rules, duties, or accepted standards of conduct —**an′ar·chis′tic** (-ər kis′tik, -är-) *adj.*

an·ar·chy (an′ər kē, -är′-) *n., pl.* **-chies** ⟦Gr *anarchia*: see ANARCH⟧ 1 the complete absence of government 2 political disorder and violence; lawlessness 3 disorder in any sphere of activity

an·ar·thri·a (an är′thrē ə) *n.* ⟦ModL < Gr < *anarthros*, inarticulate (< *an-*, without + *arthron*, articulation, joint: see ARTHRO-) + -IA⟧ complete inability to produce articulate speech

an·a·sar·ca (an′ə sär′kə) *n.* ⟦ME < ML < Gr *ana*, throughout + *sarx*, flesh: see SARCASM⟧ generalized edema, or dropsy —**an′a·sar′cous** *adj.*

A·na·sa·zi (ä′nə sä′zē, an′ə-) *n., pl.* **-zi** ⟦< Navajo name, ancient ones or enemy ancestors⟧ a member of an ancient, cliff-dwelling North American Indian people of the SW U.S. that built multistory adobe houses —*adj.* designating or of this people

An·a·sta·si·a (an′ə stā′zhə, -shə; -zhē ə, -shē ə) *n.* ⟦LL, fem. of *Anastasius* < Gr *Anastasias*, lit., of the resurrection⟧ a feminine name: dim. *Stacey*, *Stacy*

an·as·tig·mat (an as′tig mat′) *n.* ⟦Ger, back-form. < *anastigmatisch*, anastigmatic⟧ an anastigmatic lens

an·as·tig·mat·ic (an as′tig mat′ik, an′ə stig-) *adj.* free from, or corrected for, astigmatism; specif., designating a compound lens made up of one converging and one diverging lens so that the astigmatism of one is neutralized by the equal and opposite astigmatism of the other

a·nas·to·mose (ə nas′tə mōz′, -mōs′) *vt., vi.* **-mosed′**, **-mos′ing** ⟦Fr *anastomoser*, ult. < Gr *anastomōsis*: see fol.⟧ to join by anastomosis

a·nas·to·mo·sis (ə nas′tə mō′sis) *n., pl.* **-ses′** (-sēz′) ⟦ModL < Gr *anastomōsis*, opening < *ana-*, again + *stomoein*, to provide with a mouth < *stoma*, mouth⟧ 1 interconnection between blood vessels, nerves, veins in a leaf, channels of a river, etc. 2 a surgical joining of one hollow or tubular organ to another, as of the severed ends of the intestine after resection, or of two nerves —**a·nas′to·mot′ic** (-mät′ik) *adj.*

a·nas·tro·phe (ə nas′trə fē) *n.* ⟦Gr *anastrophē* < *anastrephein* < *ana-*, back + *strephein*, to turn: see STROPHE⟧ reversal of the usual order of the parts of a sentence; inversion (Ex.: "Came the dawn")

anat *abbrev.* 1 anatomical 2 anatomy

an·a·tase (an′ə tāz′) *n.* ⟦Fr < Gr *anatasis*, prolongation < *ana-*, up + *tasis*, a stretching < stem of *teinein*: see TEND[2]; so named because of its long crystals⟧ a dark-colored, hard, tetragonal form of titanium dioxide, usually found in schist and gneiss

a·nath·e·ma (ə nath′ə mə) *n., pl.* **-mas** ⟦LL(Ec) < Gr, thing devoted to evil; previously, anything devoted < *anatithenai*, to dedicate < *ana-*, up + *tithenai*, to place: see DO[1]⟧ 1 a thing or person accursed or damned 2 a thing or person greatly detested 3 *a)* a solemn ecclesiastical condemnation of a teaching judged to be gravely opposed to accepted church doctrine, or of the originators or supporters of such a teaching *b)* the excommunication often accompanying or following this condemnation —*adj.* 1 greatly detested 2 viewed as accursed or damned 3 subjected to an ecclesiastical anathema

a·nath·e·ma·tize (ə nath′ə mə tīz′) *vt., vi.* **-tized′**, **-tiz′ing** to utter an anathema (against); curse —**SYN.** CURSE —**a·nath′e·ma·ti·za′tion** *n.*

An·a·to·li·a (an′ə tō′lē ə) 1 [Obs.] Asia Minor 2 the part of modern Turkey that is in Asia

An·a·to·li·an (-ən) *adj.* 1 of Anatolia or its peoples, languages, or cultures 2 designating or of a group of extinct Indo-European languages of ancient Anatolia, including Hittite —*n.* a person born or living in Anatolia

an·a·tom·i·cal (an′ə täm′i kəl) *adj.* ⟦< Gr *anatomikos*, skilled in anatomy (see ANATOMY) + -ICAL⟧ 1 of or connected with anatomy 2 structural Also **an′a·tom′ic** —**an′a·tom′i·cal·ly** *adv.*

a·nat·o·mist (ə nat′ə mist) *n.* ⟦Fr *anatomiste*⟧ 1 a person skilled in anatomy 2 a person who analyzes in great detail

a·nat·o·mize (ə nat′ə mīz′) *vt., vi.* **-mized′**, **-miz′ing** ⟦ME *anatomisen* < ML *anatomizare*: see fol.⟧ 1 to dissect (an animal or plant) in order to examine the structure 2 to analyze in great detail —**a·nat′o·mi·za′tion** (-mə zā′shən, -mī′-) *n.*

a·nat·o·my (ə nat′ə mē) *n., pl.* **-mies** ⟦ME & OFr *anatomie* < LL *anatomia* < Gr *anatomia*, *anatomē*, a cutting up < *anatemnein* < *ana-*, up + *temnein*, to cut: see -TOMY⟧ 1 the dissecting of an animal or plant in order to determine the position, structure, etc. of its parts 2 the science of the morphology or structure of animals or plants 3 the structure of an organism or body 4 a detailed analysis 5 [Archaic] a skeleton

a·nat·ro·pous (ə na′trə pəs) *adj.* ⟦ModL *anatropus*: see ANA- & -TROPOUS⟧ *Bot.* having a flower ovule with an inverted structure, with the stalk attachment near the top and the opening near the bottom: the most common form for angiosperms

a·nat·to (ə nät′ō, ä-) *n.* ANNATTO

An·ax·ag·o·ras (an′aks ag′ə rəs) 500?-428? B.C.; Gr. philosopher from Ionia who taught in Athens

A·nax·i·man·der (ə naks′ə man′dər) 611?-547? B.C.; Gr. philosopher, astronomer, & mathematician

anc *abbrev.* 1 ancient 2 anciently

ANC *abbrev.* African National Congress

-ance (əns, ′ns; ənts, ′nts) ⟦ME < OFr *-ance* (< L *-antia*, *-entia*) or directly < L⟧ *suffix forming nouns* 1 the act or process of ___ing [*discontinuance*] 2 the quality or state of being [*forbearance*] 3 a thing that ___s [*hindrance*] 4 a thing that is ___ed [*utterance, remittance*]

an·ces·tor (an′ses′tər; *also*, -səs-, -sis-) *n.* ⟦ME & OFr *ancestre* < L *antecessor*, one who goes before < pp. of *antecedere* < *ante-*, before + *cedere*, to go⟧ 1 any person from whom one is descended, esp. one earlier in a family line than a grandparent; forefather; forebear 2 an early type of animal from which later kinds have evolved 3 anything regarded as a precursor or forerunner of a later thing 4 *Law* the deceased person from whom an estate has been inherited —*vt.* to be an ancestor of

an·ces·tral (an ses′trəl) *adj.* of or inherited from an ancestor or ancestors —**an·ces′tral·ly** *adv.*

an·ces·tress (an′ses′trəs) *n.* a female ANCESTOR (*n.* 1 & 4)

an·ces·try (an′ses′trē; *also*, -səs-, -sis-) *n., pl.* **-tries** ⟦ME *ancestrie* < OFr *ancesserie* < *ancestre*, ANCESTOR⟧ 1 family descent or lineage 2 ancestors collectively: opposed to POSTERITY 3 noble or distinguished descent

An·chi·ses (an kī′sēz′) *n.* ⟦L < Gr *Anchisēs*⟧ *Class. Myth.* the father of Aeneas

an·cho chili (än′chō′) ⟦< MexSp *chile ancho*, lit., wide (chili) pepper: so named from its shape⟧ a dried poblano pepper, reddish-brown in color, used esp. in Mexican cooking: also **an′cho′** *n., pl.* **-chos′**

an·chor (aŋ′kər) *n.* ⟦ME *anker* < OE *ancor* < L *anc(h)ora* < Gr *ankyra*, an anchor, hook < IE base **ank-*, to bend > ANKLE⟧ 1 a heavy object, usually a shaped iron weight with flukes, lowered by cable or chain to the bottom of a body of water to keep a vessel from drifting 2 any device that holds something else secure 3 anything that gives or seems to give stability or security 4 a person who anchors a team, newscast, etc. 5 a major retail store, corporate headquarters, etc. that stabilizes or stimulates the economic activity of the shopping center, office building, etc. where it is located —*adj.* designating the final leg, or stage, of a relay race —*vt.* 1 to keep from drifting, giving way, etc., by or as by an anchor 2 to serve as the end person for (a tug-of-war team) 3 to serve as the final contestant for (a relay team, bowling team, etc.) 4 to serve as coordinator of the various reports and as chief reporter for (a newscast) 5 to serve as an anchor for (a shopping center, etc.) —*vi.* 1 to lower the anchor overboard so as to keep from drifting 2 to be or become fixed —**at anchor** anchored —**drop (or cast) anchor** 1 to lower the anchor overboard 2 to stay or settle (*in* a place) —**drag anchor** 1 to drift because of the failure of the anchor to hold 2 to lose ground; slip or fail —**ride at anchor** to be anchored: said of ships —**weigh anchor** 1 to hoist a ship's anchor off the bottom preparatory to sailing 2 to leave; go away

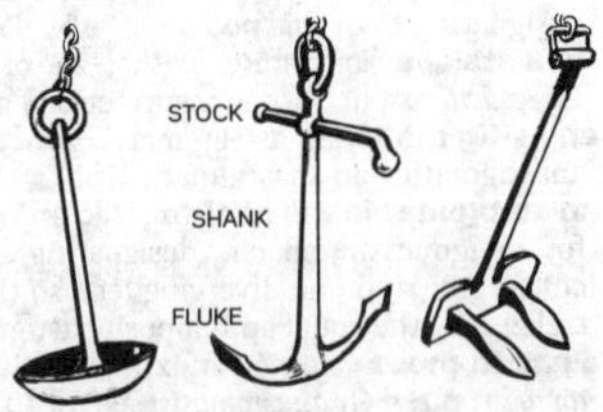

mush-room anchor stocked anchor stock-less anchor

an·chor·age (aŋ′kər ij) *n.* 1 money charged for the right to anchor, as in a port 2 an anchoring or being anchored 3 a place to anchor 4 something that can be firmly held on to or relied on

An·chor·age (aŋ′kər ij) ⟦from the anchoring there of early supply ships⟧ seaport in S Alas., on Cook Inlet

an·cho·ress (aŋ′kə rəs) *n.* a female anchorite

☆**anchor ice** ice found attached to the bottom of an otherwise unfrozen stream or lake, often covering stones, etc.

an·cho·rite (aŋ′kə rīt′) *n.* ⟦ME < OFr *anachorete* < LL(Ec) *anachoreta* < LGr *anachōrētēs*, one retired < Gr *anachōrein* < *ana-*, back + *chōrein*, to retire < IE base **ĝhē-*, *ĝhēi*, leave behind, GO[1]⟧ a person who lives alone and apart from society for religious meditation; hermit; recluse: also **an′cho·ret′** (-ret′, -rit′) —**an′cho·rit′ic** (-rit′ik) *adj.*, **an′cho·ret′ic** (-ret′ik)

an·chor·man (aŋ′kər man′) *n., pl.* **-men′** (-men′) a man or, occas., woman who anchors a team, newscast, etc.

an·chor·per·son (-pur′sən) *n.* a person who anchors a newscast

an·chor·wom·an (-woom′ən) *n., pl.* **-wom′en** (-wim′in) a female anchorperson

an·cho·vy (an′chō′vē, -chə-; an′chō′vē) *n., pl.* **-vies** or **-vy** ⟦Port *anchova* < VL **apiua* < L *aphya* < Gr *aphyē*, small fry⟧ any of a family (Engraulidae) of very small fishes (order Clupeiformes) with large mouths, found mostly in warm seas: anchovies, esp. the European species (*Engraulis encrasicholus*), are used as a relish, either canned in oil or made into a salty paste

anchovy pear ⟦< prec.: the fish is a common hors d'oeuvre, and the pickled fruit has been used in this way⟧ 1 a West Indian fruit that tastes like a mango 2 the tree (*Grias cauliflora*) of the lecythis family that it grows on

an·chu·sa (an kyoo͞′sə, -zə; aŋ-) *n.* ⟦L < Gr *anchousa*⟧ ALKANET (senses 1*a* & 2)

an·chu·sin (an kyoo͞′sin, -zin; aŋ-) *n.* ALKANET (sense 1*c*)

an·chy·lose (aŋ′kə lōs′, -lōz′) *vt., vi.* **-losed′**, **-los′ing** ANKYLOSE —**an′chy·lo′sis** (-lō′sis) *n.*

an·cien ré·gime (än′syan rā zhēm′; *Fr* än syan rā zhēm′) ⟦Fr, old order⟧ [*often in italics*] 1 the social and governmental system of France before the Revolution of 1789 2 any former political or social system

an·cient[1] (ān′chənt, -shənt) *adj.* ⟦ME *auncien* < OFr *ancien* < VL **anteanus* < L *ante*, before: *-t* by infl. of -ENT⟧ 1 of times long past; belonging to the early history of the world, esp. before the end of the Western Roman Empire (A.D. 476) 2 having existed a long time; very old 3 old-fashioned; antiquated 4 [Archaic] having the wisdom, dignity, etc. of age; venerable —*n.* 1 a person who lived in ancient times 2 an aged person —**SYN.** OLD —**the ancients** 1 the people who lived in ancient times 2 the ancient or classical writers and artists, esp. of Greco-Roman times —**an′cient·ness** *n.*

an·cient[2] (ān′chənt, -shənt) *n.* ⟦confusion of ENSIGN with earlier *ancien*, prec.⟧ [Archaic] 1 an ensign, or flag 2 a person carrying an ensign

ancient history 1 history from the earliest recorded events to the end of the Western Roman Empire in A.D. 476 2 [Informal] something of the recent past that is well known or no longer important

an·cient·ly (-lē) *adv.* in ancient times

Ancient of Days God or a heavenly judge: cf. Dan. 7:13

an·cient·ry (-rē) *n.* [Archaic] a being ancient; antiquity

an·cil·la (an sil′ə) *n.* ⟦see fol.⟧ an aid for use as in understanding or accomplishing something; often, specif., a handbook, or manual

an·cil·lar·y (an′sə ler′ē, an sil′ər ē) *adj.* ⟦< L *ancillaris* < *ancilla*, maidservant, dim. of fem. of *anculus*, servant⟧ 1 subordinate: often with *to* 2 that serves as an aid; auxiliary

an·cip·i·tal (an sip′it əl) *adj.* ⟦< L *anceps* (gen. *ancipitis*), two-headed, two-sided < *an-* for *ambi-*, on both sides (see AMBI-) + *caput*, HEAD⟧ *Bot.* two-edged, as the flat stems of certain grasses: also **an·cip′i·tous** (-it əs)

an·con (an′kän′, aŋ′-) *n., pl.* **an·co·nes** (an kō′nēz′, aŋ-) ⟦L < Gr *ankōn*, elbow: see ANKLE⟧ *Archit.* a bracketlike projection supporting a cornice; console

An·co·na (än kō′nə) seaport in central Italy, on the Adriatic

-an·cy (ən sē, ′n sē; ənt sē, ′nt sē) *suffix* -ANCE

an·cy·los·to·mi·a·sis (an′sə läs′tə mī′ə sis, -lō′stə-; aŋ′kə-) *n., pl.* **-ses′** (-sēz′) ⟦ModL < *Ancylostoma*, genus of hookworms < Gr *ankylos*, crooked (see ANKLE) + *stoma*, the mouth + -IASIS⟧ *technical term for* HOOKWORM DISEASE

and (and; *unstressed*, ənd, ən, ′n) *conj.* ⟦ME *and*, *an* < OE *and*, *ond;* akin to Ger *und*, OHG *unti*, OS *endi*, ON *enn*: orig. meaning, thereupon, then, next⟧ 1 in addition; also; as well as: used to join elements of similar syntactic structure [apples *and* pears; a red *and* white dress; he begged *and* borrowed] **2** plus; added to [6 *and* 2 equals 8] **3** but; yet; in contrast [vegetable oil is digestible *and* mineral oil is not] **4** then again; then in addition: used between two instances of the same word to express repetition or continuity [we talked *and* talked] **5** as a consequence or result [he told her *and* she wept] **6** then; following this [she drove to the store *and* bought groceries] **7** [Informal] to: used as a sign of the inf. [try *and* understand] **8** as well as other kinds of: used between two instances of the same word to express difference in kind or quality [there are painters *and* painters, my friend] **9** [Archaic] then: used before a sentence [*and* it came to pass] **10** [Obs.] if

USAGE—*and* is also used correlatively with *both*, indicating inclusion of all of the items mentioned *And* is sometimes also used informally as a superfluous element connecting clauses in conversation

An·da·lu·si·a (an′də lo͞o′zhə, -shə; -zhē ə, -shē ə) region of S Spain on the Mediterranean & the Atlantic: 33,694 sq mi (87,268 sq km); cap. Seville: Sp. name **An·da·lu·cí·a** (än′dä lo͞o thē′ä)

An·da·lu·si·an (-zhən, -shən; -zhē ən, -shē ən) *adj.* of Andalusia or its people, language, or culture —*n.* **1** a person born or living in Andalusia **2** the variety of Spanish spoken in Andalusia

an·da·lu·site (an′də lo͞o′sīt′) *n.* ⟦after ANDALUSIA, where it was discovered⟧ a very hard, orthorhombic silicate of aluminum, Al_2SiO_5, usually found in schist, slate, or other metamorphic rocks and used to make various high-temperature materials and as a gem

An·da·man Islands (an′də mən) group of islands in the Bay of Bengal, west of the Malay Peninsula: with the Nicobar Islands, constituting a territory of India (**Andaman and Nicobar Islands**), 3,185 sq mi (8,249 sq km)

Andaman Sea part of the Indian Ocean, west of the Malay Peninsula and east of the Andaman and Nicobar Islands: *c.* 218,100 sq mi (564,877 sq km)

an·dan·te (än dän′tā, an dan′tē) [*also in italics*] *Music adj., adv.* ⟦It, prp. of *andare*, to walk < VL *ambitare*, to go about < L *ambitus*: see AMBIT⟧ moderate in tempo; slower than allegretto but faster than adagio: often used as a musical direction —*n.* an andante movement or passage

an·dan·ti·no (än′dän tē′nō, an′dan-) [*also in italics*] *Music adj., adv.* ⟦It, dim. of prec.⟧ slightly faster than andante; previously, slightly slower than andante: often used as a musical direction —*n., pl.* **-nos** an andantino movement or passage

An·de·an (an dē′ən, an′dē ən) *adj.* of the Andes or the peoples of the region

An·der·sen (an′dər sən), **Hans Christian** 1805-75; Dan. novelist, poet, & writer of fairy tales

An·der·son (an′dər sən) **1 Carl David** 1905-91; U.S. physicist; discovered the positron (1932) **2** Dame **Judith** 1898-1992; U.S. actress, born in Australia **3 Marian** 1897-1993; U.S. contralto **4 Max·well** (maks′wel, -wəl) 1888-1959; U.S. playwright **5 Sher·wood** (shur′wood) 1876-1941; U.S. novelist & short-story writer

An·der·son·ville (an′dər sən vil′) ⟦after Major Robt. *Anderson* (1805-71), U.S. Army⟧ town in SW central Ga.: site of a Confederate prison in the Civil War

an·des·ite (an′də zīt′) *n.* ⟦after fol.⟧ a dark-colored, fine-grained, extrusive igneous rock consisting chiefly of plagioclase feldspars with some biotite, hornblende, or pyroxene

An·des (Mountains) (an′dēz′) mountain system extending the length of W South America: highest peak, Aconcagua

An·dhra Pra·desh (än′drə prə desh′) state of SE India, on the Bay of Bengal: 106,195 sq mi (275,044 sq km); cap. Hyderabad

and·i·ron (and′ī′ərn) *n.* ⟦ME *aundiren* (with ending altered by assoc. with IRON) < OFr *andier* < Gaul **andera*, andiron, heifer (so named from use of bull's head as ornamentation on andirons) < IE base **andh-*, to sprout, bloom > Gr *anthos*: see ANTHO-⟧ either of a pair of metal supports with ornamented front uprights, used to hold the wood in a fireplace

andirons

An·di·zhan (än′di zhän′, an′di zhan′) city in E Uzbekistan, on the upper Syr Darya

and/or (and′ôr′, -ôr′) *conj.* either *and* or *or*, according to what is meant [personal *and/or* real property]

An·dor·ra (an dôr′ə) **1** country in the E Pyrenees, between Spain and France: 181 sq mi (468 sq km) **2** its capital: in full **Andorra la Vel·la** (lä väl′yə) —**An·dor′ran** *adj., n.*

an·dou·ille (än do͞o′ē; *Fr* än do͞o′y′) *n.* **1** in France, a large sausage containing mainly pork tripe and chitterlings **2** in the cooking of the Cajuns, a smoked pork sausage that is flavored with garlic and highly spiced Also **andouille sausage**

an·douill·ette (än do͞o yet′) *n.* ⟦Fr, dim. of *andouille*: see prec.⟧ a small sausage, variously flavored, containing mainly pork chitterlings and not smoked

an·dra·dite (an′drə dīt′) *n.* ⟦after J. B. de *Andrada* (*c.* 1763-1838), Brazilian geologist⟧ a variety of garnet, $Ca_3Fe_2(SiO_4)_3$, sometimes used as a gem

An·dré (än′drā′, an′drē′), Major **John** 1750-80; Brit. officer hanged as a spy in the American Revolution

An·dre·a (än drā′ə; an′drē ə, än′-) *n.* ⟦fem. of ANDREW⟧ a feminine name: see ANDREW

Andrea del Sarto *see* SARTO, Andrea del

An·drew (an′dro͞o′) *n.* ⟦ME *Andreas* (< LL(Ec) *Andreu*) < OFr *Andrieu* < LL(Ec) *Andreas* < Gr(Ec) < Gr *andreios*, manly < *anēr*: see ANDRO-⟧ **1** a masculine name: dim. *Andy, Drew*; equiv. L. *Andreas*, Fr. *André*, It. *Andrea*, Sp. *Andrés*; fem. *Andrea* **2** *Bible* one of the twelve apostles; brother of Simon Peter: his day is Nov. 30: also **Saint Andrew**

An·drews (an′dro͞oz′), **Roy Chapman** 1884-1960; U.S. naturalist, explorer, & writer

An·dre·yev (än drā′yef), **Le·o·nid Ni·ko·la·ye·vich** (le′ô nēd′ nē′kô lä′yə vich) 1871-1919; Russ. playwright, novelist, & short-story writer

an·dro (an′drō) *n. short for* ANDROSTENEDIONE

an·dro- (an′drō, -drə) ⟦< Gr *anēr* (gen. *andros*), man, male < IE base **aner*, **ner-*, vital force, man > Sans *nár-*, man, human being, Welsh *ner*, hero, L *Nero*, lit., strong⟧ *combining form* **1** man, male, masculine [*androgynous*] **2** anther, stamen

An·dro·cles (an′drə klēz′) *n.* ⟦L < Gr *Androklēs*⟧ *Rom. Legend* a slave who escapes death when thrown into the arena with a lion because the lion recognizes him as the man who once extracted a thorn from its foot: also **An′dro·clus** (-kləs)

an·droe·ci·um (an drē′shē əm, -sē əm) *n., pl.* **-ci·a** (-shē ə, -sē ə) ⟦ModL < ANDRO- + Gr *oikos*, house: see ECONOMY⟧ *Bot.* the stamens and the parts belonging to them, collectively; all the microsporophylls of a flower

an·dro·gen (an′drō jən, -drə-) *n.* a type of natural or artificial steroid that acts as a male sex hormone —**an′dro·gen′ic** (-jen′ik) *adj.*

an·dro·gen·e·sis (an′drō jen′ə sis) *n.* ⟦ModL < ANDRO- + -GENESIS⟧ the development of an embryo solely from a male reproductive cell, without the active participation of the chromosomes from the nucleus of an egg: opposed to PARTHENOGENESIS —**an′dro·ge·net′ic** (-jə net′ik) *adj.*

an·drog·e·nous (an dräj′ə nəs) *adj.* ⟦ANDRO- + -GENOUS⟧ *Biol.* producing only male offspring

an·dro·gyne (an′drə jin, -jīn′) *n.* an androgynous plant or animal

an·drog·y·nous (an dräj′ə nəs) *adj.* ⟦L *androgynus* < Gr *androgynos*: see ANDRO- & -GYNOUS⟧ **1** both male and female in one; hermaphroditic **2** *Bot.* bearing both staminate and pistillate flowers in the same inflorescence or cluster **3** *a)* of or marked by a blend of male and female characteristics, roles, etc. [an *androgynous* culture] *b)* designating or of something that is not differentiated as to sex [*androgynous* clothing] —**an·drog′y·ny** (-jə nē) *n.*

an·droid (an′droid′) *n.* ⟦ANDR(O)- + -OID⟧ in science fiction, a robot made to resemble a human being closely

An·drom·a·che (an dräm′ə kē) *n.* ⟦L < Gr *Andromachē*⟧ *Gr. Myth.* the wife of Hector

An·drom·e·da (an dräm′ə də) *n.* ⟦L < Gr *Andromedē*⟧ **1** *Gr. Myth.* an Ethiopian princess whom Perseus rescues from a sea monster and then marries **2** *Astron.* a N constellation between Cassiopeia and Pisces containing the nearest spiral galaxy (**Andromeda Galaxy**) which is just visible to the naked eye **3** [**a-**] any of several species of two genera (*Andromeda* and *Pieris*) of evergreen shrubs of the heath family

☆**Andromeda strain** ⟦ref. to outer-space bacteria in *The Andromeda Strain*, science fiction novel (1969) by U.S. writer M. Crichton (1942-2008)⟧ a hypothetical microorganism, as might be developed from biological research, that if released would uncontrollably kill living things on earth

An·dro·pov (än drō′pôf′) *name* (1984-88) *for* RYBINSK (the city)

An·dros (an′drəs), Sir **Edmund** 1637-1714; Eng. gov. of colonies in America

an·dro·stene·di·one (an′drə stēn′dī′ōn) *n.* ⟦fol. + -ENE + DI-[1] + -ONE⟧ a weak hormone, $C_{19}H_{26}O_2$, produced by the ovaries, testes, and adrenal glands as a precursor to estrogen, testosterone, etc.: formerly taken in a concentrated tablet or capsule form as by some bodybuilders

an·dros·ter·one (an dräs′tər ōn′) *n.* ⟦ANDRO- + STER(OL) + -ONE⟧ a weak androgen, $C_{19}H_{30}O_2$, produced by the metabolism of certain hormones and found in the normal urine of both males and females

-an·drous (an′drəs) ⟦< Gr *anēr*: see ANDRO-⟧ *combining form forming adjectives* having stamens [*monandrous*]

An·dva·ri (än′dvä rē) *n. Norse Myth.* a dwarf from whom Loki steals gold and a magic ring

ane (ān) *adj., pron.* ⟦OE *an*, one⟧ [Scot.] one

-ane (ān) ⟦arbitrary formation⟧ *suffix* **1** an alkane [*methane, ethane*] **2** any of certain cyclic compounds [*cyclohexane*]

an·ec·dot·age (an′ik dōt′ij) *n.* **1** ⟦ANECDOT(E) + -AGE⟧ a collection of anecdotes **2** ⟦blend of ANECDOTE & DOTAGE⟧ senility, as characterized by the telling of rambling anecdotes: a humorous usage

an·ec·dot·al (an′ik dōt′'l) *adj.* **1** of or like an anecdote **2** full of anecdotes **3** based on personal experience or reported observations unverified by controlled experiments [*anecdotal* evidence]

an·ec·dote (an′ik dōt′) *n.* ⟦Fr < ML *anecdota* < Gr *anekdota*, neut. pl. of *anekdotos*, unpublished < *an-*, not + *ekdotos*, published < *ekdidonai*, to give out, publish < *ek-*, out + *didonai*, to give: see DATE[1]⟧ **1** [*pl.*] [Obs.] little-known, entertaining facts of history or biography **2** a short, entertaining account of some happening, usually personal or biographical —***SYN.*** STORY[1]

an·ec·dot·ic (än′ik dät′ik) *adj.* **1** anecdotal **2** fond of telling anecdotes Also **an′ec·dot′i·cal**

an·ec·dot·ist (an′ik dōt′ist) *n.* a person who tells or collects anecdotes: also **an′ec·dot′al·ist** (-dōt′'l ist)

an·e·cho·ic (an′e kō′ik) *adj.* ⟦AN-[1] + ECHOIC⟧ free from echoes; completely absorbing sound or radar waves [an *anechoic* chamber]

a·nele (ə nēl′) *vt.* **-neled′**, **-nel′ing** ⟦ME *anelien* < *an-* (< OE *an-*, on) + *elien*, anoint < *ele*, oil < OE < L *oleum*, OIL⟧ [Archaic] to anoint, esp. in the last rites

a·ne·mi·a (ə nē′mē ə) *n.* ⟦ModL < Gr *anaimia* < *an-*, without + *haima*, blood: see HEMO-⟧ **1** *Med.* a condition in which there is a reduction of the number, or volume, of red blood corpuscles or of the total amount of hemoglobin in the bloodstream, resulting in paleness, generalized weakness, etc. **2** lack of vigor or vitality; lifelessness —**a·ne′mic** (-mik) *adj.* —**a·ne′mi·cal·ly** *adv.*

a·ne·mo- (an′ə mō′, -mə; ə nem′ō, ə nem′ə) ⟦< Gr *anemos*, the wind: see ANIMAL⟧ *combining form* wind [*anemometer*]

a·nem·o·graph (ə nem′ə graf′) *n.* an instrument for recording the velocity and direction of the wind —**a·nem′o·graph′ic** *adj.*

an·e·mol·o·gy (an′ə mäl′ə jē) *n.* the study of winds

an·e·mom·e·ter (an′ə mäm′ət ər) *n.* a gauge for determining the force or speed of the wind, and sometimes its direction; wind gauge

an·e·mom·e·try (an′ə mäm′ə trē) *n.* the process of determining the speed and direction of the wind with an anemometer —**an′e·mo·met·ric** (an′ə mō me′trik) *adj.*

a·nem·o·ne (ə nem′ə nē′) *n.* ⟦L < Gr *anemōnē*, altered, after *anemos*, wind < ?⟧ **1** *Bot.* any of a number of related plants of a genus (*Anemone*) of the buttercup family, with cup-shaped flowers that are usually white, pink, red, or purple **2** *Zool.* SEA ANEMONE

an·e·moph·i·lous (an′ə mä′fə ləs) *adj.* pollinated by the wind —**an′e·moph′i·ly** *n.*

a·nem·o·scope (ə nem′ə skōp′) *n.* an instrument for showing or recording the direction of the wind

an·e·mo·sis (an′ə mō′sis) *n.* ⟦ModL < ANEM(O)- + -OSIS⟧ WIND SHAKE

an·en·ceph·a·ly (an′en sef′ə lē) *n.* ⟦< AN-[1] + Gr *enkephalos*: see ENCEPHALON⟧ congenital malformation of the skull with absence of all or part of the brain —**an′en·ce·phal′ic** (-sə fal′ik) *n., adj.*

a·nent (ə nent′) *prep.* ⟦ME *anent* (with unhistoric *-t*) < OE *onemn, on efen*, lit., on even (with), level (with)⟧ [Now Rare] concerning; as regards; about

an·er·gy (an′ər jē) *n.* ⟦ModL *anergia* < Gr *an-*, without + *ergon*, WORK⟧ *Med.* a condition in which the body of a sensitized person fails to respond to an antigen —**an·er·gic** (an ʉr′jik) *adj.*

an·er·oid (an′ər oid′) *adj.* ⟦< Gr *a-*, without + *nēros*, liquid + -OID⟧ not using liquid —*n.* ANEROID BAROMETER

aneroid barometer a barometer with a needle connected by mechanical linkages and springs to a thin, hollow metal disk in which a partial vacuum is maintained: a change in atmospheric pressure changes the shape of the disk, thus moving the needle

an·es·the·si·a (an′es thē′zhə, -zhē ə, -zē ə; an′is-) *n.* ⟦ModL < Gr *anaisthēsia* < *an-*, without + *aisthēsis*, feeling < *aisthanesthai*: see AESTHETIC⟧ **1** a partial or total loss of the sense of pain, temperature, touch, etc., produced by disease ☆**2** a loss of sensation induced by an anesthetic, hypnosis, or acupuncture and limited to a specific area (**local anesthesia**) or involving a loss of consciousness (**general anesthesia**)

☆**an·es·the·si·ol·o·gist** (an′es thē′zē äl′ə jist, an′is-) *n.* a doctor who specializes in anesthesiology: see ANESTHETIST

☆**an·es·the·si·ol·o·gy** (-jē) *n.* the science of anesthesia and anesthetics

☆**an·es·thet·ic** (an′es thet′ik, an′is-) *adj.* ⟦< Gr *anaisthētos* + -IC⟧ **1** relating to, with, or characterized by anesthesia **2** producing anesthesia —*n.* a drug, gas, etc. used to produce anesthesia, as before surgery —**anesthetic to** incapable of feeling or responding to —**an′es·thet′i·cal·ly** *adv.*

an·es·the·tist (ə nes′thə tist′) *n.* a nurse or other person trained to administer anesthetics: see ANESTHESIOLOGIST

an·es·the·tize (ə nes′thə tīz′) *vt.* **-tized′**, **-tiz′ing** to cause anesthesia in; give an anesthetic to —**an·es′the·ti·za′tion** *n.*

an·es·trus (an es′trəs) *n.* ⟦AN-[1] + ESTRUS⟧ in the breeding cycle of many mammals, the period of sexual inactivity between two periods of estrus —**an·es′trous** (-trəs) *adj.*

A·ne·to (ä nā′tō), **Pi·co de** (pē′kō dā′) highest mountain in the Pyrenees, in Spain: 11,168 ft (3,404 m)

an·eu·ploid (an′yo͞o ploid′) *adj.* ⟦AN-[1] (var. of A-[2], sense 3) + EUPLOID⟧ having an abnormal number of chromosomes —*n.* an aneuploid cell or organism —**an′eu·ploid′y** (-ploi′dē) *n.*

an·eu·rin (an′yo͞o rin′, -yə-) *n.* ⟦A(NTI)- + (POLY)NEUR(ITIS) + (VITAM)IN⟧ THIAMINE

an·eu·rysm or **an·eu·rism** (an′yo͞o riz′əm, -yə-) *n.* ⟦ModL *aneurisma* < Gr *aneurysma* < *ana-*, up + *eurys*, broad: see EURY-⟧ a sac formed by local enlargement of the weakened wall of an artery, a vein, or the heart, caused by disease or injury —**an′eu·rys′mal** *adj.*, **an′eu·ris′mal** (-riz′məl)

a·new (ə no͞o′, -nyo͞o′) *adv.* ⟦ME *aneue* < *of neue*: see A-[1] & NEW⟧ **1** once more; again **2** in a new manner or form

an·frac·tu·os·i·ty (an frak′cho͞o äs′ə tē) *n.* **1** the quality or state of being anfractuous **2** *pl.* **-ties** a winding channel, passage, etc.

an·frac·tu·ous (an frak′cho͞o əs) *adj.* ⟦LL(Ec) *anfractuosus* < L *anfractus*, pp. of *anfringere* < *an-* (for *ambi-*), around + *frangere*, BREAK⟧ full of twists, turns, and windings; roundabout; tortuous

an·ga·kok (aŋ′gə käk′) *n.* ⟦prob. via Dan < Greenland Esk⟧ an Eskimo medicine man

An·ga·ra (än′gə rä′) river in SC Siberia, flowing from Lake Baikal north & west to the Yenisei River: 1,150 mi (1,851 km)

An·garsk (än gärsk′) city in S Asian Russia, near Irkutsk

an·ga·ry (aŋ′gə rē) *n.* ⟦LL *angaria*, enforced service < Gr *angareia*, impressment < *angaros*, a mounted courier; prob. < OPers term⟧ *International Law* the right of a belligerent to use or destroy a neutral's property if necessary, with the obligation of full indemnification

an·gel (ān′jəl) *n.* ⟦ME *aungel* < OFr *angele* or OE *engel*, or directly < LL(Ec) *angelus* (> OFr & OE forms) < Gr(Ec) *angelos*, messenger < ?⟧ **1** *Theol.* *a)* a messenger of God *b)* a supernatural being, either good or bad, to whom are attributed greater than human power, intelligence, etc. **2** a guiding spirit or influence [one's good *angel*] **3** a conventionalized image of a white-robed figure in human form with wings and a halo **4** a person regarded as being as beautiful, good, innocent, etc. as an angel: said esp. of women and children **5** an English gold coin, last issued in 1634, stamped with an image of the archangel Michael and the dragon ☆**6** [Informal] a supporter who provides money, as for producing a play **7** a radar echo from something other than an aircraft, as from birds or rain —*vt.* [Slang] to support with money —*SYN.* SPONSOR

An·ge·la (an′jə lə) *n.* ⟦contr. of *Angelica* < ML *angelica*, angelic < LL(Ec) *angelicus*: see ANGELIC⟧ a feminine name: dim. *Angie*; var. *Angelica, Angelina, Angeline*

angel dust [Slang] PCP[1]

☆**An·ge·le·no** (an′jə lē′nō) *n., pl.* **-nos** ⟦AmSp < (LOS) ANGEL(ES) + Sp *-eño*, suffix denoting inhabitant of given location < L *-enus* < Gr *-ēnos*⟧ a person born or living in Los Angeles

An·ge·les (än′hə läs′) city in WC Luzon, the Philippines

Angel Falls (*or* **Fall**) waterfall in SE Venezuela: over 3,200 ft (975 m)

an·gel·fish (ān′jəl fish′) *n., pl.* **-fish′** or **-fish′es** (see FISH) **1** any of a percoid family (Pomacanthidae) of bright-colored, tropical reef fishes with long, trailing spiny fins **2** SCALARE

☆**angel food cake** a light, spongy white cake made with egg whites and no shortening: also **angel cake**

an·gel-hair pasta (ān′jəl her′) spaghetti made in very fine strands: also called **angel's hair**

an·gel·ic (an jel′ik) *adj.* ⟦LL(Ec) *angelicus* < Gr *angelikos* < *angelos*: see ANGEL⟧ **1** of an angel or the angels; spiritual; heavenly **2** like an angel in beauty, goodness, innocence, etc. Also **an·gel′i·cal** (-i kəl) —**an·gel′i·cal·ly** *adv.*

an·gel·i·ca (an jel′i kə) *n.* ⟦ModL < ML (*herba*) *angelica*, lit., the angelic (herb) < LL(Ec) *angelicus* (see prec.): so named from its medical uses⟧ any of a number of related plants (genus *Angelica*) of the umbel family, with tall stalks, large divided leaves, clusters of white or greenish flowers, and roots and fruit used in flavoring, perfumes, medicine, etc.

angelica tree ☆**1** HERCULES'-CLUB **2** any of several exotic, Asian trees (genus *Aralia*) of the ginseng family, now in the U.S., with large leaves and small, black, berrylike fruit

An·gel·i·co (an jel′i kō′), **Fra** (frä) (born *Guido di Pietro*, also named *Giovanni da Fiesole*) 1387-1455; It. painter

An·ge·li·na (an′jə lē′nə, -lī′-) *n.* a feminine name: see ANGELA

an·gel·ol·o·gy (ān′jəl äl′ə jē) *n.* the branch of theology dealing with angels

An·ge·lus (an′jə ləs) *n.* ⟦L (see ANGEL): so named from the opening words, "*Angelus Domini*"⟧ [*also* **a-**] *R.C.Ch.* **1** a prayer said at morning, noon, and evening in commemoration of the Incarnation **2** the bell rung to announce the time for this prayer

an·ger (aŋ′gər) *n.* ⟦ME < ON *angr*, distress < IE base **angh-*, constricted > L *angustus*, narrow, *angustia*, tightness, Gr *anchein*, to squeeze, *anchonē*, a strangling, Ger *angst*, fear⟧ **1** a feeling of displeasure resulting from injury, mistreatment, opposition, etc., and usually showing itself in a desire to fight back at the supposed cause of this feeling **2** [Obs.] pain or trouble —*vt.* ⟦ME *angren* < ON *angra*, to distress⟧ to make angry; enrage —*vi.* to become angry

SYN.—**anger** is broadly applicable to feelings of resentful or revengeful displeasure; **indignation** implies righteous anger aroused by what seems unjust, mean, or insulting; **rage** suggests a violent outburst of anger in which self-control is lost; **fury** implies a frenzied rage that borders on madness; **ire**, chiefly a literary word, suggests a show of great anger in acts, words, looks, etc.; **wrath** implies deep indignation expressing itself in a desire to punish or get revenge —*ANT.* **pleasure, forbearance**

An·gers (än zhā′) city in NW France

An·ge·vin (an′jə vin′) *adj.* ⟦Fr⟧ **1** of or from Anjou **2** of or belonging to the Plantagenet line of English kings (1154-1399) —*n.* **1** a person born or living in Anjou **2** a person of the Plantagenet royal line Also sp. **An′ge·vine′**

an·gi·na (an jī′nə, an′jə nə) *n.* ⟦L, quinsy < Gr *anchonē*: see ANGER⟧ **1** any inflammatory disease of the throat or mouth, esp. one characterized by spasmodic suffocation **2** a localized spasm of pain or any condition marked by such spasms; specif., ANGINA PECTORIS —**an·gi′nal** *adj.*

angina pec·to·ris (pek′tər is) ⟦L, lit., angina of the breast⟧ a condition marked by recurrent pain, usually in the chest and left arm, caused by a sudden decrease of the blood supply to the heart muscle

an·gi·o- (an′jē ō, -ə) ⟦< Gr *angeion*, case, capsule < *angos*, vessel⟧ *combining form* **1** seedcase **2** blood vessel or lymph vessel

an·gi·o·car·di·og·ra·phy (an′jē ō kär′dē äg′rə fē) *n.* the making of X-ray pictures of the heart and its blood vessels after injecting a radiopaque substance —**an′gi·o·car′di·o·graph′ic** *adj.*

an·gi·o·gen·e·sis (an′jē ō jen′ə sis) *n.* ⟦ModL⟧ the formation and growth of new blood vessels

an·gi·o·gram (an′jē ō gram′) *n.* an X-ray picture produced by angiography

an·gi·og·ra·phy (an′jē äg′rə fē) *n.* ⟦ANGIO- + -GRAPHY⟧ the process of making X-ray pictures of blood vessels after first injecting a radiopaque substance —**an′gi·o·graph·ic** (an′jē ə graf′ik) *adj.*

an·gi·ol·o·gy (an′jē äl′ə jē) *n.* the study of blood vessels and lymph vessels

an·gi·o·ma (an′jē ō′mə) ***n.***, *pl.* **-ma·ta** (-mə tə) or **-mas** ⟦ANGI(O)- + -OMA⟧ a tumor made up mainly of blood vessels or lymph vessels

an·gi·o·plas·ty (an′jē ō plas′tē) ***n.*** ⟦ANGIO- + -PLASTY⟧ the repair or replacement of damaged blood vessels by surgery or by a nonsurgical technique such as balloon angioplasty

an·gi·o·sar·co·ma (an′jē ō′sär kō′mə) ***n.***, *pl.* **-mas** or **-ma·ta** (-mə tə) a sarcoma containing many vessel-like structures

an·gi·o·sperm (an′jē ō spʉrm′) ***n.*** ⟦< ANGIO- + Gr *sperma*, seed: see SPERM[1]⟧ any of a division (Magnoliophyta) of flowering plants having seeds produced within a closed pod or ovary, including monocotyledons and dicotyledons: see GYMNOSPERM —**an′gi·o·sper′mous** ***adj.***

an·gi·o·ten·sin (an′jē ō ten′sin) ***n.*** ⟦ANGIO- + TENS(ION) + -IN[1]⟧ a polypeptide that is a powerful vasopressor, formed in the blood by the action of renin on a plasma protein

Ang·kor (aŋ′kôr′) an accumulation of Khmer ruins in NW Cambodia, consisting mainly of **Angkor Thom** (tôm), the capital of the ancient Khmer civilization, and including **Angkor Vat** (vät) or **Angkor Wat** (wät), an ancient Khmer temple

an·gle[1] (aŋ′gəl) ***n.*** ⟦ME & OFr < L *angulus*, a corner, angle < Gr *ankylos*, bent, crooked: see ANKLE⟧ **1** *a)* the shape made by two straight lines meeting at a common point, the vertex, or by two planes meeting along an edge (see DIHEDRAL, SPHERICAL ANGLE) *b)* SOLID ANGLE **2** the space between, or within, such lines or planes **3** the measure of this space, expressed in degrees, radians, or steradians **4** a sharp or projecting corner **5** an aspect, as of something viewed or considered; point of view [to examine a problem from all *angles*] **6** [Informal] *a)* a motive *b)* a tricky method for achieving a purpose — ***vt., vi.*** **-gled, -gling 1** to move or bend at an angle or by means of angles **2** [Informal] to give a specific point of view to (a story, report, etc.) —***SYN.*** PHASE[1]

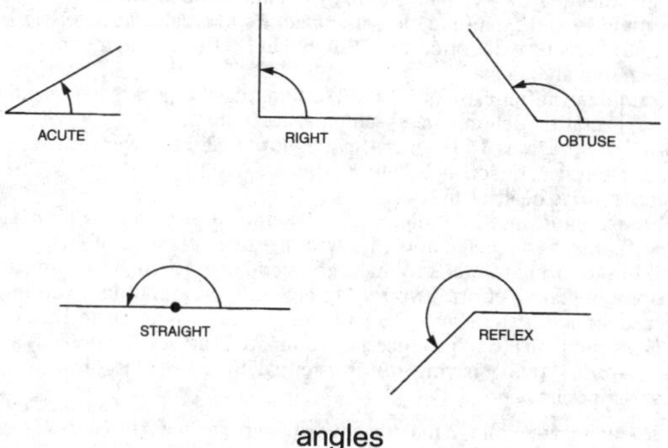

angles

an·gle[2] (aŋ′gəl) ***vi.*** **-gled, -gling** ⟦< ME *angel* < OE *angul*, fishhook, hook: see ANKLE⟧ **1** to fish with a hook and line **2** to scheme or use tricks to get something [to *angle* for a promotion]

An·gle (aŋ′gəl) ***n.*** ⟦L *Anglus*, sing. of *Angli* < PGmc source of OE *Angle*, *Ængle*, the Angles < *Angel, Angul*, district in Holstein, lit., hook (see prec.): so named from its shape⟧ a member of a Germanic people of the northern lowlands that settled in E England in the 5th cent. A.D.: the name *England* is from *Englaland* (land of the Angles), and *English* is from *Englisc* (of the Angles)

an·gled (aŋ′gəld) ***adj.*** **1** set at an angle **2** having an angle

angle iron a piece of structural iron or steel in the form of an angle; esp., such a piece in a right angle, used for joining or reinforcing two beams, girders, etc.

angle iron

angle of attack *Aeron.* the acute angle between the chord of an airfoil and the line of relative air flow

angle of incidence 1 the angle that a light ray or electromagnetic wave striking a surface makes with a line perpendicular to the reflecting surface **2** [Chiefly Brit.] ANGLE OF ATTACK **3** *Aeron.* a permanent angle between the chord of an airfoil and the horizontally level fuselage

angle of repose the maximum angle of slope at which sand, loose rock, etc. will remain in place without sliding, as on a hillside

angle of view *Optics* the angle that corresponds to the field of view provided by a lens

☆**an·gle·pod** (aŋ′gəl päd′) ***n.*** any of a genus (*Cynanchum*) of the milkweed family; esp., a vine (*C. laeve*) of the SE U.S., bearing angular pods

an·gler (aŋ′glər) ***n.*** ⟦< ANGLE[2]⟧ **1** a fisherman who uses hook and line **2** a person who schemes and uses tricks to get something **3** any of an order (Lophiiformes) of bony fishes that feed on other fish, attracting them by means of a movable lure that grows from the head: often **an′gler·fish′** (-fish′), *pl.* **-fish′** or **-fish′es** (see FISH)

An·gle·sey or **An·gle·sea** (aŋ′gəl sē′) **1** former county of NW Wales, now part of Gwynedd county **2** large island in the Irish Sea off the NW coast of Wales: part of Gwynedd county: 276 sq mi (715 sq km)

an·gle·site (aŋ′gəl sīt′, -glə sīt′) ***n.*** ⟦after prec., where it was discovered⟧ a usually white, orthorhombic mineral, $PbSO_4$, often found with galena; lead sulfate

☆**an·gle·worm** (aŋ′gəl wʉrm′) ***n.*** an earthworm: so called because used as fishing bait

An·gli·a (aŋ′glē ə) ⟦see ANGLE⟧ *Latin name for* ENGLAND

An·gli·an (aŋ′glē ən) ***adj.*** of the Angles or their language or culture —***n.*** **1** a member of the Angles **2** Old English as spoken in the dialects of Mercia and Northumbria

An·gli·can (aŋ′gli kən) ***adj.*** ⟦ML *Anglicanus* < *Anglicus*, of England, of the Angles (see ANGLE)⟧ **1** of England or its people or culture **2** of the Church of England or of any other church in the Anglican Communion —***n.*** any member of the Church of England or of another church in the Anglican Communion —**An′gli·can·ism′** ***n.***

Anglican Communion the informal organization of the Church of England and derived churches with closely related beliefs and practices, including the Anglican Church of Canada, the Protestant Episcopal Church in the U.S., the Episcopal Church of Scotland, etc.

An·gli·ce (aŋ′glə sē) ***adv.*** ⟦ML < *Anglicus*: see ANGLICAN⟧ in English; as the English term is [Livorno, *Anglice* Leghorn]

An·gli·cism (aŋ′glə siz′əm) ***n.*** ⟦< ML *Anglicus* (see ANGLICAN) + -ISM⟧ **1** a word, phrase, grammatical construction, etc. originating in or peculiar to English, esp. British English; Briticism **2** a typically English trait, custom, etc. **3** the quality of being English

An·gli·cist (-sist) ***n.*** a student of or authority on the English language and literature

An·gli·cize (aŋ′glə sīz′) ***vt., vi.*** **-cized′, -ciz′ing** ⟦< ML *Anglicus* (see ANGLICAN) + -IZE⟧ [*also* **a-**] to change to English idiom, pronunciation, customs, manner, etc. —**An′gli·ci·za′tion** ***n.***

☆**An·gli·fy** (-fī′) ***vt.*** **-fied′, -fy′ing** to Anglicize

an·gling (aŋ′gliŋ) ***n.*** ⟦< ANGLE[2]⟧ the act or skill of fishing with hook and line

An·glo (aŋ′glō′) [*also* **a-**] ***n.***, *pl.* **-glos′** (-glōz′) ⟦AmSp⟧ a white citizen or inhabitant of the U.S. who is of non-Hispanic descent —***adj.*** of or relating to Anglos

An·glo- (aŋ′glō′, -glə) ⟦< L *Anglus*, sing. of *Angli*, Angles (see ANGLE)⟧ *combining form* **1** English, English and [*Anglophone, Anglo-*American] **2** Anglican [*Anglo-*Catholic]

☆**An·glo-A·mer·i·can** (aŋ′glō ə mer′i kən) ***adj.*** **1** English and American; of or between England and the U.S. **2** of Anglo-Americans —***n.*** an American of English birth or ancestry

An·glo-Cath·o·lic (-kath′ə lik) ***n.*** a member of the Anglican Communion who stresses its continuous tradition with the Catholic Church before and after the Reformation —***adj.*** of Anglo-Catholics or their beliefs and practice

An·glo-E·gyp·tian Sudan (-ē jip′shən) territory jointly administered by Egypt & Great Britain (1899-1956): see SUDAN

An·glo-French (-french′) ***adj.*** **1** English and French; of or between England and France **2** of Anglo-French —***n.*** the French spoken in England from the Norman Conquest through the Middle Ages: see NORMAN FRENCH

An·glo-In·di·an (-in′dē ən) ***adj.*** **1** English and Indian; of or between England and India **2** of Anglo-Indians **3** designating or of the dialect of English used by Anglo-Indians in India —***n.*** **1** an English citizen living in India **2** a person of both English and Indian ancestry

☆**An·glo·ma·ni·a** (-mā′nē ə) ***n.*** an exaggerated liking for and imitation of English customs, manners, institutions, etc.

An·glo-Nor·man (-nôr′mən) ***adj.*** **1** English and Norman **2** of the Anglo-Normans or their language or culture —***n.*** **1** a Norman settler in England after the Norman Conquest **2** the Anglo-French dialect spoken by such settlers

An·glo·phile (aŋ′glō fīl′, -glə-) ***n.*** [*often* **a-**] a person who strongly admires England or its people, culture, customs, influence, etc.

An·glo·phil·i·a (aŋ′glō fil′ē ə, -glə-) ***n.*** [*often* **a-**] extreme admiration for England or its people, culture, customs, influence, etc.

An·glo·phobe (aŋ′glō fōb′, -glə-) ***n.*** [*often* **a-**] a person who hates or fears England or its people, culture, customs, influence, etc.

☆**An·glo·pho·bi·a** (aŋ′glō fō′bē ə) ***n.*** [*often* **a-**] hatred or fear of England or its people, culture, customs, influence, etc. —**An′glo·pho′bic** (-fō′bik) ***adj.***

An·glo·phone (aŋ′glō fōn′, -glə-) [*also* **a-**] ***adj.*** ⟦Fr *anglophone*: see ANGLO- & PHONE[1]⟧ of or having to do with speakers of English —***n.*** a person who speaks English —**An′glo·phon′ic** (-fän′ik) ***adj.***

An·glo-Sax·on (aŋ′glō sak′sən) ***n.*** ⟦< ML *Anglo-Saxones*: see ANGLE & SAXON⟧ **1** a member of the Germanic peoples (Angles, Saxons, and Jutes) that invaded England (5th-6th cent. A.D.) and were there at the time of the Norman Conquest **2** the language of these peoples, OLD ENGLISH **3** modern English, esp. plain, blunt language of Old English origin **4** a person of English nationality or descent —***adj.*** **1** of the Anglo-Saxons or their language or culture **2** of their descendants; English

An·go·la (aŋ gō′lə, an-) country on the SW coast of Africa: formerly a Portuguese territory, it became independent in 1975: 481,354 sq mi (1,246,700 sq km); cap. Luanda —**An·go′lan** ***adj., n.***

An·go·ra (aŋ gôr′ə, an-) ***n.*** ⟦after *Angora*, former name of ANKARA⟧ **1** a kind of cat with long, silky fur: in full **Angora cat 2** *a)* a kind of goat raised for its long, silky hair (in full **Angora goat**) *b)* this hair (**Angora wool**) or the cloth made from this hair; mohair **3** *a)* a long-eared rabbit, raised for its long, silky hair (in full **Angora rabbit**) *b)* this hair *c)* a soft yarn made from this hair and used esp. for sweaters, etc. Also, for senses 2*b*, 3*b*, 3*c*, **angora**

an·gos·tu·ra (bark) (aŋ′gəs to͝or′ə, -tyo͝or′-; an′-) ⟦after *Angostura* (former name of CIUDAD BOLÍVAR), lit. (in Sp), narrow pass: so named because located on the narrows of the Orinoco River⟧ the bitter aromatic bark of either of two South American trees (*Galipea officinalis* or *Cusparia trifoliata*) of the rue family, used as a medicinal tonic and as a flavoring in bitters

An·gou·lême (än go͞o lem′) city in SW France

an·gry (aŋ′grē) ***adj.*** **-gri·er, -gri·est** ⟦ME *angri*, troubled < ANGER⟧ **1** feeling, showing, or resulting from anger [an *angry* reply] **2** wild and stormy, as if angry [an *angry* sea] **3** inflamed and sore [an *angry* wound] **—an′gri·ly** (-grə lē) ***adv.*** **—an′gri·ness** (-grē nis) ***n.***

angry young men [*often* **A- Y- M-**] a group of young writers in Great Britain after WWII, bitterly critical of upper-class and middle-class values, practices, etc.

angst (äŋst, aŋst) ***n.*** ⟦Ger: see ANGER⟧ [*occas.* **A-**] a gloomy, often neurotic feeling of generalized anxiety and depression

ang·strom (aŋ′strəm) ***n.*** ⟦after fol.⟧ one hundred-millionth of a centimeter: a unit used in measuring the length of light waves: symbol, Å: also **angstrom unit**

Ång·ström (aŋ′strəm, ôŋ′-), **An·ders Jo·nas** (än′dərs yo͞o′näs′; -dərsh-) 1814-74; Swed. physicist

An·guil·la (aŋ gwil′ə) island of the Leeward group in the West Indies: with nearby islands, it constitutes a dependency of the United Kingdom: 60 sq mi (155 sq km) **—An·guil′lan *adj., n.***

an·guish (aŋ′gwish) ***n.*** ⟦ME *angwisshe* < OFr *anguisse* < L *angustia*, tightness, distress: see ANGER⟧ great suffering, as from worry, grief, or pain; agony **—*vt.*** to cause to feel anguish **—*vi.*** to feel anguish **—*SYN.*** DISTRESS

an·guished (aŋ′gwisht) ***adj.*** **1** feeling anguish **2** showing or resulting from anguish

an·gu·lar (aŋ′gyo͞o lər, -gyə-) ***adj.*** ⟦L *angularis* < *angulus*, ANGLE¹⟧ **1** having or forming an angle or angles; having sharp corners **2** measured by an angle [*angular* distance] **3** with bones that jut out **4** without ease or grace [*angular* strides] **—an′gu·lar·ly *adv.***

an·gu·lar·i·ty (aŋ′gyo͞o lar′ə tē, -gyə-) ***n., pl.*** **-ties 1** the quality or condition of being angular **2** [*pl.*] angular forms; sharp corners

angular momentum the momentum characteristic of a rotating object; the product of linear momentum and the perpendicular distance from the origin of coordinates to the path of the object: the conservation of angular momentum causes a spinning skater, star, etc. to increase (or decrease) in velocity as the radius is reduced (or increased): symbol, Ω

an·gu·late (aŋ′gyo͞o lit, -gyə-; *also, and for v. always*, -lāt′) ***adj.*** ⟦L *angulatus*, pp. of *angulare*, to make angular < *angulus*, ANGLE¹⟧ having angles or corners **—*vt., vi.*** **-lat′ed, -lat′ing** to make or become angular **—an′gu·late·ly *adv.***

an·gu·la·tion (aŋ′gyo͞o lā′shən, -gyə-) ***n.*** **1** the act of angulating **2** an angular form, part, or position

An·gus¹ (aŋ′gəs) ***n.*** ⟦Gael *Aonghas* & Ir *Aonghus* < *aon*, ONE⟧ **1** a masculine name **2** *Celt. Myth.* the god of love

An·gus² (aŋ′gəs) administrative division of E Scotland: formerly a county & district

ang·wan·ti·bo (aŋ wän′tə bō′) ***n., pl.*** **-bos′** ⟦Efik⟧ a small, rare prosimian primate (*Arctocebus calabarensis*) of W African forests, with a long, sharp nose and a small tail: it is in the same family with the lorises and pottos

An·halt (än′hält′) region of central Germany, formerly a German state and now part of the state of Saxony-Anhalt

an·he·do·ni·a (an′hē dō′nē ə, -dōn′yə) ***n.*** ⟦Fr *anhédonie* < Gr *an-*, not + *hēdonē*, pleasure⟧ a psychological condition marked by an inability to experience pleasure **—an′he·don′ic** (-dän′ik) ***adj., n.***

an·hin·ga (an hiŋ′gə) ***n.*** ⟦Port < Tupí *áyinga*⟧ any of a family (Anhingidae) of pelecaniform birds of tropical and subtropical regions, with a long, sharp-pointed bill and long neck

An·hui (än′hwē′) province of E China: 54,016 sq mi (139,901 sq km); cap. Hefei: former transliteration **An′hwei′** (-hwā′)

an·hy·dride (an hī′drīd′) ***n.*** ⟦< Gr *anydros* (see ANHYDROUS) + -IDE⟧ **1** an oxide that reacts with water to form an acid or a base **2** any compound formed by the removal of water

an·hy·drite (an hī′drīt′) ***n.*** ⟦< Gr *anydros* (see fol.) + -ITE¹⟧ a soft, light-colored, orthorhombic mineral, $CaSO_4$, that changes into gypsum with the absorption of water; anhydrous calcium sulfate

an·hy·drous (an hī′drəs) ***adj.*** ⟦Gr *anydros* < *an-*, without + *hydōr*, WATER⟧ **1** without water **2** *Chem.* having no water of crystallization; not hydrated

a·ni (ä′nē) ***n., pl.*** **a′nis′** (-nēz′) ⟦Port < Guaraní⟧ a tropical American cuckoo bird (genus *Crotophaga*), generally black, with a long tail

an·il (an′il) ***n.*** ⟦Fr < Port < Ar *an-nīl* < *al*, the + *nīl*, indigo plant < Sans *nīlaḥ*, dark blue⟧ **1** a West Indian shrub (*Indigofera suffruticosa*) of the pea family, from which indigo is made **2** INDIGO

an·ile (an′īl′, ā′nīl′; an′il) ***adj.*** ⟦L *anilis* < *anus*, old woman < IE base **an-*, designation of male or female ancestor (> Ger *ahn*, grandfather); orig. < baby talk⟧ of or like an old woman; infirm; weak **—a·nil·i·ty** (ə nil′ə tē) ***n.***

an·i·line (an′ə lin, -lēn′, -līn′) ***n.*** ⟦Ger *anilin*: see ANIL & -INE³⟧ a colorless, poisonous, oily liquid, $C_6H_5NH_2$, a derivative of benzene used in making dyes, resins, rubber additives, fungicides, herbicides, etc., and in organic synthesis

aniline dye 1 any dye made from aniline **2** any dye that is chemically like aniline; commonly, any dye produced synthetically from coal-tar products

an·i·ma (an′i mə) ***n.*** ⟦L⟧ **1** life principle; soul **2** in Jungian psychology, the feminine component of the unconscious of a man, specif. when apprehended as a female figure by the psyche: cf. ANIMUS

an·i·mad·ver·sion (an′i mad vur′zhən, -shən; -mad′-) ***n.*** ⟦L *animadversio* < pp. of *animadvertere*: see fol.⟧ **1** a critical, esp. unfavorable, comment (*on* or *upon* something) **2** the act of criticizing adversely

an·i·mad·vert (an′i mad vurt′, -mad′-) ***vi.*** ⟦L *animadvertere*, to observe, censure < *animum* (acc. of *animus*, mind) + *advertere*, to turn: see ANIMUS & ADVERT¹⟧ to comment (*on* or *upon*), esp. with disapproval; criticize adversely

an·i·mal (an′i məl) ***n.*** ⟦L, living being < *anima, animus*, breath, air, life principle, soul < IE base **an(e)-*, to breathe, exhale > Gr *anemos*, Sans *anilas*, wind, breath, OE *antha*, excitement, anger⟧ **1** any of a kingdom (Animalia) of eukaryotes generally characterized by a multicellular body, the ability to move quickly and obtain food, specialized sense organs, and sexual reproduction **2** any such organism other than a human being, esp. a mammal or, often, any four-footed creature **3** a brutish, debased, or inhuman person **4** [Informal] a person, thing, concept, etc. thought of as a kind or type [today's athlete is another *animal* altogether] **—*adj.*** **1** of, like, or derived from animals **2** physical rather than mental or spiritual; specif., sensual, gross, bestial, etc. **—*SYN.*** CARNAL **—the animal** animal nature; animality [it's *the animal* in him] **—an′i·mal·ly *adv.***

☆**animal cracker** a small cookie shaped like any of various animals

an·i·mal·cule (an′i mal′kyo͞ol′) ***n.*** ⟦ModL *animalculum*, dim. of ANIMAL⟧ [Obs.] a microscopic animal; protozoan: also **an′i·mal′cu·lum** (-kyo͞o ləm), *pl.* **-la** (-lə) **—an′i·mal′cu·lar** (-kyo͞o lər) ***adj.***

animal heat heat produced in the body of an animal by chemical changes that occur when food is assimilated: see BASAL METABOLISM

animal husbandry the care and raising of domesticated animals, as cattle, horses, sheep, etc.

an·i·mal·ism (an′i məl iz′əm) ***n.*** **1** the activity, appetites, nature, etc. of animals **2** the doctrine that human beings are mere animals with no soul or spiritual quality **—an′i·mal·ist *n.*** **—an′i·mal·is′tic *adj.***

an·i·mal·i·ty (an′i mal′ə tē) ***n.*** ⟦Fr *animalité* < LL *animalitas*: see ANIMAL⟧ **1** animal characteristics or nature **2** animal life **3** the animal instincts or nature in human beings

an·i·mal·ize (an′i məl īz′) ***vt.*** **-ized′, -iz′ing** to make (a person) resemble a beast; brutalize; dehumanize **—an′i·mal·i·za′tion *n.***

animal magnetism 1 *former term for* HYPNOTISM **2** the power to attract others in a physical or sensual way

animal spirits healthy, lively vigor

an·i·mate (an′i māt′; *for adj.*, -mit) ***vt.*** **-mat′ed, -mat′ing** ⟦< L *animatus*, pp. of *animare*, to make alive, fill with breath < *anima*: see ANIMAL⟧ **1** to give life to; bring to life **2** to make energetic or spirited **3** to stimulate to action or creative effort; inspire **4** to give motion to; put into action [the breeze *animated* the leaves] **5** to make move so as to seem lifelike [to *animate* puppets] **6** to produce as an animated cartoon [to *animate* a fairy tale] **—*adj.*** **1** living; having life, esp. animal life **2** lively; vigorous; spirited **—an′i·mate·ness *n.***

***SYN.*—animate** implies a making alive or lively [an *animated* conversation] or an imparting of motion or activity [an *animated* doll]; to **quicken** is to rouse to action that which is lifeless or inert [the rebuff *quickened* his resolution]; **exhilarate** implies an enlivening or elevation of the spirits; **stimulate** implies a rousing from inertia, inactivity, or lethargy, as if by goading; **invigorate** means to fill with vigor or energy in a physical sense [an *invigorating* tonic]; **vitalize** implies the imparting of vigor or animation in a nonphysical sense [to *vitalize* a dull story] See also **living —*ANT.* deaden, depress, enervate**

an·i·mat·ed (-māt′id) ***adj.*** **1** alive or seeming alive; living or lifelike **2** showing animation; lively **3** of or having to do with an ANIMATED CARTOON or its preparation **—*SYN.*** LIVELY, LIVING **—an′i·mat′ed·ly *adv.***

☆**animated cartoon** a film made by photographing a series of images, as drawings or cels, each showing a stage of movement slightly changed from the one before, so that the figures in them seem to move when the images are projected in rapid succession

an·i·mat·er (an′i māt′ər) ***n.*** *alt. sp. of* ANIMATOR

an·i·ma·tion (an′i mā′shən) ***n.*** **1** an animating or being animated **2** an animate condition; life **3** vivacity; brisk, lively quality **4** the preparation of animated cartoons **5** ANIMATED CARTOON

an·i·ma·tism (an′i mə tiz′əm) ***n.*** the belief that inanimate things have consciousness or personality

a·ni·ma·to (ä′nē mä′tō′) ***adj., adv.*** ⟦It⟧ *Musical Direction* with animation

an·i·ma·tor (an′i māt′ər) ***n.*** ⟦L⟧ **1** a person or thing that animates **2** an artist who draws animated cartoons; specif., one who draws the progressive changes in movement

an·i·ma·tron·ics (an′i mə trän′iks) ***n.*** ⟦shortened < *Audio-Animatronics*, service mark for a type of entertainment using robotics in this way; prob. < blend of ANIMATION & ELECTRONICS⟧ the use of electronic mechanisms in puppets, dolls, and other figures, for the purpose of simulating lifelike motion **—an′i·ma·tron′ic *adj.***

an·i·me (an′i mā′) ***n.*** ⟦Jpn, ? ult. < Eng ANIMATION⟧ a style of Japanese film animation, strongly influenced by MANGA, often featuring stories with science-fiction and fantasy themes sometimes emphasizing sex and violence

a·ni·mé (an′i mā′, -mē′) ***n.*** ⟦Fr < Port or Sp *anime*, < ? Tupí name⟧ any of various resins, obtained from certain tropical trees and used in making varnish; esp., a variety of copal: also **a′ni·mi′** (-mē′)

an·i·mism (an′i miz′əm) ***n.*** ⟦Fr *animisme* & Ger *animismus*, both < L *anima*, soul: see ANIMAL & -ISM⟧ **1** the doctrine that all life is produced by a spiritual force separate from matter **2** the belief that all natural phenomena have souls independent of their physical being **3** a belief in the existence of spirits, demons, etc. —**an′i·mist** *n.* —**an′i·mis′tic** *adj.*

an·i·mos·i·ty (an′ə mäs′ə tē) *n., pl.* **-ties** ⟦ME *animosite* < L *animositas*, boldness, spirit < *animosus*, spirited < *animus*: see fol.⟧ a feeling of strong dislike or hatred; ill will; hostility —**SYN.** ENMITY

an·i·mus (an′ə məs) *n.* ⟦L, soul, mind, disposition, passion, akin to *anima*: see ANIMAL⟧ **1** an animating force or underlying purpose; intention **2** in Jungian psychology, the masculine component of the unconscious of a woman, specif. when apprehended as a male figure by the psyche: cf. ANIMA **3** a feeling of strong ill will or hatred; animosity

an·i·on (an′ī′ən) *n.* ⟦coined by Michael FARADAY < Gr *anion*, thing going up, neut. prp. of *anienai*, to go up < *ana-*, up + *ienai*, to go: see VIA⟧ a negatively charged ion, esp. one that moves toward the anode during electrolysis: opposed to CATION —**an′i·on′ic** (-än′ik) *adj.*

a·nis (*Fr* å nē′; *Sp* ä′nēs′) *n.* a French or Spanish liqueur flavored with aniseed

an·ise (an′is) *n.* ⟦ME & OFr *anis* < L *anisum* < Gr *anison*⟧ **1** a plant (*Pimpinella anisum*) of the umbel family, with small, white or yellow flowers **2** its fragrant seed, used for flavoring and as a medicine for expelling intestinal gas

an·i·seed (an′i sēd′) *n.* ANISE (sense 2)

an·i·sette (an′i zet′, -set′) *n.* ⟦Fr, dim. < *anis*: see ANISE⟧ a sweet, usually colorless anise-flavored liqueur, lower in proof than anis

an·i·so- (an ī′sō, -sə) ⟦ModL < Gr *anisos*, unequal < *an-*, not + *isos*, equal⟧ *combining form* not equal, not alike [*anisomerous*]: also, before a vowel, **anis-**

an·i·so·gam·ete (an ī′sō gam′ēt′, -gə mēt′) *n.* HETEROGAMETE —**an·i·sog·a·mous** (an′ī säg′ə məs) *adj.* —**an′i·sog′a·my** (-mē) *n.*

an·i·sole (an′i sōl′) *n.* ⟦Fr *anisol* < *anis* (see ANISE) + *-ol*, -OLE⟧ a colorless, fragrant liquid, $C_6H_5OCH_3$, made by heating phenol with methyl alcohol: it is used in making perfumes

an·i·som·er·ous (an′ī säm′ər əs) *adj.* ⟦ANISO- + -MEROUS⟧ *Bot.* of or describing a flower having an unequal number of petals, stamens, or other floral parts

an·i·so·met·ric (an ī′sō me′trik) *adj.* ⟦AN-[1] + ISOMETRIC⟧ not isometric; with asymmetrical parts

an·i·so·me·tro·pi·a (an ī′sō mə trō′pē ə) *n.* ⟦ANISO- + METR(O)- + -OPIA⟧ a condition of the eyes in which they have unequal refractive power —**an·i′so·me·trop′ic** (-träp′ik) *adj.*

an·i·so·trop·ic (an ī′sō träp′ik) *adj.* ⟦AN-[1] + ISOTROPIC⟧ **1** *Bot.* assuming a new position in response to external stimuli **2** *Physics* having properties, such as conductivity or speed of transmission of light, etc., that vary according to the direction in which they are measured —**an·i·sot·ro·py** (an′ī sä′trə pē) *n.*, **an′i·sot′ro·pism′** (-piz′əm) —**an·i′so·trop′i·cal·ly** *adv.*

A·ni·ta (ə nēt′ə) *n.* ⟦Sp dim. of *Ana*: see ANNA⟧ a feminine name: dim. *Nita*

An·jou (an′jo͞o′; *Fr* än zho͞o′) historical region of W France: the ruling family of Anjou gave rise to the Plantagenets of England

An·jou pear (an′jo͞o′) a thick, green, oval-shaped pear that ripens during the winter

An·ka·ra (aŋ′kər ə, äŋ′-) capital of Turkey, in the central part

an·ker·ite (aŋ′kər īt′) *n.* ⟦Ger *ankerit*, after M. J. *Anker*, 19th-c. Austrian mineralogist⟧ a variety of dolomite, $Ca(Fe,Mg,Mn)(CO_3)_2$, with more iron than magnesium

ankh (aŋk, äŋk) *n.* ⟦Egypt, life, soul⟧ a cross with a top loop, an ancient Egyptian symbol of life

ankh

an·kle (aŋ′kəl) *n.* ⟦ME *ancle, ancleou* < OE *ancleow* (& ? ON *ǫkkla*) < IE base **ang-*, limb, var. of **ank-*, to bend > ANGLE[1], ANGLE[2], Gr *ankōn*, elbow, *ankylos*, crooked⟧ **1** the joint that connects the foot and the leg **2** the area of the leg between the foot and calf —*vi.* **-kled, -kling** [Slang] **1** to walk ☆**2** to fail to go on with (an agreement, job, contract, etc.)

an·kle·bone (-bōn′) *n.* the bone of the ankle; talus

ankle bracelet **1** an ornamental band or chain worn around the ankle **2** an electronic device worn around the ankle, as of someone under house arrest, used to monitor that person's whereabouts

an·klet (aŋk′lit) *n.* **1** anything worn around the ankle as a fetter, ornament, or support **2** a short sock that rises to or just above the ankle

an·ky·lo·saur (aŋ′kə lō sôr′) *n.* ⟦< ModL < Gr *ankylos*, crooked (see ANKLE) + -SAUR⟧ any of a suborder (Ankylosauria) of heavily armored, short-legged ornithischian dinosaurs of the Cretaceous: also **an′ky·lo·sau′rus**

an·ky·lose (aŋ′kə lōs′, -lōz′) *vt., vi.* **-losed′, -los′ing** ⟦< fol.⟧ to stiffen or join by ankylosis

an·ky·lo·sis (aŋ′kə lō′sis) *n., pl.* **-ses′** (-sēz′) ⟦Gr *ankylōsis* < *ankyloun*, to crook, stiffen < *ankylos*, crooked: see ANKLE⟧ **1** *Med.* a stiffening of a joint, caused by the pathological joining of bones or fibrous parts, as from an injury **2** *Zool.* a joining of bones or fibrous parts into a single part —**an′ky·lot′ic** (-lät′ik) *adj.*

an·ky·los·to·mi·a·sis (aŋ′kə läs′tə mī′ə sis, -lō′stə-) *n., pl.* **-ses′** (-sēz′) ANCYLOSTOMIASIS

☆**an·la·ge** (än′lä′gə) *n., pl.* **-gen** (-gən) or **-ges** (-gəz) ⟦Ger, foundation < *anlegen*, lay out⟧ [*occas.* **A-**] **1** the basis of a later development; foundation **2** PRIMORDIUM

ann *abbrev.* **1** annual **2** annuity

Ann (an) *n.* a feminine name: see ANNA

An·na (an′ə) *n.* ⟦L *Anna* < Gr < Heb *chana* lit., grace⟧ a feminine name: dim. *Annie, Nan, Nancy*; var. *Ann, Anne, Hannah*; equiv. Fr. *Anne, Annette, Nannette*, Sp. *Ana*

An·na·ba (an ä′bə) seaport in NE Algeria, on the Mediterranean

An·na·bel or **An·na·belle** (an′ə bel′) *n.* ⟦? altered < *Amabel* < L *amabilis*, lovable < *amare*, to love: now assoc. with ANNA & BELLE⟧ a feminine name

an·na·berg·ite (an′ə bʉrg′īt′) *n.* ⟦after *Annaberg*, town in Germany + -ITE[1]⟧ the light-green variety of erythrite, $(Ni,Co)_3(AsO_4)_2{\cdot}8H_2O$, in which nickel replaces the cobalt; hydrous cobalt-nickel arsenate

An·nales (å nål′) *adj.* ⟦< Fr *Annales d'histoire économique et sociale*, annals of economic and social history, Fr journal founded 1929⟧ designating or of a group of Fr. historians using a variety of materials and methods to detail the structure and patterns of everyday life, as of a town or region, so as to identify underlying processes of cultural development

an·nal·ist (an′əl ist) *n.* a writer of annals —**an′nal·is′tic** *adj.*

an·nals (an′əlz) *pl.n.* ⟦L *annalis*, pl. *annales* < *annus*, year: see ANNUAL⟧ **1** a written account of events year by year in chronological order **2** historical records or chronicles; history **3** any journal reporting discoveries in some field, meetings of a society, etc.

An·nam (a nam′, an′am′) historic region and former French protectorate in EC Indochina: the central part of Vietnam

An·na·mese (an′ə mēz′, -mēs′) *n.* ⟦Chin *ahn-nahm*, pacified South⟧ **1** *pl.* **-mese′** *a)* a person born or living in Vietnam; Vietnamese *b)* a person born or living in Annam **2** *a)* the Vietnamese language *b)* the language of Annam —*adj.* of Annam or its people, language, or culture Also **An′na·mite′** (-mīt′)

An·nap·o·lis (ə nap′ə lis) ⟦after *Anna*, Princess, later Queen, ANNE + Gr *polis*, city⟧ capital of Md., on Chesapeake Bay: site of U.S. Naval Academy

An·na·pur·na (an′ə po͝or′nə, ä′nə-; -pʉr′-) massif of the Himalayas, in central Nepal: highest peak, *c.* 26,500 ft (8,077 m)

Ann Ar·bor (an är′bər) ⟦prob. after *Ann* Allen, early settler, and the woody site⟧ city in SE Mich.

an·nat·to (ə nät′ō, ä-) *n.* ⟦of WInd orig.⟧ a dye of reddish yellow made from the pulp around the seeds of a tropical dicotyledonous tree (*Bixa orellana*, family Bixaceae): it is used for coloring butter, cheese, varnishes, etc.

Anne[1] (an) *n.* **1** a feminine name: see ANNA **2** according to Christian tradition, the mother of the Virgin Mary: her day is July 26

Anne[2] (an) 1665-1714; queen of Great Britain and Ireland (1702-14): last of the Stuart monarchs

an·neal (ə nēl′) *vt.* ⟦ME *anelen* < OE *anælan*, to burn < *an-*, ON + *ælan*, to burn < *al, æl*, fire⟧ **1** [Obs.] to fire or glaze, as in a kiln **2** to heat (glass, metals, etc.) and then cool, sometimes slowly, to prevent brittleness **3** to strengthen and temper (the mind, will, etc.) —**an·neal′er** *n.*

Anne Boleyn *see* BOLEYN, Anne

an·ne·lid (an′ə lid′) *n.* ⟦< ModL *Annelida* (pl.) < Fr *annélides* < (*animaux*) *annelés*, ringed (animals) < pp. of *anneler*, to encircle < OFr *anel*, a ring < L *annellus*, dim. of *anulus*, a ring: see ANNULAR⟧ any of a phylum (Annelida) of roundish, wormlike animals having long, segmented bodies, a brain and ventral nerve cord, and a closed circulatory system, including polychaetes, oligochaetes, and leeches —*adj.* of this phylum —**an·nel·i·dan** (ə nel′i dən) *adj.*

Anne of Austria 1601-66; wife of Louis XIII of France: regent (1643-61) during minority of Louis XIV

Anne of Cleves (klēvz) 1515-57; 4th wife of Henry VIII of England

An·nette (an et′, ə net′) *n.* a feminine name: see ANNA

an·nex (ə neks′, a-; *for n.* an′eks′) *vt.* ⟦ME *annexen* < OFr *annexer* < L *annexus*, pp. of *annectere* < *ad-*, to + *nectere*, to tie, bind: see NET[1]⟧ **1** to add on or attach, as a smaller thing to a larger; append **2** to add to as a condition, consequence, etc. **3** to incorporate into a country, state, etc. the territory of (another country, state, etc.) **4** to take or appropriate, esp. without asking **5** [Archaic] to join; connect —*n.* something added on; specif., *a)* a wing added to a building *b)* a nearby building used as an addition to the main building *c)* a section added as to a document; addendum —**an·nex·a·tion** (an′ek sā′shən, -iks-) *n.* —**an′nex·a′tion·ist** *n.*

an·nexe (an′eks′) *n.* ⟦Fr⟧ *Brit. sp. of* ANNEX

☆**An·nie Oak·ley** (an′ē ōk′lē) ⟦after Annie OAKLEY ? because her small targets resembled punched tickets⟧ [Slang] a free ticket; pass

an·ni·hi·la·ble (ə nī′ə lə bəl) *adj.* that can be annihilated

an·ni·hi·late (ə nī′ə lāt′) *vt.* **-lat′ed, -lat′ing** ⟦< LL(Ec) *annihilatus*, pp. of *annihilare*, to bring to nothing < L *ad*, to + *nihil*, nothing⟧ **1** to destroy completely; put out of existence; demolish [*an atomic bomb can annihilate a city*] **2** to consider or cause to be of no importance or without effect; nullify [*to annihilate another's ambition*] **3** to kill **4** to conquer decisively; crush —**SYN.** DESTROY —**an·ni′hi·la′tion** *n.* —**an·ni′hi·la′tive** *adj.* —**an·ni′hi·la′tor** *n.*

an·ni·ver·sa·ry (an′ə vʉr′sə rē) *n., pl.* **-ries** ⟦ME *anniversarie* < ML *anniversaria (dies)*, anniversary (day) < L *anniversarius* < *annus*, year + *versum*, pp. of *vertere*, to turn: see VERSE⟧ **1** the annually recurring date on which some event took place **2** the commemoration of such an event on that date in following years **3** loosely, any commemoration, not based on years, of the date of an event [*the six-month anniversary of their wedding*] —*adj.* **1** that is an anniversary **2** of or connected with an anniversary

an·no Do·mi·ni (ä′nō dō′mē nē′, an′ō däm′ə nē′) ⟦L, in the year of the Lord⟧ [*often* **A- D-**] in the (given) year since the beginning of the Christian Era

an·no·tate (an′ə tāt′, an′ō-) *vt., vi.* **-tat′ed, -tat′ing** ⟦< L *annotatus*, pp. of *annotare* < *ad-*, to + *notare*, to note, mark < *nota*: see NOTE⟧ to provide critical or explanatory notes for (a literary work, etc.) **—an′no·ta′tive** *adj.* **—an′no·ta′tor** *n.*

an·no·ta·tion (an′ə tā′shən, an′ō-) *n.* **1** an annotating or being annotated **2** a critical or explanatory note or notes

an·nounce (ə nouns′) *vt.* **-nounced′, -nounc′ing** ⟦ME *announcen* < OFr *anoncier* < L *annuntiare*, to make known < *ad-*, to + *nuntiare*, to report < *nuntius*, messenger: see NUNCIO⟧ **1** to declare publicly; give notice of formally; proclaim **2** to say or tell **3** to make known the arrival of **4** to make known through the senses [footsteps *announced* his return] **5** *Radio, TV* to be an announcer for **—*vi.*** **1** to serve as a radio or television announcer ☆**2** to make known publicly one's candidacy or one's political endorsement of another: with *for* **—*SYN.*** DECLARE

an·nounce·ment (ə nouns′mənt) *n.* **1** an announcing or being announced **2** something announced **3** a written or printed notice [an engraved wedding *announcement*]

an·nounc·er (ə noun′sər) *n.* a person who announces; specif., one who introduces radio or television programs, identifies the station, reads the news, etc.

an·no ur·bis con·di·tae (an′ō ur′bis kän′di tē′, -tī′; än′-) ⟦L⟧ in a (specified) year from the founding of the city: the ancient Romans reckoned dates from Rome's founding, *c.* 753 B.C.

an·noy (ə noi′) *vt.* ⟦ME *anoien* < OFr *anoier* < VL *inodiare* < *in odio habere* (or *esse*), to have (or be) in hate: see ODIUM⟧ **1** to irritate, bother, or make somewhat angry, as by a repeated action, noise, etc. **2** to harm by repeated attacks; harry; molest **—*vi.*** to be annoying **—an·noy′er** *n.*

SYN.—**annoy** implies temporary disturbance of mind caused by something that displeases one or tries one's patience; **vex** implies a more serious source of irritation and greater disturbance, often intense worry; **irk** stresses a wearing down of one's patience by persistent annoyance; **bother** implies minor disturbance of one's peace of mind and may suggest mild perplexity or anxiety; to **tease** is to annoy by persistent mocking or playful fooling; **plague** suggests mental torment comparable to the physical suffering caused by an affliction **—*ANT.*** **comfort, soothe**

an·noy·ance (ə noi′əns) *n.* **1** an annoying or being annoyed **2** a thing or person that annoys

an·noy·ing (ə noi′iŋ) *adj.* irritating; vexing; bothersome **—an·noy′ing·ly** *adv.*

an·nu·al (an′yo͞o əl; -yool, -yəl) *adj.* ⟦ME & OFr *annuel* < LL *annualis*, a year old < L *annus*, year < IE **atnos* < base **at-*, to go, year > Goth *athnam* (dat. pl.), years, Sans *átati*, (he) goes⟧ **1** of or measured by a year **2** happening or appearing once a year; yearly **3** for a year's time, work, etc. [an *annual* wage] **4** lasting or living only one year or season, as some plants **—*n.*** **1** *a)* a book, magazine, or report published once a year *b)* YEARBOOK **2** a plant that lives only one year or season **—an′nu·al·ly** *adv.*

an·nu·al·ize (-īz) *vt.* **-ized′, -iz′ing** ⟦prec. + -IZE⟧ ☆to compute for lesser periods as though on the basis of a full year

annual ring any of the concentric rings seen in cross sections of the stems of most trees and shrubs: each ring is a layer of wood that normally is a year's growth

an·nu·i·tant (ə no͞o′ə tənt, -nyo͞o′-) *n.* a person receiving or entitled to receive an annuity

an·nu·i·tize (ə no͞o′ə tīz′, -nyo͞o′-) *vt.* to convert (a lump sum) into a future stream of payments under an annuity contract **—an·nu′i·ti·za′tion** *n.*

an·nu·i·ty (ə no͞o′ə tē, -nyo͞o′-) *n., pl.* **-ties** ⟦ME & OFr *annuite* < ML *annuitas* < L *annuus*, annual < *annus*: see ANNUAL⟧ **1** a payment of a fixed sum of money at regular intervals of time, esp. yearly **2** an investment yielding periodic payments during the annuitant's lifetime, for a stated number of years, or in perpetuity

an·nul (ə nul′) *vt.* **-nulled′, -nul′ling** ⟦ME *annullen* < OFr *anuller* < LL(Ec) *annullare*, to bring to nothing < L *ad-*, to + *nullum*, nothing, neut. of *nullus*: see NULL⟧ **1** to do away with; put an end to **2** to make no longer binding under the law; invalidate; cancel **—*SYN.*** ABOLISH

an·nu·lar (an′yə lər) *adj.* ⟦L *anularis* < *anulus*, a ring < *anus*: see ANUS⟧ of, like, or forming a ring **—*SYN.*** ROUND[1] **—an′nu·lar′i·ty** (-ler′ə tē) *n.* **—an′nu·lar·ly** *adv.*

annular eclipse an eclipse in which a ring of sunlight can be seen around the disk of the moon

annular ligament a circular ligament, esp. of the ankle joint, wrist joint, or inner ear

an·nu·late (an′yə lit, -lāt′) *adj.* ⟦L *anulatus* < *anulus*: see ANNULAR⟧ **1** provided or marked with rings; ringed **2** made up of rings Also **an′nu·lat′ed** (-lāt′əd)

an·nu·la·tion (an′yə lā′shən) *n.* **1** formation of rings **2** a ring or ringlike structure

an·nu·let (an′yə lit) *n.* ⟦< L *anulus*, a ring (see ANNULAR) + -ET⟧ **1** a small ring **2** *Archit.* a ringlike molding where the shaft of a column joins the capital

an·nul·ment (ə nul′mənt) *n.* **1** an annulling or being annulled **2** an invalidation, as of a marriage, by the decree of a court

an·nu·lus (an′yə ləs) *n., pl.* **-li′** (-lī′) or **-lus·es** ⟦L *annulus*, for *anulus*: see ANNULAR⟧ any ring or ringlike part, mark, etc.

an·nun·ci·ate (ə nun′sē āt′) *vt.* **-at′ed, -at′ing** ⟦< L *annuntiatus*, pp. of *annuntiare*, ANNOUNCE⟧ to announce

an·nun·ci·a·tion (ə nun′sē ā′shən) *n.* ⟦LL *annuntiatio*: see ANNOUNCE⟧ **1** an announcing or being announced **2** an announcement **—the Annunciation** **1** *Christian Theol.* the angel Gabriel's announcement to Mary that she was to give birth to Jesus: Luke 1:26-38 **2** *Eccles.* the church festival on March 25 commemorating this

an·nun·ci·a·tor (ə nun′sē āt′ər) *n.* ⟦LL(Ec) *annuntiator*⟧ **1** a person or thing that announces **2** an electric indicator, as a light or buzzer, used in hotels, offices, etc. to show the source of calls

Annunzio, Gabriele d′ *see* D'ANNUNZIO

an·nus hor·ri·bi·lis (an′əs hə rib′ə lis, än′-) ⟦ModL, horrible year, after fol.: used by Queen ELIZABETH II in ref. to the year 1992⟧ [*also in roman type*] a year of misfortune or disaster

an·nus mi·ra·bi·lis (an′əs mə räb′ə lis, än′-) *pl.* ***an·ni mi·ra·bi·les*** (an′ī′ mə räb′ə lēz′, än′-) ⟦ModL, lit., wonderful year⟧ a year regarded as pivotal, crucial, etc.

an·ode (an′ōd′) *n.* ⟦coined by Michael FARADAY < Gr *anodos*, a way up < *ana-*, up + *hodos*, way: see -ODE[1]⟧ **1** in an electroplating cell, the positively charged electrode, toward which current flows **2** in an electron tube, the principal electrode for collecting electrons, operated at a positive potential with respect to the cathode **3** in a battery that is a source of electric current, as a dry cell or storage battery, the negative electrode from which the electrons are released to the external circuit See CATHODE **—an·o·dal** (an ōd′′l) *adj.*, **an·od·ic** (an äd′ik)

an·o·dize (an′ə dīz′) *vt.* **-dized′, -diz′ing** to put a protective, often colored, oxide film on (a light metal) by an electrolytic process in which the metal serves as the anode

an·o·dyne (an′ə dīn′) *adj.* ⟦L *anodynus* < Gr *anōdynos* < *an-*, without + *odynē*, pain⟧ **1** relieving or lessening pain; soothing **2** lacking zest, vigor, etc.; bland; insipid **—*n.*** anything that relieves pain or soothes **—an′o·dyn′ic** (-din′ik) *adj.*

a·noint (ə noint′) *vt.* ⟦ME *anointen* < OFr *enoindre* < L *inunguere* < *in-*, on + *unguere*, to smear: see UNGUENT⟧ **1** to rub oil or ointment on **2** to put oil on in a ceremony of consecration **—a·noint′er** *n.* **—a·noint′ment** *n.*

Anointing of the Sick *R.C.Ch.* a sacrament in which a priest anoints with oil and prays for a person dying, in danger of death, or otherwise critically ill, infirm, or disturbed

a·no·le (ə nō′lē) *n.* any of a genus (*Anolis*, esp. *A. carolinensis*) of New World, tropical, arboreal lizards that can change color: see AMERICAN CHAMELEON

a·nom·a·lis·tic (ə näm′ə lis′tik) *adj.* **1** tending to be anomalous **2** of an anomaly

a·nom·a·lous (ə näm′ə ləs) *adj.* ⟦LL *anomalus* < Gr *anōmalos* < *an-*, not + *homalos* < *homos*, SAME⟧ **1** deviating from the regular arrangement, general rule, or usual method; abnormal **2** being or seeming to be inconsistent, contradictory, or improper **—*SYN.*** IRREGULAR **—a·nom′a·lous·ly** *adv.* **—a·nom′a·lous·ness** *n.*

a·nom·a·ly (ə näm′ə lē) *n., pl.* **-lies** ⟦L *anomalia* < Gr *anōmalia*, inequality: see prec. ⟧ **1** departure from the regular arrangement, general rule, or usual method; abnormality **2** anything anomalous **3** *Astron.* a measurement used for any orbiting body, as a planet's angular distance around its orbit from its perihelion, taken as if viewed from the sun

an·o·mie or **an·o·my** (an′ə mē) *n.* ⟦Fr < Gr *anomia*, lawlessness < *a-*, without + *nomos*, law: see -NOMY⟧ lack of purpose, identity, or ethical values in a person or in a society; rootlessness **—a·nom·ic** (ə näm′ik) *adj.*

a·non (ə nän′) *adv.* ⟦ME < OE *on an* acc., into one, together, straightway⟧ **1** [Archaic] immediately; at once **2** *a)* soon; shortly *b)* at another time: now nearly archaic or a self-conscious usage **—ever and anon** now and then

Anon or **anon** *abbrev.* anonymous

an·o·nym (an′ə nim′) *n.* ⟦Fr *anonyme* < LL *anonymus*, ANONYMOUS⟧ **1** an anonymous person **2** a pseudonym

an·o·nym·i·ty (an′ə nim′ə tē) *n.* the condition or fact of being anonymous

a·non·y·mous (ə nän′ə məs) *adj.* ⟦LL *anonymus* < Gr *anōnymos* < *an-*, without + *onyma*, NAME⟧ **1** with no name known or acknowledged **2** given, written, etc. by a person whose name is withheld or unknown **3** not easily distinguished from others or from one another because of a lack of individual features or character **—a·non′y·mous·ly** *adv.*

a·noph·e·les (ə näf′ə lēz′) *n.* ⟦ModL < Gr *anōphelēs*, harmful < *an-*, without + *ophelos*, use, help⟧ any of a genus (*Anopheles*) of mosquitoes that can carry and transmit various diseases, esp. malaria **—a·noph′e·line′** (-līn′, -lin) *adj.*

a·no·rak (an′ə rak′) *n.* ⟦Esk (Greenland) *ánorâq*⟧ a heavy jacket with a hood

an·o·rex·i·a (an′ə rek′sē ə) *n.* ⟦ModL < Gr < *an-*, without + *orexis*, a desire for < *oregein*, to reach after < IE base **reg-*: see RIGHT⟧ **1** lack of appetite for food **2** an eating disorder, chiefly in young women, characterized by aversion to food and obsession with weight loss, and manifested in self-induced starvation and excessive exercise, etc.: in full **anorexia ner·vo·sa** (nər vō′sə): cf. BULIMIA

an·o·rex·ic (an′ə rek′sik) *adj.* **1** suffering from anorexia **2** suppressing appetite for food **—*n.*** **1** an anorexic person **2** an anorexic drug Also **an′o·rec′tic** (-rek′tik) or **an′o·ret′ic** (-ret′ik)

an·or·thite (an ôr′thīt′) *n.* ⟦< Gr *an-*, not + *orthos*, straight (see ORTHO-) + -ITE[1]⟧ a white or grayish variety of plagioclase, $CaAl_2Si_2O_8$, found in basic igneous rocks **—an′or·thit′ic** (-thit′ik) *adj.*

an·or·tho·site (an ôr′thō sīt′; -thə-) *n.* ⟦< Fr *anorthose* < Gr *an-*, not + *orthos* (see prec.) + -ITE[1]⟧ a type of gabbro, usually light-colored, made up almost entirely of plagioclase feldspars, esp. labradorite

an·os·mi·a (an äz′mē ə, -äs′-) ***n.*** ⟦ModL < Gr *an-*, without + *osmē*, smell (see ODOR) + -IA⟧ total or partial loss of the sense of smell —**an·os′mic** (-mik) ***adj.***

an·oth·er (ə nuth′ər) ***adj.*** ⟦ME *an other*; OE uses solid *ōther* in same sense⟧ **1** one more; an additional [have *another* cup of tea] **2** a different; not the same [in *another* city, at *another* time] **3** one of the same sort as; some other [*another* Caesar] —***pron.*** **1** one additional **2** a different one [anger is one thing, but rage is *another*] **3** one of the same kind

A·nouilh (à no͞o′y′; *E* än wē′), **Jean** (zhän) 1910-87; Fr. playwright

an·ov·u·la·tion (an′äv′yo͞o lā′shən, -yə-; an′ō′vyo͞o-, -vyə-) ***n.*** the failure of an ovary to release an egg at the appropriate time —**an′ov′u·lar** (-lər) ***adj.***, **an′ov′u·la·to′ry** (-tôr′ē)

an·ox·e·mi·a (an′äks ē′mē ə) ***n.*** ⟦AN-[1] (var. of A-[2]) + OX(YGEN) + -EMIA⟧ a reduction in the normal amount of oxygen in the blood, as at high altitudes —**an′ox·e′mic** (-mik) ***adj.***

an·ox·i·a (an äks′ē ə) ***n.*** ⟦AN-[1] (var. of A-[2]) + OX(YGEN) + -IA⟧ *Med.* **1** total deprivation of oxygen **2** HYPOXIA —**an·ox′ic** (-ik) ***adj.***

ans *abbrev.* answer

an·sate (an′sāt′) ***adj.*** ⟦L *ansatus* < *ansa*, a handle < IE **ansā*, noose > Ger *öse*, eyelet⟧ having a handle or handlelike part

ansate cross ANKH

An·schluss (än′shlo͝os) ***n.*** ⟦Ger, addition, union < *anschliessen*, to join⟧ [*often in roman type*] political or economic union; specif., the annexation of Austria by Germany in 1938

An·selm (an′selm′), Saint (1033-1109); theologian, philosopher, & archbishop of Canterbury (1093-1109), born in Italy: his day is April 21

an·ser·ine (an′sər īn′, -in) ***adj.*** ⟦L *anserinus* < *anser*, GOOSE⟧ **1** of or like a goose **2** stupid; foolish

An·shan (än′shän′) city in NE China, in central Liaoning province

ANSI (an′sē) *trademark* American National Standards Institute

an·swer (an′sər, än′-) ***n.*** ⟦ME *andsware* < OE *andswaru* < *and-*, against + *swerian*, SWEAR⟧ **1** something said or written in return to a question, argument, letter, etc. **2** any act in response or retaliation [his *answer* was a well-aimed blow] **3** one that is a counterpart or equivalent of another, often as the result of imitation **4** a solution to a problem **5** *Law* a written pleading by which the defendant replies to the plaintiff's charges; defense **6** *Music* in a fugue, the second or fourth restatement of the subject in another voice and transposed to another key, usually at the interval of a fourth or fifth —***vi.*** **1** *a)* to reply in words, by an action, etc. *b)* to respond in kind (*with*) [the team *answered* with a touchdown of their own] **2** to react to a stimulus; respond (*to*) [the horse *answered* to its rider's touch] **3** to serve the purpose; be sufficient **4** to be responsible or liable (*to* a person *for* an action, accusation, etc.) **5** to be in conformity; correspond (*to*) [he *answers* to the description] —***vt.*** **1** *a)* to reply to in words, by an action, etc. *b)* to say or write in reply *c)* to respond in kind to **2** to respond to the signal of (a telephone, doorbell, etc.) **3** to fulfill satisfactorily; comply with; be sufficient for; serve [the makeshift tent *answered* their purpose] **4** to defend oneself against (an accusation, criticism, etc.); refute **5** to agree with; conform to; suit [he *answers* the description] **6** [Obs.] to atone for —**answer back** [Informal] to reply forcefully, rudely, or impertinently; talk back

SYN.—**answer** implies a saying, writing, or acting in return, as required by the situation or by courtesy [to *answer* a letter, the phone, etc.]; **respond** implies an appropriate reaction made voluntarily or spontaneously to that which serves as a stimulus [to *respond* to an appeal]; **reply** in its strictest application refers to an answer that satisfies in detail the question asked; **retort** suggests a reply, esp. one that is sharp or witty, provoked by a charge or criticism; **rejoin** implies an answer, originally to a reply, now often to an objection —***ANT.*** **question, ask, inquire**

an·swer·a·ble (an′sər ə bəl) ***adj.*** **1** subject to being called to account; responsible **2** that can be answered or shown to be wrong [an *answerable* argument] **3** [Archaic] in proportion; corresponding —***SYN.*** RESPONSIBLE —**an′swer·a·bil′i·ty *n.***

answering machine an electronic device using recording tape or a semiconductor chip to take or give telephone messages automatically: also [Brit.] **an·swer·phone** (an′sər fōn′) ***n.***

answering service a business whose function is to answer telephone calls for its clients and transmit messages to them

ant[1] (ant) ***n.*** ⟦ME *ante*, *amete* < OE *æmet(t)e*: akin to OHG *âmeiza* < *â-*, off + *meizen*, Goth *maitan*, OE **mætan*, to cut; hence, lit., "the cutter off"⟧ any of a widespread family (Formicidae) of black, brown, or red hymenopteran insects, generally wingless, that live in colonies with a complex division of labor by castes, including workers, males, and a queen

worker ant

ant[2] *abbrev.* **1** antenna **2** antonym

Ant *abbrev.* **1** Antarctica **2** antonym

an't (ant, änt, ānt) *contraction* [Chiefly Dial. or Brit. Informal] are not: also variously heard at different levels of usage as an assimilated form for *am not*, and as a contracted form for *is not*, *have not*, and *has not*: see also AIN'T, AMN'T

ant- (ant) *prefix* ANTI-: used before a vowel

-ant (ənt, ′nt) ⟦ME < OFr < L *-antem* or *-entem*, acc. prp. ending⟧ *suffix* **1** *forming adjectives* that has, shows, or does [*defiant, radiant*] **2** *forming nouns* a person or thing that ___s [*occupant, accountant*]

an·ta (an′tə) ***n.***, *pl.* **-tae′** (-tē′) or **-tas** ⟦L⟧ *Archit.* a pilaster built out from the end of a wall, as on either side of a doorway

ANTA (an′tə) *abbrev.* American National Theatre and Academy

ant·ac·id (ant′as′id) ***adj.*** ⟦ANT(I)- + ACID⟧ that neutralizes acids; counteracting acidity —***n.*** an antacid substance, such as sodium bicarbonate

An·tae·us (an tē′əs) ***n.*** ⟦L < Gr *Antaios*⟧ *Gr. Myth.* a giant wrestler who is invincible as long as he is touching his mother, the earth —**An·tae′an *adj.***

an·tag·o·nism (an tag′ə niz′əm) ***n.*** ⟦Gr *antagōnisma* < *antagōnizesthai*: see ANTAGONIZE⟧ **1** the state of being opposed or hostile to another or to each other; opposition or hostility **2** an opposing force, principle, etc.; specif., a mutually opposing action that can take place between organisms, muscles, drugs, etc. —***SYN.*** ENMITY

antae

an·tag·o·nist (an tag′ə nist) ***n.*** **1** a person who opposes or competes with another; adversary; opponent **2** a muscle that counteracts or opposes the action of another muscle (called the *agonist*) **3** a substance in the body, or a drug, that counteracts or blocks the effect of another substance or drug (called the *agonist*) —***SYN.*** OPPONENT

an·tag·o·nis·tic (an tag′ə nis′tik) ***adj.*** showing antagonism; acting in opposition —**an·tag′o·nis′ti·cal·ly *adv.***

an·tag·o·nize (an tag′ə nīz′) ***vt.*** **-nized′**, **-niz′ing** ⟦Gr *antagōnizesthai*, to struggle against < *anti-*, against + *agōnizesthai*: see AGONIZE⟧ **1** to oppose or counteract **2** to incur the dislike of; make an enemy of

An·ta·kya (än′tə kyä′) *Turk. name for* ANTIOCH (ancient Syria)

ant·al·ka·li (ant al′kə lī′) ***n.***, *pl.* **-lies′** or **-lis′** a substance that neutralizes an alkali or counteracts alkalinity

ant·al·ka·line (-lin′, -līn′) ***adj.*** neutralizing an alkali or counteracting alkalinity —***n.*** an antalkali

An·tal·ya (än′təl yä′) seaport in SW Turkey, on the Mediterranean

An·ta·na·na·ri·vo (an′tə nan′ə rē′vō′) capital of Madagascar, in the central part

Antarc *abbrev.* Antarctica

ant·arc·tic (ant ärk′tik, -är′-) ***adj.*** ⟦ME *antarik* < OFr *antartique* < L *antarcticus* < Gr *antarktikos*, southern < *anti-*, opposite + *arktikos*, ARCTIC⟧ of or near the South Pole or the region around it —**the Antarctic** the region including Antarctica & the Antarctic Ocean

Ant·arc·ti·ca (ant ärk′ti kə, -är′-) land area about the South Pole, completely covered by an ice shelf: *c.* 5,100,000 sq mi (13,209,000 sq km): now usually classified as a continent

Antarctic Circle [*also* **a- c-**] an imaginary circle parallel to the equator, *c.* 66°34′ south of it

Antarctic Ocean popularly, the S parts of the Atlantic, Pacific, and Indian oceans surrounding Antarctica

Antarctic Peninsula peninsula in Antarctica, extending toward South America: *c.* 800 mi (1,287 km) long

An·tar·es (an ter′ēz′) ***n.*** ⟦Gr *Antarēs* < *anti-*, like + *Arēs*, Gr god of war: so named because of its color⟧ a red, supergiant, binary, variable star, the brightest star in the constellation Scorpius: magnitude, 1.06

ant bear **1** a large, ant-eating, edentate mammal (*Myrmecophaga tridactyla*) of Central America and tropical South America, with a long, shaggy tail; giant anteater **2** AARDVARK

ant cow any aphid from which ants get honeydew

☆**an·te** (an′tē) ***n.*** ⟦L, before⟧ **1** *Poker* the stake that each player must put into the pot before receiving cards **2** [Informal] the amount one must pay as one's share — ***vt., vi.*** **-ted** or **-teed**, **-te·ing** **1** *Poker* to put in (one's ante) **2** [Informal] to pay (one's share) —**ante up** to ante; pay —**up** (or **raise**) **the ante** [Informal] to increase the seriousness or risk, as in a competition

an·te- (an′ti, -tə, -tē) ⟦< L *ante*, before⟧ *prefix* **1** before, prior (to) [*antecede, ante-*Victorian] **2** before, in front (of) [*anteroom, antepenult*]

ant·eat·er (ant′ēt′ər) ***n.*** any of several mammals of various orders that feed mainly on ants, as the pangolins, echidnas, and esp. ant bears: anteaters have a long, sticky tongue and a long snout

☆**an·te·bel·lum** (an′tē bel′əm, -ti-) ***adj.*** ⟦L *ante bellum*⟧ before the war; specif., before the American Civil War

an·te·cede (an′tə sēd′) ***vt., vi.*** **-ced′ed**, **-ced′ing** ⟦L *antecedere*: see ANTE- & CEDE⟧ to go before in rank, place, or time; precede

an·te·ced·ence (an′tə sed′ns) ***n.*** ⟦L *antecedentia*⟧ **1** the act of going before or the fact of being prior; precedence **2** *Astron.* retrograde motion

an·te·ced·en·cy (an′tə sēd′n sē) ***n.*** being antecedent

an·te·ced·ent (an′tə sēd′nt) ***adj.*** ⟦ME & OFr < L *antecedens*, prp. of *antecedere*, ANTECEDE⟧ going or coming before in time, order, or logic; prior; previous; preceding —***n.*** **1** any happening or thing prior to another **2** anything logically preceding **3** [*pl.*] one's ancestry, past life, training, etc. **4** *Gram.* the word, phrase, or clause to which a pronoun refers ["man" is the *antecedent* of "who" in "the man who spoke"] **5** *Logic* the part of a conditional proposition that states the condition **6** *Math.* the first term or numerator of a ratio: distinguished from CONSEQUENT —***SYN.*** CAUSE, PREVIOUS —**an′te·ced′ent·ly *adv.***

an·te·ces·sor (an′tə ses′ər) ***n.*** ⟦ME *antecessour* < L *antecessor* < pp. of *antecedere*, ANTECEDE⟧ [Rare] a predecessor

an·te·cham·ber (an′tē chām′bər, -ti-) ***n.*** ⟦Fr *antichambre* < *anti-* (for L *ante*, before) + *chambre*, CHAMBER⟧ a smaller room leading into a larger or main room

an·te·choir (-kwīr′) *n.* a partially or wholly enclosed part of a chapel in front of the choir

an·te·date (an′ti dāt′) *vt.* **-dat′ed, -dat′ing 1** to put a date on that is earlier than the actual date [to *antedate* a check] **2** to come or happen at an earlier date than; come before **3** to make happen earlier; accelerate **4** to set an earlier date for **5** [Archaic] to anticipate —*n.* a date fixed for a historical event, writing, etc. that is earlier than the actual one

an·te·di·lu·vi·an (an′tē də lo͞o′vē ən, -ti-) *adj.* ⟦< ANTE- + L *diluvium*, a flood (see DILUVIUM) + -AN⟧ **1** of the time before the biblical Flood **2** very old, old-fashioned, or primitive —*n.* an antediluvian person or thing

an·te·fix (an′ti fiks′) *n., pl.* **-fix′es** ⟦L *antefixus*: see ANTE- & FIX⟧ a small decorative fixture put at the eaves of a roof of a classic building to hide the ends of the tiles —**an′te·fix′al** *adj.*

an·te·lope (an′tə lōp′) *n., pl.* **-lopes′** or **-lope′** ⟦ME & OFr *antelop*, a fabulous horned animal < ML *antalopus* < MGr *antholops*, deer⟧ **1** *a)* any of a group of swift, bovid ruminants usually living in wild herds on the plains of Africa and Asia, including the gnu, impala, and kudu ☆*b)* PRONGHORN **2** leather made from the hide of an antelope

an·te·me·rid·i·an (an′tē mə rid′ē ən, -ti-) *adj.* ⟦L *antemeridianus* < *ante-*, before + *meridianus*, of midday: see MERIDIAN⟧ before noon; of or in the forenoon [an *antemeridian* repast]

an·te me·ri·di·em (an′tē mə rid′ē əm, -ti-) ⟦L⟧ before noon: abbrev. *A.M., a.m., AM,* or *am*

an·te·mor·tem (an′tē môr′təm) *adj.* ⟦L *ante mortem*, before death⟧ made or done just before one's death

an·te·na·tal (an′tē nāt′'l) *adj.* before birth; prenatal

an·ten·na (an ten′ə) *n.* ⟦L, earlier *antemna*, sail yard⟧ **1** *pl.* **-nae** (-ē) or **-nas** either of a pair of movable, jointed sense organs on the head of most arthropods, as insects, crabs, or lobsters; feeler **2** *pl.* **-nas** *Radio, TV a)* an arrangement of wires, metal rods, etc. used in sending and receiving electromagnetic waves; aerial *b)* a single rod or wire acting as such an antenna for a small television or radio receiver, cell phone, etc.

an·ten·nule (an ten′yo͞ol′) *n.* ⟦prec. + -ULE⟧ *Zool.* a small antenna, esp. a crustacean's secondary, smaller antenna

an·te·pen·di·um (an′ti pen′dē əm) *n., pl.* **-di·a** (-ə) or **-di·ums** ⟦ML < L *ante*, before + *pendere*, hang⟧ a screen or veil hanging from the front of an altar, pulpit, etc.

an·te·pe·nult (an′tē pē′nult′, -ti-) *n.* ⟦contr. < L (*syllaba*) *antepaenultima* < *ante-*, before + *paenultima*, the last but one < *paene*, almost + fem. of *ultimus*, last⟧ the third last syllable in a word, as *-lu-* in *an·te·di·lu·vi·an*

an·te·pe·nul·ti·mate (an′tē pē nul′tə mət, -pi-; -ti-) *adj.* ⟦< prec. (by assoc. with ULTIMATE)⟧ third last; third from the end —*n.* **1** anything third from the end **2** an antepenult

an·te·ri·or (an tir′ē ər) *adj.* ⟦L, compar. of *ante*, before⟧ **1** at or toward the front; forward; specif., ventral: opposed to POSTERIOR **2** coming before in time, order, or logic; previous; earlier **3** *Bot.* on the side away from the main stem —**an·te′ri·or·ly** *adv.*

an·te·room (an′tē ro͞om′, -ti-) *n.* a room leading to a larger or more important room; waiting room

an·te·type (an′tē tīp′, -ti-) *n.* an earlier form; prototype

an·te·ver·sion (an′tē vʉr′zhən, -shən; -ti-) *n.* ⟦LL *anteversio* < L *anteversus*, pp. of *antevertere*, fol.⟧ an abnormal, forward displacement of a bodily organ, esp. the uterus

an·te·vert (an′tē vʉrt′, -ti-) *vt.* ⟦L *antevertere* < *ante-*, before + *vertere*, to turn: see VERSE⟧ to cause anteversion of

ant·he·li·on (ant hē′lē ən, an thē′-) *n., pl.* **-li·a** (-ə) or **-li·ons** ⟦ModL < Gr *anthēlion* < *anti-*, against + *hēlios*, SUN[1]⟧ a rarely seen, hazy white spot at the same altitude as the sun, but opposite in the sky, caused by a reflection from the atmosphere, snow, or ice

ant·he·lix (ant hē′liks′) *n., pl.* **-he′lix·es′** (-hē′liks iz′) or **-hel′i·ces′** (-hel′i sēz′) ANTIHELIX

ant·hel·min·tic (ant′hel min′tik, an′thel-) *adj.* ⟦ANT(I)- + Gr *helmins* (gen. *helminthos*), worm + -IC⟧ killing or ejecting intestinal worms —*n.* an anthelmintic medicine

an·them (an′thəm) *n.* ⟦ME *antefne* < OE *antefn* < ML *antifona, antiphona* < Gr *antiphōna* < *antiphōnos*, sounding back < *anti-*, over against + *phōnē*, voice: see PHONO-⟧ **1** [Archaic] a religious song sung antiphonally **2** a religious choral song usually based on words from the Bible **3** a song of praise or devotion, as to a nation, college, etc. **4** any well-known song or recording regarded as being inspirational or iconic [a rock *anthem* played often by marching bands]

an·the·mi·on (an thē′mē ən) *n., pl.* **-mi·a** (-ə) ⟦Gr, a flower < *anthos*: see ANTHO-⟧ a flat decoration of floral or leaf forms, used in painting and relief sculpture

an·ther (an′thər) *n.* ⟦Fr *anthère* < ModL *anthera* (in L, medicine composed of flowers) < Gr *anthēros*, blooming < IE **andher-*, a sprout, stalk < base **andh-*: see ANTHO-⟧ the part of a stamen that produces and releases the pollen

an·ther·id·i·um (an′thər id′ē əm) *n., pl.* **-id′i·a** (-ə) ⟦ModL < *anthera* (see prec.) + Gr dim. suffix *-idion*⟧ in flowerless and seedless plants (cryptogams), the organ in which the male sex cells are developed —**an′ther·id′i·al** *adj.*

an·ther·o·zo·id (an′thər ə zō′id, an′thər ə zoid′) *n.* ⟦< ModL *anthera*, ANTHER + -O- + ZO(O)ID⟧ a spermatozoid developing in the antheridium

an·the·sis (an thē′sis) *n.* ⟦Gr *anthēsis* < *anthein*, to bloom < *anthos*: see ANTHO-⟧ the state of full bloom in a flower

ant·hill (ant′hil′) *n.* the soil carried away by ants in digging their underground nest, heaped in a mound around its entrance

an·tho- (an′thō, -thə) ⟦< Gr *anthos*, a flower < IE **andhos*, flower, vegetation < base **andh-*, to sprout, bloom⟧ *combining form* flower [*anthocarpous*]

an·tho·car·pous (an′thō kär′pəs, -thə-) *adj.* designating or of a false fruit, as the pineapple or strawberry, formed from the separate ovaries of one or several blossoms

an·tho·cy·a·nin (an′thō sī′ə nin′) *n.* ⟦ANTHO- + Gr *kyan(os)*, blue (see CYANO-) + -IN[1]⟧ a water-soluble, reddish or blue pigment in flowers, plants, and some insects: also **an′tho·cy′an** (-sī′ən)

an·tho·di·um (an thō′dē əm) *n., pl.* **-di·a** (-ə) ⟦ModL < Gr *anthōdēs*, flowerlike < *anthos*: see ANTHO-⟧ the flower head or bracts of a composite plant, as in daisies or asters

an·thol·o·gize (an thäl′ə jīz′) *vi.* **-gized′, -giz′ing** to make anthologies —*vt.* to make an anthology of or include in an anthology —**an·thol′o·gist** (-jist) *n.*, **an·thol′o·giz′er**

an·thol·o·gy (an thäl′ə jē) *n., pl.* **-gies** ⟦Gr *anthologia*, a garland, collection of short poems < *anthologos*, gathering flowers < *anthos* (see ANTHO-) + *legein*, to gather (see LOGIC)⟧ a published collection of poems, stories, songs, excerpts, etc. —**an·tho·log·i·cal** (an′thə läj′i kəl) *adj.*

An·tho·ny[1] (an′thə nē; *Brit usually* -tə-) *n.* ⟦with unhistoric *-h-* < L *Antonius*, name of a Roman gens⟧ a masculine name: dim. *Tony;* var. *Antony;* equiv. L. *Antonius*, It. & Sp. *Antonio*, Fr. *Antoine*, Ger. & Russ. *Anton;* fem. *Antonia*

An·tho·ny[2] (an′thə nē; *for 1, 2, 3, also,* -tə-) **1** Saint (A.D. 251?-356?); Egypt. hermit: founder of Christian monasticism: his day is Jan. 17: called *the Great* **2** Saint (1195-1231); Franciscan friar in France & Italy, born in Portugal: his day is June 13: also called **Saint Anthony of Padua** **3 Mark** *see* ANTONY[2], Mark **4 Susan B(rownell)** 1820-1906; U.S. leader in the movement for women's suffrage

an·tho·phore (an′thō fôr′, -thə-) *n.* ⟦ANTHO- + -PHORE⟧ an elongated stalk between the sepals and the petals of some flowers that supports the flowering parts

-an·thous (an′thəs) ⟦< Gr *anthos*: see ANTHO-⟧ *combining form forming adjectives* having flowers (of a specified kind or number) [*monanthous*]

an·tho·zo·an (an′thə zō′ən) *n.* ⟦< ModL *Anthozoa* (see ANTHO- & -ZOA) + -AN⟧ any of a class (Anthozoa) of sessile saltwater cnidarians with a dominant polyp stage, including corals, sea anemones, and gorgonians; actinozoan —*adj.* of the anthozoans

an·thra·cene (an′thrə sēn′) *n.* ⟦< Gr *anthrax*, coal + -ENE⟧ a crystalline cyclic hydrocarbon, $C_6H_4(CH)_2C_6H_4$, a product of coal-tar distillation used in making alizarin dyes and as a detector of radiation

an·thra·cite (an′thrə sīt′) *n.* ⟦Gr *anthrakitis*, kind of coal < *anthrax*, coal⟧ a shiny black, hard, metamorphic coal that contains a low percentage of volatile matter and burns with a smokeless flame: also called *hard coal*: see BITUMINOUS COAL —**an′thra·cit′ic** (-sit′ik) *adj.*

an·thrac·nose (an thrak′nōs′) *n.* ⟦< Gr *anthrax*, coal, carbuncle + *nosos*, disease⟧ any of various fungus diseases of plants, in which roundish dead spots appear chiefly on leaves or fruit

an·thra·coid (an′thrə koid′) *adj.* resembling anthrax

an·thra·co·sis (an′thrə kō′sis) *n.* ⟦ModL < Gr *anthrax*, coal + -OSIS⟧ BLACK LUNG (DISEASE)

an·thra·nil·ic acid (an′thrə nil′ik) ⟦ANTHR(ACENE) + ANIL(INE) + -IC⟧ a yellow crystalline compound, $NH_2C_6H_4COOH$, used in the manufacture of dyes, drugs, etc.

an·thra·qui·none (an′thrə kwi nōn′, -kwin′ōn′) *n.* ⟦ANTHRA(CENE) + QUINONE⟧ a yellow crystalline ketone, $C_6H_4(CO)_2C_6H_4$, produced from anthracene by oxidation or the reaction of phthalic anhydride with benzene: it is used in the manufacture of certain dyes and dye intermediates

an·thrax (an′thraks′) *n., pl.* **-thra·ces′** (-thrə sēz′) ⟦ME *antrax* < L *anthrax*, virulent ulcer < Gr, (burning) coal, hence ulcer, carbuncle⟧ **1** an infectious hemorrhagic disease of wild and domesticated animals, esp. cattle and sheep, that is caused by a bacillus (*Bacillus anthracis*) and can be transmitted to people: it is characterized by black pustules **2** any such pustule **3** BLACKLEG (sense 1)

anthrop *abbrev.* **1** anthropological **2** anthropology

an·throp·ic principle (an thräp′ik) ⟦< *anthropic* < Gr *anthrōpikos*, human (adj.) < *anthrōpos*: see fol.⟧ a cosmological theory according to which the universe is so constituted as to ensure the emergence of conscious beings

an·thro·po- (an′thrə pō′, -pə) ⟦< Gr *anthrōpos*, man, orig., ? one with bearded face < **anthro-* (< ? IE **andher-*: see ANTHER) + *ōps*, face, EYE⟧ *combining form* man, human [*anthropology*]: also, before a vowel, **an·throp-** (an′thrəp)

an·thro·po·cen·tric (an′thrə pō′sen′trik, -pə-) *adj.* ⟦prec. + -CENTRIC⟧ **1** that considers humankind as the central focus, or final goal, of the universe **2** conceiving of everything in the universe in terms of human values

an·thro·po·gen·e·sis (an′thrə pō′jen′ə sis) *n.* the study of man's origin and development: also **an·thro·pog·e·ny** (an′thrō päj′ə nē, -thrə-) —**an′thro·po′ge·net′ic** (-pō′jə net′ik) *adj.*

an·thro·po·gen·ic (an′thrə pō′jen′ik) *adj.* **1** of anthropogenesis **2** caused by man, as air pollution

an·thro·pog·ra·phy (an′thrō päg′rə fē, -thrə-) *n.* the branch of anthropology that deals with the distribution of humans according to their physical characteristics, languages, etc.

an·thro·poid (an′thrə poid′) *adj.* ⟦Gr *anthrōpoeidēs*: see ANTHROPO- & -OID⟧ 1 resembling a human 2 apelike [a brutish man with *anthropoid* features] —*n.* any of certain highly developed primates, esp. the chimpanzee, gorilla, orangutan, and gibbon: in some classification systems, any of a suborder (Anthropoidea) of primates —**an′thro·poi′dal** *adj.*

an·thro·pol·o·gist (an′thrō päl′ə jist, -thrə-) *n.* a person who specializes in anthropology

an·thro·pol·o·gy (an′thrō päl′ə jē, -thrə-) *n.* ⟦ANTHROPO- + -LOGY⟧ the study of humans, esp. of the variety, physical and cultural characteristics, distribution, customs, social relationships, etc. of humanity —**an′thro·po·log′i·cal** (-pō läj′i kəl, -pə-) *adj.*, **an′thro·po·log′ic** —**an′thro·po·log′i·cal·ly** *adv.*

an·thro·pom·e·try (an′thrō päm′ə trē, -thrə-) *n.* a branch of anthropology dealing with measurement of the human body to determine differences in individuals, groups, etc.: it is used in medicine, space programs, archaeology, etc. —**an′thro·po·met′ric** (-pō mə′trik, -pə-) *adj.*, **an′thro·po·met′ri·cal** —**an′thro·po·met′ri·cal·ly** *adv.*

an·thro·po·mor·phic (an′thrə pō′môr′fik, -pə-) *adj.* of, characterized by, or resulting from anthropomorphism —**an′thro·po′mor′phi·cal·ly** *adv.*

an·thro·po·mor·phism (an′thrə pō′môr′fiz′əm, -pə-) *n.* the attributing of human shape or characteristics to a god, animal, or inanimate thing —**an′thro·po·mor′phist** (-fist) *n.*

an·thro·po·mor·phize (-môr′fīz′) *vt., vi.* **-phized′, -phiz′ing** to attribute human shape or characteristics to (a god, animal, etc.)

an·thro·po·mor·pho·sis (an′thrə pō′môr′fə sis, -pə-) *n.* ⟦ANTHROPO- + (META)MORPHOSIS⟧ a changing into human form

an·thro·po·mor·phous (an′thrə pō′môr′fəs, -pə-) *adj.* ⟦Gr *anthrōpomorphos* < *anthrōpos* (see ANTHROPO-) + *morphē*, form, shape⟧ having human shape and appearance

an·thro·pop·a·thy (an′thrō päp′ə thē, -thrə-) *n.* ⟦ML *anthropopathia* < Gr *anthrōpopatheia*, humanity: see ANTHROPO- & -PATHY⟧ the attributing of human feelings and passions to a god, animal, etc.: also **an′thro·pop′a·thism′** (-thiz′əm)

an·thro·poph·a·gi (an′thrō päf′ə jī′, -thrə-) *pl.n., sing.* **-a·gus** (-ə gəs) ⟦L, pl. of *anthropophagus* < Gr *anthrōpophagos*, a man-eater < *anthrōpos* (see ANTHROPO-) + *phagos* (see -PHAGOUS)⟧ cannibals

an·thro·poph·a·gite (-jīt′) *n.* ⟦see prec.⟧ a cannibal

an·thro·poph·a·gy (an′thrō päf′ə jē, -thrə-) *n.* ⟦see ANTHROPOPHAGI⟧ cannibalism —**an′thro·poph′a·gous** (-päf′ə gəs) *adj.*, **an·thro·po·phag·ic** (an′thrə pō′faj′ik, -pə-)

an·thro·pos·o·phy (an′thrō päs′ə fē, -thrə-) *n.* ⟦ANTHROPO- + -SOPHY: orig., knowledge of human nature; used for Ger *Anthroposophie*⟧ a religious or mystical system or movement similar to theosophy, founded by Rudolf Steiner about 1912 —**an·thro·po·soph·i·cal** (an′thrə pō′säf′i kəl, -pə-) *adj.*

an·thu·ri·um (an thyoor′ē əm, -thoor′-) *n.* ⟦ModL < Gr *anthos* (see ANTHO-) + *oura*, tail (see URO-²)⟧ any of a genus (*Anthurium*) of tropical American plants of the arum family, having a spadix surrounded at the base by a flaring, heart-shaped, white or colored spathe

an·ti (an′tī′, -tē) *n., pl.* **-tis′** ⟦< fol., in various compounds⟧ [Informal] a person opposed to some policy, proposal, action, etc. —*prep.* [Informal] opposed to; against

an·ti- (an′ti′, -tē, -ti, -tə) ⟦Gr *anti-*, *ant-* < *anti*, against < IE **anti*, facing, opposite, near (> L *ante*, opposite, before) < base **ant-s*, front, forehead⟧ *prefix* 1 against, hostile to, opposed to [*antilabor, antislavery*] 2 that counteracts, that operates against [*antiaircraft*] 3 that prevents, cures, or neutralizes [*antitoxin*] 4 opposite, reverse [*antiperistalsis*] 5 rivaling [*antipope*] 6 having the superficial aspect, but not the usual characteristics, of [*antihero*]

an·ti·a·bor·tion (an′tī ə bôr′shən, -tē-) *adj.* opposed to a legal right to obtain an abortion —**an′ti·a·bor′tion·ist** *n.*

an·ti·air·craft (-er′kraft′) *adj.* used for defense against hostile aircraft [an *antiaircraft* gun]

an·ti·ar (an′tē är′) *n.* ⟦Javanese *antjar*⟧ 1 the upas tree of Java 2 a poison made from its gum resin: also called **an′ti·a·rin′** (-tē ə rin′)

an·ti·bac·te·ri·al (an′tī bak tir′ē əl; an′tē-, an′ti-) *adj.* that destroys bacteria or inhibits their growth —*n.* any antibacterial drug or medicine

an·ti·bal·lis·tic missile (-bə lis′tik) a missile intended to intercept and destroy a ballistic missile in flight: see GUIDED MISSILE

an·ti·bar·y·on (-bar′ē än′) *n.* an antiparticle of the baryon, as an antineutron, antiproton, or antihyperon

an·ti·bi·o·sis (-bī ō′sis) *n.* ⟦ModL < ANTI- + -BIOSIS⟧ *Biol.* an association between organisms that is harmful to one of them, as a fungus producing an antibiotic that inhibits neighboring bacteria

☆**an·ti·bi·ot·ic** (-bī ät′ik, -bē-) *adj.* 1 of antibiosis 2 destroying bacteria and other microorganisms or inhibiting their growth 3 of antibiotics —*n.* any of certain chemical substances produced by various microorganisms, specif. bacteria, fungi, and actinomycetes, and having the capacity, in dilute solutions, to inhibit the growth of or to destroy bacteria and other microorganisms: the antibiotics, including penicillin, streptomycin, and tetracycline, are used in the treatment of various infectious diseases

☆**an·ti·bod·y** (an′ti bäd′ē, -tə-) *n., pl.* **-bod′ies** ⟦transl. of Ger *antikörper* < *anti-*, ANTI- + *körper*, body⟧ a specialized protein produced by certain lymphocytes, esp. in response to the presence of an antigen, to neutralize, thus creating immunity to, specific antigens; immunoglobulin

an·ti·bus·ing (an′tī bus′iŋ, -tē-) *adj.* opposed to the court-ordered busing of schoolchildren as a means of desegregation

an·tic (an′tik) *adj.* ⟦It *antico* < L *antiquus*: see ANTIQUE⟧ 1 [Archaic] fantastic and queer; grotesque: also **an′tick** 2 odd and funny; ludicrous —*n.* 1 a playful, silly, or ludicrous act, trick, etc.; prank: *usually used in pl.* 2 [Archaic] a clown or buffoon

an·ti·cat·a·lyst (an′tī kat′ə list′, -tē-, -ti-) *n.* a substance that slows down a chemical reaction by acting directly on the catalyst

an·ti·cath·ode (-kath′ōd′) *n.* in an X-ray tube, the piece opposite the cathode, serving as the target for the cathode's discharge

an·ti·chlor (an′ti klôr′) *n.* ⟦ANTI- + CHLOR(INE)⟧ any substance for removing excess hypochlorite or chlorine from textiles or other substances that have been bleached

an·ti-choice (an′tē chois′, -tī-) *adj.* opposed to the legal right to obtain an abortion; pro-life: used disparagingly by pro-choice advocates

an·ti·cho·lin·er·gic (an′tī kō′lin ʉr′jik; -tē-, -ti-) *adj.* ⟦ANTI- + CHOLINERGIC⟧ having the ability to retard or block the activity of organs that receive their nerve impulses through the parasympathetic nervous system by opposing the action of acetylcholine —*n.* an anticholinergic drug, as atropine

an·ti·cho·lin·es·ter·ase (-es′tər ās′) *n.* a substance that inhibits the action of a cholinesterase, as the drug physostigmine or the insecticide parathion

an·ti·christ (an′ti krīst′, -tī-) *n.* ⟦ME *anticrist* < OFr *antecrist* < LL(Ec) *antichristus* < Gr(Ec) *antichristos* < *anti-*, against + *Christos*, Christ⟧ 1 an opponent of or disbeliever in Christ 2 [A-] *Bible* the great antagonist of Christ, expected to spread universal evil before the end of the world but finally to be conquered at Christ's second coming: 1 John 2:18 3 a false Christ

an·tic·i·pant (an tis′ə pənt) *adj.* ⟦L *anticipans*, prp. of *anticipare*: see fol.⟧ expecting; anticipating: with *of* —*n.* a person who anticipates

an·tic·i·pate (an tis′ə pāt′) *vt.* **-pat′ed, -pat′ing** ⟦< L *anticipatus*, pp. of *anticipare* < *ante-*, before + **capare* < *capere*, to take: see HAVE⟧ 1 to look forward to; expect [to *anticipate* a pleasant vacation] 2 to make happen earlier; precipitate 3 to prevent by action in advance; forestall [to *anticipate* an opponent's blows] 4 to foresee (a command, wish, etc.) and perform in advance [to *anticipate* a request] 5 to use or enjoy in advance [to *anticipate* a legacy] 6 to be ahead of in doing or achieving [did the Vikings *anticipate* Columbus in discovering America?] 7 to pay (a debt) before due —*vi.* to speak of or consider a matter prematurely —SYN. EXPECT —**an·tic′i·pat′a·ble** *adj.* —**an·tic′i·pa′tor** (-ər) *n.*

an·tic·i·pa·tion (an tis′ə pā′shən) *n.* 1 an anticipating or being anticipated 2 something anticipated or expected 3 foreknowledge; presentiment 4 *Law* the assignment or taking of income from a trust fund before it is due 5 *Music* the sounding of a tone in advance of the chord to which the tone belongs

an·tic·i·pa·tive (an tis′ə pāt′iv, -pə tiv′) *adj.* inclined to anticipate; of or full of anticipation —**an·tic′i·pa′tive·ly** *adv.*

an·tic·i·pa·to·ry (an tis′ə pə tôr′ē) *adj.* anticipating; of or expressing anticipation —**an·tic′i·pa·to′ri·ly** *adv.*

an·ti·cler·i·cal (an′tī kler′i kəl; -tē-, -ti-) *adj.* opposed to the clergy or church hierarchy, esp. to its influence in public affairs —**an′ti·cler′i·cal·ist** *adj., n.* —**an′ti·cler′i·cal·ism′** *n.*

an·ti·cli·mac·tic (-klī mak′tik) *adj.* of, having, or like an anticlimax —**an′ti·cli·mac′ti·cal·ly** *adv.*

an·ti·cli·max (-klī′maks′) *n.* 1 a sudden drop from the dignified or important in thought or expression to the commonplace or trivial, sometimes for humorous effect 2 a descent, as in a series of events, which is in ludicrous or disappointing contrast to a preceding rise

an·ti·cli·nal (an′ti klī′nəl) *adj.* ⟦< ANTI- + Gr *klinein*, to LEAN¹ + -AL⟧ 1 inclined in opposite directions 2 of or like an anticline

an·ti·cline (an′ti klīn′) *n.* ⟦< prec., modeled on INCLINE, DECLINE⟧ *Geol.* a sharply arched fold of stratified rock from whose central axis the strata slope downward in opposite directions: opposed to SYNCLINE

an·ti·cli·no·ri·um (an′ti klī nôr′ē əm) *n., pl.* **-ri·a** (-ə) ⟦ModL < prec. + Gr *oros*, mountain: see ORIENT⟧ *Geol.* a large, generally anticlinal structure consisting of a succession of anticlines and synclines: opposed to SYNCLINORIUM

an·ti·clock·wise (an′tē kläk′wīz′) *adj., adv.* [Brit.] COUNTERCLOCKWISE

an·ti·co·ag·u·lant (an′tī kō ag′yoo lənt; -tē-, -ti-) *n.* a drug or substance that delays or prevents the clotting of blood, as heparin

an·ti·con·vul·sant (-kən vul′sənt) *adj.* able to inhibit or control convulsions or seizures: also **an′ti·con·vul′sive** —*n.* such a substance or drug

An·ti·cos·ti (an′ti käs′tē) ⟦< ? AmInd *natiscotec*, lit., where bears are hunted⟧ island at the mouth of the St. Lawrence River, in Quebec, Canada: 3,066 sq mi (7,941 sq km)

an·ti·cy·clone (an′tī sī′klōn′; -tē-, -ti-) *n.* *Meteorol.* a system of rotating winds over a vast area spinning out from a high pressure center (clockwise in the Northern Hemisphere) and generally causing fair weather: commonly called a high since it coexists with high barometric pressure —**an′ti·cy·clon′ic** (-sī klän′ik) *adj.*

an·ti·dem·o·crat·ic (an′tē dem ə krat′ik, -tī-) *adj.* opposed or hostile to democracy as a form of government or to certain of its features, as majority rule or political equality —**an′ti·dem′o·crat′** *n.*

an·ti·de·pres·sant (-dē pres′ənt, -di-) *adj.* *Psychiatry* designating or of any drug used primarily to treat emotional depression —*n.* an antidepressant drug

an·ti·dote (an′tə dōt′) *n.* ⟦ME & OFr *antidote* < L *antidotum* < Gr *antidoton* < *anti-*, against + *dotos*, given < *didonai*, to give: see DATE¹⟧ 1 a remedy to counteract a poison 2 anything that works against an evil or unwanted condition —**an′ti·dot′al** *adj.*

an·ti·drom·ic (an′ti dräm′ik) *adj.* ⟦< ANTI- + Gr *dromos*, a running (see

DROMEDARY) + -IC] *Physiol.* conveying nerve impulses in a direction opposite to the normal

an·ti·dump·ing (an′tī dump′iŋ, -tē-) ***adj.*** designating or of laws, tariffs, etc. that ban or counteract the dumping of goods by a foreign manufacturer: see DUMP[1] (*vt.* 3)

an·ti·e·lec·tron (-ē lek′trän′) ***n.*** POSITRON

an·ti·en·er·gis·tic (-en′ər jis′tik) ***adj.*** resisting applied energy

an·ti·es·tab·lish·ment (an′tē ə stab′lish mənt) ***adj.*** opposed to THE ESTABLISHMENT (senses 1 & 2) (see phrase under ESTABLISHMENT): often sp. **an′ti·es·tab′lish·ment**

An·tie·tam (an tēt′əm) ⟦AmInd < ?⟧ creek in W Md.: its juncture with the Potomac is the site of a bloody, but indecisive, Civil War battle (1862)

an·ti·fe·brile (an′tī fē′brəl, -feb′rəl; -tē-, -ti-) ***adj.*** reducing or relieving fever —***n.*** an antifebrile drug

☆**an·ti·fed·er·al·ist** (-fed′ər əl ist) ***n.*** **1** a person opposed to federalism **2** [**A-**] a person who opposed the adoption of the U.S. Constitution —***adj.*** [**A-**] designating or of a former political party, later allied with the Jeffersonian Republican party, which opposed the Federalists

an·ti·fer·til·i·ty (-fər til′ə tē) ***adj.*** that prevents or is intended to prevent fertility; contraceptive

an·ti·foul·ing (-foul′iŋ) ***adj.*** designating or of a paint or other protective coating that prevents the fouling of a boat's hull with barnacles, seaweed, etc.

☆**an·ti·freeze** (an′ti frēz′, -tī-) ***n.*** a substance of low freezing point added to a liquid, esp. to the water in the radiator of an automobile or to gasoline in the tank, to prevent freezing

an·ti·fric·tion (an′tī frik′shən; -tē-, -ti-) ***adj.*** reducing friction —***n.*** a device, lubricant, etc. for reducing friction

an·ti·fun·gal (an′tē fuŋ′gəl, -tī-) ***adj.*** designating or of a medication used to treat a fungus infection —***n.*** a medicine that is or that contains a fungicide Also **an′ti-fun′gal**

☆**an·ti·gen** (an′tə jən, -jen′) ***n.*** ⟦ANTI- + -GEN⟧ a protein, toxin, or other substance of high molecular weight, to which the body reacts by producing antibodies —**an′ti·gen′ic** (-jen′ik) ***adj.***

An·tig·o·ne (an tig′ə nē′) ***n.*** ⟦L < Gr *Antigonē*⟧ *Gr. Myth.* a daughter of Oedipus and Jocasta: she defies the king of Thebes, Creon, by performing funeral rites for her brother, Polynices

An·tig·o·nus (I) (an tig′ə nəs) 382-301 B.C.; Macedonian general under Alexander the Great: king of Macedonia (306-301): called *Cyclops*

an·ti·grav·i·ty (an′tē grav′ə tē, an′tī-) ***n.*** a hypothetical force that acts against gravity, thus causing objects to move away from each other

An·ti·gua (an tē′gwə, -gə; -tig′wə, -tig′ə) island of the Leeward group in the West Indies: 108 sq mi (280 sq km): see ANTIGUA AND BARBUDA —**An·ti′guan** ***adj., n.***

Antigua and Barbuda country in the E West Indies, consisting of three islands, including Antigua and Barbuda: formerly a British colony, it became independent in 1981 & a member of the Commonwealth: 171 sq mi (443 sq km); cap. St. John's (on Antigua)

an·ti·he·lix (an′tī hē′liks′; -tē-, -ti-) ***n.***, *pl.* **-he′lix·es′** (-hē′liks iz′) or **-hel′i·ces′** (-hel′i sez′) the rounded piece of cartilage inside the outer rim (helix) of the ear; anthelix

an·ti·he·ro (an′tī hir′ō; -tē-, -ti-) ***n.***, *pl.* **-roes** the protagonist of a novel, play, etc. who lacks the virtues and estimable traits of a traditional hero —**an′ti·he·ro′ic** ***adj.***

an·ti·her·o·ine (-her′ō in) ***n.*** a female antihero

an·ti·his·ta·mine (an′tī his′tə mēn′; an′tē-, -ti-; -min′) ***n.*** any of several synthetic drugs used to minimize or prevent the action of histamine, as in an allergic condition —**an′ti·his′ta·min′ic** (-his′tə min′ik) ***adj.***

an·ti·hy·per·on (-hī′pər än′) ***n.*** the antiparticle of the hyperon

an·ti·hy·per·ten·sive (-hī′pər ten′siv) ***adj.*** able to inhibit or control hypertension —***n.*** an antihypertensive substance or drug

an·ti-in·flam·ma·to·ry (an′tē in flam′ə tôr′ē, -tī-) ***adj.*** designating or of a medication that suppresses or reduces inflammation —***n.***, *pl.* **-ries** an anti-inflammatory medication, as ibuprofen or aspirin

an·ti-in·tel·lec·tu·al (an′tī in′tə lek′choo əl, -tē-) ***adj.*** hostile to or opposed to intellectual persons or matters, ideas, activities, etc. —***n.*** a person who is anti-intellectual —**an′ti-in′tel·lec′tu·al·ism′** ***n.*** —**an′ti-in′tel·lec′tu·al·ly** ***adv.***

an·ti-Jew·ish (an′tī jōō′ish; -tē-, -ti-) ***adj.*** ANTI-SEMITIC

☆**an·ti·knock** (an′tī näk′; -tē-, -ti-) ***adj.*** of or having to do with a substance added to the fuel of internal-combustion engines to reduce or eliminate explosive noise resulting from too rapid combustion

an·ti·la·bor (-lā′bər) ***adj.*** opposed to labor unions or to the interests of workers

An·ti-Leb·a·non (an′ti leb′ə nän′, -nən) mountain range in W Syria, east of and parallel to the Lebanon Mountains: highest peak, Mt. Hermon

an·ti·lep·ton (an′tī lep′tän′; -tē-, -ti-) ***n.*** an antiparticle (positron, positive muon, or antineutrino) of the lepton

an·ti·lith·ic (-lith′ik) ***adj.*** ⟦ANTI- + LITHIC⟧ *Med.* preventing the formation or development of calculi, as of the urinary tract —***n.*** an antilithic substance

An·til·les (an til′ēz′) main island group of the West Indies, including all but the Bahamas: see GREATER ANTILLES, LESSER ANTILLES —**An·til′le·an** (-ē ən; an′tə lē′ən) ***adj.***

an·ti-lock (an′tē läk′, -tī-) ***adj.*** designating or of an automotive braking system that prevents the wheels from locking during a sudden stop: also **an′ti·lock′**

an·ti·log (-lôg′) ***n.*** *short for* ANTILOGARITHM

an·ti·log·a·rithm (an′tī lôg′ə rith′əm; -tē-, -ti-) ***n.*** the number that results when a base is raised to a power by a logarithm [10^3 = 1,000 is expressed by: the *antilogarithm* of 3 to the base 10 is 1,000, or antilog 3 = 1,000, or log 1,000 = 3]

an·til·o·gy (an til′ə jē) ***n.***, *pl.* **-gies** ⟦Gr *antilogia*: see ANTI- & -LOGY⟧ a contradiction in ideas, statements, or terms

an·ti·ma·cas·sar (an′ti mə kas′ər) ***n.*** ⟦ANTI- + *macassar (oil)*, an oil, orig. imported from MACASSAR, used as a hair dressing⟧ a small cover on the back or arms of a chair, sofa, etc. to prevent soiling

an·ti·mag·net·ic (an′tī mag net′ik; -tē-, -ti-) ***adj.*** constructed of metals that resist magnetism or designed to prevent or limit the influence of a magnetic field [an *antimagnetic* watch]

an·ti·ma·lar·i·al (-mə ler′ē əl) ***adj.*** preventing or relieving malaria —***n.*** an antimalarial drug

an·ti·masque or **an·ti·mask** (an′ti mask′) ***n.*** a comic sketch, often a burlesque, between the acts of a masque

an·ti·mat·ter (an′ti mat′ər; -tī-, -tē-) ***n.*** a form of matter in which the electrical charge or other property of each constituent particle is the reverse of that in the corresponding particle of the usual matter of the universe: an atom of antimatter has a nucleus of antiprotons and antineutrons surrounded by positrons

an·ti·mere (an′ti mir′) ***n.*** ⟦ANTI- + -MERE⟧ *Zool.* either of the corresponding parts opposite each other on a symmetrical animal —**an′ti·mer′ic** (-mer′ik) ***adj.***

an·ti·me·tab·o·lite (an′tī mə tab′ə līt′; an′tē-, -ti-) ***n.*** a drug or biochemical that inhibits a metabolic process by competing with a similarly shaped metabolite for a particular enzyme

an·ti·mi·cro·bi·al (-mī krō′bē əl) ***adj.*** able to inhibit or control microbes —***n.*** an antimicrobial substance or drug

an·ti·mis·sile (an′tī mis′əl; -tē-, -ti-) ***adj.*** designed as a defense against ballistic missiles

an·ti·mo·ni·al (an′tə mō′nē əl) ***adj.*** of or containing antimony —***n.*** a medicine, etc. containing antimony

an·ti·mon·ic (-män′ik, -mō′nik) ***adj.*** **1** of or containing antimony **2** of or containing pentavalent antimony

an·ti·mo·nous (an′tə mə nəs) ***adj.*** **1** of or like antimony **2** of or containing trivalent antimony Also **an′ti·mo′ni·ous** (-mō′nē əs)

an·ti·mon·soon (an′tī män sōōn′; -tē-, -ti-) ***n.*** the air current above a monsoon, moving in the opposite direction

an·ti·mo·ny (an′tə mō′nē) ***n.*** ⟦ME *antimonie* < OFr *antimoine* < ML *antimonium* < ? Ar *al ithmid*, antimony < Gr *stimi* (> L *stibium*) < Coptic *stēm* < Egypt *sdmt*, orig., mixture used to protect the eyes from flies⟧ a silvery-white, brittle, nonmetallic chemical element of crystalline structure, found only in combination: used in alloys with metals to harden them and increase their resistance to chemical action; compounds of antimony are used in medicines, pigments, and matches, and for fireproofing: symbol, Sb; at. no. 51: see the periodic table of elements in the Reference Supplement

antimony glance STIBNITE

an·ti·mo·nyl (an′tə mə nil′) ***n.*** ⟦ANTIMON(Y) + -YL⟧ the monovalent radical SbO, found in certain salts, notably antimony potassium tartrate

antimony potassium tartrate TARTAR EMETIC: also **antimonyl potassium tartrate**

antimony trisulfide a black or orange-red crystalline compound, Sb_2S_3, used as a pigment, in pyrotechnics and matches, for fireproofing fabrics and paper, etc.

an·ti·neu·tri·no (an′tī nōō trē′nō; -tē-, -ti-) ***n.*** the antiparticle of the neutrino, with no charge and a rest mass close to zero: it is emitted during radioactive decay

☆**an·ti·neu·tron** (-nōō′trän′) ***n.*** the antiparticle of the neutron, with the same mass and spin as the neutron, but with a positive magnetic moment (the neutron has a negative magnetic moment)

an·ti·node (an′ti nōd′; -tī-, -tē-) ***n.*** *Physics* the point of maximum vibration located between two adjacent nodes in a vibrating body

an·ti·no·mi·an (an′ti nō′mē ən, -tī-) ***n.*** ⟦< fol. + -AN⟧ [*also* **A-**] *Christian Theol.* one who believes in the doctrine that, because of GRACE (***n.*** 11*b*), right conduct is unnecessary for salvation —***adj.*** of this doctrine —**an′ti·no′mi·an·ism′** ***n.***

an·tin·o·my (an tin′ə mē) ***n.***, *pl.* **-mies** ⟦L *antinomia* < Gr *antinomia*: see ANTI- & -NOMY⟧ **1** the opposition of one law, regulation, etc. to another **2** a contradiction or inconsistency between two apparently reasonable principles or laws, or between conclusions drawn from them

an·ti·nov·el (an′tī näv′əl; -tē-, -ti-) ***n.*** ⟦transl. of Fr *antiroman*, term coined by Jean-Paul SARTRE⟧ a work of prose fiction in which such characteristics of the traditional novel as character development, the realistic description of society, and, esp., a clearly developed narrative are deliberately de-emphasized or rejected

an·ti·nu·cle·ar or **an·ti·nu·cle·ar** (an′tī nōō′klē ər, -tē-; -nyōō′-) ***adj.*** opposed to military and industrial applications of nuclear energy and to technologies which produce radioactive waste products

an·ti·nu·cle·on (an′tī nōō′klē än′; -tē-, -ti-) ***n.*** the antiparticle of a nucleon; an antiproton or antineutron

An·ti·och (an′tē äk′) **1** capital of ancient Syria (until 64 B.C.), an early center of Christianity: now, a city in S Turkey: Turk. name ANTAKYA **2** city in ancient Pisidia, Asia Minor **3** city in W Calif.

An·ti·o·chus[1] (an tī′ə kəs) *n.* name of thirteen kings of the Seleucid dynasty of Syria

An·ti·o·chus[2] (an tī′ə kəs) 1 **Antiochus III** 242-187 B.C.; Syrian king (223-187): called **Antiochus the Great** 2 **Antiochus IV** died 163? B.C.; Syrian king (175?-163?): his suppression of the Jews led to the Maccabean revolt: called **Antiochus E·piph·a·nes** (ē pif′ə nēz, i pif′-)

an·ti·ox·i·dant (an′tī äks′i dənt, an′tē-) *n.* a substance that slows down the oxidation of hydrocarbons, oils, fats, etc. and thus helps to check deterioration: antioxidants are added to many products, esp. foods and soaps —*adj.* serving to check oxidation

an·ti·par·al·lel (an′tī par′ə lel′; -tē-, -ti-) *adj.* designating vectors that are parallel but opposite in direction

an·ti·par·ti·cle (an′tī pärt′i kəl, -tē-, -ti-) *n.* any of the constituent particles of antimatter: see ANTIMATTER

an·ti·pas·to (an′ti päs′tō, -pas′-; än′ti päs′tō) *n., pl.* **-ti** (-tē) or **-tos** ⟦It < *anti-* (L *ante*), before + *pasto* < L *pastus*, food < *pascere*, to feed: see FOOD⟧ 1 an assortment, as of salted fish, marinated vegetables, meats, cheeses, and olives, served as an appetizer 2 any single dish in such an assortment, or one such dish served alone

An·tip·a·ter (an tip′ə tər) 397?-319 B.C.; Macedonian general under Alexander the Great

an·ti·pa·thet·ic (an′tə pə thet′ik, an tip′ə-) *adj.* ⟦< fol., infl. by PATHETIC⟧ 1 having antipathy 2 opposed or antagonistic in character, tendency, etc. Also **an′ti·pa·thet′i·cal** —**an′ti·pa·thet′i·cal·ly** *adv.*

an·tip·a·thy (an tip′ə thē) *n., pl.* **-thies** ⟦L *antipathia* < Gr *antipatheia* < *anti-*, ANTI- + *patheia* < *pathein*, to suffer: see PATHOS⟧ 1 strong or deep-rooted dislike; aversion 2 the object of such dislike 3 [Obs.] an opposition in character, nature, tendency, etc. —**SYN.** AVERSION

an·ti·pe·ri·od·ic (an′tī pir′ē äd′ik; -tē-, -ti-) *adj.* preventing the periodic return of attacks of disease, as of certain fevers, esp. malaria —*n.* an antiperiodic substance or drug

an·ti·per·i·stal·sis (-per′i stal′sis) *n. Physiol.* reverse peristaltic action in which the contents of the intestines, etc. are moved backward

an·ti·per·son·nel (an′tī pʉr′sə nel′; -tē-, -ti-) *adj.* directed against, or intended to destroy, people rather than material objects [*antipersonnel* mines]

an·ti·per·spi·rant (an′tī pʉr′spə rənt; -tē-, -ti-; *also*, -pər′spī′rənt) *n.* an astringent substance applied to the skin to reduce perspiration

an·ti·phlo·gis·tic (an′tī flō jis′tik; -tē-, -ti-) *adj.* counteracting inflammation and fever —*n.* an antiphlogistic substance

an·ti·phon (an′tə fən, -fän′) *n.* ⟦ML(Ec) *antiphona*: see ANTHEM⟧ 1 a hymn, psalm, etc. chanted or sung in responsive, alternating parts 2 anything composed for responsive chanting or singing 3 verses chanted or a piece of plainsong sung before or after a psalm, canticle, etc.

an·tiph·o·nal (an tif′ə nəl) *adj.* of or like an antiphon; sung or chanted in alternation: also **an·ti·phon·ic** (an′tə fän′ik) —*n.* an antiphonary —**an·tiph′on·al·ly** *adv.*

an·tiph·o·nar·y (an tif′ə ner′ē) *n., pl.* **-nar′ies** ⟦ME *antiphonere* < OFr *antifonier* < ML(Ec) *antiphonarium*: see ANTIPHON⟧ a collection of antiphons, esp. a book of responsive prayers

an·tiph·o·ny (an tif′ə nē) *n., pl.* **-nies** ⟦< Gr *antiphōnos* (see ANTHEM), by assoc. with SYMPHONY⟧ 1 the opposition of sounds 2 harmony produced by this 3 an antiphon 4 antiphonal chanting or singing 5 any response or echo

an·tiph·ra·sis (an tif′rə sis) *n.* ⟦L < Gr < *anti-*, against + *phrazein*, to speak⟧ the use of words or phrases in a sense opposite to the usual one, as for ironic effect

an·ti·pode (an′tə pōd′) *n.* 1 *sing. of* ANTIPODES 2 anything diametrically opposite; exact opposite

an·tip·o·des (an tip′ə dēz′) *pl.n.* ⟦ML < L < Gr, pl. of *antipous*, with the feet opposite < *anti-*, opposite + *pous*, FOOT⟧ 1 any two places directly opposite each other on the earth 2 [*with pl. or sing. v.*] a place on the opposite side of the earth 3 two opposite or contrary things —**an·tip′o·dal** *adj.* —**an·tip′o·de′an** (-dē′ən) *adj., n.*

An·tip·o·des (an tip′ə dēz′) [*sometimes* **a-**] [Brit.] New Zealand and Australia: with *the*

an·ti·pol·lu·tion (an′tī pə lo͞o′shən, -tē-, -ti-) *adj.* designating or of devices, laws, etc. intended to prevent, lessen, or remove pollutants or pollution —**an′ti·pol·lu′tion·ist** *n.*

an·ti·pope (an′ti pōp′; -tē-, -tī-) *n.* a pope set up against the one chosen by church laws, as in a schism

an·ti·pro·ton (an′tī prō′tän′; -tē-, -ti-) *n.* the antiparticle of the proton, with the same mass as the proton but a negative charge

an·ti·psy·chot·ic (an′tī sī kät′ik; -tē-, -tī-) *adj.* tranquilizing; neuroleptic —*n.* an antipsychotic drug

an·ti·py·ret·ic (-pī ret′ik) *adj.* reducing fever —*n.* anything that reduces fever

an·ti·py·rine (-pī′rēn′, -rin′) *n.* ⟦< prec. + -INE[3]⟧ a white, crystalline powder, $(CH_3)_2(C_6H_5)C_3HN_2O$, formerly used to relieve pain and to reduce fever, and currently used in solution with benzocaine for acute otitis media

antiq *abbrev.* 1 antiquarian 2 antiquity; antiquities

an·ti·quar·i·an (an′ti kwer′ē ən) *adj.* 1 of antiques or antiquities 2 of antiquaries 3 of, or dealing in, old books —*n.* an antiquary —**an′ti·quar′i·an·ism′** *n.*

an·ti·quark (an′tē kwôrk′, -tī-; -kwärk′) *n.* an antiparticle of a quark

an·ti·quar·y (an′ti kwer′ē) *n., pl.* **-quar′ies** ⟦L *antiquarius* < *antiquus*: see ANTIQUE⟧ a person who collects or studies relics and ancient works of art

an·ti·quate (an′ti kwāt′) *vt.* **-quat′ed, -quat′ing** ⟦< L *antiquatus*, pp. of *antiquare* < *antiquus*: see ANTIQUE⟧ 1 to make old or obsolete; cause to become old-fashioned 2 to give an antique look to —**an′ti·qua′tion** *n.*

an·ti·quat·ed (-id) *adj.* 1 no longer used or useful; obsolete, old-fashioned, out-of-date, etc. 2 aged —**SYN.** OLD

an·tique (an tēk′) *adj.* ⟦Fr < L *antiquus*, ancient, old < *ante*, before⟧ 1 of ancient times; ancient; old 2 out-of-date; old-fashioned 3 in the style of classical antiquity 4 of, or in the style of, a former period 5 dealing in antiques —*n.* 1 anything from ancient times; relic 2 the ancient style, esp. of Greek or Roman sculpture, architecture, etc. 3 a piece of furniture, silverware, etc. made in a former period, generally more than 100 years ago —*vt.* **-tiqued′, -tiqu′ing** to make look antique, as in the style of a former period —*vi.* to look for or shop for antique furniture, articles, etc. —**SYN.** OLD —**an·tique′ly** *adv.* —**an·tique′ness** *n.*

an·tiq·ui·ty (an tik′wə tē) *n., pl.* **-ties** ⟦ME & OFr *antiquite* < L *antiquitas* < *antiquus*: see prec.⟧ 1 the early period of history, esp. before the Middle Ages 2 the quality of being ancient or old [a statue of great *antiquity*] 3 the people of ancient times 4 [*pl.*] *a)* relics, monuments, etc. of the distant past *b)* ancient manners, customs, etc.

an·ti·ra·chit·ic (an′tī rə kit′ik; -tē-, -ti-) *adj.* that cures or prevents rickets —*n.* a remedy or preventive for rickets

an·ti·ret·ro·vi·ral (an′tē re′trō vī′rəl, an′tī-) *adj.* designating or of a medication or process effective in destroying or slowing the growth of a retrovirus —*n.* such a medication or process

an·ti·roll bar (an′tē rōl′, -tī-) a horizontal bar in the suspension system of some automotive vehicles, that stabilizes the body of the vehicle and thereby reduces sway, esp. during turns

an·tir·rhi·num (an′tə rī′nəm) *n.* ⟦ModL < Gr *antirrhinon*, snapdragon < *anti-*, equivalent to, imitating + *rhis* (gen. *rhinos*), nose: from seeming resemblance to an animal's snout⟧ SNAPDRAGON (sense 1)

An·ti·sa·na (an′ti sä′nə, än′-) volcanic mountain of the Andes, in NC Ecuador: *c.* 18,700 ft (5,700 m)

an·ti·sat·el·lite (an′tī sat′′l īt′; -tē-, -ti-) *adj.* designating or of a weapon, weapons system, technology, etc. designed to destroy or damage a SATELLITE (*n.* 2*b*)

an·ti·scor·bu·tic (-skôr byo͞ot′ik) *adj.* that cures or prevents scurvy —*n.* a remedy or preventive for scurvy, as vitamin C

antiscorbutic acid VITAMIN C

an·ti-Sem·ite (an′tī sem′īt′; -tē-, -ti-) *n.* an anti-Semitic person

an·ti-Se·mit·ic (-sə mit′ik) *adj.* ⟦< *anti-Semitism* < Ger *Antisemitismus*, coined (1879) by Wilhelm Marr, Ger writer⟧ 1 having or showing prejudice against Jews 2 discriminating against or persecuting Jews 3 of or caused by such prejudice or hostility Also written **an′ti·se·mit′ic** —**an′ti-Se·mit′i·cal·ly** *adv.* —**an′ti-Sem′i·tism′** (-sem′ə tiz′əm) *n.*

USAGE—some writers and scholars prefer the alternate form *antisemitic* because they contend that the form *anti-Semitic* suggests being opposed to (the) *Semites*, a term that could include Arabs and other peoples, when in fact the word means "anti-Jewish"

an·ti·sense (an′tē sens′, -tī-) *adj. Genetics* of, having, being, or based on a nucleotide sequence that blocks DNA protein synthesis by binding with and inhibiting the action of specific MESSENGER RNA

an·ti·sep·sis (an′tə sep′sis) *n.* ⟦ANTI- + SEPSIS⟧ 1 the technique of preventing infection, the growth of microorganisms, etc. 2 the condition of being antiseptic 3 the use of antiseptics

an·ti·sep·tic (-tik) *adj.* 1 preventing infection, decay, etc. by inhibiting the action of microorganisms 2 using antiseptics 3 free from infection or infectious agents; sterile 4 very clean or tidy 5 untouched by life, its problems, emotions, etc. [an *antiseptic* mind] —*n.* any substance that inhibits the action of microorganisms —**an′ti·sep′ti·cal·ly** *adv.*

an·ti·se·rum (an′ti sir′əm, -tī-) *n., pl.* **-rums** or **-ra** a serum containing antibodies specific for one or more antigens

☆**an·ti·slav·er·y** (an′tī slā′vər ē; -tē-, -ti-) *adj.* against slavery

an·ti·smok·ing (an′tī smō′kiŋ, -tē-) *adj.* in opposition to or prohibiting the smoking of tobacco, esp. in public places

an·ti·so·cial (-sō′shəl) *adj.* 1 avoiding association with others; unsociable 2 against the basic principles of society; harmful to the welfare of the people generally —**SYN.** UNSOCIAL —**an′ti·so′cial·ly** *adv.*

an·ti·spas·mod·ic (-spaz mäd′ik) *adj.* relieving or preventing spasms, esp. of smooth muscle —*n.* an antispasmodic drug See ANTISPASTIC

an·ti·spas·tic (-spas′tik) *adj.* relieving or preventing spasms, esp. of voluntary skeletal muscles —*n.* an antispastic drug See ANTISPASMODIC

an·ti·stat·ic (-stat′ik) *adj.* reducing static electric charges, as on textiles, waxes, polishes, etc., by retaining enough moisture to provide electrical conduction

An·tis·the·nes (an tis′thə nēz′) 444?-365? B.C.; Gr. philosopher; founder of Cynicism

an·tis·tro·phe (an tis′trə fē) *n.* ⟦LL < Gr *antistrophē* < *antistrephein*, to turn about < *anti-*, against, opposite + *strephein*, to turn: see STROPHE⟧ 1 in the ancient Greek theater, *a)* the return movement, from left to right of the stage, made by the chorus in answering the previous strophe *b)* the part of the choric song performed during this 2 in a Pindaric ode, the stanza, usually in the same or similar form, which follows the strophe 3 in poems with contrasting or parallel stanza systems, a stanza of the second system —**an·ti·stroph·ic** (an′tə sträf′ik) *adj.*

an·ti-sway bar (an′tē swā′) ANTIROLL BAR

an·ti·tank (an′tī taŋk′; -tē-, -ti-) *adj.* for use against tanks in war

an·tith·e·sis (an tith′ə sis) ***n.***, *pl.* **-ses′** (-sēz′) ⟦ME *antitesis* < LL *antithesis* < Gr < *antithenai* < *anti-*, against + *tithenai*, to place: see DO[1]⟧ **1** a contrast or opposition of thoughts, usually in two phrases, clauses, or sentences (Ex.: you are going; I am staying) **2** the second part of such an expression **3** a contrast or opposition: see also DIALECTIC (sense 3) **4** the exact opposite [joy is the *antithesis* of sorrow]

an·ti·thet·i·cal (an′tə thet′i kəl) ***adj.*** ⟦obs. *antithetic*, opposite (< Gr *antithetikos* < *antithenai*: see prec.) + -AL⟧ **1** of or containing antithesis **2** exactly opposite Also **an′ti·thet′ic** **—SYN.** OPPOSITE **—an′ti·thet′i·cal·ly** ***adv.***

an·ti·tox·ic (an′ti täk′sik) ***adj.*** of, containing, or acting as an antitoxin

an·ti·tox·in (-täks′in) ***n.*** **1** a circulating antibody formed by the body, as active immunity, to act against a specific toxin **2** a sterile solution containing an antitoxin: it is taken from the blood serum of an immunized animal or person and injected into a person to prevent a specific disease, as tetanus or diphtheria, by creating a passive immunity

an·ti·trades (an′ti trādz′, -tī-) ***pl.n.*** winds moving above and opposite to the tropical trade winds: as they reach the Temperate Zones, they descend to the surface, forming a deep layer of prevailing westerlies

an·ti·tra·gus (an ti′trə gəs, an′tə trā′gəs) ***n.***, *pl.* **-gi′** (-jī′) the fleshy, cartilaginous protrusion of the external ear, opposite and just below the tragus

☆**an·ti·trust** (an′tī trust′, -tē-) ***adj.*** opposed to or regulating trusts; specif., designating or of federal laws, suits, etc. designed to prevent restraints on trade, as by business monopolies, cartels, etc.

an·ti·tus·sive (an′tī tus′iv; -tē-, -ti-) ***adj.*** reducing the severity of coughing ***—n.*** an antitussive preparation

an·ti·type (an′ti tīp′) ***n.*** ⟦LL *antitypus* < LGr *antitypos* < Gr, resembling, corresponding to + *typos*, figure: see TYPE⟧ **1** the person or thing represented or foreshadowed by an earlier type or symbol **2** an opposite type **—an′ti·typ′i·cal** (-tip′i kəl) ***adj.***, **an′ti·typ′ic** **—an′ti·typ′i·cal·ly** ***adv.***

an·ti-u·ni·verse (an′tī yōō′nə vʉrs′; -tē-, -ti-) ***n.*** a universe made up of antimatter, postulated to exist far out in space

an·ti·ven·in (an′tī ven′in; -tē-, -ti-) ***n.*** ⟦ANTI- + VENIN⟧ **1** an antitoxin for venom, as of snakes, produced in animals by gradually increased injections of the specific venom **2** a serum, taken from these animals, containing this antitoxin, used for emergencies: also called **an′ti·ven′om** (-ven′əm)

an·ti·vi·ral (-vī′rəl) ***adj.*** capable of checking the growth or effect of a virus

an·ti·viv·i·sec·tion (-viv′ə sek′shən) ***n.*** opposition to medical research on living animals **—an′ti·viv′i·sec′tion·ist** ***n., adj.***

an·ti·war or **an·ti-war** (an′tē wôr′, -tī-) ***adj.*** opposed to war or to a particular war

ant·ler (ant′lər) ***n.*** ⟦ME *aunteler* < OFr *antoillier* < ?⟧ **1** the branched, annually shed, bony growth on the head of any animal of the deer family **2** any branch of such a growth **—ant′lered** ***adj.***

Ant·li·a (ant′lē ə) ***n.*** ⟦ModL *Antlia (Pneumatica)*, lit., (air) pump < L *antlia*, water pump < Gr, bilge water < *antlos*, hold (of a ship)⟧ a S constellation between Hydra and Centaurus

ant lion ⟦transl. of Gr *myrmēkoleōn* in LXX, Job 4:11⟧ any of a family (Myrmeleontidae) of neuropteran insects, some of which have large-jawed larvae (doodlebugs) that lie hidden in cone-shaped pits where they feed on ants and other insects that fall in: also written **ant′li′on** ***n.***

An·to·fa·gas·ta (än′tô fə gäs′tə) seaport in N Chile

An·toi·nette[1] (an′twə net′, -tə-; *Fr* än twȧ net′) ***n.*** a feminine name: dim. *Nettie, Netty, Toni, Tony*: see ANTONIA

Antoinette[2], **Marie** *see* MARIE ANTOINETTE

An·to·ni·a (an tō′nē ə) ***n.*** ⟦L, fem. of *Antonius*: see ANTHONY[1]⟧ a feminine name: var. *Antoinette, Tonya*

An·to·nine (an′tə nīn′) ***adj.*** designating or having to do with a succession of Roman emperors (**the Antonines**) of the 2d cent. A.D., including Antoninus Pius and Marcus Aurelius

An·to·ni·nus (an′tə nī′nəs), **Marcus Aurelius** *see* AURELIUS, Marcus

Antoninus Pius A.D. 86-161; Rom. emperor (138-161)

an·to·no·ma·sia (an′tə nō′mā′zhə) ***n.*** ⟦L < Gr < *antonomazein*, to call by another name < *anti-*, instead of + *onomazein*, to name < *onoma*, NAME⟧ **1** the use of an epithet or title in place of a name, as in calling a judge *his honor* **2** the use of a proper name in place of a common noun which it represents, as in calling a philanderer a *Don Juan*

An·to·ny[1] (an′tə nē) ***n.*** a masculine name: see ANTHONY[1]

An·to·ny[2] (an′tə nē), **Mark** (or **Marc**) (Latin name *Marcus Antonius*) 83?-30 B.C.; Rom. general & member of the second triumvirate

an·to·nym (an′tə nim′) ***n.*** ⟦with altered sense (as if < ANTI-) < Gr *antōnymia*, a pronoun < *anti-*, equal to, instead of, opposite (see ANTI-) + *onyma*, NAME⟧ a word that is opposite in meaning to another word ["sad" is an *antonym* of "happy"]

an·ton·y·mous (an tän′ə məs) ***adj.*** of, or having the nature of, an antonym; opposite in meaning: also **an′to·nym′ic** **—SYN.** OPPOSITE

An·trim (an′trim′) **1** former county of NE Northern Ireland: *c.* 1,176 sq mi (3,046 sq km) **2** district in NE Northern Ireland, in the S part of the former county: 221 sq mi (572 sq km)

☆**An·tron** (an′trän′) ⟦arbitrary formation⟧ *trademark for* a strong, shiny, silklike nylon fiber made into clothing, carpet, upholstery fabric, etc.

an·trorse (an trôrs′) ***adj.*** ⟦ModL *antrorsus*: see ANTERIOR & VERSE⟧ *Biol.* upward or forward **—an·trorse′ly** ***adv.***

an·trum (an′trəm) ***n.***, *pl.* **-tra** (-trə) or **-trums** ⟦L < Gr *antron*, cave < IE **antrom*⟧ *Anat.* a cavity, esp. one within a bone, as either of a pair of sinuses in the upper jaw

☆**ant·sy** (ant′sē) ***adj.*** **-si·er**, **-si·est** ⟦< ANT[1] + -Y[2]: prob. < phr. *have ants in one's pants*, be full of nervous energy⟧ [Slang] fidgety, nervous, impatient, etc.

☆**ANTU** (an′tōō′) ***n.*** ⟦*a*(*lpha*-)*n*(*aphthyl*-)*t*(*hio*)*u*(*rea*)⟧ an odorless gray powder, $C_{10}H_7NHCSNH_2$, used to kill rats

An·tung (än′dooŋ′; *E* an tooŋ′) *a former transliteration of* DANDONG

Ant·werp (an′twʉrp′) **1** province of N Belgium: 1,107 sq mi (2,867 sq km) **2** its capital, on the Scheldt River Fl. name **Ant·wer·pen** (änt′ver′pən)

A·nu·bis (ə nōō′bis, -nyōō′-) ***n.*** ⟦L < Gr *Anoubis* < Egypt *Anpu*⟧ *Egypt. Myth.* the god who leads the dead to judgment: usually represented with the head of a jackal

a·nu·ran (ə noor′ən, -nyōō′rən) ***n.*** ⟦< Gr *an-*, not + *oura*, tail (see URO-[2]) + -AN⟧ any of an order (Anura) of tailless, jumping amphibians with a broad body and well-developed hind legs, consisting of frogs and toads ***—adj.*** of or pertaining to the anurans

an·u·re·sis (an′yōō rē′sis, -yə-) ***n.***, *pl.* **-ses** (-sēz) ⟦ModL < AN-[1] + Gr *ourēsis*, urination < *ourein*: see URINE⟧ ANURIA **—an′u·ret′ic** (-ret′ik) ***adj.***

a·nu·ri·a (ə nyōō′rē ə, -noor′ē ə) ***n.*** ⟦ModL: see AN-[1] & -URIA⟧ partial or total failure of the kidneys to secrete urine, or blockage which prevents or limits the normal excretion of urine **—a·nu′ric** ***adj.***

a·nu·rous (ə nyōō′rəs, -noor′əs) ***adj.*** ⟦see ANURAN & -OUS⟧ having no tail, as a frog or toad: also **a·nu′ral**

a·nus (ā′nəs) ***n.***, *pl.* **a′nus·es** or **a′ni′** (-nī′) ⟦L, ring, anus < IE base **āno-*, ring⟧ the opening at the lower end of the alimentary canal

an·vil (an′vəl) ***n.*** ⟦ME *anvelt* < OE *anfilt* < *an*, ON + **filtan*, to hit, beat < IE base **pel-*, to beat > (IM)PEL, FELT[1]⟧ **1** an iron or steel block on which metal objects are hammered into shape **2** the incus, one of the three bones of the middle ear

anvil

anx·i·e·ty (aŋ zī′ə tē) ***n.***, *pl.* **-ties** ⟦L *anxietas* < *anxius*, ANXIOUS⟧ **1** a state of being uneasy, apprehensive, or worried about what may happen; concern about a possible future event **2** *Psychiatry* an abnormal state like this, characterized by a feeling of being powerless and unable to cope with threatening events, typically imaginary, and by physical tension, as shown by sweating, trembling, etc. **3** an eager but often uneasy desire [*anxiety* to do well] **—SYN.** CARE

anx·i·o·lyt·ic (aŋ′zē ō lit′ik, aŋk′sē-) ***adj.*** ⟦< prec. + -O- + LYTIC (sense 2)⟧ relieving tension or anxiety ***—n.*** any anxiolytic drug or substance

anx·ious (aŋk′shəs, aŋ′-) ***adj.*** ⟦L *anxius* < *angere*, to choke, give pain < IE base **angh-*: see ANGER⟧ **1** having or showing anxiety; uneasy in mind; apprehensive; worried **2** causing or full of anxiety [an *anxious* hour] **3** eagerly wishing [*anxious* to do well] **—SYN.** EAGER[1] **—anx′ious·ly** ***adv.*** **—anx′ious·ness** ***n.***

☆**anxious seat** a bench near the preacher at revival meetings, for those with a troubled conscience who seek salvation: also **anxious bench**

an·y (en′ē) ***adj.*** ⟦ME *ani* < OE *ænig* < *an*, ONE; akin to Ger *einig*, ON *einigr*⟧ **1** one, no matter which, of more than two [*any* pupil may answer] **2** some, no matter how much or how little, how many, or what kind [he can't tolerate *any* criticism] **3** without limit [entitled to *any* number of admissions] **4** even one; the least amount or number of [I haven't *any* dimes] **5** every [*any* child can do it] **6** of considerable size or extent [we won't be able to travel *any* distance before nightfall] ***—pron.*** (*sing. & pl.*) any one or ones; any amount or number ***—adv.*** to any degree or extent; at all [is he *any* better this morning?] **—any day (or minute, etc.) (now)** sometime in the next several days (or minutes, etc.) **—any time (now)** sometime soon

an·y·bod·y (-bäd′ē, -bud′ē) ***pron.*** any person; anyone ***—n.***, *pl.* **-bod′ies** a person of some fame, importance, etc. [no one who was *anybody* missed the party]

an·y·how (-hou′) ***adv.*** **1** no matter in what way **2** no matter what else may be true; in any case **3** in a careless way; haphazardly

an·y·more (-môr′) ***adv.*** now; nowadays; at present: usually used in a negative clause [he doesn't live here *anymore*]: also **any more**

an·y·one (-wun′) ***pron.*** any person; anybody

any one **1** any single **2** any single person or thing

☆**an·y·place** (-plās′) ***adv.*** [Informal] in or to any place; anywhere

an·y·thing (-thiŋ′) ***pron.*** any object, event, fact, etc. [do you know *anything* about it?] ***—n.*** a thing, no matter of what kind [do *anything* you want] ***—adv.*** in any way; at all [is he *anything* like his father?] **—anything but** by no means; not at all

an·y·time (-tīm′) ***adv.*** at any time ***—conj.*** WHENEVER (***conj.*** 1)

an·y·way (-wā′) ***adv.*** **1** in any manner or way **2** at least; nevertheless; anyhow **3** haphazardly; carelessly Also [Dial.] **an′y·ways′**

an·y·where (-hwer′, -wer′) ***adv.*** **1** in, at, or to any place **2** [Informal] at all; to any extent Also [Informal or Dial.] **an′y·wheres′** (-hwerz′, -werz′) —☆**anywhere from** [Informal] any amount, rate, time, etc. between (stated limits) [*anywhere from* five to ten dollars]

an·y·wise (-wīz′) ***adv.*** ⟦ME *ani wise* < OE (*on*) *ænige wīsan*: see ANY & WISE[2]⟧ in any manner or way; at all

An·zac (an′zak′) ***n.*** ⟦acronym formed from the name of the corps⟧ **1** in WWI, a soldier in the Australian and New Zealand Army Corps **2** any soldier from Australia or New Zealand

An·zi·o (an′zē ō′; *It* än′tsyô) port on the W coast of Italy, south of Rome: site of Allied beachhead (Jan., 1944) in the invasion of Italy in WWII

ANZUS (an′zəs) ***n.*** Australia, New Zealand, and the United States, allied by treaty in 1951 for the purpose of mutual defense in the Pacific: also written **An′zus**

A/o or **a/o** *abbrev.* account of

ao dai (ou′zī′) ⟦Vietnamese < *áo*, jacket + *dài*, to be long⟧ the traditional costume of Vietnamese women, consisting of a long, high-necked, closefitting tunic split along the sides from waist to hem: it is worn over loosefitting trousers

☆**A-OK** (ā′ō kā′) ***adj.*** ⟦A(LL) OK[1]⟧ [Informal] excellent, fine, in working order, etc.: a generalized term of commendation: also **A′-O·kay′**

Ao·mo·ri (ou′mə rē′) seaport in northernmost Honshu, Japan, on an inlet of the Sea of Japan

A one (ā′ wun′) ⟦orig. a designation of first-class ships, as in Lloyd's Register: *A* indicating the excellent condition of the hull, *1* that of the equipment⟧ [Informal] first-class; first-rate; superior: also **A 1, A-1,** or **A number 1**

A1C *abbrev.* airman first class

AOR *abbrev.* album-oriented rock (or radio)

A·o·ran·gi (ou räŋ′ē) *former name for* Mount COOK[2]

a·o·rist (ā′ə rist, er′ist) ***n.*** ⟦Gr *aoristos*, indefinite < *a-*, not + *horistos*, definable < *horizein*, to define < *horos*, a limit: see HORIZON⟧ a past tense of Greek verbs, denoting an action without indicating whether completed, continued, or repeated —***adj.*** designating or in this tense —**a′o·ris′tic** ***adj.***

a·or·ta (ā ôr′tə) ***n., pl.*** **-tas** or **-tae** (-tē) ⟦ModL < Gr *aortē* < *aeirein*, to raise⟧ the main artery of the body, carrying blood from the left ventricle of the heart to all the main arteries —**a·or′tic** ***adj.***, **a·or′tal**

Aosta, Valle d′ *see* VALLE D'AOSTA

a·ou·dad (ä′oo dad′, ou′dad′) ***n.*** ⟦Fr < Moorish *audad*⟧ a wild N African sheep (*Ammotragus lervia*) with large curved horns and a heavy growth of hair from the throat to the knees; Barbary sheep

à ou·trance (ä o͞o träns′) ⟦Fr⟧ to the utmost; to the bitter end; to the death

ap (ap) ***n.*** *Comput. alt. sp. of* APP[1]

Ap *abbrev.* April

AP *trademark* **1** Advanced Placement **2** Associated Press

ap- (ap, əp) *prefix* **1** AD-: used before a vowel **2** APO-: used before a vowel

APA *abbrev.* **1** American Pharmaceutical Association **2** American Psychiatric Association **3** American Psychological Association

a·pace (ə pās′) ***adv.*** ⟦ME *apas*: see A-[1] & PACE[1]⟧ at a fast pace; with speed; swiftly

a·pache (ə pash′, -päsh′; *Fr* à pàsh′) ***n., pl.*** **a·pach′es** (-iz; *Fr* à pàsh′) ⟦Fr, lit., Apache: first used of Parisian thieves (1902) by Victor Moris, Fr journalist⟧ a gangster or thug of Paris —***adj.*** designating a dance, performed typically as an exhibition in cabarets, that represents an apache handling his girl in a brutal, masterful way

A·pach·e (ə pach′ē) ***n.*** ⟦AmSp, prob. < Yavapai (a Yuman language) *ʔəpá·čə*, people⟧ **1** *pl.* **A·pach′es** or **A·pach′e** a member of a group of North American Indian peoples of the SW U.S. and N Mexico **2** any of several Athabaskan languages and dialects spoken by these peoples

Ap·a·lach·ee Bay (ap′ə lach′ē) ⟦< AmInd (? Choctaw) tribal name⟧ inlet of the Gulf of Mexico, on the NW coast of Florida

Ap·a·lach·i·co·la (ap′ə lach′i kō′lə) ⟦< AmInd, ? a tribal name⟧ river in NW Fla., flowing from the Fla.-Ga. border southward into the Gulf of Mexico: 90 mi (145 km)

a·pa·nage (ap′ə nij′) ***n.*** APPANAGE

☆**a·pa·re·jo** (ap′ə rā′hō′) ***n., pl.*** **-jos′** ⟦Sp⟧ [Chiefly Southwest] a kind of packsaddle made of a stuffed leather pad

a·part (ə pärt′) ***adv.*** ⟦ME < OFr *a part* < L *ad*, to, at + *partem*, acc. of *pars*, a side, PART[2]⟧ **1** to one side; at a little distance; aside **2** separately or away in place or time [*born two years apart*] **3** reserved for a particular purpose **4** separately or independently in function, use, etc. [*viewed apart*] **5** in or to pieces [*to take a motor apart*] **6** aside; notwithstanding [*all joking apart*] —***adj.*** separated; not together: used in the predicate —**apart from** other than; besides —**take apart** to reduce (a whole) to its parts —**tell apart** to distinguish one from another

a·part·heid (ə pär′tāt′; -tīt′, -tīd′) ***n.*** ⟦Afrik, the state of being separate < *apart*, prec. + *-heid*, noun suffix akin to -HOOD⟧ **1** the official policy (*c.* 1950-91) of strict racial segregation and discrimination against nonwhites practiced in South Africa **2** any policy or condition of discriminatory segregation or separation

a·part·ment (ə pärt′mənt) ***n.*** ⟦Fr *appartement* < It *appartamento* < *appartare*, to separate < *a*, to + *parte*, PART[2]⟧ **1** a room or suite of rooms to live in; esp., one suite in an apartment house ☆**2** an apartment house —***adj.*** of, in, or for an apartment or apartments

☆**apartment building** a building in which the rooms are arranged in suites as apartments: also **apartment house**

ap·a·tet·ic (ap′ə tet′ik) ***adj.*** ⟦Gr *apatētikos*, deceiving < *apatē*, deceit⟧ serving to mislead potential attackers: said of an animal's protective coloration: see APOSEMATIC

ap·a·thet·ic (ap′ə thet′ik) ***adj.*** ⟦< fol., modeled on PATHETIC⟧ **1** feeling little or no emotion; unmoved **2** not interested; indifferent; listless —***SYN.*** IMPASSIVE —**ap′a·thet′i·cal·ly** ***adv.***

ap·a·thy (ap′ə thē) ***n., pl.*** **-thies** ⟦Fr *apathie* < L *apathia* < Gr *apatheia* < *a-*, without + *pathos*, emotion: see PATHOS⟧ **1** lack of emotion **2** lack of interest; listless condition; unconcern; indifference

ap·a·tite (ap′ə tīt′) ***n.*** ⟦Ger *apatit* < Gr *apatē*, deceit + -ITE[1]: so named from being mistaken for other minerals⟧ any of a group of variously colored, hard, hexagonal calcium minerals, $Ca_5(PO_4,CO_3)_3$ (F,OH,Cl), found mainly in sedimentary rocks, esp. phosphate rock, and in teeth and bones: see MOHS SCALE

a·pa·to·saur·us (ə pat′ə sôr′əs, ap′ət ə-) ***n.*** ⟦ModL < Gr *apatē*, deceit + *sauros*, lizard: so named by O. C. Marsh (1831-99), U.S. paleontologist⟧ any of a genus (*Apatosaurus*) of huge sauropod dinosaurs of the Late Cretaceous, weighing more than 18,000 kg (20 tons)

APB (ā′pē′bē′) ***n.*** all-points bulletin: a general bulletin sent to law-enforcement agencies, as one describing a wanted person

APC[1] (ā′pē′sē′) ***n.*** ⟦*a*(*cetylsalicylic acid*), *p*(*henacetin*), and *c*(*affeine*)⟧ aspirin, phenacetin, and caffeine, usually in a white tablet (**APC tablet**) used for reducing fevers, relieving headaches, etc.

APC[2] *abbrev.* armored personnel carrier

ape (āp) ***n.*** ⟦ME < OE *apa*; akin to Ger *affe* < Gmc **apan*, prob. < OSlav *opica*⟧ **1** any gibbon or great ape **2** loosely, any Old or New World monkey **3** a person who imitates; mimic **4** a person who is uncouth, gross, clumsy, etc. —***vt.*** **aped, ap′ing** to imitate or mimic —***SYN.*** IMITATE —**go ape** [Slang] **1** to express unrestrained anger; rage **2** to become wildly enthusiastic: often with *over* —**ape′like′** ***adj.*** —**ap′er** ***n.***

a·peak (ə pēk′) ***adv., adj.*** *Naut.* in a vertical position

A·pel·doorn (ä′pəl dōrn′) city in EC Netherlands

A·pel·les (ə pel′ēz′) fl. 4th cent. B.C.; Gr. painter

ape-man (āp′man′) ***n., pl.*** **-men′** (-men′) any of several extinct primates, as a pithecanthropine, with structural characteristics intermediate between ape and man

Ap·en·nines (ap′ə nīnz′) mountain range of central Italy, extending the full length of the peninsula: highest peak, 9,560 ft (2,914 m)

a·per·çu (à per sü′; *E* ap′ər so͞o′) ***n., pl.*** **-çus′** (-sü′; *E*, -so͞oz′) ⟦Fr < pp. of *apercevoir*, to perceive⟧ **1** a quick impression or insight **2** a brief digest or survey

a·pe·ri·ent (ə pir′ē ənt) ***adj., n.*** ⟦L *aperiens*, prp. of *aperire*: see APERTURE⟧ laxative —***SYN.*** PHYSIC

a·pe·ri·od·ic (ā′pir′ē äd′ik) ***adj.*** **1** not periodic; occurring irregularly **2** *Physics* without periodic vibrations

a·pe·ri·tif (ə per′ə tēf′, ä′-, ap′ər ə-; *Fr* à pà rē tēf′) ***n.*** ⟦Fr *apéritif* < L *apertus*: see APERTURE⟧ **1** an alcoholic drink taken before a meal to stimulate the appetite **2** any of certain wines flavored with herbs and other substances, used as a cocktail ingredient or drunk before meals

a·pe·ri·ti·vo (ä per i tē′vō) ***n., pl.*** **-vi** (-vē) ⟦It, akin to Fr *apéritif*: see prec.⟧ APERITIF (sense 2), esp. any of those produced in Italy

ap·er·ture (ap′ər chər) ***n.*** ⟦L *apertura* < *apertus*, pp. of *aperire*, to open < IE **ap-wer-*, to uncover < base **ap(o)-*, away + **wer-*, to close, cover > WARN⟧ **1** an opening; hole; gap **2** the opening, or the diameter of the opening, in a camera, telescope, etc. through which light passes into the lens

ap·er·y (āp′ər ē) ***n., pl.*** **-er·ies** **1** an aping; mimicking **2** a silly or mischievous act

a·pet·a·lous (ā pet′'l əs) ***adj.*** *Bot.* without petals

a·pex (ā′peks′) ***n., pl.*** **a′pex′es** or **ap·i·ces** (ap′ə sēz′, ā′pə-) ⟦L, a point; prob. < *apere*, to fasten: see APT[1]⟧ **1** the highest point; peak; vertex **2** the pointed end; tip **3** the highest point of interest, excitement, etc.; climax ☆**4** *Mining* the edge or outcrop of a vein nearest the surface —***SYN.*** SUMMIT

Ap·gar score (ap′gär′) ⟦after V. *Apgar* (1909-74), U.S. anesthesiologist⟧ a quantitative rating test with a maximum of ten used to measure the vital signs of a newborn a minute or so after birth: a score greater than seven signifies good health

aph- (af) *prefix* APO-

aph·a·nite (af′ə nīt′) ***n.*** ⟦Gr *aphanēs*, invisible < *a-*, not + base of *phainein*, to appear (see FANTASY) + -ITE[1]⟧ rock so closely grained that its individual crystals cannot be seen by the unaided eye —**aph′a·nit′ic** (-nit′ik) ***adj.***

a·pha·si·a (ə fā′zhə, -zhē ə, -zē ə) ***n.*** ⟦ModL < Gr < *aphatos*, unuttered < *a-*, not + *phatos* < *phanai*, to say: see PHONO-⟧ total or partial loss of the power to use or understand words, usually caused by brain disease or injury —**a·pha′sic** (-zik) ***adj., n.***, **a·pha′si·ac′** (-zē ak′)

a·phe·li·on (ə fē′lē ən, -fēl′yən) ***n., pl.*** **-li·ons** or **-li·a** (-ə) ⟦ModL, altered (as if Gr) by Johannes KEPLER < earlier *aphelium* < Gr *apo-*, from + *hēlios*, SUN[1]; modeled on L *apogaeum*, APOGEE⟧ the point farthest from the sun in the orbit of a planet or comet, or of a man-made satellite in orbit around the sun: opposed to PERIHELION

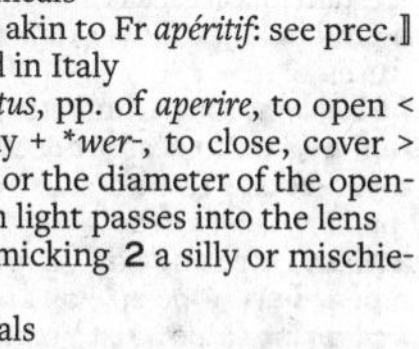

SUN
P
A

aphelion
(planet at aphelion A and at perihelion P)

a·phe·li·ot·ro·pism (ə fē′lē ä′trə piz′əm) ***n.*** ⟦AP- + HELIOTROPISM⟧ a tendency of certain plants to turn away from the sun; negative heliotropism —**a·phe′li·o·trop′ic** (-ə träp′ik) ***adj.***

a·pher·e·sis (ə fer′ə sis) ***n.*** ⟦LL *aphaeresis* < Gr *aphairesis* < *aphairein*, to take away < *apo-*, away + *hairein*, to take⟧ **1** the dropping of a letter, syllable, or phoneme at the beginning of a word (Ex.: *'cause* for *because*): also sp. **a·phaer′e·sis** **2** a medical procedure in which blood is taken from a donor, and some component, as the plasma or platelets, is separated from the blood cells in a centrifuge: the blood cells are then returned to the donor's circulatory system

aph·e·sis (af′ə sis) ***n.*** ⟦ModL < Gr, a letting go < *apo-* from + *hienai*, to send: see JET[1]⟧ loss of a short unaccented vowel at the beginning of a word, a form of apheresis (Ex.: *squire* for *esquire*) —**a·phet·ic** (ə fet′ik) ***adj.*** —**a·phet′i·cal·ly** ***adv.***

a·phid (ā′fid, af′id) ***n.*** ⟦< ModL *aphis* (pl. *aphides*); first applied by LINNAEUS prob. < MGr, misreading of Gr *koris*, a bug⟧ any of a large family (Aphididae) of small, soft-bodied homopteran insects that suck the juice from plants; plant louse —**a·phid·i·an** (ə fid′ē ən) ***adj., n.***

a·phis (ā′fis, af′is) ***n., pl.*** **aph·i·des** (af′ə dēz′) ⟦ModL⟧ an aphid; specif., one of a widespread genus (*Aphis*)

aphis lion any of the larvae of a family (Chrysopidae) of lacewings: a useful insect that feeds on aphids

a·pho·ni·a (ā fō′nē ə) ***n.*** ⟦ModL < Gr *aphōnia* < *aphōnos*, voiceless < *a-*, without + *phōnē*, sound, voice < *phanai*, to say: see PHONO-⟧ loss of voice due to an organic or functional disorder

a·phon·ic (ā fän′ik) ***adj.*** **1** of or having aphonia **2** *Phonet.* *a)* not pronounced *b)* voiceless

aph·o·rism (af′ə riz′əm) ***n.*** ⟦< OFr & ML: OFr *aufforisme* < ML *aphorismus* < LGr *aphorismos* < Gr, a distinction, determination < *aphorizein*, to divide, mark off < *apo-*, from + *horizein*, to bound: see HORIZON⟧ **1** a short, concise statement of a principle **2** a short, pointed sentence expressing a wise or clever observation or a general truth; maxim; adage —***SYN.*** SAYING

aph·o·ris·tic (af′ə ris′tik) ***adj.*** **1** of or like an aphorism **2** full of or using aphorisms —**aph′o·ris′ti·cal·ly** ***adv.***

aph·o·rize (af′ə rīz′) ***vi.*** **-rized′**, **-riz′ing** to write or speak in aphorisms —**aph′o·rist** ***n.***

a·pho·tic (ā fōt′ik) ***adj.*** ⟦A-[2] + PHOTIC⟧ without light; specif., pertaining to that part (**aphotic zone**) of the ocean below a depth of *c.* 100 m (*c.* 328 ft) which does not receive sufficient sunlight for photosynthesis: see EUPHOTIC

aph·ro·di·si·ac (af′rə dē′zē ak′, -diz′ē-) ***adj.*** ⟦Gr *aphrodisiakos*, ult. < fol.⟧ arousing or increasing sexual desire: also **aph′ro·di·si′a·cal** (-di zī′ə kəl) —***n.*** any aphrodisiac drug or other agent

Aph·ro·di·te (af′rə dīt′ē) ***n.*** ⟦? altered < Heb-Phoen *Ashtoreth*, ASHTORETH⟧ **1** *Gr. Myth.* the goddess of love and beauty: identified with the Roman Venus **2** [**a-**] a silver-spotted, large, brown butterfly (*Speyeria aphrodite*) of NE North America

aph·tha (af′thə) ***n., pl.*** **-thae** (-thē) ⟦ModL < L *aphthae* (occurring only in pl.) < Gr *aphtha* (pl. *aphthai*), eruption, thrush < *haptein*, to inflame⟧ a small, white spot or pustule, caused by either viral or fungal infections, that appears in the mouth, on the lips, or in the gastrointestinal tract in certain diseases, as thrush —**aph′thous** (-thəs) ***adj.***

a·phyl·lous (ā′fil′əs) ***adj.*** ⟦A-[2] + -PHYLLOUS⟧ lacking leaves, as most cactuses

API *abbrev.* American Petroleum Institute

A·pi·a (ä pē′ə) seaport & capital of Samoa, on Upolu island

a·pi·a·ceous (ā′pē ā′shəs) ***adj.*** ⟦< ModL *apiaceae*, carrot family < L *apium*, parsley, celery + -OUS⟧ UMBELLIFEROUS

a·pi·an (ā′pē ən) ***adj.*** ⟦L *apianus* < *apis*, bee⟧ of a bee or bees

a·pi·ar·i·an (ā′pē er′ē ən) ***adj.*** having to do with bees or the care of bees

a·pi·a·rist (ā′pē ə rist) ***n.*** a person who keeps bees

a·pi·ar·y (ā′pē er′ē) ***n., pl.*** **-ar′ies** ⟦L *apiarium*, beehive < *apis*, bee⟧ a place where bees are kept for their honey, generally consisting of a number of hives

ap·i·cal (ap′i kəl, ā′pi-) ***adj.*** ⟦ModL *apicalis* < L *apex* (gen. *apicis*), APEX + *-alis*, -AL⟧ **1** of, at, or constituting the apex **2** *Phonet.* articulated with the apex, or tip, of the tongue, as the (l), (t), and (d) of *lighted* —***n.*** a sound so articulated

ap·i·ces (ap′ə sēz′, ā′pə-) ***n.*** *alt. pl. of* APEX

ap·i·co-al·ve·o·lar (ap′i kō′al vē′ə lər) ***adj.*** *Phonet.* articulated with the apex of the tongue touching or near the alveolar ridge, as (t), (z), (n), and (l) —***n.*** an apico-alveolar consonant

ap·i·co·den·tal (ap′i kō dent′'l) ***adj.*** ⟦< *apico-*, APICAL (and)⟧ *Phonet.* articulated with the apex of the tongue near the upper front teeth, as (th) and (*th*) —***n.*** an apicodental consonant

a·pic·u·late (ə pik′yoo lit, -lāt′; ā-) ***adj.*** ⟦ModL *apiculatus* < *apiculus*, dim. of L *apex*, APEX⟧ ending abruptly in a small point, as some leaves

a·pi·cul·ture (ā′pi kul′chər) ***n.*** ⟦< L *apis*, bee + CULTURE⟧ the raising and care of bees; beekeeping —**a′pi·cul′tur·al** ***adj.*** —**a′pi·cul′tur·ist** ***n.***

a·piece (ə pēs′) ***adv.*** ⟦ME *a pece*: see A-[1] & PIECE⟧ for each one; each

à pied (à pyā′) ⟦Fr⟧ on foot; afoot

A·pis (ā′pis) ***n.*** ⟦L < Gr < Egypt *Ḥāpi*, lit., hidden⟧ *Egypt. Myth.* the sacred bull worshiped as the embodiment of Osiris

ap·ish (āp′ish) ***adj.*** **1** like an ape **2** imitative in an unreasoning way **3** silly, affected, mischievous, etc. —**ap′ish·ly** ***adv.*** —**ap′ish·ness** ***n.***

a·piv·o·rous (ā piv′ə rəs) ***adj.*** ⟦< L *apis*, bee + -VOROUS⟧ feeding on bees, as some birds

APL (ā′pē′el′) ***n.*** ⟦*a p(rogramming) l(anguage)*⟧ a high-level computer language employing a large number of special symbols, used esp. in mathematical applications

a·pla·cen·tal (ā′plə sent′'l) ***adj.*** having no true placenta, as any marsupial

ap·la·nat·ic (ap′lə nat′ik) ***adj.*** ⟦< Gr *aplanētos*, unerring < *a-*, not + *planan*: see PLANET⟧ *Optics* corrected for spherical aberration and coma: said of a lens

a·plas·tic anemia (ā plas′tik) ⟦< ModL *aplasia*, incomplete development (see A-[2] & -PLASIA) + -IC⟧ a form of anemia resulting from a failure of the bone marrow to produce adequate quantities of the essential blood components, including leukocytes and platelets

☆**a·plen·ty** (ə plen′tē) ***adj., adv.*** ⟦A-[1] + PLENTY⟧ [Informal] in abundance: used postpositively [*he's got problems aplenty*]

ap·lite (ap′līt′) ***n.*** ⟦Ger *aplit* < Gr *haploos*, simple (see HAPLO-) + -ITE[1]⟧ a light-colored, fine-grained igneous rock, similar to granite, that often forms in and near dikes, consisting mainly of quartz and feldspar —**ap·lit·ic** (ap lit′ik) ***adj.***

a·plomb (ə pläm′, -plum′) ***n.*** ⟦Fr, lit., perpendicularity, equilibrium < *à*, to + *plomb*, the metal lead: see PLUMB⟧ self-possession; assurance; poise —***SYN.*** CONFIDENCE

ap·ne·a or **ap·noe·a** (ap′nē ə) ***n.*** ⟦ModL < Gr *apnoia* < *a-*, without + *pnoiē*, wind: see PNEUMATIC & SNEEZE⟧ **1** temporary stopping of breathing **2** asphyxia See DYSPNEA —**ap·ne′ic** ***adj.***, **ap·noe′ic**

APO *abbrev.* Army and Air Force Post Office (overseas)

ap·o- (ap′ō, -ə) ⟦< Gr *apo*, off, from⟧ *prefix* **1** off, from, or away from [*apogamy*] **2** detached [*apocrine*]

ap·o·ap·sis (ap′ō ap′sis) ***n.*** *Astron.* the farthest point from the gravitational center in the orbit of any satellite: see PERIAPSIS

Apoc *abbrev.* **1** Apocalypse **2** Apocrypha

a·poc·a·lypse (ə päk′ə lips′) ***n.*** ⟦LL(Ec) *apocalypsis* < Gr *apokalypsis* < *apokalyptein*, to disclose < *apo-*, from + *kalyptein*, to cover < IE base **kel-* > HALL⟧ **1** any of various Jewish and Christian pseudonymous writings (*c.* 200 B.C.-*c.* A.D. 300) depicting symbolically the ultimate destruction of evil and triumph of good **2** a disclosure regarded as prophetic; revelation **3** a cataclysmic event, esp. the sudden and violent end of the world **4** [**A-**] the last book of the New Testament; Revelation

a·poc·a·lyp·tic (-lip′tik) ***adj.*** **1** of or like an apocalypse **2** of or relating to a sudden and violent end of the world **3** of or constituting a culminating or decisive event, turning point, etc., esp. one that is unsettling or threatening Also **a·poc′a·lyp′ti·cal** —***n.*** a system of beliefs about the end of the world, esp. that it will be sudden, violent, and destructive —**a·poc′a·lyp′ti·cal·ly** ***adv.***

a·poc·a·lyp·ti·cism (-lip′tə siz′əm) ***n.*** the belief that the world will end, esp. soon, in a series of events foretold in prophecy and marked by special signs and omens

ap·o·car·pous (ap′ō kär′pəs, ap′ə-) ***adj.*** *Bot.* having separate carpels, as the strawberry: see SYNCARPOUS

ap·o·chro·mat·ic (ap′ō krō mat′ik, ap′ə-) ***adj.*** *Optics* corrected to prevent distortion of the image and the occurrence of refracted colors along its edges: said of a lens

a·poc·o·pate (ə päk′ə pāt′) ***vt.*** **-pat′ed**, **-pat′ing** to shorten by apocope —**a·poc′o·pa′tion** ***n.***

a·poc·o·pe (-ə pē′) ***n.*** ⟦LL < Gr *apokopē*, a cutting off < *apokoptein*, to cut off < *apo-*, from + *koptein*, to cut off⟧ the cutting off or dropping of the last sound or sounds of a word (Ex.: *mos'* for *most*)

ap·o·crine (ap′ə krīn′, -krin) ***adj.*** ⟦< APO- + Gr *krinein*, to separate: see CRISIS⟧ designating a type of glandular secretion in which part of the secreting cell is thrown off along with the secretion, as a type of sweat with a strong odor from large, deep glands in the armpit and anal areas: see ECCRINE

a·poc·ry·pha (ə päk′rə fə) ***pl.n.*** ⟦ME *apocrifa* < LL(Ec) *apocrypha* (pl. of *apocryphus*) < Gr *apokryphos*, hidden, obscure < *apokryptein* < *apo-*, away + *kryptein*, to hide: see CRYPT⟧ [*with sing. or pl. v.*] **1** any writings, anecdotes, etc., of doubtful authenticity or authorship **2** [**A-**] fourteen books of the Septuagint that are rejected in Judaism and regarded by Protestants as not canonical: eleven of them are fully accepted in the Roman Catholic canon **3** [**A-**] various writings falsely attributed to Biblical characters or kept out of the New Testament because not accepted as resulting from revelation

a·poc·ry·phal (-fəl) ***adj.*** **1** of doubtful authorship or authenticity **2** not genuine; spurious; counterfeit **3** [**A-**] of or like the Apocrypha —***SYN.*** FICTITIOUS

a·poc·y·na·ceous (ə päs′ə nā′shəs) ***adj.*** of the dogbane family of plants, which are mainly tropical, with simple leaves and a milky, often poisonous juice

ap·o·cyn·thi·on (ap′ō sin′thē än′, -ən; ap′ə-) ***n.*** ⟦< APO- + Gr *Kynthion*, neut. of *Kynthios*: see CYNTHIA⟧ the point farthest from the moon in the orbit of a lunar satellite

ap·od (ap′əd) ***adj.*** APODAL —***n.*** an apodal animal, such as a snake or a legless lizard

ap·o·dal (ap′ə dəl) ***adj.*** ⟦< Gr *apous* (gen. *apodos*), footless < *a-*, without + *pous*, FOOT + -AL⟧ *Zool.* **1** lacking feet or legs, as snakes **2** lacking ventral fins Also **ap′o·dous** (-dəs)

ap·o·dic·tic (ap′ə dik′tik) ***adj.*** ⟦L *apodicticus* < Gr *apodeiktikos*, proving clearly < *apodeiknynai*, to show by argument < *apo-*, from + *deiknynai*, to show⟧ that can clearly be shown or proved; absolutely certain or necessarily true: also **ap′o·deic′tic** (-dīk′tik) —**ap′o·dic′ti·cal·ly** ***adv.***

a·pod·o·sis (ə päd′ə sis) ***n., pl.*** **-ses′** (-sēz′) ⟦LL < Gr, a giving back < *apo-*, back + *didonai*, to give⟧ the clause that expresses the conclusion or result in a conditional sentence: opposed to PROTASIS

ap·o·en·zyme (ap′ō en′zīm′) ***n.*** the part of an enzyme that consists wholly of protein and that, together with a coenzyme or prosthetic group, forms a complete enzyme (*holoenzyme*)

a·pog·a·my (ə päg′ə mē) ***n.*** ⟦APO- + -GAMY⟧ the development of a plant without the union of gametes; development of a sporophyte from a gametophyte without fertilization —**ap·o·gam·ic** (ap′ə gam′ik) ***adj.***, **a·pog′a·mous** (-məs)

ap·o·gee (ap′ə jē′) ***n.*** ⟦Fr *apogée* < ML *apogaeum* < Gr *apogaion* < *apo-*, from + *gaia*, *gē*, earth⟧ **1** the point farthest from the earth in the orbit of the moon or of a man-made satellite: opposed to PERIGEE **2** the highest or farthest point —**ap′o·ge′an** *adj.*, **ap′o·ge′al**

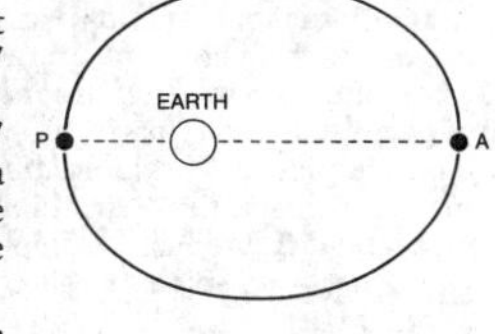

apogee
(moon at apogee A and at perigee P)

ap·o·ge·ot·ro·pism (ap′ō jē ä′trə piz′əm, ap′ə-) ***n.*** ⟦APO- + GEOTROPISM⟧ *Bot.* a tendency to grow or move away from the earth or from the pull of gravity; negative geotropism

ap·o·lip·o·pro·tein (ap′ə lip′ō prō′tēn′, -lī′pō-) ***n.*** the protein component of a lipoprotein, as HDL or LDL, that binds with a plasma lipid thus enabling it to circulate through the bloodstream

a·po·lit·i·cal (ā′pə lit′i kəl) ***adj.*** not concerned or connected with political matters —**a′po·lit′i·cal·ly** ***adv.***

A·pol·li·naire (ȧ pô lē ner′), **Guil·laume** (gē yōm′) (born *Wilhelm Apollinaris de Kostrowitzki*) 1880-1918; Fr. poet & essayist

A·pol·lo (ə päl′ō) ***n.*** ⟦L < Gr *Apollōn*⟧ **1** *Class. Myth.* the god of music, poetry, prophecy, and medicine, represented as exemplifying manly youth and beauty: later identified with Helios **2** *pl.* **-los** any handsome young man

Ap·ol·lo·ni·an (ap′ə lō′nē ən) ***adj.*** **1** of, like, or having to do with Apollo **2** well-ordered, rational, and serene: distinguished from DIONYSIAN Sometimes **Ap′ol·lin′i·an** (-lin′-)

A·pol·lyon (ə päl′yən) ***n.*** ⟦Gr *apollyōn*, destroying, ruining < *apollyein*, to destroy < *apo-*, from + *lyein*, to LOOSE⟧ *Bible* in Revelation, the angel of the abyss; Abaddon: Rev. 9:11

a·pol·o·get·ic (ə päl′ə jet′ik) ***adj.*** ⟦Fr *apologétique* < LL(Ec) *apologeticus* < Gr *apologētikos*, suitable for defense < *apologeisthai*: see APOLOGY⟧ **1** defending in writing or speech; vindicating **2** showing realization of and regret for a fault, wrong, etc.; making an apology Also **a·pol′o·get′i·cal** —***n.*** a formal defense, often written, of a belief, cause, etc. —**a·pol′o·get′i·cal·ly** ***adv.***

a·pol·o·get·ics (-iks) ***n.*** ⟦see prec.⟧ the branch of theology having to do with the defense and proofs of Christianity

ap·o·lo·gi·a (ap′ə lō′jē ə) ***n.*** ⟦LL(Ec): popularized by J. H. NEWMAN in *Apologia Pro Vita Sua*, his defense of his conversion from Anglicanism to Roman Catholicism⟧ an apology or formal defense of an idea, religion, etc., esp. such a defense of one's own beliefs or conduct

a·pol·o·gist (ə päl′ə jist) ***n.*** ⟦Fr *apologiste*: see APOLOGY⟧ a person who writes or speaks in defense or justification of a doctrine, faith, action, etc.

a·pol·o·gize (-jīz′) ***vi.*** **-gized′**, **-giz′ing** **1** to make an apology; acknowledge, and express regret for, a fault, wrong, etc. **2** to make a formal defense in speech or writing —**a·pol′o·giz′er** ***n.***

ap·o·logue (ap′ə lôg′, -läg′) ***n.*** ⟦Fr < L *apologus* < Gr *apologos*⟧ [Now Rare] a short allegorical story with a moral; fable

a·pol·o·gy (ə päl′ə jē) ***n.***, *pl.* **-gies** ⟦LL(Ec) *apologia* < Gr, a speaking in defense < *apologeisthai*, to speak in defense < *apo-*, from + *logos*, speech: see LOGIC⟧ **1** a formal spoken or written defense of some idea, religion, philosophy, etc. **2** an acknowledgment of some fault, injury, insult, etc., with an expression of regret and a plea for pardon **3** an inferior substitute; makeshift: usually used with a pejorative adjective [he is a poor *apology* for an actor]

ap·o·mict (ap′ō mikt′, ap′ə-) ***n.*** ⟦< *apomictic*, of apomixis < fol., with suffix as if < Gr *miktos*, mixed + -IC⟧ a plant that reproduces by apomixis or that has been produced by apomixis —**ap′o·mic′tic** ***adj.***

ap·o·mix·is (ap′ō mik′sis, ap′ə-) ***n.*** ⟦ModL < Gr *apo-*, from + *mixis*, a mingling: see MIX⟧ asexual reproduction of plants; esp., the formation of seed from the tissues of the maternal parent

ap·o·mor·phine (ap′ō môr′fēn′, ap′ə-) ***n.*** a crystalline alkaloid, $C_{17}H_{17}NO_2$, produced by synthesis from morphine: used as an emetic and expectorant

ap·o·neu·ro·sis (ap′ō nōō rō′sis, -nyōō-; ap′ə-) ***n.***, *pl.* **-ses′** (-sēz′) ⟦ModL < Gr *aponeurōsis* < *apo-*, from + *neuron*, NERVE⟧ a fibrous membrane that covers certain muscles or connects them to their origins or insertions —**ap′o·neu·rot′ic** (-rät′ik) ***adj.***

a·poph·o·ny (ə päf′ə nē) ***n.***, *pl.* **-nies** ⟦Fr *apophonie*: see APO- & -PHONY⟧ ABLAUT

ap·o·phthegm (ap′ə them′) ***n.*** APOTHEGM

a·poph·y·ge (ə päf′ə jē′) ***n.*** ⟦Gr *apophygē* < *apopheugein*, to flee away < *apo-*, from + *pheugein*, to flee < IE base **bheug-* > FUGITIVE⟧ *Archit.* the concave curve where the end of a column spreads into its base or capital

a·poph·yl·lite (-ə līt′) ***n.*** ⟦< APO- + Gr *phyllon*, a leaf + -ITE[1]: so named from its flaking off under the blowpipe⟧ a semihard, hydrous, tetragonal mineral, $KCa_4Si_8O_{20}(F,OH)\cdot 8H_2O$, usually found as variously colored crystals or flat, sheetlike plates

a·poph·y·sis (-ə sis) ***n.***, *pl.* **-ses′** (-sēz′) ⟦ModL < Gr, an offshoot < *apo-*, from + *phyein*, grow: see BE⟧ **1** *Anat.* any natural outgrowth or process, esp. on a vertebra or other bone **2** *Bot.* a swelling at the base of the capsule in some mosses —**a·poph′y·se′al** (-sē′al) ***adj.***

ap·o·plec·tic (ap′ə plek′tik) ***adj.*** ⟦LL *apoplecticus* < Gr *apoplēktikos* < *apoplēktos*, stricken: see fol. ⟧ **1** of, like, or causing apoplexy **2** having apoplexy **3** extremely angry, upset, etc. [he was *apoplectic* over the missed deadline] Also **ap′o·plec′ti·cal** —***n.*** a person having or likely to have apoplexy —**ap′o·plec′ti·cal·ly** ***adv.***

ap·o·plex·y (ap′ə plek′sē) ***n.*** ⟦ME & OFr *apoplexie* < LL *apoplexia* < Gr *apoplēxia* < *apoplēssein*, to strike down, disable by a stroke < *apo-*, from + *plēssein*, to strike < IE base **plāg-* > PLAGUE⟧ **1** [Old-fashioned] a cerebrovascular accident, or stroke **2** a condition in any organ of severe hemorrhage or infarction

ap·op·to·sis (ap′ə tō′sis, ap′əp-, ā′päp-) ***n.*** ⟦< Gr *apoptōsis*, a falling away < *apo-*, from + *ptōsis*, a fall: see PTOSIS⟧ a natural cytolytic process in which cells disintegrate and other cells nearby use the resulting cell parts —**ap′op·tot′ic** (-tät′ik) ***adj.***

a·po·ri·a (ə pôr′ē ə) ***n.*** ⟦L, doubt < Gr, perplexity < *aporos*, impassable < *a-*, A-[2] (sense 3) + *poros*, passage: see PORE[2]⟧ **1** a difficulty, as in a philosophical or literary text, caused by an indeterminacy of meaning for which no resolution seems possible **2** a condition of uncertainty or skeptical doubt resulting from this —**ap′o·ret·ic** (ap′ə ret′ik) ***adj.***

a·port (ə pôrt′) ***adv.*** *Naut.* on or to the left, or port, side

ap·o·se·mat·ic (ap′ō si mat′ik, ap′ə-) ***adj.*** ⟦APO- + SEMATIC⟧ *Zool.* serving to warn off potential attackers: said of an animal's warning coloration: see APATETIC —**ap′o·se·mat′i·cal·ly** ***adv.***

ap·o·si·o·pe·sis (ap′ō sī′ō pē′sis, ap′ə sī′ə-) ***n.*** ⟦L < Gr *aposiōpēsis* < *aposiōpan*, to be silent < *apo-*, from + *siōpan*, to be silent⟧ a sudden breaking off of a thought in the middle of a sentence as if one were unable or unwilling to continue (Ex.: the horrors I saw there—but I dare not tell them) —**ap′o·si′o·pet′ic** (-pet′ik) ***adj.***

ap·o·spor·y (ap′ō spôr′ē, ap′ə-) ***n.*** ⟦APO- + SPOR(E) + -Y[3]⟧ the formation of a gametophyte from a sporophyte cell which has not undergone reduction division: apomixis without spore formation

a·pos·ta·sy (ə päs′tə sē) ***n.***, *pl.* **-sies** ⟦ME *apostasie* < LL(Ec) *apostasia* < Gr *apo-*, away + *stasis*, a standing: see STASIS⟧ an abandoning of what one has believed in, as a faith, cause, or principles

a·pos·tate (-tāt′, -tit) ***n.*** ⟦ME *apostate, apostata* < OFr *apostate* & ML *apostata* < LL(Ec) *apostata* < Gr(Ec) *apostates* < Gr, deserter, rebel: see prec.⟧ a person guilty of apostasy —***adj.*** guilty of apostasy

a·pos·ta·tize (-tə tīz′) ***vi.*** **-tized′**, **-tiz′ing** ⟦ML *apostatizare*⟧ to become an apostate

a pos·te·ri·o·ri (ā′ päs tir′ē ôr′ī′, -ôr′ē) ⟦L, lit., from what comes later < *a*, *ab*, from + *posteriori*, abl. of *posterior*: see POSTERIOR⟧ **1** from effect to cause, or from particular instances to a generalization; inductive or inductively **2** based on observation or experience; empirical Opposed to A PRIORI

a·pos·til or **a·pos·tille** (ə päs′til) ***n.*** ⟦Fr *apostille* < *à*, to + *postille*, marginal note < ML *postilla* < L *post illa*, lit., after these⟧ an annotation, esp. one in the margin of a page

a·pos·tle (ə päs′əl) ***n.*** ⟦ME < OE *apostol* < LL(Ec) *apostolus* < Gr *apostolos*, person sent forth < *apostellein* < *apo-*, from + *stellein*, to send: see STILL[1]⟧ **1** a person sent out on a special mission **2** [*usually* **A-**] any of the early disciples of Christ who spread the gospel; specif., the twelve companions of Christ, originally, Andrew, Bartholomew, James (the younger, son of Alphaeus), James (the elder) and John (sons of Zebedee), Jude (or Lebbaeus or Thaddaeus), Judas Iscariot, Matthew (or Levi), Philip, Simon the Canaanite, Simon (called Peter), and Thomas (or Didymus): Paul, the "Apostle to the Gentiles," was not among the original twelve; Judas was replaced by Matthias **3** the first Christian missionary in a place **4** any of a group of early Christian missionaries **5** an early advocate or leader of a new principle or movement, esp. one aimed at reform **6** any of the twelve administrative officials of the Mormon Church

Apostles' Creed an ancient Christian statement of belief traditionally attributed to the Twelve Apostles: it begins, "I believe in God, the Father Almighty"

a·pos·to·late (ə päs′tə lit, -lāt′) ***n.*** ⟦ME *apostolat* < LL(Ec) *apostolatus* < *apostolus*: see APOSTLE⟧ the office, duties, or period of activity of an apostle

ap·os·tol·ic (ap′ə stäl′ik) ***adj.*** ⟦ME *apostolik* < LL(Ec) *apostolicus* < Gr *apostolikos*⟧ **1** of an apostle **2** of the Apostles or their teachings, work, or times **3** held to derive from the Apostles in a direct line of succession **4** [*often* **A-**] of the pope; papal Also **ap′os·tol′i·cal** —**a·pos·to·lic·i·ty** (ə päs′tə lis′ə tē) ***n.***

apostolic delegate a church official empowered to represent the pope, specif. in a country that does not have diplomatic relations with the Vatican

Apostolic Fathers **1** a group of early Christian writers of the late first and early second century traditionally believed to have known some of the Apostles **2** the writings attributed to them

apostolic see **1** a see, or bishopric, founded by an apostle **2** [**A- S-**] *R.C.Ch.* the Pope's see, regarded as having been founded at Rome by Peter

apostolic succession the doctrine that the religious authority and mission conferred by Jesus on Saint Peter and the other Apostles have come down through an unbroken succession of bishops

a·pos·tro·phe[1] (ə päs′trə fē) ***n.*** ⟦L < Gr *apostrophē*, a turning away from the audience to address one person < *apostrephein* < *apo-*, from + *strephein*, to turn: see STROPHE⟧ words addressed to a person or thing, whether absent or present, generally in an exclamatory digression in a speech or literary writing —**ap·os·troph·ic** (ap′ə sträf′ik) ***adj.***

a·pos·tro·phe[2] (ə päs′trə fē) ***n.*** ⟦Fr < LL *apostrophus* < Gr *apostrophos* (*prosōidia*), averted (accent): see prec. ⟧ a mark (') used: *a)* to indicate the omission of a letter or letters from a word or phrase (Ex.: *o'* for *of*, *it's* for *it is*) *b)* to form the possessive case of English nouns and some pronouns (Ex.: *Mary's* dress, the *girls'* club, *one's* duty) *c)* to form some plurals, as of figures and letters (Ex.: five *6's*, dot the *i's*) —**ap·os·troph·ic** (ap′ə sträf′ik) ***adj.***

a·pos·tro·phize (-fīz′) *vt., vi.* **-phized′, -phiz′ing** to speak or write an apostrophe (to)

apothecaries' measure *Pharmacy* a system of fluid measure using minims, fluid drams, and fluid ounces: see the table of weights and measures in the Reference Supplement

apothecaries' weight a system of weights no longer used in modern pharmacy: see the table of weights and measures in the Reference Supplement

a·poth·e·car·y (ə päth′ə ker′ē) *n., pl.* **-car′ies** ⟦ME *apotecarie* < OFr < ML *apothecarius*, shopkeeper, apothecary (in LL, warehouseman) < L *apotheca*, storehouse < Gr *apothēkē* < *apo-*, away + *tithenai*, to put: see DO[1]⟧ [Old-fashioned] **1** a pharmacist or druggist **2** a drugstore or pharmacy

ap·o·the·ci·um (ap′ō thē′shē əm, -sē əm; ap′ə-) *n., pl.* **-ci·a** (-ə) ⟦ModL < L *apotheca* (see prec.) + -IUM⟧ *Bot.* an open cuplike structure containing sacs in which sexual spores are developed, as in lichens and certain fungi —**ap′o·the′ci·al** (-shəl, -shē əl) *adj.*

ap·o·thegm (ap′ə them′) *n.* ⟦Gr *apophthegma*, a terse, pointed saying < *apophthengesthai* < *apo-*, from + *phthengesthai*, to utter⟧ a short, pithy saying (Ex.: "Brevity is the soul of wit") —**ap·o·theg·mat·ic** (ap′ə theg mat′ik) *adj.*, **ap′o·theg·mat′i·cal**

ap·o·them (ap′ə them′) *n.* ⟦ModL < APO- + Gr *thema*, that which is placed: see THEME⟧ *Math.* the perpendicular from the center of a regular polygon to any one of its sides

a·poth·e·o·sis (ə päth′ē ō′sis, ap′ə thē′ə sis) *n., pl.* **-ses′** (-sēz′) ⟦LL(Ec) < Gr *apotheōsis* < *apotheoun*, to deify < *apo-*, from + *theos*, god: see THEO-⟧ **1** the act of raising a person to the status of a god; deification **2** the glorification of a person or thing **3** a glorified ideal

a·poth·e·o·size (ə päth′ē ə sīz′, ap′ə thē′ə sīz′) *vt.* **-sized′, -siz′ing** ⟦prec. + -IZE⟧ **1** to make a god of; deify **2** to glorify; idealize

ap·o·tro·pa·ic (ap′ō trō pā′ik, ap′ə-) *adj.* ⟦< Gr *apotropaios*, averting evil (< *apotrepein*, to turn away) + -IC⟧ safeguarding against evil —**ap′o·tro·pa′i·cal·ly** *adv.*

app[1] (ap) *n. Comput. short for* APPLICATION (sense 8), specif., one designed to be downloaded to a computer, smartphone, etc. and having specific Web interface functions

app[2] *abbrev.* **1** appendix **2** applied **3** appointed **4** apprentice **5** approved

ap·pal (ə pôl′) *vt.* **-palled′, -pal′ling** *alt. sp. of* APPALL

Ap·pa·la·chi·a (ap′ə lā′chə, -chē ə; -lach′ə) the highland region of the E U.S. including the central and S Appalachian Mountains and the Piedmont plateau —**Ap′pa·la′chi·an** *adj.*

Appalachian Mountains ⟦< ? *Apalachee* Indians < ? AmInd (Choctaw)⟧ mountain system located in E North America, extending from S Quebec to N Ala.: *c.* 1,600 mi (2,575 m); highest peak, Mt. Mitchell: also **Appalachians**

☆**Appalachian tea** any of various plants, as withe rod, whose leaves were used locally for tea in pioneer times

Appalachian Trail hiking trail extending from central Me. to N Ga., along the Appalachian Mountains: *c.* 2,174 mi (3,499 km)

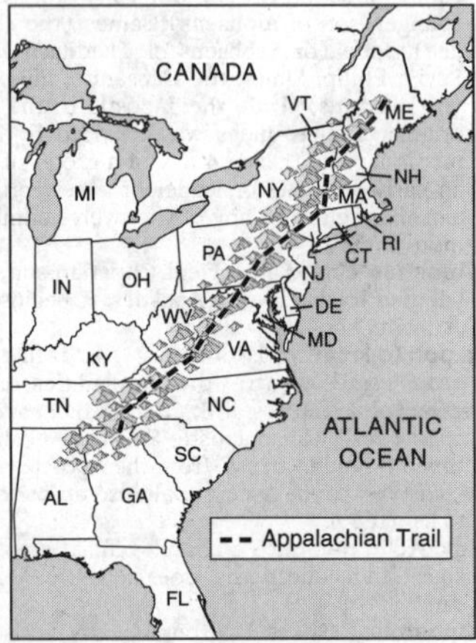

Appalachian Trail

ap·pall (ə pôl′) *vt.* ⟦ME *apallen* < OFr *apalir* < *a-*, to + *palir*, to grow pale < L *pallescere* < *pallere*, to be pale: see PALE[1]⟧ to fill with horror or dismay; shock —*SYN.* DISMAY

ap·pall·ing (-iŋ) *adj.* causing horror, shock, or dismay —**ap·pall′ing·ly** *adv.*

☆**Ap·pa·loo·sa** (ap′ə lo͞o′sə) *n.* ⟦altered < *a palouse*: so named after the *Palouse* Indians or the *Palouse* River (in NW Idaho and SE Washington), near which the horses were raised; ult. < a Nez Percé word⟧ [*also* **a-**] any of a sturdy breed of Western saddle horses distinguished by black and white spotted markings on the rump and loins

ap·pa·nage (ap′ə nij′) *n.* ⟦Fr *apanage* < ML *appanagium* < *appanare*, equip, lit., provide with bread < L *ad-*, to + *panis*, bread: see FOOD⟧ **1** money, land, etc. granted by a monarch for the support of his younger children **2** a person's rightful extra gain; perquisite **3** an accompanying endowment; adjunct

ap·pa·rat (äp′ə rät′, ap′ə rat′) *n.* ⟦Russ < Ger < L *apparatus*, APPARATUS⟧ an organization; esp., a political organization

ap·pa·rat·chik (äp′ə rä′chik) *n., pl.* **-chiks** or **-chi·ki** (-chi kē) ⟦Russ *apparatčik* < *apparat*: see prec.⟧ **1** a member, esp. an official, of a Communist Party **2** a member of any political organization; esp., a bureaucrat

ap·pa·ra·tus (ap′ə rat′əs, -rāt′-) *n., pl.* **-ra′tus** or **-ra′tus·es** ⟦L, a making ready, preparation < *apparare*, to make ready for < *ad-*, to + *parare*, PREPARE⟧ **1** the instruments, materials, tools, etc. needed for a specific use **2** any complex device or machine for a specific use **3** *Physiol.* a set of organs having a specific function [the digestive *apparatus*] **4** the means or system by which something is kept in action or a desired result is obtained; organization [the *apparatus* of government] **5** the notes, indexes, glossaries, etc. of a scholarly edition of a text: in full **apparatus crit·i·cus** (krit′i kəs)

ap·par·el (ə per′əl, -par′-) *n.* ⟦ME *appareil* < OFr *apareil* < VL **appariculum*, equipment < **appariculare*, to clothe < L *apparare*: see prec.⟧ **1** clothing; garments; attire **2** anything that clothes or adorns [the white *apparel* of winter] **3** [Archaic] a ship's outfit or furnishings, as rigging, anchor, guns, etc. —*vt.* **-eled** or **-elled, -el·ing** or **-el·ling 1** to clothe; dress **2** to adorn; bedeck

ap·par·ent (ə per′ənt, -par′-) *adj.* ⟦ME *aparaunt* < OFr *aparant* < L *apparens*, prp. of *apparere*, APPEAR⟧ **1** readily seen; visible **2** readily understood or perceived; evident; obvious **3** appearing real or true without necessarily being so; seeming See also HEIR APPARENT —*SYN.* EVIDENT —**ap·par′ent·ly** *adv.* —**ap·par′ent·ness** *n.*

apparent magnitude MAGNITUDE (sense 3)

ap·pa·ri·tion (ap′ə rish′ən) *n.* ⟦ME *apparicioun* < OFr *apparition* < ML *apparitio*, epiphany, appearance (in L, attendance, service) < *apparere*, APPEAR⟧ **1** anything that appears unexpectedly or in an extraordinary way **2** a phantom or ghost **3** the act of appearing or becoming visible —**ap′pa·ri′tion·al** *adj.*

ap·par·i·tor (ə per′ə tər, -par′-; -tôr′) *n.* ⟦L < *apparere*, APPEAR⟧ an officer formerly sent out to carry out the orders of a civil or ecclesiastical court

ap·pas·si·o·na·to (äp pä′syô nä′tô; *E* ə pä′sē ə nä′tō) *adj., adv.* ⟦It⟧ *Musical Direction* (in an) impassioned (manner): also **ap·pas′si·o·na′ta** (-tä; *E*, -tə)

ap·peal (ə pēl′) *vt.* ⟦ME *apelen* < OFr *apeler* < L *appellare*, to accost, apply to, appeal; iterative < *appellere*, to prepare < *ad-*, to + *pellere*: see FELT[1]⟧ **1** to submit (a lower court's ruling, verdict, etc.) to a higher court for review **2** [Obs.] to accuse of a crime —*vi.* **1** to appeal a law case to a higher court **2** to make an urgent request (*to* a person *for* help, sympathy, etc.) **3** to resort or turn (*to*) for decision, justification, etc. [to *appeal* to logic] **4** to be attractive, interesting, etc.; arouse a favorable response [her argument *appealed* to me] —*n.* **1** a call upon some authority or person for a decision, opinion, etc. **2** an urgent request for help, sympathy, etc. **3** a quality in a person or thing that arouses interest, sympathy, desire, etc.; attraction **4** [Obs.] an accusation **5** *Law a)* the submission of a lower court's ruling, verdict, etc. to a higher court for review *b)* a request for this *c)* the right to do this *d)* a court decision thus submitted —**on appeal** being reviewed or pending review by an appellate court: said as of a ruling or verdict of a trial court —**ap·peal′a·ble** *adj.* —**ap·peal′ing** *adj.* —**ap·peal′ing·ly** *adv.*

SYN.—**appeal** implies an earnest, sometimes urgent request and in legal usage connotes resort to a higher court or authority; **plead**, applied to formal statements in court answering to allegations or charges, carries into general usage the implication of entreaty by argument [he *pleaded* for tolerance]; **sue** implies respectful or formal solicitation for relief, a favor, etc.; **petition** implies a formal request, usually in writing and in accordance with established rights; **pray** and **supplicate** suggest humility in entreaty and imply that the request is addressed to God or to a superior authority, **supplicate** in addition suggesting a kneeling or other abjectly prayerful attitude

ap·pear (ə pir′) *vi.* ⟦ME *aperen* < OFr *aparoir* < L *apparere* < *ad-*, to + *parere*, to come forth, be visible; akin to Gr *peparein*, to display⟧ **1** to come into sight **2** to come into being [freckles *appear* on his face every summer] **3** to become understood or apparent [it *appears* he's right] **4** to seem; look [to *appear* to be in good health] **5** to present oneself formally, as in court **6** to come before the public [he will *appear* in *Hamlet*] **7** to be published [the magazine *appears* monthly]

ap·pear·ance (-əns) *n.* ⟦ME *aparaunce* < OFr *aparance* < LL *apparentia* < *apparere*, prec.⟧ **1** the act or an instance of appearing **2** the look or outward aspect of a person or thing **3** anything that appears; thing seen **4** [Archaic] an apparition **5** an outward show; pretense [to give the *appearance* of being busy] **6** [*pl.*] the way things seem to be [from all *appearances* he's innocent] —**keep up appearances** to maintain an outward show of being proper, decorous, well-off, etc. —**make an appearance 1** to put in an appearance **2** to appear publicly —**put in an appearance** to be present for a short time, as at a party, meeting, etc.

SYN.—**appearance** and **look** refer generally to the outward impression of a thing, but the former often implies mere show or pretense [an *appearance* of honesty], and the latter (often in the plural) refers specifically to physical details [the *look* of an abandoned house, good *looks*]; **aspect** also refers to physical details, esp. to facial features or expression [a man of handsome *aspect*] or to the distinguishing features at a given time or place [in spring the yard had a refreshing *aspect*]; **semblance**, which also refers to the outward impression as contrasted with the inner reality, usually does not imply deception [a *semblance* of order]; **guise** is usually used of a deliberately misleading appearance [under the *guise* of patriotism]

ap·pease (ə pēz′) *vt.* **-peased′, -peas′ing** ⟦ME *apaisen* < OFr *apaisier* < *a-*, to + *pais* < L *pax*, PEACE⟧ **1** to pacify or quiet, esp. by giving in to the demands of **2** to satisfy or relieve [water *appeases* thirst] —*SYN.* PACIFY —**ap·peas′a·ble** *adj.* —**ap·peas′er** *n.*

ap·pease·ment (-mənt) *n.* **1** an appeasing or being appeased **2** the policy of giving in to the demands of a hostile or aggressive power in an attempt to keep the peace

ap·pel (à pel′) ***n.*** ⟦Fr, lit., an appeal, call < *appeler*, APPEAL⟧ *Fencing* a slap or tap of the ball of the front foot as the first of two advancing steps in making a lunge

ap·pel·lant (ə pel′ənt) ***adj.*** ⟦Fr < prp. of *appeler*, APPEAL⟧ *Law* relating to appeals; appealing —***n.*** a person who appeals, esp. to a higher court

ap·pel·late (-it) ***adj.*** ⟦L *appellatus*, pp. of *appellare*, APPEAL⟧ *Law* relating to or having jurisdiction to review appeals [*an appellate court*]

ap·pel·la·tion (ap′ə lā′shən) ***n.*** ⟦L *appellatio* < pp. of *appellare*, APPEAL⟧ **1** the act of calling by a name **2** a name or title that describes or identifies a person or thing; designation

ap·pel·la·tion con·trô·lée (à pel lä syōn kôn trō lā′) ⟦Fr, controlled name⟧ [*often* **A- C-**] a designation on the label of certain French wines, brandies, etc. guaranteeing that the contents meet established standards, as type of grape and location of vineyard

ap·pel·la·tive (ə pel′ə tiv) ***adj.*** ⟦L *appellativus* < pp. of *appellare*, APPEAL⟧ **1** having to do with the giving of names; naming **2** relating to a common noun: an earlier usage —***n.*** **1** a name or title **2** a common noun: an earlier usage

ap·pel·lee (ap′ə lē′, ə pel′ē′) ***n.*** ⟦Fr *appelé*, pp. of *appeler*, APPEAL⟧ *Law* the respondent in an appeal

ap·pend (ə pend′) ***vt.*** ⟦ME *appenden* < OFr *apendre* < L *appendere* < *ad-*, to + *pendere*, hang: see SPIN⟧ to attach or affix; add as a supplement or appendix

ap·pend·age (ə pen′dij) ***n.*** **1** anything appended; adjunct **2** any subordinate or external organ or part of a plant or animal, as a branch, tail, or limb

ap·pend·ant or **ap·pend·ent** (-dənt) ***adj.*** ⟦Fr, prp. of *appendre*, APPEND⟧ **1** attached or added as an appendage **2** associated with as a consequence **3** *Law* belonging to as a subsidiary right —***n.*** **1** an appendage **2** *Law* a subsidiary right attached to and passing with a major one

☆**ap·pen·dec·to·my** (ap′ən dek′tə mē) ***n., pl.* -mies** ⟦APPEND(IX) + -ECTOMY⟧ the surgical removal of the vermiform appendix

☆**ap·pen·di·ci·tis** (ə pen′də sīt′is) ***n.*** ⟦< APPENDIX + -ITIS⟧ inflammation of the vermiform appendix: usually, the infected appendix must be surgically removed

ap·pen·di·cle (ə pen′di kəl) ***n.*** ⟦L *appendicula*, dim. of *appendix*, APPENDIX⟧ a small appendage or appendix

ap·pen·dic·u·lar (ap′ən dik′yoo lər, -yə-) ***adj.*** of an appendix or appendage; specif., of a limb or the limbs of a vertebrate

ap·pen·dix (ə pen′diks) ***n., pl.* -dix·es** or **-di·ces′** (-də sēz′) ⟦L, appendage < *appendere*, APPEND⟧ **1** additional or supplementary material at the end of a book or other writing **2** *Anat.* an outgrowth of an organ; esp., the VERMIFORM APPENDIX

Ap·pen·zell (ap′ən zel′; *Ger* ä′pən tsel′) canton of NE Switzerland: 161 sq mi (417 sq km): divided into two politically independent half cantons

ap·per·ceive (ap′ər sēv′) ***vt.* -ceived′, -ceiv′ing** ⟦ME *aperceiven* < OFr *aperceivre* < L *ad-*, to + *percipere*, PERCEIVE⟧ **1** *Psychol.* to assimilate and interpret (new ideas, impressions, etc.) by the help of past experience **2** [Obs.] to perceive

ap·per·cep·tion (-sep′shən) ***n.*** ⟦Fr *aperception* < *apercevoir*, prec.⟧ **1** the act or process of apperceiving **2** the state or fact of the mind in being conscious of its own consciousness —**ap′per·cep′tive** ***adj.***

ap·per·tain (ap′ər tān′) ***vi.*** ⟦ME *apertenen* < OFr *apertenir* < LL *appertinere* < *ad-*, to + *pertinere*: see PERTAIN⟧ to belong properly as a function, part, etc.; have to do with; relate; pertain

ap·pe·stat (ap′ə stat′) ***n.*** ⟦APPE(TITE) + -STAT⟧ a mechanism or region of the brain that regulates the desire for, and intake of, food: thought to be in the hypothalamus

ap·pe·ten·cy (ap′ə tən sē) ***n., pl.* -cies** ⟦L *appetentia*, a longing after < prp. of *appetere*: see fol.⟧ **1** a strong desire; craving; appetite **2** [Now Rare] *a)* an instinctive tendency; propensity *b)* a natural attraction; affinity Also **ap′pe·tence** (-təns)

ap·pe·tite (ap′ə tīt′) ***n.*** ⟦OFr *apetit* < L *appetitus*, eager desire for < *appetere*, to strive after < *ad-*, to + *petere*, to desire: see FEATHER⟧ **1** a desire to satisfy some craving of the body; specif., a desire for food, or, sometimes, a desire for some specific food **2** any strong desire or craving [*an appetite for knowledge*] —**ap′pe·ti′tive** (-tīt′iv) ***adj.***

ap·pe·tiz·er (-tī′zər) ***n.*** ⟦< fol. + -ER⟧ **1** a small portion of a tasty food or a drink to stimulate the appetite at the beginning of a meal **2** a bit of something that excites a desire for more

ap·pe·tiz·ing (-tī′ziŋ) ***adj.*** ⟦transl. of Fr *appétissant*, formed as if prp. of **appetissier* < base of *appétit*, APPETITE⟧ **1** stimulating the appetite **2** savory; delicious —**ap′pe·tiz′ing·ly** ***adv.***

Ap·pi·an Way (ap′ē ən) ⟦after the Roman censor *Appius* Claudius Caecus, by whom it was begun in 312 B.C.⟧ ancient Roman paved highway from Rome to Capua to Brundisium (Brindisi): *c.* 350 mi (563 km)

ap·plaud (ə plôd′) ***vt.*** ⟦L *applaudere* < *ad-*, to + *plaudere*, to clap hands, strike⟧ **1** to show approval of by clapping, cheering, etc. **2** to praise; commend [*I applaud your efforts*] —***vi.*** to show approval by clapping, etc. —**ap·plaud′er** ***n.*** —**ap·plaud′ing·ly** ***adv.***

ap·plause (ə plôz′) ***n.*** ⟦L *applausus*, pp. of *applaudere*, prec.⟧ approval or praise, esp. as shown by clapping hands, cheering, etc.

ap·ple (ap′əl) ***n.*** ⟦ME *appel* < OE *æppel*, fruit, apple (also, eyeball, anything round); akin to OIr *aball* (Welsh *afall*), apple tree⟧ **1** a round, firm, fleshy, edible fruit with a green, yellow, or red skin and small seeds **2** any of the trees (genus *Malus*) of the rose family bearing this fruit, widely distributed in temperate regions **3** any of various plants bearing applelike fruits, or growths, as the May apple, love apple, etc. **4** [*pl.*] [Slang] a troublesome response, fact, or state of affairs: in such sarcastic or reproving phrases as **how do you like them (or those) apples?** and **how about them (or those) apples?** —☆**(compare) apples and (or to) oranges** (to attempt to draw an analogy between) things regarded as not legitimately comparable —**the Apple** the BIG APPLE

☆**apple butter** a smooth, sweet, thick spread made from apples stewed with sugar and spices

apple cart a handcart from which a peddler sells apples in the street —**upset the (or someone's) apple cart** to disrupt a procedure, spoil someone's plans, etc.

ap·ple-cheeked (ap′əl chēkt′) ***adj.*** [Informal] **1** having rosy cheeks; ruddy **2** showing childlike innocence, freshness, enthusiasm, etc.

apple green a clear yellowish-green color

☆**ap·ple·jack** (-jak′) ***n.*** ⟦APPLE + JACK⟧ brandy distilled from fermented cider

☆**ap·ple-knock·er** (-näk′ər) ***n.*** ⟦? in ref. to another sense, apple picker or seller: from the erroneous idea that *apples* are *knocked* from trees⟧ [Slang] **1** a person living outside large urban areas, regarded as being unsophisticated, narrow-minded, etc. **2** an inexperienced person; greenhorn Also written **ap′ple·knock′er**

☆**apple maggot** **1** a fruit fly larva (*Rhagoletis pomonella*) that infests apples and other fruits **2** the winged adult stage of this fruit fly

apple of discord **1** *Gr. Myth.* a golden apple marked "For the most beautiful," claimed by Athena, Hera, and Aphrodite, and awarded by Paris to Aphrodite: in return, she helps him kidnap the beautiful Helen, thus starting the Trojan War **2** anything causing trouble, discord, or jealousy

apple of someone's eye ⟦from obs. sense of APPLE, pupil (of the eye), iris and pupil⟧ a person or thing that someone cherishes

ap·ple-pie (ap′əl pī′) ***adj.*** [Informal] of or characteristic of certain values, as wholesomeness or decency, esp. when regarded as being particularly American

ap·ple-pie order [Informal] neat, orderly condition

☆**apple polisher** ⟦in allusion to the former practice of a child giving his or her teacher an apple⟧ [Informal] a person who seeks to curry favor with a superior through gifts, flattery, etc.

ap·ple·sauce (-sôs′) ***n.*** **1** a dessert or relish made of apples simmered in water and puréed, often containing sugar, cinnamon, etc. ☆**2** [Slang] nonsense; hokum

Ap·ple·seed (ap′əl sēd′), **Johnny** (name for *John Chapman*) 1774-1845; U.S. frontiersman who planted apple trees throughout the Midwest

ap·plet (ap′lit) ***n.*** ⟦blend of APPLICATION & -LET⟧ *Comput.* a small APPLICATION (sense 8*b*) that performs a simple function and operates only within or in association with another program or device

Ap·ple·ton layer (ap′əl tən) ⟦after Sir Edward *Appleton* (1892-1965), Eng scientist⟧ the F_2 layer of the ionosphere: see F LAYER

ap·pli·ance (ə plī′əns) ***n.*** **1** [Rare] the act of applying; application **2** a device or machine for performing a specific task [*stoves, irons, etc. are household appliances*] —***SYN.*** IMPLEMENT

ap·pli·ca·ble (ap′li kə bəl, ə plik′ə-) ***adj.*** ⟦ML *applicabilis*: see APPLY & -ABLE⟧ that can be applied; appropriate —***SYN.*** RELEVANT —**ap′pli·ca·bil′i·ty** (-bil′ə tē) ***n.***

ap·pli·cant (ap′li kənt) ***n.*** ⟦< L *applicans*, prp. of *applicare*, APPLY⟧ a person who applies for employment, help, etc.

ap·pli·ca·tion (ap′li kā′shən) ***n.*** ⟦ME *applicacioun* < L *applicatio*, a binding on, joining to < pp. of *applicare*, APPLY⟧ **1** the act of applying; specif., *a)* the act of putting something on [*the application of cosmetics*] *b)* the act of putting something to use [*a job calling for the application of many skills*] **2** anything applied, esp. a remedy **3** a way of applying or method of applying or using; specific use [*a scientific principle having many applications in industry*] **4** an asking for something; request [*an application for employment*] **5** a form to be filled out with pertinent data in applying for something, as for employment **6** continued mental or physical effort; close attention; diligence **7** relevance or practicality [*this idea has no application to the case*] **8** *Comput.* *a)* any specific task, as billing, inventory, or Web interface, to be performed by a program *b)* a program for performing such a task: often in the pl. form when used attributively [*an application program, applications software*]

ap·pli·ca·tive (ap′li kāt′iv, -kə tiv) ***adj.*** applying or capable of being applied, as to some practical use; applicatory

ap·pli·ca·tor (-kāt′ər) ***n.*** ⟦< L *applicatus*, pp. of *applicare*, APPLY + -OR⟧ **1** any device for applying medicine or paint, polish, etc. **2** a person who applies a substance

ap·pli·ca·to·ry (-kə tôr′ē) ***adj.*** that can be applied or used; practical

ap·plied (ə plīd′) ***adj.*** used in actual practice or to work out practical problems [*applied science*]

ap·pli·qué (ap′li kā′) ***n.*** ⟦Fr, pp. of *appliquer* < L *applicare*: see fol.⟧ a decoration or trimming made of one material attached by sewing, gluing, etc. to another —***adj.*** applied as such a decoration —***vt.* -quéd′, -qué′ing** **1** to decorate with appliqué **2** to put on as appliqué

ap·ply (ə plī′) ***vt.* -plied′, -ply′ing** ⟦ME *applien* < OFr *aplier* < L *applicare*, to attach to < *ad-*, to + *plicare*, to fold: see PLY[1]⟧ **1** to put on or spread on; place so as to be touching [*to apply a salve to the skin*] **2** to put to some practical or specific use [*to apply one's knowledge to a problem*] **3** to refer to a person or thing with (an epithet or suitable term) **4** to concentrate (one's faculties) on; employ (oneself) diligently [*to apply oneself to one's work*] —***vi.*** **1** to make a formal request (*to* someone *for* something) **2** to be appropriate, suitable, or relevant [*this principle always applies*] —**ap·pli′er** ***n.***

ap·pog·gia·tu·ra (ə päj′ə toor′ə) ***n.*** ⟦It < *appoggiare*, to rest, lean < VL *appodiare*, to support < L *ad-*, to + **podiare*, to support < *podium*, PODIUM⟧ *Music* a rhythmically strong dissonant grace note used melodically and resolving to a principal harmonic tone, usually by a single scale step

ap·point (ə point′) ***vt.*** ⟦ME *apointen* < OFr *apointer*, to arrange, make ready < ML *appunctuare* < L *ad*, to + *punctum*, POINT⟧ **1** to set (a date, place, etc.); decide upon officially; decree *[*to *appoint* a time for a meeting*]* **2** to name or select officially for an office, position, etc. *[*to *appoint* a chairman*]* **3** to furnish and arrange: now usually in *well-appointed*, etc. **4** *Law* to decide the disposition of (property) by special authority —***vi.*** to make appointments to an office, position, etc. —***SYN.*** FURNISH

ap·point·ee (ə poin′tē′, ap′oin tē′) ***n.*** a person appointed to some position

ap·point·ive (ə point′iv) ***adj.*** of or filled by appointment *[*an *appointive* position*]*

ap·point·ment (ə point′mənt) ***n.*** **1** an appointing or being appointed; specif., a naming or selecting for an office, position, etc. **2** a person so selected **3** a position held in this way **4** an arrangement to meet someone or be somewhere at a set time; engagement **5** [*pl.*] furniture; equipment **6** *Law* the designation of beneficiaries and the assignment of property to them by an appointor

ap·poin·tor (ə poin′tər, -tôr′) ***n.*** *Law* a person given special authority (power of appointment) by a will or deed to dispose of property

Ap·po·mat·tox (ap′ə mat′əks) ⟦< Algonquian tribal name⟧ town in central Va., near Lynchburg: at a former nearby village (**Appomattox Court House**) Lee surrendered to Grant (April 9, 1865), ending the Civil War

ap·por·tion (ə pôr′shən) ***vt.*** ⟦OFr *apportionner*: see AD- & PORTION⟧ to divide and distribute in shares according to a plan —***SYN.*** ALLOT

ap·por·tion·ment (-mənt) ***n.*** **1** an apportioning or being apportioned **2** a proportional distribution or assignment, as of U.S. Representatives among the states, or of state legislators among counties, etc.

ap·pos·a·ble (ə pōz′ə bəl) ***adj.*** that can be apposed; opposable

ap·pose (ə pōz′) ***vt.*** **-posed′**, **-pos′ing** ⟦Fr *apposer* < L *appositus*, pp. of *apponere*, to put near to < *ad-*, to + *ponere*, to put⟧ **1** to put side by side; place opposite or near **2** [Archaic] to put or apply (something) *to* another thing

ap·po·site (ap′ə zit) ***adj.*** ⟦L *appositus*: see prec.⟧ suited to the purpose; appropriate; apt —***SYN.*** RELEVANT —**ap′po·site·ly** ***adv.*** —**ap′po·site·ness** ***n.***

ap·po·si·tion (ap′ə zish′ən) ***n.*** ⟦L *appositio*, a setting before < *appositus*: see APPOSE⟧ **1** an apposing or being apposed; putting side by side **2** the position resulting from this **3** *Gram. a)* the placing of a word or expression beside another so that the second explains and has the same grammatical construction as the first *b)* the relationship between such terms *[*"my cousin" is in *apposition* to "Mary" in "Mary, my cousin, is here"*]* —**ap′po·si′tion·al** ***adj.*** —**ap′po·si′tion·al·ly** ***adv.***

ap·pos·i·tive (ə päz′ə tiv) ***adj.*** of or in apposition —***n.*** a word, phrase, or clause in apposition —**ap·pos′i·tive·ly** ***adv.***

ap·prais·al (ə prāz′əl) ***n.*** **1** an appraising or being appraised **2** an appraised value or price; esp., an expert valuation for taxation, tariff duty, sale, etc.; estimate Also **ap·praise′ment**

ap·praise (ə prāz′) ***vt.*** **-praised′**, **-prais′ing** ⟦ME *apreisen* < OFr *apreiser* < LL(Ec) *appretiare* < L *ad*, to + *pretium*, PRICE; sp. infl. by PRAISE⟧ **1** to set a price for; decide the value of, esp. officially **2** to estimate the quantity of **3** to judge the quality or worth of —***SYN.*** ESTIMATE —**ap·prais′a·ble** ***adj.*** —**ap·prais′er** ***n.*** —**ap·prais′ing·ly** ***adv.***

ap·pre·ci·a·ble (ə prē′shə bəl, -shē ə-) ***adj.*** ⟦ME & OFr < ML *appretiabilis*: see fol. & -ABLE⟧ enough to be perceived or estimated; noticeable; measurable *[*an *appreciable* difference*]* —***SYN.*** PERCEPTIBLE —**ap·pre′ci·a·bly** ***adv.***

ap·pre·ci·ate (ə prē′shē āt′) ***vt.*** **-at′ed**, **-at′ing** ⟦< LL(Ec) *appretiatus*, pp. of *appretiare*, APPRAISE⟧ **1** to think well of; understand and enjoy; esteem **2** to recognize and be grateful for; be thankful for **3** to estimate the quality or worth of, esp. favorably **4** to be fully or sensitively aware of; notice with discrimination ☆**5** to raise the price or value of: opposed to DEPRECIATE —☆***vi.*** to rise in value —**ap·pre′ci·a′tor** ***n.*** —**ap·pre′ci·a·to′ry** (-shə tôr′ē, -shē ə-) ***adj.***

SYN.**—appreciate**, in this comparison, implies sufficient critical judgment to see the value of or to enjoy *[*he *appreciates* good music*]*; to **value** is to rate highly because of worth *[*I *value* your friendship*]*; to **prize** is to value highly or take great satisfaction in *[*he *prizes* his Picasso collection*]*; to **treasure** is to regard as precious and implies special care to protect from loss; to **esteem** is to hold in high regard and implies warm attachment or respect *[*an *esteemed* statesman*]*; to **cherish** is to prize or treasure, but connotes greater affection for or attachment to the thing cherished *[*she *cherished* her friends*]* See also **understand** —***ANT.*** **despise, disdain**

ap·pre·ci·a·tion (ə prē′shē ā′shən) ***n.*** **1** the act or fact of appreciating; specif., *a)* proper estimation or enjoyment *b)* grateful recognition, as of a favor *c)* sensitive awareness or enjoyment, as of art **2** a judgment or evaluation ☆**3** a rise in value or price: opposed to DEPRECIATION

ap·pre·ci·a·tive (ə prē′shə tiv, -shē ə-; -shē āt′iv) ***adj.*** feeling or showing appreciation —**ap·pre′ci·a·tive·ly** ***adv.*** —**ap·pre′ci·a·tive·ness** ***n.***

ap·pre·hend (ap′rē hend′, -ri-) ***vt.*** ⟦ME *apprehenden* < LL *apprehendere*, to understand < L, to take hold of < *ad-*, to + *prehendere*: see PREHENSILE⟧ **1** to take into custody; capture or arrest **2** to take hold of mentally; perceive; understand **3** to anticipate with fear or alarm: now rare, except in legal usage **4** [Obs.] to seize —***vi.*** to understand

ap·pre·hen·si·ble (-hen′sə bəl) ***adj.*** ⟦ME < LL *apprehensibilis*: see prec. & -IBLE⟧ that can be apprehended —**ap′pre·hen′si·bil′i·ty** (-bil′ə tē) ***n.***

ap·pre·hen·sion (-hen′shən) ***n.*** ⟦ME *apprehencioun* < LL *apprehensio*: see APPREHEND⟧ **1** capture or arrest **2** mental grasp; perception or understanding **3** a judgment or opinion **4** an anxious feeling of foreboding; dread

ap·pre·hen·sive (-hen′siv) ***adj.*** ⟦ME < ML *apprehensivus* < pp. of L *apprehendere*, APPREHEND⟧ **1** able or quick to apprehend or understand **2** having to do with perceiving or understanding **3** anxious or fearful about the future; uneasy —**ap′pre·hen′sive·ly** ***adv.*** —**ap′pre·hen′sive·ness** ***n.***

ap·pren·tice (ə pren′tis) ***n.*** ⟦ME *aprentis* < OFr *aprentiz* < *aprendre*, learn < L *apprehendere*, APPREHEND⟧ **1** a person under legal agreement to work a specified length of time for a master craftsman in a craft or trade in return for instruction and, formerly, support **2** a person who is acquiring a trade, craft, or skill under specified conditions, usually as a member of a labor union **3** any learner or beginner; novice —***vt.*** **-ticed**, **-tic·ing** to place or accept as an apprentice —***vi.*** to work or train as an apprentice —**ap·pren′tice·ship′** ***n.***

ap·pressed (ə prest′, a-) ***adj.*** ⟦< L *appressus*, pp. of *apprimere* < *ad-*, to + *primere*, to press⟧ pressed close to or flat against a surface: said esp. of a leaf or plant part

ap·prise or **ap·prize** (ə prīz′) ***vt.*** **-prised′** or **-prized′**, **-pris′ing** or **-priz′ing** ⟦< Fr *appris*, pp. of *apprendre*, to teach, inform < L *apprehendere*, APPREHEND⟧ to inform or notify —***SYN.*** NOTIFY

ap·proach (ə prōch′) ***vi.*** ⟦ME *aprochen* < OFr *aprochier* < LL(Ec) *appropiare* < L *ad-*, to + *propius*, compar. of *prope*, near⟧ to come closer or draw nearer —***vt.*** **1** to come near or nearer to **2** to be like or similar to; approximate **3** to make advances, a proposal, or a request to **4** to begin dealing with *[*to *approach* a task*]* —***n.*** **1** a coming closer or drawing nearer **2** an approximation or similarity **3** an advance or overture (*to* someone): *usually used in pl.* **4** a path, road, or other means of reaching a person or place; access **5** a means of attaining a goal or purpose *[*let's take a new *approach* to the problem*]* **6** *Aeron.* the act of bringing an aircraft into position for landing, bombing a target, etc. **7** *Golf* a shot from the fairway, meant to hit the ball onto the putting green

ap·proach·a·ble (-ə bəl) ***adj.*** **1** that can be approached; accessible **2** easily approached; friendly; receptive —**ap·proach′a·bil′i·ty** ***n.***

ap·pro·bate (ap′rə bāt′) ***vt.*** **-bat′ed**, **-bat′ing** ⟦ME *approbaten* < L *approbatus*, pp. of *approbare*, APPROVE⟧ [Now Rare] to approve or sanction

ap·pro·ba·tion (ap′rə bā′shən) ***n.*** **1** approval, sanction, or commendation **2** [Obs.] proof

ap·pro·ba·tive (ap′rə bāt′iv) ***adj.*** ⟦Fr *approbatif* < LL *approbativus*⟧ showing approbation or approval: also **ap·pro·ba·to·ry** (ə prō′bə tôr′ē)

ap·pro·pri·a·ble (ə prō′prē ə bəl) ***adj.*** that can be appropriated

ap·pro·pri·ate (ə prō′prē āt′; *for adj.*, -it) ***vt.*** **-at′ed**, **-at′ing** ⟦ME *appropriaten* < LL *appropriatus*, pp. of *appropriare*, to make one's own < L *ad-*, to + *proprius*, one's own⟧ **1** to take for one's own or exclusive use **2** to take improperly, as without permission **3** to set aside for a specific use or certain person *[*to *appropriate* funds for the schools*]* —***adj.*** right for the purpose; suitable; fit; proper: often in comb. *[*age-*appropriate* TV shows for preschoolers*]* —***SYN.*** FIT[1] —**ap·pro′pri·ate·ly** ***adv.*** —**ap·pro′pri·ate·ness** ***n.*** —**ap·pro′pri·a′tive** ***adj.*** —**ap·pro′pri·a′tor** ***n.***

ap·pro·pri·a·tion (ə prō′prē ā′shən) ***n.*** **1** an appropriating or being appropriated **2** [*often pl.*] a thing appropriated; esp., money set aside for a specific use

ap·prov·al (ə proo̅′vəl) ***n.*** **1** the act of approving **2** favorable attitude or opinion **3** formal consent or sanction **4** [*pl.*] *Philately* stamps sent on request by mail to potential buyers —**on approval** for the customer to examine and decide whether to buy or return

ap·prove (ə proo̅v′) ***vt.*** **-proved′**, **-prov′ing** ⟦ME *aproven* < OFr *aprover* < L *approbare* < *ad-*, to + *probare*, to try, test < *probus*, good⟧ **1** to give one's consent to; sanction; confirm **2** to be favorable toward; think or declare to be good, satisfactory, etc. **3** [Archaic] to prove or show: often used reflexively **4** [Obs.] to prove by testing —***vi.*** to give approval; have a favorable opinion (*of*) —**ap·prov′a·ble** ***adj.*** —**ap·prov′er** ***n.*** —**ap·prov′ing·ly** ***adv.***

SYN.**—approve**, the most general of the following terms, means simply to regard as good or satisfactory; **endorse** adds the further implication of active support or advocacy *[*to *endorse* a candidate for office*]*; **sanction** implies authoritative approval *[*a practice *sanctioned* by the charter*]*; **certify** implies official approval because of compliance with the requirements or standards *[*a *certified* public accountant*]*; **ratify** implies official approval of that which has been done by one's representative *[*to *ratify* a peace treaty*]* —***ANT.*** **disapprove, reject**

approx *abbrev.* **1** approximate **2** approximately

ap·prox·i·mal (ə präk′sə məl) ***adj.*** ⟦< L *approximare* (see fol.) + -AL⟧ *Anat.* side by side; adjoining

ap·prox·i·mate (ə präk′sə mit; *for v.*, -māt′) ***adj.*** ⟦ME < LL *approximatus*, pp. of *approximare*, to come near < L *ad-*, to + *proximus*, superl. of *prope*, near⟧ **1** near in position; close together **2** much like; resembling **3** more or less correct or exact —***vt.*** **-mat′ed**, **-mat′ing** **1** to come near to; approach or be almost the same as *[*this painting *approximates* reality*]* **2** to bring near; make approach (*to* something) **3** to estimate roughly —***vi.*** to come near; be almost the same —**ap·prox′i·mate·ly** ***adv.***

ap·prox·i·ma·tion (ə präk′sə mā′shən) ***n.*** **1** the act or state of approximating, or coming close **2** a calculation, assessment, etc. intended to be no more than approximately accurate; rough estimate

ap·pur·te·nance (ə purt′'n əns) ***n.*** ⟦ME < Anglo-Fr *apurtenance* < OFr *apertenance* < prp. of LL *appertinere*, APPERTAIN⟧ **1** anything that appertains; thing added to a more important thing; adjunct **2** [*pl.*] apparatus or equipment; accessories **3** an incidental right, privilege, etc., attached to some thing and passing with it, as by conveyance or sale

ap·pur·te·nant (-ənt) ***adj.*** appertaining or pertinent; accessory —***n.*** an appurtenance

Apr *abbrev.* April

APR *abbrev.* annual percentage rate

a·prax·i·a (ā prak′sē ə, ə-) ***n.*** ⟦ModL < Gr, inaction; see A-[2] & PRAXIS⟧ complete or partial loss of the ability to perform complex muscular movements, resulting from damage to certain areas of the brain without any paralysis or damage to normal motor functions —**a·prax′ic** (-prak′sik) ***adj.***, **a·prac′tic** (-prak′tik)

a·près (a′prā′; *Fr* å pre′) ***prep.*** ⟦Fr⟧ after: often used in hyphenated compounds [an *après*-ski party]

a·près moi le dé·luge (å pre mwå lə dā lüzh′) ⟦Fr⟧ after me the deluge: a saying attributed to Louis XV of France

ap·ri·cot (ap′ri kät′, ā′pri-) ***n.*** ⟦Fr *abricot* < Port *albricoque* < Ar *al-birqūq* < LGr *praikokion* < L *praecoquum*, early matured (fruit) < *prae-*, beforehand + *coquere*, ripen, COOK⟧ **1** a small, yellowish-orange fruit that is closely related to the peach and plum **2** any of various prunus trees bearing this fruit **3** a yellowish-orange color

A·pril[1] (ā′prəl) ***n.*** ⟦altered, infl. by the L, from ME *Avril* < OFr *avrill* < L *aprilis* < **apero-*, latter, second (in the ancient Roman calendar, the year began with March); akin to Sans *aparah*, latter, Goth *afar*, after⟧ the fourth month of the year, having 30 days: abbrev. *Apr* or *Ap*

A·pril[2] (ā′prəl) ***n.*** a feminine name: equiv. Fr. *Avril*

April fool victim of jokes played on April Fools' Day

April Fools' Day April 1; All Fools' Day, when practical jokes are played on the unsuspecting

a pri·o·ri (ā′ prī ôr′ī, -ôr′ē; ä′-) ⟦L, lit., from what precedes < *a, ab*, from + *priori*, abl. of *prior*: see PRIOR⟧ **1** from cause to effect or from a generalization to particular instances; deductive or deductively **2** based on theory, logic, fixed rules or forms, etc. instead of on experience or experiment **3** before examination or analysis Opposed to A POSTERIORI

a·pri·or·i·ty (ā′prī ôr′ə tē) ***n.*** **1** the quality or fact of being a priori **2** the use of a priori reasoning

a·pron (ā′prən) ***n.*** ⟦by faulty separation of *a napron* < ME *napron* < OFr *naperon* < *nape*, a cloth < L *mappa*, napkin⟧ **1** a garment of cloth, leather, etc. worn over the front part of the body, usually to protect one's clothes **2** anything like an apron in appearance or use; specif., *a)* a covering or extending part for protecting or shielding a structure, machine, etc. *b)* a waterproof protecting shield in an open vehicle *c)* the hard-surfaced area, often paved, in front of or next to the terminal or hangars of an airport *d)* a broadened part of an automobile driveway, as where it joins the roadway *e)* the part of a proscenium stage in front of the arch *f)* an endless belt for carrying things *g)* a protective work of planking or other material along a river bank, below a dam, etc. —***vt.*** to put an apron on or provide an apron for —**a′pron·like′** ***adj.***

apron string a cloth tie, typically attached to an apron, for securing it about the waist: *usually used in pl.* —**tied to one's mother's** (or **wife's,** etc.) **apron strings** dominated by one's mother (or wife, etc.)

ap·ro·pos (ap′rə pō′) ***adv.*** ⟦Fr *à propos*, to the purpose < L *ad*, to + *propositus*, pp. of *proponere*, PROPOSE⟧ **1** at the right time; opportunely **2** by the way: used to introduce a remark —***adj.*** fitting the occasion; relevant; apt —***prep.*** in connection with; with regard to —***SYN.*** RELEVANT —**apropos of** in connection with; with regard to

A-prop·o·si·tion (ā′präp′ə zish′ən) ***n.*** *Logic* a universal, affirmative proposition

apse (aps) ***n.*** ⟦L *apsis*, APSIS⟧ **1** a semicircular or polygonal projection of a building, esp. one at the east end of a church, with a domed or vaulted roof **2** APSIS (sense 1)

ap·si·dal (ap′si dəl) ***adj.*** of an apse or apsis

ap·sis (ap′sis) ***n., pl.*** **-si·des′** (-sə dēz′) ⟦L, an arch < Gr *hapsis*, a fastening < *haptein*: see fol.⟧ **1** that point in the elliptical orbit of the moon, a planet, etc. nearest to (**lower apsis**), or that farthest from (**higher apsis**), the gravitational focus point **2** APSE (sense 1) —**line of apsides** a line joining the lower and higher apsides, forming the major axis of the orbit

apt[1] (apt) ***adj.*** ⟦ME & OFr *apte* < L *aptus*, pp. of *apere*, to fasten < IE base **ap-*, to grasp, reach > Gr *haptein*, to fasten⟧ **1** suited to its purpose; appropriate; fitting [an *apt* remark] **2** tending or inclined; likely [*apt* to rain] **3** quick to learn or understand [an *apt* student] **4** [Archaic] ready; prepared —***SYN.*** FIT[1], LIKELY, QUICK —**apt′ly** ***adv.*** —**apt′ness** ***n.***

apt[2] *abbrev.* apartment

ap·ter·al (ap′tər əl) ***adj.*** ⟦Gr *apteros* (see APTEROUS) + -AL⟧ **1** *Archit.* having columns at one or both ends, but not along the sides **2** *Zool.* APTEROUS

ap·te·ri·um (ap tir′ē əm) ***n., pl.*** **-te′ri·a** (-ē ə) ⟦ModL: see fol. & -IUM⟧ *Ornithology* a bare area of skin between feather tracts on the body of a bird

ap·ter·ous (ap′tər əs) ***adj.*** ⟦Gr *apteros* < *a-*, without + *pteron*, a wing, FEATHER⟧ *Biol.* having no wings or winglike parts

ap·ter·yg·i·al (ap′tər ij′ē əl) ***adj.*** ⟦< Gr *apterygos* < *a-*, without + *pteryx*, wing + -AL⟧ *Zool.* lacking fins, limbs, or wings

ap·ter·yx (ap′tər iks′) ***n.*** ⟦ModL < Gr *a-*, without + *pteryx*, wing⟧ KIWI

ap·ti·tude (ap′tə to͞od′, -tyo͞od′) ***n.*** ⟦ME < LL *aptitudo* < L *aptus*: see APT[1]⟧ **1** [Archaic] the quality of being apt, or appropriate; fitness **2** a natural tendency or inclination **3** a natural ability or talent **4** quickness to learn or understand —***SYN.*** TALENT

☆**aptitude test** a test for determining the probability of a person's success in some activity in which he is not yet trained

A·pu·le·ius (ap′yo͞o lē′əs), **Lucius** fl. 2d cent. A.D.; Rom. satirist: author of *The Golden Ass*

A·pu·li·a (ə pyo͞ol′yə, -ē ə) region on the SE coast of Italy, on the Adriatic Sea & the Gulf of Taranto: 7,469 sq mi (19,357 sq km); cap. Bari: It. name PUGLIA

A·pu·re (ä po͞o′re) river in WC Venezuela, flowing from the Andes into the Orinoco: *c.* 500 mi (805 km)

A·pus (ā′pəs) ***n.*** ⟦ModL, the Old World swift (genus name) < Gr *apous*, lit., footless: see APODAL⟧ a S constellation near the celestial pole

APY *abbrev.* annual percentage yield

a·py·ret·ic (ā′pī ret′ik) ***adj.*** ⟦Gr *apyretos*: see A-[2] & PYRETIC⟧ *Med.* without fever

aq *abbrev.* ⟦L *aqua*⟧ *Pharmacy* water

A·qa·ba (ä′kə bä′), **Gulf of** arm of the Red Sea between the Sinai Peninsula and NW Saudi Arabia

aq·ua (äk′wə, ak′wə) ***n., pl.*** **aq′uas** or **aq′uae′** (-wē′) ⟦L < IE **akwa-*: see ISLAND⟧ **1** water; esp., in pharmacy, a solution of a substance in water **2** a bluish-green color —***adj.*** ⟦< AQUAMARINE⟧ bluish-green

aqua ammonia ⟦ModL, lit., water of ammonia⟧ a water solution of ammonia; ammonia water; ammonium hydroxide

☆**aq·ua·cade** (äk′wə kād′, ak′-) ***n.*** ⟦AQUA(TIC) + -CADE⟧ an aquatic exhibition or entertainment consisting of swimming, diving, etc., often to music

aq·ua·cul·ture (-kul′chər) ***n.*** ⟦AQUA + CULTURE⟧ the regulation and cultivation of water plants and animals for human use or consumption —**aq′ua·cul′tur·al** ***adj.***

aqua for·tis (fôr′tis) ⟦L, strong water⟧ NITRIC ACID

aq·ua·lung (-luŋ′) ***n.*** ⟦< *Aqua-Lung*, a trademark: see fol.⟧ [*also* **A-**] a type of scuba apparatus like an Aqua-Lung

Aq·ua-Lung (-luŋ′) ⟦AQUA + LUNG⟧ *trademark for* a type of scuba apparatus no longer much used

aq·ua·ma·rine (äk′wə mə rēn′, ak′-) ***n.*** ⟦L *aqua marina*, sea water⟧ **1** a transparent, pale bluish-green variety of beryl, used in jewelry **2** its color —***adj.*** bluish-green

☆**aq·ua·naut** (äk′wə nôt′, ak′-) ***n.*** ⟦AQUA + (ASTRO)NAUT⟧ **1** a person trained to live and work in a watertight underwater chamber in and from which oceanographic experiments can be conducted **2** a skin diver: see SKIN DIVING

☆**aq·ua·plane** (äk′wə plān′, ak′-) ***n.*** ⟦AQUA + PLANE[4]⟧ a board or small platform towed by a speedboat while a person stands on it, often holding onto ropes attached to the board or platform for support —***vi.*** **-planed′**, **-plan′ing** **1** to ride on such a board or platform as a sport **2** HYDROPLANE (***vi.*** 2)

aqua pu·ra (pyoor′ə, poor′ə) ⟦L⟧ pure water; esp., distilled water

aqua re·gi·a (rē′jē ə) ⟦L, lit., kingly water: it dissolves the "noble metals," gold and platinum⟧ a mixture of nitric and hydrochloric acids

aq·ua·relle (äk′wə rel′, ak′-) ***n.*** ⟦Fr < It *acquerella*, watercolor < *acqua* < L *aqua*, water⟧ a kind of painting in transparent watercolors —**aq′ua·rel′list** ***n.***

A·quar·i·an (ə kwer′ē ən) ***n.*** *var. of* AQUARIUS (***n.*** 3)

☆**a·quar·ist** (ə kwer′ist) ***n.*** **1** a person who keeps an aquarium as a hobby **2** the curator or director of an AQUARIUM (sense 2)

a·quar·i·um (ə kwer′ē əm) ***n., pl.*** **-i·ums** or **-i·a** (-ə) ⟦L, watering place for cattle, neut. of *aquarius*, of water < *aqua*, water⟧ **1** a tank, usually with glass sides, or a pool, bowl, etc. for keeping live water animals and water plants **2** a building where such collections are exhibited

A·quar·i·us (ə kwer′ē əs) ***n.*** ⟦L, water carrier: see prec.⟧ **1** a large S constellation, near the celestial equator between Cetus and Capricornus; the Water Bearer **2** the eleventh sign of the zodiac, entered by the sun about January 21: also called *the Water Bearer* **3** a person born under this sign

a·quat·ic (ə kwät′ik, -kwat′-) ***adj.*** ⟦L *aquaticus* < *aqua*, water⟧ **1** growing or living in or upon water [*aquatic* plants] **2** done in or upon the water [*aquatic* sports] —***n.*** **1** an aquatic plant or animal **2** [*pl., often with sing. v.*] aquatic sports or performances —**a·quat′i·cal·ly** ***adv.***

aq·ua·tint (äk′wə tint′, ak′-) ***n.*** ⟦Fr *aquatinte* < It *acqua tinta*, dyed in water < L *aqua*, water + *tintus*, pp. of *tingere*, to dye, TINGE⟧ **1** a process by which spaces rather than lines are etched with acid, producing tones that give the effect of a wash drawing or watercolor **2** an etching made in this way —***vt.*** to etch in this way

aq·ua·vit (äk′wə vēt′, ak′-) ***n.*** ⟦Ger < L *aqua vitae*: see fol. ⟧ a Scandinavian alcoholic liquor distilled from grain or potatoes, flavored with caraway seeds, and usually drunk as an aperitif

aqua vi·tae (vīt′ē) ⟦ML, spirit distilled from wine and herbs, alcohol, lit., water of life (> ME *aqua vite*, brandy, Dan *akvavit*, Ger *aquavit*) < L *aqua*, water + gen. of *vita*, life: see VITAL & WHISKEY⟧ **1** *Alchemy* alcohol **2** brandy or other strong liquor

aq·ue·duct (ak′wə dukt′) ***n.*** ⟦L *aquaeductus* < *aquae*, gen. of *aqua*, water + *ductus*: see DUCT⟧ **1** a large pipe or conduit made for bringing water from a distant source **2** a bridgelike structure for carrying a water conduit or canal across a river or valley **3** *Anat.* a passage or canal

a·que·ous (ā′kwē əs, ak′wē-) ***adj.*** ⟦ML *aqueus*: see AQUA & -OUS⟧ **1** of, like, or containing water; watery **2** formed by the action of water, as certain rocks made of sediment **3** of or having to do with the aqueous humor

aqueous humor a watery fluid in the space between the cornea and the lens of the eye

aq·ui·cul·ture (ăk′wə kul′chər, ak′-) ***n.*** AQUACULTURE —**aq′ui·cul′tur·al** ***adj.***

☆**aq·ui·fer** (ăk′wə fər, ak′-) ***n.*** ⟦ModL: see AQUA & -FER⟧ an underground layer of porous rock, sand, etc. containing water, into which wells can be sunk —**a·quif·er·ous** (ə kwif′ər əs) ***adj.***

aq·ui·fo·li·um (ăk′wə fōl′ē əm) ***n., pl.*** **-li·a** (-ə) or **-li·ums** ⟦ModL < L *aqua*, water + *folium*, leaf (see FOLIATE)⟧ any of the family (Aquifoliaceae) of trees and shrubs that includes the holly

Aq·ui·la (ak′wi lə) ***n.*** ⟦L, eagle⟧ a N constellation in the Milky Way, nearly centered on the celestial equator

aq·ui·le·gi·a (ak′wə lē′jē ə) ***n.*** ⟦ModL < ML *aquileia* < L *aquila*, eagle: so named because of the spurred flower⟧ COLUMBINE

aq·ui·line (ak′wə līn′, -lin) ***adj.*** ⟦L *aquilinus* < *aquila*, eagle⟧ **1** of or like an eagle **2** curved or hooked like an eagle's beak [*an aquiline nose*]

A·qui·nas (ə kwī′nəs), Saint **Thomas** (1225?-74); It. theologian & philosopher: his day is March 7: called *the Angelic Doctor*: cf. THOMISM

Aq·ui·taine (ak′wə tān′) **1** historical region of SW France: orig., a division of Gaul; later, a duchy under the French crown, passed to English control when Eleanor of Aquitaine married Henry II; returned to France after Hundred Years' War **2** metropolitan region of modern France of much smaller size: 15,949 sq mi (41,308 sq km); chief city, Bordeaux: Latin name **Aq′ui·ta′ni·a** (-tā′nē ə)

ar *abbrev.* **1** arrival **2** arrives

Ar[1] *abbrev.* Arabic

Ar[2] *Chem. symbol for* argon

AR *abbrev.* **1** airman recruit **2** Arkansas **3** Army Regulation **4** Autonomous Republic

ar- (er, ar) *prefix* AD-: used before *r*

-ar (ər) ⟦< ME *-er* < OFr *-er, -ier, -air* < L *-aris*; or directly < L *-aris*; also < L *-arius*, a suffix of nouns of agency⟧ *suffix* **1** *forming adjectives* of, relating to, like, of the nature of [*singular, polar*] **2** *forming nouns* the agent of a particular action [*registrar*] **3** ⟦modeled on SCHOLAR, etc.⟧ -ER

A·ra (ā′rə) ***n.*** ⟦L, altar⟧ a S constellation between Scorpius and Pavo

ar·a-A (ar′ə ā′, er′-) ***n.*** ⟦< ARA(BINOSE) + A(DENINE)⟧ an antiviral drug, $C_{10}H_{13}N_5O_4H_2O$, that prevents DNA synthesis: used to treat certain herpes infections

Ar·ab[1] (ar′əb, er′-) ***n.*** ⟦ME *Arabes* (pl.) < L *Arabes, Arabs*, an Arab < Gr *Araps*, pl. *Arabes* < Ar *ʿarab*⟧ **1** a person born or living in Arabia **2** a member of a Semitic people originating in Arabia but now widely scattered throughout surrounding lands **3** a member of a people whose native language is Arabic **4** ARABIAN (*n.* 2) **5** [Archaic] a waif left to roam the streets; street Arab —***adj.*** ARABIAN

Arab[2] *abbrev.* **1** Arabian **2** Arabic

Ar·a·bel·la (ar′ə bel′ə, er′-) ***n.*** ⟦? by dissimilation < ANNABEL⟧ a feminine name: dim. *Bella*

ar·a·besque (ar′ə besk′, er′-) ***n.*** ⟦Fr < It *arabesco* < *Arabo*, Arab < Ar *ʿarab*: with reference to the designs in Moorish architecture⟧ **1** a complex and elaborate decorative design of intertwined lines suggesting flowers, foliage, animals, geometric patterns, etc., used in drawing, painting, low relief, metalwork, etc. **2** *Ballet* a position in which one leg is extended straight backward and the arms are extended, usually one forward and one backward **3** *Music a)* a light, whimsical composition with many delicately ornamental passages *b)* any ornamental passage typical of such a composition —***adj.*** of, done in, or like arabesque; fantastic and elaborate

arabesque

A·ra·bi·a (ə rā′bē ə) peninsula in SW Asia, between the Red Sea and the Persian Gulf: largely an arid desert plateau: *c.* 1,000,000 sq mi (2,590,000 sq km): also **Arabian Peninsula**

A·ra·bi·an (-ən) ***adj.*** of Arabia or the Arabs —***n.*** **1** ARAB[1] (*n.* 1) **2** any of a breed of swift, graceful horses native to Arabia

Arabian camel the one-humped camel (*Camelus dromedarius*) ranging from N Africa to India

Arabian coffee ARABICA (*n.*)

Arabian Desert **1** desert in E Egypt, between the Nile valley and the Red Sea **2** popularly, the desert area of Arabia

Arabian Nights, The a medieval collection of tales from Arabia, India, Persia, etc.: also **The Arabian Nights' Entertainment**

Arabian Sea part of the Indian Ocean, between India and Arabia

Ar·a·bic (ar′ə bik, er′-) ***adj.*** **1** of Arabia **2** of the Arabs or their language or culture **3** [**a-**] designating an acid, $C_5H_{10}O_6$, found in gum arabic —***n.*** the Semitic language of the Arabs, spoken in Arabia, Syria, Jordan, Israel, Iraq, N Africa, etc. in various dialects

a·rab·i·ca (ə rab′i kə) ***adj.*** ⟦ModL, species name < L, fem. of *Arabicus*, of Arabia⟧ designating or of one of the two main types of coffee (*Coffea arabica*) produced commercially, which grows at high altitudes, mainly in Latin America, and is prized for its aromatic qualities and complex flavor: see also ROBUSTA —***n.*** this coffee

Arabic numerals the figures 1, 2, 3, 4, 5, 6, 7, 8, 9, and the 0 (zero) that originated in India; Hindu-Arabic numerals

a·rab·i·nose (ə rab′ə nōs′, ar′ə bə-) ***n.*** ⟦ARAB(IC) + -IN[1] + -OSE[1]⟧ a pentose sugar, $C_5H_{10}O_5$, obtained esp. from certain vegetable gums

Ar·ab·ist (ar′ə bist, er′-) ***n.*** a specialist in the study of the Arabic language or of Arabic literature, culture, etc.

ar·a·ble (ar′ə bəl, er′-) ***adj.*** ⟦Fr < L *arabilis* < *arare*, to plow < IE base **ar-* > Gr *aroun*, Goth *arjan*, to plow⟧ suitable for plowing, hence for producing crops —***n.*** arable land —**ar′a·bil′i·ty** (-bil′ə tē) ***n.***

Arab League a confederation of 22 Arab administrations, including the Arab countries of SW Asia and N Africa, established in 1945 to promote political, economic, and military cooperation among its members

Ar·a·by (ar′ə bē, er′-) *archaic and old poet. name for* ARABIA

A·ra·ca·ju (är′ə kə zhōō′) seaport in NE Brazil; capital of Sergipe

A·rach·ne (ə rak′nē) ***n.*** ⟦L < Gr *Arachnē* < *arachnē*, spider⟧ *Gr. Myth.* a girl turned into a spider by Athena for challenging the goddess to a weaving contest

a·rach·nid (ə rak′nid) ***n.*** ⟦< Gr *arachnē*, spider, akin to L *araneus*⟧ any of a large class (Arachnida) of chiefly terrestrial arthropods, including spiders, scorpions, mites, and ticks, typically with four pairs of legs, either lungs or tracheae, a liquid diet, no antennae, simple eyes, sensory pedipalps, and a body divided into cephalothorax and abdomen —**a·rach′ni·dan** (-ni dən) ***adj., n.***

a·rach·nid·ism (ə rak′nid iz′əm) ***n.*** *Med.* a condition resulting from the bite or sting of a venomous arachnid

a·rach·noid (-noid′) ***adj.*** ⟦ModL *arachnoides* < Gr *arachnoeidēs*, like a cobweb < *arachnē*, spider (see ARACHNID) + *-eidēs*, -OID⟧ **1** *Anat.* designating the middle of three membranes covering the brain and the spinal cord: see DURA MATER, PIA MATER **2** *Bot.* covered with or consisting of soft, fine hairs or fibers **3** *Zool.* of or like an arachnid —***n.*** **1** *Anat.* the arachnoid membrane **2** *Zool.* an arachnid

A·rad (ä räd′) city in W Romania, on the Mureş River

A·ra·fu·ra Sea (ä′rə fōō′rə) part of the South Pacific Ocean, between Australia and New Guinea

A·ra·gats (ä′rä gäts′) extinct volcano in NW Armenia: 13,435 ft (4,095 m)

A·ra·gon[1] (à rà gōn′), **Louis** (lwē) 1897-1982; Fr. poet, novelist, & journalist

Ar·a·gon[2] (ar′ə gän′, er′-) region in NE Spain: from the 11th to the 15th cent., a kingdom which at various times included the Balearic Islands, Sardinia, Sicily, & several other Mediterranean areas; united with Castile, 1479: 18,405 sq mi (47,669 sq km)

Ar·a·go·nese (ar′ə gə nēz′, er′-) ***adj.*** of Aragon or its people, language, or culture —***n.*** **1** *pl.* **-nese′** a person born or living in Aragon **2** the variety of Spanish spoken in Aragon

a·rag·o·nite (ə rag′ə nīt′, ar′ə gə-) ***n.*** ⟦after ARAGON[2], in Spain⟧ a semihard, orthorhombic mineral resembling calcite, made up of calcium carbonate, $CaCO_3$: it is found in sedimentary and metamorphic rocks and in the skeletons of marine organisms

A·ra·gua·ia (ä′rə gwä′yə) river in central Brazil, flowing north into the Tocantins: *c.* 1,300 mi (2,092 km)

ar·ak (ar′ək) ***n.*** ARRACK

A·rak (ə räk′) city in WC Iran

A·ra·kan Yo·ma (ar′ə kan′ yō′mə) mountain range in W Myanmar, along the Indian border: highest peak, over 10,000 ft (3,048 m)

A·raks (ä räks′) river flowing from E Turkey along the S border of Armenia & Azerbaijan, into the Kura River and the Caspian Sea: *c.* 600 mi (966 km)

Ar·al Sea (ar′əl) inland body of salt water in SW Asia, east of the Caspian Sea: rapidly decreasing in area, chiefly from man-made diversion of its sources: are now approximately one tenth that of the 1960s

Ar·am[1] (er′əm) ⟦Heb⟧ ancient country in SW Asia, generally identified as Syria

Aram[2] *abbrev.* Aramaic

-a·ram·a (ə ram′ə, -rä′mə) *combining form* -ORAMA [*snackarama*]: also **-a·ram′a**

Ar·a·mae·an or **Ar·a·me·an** (ar′ə mē′ən, er′-) ***n.*** **1** a member of a people that lived in ancient Syria (Aram) and Mesopotamia **2** ARAMAIC —***adj.*** of the Aramaeans or their language or culture

Ar·a·ma·ic (-mā′ik) ***n.*** a Northwest Semitic language that was the lingua franca throughout the Near East from *c.* 300 B.C. to *c.* A.D. 650: it replaced Hebrew as the language of the Jews, and one of its dialects was spoken by Jesus and his disciples

☆**ar·a·mid** (ar′ə mid′) ***n.*** ⟦*ar(omatic) (poly)amid(e)*⟧ any of a group of very strong, lightweight, synthetic fibers used in making radial tires, bulletproof vests, etc.

a·ra·ne·id (ə rā′nē id′) ***n.*** ⟦< ModL < L *aranea* (akin to Gr *arachnē*, spider) + -ID⟧ *Zool.* a spider —**ar·a·ne·i·dan** (ar′ə nē′i dən) ***adj.***

☆**A·rap·a·ho** (ə rap′ə hō′) ***n.*** ⟦< Crow *aaraxpéahu*, lit., (one with) many tattoos⟧ **1** *pl.* **-ho′** a member of a North American Indian people formerly living in the area between the North Platte and Arkansas rivers and now living in Wyoming and Oklahoma **2** the Algonquian language of this people

ar·a·pai·ma (ar′ə pī′mə) ***n.*** ⟦ModL < Port < a Tupí word⟧ a very long, edible, large-scaled bony fish (*Arapaima gigas*) of the rivers of the Amazon region, sometimes reaching a weight of *c.* 180 kg (*c.* 400 lb)

Ar·a·rat (ar′ə rat′, er′-), **Mount** mountain in E Turkey, near the Armenian and Iranian borders: supposed landing place of Noah's Ark (Gen. 8:4): higher of its two peaks, *c.* 17,000 ft (5,182 m)

ar·a·ro·ba (ar′ə rō′bə, är′-) ***n.*** ⟦Port < Tupí name⟧ **1** a bitter, yellow powder obtained from cavities in the trunk of a Brazilian tree (*Andira araroba*) of the pea family and used to make the drug chrysarobin; Goa powder **2** this tree

A·ras (ä räs′) *Turk. name for* ARAKS

Ar·au·ca·ni·an (ar′ô kā′nē ən, ə rô′-) ***n.*** ⟦< Sp *Araucano,* after *Arauco,* region (now a province) in Chile < Araucanian *rau,* clay + *ko,* water⟧ **1** a member of a group of South American Indian peoples of Chile and the Argentine pampas **2** the language of these peoples —***adj.*** of these peoples or their language or culture

ar·au·car·i·a (ar′ô ker′ē ə, er′-) ***n.*** ⟦ModL < Sp *Arauco:* see prec.⟧ any of a genus (*Araucaria*) of the araucaria family of cone-bearing trees with flat, scalelike needles, native to the Southern Hemisphere and grown as ornamentals in other areas; esp., the monkey puzzle tree and the Norfolk Island pine —***adj.*** designating a family (Araucariaceae) of unusual conifers found esp. in Chile, Australia, and S U.S. Also **ar′au·car′i·an**

A·ra·wak (ä′rä wäk′, ar′ə wak′) ***n.*** **1** a member of a South American Indian people living chiefly in NE South America and formerly in the West Indies **2** the language of this people

A·ra·wa·kan (ä′rä wä′kən) ***n.*** a family of South American Indian languages, including Arawak —***adj.*** designating or of this family of languages

A·rax·es (ə rak′sēs′) *ancient name for* ARAKS

arb (ärb) ***n.*** [Informal] *short for* ARBITRAGEUR

ar·ba·lest (är′bə lest′) ***n.*** ⟦ME *arbelaste* < OFr *arbaleste* < LL *arcuballista* < L *arcus,* a bow (see ARC) + *ballista,* BALLISTA⟧ a medieval crossbow consisting of a steel bow set crosswise in a wooden shaft with a mechanism to bend the bow: it propelled arrows, balls, or stones: also **ar′ba·list** (-list) —**ar′ba·lest′er** ***n.***

Ar·be·la (är bē′lə) ancient city in Assyria, often erroneously identified as the site of a battle (331 B.C.) in which Alexander the Great defeated Darius III of Persia: modern name IRBIL

ar·bi·ter (är′bət ər) ***n.*** ⟦L, orig., one who goes to a place, a witness, judge < *ad-,* to + *baetere,* to come, go⟧ **1** a person selected to judge a dispute; umpire; arbitrator **2** a person fully authorized or qualified to judge or decide —***SYN.*** JUDGE

ar·bi·tra·ble (är′bə trə bəl) ***adj.*** that can be arbitrated; subject to arbitration

ar·bi·trage (är′bə träzh′) ***n.*** ⟦LME < Fr < *arbitrer,* to judge < L *arbitrari:* see ARBITRATE; for 2, < Fr *arbitrage*⟧ **1** a simultaneous purchase and sale in two separate financial markets in order to profit from a price difference existing between them **2** a buying of a large number of shares in a corporation in anticipation of, and with the expectation of making a profit from, a merger or takeover: in full **risk arbitrage** —***vi.*** **-traged′, -trag′ing** to engage in arbitrage

ar·bi·trag·eur (är′bə träzh′ər) ***n.*** ⟦Fr⟧ a person who engages in arbitrage: also sp. **ar′bi·trag′er**

ar·bi·tral (är′bə trəl) ***adj.*** ⟦Fr < L *arbitralis:* see ARBITER⟧ of arbiters or arbitration

ar·bit·ra·ment (är bi′trə mənt) ***n.*** ⟦ME & OFr *arbitrement* < L *arbitrari:* see ARBITRATE⟧ **1** arbitration **2** an arbitrator's verdict or award **3** the power to judge or right to decide

ar·bi·trar·y (är′bə trer′ē) ***adj.*** ⟦L *arbitrarius* < *arbiter,* ARBITER⟧ **1** not fixed by rules, but left to one's judgment or choice; discretionary [*arbitrary* decision, *arbitrary* judgment] **2** based on one's preference, notion, whim, etc.; capricious [young children and their *arbitrary* rules for games] **3** absolute; despotic —***SYN.*** DICTATORIAL —**ar′bi·trar′i·ly** ***adv.*** —**ar′bi·trar′i·ness** ***n.***

ar·bi·trate (är′bə trāt′) ***vt.*** **-trat′ed, -trat′ing** ⟦< L *arbitratus,* pp. of *arbitrari,* to give a decision < *arbiter,* ARBITER⟧ **1** to give to an arbitrator to decide; settle by arbitration **2** to decide (a dispute) as an arbitrator —***vi.*** **1** to act as an arbitrator (*in* a dispute, *between* persons) **2** to submit a dispute to arbitration —**ar′bi·tra′tive** ***adj.***

ar·bi·tra·tion (är′bə trā′shən) ***n.*** the act of arbitrating; specif., the settlement of a dispute by a person or persons chosen to hear both sides and come to a decision —**ar′bi·tra′tion·al** ***adj.***

ar·bi·tra·tor (är′bə trāt′ər) ***n.*** **1** a person selected to judge a dispute; arbiter, esp. one, as in collective bargaining negotiations, named with the consent of both sides **2** a person authorized to judge or decide

ar·bi·tress (är′bə tris) ***n.*** a woman arbiter: see -ESS

ar·bor[1] (är′bər) ***n.*** ⟦ME *erber* < OFr *erbier, herbier* < LL *herbarium,* HERBARIUM⟧ **1** a place shaded by trees or shrubs or, esp., by vines on a latticework; bower **2** [Obs.] *a)* a garden or lawn *b)* an orchard

ar·bor[2] (är′bər) ***n., pl.*** **ar′bo·res′** (-bə rēz′) ⟦L, a tree, beam: see ARDUOUS⟧ *Bot.* a tree, in contrast to a shrub

ar·bor[3] (är′bər) ***n.*** ⟦Fr *arbre,* tree, axis < L *arbor:* see prec.⟧ *Mech.* **1** a shaft; beam **2** a spindle; axle **3** a round bar that holds a cutting tool or an article being turned on a lathe

Arbor Day a tree-planting day observed individually by the states of the U.S., usually in spring

ar·bo·re·al (är bôr′ē əl) ***adj.*** ⟦L *arboreus,* of a tree < *arbor,* tree + -AL⟧ **1** of or like a tree **2** living in trees or adapted for living in trees

ar·bored (är′bərd) ***adj.*** **1** having an arbor, or bower **2** having trees on both sides or all around

ar·bo·re·ous (är bôr′ē əs) ***adj.*** **1** ARBOREAL **2** full of trees **3** ARBORESCENT

ar·bo·res·cent (är′bə res′ənt) ***adj.*** ⟦L *arborescens,* prp. of *arborescere,* to become a tree < *arbor,* tree: see ARBOR[2]⟧ treelike in shape or growth; branching —**ar′bo·res′cence** ***n.***

ar·bo·re·tum (-rēt′əm) ***n., pl.*** **-re′tums** or **-re′ta** (-rēt′ə) ⟦L < *arbor,* tree⟧ a place where many kinds of trees and shrubs are grown for exhibition or study

ar·bo·ri·cul·ture (är′bə rə kul′chər, är bôr′-) ***n.*** ⟦< L *arbor,* tree + (AGRI)CULTURE⟧ the scientific cultivation of trees and shrubs —**ar′bo·ri·cul′tur·ist** ***n.***

ar·bo·ri·o rice (är bôr′ē ō) ⟦after *Arborio,* town in NW Italy⟧ a type of short-grained rice, grown mainly in Italy, used esp. for making risotto

ar·bor·ist (är′bər ist) ***n.*** a specialist in the planting and maintenance of trees

ar·bor·i·za·tion (är′bər i zā′shən) ***n.*** ⟦ARBOR[2] + -IZATION⟧ **1** a treelike formation or arrangement **2** the forming of such an arrangement

ar·bor·vi·tae (är′bər vīt′ē) ***n.*** ⟦L, lit., tree of life⟧ **1** *Bot.* any of several trees or shrubs (genus *Thuja*) of the cypress family, with flattened sprays of scalelike leaves **2** *Anat.* the treelike structure of the white substance in a longitudinal section of the cerebellum Also, esp. for sense 2, **arbor vitae**

ar·bour (är′bər) ***n.*** *Brit. sp. of* ARBOR[1]

ar·bo·vi·rus (är′bə vī′rəs) ***n.*** ⟦AR(THROPOD) + BO(RNE) + VIRUS⟧ any of a group of RNA viruses, including those that cause yellow fever and viral encephalitis, which are transmitted to people by certain bloodsucking arthropods, esp. mosquitoes and ticks

Ar·buth·not (är buth′nət, är′bəth nät′), **John** 1667-1735; Scot. writer & physician

ar·bu·tus (är byo͞ot′əs) ***n.*** ⟦L, wild strawberry tree⟧ **1** any of a genus (*Arbutus*) of trees or shrubs of the heath family, with dark-green leaves, clusters of white or pinkish flowers, and small strawberrylike fruit; esp., the madroño and the strawberry trees **2** a trailing plant (*Epigaea repens*) of the heath family, with clusters of white or pink flowers

arc (ärk) ***n.*** ⟦ME *ark* < OFr *arc* < L *arcus,* a bow, arch < IE base **arqu-,* bowed, curved > ARROW⟧ **1** [Historical] the part of a circle that is the apparent path of a heavenly body above and below the horizon **2** a bowlike curved line or object **3** *Elec.* the band of sparks or incandescent light formed when an electric discharge is conducted from one electrode or conducting surface to another, characterized by relatively high current and low potential difference between electrodes **4** *Geom.* *a)* any part of a curve, esp. of a circle *b)* the angular measurement of this —***adj.*** designating an inverse trigonometric function [*arc sine x* is an angle whose sine is *x*] —***vi.*** **arced, arc′ing** **1** to move in a curved course **2** *Elec.* to form an arc

Arc, Jeanne d′ *see* D'ARC

ARC[1] (ärk) ***n.*** AIDS-RELATED COMPLEX

ARC[2] *abbrev.* American Red Cross

ar·cade (är kād′) ***n.*** ⟦Fr < Prov *arcada* < ML *arcata* < L *arcus,* arch: see ARC⟧ **1** a passage having an arched roof **2** any covered passageway, esp. one with shops along the sides **3** *a)* PENNY ARCADE *b)* a place somewhat like a penny arcade, containing coin-operated video games **4** *Archit.* *a)* a line of arches and their supporting columns *b)* an arched building —***vt.*** **-cad′ed, -cad′ing** to make into or provide with an arcade

Ar·ca·di·a[1] (är kā′dē ə) ***n.*** ⟦after fol.⟧ any place of rural peace and simplicity

Ar·ca·di·a[2] (är kā′dē ə) **1** ancient, relatively isolated pastoral region in the central Peloponnesus **2** department of modern Greece occupying the same general area

Ar·ca·di·an (-ən) ***adj.*** **1** of Arcadia **2** rustic, peaceful, and simple; pastoral —***n.*** **1** a person born or living in Arcadia **2** a person of simple habits and tastes

Ar·ca·dy (är′kə dē) *old poet. name for* ARCADIA[2] (the ancient region)

ar·cane (är kān′) ***adj.*** ⟦< L *arcanus:* see fol.⟧ **1** hidden or secret **2** understood by only a few; esoteric

ar·ca·num (-kā′nəm) ***n., pl.*** **-na** (-nə) ⟦L, neut. of *arcanus,* shut in, hidden < *arcere,* to enclose: see EXERCISE⟧ **1** a secret, typically one understood by or revealed to only a few; mystery: *usually used in pl.* **2** [Archaic] a secret remedy; elixir

arc furnace an electric furnace in which the heat comes from an arc, as between electrodes

arch[1] (ärch) ***n.*** ⟦ME < OFr *arche* < ML *arca* < L *arcus,* arch: see ARC⟧ **1** a curved structure, as of masonry, that supports the weight of material over an open space, as in a bridge, doorway, etc. **2** any similar structure, as a monument **3** the form of an arch **4** anything shaped like an arch **5** an archlike anatomical part; specif., the natural arch of the human foot, formed by the INSTEP (sense 1) and the central, concave portion of the sole —***vt.*** **1** to provide with an arch or arches **2** to cause to take the form of an arch; curve or bend **3** to span as an arch —***vi.*** to form an arch

KEYSTONE
EXTRADOS
INTRADOS
SPRINGERS

parts of an arch

arch[2] (ärch) ***adj.*** ⟦< ARCH-; with changed meaning because of use in *archknave, archrogue*⟧ **1** main; chief; principal [the *arch* villain] **2** clever; crafty **3** gaily mischievous; pert [an *arch* look]

Arch or **arch** *abbrev.* **1** archaic **2** archipelago **3** architecture

arch- (ärch; *in "archangel" & its derivatives,* ärk) ⟦ME *arche-* < OE *arce-* < L *archi-, arch-* < Gr *archos,* first, ruler < *archein,* begin, rule⟧ *prefix* **1** main, chief, principal: often used in forming titles of rank [*archangel, archenemy; archduke*] **2** prototypical or extreme [*archconservative*]

-arch (ärk; *occas.,* ərk) ⟦< Gr *archos:* see prec.⟧ *suffix* ruler [*matriarch, monarch*]

ar·chae·a (är kē′ə) *pl.n.* any of a domain of primitive microorganisms lacking internal membranes and, often, living in anaerobic, extremely hot, salty, or acidic environments —**ar·chae′al** *adj.*
Ar·chae·an (är kē′ən) *adj.* ARCHEAN —*n.* [a-] any archaebacterium
ar·chae·bac·te·ri·a (är′kē bak tir′ē ə) *pl.n., sing.* **-ri·um** (-əm) or **-ri·a** ARCHAEA
ar·chae·o- (är′kē ō′, -ə) ⟦< Gr *archaios,* ancient < *archē,* the beginning⟧ *combining form* ancient, original [*archaeology*]
ar·chae·o·as·tron·o·my (är′kē ō ə strän′ə mē) *n.* the scientific study of archaeological artifacts, sites, etc. to determine the astronomical knowledge of ancient, esp. prehistoric, peoples and what they believed about the sun, moon, etc. —**ar′chae·o·as·tron′o·mer** (-mər) *n.* —**ar′chae·o·as′tro·nom′i·cal** (-as′trə näm′i kel) *adj.*
ar·chae·ol·o·gy (är′kē äl′ə jē) *n.* ⟦ARCHAEO- + -LOGY⟧ the scientific study of the life and culture of past, esp. ancient, peoples, as by excavation of ancient cities, artifacts, etc. —**ar′chae·o·log′i·cal** (-ə läj′i kəl) *adj.* —**ar′chae·o·log′i·cal·ly** *adv.* —**ar′chae·ol′o·gist** *n.*
ar·chae·op·ter·yx (-äp′tər iks′) *n.* ⟦ModL < ARCHAEO- + Gr *pteryx,* wing: see FEATHER⟧ a reptilian bird (genus *Archaeopteryx*) of the Jurassic Period, that had teeth and feathers, a lizardlike tail, and well-developed wings
ar·chae·or·nis (-ôr′nis) *n.* ⟦ModL < ARCHAE(O)- + Gr *ornis,* bird: see ORNITHO-⟧ a bird (genus *Archaeornis*) of the Jurassic Period, that resembled the archaeopteryx
Ar·chae·o·zo·ic (-ə zō′ik) *adj.* ARCHEOZOIC
ar·cha·ic (är kā′ik) *adj.* ⟦Gr *archaikos* < *archaios,* old, ancient < *archein,* begin⟧ **1** belonging to an earlier period; ancient **2** antiquated; old-fashioned **3** that has ceased to be used except for special purposes, as in poetry, church ritual, etc. [*thou* is an *archaic* form of *you*] —***SYN.*** OLD —**ar·cha′i·cal·ly** *adv.*
ar·cha·ism (är′kā iz′əm, -kē-) *n.* ⟦ModL *archaismus* < Fr *archaisme* < Gr *archaismos* < *archaios,* old⟧ **1** the use or imitation of archaic words, technique, etc. **2** an archaic word, usage, style, practice, etc. —**ar′cha·ist** *n.* —**ar′cha·is′tic** (-is′tik) *adj.* —**ar′cha·is′ti·cal·ly** *adv.*
ar·cha·ize (-īz′) *vt.* **-ized′, -iz′ing** to make archaic or make seem archaic —*vi.* to use archaisms
arch·an·gel (ärk′ān′jəl) *n.* ⟦ME < OFr *archangel* or LL(Ec) *archangelus* < LGr(Ec) *archangelos* < Gr *archos* (see ARCH-) + *angelos,* ANGEL⟧ **1** a chief angel; angel of high rank **2** an angelica plant (*Angelica archangelica*)
Arch·an·gel (ärk′ān′jəl) *var. of* ARKHANGELSK
arch·bish·op (ärch′bish′əp) *n.* ⟦ME *archebishop* < OE *arcebisceop* < LL(Ec) *archiepiscopus* < LGr(Ec) *archiepiskopos* < Gr *archos* (see ARCH-) + *episkopos,* overseer: see BISHOP⟧ a bishop of the highest rank, who presides over an archbishopric or archdiocese
arch·bish·op·ric (-rik) *n.* ⟦ME *archebishopriche* < OE *arcebiscoprice* < *arcebisceop* (see prec.) + *rice,* jurisdiction < PGmc **rikja* (> Ger *reich,* realm): for IE base see REGAL⟧ **1** the office, rank, duties, or term of an archbishop **2** the church district over which an archbishop has jurisdiction
arch·dea·con (-dē′kən) *n.* ⟦ME *archedeken* < OE *arcediacon* < LL(Ec) *archidiaconus* < LGr(Ec) *archidiakonos* < Gr *archos* (see ARCH-) + *diakonos,* servant: see DEACON⟧ a church official ranking just below a bishop or an archpriest: in the Anglican Church, an archdeacon has supervisory duties under the bishop
arch·dea·con·ry (-rē) *n., pl.* **-ries 1** the office, rank, duties, or jurisdiction of an archdeacon **2** an archdeacon's residence
arch·di·o·cese (ärch′dī′ə sis, -sēz′) *n.* the diocese of an archbishop —**arch′di·oc′e·san** (-dī äs′ə sən) *adj.*
arch·du·cal (-do͞o′kəl, -dyo͞o′kəl) *adj.* of an archduke or archduchy
arch·duch·ess (-duch′is) *n.* **1** the wife or widow of an archduke **2** a princess of the former Austrian imperial family
arch·duch·y (-duch′ē) *n., pl.* **-ies** ⟦Fr *archiduché:* see ARCH- & DUCHY⟧ the territory ruled by an archduke or archduchess
arch·duke (-do͞ok′, -dyo͞ok′) *n.* a sovereign prince, esp. a prince of the former Austrian imperial family
Ar·che·an (är kē′ən) *adj.* ⟦< Gr *archaios,* ARCHAIC⟧ [*sometimes* a-] designating or of the geologic eon characterized by the development of the first igneous and metamorphic rocks and the first marine microorganisms; Precambrian, esp. early Precambrian —**the Archean** the Archean Eon or its rocks: see the geologic time chart in the Reference Supplement
arched (ärcht) *adj.* **1** furnished or covered with an arch or arches **2** having the form of an arch; curved
ar·che·go·ni·ate (är′kə gō′nē it) *adj.* having archegonia —*n.* a plant having archegonia
ar·che·go·ni·um (-nē əm) *n., pl.* **-ni·a** (-nē ə) ⟦ModL, dim. < Gr *archegonos,* the first of a race: see ARCH- & -GONIUM⟧ the flask-shaped female reproductive organ in mosses, ferns, and other related plants —**ar′che·go′ni·al** *adj.*
arch·en·e·my (ärch′en′ə mē) *n., pl.* **-mies** a chief enemy —**the archenemy** Satan
ar·chen·ter·on (är ken′tər än′) *n.* ⟦ARCH- + Gr *enteron,* intestine⟧ the cavity at the center of an embryo in the gastrula stage of development, forming a primitive digestive tract —**ar·chen·ter·ic** (är′kən ter′ik) *adj.*
ar·che·o- (är′kē ō, -ə) *combining form* ARCHAEO-
ar·che·ol·o·gy (är′kē äl′ə jē) *n. alt. sp. of* ARCHAEOLOGY —**ar′che·o·log′i·cal** (-ə läj′i kəl) *adj.* —**ar′che·o·log′i·cal·ly** *adv.* —**ar′che·ol′o·gist** *n.*
Ar·che·o·zo·ic (är′kē ə zō′ik) *adj.* ⟦ARCHEO- + -ZOIC⟧ early Precambrian; Archean —**the Archeozoic** THE ARCHEAN (see phrase under ARCHEAN)
arch·er (är′chər) *n.* ⟦ME < OFr *archier* < ML *arcarius* < L *arcus,* bow (see ARC) + *-arius,* -ER⟧ a person who shoots with bow and arrow; bowman —**the Archer** Sagittarius, the constellation and ninth sign of the zodiac
arch·er·fish (är′chər fish′) *n., pl.* **-fish′** or **-fish′es** (see FISH) any of a family (Toxotidae) of freshwater percoid fishes of Australasia
arch·er·y (är′chər ē) *n.* ⟦ME & OFr *archerie:* see ARCHER & -ERY⟧ **1** the practice, art, or sport of shooting with bow and arrow **2** an archer's bows, arrows, and other equipment **3** archers collectively
ar·che·spore (är′kə spôr′) *n.* ⟦ModL *archesporium:* see ARCH- & SPORE⟧ a cell or group of cells from which the spore mother cells develop: also **ar′che·spo′ri·um** (-spôr′ē əm) —**ar′che·spo′ri·al** *adj.*
ar·che·type (är′kə tīp′) *n.* ⟦L *archetypus* < Gr *archetypon* < *archos* (see ARCH-) + *typos* (see TYPE)⟧ **1** the original pattern, or model, from which all other things of the same kind are made; prototype **2** a perfect example of a type or group **3** in Jungian psychology, any of several innate ideas or patterns in the psyche, expressed in dreams, art, etc. as certain basic symbols or images —***SYN.*** MODEL —**ar′che·typ′al** (-tīp′əl) *adj.*, **ar′che·typ′i·cal** (-tip′i kəl) —**ar′che·typ′al·ly** *adv.*, **ar′che·typ′i·cal·ly**
arch·fiend (ärch′fēnd′) *n.* a chief fiend —**the archfiend** Satan
ar·chi- (är′ki, -kə, -kē) ⟦see ARCH-⟧ *prefix* **1** chief, first [*archiepiscopal*] **2** *Biol.* primitive, original [*archiblast*]
Ar·chi·bald (är′chə bôld′) *n.* ⟦of Gmc orig. (akin to OHG *Erchanbald*), prob., nobly bold⟧ a masculine name: dim. *Archie, Archy*
ar·chi·blast (är′kə blast′) *n.* ⟦ARCHI- + -BLAST⟧ *Biol.* **1** egg protoplasm **2** the outer of the two layers of an embryo in an early stage of development
ar·chi·carp (-kärp′) *n.* ⟦ARCHI- + -CARP⟧ *Bot.* the female reproductive organ in an ascomycetous fungus, giving rise to spore sacs (*asci*) after fertilization
ar·chi·di·ac·o·nal (är′kə dī ak′ə nəl) *adj.* ⟦ME < ML *archidiaconalis*⟧ of an archdeacon or archdeaconry —**ar′chi·di·ac′o·nate** (-ak′ə nit) *n.*
ar·chi·e·pis·co·pal (är′kē ē pis′kə pəl) *adj.* ⟦see ARCHI- & EPISCOPACY⟧ of an archbishop or archbishopric —**ar′chi·e·pis′co·pate** (-pət) *n.*
ar·chil (är′kil, -chil) *n.* ⟦ME *orchell* < OFr *orchel* < It *orcello* < L *urceolaris* (*herba*), (plant) used for polishing glass pitchers < *urceolus,* dim. of *urceus,* pitcher⟧ ORCHIL
ar·chi·man·drite (är′kə man′drīt′) *n.* ⟦LL(Ec) *archimandrita* < LGr(Ec) *archimandritēs* < *archi-,* ARCH- + *mandra,* monastery (in Gr, pen, stall)⟧ *Eastern Orthodox Ch.* the head of a monastery or of a number of monasteries
Ar·chi·me·des (är′kə mē′dēz′) 287?-212 B.C.; Gr. mathematician & inventor, born in Syracuse (Sicily) —**Ar·chi·me·de·an** (är′kə mē′dē ən, är′kə mi dē′ən) *adj.*
Archimedes' (*or* **Archimedean**) **screw** an ancient water-raising device attributed to Archimedes, made up of a spiral tube coiled about a shaft or of a large screw in a cylinder, revolved by hand

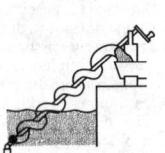

Archimedes' screw

arch·ing (är′chiŋ) *adj.* forming an arch —*n.* **1** an arched part **2** a series of arches
ar·chi·pel·a·go (är′kə pel′ə gō′) *n., pl.* **-goes′** or **-gos′** ⟦It *arcipelago* < MGr *archipelagos,* orig., the Aegean Sea < Gr *archi-,* chief + *pelagos,* sea: see PELAGIC⟧ **1** a sea with many islands **2** a group or chain of many islands —**ar′chi·pe·lag′ic** (-pə laj′ik) *adj.*
Ar·chi·pen·ko (är′ki peŋ′kō), **Alexander** 1887-1964; U.S. sculptor, born in Russia
ar·chi·plasm (är′kə plaz′əm) *n.* ARCHOPLASM
ar·chi·tect (är′kə tekt′) *n.* ⟦L *architectus* < Gr *architektōn* < *archi-,* chief + *tektōn,* carpenter: see TECHNIC⟧ **1** a person whose profession is designing and drawing up plans for buildings, bridges, etc. and generally supervising the construction **2** any similar designer in a specialized field [a naval *architect*] **3** any planner or creator [the *architects* of our Constitution]
ar·chi·tec·ton·ic (är′kə tek tän′ik) *adj.* ⟦L *architectonicus* < Gr *architektonikos* < *architektōn,* prec.⟧ **1** of or relating to architecture or architectural methods, principles, etc. **2** having structure or design of a kind thought of as architectural —*n.* ARCHITECTONICS —**ar′chi·tec·ton′i·cal·ly** *adv.*
ar·chi·tec·ton·ics (-iks) *pl.n.* [*usually with sing. v.*] **1** the science of architecture **2** structural design [the *architectonics* of a symphony]
ar·chi·tec·tur·al (-tek′chər əl) *adj.* **1** of or connected with architecture **2** having the qualities of architecture —**ar′chi·tec′tur·al·ly** *adv.*
ar·chi·tec·ture (är′kə tek′chər) *n.* ⟦Fr < L *architectura:* see ARCHITECT⟧ **1** the science, art, or profession of designing and constructing buildings, bridges, etc. **2** a building, or buildings collectively **3** a style of construction [Gothic *architecture*] **4** design and construction [the *architecture* of a beehive] **5** any framework, system, etc. **6** the design and interaction of components of a computer or computer system
ar·chi·trave (är′kə trāv′) *n.* ⟦Fr < It < L *archi-,* ARCHI- + *trabs,* a beam: see TAVERN⟧ *Archit.* **1** the lowest part of an entablature, a beam resting directly on the tops, or capitals, of the columns; epistyle **2** the molding around a doorway, window, etc.
ar·chi·val (är kī′vəl, är′kī′vəl; är′kə-) *adj.* of, in, or containing archives
ar·chive (är′kīv′) *n.* ⟦Fr *archif* < LL *archivum* < Gr *archeion,* town hall < *archē,* the beginning, government⟧ [*usually pl.*] **1** *a)* a place where public records, documents, etc. are kept *b)* a place where material having documentary interest, as private papers, institutional records, memorabilia, or photographs, is kept **2** the records, material, etc. kept in either of such

places —*vt.* **-chived′, -chiv′ing** to place or keep (records, papers, etc.) in or as in archives

ar·chi·vist (är′kə vist, är′kī′vist) *n.* ⟦ML *archivista*⟧ a person having charge of archives

ar·chi·volt (är′kə vōlt′) *n.* ⟦It *archivolto* < ML *archivoltum*: see ARCH[1] & VAULT[1]⟧ *Archit.* **1** the inner curve of an arch or the structural parts of this **2** an ornamental molding on the face of an arch

arch·ly (ärch′lē) *adv.* in an arch manner; pertly and mischievously

arch·ness (-nis) *n.* the quality of being arch, or saucily mischievous

ar·chon (är′kän′, -kən) *n.* ⟦Gr *archōn* < *archein*: see ARCH-⟧ **1** one of the chief magistrates of ancient Athens **2** a ruler or chief officer

ar·cho·plasm (är′kə plaz′əm) *n.* ⟦ModL *archoplasma* < ARCH- (with *-o-*, as if Gr *archōn*, prec.) + -PLASM⟧ a specialized portion of the cytoplasm involved in the formation of the aster and spindle during mitosis

ar·cho·saur (är′kə sôr′) *n.* ⟦< ModL *Archosauria* < Gr *archōn* (see ARCHON) + *sauros*, lizard⟧ any of a subclass (Archosauria) of reptiles, including the dinosaurs, pterosaurs, crocodilians, and thecodonts

arch·priest (ärch′prēst′) *n.* **1** [Archaic] a priest who acts as a bishop's chief assistant; dean **2** a chief priest

arch·ri·val (ärch′rī′vəl) *n.* a chief rival

arch·way (ärch′wā′) *n.* **1** a passageway under an arch **2** an arch framing a passage

-ar·chy (är kē, ər kē) ⟦via ME *-archy* or OFr *-archie* or L *-archia* < Gr *archein*, to rule⟧ *combining form forming nouns* rule or government [*matriarchy, monarchy*]

arc lamp a lamp in which brilliant light is produced by maintaining an arc between two electrodes, used as a spotlight, searchlight, etc.: also called **arc light**

ar·co (är′kō) [*also in italics*] *Music adj.* ⟦It < L *arcus*, a bow: see ARC⟧ bowed: often used as a musical direction to performers on stringed instruments to resume using the bow after plucking the strings —*adv.* in an *arco* manner; with a bow

arc·tic (ärk′tik, är′-) *adj.* ⟦ME *artik* < OFr *artique* < L *arcticus* < Gr *arktikos*, lit., of the (constellation of the) Bear (Gr *arktos*), northern, arctic⟧ **1** of, characteristic of, or near the North Pole or the region around it **2** very cold; frigid —**the Arctic** the region around the North Pole, including the Arctic Ocean and the lands in it north of the 70° latitude

Arctic Archipelago group of mostly large islands in the Arctic Ocean off the N coast of Canada

arctic char a trout (*Salvelinus alpinus*) of N Canada and Alaska

Arctic Circle [*also* **a- c-**] an imaginary circle parallel to the equator, *c.* 66°34′ north of it

arctic fox any of a widespread species (*Alopex lagopus*) of foxes of the Arctic region, having fur almost pure white in winter and smoky-gray in summer: see BLUE FOX

Arctic Ocean ocean surrounding the North Pole, north of the Arctic Circle: 5,105,700 sq mi (13,223,711 sq km)

☆**arc·tics** (ärt′iks, ärk′tiks) *pl.n.* ⟦< *arctic boots*⟧ high, warm, waterproof overshoes, usually with buckles

Arc·tu·rus (ärk toor′əs, -tyoor′-) *n.* ⟦L < Gr *Arktouros*, guardian of the bear < *arktos*, a bear + *ouros*, a guard < IE **woros*, heedful < base **wer-* (see WARN): so named from its position behind the tail of URSA MAJOR in ancient diagrams of the constellation⟧ a giant, orange, variable star in the constellation Boötes, the brightest star in the N celestial sphere: magnitude, −0.05

ar·cu·ate (är′kyoo͞ it, -āt′) *adj.* ⟦L *arcuatus*, pp. of *arcuare*, bend like a bow < *arcus*, a bow: see ARC⟧ curved like a bow; arched —**ar′cu·ate·ly** *adv.*

ar·cu·a·tion (är′kyoo͞ ā′shən) *n.* **1** a curving or being curved like a bow **2** the use of arches in building **3** a row of arches

arc welding a method of fusing metal parts together under the extreme heat produced by an electric arc

-ard (ərd) ⟦ME < OFr < MHG *-hart* < *hart*, bold, HARD⟧ *suffix* one that carries some action, or possesses some quality, to excess [*sluggard, drunkard*]

Ar·da·bil (ard′ə bēl′) city in NW Iran, near the Caspian Sea: also sp. **Ar′de·bil′**

ar·deb (är′deb′) *n.* ⟦informal Ar *ardabb*, for *al irdabb*; prob. ult. < Gr *artabē*, a Persian measure⟧ a unit of dry measure used in Egypt, equal to 198 liters (5.619 bushels)

Ar·den (ärd′'n) wooded area in Warwickshire, Eng.: the "Forest of Arden" of Shakespeare's *As You Like It*

Ar·dennes (är den′) wooded plateau in NE France, S Belgium, and Luxembourg: scene of heavy fighting in WWI and, esp., at the "Battle of the Bulge" (Dec., 1944–Jan., 1945) in WWII

ar·dent (är′dənt) *adj.* ⟦ME < OFr *ardant* < L *ardens*, prp. of *ardere*, to burn; akin to *aridus*, ARID⟧ **1** warm or intense in feeling; passionate [*ardent* love] **2** intensely enthusiastic or devoted; zealous [an *ardent* disciple] **3** glowing; radiant **4** burning; aflame —***SYN.*** PASSIONATE —**ar′den·cy** (-dən sē) *n.* —**ar′dent·ly** *adv.*

ardent spirits [Now Rare] strong alcoholic liquor; whiskey, gin, etc.

ar·dor (är′dər) *n.* ⟦ME & OFr *ardour* < L *ardor*, a flame, fire < *ardere*: see ARDENT⟧ **1** emotional warmth; passion **2** eagerness; enthusiasm; zeal **3** intense heat; fire —***SYN.*** PASSION

ar·dour (är′dər) *n. Brit. sp. of* ARDOR

ar·du·ous (är′joo͞ əs) *adj.* ⟦L *arduus*, steep < IE **er(ə)dh-*, high, to grow (> L *arbor*, tree) < base **er-*, to set in motion, RUN⟧ **1** difficult to do; laborious; onerous **2** using much energy; strenuous **3** steep; hard to climb —***SYN.*** HARD —**ar′du·ous·ly** *adv.* —**ar′du·ous·ness** *n.*

are[1] (är; *unstressed*, ər) *vi.* ⟦OE (Northumbrian) *aron* < base found also in AM & ART[2]⟧ *pl. & 2d pers. sing., pres. indic., of* BE

are[2] (ar, är) *n.* ⟦Fr < L *area*: see AREA⟧ the basic unit of land area in the metric system, equal to 100 square meters or 0.01 hectare (119.6 square yards or 0.0247 acre): abbrev. *a*

ARE *abbrev.* Arab Republic of Egypt

ar·e·a (er′ē ə) *n.* ⟦L, vacant place, courtyard, prob. (in sense "arid, bare place") < *arere*, to be dry: see ASH[1]⟧ **1** a level surface or piece of ground **2** a part of the earth's surface; region; tract **3** the measure of a bounded region on a plane or of the surface of a solid: see SQUARE MEASURE **4** a yard of a building **5** a part of a house, lot, district, city, etc. having a specific use or character [dining *area*, play *area*, commercial *area*] **6** a part of any surface, as of an organism, or a particular zone, as of the cerebral cortex **7** scope or extent, as of an operation —**ar′e·al** *adj.*

☆**area code** any of the three-digit telephone codes assigned to each of the areas into which the U.S., Canada, etc. are divided

☆**area rug** a rug intended to cover only part of a floor

☆**ar·e·a·way** (-wā′) *n.* **1** a sunken area next to a building, for providing access or light and air to a basement **2** a passageway between buildings or parts of a building

ar·e·ca (ar′i kə, er′-; ə rē′kə) *n.* ⟦ModL < Port; prob. < Malayalam *adekka*⟧ any of a genus (*Areca*) of palm trees, native to Asia and Australia, with a smooth, slender trunk and feathery compound leaves; esp., the betel palm

A·re·ci·bo (ä′re sē′bô) ⟦after *Arasibo*, local Indian chief⟧ seaport in N Puerto Rico

a·re·na (ə rē′nə) *n.* ⟦L *arena, harena*, sand, sandy place, arena⟧ **1** the central part of an ancient Roman amphitheater, where gladiatorial contests and shows took place **2** *a)* a central area used for entertainment or sports events and usually surrounded by seats *b)* a building containing such an area [an *arena* for boxing matches] **3** any sphere of struggle or conflict [the *arena* of politics] **4** the central stage in an arena theater

ar·e·na·ceous (ar′ə nā′shəs, er′-) *adj.* ⟦L *arenaceus*: see prec.⟧ **1** sandy **2** growing in sand

☆**arena theater 1** a theater having a central stage without a proscenium, surrounded by seats **2** the techniques, methods, etc. used in such a theater

A·rendt (ar′ənt, är′-), **Hannah** 1906-75; U.S. writer & political philosopher, born in Germany

ar·e·nic·o·lous (ar′ə nik′ə ləs, er′-) *adj.* ⟦< L *arena*, sand + -I- + -COLOUS⟧ living or growing in sand

ar·e·nite (ar′ə nīt′, er′-) *n.* ⟦L *arena*, sand, ARENA + -ITE[1]⟧ sandstone or other sedimentary rock made up chiefly of sand grains

aren't (ärnt) *contraction* **1** are not **2** am not: used occasionally in questions [I'm helping you, *aren't* I?]

a·re·o·la (ə rē′ə lə) *n., pl.* **-lae′** (-lē′) or **-las** ⟦ModL < L, dim. of *area*: see AREA⟧ **1** a small space, as between the veins of a leaf or the ribs of an insect's wing **2** *Anat.* a small area around something, as the dark ring around a nipple **3** *Biol.* a small hollow in a surface —**a·re′o·lar** (-lər) *adj.* —**a·re′o·late** (-lit) *adj.* —**ar·e·o·la·tion** (ar′ē ə lā′shən, ə rē′ə-) *n.*

ar·e·ole (ar′ē ōl′, er′-) *n.* ⟦Fr⟧ AREOLA

Ar·e·op·a·gite (ar′ē äp′ə jīt′, er′-; -gīt′) *n.* ⟦L *Areopagites* < Gr *Areiopagitēs*⟧ any member of the Areopagus in ancient Athens

Ar·e·op·a·gus[1] (-äp′ə gəs) *n.* **1** the high court of justice in ancient Athens that met on Areopagus **2** any supreme court

Ar·e·op·a·gus[2] (-äp′ə gəs) ⟦L < Gr *Areiopagos* < *Areios*, of Ares + *pagos*, hill⟧ rocky hill northwest of the Acropolis, Athens

a·re·pa (ə rā′pə) *n.* ⟦AmSp⟧ a kind of cornmeal cake esp. of Colombia and Venezuela, usually baked on a griddle

A·re·qui·pa (ä′re kē′pä) city in S Peru

Ar·es (er′ēz′) *n.* ⟦L < Gr *Arēs*⟧ *Gr. Myth.* the god of war, son of Zeus and Hera: identified with the Roman Mars

ar·e·te (ar′ə tā′, är′-) *n.* ⟦Gr *aretē*⟧ excellence; specif., *a)* excellence of character; virtue *b)* superior ability or skill; prowess

a·rête (ə rāt′) *n.* ⟦Fr, lit., fish skeleton, awn of wheat, ridge < OFr *areste* < VL **aresta* < L *arista*, awn of grain⟧ a sharp, narrow ridge or crest of a mountain, formed by glacial erosion

Ar·e·thu·sa (ar′ə thoo͞′zə, er′-; -thyoo͞′-; -sə) *n.* ⟦L < Gr. *Arethousa*⟧ **1** *Gr. Myth.* a woodland nymph, changed into a stream by Artemis so that she might escape her pursuer, Alpheus **2** [**a-**] a North American orchid (*Arethusa bulbosa*) with one pink flower and one long leaf that grows only with the fruit

A·re·ti·no (ä′re tē′nô), **Pie·tro** (pye′trô) 1492-1556; It. satirical writer

arf (ärf) *interj., n.* ⟦echoic⟧ (used to suggest) a barking sound of or like that of a dog

Arg *abbrev.* Argentina

ar·gal (är′gəl) *n.* ARGOL

ar·ga·la (är′gə lə) *n.* ⟦Hindi *hargīla*⟧ **1** the adjutant, a stork of India **2** the marabou, an African stork

ar·ga·li (är′gə lē) *n., pl.* **-lis** or **-li** ⟦Mongolian *aryali*⟧ a wild sheep (*Ovis ammon*) of Asia, with large, curved horns

Ar·gand burner (är′gənd) ⟦after its inventor, Aimé *Argand* (1755-1803), Swiss chemist⟧ a gas or oil burner designed to let air flow inside and outside a cylindrical wick

ar·gent (är′jənt) *n.* ⟦OFr < L *argentum* < IE base **ar(e)g-*, gleaming, whitish > Gr *argos*, white, *argyros*, silver⟧ **1** [Archaic] silver **2** [Obs.] silver coin; money **3** *Heraldry* the representation of the metal silver: indicated in engravings by a plain white field —*adj.* [Old Poet.] silvery

ar·gen·tic (är jen′tik) *adj.* ⟦< L *argentum* (see prec. + -IC⟧ of or containing divalent silver

ar·gen·tif·er·ous (är′jən tif′ər əs) *adj.* ⟦< L *argentum* (see ARGENT) + -FEROUS⟧ containing or yielding silver [*argentiferous* ore]

Ar·gen·ti·na (är′jən tē′nə) country in S South America: 1,068,302 sq mi (2,766,890 sq km); cap. Buenos Aires

ar·gen·tine (är′jən tin, -tīn′, -tēn′) *adj.* ⟦Fr & OFr *argentin* < *argent*, ARGENT⟧ of or like silver; silvery —*n.* silver or any silvery substance

Ar·gen·tine (är′jən tēn′, -tīn′; *Brit*, -tīn′) *adj.* of Argentina or its people or culture —*n.* a person born or living in Argentina Also **Ar′gen·tin′i·an** or **Ar′gen·tin′e·an** (-tin′ē ən) —**the Argentine** [Now Chiefly Brit.] Argentina

ar·gen·tite (-tīt′) *n.* ⟦< L *argentum* (see ARGENT) + -ITE[1]⟧ native silver sulfide, a lead-gray cubic mineral, Ag_2S, that is an important ore of silver

ar·gen·tous (är jen′təs) *adj.* ⟦< L *argentum* (see ARGENT) + -OUS⟧ of or containing monovalent silver

ar·gil·la·ceous (är′jə lā′shəs) *adj.* ⟦L *argillaceus* < *argilla*, clay < Gr < *argos*, white: see ARGENT⟧ of, like, or containing clay

ar·gil·lite (är′jə līt′) *n.* ⟦L *argilla* (see prec.) + -ITE[1]⟧ a hardened mudstone showing no slatelike cleavage

ar·gi·nase (är′jə nās′) *n.* ⟦< fol. + -ASE⟧ an animal enzyme, found esp. in the liver of mammals, important in the hydrolysis of arginine to form urea and ornithine

ar·gi·nine (-nēn′, -nin, -nīn′) *n.* ⟦Ger *arginin* < ? Gr *arginoeis*, white, gleaming (its first discovered salts were silvery) + *-in*, -INE[3]⟧ a nonessential amino acid, $NHC(NH_2)NH(CH_2)_3CH(NH_2)COOH$, considered essential during periods of rapid growth: see AMINO ACID

Ar·give (är′gīv′, -jīv′) *adj.* **1** of ancient Argos or Argolis **2** GREEK (*adj.* 1): term used by Homer —*n.* **1** a native of Argos or Argolis **2** any GREEK (*n.* 1): Homeric name

ar·gle-bar·gle (är′gəl bär′gəl) *n.* [Informal or Dial.] ARGY-BARGY

Ar·go (är′gō) *n.* ⟦L < Gr *Argō*⟧ **1** *Gr. Myth.* the ship on which Jason sails to find the Golden Fleece **2** *former name for* a large S constellation between Canis Major and Crux; the Ship: now subdivided into the constellations Carina, Puppis, Pyxis, and Vela

ar·gol (är′gəl) *n.* ⟦ME *argoile* < Anglo-Fr *argoil*⟧ tartar in its crude form as deposited in wine casks

Ar·go·lis (är′gə lis) department on the NE coast of the Peloponnesus, Greece: in ancient times, a region dominated by the city-state of Argos

ar·gon (är′gän′) *n.* ⟦Gr, neut. of *argos*, inert, idle < *a-*, without + *ergon*, WORK⟧ a colorless, odorless chemical element, one of the noble gases, constituting nearly 1% of the atmosphere: it is used in incandescent lightbulbs, electron tubes, welding, etc.: symbol, Ar; at. no. 18: see the periodic table of elements in the Reference Supplement

Ar·go·naut (är′gə nôt′, -nät′) *n.* ⟦L *Argonauta* < Gr *Argonautēs* < *Argō*, Jason's ship + *nautēs*, sailor < *naus*, ship⟧ **1** *Gr. Myth.* any of the men who sail with Jason to search for the Golden Fleece ☆**2** [*also* **a-**] a person who took part in the California gold rush of 1848-49 **3** [**a-**] *Zool.* PAPER NAUTILUS

Ar·gonne (är′gän′) wooded region in NE France, near the Belgian border

Ar·gos (är′gäs′, -gəs) ancient city-state in the NE Peloponnesus: it dominated the Peloponnesus from the 7th cent. B.C. until the rise of Sparta

ar·go·sy (är′gə sē) *n., pl.* **-sies** ⟦earlier *ragusy* < It (*nave*) *Ragusea*, (vessel of) RAGUSA (in Croatia); sp. infl. by the ARGO⟧ [Old Poet.] **1** a large ship, esp. a merchant ship **2** a fleet of such ships

ar·got (är′gō, -gət) *n.* ⟦Fr, orig. (in thieves' jargon), the company of beggars (*argoter*, to beg, prob. < *ergot*, claw, spur, hence orig., "get one's claws into")⟧ the specialized vocabulary and idioms of those in the same work, way of life, etc., as the language used by computer hackers: see SLANG —*SYN.* DIALECT

Ar·go·vie (år gô vē′) *Fr. name for* AARGAU

ar·gu·a·ble (är′gyo͞o ə bəl) *adj.* **1** that can be argued about **2** that can be supported by argument

ar·gu·a·bly (-blē) *adv.* as can be supported by argument

ar·gue (är′gyo͞o) *vi.* **-gued, -gu·ing** ⟦ME *arguen* < OFr *arguer* < VL *argutare*, for L *argutari*, to prattle, freq. of *arguere*, to make clear, prove < IE base **ar(e)g-*, gleaming (see ARGENT); OFr meaning and form infl. by *arguere*⟧ **1** to give reasons (*for* or *against* a proposal, proposition, etc.) **2** to have a disagreement; quarrel; dispute —*vt.* **1** to give reasons for and against; discuss; debate **2** to try to prove by giving reasons; maintain; contend **3** to give evidence of; seem to prove; indicate [his manners *argue* a good upbringing] **4** to persuade (*into* or *out of* an opinion, etc.) by giving reasons —*SYN.* DISCUSS —**ar′gu·er** *n.*

ar·gu·fy (är′gyə fī′) *vt., vi.* **-fied′, -fy′ing** ⟦< prec. + -FY⟧ [Informal or Dial.] to argue, esp. about something petty or merely for the sake of arguing; wrangle —**ar′gu·fi′er** *n.*

ar·gu·ment (är′gyo͞o mənt, -gyə-) *n.* ⟦ME < OFr or L: OFr < L *argumentum*, evidence, proof < *arguere*: see ARGUE⟧ **1** [Archaic] proof or evidence **2** a reason or reasons offered for or against something **3** the offering of such reasons; reasoning **4** a discussion in which there is disagreement; dispute; debate **5** a short statement of subject matter, or a brief synopsis of a plot; summary **6** [Obs.] a topic; theme **7** *Math.* INDEPENDENT VARIABLE

***SYN.*—argument** refers to a discussion in which there is disagreement and suggests the use of logic and the bringing forth of facts to support or refute a point; **dispute** basically refers to a contradiction of an assertion and implies vehemence or anger in debate; **controversy** connotes a disagreement of lengthy duration over a matter of some weight or importance [the Darwinian *controversy*]

ar·gu·men·ta·tion (är′gyo͞o men tā′shən, -mən-; -gyə-) *n.* ⟦Fr < L *argumentatio* < *argumentari*, to adduce as proof < *argumentum*: see prec.⟧ **1** the process of arriving at reasons and conclusions; arguing or reasoning **2** discussion in which there is disagreement; debate

ar·gu·men·ta·tive (-men′tə tiv) *adj.* **1** of or containing argument; controversial **2** apt to argue; contentious Also **ar′gu·men′tive** —**ar′gu·men′ta·tive·ly** *adv.*

ar·gu·men·tum (-men′təm) *n.* ⟦L⟧ an argument: used with Latin phrases AD HOMINEM, AD REM, etc.

Ar·gus (är′gəs) *n.* ⟦L < Gr *Argos* < *argos*, white: see ARGENT⟧ **1** *Gr. Myth.* a giant with a hundred eyes, ordered by Hera to watch Io: after he is killed by Hermes, his eyes are put in the tail of the peacock **2** any alert watchman **3** [**a-**] an East Indian pheasant (genus *Argusianus*) resembling the peacock

Ar·gus-eyed (-īd′) *adj.* keenly observant; vigilant

ar·gy-bar·gy (är′gē bär′gē) *n.* ⟦earlier dial. *argle-bargle*, redupl. alteration (? after HAGGLE) < ARGUE + BARGAIN⟧ [Informal, Chiefly Brit.] argument; squabble

ar·gyle (är′gīl′) *adj.* ⟦after fol.: the pattern is adapted from a clan tartan of Argyll⟧ knitted or woven in a pattern of diamond-shaped figures of different colors —*n.* [*pl.*] argyle socks

Ar·gyll (är′gīl′) former county of W Scotland: also **Ar′gyll·shire′** (-shir′)

Argyll and Bute administrative division of Scotland: formerly a district

ar·gyr·o·dite (är jir′ə dīt′) *n.* ⟦< Gr *argyrōdēs*, rich in silver < *argyros* (see ARGENT) + -ITE[1]⟧ a dark gray, soft mineral, Ag_8GeS_6, found in silver veins, and used as a major source of germanium

ar·hat (är′hət) *n.* ⟦Sans < *arhat*, adj., deserving (respect)⟧ *Buddhism* one who has attained nirvana and, thus, is no longer subject to the cycle of rebirth

År·hus (ôr′ho͞os′) seaport in E Jutland, Denmark, on the Kattegat

a·ri·a (ä′rē ə; ar′ē ə, er′-) *n.* ⟦It < L *aer*, AIR⟧ an air or melody in an opera, cantata, or oratorio, esp. for solo voice with instrumental accompaniment

-a·ri·a (er′ē ə, ä′rē ə) ⟦ModL < L, neut. pl. of *-arius*, -ARY⟧ *suffix Bot., Zool.* forming the scientific names of taxonomic groups

Ar·i·ad·ne (ar′ē ad′nē, er′-) *n.* ⟦L < Gr *Ariadnē*⟧ *Gr. Myth.* King Minos' daughter, who gives Theseus the thread by which he finds his way out of the labyrinth

Ar·i·an[1] (er′ē ən, ar′-) *adj.* ⟦L *Arianus* < *Arius*⟧ of Arius or Arianism —*n.* a believer in Arianism

Ar·i·an[2] (er′ē ən, ar′-) *n. var. of* ARIES (sense 3)

-ar·i·an (er′ē ən, ar′-) ⟦L *-arius*, -ARY + *-anus*, -AN⟧ *suffix forming adjectives and nouns* **1** (one) characterized by or having [*octogenarian, centenarian*] **2** *a)* (one) believing in [*Unitarian*] *b)* (one) advocating [*disciplinarian*] **3** (one) associated with [*antiquarian, agrarian*]

Ar·i·an·ism (er′ē ən iz′əm, ar′-) *n.* the doctrines of Arius, who taught that Jesus was not of the same substance as God, but a created being exalted above all other creatures

a·ri·a·ry (ä′rē ä′rē) *n., pl.* **-ries** ⟦Malagasy⟧ the basic monetary unit of Madagascar: see the table of monetary units in the Reference Supplement

A·ri·ca[1] (ə rē′kə) *n.* a technique or program for increasing self-awareness, consciousness, etc., featuring physical and mental exercises, meditation, diet, etc.

A·ri·ca[2] (ə rē′kə) seaport in N Chile, just south of the Peruvian border: see also TACNA

ar·id (ar′id, er′-) *adj.* ⟦L *aridus* < *arere*, to be dry: see ASH[1]⟧ **1** lacking enough water for things to grow; dry and barren **2** not interesting; lifeless; dull —*SYN.* DRY —**a·rid·i·ty** (ə rid′ə tē) *n.*, **ar′id·ness** —**ar′id·ly** *adv.*

Ar·i·el (er′ē əl, ar′-) *n.* ⟦< Gr(Ec) *ariēl* < Heb *ariel*, lion of God: a name applied to Jerusalem in the Bible⟧ **1** in Shakespeare's *The Tempest*, an airy spirit who is the servant of Prospero **2** a satellite of the planet Uranus

Ar·ies (er′ēz′, ar′-; -ē ēz′) *n.* ⟦L, a ram (male sheep)⟧ **1** a N constellation between Pisces and Taurus; the Ram **2** the first sign of the zodiac, entered by the sun about March 21: also called *the Ram* **3** a person born under this sign

ar·i·et·ta (ä′rē et′ə; ar′ē-, er′ē-) *n.* ⟦It, dim. of *aria*, ARIA⟧ a short aria: also **ar′i·ette′** (-et′)

a·right (ə rīt′) *adv.* ⟦ME < *on right*⟧ **1** [Dial.] correctly; rightly **2** into a correct state or position [a new mayor should finally set things *aright*]

☆**A·ri·ka·ra** (ə rē′kə rə, -rik′ə-) *n.* ⟦Fr *Aricara* < Pawnee *arikará·ru'*, elk, lit., horns; explained as an allusion to a hairstyle formerly worn by male members of this people⟧ **1** a member of a North American Indian people living along the Missouri River in W North Dakota **2** the Caddoan language of this people

ar·il (ar′il, er′-) *n.* ⟦ModL *arillus* < ML, dried grape < L *aridus*, ARID⟧ an additional covering that forms on certain seeds after fertilization, developing from the stalk of the ovule —**ar′il·late′** (-ə lāt′) *adj.*

ar·il·lode (ar′ə lōd′, er′-) *n.* ⟦< ModL *arillus* (see prec.) + -ODE[2]⟧ a false aril, developing from an opening in the covering of the ovule instead of from its stalk

Ar·i·ma·the·a or **Ar·i·ma·thae·a** (ar′ə mə thē′ə) town in ancient Palestine, possibly in Samaria

A·rim·i·num (ə rim′ə nəm) *ancient name for* RIMINI

a·ri·o·so (ä′rē ō′sō′) *n., pl.* **-si′** (-sē′) or **-sos′** (-sōz′) ⟦It < *aria*, ARIA⟧ *Mu-*

sic 1 a vocal style between aria and recitative 2 a composition or passage in this style — *adj., adv.* in the style of an arioso

A·ri·o·sto (ä′rē ô′stô′), **Lu·do·vi·co** (lo͞o′də vē′kô) 1474-1533; It. poet: author of *Orlando Furioso*

-ar·i·ous (er′ē əs, ar′-) ⟦< -ARY + -OUS⟧ *suffix forming adjectives* relating to, connected with [*hilarious, vicarious*]

a·rise (ə rīz′) *vi.* **a·rose′** (-rōz′), **a·ris′en** (-riz′ən), **a·ris′ing** ⟦ME *arisen* < OE *arisan* < *a-*, out (see A-²) + *risan*, to RISE⟧ 1 to get up, as from sleeping or sitting; rise 2 to move upward; ascend 3 to come into being; originate 4 to result or spring (*from*) —SYN. RISE

a·ris·ta (ə ris′tə) *n., pl.* **-tae** (-tē) ⟦L⟧ 1 a bristle-like fiber on the spikelet of some grains or grasses; awn 2 a bristle that extends from the antenna of certain dipterous insects: used in flight for monitoring air speed and for wing control —**a·ris′tate** (-tāt) *adj.*

Ar·is·tar·chus of Samos (ar′is tär′kəs) fl. 3d cent. B.C.; Gr. astronomer

Ar·is·ti·des (ar′is tī′dēz′) 530?-468? B.C.; Athenian general & statesman: called *the Just*

Ar·is·tip·pus (ar′is tip′əs) 435?-365? B.C.; Gr. philosopher: founder of the Cyrenaic school

a·ris·to (ə ris′tō) *n.* ⟦Fr, shortened < *aristocrate*⟧ [Informal, Chiefly Brit.] an aristocrat

ar·is·toc·ra·cy (ar′i stäk′rə sē, er′-) *n., pl.* **-cies** ⟦L *aristocratia* < Gr *aristokratia* < *aristos*, best + *-kratia*, rule < *kratos*, power, rule: see HARD⟧ 1 [Historical] government by the best citizens 2 government by a privileged minority or upper class, usually of inherited wealth and social position 3 a country with this form of government; oligarchy 4 a privileged ruling class; nobility 5 those considered the best in some way [*an aristocracy* of scientists] 6 aristocratic quality or spirit

a·ris·to·crat (ə ris′tə krat′; *chiefly Brit* ar′is tə-) *n.* ⟦Fr *aristocrate*: term popularized during Fr Revolution⟧ 1 a member of the aristocracy; nobleman 2 a person with the tastes, manners, beliefs, etc. of the upper class 3 a person who believes in aristocracy as a form of government

a·ris·to·crat·ic (ə ris′tə krat′ik; *chiefly Brit* ar′is tə-) *adj.* 1 of, characteristic of, or favoring aristocracy as a form of government 2 of an aristocracy or upper class 3 like or characteristic of an aristocrat: used in either a favorable sense (proud, distinguished, etc.) or an unfavorable (snobbish, haughty, etc.) —**a·ris′to·crat′i·cal·ly** *adv.*

Ar·is·toph·a·nes (ar′i stäf′ə nēz′) 450?-388? B.C.; Gr. writer of satirical comic dramas —**Ar′is·to·phan′ic** (-stə fan′ik) *adj.*

Ar·is·to·te·li·an (ar′is tə tēl′yən, -tē′lē ən) *adj.* of or characteristic of Aristotle or his philosophy —*n.* 1 a follower of Aristotle or his philosophy 2 a person who tends to be empirical or practical in outlook, rather than abstract, speculative, or idealistic: distinguished from PLATONIST —**Ar′is·to·te′li·an·ism′** *n.*

Aristotelian logic 1 Aristotle's method of deductive logic, characterized by the syllogism 2 the formal logic developed from Aristotle's

Ar·is·tot·le (ar′is tät′'l, er′-) 384-322 B.C.; Gr. philosopher; pupil of Plato: noted for works on logic, metaphysics, ethics, politics, etc.

a·rith·me·tic (ə rith′mə tik; *for adj.*, ar′ith met′ik, er′-) *n.* ⟦ME *arsmetrike* < OFr *arismetrique* (infl. in form by L *ars metrica*, the art of measurement) < L *arithmetica* < Gr (*hē*) *arithmētikē* (*technē*), (the) counting (art) < *arithmētikos*, arithmetical < *arithmein*, to count < *arithmos*, number⟧ 1 the science or art of computing by positive real numbers, specif. by adding, subtracting, multiplying, and dividing 2 knowledge of or skill in this science [her *arithmetic* is poor] —*adj.* of, based on, or using arithmetic: also **ar′ith·met′i·cal** —**ar′ith·met′i·cal·ly** *adv.*

ar·ith·me·ti·cian (ar′ith mə tish′ən, ə rith′mə-) *n.* a person skilled in arithmetic

arithmetic mean the average obtained by dividing a sum by the number of its addends

arithmetic progression a sequence of terms each of which, after the first, is derived by adding to the preceding one a common difference [5, 9, 13, 17, etc. form an *arithmetic progression*]

-ar·i·um (er′ē əm, ar′-) ⟦L, neut. sing. of *-arius*, -ARY⟧ *suffix* a place for or connected with [*oceanarium*]

A·ri·us (ar′ē əs; *also*, ə rī′əs) A.D. 250?-336; Alexandrian theologian, born in Libya: see ARIANISM

Ariz *abbrev.* Arizona

Ar·i·zo·na (ar′ə zō′nə, er′-) ⟦AmSp < Papago *Arizonac*, lit., little springs⟧ Mountain State of the SW U.S., on the Mexican border: admitted 1912: 113,635 sq mi (294,312 sq km); cap. Phoenix: abbrev. AZ or *Ariz*

Ar·i·zo·nan (-nən) *adj.* of Arizona: usually used in the predicate —*n.* a person born or living in Arizona Also **Ar′i·zo′ni·an** (-nē ən)

Ar·ju·na (är′jo͞o nə, ʊr′-) *n.* the hero of the Sanskrit epic, the *Mahabharata*

ark (ärk) *n.* ⟦OE *earc* < LL(Ec) *arca* < L, a box < *arcere*, to shut up, enclose: see EXERCISE⟧ 1 [Archaic] a chest or coffer 2 an enclosure in a synagogue or temple for the scrolls of the Torah 3 a place or thing furnishing protection; refuge 4 *a)* the huge boat in which Noah, his family, and two of every kind of creature survived the Flood: Gen. 6 *b)* ARK OF THE COVENANT ☆5 a large, flat-bottomed boat formerly used on rivers

Ark *abbrev.* Arkansas

Ar·kan·san (är kan′zən) *adj.* of Arkansas: usually used in the predicate —*n.* a person born or living in Arkansas

Ar·kan·sas (är′kən sô′; *for 2, sometimes,* är kan′zəs) ⟦< Fr (*la rivière des*) *Arkansas* < Illinois *Akansea, Akansa*, Quapaw (a Siouan people of this river valley)⟧ 1 state of the SC U.S.: admitted 1836: 52,068 sq mi (134,856 sq km); cap. Little Rock: abbrev. AR or *Ark* 2 river flowing from Colorado southeast into the Mississippi: 1,450 mi (2,333 km)

Ar·khan·gelsk (är khän′gelsk′) seaport in NW Russia, at the mouth of the Northern Dvina River

ark of the covenant the chest containing the two stone tablets inscribed with the Ten Commandments, kept in the holiest part of the ancient Jewish Tabernacle: Ex. 25:10

ar·kose (är′kōs′, är kōs′) *n.* ⟦Fr⟧ a medium-grained sandstone containing feldspar, derived from the erosion of igneous rock, esp. granite

Ark·wright (ärk′rīt′), Sir **Richard** 1732-92; Eng. inventor of a cotton-spinning machine

Ar·len (är′lən), **Harold** (born *Hymen Arluck*) 1905-1986; U.S. composer of popular songs

Ar·lene (är lēn′) *n.* a feminine name: var. *Arleen, Arline*

Ar·ling·ton (är′liŋ tən) ⟦orig. after an Eng place name⟧ 1 urban county in NE Va., across the Potomac from Washington, D.C.: site of a national cemetery (**Arlington National Cemetery**) 2 city in NE Tex.: suburb of Fort Worth

arm¹ (ärm) *n.* ⟦ME < OE *earm*; akin to L *armus*, Goth *arms*, OHG *arm*: see ART¹⟧ 1 *a)* an upper limb of the human body *b)* in anatomy, the part of the upper limb between the shoulder and the elbow *c)* in nontechnical use, the part of the upper limb between the shoulder and the wrist 2 anything resembling this in structure or function; esp., *a)* the forelimb of some vertebrate animals *b)* any limb of an invertebrate animal 3 anything commonly in contact with the human arm; esp., *a)* a sleeve of a garment *b)* a support for the arm on a chair, sofa, etc. 4 anything thought of as armlike, esp. in being attached or connected to something larger [an *arm* of the sea, a yard*arm*, the *arm* of a balance, an *arm* of the government, etc.] 5 power to seize, control, etc. [the long *arm* of the law] ☆6 [Slang] *Baseball* a pitcher [a team with several young *arms*] ☆7 *Baseball, Football* the ability to pitch or throw a ball —**an arm and a leg** [Informal] a very great amount of money [it cost me *an arm and a leg*] —**arm in arm** with arms interlocked, as two persons walking together —**at arm's length** at an emotional or relational distance so as to avoid or prevent intimacy, the appearance of favoritism, etc. —☆**put the arm on** [Slang] 1 to arrest or restrain 2 to request a loan or donation from —**under one's arm** between one's arm and side; specif., at the armpit [carrying a box *under his arm*] —**with open arms** in a warm and friendly way —**arm′less** *adj.* —**arm′like′** *adj.*

arm² (ärm) *n.* ⟦ME < OFr *armes*, pl. < L *arma*, implements, weapons; akin to *armus*, shoulder, upper arm (see ART¹): for semantic development see prec.⟧ 1 any instrument used in fighting; weapon: *usually used in pl.*: see also SMALL ARMS 2 [*pl.*] warfare; fighting 3 [*pl.*] *a)* COAT OF ARMS *b)* insignia of countries, corporations, etc. 4 ⟦a merging with prec.⟧ any combatant branch of the military forces —*vt.* ⟦ME *armen* < OFr *armer* < L *armare*, to arm < *arma*: see the *n.*⟧ 1 to provide with weapons, tools, etc. 2 to provide with something that protects or fortifies 3 to prepare to attack or to meet attack [reporters *armed* with questions] 4 to make ready or equip with parts needed for operation [to *arm* a missile with a warhead] —*vi.* 1 to equip oneself with weapons, as in preparing for war 2 to prepare for any struggle —SYN. FURNISH —**bear arms** 1 to carry or be equipped with weapons 2 to serve as a combatant in the armed forces —**take up arms** 1 to go to war or rise in rebellion 2 to enter a dispute —**to arms!** get ready to fight! —**under arms** equipped with weapons; ready for war —**up in arms** 1 prepared to fight 2 indignant

ARM (*often* ärm) *abbrev.* adjustable-rate mortgage

ar·ma·da (är mä′də, -mā′-) *n.* ⟦Sp, an armed force < L *armata*, fem. of *armatus*, pp. of *armare*: see ARM², *vt.*⟧ 1 a fleet of warships 2 a fleet of military aircraft 3 [A-] a fleet of warships sent against England by Spain in 1588 but destroyed: also SPANISH ARMADA

ar·ma·dil·lo (är′mə dil′ō) *n., pl.* **-los** ⟦Sp, dim. of *armado*, armored < L *armatus*: see prec.⟧ any of a family (Dasypodidae) of burrowing edentate mammals with an armorlike covering of bony plates, ranging from the S U.S. to Argentina: they are mostly nocturnal, and a few species roll up into a ball when attacked

Ar·ma·ged·don (är′mə ged′'n) *n.* ⟦LL(Ec) *Armagedon* < Gr *Harmagedōn* < ? Heb *har*, mountain + *megido*, the plain of MEGIDDO⟧ 1 *Bible a)* the place where the last, decisive battle between the forces of good and evil is to be fought before Judgment Day: Rev. 16:16 *b)* this battle 2 any great, decisive battle

Ar·magh (är mä′) 1 former county of S Northern Ireland: *c.* 512 sq mi (1,326 sq km) 2 district in S Northern Ireland, in the N part of the former county: 261 sq mi (676 sq km)

Ar·ma·gnac (är′mən yak′; *Fr* år må nyåk′) *n.* [*sometimes* **a-**] brandy distilled from wine in the district of Armagnac in Gascony, France

ar·ma·ment (är′mə mənt) *n.* ⟦L *armamentum*, pl. *armamenta*, implements, ship's tackle < *armare*: see ARM², *vt.*⟧ 1 [*often pl.*] all the military forces and equipment of a nation 2 a large force for offense or defense 3 all the guns and other military equipment of a warship, warplane, tank, fortification, etc. 4 an arming or being armed for war 5 anything serving to protect or defend

☆**ar·ma·men·tar·i·um** (är′mə men ter′ē əm) *n., pl.* **-i·a** (-ē ə) ⟦L, an arsenal < *armamenta*: see prec.⟧ an aggregate of resources, apparatus, etc., specif. for work in the field of medicine

ar·ma·ture (är′mə chər) *n.* ⟦L *armatura*, arms, equipment < *armatus*, pp. of *armare*; all senses from that of "armored, protected": see ARM², *vt.*⟧ 1 any protective covering: see ARMOR (senses 1 & 2) 2 any part or structure of an organism useful for defense or offense, as claws, teeth, burs, or thorns **3** a soft iron bar placed across the poles of a magnet to keep it from losing magnetic power **4** *a)* the laminated iron core with wire wound around it in which electromotive force is produced by magnetic induction in a generator or motor: usually a revolving part, but in an alternating-current machine often stationary *b)* the moving or vibrating part in an electric relay or bell **5** *Sculpture* a framework for supporting the clay or other plastic material in modeling

Ar·ma·vir (är′mə vir′) city in SW Russia, in the Caucasus, on the Kuban River

☆**arm·band** (ärm′band′) ***n.*** a cloth band worn around the upper arm, as in mourning or as a symbol of rank, membership, etc.

arm candy [Informal] a very attractive person who accompanies someone, usually of the opposite sex, at a social gathering

arm·chair (ärm′cher′) ***n.*** a chair with supports at the sides for one's arms or elbows —***adj.*** not based on or working from firsthand experience, direct investigation, etc. *[armchair* strategy, an *armchair* detective*]* —☆**armchair quarterback** (or **general**) someone, as a spectator or fan, who lacks experience in a particular field yet criticises the performance or decisions of a professional in that field

armed (ärmd) ***adj.*** **1** provided with arms (weapons), armor, etc. **2** having arms (limbs) of a specified kind *[*long-*armed]*

armed forces all the military, naval, and air forces of a country or group of countries

Ar·me·ni·a (är mēn′yə, -mē′nē ə; *for 4,* -mā′nē ə, -mān′yə) **1** region & former kingdom of W Asia, south of the Caucasus Mts.: now divided between Turkey, Iran, and present-day Armenia **2** ARMENIAN SOVIET SOCIALIST REPUBLIC **3** country in W Asia: became independent upon the breakup of the U.S.S.R. (1991): 11,506 sq mi (29,800 sq km); cap. Yerevan: formerly, *Armenian Soviet Socialist Republic* **4** city in WC Colombia

Ar·me·ni·an (är mēn′yən, -mē′nē ən) ***adj.*** of Armenia or its people, language, or culture —***n.*** **1** a person born or living in Armenia **2** the language spoken in Armenia, constituting a branch of the Indo-European family of languages

Armenian Soviet Socialist Republic a republic of the U.S.S.R.: now ARMENIA (the country)

Ar·men·tières (är′mən tirz′; *Fr* år män tyer′) town in N France, near the Belgian border

arm·ful (ärm′fo͝ol) ***n.,*** *pl.* **-fuls** as much as the arms or one arm can hold

arm·hole (ärm′hōl′) ***n.*** an opening for the arm in a garment

ar·mi·ger (är′mə jər) ***n.*** ⟦L < *arma,* arms (see ARM[2]) + *gerere,* to carry⟧ **1** an armorbearer for a knight; squire **2** a person entitled to display armorial bearings

ar·mig·er·ous (är mij′ər əs) ***adj.*** ⟦see prec. & -OUS⟧ of, having, or entitled to have a coat of arms

ar·mil·lar·y sphere (är′mə ler′ē) ⟦< L *armilla,* armlet, bracelet < *armus*: see ARM[2]⟧ an ancient astronomical sighting instrument representing the great circles of the horizon, the ecliptic, the meridian, etc.

Ar·min·i·an·ism (är min′ē ən iz′əm) ***n.*** a liberal Christian movement based on the doctrines of Jacobus Arminius, that stressed free will as opposed to Calvinistic predestination —**Ar·min′i·an** ***adj., n.***

Ar·min·i·us (är min′ē əs) **1** (Ger. name *Hermann*) 17? B.C.-A.D. 21?; Germanic tribal leader **2 Ja·co·bus** (yä kō′bəs) (born *Jacob Harmensen*) 1560-1609; Du. theologian: see ARMINIANISM

ar·mi·stice (är′mə stis) ***n.*** ⟦Fr < L *arma,* arms (see ARM[2]) + *-stitium* (as in *solstitium,* SOLSTICE) < *sistere,* to cause to stand, redupl. < *stare,* STAND⟧ a temporary stopping of warfare by mutual agreement, as a truce preliminary to the signing of a peace treaty

Armistice Day Nov. 11, the anniversary of the armistice of WWI in 1918: see VETERANS DAY

arm·let (ärm′lət) ***n.*** ⟦ARM[1] + -LET⟧ **1** a band worn for ornament around the arm, esp. the upper arm **2** a small, narrow, deep arm or inlet of the sea

arm·load (ärm′lōd′) ***n.*** as much as can be held or carried with the arms or one arm; armful

arm·lock (ärm′läk′) ***n.*** *Wrestling* a hold in which one contestant's arm is locked by an arm and a hand of the other

ar·moire (är mwär′) ***n.*** ⟦Fr < OFr *armarie,* AMBRY⟧ a large, usually ornate cupboard or clothespress

ar·mor (är′mər) ***n.*** ⟦ME *armure* < OFr < L *armatura*: see ARMATURE⟧ **1** covering worn to protect the body against weapons **2** any defensive or protective covering, as on animals or plants, or the metal plating on warships, warplanes, etc. **3** the armored forces and vehicles of an army; tanks, reconnaissance cars, etc. **4** a quality or condition serving as a defense difficult to penetrate — ***vt., vi.*** to put armor or armor plate on

ar·mor·bear·er (-ber′ər) ***n.*** a person who carried the armor or weapons of a warrior

ar·mor-clad (-klad′) ***adj.*** covered with armor

ar·mored (är′mərd) ***adj.*** **1** covered with armor or armor plate **2** equipped with armored vehicles *[*an *armored* division*]*

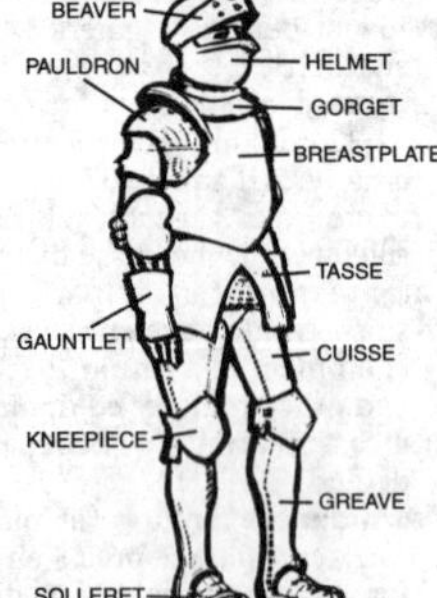

suit of armor

armored cable an electric cable having a metal protective covering

☆**armored car** **1** any of various vehicles covered with armor plate, as a truck for carrying money to or from a bank **2** *Mil.* a wheeled motor vehicle with armor plate, usually carrying a mounted machine gun and used esp. for reconnaissance

☆**armored scale** any of a family (Diaspididae) of scale insects characterized by a hard, waxy secretion that covers the body: many armored scales are serious pests of trees and shrubs

ar·mor·er (är′mər ər) ***n.*** **1** [Historical] a person who made or repaired armor and arms **2** a maker of firearms **3** *Mil.* an enlisted person in charge of the maintenance and repair of the small arms of a unit, warship, etc.

ar·mo·ri·al (är môr′ē əl) ***adj.*** ⟦< ARMORY + -AL⟧ of coats of arms; heraldic

Ar·mor·i·ca (är môr′i kə) region of ancient Gaul, between the mouths of the Loire and Seine rivers: invaded by Britons in the 5th cent. & thereafter known as *Brittany*

Ar·mor·i·can (är môr′i kən) ***adj.*** of Armorica or its people, language, or culture —***n.*** **1** a person born or living in Armorica **2** the language of Armorica; Breton Also **Ar·mor′ic** (-ik)

armor plate a protective covering of specially hardened steel plates, as on a tank —**ar′mor-plat′ed** ***adj.***

ar·mor·y (är′mər ē) ***n.,*** *pl.* **-mor·ies** ⟦altered, by assoc. with ARMOR < OFr *armoierie,* science of heraldry < *armoier,* to blazon coats of arms < *arme,* ARM[2]⟧ **1** [Obs.] armor or armorial bearings **2** a storehouse for weapons; arsenal **3** an aggregate of resources, etc. ☆**4** a building housing the drill hall and offices of a National Guard unit ☆**5** a place where firearms are made **6** heraldry

ar·mour (är′mər) ***n., vi., vt.*** *Brit. sp. of* ARMOR

arm·pit (ärm′pit′) ***n.*** the hollow under the arm at the shoulder; axilla

arm·rest (-rest′) ***n.*** a support on which to rest one's arm, as on the inside of an automobile door

arm's-length (ärmz′leŋkth′) ***adj.*** ⟦< AT ARM'S LENGTH (see phr. under ARM[1])⟧ conducted or effected in a manner that is formal, impersonal, etc. *[arm's-length* negotiations*]*

Arm·strong (ärm′strôŋ′) **1 Louis** 1901-71; U.S. jazz trumpeter & singer: also called *Satchmo* **2 Neil (Alden)** 1930-2012; U.S. astronaut: first man to step onto the moon

☆**arm-twist·ing** (ärm′twis′tiŋ) ***n.*** [Informal] the use of extreme or unethical pressure or influence in an effort to compel someone to act in a certain way —**arm′-twist′er** ***n.***

ar·mure (är′myo͝or) ***n.*** ⟦Fr, ARMOR⟧ a woven fabric with a small pebbled pattern

☆**arm-wres·tling** (ärm′res′liŋ) ***n.*** a contest in which two persons grasp each other's hand, with their elbows resting on a flat surface: the one who forces the other's arm down to the surface wins

ar·my (är′mē) ***n.,*** *pl.* **-mies** ⟦ME & OFr *armee* < *armer,* ARM[2], v.⟧ **1** a large, organized body of soldiers for waging war, esp. on land **2** a military unit, usually two or more army corps, together with auxiliary troops **3** STANDING ARMY **4** *[often* **A-***]* a large organization of persons for a specific cause *[*the Salvation *Army]* **5** any large number of persons, animals, etc. considered as a whole *[*the *army* of the unemployed*]*

army ant any of a number of carnivorous ants that travel in long lines and prey on insects and animals in their path; esp., any of a genus (*Eciton*) of such ants of the American tropics and S U.S.

army brat [Slang] a daughter or son of a career U.S. Army officer or enlisted person, esp. one raised in military communities: also written **Army brat**

army of occupation an army that goes into a defeated country to enforce peace terms, keep order, etc.

Army of the United States during WWII, the overall army forces of the U.S., including the Regular Army, the Organized Reserves, the National Guard, and Selective Service personnel: cf. UNITED STATES ARMY

☆**army worm** any of the larvae of certain noctuid moths, esp. of the moth (*Pseudaletia unipuncta*) of which the caterpillar is dark-striped green and yellow: these larvae travel in large groups, ruining crops and grass

Arne (ärn), **Thomas Augustine** 1710-78; Eng. composer

Arn·hem (ärn′hem′, är′nəm) city in the E Netherlands, on the Rhine

ar·ni·ca (är′ni kə) ***n.*** ⟦ModL⟧ **1** any of a number of plants (genus *Arnica*) of the composite family, bearing bright yellow flowers on long stalks with clusters of leaves at the base **2** a preparation made from certain of these plants (esp. *A. montana* or *A. cordifolia*), once used for treating sprains, bruises, etc.

Ar·no (är′nō) river in Tuscany, central Italy, flowing west into the Ligurian Sea: *c.* 150 mi (241 km)

Ar·nold[1] (är′nəld) ***n.*** ⟦Ger < OHG *Aranold* < Gmc **Arnwald,* lit., strong as an eagle < **aran,* eagle (> MLowG *arn*: see ERNE) + **waltan,* to rule (> Ger *walten*: see WIELD) > ML *Arnoldus,* Fr *Arnaud,* ME *Arnett*⟧ a masculine name

Ar·nold[2] (är′nəld) **1 Benedict** 1741-1801; Am. Revolutionary general who became a traitor **2 Matthew** 1822-88; Eng. poet, essayist, & critic **3 Thomas** 1795-1842; Eng. educator: father of Matthew

ar·oid (ar′oid′, er′-) ***n.*** any plant of the arum family

a·roint (ə roint′) ***vt.*** ⟦< ?; earliest known occurrence in Shakespeare's *Macbeth* I, iii, 6⟧ [Obs.] begone; avaunt: usually followed by *thee*: used in the imperative

a·ro·ma (ə rō′mə) ***n.*** ⟦L < Gr *arōma,* sweet spice⟧ **1** a pleasant, often spicy odor; fragrance, as of a plant, a wine, cooking, etc. **2** any smell or odor **3** a characteristic quality or atmosphere *[*a city with the *aroma* of Paris*]* —***SYN.*** SMELL

a·ro·ma·ther·a·py (ə rō′mə ther′ə pē) ***n.*** the use of aromatic oils from herbs, flowers, etc. as an alternative therapeutic technique, either by application to the skin, as in massage, or by inhalation of the scent

ar·o·mat·ic (ar′ə mat′ik, er′-) ***adj.*** ⟦ME *aromatik* < OFr *aromatique* < LL *aromaticus* < Gr *arōmatikos* < *arōma*, sweet spice⟧ **1** of or having an aroma; smelling sweet or spicy; fragrant or pungent **2** *Chem.* of or designating certain cyclic compounds, including benzene, derivatives of benzene, and compounds containing one or more benzene rings: many of these derivatives and compounds have a recognizable odor: see ALIPHATIC (sense 2), ALICYCLIC —***n.*** an aromatic plant, chemical, etc. —**ar′o·mat′i·cal·ly** ***adv.***

a·ro·ma·tize (ə rō′mə tīz′) ***vt.*** **-tized′**, **-tiz′ing** **1** to make aromatic **2** *Chem.* to change into an aromatic compound —**a·ro′ma·ti·za′tion** ***n.***

A·roos·took (ə ro͞os′tək) ⟦< an Eastern Algonquian language: meaning unknown⟧ river in N Me., flowing into the St. John River in New Brunswick, Canada: *c.* 140 mi (225 km)

a·rose (ə rōz′) ***vi. pt. of*** ARISE

a·round (ə round′) ***adv.*** ⟦ME < *a-*, on + ROUND[1]: all senses derive from those of "circling, within a circle"⟧ **1** round; esp., *a)* in a circle; along a circular course or circumference *b)* in or through a course or circuit, as from one place to another *c)* on all sides; in every direction *d)* in circumference *e)* in or to the opposite direction, belief, etc. *f)* in various places; here and there *g)* in succession or sequence [his turn came *around*] *h)* in every part; throughout [the year *around*] **2** [Informal] within a close periphery; nearby [stay *around*] ☆**3** [Informal] to a (specified or understood) place [come *around* to see us] **4** [Informal] nearly; approximately; about [*around* five pounds] —***prep.*** **1** *a)* on the circumference, border, or outer part of *b)* so as to encircle **2** so as to surround or envelop **3** from the beginning to the end of (a period of time); throughout **4** so as to rotate or revolve about (an axis or center) **5** on all sides of; in every direction from **6** *a)* in various places in or on; here and there in; all about *b)* to or through every part or various parts of; in a circuit or course through **7** *a)* so as to make a curve or partial circuit about *b)* at a point reached by making such a circuit about [the house *around* the corner] **8** so as to master or overcome (an obstacle or problem) [we got *around* the boss by finding a substitute] **9** in the vicinity of; near to [somewhere *around* the building] ☆**10** somewhat close to; about [it happened *around* 1965] **11** so as to be based on [a speech written *around* a favorite concept] —***adj.*** **1** on the move; about [he's up and *around* now] **2** existing; living [when dinosaurs were *around*] ➥As an adjective, used only in the predicate Cf. ROUND[1] —☆**have been around** [Informal] to have had wide experience; be sophisticated: see also phrases under BRING, COME, GET, etc.
USAGE—See usage note at ROUND[1]

a·round-the-clock (-*thə* kläk′) ***adj., adv.*** ROUND-THE-CLOCK

a·rouse (ə rouz′) ***vt.*** **a·roused′**, **a·rous′ing** ⟦A-[2], intens. + ROUSE[1]⟧ **1** to awaken, as from sleep **2** to stir, as to action or strong feeling **3** to evoke (some action or feeling); excite [to *arouse* pity] —***vi.*** to become aroused —***SYN.*** INCITE, STIR[1] —**a·rous′al** ***n.***

Arp (ärp), **Jean** (zhän) 1887-1966; Fr. painter & sculptor, born in Alsace: also **Hans Arp**

Ar·pad (är′päd) died A.D. 907; Magyar leader: national hero of Hungary

ar·peg·gi·ate (är pej′ē āt′) ***vt.*** **-at′ed**, **-at′ing** to play the notes of (a chord) in quick succession

ar·peg·gi·o (är pej′ō, -pej′ē ō) ***n.***, *pl.* **-gi·os** (-ōz) ⟦It < *arpeggiare*, to play on a harp < *arpa*, a harp < LL *harpa*, of Gmc orig.: see HARP⟧ **1** the playing of the notes of a chord in quick succession instead of simultaneously **2** a chord so played

ar·pent (är′pənt; *Fr* ȧr pän′) ***n.*** ⟦Fr, ult. < Gaul *arepenis*⟧ an old French unit of land measure, formerly used in parts of Quebec and Louisiana, equal to about 5⁄6 acre

ar·que·bus (är′kwə bəs) ***n.*** HARQUEBUS

arr *abbrev.* **1** arranged **2** arrangements **3** arrival

ar·rack (ar′ək) ***n.*** ⟦Fr *arak* < Ar *ʿaraq*, sweat, palm sap, liquor⟧ in Muslim countries, strong alcoholic liquor, esp. that which is distilled from rice and molasses, and, sometimes, palm sap

ar·raign (ə rān′) ***vt.*** ⟦ME *arreinen* < OFr *araisnier* < ML *adrationare* < L *ad*, to + *ratio*, REASON⟧ **1** to bring before a law court to hear and answer charges **2** to call to account; accuse —***SYN.*** ACCUSE —**ar·raign′ment** ***n.***

Ar·ran (ar′ən) island in the Firth of Clyde, SW Scotland: 165 sq mi (427 sq km)

ar·range (ə rānj′) ***vt.*** **-ranged′**, **-rang′ing** ⟦ME *arengen* < OFr *arengier* < *a-*, to + *rengier*, RANGE⟧ **1** to put in the correct, proper, or suitable order **2** to sort systematically; classify **3** to make ready; prepare or plan [to *arrange* a program of entertainment] **4** to arrive at an agreement about; settle **5** *Music* to adapt (a composition) to other instruments or voices than those for which it was written, or to the style of a certain band or orchestra —***vi.*** **1** to come to an agreement (*with* a person, *about* a thing) **2** to make plans; prepare [*arrange* to be here later] **3** *Music* to write arrangements, esp. as a profession —**ar·rang′er** ***n.***

arranged marriage a nuptial match traditionally arranged by the families of a young man and woman

ar·range·ment (-mənt) ***n.*** **1** an arranging or being arranged **2** the way in which something is arranged **3** something made by arranging parts in a particular way **4** [*usually pl.*] a preparation; plan [*arrangements* for the party, *arrangements* for a funeral] **5** a settlement or adjustment, as of a dispute, difference, etc. **6** *Music a)* adaptation of a composition to other instruments or voices than those for which it was originally written, or to the style of a certain band or orchestra *b)* the composition as thus adapted

ar·rant (ar′ənt, er′-) ***adj.*** ⟦var. of ERRANT⟧ that is plainly such; out-and-out; notorious [an *arrant* fool] —**ar′rant·ly** ***adv.***

ar·ras (ar′əs, er′-) ***n.*** ⟦ME, after *Arras*, city in France, where it was made⟧ **1** an elaborate kind of tapestry **2** a wall hanging, esp. of tapestry

ar·ray (ə rā′) ***vt.*** ⟦ME *arraien* < OFr *areer* < ML **arredare*, to put in order < L *ad-*, to + Gmc **raid-*: for IE base see RIDE⟧ **1** to place in order; marshal (troops for battle, etc.) **2** to dress in fine or showy attire; deck out —***n.*** **1** an orderly grouping or arrangement, esp. of troops **2** troops in order; military force **3** *a)* an impressive display of assembled persons or things *b)* any wide or varied assortment **4** fine clothes; finery **5** *Comput.* a group of two or more logically related elements, identified by a single name and usually stored in consecutive storage locations in main memory **6** *Math., Statistics* a systematic arrangement of numbers or symbols in rows and columns

ar·ray·al (-əl) ***n.*** **1** the act or process of arraying **2** something arrayed

ar·rear·age (ə rir′ij) ***n.*** ⟦ME *arerage* < OFr *arierage* < *ariere*: see fol.⟧ **1** the state of being in arrears **2** arrears

ar·rears (ə rirz′) ***pl.n.*** ⟦ME *arrers* < *arrere*, backward < OFr *ariere* < VL *aretro* < L *ad*, to + *retro*, behind⟧ **1** unpaid and overdue debts **2** unfinished business, work, etc. —**in arrears** (or **arrear**) behind in paying a debt, doing one's work, etc.

ar·rest (ə rest′) ***vt.*** ⟦ME *aresten* < OFr *arester* < VL **arrestare* < L *ad-*, to + *restare*, to stop, REST[2]⟧ **1** to stop or check the motion, course, or spread of **2** to seize or take into custody by authority of the law **3** to catch and keep (one's attention, sight, etc.) —***n.*** ⟦ME & OFr *arest* < the v.⟧ **1** an arresting or being arrested; esp., a taking or being taken into custody by authority of the law **2** a thing for checking motion —**under arrest** in legal custody, as of the police —**ar·rest′ee** ***n.*** —**ar·rest′er** ***n.***, **ar·res′tor**

ar·rest·ing (-iŋ) ***adj.*** attracting attention; interesting; striking —**ar·rest′ing·ly** ***adv.***

Ar·rhe·ni·us (ä rā′nē o͝os; *E* ə rā′nē əs), **Svan·te Au·gust** (svän′te ou′go͝ost) 1859-1927; Swed. physical chemist: first to present the theory of ionization

ar·rhyth·mi·a (ə rith′mē ə) ***n.*** ⟦ModL < Gr, lack of rhythm < *a-*, without + *rhythmos*, measure⟧ any irregularity in the rhythm of the heart's beating —**ar·rhyth′mic** ***adj.***, **ar·rhyth′mi·cal** —**ar·rhyth′mi·cal·ly** ***adv.***

ar·rière-ban (ar′ē er′ban′; *Fr* ȧ ryer bän′) ***n.*** ⟦Fr, altered by folk etym., after *arrière* (see ARREARS) < OFr *harbon* < OHG *hariban*, conscription < *hari*, army + *ban*, command under penalty⟧ **1** in medieval France, a king's summoning of his vassals to do their military duty **2** the vassals so summoned

ar·rière-pen·sée (ȧ ryer pän sā′) ***n.*** ⟦Fr, lit., back-thought⟧ **1** a mental reservation **2** an ulterior motive

ar·ris (ar′is, er′-) ***n.*** ⟦OFr *areste*: see ARÊTE⟧ *Archit.* the edge made by two straight or curved surfaces coming together at an angle, as in a molding

ar·riv·al (ə rī′vəl) ***n.*** **1** the act of arriving **2** a person or thing that arrives or has arrived

ar·rive (ə rīv′) ***vi.*** **-rived′**, **-riv′ing** ⟦ME *ariven* < OFr *ariver* < VL **arripare*, come to shore, land < L *ad-*, to + *ripa*, shore⟧ **1** to reach one's destination; come to a place **2** to come [the time has *arrived* for action] **3** to attain success, fame, etc. [he has *arrived* professionally] —***vt.*** to reach [this flight *arrives* Atlanta at 6 P.M.] —**arrive at** **1** to reach by traveling **2** to reach by work, thinking, development, etc.

ar·ri·ve·der·ci (är rē′ve der′chē) ***interj.*** ⟦It, lit., to the seeing again⟧ until we meet again; goodbye: implies temporary parting

ar·ri·viste (ar′ē vēst′, er′-; *Fr* ȧ rē-) ***n.*** ⟦Fr < *arriver* (see ARRIVE) + *-iste*, -IST[1]⟧ a person who has recently gained power, wealth, success, etc. and is regarded as an upstart; parvenu

ar·ro·ba (ə rō′bə; *Sp* ä rô′bä) ***n.*** ⟦Sp < Ar *al rubʿ*, the quarter (of the Sp quintal)⟧ [Historical] **1** a unit of weight used in Spanish-speaking countries, equal to 25.36 pounds (11.5 kg) **2** a unit of weight used in Portugal and Brazil, equal to 32.38 pounds (14.7 kg) **3** a unit of liquid measure used in Spanish-speaking countries, varying from 13 quarts (for oil) to 17 quarts (for wine) (12 to 16 liters)

ar·ro·gance (ar′ə gəns, er′-) ***n.*** the quality or state of being arrogant; overbearing pride or self-importance: also **ar′ro·gan·cy**

ar·ro·gant (-gənt) ***adj.*** ⟦ME & OFr < L *arrogans*, prp. of *arrogare*, fol.⟧ full of or due to unwarranted pride and self-importance; overbearing; haughty —***SYN.*** PROUD —**ar′ro·gant·ly** ***adv.***

ar·ro·gate (-gāt′) ***vt.*** **-gat′ed**, **-gat′ing** ⟦< L *arrogatus*, pp. of *arrogare*, to claim < *ad-*, to, for + *rogare*, to ask: see ROGATION⟧ **1** to claim or seize without right; appropriate (to oneself) arrogantly **2** to ascribe or attribute without reason —**ar′ro·ga′tion** ***n.***

ar·ron·disse·ment (ȧ rōn dēs män′) ***n.***, *pl.* **-ments′** (-män′) ⟦Fr < *arrondir*, to make round⟧ in France, *a)* the largest administrative subdivision of a department *b)* a municipal subdivision, as of Paris

ar·row (ar′ō, er′-) ***n.*** ⟦OE *earh*, *arwe*; akin to Goth *arhwa-* (for IE base see ARC); orig. sense of *arrow* was "belonging to the bow"⟧ **1** a slender shaft, usually pointed at one end and feathered at the other, for shooting from a bow **2** anything like an arrow in form, speed, purpose, etc. **3** a sign (←), used to indicate direction or position

ar·row·head (-hed′) ***n.*** **1** the separable, pointed head or tip of an arrow, made formerly of flint or stone, now usually of metal **2** anything shaped like an arrowhead; specif., an indicating mark, part of a cuneiform character, etc.: the sign (<) as used throughout this dictionary marks the derivation of a word or word form from another **3** any of various marsh plants (genus *Sagittaria*) of the water plantain family, with arrow-shaped leaves and small, white, open flowers

ar·row·root (-ro͞ot′, -ro͝ot′) ***n.*** ⟦altered, from use as antidote for poisoned arrows < Arawakan *aru-aru*, lit., meal of meals⟧ **1** any of a number of tropical plants of various families with clumplike roots; esp., a West Indian plant (*Maranta arundinacea*) of the arrowroot family with large leaves, white flowers, and starchy roots **2** an easily digestible starch derived from an arrowroot (esp. *M. arundinacea*) **—*adj.*** designating a family (Marantaceae, order Zingiberales) of monocotyledonous, tropical American plants

☆**ar·row·wood** (-wo͝od′) ***n.*** any of various trees or shrubs of several families, as certain viburnums, with long straight stems used by North American Indians to make arrows

ar·row·worm (-wurm′) ***n.*** any of a phylum (Chaetognatha) of small, wormlike marine animals with an arrow-shaped, finned, almost completely transparent body: they feed on plankton

☆**ar·roy·o** (ə roi′ō) ***n.***, *pl.* **-os** ⟦Sp < L *arrugia*, shaft or pit (in a gold mine)⟧ [Southwest] **1** a dry gully **2** a rivulet or stream

a·rroz con po·llo (ä rôs′kôn pô′lyô) ⟦Sp⟧ a Spanish and Latin American dish consisting of chicken and rice cooked usually with saffron

arse (äs; *in the U.S., typically*, ärs, as) ***n.*** ⟦ME *ars* < OE *ears, ærs* < IE base **orsos* > Gr *oura*, tail⟧ [Brit. Slang] the buttocks; ass: now mildly vulgar

ar·se·nal (är′sə nəl) ***n.*** ⟦It *arsenale*, a dock < Ar *dār aṣṣināʿa*, wharf, workshop < *dār*, house + *al-ṣināʿa*, craft, skill⟧ **1** a place for making or storing weapons and other munitions **2** a nation's or military organization's stockpile of weapons **3** any collection of things to be used in a conflict or struggle [a debater's *arsenal* of facts]

ar·se·nate (är′sə nāt′, -nit′) ***n.*** **1** a salt of arsenic acid containing the trivalent, negative radical AsO_4 **2** an uncharged ester of arsenic acid

ar·se·nic (är′sə nik′; *for adj.* är sen′ik) ***n.*** ⟦ME < OFr < L *arsenicum* < Gr *arsenikon*, yellow orpiment; ult. (? via Syr *zarnīk(ā)*) < Iran **zarnīk*, gold-colored (> Pers *zarnīq*, arsenic); assoc. in Gr with *arsenikos*, strong, masculine⟧ **1** a silvery-white, brittle, very poisonous chemical element, compounds of which are used in making insecticides, glass, medicines, semiconductors, etc.: symbol, As; at. no. 33: see the periodic table of elements in the Reference Supplement **2** loosely, arsenic trioxide, As_2O_3, a poisonous compound of arsenic used to exterminate insects and rodents: it is a white powder and has no taste **—*adj.*** of or containing arsenic, esp. pentavalent arsenic

arsenic acid a white, poisonous, crystalline compound, H_3AsO_4, used to make insecticides, medicines, etc.

ar·sen·i·cal (är sen′i kəl) ***adj.*** ⟦ML *arsenicalis*⟧ of or containing arsenic **—*n.*** a drug, fungicide, insecticide, etc. whose effect depends on its arsenic content

ar·se·nide (är′sə nīd′) ***n.*** a binary compound containing trivalent, negative arsenic

ar·se·ni·ous (är sē′nē əs) ***adj.*** ARSENOUS

ar·se·nite (är′sə nīt′) ***n.*** a salt or ester of arsenous acid

ar·se·niu·ret·ed or **ar·se·niu·ret·ted** (är sēn′yə ret′id, -sen′-) ***adj.*** ⟦< *arseniuret*, old name for arsenide < L *arsenicum*, ARSENIC + -URET⟧ combined with arsenic

ar·se·no- (är′sə nō′, är sen′ə) *combining form* having arsenic as a constituent [*arsenopyrite*]: also **arsen-**

ar·se·no·py·rite (är′sə nō′pī′rīt′) ***n.*** a silvery-white, hard, brittle, monoclinic mineral, FeAsS; iron arsenic sulfide: it is an ore of arsenic found as a twinned crystal in veins of metamorphic rock

ar·se·nous (är′sə nəs) ***adj.*** of or containing trivalent arsenic

arsenous acid a toxic white powder, As_2O_3, used to make other arsenic compounds, insecticides, and preservatives; white arsenic: also called **arsenic trioxide** or **arsenious acid**

ars gra·ti·a ar·tis (ärz′ grä′shē ə är′tis) ⟦L⟧ art for art's sake

ar·sine (är sēn′; är′sēn, -sin) ***n.*** ⟦ARS(ENIC) + -INE³⟧ **1** a very poisonous, flammable gas, AsH_3, that smells like garlic **2** any of its derivatives

ar·sis (är′sis) ***n.***, *pl.* **-ses′** (-sēz′) ⟦LL < Gr, a lifting up, omission < *airein*, to lift, raise up⟧ **1** in classical Greek poetry, the short syllable or syllables of a foot **2** in later poetry, the long or accented syllable of a foot **3** *Music* the unaccented part of a measure; upbeat Cf. THESIS (sense 1)

ars lon·ga, vi·ta bre·vis (ärz′ lôŋ′gə vēt′ə brev′is, -vīt′ə brē′vis) ⟦L⟧ art is long, life is short

ar·son (är′sən) ***n.*** ⟦OFr < LL *arsio*, fire < L *arsus*, pp. of *ardere*, to burn: see ASH¹⟧ the crime of purposely setting fire to another's building or property, or to one's own, as to collect insurance **—ar′son·ist *n.***

ars·phen·a·mine (ärs fen′ə mēn′, -min′) ***n.*** ⟦ARS(ENIC) + PHEN(YL) + AMINE⟧ a yellowish arsenical powder, $[OH{\cdot}C_6H_3(NH_2{\cdot}HCl){\cdot}As]_2$, formerly used in treating syphilis

ars po·e·ti·ca (ärz′ pō et′i kə) ⟦L⟧ the art of poetry

art¹ (ärt) ***n.*** ⟦ME < OFr *arte* < L *ars* (gen. *artis*), art < IE base **ar-*, to join, fit together > ARM¹, ARM², ARTICULATE, RATIO, L *artus*, joint⟧ **1** human ability to make things; creativity of man as distinguished from the world of nature **2** skill; craftsmanship **3** any specific skill or its application [the *art* of making friends] **4** any craft, trade, or profession, or its principles [the cobbler's *art*, the physician's *art*] **5** creative work or its principles; a making or doing of things that display form, beauty, and unusual perception: art includes painting, sculpture, architecture, music, literature, drama, the dance, etc.: see also FINE ART **6** any branch of creative work, esp. painting, drawing, or work in any other graphic or plastic medium **7** products of creative work; paintings, statues, etc. **8** pictorial and decorative material accompanying the text in a newspaper, magazine, or advertising layout **9** *a)* [Archaic] learning *b)* a branch of learning *c)* [*pl.*] the liberal arts (literature, music, philosophy, etc.) as distinguished from the sciences **10** artful behavior; cunning **11** sly or cunning trick; wile: *usually used in pl.* **—*adj.*** of or for works of art or artists [*art* gallery, *art* colony]

SYN.—**art**, the word of widest application in this group, denotes in its broadest sense merely the ability to make something or to execute a plan; **skill** implies expertness or great proficiency in doing something; **artifice** implies skill used as a means of trickery or deception; **craft** implies ingenuity in execution, sometimes even suggesting trickery or deception; in another sense, **craft** is distinguished from **art** in its application to a lesser skill involving little or no creative thought

art² (ärt) ***vi.*** *archaic 2d pers. sing., pres. indic., of* BE: used with *thou*

art³ *abbrev.* **1** article **2** artificial

-art (ərt) *suffix* -ARD [*braggart*]

ar·tal (är′täl′) ***n.*** *alt. pl. of* ROTL

Ar·taud (ȧr tō′), **An·to·nin** (än tô nan′) 1896-1948; Fr. dramatic theorist, dramatist, & poet

Ar·ta·xer·xes (är′tə zurk′sēz) **1 Artaxerxes I** 465?-424? B.C.; king of ancient Persia: son of Xerxes I **2 Artaxerxes II** 404?-358 B.C.; king of ancient Persia

art dec·o (dek′ō, dā′kō) [*also* **A- D-**] a decorative style of the late 1920s and the 1930s derived from cubism, based generally on geometric forms, and applied to furnishings, textiles, graphic arts, etc.: revived in the mid-1960s

ar·te·fact (ärt′ə fakt′) ***n.*** *Brit. var. of* ARTIFACT

ar·tel (är tel′) ***n.*** ⟦Russ *artel′* < It *artieri* (pl. of *artiere*), workmen, artisans⟧ in Russia, a group of people working collectively and sharing the income and liability

Ar·te·mis (är′tə mis) ***n.*** ⟦L < Gr *Artemis*⟧ *Gr. Myth.* the goddess of the moon, wild animals, and hunting, twin sister of Apollo: identified with the Roman Diana

ar·te·mis·i·a (ärt′ə miz′ē ə, -mē′zē ə; -mish′ə, -mizh′ə) ***n.*** ⟦L, a plant of this genus < Gr: said to be named after *Artemisia*, wife of Mausolus, king of Caria⟧ any of a genus (*Artemisia*) of aromatic herbs or shrubs of the composite family, with small yellowish flowers, including wormwood and sagebrush

ar·te·ri·al (är tir′ē əl) ***adj.*** ⟦Fr *artérial* (now *artériel*) < ML *arterialis*: see ARTERY⟧ **1** of or like an artery or arteries **2** designating or of the blood in the arteries, which has been oxygenated in the lungs or gills and is brighter red than that in the veins **3** of or being a main road or channel with many branches **—ar·te′ri·al·ly *adv.***

ar·te·ri·al·ize (-īz′) ***vt.*** **-ized′**, **-iz′ing** to change (venous blood) into arterial blood by oxygenation **—ar·te′ri·al·i·za′tion *n.***

ar·te·ri·o- (är tir′ē ō, -ə) ⟦< Gr *artēria*, ARTERY⟧ *combining form* artery, arteries [*arteriosclerosis*]: also **arteri-**

ar·te·ri·o·gram (är tir′ē ō gram′) ***n.*** ⟦prec. + -GRAM⟧ an X-ray obtained by arteriography

ar·te·ri·og·ra·phy (är tir′ē äg′rə fē) ***n.*** ⟦ARTERIO- + -GRAPHY⟧ X-ray examination of arteries after injection of radiopaque dyes

ar·te·ri·ole (är tir′ē ōl′) ***n.*** ⟦ModL *arteriola*, dim. of L *arteria*, ARTERY⟧ any of the smaller blood vessels, intermediate in size and position between arteries and capillaries **—ar·te′ri·o′lar** (-ō′lər) ***adj.***

ar·te·ri·o·scle·ro·sis (är tir′ē ō′sklə rō′sis) ***n.*** ⟦ARTERIO- + SCLEROSIS⟧ an abnormal thickening, and loss of elasticity, of the walls of the arteries **—ar·te′ri·o·scle·rot′ic** (-rät′ik) ***adj.***

ar·te·ri·o·ve·nous (-vē′nəs) ***adj.*** designating or of arteries and veins or arterioles and venules

ar·te·ri·tis (ärt′ə rīt′is) ***n.*** ⟦ModL: see fol. & -ITIS⟧ any inflammatory disorder of the arteries

ar·ter·y (ärt′ər ē) ***n.***, *pl.* **-ter·ies** ⟦ME *arterie* < L *arteria*, windpipe, artery < Gr *artēria*, prob. < *aeirein*, to lift, take up⟧ **1** any one of the system of thick-walled blood vessels that carry blood away from the heart: cf. VEIN, CAPILLARY **2** a main road or channel

ar·te·sian well (är tē′zhən) ⟦Fr *artésien*, lit., of ARTOIS (OFr *Arteis*), where such wells were bored⟧ a well drilled deep enough to reach water that is draining down from higher surrounding ground above the well so that the pressure will force a flow of water upward

artesian well

Ar·te·vel·de (är′tə vel′də) **1 Jacob van** 1290?-1345; Fl. statesman **2 Philip van** 1340-81; Fl. leader: son of Jacob

art film a film characterized primarily by content and technique that reflect an artistic sensibility, by psychological or social realism, etc.

art form **1** a means of creative expression, as poetry, or a specific creative genre, as the sonnet, based on traditional structures, standards, and principles **2** any activity or medium similarly regarded as a means for the expression of creative impulses or professional expertise [diplomacy as an *art form*]

art·ful (ärt′fəl) ***adj.*** **1** skillful or clever, esp. in achieving a purpose **2** sly or cunning; crafty [an *artful* swindle] **3** done with, using, or showing much art or skill **4** artificial; imitative **—art′ful·ly *adv.*** **—art′ful·ness *n.***

art·his·tor·i·cal (ärt′his tôr′i kəl) ***adj.*** of or concerned with the history of art

art house a theater chiefly for the exhibition of art films, film classics, etc.

ar·thral·gia (är thral′jə) ***n.*** ⟦ARTHR(O)- + -ALGIA⟧ pain in a joint or joints

ar·thri·tis (är thrīt′is) ***n.*** ⟦L < Gr < *arthron* (see fol.) + -ITIS⟧ inflammation of a joint or joints, esp. as in rheumatoid arthritis —**ar·thrit·ic** (är thrit′ik) ***adj.***

ar·thro- (är′thrō, -thrə) ⟦< Gr *arthron*, a joint < var. of IE base **ar-*: see ART[1]⟧ *combining form* joint, joints [*arthropod*]: also, before a vowel, **arthr-**

ar·thro·mere (är′thrō mir′, -thrə-) ***n.*** ⟦prec. + -MERE⟧ any of the body segments of an arthropod

ar·thro·pod (-päd′) ***n.*** ⟦ARTHRO- + -POD⟧ any of the largest phylum (Arthropoda) of invertebrate animals with jointed legs, a segmented body, and an exoskeleton, including insects, crustaceans, arachnids, and myriapods —**ar·throp·o·dal** (är thräp′ə dəl) ***adj.***, **ar·throp′o·dan** (-dən), or **ar·throp′o·dous** (-dəs)

ar·thro·scope (-skōp′) ***n.*** ⟦ARTHRO- + -SCOPE⟧ a fiber-optic endoscope used inside a joint for diagnostic or surgical procedures —**ar′thro·scop′ic** (-skäp′ik) ***adj.*** —**ar·thros·co·py** (är thräs′kə pē) ***n.***

ar·thro·spore (-spôr′) ***n.*** ⟦ARTHRO- + SPORE⟧ a spore produced by the breaking up of a fungus hypha into cells

Ar·thur[1] (är′thər) ***n.*** ⟦ML *Arthurus*⟧ **1** a masculine name: dim. *Art, Artie*; equiv. It. *Arturo* **2** *Arthurian Legend* a king of Britain and leader of the knights of the Round Table: such a king is supposed to have lived in the 6th cent.

Ar·thur[2] (är′thər), **Chester A(lan)** 1829-86; 21st president of the U.S. (1881-85)

Ar·thu·ri·an (är thoor′ē ən) ***adj.*** of King Arthur and his knights (see ARTHUR[1], sense 2)

ar·ti·choke (ärt′ə chōk′) ***n.*** ⟦It dial. *articiocco* < OSp *alcarchofa* < Ar *al-ḥarshaf* (var. *kharshūf*)⟧ **1** *a)* a thistlelike plant (*Cynara scolymus*) of the composite family *b)* its flower head, cooked as a vegetable **2** *short for* JERUSALEM ARTICHOKE

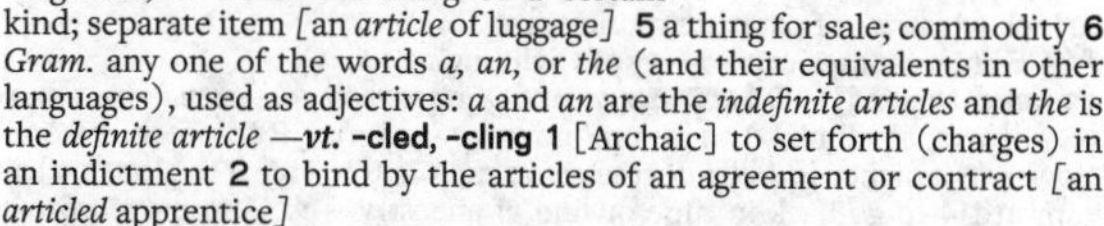

artichoke

ar·ti·cle (ärt′ə kəl) ***n.*** ⟦ME & OFr < L *articulus*, dim. of *artus*, a joint: see ART[1]⟧ **1** one of the sections or items of a written document, as of a constitution, treaty, contract, etc. **2** [*pl.*] the parts of a formal declaration, or of a body of rules, beliefs, etc., considered as a whole **3** a complete piece of writing, as a report or essay, that is part of a newspaper, magazine, or book **4** a thing of a certain kind; separate item [an *article* of luggage] **5** a thing for sale; commodity **6** *Gram.* any one of the words *a, an,* or *the* (and their equivalents in other languages), used as adjectives: *a* and *an* are the *indefinite articles* and *the* is the *definite article* —***vt.*** **-cled, -cling 1** [Archaic] to set forth (charges) in an indictment **2** to bind by the articles of an agreement or contract [an *articled* apprentice]

article of faith 1 a basic religious belief held by a group or person **2** any basic belief strongly held

Articles of Confederation the first constitution of the thirteen original states, in effect from 1781 to 1789

Articles of War the former code of laws governing members of the U.S. Army: see UNIFORM CODE OF MILITARY JUSTICE

ar·tic·u·lar (är tik′yoo lər, -yə-) ***adj.*** ⟦L *articularis* < *articulus*: see ARTICLE⟧ of a joint or joints [an *articular* inflammation]

ar·tic·u·late (är tik′yoo lit, -yə-; *for v.,* -lāt′) ***adj.*** ⟦L *articulatus*, pp. of *articulare*, to separate into joints, utter distinctly < *articulus*: see ARTICLE⟧ **1** having parts connected by joints; jointed: now usually *articulated* **2** made up of distinct syllables or words that have meaning, as human speech **3** able to speak **4** expressing oneself easily and clearly **5** well formulated; clearly presented [an *articulate* argument] —***vt.*** **-lat′ed, -lat′ing 1** to connect by forming a joint or joints **2** to arrange in connected sequence; fit together; correlate [to *articulate* a middle-school science program with high-school courses] **3** to utter distinctly; pronounce carefully; enunciate **4** to express clearly **5** *Music* to play or sing (a note, passage, etc.) in a particular, usually the indicated, manner **6** *Phonet.* to produce (a speech sound) by moving an articulator —***vi.*** **1** to speak distinctly; pronounce clearly **2** to be jointed or connected **3** *Phonet.* to produce a speech sound —**ar·tic′u·late·ly** ***adv.*** —**ar·tic′u·late·ness** ***n.***, **ar·tic′u·la·cy** (-lə sē) —**ar·tic′u·la′tive** (-lāt′iv) ***adj.***

ar·tic·u·lat·ed (är tik′yoo lāt′id, -yə-) ***adj.*** having parts connected by joints; jointed

ar·tic·u·la·tion (är tik′yoo lā′shən, -yə-) ***n.*** **1** a jointing or being jointed **2** the way in which parts are joined together **3** *a)* utterance or enunciation; way of talking or pronouncing *b)* the moving of articulators to produce speech sounds **4** a spoken sound, esp. a consonant **5** a joint between bones or similar parts **6** *Bot. a)* a joint in a stem or between two separable parts, as a branch and leaf *b)* a node or space between two nodes **7** *Music* a particular manner of playing or singing a passage or piece [legato *articulation*]

ar·tic·u·la·tor (är tik′yoo lāt′ər, -yə-) ***n.*** **1** a person or thing that articulates **2** *Phonet.* any organ in the mouth or throat whose movement produces speech sounds, as the tongue, uvula, or teeth —**ar·tic′u·la·to′ry** ***adj.***

ar·ti·fact (ärt′ə fakt′) ***n.*** ⟦L *arte*, by skill (abl. of *ars*, ART[1]) + *factum*, thing made (see FACT)⟧ **1** any object made by human work; esp., a simple or primitive tool, weapon, vessel, etc. **2** *Histology, Med., etc.* any nonnatural feature or structure accidentally introduced into something being observed or studied

ar·ti·fice (ärt′ə fis) ***n.*** ⟦OFr < L *artificium*, craft < *artifex*, artist, master of a trade < *ars*, ART[1] + *facere*, DO[1]⟧ **1** skill or ingenuity **2** a clever expedient **3** trickery or craft **4** a sly or artful trick —***SYN.*** ART[1], TRICK

ar·tif·i·cer (är tif′ə sər; *also* ärt′ə fə-) ***n.*** **1** a skillful maker of things; skilled craftsman **2** a person who devises; inventor

ar·ti·fi·cial (ärt′ə fish′əl) ***adj.*** ⟦ME < OFr < L *artificialis* < *artificium*, ARTIFICE⟧ **1** made by human work or art, not by nature; not natural **2** made in imitation of or as a substitute for something natural; simulated [*artificial* teeth] **3** unnatural in an affected way [an *artificial* smile] **4** pretended **5** *Biol.* designating or of a system of classification based on only a few characteristics, as color —**ar′ti·fi′ci·al′i·ty** (-fish′ē al′ə tē) ***n.***, *pl.* **-ties** —**ar′ti·fi′cial·ly** ***adv.***

SYN.*—artificial** is applied to anything made by human work, esp. if in imitation of something natural [*artificial* hair]; **synthetic** is applied to a substance that is produced by chemical synthesis and is used as a substitute for a natural substance which it resembles [*synthetic* dyes]; **ersatz**, which refers to an artificial substitute, always implies an inferior substance [*ersatz* coffee made of acorns]; **counterfeit** and **spurious** are applied to a careful imitation deliberately intended to deceive [*counterfeit* money, a *spurious* signature] —ANT.*** **natural**

artificial horizon a gyroscopic instrument on an aircraft for indicating the true horizon and the position of the craft with reference to it; flight indicator

artificial insemination the impregnation of a female by artificially injecting semen into the vagina, uterus, etc. rather than by sexual intercourse

☆**artificial intelligence 1** the capability of computers or programs to operate in ways believed to mimic human thought processes, such as reasoning and learning **2** the branch of computer science dealing with this

artificial respiration the maintenance of breathing by artificial means, as by forcing breath into the mouth or by creating and relaxing pressure externally on the chest cavity at regular intervals

ar·til·ler·y (är til′ər ē) ***n.*** ⟦ME < OFr *artillerie* < *artillier* (prob. altered by assoc. with *arte*, ART[1]) < *atillier*, to equip; dissimilated var. of *atirier*: see ATTIRE⟧ **1** [Archaic] apparatus, as catapults or arbalests, for hurling heavy missiles **2** guns of large caliber, too heavy to carry; mounted guns (excluding machine guns), as cannons or missile launchers: artillery may be mobile, stationary, or mounted on ships, airplanes, etc. **3** the science of guns; gunnery —**the artillery** the branch of an army specializing in the use of heavy mounted guns —**ar·til′ler·y·man** (-mən) ***n.***, *pl.* **-men** (-mən), **ar·til′ler·ist** (-ər ist)

ar·ti·o·dac·tyl (ärt′ē ō dak′təl) ***n.*** ⟦< ModL < Gr *artios*, even + *daktylos*, finger or toe⟧ any of an order (Artiodactyla) of hoofed mammals having an even number of toes, including swine, hippopotamuses, and all ruminants —**ar′ti·o·dac′ty·lous** (-tə ləs) ***adj.***

ar·ti·san (ärt′ə zən, -sən) ***n.*** ⟦Fr < It *artigiano*; ult. < L *ars*, ART[1]⟧ a worker in a skilled trade; craftsman —**ar·tis·a·nal** (är tiz′ə nəl; ärt′ə zə nəl, -sə-) ***adj.*** —**ar′ti·san·ship′** ***n.***

art·ist (ärt′ist) ***n.*** ⟦ML *artista*, craftsman, artisan < L *ars*, ART[1]⟧ **1** a person who works in, or is skilled in the techniques of, any of the fine arts, esp. in painting, drawing, sculpture, etc. **2** a person who does anything very well, with imagination and a feeling for form, effect, etc. **3** a professional person in any of the performing arts

ar·tiste (är tēst′) ***n.*** ⟦Fr, prec.⟧ **1** ARTIST (sense 3) **2** a person very skilled in a particular occupation: often humorous or facetious

ar·tis·tic (är tis′tik) ***adj.*** ⟦Fr *artistique*⟧ **1** of art or artists **2** done skillfully and tastefully; aesthetically satisfying **3** keenly sensitive to aesthetic values —**ar·tis′ti·cal·ly** ***adv.***

art·ist·ry (ärt′is trē) ***n.*** artistic quality, ability, or work

art·less (ärt′lis) ***adj.*** **1** lacking skill or art **2** uncultured; ignorant **3** not artistic; clumsy; crude **4** without artificiality; simple; natural **5** without guile or deceit; ingenuous; innocent —***SYN.*** NAIVE —**art′less·ly** ***adv.*** —**art′less·ness** ***n.***

art mo·derne (mō dern′) ⟦Fr, lit., modern art⟧ [*also* **A- M-**] **1** an architectural style of the 1930s and 1940s characterized by streamlined, horizontal structures with flat roofs and, often, curved walls or rounded corners **2** a decorative style somewhat like art deco

art music that form of music in a culture, as European classical music, having an established theoretical basis handed down by rote or through notation, a traditional repertoire, and a high standard of performance, usually by professional musicians

art nou·veau (ärt′noo vō′, är′-; *Fr* år-) ⟦Fr, from the name of an art gallery (*c.* 1895) carrying examples of the work⟧ [*also* **A- N-**] a movement in arts and crafts of the late 19th and early 20th cent., characterized by curvilinear designs styled from nature

Ar·tois (är twä′) historical region of N France, on the Strait of Dover

arts and crafts work done or articles made by hand

Arts and Crafts (movement) a social and artistic movement of the second half of the 19th cent. emphasizing a return to handwork, skilled craftsmanship, and attention to design in the decorative arts, from the mechanization and mass production of the Industrial Revolution: also written **Arts and Crafts Movement**

art song a song written by a trained composer to convey a specific artistic idea, as in projecting the mood and meaning of a poetic text: cf. FOLK SONG

art·sy (ärt′sē) *adj.* **-si·er, -si·est** ⟦see -SY⟧ [Informal] having or showing artistic pretensions: often seen as more pejorative than ARTY[1]

art·sy-craft·sy (-kraft′sē, -kräft′-) *adj.* ⟦redupl. < ARTS AND CRAFTS + -SY⟧ [Informal] having to do with arts and crafts: usually used disparagingly to connote faddishness, dilettantism, superficiality, etc.

art·sy-fart·sy (ärt′sē färt′sē) *adj.* ⟦jocular redupl. < ART[1] + FART, with pejorative dim. suffix -SY, prob. after prec. ⟧ [Slang] pretentiously artistic, sophisticated, etc.: also **art·y-fart·y** (ärt′ē färt′ē)

art theater ART HOUSE

art·work (-wurk′) *n.* **1** *a)* a WORK OF ART (sense 1) *b)* works of art collectively ☆**2** ART[1] (*n.* 8)

art·y[1] (ärt′ē) *adj.* **art′i·er, art′i·est** [Informal] having or showing artistic pretensions; artsy —**art′i·ness** *n.*

arty[2] *abbrev.* artillery

A·ru·ba (ə ro͞o′bə) self-governing island in the Caribbean, off the NW coast of Venezuela, under the protection of the Netherlands: formerly (until 1986) part of the Netherlands Antilles: 75 sq mi (194 sq km) —**A·ru′ban** *adj., n.*

a·ru·gu·la (ə ro͞o′gə lə) *n.* ⟦It dial., dim. < Prov *auruga*, ROCKET[2], ult. < L *eruca*, kind of colewort⟧ a European annual (*Eruca vesicaria sativa*) of the crucifer family, sometimes cultivated as a pungent salad herb; rocket: also **a·ru′go·la**

A·ru Islands (ä′ro͞o) group of islands of Indonesia, part of the Moluccas, in the Arafura Sea southwest of New Guinea: *c.* 3,300 sq mi (8,547 sq km)

ar·um (ar′əm, er′-) *n.* ⟦ModL < L < Gr *aron*, the cuckoopint⟧ any plant of the arum family (esp. genus *Arum*) which is characterized by small flowers on a thick spike, within a hoodlike leaf —*adj.* designating a family (Araceae, order Arales) of monocotyledonous plants growing throughout the world, including the jack-in-the-pulpit and skunk cabbage

a·run·di·na·cea (ə run′di nā′shə, -sē ə) *n.* ⟦ModL < L *arundo*, reed, cane⟧ any of a number of reeds or grasses, specif., *a)* a species of fescue (*Festuca arundinacea*) *b)* a common ornamental grass (*Phalaris arundinacea*)

a·run·di·na·ceous (ə run′di nā′shəs) *adj.* ⟦L *arundinaceus* < *arundo*, reed, cane⟧ of or like a reed

ARV *abbrev.* American (Standard) Revised Version (of the Bible), printed in 1901

Ar·vad·a (är vad′ə) ⟦after Hiram *Arvada* Haskins, a member of the founding family⟧ city in NC Colo.: suburb of Denver

-ar·y (er′ē; *chiefly Brit* ər i) ⟦L *-arius, -aria, -arium*⟧ *suffix* **1** *forming adjectives* relating to, connected with *[urinary]* **2** *forming nouns a)* a person or thing connected with *[dictionary] b)* a place for *[granary]* **3** ⟦L *-aris*⟧ *forming adjectives* like, of the same kind

Ar·y·an (ar′ē ən, er′-) *adj.* ⟦< Sans *āzya-*, noble (used as tribal name to distinguish from indigenous races) > Avestan *airya-nam*, IRAN[1]; ? akin to Gr *aristos*, best or Hittite *arawa-*, free⟧ **1** [Obs.] designating or of the Indo-European language family **2** *obs. term for* INDO-IRANIAN **3** of the Aryans —*n.* **1** [Obs.] the hypothetical parent language of the Indo-European family **2** a person belonging to, or supposed to be a descendant of, the prehistoric peoples that spoke this language: *Aryan* has no technical currency as an ethnological term, but it has been so used, notoriously by the Nazis, to mean "a Caucasoid of non-Jewish descent," "a person of Nordic descent," etc.

ar·yl (ar′il, er′-) *n.* ⟦Ger < *aromatisch*, aromatic + *-yl*, -YL⟧ an organic radical derived from an aromatic hydrocarbon by the removal of one hydrogen atom

ar·y·te·noid (ar′ə tē′noid, ə rit′n oid′) *adj.* ⟦Gr *arytainoeidēs*, ladle-shaped < *arytaina*, a ladle, cup < *aryein*, to draw (water) + *eidos*, form: see -OID⟧ **1** designating or of either of two small cartilages at the back of the larynx, connected with the vocal cords **2** relating to any of certain muscles in the larynx —*n.* an arytenoid cartilage or muscle

as[1] (az; *unstressed* əz) *adv.* ⟦weakened form of ALSO; ME *as, ase* < OE *eallswa* (see ALSO); lit., wholly so, just as⟧ **1** to the same amount or degree; equally *[I'm just as happy at home]* **2** for instance; thus *[a card game, as bridge]* **3** when set off or related in a specified way *[romanticism as contrasted with classicism]* —*conj.* **1** in the same amount in which or to the same degree to which *[it flew straight as an arrow]* **2** in the same manner that; according to the way that *[do as you are told]* **3** at the same time that; while *[she laughed as she spoke]* **4** because; since *[as you object, we won't go]* **5** that the consequence is *[the question is so obvious as to need no reply]* **6** though *[tall as he was, he couldn't reach it]* **7** [Informal] that *[I don't know as I should]* —*pron.* **1** a fact that *[we are tired, as anyone can see]* **2** that: preceded by *such* or *the same [the same color as yours is]* **3** [Dial.] who; which; that *[them as likes pork chops will be there]* —*prep.* **1** in the role, function, capacity, or sense of *[he poses as a friend]* **2** like *[the risk is as nothing compared to the gain]* —**as ... as** a correlative construction used to indicate the equality or sameness of two things *[as large as, as heavy as, as many as, etc.]*: see also GOOD, WELL[2], MUCH, FAR, etc. for certain idiomatic phrases with *as* —**as for** with reference to; concerning —**as if 1** as it (or one) would if **2** that *[it seems as if you're never happy]* —☆**as is** [Informal] just as it is; without any changes: said esp. of damaged goods that are being sold —**as it were** as if it were so; so to speak —☆**as of** up to, on, or from (a specified time) —**as though** AS IF —**as to 1** with reference to **2** as if to

as[2] (as) *n., pl.* **as′ses** (-iz, -ēz′) ⟦L⟧ **1** an ancient Roman unit of weight, equal to about twelve ounces; libra, or Roman pound **2** an ancient Roman coin of copper alloy

As *Chem. symbol for* arsenic

AS *abbrev.* **1** American Samoa **2** Anglo-Saxon **3** Associate in (or of) Science

as- (as, əs) *prefix* AD-: used before *s*

A·sa (ā′sə) *n.* ⟦Heb *asa*, lit., healer⟧ **1** a masculine name **2** *Bible* a king of Judah, who opposed idolatry: I Kings 15:8-24

ASA *abbrev.* **1** *service mark* Amateur Softball Association of America **2** American Sociological Association

as·a·fet·i·da or **as·a·foet·i·da** (as′ə fet′ə də) *n.* ⟦ME < ML *asa* (< Pers *āzā*, gum) + L *foetida*, fem. of *foetidus*, FETID⟧ a bad-smelling gum resin obtained from various Asian plants (genus *Ferula*) of the umbel family: it was formerly used to treat some illnesses or, in folk medicine, to repel disease

A·sa·hi·ka·wa (ä sä′hē kä′wə) city in central Hokkaido, Japan

a·sa·na (ä′sə nə) *n.* ⟦Sans *āsana*, way of sitting⟧ any of various traditional sitting positions assumed during the practice of yoga

A·san·sol (äs′ən sōl) city in E India, in the state of West Bengal

ASAP (ā′es′ā′pē′, ā′sap′) *abbrev.* as soon as possible: also **a.s.a.p.**

as·a·rum (as′ə rəm) *n.* ⟦ModL < L, wild spikenard < Gr *asaron*⟧ the dried rhizomes and roots of certain wild ginger plants (esp. *Asarum canadense*), from which an aromatic oil used in perfumery and flavorings is extracted

☆**ASAT** (ā′sat) *adj.* antisatellite

as·bes·tos (as bes′təs, az-) *n.* ⟦ME *asbestus* < L *asbestos* < Gr, inextinguishable < *a-*, not + *sbestos* < *sbennynai*, to extinguish: first applied in Gr & L to unslaked lime or a mineral other than asbestos⟧ any of several grayish minerals, as amphiboles (esp. actinolite) or serpentines (esp. chrysotile), that separate into long, threadlike fibers that do not burn or conduct heat or electricity and are often resistant to chemicals: used, esp. formerly, to make fireproof materials, electrical insulation, roofing, etc.: occas. sp. **as·bes′tus** —*adj.* woven of or containing asbestos —**as·bes′tine** (-tin) *adj.*

as·bes·to·sis (as′bes tō′sis, az′-) *n.* ⟦ModL: see prec. & -OSIS⟧ a form of pneumoconiosis caused by inhaling asbestos particles

As·bur·y (az′ber′ē, -bər-), **Francis** 1745-1816; 1st Methodist bishop in U.S.

Asbury Park ⟦after prec.⟧ city in EC N.J., on the Atlantic: an ocean resort

ASC *abbrev.* American Society of Cinematographers

As·ca·ni·us (as kā′nē əs) *n.* ⟦L⟧ *Rom. Myth.* son of Aeneas

ASCAP (as′kap′) *abbrev.* American Society of Composers, Authors, and Publishers

as·ca·ri·a·sis (as′kə rī′ə sis) *n., pl.* **-ses′** (-sēz′) ⟦ModL: see fol. & -IASIS⟧ infestation with ascarids or a disease caused by this; esp., infestation of the intestines by a particular roundworm (*Ascaris lumbricoides*)

as·ca·rid (as′kə rid′) *n.* ⟦< ModL < Gr *askaris* (gen. *askaridos*), intestinal worm; akin to *askairein*, to jump, dance: for IE base see SCREAM⟧ any of a genus (*Ascaris*) of parasitic roundworms

ASCE *abbrev.* American Society of Civil Engineers

as·cend (ə send′) *vi.* ⟦ME *ascenden* < OFr *ascendre* < L *ascendere* < *ad-*, to + *scandere*, to climb⟧ **1** to go up; move upward; rise **2** to proceed from a lower to a higher level or degree, as in rank, pitch, etc. **3** to slope or lead upward **4** to go back in time or line of ancestry —*vt.* **1** to move upward along; mount; climb *[to ascend stairs]* **2** to move toward the source of *[to ascend a river]* **3** to succeed to (a throne) —**as·cend′a·ble** *adj.*, **as·cend′i·ble**

as·cend·an·cy or **as·cend·en·cy** (ə sen′dən sē) *n.* a position in which one has control or power; supremacy; domination: also **as·cend′ance** or **as·cend′ence**

as·cend·ant or **as·cend·ent** (-dənt) *adj.* ⟦OFr < L *ascendens*, prp. of *ascendere*, ASCEND⟧ **1** rising; ascending **2** in control; dominant; superior **3** [*often* **A-**] *Astrol.* designating or of the ASCENDANT (*n.* 3); rising **4** *Bot.* ASCENDING (sense 2) —*n.* **1** a dominating position; ascendancy **2** an ancestor: opposed to DESCENDANT **3** [*often* **A-**] *Astrol.* the sign of the zodiac just above the eastern horizon at any given moment, specif. at the time of one's birth —**in the ascendant** at or heading toward the height of power, influence, fame, etc.

as·cend·er (-dər) *n.* **1** a person or thing that ascends **2** *Typography a)* the extension or upward stroke of any of the tall lowercase letters such as *b, d,* or *k b)* any such letter

as·cend·ing (-diŋ) *adj.* **1** that ascends **2** *Bot.* rising or curving upward from a trailing position, as the stems of certain vines and shrubs

as·cen·sion (ə sen′shən) *n.* ⟦ME *ascensioun* < OFr *ascension* < L *ascensio*, a rising < pp. of *ascendere*, ASCEND⟧ **1** the act of ascending; ascent **2** [**A-**] Ascension Day —**the Ascension** *Bible* the bodily ascent of Jesus into heaven on the fortieth day after the Resurrection: Acts 1:9 —**as·cen′sion·al** *adj.*

As·cen·sion (ə sen′shən) ⟦so named because discovered on *Ascension Day* (1501)⟧ small island in the S Atlantic: part of the British territory of St. Helena: 34 sq mi (88 sq km)

Ascension Day the fortieth day after Easter, celebrating the Ascension

as·cen·sive (ə sen′siv) *adj.* ascending; rising

as·cent (ə sent′) *n.* ⟦< ASCEND, modeled on DESCENT⟧ **1** the act of ascending, rising, or climbing **2** an advancement, as in rank, fame, etc. **3** *a)* a way leading up; upward slope; acclivity *b)* the amount of such slope *[an ascent of three degrees]* **4** a going back in time or in line of ancestry

as·cer·tain (as′ər tān′) *vt.* ⟦ME *acertainen* < OFr *acertainer* < *a-*, to + *certain*, CERTAIN⟧ **1** [Archaic] to make certain or definite **2** to find out with certainty —*SYN.* LEARN —**as′cer·tain′a·ble** *adj.* —**as′cer·tain′ment** *n.*

as·ce·sis (ə sē′səs) *n., pl.* **-ses′** (-sēz′) ⟦< Gr *askēsis*, exercise < *askein*, to exercise⟧ the practice of self-discipline, esp. for spiritual purposes; asceticism

as·cet·ic (ə set′ik) ***adj.*** ⟦Gr(Ec) *askētikos*, austere < Gr, laborious, exercised < *askein*, to exercise, train (for athletic competition)⟧ of or characteristic of ascetics or asceticism; self-denying; austere: also **as·cet′i·cal** —***n.*** ⟦< Gr *askētēs*, monk, hermit⟧ **1** a person who leads a life of contemplation and rigorous self-denial for religious purposes **2** anyone who lives with strict self-discipline and without the usual pleasures and comforts —*SYN.* SEVERE —**as·cet′i·cal·ly** ***adv.***

as·cet·i·cism (ə set′ə siz′əm) ***n.*** **1** the practices or way of life of an ascetic **2** the religious doctrine that one can reach a higher spiritual state by rigorous self-discipline and self-denial

Asch (ash), **Sho·lem** (shō′ləm) 1880-1957; U.S. novelist & playwright in Yiddish, born in Poland

As·cham (as′kəm), **Roger** 1515-68; Eng. writer & classical scholar: tutor of Queen Elizabeth I

asc·hel·minth (ask′hel minth) ***n.*** in some systems of classification, any of a phylum (Aschelminthes) of wormlike animals, including rotifers, gastrotrichs, gordian worms, and nematodes: these animals are usually considered to be in separate phyla

as·ci (as′ī′) ***n.*** *pl. of* ASCUS

as·cid·i·an (ə sid′ē ən) ***n.*** ⟦< ModL < Gr *askidion*: see fol.⟧ any of a class (Ascidiacea) of fixed tunicates; sea squirt

as·cid·i·um (-əm) ***n.***, *pl.* **-i·a** (-ə) ⟦ModL < Gr *askidion*, dim. of *askos*: see ASCO-⟧ *Bot.* a pitcherlike leaf or structure, as of the pitcher plant or bladderwort

☆**ASCII** (as′kē) ***n.*** ⟦*A(merican) S(tandard) C(ode for) I(nformation) I(nterchange)*⟧ a standard computer code used to facilitate the interchange of information among various types of data-processing equipment

as·ci·tes (ə sīt′ēz′) ***n.***, *pl.* **-tes′** ⟦LL < Gr *askitēs*, kind of dropsy < *askos*: see ASCO-⟧ an accumulation of fluid in the peritoneal cavity of the abdomen

as·cle·pi·a·da·ceous (as klē′pē ə dā′shəs) ***adj.*** ⟦< ModL *Asclepias*, genus name (< Gr *asklēpias* < *Asklēpios*: see fol.) + -ACEOUS⟧ belonging to the milkweed family of plants —**as·cle′pi·ad′** (-ad′) ***n.***

As·cle·pi·us (as klē′pē əs) ***n.*** ⟦L < Gr *Asklēpios*⟧ *Gr. Myth.* the god of healing and medicine: identified with the Roman Aesculapius

as·co- (as′kō, -kə) ⟦ModL < Gr *askos*, wineskin, bladder⟧ *combining form* bag, bladder [*ascocarp*]: also, before a vowel, **asc-**

as·co·carp (as′kō kärp′) ***n.*** ⟦prec. + -CARP⟧ *Bot.* a structure shaped like a globe, cup, or disk, containing spore sacs; sac fruit of an ascomycetous fungus —**as′co·car′pous** (-kär′pəs) ***adj.***

as·co·go·ni·um (as′kō gō′nē əm) ***n.***, *pl.* **-ni·a** (-ə) ⟦ModL < ASCO- + -GONIUM⟧ *Bot.* the female reproductive structure in an ascomycetous fungus

as·co·my·cete (as′kō mī′sēt′, -mī sēt′) ***n.*** ⟦ModL < ASCO- + -MYCETE⟧ any of a subdivision (Ascomycotina) of fungi, including the mildews, yeasts, and truffles, that produce spores in asci; sac fungus: cf. BASIDIOMYCETE —**as′co·my·ce′tous** ***adj.***

a·scor·bate (ə skôr′bāt′) ***n.*** a salt of ascorbic acid

a·scor·bic acid (ə skôr′bik) ⟦A-[2] + SCORB(UTIC) + -IC⟧ a colorless, crystalline, water-soluble vitamin, $C_6H_8O_6$, found in many foods, esp. citrus fruits, vegetables, and rose hips, and also made synthetically; vitamin C: it is required for proper nutrition and metabolism, and a deficiency produces scurvy

as·co·spore (as′kō spôr′) ***n.*** ⟦ASCO- + SPORE⟧ any of the spores in an ascus

as·cot (as′kət, -kät′) ***n.*** ⟦from being the fashionable neckwear for men of means attending horse races at *Ascot* Heath, racetrack near *Ascot*, village in Berkshire, England⟧ a kind of necktie or scarf with very broad ends hanging from the knot, one upon the other

ascot

as·cribe (ə skrīb′) ***vt.*** **-cribed′**, **-crib′ing** ⟦ME *ascriben* (also *ascriven* < OFr *ascriv-*, stem of *ascrire*) < L *ascribere* < *ad-*, to + *scribere*, to write: see SCRIBE⟧ **1** to assign (something) *to* a supposed cause; impute; attribute **2** to regard (something) as belonging *to* or coming from someone [poems that were *ascribed* to Homer] —**as·crib′a·ble** ***adj.***

SYN.—**ascribe**, in this comparison, implies assignment to someone of something that may reasonably be deduced [to *ascribe* a motive to someone]; **attribute** implies assignment of a quality, factor, or responsibility that may reasonably be regarded as applying [to *attribute* an error to carelessness]; **impute** usually implies the assignment of something unfavorable or accusatory [to *impute* evil to someone]; **assign** implies the placement of something in a particular category because of some quality, etc. attributed to it [to *assign* a poem to the 17th century]; **credit** implies belief in the possession by someone of some quality, etc. [to *credit* someone with intelligence]; **attach** implies the connection of something with something else as being appropriate to it [different people *attach* different meanings to words]

as·crip·tion (ə skrip′shən) ***n.*** ⟦L *ascriptio* < pp. of *ascribere*, prec.⟧ **1** the act of ascribing or being ascribed **2** a statement that ascribes; specif., a prayer or text ascribing glory to God

as·crip·tive (ə skrip′tiv) ***adj.*** ⟦L *ascriptivus* < *ascriptus*, pp. of *ascribere*, ASCRIBE⟧ designating or of a society, group, etc. in which status is based on a predetermined factor, as age, sex, or race, and not on individual achievement —**as·crip′tive·ly** ***adv.***

ASCS *abbrev.* Agricultural Stabilization and Conservation Service

as·cus (as′kəs) ***n.***, *pl.* **as·ci** (as′ī′) ⟦ModL < Gr *askos*: see ASCO-⟧ in ascomycetous fungi, a sac in which spores (usually eight) are produced and meiosis occurs

as·dic or **ASDIC** (az′dik) ***n.*** ⟦*a(nti-)s(ubmarine) d(etection) i(nvestigation) c(ommittee)*⟧ [Brit.] *orig. term for* SONAR

ASE *abbrev.* American Stock Exchange

-ase (ās, āz) ⟦abstracted < (DIAST)ASE⟧ *suffix forming nouns* an enzyme, esp. one of vegetable origin [*amylase*]

ASEAN (ä′sē än′) *abbrev.* Association of Southeast Asian Nations

a·sep·sis (ā sep′sis, ə-) ***n.*** **1** the condition of being aseptic **2** aseptic treatment or technique

a·sep·tic (-tik) ***adj.*** not septic; free from or keeping away disease-producing or putrefying microorganisms —**a·sep′ti·cal·ly** ***adv.***

a·sex·u·al (ā sek′shoo͞ əl) ***adj.*** **1** having no sex or sexual organs; sexless **2** designating or of reproduction without the union of male and female germ cells: budding and fission are types of asexual reproduction **3** having little or no sexual activity, desire, character, etc. —**a·sex′u·al′i·ty** (-shoo͞ al′ə tē) ***n.*** —**a·sex′u·al·ly** ***adv.***

As·gard (äs′gärd′) ***n.*** ⟦ON *Āsgarthr* < *āss*, god (see AESIR) + *garthr*, YARD[2]⟧ *Norse Myth.* the home of the gods and slain heroes: also **As·garth** (äs′gärth′)

ash[1] (ash) ***n.*** ⟦ME *asshe* (usually in pl.) < OE *æsce* < IE base **as-*, to burn > L *arere*, to be dry, burn, Goth *azgo*, ON *aska*, ash⟧ **1** the white or grayish powder remaining after something has been thoroughly burned **2** fine volcanic dust **3** the silvery-gray color of wood ash See also ASHES

ash[2] (ash) ***n.*** ⟦ME *asshe* < OE *æsc* < IE **os-ko* < base **ōs-*, ash > Ger *esche*, L *ornus*, mountain ash, ON *askr*⟧ **1** any of a genus (*Fraxinus*) of timber and shade trees of the olive family, having odd-pinnate leaves, winged fruit, and tough, springy wood **2** the wood **3** a letter of the Old English alphabet (æ or Æ), used to represent the sound (a)

a·shamed (ə shāmd′) ***adj.*** ⟦ME < OE *asceamod*, pp. of *ascamian*, to be ashamed < *a-*, A-[2] + *scamian* < *scamu*, SHAME⟧ **1** feeling shame because something bad, wrong, or foolish was done **2** feeling humiliated or embarrassed, as from a sense of inadequacy or inferiority **3** reluctant because fearing shame beforehand —**a·sham·ed·ly** (ə shām′id lē) ***adv.***

SYN.—**ashamed** implies embarrassment, and sometimes guilt, felt because of one's own or another's wrong or foolish behavior, appearance, etc. [*ashamed* of my tattered clothing]; **humiliated** implies a sense of being humbled or disgraced [a team *humiliated* after a game with a much stronger opponent]; **mortified** suggests humiliation so great as to seem almost fatal to one's pride or self-esteem [*mortified* after his public outburst]; **chagrined** suggests embarrassment coupled usually with regret over what might have been prevented [*chagrined* at my many past mistakes] —*ANT.* **proud**

A·shan·ti[1] (ə shän′tē, -shan′-) ***n.*** **1** *pl.* **-ti** a member of a W African people living mainly in Ashanti, in Ghana **2** the variety of Akan spoken by this people

A·shan·ti[2] (ə shän′tē, -shan′-) region in central Ghana: orig. a native kingdom, it was a protectorate in the Gold Coast from 1901 to 1957: 9,417 sq mi (24,390 sq km); cap. Kumasi

ash blond a silvery-blond or light brownish-gray color —**ash′-blond′** ***adj.***

☆**ash·can** (ash′kan′) ***n.*** **1** a large can for ashes and trash **2** [Slang] *U.S. Navy* DEPTH CHARGE: also **ash can**

☆**Ashcan School** ⟦orig. hostile critical term⟧ a group (formed *c.* 1908) of U.S. painters who promoted realistic painting based on the direct observation of everyday, esp. urban, events

ash·en[1] (ash′ən) ***adj.*** **1** of ashes **2** like ashes, esp. in color; pale; pallid —*SYN.* PALE[1]

ash·en[2] (ash′ən) ***adj.*** [Archaic] **1** of the ash tree **2** made of its wood

Ash·er (ash′ər) ***n.*** *Bible* **1** Jacob's eighth son, whose mother was Zilpah: Gen. 30:12-13 **2** the tribe of Israel descended from him: Num. 1:40

ash·es (ash′iz) ***pl.n.*** ⟦see ASH[1]⟧ **1** the unburned particles and white or grayish powder remaining after a thing has been burned **2** the part of the body left after cremation **3** a dead person; human remains **4** ruins or remains, as of a destroyed civilization

Ash·ga·bat (äsh′gä bät′) capital of Turkmenistan, in the SC part, near the Iranian border

Ash·ke·lon (ash′kə län′) *alt. sp. of* ASHQELON

Ash·ke·naz·i (äsh′kə näz′ē; ash′kə naz′ē) ***n.***, *pl.* **-naz′im** (-näz′im, -naz′im) ⟦Heb, a German Jew; earlier, a German, after *ashkenaz*, name of an ancient kingdom (see Jer. 51:27), after *ashkenaz*, second son of Gomer (see Gen. 10:3); prob. akin to Akkadian *ishkuzai* (> Gr *Skythoi*, the Scythians)⟧ **1** a member of the group of Jews that, after the Diaspora, settled in central, northern, and, later, eastern Europe and developed Yiddish as their spoken language **2** a descendant of this group which has some traditions of ritual and prayer, culture and customs, and Hebrew pronunciation that differ from those of a Sephardi Distinguished from SEPHARDI —**Ash′ke·naz′ic** ***adj.***

Ash·kha·bad (äsh′khä bäd′) *former name for* ASHGABAT

ash·lar or **ash·ler** (ash′lər) ***n.*** ⟦ME *assheler* < OFr *aisseler* < *aissele*, shingle, dim. < *ais*, board < L *assis*, board, akin to *asser*, beam, plank⟧ **1** a square-cut building stone **2** a thin, dressed, square stone used for facing masonry walls **3** masonry made of either kind of ashlar

Ash·ley (ash′lē) ***n.*** ⟦< the surname *Ashley* < the place name *Ashley*, ult. < OE *æsc*, ASH[2] + *lēah*: see LEA[1]⟧ a feminine and masculine name

a·shore (ə shôr′) ***adv.*** ⟦A-[1] + SHORE[1]⟧ **1** to the shore [rowing the boat *ashore*] **2** on land [an old sailor in sad retirement *ashore*]

Ash·qe·lon (ash′kə län′) city in SW Israel, on the Mediterranean: nearby is the site of an ancient city-state (often sp. *Ashkelon*) of the Philistines, 12th cent. B.C. (cf. I Sam. 6:17; Jer. 25:20)

ash·ram (äsh′rəm) ***n.*** ⟦Sans *āśrama* < *ā*, toward + *śrama*, fatigue, religious penance < IE base **klem-*, tired, weak > Welsh *claf*, sick⟧ **1** a secluded place for a community of Hindus leading a life of simplicity and religious meditation **2** such a religious community

Ash·to·reth (ash′tə reth′) ***n.*** ⟦Heb *ashtoret*; akin to Phoen *'shtrt*, Akkadian *Ishtar*, also South Ar *'thtr* (the only manifestation of the deity as a male)⟧ the ancient Phoenician and Syrian goddess of love and fertility: identified with ASTARTE

ash·tray (ash′trā′) ***n.*** a container for smokers' tobacco ashes and cigarette butts, etc.: also **ash tray**

A·shur[1] (ä′shoor′) ***n.*** ⟦Akkadian⟧ *Assyr. Myth.* the chief deity, god of war and empire

A·shur[2] (ä′shoor′) **1** ancient Sumerian city on the upper Tigris River in what is now N Iraq: the original capital of Assyria **2** *orig. name for* ASSYRIA

A·shur·ba·ni·pal (ä′shoor bän′i päl′) died 626? B.C.; king of Assyria (668?-626?)

Ash Wednesday the first day of Lent and seventh Wednesday before Easter: so named from the practice of putting ashes on the forehead, to be worn as a sign of penitence

ash·y (ash′ē) ***adj.*** **ash′i·er, ash′i·est 1** of, like, or covered with ashes **2** of ash color; pale; pallid

A·sia (ā′zhə; *chiefly Brit*, -shə) ⟦L < Gr < ? Akkadian *āṣū*, to rise (of the sun), go out⟧ largest continent, situated in the Eastern Hemisphere, bounded by the Arctic, Pacific, and Indian oceans, and separated from N Europe by the Ural Mountains: it includes, in addition to the nations on the land mass, Japan, the Philippines, Taiwan, Malaysia, & Indonesia: *c.* 17,212,000 sq mi (44,579,000 sq km)

A·si·a·go (cheese) (ä′sē ä′gō, ä syä′gō) ⟦after *Asiago*, town in N Italy⟧ a hard, dry, sharply flavored cheese originally of N Italy: also **asiago (cheese)**

Asia Minor large peninsula in W Asia that includes Asiatic Turkey west of a line (*c.* 36° longitude) between the Black Sea and the Mediterranean: cf. ANATOLIA

A·sian (ā′zhən; *chiefly Brit*, -shən) ***adj.*** of Asia or its peoples, languages, or cultures **—*n.*** a person born or living in Asia Term now generally preferred over *Asiatic* for the *n.*

Asian elephant *see* ELEPHANT: often called **Asiatic elephant**

Asian influenza pandemic influenza caused by a strain of the influenza virus first isolated in Singapore in 1957: also **Asian flu**

A·si·at·ic (ā′zhē at′ik, -zē-; *chiefly Brit*, -shē-) ***adj., n.*** ASIAN: the *n.* is now often a mild term of contempt or disparagement

Asiatic cholera *see* CHOLERA

ASID *abbrev.* American Society of Interior Designers

a·side (ə sīd′) ***adv.*** ⟦ME < *on side*: see A-[1] & SIDE⟧ **1** on or to one side [pull the curtains *aside*] **2** away; in reserve [put the book *aside* for me] **3** out of the way; out of one's mind [lay the proposal *aside* temporarily] ☆**4** apart; notwithstanding [joking *aside*, I mean it] **—*n.* 1** words spoken by an actor in such a way that they are heard by the audience but supposedly not by the other actors **2** a written digression [a novelist's *aside* to the reader] ☆**aside from 1** with the exception of **2** apart from; besides

As·i·mov (az′ə môf, -môv), **Isaac** 1920-92; U.S. science & science-fiction writer

as·i·nine (as′ə nīn′) ***adj.*** ⟦L *asininus* < *asinus*, ass⟧ of or like an ass; esp., having qualities regarded as characteristic of asses; stupid, silly, obstinate, etc. **—*SYN.*** SILLY **—as′i·nine′ly *adv.***

as·i·nin·i·ty (as′ə nin′ə tē) ***n.*** **1** the quality or state of being asinine; stupidity **2** *pl.* **-ties** an asinine act or remark

A·sir (ä sir′) region of SW Saudi Arabia, on the Red Sea

-a·sis (ə sis, -səs) ⟦L < Gr⟧ *suffix* a condition resembling or a condition characterized by [*elephantiasis*]

ask (ask, äsk) ***vt.*** ⟦ME *askien* < OE *āscian* < IE base **ais-*, to wish, desire > Sans *iccháti*, (he) seeks, OHG *eiscōn*, inquire, demand⟧ **1** to use words in seeking the answer to (a question); try to find out about by inquiring **2** to put a question to (a person); inquire of **3** to request; solicit; beg **4** to demand or expect as a price [they *ask* ten dollars for it] **5** to be in need of or call for (a thing) **6** to invite **—*vi.* 1** to request information **2** to make a request (*for*) **3** to inquire (*about, after,* or *for*) **4** to behave in such a way that one appears to be looking (*for* trouble, punishment, etc.) **—ask′ing *n.* —ask′er *n.***

SYN.—ask and the more formal **inquire** and **query** usually denote no more than the seeking of an answer or information, but **query** also often implies doubt as to the correctness of something [the printer *queried* the spelling of several words]; **question** and **interrogate** imply the asking of a series of questions [to *question* a witness], **interrogate** adding the further implication of systematic examination [to *interrogate* a prisoner of war]; **catechize** is equivalent to **interrogate** but implies the expectation of certain fixed answers, esp. with reference to religious doctrine; **quiz**, used esp. in schools, implies a short, selective questioning to test factual knowledge of some subject **—*ANT.* answer, tell**

a·skance (ə skans′) ***adv.*** ⟦ME *ascaunce*; form < *ase quances* < *as(e)*, AS[1] + OFr *quanses*, how if < VL *quam si* < L *quam*, how + *si*, if; meaning < ME *askoin* < *a-*, A-[1] + *skwyn* < Du *schuin*, sideways⟧ **1** with a sideways glance **2** with suspicion, disapproval, etc.

a·skant (ə skant′) ***adv.*** [Archaic] askance

As·ke·lon or **As·ka·lon** (äs′kə län′) ASHQELON

a·skew (ə skyōō′) ***adv.*** ⟦A-[1] + SKEW⟧ to one side; awry; crookedly **—*adj.*** on one side; awry

asking price the price asked by a seller, esp. when willing to accept less after bargaining

ASL *abbrev.* AMERICAN SIGN LANGUAGE

a·slant (ə slant′) ***adv.*** on a slant; slantingly; obliquely **—*prep.*** on a slant across **—*adj.*** slanting

a·sleep (ə slēp′) ***adj.*** **1** in a condition of sleep; sleeping **2** inactive; dull; sluggish **3** numb except for a prickly feeling [my arm is *asleep*] **4** dead **—*adv.*** into a sleeping or inactive condition

a·slope (ə slōp′) ***adv., adj.*** at a slant

As·ma·ra (äs mä′rä) capital of Eritrea, in the W part

ASME *abbrev.* American Society of Mechanical Engineers

As·mo·de·us (az′mə dē′əs, as′-) ***n.*** ⟦L *Asmodaeus* < Gr *Asmodaios* < Talmudic Heb *ashmeday* < Avestan *Aēšmā daēva*, Aeshma the deceitful⟧ *Jewish Folklore* an evil spirit or chief demon

A·so (ä′sō) large volcanic crater in central Kyushu, Japan, with five cones: highest cone, 5,223 ft (1,592 m); crater, *c.* 15 mi (24 km) wide: also **A·so-san** (ä′sō sän′)

a·so·cial (ā sō′shəl) ***adj.*** **1** not social; not gregarious; characterized by withdrawal from others **2** showing little concern for the welfare of others; selfish **—*SYN.*** UNSOCIAL

A·so·ka (ə sō′kə) died 232? B.C.; king of India (273?-232?): 1st Indian ruler to embrace Buddhism

asp[1] (asp) ***n.*** ⟦ME < OFr *aspe* < L *aspis* < Gr; prob. < *aspis*, shield (in reference to the shape of the hood)⟧ any of several small, poisonous snakes of Africa, Arabia, and Europe, as the horned viper, Egyptian cobra, or a European viper (*Vipera aspis*)

asp[2] (asp) ***n.*** [Archaic] an aspen

as·par·a·gine (as par′ə jēn′, -per′-; -jin′) ***n.*** ⟦Fr < L *asparagus* (see fol.) + Fr *-ine*, -INE[3]⟧ a nonessential amino acid, $NH_2COCH_2CH(NH_2)COOH$

as·par·a·gus (ə spar′ə gəs, -sper′-) ***n.*** ⟦ModL < L < Gr *asparagos* < IE base **sp(h)er(e)g-*, to spring up, sprout > SPRING, SPARK[1]⟧ **1** any of a genus (*Asparagus*) of plants of the lily family, with small, scalelike leaves, many flat or needlelike branches, and whitish flowers, including several plants (asparagus ferns) having fleshy roots and fine fernlike leaves **2** the tender shoots of one of these plants (*A. officinalis*), used as a vegetable

asparagus fern an ornamental vine (*Asparagus setaceus*) of the lily family, having long branches with short, evergreen needles and dark berries

a·spar·kle (ə spär′kəl) ***adj.*** sparkling

as·par·tame (as′pər tām′) ***n.*** ⟦fol. + *(phenyl)a(lanine) m(ethyl) e(ster)*⟧ an artificial, low-calorie sweetener, $C_{14}H_{18}N_2O_5$, about 200 times sweeter than sucrose, used in the manufacture of soft drinks, packaged cereals, etc.

as·par·tic acid (as pär′tik) ⟦coined from ASPARAGUS⟧ a nonessential amino acid, $COOHCH_2CH(NH_2)COOH$

As·pa·si·a (as pā′zhē ə, -zhə) fl. 5th cent. B.C.; woman of Athens celebrated for her beauty and intellect: paramour of Pericles

ASPCA *abbrev.* American Society for the Prevention of Cruelty to Animals

as·pect (as′pekt′) ***n.*** ⟦ME < L *aspectus*, pp. of *aspicere*, to look at < *ad-*, to, at + *specere*, to look: see SPY⟧ **1** the way a person appears; looks; mien **2** the appearance of a thing as seen from a specific point; view **3** *a)* any of the possible ways in which an idea, problem, etc. may be regarded [consider all *aspects* of the war] *b)* a component part or quality; element [*aspects* of her personality] **4** a facing in a given direction **5** a side facing in a given direction; exposure [the eastern *aspect* of the house] **6** [Archaic] a glance; gaze **7** *Astrol.* the position of stars, planets, etc. in relation to each other or to the observer, as an influence on human affairs **8** *Gram. a)* a characteristic of verbs, expressed in some languages by inflection, indicating the nature of an action as being completed or single (called *perfective* or *nonprogressive aspect*), or as being uncompleted, repeated, or habitual (called *imperfective* or *progressive aspect*); also, an analytic category based on this characteristic *b)* any of the forms a verb takes to indicate this characteristic **9** *Physics* the position of a plane (flat surface) in relation to a liquid or gaseous substance through which it is moving or which is moving past it **—*SYN.*** APPEARANCE, PHASE[1]

aspect ratio the ratio between any two dimensions, as width and height: it is used in describing airplane wings, movie film, etc.

as·pen (as′pən) ***n.*** ⟦ME *aspe* (in compounds, *aspen*) < OE *æspe* < IE base **apsa* > Lith *ãpušė*, OPrus *abse*⟧ any of several kinds of poplar tree (genus *Populus*) with flattened leafstalks that cause the leaves to flutter in the least breeze **—*adj.*** of or like an aspen

As·pen (as′pən) ⟦< prec.: so named for the trees common in the area⟧ city in central Colorado: ski resort

as·per (as′pər) ***n.*** ⟦< Fr *aspre* < MGr *aspron* < L *asper (nummus)*, rough (coin): see ASPERITY⟧ a former silver coin of Turkey and Egypt, later a money of account equal to $\frac{1}{120}$ of a piaster

As·per·ger's syndrome (as′pər gərz) ⟦after H. *Asperger* (1906-80), Austrian pediatrician⟧ *Psychol.* a developmental disorder characterized by social and emotional deficiencies, but accompanied by normal or above-average verbal skills and cognitive ability

As·per·ges (äs per′jez′, ə spur′jēz′) *n.* ⟦2d pers. sing., fut. indic. of L *aspergere*: see ASPERSE⟧ *R.C.Ch.* **1** [*also* **a-**] the sprinkling of altar, clergy, and people with holy water before High Mass **2** a hymn sung during this ceremony, beginning *Asperges me*

as·per·gil·lo·sis (as′pər ji lō′sis) *n., pl.* **-ses′** (-sēz′) an infection caused by a fungus (genus *Aspergillus*), characterized by small, inflamed lesions of the skin, respiratory tract, bones, etc.

as·per·gil·lum (as′pər jil′əm) *n., pl.* **-gil′la** (-ə) or **-gil′lums** ⟦ModL < L *aspergere* (see ASPERSE) + neut. dim. suffix *-illum*⟧ *R.C.Ch.* a brush or perforated container for sprinkling holy water: also **as′per·gill′** (-jil′)

as·per·gil·lus (-jil′əs) *n., pl.* **-gil′li′** (-ī′) ⟦ModL < prec.: so named from appearing similar to the aspergillum⟧ any of a widespread genus (*Aspergillus*) of ascomycetous fungi bearing chains of spores attached to stalks on the swollen end of a threadlike branch: their purified enzymes are used in food production

as·per·i·ty (ə sper′ə tē) *n., pl.* **-ties** ⟦ME & OFr *asprete* < L *asperitas*, roughness < *asper*, rough < IE **apo-spero-*, repellent < base **apo-*, away + **sper-*, to flick away, push⟧ **1** roughness or harshness, as of surface, sound, weather, etc. or of circumstances **2** harshness or sharpness of temper

as·perse (ə spurs′) *vt.* **-persed′, -pers′ing** ⟦< L *aspersus*, pp. of *aspergere*, to sprinkle on < *ad-*, to + *spargere*, to sprinkle, strew: see SPARK[1]⟧ **1** [Rare] to sprinkle water on, as in baptizing **2** to spread false or damaging charges against; slander

as·per·sion (ə spur′zhən, -shən) *n.* ⟦L *aspersio*: see prec.⟧ **1** [Now Rare] a sprinkling with water, as in baptizing **2** the act of defaming **3** a damaging or disparaging remark; slander; innuendo

as·per·so·ri·um (as′pər sôr′ē əm) *n., pl.* **-ri·a** (-ə) or **-ri·ums** (-əmz) ⟦ML < L *aspersus*: see ASPERSE⟧ *R.C.Ch.* **1** a basin, font, etc. for holy water **2** ASPERGILLUM

as·phalt (as′fôlt′; *often* ash′-) *n.* ⟦ML *asphaltus* < Gr *asphaltos*, prob. < *a-*, not + *sphallein*, to cause to fall, injure (< IE base **(s)p(h)el-*, to split off > SPILL[1]): ? so named because of use as protective substance for walls⟧ **1** a brown or black, tarlike, bituminous substance that consists mainly of hydrocarbons, found in large flat beds or made by refining petroleum **2** a mixture of this with sand or gravel, for cementing, paving, roofing, etc. —*vt.* to pave, roof, etc. with asphalt —**as·phal′tic** *adj.*

as·phal·tite (as fôl′tīt′, -fal′-; as′fôl tīt′) *n.* any of the pure, solid, usually black forms of asphalt found in natural deposits, as uintahite

☆**asphalt jungle** the crowded city, esp. regarded as a place of predatory behavior in a struggle for survival

a·spher·ic (ā′sfir′ik) *adj.* designating or of a lens or mirror made so that it is not perfectly spherical, as to minimize spherical aberration: also **a′spher′i·cal**

as·pho·del (as′fə del′) *n.* ⟦< ModL < L *asphodelus* < Gr *asphodelos*⟧ **1** any of a genus (*Asphodeline*) of plants of the lily family, having fleshy roots, narrow leaves, and white or yellow, lilylike flowers; esp. the classic flower of death (*A. lutea*) **2** any of a similar genus (*Asphodelus*) of plants of the lily family, having leafless flower stems

as·phyx·i·a (as fik′sē ə) *n.* ⟦ModL < Gr, stopping of the pulse < *a-*, not + *sphyzein*, to throb⟧ loss of consciousness as a result of too little oxygen and too much carbon dioxide in the blood: suffocation causes asphyxia

as·phyx·i·ant (-sē ənt) *adj.* causing or tending to cause asphyxia —*n.* an asphyxiant substance or condition

as·phyx·i·ate (-sē āt′) *vt.* **-at′ed, -at′ing 1** to cause asphyxia in **2** to suffocate —*vi.* to undergo asphyxia —**as·phyx′i·a′tion** *n.* —**as·phyx′i·a′tor** *n.*

as·pic (as′pik′) *n.* ⟦Fr < OFr *aspe*, ASP[1]; *-ic* prob. by assoc. with *basilic*, basilisk⟧ **1** [Archaic] an asp **2** a cold jelly of meat juice, tomato juice, etc., served as a garnish or molded, often with meat, seafood, etc.

as·pi·dis·tra (as′pi dis′trə) *n.* ⟦ModL < Gr *aspis*, a shield + *astron*, a star: see ASTRAL⟧ any of a genus (*Aspidistra*) of plants of the lily family, with dark, inconspicuous flowers and stiff, glossy, evergreen leaves: cultivated as a houseplant

as·pi·rant (as′pə rənt, ə spī′rənt) *adj.* aspiring —*n.* a person who aspires, as after honors, high position, etc.

as·pi·rate (as′pə rāt′; *for n. & adj.*, -pər it) *vt.* **-rat′ed, -rat′ing** ⟦< L *aspiratus*, pp. of *aspirare*: see ASPIRE⟧ **1** to begin (a word) or precede (a sonorous speech sound) with a puff of breath resulting in the sound (h) **2** to follow (a consonant, esp. a stop) with a puff of suddenly released breath [in English we usually *aspirate* the sound represented by *p*, *t*, or *k* when it begins a word] **3** to suck in or draw in, as by inhaling [*aspirating* dust into the lungs] **4** *Med.* to remove (an abnormal accumulation of fluid or gas), as from a body cavity, by suction —*n.* **1** the speech sound (h) **2** an expiratory breath puff such as follows initial (p), (t), or (k) in English **3** a consonant articulated with a following puff of breath —*adj.* articulated with a preceding or following puff of breath: also **as′pi·rat′ed**

as·pi·ra·tion (as′pə rā′shən) *n.* ⟦L *aspiratio*, a blowing or breathing < pp. of *aspirare*, ASPIRE⟧ **1** *a)* strong desire or ambition, as for advancement, honor, etc. *b)* the thing so desired **2** the act of breathing in; inhalation **3** *Med.* removal of fluid or gas by suction, as from a body cavity **4** *Phonet. a)* the act of pronouncing with an aspirate *b)* ASPIRATE (*n.* 1 & 2) —**as′pi·ra′tion·al** *adj.*

as·pi·ra·tor (as′pə rāt′ər) *n.* ⟦see ASPIRATE⟧ any apparatus for moving air, fluids, etc. by suction; specif., an apparatus using suction to remove a fluid or gas from a body cavity

as·pi·ra·to·ry (ə spī′rə tôr′ē) *adj.* ⟦ASPIRAT(E) + -ORY⟧ of or suited for breathing or suction

as·pire (ə spīr′) *vi.* **-pired′, -pir′ing** ⟦ME *aspiren* < L *aspirare*, to breathe upon, aspire to < *ad-*, to + *spirare*, to breathe: see SPIRIT⟧ **1** to be ambitious (*to* get or do something, esp. something grand); seek (*after*) **2** [Archaic] to rise high; tower —**as·pir′er** *n.*

as·pi·rin (as′prin, as′pə rin) *n.* ⟦Ger < Gr *a-*, without + ModL *Spiraea*, SPIREA + -IN[1]: so named (1899) by H. Dreser, Ger chemist, because compounded without use of spirea (in which the natural acid is found)⟧ **1** a white, crystalline powder, acetylsalicylic acid, $CH_3COOC_6H_4COOH$, used as an anti-inflammatory drug and for reducing fever, relieving headaches, etc. **2** *pl.* **-rin** or **-rins** a tablet of this powder

as·pir·ing (ə spīr′iŋ) *adj.* striving for or desirous of reaching some (usually lofty) goal —**SYN.** AMBITIOUS —**as·pir′ing·ly** *adv.*

a·squint (ə skwint′) *adv., adj.* ⟦ME *on skwyn* (see ASKANCE): infl. by SQUINT⟧ with a squint; out of the corner of the eye

As·quith (as′kwith), **Herbert Henry** 1st Earl of Oxford and Asquith 1852-1928; Brit. statesman: prime minister (1908-16)

ass[1] (as) *n.* ⟦ME *asse* < OE *assa, assen*: prob. < OIr *assan* or Welsh *asyn*, both < L *asinus*⟧ **1** any of a number of horselike perissodactylous mammals (family Equidae) having long ears and a short mane, esp. the common wild ass (*Equus asinus*) of Africa: donkeys and burros are domesticated asses: in fables the ass is represented as obstinate and stupid **2** a stupid or silly person; fool

ass[2] (as) *n.* ⟦var. of ARSE⟧ [Slang] the buttocks or anus: somewhat vulgar

-ass (as) *combining form* ⟦< prec.⟧ [Slang] added to adjectives as an intensifier: mildly vulgar [a big-*ass* pickup truck]

As·sad (ä säd′), **Ha·fez al-** (hä fez′ al) 1928-2000; president of Syria (1971-2000)

as·sa·fet·i·da or **as·sa·foet·i·da** (as′ə fet′ə də) *n. alt. sp. of* ASAFETIDA

as·sa·gai (as′ə gī′) *n. alt. sp. of* ASSEGAI

as·sai[1] (ə sī′) *n.* ⟦BrazPort *assahy* < Tupí *assaí*⟧ any of a genus (*Euterpe*, esp. *E. edulis*) of palm trees native to Brazil, bearing a small, dark-purple, fleshy, edible fruit

as·sa·i[2] (äs sä′ē) *adv.* ⟦It, enough, very < L *ad satis* < *ad*, to + *satis*, enough; akin to Fr *assez*, enough⟧ *Musical Direction* very: used in indicating tempo [allegro *assai*]

as·sail (ə sāl′) *vt.* ⟦ME *assailen* < OFr *asaillir* < VL *assalire*, for L *assilire*, to leap on < *ad-*, to + *salire*, to leap: see SALIENT⟧ **1** to attack physically and violently; assault **2** to attack with arguments, questions, doubts, etc. **3** to begin working on (a task, problem, etc.) with vigor and determination **4** to have a forceful effect on [a loud noise *assailed* her ears] —**SYN.** ATTACK —**as·sail′a·ble** *adj.* —**as·sail′er** *n.* —**as·sail′ment** *n.*

as·sail·ant (-ənt) *n.* ⟦< Fr⟧ one who assails or attacks; attacker

As·sam (a sam′, as′am) state of NE India, south of Bhutan, west of Myanmar, & almost completely separated from the rest of India by Bangladesh: 30,285 sq mi (78,438 sq km); cap. Dispur

As·sa·mese (as′ə mēz′, -mēs′) *n.* **1** *pl.* **-mese′** a person born or living in Assam **2** the Indo-Aryan language spoken in Assam —*adj.* of Assam or its people, language, or culture

as·sas·sin (ə sas′ən) *n.* ⟦Fr < ML *assassinus* < Ar *ḥashshāshīn*, hashish users < *ḥashīsh*, hemp⟧ **1** [**A-**] a member of a secret terrorist sect of Muslims of the 11th-13th cent., who killed their political enemies as a religious duty, allegedly while under the influence of hashish **2** a murderer who strikes suddenly and by surprise **3** the murderer of a person who is politically important or is prominent, typically by surprise attack and usually for payment or from zealous belief **4** a person who harms or ruins someone's reputation, as by slander, vilification, etc. [a character *assassin*]

as·sas·si·nate (-āt′) *vt.* **-nat′ed, -nat′ing 1** to murder (esp. a person who is politically important or is prominent), typically by surprise attack and usually for payment or from zealous belief **2** to harm or ruin (someone's reputation, etc.), as by slander, vilification, etc. —**SYN.** KILL[1] —**as·sas′si·na′tion** *n.*

☆**assassin bug** any of a family (Reduviidae) of large brownish hemipteran insects that kill other insects and suck the life fluids from them: some species suck blood from mammals and may transmit Chagas' disease to humans

as·sault (ə sôlt′) *n.* ⟦ME *assaut* < OFr *assaut, assalt* < VL **assaltus* < *assalire*: see ASSAIL⟧ **1** a violent attack, either physical or verbal **2** *euphemism for* RAPE[1] **3** *Law* an unlawful threat or unsuccessful attempt to do physical harm to another, causing a present fear of immediate harm **4** *Mil. a)* a sudden attack upon a fortified place *b)* the close-combat phase of an attack — *vt., vi.* to make an assault (upon) —*adj.* designating a rifle or other firearm, either automatic or semiautomatic, designed especially for military use —**SYN.** ATTACK —**as·saul′tive** *adj.*

assault and battery *Law* the carrying out of threatened physical harm or violence; an unlawful beating

as·say (as′ā, a sā′; *for v.* a sā′, ə-) *n.* ⟦ME & Anglo-Fr *assai* < OFr *essai*, trial: see ESSAY, *n.*⟧ **1** an examination or testing **2** the analysis of an ore, alloy, drug, etc. to determine the nature, proportion, or purity of the ingredients **3** a substance to be thus tested or analyzed **4** the result or report of such an analysis **5** [Now Rare] an attempt —*vt.* **1** to make an assay of; test; analyze **2** to attempt —☆*vi.* to be shown by analysis to contain a specified proportion of some component [this ore *assays* high in gold] —**as·say′er** *n.*

☆**ass-back·wards** (as′bak′wərdz) *adj., adv.* [Slang] of or in a way that is particularly contrary to the usual way, confusing, etc.

-assed (ast) *combining form* [Slang] -ASS [a sorry-*assed* excuse for a novel]

as·se·gai (as′ə gī′) *n.* ⟦Port *azagaia* < colloquial Ar *az-zaghāya* < *az*, for *al*, the + Berber *zaghāyah*, spear, prob. < Berber (cf. Tuareg *(a)zegiz*, long-armed dagger)⟧ 1 a slender spear or javelin with an iron tip, used in S Africa 2 a tree (*Curtisia faginea*) of the dogwood family, whose hard wood is used to make such spears

as·sem·blage (ə sem′blij; *for 3, also* ä′sem bläzh′) ***n.*** ⟦Fr⟧ 1 an assembling or being assembled 2 a group of persons or things gathered together; assembly 3 a form of art involving the assembly and arrangement of unrelated objects, parts, and materials in a kind of sculptured collage

as·sem·ble (-bəl) ***vt., vi.*** **-bled, -bling** ⟦ME *assemblen* < OFr *assembler* < VL **adsimulare* < L *ad-*, to + *simul*, together: see SAME⟧ 1 to gather into a group; collect ☆2 to fit or put together the parts of (a machine, etc.) 3 to translate (a computer program, instruction, etc. in assembly language) into machine language: said of an assembly program —***SYN.*** GATHER

as·sem·bler (-blər) ***n.*** one that assembles; specif., a computer program that translates a low-level programming language into machine language

as·sem·bly (-blē) ***n.***, *pl.* **-blies** ⟦ME *assemble* < OFr *assemblee* < *assembler*: see ASSEMBLE⟧ 1 an assembling or being assembled 2 a group of persons gathered together, as for worship, instruction, or entertainment 3 *a)* a legislative body *b)* [**A-**] in some states of the U.S., the lower house of the legislature 4 a fitting together of parts to make a whole, as in manufacturing automobiles 5 the parts to be thus fitted together 6 a call, as by bugle or drum, for soldiers to assemble in ranks 7 the process of translating a computer program, written in assembly language, into machine language —***adj.*** designating or of a low-level computer language that uses words, abbreviations, etc. that are translated into machine language

☆**assembly line** in many factories, an arrangement whereby each worker performs a specialized operation in assembling the work as it is passed along, often on a slowly moving belt or track

as·sem·bly·man (-mən) ***n.***, *pl.* **-men** (-mən) 1 a member of a legislative assembly 2 [**A-**] in some states of the U.S., a member of the Assembly

as·sem·bly·wom·an (-woom′ən) ***n.***, *pl.* **-wom′en** (-wim′in) a female assemblyman

as·sent (ə sent′) ***vi.*** ⟦ME *assenten* < OFr *assenter* < L *assentari* < *assentire* < *ad-*, to + *sentire*, to feel: see SEND⟧ to express acceptance of an opinion, proposal, etc.; agree (*to*); concur —***n.*** consent or agreement; concurrence —***SYN.*** CONSENT —**as·sent′er** ***n.***

as·sen·ta·tion (as′en tā′shən) ***n.*** immediate and usually flattering or hypocritical assent

as·sert (ə surt′) ***vt.*** ⟦< L *assertus*, pp. of *asserere*, to join to, claim < *ad-*, to + *serere*, join: see SERIES⟧ 1 to state positively; declare; affirm 2 to maintain or defend (rights, claims, etc.) —**assert oneself** to insist on one's rights, or on being recognized —**as·sert′er** ***n.***, **as·ser′tor**

SYN.—to **assert** is to state positively with great confidence but with no objective proof [she *asserted* that human nature would never change]; to **declare** is to assert openly or formally, often in the face of opposition [they *declared* their independence]; **affirm** implies deep conviction in one's statement and the unlikelihood of denial by another [I cannot *affirm* that she was there]; **aver** connotes implicit confidence in the truth of one's statement from one's own knowledge of the matter; **avouch** implies firsthand knowledge or authority on the part of the speaker; **warrant**, in this comparison, is informal, and implies positiveness by the speaker [I *warrant* he'll be late again] —***ANT.*** **deny, controvert**

as·ser·tion (ə sur′shən) ***n.*** 1 the act of asserting 2 something asserted; positive statement; declaration

as·ser·tive (ə surt′iv) ***adj.*** ⟦ML *assertivus*⟧ characterized by assertion; persistently, forcefully, or boldly positive or confident —***SYN.*** AGGRESSIVE —**as·ser′tive·ly** ***adv.*** —**as·ser′tive·ness** ***n.***

asses' bridge PONS ASINORUM

as·sess (ə ses′) ***vt.*** ⟦ME *assessen* < OFr *assesser* < ML *assessare*, to impose a tax, set a rate < L *assessus*, pp. of *assidere*, to sit beside, assist in the office of judge < *ad-*, to + *sedere*, to SIT⟧ 1 to set an estimated value on (property, etc.) for taxation 2 to set the amount of (a tax, a fine, damages, etc.) 3 to impose a fine, tax, or special payment on (a person or property) 4 to impose (an amount) as a fine, tax, etc. 5 to estimate or determine the significance, importance, or value of; evaluate —**as·sess′a·ble** ***adj.***

as·sess·ment (-mənt) ***n.*** 1 the act or an instance of assessing 2 an amount assessed See also SPECIAL ASSESSMENT

as·ses·sor (-ər) ***n.*** 1 a person who sets valuations, as on property, for taxation 2 a person with special knowledge in some field who serves as a consultant to a judge in a legal proceeding —**as·ses·so·ri·al** (as′ə sôr′ē əl) ***adj.***

as·set (as′et) ***n.*** ⟦earlier *assets* < Anglo-Fr *assetz* (in legal phrase *aver assetz*, to have enough) < OFr *assez*, enough < VL **ad satis*, sufficient < L *ad*, to + *satis*, enough: see SAD⟧ 1 anything owned that has exchange value 2 a valuable or desirable thing to have [charm is your chief *asset*] 3 [*pl.*] *Accounting* all the entries on a balance sheet showing the entire resources of a person or business, tangible and intangible, including accounts and notes receivable, cash, inventory, equipment, real estate, goodwill, etc. 4 [*pl.*] *Law a)* property, as of a business, a bankrupt, etc. *b)* the property of a deceased person available to his or her estate for the payment of debts and legacies

as·sev·er·ate (ə sev′ə rāt′) ***vt.*** **-at′ed, -at′ing** ⟦< L *asseveratus*, pp. of *asseverare*, to assert strongly < *ad-*, to + *severus*, earnest, SEVERE⟧ to state seriously or positively; assert —**as·sev′er·a′tion** ***n.***

ass·hole (as′hōl′) ***n.*** [Slang] 1 the anus 2 a person who is stupid, foolish, despicable, etc. Somewhat vulgar

As·shur (ä′shoor′) *alt. sp. of* ASHUR[1]

as·sib·i·late (ə sib′ə lāt′) ***vt.*** **-lat′ed, -lat′ing** ⟦AS- + SIBILATE⟧ *Phonet.* to change into or accompany with a hissing sound

as·si·du·i·ty (as′ə dyoo′ə tē, -doo′-) ***n.***, *pl.* **-ties** ⟦L *assiduitas*, constant presence < *assidere*, to assist: see ASSESS⟧ 1 the quality or condition of being assiduous; diligence 2 [*also pl.*] constant personal attention

as·sid·u·ous (ə sij′oo əs) ***adj.*** ⟦L *assiduus* < *assidere*: see prec.⟧ 1 done with constant and careful attention 2 diligent; persevering —***SYN.*** BUSY —**as·sid′u·ous·ly** ***adv.*** —**as·sid′u·ous·ness** ***n.***

as·sign (ə sīn′) ***vt.*** ⟦ME *assignen* < OFr *assigner* < L *assignare*, mark out, allot < *ad-*, to + *signare*, SIGN⟧ 1 to set apart or mark for a specific purpose; designate [*assign* a day for the meeting] 2 to place at some task or duty; appoint [I was *assigned* to watch the road] 3 to give out as a task; allot [the teacher *assigned* a new lesson] 4 to ascribe; attribute [jealousy was *assigned* as the motive for the crime] 5 *Law* to transfer (a claim, right, property, etc.) to another —***vi.*** *Law* to transfer property, etc. to another —***n.*** [*usually pl.*] an assignee —***SYN.*** ALLOT, ASCRIBE —**as·sign′a·bil′i·ty** ***n.*** —**as·sign′a·ble** ***adj.*** —**as·sign′er** ***n.***, *Law* **as·sign·or** (ə sīn′ôr′)

as·sig·nat (as′ig nat′; *Fr* á sē nyá′) ***n.*** ⟦Fr < L *assignatus*, pp. of *assignare*, prec.⟧ a piece of paper currency issued during the French Revolution with confiscated lands as the security

as·sig·na·tion (as′ig nā′shən) ***n.*** 1 an assigning or being assigned 2 anything assigned 3 an appointment to meet, esp. one made secretly by lovers, or the meeting itself; tryst; rendezvous

as·sign·ee (ə sīn′ē′) ***n.*** ⟦Fr *assigné*: see ASSIGN⟧ *Law* 1 a person to whom a claim, right, property, etc. is transferred 2 a person appointed to act for another

as·sign·ment (ə sīn′mənt) ***n.*** 1 an assigning or being assigned; appointment; allotment 2 anything assigned or allotted, as a lesson, task, etc. 3 *Law a)* a transfer of a claim, right, property, etc. *b)* an instrument, as a deed, authorizing this —***SYN.*** TASK

as·sim·i·late (ə sim′ə lāt′) ***vt.*** **-lat′ed, -lat′ing** ⟦ME *assimilaten* < L *assimilatus*, pp. of *assimilare* < *ad-*, to + *similare*, make similar < *similis*, like: see SAME⟧ 1 to change (food) into a form that can be taken up by, and made part of, the bodily tissues; absorb into the body 2 to absorb and incorporate into one's thinking 3 to absorb (groups of different cultures) into the main cultural body 4 to make like or alike; cause to resemble: with *to* or, sometimes, *with* 5 [Now Rare] to compare or liken 6 *Linguis.* to cause to undergo assimilation —***vi.*** 1 to become like or alike 2 to become absorbed and incorporated 3 *Linguis.* to undergo assimilation —**as·sim′i·la·ble** (-ə lə bəl) ***adj.***

as·sim·i·la·tion (ə sim′ə lā′shən) ***n.*** an assimilating or being assimilated; specif., *a)* the cultural absorption of a minority group into the main cultural body *b)* *Linguis.* a process in which a sound, influenced by a neighboring sound, tends to become like it in articulation [the (n) in "in-" meaning "not" becomes (l) by *assimilation* in forming "illiterate"] *c)* *Physiol.* the change of digested food into the protoplasm of an animal; also, the absorption and incorporation of nutritive elements by plants, as in photosynthesis

as·sim·i·la·tion·ism (-iz′əm) ***n.*** the policy of completely absorbing minority cultural groups into the main cultural body, esp. by intermarriage —**as·sim′i·la′tion·ist** ***n.***

as·sim·i·la·tive (ə sim′ə lāt′iv) ***adj.*** of or causing assimilation; assimilating: also **as·sim·i·la·to·ry** (ə sim′′l ə tôr′ē)

As·sin·i·boine (ə sin′ə boin′) ⟦< Fr < Ojibwa *asinii-bwaan*, lit., stone Sioux⟧ river in SC Canada flowing from E Saskatchewan through S Manitoba into the Red River at Winnipeg: *c.* 600 mi (966 km)

As·si·si (ə sē′zē, -sē′sē; *It* äs sē′zē) town in Umbria, central Italy: birthplace of St. Francis

as·sist (ə sist′) ***vt.*** ⟦ME *assisten* < OFr *assister* < L *assistere* < *ad-*, to + *sistere*, to make stand < *stare*, to STAND⟧ 1 to give help to; aid 2 to work with as a helper or assistant —***vi.*** to give help; aid —***n.*** 1 an instance or act of helping 2 *Baseball* the act of a player who throws or deflects a batted ball in such a way that a teammate can make a putout 3 *Basketball, Ice Hockey* the act of a player who passes the ball or puck in such a way that a teammate scores —***SYN.*** HELP —**assist at** to be present at; attend

as·sist·ance (ə sis′təns) ***n.*** ⟦ME & OFr < ML *assistentia*: see prec.⟧ the act of assisting or the help given; aid

as·sist·ant (-tənt) ***adj.*** assisting; helping; that serves as a helper —***n.*** 1 a person who assists or serves in a subordinate position; helper 2 a thing that aids

☆**assistant professor** a college teacher ranking above an instructor and below an associate professor

as·sist·ant·ship (ə sis′tənt ship′) ***n.*** a temporary job teaching or doing research at a university, given to graduate students as a form of financial aid

assisted living a housing or living arrangement for elderly or disabled persons in which assistance with cooking, cleaning, shopping, etc. is provided as a service

assisted suicide suicide committed with the assistance of a physician by a person terminally ill or in unmanageable pain

As·siut (ä syoot′) *alt. sp. of* ASYUT

as·size (ə sīz′) ***n.*** ⟦ME & OFr *assise*, court session < *asseoir* < L *assidere*: see ASSESS⟧ 1 [Historical] a legislative assembly or any of its decrees 2 [*pl.*] court sessions held periodically in each county of England to try civil and criminal cases 3 [*pl.*] the time or place of such sessions 4 an inquest, the writ instituting it, or the verdict 5 [Archaic] *a)* a law regulating standards of price, measure, weight, ingredients, etc. for goods to be sold *b)* these standards

assn *abbrev.* association

assoc *abbrev.* **1** associate(s) **2** association

as·so·ci·a·ble (ə sō′shē ə bəl, -shə bəl) *adj.* ⟦Fr⟧ that can be associated or connected in the mind

as·so·ci·ate (ə sō′shē āt′, -sē-; *for n. & adj.,* -sōsh′it, -sō′shē it) *vt.* **-at′ed, -at′ing** ⟦< L *associatus,* pp. of *associare,* join to < *ad-,* to + *sociare,* unite with < *socius,* companion: see SOCIAL⟧ **1** to join together; connect; combine **2** to bring (a person) into relationship with oneself or another as companion, partner, friend, etc. **3** to connect in the mind [to *associate* rain with grief] —*vi.* **1** to join (*with* another or others) as a companion, partner, friend, etc. **2** to join together; unite —*n.* **1** a person with whom one is associated; friend, partner, fellow worker, etc. **2** a member of less than full status, as of a society, institute, etc. ☆**3** a degree or certificate granted by a junior college to those who have completed the regular two-year course [an *Associate* in (or of) Arts] ☆**4** a person employed in a retail store, esp. in selling goods or services; salesclerk —*adj.* **1** joined with others in some venture, work, etc. [an *associate* justice] **2** having less than full status [an *associate* membership] **3** accompanying; connected

SYN.—**associate** refers to a person who is frequently in one's company, usually because of shared work [business *associates*]; **colleague** denotes a co-worker, esp. in one of the professions, and may or may not imply a personal relationship [her *colleagues* at the university]; **companion** always refers to a person who actually accompanies one and usually implies a close, personal relationship [a dinner *companion,* the *companions* of one's youth]; **comrade** refers to a close associate and implies a sharing in activities and fortunes [*comrades* in arms]; **ally** now usually refers to a government joined with another or others in a common pursuit, esp. war; a **confederate** is one who joins with another or others for some common purpose, esp. in some unlawful act; an **accomplice** is one who unites with another or others in an unlawful act See also **join**

☆**associate professor** a college teacher ranking above an assistant professor and below a full professor

as·so·ci·a·tion (ə sō′sē ā′shən, -shē-) *n.* ⟦ML *associatio,* a joining with: see ASSOCIATE⟧ **1** the act of associating **2** the state of being associated; companionship; fellowship; partnership **3** an organization of persons having common interests, purposes, etc.; society; league **4** a connection in the mind between ideas, sensations, memories, etc. **5** the use of such connections as a literary device or psychoanalytic technique **6** a group of organisms living together in the same environment and forming a large, distinct component of a biome [an oak forest *association* within a deciduous forest biome] **7** *Chem.* the joining by relatively weak chemical bonds of two or more molecules of the same or different substances into a larger aggregate, as in polymerization —**as·so′ci·a′tion·al** *adj.*

association football soccer: so called from the Football Association established in England (1863) to set up rules for the game

as·so·ci·a·tive (ə sō′shē āt′iv, -sē-; -shə tiv) *adj.* ⟦ML *associativus*⟧ **1** of, characterized by, or causing association, as of ideas **2** *Math.* of or pertaining to an operation in which the result is the same regardless of the way the elements are grouped, as, in addition, $2 + (3 + 4) = (2 + 3) + 4$ and in multiplication, $2(3 \times 4) = (2 \times 3)4$

as·soil (ə soil′) *vt.* ⟦ME *assoilen* < OFr *assoil-,* pres. stem of *assoldre* < L *absolvere,* ABSOLVE⟧ [Archaic] **1** to absolve or acquit **2** to atone for

as·so·nance (as′ə nəns) *n.* ⟦Fr < L *assonans,* prp. of *assonare,* to sound in answer < *ad-,* to + *sonare,* SOUND[1], v.⟧ **1** likeness of sound, as in a series of words or syllables **2** *Prosody* repetition of a vowel sound in stressed syllables in which the consonant sounds are unlike (Ex.: l*a*te, m*a*ke) —**as′so·nant** (-nənt) *adj., n.*

as·sort (ə sôrt′) *vt.* ⟦OFr *assorter* < *a-* (L *ad-*), to + *sorte,* SORT⟧ to sort or classify —*vi.* to be of the same sort; match (*with*) —**as·sort′a·tive** (-ə tiv) *adj.* —**as·sort′er** *n.*

as·sort·ed (-id) *adj.* **1** of different sorts; of various kinds; miscellaneous **2** sorted into groups according to kind **3** matched [a poorly *assorted* pair]

as·sort·ment (-mənt) *n.* **1** an assorting or being assorted; classification **2** an assorted, or miscellaneous, group or collection; variety

ASSR *abbrev.* Autonomous Soviet Socialist Republic

asst *abbrev.* assistant

asstd *abbrev.* **1** assisted **2** assorted

as·suage (ə swāj′, a-) *vt.* **-suaged′, -suag′ing** ⟦ME *aswagen* < OFr *assouagier* < L *ad-,* to + *suavis,* SWEET⟧ **1** to lessen (pain, distress, etc.); allay **2** to calm (passion, anger, etc.); pacify **3** to satisfy or slake (thirst, appetite, etc.) —*SYN.* RELIEVE —**as·suage′ment** *n.*

As·suan (as′wän′, äs′wän′) *alt. sp. of* ASWAN

as·sua·sive (ə swā′siv) *adj.* ⟦< ASSUAGE, after PERSUASIVE⟧ soothing; allaying

as·sume (ə so͞om′, -syo͞om′) *vt.* **-sumed′, -sum′ing** ⟦ME *assumen* < L *assumere,* to take up, claim < *ad-,* to + *sumere,* to take: see CONSUME⟧ **1** *a)* to take on or put on (a certain appearance, form, role, etc.) *b)* to put oneself into [please *assume* a standing position] **2** to seize; usurp [to *assume* control] **3** to take upon oneself; undertake [to *assume* an obligation] **4** to take for granted; suppose (something) to be a fact **5** to pretend to have; feign [to *assume* an air of innocence] **6** [Archaic] *a)* to take in or receive *b)* to take into association —**as·sum′a·ble** *adj.* —**as·sum′er** *n.*

SYN.—**assume** implies the putting on of a false appearance but suggests a harmless or excusable motive [an *assumed* air of bravado]; **pretend** and **feign** both imply a profession or display of what is false, the more literary **feign** sometimes suggesting an elaborately contrived situation [to *pretend* not to hear, to *feign* deafness]; to **affect** is to make a show of being, having, using, wearing, etc., usually for effect [to *affect* a British accent]; **simulate** emphasizes the imitation of typical signs involved in assuming an appearance or characteristic not one's own [to *simulate* interest] See also **presume**

as·sumed (ə so͞omd, -syo͞omd′) *adj.* **1** pretended; put on; fictitious **2** taken for granted

as·sum·ing (ə so͞om′iŋ, -syo͞om′-) *adj.* taking too much for granted; presumptuous

as·sump·sit (ə sump′sit) *n.* ⟦ModL < L, he has undertaken; 3d pers. sing., perf. indic., of *assumere,* ASSUME⟧ *Law* **1** an agreement or promise, written, spoken, or implied, and not under seal **2** an action to recover damages for the nonfulfillment of such an agreement

as·sump·tion (ə sump′shən) *n.* **1** *Religion* the taking up of a person into heaven **2** [**A-**] *R.C.Ch. a)* the taking up of the body and soul of the Virgin Mary into heaven after her death *b)* a church festival on Aug. 15 celebrating this **3** the act of assuming; a taking upon oneself, taking over, or taking for granted **4** anything taken for granted; supposition **5** presumption —**as·sump′tive** *adj.*

As·sur (ä′so͝or) *var. of* ASHUR[2] (in both senses)

as·sur·ance (ə sho͝or′əns) *n.* **1** the act of assuring **2** the state of being assured; sureness; confidence; certainty **3** something said or done to inspire confidence, as a promise, positive statement, etc.; guarantee **4** belief in one's own abilities; self-confidence **5** impudent forwardness; presumption **6** [Chiefly Brit.] insurance, esp. life insurance —*SYN.* CERTAINTY, CONFIDENCE

As·sur·ba·ni·pal (ä′so͝or bän′i päl′) *var. of* ASHURBANIPAL

as·sure (ə sho͝or′) *vt.* **-sured′, -sur′ing** ⟦ME *assuren* < OFr *asseurer* < ML *assecurare* < L *ad-,* to + *securus,* SECURE⟧ **1** to make (a person) sure of something; convince **2** to give confidence to; reassure [the news *assured* us] **3** to declare to or promise confidently [I *assure* you I'll be there] **4** to make (a doubtful thing) certain; guarantee **5** to make safe or secure **6** [Chiefly Brit.] to insure against loss, esp. of life

as·sured (ə sho͝ord′) *adj.* **1** made sure; certain **2** confident; sure of oneself **3** [Chiefly Brit.] insured —*n.* **1** the person to whom an insurance policy is payable **2** [Chiefly Brit.] the person whose life or property is insured —**as·sur·ed·ly** (ə sho͝or′id lē) *adv.* —**as·sur′ed·ness** *n.*

as·sur·er (ə sho͝or′ər) *n.* **1** a person or thing that gives assurance **2** [Brit.] an insurance underwriter

as·sur·gent (ə sʉr′jənt) *adj.* ⟦L *assurgens,* prp. of *assurgere,* to rise up, swell < *ad-,* to + *surgere,* to rise: see SURGE⟧ **1** rising **2** *Bot.* ASCENDING

Assyr *abbrev.* Assyrian

As·syr·i·a (ə sir′ē ə) ancient empire in SW Asia in the region of the upper Tigris River: at its height (7th cent. B.C.), it extended from the head of the Persian Gulf to Egypt and Asia Minor: original cap. Ashur; later cap. Nineveh

As·syr·i·an (-ən) *adj.* ⟦< Sem, as in Heb *ashur,* ASHUR[2]⟧ of Assyria or its people, language, or culture —*n.* **1** a person born or living in Assyria **2** the Akkadian dialect of the Assyrians

As·syr·i·ol·o·gy (ə sir′ē äl′ə jē) *n.* the study of the civilization of ancient Assyria —**As·syr′i·ol′o·gist** *n.*

AST *abbrev.* Atlantic Standard Time

A·staire (ə ster′), **Fred** (born *Frederick Austerlitz*) 1899-1987; U.S. dancer, choreographer, & film actor

A·sta·na (ä stä nä′) capital of Kazakhstan, in the N part

As·tar·te (as tär′tē) *n.* ⟦L < Gr *Astartē* < Heb *ashtoret,* ASHTORETH⟧ a Semitic goddess of fertility and sexual love, worshiped by the Phoenicians and others: see also ASHTORETH, ISHTAR

a·stat·ic (ā stat′ik) *adj.* ⟦A-[2] (not) + STATIC⟧ **1** unstable; unsteady **2** *Physics* not taking a definite position or direction [an *astatic* needle on a galvanometer is not affected by the earth's magnetism] —**a·stat′i·cal·ly** *adv.* —**a·stat′i·cism′** (-ə siz′əm) *n.*

☆**as·ta·tine** (as′tə tēn′, -tin) *n.* ⟦< Gr *astatos,* unstable + -INE[3]⟧ a radioactive chemical element, one of the halogens, formed from bismuth when it is bombarded by alpha particles: it resembles iodine in its chemical properties: symbol, At; at. no. 85: see the periodic table of elements in the Reference Supplement

as·ter (as′tər) *n.* ⟦ModL < L < Gr *astēr,* STAR⟧ **1** any of a large genus (*Aster*) of plants of the composite family, with purplish, blue, pink, or white daisylike flowers **2** CHINA ASTER **3** a structure shaped like a star, formed during mitosis around the centrosome in the cytoplasm of a cell: not formed in seed plant cells

-as·ter[1] (as′tər) ⟦< Gr *astēr,* STAR⟧ *combining form forming nouns* star or starlike structure [*diaster*]

-as·ter[2] (as′tər) ⟦L dim. suffix⟧ *suffix forming nouns* a (specified) person or thing that is inferior or not genuine [*poetaster*]

as·te·ri·at·ed (as tir′ē āt′id) *adj.* ⟦< Gr *asterios,* starred (< *astēr,* STAR) + -AT(E) + -ED⟧ **1** having radiate form; star-shaped **2** *Mineralogy* having a structure that produces an asterism

as·ter·isk (as′tər isk′) *n.* ⟦LL *asteriscus* < Gr *asteriskos,* dim. of *astēr,* STAR⟧ a starlike sign (*) used in printing to indicate footnote references, omissions, etc. —*vt.* to mark with this sign

as·ter·ism (-iz′əm) *n.* ⟦Gr *asterismos*, a marking with stars < *asterizein*, to mark with stars < *astēr*, STAR⟧ 1 a group or cluster of stars that may or may not form a constellation 2 *Mineralogy* a starlike figure produced in some crystals by reflected or transmitted light 3 *Printing* three asterisks placed in triangular form (⁂ or ⁂) to call attention to a passage

a·stern (ə sturn′) *adv.* ⟦A-[1] + STERN[2]⟧ 1 behind a ship or aircraft [a keg bobbed up *astern*] 2 AFT[1]: not a nautical usage 3 backward; in a reverse direction [full speed *astern*]

a·ster·nal (ā stur′nəl) *adj.* ⟦A-[2] + STERNAL⟧ 1 not joined to the sternum 2 without a sternum

as·ter·oid (as′tər oid′) *adj.* ⟦Gr *asteroeidēs* < *astēr*, STAR + *eidēs*, -OID⟧ starlike; shaped like a star or starfish —*n.* 1 any of the thousands of relatively small, irregularly shaped objects orbiting the sun typically between Mars and Jupiter 2 *Zool.* STARFISH

as·the·ni·a (as thē′nē ə) *n.* ⟦ModL < Gr *astheneia*, weakness < *a-*, without + *sthenos*, strength⟧ a lack or loss of bodily strength; bodily weakness

as·then·ic (as then′ik) *adj.* ⟦Gr *asthenikos*⟧ 1 of or having asthenia 2 *former term for* ECTOMORPHIC

as·the·no·pi·a (as′thə nō′pē ə) *n.* ⟦ModL < Gr *asthenēs*, weak (see ASTHENIA) + -OPIA⟧ a strained condition of the eyes, often with headache, dizziness, etc. —**as′the·nop′ic** (-näp′ik) *adj.*

as·then·o·sphere (as then′ə sfir′) *n.* ⟦< Gr *asthenēs*, weak (see ASTHENIA) + -O- + -SPHERE⟧ a zone in the upper mantle of the earth, consisting of hot, plastic rock, that underlies the solid lithosphere

asth·ma (az′mə; *chiefly Brit* as′-) *n.* ⟦ME *asma* < ML < Gr *asthma*, a panting, asthma⟧ a generally chronic disorder characterized by wheezing, coughing, difficulty in breathing, and a suffocating feeling, caused by an allergy to ingested substances, stress, etc.

asth·mat·ic (az mat′ik; *chiefly Brit* as-) *adj.* of or having asthma: also **asth·mat′i·cal** —*n.* a person who has asthma —**asth·mat′i·cal·ly** *adv.*

As·ti (äs′tē) city in Piedmont, NW Italy: center of a winegrowing region

as·tig·mat·ic (as′tig mat′ik) *adj.* 1 of or having astigmatism 2 correcting astigmatism 3 having or resulting from a distorted view or judgment —**as′tig·mat′i·cal·ly** *adv.*

a·stig·ma·tism (ə stig′mə tiz′əm) *n.* ⟦< Gr *a-*, without + *stigma* (gen. *stigmatos*) a mark, puncture (see STICK) + -ISM⟧ 1 an irregularity in the curvature of a lens, including the lens of the eye, so that light rays from an object do not meet in a single focal point, resulting in an indistinct or distorted image 2 distorted view or judgment, as because of bias

a·stil·be (ə stil′bē) *n.* ⟦ModL < Gr *a-*, A-[2] (sense 3) + *stilbē*, glittering, fem. of *stilbos*: so named from its tiny white flowers⟧ any of a genus (*Astilbe*) of herbaceous, perennial plants of the saxifrage family, usually having spikes of white, pink, or red flowers

a·stir (ə stur′) *adv., adj.* ⟦A-[1] + STIR[2]⟧ 1 in motion; in excited activity 2 out of bed

As·ti Spu·man·te (äs′tē spo͞o män′tē) ⟦It, after ASTI + *spumante*, effervescent < *spumare*, to foam⟧ an effervescent white wine, typically sweet, from the area around Asti, Italy

ASTM *abbrev.* American Society for Testing and Materials

a·stom·a·tous (ā stäm′ə təs, -stō′mə-) *adj.* ⟦A-[2] + STOMATOUS⟧ *Biol.* without a stoma

As·ton (as′tən), **Francis William** 1877-1945; Eng. chemist & physicist: noted for his work on isotopes

as·ton·ied (ə stän′ēd) *adj.* ⟦pp. of ME *astonien*, fol. ⟧ [Obs.] bewildered, dazed, astounded, etc.

as·ton·ish (ə stän′ish) *vt.* ⟦altered < ME *astonien* < OFr *estoner* < VL **extonare* (for L *attonare*) < *ex-*, intens. + *tonare*, to THUNDER⟧ to fill with sudden wonder or great surprise; amaze —**SYN.** SURPRISE —**as·ton′ish·ing** *adj.* —**as·ton′ish·ing·ly** *adv.*

as·ton·ish·ment (-mənt) *n.* 1 the state of being astonished; great amazement 2 anything that astonishes

As·tor (as′tər) 1 Viscountess (born *Nancy Witcher Langhorne*) 1879-1964; 1st woman member of the Brit. House of Commons (1919-45): born in the U.S. 2 **John Jacob** 1763-1848; U.S. fur merchant & financier, born in Germany

as·tound (ə stound′) *vt.* ⟦< ME *astouned*, *astoned*, pp. of *astonien*, ASTONISH⟧ to bewilder with sudden surprise; astonish greatly; amaze —*adj.* [Old Poet.] amazed; astonished —**SYN.** SURPRISE —**as·tound′ing** *adj.* —**as·tound′ing·ly** *adv.*

a·strad·dle (ə strad′'l) *adv.* in a straddling position

As·trae·a (as trē′ə) *n.* ⟦L < Gr *Astraia* < *astraios*, starry < *astron*, STAR⟧ *Gr. Myth.* a goddess of justice, later also of innocence and purity: she is the last deity to leave the earth after the Golden Age

as·tra·gal (as′trə gəl) *n.* ⟦L *astragalus* < Gr *astragalos*, anklebone, vertebra, architectural molding⟧ 1 *Anat.* ASTRAGALUS 2 *Archit.* a small, convex molding, sometimes cut like beading

as·trag·a·lus (ə strag′ə ləs) *n.* ⟦L, prec.⟧ 1 *pl.* **-li′** (-lī′) *Anat. former term for* the talus, or anklebone, in humans 2 an herb used in Chinese medicine to strengthen the immune system, derived from the dried roots of a milk vetch (*Astragalus membranaceus*)

as·tra·khan (as′trə kən) *n.* 1 a loosely curled fur, a kind of karakul, made from the pelt of very young lambs originally bred near Astrakhan 2 a wool fabric with a pile cut and curled to look like this

As·tra·khan (as′trə kan′; *Russ* äs′trə khän′y′) city & port in SW Russia, on the Volga River delta near the Caspian Sea

as·tral (as′trəl) *adj.* ⟦L *astralis* < *astrum*, star < Gr *astron* < *astēr*, STAR⟧ 1 of, from, or like the stars 2 *Zool.* of an aster in mitosis 3 in theosophy, designating or of a universal substance supposedly existing at a level just beyond normal human perception

a·stray (ə strā′) *adv., adj.* ⟦ME < pp. of OFr *estraier*, STRAY⟧ 1 off the right path or way; wandering 2 in error

a·stride (ə strīd′) *adv.* ⟦A-[1] + STRIDE⟧ 1 with a leg on either side; astraddle 2 with legs far apart —***prep.*** 1 with a leg on either side of (a horse, etc.) 2 lying on both sides of [a town *astride* the river] 3 extending over or across

as·trin·gent (ə strin′jənt) *adj.* ⟦L *astringens*, prp. of *astringere*, to contract < *ad-*, to + *stringere*, draw tight: see STRICT⟧ 1 that contracts bodily tissue and checks secretions, capillary bleeding, etc.; styptic 2 having a harsh, biting quality [an *astringent* style of writing] —*n.* an astringent substance, drug, etc. —**as·trin′gen·cy** *n.* —**as·trin′gent·ly** *adv.*

as·tro- (as′trō, -trə) ⟦< Gr *astron*, STAR⟧ *combining form* 1 star or stars [*astrophysics*] 2 *Zool.* of an aster in mitosis [*astrosphere*]

as·tro·bi·ol·o·gy (as′trō bī äl′ə jē) *n.* the branch of biology that investigates the existence of living organisms on planets other than earth

as·tro·chem·is·try (as′trō kem′is trē) *n.* the study of the chemistry of celestial bodies —**as′tro·chem′ist** *n.*

as·tro·com·pass (as′trō kum′pəs, -trə-) *n.* an instrument for determining the direction of an aircraft by sighting upon a celestial body

as·tro·cyte (-sīt′) *n.* ⟦ASTRO- + -CYTE⟧ a star-shaped cell of the brain and spinal cord —**as′tro·cyt′ic** (-sit′ik) *adj.*

as·tro·dome (-dōm′) *n.* a domelike transparent structure for housing astronomical or navigational instruments; specif., such a structure mounted on top of an aircraft fuselage for the navigator

as·tro·dy·nam·ics (as′trō dī nam′iks) *n.* the branch of dynamics dealing with the motion and gravitation of natural and artificial objects in space

astrol *abbrev.* astrology

as·tro·labe (as′trō lāb′, -trə-) *n.* ⟦ME *astrelabie* < OFr *astrelabe* < ML *astrolabium* < Gr *astrolabon* < *astron*, STAR + *lambanein*, to take: see LATCH⟧ an instrument formerly used to find the altitude of a star, etc.: it was replaced by the sextant

as·trol·o·gy (ə sträl′ə jē) *n.* ⟦ME *astrologie* < L & Gr *astrologia*, astronomy, astrology < *astron*, STAR + *-logia*, -LOGY⟧ 1 [Historical] primitive astronomy 2 a system of methods, theories, etc. based on the assumption that the positions of the moon, sun, and stars affect human affairs and that one can foretell the future by studying the stars, etc. —**as·trol′o·ger** *n.*, **as·trol′o·gist** —**as·tro·log·i·cal** (as′trə läj′i kəl) *adj.* —**as′tro·log′i·cal·ly** *adv.*

as·trom·e·try (ə sträm′ə trē) *n.* ⟦ASTRO- + -METRY⟧ the branch of astronomy dealing with the measurement of the positions, motions, and distances of planets, stars, etc. —**as·tro·met·ric** (as′trō me′trik) *adj.*

astron *abbrev.* 1 astronomer 2 astronomy

as·tro·naut (as′trə nôt′, -nät′) *n.* ⟦< Fr *astronaute*: see ASTRO- & AERONAUT⟧ a person trained to make rocket flights in outer space

as·tro·nau·tics (as′trə nôt′iks, -nät′-) *n.* ⟦< Fr *astronautique* (coined 1927): see ASTRO- & AERONAUTICS⟧ the science that deals with spacecraft and with travel in outer space, esp. to the moon and to other planets —**as′tro·nau′ti·cal** *adj.* —**as′tro·nau′ti·cal·ly** *adv.*

as·tro·nav·i·ga·tion (as′trō nav′ə gā′shən) *n.* CELESTIAL NAVIGATION —**as′tro·nav′i·ga′tor** *n.*

as·tron·o·mer (ə strän′ə mər) *n.* an expert in astronomy

as·tro·nom·i·cal (as′trə näm′i kəl) *adj.* 1 of or having to do with astronomy 2 extremely large, like the numbers or quantities used in astronomy Also **as′tro·nom′ic** —**as′tro·nom′i·cal·ly** *adv.*

astronomical latitude the angle between the direction of gravity at the observer's position and the plane of the celestial equator

astronomical unit *Astron.* a unit of length based on the mean distance of the earth from the sun, *c.* 149.6 million km (*c.* 93 million mi): light travels this distance in *c.* 8.3 minutes: abbrev. *AU*

as·tron·o·my (ə strän′ə mē) *n.* ⟦ME & OFr *astronomie* < L *astronomia* < Gr < *astron*, STAR + *nomos*, law: see -NOMY⟧ 1 the science of the universe in which the stars, planets, etc. are studied, including their origins, evolution, composition, motions, relative positions, sizes, etc. 2 *pl.* **-mies** a book or treatise on this

as·tro·pho·tog·ra·phy (as′trō fə täg′rə fē) *n.* photography of celestial objects and events

as·tro·phys·ics (-fiz′iks) *n.* the main branch of astronomy which deals primarily with the physical properties of the universe, including luminosity, density, temperature, and chemical composition —**as′tro·phys′i·cal** *adj.* —**as′tro·phys′i·cist** (-ə sist) *n.*

as·tro·sphere (as′trō sfir′) *n.* ⟦ASTRO- + -SPHERE⟧ *Biol.* 1 CENTROSPHERE 2 all of an aster except the centrosome

As·tro·Turf (-turf′) *trademark for* a durable, grasslike synthetic outdoor carpet used in stadiums, as a floor covering, etc.

As·tu·ri·as (as toor′ē əs; *Sp* äs to͞or′yäs) region of NW Spain, on the Bay of Biscay: formerly (8th-9th cent.), a kingdom: 4,079 sq mi (10,565 sq km); cap. Oviedo —**As·tu′ri·an** *adj., n.*

as·tute (ə sto͞ot′, -styo͞ot′) *adj.* ⟦L *astutus* < *astus*, craft, cunning⟧ having or showing a clever or shrewd mind; cunning; crafty; wily —**SYN.** SHREWD —**as·tute′ly** *adv.* —**as·tute′ness** *n.*

As·ty·a·nax (as tī′ə naks′) *n.* ⟦L < Gr⟧ *Gr. Myth.* the young son of Hector and Andromache: he is killed at Troy by the Greek conquerors

a·sty·lar (ā stīʹlər) ***adj.*** ⟦< A-² + Gr *stylos*, pillar (see STYLITE) + -AR⟧ *Archit.* having no columns or pilasters

A·sun·ción (ä so͞on syônʹ) capital of Paraguay: port on the Paraguay River

a·sun·der (ə sunʹdər) ***adv.*** ⟦ME < OE *on sundran* < *on*, on + *sundor*: see SUNDER⟧ **1** into parts or pieces **2** apart or separate in direction or position

ASV *abbrev.* American Standard Version (of the Bible)

As·wan (asʹwän′, äsʹwän′) city in S Egypt, on the Nile: 3 mi (4.5 km) south is a dam (completed 1902) providing irrigation for the surrounding region: a larger dam (**Aswan High Dam**, completed 1970) is 4 mi (6.4 km) farther south

a·swarm (ə swôrmʹ) ***adj.*** ⟦A-¹ + SWARM¹⟧ filled or crowded (*with*); swarming [the park *aswarm* with people]

a·syl·lab·ic (āʹsə labʹik) ***adj.*** not syllabic; specif., incapable of forming a syllable or the nucleus of a syllable

a·sy·lum (ə sīʹləm) ***n.*** ⟦L < Gr *asylon* < *asylos*, inviolable < *a-*, without + *sylon*, right of seizure⟧ **1** [Obs.] a sanctuary, as a temple, where criminals, debtors, etc. were safe from arrest **2** a place where one is safe and secure; refuge **3** the protection given by a sanctuary or refuge or by one country to refugees from another country **4** an institution for the care of the mentally ill, or of the aged, the poor, etc.: in this sense, largely replaced by such terms as *mental* (or *psychiatric*) *hospital, nursing home,* etc. —***SYN.*** SHELTER

asymmetrical bars a set of parallel bars, having one bar fixed at 230 cm (7 ft, 6 in) and the other at 150 cm (4 ft, 11 in), used by women gymnasts

a·sym·me·try (ā simʹə trē) ***n.*** ⟦Gr *asymmetria* < *a-*, without + *symmetria*: see SYMMETRY⟧ **1** lack of symmetry **2** *Chem.* the asymmetrical structure of a molecule, esp. of stereoisomers containing carbon atoms **3** *Mil.* lack of essential parity between adversarial forces, as between a highly mechanized army and a group of guerillas —**a·sym·met·ri·cal** (āʹsə meʹtri kəl) ***adj.***, **a′sym·metʹric** —**a′sym·metʹri·cal·ly** ***adv.***

a·symp·to·mat·ic (āʹsimp tə matʹik) ***adj.*** without symptoms

as·ymp·tote (asʹim tōt′, -imp-) ***n.*** ⟦ModL *asymptota* < Gr *asymptōtos* < *a-*, not + *symptōtos*, self-intersecting < *syn-*, together + *piptein*, to fall: see FEATHER⟧ *Math.* a straight line always approaching but never meeting a curve; tangent to a curve at infinity —**as′ymp·totʹic** (-tätʹik) ***adj.***, **as′ymp·totʹi·cal** —**as′ymp·totʹi·cal·ly** ***adv.***

A
C

asymptote
(A, asymptote of curve C)

a·syn·chro·nism (ā siŋʹkrə niz′əm) ***n.*** lack of synchronism; failure to occur at the same time —**a·synʹchro·nous** ***adj.*** —**a·synʹchro·nous·ly** ***adv.***

asynchronous transfer mode a set of rules for transferring data, sound, and images in small, fixed groups at very high rates of speed over computer networks

a·syn·de·ton (ə sinʹdə tän′) ***n.*** ⟦LL < Gr < *a-*, not + *syndetos*, united with < *syndein*, to bind together < *syn-*, together + *dein*, to bind: see DIADEM⟧ the practice of leaving out the usual conjunctions between coordinate sentence elements (Ex.: smile, shake hands, part) —**as·yn·det·ic** (as′ən detʹik) ***adj.*** —**as′yn·detʹi·cal·ly** ***adv.***

As·yut (ä syo͞otʹ) city in central Egypt, on the Nile

at¹ (at; *unstressed* ət) ***prep.*** ⟦ME < OE *æt*; akin to Goth, OS, ON *at* & L *ad* at, in, to⟧ **1** on; in; near; by: *at* is the preposition of general (usually static) location, and is replaced by *in, on,* etc. when a more precise indication of location is needed [*at* the office, *at* the edge of town] **2** *a)* to or toward as the goal or object [look *at* her, swing *at* the ball, don't shout *at* me] *b)* criticizing, attacking, pestering, etc. [the critics are *at* him again] **3** through [come in *at* the front door] **4** from [get the facts *at* their source] **5** attending [*at* the party] **6** occupied in; busy with [*at* work] **7** in a condition or state of [*at* war] **8** in the manner of [*at* a trot] **9** because of; in response to [terrified *at* the sight, to smile *at* a remark] **10** according to [*at* his discretion] **11** with reference to [good *at* tennis] **12** in the amount or number, to the degree, for the price, etc. of: symbol, @ [*at* twenty miles per hour, *at* five cents each] **13** from an interval or distance of [visible *at* half a mile, *at* arm's length] **14** *a)* occurring on the hour, minute, etc. of [*at* five fifteen] *b)* being of the age of [*at* sixty-five] **15** during the period of [it happened *at* night] **16** *Comput.* located at: used in an internet address to separate a username from the DOMAIN NAME: usually written @

at² (ät, at) ***n.***, *pl.* **at** ⟦Thai⟧ a monetary unit of Laos, equal to $\frac{1}{100}$ of a kip

at³ *abbrev.* **1** airtight **2** atmosphere **3** atomic

At *Chem. symbol for* astatine

at- (ət, at) *prefix* AD-: used before *t*

☆**At·a·brine** (atʹə brin′, -brēn′) ***n.*** ⟦former trademark < Ger *atebrin* < ? *a(n)-t(if)ebrin*; see ANTI- & FEBRILE & -INE³⟧ [*sometimes* **a-**] quinacrine hydrochloride, $C_{23}H_{30}ClN_3O{\cdot}2HCl{\cdot}2H_2O$, a synthetic drug used in treating malaria and other diseases

A·ta·ca·ma Desert (äʹtä käʹmä) desert area in N Chile: its nitrate deposits were once a chief source of the world's supply: 30,000 sq mi (77,700 sq km)

A·ta·hual·pa (äʹtə wälʹpə) 1502?-33; last Inca king of Peru (1525-33)

At·a·lan·ta (at′ə lanʹtə) ***n.*** ⟦L < Gr *Atalantē*⟧ *Gr. Myth.* a beautiful, swift-footed maiden who offers to marry any man able to defeat her in a race: Hippomenes wins by dropping three golden apples, which she stops to pick up, along the way

at·a·man (atʹə man′) ***n.***, *pl.* **-mans′** ⟦Russ⟧ HETMAN

☆**at·a·mas·co lily** (at′ə masʹkō) ⟦Virginia Algonquian *attamusco*⟧ any of a genus (*Zephyranthes*) of bulbous plants of the lily family, with hollow stems, grassy leaves, and funnel-shaped flowers of yellow, pink, red, or purple-tinged white

at·ap (atʹap′) ***n.*** ⟦Malay, roof, thatch⟧ **1** thatch for native huts in Malaya, made of leaves of the nipa palm **2** NIPA

at·a·rac·tic (at′ə rakʹtik) ***n.*** ⟦< Gr *ataraktos*, calm, undisturbed < *ataraxia*: see fol.⟧ a tranquilizing drug —***adj.*** of or having to do with tranquilizing drugs or their effects Also **at′a·raxʹic** (-rakʹsik)

at·a·rax·i·a (at′ə rakʹsē ə) ***n.*** ⟦Gr < *a-*, not + *tarassein*, to disturb: for IE base see DARK⟧ calmness of the mind and emotions; tranquillity: also **atʹa·raxʹy** (-rakʹsē)

Atatürk *see* KEMAL ATATÜRK

at·a·vism (atʹə viz′əm) ***n.*** ⟦Fr *atavisme* < L *atavus*, father of a great-grandfather, ancestor < *at-*, beyond + *avus*, grandfather < IE **ati*, beyond + **awos*, maternal grandfather⟧ **1** appearance in an individual of some characteristic found in a remote ancestor but not in nearer ancestors **2** *a)* such a characteristic *b)* an individual with such a characteristic (also **atʹa·vist**) —**at′a·visʹtic** ***adj.***, **a·tav·ic** (ə tavʹik) —**at′a·visʹti·cal·ly** ***adv.***

a·tax·i·a (ə takʹsē ə) ***n.*** ⟦Gr, disorder < *ataktos*, disorderly < *a-*, not + *taktos* < *tassein*, arrange: see TACTICS⟧ total or partial inability to coordinate voluntary bodily movements, as in walking —**a·taxʹic** ***adj., n.***

At·ba·ra (ätʹbä rä) river flowing from N Ethiopia into the Nile in NE Sudan: 500 mi (805 km)

☆**at-bat** (atʹbatʹ) ***n.*** *Baseball* **1** an official turn as a batter: a turn as a batter is not recognized as being official if the batter walks, sacrifices, or is hit by a pitch or interfered with by the catcher: see also BATTING AVERAGE (sense 1) **2** any turn as a batter Also written **at bat**

ate (āt, *dial.* et; *Brit* et, *also* āt) ***vt., vi.*** *pt. of* EAT

A·te (āʹtē) ***n.*** ⟦Gr *Atē*⟧ *Gr. Myth.* the goddess personifying criminal folly or reckless ambition in human beings, which brings on punishment by Nemesis

-ate¹ (āt; *for 2 & 3 it,* ət) *suffix* **1** *forming verbs a)* to become [*evaporate, maturate*] *b)* to cause to become [*invalidate, rejuvenate*] *c)* to form or produce [*ulcerate*] *d)* to provide or treat with [*vaccinate*] *e)* to put in the form of, or form by means of [*delineate, triangulate*] *f)* to arrange for [*orchestrate*] *g)* to combine, infuse, or treat with [*oxygenate*] **2** *forming adjectives a)* of or characteristic of [*collegiate, roseate*] *b)* having or filled with [*foliolate, passionate*] *c) Biol.* having or characterized by [*caudate*] **3** forming adjectives roughly equivalent to corresponding past participles ending in -ED [*animate* (*animated*), *determinate* (*determined*)]

-ate² (āt, it) *suffix forming nouns* **1** an office, function, agent, official, or group of officials [*episcopate, potentate, directorate*] **2** the land, territory, or dominion of (a person or office) [*priorate, sultanate*] **3** a person or thing that is the object of (an action) [*legate, mandate*] **4** *Chem. a)* salt made from any of certain acids with names ending in -IC: its metal or nonmetal is in its highest oxidation state [ammonium *nitrate*] *b)* a result of some process [*distillate*]

at·e·lec·ta·sis (at′ə lekʹtə sis) ***n.***, *pl.* **-ses′** (-sēz′) ⟦ModL < Gr *atelēs*, incomplete (< *a-*, without + *telos*, end: see WHEEL) + *ektasis*, a stretching out < *ek-*, out + *teinein*, to stretch: see THIN⟧ the collapse of all or part of a lung

a·te·lic (ā tēʹlik, -telʹik) ***adj.*** *Linguis.* IMPERFECTIVE: opposed to TELIC (sense 2)

at·el·ier (atʹʹl yā′; *Fr* à tə lyāʹ) ***n.*** ⟦Fr < OFr *astelier* < *astele*, a shaving, splinter < VL *astella* < L *assula*, dim. of *assis*, board⟧ a studio or workshop, esp. one used by an artist

a tem·po (ä temʹpō) ⟦It⟧ *Musical Direction* in time: a note to the performer to return to the preceding tempo

A·te·ri·an (ə tirʹē ən) ***adj.*** ⟦Fr *atérien*, after Bir-el-*Ater*, Algeria⟧ designating or of the Middle or Upper Paleolithic culture of N Africa, characterized by arrowheads with barbs and tangs, etc.

ATF *abbrev.* Bureau of Alcohol, Tobacco, Firearms and Explosives

Ath·a·bas·ca (ath′ə basʹkə) ⟦Cree dial. *ahthapaskaaw*, name of lake, lit., there are reeds here and there < *ahthap-*, net(like) + *-ask-*, vegetation + formative suffixes⟧ **1** river rising in the Rocky Mountains of SW Alberta, Canada, and flowing northeast into Lake Athabasca: 765 mi (1,231 km) **2 Lake** lake extending across the N Alberta-Saskatchewan, Canada, border: 3,100 sq mi (8,029 sq km)

Ath·a·bas·kan or **Ath·a·bas·can** (ath′ə basʹkən) ***n.*** **1** a family of North American Indian languages, including Chipewyan, Hupa, and Navajo **2** a member of any of the peoples speaking these languages —***adj.*** designating or of these peoples or their languages or cultures

Athanasian Creed a 4th-5th cent. statement of Christian beliefs of unknown authorship, formerly attributed to Athanasius: as opposed to Arianism, it emphasizes faith in the Trinity

Ath·a·na·sius (ath′ə nāʹshəs), Saint (A.D. 296?-373); Alexandrian bishop: patriarch of Alexandria (328-373) & opponent of Arianism: his day is May 2: called *the Great* —**Ath′a·naʹsian** (-zhən) ***adj.***

Ath·a·pas·can or **Ath·a·pas·kan** (ath′ə pasʹkən) ***n., adj.*** ATHABASKAN

a·the·ism (āʹthē iz′əm) ***n.*** ⟦MFr *athéisme* < Gr *atheos*, godless < *a-*, without + *theos*, god: see THEO-⟧ **1** the belief that there is no God, or denial that God or gods exist **2** godlessness —**a′the·isʹtic** ***adj.***, **a′the·isʹti·cal** —**a′the·isʹti·cal·ly** ***adv.***

a·the·ist (-ist) ***n.*** ⟦MFr *athéiste*: see prec.⟧ a person who believes that there is no God

SYN.—an **atheist** rejects all religious belief and denies the existence of God; an **agnostic** questions the existence of God, heaven, etc. in the absence of material proof and in unwillingness to accept supernatural revelation; **deist**, a historical term, was applied to 18th-cent. rationalists who believed in God as a creative, moving force but who otherwise rejected formal religion and its doctrines of revelation, divine authority, etc.; **freethinker**, the current parallel term, similarly implies rejection of the tenets and traditions of formal religion as incompatible with reason; **unbeliever** is a more negative term, simply designating, without further qualification, one who does not accept any religious belief; **infidel** is applied to a person not believing in a certain religion or the prevailing religion —*ANT.* **theist**

ath·el·ing (ath′əl iŋ) ***n.*** ⟦ME < OE *ætheling* < *æthele*, noble⟧ a nobleman or prince of the Anglo-Saxons

Ath·el·stan (ath′əl stan′) ⟦ME < OE *ætheling* < *æthele*, noble⟧ A.D. 895?-940; king of the Mercians & West Saxons (925-940): assumed the title of king of England: grandson of Alfred the Great

A·the·na (ə thē′nə) ***n.*** ⟦Gr *Athēnē*⟧ *Gr. Myth.* the goddess of wisdom, skills, and warfare: identified with the Roman Minerva: also **A·the′ne** (-nē)

Ath·e·nae·um or **Ath·e·ne·um** (ath′ə nē′əm) ***n.*** ⟦LL *Athenaeum* < Gr *Athēnaion*⟧ **1** the temple of Athena at Athens, where writers and scholars met **2** the Roman academy of law, literature, etc. founded by Hadrian **3** [**a-**] a literary or scientific club **4** [**a-**] any building or hall used as a library or reading room

A·the·ni·an (ə thē′nē ən) ***adj.*** of Athens, esp. ancient Athens, or its people or culture —***n.*** **1** a person born or living in Athens **2** a citizen of ancient Athens

Ath·ens (ath′ənz) **1** capital of Greece, in the SE part: became established as the center of Greek culture in the 5th cent. B.C., when it was the capital of ancient Attica **2** ⟦after the Greek city: so named as an early center of higher learning, from being the site of the University of Ga.⟧ city in NE Ga., in Clarke county, with which it constitutes a metropolitan government (**Athens-Clarke County**)

a·ther·man·cy (ā thur′mən sē) ***n.*** ⟦< Gr *a-*, not + *thermansis*, heating (< *thermainein*, to heat < *thermē*, heat: see WARM) + -CY⟧ the property of not transmitting infrared or heat rays —**a·ther′ma·nous** (-mə nəs) ***adj.***

ath·er·o·ma (ath′ər ō′mə) ***n.***, *pl.* **-mas** or **-ma·ta** (-mə tə) ⟦ModL < Gr *atherōma*, tumor filled with grainy matter < *athēr*, awn, chaff + *-ōma*, -OMA⟧ a condition marked by deposits of small fatty nodules on the inner walls of the arteries, often accompanied by degeneration of the affected areas; also, such a nodule or arterial plaque —**ath′er·om′a·tous** (-äm′ə təs, -ō′mə-) ***adj.***

ath·er·o·scle·ro·sis (ath′ər ō′sklə rō′sis) ***n.*** ⟦ModL < prec. + SCLEROSIS⟧ a form of arteriosclerosis associated with the formation of atheromas —**ath′er·o′scle·rot′ic** (-rät′ik) ***adj.***

ath·e·to·sis (ath′ə tō′sis) ***n.***, *pl.* **-ses′** (-sēz′) ⟦< Gr *athetos*, without position or place + -OSIS⟧ a muscular disorder characterized by continuous, slow, twisting motions of the hands, feet, etc., as in cerebral palsy —**ath′e·toid′** (-toid′) ***adj.***, **ath′e·tot′ic** (-tät′ik)

A·thí·nai (ä thē′ne) *Gr. name for* ATHENS

a·thirst (ə thurst′) ***adj.*** ⟦ME *ofthurst* < OE *ofthyrsted*, pp. of *ofthyrstan* < *of-*, intens. + *thyrstan*, THIRST⟧ **1** [Archaic] thirsty **2** eager; longing (*for* a thing)

ath·lete (ath′lēt′) ***n.*** ⟦L *athleta* < Gr *athlētēs*, contestant in the games < *athlein*, to contest for a prize < *athlos*, a contest, *athlon*, a prize⟧ a person trained in exercises, games, or contests requiring physical strength, skill, stamina, speed, etc.

athlete's foot a common fungous infection of the skin of the feet; ringworm of the feet

athlete's heart enlargement of the heart, caused by continued, heavy physical exertion

ath·let·ic (ath let′ik) ***adj.*** **1** of, like, or proper to athletes or athletics **2** physically strong, fit, skillful, active, etc. **3** *former term for* MESOMORPHIC (sense 2) —**ath·let′i·cal·ly** ***adv.***

ath·let·i·cism (ath let′ə siz′əm) ***n.*** physical prowess consisting variously of coordination, dexterity, vigor, stamina, etc.

ath·let·ics (-iks) ***pl.n.*** [*sometimes with sing. v.*] sports, games, exercises, etc. requiring physical strength, skill, stamina, speed, etc.

athletic supporter an elastic belt with a pouch for supporting the genitals, worn by men while engaging in athletics

ath·o·dyd (ath′ə did′) ***n.*** ⟦*a(ero)th(erm)ody(namic) d(uct)*⟧ RAMJET (ENGINE)

at-home (at hōm′) ***n.*** an informal reception at one's home, usually in the afternoon

-a·thon (ə thän′) ⟦< (MAR)ATHON⟧ *suffix* an event marked by length or endurance: used freely to form nonce compounds [*walkathon, drinkathon*; sale-*a-thon*]: also **-a-thon**

Ath·os (ath′äs, ā′thäs), **Mount 1** autonomous monastic district occupying the tip of the easternmost prong of the Chalcidice peninsula, NE Greece: 130 sq mi (337 sq km) **2** mountain in this district: 6,670 ft (2,033 m)

a·thwart (ə thwôrt′) ***prep.*** ⟦A-^{1} + THWART⟧ **1** across; from one side to the other of **2** against; opposed to **3** *Naut.* at right angles to the keel of —***adv.*** **1** crosswise; esp., across at a slant **2** so as to block or thwart

-at·ic (at′ik) ⟦< Fr or L; Fr *-atique* < L *-aticus* < Gr *-atikos* < base ending *-at* + suffix *-ikos*, -IC⟧ *suffix forming adjectives* of, of the kind of: used in words of Greek and Latin origin [*lymphatic*]

a·tilt (ə tilt′) ***adj., adv.*** ⟦A-^{1} + TILT^1⟧ **1** in a tilted, or inclined, position **2** tilting, or jousting, with or as with a lance

a·tin·gle (ə tiŋ′gəl) ***adj.*** ⟦A-^{1} + TINGLE⟧ tingling, as with excitement or pleasure

-a·tion (ā′shən) ⟦< Fr or L; Fr *-ation* < L *-ation(em)*, suffix formed from *-at-* of pp. of *-are* verbs (1st conjugation)⟧ *suffix forming nouns* **1** the act of ____ing [*alteration*] **2** the condition of being ____ed [*starvation*] **3** the result of ____ing [*compilation*]

-a·tive (ə tiv, āt′iv) ⟦< Fr or L; Fr *-atif*, fem. *-ative* < L *-ativus*⟧ *suffix forming adjectives* of or relating to, serving to, tending to [*demonstrative, informative, talkative*]

☆**At·ka mackerel** (at′kə) ⟦after *Atka* Island, in the Aleutians⟧ a commercially important ocean greenling (*Pleurogrammus monopterygius*) of the N Pacific, esp. the area off the Aleutian Islands: also called **Atka fish**

At·kin·son (at′kin sən), **(Justin) Brooks** (broo͝ks) 1894-1984; U.S. journalist & drama critic

Atl *abbrev.* Atlantic

At·lan·ta (at lan′tə) ⟦after Western & *Atlantic* Railroad, of which it was the terminus⟧ capital of Ga., in the NC part —**At·lan′tan** ***n.***

At·lan·te·an (at′lan tē′ən) ***adj.*** ⟦L *Atlanteus*, of Atlas, of the Atlantic < *Atlas*, ATLAS⟧ **1** of or like Atlas; strong **2** of Atlantis

at·lan·tes (at lan′tēz′) ***pl.n.***, *sing.* **at·las** (at′ləs) ⟦L < Gr *Atlantes*, pl. of *Atlas*⟧ *Archit.* supporting columns for an entablature, carved in the form of standing or kneeling figures of men

At·lan·tic (at lan′tik) ***adj.*** of, in, on, or near the Atlantic Ocean

Atlantic City city in SE N.J., on the Atlantic: an ocean resort

At·lan·ti·cism (at lan′tə siz′əm) ***n.*** a belief in the importance of maintaining cordial relations and a policy of close cooperation in economic and political matters between the U.S. and Europe —**At·lan′ti·cist** ***adj., n.***

Atlantic Ocean ⟦L *Atlanticum (mare)*, Atlantic (ocean) < *Atlanticus*, of the Atlas Mountains < *Atlas*, ATLAS⟧ ocean touching the American continents to the west and Europe and Africa to the east: *c.* 33,420,000 sq mi (86,557,466 sq km); greatest known depth, *c.* 28,000 ft (8,500 m): often **Atlantic**

Atlantic Standard Time a standard time used in the zone which includes Bermuda, Nova Scotia, New Brunswick, and E Quebec, corresponding to the mean solar time of the 60th meridian west of Greenwich, England: it is four hours behind Greenwich time

At·lan·tis (at lan′tis) ***n.*** ⟦L < Gr⟧ legendary island or continent supposed to have existed in the Atlantic west of Gibraltar and to have sunk into the ocean

-at-large (at′lärj′) *combining form see* AT LARGE (senses 4-5) at LARGE [*councillor-at-large*]

At·las (at′ləs) ***n.*** ⟦L < Gr < prothetic *a-* + *tlan*, bearing < IE base **tel-*, **tla-*, to lift, bear > TOLERATE, THOLE^2⟧ **1** *Gr. Myth.* a Titan compelled to support the heavens on his shoulders **2** any person who carries a great burden **3** [**a-**] *a)* a book of maps: Atlas supporting the earth was often pictured on the front page of such books *b)* a book of tables, charts, illustrations, etc. on a specific subject or subjects [an anatomical *atlas*] **4** [**a-**] *Anat.* the topmost vertebra of the neck **5** [**a-**] *Archit. sing. of* ATLANTES

Atlas Mountains mountain system in NW Africa, extending *c.* 1,500 mi (2,414 km) across Morocco, Algeria, and Tunisia: highest peak (in Morocco), *c.* 13,600 ft (4,145 m)

At·li (ät′lē) ***n.*** ⟦ON < Goth *Attila*, ATTILA⟧ *Norse Myth.* a king of the Huns: he is killed by his wife, Gudrun, because he has killed her brothers for Sigurd's treasure

atm *abbrev.* atmosphere

ATM^1 (ā′tē em′) ***n.*** ⟦*a(utomated) t(eller) m(achine)*⟧ a computer terminal that allows a bank customer to deposit, withdraw, or transfer funds automatically

ATM^2 *abbrev.* asynchronous transfer mode

at·man (ät′mən) ***n.*** ⟦Sans *ātmā*, breath, soul, Supreme Spirit < IE **ēt-men*, breath > OE *æthm*, Ger *atem*⟧ *Hinduism* **1** the individual soul or ego **2** [**A-**] the universal soul; source of all individual souls

at·mom·e·ter (at mäm′ət ər) ***n.*** ⟦fol. + -METER⟧ an instrument for measuring the rate of evaporation of water into the atmosphere under varying conditions

at·mos·phere (at′məs fir′) ***n.*** ⟦ModL *atmosphaera* < Gr *atmos*, vapor + *sphaira*, sphere⟧ **1** the gaseous envelope (air) surrounding the earth to a height of *c.* 1,000 km (*c.* 621 mi): it is *c.* 21% oxygen, 78% nitrogen, and 1% other gases, and rotates with the earth, because of gravity **2** the gaseous mass surrounding any star, planet, etc. **3** the air in any given place **4** a pervading or surrounding influence or spirit; general mood or social environment **5** the general tone of a work of art [a play with a fateful *atmosphere*] **6** an interesting, often exotic, effect produced by decoration, furnishings, etc. [a restaurant with *atmosphere*] **7** *Physics* a standard unit of pressure used to measure atmospheric pressure, equal to the pressure exerted by a column of mercury that is 760 millimeters (29.9213 inches) high at 0°C at sea level (101,325 pascals, 1,013.25 millibars, or 14.70 pounds per square inch): abbrev. *atm*

at·mos·pher·ic (at′məs fer′ik, -fir′-) ***adj.*** **1** of or in the atmosphere [*atmospheric* lightning] **2** caused or produced by the atmosphere [*atmospheric* pressure] **3** having or giving an atmosphere [*atmospheric* music] —**at′mos·pher′i·cal·ly** ***adv.***

atmospheric pressure the pressure due to the weight of the earth's atmosphere, usually measured by a standard unit: see ATMOSPHERE (sense 7)

at·mos·pher·ics (-iks) ***pl.n.*** **1** *Radio a)* disturbances in reception, produced by natural electric discharges, as in a storm; static *b)* the phenomena producing these disturbances **2** prevailing mood or influence

at. no. *abbrev.* atomic number

at·oll (a′tôl′, -täl′) ***n.*** ⟦< *atolu,* in Maldive Is-lands dial. of Malayalam⟧ a ring-shaped coral island nearly or completely surrounding a lagoon

atoll

at·om (at′əm) ***n.*** ⟦ME *attome* < OFr *atome* < L *atomus* < Gr *atomos,* uncut, indivisible, atom < *a-,* not + *tomos* < *temnein,* to cut: see -TOMY⟧ **1** [Obs.] any of the indivisible particles postulated by philosophers as the basic component of all matter **2** a tiny particle of anything; jot **3** *Chem., Physics* any of the smallest particles of an element that combine with similar particles of other elements to produce compounds: atoms combine to form molecules, and consist of a complex arrangement of electrons revolving about a positively charged nucleus containing (except for hydrogen) protons and neutrons and other particles —**the atom** nuclear energy

atom bomb ATOMIC BOMB —**at′om-bomb′** ***vt.***

a·tom·ic (ə täm′ik) ***adj.*** **1** of an atom or atoms **2** of, using, or powered by nuclear energy *[*an *atomic* submarine*]* **3** involving the use of nuclear weapons *[atomic* warfare*]* **4** having its atoms in an uncombined form *[atomic* oxygen*]* **5** very small; minute —**a·tom′i·cal·ly** ***adv.***

☆**Atomic Age** [*also* **a- a-**] the period characterized by the use of atomic energy: regarded as beginning with the creation of the first self-sustaining nuclear chain reaction on December 2, 1942

☆**atomic bomb** an extremely destructive type of bomb, the power of which results from the immense quantity of energy suddenly released when a very rapid chain reaction of nuclear fission is set off by neutron bombardment in the atoms of a charge of plutonium (primarily Pu-239) or uranium (U-235)

atomic clock an extremely accurate clock whose precision depends upon the very constant frequency at which atoms (or molecules) of certain substances, as of cesium, rubidium, or ammonia, absorb or emit electromagnetic radiation

☆**atomic cocktail** a dose of medicine to be swallowed, containing a radioactive element, used in medical treatment and diagnosis, as of cancer

atomic disintegration a process resulting in the change of a radioactive nucleus, either by emission of an alpha, beta, or gamma ray or by fission, and producing a change in the original mass, atomic number, or energy

atomic energy NUCLEAR ENERGY

at·o·mic·i·ty (at′ə mis′ə tē) ***n.*** **1** the condition of being made up of atoms **2** *Chem. a)* the number of atoms in a molecule *b)* the number of replaceable atoms or groups of atoms in the molecule of a compound *c)* VALENCE

atomic mass the mass of a given atom, usually expressed in atomic mass units: it is the atomic weight multiplied by the atomic mass unit

atomic mass unit a unit of mass, exactly one twelfth the mass of a neutral atom of the most abundant isotope of carbon, carbon-12: one atomic mass unit equals 1.6605 x 10^{-24} gram and is equivalent to 931.48 MeV in energy: symbol *amu* or *u*

atomic number *Chem.* a number representing the relative position of an element in the periodic table, in which the elements are arranged in the order of their nuclear charges; a number representing the positive charge or the number of protons in the nucleus of the atom of an element: isotopes have the same atomic number but different mass numbers

☆**atomic pile** *former name for* NUCLEAR REACTOR

a·tom·ics (ə täm′iks) ***n.*** the science dealing with atomic structure and, esp., nuclear energy

atomic structure *Physics* a conventionalized, hypothetical concept of an atom, regarded as consisting of a central, positively charged nucleus and a number of negatively charged electrons revolving about it in various orbits: the number and arrangement of the electrons vary in the different elements

atomic theory the theory that all material objects and substances are composed of atoms, and that various phenomena are explained by the properties and interactions of these atoms

atomic volume *Chem.* the quotient obtained by dividing the atomic weight of an element by its density

atomic weight *Chem.* the weight of one atom of an element expressed in atomic mass units: it is the average weight of all the isotopes of the element

at·om·ism (at′əm iz′əm) ***n.*** ⟦ATOM + -ISM⟧ *Philos.* a theory that the universe is made up of tiny, simple, indivisible particles that cannot be destroyed —**at′om·ist** ***n., adj.***

at·om·is·tic (at′əm is′tik) ***adj.*** **1** of atoms or atomism **2** made up of a number of unrelated elements —**at′om·is′ti·cal·ly** ***adv.***

at·om·ize (at′əm īz′) ***vt.*** **-ized′, -iz′ing** **1** to separate into atoms **2** to reduce (a liquid) to a fine spray **3** to destroy by nuclear weapons **4** to separate into many parts or fragments; disintegrate —**at·om·i·za·tion** (at′ə mə zā′shən, -mī′-) ***n.***

at·om·iz·er (-ī′zər) ***n.*** a device used to shoot out a fine spray, as of medicine or perfume

☆**atom smasher** ACCELERATOR (sense 3)

at·o·my[1] (at′ə mē) ***n., pl.*** **-mies** ⟦faulty separation of *anatomy* as *an atomy,* by assoc. with ATOM⟧ [Archaic] a skeleton

at·o·my[2] (at′ə mē) ***n., pl.*** **-mies** ⟦< L *atomi,* pl. of *atomus,* ATOM⟧ [Archaic] **1** an atom; tiny thing **2** a tiny being; pygmy

a·ton·al (ā tōn′əl) ***adj.*** *Music* without a tonal center or key —**a·ton′al·ism′** ***n.*** —**a·ton′al·ist** ***n.*** —**a·ton′al·is′tic** ***adj.*** —**a·ton′al·ly** ***adv.***

a·to·nal·i·ty (ā′tō nal′ə tē) ***n.*** *Music* in composition, the organization of tones in which all tones of the chromatic scale have equal importance, without relation to a tonal center or key; the absence of tonality

a·tone (ə tōn′) ***vi.*** **a·toned′, a·ton′ing** ⟦ME *at-onen,* become reconciled < *at one,* in accord: see AT[1] & ONE⟧ **1** to make amends or reparation (*for* a wrongdoing, a wrongdoer, etc.) **2** [Obs.] to be in agreement —***vt.*** [Obs.] **1** to make amends for; expiate **2** to bring into agreement; reconcile

a·tone·ment (-mənt) ***n.*** **1** the act of atoning **2** satisfaction given for wrongdoing, injury, etc.; amends; expiation **3** [Obs.] agreement or reconciliation —**the Atonement** *Christian Theol.* humanity's reconciliation with God brought about by Christ's Redemption

a·ton·ic (ə tän′ik, ā-) ***adj.*** ⟦Fr *atonique* < Gr *atonia* (see fol. + Fr *-ique,* -IC⟧ **1** caused or characterized by atony **2** unaccented: said of a word or syllable —***n.*** ⟦< A-[2] + Gr *tonos,* accent, pitch; see TONE⟧ an unaccented syllable or word —**at·o·nic·i·ty** (at′ə nis′ə tē, ā′tō nis′-) ***n.***

at·o·ny (a′tə nē) ***n.*** ⟦Fr *atonie* < LL *atonia* < Gr *atonia,* languor < *a-,* not + *tonos,* tone < *teinein,* to stretch: see THIN⟧ lack of bodily tone or muscle tone

a·top (ə täp′) ***adv.*** on the top; at the top —***prep.*** on the top of

a·top·ic (ā täp′ik, ə-) ***adj.*** ⟦< *atopy,* a certain type of allergy < Gr *atopia,* strangeness < *atopos,* uncommon < *a-,* A-[2] (sense 3) + *topos,* a place⟧ designating or of any of various allergic conditions, including a type of dermatitis and a type of asthma, that are thought to be inherited

-a·tor (āt′ər) ⟦ME *-atour* < OFr < L *-ator:* see -ATE[1] & -OR⟧ *suffix forming nouns* one who or that which acts or does *[improvisator]*

-a·to·ry (ə tôr′ē, ə tō′rē) ⟦L *-atorius* < *-ator,* n. ending + *-ius,* adj. suffix⟧ *suffix* -ORY

ATP (ā′tē′pē′) ***n.*** ⟦A(DENOSINE) T(RI)P(HOSPHATE)⟧ a nucleotide, $C_{10}H_{16}P_3O_{13}N_5$, present in, and vital to the energy processes of, all living cells: see ADP[1]

at·ra·bil·i·ous (a′trə bil′ē əs, -bil′yəs) ***adj.*** ⟦< L *atra bilis,* black bile; sp. after BILIOUS: cf. MELANCHOLY⟧ melancholy, morose, cross, etc.: also **at′ra·bil′i·ar** (-ē ər)

at·ra·zine (a′trə zēn′) ***n.*** ⟦A(MINO) + TR(I)AZINE⟧ a white, crystalline compound, $C_8H_{14}ClN_5$, widely used as a herbicide to control grassy weeds

a·trem·ble (ə trem′bəl) ***adv.*** ⟦A-[1] + TREMBLE⟧ [Old Poet.] trembling

a·tre·sia (ə trē′zhə) ***n.*** ⟦ModL, ult. < Gr *a-,* A-[2] (sense 3) + *trēsis,* perforation⟧ an abnormality of the structure of a canal, duct, or body opening caused by a failure to develop properly or by an acquired closure, as with scar tissue

A·tre·us (ā′trē əs) ***n.*** ⟦L < Gr⟧ *Gr. Myth.* a king of Mycenae and father of Agamemnon and Menelaus: to avenge the treachery of his brother, Thyestes, he kills Thyestes' sons and serves their flesh to him at a banquet

a·tri·o·ven·tric·u·lar (ā′trē ō ven trik′yə lər) ***adj.*** of or having to do with an atrium and a ventricle of the heart

a·tri·um (ā′trē əm) ***n., pl.*** **a′tri·a** (-ə) or **a′tri·ums** ⟦L⟧ **1** the central court or main room of an ancient Roman house **2** a hall or court at the center or entrance of a building, usually rising through more than one story or all the stories and having a skylight or glass on one side and the roof **3** *Anat.* a chamber or cavity, esp. either of the thin-walled upper chambers of the heart that receive blood; auricle —**a′tri·al** (-əl) ***adj.***

a·tro·cious (ə trō′shəs) ***adj.*** ⟦< L *atrox* (gen. *atrocis*), fierce, cruel < *ater,* black + *-ox* < ? base of *oculus,* EYE⟧ **1** very cruel, evil, brutal, etc. **2** appalling or dismaying **3** very bad, unpleasant, offensive, inferior, etc. *[*an *atrocious* joke*]* —**SYN.** OUTRAGEOUS —**a·tro′cious·ly** ***adv.*** —**a·tro′cious·ness** ***n.***

a·troc·i·ty (ə träs′ə tē) ***n., pl.*** **-ties** ⟦L *atrocitas* < *atrox:* see prec. ⟧ **1** atrocious behavior or condition; brutality, cruelty, etc. **2** an atrocious act **3** [Informal] a very displeasing or tasteless thing

at·ro·phy (a′trə fē) ***n.*** ⟦< LL *atrophia* < Gr, a wasting away < *a-,* not + *trephein,* to feed: see TROPHIC⟧ a wasting away, esp. of bodily tissue, an organ, etc., or the failure of an organ or part to grow or develop, as because of insufficient nutrition —***vi.*** **-phied, -phy·ing** to waste away or fail to develop —***vt.*** to cause atrophy in —**a·troph·ic** (ə träf′ik) ***adj.***

at·ro·pine (at′rə pēn′, -pin) ***n.*** ⟦< ModL *Atropa,* genus name of belladonna < Gr *Atropos* (see fol.) + -INE[3]⟧ a poisonous, crystalline alkaloid, $C_{17}H_{23}NO_3$, obtained from belladonna and similar plants: used to relieve spasms and dilate the pupil of the eye: also **at′ro·pin** (-pin)

At·ro·pos (a′trə päs′) ***n.*** ⟦L < Gr lit., not to be turned < *a-,* not + *trepein,* to turn: see TROPE⟧ *Class. Myth.* that one of the three Fates who cuts the thread of life

att *abbrev.* **1** attached **2** attention **3** attorney

at·ta·boy (at′ə boi′) ***interj.*** ⟦prob. < *that's the boy!*⟧ [Informal] indicating approval or encouragement: said to a man or boy: also written **atta boy**

at·tach (ə tach′) ***vt.*** ⟦ME *attachen* < OFr *atacher,* altered by substitution of prefix < *estachier,* to attach < *estache,* a post, stake < Frank **stakka:* see STICK⟧ **1** to fasten by sticking, tying, etc. **2** to make (a person or thing) part of; join: often used reflexively *[*he *attached* himself to us*]* **3** to connect by ties of affection, attraction, etc. **4** to add or affix (a signature, codicil, etc.) **5** to ascribe *[*I *attach* great significance to the news*]* **6** to appoint by authority or order **7** *Law* to take (property) into custody of a court by writ **8** *Mil.* to join (troops, a unit, etc.) temporarily to some other unit —***vi.*** to be fastened or joined; adhere; belong *[*the advantages that *attach* to wealth*]* —**SYN.** ASCRIBE, TIE —**at·tach′a·ble** ***adj.***

at·ta·ché (at′ə shā′; *chiefly Brit* ə tash′ā) ***n.*** ⟦Fr, pp. of *attacher,* prec.⟧ a person with special duties on the diplomatic staff of an ambassador or minister to another country

attaché case a flat, rectangular case, as for carrying documents

at·tach·ment (ə tach′mənt) *n.* **1** the act of attaching something **2** anything used for attaching; fastening **3** affectionate regard or devotion **4** anything added or attached **5** an accessory for an electrical appliance, machine, etc. **6** *Law a)* a taking of property into the custody of a court *b)* a writ authorizing this —**SYN.** LOVE

at·tack (ə tak′) *vt.* ⟦Fr *attaquer* < It *attaccare* < **estaccare* < Goth **stakka*, stake: see STICK⟧ **1** to use force against in order to harm; start a fight with; strike out at with physical or military force; assault **2** to speak or write against, esp. with vigor; criticize, denounce, censure, etc. **3** to begin working on energetically; undertake (a problem, task, etc.) vigorously **4** to begin acting upon harmfully or destructively [the disease *attacked* him suddenly] —*vi.* to make an assault —*n.* **1** the act of attacking **2** any hostile offensive action, esp. with armed forces; onslaught **3** the onset of a disease, or the recurrence of a chronic disease **4** a beginning of any task, undertaking, etc. **5** act or manner of such beginning **6** *Music* promptness and precision in beginning a passage or phrase —*adj.* **1** designed or used for carrying out a hostile or aggressive attack [a political *attack* ad] **2** trained to attack on command [an *attack* dog] —**at·tack′er** *n.*

SYN.—attack implies vigorous, aggressive action, whether in actual combat or in an undertaking [to *attack* a city, a problem, etc.]; **assail** means to attack by repeated blows, thrusts, etc. [*assailed* by reproaches]; **assault** implies a sudden, violent attack or onslaught and suggests direct contact and the use of force; **beset** implies an attack or onset from all sides [*beset* with fears]; **storm** suggests a rushing, powerful assault that is stormlike in its action and effect; **bombard** means to attack with artillery or bombs, and in figurative use suggests persistent, repetitious action [to *bombard* a speaker with questions] —**ANT. defend, resist**

at·ta·girl (at′ə gurl′) *interj.* ⟦prob. < *that's the girl!* by analogy with ATTABOY⟧ [Informal] indicating approval or encouragement: said to a woman or girl: also written **atta girl**

at·tain (ə tān′) *vt.* ⟦ME *attainen* < OFr *ataindre* < L *attingere* < *ad-*, to + *tangere*, to touch: see TACT⟧ **1** to gain through effort; accomplish; achieve **2** to reach or come to; arrive at [he *attained* the age of ninety] —*vi.* to succeed in reaching or coming (*to* a goal) —**SYN.** REACH —**at·tain′a·bil′i·ty** *n.* —**at·tain′a·ble** *adj.*

at·tain·der (ə tān′dər) *n.* ⟦ME *atteindre* < Anglo-Fr *atteinder*, inf. used as n. < OFr *ataindre* (see prec.); sense infl. by ME *atteinten*, ATTAINT⟧ **1** forfeiture of property and loss of civil rights of a person sentenced to death or outlawed: see BILL OF ATTAINDER **2** [Obs.] dishonor

at·tain·ment (ə tān′mənt) *n.* **1** an attaining or being attained **2** anything attained, as an acquired skill; accomplishment

at·taint (ə tānt′) *vt.* **-taint′ed, -taint′ing** ⟦ME *atteinten*, to convict < OFr *ateint*, pp. of *ataindre* (see ATTAIN); sense infl. by Anglo-Fr *teinte*, TAINT⟧ **1** to punish by attainder **2** [Archaic] to disgrace or dishonor **3** [Archaic] to infect **4** [Archaic] to accuse **5** [Obs.] to prove guilty —*n.* **1** an attainder **2** [Archaic] a taint; disgrace **3** [Obs.] a touch or hit in tilting

at·tain·ture (ə tān′chər) *n.* [Obs.] **1** attainder **2** dishonor

at·tar (at′ər) *n.* ⟦Pers *ʿatar*, fragrance < Ar *ʿuṭūr*, *ʿoṭār*, pl. of *ʿiṭr*, perfume⟧ an essential oil or perfume made from the petals of flowers, esp. of damask roses (**attar of roses**)

at·tempt (ə tempt′) *vt.* ⟦ME *attempten* < OFr *attempter* < L *attemptare*, to try, solicit < *ad-*, to + *temptare*, to try: see TEMPT⟧ **1** to make an effort to do, get, have, etc.; try; endeavor **2** [Archaic] to tempt —*n.* **1** a try **2** an attack, as on a person's life —**SYN.** TRY —**attempt the life of** to try to kill —**at·tempt′a·ble** *adj.*

at·tend (ə tend′) *vt.* ⟦ME *attenden* < OFr *atendre*, to wait, expect < L *attendere*, to stretch toward, give heed to < *ad-*, to + *tendere*, stretch: see THIN⟧ **1** [Now Rare] to take care or charge of; look after **2** *a)* to wait on; minister to; serve *b)* to serve as doctor to during an illness **3** to accompany; go with **4** to accompany as a circumstance or result [success *attended* his efforts] **5** to be present at [to *attend* a concert] **6** [Archaic] to await **7** [Archaic] to pay attention to —*vi.* **1** to pay attention; give heed **2** to be in readiness; wait: with *on* or *upon* **3** to devote or apply oneself (*to*) **4** to give the required care or attention (*to*) **5** [Obs.] to wait or delay —**SYN.** ACCOMPANY

at·tend·ance (ə ten′dəns) *n.* **1** the act of attending **2** the persons or number of persons attending **3** the degree of regularity in attending

attendance officer a school official who deals with cases of truancy

at·tend·ant (-dənt) *adj.* **1** attending or serving [an *attendant* nurse] **2** being present **3** accompanying as a circumstance or result [*attendant* difficulties] —*n.* **1** a person who attends or serves [an *attendant* at the zoo, a queen's *attendants*] **2** a person present **3** an accompanying thing; concomitant

at·ten·dee (ə ten dē′, -ten′dē; at′en dē) *n.* a person who attends or is present at a meeting, gathering, etc.

at·ten·tat (á tän tá′) *n.* ⟦Fr⟧ an attempt, esp. an unsuccessful one, at an act of political violence

at·ten·tion (ə ten′shən) *n.* ⟦L *attentio* < pp. of *attendere*: see ATTEND⟧ **1** *a)* the act of keeping one's mind closely on something or the ability to do this; mental concentration *b)* mental readiness for such concentration **2** notice or observation [her smile caught my *attention*] **3** care or consideration [the matter will receive his immediate *attention*] **4** *a)* thoughtful consideration for others *b)* [*pl.*] acts of consideration, courtesy, or devotion [a suitor's *attentions* to a woman] **5** *Mil. a)* the erect, motionless posture of soldiers in readiness for another command *b)* a command to assume this posture

attention deficit (hyperactivity) disorder a psychological disorder, assessed on the basis of behavior appropriate to a given mental age, characterized by inability to concentrate, hyperactivity, impulsiveness, etc.: also written **attention-deficit (hyperactivity) disorder**

attention span the duration of a person's ability to concentrate or pay attention

at·ten·tive (ə ten′tiv) *adj.* ⟦ME & OFr *attentif* < ML *attentivus*: see ATTEND⟧ **1** paying attention; observant **2** considerate, courteous, devoted, etc. [an *attentive* husband] —**SYN.** THOUGHTFUL —**at·ten′tive·ly** *adv.* —**at·ten′tive·ness** *n.*

at·ten·u·ate (ə ten′yo͞o āt′; *for adj.*, -it, -āt′) *vt.* **-at′ed, -at′ing** ⟦< L *attenuatus*, pp. of *attenuare*, to make thin < *ad-* to + *tenuare* < *tenuis*, THIN⟧ **1** to make slender or thin **2** to dilute or rarefy **3** to lessen in severity, value, amount, intensity, etc.; weaken **4** *Electronics* to reduce the amplitude or strength of (an electrical signal) **5** *Microbiol.* to reduce the virulence of (a bacterium or virus) usually to make a vaccine —*vi.* to become thin, weak, etc. —*adj.* **1** attenuated **2** *Bot.* tapering gradually to a point, as the base of a leaf —**at·ten′u·a′tion** *n.* —**at·ten′u·a′tor** *n.*

at·test (ə test′) *vt.* ⟦Fr *attester* < L *attestari* < *ad-*, to + *testari*, to bear witness < *testis*, a witness: see TESTIFY⟧ **1** to declare to be true or genuine **2** to certify by oath or signature **3** to serve as proof of; demonstrate; make clear **4** to place (a person) under oath **5** *Linguis.* to verify the existence of (a form believed to have occurred in a language) [an *attested* form is written in an etymology without an asterisk before it] —*vi.* to bear witness; certify or testify (*to*) —**at·test′er** *n.*, **at·tes′tor**

at·tes·ta·tion (at′əs tā′shən, -es-) *n.* **1** the act of attesting **2** testimony

at·tic (at′ik) *n.* ⟦Fr *attique*, an attic < *Attique*, ATTIC, used as an architectural term⟧ **1** a low wall or story above the cornice of a classical facade **2** the room or space just below the roof of a house; garret

At·tic (at′ik) *adj.* ⟦L *Atticus* < Gr *Attikos*⟧ **1** of Attica **2** of or characteristic of Athens, esp. ancient Athens, or its people, language, or culture; Athenian **3** classical; simple, restrained, etc.: said of a style —*n.* the variety of Greek spoken in ancient Attica, which became the literary language of ancient Greece

At·ti·ca (at′i kə) ⟦Gr *Attikē*⟧ **1** state of ancient Greece, occupying a peninsula in the SE part &, after the 5th cent. B.C., a region dominated by Athens **2** region of modern Greece, in the same general area

Attic faith unshakable faith

At·ti·cism (at′ə siz′əm) *n.* ⟦Gr *Attikismos* < *Attikos*, ATTIC⟧ [*also* **a-**] **1** an Attic idiom, style, custom, etc. **2** a graceful, restrained phrase —**At′ti·cize′** (-sīz′) *vt., vi.* **-cized′, -ciz′ing**

Attic salt (or wit) graceful, piercing wit

At·ti·la (at′'l ə, ə til′ə) ⟦Goth *atta*, father (< baby talk) + *-ila*, dim. suffix⟧ A.D. 406?-453; king of the Huns (433?-453): called *Attila the Hun*

at·tire (ə tīr′) *vt.* **-tired′, -tir′ing** ⟦ME *atiren* < OFr *atirier*, to put in order, arrange < *a tire*, in a row, in order; *a* (L *ad*), to + *tire*, order, row, dress: see TIER[1]⟧ to dress, esp. in fine garments; clothe; array —*n.* clothes, esp. fine or rich apparel; finery

at·ti·tude (at′ə to͞od′, -tyo͞od′) *n.* ⟦Fr < It *attitudine*, attitude, aptness < LL *aptitudo* (gen. *aptitudinis*) < L *aptus*, APT[1]⟧ **1** the position or posture assumed by the body in connection with an action, feeling, mood, etc. [to kneel in an *attitude* of prayer] **2** a manner of acting, feeling, or thinking that shows one's disposition, opinion, etc. [a friendly *attitude*] **3** one's disposition, opinion, mental set, etc. **4** *Aeron.* the position of an aircraft or spacecraft in relation to a given line or plane, as the horizon **5** *Ballet* a position in which one leg is raised with the knee bent and the arms are extended **6** [Slang] *a)* a quarrelsome or sullen disposition or temperament *b)* a posture or pose of being cocky, haughty, etc. —**SYN.** POSTURE —**strike an attitude** to assume a posture or pose, often an affected or theatrical one —**at′ti·tu′di·nal** (-to͞od′'n əl, -tyo͞od′-) *adj.*

at·ti·tu·di·nize (at′ə to͞od′'n īz′, -tyo͞od′-) *vi.* **-nized′, -niz′ing** ⟦see prec. & -IZE⟧ to strike an attitude; pose

Att·lee (at′lē), **Clement Richard** 1st Earl Attlee 1883-1967; Brit. statesman: prime minister (1945-51)

Attn or **attn** *abbrev.* attention

at·to- (at′ō) ⟦< Dan *atten*, eighteen < ODan *attan* < *atta*, EIGHT + *-tjan*; akin to OE *-tyne*, -TEEN⟧ *combining form* one quintillionth part of; the factor 10^{-18} [*attosecond*]

at·torn (ə turn′) *vi.* ⟦ME *attournen* < OFr *atourner* < *a-* (L *ad*), to + *torner*, TURN⟧ **1** *Feudal Law* to transfer homage and service from one feudal lord to another **2** to agree to continue as tenant under a new landlord —**at·torn′ment** *n.*

at·tor·ney (ə tur′nē) *n., pl.* **-neys** ⟦ME *attourne* < OFr *atourne*, (one) appointed, pp. of *atourner*: see prec.⟧ any person legally empowered to act as agent for, or in behalf of, another; esp., a lawyer —**SYN.** LAWYER

attorney at law a lawyer

attorney general *pl.* **attorneys general** or **attorney generals** **1** the chief law officer and representative in legal matters of a national or state government, and the legal advisor to the chief executive **2** [**A- G-**] the head of the U.S. Department of Justice and member of the President's Cabinet

at·tract (ə trakt′) *vt.* ⟦ME *attracten* < L *attractus*, pp. of *attrahere*, to draw to < *ad-*, to + *trahere*, DRAW⟧ **1** to draw to itself or oneself; make approach or adhere [magnets *attract* iron] **2** to get the admiration, attention, etc. of;

allure [his smile *attracted* her] —*vi.* to be attractive —**at·tract′a·ble** *adj.* —**at·tract′er** *n.*, **at·trac′tor**

SYN.—**attract** implies the exertion of a force such as magnetism to draw a person or thing and connotes susceptibility in the thing drawn; **allure** implies attraction by that which seductively offers pleasure, delight, reward, etc.; **charm** suggests the literal or figurative casting of a spell and implies very pleasing qualities in the agent; **fascinate** and **enchant** both also suggest a magical power, **fascinate** stressing irresistibility and **enchant** the evoking of great delight; **captivate** implies a capturing of the attention or affection, but suggests a light, passing influence —*ANT.* **repel**

at·tract·ant (ə trak′tənt) *n.* something that attracts; esp., a chemical pheromone that attracts insects

at·trac·tion (ə trak′shən) *n.* **1** the act of attracting or condition of being attracted **2** power to attract; charm or fascination **3** anything that attracts or is meant to attract ["coming *attractions*" at the movies] **4** *Physics* the mutual action by which bodies or particles of matter tend to draw together or cohere: opposed to REPULSION

attraction sphere CENTROSPHERE (sense 1)

at·trac·tive (ə trak′tiv) *adj.* ⟦ME < LL *attractivus*⟧ that attracts or has the power to attract; esp., pleasing, charming, pretty, handsome, etc. —**at·trac′tive·ly** *adv.* —**at·trac′tive·ness** *n.*

attrib *abbrev.* attributive

at·trib·ute (ə trib′yo͞ot; *for n.* a′trə byo͞ot′) *vt.* **-ut·ed, -ut·ing** ⟦< L *attributus*, pp. of *attribuere*, to assign < *ad-*, to + *tribuere*, to assign < *tribus*: see TRIBE⟧ **1** to set down or think of as belonging to, produced by, resulting from, or originating in; assign or ascribe (*to*) [the play is *attributed* to Shakespeare] **2** to ascribe as a quality or characteristic —*n.* **1** a characteristic or quality of a person or thing **2** an object used in literature or art as a symbol for a person, office, etc. [winged feet are the *attribute* of Mercury] **3** *Gram.* a word or phrase used adjectivally —*SYN.* ASCRIBE, QUALITY —**at·trib′ut·a·ble** (-yo͞ot ə bəl) *adj.* —**at·tri·bu·tion** (a′trə byo͞o′shən) *n.*

at·trib·u·tive (ə trib′yo͞o tiv, -yə-) *adj.* ⟦Fr *attributif*⟧ **1** attributing **2** of or like an attribute **3** *Gram.* joined directly to (in English, generally preceding) the substantive that it modifies: said of an adjective —*n. Gram.* an attributive adjective ["black" in "black cat" is an *attributive*] —**at·trib′u·tive·ly** *adv.*

NOTE—in this dictionary the phrase "used attributively" is used of certain nouns that frequently function as adjectives

at·trit·ed (ə trīt′id) *adj.* ⟦< L *attritus*: see fol.⟧ worn down by friction or attrition

at·tri·tion (ə trish′ən) *n.* ⟦ME *attricioun* < L *attritio* < *attritus*, pp. of *atterere*, to wear, rub away < *ad-*, to + *terere*, to rub: see THROW⟧ **1** the act or process of wearing away or grinding down by friction **2** any gradual wearing or weakening, esp. to the point of exhaustion [a siege is a battle of *attrition*] **3** loss of personnel in an organization in the normal course of events, as by retirement **4** *Theol.* repentance that is not perfect because not prompted solely by sorrow for having offended God: cf. CONTRITION (sense 2)

At·tu (at′o͞o) westernmost island of the Aleutians: 338 sq mi (875 sq km)

at·tune (ə to͞on′, -tyo͞on′) *vt.* **-tuned′, -tun′ing** ⟦AT- (var. of AD-) + TUNE⟧ **1** to tune **2** to bring into harmony or agreement [old methods not *attuned* to the times]

atty *abbrev.* attorney

Atty Gen *abbrev.* Attorney General

☆**ATV** (ā′tē′vē′) *n.*, *pl.* **ATVs** ⟦*a*(*ll-*)*t*(*errain*) *v*(*ehicle*)⟧ a small, amphibious motor vehicle with wheels or tractor treads for traveling over rough ground, snow, and ice, and through shallow water

at vol *abbrev.* atomic volume

a·twain (ə twān′) *adv.* ⟦ME: see A-[1] & TWAIN⟧ [Archaic] in two [cut *atwain*]

a·twit·ter (ə twit′ər) *adj.* in a state of nervous excitement

at wt *abbrev.* atomic weight

a·typ·i·cal (ā tip′i kəl) *adj.* not typical; not characteristic; abnormal: also **a·typ′ic** —**a·typ′i·cal·ly** *adv.*

Au[1] *abbrev.* author

Au[2] ⟦L *aurum*⟧ *Chem. symbol for* gold

AU *abbrev.* **1** African Union **2** angstrom unit(s) **3** astronomical unit(s)

au·bade (ō bäd′; *Fr* ō bȧd′) *n.* ⟦Fr < Sp *albada* < Prov *alba*, dawn: see ALBA⟧ **1** a piece of music composed for performance in the morning: cf. SERENADE **2** a lyric love poem about or suitable for dawn

Au·ber (ō ber′), **Da·niel (François Esprit)** (dȧ nyel′) 1782-1871; Fr. composer of operas

au·berge (ō berzh′) *n.* ⟦Fr⟧ an inn

au·ber·gine (ō′bər zhēn′, -jēn′) *n.* ⟦Fr < Catalan *albergínia* < Ar *al-bādhinjān* < Pers *bādindjan*⟧ **1** [Brit.] eggplant **2** dark purple

Au·brey[1] (ô′brē) *n.* ⟦Fr *Aubri* < Ger *Alberich* < OHG *alb*, ELF + *rihhi*, ruler, realm: see REICH⟧ a masculine name

Au·brey[2] (ô′brē), **John** 1626-97; Eng. biographer & antiquary

au·brie·ta (ô brēt′ə) *n.* ⟦ModL, after Claude *Aubriet*, 18th-c. Fr painter of floral and animal subjects⟧ any of a genus (*Aubrieta*) of plants of the crucifer family native to the Middle East, with showy, purplish flowers: often grown in rock gardens: also **au·bre′ti·a** or **au·brie′ti·a** (-brē′shə, -shē ə)

au·burn (ô′bərn) *adj.*, *n.* ⟦ME *auburne* < OFr *auborne* < ML *alburnus* < L *albus*, white (see ELF); meaning infl. by ME *brun*, BROWN⟧ reddish brown

Au·bus·son (ō′bə sən; *Fr* ō bü sōn′) *adj.* ⟦after *Aubusson*, town in central France⟧ designating or of tapestries or tapestrylike rugs of a kind made in the Aubusson region of France

A.U.C. or **AUC** *abbrev.* ⟦L *ab urbe condita* or *anno urbis conditae*⟧ used by the ancient Romans to identify a particular year in terms of the founding of the city of Rome, traditionally 753 B.C. (Ex.: 754 A.U.C. = the year A.D. 1)

Auck·land (ôk′lənd) seaport of N North Island, New Zealand

au con·traire (ō kōn trer′) ⟦Fr⟧ on the contrary

au cou·rant (ō ko͞o rän′; *Fr*, -rän′) ⟦Fr, lit., with the current⟧ fully informed on current matters; up-to-date

auc·tion (ôk′shən) *n.* ⟦L *auctio*, an increasing, sale by increase of bids < *auctus*, pp. of *augere*, to increase: see WAX[2]⟧ **1** a public sale at which items are sold one by one, each going to the last and highest of a series of competing bidders **2** AUCTION BRIDGE **3** the bidding in bridge **4** *Finance* a sale of government securities in which competitive bidding determines their yield —*vt.* to sell at an auction —*SYN.* SELL —**auction off** to sell at auction —☆**put up at auction** to offer for sale at an auction

auction bridge a variety of the game of bridge in which the players bid for the right to say what suit shall be trump or to declare no-trump: the extra tricks the declarer wins beyond his or her bid count toward a game: see also CONTRACT BRIDGE

auc·tion·eer (ôk′shən ir′) *n.* a person whose work is selling things at an auction —*vt.* to sell at an auction

auc·to·ri·al (ôk tôr′ē əl) *adj.* ⟦< L *auctor*, AUTHOR + -AL⟧ of or by an author

au·cu·ba (ô′kyo͞o bə) *n.* ⟦ModL, prob. < Jpn < *ao*, green + *ki*, tree + *ha*, leaf⟧ any of a genus (*Aucuba*) of evergreen shrubs of the dogwood family, grown for their variegated foliage and red berries

aud *abbrev.* **1** audit **2** auditor

au·da·cious (ô dā′shəs) *adj.* ⟦< L *audacia*, audacity < *audax* (gen. *audacis*), bold < *audere*, to dare, be bold⟧ **1** bold or daring; fearless **2** not restrained by a sense of shame or propriety; rudely bold; brazen —*SYN.* BRAVE —**au·da′cious·ly** *adv.* —**au·da′cious·ness** *n.*

au·dac·i·ty (ô das′ə tē) *n.* ⟦ME *audacite* < L *audacia*: see prec. ⟧ **1** bold courage; daring **2** shameless or brazen boldness; insolence **3** *pl.* **-ties** an audacious act or remark —*SYN.* TEMERITY

Au·den (ôd′′n), **W(ystan) H(ugh)** 1907-73; Brit. poet, in the U.S. 1939-70

au·di·ble (ô′də bəl) *adj.* ⟦LL *audibilis* < L *audire*: see fol.⟧ that can be heard; loud enough to be heard —*n.* ☆*Football* a play decided upon and called by the quarterback at the line of scrimmage —**au′di·bil′i·ty** (-bil′ə tē) *n.* —**au′di·bly** *adv.*

au·di·ence (ô′dē əns) *n.* ⟦ME & OFr < L *audientia*, a hearing, listening < *audiens*, prp. of *audire*, to hear < IE **awiz-dh-io* < base **awis-*, to perceive physically, grasp > AESTHETE⟧ **1** [Obs.] the act or state of hearing **2** a group of persons assembled to hear and see a speaker, a play, a concert, etc. **3** all those persons who are tuned in to a particular radio or TV program ☆**4** all those persons who read what one writes or hear what one says; one's public **5** an opportunity to have one's ideas heard; a hearing **6** a formal interview with a person in a high position

au·dile (ô′dīl′, -dil′) *adj.* ⟦< L *audire* (see prec.) + -ILE⟧ auditory

au·di·o (ô′dē ō′) *adj.* ⟦< L *audire*: see AUDIENCE⟧ **1** of frequencies corresponding to sound waves that can normally be heard by the human ear ☆**2** of or relating to the reproduction of sound, esp. as distinguished from video, as in a telecast or videotape —*n.* **1** the sound portion of a telecast, webcast, recording, etc. **2** *short for* AUDIOCASSETTE, AUDIOTAPE, etc. Cf. VIDEO

au·di·o- (ô′dē ō) ⟦see prec.⟧ *combining form* hearing or sound

au·di·o·book (ô′dē ō bo͝ok′) *n.* a recording, as for use on a portable listening device, of a reading of a book by the author or by an actor

au·di·o·cas·sette (ô′dē ō kə set′) *n.* a cassette containing audiotape: also written **audio cassette**

au·di·o-fre·quen·cy (ô′dē ō frē′kwən sē) *adj.* of the band of audible sound frequencies or corresponding electric current frequencies, about 20 to 20,000 hertz

au·di·o·gram (ô′dē ō gram′, -dē ə-) *n.* a graph showing the percentage of hearing loss in a particular ear, as indicated by an audiometer

au·di·ol·o·gy (ô′dē äl′ə jē) *n.* **1** the science of hearing **2** the evaluation of hearing defects and the rehabilitation of those who have such defects —**au′di·o·log′i·cal** (-ə läj′i kəl) *adj.* —**au′di·ol′o·gist** *n.*

au·di·om·e·ter (ô′dē äm′ət ər) *n.* an instrument for measuring the sharpness and range of hearing through the use of controlled amounts of sound —**au′di·o·met′ric** (-ō me′trik) *adj.* —**au′di·om′e·trist** *n.* —**au′di·om′e·try** (-trē) *n.*

au·di·o·phile (ô′dē ō fīl′, -dē ə-) *n.* a devotee of high-fidelity sound reproduction, as from recordings

au·di·o·tape (ô′dē ō tāp′) *n.* a magnetic tape for recording and playing back sound: cf. VIDEOTAPE: also written **audio tape**

au·di·o·vis·u·al (ô′dē ō vizh′o͞o əl) *adj.* **1** involving both hearing and sight **2** designating or of teaching materials or aids other than books, such as films, videos, filmstrips, recordings, etc. —*n.* [*pl.*] audiovisual teaching materials or aids

☆**au·di·phone** (ô′də fōn′) *n.* ⟦AUDI(O)- + -PHONE⟧ a device for the hard of hearing that transmits sound to the auditory nerves through the bones of the head, as by being placed against the teeth

au·dit (ôd′it) *n.* ⟦ME < L *auditus*, a hearing, pp. of *audire*: see AUDIENCE⟧ **1** a formal, often periodic examination and checking of accounts or financial records to verify their correctness **2** a settlement or adjustment of accounts **3** an account thus examined and adjusted **4** a final statement

of account by auditors **5** any thorough examination and evaluation of a problem —*vt., vi.* **1** to examine and check (accounts, claims, etc.) **2** to attend (a college course) simply to hear the lectures without receiving credit
au·di·tion (ô dish′ən) *n.* ⟦L *auditio* < pp. of *audire*: see AUDIENCE⟧ **1** the act or sense of hearing **2** a hearing to test the fitness of an actor, musician, etc., as for a particular job —☆*vt.* to give an audition to —☆*vi.* to perform in an audition
au·di·tor (ô′dit ər) *n.* ⟦ME < L < *audire*: see AUDIENCE⟧ **1** a hearer or listener **2** *a)* a person authorized to audit accounts *b)* a public official who audits government accounts, distributes revenues, assesses real estate, inspects scales, etc. ☆**3** a person who audits a college course
au·di·to·ri·um (ô′də tôr′ē əm) *n., pl.* **-ri·ums** or **-ri·a** ⟦L, neut. of *auditorius*: see fol.⟧ **1** a room for the gathering of an audience, as in a school, library, etc. ☆**2** a building or hall for speeches, concerts, etc.
au·di·to·ry (ô′də tôr′ē) *adj.* ⟦L *auditorius* < *auditor*, AUDITOR⟧ of or having to do with hearing or the organs of hearing —*n., pl.* **-ries** ⟦L *auditorium*⟧ [Archaic] **1** an assembly of hearers; audience **2** an auditorium —**au′di·to′ri·ly** *adv.*
auditory nerve either of the eighth pair of cranial nerves, which connect the ear with the brain and carry impulses relating to sound and balance
Au·drey (ô′drē) *n.* ⟦ult. < OE *æthelthryth*, lit., noble might < *æthel*, noble + *thryth*, might, strength⟧ a feminine name
Au·du·bon (ô′də bän′), **John James** 1785-1851; U.S. ornithologist, naturalist, & painter, born in Haiti: famed for his paintings of North American birds
au fait (ō fe′) ⟦Fr, lit., to the fact, in fact⟧ **1** acquainted with the facts; well-informed **2** proficient; expert
Auf·klä·rung (ouf′kler′ooŋ) *n.* ⟦Ger < *aufklären*, to enlighten < *auf-*, up + *klären*, to clear < *klar* < L *clarus*, CLEAR⟧ the Enlightenment
au fond (ō fōn′) ⟦Fr⟧ at bottom; basically
auf Wie·der·seh·en (ouf vē′dər zā′ən) ⟦Ger⟧ until we see each other again; goodbye: implies temporary parting
aug *abbrev.* augmentative
Aug *abbrev.* August
Au·ge·an (ô jē′ən) *adj.* ⟦< L *Augeas* < Gr *Augeias*⟧ **1** *Gr. Legend* of Augeas, king of Elis, or his stable, which holds 3,000 oxen and remains uncleaned for 30 years until Hercules, as one of his twelve labors, cleans it in one day by diverting a river (or two rivers) through it **2** very filthy or corrupt
au·ger (ô′gər) *n.* ⟦by faulty separation of ME *a nauger* < OE *nafogar*, nave drill < *nafu*, NAVE[2] + *gar*, a spear: see GORE[3]⟧ **1** a narrow tool for boring holes in wood, etc., with a sharp end for cutting and spiral grooves for channeling the shavings out of the hole: it is larger than a gimlet **2** a similar but larger tool, as for boring holes in the earth
Au·ger effect (ō zhā′) ⟦after P. V. *Auger* (1899-1993), Fr physicist⟧ the excitation of electrons within an atom initiated by the absorption of energy and accompanied by the emission of an electron
Auger shower a shower of electrons, photons, etc. resulting from the collision of primary cosmic rays with atomic nuclei in the atmosphere
aught (ôt) *n.* ⟦ME < OE *awiht* < *a*, ever + *wiht*, a creature, WIGHT[1]⟧ **1** anything whatever [for *aught* I know] **2** ⟦< *a naught* (see NAUGHT), by faulty separation into *an aught*⟧ a zero —*adv.* [Archaic] to any degree; at all —**the aughts** the numbers or years, as of a century, from zero through nine
au·gite (ô′jīt′) *n.* ⟦L *augites* < Gr *augitēs*, a precious stone < *augē*, sunlight, brightness < IE base **aug-*, to gleam⟧ any of various dark-colored, hard, monoclinic pyroxenes, $(Ca,Na)(Mg,Fe,Al,Ti)(Si,Al)_2O_6$, found in basic igneous rocks
aug·ment (ôg ment′; *for n.* ôg′ment′) *vt.* ⟦ME *augmenten* < OFr *augmenter* < LL *augmentare* < *augmentum*, an increase < L *augere*, to increase: see WAX[2]⟧ **1** to make greater, as in size, quantity, or strength; enlarge **2** to add an augment to —*vi.* to become greater; increase —*n.* **1** [Obs.] an increase **2** *Gram.* a prefixed vowel or a lengthening or diphthongization of the initial vowel to show past time in Greek and Sanskrit verbs —***SYN.*** INCREASE —**aug·ment′a·ble** *adj.* —**aug·ment′er** *n.*
aug·men·ta·tion (ôg′men tā′shən, -mən-) *n.* **1** an augmenting or being augmented **2** a thing that augments; addition; increase **3** *Music* variation of a theme by lengthening, usually doubling, the time value of the notes: cf. DIMINUTION
aug·ment·a·tive (ôg men′tə tiv′) *adj.* **1** augmenting or capable of augmenting **2** *Gram.* increasing the force of an idea expressed by a word or denoting increased size, intensity, etc. —*n.* an augmentative affix, word, etc. (Ex.: *per-* in *perdurable*, *up* in *eat up*)
aug·ment·ed interval (ôg ment′id) *Music* an interval that is a half step greater than the corresponding major or perfect interval
au gra·tin (ō grät′'n, -grat′-; *Fr* ō grȧ tan′) ⟦Fr, lit., with scrapings: see GRATIN⟧ having a lightly browned crust of bread crumbs and grated cheese
Augs·burg (ôgz′bərg; *Ger* ouks′boork) city in S Germany, in the state of Bavaria
au·gur (ô′gər) *n.* ⟦L, orig., a priest at rituals of fertility and increase, prob. < OL **augos* (gen. **augeris*), increase, growth < *augere* (see WAX[2]); meaning infl. by *auspex*, AUSPEX⟧ **1** in ancient Rome, any of a body of officials who interpreted omens as being favorable or unfavorable in connection with an undertaking **2** a fortuneteller; prophet; soothsayer — *vt., vi.* ⟦L *augurari* < the n.⟧ **1** to foretell or prophesy from omens **2** to be an omen (of); presage [cloudy skies *augur* rain] —**augur ill** (or **well**) to be a bad (or good) omen
au·gu·ry (ô′gyoo rē, -gyə-) *n.* ⟦ME *augurie* < L *augurium*, divination < *augur*, prec.⟧ **1** divination from omens **2** *pl.* **-ries** an omen; portent; indication
au·gust (ô gust′) *adj.* ⟦L *augustus* < *augere*, to increase: see WAX[2]⟧ **1** inspiring awe and reverence; imposing and magnificent **2** worthy of respect because of age and dignity, high position, etc.; venerable —***SYN.*** GRAND —**au·gust′ly** *adv.* —**au·gust′ness** *n.*
Au·gust (ô′gəst) *n.* ⟦ME < L *Augustus*, after AUGUSTUS[2] Caesar: for the adj., see prec.⟧ **1** a masculine name: see AUGUSTUS[1] **2** the eighth month of the year, having 31 days: abbrev. *Aug, Ag, A*
Au·gus·ta[1] (ô gus′tə, ə-) *n.* ⟦L, fem. of AUGUSTUS[1]⟧ a feminine name
Au·gus·ta[2] (ô gus′tə, ə-) ⟦after Princess *Augusta* of Saxe-Gotha, mother of GEORGE III⟧ **1** city in EC Ga., in Richmond county, with which it constitutes a metropolitan government (**Augusta-Richmond County**) **2** ⟦prob. after Pamela *Augusta* Dearborn, daughter of a general in the Am Revolution⟧ capital of Me., on the Kennebec River
Au·gus·tan (ô gus′tən) *adj.* **1** of or characteristic of Augustus Caesar, his reign (27 B.C.- A.D. 14), or its Latin literature **2** designating or characteristic of any age like Augustus' age, esp. in having standards or tastes that are classic, as the period of Pope and Addison in English literature —*n.* a person writing in an Augustan age
Au·gus·tine[1] (ô′gəs tēn′; ə gus′tin, ô-) *n.* ⟦L *Augustinus*, dim. of AUGUSTUS[1]⟧ a masculine name: var. *Austin, Augustin*; equiv. Ger. & Fr. *Augustin*, It. *Agostino*
Au·gus·tine[2] (ô′gəs tēn′; ə gus′tin, ô-) **1** Saint (A.D. 354-430); early Christian church father, born in Numidia: bishop of Hippo in N Africa: his day is Aug. 28 **2** Saint (died A.D. 604); Rom. monk sent to convert the English to Christianity: 1st archbishop of Canterbury: his day is May 27
Au·gus·tin·i·an (ô′gəs tin′ē ən) *adj.* **1** of Saint Augustine of Hippo or his doctrines **2** designating or of any of several orders named for him —*n.* **1** a follower of Saint Augustine of Hippo **2** a member of an Augustinian religious order —**Au′gus·tin′i·an·ism′** *n.*, **Au·gus·tin·ism** (ô gus′tə niz′əm)
Au·gus·tus[1] (ô gus′təs, ə-) *n.* ⟦L, AUGUST⟧ a masculine name: dim. *Gus;* fem. *Augusta;* equiv. Fr. *Auguste*, Ger. *August*, It. *Augusto*
Au·gus·tus[2] (ô gus′təs, ə-) (*Gaius Julius Caesar Octavianus*) 63 B.C.-A.D. 14; 1st Rom. emperor (27 B.C.-A.D. 14): grandnephew of Julius Caesar: also called *Octavian*
au jus (ō zhoo′, ō joos′; *Fr* ō zhü′) ⟦Fr, with the juice⟧ served in its natural juice or gravy: said of meat
auk (ôk) *n.* ⟦dial. *alk* < ON *alka* < IE base **el-*, **ol-*, echoic of water-bird cry > L *olor*, swan⟧ any of a number of related diving alcidine shorebirds of northern seas, with a heavy body, webbed feet, a short tail, and short wings used as paddles
auk·let (ôk′lit) *n.* ⟦prec. + -LET⟧ any of several small kinds of auk
au lait (ō le′) ⟦Fr⟧ with milk
auld (ôld, äld) *adj.* [Scot.] old
auld lang syne (ôld′ laŋ′ zīn′, -sīn′) ⟦Scot, lit., old long since⟧ old times; the good old days (of one's youth, etc.)
au na·tu·rel (ō nach′ə rel′, -nat′yə-; *Fr* ō nȧ tü rel′) ⟦Fr⟧ **1** in the natural state **2** naked **3** cooked or served simply
aunt (ant, änt) *n.* ⟦ME & OFr *aunte* < L *amita*, paternal aunt, dim. of **amma*, mother (< baby talk)⟧ **1** a sister of one's mother or father **2** the wife of one's uncle
aunt·ie or **aunt·y** (an′tē, än′-) *n., pl.* **-ies** aunt: a familiar or affectionate form
Aunt Sally *pl.* **-lies** or **-lys** ⟦after the figure of a woman's head at which balls are thrown, as in a sideshow⟧ [Brit.] a person or idea seen or set up as an easy target for criticism
au pair (ō per′) ⟦Fr, lit., as an equal⟧ a young person from another country, typically a young woman, who agrees to live with a family and help with child-care duties, housework, etc. in exchange for room and board
au poi·vre (ō pwäv′rə) ⟦Fr, lit., with pepper⟧ coated with crushed black peppercorns, sautéed, and usually flamed with brandy and served with a sauce [steak *au poivre*]
au·ra (ô′rə) *n., pl.* **-ras** or **-rae** (-rē) ⟦ME < L < Gr < IE **awer-*: for base see WIND[2]⟧ **1** an invisible emanation or vapor, as the aroma of flowers **2** a particular atmosphere or quality that seems to arise from and surround a person or thing [enveloped in an *aura* of grandeur] **3** a field of energy thought by some to emanate from all things in nature and to be visible to certain persons with psychic powers **4** *Med.* a warning sensation that precedes a seizure or other neurological disorder
au·ral[1] (ô′rəl) *adj.* of an aura
au·ral[2] (ô′rəl) *adj.* ⟦< L *auris*, EAR[1] + -AL⟧ of or received through the ear or the sense of hearing —**au′ral·ly** *adv.*
Au·rang·a·bad (ou ruŋ′ə bäd′) city in central Maharashtra, W India
Au·rang·zeb (ôr′əŋ zeb′) 1618-1707; last influential Mogul emperor of Hindustan (1658-1707): also **Au′rang·zib′** (-zib′) or **Au′rang·zebe′** (-zēb′)
au·rar (ou′rär′) *n. pl. of* EYRIR
au·re·ate (ô′rē it) *adj.* ⟦ME *aureat* < LL *aureatus* < L *aureus* < *aurum*, gold: see EAST⟧ **1** golden; gilded **2** splendid or brilliant, often affectedly so
Au·re·li·a (ô rē′lē ə, -rēl′yə) *n.* ⟦L, lit., golden < *aurum*, gold: see EAST⟧ a feminine name
Au·re·li·an (ô rē′lē ən, -rēl′yən) (*Lucius Domitius Aurelianus*) A.D. 212?-275; Rom. emperor (270-275)
Au·re·li·us (ô rē′lē əs, -rēl′yəs), **Marcus** (*Marcus Aurelius Antoninus*) A.D. 121-180; Rom. emperor (161-180) & Stoic philosopher

au·re·ole (ô′rē ōl′) ***n.*** ⟦ME < LL *aureola (corona),* golden (crown) < L *aureolus,* dim. of *aureus:* see AUREATE⟧ **1** a radiance encircling the head or body, as in religious paintings; halo; glory **2** the illuminated area around the sun, etc., as when seen in a mist or during an eclipse; sun's corona Also **au·re·o·la** (ô rē′ə lə)

☆**Au·re·o·my·cin** (ô′rē ō mī′sin) ⟦< L *aureus,* golden (from its color) + -MYCIN⟧ *trademark for* CHLORTETRACYCLINE

au re·voir (ōr vwär′; E ō′rə vwär′) ⟦Fr < *au,* to the + *revoir,* seeing again < L *revidere,* see again < *re-,* again + *videre,* see: see VISION⟧ *[also in roman type]* until we meet again; goodbye: implies temporary parting

au·ric (ô′rik) ***adj.*** ⟦< L *aurum,* gold: see EAST⟧ **1** of or containing gold **2** of or containing trivalent gold

au·ri·cle (ô′ri kəl) ***n.*** ⟦ME < L *auricula,* dim. of *auris,* EAR[1]⟧ **1** *Anat. a)* the external part of the ear; pinna *b)* [Obs.] an atrium of the heart **2** *Biol.* an earlike part or organ

au·ric·u·la (ô rik′yoo͞ lə, -yə-) ***n., pl.*** **-las** or **-lae′** (-lē′) ⟦ModL: see prec.⟧ **1** a species of primrose (*Primula auricula*) with leaves shaped like a bear's ear **2** AURICLE

au·ric·u·lar (-lər) ***adj.*** ⟦ME *auriculer* < ML *auricularis* < L *auricula:* see AURICLE⟧ **1** of or near the ear, or having to do with the sense of hearing **2** received by or spoken directly into the ear; private *[an auricular confession]* **3** shaped like an ear **4** of an auricle —***n.*** any of the feathers covering the opening of a bird's ear: *usually used in pl.* —**au·ric′u·lar·ly** ***adv.***

au·ric·u·late (-lit, -lāt′) ***adj.*** ⟦< L *auricula* (see AURICLE) + -ATE[1]⟧ having auricles, ears, or earlike parts, as the base of a leaf

au·rif·er·ous (ô rif′ər əs) ***adj.*** ⟦L *aurifer* (< *aurum,* gold: see EAST + *ferre,* BEAR[1]) + -OUS⟧ bearing or yielding gold

au·ri·form (ô′rə fôrm′) ***adj.*** ⟦< L *auris,* EAR[1] + -FORM⟧ ear-shaped

Au·ri·ga (ô rī′gə) ***n.*** ⟦ME < L, lit., charioteer < *aurea,* bridle + *agere,* to drive: see ACT[1]⟧ a N constellation between Perseus and Gemini; the Charioteer

Au·rig·na·cian (ô′rig nā′shən) ***adj.*** ⟦Fr *Aurignacien,* after *Aurignac,* village in S France, in whose caves artifacts were discovered⟧ designating or of an Upper Paleolithic culture, characterized by stone tools called burins which were used for carving wood, bone, and ivory: Aurignacian peoples are credited with producing the earliest cave paintings in W Europe

au·rochs (ô′räks′) ***n., pl.*** **au′rochs′** ⟦Ger *auerochs* < OHG *ūrohso* < *ūr,* aurochs (< IE base *wer-, damp > URINE & names of male animals, as L *verres,* boar, Sans *vṛṣabháḥ,* bull) + *ohso,* OX⟧ an extinct, shaggy, long-horned wild ox of Eurasia: it is the ancestor of modern domestic cattle

Au·ro·ra[1] (ô rôr′ə, ə-) ***n., pl.*** for 2-4 **-ras** or **-rae** (ē) ⟦L, lit., dawn: for IE base see EAST⟧ **1** *Rom. Myth.* the goddess of dawn: identified with the Greek Eos **2** [**a-**] the dawn **3** [**a-**] AURORA AUSTRALIS or AURORA BOREALIS **4** [**a-**] any of various luminous phenomena, similar to the aurora borealis, in the atmosphere of a planet —**au·ro′ral** ***adj.,*** **au·ro′re·an** (-ē ən)

Au·ro·ra[2] (ô rôr′ə, ə-) **1** ⟦after the goddess *Aurora,* prob. because of pleasant connotations⟧ city in NC Colo., near Denver **2** ⟦after the goddess *Aurora*⟧ city in NE Ill., near Chicago

aurora aus·tra·lis (ô strā′lis) ⟦L, lit., southern aurora: see AURORA[1] & AUSTRAL⟧ luminous phenomena similar to the aurora borealis, visible in a zone around the south magnetic pole; southern lights

aurora bo·re·al·is (bôr′ē al′is, -ā′lis) ⟦L, lit., northern aurora: see AURORA[1] & BOREAS⟧ irregular, luminous phenomena, as streamers, visible at night in a zone surrounding the north magnetic pole and produced in the ionosphere when atomic particles strike and excite atoms; northern lights

au·rous (ô′rəs) ***adj.*** ⟦< L *aurum,* gold (see EAST) + -OUS⟧ **1** of or containing gold **2** of or containing monovalent gold

Au·rung·zeb (ôr′əŋ zeb′) *alt. sp. of* AURANGZEB

Aus *abbrev.* Austria

Ausch·witz (oush′vits′) city in S Poland: in WWII, site of a Nazi concentration camp notorious as an extermination center: Pol. name OŚWIĘCIM

aus·cul·tate (ôs′kəl tāt′) ***vt., vi.*** **-tat′ed, -tat′ing** ⟦< pp. of L *auscultare*⟧ to examine by auscultation —**aus′cul·ta′tor** ***n.*** —**aus·cul·ta·to·ry** (ôs kul′tə tôr′ē) ***adj.***

aus·cul·ta·tion (ôs′kəl tā′shən) ***n.*** ⟦L *auscultatio,* a listening < *auscultare,* to listen < *aus-,* base of *auris,* EAR[1] + *cultare,* by metathesis < **clutare* < IE base **kel-,* to incline⟧ **1** a listening **2** a listening, often with the aid of a stethoscope, to sounds in the chest, abdomen, etc. so as to determine the condition of the heart, lungs, etc.

aus·land·er (ous′lan′dər) ***n.*** ⟦Ger *ausländer* < *aus,* OUT + *land,* LAND⟧ a foreigner; outsider; alien

aus·pex (ôs′peks′) ***n., pl.*** **aus′pi·ces′** (-pə sēz′) ⟦L, contr. of *avispex* < *avis,* bird + *specere,* see: see SPY⟧ in ancient Rome, an augur, or diviner, esp. one who watched for omens in the flight of birds

aus·pice (ôs′pis) ***n., pl.*** **aus′pi·ces** (-pə siz, -sēz′; *for 3 usually,* -siz) ⟦Fr < L *auspicium,* omen < *auspex,* prec. ⟧ **1** a watching for omens in the flight of birds; divination **2** an omen, esp. a favorable one **3** [*pl.*] approval and support; guiding sponsorship; patronage *[a plan under government auspices]*

aus·pi·cious (ô spish′əs) ***adj.*** ⟦< L *auspicium* (see prec.) + -OUS⟧ **1** of good omen; boding well for the future; favorable; propitious **2** favored by fortune; successful —**SYN.** FAVORABLE —**aus·pi′cious·ly** ***adv.*** —**aus·pi′cious·ness** ***n.***

Aus·sie (ôs′ē) ***adj., n.*** [Informal] Australian

Aust *abbrev.* **1** Australia **2** Austria

Aus·ten (ôs′tən), **Jane** 1775-1817; Eng. novelist

aus·ten·ite (ôs′tən īt′) ***n.*** ⟦Fr, after Sir W. C. Roberts-*Austen* (1843-1902), Eng metallurgist⟧ a nonmagnetic solid solution of carbon or iron carbide in some iron, obtained in high carbon steels by rapid quenching and deformation at high temperatures

aus·tere (ô stir′) ***adj.*** ⟦ME < OFr < L *austerus,* harsh < Gr *austēros,* dry, harsh < *auein,* to dry < *auos,* dry < IE base **saus,* dry > SEAR[1]⟧ **1** having a severe or stern look, manner, etc.; forbidding **2** showing strict self-discipline and self-denial; ascetic **3** very plain; lacking ornament or luxury *[austere surroundings]* **4** [Rare] grave; sober —**SYN.** SEVERE —**aus·tere′ly** ***adv.***

aus·ter·i·ty (ô ster′ə tē) ***n., pl.*** **-ties** **1** the quality or condition of being austere **2** an austere act, habit, practice, or manner **3** tightened economy, as because of shortages of consumer goods

Aus·ter·litz (ous′tər lits′, ôs′-) town in the SE Czech Republic, near Brno: scene of Napoleon's victory (1805) over the combined Russian and Austrian armies: Czech name SLAVKOV

Aus·tin[1] (ôs′tən) ***n.*** **1** a masculine name: see AUGUSTINE[1] **2** [Chiefly Brit.] AUGUSTINIAN —***adj.*** [Chiefly Brit.] AUGUSTINIAN

Aus·tin[2] (ôs′tən) **1 Alfred** 1835-1913; Eng. poet: poet laureate (1896-1913) **2 John** 1790-1859; Eng. jurist **3 Stephen (Fuller)** 1793-1836; U.S. pioneer: founded 1st U.S. colony in Tex. in early 1820s

Aus·tin[3] (ôs′tən) ⟦after Stephen AUSTIN[2]⟧ capital of Tex., on the Colorado River

Austl or **Austral** *abbrev.* Australia

aus·tral (ôs′trəl; *for n.* ôs träl′) ***adj.*** ⟦L *australis,* southern < *auster,* south wind, the south: for IE base see EAST; shift in meaning from "east" prob. due to false assumption concerning direction of axis of Italy⟧ **1** southern; southerly **2** [**A-**] Australian —***n., pl.*** **-tra′les** (-trä′lās) the former basic monetary unit of Argentina

Aus·tral·a·sia (ôs′trə lā′zhə) **1** generally, the islands of the SW Pacific **2** Australia, New Zealand, New Guinea, the Malay Archipelago, and all islands south of the equator and between E longitudes 100 and 180 **3** Oceania —**Aus′tral·a′sian** ***adj., n.***

Aus·tral·ia (ô strāl′yə) ⟦ModL < L *(terra) australis,* southern (land): see AUSTRAL⟧ **1** large island in the Southern Hemisphere between the S Pacific and Indian oceans: traditionally regarded as a continent, but now often considered by geographers to be part of a larger continent called *Oceania:* see the table of continents in the Reference Supplement **2** country comprising this island, Tasmania, and many smaller islands: a member of the Commonwealth: 2,967,909 sq mi (7,686,850 sq km); cap. Canberra

Australia antigen ⟦so named because first identified in an *Australian* Aborigine⟧ an antigen present in the blood of some persons with one form of hepatitis

Aus·tral·i·an (ô strāl′ē ən, -strāl′yən) ***adj.*** **1** of Australia or its people **2** designating or of the biogeographic realm that includes Australia, New Zealand, and New Guinea —***n.*** a person born or living in Australia

Australian Alps mountain range in SE Australia, in the states of Victoria and New South Wales: S end of the Great Dividing Range: highest peak, Mt. Kosciusko

Australian Antarctic Territory region in Antarctica, claimed by Australia, between E longitudes 45 and 160, exclusive of the Adélie Coast

☆**Australian ballot** an official ballot listing candidates for election to public office and issues, levies, etc., distributed inside the polling place to be marked by the voter in secret: it originated in Australia and is widely used in the U.S.

Australian Capital Territory federal territory in the SE part of New South Wales: site of Canberra, Australian capital: 911 sq mi (2,360 sq km)

Australian cattle dog any of a breed of medium-sized dog developed in Australia for herding cattle and obtained by crossing various breeds, principally the dingo, collie, and Dalmatian, characterized by pointed ears and a moderately short, straight coat that is blue, blue with tan markings, or red speckled

Australian crawl *Swimming* an earlier form of the crawl

Australian pine CASUARINA

Australian terrier a small terrier with a wire-haired, blue-black or silver-black coat with tan markings: first bred in Australia

Aus·tra·loid (ôs′trə loid′) ***adj.*** ⟦AUSTRAL(IA) + -OID⟧ designating or of one of the major geographical varieties of human beings, including the Australian Aborigines, the Veddas of Sri Lanka, possibly the Ainu, etc., who are generally characterized by dark skin, curly hair, large teeth and jaws, etc. —***n.*** a member of the Australoid population See RACE[2]

aus·tra·lo·pith·e·cine (ô strā′lō pith′ə sīn′, -sēn′; ô′strə lō-) ***adj.*** ⟦< ModL < L *australis* (see AUSTRAL) + ModL *-pithecus* (see PITHECANTHROPUS ERECTUS)⟧ of or relating to a genus (*Australopithecus*) of extinct hominids from E and S Africa that walked upright —***n.*** an australopithecine hominid

Aus·tra·sia (ôs trā′zhə) ⟦ML < OHG *ostarrih:* see fol.⟧ easternmost part of the kingdom of the Merovingian Franks from the 6th to the 8th cent., composed of what is now NE France, Belgium, and W Germany

Aus·tri·a (ôs′trē ə) ⟦ML < OHG *ostarrih* < *ostan,* EAST + *rihhi,* realm⟧ country in central Europe: 32,382 sq mi (83,870 sq km); cap. Vienna —**Aus′tri·an** ***adj., n.***

Aus·tri·a-Hun·ga·ry (-huŋ′gə rē) former monarchy in central Europe (1867-1918) consisting of territory that became Austria, Hungary, and Czechoslovakia, as well as parts of Poland, Romania, Yugoslavia, and Italy —**Aus·tro-Hun·gar·i·an** (ôs′trō huŋ ger′ē ən) ***adj., n.***

Aus·tro-[1] (ôs′trō) *combining form* Austrian, Austrian and *[Austro-Hungarian]*

Aus·tro-[2] (ôs′trō) ⟦< L *auster:* see AUSTRAL⟧ *combining form* **1** southern **2** Australian, Australian and

Aus·tro-A·si·at·ic (ôs′trō ā′zhē at′ik) ***n.*** ⟦prec. + ASIATIC⟧ a family of languages scattered widely throughout S Asia, including Mon, Khmer, Vietnamese, and the Munda languages of NE India —***adj.*** designating or of this family of languages

Aus·tro·ne·sia (ôs′trō nē′zhə) ⟦< AUSTRO-[2] (sense 1) + Gr *nēsos*, island + -IA⟧ the islands of the central and S Pacific

Aus·tro·ne·sian (-zhən) ***n.*** **1** a family of languages spoken over a large area extending from Hawaii south to New Zealand and west to Madagascar **2** a member of any of the peoples speaking these languages —***adj.*** designating or of these languages, the peoples that speak them, or their cultures

au·su·bo (ou so͞o′bō) ***n.*** BALATA

aut- (ôt) *combining form* AUTO-: used before a vowel [*autecology*]

au·ta·coid (ôt′ə koid′) ***n.*** ⟦AUT(O)- + Gr *akos*, cure, remedy + -OID⟧ **1** HORMONE **2** any of a group of natural biochemicals, as serotonin, angiotensin, or histamine, that activate changes in the blood, nerves, etc., similar to those caused by drugs

au·tar·chy (ô′tär′kē) ***n., pl.*** **-chies** ⟦Gr *autarchia* < *autarchos*, autocrat, absolute ruler < *autos*, self + *archos*: see ARCH-⟧ **1** absolute rule or sovereignty; autocracy **2** a country under such rule **3** AUTARKY —**au·tar′chic** ***adj.***, **au·tar′chi·cal**

au·tar·ky (ô′tär′kē) ***n.*** ⟦Gr *autarkeia*, self-sufficiency < *autos*, self + *arkein*, to achieve, suffice: see EXERCISE⟧ **1** self-sufficiency; independence **2** economic self-sufficiency, esp. on a national basis; national policy of getting along without imports —**au·tar′kic** ***adj.***, **au·tar′ki·cal**

au·te·cious (ô tē′shəs) ***adj.*** AUTOECIOUS

aut·e·col·o·gy (ôt′ē käl′ə jē) ***n.*** ⟦AUT(O)- + ECOLOGY⟧ the ecological study of a single organism, or of a single species of organism: cf. SYNECOLOGY

au·teur (ō tʉr′) ***n., pl.*** **-teurs′** (-tʉr′) ⟦Fr, author⟧ **1** the primary creator of a film, esp. the director **2** a film director with a distinctive personal style

au·teur·ism (ō tʉr′iz′əm) ***n.*** in film criticism, the theory according to which the primary creator of a film is the director, all of whose works are said to reflect to a certain degree the characteristics of a personal style: also **auteur theory** —**au·teur′ist** ***n.***

auth *abbrev.* **1** authentic **2** author **3** authorized

au·then·tic (ô then′tik) ***adj.*** ⟦ME *autentike* < OFr *autentique* < LL *authenticus* < Gr *authentikos*, genuine < *authentēs*, one who does things himself < *autos*, self + *-hentēs* < IE base **sen-*, to prepare, achieve⟧ **1** that can be believed or accepted; trustworthy; reliable [an *authentic* news report] **2** that is in fact as represented; genuine; real [an *authentic* antique] **3** legally attested or executed, as a deed, affidavit, etc. **4** true to its type; conforming to an original in style, methods, etc. [*authentic* Japanese cooking] **5** [Obs.] authoritative —**au·then′ti·cal·ly** ***adv.***

SYN.—**authentic** implies reliability and trustworthiness, stressing that the thing considered is in agreement with fact or actuality [an *authentic* report]; **genuine** is applied to that which really is what it is represented to be, emphasizing freedom from admixture, adulteration, sham, etc. [*genuine* silk; *genuine* grief]; **bona fide** is properly used when a question of good faith is involved; **veritable** implies correspondence with the truth and connotes absolute affirmation [a *veritable* fool] —*ANT.* **spurious, counterfeit, sham**

au·then·ti·cate (ô then′ti kāt′) ***vt.*** **-cat′ed, -cat′ing** ⟦< ML *authenticatus*, pp. of *authenticare* < LL *authenticus*⟧ **1** to make authentic or valid **2** to establish the truth of; verify **3** to prove to be genuine or as represented —*SYN.* CONFIRM —**au·then′ti·ca′tion** ***n.*** —**au·then′ti·ca′tor** ***n.***

au·then·tic·i·ty (ô′thən tis′ə tē) ***n.*** the quality or state of being authentic; reliability; genuineness

au·thor (ô′thər) ***n.*** ⟦ME *autour* < OFr *autor* < L *auctor*, enlarger, author < *augere*, to increase: see WAX[2]⟧ **1** a person who makes or originates something; creator; originator [*"author* of liberty"] **2** a writer of a book, article, etc.; often specif., a person whose profession is writing books —***vt.*** to be the author of —**au·tho·ri·al** (ô thôr′ē əl) ***adj.***

au·thor·ess (ô′thər is) ***n.*** a woman writer: see -ESS

au·thor·i·tar·i·an (ə thôr′ə ter′ē ən, -thär′-) ***adj.*** ⟦AUTHORIT(Y) + -ARIAN⟧ believing in, relating to, characterized by, or enforcing unquestioning obedience to authority, as that of a dictator, rather than individual freedom of judgment and action —***n.*** a person who advocates, practices, or enforces such obedience —**au·thor′i·tar′i·an·ism′** ***n.***

au·thor·i·ta·tive (ə thôr′ə tāt′iv, -thär′-; *also*, -ə tə tiv′) ***adj.*** ⟦ML *auctoritativus*⟧ **1** having or showing authority; official **2** based on competent authority; reliable because coming from one who is an expert or properly qualified [an *authoritative* biography] **3** asserting authority; fond of giving orders; dictatorial —**au·thor′i·ta′tive·ly** ***adv.*** —**au·thor′i·ta′tive·ness** ***n.***

au·thor·i·ty (ə thôr′ə tē, -thär′-) ***n., pl.*** **-ties** ⟦ME *autorite* < OFr *autorité, auctorité* < L *auctoritas* < *auctor*, AUTHOR⟧ **1** *a)* the power or right to give commands, enforce obedience, take action, or make final decisions; jurisdiction *b)* the position of one having such power [a person in *authority*] **2** such power as delegated to another; authorization; warrant [he has my *authority* to do it] **3** power or influence resulting from knowledge, prestige, etc. **4** *a)* the citation of a writing, decision, etc. in support of an opinion, action, etc. *b)* the writing, etc. cited **5** reliability of a source or witness **6** *a)* [*pl.*] persons, esp. in government, having the power or right to enforce orders, laws, etc. *b)* a government agency that administers a project **7** a person with much knowledge or experience in some field, whose information or opinion is hence reliable; expert **8** self-assurance and expertness that come with experience [the pianist's performance lacked *authority*] —*SYN.* INFLUENCE, POWER

au·thor·i·za·tion (ô′thər i zā′shən) ***n.*** **1** an authorizing or being authorized **2** legal power or right; sanction

au·thor·ize (ô′thər īz′) ***vt.*** **-ized′, -iz′ing** ⟦ME *autorisen* < OFr *autoriser* < ML *auctorizare* < L *auctor*, AUTHOR⟧ **1** to give official approval to or permission for [a housing project *authorized* by the city] **2** to give power or authority to; empower; commission **3** to give justification for; warrant —**au′thor·iz′er** ***n.***

SYN.—**authorize** implies the giving of power or right to act, ranging in application from a specific legal power to discretionary powers in dealings of any kind; to **commission** a person is to authorize as well as instruct to perform a certain duty, as the execution of an artistic work, or to appoint to a certain rank or office; **accredit** implies the sending of a person, duly authorized and with the proper credentials, as an ambassador, delegate, etc.; **license** implies the giving of formal legal permission to do some specified thing and often emphasizes regulation [to *license* hunters]

au·thor·ized (-īzd′) ***adj.*** **1** established or justified by authority **2** given authority [my *authorized* agent]

Authorized Version the revised English translation of the Bible published in England in 1611 with the authorization of King James I: also called *King James Version*

au·thor·ship (-ship′) ***n.*** **1** the profession or occupation of a writer **2** the origin (of a book, etc.) with reference to its author [a story of unknown *authorship*] **3** the source (of an idea, deed, etc.) with reference to its originator

☆**au·tism** (ô′tiz′əm) ***n.*** ⟦AUT(O)- + -ISM⟧ *Psychol.* a developmental disorder characterized variously by impaired social interaction, difficulties in communicating, problems with seeing and hearing, repetitive behavior, etc. —**au·tis·tic** (ô tis′tik) ***adj.***

☆**au·to**[1] (ôt′ō, ät′ō) ***n., pl.*** **-tos** an automobile —***vi.*** **-toed, -to·ing** to go by automobile: an earlier usage

au·to[2] (ôt′ō, ät′ō) ***adj., n.*** *short for* AUTOMATIC

au·to- (ôt′ō, -ə; ät′-) ⟦< Gr *autos*, self⟧ *combining form* **1** of or for oneself; self [*autobiography*] **2** by oneself or itself [*automobile*] **3** automatic [*autofocus*]

au·to·an·a·lyz·er (ôt′ō an′ə lī′zər) ***n.*** any of various automatic devices that test and analyze chemicals, blood, etc.

au·to·an·ti·bod·y (ôt′ō an′ti bäd′ē) ***n. pl.*** **-bod′ies** an antibody that acts against the body's own molecules and tissues and may cause an autoimmune disorder

au·to·bahn (ôt′ō bän′, ôt′ə-; *Ger* ou′tō bän′) ***n., pl.*** **-bahns′** or **-bahn′en** (-bän′ən) ⟦Ger < *auto(mobil)*, AUTOMOBILE + *bahn*, a course, highway⟧ in Germany and Austria, an expressway

au·to·bi·og·ra·pher (ôt′ō bī äg′rə fər, -bē-) ***n.*** a person who writes the story of his or her own life

au·to·bi·og·ra·phy (-fē) ***n., pl.*** **-phies** ⟦AUTO- + BIOGRAPHY: coined (1809) by Robert SOUTHEY⟧ **1** the art or practice of writing one's own biography **2** the story of one's own life written or dictated by oneself —**au′to·bi′o·graph′i·cal** (-bī′ə graf′i kəl) ***adj.***, **au′to·bi′o·graph′ic** —**au′to·bi′o·graph′i·cal·ly** ***adv.***

☆**au·to·bus** (ôt′ō bus) ***n.*** BUS (sense 1)

au·to·ca·tal·y·sis (ôt′ō kə tal′ə sis) ***n.*** a chemical reaction in which one or more of the products act as catalysts to accelerate the reaction

au·to·ceph·a·lous (-sef′ə ləs) ***adj.*** ⟦see AUTO- & -CEPHALOUS⟧ self-governing; independent: said of certain churches within the communion of the Eastern Orthodox Church

au·toch·thon (ô täk′thən) ***n., pl.*** **-thons** or **-tho·nes′** (-thə nēz′) ⟦Gr *autochthōn*, sprung from the land itself < *autos*, self + *chthōn*, earth: see HOMAGE⟧ **1** any of the earliest known inhabitants of a place; aborigine **2** any indigenous animal or plant —**au·toch′tho·nous** (-thə nəs) ***adj.***, **au·toch′tho·nal** —**au·toch′tho·nous·ly** ***adv.***

au·to·clave (ôt′ə klāv′) ***n.*** ⟦Fr < *auto-*, AUTO- + L *clavis*, key: see CLOSE[3]⟧ a container for sterilizing, cooking, etc. by superheated steam under pressure —***vt.*** **-claved′, -clav′ing** to sterilize or cook by means of such a device

au·toc·ra·cy (ô tä′krə sē) ***n.*** ⟦Gr *autokrateia*, absolute power: see AUTO- & -CRACY⟧ **1** government in which one person has absolute power; dictatorship; despotism **2** *pl.* **-cies** a country with this kind of government **3** unlimited power or authority of one person over others

au·to·crat (ôt′ə krat′) ***n.*** ⟦Fr *autocrate* < Gr *autokratēs*, absolute ruler < *autos*, self + *kratos*, power, rule: see -CRAT⟧ **1** a ruler with absolute power; dictator; despot **2** anyone having unlimited power over others **3** any domineering, self-willed person —**au′to·crat′ic** ***adj.***, **au′to·crat′i·cal** —**au′to·crat′i·cal·ly** ***adv.***

au·to-da-fé (ôt′ō də fā′, out′-) ***n., pl.*** **au′tos-da-fé′** ⟦Port, lit., act of the faith < *auto* (< L *actus*, ACT[1]) + *da*, of the + *fé* (< L *fides*, faith)⟧ **1** the public ceremony in which the Inquisition pronounced judgment and passed sentence on those tried as heretics **2** the execution by the secular power of the sentence thus passed; esp., the public burning of a heretic

au·to de fe (ou′tō de fe′) *pl.* ***au·tos de fe*** (ou′tôs) ⟦Sp⟧ AUTO-DA-FÉ

au·to-di·al (ôt′ō dī′əl) ***n.*** an automated system or device designed to dial a programmed telephone number or a series of numbers — ***vt., vi.*** **-aled** or **-alled, -al·ing** or **-al·ling** to dial or call using auto-dial —**au′to-di′al·er** ***n.***, **au′to-di′al·ler**

au·to·di·dact (ôt′ō dī′dakt′) *n.* ⟦ML *autodidactus* < Gr *autodidaktos*, self-taught: see AUTO- & DIDACTIC⟧ a person who is self-educated —**au′to·di·dac′tic** (-dī dak′tik) *adj.*

au·to·dyne (ôt′ə dīn′) *adj.* ⟦AUTO- + DYNE⟧ designating or of a system of heterodyne radio reception in which a single tube serves both as oscillator and first detector —*n.* **1** an autodyne system **2** an autodyne receiver

au·toe·cious (ô tē′shəs) *adj.* ⟦AUTO- + Gr *oikos*, house (see ECONOMY) + -OUS⟧ *Biol.* passing the entire life cycle on one host, as certain parasites do, esp. rust fungi —**au·toe′cious·ly** *adv.* —**au·toe′cism′** (-siz′əm) *n.*

au·to·er·o·tism (ôt′ō er′ə tiz′əm) *n.* ⟦AUTO- + EROTISM: coined by Havelock ELLIS[2]⟧ **1** pleasurable sensations or tensions arising in the erogenous body zones without external stimulation **2** self-initiated activity aimed at reducing sexual excitations, as in masturbation Also **au′to·e·rot′i·cism′** (-ē rät′ə siz′əm) —**au′to·e·rot′ic** (-ē rät′ik) *adj.* —**au′to·e·rot′i·cal·ly** *adv.*

au·to·fo·cus (ôt′ō fō′kəs, ät′-) *n.* a device that focuses a lens, camera, etc. automatically: also written **auto focus** or **au′to-fo′cus**

au·tog·a·my (ô täg′ə mē) *n.* ⟦AUTO- + -GAMY⟧ **1** self-fertilization, as in a flower receiving pollen from its own stamens **2** internal self-fertilization in algae, fungi, protozoans, etc. by the fusion of gametes or nuclei within the same individual —**au·tog′a·mous** (-məs) *adj.*

au·to·gen·e·sis (ôt′ō jen′ə sis) *n.* ⟦AUTO- + -GENESIS⟧ SPONTANEOUS GENERATION —**au′to·ge·net′ic** (-jə net′ik) *adj.* —**au′to·ge·net′i·cal·ly** *adv.*

au·tog·e·nous (ô täj′ə nəs) *adj.* ⟦Gr *autogenēs* (< *autos*, self + *genesis*, birth: see GENUS) + -OUS⟧ **1** self-generated or self-generating **2** produced in or obtained from one's own body: said esp. of a vaccine or tissue transplant Also **au·to·gen·ic** (ôt′ə jen′ik) —**au·tog′e·nous·ly** *adv.*

au·to·gi·ro (ôt′ə jī′rō) *n., pl.* **-ros** ⟦Sp, orig. a trademark, *Autogiro* < *auto-*, AUTO- + Gr *gyros*, a circle: see GYRATE⟧ an aircraft that moves forward by means of a propeller and is supported in the air mainly by means of a large rotor mounted horizontally above the fuselage and turned by air pressure rather than motor power: largely superseded by the HELICOPTER

au·to·graft (ôt′ō graft′) *n.* any tissue grafted from one location to another on the same individual: see ALLOGRAFT, XENOGRAFT

au·to·graph (ôt′ə graf′) *n.* ⟦L *autographum*, neut. of *autographus* < Gr *autographos*, written with one's own hand < *autos*, self + *graphein*: see GRAPHIC⟧ **1** a signature, handwritten inscription, etc., esp. that of a famous person which is valued as a memento **2** a thing written in one's own handwriting; original manuscript; holograph —*vt.* **1** to write (something) with one's own hand **2** to write one's signature on or in

au·to·graph·ic (ôt′ə graf′ik) *adj.* **1** of, for, or like an autograph or autographs **2** written in one's own handwriting —**au′to·graph′i·cal·ly** *adv.*

au·tog·ra·phy (ô täg′rə fē) *n.* ⟦< AUTOGRAPH⟧ **1** the writing of something with one's own hand **2** a person's own handwriting **3** autographs in general

au·to·gy·ro (ôt′ə jī′rō) *n., pl.* **-ros** *alt. sp. of* AUTOGIRO

☆**au·to·harp** (ôt′ō härp′) *n.* ⟦< *Autoharp*, a former trademark < AUTO- + HARP⟧ a type of zither for playing chordal accompaniments by means of a series of dampers worked by keys

au·to·hyp·no·sis (ôt′ō hip nō′sis) *n.* the act of hypnotizing oneself or the state of being so hypnotized —**au′to·hyp·not′ic** (-nät′ik) *adj.*

au·to·im·mune (-i myo͞on′) *adj.* initiating or resulting from the production of autoantibodies, sometimes with damage to normal components of the body —**au′to·im·mu′ni·ty** *n.*

au·to·in·fec·tion (-in fek′shən) *n.* infection from a source within the organism itself, as from harmful bacteria previously present but not in contact with vulnerable areas

au·to·in·oc·u·la·tion (-in äk′yo͞o lā′shən) *n.* **1** inoculation of a patient with a vaccine prepared from microorganisms from the patient's own body **2** a spreading of infection from one part to other parts in the body

au·to·in·tox·i·ca·tion (-in täks′i kā′shən) *n.* poisoning by toxic substances generated within the body

☆**au·to·load·ing** (ôt′ō lōd′iŋ) *adj.* SEMIAUTOMATIC (sense 2)

au·tol·o·gous (ô täl′ə gəs) *adj.* ⟦AUTO- + (HOMO)LOGOUS⟧ derived from the same organism or from one of its parts [an *autologous* graft]: see HOMOLOGOUS (sense 5)

au·tol·y·sate (ô täl′ə sāt′, ôt′ə lī′sāt) *n.* ⟦AUTOLYS(IS) + -ATE[2]⟧ a product of autolysis

au·to·ly·sin (ôt′ə lī′sin, ô täl′ə sin) *n.* ⟦< fol. + -IN[1]⟧ a substance that produces autolysis

au·tol·y·sis (ô täl′ə sis) *n.* ⟦AUTO- + -LYSIS⟧ the destruction of cells or tissues by their own enzymes, as after death or in some diseases —**au·to·lyt·ic** (ôt′ə lit′ik) *adj.*

au·to·lyze (ôt′ə līz′) *vt., vi.* **-lyzed′**, **-lyz′ing** to affect with or undergo autolysis

au·to·mak·er (ôt′ō mā′kər, ät′-) *n.* a manufacturer of automotive vehicles

au·to·mat (ôt′ə mat′) *n.* ⟦Ger < Gr *automatos*: see AUTOMATIC⟧ a restaurant in which patrons get food from small compartments with doors that open when coins are put into slots

au·tom·a·ta (ô täm′ə tə) *n. alt. pl. of* AUTOMATON

☆**au·to·mate** (ôt′ə māt′) *vt.* **-mat′ed**, **-mat′ing** ⟦back-form. < AUTOMATION⟧ to modernize, improve, etc. (a system, process, facility, etc.) by means of automation [to *automate* a company's payroll system, to *automate* a factory]

au·to·mat·ic (ôt′ə mat′ik) *adj.* ⟦< Gr *automatos*, self-moving, self-thinking (< *autos*, self + component < IE **mntos*, thinking < base **men-*, to think > MIND, MEMORY) + -IC⟧ **1** done without conscious thought or volition, as if mechanically **2** involuntary or reflex, as some muscle or gland action **3** *a)* moving, operating, etc. by itself; regulating itself [*automatic* machinery] *b)* done with automatic equipment [an *automatic* landing] **4** *Firearms a)* using the force of the explosion of a shell to eject the empty cartridge case, place the next cartridge into the breech, and fire it, so that shots continue in rapid succession until the trigger is released *b) nontechnical name for* SEMIAUTOMATIC (sense 2) **5** *Mech.* of or pertaining to a transmission, specif. an automotive transmission, designed to change gears automatically —*n.* **1** an automatic (or, popularly, semiautomatic) firearm **2** any automatic machine **3** an automotive vehicle having a transmission that changes gears automatically —**SYN.** SPONTANEOUS —**au′to·mat′i·cal·ly** *adv.*

automatic direction finder a type of radio compass that indicates automatically the direction of the station to which it is tuned, used esp. on aircraft

au·to·ma·tic·i·ty (ôt′ə mə tis′ə tē, ô täm′ə-) *n.* the condition of being automatic, or the degree of this

automatic pilot **1** a gyroscopic instrument that automatically keeps an aircraft, missile, etc. to a predetermined course and attitude **2** a way of acting that involves habit and little or no thought or concentration [a bedtime routine performed largely on *automatic pilot*]

☆**au·to·ma·tion** (ôt′ə mā′shən) *n.* ⟦AUTOMA(TIC) + -TION⟧ **1** the use of self-regulating machinery, electronic equipment, etc. to make a manufacturing system or process operate at greater speed and with little or no human intervention **2** the use of equipment or devices, esp. computers, in any system or process so as to improve its efficiency or effectiveness [*automation* in education] **3** the science or technique of automating systems, processes, etc.

au·tom·a·tism (ô täm′ə tiz′əm) *n.* ⟦AUTOMAT(IC) + -ISM⟧ **1** the quality or condition of being automatic **2** automatic action **3** *Philos.* the theory that the human or animal body is a machine governed by physical laws and that consciousness does not control but only accompanies its actions **4** *Physiol. a)* action independent of outside stimulus, as sleepwalking *b)* action not controlled by the will, as the heartbeat *c)* the power of such action **5** *Psychol.* an automatic or unconscious action, as a tic **6** free expression of the unconscious mind by releasing it from the control of the conscious: a surrealist concept —**au·tom′a·tist** *n.*

au·tom·a·tize (-tīz′) *vt.* **-tized′**, **-tiz′ing** **1** to make automatic **2** AUTOMATE —**au·tom′a·ti·za′tion** *n.*

au·tom·a·ton (ô täm′ə tän′, -tən) *n., pl.* **-tons′** or **-ta** (-tə) ⟦L < Gr, neut. of *automatos*: see AUTOMATIC⟧ **1** anything that can move or act of itself **2** an apparatus that automatically performs certain actions by responding to preset controls or encoded instructions **3** an electronic machine, control device, etc. equipped with a computer and designed to operate automatically in response to instructions previously fed into the computer **4** a person or animal acting in an automatic or mechanical way

☆**au·to·mo·bile** (ôt′ə mə bēl′, ôt′ə mə bēl′) *n.* ⟦Fr: see AUTO- & MOBILE⟧ a passenger vehicle, usually four-wheeled, propelled by an engine or motor that is part of it, esp. an internal-combustion engine, and meant for traveling on streets or roads; motorcar

au·to·mo·tive (ôt′ə mōt′iv) *adj.* ⟦AUTO- + -MOTIVE⟧ **1** moving by means of its own power; self-moving **2** of or having to do with automobiles or other motor vehicles

au·to·nom·ic (-näm′ik) *adj.* **1** occurring involuntarily; automatic **2** of or controlled by the autonomic nervous system **3** *Biol.* resulting from internal causes, as through a mutation —**au′to·nom′i·cal·ly** *adv.*

autonomic nervous system the part of the nervous system that is responsible for control and regulation of the involuntary bodily functions, including those of the heart, blood vessels, visceral smooth muscles, and glands: it consists of the sympathetic system which, in general, stimulates the body to prepare for physical action or emergency, and the parasympathetic system which, in general, stimulates the opposite responses: see CENTRAL NERVOUS SYSTEM

au·ton·o·mist (ô tän′ə mist) *n.* a person desiring or advocating autonomy

au·ton·o·mous (-məs) *adj.* ⟦Gr *autonomos*, independent < *autos*, self + *nomos*, law: see -NOMY⟧ **1** of or having to do with an autonomy **2** *a)* having self-government *b)* functioning independently without control by others **3** *Biol. a)* existing, functioning, or developing independently of other parts or forms *b)* autotrophic *c)* resulting from internal causes; autonomic —**au·ton′o·mous·ly** *adv.*

au·ton·o·my (-mē) *n.* ⟦Gr *autonomia*⟧ **1** the fact or condition of being autonomous; self-government; independence **2** *pl.* **-mies** any state that governs itself

au·to·phyte (ôt′ə fīt′) *n.* ⟦AUTO- + -PHYTE⟧ any plant that makes its own food from inorganic matter —**au′to·phyt′ic** (-fit′ik) *adj.* —**au′to·phyt′i·cal·ly** *adv.*

au·to·pi·lot (-pī′lət) *n.* AUTOMATIC PILOT

au·to·plas·ty (-plas′tē) *n.* ⟦AUTO- + -PLASTY⟧ the repairing of injuries by grafting in tissue from another part of the patient's body: see HOMOPLASTIC (sense 2), HETEROPLASTY —**au′to·plas′tic** *adj.*

au·top·sy (ô′täp′sē, ôt′əp sē) *n., pl.* **-sies** ⟦ML & Gr *autopsia*, a seeing with one's own eyes < Gr *autos*, self + *opsis*, a sight < *ōps*, EYE⟧ **1** an examination and dissection of a dead body to discover the cause of death, damage done by disease, etc.; postmortem **2** a detailed critical analysis of a book, play, etc., or of some event —*vt.* **-sied**, **-sy·ing** to examine (a body) in this manner

au·to·ra·di·o·graph (ôt′ō rā′dē ə graf′) *n.* ⟦AUTO- + RADIOGRAPH⟧ an X-ray photograph made by bringing an object containing radioactive material into close contact with the emulsion on a film or plate: it shows the pattern of radioactivity in the object: also **au′to·ra′di·o·gram′** —**au′to·ra′di·o·graph′ic** *adj.* —**au′to·ra′di·og′ra·phy** (-äg′rə fē) *n.*

au·to·some (ôt′ə sōm′) *n.* ⟦AUTO- + (CHROMO)SOME⟧ any chromosome that is not a sex chromosome; specif., either of a pair of like chromosomes in a diploid cell —**au′to·so′mal** (-sō′məl) *adj.*

au·to·stra·da (ôt′ō strä′də; *It* ou′tô strä′dä) *n., pl.* **-das** or **-de** (-de) ⟦It < *auto*, contr. < *automobile* (< Fr: see AUTOMOBILE) + *strada*, road < LL *strata*: see STREET⟧ in Italy, an expressway

au·to·sug·ges·tion (ôt′ō səg jes′chən) *n.* suggestion to oneself arising within one's own mind and having effects on one's thinking and bodily functions

au·to·tel·ic (-tel′ik) *adj.* ⟦< Gr *autotelēs*, complete in itself (see AUTO- & TELEOLOGY) + -IC⟧ having an end in itself; engaged in for its own sake, as some creative art —**au′to·tel′ism′** *n.*

au·tot·o·mize (ô tät′ə mīz′) *vi., vt.* **-mized′**, **-miz′ing** to undergo or cause to undergo autotomy

au·tot·o·my (-mē) *n.* ⟦AUTO- + -TOMY⟧ the reflex action by which a leg, claw, tail, etc., as of a lobster, starfish, or lizard, is broken off at a special joint when the part is damaged, seized, etc.: the missing part then regenerates —**au·to·tom·ic** (ôt′ə täm′ik) *adj.*

au·to·tox·e·mi·a or **au·to·tox·ae·mi·a** (ôt′ō täks ē′mē ə) *n.* ⟦AUTO- + TOXEMIA⟧ AUTOINTOXICATION

au·to·tox·in (ôt′ō täk′sin) *n.* any toxin or poison produced within the body —**au′to·tox′ic** *adj.*

au·to·trans·form·er (ôt′ō trans′fôrm′ər) *n. Elec.* a transformer with at least part of the windings common to both the primary and the secondary circuits

au·to·troph·ic (ôt′ō träf′ik) *adj.* ⟦AUTO- + TROPHIC⟧ making its own food by photosynthesis, as a green plant does, or by chemosynthesis, as any of certain bacteria do: cf. HETEROTROPHIC —**au′to·troph′** (-träf′) *n.* —**au′to·troph′i·cal·ly** *adv.*

au·to·work·er (ôt′ō wurk′ər, ät′-) *n.* a worker in a factory where automobiles are manufactured

au·tox·i·da·tion (ô täks′ə dā′shən) *n.* ⟦AUT(O)- + OXIDATION⟧ *Chem.* the oxidation of a substance by its exposure to air —**au·tox′i·da′tive** (-tiv) *adj.*

au·tres temps, au·tres moeurs (ō trə tän ō trə mërs′) ⟦Fr⟧ other times, other customs

au·tumn (ôt′əm) *n.* ⟦ME *autumpne* < OFr *autompne* < L *autumnus, auctumnus*; prob. of Etr orig.⟧ **1** the season that comes between summer and winter; fall: in the astronomical year, that period between the autumnal equinox and the winter solstice **2** any period of maturity or of beginning decline —*adj.* of, in, for, or characteristic of fall —**au·tum·nal** (ô tum′nəl) *adj.* —**au·tum′nal·ly** *adv.*

autumn crocus COLCHICUM (sense 1)

autumn olive a spiny shrub (*Elaeagnus umbellata*) of the oleaster family, having leaves covered with silvery or brown scales: see RUSSIAN OLIVE

au·tun·ite (ô′tən īt′) *n.* ⟦after *Autun*, town in France + -ITE[1]⟧ a hydrous, radioactive, tetragonal mineral, $Ca(UO_2)_2(PO_4)_2 \cdot 10\text{-}12H_2O$: it is an ore of uranium

Au·vergne (ō vurn′; *Fr* ō ver′ny′) **1** historical region of SC France **2** metropolitan region in SC France: 10,044 sq mi (26,014 sq km); chief city, Clermont-Ferrand **3** mountain range running north to south through this region: highest peak, 6,188 ft (1,886 m): in full **Auvergne Mountains**

aux or **Aux** *abbrev.* auxiliary

aux·e·sis (ôks ē′sis) *n.* ⟦ModL < Gr *auxēsis*, growth < *auxein*, to increase: see WAX[2]⟧ *Biol.* the process of cell growth caused by the increase of cell volume prior to cell division —**aux·et′ic** (-et′ik) *adj.*

aux·il·ia·ry (ôg zil′yə rē; -zil′ē ə rē, -ē er′ē; *often*, -zil′ə rē) *adj.* ⟦L *auxiliaris*, helpful < *auxilium*, aid < pp. of *augere*, to increase: see WAX[2]⟧ **1** giving help or aid; assisting or supporting **2** acting in a subsidiary, or subordinate, capacity **3** additional; supplementary; reserve **4** having an engine that can be used for supplementary power, as a sailing vessel **5** designating or of any of the noncombat ships, as tankers or tenders, that form the service fleet of a navy —*n., pl.* **-ries** **1** an auxiliary person or thing **2** [*pl.*] foreign or allied armed forces aiding those of a country at war **3** an assisting or supplementary group or organization [this club has a women's *auxiliary*] **4** an auxiliary vessel or ship **5** *Gram.* AUXILIARY VERB

auxiliary verb *Gram.* a verb used to help form the tenses, aspects, voices, or moods of other verbs, as *will, have, do, be, should, must*

aux·in (ôk′sin) *n.* ⟦< Gr *auxein*, to increase (see WAX[2]) + -IN[1]⟧ a plant hormone, esp. indoleacetic acid, produced in the fruits, seeds, leaves, or stem tips, to promote longitudinal growth and to control bud growth, root formation, leaf abscission, etc.: also produced synthetically —**aux·in·ic** (ôks in′ik) *adj.*

aux·o·chrome (ôk′sə krōm′) *n.* ⟦< Gr *auxanein*, to increase (< *auxein*: see prec.) + CHROME⟧ a radical or atom group, as NH_2 or OH, needed to bond organic dyes to fabric fibers

aux·o·troph·ic (ôk′sə träf′ik) *adj.* ⟦< Gr *auxein*, to increase + -TROPHIC⟧ designating or of a mutant organism requiring more nutritional substances than its prototrophic parent because it has lost the ability to make a certain enzyme —**aux′o·troph′** (-träf′) *n.*

av *abbrev.* **1** ad valorem: also **a/v** or **A/V** **2** average **3** avoirdupois

Av[1] (äv) *n. var. of* AB

Av[2] *abbrev.* **1** Avenue **2** avoirdupois

AV *abbrev.* **1** audiovisual **2** Authorized Version (of the Bible)

av·a·da·vat (av′ə də vat′) *n.* a small waxbill (*Estrilda amandava*) of Southeast Asia, kept as a caged bird for its singing ability

a·vail (ə vāl′) *vi., vt.* ⟦ME *availen* < OFr *a* (L *ad*), to + *valoir*, to be worth < L *valere*, to be strong: see VALUE⟧ to be of use, help, worth, or advantage (to), as in accomplishing an end [will force alone *avail* us?] —*n.* **1** effective use or help; advantage [he tried, but to no *avail*] **2** [*pl.*] [Obs.] net proceeds; profits —**avail oneself of** to take advantage of (an opportunity, etc.); utilize

a·vail·a·bil·i·ty (ə vāl′ə bil′ə tē) *n.* **1** the quality or condition of being available **2** *pl.* **-ties** an available person or thing

a·vail·a·ble (ə vāl′ə bəl) *adj.* **1** that one can avail oneself of; that can be used; usable **2** that can be gotten, had, or reached; handy; accessible **3** able to be understood or generally appreciated [one of Shakespeare's more *available* plays] **4** not married, engaged, etc., and therefore a potential romantic or sexual partner **5** [Obs.] that can avail ☆**6** *Politics a)* having qualifications that would make one a strong candidate for an elective office *b)* willing and able to run for office —**a·vail′a·bly** *adv.*

av·a·lanche (av′ə lanch′) *n.* ⟦Fr (altered after *avaler*, to descend) < *lavanche* < Prov *lavanca* < **lavenca*, prob. a pre-Roman word in a non-IE language of N Italy⟧ **1** a mass of loosened snow, earth, rocks, etc. suddenly and swiftly sliding down a mountain, often growing as it descends **2** any large, overwhelming quantity that comes suddenly [an *avalanche* of mail, of blows, etc.] —*vi., vt.* **-lanched′**, **-lanch′ing** to come down (on) like an avalanche

☆**avalanche lily** a wildflower (*Erythronium montanum*) of the lily family, native to the mountain meadows of Washington and Oregon and blooming in June among the melting snowbanks

Av·a·lon or **Av·al·lon** (av′ə län′) *n.* ⟦Fr < ML *Avallonis (insula)* < Welsh (*ynys yr*) *Afallon*, (island of) apples: cf. APPLE⟧ *Celt. Legend* the isle of the dead, an island paradise in the west where King Arthur and other heroes are taken after death

Avalon Peninsula peninsula forming the SE corner of Newfoundland, Canada

a·vant-garde (ə vänt′gärd′, ä′-, a′-; *Fr* ȧ vän gȧrd′) *n.* ⟦Fr, lit., advance guard⟧ the leading position or persons in new or unconventional movements, esp. in the arts; vanguard —*adj.* of such movements, ideas, etc. —**a·vant′-gard′ism′** *n.* —**a·vant′-gard′ist** *n.*

a·vant la let·tre (ȧ vän lȧ le′tr′) ⟦Fr⟧ before the (specified) concept, word, person, etc. existed [a mid-Victorian matron who was a feminist *avant la lettre*]

av·a·rice (av′ə ris) *n.* ⟦ME & OFr < L *avaritia* < *avarus*, greedy < *avere*, to desire⟧ too great a desire to have wealth; cupidity

av·a·ri·cious (av′ə rish′əs) *adj.* full of avarice; greedy for riches —*SYN.* GREEDY —**av′a·ri′cious·ly** *adv.* —**av′a·ri′cious·ness** *n.*

a·vast (ə vast′) *interj.* ⟦< Du *hou'vast, houd vast*, hold fast⟧ *Naut.* stop; cease; halt

av·a·tar (av′ə tär′) *n.* ⟦Sans *avatāra* < *ava-*, down + base of *tarati*, (he) crosses over: see TERM[2]⟧ **1** *Hinduism* a god appearing on earth in bodily form; incarnation of a god **2** any incarnation or embodiment, as of a quality or concept in a person

a·vaunt (ə vônt′, -vänt′) *interj.* ⟦ME < OFr *avant*, forward < LL *abante* < L *ab*, from + *ante*, before⟧ [Archaic] begone; go away

avdp *abbrev.* avoirdupois

a·ve (ä′vā, ā′vē) *interj.* ⟦L, prob. of Punic orig., lit., live!⟧ **1** hail **2** farewell —*n.* **1** the salutation *ave* **2** [**A-**] the prayer AVE MARIA

Ave *abbrev.* Avenue

a·ve at·que va·le (ä′vā ät′kwā vä′lā) ⟦L⟧ hail and farewell: from an ode of Catullus in commemoration of his dead brother

A·vel·la·ne·da (ä ve′yä ne′thä; *locally, also* ä ve′zhä-) city in E Argentina, on the Río de la Plata: suburb of Buenos Aires

A·ve Ma·ri·a (ä′vā mə rē′ə, ä′vē-) ⟦ME < L, "Hail, Mary" (Luke 1:28)⟧ **1** a prayer to the Virgin Mary used in the Roman Catholic Church **2** a musical setting of this prayer

a·venge (ə venj′) *vt.* **a·venged′**, **a·veng′ing** ⟦ME *avengen* < OFr *avengier* < *a-* (L *ad*), to + *vengier*, *venger* < L *vindicare*, to claim: see VINDICATE⟧ **1** to get revenge for (an injury, wrong, etc.) **2** to take vengeance on behalf of, as for a wrong —**a·veng′er** *n.*

SYN.—**avenge** implies the infliction of deserved or just punishment for wrongs or oppressions; **revenge** implies the infliction of punishment as an act of retaliation, usually for an injury against oneself, and connotes personal malice, bitter resentment, etc. as the moving force

av·ens (av′ənz) *n.* ⟦ME & OFr *avence*⟧ any of a genus (*Geum*) of herbaceous plants of the rose family, with compound leaves and variously colored, usually yellow, flowers

Av·en·tine (av′en tīn′, -tēn′) *see* SEVEN HILLS OF ROME

a·ven·tu·rine (ə ven′chə rin) *n.* ⟦Fr < It (*vetro*) *avventurino*, aventurine (glass): so named from resembling the mineral *avventurina* (< *avventura*, chance), so named from its rarity: see ADVENTURE⟧ **1** a kind of glass flecked with spangles, as from copper filings or bits of chromic oxide **2** a translucent mineral containing reflective particles; specif., a variety of chert that contains sparkling bits of mica, hematite, etc.

av·e·nue (av′ə no͞o′, -nyo͞o′) *n.* ⟦Fr < *avenir*, to happen, come < L *advenire*: see ADVENT⟧ **1** *a)* a roadway, pathway, or drive, often bordered with trees *b)* [Brit.] such a roadway, etc. leading from the main road to the house on an estate **2** a way of approach to something [books are *avenues* to knowledge] ☆**3** a street, esp. a wide, principal one; often, one running at right angles to others called "streets"

a·ver (ə vʉr′) *vt.* **a·verred′**, **a·ver′ring** ⟦ME *averren* < OFr *averer*, to confirm < L *ad-*, to + *verus*, true: see VERY⟧ **1** to declare to be true; state positively; affirm **2** *Law* to state or declare formally; assert; allege —***SYN.*** ASSERT —**a·ver′ment** *n.*

av·er·age (av′ər ij, av′rij) *n.* ⟦altered (by assoc. with ME *average*, money rent paid in place of service by the tenant with his horses < *aver*, draft horse) < OFr *avarie*, damage to ship or goods, mooring charges < OIt *avaria* < Ar ʿ*awār*, damaged goods; order of main sense development (in ***n.***), 6*a*, 6*c*, 1, 2, etc.⟧ **1** the numerical result obtained by dividing the sum of two or more quantities by the number of quantities; an arithmetic mean **2** *a)* GRADE-POINT AVERAGE *b)* an approximation of this [an *average* of C in French] **3** usual or normal kind, amount, quality, rate, etc. [an intelligence above the *average*] **4** a number or value of a set of values carefully defined to typify the set, as a median or mode ☆**5** BATTING AVERAGE **6** *Maritime Law a)* a loss incurred by damage to a ship at sea or to its cargo *b)* an incurring of such loss *c)* the equitable division of such loss among the interested parties *d)* a charge arising from such loss *e)* any of various small charges paid by the master of a ship, as for pilotage or towage —***adj.*** **1** constituting an average [the *average* speed is high] **2** intermediate in value, rate, etc.; hence, normal or ordinary [an *average* student] —***vi.*** **-aged**, **-ag·ing** **1** to be or amount to on an average [the children *average* six years of age] **2** to buy or sell additional fixed amounts, as of shares of stock, at lower or higher prices over time so as to get a better average price: usually with *down* or *up* **3** to invest, as in shares of stock, fixed amounts of money at regular intervals so as to buy more at lower prices and less at higher prices: usually in phrase *dollar (cost) averaging* —***vt.*** **1** to calculate the average or mean of **2** to do, take, etc. on an average [to *average* six hours of sleep a night] **3** to divide proportionately among more than two [they *averaged* the loss among themselves] —**average out** to arrive at an average eventually —**on (the) average** as an average quantity, rate, etc.

SYN.—**average** refers to the result obtained by dividing a sum by the number of quantities added [the *average* of 7, 9, 17 is 33 ÷ 3, or 11] and in extended use is applied to the usual or ordinary kind, instance, etc.; **mean** commonly designates a figure intermediate between two extremes [the *mean* temperature for a day with a high of 56° and a low of 34° is 45°] and figuratively implies moderation [the golden *mean*]; the **median** is the middle number or point in a series arranged in order of size [the *median* grade in the group 50, 55, 85, 88, 92 is 85; the average is 74]; **norm** implies a standard of average performance for a given group [a child below the *norm* for his age in reading comprehension] See also **normal**

A·ver·nus[1] (ə vʉr′nəs) *n.* ⟦see fol.⟧ Hades; hell

A·ver·nus[2] (ə vʉr′nəs) ⟦L⟧ small lake in an extinct volcano near Naples, Italy, at the edge of which the entrance to Hades was anciently said to be: It. name ***A·ver·no*** (ä ver′nô)

A·ver·ro·ës or **A·ver·rho·ës** (ə ver′ō ēz′) (Ar. *ibn-Rushd*) 1126-98; Arab philosopher & physician in Spain & Morocco

a·verse (ə vʉrs′) *adj.* ⟦L *aversus*, pp. of *avertere*, AVERT⟧ **1** not willing or inclined; opposed (*to*) **2** *Bot.* turned away from the main stem —***SYN.*** RELUCTANT —**a·verse′ly** *adv.* —**a·verse′ness** *n.*

a·ver·sion (ə vʉr′zhən, -shən) *n.* ⟦L *aversio* < *aversus*, pp. of *avertere*: see AVERT⟧ **1** [Obs.] the act of turning away **2** an intense or definite dislike; antipathy; repugnance **3** the object arousing such dislike

SYN.—**aversion** and **antipathy** both imply an ingrained feeling against that which is disagreeable or offensive, **aversion** stressing avoidance or rejection, and **antipathy**, active hostility; **repugnance** emphasizes the emotional resistance or opposition one offers to that which is incompatible with one's ideas, tastes, etc.; **loathing** suggests a feeling of extreme disgust or intolerance; **revulsion** suggests a drawing back or away from in disgust, horror, etc.; **abhorrence** implies a feeling of extreme aversion or repugnance —***ANT.*** **attraction, affinity**

aversion therapy therapy designed to suppress undesirable behavior, as a compulsion or addiction, by conditioning a person to associate the behavior with an unpleasant or painful stimulus

a·ver·sive (ə vʉr′siv) *adj.* ⟦AVERS(ION) + -IVE⟧ **1** characterized by aversion **2** *Psychol.* designating or having to do with conditioning, therapy, etc. intended to produce an aversion to a certain kind of undesirable behavior

a·vert (ə vʉrt′) *vt.* ⟦L *avertere*, to turn away < *a-* (*ab-*), from + *vertere*, to turn: see VERSE⟧ **1** to turn away [to *avert* one's glance from an ugly sight] **2** to keep from happening; ward off; prevent [he apologized in order to *avert* trouble] —***SYN.*** PREVENT

A·ves·ta (ə ves′tə) *n.* ⟦Pers < earlier *Avistāk*, lit., original text⟧ the sacred writings of the Zoroastrian religion

A·ves·tan (-tən) *n.* the Iranian language in which the Avesta was written: it is closely related to Old Persian —***adj.*** of the Avesta or Avestan

avg *abbrev.* average

☆**av·gas** (av′gas′) *n.* ⟦*av(iation) gas(oline)*⟧ gasoline for aircraft

av·go·lem·o·no (äv′gō lem′ə nō′) *n.* ⟦ModGr < *augon*, egg + *lemōnion*, lemon⟧ **1** a Greek soup of lemon juice and beaten eggs blended into a meat stock, containing rice, noodles, etc. **2** a sauce of lemon juice, beaten eggs, and meat stock

a·vi·an (ā′vē ən) *adj.* ⟦< L *avis*, bird + -AN⟧ of or having to do with birds —***n.*** a bird

avian flu BIRD FLU: also **avian influenza**

a·vi·ar·y (ā′vē er′ē) *n.*, *pl.* **-ar′ies** ⟦L *aviarium* < *avis*, bird⟧ a large cage or building for keeping many birds

a·vi·a·tion (ā′vē ā′shən; *occas.* av′ē-) *n.* ⟦Fr < L *avis*, bird⟧ **1** the art or science of flying airplanes **2** the development and operation of heavier-than-air craft, including airplanes and piloted or guided rocket ships **3** aircraft, esp. military aircraft, collectively

aviation medicine a branch of medicine that embraces aeromedicine and space medicine; aerospace medicine

a·vi·a·tor (ā′vē āt′ər; *occas.* av′ē-) *n.* ⟦Fr *aviateur*⟧ an airplane pilot; flyer

aviator glasses sunglasses with large tinted, reflective lenses of a modified oval shape, held in a thin metal frame

a·vi·a·trix (ā′vē ā′triks) *n.*, *pl.* **-trix·es** or **-tri·ces′** (-tri sēz′) a female aviator

Av·i·cen·na (av′i sen′ə) (Ar. *ibn-sīnā*) A.D. 980-1037; Islamic physician & philosopher, born in Persia

a·vi·cul·ture (ā′vi kul′chər, av′ə-) *n.* ⟦< L *avis*, bird + *cultura*, CULTURE⟧ the raising and care of birds —**a′vi·cul′tur·ist** *n.*

av·id (av′id) *adj.* ⟦L *avidus* < *avere*, to desire⟧ **1** having an intense craving; greedy [*avid* for power] **2** eager and enthusiastic [an *avid* reader] —***SYN.*** EAGER[1] —**a·vid·i·ty** (ə vid′ə tē) *n.* —**av′id·ly** *adv.*

av·i·din (av′ə din) *n.* ⟦prec. + -IN[1]: so named because of its peculiar biotin-binding capacity⟧ a protein in raw egg white that binds to biotin, making the biotin inactive in the body

a·vi·fau·na (ā′və fô′nə) *n.* ⟦< L *avis*, bird + FAUNA⟧ the birds of a specified region or time —**a′vi·fau′nal** *adj.*

A·vi·gnon (à vē nyōn′) city in SE France, on the Rhone River: seat of the papacy (1309-77)

a·vi·on·ics (ā′vē än′iks; *occas.* av′ē-) *n.* ⟦AVI(ATION) + (ELECTR)ONICS⟧ the branch of electronics dealing with the development and use of electronic equipment in aviation and astronautics —***pl.n.*** the electronic devices, systems, etc. used in an aircraft or spacecraft [the plane's *avionics* need upgrading] —**a′vi·on′ic** *adj.*

a·vir·u·lent (ā′vir′yoo lənt) *adj.* not virulent or no longer virulent

a·vi·ta·min·o·sis (ā′vīt′ə mi nō′sis) *n.*, *pl.* **-ses** (-sēz) ⟦A-[2] + VITAMIN + -OSIS⟧ any disease caused by a deficiency of vitamins

☆**av·o·ca·do** (av′ə kä′dō, ä′və-) *n.*, *pl.* **-dos** ⟦altered (infl. by earlier Sp *avocado*, now *abogado*, advocate) < MexSp *aguacate* < Nahuatl *a:wakaλ*, avocado, lit., testicle; so named from its shape⟧ **1** a widespread, thick-skinned, pear-shaped tropical fruit, yellowish green to purplish black, with a single large seed and yellow, buttery flesh, used in salads; alligator pear **2** the tree (*Persea americana*) of the laurel family on which it grows **3** a yellowish-green color

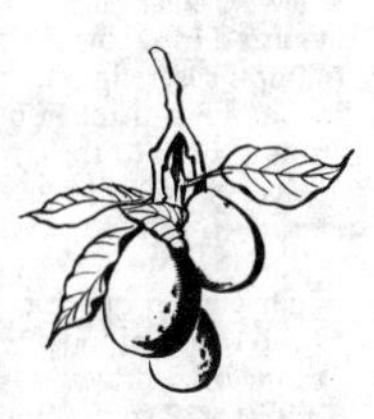
avocado

av·o·ca·tion (av′ə kā′shən) *n.* ⟦L *avocatio*, a calling away < pp. of *avocare* < *a-* (*ab-*), away + *vocare*, to call < *vox*, VOICE⟧ **1** [Obs.] the fact of being called away or distracted from something **2** something one does in addition to a vocation or regular work, and usually for pleasure; hobby **3** [Now Rare] one's regular work; vocation —**av′o·ca′tion·al** *adj.*

av·o·cet (av′ə set′) *n.* ⟦Fr *avocette* < It *avocetta*⟧ any of a genus (*Recurvirostra*, family Recurvirostridae) of long-legged shorebirds with webbed feet and a slender bill that curves upward

A·vo·ga·dro (ä′vô gä′drô; *E* äv′ə gä′drō), **A·me·de·o** (ä′me de′ô) (*Conte di Quaregna e Ceretto*) 1776-1856; It. chemist & physicist

Avogadro constant (*or* number) the number of molecules contained in one mole (molecular weight in grams) of a substance, equal to 6.02214179 × 10^{23}: symbol, N, N_A, or L: often **Avogadro's number**

Avogadro's law the principle, formulated by Avogadro, that equal volumes of all gases under identical conditions of temperature and pressure contain equal numbers of molecules

a·void (ə void′) *vt.* ⟦ME *avoiden* < Anglo-Fr *avoider* < OFr *esvuidier*, to empty < *es-* (< L *ex-*), out + *vuidier*: see VOID⟧ **1** *Law* to make void; annul, invalidate, or quash (a plea, etc.) **2** to keep away from; evade; shun [to *avoid* crowds] **3** to keep from happening [to *avoid* breakage] **4** [Obs.] to void; empty **5** [Obs.] to go away from; leave —***SYN.*** ESCAPE —**a·void′a·ble** *adj.* —**a·void′a·bly** *adv.*

a·void·ance (-'ns) *n.* **1** the act of avoiding, or shunning something **2** *Law* the act of making void; annulment

av·oir·du·pois (av′ər də poiz′) *n.* ⟦ME *aver de poiz* < OFr *aveir de peis* < *aveir*, goods (< L *habere*, to have) + *de* (< L *de*), of + *peis* (< L *pensum*), weight⟧ **1** AVOIRDUPOIS WEIGHT ☆**2** [Informal] heaviness or weight, esp. of a person

avoirdupois weight a British and American system of weights based on a pound of 16 ounces: see the table of weights and measures in the Reference Supplement

A·von (ā′vän′, ā′vən) **1** former county of SW England, on the Severn estuary & Bristol Channel: 514 sq mi (1,331 sq km) **2** any of three rivers in S & SW England, esp. the one flowing from Northamptonshire into the Severn, on which lies Stratford-upon-Avon: 96 mi (154 km)

à vo·tre san·té (à vô′tr′ sän tā′) ⟦Fr⟧ to your health: used as a toast

a·vouch (ə vouch′) *vt.* ⟦ME *avouchen* < OFr *avochier*, to affirm positively < L *advocare*: see ADVOCATE⟧ **1** to vouch for; guarantee **2** to declare the truth of; assert; affirm **3** to acknowledge openly; avow —*SYN.* ASSERT —**a·vouch′ment** *n.*

a·vow (ə vou′) *vt.* ⟦ME *avowen* < OFr *avouer* < L *advocare*: see ADVOCATE⟧ **1** to declare openly or admit frankly **2** to acknowledge or claim (oneself) to be [he *avowed* himself a patriot] —*SYN.* ACKNOWLEDGE —**a·vow′er** *n.*

a·vow·al (ə vou′əl) *n.* open acknowledgment or declaration

a·vowed (ə voud′) *adj.* openly declared or frankly acknowledged [her *avowed* purpose] —**a·vow·ed·ly** (ə vou′id lē) *adv.*

a·vul·sion (ə vul′shən) *n.* ⟦L *avulsio* < *a-*, from + pp. of *vellere*, to pull: see REVULSION⟧ **1** a separation by force **2** *Med.* the tearing away of a structure or part by surgical traction or by accident **3** a structure, part, etc. separated by force **4** the sudden removal of a person's land by the action of water, as by flood or change in the course of a stream, without a resulting loss of ownership

a·vun·cu·lar (ə vuŋ′kyo͞o lər) *adj.* ⟦< L *avunculus*, maternal uncle, dim. of *avus*, ancestor (see ATAVISM) + -AR⟧ **1** of an uncle **2** having traits considered typical of uncles; jolly, indulgent, stodgy, etc.

aw (ô, ä) *interj.* used to express *a)* mild protest, dislike, or disgust *b)* mild sympathy or commiseration

☆**AWACS** or **A·wacs** (ā′waks′) *n.* ⟦*A(irborne) W(arning) A(nd) C(ontrol) S(ystem)*⟧ a system employing high-flying reconnaissance aircraft equipped with a special radar system that can detect and track approaching aircraft, missiles, etc.

a·wait (ə wāt′) *vt.* ⟦ME *awaiten* < Anglo-Norm *awaitier* < *a-* (L *ad*), to + *waitier*, WAIT)⟧ **1** to wait for; expect **2** to be in store for; be ready for **3** [Obs.] to watch for so as to confront —*vi.* to wait —*SYN.* EXPECT

a·wake (ə wāk′) *vt.* **a·woke′** or **a·waked′**, **a·waked′** or **a·wok′en**, **a·wak′ing** ⟦a merging of two words: ME *awaken* < OE *awacan* (*on-*, out + *wacan*, to arise, awake) & ME *awakien* < OE *awacian* (*on-*, out + *wacian*, to be awake, watch): see WAKE[1]⟧ **1** to rouse from sleep; wake **2** to rouse from inactivity; stir up **3** to call forth (memories, fear, etc.) **4** to make aware: with *to* —*vi.* **1** to come out of sleep; wake **2** to become active **3** to become aware: with *to* —*adj.* ⟦< obs. pp. *awaken*⟧ **1** not asleep **2** active or alert; aware

a·wak·en (ə wā′kən) *vt., vi.* ⟦ME *awakenen* < OE *awæcnian*, to awaken < *on-*, out + *wæcnian*, to WAKEN⟧ to awake; wake up; rouse —*SYN.* STIR[1] —**a·wak′en·er** *n.*

a·wak·en·ing (-iŋ) *n., adj.* **1** (a) waking up **2** (an) arousing or reviving, as of impulses, religion, etc. —☆**the Great Awakening** any of several American movements of religious revival, specif., *a)* one in the American Colonies from *c.* 1720 to the time of the Revolution *b)* one in the U.S. in the late 19th & early 20th cent.

a·ward (ə wôrd′) *vt.* ⟦ME *awarden* < Anglo-Fr *awarder* < Anglo-Norm *eswarder* < *es-* (< L *ex*) + Gmc **wardon*: see WARN⟧ **1** to give by the decision of a law court or arbitrator [the plaintiff was *awarded* damages] **2** to give as the result of judging the relative merits of those in competition; grant [to *award* a prize for the best essay] —*n.* **1** a decision, as by a judge or arbitrator **2** something that is awarded; prize —*SYN.* REWARD —**a·ward′a·ble** *adj.* —**a·ward′ee′** *n.*

a·ware (ə wer′) *adj.* ⟦ME < OE *gewær* < *wær*, cautious: see WARN⟧ **1** [Obs.] on one's guard; vigilant **2** knowing or realizing; conscious; informed —**a·ware′ness** *n.*

SYN.—**aware** implies having knowledge of something through alertness in observing or in interpreting what one sees, hears, feels, etc. [to be *aware* of a fact]; **conscious** implies awareness of a sensation, feeling, fact, condition, etc. and may suggest mere recognition or a focusing of attention [*conscious* of a draft in the room, *conscious* humor]; one is **cognizant** of something when one has certain or special knowledge of it through observation or information [*cognizant* of the terms of the will]; **sensible** implies awareness of something that is not expressed directly or explicitly [*sensible* of their solemn grief]

a·wash (ə wôsh′) *adv., adj.* **1** just above the surface of the water so that breakers, tide, etc. flow over **2** floating on the water **3** flooded with water

a·way (ə wā′) *adv.* ⟦ME < OE *aweg* < phr. *on weg* < *on*, on + *weg*, WAY, in the sense "from this (that) place"⟧ **1** from any given place; off [to run *away*] **2** in another place, esp. the proper place [to put one's tools *away*] **3** in another direction [look *away*, turn *away*] **4** by a considerable time or distance; far [*away* behind] **5** so as to be removed; aside [to clear snow *away*, to get *away* from the subject] **6** from one's possession [to give *away* a secret] **7** out of existence [the sound faded *away*] **8** at once [fire *away*] **9** without stopping; continuously [he worked *away* all night] **10** into action or movement [*away* we go!] —*adj.* **1** not present; absent; gone [he is *away*] **2** at a distance [a mile *away*] ☆**3** played or playing on a competing team's field, court, etc. [an *away* game] ☆**4** *Baseball* out [one *away* in the last half of the 4th] **5** *Golf* designating the player (or the ball) that is farthest from the cup and hence is required to shoot (or be shot) first —*interj.* **1** begone **2** let's go —**away with 1** take away **2** go or come away Used generally as an imperative expression without a verb —**do away with 1** to get rid of; put an end to **2** to kill —**where away?** *Naut.* in what direction?: usually said in response to a lookout's report of sighting something

AWD *abbrev.* **1** all-wheel drive **2** all-wheel-drive vehicle

awe (ô) *n.* ⟦ME *age, aghe, awe* < ON *agi* < IE base **agh-*, to be depressed, afraid > OE *ege*, Goth *agis*, Gr *achos*⟧ **1** a mixed feeling of reverence, fear, and wonder, caused by something majestic, sublime, sacred, etc. **2** [Archaic] the power of inspiring intense fear or fearful reverence **3** [Obs.] terror; dread —*vt.* **awed**, **aw′ing** to inspire awe in; fill with awe —**stand** (or **be**) **in awe of** to respect and fear

SYN.—**awe** refers to a feeling of fearful or profound respect or wonder inspired by the greatness, superiority, grandeur, etc. of a person or thing and suggests an immobilizing effect; **reverence** is applied to a feeling of deep respect mingled with love for something one holds sacred or inviolable and suggests a display of homage, deference, etc.; **veneration** implies worshipful reverence for a person or thing regarded as hallowed or sacred and specifically suggests acts of religious devotion; **dread**, as it comes into comparison here, suggests extreme fear mixed with awe or reverence [a *dread* of divine retribution]

a·wear·y (ə wir′ē) *adj.* [Old Poet.] weary; tired (*of*)

a·weath·er (ə weth′ər) *adv., adj.* ⟦A-[1] + WEATHER⟧ *Naut.* on or toward the weather side of a ship; windward

a·weigh (ə wā′) *adj.* ⟦A-[1] + WEIGH[2]⟧ *Naut.* just clear of the bottom: said of an anchor that is being weighed

awe·less or **aw·less** (ô′lis) *adj.* feeling no awe

awe·some (ô′səm) *adj.* ⟦AWE + -SOME[1]⟧ **1** inspiring awe **2** [Now Rare] showing awe **3** [Slang] wonderful; impressive; excellent —**awe′some·ly** *adv.* —**awe′some·ness** *n.*

awe·struck (ô′struk′) *adj.* filled with awe: also **awe′strick′en** (-strik′ən)

aw·ful (ô′fəl) *adj.* ⟦ME *awful, agheful*: see AWE & -FUL⟧ **1** inspiring awe; highly impressive **2** causing fear; terrifying **3** dreadful; appalling **4** full of awe; reverential **5** very bad, ugly, unpleasant, etc. [an *awful* joke] **6** [Informal] great [an *awful* lot of laughing] —☆*adv.* [Informal] very; extremely —**aw′ful·ness** *n.*

aw·ful·ly (ô′fə lē, ô′flē) *adv.* **1** in a way to inspire awe ☆**2** in a bad or offensive way [to behave *awfully*] **3** [Informal] very; very much; extremely

a·while (ə wīl′, -hwīl′) *adv.* ⟦ME < OE *ane hwile*, a while⟧ for a while; for a short time —*n.* a while; an unspecified period of time, often, specif., a lengthy one: used as an object of a preposition: sp. objected to by many [he lingered for *awhile*]

awk·ward (ôk′wərd) *adj.* ⟦ME *aukward* < ON *ǫfugr*, turned backward + OE *-weard*, -WARD⟧ **1** not having grace or skill; clumsy, as in form or movement; bungling [an *awkward* dancer, an *awkward* style] **2** inconvenient to use; hard to handle; unwieldy [an *awkward* tool] **3** inconvenient; uncomfortable; cramped [an *awkward* position] **4** showing or resulting from lack of social poise; embarrassed or embarrassing [an *awkward* remark] **5** not easy to deal with; delicate [an *awkward* situation] **6** [Obs.] perverse or untoward —**awk′ward·ly** *adv.* —**awk′ward·ness** *n.*

SYN.—**awkward** implies unfitness for smooth, easy functioning and has the broadest application of the terms here, suggesting ungracefulness, inconvenience, tactlessness, embarrassment, etc. [an *awkward* implement, step, position, remark, etc.]; **clumsy**, emphasizing stiffness or bulkiness, suggests a lack of flexibility or dexterity, unwieldiness, etc. [a *clumsy* build, *clumsy* galoshes]; **maladroit** and **inept** both imply tactlessness in social relations, **maladroit** often emphasizing this as a tendency and **inept** stressing inappropriateness of a particular act or remark —*ANT.* **deft, handy, graceful**

awl (ôl) *n.* ⟦earlier (16th c.) *aule* < ME *alle* < OE *æl* < IE base **ēlā* (> ON *alr*), **ēlā* (> Sans *ārā*)⟧ a small, pointed tool for making holes in wood, leather, etc.

awl-shaped (-shāpt′) *adj. Bot.* shaped like an awl

awl·wort (ôl′wurt′) *n.* a small water plant (*Subularia aquatica*) of the crucifer family, bearing clusters of awl-shaped leaves around the root

awn (ôn) *n.* ⟦ME *aune* < ON *ǫgn* (pl. *agnir*) < IE **aken* < base **ak-* (see ACID) > OE *egenu*, Goth *ahana*, L *agna*⟧ *Bot.* any bristlelike fiber or fibers, as on the head of barley, oats, or wheat; beard —**awned** *adj.* —**awn′less** *adj.*

awns

awn·ing (ô′niŋ) *n.* ⟦< ? MFr *auvans*, (pl. of *auvent*, a sloping roof < OProv *amban*, parapet of a fortification) + -ING⟧ a structure of canvas, metal, etc. projecting from above a window or door or over a patio, deck, etc. as a protection from the sun or rain

a·woke (ə wōk′) *vt., vi. pt. of* AWAKE

a·wok·en (ə wō′kən) *vt., vi. alt. pp. of* AWAKE

☆**AWOL** or **a·wol** (ā′wôl′) *adj., adv.* **1** *Mil.* ABSENT WITHOUT LEAVE **2** [Informal] absent from one's proper or designated place without permission —*n.* one who is AWOL

a·wry (ə rī′) *adv., adj.* ⟦ME *a wrie*: see A-[1] & WRY⟧ **1** with a twist to a side; not straight; askew **2** wrong; amiss [our plans went *awry*]

☆**aw-shucks** (ô′shuks′) *adj.* [Informal] unsophisticated, bashful, socially awkward, etc., often winningly so [his *aw-shucks* manner]

ax[1] or **axe** (aks) *n., pl.* **ax′es** ⟦ME < OE *eax, æx* < IE base **agw(e)si* > Goth *aqizi*, Gr *axinē*, L *ascia*⟧ **1** a tool for chopping trees and splitting wood: it has a long wooden handle and a metal head with a

ax

blade usually on only one side **2** any similar tool or weapon, as a battle-ax, headsman's ax, etc. **3** ⟦allusion to execution by beheading⟧ [Informal] *a)* dismissal from one's job, from a team roster, etc. *b)* any elimination, esp. as a cost-cutting measure: with *the* and often in phrases like ☆**get the ax** [government programs that are *getting the ax* in the next fiscal year] ☆**4** [Slang] in jazz or popular music, an instrument, as a saxophone or guitar —*vt.* **axed, ax′ing 1** to trim, split, etc. with an ax **2** to cut off, remove, get rid of, etc. —☆**have an ax to grind** to have an object of one's own to gain or promote

ax² *abbrev.* **1** axiom **2** axis

ax·el (ak′səl) *n.* ⟦after *Axel* Paulsen (1865-1938), Norw figure skater⟧ *Figure Skating* a jump in which the skater takes off from one skate, does one and a half turns in the air, and lands on the other skate, facing in the opposite direction but moving in the same direction: cf. LUTZ

a·xe·nic (ā zē′nik, -zen′ik) *adj.* ⟦< A-² + XEN(O)- + -IC⟧ not contaminated; gnotobiotic: said esp. of a culture medium devoid of all living organisms except those of a single species

ax·es¹ (ak′siz′) *n. pl. of* AX¹

ax·es² (ak′sēz′) *n. pl. of* AXIS¹

ax·i·al (ak′sē əl) *adj.* ⟦< AXIS¹ + -AL⟧ **1** of or like an axis **2** forming an axis **3** around, on, or along an axis

axial flow the flow of air parallel to the longitudinal axis of the engine of a jet aircraft

ax·i·al·ly (ak′sē ə lē) *adv.* in the direction or line of the axis

axial skeleton in vertebrates, the skull, vertebral column, sternum, and ribs without the arms and legs

ax·il (ak′sil) *n.* ⟦< L *axilla,* AXILLA⟧ the upper angle formed by a leaf, twig, etc. and the stem from which it grows

ax·ile (ak′sil, -sīl′) *adj.* ⟦AX(IS) + -ILE⟧ *Bot.* in or of the axis

axile placentation *Bot.* a type of placenta structure in an ovary with the ovules forming at the angles where the septa join the central placenta

ax·il·la (ak sil′ə) *n., pl.* **-il′lae** (-ē) or **-il′las** ⟦L, armpit: see AXIS¹⟧ **1** the armpit **2** *Bot.* an axil

ax·il·lar (ak′sə lər, ak sil′ər) *adj.* AXILLARY —*n.* any of the innermost feathers on the underside of a bird's wing

ax·il·lar·y (ak′sə ler′ē, ak sil′ə rē) *adj.* ⟦Fr *axillaire*⟧ **1** *Anat.* of or near the axilla **2** *Bot.* of, in, or growing from an axil —*n.* AXILLAR

ax·i·ol·o·gy (ak′sē äl′ə jē) *n.* ⟦< Gr *axios,* worthy (see fol.) + -LOGY⟧ the branch of philosophy dealing with the nature of value and the types of value, as in morals, aesthetics, religion, and metaphysics —**ax′i·o·log′i·cal** (-ə läj′i kəl) *adj.* —**ax′i·o·log′i·cal·ly** *adv.*

ax·i·om (ak′sē əm) *n.* ⟦Fr *axiome* < L *axioma* < Gr *axiōma,* authority, authoritative sentence < *axioun,* to think worthy < *axios,* worthy < base of *agein,* to weigh, orig., to lend: see ACT¹⟧ **1** a statement universally accepted as true; maxim **2** an established principle or law of a science, art, etc. **3** *Logic, Math.* a statement or proposition that needs no proof because its truth is obvious, or one that is accepted as true without proof [Euclid's *axiom* that things equal to the same thing are equal to each other]

ax·i·o·mat·ic (ak′sē ə mat′ik) *adj.* ⟦Gr *axiōmatikos*⟧ **1** of or like an axiom **2** self-evident or aphoristic —**ax′i·o·mat′i·cal·ly** *adv.*

ax·i·on (ak′sē än′) *n.* a hypothetical subatomic particle thought to be a lightweight, electrically neutral boson essential to the strong interaction

ax·is¹ (ak′sis) *n., pl.* **ax′es′** (-sēz′) ⟦L, axle, axis < IE **aks-* < base **aĝ-* (see ACT¹) > OE *eax,* ON *ǫxull,* Gr *axōn,* L *axilla*⟧ **1** a real or imaginary straight line on which an object rotates or is regarded as rotating [the *axis* of a planet] **2** a real or imaginary straight line around which the parts of a thing, system, etc. are symmetrically or evenly arranged or composed [the *axis* of a picture] **3** a main line of motion, development, etc. **4** an alignment between countries, groups, etc. for promoting their purposes **5** *Aeron.* any of the three straight lines, perpendicular to each other, passing through the center of gravity of an aircraft, namely the longitudinal axis from nose to tail, the lateral axis from side to side, and the vertical axis from above to below **6** *Anat. a)* the second cervical vertebra *b)* any of various axial or central parts **7** *Bot. a)* the main stem of a plant *b)* the central system of a cluster **8** *Geom. a)* a straight line through the center of a plane figure or solid, esp. one around which the parts are symmetrically arranged *b)* a straight line for measurement or reference, as in a graph **9** *Optics a)* a straight line through the centers of both surfaces of a lens *b)* a straight line from the object of vision to the fovea of the eye —**the Axis** the countries aligned against the Allies in WWII: originally applied to Nazi Germany and Fascist Italy (**Rome-Berlin Axis**), later extended to include Japan, etc. (**Rome-Berlin-Tokyo Axis**)

ax·is² (ak′sis) *n.* ⟦ModL < L⟧ any of a genus (*Axis*) of small deer of India and S Asia, with slender, sparsely branched antlers

ax·le (ak′səl) *n.* ⟦ME *axel* (only in comp. *axeltre*): see fol.⟧ **1** a rod on which a wheel turns, or one connected to a wheel so that they turn together **2** *a)* a bar connecting two opposite wheels, as of an automobile *b)* the spindle at either end of such a bar

ax·le·tree (-trē′) *n.* ⟦ME *axeltre* < ON *ǫxultre* < *ǫxull,* axle (see AXIS¹) + *tre,* beam, TREE⟧ a bar connecting two opposite wheels of a carriage, wagon, etc.

Ax·min·ster (aks′min′stər) *n.* ⟦after *Axminster,* a town in SW England, where it was first made by hand⟧ a type of carpet with a cut pile, woven in various colors and patterns

ax·o·lotl (ak′sə lät′'l) *n.* ⟦Sp < Nahuatl *a:šo:loλ* < *a:λ,* water + *šo:lo:λ,* naked⟧ any of various members of a genus (*Ambystoma*) of dark salamanders of Mexico and the W U.S. that mature sexually and breed while remaining in the gilled larval stage due to a thyroid deficiency

ax·on (ak′sän′) *n.* ⟦ModL < Gr *axōn,* AXIS¹⟧ that part of a nerve cell through which impulses travel away from the cell body —**ax·o·nal** (ak′sə nəl) *adj.*

ax·o·no·met·ric projection (ak′sə nə me′trik) ⟦ult. < Gr *axōn,* AXIS¹ + *metron,* MEASURE⟧ a two-dimensional pictorial representation of a three-dimensional object, used as in showing three sides of a six-sided object, in which the three principal axes of the object are tilted from the plane of viewing, the edges of the object are shown as being projected on the plane of viewing, and the dimensions are foreshortened in the direction of the axes

ax·seed (aks′sēd′) *n.* ⟦AX¹ + SEED: so named from the shape of the pods⟧ CROWN VETCH

Ax·um (äk′so͝om) *alt. sp. of* AKSUM

ay (ā) *interj.* [Chiefly North Eng.] used to express sorrow, distress, etc.: used chiefly in the phrase **ay me!**

A·ya·cu·cho (ä′yä ko͞o′chô) city in SC Peru: site of a battle (1824) which marked the end of Spanish rule in South America

ay·ah (ä′yə) *n.* ⟦Anglo-Ind < Hindi *āya* < Port *aia,* governess⟧ a native nursemaid or lady's maid in India

a·ya·huas·ca (ä′yä wäs′kä) *n.* ⟦AmSp < Quechua, lit., vine of the dead < *aya,* cadaver + *huasca,* vine⟧ **1** a hallucinogenic drink containing harmine, $C_{13}H_{12}N_2O$, prepared by Amazonian Indians from the bark of various vines of a genus (*Banisteriopsis,* esp. *B. caapi*) of the malpighia family **2** any of these vines

a·ya·tol·lah (ī′yə tō′lə, -tō lä′; ä′yä-) *n.* ⟦Ar, lit., sign of God < *āyat,* sign + *Allah,* ALLAH⟧ **1** a leader of the Shiite sect of the Muslim religion, serving as teacher, judge, and administrator **2** a leader, authority, etc. having much power or influence

aye¹ (ā) *adv.* ⟦ME *ai, ay* < ON *ei* < IE base **aiw-,* vital force > AGE⟧ [Old Poet.] always; ever: also sp. **ay**

aye² (ī) *adv., interj.* ⟦prob. < *I,* pers. pron.⟧ yes; yea —*n.* an affirmative vote or a person voting affirmatively Also sp. **ay** —**aye, aye** *Naut.* I understand and will obey: used in response to a command

aye-aye (ī′ ī′) *n.* ⟦Fr < Malagasy; echoic of its cry⟧ an arboreal, nocturnal prosimian primate (*Daubentonia madagascariensis*) of Madagascar, with shaggy, generally dark-brown fur, large ears, fingerlike claws, and a long, bushy tail

Ay·er (ā′ər), Sir **A(lfred) J(ules)** 1910-89; Brit. philosopher

A·ye·sha or **A·ye·shah** (ä′ē shä′) *alt. sp. of* AISHA

a·yin (ä′yin) *n.* ⟦Heb *ayin,* lit., eye⟧ the sixteenth letter of the Hebrew alphabet (ע)

Ay·ma·ra (ī′mə rä′) *n.* ⟦AmSp, prob. < Quechua⟧ **1** *pl.* **-ras′** or **-ra′** a member of a South American Indian people living mainly in Bolivia and Peru and believed to have been the builders of a great ancient culture that was later supplanted by that of the Incas **2** the language of this people —**Ay′ma·ran′** *adj., n.*

Ayr (er, ar) **1** former county of Scotland **2** seaport in SW Scotland, on the Firth of Clyde

Ayr·shire¹ (-shir) *n.* any of a breed of medium-sized dairy cattle which are brownish-red and white: originally from the county of Ayr

Ayr·shire² (-shir) AYR (the former county)

a·yur·ve·da (ä′yo͝or vā′də) *n.* ⟦Sans *āyurveda* < *āyur,* life + *veda,* knowledge: see WISE¹⟧ a traditional Hindu system of medicine practiced in India since the first century A.D. and using combinations of herbs, purgatives, rubbing oils, etc. in treating diseases —**a′yur·ve′dic** (-vā′dik) *adj., n.*

A·yut·tha·ya (ä yo͞o′tä yä) city in central Thailand, on the Chao Phraya River: capital (1350-1767) of a former Thai kingdom: in full **Phra Na·khon Si Ayutthaya** (prä′nä kôn′sē)

az *abbrev.* azimuth

AZ *abbrev.* Arizona

az- (az) *combining form* AZO- [*azide*]

a·za·lea (ə zāl′yə) *n.* ⟦ModL < Gr, fem. of *azaleos,* dry: so called because it thrives in dry soil⟧ **1** any of various flowering shrubs (genus *Rhododendron*) of the heath family: the flowers are of various colors, and the leaves are usually shed each season **2** the flower of any of these shrubs

a·zan (ä zän′) *n.* ⟦< Ar *adhān*⟧ the Muslim summons to prayer: it is called five times a day by a muezzin

az·a·thi·o·prine (az′ə thī′ə prēn′) *n.* ⟦*aza-* (< AZO-) + THIO- + P(U)RINE⟧ an immunosuppressive drug, $C_9H_7N_7O_2S$, used to prevent rejections in transplant surgery

A·za·zel (ə zā′zəl, az′ə zel′) *n.* ⟦Heb *azazel,* lit., removal: in KJV (Lev 16: 7-10, 21-26) transl. as "scapegoat"⟧ in ancient Hebrew tradition, a place in the wilderness or an evil spirit in the desert to which a scapegoat is to be sent on the Day of Atonement

a·zed·a·rach (ə zed′ə rak′) *n.* ⟦< Fr *azédarac* < Sp *acedaraque* < Ar *āzādirakht* < Pers *azād diraḫt,* lit., free tree⟧ **1** the chinaberry tree **2** the bark of this tree, formerly used as a cathartic, emetic, etc.

a·ze·o·trope (ə′zē′ə trōp′) *n.* ⟦< A-² + Gr *zein,* to boil (see YEAST) + -TROPE⟧ a liquid mixture that maintains a constant boiling point and that produces a vapor of the same composition as the mixture —**az·e·o·trop·ic** (āz′ē ō träp′ik) *adj.*

Az·er·bai·jan (äz′ər bī jän′, az′-) **1** region of NW Iran **2** AZERBAIJAN SOVIET SOCIALIST REPUBLIC **3** country in W Asia, south of the Caucasus Mountains: became independent upon the breakup of the U.S.S.R. (1991): 33,436 sq mi (86,600 sq km); cap. Baku: formerly, *Azerbaijan Soviet Socialist Republic*

Az·er·bai·ja·ni (-jä′nē) *n.* **1** *pl.* **-nis** or **-ni** a member of a people living in Azerbaijan and NW Iran **2** the Turkic language of this people

Azerbaijan Soviet Socialist Republic a republic of the U.S.S.R.: now AZERBAIJAN

A·zer·i (ə zer′ē) *n.* ⟦< Turk⟧ AZERBAIJANI (sense 1)

az·ide (az′īd, ā′zīd, az′id) *n.* ⟦AZ(O)- + -IDE⟧ a compound containing the group N_3

a·zid·o·thy·mi·dine (ə zī′dō thī′mə dēn′) *n.* ⟦prec. + -O- + THYMIDINE⟧ *former term for* ZIDOVUDINE

A·zil·ian (ə zil′yən) *adj.* ⟦after Mas d'*Azil*, cavern in the French Pyrenees, where traces were found⟧ denoting or of a stage of Mesolithic culture following the Magdalenian and characterized by painted stone pebbles and by harpoon heads made from antlers

az·i·muth (az′ə məth) *n.* ⟦ME & OFr *azimut* < Ar *as-sumūt* < *as* < *al*, the + *sumūt*, pl. of *samt*, way, path⟧ *Astron., Surveying, etc.* an angular measurement used to locate an object, star, etc.: it is measured clockwise around the horizon from the north, or south, to the object or the intersection of the object's vertical circle with the horizon —**az′i·muth′al** (-muth′əl) *adj.*

az·ine (az′ēn, ā′zēn′, az′in) *n.* ⟦AZ(O)- + -INE[3]⟧ any of a group of organic chemical compounds with a 6-membered ring containing one or more nitrogen atoms: the group consists of the diazines, triazines, etc.

a·zith·ro·my·cin (ə zith′rō mī′sin) *n.* an antibiotic derived from erythromycin and used in treating various bacterial infections

az·lon (az′län′) *n.* ⟦AZ(O)- + (NY)LON⟧ any of a group of textile fibers made from a regenerated protein such as casein

az·o (az′ō, ā′zō) *adj.* ⟦< AZOTE⟧ pertaining to or containing the divalent radical N:N *[azo* dyes*]*

az·o- (az′ō, ā′zō) ⟦< AZOTE⟧ *combining form* **1** containing nitrogen *[azole]* **2** containing the divalent radical N:N *[azobenzene]*

az·o·ben·zene (az′ō ben′zēn′, -ben zēn′) *n.* an orange-red crystalline compound, $C_6H_5N{:}NC_6H_5$, derived from nitrobenzene in an alkaline solution and used in organic synthesis

a·zo·ic (ə zō′ik, ā-) *adj.* ⟦Gr *azōos* (< *a-*, without + *zōē*, life: see BIO) + -IC⟧ **1** without any life *[an azoic* ecological zone*]* **2** *[usually* **A-***]* designating or of the earliest part of the Archean Eon, when there was no life on earth

az·ole (az′ōl′, ə zōl′) *n.* ⟦AZ(O)- + -OLE⟧ any of a group of chemical compounds with a 5-membered ring containing one or more nitrogen atoms: the group consists of the diazoles, triazoles, etc.

a·zon·al (ā′zōn′əl) *adj.* designating or of zones, or layers, of soil that cannot be sharply distinguished from one another because, for example, they are of recent formation

A·zores (ā′zôrz′, ə zôrz′) group of islands in the N Atlantic, *c.* 800 mi (1,287 km) west of Portugal and constituting an autonomous region of that country: 900 sq mi (2,331 sq km); chief city, Ponta Delgada

az·ote (az′ōt, ə zōt′) *n.* ⟦Fr < Gr *a-*, without + *zōē* (see AZOIC); the gas does not support life: coined by Gayton de Morveau (1737-1816) & LAVOISIER, Fr chemists⟧ *former term for* NITROGEN

az·o·te·mi·a (az′ō tē′mē ə) *n.* ⟦ModL: see prec. & -EMIA⟧ the accumulation of nitrogenous substances in the blood, resulting from failure of the kidneys to remove them —**az′o·te′mic** (-tē′mik, -tem′ik) *adj.*

az·oth (az′äth′) *n.* ⟦< Ar *az zā'uq* < *al*, the + *zā'ūq*, mercury⟧ *Alchemy* **1** the metal mercury; quicksilver **2** Paracelsus' universal remedy

az·o·tize (az′ə tīz′) *vt.* **-tized′, -tiz′ing** ⟦AZOT(E) + -IZE⟧ **1** to nitrogenize **2** to change to an azo compound

a·zo·to·bac·ter (ə zōt′ō bak′tər) *n.* ⟦ModL: see AZOTE & BACTERIA⟧ any of a genus (*Azotobacter*) of large, rod-shaped, nitrogen-fixing bacteria found in certain soils

A·zov (ā′zôf; *Russ* ä′zôf), **Sea of** northern arm of the Black Sea, in SE Europe: *c.* 14,000 sq mi (36,260 sq km)

Az·ra·el (az′rā əl) *n.* ⟦Heb *azrael*, lit., help of God⟧ *Jewish & Muslim Folklore* the angel who parts the soul from the body at death

AZT (ā′zē′tē′) *n.* ⟦AZ(IDO)T(HYMIDINE)⟧ ZIDOVUDINE

Az·tec (az′tek′) *n.* ⟦Sp *Azteca* < Nahuatl *aste:kaλ*, after *as-λa:n*, ? name of their legendary place of origin⟧ **1** a member of an Amerindian people of what is now Mexico, that had an advanced civilization before the conquest of Mexico by Cortés in 1519 **2** the language of this people; Nahuatl **3** the branch of the Uto-Aztecan language family to which Nahuatl belongs —*adj.* of the Aztecs or their language or culture: also **Az′tec·an**

Aztec two-step ⟦jocular euphemism: apparently in allusion to MONTEZUMA (II) & in ref. to a run for the bathroom⟧ MONTEZUMA'S REVENGE

a·zu·ki bean (ä zoo′kē, ə-) *var. of* ADZUKI BEAN

az·ure (azh′ər) *adj.* ⟦ME *asur* < OFr *azur* (with omission of initial *l-*, as if *l'azur*) < Ar *lāzaward* < Pers *lāzhuward*, lapis lazuli⟧ of or like the color of a clear sky; sky-blue —*n.* **1** sky blue or any similar blue color **2** [Old Poet.] the blue sky

az·ur·ite (azh′ər īt′) *n.* ⟦prec. + -ITE[1]⟧ **1** a brilliantly blue or violet, monoclinic mineral, $Cu_3(CO_3)_2(OH)_2$, an ore of copper **2** a semiprecious gem made from this mineral

az·y·gous (az′i gəs) *adj.* ⟦Gr *azygos*, unmatched < *a-*, not + *zygon*, YOKE⟧ not one of a pair; having no mate; odd *[an azygous* muscle*]*

b[1] or B (bē) ***n.**, pl.* **b's, B's 1** the second letter of the English alphabet: from the Greek *beta,* a borrowing from the Phoenician **2** any of the speech sounds that this letter represents, as, in English, the (b) of *boat* **3** a type or impression for *b* or *B* **4** the second in a sequence or group **5** an object shaped like B —***adj.* 1** of *b* or *B* **2** second in a sequence or group **3** shaped like B

b[2] *abbrev.* **1** *Physics a)* bar(s) *b)* barn(s) **2** boliviano

B[1] (bē) ***n.* 1** a blood type: see ABO SYSTEM ☆**2** *Educ.* a grade indicating above-average but not outstanding work *[a B in French]* **3** *Music a)* the seventh note or tone in the ascending scale of C major *b)* the scale having this tone as the keynote *c)* a note representing this tone *d)* a key, string, etc. producing this tone —***adj.*** ☆second-class; inferior to the best *[a B film]*

B[2] *abbrev.* **1** bachelor **2** bacillus **3** *Football* back: sometimes written **b 4** *Baseball a)* base *b)* baseman *c)* batter **5** *Music a)* bass *b)* basso **6** battery **7** Baumé **8** bay **9** *Physics* bel(s) **10** Bible **11** billion(s) **12** *Chess* bishop **13** bolívar **14** book **15** born **16** brightness **17** breadth **18** British **19** brother **20** Brotherhood Also, for 1-2, 4-6, 8, 10, 12-13, 15-17, & 19, **b**

B[3] *symbol* **1** *Chem.* boron **2** *Physics* magnetic flux density

B- (bē) *prefix* bomber: used in designations for aircraft *[B-52]*

ba (bä) ***n.*** *Egypt. Myth.* the soul, symbolized by a bird with a human head

Ba[1] *abbrev. Bible* Baruch

Ba[2] *Chem. symbol for* barium

BA *abbrev.* **1** ⟦ModL *Baccalaureus Artium*⟧ Bachelor of Arts: also **B.A. 2** *Baseball* batting average

baa (bä) ***n.*** ⟦echoic⟧ the cry of a sheep or goat —***vi.*** to make this cry; bleat

Ba·al (bā′əl) ***n.**, pl.* **Ba′al·im** (-im) or **Ba′als** ⟦LL < Heb *baal*⟧ **1** among some ancient Semitic peoples, orig., any of a number of local fertility gods; later, a chief god **2** a false god; idol —**Ba′al·ism′** ***n.*** —**Ba′al·ite′** (-īt′) ***n.***

Baal·bek (bäl′bek′) town in NE Lebanon: site of ruins of HELIOPOLIS

Baal Shem Tov (bäl′ shem′ tōv′) (born *Israel ben Eliezer*) 1700?-60; Jewish religious leader in Poland: founder of Hasidism: also **Baal Shem Tob**

baas (bäs, bôs) ***n.*** ⟦Afrik < Du, master, foreman, BOSS[1]⟧ [Historical] master; sir: term of address used in South Africa for a white man

baas·kap or **baas·skap** (bäs′käp′) ***n.*** ⟦Afrik < *baas* (see prec.) + MDu *-scap,* -SHIP⟧ the policy of absolute domination of the native peoples by white settlers in South Africa: cf. APARTHEID

Baath (bäth, bath) ***adj.*** ⟦< Ar, rebirth, resurrection⟧ designating or of a political party formed in Syria in the 1940s: separate factions of the party have ruled Syria since 1970 and ruled Iraq from 1968 to 2003: also written Ba'ath —**Baath′ism′** ***n.*** —**Baath′ist** ***adj., n.***

Bab[1] (bäb) ***n.*** ⟦Pers, contr. < *Bāb-ud-Dīn,* lit., Gate of the Faith⟧ a Persian title taken by the founder of Babism

Bab[2] *abbrev.* Babylonian

ba·ba au rhum (bȧ bȧ ō rôm′) ⟦Fr < Pol *baba,* lit., old woman + Fr *au,* in or with the + *rhum,* rum⟧ a light cake raised with yeast, containing raisins and dried fruits and soaked in a rum syrup

ba·ba gha·nouj (bä′bä gä no͞ozh′) ⟦Ar *bābā ghannūj,* lit., father of flirtation: ? so called from having been invented by a member of a harem⟧ a Middle Eastern dish, a puree of broiled eggplant usually with garlic, lemon juice, and tahini, eaten with pita as an appetizer: also **ba′ba ga·noush′** (-no͞osh′)

Ba·bar (bä′bər) *alt. sp. of* BABUR

ba·bas·su (bä′bə so͞o′) ***n.*** ⟦Port *babaçú*⟧ any of a genus (*Orbignya*) of Brazilian palms whose edible nuts furnish an oil used in making soap, margarine, etc.

Bab·bage (bab′ij), **Charles** 1792-1871; Eng. mathematician & computer pioneer

☆**bab·bitt**[1] (bab′it) ***n.*** Babbitt metal —***vt.*** to line or cover with Babbitt metal

☆**bab·bitt**[2] or **Bab·bitt** (bab′it) ***n.*** ⟦after George *Babbitt,* title character of a satirical novel (1922) by Sinclair Lewis⟧ a smugly narrow and conventional person interested chiefly in business and social success; philistine —**bab′bitt·ry** ***n.***, **Bab′bitt·ry**

Bab·bitt (bab′it), **Milton (Byron)** 1916-2011; U.S. composer

☆**Babbitt metal** ⟦after Isaac *Babbitt* (1799-1862), U.S. inventor⟧ a soft white metal of tin, lead, copper, and antimony in various proportions, used to reduce friction as in bearings

bab·ble (bab′əl) ***vi.*** **-bled, -bling** ⟦ME *bablen;* akin to Norw *bable,* Swed *babbla,* Ger *babbeln,* to prattle, L *balbutire,* to stammer, Sans *balbuthah,* stammerer: of echoic orig.⟧ **1** to make incoherent sounds, as a baby does; prattle **2** to talk foolishly or too much; blab **3** to make a low, bubbling sound, as a brook does when flowing over stones —***vt.* 1** to say indistinctly or incoherently **2** to say foolishly or unadvisedly; blab —***n.* 1** confused, incoherent talk or vocal sounds **2** foolish or meaningless talk **3** a low, bubbling sound —**bab′bler** ***n.***

-bab·ble (bab′əl) *combining form* jargon or wordy and confusing language related to or characteristic of a (specified) field, group, etc.: often used in nonce compounds *[technobabble]*

babe (bāb) ***n.*** ⟦ME; similar or akin to Welsh *baban,* Alb *bebe,* MHG *babe,* old woman, Lith *boba,* mother: ult. imitation of baby talk⟧ **1** a baby; infant **2** a naive, gullible, or helpless person: also **babe in the woods** ☆**3** [Slang] a young woman, esp. an attractive one

Ba·bel[1] (bā′bəl, bab′əl) ***n.*** ⟦Heb *bavel* < Akkadian *bābilu,* altered (by folk-etym. assoc. with *bāb,* gate & *ili,* god) < pre-Akkadian city name *babila,* Babylon⟧ **1** *Bible* a city in Shinar in which Noah's descendants tried to build a very high tower to reach heaven and were prevented by God from doing so by a confusion of tongues: Gen. 11:1-9 **2** an impracticable scheme **3** [*also* **b-**] *a)* any confusion of voices or sounds; tumult *b)* a place of such confusion

Ba·bel[2] (bä′bəl), **I·saak (Emmanuilovich)** (ē säk′) 1894-1940; Russ. writer

Bab el Man·deb (bab′ el man′deb′) strait joining the Red Sea and the Gulf of Aden: 20 mi (32 km) wide

Ba·ber (bä′bər) *alt. sp. of* BABUR

bab·e·si·o·sis (bab′ə zī′ə sis, -sī′-) ***n.**, pl.* **-ses** ⟦after V. *Babeş* (1854-1926), Romanian bacteriologist⟧ TEXAS FEVER: also **bab′e·si′a·sis**

Ba·bi (bä′bē) ***n.*** BABISM, BABIST

ba·biche (bä bēsh′) ***n.*** ⟦CdnFr < Micmac *aapapiich,* cord, thread, lit., net string⟧ [Chiefly Cdn.] rawhide thongs or lacings, used for tying or weaving, esp. in snowshoes

babies' breath BABY'S BREATH

bab·i·ru·sa, bab·i·rous·sa, *or* **bab·i·rus·sa** (bab′ə ro͞os′ə, bä′bə-) ***n.*** ⟦Malay *babi,* hog + *rusa,* deer⟧ a wild pig (*Babyrousa babyrussa*) of the East Indies with backward-curving tusks: the upper pair grow through the middle of the snout

Bab·ism (bäb′iz′əm) ***n.*** a Persian religion founded *c.* 1844 by the Bab (Mirza Ali Mohammed): it forbids begging, drinking alcoholic liquors, buying and selling slaves, having more than one wife, etc.: cf. BAHAISM —**Bab′ist** ***n., adj.***, **Bab′ite**

bab·ka (bäb′kə) ***n.*** ⟦Pol dim. of *baba,* lit., old woman⟧ a light, sweet, usually cylindrical cake raised with yeast and containing raisins, often glazed and flavored with rum

ba·boon (ba bo͞on′, bə-) ***n.*** ⟦ME *babewyne* < OFr *babuin,* ape, fool < *baboue,* lip (of animals) < *bab,* echoic: see BABBLE⟧ any of various large, fierce, short-tailed Old World monkeys (mainly genus *Papio*) of Africa and Arabia, having a doglike snout and long teeth, a large head with cheek pouches, and bare calluses on the rump —**ba·boon′er·y** ***n.*** —**ba·boon′ish** ***adj.***

baboon

ba·bu or **ba·boo** (bä′bo͞o′) ***n.*** ⟦Hindi *bābū,* lit., father⟧ **1** in India, a title equivalent to *Mr.* or *sir* used in addressing a man who is a Hindu **2** in India, an indigenous clerk who can write English: used disparagingly, esp. in the phrase **Babu English,** to suggest a less-than-adequate command of the language

ba·bul (bä bo͝ol′, bä′bo͝ol′) ***n.*** ⟦Anglo-Ind < Hindi *babūl, babūr*⟧ any of several trees (genus *Acacia*) of the mimosa family, found in N Africa and parts of Asia, that furnish gum arabic, tannin, and wood for carving

Ba·bur (bä′bər) (born *Zahir ud-Din Mohammed*) 1483-1530; founder & 1st emperor (1526-30) of the Mogul dynasty of India

ba·bush·ka (bə bo͞osh′kə, -bo͞osh′-; *for 1, often* bä′bo͞osh kə) ***n.*** ⟦Russ, grandmother, dim. of *baba,* old woman, orig. < baby talk: so named as frequent garb of old women⟧ **1** an old Russian woman or grandmother **2** a kerchief or scarf worn on the head by a woman or girl and tied under the chin

babushka

ba·by (bā′bē) ***n.**, pl.* **-bies** ⟦ME *babi,* dim.: see BABE⟧ **1** a very young child; infant **2** a person who behaves like an infant; helpless or timid person **3** a very young animal **4** the youngest or smallest in a group ☆**5** [Slang] darling; honey: often a casual term of address ☆**6** [Slang] any person or thing *[this car is a tough baby to drive]* —***adj.* 1** of or for an infant [*baby* food] **2** extremely young **3** small of its kind **4** infantile or childish **5** small and delicate because immature [*baby* corn, *baby* lettuces] —*vt.* **-bied, -by·ing 1** to treat like a baby; pamper; coddle **2** [Informal] to handle with great care [to *baby* a new car] —*SYN.* INDULGE —**ba′by·hood′** *n.* —**ba′by·ish** *adj.* —**ba′by·ish·ly** *adv.*

☆**baby beef** meat from a prime heifer or steer fattened for butchering when one to two years old

☆**baby blue-eyes** (blo͞o′īz′) ⟦so named from the color of the flowers⟧ a California wildflower (*Nemophila menziesii*) of the waterleaf family with bell-shaped flowers: also written **baby blue eyes**

baby blues[1] ⟦prob. shortened < *baby-blue eyes* < *baby blue,* a pale-blue color⟧ [Informal] blue eyes

baby blues[2] ⟦< BLUES (sense 1), ? after *baby blue* (the color: see prec.)⟧ [Informal] a mild form of POSTPARTUM DEPRESSION commonly experienced by women in the early days after childbirth

☆**baby boomer** ⟦see BOOM[3] (*n.* 1)⟧ a person born in the U.S. during the great increase in birthrate (the **baby boom**) in the years following WWII

baby bust ⟦by analogy with *baby boom* (see prec.) & BUST[2] (*n.* 2)⟧ a marked decline in birthrate, esp., in the U.S., that of persons born in the 1960s and 1970s, the children of the baby boomers —**baby buster**

☆**baby carriage** a small, wheeled vehicle, pushed by hand, for carrying a baby around, often with a partial hood that can fold back; perambulator: also **baby buggy**

☆**ba·by·doll** (-däl′) *n.* a short, sheer woman's nightgown or pajamas, ending usually around the hips and worn with a bikini panty —*adj.* **1** designating a short dress having a high waist, low neckline, and, usually, thin shoulder straps **2** designating a woman's form-fitting T-shirt, often with very short or cap sleeves Also, and for the *n.* usually, **baby doll**

baby grand a small grand piano, about five feet long

Bab·y·lon (bab′ə län′, -lən) ⟦L < Gr *Babylōn* < Heb *bavel*: see BABEL[1]⟧ ancient city on the lower Euphrates River (in what is now central Iraq), the capital of Babylonia: noted for wealth, luxury, and wickedness

Bab·y·lo·ni·a (bab′ə lō′nē ə) ⟦L < Gr *Babylōnia* < *Babylōn*: see prec.⟧ ancient empire in SW Asia, in the lower valley of the Tigris & Euphrates rivers: it flourished *c.* 2100-689 B.C. and again, as Chaldea or "New Babylonia," *c.* 625-538 B.C.

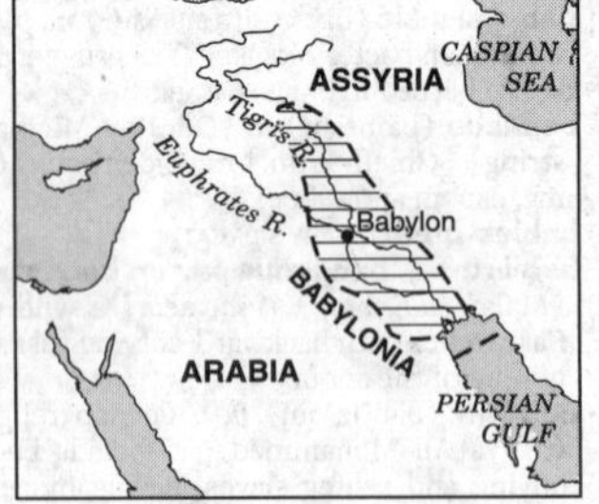

Babylonia (c. 2100 B.C.)

Bab·y·lo·ni·an (bab′ə lō′nē ən) *adj.* **1** of Babylon or its people, language, or culture **2** of Babylonia **3** luxurious, unrestrained, wicked, etc. —*n.* **1** a person born or living in Babylon or Babylonia **2** the variety of Akkadian spoken by the ancient Babylonians

Babylonian Captivity 1 BABYLONIAN EXILE **2** the period of forced residence of the popes at Avignon, France (1309-77): so called after the exile of the Jews

Babylonian Exile the exile of the Jews, deported by Nebuchadnezzar from Judah (Judea) into Babylonia in 597 B.C. and permitted to return by Cyrus in 538 B.C.

baby's breath any of a genus (*Gypsophila*) of the pink family, having small, delicate, white or pink flowers

☆**ba·by-sit** or **ba·by-sit** (bā′bē sit′) *vi.* **-sat′** or **-sit′ted, -sit′ting** ⟦back-form. < fol.⟧ to act as a babysitter, either for pay or in a more informal arrangement, as one involving a sibling or grandparent —*vt.* to babysit for (a specified child or children)

☆**ba·by·sit·ter** (-sit′ər) a person hired to take care of a child or children, as when the parents are away for the evening: also **ba′by-sit′ter** or **baby sitter**

baby talk playful, often nonsensical talk used to amuse or imitate a baby

baby tooth MILK TOOTH

ba·ca·lao (bä′kə lou′) *n.* ⟦< Sp *bacalao, bacallao* or Port *bacalhau*⟧ codfish, esp. when dried or salted for use as food: Port. sp. **ba·ca·lhau**

Ba·cău (bə kou′) city in E Romania

bac·ca·lau·re·ate (bak′ə lôr′ē it) *n.* ⟦ML *baccalaureatus;* as if < L *bacca laureus,* laurel berry, but actually < ML *baccalaris,* vassal farmer, young nobleman seeking to become a knight < ? Gaul **bakalākos,* a staff-bearer, shepherd < L *baculum,* staff⟧ **1** the degree of Bachelor of Arts, Bachelor of Science, etc. ☆**2** an address or sermon delivered to a graduating class at commencement: also **baccalaureate address (**or **sermon)**

bac·ca·rat or **bac·ca·ra** (bak′ə rä′, bak′ə rä′) *n.* ⟦Fr *baccara* < ?⟧ a gambling game played with cards, in which players may bet that either or both of the two other hands will beat the dealer's hand: the dealer typically uses a paddle to deal the cards and move the chips

bac·cate (bak′āt′) *adj.* ⟦L *baccatus* < *bacca,* berry⟧ **1** like a berry, as in form **2** bearing berries

Bac·chae (bak′ē) *pl.n.* ⟦L < Gr *Bakchai* < *Bakchos,* BACCHUS⟧ **1** *Gr. Myth.* women companions of Bacchus **2** priestesses of Bacchus **3** the women who took part in the Bacchanalia

bac·cha·nal (bak′ə nal′) *n.* ⟦L, place devoted to BACCHUS⟧ **1** a worshiper of Bacchus; bacchant or bacchante **2** a drunken carouser **3** [*pl.*] the Bacchanalia **4** a dance or song in honor of Bacchus **5** a drunken party; orgy —*adj.* **1** of Bacchus or his worship; bacchanalian **2** carousing

Bac·cha·na·li·a (bak′ə nā′lē ə) *n., pl.* **-li·as** or **-li·a** ⟦L⟧ **1** an ancient Roman festival in honor of Bacchus **2** [**b-**] a drunken party; orgy —**bac′cha·na′li·an** *adj., n.*

bac·chant (bak′ənt) *n., pl.* **bac′chants** or **bac·chan·tes** (bə kan′tēz, -kän′-) ⟦< L *bacchans,* prp. of *bacchari,* to celebrate the feast of BACCHUS⟧ **1** a priest or worshiper of Bacchus **2** a drunken carouser —*adj.* **1** worshiping Bacchus **2** given to carousing —**bac·chan·tic** (bə kant′ik) *adj.*

bac·chan·te (bə kant′, -kant′ē) *n.* ⟦Fr: see prec.⟧ **1** a priestess or woman votary of Bacchus **2** a woman who carouses

Bac·chus (bak′əs) *n.* ⟦L < Gr *Bakchos*⟧ *Class. Myth.* the god of wine and revelry: identified with the Greek Dionysus —**Bac′chic** *adj.*, **bac′chic**

bac·ci- (bak′si, -sə) ⟦< L *bacca, baca,* berry⟧ *combining form* berry [*baccivorous*]

bac·cif·er·ous (bak sif′ər əs) *adj.* ⟦L *baccifer* < *bacca,* berry + *ferre,* BEAR[1] + -OUS⟧ producing berries

bac·ci·form (bak′sə fôrm′) *adj.* shaped like a berry

bac·civ·or·ous (bak siv′ər əs) *adj.* feeding on berries

☆**bach** (bach) [Slang] *v.* ⟦< BACHELOR⟧ *used only in the phrase* **bach it**, to live alone or keep house for oneself, as a bachelor does —*n.* a bachelor

Bach (bäkh; *E* bäk) **1 Carl Phi·lipp E·ma·nu·el** (kärl fē′lip ā mä′no͞o el′) 1714-88; Ger. composer: son of Johann Sebastian **2 Jo·hann Chris·ti·an** (yō′hän′ kris′tē än′) 1735-82; Ger. organist & composer: son of Johann Sebastian **3 Johann Se·bas·ti·an** (zā bäs′tē än′) 1685-1750; Ger. organist & composer

bach·e·lor (bach′ə lər, bach′lər) *n.* ⟦ME *bacheler* < OFr *bachelier* < ML *baccalaris:* see BACCALAUREATE⟧ **1** in the feudal system, a young knight and landholder who served under another's banner: also **bach′e·lor-at-arms′ 2** a man who has not married **3** a young male animal, specif. a fur seal, that has not yet mated —*adj.* of or for a bachelor —**bach′e·lor·hood′** *n.*, **bach′e·lor·ship′**

bachelor apartment EFFICIENCY APARTMENT

bachelor chest a chest of drawers, esp., one for men's shirts, sweaters, underwear, etc.

bach·e·lor·ette (bach′lər et′, bach′ə-) *n.* [Informal] an unmarried, usually young woman

☆**bachelor girl** [Informal] an unmarried young woman who works and leads an independent life: an old-fashioned usage

Bachelor of Arts (or **Science,** etc.**) 1** a degree given by a college or university to a person who has completed a four-year course or its equivalent in the humanities or related studies (or in science, etc.): also **bachelor's (degree) 2** a person who holds this degree

bachelor party a party for a man who is about to be married, given by his male friends and frequently involving raucous behavior

bachelor's button any of several plants of a genus (*Centaurea*) of the composite family, that have scaly, vase-shaped bracts below the white, pink, or blue flowers; esp., the cornflower and knapweed

bac·il·lar·y (bas′ə ler′ē, bə sil′ər ē) *adj.* ⟦ModL *bacillarius:* see BACILLUS⟧ **1** rod-shaped; bacilliform **2** consisting of rodlike structures **3** of, like, characterized by, or caused by bacilli Also **ba·cil·lar** (bə sil′ər, bas′ə lər)

ba·cil·li (bə sil′ī′) *n. pl. of* BACILLUS

ba·cil·li·form (bə sil′ə fôrm′) *adj.* rod-shaped; shaped like a bacillus

ba·cil·lus (bə sil′əs) *n., pl.* **-cil′li′** (-ī′) ⟦ModL < LL, little rod < L *bacillum,* dim. of *baculus,* var. of *baculum,* a stick < IE base **bak-,* staff > PEG, Gr *baktron*⟧ **1** any of a genus (*Bacillus*) of rod-shaped bacteria that occur in chains, produce spores, and are active only in the presence of oxygen **2** any rod-shaped bacterium: distinguished from COCCUS, SPIRILLUM **3** [*usually pl.*] loosely, any of the bacteria, esp. those causing disease

☆**bac·i·tra·cin** (bas′i trā′sin) *n.* ⟦< arbitrary blend of prec. & *Tracy,* after Margaret *Tracy* (1936-94), Am child from whose wounds the strain was isolated⟧ an antibiotic obtained from a strain of bacteria (*Bacillus subtilis*) and used in the treatment of certain bacterial infections, esp. of the body surfaces

back[1] (bak) *n.* ⟦ME *bak* < OE *baec;* akin to ON *bak,* OHG *bahho*⟧ **1** the part of the body opposite to the front; in humans and many other animals, the part to the rear or top reaching from the nape of the neck to the end of the spine **2** the backbone or spine **3** the part of a chair that supports one's back **4** the part of a garment or harness that fits on the back of a person or animal **5** physical strength [put some *back* into the work] **6** the rear or hind part of anything; part behind or opposite the front [the *back* of the room, the *back* of his leg] **7** the part or side of anything that is less often used, seen, etc. [the *back* of the hand; the *back* of a carpet, textile, etc.; the *back* of a knife] **8** *a)* the part of a book where the sections are sewed or glued together; part covered by the spine *b)* the spine of a book **9** *Mining* the roof or overhead part of an underground passage **10** *Sports* a player positioned behind many of his or her teammates, as a running back in football or a halfback in soccer —*adj.* **1** at the rear or back; behind **2** distant or remote [*back* country] **3** of or for a time in the past [a *back* copy of a newspaper, *back* pay] **4** in a backward direction; returning; reversed [a *back* step] **5** *Phonet.* articulated with the tongue in a position toward the back of the mouth: said of certain vowels, as (o͞o) in *cool* —*adv.* ⟦ME *bac* < *abac* < OE *on bæc,* backward⟧ **1** at, to, or toward the rear; backward **2** to or toward a former position or location **3** into or toward a previous condition **4** *a)* to or toward an earlier time [set your clocks *back* one hour] *b)* to or toward a later time [the snowstorm pushed the meeting *back* two days] **5** so as to keep in reserve or concealment [to hold *back* information] **6** *a)* in return or requital [to pay someone *back*] *b)* in opposition or resistance [consumers fighting *back* against unfair lending practices] —*vt.* **1** to cause to move backward, or to the rear: often with *up* **2** to be at the back of; stand behind **3** to support or help, as with money, endorsement, etc. **4** to make a wager in support of; bet on **5** to get on the back of; mount **6** to provide with a back or backing **7** to form the back of **8** to sign on the back; endorse **9** to provide security for (a currency, loan, etc.) —*vi.* **1** *a)* to move or go backward [to *back* into a room] *b)* to move (*into* a desired position) through the faulty performance of an opponent [to *back* into a championship] **2** to have the back in a certain place or direction [the house *backs* on a lake] **3** *Meteorol.* to shift counterclockwise (in the Northern Hemisphere): said of the changing direction of a wind: opposed to VEER[1] (*vi.* 3) —**SYN.** SUPPORT —**back and fill 1** to handle sails so that they alternately spill wind and fill with wind, as in maneuvering in a narrow channel **2** to zigzag ☆**3** to vacillate, as in a decision —**back and forth 1** to and fro **2** from side to side —**back away 1** to move or go backward **2** to withdraw from a position, stop holding to an attitude, etc. —☆**back down** to withdraw from a position or a claim —☆**(in) back of** at or to the rear of; behind —**back off 1** to move back a short distance **2** [Informal] BACK DOWN **3** [Informal] to refrain or cease from pursuing or annoying; lay off **4** [Informal] to stop supporting a position, holding to an attitude, etc. —**back out 1** to withdraw from an enterprise **2** to refuse to keep a promise —**back out of 1** to withdraw from (an enterprise) **2** to refuse to keep (a promise) —**back up 1** to support or help **2** to move or go backward **3** to accumulate as the result of a stoppage [traffic *backed up* for a mile] **4** *Baseball* to take a position behind (a teammate) in case there should be a mishandled or erratically thrown ball **5** *Comput.* to make a standby or alternate copy of (data, a file, etc.) —**back water 1** to use oars, a propeller, etc. to move backward or prevent drifting ☆**2** to withdraw from a position or a claim —**behind someone's back** without someone's knowledge or consent —**be (flat) on one's back** to be ill, bedridden, or helpless —☆**get off someone's back** [Slang] to stop nagging or harassing someone —**get one's back up** [Informal] to become angry —☆**go back on** [Informal] **1** to be faithless or disloyal to; betray **2** to fail to keep (a promise, one's word, etc.) —**have someone's back** [Informal] to watch over, defend, or support someone who is in a vulnerable position —**put someone's back up** [Informal] to make someone angry —**turn one's back on 1** to show anger, contempt, etc. toward by turning away from **2** to ignore the plight of; desert; fail —**watch one's back** [Informal] to be wary against an attack, specif. a treacherous attack —**with one's back to the wall** in a desperate or awkward position or situation, often one in which one finally has to act in response to an attack or demand

back[2] (bak) *n.* ⟦Du *bak* < LL *bacca,* water bowl⟧ a vat or tub used in certain industrial processes

Back (bak) ⟦after George *Back* (1796-1878), Arctic navigator⟧ river in N Canada, flowing northeast into the Arctic Ocean: *c.* 600 mi (966 km)

back·ache (bak′āk′) *n.* an ache or pain in the back, esp. in the lower back

back-and-forth (bak′ən fôrth′) *adj.* moving forward and backward; to-and-fro

back·beat (bak′bēt) *n.* in popular music, a primary accent on the second and fourth beats of a four-beat measure

back·bench·er (-ben′chər) *n.* a legislator, esp. in the British House of Commons, who is not a leader in his or her party

back·bend (-bend′) *n.* an acrobatic stunt in which the body is bent backward from a standing position until the hands touch the ground

back·bite (-bīt′) *vt., vi.* **-bit′** (-bit′), **-bit′ten** (-bit″n) or **-bit′**, **-bit′ing** ⟦ME *bakbiten:* see BACK[1] & BITE⟧ to speak maliciously about (an absent person); slander —**back′bit′er** (-bīt′ər) *n.* —**back′bit′ing** *n.*

back·board (-bôrd′) *n.* **1** a board that forms or supports the back of something ☆**2** *Basketball* a flat, rigid piece of material, often fiberglass and usually rectangular, to which the basket is attached

back·bone (-bōn′) *n.* ⟦ME *bakbon:* see BACK[1] & BONE⟧ **1** the column of bones along the center of the back of vertebrate animals, including humans, made up of separate bones connected by the spinal cord, ligaments, and disk-shaped cartilage; spine **2** main support; firmest part **3** a main ridge or range of mountains **4** willpower, courage, determination, etc. **5** BACK[1] (*n.* 8) —**SYN.** FORTITUDE

back·break·ing (-brāk′iŋ) *adj.* requiring great physical exertion

back burner ⟦from the idea of putting a pot on a *back burner* of a stove to keep its contents warm⟧ a state of temporary suspension, low priority, etc.: usually in the phrase **on the back burner**, in or into such a state

back·cast (-kast′) *n.* *Fishing* that part of a cast in which the rod is swung backward preparatory to the forward motion during which the bait, plug, fly, etc. is sent toward a desired location

back channel an unofficial, often secret, means of communication

back·chat (bak′chat′) *n.* [Informal, Chiefly Brit.] **1** BACK TALK **2** REPARTEE

back·check (-chek′) *vt.* *Hockey* to check (an opponent) in the area around one's own goal, usually in an effort to prevent that player from joining others in developing an offensive threat: cf. FORECHECK

back·cloth (bak′klôth′) *n.* [Chiefly Brit.] BACKDROP

back·coun·try (-kun′trē) *n.* thinly populated and largely undeveloped land far from cities and towns; hinterland —*adj.* in, from, or characteristic of backcountry

back·court (-kôrt′) *n.* ☆**1** *Basketball* *a)* the half of the court with the basket a team is defending *b)* the players on a team who play guard **2** *Tennis* the area at either end of the court between the service line and the base line

back·cross (-krôs′) *vt., vi.* to cross, or breed (a hybrid) with one of its parents or with a genetic equivalent to such a parent —*n.* an instance or result of such a breeding

☆**back·date** (-dāt′) *vt.* **-dat′ed**, **-dat′ing** to date before the actual date; predate

back·door (-dôr′) *adj.* **1** of a rear entrance **2** secret; underhanded

☆**back·drop** (-dräp′) *n.* **1** a curtain hung at the back of a stage, often painted to represent some scene **2** background or setting, as of an event

backed (bakt) *adj.* having a back or backing: *often used in hyphenated compounds meaning* having a (specified kind of) back [canvas-*backed*]

back-end (bak′end′) *adj.* designating or of a deferred charge payable at the end of a financial arrangement, as a LOAD (*n.* 9) paid by an investor in certain mutual funds when the shares are sold

back·er (bak′ər) *n.* **1** a person who supports or gives help, as to a protégé or undertaking; patron; sponsor **2** a person who bets on a contestant —**SYN.** SPONSOR

☆**back·field** (bak′fēld′) *n.* *Football* **1** *a)* the set of four offensive backs, including the quarterback and some combination of running backs and flankers *b)* the set of defensive backs, usually three, four, or five, who are primarily responsible for covering the pass receivers **2** either of the areas where the backs are positioned

back·fill (-fil′) *vt., vi.* to refill (an excavation) as with earth, etc. previously removed —*n.* material used in refilling an excavation

back·fire (-fīr′) *n.* ☆**1** a fire started to stop an advancing prairie fire or forest fire by creating a burned area in its path **2** a premature ignition of fuel or an explosion of unburned exhaust gases in an internal-combustion engine, sometimes preventing the completion of the compression stroke and reversing the direction of the piston **3** an explosive force toward the breech, rather than through the muzzle, of a firearm —*vi.* **-fired′**, **-fir′ing** ☆**1** to use or set a backfire **2** to explode as a backfire **3** to have an unexpected and unwelcome result; go awry; boomerang [his plan *backfired*]

back·flip (-flip′) *n.* a backward somersault, dive, or jump —*vi.* **-flipped′**, **-flip′ping** to perform or complete a backflip

back-for·ma·tion (-fôr mā′shən) *n.* **1** a word actually formed from, but seeming to be the base of, another word (Ex.: *burgle* from *burglar*) **2** the process of forming such a word

back·gam·mon (-gam′ən) *n.* ⟦BACK[1] + GAMMON[2]⟧ a game played on a special board by two people: each has fifteen pieces, which are moved according to the throw of dice

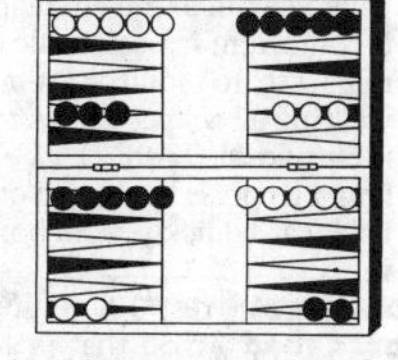
backgammon board

back·ground (-ground′) *n.* **1** the part of a scene or picture that is or seems to be toward the back **2** surroundings, esp. those behind something and providing harmony or contrast; surface against which something is seen **3** a less important or unobtrusive place or position [to stay in the *background*] **4** the whole of one's study, training, and experience [the right *background* for the job] **5** *a)* the circumstances or conditions surrounding something *b)* the events leading up to something *c)* information which will help to explain something **6** music (in full **background music**) or sound effects used as a subordinated accompaniment to dialogue or action, as in movies **7** any of various unwanted, interfering effects produced or registered by apparatus of various kinds, as static in radio or radiation due to cosmic rays —*vt.* to provide a background for

back·ground·er (-ground′ər) *n.* **1** a briefing, as by a government official, specif. of newspersons who agree not to name that official in their reports **2** a printed handout containing background information

background radiation **1** *Astron.* low-intensity, multidimensional microwave radiation present in space: its existence is used to support the validity of the big-bang theory since it is thought to be a remnant of the original explosion **2** *Physics* low levels of natural radiation existing on earth as a result of high-energy cosmic rays, the radioactive decay of rock, etc.

back·hand (-hand′) *n.* **1** handwriting that slants backward, up to the left **2** a kind of stroke, as in tennis, with the back of the hand turned forward, the arm being brought forward from across the body —*adj.* **1** done with the back of the hand turned inward, as for a baseball catch, or forward, as for a tennis stroke, and with the arm across the body **2** written in backhand —*adv.* with a backhand —*vt.* ☆**1** to catch (a ball) with the back of the hand turned inward and arm extended across the body **2** to hit (a ball) with a backhand stroke

back·hand·ed (-han′did) *adj.* **1** BACKHAND **2** designating an insincere or ambiguous compliment, esp. one that is indirectly unflattering or derogatory [a *backhanded* compliment] **3** *Sports* performed by backhanding the ball [a *backhanded* catch] —*adv.* with a backhand

back·hand·er (-han′dər) *n.* [Brit. Informal] **1** an uncomplimentary remark **2** BRIBE (*n.* 1)

back·haul (-hôl′) *n.* the return trip made, as by a truck or cargo ship, after delivering a load to a specified destination —*vi.* to make such a trip, often with no load as required by regulations

back·hoe (-hō′) *n.* **1** a power-driven excavating vehicle with a hinged bucket at the end of a long, jointed arm: it digs by drawing the bucket toward the power unit **2** the digging mechanism of this vehicle

back·house (-hous′) *n.* an outdoor privy; outhouse
back·ing (-iŋ) *n.* **1** something placed in back or forming a back for support or strength, adhesion, etc. **2** support given to a person or cause **3** those giving such support **4** [Slang] a musical accompaniment
back judge *Football* an official who makes rulings regarding pass receptions, field goals, etc.
back·land (-land′) *n.* [*usually pl.*] BACKCOUNTRY —*adj.* of, in, or from the backlands
back·lash (-lash′) *n.* **1** a quick, sharp recoil **2** any sudden or violent reaction; specif., strong political or social reaction resulting from fear or resentment of a movement, candidate, etc. **3** a snarl in a reeled fishing line, resulting from an imperfect cast **4** the jarring reaction of loose or worn parts; also, the play in these parts
back·less (-lis) *adj.* made without a back [*a backless dress*]
back·light (-līt′) *vt.* **-lit′** (-lit′) or **-light′ed**, **-light′ing** to light, or illuminate, from the rear or from the side away from the camera or the viewer —*n.* light or illumination from behind the person or thing being viewed: also **back′light′ing**
back·list (-list′) *n.* all the books of a publisher that are kept in print over a relatively long period of time —*vt.* to include in a backlist
back·load or **back-load** (-lōd′) *vt.* to defer or postpone (all or the greater part of a financial obligation) until the end of (a contract, budget, etc.)
☆**back·log** (-lôg′) *n.* **1** a large log at the back of a fire, as in a fireplace **2** a reserve of something stored, saved, etc. **3** an accumulation of unfilled orders, unfinished work, etc. —*vi., vt.* **-logged′**, **-log′ging** **1** to accumulate as a backlog **2** to have or cause to have a backlog
back·lot (-lät′) *n.* the section of a film studio containing large outdoor sets, as buildings, streets, etc.
back nine those holes of a golf course numbered 10 through 18, regarded as a unit: cf. FRONT NINE
☆**back number** **1** an old issue of a periodical **2** [Informal] an old-fashioned person or thing
back-of·fice (-ôf′is) *adj.* ⟦as distinguished from functions of the FRONT OFFICE⟧ of or having to do with the routine internal functions of a business or institution
back order an order to be filled when stock is renewed
back-or·der (-ôrd′ər) *vt.* to deal with as a back order
☆**back·pack** (-pak′) *n.* **1** a kind of knapsack, specif. one attached to a lightweight frame and worn by campers or hikers **2** a piece of equipment, as a radio transmitter, used while being carried on the back **3** an astronaut's pack used in extravehicular activities to provide a life support system and locomotion **4** a scientific instrument pack attached to people, wild animals, etc. to monitor their physical conditions, locations, etc. —*vi.* to hike wearing a backpack —*vt.* to carry in a backpack —**back′pack′er** *n.*
back·ped·al (-ped′'l) *vi.* **-ped′aled** or **-ped′alled**, **-ped′al·ing** or **-ped′al·ling** **1** to press backward on the pedals of a bicycle, as to brake ☆**2** to move backward quickly, as in boxing to avoid blows ☆**3** to retract an earlier opinion
back·rest (-rest′) *n.* a support for or at the back
☆**back road** a road that is away from the main road; country road, esp. an unpaved one
back·room (bak′ro͞om′; *for adj.* bak′ro͞om′) *n.* a place outside the purview of the public where political or business deals are brokered: also **back room** —*adj.* designating or of an activity carried on in or as in a backroom; behind-the-scenes: also **back′-room′**
back·saw (bak′sô′) *n.* a saw with a metal strip along the back of the blade and many small teeth, used for precision work
back·scat·ter·ing (-skat′ər iŋ) *n.* the scattering of rays or particles at angles to the original direction of motion of greater than 90°: also **back′scat′ter**
back-scratch·ing (-skrach′iŋ) *n.* ⟦< the saying, "You *scratch* my *back*; I'll *scratch* yours"⟧ [Informal] a reciprocal exchange of favors, aid, or compliments
back seat a secondary or inconspicuous position: also written **back′seat′** *n.*
☆**back-seat driver** (-sēt′) a passenger in an automobile who offers unwanted advice about driving
back·set (-set′) *n.* a setback; relapse; reverse
back·side (-sīd′) *n.* ⟦ME *bak side*⟧ **1** the back or hind part **2** the rump; buttocks
☆**back·slap·per** (-slap′ər) *n.* [Informal] a person who is friendly in a way that is effusive or too hearty —**back′slap′** *vt.* **-slapped′**, **-slap′ping**
back·slash (-slash′) *n.* a short diagonal line (\): a character commonly found on computer keyboards: cf. SLASH[1] (*n.* 3)
back·slide (-slīd′) *vi.* **-slid′** (-slid′), **-slid′** or **-slid′den** (-slid′'n), **-slid′ing** to slide backward in morals or religious enthusiasm; become less virtuous, less pious, etc. —**back′slid′er** *n.*
back·space (-spās′) *vi.* **-spaced′**, **-spac′ing** to move a typewriter carriage, cursor, etc. back along the same line one space at a time by depressing a special key (**back′spac′er**)
back·spin (-spin′) *n.* a backward spin given to a ball, wheel, etc. that causes it, upon hitting a surface, to change, esp. to reverse, its normal direction
back·splash (bak′splash′) *n.* a washable surface, as of ceramic tile, extending behind and above a sink, stove, or countertop, that protects a wall from liquid splashes
back·stab (bak′stab′) *vi., vt.* **-stabbed′**, **-stab′bing** ⟦back-form. < fol.⟧ to harm (a friend, partner, etc.) by treachery
back·stab·ber (-stab′ər) *n.* ⟦< STAB IN THE BACK (sense 1) (see phr. under STAB)⟧ a person who backstabs
back·stage (-stāj′) *adv.* in or to that part of the stage or theater behind the proscenium, esp. the wings, the dressing rooms, etc. —*adj.* **1** situated backstage **2** of or relating to the life of people in show business **3** of or relating to secret or private activities or dealings
back·stairs (-sterz′) *adj.* involving intrigue or scandal; secret: also **back′stair′**
back·stamp (-stamp′) *n.* a postmark on the back of a piece of mail to record place and date of arrival —*vt.* to apply such a mark to
back·stay (-stā′) *n.* a stay extending aft from a masthead to the side or stern of a vessel
back·stitch (-stich′) *n.* a stitch made by doubling the thread back on part of the previous stitch — *vt., vi.* to sew with backstitches
back·stop (-stäp′) *n.* ☆**1** *Sports* a fence, screen, etc., esp. one behind the catcher in baseball, serving to stop balls from leaving the playing area **2** anything that supports or bolsters —*vt.* **-stopped′**, **-stop′ping** to act as a backstop for
back story background information provided, often in narrative form, to give help in understanding something, as the behavior of a character in a film: also written **back′sto′ry** *n.*
back·street (-strēt′) *n.* a street in an area away from the main roads: also written **back street** —*adj.* **1** located on a backstreet **2** of or having to do with a place or person that is disreputable, engaged in an illegal activity, etc.: also written **back′-street′**
☆**back·stretch** (-strech′) *n.* **1** the part of a racetrack farthest from the grandstand and opposite and parallel to the homestretch **2** the barn area adjacent to a racetrack where horses are stabled and grooms and other horse attendants have temporary living quarters
back·stroke (-strōk′) *n.* **1** a stroke backward, or a backhanded stroke **2** *Swimming a)* a stroke made by lying face upward; esp., a racing stroke in which the arms are stretched alternately over the head and the legs are moved in a flutter kick *b)* a contest in which each participant uses such a stroke —*vi.* **-stroked′**, **-strok′ing** to perform a backstroke —*vt.* to hit with a backstroke
back·swept (-swept′) *adj.* sloping, brushed, etc. away from the front
back·swim·mer (-swim′ər) *n.* any of a family (Notonectidae) of hemipterous water bugs that swim rapidly on their back by use of their long, oarlike legs
back·swing (-swiŋ′) *n.* *Golf, Racket Sports, etc.* that part of a player's swing in which the club, racket, etc. is swung backward preparatory to the forward part of the swing
back·sword (-sôrd′) *n.* **1** a sword sharpened on only one edge **2** a hilted, saberlike stick used in fencing practice or as a singlestick
back talk [Informal] disrespectful or insolent replies —**back′-talk′** *vi., vt.*
back-to-back (bak′tə bak′) *adj.* ⟦from use in stud poker to describe a pair dealt consecutively, one face down and the next face up⟧ ☆**1** [Informal] one right after another; consecutive **2** facing in opposite directions, with the backs touching
☆**back·track** (-trak′) *vi.* **1** to return by the same path **2** to withdraw from a position, attitude, etc.
back·up or **back-up** (-up′) *adj.* **1** standing by as an alternate or auxiliary [*a backup pilot*] **2** supporting [*a backup effort*] **3** of or having to do with the backing up of computer data, files, etc.: see the phrase BACK UP (sense 5) under BACK[1] —*n.* **1** the act or result of backing up; specif., *a)* an accumulation because of a stoppage *b)* a support or help; specif., a person or thing available for service on an emergency basis or as a substitute *c)* in jazz and popular music, musical accompaniment, as that provided by a singer or instrumentalist; also, such a singer or instrumentalist **2** *Bowling* a ball that follows a path opposite to that of a hook: in full **backup ball** **3** *Comput. a)* the act or an instance of backing up computer data, files, etc. *b)* a backup copy of data, a file, etc.: see the phrase BACK UP (sense 5) under BACK[1]
back·ward (-wərd) *adv.* ⟦ME *bakward*, for *abakward* < *abak* (< OE *on bæc*, back) + *-ward* (< OE *-weard*, toward)⟧ **1** toward the back or rear; behind **2** with the back or rear foremost **3** in reverse [*to spell a word backward*] **4** in a way contrary to the normal or usual way **5** toward earlier times; into the past **6** from a better to a worse state —*adj.* **1** turned or directed toward the rear or in the opposite way **2** hesitant, bashful, or shy, as in meeting people **3** late in developing or growing; retarded; slow —☆**bend (or lean) over backward (or backwards)** **1** to try to an unusual degree (to please, pacify, etc.) **2** to attempt to compensate, as for one's own bias, tendency, etc., with an extreme effort in the opposite direction —**back′ward·ly** *adv.* —**back′ward·ness** *n.*
back·wards (-wərdz) *adv.* BACKWARD
back·wash (-wôsh′) *n.* **1** water moved backward, as by a ship or an oar **2** a backward current or flow, as of air from an airplane propeller **3** a reaction or commotion caused by some event
back·wa·ter (-wôt′ər) *n.* **1** water moved backward or held back by a dam, tide, etc. **2** stagnant water in a small stream or inlet **3** a place or condition regarded as stagnant, backward, etc. [*a cultural backwater*] —*adj.* like a backwater; backward
☆**back·woods** (-wo͝odz′) *pl.n.* [*occas. with sing. v.*] **1** heavily wooded areas far from centers of population **2** any remote, thinly populated place —*adj.* in, from, or characteristic of backwoods: also **back′wood′** —**back′woods′man** (-mən) *n., pl.* **-men** (-mən)

back·yard (bak′yärd′; *for adj.*, -yärd′) ***n.*** a yard adjoining the back of a house: also **back yard** —***adj.*** of or in a backyard

Ba·co·lod (bä kô′lôd) seaport on Negros, the Philippines

ba·con (bā′kən) ***n.*** ⟦ME & OFr < OS *baco*, side of bacon; akin to OHG *bahho*, BACK[1]⟧ salted and smoked meat from the back or sides of a hog —**bring home the bacon** [Informal] **1** to earn a living **2** to succeed; win

Ba·con (bā′kən) **1 Francis** Baron Verulam, Viscount St. Albans 1561-1626; Eng. philosopher, essayist, & statesman **2 Francis** 1909-92; Brit. painter, born in Ireland **3 Nathaniel** 1647-76; Am. colonist born in England: leader of a rebellion (1676) which sought social reform **4 Roger** 1214?-94; Eng. philosopher & scientist

Ba·co·ni·an (bā kō′nē ən) ***adj.*** **1** of or having to do with Francis Bacon or his philosophy, esp. his belief that truth is discovered through empirical observation and induction **2** designating or of the theory alleging that Francis Bacon wrote Shakespeare's works —***n.*** **1** one who accepts the Baconian philosophy **2** one who supports the Baconian theory

bact *abbrev.* **1** bacteriology **2** bacterium

bac·te·re·mi·a (bak′tə rē′mē ə) ***n.*** ⟦fol. + -EMIA⟧ the presence of bacteria in the bloodstream

bac·te·ri·a (bak tir′ē ə) ***pl.n.***, *sing.* **-ri·um** (-əm) or **-ri·a** ⟦ModL, pl. of *bacterium* < Gr *baktērion*, dim. of *baktron*, a staff: see BACILLUS⟧ any of a division (Bacteria) of monerans, microorganisms which are typically one-celled, have no chlorophyll, multiply by simple division, and can be seen only with a microscope: they occur in three main forms, spherical (*cocci*), rod-shaped (*bacilli*), and spiral (*spirilla*): some bacteria cause diseases such as pneumonia and anthrax, and others are necessary for fermentation, nitrogen fixation, etc. —**bac·te′ri·al** ***adj.*** —**bac·te′ri·al·ly** ***adv.***

bac·te·ri·cide (bak tir′ə sīd′) ***n.*** ⟦fol. + -CIDE⟧ an agent or substance that destroys bacteria —**bac·te′ri·cid′al** ***adj.***

bac·te·ri·o- (bak tir′ē ō, -ə) ⟦< BACTERIUM⟧ *combining form* bacteria [*bacteriostasis*]: also **bac·te′ri-**

bac·te·ri·ol·o·gy (bak tir′ē äl′ə jē) ***n.*** the study of bacteria, either as a branch of medicine or as a science, important in food processing, agriculture, industry, etc. —**bac·te′ri·o·log′ic** (-ē ə läj′ik) ***adj.***, **bac·te′ri·o·log′i·cal** —**bac·te′ri·o·log′i·cal·ly** ***adv.*** —**bac·te′ri·ol′o·gist** ***n.***

bac·te·ri·ol·y·sis (bak tir′ē äl′ə sis) ***n.*** ⟦BACTERIO- + -LYSIS⟧ the dissolution or destruction of bacteria —**bac·te′ri·o·lyt′ic** (-ə lit′ik) ***adj.***

bac·te·ri·o·phage (bak tir′ē ə fāj′) ***n.*** ⟦BACTERIO- + -PHAGE⟧ any virus that infects bacteria

bac·te·ri·o·rho·dop·sin (bak tir′ē ō′rō däp′sin) ***n.*** a purple protein containing retinal and found in the plasma membrane of certain bacteria (genus *Halobacterium*): it directly supplies electrochemical energy from sunlight

bac·te·ri·o·sta·sis (bak tir′ē ō stā′sis) ***n.*** ⟦ModL: see BACTERIO- & STASIS⟧ an arresting of the growth or multiplication of bacteria —**bac·te′ri·o·stat′** (-stat′) ***n.***

bac·te·ri·um (bak tir′ē əm) ***n.*** *sing. of* BACTERIA

bac·te·ri·u·ri·a (bak tir′ē yoor′ē ə) ***n.*** ⟦*bacteri(um)* (see BACTERIA) + -URIA⟧ the presence of bacteria in the urine: also **bac·ter·u·ri·a** (bak′tər yoor′ē ə)

bac·te·rize (bak′tə rīz′) ***vt.*** **-rized′**, **-riz′ing** to affect by bacterial action —**bac′te·ri·za′tion** ***n.***

bac·te·roid (-roid′) ***adj.*** resembling bacteria: also **bac′te·roi′dal** —***n.*** a structurally modified form of bacterium

Bac·tri·a (bak′trē ə) ancient country between the Hindu Kush & the Oxus River in what is now NE Afghanistan (fl. 250-130 B.C.) —**Bac′tri·an** ***adj.***, ***n.***

Bactrian camel a camel (*Camelus bactrianus*) with two humps, native to central Asia: it is shorter, heavier, and hairier than the Arabian camel

ba·cu·li·form (ba kyōō′lə fôrm′, bak′yōō-) ***adj.*** ⟦< L *baculus*, a stick (see BACILLUS) + -FORM⟧ shaped like a rod

bac·u·lum (bak′yōō ləm) ***n.***, *pl.* **-la** (-lə) or **-lums** ⟦L, a stick: see BACILLUS⟧ a slim bone that supports rigidity of the penis in many mammals, including rodents, carnivores, and primates

bad[1] (bad) ***adj.*** **worse**, **worst** ⟦ME *bad*, *badde* < ? OE *bœddel*, hermaphrodite⟧ **1** *a)* not good; not as it should be [*a bad* attitude, a *bad* deal] *b)* defective in quality; below standard; inadequate [*bad* plumbing] **2** showing a lack of talent, judgment, aptitude, skill, etc. [a *bad* painting, a *bad* writer] **3** *a)* not pleasant; unfavorable; disagreeable [*bad* news] *b)* sour; irritable; cross [a *bad* temper] **4** rotten; spoiled [a *bad* apple] **5** incorrect; faulty; erroneous [*bad* spelling] **6** *a)* wicked; immoral *b)* not behaving properly; mischievous **7** causing injury; harmful [*bad* for one's health] **8** severe [a *bad* storm] **9** ill; in poor health **10** sorry; distressed [he feels *bad* about it]: cf. BADLY **11** offensive; disgusting [a *bad* smell] **12** unpaid and not collectible [a *bad* debt] **13** *Law* defective; not valid; void [a *bad* title] ☆**14** **bad′der**, **bad′dest** [Slang] very good, stylish, effective, etc. —***adv.*** **worse**, **worst** [Informal] badly —***n.*** **1** anything that is bad; bad quality or state **2** wickedness —**go to the bad** [Informal] to become wicked, shiftless, etc.; degenerate —☆**in bad** [Informal] **1** in trouble **2** in disfavor —☆**my bad!** [Slang] that's my mistake! it's my fault! —**not bad** [Informal] good; fairly good; not unsatisfactory: also **not half bad** or **not so bad** —**the bad** those who are wicked —**too bad** **1** regrettable **2** that is regrettable! —**bad′ness** ***n.***

SYN.—**bad**, in this comparison, is the broadest term, ranging in implication from merely unsatisfactory to utterly depraved; **evil** and **wicked** connote willful violation of a moral code, but **evil** often has ominous or malevolent implications [an *evil* hour], and **wicked** is sometimes weakened in a playful way to mean mischievous [*wicked* wit]; **ill**, which is slightly weaker than **evil** in its implications of immorality, is now used chiefly in certain idiomatic phrases [*ill*-gotten gains]; **naughty** today implies mere mischievousness or disobedience [a *naughty* child] —**ANT. good, moral**

bad[2] (bad) ***vt.***, ***vi.*** **1** *archaic pt. of* BID[1] **2** *obs. pt. of* BIDE

Ba·da·joz (bä′thä hôth′) city in SW Spain, on the Guadiana at the Portuguese border

Ba·da·lo·na (bä′thä lô′nä) seaport in NE Spain, on the Mediterranean: suburb of Barcelona

bad apple [Slang] a mean or dishonest person

Ba·da·ri·an (bə dä′rē ən) ***adj.*** ⟦after *Badari* (village in Egypt where artifacts were found) + -AN⟧ designating or of a Neolithic culture of Egypt, characterized by cattle-breeding, fine pottery, and a large range of ornaments

bad·ass (bad′as′) [Slang] ***n.*** a troublemaker, esp. one who is rough, tough, mean, or, sometimes, violent —***adj.*** of or characteristic of a badass: also **bad′assed′** (-ast′)

bad blood a feeling of (mutual) enmity

bad boy [Informal] a man who publicly engages in daring or unseemly behavior, self-expression, etc. —**bad′-boy′** ***adj.***

bad·der·locks (bad′ər läks′) ***n.*** ⟦< ?⟧ dark-brown kelp (*Alaria esculenta*, family Alariaceae) used as a food for humans and as a fodder in N Europe

☆**bad·die** or **bad·dy** (bad′ē) ***n.***, *pl.* **-dies** [Slang] a bad or wicked person, esp. such a character in a play, film, etc.

bade (bad) ***vt.***, ***vi.*** *alt. pt. of* BID[1]

Ba·den (bäd′′n) **1** region of SW Germany that, since the 12th cent., has taken the form of several political units, including duchy, electorate, state of West Germany, etc.: now mostly in the state of Baden-Württemberg **2** BADEN-BADEN

Ba·den-Ba·den (bäd′′n bäd′′n) city in SW Germany, in the state of Baden-Württemberg: health resort

Ba·den-Pow·ell (bād′′n pō′əl), Sir **Robert Stephenson Smyth** 1st Baron Baden-Powell of Gilwell 1857-1941; Brit. general: founder of Boy Scouts & Girl Guides

Ba·den-Würt·tem·berg (bäd′′n wurt′′m burg′; *Ger*, -vür′təm berk′) state of SW Germany: 13,804 sq mi (35,752 sq km); cap. Stuttgart

bad faith insincerity; dishonesty; duplicity

badge (baj) ***n.*** ⟦ME *bage*, *bagge*⟧ **1** a distinctive token, emblem, or sign worn to show rank, membership, achievement, etc. **2** any distinguishing mark, sign, or symbol —***vt.*** **badged**, **badg′ing** to mark or provide with a badge

badg·er (baj′ər) ***n.***, *pl.* **-ers** or **-er** ⟦16th-c. term for earlier *brock* < *bageard* < ? ME *bage*, prec. + *-ard*, -ARD, in allusion to white spot on face⟧ **1** any of certain mammals of a family (Mustelidae) of burrowing carnivores (esp. genera *Taxidea* and *Meles*) of North America, Europe, and Asia, with a broad back, thick, short legs, and long claws on the forefeet **2** the fur of a badger **3** [Austral.] *a)* WOMBAT *b)* BANDICOOT ☆**4** [**B-**] [Informal] a person born or living in Wisconsin, called the **Badger State** —***vt.*** ⟦by analogy with the former sport of baiting *badgers*⟧ to annoy or harass persistently; pester; nag —**SYN.** BAIT

American badger

☆**badger game** [Slang] the blackmailing of a man by maneuvering him into a compromising situation with a woman

bad girl [Informal] a young woman who flagrantly engages in daring or unseemly behavior, self-expression, etc. —**bad′-girl′** ***adj.***

bad·i·nage (bad′′n äzh′) ***n.*** ⟦Fr < *badiner*, to jest, make merry < *badin*, fool < Prov *badar*, to gape < VL **batare*, to gape, trifle⟧ playful, teasing talk; banter

☆**bad·lands** (bad′landz′) ***pl.n.*** any section of barren land where rapid erosion has cut the loose, dry soil or soft rocks into strange shapes, as in various places in the W U.S. —**SYN.** WASTE

Bad·lands (bad′landz′) barren plateau in SW South Dakota east of the Black Hills; marked by dramatically eroded hills and containing many fossil deposits

bad·ly (bad′lē) ***adv.*** **worse**, **worst** **1** in a bad manner; harmfully, unpleasantly, incorrectly, wickedly, etc. **2** [Informal] very much; greatly [to want something *badly*]

USAGE—*badly* is also used informally as an adjective meaning "sorry," although *bad* is preferred in formal use [she feels *bad* (or *badly*) about the loss]

☆**bad·man** (bad′man′) ***n.***, *pl.* **-men′** (-men′) a cattle thief, desperado, or hired gunman of the Old West

bad·min·ton (bad′mint′′n; *often*, -mit′′n) ***n.*** ⟦after *Badminton*, estate of the Duke of Beaufort⟧ a game in which a shuttlecock is batted back and forth with light rackets across a net by opposing players or pairs of players

☆**bad-mouth** (bad′mouth′) ***vt.***, ***vi.*** [Slang] to find fault (with); criticize or disparage

bad-tem·pered (bad′tem′pərd) ***adj.*** having a bad temper or cranky disposition; irritable

Bae·de·ker (bā′də kər) ***n.*** **1** any of a series of guidebooks to foreign countries, first published in Germany by Karl Baedeker (1801-59) **2** loosely, any guidebook

Baf·fin[1] (baf′in), **William** 1584-1622; Eng. navigator & explorer
Baf·fin[2] (baf′in) region in the territory of Nunavut, Canada, in the N & E part
Baffin Bay ⟦after William BAFFIN[1], its discoverer⟧ arm of the N Atlantic, between Greenland & Baffin Island
Baffin Island island off the NE coast of Canada, north of Hudson Strait: part of Baffin region of Nunavut: *c.* 195,928 sq mi (507,452 sq km)
baf·fle (baf′əl) *vt.* **-fled, -fling** ⟦16th-c. Scot; prob. respelling (as *duff* for *dough, Affleck* for *Auchinleck*) of obs. *bauchle*⟧ **1** to confuse so as to keep from understanding or solving; puzzle; confound **2** to interfere with; hinder; impede **3** to check the interference of (low-frequency sound waves) in a radio, phonograph, etc. by the use of a baffle —*n.* **1** [Rare] a baffling or being baffled **2** an obstructing device; specif., *a)* a wall or screen to hold back or turn aside the flow of liquids, gases, etc. (also **baf′fle·plate′**) *b)* any of various devices designed to obstruct a rodent's access to a bird feeder **3** a mounting or partition used to check the transmission of sound waves between the front and rear of the speaker of a radio, phonograph, etc. —SYN. FRUSTRATE —**baf′fle·ment** *n.* —**baf′fler** *n.* —**baf′fling** *adj.*
☆**baf·fle·gab** (-gab′) *n.* ⟦prec. + GAB (*n.*)⟧ [Informal] pretentious, confusing language, esp. the jargon of a specific profession or a government agency
bag (bag) *n.* ⟦ME *bagge* < ON *baggi*⟧ **1** a nonrigid container made of fabric, paper, plastic, leather, etc., typically with an opening at the top that can be closed as by folding the sides; sack or pouch **2** a piece of hand luggage; suitcase **3** a woman's handbag or purse **4** *a)* a container for game *b)* the amount of game caught or killed **5** a bagful **6** anything shaped like a bag **7** any thing or part shaped or bulging like a bag [*bags* under the eyes, *bags* at trouser knees] **8** an udder or similar pouchlike membrane or sac **9** [*pl.*] [Brit. Informal] trousers ☆**10** [Slang] one's special sphere of interest, milieu, talent, obsession, etc. ☆**11** ⟦< BAGGAGE, sense 3*a*⟧ [Slang] an unattractive woman **12** *Baseball* a base —*vt.* **bagged, bag′ging 1** to make bulge **2** to enclose within a bag **3** to seize; capture **4** to kill in or as in hunting **5** [Slang] to obtain or collect **6** [Slang] to quit, forgo, or give up on [*I bagged* retail for a sales job]: also in the phrase **bag it!** —*vi.* **1** to swell like a full bag **2** to hang loosely —**bag and baggage** [Informal] **1** with all one's possessions **2** completely; entirely —**be left holding the bag** [Informal] to be left to suffer the bad consequences or the blame —**in the bag** ☆**1** [Slang] having its success assured; certain ☆**2** [Slang] drunk; intoxicated
-bag (bag) *combining form* [Slang] a person characterized, usually figuratively, by (a specified negative quality)
☆**ba·gasse** (bə gas′) *n.* ⟦Fr < Prov *bagasso,* refuse from processing of grapes or olives < Gallo-Roman **bacacea* < L *baca,* berry⟧ the part of sugar cane left after the juice has been extracted, or the residue from processing certain other plants, used for fuel and in making paper, fiberboard, etc.
bag·a·telle (bag′ə tel′) *n.* ⟦Fr < It *bagatella,* dim. < L *baca,* berry⟧ **1** something of little importance or value; trifle **2** a game somewhat like billiards, played with nine balls on a table having nine holes in a circular arrangement at one end **3** a short musical composition, esp. for the piano
Bag·dad (bag′dad′, bäg däd′) *alt. sp. of* BAGHDAD
Bage·hot (baj′ət), **Walter** 1826-77; Eng. economist, journalist, & critic
ba·gel (bā′gəl) *n.* ⟦Yiddish *beygl* < MHG **bougel* (> Austrian Ger *beugel,* kind of croissant); akin to Ger *bügel,* stirrup, orig. ring < *beugen,* to bend: for IE base see BOW[1]⟧ a chewy bread roll made of yeast dough twisted into a doughnutlike shape, cooked in simmering water, then baked
bag·ful (bag′fool′) *n., pl.* **-fuls′ 1** the amount that a bag will hold **2** a large amount
bag·gage (bag′ij) *n.* ⟦ME & OFr *bagage* < *bagues,* baggage < ML *bagga,* chest, bag, prob. < ON *baggi,* bag⟧ **1** the trunks, bags, etc. of a traveler, esp. when packed and being used on a trip; luggage **2** the supplies and gear of an army **3** ⟦assoc., in sense "camp follower," with "army baggage," but < ? Fr *bagasse,* harlot < OFr *baiasse,* ult. < Ar *baghīy,* pl. *baghāyā,* whore, prostitute⟧ *a)* a prostitute or wanton *b)* a saucy, impudent, or lively girl **4** *a)* burdensome, superfluous, or outdated ideas, practices, etc. *b)* past experiences or behavior, emotional or psychological characteristics, etc. that may affect a person's behavior or relations with others, usually in a limiting or destructive way
bag·ger (bag′ər) *n.* a person whose job is filling bags, as with food purchased in a supermarket
bag·gie (bag′ē) *n.* ⟦< *Baggies,* a trademark for such bags⟧ a thin, strong plastic bag, used for storing food, etc.
bag·ging (bag′iŋ) *n.* cloth for making bags; sacking
bag·gy (bag′ē) *adj.* **-gi·er, -gi·est 1** puffed out in a baglike way **2** hanging loosely [*baggy* trousers] —**bag′gi·ly** *adv.* —**bag′gi·ness** *n.*
Bagh·dad (bag′dad′, bäg däd′) capital of Iraq, on the Tigris River: as the capital of a caliphate, it flourished (8th-9th cent.) as a commercial & cultural center and the chief city of Islam
☆**bag lady** [Slang] a homeless, destitute, usually elderly woman who wanders the streets of a city carrying her possessions with her, as in shopping bags
bag·man (-mən; *for 2,* -man′) *n., pl.* **-men** (-mən; *for 2,* -men′) **1** [Brit.] a traveling salesman: an old-fashioned usage ☆**2** [Slang] a go-between in offering bribes, collecting money as for the numbers racket, etc.
bagn·io (ban′yō, bän′-) *n., pl.* **-ios** ⟦It *bagno* < L *balneum,* bathing place: see BALNEOLOGY⟧ **1** [Obs.] a Turkish or Italian bathhouse **2** [Obs.] in the Near East and N Africa, a prison **3** a house of prostitution; brothel
bag·pipe (bag′pīp′) *n.* [*often pl.*] a shrill-toned musical instrument with one double-reed pipe operated by finger stops and one or more drone pipes, all of them sounded by air forced with the arm from a leather bag, which is kept filled by the breath: now played chiefly in Scotland —**bag′pip′er** *n.*

bagpipe

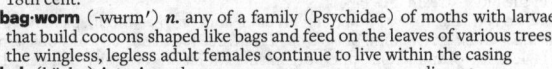

ba·guette or **ba·guet** (ba get′) *n.* ⟦Fr *baguette,* a rod < It *bacchetta,* dim. of *bacchio,* a pole, cudgel < L *baculum,* a stick: see BACILLUS⟧ **1** a gem, etc. cut in the shape of a narrow oblong, often tapered at one end **2** this shape **3** a long, thin loaf of bread **4** *Archit.* a small, convex molding
Ba·gui·o (bä′gē ō′; *Sp* bä′gyô) city in NW Luzon: summer capital of the Philippines
bag·wig (bag′wig′) *n.* a wig with the back hair held in a cloth bag or snood: worn in the 18th cent.
☆**bag·worm** (-wurm′) *n.* any of a family (Psychidae) of moths with larvae that build cocoons shaped like bags and feed on the leaves of various trees: the wingless, legless adult females continue to live within the casing
bah (bä, ba) *interj.* used to express contempt, scorn, or disgust
Ba·hā' Al·lah (bä hä′ä lä′) (born *Mirzā Ḥoseyn 'Ali Nūrī*) 1817-92; Iran. Muslim religious leader: founder of Bahaism
Ba·ha·i (bə hī′, -hä′ē; bä-) *n., pl.* **Ba·ha·is** (bə hīz′, -hä′ēz; bä-) ⟦Pers *bahā'ī,* lit., of splendor < *bahā,* splendor < Ar *bahā',* beauty⟧ **1** a believer in Bahaism **2** BAHAISM —*adj.* of Bahaism or a Bahai Also written **Bahá'í**
Ba·ha·ism (bə hä′iz′əm, -hī′-; bä-) *n.* a modern religion, developed originally in Iran from Babism, that stresses principles of universal brotherhood, social equality, etc. —**Ba·ha′ist** (-ist) *n., adj.*
Ba·ha·mas (bə hä′məz, -hā′-) country on a group of islands (**Bahama Islands**) in the West Indies, southeast of Fla. & north of Cuba: formerly a British possession, it became independent (1973) & a member of the Commonwealth: 5,382 sq mi (13,940 sq km); cap. Nassau —**Ba·ha′mi·an** (-hā′mē ən) *adj., n.*
Ba·ha·sa Indonesia (bä hä′sä) ⟦< Indonesian *bahasa,* language < Sans *bhāṣā*⟧ Indonesian (the language)
Ba·hi·a (bə hē′ə; *Port* bä ē′ə) state on the EC coast of Brazil: 219,034 sq mi (567,296 sq km); cap. Salvador
Ba·hí·a Blan·ca (bä ē′ə bläŋ′kä) seaport on the E coast of Argentina
Bah·rain (bä rān′) country on a group of islands in the Persian Gulf, between Qatar & the E coast of Saudi Arabia: formerly a British protectorate, it became an independent state in 1971: 257 sq mi (665 sq km); cap. Manama: also sp. **Bah·rein′** —**Bah·rain′i** (-rān′ē) *adj., n.*
baht (bät) *n., pl.* **bahts** or **baht** ⟦Thai *bāt*⟧ the basic monetary unit of Thailand: see the table of monetary units in the Reference Supplement
Ba·hu·tu (bə hōō′tōō′) *n. alt. pl. of* HUTU
Ba·ia-Ma·re (bä′yə mär′ə) city in NW Romania
Bai·kal (bī käl′), **Lake** large lake in SE Siberia: deepest lake in the world, *c.* 5,316 ft (1,620 m) at maximum depth; 12,162 sq mi (31,499 sq km)
bail[1] (bāl) *n.* ⟦ME & OFr, power, control, custody < OFr *baillier,* to keep in custody, deliver < L *bajulare,* to bear a burden < *bajulus,* porter, carrier⟧ **1** money, a bond, etc. deposited with the court to obtain the temporary release of an arrested person on the assurance that the person will obey the court's orders, as by appearing for trial **2** the release thus brought about **3** the person or persons giving bail —*vt.* **1** to deliver (goods) in trust for a special purpose **2** to set (an arrested person) free on bail or have (an arrested person) set free by giving bail: often with *out* **3** to help out of financial or other difficulty: often with *out* —**go bail for** to furnish bail for
bail[2] (bāl) *n.* ⟦ME & OFr *baille,* bucket < VL **bajula,* vessel < *bajulare*: see prec.⟧ a bucket or scoop for dipping up water and removing it from a boat —*vi., vt.* **1** to remove water from (a boat) as with a bail **2** to dip out (water, etc.) as with a bail Usually with *out* —☆**bail out 1** to parachute from an aircraft in an emergency **2** [Informal] to flee a difficult or dangerous situation —**bail′er** *n.*
bail[3] (bāl) *n.* ⟦ME *beil* < ON *beygla* < *beygja,* to bend, arch; ult. < IE base **bheugh-* > BOW[1]⟧ **1** a hoop-shaped support for holding up the cloth of a canopy, etc. **2** a hoop-shaped handle for a bucket, kettle, etc. **3** a device on certain fishing rods for controlling the unwinding and rewinding of the line **4** a bar on a typewriter to hold the paper against the platen
bail[4] (bāl) *n.* ⟦ME < OFr *baile* < ?⟧ **1** [Chiefly Brit.] a bar or pole to keep animals separate in a barn **2** *Cricket* either of two sticks laid across the three stumps to form a wicket
bail·a·ble (-ə bəl) *adj.* **1** that may be released on bail **2** allowing payment of bail
bail bond a surety bond (money or property) offered or deposited by a defendant or other persons to ensure the defendant's appearance at trial
Baile Átha Cliath (blä′klē′ə) *Ir. name for* DUBLIN
bail·ee (bāl ē′) *n.* ⟦BAIL[1] + -EE[1]⟧ the party to whom property is delivered under contract of bailment
bai·ley (bā′lē) *n., pl.* **-leys** ⟦ME *baili,* var. of *baile,* BAIL[4]⟧ the outer wall or court of a medieval castle: term still kept in some proper names, as in OLD BAILEY
Bai·ley (bā′lē), **Nathan(iel)** died 1742; Eng. lexicographer
Bai·ley bridge (bā′lē) ⟦after Sir D. C. *Bailey* (1901-85), Eng inventor⟧ in

military engineering, a portable bridge consisting of a series of prefabricated steel sections in the form of lattices

bail·ie (bā′lē) ***n.*** ⟦Scot < ME *baili* < OFr < *bailif,* fol.⟧ **1** in Scotland, a municipal official corresponding to alderman in England **2** [Now Dial.] a bailiff

bail·iff (bā′lif) ***n.*** ⟦ME *bailif* < OFr *bailif* < *baillier,* to govern, keep in custody: see BAIL[1]⟧ **1** a deputy sheriff who serves processes, etc. **2** a court officer who guards the jurors, maintains order in the courtroom, etc. **3** in England, an administrative official of a district, with power to collect taxes, serve as a magistrate, etc. **4** [Chiefly Brit.] an overseer or steward of an estate

bail·i·wick (bā′lə wik) ***n.*** ⟦ME < *baili,* BAILIE + *wik* < OE *wic,* village⟧ **1** the district of a bailiff ☆**2** one's particular area of activity, authority, interest, etc.

bail·ment (bāl′mənt) ***n.*** **1** the providing of bail for an arrested person **2** the delivering of goods by one party to another to be held in trust for a specific purpose and returned when that purpose is ended

bail·or (bāl′ôr′, bāl′ər) ***n.*** *Law* the party who delivers property to another under contract of bailment

bail·out (bāl′out′) ***n.*** ⟦see BAIL[1], *vt.* 3⟧ **1** a helping out of one in difficulty ☆**2** a providing of government financial aid to a failing company, city, etc.

bails·man (bālz′mən) ***n.,*** *pl.* **-men** (-mən) a person who acts as surety or gives bail for another

Bai·ly's beads (bā′lēz) ⟦after F. *Baily* (1774-1844), Eng astronomer⟧ bright spots visible along the rim of the moon during a total eclipse of the sun, just before or after totality, caused by sunlight passing through the moon's valleys and clefts

Baird (berd), **John Lo·gie** (lō′gē) 1888-1946; Scot. inventor & television pioneer

bairn (bern) ***n.*** ⟦ME *bearn* < OE < *beran,* BEAR[1]⟧ [Scot.] a son or daughter; child

bait (bāt) ***vt.*** ⟦ME *baiten* < ON *beita* < Gmc **baitian,* caus. of **bitan:* for base see BITE⟧ **1** *a)* to set attacking dogs against [people formerly *baited* chained bears for sport] *b)* to attack as such dogs do **2** to torment or harass with unprovoked, vicious, repeated attacks **3** to tease or goad, esp. so as to provoke a reaction **4** to put food, etc. on (a hook or trap) to lure animals or fish **5** to lure; tempt; entice **6** [Archaic] to feed (animals) during a break in a journey —***vi.*** [Archaic] to stop for food during a journey —***n.*** ⟦ON *beita,* lure, fish bait⟧ **1** food, etc. put on a hook or trap to lure fish or animals **2** anything used as a lure; enticement ☆**3** [Dial.] a large amount [we wolfed down a *bait* of huckleberries] **4** [Archaic] a stop for rest or food during a journey —**bait′er** ***n.***

SYN.—to **bait** is to harass or goad and implies that the persecutor gets malicious pleasure from the act; to **badger** is to pester so persistently as to bring to a state of frantic confusion; to **hound** is to pursue or attack relentlessly until the victim succumbs [he was *hounded* out of office]; **heckle** denotes the persistent questioning and taunting of a public speaker so as to annoy or confuse him or her; **hector** implies a continual bullying or nagging in order to intimidate or break down resistance; **torment,** in this comparison, suggests continued harassment so as to cause acute suffering [*tormented* by her memories]; **ride** is informal and implies harassment or teasing by ridiculing, criticizing, etc. [they were *riding* the rookie unmercifully from the dugout]

☆**bait-and-switch** (bāt′'n swich′) ***adj.*** of, related to, or employing an illegal or unethical sales technique in which a seller lures customers by advertising an often nonexistent item at a bargain price and then attempts to switch their attention to more expensive items

bait-cast·ing (bāt′kas′tiŋ) ***adj.*** designating fishing equipment designed for use with live bait or artificial lures, in which the weight of the bait or lure pulls the line from a winch-type reel, as during casting or trolling

☆**bait·fish** (bāt′fish′) ***n.,*** *pl.* **-fish′** or **-fish′es** (see FISH) any of various small fishes used commonly as bait in fishing

bai·za (bī′zä) ***n.,*** *pl.* **-zas** (-zəz) ⟦Ar⟧ a monetary unit of Oman, equal to $\frac{1}{1000}$ of a rial

baize (bāz) ***n.*** ⟦OFr *baie,* pl. *baies,* baize < L *badius,* chestnut-brown⟧ a thick woolen cloth made to resemble felt and often dyed green, used to cover billiard tables, etc.

Ba·ja Ca·li·for·nia (bä′hä kä′lē fôr′nyä) ⟦Sp, lit., lower California⟧ peninsula in Mexico, between the Pacific & the Gulf of California: divided into a northern state (**Baja California**), 27,071 sq mi (70,114 sq km), cap. Mexicali; and a southern state (**Baja California Sur**), 28,447 sq mi (73,677 sq km), cap. La Paz: also [Informal] **the Baja**

bake (bāk) ***vt.*** **baked, bak′ing** ⟦ME *baken* < OE *bacan* < IE **bhog-* < base **bhe-,* to warm, bake > BATH[1], Gr *phōgein,* to roast⟧ **1** to cook (food) by dry heat, esp. in an oven **2** to make dry and hard by heat; fire (bricks, earthenware, etc.) **3** to expose (oneself) to the rays of the sun, a lamp, etc. **4** [Obs.] to harden or cake —***vi.*** **1** to bake bread, pastry, etc. **2** to become baked **3** to become dry and hard in the sun: said of soil —***n.*** **1** the act of baking **2** a product of baking ☆**3** a social affair at which a certain kind of food, often baked, is served **4** [Scot.] a cracker

☆**baked Alaska** ⟦so named in allusion to the cold, unmelted ice cream, insulated by the meringue, likened to the cold climate of ALASKA⟧ a dessert consisting of a cake layer covered with ice cream, topped with sweetened, stiffly beaten egg whites, and browned quickly in an oven

☆**baked beans** Boston baked beans or other similar preparations variously seasoned

baked goods foods made from a flour dough or batter and baked until firm, browned, crusty, etc.; breads, cakes, cookies, etc.

☆**Ba·ke·lite** (bā′kə līt′, bāk′-) ⟦after L. H. *Baekeland* (1863-1944), U.S. chemist, born in Belgium⟧ *trademark for* any of various synthetic resins and plastics, esp. ones made from formaldehyde and phenol —***n.*** [**b-**] such a resin

bake-off (bāk′ôf′) ***n.*** ⟦prob. < *Bake-Off,* trademark for an annual baking contest first conducted by the Pillsbury Company in 1949, although similar formations such as *playoff* and *runoff* date from the 19th c.⟧ a cooking contest in which participants prepare their own recipes, as for a specified kind of cake

bak·er (bā′kər) ***n.*** ⟦ME *bakere* < OE *bæcere* < *bacan,* BAKE⟧ **1** a person whose work or business is baking bread, pastry, etc. ☆**2** a small, portable oven

baker's dozen a group of thirteen: supposedly from bakers' former practice of adding an extra roll to each dozen sold to avoid any risk of penalty for short measure

Bak·ers·field (bā′kərz fēld′) ⟦after Col. T. *Baker,* early landowner⟧ city in SC Calif.

baker's yeast a yeast (*Saccharomyces cerevisiae*) used in baking as a leavening, as for certain breads

☆**bak·er·y** (bā′kər ē) ***n.*** **1** *pl.* **-er·ies** a place where bread, pastries, etc. are baked or sold: also **bake′house′** or **bake′shop′** **2** [Dial.] baked goods; bread, pastries, etc.

bake sale an event at which baked goods, often homemade, are sold, as to raise funds for a club, school, or charity

bake·ware (bāk′wer′) ***n.*** cake pans, cookie sheets, casseroles, etc., used for baking

Bakh·ta·ran (bak′tə rän′) city in W Iran

Bakh·tin (bäkh′tin), **Mi·kha·il** (mē′khä ēl′) 1895-1975; Russ. literary critic & theoretician

☆**baking powder** a leavening agent that raises dough by the gas (carbon dioxide) produced when baking soda and acid react in the presence of water: it usually contains baking soda mixed with either starch or flour, plus cream of tartar or another acid-forming substance such as anhydrous sodium aluminum sulfate

☆**baking soda** a white powder, sodium bicarbonate, $NaHCO_3$, used as a leavening agent, antacid, and mouthwash, and in fire extinguishers

bak·la·va (bäk′lə vä′) ***n.*** ⟦Turk⟧ a rich Greek and Middle Eastern pastry consisting of sheets of phyllo layered with chopped nuts, butter, and cinnamon, baked, and soaked in a honey or sugar syrup

bak·sheesh (bak′shēsh′) ***n.*** ⟦prob. via Ar *baqshīsh* or Anglo-Ind *buck-sheesh* < Pers *bahšiš* < *bahšīdan,* to give; akin to Sans *bhájah,* (he) allots: see -PHAGOUS⟧ in Egypt, India, etc., a tip, a gratuity, or alms

Bakst (bäkst), **Lé·on Ni·ko·la·ye·vich** (lā′ôn ni′kô lä′yə vich) (born *Lev Samoylovich Rosenberg*) 1866-1924; Russ. painter and stage designer

Ba·ku (bä ko͞o′) seaport & capital of Azerbaijan, on the Caspian Sea

Ba·ku·nin (bä ko͝o′nyin; *E* bə kyo͞o′nin), **Mi·kha·il A·lek·san·dro·vich** (mē′ khä ēl′ ä′lyik sän′drô vich) 1814-76; Russ. anarchist

bal *abbrev.* balance

Ba·laam (bā′ləm) ***n.*** *Bible* a prophet hired to curse the Israelites: when he beat his donkey, the animal rebuked him: Num. 22-24

ba·la·cla·va (bäl′ə klä′və) ***n.*** ⟦after BALAKLAVA: prob. because worn by soldiers in the Crimean War⟧ a knitted covering for the head and neck, with an opening for the nose and eyes, worn for protection against wind and extreme cold: also **balaclava helmet**

Ba·la·ki·rev (bä lä′kē ryef, bä′lä kē′-), **Mi·li A·lek·sey·e·vich** (mē′lē ä′lyik sā′yə vich) 1837-1910; Russ. composer

Ba·la·kla·va (bäl′ə klä′və) seaport in the Crimea, now part of Sevastopol: site of the incident (1854) in the Crimean War celebrated in Tennyson's "Charge of the Light Brigade"

bal·a·lai·ka (bal′ə līk′ə) ***n.*** ⟦Russ *balalajka*⟧ a Russian stringed instrument somewhat like a guitar but with a triangular body and usually three strings

balalaika

bal·ance (bal′əns) ***n.*** ⟦ME & OFr, prob. via ML < VL **bilancia* < LL *bilanx,* having two scales < L *bis,* twice + *lanx,* a dish, scale < IE **elek-,* extended stem of base **el-,* to bend > ELBOW⟧ **1** an instrument for weighing, esp. one that opposes equal weights, as in two matched shallow pans hanging from either end of a lever supported exactly in the middle; scales **2** the imaginary scales of fortune or fate, as an emblem of justice or the power to decide **3** the power or ability to decide **4** a state of equilibrium or equipoise; equality in amount, weight, value, or importance, as between two things or the parts of a thing **5** bodily equilibrium or stability [he kept his *balance* on the tightrope] **6** mental or emotional stability **7** *a)* the pleasing harmony of various elements in a design, painting, musical composition, etc.; harmonious proportion *b)* a setting of clauses, phrases, ideas, etc. in parallel constructions for rhetorical effect **8** a weight, force, effect, etc. that counteracts another or causes equilibrium; counterpoise **9** the point along an object's length at which there is equilibrium: in full **balance point** **10** *a)* equality of debits and credits in an account *b)* the excess of credits over debits or of debits over credits **11**

the amount still owed after a partial settlement ☆12 whatever is left over; remainder **13** the act of balancing **14** BALANCE WHEEL —*vt.* **-anced, -anc·ing 1** to weigh in or as in a balance **2** to compare as to relative importance, value, etc. **3** to counterpoise or counteract; make up for; offset **4** to bring into or keep in a state of equilibrium or equipoise; keep steady; poise [to *balance* oneself on stilts] **5** to bring into proportion, harmony, etc. **6** to make or be proportionate to; make or be equal to in weight, force, effect, etc. **7** *a)* to find any difference that may exist between the debit and credit sides of (an account); also, to equalize the debit and credit sides of (an account) *b)* to settle (an account) by paying debts **8** *Dancing* to move toward and then back from (a partner) —*vi.* **1** to be in equilibrium **2** to be equal in value, weight, etc. **3** to have the credit and debit sides equal to each other **4** to waver slightly; tilt and return to equilibrium **5** *Dancing* to balance partners —*SYN.* REMAINDER, SYMMETRY —**in the balance** in a critical, undecided state —**off balance 1** while in an awkward or unbalanced position [to throw a ball *off balance*] **2** not proportional or harmonious; not in equilibrium **3** unready; unprepared [a question that catches someone *off balance*] —**on balance** considering everything; all in all —**the Balance** Libra, the constellation and seventh sign of the zodiac —**bal′ance·a·ble** *adj.*

balance beam *Gym.* **1** a long, narrow, horizontal wooden beam raised about 4 feet (1.2 m) above the floor, on which women gymnasts perform balancing routines consisting of jumps, tumbles, turns, running steps, etc. **2** an event in which such routines are performed, usually with recorded musical accompaniment

balanced fund a mutual fund made up of both stocks and bonds

balance of (international) payments a balance estimated for a given time period showing an excess or deficit in total payments of all kinds between one country and another country or other countries, including exports and imports, grants, debt payments, etc.

balance of power 1 a distribution of military and economic power among nations that is sufficiently even to keep any one of them from being too strong or dangerous **2** the power of a minority to give control to a larger group by allying with it

balance of trade the difference in value between a country's exports and imports

bal·anc·er (bal′ən sər) *n.* **1** a person or thing that balances **2** HALTER[2]

balance sheet a statement summarizing the financial status of an individual or a business by showing assets, liabilities, etc. at a given date

balance wheel a wheel that swings back and forth to regulate the movement of a timepiece, music box, etc.

Bal·an·chine (bal′ən shēn′), **George** (born *Georgy Melitonovich Balanchivadze*) 1904-83; U.S. choreographer, born in Russia

bal·as (bal′əs, bāl′-) *n.* ⟦ME *baleis* < OFr *balais* < ML *balascius* < Ar *balakhsh*, after Pers *Badaḫšān*, name of province in Afghanistan where the gem occurs⟧ a pink or orange type of ruby spinel, a semiprecious stone

ba·la·ta (bə lät′ə, bal′ə tə) *n.* ⟦Sp < Tupí or Galibi⟧ **1** any of a genus (*Manilkara*, esp. *M. bidentata*) of tropical American trees of the sapodilla family with hard, heavy, dark-red wood used for flooring, furniture, etc. **2** the dried milky sap of these trees, a rubberlike gum

Ba·la·ton (bä′lä tôn), **Lake** lake in W Hungary: largest lake in central Europe: *c.* 230 sq mi (596 sq km)

ba·lay·age (bä′lā äzh′, bä′lā äzh′) *n.* ⟦Fr < *balayer*, to sweep; ult. < LL *ballare* (see BALL[2])⟧ a hair-coloring technique in which color is applied by hand to create natural-looking, graduated layers of highlighting

bal·bo·a (bal bō′ə) *n.* ⟦Sp, after fol.⟧ the basic monetary unit of Panama: see the table of monetary units in the Reference Supplement

Bal·bo·a[1] (bal bō′ə; *Sp* bäl bô′ä), **Vas·co Nú·ñez de** (väs′kô no͞o′nyeth *the*) 1475?-1519; Sp. explorer: 1st European to discover the Pacific Ocean (1513)

Bal·bo·a[2] (bal bō′ə) seaport in Panama, at the Pacific entrance to the Panama Canal

bal·brig·gan (bal brig′ən) *n.* ⟦after *Balbriggan*, town in Ireland⟧ a knitted cotton material used for hosiery, underwear, etc.

bal·co·ny (bal′kə nē) *n., pl.* **-nies** ⟦It *balcone* < Langobardic **balko-*, akin to OHG *balcho*, beam: for IE base see BALK⟧ **1** a platform projecting from the wall of an upper floor of a building and enclosed by a railing **2** an upper floor of rows of seats in a theater or auditorium, often jutting out over the main floor; gallery —**bal′co·nied** *adj.*

balcony

bald (bôld) *adj.* ⟦ME *balled*, assoc. with *bal*, BALL[1], but prob. ult. < IE base **bhel-*, gleaming, white > Gr *phalos*, white, *phalakros*, bald, OPrus *ballo*, forehead⟧ **1** having white fur or feathers on the head, as some animals and birds **2** having no hair on all or part of the scalp **3** not covered by natural growth [*bald* hills] **4** having the tread nearly or completely worn off [a *bald* tire] **5** bare; plain; unadorned [the *bald* facts] **6** frank and blunt [a *bald* statement] —*SYN.* BARE[1] —**bald′ly** *adv.* —**bald′ness** *n.*

bal·dac·chi·no or **bal·da·chi·no** (bal′də kē′nō) *n.* ⟦see fol.⟧ BALDACHIN

bal·da·chin or **bal·da·quin** (bal′də kin) *n.* ⟦< It or Fr: Fr *baldaquin* < It *baldacchino*, after *Baldacco*, BAGHDAD, where the cloth was manufactured⟧ **1** a rich brocade, formerly made of silk and gold **2** a canopy of this or other material, carried in church processions or placed over an altar or throne **3** a stone or wooden structure like a canopy, built over an altar

☆**bald·cy·press** (bôld′sī′prəs) *n.* any of a genus (*Taxodium*, esp. *T. distichum*) of cone-bearing trees of the baldcypress family, that grows in the swamps of the SE U.S. and normally sheds its small, pointed needles in the fall: also **bald cypress** —*adj.* designating a family (Taxodiaceae) of conifers including the redwoods

☆**bald eagle** a large, strong eagle (*Haliaeetus leucocephalus*) of North America: the adult has a white-feathered head and neck and a white tail: the national bird of the U.S.

Bal·der (bôl′dər) *n.* ⟦ON *Baldr*, lit., bold, dangerous⟧ *Norse Myth.* the god of light, peace, virtue, and wisdom, son of Odin and Frigg: he is killed by the trickery of Loki: also sp. **Baldr**

bal·der·dash (bôl′dər dash′) *n.* ⟦orig. (17th c.), a senseless mixture of liquids, as of milk and ale⟧ senseless talk or writing; nonsense

bald·faced (bôld′fāst′) *adj.* ☆brazen; shameless [a *baldfaced* lie]

bald·head (-hed′) *n.* **1** a person with a bald head **2** any of various birds with a patch of white on the head —**bald′head′ed** *adj.*

bald·ing (bôl′diŋ) *adj.* becoming bald

bald·pate (bôld′pāt′) *n.* **1** a baldheaded person **2** AMERICAN WIGEON

bal·dric (bôl′drik′) *n.* ⟦ME *bauderik* < OFr *baudrei* < Frank **balti*, belt < ? L *balteus* > BELT⟧ a belt worn over one shoulder and across the chest to support a sword, bugle, etc.

Bald·win[1] (bôld′win′) *n.* **1** ⟦ME < OFr *Baldewin, Baudoïn* < MHG *Baldewin*, lit., bold friend < OHG *bald* (akin to OE *beald*, BOLD) + *wini*, friend⟧ a masculine name ☆**2** ⟦after Col. Loammi *Baldwin* (1740-1807), Mass. apple grower⟧ a moderately tangy, red winter apple

Bald·win[2] (bôld′win′) **1 Baldwin I** 1058?-1118; crusader & king of Jerusalem (1100-18) **2 James (Arthur)** 1924-87; U.S. novelist & essayist **3 Stanley** 1st Earl Baldwin of Bewdley 1867-1947; Brit. statesman: prime minister (1923-24; 1924-29; 1935-37)

bale[1] (bāl) *n.* ⟦ME < OFr < OHG *balla*, BALL[1]⟧ a large bundle, esp. a standardized quantity of goods, as ginned cotton, hay, straw, etc., compressed, bound, and sometimes wrapped —*vt.* **baled, bal′ing** to make into a bale or bales —*SYN.* BUNDLE —**bal′er** *n.*

bale[2] (bāl) *n.* ⟦ME < OE *bealu*, akin to OHG *bal*, evil, ON *bǫl*, harm < IE base **bheleu-*, to beat > BLOW[2]⟧ [Old Poet.] **1** evil; disaster; harm **2** sorrow; woe

bale[3] (bāl) *n.* [Archaic] BALEFIRE

Bâle (bäl) *Fr. name for* BASEL

Ba·le·a·res (bä′le ä′res) region of Spain comprising the Balearic Islands: 1,927 sq mi (4,992 sq km); cap. Palma

Bal·e·ar·ic Islands (bal′ē er′ik) group of islands in the W Mediterranean, off the E coast of Spain: see BALEARES: also **Balearics**

ba·leen (bə lēn′) *n.* ⟦ME & OFr *baleine* < L *ballaena* < Gr *phallaina*, whale < *phallos* (see PHALLUS): so named from the shape of the whale⟧ the horny, elastic plates that hang down in fringed, parallel columns from the upper jaw or palate of baleen whales and serve as a strainer that catches plankton while a whale is feeding; whalebone

baleen whale any of an order (Mysticeta) of whales with toothless jaws, baleen in the mouth, and a symmetrical skull, consisting of the gray whale, the right whales, and rorquals

bale·fire (bāl′fīr′) *n.* ⟦ME *balefir* < OE *bælfyr*, fire of the funeral pyre < *bæl*, great fire (for IE base see BLACK) + *fyr*, FIRE⟧ **1** an outdoor fire; bonfire **2** a beacon fire **3** [Obs.] a funeral pyre

bale·ful (bāl′fəl) *adj.* ⟦ME < OE *bealoful* < *bealu*, BALE[2] + *-ful*, full⟧ **1** harmful or threatening harm or evil; ominous; deadly **2** [Archaic] sorrowful; wretched —*SYN.* SINISTER —**bale′ful·ly** *adv.* —**bale′ful·ness** *n.*

Bal·four (bal′fo͝or′), **Arthur James** 1st Earl of Balfour 1848-1930; Brit. statesman & philosopher: prime minister (1902-05)

Balfour Declaration a declaration by the British government (Nov., 1917) favoring the establishment in Palestine of a Jewish "national home"

Ba·li (bä′lē, bal′ē) island of Indonesia, east of Java: 2,147 sq mi (5,561 sq km)

Ba·li·ke·sir (bäl′i ke sir′) city in NW Asiatic Turkey

Ba·li·nese (bä′lə nēz′, bal′ə-) *adj.* of Bali or its people, language, or culture —*n., pl.* **-nese′ 1** a person born or living on Bali **2** the Western Austronesian language spoken on Bali **3** any of a breed of long-haired domestic cat, developed from the Siamese, with blue, almond-shaped eyes and a light-colored coat shading to a darker color at the face, ears, feet, and tail

balk (bôk) *n.* ⟦ME *balke* < OE *balca*, a bank, ridge < IE **bhelg-* (extended stem of **bhel-*, a beam) > Ger *balken*, beam, Gr *phalanx*, L *fulcrum*⟧ **1** a ridge of unplowed land between furrows **2** a roughly hewn piece of timber **3** a beam used in construction **4** something that obstructs or thwarts; check, hindrance, disappointment, etc. **5** [Obs.] a blunder; error **6** *Baseball* an illegal motion by the pitcher, such as an uncompleted motion to throw to a base, while one foot is on the rubber: it entitles each base runner to advance one base —*vt.* **1** [Obs.] to make balks in (land) **2** to obstruct or thwart; foil **3** [Archaic] to miss or let slip by **4** *Baseball* to force (a base runner to score from third base) by committing a balk —*vi.* **1** to stop and obstinately refuse to move or act **2** to hesitate or recoil (*at*) **3** to make a balk in baseball —*SYN.* FRUSTRATE —**balk′er** *n.*

Bal·kan (bôl′kən) *adj.* **1** of the Balkan States or their peoples, languages, or cultures **2** of the Balkan Mountains

Bal·kan·ize (bôl′kən īz′) *vt., vi.* **-ized′**, **-iz′ing** [*often* **b-**] to break up into small, mutually hostile political units, as the Balkans after WWI —**Bal′kan·i·za′tion** *n.*

Balkan Mountains mountain range extending across central Bulgaria, from the W border to the Black Sea: highest peak, *c.* 7,800 ft (2,377 m)

Balkan Peninsula peninsula in SE Europe, between the Adriatic & Ionian seas on the west & the Black & Aegean seas on the east

Balkan Peninsula

Bal·kans (bôl′kənz) countries of the Balkan Peninsula (Albania, Bosnia and Herzegovina, Bulgaria, Croatia, Greece, Macedonia, Montenegro, Romania, Serbia, Slovenia, & the European part of Turkey and the republic of Kosovo): also **Balkan States**

Balkh (bälkh) town in N Afghanistan: site of an ancient city that flourished as the capital of Bactria &, later (7th-13th cent.), as a center of Islam

Bal·khash (bäl khäsh′), **Lake** large lake in SE Kazakhstan, half saline & half freshwater, the halves separated by a sandbar: *c.* 6,500 sq mi (16,835 sq km)

balk·line (bôk′līn′) *n. Billiards* a line at one end of a table from behind which opening shots with the cue ball are made

balk·y (bôk′ē) *adj.* **balk′i·er**, **balk′i·est** in the habit of balking; stubbornly resisting —**SYN.** CONTRARY

ball[1] (bôl) *n.* ⟦ME *bal* < OE **beallu* < IE base **bhel-*, to swell > BOWL[1], BLADDER, ON *bǫllr*, OHG *balla*, Gr *phallos*, L *follis* & *flare*⟧ **1** any round, or spherical, object; sphere; globe **2** a planet or star, esp. the earth **3** *a)* a round or egg-shaped object used in various games *b)* any of several such games, esp. baseball **4** a throw or pitch of a ball **5** *a)* a solid missile or projectile for a cannon or firearm *b)* such projectiles for firearms, collectively **6** a rounded part of the body; specif., the rounded area (**ball of the foot**) formed along the first joints of the toes when the foot is arched **7** [Slang] *a)* a testicle (*usually used in pl.*) (somewhat vulgar) *b)* [*pl.*] daring or courage ☆**8** *Baseball* a pitch that is wide of the plate or goes above the armpit (or shoulder in slow-pitch softball) or below the knee of the batter, who does not swing at it: four balls allow the batter to go to first base **9** *Hort.* the roots of a plant, bound and packed for shipping — *vi., vt.* **1** to form into a ball **2** [Slang] to have sexual intercourse (with): somewhat vulgar —**ball up** ⟦see BOLLIX⟧ ☆[Slang] to muddle or bungle —☆**be on the ball** [Slang] to be alert; be efficient —☆**carry the ball** [Informal] to assume responsibility; take command —☆**get** (or **keep**) **the ball rolling** [Informal] to start (or maintain) some action —☆**have something on the ball** [Slang] to have ability —**play ball** ☆**1** to begin or resume playing a ballgame ☆**2** to begin or resume any activity ☆**3** [Informal] to cooperate

ball[2] (bôl) *n.* ⟦Fr *bal* < OFr *baller*, to dance < LL *ballare* < Gr *ballein*, to throw (with sense of *ballizein*, to dance, jump about) < IE base **gwel-*, to drip, spring forth, throw > Ger *quelle*, a spring⟧ **1** a formal social dance **2** [Slang] an enjoyable time, event, or experience

Ball (bôl) **1 John** died 1381; Eng. priest: executed as an instigator of the Peasants' Revolt of 1381 **2 Lucille (Desiree)** 1911-89; U.S. comedienne and actress

-ball (bôl) *combining form* [Slang] a person characterized, usually figuratively, by (a specified negative quality): often used attributively [*a slimeball* gambler]

bal·lad (bal′əd) *n.* ⟦ME *balad* < OFr *ballade*, dancing song < OProv *ballada*, (poem for a) dance < *balar*, to dance < LL *ballare*: see BALL[2]⟧ **1** a romantic or sentimental song with the same melody for each stanza **2** a song or poem that tells a story in short stanzas and simple words, with repetition, refrain, etc.: most old ballads are of unknown authorship and have been handed down orally in more than one version **3** a slow, sentimental popular song, esp. a love song

bal·lade (bə läd′, ba-) *n.* ⟦Fr: see prec.⟧ **1** a verse form that has three stanzas of eight or ten lines each and an envoy of four or five lines: the last line of each stanza and of the envoy is the same **2** a musical composition of a romantic or narrative nature, esp. for piano

bal·lad·eer (bal′ə dir′) *n.* a ballad singer

bal·lad·mon·ger (bal′əd muŋ′gər) *n.* **1** [Historical] a person who sells printed popular ballads, esp. in the streets **2** an inferior poet; poetaster

bal·lad·ry (bal′əd rē) *n.* **1** ballads in general **2** the art of composing ballads

ballad stanza the four-line stanza commonly used in ballads, generally rhymed *abcb*

☆**ball and chain** a metal ball fastened by a chain to a prisoner's body to prevent escape

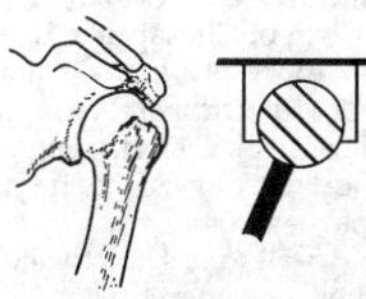
ball-and-socket joints

ball-and-sock·et joint (bôl′ən säk′it) a joint, as that of the hip or shoulder, formed by a ball in a socket, allowing limited movement in any direction

bal·last (bal′əst) *n.* ⟦LowG < MDu < *bal*, bad, useless (akin to OE *bealu*, BALE[2]) + *last*, a load⟧ **1** anything heavy carried in a ship, aircraft, or vehicle to give stability or in a balloon or airship to help control altitude **2** anything giving stability and firmness to character, human relations, etc. **3** crushed rock or gravel, as that placed between and below railroad ties **4** an electrical device used to supply and regulate electricity in fluorescent lamps, mercury-vapor lamps, etc. —*vt.* **1** to furnish with ballast; stabilize **2** to fill in (a railroad bed) with ballast

ball bearing 1 a bearing in which the moving parts revolve or slide on freely rolling metal balls so that friction is reduced **2** any of such metal balls

ball boy *Sports* a boy who retrieves balls that have gone out of play, as in tennis and baseball, or a boy in charge of the extra balls used in practice, as in basketball and football

☆**ball·bust·er** (bôl′bus′tər) *n.* ⟦see BALL[1] (*n.* 7*a*)⟧ [Slang] **1** an extremely difficult or trying problem, job, etc. **2** *a)* an aggressive or tyrannical person *b)* a woman seen as domineering Also **ball′-break′er** (-brāk′ər)

☆**ball·car·ri·er** (bôl′kar′ē ər) *n. Football* the player carrying the ball on an offensive play

ball cock a device consisting of a valve connected by a lever to a floating ball that shuts the valve when raised and opens it when lowered, as in flush toilets

ball-con·trol (bôl′kən trōl′) *adj. Football* designating a style of offensive play designed to gain yardage in small amounts, thereby consuming playing time and keeping the opposing team from using its offensive unit

bal·le·ri·na (bal′ə rē′nə) *n.* ⟦It < *ballare*: see BALL[2]⟧ a girl or woman ballet dancer

bal·let (ba lā′, bal′ā) *n.* ⟦Fr *ballette* < It *balletto*, dim. < *ballo*, a dance: see BALL[2]⟧ **1** an artistic dance form based on an elaborate formal technique, characterized by gestures and movements of grace, precision, and fluidity **2** *a)* a theatrical presentation of ballet dancing performed to music and presenting a story, idea, or mood, usually with costumes and scenery *b)* the music for such a presentation **3** a company of dancers of ballet —**bal·let·ic** (ba let′ik) *adj.*

bal·let·o·mane (bə let′ə mān′) *n.* ⟦Fr < It *balletto* (see prec.) + Fr *manie*, mania⟧ a person enthusiastic about the ballet —**bal′let·o·ma′ni·a** (-mā′nē ə) *n.*

ball-flow·er (bôl′flou′ər) *n. Archit.* a decoration in a molding that looks like a ball held in the petals of a flower

☆**ball·game** (bôl′gām′) *n.* **1** a game played with a ball; specif., a baseball game **2** any contest **3** [Informal] a set of circumstances [*a different ballgame*] —**(whole) new ballgame** ⟦? from use in baseball, as when a score has become tied⟧ [Informal] a situation changed so drastically as to need new approaches or solutions —**the (whole) ballgame** [Informal] the main or decisive factor, event, etc.

ball girl *Sports* a girl who retrieves balls that have gone out of play, as in tennis and baseball, or a girl in charge of the extra balls used in practice, as in basketball and football

ball·han·dler (bôl′hand′lər) *n. Basketball* a player particularly skilled at passing and dribbling

ball·hawk (bôl′hôk′) *n.* [Slang] **1** *Baseball* a skillful outfielder **2** *Football a)* a defensive player adept at intercepting passes and recovering fumbles *b)* a skillful pass receiver

bal·lis·ta (bə lis′tə) *n., pl.* **-tae** (-tē) ⟦L < Gr **ballistēs* < *ballein*, to throw: see BALL[2]⟧ a device, resembling a large mounted crossbow, used in ancient warfare to hurl heavy stones and similar missiles

bal·lis·tic (bə lis′tik) *adj.* ⟦< prec.⟧ **1** of or connected with ballistics **2** of the motion and force of projectiles —☆**go ballistic** [Slang] to react with an outburst of uncontrolled anger

ballistic missile a long-range missile that is propelled to high speed and may be guided for a part of its flight, but is a free-falling object as it approaches its target: see GUIDED MISSILE

bal·lis·tics (bə lis′tiks) *n.* ⟦formed < BALLISTIC, as in names of other sciences and areas of study: see -ICS⟧ **1** the science dealing with the motion and impact of projectiles, such as bullets, rockets, bombs, etc. **2** the study of the effects of firing on a firearm or bullet, cartridge, etc.

☆**bal·lis·to·car·di·o·gram** (bə lis′tō kär′dē ə gram′) *n.* a tracing made by a ballistocardiograph

☆**bal·lis·to·car·di·o·graph** (-graf′) *n.* ⟦< BALLISTIC + CARDIOGRAPH⟧ an instrument that records the slight recoil of the body, while on a special bed, caused by the contractions of the heart: used to measure cardiac pumping power and the elasticity of the aorta

ball joint a mechanical ball-and-socket joint, esp. one used in the steering linkage of certain automotive vehicles to connect the tie rod to either of the wheels that turn

ball lightning a short-lived, glowing ball of light observed floating in the air or moving rapidly along the ground: generally assumed to be a rare form of lightning

bal·lon (ba lōn′; *Fr* bȧ lōn′) *n.* ⟦Fr, lit., BALLOON⟧ a special quality of movement that enables a dancer to create the illusion of floating briefly in midair

bal·lo·net (bal′ə net′) *n.* ⟦Fr *ballonnet*, dim. of *ballon*, fol.⟧ any of several auxiliary air containers within a balloon or airship, that can be inflated or deflated to compensate for changing gas pressure during flight: used to control altitude and maintain proper structure

bal·loon (bə lo͞on′) *n.* ⟦Fr *ballon*, altered (after *balle*) < It *pallone*, large ball

< *palla,* ball < Langobardic **palla* (OHG *balla*), BALL[1]] 1 an airtight bag that rises and floats above the earth when filled with hot air or a gas lighter than air, such as hydrogen or helium 2 a bag of this sort with an attached car or gondola for carrying passengers or instruments 3 any of various small rubber bags that are inflated for use, as a toy or decoration, in a type of catheter, etc. 4 the outline enclosing the words or thoughts of a character in a cartoon, as in comic strips 5 *a)* an installment loan, mortgage loan, etc. allowing small, regular payments during the term of the loan, but having a large, final payment *b)* the final payment —*vt.* to cause to swell like a balloon; inflate —*vi.* 1 to ride in a balloon 2 to swell; expand 3 to fall due as a balloon payment —*adj.* 1 of or having to do with a balloon or balloons 2 like a balloon; round and soft, inflatable, etc. —**bal·loon′ist** *n.*

balloon angioplasty angioplasty in which a balloon catheter is moved to a blocked area of a blood vessel where the balloon is inflated to expand or force open the vessel

balloon catheter a type of catheter with a tiny, inflatable balloon at the tip, used in various surgical procedures

balloon sail a large, light sail, as a jib, used on yachts together with or instead of the customary working sails

balloon tire a wide, deep-walled pneumatic tire with relatively low air pressure to lessen the shock of bumps

☆**balloon vine** a tropical American vine (*Cardiospermum halicacabum*) of the soapberry family, bearing inflated triangular pods

bal·lot (bal′ət) *n.* ⟦It *ballotta, pallotta,* dim. of *palla*: see BALLOON⟧ 1 *a)* [Obs.] a ball *b)* now, a paper, form, electronic document, etc., by which a vote is registered 2 the act or a method of voting; esp., secret voting by the use of ballots or voting machines 3 the right to vote 4 the total number of votes cast in an election 5 a list of people running for office; ticket —*vi.* to decide by means of the ballot; vote —**bal′lot·er** *n.*

ballot box 1 a box into which ballots are placed 2 BALLOT (*n.* 2)

bal·lotte·ment (bə lät′mənt) *n.* ⟦Fr < *ballotter,* to toss < *ballotte*: see BALLOT⟧ *Med.* a technique for palpating internal organs, as to check for pregnancy or a floating kidney

☆**ball·park** (bôl′pärk′) *n.* a stadium, outdoor arena, or other facility for contests between athletic teams, esp. baseball or football teams —*adj.* [Informal] designating an estimate, figure, etc. that is thought to be fairly accurate —**in the ballpark** [Informal] 1 fairly accurate 2 fairly close to what is required

ball-peen hammer (bôl′pēn′) a hammer with one end of the head rounded and the other end flat: see HAMMER, illus.

ball·play·er (bôl′plā′ər) *n.* a player in any of several games in which a ball is used, esp. baseball

ball·point (pen) (-point′) a pen having, instead of a point, a small ball bearing that picks up its ink by rolling against an interior ink reservoir: also **ball′-point′** *n.*

ball·room (-ro͞om′) *n.* a large hall for dancing

ballroom dance a kind of dance in which two people dance as partners to a waltz, fox trot, etc. —**ballroom dancing**

balls (bôlz) *interj.* ⟦< pl. of BALL[1] (*n.* 7*a*)⟧ [Slang] nonsense

balls·y (bôl′zē) *adj.* **-i·er, -i·est** ⟦< BALL[1], *n.* 7*b* + -Y[2]⟧ [Slang] daring, courageous, aggressive, etc.

☆**bal·lute** (ba lo͞ot′) *n.* ⟦BALL(OON) + (PARACH)UTE⟧ a balloonlike device made of heat-resistant materials and inflated by stored gas, used for deceleration, as of a spacecraft reentering the earth's atmosphere

ball valve a valve that works by the action of a ball resting on the outlet hole: use of external pressure raises the ball and opens the hole; when the pressure is removed, the ball drops and closes the hole

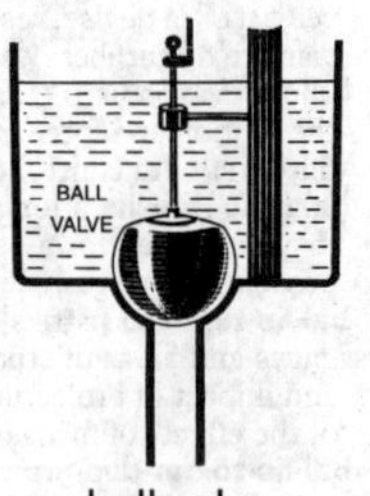

ball valve

bal·ly (bal′ē) *n.* BALLYHOO

ball·yard (bôl′yärd′) *n.* a ballpark, esp. one used for baseball games

☆**bal·ly·hoo** (bal′ē ho͞o′; *for v. also* bal′ē ho͞o′) *n.* ⟦orig. obscure⟧ 1 loud talk; noisy uproar 2 loud, exaggerated, or sensational advertising or propaganda — *vt., vi.* **-hooed′, -hoo′ing** [Informal] to advertise or promote by sensational methods —**bal′ly·hoo′er** *n.*

balm (bäm, bälm) *n.* ⟦ME *baume* < OFr *basme* < L *balsamum,* balsam < Gr *balsamon* < Sem (cf. Heb *basam,* Ar *bašām*⟧ 1 an aromatic gum resin obtained from certain trees and plants (esp. genus *Commiphora* of the bursera family) and used in the manufacture of perfume, medicine, etc.; balsam 2 any fragrant ointment or aromatic oil for healing or anointing 3 anything healing or soothing, esp. to the mind or temper 4 any of various aromatic plants of the mint family, as the lemon balm 5 pleasant odor; fragrance

bal·ma·caan (bal′mə kan′) *n.* ⟦after *Balmacaan,* estate in Inverness, Scotland⟧ a loose overcoat with raglan sleeves

balm of Gilead ⟦in allusion to Jer. 8:22⟧ 1 *a)* a small evergreen tree (*Commiphora opobalsamum*) of the bursera family native to Asia and Africa *b)* the resinous juice of this tree, used in ancient times in an aromatic ointment 2 anything healing or soothing 3 BALSAM FIR 4 BALSAM POPLAR

Bal·mor·al (bal môr′əl, -mär′-) *n.* ⟦after *Balmoral* Castle, Scotland⟧ 1 a striped or figured woolen petticoat formerly worn beneath a skirt that was looped up in front 2 [*also* **b-**] *a)* a kind of laced walking shoe *b)* a round, brimless Scottish cap, flat on top

balm·y (bäm′ē; *also, for sense 1,* bäl′mē) *adj.* **balm′i·er, balm′i·est** 1 *a)* having the qualities of balm; soothing, fragrant, etc. *b)* pleasantly warm and breezy [*a balmy* day] 2 ⟦var. of BARMY⟧ [Slang, Chiefly Brit.] crazy or foolish —**balm′i·ly** *adv.* —**balm′i·ness** *n.*

bal·ne·ol·o·gy (bal′nē äl′ə jē) *n.* ⟦< L *balneum,* bath < Gr *balaneion* (for IE base see BALL[2]) + -LOGY⟧ the study of the therapeutic use of various sorts of bathing, as in mineral springs, etc.

Ba·loch·i·stan (bə lō′chə stan′, -stän′) *var. of* BALUCHISTAN (the province)

☆**ba·lo·ney** (bə lō′nē) *n.* ⟦altered < *bologna,* sausage⟧ 1 bologna sausage 2 [Slang] foolish or exaggerated talk or behavior; nonsense —*interj.* [Slang] nonsense

☆**bal·sa** (bôl′sə) *n.* ⟦Sp⟧ 1 any of several tropical American trees (genus *Ochroma*) of the bombax family that yield an extremely light and buoyant wood used for rafts, model airplanes, etc. 2 the wood 3 a raft, esp. one made up of a frame resting on cylindrical floats

bal·sam (bôl′səm) *n.* ⟦OE < L *balsamum*: see BALM⟧ 1 any of various oily or gummy aromatic resins obtained from various plants and containing either benzoic or cinnamic acid 2 any of various aromatic, resinous oils or fluids 3 any aromatic preparation made with balsam, as certain medical dressings 4 anything healing or soothing; balm 5 any of various plants or trees of various families that yield balsam, as the balsam fir 6 any of various species of the impatiens, esp. the garden balsam —*adj.* designating a family (Balsaminaceae, order Geraniales) of dicotyledonous plants, including jewelweed and impatiens —**bal·sam′ic** (-sam′ik) *adj.*

☆**balsam fir** a flat-needled evergreen tree (*Abies balsamea*) of the pine family, native to Canada and the N U.S.: it yields Canada balsam and a soft wood, and is used as a Christmas tree

balsamic vinegar ⟦transl. of It *aceto balsamico,* a vinegar with "healing" qualities: term first applied to vinegar made from unfermented white grapes in EMILIA-ROMAGNA⟧ an aromatic, dark-brown, viscous vinegar, used in salad dressings, marinades, etc.

balsam of Peru a viscous liquid resin obtained from a leguminous Central American tree (*Myroxylon pereirae*), used in medical preparations, flavorings, perfumes, etc.

balsam of To·lu (tō lo͞o′) TOLU

☆**balsam poplar** a poplar (*Populus balsamifera*) of N North America, having buds that are coated with a fragrant resin

Bal·sas (bäl′säs) river in SC Mexico, flowing into the Pacific: *c.* 450 mi (724 km): in full **Río (de las) Balsas**

Bal·thus (-thəs) (pseud. of *Balthasar Klossowski de Rola*) 1908-2001; Fr. painter

Bal·tic[1] (bôl′tik) *adj.* 1 of the Baltic Sea 2 of the Baltic States 3 designating or of a branch of the Indo-European language family that includes Lithuanian, Latvian, and Old Prussian —*n.* the Baltic branch of the Indo-European family of languages

Bal·tic[2] (bôl′tik) BALTIC SEA

Baltic Sea sea in N Europe, south & east of the Scandinavian Peninsula, west of the Baltic States, & north of Poland, connecting with the North Sea through the Kattegat & the Skagerrak: 147,500 sq mi (382,024 sq km)

Baltic Sea

Baltic States Estonia, Latvia, & Lithuania, countries on the Baltic Sea: also **Baltics**

Bal·ti·more[1] (bôl′tə môr′), Lord 1st Baron Baltimore (*George Calvert*) 1580?-1632; Eng. statesman: founder of Maryland

Bal·ti·more[2] (bôl′tə môr′; *locally,* -mər) ⟦after prec.⟧ seaport in N Md., on an arm of Chesapeake Bay on its W shore

☆**Baltimore oriole** ⟦so named from having the colors of the coat of arms of Lord *Baltimore* (son of 1st Baron Baltimore), colonial proprietor of Maryland⟧ a North American oriole (*Icterus galbula*) that has an orange body with black on the head, wings, and tail: now more properly called NORTHERN ORIOLE

Bal·to-Sla·vic (bôl′tō slä′vik, -slav′ik) *n.* the Baltic and Slavic languages, when considered as constituting a subfamily within the Indo-European family of languages: the Baltic and Slavic branches are now generally considered by scholars as independently derived from Indo-European —*adj.* designating or of such a language subfamily

Ba·lu·chi (bə lo͞o′chē) ***n.*** **1** the Iranian language spoken in Baluchistan **2** *pl.* **-chis** or **-chi** a person born or living in Baluchistan

Ba·lu·chi·stan (bə lo͞o′chə stan′, -stän′) **1** region in SW Pakistan and SE Iran, on the Arabian Sea **2** province of W Pakistan: 134,051 sq mi (347,191 sq km); cap. Quetta

bal·us·ter (bal′əs tər) ***n.*** ⟦Fr *balustre* < It *balaustro,* pillar < *balausta,* flower of the wild pomegranate < L *balaustium* < Gr *balaustion:* from some resemblance in shape⟧ any of the small posts that support the handrail of a railing, as on a staircase

bal·us·trade (bal′əs trād′) ***n.*** ⟦Fr *balustrade* < It *balaustrata* < *balaustro:* see prec.⟧ a structure, as along a stairway, consisting of a handrail supported by balusters

Bal·zac (bȧl zȧk′; *E* bôl′zak), **Ho·no·ré de** (ô nô rā′ də) 1799-1850; Fr. novelist

bam (bam) ***interj.*** ⟦echoic⟧ used to suggest the sound of a sudden, hard impact **—*n.*** such a sound **—*vt.* bammed, bam′ming** to strike with a hard impact

Ba·ma·ko (bä mä kō′) capital of Mali, in the SW part: port on the upper Niger River

bam·bi·no (bam bē′nō, bäm-) ***n., pl.*** **-nos** or **-ni** (-nē) ⟦It, dim. of *bambo,* childish, lit., stupid, of echoic orig.⟧ **1** a child; baby **2** any image of the infant Jesus

bam·boo (bam bo͞o′) ***n.*** ⟦Malay *bambu* < ? a Dravidian language⟧ any of a number of semitropical or tropical grasses (subfamily Bambusoideae) often resembling trees, with perennial, jointed stems that are woody, hard, springy, and often hollow and sometimes grow to a height of *c.* 36 m (*c.* 120 feet): the stems are used in light construction and for furniture, canes, etc., and the young shoots of some species are eaten **—*adj.*** **1** of bamboo **2** made of bamboo stems

bamboo

bamboo curtain ⟦formed by analogy with IRON CURTAIN⟧ [*often* **B- C-**] the barrier of political and ideological differences that separated China from the West, esp. between 1949 and 1972

bam·boo·zle (bam bo͞o′zəl) ***vt.*** **-zled, -zling** ⟦*c.* 1700; cant form: < ?⟧ **1** to deceive or cheat by trickery; dupe **2** to confuse or puzzle **—bam·boo′zle·ment *n.* —bam·boo′zler *n.***

ban[1] (ban) ***vt.*** **banned, ban′ning** ⟦ME *bannen* < OE *bannan,* to summon, proclaim < *ban,* a command < IE base **bha-,* to speak: see PHONO-⟧ **1** to prohibit, as by official order, from doing, using, appearing, happening, etc.; forbid; censor [*to ban fraternities, to ban a book*] **2** [Archaic] to curse; condemn **—*n.*** ⟦ME < the v.; also < OFr *ban,* decree < OHG *bann*⟧ **1** in medieval times, a proclamation, esp. an official calling of vassals to arms **2** an excommunication or condemnation by church authorities **3** a curse **4** an official order forbidding something; prohibition **5** strong public disapproval or condemnation intended to prevent something **6** a sentence or decree of outlawry **—*SYN.*** FORBID

ban[2] (bän) ***n., pl.*** **ba·ni** (bä′nē) ⟦after *ban,* title of provincial governors of Slavonia⟧ a monetary unit of Romania, equal to 1/100 of a leu

ba·nal (bā′nəl; bə nal′, -näl′) ***adj.*** ⟦Fr < OFr, designating objects (such as ovens or mills) belonging to feudal serfs (hence common, ordinary) < *ban,* decree, legal control: see BAN[1]⟧ dull or stale as because of overuse; trite; hackneyed; commonplace **—*SYN.*** INSIPID **—ba·nal·i·ty** (bə nal′ə tē, bā-) ***n., pl.*** **-ties —ba′nal·ly *adv.***

ba·nan·a (bə nan′ə) ***n.*** ⟦Sp & Port < native name in W Africa, as in Mande *banäna*⟧ **1** any of a genus (*Musa*) of treelike tropical plants of the banana family, with long, broad leaves and large clusters of edible fruit; esp., any of the various hybrids widely cultivated in the Western Hemisphere **2** the long, curved fruit of these plants which usually has a soft, sweet, whitish pulp and a thick, usually yellowish skin See PLANTAIN[2] **—*adj.*** designating a family (Musaceae, order Zingiberales) of monocotyledonous tropical plants, including heliconia and bird of paradise

banana oil **1** amyl acetate, $CH_3CO_2C_5H_{11}$, a colorless liquid with a bananalike odor, used in flavorings, in making lacquers, etc. **2** [Old Slang] insincere talk

banana

☆**banana republic** ⟦coined by O. HENRY[2] in his short-story collection *Cabbages and Kings* (1904)⟧ any small, typically Latin American, country characterized by political instability and a one-crop economy controlled by foreign capital

☆**ba·nan·as** (bə nan′əz) ***adj.*** [Slang] **1** crazy or eccentric **2** wildly enthusiastic, excited, etc.

☆**banana seat** ⟦so called from its shape⟧ a narrow, tapered, elongated bicycle seat that curves upward at the rear

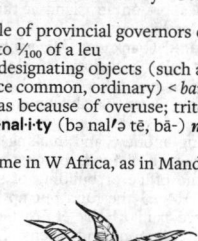

☆**bananas Foster** ⟦after R. *Foster,* patron of Brennan's, New Orleans restaurant where first made (1950s)⟧ a dessert consisting of sliced bananas sautéed in brown sugar, banana liqueur, and rum, then flamed and served over ice cream

banana spider a large, yellowish, tropical crab spider (*Heteropoda venatoria*) occasionally found in bunches of bananas shipped to the Temperate Zones

banana split a type of sundae consisting of a banana halved lengthwise, topped with several scoops of ice cream, sauces, nuts, whipped cream, etc.

Ba·nat (bä nät′) agricultural region in SE Europe, in the Danube River basin: formerly a part of Hungary (1779-1919?), it was divided among Hungary, Romania, & Yugoslavia in 1920

ba·nau·sic (bə nô′sik, -zik) ***adj.*** ⟦Gr *banausikos,* for artisans or mechanics⟧ **1** merely mechanical **2** materialistic **3** mundane or utilitarian

Ban·bur·y tarts (ban′ber′ē, -bər ē) ⟦after *Banbury,* town in England noted for its cakes⟧ small baked pastries filled with raisins, currants, etc.

Ban·croft (ban′krôft′, baŋ′-; -kräft′), **George** 1800-91; U.S. historian & statesman

band[1] (band) ***n.*** ⟦ME < ON *band* (akin to OE *bend*); also (in meaning "thin strip") < Fr *bande,* flat strip < OFr *bende* < ML *benda* < Goth *binda* < *bindan,* BIND⟧ **1** something that binds, ties together, restrains, etc. **2** *a)* a strip or ring of wood, metal, rubber, etc. fastened around something, as to bind or tie it together *b)* a finger ring [*a wedding band*] **3** a contrasting strip or stripe running across or along the edge of a material, or separating different sorts of material **4** a narrow strip of cloth used to bind, line, decorate, etc.; binding; banding [*hatband, neckband*] **5** [*usually pl.*] two strips hanging in front from the neck, as part of certain academic, legal, or clerical dress **6** a belt to drive wheels or pulleys in machinery **7** any of the separate divisions on a phonograph record containing individual selections **8** *a)* a specific range of wavelengths or frequencies, as in radio broadcasting or sound or light transmission *b)* any of the stripes of color in a spectrum **9** *Archit.* a thin layer or molding **10** *Geol.* a thin layer of distinctive rock, ore, etc. **—*vt.*** ⟦OFr *bander* < the n.⟧ **1** to put a band on or around; tie with a band ☆**2** to mark with a band for identification [*to band migratory birds*]

band[2] (band) ***n.*** ⟦LME *bande* < MFr < OFr < OProv < Goth *bandwa,* a sign < ?⟧ **1** a group of people joined together for a common purpose **2** a group of musicians playing together, esp. upon wind and percussion instruments [*a dance band*] **—*vi., vt.*** to gather or unite for a common purpose: usually with *together* **—*SYN.*** TROOP

band·age (ban′dij) ***n.*** ⟦Fr < *bande,* BAND[1]⟧ a strip of cloth, esp. gauze, or other dressing used to bind or cover an injured part of the body **—*vt.*** **-aged, -ag·ing** to put a bandage on (an injured part or person)

☆**Band-Aid** (band′ād′) ⟦prec. + AID⟧ *trademark for* a small prepared bandage of gauze and adhesive tape for minor wounds **—*n.*** [*also* **band-aid**] **1** a bandage of this type **2** a temporary, superficial remedy for a serious or complex problem **—*adj.*** [*also* **band-aid**] providing only temporary, superficial relief Also, for *n.* & *adj.,* **band′aid′**

ban·dan·na or **ban·dan·a** (ban dan′ə) ***n.*** ⟦Hindi *bāndhnū,* a method of dyeing < Sans *bándhana-,* tying (so named because the cloth is tied to prevent certain parts from receiving the dye) < IE **bhendh-,* BIND⟧ a large, colored handkerchief, usually with a figure or pattern

Ban·dar Se·ri Be·ga·wan (bun′dər ser′ē bə gä′wən) capital of Brunei, on the N coast

Ban·da Sea (bän′də) part of the S Pacific Ocean, within E Indonesia, between Sulawesi & New Guinea, south of most of the Molucca group

B & B[1] or **B and B** [Informal] BED-AND-BREAKFAST

B & B[2] or **B and B** an after-dinner drink consisting of benedictine and brandy

band·box (band′bäks′) ***n.*** ⟦orig. made to hold *neckbands,* or collars⟧ **1** a light, round box to hold hats, collars, etc. **2** a building or structure, often specif. a ballpark, regarded as undersized

B & E or **B and E** *abbrev.* breaking and entering

ban·deau (ban dō′, ban′dō) ***n., pl.*** **-deaux′** (-dōz′) ⟦Fr < OFr *bendel,* dim. of *bende,* BAND[1]⟧ **1** a narrow ribbon, esp. one worn around the head to hold the hair in place **2** a band of material covering the breasts, as a strapless bikini top

ban·de·ri·lla (bän′de rēl′yä) ***n., pl.*** ***-ri′llas*** (-rēl′yäs) ⟦Sp, dim. of *bandera,* akin to Fr *bannière* < VL **bandaria:* see BANNER⟧ any of several barbed darts with little streamers attached to them, that the *banderillero* sticks into the neck and shoulders of the bull

ban·de·ri·lle·ro (-rē lye′rô) ***n., pl.*** ***-ri·lle′ros*** (-rē lye′rôs) ⟦Sp < prec.⟧ the person whose task in a bullfight is to stick *banderillas* into the neck and shoulders of the bull

ban·de·role or **ban·de·rol** (ban′də rōl′) ***n.*** ⟦Fr *banderole* < It *banderuola,* dim. of *bandiera* < VL **bandaria:* see BANNER⟧ **1** a narrow flag or pennant, esp. one attached to a lance or carried at the masthead of a ship **2** a ribbonlike scroll, or a representation of one, carrying an inscription or symbol

ban·di·coot (ban′di ko͞ot′) ***n.*** ⟦< Telugu *pandikokku,* lit., pig rat⟧ **1** a member of either genus (*Bandicota* and *Nesokia,* family Muridae) of large rats, found esp. in India and Sri Lanka, that destroy grain and root crops **2** any of an order (Peramelina) of ratlike marsupials of Australia and nearby islands, which feed on insects and plants

ban·dit (ban′dit) ***n., pl.*** **-dits** or [Rare] **ban·dit·ti** (ban dit′ē) ⟦It *bandito* < *bandire,* to outlaw < Gmc **bann* (see BAN[1]), with sp. infl. by It *banda,* BAND[2]⟧ **1** a robber, esp. one who robs travelers on the road; brigand; highwayman **2** anyone who steals, cheats, exploits, etc. **—ban′dit·ry *n.***

Ban·djar·ma·sin (bän′jər mä′sin) *alt. sp. of* BANJARMASIN

band·lead·er (band′lēd′ər) ***n.*** a person who leads, or conducts, a dance band, marching band, etc.

band·mas·ter (band′mas′tər) *n.* the leader or conductor of a military or brass band

ban·dog (ban′dôg′) *n.* ⟦ME *bande dogge:* see BAND[1] & DOG⟧ **1** [Obs.] a dog kept tied up as a watchdog or because it is ferocious **2** any mastiff or bloodhound

ban·do·leer or **ban·do·lier** (ban′də lir′) *n.* ⟦Fr *bandoulière* < Sp *bandolera* < *banda,* a scarf, sash, ult. < Goth *bandwa*⟧ a broad belt worn over one shoulder and across the chest, with pockets for ammunition or loops for holding cartridges

bandoleer

ban·dore (ban dôr′, ban′dôr′) *n.* ⟦Sp *bandurria* < LL *pandura* < Gr *pandoura,* three-stringed instrument⟧ an ancient musical instrument somewhat like a guitar

band-pass filter (band′pas′) *Electronics* a filter which will pass frequencies within a desired range but will virtually cut out all other frequencies

☆**band saw** a power saw consisting of an endless toothed steel belt that runs over pulleys

band shell an outdoor platform for concerts, having a concave, nearly hemispherical back serving as a sounding board

bands·man (bandz′mən) *n., pl.* **-men** (-mən) a member of a band of musicians

band·stand (band′stand′) *n.* **1** an outdoor platform for a band or orchestra, usually with a roof **2** any platform for a band of musicians, as in a ballroom

Ban·dung (bän′dooŋ′, ban′-) city in W Java, Indonesia

B & W or **b & w** *abbrev.* BLACK-AND-WHITE (sense 3)

☆**band·wag·on** (band′wag′ən) *n.* a decorated wagon for a band of musicians to ride in, as in a parade —**on the bandwagon** [Informal] on the popular or apparently winning side, as in an election

band·width (band′width′, -witth′) *n.* **1** the range of frequencies within a BAND[1] (*n.* 8*a*), as that required to transmit a particular signal **2** *Comput.* the rate at which information can be transmitted along a communications line, to a device, etc.

ban·dy[1] (ban′dē) *vt.* **-died, -dy·ing** ⟦Fr *bander,* to bandy at tennis, lit., connect by binding: see BAND[1], *vt.*⟧ **1** to toss or hit back and forth, as a ball **2** to pass (gossip, rumor, etc.) about freely and carelessly **3** to give and take; specif., to exchange (words) in an angry or argumentative manner

ban·dy[2] (ban′dē) *n., pl.* **-dies** ⟦Fr *bandé,* pp. of *bander,* to tie, bend (as a bow): see BAND[1], *vt.*⟧ **1** an old game, much like field hockey, still played in parts of Europe **2** a club bent at one end, used to strike the ball in this game —*adj.* bent or curved outward; bowed

ban·dy-leg·ged (-leg′id, -legd′; -lā′gid, -lāgd′) *adj.* having bandy legs; bowlegged

bane (bān) *n.* ⟦ME < OE *bana* < IE base **bhen-,* to strike, wound > Avestan *banta-,* sick, weak, Goth *banja,* wound, blow⟧ **1** [Old Poet.] deadly harm; ruin; death **2** the cause of distress, death, or ruin **3** deadly poison: now obsolete except in *ratsbane,* etc.

bane·ber·ry (bān′ber′ē) *n., pl.* **-ries 1** any of a genus (*Actaea*) of plants of the buttercup family, with clusters of fleshy, white or red, poisonous berries **2** the berry of any of these plants

bane·ful (bān′fəl) *adj.* causing distress, death, or ruin; deadly —*SYN.* PERNICIOUS —**bane′ful·ly** *adv.*

Banff (bamf) **1** former county of NE Scotland: also **Banffshire** (-shir) **2** ⟦after the county, birthplace of an early pres. of the Canadian Pacific Railway⟧ town in SW Alberta, Canada: summer & winter resort

bang[1] (baŋ) *vt.* ⟦ON *banga,* to pound, hammer; akin to Ger *bengel,* cudgel, of echoic orig.⟧ **1** to hit with a resounding blow; strike hard and noisily **2** to shut (a door, window, etc.) noisily **3** to handle violently **4** [Slang] to engage in sexual intercourse with: somewhat vulgar —*vi.* **1** to make a loud noise, as through concussion or explosion **2** to move noisily or strike sharply (*against* something) —*n.* **1** a hard, noisy blow or impact **2** a loud, sudden noise, as of hitting or exploding ☆**3** *a)* [Informal] a display of enthusiasm or vigor [to start with a *bang*] *b)* [Slang] a thrill; excitement *c)* [Informal] sudden force or effectiveness [the idea hit him with a *bang*] **4** [Slang] the act or an instance of sexual intercourse: somewhat vulgar —*adv.* **1** hard, noisily, and suddenly [to run *bang* against a wall] **2** suddenly or exactly [be stopped *bang* in the middle] —*interj.* used to suggest the sound of a shot or explosion —**bang up** to do physical damage to

☆**bang**[2] (baŋ) *vt.* ⟦< prec.⟧ to cut (hair) short and straight across —*n.* [*usually pl.*] banged hair across the forehead

bang[3] (baŋ) *n. alt. sp. of* BHANG

Ban·ga·lore (baŋ′gə lôr′) city in S India

ban·ga·lore torpedo (baŋ′gə lôr′) ⟦? after prec.⟧ *Mil.* a piece of metal tubing filled with a high explosive, used esp. to blast through barbed wire or to detonate buried mines

bang·er (-ər) *n.* ⟦BANG[1] + -ER: ? from resemblance to a thick club used for banging⟧ [Brit. Informal] a sausage

Bang·ka (bäŋ′kä) island of Indonesia, off the SE coast of Sumatra: tin-mining center: 4,600 sq mi (11,914 sq km)

Bang·kok (baŋ′käk′) capital of Thailand; seaport on the Chao Phraya River, near its mouth on the Gulf of Thailand

Ban·gla·desh (bäŋ′glə desh′, baŋ′-) country in S Asia, at the head of the Bay of Bengal: formerly (1955-71) the province of East Pakistan, it became independent (1971) & a member of the Commonwealth (1972): 55,599 sq mi (144,000 sq km); cap. Dhaka —**Ban′gla·desh′i** (-desh′ē) *n., pl.* **-is**

ban·gle (baŋ′gəl) *n.* ⟦Hindi *bangrī,* glass bracelet⟧ **1** a decorative bracelet, armlet, or anklet **2** a disk-shaped ornament, esp. one hanging from a bracelet

bang on [Brit. Informal] precisely accurate or thoroughly appropriate

Bang's disease (baŋz) ⟦after B. L. F. *Bang* (1848-1932), Dan veterinarian⟧ a type of infectious brucellosis affecting cattle, caused by a bacterium (*Brucella abortus*) and often resulting in abortion

bang·tail (baŋ′tāl′) *n.* ☆[Slang] a racehorse

Ban·gui (bäŋ gē′) capital of the Central African Republic, on the Ubangi River

bang-up (baŋ′up′) *adj.* ⟦< BANG[1] (*adv.* 2): ? from the idea of being up to the mark, meeting a standard of excellence, etc.⟧ [Informal] very good; excellent

Bang·we·u·lu (baŋ′wē oo′loo) shallow lake in N Zambia: including swamps, 3,800 sq mi (9,842 sq km)

ba·ni (bä′nē) *n. pl. of* BAN[2]

ban·ian[1] (ban′yən) *n.* BANYAN

ban·ian[2] (ban′yən) *n.* ⟦Port < Ar *banyān* < Gujarati *vaniyo* < Sans *vanij,* merchant⟧ a Hindu merchant

ban·ish (ban′ish) *vt.* ⟦ME *banischen* < extended stem of OFr *banir* < ML **bannire* < Frank **bannjan,* to order or prohibit under penalty < *ban,* akin to BAN[1]⟧ **1** to exile **2** to send or put away; get rid of [to *banish* cares, to *banish* wrinkles] —**ban′ish·ment** *n.*

SYN.—**banish** implies removal from a country (not necessarily one's own) as a formal punishment; **exile** implies compulsion to leave one's own country, either because of a formal decree or through force of circumstance; **expatriate** suggests more strongly voluntary exile and often implies the acquiring of citizenship in another country; to **deport** is to send (an alien) out of the country, because the alien either entered unlawfully or is regarded as undesirable; to **transport** is to banish (a convict) to a penal colony; **ostracize** today implies forced exclusion from society, or a certain group, as because of disgrace [*ostracized* for scandalous behavior]

ban·is·ter (ban′is tər) *n.* ⟦altered < BALUSTER⟧ **1** [Now Rare] a baluster **2** *a)* a handrail together with the balusters that support it, as along a staircase *b)* the handrail itself

Ba·nja Lu·ka (bän′yə loo′kə) city in N Bosnia and Herzegovina

Ban·jar·ma·sin (bän′jər mä′sin) seaport in S Borneo, Indonesia, near the Java Sea

☆**ban·jo** (ban′jō′) *n., pl.* **-jos′** or **-joes′** ⟦of Afr orig., prob. akin to Kimbundu (a Bantu language) *mbanza,* an instrument resembling the banjo⟧ a stringed musical instrument having a long neck and a circular body covered on top with tightly stretched skin: the strings, usually four or five, are plucked with the fingers or a plectrum —**ban′jo·ist** *n.*

Ban·jul (bän′jool′) capital of Gambia; seaport on an island at the mouth of the Gambia River

banjo

bank[1] (baŋk) *n.* ⟦ME *banke* < MFr *banque* < OIt *banca,* orig., table, moneylenders' exchange table < OHG *bank,* bench: see fol.⟧ **1** an establishment for receiving, keeping, lending, or, sometimes, issuing money, and making easier the exchange of funds by checks, notes, etc. **2** the office or building of such an establishment **3** SAVINGS BANK (sense 2) **4** *a)* the fund put up by the dealer in baccarat, out of which losses are paid *b)* the entire monetary pool of a gambling establishment *c)* a common fund of chips, pieces, etc. used in playing a game, as poker or dominoes ☆**5** a reserve of things for later distribution or use, or a place for this; specif., *a)* a store of blood for transfusions, body organs for transplantation, etc. *b)* a store or a device for keeping retrievable data [a memory *bank*] —*vi.* **1** to deposit money in or do business with a bank **2** to operate or manage a bank **3** to be in charge of the bank, as in some gambling games —*vt.* to deposit (money) in a bank —*SYN.* RELY —☆**bank on** [Informal] to depend on; rely on

bank[2] (baŋk) *n.* ⟦ME *banke* < (prob. via Anglo-Norm **banki*) ON *bakki,* akin to OHG & Du *bank* & OE *benc,* BENCH⟧ **1** a long mound or heap, as of ground, clouds, or snow; ridge **2** a steep rise or slope, as of a hill **3** a stretch of rising land at the edge of a body of water, esp. a stream **4** a shoal or shallow place, as in a sea or lake; esp., a raised part of a continental shelf **5** the sloping of an airplane laterally to avoid slipping sideways on a turn **6** the sloping of a road, racing track, etc. laterally along a curve **7** *Billiards* CUSHION (sense 4) **8** *Mining* the face or top end of a body of ore —*vt.* **1** to heap dirt around for protection from cold, light, etc.; embank **2** to arrange (a fire) by covering with ashes, adding fuel, etc. so that it will burn low and keep longer **3** to heap or pile up so as to form a bank **4** to construct (a curve in a road, etc.) so that it slopes up from the inside edge **5** to slope (an airplane) laterally on a turn, with the inside wing low and the outside wing high so as to prevent slipping sideways **6** *Basketball* to shoot (the ball) so that it bounces from the backboard into the basket **7** *Billiards a)* to stroke (a ball) so that it recoils from a cushion *b)* to make (a shot) in this way —*vi.* **1** to take the form of a bank or banks **2** to fly an airplane with lateral slope on a turn —**SYN.** SHOAL[2], SHORE[1]

bank[3] (baŋk) *n.* ⟦ME *banke* < OFr *banc,* bench < Frank or OHG *bank:* see prec.⟧ **1** *a)* a bench for rowers in a galley *b)* the rowers **2** a row or tier of oars **3** a row or tier of objects [*a bank of lights*] **4** a row of keys in a keyboard or console **5** any of the subheads under a newspaper headline —*vt.* to arrange in a bank

Ban·ka (bäŋ′kä) *alt. sp. of* BANGKA

☆**bank·a·ble** (baŋk′ə bəl) *adj.* **1** acceptable to a bank **2** that is likely to attract investment [*a bankable motion-picture star*]

bank acceptance BANKER'S ACCEPTANCE

☆**bank account** money deposited in a bank and subject to withdrawal by the depositor

bank annuities British government bonds; consols

bank bill BANK NOTE

bank·book (baŋk′boŏk′) *n.* a booklet providing a personal record of a depositor's bank transactions

bank card an identification card with a magnetically coded strip, issued by a bank; specif., *a)* CREDIT CARD *b)* a card used for deposits, withdrawals, etc., as at an ATM[1]

bank discount interest deducted in a lump sum by a bank from a loan when the loan is made: it is computed from the date of the loan to the date of the final payment on the basis of the original amount of the loan

bank draft a draft or bill of exchange drawn by a bank on another bank

bank·er[1] (baŋk′ər) *n.* ⟦< BANK[1], by analogy with Fr *banquier*⟧ **1** a person who owns or manages a bank **2** the person in charge of the bank in some gambling games

bank·er[2] (baŋk′ər) *n.* ⟦< BANK[2]⟧ a person or boat engaged in cod fishing on the Newfoundland banks

bank·er[3] (baŋk′ər) *n.* ⟦BANK[3], in obs. sense "bench" + -ER⟧ the workbench of a bricklayer, mason, or sculptor

banker's acceptance a draft or bill of exchange drawn on a bank and accepted by it

bank holiday **1** any weekday on which banks are closed, as for a legal holiday **2** any period during which banks are closed by government order, as during a financial crisis **3** [Brit.] any of several legal holidays, usually on a Monday, when banks, schools, etc. are closed

bank·ing (baŋk′iŋ) *n.* **1** the business of operating a bank **2** any transaction with a bank involving one's checking account, savings account, etc.

banking house a company in the business of banking

bank note a promissory note issued by a bank, payable on demand: it is a form of paper money

bank paper **1** bank notes collectively **2** any bankable notes, bills, etc.

☆**bank·roll** (baŋk′rōl′) *n.* ⟦BANK (NOTE) + ROLL (*n.*)⟧ a supply of money; available funds —*vt.* [Informal] to supply with money; finance

bank·rupt (baŋk′rupt′, -rəpt) *n.* ⟦Fr *banqueroute* < It *banca rotta* < *banca,* bench (see BANK[1]) + *rotta,* broken < L *rupta,* fem. pp. of *rumpere,* to break: see RUPTURE⟧ **1** a person legally declared unable to pay his or her debts: the property of a bankrupt is administered for the benefit of his or her creditors and divided among them **2** anyone unable to pay his or her debts **3** a person who lacks a certain quality or has failed completely in some way [*a political bankrupt*] —*adj.* **1** that is a bankrupt; insolvent **2** lacking in some quality; destitute [*morally bankrupt*] **3** that has failed completely [*a bankrupt foreign policy*] —*vt.* to cause to become bankrupt

bank·rupt·cy (-rupt′sē, -rəp sē) *n., pl.* **-cies** **1** the state or an instance of being bankrupt **2** complete failure; ruin

bank·si·a (baŋk′sē ə) *n.* ⟦ModL, after Sir Joseph *Banks:* see fol.⟧ any of a genus (*Banksia*) of Australian evergreen shrubs of the protea family, with showy, dense clusters of small flowers and spiny leaves

Banks Island (baŋks) ⟦after Sir Joseph *Banks* (1743-1820), Eng botanist & explorer⟧ westernmost island of the Arctic Archipelago, Canada: part of Inuvik region, Northwest Territories: 27,038 sq mi (70,028 sq km)

Ban-Lon (ban′län′) *trademark for* a smooth synthetic knitted fabric that resists wrinkling

ban·ner (ban′ər) *n.* ⟦ME *banere* < OFr *baniere* < VL **bandaria,* ult. < Goth *bandwa,* a sign⟧ **1** a piece of cloth bearing a design, motto, slogan, etc., sometimes attached to a staff and used as a battle standard **2** a flag [*the Star-Spangled Banner*] **3** a headline extending across a newspaper page **4** a long strip of cloth with an advertisement, greeting, etc. lettered on it **5** an advertisement appearing on a Web page and typically containing a hyperlink to the advertiser's website: in full **banner ad** —*adj.* foremost; leading; outstanding [*a banner year in sales*] —*vt.* to publish or proclaim with or as with a banner headline

ban·ner·et[1] (ban′ər et′) *n.* a small banner: also **ban′ner·ette′**

ban·ner·et[2] (ban′ər ət′) *n.* ⟦ME & OFr *baneret* < *baniere,* BANNER⟧ [Historical] a knight allowed to lead his men into a battle under his own banner and ranking just above a knight bachelor

ban·ner·ol (ban′ər ōl′) *n.* BANDEROLE

ban·nis·ter (ban′is tər) *n.* BANISTER

ban·nock (ban′ək) *n.* ⟦ME *bannok* < Gael *bannach,* a cake⟧ [Scot.] a thick, flat cake made of oatmeal or barley meal baked on a griddle

Ban·nock·burn (ban′ək burn′) town in central Scotland: site of a battle (1314) in which the Scots under Robert Bruce defeated a much larger English force led by Edward II, thereby securing Scottish independence

banns (banz) *pl.n.* ⟦see BAN[1]⟧ the proclamation, generally made in church on three successive Sundays, of an intended marriage

ban·quet (baŋ′kwət) *n.* ⟦LME *banket* < MFr *banquet* < OIt *banchetto,* dim. of *banca:* see BANK[1]⟧ **1** an elaborate meal; feast **2** a formal dinner for many people, usually with toasts and speeches —*vt.* to honor with a banquet —*vi.* to dine at a banquet

ban·quette (baŋ ket′) *n.* ⟦Fr, dim. of Norm *banque,* earthwork < Du *bank,* BANK[2]⟧ **1** a gunners' platform extending along the inside of a trench or parapet ☆**2** [South] a raised way; sidewalk **3** an upholstered bench, esp. one along a wall in a restaurant

Ban·quo (baŋ′kwō) *n.* a character in Shakespeare's *Macbeth:* the ghost of Banquo appears to Macbeth, who had ordered his murder

ban·shee or **ban·shie** (ban′shē) *n.* ⟦Ir *bean sidhe* < *bean,* woman (see GYNO-) + *sith,* fairy⟧ *Celt. Folklore* a female spirit believed to wail outside a house as a warning that a death will occur soon in the family

ban·tam (ban′təm) *n.* ⟦after *Bantam,* early Du settlement in Java⟧ **1** any of various small, domestic fowls **2** a small but aggressive person —*adj.* like a bantam; small and aggressive

ban·tam·weight (-wāt′) *n.* a boxer between a flyweight and a junior featherweight, with a maximum weight of 118 pounds (53.53 kg)

ban·ter (ban′tər) *vt.* ⟦17th-c. slang < ?⟧ to tease or make fun of in a playful, good-natured way —*vi.* to exchange banter (*with* someone) —*n.* good-natured teasing, ridicule, or joking —**ban′ter·er** *n.* —**ban′ter·ing·ly** *adv.*

Ban·ting (ban′tiŋ), Sir **Frederick Grant** 1891-1941; Cdn. physiologist: codiscoverer of insulin (1922)

bant·ling (bant′liŋ) *n.* ⟦< Ger *bänkling,* bastard < *bank,* a bench: cf. BASTARD⟧ [Archaic] a young child; brat: a term of contempt

Ban·tu (ban′too͞′) *n.* ⟦Bantu *ba-ntu,* the men < *ba,* var. of *aba,* pl. prefix + *-ntu,* man: coined (1850s) by W. H. I. Bleek, librarian of the Brit gov. of the Cape Colony⟧ **1** a group of more than 200 languages belonging to the Niger-Congo language subfamily, including Swahili, Xhosa, and Zulu **2** *pl.* **-tus′** or **-tu′** a member of any of the Bantu-speaking peoples living throughout the S half of the African continent —*adj.* of the Bantus or their languages or cultures

Ban·tu·stan (ban′too͞ stan′) *n.* ⟦prec. + *-stan,* as in HINDUSTAN⟧ [*also* **b-**] **1** any of the enclaves established for the indigenous African peoples of South Africa under apartheid **2** any place in which an ethnic or religious group is segregated from the larger society

☆**ban·ty** (ban′tē) *n., pl.* **-ties** [Informal] **1** BANTAM (sense 1): also **banty rooster** or **banty hen** **2** a short or small, often aggressive person —*adj.* [Informal] short or small, and, often, aggressive

ban·yan (ban′yən) *n.* ⟦so called in allusion to such a tree on the S Iranian coast at the eastern end of the Persian Gulf, under which the *banians* (see BANIAN[2]) had built a pagoda⟧ a widespread, tropical fig tree (*Ficus benghalensis*) that is native to India: shoots that grow from its branches take root and form new trunks over a relatively wide area

banyan

ban·zai (bän′zī′) *interj.* ⟦Jpn < SinoJpn *ban,* ten thousand + *sai,* year, age⟧ used as a Japanese greeting, cheer, and battle cry

ba·o·bab (bā′ō bab′, bä′-) *n.* ⟦< ? name in a language of Ethiopia⟧ a thick-trunked tree (*Adansonia digitata*) of the bombax family, native to Africa: fiber from its bark is used for making rope, paper, etc., and the gourdlike fruit has an edible pulp

Bao·tou (bou′dō′) city in SW Inner Mongolia, China

bap or **bapt** *abbrev.* baptized

Bap or **Bapt** *abbrev.* Baptist

bap·ti·si·a (bap tiz′ē ə, -tizh′ə) *n.* ⟦ModL < Gr *baptisis,* a dipping: see BAPTIZE⟧ any of a genus (*Baptisia*) of herbs of the pea family, including a common wildflower of the E U.S.; wild indigo

bap·tism (bap′tiz′əm) *n.* ⟦ME & OFr *baptesme* < LL(Ec) *baptisma,* Christian baptism < L, a dipping under < Gr < *baptizein:* see BAPTIZE⟧ **1** a baptizing or being baptized; specif., the ceremony or sacrament of admitting a person into Christianity or a specific Christian church by immersing the individual in water or by pouring or sprinkling water on the individual, as a symbol of washing away sin and of spiritual purification **2** any experience or ordeal that initiates, tests, or purifies —**bap·tis′mal** (-tiz′məl) *adj.* —**bap·tis′mal·ly** *adv.*

baptism of fire ⟦transl. of Gr *baptisma pyros* (see Matt. 3:11)⟧ **1** the first time that new troops are under fire or in combat **2** any experience that tests one's courage, strength, etc. for the first time

bap·tist (bap′tist) *n.* ⟦ME & OFr *baptiste* < LL (Ec) *baptista,* a baptizer (esp. John the Baptist) < Gr *baptistēs:* see BAPTIZE⟧ **1** a person who baptizes **2** [**B-**] a member of a Protestant denomination holding that baptism should be given only to believers after confession of faith and by immersion rather than sprinkling —**the Baptist** John the Baptist

bap·tis·ter·y (bap′tis tər ē, -trē) *n., pl.* **-ter·ies** ⟦LL (Ec) *baptisterium,* baptismal font < L, place for bathing < Gr *baptistērion* < *baptizein,* fol.⟧ **1** a place, esp. a part of a church, used for baptizing **2** a baptismal font or tank Also **bap′tis·try** (-trē) *pl.* **-tries**

bap·tize (bap tīz′, bap′tīz) *vt.* **-tized′, -tiz′ing** ⟦ME *baptisen* < OFr *bap-*

tiser < LL(Ec) *baptizare* < Gr *baptizein,* to immerse, baptize, substituted for earlier *baptein,* to dip (used in post-classical Gr chiefly in sense "to dip in dye") < IE base **gwēbh-,* to dip, plunge > ON *kvefja,* to plunge⟧ **1** to immerse (an individual) in water, or pour or sprinkle water over (the individual), as a symbol of admission into Christianity or a specific Christian church **2** to subject to an initiation or an ordeal that purifies or cleanses **3** to give a first name to as part of the baptismal ceremony; christen —*vi.* to administer baptism —**bap·tiz′er** *n.*

bar[1] (bär) *n.* ⟦ME & OFr *barre* < ML *barra,* bar, barrier, prob. < Gaul **barros,* the bushy end, akin to Ir *bar,* branch < IE **bhoros,* cut wood < base **bher-,* to cut with a sharp tool⟧ **1** any piece of wood, metal, etc. longer than it is wide or thick, often used as a barrier, fastening, lever, etc.; specif., one of a series of such pieces enclosing a cage, jail cell, etc. **2** *a)* an oblong piece or mass of something solid [*bar* of soap, chocolate *bar*] *b)* any of various small metal strips worn to show military or other rank **3** a thing that blocks the way or prevents entrance, departure, or further movement; specif., SANDBAR **4** anything that hinders or prevents [illiteracy is a *bar* to success] **5** a strip, stripe, band, or broad line, as of light or color **6** *a)* the railing enclosing the part of a law court where the judges or lawyers sit, or where prisoners are brought to trial *b)* this part of the law court **7** *a)* a law court or system of courts *b)* any place of judgment [the *bar* of public opinion] **8** *a)* lawyers collectively *b)* the legal profession **9** *a)* a counter at which alcoholic drinks and sometimes food are served *b)* an establishment or room with such a counter *c)* a counter, or an establishment or room with such a counter, at or in which a specified beverage or food is served [a juice *bar,* espresso *bar,* sushi *bar*] **10** BARRE **11** the mouthpiece of a horse's bit, or the part of a horse's mouth into which it is fitted **12** in lace making and other needlework, a loop or tie that connects parts of a pattern **13** *Comput.* a horizontal box, as in a GUI screen, for displaying or typing text **14** *Heraldry* a horizontal stripe on a shield or bearing **15** *Law a)* the defeat or nullifying of a claim or action *b)* anything that brings this about **16** *Music a)* a vertical line across a staff, dividing it into measures *b)* a measure *c)* DOUBLE BAR **17** *Track & Field* the horizontal bar used in the HIGH JUMP or POLE VAULT **18** *Zool.* either of the ends of the wall of a horse's hoof, curving inward toward the center of the sole —*vt.* **barred, bar′ring 1** to fasten with or as with a bar **2** to obstruct by means of a bar or bars; shut off; close **3** to oppose, prevent, or forbid, as by legal action **4** to keep out; exclude [he was *barred* from the contest] **5** to set aside [*barring* certain possibilities] **6** to mark with stripes —*prep.* excluding; excepting [the best *bar* none] —*SYN.* HINDER[1], SHOAL[2] —**behind bars** in prison or jail —**raise** (or **lower**) **the bar** ⟦< *n.* 17⟧ raise (or lower) a limit, standard, etc.

bar[2] (bär) *n.* ⟦Ger < Gr *baros,* weight, akin to *barys,* heavy: see GRAVE[1]⟧ **1** the basic unit of pressure in the CGS system, equal to the pressure of a force of one million dynes per square centimeter: abbrev. *b* **2** *former name for* MICROBAR

bar[3] *abbrev.* **1** *a)* barometer *b)* barometric **2** barrel

Bar *abbrev. Bible* Baruch

BAR *abbrev.* Browning automatic rifle

Bar·ab·bas (bə rab′əs) *n.* ⟦L(Ec) < Aram < *baraba,* son of Abba⟧ *Bible* the prisoner whom the people wanted freed rather than Jesus: Matt. 27:16-21

Ba·ra·cal·do (bar′ə käl′dō, bär′-) city in The Basque Country, N Spain

Bar·a·nof (bar′ə nôf′) ⟦after A. A. *Baranov* (1745-1819), 1st gov. of the Russ colonies in America⟧ island in Alexander Archipelago, Alas.: *c.* 1,600 sq mi (4,144 sq km): largest city, Sitka

bar·a·the·a (bar′ə thē′ə) *n.* ⟦orig., a trademark < ?⟧ a soft fabric made of silk and wool or rayon and cotton

barb[1] (bärb) *n.* ⟦ME & OFr *barbe* < L *barba,* BEARD⟧ **1** a thin, somewhat beardlike growth near the mouth of certain animals, as the barbel of a fish **2** a piece of white linen for covering the throat and sometimes the chin, worn by certain nuns **3** a sharp point curving or projecting in an opposite direction from the main point of a fishhook, arrow, etc. **4** a cutting remark **5** one of the hairlike branches on the shaft of a feather **6** *Bot.* a hooked hair or bristle —*vt.* to provide with a barb

barb[2] (bärb) *n.* ⟦Fr *barbe,* Barbary horse < It *barbero* < Ar *Barbar,* BERBER⟧ **1** a horse of a breed native to N Africa, noted for speed and strength **2** a breed of pigeon similar to the carrier pigeon

bar·back (bär′bak′) *n.* a bartender's assistant

Bar·ba·dos (bär bā′dōs, -dōz) country on the easternmost island of the West Indies: formerly (1663-1966) a British dependency, it became independent & a member of the Commonwealth in 1966: 166 sq mi (431 sq km); cap. Bridgetown —**Bar·ba′di·an** (-dē ən) *adj., n.*

Bar·ba·ra (bär′bə rə, -brə) *n.* ⟦L, fem. of *barbarus* (see BARBAROUS), lit., foreign, strange⟧ a feminine name: dim. *Babs, Barb, Barbie*; var. *Barbra, Babette*

Bar·ba·res·co (bär′bə res′kō) *n.* ⟦after *Barbaresco,* village where produced⟧ a dark, dry red wine from the Piedmont region of Italy

bar·bar·i·an (bär ber′ē ən) *n.* ⟦< L *barbarus,* BARBAROUS⟧ **1** [Obs.] an alien or foreigner: in the ancient world applied esp. to non-Greeks, non-Romans, or non-Christians **2** a member of a people or group with a civilization regarded as primitive, savage, etc. **3** *a)* a person who lacks culture *b)* a coarse or unmannerly person; boor **4** a savage, cruel person; brute —*adj.* of or like a barbarian; esp., *a)* uncivilized; crude *b)* cruel; barbarous —**bar·bar′i·an·ism′** *n.*

SYN.—**barbarian** basically refers to a civilization regarded as primitive, usually without further connotation [the Anglo-Saxons were a *barbarian* people]; **barbaric** suggests the crudeness and lack of restraint regarded as characteristic of primitive peoples [*barbaric* splendor]; **barbarous** connotes the cruelty and brutality regarded as characteristic of primitive people [*barbarous* warfare]; **savage** implies a more primitive civilization than **barbarian** and connotes even greater fierceness and cruelty [a *savage* inquisition] —*ANT.* **civilized**

bar·bar·ic (bär ber′ik) *adj.* ⟦ME *barbarik* < L *barbaricus* < Gr *barbarikos*: see BARBAROUS⟧ **1** of, like, or characteristic of barbarians; uncivilized; primitive **2** wild, crude, and unrestrained —*SYN.* BARBARIAN —**bar·bar′i·cal·ly** *adv.*

bar·ba·rism (bär′bə riz′əm) *n.* ⟦L *barbarismus* < Gr *barbarismos*: see BARBAROUS⟧ **1** *a)* the use of words and expressions not standard in a language *b)* a word or expression of this sort (Ex.: "youse" for "you"): see also IMPROPRIETY, SOLECISM **2** the state of being primitive or lacking civilization **3** a barbarous action, custom, etc. **4** brutal behavior; barbarity; cruelty

bar·bar·i·ty (bär ber′ə tē) *n., pl.* **-ties 1** cruel or brutal behavior; inhumanity **2** a cruel or brutal act **3** a crude or coarse taste, manner, form, etc.

bar·ba·rize (bär′bə rīz′) *vt.* **-rized′, -riz′ing** ⟦ML *barbarizare* < Gr *barbarizein,* to behave like a barbarian⟧ to make barbarous; coarsen, brutalize, etc. —*vi.* to become barbarous —**bar′ba·ri·za′tion** *n.*

Bar·ba·ros·sa (bär′bə rôs′ə, -räs′ə), **Frederick** ⟦It < *barba,* beard + *rossa,* red: so named from his beard⟧ *see* FREDERICK I (of the Holy Roman Empire)

bar·ba·rous (bär′bə rəs) *adj.* ⟦L *barbarus* < Gr *barbaros,* foreign, strange, ignorant < IE echoic base **barbar-,* used for unintelligible speech of foreigners > Sans *barbara-,* stammering, non-Aryan⟧ **1** [Obs.] foreign or alien; in the ancient world, non-Greek, non-Roman, or non-Christian **2** characteristic of barbarians; primitive or lacking in civilization **3** uncultured, crude, coarse, rough, etc.: often used specifically of language regarded as lacking in refinement or good taste **4** cruel; brutal —*SYN.* BARBARIAN —**bar′ba·rous·ly** *adv.* —**bar′ba·rous·ness** *n.*

Bar·ba·ry (bär′bə rē) ⟦< L *Barbaria,* lit., a foreign country: see prec.⟧ BARBARY COAST (region of N Africa)

Barbary ape a tailless, apelike macaque monkey (*Macaca sylvana*) of N Africa and Gibraltar: the only surviving wild monkey in Europe

Barbary Coast 1 coastal region of N Africa, extending from Egypt to the Atlantic, inhabited chiefly by Berbers and once (until early 19th cent.) dominated by pirates **2** ⟦after the region of N Africa⟧ the waterfront district in San Francisco from the gold rush of 1849 to the earthquake of 1906, known for its saloons, gambling places, & brothels

Barbary sheep AOUDAD

Barbary States semi-independent Turkish provinces along the coast of N Africa (16th-19th cent.); Tripoli, Tunisia, Algeria, & Morocco

bar·bas·co (bär bas′kō) *n., pl.* **-cos** or **-coes** ⟦AmSp, altered < *verbasco,* mullein < L *verbascum*⟧ any of several Mexican plants (genus *Dioscorea*) of the yam family having a large, inedible root that yields extracts used in making synthetic steroidal hormones

bar·bate (bär′bāt′) *adj.* ⟦L *barbatus* < *barba,* BEARD⟧ **1** bearded **2** *Bot.* having hairlike tufts, or awns, as oats, barley, etc.

bar·be·cue (bär′bə kyo͞o′) *n.* ⟦AmSp *barbacoa* < Taino, lit., framework of sticks⟧ **1** [Obs.] a raised framework for smoking, drying, or broiling meat **2** a hog, steer, etc. broiled or roasted whole over an open fire, sometimes in an open pit **3** *a)* any meat broiled over an open fire *b)* any meat prepared and broiled with a barbecue sauce ☆**4** a party or picnic at which such meat is served **5** a restaurant that specializes in barbecuing **6** *a)* an outdoor structure for cooking or, esp., roasting over an open fire *b)* a portable outdoor grill —*vt., vi.* **-cued′, -cu′ing 1** to prepare (meat) outdoors by roasting on a spit or broiling on a grill, usually over a charcoal fire **2** to broil or cook (meat) with a highly seasoned sauce (**barbecue sauce**) containing vinegar, tomatoes, spices, etc. —*adj.* **1** of or for a barbecue **2** prepared by barbecuing [*barbecue* ribs]

barbed (bärbd) *adj.* **1** having a barb or barbs **2** stinging; cutting [*barbed* words]

☆**barbed wire** strands of wire twisted together, with barbs at regular, close intervals, used for fencing or military barriers

bar·bel (bär′bəl) *n.* ⟦ME & OFr < ML *barbellus* < L *barbula,* dim. of *barbus* < *barba,* BEARD⟧ **1** a threadlike growth from the lips or jaws of certain fishes: it is an organ of touch **2** any of a genus (*Barbus*) of large, European, freshwater cyprinoid fishes with such growths

bar·bell (bär′bel′) *n.* ⟦BAR[1] + (DUMB)BELL⟧ a long metal bar or rod to which disks of varying weights are attached at each end, used for weight-lifting exercises and in weight-lifting contests: also **bar bell** or **bar-bell**

barbell

bar·bel·late (bär′bə lāt′, bär bel′it) *adj.* ⟦ModL *barbellatus* < *barbella,* dim. < L *barbula*: see BARBEL⟧ *Bot.* covered with short, hooked bristles or hairs

☆**bar·be·que** (bär′bə kyo͞o′) *n., adj., vt., vi.* **-qued′, -qu′ing** BARBECUE

bar·ber (bär′bər) *n.* ⟦ME & OFr *barbour*; ult. < ML *barbator* < L *barba*, BEARD⟧ a person whose work is cutting hair, shaving and trimming beards, etc. —*vt.* to cut the hair of, shave, etc. —*vi.* to work as a barber

Bar·ber (bär′bər), **Samuel** 1910-81; U.S. composer

bar·be·ra (bär ber′ə) ***n.*** ⟦It⟧ [*also* **B-**] **1** a red grape originating in Italy, now grown also in California **2** the dry red wine made from this grape

☆**barber college** a school for training barbers

barber pole a pole with spiral stripes of red and white, used as a symbol of the barber's trade

bar·ber·ry (bär′ber′ē, -bə rē) ***n.***, *pl.* **-ries** ⟦ME *berberie* (infl. by *berie*, BERRY) < ML *barberis* < Ar *barbāris*⟧ **1** any of a genus (*Berberis*) of spiny shrubs of the barberry family, with sour, red berries and yellow flowers: it is often used for hedges **2** the berry —***adj.*** designating a family (Berberidaceae) of mostly spiny dicotyledonous plants (order Ranunculales), including the May apple and mahonia

☆**bar·ber·shop** (bär′bər shäp′) ***n.*** a barber's place of business —***adj.*** of or characterized by a style of singing traditional popular songs in close, four-part harmony, typically by an unaccompanied male quartet

barber's itch an inflammation of the hair follicles of the face and neck, caused by various fungi (genera *Trichophyton* and *Microsporum*); tinea barbae

bar·bet (bär′bət′, -bit) ***n.*** ⟦Fr, dim. of *barbe*, BEARD⟧ any of a tropical family (Capitonidae) of brightly colored piciform birds having a large, strong bill with bristles at its base

bar·bette (bär bet′) ***n.*** ⟦Fr, after St. *Barbara*, patron saint of artillerymen + *-ette*, -ET⟧ **1** a platform for guns in a fort, high enough to permit firing over the walls **2** the armored structure around a gun platform on a warship

bar·bi·can (bär′bi kən) ***n.*** ⟦ME < OFr *barbacane* < ML *barbacana* < ?⟧ a defensive tower or similar fortification at a gate or bridge leading into a town or castle

bar·bi·cel (bär′bə sel′) ***n.*** ⟦ModL *barbicella*, dim. of L *barba*, BEARD⟧ any of the tiny, hairlike extensions growing from the barbules of a feather, that hook the barbules together

☆**Bar·bie** (bär′bē) *trademark for* a plastic doll made in the image of a conventionally attractive, slim, and shapely young woman or girl —***n.*** [Informal] BARBIE DOLL

☆**Barbie doll** ⟦see prec.⟧ [Informal] any young woman or girl regarded variously as being superficial, vacuous, blandly attractive, etc. —**Bar′bie-doll′** ***adj.***

☆**bar·bi·tal** (bär′bi tôl′, -tal′) ***n.*** ⟦BARBIT(URIC ACID) + -AL⟧ diethylbarbituric acid, $C_8H_{12}N_2O_3$, a drug in the form of a white powder, used as a hypnotic and sedative: it is habit-forming and toxic

bar·bi·tu·rate (bär bich′ər it, -ə rāt′; bär′bə tyoor′it, -toor′-, -āt′; *often*, -bich′ə wit) ***n.*** ⟦fol. + -ATE[2]⟧ any depressant drug, as phenobarbital, derived from barbituric acid and used as a sedative, sleeping pill, anticonvulsant, etc.

bar·bi·tu·ric acid (bär′bə tyoor′ik, -toor′-) ⟦< Ger *barbitursäure* (< ModL *Usnea barbata*, lit., bearded moss + *ursäure*, a ureide of acid character < *urea*, urea + *säure*, acid) + -IC⟧ a white, odorless, crystalline acid, $C_4H_4O_3N_2$, used in the manufacture of sedatives and hypnotics, in making dyes, and as a polymerization catalyst

Bar·bi·zon School (bär′bə zän′; *Fr* bȧr bē zōn′) a group of French Romantic landscape painters (including Millet, Corot, Théodore Rousseau, and Daubigny) who settled in Barbizon, a village in N France, in the mid-19th cent.

Bar-B-Que (bär′bə kyoo′) ***n.***, ***adj.***, ***vt.***, ***vi.*** **-Qued′**, **-Qu′ing** ⟦partial phonetic sp.⟧ BARBECUE: also sp. **Bar-B-Q**, **-Qed**, **-Qing**

Bar·bu·da (bär byoo′də, -boo′-) island of the Leeward group in the West Indies: 62 sq mi (161 sq km): see ANTIGUA AND BARBUDA

bar·bule (bär′byool′) ***n.*** ⟦L *barbula*, dim. of *barba*, BEARD⟧ any of the threadlike parts fringing each side of the barb of a feather: cf. BARBICEL

barb·wire (bärb′wīr′) ***n.*** BARBED WIRE

bar·ca·role or **bar·ca·rolle** (bär′kə rōl′) ***n.*** ⟦Fr *barcarolle* < It (Venetian) *barcarola* < *barcarolo*, gondolier < *barca*, BARK[3]⟧ **1** a song sung by Venetian gondoliers, in moderate 6/8 or 12/8 time **2** any piece of music imitating this

Bar·ce·lo·na (bär′sə lō′nə) **1** seaport in NE Spain, on the Mediterranean **2** city in N Venezuela

Barcelona chair ⟦after BARCELONA, Spain, where exhibited in 1929 by MIES VAN DER ROHE⟧ an armless, padded leather chair on a steel frame shaped like a pair of curved X's: *Barcelona* is a trademark for this chair

BArch or **B.Arch.** *abbrev.* Bachelor of Architecture

bar·chan (bär kän′, bär′kän′) ***n.*** ⟦Russ *barxan*⟧ a crescent-shaped sand dune formed in certain inland desert regions, with the convex side facing into the wind

bar chart BAR GRAPH

bar code any of the patterned sets of vertical bars of varying widths imprinted on consumer products, mail, etc. and containing coded information that can be read by a computerized scanner: cf. UNIVERSAL PRODUCT CODE

bard[1] (bärd) ***n.*** ⟦Gael & Ir: see GRACE⟧ **1** an ancient Celtic poet and singer of epic poems, who accompanied himself on the harp **2** any of various other national minstrels or epic poets **3** a poet —**the Bard** ⟦see BARD OF AVON⟧ *name for* William SHAKESPEARE —**bard′ic** ***adj.***

bard[2] (bärd) ***n.*** ⟦Fr *barde* < Sp or It *barda*, leather armor for horses < Ar *barda′a*, saddle, packsaddle⟧ a piece of armor for a horse —***vt.*** to put bards on (a horse) Also sp. **barde**

Bard of Avon *name for* William SHAKESPEARE: so called after his birthplace, STRATFORD-UPON-AVON

bard·ol·a·try (bär däl′ə trē) ***n.*** ⟦prob. coined by G. B. SHAW: see prec. & -LATRY⟧ devotion, esp. excessive devotion, to Shakespeare or his works —**bard·ol′a·ter** (-ə tər) ***n.***

Bar·do·li·no (bär′dō lē′nō) ***n.*** ⟦after *Bardolino*, village in N Italy, where produced⟧ a light, fruity Italian red wine

bare[1] (ber) ***adj.*** **bar′er**, **bar′est** ⟦ME *bar* < OE *bær* < IE **bhoso-s* < ? base **bhes-*, to rub off > SAND⟧ **1** *a)* without the natural or customary covering [*bare* wooden floors] *b)* without clothing; naked [*bare* legs] **2** without equipment, supplies, or furnishings; empty [a *bare* room, a *bare* larder] **3** without embellishment; unadorned; simple; plain [the *bare* facts] **4** without tools or weapons: obsolete except in *bare hands* **5** threadbare **6** no more than; mere [a *bare* subsistence wage] —***vt.*** **bared**, **bar′ing** to make bare; uncover; strip; expose —**lay bare** to open to view; uncover; expose —**bare′ness** ***n.***

SYN.—**bare**, in this comparison, implies the absence of the conventional or appropriate covering [*bare* legs, *bare*headed]; **naked** implies the absence of clothing, either entirely or from some part, and connotes a revealing of the body [a *naked* chest]; **nude**, which is somewhat euphemistic for **naked**, is commonly applied to the undraped human figure in art; **bald** suggests a lack of natural covering, esp. of hair on the head; **barren** implies a lack of natural covering, esp. vegetation, and connotes destitution and fruitlessness [*barren* lands] See also **strip**

bare[2] (ber) ***vt.***, ***vi.*** *archaic pt. of* BEAR[1]

bare·back (ber′bak′) ***adv.***, ***adj.*** on a horse with no saddle

bare·boat (-bōt′) ***n.*** ⟦so called because it lacks what is usual, the crew⟧ a pleasure boat, esp. a yacht, with no personnel, rented to someone who will provide a captain and a crew

bare-bones (-bōnz′) ***adj.*** reduced to the essential; simple; basic

bare·faced (-fāst′) ***adj.*** **1** with the face uncovered, unmasked, or beardless **2** unconcealed; open **3** shameless; brazen; audacious; impudent [a *barefaced* lie] —**bare′fac′ed·ly** (-fās′id lē) ***adv.*** —**bare′fac′ed·ness** ***n.***

bare·foot (-foot′) ***adj.***, ***adv.*** with bare feet; without shoes and stockings or socks: also **bare′foot′ed** (-foot′id)

barefoot doctor a healthcare worker in China trained to attend to the basic medical needs of villagers in rural areas

ba·rège or **ba·rege** (bə rezh′) ***n.*** ⟦Fr, after *Barèges*, town in France⟧ a gauzy cloth of silk and wool, or cotton and wool, used for veils, dresses, etc.

bare·hand·ed (ber′han′did) ***adj.***, ***adv.*** **1** with hands uncovered or unprotected **2** without weapons, appropriate means, etc.

bare·head·ed (-hed′id) ***adj.***, ***adv.*** wearing no hat or other covering on the head

Ba·reil·ly or **Ba·re·li** (bə rā′lē) city in central Uttar Pradesh, N India

bare-knuck·le (ber′nuk′əl) ***adj.***, ***adv.*** **1** using bare fists rather than boxing gloves [a *bare-knuckle* prizefight, to fight *bare-knuckle*] **2** without refinement, compromise, etc.; rough [a *bare-knuckle* legal battle] Also **bare′-knuck′led** or occas. **bare′-knuck′les**

bare·leg·ged (ber′leg′id, -legd′; -lā′gid, -lāgd′) ***adj.***, ***adv.*** with the legs bare; without stockings on

bare·ly (ber′lē) ***adv.*** **1** without covering or disguise; plainly [stating the unpleasant facts *barely*] **2** only just; no more than; scarcely [*barely* enough to eat] **3** meagerly; scantily [a *barely* furnished room]

Bar·ents Sea (bar′ənts, bär′-) part of the Arctic Ocean, north of Norway & W Russia, between Svalbard & Novaya Zemlya

bare·sark (ber′särk′) ***n.*** ⟦altered (by assoc. with BARE[1] + SARK) < BERSERK⟧ BERSERKER

☆**barf** (bärf) ***vi.***, ***vt.*** ⟦echoic⟧ [Slang] to vomit

☆**bar·fly** (bär′flī′) ***n.***, *pl.* **-flies′** [Slang] a person who spends much time drinking in bars

bar·gain (bär′gən) ***n.*** ⟦ME & OFr *bargaine* < OFr *bargaignier*, to haggle < Frank **borganjan*, to lend, akin to OE *borgian*, BORROW⟧ **1** a mutual agreement or contract in which the parties settle on what should be given or done by each **2** the terms of such an agreement **3** such an agreement considered in terms of its worth to one of the parties [to make a bad *bargain*] **4** something offered, bought, or sold at a price favorable to the buyer —***vi.*** **1** to discuss the details of a transaction, contract, treaty, etc., trying to get the best possible terms **2** to make a bargain or agreement —***vt.*** to sell or trade to another by bargaining; barter —**bargain for 1** to try to get cheaply **2** to expect; anticipate; count on: also **bargain on** —**into (or in) the bargain** beyond what has been agreed on; in addition —**bar′gain·er** ***n.***

bar·gain-base·ment (bär′gən bās′mənt) ***adj.*** ⟦with reference to the area, in some stores, where goods on sale are displayed and sold⟧ **1** very low or greatly reduced [*bargain-basement* prices] **2** cheap, inferior, etc.

☆**bargain counter** a store counter on which goods are displayed for sale at reduced prices

☆**bargaining chip** something which can be helpful in negotiation, specif. in eliciting a concession

barge (bärj) ***n.*** ⟦ME & OFr < ML *barga* < LL *barca* < **barica* < Gr *baris*, Egyptian boat < Coptic *barī*, small boat⟧ **1** a large boat, usually flat-bottomed, for carrying heavy freight on rivers, canals, etc. **2** a large pleasure boat, esp. one used for state ceremonies, pageants, etc. **3** a boat reserved for the use of a flag officer **4** [Slang] any clumsy boat —***vt.*** **barged**, **barg′ing** to carry by barge —***vi.*** **1** to move slowly and clumsily **2** to come or go (*in* or *into*) in a rude, abrupt, or clumsy way **3** to collide heavily or clumsily; run (*into*)

barge·board (bärj′bôrd′) *n.* ⟦see fol.⟧ a board, often ornate, attached along the barge couples of a gabled roof, as in Tudor and Gothic architecture

barge couple ⟦ME *berge,* a sloping roof (< ? OFr, a slope) + COUPLE⟧ either of the pair of outside rafters forming the projection of a gabled roof

bar·gee (bär jē′) *n.* ⟦BARG(E) + -EE[1]⟧ [Brit.] a bargeman

bar·gel·lo (bär jel′ō; *often,* -zhel′ō) *n.* ⟦after *Bargello,* a museum in Florence, Italy, where it appears in upholstery⟧ **1** a long, straight stitch in needlepoint, arranged so as to produce a zigzag pattern **2** the pattern produced by using this stitch, esp. a modified zigzag or flamelike design, or any pattern like this **3** this type of embroidery

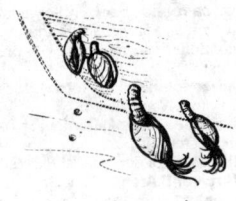

bargeboard

barge·man (bärj′mən) *n., pl.* **-men** (-mən) a man who operates, or works aboard, a barge

bar·ghest (bär′gest′) *n.* ⟦< ? Ger *berg geist,* mountain spirit⟧ *Eng. Folklore* a doglike goblin whose appearance supposedly foreshadows death or bad luck

☆**bar girl** a woman employed by a bar to entice men into buying drinks freely

bar graph a graph in which the lengths of parallel bars are used to compare statistical frequencies, quantities, etc.

Bar Harbor ⟦so named from a *(sand) bar* connecting Mount Desert Island with a nearby island⟧ resort town on Mount Desert Island, Me.

☆**bar·hop** (bär′häp′) *vi.* **-hopped′, -hop′ping** [Informal] to drink at a series of bars in a single evening or on a single occasion

Ba·ri (bä′rē) seaport in SE Italy, on the Adriatic

☆**bar·i·at·rics** (bar′ē a′triks) *n.* ⟦< Gr *baros,* weight + -IATRICS⟧ the study of obesity and its treatment —**bar′i·at′ric** *adj.* —**bar′i·a·tri′cian** *n.*

bar·ic (ber′ik) *adj.* ⟦< Gr *barys,* weighty (see GRAVE[1]) + -IC⟧ *Physics* of weight or pressure, esp. that of the atmosphere; barometric

ba·ril·la (bə ril′ə) *n.* ⟦Sp *barrilla* < Galician *baril,* very good < Ar *bari′*, free, healthy⟧ crude soda ash, formerly used in glassmaking and obtained by burning various saltworts and related plants (genera *Salsola* and *Halogeton*) native to the Mediterranean area

Ba·ri·sal (bar′ə sôl′) river port in S Bangladesh, in the Ganges delta

ba·ris·ta (bə rēs′tə, -ris′-) *n.* ⟦It, person who brews espresso; orig., bartender⟧ a person who brews and sells coffee, as in a coffeehouse

bar·ite (ber′īt′) *n.* ⟦< Gr *barys,* weighty (see GRAVE[1]) + -ITE[1]⟧ a soft, heavy, orthorhombic mineral, barium sulfate, $BaSO_4$, that is the chief ore of barium, used in making paint, DRILLING MUD, etc.

bar·i·tone (bar′ə tōn′, ber′-) *n.* ⟦It *baritono* < Gr *barytonos,* deep-toned < *barys,* heavy, deep (see GRAVE[1]) + *tonos,* TONE⟧ **1** the range of a male voice between tenor and bass **2** *a)* a voice or singer with such a range *b)* an instrument with a similar range within its family, as a baritone saxophone *c)* a part for such a voice or instrument **3** a valved brass instrument of the saxhorn family pitched in B♭ and often used in brass bands —*adj.* of, for, or having the range of a baritone

bar·i·um (ber′ē əm) *n.* ⟦ModL < Gr *barys,* heavy (see GRAVE[1]) + -IUM⟧ a silver-white, slightly malleable, metallic chemical element, one of the alkaline-earth metals, found as a carbonate or sulfate and used in alloys: symbol, Ba; at. no. 56: see the periodic table of elements in the Reference Supplement

barium chloride a poisonous compound, $BaCl_2$, consisting of flat white crystals that are soluble in water: it is used to treat water, metals, leather, etc.

barium hydroxide a toxic, white powder or crystalline material, $Ba(OH)_2$, used in making lubricating oils and greases, soaps, and insecticides and in sugar refining, water softening, etc.

barium oxide a toxic, white powder, BaO, formed by decomposing barium carbonate at high temperature: it reacts vigorously with water to form the hydroxide

barium peroxide a gray-white powder, BaO_2, used as a bleach and in making hydrogen peroxide: also **barium dioxide**

barium sulfate an odorless, tasteless, white powder, $BaSO_4$, insoluble in water: it is used as a paint pigment, as a filler for paper, textiles, etc., and as an opaque substance that is ingested to aid in making diagnostic X-rays of the stomach and intestine

bark[1] (bärk) *n.* ⟦ME < ON *bǫrkr,* akin to MLowG *borke*⟧ **1** the outside covering of the stems and roots of trees and woody plants **2** some kinds of this matter used in tanning, dyeing, etc. **3** CINCHONA —*vt.* **1** to treat with a bark infusion, as in leather tanning **2** to take the bark off; specif., to girdle (a tree) **3** [Informal] to scrape some skin off *[to bark one's shin]* —*SYN.* SKIN

bark[2] (bärk) *vi.* ⟦ME *berken* < OE *beorcan,* akin to ON *berkja,* of echoic orig.⟧ **1** to make the characteristic sharp, abrupt cry of a dog **2** to make a sound like this *[the engine barked]* **3** to speak or shout sharply; snap **4** [Informal] to cough ☆**5** [Slang] to advertise a show, sale, etc. by shouting about it in public —*vt.* to say or advertise with a bark or shout —*n.* **1** the sharp, abrupt sound made by a dog **2** any sharp, abrupt sound or utterance like this —☆**bark up the wrong tree** to misdirect one's attack, energies, etc.

bark[3] (bärk) *n.* ⟦ME *barke,* prob. via Port or ML *barca* (> OFr *barque*) < LL, small boat: see BARGE⟧ **1** [Old Poet.] any boat, esp. a small sailing boat **2** a sailing vessel with its two forward masts square-rigged and its rear mast rigged fore and aft

☆**bark beetle** any of a number of small weevils (family Curculionidae), the larvae and adults of which burrow under the bark of trees, esp. conifers, and feed on the inner bark, sometimes causing extensive damage

bar·keep·er (bär′kē′pər) *n.* **1** an owner of a bar where alcoholic drinks are sold **2** a bartender Also ☆**bar′keep′**

☆**bark·en·tine** (bär′kən tēn′) *n.* ⟦< BARK[3], modeled on BRIGANTINE⟧ a sailing vessel with its foremast square-rigged and its two other masts rigged fore and aft

bark·er[1] (bär′kər) *n.* a person or machine that takes bark off a tree, log, etc.

bark·er[2] (bär′kər) *n.* **1** an animal, person, or thing that makes a barking sound **2** a person in front of a side show, theater, store, etc. who tries to attract customers by loud, animated talking

Bar·king (bär′kiŋ) former municipal borough of SE England: now, with Dagenham, constituting a borough (**Barking and Dagenham**) of Greater London

bar·ley (bär′lē) *n.* ⟦ME *barli* < OE *bærlic,* of barley < *bere,* barley + *-lic* (-LY[1]) < IE base **bhares-* > FARINA, ON *barr,* grain⟧ **1** a cereal grass (*Hordeum vulgare* and related species) with dense, bearded spikes of flowers, each made up of three single-seeded spikelets **2** its grain, used in making malt, soups, etc.

bar·ley·corn (-kôrn′) *n.* ⟦ME *barli-corn*⟧ **1** barley or a grain of barley **2** an old unit of linear measure equal to ⅓ inch

Barleycorn, John *see* JOHN BARLEYCORN

barley sugar a clear, hard candy made by melting sugar, formerly with a barley extract added

barley water [Chiefly Brit.] a nourishing drink, given esp. to children and sick persons, made by boiling barley in water, then straining and cooling the liquid

barm (bärm) *n.* ⟦ME *berme* < OE *beorma,* yeast < IE base **bher-,* to boil up > FERMENT, BREATH⟧ the yeast foam that appears on the surface of malt liquors as they ferment

bar·maid (bär′mād′) *n.* **1** [Chiefly Brit.] a woman bartender **2** a waitress who serves alcoholic drinks in a bar

bar·man (-mən) *n., pl.* **-men** (-mən) [Chiefly Brit.] a male bartender

Bar·me·cide (feast) (bär′mə sīd′) ⟦after a prince in *The Arabian Nights* who served such a feast⟧ **1** a pretended feast with no food **2** any pretended or illusory generosity or hospitality —**Bar′me·cid′al** (-sīd′′l) *adj.*

bar mitz·vah or **bar miz·vah** (bär mits′və; *Heb* bär′mits vä′) [*also* **B-M-**] ⟦Yiddish *bar-mitsve* < Heb-Aram < Aram *bar,* son of + Heb *mitsva,* commandment⟧ **1** a Jewish boy who has arrived at the age of religious responsibility, thirteen years ☆**2** the ceremony celebrating this event, with its attendant festivities —*vt.* **-vahed, -vah·ing** to confirm (a boy) as a bar mitzvah

barm·y (bärm′ē) *adj.* **barm′i·er, barm′i·est 1** full of barm; yeasty or foamy **2** [Brit. Slang] crazy

barn (bärn) *n.* ⟦ME < OE *bern, berern* < *bere,* BARLEY + *ærn,* house: see REST[1]⟧ **1** a farm building for sheltering harvested crops, livestock, machines, etc. ☆**2** a large building for streetcars, trucks, etc. ☆**3** ⟦arbitrary use, from phr. *as big as a barn*⟧ *Nuclear Physics* a unit of area used to show the degree of probability that a nuclear reaction will occur: 1 barn = a magnitude of 10^{-24} sq cm per nucleus: abbrev. *b*: see CROSS SECTION

Bar·na·bas (bär′nə bəs) *n.* ⟦ME < LL (Vulg.: Acts 4:36) < Gr < Aram *barnebhū′āh,* son of exhortation⟧ **1** a masculine name: dim. *Barney;* var. *Barnaby* **2** *Bible* (original name *Joses* or *Joseph*) a Levite of Cyprus, a Christian apostle & missionary companion of Paul: Acts 4:36

Bar·na·by (bär′nə bē) *n.* a masculine name: see BARNABAS

bar·na·cle (bär′nə kəl) *n.* ⟦ME *bernacle,* earlier *bernak* < MIr *bairnech* & Bret *bernik,* kind of shellfish: ult. via Gaul **berna,* split < IE base **bher-,* to slit⟧ **1** BARNACLE GOOSE **2** any member of various orders of saltwater cirriped crustaceans that cement themselves to rocks, wharves, ship bottoms, etc. and to other animals, as whales, after a free-swimming larval stage **3** a person or thing hard to get rid of —**bar′na·cled** *adj.*

barnacle goose ⟦so named from the popular notion that it grew from the crustacean: see prec.⟧ a European wild goose (*Branta leucopsis*)

goose barnacles

bar·na·cles (-kəlz) *pl.n.* ⟦ME & OFr *bernac,* kind of bit⟧ **1** nose pincers for controlling an unruly horse **2** an instrument of torture like such pincers

Bar·nard[1] (bär′nərd) *n.* a masculine name: see BERNARD[1]

Bar·nard[2] (bär′nərd), **George Grey** 1863-1938; U.S. sculptor

Bar·na·ul (bär′nä o͞ol′) city in SC Russia, on the Ob River

☆**barn·burn·er** (bärn′burn′ər) *n.* [Slang] something, esp. a closely contested sports event, that is very exciting, intense, dramatic, etc.

☆**barn dance** a party, originally held in a barn, at which people dance square dances

Barnes (bärnz), **William** 1801-86; Eng. dialect poet

Bar·net (bär′nət) borough of Greater London, England

Bar·ne·veldt (bär′nə velt′), **Jan van Ol·den** (yän′vän ôl′dən) 1547-1619; Du. statesman & patriot

bar·ney (bär′nē) *n.* [Brit. Informal] a loud argument or quarrel; altercation

barn owl any of a family (Tytonidae) of owls, esp. a widely distributed species (*Tyto alba*), usually brown and gray with a spotted white breast, found chiefly in hollow trees or barns, that feeds on rats and mice

Barns·ley (bärnz′lē) city in South Yorkshire, N England

barn·storm (bärn′stôrm′) *vi., vt.* ⟦BARN + STORM, *vi.* 3: from occas. use of barns as auditoriums⟧ **1** to go about (the country) performing plays, giving lectures or campaign speeches, playing exhibition games, etc., esp. in small towns and rural districts **2** ⟦from the use of barns as hangars⟧ in the early days of aviation, to tour (the country) giving short airplane rides, exhibitions of stunt flying, etc. —**barn′storm′er** *n.*

barn swallow a common swallow (*Hirundo rustica*) with a long, deeply forked tail: it often nests in barns and other structures

Bar·num (bär′nəm), **P(hineas) T(aylor)** 1810-91; U.S. showman & circus operator

barn·yard (bärn′yärd′) *n.* the yard or ground near a barn, often enclosed —*adj.* **1** of a barnyard **2** like or fit for a barnyard; earthy, smutty, etc.

bar·o- (bar′ō, ber′-; -ə) ⟦< Gr *baros,* weight < *barys,* heavy: see GRAVE[1]⟧ *combining form* weight or pressure, esp. atmospheric pressure [*barograph*]

Ba·ro·da (bə rō′də) *former name for* VADODARA (the city)

bar·o·gram (bar′ə gram′) *n.* a linear record traced by a barograph

bar·o·graph (-graf′) *n.* a barometer that records changes in atmospheric pressure on a revolving cylinder —**bar′o·graph′ic** *adj.*

Ba·ro·ja (bä rô′hä), **Pí·o** (pē′ô) 1872-1956; Sp. novelist

Ba·ro·lo (bä rō′lō) *n.* ⟦after *Barolo,* main village of district where produced⟧ a dark, dry red wine from the Piedmont region of Italy

ba·rom·e·ter (bə räm′ət ər) *n.* ⟦BARO- + -METER⟧ **1** an instrument for measuring atmospheric pressure, esp. an aneroid barometer or an evacuated and graduated glass tube (**mercury barometer**) in which a column of mercury rises or falls as the pressure of the atmosphere increases or decreases: barometers are used in forecasting changes in the weather or finding height above sea level **2** anything that reflects or indicates change [the stock market is a *barometer* of business] —**bar·o·met·ric** (bar′ə met′rik) *adj.*, **bar′o·met′ri·cal** —**bar′o·met′ri·cal·ly** *adv.*

barometric gradient PRESSURE GRADIENT

barometric pressure the pressure of the atmosphere as indicated by a barometer: see ATMOSPHERIC PRESSURE

bar·on (bar′ən, ber′-) *n.* ⟦ME & OFr < Frank **baro,* freeman, man < IE base **bher-,* to carry > BEAR[1]⟧ **1** in the Middle Ages, a feudal tenant of the king or of any higher-ranking lord; nobleman **2** a member of the lowest rank of the British hereditary peerage **3** this rank or its title **4** a European or Japanese nobleman of like rank ☆**5** a man having great or absolute power in some field of business or industry; magnate [an oil *baron*] **6** a large joint of meat, including the whole sirloin or both loins, with the backbone between

bar·on·age (bar′ən ij, ber′-) *n.* ⟦ME & OFr *barnage* < prec.⟧ **1** the barons as a class **2** the peerage **3** BARONY (sense 2)

bar·on·ess (-is) *n.* ⟦ME & OFr *baronesse*⟧ **1** a baron's wife, widow, or (in some European countries) daughter **2** a woman with a barony in her own right

bar·on·et (-ət) *n.* ⟦ME, dim. of BARON⟧ **1** a man holding the lowest hereditary British title, below a baron but above a knight: a baronet is addressed as "Sir," and may add "Bart." to his name, as Sir John Doe, Bart. **2** this title

bar·on·et·age (-ij) *n.* **1** baronets as a class **2** BARONETCY

bar·on·et·cy (-sē) *n., pl.* **-cies** the title, rank, or status of a baronet

ba·rong (bə rôn′, -räŋ′) *n.* ⟦< name in a language of the Philippines; prob. akin to PARANG⟧ a heavy knife with an ornate pommel, used by the Moros of the Philippines

ba·ro·ni·al (bə rō′nē əl) *adj.* **1** of a baron or barons **2** fit for a baron; grand, showy, etc. [a *baronial* mansion]

ba·ronne (bȧ rôn′) *n.* ⟦Fr⟧ baroness

bar·o·ny (bar′ə nē, ber′-) *n., pl.* **-nies** ⟦ME & OFr *baronie*⟧ **1** a baron's domain **2** the rank, title, or status of a baron or baroness

ba·roque (bə rōk′) *adj.* ⟦Fr, orig., irregular < Port *barroco,* imperfect pearl⟧ **1** [*often* **B-**] *a)* of, characteristic of, or like a style of art and architecture characterized by much ornamentation and curved rather than straight lines *b)* of, characteristic of, or like a style of music characterized by highly embellished melodies and fugal or contrapuntal forms **2** [*often* **B-**] designating or of the period in which these styles flourished (*c.* 1600-1750) **3** fantastically overdecorated; gaudily ornate **4** irregular in shape: said of pearls —*n.* [*often* **B-**] the period of the Baroque style of art: cf. ROCOCO

bar·o·re·cep·tor (bar′ō ri sep′tər) *n.* a nerve ending sensitive to pressure: in the circulatory system they help regulate the dilation of blood vessels by reacting to blood pressure: also **bar′o·cep′tor**

bar·o·scope (bar′ə skōp′) *n.* ⟦BARO- + -SCOPE⟧ an instrument for indicating changes in atmospheric pressure —**bar′o·scop′ic** (-skäp′ik) *adj.*

ba·rouche (bə ro͞osh′) *n.* ⟦Ger *barutsche* < It *baroccio* altered < *biroccio* < ML **birotium,* two-wheeled cart < LL *birotus,* two-wheeled < L *bi-,* BI-[1] + *rota,* wheel: see ROLL⟧ a four-wheeled carriage with a collapsible hood, two double seats facing each other, and a box seat in front for the driver

barque (bärk) *n.* BARK[3]

bar·quette (bär ket′) *n.* ⟦Fr, dim. of *barque,* boat⟧ a pastry shell shaped like a little boat, filled with fruit, vegetables, custard, etc.

Bar·qui·si·me·to (bär kē′sē mā′tô) city in NW Venezuela

bar·rack[1] (bar′ək, ber′-) *n.* ⟦Fr *baraque* < Sp *barraca,* cabin, mud hut < *barro,* clay, mud < VL **barrum,* clay⟧ **1** [Rare] an improvised hut **2** [*pl., often with sing. v.*] *a)* a building or group of buildings for housing soldiers *b)* a large, plain, often temporary building for housing workmen, police, etc. — *vt., vi.* to house in barracks

bar·rack[2] (bar′ək, ber′-) *vt., vi.* [Chiefly Austral.] to jeer or shout at (a player, team, performer, etc.)

barracks bag a large cloth bag to hold a soldier's equipment and personal possessions

bar·ra·coon (bar′ə ko͞on′) *n.* ⟦Sp *barracón,* aug. of *barraca*: see BARRACK[1]⟧ an enclosure or barracks, formerly used for temporarily confining slaves or convicts awaiting transportation

bar·ra·cu·da (bar′ə ko͞o′də, ber′-) *n., pl.* **-da** or **-das** ⟦AmSp, prob. < name in a language of the West Indies⟧ **1** any of a family (Sphyraenidae) of fierce, pikelike percoid fishes of tropical seas: some species are edible **2** [Informal] a person who is ruthlessly aggressive, esp. in business or professional matters

bar·rage[1] (bə räzh′, -räj′) *n.* ⟦Fr, in *tir de barrage,* barrier fire: see fol.⟧ **1** a curtain of artillery fire laid down to keep enemy forces from moving, or to cover or prepare the way for one's own forces, esp. in attack **2** a heavy, prolonged attack of words, blows, etc. — *vi., vt.* **-raged′**, **-rag′ing** to lay down a barrage (against); subject to a barrage

bar·rage[2] (bär′ij, bar′-) *n.* ⟦Fr < *barrer,* to stop < *barre,* BAR[1]⟧ a man-made barrier in a stream, river, etc. to deepen the water or channel it for irrigation; dam

barrage balloon (bə räzh′, -räj′) any of a number of anchored balloons with cables or nets attached for entangling low-flying attacking airplanes

bar·ra·mun·da (bar′ə mun′də, ber′-) *n., pl.* **-da** or **-das** ⟦< native name⟧ BARRAMUNDI

bar·ra·mun·di (-dē) *n., pl.* **-di**, **-dis**, **-dies** **1** the Australian lungfish (*Neoceratodus forsteri*): the only existing species of an order (Ceratodiformes) of bony fishes having one lung, large scales, and paddlelike fins **2** any of various edible, freshwater, Australian percoid fishes (esp. genus *Scleropages*)

☆**bar·ran·ca** (bə raŋ′kə) *n.* ⟦Sp < VL < Gr *pharanx,* chasm < **pharein*: see BORE[1]⟧ a deep ravine or a steep cliff, esp. in the Southwest: also **bar·ran′co** (-kō) *pl.* **-cos**

Bar·ran·quil·la (bä′rän kē′yä) seaport in NW Colombia, on the Magdalena River

bar·ra·tor or **bar·ra·ter** (bar′ə tər, ber′-) *n.* ⟦ME *baratour* < OFr *barateor,* swindler < *barater,* to cheat < *barate,* fraud, strife < ON *baratta,* quarrel < *berja,* to beat < IE base **bher-,* to cut > L *ferire,* to strike, kill⟧ a person guilty of barratry

bar·ra·try (-trē) *n.* ⟦Fr *baraterie,* orig., misuse of office < *barater*: see prec.⟧ **1** [Obs.] the buying or selling of ecclesiastical or civil positions **2** the criminal offense of habitually bringing about quarrels or lawsuits **3** *Maritime Law* wrongful conduct on the part of a ship's officer or crew that results in loss to the owners —**bar′ra·trous** (-trəs) *adj.*

Barr body (bär) ⟦after M. L. *Barr* (1908-95), Cdn anatomist⟧ a structure found on the inside of the nuclear membrane of female cells that takes a dark stain and indicates by its presence the sex of the individual

barre (bär) *n.* ⟦Fr⟧ a horizontal handrail held onto while doing ballet exercises

barred (bärd) *adj.* **1** having bars or stripes **2** closed off with bars **3** forbidden or excluded

barred owl a large, North American owl (*Strix varia*) with bars of brown feathers across the breast

bar·rel (bar′əl, ber′-) *n.* ⟦ME *barel* < OFr *baril* < ML *barillus* < ?⟧ **1** *a)* a large, wooden, cylindrical container with flat, circular ends and sides that bulge outward, made usually of staves bound together with hoops *b)* any similarly shaped container made as of steel **2** *a)* the capacity or contents of a barrel *b)* a unit of measure: in the U.S., 31½ gal, but for petroleum, 42 gal and for fermented beverages, 31 gal; in Gr. Brit., 36 imperial gal; in dry measure, various amounts, as 196 lb of flour, 200 lb of pork or fish, etc. **3** something barrel-shaped; specif., any of the large, typically brightly colored cylinders used as a barrier to divert traffic from roadwork, from a chuckhole, etc.: in full **traffic barrel** **4** a revolving cylinder, wound with a chain or rope [the *barrel* of a windlass] **5** any hollow or solid cylinder [the *barrel* of a fountain pen] **6** the tube of a gun, through which the projectile is fired **7** the cylindrical case containing the mainspring of a clock or watch **8** the piston chamber of a pump **9** the quill of a feather **10** [Informal] a great amount [a *barrel* of fun] —*vt.* **-reled** or **-relled**, **-rel·ing** or **-rel·ling** to put or pack in a barrel or barrels —☆*vi.* [Informal] to go at high speed —☆**have someone over a barrel** [Informal] to have someone completely at one's mercy, esp. financially

☆**barrel chair** a kind of upholstered chair with an upright, rounded back

bar·rel-chest·ed (-ches′tid) *adj.* having an especially broad, deep chest for one's height

bar·rel·ful (-fo͝ol′) *n.* **1** as much or as many as a barrel will hold **2** [Informal] any great amount or number

bar·rel·head (-hed′) *n.* the flat, circular end of a barrel —**on the barrelhead** upon being presented for sale; at the time of delivery [to pay cash *on the barrelhead*]

☆**bar·rel·house** (-hous′) *n.* **1** a small, cheap old-time saloon with a row of racked barrels along the wall **2** a raucous, driving, unsophisticated style of playing jazz

barrel organ a mechanical musical instrument having a cylinder studded with pins which open pipe valves or strike metal tongues when the cylinder is revolved, producing a tune; hand organ

barrel roll a complete roll made by an airplane around its longitudinal axis while it simultaneously completes one spiral revolution in the air

barrel vault *Archit.* a vault shaped like half a cylinder

bar·ren (bar′ən, ber′-) ***adj.*** ⟦ME *barain* < OFr *baraigne, brehaigne,* orig. used of land⟧ **1** that cannot produce offspring; sterile *[a barren woman]* **2** not bearing or pregnant at the regular time: said of animals or plants **3** not producing crops or fruit; having little or no vegetation *[barren soil]* **4** not bringing useful results; unproductive; unprofitable *[a barren plan]* **5** lacking appeal, interest, or meaning; dull; boring **6** empty; devoid *[barren of creative spirit]* **—*n.*** **1** an area of unproductive land **2** *[usually pl.]* land with poor soil and very few shrubs, trees, etc. **—*SYN.*** BARE[1], STERILE **—bar′ren·ly *adv.*** **—bar′ren·ness *n.***

ba·rre·ra (bä rā′rä) ***n., pl.* -ras** (-räs) ⟦Sp < *barra,* a bar < ML, BAR[1]⟧ **1** the protecting wall enclosing the floor of a bull ring at bullfights **2** *[pl.]* the first row of seats in a bullfight arena

Bar·rès (bȧ *res′*), **(Auguste) Mau·rice** (mō *rēs′*) 1862-1923; Fr. novelist, essayist, & politician

bar·re·try (bar′ə trē, ber′-) ***n.*** BARRATRY

Barrett, Elizabeth *see* BROWNING, Elizabeth Barrett

bar·rette (bə ret′) ***n.*** ⟦Fr, dim. of *barre,* BAR[1]⟧ a small bar or clasp for holding a girl's or woman's hair in place

bar·ri·cade (bar′i kād′, ber′-) ***n.*** ⟦Fr < It *barricata,* pp. of *barricare,* to fortify (< ? Fr or Sp *barrica,* barrel, akin to BARREL: from use of casks as barriers)⟧ **1** a barrier thrown up hastily for defense, as in street fighting **2** any barrier or obstruction **—*vt.* -cad′ed, -cad′ing** **1** to shut in or keep out with a barricade **2** to put up barricades in; obstruct

Bar·rie[1] (bar′ē, ber′-), Sir **James M(atthew)** 1860-1937; Brit. novelist & playwright, born in Scotland

Bar·rie[2] (bar′ē, ber′-) city in SE Ontario, Canada

bar·ri·er (bar′ē ər, ber′-) ***n.*** ⟦ME *barrere* < OFr *barriere* < *barre,* BAR[1]⟧ **1** [Obs.] a fortress, stockade, etc. for defending an entrance or gate **2** a thing that prevents passage or approach; obstruction, as a fence, wall, etc. **3** anything that holds apart, separates, or hinders *[racial barriers, barriers to progress]* **4** a customs gate on a country's border **5** *[sometimes* **B-***]* *former term for* ICE SHELF **6** *[pl.]* a high fence of stakes enclosing the area in which a tournament of knights was held; lists **7** *Horse Racing* the movable gate used to keep the horses in line at the starting point **—*SYN.*** OBSTACLE

barrier beach a lengthy sandbar above high tide, formed by the buildup of sand by waves

barrier island a long, narrow island, parallel to the coastline, formed from deposits of sand and sediment thrown up by the waves, that serves the shore as a protective barrier against tidal waves, storms, etc.

barrier reef a long coral reef that is parallel to the shoreline, separated from the shore by a deep, wide lagoon: see GREAT BARRIER REEF

bar·ring (bär′iŋ) ***prep.*** unless there should be; excepting *[barring rain, we leave tonight]*

bar·ri·o (bär′ē ō) ***n., pl.* -os** ⟦Sp < Ar *barrī,* rural < *barr,* land, open country⟧ **1** in Spanish-speaking countries, a district or suburb of a city **2** in the U.S., a Spanish-speaking quarter, esp. one inhabited by Chicanos

bar·ris·ter (bar′is tər, ber′-) ***n.*** ⟦< BAR[1] (*n.* 6) + *-ister,* as in MINISTER, CHORISTER⟧ in England, a qualified member of the legal profession who presents and pleads cases in court; counselor-at-law: distinguished from SOLICITOR **—*SYN.*** LAWYER

☆**bar·room** (bär′ro͞om′) ***n.*** a room with a bar or counter at which alcoholic drinks are sold

bar·row[1] (bar′ō, ber′-) ***n.*** ⟦ME *barwe* < OE *bearwe,* basket, barrow < *beran,* BEAR[1]⟧ **1** HANDBARROW **2** WHEELBARROW **3** [Chiefly Brit.] a small cart with two wheels, pushed by hand; pushcart

bar·row[2] (bar′ō, ber′-) ***n.*** ⟦ME *berwe* < OE *beorg,* hill < IE base **bhereĝh-*, high, elevated > Ger *berg, burg,* L *fortis*⟧ **1** a heap of earth or rocks covering a grave, esp. an ancient one; tumulus **2** a mountain; hill: now used only in English place names

bar·row[3] (bar′ō, ber′-) ***n.*** ⟦ME *barow* < OE *beorg* < IE base **bher-*: see BARRATOR⟧ a pig castrated before maturing: see STAG (sense 2)

Bar·row (bar′ō, ber′-), **Point** ⟦after Sir John *Barrow* (1764-1848), Eng geographer: he promoted Arctic exploration⟧ northernmost point of Alas.: cape on the Arctic Ocean

Bar·ry (bar′ē, ber′-) ***n.*** a masculine name

Bar·ry·more (bar′ə môr′, ber′-) **1 Ethel** 1879-1959; U.S. actress: sister of John **2 John** 1882-1942; U.S. actor **3 Lionel** 1878-1954; U.S. actor: brother of John **4 Maurice** (born *Herbert Blythe*) 1847-1905; U.S. actor: father of Ethel, John, & Lionel

bar sinister *nontechnical or literary term for* BEND SINISTER

Bart *abbrev.* Baronet

bar·tend (bär′tend′) ***vi.*** ⟦back-form. < fol.⟧ to be employed or serve as a bartender **—bar′tend′ing *n.***

☆**bar·tend·er** (bär′ten′dər) ***n.*** a person who mixes and serves alcoholic drinks at a bar

bar·ter (bärt′ər) ***vi.*** ⟦ME *bartren* < OFr *barater,* to barter, cheat: see BARRATOR⟧ to trade by exchanging goods or services without using money **—*vt.*** to give (goods or services) in return for other goods or services; trade **—*n.*** **1** the act or practice of bartering **2** anything bartered **—*SYN.*** SELL **—barter away** to give or trade for too small a return **—bar′ter·er *n.***

Barth (bärt), **Karl** 1886-1968; Swiss theologian **—Barth′i·an *adj.***

Barthes (bärt), **Roland** 1915-80; Fr. writer & critic

Bar·thol·di (bȧr tôl dē′), **Fré·dé·ric Au·guste** (frā dā rēk′ ō güst′) 1834-1904; Fr. sculptor of the Statue of Liberty

Bar·tho·lin's gland (bärt′'l inz, bär tō′linz) ⟦after C. T. *Bartholin* (1655-1738), Dan anatomist⟧ either of two small glands near the vaginal opening: during sexual excitement they secrete a mucous lubricating substance: see COWPER'S GLAND

Bar·thol·o·mew (bär thäl′ə myo͞o′) ***n.*** ⟦ME *Bartelmeus* < LL (Vulg.) *Bartholomaeus* < Gr *Bartholomaios* < Aram *bar talmay,* lit., son of Talmay⟧ **1** a masculine name: dim. *Bart;* equiv. Fr. *Bartholomé,* It. *Bartolomeo,* Ger. *Bartholomäus,* Sp. *Bartolomé* **2** *Bible* one of the twelve Apostles: his day is Aug. 24: identified by some authorities with NATHANAEL: also **Saint Bartholomew**

bar·ti·zan (bär′tə zən, bär′tə zan′) ***n.*** ⟦revived by Sir Walter SCOTT[2] from a Scot form altered < ME *bretasce,* BRATTICE⟧ a small, overhanging turret on a tower or battlement, originally for defense or as a lookout

Bart·lett (bärt′lət), **John** 1820-1905; U.S. editor & publisher: compiler of a book of quotations

☆**Bartlett pear** ⟦after Enoch *Bartlett* (1779-1860) of Roxbury, Mass., the distributor⟧ a large, juicy variety of pear

Bar·tók (bär′tôk′), **Bé·la (Viktor János)** (bā′lä) 1881-1945; Hung. composer

Bar·to·lom·me·o (bär′tô lôm mā′ô), Fra (born *Bartolommeo di Pagholo del Fattorino*) 1475?-1517; Florentine painter

Bar·ton (bärt′'n), **Clara** (born *Clarissa Harlowe Barton*) 1821-1912; U.S. philanthropist: founder of the American Red Cross (1881)

Bar·tram (bär′trəm) **1 John** 1699-1777; Am. botanist **2 William** 1739-1823; Am. naturalist: son of John

Bar·uch[1] (ber′ək, bə ro͞ok′) ***n.*** ⟦Heb, lit., blessed⟧ *Bible* **1** Jeremiah's scribe: Jer. 36:4-6 **2** a book of the Old Testament Apocrypha ascribed to him: abbrev. *Ba, Bar*

Ba·ruch[2] (bə ro͞ok′), **Bernard (Mannes)** 1870-1965; U.S. financier & statesman

bar·ware (bär′wer′) ***n.*** glassware, utensils, etc. for use in serving wines and alcoholic drinks, as at a bar

bar·y·on (bar′ē än′, ber′-) ***n.*** ⟦< Gr *barys,* heavy (see GRAVE[1]) + (ELECTR)ON⟧ *Particle Physics* a subatomic particle that is both a hadron and a fermion, as a nucleon or hyperon: the proton is the baryon with the smallest mass

ba·ry·ta (bə rīt′ə) ***n.*** ⟦ModL < fol.⟧ any of several compounds of barium, esp. barium oxide and barium hydroxide **—ba·ryt′ic** (-rit′ik) ***adj.***

ba·ry·tes (bə rī′tēz) ***n.*** ⟦ModL < Gr *barytēs,* weight < *barys,* heavy: see GRAVE[1]⟧ BARITE: also called **bar·yte** (bar′īt′, ber′-)

bar·y·tone (bar′ə tōn′, ber′-) ***adj., n.*** BARITONE

ba·sal (bā′səl) ***adj.*** **1** of, at, or forming the base **2** being the base or basis; basic; fundamental **3** *Bot.* growing from the base of a stem **—ba′sal·ly *adv.***

basal anesthesia *Med.* anesthesia induced as a preliminary to further and deeper anesthesia

basal cell a cell of the basal, or deepest, layer of the epidermis

basal metabolism the minimum quantity of energy used or required to sustain life in an organism at rest: it is measured, in people, by the rate (**basal metabolic rate**) at which heat is given off by a conscious, resting person in a warm place 12 to 18 hours after eating, and is expressed in large calories per hour per square meter of skin surface

ba·salt (bə sôlt′; bā′sôlt′, bas′ôlt′) ***n.*** ⟦earlier *basaltes* < L, a dark Ethiopian marble: term used by PLINY for *basanites* < Gr *basanitēs,* species of slate used to test gold < *basanos,* touchstone, test (ult. < Egypt *bḫnw*) + *-itēs,* -ITE[1]⟧ **1** a dark, fine-grained, usually extrusive igneous rock that is more basic than andesite, consisting chiefly of plagioclase feldspars and pyroxene: often found in vast sheets, it is the most common extrusive igneous rock **2** a kind of unglazed, black pottery designed by Josiah Wedgwood: also **ba·salt′ware′** **—ba·sal·tic** (bə sôlt′ik) ***adj.***

bas·cule (bas′kyo͞ol′) ***n.*** ⟦Fr, a seesaw < *bacule* < *baculer,* lit., to strike the posterior < stem of *battre* (see BATTER[1]) + *cul* < L *culus,* the posterior⟧ a device balanced so that when one end is lowered the other end is raised

bascule bridge a kind of drawbridge counterweighted so that it can be raised and lowered easily

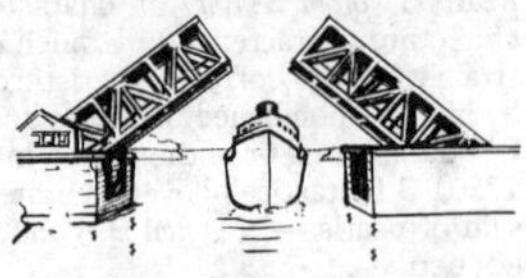
bascule bridge

base[1] (bās) ***n.*** ⟦ME < OFr *bas* < L *basis,* BASIS⟧ **1** the thing or part on which something rests; lowest part or bottom; foundation **2** the fundamental or main part, as of a plan, organization, system, theory, etc.; specif., the most loyal supporters of a political candidate or party, a sports team, etc. **3** the principal or essential ingredient, or the one serving as a vehicle *[paint with an oil base]* **4** anything from which a start is made; basis **5** the point of attachment of a part of the body *[the base of the thumb]* **6** a center of operations or source of supply; headquarters, as of a military operation or exploring expedition **7** *a)* the bottommost layer or coat, as of paint *b)* a makeup cream to give a desired color to the skin, esp. in the theater **8** *Archit.* the lower part, as of a column, pier, or wall, regarded as a separate unit **9** *Baseball* any of the four objects at the four corners of the infield that must be reached safely one after the other to score a run: three (*first base, second base,* and *third base*) are set above the ground while the fourth (*home plate*) is set flush with the ground **10** *Chem.* *a)* any compound that can react with an acid to form a salt, the hydroxyl of the base being replaced by a negative ion: in modern theory, any substance that produces a negative ion and donates electrons to an acid to form covalent bonds: in water solution a base tastes bitter, turns red litmus paper blue, and, in dissociation theory, produces free hydroxyl ions (see PH) *b)* any of the two purines (adenine or guanine) or three pyrimidines (thymine, cytosine, or uracil) that are the key building blocks of nucleic acid (see BASE PAIR) **11** *Dyeing* a substance used for fixing colors **12** *Electronics* in some transistors, the region or layer of semiconductor material, acting as an electrode, that separates the emitter from the collector and receives an electric current of electrons or holes **13** *Geom.* the line or plane upon which a figure is thought of as resting [the *base* of a triangle] **14** *Heraldry* the lower portion of a shield **15** *Linguis.* any morpheme to which prefixes, suffixes, etc. are or can be added; stem or root **16** *Math.* *a)* a whole number, esp. 10 or 2, made the fundamental number, and raised to various powers to produce the major counting units, of a number system; radix *b)* any number raised to a power by an exponent (see LOGARITHM) *c)* a starting or reference figure or sum upon which certain calculations are made —*adj.* forming a base —*vt.* **based**, **bas′ing 1** to make or form a base or foundation for **2** to put or rest (*on*) as a base or basis [to *base* a guess on past experience] **3** to place or station (*in* or *at* a base) —☆**off base 1** *Baseball* not touching the base **2** [Slang] taking a position or attitude that is unsound or in error —☆**on base** *Baseball* at a base, having reached it safely with a base hit, walk, etc. —☆**touch all the bases** to deal with all related details —☆**touch base** (or **bases**) to be in communication or contact

SYN.—**base**, as compared here, refers to a part or thing at the bottom acting as a support or underlying structure [the *base* of a lamp]; **basis**, conveying the same idea, is the term preferred for nonphysical things [the *basis* of a theory]; **foundation** stresses solidity in the underlying or supporting thing and often suggests permanence and stability in that which is built on it [the *foundation* of a house]; **groundwork**, closely synonymous with **foundation**, is principally applied to nonphysical things [the *groundwork* of a good education]

base² (bās) *adj.* **bas′er**, **bas′est** ⟦ME & OFr *bas* < VL *bassus*, thick, stumpy, low⟧ **1** having or showing little or no honor, courage, or decency; mean; ignoble; contemptible [a *base* coward, *base* ingratitude] **2** of a menial or degrading kind [*base* servitude] **3** inferior in quality **4** [Now Rare] not classical or cultivated [*base* Latin] **5** of comparatively low worth [iron is a *base* metal, gold a precious one] **6** debased or counterfeit [*base* coin] **7** *a)* having the low feudal status of villein *b)* held by one having this status [*base* tenure] **8** [Archaic] low in height; short **9** [Archaic] of servile, humble, or illegitimate birth **10** [Obs.] low or inferior in place or position **11** [Obs.] BASS¹ —*n.* [Obs.] BASS¹ —**base′ly** *adv.* —**base′ness** *n.*

SYN.—**base** implies a putting of one's own interests ahead of one's obligations, as because of greed or cowardice [*base* motives]; **mean** suggests a contemptible pettiness of character or conduct [his *mean* attempts to slander her]; **ignoble** suggests a lack of high moral or intellectual qualities [to work for an *ignoble* end]; **abject** implies debasement and a contemptible lack of self-respect [an *abject* servant]; **sordid** connotes the depressing drabness of that which is mean or base [the *sordid* details of their affair]; **vile** suggests disgusting foulness or depravity [*vile* epithets]; **low** suggests rather generally coarseness, vulgarity, depravity, etc., specif. in reference to taking grossly unfair advantage [so *low* as to steal from one's own mother]; **degrading** suggests a lowering or corruption of moral standards [the *degrading* aspects of prison life] —*ANT.* **noble, moral, virtuous**

base·ball (bās′bôl′) *n.* ☆**1** a game (esp. HARDBALL, *n.* 1*a*) played with a bat and a ball by two opposing teams of nine or ten players on a field with four bases: each team takes turns batting against the opponent's pitcher and tries to score more runs than the other team ☆**2** the ball used in playing hardball: it is hard, usually white and rawhide-covered, and smaller than a softball Cf. SOFTBALL

☆**baseball cap** a cap worn by or like that worn by baseball players, with a stiff visor and a soft, rounded crown, the front of which typically displays a stylized team logo, name, etc.

☆**base·board** (-bôrd′) *n.* a board or molding covering the edge of a wall next to the floor

baseboard heating 1 a heating system by pipes, through which steam or hot water circulates, near the base of the walls of rooms **2** the pipes used for this, or their metal covering

base·born (-bôrn′) *adj.* **1** of humble birth or origin **2** of illegitimate birth **3** mean or ignoble in character or spirit

☆**base·burn·er** or **base-burn·er** (-burn′ər) *n.* any stove or furnace in which more coal is fed automatically from above when that at the base is consumed

-based (bāst) *combining form* **1** based on; having as its basis [paper-*based*, milk-*based*] **2** based in or at (a specified place); having headquarters in or at [space-*based* weapons, a Cleveland-*based* company]

☆**Base Exchange** *service mark for* a nonprofit general store at a military base, for the sale of merchandise for personal use, refreshments, etc.

☆**base hit** *Baseball* a play in which the batter hits a fair ball and gets on base without benefit of an opponent's error and without forcing out a runner already on base

Ba·sel (bä′zəl) **1** city in NW Switzerland, on the Rhine **2** canton of NW Switzerland: *c.* 180 sq mi (466 sq km): divided into two politically independent half-cantons

base·less (bās′lis) *adj.* having no basis in fact; unfounded —**base′less·ness** *n.*

base level *Geol.* the lowest level to which land can be eroded, esp. by a river; sea level

base line 1 *a)* a line serving as a base *b)* any starting or reference point, figure, amount, level, etc. with which others can be measured or compared *c)* *Surveying* a horizontal line measured with special accuracy to provide a base for survey by triangulation ☆**2** *Baseball* the unmarked lane, six feet (1.8 m) wide, between any two consecutive bases: a base runner who does not stay within this lane may, in certain situations, be called out by an umpire **3** *Basketball* END LINE; esp., an area of the court just inside this line **4** *Tennis* the line at the back at either end of the court Also **base·line** (bās′līn′) *n.*

☆**base·man** (-mən) *n., pl.* **-men** (-mən) *Baseball* any of three infielders; first baseman, second baseman, or third baseman

base map an outline map on which data may be plotted

base·ment (bās′mənt) *n.* ⟦BASE¹ + -MENT⟧ **1** the foundation or lower part of a wall or structure **2** the lowest story of a building, below the main floor and wholly or partly below the surface of the ground **3** *Geol.* the oldest layer of igneous and metamorphic rocks in the crust of the earth, covered by layers of more recent, usually sedimentary rocks: in full **basement complex**

ba·sen·ji (bə sen′jē) *n.* ⟦Bantu < *ba-*, pl. prefix + **senji*, altered < ? Fr *singe*, a monkey: so named because of the monkeylike tail and face⟧ any of an African breed of small dog that has a silky, reddish-brown coat and does not make a true barking sound

☆**base on balls** *Baseball* WALK

base pair a pair of bases consisting of the pyrimidine base of one nucleotide joined by a hydrogen bond to the complementary purine base of another nucleotide: such pairs form the links between the two strands of DNA and of double-stranded RNA

base path *Baseball* BASE LINE (sense 2): also written **base′path′** *n.*

base pay the basic rate of pay for a particular job exclusive of overtime pay, bonuses, etc.

☆**base runner** *Baseball* any member of the team at bat who has reached first, second, or third base safely or is trying to reach a base or home plate

bas·es¹ (bās′iz) *n. pl. of* BASE¹

ba·ses² (bā′sēz′) *n. pl. of* BASIS

bash (bash) *vt.* ⟦echoic; akin to or < ? ON **basca*, to strike⟧ [Informal] **1** to strike with a violent blow; smash (*in*) **2** to attack or abuse, as with blows or with words —*n.* **1** [Informal] a violent blow ☆**2** [Slang] a gala event or party —**have a bash at** [Slang] to make an attempt at

Ba·shan (bā′shan) *n. Bible* fertile region east & northeast of the Sea of Galilee, in ancient Palestine

ba·shaw (bə shô′) *n.* ⟦see PASHA⟧ PASHA

bash·ful (bash′fəl) *adj.* ⟦(A)BASH + -FUL⟧ **1** timid, shy, and easily embarrassed **2** showing an embarrassed timidity —*SYN.* SHY¹ —**bash′ful·ly** *adv.* —**bash′ful·ness** *n.*

bash·i-ba·zouk (bash′ē bə zo͞ok′) *n.* ⟦Turk *bashi-bozuq* < *bashi*, head + *bozuq*, disorderly, unkempt⟧ a member of the notoriously brutal 19th-cent. Turkish irregulars

-bashing (bash′iŋ) *combining form* the act or process of attacking or abusing, as with blows or, esp., with words: used freely in nonce constructions [union-*bashing*]

Bash·kir (bash kir′) *n.* **1** *pl.* **-kirs′** or **-kir′** a member of a people of SW Russia **2** the Turkic language of this people

bas·ic (bā′sik) *adj.* **1** of, at, or forming a base; fundamental; essential **2** constituting a basis or introduction; elementary [*basic* military training] **3** *a)* *Chem.* of, having the nature of, or containing a base; alkaline *b)* designating, of, or resulting from a process of manufacturing steel from high-phosphorus iron, in which the refining agent is a basic slag formed from a basic furnace lining and the addition of lime **4** *Geol.* designating or of igneous rocks with 45-52% silica —*n.* **1** a basic principle, factor, etc.: *usually used in pl.* **2** basic military training —**bas′i·cal·ly** *adv.*

BASIC (bā′sik) *n.* ⟦*B(eginner's) A(ll-purpose) S(ymbolic) I(nstruction) C(ode)*⟧ a simplified computer language that utilizes common English words and algebra

Basic English ⟦*B(ritish) A(merican) S(cientific) I(nternational) C(ommercial)*⟧ a simplified form of the English language, devised around 1930 by Brit. linguist and writer C. K. Ogden (1889-1957), and proposed for use as an international auxiliary language and for beginning studies in English: it consists of a selected vocabulary of 850 essential words and is copyrighted

ba·sic·i·ty (bə sis′ə tē) *n. Chem.* **1** the quality or condition of being a base **2** the capacity of an acid to react with a base, measured by the number of hydrogen atoms that can be replaced by a base: cf. MONOBASIC, DIBASIC

basic oxygen process a process for refining steel in which oxygen is blown into the molten iron

basic slag an alkaline slag that is formed while making steel, used as a fertilizer, in cement, etc.

ba·sid·i·o·my·cete (bə sid′ē ō mī′sēt′, -mī sēt′) *n.* ⟦< ModL < BASIDIUM + -MYCETE⟧ any of a subdivision (Basidiomycotina) of fungi, including the mushrooms, rusts, smuts, and puffballs, that produce spores on basidia; club fungus: cf. ASCOMYCETE —**ba·sid′i·o·my·ce′tous** (-mī sēt′əs) *adj.*

ba·sid·i·o·spore (bə sid′ē ō spôr′) ***n.*** ⟦< fol. + SPORE⟧ a spore produced on a basidium —**ba·sid′i·o·spor′ous** (-spôr′əs) ***adj.***

ba·sid·i·um (bə sid′ē əm) ***n.***, *pl.* **-sid′i·a** (-ə) ⟦ModL < Gr *basis*, BASIS + ModL dim. suffix *-idium*⟧ *Bot.* any of a number of oblong cells in basidiomycetous fungi, bearing a definite number of external spores (usually four) on short, slender stalks —**ba·sid′i·al** ***adj.***

Ba·sie (bā′sē), **William** 1904-84; U.S. jazz pianist & bandleader: called *Count Basie*

bas·i·fixed (bās′ə fikst′) ***adj.*** *Bot.* attached at the base

bas·i·fy (bās′ə fī′) ***vt.*** **-fied′**, **-fy′ing** to change into a base; alkalize

bas·il (bā′zəl, baz′əl) ***n.*** ⟦ME & OFr *basile* < ML *basilicum* < Gr *basilikon* (*phyton*), basil, lit., royal (plant) < *basileus*, king⟧ any of a genus (*Ocimum*) of fragrant plants of the mint family, esp. a white-flowered garden herb (*O. basilicum*) whose leaves are used for flavoring in cooking

Bas·il[1] (bā′zəl, baz′əl) ***n.*** ⟦L *Basilius* < Gr *Basileios*, lit., kingly < *basileus*, king⟧ a masculine name

Bas·il[2] (bā′zəl, baz′əl), Saint (A.D. 330?-379); Gr. prelate, born in Cappadocia: bishop of Caesarea: his day is Jan. 2: called *the Great*

Ba·si·lan (bä sē′län) largest island of the Sulu Archipelago, the Philippines, southwest of Mindanao: 495 sq mi (1,282 sq km)

bas·i·lar (bas′ə lər) ***adj.*** ⟦ModL *basilaris* < L *basis*, BASIS⟧ of or at the base, esp. of the skull: also **bas′i·lar′y** (-ler′ē)

Bas·il·don (baz′əl dən) city in Essex, SE England

ba·sil·ic (bə sil′ik) ***adj.*** ⟦Fr *basilique* < L *basilicus* < Gr *basilikos*: see BASIL⟧ **1** designating or of a large vein of the upper arm, on the inner side of the biceps muscle **2** of a basilica; basilican: also **ba·sil′i·cal** **3** [Obs.] kingly

ba·sil·i·ca (bə sil′i kə; *also*, -zil′-) ***n.***, *pl.* **-cas** ⟦L < Gr *basilikē* (*stoa*), royal (portico) < *basilikos*: see BASIL⟧ **1** [Obs.] a royal palace **2** in ancient Rome, a rectangular building with a broad nave ending in an apse, and flanked by colonnaded aisles, used as a courtroom, public hall, etc. **3** a Christian church built in this style **4** *R.C.Ch.* a church granted certain ceremonial rights —**ba·sil′i·can** (-kən) ***adj.***

Ba·sil·i·ca·ta (bä sē′lē kä′tä) region in S Italy, on the Gulf of Taranto: 3,858 sq mi (9,992 sq km)

bas·i·lisk (bas′ə lisk′, baz′-) ***n.*** ⟦ME < L *basiliscus* < Gr *basiliskos*, dim. of *basileus*, king⟧ **1** a mythical lizardlike monster with supposedly fatal breath and glance, fabled to have been hatched by a serpent from a cock's egg: see also COCKATRICE **2** any of a genus (*Basiliscus*) of iguanas with an erectile crest on the back and tail and an inflatable pouch on the head **3** an obsolete kind of cannon

ba·sin (bā′sin) ***n.*** ⟦ME & OFr *bacin* < VL **baccinum* < **bacca*, water vessel⟧ **1** a round, wide, shallow container, as for holding water to wash in **2** its contents or capacity **3** a washbowl or sink **4** any shallow, rounded hollow or depression, often containing water, as a pond **5** a bay or harbor [*yacht basin*] **6** all the land drained by a river and its branches **7** a great hollow in the earth's surface filled by an ocean **8** *Geol.* a wide, depressed area in which the rock layers all incline toward a central area

bas·i·net (bas′i net′) ***n.*** ⟦ME & OFr *bacinet*, dim. of *bacin*, prec.⟧ a light, steel, medieval helmet

ba·si·on (bā′sē ən) ***n.*** ⟦ModL < Gr *basis*: see BASIS⟧ the midpoint of the front border of the foramen magnum

ba·sip·e·tal (bā sip′i təl) ***adj.*** ⟦< BASIC + -PETAL⟧ developing or moving from the apex toward the base of the stem: used to describe the development of tissues or movement of hormones in plants: opposed to ACROPETAL

ba·sis (bā′sis) ***n.***, *pl.* **ba′ses′** (-sēz′) ⟦L < Gr, a base, pedestal < *bainein*, to go < IE base **gwem-*, COME⟧ **1** the base, foundation, or chief supporting factor of anything **2** the principal constituent of anything **3** the fundamental principle or theory, as of a system of knowledge **4** *a)* a procedure or timed plan [*paid on a weekly basis*] *b)* a specified attitude [*a friendly basis*] —**SYN.** BASE[1]

basis point a unit equal to ¹⁄₁₀₀ of 1 percent: used in measuring changes in interest rates, exchange rates, etc.

bask (bask, bäsk) ***vi.*** ⟦ME *basken*, to wallow (in blood): found only in Gower & Lydgate; < ?: modern use apparently due to Shakespeare's misunderstanding of Lydgate⟧ **1** to warm oneself pleasantly, as in the sunlight **2** to enjoy a warm or pleasant feeling from being in a certain environment or situation [*to bask in someone's favor*] —***vt.*** [Archaic] to expose to warmth

Bas·ker·ville (bas′kər vil), **John** 1706-75; Eng. printer & type designer

bas·ket (bas′kit, bäs′-) ***n.*** ⟦ME < ?⟧ **1** a container made of interwoven cane, rushes, strips of wood, etc. and often having a handle or handles **2** the amount that a basket will hold **3** anything like a basket in shape or use **4** the structure hung from a balloon to carry personnel and equipment ☆**5** *Basketball a)* the goal, consisting of a round, open net hanging from a metal ring attached to a raised backboard *b)* FIELD GOAL **6** *Finance a)* a selected group of goods, currencies, etc. whose value is used as an index or standard (cf. MARKETBASKET) *b)* a large group of stocks in the same proportions as those of a stock index: used in program trading

☆**bas·ket·ball** (-bôl′) ***n.*** ⟦invented & named (1891) by James A. Naismith (1861-1939) at Y.M.C.A. College, Springfield, Mass.⟧ **1** a game played by two opposing teams of usually five players on a rectangular, often wooden, court with a raised basket at each end: points are scored by tossing or throwing a ball through the basket at the opponent's end **2** the large, round, inflated ball used in this game

basket case ⟦from such a person's inability to move independently and the need to be carried and cared for by others⟧ [Slang] **1** a person lacking all four limbs **2** a person unable to function, esp. because of emotional disturbance **3** anything that does not function properly

basket hilt a hilt with a basketlike guard for the hand, as on some swords —**bas′ket-hilt′ed** ***adj.***

Basket Maker **1** any of several early American Indian cultures of the SW U.S. (*c.* A.D. 100-700) characterized by great skill in basket making and by the later development of basket molds for the construction and drying of mud pottery **2** a member of the people who produced this culture

bas·ket-of-gold (-əv gōld′) ***n.*** a yellow-flowered perennial plant (*Alyssum saxatile*, now more properly *Aurinia saxatilis*) of the crucifer family, often used in rock gardens

bas·ket·ry (bas′kə trē) ***n.*** **1** the craft of making baskets **2** baskets collectively **3** basketwork

basket star any of a family (Gorgonocephalidae) of brittle stars with many tangled, rootlike arms: also called **basket fish**

basket weave a weave of fabrics resembling the weave used in basket making

bas·ket·work (bas′kit wurk′) ***n.*** work that is interlaced or woven like a basket; wickerwork

basking shark any of a family (Cetorhinidae) of plankton-eating giant sharks (order Lamniformes) with small, weak teeth: often found feeding along the surface in northern seas

Basle (bäl) *former name for* BASEL

bas·ma·ti rice (bas mät′ē, baz-) ⟦< Hindi *bāsmatī*, lit., fragrant⟧ a type of long-grained rice, grown mainly in India and Pakistan, that has a distinctive fragrance and a delicate flavor

bas mitz·vah or **bas miz·vah** (bäs mits′və) [*also* **B- M-**] BAT MITZVAH

ba·so·phil (bā′sə fil′) ***n.*** ⟦< BASIC + -PHILE⟧ a cell, substance, or tissue easily stained by basic dyes, as the beta cells in the anterior pituitary or certain white blood cells: also **ba′so·phile′** (-fīl′, -fil′) —**ba′so·phil′ic** (-fil′ik) ***adj.***

basque (bask) ***n.*** ⟦Fr < Prov *basto* < ?; altered by assoc. with Fr *basquine*, kind of petticoat < Sp *basquiña* < *basco*, *vasco*, fol.⟧ a woman's tightfitting bodice or tunic

Basque (bask, bäsk) ***n.*** ⟦Fr < Sp *Vasco*; ult. < L *Vascones*, the Basques⟧ **1** a member of a people living in the W Pyrenees of Spain and France **2** the language of this people: it is not known to be related to any other language —***adj.*** of the Basques or their language or culture

Basque Country, The region comprising three provinces in N Spain, on the Bay of Biscay, inhabited by Basques: 2,803 sq mi (7,260 sq km): also called **Basque Provinces**

Bas·ra (bäs′rə, bäz′-, bus′-) port in SE Iraq, at the head of the Shatt-al-Arab: Arabic name **Al-Bas′rah** (al-)

bas-re·lief (bä′ri lēf′, bas′-) ***n.*** ⟦Fr < It *basso-rilievo*: see BASSO & RELIEF⟧ sculpture in which figures are carved in a flat surface so that they project only a little from the background

bass[1] (bās) ***n.*** ⟦ME *bas*, BASE[2]; sp. infl. by It *basso*⟧ **1** the range of the lowest male voice, usually from middle C to two or more octaves below **2** *a)* a voice or singer with such a range *b)* an instrument with a similar range within its family; specif., a double bass *c)* a part for such a voice or instrument **3** a low, deep sound or tone, as of a voice with this range **4** in four-part harmony, the lowest part **5** the lower part of the audio-frequency band in sound reproduction —***adj.*** of, for, or having the range of a bass

bass[2] (bas) ***n.***, *pl.* **bass** or **bass′es** ⟦ME *bas*, earlier *baers* < OE *bærs* < IE **bhors-*, point, bristle (in reference to the dorsal fins) < base **bhar-* > BUR[1]⟧ any of various families of spiny-finned percoid, food and game fishes of fresh or salt water, including black bass, rock bass, and striped bass

bass[3] (bas) ***n.*** **1** BAST **2** BASSWOOD

bass clef (bās) *Music* **1** a sign on a staff, indicating the position of F below middle C on the fourth line **2** the range of notes on a staff so marked

bass drum (bās) the largest and lowest-toned of the double-headed drums

Bas·sein (bə sān′) river port in S Myanmar, on the Irrawaddy delta

Basse-Nor·man·die (bâs nôr män dē′) metropolitan region of NW France, on the English Channel, including the historic region of Normandy: 6,791 sq mi (17,589 sq km); chief city, Caen

bas·set[1] (bas′it) ***n.*** ⟦OFr, short-legged dog, orig., short, dim. of *basse*, fem. of *bas*, BASE[2]⟧ a kind of hound with a long body, short, crooked forelegs, and long, drooping ears, used in hunting: also **basset hound**

bas·set[2] (bas′it) ***n.*** ⟦< ? Fr *basset*, dim. of *basse*: see prec.⟧ *Geol., Mining* OUTCROP —***vi.*** to appear at or emerge above the surface

Basse·terre (bäs ter′) capital & seaport of St. Kitts and Nevis, on the SW coast of St. Kitts island in the Leeward Islands, West Indies

Basse-Terre (bäs ter′) **1** W island of the two major islands of Guadeloupe, West Indies: 327 sq mi (848 sq km) **2** seaport on this island: capital of Guadeloupe

basset horn a kind of clarinet pitched in F and ending in a brass bell: its range lies between those of the common clarinet and the bass clarinet

bass horn (bās) **1** [Historical] a brass instrument related to the serpent **2** a tuba

bas·si·net (bas′ə net′) ***n.*** ⟦altered (after Fr *bassin*, BASIN) < Fr *berceonnette*, dim. of *berceau*, cradle⟧ a basketlike bed for an infant: it is often hooded and set on a stand having casters

bass·ist (bās′ist) ***n.*** a person who plays the double bass

bas·so (bas′ō, bäs′-; *It* bäs′sô) ***n.***, *pl.* **bas′sos** or **bas′si** (-sē) ⟦It < adj., low < VL *bassus*: see BASE[2]⟧ a bass voice or singer

bas·soon (ba so͞on′, bə-) ***n.*** ⟦Fr *basson* < It *bassone* < prec.⟧ a double-reed bass woodwind instrument having a long, curved stem attached to the mouthpiece —**bas·soon′ist** ***n.***

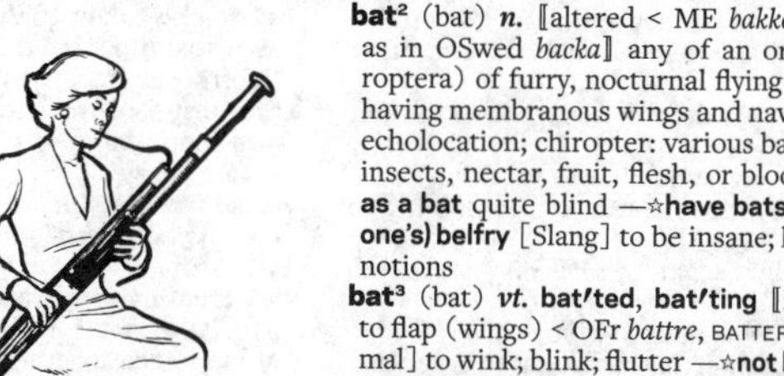
bassoon

basso pro·fun·do (prō fun′dō, -fo͞on′-) ⟦< It *basso*, BASSO + *profondo*, deep < L *profundus*, PROFOUND⟧ **1** a very deep bass voice **2** a man with such a voice

bas·so-re·lie·vo (-ri lē′vō) ***n., pl.*** **-vos** ⟦It *basso-rilievo*⟧ BAS-RELIEF

bas·so-ri·lie·vo (bäs′sô rē lye′vô) ***n., pl. bas·si-ri·lie·vi*** (bäs′sē rē lye′vē) ⟦It⟧ BAS-RELIEF

Bass Strait (bas) strait separating Victoria, SE Australia from Tasmania: 80-150 mi (129-241 km) wide

bass viol (bās) **1** VIOLA DA GAMBA **2** DOUBLE BASS

☆**bass·wood** (bas′wood′) ***n.*** **1** any of a genus (*Tilia*) of trees of the linden family, with light, soft, durable wood; linden **2** its wood

bast (bast) ***n.*** ⟦ME < OE *bæst*, inner bark of trees; akin to Ger & ON *bast*⟧ **1** *Bot.* any type of phloem **2** fiber obtained from phloem, used in making ropes, mats, etc.

bas·ta (bäs′tä) ***interj.*** ⟦It⟧ (it is) enough

bas·tard (bas′tərd) ***n.*** ⟦ME < OFr < *bast-* (also in *fils de bast*) (< ? Goth *bansts*, barn) + *-ard*, -ARD: hence, one conceived in a barn⟧ **1** a person born of parents not married to each other; illegitimate child **2** anything spurious, inferior, or varying from standard **3** [Slang] a person regarded with contempt, hatred, pity, resentment, etc. or, sometimes, with playful affection: sometimes considered a mildly offensive term —***adj.*** **1** of illegitimate birth or of uncertain origin **2** of a size or shape that differs from the normal or standard **3** that is not truly the designated thing but that closely resembles it [gneiss is called *bastard* granite] **4** not genuine; sham; inferior —**bas′tard·ly** ***adj.***

bas·tard·ize (bas′tər dīz′) ***vt.*** **-ized′, -iz′ing** **1** to make, declare, or show to be a bastard **2** to make corrupt or inferior; debase —***vi.*** [Rare] to become inferior —**bas′tard·i·za′tion** ***n.***

bastard wing ALULA

bas·tar·dy (bas′tər dē) ***n., pl.*** **-ies** **1** the state of being a bastard; illegitimacy **2** the begetting of a bastard

baste[1] (bāst) ***vt.*** **bast′ed, bast′ing** ⟦ME *basten* < OFr *bastir* < Gmc **bastjan*, make with bast⟧ to sew with long, loose stitches so as to keep the parts together until properly sewn; tack

baste[2] (bāst) ***vt.*** **bast′ed, bast′ing** ⟦< OFr *basser*, to moisten < *bassiner* < *bassin*, BASIN⟧ to moisten (meat) with melted butter, drippings, etc. during roasting —**bast′er** ***n.***

baste[3] (bāst) ***vt.*** **bast′ed, bast′ing** ⟦ON *beysta*⟧ **1** to beat soundly; thrash **2** to attack with words; abuse

bas·tille or **bas·tile** (bas tēl′) ***n.*** ⟦ME *bastile* & Fr *bastille*, both < OFr *bastille*, altered < *bastide* < *bastida* < fem. pp. of *bastir*, build, orig., make with bast: see BASTE[1]⟧ **1** in ancient warfare, a tower for defense or attack; small fortress **2** a prison —**the Bastille** a state prison in Paris that was stormed and destroyed (1789) in the French Revolution: its destruction is commemorated on Bastille Day, July 14

bas·ti·na·do (bas′tə nād′ō, -nä′dō) ***n., pl.*** **-does** ⟦Sp *bastonada* < *bastón*, a stick⟧ **1** a beating or blow with a stick, usually on the soles of the feet, esp. as a method of punishment **2** a rod, stick, or cudgel Also **bas′ti·nade′** (-nād′) —***vt.*** **-doed, -do·ing** to inflict the bastinado on

bast·ing (bās′tiŋ) ***n.*** ⟦< BASTE[1]⟧ **1** the act of sewing with loose, temporary stitches **2** loose, temporary stitches or the thread used for them

bas·tion (bas′chən, -tē ən) ***n.*** ⟦Fr < MFr *bastillon* < OFr *bastille*: see BASTILLE⟧ **1** a projection from a fortification, arranged to give a wider firing range **2** any fortified place; strong defense or bulwark: often used fig. —**bas′tioned** ***adj.***

Bas·togne (bas tōn′; *Fr* bȧ stôn′y′) town in SE Belgium: besieged by the German Army (Dec., 1944–Jan., 1945) during a counteroffensive in WWII, but relieved after fierce fighting (Battle of the Bulge)

Ba·su·to·land (bə so͞ot′ō land′) *former name for* LESOTHO

bat[1] (bat) ***n.*** ⟦ME < OE *batt*, cudgel (prob. < Welsh *bat* < IE base **bhat-*, to strike) & < OFr *batte*, pestle < *battre*, BATTER[1]⟧ **1** any stout club, stick, or cudgel **2** a club used to strike the ball in baseball and cricket **3** a ping-pong paddle, squash racket, etc. ☆**4** a turn at batting, as in baseball: see also AT-BAT **5** [Brit.] a batsman at cricket **6** [*usually pl.*] cotton batting, esp. of an inferior quality; batt **7** the whip used by a jockey **8** [Informal] a blow or hit ☆**9** [Slang] a drinking bout; spree **10** [Brit. Informal] fast pace; speed **11** *Ceramics* a disk made of plastic, plaster, etc. attached to the top of a potter's wheel and upon which clay is placed for shaping —***vt.*** **bat′ted, bat′ting** **1** to strike with or as with a bat **2** to have a batting average of: see BATTING AVERAGE —***vi.*** **1** to use a bat [to *bat* left-handed] **2** to take a turn at batting [to *bat* third in the lineup] —☆**at bat** *Baseball* taking a turn at batting: see also AT-BAT —☆**bat around** [Slang] **1** to travel or roam about **2** to consider or discuss (an idea, plan, etc.) freely and informally **3** *Baseball* to have all the batters in the lineup come to bat in a single inning —☆**bat out** [Slang] to create or compose quickly or hastily —☆**go to bat for** [Informal] to intervene on behalf of; defend —☆**(right) off the bat** [Informal] immediately

bat[2] (bat) ***n.*** ⟦altered < ME *bakke* < Scand, as in OSwed *backa*⟧ any of an order (Chiroptera) of furry, nocturnal flying mammals having membranous wings and navigating by echolocation; chiropter: various bats feed on insects, nectar, fruit, flesh, or blood —**blind as a bat** quite blind —☆**have bats in the** (or **one's**) **belfry** [Slang] to be insane; have crazy notions

brown bat

bat[3] (bat) ***vt.*** **bat′ted, bat′ting** ⟦ME *baten*, to flap (wings) < OFr *battre*, BATTER[1]⟧ [Informal] to wink; blink; flutter —☆**not bat an eye** (or **eyelash**) [Informal] not show surprise

Ba·taan (bə tan′, -tän′) peninsula on SW Luzon, the Philippines: in WWII (1942), scene of a Japanese victory over American-Philippine forces, marking the completion of the Japanese conquest of the Philippines

Ba·tan·gas (bə taŋ′gəs, -täŋ′-) city on the S coast of Luzon, the Philippines

Ba·ta·vi·a (bə tā′vē ə) *former name for* JAKARTA

bat·boy (bat′boi′) ***n.*** *Baseball* a boy or young man who serves as a general assistant during practice and around the clubhouse and retrieves bats as they are used during a game

batch[1] (bach) ***n.*** ⟦ME *bache* < OE *bacan*, BAKE⟧ **1** the amount (of bread, etc.) produced at one baking **2** the amount of material, as dough, needed for one operation **3** the quantity of anything made in one operation or lot **4** a number of things or persons taken as a group; lot; set **5** a group of programs, instructions, etc. for processing by a computer in a single run —***vt.*** to treat, process, etc. as part of a batch or together as a batch: informal except in technical use

☆**batch**[2] (bach) ***vi.*** BACH

bate[1] (bāt) ***vt.*** **bat′ed, bat′ing** ⟦ME *baten*, aphetic for *abaten*, ABATE⟧ **1** to abate, lessen, lower, etc. **2** [Archaic] to deprive (of) —**with bated breath** with the breath held in because of fear, excitement, etc.

bate[2] (bāt) ***vt., vi.*** **bat′ed, bat′ing** ⟦prob. var. of BAIT; akin to Ger *beiszen*, to soak in lye⟧ *Tanning* to soften by soaking in an enzyme solution after the hair has been removed —***n.*** an enzyme solution for this purpose

☆**ba·teau** (ba tō′) ***n., pl.*** **-teaux′** (-tōz′) ⟦CdnFr < Fr < OFr *batel* < OE *bat*, BOAT⟧ a lightweight, flat-bottomed riverboat with tapering ends, used chiefly in Canada and Louisiana —***adj.*** designating a wide, shallow neckline, as on a woman's dress, extending to the shoulders

Bates·i·an mimicry (bāt′sē ən) ⟦after H. W. *Bates* (1825-92), Eng naturalistl⟧ a kind of mimicry in which one species, to make itself less vulnerable to a particular predator, imitates the structure and coloration of another species that is unpalatable, difficult to capture, etc.

bat·fish (bat′fish′) ***n., pl.*** **-fish′** or **-fish′es** (see FISH) ⟦BAT[2] + FISH⟧ any of various strangely shaped marine fishes; esp., *a)* any of a family (Ogcocephalidae) of angler fishes *b)* a batlike ray (*Myliobatis californica*) of the E Pacific *c)* FLYING GURNARD

bat·fowl (bat′foul′) ***vi.*** ⟦BAT[1] + FOWL⟧ to catch birds at night by blinding them with a light, and netting or hitting them when they fly toward it —**bat′fowl′er** ***n.***

bat·girl (bat′gurl′) ***n.*** *Baseball* a girl or young woman who serves as a general assistant during practice and around the clubhouse and retrieves bats as they are used during a game

bath[1] (bath, bäth) ***n., pl.*** **baths** (ba*th*z, bä*th*z; baths, bäths) ⟦ME < OE *bæth* < IE base **bhe-*, to warm > BAKE⟧ **1** a washing or dipping of a thing, esp. the body, in water or other liquid, steam, etc. **2** water or other liquid for bathing, or for dipping, cleaning, soaking, regulating temperature, etc. **3** a container for such liquid **4** a bathtub **5** a bathroom **6** *a)* [*often pl.*] a building or set of rooms for bathing *b)* [*pl.*] in ancient Greece and Rome, a building used for public bathing, relaxation, etc. and as a social center **7** [*often pl.*] a resort where bathing is part of the medical treatment; spa **8** the condition of being covered with a liquid **9** *Chem.* *a)* a material that acts as a medium for regulating the temperature of things put in or on it *b)* the container for this **10** *Metallurgy* molten metal in a furnace **11** *Photog.* a solution used in developing, fixing, etc. — ***vt., vi.*** [Brit.] BATHE —**take a bath** [Slang] to suffer a heavy financial loss

bath[2] (bath) ***n.*** ⟦Heb *bat*⟧ an ancient Hebrew unit of liquid measure, variously estimated as equaling from 6 to 10 gal

Bath (bath, bäth) city in SW England: health resort known for its hot springs

Bath brick ⟦after prec., where first made⟧ a brick-shaped piece of calcareous earth, used for cleaning polished metal

Bath chair ⟦after BATH, where first used⟧ a hooded wheelchair

bathe (bā*th*) ***vt.*** **bathed, bath′ing** ⟦ME *bathen* < OE *bathian* < *bæth*, BATH[1]⟧ **1** to put into a liquid; immerse **2** to give a bath to; wash **3** to wet or moisten [sweat *bathed* his brow] **4** to cover or envelop as if with liquid [the trees are *bathed* in moonlight] —***vi.*** **1** to bathe oneself; take a bath or shower **2** to go into or be in a body of water so as to swim, cool oneself, etc. **3** to soak oneself in some substance or influence —***n.*** [Brit.] a bathing in the sea, a pool, etc.; a swim —**bath·er** (bā′*th*ər) ***n.***

ba·thet·ic (bə thet′ik) ***adj.*** ⟦< BATHOS by analogy with PATHETIC⟧ characterized by bathos —**ba·thet′i·cal·ly** ***adv.***

bath·house (bath′hous′) ***n.*** **1** a public building where people can take baths ☆**2** a building used by bathers for changing clothes, as at the seashore

☆**bath·i·nette** (bath′ə net′) ***n.*** ⟦< *Bathinette,* former trademark⟧ a portable folding bathtub for babies, made of or covered with rubberized or other waterproof cloth

bathing cap a tightfitting cap of rubber, plastic, etc. worn to keep the hair from getting wet in swimming

bathing suit a garment worn for swimming, sunbathing, etc.; swimsuit

bath·mat (bath′mat′) ***n.*** a mat placed inside or next to a bathtub, as to prevent slipping or keep the floor dry

bath·o- (bath′ō, -ə) ⟦< Gr *bathos,* depth: see BATHY-⟧ *combining form* depth *[bathometer]*

bath·o·lith (bath′ō lith′) ***n.*** ⟦prec. + -LITH⟧ a massive, dome-shaped formation of intrusive igneous rock, usually granite, that is thought to have originated far beneath the earth's surface, forms the base of mountain ranges, and is often found exposed as the result of long periods of erosion: cf. LACCOLITH: often called **bath′o·lite′** (-lit′)

ba·thom·e·ter (bə thäm′ət ər) ***n.*** ⟦BATHO- + -METER⟧ an instrument for measuring water depths

ba·thos (bā′thäs′, -thôs′) ***n.*** ⟦Gr *bathos,* depth < *bathys:* see BATHY-⟧ **1** an abrupt, often ludicrous change from the lofty to the ordinary or trivial in writing or speech; unintentional anticlimax **2** false pathos; sentimentality **3** hackneyed quality; triteness —**SYN.** PATHOS

☆**bath·robe** (bath′rōb′) ***n.*** a loose robe for wearing to and from the bath or for lounging

bath·room (-ro͞om′) ***n.*** **1** a room with a bathtub, toilet, washstand, etc. ☆**2** LAVATORY (sense 2*a*) —☆**go to the bathroom** [Informal] to urinate or defecate

Bath·she·ba (bath shē′bə, bath′shi bə) ***n.*** ⟦Heb *batsheva,* lit., daughter of Sheba, daughter of the oath⟧ *Bible* the mother of Solomon by King David, whom she married after he had sent her first husband, Uriah, to his death in battle: 2 Sam. 11

☆**bath·tub** (bath′tub′) ***n.*** a tub, now usually a bathroom fixture, in which to take a bath

Bath·urst (bath′ərst, bäth′-) *former name for* BANJUL

bath·wa·ter (bath′wôt′ər) ***n.*** water drawn or used for a bath

bath·y- (bath′ə) ⟦< Gr *bathys,* deep < IE base **gwadh-,* plunge into, sink > Cornish *bedhy,* drown⟧ *combining form* deep; of the sea depths: see BATHO- *[bathysphere]*

bath·y·al (bath′ē əl) ***adj.*** ⟦prec. + -AL⟧ designating or of the ecological zone (**bathyal zone**) along the continental slope of the ocean floor between *c.* 660 and 13,000 ft (*c.* 200 and 3,960 m)

ba·thym·e·try (ba thim′ə trē) ***n.*** ⟦BATHY- + -METRY⟧ **1** the science of measuring the depths of oceans, seas, etc. **2** the topographic maps of the sea floor resulting from such measurements —**bath·y·met·ric** (bath′ə met′rik) ***adj.,*** **bath′y·met′ri·cal**

bath·y·scaph (bath′ə skaf′) ***n.*** ⟦< Fr, coined by Auguste PICCARD < Gr *bathys,* deep + *skaphē,* boat⟧ a deep-sea diving apparatus for reaching great depths, nearly 11 km (*c.* 6.8 mi), without a cable: it consists of a navigable, ballasted, submarine-shaped float filled with a fluid lighter than water, and a steel observation cabin: also **bath′y·scaphe′** (-skaf′, -skāf′)

☆**bath·y·sphere** (-sfir′) ***n.*** ⟦BATHY- + -SPHERE; coined (*c.* 1930) by William BEEBE⟧ a round, watertight observation chamber lowered by cables into the sea to a depth of *c.* 900 m (*c.* 2,950 ft)

bath·y·ther·mo·graph (bath′ə thur′mə graf′) ***n.*** ⟦BATHY- + THERMOGRAPH⟧ a device for measuring the temperature of the ocean at any specific depth down to *c.* 1,800 m (*c.* 5,900 ft)

ba·tik (bə tēk′, bä′tēk′) ***n.*** ⟦< Javanese, lit., painted⟧ **1** a method of dyeing designs on cloth by coating the parts that are not to be dyed with removable wax **2** cloth so decorated or a design made in this way —***adj.*** of or like batik

bat·ing (bāt′iŋ) ***prep.*** ⟦prp. of BATE[1]⟧ [Archaic] except for; excluding

ba·tiste (bə tēst′, ba-) ***n.*** ⟦Fr < OFr *baptiste:* after the supposed original maker, *Baptiste* of Cambrai: see CAMBRIC⟧ a fine, thin cloth of cotton, linen, rayon, wool, etc.

bat·man (bat′mən) ***n., pl.*** **-men** (-mən) ⟦*bat,* packsaddle (only in comb.) < Fr *bât* < OFr *bast* < ML **bastum* + MAN⟧ the orderly of an officer in the British army

☆**bat mitz·vah** or **bat miz·vah** (bät mits′və; *Heb* bät′mits vä′) [*also* **B- M-**] ⟦< Heb *bat,* daughter + *mitsva,* commandment⟧ **1** a Jewish girl who has arrived at the age of religious responsibility, usually 13 years **2** the ceremony celebrating this event, with its attendant festivities —***vt.*** **-vahed, -vah·ing** to confirm (a girl) as a bat mitzvah

Bat·na (bat′nə) city in NE Algeria

ba·ton (bə tän′, ba-; *Brit* ba′tän′) ***n.*** ⟦Fr *bâton* < OFr *baston* < VL **basto* < LL *bastum,* stick, prob. of Gaul orig.⟧ **1** a staff serving as a symbol of office **2** *Heraldry* a short, narrow bend: in England, a baton placed diagonally right to left (as seen by the viewer) and cut short at both ends signifies bastardy: cf. BEND SINISTER **3** a slender stick used by a conductor in directing an orchestra, choir, etc. ☆**4** a hollow metal rod, with a knob at one or at each end, twirled in a showy way by a drum major or drum majorette **5** the short, light rod passed from one runner to the next in a relay race **6** a policeman's club; billy; truncheon

Bat·on Rouge (bat′'n ro͞ozh′) ⟦Fr transl. of Choctaw *ítu-úma,* red pole, a boundary mark, prob. between the hunting grounds of two tribes⟧ capital of La., on the Mississippi

ba·tra·chi·an (bə trā′kē ən) ***adj.*** ⟦< ModL *Batrachia* (former group name) < Gr *batracheios,* relating to frogs < *batrachos,* frog⟧ of, like, or concerning frogs and toads —***n.*** a frog or toad

bat·ra·cho·tox·in (ba′trə kō täks′in; bə trak′ō-) ***n.*** ⟦< Gr *batrachos,* frog + -O- + TOXIN⟧ a steroidal alkaloid, $C_{31}H_{42}N_2O_6$, found in the skin of certain Neotropical frogs (genus *Phyllobates*) and used on poison arrows: one of the most powerful natural neurotoxins known

bats (bats) ***adj.*** ⟦< HAVE BATS IN THE BELFRY (see phr. under BAT[2])⟧ [Slang] insane; crazy

bats·man (bats′mən) ***n., pl.*** **-men** (-mən) **1** *Baseball* BATTER[2] **2** *Cricket* the player whose turn it is to bat

batt (bat) ***n.*** BAT[1] (*n.* 6)

bat·tal·ion (bə tal′yən) ***n.*** ⟦MFr *bataillon* < It *battaglione* < *battaglia* < VL *battalia,* BATTLE[1]⟧ **1** a large group of soldiers arrayed for battle **2** any large group joined together in some activity **3** *U.S. Army* a tactical unit made up of three or more companies, batteries, or analogous units: it is normally commanded by a lieutenant colonel and is the basic building unit of a division

batte·ment (bat′mənt; *Fr* bȧt män′) ***n.*** ⟦Fr, lit., the act of beating < *battre,* to beat < OFr: see BATTER[1]⟧ *Ballet* any of various movements in which one leg is extended away from the body and then brought back toward the other leg

bat·ten[1] (bat′'n) ***n.*** ⟦var. of BATON⟧ **1** a sawed strip of wood, flooring, etc. **2** a strip of wood put over a seam between boards as a fastening or covering **3** a short piece of wood or plastic inserted in a sail to keep it taut **4** a strip of steel or wood used to fasten canvas over a ship's hatchways —***vt.*** **1** to fasten with battens **2** to supply or strengthen with battens —**batten down the hatches** to fasten canvas over the hatches, esp. in preparing for a storm

bat·ten[2] (bat′'n) ***vi.*** ⟦ON *batna,* improve < IE base **bhad-,* good > BETTER[1]⟧ **1** to grow fat; thrive **2** to be well fed or wealthy at another's expense —***vt.*** to fatten up; overfeed

bat·ten[3] (bat′'n) ***n.*** ⟦Fr *battant,* orig. prp. of *battre* < OFr: see fol.⟧ in a loom, the movable frame that presses into place the threads of a woof

bat·ter[1] (bat′ər) ***vt.*** ⟦ME *bateren* < OFr *battre* < VL *battere* < L *battuere,* to beat, via Gaul < IE base **bhāt-,* to strike > L *fatuus,* foolish & Sans *bátati,* (he) strikes; also, in part, freq. of BAT[1], v.⟧ **1** *a)* to beat or strike with blow after blow; pound *b)* to subject (a smaller or weaker person) to frequent beatings **2** to break to bits by pounding **3** to injure or damage by pounding, by hard wear or use, etc. —***vi.*** to pound noisily and repeatedly

bat·ter[2] (bat′ər) ***n.*** **1** *Baseball* the player who is batting or whose turn it is to bat **2** *Cricket* BATSMAN

bat·ter[3] (bat′ər) ***n.*** ⟦ME & OFr *bature,* prob. < *battre:* see BATTER[1]⟧ a flowing mixture of flour, milk, eggs, etc. for making cakes or pancakes, coating food before frying, etc. —***vt.*** to coat with batter

bat·ter[4] (bat′ər) ***vt., vi.*** ⟦< ?⟧ to slope gradually upward and backward —***n.*** a gradual upward and backward slope, as of the outer face of a wall

bat·ter·ie (bat′ə rē; *Fr* bȧ trē′) ***n.*** ⟦Fr: see BATTERY⟧ *Ballet* any of various movements in which the legs move rapidly and repeatedly toward and away from each other, esp. in the air

battering ram **1** an ancient military machine having a heavy wooden beam, sometimes with an iron ram's head at its end, for battering down gates, walls, doors, etc. **2** any bar, log, etc. used like this to force entrance

Bat·ter·sea (bat′ər sē) former district of London, on the south bank of the Thames, now part of Wandsworth

bat·ter·y (bat′ər ē) ***n., pl.*** **-ter·ies** ⟦Fr *batterie* < OFr *battre:* see BATTER[1]⟧ **1** the act of battering, beating, or pounding **2** machinery used in battering **3** a group of similar things arranged, connected, or used together; set or series; array [*a battery* of microphones, a *battery* of school achievement tests] **4** [Chiefly Brit.] a series of cages or other restrictive compartments used as to confine hens for intensive laying: often used attributively ☆**5** *Baseball* the pitcher and the catcher **6** *Elec. a)* a connected group of electrochemical cells that store electric charges and generate direct current *b)* a single cell of this type *c)* a similar nuclear, solar, or thermal device that stores and generates electrical energy **7** *Law* any illegal beating or touching of another person, either directly or with an object: see ASSAULT AND BATTERY **8** *Mil. a)* an emplacement for heavy guns or a fortification equipped with such guns *b)* a set of heavy guns, rockets, etc. *c)* the personnel who operate such guns: usually the basic unit of artillery, corresponding to an infantry company **9** *U.S. Navy* a group of guns of the same caliber or used for the same purpose on a warship [an antiaircraft *battery*] **10** *Music* the percussion instruments of an orchestra —**in battery** in firing position after recovery from the recoil of a previous discharge: said of a heavy gun —**the Battery** a park in New York City, at the S tip of Manhattan: 21 acres: also called **Battery Park**

bat·ting (bat′iŋ; *for 2, usually* bat′'n) ***n.*** **1** the action of a person who bats, as in baseball ☆**2** ⟦see BATT⟧ cotton, wool, or synthetic fiber wadded into sheets and used in bandages, quilts, quilted garments, etc.

☆**batting average** **1** in baseball, a figure expressing the average batting efficiency of a player or team, figured by dividing the number of base hits by the number of official at-bats: see AT-BAT **2** [Informal] the average level of competence or success reached by a person in any activity

batting cage *Baseball* a screen with three sides and a top, in which batters practice: it keeps missed and fouled pitches within its enclosure

batting helmet *Baseball* a rigid plastic cap with a sidepiece extending down over the ear, worn for protection while batting

bat·tle[1] (bat′'l) ***n.*** ⟦ME & OFr *bataille* < VL *battalia* < L *battualia,* exercises of gladiators and soldiers in fighting and fencing < *battuere:* see BATTER[1]⟧ **1** a fight, esp. a large-scale engagement, between armed forces on land, at sea, or in the air **2** armed fighting; combat or war **3** any fight or struggle; conflict **4** [Archaic] a battalion —*vt.* **-tled**, **-tling 1** to oppose as in a battle; fight **2** to try to overcome; struggle against or contend with [*a patient battling cancer*] —*vi.* **1** to take part in a battle; fight **2** to struggle; contend —**give** (or **do**) **battle** to engage in battle; fight —**bat′tler** *n.*

SYN.—**battle** denotes a conflict between armed forces in a war and implies a large-scale, prolonged contest over a particular area; **engagement**, the more formal term, stresses the actual meeting of opposing forces, with no restrictive connotation as to duration; a **campaign** is a series of military operations with a particular objective and may involve a number of battles; **encounter** usually suggests a chance meeting of hostile forces; **skirmish** refers to a brief, light encounter between small detachments; **action** stresses the detailed operations of active fighting [*killed in action*]; **combat**, the most general of these terms, simply implies armed fighting, without further qualification

bat·tle[2] (bat′'l) *vt.* **-tled**, **-tling** [Archaic] to build battlements on

bat·tle-ax or **bat·tle-axe** (-aks′) *n.* **1** a heavy ax with a wide blade, formerly used as a weapon of war ☆**2** [Slang] a woman who is harsh, domineering, etc.

battle cry a cry or slogan used to encourage those in a battle, struggle, contest, etc.

bat·tle·dore (bat′'l dôr′) *n.* ⟦ME *batildore* < OProv *batedor,* beater < OFr *battre* (see BATTER[1]): sp. infl. by ME *betel,* BEETLE[2]⟧ **1** a flat paddle or racket used to hit a shuttlecock back and forth in a game (called **battledore and shuttlecock**) from which badminton developed **2** this game

battle fatigue COMBAT FATIGUE

bat·tle·field (bat′'l fēld′) *n.* **1** the site of a battle **2** any area of conflict Also **bat′tle·ground′** (-ground′)

battle group a military or naval task force, esp. aircraft carriers with their aircraft and support vessels

☆**battle jacket** ⟦from a style of military jacket worn in combat⟧ a closefitting jacket reaching to the waist

bat·tle·ment (-mənt) *n.* ⟦ME *batelment* < OFr *bataillier,* to fortify < *bataille,* fortification on a wall or tower < ? VL **battacula,* place of battle < *battere,* BATTER[1]⟧ **1** a parapet with open spaces for shooting, built on top of a castle wall, tower, or fort **2** an architectural decoration like this —**bat′tle·ment′ed** (-men′tid) *adj.*

BATTLEMENT

battlement (sense 1)

battle royal *pl.* **battles royal 1** a fight or bout involving several or many contestants; free-for-all **2** a long, bitterly fought battle **3** a heated dispute

bat·tle-scarred (-skärd′) *adj.* having scars from wounds received in combat or in fights

☆**bat·tle·ship** (-ship′) *n.* any of a class of large warships with the biggest guns and very heavy armor

☆**battle star 1** a small star worn on a campaign ribbon, awarded to a member of the armed forces for participation in a particular battle or campaign: after 1962 officially termed *service star* **2** a star awarded to, and often painted on the side of, a ship, submarine, etc. for specific combat activities

battle stations the places to which soldiers, sailors, warships, etc. are assigned for a battle or an emergency

☆**bat·tle·wag·on** (-wag′ən) *n.* [Slang] a battleship

bat·tue (ba to͞o′, -tyo͞o′; bə-) *n.* ⟦Fr, fem. pp. of OFr *battre,* to beat: see BATTER[1]⟧ **1** a beating of underbrush and woods to drive game out toward hunters **2** a hunt of this kind **3** any mass killing

bat·ty (bat′ē) *adj.* **-ti·er**, **-ti·est** ⟦< BAT[2] + -Y[2]: see BATS⟧ [Slang] crazy or eccentric

Ba·tu·mi (bä to͞o′mē) seaport in Georgia, on the Black Sea, near the Turkish border: formerly called **Ba·tum′** (-to͞om′)

bat·wing (bat′wiŋ′) *adj.* shaped like a bat's wing

Bat-Yam (bät′yäm′) city in W Israel, on the Mediterranean, near Tel Aviv

bau·ble (bô′bəl) *n.* ⟦ME *babel* < OFr *baubel, belbel,* prob. redupl. of *bel* < L *bellus,* pretty⟧ **1** a showy but worthless or useless thing; trinket, trifle, etc. **2** [Archaic] a jester's baton with an ornament at the end

Bau·cis (bô′sis) *n. Gr. Myth.* a poor old woman who, with her husband, Philemon, shows such hospitality to the disguised Zeus and Hermes that the grateful gods turn their humble cottage into a temple

baud (bôd) *n.* ⟦after J. M. E. *Baudot* (1845-1903), Fr inventor⟧ **1** a unit of signaling speed in telegraphic code **2** *Comput. a)* a unit of data-transmission speed equal to the number of changes per second in a signal *b)* loosely, the number of bits per second transmitted in a given computer system

bau·de·kin (bô′də kin) *n.* ⟦ME < OFr *baudequin*⟧ [Archaic] BALDACHIN

Bau·de·laire (bōd ler′), **(Pierre) Charles** (shȧrl) 1821-67; Fr. poet & essayist

Bau·douin (bō dwen′) 1930-93; king of Belgium (1951-93): son of Leopold III

bau·drons (bô′drənz) *n.* [Scot.] cat: a name for the cat used in folklore

Bau·haus (bou′hous′) *n.* ⟦Ger < *bauen,* to build + *haus,* a house⟧ the architectural school of Walter Gropius, founded in Germany, 1919: it promoted a synthesis of painting, sculpture, and architecture, the adaptation of science and technology to architecture, and an emphasis on functionalism

bau·hin·i·a (bô hin′ē ə, -yə) *n.* ⟦after J. *Bauhin* (1541-1613) & G. *Bauhin* (1560-1624), Swiss botanists⟧ any of a genus (*Bauhinia*) of small tropical trees of the caesalpinia family having two-lobed leaves and large, flat, white or lavender flowers

baulk (bôk) *n., vt., vi.* BALK

Baum (bôm, bäm), **L(yman) Frank** 1856-1919; U.S. writer of children's books, including the Oz books

Bau·mé (bō mā′) *adj.* ⟦after A. *Baumé* (1728-1804), Fr chemist⟧ designating or of either of two hydrometer scales used to indicate specific gravity

baum marten (boum) ⟦partial transl. of Ger *baummarder* < *baum,* tree + *marder,* marten⟧ a dark brown European marten (esp. *Martes martes*) or its fur

baux·ite (bôks′īt′, bō′zīt′) *n.* ⟦Fr, after *(Les) Baux,* town near Arles, France⟧ a soft, claylike sedimentary rock, mainly hydrous aluminum hydroxide, that is the chief ore of aluminum

Ba·var·i·a (bə ver′ē ə) state of SW Germany: formerly (1918-33) a republic and, before that, a duchy, an electorate, & a kingdom with varying boundaries: 27,241 sq mi (70,554 sq km); cap. Munich

Ba·var·i·an (-ən) *adj.* of Bavaria or its people, language, or culture —*n.* **1** a person born or living in Bavaria **2** the variety of German spoken in Bavaria and Austria

Bavarian cream a dessert made with gelatin, whipped cream, eggs, and fruit flavoring

baw·bee (bô bē′, bô′bē) *n.* ⟦prob. < *siller* (Scot for SILVER) *bawby,* jocular for name of the laird of *Sillebawby,* a mint master⟧ [Scot.] a halfpenny or any small coin

baw·cock (bô′käk′) *n.* ⟦< Fr *beau,* pretty + *coq,* COCK[2]⟧ [Archaic] a good fellow

bawd (bôd) *n.* ⟦ME *baude,* lewd person < ? OFr *baud,* merry, licentious (< Frank *bald,* bold) > Fr *baudet,* donkey, also (in Picardy) loose woman⟧ **1** [Literary] a person, now esp. a woman, who keeps a brothel; madam **2** [Rare] a prostitute

bawd·ry (bô′drē) *n.* ⟦ME & OFr *bauderie,* gaiety: see prec.⟧ **1** lewd language; bawdiness **2** [Archaic] the occupation of a bawd

bawd·y (bô′dē) *adj.* **bawd′i·er**, **bawd′i·est** characteristic of a bawd; indecent or humorously coarse; lewd —*n.* bawdy language —**bawd′i·ly** *adv.* —**bawd′i·ness** *n.*

bawd·y·house (-hous′) *n.* [Old-fashioned] a house of prostitution

bawl (bôl) *vi., vt.* ⟦ME *baulen* (found only in ger.) < ML *baulare,* to bark & ? ON *baula,* to low like a cow; both of echoic orig.⟧ **1** to shout or call out noisily; bellow; yell **2** to weep and wail loudly —*n.* **1** an outcry; bellow **2** a noisy weeping —**bawl out 1** to shout or call out ☆**2** [Slang] to scold angrily —**bawl′er** *n.*

bay[1] (bā) *n.* ⟦ME *bai* < OFr *baie* < ML *baia,* prob. < Iberian⟧ **1** *a)* a part of a sea or lake that cuts into the shoreline; wide inlet: usually smaller than a gulf *b) International Law* a small gulf with an opening to the sea of less than 24 nautical miles and a strictly defined minimum area: used to determine territorial waters ☆**2** any level land area making an indentation, as into a woods, range of hills, etc.

bay[2] (bā) *n.* ⟦ME *bai* < OFr *baée* < *baer, bayer,* to gape, yawn < VL *batare,* to gape⟧ **1** *a)* an opening or alcove marked off by pillars, columns, etc. *b)* a recess in a wall, as for a window *c)* BAY WINDOW **2** a part of a building projecting from the main part; wing **3** a compartment or space; specif., *a)* a bin in a barn, for storing hay or grain *b)* a compartment in an aircraft or spacecraft [*bomb bay, cargo bay*] *c)* in a service station, the area for one car **4** SICK BAY

bay[3] (bā) *vi.* ⟦ME *baien, abaien* < OFr *baiier, abaiier* < IE base **bai-,* echoic of howling⟧ to bark or howl in long, deep tones —*vt.* **1** to bark at; howl at **2** to chase with yelps and barks **3** to bring to or hold at bay **4** to utter in long, deep tones —*n.* **1** the sound of baying **2** the situation of or as of a hunted animal forced to turn and fight —**at bay 1** with escape cut off; cornered **2** unable to advance; held off [*the bear kept the hunters at bay*] —**bring to bay** to force into a situation that makes escape impossible; corner

bay[4] (bā) *n.* ⟦ME *bai* < OFr *baie* < L *baca,* berry⟧ **1** LAUREL (*n.* 1) **2** [*pl.*] *a)* a wreath of bay leaves, a classical token of honor given to poets and conquerors *b)* honor; fame **3** any of various trees or shrubs of various families, as rosebay or bayberry

bay[5] (bā) *adj.* ⟦ME *bai* < OFr *baie* < L *badius*⟧ reddish-brown: said esp. of horses —*n.* **1** a horse or, sometimes, some other animal of this color **2** reddish brown

ba·ya·dere or **ba·ya·deer** (bä′yə dir′) *n.* ⟦Fr *bayadère,* Hindu dancing girl < Port *bailadeira,* dancer < *bailar,* to dance < LL *ballare*: see BALL[2]⟧ a fabric or design with horizontal stripes, usually brightly colored —*adj.* striped horizontally

Ba·ya·món (bä′yä môn′) city in NE Puerto Rico, near San Juan

bay antler the second branch from the base of a deer's horn

Ba·yard (bȧ yȧr′; *E* bā′ərd), Chevalier de (born *Pierre Terrail*) 1473?-1524; Fr. military hero: known as *chevalier sans peur et sans reproche* (the fearless & irreproachable knight)

Bay Area region in W Calif., generally consisting of the counties surrounding San Francisco Bay

bay·ber·ry (bā′ber′ē, -bər ē) *n., pl.* **-ries** ⟦BAY[4] + BERRY: orig. used of the laurel and its berries⟧ ☆**1** *a)* any of a genus (*Myrica*) of shrubs of the bayberry family, as the wax myrtle, having a small, berrylike fruit covered with a wax used in making candles *b)* the fruit **2** a tropical American tree (*Pimenta racemosa*) of the myrtle family, that yields an aromatic oil used in making bay rum —*adj.* designating a family (Myricaceae) of aromatic, dicotyledonous trees and shrubs (order Myricales)

Bay·ern (bī′ərn) *Ger. name for* BAVARIA

Bayes·i·an (bā′zē ən) *adj.* of or having to do with BAYES' THEOREM or its application [*Bayesian* statistics]

Bayes' theorem (bāz) ⟦after T. *Bayes* (1702-61), Eng theologian and mathematician known for his early work in modern probability theory⟧ a theorem establishing a method of calculating CONDITIONAL (*adj.* 1*b*) statistical probabilities, in which a known probability is modified in the light of later events that affect the data under consideration (Ex.: the probability of selecting a heart from a deck of cards is 13/52; if a card is selected from a full deck and that card is a heart, the probability that the next card selected will also be a heart becomes 12/51, but if that first selected card is not a heart, the probability for the next card becomes 13/51)

Ba·yeux Tapestry (bā yo͞o′; *Fr* bȧ yö′) an embroidered length of linen, 231 feet (70 m) long and 19½ inches (51 cm) wide, probably of the 11th cent., in the museum of Bayeux, in NW France, picturing incidents of the Norman conquest and events leading up to it

Bay·kal (bī käl′), **Lake** *alt. sp. of* Lake BAIKAL

Bayle (bel), **Pierre** (pyer) 1647-1706; Fr. critic & philosopher

bay leaf the dried, aromatic leaf of certain plants (esp. *Laurus nobilis*) of the laurel family, used as a seasoning in cooking

☆**bay lynx** BOBCAT

Bay of Pigs bay on the SW coast of Cuba: site of an unsuccessful invasion (1961) by exiled Cubans trained & funded by the U.S.

bay·o·net (bā′ə net′; *also* bā′ə nət) *n.* ⟦Fr *bayonnette,* after *Bayonne,* France (see BAYONNE), where first made⟧ **1** a detachable, daggerlike blade put on the muzzle end of a rifle, for hand-to-hand fighting **2** a part like a bayonet in shape, manner of attachment, etc. — *vt., vi.* **-net′ed** or **-net′ted, -net′ing** or **-net′ting** to stab, prod, or kill with a bayonet

☆**bay·ou** (bī′o͞o′; *also* bī′ō′) *n.* ⟦AmFr < Choctaw *bayuk,* small stream⟧ in some parts of the S U.S., a sluggish, marshy inlet or outlet of a lake, river, etc.

Bay·reuth (bī roit′, bī′roit) city in SE Germany, in the state of Bavaria: known for its annual Wagnerian music festivals, begun in 1876

bay rum **1** BAYBERRY (sense 2) **2** an aromatic liquid formerly obtained from leaves of the bayberry tree, now made of certain oils, water, and alcohol: it is used in medicines and cosmetics

Bay State *name for* MASSACHUSETTS —**Bay Stat′er**

bay window **1** a window or set of windows jutting out from the wall of a building and forming an alcove within ☆**2** [Slang] a large, protruding belly

bay·wood (bā′wood′) *n.* a soft, light kind of mahogany (*Swietenia macrophylla*) that grows from the bay region of SE Mexico to South America

ba·zaar (bə zär′) *n.* ⟦Pers *bāzār,* a market⟧ **1** a market or street of shops and stalls, esp. in Middle Eastern countries **2** a shop for selling various kinds of goods **3** a sale of various articles, usually to raise money for a club, church, etc.

☆**ba·zil·lion** (bə zil′yən) *n.* ⟦arbitrary coinage < ZILLION⟧ [Slang] a very large, indefinite number

☆**ba·zoo** (ba zo͞o′) *n.* ⟦prob. < Du *bazuin,* trumpet⟧ [Slang] **1** the mouth **2** the nose **3** loud or boastful talk

☆**ba·zoo·ka** (bə zo͞o′kə) *n.* ⟦extension of prec.: name applied by Bob Burns (1896-1956), U.S. comedian, to a comic musical horn made of two gas pipes and a whiskey funnel⟧ a portable weapon of metal tubing, for aiming and launching armor-piercing rockets

ba·zooms (bə zo͞omz′) *pl.n.* ⟦altered < pl. of BOSOM⟧ [Slang] a woman's breasts; bosom

☆**BB**[1] (bē′bē′) *n., pl.* **BB's** ⟦size designation⟧ **1** a small pellet of shot, .175 inch in diameter, fired from an air gun (**BB gun**) **2** a small pellet of shot, .18 inch in diameter, used in shotgun cartridges

BB[2] or **bb** *abbrev. Baseball* base(s) on balls

BBA or **B.B.A.** *abbrev.* Bachelor of Business Administration

BBB *service mark* Better Business Bureau

BBC *service mark* British Broadcasting Corporation

bbl *abbrev.* barrel

bbls *abbrev.* barrels

B-boy (bē′boi′) *n.* ⟦< ? *b(reak dancer), b(eat),* etc. + *boy*⟧ a young male performer or fan of hip hop, rap, etc.

BBQ (bär′bə kyo͞o′) *n., pl.* **BBQ's**, *adj., vt., vi.* **BBQed, BBQing** *informal sp. of* BARBECUE

BBS *abbrev. Comput.* bulletin board system

BC or **B.C.** *abbrev.* **1** before Christ: used with dates **2** British Columbia

bcc *abbrev.* blind carbon copy

BCE or **B.C.E.** *abbrev.* **1** Bachelor of Civil Engineering **2** before the COMMON ERA: used with dates as an alternative to B.C.

B cell ⟦< *b(ursa of Fabricius),* a structure in birds analogous to the human thymus < Latinized surname of G. Fabrici (1537–1619), It anatomist⟧ any of the lymphocytes not derived from the thymus, that mature in the bone marrow and help to build antibodies: cf. T CELL

BCG (vaccine) (bē′sē′jē′) ⟦*b(acillus) C(almette-)G(uérin),* after A. L. C. *Calmette* (1863-1933) & Camille *Guérin* (1872-1961), Fr physicians who developed it⟧ a vaccine prepared from an attenuated strain of the tubercle bacillus, used for immunization against tuberculosis

BChE or **B.Ch.E.** *abbrev.* Bachelor of Chemical Engineering

BCL or **B.C.L.** *abbrev.* **1** Bachelor of Canon Law **2** Bachelor of Civil Law

BCME (bē′sē′em′ē′) *n.* ⟦< *b(is)c(hloro)m(ethyl) e(ther)*⟧ a colorless liquid, CH_2ClOCH_2Cl, that forms spontaneously from hydrochloric acid and formaldehyde: a known carcinogen

B complex VITAMIN B (COMPLEX)

BC soil a soil that contains the B and C horizons only: see ABC SOIL

bd *abbrev.* **1** board **2** bond

BD or **B.D.** *abbrev.* Bachelor of Divinity

B/D or **b/d** *abbrev.* **1** bank draft **2** bills discounted

bdel·li·um (del′ē əm) *n.* ⟦ME < L < Gr *bdellion;* of Sem orig. (as in Assyr *budulḫu,* Heb *bedolach*)⟧ **1** a myrrhlike gum resin **2** any of a genus (*Commiphora*) of trees of the bursera family yielding this **3** *Bible* a jewel variously interpreted as being a carbuncle (Gen. 2:12), a crystal (Num. 11:7), or a pearl (rabbinical interpretation)

bd ft *abbrev.* board foot (or feet)

bdl *abbrev.* bundle

bdrm *abbrev.* bedroom

be (bē; *unstressed* bi) *vi.* **was** or **were, been, be′ing** ⟦ME *been, beon* < OE *beon*: *be* is a defective verb with parts from three unrelated stems: 1) the IE substantive verb, base **es-,* as in AM, IS[1], Sans *ásmi, asti,* Goth *im, ist;* 2) IE base **wes-,* stay, remain, as in WAS, WERE, Sans *vasati,* (he) lingers, stays, Goth *wisan, was, wēsum,* remain, be; 3) IE base **bheu-,* grow, become, (it) occurs, is there, L *fieri,* as in BE, BEEN, Sans *bhávati,* be, become: see BONDAGE⟧ **I.** as a substantive verb, *be* means: **1** to exist; live [Caesar *is* no more] **2** to happen or occur [when will the wedding *be*?] **3** to remain or continue [will he *be* here long?] **4** to come to; belong [peace *be* with you] **5** to have a place or position [the door *is* on your left] **II.** as a copula, *be* links its subject to a predicate nominative, adjective, or pronoun so as to express attribution or identity, and by extension, value, cause, or signification: it is sometimes equivalent to the equal sign (=) in mathematics [Mrs. Siddons *was* an actress; he *is* handsome; that hat *is* fifty dollars; let x *be* y] —***v.aux.*** **1** used with the past participle of a transitive verb to form the passive voice [he will *be* sued] **2** [Archaic] used with the past participle of certain intransitive verbs to form a perfect tense [Christ *is* risen] **3** used with the present participle of another verb to express continuation [the player *is* running with the ball] **4** used with the present participle or infinitive of another verb to express futurity, possibility, obligation, intention, etc. [he *is* starting next week; you *are* to help him] —**be off!** [Archaic] go away!

NOTE—*Be* is conjugated in the present indicative: (I) *am,* (he, she, it) *is,* (we, you, they) *are;* in the past indicative: (I, he, she, it) *was,* (we, you, they) *were;* archaic forms are (thou) *art, wert, wast;* the present subjunctive is *be,* the past subjunctive *were*

Be[1] *abbrev.* Baumé: also **Bé**

Be[2] *Chem. symbol for* beryllium

BE *abbrev.* **1** Bachelor of Education **2** Bachelor of Engineering **3** bill of exchange: also **be** or **B/E** Also, for 1 & 2, **B.E.**

be- (bē, bi, bə) ⟦ME *bi-, be-* < OE (akin to Goth *bi-,* Ger *be-*), at, near < Gmc base of BY⟧ *prefix* **1** *forming verbs a)* around [*besprinkle, beset*] *b)* completely, thoroughly, excessively (used as an intensifier) [*bedeck, besmear*] *c)* away (used as a privative) [*bereave, betake*] *d)* about (used as a transitive prefix) [*bethink, bemoan*]: added to other verbs **2** *forming transitive verbs a)* make [*besot, bedim*] *b)* furnish with, cover with, affect by, treat as [*befriend, bedizen, becloud*]: added to nouns and, sometimes, adjectives **3** *forming adjectives* covered with, furnished with, furnished with to excess: added to past participles in -ED [*bemedaled, bewhiskered*]

beach (bēch) *n.* ⟦E dial., orig., pebbles, shingle < ?⟧ **1** a nearly level stretch of pebbles and sand beside a sea, lake, etc., often washed by high water; sandy shore; strand **2** an area of shore as a place for swimming, sunbathing, etc. — *vt., vi.* to ground (a boat, whale, etc.) on or as if on a beach —*adj.* appropriate for the beach or sunbathing; specif., designating or of a novel, etc. regarded as entertaining and easy to read —**SYN.** SHORE[1]

☆**beach ball** a large, inflated ball for playing with as on beaches

beach·comb·er (-kōm′ər) *n.* **1** COMBER (sense 2) **2** a person who loafs on beaches or wharves, typically on a South Sea island, living on what he or she can beg or find **3** a person who spends time on a beach looking for lost or discarded items, natural specimens, etc. that are useful or interesting —**beach′comb′ing** *n.*

beached (bēcht) *adj.* grounded or stranded on a beach or shore [a *beached* whale]

☆**beach flea** SAND HOPPER

beach·front (-frunt′) *n.* a strip of land bordering on a beach —*adj.* located next to a beach [a *beachfront* hotel]

beach grass any of a genus (*Ammophila*) of deeply rooted, tough, perennial grasses that grow on sandy beaches and are often planted to combat beach erosion

beach·head (-hed′) *n.* **1** a position established by invading troops on an enemy shore **2** a position gained as a secure starting point for any action; foothold

beach-la-mar (bēch′lə mär′) *n.* BÊCHE-DE-MER (sense 2)

beach ridge a ridge just inland from a beach, consisting of sand and gravel built up by storm waves

☆**beach umbrella** a large umbrella used as a sunshade on beaches, in gardens, etc.

beach·wear (bēch′wer′) *n.* garments for wearing at the beach, poolside, etc. in warm weather; esp., swimsuits and coverups

bea·con (bē′kən) *n.* ⟦ME *beken* < OE *beacen, becen* < Gmc **baukna,* prob. < IE **bhāu-,* var. of base **bhā-,* to gleam, shine > Gr *phainein,* to show, appear⟧ **1** a signal fire, esp. one on a hill, pole, etc. **2** any light or radio signal for warning or guiding **3** a lighthouse **4** a radio transmitter that sends out signals for the guidance of aircraft, as at night or in fog **5** a person or thing that warns, offers encouragement or guidance, etc. —***vt.*** **1** to light up (darkness, etc.) **2** to provide or mark with beacons —***vi.*** to shine or serve as a beacon

Bea·cons·field (bē′kənz fēld′), Earl of *see* DISRAELI, Benjamin

bead (bēd) ***n.*** ⟦ME *bede,* prayer, prayer bead < OE *bed* < *biddan,* to pray, ask: see BID[1]⟧ **1** a small, usually round piece of glass, wood, metal, etc., pierced for stringing **2** [*pl.*] ROSARY (sense 1*a*) **3** [*pl.*] a string of beads; necklace **4** any small, round object, as the sight at the muzzle end of a gun barrel **5** a drop or bubble [*beads* of sweat] **6** *a)* a bubble in an effervescing liquid *b)* foam or a head, as on beer **7** a globule of metal, as gold or silver, obtained by refining in a cupel **8** the liplike region around a pneumatic tire that seals to the rim **9** *Archit. a)* a narrow, half-round molding *b)* a molding composed of small rounded ornaments, like a string of beads **10** *Chem.* a beadlike mass usually formed inside the loop of a platinum wire by the action of a flux, such as borax, upon the oxide or salt of certain metals: used in identifying metals in their compounds, since the metal determines the color of the bead —***vt.*** **1** to decorate or string with beads or beading **2** to string like beads —***vi.*** to form a bead or beads —☆**draw a bead on** to take careful aim at —**say** (**or tell** or **count**) **one's beads** to pray with a rosary —**bead′ed** ***adj.***

bead·house (-hous′) ***n.*** an almshouse where the inmates were required to pray for its benefactors

bead·ing (-iŋ) ***n.*** **1** decorative work in beads on dresses, purses, etc. **2** a molding, edge, or pattern resembling a row of beads **3** a narrow, half-round molding **4** *a)* a narrow trimming of lacelike loops *b)* an openwork trimming through which a ribbon can be run

bea·dle (bēd′'l) ***n.*** ⟦ME *bidel* (< OE *bydel,* akin to *beodan,* to BID[1], order), *bedel* < OFr *bedel* < Frank **bidal,* akin to OE form⟧ **1** [Historical] a minor parish officer in the Church of England, who kept order in church **2** [Obs.] a messenger of a law court

bea·dle·dom (-dəm) ***n.*** ⟦prec. + -DOM⟧ fussiness and stupidity of minor officials; petty bureaucracy

bead·roll (bēd′rōl′) ***n.*** ⟦orig., a list of the names of people to be prayed for: see BEAD⟧ [Archaic] a long list, series, or catalog

☆**bead-ru·by** (-ro͞o′bē) ***n.,*** *pl.* **-bies** CANADA MAYFLOWER

beads·man (bēdz′mən) ***n.,*** *pl.* **-men** (-mən) ⟦ME *bedeman* < *bede,* prayer (see BEAD) + *man,* MAN⟧ [Obs.] **1** a person who prays for another, esp. one paid to do so **2** a person in a poorhouse

beads·wom·an (-woom′ən) ***n.,*** *pl.* **-wom′en** (-wim′in) a female beadsman

bead·work (bēd′wurk′) ***n.*** **1** decorative work in beads **2** beaded molding; beading

bead·y (bēd′ē) ***adj.*** **bead′i·er, bead′i·est** **1** small, round, and glittering like a bead [*beady* eyes] **2** decorated with beads

bea·gle (bē′gəl) ***n.*** ⟦ME *begle* < ? MFr *bee gueule,* lit., wide throat < OFr *béer, baer, baier* (see BAY[3]), to gape + *gueule,* throat < L *gula:* see GULLET⟧ a small hound with a smooth coat, short legs, and drooping ears, used in hunting small game

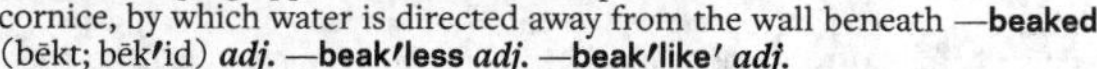

beagle

beak (bēk) ***n.*** ⟦ME *bek* < OFr *bec* < L *beccus* < Gaul⟧ **1** a bird's bill, esp. the large, sharp, horny bill of a bird of prey **2** a beaklike part or thing, as the protruding mouthpart of various insects, fishes, etc., or the spout of a pitcher **3** the metal-covered ram projecting from the prow of an ancient warship **4** [Slang] the nose, esp. if large and hooked **5** *Archit.* the outward-sloping upper surface of the drip of a cornice, by which water is directed away from the wall beneath —**beaked** (bēkt; bēk′id) ***adj.*** —**beak′less** ***adj.*** —**beak′like′** ***adj.***

beaked whale (bēkt) any of a worldwide family (Ziphiidae) of medium-sized toothed whales characterized by a long, narrow snout

beak·er (bēk′ər) ***n.*** ⟦ME *biker* < ON *bikarr,* a cup < VL *bicarium* < ? Gr *bikos,* vessel with handles⟧ **1** a large or ornate cup; goblet **2** a jarlike container of glass or metal with a lip for pouring, used by chemists, druggists, etc. **3** the contents or capacity of a beaker

beak·y (bē′kē) ***adj.*** **1** having a large beak **2** [Informal] designating or having a prominent nose: also **beak′y-nosed′** (-nōzd′)

be-all and end-all (bē′ôl′ ənd end′ôl′) [Informal] **1** a thing or person regarded as being the ultimate or utmost **2** chief or all-important element

beam (bēm) ***n.*** ⟦ME < OE, a tree, piece of wood, column; akin to Ger *baum,* Du *boom,* tree⟧ **I. 1** [Obs.] the squared-off trunk of a tree **2** *a)* a long, thick piece of wood, metal, or stone, used in building *b)* such a piece used as a horizontal support for a roof, ceiling, etc. **3** one of the two large rollers of a loom **4** the barlike, horizontal part of a plow, to which the handles, share, etc. are attached **5** the crossbar of a balance; also, occasionally, the balance itself **6** the main shaft of a deer's antler: see BAY ANTLER **7** any of the heavy, horizontal crosspieces of a ship **8** a ship's breadth at its widest point **9** the side of a ship or the direction extending outward on either side at right angles to the fore-and-aft line of a ship, aircraft, etc. **10** [Slang] the width of the hips **11** *Gym.* BALANCE BEAM **12** *Mech.* a lever that is moved back and forth by a piston rod and transmits its motion to the crank, etc. as in some early steam engines **II.** ⟦orig. transl. of L *columna lucis,* column of light⟧ **1** a shaft or stream of light or other radiation, as of X-rays or nuclear particles: also used fig. **2** a radiant look, smile, etc. **3** a stream of radio or radar signals sent continuously in one direction from a landing field, harbor, etc. as a guide for incoming aircraft or ships —***vt.*** **1** to give out (shafts of light); radiate in a beam or beams **2** to direct or aim (a radio signal, program, etc.) **3** to construct (a ceiling) so that the beams are exposed —***vi.*** **1** to shine brightly; be radiant **2** to smile warmly —**beam in one's own eye** ⟦after Matt. 7:3, Luke 6:41⟧ a major moral flaw in oneself which one ignores while criticizing minor faults in others —**off the beam** **1** not following the direction of a guiding beam, as an airplane ☆**2** [Informal] *a)* going in the wrong direction *b)* wrong; incorrect —**on the beam** **1** in a direction at right angles to the keel of a ship; abeam **2** following the direction of a guiding beam, as an airplane ☆**3** [Informal] *a)* going in the right direction *b)* working or functioning well; alert, keen, quick, etc.

beam-ends (bēm′endz′) ***pl.n.*** the ends of a ship's beams: see BEAM (*n.* I, 7) —**on the beam-ends** tipping so far to the side as to be in danger of capsizing

beam·ing (-iŋ) ***adj.*** **1** sending out beams; shining **2** radiant as with joy; bright; cheerful —**beam′ing·ly** ***adv.***

beam·ish (-ish) ***adj.*** ⟦BEAM + -ISH; used (? in sense of *happy*) by Lewis CARROLL in *Through the Looking-Glass*⟧ beaming; radiant; cheerful

beam splitter an optical device with a special mirror or prism system that separates a beam of light into component beams, used in making holograms, separating colors in a color TV camera, etc.: occasionally written **beam′split′ter** ***n.***

beam·y (-ē) ***adj.*** **beam′i·er, beam′i·est** **1** sending out beams of light; radiant; bright **2** beamlike; broad; massive **3** *Naut.* having a broad BEAM (*n.* I, 8)

bean (bēn) ***n.*** ⟦ME *ben* < OE *bean;* akin to ON *baun,* Ger *bohne* < ? IE **bhabhā-* > L *faba,* bean⟧ **1** any of various leguminous plants; esp., any of several species of a genus (*Phaseolus*) of the pea family, including the kidney bean and lima bean **2** the edible, smooth, kidney-shaped seed of any of these plants **3** a pod with such seeds, eaten as a vegetable when still unripe **4** the bean-shaped seed of some other plants [coffee *bean*] **5** any of these other plants [castor *bean* tree] ☆**6** [Slang] the head, brain, or mind ☆**7** [*pl.*] [Slang] even a small amount: used in negative constructions [not to know *beans* about something] —☆***vt.*** **1** [Slang] to hit on the head **2** *Baseball* to hit (a batter) on the head with a pitched ball —**full of beans** [Slang] **1** full of energy and vitality; lively ☆**2** mistaken; in error —☆**spill the beans** [Informal] to divulge secret information

☆**bean·bag** (-bag′) ***n.*** **1** a small cloth bag filled with beans, for throwing in certain games **2** such a game

☆**beanbag chair** a chair like a large beanbag covered with vinyl, fabric, etc. and filled with foam pellets, as of polystyrene, that shift about to fit one's body

☆**bean ball** ⟦see BEAN (*n.* 6)⟧ [Slang] *Baseball* a pitch aimed at the batter's head, in violation of the rules

☆**bean beetle** any of a number of beetles and weevils attacking legumes, esp. the Mexican bean beetle

bean caper any of a genus (*Zygophyllum*) of plants of the caltrop family having buds used as capers

☆**bean counter** [Informal] a person, esp. an accountant, who is regarded as concentrating on quantitative details to the exclusion of other factors

bean curd TOFU

☆**bean·er·y** (bēn′ər ē) ***n.,*** *pl.* **-er·ies** ⟦BEAN + -ERY: so named from serving baked beans as a chief dish⟧ [Informal] a cheap restaurant

☆**bean·ie** (bē′nē) ***n.*** ⟦BEAN (*n.* 6) + -IE⟧ any of various kinds of skullcap worn as by children

☆**bean·o**[1] (bē′nō) ***n.*** ⟦altered < BINGO⟧ BINGO

bean·o[2] (bē′nō) ***n.*** ⟦*bean* (*feast*), orig., an annual dinner for employees at which *beans* were traditionally served + -O⟧ [Brit. Informal] a festive party, banquet, or celebration

☆**bean·pole** (bēn′pōl′) ***n.*** **1** a long stick put upright for bean plants to climb on **2** [Informal] a tall, lean person

bean·shoot·er (-sho͞ot′ər) ***n.*** PEASHOOTER

bean sprout a sprout from a seed of the soybean or esp. the mung bean, used in salads, chop suey, etc.

bean·stalk (-stôk′) ***n.*** the main stem of a bean plant

☆**Bean·town** (bēn′toun′) ⟦so called in allusion to BOSTON BAKED BEANS⟧ *name for* BOSTON

☆**bean tree** any of various trees, as the catalpa or carob, bearing podlike fruit

☆**bean weevil** any of a family (Bruchidae) of small, hardy beetles (esp. *Acanthoscelides obtectus*) whose larvae feed inside seeds, esp. beans and peas; seed beetle

bear[1] (ber) ***vt.*** **bore, borne** (see vt. 3), **bear′ing** ⟦ME *beren* < OE *beran* < IE base **bher-,* to carry, bring > L *ferre,* Gr *pherein,* Sans *bharati,* (he) bears⟧ **1** *a)* to hold and take along; carry; transport *b)* to hold in the mind [to *bear* a secret] **2** to possess as a part, characteristic, attribute, etc.; have or show [the letter *bore* his signature] **3** to give birth to: the passive past participle in this sense is *born* when *by* does not follow **4** to bring forth; produce or yield [fruit-*bearing* trees, coal-*bearing* strata] **5** to support or hold up; sustain **6** to sustain the burden of; take on; take care of [to *bear* the cost] **7** *a)* to undergo successfully; withstand; endure [her work won't *bear* scrutiny] *b)* to put up with; tolerate [she can't *bear* him] **8** to call for; require [his actions *bear* watching] **9** to carry or conduct (oneself) **10** to carry over or hold (a sentiment) [to *bear* a grudge] **11** to bring and tell (a message, tales, etc.) **12** to move or push as if carrying [the crowd *bore* us along] **13** to give, offer, or supply [to *bear* witness] —*vi.* **1** to be productive [the tree *bears* well] **2** *a)* to lie in a given direction [the lighthouse *bears* due east] *b)* to point or be aimed toward (with *on* or *upon*) [artillery deployed to *bear* on the fort] *c)* to move in a given direction [*bear* right at the corner] **3** to have bearing (*on*); have a relation [his story *bears* on the crime] **4** to tolerate; put up patiently (*with*) **5** to be oppressive; weigh [grief *bears* heavily on her] —**bear a hand 1** to give help **2** *Naut.* get to work! help out! work faster! —**bear down 1** to press or push down; exert pressure **2** to make a strong effort —**bear down on 1** to press down on; exert pressure on **2** to make a strong effort toward accomplishing **3** to come or go toward; closely approach —**bear out** to show to be true; support or confirm —**bear up** to endure, as under a strain; keep up one's spirits —**bring to bear on** (or **upon**) to cause to have an effect on [he *brought* his influence *to bear on* the lawmakers]

SYN.—**bear** implies a putting up with something that distresses, annoys, pains, etc., without suggesting the way in which one sustains the imposition; **suffer** suggests passive acceptance of or resignation to that which is painful or unpleasant; **endure** implies a holding up against prolonged pain, distress, etc. and stresses stamina or patience; **tolerate** and the more informal **stand** both imply self-imposed restraint of one's opposition to what is offensive or repugnant; **brook**, a literary word, is usually used in the negative, suggesting determined refusal to put up with what is distasteful See also **carry**

bear[2] (ber) *n., pl.* **bears** or **bear** ⟦ME *bere* < OE *bera* < IE **bheros*, brown animal < base **bher-*, brown (> BROWN, BEAVER[1], L *fiber*): orig. euphemism for taboo name prob. seen in L *ursus*⟧ **1** any of a family (Ursidae) of large, heavy, omnivorous carnivores that walk flat on the soles of their feet and have shaggy fur and a very short tail: bears are native to temperate and arctic zones **2** a person who is clumsy, rude, gruff, churlish, etc. **3** ⟦short for *bearskin jobber* < phr. *to sell the bearskin*, i.e., to sell the skin before the bear is caught⟧ an investor who sells stocks, commodities, etc. in the belief that their price will fall: opposed to BULL[1] (sense 3) ☆**4** [Slang] a difficult task [checking these computer files is a real *bear*] —*adj.* falling in price [a *bear* market] —**be a bear for punishment** to be able to withstand much rough treatment; be rugged, tough, determined, etc. —**the Bear** the constellation Ursa Major or Ursa Minor —**bear′like′** *adj.*

Bear (ber) ⟦so named from the grizzly *bears* once abundant in the region⟧ river flowing from the Uinta Mountains through Utah, Wyo., & Ida. into Great Salt Lake: *c.* 350 mi (563 km)

bear·a·ble (-ə bəl) *adj.* that can be borne or endured; tolerable —**bear′a·bly** *adv.*

bear·bait·ing (-bāt′iŋ) *n.* an old form of diversion in which dogs were made to torment a chained bear

bear·ber·ry (-ber′ē) *n., pl.* **-ries** any of a genus (*Arctostaphylos*, esp. *A. uva-ursi*) of trailing plants of the heath family, having small, leathery leaves, white or pinkish flowers, and red berries

bear·cat (-kat′) *n.* ⟦BEAR[2] + CAT[1] (descriptive)⟧ [Informal] **1** any of various medium-sized carnivores, esp. the wolverine or binturong: not a technical term ☆**2** a person or thing having exceptional power, energy, ferocity, etc.

beard (bird) *n.* ⟦ME & OE < IE **bhardhā* > L *barba*, Russ *boroda*, Gmc **barda*, Ger *bart*⟧ **1** the hair growing on the lower part of a man's face; whiskers **2** this hair, esp. on the chin and cheek, when worn long or trimmed in various shapes **3** any beardlike part, as of certain animals **4** a hairy outgrowth on the head of certain grains, grasses, etc.; awn **5** anything that projects like a beard, as a barb or hook **6** the part of a printing type that lies between the face and shoulder ☆**7** [Slang] a person who acts as a COVER (*n.* 7) for another in public settings; specif., one who assumes the role of spouse or sweetheart so as to conceal the homosexuality of a well-known person —*vt.* **1** to face or oppose courageously or brazenly, as if grasping by the beard; defy **2** to provide with a beard —**beard′ed** *adj.*

Beard (bird) **1 Charles Austin** 1874-1948; U.S. historian **2 Daniel Carter** 1850-1941; U.S. writer & illustrator: a founder of the Boy Scouts of America **3 Mary** 1876-1958; U.S. historian: collaborated with husband Charles Austin

bearded collie any of a breed of sturdy, medium-sized dogs, having a shaggy coat and a beardlike growth of hair on the chin: originally bred in Scotland for herding

bearded vulture LAMMERGEIER

beard·less (bird′lis) *adj.* **1** having no beard **2** too young to have a beard **3** young, callow, etc.

Beards·ley (birdz′lē), **Aubrey (Vincent)** 1872-98; Eng. artist & illustrator

☆**beard·tongue** (bird′tuŋ′) *n.* ⟦so named from the bearded, tonguelike stamen⟧ PENSTEMON

bear·er (ber′ər) *n.* **1** a person or thing that bears, carries, or supports **2** a plant or tree that produces fruit or blooms **3** [Rare] a pallbearer **4** a person presenting for payment a check, note, money order, etc. —*adj.* payable to the bearer [*bearer* bonds]

bear garden 1 a place for bearbaiting or similar pastimes **2** any rough, noisy, rowdy place

☆**bear·grass** (ber′gras′) *n.* **1** any of several plants (esp. genera *Yucca* and *Nolina*) of the agave family, with a thick tuft of swordlike leaves at the base of a flowering stalk **2** a Western American plant (*Xerophyllum tenax*) of the lily family, with stiff, grasslike leaves and spikes of small, white flowers

bear hug an extremely tight, rough embrace with the arms: often written **bear′hug′** *n.*

bear·ing (ber′iŋ) *n.* **1** way of carrying and conducting oneself; carriage; manner; mien **2** a support or supporting part **3** *a)* the act, power, or period of producing young, fruit, etc. *b)* ability to produce *c)* anything borne or produced, as a crop, fruit, etc. **4** an enduring; endurance **5** *a)* direction relative to one's own position or to the compass *b)* [*pl.*] position, as of a ship, established by determining the bearing from it of several known points *c)* [*pl.*] awareness or recognition of one's position or situation [to lose one's *bearings*] **6** relevant meaning; application; relation [the evidence had no *bearing* on the case] **7** *Archit.* the part of a lintel or beam that rests on supports **8** *Heraldry* any figure on the field; charge **9** *Mech.* any part of a machine in or on which another part revolves, slides, etc. —*adj.* that bears, or supports, weight [a *bearing* wall]

SYN.—**bearing**, in this comparison denoting manner of carrying or conducting oneself, refers to characteristic physical and mental posture; **carriage**, also applied to posture, specif. stresses the physical aspects of a person's bearing [an erect *carriage*]; **demeanor** refers to behavior as expressing one's attitude or a specified personality trait [a demure *demeanor*]; **mien**, a literary word, refers to one's bearing and manner [a man of melancholy *mien*]; **deportment** refers to one's behavior with reference to standards of conduct or social conventions; **manner** is applied to customary or distinctive attitude, actions, speech, etc. and, in the plural, refers to behavior conforming with polite conventions

bearing rein CHECKREIN

bear·ish (ber′ish) *adj.* **1** bearlike; rude, rough, surly, etc. **2** *a)* of, causing, or resulting from expectations of lower prices for stocks, bonds, etc. *b)* pessimistic —**bear′ish·ly** *adv.* —**bear′ish·ness** *n.*

Bé·arn (bā ärn′, -är′) historical region in SW France, in the Pyrenees

bé·ar·naise sauce (bā′är nāz′) ⟦< Fr *béarnaise*, fem. of *béarnais*, of prec.⟧ a creamy sauce, esp. for meat or fish, made of butter and egg yolks and flavored with wine, vinegar, shallots, and herbs

bear's-breech (berz′brēch′) *n.* ACANTHUS (sense 1): also **bear's breech**

bear's-ear (-ir′) *n.* AURICULA: also **bear's ear**

bear·skin (ber′skin′) *n.* **1** the pelt, fur, or hide of a bear **2** anything made from this, as a rug or coat **3** a tall fur cap worn as part of some uniforms

☆**bear·wood** (-wood′) *n.* CASCARA (sense 1)

beast (bēst) *n.* ⟦ME & OFr *beste* < L *bestia* < ? IE base **dheus-* > DEER⟧ **1** any animal as distinguished from a human being [neither man nor *beast*] **2** any large, four-footed animal; sometimes, specif., a domesticated animal **3** qualities or impulses like an animal's [to bring out the *beast* in him] **4** a person who is gross, brutal, vile, etc.

beast·ie (bēs′tē) *n.* [Chiefly Scot.] a little animal

beast·ings (bēs′tiŋz) *pl.n. alt. sp. of* BEESTINGS

beast·ly (bēst′lē) *adj.* **-li·er, -li·est 1** of, like, or characteristic of a beast; bestial, brutal, etc. **2** [Informal] disagreeable; unpleasant —*adv.* **-li·er, -li·est** [Brit. Informal] very [*beastly* bad news] —**beast′li·ness** *n.*

beast of burden any animal, as a donkey, used for carrying loads

beast of prey any animal, esp. a mammal, that kills other animals for food

beat (bēt) *vt.* **beat, beat′en, beat′ing** ⟦ME *beten* < OE *beatan* < IE **bhaut-* < base **bhau-*, **bhū-*, to strike, beat > BEETLE[2], BUTT[1] & BUTT[2], L *fustis*, a club⟧ **1** to hit or strike repeatedly; pound **2** to punish by striking repeatedly and hard; whip, flog, spank, etc. **3** to dash repeatedly against [waves *beat* the shore] **4** *a)* to form by repeated treading or riding [to *beat* a path through grass] *b)* to keep walking on [to *beat* the pavements] **5** to shape or flatten by hammering; forge **6** to mix by stirring or striking repeatedly with a utensil; whip (an egg, cream, etc.) **7** to move (esp. wings) up and down; flap; flail **8** to hunt through; search [the posse *beat* the countryside for the fugitive] **9** to make, force, or drive by or as by hitting, flailing, or pounding [to *beat* one's way through a crowd, to *beat* chalk dust from erasers] **10** *a)* to defeat in a race, contest, or struggle; overcome *b)* to outdo or surpass *c)* to act, arrive, or finish before **11** to mark (time or rhythm) by tapping, etc. **12** to sound or signal, as by a drumbeat **13** [Informal] to baffle or puzzle ☆**14** [Informal] to cheat or trick ☆**15** [Slang] to avoid the penalties associated with (a charge, indictment, etc.); escape (a rap) —*vi.* **1** to strike, hit, or dash repeatedly and, usually, hard **2** to move or sound rhythmically; throb, pulsate, vibrate, tick, etc. **3** to strike about in or hunt through underbrush, woods, etc. for game **4** to take beating or stirring [this cream doesn't *beat* well] **5** *a)* to make a sound by being struck, as a drum *b)* to beat a drum, as to sound a signal **6** [Informal] to win **7** *Naut.* to progress by tacking into the wind **8** *Radio* to combine two waves of different frequencies, thus producing an additional frequency equal to the difference between these —*n.* **1** a beating, as of the heart **2** any of a series of blows or strokes **3** any of a series of movements or sounds; throb **4** *a)* a habitual path or round of duty [a policeman's *beat*] *b)* the subject or area assigned regularly to a news writer **5** *a)* the unit of musical rhythm [four *beats* to a measure] *b)* the accent or stress in the rhythm of verse or music *c)* the gesture of the hand, baton, etc. used to mark this ☆**6** [Informal] a person or thing that surpasses [you never saw the *beat* of it] ☆**7** *a)* BEATNIK *b)* [*often* **B-**] any of a group of U.S. writers in the 1950s and 1960s whose work grew out of and expressed beat attitudes: see BEAT (*adj.* 2) **8** *Acoustics* the regularly recurring fluctuation in loudness of sound produced by two simultaneous tones of nearly equal frequency **9** *Ballet* a movement in which one leg is brought in contact with the other or both legs are brought together in the air ☆**10** *Journalism* a reporting of a news item ahead of all rivals;

scoop 11 *Naut.* a tack into the wind 12 *Radio* one cycle of a frequency formed by beating —*adj.* 1 [Informal] tired out; exhausted, physically or emotionally ☆2 of or belonging to a group of young persons, esp. of the 1950s, rebelling against conventional attitudes, dress, speech, etc., largely as an expression of social disillusionment —**beat about** to hunt or look through or around —**beat back** to force to retreat; drive back —**beat down** 1 to shine steadily with dazzling light and intense heat, as the sun 2 to put down; suppress 3 [Informal] to force to a lower price —☆**beat it!** [Slang] go away! —**beat off** 1 to drive back; repel ☆2 [Slang] to masturbate: said of a male: somewhat vulgar —**beat one's meat** [Slang] to masturbate: said of a male: considered vulgar by many —☆**beat out** *Baseball* to reach first base safely on (a bunt or grounder), as before an infielder's throw —☆**beat up (on)** [Slang] to give a beating to; thrash —**on the beat** in tempo —**to beat the band (**or **hell, the devil,** etc.**)** [Slang] with great energy and vigor; fast and furiously

SYN.—**beat**, the most general word in this comparison, conveys the basic idea of hitting or striking repeatedly, whether with the hands, the feet, an implement, etc.; **pound** suggests heavier, more effective blows than **beat** [to *pound* with a hammer]; **pummel** implies the beating of a person with the fists and suggests a continuous, indiscriminate rain of damaging blows; **thrash**, originally referring to the beating of grain with a flail, suggests similar broad, swinging strokes, as in striking a person repeatedly with a stick, etc.; **flog** implies a punishing by the infliction of repeated blows with a stick, strap, whip, etc.; **whip**, often used as an equivalent of **flog**, specifically suggests lashing strokes or motions; **maul** implies the infliction of repeated heavy blows so as to bruise or lacerate. Most of these terms are used loosely, esp. by journalists, in describing a decisive victory in a contest

☆**beat·box** (bēt′bäks′) *n.* 1 [Slang] DRUM MACHINE 2 [Slang] BOOMBOX 3 a form of HIP HOP (sense 1) in which vocal imitations of the beats of percussive rhythms are produced by using the mouth and tongue to make thumping, popping, or hissing sounds —*vi.* to perform beatbox Sometimes written **beat box**

beat·en (bēt′'n) *adj.* ⟦pp. of BEAT⟧ 1 struck with repeated blows; whipped 2 shaped or made thin by hammering 3 flattened by treading; much traveled [a *beaten* path] 4 *a)* defeated *b)* crushed in spirit by defeat 5 tired out 6 searched through for game —**off the beaten track (**or **path)** 1 away or apart from others of its kind 2 unusual, unfamiliar, original, etc.

beat·er (bēt′ər) *n.* 1 a person or thing that beats 2 an implement or utensil for beating 3 any of various implements for playing a percussion instrument, as a drumstick or mallet 4 a person employed to drive game from cover for hunters ☆5 [Slang] an automobile characterized by the effects of much hard use

be·a·tif·ic (bē′ə tif′ik) *adj.* ⟦ME < ML(Ec) *beatificus* < LL(Ec) *beatificare*: see BEATIFY⟧ 1 making blissful or blessed 2 showing happiness or delight; blissful [a *beatific* smile] —**be′a·tif′i·cal·ly** *adv.*

be·at·i·fi·ca·tion (bē at′ə fi kā′shən) *n.* ⟦Fr *béatification* < MFr: see fol.⟧ 1 a beatifying or being beatified 2 *R.C.Ch.* *a)* investigation, now formal, of whether a deceased person should be publicly declared to be in heaven and so entitled to some public veneration: an affirmative decision may lead to canonization *b)* a public declaration, now made only by the pope, ratifying an affirmative decision arrived at through this investigation

be·at·i·fy (bē at′ə fī′) *vt.* **-fied′**, **-fy′ing** ⟦MFr < ML(Ec) *beatificare* < LL(Ec) < *beatus*, happy, blessed < L (see BONUS) + *facere*, to make, DO[1]⟧ 1 to make blissfully happy 2 *R.C.Ch.* to declare (a deceased person), by public statement, to be in heaven and entitled to some public veneration: see BEATIFICATION (sense 2*b*)

beat·ing (bēt′iŋ) *n.* 1 the act of a person or thing that beats 2 a whipping or thrashing 3 a throbbing; pulsation 4 a defeat

be·at·i·tude (bē at′ə to͞od′, -tyo͞od′) *n.* ⟦LME < MFr *béatitude* or ML(Ec) *beatitudo*, happiness, beatitude < LL(Ec) < L, happiness < *beatus*, happy, blessed: see BONUS⟧ perfect blessedness or happiness —**the Beatitudes** the pronouncements in the Sermon on the Mount, which begin "Blessed are the poor in spirit": Matt. 5:3-12

Beat·les (bēt′'lz), **The** Brit. rock group (1961-70) including John Lennon (1940-80), Ringo Starr (born *Richard Starkey*) (1940-), (James) Paul McCartney (1942- ; knighted 1997), & George Harrison (1943-2001)

☆**beat·nik** (bēt′nik) *n.* ⟦BEAT, *adj.* 2 + -NIK⟧ a member of a group of young persons, esp. of the 1950s, rebelling against conventional attitudes, dress, speech, etc., largely as an expression of social disillusionment

Bea·ton (bēt′'n), Sir **Cecil (Walter Hardy)** 1904-80; Brit. photographer & theatrical designer

Be·a·trice[1] (bē′ə tris) *n.* ⟦It < L *beatrix*, she who makes happy < *beatus*, happy, blessed: see BEATITUDE⟧ a feminine name: dim. *Bea*; var. *Beatrix*

Be·a·trice[2] (bē′ə tris; *It* be′ä trē′che) Florentine woman (*Beatrice Portinari*, 1266-90) loved by Dante and immortalized in his *Divine Comedy*

Beat·ty (bēt′ē), **David** 1st Earl Beatty 1871-1936; Brit. admiral

☆**beat-up** (bēt′up′) *adj.* [Slang] dilapidated, battered, shabby, deteriorated, etc.

beau (bō) *n., pl.* **beaus** or **beaux** (bōz, bō) ⟦Fr, a dandy < *beau, bel*, pretty < L *bellus*, pretty⟧ 1 [Archaic] a dandy 2 [Old-fashioned] the sweetheart or courter of a woman or girl

Beau Brum·mell[1] (bō′ brum′əl) ⟦after fol.⟧ any dandy or fop

Beau Brummell[2] (name for *George Bryan Brummell*) 1778-1840; Eng. gentleman famous for his fashionable dress and manners

beau·coup[1] (bō ko͞o′) *n.* ⟦Fr⟧ very much; very many —*adv.* very much

beau·coup[2] (bō′ko͞o′) *adj.* ⟦< prec.⟧ [Slang] a lot of; much or many [*beaucoup* dollars in the bank]

Beau·fort scale (bō′fərt) ⟦after Sir Francis *Beaufort* (1774-1857), Brit naval officer who devised the original scale (1806)⟧ a scale of wind force and speed: see the Reference Supplement

Beau·fort Sea (bō′fərt) ⟦named in honor of Sir Francis *Beaufort* (see prec.)⟧ part of the Arctic Ocean, north of Alaska & northwest of Canada

beau geste (bō zhest′) *pl.* ***beaux gestes*** (bō zhest′) ⟦Fr⟧ 1 a fine or beautiful gesture 2 an act or offer that seems fine, noble, etc., but is empty

Beau·har·nais (bō är ne′), **Josephine de** *see* JOSEPHINE[2]; *see also* HORTENSE[2]

beau i·de·al ⟦Fr *beau idéal*⟧ 1 ideal beauty 2 the perfect type or conception: a sense due to mistranslation [the *beau ideal* of fashion]

Beau·jo·lais (bō′zhə lā′) *n.* [*occas.* **b-**] 1 a light, fruity red wine from the Beaujolais district in S Burgundy 2 a similar type of red wine made elsewhere

Beau·mar·chais (bō mär she′), **Pierre Au·gus·tin Ca·ron de** (pyer ō güs tan′ kä rôn′ də) 1732-99; Fr. dramatist

beau monde (bō′ mänd′; *Fr* bō mōnd′) ⟦Fr, lit., elegant world⟧ fashionable society

Beau·mont[1] (bō′mänt′), **Francis** 1584-1616; Eng. dramatist who collaborated with John Fletcher

Beau·mont[2] (bō′mänt′) ⟦after J. *Beaumont*: so named by his brother-in-law, Henry Millard, who purchased land for a town site (1835)⟧ city in SE Tex., on the Neches River

Beau·port (bō pôr′) borough of Quebec City

Beau·re·gard (bō′rə gärd′, bôr′ə-), **P(ierre) G(ustave) T(outant) de** 1818-93; Confederate general

☆**beaut** (byo͞ot′) *n.* [Slang] one that is beautiful or superlative: often used ironically [his alibi was a *beaut*]

beau·te·ous (byo͞ot′ē əs) *adj.* ⟦ME: see BEAUTY & -OUS⟧ beautiful —*SYN.* BEAUTIFUL —**beau′te·ous·ly** *adv.*

☆**beau·ti·cian** (byo͞o tish′ən) *n.* a person who does or is trained to do hairstyling, manicures, etc. in a beauty salon; cosmetologist

beau·ti·ful (byo͞ot′ə fəl; *often* byo͞ot′ē-) *adj.* having beauty; very pleasing to the eye, ear, mind, etc. —*interj.* used to express approval or pleasure —**the beautiful** 1 the quality of beauty 2 those who are beautiful —**beau′ti·ful·ly** *adv.*

SYN.—**beautiful** is applied to that which gives the highest degree of pleasure to the senses or to the mind and suggests that the object of delight approximates one's conception of an ideal; **lovely** refers to that which delights by inspiring affection or warm admiration; **handsome** implies attractiveness by reason of pleasing proportions, symmetry, elegance, etc. and carries connotations of masculinity, dignity, or impressiveness; **pretty** implies a dainty, delicate, or graceful quality in that which pleases and carries connotations of femininity or diminutiveness; **comely** applies to persons only and suggests a wholesome attractiveness of form and features rather than a high degree of beauty; **fair** suggests beauty that is fresh, bright, or flawless and, when applied to persons, is used esp. of complexion and features; **good-looking** is closely equivalent to **handsome** or **pretty**, suggesting a pleasing appearance but not expressing the fine distinctions of either word; **beauteous**, equivalent to **beautiful** in poetry and lofty prose, is now often used in humorously disparaging references to beauty —*ANT.* **ugly**

beautiful people [*also* **B- P-**] wealthy, fashionable people of the leisure class: with *the*

beau·ti·fy (byo͞ot′ə fī′) *vt.* **-fied′**, **-fy′ing** to make beautiful or more beautiful —*vi.* to become beautiful —*SYN.* ADORN —**beau′ti·fi·ca′tion** (-fi kā′shən) *n.* —**beau′ti·fi′er** *n.*

beau·ty (byo͞ot′ē) *n., pl.* **-ties** ⟦ME *beaute* < OFr *bealte* < VL **bellitas* < L *bellus*, pretty, lovely⟧ 1 the quality attributed to whatever pleases or satisfies the senses or mind, as by line, color, form, texture, proportion, rhythmic motion, tone, etc., or by behavior, attitude, etc. 2 a thing or person having this quality; specif., a very good-looking woman 3 good looks 4 any very attractive feature —*adj.* of or having to do with cosmetics, hairstyling, etc. [*beauty* products]

beauty bush a hardy shrub (*Kolkwitzia amabilis*) of the honeysuckle family, having tubular pink flowers with white bristly hairs on the ovary

beauty contest 1 a competition in which women are rated on the basis of physical beauty, and often also talent, personality, etc.: also **beauty pageant** 2 any competition based on superficial criteria

☆**beauty culture** the skill or occupation of a beautician

beauty mark a natural mark or mole on the skin

beauty quark *Particle Physics* BOTTOM QUARK

beauty queen a woman who has won a beauty contest

☆**beauty salon (***or* **shop, parlor,** *etc.***)** a place where people, esp. women, go for hair styling and tinting, manicures, etc.

beauty sleep any extra sleep regarded as necessary to sustain a healthy, attractive appearance: typically a humorous usage

beauty spot 1 a tiny black patch applied to the face or back to emphasize the beauty or whiteness of the skin: a former fashion among women 2 BEAUTY MARK 3 any place noted for its beauty

Beau·voir (bō vwär′), **Si·mone de** (sē môn′ də) 1908-86; Fr. existentialist writer & feminist

beaux (bōz; *Fr* bō) *n.* ⟦Fr⟧ *alt. pl. of* BEAU

Beaux Arts (bō zär′) ⟦after the *École des Beaux-Arts*, School of (the) Fine

Arts, in Paris, influential in promoting this style: see fol.⟧ [*also* **b- a-**] designating or of an ornate style of architecture of the late 19th and early 20th cent. characterized by classical forms, massive proportions, and lavish, usually symmetrical, detailing

beaux-arts (bō zär′; *E* bō zär′) ***pl.n.*** ⟦Fr⟧ the fine arts

beaux es·prits (bō zes prē′) ⟦Fr⟧ *pl. of* BEL ESPRIT

bea·ver[1] (bē′vər) ***n.*** ⟦ME *bever* < OE *beofor:* for IE base see BEAR[2]⟧ **1** *a) pl.* **-vers** or **-ver** any of a family (Castoridae) of large rodents with soft, brown fur, chisel-like teeth, webbed hind feet, and a flat, broad tail: they often gnaw trees down and build canals and dams to form **beaver ponds** in which they build dry, dome-shaped, island lodges having underwater entrances *b)* its fur **2** a man's high silk hat, originally made of this fur **3** a heavy cloth of felted wool, used for overcoats, etc. ☆**4** [Slang] the female genitals: usually considered somewhat vulgar —***adj.*** ☆[Slang] designating or of a film sequence, photograph, etc. in which the female genitals are exposed: usually considered somewhat vulgar [*beaver* shot] —***vi.*** ☆to work hard, constantly, conscientiously, etc.: usually with *away*

bea·ver[2] (bē′vər) ***n.*** ⟦ME *bavier* < OFr *baviere,* beaver of a helmet, orig., bib < *baver,* to drivel < *bave,* saliva, foam⟧ **1** a movable piece of armor on the lower part of a medieval helmet, for protecting the mouth and chin **2** later, the visor of a helmet

☆**bea·ver·board** (-bôrd′) ***n.*** ⟦< *Beaverboard,* former trademark⟧ [*sometimes* **B-**] board made of compressed wood fiber, used for walls, partitions, etc.

Bea·ver·brook (bē′vər bro͝ok′), 1st Baron (*William Maxwell Aitkin*) 1879-1964; Brit. newspaper publisher & statesman, born in Canada

be·bee·rine (bi bē′rēn′, -rin) ***n.*** ⟦< fol. + -INE[3]⟧ an antimalarial, alkaloid drug, $C_{36}H_{38}N_2O_6$, similar to quinine, obtained from the bark of the bebeeru tree

be·bee·ru (bi bē′ro͞o′) ***n.*** ⟦< native name in Guiana⟧ a tropical South American evergreen tree (*Nectandra rodioei*) of the laurel family

Be·bel (bā′bəl), **(Ferdinand) Au·gust** (ou go͞ost′) 1840-1913; Ger. socialist leader & writer

☆**be·bop** (bē′bäp′) ***n.*** ⟦? echoic of sound made on a trumpet⟧ BOP[2]

be·calm (bē käm′, bi-) ***vt.*** **1** to make quiet or still; calm **2** to make (a sailing vessel) motionless from lack of wind: usually in passive voice

be·came (bē kām′, bi-) ***vi., vt. pt. of*** BECOME

be·cause (bē kôz′, -kuz′; bi-) ***conj.*** ⟦ME *bi cause* < *bi,* BY + CAUSE⟧ **1** for the reason or cause that; on account of the fact that; since **2** the reason that; that: used to introduce a noun clause —**because of** by reason of; on account of

bec·ca·fi·co (bek′ə fē′kō) ***n., pl.*** **-cos** ⟦It < *beccare,* to peck + *fico,* a fig⟧ any of several small European songbirds, esp. certain warblers (genus *Sylvia*), eaten as a delicacy esp. in Italy

bé·cha·mel (bā′shə mel′) ***n.*** ⟦Fr, after Louis de *Béchamel,* steward to Louis XIV⟧ a basic white sauce made of milk, butter, flour, and, sometimes, cream

be·chance (bē chans′, bi-) ***vt., vi.*** **-chanced′**, **-chanc′ing** [Archaic] to happen (to); befall

bêche-de-mer (besh də mer′) ***n.*** ⟦Fr, worm of the sea; altered < Port *bicho do mar,* sea slug⟧ **1** *pl.* **bêches-de-mer** (besh də mer′) TREPANG **2** a mixed trade language, largely a pidgin based on English, spoken in island areas of the SW Pacific

Be·chet (bə shā′), **Sidney (Joseph)** 1897-1959; U.S. jazz saxophonist & composer

Bech·u·a·na (bech′o͞o ä′nə) ***n.*** **1** *pl.* **-nas** or **-na** a member of a people living in Botswana **2** the Bantu language of this people

Bech·u·a·na·land (bech′o͞o än′ə land′) former British territory (1884-1966) in S Africa: now the country of BOTSWANA

beck[1] (bek) ***n.*** ⟦< BECKON⟧ a gesture of the hand, head, etc., meant to summon — ***vt., vi.*** [Archaic] to summon by a beck; beckon —**at the beck and call of** at the service of; obedient to the wishes of

beck[2] (bek) ***n.*** ⟦ME *bek* < ON *bekkr,* a brook < IE base **bhog-,* flowing water > Ger *bach,* MIr *bual,* E dial. *bache*⟧ [Dial., Chiefly Brit.] a little stream, esp. one with a rocky bottom

beck·et (bek′ət) ***n.*** ⟦< ?⟧ a contrivance, as a looped rope, large hook and eye, or grommet, used for securing loose ropes, oars, spars, etc.

Beck·et (bek′ət), Saint **Thomas** (1118?-70); Eng. prelate: archbishop of Canterbury: murdered after opposing Henry II: his day is Dec. 29: sometimes **Saint Thomas à Becket**

becket bend SHEET BEND

Beck·ett (bek′ət), **Samuel** 1906-89; Ir. poet, novelist, & playwright in France, writing mostly in French

Beck·ford (bek′fərd), **William** 1759?-1844; Eng. writer

beck·on (bek′ən) ***vi., vt.*** ⟦ME *beknen* < OE *beacnian, becnian;* akin to OS *boknian,* OHG *bouhnen* < Gmc **bauhnan* < **baukna,* BEACON⟧ **1** to call or summon by a silent gesture **2** to seem enticing (to); attract; lure [the woods *beckon*] —***n.*** a summoning gesture

be·cloud (bē kloud′, bi-) ***vt.*** **1** to cloud over; darken **2** to confuse; muddle

be·come (bē kum′, bi-) ***vi.*** **-came′**, **-come′**, **-com′ing** ⟦ME *bicumen* < OE *becuman:* see BE- & COME⟧ **1** to come to be [to *become* ill] **2** to grow to be; change or develop into by growth [the tadpole *becomes* a frog] —***vt.*** **1** to befit; suit [modesty *becomes* her] **2** to be right for or suitable to in appearance [that hat *becomes* you] —**become of** to happen to; be the fate of

be·com·ing (bē kum′iŋ, bi-) ***adj.*** **1** that is suitable or appropriate; fit **2** suitable to the wearer [a *becoming* gown] —***n.*** the fact of coming into existence —**be·com′ing·ly** ***adv.***

bec·que·rel (bek′ə rel′) ***n.*** ⟦after Antoine Henri BECQUEREL⟧ the basic unit of radioactivity in the SI system, equal to a rate of decay of one disintegration per second (2.7×10^{-11} curies): abbrev. *Bq*

Bec·que·rel (be krel′; *E* bek′ə rel′) **1 A·lex·an·dre Ed·mond** (á lek sändr′ ed mōn′) 1820-91; Fr. physicist: father of Antoine Henri **2 An·toine Cé·sar** (än twán′ sā zár′) 1788-1878; Fr. physicist: pioneer in electrochemistry: father of Alexandre **3 Antoine Hen·ri** (än rē′) 1852-1908; Fr. physicist: discoverer of radioactivity in uranium

Becquerel rays ⟦after Antoine Henri BECQUEREL⟧ rays given off by radioactive substances: now called **gamma rays**

bed (bed) ***n.*** ⟦ME & OE < IE base **bhedh-,* to dig > Ger *bett,* L *fossa,* ditch, Welsh *bedd,* Bret *béz,* a grave; orig. sense, "a hollow in the ground for sleeping"⟧ **1** a thing for sleeping or resting on; specif., a piece of furniture consisting usually of a bedstead, bedspring, mattress, and bedding **2** BEDSTEAD **3** BEDTIME **4** *a)* any place used for sleeping or reclining *b)* such a place regarded as the scene of sexual intercourse or procreation **5** accommodations for an occupant: often used in comb. [a 100-*bed* hospital] **6** *a)* a plot of soil where plants are raised *b)* the flowers or vegetables growing in this **7** *a)* the bottom of a river, lake, etc. *b)* a place on the ocean floor where something grows in abundance [oyster *bed*] **8** an enclosing substance, as rock in which shells, minerals, etc. are lodged **9** any flat surface used as a foundation or support, as the earth, gravel, etc. under the rails and ties of a railroad **10** *a)* a layer of cement or mortar in which stone or brick is laid *b)* the underside of a brick, slate, or tile **11** a pile or heap resembling a bed, esp. in softness or shape [a *bed* of leaves] **12** a geologic layer; stratum [a *bed* of coal] ☆**13** the flat surface on which cargo is placed, as in a pickup or flatbed —***vt.*** **bed′ded, bed′ding** **1** to provide with a sleeping place **2** to put to bed **3** to have sexual intercourse with **4** to fix or place firmly; embed **5** to plant or arrange in a bed of earth **6** to make (earth) into a bed for plants **7** to lay out flat like a bed; arrange in layers —***vi.*** **1** to go to bed; rest; sleep **2** to form in layers; stratify —**be brought to bed (of)** [Archaic] to give birth (to) —**bed and board** **1** sleeping accommodations and meals **2** home; the married state —☆**bed down** to prepare and use a sleeping place —**get up on the wrong side of the bed** to be cross or grouchy —**in (or into) bed** [Informal] in (or into) a close, collaborative relationship regarded as improper, undesirable, etc. [city officials *in bed* with organized crime] —**put to bed** **1** to get (a child, invalid, etc.) ready for sleep, as in a bed **2** to lock (type, plates, etc.) into a form and place on a printing press **3** to get an edition (of a newspaper, etc.) ready for printing —**take to one's bed** to go to bed because of illness, etc.

BEd or **B.Ed.** *abbrev.* Bachelor of Education

bed-and-break·fast (bed′n brek′fəst) ***adj.*** designating or of accommodations, as in a hotel or private home, in which breakfast is provided as part of the price —***n.*** an establishment featuring such accommodations Also **bed and breakfast**

be·daub (bē dôb′, bi-) ***vt.*** **1** to make daubs on; smudge or smear over **2** to ornament showily; overdecorate

be·daz·zle (bē daz′əl, bi-) ***vt.*** **-daz′zled**, **-daz′zling** to dazzle thoroughly; bewilder; confuse

☆**bed board** a thin, stiff board placed on a bed under the mattress to lend added support for the body

bed·bug (bed′bug′) ***n.*** any of various members of a family (Cimicidae) of wingless, bloodsucking hemipteran insects, esp. the species (*Cimex lectularius*) with a broad, flat, reddish-brown body and an unpleasant odor that infests beds, furniture, walls, etc., is active mainly at night, and may transmit a variety of diseases

bed·cham·ber (-chām′bər) ***n.*** [Now Rare] a bedroom

bed check the act or an instance of checking that all persons are in their beds [a nightly *bed check* in the dormitory]

bed·clothes (-klōthz′, -klōz′) ***pl.n.*** sheets, blankets, comforters, etc. used on a bed

bed·cov·er (-kuv′ər) ***n.*** a cover for a bed; coverlet; bedspread

bed·der (-ər) ***n.*** a plant suitable for a garden bed

bed·ding (-iŋ) ***n.*** **1** mattresses and bedclothes **2** straw, grass, etc., used to bed animals **3** a bottom layer; base **4** *Geol.* stratification —***adj.*** suitable for planting in a garden bed

bedding plane *Geol.* the surface separating two successive layers of stratified rock

bed·dy-bye (bed′ē bī′) ***n.*** ⟦< BED + -Y[1] + BYE(-BYE)⟧ bed or bedtime: originally a nursery word, now facetious

Bede (bēd), Saint (A.D. 673-735); Eng. historian & theologian: his day is May 27: called *the Venerable Bede*

be·deck (bē dek′, bi-) ***vt.*** to cover with decorations; adorn —***SYN.*** ADORN

bede·house (bēd′hous′) ***n.*** BEADHOUSE

bedes·man (bēdz′mən) ***n., pl.*** **-men** (-mən) BEADSMAN

bedes·wom·an (-wo͝om′ən) ***n., pl.*** **-wom′en** (-wim′in) BEADSWOMAN

be·dev·il (bē dev′əl, bi-) ***vt.*** **-iled** or **-illed**, **-il·ing** or **-il·ling** **1** to plague diabolically; torment; harass **2** to possess as with a devil; bewitch **3** to confuse completely; muddle **4** to corrupt; spoil —**be·dev′il·ment** ***n.***

be·dew (bē do͞o′, -dyo͞o′; bi-) ***vt.*** to make wet with or as if with drops of dew

bed·fast (bed′fast′, -fäst′) ***adj.*** BEDRIDDEN

bed·fel·low (-fel′ō) ***n.*** **1** a person who shares one's bed **2** an associate, ally, confederate, etc.

Bed·ford (bed′fərd) **1** county seat of Bedfordshire **2** BEDFORDSHIRE

Bedford cord ⟦? after prec. or NEW BEDFORD⟧ a heavy cloth with vertical ribs, like corduroy

Bed·ford·shire (bed′fərd shir′, -shər) county in SE England: 477 sq mi (1,235 sq km)

be·dight (bē dīt′) *adj.* ⟦pp. of obs. *bedight* < ME *bidighten,* to equip, deck out < *bi-,* BE- + *dighten,* to prepare, set in order < OE *dihtan,* to arrange, compose, write < L *dictare*: see DICTATE⟧ [Archaic] bedecked; arrayed

be·dim (bē dim′, bi-) *vt.* **-dimmed′, -dim′ming** to make (the eyes or the vision) dim; darken or obscure

Bed·i·vere (bed′ə vir′) *n. Arthurian Legend* the loyal knight who is with the dying King Arthur and sees him off to Avalon

be·di·zen (bē dī′zən, bi-; *also,* -diz′ən) *vt.* ⟦BE- + DIZEN⟧ [Now Rare] to dress or decorate in a cheap, showy way —**be·di′zen·ment** *n.*

bed jacket a woman's short, loose upper garment sometimes worn in bed over a nightgown

bed·lam (bed′ləm) *n.* ⟦ME *Bedlam, Bethlem,* var. of BETHLEHEM⟧ **1** [**B-**] an old insane asylum (in full, *St. Mary of Bethlehem*), later a hospital for the mentally ill, in London **2** [Archaic] any insane asylum **3** any place or condition of noise and confusion

bed·lam·ite (-īt′) *n.* ⟦prec. + -ITE[2]⟧ [Archaic] an insane person; madman

bed linen bedsheets, pillowcases, etc., whether of linen or not

☆**bed liner** a stiff, durable plastic lining used to protect the bed and side walls of the cargo space of some pickup trucks

Bed·ling·ton terrier (bed′liŋ tən) ⟦after *Bedlington,* a town in England⟧ a blue or liver-colored, woolly-coated terrier resembling a small lamb

Bed·loe's Island (bed′lōz) ⟦after Isaac *Bedloe,* first owner⟧ *former name for* LIBERTY ISLAND

bed molding *Archit.* a molding below a projecting part, esp. between the corona and frieze

bed of roses [Informal] a situation or position of ease and luxury

Bed·ou·in (bed′o͞o in′) *n., pl.* **-ins** or **-in** ⟦Fr *bédouin* < Ar *badāwīn,* pl. of *badawī,* desert dweller < *badw,* desert⟧ [*also* **b-**] **1** an Arab of any of the nomadic desert peoples of Arabia, Syria, or N Africa **2** any wanderer or nomad —*adj.* of the Bedouins or their culture

bed·pan (bed′pan′) *n.* ☆a shallow pan for use as a toilet by a person confined to bed

bed·plate (-plāt′) *n.* a plate forming the base, as of a machine

bed·post (-pōst′) *n.* any of the vertical posts at the corners of some beds, often tall enough to support a canopy

be·drag·gle (bē drag′əl, bi-) *vt.* **-gled, -gling** to make wet, limp, and dirty, as by dragging through mire —**be·drag′gled** *adj.*

bed·rail (bed′rāl′) *n.* a rail along the side of a bed

bed rest a period of resting in bed

bed·rid·den (-rid′'n) *adj.* ⟦ME *bedrede(n)* < OE *bedreda* < *bed,* BED + *rida,* rider < *ridan,* to RIDE⟧ having to stay in bed, usually for a long period, because of illness, infirmity, etc.: sometimes **bed′rid′**

☆**bed·rock** (-räk′) *n.* **1** solid rock beneath the soil and superficial rock **2** a secure foundation **3** the very bottom **4** basic principles or facts

☆**bed·roll** (-rōl′) *n.* a portable roll of bedding, generally for sleeping outdoors

bed·room (-ro͞om′) *n.* a room with a bed, for sleeping in —*adj.* **1** having to do with sex or sexual affairs [*a bedroom* farce] **2** housing those who spend their days at work in a nearby metropolis [*bedroom* suburbs]

bed·sheet (-shēt′) *n.* a sheet for use on a bed

bed·side (-sīd′) *n.* the side of a bed; space beside a bed [a nurse at his *bedside*] —*adj.* near a bed [a *bedside* table]

bedside manner the way that a particular physician acts or behaves with his or her patients in treating them medically

bed-sit·ting room (bed′sit′iŋ) [Brit.] a combined bedroom and sitting room serving as a one-room apartment: also [Informal] **bed′-sit′** or **bed′-sit′ter** *n.*

bed skirt a decorative SKIRT (*n.* 3) hanging from the sides of a bed

bed·sore (-sôr′) *n.* a sore on the body of a bedridden person, caused by chafing or pressure

☆**bed·spread** (-spred′) *n.* a cover spread over the blanket on a bed, mainly for ornament

☆**bed·spring** (-spriŋ′) *n.* **1** a framework of springs placed in a bedstead to support the mattress **2** any of these springs

bed·stead (-sted′) *n.* ⟦BED + STEAD: orig., place occupied by a bed⟧ a framework for supporting the bedspring and mattress of a bed

bed·straw (-strô′) *n.* ⟦from its former use as straw for beds⟧ any of a genus (*Galium*) of small plants of the madder family, with whorled leaves and small flowers

bed·time (-tīm′) *n.* a person's usual time for going to bed

bedtime story a story told to children at bedtime

bed-wet·ting (-wet′iŋ) *n.* involuntary urination in bed while asleep, especially as a habitual problem —**bed′-wet′ter** *n.*

bee[1] (bē) *n.* ⟦ME < OE *beo* < IE base *bhei- > Ger *biene,* OPrus *bitte,* OIr *bech*⟧ any of a large superfamily (Apoidea) of broad-bodied, four-winged, hairy hymenopteran insects that gather pollen and nectar, have biting as well as sucking mouthparts, and often live in organized colonies; esp., the honeybee —**have a bee in one's bonnet 1** to be obsessed with one idea **2** to be not quite sane

bee[2] (bē) *n.* ⟦altered (prob. after prec.) < dial *bean,* a social gathering to assist < ME *bene,* extra feudal service, a favor, boon < OE *ben,* compulsory service, request; akin to ON *bon*: see BOON[1]⟧ ☆a meeting of people to work together or to compete [a sewing *bee,* spelling *bee*]

bee[3] (bē) *n.* ⟦ME *bei,* bracelet < OE *beah* < *bugen,* to bend: see BOW[1]⟧ *Naut.* a piece of wood on each side of the bowsprit of a ship, used for fastening stays from the mast or foremast: in full **bee block**

bee[4] (bē) *n.* the letter B

☆**bee balm 1** OSWEGO TEA **2** LEMON BALM

Bee·be (bē′bē), **(Charles) William** 1877-1962; U.S. naturalist, explorer, & writer

bee·bread (-bred′) *n.* a yellowish-brown mixture of pollen and honey, made by honeybees to feed larvae

beech (bēch) *adj.* ⟦ME *beche* < OE *boece, bece*: see BOOK⟧ designating a family (Fagaceae, order Fagales) of dicotyledonous trees, including the oaks and chestnuts —*n.* **1** any of a genus (*Fagus*) of trees of the beech family, with smooth, gray bark, hard wood, dark-green leaves, and edible three-cornered nuts **2** the wood of the trees of this genus —**beech′en** *adj.*

Bee·cham (bē′chəm), Sir **Thomas** 1879-1961; Eng. orchestra conductor

☆**beech·drops** (bēch′dräps′) *pl.n.* [*with sing. v.*] a wiry North American plant (*Epifagus virginiana*) of the broomrape family with brown stems and small purplish flowers, parasitic on beech roots

Bee·cher (bē′chər) **1 Henry Ward** 1813-87; U.S. clergyman & lecturer: brother of Harriet Beecher Stowe **2 Ly·man** (lī′mən) 1775-1863; U.S. clergyman & theologian: father of Henry & of Harriet Beecher Stowe

beech·mast (bēch′mast′) *n.* beechnuts, esp. those lying on the ground

beech·nut (-nut′) *n.* the small, three-cornered, edible nut of the beech tree

beech·wood (-wood′) *n.* the wood of the beech tree

bee eater any of a family (Meropidae) of small, brightly colored, tropical Old World coraciiform birds that feed on bees and other insects

beef (bēf) *n., pl.* for 1 & 5, **beefs**; for 1, also, **beeves** ⟦ME < OFr *boef* < L *bos* (gen. *bovis*), ox (apparently an Osco-Umbrian cognate form, replacing L *vos) < IE *gwōus < base *gwou-: see COW[1]⟧ **1** a full-grown ox, cow, bull, or steer, esp. one bred and fattened for meat **2** meat from such an animal; specif., a whole dressed carcass **3** such animals collectively ☆**4** [Informal] *a)* human flesh or muscle *b)* strength; brawn ☆**5** [Slang] a complaint or grievance —☆*vi.* [Slang] to complain or protest —**beef up** [Informal] to strengthen by addition, reinforcement, etc.

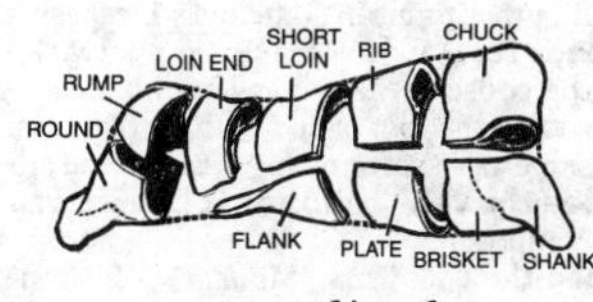

cuts of beef

beef·a·lo (bēf′ə lō′) *n., pl.* **-loes′, -los′, -lo′** ⟦prec. + (BUFF)ALO⟧ an animal developed by crossing the American buffalo, or bison, with beef cattle: supposedly better able to reproduce, grow rapidly, and provide lean meat on a grass diet

beef bour·gui·gnon (boor gē nyōn′) BOEUF BOURGUIGNON

beef·cake (-kāk′) *n.* ⟦BEEF (*n.* 4*a*) + (CHEESE)CAKE⟧ [Informal] display of the figure of a nude, or partly nude, muscular man, as in a magazine photograph

☆**beef cattle** cattle bred and fattened for meat

beef·eat·er (-ēt′ər) *n.* **1** a person who eats beef, typified as a large, well-fed, red-faced person **2** a guard at the Tower of London **3** popularly, YEOMAN OF THE (ROYAL) GUARD

☆**bee fly** any of a family (Bombyliidae) of dipterous flies that look like bees and feed on nectar and pollen

beef·steak (bēf′stāk′) *n.* a slice of beef, esp. from the loin, cut thick for broiling or frying

beefsteak tomato any very large, red tomato

beef tea a drink made from beef extract or by boiling lean strips of beef

beef Wellington ⟦after the 1st Duke of WELLINGTON[2]⟧ a lightly roasted beef fillet covered with pâté de foie gras, wrapped in pastry, and then baked

beef·wood (-wood′) *n.* CASUARINA

beef·y (bēf′ē) *adj.* **beef′i·er, beef′i·est** fleshy and solid; muscular and heavy; brawny —**beef′i·ness** *n.*

☆**bee gum 1** [Chiefly South] a hollow gum tree or log used as a hive by bees **2** a beehive, esp. one made from such a tree

bee·hive (bē′hīv′) *n.* **1** a hive of or for bees, esp., a box or other shelter for a colony of domesticated bees, in which they make and store honey **2** a place of great activity **3** a woman's hairdo in which the hair is worn teased on top of the head, resembling a domed beehive

bee·keep·er (-kē′pər) *n.* a person who keeps bees for producing honey; apiarist —**bee′keep′ing** *n.*

☆**bee·line** (-līn′) *n.* ⟦from the belief that a bee usually flies straight back to its hive after getting nectar⟧ a straight line or direct route from one place to another: now chiefly in the phrase **make a beeline for,** to go straight toward

Be·el·ze·bub (bē el′zə bub′) *n.* ⟦LL(Ec) < Gr(Ec) *Beelzeboub* < Heb *baal-zevuv,* lit., god of flies < *baal* (see BAAL) + *zevuv,* a fly: prob. deliberate pejorative alteration < *Ba'al zebul*; cf. Ugaritic *zbl b'l 'rs,* the exalted one, the lord of the earth⟧ **1** *Bible* the chief devil; Satan **2** in Milton's *Paradise Lost,* Satan's chief lieutenant among the fallen angels

☆**bee moth** any of various moths; esp., a pest moth (*Galleria melonella*) whose larvae, hatched in beehives, eat the wax of the honeycomb

been (bin; *often* ben; *Cdn also and Brit usually* bēn) *vi.* ⟦ME *ben* < OE *beon*: see BE⟧ *pp. of* BE

beep (bēp) ***n.*** ⟦echoic⟧ **1** the brief, high-pitched sound of a horn, as on an automobile or bicycle **2** a brief, high-pitched electronic signal, used in warning, direction-finding, etc. —***vi.*** to make such a sound —***vt.*** to cause to make such a sound

beep·er (bēp′ər) ***n.*** [Informal] PAGER

☆**bee plant** any plant that particularly attracts bees; esp., a pungent plant (*Cleome serrulata*) of the caper family

beer (bir) ***n.*** ⟦ME & OE *beor,* akin to Ger *bier;* only in WGmc; a monastic (6th c.) borrowing < VL *biber,* beverage (< L *bibere,* IMBIBE): orig. used for the drink made with hops, as distinct from the older drink, ale, then made without⟧ **1** an alcoholic beverage made from grain, esp. malted barley, fermented by yeast and flavored with hops; esp., such a beverage produced by slow fermentation at a relatively low temperature: cf. ALE **2** any of several soft drinks made from extracts of roots and plants [ginger *beer*]

beer belly [Informal] a man's protruding belly, as from the excessive consumption of beer: sometimes **beer gut**

Beer·bohm (bir′bōm′), Sir **(Henry) Max(imilian)** 1872-1956; Eng. satirist, caricaturist, & critic

Beer·she·ba (bir shē′bə, ber-) city in S Israel, the principal city of the Negev: in ancient times, it marked the southernmost extremity of Israelite territory: cf. DAN[3]

beer·y (bir′ē) ***adj.*** **beer′i·er, beer′i·est** **1** of, like, or suggestive of beer **2** showing the effects of drinking beer; drunken, tipsy, maudlin, etc. —**beer′i·ness** ***n.***

beest·ings (bēs′tiŋz) ***pl.n.*** ⟦ME *bestinge* < OE *bysting* < *beost,* beestings⟧ [*often with sing. v.*] colostrum, esp. that of a cow

bees·wax (bēz′waks′) ***n.*** a tallowlike substance that honeybees secrete and use for building their honeycomb: it is used in candles, polishes, etc.

bees·wing (-wiŋ′) ***n.*** ⟦descriptive of its diaphanous appearance⟧ a gauzy film that forms in some old wines, esp. port

beet (bēt) ***n.*** ⟦ME & OE *bete* < L *beta*⟧ **1** any of a genus (*Beta*) of plants of the goosefoot family, with edible leaves and a thick, fleshy, white or red root **2** the root of any of these plants: some are eaten as a vegetable, some serve as a source of sugar, and some are used for fodder

Bee·tho·ven (bā′tō′vən), **Lud·wig van** (lo͞ot′viH vän) 1770-1827; Ger. composer

bee·tle[1] (bēt′'l) ***n.*** ⟦ME *bitil* < OE *bitela* < *bītan,* BITE⟧ **1** any of a large order (Coleoptera) of insects, including weevils, with biting mouthparts and hard front wings (*elytra*) that cover the membranous hind wings when the hind wings are folded **2** any insect resembling a beetle —***vi.*** to move or run hastily; scurry; scuttle

bee·tle[2] (bēt′'l) ***n.*** ⟦ME & OE (Anglian) *betel,* mallet, hammer: ult. connected with BEAT⟧ **1** a heavy mallet, usually wooden, for driving wedges, tamping earth, etc. **2** a household mallet or pestle for mashing or beating **3** a club used in finishing handmade linen **4** a machine for finishing cloth by beating it over or between rollers —***vt.*** **-tled, -tling** **1** to pound with a beetle **2** to put a glossy finish on (cloth) by flattening the fibers with a beetle

bee·tle[3] (bēt′'l) ***vi.*** **-tled, -tling** ⟦prob. back-form. < BEETLE-BROWED⟧ to project or jut; overhang —***adj.*** jutting; overhanging: also **bee′tling**

☆**beet leaf·hop·per** (lēf′häp′ər) a small leafhopper (*Circulifer tenellus*) that transmits a very destructive virus to sugar beets

bee·tle-browed (bēt′'l broud′) ***adj.*** ⟦ME *bitelbrouwed* < ? *bitel,* sharp, cruel + *brouwe,* BROW⟧ **1** having bushy or overhanging eyebrows **2** frowning; scowling

☆**bee tree** **1** a hollow tree used as a hive by bees **2** BASSWOOD (sense 1)

beet sugar sugar extracted from sugar beets

beeves (bēvz) ***n.*** *alt. pl. of* BEEF

bee·zer (bē′zer) ***n.*** ⟦orig., prize-fight slang⟧ [Slang] the nose

bef *abbrev.* before

BEF *abbrev.* British Expeditionary Force (or Forces)

be·fall (bē fôl′, bi-) ***vi.*** **-fell′, -fall′en, -fall′ing** ⟦ME *bifallen* < OE *befeallan,* to fall, fall to as a share or right < *be-,* BE- + *feallan,* FALL⟧ **1** to come to pass; happen; occur **2** [Archaic] to be fitting; pertain —***vt.*** to happen to [what *befell* them?]

be·fit (bē fit′, bi-) ***vt.*** **-fit′ted, -fit′ting** to be suitable or proper for; be suited or becoming to

be·fit·ting (-iŋ) ***adj.*** proper or right; suitable —**be·fit′ting·ly** ***adv.***

be·fog (bē fôg′, -fäg′; bi-) ***vt.*** **-fogged′, -fog′ging** **1** to cover with or envelop in fog; make foggy **2** to make obscure or muddled; confuse; bewilder [to *befog* an issue, to *befog* someone's mind]

be·fool (bē fo͞ol′, bi-) ***vt.*** **1** to play a trick on; fool or deceive **2** to treat as a fool

be·fore (bē fôr′, bi-) ***adv.*** ⟦ME *biforen* < OE *beforan* < *be-,* BY + *foran,* FORE⟧ **1** in advance; in front; ahead **2** in the past; previously [I've heard that song *before*] **3** at an earlier time; sooner [come at ten, not *before*] —***prep.*** **1** ahead of in time, space, order, rank, or importance **2** located just to the front of [he paused *before* the door] **3** in or into the sight, notice, presence, etc. of [a thought flashed *before* her mind; he stood *before* his accuser] **4** being considered, judged, or decided by [the matter *before* the committee] **5** earlier than; prior to [he left *before* noon] **6** still to be reached, accomplished, etc. by [the hardest task was *before* them] **7** in preference to; rather than [to choose death *before* dishonor] —***conj.*** **1** earlier than the time that [drop in *before* you go] **2** sooner than; rather than [I'd die *before* I'd tell]

be·fore·hand (-hand′) ***adv., adj.*** **1** ahead of time; in advance **2** in anticipation; exercising forethought

be·fore·time (-tīm′) ***adv.*** [Archaic] formerly

be·foul (bē foul′, bi-) ***vt.*** ⟦ME *befoulen* < OE *befylan:* see BE- & FOUL⟧ **1** to make filthy; dirty; soil **2** to cast aspersions on; slander —**be·foul′ment** ***n.***

be·friend (bē frend′, bi-) ***vt.*** to act as a friend to; help

be·fud·dle (bē fud′'l, bi-) ***vt.*** **-dled, -dling** **1** to fuddle or confuse (the mind, a person, etc.) **2** to stupefy with alcoholic liquor —**be·fud′dle·ment** ***n.***

beg (beg) ***vt.*** **begged, beg′ging** ⟦ME *beggen* < Anglo-Fr *begger* < *begart* < OFr *begard,* religious mendicant < MDu *beggaert*⟧ **1** to ask for as charity or as a gift [he *begged* a dime] **2** to ask for earnestly as a kindness or favor —***vi.*** **1** to ask for alms; be a beggar **2** to ask humbly; entreat —**beg off** to ask to be released from some obligation —**beg the question** **1** to use an argument that assumes as proved the very thing one is trying to prove **2** loosely, to evade the issue **3** to lead naturally or logically to the following: phrase used as a rhetorical bridge between a point made and a question that results from it [the employee's incompetence *begs the question:* who hired him in the first place?] —**go begging** to be available but unwanted

SYN.—**beg** implies humbleness or earnestness in asking for something and is now often used in polite formulas [I *beg* to differ; I *beg* to report]; **solicit** stresses courtesy and formality in requesting something [we *solicit* your aid; he *solicits* our trade]; **entreat** implies the use of all the persuasive power at one's command; **beseech** suggests fervor or passion in the asking and connotes anxiety over the outcome; **implore** is stronger still, suggesting desperation or great distress; **importune** suggests persistence in entreating, often to the point of becoming offensive

be·gan (bē gan′, bi-) ***vi., vt.*** *pt. of* BEGIN

be·get (bē get′, bi-) ***vt.*** **be·got′** or [Archaic] **be·gat′** (-gat′), **be·got′ten** or **be·got′**, **be·get′ting** ⟦ME *begeten,* to obtain, beget < OE *begietan,* to acquire: see BE- & GET⟧ **1** to be the father or sire of; procreate **2** to bring into being; produce [tyranny *begets* rebellion] —**be·get′ter** ***n.***

beg·gar (beg′ər) ***n.*** ⟦ME *beggere* < OFr *begard:* see BEG⟧ **1** a person who begs, or asks for charity, esp. one who lives by begging; mendicant **2** a person who is very poor; pauper **3** [Chiefly Brit.] a person; fellow: often used jokingly or affectionately —***vt.*** **1** to make a beggar of; make poor **2** to render (one's ability to do something) ultimately inadequate or pointless: usually in the phrases **beggar description** or **beggar belief** [her dazzling beauty *beggars* description; your outrageous story *beggars* belief] —**beg′gar·dom** (-dəm) ***n.***

beg·gar·ly (-lē) ***adj.*** like or fit for a beggar; very poor, worthless, inadequate, etc. —**beg′gar·li·ness** ***n.***

☆**beg·gar's-lice** (beg′erz līs′) ***n.,*** *pl.* **beg′gar's-lice′** **1** any of several plants (esp. the genus *Lappula* of the borage family) with dry, prickly fruits that adhere to fur or clothing **2** the fruit Also **beg′gar-lice′**

☆**beg·gar's-ticks** (-tiks′) ***n.,*** *pl.* **beg′gar's-ticks′** **1** *a)* TICK TREFOIL *b)* the prickly seed pod of a tick trefoil **2** *a)* BUR MARIGOLD *b)* the prickly seed of a bur marigold **3** BEGGAR'S-LICE Also **beg′gar-ticks′**

☆**beg·gar·weed** (beg′ər wēd′) ***n.*** any of several plants, esp. a leguminous West Indian plant (*Desmodium purpureum*), grown in the SE U.S. for soil improvement

beg·gar·y (beg′ər ē) ***n.,*** *pl.* **-gar·ies** ⟦ME *beggerie* < *beggere,* BEGGAR⟧ **1** extreme poverty **2** the act of begging or state of being a beggar **3** beggars as a group

be·gin (bē gin′, bi-) ***vi.*** **be·gan′, be·gun′, be·gin′ning** ⟦ME *biginnen* < OE *beginnan;* akin to Ger *beginnen,* Goth *duginnan*⟧ **1** to start doing, acting, going, etc.; get under way **2** to come into being; arise **3** to have a first part or element [the Bible *begins* with Genesis] **4** to be or do in the slightest degree: used with an infinitive [they don't *begin* to compare] —***vt.*** **1** to cause to start; set about; commence **2** to cause to come into being; originate **3** to be the first part or element of —**to begin with** as the first point or consideration

SYN.—**begin,** the most general of these terms, indicates merely a setting into motion of some action, process, or course [to *begin* eating]; **commence,** the more formal term, is used with reference to a ceremony or an elaborate course of action [to *commence* a court action]; **start** carries the particular implication of leaving a point of departure in any kind of progression [to *start* a journey, the boulder *started* a landslide]; **initiate,** in this connection, refers to the carrying out of the first steps in some course or process, with no indication of what is to follow [to *initiate* peace talks]; **inaugurate** suggests a formal or ceremonial beginning or opening [to *inaugurate* a new library] —*ANT.* **end, finish, conclude**

Be·gin (bā′gin), **Me·na·chem** (mə näkh′əm) 1913-92; prime minister of Israel (1977-83), born in Poland

be·gin·ner (bē gin′ər, bi-) ***n.*** **1** a person who begins anything **2** a person just beginning to do or learn something; inexperienced, unskilled person; novice

be·gin·ning (-iŋ) ***n.*** **1** a starting or commencing **2** the time or place of starting; birth; origin; source [English democracy had its *beginning* in the Magna Carta] **3** the first part [the *beginning* of a book] **4** [*usually pl.*] an early stage or example [the *beginnings* of scientific agriculture] —*SYN.* ORIGIN

be·gird (bē gurd′, bi-) ***vt.*** **-girt′** (-gurt′) or **-gird′ed, -girt′, -gird′ing** ⟦ME *bigirden* < OE *begyrdan* < *be-* + *gyrdan:* see BE- & GIRD[1]⟧ **1** to bind around; gird **2** to encircle; surround; encompass

be·gone (bē gôn′, bi-) ***interj., vi.*** (to) be gone; go away; get out

be·gon·ia (bi gōn′yə) ***adj.*** ⟦ModL, after M. *Bégon* (1638-1710), Fr governor of Santo Domingo & a patron of science⟧ designating a family (Begoniaceae, order Violales) of dicotyledonous tropical plants —***n.*** any of a genus (*Begonia*) of plants of this family, grown for their handsome, ornamental leaves or their clustered, showy flowers

be·gor·ra (bi gôr′ə) ***interj.*** ⟦altered < *by God*⟧ used to express surprise or add emphasis: usage attributed to the Irish [faith and *begorra!*]

be·got (bē gät′, bi-) ***vt. pt. & alt. pp. of*** BEGET

be·got·ten (-gät′'n) ***vt. alt. pp. of*** BEGET

be·grime (bē grīm′, bi-) ***vt.*** **-grimed′**, **-grim′ing** to cover with grime; make dirty; soil

be·grudge (bē gruj′, bi-) ***vt.*** **-grudged′**, **-grudg′ing** **1** to feel ill will or resentment at the possession or employment of (something) by another [to *begrudge* another's fortune] **2** to give with ill will or reluctance [he *begrudges* them every cent] **3** to regard with displeasure or disapproval —**SYN.** ENVY —**be·grudg′ing·ly** ***adv.***

be·guile (bē gīl′, bi-) ***vt.*** **-guiled′**, **-guil′ing** **1** to mislead by cheating or tricking; deceive **2** to deprive (someone) *of* or *out of* something by deceit; cheat [he was *beguiled* of his money] **3** to pass (time) pleasantly; while away [she *beguiled* her days with reading] **4** to charm or delight —**SYN.** AMUSE, DECEIVE, LURE —**be·guile′ment** ***n.*** —**be·guil′er** ***n.***

be·guine (bi gēn′) ***n.*** ⟦AmFr *béguine* < Fr *béguin,* infatuation, fancy (< phr. *avoir un béguin pour,* to have a fancy for); earlier, a child's cap with strings, orig., a nun's cap < OFr *Béguine*: see fol.⟧ a rhythmic native dance of Martinique or its music

Beg·uine (beg′ēn′; *Fr* bā gēn′) ***n.*** ⟦MFr *beguine* < OFr < *begard*: see BEG⟧ a member of certain lay sisterhoods, not under permanent vows, begun in the Low Countries in the 12th cent.

be·gum (bē′gəm) ***n.*** ⟦Anglo-Ind < Hindi *begam,* lady < Turk, princess, fem. of *beg,* BEY⟧ in Pakistan and certain other Muslim countries, a lady of high rank

be·gun (bē gun′, bi-) ***vi., vt. pp. of*** BEGIN

be·half (bē haf′, -häf′; bi-) ***n.*** ⟦ME, in phrase *on (mi) behalfe,* on (my) side < OE *be,* BY + *healf,* HALF, side⟧ support, interest, side, etc. [I speak in his *behalf*] —**in** (or **on**) **behalf of** in the interest of; for —**on behalf of** speaking for; representing

Be·han (bē′ən), **Bren·dan (Francis)** (bren′dən) 1923-64; Ir. playwright

be·have (bē hāv′, bi-) ***vt., vi.*** **-haved′**, **-hav′ing** ⟦see BE- & HAVE⟧ **1** to conduct (oneself or itself) in a specified way; act or react **2** to conduct (oneself) in a correct or proper way

SYN.—**behave**, used reflexively (as also the other words in this comparison), implies action in conformity with the required standards of decorum [did the children *behave* themselves?]; **conduct** implies the direction or guidance of one's actions in a specified way [he *conducted* himself well at the trial]; **demean** suggests behavior or appearance that is indicative of the specified character trait [she *demeaned* herself like a gracious hostess]; **deport** and **comport** suggest behavior in accordance with the fixed rules of society [they always *deport* themselves like ladies]; **acquit** suggests behavior in accordance with the duties of one's position or with one's obligations [the rookie *acquitted* himself like a major leaguer]

be·hav·ior (bē hāv′yər, bi-) ***n.*** ⟦< prec. by analogy with ME *havior,* property < OFr *aveir* < *avoir,* to have⟧ **1** the way a person behaves or acts; conduct; manners **2** *a)* an organism's responses to stimulation or environment, esp. those responses that can be observed *b)* an instance of behavior; specif., one of a recurring or characteristic pattern of observable actions or responses **3** the way a machine, element, etc. acts or functions —**be·hav′ior·al** ***adj.*** —**be·hav′ior·al·ly** ***adv.***

behavioral science any of several studies, as sociology, psychology, or anthropology, that examine human activities in an attempt to discover recurrent patterns and to formulate rules about social behavior

☆**be·hav·ior·ism** (-iz′əm) ***n.*** ⟦BEHAVIOR + -ISM: coined (1913) by John B. Watson (1878-1958), U.S. psychologist⟧ the doctrine that observed behavior provides the only valid data of psychology: it rejects the concept of mind and consciousness —**be·hav′ior·ist** ***n., adj.*** —**be·hav′ior·is′tic** ***adj.***

behavior modification *Psychol.* a technique that seeks to modify animal and human behavior through application of the principles of conditioning, in which rewards and reinforcements, or punishments, are used to establish desired habits, or patterns of behavior: see also CONDITIONED RESPONSE: also called **behavioral modification**

behavior therapy therapy employing behavior modification

be·hav·iour (bē hāv′yər, bi-) ***n. Brit. sp. of*** BEHAVIOR

be·head (bē hed′, bi-) ***vt.*** ⟦ME *bihevden* < OE *beheafdian* < *be,* BE- + *heafod,* HEAD⟧ to cut off the head of; decapitate

be·held (bē held′, bi-) ***vt. pt. & pp. of*** BEHOLD

be·he·moth (bə hē′məth, bē′ə məth) ***n.*** ⟦Heb *behemot,* intens. pl. of *behema,* beast; akin to Ethiopic *bəhma,* dumb, speechless & Ar *ʿabham* (> *bahma(t), bahīma(t),* animal)⟧ **1** *Bible* a huge animal, assumed to be the hippopotamus: Job 40:15-24 **2** any animal or thing that is huge or very powerful

be·hest (bē hest′, bi-) ***n.*** ⟦ME *bihest* (with unhistoric *-t*) < OE *behæs,* a vow: see BE- & HEST⟧ an order, command, or request

be·hind (bē hīnd′, bi-) ***adv.*** ⟦ME *bihinden* < OE *behindan*: see BE- & HIND[1]⟧ **1** in or to the rear or back [to walk *behind,* to look *behind*] **2** at an earlier time; in the past [my joy lies *behind*] **3** in a former place, condition, etc. [the girl he left *behind*] **4** in or into a retarded state [to drop *behind* in one's studies] **5** in or into arrears [to fall *behind* in one's dues] **6** slow in time; late [the train was running *behind*] **7** [Archaic] in reserve; yet to come —***prep.*** **1** remaining after [the dead leave their wealth *behind* them] **2** *a)* in the rear of; in back of [he sat *behind* me] *b)* following at the rear of **3** inferior to in position, achievement, etc. **4** later than; delayed with respect to [to be *behind* schedule] **5** on the other or farther side of; beyond [*behind* the hill] **6** gone by or ended for; out of the attention or concern of [his apprenticeship was *behind* him] **7** *a)* supporting [fans solidly *behind* their team] *b)* prompting or instigating [the mastermind *behind* the plot] **8** *a)* hidden by; not yet revealed about [there's something *behind* this news] *b)* in the circumstances surrounding or antecedent to —***adj.*** that follows, as in a line [the person *behind*] —***n.*** [Informal] the buttocks

be·hind·hand (-hand′) ***adv., adj.*** **1** behind in paying debts, rent, etc. **2** behind time; slow; late **3** behind or slow, as in progress

Behn (bān, ben), **Aph·ra** (af′rə) 1640-89; Eng. dramatist & novelist

be·hold (bē hōld′, bi-) ***vt.*** **-held′**, **-hold′ing** ⟦ME *biholden* < OE *bihealdan,* to hold, keep hold of: see BE- & HOLD[1]⟧ to hold in view; look at; see; regard —***interj.*** look; see —**SYN.** SEE[1] —**be·hold′er** ***n.***

be·hold·en (-ən) ***vt.*** ⟦ME, pp. of prec.⟧ *archaic pp. of* BEHOLD —***adj.*** obliged to feel grateful; owing thanks; indebted

be·hoof (bē ho͞of′, bi-) ***n.*** ⟦ME *bihove,* profit, benefit < OE *behofe* (dat. of **bihof*) < WGmc **behafjan* < *be-* + **hafjan*: see HEAVE⟧ behalf, benefit, interest, sake, etc.

be·hoove (bē ho͞ov′, bi-) ***vt.*** **-hooved′**, **-hoov′ing** ⟦ME *bihofian* < OE *behofian,* to have need of < prec.⟧ to be necessary for or incumbent upon [it *behooves* you to think for yourself] —***vi.*** [Now Rare] to be morally necessary or proper Brit. **be·hove′** (-hōv′) **-hoved′**, **-hov′ing**

Beh·ring (bā′riŋ), **E·mil A·dolf von** (ā′mēl ä′dôlf fôn) 1854-1917; Ger. bacteriologist: developed tetanus & diphtheria antitoxins

Bei·der·becke (bī′dər bek′), **(Leon) Bix** (biks) 1903-31; U.S. jazz cornetist

beige (bāzh) ***n.*** ⟦Fr, orig., natural color of wool < ?⟧ **1** a soft wool fabric, formerly undyed and unbleached **2** its characteristic sandy color; grayish tan —***adj.*** grayish-tan

bei·gnet (bā nyā′) ***n.*** ⟦Fr, fritter⟧ **1** a fritter with a filling of fruit, vegetables, meat, fish, cheese, etc. **2** a square doughnut or friedcake coated with powdered sugar

Bei·jing (bā jiŋ′, -zhiŋ′) ⟦Chin, northern capital (as contrasted with NANJING)⟧ capital of China, in the NE part: formerly *Peking*

be·ing (bē′iŋ) ***n.*** ⟦see BE⟧ **1** the state or fact of existing or living; existence or life **2** fundamental or essential nature **3** one who lives or exists, or is assumed to do so [a human *being,* a divine *being*] **4** all the physical and mental qualities that make up a person; personality **5** *Philos.* *a)* fulfillment of possibilities; essential completeness *b)* that which exists, can exist, or can be logically conceived —**being as** (or **that**) [Informal or Dial.] since; because —**for the time being** for the present; for now

Bei·ra (bā′rə) seaport on the SE coast of Mozambique

Bei·rut (bā ro͞ot′) seaport & capital of Lebanon, on the Mediterranean

be·jab·bers (bi jab′ərz) ⟦euphemism for *by Jesus*⟧ ***interj., n.*** BEJESUS: also **be·ja′bers** (-jā′bərz)

Be·jaï·a (bə jī′ə) seaport in NE Algeria, on the Mediterranean

be·je·sus (bi jē′zəs) ⟦euphemism for *by Jesus*⟧ ***interj.*** used variously to express surprise, pleasure, anger, annoyance, etc. —***n.*** [Slang] a term of indefinite meaning, often used to provide emphasis, esp. in such phrases as **beat** (or **scare**) **the bejesus out of**

be·jew·el (bē jo͞o′əl, bi-) ***vt.*** **-eled** or **-elled**, **-el·ing** or **-el·ling** to cover or decorate with or as with jewels

☆**bel** (bel) ***n.*** ⟦after Alexander Graham BELL⟧ *Physics* a unit used for measuring sound intensity, equal to 10 decibels: abbrev. *B*

Bel[1] (bāl) ***n.*** ⟦Akkadian form of BAAL⟧ *Bab. Myth.* the god of heaven and earth

Bel[2] *abbrev.* Belgium

be·la·bor (bē lā′bər, bi-) ***vt.*** **1** to beat severely; hit or whip **2** to attack with words; scold **3** to spend too much time and effort on; develop in too great detail [to *belabor* the issue]

Bel·a·rus (bel′ə ro͞os′) country in central Europe: became independent upon the breakup of the U.S.S.R. (1991): 80,155 sq mi (207,600 sq km); cap. Minsk: formerly, *Belorussian Soviet Socialist Republic*

Be·las·co (bə las′kō), **David** 1853-1931; U.S. theatrical producer, playwright, & actor

be·lat·ed (bē lāt′id, bi-) ***adj.*** ⟦BE- + LAT(E) + -ED⟧ late or too late; tardy —**be·lat′ed·ly** ***adv.*** —**be·lat′ed·ness** ***n.***

Be·lau (bə lou′) PALAU

be·lay (bi lā′) ***vt., vi.*** **-layed′**, **-lay′ing** ⟦ME *bileggen* < OE *belecgan,* to make fast < *be-,* BE- + *lecgan,* LAY[2]⟧ **1** to make (a rope) secure by winding around a belaying pin, cleat, piton, etc.; hold fast **2** [Informal] *Naut.* *a)* to hold; stop [*belay* there!] *b)* to cancel [*belay* the last order] **3** to secure (a person, as a mountain climber, or thing) by a rope —***n.*** action, method, or place of securing a hold for a rope in mountain climbing

Be·la·ya Tser·kov (bel′ə yə ser′kôf) city in WC Ukraine

belaying pin a removable wooden or metal pin in the rail of a ship, around which ropes can be fastened

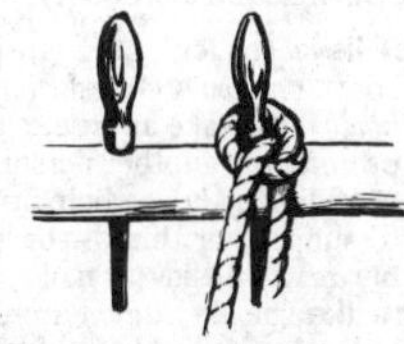

belaying pins

bel can·to (bel′kän′tō) ⟦It, lit., beautiful song⟧ a style of singing characterized by brilliant vocal display and purity of tone

belch (belch) *vi., vt.* ⟦ME *belchen* < OE *bealcian,* to bring up, emit, splutter out⟧ **1** to expel (gas) through the mouth from the stomach; eruct **2** to utter (curses, orders, etc.) violently **3** to throw forth (its contents) violently, often in spasms [the volcano *belched* flame] —*n.* **1** the act of belching; eructation **2** a thing belched

bel·dam or **bel·dame** (bel′dəm) *n.* ⟦ME, grandmother < *bel,* good, beautiful < OFr *bel,* used as term of affection and respect in the Middle Ages (see BEAU) + DAME⟧ **1** [Obs.] a grandmother **2** an old woman; esp., a hideous old woman; hag

be·lea·guer (bē lē′gər, bi-) *vt.* ⟦Du *belegeren,* to besiege < *be-,* around + *legeren,* to camp < *leger* (akin to LAIR), a camp⟧ **1** to besiege by encircling, as with an army **2** to beset, as with difficulties; harass

Be·lém (bə len′) seaport in NE Brazil, in the Amazon delta, on the Pará River: capital of Pará state

bel·em·nite (bel′əm nīt′) *n.* ⟦< Gr *belemnon,* a dart, arrow, prob. akin to *ballein,* to throw (see BALL[2]) + -ITE[1]⟧ the cigar-shaped fossilized internal shell of extinct cephalopods (order Belemnoidea) of the Mesozoic Era

bel es·prit (bel es prē′) *pl.* ***beaux es·prits*** (bō zes prē′) ⟦Fr, lit., beautiful spirit⟧ a clever, cultured person

Bel·fast (bel′fast′, bel fast′) seaport & capital of Northern Ireland, on the North Channel

bel·fry (bel′frē) *n., pl.* **-fries** ⟦ME *belfrei,* altered by assoc. with *belle* (BELL[1]) < *berfrai* < OFr *berfroi* < OHG *bergfrid,* lit., protector of peace < *bergen,* to protect (see BURY) + *frid,* peace⟧ **1** a movable tower used in ancient warfare for attacking walled positions **2** a bell tower, esp. one that is part of a building, placed at the top **3** the part of a tower or steeple that holds the bell or bells

Belg *abbrev.* Belgium

Bel·gae (-jē) *pl.n.* ⟦L < Gaul, lit., the angry ones⟧ the members of an ancient Gallic people of N France and Belgium

Bel·gaum (bel goum′) city in SW India

Bel Geddes *see* GEDDES, Norman Bel

Bel·gian (bel′jən) *adj.* of Belgium or its people or culture —*n.* a person born or living in Belgium

Belgian Congo former Belgian colony (1908-60) in central Africa: now the country of *Democratic Republic of the Congo*: see CONGO

Belgian hare a large, reddish-brown domestic variety of Old World rabbit (*Oryctolagus cuniculus*)

Belgian sheepdog any of a Belgian breed of large herding dog with a black coat, sometimes used as a guide dog

Bel·gic (bel′jik′) *adj.* ⟦L *Belgicus* < *Belgae*⟧ **1** of Belgium **2** of the Netherlands **3** of the Belgae

Bel·gium (bel′jəm) kingdom in W Europe, on the North Sea: independence established in 1831: 11,787 sq mi (30,528 sq km); cap. Brussels: Fr. name **Bel·gique** (bel zhēk′); Fl. name **Bel·gi·ë** (bel′gē ə)

Bel·go·rod (bel′gə räd′) city in W European Russia, on the Donets River

Bel·grade (bel′grād′, -grad′) capital of Serbia, on the Danube

Bel·gra·vi·a (bel grā′vē ə) a fashionable residential area surrounding Belgrave Square in Westminster, London —**Bel·gra′vi·an** *adj., n.*

Be·li·al (bē′lē əl, bēl′yəl) *n.* ⟦ME < LL (Vulg.: Deut. 13:13) < Heb *beliyaal,* worthlessness⟧ **1** *Bible a)* wickedness as an evil force: Deut. 13:13 *b)* Satan: 2 Cor. 6:15 **2** in Milton's *Paradise Lost,* one of the fallen angels

be·lie (bē lī′, bi-) *vt.* **-lied′, -ly′ing** ⟦ME *bilien* < OE *beleogan,* to deceive by lying < *be-,* BE- + *leogan,* LIE[2]⟧ **1** [Archaic] to tell lies about **2** to give a false idea of; disguise or misrepresent [his smile *belies* his anger] **3** to leave unfulfilled; disappoint [war *belied* hopes for peace] **4** to show to be untrue; prove false [her cruelty *belied* her kind words] —**be·li′er** *n.*

be·lief (bə lēf′, bē-) *n.* ⟦ME *bileve* < *bi-,* BE- + *-leve,* contr. < *ileve* < OE *geleafa*: see fol.⟧ **1** the state of believing; conviction or acceptance that certain things are true or real **2** faith, esp. religious faith **3** trust or confidence [I have *belief* in his ability] **4** anything believed or accepted as true; esp., a creed, doctrine, or tenet **5** an opinion; expectation; judgment [my *belief* is that he'll come]

SYN.—**belief,** the term of broadest application in this comparison, implies mental acceptance of something as true, even though absolute certainty may be absent; **faith** implies complete, unquestioning acceptance of something even in the absence of proof and, esp., of something not supported by reason; **trust** implies assurance, often apparently intuitive, in the reliability of someone or something; **confidence** also suggests such assurance, esp. when based on reason or evidence; **credence** suggests mere mental acceptance of something that may have no solid basis in fact See also **opinion** —*ANT.* **doubt, incredulity**

be·lieve (bə lēv′, bē-) *vt.* **-lieved′, -liev′ing** ⟦ME *bileven* < *bi,* BE- + *-leven,* contr. < *ileven* < OE *geliefan* < IE base **leubh-,* to like, desire > LOVE, LIEF, L *libido*⟧ **1** to take as true, real, etc. **2** to have confidence in a statement or promise of (another person) **3** to suppose or think —*vi.* **1** to have trust or confidence (*in*) as being true, real, good, etc. **2** to have religious faith **3** to suppose or think —**be·liev′a·ble** *adj.* —**be·liev′a·bil′i·ty** *n.* —**be·liev′a·bly** *adv.* —**be·liev′er** *n.*

be·like (bē līk′) *adv.* [Archaic] quite likely; probably

Be·lin·da (bə lin′də) *n.* ⟦< Gmc *Betlindis*: *Bet-* (< ?) + *-lindis,* prob. akin to OHG *lind,* gentle < IE base **lento-,* flexible > L *lentus*⟧ a feminine name: dim. *Linda*

Bel·i·sa·ri·us (bel′ə ser′ē əs) A.D. 505?-565; Byzantine general under Justinian I

☆**be·lit·tle** (bē lit′'l, bi-) *vt.* **-tled, -tling** ⟦coined (*c.* 1780) by Thomas JEFFERSON⟧ to make seem little, less important, etc.; speak slightingly of; depreciate —*SYN.* DISPARAGE —**be·lit′tle·ment** *n.* —**be·lit′tler** *n.*

Be·li·tung (bə lē′tooŋ) island of Indonesia, in the Java Sea, between Borneo & Sumatra: 1,866 sq mi (4,833 sq km)

Be·lize (bə lēz′) **1** country in Central America, on the Caribbean: formerly a British colony & territory, it became independent & a member of the Commonwealth (1981): 8,867 sq mi (22,966 sq km); cap. Belmopan **2** seaport on the coast of this country: also called **Belize City** —**Be·liz′e·an** *adj., n.*

bell[1] (bel) *n.* ⟦ME & OE *belle* < IE base **bhel-,* to sound, roar (orig. ? echoic) > BELLOW, ON *belja,* to roar⟧ **1** a hollow object, usually cuplike, made of metal or other hard material which rings when struck, as by a clapper inside **2** such an object rung to mark the hours or the beginning and end of a period of time **3** the sound made by a bell **4** anything shaped like a bell, as a flower, the flare of a horn, etc. **5** [*pl.*] a musical instrument made up of a series of tuned metal bars or hollow tubes that are sounded by striking; specif., *a)* GLOCKENSPIEL *b)* chimes (see CHIME[1], *n.* 2) **6** *Naut. a)* a bell rung every half hour during each of the five four-hour watches and during the four-hour period comprising the two dog watches: the series of rings begins at *one bell* (12:30, 4:30, and 8:30 o'clock) and ends at *eight bells* (4:00, 8:00, and 12:00 o'clock) *b)* any of these half-hour periods —*vt.* **1** to attach a bell or bells to **2** to shape like a bell —*vi.* to flare out like a bell

bell[2] (bel) *n.* ⟦ME *bellen* < OE *bellan*: see prec.⟧ a bellow; roar —*vi.* to utter long, deep sounds, as a hound in pursuit of game; bay; bellow

Bell (bel) **1 Alexander Graham** 1847-1922; U.S. inventor of the telephone, born in Scotland **2** pseudonym used variously by the Brontë sisters: see BRONTË

Bel·la (bel′ə) *n.* a feminine name: see ARABELLA, ISABELLA[1]

bel·la·don·na (bel′ə dän′ə) *n.* ⟦ModL < It *bella donna,* lit., beautiful lady: a folk etym. (infl. by cosmetic use for dilating the eye) for ML *bladona,* nightshade, prob. < Gaul⟧ **1** a poisonous European plant (*Atropa belladonna*) of the nightshade family, with purplish or reddish bell-shaped flowers and shiny black berries; deadly nightshade: it is a source of atropine **2** ATROPINE

belladonna lily a tropical bulbous plant (*Amaryllis belladonna*) of the lily family, grown for its large pink, white, or red flowers and native to S Africa

bel·la fi·gu·ra (bel′lä fē goo′rä) ⟦It⟧ a good impression; fine appearance

Bel·la·my (bel′ə mē), **Edward** 1850-98; U.S. writer & political theoretician: author of *Looking Backward*

bell·bird (bel′burd′) *n.* any of various birds that make bell-like sounds, as certain honeyeaters

bell-bot·tom (-bät′əm) *adj.* designating trousers or slacks having a pronounced flare from the knee or mid-calf downward: also **bell′-bot′tomed** —*n.* [*pl.*] bell-bottom trousers or slacks

☆**bell·boy** (-boi′) *n.* BELLHOP

bell buoy a buoy with a warning bell rung by the motion of the waves

☆**bell captain** a person in charge of a group of bellhops

bell curve *Statistics* a curve resembling the outline of a flared bell, usually representing a normal distribution

belle (bel) *n.* ⟦Fr, fem. of *beau*: see BEAU⟧ a pretty woman or girl; often, one who is the prettiest or most popular [the *belle* of the ball]

Belle (bel) *n.* ⟦Fr: see prec.⟧ a feminine name

Bel·leau Wood (be lō′) small forest in N France: site of a battle (1918) in WWI in which U.S. forces stopped a German advance on Paris

Bel·leek (ware) (bə lēk′) ⟦after *Belleek,* town in Northern Ireland, where it is made⟧ a fine, glossy, often iridescent pottery resembling porcelain

bell curve

belle é·poque or **belle é·poque** (be lā pôk′) ⟦Fr⟧ [*also* **B- E-**] the era of elegance and gaiety that characterized fashionable Parisian life in the period preceding WWI

Belle Isle, Strait of ⟦after the small island, *Belle Isle* (Fr, beautiful island), at its Atlantic entrance, the first land seen by incoming ships⟧ strait between Labrador & Newfoundland: 10-15 mi (16-24 km) wide

Bel·ler·o·phon (bə ler′ə fän′) *n.* ⟦L < Gr *Bellerophōn*⟧ *Gr. Myth.* the hero who kills the monster Chimera, aided by the winged horse Pegasus

belles-let·tres (bel le′tr′, -trə) *pl.n.* ⟦Fr, lit., beautiful letters, fine literature⟧ **1** imaginative writings as distinguished from technical and scientific writings, esp. when characterized by a polished, highly literary style and, often, a somewhat dilettantish manner **2** essays written in a polished, literary style

bel·let·rist (bel le′trist) *n.* a writer of belles-lettres —**bel·le·tris·tic** (bel′ le tris′tik) *adj.*

Belle·vue (bel′vyoo′) ⟦Fr, lit., beautiful view⟧ city in NW Wash.: suburb of Seattle

bell·flow·er (bel′flou′ər) *adj.* designating a large family (Campanulaceae, order Campanulales) of dicotyledonous flowering plants —*n.* any of a genus (*Campanula*) of plants of this family, with showy, bell-shaped flowers of white, pink, or blue, widely distributed in the temperate zones

☆**bell·hop** (-häp′) ***n.*** a person employed by a hotel, club, etc. to carry luggage and do errands

bel·li·cose (bel′i kōs′) ***adj.*** ⟦ME < L *bellicosus* < *bellicus,* of war < *bellum,* war < OL *duellum:* for IE base see DUEL⟧ of a quarrelsome or hostile nature; eager to fight or quarrel; warlike —***SYN.*** BELLIGERENT —**bel′li·cose′ly** ***adv.*** —**bel·li·cos·i·ty** (bel′i käs′ə tē) ***n.***

bel·lied (bel′ēd) ***adj.*** having a belly, esp. of a specified kind [the yellow-*bellied* sapsucker]

bel·lig·er·ence (bə lij′ər əns) ***n.*** a belligerent or aggressively hostile attitude, nature, or quality

bel·lig·er·en·cy (-ən sē) ***n.*** **1** the state of being at war or of being recognized as a belligerent **2** BELLIGERENCE

bel·lig·er·ent (bə lij′ər ənt) ***adj.*** ⟦L *belligerans,* prp. of *belligerare,* to wage war < *bellum,* war (see BELLICOSE) + *gerere,* to carry on⟧ **1** at war; designating or of a state recognized under international law as being engaged in a war **2** of war; of fighting **3** seeking war; warlike **4** showing a readiness to fight or quarrel [a *belligerent* gesture or tone] —***n.*** a belligerent person, group, or nation —**bel·lig′er·ent·ly** ***adv.***

SYN.—**belligerent** implies a taking part in war or fighting or in actions that are likely to provoke fighting [*belligerent* nations]; **bellicose** implies a warlike or hostile nature, suggesting a readiness to fight [a *bellicose* mood]; **pugnacious** and **quarrelsome** both connote aggressiveness and a willingness to initiate a fight, but **quarrelsome** more often suggests pettiness and eagerness to fight for little or no reason; **contentious** suggests an inclination to argue or quarrel, usually with annoying persistence —***ANT.*** **peaceful, friendly**

Bel·lings·hau·sen Sea (bel′iŋz hou′zən) part of the S Pacific Ocean, west of the Antarctic Peninsula

Bel·li·ni[1] (bə lē′nē) ***n.*** ⟦after Giovanni BELLINI[2]⟧ a cocktail consisting of champagne or other sparkling wine with peach juice

Bel·li·ni[2] (bə lē′nē; *It* bel-) **1 Gen·ti·le** (jen tē′le) 1429?-1507; Venetian painter: son of Jacopo **2 Gio·van·ni** (jô vän′nē) 1430?-1516; Venetian painter: teacher of Titian: son of Jacopo **3 Ja·co·po** (yä′kô pô) 1400?-70?; Venetian painter **4 Vin·cen·zo** (vēn chen′tsô) 1801-35; It. operatic composer

bell jar a bell-shaped container or cover made of glass, used to keep gases, air, moisture, etc. in or out: also **bell glass**

bell·man (bel′mən) ***n., pl.*** **-men** (-mən) **1** TOWN CRIER ☆**2** BELLHOP

bell metal an alloy of copper and tin used in bells

bell·mouthed (-mouthd′, -moutht′) ***adj.*** having a flaring mouth or opening like that of a bell

Bel·loc (bel′äk), **(Joseph) Hi·laire (Pierre)** (hi ler′) 1870-1953; Eng. writer, born in France

Bel·lo·na (bə lō′nə) ***n.*** ⟦L < *bellum:* see BELLICOSE⟧ *Rom. Myth.* the goddess of war, wife or sister of Mars

bel·low (bel′ō) ***vi.*** ⟦ME *belwen* < OE *bylgan:* for IE base see BELL[1]⟧ **1** to roar with a powerful, reverberating sound, as a bull does **2** to cry out loudly, as in anger or pain —***vt.*** to utter loudly or powerfully —***n.*** the sound of bellowing

Bel·low (bel′ō), **Saul** (born *Solomon Bellows*) 1915-2005; U.S. novelist, born in Canada

bel·lows (bel′ōz′) ***n.*** ⟦ME *belwes,* orig. pl. of *beli:* see BELLY⟧ [*with sing. or pl. v.*] **1** a device that produces a stream of air through a narrow tube when its sides are pressed together: used in pipe organs, for blowing fires, etc. **2** anything like a bellows, as the lungs, the compressible part of an accordion, etc.

ENTRANCE FOR AIR
VALVE
NOZZLE

bellows

Bel·lows (bel′ōz′), **George (Wesley)** 1882-1925; U.S. painter

bell pepper **1** the large, sweet, bell-shaped, tropical American pepper used as a vegetable **2** the plant (*Capsicum frutescens* var. *grossum*) on which it grows: see CAPSICUM (sense 1)

bells and whistles [Informal] inessential, usually showy features or additions; frills

bell-shaped curve (bel′shāpt′) BELL CURVE

Bell's palsy ⟦after Charles *Bell* (1774-1842), Scot anatomist who identified it⟧ a usually temporary, sudden paralysis of the facial nerve resulting in weakened or paralyzed muscles on one side of the face

bell tower a tower in which a bell or set of bells is hung

bell·weth·er (bel′weth′ər) ***n.*** ⟦ME: see BELL[1] & WETHER⟧ **1** a male sheep, usually wearing a bell, that leads the flock **2** a leader, esp. of a sheeplike crowd **3** anything suggesting the general tendency or direction of events, style, etc.

bell·wort (-wurt′) ***n.*** **1** any of a genus (*Uvularia*) of perennial woodland plants of the lily family, native to North America, with conspicuous, drooping, bell-shaped yellow flowers **2** [Chiefly Brit.] any of various bellflowers (esp. genus *Campanula*)

bel·ly (bel′ē) ***n., pl.*** **-lies** ⟦ME *beli* < OE *belg,* leather bag, purse, bellows < IE base **bhelĝh-,* to swell, bag (< **bhel-,* to inflate) > Ir *bolg,* sack, belly, ON *bylgja,* billow, Goth *balgs,* leather bottle⟧ **1** the lower front part of the human body between the chest and thighs; abdomen **2** the underside of an animal's body **3** the abdominal cavity **4** the stomach **5** an appetite for food **6** the deep interior [the *belly* of a ship] **7** any part, surface, or section that curves outward or bulges, as the swelling part of a sail in the wind, the fleshy middle part of a muscle, or the upper surface of a violin **8** the front part or underside of anything **9** [Archaic] the womb —***vt., vi.*** **-lied, -ly·ing** to swell out; curve out; bulge —☆**belly up** [Slang] to stand or step close as to a counter or railing —**go belly up** [Slang] ⟦from the way in which a dead fish floats in the water⟧ **1** to die: said as of a fish **2** to fail; often, specif., to become bankrupt

bel·ly·ache (-āk′) ***n.*** pain in the abdomen or bowels —☆***vi.*** **-ached′, -ach′ing** [Slang] to complain or grumble

bel·ly·band (-band′) ***n.*** **1** a girth or cinch around an animal's belly, as for keeping a saddle or harness in place: see HARNESS, illus. **2** a cloth band formerly put around a baby's abdomen to prevent protrusion of the navel

bel·ly·but·ton (-but′′n) ***n.*** [Informal] the navel

belly dance a dance of E Mediterranean origin, typically performed by a woman, characterized by a twisting of the abdomen, sinuous hip movements, etc. —**bel′ly-dance′** ***vi.*** **-danced′, -danc′ing** —**belly dancer**

☆**bel·ly-flop** (-fläp′) ***vi.*** **-flopped′, -flop′ping** to dive awkwardly so that the belly strikes flat against the water or other surface —***n.*** an instance or the act of so diving Also **bel′ly-bump′, bel′ly-whop′,** or **bel′ly-slam′**

bel·ly·ful (-fool′) ***n.*** **1** enough or more than enough to eat **2** [Slang] enough or more than enough of anything; all that one can bear

☆**belly laugh** **1** [Informal] a hearty laugh **2** anything that provokes such a laugh, as a line in a play

Bel·mo·pan (bel′mō pan′) capital of Belize, in the central part

Be·lo Ho·ri·zon·te (bā′lō hôr′ə zän′tē; *Port* be′lô rē zôn′te) city in SE Brazil: capital of Minas Gerais state

be·long (bē lôŋ′, bi-) ***vi.*** ⟦ME *bilangen* < *be-,* intens. + *longen,* to be suitable < OE *langian,* to belong⟧ **1** to have a proper or suitable place [the chair *belongs* in the corner; she *belongs* in the movies] **2** to be part of; be related or connected (*to*) **3** to be a member: with *to* **4** to be owned: with *to* **5** [Slang] to be the owner: with *to* [who *belongs* to this toothbrush?]

be·long·ing (-iŋ) ***n.*** **1** a thing that belongs to one **2** [*pl.*] possessions; property **3** close relationship; familiarity; camaraderie [a feeling of *belonging*]

Bel·o·rus·sia (bel′ō rush′ə, bye′lō-) **1** historical region in central Europe corresponding to present-day Belarus **2** BELORUSSIAN SOVIET SOCIALIST REPUBLIC **3** BELARUS

Bel·o·rus·sian (-ən) ***adj.*** of Belarus or its people, language, or culture —***n.*** **1** a person born or living in Belarus **2** the East Slavic language spoken in Belarus

Belorussian Soviet Socialist Republic a republic of the U.S.S.R.: now BELARUS

be·lov·ed (bi luv′id, -luvd′) ***adj.*** ⟦ME *biloved* < *biloven:* see BE & LOVE⟧ dearly loved —***n.*** a beloved person

be·low (bi lō′) ***adv.*** ⟦see BE- & LOW[1]⟧ **1** in or to a lower place; beneath **2** in a lower place on the page or on a later page (of a book, etc.) **3** in or to hell **4** on earth **5** on or to a lower floor or deck **6** in or to a lesser rank, amount, etc. **7** at a temperature lower than zero [it reached 13 *below*] —***prep.*** **1** lower than, as in position, rank, or worth **2** unworthy of [it is *below* her to say that]

below stairs [Chiefly Brit.] **1** DOWNSTAIRS (*adv.* 2) **2** in the servants' area in the basement of a wealthy household Also written **be·low′stairs′** ***adv.*** —**be·low′-stairs′** ***adj.***

Bel·sen (bel′zən) village in W Germany, near Hanover: with the nearby village of Bergen, it was the site of a Nazi prisoner-of-war camp and, later, a concentration camp (called **Ber′gen-Bel′sen**)

Bel·shaz·zar (bel shaz′ər) ***n.*** ⟦Heb *belshatsar* < Akkadian *bēl-sharra-uṣur,* lit., "Bel, protect the king"⟧ *Bible* the last king of Babylon, who was warned of defeat by the handwriting on the wall: Dan. 5

belt (belt) ***n.*** ⟦OE, akin to OHG *balz,* ult. < L *balteus* < ? Etr⟧ **1** a strip or band of leather or other material worn around the waist to hold clothing up, support tools, etc., or as an ornament or sign of rank: see also SAFETY BELT **2** any encircling thing like this **3** a long, flexible band used to feed bullets into a machine gun **4** an endless strap or band for transferring motion from one wheel or pulley to another, or for conveying things **5** a region distinguished from others in some way [the Corn *Belt*] **6** [Informal] a hard blow; cuff **7** [Slang] *a)* a drink or big gulp, esp. of liquor *b)* pleasurable excitement; thrill —***vt.*** **1** to encircle with or as with a belt; girdle **2** to fasten or attach with or as with a belt **3** to strike with a belt ☆**4** [Informal] to sing loudly and lustily with a driving rhythm: usually with *out* **5** [Informal] to strike with force ☆**6** [Slang] *a)* to take one or more drinks of (liquor) (often with *down*) *b)* to drink heavily —***vi.*** [Informal] to move at high speed —**below the belt** unfair(ly); foul: originally said of a blow to the groin in boxing —**tighten one's belt** **1** to endure hunger, privation, etc. as best one can **2** to live more thriftily —☆**under one's belt** [Informal] as part of one's experience [ten years of service *under his belt*]

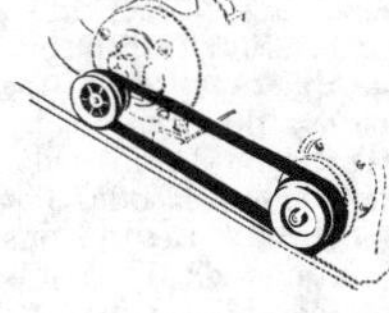

transmission belt

Bel·tane (bel′tān′) ***n.*** ⟦Scot < Gael *Bealtainn*⟧ Celtic May Day

belt·ed (bel′tid) ***adj.*** **1** wearing a belt, esp. as a mark of distinction [*a belted* knight] **2** furnished with a belt or belts [*a belted* jacket, a *belted* tire] **3** having or marked by a band or stripe

belt·ing (-tiŋ) ***n.*** **1** material for making belts **2** belts collectively **3** [Slang] a beating

belt-tight·en·ing (belt′tīt′′n iŋ) ***n.*** a reduction of expenditures; economizing —***adj.*** of or involving the reduction of expenditures [*belt-tightening* measures]

☆**belt·way** (belt′wā′) ***n.*** an expressway passing around an urban area —**the Beltway** Washington, D.C., esp. as regarded as the center of U.S. government and politics: so called from the expressway around the District of Columbia & nearby areas

be·lu·ga (bə lo͞o′gə) ***n.***, *pl.* **-ga** or **-gas** **1** ⟦Russ < *belyj,* white⟧ a large, white sturgeon (*Huso huso*) of the Black Sea and the Caspian Sea **2** ⟦Russ *beluxa* < *belyj,* white⟧ a large, white toothed whale (*Delphinapterus leucas*) of northern seas: it is in the same family (Monodontidae) as the narwhal **3** caviar prepared from the eggs of the white sturgeon: also called **beluga caviar**

bel·ve·dere (bel′və dir′, bel′və dir′) ***n.*** ⟦It, beautiful view < *bel,* beautiful (< L *bellus*) + *vedere* (< L *videre,* to see: see VISION)⟧ **1** a summerhouse on a height, or an open, roofed gallery in an upper story, built for giving a view of the scenery **2** [**B-**] a court in the Vatican, housing a collection of classical art

be·ma (bē′mə) ***n.***, *pl.* **be′ma·ta** (-mə tə) or **be′mas** ⟦Gr *bēma,* platform, lit., a step < base of *bainein,* to go: see COME⟧ **1** in ancient Greece, a speaker's platform **2** BIMAH **3** *Eastern Orthodox Ch.* the enclosed area surrounding the altar

Bem·ba (bem′bə) ***n.*** **1** *pl.* **-bas** or **-ba** a member of a people of N Zambia **2** the Bantu language of this people

be·mire (bē mīr′, bi-) ***vt.*** **-mired′**, **-mir′ing** **1** to make dirty with or as with mire **2** to cause to bog down in mud

be·moan (bē mōn′, bi-) ***vt., vi.*** ⟦ME *bimaenen* < OE *bemaenan:* see BE- & MOAN⟧ to moan about or deplore (a loss, grief, etc.); lament [to *bemoan* one's fate]

be·muse (bē myo͞oz′, bi-) ***vt.*** **-mused′**, **-mus′ing** ⟦BE- + MUSE⟧ **1** to muddle or stupefy **2** to plunge in thought; preoccupy: usually in the passive voice —**be·muse′ment** ***n.***

ben[1] (ben) ***n.*** ⟦Heb *ben*⟧ son (of) [Rabbi *Ben* Ezra]

ben[2] (ben) ***n.*** ⟦Scot < Gael *beann,* akin to MIr *benn,* a peak: see PIN⟧ [Scot. or Irish] a mountain peak [*Ben* Nevis]

ben[3] (ben) [Scot.] ***adv., prep.*** ⟦Scot < ME *binne* < OE *be-,* BY + *innan,* in⟧ within; inside —***n.*** the inner room or living room of a cottage

ben·act·y·zine (bən ak′tə zēn′, -zin′) ***n.*** ⟦arbitrary coinage⟧ a crystalline drug, $C_{20}H_{25}NO_3$, used to make tranquilizers

☆**Ben·a·dryl** (ben′ə dril′) *trademark for* DIPHENHYDRAMINE —***n.*** [**b-**] this antihistamine

Be·na·res (bə nä′rēz′) *former name for* VARANASI

Be·na·ven·te (y Mar·tí·nez) (be′nä ven′te ē mär tē′neth), **Ja·cin·to** (hä thēn′tô) 1866-1954; Sp. playwright

bench (bench) ***n.*** ⟦ME < OE *benc:* see BANK[2]⟧ **1** a long seat for several persons, with or without a back and often made of wood or stone **2** a seat between the two sides of a boat **3** the place where judges sit in a court **4** [*sometimes* **B-**] *a)* the status or office of a judge *b)* judges collectively *c)* a law court **5** *a)* an official's seat or his office, status, etc. *b)* the officials in this office ☆**6** *a)* a seat on which the players on a sports team sit when not participating in the action *b)* auxiliary players collectively **7** a stand upon which dogs, or cats, are exhibited and judged at a show **8** a strong table on which work with tools is done, often one that is part of a machine; worktable **9** a terrace along the bank of a body of water, often marking a former shoreline **10** a shelflike layer of rock formed by erosion, mining, etc. **11** a low, usually padded platform used in weight lifting —***vt.*** **1** to provide with benches **2** to place on a bench, esp. an official one **3** to exhibit at a dog, or cat, show **4** [Informal] BENCH-PRESS ☆**5** *Sports* to take or keep (a player) out of a game —**on the bench** **1** presiding in a law court; serving as a judge ☆**2** *Sports* not taking part in the game, as an auxiliary player

bench·er (ben′cher) ***n.*** a person who sits on a bench, as a judge or member of the British Parliament

☆**bench jockey** [Slang] *Sports* a player on the bench who taunts opposing players, the officials, etc.

bench·land (bench′land′) ***n.*** BENCH (sense 9)

Bench·ley (bench′lē), **Robert (Charles)** 1889-1945; U.S. humorist

bench mark **1** a surveyor's mark made on a permanent landmark of known position and altitude: it is used as a reference point in determining other altitudes **2** a standard or point of reference in measuring or judging quality, value, etc. Also, and for *2* usually, written **bench′mark′** ***n.***

bench press ⟦see PRESS[1], *n.* 9⟧ a weight-lifting exercise, performed while one is lying on a bench with the feet on the floor, in which a barbell is pushed upward from the chest until the arms are fully extended —**bench′-press′** ***vt.***

☆**bench show** an exhibition of small animals, esp. dogs, or cats, displayed on benches and competing for awards on the basis of how closely they conform to ideal standards for the breed

bench trial a trial before a judge, without a jury

☆**bench·warm·er** (bench′wôr′mər) ***n.*** [Informal] in team sports, an auxiliary player who is seldom called upon to participate in games and hence spends much time on the bench

bench warrant an order issued by a judge or law court for the arrest of a person, as one charged with contempt of court or a criminal offense

bend[1] (bend) ***vt.*** **bent**, **bend′ing** ⟦ME *benden* < OE *bendan,* to confine with a string (< Gmc **bandjan* < **bindan* > BIND); hence, to fetter, bend (a bow)⟧ **1** [Obs.] to cause tension in (a bow, etc.), as by drawing with a string **2** to force (an object) into a curved or crooked form, or (*back*) to its original form, by turning, pulling, pressing, etc. **3** to turn from a straight line [light rays are *bent* by refraction] **4** to flex a limb at (a joint, as the knee or elbow) **5** to make submit or give in [to *bend* another's will to one's wishes] **6** to turn or direct (one's eyes, attention, energy, etc. *to*) **7** to cause to have a fixed purpose; determine: used in the passive voice [he was *bent* on success] **8** to incline or tend (*to* or *toward*) **9** to interpret or apply (a rule) in a way calculated to gain a desired end **10** *Naut.* to attach; fasten [to *bend* a signal flag onto a halyard] —***vi.*** **1** to turn or be turned from a straight line or from some direction or position **2** to yield by curving or crooking, as from pressure **3** to crook or curve the body from a standing position; stoop (*over* or *down*) **4** to give in; yield [he *bent* to her wishes] **5** [Archaic] to direct one's attention, energy, etc. (*to* something) —***n.*** **1** a bending or being bent **2** a bent or curving part, as of a river **3** *Naut.* a wale: *usually used in pl.* —**SYN.** CURVE —**round the bend** [Brit. Informal] crazy, mad, insane, etc. —**bend′a·ble** ***adj.***

bend[2] (bend) ***n.*** ⟦ME < prec.⟧ **1** any of various knots used to tie one rope to another or to something else **2** *Tanning* one half of a trimmed hide

bend[3] (bend) ***n.*** ⟦OFr *bende:* see BAND[1]⟧ *Heraldry* a diagonal stripe or band on a shield from the upper left to the lower right corner (as seen by the viewer)

☆**Ben·day process** (ben′dā′) ⟦after *Benjamin Day* (1838-1916), N.Y. printer⟧ [*often* **b- p-**] *Photoengraving* a process for adding tone or shading, as in reproducing drawings, by the overlay on the plate of patterns, as of dots: also written **Ben Day process**

bend·ed (ben′did) ***vt.*** *archaic pt. & pp. of* BEND[1] —**on bended knee** in a humble, contrite, or beseeching manner

bend·er (ben′dər) ***n.*** **1** a person or thing that bends ☆**2** [Slang] a drinking bout; spree

bends (bendz) ***pl.n.*** ⟦so called from the involuntary flexing of the limbs in response to the pain⟧ [*with sing. or pl. v.*] the severe pain in the limbs, joints, and abdomen during decompression sickness: preceded by *the*

bend sinister *Heraldry* a diagonal band or stripe on a shield, from the upper right to the lower left corner (as seen by the viewer): popularly understood to signify bastardy in the family line

be·neath (bē nēth′, bi-) ***adv.*** ⟦ME *binethe* < OE *beneothan* < *be-,* BY + *neothan,* down: see NETHER⟧ **1** in a lower place; below **2** just below something; underneath —***prep.*** **1** below; lower than **2** directly under; underneath **3** covered by [*beneath* a blanket of snow] **4** under the influence or control of **5** inferior to or lower than in rank, quality, worth, etc. **6** unworthy of [it is *beneath* him to cheat]

ben·e·dict (ben′ə dikt′) ***n.*** ⟦alteration of *Benedick,* the bachelor in Shakespeare's *Much Ado About Nothing* who marries Beatrice⟧ a recently married man, esp. one who seemed to be a confirmed bachelor

Ben·e·dict[1] (ben′ə dikt′) ***n.*** ⟦LL(Ec) *Benedictus,* lit., blessed: see BENEDICTION⟧ a masculine name: dim. *Ben;* var. *Bennet, Bennett*

Ben·e·dict[2] (ben′ə dikt′) **1** Saint (A.D. 480?-543?); It. monk: founder of the Benedictine order: his day is July 11: also called **Saint Benedict of Nur·si·a** (nʉr′sē ə) **2** (born *Prospero Lambertini*) 1675-1758; pope (1740-58) **3** **Benedict XV** (born *Giacomo della Chiesa*) 1854-1922; pope (1914-22) **4** **Benedict XVI** (born *Joseph Alois Ratzinger*) 1927- ; pope (2005-13) **5** **Ruth (Fulton)** 1887-1948; U.S. anthropologist

Ben·e·dic·tine (ben′ə dik′tin; *also, and for n. 2 usually,* -tēn) ***adj.*** ⟦< Fr *bénédictin* or ModL *benedictinus,* masc. adjs., after *Benedictus,* Saint BENEDICT[2]⟧ **1** of Saint Benedict **2** designating or of the monastic order based on his teachings, founded *c.* A.D. 529 —***n.*** **1** a Benedictine monk or nun **2** ⟦< *Bénédictine,* trademark < fem. of Fr adj.⟧ [**b-**] a liqueur, containing aromatic herbs and spices, originally made by Benedictine monks in France

ben·e·dic·tion (ben′ə dik′shən) ***n.*** ⟦ME *benediccioun* < LL(Ec) *benedictio* < *benedicere,* to bless < L, to commend < *bene,* well + *dicere,* to speak: see DICTION⟧ **1** a blessing **2** an invocation of divine blessing, esp. at the end of a religious service **3** blessedness **4** [**B-**] *R.C.Ch.* a devotional service during which a consecrated Host is exposed in a monstrance and a solemn blessing is given with the Host —**ben′e·dic′to·ry** (-tə rē) ***adj.***

Ben·e·dic·tus (-təs) ***n.*** ⟦LL (Ec), blessed, pp. of *benedicere:* see prec.⟧ **1** Zacharias' hymn (Luke 1:68-79) beginning "Blessed," a part of Lauds **2** a short hymn of praise (Matt. 21:9), also beginning "Blessed," used in the Mass: term used esp. in ref. to the traditional Latin Mass **3** music for either of these hymns

ben·e·fac·tion (ben′ə fak′shen, ben′ə fak′shən) ***n.*** ⟦LL *benefactio* < L *benefacere,* to do (something) well, do a good deed < *bene,* well + *facere,* DO[1]⟧ **1** the act of doing good or helping others, esp. by giving money as a charitable donation **2** the money or help so given

ben·e·fac·tor (ben′ə fak′tər) ***n.*** ⟦ME < LL: see prec.⟧ a person who has given help, esp. financial help; patron

ben·e·fac·tress (-tris) ***n.*** a female benefactor: see -ESS

be·nef·ic (bə nef′ik) ***adj.*** ⟦L *beneficus* < *benefacere:* see BENEFACTION⟧ BENEFICENT

ben·e·fice (ben′ə fis) ***n.*** ⟦ME < OFr < ML *beneficium* < L, a kindness, service, promotion < prec.⟧ **1** land held by a feudal tenant for services rendered the owner **2** an endowed church office providing a living for a vicar, rector, etc. **3** its income —*vt.* **-ficed**, **-fic·ing** to provide with a benefice

be·nef·i·cence (bə nefʹə səns) *n.* ⟦ME < L *beneficentia* < *benefacere*: see BENEFACTION⟧ **1** the fact or quality of being kind or doing good; charity **2** a charitable act or generous gift

be·nef·i·cent (-sənt) *adj.* **1** showing beneficence; doing good **2** resulting in benefit —**be·nefʹi·cent·ly** *adv.*

ben·e·fi·cial (benʹə fishʹəl) *adj.* ⟦ME < OFr < LL *beneficialis* < L *benefacere*: see BENEFACTION⟧ **1** producing benefits; advantageous; favorable **2** receiving benefit **3** *Law* for one's own benefit [*beneficial* interest] —**benʹe·fiʹcial·ly** *adv.*

ben·e·fi·ci·ar·y (benʹə fishʹē erʹē, -fishʹər ē) *adj.* ⟦L *beneficiarius*⟧ of or holding a benefice —*n., pl.* **-arʹies 1** a holder of a benefice **2** anyone receiving benefit **3** a person named to receive the income or inheritance from a will, insurance policy, trust, etc. **4** *Law* a person for whose benefit a trust has been created

ben·e·fit (benʹə fit) *n.* ⟦ME *benefet* < OFr *bienfait*, a kindness < L *benefactum*, meritorious act < *benefacere*: see BENEFACTION⟧ **1** [Archaic] a kindly, charitable act; benefaction **2** *a)* gain or advantage [tax legislation for the *benefit* of the rich] *b)* a favorable or beneficial circumstance, condition, or result [several *benefits* to good nutrition] **3** FRINGE BENEFIT **4** [*often pl.*] payments made by an insurance company, public agency, welfare society, etc. as during sickness, retirement, unemployment, etc. or for death **5** any public performance, bazaar, dance, etc. the proceeds of which are to help a certain person, group, or cause —*vt.* **-fit·ed** or **-fit·ted**, **-fit·ing** or **-fit·ting** to do good to or for; aid —*vi.* to receive advantage; profit

benefit of clergy 1 the exemption of the medieval clergy from trial or punishment except in a church court **2** an administering or sanctioning by the church [a couple that is married without *benefit of clergy*]

benefit society (*or* association) an organization which, by means of dues, secures for its members certain benefits, such as life insurance, hospitalization, etc.

Be·ne·lux (benʹə luksʹ) *n.* ⟦< BE(LGIUM), NE(THERLANDS), LUX(EMBOURG)⟧ the economic union of Belgium, Netherlands, & Luxembourg, established by treaty in 1948: in full **Benelux Economic Union**

Be·neš (benʹesh), **Ed·vard** (edʹvärt) 1884-1948; Czech statesman: president of Czechoslovakia (1935-38; 1946-48): president of government in exile (1939-45)

Be·nét (bi nāʹ, bə-), **Stephen Vincent** 1898-1943; U.S. poet & writer

be·nev·o·lence (bə nevʹə ləns) *n.* ⟦ME & OFr < L *benevolentia*: see fol.⟧ **1** an inclination to do good; kindliness **2** a kindly, charitable act or gift; beneficence **3** a forced loan formerly levied by some English kings on their subjects

be·nev·o·lent (-lənt) *adj.* ⟦ME & OFr < L *benevolens* < *bene*, well + *volens*, prp. of *velle*, to wish: see WILL[1]⟧ **1** doing or inclined to do good; kindly; charitable **2** characterized by or resulting from benevolence —**SYN.** KIND —**be·nevʹo·lent·ly** *adv.*

Ben·gal (ben gôlʹ, beŋ-; beŋʹgəl, benʹ-) **1** region in the NE part of the Indian peninsula, divided between the Indian state of West Bengal & Bangladesh **2 Bay of** part of the Indian Ocean, east of India & west of Myanmar & the Malay Peninsula

Ben·ga·lese (benʹgə lēzʹ, beŋʹ-; -lēsʹ) *adj.* BENGALI (*adj.*) —*n., pl.* **-leseʹ** BENGALI (*n.* 1)

Ben·gal·i (ben gôlʹē, beŋ-) *n.* **1** a person born or living in Bengal **2** the Indo-Aryan language spoken in Bengal —*adj.* of Bengal or its people, language, or culture

ben·ga·line (beŋʹgə lēnʹ, beŋʹgə lēnʹ) *n.* ⟦Fr, after BENGAL, area from which the cloth was imported⟧ a heavy, corded cloth of silk, rayon, or the like and either wool or cotton

Ben·gal light (beŋʹgəl, benʹ-) a firework or flare with a steady blue light, used, esp. formerly, as a signal, etc.

Ben·gal tiger (beŋʹgəl, benʹ-) a large, fierce tiger native to Bengal or the adjacent regions: formerly thought to be a separate subspecies or species because of its large size

Ben·gha·zi or **Ben·ga·si** (ben gäʹzē, beŋ-) seaport in NE Libya, on the Gulf of Sidra: formerly (1951-72) one of the country's two capitals

Ben·gue·la Current (ben gāʹlə) ⟦after *Benguela*, city in W Angola⟧ a strong ocean current in the South Atlantic, flowing northward along the SW coast of Africa

Ben-Gu·ri·on (ben goorʹē ən), **David** 1886-1973; Israeli statesman, born in Poland: prime minister of Israel (1948-53; 1955-63)

Be·ni (bāʹnē) river in NW Bolivia, rising in the Andes, flowing northward to join the Mamoré and form the Madeira: *c.* 1,000 mi (1,609 km)

be·night·ed (bē nītʹid, bi-) *adj.* ⟦ME, pp. of *binighten*: see BE- & NIGHT⟧ **1** caught or surrounded by darkness or night **2** intellectually or morally backward; unenlightened

be·nign (bi nīnʹ) *adj.* ⟦ME & OFr *benigne* < L *benignus*, good, lit., well-born < *bene*, well (cf. sense development of GENTLE) + *genus*, birth: see GENUS⟧ **1** good-natured; kindly **2** favorable; beneficial **3** *Med.* doing little or no harm; not malignant; specif., not cancerous [*benign* tumors] —**SYN.** KIND —**be·nignʹly** *adv.*

be·nig·nant (bi nigʹnənt) *adj.* ⟦< prec., by analogy with MALIGNANT⟧ **1** kindly or gracious, sometimes in a patronizing way **2** BENIGN (senses 2 & 3) —**be·nigʹnan·cy** *n., pl.* **-cies** —**be·nigʹnant·ly** *adv.*

be·nig·ni·ty (-nə tē) *n.* ⟦ME & OFr *benignite* < L *benignitas*: see BENIGN⟧ **1** benignancy; kindliness **2** *pl.* **-ties** a kind or generous act

Be·nin (be nēnʹ, -ninʹ) **1** former native kingdom (fl. 14th-17th cent.) in W Africa, including what came to be known as the Slave Coast **2** country in WC Africa, on the Bight of Benin: formerly a French territory, it became independent in 1960: 43,483 sq mi (112,620 sq km); caps. Porto Novo (constitutional), Cotonou (administrative) **3 Bight of** N part of the Gulf of Guinea, just west of the Niger delta —**Be·ninʹese** (-ēz) *adj., n., pl.* **-ese**

ben·i·son (benʹə zən, -sən) *n.* ⟦ME *benisoun* < OFr *beneisson* < LL(Ec) *benedictio*, BENEDICTION⟧ [Archaic] a blessing; benediction

Ben·i Su·ef (benʹē soo āfʹ) city in NE Egypt, on the Nile

ben·ja·min (benʹjə mən) *n.* ⟦altered < Fr *benjoin*, BENZOIN⟧ BENZOIN (sense 1)

Ben·ja·min[1] (benʹjə mən) *n.* ⟦Heb *binyamin*, lit., son of the right hand; hence, favorite son⟧ **1** a masculine name: dim. *Ben, Benny* **2** *Bible a)* Jacob's youngest son, whose mother was Rachel: Gen. 35:18 *b)* the tribe of Israel descended from him: Num. 1:36

Ben·ja·min[2] (benʹjə mən) **1 Judah Philip** 1811-84; U.S. lawyer: Confederate secretary of state (1862-65) **2 Walter** 1892-1940; Ger. philosopher & critic

☆**ben·ne** or **ben·e** (benʹē) *n.* ⟦< Mende (Sierra Leone) *bene*⟧ SESAME

Ben·nett[1] (benʹit) *n.* a masculine name: see BENEDICT[1]

Ben·nett[2] (benʹit) **1 (Enoch) Arnold** 1867-1931; Eng. novelist **2 James Gordon** 1795-1872; U.S. journalist, born in Scotland: founder of the New York *Herald* **3 Richard Bedford** 1st Viscount Bennett 1870-1947; Cdn. statesman: prime minister of Canada (1930-35)

Ben Ne·vis (ben nēʹvis, -nevʹəs) mountain in the Grampian Mountains, WC Scotland: highest peak in the British Isles: 4,406 ft (1,343 m)

Ben·ning·ton (benʹiŋ tən) ⟦after *Benning* Wentworth (1696-1770), 1st gov. of New Hampshire⟧ town in SW Vt.: in a Revolutionary battle (1777) fought nearby, Hessians sent by Burgoyne were defeated by colonial forces

☆**ben·ny** (benʹē) *n., pl.* **-nies** ⟦< BEN(ZEDRINE) + -Y[1]⟧ [Slang] an amphetamine pill, esp. Benzedrine, used as a stimulant

Ben·ny (benʹē), **Jack** (born *Benjamin Kubelsky*) 1894-1974; U.S. radio, television, & film comedian

bent[1] (bent) *vt., vi. pt. & pp. of* BEND[1] —*adj.* **1** made curved or crooked; not straight **2** strongly inclined or determined: with *on* [*bent* on going] **3** set in a course; bound [westward *bent*] **4** [Slang] *a)* dishonest; crooked *b)* eccentric; odd —*n.* **1** an inclination; tendency **2** a natural leaning or tendency; propensity [a *bent* for music, a criminal *bent*] **3** a framework transverse to the length of a structure, for supporting lateral as well as vertical loads —**SYN.** INCLINATION —☆**bent out of shape** [Slang] very angry, upset, or agitated —**to (or at) the top of one's bent** to (or at) the limit of one's capacity or ability

bent[2] (bent) *n.* ⟦ME < OE *beonot*, bent, a rush < WGmc **binut* > Ger *binse*⟧ **1** any of a genus (*Agrostis*) of dense, low-growing perennial grasses that spread by putting out runners and are often used for lawns and golf greens: also called **bentʹgrassʹ 2** the stiff flower stalk of certain grasses **3** [Now Dial., Chiefly Brit.] a heath; moor

Ben·tham (benʹthəm, -təm), **Jeremy** 1748-1832; Eng. philosopher, economist, & jurist

Ben·tham·ism (-izʹəm) *n.* the utilitarian philosophy of Jeremy Bentham, which holds that the greatest happiness of the greatest number should be the ultimate goal of society and of the individual —**Benʹtham·iteʹ** (-īt') *n.*

ben·thos (benʹthäsʹ) *n.* ⟦ModL < Gr, depth of the sea; akin to *bathos*: see BATHY-⟧ all the plants and animals living on or closely associated with the bottom of a body of water, esp. the ocean —**benʹthic** (-thik) *adj.*, **ben·thonʹic** (-thänʹik)

ben·to (benʹtō) *n., pl.* **-tos** ⟦Jpn < Chin⟧ **1** a small box with compartments, of a type popular in Japan and SE Asia, for holding several courses of a single meal: also **bento box 2** a packed meal, esp. a lunch, of a kind traditionally stored or served in such a box

Ben·ton (benʹtən) **1 Thomas Hart** 1782-1858; U.S. senator (1821-51) **2 Thomas Hart** 1889-1975; U.S. painter; grandnephew of the senator

☆**ben·ton·ite** (benʹtən īt') *n.* ⟦after Fort *Benton* (named for Senator BENTON) in Montana, where it is found⟧ a porous clay consisting mainly of the mineral montmorillonite, which swells greatly when it absorbs water

bent·wood (bentʹwoodʹ) *adj.* designating furniture made of wood permanently bent into various forms by the application of heat, moisture, and pressure

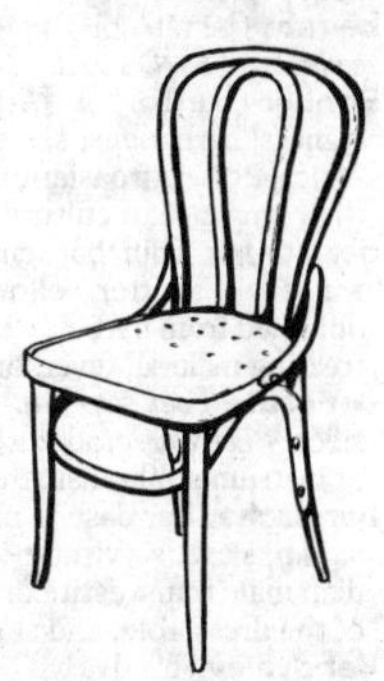
bentwood chair

Be·nue (bāʹnwā) river in W Africa, a tributary of the Niger, flowing through Cameroon and Nigeria: *c.* 900 mi (1,448 km)

be·numb (bē numʹ, bi-) *vt.* ⟦< ME *binumen*, pp. of *binimen*, to take away < OE *beniman* < *be-*, BE- + *niman*, to take (see -NOMY); *-b* by analogy with DUMB⟧ **1** to make numb physically **2** to deaden the mind, will, or feelings of [my mind was *benumbed* by grief]

Ben·xi (bunʹshēʹ) city in Liaoning province, NE China, near Shenyang

benz- (benz) *combining form* BENZO-: used before a vowel

benz·al·de·hyde (ben zalʹdə hīdʹ) *n.* ⟦BENZ(O)- + ALDEHYDE⟧ a clear, volatile, pleasant-smelling liquid, C_6H_5CHO, found in the oil of the bitter almond and used in making dyes, perfumes, chemicals, etc.

☆**ben·ze·drine** (ben′zə drēn′) ***n.*** ⟦< *Benzedrine,* former trademark < BENZ(O)- + (EPH)EDRINE⟧ [*also* **B-**] AMPHETAMINE

ben·zene (ben′zēn, ben zēn′) ***n.*** ⟦BENZ(OIC) + -ENE⟧ a clear, flammable, poisonous, aromatic liquid, C_6H_6, obtained by scrubbing coal gas with oil and by the fractional distillation of coal tar: it is used as a solvent and in making a vast number of derivatives used in plastics, insecticides, detergents, paints, dyes, etc.

benzene hex·a·chlo·ride (hek′sə klôr′īd′) a compound, $C_6H_6Cl_6$, used as an insecticide: see also LINDANE

benzene ring a structural unit in the molecules of aromatic organic compounds, represented by a ring of six atoms of carbon with alternate double bonds between the carbon atoms: in the molecule of benzene six atoms of hydrogen are attached to the ring, one to each atom of carbon, but in derivatives of benzene one or more atoms of hydrogen are replaced by atoms of other elements or by groups of atoms: also called **benzene nucleus**

ben·zi·dine (ben′zə dēn′) ***n.*** ⟦< BENZENE⟧ a white or reddish crystalline organic base, $NH_2C_6H_4C_6H_4NH_2$, used in the manufacture of dyes

ben·zine (ben′zēn, ben zēn′) ***n.*** ⟦BENZ(OIC) + -INE[3]⟧ [Archaic] LIGROIN

ben·zo- (ben′zō, -zə) ⟦see BENZENE⟧ *combining form* **1** relating to benzene [*benzopyrene*] **2** the divalent radical C_6H_4 [*benzocaine*]

ben·zo·ate (ben′zō āt′) ***n.*** ⟦prec. + -ATE[2]⟧ a salt or ester of benzoic acid

benzoate of soda SODIUM BENZOATE

ben·zo·caine (ben′zō kān′, -zə-) ***n.*** ⟦BENZO- + (CO)CAINE⟧ a white, crystalline, odorless powder, $C_6H_4NH_2COOC_2H_5$, used in ointments as a local anesthetic and for protection against sunburn; ethyl-para-aminobenzoate

ben·zo·di·az·e·pine (ben′zō dī az′ə pēn′) ***n.*** ⟦BENZO- + DI-[1] + AZ(O)- + *-epine* < (H)EP(TA)- + -INE[3]⟧ any of a class of synthetic, potentially addictive, tranquilizers and sleeping pills, including Valium, Librium, and Dalmane

ben·zo·ic (ben zō′ik) ***adj.*** ⟦BENZO(IN) + -IC⟧ [Archaic] of or derived from benzoin

benzoic acid a white, crystalline organic acid, C_6H_5COOH, produced commercially from toluene and used as an antiseptic and preservative and in the making of perfumes, flavorings, etc.

ben·zo·in (ben′zō in′, ben zō′in; ben′zoin′) ***n.*** ⟦Fr *benjoin* < It *benzoino* < Ar *lubān jāwī,* incense of Java: *lu-* dropped because falsely assumed to be the article⟧ **1** a balsamic resin obtained from certain tropical Asian trees (genus *Styrax* of the storax family) and used in medicine and perfumery and as incense **2** any of a genus (*Lindera*) of aromatic plants of the laurel family; esp., the spicebush of E North America **3** *Chem.* a white, crystalline substance, $C_6H_5CHOHCOC_6H_5$, used in making antiseptic ointments and in respiration inhalants

ben·zol (ben′zôl′, -zōl′) ***n.*** ⟦BENZ(O)- + -OL[1]⟧ [Now Chiefly Brit.] a name used for products that consist mostly of benzene

ben·zo·phe·none (ben′zō fi nōn′, -fē′nōn′) ***n.*** ⟦BENZO- + PHEN(OL) + -ONE⟧ a white, sweet-smelling crystalline ketone, $C_6H_5COC_6H_5$, used as an intermediate compound in making flavorings, fragrances, etc.

ben·zo·py·rene (ben′zō pī′rēn′) ***n.*** ⟦BENZO- + PYRENE[2]⟧ an aromatic hydrocarbon, $C_{20}H_{12}$, found in coal tar, cigarette smoke, etc. and known to be a cause of cancer in animals: sometimes called **benz·py·rene** (benz′pī′rēn)

ben·zo·yl (ben′zō il′) ***n.*** ⟦BENZO- + -YL⟧ the radical C_6H_5CO, found in benzoic acid and some of its derivatives

ben·zyl (ben′zil′) ***n.*** ⟦BENZ(O)- + -YL⟧ the radical $C_6H_5CH_2$, found in organic compounds derived from toluene

Be·o·grad (be′ō grād′) *Serbo-Croatian name for* BELGRADE

Be·o·wulf (bā′ə woolf′) ***n.*** ⟦< ?; prob. understood in OE as *beo,* BEE[1] + *wulf,* WOLF, hence as a kenning for "bear"⟧ hero of the Old English folk epic of that name, an Anglian poem probably composed during the first half of the 8th cent. A.D.

be·queath (bē kwēth′, -kwēth′; bi-) ***vt.*** ⟦ME *bequethen* < OE *becwethan,* to declare, give by will < *be-,* BE- + *cwethan,* to say: see QUOTH⟧ **1** to leave (property) to another by last will and testament **2** to hand down; pass on [*he bequeathed* his talent to his son] —**be·queath′al** ***n.***

be·quest (-kwest′) ***n.*** ⟦ME *biquest* < *be-,* BE- + OE *-quiss,* a saying < *cwethan,* to speak (see QUOTH); *-t* is unhistoric⟧ **1** the act of bequeathing **2** anything bequeathed

be·rate (bē rāt′, bi-) ***vt.*** **-rat′ed, -rat′ing** ⟦BE- + RATE[2]⟧ to scold or rebuke severely —***SYN.*** SCOLD

Ber·ber (bur′bər) ***n.*** ⟦Ar, earlier *Barbar* < L *Barbari* < Gr *barbaroi,* lit., foreigners, barbarians: see BARBAROUS⟧ **1** a member of a Muslim people of N Africa **2** the Afroasiatic language of this people —***adj.*** of the Berbers or their language or culture

ber·ber·ine (bur′bər ēn′, -in′) ***n.*** ⟦< ModL *berberina* < ML *barberis,* BARBERRY⟧ a bitter, yellow alkaloid, $C_{20}H_{17}NO_4 \cdot 6H_2O$ or $C_{20}H_{19}NO_5 \cdot 6H_2O$, obtained from barberry and other plants: it is used as a dye and as a drug in treating malaria, fever, or skin ulcers

ber·ceuse (ber söz′) ***n.,*** *pl.* **-ceuses′** (-söz′) ⟦Fr < *bercer,* to rock, lull to sleep < *berceau,* cradle < VL **bertium,* woven basket⟧ **1** a lullaby **2** a piece of instrumental music that has a rocking or lulling effect

ber·dache (bər dash′) ***n.*** ⟦? via CdnFr < MFr *bardache* < It *bardascia* < Ar *bardaj,* slave, servitude < Pers *bardah,* slave, page⟧ a North American Indian male transvestite or homosexual who was accepted in his assumption of the dress, role, and status of a woman

Ber·dya·ev (bir dyä′yif), **Ni·ko·lai (Aleksandrovich)** (nē kô lī′) 1874-1948; Russ. religious philosopher, in France after 1922

be·reave (bē rēv′, bi-) ***vt.*** **-reaved′** or **-reft′** (-reft′), **-reav′ing** ⟦ME *bireven* < OE *bereafian,* to deprive, rob < *be-,* BE- + *reafian,* akin to Ger *rauben:* see REAVE[1]⟧ **1** to deprive or rob; dispossess: now usually in the pp. *bereft* [*she was bereft* of hope or happiness] **2** to leave in a sad or lonely state, as by loss or death **3** [Obs.] to take away by force —**be·reave′ment** ***n.***

be·reaved (-rēvd′) ***adj.*** grieving over the death of a relative or friend —**the bereaved** the survivors of a person who has died recently

be·reft (-reft′) ***vt. alt. pt. & pp. of*** BEREAVE —***adj.*** **1** deprived, robbed, or devoid, as of life, hope, or happiness **2** BEREAVED

Ber·e·ni·ce (bər nēs′, bur′nis, ber′ə nī′sē) ***n.*** a feminine name: see BERNICE

Ber·e·ni·ce's Hair (ber′ə nī′sēz′) the constellation Coma Berenices

Ber·en·son (ber′ən sən), **Bernard** 1865-1959; U.S. art critic, born in Lithuania

be·ret (bə rā′) ***n.*** ⟦Fr *béret* < Prov *berret* < LL *birrettum:* see BIRETTA⟧ a round, flat cap of felt, wool, etc.

be·ret·ta (bə ret′ə) ***n.*** BIRETTA

Be·re·zi·na (bə rez′i nə) river in Belarus, flowing into the Dnieper: *c.* 365 mi (587 km): site of a battle (1812) in which Napoleon's army suffered severe losses while making its retreat from Moscow

Be·rez·ni·ki (bər yôz′nə kē) city in E European Russia, at the foot of the Urals, on the Kama River

beret

berg (burg) ***n.*** ICEBERG

Berg (berk; *E* berg), **Al·ban** (äl′bän) 1885-1935; Austrian composer

Ber·ga·ma (ber′gə mä′) town in W Turkey, on the site of ancient Pergamum

Ber·ga·mo (ber′gä mō′) commune in Lombardy, N Italy

ber·ga·mot (bur′gə mät′) ***n.*** ⟦Fr *bergamote* < It *bergamotta* < Turk *begarmûdi,* prince's pear (< *beg,* BEY + *armûdi,* pear); form infl. by prec.⟧ **1** a small evergreen tree (*Citrus bergamia*) of the rue family, grown in S Europe **2** its pear-shaped, inedible citrus fruit **3** an oil extracted from the rind of this fruit, used widely in perfumery **4** any of several aromatic North American herbs (genera *Monarda* and *Mentha*) of the mint family, as horsemint or Oswego tea

Ber·gen (ber′gən; *E* bur′-) **1** seaport in SW Norway, on an inlet of the North Sea **2** village in NW Germany: see BELSEN

Bergerac, Cyrano de *see* CYRANO DE BERGERAC

ber·gère or **ber·gere** (ber zher′) ***n.*** ⟦Fr, lit., shepherdess, fem. of *berger,* shepherd < OFr *bergier* < VL *berbecarius,* altered < **vervecarius* < L *vervex,* a wether⟧ an upholstered armchair, or one with caned seat, back, and sides and loose cushions, esp. in an 18th-cent. French style

Ber·gisch Glad·bach (ber′gish glät′bäk′) city in W Germany, in the state of North Rhine-Westphalia

Berg·man (burg′mən; *Swed* bar′y′ män) **1 (Ernst) Ing·mar** (iŋ′mär) 1918-2007; Swed. film director **2 Ingrid** 1915-82; U.S. actress, born in Sweden

berg·schrund (berk′shroont, burg′shroond) ***n.*** ⟦Ger < *berg,* mountain (see BARROW[2]) + *schrund,* crevice⟧ a type of glacial crevasse that separates the moving ice and snow from the snowfield at the top of a mountain valley

Berg·son (berk sōn′; *E* berg′sən), **Hen·ri** (än rē′) 1859-1941; Fr. philosopher —**Berg·so·ni·an** (berg sō′nē ən) ***adj., n.***

Berg·son·ism (berg′sən iz′əm) ***n.*** the philosophy of Bergson, which maintains that there is an original life force (*élan vital*) that is carried through all successive generations and that is the substance of consciousness and nature: see also ÉLAN VITAL

be·rib·boned (bē rib′ənd) ***adj.*** ⟦see BE- (sense 3)⟧ decorated with ribbons

ber·i·ber·i (ber′ē ber′ē) ***n.*** ⟦Sinhalese, intens. redupl. of *beri,* weakness⟧ a deficiency disease caused by lack of vitamin B_1, thiamine, in the diet: it is characterized by nerve disorders and, sometimes, by edema due to heart dysfunction

Be·ring (bā′riŋ; *E* ber′iŋ, bir′-), **Vi·tus** (vē′toos) 1680?-1741; Dan. navigator & explorer, in the service of Russia

Be·rin·gi·a (bə rin′jē ə) ⟦prob. after prec. + -IA⟧ the former land bridge between Siberia & Alas., over which Asian animals and peoples migrated into North America

Ber·ing Sea (ber′iŋ, bir′-) ⟦after V. BERING⟧ part of the N Pacific Ocean, between NE Siberia & Alas.: *c.* 873,000 sq mi (2,261,061 sq km)

Ber·ing Strait (ber′iŋ, bir′-) ⟦after V. BERING⟧ strait between Siberia & Alas., joining the Pacific & Arctic oceans: *c.* 55 mi (89 km) wide

berk (burk) ***n.*** [Brit. Slang] a stupid person; fool

Berke·le·ian (bärk′lē ən, burk′-) ***adj.*** of George Berkeley or his philosophy —***n.*** a person who believes in Berkeley's philosophy Also **Berke′le·yan**

Berke·le·ian·ism (-iz′əm) ***n.*** the philosophy of George Berkeley, which holds that what are called physical objects exist only as ideas in God's mind and, in other minds, as perceptions of those ideas

Berke·ley[1] (bärk′lē, burk′-) **1 George** 1685-1753; Ir. philosopher & bishop **2 Sir William** 1606-77; Brit. colonial governor of Virginia (1641-52; 1660-76)

Berke·ley[2] (burk′lē) ⟦after George BERKELEY[1]⟧ city in W Calif., on San Francisco Bay, just north of Oakland

☆**berke·li·um** (burk′lē əm) ***n.*** ⟦ModL, after prec. + -IUM: so named by G. T. SEABORG, one of its discoverers, by analogy with TERBIUM⟧ a radioactive, metallic chemical element, one of the actinides, initially produced by bombarding americium with high-energy alpha particles in a cyclotron, and now prepared by intense neutron bombardment of plutonium: symbol, Bk; at. no. 97: see the periodic table of elements in the Reference Supplement

Berk·shire[1] (burk′shir, -shər; *Brit* bärk′-) ***n.*** ⟦after fol.⟧ any of a breed of medium-sized hogs, black with white spots

Berk·shire[2] (burk′shir, -shər; *Brit* bärk′-) county in SC England: 485 sq mi (1,256 sq km): also **Berks** (bärks)

Berk·shire Hills (burk′shir, -shər) ⟦after prec.⟧ region of wooded hills in W Mass.: resort area: also called **Berk′shires**

ber·lin (bər lin′, bur′lin′) ***n.*** ⟦after BERLIN[2], where first used, made, etc.⟧ **1** a four-wheeled closed carriage with a footman's platform behind, separate from the body **2** [*sometimes* **B-**] a fine, soft wool yarn: also called **Berlin wool**

Ber·lin[1] (bər lin′), **Irving** (born *Israel Baline*) 1888-1989; U.S. composer of popular songs, born in Russia

Ber·lin[2] (bər lin′) city and state of E Germany: capital of Germany (1871-1945; 1990-): after WWII and before reunification of Germany in 1990, it was divided into four sectors of occupation (U.S., British, French, and Soviet); the eastern (Soviet) sector (**East Berlin**) was the capital of East Germany; the three western sectors (**West Berlin**) constituted an exclave state of West Germany: 344 sq mi (892 sq km) —**Ber·lin′er** ***n.***

Berlin Wall the heavily fortified barrier that closed off West Berlin, erected by the Communists in 1961 to prevent East Germans from escaping to the West: it was opened in 1989 and subsequently demolished

Ber·li·oz (ber′lē ōz′; *Fr* ber lyôz′), **(Louis) Hector** 1803-69; Fr. composer

berm (burm) ***n.*** ⟦Fr *berme* & Du *berm* < MDu *baerm*: for IE base see BROOM⟧ **1** a ledge or space between the ditch and parapet in a fortification: also sp. **berme** ☆**2** [Dial.] the shoulder of a road **3** a narrow ledge or path as at the top or bottom of a slope, or along a beach **4** a wall or mound of earth

Ber·me·jo (ber me′hô) river flowing southeastward across N Argentina into the Paraguay River: *c.* 650 mi (1,046 km)

Ber·mu·da (bər myōō′də) ⟦after Juan de *Bermúdez*, Sp explorer who discovered it (*c.* 1515)⟧ group of islands in the W Atlantic, 584 mi (940 km) southeast of N.C.: a self-governing colony under British control since 1684: 21 sq mi (54 sq km); cap. Hamilton —**Ber·mu′dan** ***adj., n.,*** **Ber·mu′di·an** (-dē ən)

Bermuda collar a narrow, pointed collar on a woman's dress or blouse

☆**Bermuda grass** a creeping perennial grass (*Cynodon dactylon*) widely grown in warm climates as a lawn or pasture grass, esp. in the S U.S.

☆**Bermuda onion** a large white or yellow onion with a mild flavor, grown in Texas, California, etc.

☆**Bermuda shorts** short pants extending to just above the knee: also **ber·mu′das** ***pl.n.***

Bermuda Triangle a triangular region in the Atlantic Ocean, bounded by Bermuda, Puerto Rico, and Florida: in this area, many ships and aircraft have been reputed to have disappeared mysteriously, esp. since the 1940s

Bern (burn; *Fr* bern) **1** capital of Switzerland & of Bern canton, on the Aare River **2** canton of WC Switzerland: 2,336 sq mi (6,050 sq km) —**Ber·nese** (bər nēz′, -nēs′) ***adj., n., pl.*** **-nese′**

Ber·na·dette (bur′nə det′) ***n.*** ⟦Fr, fem. of *Bernard*: see BERNARD[1]⟧ a feminine name

Ber·na·dotte (bur′nə dät′; *Fr* ber nȧ dôt′), **Jean Bap·tiste Jules** (zhän bȧ tēst zhül′) 1763-1844; Fr. marshal under Napoleon I: as Charles XIV John he was king of Sweden & Norway (1818-44)

Ber·nard[1] (bər närd′, bur′nərd) ***n.*** ⟦OFr < OHG *Berinhard*, lit., bold as a bear < *bero*, BEAR[2] + *hart*, bold, HARD⟧ a masculine name: dim. *Barney, Bernie*; var. *Barnard*; equiv. Ger. *Bernhard*

Ber·nard[2] (ber nȧr′), **Claude** (klōd) 1813-78; Fr. physiologist

Ber·nar·din de Saint-Pierre (ber nȧr dan′ də san pyer′), **Jacques Hen·ri** (zhäk än rē′) 1737-1814; Fr. writer

Ber·nard·ine (bur′nər din, -dēn′) ***adj.*** **1** of Saint Bernard of Clairvaux **2** of the order of Cistercian monks founded by him in 1115 —***n.*** a monk belonging to this order

Bernard of Clair·vaux (kler vō′), Saint (1090?-1153); Fr. monk & theological writer: founder of the Cistercian order: his day is Aug. 20

Bernard of Men·thon (män tōn′), Saint (11th cent.); Fr. monk who founded hospices in the Swiss Alps: his day is May 28

Berne (burn; *Fr* bern) *alt. sp. of* BERN

Bern·ese Alps (bər nēz′) range of the Alps, in SW Switzerland: highest peak, Finsteraarhorn

Bern·hardt (burn′härt′; *Fr* ber nȧr′), **Sarah** (born *Rosine Bernard*) 1844-1923; Fr. actress

Ber·nice (bər nēs′, bur′nis) ***n.*** ⟦L *Berenice* < Gr *Berenikē*, Macedonian var. of *Pherenikē*, lit., bringer of victory < *pherein*, to BEAR[1] + *nikē*, victory⟧ a feminine name: var. *Berenice*

ber·ni·cle goose (bur′ni kəl) BARNACLE GOOSE

Ber·ni·ni (ber nē′nē), **Gio·van·ni Lo·ren·zo** (jô vän′nē lô ren′tsô) 1598-1680; It. baroque sculptor, architect, & painter

Ber·noul·li or **Ber·nouil·li** (ber nōō′lē; *Fr* ber nōō yē′) **1 Daniel** 1700-82; Swiss scientist, known for his work on hydrodynamics: son of Jean **2 Jacques** (zhäk) 1654-1705; Swiss mathematician, known for his work on calculus: brother of Jean **3 Jean** (zhän) 1667-1748; Swiss mathematician, known for his work on calculus

Bernoulli's principle ⟦after Daniel BERNOULLI⟧ the statement that an increase in the speed of a fluid produces a decrease in pressure and a decrease in the speed produces an increase in pressure

Bern·stein (burn′stēn′; *for 2*, -stīn′) **1 Elmer** 1922-2004; U.S. composer of film scores **2 Leonard** 1918-90; U.S. conductor & composer

ber·ret·ta (bə ret′ə) ***n.*** BIRETTA

ber·ried (ber′ēd) ***adj.*** **1** producing or covered with berries **2** like a berry, as in shape **3** bearing eggs: said of lobsters, crayfish, etc.

ber·ry (ber′ē) ***n., pl.*** **-ries** ⟦ME & OE *berie*, a berry, grape, akin to ON *ber*, Goth *weina-basi*, lit., wine berry⟧ **1** any small, juicy, fleshy fruit, as a strawberry or raspberry **2** the dry seed or kernel of various plants, as a coffee bean or wheat grain **3** an egg of a lobster, crayfish, etc. **4** *Bot.* a fleshy fruit with a soft wall and thin skin, as the tomato, grape, or cranberry: see DRUPE, POME —***vi.*** **-ried, -ry·ing 1** to produce berries **2** to look for and pick berries —**ber′ry·like′** ***adj.***

Ber·ry or **Ber·ri** (be rē′) historical region in central France: chief city, Bourges

ber·seem (bər sēm′) ***n.*** ⟦Ar *birsīm* < Coptic *bersim* < *ebra*, seed + *sim*, herbs⟧ an Egyptian clover (*Trifolium alexandrinum*) grown as a forage crop

ber·serk (bər surk′, -zurk′; bə-) ***n.*** ⟦see fol.⟧ a berserker — ***adj., adv.*** in or into a state of violent or destructive rage or frenzy

ber·serk·er (-sur′kər, -zur′-) ***n.*** ⟦ON *berserkr*, warrior clothed in bearskin < *bera*, BEAR[2] + *serkr*, coat⟧ **1** one of a group of early Norse warriors known for their ferocity in battle **2** one who is like a berserker, as in behaving violently, with frenzy or rage, etc.

berth (burth) ***n.*** ⟦< base of BEAR[1] + -TH[1]⟧ **1** enough space at sea to keep clear of another ship, the shore, etc. **2** space for anchoring or tying up **3** a ship's place of anchorage **4** a position, place, office, job, etc. [*a berth* as chief engineer on the ship] **5** *a)* a built-in bed or bunk, as in a ship's cabin or a Pullman car *b)* any sleeping place —***vt.*** **1** to put into a berth **2** to furnish with a berth —***vi.*** to come into or occupy a berth —**give (a) wide berth to** to stay at a prudent distance from; keep well clear of

Ber·tha (bur′thə) ***n.*** ⟦Ger < OHG *Berahta*, lit., bright one < *beraht*, bright, shining, akin to OE *beorht, bryht*, BRIGHT⟧ **1** a feminine name **2** ⟦Fr < *Berthe*, Bertha: after Charlemagne's mother, noted for modesty: the collar concealed décolletage⟧ [**b-**] a woman's wide collar, often made of lace and usually extending over the shoulders

Ber·til·lon system (bur′tə län′; *Fr* ber tē yōn′) ⟦after A. *Bertillon* (1853-1914), Fr criminologist who developed it⟧ a system of identifying people, esp. criminals, through records of body measurements, markings, coloring, etc., used before fingerprinting was adopted

Ber·tram (bur′trəm) ***n.*** ⟦Ger < OHG *Berahtram, Berahthraban* < *beraht*, bright + *hraban*, RAVEN[1]⟧ a masculine name: dim. *Bertie*; var. *Bertrand*

Ber·trand (-trənd) ***n.*** a masculine name: see BERTRAM

Ber·wick (ber′ik) former county of SE Scotland, on the English border: also **Ber′wick·shire** (-shir, -shər)

ber·yl (ber′əl) ***n.*** ⟦ME & OFr *beril* < L *beryllus* < Gr *bēryllos*, sea-green gem < Prakrit *veruliya* < *veḷuriya*, of Dravidian orig., prob. after *Vēlūr* (now *Bēlūr*), city in S India⟧ a very hard, lustrous, hexagonal mineral, $Be_3Al_2Si_6O_{18}$, that is an ore of beryllium; beryllium aluminum silicate: emerald and aquamarine are two varieties used as a gem

Beryl (berl) ***n.*** ⟦< prec., with ref. to gems⟧ a feminine name

be·ryl·li·o·sis (bə ril′ē ō′sis) ***n., pl.*** **-ses′** (-sēz′) a serious disease caused by beryllium poisoning, usually found in the lungs from the inhalation of beryllium fumes or particles

be·ryl·li·um (bə ril′ē əm) ***n.*** ⟦< *beryllia*, beryllium oxide (< L *beryllus*, BERYL + -IA) + -IUM: discovered (1798) by L. N. Vauquelin (1763-1829), Fr chemist⟧ a hard, silver-white, metallic chemical element, one of the alkaline-earth metals, found only in combination with others: it forms strong, hard, lightweight alloys with several metals: symbol, Be; at. no. 4: see the periodic table of elements in the Reference Supplement

Ber·ze·li·us (ber sā′lē oos; *E* bər zē′lē əs), Baron **Jöns Ja·kob** (yöns′ yä′kôp) 1779-1848; Swed. chemist

Bes (bes) ***n.*** ⟦Egypt *besa*⟧ *Egypt. Myth.* a god of pleasure and a protector of women in childbirth and of children

Be·san·çon (bə zän sōn′) city in E France, on the Doubs River

Bes·ant (bes′ənt), **Annie** (born *Annie Wood*) 1847-1933; Brit. theosophist: leader in India's movement for independence

be·seech (bē sēch′, bi-) ***vt.*** **-sought′** or **-seeched′**, **-seech′ing** ⟦ME *bisechen* < OE *besecan*; see BE- & SEEK⟧ **1** to ask (someone) earnestly; entreat; implore **2** to ask for earnestly; solicit eagerly; beg for —***SYN.*** BEG —**be·seech′ing·ly** ***adv.***

be·seem (bē sēm′, bi-) ***vi.*** ⟦ME *bisemen*: see BE- & SEEM⟧ [Archaic] to be suitable or appropriate (to): what appears to be the direct object of the verb (e.g., *him* in "it ill beseems him") is really the indirect object

be·set (bē set′, bi-) ***vt.*** **-set′**, **-set′ting** ⟦ME *bisetten* < OE *besettan*: see BE- & SET⟧ **1** to cover or set thickly with; stud **2** to attack from all sides; harass or besiege **3** to surround or hem in —***SYN.*** ATTACK —**be·set′ment** ***n.***

be·set·ting (-iŋ) ***adj.*** constantly harassing or attacking [*a besetting* temptation]

be·shrew (bē shrōō′) ***vt.*** ⟦ME *bishrewen*: see BE- & SHREW⟧ [Archaic] to curse: mainly in mild imprecations [*beshrew* thee]

be·side (bē sīd′, bi-) ***prep.*** ⟦ME < OE *bi sidan* (dat. of *side*): see BY & SIDE⟧ **1** by or at the side of; alongside; near **2** in comparison with [*beside* yours my share seems small] **3** BESIDES **4** not pertinent to [that's *beside* the point] —***adv.*** [Archaic] in addition —**beside oneself** wild or upset, as with fear, rage, etc.

be·sides (-sīdz′) ***adv.*** ⟦ME < prec. + -(*e*)*s*, adverbial genitive: see -S (sense 3)⟧ **1** in addition; as well **2** except for that mentioned; else **3** moreover; furthermore —***prep.*** **1** in addition to; as well as **2** other than; except [who, *besides* him, is qualified?]

be·siege (bē sēj′, bi-) ***vt.*** **-sieged′, -sieg′ing** ⟦ME *bisegen* < *be-*, BE- + *segen,* to lay siege to < *sege,* seat, SIEGE⟧ **1** to hem in with armed forces, esp. for a sustained attack; lay siege to **2** to close in on; crowd around **3** to overwhelm, harass, or beset [*besieged* with queries] **—be·sieg′er** ***n.***

be·smear (bē smir′, bi-) ***vt.*** ⟦ME *bismeren* < OE *bismerian:* see BE- & SMEAR⟧ to smear over; bedaub; soil

be·smirch (bē smurch′, bi-) ***vt.*** ⟦BE- + SMIRCH⟧ **1** to make dirty; soil **2** to bring dishonor to; sully

be·som (bē′zəm) ***n.*** ⟦ME *besme* < OE *besma,* broom, rod < WGmc **besman* > Ger *besen*⟧ a broom, esp. one made of twigs tied to a handle

besom pocket ⟦< ?⟧ an inset, flapless pocket, often in a jacket or trousers, having a slit opening trimmed with a welt or with reinforced stitching

be·sot (bē sät′, bi-) ***vt.*** **-sot′ted, -sot′ting** **1** to make a sot of; stupefy or confuse, as with alcoholic drink **2** to make silly or foolish Usually in the pp.

be·sought (bē sôt′, bi-) ***vt.*** *alt. pt. & alt. pp. of* BESEECH

be·span·gle (bē spaŋ′gəl, bi-) ***vt.*** **-span′gled, -span′gling** to cover with or as with spangles

be·spat·ter (bē spat′ər, bi-) ***vt.*** to spatter, as with mud or slander; soil or sully by spattering

be·speak (bē spēk′, bi-) ***vt.*** **-spoke′, -spo′ken** or **-spoke′, -speak′ing** ⟦ME *bispeken* < OE *besprecan:* see BE- & SPEAK⟧ **1** to speak for in advance; engage beforehand; reserve [that room is *bespoken*] **2** to be indicative of; show [a mansion that *bespeaks* wealth] **3** to foreshadow; point to [her talent *bespeaks* success] **4** [Archaic] to speak to; address

be·spec·ta·cled (bē spek′tə kəld) ***adj.*** wearing spectacles

be·spoke (bē spōk′, bi-) ***vt. pt. & alt. pp. of*** BESPEAK **—*adj.*** [Brit.] **1** custom or custom-made **2** making or made to order

be·spread (bē spred′, bi-) ***vt.*** **-spread′, -spread′ing** to spread over or cover

be·sprent (bē sprent′) ***adj.*** ⟦ME *bespreynt,* pp. of *besprengen* < OE *besprengan* < *be-*, BE- + *sprengan,* caus. < *springan,* SPRING⟧ [Old Poet.] sprinkled; strewed

be·sprin·kle (bē spriŋ′kəl, bi-) ***vt.*** **-kled, -kling** to sprinkle over (*with* something)

Bess (bes) ***n.*** a feminine name: see ELIZABETH[1]

Bes·sa·ra·bi·a (bes′ə rā′bē ə) region in SE Europe, between the Dniester & Prut rivers: historically associated with Moldavia since the 14th cent.; ceded by Romania to the U.S.S.R. in 1940 & incorporated into the Moldavian S.S.R. (now Moldova) **—Bes′sa·ra′bi·an** ***adj., n.***

Bes·se·mer process (bes′ə mər) ⟦after Sir Henry *Bessemer* (1813-98), Eng engineer who developed it⟧ a method of making steel by blasting air through molten pig iron in a large container (**Bessemer converter**) to burn away the carbon and other impurities

best (best) ***adj.*** ⟦ME *best, betst* < OE *betst* (akin to Goth *batists*) < ? IE base **bhad-,* good > Sans *bhadrá-ḥ,* fortunate, good⟧ **1** *superl. of* GOOD **2** of the most excellent sort; surpassing all others **3** most suitable, most desirable, most favorable, most profitable, etc. **4** being almost the whole; largest [it took the *best* part of an hour] **—*adv.* 1** *superl. of* WELL[2] **2** in the most excellent manner; in the most suitable way **3** in the highest degree; to the greatest extent; most **—*n.* 1** people of the highest worth, ability, or reputation [among the *best* in his profession] **2** the thing, condition, circumstance, action, etc. that is most excellent, most suitable, etc. **3** the most one can do; utmost [to do one's *best*] **4** one's finest clothes **—*vt.*** to win out over; defeat or outdo **—all for the best** turning out to be good or fortunate after all **—as best one can** as well as one can **—at best 1** under the most favorable conditions or interpretation **2** at most **—at one's best** in one's best mood, form, health, etc. **—get the best of 1** to outdo, overcome, or defeat **2** to outwit **—had best** ought to; would be prudent or wise to **—make the best of** to do as well as one can with **—with the best** as ably as the most able

best-ball (best′bôl′) ***adj.*** *Golf* designating a type of team competition for partners in which the lower score of either partner is recorded as the team score on each hole: also called **bet′ter-ball′**

best boy the principal assistant to the gaffer or grip on a film crew

best-case (best′kās′) ***adj.*** being the best that can possibly be expected; optimal [a *best-case* scenario]

be·stead (bē sted′) ***adj.*** ⟦ME *bistad* < *bi,* BE- + *stad,* placed < ON *staddr,* pp. of *stethja,* to fix, place⟧ [Archaic] situated; placed **—*vt.* -stead′ed, -stead′, -stead′ing** [Archaic] to help; avail

bes·tial (bes′chəl, -tyəl; *often* bēs′-) ***adj.*** ⟦ME & OFr < LL *bestialis* < L *bestia,* BEAST⟧ **1** of beasts or lower animals **2** like a beast in qualities or behavior; brutish or savage; brutal, coarse, vile, etc.

bes·ti·al·i·ty (bes′chē al′ə tē, -tē-; *often* bēs′-) ***n., pl.*** **-ties 1** bestial quality, character, or behavior **2** a bestial act or practice **3** sexual relations between a person and an animal

bes·tial·ize (bes′chəl īz′, -tyəl-; *often* bēs′-) ***vt.*** **-ized′, -iz′ing** to make bestial; brutalize

bes·ti·ar·y (bes′tē er′ē) ***n., pl.*** **-ar′ies** ⟦ML *bestiarium* < L *bestiarius,* relating to beasts < *bestia,* BEAST⟧ a type of medieval natural-history book with descriptions and moralistic and religious interpretations of actual and mythical animals

best·ie (bes′tē) ***n.*** [Slang] one's best friend

be·stir (bē stur′, bi-) ***vt.*** **-stirred′, -stir′ring** ⟦ME *bistiren* < OE *bestyrian:* see BE- & STIR[1]⟧ to stir to action; exert or busy (oneself)

☆**best man** the principal attendant of the bridegroom at a wedding

be·stow (bē stō′, bi-) ***vt.*** ⟦ME *bistowen:* see BE- & STOW⟧ **1** to give or present as a gift: often with *on* or *upon* **2** to apply; devote [to *bestow* much time on a project] **3** [Archaic] to put or place, as in storage **4** [Archaic] to provide lodgings for; house **5** [Obs.] to give in marriage **—*SYN.*** GIVE **—be·stow′al** ***n.***

be·strew (bē stro͞o′, bi-) ***vt.*** **-strewed′, -strewed′** or **-strewn′, -strew′ing** ⟦ME *bistrewen* < OE *bestreowian:* see BE- & STREW⟧ **1** to cover over (a surface) *with* something; strew **2** to scatter (things) over or about a surface **3** to lie scattered over or about (a surface) [papers *bestrewed* the streets]

be·stride (bē strīd′, bi-) ***vt.*** **-strode′** (-strōd′), **-strid′den** (-strid′'n), **-strid′ing** ⟦ME *bistriden* < OE *bestridan:* see BE- & STRIDE⟧ **1** to sit on, mount, or stand over with a leg on each side; straddle **2** [Archaic] to stride over or across

☆**best·sell·er** (best′sel′ər) ***n.*** a book, recording, etc. currently outselling most others: also **best′-sell′er** or **best seller —best′sell′er·dom** ***n.***, **best′-sell′er·dom**

best·sell·ing (best′sel′iŋ) ***adj.*** **1** currently outselling most others [a *bestselling* novel] **2** having written, recorded, etc. a bestseller [a *bestselling* author]

bet[1] (bet) ***n.*** ⟦prob. aphetic < ABET⟧ **1** an agreement between two persons that the one proved wrong about the outcome of something will do or pay what is stipulated; wager **2** *a)* the proposition or terms of such an agreement *b)* the thing or sum thus staked ☆*c)* the thing or person that something is or may be thus staked on [this team is a poor *bet*] ☆**3** a person, thing, or action with a (specified) likelihood of achieving success or bringing about a desired result [he's the best *bet* for the job] **—*vt.* bet** or [Now Brit.] **bet′ted, bet′ting 1** to declare in or as in a bet [I *bet* he'll be late] **2** to stake (money, etc.) in a bet **3** to wager with (someone) **—*vi.*** to make a bet or bets (*on, against, with*); wager **—☆you bet (you)!** [Informal] certainly!

bet[2] (bāt, bet) ***n.*** BETH

bet[3] *abbrev.* between

be·ta (bāt′ə; *chiefly Brit* bēt′ə) ***n.*** ⟦L < Gr *bēta* < Heb *bet,* lit., house; prob. of Phoen orig.⟧ **1** the second letter of the Greek alphabet (Β, β) **2** the second of a group or series **3** [**B-**] *Astron.* the name assigned to the second brightest star in each constellation: followed by the constellation's name in the genitive case, as *Beta Geminorum* **4** *Comput.* a version of software distributed to selected users for testing before sale **5** *Finance* a measure of the impact of a change in the stock market on the probable price change of a stock or stocks **—*adj.*** *Chem.* designating an organic structural position See ALPHA

Beta (bāt′ə) *trademark for:* **1** an electronic system for recording and playing back videocassettes **2** a videocassette recorder using this system In full **Be′ta·max′** (-maks′)

be·ta-ad·re·ner·gic (bāt′ə ad′rə nur′jik) ***adj.*** pertaining to or involving beta receptors

be·ta-am·y·loid (bāt′ə am′ə loid′) ***n.*** a complex, sticky AMYLOID (sense 2) found in the tangled masses of nerve cells in the brains of people with Alzheimer's disease: sometimes written **beta amyloid**

beta blocker any of a class of drugs used to control heartbeat, relieve angina pectoris, treat hypertension, etc. by blocking the nerve impulses that normally excite the beta receptors

beta carotene a yellowish form of carotene: a dietary deficiency of this is associated with a greater risk of certain cancers

beta decay radioactive disintegration of a nucleus with the accompanying emission of a beta particle: the residual nucleus has one more unit of positive charge after electron emission and one less after positron emission

beta emitter a radioactive element, either natural or artificial, which changes into another element by emitting a beta particle

Be·ta fiber ⟦< *Beta,* formerly a trademark for this fiber⟧ a nonflammable glass fiber made into fabrics, insulation, etc.

Beta Gem·i·nor·um (jem′ə nôr′əm) ⟦< L *geminorum,* gen. of *gemini:* see GEMINI⟧ *Astron.* POLLUX

be·ta·ine (bēt′ə ēn′, -in′) ***n.*** ⟦L *beta,* beet + -INE[3]⟧ a crystalline, basic organic compound, $(CH_3)_3NCH_2COO$, obtained from beet sugar or prepared synthetically

be·take (bē tāk′, bi-) ***vt.*** **-took′** (-to͝ok′), **-tak′en, -tak′ing** ⟦ME *bitaken:* see BE- & TAKE⟧ **1** to go: used reflexively [he *betook* himself to his own kingdom] **2** [Archaic] to direct or devote (oneself)

be·ta·naph·thol (bāt′ə naf′thôl′, -thōl) ***n.*** a colorless, crystalline isomer of naphthol, $C_{10}H_8O$, used as an antiseptic and parasiticide

Beta O·ri·o·nis (ō rī′ə nis) *Astron.* RIGEL

beta particle an electron or positron ejected at high velocity from the nucleus of an atom undergoing beta decay

beta ray a stream of beta particles

beta receptor a receptor, found on the surface of some cells of the sympathetic nervous system, that is stimulated by certain adrenergic substances: such stimulation results in certain physiological responses, such as acceleration of the action of the heart and dilatation of the arteries supplying heart and skeletal muscles: cf. ALPHA RECEPTOR

☆**be·ta·tron** (bāt′ə trän′) ***n.*** ⟦< BETA (as in BETA RAY, BETA PARTICLE) + -TRON⟧ an electron accelerator which uses a rapidly changing magnetic field to accelerate the particles and maintain them in a focused circular path

beta wave any of the electrical waves from the parietal-frontal regions of the brain, having frequencies from 13 to 30 hertz: a sign of mental activity and alertness: also **beta rhythm**

Be·tel·geuse (bēt′'l jo͞oz′, bet′-) ***n.*** ⟦Fr *Bételgeuse* < Ar *baytal-jauzā′*, lit., house of the middle (of the sky)⟧ a reddish, supergiant variable star in the constellation Orion: magnitude, 0.45: sometimes sp. **Be′tel·geux′**

betel nut ⟦because chewed with betel pepper leaves⟧ the fruit of the betel palm, chewed with lime and the leaves of the betel pepper by some Southeast Asian peoples as a mild stimulant

be·tel palm (bēt′′l) a palm tree (*Areca catechu*) grown in Southeast Asia

be·tel pepper (bēt′′l) ⟦Port < Malayalam *veṭṭilai*⟧ a tropical Asian climbing plant (*Piper betle*) of the pepper family

bête noire (bāt′ nwär′; *Fr* bet nwȧr′) *pl.* **bêtes noires** (bāt′nwärz′; *Fr* bet nwȧr′) ⟦Fr, lit., black beast⟧ a person or thing that one especially or obsessively dislikes or fears

beth (beth, bāth; *Heb* bāt, bās) *n.* ⟦Heb *bet*, lit., house: see BETA⟧ **1** the second letter of the Hebrew alphabet (ב): in a text containing points, this letter written with a dot is designated *beth* or *bet*; without a dot it is *vet* **2** [*often* **B-**] house (of): used in the names of Jewish institutions, houses of worship, etc. [*Beth* Din, *Beth* Jacob School]

Beth·a·ny (beth′ə nē) ⟦LL (Vulg.) *Bethania* < Gr *Bēthania* < Heb *betanya* < *bet*, house + ? *hayan*, late-season green figs⟧ ancient town in Palestine, near Jerusalem, at the foot of the Mount of Olives (Luke 19:29; John 11:1): now a village in the West Bank

Be·the (bā′tə), **Hans Al·brecht** (häns äl′breHt) 1906-2005; U.S. theoretical physicist, born in Germany

beth·el (beth′əl) *n.* ⟦LL (Vulg.) < Heb *bet-el*, house of God⟧ **1** a spot where God is worshiped, marked by a pillar: Gen. 28:17-19 **2** a holy place ☆**3** a church or other place of worship for seamen **4** [Brit.] a place of worship for non-Anglican Protestants

Beth·el (beth′əl) ancient city in Palestine, just north of Jerusalem (Gen. 35:1-15; Judg. 20:26)

Be·thes·da (bə thez′də) ⟦after the biblical *Bethesda* (in RSV, *Bethzatha*): John 5:2⟧ suburb of Washington, D.C., in central Md.

be·think (bē thiŋk′, bi-) [Archaic] *vt.* **-thought′** (-thôt′), **-think′ing** ⟦ME *bithenchen* < OE *bethencan*: see BE- & THINK[1]⟧ to bring (oneself) to think of or recollect; remind (oneself) —*vi.* to ponder

Beth·le·hem (beth′lə hem′, -həm; *occas.*, -lē-) ⟦LL (Vulg.) < Gr *Bēthleem* < Heb *bet-lechem*, lit., house of bread⟧ ancient town in Judea; traditionally regarded as the birthplace of Jesus (Matt. 2:1): now a town in the West Bank: Ar. name *Bayt Lahm* or *Beit Lahm*

Beth·mann-Holl·weg (bāt′män hôl′vāk), **The·o·bald von** (tā′ô bält′ fôn) 1856-1921; chancellor of Germany (1909-17)

Be·thune (bə thyo͞on′), **Mary** (born *Mary McLeod*) 1875-1955; U.S. educator

be·tide (bē tīd′, bi-) *vi., vt.* **-tid′ed, -tid′ing** ⟦ME *bitiden* < *be-*, BE- + *tiden*, happen < OE *tidan* < *tid*, time: see TIDE[1]⟧ [Archaic] to happen (to); befall

be·times (bē tīmz′, bi-) *adv.* ⟦ME *bitimes* < *bi*, BY + *time*, TIME + *-(e)s*, adverbial genitive: see -S (sense 3)⟧ [Archaic] **1** early or early enough [he awoke *betimes*] **2** promptly; quickly

bê·tise (be tēz′) *n.* ⟦Fr < *bête*, beast, foolish < OFr *beste*, BEAST⟧ **1** *pl.* **-tises′** (-tēz′) a foolish act, remark, etc. **2** stupidity or foolishness

Bet·je·man (bech′ə mən), Sir **John** 1906-84; Eng. poet: poet laureate (1972-84)

be·to·ken (bē tō′kən, bi-) *vt.* ⟦ME *betocnen* < *be-*, BE- + *toknen* < OE *tacnian*, to mark < *tacen, tacn*, TOKEN⟧ **1** to be a token or sign of; indicate; show **2** to show beforehand; presage

bet·o·ny (bet′′n ē) *n., pl.* **-nies** ⟦ME *betonike* < OE *betonice* < LL *betonica*, altered < L *vettonica*, after the *Vettones*, an ancient Iberian people⟧ **1** any of a genus (*Stachys*) of plants of the mint family, having spikes of white, yellow, or lavender flowers and formerly used in medicine **2** *short for* WOOD BETONY

be·tray (bē trā′, bi-) *vt.* ⟦ME *bitraien* < *be-*, intens. + *traien*, betray < OFr *trair* < L *tradere*, to hand over: see TREASON⟧ **1** *a)* to help the enemy of (one's country, cause, etc.); be a traitor to *b)* to deliver or expose to an enemy traitorously **2** to break faith with; fail to meet the hopes of [he *betrayed* my trust in him] **3** to lead astray; deceive; specif., to seduce and then desert **4** to reveal unknowingly or against one's wishes [his face *betrays* his fear] **5** to reveal or show signs of; indicate [the house *betrays* its age] **6** to disclose (secret information, confidential plans, etc.) —**SYN.** DECEIVE, REVEAL[1] —**be·tray′al** *n.* —**be·tray′er** *n.*

be·troth (bē trōth′, -trôth′; bi-) *vt.* ⟦ME *bitrouthen* < *be-*, BE- + *treuthe*, TRUTH⟧ **1** [Obs.] to promise to marry **2** to promise in marriage [to *betroth* a daughter]

be·troth·al (-əl) *n.* a betrothing or being betrothed; mutual pledge to marry; engagement

be·trothed (-trōthd′, -trôtht′) *adj.* engaged to be married —*n.* the person to whom one is betrothed

Bet·sy (bet′sē) *n.* ⟦shortened & altered < ELIZABETH[1]⟧ a feminine name: see ELIZABETH[1]

bet·ta (bet′ə) *n.* ⟦ModL⟧ any of a genus (*Betta*) of brightly colored gouramies of Southeast Asia, esp. a species (*B. splendens*) kept in aquariums

bet·ter[1] (bet′ər) *adj.* ⟦ME *bettere, betere* < OE *betera*: see BEST⟧ **1** *compar. of* GOOD **2** of a more excellent sort; surpassing another or others **3** more suitable, more desirable, more favorable, more profitable, etc. **4** being more than half; larger [it cost the *better* part of her pay] **5** improved in health or disposition —*adv.* **1** *compar. of* WELL[2] **2** in a more excellent manner; in a more suitable way **3** in a higher degree; to a greater extent **4** more [it took *better* than an hour] **5** [Informal] HAD BETTER (see phrase below) [you *better* behave yourself] —*n.* **1** a person superior in authority, position, etc. [obey your *betters*] **2** the thing, condition, circumstance, action, etc. that is more excellent, more suitable, etc. **3** advantage [to get the *better* of a rival] —*vt.* **1** to outdo; surpass **2** to make better; improve —*vi.* to become better —**SYN.** IMPROVE —**better off 1** in a better situation or condition **2** having more income, wealth, etc. —**for the better** to a better or improved condition —**get (or have) the better of 1** to outdo **2** to outwit —**had better** ought to; would be prudent or wise to

bet·ter[2] (bet′ər) *n. alt. sp. of* BETTOR

better half one's spouse; esp., one's wife: a humorous usage

bet·ter·ment (-mənt) *n.* **1** a making or being made better; improvement ☆**2** *Law* an improvement that increases the value of property and is more extensive than mere repairs

bet·tor (bet′ər) *n.* a person who bets

Bet·ty (bet′ē) *n.* ⟦shortened & altered < ELIZABETH[1]⟧ a feminine name: see ELIZABETH[1]

be·tween (bē twēn′, bi-) *prep.* ⟦ME *bitwene* < OE *betweonum* < *be*, BY + *tweonum* (dat. of **tweon*); akin to Goth *tweihnai*, by twos, in pairs: for IE base see TWO⟧ **1** in or through the space that separates (two things) [*between* the house and the garage] **2** in or of the time, amount, or degree that separates (two things); intermediate to [*between* blue and green] **3** that connects or relates to [a bond *between* friends, the difference *between* right and wrong] **4** along a course that connects [the road runs *between* here and there] **5** *a)* by the joint action of [*between* them they landed the fish] *b)* because of the combined effect of [*between* work and studies she has no time left] *c)* in or into the combined possession of [they had fifty dollars *between* them] **6** with equal parts shared by each of [they divided it *between* them] **7** to the exclusion of all but both of [let's keep this matter *between* us] **8** from one or the other of [choose *between* love and duty] —*adv.* **1** in an intermediate space, position, or function **2** in an intermediate time; in the interval —**between ourselves** in confidence; as a secret: also **between you and me** —**in between 1** in an intermediate position **2** in the midst of

USAGE—*between* is sometimes used, instead of *among*, in relationships of more than two persons or things, if the relationship is thought of as involving each one individually with each of the others [a treaty *between* four powers]

be·tween·brain (-brān′) *n.* DIENCEPHALON

be·tween·times (-tīmz′) *adv.* at intervals: also **be·tween′whiles′** (-hwīlz′, -wīlz′)

be·twixt (bē twikst′, bi-) *prep., adv.* ⟦ME *bitwix* < OE *betwix* < *be*, BY + a form related to *twegen*, TWAIN; *-t* is unhistoric⟧ between: archaic except in the phrase **betwixt and between**, in an intermediate position; neither altogether one nor altogether the other

Beu·lah (byo͞o′lə) *n.* ⟦name for Israel (Isa. 62:4) < Heb *beula*, married⟧ **1** in Bunyan's *Pilgrim's Progress*, a country of peace near the end of life's journey: in full **Land of Beulah** **2** a feminine name

beurre blanc (bur′blän′, -bläŋk′; *Fr* bër blän′) ⟦Fr < *beurre* (< L *butyrum*, BUTTER) + *blanc*, white: see BLANK⟧ a creamy sauce, especially for fish and seafood, made with butter, shallots, and lemon juice or vinegar

BeV or **bev** (bev) *abbrev.* one billion (10^9) electron volts

☆**Bev·a·tron** (bev′ə trän′) *n.* ⟦< prec. + *-tron*, as in CYCLOTRON⟧ the synchrotron at the University of California, Berkeley, used to accelerate protons and other charged particles to an energy level of 6 GeV or more

bev·el (bev′əl) *n.* ⟦prob. < OFr **baivel*, dim. < *baif*, gaping: see BAY[2]⟧ **1** a tool consisting of a rule with a movable arm, used in measuring or marking angles and in fixing surfaces at an angle: also **bevel square** **2** an angle other than a right angle **3** sloping part or surface, as the angled edge of plate glass —*adj.* sloped; beveled —*vt.* **-eled** or **-elled**, **-el·ing** or **-el·ling** to cut to an angle other than a right angle —*vi.* to slope at an angle; slant

bevel

bevel gear a toothed-wheel gear meshed with another so that their shafts are at an angle of less than 180°

bev·er·age (bev′ər ij, bev′rij) *n.* ⟦ME < OFr *bevrage* < *bevre* < L *bibere*, IMBIBE⟧ any liquid for drinking, esp. one other than water

Bev·er·ly or **Bev·er·ley** (bev′ər lē) *n.* ⟦< ME *bever*, BEAVER[1] + *ley*, LEA[1]⟧ a feminine name

Beverly Hills ⟦after *Beverly* Farms, in Mass.⟧ city in Calif., surrounded by Los Angeles

bev·y (bev′ē) *n., pl.* **bev′ies** ⟦ME *bevey* < Anglo-Fr *bevée* < OFr, a drinking bout < *bevre*: see BEVERAGE⟧ **1** a group, esp. of girls or women **2** a flock: now said chiefly of quail **3** any group or collection —**SYN.** GROUP

be·wail (bē wāl′, bi-) *vt.* ⟦ME *biwailen*: see BE- & WAIL⟧ to wail over or complain about; lament; mourn

be·ware (bē wer′, bi-) *vi., vt.* ⟦assoc. with BE, imper. + WARE[2], but prob. < OE *bewarian*, to keep watch < *be-* + *warian*, to watch, be wary⟧ to be wary or careful (*of*); be on one's guard (against): used in the imperative or infinitive

be·wigged (bē wigd′, bi-) *adj.* wearing a wig

be·wil·der (bē wil′dər, bi-) *vt.* ⟦BE- + WILDER⟧ **1** to confuse hopelessly, as by something complicated or involved; befuddle; puzzle **2** [Archaic] to cause to be lost, as in a wilderness —*SYN.* PUZZLE —**be·wil′der·ing·ly** *adv.*

be·wil·der·ment (-mənt) *n.* **1** the fact or condition of being bewildered **2** a confusion; jumble

be·witch (bē wich′, bi-) *vt.* ⟦ME *biwicchen* < BE-, intens. + *wicchen* < OE *wiccian* < *wicca,* WITCH⟧ **1** to use witchcraft or magic on; cast a spell over **2** to attract and delight irresistibly; enchant; fascinate; charm —**be·witch′ing** *adj.* —**be·witch′ing·ly** *adv.*

be·witch·ment (-mənt) *n.* **1** power to bewitch **2** a bewitching or being bewitched **3** a spell that bewitches Also **be·witch′er·y** (-ər ē) *pl.* **-er·ies**

be·wray (bē rā′) *vt.* ⟦ME *biwreien* < BE-, intens. + OE *wregan,* to inform; akin to Ger *rügen,* to blame⟧ [Archaic] to divulge; reveal; betray

Bex·ley (beks′lē) borough of Greater London, England, on the Thames

bey (bā) *n.* ⟦Turk *bey, beg*⟧ a Turkish title of respect and former title of rank

Beyle (bel), **Ma·rie Hen·ri** (mȧ rē′ än rē′) *see* STENDHAL

be·yond (bē änd′) *prep.* ⟦ME *biyonde* < OE *begeondan* < *be,* BY + *geond,* YONDER⟧ **1** on or to the far side of; farther on than; past [*beyond* the river] **2** farther on in time than; later than [*beyond* the visiting hours] **3** outside the reach, possibility, or understanding of [*beyond* help, *beyond* belief] **4** more or better than; exceeding; surpassing [a success *beyond* one's expectations] **5** in addition to [he had no experience *beyond* school training] —*adv.* **1** farther out; farther away **2** in addition; besides —**the beyond 1** whatever is beyond or far away **2** whatever follows death; afterlife: often **the great beyond**

bez·ant (bez′ənt, bi zant′) *n.* ⟦ME *besant* < OFr < L *Byzantius (nummus),* Byzantine (coin)⟧ **1** the solidus, a gold coin issued in Byzantium: see SOLIDUS (sense 1) **2** *Archit., Heraldry* an ornamental flat disk or circular figure representing such a coin

bez antler (bez, bāz) ⟦< OFr *bes-* < L *bis,* twice + ANTLER⟧ BAY ANTLER

☆**be·zazz** (bi zaz′) *n. var. of* PIZAZZ

bez·el (bez′əl) *n.* ⟦< MFr **besel* (> Fr *biseau*) < ? OFr *biais,* BIAS⟧ **1** a sloping surface, as the cutting edge of a chisel **2** the slanting faces of the upper part of a cut gem, esp. a brilliant; also, this part of a gem **3** *a)* the groove and flange holding a gem, watch crystal, etc. in place *b)* a rotatable rim on a watch or clock, that can be moved to indicate certain kinds of data [an elapsed-time *bezel*]

be·zique (bə zēk′) *n.* ⟦Fr *bésigue* < ?⟧ a card game resembling pinochle, but using a double deck of 64 cards, two of each card above the six

be·zoar (bē′zôr′) *n.* ⟦Fr *bézoard* < Sp *bezoar* < Ar *bāzahr* < Pers *pādzahr* < *pād,* protecting (against) + *zahr,* poison⟧ a concretion found in the stomach or intestines of some animals, esp. ruminants, and sometimes humans, formerly thought to be an antidote for poisons

bf *abbrev.* boldface

B/F or **b/f** *abbrev. Bookkeeping* brought forward

BFA or **B.F.A.** *abbrev.* Bachelor of Fine Arts

bg *abbrev.* bag

BG *abbrev.* Brigadier General

BGH or **bGH** *abbrev.* bovine growth hormone

☆**B-girl** (bē′gʉrl′) *n.* ⟦short for *bar girl*⟧ a woman employed by a bar to entice men into buying drinks freely

Bh *Chem. symbol for* bohrium (element 107)

BHA (bē′āch′ā′) *n.* ⟦*b(utylated) h(ydroxy)a(nisole)*⟧ a waxy, white, synthetic antioxidant, $(CH_3)_3CC_6H_3OHOCH_3$, used as a preservative in foods containing fats and oils

Bha·ga·vad-Gi·ta (bug′ə vəd gē′tä) *n.* ⟦Sans *Bhagavad-gītā,* Song of the Blessed One⟧ a philosophic dialogue that is a sacred Hindu text, found in the *Mahabharata,* one of the ancient Sanskrit epics

bhak·ti (buk′tē) *n.* ⟦Sans *bhaktí-,* lit., a share < *bhájati,* (he) distributes < IE base **bhag-,* to allot: see -PHAGOUS⟧ *Hinduism* personal devotion to a particular deity

bhang (baŋ) *n.* ⟦Hindi < Sans *bhaṅgáḥ, bhaṅgā,* hemp⟧ HEMP (sense 1)

Bha·rat (bu′rut) *Sans. name for* INDIA (the republic)

Bhav·na·gar (bou nug′ər) seaport in Gujarat state, W India, on the Arabian Sea: sometimes sp. **Bhau·na′gar**

BHC *abbrev.* benzene hexachloride

Bhn *abbrev.* Brinell hardness number

Bho·pal (bō päl′) city in central India: site of a U.S.-owned pesticide plant where a major industrial accident occurred in 1984

B-ho·ri·zon (bē′hə rī′zən) *n.* the second soil zone, in which material leached from the overlying zone is concentrated: see ABC SOIL

bhp *abbrev.* brake horsepower

BHT (bē′āch′tē′) *n.* ⟦*b(utylated) h(ydroxy)t(oluene)*⟧ a white, synthetic antioxidant, $[C(CH_3)_3]_2CH_3C_6H_2OH$, used as an additive in foods, fuels, rubber, etc.

Bhu·ba·nes·war (bo͞o′bə nesh′wər) city in E India, noted for its Hindu shrines

Bhu·tan (bo͞o tän′) independent kingdom in the Himalayas, north of the Indian state of Assam: monarchy established in 1907: 18,147 sq mi (47,000 sq km); cap. Thimphu —**Bhu·tan·ese** (bo͞ot′′n ēz′) *adj., n., pl.* **-ese′**

bi (bī) *adj., n.* [Slang] *short for* BISEXUAL

Bi *Chem. symbol for* bismuth

bi-[1] (bī) ⟦L *bi-* < OL *dui-* < IE **dwi-* < base **dwo-,* TWO⟧ *prefix* **1** having two [*biangular, bicapsular*] **2** doubly, on both sides, in two ways or directions [*biconvex, bilingual*] **3** coming, happening, or issued every two (specified periods) [*biennial, biweekly*] **4** coming, happening, or issued twice during every (specified period): often replaced by SEMI- or *half-,* to avoid confusion with preceding sense [*bimonthly, biyearly*] **5** using two or both [*bilabial, bimanual*] **6** joining two, combining or involving two [*bilateral, bipartisan*] **7** *Bot., Zool.* twice, doubly, in pairs [*bifurcate, bipinnate*] **8** *Chem. a)* having twice as many atoms or chemical equivalents for a definite weight of the other constituent of the compound [sodium *bicarbonate*] *b)* in organic compounds, having a combination of two radicals of the same composition [*biphenyl*]: usually replaced by DI-[1] (sense 2) except in the names of acid salts [potassium *bitartrate*] It becomes *bin-* before a vowel and *bis-* before *c* or *s*

bi-[2] (bī) *combining form* BIO-

BIA *abbrev.* Bureau of Indian Affairs

Bi·a·fra (bē äf′rə, -af′-) **1** region of SE Nigeria, on the Bight of Biafra: seceded from Nigeria (1967-70) during unsuccessful war for independence **2 Bight of** eastern part of the Gulf of Guinea, on the W coast of Africa —**Bi·a′fran** *adj., n.*

bia·ly (byä′lē) *n., pl.* **-lys** ⟦< Yiddish *byali,* short for *byalistoker pletsl,* flat roll from BIAŁYSTOCK, where orig. made⟧ a flat bread roll made with gluten flour and topped with chopped onions, etc.: also sp. **bia′li**

Bia·lys·tok (byä′lis tôk′) city in NE Poland

bi·an·nu·al (bī an′yo͞o əl) *adj.* coming twice a year; semiannual: see also BIENNIAL —**bi·an′nu·al·ly** *adv.*

bi·an·nu·late (bī an′yo͞o lit, -lāt′) *adj. Zool.* having two rings or bands of color, etc.

Bi·ar·ritz (bē′ə rits′; *Fr* byȧ rēts′) resort town in SW France, on the Bay of Biscay

bi·as (bī′əs) *n., pl.* **bi′as·es** ⟦MFr *biais,* a slope, slant < OFr < OProv < ?⟧ **1** a line, cut or sewn diagonally across the weave of cloth, as in making seams, binding tape, etc. **2** a mental leaning or inclination; partiality; bent **3** in lawn bowling, *a)* the bulge in the side of the ball (the *bowl*) that causes it to roll in a curve *b)* this curve or tendency to curve *c)* the force causing this **4** *Electronics* a high-frequency signal or tone added to a tape during the recording process so as to reduce distortion and increase frequency response **5** *Radio* the fixed voltage applied to an electrode circuit to control the mode of operation, usually measured with the cathode voltage as reference **6** *Statistics* any systematic error contributing to the difference between statistical values in a population and a sample drawn from it —*adj.* slanting; diagonal —*adv.* **1** diagonally **2** [Obs.] awry —*vt.* **-ased** or **-assed, -as·ing** or **-as·sing 1** to cause to have a bias; influence; prejudice **2** *Radio* to apply a bias to (an electrode) —*SYN.* PREJUDICE —**on the bias** diagonally; obliquely; specif., cut or sewn diagonally across the weave

bias (ply) tire a motor vehicle tire having a foundation of plies of rubberized cords in a crisscross pattern of lines diagonal to the center line of the tread: see RADIAL (PLY) TIRE

bi·ath·lete (bī ath′lēt′) *n.* ⟦blend of fol. & ATHLETE⟧ a person who competes in a biathlon

bi·ath·lon (bī ath′län′, -lən) *n.* ⟦BI-[1] + Gr *athlon,* a contest⟧ a winter sports event combining cross-country skiing and rifle marksmanship

bi·au·ric·u·late (bī′ô rik′yo͞o lit) *adj.* ⟦BI-[1] + AURICULATE⟧ *Anat.* having two ears or earlike parts: also **bi′au·ric′u·lar** (-lər)

bi·ax·i·al (bī ak′sē əl) *adj.* **1** having two axes [a *biaxial* joint] **2** designating a monoclinic, orthorhombic, or triclinic crystal that does not have birefringence along two axes —**bi·ax′i·al·ly** *adv.*

bib[1] (bib) *vt., vi.* **bibbed, bib′bing** ⟦ME *bibben* < L *bibere,* IMBIBE⟧ [Archaic] to drink; imbibe; tipple —*n.* **1** an apron-like cloth or plastic napkin tied under a child's chin at meals **2** the front upper part of an apron or overalls

bib[2] *abbrev.* ⟦L *bibe*⟧ *Pharmacy* drink

Bib *abbrev.* **1** Bible **2** Biblical

bib and tucker [Informal] an outfit of clothes; esp., **best bib and tucker,** best, or most formal, clothes

bi·ba·sic (bī bā′sik) *adj.* [Rare] *Chem.* DIBASIC

bibb (bib) *n.* ⟦< BIB[1], *n.*: so named because in position it resembles a child's bib⟧ **1** a bibcock **2** a wooden bracket fastened to a ship's mast to support the trestletrees

bib·ber (bib′ər) *n.* a person who bibs; drinker; toper

☆**bibb lettuce** (bib) ⟦after Jack *Bibb* (1789-1884), Kentucky horticulturist who developed it⟧ a type of butterhead lettuce, formed in loose heads of very crisp, dark-green leaves

bib·cock (bib′käk′) *n.* ⟦BIB[1] + COCK[1]: from the position of the nozzle⟧ a faucet whose nozzle is bent downward

bi·be·lot (bib′lō′, -ə lō′; *Fr* bē blō′) *n.* ⟦Fr < OFr *beubelot* < *belbel,* BAUBLE⟧ **1** a small object whose value lies in its beauty or rarity; trinket **2** a book of unusually small size

bi-bi·va·lent (bī′bī vā′lənt) *adj. Chem.* separating into two bivalent ions: said of electrolytes

Bibl or **bibl** *abbrev.* Biblical

Bi·ble (bī′bəl) *n.* ⟦ME & OFr < ML *biblia* < Gr, collection of writings, in LGr(Ec), the Scriptures (pl. of *biblion,* book) < *biblos,* papyrus, after *Byblos* (now *Dschebēl*), Phoen city from which papyrus was imported⟧ **1** the sacred book of Christianity; Old Testament and New Testament: some Roman Catholic versions also include all or part of the Apocrypha **2** the Holy Scriptures of Judaism, identical with the Old Testament of Christianity **3** a copy or particular edition of the Scriptures **4** any collection or book of writings sacred to a religion [the Koran is the Muslim *Bible*] **5** [**b-**] any book regarded as authoritative or official See also AMERICAN STANDARD VERSION, APOCRYPHA, AUTHORIZED VERSION, DOUAY BIBLE, JERUSALEM BIBLE,

NEW AMERICAN BIBLE, NEW ENGLISH BIBLE, REVISED STANDARD VERSION, SEPTUAGINT, VULGATE

☆**Bible Belt** ⟦coined (1924) by H. L. MENCKEN⟧ those regions of the U.S., particularly areas in the South, where fundamentalist beliefs prevail and Christian clergy are especially influential

Bi·ble-thump·ing (-thum′piŋ) *adj.* ⟦from the image of an old-time evangelist pounding the Bible on his pulpit, for emphasis, in the intensity of his preaching⟧ [Informal] designating or characteristic of an evangelistic Christian, esp. a fundamentalist, often variously regarded as being sanctimonious, self-righteously pious, dogmatically moralizing, etc. —**Bi′ble-thump′er** *n.*

bib·li·cal (bib′li kəl) *adj.* [*also* **B-**] **1** of or in the Bible **2** in keeping with or according to the Bible; like that in the Bible —**bib′li·cal·ly** *adv.*

bib·li·cist (-sist) *n.* [*also* **B-**] a person who takes the words of the Bible literally —**bib′li·cism′** *n.*

bib·li·o- (bib′lē ō, -ə) ⟦< Gr *biblion*: see BIBLE⟧ *combining form* **1** book, books [*bibliophile*] **2** of the Bible [*bibliolatry*]

bibliog *abbrev.* **1** bibliographic **2** bibliography

bib·li·og·ra·pher (bib′lē äg′rə fər) *n.* ⟦< Gr *bibliographos*, writer of books < *biblion*, a book (see BIBLE) + *graphos* < *graphein*, to write (see GRAPHIC) + -ER⟧ **1** an expert in bibliography **2** a person who compiles a bibliography

bib·li·og·ra·phy (bib′lē äg′rə fē) *n., pl.* **-phies** ⟦Gr *bibliographia*: see BIBLIO- & -GRAPHY⟧ **1** the study of the editions, dates, authorship, etc. of books and other writings **2** a book containing such information **3** a list of sources of information on a given subject, period, etc., or of the literary works of a given author, publisher, etc. **4** a list of the books, articles, etc. used or referred to by an author —**bib′li·o·graph′ic** (-ə graf′ik) *adj.*, **bib′li·o·graph′i·cal** —**bib′li·o·graph′i·cal·ly** *adv.*

bib·li·ol·a·try (bib′lē äl′ə trē) *n.* ⟦BIBLIO- + -LATRY⟧ **1** excessive adherence to a literal interpretation of the Bible **2** excessive veneration of books —**bib′li·ol′a·ter** *n.* —**bib′li·ol′a·trous** *adj.*

bib·li·o·man·cy (bib′lē ə man′sē) *n.* ⟦BIBLIO- + -MANCY⟧ divination based on a Bible verse or a literary passage chosen at random

bib·li·o·ma·ni·a (bib′lē ə mā′nē ə) *n.* ⟦BIBLIO- + -MANIA⟧ a craze for collecting books, esp. rare ones —**bib′li·o·ma′ni·ac** *n., adj.*

bib·li·op·e·gy (bib′lē äp′ə jē) *n.* ⟦BIBLIO- + Gr *pēgia* < *pēgnynai*, to fasten, bind: see PEACE⟧ the art of bookbinding

bib·li·o·phile (bib′lē ə fīl′) *n.* ⟦BIBLIO- + -PHILE⟧ **1** a person who loves or admires books, esp. for their style of binding, printing, etc. **2** a collector of books Also **bib·li·oph·i·list** (bib′lē äf′ə list) —**bib′li·o·phil′ic** (-ə fil′ik) *adj.* —**bib′li·oph′i·lism′** (-äf′ə liz′em) *n.*, **bib′li·oph′i·ly** (-äf′ə lē)

bib·li·o·pole (bib′lē ə pōl′) ⟦L *bibliopola* < Gr *bibliopōlēs* < *biblion*, a book (see BIBLE) + *pōlein*, to sell: see MONOPOLY⟧ *n.* a bookseller, esp. one dealing in rare works: also **bib·li·op·o·list** (bib′lē äp′ə list) —**bib′li·o·pol′ic** (-ə päl′ik) *adj.*

bib·li·o·the·ca (bib′lē ə thē′kə) *n.* ⟦L < Gr *bibliothēkē*, library, bookcase < *biblion*, a book (see BIBLE) + *thēkē* < *tithenai*, to place, DO[1]⟧ **1** a book collection; library **2** a bookseller's catalog —**bib′li·o·the′cal** *adj.*

bib·list (bib′list, bī′blist) *n.* BIBLICIST

bib·u·lous (bib′yoo̅ ləs) *adj.* ⟦L *bibulus* < *bibere*, IMBIBE⟧ **1** highly absorbent **2** addicted to or fond of alcoholic beverages —**bib′u·lous·ly** *adv.* —**bib′u·lous·ness** *n.*

bi·cam·er·al (bī kam′ər əl) *adj.* ⟦BI-[1] + CAMERAL⟧ made up of or having two legislative chambers [Congress is a *bicameral* legislature] —**bi·cam′er·al·ism′** *n.*

bi·cap·su·lar (bī kap′sə lər, -syoo lər) *adj. Bot.* having two capsules or a capsule with two cells

bi·carb (bī′kärb′) *n.* [Informal] SODIUM BICARBONATE

bi·car·bon·ate (bī kär′bən it, -āt′) *n.* an acid salt of carbonic acid containing the monovalent, negative radical HCO_3

bicarbonate of soda SODIUM BICARBONATE

bi·cen·te·nar·y (bī′sen ten′ər ē, bī sen′tə ner′ē) *adj., n., pl.* **-nar·ies** BICENTENNIAL

bi·cen·ten·ni·al (bī′sen ten′ē əl) *adj.* **1** happening once in a period of 200 years **2** lasting 200 years **3** of a 200th anniversary —☆*n.* a 200th anniversary or its commemoration

bi·cep (bī′sep′) *adj.* of or having to do with the biceps muscle in the front of the upper arm or at the back of the thigh [a *bicep* injury]

bi·ceph·a·lous (bī sef′ə ləs) *adj.* ⟦BI-[1] + CEPHALOUS⟧ two-headed: also **bi·ce·phal·ic** (bī′sə fal′ik)

bi·ceps (bī′seps′) *n., pl.* **-ceps′** ⟦ModL < L < *bis*, two + *caput*, HEAD⟧ **1** a muscle having two heads, or points of origin; esp., the large muscle in the front of the upper arm or the corresponding muscle at the back of the thigh **2** loosely, strength or muscular development, esp. of the arm

bi·chlo·ride (bī klôr′īd′) *n.* **1** a binary compound containing two atoms of chlorine for each atom of another element; dichloride **2** MERCURIC CHLORIDE

bichloride of mercury MERCURIC CHLORIDE

bi·chon fri·sé (bē shōn frē zā′) ⟦Fr *bichon*, lap dog + *frisé*, curly⟧ a variety of toy spaniel with curly white hair, originally from Tenerife

bi·chro·mate (bī krō′māt) *n.* DICHROMATE

bi·cip·i·tal (bī sip′ət ′l) *adj.* ⟦< ModL < L *biceps* (gen. *bicipitis*), BICEPS⟧ *Anat.* **1** with two heads or points of origin, as a biceps muscle **2** of a biceps

bick·er (bik′ər) *vi.* ⟦ME *bikeren*, ? akin to Fris *bikkern*, hack, gnaw⟧ to have a petty quarrel; squabble —*n.* [Archaic] a skirmish or quarrel —**bick′er·er** *n.*

bi·coast·al (bī kōs′təl) *adj.* of or involving both the east and west coasts of the U.S.; specif., *a)* traveling back and forth from coast to coast, or entailing such travel *b)* with offices, homes, etc. on both coasts

bi·col·or (bī′kul′ər) *adj.* ⟦L: see BI-[1] & COLOR⟧ of two colors: also **bi′col′ored**

bi·con·cave (bī kän′kāv′, bī′kän kāv′) *adj.* concave on both surfaces [a *biconcave* lens]

bi·con·vex (bī kän′veks′, bī′kän veks′) *adj.* convex on both surfaces [a *biconvex* lens]

bi·corn (bī′kôrn′) *adj.* ⟦L *bicornis* < *bi-*, BI-[1] + *cornu*, HORN⟧ **1** having two horns or hornlike parts **2** crescent-shaped Also **bi·cor·nu·ate** (bī kôr′nyoo̅ it)

☆**bi·cul·tur·al** (bī kul′chər əl) *adj.* of or combining two distinct cultures in a single region —**bi·cul′tur·al·ism′** *n.*

bi·cus·pid (bī kus′pid) *adj.* ⟦ModL *bicuspis* < BI-[1] + L *cuspis* (gen. *cuspidis*), CUSP⟧ having two points [a *bicuspid* tooth]: also **bi·cus′pi·date′** (-pi dāt′) —*n.* any of eight adult teeth with two-pointed crowns; premolar tooth

bicuspid valve MITRAL VALVE

bi·cy·cle (bī′sik′əl, -si kəl) *n.* ⟦Fr: see BI-[1] & CYCLE⟧ a vehicle consisting of a tubular metal frame mounted on two large, wire-spoked wheels, one behind the other, and equipped with handlebars, a saddlelike seat, and foot pedals —*vi.* **-cled, -cling** to ride or travel on a bicycle —*vt.* **1** to carry on or as on a bicycle **2** to travel over on a bicycle —**bi·cy·clist** (bī′sik′əl ist; -si kəl ist, -klist) *n.*, **bi·cy·cler** (bī′sik′əl ər; -si kəl ər, -klər)

bi·cy·clic (bī sīk′lik) *adj.* **1** of or forming two cycles **2** *Chem.* containing only two fused rings in the molecule Also **bi·cy′cli·cal**

bid[1] (bid) *vt.* **bade, bid′den, bid′ding**; for vt. 3, 6, 8 & for vi., the pt. & pp. are always **bid** ⟦ME *bidden*, to ask, plead, pray < OE *biddan* < IE base **bheidh-*, to urge, compel; meaning and form merged with ME *beden*, to offer, present < OE *beodan*, to command, decree < IE base **bheudh-*, to be alert, announce⟧ **1** [Obs.] to beseech or implore **2** to command, ask, or tell [do as you are *bidden*] **3** to offer (a certain amount) as the price one will pay, the fee one will charge, or the amount one will accept **4** to declare openly [to *bid* defiance] **5** to express in greeting or taking leave [*bid* farewell to your friends] ☆**6** [Informal] to offer membership to [the fraternity may *bid* five new men] **7** [Now Chiefly Dial.] to invite **8** *Card Games* to state (the number of tricks or points one proposes to take and, in bridge, whether one proposes to play the hand with a specified suit as trump or with no suit as trump) in an effort to win the right to name trump —*vi.* to make a bid —*n.* **1** a bidding of an amount **2** the amount bid **3** a chance to bid **4** an attempt or try [a *bid* for fame] ☆**5** [Informal] an invitation, esp. to become a member **6** *Card Games* *a)* the act of bidding *b)* the number of tricks, suit, etc. stated in a bid *c)* a player's turn to bid —**bid fair** to seem likely (to be or do something) —☆**bid in** at an auction, to bid more than the best offer on one's own property in order to keep it —**bid up** to raise the amount bid —**bid′der** *n.*

bid[2] (bid) *vi. obs. pp. of* BIDE

b.i.d. *abbrev.* ⟦L *bis in die*⟧ *Pharmacy* twice daily

bid·da·ble (bid′ə bəl) *adj.* **1** ready to do as bidden; obedient **2** worth bidding on [a *biddable* bridge hand]

bid·den[1] (bid′′n) *vt., vi. alt. pp. of* BID[1]

bid·den[2] (bid′′n) *vi. obs. pp. of* BIDE

bid·ding (-iŋ) *n.* **1** a command or request **2** an invitation or summons **3** the bids or the making of bids in a card game or auction —**do the bidding of** to be obedient to; carry out the orders of

Bid·dle (bid′′l) **1 John** 1615-62; Eng. theologian: founder of Eng. Unitarianism **2 Nicholas** 1786-1844; U.S. financier

bid·dy (bid′ē) *n., pl.* **-dies** ⟦< ?⟧ **1** a chicken or chick; esp., a hen **2** [Informal] a woman; esp., an elderly woman (usually **old biddy**) regarded contemptuously as annoying, gossipy, etc.

bide (bīd) *vi.* **bid′ed** or **bode, bid′ed, bid′ing** ⟦ME *biden* < OE *bidan*, to stay, wait < IE base **bheidh-* (see BID[1]), prob. in sense "compel oneself," hence, delay⟧ [Archaic] **1** to stay; continue **2** to dwell; reside **3** to wait —*vt.* [Archaic] to endure or tolerate —**bide one's time** to wait patiently for a chance

Bi·den (bī′dən), **Joe** (born *Joseph Robinette Biden, Jr.*) 1942-   ; vice president of the U.S. (2009-   )

bi·den·tate (bī den′tāt′) *adj.* ⟦BI-[1] + DENTATE⟧ having two teeth or toothlike parts

bi·det (bē dā′, bi-) *n.* ⟦Fr, lit., small pony, nag (prob. < Gaul *bid*, small): fig. use from straddling stance assumed by the user⟧ a low, bowl-shaped, porcelain bathroom fixture equipped with running water, used for bathing the crotch

bi·di·rec·tion·al (bī′də rek′shə nəl) *adj.* moving, functioning, or receiving signals in or from two, usually opposite, directions

bi·don·ville (bē′dōn vēl′) *n.* ⟦Fr slang < *bidonner*, to guzzle, swig < *bidon*, wine jug, orig. soldier's water bottle + *ville*, city⟧ a shantytown on the outskirts of a city, characterized by squalor and extreme poverty, as in France and formerly Algeria or Tunisia

Bie·der·mei·er (bē′dər mī′ər) *adj.* ⟦Ger, after (*Gottlieb*) *Biedermeier*, fictitious author of stodgy poems published (1855-57, and later) by Adolf Kussmaul and Ludwig Eichrodt to satirize Ger bourgeois tastes⟧ **1** designating or of a style of chiefly middle-class German & Austrian furniture and interior design in the first half of the 19th cent., characterized by solidity, comfort, and deliberate simplicity of decoration **2** designating or of the general middle-class German & Austrian culture of this period

Bie·le·feld (bē′lə felt′) city in NW Germany, in North Rhine-Westphalia

Bi·el·sko-Bi·a·ła (bē el′skô bē äl′ə) city in S Poland, at the foot of the Carpathian Mountains

bien en·ten·du (byan nän tän dü′) ⟦Fr, lit., well understood⟧ certainly; to be sure

bi·en·na·le (bē′ə nä′lē) ***n.*** ⟦It, prob. after *la Biennale di Venezia,* the Biennial (Exhibition of Modern Art) of Venice < *biennale,* adj. < L *biennium:* see fol.⟧ a biennial show; esp., an art show held every two years

bi·en·ni·al (bī en′ē əl) ***adj.*** ⟦< L *biennium,* period of two years < *bi-,* BI-[1] + *annus,* year + -AL⟧ **1** happening every two years **2** lasting or living two years —***n.*** **1** a biennial event or occurrence **2** *Bot.* a plant that lasts two years, usually producing flowers and seed the second year —**bi·en′ni·al·ly** ***adv.***

bi·en·ni·um (bī en′ē əm) ***n.,*** *pl.* **-ni·ums** or **-ni·a** (-ə) ⟦L, see prec.⟧ a period of two years

bien-pen·sant (byan pän sän′) ***adj.*** ⟦Fr < *bien,* well + prp. of *penser,* to think⟧ right-minded; accepting or based on ideas regarded as sound or correct; orthodox, doctrinaire, conventional, etc. —***n.*** one who is orthodox, conventional, etc. Also ***bien pensant***

bien·ve·nue (byan və nü′) ***n.*** ⟦Fr, lit., well come⟧ a welcome

Bien·ville (byan vēl′), Sieur de (born *Jean Baptiste Le Moyne*) 1680-1768; Fr. colonizer & governor of Louisiana: founder of New Orleans

bier (bir) ***n.*** ⟦ME *bere* < OE *bær:* for IE base see BEAR[1]⟧ **1** a platform or portable framework on which a coffin or corpse is placed **2** a coffin and its supporting platform

Bierce (birs), **Ambrose (Gwinett)** 1842-1914?; U.S. writer

Bier·stadt (bir′stat), **Albert** 1830-1902; U.S. painter, born in Germany

biest·ings (bēs′tiŋz) ***pl.n.*** *alt. sp. of* BEESTINGS

bi·fa·cial (bī fā′shəl) ***adj.*** **1** having two faces or main surfaces **2** *Bot.* having two unlike opposite surfaces

bi·far·i·ous (bī fer′ē əs) ***adj.*** ⟦L *bifarius,* twofold < *bifariam,* in two directions < *bis,* twice + *fas,* (divine) law, lawful, possible⟧ *Bot.* arranged in two rows

☆**biff** (bif) [Old Slang] ***n.*** ⟦prob. echoic⟧ a blow; strike; hit —***vt.*** to strike; hit

bif·fy (bif′ē) ***n.,*** *pl.* **-fies** [Slang, Chiefly Cdn.] TOILET (sense 4)

bi·fid (bī′fid′) ***adj.*** ⟦L *bifidus,* forked: see BI-[1] & -FID⟧ divided into two equal parts by a cleft, as the end of a snake's tongue; forked —**bi·fid′i·ty** (-fid′ə tē) ***n.*** —**bi′fid′ly** (-fid′lē) ***adv.***

bi·fi·lar (bī fī′lər) ***adj.*** ⟦BI-[1] + FILAR⟧ having two threads, wires, etc. as certain sensitive measuring instruments —**bi·fi′lar·ly** ***adv.***

bi·flag·el·late (bī flaj′ə lit, -lāt′) ***adj.*** ⟦BI-[1] + FLAGELLATE⟧ *Biol.* having two whiplike parts, as certain protozoans

☆**bi·fo·cal** (bī fō′kəl, bī′fō′-) ***adj.*** adjusted to two different focal lengths —***n.*** a lens, esp. for eyeglasses, with one part ground for close focus, as for reading, and the other ground for distance

☆**bi·fo·cals** (bī′fō′kəlz) ***pl.n.*** eyeglasses with bifocal lenses

bi-fold (bī′fōld′) ***adj.*** designed to fold in half, as at a hinge or crease [*a bi-fold* door, *bi-fold* wallet] —***n.*** any of various products designed to fold in half, as at a hinge or crease; esp., *a)* a hinged, often louvered door, as for a closet *b)* a man's wallet Also written **bi′fold′**

bi·fo·li·ate (bī fō′lē it, -āt′) ***adj.*** ⟦BI-[1] + FOLIATE⟧ *Bot.* having two leaves

bi·fo·li·o·late (bī fō′lē ə lit, -lāt′) ***adj.*** ⟦BI-[1] + FOLIOLATE⟧ *Bot.* having two leaflets

bi·form (bī′fôrm′) ***adj.*** ⟦L *biformis:* see BI-[1] & FORM⟧ having, or incorporating the features of, two forms

Bif·rost (bēf′räst′) ***n.*** ⟦ON *bifrost,* lit., the tremulous way: *bif-* < *bifask,* to tremble + *rǫst,* a distance⟧ *Norse Myth.* the rainbow bridge of the gods from Asgard, their home, to Midgard, the earth

bif·teck (bēf tek′) ***n.*** ⟦Fr⟧ beefsteak: also **bif′tek**

bi·fur·cate (bī′fər kāt′, bī fur′kāt′; *for adj. also,* -kit) ***adj.*** ⟦ML *bifurcatus* < L *bifurcus* < *bi-,* BI-[1] + *furca,* FORK⟧ having two branches or peaks; forked — ***vt., vi.*** **-cat′ed, -cat′ing** to divide into two parts or branches

bi·fur·ca·tion (bī′fər kā′shən) ***n.*** **1** the act or fact of bifurcating **2** the place where this occurs

big (big) ***adj.*** **big′ger, big′gest** ⟦ME < Gmc **bugja,* swollen up, thick (> BUG[2] & Norw dial. *bugge,* big man) < IE base **beu-,* **bheu-,* to blow up, swell > PUCK[2], L *bucca,* puffed cheek⟧ **1** *a)* of great size, extent, or capacity; large *b)* great in amount or quantity *c)* great in force or intensity [*a big* wind] **2** *a)* full-grown *b)* elder [his *big* sister] **3** *a)* far advanced in pregnancy (*with*) *b)* filled or swelling (*with*) **4** loud **5** *a)* important or outstanding [to do *big* things] *b)* very well known; famous *c)* popular; very well liked **6** boastful; pompous; extravagant [*big* talk] ☆**7** generous; noble [*a big* heart] **8** [*often* **B-**] designating an industry or other organized, large-scale activity regarded as having distinct political and economic interests [*big* oil, *big* labor, etc.] ➥*Big* is much used in comb. to form adjectives [*big*-bodied, *big*-headed, *big*-souled, etc.] —***adv.*** **big′ger, big′gest** [Informal] **1** pompously; boastfully; extravagantly [to talk *big*] **2** impressively **3** in a broad way; showing imagination [think *big!*] —***SYN.*** LARGE —**big′ness** ***n.***

big·a·mist (big′ə mist) ***n.*** a person who commits bigamy

big·a·mous (-məs) ***adj.*** ⟦LL *bigamus*⟧ **1** constituting or involving bigamy **2** guilty of bigamy —**big′a·mous·ly** ***adv.***

big·a·my (-mē) ***n.,*** *pl.* **-mies** ⟦ME & OFr *bigamie* < LL *bigamus* < L *bi-,* BI-[1] + Gr *gamos,* marriage: see GAMO-⟧ the act of marrying a second time while a previous marriage is still legally in effect: when done knowingly, it is a criminal offense

☆**Big Apple, the** ⟦orig., jazzmen's slang for the BIG TIME < ?⟧ *name for* NEW YORK (City)

big·ar·reau (big′ə rō′, big′ə rō′) ***n.*** ⟦Fr < Prov *bigarreu* < *bigarra,* fleck⟧ [*also* **B-**] any of several heart-shaped, firm-fleshed varieties of sweet cherry: cf. HEART CHERRY: also **big′a·roon′** (-ro͞on′)

big band an ensemble of ten or more players, usually 16 to 20, including sections of rhythm, brass, and reeds, playing arrangements of jazz, popular dance music, etc.

big-band (big′band′) ***adj.*** **1** of or characteristic of jazz as played by large bands and, specif., of dance music as played by large swing bands of the 1930s and 1940s **2** of or relating to a BIG BAND

big-bang theory (big′baŋ′) ⟦< *big bang,* dismissive term coined by F. Hoyle (1915-2001), Brit astronomer and proponent of STEADY-STATE THEORY⟧ a theory of cosmology holding that the expansion of the universe began with a gigantic explosion (**big bang**) between 12 and 14 billion years ago: see STEADY-STATE THEORY

Big Ben ⟦prob. < nickname of Sir *Benjamin* Hall (1802-67), Brit commissioner of public works at time of installation (1859)⟧ **1** the great bell in the clock tower of the Houses of Parliament in London **2** the clock in this tower **3** the tower itself

☆**Big Board** **1** the listing of the securities that are bought and sold on the New York Stock Exchange **2** the New York Stock Exchange

big-box (big′bäks′) ***adj.*** designating or of a large retail store that is typically a spacious boxlike building with an extensive ground-level sales floor: also written **big box**

big brother **1** one's older brother ☆**2** [*often* **B- B-**] a man who undertakes the role of friend and mentor to a disadvantaged boy, as through a social agency **3** ⟦after personified concept in *1984,* novel (published 1949) by George ORWELL⟧ [*usually* **B- B-**] the state or some other organization regarded as ruthlessly invading the privacy of individuals in seeking to exercise control over them

big business the largest business organizations regarded collectively and, usually, in terms of having distinctive political and economic interests

Big C [Slang] CANCER (***n.*** 4): usually preceded by *the*

☆**big cheese** ⟦see CHEESE[2]⟧ [Slang] the most important person

Big D *name for* DALLAS

Big Daddy [Informal] someone or something dominantly important, powerful, wealthy, or, often, paternalistic

big data data sets that are too large to be processed easily by standard software

Big Diomede *see* DIOMEDE ISLANDS

☆**Big Dipper, the** a dipper-shaped group of stars in the constellation Ursa Major

Big Easy, the *name for* NEW ORLEANS

bi·gem·i·ny (bī jem′ə nē) ***n.*** ⟦< *bigemin(ate),* in two pairs (< BI-[1] + GEMINATE) + -Y[3]⟧ the state of occurring in pairs, as a rhythm of the heartbeat consisting of pairs of beats —**bi·gem′i·nal** ***adj.***

bi·ge·ner·ic (bī′jə ner′ik) ***adj.*** designating or of hybrids derived from two different genera

big·eye (big′ī′) ***n.*** any of a family (Priacanthidae) of small, red, tropical percoid fishes with large eyes and a short body

Big·foot (big′fo͝ot′) ***n.*** [*also* **b-**] SASQUATCH

big game **1** large wild animals hunted for sport, as lions or moose **2** the object of any important or dangerous undertaking

big·ger-than-life (big′ər *than′*līf′) ***adj.*** *var. of* LARGER-THAN-LIFE

☆**big·gie** (big′ē) ***n.*** [Informal] an important person or thing

big·gin (big′in) ***n.*** ⟦MFr < OFr, orig. cap worn by the *Beguines,* a lay sisterhood⟧ [Archaic] **1** a cap or hood, esp. for a child **2** a nightcap

big·gish (big′ish) ***adj.*** somewhat big

☆**big·gi·ty** (big′ət ē) ***adj.*** [Chiefly South] self-important, conceited, vain, etc.

big gun [Slang] **1** an important and influential person **2** a high-ranking military officer

big hair hair styled in such a way as to appear very full, esp. when regarded as being stiff from overuse of styling products or excessively teased or curled

☆**big·head** (-hed′) ***n.*** **1** [Slang] a conceited or egotistical person **2** any of certain diseases of animals, esp. sheep, characterized by the swelling of tissues about the head —**big′head′ed** ***adj.***

big head [Informal] a personality characterized by conceit and egotism: often with *a* [his rapid rise in the company has given him a *big head*]

big·heart·ed (-härt′id) ***adj.*** quick to give or forgive; generous or magnanimous —**big′heart′ed·ly** ***adv.***

☆**big·horn** (-hôrn′) ***n.,*** *pl.* **-horns′** or **-horn′** any of a number of sheep with large horns, esp. a large, wild, hairy species (*Ovis canadensis*) of the Rocky Mountains

Big·horn (big′hôrn′) ⟦after the *bighorn* sheep⟧ river in WC Wyo. flowing northward into the Yellowstone River in S Mont.: *c.* 450 mi (724 km)

Bighorn Mountains range of the Rocky Mountains in N Wyo. and S Mont.: highest peak, 13,165 ft (4,013 m)

☆**big house, the** [Slang] a penitentiary

bight (bīt) ***n.*** ⟦ME < OE *byht* < base of *bugan* (see BOW[1]); akin to Du & Ger *bucht*⟧ **1** [Obs.] a bend, angle, or hollow, specif. of a body structure **2** a loop or slack part in a rope **3** a curve in a river, coastline, etc. **4** a bay formed by such a curve —***vt.*** to fasten with a bight of rope

☆**big-league** (big′lēg′) ***adj.*** ⟦after the *big* (i.e., major) *leagues* in professional baseball⟧ [Informal] of or at the highest level in one's profession or field of activity

big lie, the 1 a gross falsification or misrepresentation of the facts that is repeated and embellished to lend it credibility 2 the propaganda technique, as in politics, of using this device

big·mouth (big′mouth′) *n.* ☆[Slang] a person who talks too much, esp. in an opinionated or gossipy way —**big′-mouthed′** (-mouthd′, -moutht′) *adj.*

big·no·ni·a (big nō′nē ə) *n.* ⟦after the Abbé *Bignon* (1662-1743), librarian to LOUIS XV⟧ a tropical American evergreen vine (*Bignonia capreolata*) of the bignonia family that bears tendrils, compound leaves, and trumpet-shaped, yellow or reddish flowers —*adj.* designating a family (Bignoniaceae, order Scrophulariales) of dicotyledonous trees, shrubs, and woody vines

big·ot (big′ət) *n.* ⟦Fr < OFr, a term of insult used of Normans, apparently a Norman oath < ? ME *bi god,* by God⟧ 1 a person who holds blindly and intolerantly to a particular creed, opinion, etc. 2 a narrow-minded, prejudiced person —**SYN.** ZEALOT —**big′ot·ed** *adj.* —**big′ot·ed·ly** *adv.*

big·ot·ry (big′ə trē) *n., pl.* **-ries** ⟦Fr *bigoterie*⟧ the behavior, attitude, or beliefs of a bigot; intolerance; prejudice

big picture, the a long-range or overall view or account of some complex matter

☆**bigs, the** [Slang] THE MAJOR LEAGUES (see phrase under MAJOR LEAGUE)

big science scientific research or projects requiring considerable funding and personnel

big screen [Informal] the medium of film, or the industry of filmmaking, esp. as distinguished from television: with *the* —**big′-screen′** *adj.*

☆**big shot** [Slang] a person regarded as important or influential

☆**big stick** ⟦from "speak softly and carry a *big stick,*" portion of Afr proverb quoted by T. ROOSEVELT[2]⟧ [*also* **B- S-**] a policy of acting or negotiating from a position backed by a show of strength

Big Ten ⟦so called from orig. having *ten* members⟧ a group of large universities, located chiefly in the Midwestern U.S., forming a league for intercollegiate sports

big-tent (big′tent′) *adj.* designating or of a political party, religious denomination, etc. that is open to a wide range of beliefs and opinions; not doctrinaire or narrowly ideological

☆**big-tick·et** (big′tik′it) *adj.* [Informal] having a high price

☆**big time** [Slang] 1 vaudeville performed in the top-ranking, big-city theatrical circuits, at high pay 2 the level regarded as highest in any profession, occupation, etc. Used with *the*

☆**big-time** (big′tīm′) *adj., adv.* ⟦< prec.⟧ [Slang] at, of, or to a very great degree, extent, etc. [*a big-time* swindle, to be hurt *big-time*]

☆**big top** [Informal] 1 the main tent of a circus 2 the life or work of circus performers

☆**big tree** a giant California evergreen (*Sequoiadendron giganteum*) of the baldcypress family, found in the high Sierras and often exceeding 90 m (*c.* 300 ft) in height; giant sequoia

big·wig (-wig′) *n.* ⟦from the large wigs once worn by judges and others of distinction⟧ [Informal] an important, influential person

Bi·har (bi här′) state of NE India: 38,301 sq mi (99,200 sq km); cap. Patna

Bi·ha·ri (bi hä′rē) *n.* 1 a person born or living in Bihar 2 the group of dialects of Hindi spoken in Bihar —*adj.* of Bihar or its people, language, or culture

Biisk (bisk, bēsk) *alt. sp. of* BIYSK

bi·jou (bē′zhōō′, bē zhōō′) *n., pl.* **-joux′** (-zhōōz′) ⟦Fr < Bret *bizou,* a ring < *biz,* finger⟧ 1 a jewel 2 something small and exquisite

bi·jou·te·rie (bi zhōōt′ə rē) *n.* ⟦Fr < prec.⟧ jewelry or trinkets generally or collectively

bi·ju·gate (bī′jōō gāt′; bī jōō′git, -gāt′) *adj.* ⟦BI-[1] + JUGATE⟧ having two pairs of leaflets, as some pinnate leaves: also **bi′ju·gous** (-gəs)

Bi·kan·er (bē kə nir′, bik′ə ner′) city in NW India, in the Thar Desert

☆**bike** (bīk) *n.* ⟦shortened & altered < BICYCLE⟧ *short for* BICYCLE, MOTORCYCLE, etc. — *vt., vi.* **biked, bik′ing** to travel on a bicycle or motorcycle

bik·er (bīk′ər) *n.* a cyclist; specif., a member of a motorcycle organization or gang

☆**bike·way** (bīk′wā′) *n.* a path, lane, or route set aside for bicycle riders

bi·ki·ni (bi kē′nē) *n.* ⟦Fr, after *Bikini,* Marshall Islands atomic bomb testing site (1946); to suggest the explosive effect on the viewer⟧ 1 a very brief two-piece swimsuit for women 2 very brief, legless swimming trunks 3 very brief, legless underpants: in full **bikini briefs** (or **brief**)

bi·ki·nied (-nēd) *adj.* [Informal] dressed in a bikini

Bi·kol (bi kōl′) *n.* 1 a Western Austronesian language spoken in S Luzon and neighboring islands 2 a member of a people of this region, one of the lowland Christian groups of the Philippines

bi·la·bi·al (bī lā′bē əl) *adj.* 1 having two lips; bilabiate 2 *Phonet.* articulated with both lips, as (p) and (m) —*n.* a bilabial sound

bi·la·bi·ate (-bē it, -āt′) *adj.* ⟦BI-[1] + LABIATE⟧ *Bot.* having two lips, as the corolla of flowers of the mint family

bi·lat·er·al (bī lat′ər əl) *adj.* ⟦BI-[1] + LATERAL⟧ 1 of, having, or involving two sides, halves, factions, etc. 2 having terms affecting both sides reciprocally [*a bilateral* pact] 3 arranged symmetrically on opposite sides of an axis —**bi·lat′er·al·ism′** *n.* —**bi·lat′er·al·ly** *adv.*

Bil·ba·o (bil bä′ō, bil bou′) port in The Basque Country, N Spain, near the Bay of Biscay

bil·ber·ry (bil′ber′ē; *chiefly Brit,* -bər ē) *n., pl.* **-ries** ⟦< Scand, as in Dan *bøllebær,* lit., ball berry < ON *bollr,* BALL[1] + *ber,* BERRY⟧ 1 any of several North American species of blueberries (genus *Vaccinium*) 2 its dark-blue fruit

bil·bo (bil′bō′) *n., pl.* **-boes′** ⟦after BILBAO, once famous for its ironworks⟧ 1 [*pl.*] a long iron bar with sliding shackles, for fettering a prisoner's feet 2 [Archaic] a sword or rapier

bil·dungs·ro·man (bil′dooŋz rō män′) *n., pl.* **-mans′** ⟦Ger < *bildung,* education + *roman,* novel⟧ a novel that details the maturation, and specif. the psychological development and moral education, of the principal character: also **Bil′dungs·ro·man** (bil′dooŋks rō män′) *pl.* **-ma′ne** (-mä′nə)

bile (bīl) *n.* ⟦Fr < L *bilis*⟧ 1 the bitter, alkaline, yellow-brown or greenish fluid secreted by the liver and stored in the gallbladder: it is discharged into the duodenum and helps in digestion, esp. of fats 2 *a)* either of two bodily humors (**black bile**, or melancholy, and **yellow bile**, or choler) in ancient physiology *b)* bitterness; anger

bi·lec·tion (bī lek′shən) *n.* BOLECTION

bile duct any of the ducts that convey bile; esp., the duct conveying bile from the liver or gallbladder to the duodenum

bi-lev·el (bī′lev′əl) *adj.* 1 having two levels ☆2 designating or of a type of one-story house having a main floor situated above ground level, with a full-sized, partially underground level below, used as for a basement or additional living space —☆*n.* a bi-level house Also written **bi′lev′el**

bilge (bilj) *n.* ⟦var. of BULGE⟧ 1 the bulge of a barrel or cask 2 the rounded, lower exterior part of a ship's hull 3 *a)* [*also pl.*] the bottommost interior part of a ship *b)* water that seeps or leaks in, collects there, and becomes stagnant and dirty 4 [Slang] worthless or silly talk or writing; nonsense —*vt.* **bilged, bilg′ing** to damage the bottom of (a ship) so that water enters —*vi.* to suffer such damage

bilge keel a projecting strip of metal or wood fastened lengthwise on either side of a ship's bottom to prevent heavy rolling, damage to the bilges, etc.: also **bilge chock** or **bilge piece**

bilge water BILGE (sense 3*b*): also written **bilge′wa′ter** *n.*

bilg·y (bil′jē) *adj.* looking or smelling like bilge water

bil·har·zi·a (bil här′zē ə) *n.* ⟦ModL, after Theodor *Bilharz* (1825-62), Ger parasitologist⟧ 1 SCHISTOSOME 2 SCHISTOSOMIASIS

bil·har·zi·a·sis (bil′här zī′ə sis) *n., pl.* **-ses′** (-sēz′) ⟦see prec. & -IASIS⟧ SCHISTOSOMIASIS

bil·i·ar·y (bil′ē er′ē, -ər ē; bil′yər ē) *adj.* ⟦Fr *biliaire*⟧ 1 of or involving the bile 2 bile-carrying 3 bilious

bi·lin·e·ar (bī lin′ē ər) *adj.* of or involving two lines

bi·lin·gual (bī liŋ′gwəl) *adj.* ⟦< L *bilinguis* (< *bi-,* BI-[1] + *lingua,* tongue) + -AL⟧ 1 of or in two languages 2 using or capable of using two languages, esp. with equal or nearly equal facility 3 designating a method of education in which students who are not yet fluent in the language of the country where they live are taught in their native language —**bi·lin′gual·ism′** *n.* —**bi·lin′gual·ly** *adv.*

bil·ious (bil′yəs) *adj.* ⟦Fr *bilieux* < L *biliosus* < *bilis,* bile⟧ 1 having or resulting from some ailment of the bile or the liver 2 afflicted with nausea or vomiting; queasy 3 of or like the color of bile [*a bilious* green] 4 bad-tempered; cross —**bil′ious·ly** *adv.* —**bil′ious·ness** *n.*

bil·i·ru·bin (bil′i rōō′bin) *n.* ⟦ModL < L *bilis,* bile + *ruber,* RED + -IN[1]⟧ the yellowish-red chief pigment, $C_{33}H_{36}N_4O_6$, of human bile, derived from biliverdin and found in small quantities in blood and urine: high concentrations change the color of blood and urine and result in jaundice

bil·i·ver·din (bil′i vur′din, bī′li-) *n.* ⟦ModL < L *bilis,* bile + obs. Fr *verd,* green (see VERDURE) + -IN[1]⟧ a dark-green pigment, $C_{33}H_{34}N_4O_6$, in animal bile, that is formed by the breakdown of hemoglobin and converts to bilirubin in humans

bilk (bilk) *vt.* ⟦? altered < BALK⟧ 1 to balk or thwart 2 to cheat or swindle; defraud 3 to get away without paying (a debt, etc.) 4 to manage to get away from; elude [*to bilk* the police] —*n.* 1 a bilking or being bilked; hoax 2 a person who cheats; swindler —**bilk′er** *n.*

bill[1] (bil) *n.* ⟦ME *bille* < Anglo-L *billa,* altered < ML *bulla,* sealed document < L, knob, bubble: see BOIL[1]⟧ 1 a statement, usually itemized, of charges for goods or services; invoice 2 a statement or list, as a menu, theater program, ship's roster, etc. 3 a poster or handbill, esp. one announcing a circus, show, etc. 4 the entertainment offered in a theater 5 a draft of a law proposed to a lawmaking body 6 a bill of exchange 7 any promissory note ☆8 *a)* a bank note or piece of paper money *b)* [Slang] a hundred dollars or a hundred-dollar bill 9 [Obs.] a written document, esp. one with a seal 10 *Law* a written declaration of charges or complaints filed in a legal action —*vt.* 1 to make out a bill of (items); list 2 to present a statement of charges to 3 *a)* to advertise by bills or posters *b)* to book or engage (a performer or performance) 4 to post bills or placards throughout (a town, etc.) 5 to book for shipping —☆**fill (or fit) the bill** [Informal] to meet the requirements —**bill′a·ble** *adj.*

bill[2] (bil) *n.* ⟦ME & OE *bile* < IE base **bhei-,* to strike⟧ 1 the horny jaws of a bird, usually projecting to a point; beak 2 a beaklike mouth part, as of a turtle 3 the point of an anchor fluke ☆4 the peak, or visor, of a cap —*vi.* 1 to touch bills together 2 to caress someone lovingly: now only in the phrase **bill and coo**, to kiss, talk softly, etc. in a loving way

bill[3] (bil) *n.* ⟦ME *bil* < OE *bill:* for IE base see prec.⟧ 1 a medieval weapon having a hook-shaped blade with a spike at the back, mounted on a long staff 2 BILLHOOK

Bill (bil) *n.* a masculine name: see WILLIAM[1]

bill·a·bong (bil′ə bôŋ′) *n.* ⟦< name in a language of Australia < *billa,* water + *bong,* dead⟧ a backwater channel forming a lagoon or pool

☆**bill·board**[1] (bil′bôrd′) *n.* ⟦BILL[1] + BOARD⟧ a signboard, usually outdoors, for advertising posters

bill·board[2] (-bôrd′) *n.* ⟦BILL[2] + BOARD⟧ an inclined plane projecting from the bow of earlier ships, on which the anchor was placed before being dropped or after being raised

☆**bill·bug** (-bug′) *n.* ⟦BILL² + BUG¹⟧ any of certain stout-bodied weevils (family Curculionidae) whose larvae feed upon numerous plants, esp. cereal grasses, corn, etc.

bill·er (-ər) *n.* **1** a person whose work is making out bills **2** a machine used in making out bills

bil·let¹ (bil′it) *n.* ⟦ME < Anglo-Fr, dim. of *bille,* BILL¹⟧ **1** [Obs.] a brief document or letter **2** a written order to provide quarters or lodging for military personnel, as in private buildings **3** *a)* the quarters thus assigned or occupied *b)* the sleeping place assigned to a sailor on ship **4** a position, job, or situation —*vt.* **1** to assign to lodging by billet **2** to assign to a post **3** to serve a billet on —*vi.* to be billeted or quartered

bil·let² (bil′it) *n.* ⟦ME < OFr *billette,* dim. of *bille* < Gaul **bilia,* tree trunk, akin to Ir *bile,* tree⟧ **1** *a)* a short, thick piece of firewood *b)* [Obs.] a wooden club **2** *a)* a long, rectangular or cylindrical unfinished bar of iron or steel, usually smaller than *c.* 232 sq cm (*c.* 36 sq in) in cross section *b)* a similar, generally smaller, bar made from a nonferrous metal **3** *Archit.* a log-shaped insert in a Norman molding **4** ⟦< ? another source⟧ in saddlery, any of the straps used to fasten the saddletree to the girth

bil·let-doux (bē′yā do͞o′, bil′ā-) *n., pl.* **bil·lets-doux** (bē′yā do͞o′, bil′ā do͞o′; -do͞oz′) ⟦Fr, lit., sweet letter⟧ a love letter

☆**bill·fish** (bil′fish′) *n., pl.* **-fish′** or **-fish′es** (see FISH) any of various fishes with long, narrow jaws that resemble a beak, as many gars or swordfish; esp., any of a family (Istiophoridae) of percoid fishes, as the marlin

☆**bill·fold** (-fōld′) *n.* a flat, folding case, usually of leather, for carrying paper money, cards, etc. in the pocket; wallet

bill·head (bil′hed′) *n.* a letterhead used for statements of charges

bill·hook (bil′ho͝ok′) *n.* a tool with a curved or hooked blade at one end, for pruning and cutting

bil·liard (bil′yərd) *adj.* of or for billiards —*n. Billiards* CAROM

bil·liards (-yərdz) *n.* ⟦Fr *billard,* the game; orig., a stick, cue < OFr *bille*: see BILLET²⟧ **1** a game played with two object balls and a cue ball on a rectangular table covered with cloth, esp. baize, and having raised, cushioned edges: a long, tapering stick (called a *cue*) is used to hit and move the balls **2** any of a number of similar games: pool is sometimes called **pocket billiards**

Bil·lie (bil′ē) *n.* ⟦dim. of WILLIAM¹⟧ a feminine and masculine name

bill·ing (bil′iŋ) *n.* **1** the listing of the actors' names on a playbill, theater marquee, etc. **2** the order in which the names are listed

Bil·lings¹ (bil′iŋz), **Josh** (jäsh) (pseud. of *Henry Wheeler Shaw*) 1818-85; U.S. humorist

Bil·lings² (bil′iŋz) ⟦after F. *Billings* (1823-90), pres. of Northern Pacific railroad, which founded the town⟧ city in S Mont., on the Yellowstone River

bil·lings·gate (bil′iŋz gāt′, -git) *n.* ⟦after a London fish market, notorious for foul language⟧ foul, vulgar, abusive talk

bil·lion (bil′yən) *n.* ⟦Fr < *bi-,* BI-¹ + *(mi)llion*⟧ **1** a thousand millions (1,000,000,000) **2** *former Brit. term for* TRILLION (a million millions) —*adj.* amounting to one billion in number

bil·lion·aire (bil′yə ner′) *n.* ⟦prec. + (MILLION)AIRE⟧ a person whose wealth comes to at least a billion dollars, pounds, francs, etc.

bil·lionth (bil′yənth) *adj.* **1** coming last in a series of a billion **2** designating any of the billion equal parts of something —*n.* **1** the last in a series of a billion **2** any of the billion equal parts of something

Bil·li·ton (bi lē′tän′) *former name for* BELITUNG

bill of attainder a legislative enactment by which a person, without benefit of a trial, is pronounced guilty of a crime, orig. a capital crime, esp. treason: prohibited in the U.S. by the Constitution

bill of exchange a written order to pay a certain sum of money to the person named or to that person's account; draft

bill of fare a list of the foods served; menu

bill of goods a shipment of goods sent to an agent for sale —**sell someone a bill of goods** ☆[Informal] to persuade someone by deception or misrepresentation to accept, believe, or do something

bill of health a certificate stating whether there is infectious disease aboard a ship or in the port which the ship is leaving: it is given to the captain to show at the next port —**clean bill of health 1** a bill of health certifying the absence of infectious disease **2** [Informal] a good record; favorable report, as after an investigation

bill of lading a document issued to a shipper by a carrier describing the goods to be shipped, acknowledging their receipt, and stating the terms of the contract for their carriage

bill of particulars *Law* **1** an itemized statement of claims or counterclaims provided to the opposing party of a lawsuit **2** an itemized statement of the facts alleged in a criminal complaint, provided by the prosecution to the accused

bill of rights 1 [**B- of R-**] an act of the British Parliament passed in 1689, to confirm certain rights of the people and of Parliament ☆**2** [**B- of R-**] the first ten amendments to the Constitution of the U.S., which guarantee certain rights to the people, as freedom of speech, assembly, and worship **3** any list of basic rights, guarantees, etc. regarded as essential to a particular group of people [*a bill of rights* for consumers]

bill of sale a written statement certifying that the ownership of something has been transferred by sale

bil·lon (bil′ən) *n.* ⟦Fr < OFr *bille,* small log: see BILLET²⟧ an alloy used in some coins, consisting of gold or silver with a heavy proportion of another metal, as copper

bil·low (bil′ō) *n.* ⟦ON *bylgja*: see BELLY⟧ **1** a large wave; great swell of water **2** any large swelling mass or surge, as of smoke, sound, etc. —*vi.* to surge, swell, or rise like or in a billow —*vt.* to make billow or surge —**SYN.** WAVE

bil·low·y (bil′ō ē) *adj.* **-low·i·er, -low·i·est** swelling in or as in a billow or billows —**bil′low·i·ness** *n.*

bill·post·er (bil′pōs′tər) *n.* a person hired to fasten advertisements or notices on walls, billboards, etc.: also **bill′stick′er** (-stik′ər) —**bill′post′ing** *n.*

bil·ly¹ (bil′ē) *n., pl.* **-lies** ⟦< BILLET²⟧ a club or heavy stick; truncheon, esp. one carried by a policeman: in full **billy club**

bil·ly² (bil′ē) *n., pl.* **-lies** ⟦< Australian *billycan* < ? native term *billa,* water (as in BILLABONG) + CAN²⟧ [Austral.] a can or kettle used in outdoor cooking

Bil·ly (bil′ē) *n.* a masculine name: see WILLIAM¹

bil·ly·cock (bil′i käk′) *n.* ⟦< ?⟧ [Old Brit. Informal] a type of felt hat with a low, round crown, as a derby

billy goat ⟦< the nickname *Billy*⟧ a male goat

Billy the Kid (name for *William H. Bonney*) 1859-81; U.S. frontier outlaw

bi·lo·bate (bī lō′bāt′) *adj.* having or divided into two lobes: also **bi·lo′bat′ed** or **bi·lobed** (bī′lōbd′)

bi·lo·ca·tion (bī′lō kā′shən) *n.* the condition of being or the ability to be in two places at the same time, attributed to certain saints and others

bi·loc·u·lar (bī läk′yo͞o lər) *adj.* ⟦BI-¹ + LOCULAR⟧ *Biol.* having or divided into two cells or chambers: also **bi·loc′u·late** (-lit, -lāt′)

Bi·lox·i (bə luk′sē, -läk′sē) *n.* ⟦Fr, earlier *Bilocchy,* prob. of Muskogean orig.⟧ **1** *pl.* **-i** or **-is** a member of a North American Indian people that lived in the lower Mississippi Valley **2** the Siouan language of this people, no longer spoken

☆**bil·sted** (bil′sted′) *n.* ⟦< ?⟧ SWEET GUM

bil·tong (bil′tôŋ) *n.* ⟦Afrik < Du *bil,* rump (from which it is cut) + *tong,* tongue (from the shape)⟧ [Chiefly South Afr.] sun-dried strips of meat

bi·mah (bē′mə) *n.* a raised platform in a synagogue, from which the Torah is read

bi·ma·nous (bī mā′nəs) *adj.* ⟦ModL *bimanus* < L *bi-,* BI-¹ + *manus,* hand: see MANUAL⟧ having two hands

bi·man·u·al (bī man′yo͞o əl) *adj.* ⟦BI-¹ + MANUAL⟧ using or requiring both hands —**bi·man′u·al·ly** *adv.*

☆**bim·bo** (bim′bō) *n.* ⟦It, a child, baby, akin to BAMBINO⟧ **1** [Old Slang] a guy; fellow **2** [Slang] a silly or stupid person: used esp. of a woman **3** [Slang] a sexually promiscuous woman

bi·mes·tri·al (bī mes′trē əl) *adj.* ⟦L *bimestris* < *bi-,* BI-¹ + *mensis,* month (see MOON) + -AL⟧ **1** happening every two months; bimonthly **2** lasting two months

bi·met·al (bī′met′'l) *adj.* BIMETALLIC —*n.* a bimetallic substance

bi·me·tal·lic (bī′mə tal′ik) *adj.* ⟦Fr *bimétallique* < *bi-,* BI-¹ + *métallique,* metallic⟧ **1** of, containing, or using two metals, often two metals bonded together **2** of or based on bimetallism

bi·met·al·lism (bī met′'l iz′əm) *n.* **1** the use of two metals, usually gold and silver, as the monetary standard, with fixed values in relation to each other **2** the doctrine, actions, or policies supporting this —**bi·met′al·list** *n.*

☆**bi·mod·al** (bī mōd′'l) *adj. Statistics* having two modes —**bi·mo·dal·i·ty** (bī′mō dal′ə tē) *n.*

bi·mo·lec·u·lar (bī′mō lek′yo͞o lər) *n.* consisting of or relating to two molecules

bi·month·ly (bī munth′lē; *esp. for n.* bī′munth′-) *adj., adv.* **1** once every two months **2** [Now Rare] twice a month: in this sense, *semimonthly* is the preferred term —*n., pl.* **-lies** a publication appearing once every two months

bi·morph cell (bī′môrf′) ⟦BI-¹ + Gr *morphē,* form⟧ *Electronics* a piezoelectric transducer consisting of two crystals cemented together, used in microphones, headphones, loudspeakers, etc. to convert vibrations into a voltage output or to convert a signal voltage into vibrations that can produce audible sounds: often called **bimorph** *n.* or **bi·mor·phous cell** (bī′môr′fəs, bī môr′fəs)

bi·mor·phe·mic (bī′môr fē′mik) *adj. Linguis.* involving or consisting of two morphemes

bin (bin) *n.* ⟦ME < OE, manger, crib < Celt, as in Welsh *benn,* cart, orig., cart with woven wicker body < IE base **bhendh-*: see BIND⟧ **1** a box or other receptacle, or an enclosed space, esp. for storing foods or other articles for a time **2** [Brit.] a container for rubbish —*vt.* **binned, bin′ning 1** to put or store in a bin **2** [Brit.] to discard in or as in a rubbish bin

bin- (bīn) *prefix* BI-¹: used before a vowel [*binaural*]

b.i.n. *abbrev. Pharmacy* twice a night

bi·na·ry (bī′nə rē) *adj.* ⟦ME *binarie* < L *binarius* < *bini,* two by two < *bis,* double < IE **duis* < base **dwōu-,* TWO⟧ **1** made up of two parts or things; twofold; double **2** designating or of a number system in which the base used is two, each number being expressed in powers of two by using only two digits, specif. 0 and 1 **3** designating or of a musical form consisting of two closely related sections **4** *Chem.* composed of two elements or radicals, or of one element and one radical [*binary* compounds] —*n., pl.* **-ries 1** something made up of two parts or things **2** BINARY STAR

binary fission asexual reproduction in protists by a splitting of the cell into two approximately equal parts

binary star two stars revolving around a common center of gravity; double star

binary weapon a weapon in which two nontoxic chemicals are combined within a moving shell or bomb to produce a deadly nerve gas

bi·nate (bī′nāt′) *adj.* ⟦ModL *binatus* < L *bini*: see BINARY⟧ *Bot.* occurring in pairs *[binate* leaves*]* —**bi′nate′ly** *adv.*

bi·na·tion·al (bī nash′ə nəl) *adj.* composed of or involving two nations or two nationalities

bin·au·ral (bī nôr′əl, bin ô′rəl) *adj.* ⟦BIN- (var. of BI-[1]) + AURAL[2]⟧ **1** having two ears **2** of or involving the use of both ears **3** designating or of sound reproduction or transmission in which at least two sources of sound are used to give a stereophonic effect —**bin·au′ral·ly** *adv.*

bind (bīnd) *vt.* **bound, bind′ing** ⟦ME *binden* < OE *bindan* < IE base **bhendh-* > BAND[1], BEND[1], Sans *badhnāti,* (he) binds, Goth *bindan*⟧ **1** to tie together; make fast or tight, as with a rope or band **2** to hold or restrain as if tied or tied down *[bound* by convention*]* **3** to gird or encircle with a belt, girdle, etc.; wrap or fasten around **4** to bandage: often with *up* **5** to make stick together; make cohere **6** to tighten the bowels of; constipate **7** to strengthen, secure, or ornament the edges of by a band, as of tape **8** to fasten together the printed pages of (a book) and enclose them within a protective cover **9** to secure or make firm (a bargain, contract, etc.) **10** to obligate by duty, love, etc. **11** to compel, as by oath, legal restraint, or contract **12** to make an apprentice of; indenture: often with *out* or *over* **13** to unite or hold, as by a feeling of loyalty or love —*vi.* **1** to do the act of binding **2** to be or become tight, hard, or stiff **3** to be constricting or restricting **4** to stick together **5** to be obligatory or binding in force —*n.* **1** anything that binds ☆**2** [Informal] a difficult or restrictive situation; jam *[*to be in a *bind]* **3** *Music* TIE (*n.* 9) —**SYN.** TIE —**bind over** to put under legal bond to appear at a specified time and place, as before a law court

bind·er (bīn′dər) *n.* **1** a person who binds; specif., a bookbinder **2** a thing that binds or holds together; specif., *a)* a band, cord, etc. *b)* a material that binds things together *[*tar is a *binder* for gravel in paving*]* *c)* a detachable cover with rings or clamps for holding sheets of paper together *d)* a leaf of tobacco rolled around the filler of a cigar to bind it ☆**3** *Agric. a)* a device attached to a reaper, for tying grain in bundles *b)* a machine that both reaps and binds grain **4** *Law* a temporary memorandum of a contract, in effect pending execution of the final contract

☆**bind·er·y** (bīn′dər ē) *n., pl.* **-er·ies** a place where books are bound, pamphlets are stitched, etc.

bin·di (bin′dē) *n.* ⟦Hindi⟧ a small dot worn on the forehead by women in India

bind·ing (bīn′diŋ) *n.* **1** the action of a person or thing that binds **2** a thing that binds, as *a)* the fastenings on a ski for the boot *b)* a band or bandage *c)* tape used in sewing to strengthen seams, edges, etc. *d)* the covers and backing of a book **3** a cohesive substance for holding a mixture together —*adj.* **1** that binds; restrictive **2** that holds one to an agreement, promise, etc. —**bind′ing·ly** *adv.*

binding energy **1** the energy needed to separate a system into its constituents, esp. that needed to separate the nucleus of an atom into its neutrons and protons **2** the energy required to remove a particle from the nucleus of an atom **3** the energy required to remove an electron from its orbit in an atom or molecule

☆**bin·dle** (bin′dəl) *n.* ⟦prob. < Ger *bündel,* bundle⟧ [Slang] a bundle, as of bedding, carried by a hobo

☆**bin·dle·stiff** (-stif′) *n.* ⟦see STIFF (*n.* 5)⟧ [Slang] a migratory worker; hobo

bind·weed (bīnd′wēd′) *n.* ⟦so called from the result of its twining habit⟧ any of various twining vines, esp. any of certain vines (genus *Convolvulus*) of the morning-glory family

bine (bīn) *n.* ⟦dial. form of BIND⟧ **1** any climbing, twining stem, as of the hop **2** a plant having such stems

Bi·net-Si·mon test (bi nā′sī′mən) ⟦after A. *Binet* (1857-1911) and T. *Simon* (1873-1961), Fr psychologists who devised it⟧ an intelligence test that consists of questions, problems, and things to do, graded in terms of mental age: see also INTELLIGENCE QUOTIENT: often **Binet test**

bing (biŋ) *interj.* ⟦? echoic of the sound of a bell or a ricocheting bullet⟧ [Informal] used to signify a sudden change or occurrence *[*it happened—*bing!*—just that fast*]*

☆**Bing cherry** (biŋ) ⟦prob. after Ah Sit *Bing,* Chin-Am foreman at an Ore. nursery where a tree bearing this cherry was first cultivated in the 1870s⟧ a dark-red variety of sweet cherry

binge (binj) *n.* ⟦< ? dial. *binge,* to soak⟧ **1** a spree or bout of unrestrained imbibing or eating **2** any completely unrestrained action *[*a shopping *binge]* —*vi.* **binged, binge′ing** to indulge in an unrestrained manner *[binge-ing* on ice cream*]* —**binger** *n.*

Bing·ham (biŋ′əm), **George Caleb** 1811-79; U.S. painter

☆**bin·go** (biŋ′gō) *n.* ⟦< ?⟧ a gambling game played with cards having rows of numbered squares, no two cards being numbered alike: players use markers to cover the numbered squares on their cards corresponding to numbers drawn by lot, and the player who first gets a row covered is the winner —*interj.* **1** in the game of bingo, used to signify that one has just finished covering a row of squares **2** used to signify sudden action, change, or success

Bi·ni (bē′nē) *n., pl.* **-nis** or **-ni** EDO[1]

bin·na·cle (bin′ə kəl) *n.* ⟦formerly *bittacle* < Port *bitacola* < L *habitaculum,* dwelling < *habitare,* INHABIT⟧ the upright, cylindrical stand holding a ship's compass, usually located near the helm

bin·ocs (bi′näks′) *pl.n.* [Informal] binoculars

bin·oc·u·lar (bī näk′yə lər; *also, esp. for n.,* bi-) *adj.* ⟦< L *bini,* double (see BINARY) + *ocularis,* of the eyes < *oculus,* EYE⟧ using, or for the use of, both eyes at the same time —*n. [pl.]* a portable binocular instrument consisting of two small telescopes mounted side by side, used for viewing distant objects; field glasses, opera glasses, etc. —**bin·oc′u·lar′i·ty** (-lar′ə tē) *n.* —**bin·oc′u·lar·ly** *adv.*

bi·no·mi·al (bī nō′mē əl) *n.* ⟦< ModL *binomium* < LL *binomius* < L *bi-,* BI-[1] + Gr *nomos,* law (see -NOMY) + -AL⟧ **1** a mathematical expression consisting of two terms connected by a plus or minus sign **2** *Taxonomy* a two-word scientific name of a plant or animal, indicating genus and species —*adj.* **1** composed of two terms **2** of binomials —**bi·no′mi·al·ly** *adv.*

binomial coefficient *Math.* **1** the coefficient of any term in the expansion of $(x + a)^n$ **2** the number of combinations of a specified size that can be drawn from a given set

binomial distribution *Statistics* the distribution of the probability of a specified number of successes in a given number of independent trials, in each of which the probability of success is the same

binomial nomenclature (*or* **system)** the scientific system of giving a double name to each plant and animal, consisting of the name of the genus followed by that of the species (Ex.: *Melanitta perspicillata,* surf scoter)

binomial theorem the general formula for the expansion of any binomial when raised to a power that is a positive whole number; the expansion of $(a + b)^n$: discovered by Omar Khayyám and generalized by Sir Isaac Newton (Ex.: $(a + b)^2 = a^2 + 2ab + b^2$)

bint (bint) *n.* ⟦Ar, girl, daughter⟧ [Brit. Slang] a girl or woman: usually a term of contempt

bin·tu·rong (bin′to͞o rôŋ′, -tyo͞o-) *n.* ⟦Malay⟧ a variety of civet (*Arctictis binturong*) of Southeast Asia, with tufted ears and a long, hairy, prehensile tail

bi·nu·cle·ate (bī no͞o′klē it, -āt′) *adj.* of or having two nuclei or centers: also **bi·nu′cle·at′ed** or **bi·nu′cle·ar**

bi·o (bī′ō) [Informal] *n., pl.* **bi′os** a biography, often a very brief one —*adj.* [Informal] biographical

bi·o- (bī′ō, -ə) ⟦Gr < *bios,* life < IE base **gwei-,* to live > QUICK, L *vivere,* to live, *vita,* life, OIr *biu,* living, Gr *bioun,* to live, *zōion,* animal⟧ *combining form* life, of living things, biological *[biography, biochemistry]*

bi·o·ac·cu·mu·la·tion (bī′ō ə kyo͞om′yo͞o lā′shən, -yə-) *n.* the process in which industrial waste, toxic chemicals, etc. gradually accumulate in living tissue —**bi′o·ac·cu′mu·late′** (-lāt′) *vi.* **-lat′ed, -lat′ing** —**bi′o·ac·cu′mu·la′tive** (-lāt′iv, -lət iv) *adj.*

bi·o·a·cous·tics (-ə ko͞os′tiks) *n.* a branch of acoustics that deals with sounds produced and perceived, esp. for communication, by animals

bi·o·ac·tive (-ak′tiv) *adj.* having a capacity to interact with a living tissue or system —**bi·o′ac·tiv′i·ty** (-ak tiv′ə tē) *n.*

☆**bi·o·as·say** (bī′ō as′ā) *n.* ⟦BIO- + ASSAY⟧ a technique for determining the power of a drug or other substance by measuring its effects on a test specimen against those of a standard substance

☆**bi·o·as·tro·nau·tics** (bī′ō as′trə nôt′iks) *n.* the science that deals with the physical responses of living things to the environment of space and space travel

bi·o·a·vail·a·bil·i·ty (-ə vā′lə bil′ə tē) *n.* the rate at which a drug, trace element, etc. enters the bloodstream and is circulated to specific organs or tissues

bi·o·a·vail·a·ble (-ə vā′lə bəl) *adj.* available for use by the body *[bioavailable* iron*]*

bi·o·cat·a·lyst (-kat′ə list) *n.* a substance, as an enzyme or hormone, that activates or speeds up a biochemical reaction —**bi·o·cat·a·lyt·ic** (bī′ō kat′ə lit′ik) *adj.*

☆**bi·o·ce·no·sis** (bī′ō si nō′sis) *n.* ⟦ModL < BIO- + Gr *koinōsis,* a mingling < *koinoun,* to share < *koinos,* common: see COENO-⟧ a community of biologically integrated and interdependent plants and animals: also **bi′o·coe·no′sis** (-si nō′sis)

biochemical oxygen demand **1** the amount of dissolved oxygen needed to decompose the organic matter in waste water: a high BOD indicates heavy pollution with little oxygen remaining for fish **2** the organic matter in waste water

bi·o·chem·is·try (-kem′is trē) *n.* a science that deals with the chemistry of life processes in plants and animals —**bi′o·chem′i·cal** *adj., n.* —**bi′o·chem′ist** *n.*

bi·o·chip (bī′ō chip′) *n.* **1** a hypothetical integrated circuit or microprocessor formed on an organic molecule or designed to process information in a way that mimics certain biochemical processes **2** a microchip designed to work in a living organism **3** a MICROARRAY built on a microchip

bi·o·ci·dal (bī′ō sīd′'l) *adj.* destructive of living organisms

bi·o·cide (bī′ō sīd′) *n.* ⟦BIO- + -CIDE⟧ any substance, esp. a bactericide or fungicide, that kills or retards the growth of microorganisms

bi·o·cli·ma·tol·o·gy (bī′ō klī′mə täl′ə jē) *n.* the science that deals with climatic effects on living matter —**bi′o·cli·mat′ic** (-klī mat′ik) *adj.*

bi·o·com·pat·i·ble (-kəm pat′ə bəl) *adj.* compatible with living tissue, as a prosthetic material or device that is not rejected or does not cause infection —**bi′o·com·pat′i·bil′i·ty** *n.*

bi·o·con·ver·sion (-kən vʉr′zhən, -shən) *n.* the process of generating a fuel from biological waste matter by the action of microorganisms

bi·o·cy·ber·net·ics (-sī′bər net′iks) *n.* the branch of cybernetics that deals with the control and communication systems of living organisms —**bi′o·cy′ber·net′ic** *adj.*

bi·o·de·fense (bī′ō di fens′, -dē′fens) *n.* measures taken to prevent or counter an attack involving biological weapons

bi·o·de·grad·a·ble (-di grā′də bəl) *adj.* ⟦BIO- + DEGRAD(E) + -ABLE⟧ capable of being readily decomposed by microbial action, as some detergents: distinguished from DEGRADABLE —**bi′o·de·grad·a·bil′i·ty** *n.*, **bi′o·deg′ra·da′tion** (-deg′rə dā′shən) —**bi′o·de·grade′** *vt.* **-grad′ed, -grad′ing**

bi·o·die·sel (bī′ō dē′zəl, -səl) *n.* an automotive fuel for diesel engines derived from vegetable oils or animal fats

bi·o·di·ver·si·ty (-də vʉr′sə tē, -dī-) *n.* diversity, or variety, in the living things in a particular area, region, etc. at a particular time

☆**bi·o·e·col·o·gy** (-ē käl′ə jē) *n.* ⟦BIO- + ECOLOGY⟧ the science that deals with the interrelations of communities of animals and plants with their environment

☆**bi·o·e·lec·tric** (-i lek′trik) *adj.* of or having to do with electrical energy in living tissues: also **bi′o·e·lec′tri·cal** —**bi′o·e·lec′tric′i·ty** *n.*

bi·o·e·lec·tron·ics (-ē′lek trän′iks, -el′ek-) *n.* a branch of electronics that deals with electronic devices, implants, etc. used in medicine and biological research —**bi′o·e′lec·tron′ic** *adj.* —**bi′o·e·lec′tron′i·cal·ly** *adv.*

bi·o·en·er·get·ics (-en′ər jet′iks) *n.* a branch of energetics that deals with how a living organism converts food, sunlight, etc. into useful energy —**bi′o·en′er·get′ic** *adj.*

bi·o·en·er·gy (bī′ō en′ər jē) *n.* energy available from such organic fuel sources as animal waste, recently living plants, etc.

bi·o·en·gi·neer·ing (-en′jə nir′iŋ) *n.* a science dealing with the application of engineering science and technology to problems of biology and medicine —**bi′o·en′gi·neer′** *n.*

bi·o·e·quiv·a·lence (-ē kwiv′ə ləns, -i-) *n.* the condition of being equivalent in strength, dosage, and bioavailability, thus producing a nearly similar therapeutic effect: used in referring to certain drugs, esp. in comparing a brand-name drug and a generic version of it: also **bi′o·e·quiv′a·len·cy** —**bi′o·e·quiv′a·lent** *adj.*

bi·o·eth·ics (-eth′iks) *n.* the study of the ethical problems arising from scientific advances, esp. in biology and medicine —**bi′o·eth′i·cal** *adj.* —**bi′o·eth′i·cist** *n.*

☆**bi·o·feed·back** (-fēd′bak′) *n.* a technique of seeking to control certain emotional states, such as anxiety or depression, by training oneself, with the aid of electronic devices, to modify autonomic bodily functions, such as blood pressure or heartbeat

bi·o·fla·vo·noid (-flā′və noid′, -flav′ə-) *n.* any of a group of biologically active flavone compounds that may help maintain the blood's capillary walls, reducing the likelihood of hemorrhaging: widely found in plants, esp. citrus fruits

bi·o·fu·el (bī′ō fyo͞o′əl) *n.* any fuel derived from renewable biological sources, as plants or animal waste; esp., a liquid fuel for automotive engines made from corn or soybean oil

biog *abbrev.* **1** biographer **2** biographical **3** biography

bi·o·gas (bī′ō gas′) *n.* a fuel gas produced by fermenting organic waste, as in capturing methane from manure

bi·o·gen·e·sis (bī′ō jen′ə sis) *n.* ⟦BIO- + -GENESIS⟧ **1** the principle that living organisms originate only from other living organisms closely similar to themselves **2** the generation of organisms in this way —**bi′o·ge·net′ic** (-jə net′ik) *adj.*, **bi′o·ge·net′i·cal** —**bi′o·ge·net′i·cal·ly** *adv.*

bi·o·gen·ic (-jen′ik) *adj.* produced by, or essential to, living cells

bi·o·ge·o·chem·i·cal cycle (bī′ō jē′ō kem′i kəl) the cycle in which nitrogen, carbon, and other inorganic elements of the soil, atmosphere, etc. of a region are converted into the organic substances of animals or plants and released back into the environment

bi·o·ge·og·ra·phy (bī′ō jē ä′grə fē) *n.* the branch of biology that deals with the geographical distribution of plants and animals —**bi′o·ge′o·graph′ic** (-ə graf′ik) *adj.*

bi·og·ra·phee (bī äg′rə fē′; *also* bē-) *n.* a subject of a biography

bi·og·ra·pher (bī äg′rə fər; *also* bē-) *n.* a writer of a biography or biographies

bi·o·graph·i·cal (bī′ə graf′i kəl) *adj.* **1** of, having to do with, or characteristic of biography or biographies **2** giving the story of, or based on, a person's life Also **bi′o·graph′ic** —**bi′o·graph′i·cal·ly** *adv.*

bi·og·ra·phy (bī äg′rə fē; *also* bē-) *n.* ⟦Gr *biographia*: see BIO- & -GRAPHY⟧ **1** the histories of individual lives, considered as a branch of literature **2** *pl.* **-phies** an account of a person's life, described by another; life story

bi·o·haz·ard (bī′ō haz′ərd) *n.* ⟦BIO- + HAZARD⟧ a risk or danger to life or health, esp. that resulting from biological experimentation —*adj.* having to do with biohazards, esp. their prevention or control —**bi′o·haz′ard·ous** *adj.*

☆**bi·o·herm** (bī′ō hʉrm′) *n.* ⟦< BIO- + Gr *herma*, a reef⟧ **1** a reeflike mass or mound of limestone built by sedentary organisms, as corals: cf. BIOSTROME **2** CORAL REEF

☆**bi·o·in·stru·men·ta·tion** (bī′ō in′strə men tā′shən) *n.* the use of instruments, as sensors, to detect and measure certain bodily functions, as of persons in spaceflight, and transmit the data to a point where it is evaluated

Bi·o·ko (bē ō′kō) island of Equatorial Guinea, in the Bight of Benin, off the coast of Cameroon: 779 sq mi (2,018 sq km)

biol *abbrev.* **1** biological **2** biologist **3** biology

bi·o·log·i·cal (bī′ə läj′i kəl) *adj.* **1** of or connected with biology; of plants and animals **2** of the nature of living matter **3** used in or produced by practical biology **4** related genetically rather than by adoption [*her biological father*] —*n.* a biopharmaceutical product Also **bi′o·log′ic** —**bi′o·log′i·cal·ly** *adv.*

biological clock any of the various natural cycles in organisms that are related to the tides, sun, moon, light, temperature, etc. and that control breeding, feeding, migration, etc.: often used fig., as in ref. to the years during which a woman is able to bear children

☆**biological control** the control of destructive organisms, esp. insects, by various, usually nonchemical means, as by the use of natural predators

biological oxygen demand BIOCHEMICAL OXYGEN DEMAND

biological therapy BIOTHERAPY

biological warfare the use of biological weapons in war

biological weapon a weapon consisting of or designed to disperse a disease-spreading microorganism, a toxin, etc.

bi·ol·o·gy (bī äl′ə jē) *n.* ⟦< Fr or Ger: Fr *biologie* < Ger; coined (1802) by G. Reinhold (Treviranus), Ger physiologist < Gr *bios* (see BIO-) + *-logia*, -LOGY⟧ **1** the science that deals with the origin, history, physical characteristics, life processes, habits, etc. of living organisms, as plants and animals, and of viruses: it includes botany, zoology, and microbiology **2** animal and plant life, as of a given area **3** biological history, principles, etc. —**bi·ol′o·gist** *n.*

bi·o·lu·mi·nes·cence (bī′ō lo͞o′mə nes′əns) *n.* **1** the production of light by living organisms, as by fireflies or many deep-water cephalopods **2** such light —**bi′o·lu′mi·nes′cent** *adj.*

bi·ol·y·sis (bī äl′ə sis) *n.* ⟦ModL: see BIO- & -LYSIS⟧ the destruction of life, as by microorganisms —**bi·o·lyt·ic** (bī′ə lit′ik) *adj.*

bi·o·mag·net·ics (bī′ō mag net′iks) *n.* a branch of magnetics that deals with how magnetism is related to living organisms —**bi′o·mag·net′ic** *adj.*

bi·o·mark·er (bī′ō mär′kər) *n.* a biochemical substance, as in blood or urine, used to detect the presence of a physical condition, disease, etc. and to measure its progress and the effectiveness of treatments

bi·o·mass (bī′ō mas′) *n.* ⟦BIO- + MASS⟧ **1** the total mass or number of living organisms in a particular area or volume **2** animal waste, matter from recently living plants, etc. for use as fuel or in making biofuel

bi·o·ma·te·ri·al (-mə tir′ē əl) *n.* a synthetic or natural substance used to replace a bone, tissue, etc. in a living body

bi·o·math·e·mat·ics (bī′ō math′ə mat′iks) *n.* the science that deals with the application of mathematical methods to the structure and functions of living organisms

bi·ome (bī′ōm′) *n.* ⟦< BI(O)- + ModL *-oma*, -OMA⟧ any of several major life zones of interrelated plants and animals determined by the climate, as deciduous forest or desert: see ASSOCIATION (sense 6)

bi·o·me·chan·ics (bī′ō mə kan′iks) *n.* the application of the principles and techniques of mechanics to the structure, functions, etc. of living organisms —**bi′o·me·chan′i·cal** *adj.* —**bi′o·me·chan′i·cal·ly** *adv.*

bi·o·med·i·cine (bī′ō med′ə sən) *n.* the aspects of medicine that derive from, or relate to, the natural sciences, esp. biology, biochemistry, and biophysics —**bi′o·med′i·cal** *adj.*

bi·o·me·te·or·ol·o·gy (-mēt′ē ər äl′ə jē) *n.* the study of the interrelationships of biology and weather —**bi′o·me·te·or·o·log′i·cal** *adj.* —**bi′o·me′te·or·ol′o·gist** *n.*

bi·o·met·rics (-me′triks) *n.* **1** that branch of biology which deals with its data statistically and by mathematical analysis **2** the scientific measurement and analysis of biological data, as in identifying individuals or in forensics —**bi′o·met′ric** *adj.*, **bi′o·met′ri·cal**

bi·om·e·try (bī äm′ə trē) *n.* **1** calculation of the probable human life span **2** BIOMETRICS

bi·o·mol·e·cule (bī′ō mäl′ə kyo͝ol′) *n.* an organic compound made in a living system

bi·o·morph·ic (bī′ō môr′fik) *adj.* resembling the curving, irregular form of living organisms [*a biomorphic sculpture*]

Bi·on (bī′än, -ən) fl. 2d cent. B.C.; Gr. pastoral poet

☆**bi·on·ic** (bī än′ik) *adj.* ⟦see fol.⟧ **1** of or having to do with bionics **2** *a)* designating an artificial replacement for a body part *b)* furnished with such a replacement part or parts, specif. in science fiction, so that strength, abilities, etc. are greatly enhanced *c)* exceptionally strong, skillful, energetic, etc. —**bi·on′ic·al·ly** *adv.*

☆**bi·on·ics** (bī än′iks) *n.* ⟦BI(O)- + (ELECTR)ONICS⟧ the science of designing instruments or systems modeled after living organisms: see ROBOTICS

bi·o·nom·ics (bī′ō näm′iks) *n.* ⟦< *bionomy*, ecology (< BIO- + -NOMY) + -ICS⟧ ECOLOGY (sense 1)

bi·o·phar·ma·ceu·ti·cal (bī′ō fär′mə so͞ot′i kəl, -syo͞ot′-) *n.* any of various pharmaceuticals, as hormones, vaccines, proteins, or interferons, produced from live organisms using biotechnology —*adj.* of or having to do with such a pharmaceutical or its production, sale, etc.

bi·o·phys·ics (-fiz′iks) *n.* the study of biological phenomena using the principles and techniques of physics —**bi′o·phys′i·cal** *adj.* —**bi′o·phys′i·cist** *n.*

☆**bi·o·pic** (bī′ō pik′) *n.* ⟦BIO(GRAPHICAL) + PIC(TURE)⟧ [Informal] a film dramatizing the life of a famous person

bi·o·plasm (bī′ō plaz′əm) *n.* ⟦< BIO- + Gr *plasma*, something molded⟧ living matter; protoplasm

bi·o·pol·y·mer (bī′ō päl′ə mər) *n.* **1** a polymer formed in a living organism, as cellulose, protein, chitin, or DNA **2** such a polymer made synthetically

bi·op·sy (bī′äp′sē) *Med. n., pl.* **-sies** ⟦< BI(O)- + -OPSIS⟧ the removal of living tissue from the body for diagnostic examination —*vt.* **-sied, -sy·ing** to perform a biopsy on

bi·o·re·ac·tor (bī′ō rē ak′tər) *n.* ⟦< BIO- + REACTOR, sense 2*b*⟧ any of various devices or systems used to grow large quantities of biochemical cultures, as to produce enzymes, antibiotics, or blood cells

bi·o·re·fin·er·y (bī′ō ri fīn′ər ē) ***n., pl.* -er·ies** a refinery for converting biomass into ethanol, etc.

bi·o·re·me·di·a·tion (bī′ō ri mē′dē ā′shən) ***n.*** any process in which organisms, esp. microorganisms, are introduced into a region to counteract pollution, plant disease, destructive insects, etc.

bi·o·rhythm (bī′ō *rith′*əm) ***n.*** any biological cycle that involves periodic changes in blood pressure, body temperature, etc.: analyzed by some to predict behavior, temperament, etc.

BIOS (bī′ōs′) ***abbrev.*** *Comput.* basic input/output system

bi·o·safe·ty (bī′ō sāf′tē) ***n.*** safety procedures associated with the research and production of biological products

☆**bi·o·sat·el·lite** (bī′ō sat′'l īt′) ***n.*** a recoverable spacecraft designed for the study of the effects of cosmic radiation, weightlessness, etc. on terrestrial forms of life in space

bi·o·sci·ence (bī′ō sī′əns) ***n.*** any science that deals with the functions or problems of living organisms

bi·os·co·py (bī äs′kə pē) ***n.*** ⟦BIO- + -SCOPY⟧ *Med.* an examination to determine whether life is present in a body

bi·o·sen·sor (bī′ō sen′sər) ***n.*** a sensor device for detecting and measuring very small quantities or changes in a biochemical or chemical substance, in which a microelectronic component registers reactions related to the substance and translates them into data

bi·o·sim·i·lar (bī′ō sim′ə lər) ***adj.*** designating or of a biopharmaceutical product considered very similar but not identical to another, licensed product [*biosimilar* insulin] **—*n.*** a biosimilar medication or product

-bi·o·sis (bī ō′sis, bē-) ⟦ModL < Gr *biōsis*, way of life < *bios*: see BIO-⟧ *combining form forming nouns* a (specified) way of living [*symbiosis*]

bi·o·so·cial (bī′ō sō′shəl) ***adj.*** of or having to do with the interrelationships between biology and sociology

bi·o·sol·ids (bī′ō säl′idz) ***pl.n.*** solid waste recovered from sewage treatment, for use as in agriculture as a fertilizer **—bi′o·sol′id *adj.***

bi·o·sphere (bī′ō sfir′) ***n.*** ⟦BIO- + SPHERE⟧ **1** the zone of planet earth where life naturally occurs, extending from the deep crust to the lower atmosphere **2** the living organisms of the earth

bi·o·sta·tis·tics (bī′ō stə tis′tiks) ***n.*** the branch of biometrics dealing with demography, esp. vital statistics **—bi′o·sta·tis′ti·cal *adj.* —bi′o·stat′is·ti′cian** (-stat′is tish′ən) ***n.***

☆**bi·o·strome** (bī′ō strōm′) ***n.*** ⟦< BIO- + Gr *strōma*, a mattress, bed, rug < IE base *ster-, to spread out > STRAW, STREW⟧ a flat, thin limestone layer consisting predominantly of marine fossils, as corals: cf. BIOHERM

bi·o·syn·the·sis (bī′ō sin′thə sis) ***n.*** the formation of chemical compounds by the enzyme action of living organisms, as in protein synthesis **—bi′o·syn·thet′ic *adj.* —bi′o·syn·thet′i·cal·ly *adv.***

bi·o·sys·te·mat·ics (-sis′tə mat′iks) ***n.*** the study of morphological and other problems of taxonomic systems **—bi′o·sys′te·mat′ic *adj.***

☆**bi·o·ta** (bī ōt′ə) ***n.*** ⟦ModL: see BIOTIC⟧ the plant and animal life of a region

bi·o·tech (bī′ō tek′) ***n.*** [Informal] BIOTECHNOLOGY

bi·o·tech·nol·o·gy (bī′ō tek näl′ə jē) ***n.*** the use of the data and techniques of engineering and technology for the study and solution of problems concerning living organisms **—bi·o·tech′no·log′i·cal *adj.* —bi′o·tech·nol′o·gist *n.***

bi·o·te·lem·e·try (-tə lem′ə trē) ***n.*** the use of telemeters to monitor the physical condition or responses of animals, human beings, etc. at great distances, as in spacecraft

bi·o·ter·ror·ism (bī′ō ter′ər iz′əm) ***n.*** terrorism using deadly microorganisms, toxins, etc.: also **bi′o·ter′ror —bi′o·ter′ror·ist *n., adj.***

bi·o·ther·a·py (bī′ō ther′ə pē) ***n.*** the treatment of disease by means of substances, as serums, vaccines, penicillin, etc., secreted by or derived from living organisms

bi·ot·ic (bī ät′ik) ***adj.*** ⟦Gr *biōtikos* < *bios*: see BIO-⟧ of life or living things, or caused by living organisms: sometimes **bi·ot′i·cal**

-bi·ot·ic (bī ät′ik, bē-) *combining form forming adjectives* of or having a (specified) way of living [*photobiotic*]

bi·o·tin (bī′ə tin) ***n.*** ⟦BIOT(IC) + -IN[1]⟧ a bacterial growth factor, $C_{10}H_{16}O_3N_2S$, present in all living things; vitamin H: it is one of the vitamin B group and is found in liver, egg yolk, yeast, etc.

bi·o·tite (bī′ə tīt′) ***n.*** ⟦Ger *biotit*: so named after J. B. *Biot* (1774-1862), Fr physicist + *-it*, -ITE[1]⟧ a dark-colored, soft, monoclinic mica, $K(Mg,Fe)_3(Al,Fe)Si_3O_{10}(OH)_2$, found in igneous, metamorphic, and sedimentary rocks

bi·o·tope (bī′ə tōp′) ***n.*** ⟦< BIO- + Gr *topos*, a place: see TOPIC⟧ a small, uniform environment occupied by a community of organisms

bi·o·tox·in (bī′ō täks′in) ***n.*** a poisonous substance made by a plant or animal

bi·o·trans·for·ma·tion (-trans′fər mā′shən) ***n.*** the metabolizing of some substance, esp. a drug, in the body

bi·o·type (bī′ō tīp′) ***n.*** a group of plants or animals having the same fundamental constitution in terms of genetic or hereditary factors **—bi′o·typ′ic** (-tip′ik) ***adj.***

bi·o·war·fare (bī′ō wôr′fer′) ***n.*** BIOLOGICAL WARFARE

bi·o·weap·on (bī′ō wep′ən) ***n.*** BIOLOGICAL WEAPON

bi·pack (bī′pak′) ***n.*** *Photog.* a film having two emulsions that are exposed simultaneously and are sensitive to different colors

bi·pa·ri·e·tal (bī′pə rī′ə təl) ***adj.*** of or connected with the prominent rounded part of the two parietal bones

bip·a·rous (bip′ər əs) ***adj.*** ⟦BI-[1] + -PAROUS⟧ **1** bearing two offspring at a birth **2** *Bot.* dividing into two branches

bi·par·ti·san (bī pär′tə zən, -sən) ***adj.*** of, representing, or supported by two parties **—bi·par′ti·san·ship′ *n.***

bi·par·tite (bī pär′tīt′) ***adj.*** ⟦L *bipartitus*, pp. of *bipartire* < *bi-*, BI-[1] + *partire*, to PART[2]⟧ **1** having two parts **2** having two corresponding parts, one each for the two parties to a contract **3** with two involved [a *bipartite* alliance] **4** *Bot.* divided in two nearly to the base, as some leaves

bi·ped (bī′ped′) ***n.*** ⟦L *bipes*: see BI-[1] & -PED⟧ any two-footed animal **—*adj.*** of or having to do with bipedalism: also **bi·ped′al**

bi·pe·dal·ism (bī ped′'l iz′əm) ***n.*** the condition of having only two feet or of using two feet for locomotion

bi·pet·al·ous (bī pet′'l əs) ***adj.*** having two petals

bi·phen·yl (bī fen′əl, -fē′nəl) ***n.*** DIPHENYL

bi·pin·nate (bī pin′āt′, -it) ***adj.*** having pinnate leaflets on stems that grow opposite each other on a main stem; twice pinnate **—bi·pin′nate′ly *adv.***

bi·plane (bī′plān′) ***n.*** an airplane with two sets of wings, one above the other

bi·pod (bī′päd′) ***n.*** ⟦BI-[1] + -POD⟧ a two-legged stand, as for an automatic rifle

bi·po·lar (bī pō′lər) ***adj.*** **1** of or having two poles **2** of or involving both of the earth's polar regions **3** characterized by two directly opposite opinions, natures, etc. **4** of or affected by bipolar affective disorder [*bipolar* characteristics] **—bi·po·lar·i·ty** (bī′pō lar′ə tē) ***n.***

bipolar (affective) disorder ⟦so named in allusion to the two *poles*, or extremes, of emotion and behavior between which a person shifts due to this disorder⟧ a psychotic disorder characterized by alternating periods of mania and mental depression; manic-depressive illness: now the preferred term in psychiatry

bi·pro·pel·lant (bī′prō pel′ənt) ***n.*** a propellant system for rockets consisting of a fuel and an oxidizer kept in separate tanks, and brought together only in the combustion chamber

bi·quad·rat·ic (bī′kwäd rat′ik) ***adj.*** *Math.* of or involving the fourth power of a quantity **—*n.*** **1** such a quantity **2** an algebraic equation of the fourth power; quartic equation

bi·quar·ter·ly (bī kwôrt′ər lē) ***adj.*** occurring twice in every three-month period

bi·ra·cial (bī rā′shəl) ***adj.*** consisting of or involving two races, esp. blacks and whites

bi·ra·di·al (bī rā′dē əl) ***adj.*** *Biol.* having both bilateral and radial symmetry

bi·ra·mous (bī rā′məs) ***adj.*** ⟦BI-[1] + RAMOUS⟧ having two branches, as the appendages of crustaceans

birch (burch) ***n.*** ⟦ME *birche* < OE *beorc* < IE base *bhereĝ-, to gleam, white > BRIGHT⟧ **1** any of a genus (*Betula*) of trees and shrubs of the birch family, having smooth bark easily peeled off in thin sheets, and hard, closegrained wood: found in northern climates **2** the wood of any of these trees **3** a birch rod or bunch of twigs used for whipping **—*vt.*** to beat with a birch **—*adj.*** **1** designating a family (Betulaceae, order Fagales) of dicotyledonous shrubs and trees, including the hazels, alders, and hornbeams **2** of birch: also **birch′en**

birch partridge [Cdn.] RUFFED GROUSE

bird (burd) ***n.*** ⟦ME *bird, brid* < OE *bridd*, bird, orig., young bird⟧ **1** any of a class (Aves) of warm-blooded, two-legged, egg-laying vertebrates with feathers and wings **2** a small game bird: distinguished from WATERFOWL **3** a clay pigeon in trapshooting **4** a shuttlecock ☆**5** [Informal] a person, esp. a mildly eccentric one **6** [Slang] a sound of disapproval made by vibrating the lips **7** [Slang] any rocket, satellite, aircraft, etc. **8** [Brit. Slang] a young woman **—*vi.*** **1** to shoot or catch birds **2** to engage in bird-watching **—birds of a feather** people with the same characteristics or tastes **—eat like a bird** to eat very little food **—☆flip someone the bird** [Slang] GIVE SOMEONE THE FINGER (see phrase under FINGER) **—☆for the birds** [Slang] ridiculous, foolish, worthless, useless, etc. **—the birds and the bees** [Informal] the basic facts about sexual matters

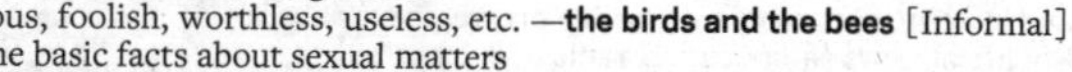

bird
(canary)

☆**bird·bath** (burd′bath′) ***n.*** a basinlike garden ornament for birds to bathe in

☆**bird·brain** (-brān′) ***n.*** [Informal] a stupid or silly person **—bird′brained′** (-brānd′) ***adj.***

bird·cage (-kāj′) ***n.*** a small cage for pet birds

bird·call (-kôl′) ***n.*** **1** the sound or song of a bird **2** an imitation of this **3** a device for imitating bird sounds

☆**bird dog** **1** a dog trained for hunting birds, as a pointer **2** [Informal] a person whose work is searching, as for missing persons

☆**bird-dog** (-dôg′) ***vt.*** **-dogged′, -dog′ging** [Informal] to search out diligently or pursue doggedly

☆**bird·er** (bur′dər) ***n.*** a person who engages in bird-watching; bird-watcher

bird flu an influenza caused by a virus that is commonly found in the intestines of birds: some deadly forms of this virus can spread to humans from infected birds, esp. poultry

☆**bird grass** *regional name for:* **1** ROUGH BLUEGRASS **2** KNOTGRASS

☆**bird·house** (-hous′) ***n.*** **1** a small box, often resembling a house, for birds to nest in **2** a building for exhibiting birds

bird·ie (burd′ē) ***n.*** **1** any small bird: a child's word ☆**2** *Golf* a score of one stroke under par for a hole —☆***vt.* bird′ied, bird′ie·ing** *Golf* to score a birdie on (a given hole)

bird·ing (burd′iŋ) ***n.*** BIRD-WATCHING

bird·lime (burd′līm′) ***n.*** **1** a sticky substance spread on twigs to catch birds **2** anything that snares —***vt.* -limed′, -lim′ing** to spread or catch with birdlime

bird louse any of an order (Mallophaga) of small, wingless insects with biting mouthparts, that live as external parasites on birds

bird·man (-man′, -mən) ***n., pl.* -men′** (-men′, -mən) **1** a person whose work deals with birds **2** [Old Informal] an aviator

bird of paradise **1** any of a family (Paradisaeidae) of brightly colored passerine birds found in and near New Guinea **2** any of several tropical plants (genus *Strelitzia*) of the banana family, native to Africa, having orange and blue flowers protruding from a green spathe in a form that resembles a bird in flight

bird of passage **1** any migratory bird **2** anyone who travels or roams about constantly

bird of prey **1** any of an order (Falconiformes) of diurnal birds with sharp claws and hooked bills that capture, kill, and eat other animals or feed chiefly on carrion, such as hawks, falcons, vultures, and the osprey **2** any such nocturnal bird, as the owl

bird pepper **1** a small, very hot, tropical American red pepper **2** the plant (*Capsicum annum* var. *glabriusculum*) on which it grows, esp. any of the native, wild forms of this plant: see CAPSICUM (sense 1)

bird·seed (-sēd′) ***n.*** seed for feeding small birds

Birds·eye (burdz′ī′), **Clarence** 1886-1956; U.S. inventor of methods of quick-freezing foods

bird's-eye (burdz′ī′) ***n.*** **1** any of several plants of various families (esp. of the genera *Primula* and *Veronica* of the primrose and figwort families) having flowers with centers and petals of contrasting colors **2** *a)* a textile pattern of small, diamond-shaped figures, each with a dot in the center *b)* a fabric with such a pattern —***adj.*** having markings that resemble birds' eyes [*bird's-eye* flowers]

bird's-eye view **1** a view or perspective from above or at a distance **2** an overall, but cursory, view

bird's-foot (-foot′) ***n., pl.* -foots′** any of various plants whose leaves or flowers resemble a bird's foot, as the bird's-foot trefoil

bird's-foot trefoil a perennial plant (*Lotus corniculatus*) of the pea family, with clusters of yellow flowers, used for forage and hay

☆**bird's-foot violet** a North American violet (*Viola pedata*) having divided leaves and large blue or purple flowers

bird·shot (burd′shät′) ***n.*** small shot, for shooting birds

bird·song (burd′sôŋ′) ***n.*** the musical sounds made by a songbird

bird-watch·ing (burd′wäch′iŋ, -wôch′-) ***n.*** the observation of wild birds in their habitat, esp. such observation when engaged in as a hobby: also **bird′ watch′ing** —**bird′-watch′er *n.*, bird′watch′er**

bi·re·frin·gence (bī′ri frin′jəns) ***n.*** ⟦BI-[1] + REFRINGENT⟧ the splitting of a light ray, generally by a crystal, into two components that travel at different velocities and are polarized at right angles to each other —**bi′re·frin′gent *adj.***

bi·reme (bī′rēm′) ***n.*** ⟦L *biremis* < *bi-*, BI-[1] + *remus*, oar: see ROW[2]⟧ a galley of ancient times, having two rows of oars on each side, one under the other

bi·ret·ta (bə ret′ə) ***n.*** ⟦It *berretta* < LL *birrettum*, dim. of L *birrus*, a hood, cloak, prob. < Celt base, as in Cymric *byrr*, MIr *berr*, short⟧ a hard, square, ceremonial hat with three or four vertical projections and sometimes with a pompom or tassel at the top, worn by Roman Catholic clergy

biretta

Bir·ken·head (bur′kən hed′) seaport in W England, at the mouth of the Mersey

Bir·ken·stock (bur′kən stäk′) ⟦trademark of *Birkenstock* Orthopadie GmbH, German firm, after Johann *Birkenstock*, 18th-c. shoemaker whose descendants founded and manage the firm⟧ *trademark for* a kind of shoe, typically, a toeless sandal with a form-fitting, cork insole and wide straps that buckle over the instep: wearers of such footwear are sometimes associated somewhat contemptuously with having progressive or liberal political views [*a Birkenstock* radical]

birl (burl) ***vt., vi.*** ⟦earlier *pirl*, to spin, ? echoic, after WHIRL, PURL[1]⟧ **1** [Scot.] to spin with a whirring sound ☆**2** to revolve (a floating log) by treading

birle or **birl** (burl, birl) ***vt.* birled, birl′ing** ⟦ME *birlen*, to serve a drink < OE *byrelian*, akin to *byrele*, cup-bearer, butler, prob. < base of *beran*, BEAR[1]⟧ [Now Scot.] to pour (a drink) or ply with drink

birl·ing (bur′liŋ) ***n.*** ☆a contest in which each of two lumberjacks, standing on the same floating log, birls the log so as to try to cause the other to fall off —**birl′er *n.***

Bir·man (bur′mən) ***n.*** ⟦var. of BURMAN⟧ any of a breed of long-haired domestic cat, originating in Burma, with round blue eyes, white paws, and a light-colored coat shaded somewhat like the Siamese

Bir·ming·ham (bur′miŋ əm; *for 2*, -ham′) **1** industrial city in West Midlands, England **2** ⟦after the English city⟧ city in NC Ala.: iron and steel center

bi·ro (bī′rō, bir′ō) ***n., pl.* -ros** ⟦< *Biro*, a trademark for a kind of ballpoint pen⟧ [Brit. Informal] a ballpoint pen

Bir·o·bi·dzhan or **Bir·o·bi·djan** (bir′ō bi jän′) autonomous republic of Khabarovsk territory, E Siberia: set aside for Jewish settlement in 1934 (current pop. is 4.2% Jewish): 13,895 sq mi (35,988 sq km): officially called *Jewish Autonomous Region*

birr[1] (bur) ***n.*** ⟦ME *bir* < ON *byrr*, impetus, strong wind < IE base **bher-*, BEAR[1]⟧ **1** onrush or driving force; impetus **2** a vibrant whirring sound —***vi.*** [Chiefly Scot.] to make or move with a birr

birr[2] (bur) ***n., pl.* birr′otch** (-äch) ⟦Amharic, silver⟧ the basic monetary unit of Ethiopia: see the table of monetary units in the Reference Supplement

birth (burth) ***n.*** ⟦ME *birthe, burthe* < ON *byrth*, akin to OE *gebyrde, byrde*, Goth *gabaurths* < IE **bhrto*, pp. of base **bher-*, BEAR[1]⟧ **1** the act of bringing forth offspring **2** the act or fact of coming into life, or of being born; nativity **3** origin or natal background [a Spaniard by *birth*] **4** good or noble lineage [a man of *birth*] **5** the beginning of anything [the *birth* of a nation] **6** an inherited or natural inclination or talent [an actress by *birth*] — ***vi., vt.*** to give birth (to) —***adj.*** relating or related biologically rather than by adoption; natural: often used in comb. [*birth* mother, *birthparent*] —**give birth** to bring forth offspring —**give birth to** **1** to bring forth (offspring) **2** to be the cause or origin of; originate; create

birth canal the passageway from the uterus of a mammal through which a fetus is pushed during birth: it consists of the cervix, vagina, and vulva

birth certificate an official document issued upon a person's birth, attesting to the date and place of birth, parentage, etc.

birth chart an astrological chart created with reference to the relative position of the planets at the time and location of a person's birth

☆**birth control** ⟦coined by M. SANGER⟧ **1** control of the number and frequency of children born, specif. through the control of conception; contraception **2** a device or method used to prevent conception

birth·day (-dā′) ***n.*** **1** the day of a person's birth or a thing's beginning **2** the anniversary of this day —**in one's birthday suit** [Informal] naked; nude: a humorous usage

birth defect any of various mental, physical, or biochemical defects present in a baby at birth

birth·ing (burth′iŋ) ***adj.*** of or having to do with birth [a *birthing* room] —***n.*** the act of giving birth

birth·mark (-märk′) ***n.*** a skin blemish or mark present at birth

birth mother a person's mother related biologically rather than by adoption: also **birth′moth′er *n.***

birth pangs **1** sharp pains associated with giving birth **2** difficulties, stress, etc. associated with the beginning or creation of something *Often used in sing.* Also written **birth′pangs′ *pl.n.***

birth·par·ent (-per′ənt) ***n.*** a person's parent related biologically rather than by adoption: also **birth parent**

birth·place (-plās′) ***n.*** **1** the place of one's birth **2** the place where something originated

birth·rate (-rāt′) ***n.*** the number of births per year per thousand of population in a given community, area, or group: sometimes other units of time or population are used: also **birth rate**

birth·right (-rīt′) ***n.*** a right or the rights that a person has because of being born in a certain family, nation, etc.

☆**birth·root** (-ro͞ot′) ***n.*** any of various trilliums whose rootstocks were traditionally used by Native Americans as an aid in childbirth

birth·stone (-stōn′) ***n.*** a precious or semiprecious gem symbolizing the month of a person's birth: the usual list (with modern variants), beginning with that of January, is as follows: garnet, amethyst, bloodstone (aquamarine), diamond, emerald, pearl (alexandrite), ruby, sardonyx (peridot), sapphire, opal (tourmaline), topaz (citrine), and turquoise (zircon)

birth·wort (-wurt′) ***n.*** any of a genus (*Aristolochia*) of vines of the birthwort family with brownish or purplish S-shaped flowers: formerly used in folk medicine as an aid in childbirth —***adj.*** designating a family (Aristolochiaceae, order Aristolochiales) of dicotyledonous plants, shrubs, and woody vines, including Dutchman's pipe

bi·ry·a·ni (bir′ē ä′nē) ***n.*** ⟦Hindi or Urdu⟧ a highly spiced dish of India, typically flavored with saffron and consisting of rice layered with lamb, chicken, or vegetables

bis (bēs; *E* bis) ***interj.*** ⟦L, double: see BINARY⟧ again; once more: used by audiences in France and Italy instead of ENCORE —***adv. Musical Direction*** again: repeat the indicated passage: a note to the performer

bis- (bis) *prefix* BI-[1]: used before *c* or *s*

Bi·sa·yan (bi sä′yən) ***n., adj.*** VISAYAN

Bis·cay (bis′kā, -kē), **Bay of** part of the Atlantic, on the N coast of Spain & the W coast of France

bis·cot·ti (bi skät′ē; *It* bē skôt′tē) ***pl.n., sing.* -to** (-ō), **-ti** ⟦It, pl. of *biscotto* < OIt: see fol.⟧ hard, plain, bar-shaped cookies containing almonds or hazelnuts

bis·cuit (bis′kit) ***n., pl.* -cuits** or **-cuit** ⟦ME *bisquit, besquit* < OFr *bescuit* (altered, under infl. of OIt *biscotto*) < ML *biscoctum* < (*panis*) *bis coctus*, (bread) twice baked < L *bis*, twice (see BINARY) + *coctus*, pp. of *coquere*, COOK⟧ **1** [Chiefly Brit.] a crisp, unleavened wafer; cracker or cookie ☆**2** *a)* a quick bread, made light by baking powder, soda, or yeast, and baked in small pieces *b)* any of these pieces **3** light brown; tan **4** pottery or porcelain after the first firing and before glazing

bise (bēz) *n.* ⟦ME < OFr < Frank **bisa* or OHG *bisa* < Gmc base **bis-,* to storm about vigorously⟧ a cold north or northeast wind blowing down from the Swiss Alps

bi·sect (bī sekt′, bī′sekt′) *vt.* ⟦< ModL *bisectus,* pp. of *bisecare* < L *bi-,* BI-[1] + *secare,* to cut: see SAW[1]⟧ 1 to cut in two 2 *Geom.* to divide into two equal parts —*vi.* to divide; fork —**bi·sec′tion** *n.* —**bi·sec′tion·al** *adj.*

bi·sec·tor (-ər) *n.* a thing that bisects; specif., a straight line that bisects an angle or line

bi·ser·rate (bī ser′āt′, -it) *adj.* 1 *Bot.* having serrations along the serrations, as some leaves; doubly serrate 2 *Zool.* notched on both sides, as some antennae

bi·sex·u·al (bī sek′sho͞o əl) *adj.* 1 of both sexes 2 having both male and female organs, as certain animals and plants; hermaphroditic 3 of or characterized by sexual desire for those of one's own sex and also those of the opposite sex —*n.* one that is bisexual —**bi·sex′u·al′i·ty** (-sho͞o al′ə tē) *n.*, **bi·sex′u·al·ism′** —**bi·sex′u·al·ly** *adv.*

Bish·kek (bish kek′) capital of Kyrgyzstan, in the NC part

bish·op (bish′əp) *n.* ⟦ME < OE *bisceop* < LL *episcopus,* an overseer (in LL(Ec), bishop) < Gr *episkopos,* overseer (in N.T., bishop) < *epi-,* upon + *skopos* < *skopein,* to look (see SCOPE)⟧ 1 *a)* a high-ranking member of the Christian clergy having authority, variously, over other clergy and usually supervising a diocese or church district *b) Mormon Ch.* a lay church officer who presides over a ward 2 a chess piece that can move in a diagonal direction only, over any number of unoccupied squares of the same color 3 a hot, sweet drink of port wine flavored with an orange stuck with cloves

Bish·op (bish′əp), **Elizabeth** 1911-79; U.S. poet

bish·op·ric (bish′əp rik) *n.* ⟦ME *bischopriche* < OE *bisceoprice* < *bisceop* (see BISHOP) + *rice*: see ARCHBISHOPRIC⟧ 1 the church district controlled by a bishop; diocese 2 the office, authority, or rank of a bishop

bish·op's-cap (bish′əps kap′) *n.* ☆any of a genus (*Mitella*) of small woodland plants of the saxifrage family, with two-lobed seedcases shaped like a bishop's hat

Bisk (bisk, bēsk) *alt. sp. of* BIYSK

Bis·marck[1] (biz′märk′), Prince **Otto (Eduard Leopold) von** 1815-98; Prus. chancellor of the German Empire (1871-90), which he unified: called the *Iron Chancellor*

Bis·marck[2] (biz′märk′) ⟦after prec., in recognition of financial aid to the local railroad by Ger investors⟧ capital of N.Dak., on the Missouri River

Bismarck Archipelago group of islands north and east of New Guinea; part of Papua New Guinea: 19,200 sq mi (49,728 sq km)

bis·muth (biz′məth) *n.* ⟦< ModL *bisemutum* < Ger *wismut,* earlier *wesemut* < ?⟧ a hard, brittle, metallic chemical element that is grayish-white with a tinge of red, used chiefly in making alloys of low melting point and in medicine: symbol, Bi; at. no. 83: see the periodic table of elements in the Reference Supplement

bis·muth·ic (biz′məth ik; biz muth′ik, -myo͞oth′-) *adj.* of or containing pentavalent bismuth

bis·muth·ous (biz′məth əs) *adj.* of or containing trivalent bismuth

bi·son (bī′sən, -zən) *n., pl.* **bi′son** ⟦Early ModE *bisontes,* pl. < L, pl. of *bison,* wild ox < Gmc **wisunt* < IE **wis-onto-* < base **weis-*: see WEASEL⟧ any of a genus (*Bison*) of bovid ruminants having a shaggy mane, short, curved horns, and a humped back, as the American buffalo (*B. bison*) or the wisent

bison

bisque[1] (bisk) *n.* ⟦Fr⟧ 1 a rich, thick, creamy soup made from shellfish or from rabbit, fowl, etc. 2 a thick, creamy soup of puréed vegetables 3 an ice cream containing ground macaroons or nuts

bisque[2] (bisk) *n.* ⟦< BISCUIT⟧ 1 biscuit ceramic ware left unglazed in the finished state 2 a red-yellow color

bisque[3] (bisk) *n.* ⟦Fr⟧ a handicap of one point per set in tennis, one turn per game in croquet, or one or more strokes per game at match play in golf

Bis·sau (bi sou′) seaport & capital of Guinea-Bissau, on the W coast

bis·sex·tile (bis seks′til, -təl, -tīl′) *adj.* ⟦LL *bisextilis,* containing an intercalary day < *bisextus* < *bis,* twice (see BI-[1]) + *sextus,* sixth: Feb. 24 (sixth day before the calends of March) was reckoned twice every fourth year⟧ 1 denoting the extra day (February 29) of a leap year 2 designating or of a leap year —*n.* [Rare] LEAP YEAR

bis·ter or **bis·tre** (bis′tər) *n.* ⟦Fr *bistre*⟧ 1 a yellowish-brown to dark-brown pigment made from the soot of burned wood 2 any of various colors in this range

bis·tort (bis′tôrt′) *n.* ⟦MFr *bistorte* < OFr < ML *bistorta,* lit., twice twisted < L *bis,* double (see BINARY) + *tortus,* pp. of *torquere,* to twist⟧ any of several perennial northern and alpine plants (genus *Polygonum*) of the buckwheat family, whose twisted roots furnish an astringent

bis·tou·ry (bis′too rē) *n., pl.* **-ries** ⟦Fr *bistouri* < *bistourner,* to deform, castrate < OFr *bestorner,* distort⟧ a surgical knife with a narrow blade used to open abscesses or fistulas

bis·tro (bē′strō′, bis′trō′) *n., pl.* **-tros′** ⟦Fr (Parisian) slang, wine shop, wine seller < *bistraud,* orig. (dial. of Anjou & Poitou), a shepherd < *biste,* goat⟧ 1 a small wine shop or restaurant where wine is served 2 a small nightclub or bar

bi·sul·cate (bī sul′kāt′) *adj.* ⟦BI-[1] + SULCATE⟧ 1 having two grooves 2 *Zool. a)* cloven *b)* cloven-footed

bi·sul·fate (bī sul′fāt′) *n.* an acid sulfate containing the monovalent negative radical HSO_4

bi·sul·fide (bī sul′fīd′) *n.* DISULFIDE

bi·sul·fite (-fīt′) *n.* an acid sulfite containing the monovalent negative radical HSO_3

bit[1] (bit) *n.* ⟦ME < OE *bite,* a bite < *bītan,* BITE⟧ 1 the part of a bridle that goes into a horse's mouth, used to control the horse 2 anything that curbs or controls 3 the part of a pipestem held in the mouth 4 the part of a key that actually turns the lock 5 the cutting part of any tool, as the blade of a plane 6 a drilling or boring tool for use in a brace, drill press, etc. —*vt.* **bit′ted, bit′ting** 1 *a)* to put a bit into the mouth of (a horse) *b)* to train to the bit 2 to check or curb 3 to make the bit on (a key) —**take (or get) the bit in one's teeth** 1 to clench the bit between the teeth, so that it fails to restrain: said of horses 2 to be beyond control

bit[2] (bit) *n.* ⟦ME *bite* < OE *bita,* a piece, morsel, bit < *bitan,* to BITE⟧ 1 *a)* a small piece or quantity *b)* a small extent or limited degree (often used with *a* and having adverbial force) [*a bit* bored] *c)* a short time; moment [wait *a bit*] ☆2 ⟦orig. used of a small silver coin worth ⅛ of the Spanish peso (hence, normally 12½ cents)⟧ [Old Informal] an amount equal to 12½ cents: usually in *two bits, four bits,* etc. ☆3 *a)* a small part or short performance in a play or entertainment *b)* [Informal] any stereotyped or repeated action, expression, etc. [resorting to the aggrieved *bit*] —*adj.* very small [a *bit* role] —**bit by bit** little by little; gradually —**do one's bit** to do one's share —**every bit** altogether; entirely

bit[3] (bit) *vt., vi. pt. & alt. pp. of* BITE

bit[4] (bit) *n.* ⟦*b(inary) (dig)it*⟧ 1 a single digit (i.e., a 0 or 1) in a binary number system 2 a unit of information equal to the amount of information obtained by learning which of two equally likely events occurred

bi·tar·trate (bī tär′trāt′) *n.* an acid tartrate containing the monovalent negative radical $C_4H_5O_6$

bitch (bich) *n.* ⟦ME *bicche* < OE *bicce;* akin to ON *bikkja*⟧ 1 the female of the dog, wolf, fox, etc. 2 [Archaic] a lewd or promiscuous woman 3 [Slang] a woman regarded as malicious, bad-tempered, or aggressive: a term of contempt 4 [Slang] anything especially unpleasant or difficult ☆5 [Slang] a complaint —*vi.* ☆[Slang] to complain —*vt.* [Slang] 1 ⟦? infl. by BOTCH⟧ to bungle: usually with *up* 2 to behave spitefully or angrily toward

bitch·er·y (bich′ər ē) *n.* [Slang] malicious or hostile remarks or behavior; spiteful complaining

bitch·y (bich′ē) *adj.* **bitch′i·er, bitch′i·est** [Slang] bad-tempered or malicious: used esp. of a woman —**bitch′i·ly** *adv.* —**bitch′i·ness** *n.*

bite (bīt) *vt.* **bit** (bit), **bit·ten** (bit′'n) or **bit, bit′ing** ⟦ME *biten* < OE *bītan* < IE base **bheid-,* to split, crack > BEETLE[1], BITTER, L *findere,* to split (see FISSION)⟧ 1 to grip, pierce, or cut with the teeth or with parts like jaws 2 to cut into, as with a sharp weapon 3 to sting, as an insect 4 to hurt in a sharp, stinging way 5 to eat into; corrode 6 to infect or possess: used esp. in the passive [*bitten* by a lust for power] 7 to cheat or trick: used esp. in the passive —*vi.* 1 *a)* to press or snap the teeth (*into, at,* etc.) *b)* to have a tendency to do this 2 to cause a biting sensation or have a biting effect 3 to get or keep a tight hold; grip [the car wheels *bit* into the snow] 4 to seize a bait 5 [Informal] *a)* to be caught, as by a trick *b)* to show interest in, or accept, something offered 6 [Slang] SUCK (*vi.* 6) —*n.* 1 the act of biting 2 biting quality; sting [*a bite* to his words] 3 a wound, bruise, or sting from biting 4 *a)* amount of food bitten off; mouthful or morsel *b)* food *c)* a meal, esp. a light meal or snack 5 a brief excerpt or other small piece of information 6 a tight hold or grip 7 an edge or surface that grips ☆8 [Informal] an amount cut off or sum deducted [the tax takes quite a *bite* from my paycheck] ☆9 [Slang] money or price asked; cost; expense: with *the*: usually used in the phrase **put the bite on,** to press for a loan, gift, or bribe of money 10 *Dentistry* the way the upper and lower teeth meet 11 *Etching* the corrosion of the metal plate by the acid —**bite down (on)** to clamp the jaws and teeth (onto something) —☆**bite off more than one can chew** [Informal] to attempt more than one is capable of —**bite the hand that feeds one** [Informal] to insult or harm a benefactor

bite-size (bīt′sīz′) *adj.* 1 being or of a size that can be eaten in one MOUTHFUL (sense 2) [*a bite-size* bar of chocolate] 2 [Informal] compact or brief enough as to be done, experienced, or understood easily [*bite-size* news reports] Also **bite′-sized′**

bite·wing (bīt′wiŋ′) *n.* ⟦so named from the winglike shape of the projecting part⟧ *Dentistry* an X-ray film with a projecting edge that is clamped by the teeth to hold the film in place for an exposure

Bi·thyn·i·a (bə thin′ē ə) ancient country in NW Asia Minor, in what is now Turkey: fl. 3d cent. B.C.–1st cent. A.D.

bit·ing (bīt′iŋ) *adj.* 1 cutting; sharp 2 sarcastic; caustic —*SYN.* INCISIVE —**bit′ing·ly** *adv.*

biting midge any of a family (Ceratopogonidae) of midges with piercing and sucking mouthparts: some species attack humans and animals in swarms

bit·map (bit′map′) *n. Comput.* a representation of a graphic image, as a letter or number, as a sequence of bits that generates a corresponding pattern of pixels on a video screen

bit·mapped (bit′mapt′) *adj.* composed of or formed by a pattern of pixels to make a bitmap

bit·stock (bit′stäk′) *n.* a handle for turning bits; brace
bit·sy (bit′sē) *adj.* [Informal] very small; tiny
bitt (bit) *n.* ⟦< ON *biti,* crossbeam⟧ any of the strong deck posts, usually in pairs, around which ropes or cables are wound and held fast, as in mooring: cf. BOLLARD (sense 1)
bit·ten (bit′'n) *vt., vi. alt. pp. of* BITE
bit·ter (bit′ər) *adj.* ⟦ME < OE *biter,* akin to *bītan,* BITE⟧ **1** designating or having a sharp, often unpleasant taste; acrid, as quinine or peach stones **2** causing or showing sorrow, discomfort, or pain; grievous **3** sharp and disagreeable; harsh; severe; piercing [*a bitter* wind] **4** characterized by strong feelings of hatred, resentment, cynicism, etc. —*adv.* **1** in a way that is bitter; bitterly **2** extremely [it was *bitter* cold] —*n.* **1** a bitter quality or thing [take the *bitter* with the sweet] **2** [Brit.] bitter, strongly hopped ale: cf. BITTERS — *vt., vi.* to make or become bitter —**bit′ter·ly** *adv.* —**bit′ter·ness** *n.*
bitter almond a variety of almond whose bitter seeds yield hydrocyanic acid upon hydrolysis
bitter apple COLOCYNTH
bitter cassava a species of cassava (*Manihot esculenta*) whose poisonous roots when processed yield tapioca starch
bitter end ⟦archaic *bitter,* turn of cable about a bitt⟧ *Naut.* the inboard end of a rope, cable, or chain —**to the bitter end** ⟦so called because with the cable out to the *bitter end,* no freedom of action remains; meaning infl. by BITTER, *adj.* 2⟧ **1** until the end, however difficult or distressing **2** until death
☆**bit·ter-end·er** (-en′dər) *n.* [Informal] a person who persists in a hopeless cause; one who will not give in
bit·tern[1] (bit′ərn) *n., pl.* **-terns** or **-tern** ⟦ME *bitor* < OFr *butor* < VL **butitaurus* < L *butio,* bittern (< echoic base **bu-*) + *taurus,* small bird that imitates the lowing of oxen, lit., bull: see STEER[1]⟧ any of a subfamily (Botaurinae) of wading birds, including a genus (*Botaurus*) noted for the resounding, thumping call of the male
bit·tern[2] (bit′ərn) *n.* ⟦prob. < dial. *bittering* < BITTER + -ING⟧ the bitter liquid left after the crystallization of salt from brine
☆**bit·ter·nut** (bit′ər nut′) *n.* a hickory tree (*Carya cordiformis*) native to the E U.S., with thin-shelled, bitter nuts
bitter principle any of various bitter substances found in plants, as lupulin, aloin, etc.
bit·ter·root (-ro͞ot′) *n.* a W North American plant (*Lewisia rediviva*) of the purslane family, having fleshy, edible roots and pink or white flowers
Bitterroot Range ⟦after prec., found esp. in the foothills⟧ range of the Rocky Mountains, along the Idaho-Montana border: highest peak, *c.* 11,000 ft (3,353 m)
bit·ters (bit′ərz) *pl.n.* a liquor containing bitter herbs, roots, etc. and usually alcohol, used as a medicine or tonic and as an ingredient in some cocktails
bit·ter·sweet (bit′ər swēt′) *n.* ☆**1** a North American twining woody vine (*Celastrus scandens*) of the staff-tree family, with poisonous leaves, and bearing clusters of small orange fruits with bright-red fleshy seeds **2** a poisonous, climbing European vine (*Solanum dulcamara*) of the nightshade family, with purple flowers and red berries, now widely found as a weed in North America **3** *a)* bitterness and sweetness combined *b)* pleasure mixed with overtones of sadness —*adj.* **1** both bitter and sweet, as dark chocolate made with little sugar **2** pleasant with overtones of sadness
☆**bit·ter·weed** (-wēd′) *n.* any of various herbs which have a bitter taste, as ragweed, sneezeweed, etc.
bit·ty (bit′ē) *adj.* **-ti·er, -ti·est** ⟦< BIT[2] + -Y[4]⟧ ☆**1** tiny: a playful term or child's term: cf. ITTY-BITTY **2** [Brit.] made up of bits, or small pieces; without unity; disjointed
bi·tu·men (bi to͞o′mən, bī-; -tyo͞o′-) *n.* ⟦L < Celt (or ? Oscan-Umbrian) < IE **gwet-,* resin > Sans *jatu,* gum, Bret *bezuen,* birch⟧ **1** [Obs.] asphalt found in a natural state **2** any of various black, combustible, solid to semisolid mixtures of hydrocarbons that are usually obtained from the distillation of petroleum, used to make roofing materials, sealants, paints, etc. —**bi·tu′mi·noid′** (-mə noid′) *adj.*
bi·tu·mi·nize (-mə nīz′) *vt.* **-nized′, -niz′ing** to impregnate with, or convert into, bitumen —**bi·tu′mi·ni·za′tion** *n.*
bi·tu·mi·nous (-mə nəs) *adj.* ⟦Fr *bitumineux* < L *bitumineus*⟧ **1** of the nature of bitumen, esp. with regard to its color and combustibility **2** containing or made from bitumen
bituminous coal a dark coal that burns easily with a smoky flame yielding pitch or tar: also called *soft coal:* see ANTHRACITE
bi·va·lence (bī vā′ləns, bi′vā′-) *n.* the quality or state of being bivalent: also **bi·va′len·cy** (-lən sē)
bi·va·lent (-lənt) *adj.* **1** *Chem.* DIVALENT: see -VALENT **2** *Biol.* double: said of a chromosome formed by two equivalent chromosomes that lie close together or appear to join completely during meiosis —*n.* a double chromosome; dyad
bi·valve (bī′valv′) *n.* any of a class (Bivalvia) of mollusks, including mussels and clams, having a shell consisting of two valves hinged together —*adj.* having a shell of two valves hinged together: also **bi′valved′**
biv·ou·ac (biv′wak′, -o͞o ak′) *n.* ⟦Fr < Ger dial. (Swiss) *biwacht,* night guard < OHG *bi-,* by, with + *wahta,* watchman < *wahhen,* watch, WAKE[1]⟧ **1** [Archaic] a night guard to avoid surprise attack **2** a temporary encampment (esp. of soldiers) in the open, with only tents or improvised shelter —*vi.* **-acked′, -ack′ing** to encamp in the open
bi·week·ly (bī wēk′lē) *adj., adv.* **1** once every two weeks **2** [Now Rare] twice a week: in this sense, *semiweekly* is the preferred term —*n., pl.* **-lies** a publication that appears once every two weeks
bi·year·ly (bī yir′lē) *adj., adv.* **1** once every two years; biennial(ly) **2** [Now Rare] twice a year: in this sense, *semiyearly, semiannual(ly),* or *biannual(ly)* is preferred
Biysk (bisk, bēsk) city in SC Siberia, in the Kuznetsk Basin
☆**biz** (biz) *n.* [Slang] business
bi·zarre (bi zär′) *adj.* ⟦Fr < It *bizarro,* angry, fierce, strange < Sp bold, knightly < Basque *bizar,* a beard⟧ **1** very odd in manner, appearance, etc.; grotesque **2** marked by extreme contrasts and incongruities of color, design, or style **3** unexpected and unbelievable; fantastic [a *bizarre* sequence of events] —*SYN.* FANTASTIC —**bi·zarre′ly** *adv.* —**bi·zarre′ness** *n.*
bi·zar·re·rie (bə zär′ə rē′) *n.* ⟦Fr⟧ **1** something bizarre **2** a bizarre quality
☆**bi·zar·ro** (bi zär′ō) *adj.* ⟦suggested by a character in the *Superman* comic books, *c.* 1950s⟧ [Informal] outlandishly bizarre —*n.* [Slang] a bizarre or weird person or thing
Bi·zer·te (bi zʉr′tə, -tē; *Fr* bē zert′) seaport in northernmost Tunisia, on the Mediterranean: also **Bi·zer′ta** (-zʉr′tə)
Bi·zet (bē zā′), **Georges** (zhôrzh) (born *Alexandre César Léopold Bizet*) 1838-75; Fr. composer
BJ or **B.J.** *abbrev.* **1** Bachelor of Journalism **2** [Slang] BLOW JOB: mildly vulgar
bk *abbrev.* **1** bank **2** book **3** brick
Bk *Chem. symbol for* berkelium
bka *abbrev.* better known as: cf. AKA: also **BKA**
bkg *abbrev.* banking
bks *abbrev.* **1** barracks **2** books
bkt *abbrev.* **1** basket(s) **2** bracket
bl *abbrev.* **1** bale(s) **2** barrel(s) **3** black **4** blue
BL or **B.L.** *abbrev.* **1** Bachelor of Laws **2** Bachelor of Letters
B/L or **b/l** *abbrev.* bill of lading
blab (blab) [Informal] *vt., vi.* **blabbed, blab′bing** ⟦ME *blabben:* see fol.⟧ **1** to give away (a secret) in idle chatter **2** to chatter; prattle —*n.* **1** loose chatter; gossip **2** a person who blabs
blab·ber (blab′ər) [Informal] *vt., vi.* ⟦ME *blabberen,* freq. of *blabben,* like ON *blabbra,* echoic⟧ to blab or babble —*n.* ⟦< prec. + -ER⟧ a person who blabs
☆**blab·ber·mouth** (-mouth′) *n.* [Informal] a person who blabs
black (blak) *adj.* ⟦ME *blak* < OE *blæc* < IE **bhleg-,* burn, gleam (> L *flagrare,* flame, burn) < base **bhel-,* to gleam, white: orig. sense, "sooted, smoke-black from flame"⟧ **1** opposite to white; of the color of coal or pitch: see COLOR (*n.* 2-4) **2** [*sometimes* **B-**] *a)* designating or of any of the dark-skinned traditional inhabitants of sub-Saharan Africa, Australia, or Melanesia or their descendants in other parts of the world *b)* by, for, or about black people as a group; specif., in the U.S., by, for, or about black Americans [*black* studies] (see AFRICAN-AMERICAN) **3** *a)* totally without light; in complete darkness *b)* very dark **4** without cream, milk, etc.: said of coffee **5** soiled; dirty **6** wearing black clothing **7** evil; wicked; harmful **8** disgraceful **9** full of sorrow or suffering; sad; dismal; gloomy **10** disastrous **11** sullen or angry [*black* looks] **12** without hope [a *black* future] **13** inveterate; confirmed; deep-dyed [a *black* villain] **14** humorous or satirical in a morbid or cynical way [*black* comedy] **15** secret; covert; hidden [a CIA *black* operator] —*n.* **1** *a)* black color *b)* a black pigment, paint, or dye **2** any substance or thing that is black **3** a spot or area that is black **4** black clothes, esp. when worn in mourning **5** [*sometimes* **B-**] a member of a black people **6** complete darkness or absence of light **7** *Chess* the player or side with the black or darker-colored pieces — *vt., vi.* **1** to make black; blacken **2** to polish with blacking —**black out** **1** to cover (writing, printing, etc.) with black pencil marks or paint **2** to cause a blackout in **3** to lose consciousness; faint **4** to lose all memory of an event or fact —☆**in the black** ⟦from the practice of entering a credit item in account books with black ink⟧ operating at a profit —☆**into the black** into a profitable condition financially —**black′ish** *adj.* —**black′ness** *n.*
Black (blak) **1 Hugo (La Fayette)** 1886-1971; associate justice, U.S. Supreme Court (1937-71) **2 Joseph** 1728-99; Scot. chemist
☆**black alder** a deciduous shrub (*Ilex verticillata*) of the holly family, native to E North America, with glossy leaves that turn black in the fall and bright-red berries
black·a·moor (blak′ə moor′) *n.* ⟦< BLACK + MOOR⟧ [Archaic] a very dark-skinned person, esp. a black African
black-and-blue (-ən blo͞o′) *adj.* ⟦descriptive⟧ discolored from congestion of blood under the skin; bruised
Black and Tan ⟦so named from wearing black caps and khaki coats, and in allusion to a famous pack of hounds in LIMERICK, where first stationed⟧ a member of the British troops sent to Ireland to help put down disturbances during the Sinn Fein rebellion (1919-21)
☆**black-and-tan terrier** (-ən tan′) MANCHESTER TERRIER
black and white ⟦with reference to *black* letters on *white* paper⟧ **1** writing or print [to put an agreement down in *black and white*] **2** a drawing or picture done in black and white **3** reproduction, as by photography or television, of images in black, white, and gray rather than in chromatic colors
black-and-white (-ən hwīt′, -wīt′) *adj.* **1** set down in writing or print **2** partly black and partly white [a *black-and-white* tie] **3** *a)* reproduced, rendered, etc. in black, white, and gray rather than in chromatic colors [a *black-and-white* print] *b)* producing images in black, white, and gray [a *black-and-white* TV set] **4** of, having to do with, or seen solely in terms

of, polar opposites [a debater framing a complex issue in *black-and-white* terms] —*n.* 1 a black-and-white photograph 2 [Informal] a police patrol car

Black Angus ABERDEEN ANGUS

black art BLACK MAGIC: with *the*

black-bag (blak′bag′) *adj.* ⟦in allusion to a burglar's bag of tools⟧ [Slang] designating or of a secret illegal break-in made by a government agency in pursuit of suspected criminals, enemy agents, etc.

black·ball (-bôl′) *n.* ⟦< a small black ball formerly used as a means of voting against a person or thing⟧ a secret ballot or vote against a person or thing —*vt.* 1 to vote against; esp., to vote against letting (a person) join one's organization 2 to bar or ostracize from social life, a particular profession, etc.

black bass any of a genus (*Micropterus*) of freshwater sunfishes of North America, highly prized as a game fish

black bear 1 the common North American bear (*Ursus americanus*) that lives in forests and feeds mainly on roots and berries 2 any of several dark-colored bears, esp. of Asia

Black·beard (blak′bird′) (name for *Edward Teach* or *Thatch*) died 1718; Eng. pirate

black belt 1 a black-colored belt or sash awarded to an advanced practitioner in many of the martial arts, as judo or karate: a beginner wears a *white belt*, and increasing degrees of skill are symbolized by belts of other colors, culminating in the black belt 2 a person who holds a black belt

Black Belt ⟦orig., as noted (1901) by B. T. WASHINGTON[1], in ref. to the fertile *black* soil of this region; now, in ref. to *black* Americans⟧ region in S and SE U.S., extending from Texas to Virginia, having a high percentage of African-Americans

black·ber·ry (blak′ber′ē, -bər ē) *n., pl.* **-ries** 1 the fleshy, purple or black, edible aggregate fruit of various brambles (genus *Rubus*) of the rose family 2 a bush or vine bearing this fruit

☆**blackberry lily** an ornamental plant (*Belamcanda chinensis*) of the iris family, bearing orange flowers and clusters of black seeds that resemble blackberries

black·bird (-burd′) *n.* 1 a common European thrush (*Turdus merula*) 2 any of various passerine birds (family Icteridae) of the New World, the males having almost entirely black plumage, as the red-winged blackbird or the grackle

black·board (-bôrd′) *n.* a large, smooth, usually dark surface of slate or other material on which to write or draw with chalk; chalkboard

black·bod·y (-bäd′ē) *n.* an ideal surface or body that can absorb completely all the radiation striking it

black book a book containing names of those blacklisted: see also LITTLE BLACK BOOK —**be in someone's black book** to be regarded unfavorably by someone

black box 1 an intricate, compact electronic component or device, such as a flight recorder, that can be quickly connected or disconnected as a unit 2 anything having a complex function that can be observed but whose inner workings are mysterious or unknown

black bread a dark, coarse bread, esp. of rye flour

black·buck (-buk′) *n.* a long-horned Indian antelope (*Antilope cervicapra*), brownish-black above and white below

Black·burn (blak′bərn) 1 city in NW England, in Lancashire: textile center 2 **Mount** mountain in the Wrangell Mountains, SE Alas.: 16,523 ft (5,036 m)

black·cap (blak′kap′) *n.* 1 any of various small passerine birds with a black crown, esp. a chickadee (*Parus atricapillus*) and a European warbler (*Sylvia atricapilla*) ☆2 BLACK RASPBERRY

black·cock (-käk′) *n., pl.* **-cocks′** or **-cock′** the male of the black grouse

black cohosh ⟦< *cohosh* < Eastern Abenaki⟧ a type of BUGBANE whose roots and rhizomes are used variously in alternative medicine

☆**black crappie** a dark, spotted crappie (*Pomoxis nigromaculatus*)

black·damp (-damp′) *n.* a suffocating gas, a mixture of carbon dioxide and nitrogen, that may occur in mines

Black Death ⟦so called from the dark spots it makes on the skin⟧ a pandemic of bubonic plague and related diseases that devastated Europe and Asia in the 14th cent.

black diamond 1 [*also pl.*] COAL (*n.* 1) 2 CARBONADO (*n.* 2)

black duck a sooty-brown wild duck (*Anas rubripes*) of E North America

black dwarf *pl.* **black dwarfs** or occas. **black dwarves** a cold, dark dwarf star

black·en (blak′ən) *vi.* ⟦ME *blaknen* < *blak*, BLACK⟧ to become black or dark —*vt.* 1 to make black; darken 2 to hurt or damage by slander, libel, etc. [to *blacken* a reputation] —**black′en·er** *n.*

black·ened (blak′ənd) *adj.* having a charred crust formed by coating with ground hot pepper and spices and frying quickly in a very hot skillet [*blackened* redfish]

black English [*often* **B- E-**] the group of related dialects of American English spoken variously by many black people in the U.S.

Black·ett (blak′it), Baron **P(atrick) M(aynard) S(tuart)** 1897-1974; Eng. nuclear physicist

black eye 1 an eye with a very dark iris 2 a discoloration of the skin or flesh surrounding an eye, resulting from a sharp blow or contusion ☆3 [Informal] shame or dishonor, or a cause or source of this

☆**black-eyed pea** (blak′īd′) COWPEA

black-eyed Su·san (so͞o′zən) ⟦so named from the dark center of the flower⟧ ☆1 any of several common North American wildflowers of several families (esp. genera *Thunbergia* and *Rudbeckia* of the acanthus and composite families) having flowers with yellow petals or bracts around a dark center 2 the flower of any of these plants

black·face (blak′fās′) *adj.* having a black or blackened face —*n.* ☆black makeup used by a performer, as in a minstrel show

black·fel·low (-fel′ō) *n.* [Archaic] Australian Aborigine: a patronizing term

black·fin (-fin′) *n.* 1 a snapper (*Lutjanus buccanella*) of the West Indies ☆2 a cisco (*Coregonus nigripinnis*) of NE North America

black·fish (-fish′) *n., pl.* **-fish′** or **-fish′es** (see FISH) ☆1 any of a genus (*Globicephala*) of large, black, migratory dolphins; pilot whale 2 any of a number of dark marine fishes, as a sea bass or tautog 3 an edible Siberian or Alaskan freshwater fish (*Dallia pectoralis*) of the same order (Salmoniformes) as trout, pike, and salmon: reputed to revive after being frozen

black flag 1 a flag that is all or mostly black, esp. such a flag flown by a pirate ship: cf. JOLLY ROGER 2 in auto racing, a signal to a driver during a race, made by waving a solid black flag, indicating that the driver must stop and consult an official

☆**black fly** any of a family (Simuliidae) of small, dark, dipterous flies of North American forests and mountains, whose larvae live attached to rocks in swift water: most species live on the blood of mammals and may transmit disease

Black·foot (blak′fo͝ot′) *n., pl.* **-feet′** or **-foot′** ⟦transl. of Blackfoot *siksīka*⟧ 1 *a)* a member of a North American Indian people consisting of three subgroups (the Blackfoot proper, the Blood, and the Piegan) and living in Montana, Saskatchewan, and Alberta *b)* a member of the subgroup 2 the Algonquian language of this people

Black Forest ⟦transl. of Ger *Schwarzwald* < *schwarz*, black (see SWART) + *wald*, wood, forest (see VOLE): so named from the dark-colored fir trees high on the mountains⟧ wooded mountain region in SW Germany

Black Forest cake ⟦after prec.⟧ a torte consisting typically of thin layers of chocolate cake spread with alternating layers of chocolate, cherry, and whipped-cream filling and covered with whipped cream

Black Friday ⟦< IN THE BLACK (see BLACK); prob. infl. by *Black Friday*, older name for Good Friday⟧ ☆the Friday after Thanksgiving, traditionally the beginning of U.S. Christmas shopping and a day of brisk retail sales

black frost a severe freezing that blackens growing plants without a visible frost

black gold ⟦from its color and its economic value⟧ [Informal] petroleum

black grouse a large grouse (*Lyrurus tetrix*) of Europe and Asia: the male is almost entirely black

black·guard (blag′ərd, -ärd′) *n.* ⟦BLACK (precise meaning or ref. uncert.) + GUARD⟧ 1 [Historical] the lowest servants of a large household, in charge of pots and pans 2 *a)* a person who uses abusive language *b)* scoundrel; villain —*adj.* 1 vulgar, low, etc. 2 abusive —*vt.* to abuse with words; rail at; revile —**black′guard·ly** *adj., adv.*

black guillemot a guillemot (*Cepphus grylle*) that is mostly black in summer and mostly white in winter

☆**black gum** a tall, deciduous tupelo (*Nyssa sylvatica*) with sour purple fruits and leaves that turn scarlet in the fall, found in moist forests of the E U.S.

Black Hand ⟦< symbol used by group in letters of extortion⟧ 1 a group of Sicilian immigrant blackmailers and terrorists in New York in the early 20th cent. 2 any similar secret society

☆**black haw** 1 any of several E U.S. shrubs or small trees (genus *Viburnum*) of the honeysuckle family, having blue-black fruits 2 SHEEPBERRY

Black Hawk 1767-1838; chief of the Sauk people

black·head (blak′hed′) *n.* 1 any of various black-headed birds, esp. the scaup duck 2 a black-tipped plug of dried fatty matter in a pore of the skin ☆3 an infectious disease of the intestines and liver of turkeys, chickens, etc. caused by a protozoan (*Histomonas meleagridis*) and characterized by a dark, discolored comb 4 the parasitic larva of a freshwater mussel (family Unionidae) encysted in the gills, etc. of a fish

black·heart (-härt′) *n.* 1 a dark, heart-shaped sweet cherry with soft, purplish flesh 2 a plant disease, esp. of potatoes, that turns the internal tissues black

black·heart·ed (-härt′id) *adj.* wicked; evil

Black Hills ⟦from their dark appearance, because heavily forested⟧ mountainous region in SW S.Dak. & NE Wyo.: highest peak, 7,242 ft (2,207 m)

black hole ⟦phr. first used with this meaning (late 1960s) by J. A. WHEELER⟧ ☆1 a celestial object or dark region in space, perhaps formed by the collapse of a large star, with such a great mass that its gravitational field will not let even light escape 2 *a)* an emptiness or void *b)* anything thought of as endlessly devouring resources, funds, etc.

Black Hole 1 a small dungeon at Calcutta: it was once believed that over 100 Europeans were confined there one night in 1756 by their Indian captors and died from heat and lack of air 2 [**b- h-**] any dungeon

black ice ⟦prob. because it appears to be the same color as the dark surface of the road⟧ a thin, nearly invisible layer of ice on a paved road

black·ing (blak′iŋ) *n.* a black polish, as for shoes

black·jack (blak′jak′) *n.* ⟦see JACK⟧ 1 a large beer mug, formerly made of leather coated with tar 2 BLACK FLAG ☆3 a small, leather-covered bludgeon with a flexible handle ☆4 a SE U.S. scrub oak (*Quercus marilandica*) with fan-shaped leaves ☆5 *a)* a gambling game at cards in which any player wins who gets cards totaling twenty-one points or less while the dealer gets either a smaller total or a total exceeding twenty-one points *b)* a combination of an ace and a face card or ten, equaling 21 points in this game **6** sphalerite, esp. a dark variety: also written **blackjack** —*vt.* **1** to hit with a blackjack **2** to force (a person) to do something by threatening, as if with a blackjack

☆**black knot** a disease of cherry and plum trees caused by a fungus (*Plowrightia morbosa*), in which hard, black swellings appear on twigs and branches

black lead (led) graphite, as used in lead pencils, etc.

black·leg (-leg′, -lāg′) *n.* **1** an acute, usually fatal, infectious disease of young cattle and sheep, caused by a bacterium (esp. *Clostridium chauvoei*) and characterized by swelling and blackening of infected muscle tissue **2** a disease of beets and related plants caused by a fungus (*Phoma betae*) **3** a disease of potatoes caused by a bacterium (*Erwinia atroseptica*) **4** [Informal] a gambler who cheats **5** [Brit.] a strikebreaker

black letter a kind of heavy-faced, ornamental printing type: also called *Gothic, Old English,* or *text*

black light ultraviolet or infrared radiation used for fluorescent effects, photography, etc. in the dark

black·list (-list′) *n.* a list of persons who have been censured and who are being discriminated against, refused employment, etc. —*vt.* to put on a blacklist

black lung (disease) a disease of the lungs caused by the inhalation of coal dust; anthracosis

black·ly (blak′lē) *adv.* **1** drearily; gloomily **2** angrily; menacingly **3** in a sinister manner

black magic magic with an evil purpose; sorcery

black·mail (blak′māl′) *n.* ⟦lit., black rent < ME *male,* rent, tribute < OE *mal,* lawsuit, terms < ON lawsuit, discussion; infl. in ME by OFr *maille,* a coin⟧ **1** [Historical] a tribute paid to freebooters and bandits along the Scottish border to assure safety from looting **2** *a)* payment extorted by threatening to disclose information that could bring disgrace or ruin *b)* extortion of such payment —*vt.* **1** to get or try to get blackmail from **2** to coerce (*into* doing something) as by threats —**black′mail′er** *n.*

☆**Black Ma·ri·a** (mə rī′ə) [Now Brit.] a patrol wagon

black mark an unfavorable item in one's record

black market a place or system for selling goods illegally, as in violation of rationing —**black′-mar′ket** *vt., vi.* —**black marketeer** (or **marketer**)

Black Mass [*also* **b- m-**] **1** a Requiem Mass, at which the clergy is dressed in black **2** a satanist ceremony that travesties the Mass

black measles a severe form of measles with intradermal hemorrhaging

black medic a widespread weedy annual plant (*Medicago lupulina*) of the pea family, with small yellow flowers and black seed pods, sometimes grown for forage

black money income, esp. from illegal activities, not reported to the government so as to avoid paying taxes on it

Black Mountains ⟦prob. < AmInd descriptive name⟧ highest range of the Appalachians, in W N.C.: branch of the Blue Ridge Mountains: highest peak, Mount MITCHELL[2]

☆**Black Muslim** a member of the NATION OF ISLAM: the term is considered derogatory by members of the group, who call themselves simply *Muslims*

☆**black nationalism** a movement advocating the establishment of a separate black nation within the U.S.

black nightshade a poisonous plant (*Solanum nigrum*) of the nightshade family, with white, star-shaped flowers and dark berries, widespread as a weed in North America

☆**black oak** any of various North American oaks (esp. *Quercus velutina*) with dark bark or foliage

black·out (blak′out′) *n.* **1** *a)* the extinguishing of all stage lights to end a play or scene *b)* a comic stage skit ending with a quick blackout **2** an elimination or concealing of all lights that might be visible to an enemy, as during an air raid, at night **3** a temporary loss of electricity in an area because of a failure in its generation or transmission **4** a temporary loss of consciousness or vision **5** a loss of memory of an event or fact **6** suppression or concealment, as of news by censorship ☆**7** the prohibition of the televising of a sports event in the locality where the event takes place, so that attendance will not be reduced

black pepper pepper ground from the whole fruits of the pepper plant, including the black outer covering: see PEPPER (*n.* 1)

☆**black·poll** (-pōl′) *n.* a North American warbler (*Dendroica striata*), the male of which has a black crown

Black·pool (blak′po͞ol′) resort city in Lancashire, NW England, on the Irish Sea

black powder gunpowder as used in sports involving modern muzzleloading firearms

☆**black power** **1** political and economic power as sought by black Americans in the struggle for civil rights **2** [*usually* **B- P-**] a movement esp. of the 1960s and 1970s, often advocating radical or violent means in an attempt to secure political and economic rights for black Americans

Black Prince *name for* EDWARD[2] (Prince of Wales)

black pudding ⟦BLACK (from the dark color of the cooked blood) + PUDDING (*n.* 1)⟧ a dark-colored sausage made with pig's blood and suet, combined with oatmeal, bread crumbs, etc.

☆**black raspberry** **1** a shrub (*Rubus occidentalis*) of the rose family, with long prickly canes that root at the tips and bear juicy, purple-black fruit **2** this fruit

Black Rod **1** in England, the chief usher to the Order of the Garter and the House of Lords: so called from his symbol of office, an ebony rod: in full, **Gentleman Usher of the Black Rod** **2** a similar official in other Commonwealth parliaments

☆**black rot** any of various bacterial or fungous diseases of plants producing discoloration and decay

Black Russian a cocktail made of vodka and coffee liqueur served over ice

☆**black rust** any of several diseases of grasses, cereals, etc. caused by a rust fungus (genus *Puccinia*)

Black Sea sea between SE Europe & Asia, north of Turkey: 196,100 sq mi (507,897 sq km)

black sheep a member of a family or group who is regarded as not so respectable or successful as the rest

Black Shirt a member of any fascist organization (specif., the former Italian Fascist party) with a black-shirted uniform

black·smith (blak′smith′) *n.* ⟦< *black metal,* former name for iron⟧ a smith who works in iron, including the making and fitting of horseshoes

☆**black·snake** (-snāk′) *n.* **1** any of various black or dark-colored snakes, esp. a slender, harmless racer (*Coluber constrictor*) found in the U.S. **2** a long, heavy whip of braided leather or rawhide Also **black snake**

black spot any of various diseases of plants, esp. roses, that produce round black spots on the leaves

☆**black spruce** **1** a small spruce (*Picea mariana*) found in the cold bogs of N North America **2** its soft, light wood

Black·stone (blak′stōn′; *Brit,* -stən), Sir **William** 1723-80; Eng. jurist & writer on law

black·strap molasses (blak′strap′) ☆dark, thick molasses with most of the sugar removed

☆**black-tailed deer** (-tāld′) a mule deer, esp. the subspecies (*Odocoileus hemionus columbianus*) found from N Calif. to British Columbia: also **black′tail′** *n.*

black tea tea that is withered and fermented before being dried: distinguished from GREEN TEA

black·thorn (-thôrn′) *n.* **1** a thorny, white-flowered prunus shrub (*Prunus spinosa*) with purple or black, plumlike fruit; sloe **2** a cane or stick made of the stem of this shrub

black tie **1** a black bow tie, properly worn with a tuxedo **2** a tuxedo and the proper accessories

black-tie (blak′tī′) *adj.* ⟦< prec.⟧ being or of a social function characterized by formalwear

black·top (-täp′) *n.* **1** a bituminous mixture, usually asphalt, used as a surface for roads, driveways, etc. **2** a road, lot, etc. covered with blacktop —*vt.* **-topped′**, **-top′ping** to cover with blacktop

Black Velvet ⟦< *black,* from its dark color + *velvet,* ? from its smoothness: said to have been invented in 1861 at a London club after the death of Prince ALBERT[2] in order to give the champagne a somber color⟧ [*sometimes* **b- v-**] a drink consisting of equal parts of champagne and stout

Black Volta *see* VOLTA[2]

black vomit **1** vomit characteristic of yellow fever, dark because of the blood in it **2** yellow fever

black·wall (blak′wôl′) *adj.* designating or of a black pneumatic tire without a colored band on the outer sidewall: also written **black-wall** —*n.* a blackwall tire

Black·wall hitch (blak′wôl′) ⟦after *Blackwall,* a shipyard in London⟧ a kind of knot

☆**black walnut** **1** a tall walnut tree (*Juglans nigra*) native to E North America **2** its hard, heavy, dark-brown wood, used in making furniture, gunstocks, etc. **3** its edible, oily nut

black·wa·ter (blak′wôt′ər) *n.* wastewater from toilets: distinguished from GREY WATER: also written **black water**

blackwater fever a severe, often fatal complication of malaria characterized by a rapid heartbeat and the passing of dark urine

Black·well (blak′wəl), **Elizabeth** 1821-1910; 1st woman physician in the U.S., born in England

☆**black widow** an American spider (*Latrodectus mactans*), the female of which has a glossy black body with an hourglass-shaped red mark underneath, and a poisonous bite which is normally not fatal: so called because the female sometimes eats its mate

blad·der (blad′ər) *n.* ⟦ME *bladre* < OE *blǣddre* < IE **bhlē-*: see BLAST⟧ **1** a bag consisting of or lined with membranous tissue in the body of many animals, capable of inflation to receive and contain liquids or gases; esp. the URINARY BLADDER in the pelvic cavity, which holds urine flowing from the kidneys **2** a thing resembling such a bag, as the inflatable rubber bag inside the leather cover of a football **3** *a)* an inflated covering of certain fruits *b)* an air sac, as in some water plants

bladder campion a perennial plant (*Silene cucubalus*) of the pink family, with an inflated calyx

bladder kelp any of various giant brown algae with air bladders that buoy up the leafy portions

bladder ket·mie (ket′mē) ⟦Fr *ketmie,* mallow < ML *ketmia* < Ar⟧ FLOWER-OF-AN-HOUR

blad·der·nose (-nōz′) *n.* HOODED SEAL

blad·der·nut (-nut′) *n.* **1** any of a genus (*Staphylea*) of shrubs or small trees of the bladdernut family, with fruit that has inflated pods **2** one of these pods —*adj.* designating or of a family (Staphyleaceae, order Sapindales) of dicotyledonous shrubs or small trees

blad·der·worm (-wurm′) *n.* CYSTICERCUS

blad·der·wort (-wurt′) *n.* any of a large genus (*Utricularia*) of chiefly aquatic plants of the bladderwort family, having finely divided leaves with bladders on them that trap small insects and crustaceans —*adj.* designating a family (Lentibulariaceae, order Scrophulariales) of dicotyledonous plants

bladder wrack any of various brown algae (genera *Ascophyllum* and *Fucus*), having a flattened body and conspicuous air bladders

blad·der·y (blad′ər ē) *adj.* **1** like a bladder **2** having a bladder or bladders

blade (blād) *n.* ⟦ME *blad* < OE *blæd*, a leaf < IE **bhlē-*, var. of base **bhel-*, to swell, sprout: see BLOOM[1]⟧ **1** *a)* the leaf of a plant, esp. of grass *b)* the flat, expanded part of a leaf; lamina **2** *a)* a broad, flat section or surface, as of an oar, propeller arm, or rotary vane *b)* the propeller arm or rotary vane itself **3** a flat bone [the shoulder *blade*] **4** *a)* the cutting part of a tool, instrument, or weapon *b)* any flat or wedge-shaped device or part for cutting, scraping, pushing, clearing, etc. **5** the metal runner of an ice skate **6** a sword **7** a swordsman **8** [Old-fashioned] a dashing young man: usually in the phrase **gay blade** ☆**9** [Slang] a knife, often, specif., a switchblade knife, intended or used as a weapon **10** *Phonet.* the flat part of the tongue, behind the tip —*adj.* designating or of a chop, roast, etc., as of beef or veal, that is cut across the shoulder blade section —**blad′ed** *adj.*

Bla·go·vesh·chensk (bläg′ə vesh′chensk′) city in SE Siberian Russia, on the Amur River, at the Chinese border

blague (bläg) *n.* ⟦Fr⟧ a practical joke, playful deception, raillery, etc.

☆**blah** (blä) [Slang] *n.* ⟦echoic of monotonous talk⟧ boring, predictable, or nonsensical talk or writing —*interj.* used, usually repeated one or more times, to suggest such talk or writing, esp. when it continues for a long time [and the speaker went on, *blah, blah, blah*, seemingly forever] —*adj.* feeling or being dull and lifeless —**the blahs** a state of weariness, boredom, or general lack of interest in life

blain (blān) *n.* ⟦ME *bleine* < OE *blegen*, a blister: for IE base see BALL[1]⟧ [Now Rare] an inflamed sore or swelling

Blaine (blān), **James G(illespie)** 1830-93; U.S. statesman: secretary of state (1881, 1889-92)

Blair (bler, blar), **Tony** (born *Anthony Charles Lynton Blair*) 1953- ; Brit. politician: prime minister (1997-2007)

Blake (blāk) **1 Robert** 1599-1657; Eng. admiral **2 William** 1757-1827; Eng. poet, artist, & mystic

Bla·key (blā′kē), **Art** 1919-90; U.S. jazz drummer & bandleader: Muslim name *Abdullah Ibn Buhaina*

blam (blam) *interj.* ⟦echoic⟧ used to suggest the sound of a shot, explosion, etc. —*n.* such a sound

blam·a·ble or **blame·a·ble** (blām′ə bəl) *adj.* ⟦ME⟧ that deserves blame; culpable —**blam′a·bly** *adv.*

blame (blām) *vt.* **blamed, blam′ing** ⟦ME *blamen* < OFr *blasmer*, to speak evil of < LL(Ec) *blasphemare*, BLASPHEME⟧ **1** to accuse of being at fault; condemn (*for* something); censure **2** to find fault with (*for* something) **3** to place responsibility for (an error, fault, etc.) *on* someone or something —*n.* **1** the act of blaming; accusation; condemnation; censure **2** responsibility for a fault or wrong **3** [Obs.] blameworthiness; fault —*SYN.* CRITICIZE —**be to blame** to be blamable; be at fault

blamed (blāmd) *adj., adv.* [Informal] damned: a mild expletive

blame·ful (blām′fəl) *adj.* **1** finding or imputing blame; blaming **2** deserving to be blamed; blameworthy —**blame′ful·ly** *adv.* —**blame′ful·ness** *n.*

blame·less (-lis) *adj.* free from blame —**blame′less·ly** *adv.* —**blame′less·ness** *n.*

blame·wor·thy (-wur′thē) *adj.* deserving to be blamed —**blame′wor′thi·ness** *n.*

Blanc (blän), **Mont** (mōn) mountain in E France, on the Italian border: highest peak in the Alps: 15,781 ft (4,810 m)

Blan·ca Peak (blaŋ′kə) ⟦Sp *blanca*, white (with snow)⟧ highest peak of the Sangre de Cristo range, S Colo.: 14,317 ft (4,364 m)

blanc de blancs (bläŋk′də bläŋk′; *Fr* blän də blän′) ⟦Fr, lit., white from whites⟧ white wine, esp. champagne, made from white grapes: also **blanc de blanc**

blanc fixe (blaŋk′ fiks′; *Fr* blän fēks′) ⟦Fr, permanent white⟧ BARIUM SULFATE

blanch (blanch, blänch) *vt.* ⟦ME *blanchen* < OFr *blanchir* < *blanc*, white: see BLANK⟧ **1** to make white; take color out of **2** to make pale **3** to bleach (endive, celery, etc.) by earthing up or covering so as to keep away light and improve the appearance, flavor, or tenderness **4** *a)* to prepare, as for freezing, by scalding (said as of vegetables) *b)* to remove the skins of (almonds) by blanching **5** *Metallurgy* to brighten with acid or by coating with tin —*vi.* to whiten; turn pale —**blanch′er** *n.*

Blanche (blanch) *n.* ⟦Fr, lit., white, fem. of *blanc*: see BLANK⟧ a feminine name

blanc·mange (blə mônzh′, -mänzh′) *n.* ⟦Fr < *blanc*, white + *manger*, to eat⟧ a sweet, molded jellylike dessert made with milk, sugar, flavoring, and a starch or gelatin to thicken it

bland (bland) *adj.* ⟦L *blandus*, mild, prob. < IE base **mḷdu-*, soft, var. of **mel-*: see MILL[1]⟧ **1** pleasantly smooth in manner; suave **2** mild and soothing; not sharp, harsh, etc. [*bland* medicine] **3** tasteless, insipid, dull, etc. —*SYN.* SOFT, SUAVE —**bland out** [Informal] to remove or omit distinctive characteristics; make or become vapid —**bland′ly** *adv.* —**bland′ness** *n.*

blan·dish (blan′dish) *vt., vi.* ⟦ME *blandishen* < OFr *blandiss-*, extended stem of *blandir*, to flatter < L *blandiri*, to flatter < prec.⟧ to flatter or coax in persuading; cajole —**blan′dish·er** *n.* —**blan′dish·ing·ly** *adv.*

blan·dish·ment (-mənt) *n.* **1** the act of blandishing; cajolery **2** a flattering or ingratiating act or remark, etc. meant to persuade: *usually used in pl.*

blank (blaŋk) *adj.* ⟦ME < OFr *blanc*, white < Frank **blank*, white, gleaming, akin to OE *blanca*, white steed < IE **bhleg-*, to shine: see BLACK⟧ **1** [Obs.] colorless or white **2** *a)* not written, recorded, etc. on; not marked; empty [a *blank* sheet of paper, a *blank* tape] *b)* having empty spaces to be filled in **3** having an empty, vacant, or monotonous look or character **4** *a)* without interest or expression [*blank* looks] *b)* showing incomprehension or confusion **5** empty of thought; lacking ideas [a *blank* mind] **6** unproductive; barren [*blank* years] **7** utter; complete [a *blank* denial] **8** lacking certain elements or characteristics, as a wall without an opening **9** [Slang] BLANKETY-BLANK —*n.* **1** an empty space, esp. one to be filled in on a printed form, school test, etc. **2** a printed form or document with such empty spaces **3** an emptiness; vacant place or time; void **4** *a)* the center spot of a target *b)* anything aimed at or pointed at **5** a manufactured article yet to be cut to a pattern or marked with a design [a key *blank*] **6** a lottery ticket that fails to win **7** a powder-filled cartridge without a bullet: in full **blank cartridge 8** a mark, usually a dash (—), indicating an omitted word, esp. an oath or curse —*vt.* ☆**1** to hold (an opponent) scoreless in a game **2** to stamp with a die from flat stock —**blank out** to cancel or obscure by covering over; void —**draw a blank 1** to draw a lottery ticket that fails to win **2** [Informal] *a)* to be unsuccessful in any attempt *b)* to be unable to remember a particular thing —**blank′ly** *adv.* —**blank′ness** *n.*

blank check 1 a check form that has not been filled in **2** a check carrying a signature only and allowing the bearer to fill in any amount **3** permission to use an unlimited amount of money, authority, etc.

blank endorsement an endorsement naming no payee, making the endorsed amount payable to the bearer

blan·ket (blaŋk′it) *n.* ⟦ME < OFr *blanchet*, dim. of *blanc*, white: see BLANK⟧ **1** a large piece of cloth, often of soft wool, used for warmth as a bed cover or a covering for animals **2** anything used as or resembling a blanket; covering [a *blanket* of leaves] —☆*adj.* covering a group of conditions or requirements; including many or all items [a *blanket* insurance policy] —*vt.* **1** to cover with or as with a blanket; overspread; overlie **2** to apply uniformly to: said of regulations or rates **3** to cut off wind from the sails of (another boat) by passing close to windward, as in yacht racing **4** to suppress; hinder; obscure [a powerful radio station *blankets* a weaker one] **5** [Archaic] to toss in a blanket, as in punishment

☆**blan·ket·flow·er** (-flou′ər) *n.* a gaillardia, esp. the common, yellow perennial species (*Gaillardia aristata*)

blanket stitch a kind of buttonhole stitch with the stitches spaced relatively far apart, used to reinforce the edge of thick material, as that used for blankets

☆**blan·ke·ty-blank** (blaŋk′it ē blaŋk′) *adj., adv.* ⟦redupl. of BLANK, *n.* 8⟧ [Slang] damned: a humorous euphemism

blank verse unrhymed verse; esp., unrhymed verse having five iambic feet per line, as in Elizabethan drama: cf. FREE VERSE

blan·quette (blän ket′) *n.* ⟦Fr⟧ a kind of stew of a light-colored meat, as chicken or veal, in a cream sauce, often with mushrooms and small onions

blare (bler) *vt., vi.* **blared, blar′ing** ⟦ME *bleren, bloren*, to wail, bellow: for IE base see BLEAR⟧ **1** to sound out with loud, harsh, trumpetlike tones **2** to announce or exclaim loudly —*n.* **1** a loud, brassy sound **2** harsh brilliance or glare, as of color

blar·ney (blär′nē) *n.* [see fol.] smooth talk used in flattering or coaxing —*vt., vi.* **-neyed, -ney·ing** to engage in blarney (with)

Blarney stone a stone in Blarney Castle in the county of Cork, Ireland, said to impart skill in blarney to those who kiss it

Blas·co I·bá·ñez (bläs′kô ē bä′nyeth), **Vi·cen·te** (vē then′te) 1867-1928; Sp. novelist

bla·sé (blä zā′, blä′zā) *adj.* ⟦Fr, pp. of *blaser*, to satiate, orig., to intoxicate⟧ **1** having indulged in pleasure so much as to be unexcited by it; satiated and bored **2** indifferent, apathetic, nonchalant, etc.

blas·pheme (blas fēm′, blas′fēm′) *vt.* **-phemed′, -phem′ing** ⟦ME *blasfemen* < OFr *blasfemer* < LL(Ec) *blasphemare* < Gr *blasphēmein*, to speak evil of, in LGr(Ec), blaspheme < *blas-* (< ?) + *phēmē*, utterance: see FAME⟧ **1** to speak irreverently or profanely of or to (God or sacred things) **2** to curse or revile —*vi.* to utter blasphemy —**blas·phem′er** *n.*

blas·phe·mous (blas′fə məs) *adj.* ⟦ME *blasfemous* < LL(Ec) *blasphemus* < Gr *blasphēmos*⟧ characterized by blasphemy; irreverent or profane —**blas′phe·mous·ly** *adv.*

blas·phe·my (blas′fə mē) *n., pl.* **-mies** ⟦ME *blasfemie* < OFr *blasphemie* < LL(Ec) *blasphemia* < Gr *blasphēmia*: see BLASPHEME⟧ **1** profane or contemptuous speech, writing, or action concerning God or anything held as divine **2** any remark or action held to be irreverent or disrespectful

SYN.—**blasphemy**, the strongest of these words, is used esp. of any remark deliberately mocking or contemptuous of God; **profanity** extends the concept to irreverent remarks referring to any person or thing regarded as sacred; **swearing** and **cursing**, in this connection, both refer to the utterance of profane oaths and imprecations, the latter, esp., to the calling down of evil upon someone or something

blast (blast, bläst) *n.* ⟦ME < OE *blæst*, puff of wind < IE **bhlē-*, var. of base **bhel-*, to swell, blow up > BALL[1], L *flare*⟧ **1** a gust of wind; strong rush of air **2** the sound of a sudden rush of air or gas, as through a trumpet **3** a strong, artificially created jet of air, steam, exhaust gases, etc. **4** the steady current of air forced into a blast furnace **5** an abrupt and damaging influence, esp. a plant blight **6** *a)* an explosion, as of dynamite *b)* a charge of explosive causing this *c)* a wave of air of increased pressure followed by one of lower pressure radiating from an explosion ☆**7** a strong, sudden outburst, as of criticism ☆**8** [Slang] *Sports* a strong, driving hit, as of a baseball ☆**9** [Slang] a pleasurable, exciting event or experience, as a wild party —*vi.* **1** to make a loud, harsh sound **2** to set off explosives, gunfire, etc. **3** to suffer or wither from a blight —*vt.* **1** to damage or destroy by or as if by a blight; wither; ruin **2** to blow up or move with or as with an explosive; explode ☆**3** to attack or criticize sharply ☆**4** [Slang] *Sports* to drive (a ball) far with a sharp blow of the bat or club —*SYN.* WIND[2] —☆**blast off** to take off with explosive force and begin its flight: said of a rocket, spacecraft, etc. —**(at) full blast** at full speed or capacity —**blast′er** *n.*

blast- (blast) *combining form* BLASTO-: used before a vowel

-blast (blast) ⟦< Gr *blastos,* a sprout⟧ *combining form* germ, embryo [*epiblast*]

blast·ed (blas′tid) *adj.* **1** blighted; withered; destroyed **2** damned; confounded: a mild expletive

blas·te·ma (blas tē′mə) *n., pl.* **-mas** or **-ma·ta** (-mə tə) ⟦ModL < Gr *blastēma,* a bud < *blastanein,* to bud < *blastos,* a sprout⟧ the undifferentiated embryonic tissue from which cells, tissues, and organs are developed —**blas·tem′ic** (-tem′ik, -tē′mik) *adj.,* **blas′te·mat′ic** (-tə mat′ik)

blast furnace a towerlike smelting furnace for separating metal, esp. iron, from the impurities in the ore: a blast of air is forced into the furnace from below to produce the intense heat needed

blas·to- (blas′tō, -tə) ⟦see -BLAST⟧ *combining form* of a germinating embryo [*blastoderm, blastogenesis*]

blas·to·coele or **blas·to·cele** (blas′tō sēl′, -tə-) *n.* ⟦prec. + -COELE⟧ the segmentation cavity of a developing ovum or of the blastula

blas·to·cyst (-sist′) *n.* ⟦BLASTO- + -CYST⟧ BLASTULA

blas·to·derm (-durm′) *n.* ⟦BLASTO- + -DERM⟧ the part of a fertilized ovum that gives rise to the germinal disk from which the embryo develops —**blas′to·der′mic** *adj.*

blas·to·disk or **blas·to·disc** (-disk′) *n.* GERMINAL DISK

☆**blast·off** or **blast-off** (blast′ôf′) *n.* the launching of a rocket, missile, spacecraft, etc.

blas·to·gen·e·sis (blas′tō jen′ə sis, -tə-) *n.* ⟦BLASTO- + -GENESIS⟧ **1** reproduction by asexual means, as by budding in corals **2** the theory that the germ plasm transmits hereditary characteristics: opposed to PANGENESIS

blas·to·ma (blas tō′mə) *n., pl.* **-mas, -ma·ta** (-mə tə) a malignant tumor that forms from the immature tissue of the blastema

blas·to·mere (blas′tō mir′, -tə-) *n.* ⟦BLASTO- + -MERE⟧ any of the cells resulting from the first few divisions of the ovum after fertilization —**blas′to·mer′ic** (-mer′ik) *adj.*

blas·to·my·cete (blas′tō mī′sēt′, -mī sēt′; -tə-) *n.* ⟦BLASTO- + -MYCETE⟧ any of a genus (*Blastomyces*) of yeastlike imperfect fungi that cause diseases in people and animals

blas·to·my·co·sis (-mī kō′sis) *n.* ⟦BLASTO- + MYCOSIS⟧ any disease caused by a blastomycete

blas·to·pore (blas′tō pôr′, -tə-) *n.* ⟦BLASTO- + PORE[2]⟧ the opening into the gastrula cavity

blas·to·sphere (-sfir′) *n.* ⟦BLASTO- + -SPHERE⟧ BLASTULA

blas·tu·la (blas′tyoo lə) *n., pl.* **-las** or **-lae′** (-lē′) ⟦ModL, dim. < Gr *blastos,* a sprout⟧ an embryo at the stage of development in which it consists of usually one layer of cells around a central cavity, forming a hollow sphere —**blas′tu·lar** (-lər) *adj.* —**blas′tu·la′tion** (-lā′shən) *n.*

blat (blat) *vi.* **blat′ted, blat′ting** ⟦var. of BLEAT⟧ ☆to bleat —☆*vt.* to blurt out; blab —*n.* a blatting sound

bla·tan·cy (blāt′'n sē) *n., pl.* **-cies** a blatant quality or thing

bla·tant (blāt′'nt) *adj.* ⟦coined by Edmund SPENSER[2], prob. < L *blaterare,* to babble, or E dial. *blate,* to bellow⟧ **1** disagreeably loud or boisterous; clamorous **2** glaringly conspicuous or obtrusive [*blatant* ignorance] —*SYN.* VOCIFEROUS —**bla′tant·ly** *adv.*

blath·er (blath′ər) *n.* ⟦ON *blathr*⟧ foolish talk; loquacious nonsense —*vi.* to talk on and on foolishly —**blath′er·er** *n.*

blath·er·skite (-skīt′) *n.* ⟦< prec. + dial. *skite,* to defecate < ON *skita*⟧ **1** blather **2** a talkative, foolish person

blau·bok (blou′bäk′) *n., pl.* **-bok′** or **-boks′** ⟦obs. Afrik *blauwbok,* lit., blue buck⟧ a large, bluish-gray antelope (*Hippotragus leucophaeus*) of South Africa: now extinct

Bla·vat·sky (blə vät′skē, -vat′-), **He·le·na Pe·trov·na** (hel ā′nə pe trōv′nə) (born *Helena Hahn*) 1831-91; Russ. theosophist in the U.S. and elsewhere: called *Madame Blavatsky*

blax·ploi·ta·tion (blaks′ploi tā′shən) *n.* ⟦< BLA(CK) + (E)XPLOITATION, as in SEXPLOITATION⟧ the exploitation of African-American characters, settings, themes, etc. in commercial films: used esp. with regard to various films in the late 1960s and early 1970s that emphasized sex, violence, crime, etc. in urban African-American communities

blaze[1] (blāz) *n.* ⟦ME *blase* < OE *blæse, blase,* a torch, flame < IE **bhles-,* shine < base **bhel-*: see BLACK⟧ **1** a brilliant mass or burst of flame; strongly burning fire **2** any very bright, often hot, light or glare [the *blaze* of searchlights] **3** a sudden, spectacular occurrence; showy outburst [a *blaze* of oratory] **4** a brightness; vivid display; flash **5** [*pl.*] hell: a euphemism, esp. in such phrases as **go to blazes!** and **what the blazes?** —*vi.* **blazed, blaz′ing 1** to burn rapidly or brightly; flame **2** to give off a strong, vivid light; shine very brightly; glare **3** to be deeply stirred or excited, as with anger —*vt.* [Rare] to cause to blaze —**blaze away 1** to fire a gun rapidly a number of times **2** to speak heatedly

SYN.—**blaze** suggests a hot, intensely bright, relatively large and steady fire [the *blaze* of a burning house]; **flame** generally refers to a single, shimmering, tonguelike emanation of burning gas [the *flame* of a candle]; **flicker** suggests an unsteady, fluttering flame, esp. one that is dying out [the last *flicker* of his oil lamp]; **flare** implies a sudden, bright, unsteady light shooting up into darkness [the *flare* of a torch]; **glow** suggests a steady, warm, subdued light without flame or blaze [the *glow* of burning embers]; **glare** implies a steady, unpleasantly bright light [the *glare* of a bare lightbulb]

blaze[2] (blāz) *n.* ⟦< ON *blesi*: for IE base see prec.⟧ **1** a light-colored spot on an animal's face ☆**2** a mark made on a tree, as by cutting off a piece of bark, esp. one made on each of a series of trees to mark a trail —☆*vt.* **blazed, blaz′ing** to mark (a tree) with a blaze or (a trail) with blazes —☆**blaze a way** (or **trail,** etc.) to pioneer, set a direction or course, etc.

blaze[3] (blāz) *vt.* **blazed, blaz′ing** ⟦ME *blasen,* to blow < OE or ON form akin to Ger < IE **bhlē-* < base **bhel-,* to swell, blow up > BALL[1]; infl. by BLAZON⟧ to make known publicly; spread the news of; proclaim

blaz·er (blā′zər) *n.* ⟦< BLAZE[1] + -ER⟧ a hip-length, single-breasted jacket, often having a notched lapel and buttons down the front

blazing star ⟦descriptive⟧ ☆**1** any of a genus (*Liatris*) of American wildflowers of the composite family, with showy, usually lavender flowers borne on wandlike spikes ☆**2** any of various plants, esp. of the lily family, having showy flower clusters

bla·zon (blā′zən) *n.* ⟦ME *blasoun* < OFr *blason,* a shield, blazon⟧ **1** a coat of arms; heraldic shield, emblem, or banner **2** a technical description or illustration of a coat of arms in accordance with the rules of heraldry **3** showy display —*vt.* ⟦< the n.; mistakenly assoc. with BLAZE[3]⟧ **1** to make known far and wide; proclaim: often with *forth, out,* or *abroad* **2** to describe technically or portray (coats of arms) **3** *a)* to portray in colors *b)* to adorn colorfully or showily —**bla′zon·er** *n.* —**bla′zon·ment** *n.*

bla·zon·ry (-rē) *n., pl.* **-ries 1** the description or illustration of coats of arms **2** a coat of arms; heraldic emblem **3** any brilliant display

bldg *abbrev.* building

bldr *abbrev.* builder

-ble (bəl) *suffix* -ABLE

bleach (blēch) *vt.* ⟦ME *blechen* < OE *blǣcan* < IE **bhleig-,* to gleam (> BLEAK[2]) < base **bhel-,* to gleam > BLACK, ON *blikja,* turn pale⟧ **1** to remove some or all color from, as by means of chemicals or by exposure to the sun's rays **2** to whiten; blanch —*vi.* to become white, colorless, or pale —*n.* **1** a bleaching or whitening **2** any substance used for bleaching **3** the degree of whiteness resulting from bleaching

bleach·er (blēch′ər) *n.* a person or thing that bleaches —*adj.* ☆of or having to do with BLEACHERS [*bleacher* tickets]

☆**bleach·er·ite** (blēch′ər īt′) *n.* one who sits in the BLEACHERS (sense 1)

☆**bleach·ers** (blēch′ərz) *pl.n.* ⟦< BLEACH, in ref. to the effects of exposure⟧ **1** a section of cheaper seats, usually bare benches in tiers without a roof, for spectators at outdoor sporting events **2** similar tiered benches indoors, as in a gymnasium

bleaching powder any powder used in bleaching; esp., chloride of lime

bleah (ble, blekh) *interj.* ⟦echoic⟧ used to express disgust, distaste, etc.

bleak[1] (blēk) *adj.* ⟦ME *bleik* < ON *bleikr,* pale: see BLEACH⟧ **1** exposed to wind and cold; unsheltered; treeless; bare **2** cold and cutting; harsh **3** not cheerful; gloomy; dreary **4** not promising or hopeful [a *bleak* future] **5** [Obs.] pale; wan —**bleak′ly** *adv.* —**bleak′ness** *n.*

bleak[2] (blēk) *n., pl.* **bleak** or **bleaks** ⟦< ON *bleikja* < *bleikr*: see prec.⟧ any of a genus (*Alburnus*) of small, slender European carp with silvery scales that are used in making artificial pearls

blear (blir) *adj.* ⟦ME *blere,* watery, rheumy < the v.⟧ **1** made dim by tears, mucus, etc.: said of eyes **2** blurred; dim; indistinct; misty —*vt.* ⟦ME *bleren,* to have watery eyes, akin to Ger *plärren,* to bawl, cry < IE base **bhlē-,* to howl, weep (of echoic orig.) > BLARE, BLEAT, L *flere,* to weep⟧ **1** to dim (the eyes) with tears, mucus, etc. **2** to blur (a surface or an outline)

blear·y (blir′ē) *adj.* **blear′i·er, blear′i·est 1** dim or blurred, as the eyes are from lack of rest or when one first awakens **2** having blurred vision —**blear′i·ly** *adv.* —**blear′i·ness** *n.*

blear·y-eyed (-īd′) *adj.* having bleary eyes: also **blear′eyed′**

bleat (blēt) *vi.* ⟦ME *bleten* < OE *blǣtan*: see BLEAR⟧ **1** to make its characteristic cry: said of a sheep, goat, or calf **2** to make a sound like this cry **3** to speak foolishly, whiningly, or querulously —*vt.* to say or express in a bleating voice —*n.* **1** the cry of a sheep, goat, or calf **2** any sound or utterance like this —**bleat′er** *n.*

bleb (bleb) *n.* ⟦echoic: to represent the sound produced in forming a bubble with the lips⟧ **1** a small swelling under the skin; a blister or vesicle **2** an air bubble, as in water or glass —**bleb′by** *adj.*

bleed (blēd) *vi.* **bled** (bled), **bleed′ing** ⟦ME *bleden* < OE *bledan* < *blod,* blood < IE **bhlē-,* var. of base **bhel-,* to swell > BALL[1], BLOOM[1]⟧ **1** to emit or lose blood **2** to suffer wounds or die in a battle or cause **3** to feel pain, grief, or sympathy; suffer **4** to ooze; esp., to ooze sap, juice, etc., as bruised plants do **5** to run together: said as of dyes in wet cloth **6** to come through a covering coat of paint: said as of certain stains **7** to be printed to the edge of a page, wrapper, etc. so that a part is later trimmed off: said of pictures, designs, etc. —*vt.* **1** to draw blood from; leech **2** to ooze (sap, juice, etc.) ☆**3** to take sap or juice from **4** *a)* to empty slowly of liquid, air, or gas *b)* to draw off (liquid, air, or gas) slowly **5** *a)* to print (a picture, design, etc.) so that a small part at the edge is cut off when the paper is trimmed *b)* to trim (a page) so as to bleed some of the printed matter **6** [Informal] to get money from, esp. by extortion —*n.* the part of a printed picture, design, etc. that overruns the margin to be trimmed

bleed·er (blēd′ər) *n.* **1** a person who draws blood from another **2** a person who bleeds profusely; hemophiliac **3** *Electronics* a resistor used to regulate the voltage in a power supply, discharge a high-voltage capacitor, etc.

bleeding heart ⟦descriptive⟧ **1** any of several dicentras, esp. a common garden perennial (*Dicentra spectabilis*) with racemes of drooping, deep-pink, heart-shaped flowers **2** a person regarded as too sentimental or too liberal in dealing with social problems

bleep (blēp) *n.* ⟦echoic⟧ **1** BEEP **2** *a)* a recording, as of an electronic tone, over a segment of a soundtrack, as for covering an expletive *b)* a word substituted as a euphemism for such an expletive, vulgar or taboo word, etc. —*vi.* BEEP —*vt.* **1** to censor (something spoken), as in a telecast, by or as by substituting a beep **2** to censor (a speaker) in this manner —*interj.* used to suggest the sound of the beep: used esp. to substitute for an expletive spoken in a broadcast or telecast

blegh (ble, blekh) *interj. alt. sp. of* BLEAH

blem·ish (blem′ish) *vt.* ⟦ME *blemishen* < OFr *blemiss-*, extended stem of *blesmir,* to injure, prob. via Frank **blesmjan,* to cause to turn pale < **blesmi,* akin to BLAZE²⟧ to mar, as by some flaw or fault; spoil the perfection of —*n.* **1** a mark that mars the appearance, as a stain, spot, scar, etc. **2** any flaw, defect, or shortcoming —*SYN.* DEFECT

blench¹ (blench) *vt., vi.* ⟦var. of BLANCH⟧ [Chiefly Brit. Dial.] to make or become pale; whiten; bleach

blench² (blench) *vi.* ⟦ME *blenchen,* move suddenly, avoid < OE *blencan,* to deceive, akin to Ger *blinken*; ult. < IE base of BLANK⟧ [Brit. Dial.] to shrink back, as in fear; flinch; quail

blend (blend) *vt.* ⟦ME *blenden* < OE *blendan* & ON *blanda,* to mix < IE base **bhlendh-*, to glimmer indistinctly > BLIND, BLUNDER⟧ **1** to mix or mingle (varieties of tea, tobacco, etc.), esp. so as to produce a desired flavor, color, grade, etc. **2** to mix or fuse thoroughly, so that the parts merge and are no longer distinct [*green results from blending* blue and yellow] —*vi.* **1** to mix, merge, or unite **2** to pass gradually or imperceptibly into each other, as colors **3** to go well together; harmonize —*n.* **1** the act of blending; thorough mixing **2** *a)* the result of blending; a mixture or merger of varieties, kinds, types, etc. [a favorite *blend* of coffee] *b)* a mixture consisting chiefly of a (specified) fabric, ingredient, etc. [a cotton *blend*] ☆**3** *Linguis.* a word formed by combining parts of other words (Ex.: *galumph, smog*) —*SYN.* MIX

blende (blend) *n.* ⟦Ger *blende* < *blenden,* to blind, deceive (akin to prec.): so named because it resembles galena, but contains no lead⟧ any of several minerals, esp. metallic sulfides, with a bright luster; specif., sphalerite

blended family a social unit consisting of two previously married parents and the children of their former marriages

☆**blended whiskey** whiskey that is a blend of straight whiskey and neutral spirits or of two or more straight whiskeys

blend·er (blen′dər) *n.* **1** a person or thing that blends ☆**2** an electrical appliance that can chop, cream, whip, mix, or liquefy foods

blending inheritance the blending of characteristics of the parents in the offspring, as in a pink flower that results from the mating of a red flower with a white one

Blen·heim (blen′əm) village in S Germany, in the state of Bavaria: site of a battle (1704) in the War of the Spanish Succession in which the English-Austrian army under Marlborough and Prince Eugene defeated the Franco-Bavarian forces

Blenheim spaniel ⟦after *Blenheim* Palace, seat of the Duke of Marlborough, where the dogs were bred⟧ a variety of toy spaniel that is white with reddish-brown spots

blen·ny (blen′ē) *n., pl.* **-nies** or **-ny** ⟦L *blennius* < Gr *blennos* < *blenna,* slime, mucus⟧ any of various small marine percoid fishes (esp. family Blenniidae) with a long, many-rayed dorsal fin and a tapering body covered with slime —**blen′ni·oid′** (-ē oid′) *adj.*

blent (blent) *vt., vi. archaic pt. & pp. of* BLEND

bleph·a·ri·tis (blef′ə rīt′is) *n.* ⟦< fol. + -ITIS⟧ inflammation of the eyelids

bleph·a·ro- (blef′ə rō′, -rə) ⟦< Gr *blepharon,* eyelid⟧ *combining form* eyelid, eyelids [*blepharoplasty*]: also, before a vowel, **blephar-**

bleph·a·ro·plas·ty (blef′ə rō′plas′tē) *n.* ⟦prec. + -PLASTY⟧ the surgical restructuring of an eyelid, as in the removal of puffy fat deposits

Blé·ri·ot (blā rē ō′, bler′ē-), **Louis** 1872-1936; Fr. aeronautical engineer & aviation pioneer

bles·bok (bles′bäk′) *n., pl.* **-bok′** or **-boks′** ⟦Afrik < *bles,* BLAZE² + *bok,* BUCK¹⟧ an antelope (*Damaliscus dorcas phillipsi*) of E South Africa, a subspecies of the bontebok, that has a large white mark on its face: also **bles′buck′** (-buk′)

bless (bles) *vt.* **blessed** or **blest, bless′ing** ⟦ME *blessen, bletsien* < OE *bletsian, bledsian* < *blod,* BLOOD: rite of consecration by sprinkling an altar with blood⟧ **1** to make or declare holy by a spoken formula or a sign; hallow; consecrate **2** to ask divine favor for [the minister *blessed* the congregation] **3** to favor or endow (*with*) [to be *blessed* with eloquence] **4** to make happy or prosperous; gladden [he *blessed* us with his leadership] **5** to think (oneself) happy; congratulate (oneself) **6** to praise or glorify [to *bless* the Lord] **7** to make the sign of the cross over or upon **8** to keep or protect from harm, evil, etc.: obsolete, except in prayers, exclamations, etc. —**bless me (**or **you, him,** etc.**)!** an exclamation of surprise, pleasure, dismay, etc. —**God bless!** may God bestow blessings on you

blessed (*for 1-2,* blest, *also* bles′id; *for 3-5,* bles′id, *also* blest) *adj.* **1** holy; sacred; consecrated **2** enjoying great happiness; blissful **3** of or in eternal bliss: a title applied to a person who has been beatified **4** bringing comfort or joy **5** confounded; cursed: an intensive —**the blessed** (*for 1,* blest *or* bles′id; *for 2,* bles′id, *also* blest) **1** people who are blessed **2** *Theol.* those dead whose souls are in heaven —**bless′ed·ly** *adv.* —**bless′ed·ness** *n.*

blessed event the birth of a child

Blessed Sacrament *R.C.Ch.* the Eucharist

Blessed Virgin the Virgin Mary

bless·ing (bles′iŋ) *n.* **1** the act or prayer of one who blesses; invocation or benediction **2** a grace said before or after eating **3** the gift of divine favor **4** good wishes or approval **5** anything that gives happiness or prevents misfortune; special benefit or favor

blest (blest) *vt. alt. pt. & pp. of* BLESS —*adj.* blessed

blet (blet) *n.* ⟦Fr *blet, blette,* overripe, soft⟧ decay in overripe fruit

bleth·er (bleth′ər) *n., vi., vt. Brit. var. of* BLATHER

bleu cheese (bloo͞) ⟦Fr *bleu,* BLUE⟧ BLUE CHEESE

blew (bloo͞) *vi., vt. pt. of* BLOW¹ & BLOW³

Bli·da (blē′dä′) city in NC Algeria

Bligh (blī), **William** 1754-1817; Eng. naval officer: commander of the *Bounty,* whose crew mutinied (1789)

blight (blīt) *n.* ⟦? akin to ME *blichening,* blight, rust (on grain) < *bliknen,* to lose color < ON *blikja,* turn pale: see BLEACH⟧ **1** any atmospheric or soil condition, parasite, or insect that kills, withers, or checks the growth of plants **2** any of several plant diseases, as rust, mildew, or smut **3** anything that destroys, prevents growth, or causes devaluation [slums are a *blight* on a city] **4** a person or thing that withers someone's hopes or ambitions **5** the condition or result of being blighted —*vt.* **1** to cause a blight in or on; wither **2** to destroy **3** to disappoint or frustrate —*vi.* to suffer blight

blight·ed (blīt′id) *adj.* **1** affected with a blight [a *blighted* crop] **2** in bad condition as a result of neglect; run-down; deteriorated [a *blighted* neighborhood]

blight·er (blīt′ər) *n.* **1** a person or thing that blights **2** [Brit. Informal] a mean or contemptible fellow

bli·mey (blī′mē) *interj.* ⟦contr. < (*God*) *blind me*⟧ [Brit.] used to express surprise, wonder, etc.

blimp (blimp) *n.* ⟦echoic of sound caused by thumping the airship bag with a finger: prob. coined (1915) by A. D. Cunningham, Brit Navy Air Force⟧ [Informal] **1** a nonrigid or semirigid airship **2** ⟦after Col. *Blimp,* creation of Sir David LOW⟧ a pompous, smug, highly conservative person ☆**3** [Informal] a very fat person: somewhat derisive or contemptuous —**blimp′ish** *adj.*

blind (blīnd) *adj.* ⟦ME & OE: see BLEND⟧ **1** without the power of sight; unable to see; sightless **2** of or for sightless persons **3** not able or willing to notice, understand, or judge **4** done without adequate directions or knowledge [a *blind* search] **5** having certain information concealed or withheld intentionally [a *blind* ad, a *blind* test] **6** disregarding evidence, sound logic, etc. [*blind* love, *blind* faith] **7** reckless; unreasonable **8** out of sight; hard to see; hidden [a *blind* driveway] **9** dense; impenetrable [a *blind* hedge] **10** closed at one end [a *blind* duct] **11** not controlled by intelligence [*blind* destiny] **12** *a)* insensible *b)* [Slang] drunk **13** illegible; indistinct [a *blind* letter] **14** not bearing flowers or fruit: said of an imperfectly developed plant **15** guided only by flight instruments, as in a storm [a *blind* landing] **16** *Archit.* having no opening [a *blind* wall] **17** *Bookbinding* designating stamping or tooling done without ink or foil —*vt.* **1** to make sightless **2** to make temporarily unable to see; dazzle **3** to deprive of the power of insight or judgment **4** to make dim; obscure **5** to outshine or eclipse **6** to hide or conceal —*n.* **1** anything that obscures or prevents sight **2** *a)* anything that keeps out light, as a window shade or shutter *b)* [*often pl.*] VENETIAN BLIND *c)* [*often pl.*] VERTICAL BLIND ☆**3** a place of concealment, as for a hunter; ambush **4** *a)* a person or thing used to deceive or mislead; decoy *b)* a person who, while appearing to act out of self-interest, really acts on behalf of another —*adv.* **1** blindly; specif., so as to be blind, insensible, etc. **2** recklessly **3** guided only by flight instruments [to fly *blind*] **4** sight unseen [to buy a thing *blind*] —**the blind** people who are blind —**blind′ly** *adv.* —**blind′ness** *n.*

blind alley **1** an alley or passage shut off at one end **2** any undertaking, idea, etc. that leads to nothing

blind carbon (copy) a carbon copy of a letter sent to someone other than the addressee, with no indication on the original letter that such a copy has been sent

☆**blind date** [Informal] **1** a DATE¹ (*n.* 6a) arranged for two persons who are strangers to each other **2** either person involved

blind·ers (blīn′dərz) *pl.n.* BLINKER (*n.* 2a): often used metaphorically

☆**blind·fish** (blīnd′fish′) *n., pl.* **-fish′** or **-fish′es** (see FISH) any of various small fishes with functionless eyes, found in underground streams, caves, etc.

blind·fold (-fōld′) *vt.* ⟦altered (infl. by FOLD¹) < ME *blindfeld,* struck blind, pp. of *blindfellen* < OE (*ge*)*blindfellian*: see BLIND + FELL²⟧ **1** to cover the eyes of with a cloth or bandage **2** to hinder the sight or understanding of —*n.* **1** a cloth used to cover the eyes **2** anything that hinders the sight or understanding —*adj.* **1** with the eyes covered **2** reckless; heedless —*adv.* **1** blindly **2** recklessly; heedlessly

blind gut **1** CECUM **2** any similar pouchlike cavity or section of the intestinal tract with only one opening, formed by surgery or disease

Blind·heim (blint′hīm′) *Ger. name for* BLENHEIM

blind·man's buff (blīnd′manz′) ⟦*buff* contr. < BUFFET[1]⟧ a game in which a blindfolded player has to catch and identify another player: also **blind′man's′ bluff′**

☆**blind pig** [Old Slang] SPEAK-EASY

☆**blind·side** (blīnd′sīd′) *vt.* **-sid′ed, -sid′ing 1** *Football* to hit or block (an opposing player) from his blind side **2** to assail (someone) from an unseen or unexpected direction

blind side the side opposite to the direction in which a person is looking

blind spot 1 the small area, insensitive to light, in the retina of the eye where the optic nerve enters **2** a portion of a field of vision that is obstructed to the viewer; specif., any area behind a vehicle that a driver cannot view with his or her rearview mirrors **3** a prejudice, or area of ignorance, that one has but is often unaware of **4** an area where radio reception is poor

☆**blind staggers** the staggers: see STAGGER (*n.* 3)

blind·sto·ry (blīnd′stôr′ē) *n., pl.* **-ries** *Archit.* **1** a windowless story **2** in Gothic churches, a gallery (triforium) without windows, above the main arches

☆**blind tiger** [Old Slang] SPEAK-EASY

blind trust an arrangement whereby a person, such as a public official, in an effort to avoid conflicts of interest, places certain personal assets under the control of an independent trustee with the provision that the person is to have no knowledge of how those assets are managed

blind·worm (-wurm′) *n.* a legless lizard (*Anguis fragilis*) of the Old World; slowworm: it has very small eyes and a snakelike body that is usually brownish

☆**bling** (bliŋ) *n.* ⟦orig. uncert.; prob. popularized through use in hip-hop music⟧ [Slang] **1** showy and expensive jewelry or other ostentatious accessories **2** flamboyant or ostentatious showiness; glitz Also **bling′-bling′**

blin·i (blin′ē) *pl.n., sing.* **blin** ⟦Russ *bliny*⟧ small, thin pancakes, commonly served with caviar and sour cream: cf. BLINTZ: also **blin′is** (-ēz)

blink (bliŋk) *vi.* ⟦ME *blenken, blenchen*: see BLENCH[2]⟧ **1** to close the eyelids and open them quickly one or more times, as either a reflex or a conscious act **2** to flash on and off; twinkle or glimmer **3** to look with eyes half-shut and winking, as in dazzling light **4** *a)* to ignore or overlook some fact or situation (with *at*) [to *blink* at a co-worker's mistake] *b)* to react with shock or astonishment (with *at*) [he didn't *blink* at the new car's sticker price] **5** [Informal] BACK DOWN (see phrase at BACK[1]) **6** [Obs.] to look with a glance —*vt.* **1** to wink (the eyes) rapidly **2** to cause (eyes, light, etc.) to wink or blink **3** to get rid of (tears, eye drops, etc.) by blinking: with *away* or *from* **4** to disregard deliberately (a fact or situation); evade awareness of **5** to signal (a message) by flashing a light, etc. —*n.* **1** a blinking of the eyes **2** a brief flash of light; twinkle or glimmer **3** [Chiefly Scot.] a quick look; glimpse **4** *short for: a)* ICEBLINK *b)* SNOWBLINK —*SYN.* WINK —☆**on the blink** [Slang] not working right; out of order

blink·er (-ər) *n.* ☆**1** *a)* a flashing warning light at traffic crossings *b)* a light for signaling messages in flashes **2** [*pl.*] *a)* two flaps on a bridle that keep the horse from seeing to the sides, esp. as worn by a racehorse that tends to shy *b)* a kind of goggles —*vt.* to put blinkers on

blink·ered (-ərd) *adj.* **1** fitted with blinkers: said of a horse **2** limited as a result of narrow-mindedness, delusion, etc.

☆**blintz** (blints) *n.* ⟦Yiddish *blintze* < Russ *blinec*, dim. of *blin*, pancake⟧ a thin pancake rolled with a filling of cottage cheese, fruit, etc.

blip (blip) *n.* ⟦echoic of a brief sound⟧ **1** a luminous image on an oscilloscope, as one on a radar screen showing the location of an aircraft, ship, etc. **2** a quick, sharp sound **3** a slight change or variation **4** a brief, temporary interruption —*vi.* **blipped, blip′ping** to make a blip or series of blips —*vt.* BLEEP

bliss (blis) *n.* ⟦ME *blisse* < OE *bliss, bliths*, joy < *blithe*, BLITHE⟧ **1** great joy or happiness **2** spiritual joy; heavenly rapture **3** any cause of bliss —☆*vi., vt.* [Slang] to experience or produce ecstasy or intense pleasure or satisfaction from or as if from a hallucinogenic drug or a mystical experience: usually with *out* —*SYN.* ECSTASY —**bliss′ful** *adj.* —**bliss′ful·ly** *adv.* —**bliss′ful·ness** *n.*

blis·ter (blis′tər) *n.* ⟦ME < Du *bluister* or OFr *blestre* < ?⟧ **1** a raised patch of skin, specif. of epidermis, filled with watery matter and caused by a burn, frostbite, rubbing, etc. **2** something used or applied to cause a blister **3** anything resembling a blister, as on a plant, a coat of paint, etc. **4** a bulging, bubblelike projection, usually transparent, used for observation, protection, etc. on an aircraft, train, car, etc. **5** a transparent, rigid shell, used to package, protect, and display an article of merchandise —*vt.* **1** to cause blisters to form on **2** to beat severely **3** to lash with words —*vi.* to have or form a blister or blisters —**blis′ter·y** *adj.*

blister beetle any of a family (Meloidae) of soft-bodied beetles, some of which are harmful to plants: the dried and ground bodies of the Spanish fly and certain other species yield a substance that is used medically as a vesicant

blister copper copper that is 96 to 99 percent pure, produced by smelting: it has a blistery surface caused by sulfur dioxide bubbles

blis·ter·ing (blis′tər iŋ) *adj.* **1** causing blisters **2** very hot [a *blistering* August afternoon] **3** extreme or intense [a *blistering* diatribe] **4** very fast [a *blistering* run]

blister pack a container for the protection and display of merchandise, consisting of a clear, rigid, bubblelike piece of plastic attached to a flat sheet of cardboard

☆**blister rust** a destructive disease of white pines, caused by a fungus (*Cronartium ribicola*) that produces orange-colored blisters on the bark and branch tips

blithe (blīth, blīth) *adj.* ⟦ME < OE; ult. < IE base **bhlei-*, to shine, gleam⟧ showing a cheerful, carefree disposition; lighthearted —**blithe′ly** *adv.* —**blithe′ness** *n.*

blith·er·ing (blith′ər iŋ) *adj.* ⟦*blither*, var. of BLATHER + -ING⟧ talking without sense; jabbering

blithe·some (blīth′səm, blīth′-) *adj.* blithe; lighthearted —**blithe′some·ly** *adv.* —**blithe′some·ness** *n.*

BLitt, BLit, B.Lit., *or* **B.Litt.** *abbrev.* ⟦L *Baccalaureus Lit(t)erarum*⟧ Bachelor of Letters (or Literature)

blitz (blits) *n.* ⟦< BLITZKRIEG⟧ **1** a sudden, destructive attack, as by aircraft or tanks **2** *a)* any sudden, overwhelming attack *b)* a concentrated effort, intensive campaign, etc. ☆**3** *Football* a sudden charge by a defensive backfield player through a gap in the line in an effort to tackle the opposing quarterback —*vt.* **1** to subject to a blitz; overwhelm and destroy ☆**2** *Football* to charge (the quarterback) in a blitz —☆*vi. Football* to make a blitz

blitzed (blitst) ☆*adj.* ⟦< prec.⟧ [Slang] drunk; intoxicated

blitz·krieg (blits′krēg′) *n.* ⟦Ger < *blitz*, lightning + *krieg*, war⟧ **1** sudden, swift, large-scale offensive warfare intended to win a quick victory **2** any sudden, overwhelming attack

☆**bliz·zard** (bliz′ərd) *n.* ⟦< ? dial. *bliz*, violent blow; ? akin to Ger *blitz*, lightning⟧ **1** a severe snowstorm characterized by cold temperatures and heavy drifting of snow **2** an overwhelming number or amount; deluge

blk *abbrev.* **1** black **2** block **3** bulk

BLM *abbrev.* Bureau of Land Management

bloat[1] (blōt) *adj.* ⟦ME *blout*, soft < ON *blautr*; ult. < IE base **bhel-*, to swell: see BALL[1]⟧ swollen or distended; puffed up — *vt., vi.* **1** to swell, as with water or air **2** to puff up, as with pride **3** to make or become overly large: often in the pp. [a *bloated* state budget] —*n.* ☆**1** a person or thing that has bloated ☆**2** *Vet.Med.* a gassy swelling of the abdomen usually caused by watery forage —**bloat′ed** *adj.*

bloat[2] (blōt) *vt.* ⟦ME *blote*, soft with moisture < ON *blautr*, soaked: see prec.⟧ to cure or preserve (herring, etc.) by soaking in salt water, smoking, and half-drying

bloat·er[1] (blōt′ər) *n.* ⟦< prec.⟧ a fat herring or mackerel that has been cured by bloating

bloat·er[2] (-ər) *n.* ⟦< BLOAT[1]⟧ a small freshwater trout (*Coregonus hoyi*) found esp. in the Great Lakes

blob (bläb) *n.* ⟦see BLEB⟧ **1** a drop or small lump of a thick, viscous substance [a *blob* of jelly] **2** a small spot or splash of color **3** something of vague or indefinite form [a hazy *blob* on the horizon] —*vt.* **blobbed, blob′bing** to splash or mark, as with blobs —**blob′by** *adj.* **-bi·er, -bi·est**

bloc (bläk) *n.* ⟦Fr & OFr < MDu *block*, log, BLOCK⟧ **1** an alliance, often temporary, of political parties in a legislature ☆**2** a group of legislators who, without regard to party affiliation, act together to advance some common interest of their constituents [the farm *bloc*] **3** a group of nations joined or acting together in mutual support

Bloch (bläk) **1 Ernest** 1880-1959; U.S. composer, born in Switzerland **2 Felix** 1905-83; U.S. physicist, born in Switzerland

block (bläk) *n.* ⟦ME *blokke* < OFr *bloc* & MDu *block* < IE **bhlugo-* < base **bhel-*, a thick plank, beam > BALK, Gr *phalanx*, L *fulcrum*⟧ **1** any large, solid piece of wood, stone, or metal, often with flat surfaces **2** a blocklike stand or platform on which hammering, chopping, etc. is done [a butcher's *block*, headsman's *block*] ☆**3** an auctioneer's platform **4** *a)* a mold upon which things are shaped, as hats *b)* the shape of a hat **5** anything that stops movement or progress; obstruction, obstacle, or hindrance **6** a pulley or system of pulleys in a frame, with a hook, loop, etc. for attachment **7** any solid piece of material used to strengthen or support **8** *a)* an oblong building unit of concrete, larger than a brick and usually not solid (in full **concrete block**) *b)* a similar unit of glass or other material *c)* such units collectively **9** a toy brick, typically cubic, of wood or plastic, and with numbers, letters, etc. displayed on the sides ☆**10** [Now Brit.] a large building with many units in it, or a group of buildings regarded as a unit ☆**11** *a)* an area bounded by streets or buildings on four sides; city square *b)* the distance along one side of such an area **12** any number of persons or things regarded as a unit [a *block* of tickets] **13** the metal casting that houses the cylinders of an internal-combustion engine; engine block **14** [Slang] a person's head **15** *Comput.* a unit of memory, consisting of one or more contiguous words, bytes, or records **16** *Med. a)* an interruption of normal function in a part of the body [heart *block*, kidney *block*] *b)* an interruption of the passage of impulses through a nerve by means of pressure or anesthetics **17** *Printing* a piece of wood, linoleum, etc. engraved with a design or picture **18** *a) Psychiatry* a sudden interruption in speech or thought processes, resulting from deep emotional conflict, repression, etc. *b)* any inability to perform as one normally can, that is attributed to an emotional cause [writer's *block*] **19** *Railroading* a length of track governed by signals: see BLOCK SYSTEM ☆**20** *Sports* an interruption, restraining, or thwarting of an opponent's play or movement **21** *Philately* a set of four or more unseparated stamps forming a rectangle **22** [*pl.*] *Track & Field* STARTING BLOCKS —*vt.* ⟦Fr *bloquer* < the n.⟧ **1** to impede the passage or progress of; obstruct **2** to blockade **3** to create difficulties for; stand in the way of; hinder **4** *a)* to shape or mold on or as on a block *b)* to stamp with a block **5** to form into blocks **6** to strengthen or support with blocks **7** to restrict or prohibit the use, conversion, or flow of (currency, assets, etc.) **8** to sketch or outline with little or no detail: often with *out* **9** *Games,*

Sports to hinder (an opponent or an opponent's play), whether legally or as a foul *[to* block *a linebacker, to* block *a shot]* **10** *Med.* to prevent the transmission of impulses in (a nerve), esp. by anesthetizing **11** *Theater* to plan or direct (the movements on stage of actors) ***—vi.*** **1** to have a mental block (*on*) ☆**2** *Sports* to block an opponent ***—adj.*** **1** made or formed in a block or blocks *[*block *coal]* **2** set out like or involving a city block **3** having no indentation in address, heading, or paragraphs **—SYN.** HINDER[1] **—block up** **1** to fill in (a passage, space, etc.) so as to obstruct **2** to elevate on blocks **—go to the block** **1** to be beheaded **2** to be up for sale in an auction **—**☆**have been around the block** [Slang] to have acquired much practical experience; specif., to be streetwise or sexually experienced **—knock someone's block off** [Slang] to give a beating to **—**☆**on the block** up for sale or auction **—out of the blocks** ⟦see *n.* 22⟧ [Informal] beginning or emerging, esp. in a competitive situation *[a company that is the first* out of the blocks *with a new technology]*

Block Island (bläk) ⟦after Adriaen *Block*, 17th-c. Du navigator who explored it⟧ island in S R.I., at the entrance to Long Island Sound

block·ade (blä kād′) ***n.*** ⟦BLOCK + -ADE⟧ **1** a shutting off of a port or region of a belligerent state by the troops or ships of the enemy in order to prevent passage in or out in time of war **2** any blocking action designed to isolate another nation and cut off communication and commerce with it **3** the force that maintains a blockade **4** any strategic barrier ***—vt.*** **-ad′ed, -ad′ing** to subject to a blockade **—**☆**run the blockade** to go past or through a blockade **—block·ad′er** ***n.***

☆**blockade runner** a ship or person that tries to go through or past a blockade

block·age (bläk′ij) ***n.*** **1** a blocking or being blocked **2** something that blocks, or obstructs; obstacle

block and tackle an arrangement of one or more pulley blocks, with rope or cables, providing significant mechanical advantage for pulling or hoisting large, heavy objects

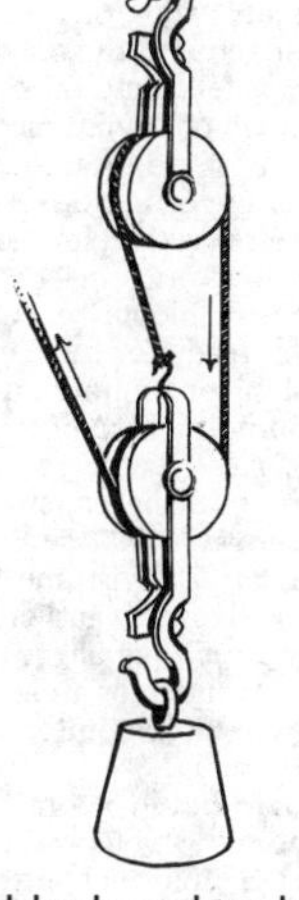

block and tackle

block association an association of residents of a small neighborhood, as a city block, formed for assisting one another, improving housing and living conditions, etc.

block·bust·er (bläk′bus′tər) ***n.*** ⟦BLOCK (*n.* 11*a*) + -BUSTER⟧ [Informal] **1** a large, aerial bomb that can demolish a large area ☆**2** a particularly powerful, forceful, or effective person or thing; specif., *a)* a film, novel, etc. that is a huge financial success, typically one that has been extensively publicized and expensively produced *b)* anything generating widespread excitement (often used attributively) *[a* blockbuster *trade between baseball teams]* ☆**3** a real-estate dealer who engages in blockbusting

☆**block·bust·ing** (-bus′tiŋ) ***n.*** [Informal] the practice of inducing homeowners in a particular neighborhood to sell their homes quickly, often at a loss, by creating the fear that actual or prospective purchases by members of a minority group will bring a loss of value

☆**block diagram** **1** *Geol.* a three-dimensional perspective representation of geologic or topographic features showing a surface area and usually two vertical cross sections **2** a kind of flowchart using geometric figures and connecting lines, as to describe the flow of data in a computer system

blocked (bläkt) *vt., vi. pt. & pp. of* BLOCK ***—adj.*** affected by a psychological BLOCK (*n.* 18)

block·er (bläk′ər) ***n.*** someone or something that blocks; specif., *a)* a drug or other substance that prevents certain biochemical reactions *[calcium* blocker*]* *b)* an offensive football player who tries to prevent the defensive players from reaching the ball carrier

block grant a grant of federal funds to a state or local government for discretionary use in funding a block of programs

block·head (bläk′hed′) ***n.*** ⟦BLOCK (*n.* 4*a*) + HEAD (*n.* 2*a*): from having no more intelligence inside than the hat mold⟧ a stupid person

block·house (-hous′) ***n.*** **1** [Historical] a strong wooden fort with a projecting second story and openings in the walls for the defenders to shoot from ☆**2** any building of squared timber or logs ☆**3** *Mil.* a small defensive structure of concrete ☆**4** a dome-shaped, heavily reinforced structure, with periscopes and detecting instruments, to protect observers of missile launchings, nuclear explosions, etc.

blockhouse (sense 1)

blocking capacitor *Elec.* a capacitor that blocks the passage of direct current but allows alternating current to pass

block·ish (-ish) ***adj.*** like a block; stupid; dull

block lava lava formed in sharp, angular, rough-surfaced blocks

block letter a printed or hand-printed letter that is simple in form, as sans-serif

block line a rope or cable used in a block and tackle

☆**block mountain** a mountain produced by faulting and the uplifting of large blocks of rock

☆**block party** a party organized by the residents of a city block or neighborhood, often one that has a street closed to traffic for the occasion

block plane a carpenter's small plane for cutting across the grain on board ends

block printing printing of designs, drawings, etc. from engraved blocks coated with ink or dyes

block system a system of dividing a railroad track into several sections (*blocks*) and regulating the trains by automatic signals (**block signals**) so that there is usually no more than one train in one section

block·work (bläk′wurk′) ***n.*** the use of concrete blocks in building

block·y (bläk′ē) ***adj.*** **block′i·er, block′i·est** **1** having contrasting blocks or patches **2** of or like a block; stocky; chunky

Bloem·fon·tein (blōōm′fän tān′) judicial capital of South Africa; capital of Orange Free State province

blog (bläg) ***n.*** ⟦(*we*)*blog* < WEB (*n.* 8) + LOG[1] (*n.* 6)⟧ a journal or diary written for public viewing on a website and consisting typically of personal reflections, commentary on current events, etc. arranged chronologically ***—vi.*** **blogged, blog′ging** to maintain or contribute to a blog **—blog′ger** ***n.***

blog·o·sphere (bläg′ə sfir′, -ō-) ***n.*** ⟦BLOG + *-osphere*, as in *stratosphere, ionosphere*, etc.⟧ internet blogs collectively, regarded as an informal social or journalistic community

Blois (blwȧ) city in central France, on the Loire River

Blok (blôk; *E* bläk), **A·lek·san·dr A·lek·san·dro·vich** (ä lyik sän′dr′ ä′lyik sän′drô vyich) 1880-1921; Russ. poet

bloke (blōk) ***n.*** ⟦< ? Shelta (Irish tinkers' argot)⟧ [Slang, Chiefly Brit.] a man; fellow; chap

blond (bländ) ***adj.*** ⟦LME *blounde* < MFr *blond* < OFr < ? Gmc **blund*⟧ **1** very light in color *[*blond *hair]* **2** having light-colored hair, often with fair skin and blue or gray eyes **3** finished in a light tone *[*blond *wood]* ***—n.*** a blond person **—blond′ness** ***n.***

blonde (bländ) ***adj.*** BLOND: esp. fem. form, but in Brit. usage preferred for all senses ***—n.*** **1** a blond woman or girl **2** a type of silk bobbin lace: so called because originally flaxen in color

☆**blond·ine** (blän dēn′) ***n.*** a preparation used to bleach hair blond ***—vt.*** **-ined′, -in′ing** to bleach (hair) with blondine

blood (blud) ***n.*** ⟦ME *blod, blode* < OE *blod*: see BLEED⟧ **1** the usually red fluid, consisting of plasma, red and white blood cells, etc., that circulates through the heart, arteries, and veins of vertebrates: blood is a tissue that carries oxygen, hormones, cell-building material, etc. to, and carbon dioxide and waste matter away from, the other tissues **2** a comparable fluid, usually colorless or bluish, in many invertebrate animals **3** the spilling of blood; murder **4** lifeblood **5** the sap or juice of a plant **6** passion, temperament, or disposition **7** parental heritage; family line; lineage **8** relationship by descent in the same family line; kinship **9** descent from nobility or royalty **10** descent from purebred stock **11** a dandy or fop **12** people, esp. youthful people *[new* blood *in an organization]* ☆**13** [Slang] *a)* a black person; esp., a black male *b)* a close male friend (used, often in direct address, esp. among black people) ***—vt.*** **1** to let (a hunting dog) taste, smell, or see the blood of its prey **2** to initiate (a hunter) by staining the hunter's face with blood of the prey **3** to initiate (a person) in any new experience **—bad blood** anger; hatred **—blood is thicker than water** family ties are stronger than others **—have (someone's) blood on one's hands** to be responsible for someone's death or misfortune **—in cold blood** **1** with cruelty; unfeelingly **2** dispassionately; deliberately **—make someone's blood boil** to make someone angry or resentful **—make someone's blood run cold** to frighten or terrify someone

Blood (blud) ***n., pl.*** **Blood** a member of a subgroup of the Blackfoot Indians

☆**blood bank** **1** a place where whole blood or blood plasma is drawn, typed, processed, and stored under refrigeration for future use **2** any reserve of blood for use in transfusion

blood bath a killing of many people; massacre

blood-brain barrier (blud′brān′) *Physiol.* the barrier created by the walls of the capillaries of the brain that prevents certain substances, as most proteins and drugs, from passing from the blood into the brain tissue and cerebrospinal fluid

blood brother **1** a brother by birth **2** a person bound to one by the ceremony of mingling his blood with one's own **—blood brotherhood**

blood count **1** a medical test to determine the number of red blood cells, white blood cells, or platelets in a given volume of blood **2** the number of blood cells or platelets so determined

blood·cur·dling (-kurd′liŋ) ***adj.*** frightening; terrifying

blood dop·ing (dō′piŋ) the practice of draining and freezing a portion of a person's blood and then restoring it just prior to intense physical effort, esp. to an athlete just before competition, so as to improve endurance by the sudden, temporary increase in red blood cells available for carrying oxygen

blood·ed (blud′id) ***adj.*** **1** having (a specified kind of) blood *[*warm-blooded*]* ☆**2** of fine stock or breed; pedigreed; thoroughbred; purebred

blood feud FEUD[1] (*n.* 1)

blood·fin (blud′fin′) ***n.*** a small, silvery South American fish (*Aphyocharax rubripinnis*, family Characidae) with red fins, often kept in aquariums

blood group **1** any of several groups, or systems, of agglutinogens present on the surface of normal red blood cells, such as the ABO SYSTEM **2** BLOOD TYPE

blood·guilt (-gilt′) *n.* the state or fact of being guilty of murder or bloodshed

blood heat the average normal temperature of the human body or blood: traditionally about 37°C (98.6°F) but now thought to be closer to *c.* 36.78°C (98.2°F)

blood·hound (blud′hound′) *n.* ⟦ME *blodhond:* see BLOOD (*n.* 10) & HOUND[1]⟧ **1** any of a breed of large dogs with a smooth coat, wrinkled face, drooping ears, and a keen sense of smell: bloodhounds are used in tracking escaped prisoners, fugitives, etc. **2** a person who pursues keenly or relentlessly

bloodhound

blood·i·ly (blud′′l ē) *adv.* **1** in a bloody manner **2** cruelly; savagely

blood·i·ness (blud′ē nis) *n.* the state of being bloody

blood·less (blud′lis) *adj.* **1** without blood **2** without bloodshed **3** not having enough blood; anemic or pale **4** having little energy or vitality **5** unfeeling; cruel —**blood′less·ly** *adv.* —**blood′less·ness** *n.*

blood·let·ting (-let′iŋ) *n.* ⟦ME *blodleting:* see BLOOD & LET[1]⟧ **1** the opening of a vein to remove blood; phlebotomy **2** bloodshed

blood libel any of various false stories, accusations, etc. that claim Jews engage in ritual murder, esp. the killing of gentile children for their blood: term used in reference to a long-standing tradition of such stories in the history of anti-Semitism

blood·line (-līn′) *n.* [*often pl.*] a direct line of descent, esp. of a domestic animal; pedigree; strain

blood·lust (-lust′) *n.* desire or enthusiasm for bloodshed

☆**blood·mo·bile** (-mō bēl′, -mə-) *n.* ⟦BLOOD + -MOBILE⟧ an automotive vehicle, typically a van or bus, equipped for collecting blood from donors for blood banks

blood money **1** money paid to a hired killer **2** money paid as compensation to the next of kin of a murdered person; wergeld **3** money gotten ruthlessly at the expense of others' lives or suffering

blood orange an orange having deep-red pulp and juice with a somewhat tart flavor

blood plasma the fluid part of blood, as distinguished from the corpuscles

blood platelet any of the minute, disklike, colorless elements of the blood that are essential for normal clotting

blood poisoning *nontechnical term for* SEPTICEMIA

blood pressure the pressure exerted by the blood against the inner walls of the blood vessels, esp. the arteries, or the heart: it varies with health, age, emotional tension, etc.

blood pudding a large sausage made of blood, esp. pig's blood, and suet, enclosed in a casing

blood-red (-red′) *adj.* **1** stained red with blood **2** having the deep-red color of blood

blood relation (*or* **relative**) a person related to another by birth rather than by marriage or adoption

blood·root (-ro͞ot′) *n.* ☆a spring-blooming, North American wildflower (*Sanguinaria canadensis*) of the poppy family, with a single white flower and lobed leaf arising from a rootstock that yields a toxic red juice

blood serum *see* SERUM (sense 1*b*)

blood·shed (-shed′) *n.* killing in a violent or bloody way

blood·shot (-shät′) *adj.* ⟦ME *blodshoten* < *blod,* BLOOD + pp. of *schoten,* SHOOT[1]⟧ red because the small blood vessels are swollen or broken: said of the eyes

blood sport any sport or contest, as fox-hunting or cockfighting, that involves killing

blood·stain (-stān′) *n.* a spot or streak of discoloration, as in fabric, caused by blood

blood·stained (-stānd′) *adj.* **1** soiled or discolored with blood **2** guilty of murder

blood·stock (-stäk′) *n.* ⟦< ? BLOOD(ED) (*adj.* 2) + STOCK⟧ Thoroughbred horses collectively

blood·stone (-stōn′) *n.* dark-green chalcedony spotted with red jasper, used as a semiprecious stone; heliotrope

blood·stream (-strēm′) *n.* the blood flowing through the circulatory system of a body

blood·suck·er (-suk′ər) *n.* **1** an animal that sucks blood, esp. a leech **2** a person who extorts or otherwise takes as much as possible from another —**blood′suck′ing** *adj., n.*

blood test **1** an examination of a small amount of a person's blood for diagnosis, classification, blood count, etc. **2** a test to detect the presence of blood that is not visible, as in feces

blood thinner any drug or substance that acts as an anticoagulant

blood·thirst·y (-thurs′tē) *adj.* eager to hurt or kill; murderous; very cruel —**blood′thirst′i·ly** *adv.* —**blood′thirst′i·ness** *n.*

☆**blood type** any of the divisions in a classification of blood based on the individual agglutinogens of a given blood group that are present in a person's red blood cells

☆**blood typing** the classification of human blood cells to determine compatible blood types as for transfusion or organ transplant

blood vessel any artery, vein, or capillary through which blood flows

blood·work (blud′wʉrk′) *n. Med.* any blood test or blood tests, esp. if used to find abnormalities that indicate the presence of a disease, infection, etc. or to discover a deficiency of an essential blood component: sometimes written **blood work**

blood·worm (-wʉrm′) *n.* **1** any of various small, red annelid worms, as the sludgeworm **2** the wormlike red larva of various midges, esp. of a genus (*Chironomus*) that lays its eggs in water

blood·wort (-wʉrt′) *n.* any of various American plants with red roots, stems, etc., as the bloodroot —*adj.* designating a family (Haemodoraceae, order Liliales) of monocotyledonous perennial plants, with red roots and juice

blood·y (blud′ē) *adj.* **blood′i·er, blood′i·est** ⟦ME *blodi* < OE *blodig*⟧ **1** of, like, or containing blood **2** covered or stained with blood; bleeding **3** involving bloodshed; with much killing or wounding **4** bloodthirsty; cruel **5** having the red color of blood **6** [Brit. Slang] cursed; damned —*adv.* [Brit. Slang] very —*vt.* **blood′ied, blood′y·ing** to cover or stain with blood

bloody mary ☆*pl.* **bloody marys** ⟦prob. < fol., in ref. to its color⟧ [*occas.* **B- M-**] a drink made of vodka, tomato juice, hot pepper sauce, etc.

Bloody Mary *name for* MARY I

blood·y-mind·ed (-mīn′did) *adj.* [Chiefly Brit.] **1** bloodthirsty; cruel **2** tending to be perverse or obstructive

bloody shirt something, as a political issue or historical event, that can be used to stir up outrage, partisan support, etc.: used chiefly in the phrase **wave the bloody shirt,** to stir up such outrage, support, etc.

☆**bloo·ey** (blo͞o′ē) *adj.* ⟦prob. echoic, as of an explosion⟧ [Slang] out of order: used chiefly in the phrase **go blooey,** to go out of order: also sp. **bloo′ie**

bloom[1] (blo͞om) *n.* ⟦ME *blom* < ON *blomi,* flowers and foliage on trees < IE **bhlō-,* var. of base **bhel-,* to swell, sprout > BLADE, BLEED, L *flos,* FLOWER, Gr *phyllon,* leaf⟧ **1** a flower; blossom **2** flowers collectively, as of a plant **3** the state or time of flowering **4** a state or time of best health or greatest beauty, vigor, or freshness; prime **5** a youthful, healthy glow (of cheeks, skin, etc.) **6** the grayish, powdery coating on various fruits, as the plum, grape, etc., and on some leaves **7** any similar coating, as on new coins **8** a mass of planktonic algae in lakes, ponds, or the sea, as in the development of red tides —*vi.* **1** to bear a flower or flowers; blossom **2** to reach a prime condition, as in health, vigor, beauty, perfection, etc.; flourish **3** to glow with color, health, etc. —*vt.* [Archaic] to cause to bloom, flower, or flourish

bloom[2] (blo͞om) *n.* ⟦OE *bloma,* lump of metal⟧ **1** a spongy mass of wrought iron ready for further working **2** a thick bar of iron or steel obtained by rolling or hammering an ingot

bloom·er[1] (blo͞om′ər) *n.* **1** a plant with reference to its blooming [*an early bloomer*] **2** a person in the bloom or prime of life **3** ⟦short for *blooming error*⟧ [Slang, Chiefly Brit.] a foolish or stupid mistake

☆**bloom·er**[2] (blo͞om′ər) *n.* ⟦after fol., who advocated the costume in the 1850s⟧ **1** a costume for women or girls, consisting of a short skirt and loose trousers gathered at the ankles: worn in the 1850s, but never popular **2** [*pl.*] *a)* baggy trousers gathered at the knee, formerly worn by girls and women for athletics *b)* an undergarment somewhat like this

Bloom·er (blo͞om′ər), **Amelia Jenks** (jeŋks) 1818-94; U.S. social reformer & feminist

Bloom·field (blo͞om′fēld′), **Leonard** 1887-1949; U.S. linguist

bloom·ing (blo͞om′iŋ) *adj.* **1** flowering; blossoming **2** thriving; flourishing **3** [Informal] utter; complete [*a blooming idiot*]

blooming mill *Metallurgy* a rolling mill for shaping ingots into blooms

Blooms·bur·y[1] (blo͞omz′bə rē, -brē; -ber′ē) *n.* a group of literary people and intellectuals residing in or associated with Bloomsbury in the early 20th cent., including Leonard and Virginia Woolf, Lytton Strachey, E. M. Forster, and John Maynard Keynes —*adj.* of or associated with this group [*the Bloomsbury set*]

Blooms·bur·y[2] (blo͞omz′bə rē, -brē; -ber′ē) district in central London, formerly an artistic and literary center

bloom·y (blo͞om′ē) *adj.* **1** full of blooms or blossoms **2** having a bloom (powdery coating)

☆**bloop** (blo͞op) *vt.* [Slang] *Baseball* **1** to hit (a pitched ball) as a blooper **2** to get (a hit) in this way

☆**bloop·er** (blo͞o′pər) *n.* ⟦*bloop,* echoic + -ER⟧ [Informal] **1** a foolish or stupid mistake; blunder **2** *Baseball* *a)* a ball batted in a low arc so that it falls between the infielders and outfielders, usually for a hit (also **bloop hit**) *b)* a ball that is pitched to the batter in a high lob: it is the basic pitch in slow-pitch softball **3** *Film, TV* an outtake containing a mistake or mishap, esp., one of a humorous series of such outtakes compiled for viewing

blos·som (bläs′əm) *n.* ⟦ME *blosme* < OE *blostma, blostm:* for IE base see BLOOM[1]⟧ **1** a flower or bloom, esp. of a fruit-bearing plant **2** a state or time of flowering —*vi.* **1** to have or open into blossoms; bloom **2** to begin to thrive or flourish; develop —**blos′som·y** *adj.*

blot[1] (blät) *n.* ⟦ME < ?⟧ **1** a spot or stain, esp. of ink **2** anything that spoils or mars, esp. by providing an unpleasant contrast [*that shack is a blot on the landscape*] **3** a moral stain; disgrace —*vt.* **blot′ted, blot′ting** **1** to make blots on; spot, stain, or blur **2** to stain (a reputation); disgrace **3** to erase or get rid of [*memories blotted from one's mind*] **4** to dry by soaking up the wet liquid, as with blotting paper —*vi.* **1** to make blots **2** to become blotted **3** to be absorbent —**blot out** **1** to darken or hide entirely; obscure **2** to kill or destroy

blot[2] (blät) *n.* ⟦prob. < MDu *bloot* or Dan *blot,* naked, uncovered⟧ **1** *Back-*

gammon an exposed piece, liable to capture **2** [Archaic] a weak point; fault; failing

blotch (bläch) ***n.*** ⟦? extension of BLOT[1]⟧ **1** a discolored patch or blemish on the skin **2** any large blot or stain —***vt.*** to cover or mark with blotches

blotch·y (bläch′ē) ***adj.*** **blotch′i·er, blotch′i·est 1** like a blotch **2** covered with blotches —**blotch′i·ness *n.***

blot·ter (blät′ər) ***n.*** **1** a piece of blotting paper ☆**2** a book for recording events as they occur [a police *blotter* is a record of arrests and charges]

blotting paper a thick, soft, absorbent paper used to dry a surface that has just been written on in ink

blot·to (blät′ō) ***adj.*** ⟦< ? BLOT[1]⟧ [Slang] very drunk; unconscious because of drinking too much —***SYN.*** DRUNK

blouse (blous, blouz) ***n.*** ⟦Fr, (18th c.) workman's smock < ?⟧ **1** a loose, smocklike outer garment of varying length, traditionally worn by certain European peasants and workmen **2** a loose garment similar to a shirt, worn esp. by women **3** the coat or jacket of a service uniform or dress uniform of the armed forces **4** a sailor's jumper — ***vi., vt.*** **bloused, blous′ing** to gather in and drape over loosely

blous·on (blo͞o′sän′; *Fr* blo͞o zōn′) ***adj.*** ⟦Fr, extended < prec.⟧ styled with a long, full, bloused top —***n.*** a blouson dress, dress top, etc.

☆**blo·vi·ate** (blō′vē āt′) ***vi.*** **-at′ed, -at′ing** ⟦< ?⟧ to speak at some length bombastically or rhetorically —**blo′vi·a′tion *n.***

blow[1] (blō) ***vi.*** **blew, blown** or [Dial.] **blowed, blow′ing** ⟦ME *blowen* < OE *blawan* < IE **bhlē-*: see BLAST⟧ **1** to move with some force: said of the wind or a current of air **2** to send forth air with or as with the mouth **3** to pant; be breathless **4** to make or give sound by blowing or being blown **5** to exhale air and condensed moisture from the lungs in a spout through the blowhole: said of whales **6** to be carried by the wind or a current of air [the paper *blew* away] **7** to be stormy **8** to burst or explode: often with *out* **9** to disrupt a circuit by melting: said of a FUSE[2] (***n.*** 3) **10** to lay eggs: said of flies **11** [Informal] to brag; boast ☆**12** [Slang] to go away; leave **13** [Slang] *Jazz* to improvise **14** [Slang] to cease functioning, esp. by overuse: said of an engine, etc. **15** ⟦see ***vt.*** 21⟧ [Slang] to be contemptible or very unsatisfying, as because of low quality: mildly vulgar [this concert *blows*] —***vt.*** **1** to cause air to come from (a bellows, blower, etc.) **2** to send out (breath, tobacco smoke, etc.) from the mouth **3** to force air onto, into, or through **4** to drive by blowing [dead leaves were *blown* by the wind] **5** *a)* to sound (a wind instrument) by blowing *b)* to make (a sound or signal) by blowing **6** to cool, warm, dry, or soothe by blowing on or toward **7** to shape or form (glass, soap bubbles, etc.) by blown air or gas **8** to clean or clear by blowing through [to *blow* one's nose] **9** to cause to burst or break by an explosion **10** to cause (a horse) to pant **11** to lay or deposit eggs in: said of flies **12** to melt (a fuse, etc.) **13** [Informal] to spend (money) freely or wastefully; squander **14** [Informal] to treat (*to* something) ☆**15** [Informal] to forget or fluff (one's lines) in a show ☆**16** [Slang] to go away from; leave [he *blew* town] ☆**17** [Slang] to bungle and fail in [we had our chance and *blew* it] **18** ***pp.*** **blowed** [Slang] to damn: used in euphemistic oaths **19** [Slang] to inhale (cocaine, marijuana, etc.) **20** [Slang] to reveal or disclose, esp. so as to compromise [they *blew* our cover] **21** [Vulgar Slang] to perform fellatio on **22** [Slang] to cause (an engine, transmission, etc.) to cease functioning, esp. by overuse —***n.*** **1** the act of blowing **2** a blast of air **3** *Metallurgy a)* the blast of air forced through molten metal to remove impurities *b)* the time or stage in metal refining in which the blast of air is forced through molten metal *c)* the amount of metal that is refined during this time **4** a strong wind; gale **5** a boast **6** [Slang] COCAINE ☆**7** [Slang] a pause, as to catch one's breath or relax; breather —**blow a kiss** to gesture affectionately to a person some distance away by puckering and smacking the lips or, esp., by kissing one's palm or fingers and then waving the hand in his or her direction [they *blew kisses* to their friends on shore] —**blow someone away** [Slang] **1** to kill by shooting **2** to overcome with emotion, surprise, etc. —☆**blow dead** [Slang] *Sports* to suspend (a play) by signaling with a whistle: said of a referee —**blow hot and cold** ⟦orig. with reference to the scent in hunting⟧ to be favorable toward something and then opposed to it; vacillate —☆**blow in** [Slang] to arrive —☆**blow someone's mind** [Slang] to astound, amaze, confuse, etc. —**blow off 1** to let steam or hot water out from (a boiler) **2** [Informal] to give vent to one's feelings, as by loud or long talking ☆**3** [Slang] to ignore, disregard, or reject —**blow out 1** to put out (a fire or flame) by blowing **2** to be put out in this way **3** to dispel (itself) after a time: said of a storm —**blow over 1** to move away, as rain clouds **2** to pass over or by; be forgotten —☆**blow one's stack** (or **top** or **lid**, etc.) [Slang] to lose one's temper; fly into a rage —**blow up 1** to fill with or as with air or gas **2** to burst or explode **3** to arise and become more intense, as a storm **4** to enlarge (a photograph) **5** to exaggerate (an incident, rumor, etc.) **6** [Informal] to lose one's temper or poise

blow[2] (blō) ***n.*** ⟦ME *blowe*, akin to Ger *bleuen*, Goth *bliggwan*, to strike⟧ **1** a hard hit or stroke with the fist, a weapon, etc. **2** a sudden attack or forcible effort **3** any sudden calamity or misfortune; shock —**at a** (or **one**) **blow** by one action —**come to blows** to begin fighting one another

blow[3] (blō) [Archaic] ***vi.*** **blew, blown, blow′ing** ⟦ME *blowen* < OE *blowan*; akin to Ger *blühen*: for IE base see BLOOM[1]⟧ to blossom —***n.*** **1** a mass of blossoms **2** the state of flowering

blow·back (blō′bak′) ***n.*** ⟦BLOW[1] + BACK[1] (***adv.***): in older sense of an explosion, expulsion of gas, etc., as from a damaged gun or backfiring engine⟧ the unforeseen negative consequences of an action or decision

☆**blow·by** (blō′bī′) ***n.*** in an internal-combustion engine, the escape of unburned gases past the piston rings into the crankcase —***adj.*** designating or of a device designed to eliminate such gases

☆**blow-by-blow** (blō′bī blō′) ***adj.*** ⟦used orig. with reference to an account of a boxing match⟧ told in great detail [a *blow-by-blow* account of a debate]

blow-dry (blō′drī′) ***vt.*** **-dried′, -dry′ing** to dry (wet hair) with an electric device (**blow-dryer**) that sends out a stream of heated air —***n.*** the act of blow-drying the hair

blow·er (blō′ər) ***n.*** **1** a person who blows **2** any device for producing a current of air or for blowing air into a room, from a furnace, etc. **3** [Brit. Slang] the telephone

☆**blow·fish** (blō′fish′) ***n., pl.*** **-fish′** or **-fish′es** (see FISH) PUFFER (sense 2)

blow·fly (-flī′) ***n., pl.*** **-flies′** ⟦BLOW[1] (***vi.*** 10) + FLY[2]⟧ any of a family (Calliphoridae) of dipterous flies that deposit eggs or maggots in carrion or meat, or in wounds or on the skin

☆**blow·gun** (-gun′) ***n.*** a long, tubelike weapon through which darts or pellets are blown

☆**blow·hard** (-härd′) ***n.*** [Slang] a loudly boastful person

blow·hole (-hōl′) ***n.*** **1** a nostril in the top of the head of whales and certain other cetaceans, through which they breathe **2** a hole through which gas or air can escape, esp. in lava **3** a hole in the ice to which seals, whales, etc. come to get air **4** a vertical opening or chimney in the roof of a sea cave through which air and water are forced by the action of the waves and the rising tides **5** a flaw in cast metal caused by an air or gas bubble

blow job [Vulgar Slang] an act or instance of fellatio: also **blow′job′ *n.***

blown[1] (blōn) ***vi., vt. pp. of*** BLOW[1] —***adj.*** **1** swollen or bloated **2** out of breath, as from exertion **3** flyblown **4** made by blowing or by using a blowpipe, etc.

blown[2] (blōn) ***vi. pp. of*** BLOW[3] —***adj.*** having bloomed; in full bloom: often FULL-BLOWN

blow·off (blō′ôf′) ***n.*** **1** a blowing off of steam, water, etc. **2** *a)* the loss of topsoil by wind erosion *b)* the soil lost by this process

blow·out (-out′) ***n.*** **1** the act or result of blowing out; specif., *a)* the bursting of a tire *b)* the melting of an electric fuse from too much current **2** [Slang] a party, banquet, or celebration **3** [Slang] an overwhelming victory or, esp. in sports, defeat

blow·pipe (-pīp′) ***n.*** **1** a small tube used to force air or gas into a flame to intensify and concentrate its heat **2** a metal tube used in glass blowing **3** BLOWGUN

blowpipe analysis a type of chemical analysis in which the intensely hot flame of a blowpipe vaporizes a mineral or other substance with a characteristically colored flame and a unique odor, so as to identify chemical elements in a substance

blows·y (blou′zē) ***adj.*** **blows′i·er, blows′i·est** ⟦< obs. *blouze*, wench⟧ **1** fat, ruddy, and coarse-looking **2** slovenly; frowzy **3** coarse and buxom: said of a woman

☆**blow·torch** (-tôrch′) ***n.*** **1** a small, liquid-fuel torch that shoots out a hot flame intensified by pressurized air: it is used to melt metal, remove old paint, etc. **2** a similar device using acetylene, propane, etc. as its fuel

blow·tube (-to͞ob′, -tyo͞ob′) ***n.*** **1** BLOWPIPE (sense 2) **2** BLOWGUN

blow·up (-up′) ***n.*** **1** an explosion ☆**2** an enlarged photograph **3** [Informal] an angry or hysterical outburst

blow·y (blō′ē) ***adj.*** **blow′i·er, blow′i·est** windy

blowz·y (blou′zē) ***adj.*** **blowz′i·er, blowz′i·est** ***alt. sp. of*** BLOWSY

BLS ***abbrev.*** **1** Bachelor of Library Science: also **B.L.S. 2** Bureau of Labor Statistics

BLT (bē′el′tē′) ***n.*** a bacon, lettuce, and tomato sandwich

blub (blub) ***vi.*** [Informal, Chiefly Brit.] BLUBBER[2]

blub·ber[1] (blub′ər) ***n.*** ⟦ME *blober*, a bubble; prob. of echoic orig.: see BLEB⟧ **1** the fat of the whale and other sea mammals, from which an oil is obtained **2** [Informal] unsightly fat on the human body

blub·ber[2] (blub′ər) ***vi.*** ⟦ME *bloberen*, to bubble: see prec.⟧ to weep loudly, like a child —***vt.*** **1** to say while blubbering **2** to wet, disfigure, or swell with weeping —***n.*** loud weeping; a blubbering —***adj.*** thick or swollen —***SYN.*** CRY

blub·ber·y (blub′ər ē) ***adj.*** **1** of or full of blubber **2** like blubber in appearance, texture, etc.; fat **3** swollen, as by blubbering

blu·cher (blo͞o′chər, -kər) ***n.*** ⟦after fol.⟧ **1** a heavy half boot **2** a kind of shoe in which the upper laps over the vamp, which is of one piece with the tongue

blucher

Blü·cher (blü′Hər; *E* blo͞o′chər, -kər), **Geb·hard Le·be·recht von** (gep′härt′ lā′bə reHt′ fôn) 1742-1819; Prus. field marshal: helped defeat Napoleon at Waterloo

bludg·eon (bluj′ən) ***n.*** ⟦? altered < MFr *bougeon*, dim. of *bouge*, a club⟧ a short club with a thick, heavy, or loaded end — ***vt., vi.*** **1** to strike with or as with a bludgeon **2** to bully or coerce

blue (blo͞o) ***adj.*** ⟦ME & OFr *bleu* < Frank **blao* < IE base **bhlē-wos*, light-colored, blue, blond, yellow > L *flavus*, yellow, Brythonic *blawr*, gray, OE *blǣwen*, blue, Ger *blau*⟧ **1** having the color of the clear sky or the deep sea **2** *a)* having a bluish cast or tinge *b)* having a grayish cast or tinge [a *blue* cat] **3** ⟦infl. by ME *blo* < ON *blā*, livid⟧ livid: said of the skin **4** sad and gloomy; depressed or depressing **5** balefully murky [the air was *blue* with oaths] **6** puritanical; rigorous **7** wearing blue garments

[*Blue* Nuns] 8 [Informal] indecent; risqué; suggestive 9 ⟦see BLUE STATE⟧ [Informal] Democratic —*n.* 1 the color of the clear sky or the deep sea; any color between green and violet in the spectrum 2 any blue pigment or dye 3 bluing 4 anything colored blue, as the third circle of an archer's target 5 *a)* blue clothing *b)* [*often* **B-**] a person or group wearing a blue uniform ☆*c)* [*often* **B-**] a Union soldier *d)* [*pl.*] a sailor's blue uniform 6 BLUESTOCKING ☆7 BLUEFISH 8 BLUELINE: *usually used in pl.* — *vt., vi.* **blued**, **blu′ing** or **blue′ing** to make or become blue —**out of the blue** as if from the sky; without being expected or foreseen —**the blue** 1 the sky 2 the sea

☆**blue baby** ⟦so called from the characteristic skin coloration⟧ a baby born with cyanosis as a result of pulmonary malfunction or of a heart malformation that allows venous blood to mix with arterial blood

Blue·beard (blo͞o′bird′) *n.* a character in an old folk tale who married and then murdered one wife after another

blue·bell (blo͞o′bel′) *n.* any of various plants (esp. of the genera *Campanula* and *Mertensia* of the bellflower and borage families) with blue, bell-shaped flowers, as the harebell or Virginia bluebell

blue·ber·ry (-ber′ē, -bər ē) *n., pl.* **-ries** ⟦ME *bloberi* < *blo,* blue + *berie,* BERRY⟧ ☆1 any of a genus (*Vaccinium*) of shrubs of the heath family, bearing small, edible, blue-black berries with tiny seeds and a whitish, waxy bloom: cf. HUCKLEBERRY ☆2 any of these berries

☆**blue·bill** (-bil′) *n.* any of various American ducks with bluish bills; esp., the scaup

blue·bird (-burd′) *n.* ☆any of a genus (*Sialia*) of small North American thrushes: the male usually has a blue or bluish back and an orange or reddish breast

blue blood ⟦transl. of Sp *sangre azul*, prob. referring to the blue veins easily visible against the pale skin of Castilian aristocrats who had not intermarried with darker-skinned people⟧ 1 descent from nobility 2 a person of such descent; aristocrat: also written **blue′blood′** *n.* —**blue′-blood′ed** *adj.*

blue·bon·net (-bän′it) *n.* 1 a broad, flat cap of blue woolen cloth, formerly worn in Scotland 2 [Archaic] a Scotsman 3 any of various blue-flowered lupines (esp. *Lupinus subcarnosus*) common in the SW U.S. 4 a cornflower with blue blossoms

blue book 1 [*also* **B- B-**] an official government report or registry, often having a blue cover ☆2 a book listing people who are socially prominent ☆3 a blank booklet with a blue paper cover, in which students can write examination answers: also **blue′book′** *n.* ☆4 ⟦< *Kelley Blue Book*, trademark for automotive price guides⟧ a book, online guide, etc. listing market values of used goods, collectibles, etc., esp. one listing such values of used vehicles

blue·bot·tle (-bät′'l) *n.* 1 any of various plants with blue, bottle-shaped flowers, as the cornflower, grape hyacinth, or closed gentian 2 any of a genus (*Calliphora*) of metallic-blue blowflies

blue cheese a strong cheese veined with bluish streaks produced by BLUE MOLD, similar to Roquefort but usually made of cow's milk

☆**blue-chip** (-chip′) *adj.* ⟦from the high-value *blue chips* used in poker⟧ 1 designating or of the high-quality stock of certain large, well-established companies with a history of financial stability, consistent profitability, etc. 2 [Informal] excellent, valuable, etc.

blue-chip·per (blo͞o′chip′ər) *n.* [Informal] a person or thing regarded as among the very best of its kind; specif., a recruited or drafted athlete regarded as an elite prospect

blue·coat (-kōt′) *n.* a person wearing a blue coat or uniform; specif., ☆*a)* a U.S. soldier of the 19th cent. ☆*b)* a policeman

☆**blue-col·lar** (-käl′ər) *adj.* ⟦from the traditional color of work shirts⟧ designating or of industrial workers, often, specif., the semiskilled or unskilled

☆**blue crab** any of a genus (*Callinectes*) of crabs, esp. a blue-legged, edible swimming species (*C. sapidus*) of the Atlantic coast of North America

☆**Blue Cross** *service mark for* a nonprofit health insurance organization offering hospitalization and medical benefits to subscribers, esp. to groups of employees and their families

☆**blue-curls** (-kurlz′) *n.* any of a genus (*Trichostema*) of plants of the mint family, with downy, narrow leaves and blue flowers: also **blue curls**

blue devils 1 delirium tremens or its hallucinations 2 a depressed feeling; the blues

☆**blue-eyed grass** (-īd′) any of a genus (*Sisyrinchium*) of small, grasslike plants of the iris family, with flat blue, blue and yellow, or white flowers

blue·fin (tuna) (blo͞o′fin′) the largest tuna (*Thunnus thynnus*): it has bright red flesh and is important as a game and food fish

☆**blue·fish** (-fish′) *n., pl.* **-fish′** or **-fish′es** (see FISH) 1 an important commercial food fish (*Pomatomus saltatrix*) of a bluish color, common along the Atlantic coast of North America: the only member of a family (Pomatomidae) of percoid fishes 2 any of various other bluish fishes

blue flag ☆any of several species of iris with blue flowers

☆**blue flu** ⟦so named from the traditional color of police uniforms⟧ a sickout, esp. by policemen

blue fox 1 *a)* the arctic fox during its smoky-gray color phase *b)* a mutant of the arctic fox having a smoky-gray cast at all seasons 2 fur from such foxes

☆**blue·gill** (-gil′) *n.* a freshwater sunfish (*Lepomis macrochirus*) of a bluish color

☆**blue·grass** (-gras′) *n.* 1 any of a large genus (*Poa*) of temperate and arctic forage grasses characterized by a bluish-green color 2 ⟦orig. in name of a band led by B. Monroe (*c.* 1945)⟧ a kind of Southern string-band music characterized by bluesy harmonies, rapid tempos, and an overall high-pitched vocal and instrumental sound

Bluegrass Country (*or* Region) region in central Ky. where there is much bluegrass: also called **the Bluegrass**

blue-green algae (-grēn′) any of a division (Cyanophycota) of photosynthetic monerans, microorganisms that contain a blue pigment which obscures the chlorophyll; cyanobacteria

blue gum a large evergreen tree (*Eucalyptus globulus*) of the myrtle family, native to Australia, having smooth, deciduous bark and aromatic leaves: grown extensively in California

☆**blue·hearts** (-härts′) *n., pl.* **-hearts′** a hairy, purple-flowered perennial plant (*Buchnera americana*) of the figwort family, found in the S U.S.

blue helmets ⟦so called from the color of their headgear⟧ [Informal] armed troops under the sponsorship of the United Nations, used for peacekeeping

blue·ing (-iŋ) *n. alt. sp. of* BLUING

blue·ish (-ish) *adj. alt. sp. of* BLUISH

blue·jack (-jak′) *n.* a small oak (*Quercus incana*) of the S U.S.

blue·jack·et (-jak′it) *n.* an enlisted person in the navy

☆**blue jay** a common, crested North American jay (*Cyanocitta cristata*) with a blue upper body and head: sometimes **blue′jay′** *n.*

blue·jeans (blo͞o′jēnz′) *pl.n.* jeans made of blue denim: also **blue jeans**

☆**blue law** ⟦said to be so named because orig. printed on blue paper⟧ 1 any of the strict puritanical laws prevalent in colonial New England 2 a law prohibiting entertainment, business, etc. on Sunday

blue·line (blo͞o′līn′) *n.* ⟦so called from the color of the image thus produced⟧ *Printing* a final proof made on photosensitive paper from negatives used in offset printing: also **blueline print**

blue line either of the two blue lines, parallel to the goal lines, that divide an ice hockey rink into three zones: cf. RED LINE

blue mold any of various species of a fungus (genus *Penicillium*) that produce bluish masses of spores: some species yield penicillin and some are used to ripen certain cheeses

blue moon a very long time: chiefly in the phrase **once in a blue moon,** very seldom; almost never: so called from a rare atmospheric condition in which layers of smoke, dust, etc., as from forest fires or volcanoes, cause the surface of the moon to look blue

Blue Mountains ⟦from their bluish appearance at a distance⟧ heavily forested mountain range of NE Oreg. & SE Wash.: highest peak, 9,105 ft (2,775 m)

Blue Nile *see* NILE

blue·nose (-nōz′) *n.* ⟦prob. after BLUE LAW, in reference to Puritan attitudes⟧ [Informal] ☆1 a puritanical person who tries to impose a strict moral code on others 2 ⟦orig. used of a potato with a bluish skin, grown in Nova Scotia; later used of the growers⟧ [**B-**] a Nova Scotian

blue note *Jazz* a note played slightly flat, esp. the third or seventh note of a major scale

blue-pen·cil (-pen′səl) *vt.* **-ciled** or **-cilled**, **-cil·ing** or **-cil·ling** to edit, cross out, or correct with or as with a blue pencil

blue peter ⟦prob. < *blue repeater,* signal flag used in Brit Navy⟧ a blue signal flag with a white square in the center, flown by a merchant ship to show it is ready to sail

☆**blue-plate special** (-plāt′) an inexpensive restaurant meal served at a fixed price on a large plate, traditionally blue

☆**blue·point** (-point′) *n.* ⟦after *Blue Point*, Long Island, near which beds of such oysters were orig. located⟧ a small oyster, usually eaten raw

blue·print (-print′) *n.* 1 a photographic reproduction in white on a blue background, as of architectural or engineering plans 2 any exact or detailed plan or outline —*vt.* to make a blueprint of

☆**blue racer** any of various long, bluish North American varieties of blacksnake that can move very rapidly

blue ribbon 1 the blue silk ribbon of the Order of the Garter 2 a blue ribbon awarded as first prize in a competition 3 first prize in a competition

blue-rib·bon (-rib′ən) *adj.* 1 [Informal] preeminent or outstanding of its kind ☆2 designating or of a panel made up of persons specially selected as for their expertise

Blue Ridge Mountains ⟦from their bluish appearance at a distance⟧ easternmost range of the Appalachians, extending from S Pa. to N Ga.: see BLACK MOUNTAINS

☆**blues** (blo͞oz) *pl.n.* ⟦short for BLUE DEVILS⟧ [*with sing. or pl. v., except 4, always with sing. v.*] 1 [Informal] a depressed, unhappy feeling: used with *the* 2 black folk music characterized by minor harmonies, a typically slow tempo, and melancholy words: often used with *the* 3 the form of jazz and popular music that evolved from this: often used with *the* 4 a song or composition in this style

blue·shift (blo͞o′shift′) *n. Astron.* the shift of spectral lines toward the shorter wavelengths and higher frequencies at the blue end of the spectrum of a luminous celestial body, indicating that the light source is moving rapidly toward the observer: cf. REDSHIFT: also **blue shift** —**blue′shift′ed** *adj.*

☆**blue-sky** (-skī′) *adj.* 1 ⟦see fol.⟧ of no value; worthless 2 ⟦prob. infl. by *out of a clear blue sky* (see phrase at SKY)⟧ *a)* taking an unrestrained approach to a problem, as in an attempt to be innovative [*a blue-sky* research team] *b)* resulting from or characterized by such an approach [*a blue-sky* scenario]

☆**blue-sky law** ⟦said to be so named from the comment made by a proponent of the first such law that certain business groups were trying to "capitalize the blue skies"⟧ [Informal] a law regulating the sale of stocks, bonds, etc., for the protection of the public from fraud

blues·man (blo͞oz′man′) ***n.***, *pl.* **-men′** (-men′) a blues musician, esp. a male one: see BLUES (sense 2)

blue spruce **1** any of several varieties of a North American spruce (*Picea pungens*) having sharply pointed, bluish-green needles: often grown as an ornamental **2** the wood of such a tree

blue state ⟦from the media's use, on maps of the states, of the color blue to designate "Democratic" and red for "Republican" in reporting on the 2004 U.S. presidential election campaign⟧ a state whose voters chose predominantly the Democratic candidate in the most recent presidential election: cf. RED STATE —**blue stat′er**

☆**blue·stem** (blo͞o′stem′) ***n.*** any of various tufted grasses (genus *Andropogon*) native to the U.S. and used for hay and forage

blue·stock·ing (-stäk′iŋ) ***n.*** ⟦from the unconventional blue (instead of black) stockings worn by Benjamin Stillingfleet at literary meetings in the home of Mrs. E. R. Montagu in London in the 1750s⟧ a learned, bookish, or pedantic woman

blue·stone (-stōn′) ***n.*** ☆**1** a blue-gray sandstone that is easily split into thin slabs, used as flagstone **2** COPPER SULFATE **3** CHALCANTHITE

☆**blue streak** [Informal] anything regarded as like a streak of lightning in speed, vividness, etc. —**talk a blue streak** to talk much and rapidly

blues·y (blo͞oz′ē) ***adj.*** **-i·er**, **-i·est** characterized by the qualities of blues music; specif., melancholy, soulful, etc.

blu·et (blo͞o′it) ***n.*** ⟦Fr *bleuet,* dim. of *bleu,* BLUE⟧ ☆a small plant (*Houstonia caerulea*) of the madder family, having little, pale-blue, four-lobed flowers

blue vitriol **1** CHALCANTHITE **2** COPPER SULFATE

blue·weed (-wēd′) ***n.*** a bristly weed (*Echium vulgare*) of the borage family with blue flowers and pink buds

blue whale a rorqual (*Balaenoptera musculus*) with a blue-gray back: the largest animal that has ever lived, reaching a length of over 30 m (100 ft) and weighing up to 136,000 kg (*c.* 150 tons)

☆**blue-winged teal** (-wiŋd′) a small North American duck (*Anas discors*) found on ponds and rivers

☆**bluff**[1] (bluf) ***vt., vi.*** ⟦17th c.: prob. < Du *bluffen,* to brag, boast or *verbluffen,* to baffle, mislead⟧ **1** to mislead or seek to mislead (a person) by a false, bold front **2** to frighten (a person) by threats not intended to be carried out **3** to manage to get (one's way) by bluffing **4** *Poker* to try to mislead (other players) by betting on one's hand when one knows or believes it is not the best hand —***n.*** **1** the act or practice of bluffing **2** a person who bluffs: usually *bluffer* —**bluff′er** ***n.***

bluff[2] (bluf) ***adj.*** ⟦orig. a naut. term, prob. < Du *blaf,* flat, broad⟧ **1** having, or ascending steeply with, a broad, flat front **2** having a rough and frank but affable manner —☆***n.*** a high, steep, broad-faced bank or cliff —***SYN.*** BLUNT —**bluff′ly** ***adv.*** —**bluff′ness** ***n.***

☆**blu·ing** (blo͞o′iŋ) ***n.*** a blue liquid, powder, etc. used in rinsing white fabrics to prevent yellowing

blu·ish (-ish) ***adj.*** somewhat blue

Blum (blo͞om), **Lé·on** (lā ōn′) 1872-1950; Fr. socialist statesman

blun·der (blun′dər) ***vi.*** ⟦ME *blunderen,* freq. < ON *blunda,* to shut the eyes, akin to Swed dial. *blundra,* to do blindly < IE base **bhlendh-*: see BLEND⟧ **1** to move clumsily or carelessly; flounder; stumble **2** to make a foolish or stupid mistake —***vt.*** **1** to say stupidly, clumsily, or confusedly; blurt: often with *out* **2** to do clumsily or poorly; bungle —***n.*** a foolish or stupid mistake —***SYN.*** ERROR —**blun′der·er** ***n.*** —**blun′der·ing·ly** ***adv.***

blun·der·buss (-bus′) ***n.*** ⟦Du *donderbus* < *donder,* THUNDER + *bus,* gun (orig., box or tube): altered by assoc. with prec.⟧ **1** [Historical] a kind of musket with a short barrel, large bore, and a broad, flaring muzzle, accurate only at close range **2** a person who blunders

blunderbuss

blunge (blunj) ***vt.*** **blunged**, **blung′ing** ⟦< ? PLUNGE⟧ *Ceramics* to mix (clay) with water —**blung′er** ***n.***

blunt (blunt) ***adj.*** ⟦ME < ?⟧ **1** slow to perceive, feel, or understand; dull **2** having a dull edge or point; not sharp **3** plain-spoken and abrupt —***vt.*** **1** to make (an edge or point) dull **2** to make dull or insensitive **3** to make less effective —***vi.*** to develop a dull edge or point —***n.*** ☆[Slang] a marijuana cigarette, specif. one made by putting marijuana into the wrapper of a hollowed-out cigar —**blunt′ly** ***adv.*** —**blunt′ness** ***n.***

SYN.—**blunt** implies a candor and tactlessness that show little regard for another's feelings [*"You're a fool," was his blunt reply*]; **bluff** suggests a coarse heartiness of manner and a good nature that causes the candor to seem inoffensive [*a bluff old gardener*]; **brusque** implies apparent rudeness, as evidenced by abruptness of speech or behavior [*a brusque rejection*]; **curt** suggests a terseness of expression that implies a lack of tact or courtesy [*a curt dismissal*]; **gruff** suggests bad temper and roughness of speech and manner, connoting, in addition, a harshness or throatiness in utterance [*a gruff sergeant*] See also **dull** —***ANT.*** **suave, tactful**

blur (blur) ***vt., vi.*** **blurred**, **blur′ring** ⟦16th c.; ? akin to BLEAR⟧ **1** to smear or stain without obliterating; blot; smudge **2** to make or become hazy or indistinct in outline or shape **3** to make or become dim or dull —***n.*** **1** the state of being blurred **2** an obscuring stain or blot **3** anything indistinct or hazy to the sight or the mind **4** [Archaic] a moral stain —**blur′ry** ***adj.*** **blur′ri·er**, **blur′ri·est** —**blur′ri·ness** ***n.***

☆**blurb** (blurb) ***n.*** ⟦coined (*c.* 1907) by Gelett BURGESS, for "self-praise, to make a noise like a publisher"⟧ a brief comment or quotation describing and, typically, praising a book, movie, etc.: blurbs appear in advertisements, on a package or book cover, etc. —***vi.*** [Informal] to state in a blurb

blurt (blurt) ***vt.*** ⟦16th-17th c.; prob. echoic⟧ to say suddenly, without stopping to think: often with *out*

blush (blush) ***vi.*** ⟦ME *blushen,* to shine brightly, blush, glance < OE *blyscan;* akin to *blyse,* torch < IE **bhles-,* shine > BLAZE[1]⟧ **1** to become red in the face from shame, embarrassment, or confusion **2** to be ashamed or embarrassed: usually with *at* or *for* **3** to be or become rosy —***vt.*** **1** to reveal by blushing **2** to redden —***n.*** **1** a reddening of the face, as from shame **2** a rosy color [*the blush of youth*] **3** any of various cosmetic powders, creams, etc., traditionally pink or reddish, applied to the face, esp. the cheeks, to give added color —***adj.*** rosy [*blush*-pink] —**at first blush** ⟦orig. ME sense⟧ at first sight; without further consideration —**blush′ful** ***adj.***

blush·er (blush′ər) ***n.*** **1** a person who blushes, esp. one who blushes readily **2** BLUSH (***n.*** 3) **3** a type of short bridal veil, typically of tulle, worn over the face

blush wine ⟦so named from its color⟧ any of certain wines similar in style to dry white wine although slightly pink in color: made like rosé from red-wine grapes, and often named by the grape's name preceded by "white," as *white zinfandel*

blus·ter (blus′tər) ***vi.*** ⟦ME *blustren,* to blow violently < or akin to LowG *blüstern, blistern:* for IE base see FLUCTUATE⟧ **1** to blow stormily: said of wind **2** to speak or conduct oneself in a noisy, swaggering, or bullying manner —***vt.*** **1** to force by blustering; bully **2** to say noisily and aggressively —***n.*** **1** stormy blowing or noisy commotion **2** noisy swaggering or bullying talk —**blus′ter·er** ***n.*** —**blus′ter·ing·ly** ***adv.*** —**blus′ter·y** ***adj.***, **blus′ter·ous**

Blvd *abbrev.* Boulevard

B lymphocyte B CELL

bm *abbrev.* board measure

BM *abbrev.* **1** beam **2** bench mark **3** [Informal] bowel movement **4** British Museum

BMI *abbrev.* BODY MASS INDEX

BMOC *abbrev.* [Slang] big man on campus

BMR *abbrev.* basal metabolism rate

BMus or **B.Mus.** *abbrev.* Bachelor of Music

BMV *abbrev.* Bureau of Motor Vehicles

bn *abbrev.* **1** battalion **2** billion

Bn *abbrev.* Baron

B.N. or **BN** *abbrev.* Bachelor of Nursing

B'nai B'rith (b'nā′ brith′) ⟦Heb, sons of the covenant: see BRITH MILAH⟧ a Jewish organization, founded in 1843, that supports cultural and educational programs, provides services, and opposes discrimination and anti-Semitism

b'nai mitz·vah (b'nā′ mits′və) ⟦Heb, lit., sons of the commandment: see prec. & BAR MITZVAH⟧ **1** a BAR MITZVAH or a BAT MITZVAH **2** bar mitzvahs and bat mitzvahs collectively

bo *abbrev.* **1** back order **2** bad order **3** buyer's option

BO *abbrev.* **1** [Informal] body odor **2** box office **3** branch office

B/O or **B/o** *abbrev. Bookkeeping* brought over

bo·a (bō′ə) ***n.*** ⟦ModL < L, a large water serpent⟧ **1** any of a number of tropical and subtropical, nonvenomous constrictor snakes (family Boidae) that use their powerful coils to squeeze their prey to cause death by suffocation, as the anaconda or boa constrictor **2** a woman's long scarf, as of fur or feathers, worn around the neck or shoulders

Bo·ab·dil (bō′əb dēl′) (Ar. name *Abu-Abdullah;* ruled as *Mohammed XI*) died 1538; last Moorish king of Granada

boa constrictor a large tropical American boa (*Boa constrictor*), pale brown with dark crosswise bars

Bo·ad·i·cea (bō′ad ə sē′ə) *var. of* BOUDICCA

Bo·a·ner·ges (bō′ə nur′jēz′) ***n.*** ⟦LL(Ec) < Gr(Ec) *boanerges;* prob. ult. < Heb *b'nāi regesh,* sons of wrath: interpreted in Gr as "sons of thunder"⟧ *Bible* the Apostles John and James: Mark 3:17: an epithet used by Jesus

boar (bôr) ***n.***, *pl.* **boars** or **boar** ⟦ME *bor* < OE *bar;* akin to Ger (dial.) *bär,* Du *beer:* only in WGmc⟧ **1** a mature uncastrated male pig **2** WILD BOAR

board (bôrd) ***n.*** ⟦ME & OE *bord,* a plank, flat surface (nautical senses via OFr *bord,* side of a ship < Frank **bord,* akin to OE *bord*) < IE **bhrdho-,* board < **bheredh-* < base **bher-,* to cut⟧ **1** a long, broad, flat piece of sawed wood ready for use; thin plank **2** a flat piece of wood or similar material, often rectangular, for some special use [*a checkerboard,* bulletin *board,* ironing *board,* diving *board*] **3** *a)* any of various construction materials manufactured in thin, flat, rectangular sheets [*fiberboard*] *b)* pasteboard or stiff paper, often used for book covers **4** *a)* a table for meals, esp. when spread with food *b)* food served at a table; esp., meals provided regularly for pay (see also ROOM AND BOARD) **5** [Archaic] a council table **6** a group of persons who manage or control a business, school system, etc.; council [*a board of trade, a board of education*] ☆**7** *a)* a posted or printed list of the stocks sold and their prices, on a particular stock exchange *b)* the stock exchange listing these stocks **8** the side of a ship: usually in compounds [*overboard*] **9** a rim, border, or coast: now only in *seaboard* ☆**10** [*pl.*] *Basketball a)* the backboards, esp. as the source of rebounds *b)* rebounds **11** [*also* **B-**] [*pl.*] *Educ. a)* a qualifying examination, esp. one for admission to an academic program [*college boards*] *b)* one's score on such an examination **12** *Electronics* CIRCUIT BOARD **13** [*pl.*] *Ice Hockey* the wooden or fiberglass wall surrounding the rink **14** *Naut.* the distance covered in one tack when sailing into the wind —*vt.* **1** to cover or close (*up*) with boards **2** to provide with meals, or room and meals, regularly for pay **3** to house (a person) where board is supplied **4** to come alongside (a ship), esp. with hostile purpose **5** to come over the rail and onto the deck of (a ship) ☆**6** to get on (a train, bus, airplane, etc.) —*vi.* **1** to receive meals, or room and meals, regularly for pay ☆**2** to get on a train, bus, airplane, etc. —☆**across the board** *see* ACROSS-THE-BOARD —**go by the board 1** to fall or be swept overboard **2** to be gotten rid of, lost, ruined, etc. —**on board 1** on, in, or into a ship ☆**2** on, in, or into an aircraft, bus, etc. **3** [Informal] *a)* in or into a group as a member, participant, employee, etc. *b)* in or into agreement or a spirit of cooperation with the viewpoint, plan, etc. of others [executives getting *on board* with the company's new business strategy] —**the boards** the stage (of a theater)

board·er (bôr′dər) *n.* **1** a person who regularly gets meals, or room and meals, at another's home for pay **2** a person who boards a ship, aircraft, etc., esp. one of the crew detailed to board a hostile ship

☆**board foot** *pl.* **board feet** a unit of linear measure of lumber, equal to a board one foot square and one inch thick

board game any of various games played by moving pieces on a board, as chess or backgammon

board·ing (bôr′diŋ) *n.* **1** a structure or covering of boards **2** boards collectively; light timber **3** the act of going on board a ship, aircraft, bus, etc. —*adj.* of or for boarding [a *boarding* pass]

board·ing·house (-hous′) *n.* a house where meals, or room and meals, can be had for pay: also written **boarding house**

boarding school a school providing lodging and meals for the pupils: cf. DAY SCHOOL

☆**board measure** measurement of lumber in board feet

board of education an elected or appointed body at the local or state level that supervises a given school system

board of health a local government agency that supervises public health

board of trade ☆**1** CHAMBER OF COMMERCE **2** [**B- of T-**] a British governmental department supervising commerce and industry **3** a commodities exchange dealing in grain, etc.

☆**board·room** (bôrd′ro͞om′) *n.* a room in which a board of administrators or directors regularly holds meetings

☆**board rule** a measuring device with a graduated scale for finding out quickly how many board feet there are in a quantity of lumber

board·sail·ing (bôrd′sāl′iŋ) *n.* WINDSURFING

☆**board·walk** (bôrd′wôk′) *n.* **1** a walk made of thick boards **2** a walk, often made of wood and elevated, placed along a beach or seafront

boar·fish (bôr′fish′) *n., pl.* **-fish′** or **-fish′es** (see FISH) any of a family (Caproidae, order Zeiformes) of small, red, deep-water marine fishes with a piglike snout

boar·hound (-hound′) *n.* a Great Dane or other large dog used in hunting wild boar

boar·ish (-ish) *adj.* like a boar; swinish, fierce, etc.

Bo·as (bō′az′, -as), **Franz** (fränts) 1858-1942; U.S. anthropologist, born in Germany

boast[1] (bōst) *vt.* ⟦< ?⟧ to do preliminary shaping on (sculpture, stonework, etc.) with a broad chisel

boast[2] (bōst) *vi.* ⟦ME *bosten* < *bost, n.* < Anglo-Fr; prob. via Gmc **bausia-* (cf. Norw *baus*, bold, haughty), ult. < IE **bhōu-*, var. of base **bheu-*, to grow, swell > BE⟧ **1** to talk proudly about deeds, abilities, etc., either one's own or those of someone close to one, esp. in a manner showing too much pride and satisfaction; brag **2** [Archaic] to be vainly proud; exult —*vt.* **1** to boast about **2** to glory in having or doing (something); be proud of [the town *boasts* a fine new library] —*n.* **1** the act of one who boasts **2** anything boasted of —**boast′er** *n.* —**boast′ing·ly** *adv.*

SYN.—**boast**, the basic term in this list, merely suggests pride or satisfaction, as in one's deeds or abilities [you may well *boast* of your efficiency]; **brag** suggests greater ostentation and overstatement [he *bragged* of what he would do in the race]; **vaunt**, a formal, literary term, implies greater suavity but more vainglory than either of the preceding [*vaunt* not in your triumph]; **swagger** suggests a proclaiming of one's superiority in an insolent or overbearing way; **crow** suggests loud boasting in exultation or triumph [*crowing* over one's victory]

boast·ful (bōst′fəl) *adj.* inclined to brag; boasting —**boast′ful·ly** *adv.* —**boast′ful·ness** *n.*

boat (bōt) *n.* ⟦ME *bot* < OE *bat* (akin to Ger & Du *boot*) < IE base **bheid-*, to split (in the sense "hollowed-out tree trunk") > FISSION⟧ **1** a small, open water vehicle propelled by oars, sails, engine, etc. **2** a large such vehicle for use in inland waters [an ore *boat* on the Great Lakes] **3** any large, seagoing water vehicle; ship: a term in popular use, but not by sailors **4** a boat-shaped dish [a gravy *boat*] —*vt.* **1** to lay or carry in the boat [to *boat* the oars] **2** to pull or lift into a boat [to *boat* a fish] —*vi.* to go in a boat; row, sail, or cruise —**in the same boat** in the same unfavorable situation —**miss the boat** [Informal] to fail to make the most of an opportunity —☆**rock the boat** [Informal] to disturb or challenge the status quo

boat-billed heron (bōt′bild′) a nocturnal, tropical American wading bird (*Cochlearius cochlearius*) with a large, broad bill: it is the only member of a family (Cochleariidae) of wading birds

boat·el (bō tel′) *n.* ⟦BOAT + (HOT)EL⟧ **1** a ship moored at a pier or wharf and used as a hotel **2** a hotel on a waterfront, with docks for use by boaters

boat·er (bōt′ər) *n.* ⟦BOAT + -ER: orig. worn when boating⟧ **1** a stiff hat of braided straw, with a flat crown and brim **2** a person who boats

boat·hook (-ho͝ok′) *n.* a long pole with a metal hook on one end, for maneuvering boats, logs, or rafts

boat·house (-hous′) *n.* a building for storing a boat or boats, sometimes equipped with recreational facilities

boat·ing (-iŋ) *n.* rowing, sailing, or cruising —*adj.* of or for boating

boat·lift (-lift′) *n.* ⟦BOAT + (AIR)LIFT⟧ a system of transporting by means of small boats, rafts, etc., as of refugees when official air or sea routes are blocked

boat·load (-lōd′) *n.* **1** all the freight or passengers that a boat can carry or contain **2** the load carried by a boat

boat·man (-mən) *n., pl.* **-men** (-mən) a person skilled in the operation of boats —**boat′man·ship′** *n.*

boat neck a bateau neckline —**boat′necked′** *adj.*

boat people refugees from a certain country or region who try to immigrate to some other country, using small boats; specif., such refugees from Southeast Asia in the late 1970s

boat shoe a shoe, usually in a style somewhat like a moccasin, with a rubber sole suitable for walking on the deck of a boat

boat·swain (bō′sən) *n.* ⟦ME *boteswayne* < OE *batswegen* < *bat*, BOAT + **swegen*, servant < or akin to ON *sveinn*: see SWAIN⟧ a ship's warrant officer or petty officer in charge of the deck crew, the rigging, anchors, boats, etc.

boat train a train scheduled to be at a port in time for prompt transfer of passengers to or from a ship

boat·yard (bōt′yärd′) *n.* a yard where boats are built, repaired, or stored

Bo·az (bō′az′) *n.* ⟦Heb *boaz*, lit., swiftness⟧ *Bible* Ruth's second husband: Ruth 4:13

bob[1] (bäb) *n.* ⟦ME *bobbe*, hanging cluster; senses 6-9, 11 < the v., 10 < BOBSLED⟧ **1** [Brit. Dial.] a hanging cluster **2** any knoblike hanging weight or pendant [a plumb *bob*] **3** a short curl or knob of hair **4** a docked tail, as of a horse **5** a short hairstyle for a woman or child, with the hair of relatively even length all around **6** a quick, jerky motion, like that of a cork on water **7** *a)* a float on a fishing line *b)* clustered bait used on a fishing line **8** a type of Scottish dance **9** a quick curtsy ☆**10** a bobsled or bob skate **11** [Archaic] a tap or light blow **12** [Archaic] a short refrain in a song —*vt.* **bobbed, bob′bing** ⟦ME *bobben*, to knock against; also < *bobbe*, hanging cluster⟧ **1** to knock against lightly; rap **2** to move, esp. up and down, with short, jerky motions **3** to cut (hair, a tail, etc.) short; dock —*vi.* **1** to move or act in a bobbing manner; move suddenly or jerkily **2** to curtsy quickly **3** to fish with a bob **4** to try to catch suspended or floating fruit with the teeth: with *for* —**bob up** to come up unexpectedly; appear suddenly

bob[2] (bäb) *n., pl.* **bob** ⟦< ? *Bob*, nickname for ROBERT[1]⟧ [Brit. Slang] a shilling

Bob (bäb) *n. nickname for* ROBERT[1]: dim. *Bobby*

bob·ber (bäb′ər) *n.* **1** a person or thing that bobs **2** a buoyant device, as a cork, attached to a fishing line to hold the baited hook at a desired depth

☆**bob·ber·y** (bäb′ər ē) *n., pl.* **-ber·ies** ⟦Anglo-Ind < Hindi *bāp-re*, O father!, exclamation of sorrow or surprise⟧ a hubbub or commotion

bob·bin (bäb′in) *n.* ⟦Fr *bobine* < ?⟧ **1** a reel or spool for thread or yarn, used in spinning, weaving, machine sewing, etc. **2** a small notched pin of wood, bone, or ivory, used in making bobbin lace

bob·bi·net (bäb′ə net′, bäb′ə net′) *n.* ⟦< prec. + NET[1]⟧ a machine-made netted fabric of hexagonal mesh

bobbin lace a lace whose design is laid out on a pillowlike pad with pins around which thread on bobbins is drawn and interlaced

bob·ble (bäb′əl) *n.* ⟦freq. of BOB[1], *vt.*⟧ **1** a bobbing, up-and-down movement **2** any of the tufted balls forming a decorative fringe, as on curtains ☆**3** [Informal] *a)* an awkward mistake; error *b)* *Sports* an awkward juggling of the ball in trying to catch or hold on to it —*vi.* **-bled, -bling 1** to move jerkily; bob ☆**2** [Informal] to make an error —☆*vt.* [Informal] to deal with awkwardly or unskillfully; specif., to make a bobble with (a ball)

bob·ble·head (doll) (bäb′əl hed′) a figurine, made variously in the likeness of a cartoon character, celebrity, famous athlete, etc., with a spring-mounted head that bobbles

bob·by (bäb′ē) *n., pl.* **-bies** ⟦after Sir Robert PEEL, nicknamed *Bobby*, who reorganized the London police force⟧ [Informal, Chiefly Brit.] a British policeman

☆**bobby pin** ⟦from use with *bobbed* hair⟧ a small metal hairpin with the sides pressing close together

☆**bobby socks** (*or* **sox**) ⟦< BOB[1] (*vt.* 3)⟧ [Informal] esp. in the 1940s and 1950s, girls' socks that reached just above the ankles

☆**bob·by-sox·er** or **bob·by·sox·er** (-säks′ər) *n.* [Informal] esp. in the 1940s, a girl in her early teens, esp. one who conformed to adolescent fads

☆**bob·cat** (bäb′kat′) *n., pl.* **-cats′** or **-cat′** ⟦so called from its short tail⟧ a small North American lynx (*Lynx rufus*) that feeds on small prey, esp. rats and rabbits

bo·beche (bō besh′) *n.* ⟦Fr⟧ a disk of glass, metal, etc. with a center hole, placed around the top of a candlestick to catch the candle drippings

☆**bob·o·link** (bäb′ə liŋk′) *n.* ⟦earlier *boblincoln*: echoic, after its call⟧ a migratory blackbird (*Dolichonyx oryzivorus*) of North American fields and meadows

Bo·bru·isk (bə bro͞o′isk) city in central Belarus: also sp. **Bo·bru′ysk** (-isk)

☆**bob skate** a skate with two parallel runners

☆**bob·sled** (bäb′sled′) *n.* **1** a long sled made of two short sleds joined together, or either of the short sleds **2** a long sled for two or four riders, equipped with steerable runners in the front, fixed runners in the back, a brake, and a protective shell, used in timed races down long, steep, winding, icy courses **3** a contest in which teams on bobsleds compete Also **bob'sleigh'** (-slā') —*vi.* **-sled'ded, -sled'ding** to ride or race on a bobsled —**bob'sled'der** *n.*

bob·stay (-stā') *n.* a rope or chain that extends upward from the stem of a ship to the bowsprit and helps hold the bowsprit in place

bob·tail (-tāl') *n.* **1** a short tail or one cut short **2** a horse or dog with a bobtail —*adj.* **1** having a bobtail **2** cut short; abbreviated —*vt.* **1** to dock the tail of **2** to cut short; curtail

☆**bob·white** (bäb'hwīt', -wīt') *n., pl.* **-whites'** or **-white'** ⟦echoic, after its call⟧ a small North American quail (*Colinus virginianus*) having markings of brown and white on a gray body; partridge

☆**bo·cac·cio** (bō kä'chō, bə-) *n.* ⟦altered (? after Giovanni BOCCACCIO) < Sp *bocacha,* var. of *bocaza,* large mouth < L *bucca:* see BUCCAL⟧ a large-mouthed marine rockfish (*Sebastes paucispinis*) found along the California coast

Bo·ca Ra·ton (bō'kə rə tōn') ⟦after nearby Lake *Boca Raton* < Sp < *boca,* mouth, inlet + *ratón,* mouse, hidden rock that frays ships' cables: with ref. to the lake's outlet to the sea⟧ city in SE Fla., near Fort Lauderdale

Boc·cac·ci·o (bō käch'ē ō'; *It* bô kä'chô), **Gio·van·ni** (jô vän'nē) 1313-75; It. author of the *Decameron*

Boc·che·ri·ni (bō'kə rē'nē; *It* bô'ke rē'nē), **Lu·i·gi** (lo͞o ē'jē) 1743-1805; It. composer

boc·cie, boc·ce, *or* **boc·ci** (bäch'ē) *n.* ⟦It *bocce,* (wooden) balls, pl. of *boccia,* akin to Fr *bosse:* see BOSS[2]⟧ an Italian game similar to lawn bowling, usually played on a long, narrow court of sand or dirt with one-foot (30-cm) boards along the sides and ends

Boc·cio·ni (bô chō'nē), **Um·ber·to** (o͝om ber'tô) 1882-1916; It. futurist painter & sculptor

Boche (bōsh) [Old Slang] *n.* ⟦Fr slang, contr. < *tête de caboche,* hard head, head of cabbage (see CABBAGE[1])⟧ a German, esp. a German soldier in WWI —**the Boche** Germans or WWI German soldiers collectively
USAGE—a hostile term

Bo·chum (bō'kəm, -kho͝om) city in W Germany, in the Ruhr valley, in the state of North Rhine-Westphalia

☆**bock** (bäk) *n.* ⟦Ger < *bockbier,* contr. < *oanbock-, ambock-,* Bavarian dial. pronun. of *Einbecker bier,* after *Einbeck,* Hanover, where first brewed⟧ a dark beer traditionally drunk in the early spring: also **bock beer**

bod (bäd) *n.* **1** [Informal] the human body **2** [Slang] a person's physique or figure **3** [Brit. Informal] a person

BOD *abbrev.* BIOCHEMICAL OXYGEN DEMAND

☆**bo·da·cious** (bō dā'shəs) *adj.* ⟦? blend of BOLD & AUDACIOUS, or < Brit dial. *boldacious,* blend of same elements⟧ [Informal or Dial.] **1** outstanding in a showy way; splendid **2** bold or blatant —**bo·da'cious·ly** *adj.*

bode[1] (bōd) *vt.* **bod'ed, bod'ing** ⟦ME *bodien* < OE *bodian* < *boda,* messenger, prob. < IE base of BID[1]⟧ **1** [Archaic] to announce in advance; predict **2** to be an omen of; presage —**bode ill (or well)** to be a bad (or good) omen

bode[2] (bōd) *vi., vt. alt. pt. of* BIDE

bo·de·ga (bō dā'gə) *n.* ⟦Sp, a grocery shop, wine cellar < L *apotheca:* see APOTHECARY⟧ in Hispanic communities *a)* a small grocery store *b)* a wine shop *c)* a bar; tavern

Bo·den·see (bōd''n zā') *Ger. name for* Lake CONSTANCE[2]

bo·dhi·satt·va (bō'di sut'və, -sät'-) *n.* ⟦Sans, lit., one enlightened in essence < *bodhi,* enlightenment (< IE base **bheudh-,* to be alert, recognize > OE *beodan,* to command: see BID[1]) + *sattva,* being, existence (< IE **sent-,* part. stem of base **es-,* BE > IS[1])⟧ *Buddhism* a person who has achieved great moral and spiritual wisdom and is a potential Buddha, esp. such a person who rejects nirvana in order to assist suffering mankind

bodh·ran (bou rän') *n.* ⟦Ir *bodhrán*⟧ a shallow, hand-held drum played by striking the single drumhead with alternate knobbed ends of a beater: used esp. in Irish folk music

bod·ice (bäd'is) *n.* ⟦altered < *bodies,* pl. of BODY, in obs. sense of "part of dress above the waist"⟧ **1** the upper part of a woman's dress **2** a kind of vest formerly worn over a blouse or dress by women or girls, usually laced in front **3** [Archaic] a corset

bod·ice-rip·per (bäd'is rip'ər) *n.* a ROMANCE (*n.* 3) set in the past and having a formulaic plot that features scenes of sexual passion and violent action: also written **bodice ripper**

-bod·ied (bäd'ēd) *combining form* having a (specified kind of) body or substance [able-*bodied,* a full-*bodied* flavor]

bod·i·less (bäd'ē lis) *adj.* without a body; having no material substance; incorporeal

bod·i·ly (bäd'ə lē) *adj.* ⟦ME *bodilich* < *bodi,* BODY⟧ **1** physical: opposed to MENTAL[1] **2** of, in, by, or to the body —*adv.* **1** in person; in the flesh [to be present *bodily*] **2** as a single body; in entirety **3** as a single group; as one unit

SYN.—**bodily** refers to the human body as distinct from the mind or spirit [*bodily* ills]; **physical,** while often interchangeable with **bodily,** suggests somewhat less directly the anatomy and physiology of the body [*physical* exercise]; **corporeal** refers to the material substance of the body and is opposed to *spiritual* [his *corporeal* remains]; **corporal** refers to the effect of something upon the body [*corporal* punishment]; **somatic** is the scientific word and refers to the body as distinct from the psyche, with no philosophic or poetic overtones [the *somatic* differences between individuals] —*ANT.* **mental, psychic, spiritual**

bod·ing (bōd'iŋ) *n.* ⟦ME *bodynge, bodunge* < OE *bodung* < *bodian,* BODE[1]⟧ an omen; foreboding —*adj.* ominous; foreboding —**bod'ing·ly** *adv.*

bod·kin (bäd'kin) *n.* ⟦ME *boidekyn, bodekin* < ?⟧ **1** [Obs.] a dagger or stiletto **2** a pointed instrument for making holes in cloth **3** a long, ornamental hairpin **4** a thick, blunt needle for drawing ribbon or tape through a hem, etc.

Bod·lei·an (Library) (bäd lē'ən, bäd'lē ən) ⟦after Sir T. *Bodley* (1545-1613), Eng statesman & scholar who restored it⟧ the Oxford University library

Bo·do·ni (bə dō'nē) *n.* a style of type designed by the Italian printer Giambattista Bodoni (1740-1813)

bod·y (bäd'ē) *n., pl.* **bod'ies** ⟦ME *bodi, bodig* < OE *bodig,* trunk, chest, orig. sense "cask," akin to MLowG *boddike,* tub for brewing, OHG *botah;* prob. < It *bottega,* shop < L *apotheca:* see APOTHECARY⟧ **1** the whole physical structure and substance of a human being, animal, or plant **2** *a)* the trunk or torso of a human being or animal *b)* the part of a garment that covers the trunk **3** a dead person; corpse **4** the flesh or material substance, as opposed to the spirit **5** [Informal] a human being; person **6** a group of people or things regarded or functioning as a unit [a *body* of soldiers, an advisory *body*] **7** the majority of a number of people or things **8** the main or central part of anything; specif., *a)* the part of an automobile, truck, etc. that holds the load or passengers; the part of a vehicle that is not the chassis *b)* the hull of a ship *c)* the fuselage of an aircraft *d)* the main part of a piece of writing as distinguished from headings and introductory or supplementary matter *e)* the sound box of a stringed instrument **9** anything having real or material substance or form; any physical or perceptible object **10** any of the natural objects seen in the visible heavens [the sun, moon, planets, stars, etc. are celestial *bodies*] **11** a separate portion or mass of matter [a *body* of land or water] **12** substance, density, or consistency, as of a liquid or fabric **13** richness or fullness of tone or flavor **14** fullness and resilience: said of the hair, specif. when long and healthy **15** *Law* a person or something legally regarded as a person **16** *Printing* the shank of a piece of type —*vt.* **bod'ied, bod'y·ing 1** to give a body or substance to; make substantial **2** to make part of; embody —**body forth 1** to give shape or form to **2** to symbolize or represent —**keep body and soul together** to stay alive

SYN.—**body** refers to the whole physical substance of a person or animal, whether dead or alive; **corpse** and the euphemistic **remains** refer to a dead human body; **carcass** is used of the dead body of an animal or, contemptuously, of a human being; **cadaver** refers primarily to a dead human body used for medical dissection

body art 1 tattoos, body piercings, and similar ornamentations of the body **2** the practice or art of ornamenting the body by means of tattooing, body piercing, etc.

body bag a rubberized bag sealed with a zipper, used for transporting a human corpse from a war zone, accident, etc.

bod·y·build·ing (-bil'diŋ) *n.* the practice of lifting weights and performing certain specific calisthenics, as sit-ups and push-ups, to develop a strong body —**bod'y·build'er** *n.*

body check *Hockey* the fair block of an opponent who has the puck by bumping with the body, shoulder to hip, from the front or side

body clock the physiological mechanisms having to do with circadian rhythms: a nontechnical usage

body corporate *Law* a corporation

☆**body count** a count made of persons killed, as in battle

☆**body English** ⟦see ENGLISH, *n.* 6⟧ a motion of the body, as after bowling a ball, in a semi-involuntary or joking effort to control the ball's movement

bod·y·guard (-gärd') *n.* a person or group of persons assigned to protect someone from harm

body language gestures, unconscious bodily movements, facial expressions, etc. which serve as nonverbal communication or as accompaniments to speech

body louse *see* LOUSE (*n.* 1*a*)

body mass index a measurement used to estimate body fat and classify persons as being underweight, overweight, or normal: it is calculated by dividing weight (in kilograms) by the square of height (in meters)

body piercing body ornamentation created by piercing a hole as in an earlobe, lip, or navel and inserting a ring or stud; also, this process or practice

body politic the people who collectively constitute a political unit under a government

☆**body shop** a garage where repair work on the body and chassis of automotive vehicles is done

bod·y-slam (-slam') *vt.* **-slammed', -slam'ming** to lift and throw (someone) to the ground, as in wrestling

body snatcher [Historical] a person who steals corpses from graves, as to sell them for anatomical dissection

☆**body stocking** a tightfitting garment, usually of one piece, that covers the torso and, sometimes, the legs

bod·y·suit (-so͞ot') *n.* a one-piece, tightfitting garment that covers the torso, usually worn with slacks, a skirt, etc.: also **body shirt**

bod·y·surf (-surf') *vi.* to engage in the sport of surfing while lying prone on a wave without the use of a surfboard

bod·y·work (bäd'ē wurk') *n.* **1** the body of a vehicle, or its design **2** the making or repairing of a vehicle body: also written **body work 3** the use of certain practices or techniques, as massage, reiki, or acupressure, for therapeutic purposes, as in alternative healing

boehm·ite (bām′īt′, bōm′-) ***n.*** ⟦Ger *böhmit,* after J. *Böhm,* 20th-c. mineralogist⟧ a soft, orthorhombic mineral, hydrous aluminum oxide, AlO(OH), that is a chief component of some bauxites

Boe·o·ti·a (bē ō′shə, bē ō′shē ə) **1** in ancient times, a region dominated by the city of Thebes (Greece): fl. from *c.* 600 B.C. until the destruction of Thebes in 336 B.C. **2** department of EC Greece, northwest of Attica —**Boe·o′tian** (-shən) ***adj., n.***

Boer (bôr, boor, bō′ər) ***n.*** ⟦Du *boer,* peasant: see BOOR⟧ a South African whose ancestors were Dutch colonists

Boer War a war (1899-1902) in which Great Britain defeated the Boers of South Africa

Bo·e·thi·us (bō ē′thē əs), **(Anicius Manlius Severinus)** A.D. 480?-524?; Rom. philosopher

boeuf bour·gui·gnon (buf′boor′gē nyōn′; *Fr* bëf boor gē nyōn′) ⟦Fr, beef of Burgundy⟧ a dish consisting of seasoned cubes of beef simmered in red wine together with onions and mushrooms

BOF *abbrev.* basic oxygen furnace

☆**boff**[1] (bäf) ***n.*** ⟦prob. < It *buffa,* a jest, or *buffo,* a gust of wind: see BUFFOON⟧ [Slang] **1** *a)* a loud, hearty laugh *b)* a joke, incident in a play, etc. meant to produce such a laugh **2** a play, song, etc. that is a great popular success; hit Also **bof·fo·la** (bə fō′lə)

☆**boff**[2] (bäf) ***vt.*** ⟦< *boff* (*n.*), a punch or blow, prob. echoic⟧ [Slang] to engage in sexual intercourse with

bof·fin (bäf′in) ***n.*** ⟦< ?⟧ [Brit. Slang] a research scientist

☆**bof·fo** (bäf′ō) ***adj.*** ⟦< BOFF[1]⟧ [Slang] very popular or successful

bog (bäg, bôg) ***n.*** ⟦< Gael & Ir *bog,* soft, moist (> Ir *bogach,* a bog) < IE **bhugh-* < base **bheugh-,* to bend > BOW[1]⟧ wet, spongy ground, characterized by decaying mosses that form peat; a small marsh or swamp — ***vt., vi.* bogged, bog′ging** to sink or become stuck in or as in a bog; mire: often with *down* —**bog′gy *adj.***

☆**bo·gart** (bō′gärt′) ***vt.*** ⟦after fol.⟧ [Slang] **1** to take over or achieve through intimidation **2** to take or use without sharing [*to bogart a marijuana joint*]

Bo·gart (bō′gärt′), **Humphrey (DeForest)** 1899-1957; U.S. film actor

bog asphodel any of several plants (genus *Narthecium*) of the lily family found in bogs, esp. a grasslike wildflower (*N. americanum*) native to New Jersey that has yellow blossoms

bog·bean (bäg′bēn′) ***n.*** BUCKBEAN

bo·gey (bō′gē; *for 1, usually* boog′ē) ***n., pl.* -geys 1** BOGY[1] **2** ⟦after Col. *Bogey* (named from a popular music hall refrain), imaginary partner assumed to play a first-rate game⟧ *Golf a)* par, esp. for an average player (a former meaning) *b)* one stroke more than par on a hole —☆***vt.* -geyed, -gey·ing** *Golf* to score one over par on (a given hole)

bo·gey·man (boog′ē man′; *also* bō′gē-) ***n., pl.* -men′** (-men′) BOOGEYMAN

bog·gle (bäg′əl) ***vi.* -gled, -gling** ⟦< Scot *bogle,* specter; prob. < ME *bugge,* specter (as in BUGBEAR); now assoc. with BUNGLE⟧ **1** to be startled or frightened (*at*); shy away **2** to hesitate (*at*); have scruples **3** to be or become confused or overwhelmed as by something very difficult, surprising, vast, etc. —***vt.* 1** to bungle or botch ☆**2** to confuse or overwhelm (the mind, imagination, etc.) —***n.*** an act or instance of boggling

bo·gie[1] (bō′gē; *for 1, usually* boog′ē) ***n., pl.* -gies 1** BOGY[1] ☆**2** BOGEY (sense 2)

bo·gie[2] (bō′gē) ***n., pl.* -gies** ⟦< N Brit dial.⟧ **1** a low, swiveled undercarriage at either end of a railroad car **2** a type of suspension unit with four wheels on two axles, used on some tanks and multiple-axle vehicles to maintain traction while moving over obstacles

BOGO (bō′gō′) *abbrev.* buy one, get one

Bo·gor (bō′gôr′) city in W Java, Indonesia

Bo·go·tá (bō′gə tä′) capital of Colombia, in the central part of the country, on an Andean plateau

bog rosemary any of several species (genus *Andromeda*) of evergreen shrubs of the heath family, native to cold bogs of North America and Europe, with pink flowers and narrow leaves

☆**bo·gus** (bō′gəs) ***adj.*** ⟦orig. (slang), counterfeiter's apparatus: < ?⟧ not genuine; spurious —**SYN.** FALSE

bo·gy[1] (bō′gē, boog′ē; *for 1, usually* boog′ē) ***n., pl.* -gies** ⟦see BOGGLE & BUG[2]⟧ **1** an imaginary evil being or spirit; goblin **2** anything one especially, and often needlessly, fears; bugbear

bo·gy[2] (bō′gē) ***n., pl.* -gies** BOGIE[2]

bo·gy·man (boog′ē man′; *also* bō′gē-) ***n., pl.* -men′** (-men′) BOOGEYMAN

Bo Hai (bō′hī′) arm of the Yellow Sea, north of Shandong peninsula in NE China: *c.* 300 mi (483 km) long

Bo·he·mi·a[1] (bō hē′mē ə, -hēm′yə) ***n.*** [*often* **b-**] a community of bohemians: see BOHEMIAN (sense 4)

Bo·he·mi·a[2] (bō hē′mē ə, -hēm′yə) former independent kingdom in central Europe (13th-15th cent.): part of Austria-Hungary until 1918 and then part of Czechoslovakia until 1993, when it was incorporated into the Czech Republic

Bohemia

Bo·he·mi·an (bō hē′mē ən, -hēm′yən) ***n.* 1** a person born or living in Bohemia **2** CZECH[1] (*n.* 2) **3** ⟦Fr *Bohémien:* from the fact that the Gypsies passed through Bohemia to reach W Europe⟧ a Gypsy **4** [*usually* **b-**] a person, esp. an artist, poet, etc., who lives in an unconventional, nonconforming way —***adj.* 1** of Bohemia or its people, language, or culture; Czech **2** [*usually* **b-**] like or characteristic of a bohemian —**Bo·he′mi·an·ism′ *n.***

Böh·me (bö′mə; *E* bā′mə), **Ja·kob** (yä′kôp) 1575-1624; Ger. theosophist & mystic: also **Böhm** (böm; *E* bām)

bo·ho (bō′hō′) [Slang] ***n.*** BOHEMIAN (*n.* 4) —***adj.*** BOHEMIAN (*adj.* 2)

Bo·hol (bə hôl′) island in the SC Philippines, between Cebu & Leyte: one of the Visayan group: 1,492 sq mi (3,864 sq km)

Bohr (bôr) **1 Aa·ge Niels** (ô′gə nēls) 1922-2009; Dan. physicist: son of Niels **2 Niels (Henrik David)** (nēls) 1885-1962; Dan. nuclear & theoretical physicist

bohr·i·um (bôr′ē əm) ***n.*** ⟦ModL, after Niels BOHR + -IUM⟧ a radioactive chemical element with a very short half-life: a transactinide produced by bombarding bismuth with high-energy nuclear particles: symbol, Bh; at. no. 107: see the periodic table of elements in the Reference Supplement

Bohr theory a theory, proposed by Niels Bohr in 1913, stating that electrons revolve in definite orbits around a nucleus, and that radiation is absorbed or emitted only when an electron is transferred from one orbit to another

☆**bo·hunk** (bō′huŋk′) ***n.*** ⟦< BO(HEMIAN) + HUN(GARIAN) + *-k*⟧ [Slang] a person from EC Europe: a derisive or contemptuous term

Bo·iar·do (bô yär′dô), **Mat·te·o Ma·ri·a** (mät tā′ô mä rē′ä) 1434?-94; It. poet

boil[1] (boil) ***vi.*** ⟦ME *boilen* < OFr *boillir* < L *bullire* < *bulla,* a bubble, knob; prob. < IE **bu-,* var. of echoic base **beu-, *bheu-,* to blow up, cause to swell⟧ **1** to bubble up and vaporize over direct heat **2** to reach the vaporizing stage **3** to seethe or churn like a boiling liquid **4** to be agitated, as with rage **5** to cook in boiling water or other liquid —***vt.* 1** to heat to the boiling point **2** to cook, process, or separate in boiling water or other liquid —***n.*** the act or state of boiling —**boil away** to evaporate as a result of boiling —**boil down 1** to lessen in quantity by boiling, esp. so as to change consistency **2** to make more terse; condense; summarize —**boil down to** to mean, when summarized; amount to [*what it all boils down to is more unemployment*] —**boil over 1** to come to a boil and spill over the rim **2** to lose one's temper; get excited

SYN.—boil, the basic word, refers to the vaporization of a liquid over direct heat or, metaphorically, to great agitation, as with rage [*it made my blood boil*]; **seethe** suggests violent boiling with much bubbling and foaming or, in an extended sense, excitement [*the country seethed with rebellion*]; **simmer** implies a gentle, continuous cooking at or just below the boiling point or, metaphorically, imminence of eruption, as in anger or revolt; **stew** refers to slow, prolonged boiling or, in an extended informal sense, unrest caused by worry or anxiety

boil[2] (boil) ***n.*** ⟦orig., & still dial., *bile* < ME *byle* < OE *byle, byl* (akin to Ger *beule*) < IE base of prec.⟧ an inflamed, painful, pus-filled swelling on the skin, caused by localized infection; furuncle

Boi·leau (bwȧ lō′), **Ni·co·las** (nē kô lä′) 1636-1711; Fr. critic & poet: in full **Nicolas Boi·leau-Des·pré·aux** (-dā prā ō′)

boiled oil any of several oils, esp. linseed, that are heated (not boiled) and mixed with driers to form a thick, dark, quick-drying oil

boil·er (boil′ər) ***n.* 1** a container in which things are boiled or heated **2** a tank or device in which water is turned to steam as for heating a building or for power, as in a steam engine **3** a tank for heating water and storing it

boil·er·mak·er (-māk′ər) ***n.* 1** a worker who makes or repairs boilers ☆**2** [Informal] a drink of whiskey in beer or with beer as a chaser

boil·er·plate (-plāt′) ***n.* 1** steel rolled in large flat plates, used in making steam boilers ☆**2** syndicated features or fillers that are relatively timeless, sent to newspapers, formerly as stereotype plates, now often by wire, mail, or computer ☆**3** a glib, hackneyed statement reflecting a generally accepted opinion or belief ☆**4** any of the standard clauses or sections of a legal document

boiler room 1 a room where a boiler is located **2** [Informal] a room equipped with telephones for the purpose of making high-pressure and often deceptive solicitations —**boil′er-room′ *adj.***

boiler suit [Brit.] coveralls

boiling point 1 the temperature at which a specified liquid boils; temperature at which the vapor pressure of a specified liquid equals the atmospheric pressure: water at sea level boils at 212°F or 100°C **2** the point at which one loses one's temper or matters get out of control

boing (boiŋ) ***n.*** ⟦echoic⟧ a sound suggesting a reverberation or vibration, as of a rebounding metal spring

boink (boiŋk) ***interj.*** ⟦echoic⟧ used to suggest the sound of something bouncing or glancing, as off the head —***vt.*** [Slang] to engage in sexual intercourse with: considered mildly vulgar by some

Boi·se (boi′zē, -sē) ⟦< Fr *boisé,* wooded: see fol.⟧ capital of Ida., in the SW part: also **Boise City**

boi·se·rie (bwä′zə rē′; *Fr* bwȧz rē′) ***n.*** ⟦Fr < *bois,* wood (< WGmc **busk* > BUSH[1]) + *-erie,* -ERY⟧ wood paneling on the walls of a room

bois·ter·ous (bois′tər əs) ***adj.*** ⟦ME *boistreous,* crude, coarse, altered < *boistous,* unmannerly, violent < ? OFr *boisteus,* limping, rough⟧ **1** rough and stormy; turbulent **2** *a)* noisy and unruly; rowdy *b)* noisy and lively; loud and exuberant **3** [Obs.] rough, coarse, or bulky —**SYN.** VOCIFEROUS —**bois′ter·ous·ly *adv.*** —**bois′ter·ous·ness *n.***

boîte (bwät) ***n.*** ⟦Fr, lit., box⟧ a small nightclub or cabaret

bok choy (bäk′ choi′) ⟦Cantonese, lit., white vegetable⟧ a variety of Chinese cabbage having pale-green stalks and dark-green leaves

bok·ken (bäk′ən) ***n., pl.*** **-kens** or **-ken** ⟦Jpn.⟧ a wooden practice sword used in kendo and other martial arts

Bok·mål (bo͝ok′môl, bōk′-) ***n.*** ⟦Norw < *bok*, book + *mål*, language⟧ the older and more widely used of the two standard varieties of Norwegian, which developed from written Danish using Norwegian pronunciation: cf. NYNORSK

Boks·burg (bäks′bərg) city in central Gauteng province, South Africa

Bol *abbrev.* Bolivia

bo·la (bō′lə) ***n.*** ⟦< AmSp *bolas*, pl. of Sp *bola*, a ball < L *bulla*: see BOIL[1]⟧ a set of cords or thongs with heavy balls at the ends, for throwing at cattle and entangling their legs: also **bo′las** (-ləs)

bola

bold (bōld) ***adj.*** ⟦ME < OE *beald*, bold, brave, akin to Ger *bald*: orig. sense, "swollen up" < IE base **bhel-*: see BALL[1]⟧ **1** showing a readiness to take risks or face danger; daring; fearless **2** too free in behavior or manner; taking liberties; impudent; shameless **3** steep or abrupt, as a cliff **4** prominent and clear; striking and sharp [*to write a bold hand*] **5** bright and vivid; rich [*bold colors*] **6** printed in boldface **7** forceful in expression **8** [Obs.] confident —***SYN.*** BRAVE —**make so bold as** to be so bold as; dare: followed by an infinitive [*he made so bold as to ask for his money back*]: also **make bold** —**bold′ly** ***adv.*** —**bold′ness** ***n.***

bold·face (-fās′) ***n.*** a printing type having heavy, dark lines: the headwords in this dictionary are in boldface —***adj.*** set or printed in boldface

bold·faced (-fāst′) ***adj.*** **1** impudent or forward in manner **2** BOLDFACE

bol·do (bôl′dō, bäl′-) ***n.*** ⟦AmSp < Araucanian⟧ any of a genus of shrubby, dicotyledenous evergreen tree (family Monimiaceae) indigenous to Chile, producing small, edible berries and leaves used in folk medicine

bole[1] (bōl) ***n.*** ⟦ME *bol*, stem, trunk < ON *bolr* < IE **bhl̥-*, var. of base **bhel-*: see BALL[1]⟧ a tree trunk

bole[2] (bōl) ***n.*** ⟦ME & OFr *bol* < ML *bolus*, clay < Gr *bōlos*, clod⟧ any of several fine, easily pulverized types of clay that are usually red, yellow, or brown —**bo·lar** (bō′lər) ***adj.***

bo·lec·tion (bō lek′shən) ***n.*** ⟦< ?⟧ *Archit.* a molding that projects beyond the surface of a panel

bo·le·ro (bō ler′ō) ***n., pl.*** **-ros** ⟦Sp < *bola*, a ball < OFr *boule* < L *bulla*, bubble: see BOIL[1]⟧ **1** a Spanish dance done to castanets and lively music in 3/4 time **2** the music for this dance **3** a sleeveless or sleeved jacket that ends at the waist and is open at the front

bo·lete (bō lēt′) ***n.*** ⟦see fol.⟧ any of a family (Boletaceae) of pore-fungus, agaric mushrooms, often edible

bo·le·tus (bō lēt′əs) ***n.*** ⟦ModL < L < Gr *bōlitēs*⟧ any of a genus (*Boletus*) of bolete mushrooms, usually with a thick, brownish stem and cap that are edible

Bol·eyn (bo͝ol′in, bə lin′), **Anne** 1507?-36; 2d wife of Henry VIII of England; mother of Elizabeth I: beheaded

bo·lide (bō′līd′, -lid′) ***n.*** ⟦Fr < L *bolis* (gen. *bolidis*), fiery meteor < Gr, missile, arrow, akin to *ballein*, to throw: see BALL[2]⟧ a brilliant meteor with a magnitude exceeding -4, esp. one that explodes; fireball

Bol·ing·broke (bo͝ol′iŋ bro͝ok′) 1st Viscount (born *Henry St. John*) 1678-1751; Eng. statesman & political writer

bo·lí·var (bō lē′vär′, bäl′ə vər) ***n., pl.*** **bo·lí·va·res** (bō lē′vä rās′, bō′li vä′res) or **bo·lí′vars′** ⟦after fol.⟧ the basic monetary unit of Venezuela: see the table of monetary units in the Reference Supplement

Bol·í·var (bäl′ə vər; *Sp* bô lē′vär), **Si·món** (sī′mən; *Sp* sē môn′) 1783-1830; South American general & revolutionary leader, born in Caracas: hero of South American fight for independence from Spain —**Bol·i·var·i·an** (bäl′ə vär′ē ən, -ver′-; bō′lē-) ***adj.***

☆**bo·liv·i·a** (bə liv′ē ə) ***n.*** ⟦after fol.⟧ a woolen cloth resembling plush

Bo·liv·i·a (bə liv′ē ə) ⟦after Simón BOLÍVAR⟧ inland country in WC South America: secured independence from Spain, 1825: 424,164 sq mi (1,098,580 sq km); caps., La Paz & Sucre —**Bo·liv′i·an** ***adj., n.***

bo·liv·i·a·no (bə liv′ē ä′nō; *Sp* bô lē′vyä′nô) ***n., pl.*** **-nos** ⟦AmSp, after prec.⟧ the basic monetary unit of Bolivia: see the table of monetary units in the Reference Supplement

boll (bōl) ***n.*** ⟦ME *bolle*, *boll*, BOWL[1]⟧ the roundish seed pod of a plant, esp. of cotton or flax

Böll (böl), **Hein·rich** (hīn′riH) 1917-85; Ger. novelist

bol·lard (bäl′ərd) ***n.*** ⟦prob. extension of BOLE[1]⟧ **1** any of the strong posts on a pier for holding fast a ship's mooring lines **2** BITT

bol·lix (bäl′iks) ***vt.*** ⟦euphemistic respelling of nautical slang < ME *ballokes* < OE *beallucas*, testicles (akin to BALL[1]), used as an extension of BALL[1]⟧ ☆[Slang] to make a muddle of; bungle; botch: usually with *up*

bol·locks (bäl′əks) [Chiefly Brit. Slang] ***pl.n.*** ⟦euphemistic respelling of ME *ballokes*: see prec.⟧ **1** testicles **2** nonsense —***interj.*** nonsense: sometimes also used to express anger, annoyance, etc. Now mildly vulgar

☆**boll weevil** **1** a small, grayish weevil (*Anthonomus grandis*) with a long snout, whose larvae, when hatched in the immature bolls of cotton plants, destroy the bolls **2** [Slang] a conservative Democratic politician from a state of the Southern U.S.

☆**boll·worm** (bōl′wurm′) ***n.*** **1** a kind of moth larva (*Platyedra gossypiella*) that feeds on developing cotton bolls, ears of corn, tomatoes, etc.: also called **pink bollworm** **2** CORN EARWORM

Bol·ly·wood (bäl′ē wo͝od′) ***n.*** ⟦blend of BOMBAY[2] & HOLLYWOOD⟧ the Hindi-language film industry of India, centered in Mumbai (formerly Bombay)

bo·lo[1] (bō′lō) ***n., pl.*** **-los** ⟦Sp < native name⟧ a large, single-edged knife used in the Philippines as a weapon or cutting tool; kind of machete

☆**bo·lo**[2] (bō′lō) ***n.*** BOLO TIE

bo·lo·gna (bə lō′nē; *also*, -nyə, -nə) ***n.*** ⟦after fol.⟧ a large smoked sausage of beef, pork, or veal, or of a mixture of these: also **bologna sausage**

Bo·lo·gna (bə lō′nyə) commune in Emilia-Romagna, NC Italy, at the foot of the Apennines

Bo·lo·gnese (bō′lə nēz′, -nēs′) ***n., pl.*** **-gnese′** a person born or living in Bologna —***adj.*** of Bologna or its people or language

☆**bo·lo·graph** (bō′lə graph′) ***n.*** ⟦*bolo-* (as in fol.) + -GRAPH⟧ a record of variations registered by a bolometer —**bo′lo·graph′ic** ***adj.***

☆**bo·lom·e·ter** (bō läm′ət ər) ***n.*** ⟦< Gr *bolē*, ray, lit., something thrown < *ballein*, to throw (see BALL[2]) + -METER⟧ *Physics* a very sensitive instrument for measuring and recording the intensity of small amounts of radiant energy —**bo·lo·met·ric** (bō′lə me′trik) ***adj.*** —**bo′lo·met′ri·cal·ly** ***adv.***

☆**bo·lo·ney** (bə lō′nē) ***n.*** *alt. sp. of* BALONEY

☆**bo·lo tie** (bō′lō) ⟦altered < *bola tie*: from its resemblance to the BOLA⟧ a cord, worn as a necktie, with an ornamented fastening for adjusting the neck loop

Bol·she·vik (bōl′shə vik′, bäl′-) [*also* **b-**] ***n., pl.*** **-viks′** or **Bol′she·vi′ki** (-vē′kē) ⟦Russ *bol′ševik* (1903) < *bol′še*, larger, compar. of *bol′šoj*, big, large⟧ **1** a member of a majority faction (*Bolsheviki*) of the Russian Social Democratic Workers' Party, which formed the Communist Party after seizing power in the 1917 Revolution **2** a Communist, esp. of the Soviet Union **3** loosely, any radical: hostile usage —***adj.*** of or like the Bolsheviks or Bolshevism —**Bol′she·vism′** ***n.*** —**Bol′she·vist** ***n., adj.*** —**Bol′she·vize′** (-vīz′) ***vt.*** **-vized′**, **-viz′ing**

bol·shie or **bol·shy** (bōl′shē) ***n., pl.*** **-shies** [Slang, Chiefly Brit.] BOLSHEVIK: a humorous or derogatory use —***adj.*** **1** [Slang, Chiefly Brit.] BOLSHEVIK: a humorous or derogatory use **2** [Brit. Informal] habitually quarrelsome, uncooperative, etc.

☆**bol·son** (bōl sōn′, bōl′sōn′) ***n.*** ⟦AmSp *bolsón* < Sp, lit., big purse < *bolsa*, purse < ML *bursa*: see BOURSE⟧ in the SW U.S., a flat desert valley surrounded by mountains and draining into a shallow lake in the center

bol·ster (bōl′stər) ***n.*** ⟦ME & OE, akin to ON *bolstr*, Ger *polster*; ult. < IE base **bhel-*, to swell: see BALL[1]⟧ **1** a long, narrow cushion or pillow **2** a soft pad for easing pressure on any part of the body **3** any bolsterlike object or support; specif., *a)* a capping piece over a post to extend the bearing area under a beam *b)* the connecting part between the volutes of an Ionic capital —***vt.*** to prop up as with a bolster; support, strengthen, or reinforce

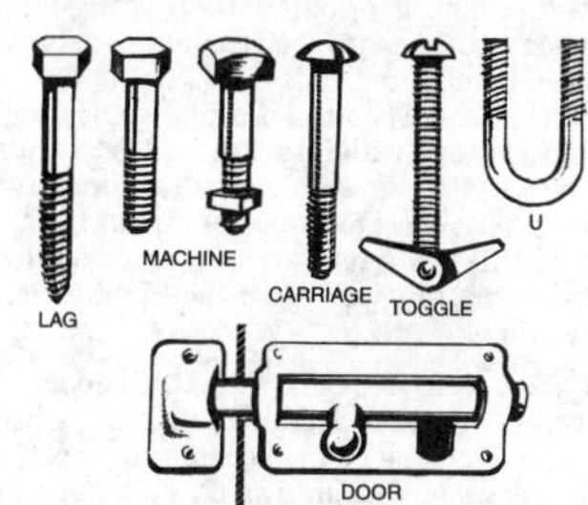

kinds of bolts

bolt[1] (bōlt) ***n.*** ⟦ME & OE, akin to Ger *bolzen* < IE base **bheld-*, to knock, strike⟧ **1** a short, heavy, often blunt arrow shot from a crossbow **2** a flash of lightning; thunderbolt **3** a sudden dash or movement **4** *a)* a sliding bar for locking a door, gate, etc. *b)* a similar bar in a lock, moved by a key **5** a threaded metal rod or pin for joining parts, having a head and usually used with a nut **6** a roll (*of* cloth, paper, etc.) of a given length **7** a jet or column (*of* some liquid) ☆**8** a bolting or withdrawal from one's party or group **9** *Firearms* a sliding bar that pushes the cartridge into place, closes the breech, and extracts the empty cartridge case after firing —***vt.*** **1** [Archaic] to shoot (an arrow, etc.) **2** to say suddenly or unexpectedly; blurt (*out*) **3** to swallow (food) hurriedly; gulp down **4** to hold together or fasten with or as with a bolt **5** to roll (cloth, etc.) into bolts ☆**6** to withdraw support from or abandon (a party, group, etc.) —***vi.*** **1** to dash out suddenly; spring; dart **2** to start suddenly and run away, as a horse ☆**3** to withdraw support from or abandon a party, group, etc. **4** *Hort.* to produce seed prematurely —**bolt from the blue** **1** a thunderbolt from a clear sky **2** a sudden, unforeseen occurrence, often an unfortunate one —**bolt upright** straight up; erect or erectly —**shoot one's bolt** to do one's utmost; exhaust one's capabilities

bolt[2] (bōlt) *vt.* ⟦ME *bulten* < OFr *buleter*, ? dissimilated < **bureter* < *bure* (< VL **bura*), coarse cloth; akin to It *burattare* < *buratto*, sieve⟧ **1** to sift (flour, grain, etc.) so as to separate and grade **2** [Archaic] to inspect and separate, as good from bad; examine closely

bolt·er[1] (bōl′tər) *n.* **1** a horse that bolts, or runs away ☆**2** a person who withdraws from a political party, group, etc.

bolt·er[2] (-tər) *n.* a device for bolting, or sifting, flour, etc.

bolt-hole (bōlt′hōl′) *n.* ⟦< *bolting-hole*, a hole through which to BOLT[1] (*vi.* 1)⟧ [Brit.] **1** a path of escape **2** a place for hiding, seclusion, etc.: also written **bolt′hole′**

Bol·ton (bōl′tən) city in Greater Manchester, NW England

☆**bol·to·ni·a** (bōl tō′nē ə) *n.* ⟦ModL, after J. *Bolton*, 18th-c. Eng naturalist⟧ any of a genus (*Boltonia*) of perennial American plants of the composite family with white or purplish asterlike heads

bolt·rope (bōlt′rōp′) *n.* ⟦BOLT[1] + ROPE⟧ a rope sewn into the edge seam of a sail to prevent tearing: also written **bolt rope**

Boltz·mann constant (bōlts′mən) ⟦after Ludwig *Boltzmann* (1844-1906), Austrian physicist⟧ *Physics* a constant used in equations involving ideal gases, equal to 1.380658×10^{-23} joules per kelvin: symbol, k: also called **Boltzmann's constant**

bo·lus (bō′ləs) *n., pl.* **bo′lus·es** ⟦ML: see BOLE[2]⟧ **1** a small, round lump or mass, as of chewed food **2** *Med.* a mass injected into a blood vessel, as an opaque contrast medium or a radioactive tracer **3** *Vet.Med.* a large pill

bomb (bäm) *n.* ⟦Fr *bombe* < It *bomba*; prob. < L *bombus*, a buzzing < Gr *bombos*, deep and hollow sound: orig. echoic⟧ **1** a container filled with an explosive, incendiary, or other chemical for dropping or hurling, or for detonating by a timing mechanism **2** BOMBSHELL (sense 2) **3** a small container with compressed gas in it [an aerosol *bomb*] **4** a heavily shielded apparatus with radioactive material in it, used in radiotherapy [a cobalt *bomb*] ☆**5** [Informal] a complete failure: said esp. of a theatrical performance **6** [Slang] *Sports a)* a long forward pass in football *b)* a long three-pointer in basketball *c)* a long home run in baseball **7** *Geol.* a mass of lava, usually globular, ejected from a volcano by explosion —*vt.* to attack, damage, or destroy with a bomb or bombs —☆*vi.* [Informal] to be a complete failure —**the Bomb** [Informal] **1** ATOMIC BOMB **2** *a)* any nuclear weapon *b)* nuclear weapons collectively

bom·bard (bäm bärd′; *for n.* bäm′bärd′) *vt.* ⟦Fr *bombarder* < *bombarde*, mortar < *bombe*, prec.⟧ **1** to attack with or as with artillery or bombs **2** to keep attacking or pressing with questions, suggestions, etc. **3** to direct a stream of particles at (atomic nuclei) to produce nuclear transmutations —*n.* the earliest type of cannon, originally for hurling stones —*SYN.* ATTACK —**bom·bard′ment** *n.*

bom·bar·dier (bäm′bər dir′) *n.* ⟦Fr < *bombarde*: see prec.⟧ **1** [Archaic] an artilleryman ☆**2** the member of the aircrew of a bomber who operates the bombsight and releases the bombs **3** a noncommissioned artillery officer, in the British and Canadian armies

bombardier beetle any of various ground beetles (esp. genus *Brachinus*) that protect themselves by discharging an irritating fluid that vaporizes with a popping sound on contact with the air

bom·bar·don (bäm′bər dən, bäm bär′-) *n.* ⟦It *bombardone* < *bombarda*, mortar < Fr *bombarde*: see BOMBARD⟧ **1** an early type of bassoon **2** a bass or contrabass tuba, used in military bands

bom·bast (bäm′bast′) *n.* ⟦ME, cotton padding < OFr *bombace* < ML *bombax*, cotton < *bambax*, cotton (with form infl. by L *bombyx*, silk, silkworm < Gr) < LGr < Gr *pambax* < Pers *pambak*, cotton⟧ talk or writing that sounds grand or important but has little meaning; pompous language

bom·bas·tic (bäm bas′tik) *adj.* using or characterized by high-sounding but unimportant or meaningless language; pompous; grandiloquent —**bom·bas′ti·cal·ly** *adv.*

SYN.—**bombastic** refers to speech or writing that is pompous and inflated and suggests extravagant verbal padding and little substance; **grandiloquent** suggests an overreaching eloquence and implies the use of grandiose, high-flown language and an oratorical tone; **flowery** language is full of figurative and ornate expressions and high-sounding words; **euphuistic** is applied to an extremely artificial style of writing in which there is a straining for effect at the expense of thought; **turgid** implies such inflation of style as to obscure meaning

bom·bax (bäm′baks′) *adj.* ⟦ModL < ML, cotton: see BOMBAST⟧ designating a family (Bombacaceae, order Malvales) of dicotyledonous tropical trees, including the kapok tree, baobab, and balsa

Bom·bay[1] (bäm bā′) *n.* ⟦named for the fol. because thought of as resembling the black leopards of India⟧ any of a breed of short-haired domestic cat with a solid black coat and round, yellowish eyes

Bom·bay[2] (bäm bā′) *former name for* MUMBAI

bom·ba·zine (bäm′bə zēn′, bäm′bə zēn′) *n.* ⟦Fr *bombasin* < ML *bombacinium*, silk texture < *bombax*: see BOMBAST⟧ a twilled cloth of silk or rayon with worsted, often dyed black

bomb bay a storage compartment in the fuselage of a bomber, with doors beneath it, for carrying bombs, fuel tanks, spare parts, etc.

bombe (bäm; *Fr* bōnb) *n.* ⟦Fr: see BOMB⟧ a frozen dessert consisting of a round mold of ice cream or sherbet with a center as of custard, mousse, or ice cream in a different flavor

bom·bé (bōn bā′; *E* bäm bā′) *adj.* ⟦Fr < *bombe*, BOMB (because of the shape)⟧ having a rounded, outward curve on the front or sides [a *bombé* china cabinet]

☆**bombed** (bämd) *adj.* [Slang] having the nervous system so affected by alcoholic liquor, a narcotic drug, etc., as to have lost control: sometimes with *out*

bomb·er (bäm′ər) *n.* **1** an airplane designed for dropping bombs **2** a person who uses bombs, as for illegal purposes

bomber jacket **1** a loose, zippered leather jacket with fitted waist and cuffs, worn by American bomber pilots in WWII **2** a casual jacket resembling this

bom·be·sin (bäm′bə sin) *n.* ⟦< ModL *Bombina bombina*, species name of the frog from whose skin it was orig. extracted⟧ a short polypeptide in some animals, esp. in the brain and stomach of a mammal, that stimulates the activity of the nervous, endocrine, and immune systems

bom·bi·nate (bäm′bə nāt′) *vi.* **-nat′ed, -nat′ing** ⟦< ModL *bombinatus*, pp. of *bombinare*, altered < L *bombitare*, to buzz < *bombus*, a buzzing: see BOMB⟧ to make a buzzing sound —**bom′bi·na′tion** *n.*

bomb·proof (bäm′pro͞of′) *adj.* capable of withstanding the force of ordinary bombs

bomb·shell (-shel′) *n.* **1** BOMB (*n.* 1) **2** any shocking surprise **3** something which arouses great interest or excitement; sensation; specif., a woman with remarkable sex appeal, typically one who is blond and buxom

bomb·sight (-sīt′) *n.* a complex instrument on a bomber which can determine when to drop a bomb in order to strike a target

bomb squad a specialized team of police technicians having expertise in disabling and removing bombs

bom·by·cid (bäm′bə sid′) *n.* ⟦< ModL < L *bombyx* (see BOMBAST) + -ID⟧ any of a family (Bombycidae) of moths found chiefly in tropical regions, as the silkworm moth —**bom′by·coid′** (-koid′) *adj.*

Bo·mu (bō′mo͞o′) river in central Africa, flowing westward along the border of the Central African Republic & the Democratic Republic of the Congo, joining the Uele to form the Ubangi: *c.* 500 mi (805 km)

☆**bo·na·ci** (bō′nä sē′) *n.* ⟦AmSp *bonasí*⟧ any of various groupers (genus *Mycteroperca*) found near Florida, the West Indies, etc.: important as food fishes

bo·na fide (bō′nə fīd′, bän′ə-; bō′nə fī′dē) ⟦L, lit., in good faith⟧ **1** in good faith; made or done without fraud or deceit [a *bona fide* offer to negotiate] **2** genuine; real [a *bona fide* Chippendale chair] —*SYN.* AUTHENTIC

bo·na fi·des (bō′nə fī′dēz′, bō′nə fīdz′) ⟦L, lit., good faith⟧ **1** good faith; honesty, sincerity, reliability, etc. **2** proof or proofs of honesty, genuineness, etc.

☆**bo·nan·za** (bə nan′zə, bō-) *n.* ⟦Sp, fair weather, prosperity < VL **bonacia*, < L *bonus*, good (see BONUS), after *malacia*, calm at sea (assumed to be < *malus*, bad) < Gr *malakia* < *malakos*, soft, akin to *mylē*, MILL[1]⟧ **1** a very rich vein or pocket of ore **2** any source of great wealth or profits

Bo·na·parte[1] (bō′nə pärt′; *Fr* bô nȧ pȧrt′) *n.* name of a Corsican family of Italian origin to which belonged Napoleon I and his four brothers

Bo·na·parte[2] (bō′nə pärt′; *Fr* bô nȧ pȧrt′) **1 Jé·rôme** (zhā rōm′) 1784-1860; king of Westphalia (1807-13) **2 Joseph** 1768-1844; king of Naples (1806-08) & of Spain (1808-13) **3 Louis** 1778-1846; king of Holland (1806-10): father of Louis Napoleon **4 Lu·cien** (lü syan′) (*Prince of Canino*) 1775-1840; Fr. government official **5 Na·po·le·on** (nə pō′lē ən, -pōl′yən) 1769-1821; Fr. military leader & emperor of France (1804-15), born in Corsica: in full *Napoleon I* See also NAPOLEON II, LOUIS NAPOLEON

Bo·na·part·ism (bō′nə pärt′iz′əm) *n.* **1** support of the Bonaparte dynasty in France **2** the methods, doctrines, etc. of any military-political dictator like Napoleon Bonaparte —**Bo′na·part′ist** *n.*

bon ap·pé·tit (bōn nȧ pā tē′) ⟦Fr, lit., good appetite⟧ enjoy your meal

Bon·a·ven·tu·ra (bō′nə ven to͝or′ə, bän′ə-), Saint (born *Giovanni Fidanza*) (1221-74); It. theologian & scholastic philosopher: his day is July 15: also **Bon·a·ven·ture** (bän′ə ven′chər)

bon·bon (bän′bän′; *Fr* bōn bōn′) *n.* ⟦Fr, redupl. of *bon*, good⟧ a small piece of candy, as a chocolate-covered cream

bond[1] (bänd) *n.* ⟦ME *bond, band*: see BAND[1]⟧ **1** anything that binds, fastens, or restrains **2** [*pl.*] *a)* fetters; shackles *b)* [Archaic] imprisonment; captivity **3** *a)* a binding or uniting force; tie; link [the *bonds* of friendship] *b)* a fastening or adhesion, as by glue, solder, etc. **4** a binding agreement; covenant **5** a duty or obligation imposed by a contract, promise, etc. **6** a substance or device, as glue, solder, or a chain, which holds things together or unites them **7** BOND PAPER **8** *Chem. a)* a unit of combining capacity equivalent to one atom of hydrogen: represented in structural formulas by a dash or dot *b)* an electrostatic attraction between atoms or groups of atoms that forms a stable aggregate unit, such as a molecule or metal **9** *Commerce a)* an agreement by an agency holding taxable or dutiable goods that taxes or duties on them will be paid before they are sold *b)* the condition of goods kept in a warehouse until taxes or duties are paid *c)* an insurance contract by which a bonding agency guarantees payment of a specified sum to the payee in the event of a financial loss caused as by the act of a specified employee or by some contingency over which the payee has no control **10** *Finance* an interest-bearing certificate issued by a government or business, promising to pay the holder a specified sum on a specified date: it is a common means of raising capital funds **11** *Law a)* a written obligation to pay specified sums, or to do or not do specified things *b)* an amount paid as surety or bail *c)* [Archaic] a bondsman, or surety **12** *Masonry* the way in which bricks, stones, etc. are lapped upon one another in building —*vt.* **1** to connect or fasten with or as with a bond; bind **2** to furnish a bond, or bail, and thus become a surety for (someone) **3** to place or hold (goods) in or under bond **4** to issue interest-bearing certificates on **5** to put under bonded debt **6** to arrange (timbers, bricks, etc.) in a pattern that gives strength —*vi.* to connect, hold together, or solidify by or as by a bond —**bottled in bond** stored in bonded warehouses for a stated length of time before being bottled, as some whiskey —**bond′a·ble** *adj.* —**bond′er** *n.*

bond[2] (bänd) [Obs.] *n.* ⟦ME *bonde* < OE *bonda*: see BONDAGE⟧ a serf or slave —*adj.* in serfdom or slavery

Bond, James *see* JAMES BOND

bond·age (bän′dij) *n.* ⟦ME < Anglo-L *bondagium* < OE *bonda* < ON *bonde,* orig. prp. of *bua,* to prepare, inhabit, akin to Ger *bauen,* to build < IE base **bheu-,* to grow, develop > BE, Sans *bhū-,* earth, Gr *phyein,* to grow⟧ **1** serfdom or slavery **2** subjection to some force, compulsion, or influence; specif., physical restraint as a sadomasochistic technique **3** VILLEINAGE —*SYN.* SERVITUDE

bond·ed (bän′did) *adj.* **1** linked or secured by a bond or bonds **2** placed in a bonded warehouse **3** having been bottled in bond

bonded warehouse a warehouse, certified by the government and guaranteed by a bonding agency, where taxable or dutiable goods may be stored, with payment of the tax or duty deferred until the goods are removed

bond·hold·er (bänd′hōl′dər) *n.* an owner of bonds issued by a company, government, or person

bond·ing (bän′diŋ) *n.* **1** the development of a close relationship as between family members or friends **2** *Dentistry* a procedure in which a synthetic resin is applied to a tooth surface to fill or cover flaws

bond·maid (bänd′mād′) *n.* a girl or woman bondservant or slave

bond·man (-mən) *n., pl.* **-men** (-mən) **1** a feudal serf **2** a man or boy bondservant

☆**bond paper 1** paper with rag content, originally used for bonds, bank notes, etc. **2** any strong, superior grade of paper used for documents, letterheads, etc.

bond·ser·vant (-sur′vənt) *n.* **1** a person bound to service without pay **2** a slave

bonds·man (bändz′mən) *n., pl.* **-men** (-mən) **1** BONDMAN **2** a person who takes responsibility for another by furnishing a bond

bond·wom·an (bänd′woom′ən) *n., pl.* **-wom′en** (-wim′in) a woman bondservant

bone (bōn) *n.* ⟦ME *bon* < OE *ban,* bone, esp. of a limb, akin to Ger *bein,* a leg; only Gmc⟧ **1** any of the separate parts of the hard connective tissue forming the skeleton of most full-grown vertebrate animals **2** this tissue, composed essentially of living cells embedded in hard calcium compounds **3** [*pl.*] the skeleton **4** [*pl.*] the body, living or dead **5** a bonelike substance or part, as whalebone **6** a thing made of bone or of bonelike material; specif., *a)* a corset stay *b)* [*pl.*] [Informal] dice **7** *a)* [*pl.*] flat sticks used as clappers in minstrel shows ☆*b)* [*pl., with sing. v.*] an end man in a minstrel show **8** BONE WHITE —*vt.* **boned, bon′ing 1** to remove the bones from **2** to put whalebone or other stiffening into **3** to fertilize with bone meal —*vi.* [Slang] ☆to study hard and hurriedly, as in preparation for an examination; cram: usually with *up* —*adv.* extremely; exceedingly [*bone* tired] —☆**feel in one's bones** to have an intuition or presentiment —**have a bone to pick** [Informal] to have something to quarrel or complain about —**make no bones about** [Informal] **1** to make no attempt to hide; admit freely **2** to have no objection to or qualms about —**throw someone a bone** ⟦in allusion to the practice of rewarding a dog with a bone⟧ [Informal] to reward someone in a meager and patronizing way —**to the bone** to the core; thoroughly and essentially [she's a conservative *to the bone*] —**work one's fingers to the bone** to work very hard

Bône (bōn) *former name for* ANNABA

bone ash a white porous ash prepared by burning bones in the open air and consisting chiefly of calcium phosphate: used in making bone china and in fertilizers: also **bone earth**

bone black a fine charcoal made by burning animal bones in closed containers: used as a pigment, in refining sugar, etc.: also written **bone·black** (bōn′blak′) *n.*

bone china translucent china made with white clay to which bone ash or calcium phosphate has been added

boned (bōnd) *adj.* **1** having (a specific kind of) bone [brittle-*boned*] **2** having the bones taken out **3** having stays of whalebone, etc.

bone-dry (bōn′drī′) *adj.* [Informal] **1** dry as a bone that has lain exposed to the air; very dry **2** absolutely abstaining from, or prohibiting the use of, alcoholic drinks

☆**bone·fish** (-fish′) *n., pl.* **-fish′** or **-fish′es** (see FISH) any of a family (Albulidae, order Elopiformes) of silvery marine fishes; esp., a game and food fish (*Albula vulpes*) of shallow tropical waters

☆**bone·head** (-hed′) *n.* [Slang] a stupid person; fool

bone·less (-lis) *adj.* without bones; specif., with the bones removed [*boneless* sardines]

☆**bone meal** crushed or finely ground bones, used as feed for stock, as fertilizer, and as a nutritional supplement for humans

bone of contention a matter for argument; subject about which there is disagreement

bone oil a thick, black oil derived from destructive distillation of bones

☆**bon·er**[1] (bōn′ər) *n.* ⟦< BONE(HEAD) + -ER⟧ [Slang] a stupid or silly blunder —*SYN.* ERROR

bon·er[2] (bōn′ər) *n.* [Slang] an erection of the penis: somewhat vulgar

☆**bone·set** (bōn′set′) *n.* ⟦prob. < BONE + SET (*vt.*), from medicinal use⟧ any of several plants of the composite family; esp., a plant (*Eupatorium perfoliatum*) with flat clusters of white flowers, used in folk medicine

bone white any of various shades of grayish or yellowish white

bone·yard (bōn′yärd′) *n.* [Slang] a cemetery; graveyard

bon·fire (bän′fīr′) *n.* ⟦ME *banefyre,* lit., bone fire; later, funeral pyre⟧ a large fire built outdoors

☆**bong**[1] (bôŋ, bäŋ) *n.* ⟦echoic⟧ a deep ringing sound, as of a large bell or gong —*vi.* to make this sound

bong[2] (bôŋ, bäŋ) *n.* ⟦< ?⟧ a water pipe for smoking marijuana, etc.

bon·go[1] (bäŋ′gō, bôŋ′-) *n., pl.* **-gos** ⟦native Afr name⟧ a large African antelope (*Tragelaphus eurycerus*) with a reddish-brown coat and white stripes

☆**bon·go**[2] (bäŋ′gō, bôŋ′-) *n., pl.* **-gos** ⟦AmSp < ?⟧ either of a pair of small joined drums, each of different pitch, struck with the fingers: in full **bongo drum**

Bon·heur (bô nër′), **Ro·sa** (rō zȧ′) (born *Marie Rosalie Bonheur*) 1822-99; Fr. painter of animal subjects

bon·ho·mie (bän′ə mē′, bän′ə mē; *Fr* bô nô mē′) *n.* ⟦Fr < *bonhomme* < *bon,* good + *homme,* man⟧ good nature; pleasant, affable manner; amiability —**bon·ho·mous** (bän′ə məs) *adj.*

bon·i·face (bän′ə fəs, -fās′) *n.* ⟦after *Boniface,* landlord in Farquhar's comedy, *The Beaux' Stratagem*⟧ an innkeeper, restaurateur, etc.

bongos

Bon·i·face (bän′ə fəs, -fās′) **1** Saint (born *Winfrid* or *Wynfrith*) (A.D. 675?-754?); Eng. monk & missionary in Germany: his day is June 5 **2 Boniface VIII** (born *Benedetto Caetani*) 1235?-1303; pope (1294-1303)

bon·i·ness (bōn′ē nis) *n.* the condition of being bony

bo·ni·to (bō nēt′ō, bə-) *n., pl.* **-tos, -toes, -to** ⟦Sp, orig. dim. of *bueno,* good < L *bonus*: see BONUS⟧ any of a genus (*Sarda*) of marine game and food scombroid fishes

bon·jour (bōn zhoor′) *interj., n.* ⟦Fr⟧ good day; good morning

☆**bonk** (bôŋk) *vt., vi.* ⟦echoic⟧ **1** to hit on the head with a hollow, resounding blow **2** to hit (one's head) against something **3** [Brit. Slang] to engage in sexual intercourse (with): mildly vulgar —*n.* **1** a blow on the head **2** the sound of this **3** [Brit. Slang] an act or instance of sexual intercourse: mildly vulgar

bonk·ers (bäŋ′kərz) *adj.* ⟦prob. < Brit *bonk,* obs. military slang, "to bomb," echoic⟧ [Slang] crazy, enraged, etc.

bon mot (bōn′ mō′; *Fr* bōn mō′) *pl.* **bons mots** (bōn′ mōz′; *Fr* bōn mō′) ⟦Fr, lit., good word: see MOT⟧ an apt, clever, or witty remark

Bonn (bän) city in W Germany, in North Rhine-Westphalia: capital of the Federal Republic of Germany (West Germany), 1949-90

Bon·nard (bô nȧr′), **Pierre** (pyer) 1867-1947; Fr. impressionist painter

bonne (bôn) *n.* ⟦Fr < fem. of *bon,* good⟧ a maidservant

bonne chance (bôn shäns′) ⟦Fr⟧ good luck: an expression of good wishes

bonne nuit (bôn nwē′) ⟦Fr⟧ good night

bon·net (bän′it) *n.* ⟦ME & OFr *bonet* < ML *bonitum* aphetic < *abonnis,* kind of cap⟧ **1** in Scotland, a flat, brimless cap, worn by men and boys **2** *a)* a hat with a chin ribbon, worn by children and women *b)* [Informal] any hat worn by women or girls **3** *a)* a metal covering, hood, or cowl, as over a fireplace, stove, or chimney for draft or ventilation *b)* [Brit.] an automobile hood **4** *Naut.* a strip of canvas fastened by lacing to the bottom of a sail to increase sail area —*vt.* to put a bonnet on

Bon·nie (bän′ē) *n.* ⟦< fol.⟧ a feminine name: var. *Bonny*

bon·ny or **bon·nie** (bän′ē) *adj.* **-ni·er, -ni·est** ⟦< Fr *bon,* good < L *bonus*: see BONUS⟧ [Now Chiefly Brit.] **1** handsome or pretty, with a healthy glow **2** fine; pleasant —**bon′ni·ly** *adv.* —**bon′ni·ness** *n.*

bon·ny·clab·ber (bän′ē klab′ər) *n.* ⟦Ir *bainne,* milk + *clabar,* clabber < *claba,* thick⟧ thickly curdled sour milk

bo·no·bo (bə nō′bō) *n., pl.* **-bos** ⟦< name in a local African language⟧ a small, long-limbed chimpanzee (*Pan paniscus*) of the rainforests of the Democratic Republic of the Congo

bon·sai (bän′sī′, bän sī′) *n.* ⟦Jpn *bon,* lit., basin or pot + *sai,* to plant⟧ **1** the art of dwarfing and shaping trees and shrubs in shallow pots by pruning, controlled fertilization, etc. **2** *pl.* **bon′sai′** such a tree or shrub

bon·soir (bōn swȧr′) *interj., n.* ⟦Fr⟧ good evening

bon·spiel (bän′spēl′, -spəl) *n.* ⟦prob. < Du *bondspel* < *bond,* league + *spel,* game⟧ [Scot.] a curling tournament

bonsai

bon·te·bok (bän′tə bäk′) *n., pl.* **-bok′** or **-boks′** ⟦Afrik < Du *bont,* variegated + *bok,* BUCK[1]⟧ a large, dark-brown antelope (*Damaliscus dorcas dorcas*) of S Africa, white on the face and rump: see BLESBOK

bon ton (bōn tōn′; *Fr* bōn tōn′) ⟦Fr, good tone⟧ **1** stylishness **2** fine manners **3** fashionable society

bo·nus (bō′nəs) *n., pl.* **bo′nus·es** ⟦L, good < OL *dvonus* < IE **du-,* var. of base **deu-,* to venerate > OE *(lang)twidig,* (long) granted, L *beare,* pp. *beatus,* to make happy⟧ anything given in addition to the customary or required amount; specif., *a)* payment over and above salary given to an employee as an incentive or reward *b)* a government payment to military veterans *c)* [Brit.] a dividend to insurance policyholders; also, an extra dividend to stockholders

SYN.—**bonus** refers to anything given over and above the regular wages, salary, remuneration, etc. [a Christmas *bonus*, a soldier's *bonus*]; a **bounty** is a reward given by a government for a specific undertaking considered in the public interest, as the production of certain crops or the destruction of vermin; **premium**, as compared here, implies a reward or prize offered as an inducement to buy, sell, or compete [a toy given as a *premium* with each package]; **dividend** refers to a prorated share in an amount distributed among stockholders or policyholders from profits or surplus

bonus stock shares of stock, usually common, given by a corporation as a bonus with the purchase of another class of security

bon vi·vant (bän′ vi vänt′; *Fr* bōn vē vän′) *pl.* **bons vi·vants** (bän′ vi vänts′; *Fr* bōn vē vän′) ⟦Fr⟧ a person who enjoys good food and drink and other luxuries

bon voy·age (bän′ voi äzh′; *Fr* bōn vwȧ yȧzh′) ⟦Fr⟧ pleasant journey: a farewell to a traveler

bon·y (bō′nē) *adj.* **bon′i·er, bon′i·est** 1 of or like bone 2 having many bones 3 having large or protruding bones 4 thin; emaciated

bony fish any of a class (Osteichthyes) of fishes with an air bladder, covered gills, and a bony inner skeleton

bonze (bänz) *n.* ⟦Fr < Port *bonzo* < Jpn *bonsō*, prob. < Chin *fan seng*, religious person⟧ a Japanese or Chinese Buddhist monk

boo[1] (bo͞o) *interj., n., pl.* **boos** ⟦echoic⟧ 1 used to express disapproval, scorn, etc.: a prolonged sound 2 used to startle someone: an abrupt exclamation — *vi., vt.* **booed, boo′ing** to shout "boo" (at) in expressing disapproval —**not say boo** to not make even the slightest comment or objection [he *didn't say boo* all evening]

boo[2] (bo͞o) *n.* [Slang] MARIJUANA

☆**boob**[1] (bo͞ob) *n.* ⟦< BOOBY⟧ [Slang] a stupid or foolish person —*vi.* [Brit. Slang] to make a stupid mistake

☆**boob**[2] (bo͞ob) *n.* ⟦prob. < *booby*, baby talk for "breast"⟧ [Slang] a woman's breast: *usually used in pl.*: also **boob·ie** (bo͞o′bē)

☆**boo-boo** or **boo·boo** (bo͞o′bo͞o′) *n., pl.* **-boos′** ⟦< baby talk⟧ 1 [Slang] a stupid or foolish mistake; blunder 2 a minor injury or bruise: chiefly a child's usage —*SYN.* ERROR

☆**boob tube** ⟦BOOB[1] + (THE) TUBE (see phr. under TUBE)⟧ [Slang] television or a television set

boo·by (bo͞o′bē) *n., pl.* **-bies** ⟦prob. < Sp *bobo*, stupid < L *balbus*, stammering < IE echoic base **bal-bal-*⟧ 1 a stupid or foolish person; nitwit 2 any of a genus (*Sula*, family Sulidae) of pelecaniform birds that dive and feed on fish of warm seas

booby hatch 1 a covering over a small hatchway on a ship ☆2 [Slang] an institution for hospitalizing the mentally ill

☆**booby prize** a prize, usually a ridiculous one, given in fun to whoever has done worst in a game, race, etc.

booby trap 1 any device or scheme, as in a practical joke, for tricking a person 2 a bomb or mine that is set to be exploded by some action of the intended victim, as when some seemingly harmless object is lifted —**boo′by-trap′** *vt.* **-trapped′, -trap′ping**

☆**boo·dle** (bo͞od′'l) *n.* ⟦< Du *boedel*, property, estate⟧ [Old Slang] 1 something given as a bribe; graft 2 the loot taken in a robbery

☆**boo·dy** (bo͞od′ē) *n.* [Slang] *var. of* BOOTY[2]

☆**boo·ger** (boog′ər) *n.* [Slang] 1 a gob or dried piece of nasal mucus 2 any person or thing, esp. one regarded as troublesome, unpleasant, etc.: often used humorously and affectionately

boo·gey·man (boog′ē man′) *n., pl.* **-men′** (-men′) a frightening imaginary being, often one used as a threat in disciplining children

boo·gie (boog′ē) *vi.* **-gied, -gie·ing** to dance to rock music —*n.* rock music

boogie board a short, lightweight surfboard, usually ridden in a prone position —**boogie boarder** —**boogie boarding**

☆**boo·gie-woo·gie** (boog′ē woog′ē, bo͞o′gē wo͞o′gē) *n.* ⟦echoic; ? suggested by the characteristic "walking" bass; ? redupl. of *boogie*, var. of *bogy* (hobgoblin)⟧ a blues-based style of jazz piano playing in which insistently repeated bass figures employing eighth notes accompany melodic variations in the treble

boo·hoo (bo͞o′ho͞o′) *vi.* **-hooed′, -hoo′ing** ⟦echoic⟧ [Informal] to weep noisily —*n., pl.* **-hoos′** [Informal] noisy weeping —*interj.* used to suggest the sound of noisy weeping

book (book) *n.* ⟦ME *bok* < OE *boc*, pl. *bec* < PGmc **bokiz*, beech, beechwood tablets carved with runes < IE **bhagos*, beech > BEECH, Gr *phagos*, L *fagus*⟧ 1 *a)* a number of sheets of paper, parchment, etc. with writing or printing on them, fastened together along one edge, usually between protective covers *b)* a literary or scientific work, anthology, etc. so prepared, distinguished by length and form from a magazine, tract, etc. 2 any of the main divisions of a long written or printed work, as of the Bible 3 *a)* a set of blank or ruled sheets or printed forms bound in a tablet, for the entry of accounts, records, notes, etc. [an account *book*] *b)* [*usually pl.*] the records or accounts, as of a business, kept in such a book or books 4 something regarded as a subject for study [the *book* of life] 5 the body of facts, traits, or circumstances connected with a person or subject, esp. as being understandable, evident, etc. [an open *book*] or obscure, done with, etc. [a closed *book*] 6 [*pl.*] studies; lessons 7 *a)* the words of an opera or musical play; libretto (distinguished from SCORE) *b)* the script of a play 8 a booklike package, as of matches or tickets 9 *a)* a list or record of bets taken and the odds given, as by bookmakers on horse races *b)* [Slang] BOOKMAKER (sense 2) 10 *Bridge* a certain number of tricks that must be won before additional tricks count in the score; specif., the first six tricks won by the declarer —*vt.* 1 to record in a book; list 2 to engage ahead of time, as rooms, transportation, performers or performances, etc. 3 to record charges against on a police record 4 to take (bets) as a bookmaker —*adj.* in, from, or according to books or accounts —**bring to book** 1 to force to explain; demand an accounting from 2 to reprimand —**by the book** according to the rules; in the prescribed or usual way —**close the book on** 1 to put an end to 2 to put an end to further consideration, discussion, etc. of —**close the books** *Bookkeeping* to make no further entries, balance the books, and draw up statements from them —**in one's book** in one's opinion —**in one's good (or bad) books** in (or out of) one's favor, or good graces —☆**in the book** in all that is known and practiced in connection with a particular activity [to know every trick *in the book*] —**keep books** to keep a record of business transactions —**know (or read) like a book** to know well or fully —☆**make book** [Slang] to make or accept a bet or bets —☆**one for the books** [Informal] something notably surprising, shocking, or unexpected —**on the books** 1 recorded 2 listed; enrolled —**the Book** the Bible —**the book** [Informal] any set of rules, pronouncements, etc. regarded as authoritative —☆**throw the book at** 1 [Slang] to place every possible pertinent charge against (an accused person) 2 to deal out the maximum in punishment, penalty, etc. to —**write the book on** [Informal] 1 to be the definitive authority or expert on 2 to be the embodiment of [she *wrote the book on* selfishness] —**book′er** *n.*

book·bind·er·y (-bīn′dər ē) *n., pl.* **-er·ies** BINDERY

book·bind·ing (-bīn′diŋ) *n.* 1 the art, trade, or business of binding books 2 the binding of a book —**book′bind′er** *n.*

book·case (-kās′) *n.* a set of shelves or a cabinet for holding books

book club ☆1 a business that sells books, usually at discounted prices, to subscribing members who agree to buy a minimum number of them annually 2 a group of people who meet periodically to discuss a particular book they have all agreed to read

book·end (-end′) *n.* a support, often ornamental and usually one of a pair, put at the end of a row of books to keep them upright —*vt.* to be located at the ends of or at one end of [a bank and a supermarket *bookend* the shopping mall]

book·ie (book′ē) *n.* [Slang] BOOKMAKER (sense 2)

book·ing (book′iŋ) *n.* an engagement, as for a lecture or concert

book·ish (book′ish) *adj.* 1 of or connected with books 2 inclined to read and study; literary; scholarly 3 having mere book learning 4 pedantic; stodgy —**book′ish·ly** *adv.* —**book′ish·ness** *n.*

book·keep·ing (-kēp′iŋ) *n.* the work of keeping a systematic record of business transactions —**book′keep′er** *n.*

book learning knowledge gained from reading or study rather than from practical experience —**book′-learn′ed** (-lur′nid) *adj.*

book·let (-lit) *n.* 1 a small book, often with paper covers 2 a light cardboard folder containing one or more panes of postage stamps

book louse any of various small, usually wingless, insects (order Psocoptera) that infest and destroy old books

book lungs primitive lungs of many arachnids, consisting of pagelike layers of tissue over which air circulates for respiration

book·mak·er (-māk′ər) *n.* 1 a compiler, publisher, or manufacturer of books 2 a person in the business of taking bets, as on horse races —**book′mak′ing** *n.*

book·man (-mən) *n., pl.* **-men** (-mən) 1 a literary or scholarly man 2 a man whose work is making, publishing, or selling books

book·mark (-märk′) *n.* 1 anything slipped between the pages of a book to mark a place 2 *Comput.* a digital pointer that a user can create for gaining easy access to a Web page, a portion of text in a file, etc. —*vt. Comput.* to create a bookmark to (a Web page, portion of text, etc.)

☆**book matches** safety matches made of paper and fastened into a small cardboard folder

☆**book·mo·bile** (-mō bēl′, -mə-) *n.* ⟦BOOK + -MOBILE⟧ a truck, bus, etc. equipped to serve as a traveling public library

book of account 1 a book to keep accounts in; ledger 2 any of the records needed for auditing the accounts of a business; journal

Book of Common Prayer ⟦< *common prayer*, public (as opposed to private) worship, in which people participate together⟧ the official book of services and prayers for the Anglican Communion

☆**Book of Mormon** the sacred book of the Mormons: see MORMON

Book of the Dead in ancient Egypt, a book of prayers and charms meant to help the soul in the afterworld

book·plate (book′plāt′) *n.* a label, often specially designed, pasted in a book to identify its owner

book·rack (-rak′) *n.* 1 a rack or shelf for books 2 BOOKSTAND (sense 1)

book·rest (-rest′) *n.* BOOKSTAND (sense 1)

book review an article or talk in which a book, esp. a new book, is discussed and critically analyzed

book scorpion any of various small arachnids (order Pseudoscorpionida) resembling a scorpion without a tail, found beneath stones, in old papers and books, etc.

book·sell·er (-sel′ər) *n.* a person who sells books; specif., the owner or manager of a bookstore

book·shelf (-shelf′) *n., pl.* **-shelves′** a shelf on which books are kept

book·shop (-shäp′) *n.* a bookstore, esp. a small or specialized one
book·stall (-stôl′) *n.* 1 a stand, booth, or counter, often one outdoors, where books are sold 2 [Brit.] a newsstand
book·stand (-stand′) *n.* 1 a stand for holding a book open before a reader 2 BOOKSTALL (sense 1)
☆**book·store** (-stôr′) *n.* a retail store specializing in books
book tour a tour of cities undertaken, typically by the author, to promote the sale of a book by means of public appearances, interviews, etc.
book value 1 the value of any of the assets of a business as shown on its account books 2 *a)* the net worth of a business, or the value of its capital stock, as shown by the excess of assets over liabilities *b)* the value, on this basis, of a single share of stock
book·worm (-wurm′) *n.* 1 any of a number of insects or insect larvae that harm books by feeding on the binding, paste, etc. 2 a person who spends much time reading or studying
Bool·e·an (bo͞o′lē ən) *adj.* ⟦after G. *Boole* (1815-64), Eng mathematician⟧ [*often* **b-**] designating or of any of a number of mathematical systems, esp. one (**Boolean algebra**) devised, using algebraic rules and symbols, for the analysis of symbolic logic and now widely used in digital computers since its true-false results are compatible with binary numbers
boom[1] (bo͞om) *vi.* ⟦ME *bummen,* to hum; like Du *bommen,* Ger *bummen,* orig. echoic⟧ to make a deep, hollow, resonant sound —*vt.* to speak or indicate with such a sound: usually with *out* [*the clock **boomed** out the hour*] —*n.* 1 a booming sound, as of thunder, heavy guns, etc. 2 the resonant cry of certain animals, as the bullfrog —**boom′er** *n.*
boom[2] (bo͞om) *n.* ⟦Du, a tree, beam, pole; same word ult. as BEAM⟧ 1 a spar extending from a mast to hold the bottom of a sail outstretched 2 ⟦from use of ship's boom for this purpose⟧ a long beam extending as from an upright to lift or carry something and guide it as needed [*the **boom** of a derrick, a microphone **boom***] 3 a barrier of chains or poles to obstruct navigation ☆4 in lumbering, *a)* a barrier across a river or around an area of water to prevent floating logs from dispersing *b)* the area in which logs are thus confined 5 *Aeron.* a retractable metal tube for transferring fuel from a tanker to another plane in flight —*vt.* to stretch out (sails) as with a boom so as to take maximum advantage of a wind abaft the beam and hence make speed —☆*vi.* to go rapidly along; move with speed or vigor: usually with *along* —☆**lower the boom** [Informal] to act suddenly and forcefully in dealing out punishment or criticism, in defeating, etc.
boom[3] (bo͞om) *vi.* ⟦< ? prec. *vi.;* later assoc. with BOOM[1]⟧ to increase suddenly in size, importance, activity, etc.; undergo swift, vigorous growth; flourish [*business **boomed***] —*vt.* to promote vigorously; popularize [*they **boomed** him for mayor*] —*n.* 1 swift, vigorous growth or development 2 a period of business prosperity, industrial expansion, etc. 3 a sudden favorable turn in business or political prospects —*adj.* of, characteristic of, or resulting from a boom in business, etc.
☆**boom·box** (bo͞om′bäks′) *n.* ⟦descriptive of its shape and the sound produced⟧ [Slang] a large, powerful portable radio and tape or CD player
boom·er[1] (bo͞om′ər) *n.* ☆⟦< BOOM[3]⟧ [Informal] a worker, as in bridge construction, who travels about, working for different employers
boom·er[2] (bo͞om′ər) *n.* ☆[Informal] *short for* BABY BOOMER
boom·er·ang (bo͞om′ər aŋ′) *n.* ⟦< name in a language of Australia⟧ 1 a flat, curved stick that can be thrown so that it will return to a point near the thrower: it is used as a weapon by Australian Aborigines 2 something that goes contrary to expectations and results in disadvantage or harm to the person doing or saying it —*vi.* to act as a boomerang; result in harm to the originator
Boom·er State (bo͞om′ər) ⟦< *boomer,* promoter (in allusion to those who promoted rapid settlement) < BOOM[3] (*vt.*)⟧ *name for* OKLAHOMA
☆**boom·let** (bo͞om′lit) *n.* a small boom, as in business
boom·town (bo͞om′toun′) *n.* a town that has sprung up or expanded rapidly as a result of an economic boom: also **boom town**
boon[1] (bo͞on) *n.* ⟦ME *bone* < ON *bon,* a petition, prayer < IE base **bha-,* to speak (see FAME); meaning prob. infl. by fol.⟧ 1 [Archaic] a request or the favor requested 2 welcome benefit; blessing
boon[2] (bo͞on) *adj.* ⟦ME & OFr *bon* < L *bonus,* good⟧ 1 [Archaic] kind, generous, pleasant, etc. 2 merry; convivial: now only in **boon companion**, a close friend
boon·docks (bo͞on′däks′) *pl.n.* ⟦orig. WWII military slang < Tagalog *bundok,* mountain⟧ [Informal] 1 a jungle or a wild, heavily wooded area; wilderness ☆2 any remote rural or provincial region; hinterland Used with *the* —**boon′dock′** *adj.*
☆**boon·dog·gle** (bo͞on′däg′əl, -dôg′-) *n.* ⟦orig. dial., ornamental leather strap; modern sense from *c.* 1935⟧ a trifling or pointless project, expenditure, etc.; now esp., one financed by public funds —*vi.* **-gled**, **-gling** to engage in a boondoggle —**boon′dog′gler** *n.*
Boone (bo͞on), **Daniel** 1734-1820; Am. frontiersman
boon·ies (bo͞o′nēz) *pl.n.* [Slang] boondocks; hinterland: used with *the*
boor (boor) *n.* ⟦Du *boer* < MDu *gheboer,* fellow dweller < *ghe-,* with, co- + *bouwen,* to build, cultivate; akin to Ger *bauer*: see BONDAGE⟧ 1 [Archaic] a peasant or farm worker 2 a rude, awkward, or ill-mannered person
boor·ish (boor′ish) *adj.* like or characteristic of a boor; rude; awkward; ill-mannered —*SYN.* RUDE —**boor′ish·ly** *adv.* —**boor′ish·ness** *n.*
☆**boost** (bo͞ost) *vt.* ⟦< ?⟧ 1 to raise by or as by a push from behind or below; push up 2 to urge others to support; promote [*to **boost** a program*] 3 to make higher or greater; increase in amount, power, etc. [*to **boost** taxes, **boost** electric current*] 4 [Slang] to steal; esp., to shoplift —*vi.* [Slang] to steal; esp., to shoplift —*n.* 1 a push to help propel a person or thing upward or forward 2 an act that helps or promotes 3 an increase in amount, power, etc. —*SYN.* LIFT
☆**boost·er** (bo͞os′tər) *n.* 1 a person who boosts; enthusiastic supporter 2 *Elec.* a device for controlling or varying the voltage in a circuit 3 *Radio, TV* an amplifier between the antenna and the receiver 4 any device that provides added power, thrust, or pressure 5 *a)* any of the early stages of a multistage rocket *b)* LAUNCH VEHICLE (also **booster rocket**) 6 BOOSTER SHOT 7 [Slang] a thief, esp. a shoplifter
booster cables JUMPER CABLES
☆**boost·er·ism** (-iz′əm) *n.* the practice of boosting or promoting a city, resort, etc.
☆**booster shot (*or* injection)** an injection of a vaccine or other antigen some time after the initial series of injections, for maintaining immunity
boot[1] (bo͞ot) *n.* ⟦ME & OFr *bote*⟧ 1 *a)* a protective covering of leather, rubber, cloth, etc., for the foot and part or all of the leg [*riding **boot***] *b)* an overshoe *c)* a man's shoe reaching at least to the ankle 2 a boot-shaped instrument of torture for crushing the foot and leg 3 [Brit.] the trunk of an automobile 4 any of various protective coverings [*a **boot** covering the base of a gearshift*] ☆5 DENVER BOOT 6 *a)* a kick *b)* [Informal] pleasurable excitement; thrill 7 *Comput.* the starting or restarting of a computer ☆8 [Slang] a Navy or Marine recruit, esp. one in a training camp —*vt.* 1 to put boots on 2 to kick 3 [Informal] to put (a person) out of a place or job; dismiss ☆4 *Baseball* to make an error in fielding (a grounder) 5 [Slang] *Horse Racing* to ride (a horse) in a race 6 *Comput.* to start (a computer) and prepare for use by loading automatically (the operating system) into memory, as from a disk: often with *up* —*vi. Comput.* to load, as from a disk, the operating system into the memory of a computer: usually with *up* —☆**bet your boots** [Informal] to be certain; rely on it —**die with one's boots on** to die in action —☆**lick the boots of** to be servile toward; fawn on —**the boot** [Slang] discharge, as from work; dismissal
boot[2] (bo͞ot) *n., vt., vi.* ⟦ME *bote* < OE *bot,* advantage, remedy; akin to BETTER[1], BEST⟧ [Archaic] remedy; profit; benefit —**to boot** besides; in addition
boot·black (bo͞ot′blak′) *n.* ⟦BOOT[1] + BLACK, *vt., vi.* 2⟧ a person whose work is shining shoes and boots
☆**boot camp** ⟦orig., *bootneck,* a Marine, in reference to the leather collar of the uniform; later contr. in use for a Marine recruit, then for a trainee more generally⟧ a station where Navy or Marine recruits receive basic training
☆**boot·ee** (bo͞o tē′; *for 2* bo͞ot′ē) *n.* ⟦BOOT[1] + -EE[1]⟧ 1 a short boot or light overshoe worn by women and children 2 a baby's soft, knitted or cloth shoe
Bo·ö·tes (bō ō′tēz′) *n.* ⟦L < Gr *boōtēs,* lit., plowman < *bous,* ox: see COW[1]⟧ a N constellation between Virgo and Draco, including the bright star Arcturus; the Herdsman
booth (bo͞oth; *chiefly Brit* bo͞oth) *n., pl.* **booths** (bo͞oths, bo͞othz) ⟦ME *both* < ON *buth,* temporary dwelling < *bua,* to prepare: see BONDAGE⟧ 1 a temporary shed or shelter 2 a stall for the sale or display of goods, as at markets and fairs 3 a small temporary structure or enclosure for voting at elections 4 a small permanent structure or enclosure to house a sentry, public telephone, etc. 5 a small, partially enclosed compartment with a table and seats, as in some restaurants
Booth (bo͞oth) 1 **Bal·ling·ton** (bal′iŋ tən) 1859-1940; founder of Volunteers of America (1896): son of William 2 **Edwin (Thomas)** 1833-93; U.S. actor: son of Junius Brutus 3 **Evangeline Cor·y** (kôr′ē) 1865-1950; U.S. general of Salvation Army, born in England: daughter of William 4 **John Wilkes** (wilks) 1838-65; U.S. actor: assassin of Abraham Lincoln: son of Junius Brutus 5 **Jun·ius Brutus** (jo͞on′yəs, -ēəs) 1796-1852; U.S. actor, born in England 6 **William** 1829-1912; Eng. revivalist: founder of the Salvation Army (1865)
Boo·thi·a (bo͞o′thē ə), **Gulf of** inlet of the Arctic Ocean between Boothia Peninsula & Baffin Island
Boothia Peninsula ⟦after Sir Felix *Booth* (1775-1850), London distiller & promoter of Arctic expeditions⟧ peninsula in Nunavut, Canada: its N tip is the northernmost point of the North American mainland
boot·ie (bo͞ot′ē) *n. alt. sp. of* BOOTEE
boot·jack (bo͞ot′jak′) *n.* ⟦BOOT[1] + JACK⟧ a device to grip a boot heel, for helping a person to pull off boots
☆**boot·leg** (bo͞ot′leg′, -läg′) *vt., vi.* **-legged′**, **-leg′ging** ⟦in allusion to concealing objects in the leg of a high boot⟧ to make, carry, or sell (esp. liquor) illegally —*adj.* bootlegged; illegal —*n.* 1 the part of a boot that covers the leg 2 something bootlegged; esp., bootlegged liquor, recordings, etc. 3 *Football* a type of play in which the quarterback fakes a handoff to a running back and then runs, usually around the defensive end, with the ball held hidden behind a hip —**boot′leg′ger** *n.*

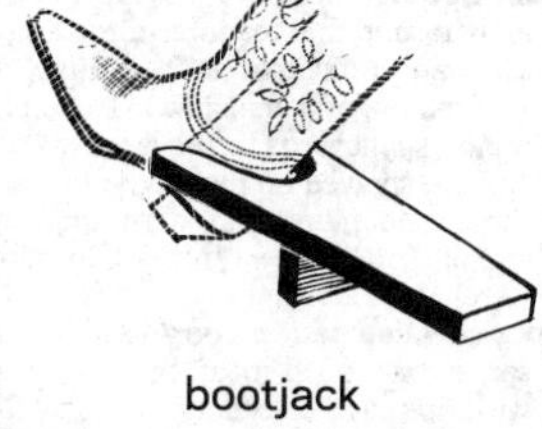
bootjack

boot·less (-lis) *adj.* ⟦BOOT[2] + -LESS⟧ without benefit; useless —**boot′less·ly** *adv.* —**boot′less·ness** *n.*
☆**boot·lick** (-lik′) *vt., vi.* ⟦< LICK THE BOOTS OF (see phr. under BOOT[1])⟧ [Informal] to try to gain favor with (someone) by fawning, servility, etc. —**boot′lick′er** *n.*

boots (bo͞ots) ***n., pl.*** **boots** [Brit.] a servant who shines shoes, as in a hotel

boots and saddles ⟦? confusion of Fr *boute-selle!*, lit., put saddle!⟧ a cavalry bugle call used as the first signal for mounted drill or other mounted formation

boot·strap (bo͞ot′strap′) ***n.*** a strap on a boot for pulling it on —***adj.*** undertaken or effected without others' help [a *bootstrap* operation] —***vt.*** **-strapped′**, **-strap′ping** [Informal] to cause (esp. oneself) to succeed without the help of others —**lift (**or **raise) oneself by the (**or **one's own) bootstraps** to achieve success by one's own unaided efforts

boo·ty[1] (bo͞ot′ē) ***n., pl.*** **-ties** ⟦MLowG *bute,* akin to Ger *beute;* infl. by BOOT[2]⟧ **1** loot taken from the enemy; spoils of war **2** anything seized by force or robbery; plunder **3** any gain, prize, or gift —***SYN.*** SPOIL

☆**boo·ty**[2] (bo͞ot′ē, bo͝od′ē) [Slang] ***n., pl.*** **-ties 1** the buttocks **2** the act or an instance of sexual intercourse —**shake one's booty** to dance

booze (bo͞oz) ***vi.*** **boozed, booz′ing** ⟦earlier *bouse, bowse* < MDu *busen;* akin to MHG *bus,* a bloating fullness; ult. < IE **bhōu-,* var. of base **bheu-,* to grow, swell: see BE⟧ [Informal] to drink too much alcoholic liquor —***n.*** [Informal] **1** an alcoholic drink; liquor **2** a drinking spree

booz·er (bo͞oz′ər) ***n.*** [Slang] **1** a person who drinks alcoholic liquor to excess; drunk **2** [Brit.] a pub; tavern

booz·y (-ē) ***adj.*** **booz′i·er, booz′i·est** [Informal] drunk, esp. habitually so —**booz′i·ly** ***adv.***

☆**bop**[1] (bäp) [Informal] ***vt.*** **bopped, bop′ping** ⟦echoic⟧ to hit or punch, as with a short, sharp blow —***n.*** a blow

☆**bop**[2] (bäp) ***n.*** ⟦shortening of BEBOP⟧ a style of jazz, esp. in its development from about 1945 to 1955, characterized by complex rhythms, experimental harmonic structures, and instrumental virtuosity —***vi.*** **bopped, bop′ping 1** [Slang] to walk, esp. in an easy but strutting way **2** to go

BOP ***abbrev.*** basic oxygen process

Bo·phu·that·swa·na (bō′po͞o tät swän′ə) former group of noncontiguous black homelands in N South Africa, on the Botswana border: granted independence in 1977, it was disbanded in 1994

BOQ ***abbrev.*** **1** bachelor officers' quarters **2** base officers' quarters

Bor ***abbrev.*** Borough

bor- (bôr) ***combining form*** BORO-: used before a vowel

bo·ra (bō′rə, bôr′ə) ***n.*** ⟦It dial. for *borea* < L *boreas,* BOREAS⟧ a fierce, cold northerly wind of lowland and coastal regions, esp. along the Adriatic Sea

bo·rac·ic (bə ras′ik) ***adj.*** ⟦< BORAX + -IC⟧ ***var. of*** BORIC

bo·ra·cite (bôr′ə sīt′) ***n.*** ⟦< BORAX + -ITE[1]⟧ a very hard, brittle, orthorhombic mineral, magnesium borate, $Mg_3B_7O_{13}Cl$, formed by the evaporation of salt water: it has a strong pyroelectric property

bor·age (bur′ij, bôr′-) ***n.*** ⟦ME < OFr *bourage* < ML *borrago, burrago;* said to be < Ar *abû ʿaraq,* "father of sweat," from diaphoretic use of the plant⟧ any of a genus (*Borago*) of plants of the borage family, esp. an annual (*B. officinalis*) with brilliant blue flowers and hairy leaves used as an herb in salads, drinks, etc. —***adj.*** designating a family (Boraginaceae, order Lamiales) of dicotyledonous plants, including Virginia cowslip, heliotrope, and forget-me-not

bo·ral (bôr′əl) ***n.*** ⟦BOR(ON) + AL(UMINUM)⟧ a mixture of boron carbide and aluminum, used in reactor control and as a shielding material

bo·rane (bôr′ān′) ***n.*** ⟦BOR(ON) + -ANE⟧ any of various compounds of boron and hydrogen, used as reducing agents in chemical reactions

bo·rate (-āt′) ***n.*** a salt or ester of boric acid —***vt.*** **-rat′ed, -rat′ing** to treat or mix with borax or boric acid

bo·rax (bôr′aks′) ***n.*** ⟦ME < ML *borax* < Ar *bauraq* < Pers *būrah*⟧ **1** sodium borate, a white, anhydrous, crystalline salt, $Na_2B_4O_7$, with an alkaline taste, used as a flux in soldering metals and in the manufacture of glass, enamel, artificial gems, soaps, antiseptics, etc. ☆**2** ⟦from the furniture formerly given as premiums by manufacturers of borax soap⟧ cheap, poorly made merchandise, esp. furniture

☆**Bo·ra·zon** (bôr′ə zän′) ⟦BOR(ON) + AZ- + -ON⟧ ***trademark for*** a crystalline modification of boron nitride, which is as hard as diamond but far more resistant to heat: it is used in many heat-resistant applications

bor·bo·ryg·mus (bôr′bə rig′məs) ***n., pl.*** **-mi′** (-mī′) ⟦ModL < Gr *borborygmos* < *borboryzein,* to rumble⟧ a rumbling sound made by gas in the intestines

Bor·deaux[1] (bôr dō′) ***n.*** [***also*** **b-**] **1** any of the red or white wines from the Bordeaux region **2** any wine of similar type made elsewhere

Bor·deaux[2] (bôr dō′) **1** seaport in SW France, on the Garonne River **2** region around this seaport, noted as a winegrowing area

Bordeaux mixture ⟦loose transl. of Fr *bouillie bordelaise* < *bouillie,* gruel (< fem. pp. of *bouillir,* BOIL[1]) + fem. of *bordelais,* of prec.: first used in the region's vineyards in the late 1800s⟧ a mixture of lime, water, and copper sulfate, sprayed on plants to kill insects and fungi: used extensively before the development of modern fungicides

bor·del (bôr′dəl) ***n.*** ⟦ME < OFr, dim. of *borde,* hut < Frank **bord,* BOARD⟧ [Archaic] a bordello

bor·de·laise sauce (bôr′də lāz′) ⟦Fr, fem. of *bordelais,* of BORDEAUX[2]⟧ a sauce for broiled meat, made from stock, wine, shallots, seasonings, etc., with flour as a thickener

bor·del·lo (bôr del′ō) ***n.*** ⟦It < OFr⟧ a house of prostitution; brothel

Bor·den (bôrd′'n), **Liz·zie (Andrew)** (liz′ē) 1860-1927; U.S. woman accused and acquitted in a sensational trial (1893) of murdering her father & stepmother (1892)

bor·der (bôr′dər) ***n.*** ⟦ME & OFr *bordure* < *border,* to border < Frank **bord,* margin: see BOARD⟧ **1** an edge or a part near an edge; margin; side **2** a dividing line between two countries, states, etc. or the land along it; frontier **3** a narrow strip, often ornamental, along an edge; fringe; edging **4** an ornamental strip of flowers or shrubs along the edge of a garden, walk, etc. —***vt.*** **1** to provide with a border **2** to extend along the edge of; bound —***adj.*** of, forming, or near a border —**border on (**or **upon) 1** to be next to or adjoining **2** to be like; almost be [his grief *borders on* madness] —**the Borders** the area surrounding the boundary between Scotland and England

SYN.—**border** refers to the boundary of a surface and may imply the limiting line itself or the part of the surface immediately adjacent to it; **margin** implies a bordering strip more or less clearly defined by some distinguishing feature [the *margin* of a printed page]; **edge** refers to the limiting line itself or the terminating line at the sharp convergence of two surfaces [the *edge* of a box]; **rim** is applied to the edge of a circular or curved surface; **brim** refers to the inner rim at the top of a vessel, etc.; **brink** refers to the edge at the top of a steep slope. All of these terms have figurative application [the *border* of good taste, a *margin* of error, an *edge* on one's appetite, the *rim* of consciousness, a mind filled to the *brim,* the *brink* of disaster]

border collie 1 a breed of medium-sized sheepdog, originally bred in the border region between Scotland and England, characterized by a coat that is usually black with white markings **2** any of this breed

bor·de·reau (bôr də rō′) ***n., pl.*** **-reaux′** (-rō′) ⟦Fr⟧ a memorandum, esp. one that gives a list of documents

bor·der·er (bôr′dər ər) ***n.*** a person living near a border

bor·der·land (-land′) ***n.*** **1** land constituting or near a border **2** a vague or uncertain condition that is not quite one thing or the other

bor·der·line (-līn′) ***n.*** a boundary; dividing line —***adj.*** on a boundary; specif., on the boundary of what is acceptable, valid, or normal; hence, having a questionable or indefinite status

borderline personality disorder a PERSONALITY DISORDER characterized by impulsiveness, intense anger, and instability in mood and behavior

Bor·ders (bôr′dərz) administrative division of S Scotland, on the English border: 1,800 sq mi (4,662 sq km)

border states slave states bordering on the free states before the Civil War: Mo., Ky., Va., Md., & Del.

bor·dure (bôr′jər) ***n.*** ⟦Fr: see BORDER⟧ *Heraldry* a border around the field of a coat of arms

bore[1] (bôr) ***vt.*** **bored, bor′ing** ⟦ME *boren* < OE *borian,* to bore < *bor,* auger < IE base **bher-,* to cut with a sharp point > Gr **pharein,* to split, L *forare,* to bore, *ferire,* to cut, kill⟧ **1** to make a hole in or through with a drill or other rotating tool **2** to make (a hole, tunnel, well, etc.) by or as by drilling **3** to force (one's way), as through a crowd **4** to weary by being dull, uninteresting, or monotonous —***vi.*** **1** to bore a hole or passage **2** to be drilled by a tool [soft materials *bore* easily] **3** to move forward slowly but steadily, as if by boring **4** to become weary and uninterested —***n.*** ⟦ME < the v.; also < ON *bora,* a hole⟧ **1** a hole made by or as by boring **2** *a)* the hollow part inside a tube, pipe, or cylinder, as of a gun barrel *b)* the inside diameter of such a hollow part; gauge; caliber **3** a tiresome, dull person or thing

bore[2] (bôr) ***n.*** ⟦ME *bare,* a wave < ON *bara,* a billow < IE **bhoros* < base **bher-* > BEAR[1]⟧ a high wall of moving water caused by a very rapid rise of the tide in shallow, narrow channels

bore[3] (bôr) ***vt., vi. pt. of*** BEAR[1]

bo·re·al (bôr′ē əl) ***adj.*** ⟦LL *borealis* < BOREAS⟧ **1** northern **2** of the north wind **3** of or pertaining to the northern zone of plant and animal life including the taiga and tundra

boreal chickadee a brown-capped, black-throated chickadee (Parus hudsonicus) found near the Atlantic coast from Labrador to N New York

Bo·re·as (-əs) ***n.*** ⟦L < Gr, north wind; ? orig., wind from the mountains < IE base **gwer-,* mountain > OSlav *gora,* mountain⟧ **1** *Gr. Myth.* the god of the north wind **2** [Old Poet.] the north wind personified

bore·dom (bôr′dəm) ***n.*** the condition of being bored; ennui

bore·hole (bôr′hōl′) ***n.*** a hole drilled in the earth to explore for or release oil, gas, water, etc. or to study the crust of the earth

bor·er (bôr′ər) ***n.*** **1** a tool for boring or drilling **2** a person whose work is to bore holes **3** an insect or its larval worm that bores holes in trees, fruit, etc. **4** a shipworm

bore·scope (bôr′skōp′) ***n.*** ⟦BORE[1] + -SCOPE⟧ an instrument, essentially a tube with a reflecting mirror and an eyepiece, used for inspecting the interior of shafts, well borings, tubing, etc., as to detect damage

☆**bore·some** (-səm) ***adj.*** BORING (sense 2)

Bor·ges (bôr′hes), **Jor·ge Lu·is** (hôr′he lo͞o ēs′) 1899-1986; Argentine poet, short-story writer, & critic

Bor·ghe·se (bôr gā′zā) ***n.*** name of a family of It. nobility, originally of Siena, later of Rome: prominent from the 16th to the 19th cent.

Bor·gia (bôr′jə, -zhə) **1 Ce·sa·re** (che′zä re) 1476?-1507; It. military leader & cardinal: son of Pope Alexander VI **2 Lu·cre·zia** (lo͞o kre′tsyä) 1480-1519; duchess of Ferrara: patron of the arts: sister of Cesare

Bor·glum (bôr′gləm), **(John) Gut·zon** (gut′sən) 1871-1941; U.S. sculptor and painter

bo·ric (bôr′ik) ***adj.*** of or containing boron, esp. its oxides

boric acid a white, crystalline compound, H_3BO_3, with the properties of a weak acid, used as a mild antiseptic and in the manufacture of glass, enamels, flame retardants, etc.

bo·ride (bôr′īd′) ***n.*** ⟦BOR(ON) + -IDE⟧ a compound consisting of boron and one other element or radical

bor·ing (bôr′iŋ) ***adj.*** **1** for making holes **2** dull, tiresome, etc. —***n.*** **1** the action of one that bores **2** a hole made by boring **3** [*pl.*] chips, flakes, etc. made by boring —**bor'ing·ly** *adv.*

boring clam PIDDOCK

boring sponge any of a family (Clionidae) of sponges that settle on and dissolve the shells of clams

Bor·is (bôr'is) *n.* ⟦Russ, lit., fight⟧ a masculine name

born (bôrn) *vt., vi. alt. pp. of* BEAR[1] —*adj.* **1** brought into life or being **2** by birth: used in hyphenated compounds [French-*born*] **3** having certain qualities or abilities innately, as if from birth; natural [*a born* athlete] **4** being as specified from birth [nobly *born*] —**in all one's born days** [Chiefly Dial.] in one's lifetime: used also as an exclamation of surprise

Born (bôrn), **Max** 1882-1970; Ger. nuclear physicist, in England (1933-53)

born-a·gain (bôrn'ə gen') *adj.* ⟦BORN + AGAIN, in allusion to spiritual rebirth in Christ: see John 3:3 & 3:7 in traditional transl.⟧ **1** having or committed to a new or renewed Christian faith, esp. as the result of a personal conversion experience **2** having a new, strong belief in some principle, movement, etc. [*a born-again* romantic]

borne (bôrn) *vt., vi. alt. pp. of* BEAR[1]

-borne (bôrn) *combining form* carried or transmitted by (the thing specified) [*foodborne* microbes, mosquito-*borne* illness]

Bor·ne·o (bôr'nē ō') large island in the Malay Archipelago, southwest of the Philippines: the S portion (KALIMANTAN) is a part of Indonesia; the N portion is composed of the Malaysian states of Sabah & Sarawak, and of BRUNEI: total area, *c.* 288,000 sq mi (745,917 sq km)

bor·ne·ol (bôr'nē ôl', -ōl') *n.* ⟦after prec. + -OL[1]⟧ a white, crystalline terpene alcohol, $C_{10}H_{17}OH$, resembling camphor, obtained from the trunk of a Southeast Asian tree: used in perfumery, as an antiseptic, etc.

born·ite (bôr'nīt') *n.* ⟦after Ignaz von *Born* (1742-91), Austrian metallurgist⟧ a reddish-brown, soft, brittle, cubic mineral, copper iron sulfide, Cu_5FeS_4, an ore of copper that tarnishes to a dark purplish color when it is fractured

bo·ro- (bôr'ō, bôr'ə) *combining form* boron

Bo·ro·din (bôr'ə dēn', bôr'ə din'; *Russ* bô'rô dyēn'), **A·lek·san·dr Por·fir·e·vich** (ä'lyik sän'dr' pôr fir'yi vich) 1833-87; Russ. composer

Bo·ro·di·no (bôr'ə dē'nō) Russian village just west of Moscow: site of a battle (1812) in which the Russian army retreated before Napoleon's army

bo·ron (bôr'än') *n.* ⟦< earlier *boracium* (< BORAX) + *-on,* as in (CARB)ON: so named by Sir Humphry DAVY, who isolated it (1808)⟧ a nonmetallic chemical element occurring only in combination, as with sodium and oxygen in borax, and produced in the form of either a brown amorphous powder or very hard, brilliant crystals: its compounds are used in the preparation of boric acid, water softeners, soaps, enamels, glass, pottery, etc.: symbol, B; at. no. 5: see the periodic table of elements in the Reference Supplement

boron carbide a black, crystalline compound of boron and carbon, B_4C, almost as hard as diamond: used as an abrasive and in control rods for nuclear reactors: see MOHS SCALE (sense 2)

boron nitride a white, powdery compound, BN, of boron and nitrogen, with high electrical resistance: it can be compressed, under a million pounds of pressure, to form Borazon

bo·ro·sil·i·cate (bôr'ō sil'i kit, -kāt') *n.* **1** any of several salts derived from both boric acid and silicic acid and found in certain minerals, such as tourmaline **2** a type of glass made of about 5% boric oxide that can withstand high temperatures: see also PYREX

bor·ough (bur'ō) *n.* ⟦ME *burgh* < OE *burg, burh,* town, fortified place, akin to Ger *burg* < IE **bhrgh,* fortified elevation < base **bheregh-,* high > BARROW[2]⟧ **1** in certain states of the U.S., a self-governing, incorporated town **2** the basic unit of local government in Alaska **3** a part of a city, having authority over certain local matters, as any of the five administrative units of New York City **4** in England *a)* a town with a municipal corporation and rights to self-government granted by royal charter *b)* a town that sends one or more representatives to Parliament *c)* [Obs.] any fortified town larger than a village

borough English a former custom in some parts of England by which the youngest son succeeded to land holdings

Bor·ro·mi·ni (bô'rô mē'nē), **Fran·ces·co** (frän ches'kô) (born *Francesco Castelli*) 1599-1667; It. architect

bor·row (bär'ō, bôr'-) *vt., vi.* ⟦ME *borwen* < OE *borgian,* to borrow, lend, be surety for, akin to *beorgan,* to protect & BOROUGH⟧ **1** to take or receive (something) with the understanding that one will return it or an equivalent **2** to adopt or take over (something) as one's own [to *borrow* a theory] **3** to adopt and naturalize (a word, etc.) from another language [the word *depot* was *borrowed* from French] **4** *Arith.* in subtraction, to take (a unit of ten) from the next higher place in the minuend and add it to the next lower place: done when the number to be subtracted in the subtrahend is greater than the corresponding number in the minuend —☆**borrow trouble** to worry about anything needlessly or before one has sufficient cause —**living on borrowed time** living past the likely or usual time of death —**bor'row·er** *n.*

bor·row·ing (-iŋ) *n.* LOANWORD

Bors (bôrs, bôrz), **Sir** *Arthurian Legend* a knight of the Round Table, nephew of Sir Lancelot

borscht (bôrsht) *n.* ⟦Russ *boršč,* orig., cow parsnip (an ingredient of the orig. recipe) < IE **bhr̥sti-* < base **bhar-,* point > BRISTLE⟧ a Russian beet soup, served either hot or cold, usually with sour cream: also **borsch** (bôrsh)

☆**borscht (*or* borsch) circuit** ⟦jocular, from the characteristic Jewish cuisine⟧ [Informal] summer resort hotels in the Catskills and White Mountains, where entertainment is provided for the guests: also **borscht belt**

bor·stal (bôr'stəl) *n.* ⟦after *Borstal,* town in England⟧ a former type of British correctional institution to which convicted young offenders (16 to 21 years old) were sent for reeducation and training

bort (bôrt) *n.* ⟦prob. via Du *boort* < OFr *bourt,* bastard < L *burdus,* hinny⟧ a flawed diamond used only for industrial purposes, esp. in crushed form for grinding and polishing: sometimes called **bortz** (bôrts)

Bo·ru·jerd (bôr'ə jerd') city in WC Iran

bor·zoi (bôr'zoi') *n.* ⟦Russ *borzoj,* masc. of *borzaja,* fem., name of the breed < *borzyj,* swift, fleet (obs. or poetic) < IE base **bheres,* quick > L *festinare,* to hurry⟧ any of a breed of large dog with a narrow head, long legs, and silky coat; Russian wolfhound

Bosc (bäsk) *n.* ⟦after L. *Bosc* d'Antic (1759-1828), Fr naturalist⟧ a sweet, russet winter pear: also **Bosc pear**

bos·cage (bäs'kij) *n.* ⟦ME *boskage* < OFr *boscage* < Frank *busk* (or OHG *busc*), forest, thicket: see BUSH[1]⟧ a natural growth of trees or shrubs; wooded place

Bosch (bäsh, bôsh; *Du* bôs), **Hi·e·ro·ny·mus** (hē'ə rō'ni məs) (born *Jerome van Aken*) 1450?-1516; Du. painter

bosch·vark (bäsh'värk') *n.* ⟦obs. Afrik < Du *bosch,* BUSH[1] + *vark,* pig: for IE base see FARROW[1]⟧ a bush pig of S Africa

Bose (bōs, bōsh), Sir **Ja·ga·dis Chan·dra** (jə gəd ēs' chun'drə) 1858-1937; Ind. physicist & plant physiologist

Bose-Ein·stein condensate (bōs'īn'stīn') ⟦after S. N. *Bose* (see BOSON) + EINSTEIN[2]; see CONDENSATE⟧ a unique state of matter, existing only at temperatures near absolute zero, in which atoms coalesce and exhibit superfluidity because they share the same quantum state

bosh[1] (bäsh) *n., interj.* ⟦Turk, empty⟧ [Informal] nonsense

bosh[2] (bäsh) *n.* ⟦< ? Ger *böschung,* slope⟧ **1** the lower part of the shaft of a blast furnace, where the walls begin to slope **2** a trough used in forging and smelting for cooling hot metal

bosk (bäsk) *n.* ⟦ME *bosk, boske,* BUSH[1]⟧ a small wooded place; grove; thicket: also **bos·kage** (bäs'kij)

bos·ket (bäs'kit) *n.* ⟦Fr *bosquet* < OFr *boschet* < OIt *boschetto,* dim. of *bosco* < ML *boscus:* see BUSH[1]⟧ a small grove; thicket

Bos·kop skull (bäs'käp') ⟦after *Boskop,* Transvaal, where fossil remains found (1913)⟧ a portion of a human skull found in South Africa, of undetermined relationship and geological age: formerly associated with a hypothetical **Boskop race**

bosk·y (bäs'kē) *adj.* ⟦BOSK + -Y[3]⟧ covered with trees or shrubs; wooded; sylvan

bo's'n (bō'sən) *n. phonetic sp. of* BOATSWAIN

Bos·ni·a (bäz'nē ə) **1** historical region & former kingdom in the NW Balkan Peninsula: now part of Bosnia and Herzegovina **2** *short for* BOSNIA AND HERZEGOVINA —**Bos'ni·an** *adj., n.*

Bosnia and Her·ze·go·vi·na (hert'sə gō vē'nə) country in SE Europe: the region came under Turkish rule in the 15th cent., under Austro-Hungarian control in 1878, and was part of Yugoslavia (1918-92): 19,741 sq mi (51,129 sq km); cap. Sarajevo: also **Bos'ni·a-Her'ze·go·vi'na**

Bos·ni·ak (bäz'nē ak') *n.* a Bosnian Muslim —*adj.* of or pertaining to Bosniaks

bos·om (booz'əm; *occas.* bōō'zəm) *n.* ⟦ME < OE *bosm;* prob. < IE base **bhou-,* **bhū-,* to grow, swell⟧ **1** *a)* [Archaic or Literary] the upper front portion of the human trunk; human breast *b)* this portion of a woman's body, including her breasts *c)* the human breast regarded as the seat of inmost thoughts or as the source of feelings **2** a thing thought of as like the human breast, as in being encompassing or affording protection, nourishment, etc. [the *bosom* of the sea] **3** *a)* the enclosing space formed by the breast and arms in embracing *b)* the human breast or an embrace, regarded as affording protection, nourishment, etc. **4** the inside; midst [in the *bosom* of one's family] **5** *a)* the part of a dress, shirt, etc. that covers the breast *b)* the space inside this part —*vt.* **1** to embrace; cherish **2** to conceal in the bosom; hide —*adj.* cherished; intimate [a *bosom* companion] —*SYN.* BREAST

bos·omed (booz əmd; *occas.* bōō'zəmd) *adj.* having a (specified kind of) bosom [small-*bosomed*]

bos·om·y (-əm ē) *adj.* having large breasts

bos·on (bō'sän) *n.* ⟦after S. N. *Bose* (1894-1974), Indian physicist + -ON⟧ *Particle Physics* any of a class of subatomic particles that do not obey the Pauli exclusion principle and have zero or integral spin, including the mesons, weakons, and classons: bosons are thought to carry the four fundamental forces of nature (electromagnetism, gravity, strong interaction, weak interaction): see FERMION

Bos·po·rus (bäs'pə rəs) strait between the Black Sea and the Sea of Marmara: *c.* 20 mi (32 km) long: also **Bos'pho·rus** (-fə rəs)

☆**bos·que** (bôs'kā') *n.* ⟦Sp < Prov *bosc* < Frank *busk,* forest: see BUSH[1]⟧ [Chiefly Southwest] a clump or grove of trees

bos·quet (bäs'kit) *n.* ⟦Fr: see BOSKET⟧ BOSKET

☆**boss**[1] (bôs, bäs) *n.* ⟦Du *baas,* a master < MDu < ?⟧ **1** a person in authority over employees, as an employer, a manager, or a foreman **2** a person who controls a political machine or organization, as in a county: often **political boss** —*vt.* **1** to act as boss of **2** [Informal] to order (a person) about; act bossy with —*adj.* **1** [Informal] chief **2** [Slang] excellent; fine

boss[2] (bôs, bäs) *n.* ⟦ME & OFr *boce* (Fr *bosse*), a hump, swelling, akin to It *boccia,* ball, bud⟧ **1** a raised part or protruding ornament on a flat surface;

a decorative knob, stud, etc. **2** *Archit.* an ornamental projecting piece, as at the intersection of the ribs of an arched roof **3** *Geol.* an exposed mass of intrusive igneous rock **4** *Mech.* the enlarged part of a shaft —*vt.* to decorate with raised ornaments, metal studs, etc.

Boss (bäs, bôs) ***n.*** ⟦< ?⟧ a traditional name for a domesticated cow: often used informally to refer to the typical cow

bos·sa no·va (bäs′ə nō′və) ⟦Port, lit., new bump, new tendency < *bossa,* a bump (akin to Fr *bosse,* BOSS[2]) + *nova* (< L, fem. of *novus,* NEW)⟧ **1** jazz samba music that originated in Brazil, with a light, flowing line **2** a dance for couples, performed to this music

☆**boss·ism** (bôs′iz′əm) ***n.*** domination or control by bosses, esp. of a political machine or party

Bos·suet (bô swā′), **Jacques Bé·ni·gne** (zhäk bā nēn′y′) 1627-1704; Fr. bishop & orator

☆**boss·y[1]** (bôs′ē) ***adj.*** **boss′i·er, boss′i·est** ⟦BOSS[1] + -Y[3]⟧ [Informal] acting like a boss, as by ordering people about; domineering —**boss′i·ness** ***n.***

boss·y[2] (bôs′ē, bäs′ē) ***adj.*** ⟦BOSS[2] + -Y[3]⟧ decorated with bosses; studded

☆**Boss·y** (bäs′ē, bôs′ē) ***n.*** ⟦Boss + -Y[2]⟧ a traditional name for a domesticated cow: often used informally to refer to the typical cow

bos·ton (bôs′tən) ***n.*** ⟦Fr⟧ ☆a kind of waltz

Bos·ton (bôs′tən, bäs′-) ⟦after *Boston,* port in NE England⟧ cap. of Mass.; seaport on an arm (**Boston Bay**) of Massachusetts Bay —**Bos·to′ni·an** (-tō′nē ən) ***adj., n.***

☆**Boston baked beans** ⟦by association with the New England Puritans, who prepared them on Saturday for consumption on the Sabbath without further cooking⟧ navy or other similar beans baked slowly with salt pork, seasonings, and molasses or brown sugar

☆**Boston brown bread** a dark, sweetened, steamed bread made of cornmeal, rye or wheat flour, etc., and molasses

☆**Boston bull** BOSTON TERRIER

☆**Boston cream pie** a split cake layer typically filled with vanilla custard and topped with chocolate frosting or powdered sugar

☆**Boston fern** a cultivated fern (*Nephrolepis exaltata* var. *bostoniensis*) with odd-pinnate leaves, used as a houseplant

☆**Boston ivy** a climbing vine (*Parthenocissus tricuspidata*) of the grape family, native to Japan and China, having shield-shaped leaves and purple berries: often grown to cover walls

Boston lettuce a type of butterhead lettuce

Boston Massacre an outbreak (1770) in Boston against British troops, in which a few citizens were killed

☆**Boston rocker** a type of 19th-cent. American rocking chair, having a curved wooden seat and a high back formed of spindles held in place by a broad headpiece

Boston Tea Party a protest (1773) against the British duty on tea imported by the American colonies: colonists boarded British ships in Boston harbor and dumped the tea overboard

☆**Boston terrier** any of a breed of small dog having a smooth coat of brindle or black with white markings: it originated as a cross between a bulldog and a bull terrier

bo·sun (bō′sən) ***n.*** *phonetic sp. of* BOATSWAIN

Bos·well[1] (bäz′wel′, -wəl) ***n.*** ⟦after fol.⟧ a biographer whose information is obtained through close observation of, or intimate association with, the subject

Bos·well[2] (bäz′wel′, -wəl), **James** 1740-95; Scot. lawyer & writer: biographer of Samuel Johnson

Bos·worth Field (bäz′wərth) field in Leicestershire, England: scene of the final battle (1485) in the Wars of the Roses, in which Richard III was killed; the crown passed to the victor, the Earl of Richmond (Henry VII)

bot[1] (bät) ***n.*** ⟦ME < ? Gael *botus,* belly worm < *boiteag,* maggot⟧ the larva of the botfly

bot[2] (bät) ***n.*** **1** *short for* ROBOT **2** a computer program that executes a specific task according to the user's instructions Often in comb. Also **'bot**

bot. *abbrev.* **1** botanical **2** botanist **3** botany

bo·tan·i·ca (bə tan′i kə) ***n.*** ⟦AmSp *botánica* < fem. of Sp *botánico,* botanical⟧ a shop selling magic charms, herbs, etc.

bo·tan·i·cal (bə tan′i kəl) ***adj.*** ⟦< obs. *botanic* (< Fr *botanique* < Gr *botanikos* < *botanē,* a plant < *boskein,* to feed, graze) + -AL⟧ **1** of plants and plant life **2** of or connected with the science of botany **3** of or belonging to a botanical species Also **bo·tan′ic** —***n.*** **1** bark or root matter, an herb, etc. used as a dietary supplement or as an ingredient in a drug, cosmetic preparation, etc. **2** a drug, cosmetic preparation, dietary supplement, etc. containing or consisting of an herb or other botanical matter —**bo·tan′i·cal·ly** ***adv.***

botanical garden a place where collections of plants and trees are kept for scientific study and exhibition

bot·a·nist (bät′'n ist) ***n.*** ⟦Fr *botaniste*⟧ a student of or specialist in botany

bot·a·nize (-īz′) ***vi.*** **-nized′, -niz′ing 1** to gather plants for botanical study **2** to study plants, esp. in their natural environment —***vt.*** to investigate the plant life of (a region) —**bot′a·niz′er** ***n.***

bot·a·ny (bät′'n ē) ***n.*** ⟦BOTAN(ICAL) + -Y[4]⟧ **1** the branch of biology that studies plants, their life, structure, growth, classification, etc. **2** the plant life of an area **3** the characteristics or properties of a plant or plant group

Botany Bay ⟦so named in ref. to the profusion of plant life found there by the botanist on the voyage of Captain COOK[1]⟧ bay on the SE coast of Australia, near Sydney: site of Captain Cook's original landing in Australia

Botany wool ⟦after prec., its original point of export from Australia⟧ merino wool of high quality

botch (bäch) ***vt.*** ⟦ME *bocchen,* to repair < ?⟧ **1** to repair or patch clumsily **2** to spoil by poor work or poor performance; bungle —***n.*** **1** a badly patched place or part **2** a bungled or unskillful piece of work —**botch′er** ***n.*** —**botch′y** ***adj.***

bo·te·co (bō tek′ōō) ***n.,*** *pl.* **-cos** ⟦Port, tavern⟧ a small nightspot or pub of a type common in Brazil, typically one serving food

bot·fly (bät′flī′) ***n.,*** *pl.* **-flies′** ⟦see BOT[1]⟧ any of a number of dipterous flies (families Cuterebridae, Gasterophilidae, and Oestridae) resembling small bumblebees: the larvae are parasitic in humans, horses, sheep, and other mammals

both (bōth) ***adj., pron.*** ⟦ME *bothe* < OE *ba tha,* both these < *ba,* fem. nom. & acc. of *begen,* both + *tha,* nom. & acc. pl. of *se,* that, the: akin to ON *bathir,* OS *bethia,* MDu *bede,* Ger *beide*: see AMBI-⟧ the two; the one and the other [*both* birds sang loudly; *both* were small; *both* of them were tired] —***conj., adv.*** together; equally; as well: used correlatively with *and* [*both* tired and hungry]

Bo·tha (bō′tə), **Louis** 1862-1919; South African statesman: 1st prime minister (1910-19)

both·er (bäth′ər) ***vt.*** ⟦earlier *bodder* (in Jonathan SWIFT); prob. Anglo-Ir for POTHER⟧ **1** to worry or trouble, esp. with petty annoyances; harass, pester, etc. **2** to bewilder or fluster **3** to cause discomfort to [her sore foot *bothers* her] **4** to disturb; interrupt —***vi.*** **1** to take the time and trouble; concern oneself [don't *bother* to reply] **2** to make a fuss —***n.*** **1** a cause or condition of worry or irritation; trouble; fuss **2** a person who gives trouble —***interj.*** used to express slight annoyance, worry, etc. —***SYN.*** ANNOY

both·er·a·tion (bäth′ər ā′shən) ***n., interj.*** [Informal] bother

both·er·some (bäth′ər səm) ***adj.*** causing bother; annoying; troublesome; irksome

Both·ni·a (bäth′nē ə), **Gulf of** arm of the Baltic Sea, between Finland & Sweden

both·y (bäth′ē) ***n.,*** *pl.* **-ies** [Chiefly Scot.] a cottage or hut

☆**Bo·tox** (bō′täks′) ⟦< *bo(tulinum) tox(in)*: see BOTULINUM (TOXIN)⟧ *trademark for* a type of purified botulin neurotoxin used in medicine as a muscle relaxant and often injected into facial muscles for cosmetic purposes, as to smooth wrinkles

bo tree (bō) ⟦Sinhalese *bo* < Pali *bodhi* < *bodhi-taru* < *bodhi,* wisdom, enlightenment < Sans *budh* (see BUDDHA[2]) + *taru,* tree⟧ the sacred fig tree (PEEPUL) of Buddhism: Gautama is believed to have received heavenly inspiration under such a tree

bot·ry·oi·dal (bä′trē oid′'l) ***adj.*** ⟦< Gr *botryoeidēs* (< *botrys,* bunch of grapes + *-eidēs,* -OID) + -AL⟧ resembling a bunch of grapes: also **bot′ry·oid′**

bot·ry·o·my·co·sis (bä′trē ō′mī kō′sis) ***n.,*** *pl.* **-ses′** (-sēz′) ⟦< Gr *botrys* (see prec.) + MYCOSIS⟧ a disease, usually of horses, caused by a bacterial infection (usually, *Staphylococcus aureus*) producing tumorous growths esp. after castration or a wound or injury

bo·try·tis (bō trī′tis) ***n.*** ⟦< Gr *botrys*: see BOTRYOIDAL⟧ a plant disease that blackens flower buds, caused by a gray mold (genus *Botrytis*) that is used in winemaking —**bo·try′tised** (-tist) ***adj.***

bots (bäts) ***n.*** a condition of horses, cattle, etc. caused by the presence of the parasitic larvae of botflies in the stomach or intestines

Bot·swa·na (bät swä′nə) country in S Africa, north of South Africa: formerly the British territory of Bechuanaland, it became independent (1966) & a member of the Commonwealth: 231,804 sq mi (600,370 sq km); cap. Gaborone

bott (bät) ***n.*** BOT[1]

Bot·ti·cel·li (bät′ə chel′ē; *It* bôt′tē chel′ē), **San·dro** (sän′drô) (born *Alessandro di Mariano dei Filipepi*) 1445?-1510; It. painter

bot·tle[1] (bät′'l) ***n.*** ⟦ME *botel* < MFr *botele* < OFr < ML *butticula,* dim. of LL *buttis,* a cask⟧ **1** a container, esp. for liquids, made of glass, plastic, etc. and having a relatively narrow neck **2** *a)* the amount that a bottle holds *b)* the volume of liquid contained in a standard U.S. wine bottle, 750 ml (25.4 oz) **3** milk from an infant's nursing bottle **4** alcoholic liquor —***vt.*** **-tled, -tling 1** to put into a bottle or bottles **2** to store (a gas, a liquefied gas, etc.) under pressure in a tank or cylinder —**bottle up 1** to shut in, as enemy troops **2** to hold in or suppress, as emotions —☆**hit the bottle** [Slang] to drink much alcohol —**bot′tle·ful′** ***n.,*** *pl.* **-fuls′** —**bot′tler** ***n.***

bot·tle[2] (bät′'l) ***n.*** ⟦ME & OFr *botel,* dim. of *botte* < MDu *bote,* bundle of flax⟧ [Brit. Dial.] a bundle, as of hay

bot·tle·brush (-brush′) ***n.*** ⟦descriptive of the tufts⟧ any of a genus (*Callistemon*) of shrubs or trees of the myrtle family, having flowers with conspicuous tufts of red or yellow stamens and cultivated in warm climates

☆**bottle club** a place where patrons are served liquor from bottles purportedly belonging to them, as to skirt liquor laws

bottle green ⟦so called from being the color of *bottle glass,* inexpensive glass used as for wine *bottles*⟧ a dark bluish-green color

bot·tle·neck (-nek′) ***n.*** **1** the neck of a bottle **2** any place, as a narrow road, where traffic is slowed up or halted **3** any point at which movement or progress is slowed up because much must be funneled through it [a *bottleneck* in production] —☆***adj.*** designating or of a style of playing blues guitar in which notes and chords are formed by stopping a string or strings with a broken-off glass bottleneck, a knife blade, etc. —***vt.*** to act as a bottleneck in

bot·tle·nose (-nōz′) ***n.*** **1** any of a genus (*Tursiops*) of marine dolphins with a bottle-shaped snout: an easily trained species (*T. truncatus*) is used in aquarium shows and scientific study: also called **bottle-nosed dolphin** **2** any of a genus (*Hyperoodon,* family Ziphiidae) of toothed whales having a similar beaklike snout: also called **bottle-nosed whale**

bot·tle·tree (-trē′) ***n.*** any of a genus (*Brachychiton*) of trees of the sterculia family, native to Australia, some of which have a swollen, bottle-shaped trunk

bot·tom (bät′əm) ***n.*** ⟦ME *botme* < OE *botm, bodan,* ground, soil < IE **bhudh-men* < base **bhudh-* > L *fundus,* ground, Gr *pythmen,* bottom, Ger *boden*⟧ **1** the lowest part **2** *a)* the lowest or last place or position *[the bottom of the class]* *b) Baseball* the second half (*of* an inning) **3** the part on which something rests; base **4** the underside or whichever end is underneath *[the bottom of a crate]* **5** the seat of a chair **6** the part farthest in; inner end, as of a bay or lane **7** the bed or ground beneath a body of water ☆**8** [*usually pl.*] BOTTOMLAND **9** *a)* the part of a ship's hull normally below water *b)* a ship; esp., a cargo ship **10** [*usually pl.*] the lower unit of a two-piece garment, as pajama trousers **11** fundamental or basic meaning or cause; source **12** endurance; stamina **13** [Informal] the buttocks —***adj.*** of, at, or on the bottom; lowest, last, undermost, basic, etc. —***vt.*** **1** to provide with a bottom **2** to place (something) *on* or *upon* a foundation; base —***vi.*** **1** to reach or rest upon the bottom **2** to be based or established —**at bottom** fundamentally; actually —**be at the bottom of** to be the underlying cause of; be the real reason for —☆**bet one's bottom dollar** [Slang] to bet one's last dollar; bet everything one has —☆**bottom out** to level off at a low point, as prices —**bottoms up!** [Informal] drink deep!: a toast

bottom feeder **1** BOTTOM FISH **2** [Slang] a person who preys upon or panders to the base qualities of others —**bot′tom-feed′ing** ***adj.***

bottom fish any fish that feeds or lives near the bottom of a body of water, as a flounder or catfish

bot·tom-fish (-fish′) ***vi.*** **1** to fish for bottom fish **2** [Informal] to make investments from among those stocks, bonds, etc. currently out of favor and selling at low prices

☆**bot·tom·land** (-land′) ***n.*** low land through which a river flows, rich in alluvial deposits; flood plain: sometimes written **bottom land**

bot·tom·less (-lis) ***adj.*** **1** having no bottom **2** seeming to have no bottom; very deep, endless, etc. ☆**3** ⟦modeled on TOPLESS, sense 2⟧ nude or characterized by nudity or nude entertainment *[a bottomless dancer, bottomless bar]* —**the bottomless pit** the underworld; hell

☆**bottom line** **1** the lowest line of the earnings report of a company, on which net profit per share of stock is shown **2** [Informal] profits or losses, as of a business **3** [Slang] *a)* the basic or most important factor, consideration, meaning, etc. *b)* the final or ultimate statement, decision, etc. —**bot′tom-line′** ***adj.***

bot·tom·most (-mōst′) ***adj.*** at the very bottom; lowest, last, most basic, etc.

bottom of the hour ⟦in ref. to the position of the minute hand on the numeral "6" at the *bottom* of a clock face⟧ thirty minutes past the beginning of any or each of the twenty-four divisions of the day; 12:30, 1:30, 2:30, etc. *[news will be broadcast at the bottom of the hour]*

bottom quark *Particle Physics* a type of quark with a mass of *c.* 4.7 to 5.3 GeV/c^2, a negative charge that is ⅓ the charge of an electron, zero charm, and zero strangeness: see FLAVOR (sense 5)

bot·tom·ry (bät′əm rē) ***n.*** ⟦< BOTTOM, *n.* 9, after Du *bodomerij,* bottomry⟧ a contract by which a shipowner borrows money for equipment, repairs, or a voyage, pledging the ship as security

Bot·trop (bä′träp) city in W Germany, in the Ruhr valley, in the state of North Rhine-Westphalia

bot·u·lin (bäch′ə lin) ***n.*** ⟦ModL < L *botulus,* sausage: see BOTULISM⟧ the toxin causing botulism

bot·u·li·num (toxin) (bäch′ə lin′əm) ⟦< ModL *botulinum,* species name < *botulinus,* former species name < L *botulus,* sausage: see BOTULISM⟧ BOTULIN

bot·u·li·nus (bäch′ə lī′nəs) ***n.*** ⟦ModL, former species name < L *botulus,* sausage: see fol.⟧ a bacterium (*Clostridium botulinum*) that produces the toxin causing botulism

bot·u·lism (bäch′ə liz′əm) ***n.*** ⟦Ger *botulismus* < L *botulus,* sausage (see BOWEL) + *-ismus,* -ISM: so named from Ger cases involving sausages⟧ poisoning resulting from the toxin produced by botulinus bacteria, sometimes found in foods improperly canned or preserved: characterized by muscular paralysis and disturbances of vision and breathing, and often fatal

Boua·ké (bwä′kā) city in central Ivory Coast

bou·bou (bo͞o′bo͞o′) ***n.*** ⟦Fr < Malinke *bubu*⟧ a loose, flowing, usually full-length garment worn in some African countries: also **bou bou**

Bou·cher (bo͞o shā′), **Fran·çois** (frän swà′) 1703-70; Fr. painter in the rococo style

Bou·ci·cault (bo͞o′sē kō′), **Di·on** (dē′än) (born *Dionysius Lardner Boursiquot*) 1820?-90; Brit. playwright & actor, born in Ireland

bou·clé or **bou·cle** (bo͞o klā′) ***n.*** ⟦Fr, pp. of *boucler,* to buckle, curl, bulge: see BUCKLE²⟧ **1** a curly wool, silk, or cotton yarn that gives the knitted or woven fabric made from it a tufted or knotted texture **2** such a fabric

Bou·dic·ca (bo͞o dik′ə) died A.D. 62; queen of the Iceni in ancient Britain, who led a vain revolt against the Romans (A.D. 61)

bou·din (bo͞o dan′; *E* bo͞o′dan) ***n.*** ⟦Fr⟧ **1** in France, *a)* a sausage boiled during manufacturing *b)* BOUDIN NOIR **2** a blood sausage similar to *boudin noir* popular in the cooking of the Cajuns

boudin blanc (blän) ⟦Fr, white boudin⟧ a boiled sausage made with light-colored meat, as veal or chicken, and without blood

boudin noir (nwàr) ⟦Fr, black boudin⟧ a dark-colored boiled sausage made with pork and blood, and often highly spiced

bou·doir (bo͞o dwär′, bo͞o′dwär′) ***n.*** ⟦Fr, lit., pouting room < *bouder,* to pout, sulk + *-oir,* as in *parloir,* parlor⟧ a woman's bedroom, dressing room, or private sitting room

bouf·fant (bo͞o fänt′) ***adj.*** ⟦Fr, prp. of *bouffer,* to puff out; akin to It *buffare,* to blow with puffed cheeks, of echoic orig.⟧ puffed out; full, as some skirts, hair styles, etc.

bouffe (bo͞of) ***n.*** ⟦Fr⟧ OPÉRA BOUFFE

Bou·gain·ville¹ (bo͞o gan vēl′), **Louis An·toine de** (lwē än twån′ də) 1729-1811; Fr. navigator & explorer

Bou·gain·ville² (bo͞o′gən vil′) largest of the Solomon Islands, in Papua New Guinea: 3,880 sq mi (10,049 sq km)

bou·gain·vil·le·a or **bou·gain·vil·lae·a** (bo͞o′gən vil′ē ə, -vil′yə, -vē′yə) ***n.*** ⟦ModL, after BOUGAINVILLE¹⟧ any of a genus (*Bougainvillea*) of woody tropical vines of the four-o'clock family, having inconspicuous flowers surrounded by large, showy purple or red bracts

bough (bou) ***n.*** ⟦ME < OE *bog,* shoulder or arm, hence twig or branch < IE **bhāgus,* elbow and forearm > BOW²⟧ branch of a tree, esp. a main branch

bought (bôt) ***vt., vi.*** *pt. & pp. of* BUY —***adj.*** [Dial.] BOUGHTEN

bought·en (bôt′'n) ***adj.*** [Dial.] bought at a store and not homemade

bou·gie (bo͞o′jē′, -zhē′) ***n.*** ⟦Fr, wax candle, after *Bougie,* Algerian seaport (< ML *Bugia* < Ar *Bujaya*) from which wax candles were imported⟧ **1** a wax candle **2** *Med.* a slender instrument introduced into a body canal, esp. the urethra or rectum, as for dilating it

bouil·la·baisse (bo͞o′yä bes′, -bās′; bo͝ol′yə-) ***n.*** ⟦Fr < Prov *boulh-abaisso,* lit., boils and settles < *bouli* (Fr *bouillir*), to boil + *abaissa* (Fr *abaisser*): see ABASE⟧ **1** a stew of various fish, crustacean shellfish, vegetables, and seasonings: the broth is served over bread slices, often with a spicy garlic sauce, and the fish and vegetables are served alongside **2** any of various similar stews or soups

bouil·lon (bo͝ol′yän′, -yən; *Fr* bo͞o yōn′) ***n.*** ⟦Fr < *bouillir,* BOIL¹⟧ a clear broth, usually of beef

bouillon cube a small cube of concentrated stock for making bouillon

Bou·lan·ger (bo͞o län zhā′), **Na·dia (Juliette)** (nå dyå′) 1887-1979; Fr. musician, composer, & teacher of composition

bou·lan·ge·rie (bo͞o länzh rē′) ***n.*** ⟦Fr⟧ a bakery shop, specif. one that specializes in breads, rolls, etc.

boul·der (bōl′dər) ***n.*** ⟦ME *bulder,* short for *bulderston* < Scand, as in Swed *bullersten,* lit., noisy stone < *bullra,* to roar (akin to BELLOW) + *sten,* STONE⟧ **1** any large rock worn smooth and round by weather and water **2** *Geol.* such a rock larger than a cobblestone with a diameter of at least 256 mm (*c.* 10 in)

Boul·der (bōl′dər) ⟦from the abundance of large rocks there⟧ city in NC Colo.

Boulder Dam *former name for* HOOVER DAM

bou·le¹ (bo͞o′lē) ***n.*** ⟦Gr *boulē;* akin to *ballein,* to throw (see BALL²); orig. sense, "to throw oneself in spirit into some effort"⟧ in ancient Greece, *a)* an advisory council of elders *b)* later, a representative assembly with legislative and administrative functions

boule² (bo͞ol) ***n.*** ⟦Fr, ball < L *bulla:* see BULL²⟧ **1** [*usually pl.*] a French game similar to boccie **2** a small rounded mass, as of synthetic sapphire or ruby, produced by the fusion of alumina, suitably tinted, in a furnace

boule³ (bo͞ol) ***n.*** *alt. sp. of* BOULLE

bou·le·vard (bo͝ol′ə värd′) ***n.*** ⟦Fr, orig., top surface of a military rampart < MDu *bolwerc,* BULWARK⟧ ☆a broad, well-made street, often one lined with trees, grass plots, etc.

bou·le·var·dier (bo͝ol′ə vär dir′, -dyā′) ***n.*** ⟦Fr⟧ a man who frequents the cafés on the boulevards of Paris; hence, any man about town

boule·verse·ment (bo͞ol vers män′) ***n.*** ⟦Fr⟧ a confused reversal of things; overthrow; upset; turmoil

boulle (bo͞ol) ***n.*** ⟦after Charles André *Boulle* (1642-1732), Fr cabinetmaker⟧ **1** decoration of furniture with designs of tortoise shell, brass, silver, etc. inlaid in wood **2** furniture so decorated

Bou·logne (bo͞o lōn′; *Fr* bo͞o lôn′y′) port in N France, on the English Channel: also **Bou·logne′-sur-Mer′** (-sür mer′)

Bou·logne-Bil·lan·court (-bē yän ko͞or′) city in France, on the Seine: SW suburb of Paris

Boult (bōlt), **Sir Adrian (Cedric)** 1889-1983; Eng. orchestra conductor

bounce (bouns) ***vt.*** **bounced, bounc′ing** ⟦ME *bounsen,* to thump; ? akin to Du *bonzen* & LowG *bunsen,* to thump, strike⟧ **1** [Archaic] to bump or thump **2** to cause to hit against a surface so as to spring back *[to bounce a ball]* ☆**3** [Informal] to have (a check) returned by one's bank to the payee as worthless because there are insufficient funds in one's account to cover it ☆**4** [Slang] to put (an undesirable person) out by force ☆**5** [Slang] to discharge from employment —***vi.*** **1** to spring back from a surface after striking it; rebound **2** to move with an up-and-down motion, as from resilience **3** to move suddenly; spring; jump *[to bounce out of bed]* ☆**4** [Informal] to be returned to the payee by a bank as worthless because there are insufficient funds in the payer's account to cover it: said of a check —***n.*** **1** *a)* a bouncing; rebound *b)* a leap or jump **2** capacity for bouncing; resilience *[the ball has lost its bounce]* **3** a temporary increase or rise, as in value or popularity *[a political candidate's post-convention bounce in the polls]* **4** [Brit.] impudence; bluster ☆**5** [Informal] *a)* energy, zest, etc. *b)* the ability to regain one's spirit or optimism —☆**bounce back** [Informal] to recover strength, good humor, etc. quickly —☆**the bounce** [Slang] dismissal or forcible ejection *[to give (or get) the bounce]* —**bounc′y** ***adj.*** **bounc′i·er, bounc′i·est**

bounc·er (boun′sər) ***n.*** **1** a person or thing that bounces ☆**2** [Informal] a person hired to remove very disorderly people from a nightclub, restaurant, etc.

bounc·ing (-siŋ) *adj.* big, healthy, strong, etc.
bouncing Bet (bet) ⟦< *Bet,* nickname for ELIZABETH[1]⟧ a perennial soapwort (*Saponaria officinalis*) with clusters of pinkish flowers
bound[1] (bound) *vi.* ⟦MFr *bondir* < OFr, to leap, make a noise, orig., to echo back < LL *bombitare,* to buzz, hum < L *bombus,* a humming: see BOMB⟧ **1** to move with a leap or series of leaps **2** to spring back from a surface after striking it, as a ball does; bounce; rebound —*vt.* to cause to bound or bounce —*n.* **1** a jump; leap **2** a springing back from a surface after striking it; bounce —*SYN.* SKIP[1]
bound[2] (bound) *vt., vi. pt. & pp. of* BIND —*adj.* **1** confined by or as by binding; tied **2** closely connected or related **3** certain; sure; destined [*bound* to lose] **4** under compulsion; obliged [legally *bound* to accept] **5** constipated **6** provided with a binding or attached cover, as a book **7** [Informal] having one's mind made up; resolved [a team *bound* on winning] **8** *Linguis.* designating a form, or morpheme, that never occurs alone as an independent word [in "singing," *-ing* is a *bound* form, but *sing* is not]: opposed to FREE (*adj.* 25) —*SYN.* LIMIT —**bound up in** (or **with**) **1** deeply devoted to **2** implicated or involved in
bound[3] (bound) *adj.* ⟦ME *boun,* ready (+ *-d,* prob. by assoc. with prec.) < ON *buinn,* pp. of *bua,* to prepare: see BONDAGE⟧ **1** ready to go or going; headed: often with *for* [*bound* for home] **2** [Archaic] ready; prepared
bound[4] (bound) *n.* ⟦ME *bounde* < OFr *bunne, bodne* < ML *bodina, butina,* boundary, boundary marker⟧ **1** a boundary; limit **2** [*pl.*] an area near, alongside, or enclosed by a boundary —*vt.* **1** to provide with bounds; limit; confine **2** to be a limit or boundary to ☆**3** to name the boundaries of (a state, etc.) —*vi.* to have a boundary (*on* another country, etc.) —**out of bounds 1** beyond the boundaries or limits, as of a playing field **2** not to be entered or used; forbidden
-bound (bound) *combining form* **1** ⟦see BOUND[3]⟧ going or headed toward [*southbound,* championship-*bound*] **2** ⟦see BOUND[2]⟧ confined by or to [*snowbound, housebound*]
bound·a·ry (boun′drē, -də rē) *n., pl.* **-ries** ⟦BOUND[4] + -ARY⟧ any line or thing marking a limit; bound; border
boundary layer a very thin layer of fluid immediately next to a solid body, that flows more slowly than the rest of the fluid
bound·en (boun′dən) *adj.* ⟦old pp. of BIND⟧ [Archaic] **1** held under obligation; indebted **2** that one is bound by; obligatory [one's *bounden* duty]
bound·er (boun′dər) *n.* ⟦BOUND[1] + -ER⟧ [Informal, Chiefly Brit.] a man whose behavior is ungentlemanly; cad
bound·less (bound′lis) *adj.* having no bounds; unlimited; vast —**bound′less·ly** *adv.* —**bound′less·ness** *n.*
boun·te·ous (boun′tē əs) *adj.* ⟦ME *bountevous* < OFr *bontive:* see BOUNTY; modern sp. as if < BOUNTY⟧ **1** giving freely and generously, without restraint **2** provided in abundance; plentiful —**boun′te·ous·ly** *adv.* —**boun′te·ous·ness** *n.*
boun·ti·ful (-tə fəl) *adj.* **1** giving freely and graciously; generous **2** provided in abundance; plentiful —**boun′ti·ful·ly** *adv.* —**boun′ti·ful·ness** *n.*
boun·ty (-tē) *n., pl.* **-ties** ⟦ME *bounte* < OFr *bonte* < L *bonitas,* goodness < *bonus,* good: see BONUS⟧ **1** generosity in giving **2** something given freely; generous gift **3** a reward, premium, or allowance, esp. one given by a government for killing certain harmful animals, raising certain crops, etc. —*SYN.* BONUS
bounty hunter a person who pursues wild animals or outlaws for whose capture a bounty is offered
☆**bounty jumper** in the U.S. Civil War, a man who accepted the cash bounty offered for enlisting and then deserted
bou·quet (bō kā′; *also, and for 2 usually,* bo͞o kā′) *n.* ⟦Fr, a plume, nosegay, older *bosquet* < OFr *boschet:* see BOSKET⟧ **1** a bunch of cut flowers **2** a fragrant smell or aroma; esp., the characteristic aroma of a wine or brandy —*SYN.* SCENT
bouquet garni ⟦Fr⟧ **1** a mixture of herbs, orig. thyme, bay leaf, and parsley, tied by the stems or placed in a cloth bag, added as to a broth or stew during cooking, and removed before serving **2** a mixture of herbs chopped fine and added directly to foods during cooking
☆**bour·bon** (bʉr′bən) [*sometimes* **B-**] *n.* ⟦after *Bourbon* County, Kentucky, where it has been produced⟧ a whiskey distilled from a fermented mash of not less than 51 percent corn grain and stored in charred new oak containers for not less than two years —*adj.* designating, of, or made with such whiskey
Bour·bon (boor′bən; *Fr* bo͞or bôn′) *n.* **1** name of the ruling family of France (1589-1793; 1814-48, from 1830 to 1848 as the ORLÉANS[1] branch); of Spain (1700-1808; 1813-1931; 1975-); of Naples and Sicily (1734-1806; 1815-60), united as the kingdom of the Two Sicilies, 1815; and of various duchies & principalities in Italy at various times within the periods 1748-1807 & 1815-60, including Parma, Piacenza, Lucca, & Etruria **2** [*also* **b-**] a political and social reactionary
☆**Bour·bon·ism** (boor′bən iz′əm) *n.* [*also* **b-**] advocacy or support of conservative government, like that of the Bourbons; extreme political and social reaction
bour·don (boor′dən) *n.* ⟦Fr < ML *burdo,* drone (bee), wind instrument: see BURDEN[2]⟧ the drone of a bagpipe
bourg (boorg) *n.* ⟦LME < MFr < OFr *borc* < Frank **burg* or OHG *burg:* see BOROUGH⟧ **1** a medieval town or village, esp. one near a castle **2** a market town in France
bour·geois (boor zhwä′, boor′zhwä′) *n., pl.* **bour·geois′** (-zhwä′) ⟦Fr < OFr *burgeis* < ML *burgensis* < *burgus, borgus,* town < OFr *borc* or Frank **burg,* prec.⟧ **1** [Obs.] a freeman of a medieval town **2** a self-employed person, as a shopkeeper or businessman **3** a member of the bourgeoisie, or middle class **4** a person whose beliefs, attitudes, and practices are conventionally middle-class —*adj.* of or characteristic of a bourgeois or the bourgeoisie; middle-class; also used variously to mean conventional, smug, materialistic, etc.
bour·geoise (-zhwäz′) *n.* a female bourgeois
bour·geoi·sie (boor′zhwä zē′) *n.* ⟦Fr < *bourgeois:* see BOURGEOIS⟧ [*with sing. or pl. v.*] **1** the social class between the aristocracy or very wealthy and the working class, or proletariat; middle class **2** in Marxist doctrine, capitalists as a social class antithetical to the proletariat
bour·geoi·si·fy (boor zhwä′zə fī′) *vt.* **-fied′**, **-fy′ing** to cause to become bourgeois in characteristics, attitudes, etc. —**bour·geoi′si·fi·ca′tion** *n.*
bour·geon (bʉr′jən) *n., vt., vi. alt. sp. of* BURGEON
Bourges (boorzh) city in central France
Bour·gogne (bo͞or gôn′y′) *Fr. name for* BURGUNDY[2]
bourguignon *n. see* BOEUF BOURGUIGNON
Bourke-White (bʉrk′hwīt′), **Margaret** 1906-71; U.S. photojournalist
bourn[1] or **bourne** (bôrn, boorn) *n.* ⟦ME *burne* < OE *burna,* metathetic for *brunna;* akin to Ger *brunnen,* a spring: see BURN[1]⟧ a brook or stream
bourn[2] or **bourne** (bôrn, boorn) *n.* ⟦Fr *borne* < OFr *bunne:* see BOUND[4]⟧ [Archaic] **1** a limit; boundary **2** a goal; objective **3** a domain
Bourne·mouth (bôrn′məth, boorn′-) resort city in Dorset, SW England, on the English Channel
bour·rée (bo͞o rā′) *n.* ⟦Fr < *bourrir,* to beat wings, whir (as a partridge)⟧ **1** a lively 17th-cent. French dance in duple time **2** music for this dance, or a composition of similar rhythm **3** *Ballet* a gliding movement across the floor by means of very small, quick steps typically while on *pointe*
bour·ride (bo͞o rēd′) *n.* ⟦Fr < Prov *bourrido* < *boulido,* something that has been boiled < *bouli,* to boil: see BOUILLABAISSE⟧ a Provençal stew containing fish, vegetables, and white wine, thickened with aioli and served over bread
bourse (boors) *n.* ⟦Fr, a purse, exchange < OFr *borse* < ML *bursa,* a bag: see PURSE⟧ **1** *a)* an exchange where securities or commodities are regularly bought and sold *b)* [**B-**] the stock exchange of Paris or of any of certain other European cities **2** a sale, as of coins or postage stamps, by dealers at a convention, exhibit, etc.
bour·sin (boor′sin) ⟦< manufacturer's name, La Fromagerie *Boursin,* Pacy-sur-Eure, France⟧ *trademark for* a spread of creamy, unripened white French cheese flavored with garlic and herbs, black pepper, etc. —*n.* [*usually* **B-**] such a spread, esp. one flavored with garlic: also **Boursin cheese**
bou·stro·phe·don (bo͞o′strō fē′dən, bou′-) *adj.* ⟦Gr *boustrophēdon,* lit., turning like oxen in plowing < *bous,* ox (see COW[1]) + *strephein,* to turn (see STROPHE)⟧ designating or of an ancient form of writing in which the lines run alternately from right to left and left to right
bout (bout) *n.* ⟦for earlier *bought* < ME *bught,* akin to MLowG *bucht,* BIGHT; form & meaning prob. infl. by *'bout* < *about*⟧ **1** a contest or match, as of boxing or wrestling **2** a period of time taken up by some specified activity, condition, etc.; spell [a *bout* of the flu]
bou·tique (bo͞o tēk′; *occas.* bō-) *n.* ⟦Fr < L *apotheca:* see APOTHECARY⟧ **1** a small shop, or a small department in a store, where fashionable, usually expensive, clothes and other articles are sold **2** a small, often exclusive agency or firm offering specialized services, as in advertising, investments, or law
bou·ton·niere or **bou·ton·nière** (bo͞o′tə nir′, -tən yer′) *n.* ⟦Fr *boutonnière,* a buttonhole⟧ a flower or flowers worn in a buttonhole, as of a lapel
bou·var·di·a (bo͞o vär′dē ə) *n.* ⟦ModL, after C. *Bouvard,* 17th-c. Fr physician⟧ any of a genus (*Bouvardia*) of plants of the madder family, grown for the showy flowers often used in brides' bouquets
bou·vi·er des Flan·dres (bo͞o′vē ā′ də flan′dərz, -dā flan′-; *Fr* bo͞o vyā dā flän′dr′) ⟦Fr, lit., cowherd of Flanders⟧ any of a breed of large, strong dog with a rough, wiry coat and pointed, erect ears: first used in Flanders for herding cattle: also called **bou·vi·er′** *n.*
bou·zou·ki (bo͞o zo͞o′kē) *n.* ⟦ModGr *mpouzouki,* prob. < Turk⟧ a stringed musical instrument of Greece, somewhat like a mandolin, used to accompany folk dances and singers
bo·vid (bō′vid′) *adj.* ⟦< ModL *Bovidae* < L *bos:* see fol.⟧ of a large family (Bovidae) of ruminants, having a pair of hollow, unbranched horns, including oxen, sheep, goats, and antelopes —*n.* any bovid animal
bo·vine (bō′vīn′, -vēn′) *adj.* ⟦LL *bovinus* < L *bos* (gen. *bovis*), ox: see COW[1]⟧ **1** of an ox **2** having oxlike qualities; thought of as oxlike; slow, dull, stupid, stolid, etc. —*n.* **1** any of a genus (*Bos*) of bovid ruminants **2** any similar bovid
bovine growth hormone a growth hormone of cattle; esp., this hormone synthesized artificially and administered to beef cattle to increase growth rate and reduce fat and to dairy cows to increase milk production: also **bovine somatotropin** or [Chiefly Brit.] **bovine somatotrophin**
Bov·ril (bäv′ril) ⟦ult. < L *bos* (gen. *bovis*), ox: see COW[1]⟧ *trademark for* a concentrated extract of beef, originating in England, used to make a drink like bouillon, and sometimes as a sandwich spread
bow[1] (bou) *vi.* ⟦ME *bouen* < OE *bugan,* to bend < IE base **bheugh-,* to bend > Ger *biegen;* the *n.* is 17th c.⟧ **1** [Dial.] to bend or stoop **2** to bend down one's head or bend one's body in respect, agreement, worship, recognition, etc. **3** to yield or submit, as to authority **4** to express assent, greeting, etc. by bowing —*vt.* **1** [Dial.] to bend **2** to bend (one's head) down in respect, prayer, shame, etc. **3** to indicate (agreement, thanks, etc.) by bowing **4** to weigh (*down*); overwhelm; crush [the president was *bowed* down by the

burdens of office] —*n.* a bending down of the head or body, as in respect or greeting —**bow and scrape** to be too polite and ingratiating —**bow out** to leave or retire formally or ceremoniously —**bow out (or in)** to usher out (or in) with a bow —**take a bow** to acknowledge an introduction, applause, etc. as by bowing

bow[2] (bō) *n.* ⟦ME *boue* < OE *boga* < PGmc **boga* < base of prec.⟧ **1** anything curved or bent [*a rainbow, oxbow*] **2** a curve; bend **3** a device for shooting arrows, made of a flexible, curved strip of wood, metal, etc. with a tightly drawn cord connecting the two ends **4** an archer **5** *a)* a slender stick strung along its length with horsehairs, drawn across the strings of a violin, cello, etc. to play it *b)* a stroke with such a bow **6** a bowknot or a decorative knot, as of ribbon, with two or more loops **7** either of the sidepieces of a pair of glasses extending over the ears; temple —*adj.* bow-shaped; curved; bent — *vt., vi.* **1** to bend or curve [the wall *bowed* outward from the pressure] **2** *Music* to play (a violin, etc.) with a bow

bow[3] (bou) *n.* ⟦ME *boue* < LowG or Scand: LowG *būg,* Du *boeg,* Swed *bog,* shoulder, shoulders of a ship, bows; akin to BOUGH⟧ **1** [*sometimes pl.*] the front part of a ship, boat, or airship; prow **2** the rower nearest the bow **3** *Naut.* a direction at a 45° angle left or right from dead ahead [a whale sighted on the port *bow*]

bow compass (bō) a pair of drawing compasses with legs joined by a flexible steel band, the angle between being adjusted by a screw

Bow·ditch (bou′dich), **Nathaniel** 1773-1838; U.S. mathematician, astronomer, & navigator

bowd·ler·ize (boud′lər īz′, bōd′-) *vt.* **-ized′**, **-iz′ing** ⟦after Thomas *Bowdler* (1754-1825), Eng editor who (1818) published an expurgated Shakespeare⟧ to remove passages considered offensive from (a book, play, etc.) —**bowd′ler·ism′** *n.* —**bowd′ler·i·za′tion** *n.*

bow·el (bou′əl) *n.* ⟦ME *bouel* < *boele* < OFr *buele* < ML *botellum,* intestine < L *botellus,* dim. of *botulus,* sausage, via Oscan or Umbrian < IE base **gwet-*, a swelling > OE *cwitha,* womb⟧ **1** an intestine, esp. of a human being; gut: *usually used in pl.* **2** [*pl.*] the interior or inner part [the *bowels* of the mountain] **3** [*pl.*] [Archaic] the inside of the body, regarded as the source of pity, tenderness, etc.; hence, tender emotions —*vt.* **-eled** or **-elled**, **-el·ing** or **-el·ling** to disembowel —**move one's bowels** to pass waste matter from the large intestine; defecate

bowel movement **1** the passing of waste matter from the large intestine **2** waste matter thus passed; feces

bow·er[1] (bou′ər) *n.* ⟦ME *bour* < OE *bur,* room, hut, dwelling, akin to Ger *bauer,* bird cage: for IE base see BONDAGE⟧ **1** a place enclosed by overhanging boughs of trees or by vines on a trellis; arbor **2** [Old Poet.] a rustic cottage or retreat **3** [Archaic] a lady's boudoir **4** a hut and platform of twigs built by a male bowerbird: used only for courtship and not as a nest —*vt.* to form into a bower; enclose with boughs, etc. —**bow′er·y** *adj.*

☆**bow·er**[2] (bou′ər) *n.* ⟦Ger *bauer,* peasant (akin to prec.): so called from the figure sometimes used as the jack⟧ the jack of trump (**right bower**) or the jack of the other suit of the same color (**left bower**), the highest card and next highest card, respectively, in euchre

bow·er[3] (bou′ər) *n.* ⟦< BOW[3]⟧ the heaviest anchor of a ship, normally carried at the bow

bow·er·bird (-burd′) *n.* any of certain passerine birds (family Ptilonorhynchidae) of Australia and New Guinea: the male builds a mating bower, variously decorated, to attract the female

☆**bow·er·y** (bou′ər ē, bou′rē) *n., pl.* **-er·ies** ⟦Du *bouwerij,* farm < *bouer, boer,* farmer: see BOOR⟧ a farm or plantation of an early Dutch settler of New York —**the Bowery** street in New York City, or the surrounding district: center of cheap hotels, bars, etc.

☆**bow·fin** (bō′fin′) *n.* a primitive freshwater fish (*Amia calva*) of E North America, with a rounded tail fin and a long, narrow fin on its back: it is the only living member of an order (Amiiformes) of bony fishes

bow-front (-frunt′) *adj.* having a front with a convex curve [a *bow-front* chest of drawers]

bow hand (bō) the hand that holds the bow in archery or in playing a violin, cello, etc.

bow·head (-hed′) *n.* a right whale (*Balaena mysticetus*) with a very large head, and an arched upper jaw: valued for its strong, elastic baleen

bow·hunt·ing (-hunt′iŋ) *n.* the practice of hunting wild animals with bow and arrow —**bow′hunt′er** *n.*

☆**bow·ie knife** (bo͞o′ē, bō′-) ⟦after Col. James *Bowie* (1799?-1836) or ? his brother, Rezin, U.S. frontiersmen⟧ a steel knife about fifteen inches long, with a single edge, usually carried in a sheath, used originally by American frontiersmen as a weapon

bowie knife

bow·ing (bō′iŋ) *n.* the manner or technique of using the bow in playing a violin, cello, etc.

bow·knot (bō′nät′) *n.* a decorative knot in a string, ribbon, etc., usually with two loops and two ends: it is untied by pulling the ends

bowl[1] (bōl) *n.* ⟦ME *bolle* < OE *bolla,* cup, bowl < IE base **bhel-*, to swell, inflate (see BALL[1]); infl. in OE by L *bulla,* bubble, ball⟧ **1** a deep, rounded container or dish, open at the top **2** the capacity or contents of a bowl **3** a thing or part shaped like a bowl; specif., *a)* the rounded or hollow part of a spoon or smoking pipe *b)* WASHBOWL *c)* the basin of a toilet *d)* a hollow land formation ☆**4** *a)* an amphitheater or stadium *b)* any of various football games played annually after the regular season between teams selected for their superior records: in full **bowl game** **5** [Archaic] a large drinking vessel —**bowl′like′** *adj.*

bowl[2] (bōl) *n.* ⟦ME & OFr *boule* < L *bulla,* bubble, knob: see BOIL[1]⟧ **1** the wooden ball rolled at the target ball, or jack, in the game of lawn bowling: it is weighted or shaped to give it a bias when rolling **2** a roll of the ball in bowling or lawn bowling **3** a roller, drum, or wheel, as in some machines —*vi.* **1** to participate or take a turn in bowling or lawn bowling **2** to roll a ball with an underhand motion, as in bowling or lawn bowling **3** to move swiftly and smoothly [the car *bowled* steadily along] **4** *Cricket* to throw a ball to the batsman —*vt.* **1** to throw so as to make roll; roll **2** to make a score of in bowling [to *bowl* 180] **3** to cause to move along swiftly and smoothly, as on wheels **4** *Cricket* to put (a batsman *out*) by bowling the balls off the wicket —**bowl over** **1** to knock over with or as with something rolled **2** [Informal] to astonish or amaze, thrill or delight, etc. [the election results *bowled* them *over*]

bowl·der (bōl′dər) *n. alt. sp. of* BOULDER

bow·leg (bō′leg′, -lāg′) *n.* **1** a leg that bows by curving outward at the knee **2** the condition or degree of such curvature

bow·leg·ged (-leg′id, -legd′; -lā′gid, -lāgd′) *adj.* having bowlegs

bowl·er[1] (bōl′ər) *n.* a person who bowls

bowl·er[2] (-ər) *n.* ⟦after J. *Bowler,* 19th-c. London hat manufacturer⟧ [Brit.] a derby hat

bow·line (bō′lin, -līn′) *n.* ⟦ME *boueline,* prob. < MDu *boeglijne* (or Dan *bovline*); for IE bases see BOW[3] & LINE[2]⟧ **1** a rope running forward from the middle of a square sail's weather edge to the bow, used to keep the sail taut when the ship is sailing into the wind **2** a knot used in making a loop that will not slip or tighten under tension: in full **bowline knot** —**on a bowline** with sails set so as to head close to the wind; closehauled

bowl·ing (bōl′iŋ) *n.* **1** a game in which a heavy ball is bowled along a wooden lane in an attempt to knock over ten large wooden pins that are set upright at the far end **2** LAWN BOWLING **3** the playing of either of these games **4** *Cricket* the act of throwing the ball to the batsman

bowling alley **1** the long, narrow wooden lane used in bowling **2** a building or hall with a number of such lanes

bowling green a smooth lawn for the game of lawn bowling

bowls (bōlz) *n.* LAWN BOWLING

bow·man[1] (bō′mən) *n., pl.* **-men** (-mən) a person who shoots with bow and arrow; archer

bow·man[2] (bou′mən) *n., pl.* **-men** (-mən) the oarsman nearest the bow of a boat

bow·shot (bō′shät′) *n.* the distance that an arrow can travel when shot from a bow

bow·sprit (bou′sprit′, bō′-) *n.* ⟦ME *bouspret,* prob. < MDu *boegspriet* < *boeg,* BOW[3] + *spriet,* SPRIT⟧ a large, tapered spar extending forward from the bow of a sailing vessel, to which stays for the masts are secured

bow·string (bō′striŋ′) *n.* **1** a cord stretched from one end of an archer's bow to the other **2** any strong, light cord

bowstring hemp **1** SANSEVIERIA **2** hemplike fiber from the leaves of certain sansevierias

bow tie (bō) a small necktie tied in a bowknot

bow window (bō) a bay window built in a curve

bow·wow (bou′wou′) *n.* ⟦echoic⟧ **1** the bark of a dog, or a sound in imitation of it **2** a dog: a child's word —*vi.* to bark as or like a dog

bow·yer (bō′yər) *n.* ⟦BOW[2] + -YER⟧ a person who makes or deals in archery bows

box[1] (bäks) *n.* ⟦ME & OE, a container, box < VL *buxis* < L *buxus,* boxwood < Gr *pyxos*⟧ **1** any of various kinds of containers, usually rectangular and lidded, made of cardboard, wood, or other stiff material; case; carton **2** the contents or capacity of a box **3** [Chiefly Brit.] a gift, esp. a Christmas present, in a box **4** ⟦< the toolbox under the seat⟧ the driver's seat on a coach **5** a boxlike thing, opening, or compartment **6** a small, enclosed group of seats, as in a theater, stadium, etc. **7** a small booth or shelter for persons on outdoor duty [a sentry *box*] **8** a small country house used by sportsmen [a grouse *box*] **9** BOX STALL **10** a space or section for a certain person or group [a press *box,* jury *box*] **11** *a)* a short newspaper article or advertisement enclosed in borders *b)* any of the enclosed sets of lines and spaces on a printed form ☆**12** [Informal, Chiefly Brit.] television or a television set: used with *the* **13** [Slang] the vulva or vagina: somewhat vulgar ☆**14** *Baseball* any of certain designated areas outlined on the playing field for the batter, catcher, and first-base and third-base coaches **15** *Mech.* a protective casing for a part [a journal *box*] —*vt.* **1** to provide with a box **2** to put into a box, etc., as for storage or shipment **3** to boxhaul —*adj.* **1** shaped or made like a box **2** packaged in a box —**box in** **1** BOX UP (sense 1) **2** to block and thus prevent (another racer) from getting ahead —**box out** *Basketball* to block (an opponent) so as to prevent that player from getting a rebound —**box the compass** **1** to name the thirty-two points of the compass in order: compasses were kept in boxes **2** to make a complete circuit, returning to the starting point —**box up** **1** to keep in; surround or confine ☆**2** to encase with sheathing boards, or laths —**in a box** [Informal] in difficulty or a dilemma —**outside (of) the box** [Informal] in a fresh, inventive, unconventional way —**box′like′** *adj.*

box[2] (bäks) *n.* ⟦ME < ?⟧ a blow struck with the hand or fist, esp. on the ear or the side of the head —*vt.* **1** to strike with such a blow **2** to engage in a boxing match with —*vi.* to fight with the fists; engage in boxing

box[3] (bäks) *n.* ⟦ME & OE < L *buxus* < Gr *pyxos*⟧ **1** any of a genus (*Buxus*) of evergreen shrubs or small trees of the box family with small, leathery leaves: some species are used as hedge plants or shaped as garden ornaments **2** BOXWOOD (sense 1) ***—adj.*** designating a family (Buxaceae, order Euphorbiales) of dicotyledonous evergreen shrubs and trees, including pachysandra

☆**box·ber·ry** (bäks′ber′ē) ***n.***, *pl.* **-ries 1** WINTERGREEN (sense 1*a*) **2** PARTRIDGEBERRY

☆**box·board** (bäks′bôrd′) ***n.*** stiff paperboard used for making boxes

☆**box calf** tanned calf leather with square markings

box camera a simple camera shaped like a box and having a fixed focus and, usually, a single shutter speed

☆**box·car** (-kär′) ***n.*** **1** a fully enclosed railroad freight car **2** [*pl.*] *Craps* a throw of twelve (two sixes)

box coat 1 a type of heavy overcoat, formerly worn by coachmen **2** an overcoat that fits loosely, hanging straight from the shoulders

box cutter a small cutting tool with a retractable blade, designed for use in opening cardboard boxes

☆**box elder** a medium-sized, fast-growing North American maple (*Acer negundo*), with compound leaves

box·er (bäk′sər) ***n.*** **1** one who boxes; pugilist; prizefighter; often, one skilled in the offensive and defensive tactics of boxing, as distinguished from a slugger ☆**2** [*pl.*] BOXER SHORTS **3** ⟦Ger < *boxen*, to BOX² (< Eng): from its aggressive appearance⟧ any of a breed of medium-sized dog with a sturdy body and a smooth fawn or brindle coat

Box·er (bäk′sər) ***n.*** ⟦< BOX²; transl. of the Chin phrase "righteous-uniting-band," misunderstood as "righteous-uniting-fists"⟧ a member of a Chinese society that led an unsuccessful uprising (the **Boxer Rebellion**, 1900) against foreign powers and foreigners in China, as a result of which China was forced to make economic and territorial concessions

☆**boxer shorts** men's undershorts with an elastic waistband and the loose, full cut of prizefighters' trunks

box·haul (bäks′hôl′) ***vt.*** to change (the course of a sailing ship) by veering around sharply instead of tacking normally

box·ing¹ (bäk′siŋ) ***n.*** the skill or sport of fighting with the fists

box·ing² (bäk′siŋ) ***n.*** **1** the act or process of packing a box or boxes **2** a boxlike covering or casing **3** material used for boxes

Boxing Day December 26, a legal holiday in most parts of the Commonwealth: so called from the former custom of giving gift boxes to employees, mail carriers, etc.

boxing glove either of a pair of padded mittens worn by a boxer

box kite a kite with an oblong, box-shaped framework, open at the ends and along the middle

☆**box lunch** an individual boxed lunch of sandwiches, fruit, etc., esp. as prepared by a caterer

box office 1 a place where admission tickets are sold, as in a theater ☆**2** [Informal] *a)* the power of a show, film, or performer to attract a paying audience *b)* a show, film, etc. considered with regard to this power *c)* the amount of money paid by audiences to see a show, film, etc.

box pleat a double pleat with the under edges folded toward each other

☆**box score** a detailed summary, printed typically in a rectangular format, of a contest, esp. a baseball or basketball game, showing the statistical performance of each contestant

box seat a seat in a box at a theater, stadium, etc.

box social a fund-raising event at which donated box meals are auctioned

☆**box spring** a bedspring consisting of a boxlike, cloth-enclosed frame containing rows of coil springs fastened together and to the frame

☆**box stall** a large, enclosed stall, for a single horse, cow, etc.

box step a basic step in ballroom dancing, in which the feet move in the form of a rectangle

☆**box supper** a social gathering, as at a church, at which box lunches donated by women are auctioned off to raise funds

box·thorn (bäks′thôrn′) ***n.*** MATRIMONY VINE

☆**box turtle (*or* tortoise)** any of several North American terrapins (genus *Terrapene*) with a hinged shell that can be completely closed: usually found on land

box·wood (-wood′) ***n.*** **1** the hard, closegrained wood of the box shrub or tree **2** the box shrub or tree

box wrench a wrench with a completely enclosed head, used to hold and turn nuts and bolts

box·y (bäk′sē) ***adj.*** **box′i·er, box′i·est** like a box, as in shape, plainness, or confining quality **—box′i·ly** ***adv.*** **—box′i·ness** ***n.***

boy (boi) ***n.*** ⟦ME *boie*, servant, commoner, knave, boy < ? OFr *embuié*, one fettered < *embuier*, to chain < *em-*, EN-¹ + L *boiae*, fetters, orig., leather collar for the neck < *bos*, ox, COW¹⟧ **1** a male child from birth to the age of physical maturity; lad; youth **2** a man regarded as immature or callow **3** any man; fellow: familiar term **4** a male domestic worker or servant: a patronizing term applied esp. by Caucasians to nonwhites **5** a bellboy, messenger boy, etc. **6** [Informal] a son [Mrs. Dill's oldest *boy*] **—**☆***interj.*** [Slang] used to express pleasure, surprise, etc.: often **oh, boy!**

bo·yar (bō yär′, boi′ər) ***n.*** ⟦Russ *bojarin*, grandee < *boj*, battle < IE base **bhei-*, to strike⟧ [Historical] **1** a member of the privileged aristocracy in czarist Russia, ranking just below the ruling princes: the rank was abolished by Peter I **2** a member of the privileged aristocracy in Romania Also **bo·yard** (bō yärd′, boi′ərd)

boy band a pop music group typically consisting of four to six young male vocalists and intended to appeal to a teenage female audience: also written **boy′band′** ***n.***

boy·chik or **boy·chick** (boi′chik′) ***n.*** ⟦Am Yiddish, dim. < E BOY⟧ [Informal] a youth; boy

boy·cott (boi′kät′) ***vt.*** ⟦after Capt. C. C. *Boycott*, land agent ostracized by his neighbors during the Land League agitation in Ireland in 1880⟧ **1** to join together in refusing to deal with, so as to punish, coerce, etc. **2** to refuse to buy, sell, or use [to *boycott* a newspaper] **—**☆***n.*** an act or instance of boycotting

☆**boy·friend** (boi′frend′) ***n.*** [Informal] **1** a sweetheart who is a boy or man **2** a boy who is one's friend

boy·hood (-hood′) ***n.*** **1** the state or time of being a boy **2** boys collectively

boy·ish (-ish) ***adj.*** of, like, or fit for a boy or boys **—boy′ish·ly** ***adv.*** **—boy′ish·ness** ***n.***

Boyle (boil), **Robert** 1627-91; Brit. chemist & physicist, born in Ireland

Boyle's law ⟦after prec.⟧ the statement that for a body of ideal gas at constant temperature the volume is inversely proportional to the pressure

Boyne (boin) river in E Ireland: site of a battle (1690) in which the forces of William III of England defeated the Jacobites of James II, resulting in his flight to France: *c.* 70 mi (113 km)

boy·o (boi′ō′) ***n.*** [Informal, Chiefly Brit.] a fellow; boy; lad; man

Boy Scout 1 a member of the **Boy Scouts**, a worldwide boys' organization, founded in England (1908), that stresses character, citizenship, outdoor life, and service to others; specif., a member of the division of **Boy Scouts of America** (1910) for boys eleven to seventeen years of age ☆**2** [**b- s-**] [Informal] a man or boy regarded as being excessively proper, conscientious, sportsmanlike, etc.

☆**boy·sen·ber·ry** (boi′zən ber′ē, boi′sən-) ***n.***, *pl.* **-ries** ⟦after Rudolph *Boysen*, U.S. horticulturist who developed it (*c.* 1935)⟧ a large berry, dark red or almost black when ripe, which is a cross of varieties of raspberry, loganberry, and blackberry

☆**boy toy** [Informal] **1** a young woman seeking to be sexually provocative to men **2** an attractive young man chosen as a partner, often, specif., by an older woman, in a superficial sexual relationship

Boz (bäz; *orig.* bōz) *pseudonym for* Charles DICKENS

Boz·caa·da (bōz′jä dä′) Turkish island in the Aegean, near the Dardanelles: 15 sq mi (39 sq km): in Greek legend, as *Tenedos*, the base of the Greek fleet in the Trojan War

☆**bo·zo** (bō′zō) ***n.***, *pl.* **-zos** ⟦< ?⟧ [Slang] **1** a fellow; guy **2** a jerk, fool, etc.

bp *abbrev.* **1** base pair **2** bills payable **3** birthplace **4** boiling point

Bp *abbrev.* Bishop

BP *abbrev.* **1** *Baseball* batting practice **2** *Geol.* before the present **3** bills payable: also **B/P** **4** blood pressure **5** blueprint: also **b/p**

BPD¹ or **bpd** *abbrev.* barrels per day

BPD² *abbrev.* borderline personality disorder

BPE or **B.P.E.** *abbrev.* Bachelor of Physical Education

BPH (bē′pē′āch′) ***n.*** ⟦*b*(*enign*) *p*(*rostatic*) *h*(*yperplasia*) or *h*(*ypertrophy*)⟧ a noncancerous enlargement of the prostate gland, often found in older men and typically resulting in obstruction of the flow of urine

BPh or **B.Ph.** *abbrev.* Bachelor of Philosophy

BPharm or **B.Pharm.** *abbrev.* Bachelor of Pharmacy

bpi *abbrev. Comput.* **1** bits per inch: see BIT⁴ **2** bytes per inch: also **BPI**

bpl *abbrev.* birthplace

BPOE *abbrev.* Benevolent and Protective Order of Elks

bps *abbrev. Comput.* bits per second: see BIT⁴

Bq *abbrev.* becquerel

br *abbrev.* **1** bedroom **2** bills receivable **3** branch **4** brass **5** brother **6** brown

Br¹ *abbrev.* **1** Branch **2** Britain **3** British **4** Brother

Br² *Chem. symbol for* bromine

BR *abbrev.* **1** bedroom **2** bills receivable: also **B/R**

☆**bra** (brä) ***n.*** ⟦< BRASSIERE⟧ an undergarment worn by women to support the breasts or give a desired contour to the bust

Bra·bant (brə bant′, -bänt′) **1** former duchy of W Europe, originating in the late 12th cent.: since 1830, divided between the Netherlands (*North Brabant* province) & Belgium (provinces *Antwerp* & *Brabant*) **2** province of central Belgium: 1,297 sq mi (3,359 sq km); cap. Brussels

brab·ble (brab′əl) ***vi.*** **-bled, -bling** ⟦< Du *brabbelen*, to jabber⟧ [Archaic] to quarrel noisily over trifles **—*n.*** quarrelsome chatter

brace¹ (brās) ***vt.*** **braced, brac′ing** ⟦ME *bracen* < OFr *bracer*, to brace, embrace < L *brachia*, pl. of *brachium*, an arm < Gr *brachiōn*, arm, upper arm < *brachys*, short (in contrast to the longer lower arm): see MERRY⟧ **1** to tie or bind on firmly **2** to tighten, esp. by stretching **3** to strengthen or make firm by supporting the weight of, resisting the pressure of, etc.; prop up **4** to equip or support with braces **5** to make ready for an impact, shock, etc.: often used reflexively **6** to give vigor or energy to; stimulate; invigorate **7** to get a firm hold with (the hands or feet) ☆**8** [Slang] to ask a loan or handout from **—*n.*** ⟦ME < OFr, armful, fathom < L *brachia*⟧ **1** two of a kind; a couple; pair, as of hounds, game animals, or pistols **2** a device that clasps or connects to keep something firmly in place; fastener **3** [*pl.*] [Brit.] suspenders **4** a device for setting up or maintaining tension, as a guy wire **5** *a)* either of the signs { }, used to connect or enclose words or items to be considered together *b)* such a sign used to connect two or more staves of a musical score *c)* the set of staves so connected **6** a device, as a beam, used as a support, to resist strain or pressure, etc.; prop **7** *a)* any of various devices for supporting a weak or malformed part of the body: often intended for permanent use in contrast to a splint or cast *b)* [*often pl.*] a device attached to the teeth in order to move them gradually into better occlusion **8** a tool for holding and rotating a drilling bit ☆**9** [Informal] a rigid position of exaggerated attention, as that assumed by underclassmen at military academies —**SYN.** PAIR —☆**brace up** to call forth one's courage, resolution, etc., as after defeat or disappointment

brace[2] (brās) ***n.*** ⟦Fr *bras (de vergue)*, brace (of a yard) < L *brachium:* see prec.⟧ *Naut.* a rope passed through a block at the end of a yard, used to swing the yard about from the deck —***vt.*** **braced, brac′ing** *Naut.* to move (a yard) by means of a brace

brace and bit a tool for boring, consisting of a removable drill (*bit*) in a rotating handle (*brace*)

brace·let (brās′lit) ***n.*** ⟦ME < OFr, dim. of *bracel, brachel* < L *brachiale,* armlet < *brachium:* see BRACE[1]⟧ **1** an ornamental band or chain worn around the wrist or arm **2** ANKLE BRACELET **3** [Slang] a handcuff: *usually used in pl.* —**brace′let·ed** ***adj.***

brac·er[1] (brā′sər) ***n.*** ⟦ME < OFr *brasseure* < *bras,* arm < L *brachium:* see BRACE[1]⟧ *Archery* a leather guard worn on the arm holding the bow, for protection against the bowstring

brac·er[2] (-sər) ***n.*** **1** a person or thing that braces ☆**2** [Slang] a drink of alcoholic liquor

☆**bra·ce·ro** (brə ser′ō) ***n., pl.*** **-ros** ⟦Sp < *brazo,* an arm < L *brachium:* see BRACE[1]⟧ a Mexican guest worker who had been permitted to enter the U.S. under a former government program

brach (brach, brak) ***n.*** ⟦ME & OFr *brache,* back-form. < OFr *brachez,* pl. of *brachet,* hunting dog < Frank **brak;* akin to OHG *brakko* < IE **bhrag-,* to smell: see FRAGRANT⟧ [Archaic] a female hound; bitch: also **brach′et** (-it)

bra·chi·al (brā′kē əl, brak′ē-) ***adj.*** ⟦L *brachialis* < *brachium:* see BRACE[1]⟧ **1** of or like an arm **2** of an armlike part, as a wing or fin

bra·chi·ate (brā′kē āt′, brak′ē-; *for adj. usually,* -it) ***adj.*** ⟦< fol. + -ATE[1]⟧ having widely spreading branches, alternately arranged —***vi.*** **-at′ed, -at′ing** to swing arm over arm from one hold to the next, as certain apes and monkeys do —**bra′chi·a′tion** ***n.*** —**bra′chi·a′tor** ***n.***

bra·chi·o- (brā′kē ō, brak′ē-; -ə) ⟦< L *brachium:* see BRACE[1]⟧ *combining form* arm, arms [*brachiopod*]: also **bra′chi-**

bra·chi·o·pod (brā′kē ō päd′, brak′ē-) ***n.*** ⟦< ModL < prec. + -POD⟧ any of a phylum (Brachiopoda) of marine animals with hinged upper and lower shells enclosing two armlike parts with tentacles that are used for guiding minute food particles to the mouth

bra·chi·o·saur (brā′kē ə sôr′, brak′ē-) ***n.*** ⟦< ModL *Brachiosaurus* < Gr *brachiōn,* an arm + *sauros,* lizard⟧ any of a genus (*Brachiosaurus*) of huge Jurassic sauropods having longer forelegs than hind legs and nostrils high on the forehead: also **bra′chi·o·saur′us** (-əs)

bra·chi·um (brā′kē əm, brak′ē-) ***n., pl.*** **-chi·a** (-ə) ⟦L: see BRACE[1]⟧ the part of the arm that extends from shoulder to elbow

brach·y- (brak′i, -ə) ⟦< Gr *brachys,* short: see MERRY⟧ *combining form* short [*brachycephalic*]

brach·y·ce·phal·ic (brak′i sə fal′ik) ***adj.*** ⟦prec. + -CEPHALIC⟧ having a relatively short or broad head; having a head whose width is 81 percent or more of its length from front to back: see also CEPHALIC INDEX: also **brach′y·ceph′a·lous** (-sef′ə ləs) —**brach′y·ceph′a·ly** (-sef′ə lē) ***n.***

brach·y·cra·ni·al (-krā′nē əl) ***adj.*** ⟦BRACHY- + CRANIAL⟧ BRACHYCEPHALIC: also **brach′y·cra′nic** (-krā′nik) —**brach′y·cra′ny** (-krā′nē) ***n.***

brach·y·dac·tyl·ic (-dak til′ik) ***adj.*** ⟦BRACHY- + DACTYL + -IC⟧ having abnormally short fingers or toes: also **brach′y·dac′ty·lous** (-dak′tə ləs) —**brach′y·dac′ty·ly** (-dak′tə lē) ***n.***

bra·chyl·o·gy (brə kil′ə jē) ***n.*** ⟦ML *brachylogia:* see BRACHY- & -LOGY⟧ **1** conciseness of speech; brevity **2** *pl.* **-gies** an abridged expression

bra·chyp·ter·ous (brə kip′tər əs) ***adj.*** ⟦BRACHY- + -PTEROUS⟧ having incompletely developed or very short wings, as certain insects

brach·y·ther·a·py (brak′i ther′ə pē) ***n., pl.*** **-pies** ⟦BRACHY- + THERAPY: so named from the short distance between tissue and radiation source⟧ radiotherapy treatment in which the radiation source is implanted in, on, or near a cancerous tumor

brach·y·u·ran (brak′ē yoor′ən) ***adj.*** ⟦< ModL *Brachyura* (< Gr *brachys,* short + *oura,* tail: see BRACHY- & URO-[2]) + -AN⟧ designating or of certain crabs with a short abdomen folded beneath the main body

brac·ing (brās′iŋ) ***adj.*** invigorating; stimulating; refreshing —***n.*** **1** a device that braces; support **2** a system of braces

bra·ci·o·la (brä′chē ō′lə, -chō′lə; brə zhōl′) ***n.*** ⟦It, cutlet, orig., braised meat < *brace,* live coal < Gmc **brasa* > BRAISE⟧ a thin slice of meat, esp. beef, rolled around a filling as of other meat, chopped vegetables, herbs, etc. and cooked in wine: also **bra′ci·o′le** (-lā)

brack·en (brak′ən) ***n.*** ⟦ME *braken* < ON **brakni* > Dan *bregne*⟧ **1** any of a genus (*Pteridium,* family Polypodiaceae) of large, coarse, weedy ferns, occurring in meadows, woods, and esp. wastelands: very closely related to the brake ferns **2** a growth of such ferns

brack·et (brak′it) ***n.*** ⟦earlier *bragget* < Fr *braguette,* codpiece, dim. of *brague,* knee pants; ult. < Gaul **braca,* pants⟧ **1** an architectural support projecting from a wall, as a corbel **2** any angle-shaped support, esp. one in the form of a right triangle **3** a wall shelf or shelves held up by brackets **4** a wall fixture, as for a small electric lamp **5** either of the pair of signs [ ], or sometimes < >, used to enclose a word or words inserted as for explanation, quantities to be taken as a single quantity, etc. **6** the part of a classified, graded grouping that falls within specified limits [the $30,000 to $40,000 income *bracket*] **7** *a)* the interval between the ranges of two rounds of artillery fire, as one over and the other short of the target, used to find the correct range *b)* such a pair of rounds **8** *Sports a)* a diagram of the matchups in a tournament *b)* a person's, specif. a bettor's, selections of winners in such a diagram —***vt.*** **1** to provide or support with brackets **2** to enclose within brackets **3** to group, classify, or associate together [Grant and Lee are *bracketed* in history] **4** to establish a bracket for (an artillery target)

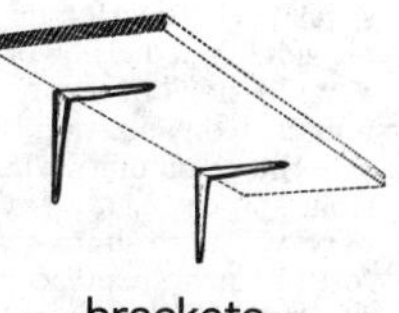

brackets

☆**bracket creep** [Informal] an advance into a higher income tax bracket resulting from an increase in nominal income: the higher taxes, when combined with the effects of inflation, may produce a decline in real income

bracket fungus ⟦so named from its shape⟧ any of various fleshy or woody basidiomycetous fungi having fruiting bodies growing like shelves from the trunk or branches of trees

brack·ish (brak′ish) ***adj.*** ⟦earlier Scot *brack* < MDu *brak,* salty (< IE **bhrogos* < base **bher-,* to cut > BRINE) + -ISH⟧ **1** somewhat salty, as the water of some marshes near the sea **2** having an unpleasant taste; nauseating —**brack′ish·ness** ***n.***

bract (brakt) ***n.*** ⟦ModL *bractea* < L, thin metal plate⟧ a modified leaf, usually small and scalelike, sometimes large and brightly colored, from whose axil grows a flower or inflorescence —**brac·te·al** (brak′tē əl) ***adj.***

brac·te·ate (brak′tē it, -āt′) ***adj.*** having bracts

brac·te·o·late (brak′tē ə lāt′) ***adj.*** having bractlets

bract·let (brakt′lit) ***n.*** a small or secondary bract at the base of a flower: also **brac·te·ole** (brak′tē ōl′)

brad (brad) ***n.*** ⟦ME *brod* < ON *broddr,* point, arrow < Gmc **bruzda:* see BROIDER⟧ a thin wire nail of uniform thickness with a small head that is sometimes off-center —***vt.*** **brad′ded, brad′ding** to fasten with brads

brad·awl (-ôl′) ***n.*** a straight awl with a chisel edge, used to make holes, as for brads

Brad·bur·y (brad′ber′ē, -bər ē), **Ray(mond Douglas)** 1920-2012; U.S. writer, esp. of science fiction

Brad·dock (brad′ək), **Edward** 1695-1755; Brit. general, born in Scotland: commander of the Brit. forces in the French & Indian War

Brad·ford[1] (brad′fərd), **William** 1590-1657; 2d governor of Plymouth Colony

Brad·ford[2] (brad′fərd) city in N England, in West Yorkshire

Brad·ley[1] (brad′lē) ***n.*** ⟦< the surname *Bradley* < the place name *Bradley* < OE *brād lēah,* broad clearing: see LEA[1]⟧ a masculine name: dim. *Brad*

Brad·ley[2] (brad′lē), **Omar (Nelson)** 1893-1981; U.S. general

Brad·street (brad′strēt), **Anne** (born *Anne Dudley*) 1612?-72; Am. poet, born in England

Bra·dy (brā′dē), **Math·ew B.** (math′yoo) 1823?-96; U.S. photographer, esp. of Lincoln & the Civil War

brad·y- (brad′i, -ē, -ə) ⟦< Gr *bradys,* slow⟧ *combining form* slow, delayed, tardy [*bradycardia*]

brad·y·car·di·a (brad′i kär′dē ə) ***n.*** ⟦< prec. + Gr *kardia,* HEART⟧ abnormally slow heartbeat: below 60 beats per minute for an adult

brad·y·ki·nin (brad′i kī′nin, -kin′in) ***n.*** ⟦< BRADY- + Gr *kinein,* to move: see KINETIC⟧ a kinin, $C_{50}H_{73}N_{15}O_{11}$, released from blood plasma by some snake venoms and certain other enzymes, which slows intestinal contractions, lowers blood pressure, etc.

brae (brā, brē) ***n.*** ⟦ME *bra, bro* < ON *bra,* eyelid, brow, river bank: see BRAID⟧ [Scot.] a sloping bank; hillside

Brae·burn (brā′burn′) ***n.*** ⟦after *Braeburn* Orchards in New Zealand⟧ a greenish-yellow to red variety of apple with crisp, mildly tart flesh

brag (brag) ***vt., vi.*** **bragged, brag′ging** ⟦ME *braggen* < ?⟧ to boast (about) in a showy way —***n.*** **1** boastful talk or manner **2** [Informal] anything boasted of; boast **3** a braggart **4** an old card game, much like poker —***adj.*** **brag′ger, brag′gest** **1** [Archaic] *a)* spirited *b)* boastful ☆**2** [Now Rare] first-rate; excellent —**SYN.** BOAST[2] —**brag′ger** ***n.***

Bragg (brag) **1 Brax·ton** (brak′stən) 1817-76; Confederate general **2 Sir (William) Lawrence** 1890-1971; Eng. physicist, born in Australia: son of William Henry **3 Sir William Henry** 1862-1942; Eng. physicist

brag·ga·do·ci·o (brag′ə dō′shē ō′, -dō′shō) ***n., pl.*** **-os′** ⟦coined by Edmund SPENSER[2], for such a character in *The Faerie Queene* (1590) < BRAG + It ending⟧ **1** a braggart **2** vain, noisy boasting or bragging

brag·gart (brag′ərt) ***n.*** ⟦BRAG + -ART⟧ an offensively boastful person

bragging rights justifiable claim to brag or boast, as of having defeated a competitor, gained distinction, won an award, etc.

Bra·gi (brä′gē) ***n.*** *Norse Myth.* the god of poetry and eloquence, son of Odin and Frigg

Bra·he (brä′ə), **Ty·cho** (tü′kō) 1546-1601; Dan. astronomer

Brah·ma[1] (brä′mə; *for sense 3 also* brā′-) ***n.*** ⟦Hindi < Sans *brahman,* worship, prayer⟧ **1** *Hinduism a)* BRAHMAN (sense 1) *b)* one of the three major gods of classical Hinduism: his role was as creator ☆**2** BRAHMAN (sense 3)

Brah·ma[2] (brä′mə, brā′-) ***n.*** ⟦after BRAHMAPUTRA⟧ [*also* **b-**] any of an Asian breed of large domestic fowl with feathered legs and small tail and wings

Brah·man (brä′mən; *for 2 also* brā′-) ***n., pl.*** **-mans** ⟦Hindi < Sans *brāhmana* < *brahman,* worship, prayer⟧ **1** the supreme and eternal essence or spirit of the universe in Hinduism **2** a member of the Hindu priestly caste, the highest of the castes **3** a breed of domestic cattle developed from the zebu of India and having a large hump over the shoulders: it is well adapted to hot climates, as of the South and Southwest, and is used in crossbreeding for beef cattle —**Brah·man·ic** (brä man′ik, brə-) ***adj.***, **Brah·man′i·cal**

Brah·man·ism (brä′mən iz′əm) ***n.*** the religious doctrines and system of the Brahmans

Brah·ma·pu·tra (brä′mə pōō′trə) river flowing from the Himalayas of SW Tibet through Assam (India) & Bangladesh, where it joins the Ganges to form a vast delta at the head of the Bay of Bengal: *c.* 1,800 mi (2,897 km)

Brah·min (brä′min) ***n.*** **1** a BRAHMAN (sense 2) **2** a cultured person from a long-established upper-class family, esp. of New England, regarded as haughty or conservative —**Brah·min·ic** (brä min′ik, brə-) ***adj.***, **Brah·min′i·cal**

Brah·min·ism (-iz′əm) ***n.*** **1** BRAHMANISM **2** the characteristic spirit, attitude, etc. of Brahmins

Brahms (brämz), **Jo·han·nes** (yō hän′əs) 1833-97; Ger. composer

braid (brād) ***vt.*** ⟦ME *breiden,* to dart, twist, pull < OE *bregdan,* to move quickly < IE base **bhereḱ-*, to gleam, flash > BREAM[1], ON *bra,* eyelid⟧ **1** to interweave three or more strands of (hair, straw, etc.) **2** to make by such interweaving [*to braid a rug*] **3** *a)* to arrange (the hair) in a braid or braids *b)* [Old Poet.] to tie up (the hair) in a ribbon or band **4** to trim or bind with braid —***n.*** **1** a band or strip formed by braiding **2** a length of braided hair **3** a woven band of cloth, tape, ribbon, etc., used to bind or decorate clothing —**braid′er** ***n.***

braid·ing (-iŋ) ***n.*** **1** braids collectively **2** trimming with or of braid

brail (brāl) ***n.*** ⟦ME < OFr *braiel,* a cincture, belt for trousers < *braie* < L *braca,* pl. *bracae,* breeches < Gaul **braca*⟧ any of the small ropes attached to the leech of a sail for hauling it in —***vt.*** to haul *(in)* with brails

Bră·i·la (brə ē′lä) city in E Romania, on the Danube

Braille (brāl) [*also* **b-**] ***n.*** ⟦after L. *Braille* (1809-52), blind Fr teacher who devised it⟧ **1** a system of printing and writing for the blind, in which characters are formed by patterns of raised dots which are felt with the fingers **2** the characters used in this system —***vt.*** **Brailled, Braill′ing** to print or write in such characters

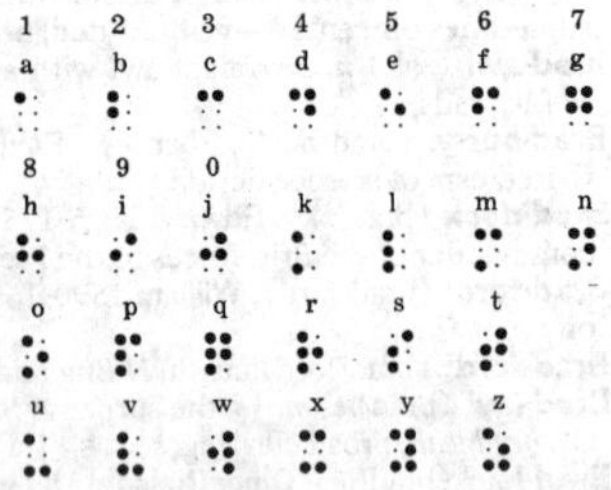

Braille alphabet and numerals

brain (brān) ***n.*** ⟦ME < OE *brægen* < IE base **mregh-m(n)o-*, skull, brain > Gr *bregma,* forehead⟧ **1** [*sometimes pl.*] the mass of nerve tissue in the cranium of vertebrate animals, an enlarged extension of the spinal cord: it is the main part of the nervous system, the center of thought, and the organ that perceives sensory impulses and regulates motor impulses: it is made up of gray matter (the outer cortex of nerve cells) and white matter (the inner mass of nerve fibers) **2** a comparable organ in invertebrate animals **3** *a)* [*often pl.*] intelligence; mental ability *b)* [Informal] a person of great intelligence **4** [*usually pl.*] [Informal] the main organizer or planner of a group activity; chief controller or director —***vt.*** **1** to dash out the brains of **2** [Slang] to hit hard on the head —**have on the brain** to be obsessed by —**pick someone's brains (**or **brain)** to extract information, ideas, etc. from someone and use to one's own advantage

brain·case (-kās′) ***n.*** BRAINPAN

brain·child (-chīld′) ***n.*** [Informal] an idea, plan, etc. regarded as produced by a person's own mental labor

brain coral a massive stony coral (genus *Diploria* or *Meandrina*) resembling the surface of a mammalian brain

brain-dead (-ded′) ***adj.*** **1** in the state of, or characterized by, brain death **2** [Informal] stupid or dull Also written **brain dead**

brain death a condition in which all vital functions of the brain are determined to have irreversibly ceased: variously accepted as a legal concept of death

brain drain [Informal] the departure from a country, industry, etc. of a large number of educated or experienced people who have better career opportunities elsewhere

☆**brain·i·ac** (brā′nē ak′) ***n.*** ⟦blend of BRAIN & MANIAC: prob. after *Brainiac,* extremely intelligent villain in the *Superman* comic books⟧ [Slang] a person of great intelligence: often a somewhat derisive or dismissive term

brain·less (-lis) ***adj.*** foolish or stupid —**brain′less·ly** ***adv.*** —**brain′less·ness** ***n.***

brain·pan (-pan′) ***n.*** the part of the skull that contains the brain; cranium

brain·pow·er (-pou′ər) ***n.*** mental ability; intellectual power

brain·sick (-sik′) ***adj.*** [Archaic] having or caused by a mental disorder —**brain′sick′ly** ***adv.*** —**brain′sick′ness** ***n.***

brain·stem (-stem′) ***n.*** a stalklike structure at the base of the brain that connects the spinal cord with the cerebrum and includes the medulla oblongata, pons, and midbrain: also written **brain stem**

☆**brain·storm** (-stôrm′) ***n.*** **1** [Archaic] a series of sudden, violent cerebral disturbances **2** [Informal] a sudden inspiration, idea, or plan —***vi.*** [Informal] to engage in brainstorming

☆**brain·storm·ing** (-stôr′miŋ) ***n.*** the unrestrained offering of ideas or suggestions by all members of a committee, conference, etc. in an effort to find a solution to a problem, generate fresh ideas, etc.

☆**brain·teas·er** (-tē′zər) ***n.*** an intellectually challenging puzzle, problem, game, etc.: also [Chiefly Brit.] **brain′-twist′er**

☆**brain trust** a group of experts unofficially acting as administrative advisers

brain·wash (brān′wôsh′) ☆***vt.*** [Informal] to indoctrinate so intensively and thoroughly as to effect a radical transformation of beliefs and mental attitudes

brain wave **1** any of a series of rhythmic electric impulses given off by nerve centers in the brain: they produce oscillations on an electroencephalogram and are usually measured during rest **2** [Informal] a sudden inspiration; brainstorm

brain·y (brā′nē) ***adj.*** **brain′i·er, brain′i·est** [Informal] having a good mind; intelligent —**brain′i·ness** ***n.***

braise (brāz) ***vt.*** **braised, brais′ing** ⟦Fr *braiser* < *braise,* live coals < Gmc **brasa,* glowing coals⟧ to cook (meat or vegetables) by browning in fat and then simmering in a covered pan with a little liquid

brake[1] (brāk) ***n.*** ⟦ME; prob. taken as sing. of BRACKEN⟧ any of a genus (*Pteris*) of coarse tropical ferns (family Polypodiaceae) used commonly as a houseplant: see BRACKEN

brake[2] (brāk) ***n.*** ⟦ME < MLowG *brake* or ODu *braeke,* flax brake < *breken,* to break; senses 2-6 variously infl. by OFr *brac* (form of *bras,* an arm) & BREAK⟧ **1** a toothed implement for beating or crushing flax or hemp so that the fiber can be separated **2** a heavy harrow for breaking up clods of earth **3** a handle or lever on a machine [*a pump brake*] **4** a machine for turning or bending the edges of sheet metal **5** *a)* any device for slowing, stopping, or preventing the motion of a vehicle or machine, as by causing a block, shoe, or band to press against a moving part *b)* anything that slows down or stops movement, activity, or progress **6** [Obs.] the rack, former instrument of torture —***vt.*** **braked, brak′ing** **1** to break up (flax, clods of earth, etc.) into smaller pieces **2** to slow down or stop with or as with a brake —***vi.*** ☆**1** to operate a brake or brakes **2** to be slowed down or stopped by a brake —**brake′less** ***adj.***

brake[3] (brāk) ***n.*** ⟦< or akin to MLowG *brake,* stumps, broken branches, akin to OE *brecan,* to BREAK⟧ a clump or area of brushwood, briers, etc.; thicket

brake[4] (brāk) ***vt., vi.*** *archaic pt. of* BREAK

brake·age (brāk′ij′) ***n.*** **1** the action or application of a brake **2** braking capacity

brake band a flexible, lined band that serves as a braking force by creating friction when tightened about a spinning shaft or drum, as in the automatic transmission of a motor vehicle

brake drum **1** a heavy metal covering fitted over an automotive brake assembly and fastened to the axle: used in a braking system (**drum brakes**) in which internal brake shoes are pushed outward to contact the spinning drum from the inside: see DISC BRAKE **2** any rim that rotates rapidly in a braking assembly

brake horsepower the actual horsepower of an engine, measured by a brake attached to the drive shaft and recorded on a dynamometer

brake light a light at the rear of a vehicle, that lights up when the brakes are applied

brake lining a material of asbestos, minerals, fine wire, etc. riveted or bonded to a brake band or shoe to create the friction necessary for braking

☆**brake·man** (-mən) ***n., pl.*** **-men** (-mən) **1** a railroad worker who operated the brakes on a train, but is now chiefly an assistant to the conductor **2** the last person on a bobsled team, who operates the brake, controlling skids and stopping the sled

☆**brake shoe** a block or plate curved to fit the shape of a wheel or drum and forced against it to act as a brake

Bra·man·te (brä män′te), **Do·na·to d'A·gno·lo** (dô nä′tô dä nyô′lô) 1444-1514; It. architect

bram·ble (bram′bəl) ***n.*** ⟦ME *brembel* < OE *bræmel* < *brom,* BROOM⟧ **1** any of a genus (*Rubus*) of generally prickly shrubs of the rose family, as the raspberry, blackberry, or dewberry **2** any prickly shrub or vine —**bram′bly** ***adj.***

bram·bling (-bliŋ) ***n.*** ⟦earlier *bramline,* prob. < prec.⟧ a brightly colored, migrating finch (*Fringilla montifringilla*) of Europe

Bramp·ton (bramp′tən, bram′-) ⟦after *Brampton,* town in NW England⟧ city in SE Ontario, Canada, west of Toronto

bran (bran) ***n.*** ⟦ME *bran, bren* < OFr *bren*⟧ the broken outer coat, or husk, of grains of wheat, rye, oats, etc. separated from the flour after grinding, as by sifting

Bran (bran) ***n.*** ⟦< ? Ir *bran,* raven⟧ *Celt. Myth.* a giant and king of ancient Britain

branch (branch, bränch) ***n.*** ⟦ME *branche* < OFr *brance* < LL *branca,* a claw, paw⟧ **1** any woody extension growing from the trunk or main stem, or from a main limb, of a tree or shrub **2** anything physically resembling a branch, as a tine of a deer's antler ☆**3** *a)* one of the streams into which a river or large creek may divide, usually near the mouth *b)* a large tributary flowing into a river ☆**4** [Chiefly South] a small stream flowing usually into a creek ☆**5** BRANCH WATER **6** any part or extension of a main body or system; specif., *a)* a division or part of a body of learning [*optics is a branch of physics*] *b)* a division of a family descending from a common ancestor *c)* a subdivision of a family of languages *d)* a division or a separately located unit of an organization [*a library branch*] *e)* a post-office subdivision outside the community where its main post office is located (distinguished from STATION, ***n.*** 1e) *f) Comput.* a JUMP (***n.*** 13), esp. one that selects one of two or more alternative instructions as the next executed —***vi.*** **1** to put forth branches; spread in or divide into branches; ramify **2** to come out (*from* the trunk or stem) as a branch **3** *Comput.* to continue at an instruction in another part of the program by means of a BRANCH (***n.*** 6f) —***vt.*** **1** to separate into branches **2** to embroider with a pattern of flowers, foliage, etc. —**branch off 1** to separate into branches; fork **2** to go off in another direction; diverge —**branch out 1** to put forth branches **2** to extend the scope of interests, activities, etc. —**branched** *adj.* —**branch′like′** *adj.*

branched chain *Chem.* a straight chain of atoms, usually carbon, with any number of secondary, straight branches; open chain

bran·chi·ae (braŋ′kē ē′) *pl.n., sing.* **-chi·a** (-ə) ⟦L, pl. of *branchia* < Gr, pl. of *branchion,* a gill⟧ the gills of an aquatic animal —**bran′chi·al** *adj.* —**bran′chi·ate** (-kē it, -āt′) *adj.*

bran·chi·o- (braŋ′kē ō, -ə) ⟦< Gr *branchia,* gills; akin to *bronchos,* windpipe⟧ *combining form* gills [*branchiopod*]

bran·chi·o·pod (braŋ′kē ō päd′) *n.* ⟦prec. + -POD⟧ any of a class (Branchiopoda) of crustaceans with many pairs of flattened, leaflike limbs, as the fairy shrimps and water fleas

branch·let (branch′lit) *n.* a small branch or twig

☆**branch water 1** water from a small stream or brook **2** water, esp. ordinary tap water, as used for mixing with whiskey, etc.

Bran·cuşi (brän′ko͞osh; *E* bran ko͞o′zē), **Con·stan·tin** (kôn′stən tēn′) 1876-1957; Romanian sculptor, in Paris after 1904

brand (brand) *n.* ⟦ME < OE *brand, brond,* a flame, torch, sword < base of *biernan, brinnan,* BURN[1]⟧ **1** a stick that is burning or partially burned **2** *a)* a mark burned on the skin with a BRANDING IRON *b)* BRANDING IRON **3** a mark of disgrace; stigma **4** *a)* an identifying mark or label on the products of a particular company; trademark *b)* the kind or make of a commodity [a new *brand* of tea] *c)* a special kind [his *brand* of nonsense] **5** [Archaic] a sword —*vt.* **1** to mark with or as with a brand **2** to put a mark of disgrace on; stigmatize **3** to market (products) by means of BRANDING —**brand′er** *n.*

bran·dade (brän däd′; *Fr* brän dȧd′) *n.* ⟦Fr < Prov *brandado* < *brandar,* to stir⟧ a purée of salted cod, olive oil, garlic, and cream, often served with toasted bread

Bran·deis (bran′dīs′, -dīz′), **Louis Dem·bitz** (dem′bits′) 1856-1941; associate justice, U.S. Supreme Court (1916-39)

Bran·den·burg (bran′dən burg′; *Ger* brän′dən boork′) **1** former province of Prussia: the region was divided between Poland & East Germany in 1947 **2** state of NE Germany: 11,383 sq mi (29,482 sq km); cap. Potsdam **3** city in E Germany, west of Berlin, in Brandenburg

Bran·des (brän′dəs), **Ge·org Mor·ris** (gē ôr′ mô′rēs) (born *Georg Morris Cohen*) 1842-1927; Dan. literary critic

bran·died (bran′dēd′) *adj.* flavored or blended with brandy

brand·ing (bran′diŋ) *n.* the practice of marketing products by associating them with a widely accepted BRAND NAME so as to distinguish them from other similar products that are sold

branding iron an iron implement designed to burn a mark onto the skin, formerly used to punish and identify criminals, now used on livestock to show ownership

bran·dish (bran′dish) *vt.* ⟦ME *brandischen* < extended stem of OFr *brandir* < Gmc **brand*: see BRAND⟧ to wave, shake, or exhibit in a menacing, challenging, or exultant way; flourish —*n.* the act of brandishing something

brand·ling (brand′liŋ) *n.* ⟦BRAND, *n.* + -LING[1]: so named from the color⟧ **1** a small, red or yellowish worm used for fish bait **2** a young salmon

☆**brand name** the name by which a certain brand or make of commodity is known; esp., the widely advertised name of a widely distributed product —**brand′-name′** *adj.*

brand-new (brand′no͞o′, -nyo͞o′; bran′-) *adj.* ⟦orig., fresh from the fire: see BRAND⟧ **1** entirely new **2** recently acquired

Bran·do (bran′dō), **Mar·lon, (Jr.)** (mär′lən) 1924-2004; U.S. film actor

Bran·don[1] (bran′dən) *n.* a masculine name

Bran·don[2] (bran′dən) ⟦prob. after a local family name⟧ village in WC Fla.: suburb of Tampa

bran·dy (bran′dē) *n., pl.* **-dies** ⟦earlier *brandywine* < Du *brandewijn,* lit., burnt wine: so called from being distilled⟧ **1** an alcoholic liquor distilled from wine **2** a similar liquor distilled from the fermented juice of a specified fruit [cherry *brandy*] —*vt.* **-died, -dy·ing** to flavor, mix, or preserve with brandy

brandy Alexander an Alexander cocktail made with brandy

Bran·dy·wine (bran′dē wīn′) ⟦< ?⟧ creek in SE Pa. & N Del.: site of a battle (1777) of the Revolutionary War, in which Washington's army failed to check the British advance on Philadelphia

brank (braŋk) *n.* ⟦< ?⟧ [*often pl., with sing. v.*] a device formerly used to punish women judged to be noisy and quarrelsome, consisting of an iron curb for the tongue, held in place by a frame around the head

☆**bran·ni·gan** (bran′ə gən) *n.* ⟦prob. after surname *Brannigan*⟧ [Slang] a noisy quarrel or fight; brawl

Bran·son (bran′sən) ⟦after Reuben *Branson,* early settler, *c.* 1882⟧ city in S Mo.

brant (brant) *n., pl.* **brants** or **brant** ⟦< ?⟧ any of a genus (*Branta*) of wild geese of Europe and North America, including the Canada goose and the barnacle goose; esp., a species (*B. bernicla*) found chiefly in the E U.S. and N Canada

Brant (brant), **Joseph** (born *Thayendanegea*) 1742-1807; Mohawk Indian chief: fought for the British in the French and Indian War & the Revolutionary War

Braque (bråk), **Georges** (zhôrzh) 1882-1963; Fr. painter

brash[1] (brash) *adj.* ⟦orig. Brit dial.; < ?⟧ **1** brittle or fragile, as some wood **2** hasty and reckless; rash; impetuous **3** offensively bold; pushing, presumptuous, impudent, etc. —*n.* **1** PYROSIS **2** [Scot.] a sudden shower —**brash′ly** *adv.* —**brash′ness** *n.*

brash[2] (brash) *n.* ⟦Fr *brèche* < OHG *brecha,* fragment < *brehhan,* to BREAK⟧ broken pieces or fragments, as of rock or floating ice

bra·sier (brā′zhər) *n.* BRAZIER[1]

Bra·sil (brä zēl′) *Port. name for* BRAZIL

bra·sil·e·in (brə zil′ē in) *n.* BRAZILEIN

Bra·sí·lia (brä zē′lyä; *E* brə zil′yə) capital of Brazil, in the EC part: constituting, with surrounding area, a federal district: 2,240 sq mi (5,802 sq km)

bras·i·lin (braz′ə lin′, brə zil′in) *n.* BRAZILIN

Bra·şov (brä shôv′) city in central Romania

brass (bras, bräs) *n., pl.* **brass′es** ⟦ME *bras* < OE *bræs,* brass, bronze⟧ **1** a yellowish metal that is essentially an alloy of copper and zinc **2** things made of brass, as fittings, ornaments, or implements **3** [*often with pl. v.*] the brass instruments of an orchestra, band, etc., or the players of these instruments **4** a brass memorial tablet **5** [Informal] bold impudence; effrontery ☆**6** [*often with pl. v.*] [Slang] *a)* military officers of high rank (see BRASS HAT) *b)* any high officials, executives, etc. **7** *Machinery* the lining or bushing of a bearing —*adj.* **1** made of or containing brass **2** designating a wind instrument, as a horn, trombone, trumpet, or tuba, made of a coiled metal tube and having a usually cup-shaped mouthpiece **3** of or for such an instrument or instruments —*vt.* to coat with brass

bras·sard (bras′ärd′) *n.* ⟦Fr < *bras,* an arm⟧ **1** armor for the arm from elbow to shoulder: also **bras·sart** (bras′ərt) **2** an armband with a distinctive design that identifies the wearer in some way

brass band a band of mainly brass instruments

brass·board (bras′bôrd′) *n.* in certain types of engineering, an experimental model at a more advanced stage of development than a BREADBOARD (sense 2)

bras·se·rie (bras′ə rē′; *Fr* brȧs rē′) *n.* ⟦Fr < MFr < *brasser,* to brew < VL **braciare* < L *brace,* grain used to prepare malt⟧ a bar serving simple meals as well as beverages

brass hat [Slang] **1** a military officer of high rank: so called from the gold braid often on the cap **2** any high official, executive, etc.

bras·si·ca (bras′i kə) *n.* ⟦ModL *Brassica,* genus name < L *brassica,* cabbage⟧ any of various mustard plants, including cabbage, cauliflower, broccoli, and various turnips

brass·ie (bras′ē) *n.* ⟦< BRASS: orig. made with a brass plate on the bottom of the head⟧ *Golf old term for* the number 2 wood: see WOOD[1] (*n.* 6)

bras·siere or **bras·sière** (brə zir′) *n.* ⟦Fr, child's chemise, shoulder strap, orig., arm guard < *bras,* an arm < L *brachium*: see BRACE[1]⟧ BRA

☆**brass knuckles** a weapon consisting of a rigid, metal framework, as of linked metal rings, with holes for the fingers, that is worn on the hand to increase greatly damage delivered by a blow with the fist

brass ring ⟦from the *brass ring* hanging beside an old-fashioned carousel, which riders would try to grasp at each pass so as to exchange it for a prize or a free ride⟧ great success or a highly valued prize; also, an opportunity for this: usually with *the*

brass tacks ☆[Informal] basic facts; practical details: chiefly in the phrase **get (or come) down to brass tacks**

brass·ware (bras′wer′) *n.* articles made of brass

brass·y (bras′ē) *adj.* **brass′i·er, brass′i·est 1** of or decorated with brass **2** like brass, as in color **3** cheap and showy **4** loud and blaring **5** impudent; brazen —**brass′i·ly** *adv.* —**brass′i·ness** *n.*

brat[1] (brat) *n.* ⟦ME, cloak of coarse cloth < OE *bratt* < Gael, mantle, cloth, rag: present sense ? from child's bib or apron⟧ **1** a child, esp. an impudent, unruly child: scornful or playful term **2** [Slang] the son or daughter of a person in a professional community, a particular company, the armed forces, etc., esp. one who has been raised in such a community, company, etc. [a Hollywood *brat*] —**brat′ty** *adj.*, **brat′tish** —**brat′ti·ness** *n.*, **brat′tish·ness**

brat[2] (brät, brat) *n.* [Informal] a link of bratwurst

Bra·ti·sla·va (brä′ti slä′və) capital of Slovakia, on the Danube

Bratsk (brätsk) city in SC Siberian Russia, on the Angara River

brat·tice (brat′is) *n.* ⟦ME *bretice, bretasce* < OFr *bretesche,* wooden tower < ML *brittisca;* prob. < OHG *brittissa,* lattice, balcony < *bret,* board⟧ **1** [Historical] a temporary breastwork or parapet put up during a siege **2** *Mining* a partition of wood, creosote-impregnated cloth, etc., used to control the flow of fresh air that is pumped into the mine —*vt.* **-ticed, -tic·ing** to furnish with a brattice

brat·tle (brat′'l) *n., vi.* **-tled, -tling** ⟦echoic⟧ [Scot.] rattle or clatter

brat·wurst (brät′wurst′) *n.* ⟦Ger < OHG < *brato,* lean meat (akin to OE *brœde,* meat) + *wurst,* sausage⟧ a highly seasoned, fresh sausage of veal and pork, made in links resembling large frankfurters and usually grilled or fried

Brau·del (brō del′), **Fer·nand Paul** (fer nän′ pôl) 1902-85; Fr. historian

Braun·schweig (broun′shvīk′) *Ger. name for* BRUNSWICK

braun·schwei·ger (broun′shwī′gər, -shvī′-) *n.* ⟦Ger *Braunschweiger (wurst),* lit., Brunswick (sausage), after prec.⟧ smoked liverwurst

bra·va (brä′vä) *interj.* ⟦It, fem. of *bravo*: see BRAVO[1]⟧ well done; very good; excellent: used to praise a female performer —*n., pl.* **-vas** a shout of "brava"

bra·va·do (brə vä′dō) *n.* ⟦altered < Sp *bravada* < *bravo,* fol.⟧ showy courage or defiant confidence, often, specif., when one is actually afraid

brave (brāv) *adj.* **brav′er, brav′est** ⟦Fr < It *bravo,* brave, bold, orig., wild, savage < L *barbarus,* BARBAROUS⟧ **1** willing to face danger, pain, or trouble;

not afraid 2 showing to good effect; having a fine appearance 3 [Archaic] fine or splendid [a *brave* new world] —*n.* 1 any brave man ☆2 ⟦< 17th-c. NAmFr⟧ a North American Indian warrior 3 [Archaic] a bully —*vt.* **braved, brav′ing** 1 to face with courage 2 to defy; dare 3 [Obs.] to make splendid, as in dress —*vi.* [Obs.] to boast —**brave′ly** *adv.* —**brave′ness** *n.*

SYN.—**brave** implies fearlessness in meeting danger or difficulty and has the broadest application of the words considered here; **courageous** suggests constant readiness to deal with things fearlessly by reason of a stout-hearted temperament or a resolute spirit; **bold** stresses a daring temperament, whether displayed courageously, presumptuously, or defiantly; **audacious** suggests an imprudent or reckless boldness; **valiant** emphasizes a heroic quality in the courage or fortitude shown; **intrepid** implies absolute fearlessness and esp. suggests dauntlessness in facing the new or unknown; **plucky** emphasizes gameness in fighting against something when one is at a decided disadvantage —ANT. **craven, cowardly**

brave new world ⟦after *Brave New World,* title of dystopian novel (1932) by Aldous HUXLEY, an allusion to a line in *The Tempest* (V, i) by SHAKESPEARE⟧ a place or situation regarded as like that of a hypothetical future society in being, variously, dehumanized, disorienting, technologically revolutionary, etc.

brav·er·y (brāv′ər ē) *n.* ⟦Fr *braverie,* gallantry, splendor < BRAVE⟧ 1 the quality of being brave; courage; valor 2 fine appearance, show, or dress; showiness

bra·vis·si·mo (brä vēs′sē mô′) *interj.* ⟦It, superl. of fol.⟧ very well done; splendid

bra·vo[1] (brä′vō) *interj.* ⟦It: see BRAVE, *adj.*⟧ well done; excellent: used to praise a performer —*n., pl.* **-vos** a shout of "bravo"

bra·vo[2] (brä′vō) *n., pl.* **-voes, -vos, -vi** (-vē) ⟦It: see BRAVE⟧ a hired killer; assassin; desperado

bra·vu·ra (brə vyoor′ə; *It* brä vōō′rä) *n.* ⟦It, bravery, spirit < *bravo,* BRAVE⟧ 1 a bold attempt or display of daring; dash 2 *Music a)* a brilliant passage or piece that displays the performer's skill and technique *b)* brilliant technique —*adj.* characterized by bravura

braw (brô, brä) *adj.* ⟦< BRAVE⟧ [Scot.] 1 well-dressed 2 splendid

brawl (brôl) *vi.* ⟦ME *braulen,* to cry out, quarrel; prob. akin to Du *brallen,* to boast⟧ 1 to quarrel or fight noisily 2 to flow noisily over rapids, falls, etc.: said of water —*n.* 1 a rough, noisy quarrel or fight; row 2 [Slang] a noisy, drunken party —**brawl′er** *n.*

brawn (brôn) *n.* ⟦ME *braun* < OFr *braon,* fleshy or muscular part, buttock < Frank *brado,* meat, calf (of leg), akin to OHG *brato,* OE *brǣde*⟧ 1 strong, well-developed muscles 2 muscular strength 3 [Brit.] cooked boar's flesh 4 HEADCHEESE

brawn·y (-ē) *adj.* **brawn′i·er, brawn′i·est** ⟦< prec.⟧ strong and muscular —**brawn′i·ness** *n.*

brax·y (brak′sē) *n.* ⟦? akin to OE *broc,* disease⟧ a fatal disease of sheep caused by a bacterium (*Clostridium septicum*) and usually characterized by an inflamed abomasum —*adj.* having braxy

bray[1] (brā) *vi.* ⟦ME *braien* < OFr *braire* < VL **bragire,* to cry out⟧ to make the loud, harsh cry of a donkey, or a sound, esp. a laugh, like this —*vt.* to utter loudly and harshly —*n.* the loud, harsh cry of a donkey, or a sound like this

bray[2] (brā) *vt.* ⟦ME *braien* < OFr *breier,* to pound, pulverize; prob. < Frank **brekan,* BREAK⟧ 1 to crush or pound into a powder, as in a mortar 2 to spread thin, as ink

bray·er (-ər) *n.* ⟦see prec.⟧ *Printing* a roller used for spreading ink by hand

Braz *abbrev.* 1 Brazil 2 Brazilian

braze[1] (brāz) *vt.* **brazed, braz′ing** ⟦Fr *braser,* to solder, var. of *braiser,* BRAISE⟧ to join (metals) by melting nonferrous metals or alloys into the joints at temperatures exceeding 800°F (426.7°C): see SOLDER, WELD[1] —**braz′er** *n.*

braze[2] (brāz) *vt.* **brazed, braz′ing** ⟦ME *brasen* < OE *brǣsian* < *brǣs,* BRASS⟧ 1 to make of, or coat with, brass or a brasslike substance 2 to make hard like brass —**braz′er** *n.*

bra·zen (brā′zən) *adj.* ⟦ME *brasen* < OE *brǣsen* < *brǣs,* BRASS⟧ 1 of brass 2 like brass in color or other qualities 3 showing no shame; bold; impudent 4 having the ringing sound of brass; harsh and piercing —**brazen it out** to act in a bold way as if one need not be ashamed —**bra′zen·ly** *adv.* —**bra′zen·ness** *n.*

bra·zen·faced (-fāst′) *adj.* having, or uttered with, a brazen expression; impudent; shameless

bra·zier[1] (brā′zhər) *n.* ⟦Fr *brasier:* see BRAISE⟧ a metal pan, bowl, etc. to hold burning coals or charcoal, as for warming a room or grilling food

bra·zier[2] (brā′zhər) *n.* ⟦ME *brasiere* < *bras:* see BRASS⟧ a person who works in brass

bra·zil (brə zil′) *n.* ⟦ME *brasile* < Sp & Port *brasil;* prob. ult. (because of color) < Gmc **brasa:* see BRAISE⟧ 1 BRAZILWOOD 2 a red or blue dye from this wood

Bra·zil (brə zil′) ⟦Port, short for *terra de brasil,* land of brazilwood: see prec.⟧ country in central & NE South America, on the Atlantic: declared independence from Portugal (1822): 3,286,488 sq mi (8,511,965 sq km); cap. Brasília —**Bra·zil′ian** (-yən) *adj., n.*

bra·zil·e·in (-ē in) *n.* ⟦< BRAZIL + -IN[1]⟧ a bright-red dye, $C_{16}H_{12}O_5$, obtained by oxidizing brazilin

braz·i·lin (braz′ə lin′, brə zil′in) *n.* ⟦BRAZIL + -IN[1]⟧ a bright-yellow compound, $C_{16}H_{14}O_5$, obtained from brazilwood as a crystalline powder and used as a dye and indicator

Brazil nut 1 a gigantic (30-45 m or 100-150 ft) South American tree (*Bertholletia excelsa*) of the lecythis family, which bears hard-shelled, triangular, oily, edible seeds that grow in large, round, hard-shelled fruits 2 this seed

bra·zil·wood (brə zil′wood′) *n.* ⟦see BRAZIL⟧ a hard, reddish wood obtained from several tropical American trees (genera *Caesalpinia* and *Haematoxylon*) of the caesalpinia family: it yields a red or blue dye and is also used in making cabinets and violin bows

Bra·zos (braz′əs, brä′zəs) ⟦Sp, lit., arms, branches (of a river)⟧ river in central & SE Tex., flowing southeastward into the Gulf of Mexico: 870 mi (1,400 km)

Braz·za·ville (braz′ə vil′, brä′zə-; -vēl′) capital of the Republic of the Congo, on the Congo River

BRE or **B.R.E.** *abbrev.* Bachelor of Religious Education

breach (brēch) *n.* ⟦ME *breche* < OE *bryce* < *brecan* (see BREAK); infl. by OFr *breche* < OHG *brecha,* of same orig.⟧ 1 [Obs.] a breaking or being broken 2 a failure to observe the terms, as of a law or promise, the customary forms, etc.; violation; infraction 3 an opening made by a breakthrough, as in a wall, line of defense, etc. 4 a broken or torn place or part 5 a breaking of waves over or upon a ship, sea wall, etc. 6 a whale's leap clear of the water 7 a break in friendly relations —*vt.* 1 to make a breach in; break open or through 2 to break or violate (a contract, covenant, etc.) —*vi.* to leap clear of the water: said of a whale

breach of promise a breaking of a promise, esp. a promise to marry

breach of the peace *Law* conduct creating or tending to create a disturbance of the public peace

breach of trust *Law* a violation of duty by a person holding property in trust

bread (bred) *n.* ⟦ME *bred* < OE *bread,* crumb, morsel < IE **bhreu-,* var. of **bhereu-,* to ferment < base **bher-,* well up, seethe > BREW, BURN[1], L *fervere,* to boil⟧ 1 *a)* a food baked from a leavened, kneaded dough made with flour or meal, water, yeast, etc. *b)* a similar food, as matzo, that is not leavened and so remains flat when baked 2 any baked food like bread but made with a batter [quick *breads,* corn *bread*] 3 food generally 4 the means of living; livelihood [to earn one's *bread*] 5 [Slang] money —*vt.* to cover with bread crumbs before cooking —**bread and butter** one's means of subsistence; livelihood —**break bread** to partake of food; eat —**cast one's bread upon the waters** to be generous or do good deeds without expecting something in return —**know which side one's bread is buttered on** to know what is to one's advantage and from what source it comes

bread-and-but·ter (-'n but′ər) *adj.* 1 relating to subsistence or to the product, work, etc. basically relied on for earnings 2 basic, commonplace, everyday, etc. ☆3 expressing thanks, as a letter sent to one's host or hostess after a visit

bread-and-butter pickles an appetizer or condiment consisting of sliced sweet pickles with onions and, often, bell peppers and flavored with mustard seed, turmeric, etc.

bread and circuses ⟦L *panem et circenses* (from *Satires,* x.80, of JUVENAL), in allusion to domestic policy of the Roman Empire⟧ something, esp. something lavish, regarded as a mindless or vulgar diversion intended to keep the masses docile

bread·bas·ket (-bas′kit) *n.* 1 a region that supplies much grain 2 [Slang] the stomach or abdomen

☆**bread·board** (-bôrd′) *n.* 1 a board on which dough is kneaded or bread is sliced 2 *a)* a board on which experimental electronic circuits or diagrams can be laid out *b)* such a circuit, model, etc. being developed or tested

bread·box (-bäks′) *n.* a container in which bread, pastry, etc. is stored to help keep it fresh

bread crumbs *Cooking* bits of dried bread, finely or coarsely ground, for breading, thickening, etc.: also written **bread′crumbs′** *pl.n.* —**bread′crumb′** *adj.*

bread·fruit (-frōōt′) *n.* 1 a tropical tree (*Artocarpus altilis*) of the mulberry family, with large, round, usually seedless fruit 2 this fruit, with a starchy pulp, which resembles bread when baked

☆**bread line** a line of people waiting to be given food as government relief or private charity

bread mold any of an order (Mucorales, esp. *Rhizopus nigricans*) of fungi often found on decaying vegetable matter or bread

bread pudding a custard dessert made with pieces of bread, raisins or other fruit, etc., often served with cream or a sauce

☆**bread·root** (-rōōt′) *n.* 1 a low-growing plant (*Psoralea esculenta*) of the pea family, with blue flowers, common on the prairies of W North America 2 its edible starchy root

bread·stick (-stik′) *n.* a thin, crisp stick of bread, often seasoned

☆**bread·stuff** (-stuf′) *n.* ⟦? coined by Thomas JEFFERSON⟧ 1 ground grain or flour for making bread 2 bread

breadth (bredth) *n.* ⟦ME *brǣde* < OE *brǣdu* < *brad,* BROAD; *-th* by analogy with LENGTH⟧ 1 the distance from side to side of a thing; width 2 a piece of a given and regular width [a *breadth* of satin] 3 extent or scope, esp. when broad or ample [a true *breadth* of learning] 4 *Art* an effect of unity and inclusiveness achieved as by subordinating details

breadth·wise (-wīz′) *adj., adv.* in the direction of the breadth: also **breadth′ways′** (-wāz′)

bread·win·ner (bred′win′ər) *n.* a working person whose earnings support his or her dependents

break (brāk) *vt.* **broke, bro′ken, break′ing** ⟦ME *breken* < OE *brecan* < IE base **bhreg-* > BREACH, BREECH, Ger *brechen,* L *frangere*⟧ 1 to cause to come apart by force; split or crack sharply into pieces; smash; burst **2** *a)* to cut open the surface of (soil, the skin, etc.) *b)* to fracture a bone of **3** to cause the failure of by force or extralegal measures [to *break* a strike] **4** to make unusable or inoperative by cracking, disrupting, etc. **5** to tame or make obedient with or as with force **6** *a)* to cause to get rid (*of* a habit) *b)* to get rid of (a habit) **7** to lower in rank or grade; demote **8** *a)* to reduce to poverty or bankruptcy *b)* to ruin the chance for success of *c)* to wreck the health, spirit, etc. of **9** to surpass (a record) **10** to fail to follow the terms of (a law, promise, agreement, etc.); violate **11** *a)* to open or enter by force (now chiefly in **break and enter**) *b)* to escape from by force [to *break* prison] **12** to disrupt the order, rhythm, or completeness of; make irregular [the troops *broke* formation and ran; the racehorse stumbled and *broke* stride] **13** to interrupt (a journey, electric circuit, etc.) **14** to reduce the force of by interrupting (a fall, the wind, etc.) **15** to bring to a sudden end [to *break* a tie] **16** *a)* to make or create (a path, way, etc.) as by removing obstructions *b)* to cut through or penetrate (silence, darkness, etc.) **17** to make known; tell; disclose **18** *a)* to decipher [to *break* a code] *b)* to succeed in solving [to *break* a criminal case] **19** to make (a will) invalid by legal process **20** to prove (an alibi) to be false **21** to begin; open; start **22** to exchange (a bill or coin) for smaller units **23** to open (a rifle or shotgun) at the breech —*vi.* **1** to split into pieces; come apart; burst **2** to scatter; disperse [to *break* and run] **3** to force one's way (*into* something or *through* obstacles or resistance) **4** to quarrel; stop associating (*with*) **5** to become unusable or inoperative; go out of order **6** to suffer a sudden fall in prices, financial condition, etc. **7** to change suddenly, as by a sharp rise, fall, turn, shift, etc. [his voice *broke*; the hot spell *broke*] **8** *a)* to move away suddenly [the base runner *broke* for second] *b)* to move apart, or withdraw, from a clinch in boxing ☆**9** to move into a gait other than the trot or pace required: said of a horse in harness racing **10** to begin suddenly to utter, perform, do, etc.: with *into, forth in,* or *out in* [to *break* into song, *break* into a sweat, *break* out in hives] **11** to come suddenly into being, evidence, or general knowledge [day was *breaking*; the story *broke*] **12** to appear suddenly above water, as a periscope, fish, etc. ☆**13** to stop activity temporarily [we *broke* for lunch] **14** *a)* to fall apart slowly; disintegrate *b)* to dash apart, as a wave on the shore **15** to suffer a collapse of health, vitality, spirit, etc. **16** to change into a diphthong: said of vowels ☆**17** to curve, dip, or rise near the plate: said of a pitched baseball ☆**18** to begin a game of pocket billiards with a BREAK (*n.* 13) **19** [Informal] to happen in a certain way [things were *breaking* badly] —*n.* **1** a breaking open or apart; breach; fracture **2** *a)* a breaking in, out, or forth ☆*b)* a sudden move away or toward; rush; dash **3** the result of a breaking; broken place; separation; crack **4** a beginning or appearance [the *break* of day] **5** an interruption of a regular or continuous arrangement, action, etc. **6** the result of this; a gap, interval, pause, omission, rest, etc. **7** a breach in friendly relations **8** a sudden change, as in weather ☆**9** an escape, as from prison ☆**10** a sudden lowering or drop, as of prices **11** an imperfection; flaw **12** an unbroken series or sequence, as of points in billiards ☆**13** the opening shot in a game of pocket billiards, in which the cue ball must come into contact with at least one ball in the rack; often, a shot that scatters the racked balls ☆**14** *Basketball* FAST BREAK ☆**15** *a)* a piece of luck, often specif. of good luck *b)* an advantage or opportunity *c)* exceptional or favorable treatment **16** *Music a)* the point where one register changes to another *b)* the abrupt change in quality of a voice or instrument at this point *c)* in jazz, a brief, usually improvised passage by one band member who continues to play while the others stop *d)* in popular music, a brief passage featuring only a drum or other rhythm instruments **17** *Printing a)* a space between paragraphs *b)* the place at which a column or page of text stops, to be continued as on another column or page *c)* a point at which a word is divided, as at the end of a line —☆**break a leg!** good luck!: said as to a performer, esp. in the theater —**break away** to leave suddenly; get away; escape —**break down 1** to go out of working order **2** to give way to tears or emotion **3** to have a physical or nervous collapse **4** to crush or overcome (opposition, etc.) **5** to separate into parts; analyze —☆**break even** [Informal] to finish as neither a winner nor a loser —**break in 1** to enter forcibly or unexpectedly **2** to interrupt **3** to train (a beginner) ☆**4** to prepare (something new) by use or wear —**break in on (**or **upon) 1** to intrude on **2** to interrupt —**break off 1** to stop abruptly, as in talking **2** to stop being friendly or intimate —**break out 1** to begin suddenly **2** to escape suddenly **3** to become covered with pimples or a rash **4** to show as a separate item, as on a financial statement **5** *a) Naut.* to bring out of stowage for use [*break out* the foul weather gear] *b)* [Informal] to bring out (anything) for use —**break service (**or **serve)** *Tennis* to win a game in which one's opponent serves —**break up 1** to separate; disperse: also, esp. as a command, **break it up 2** to take apart; dismantle and scrap **3** to put a stop to **4** [Informal] to end a relationship ☆**5** [Informal] to distress or upset greatly ☆**6** [Informal] to laugh or make laugh uncontrollably **7** [Informal] to be interrupted, as by interference or signal loss, often, specif., to the point of being unintelligible: said as of a cell-phone or radio transmission —☆**give someone a break** [Informal] to stop treating someone harshly, critically, etc. —☆**the breaks** [Informal] the ways of fortune; the way one's luck plays out: often in such phrases as **those are the breaks** or [Slang] **them's the breaks**

SYN.—**break**, the most general of these terms, expresses the basic idea of separating into pieces as a result of impact, stress, etc.; **smash** and **crash** add connotations of suddenness, violence, and noise; **crush** suggests a crumpling or pulverizing pressure; **shatter**, sudden fragmentation and a scattering of pieces; **crack**, incomplete separation of parts or a sharp, snapping noise in breaking; **split**, separation lengthwise, as along the direction of grain or layers; **fracture**, the breaking of a hard or rigid substance, as bone or rock; **splinter**, the splitting of wood, etc. into long, thin, sharp pieces. All of these terms are used figuratively to imply great force or damage [to *break* someone's heart, *smash* someone's hopes, *crush* the opposition, *shatter* someone's nerves, etc.]

break·a·ble (brāk′ə bəl) *adj.* that can be, or is liable to be, broken —*n.* a thing easily broken; fragile article

break·age (-ij) *n.* **1** an act or instance of breaking **2** things or quantity broken **3** loss or damage due to breaking **4** the sum allowed for such loss or damage

break·a·way (-ə wā′) *adj.* **1** breaking away from a given position, procedure, group, etc. ☆**2** designed to break harmlessly upon slight impact, as a theatrical prop used in staging a fight **3** *Basketball, Hockey, etc.* of a play in which the offensive player breaks free of defensive players, has control of the ball, puck, etc., and heads toward the opponent's goal —*n.* a breakaway movement, stage prop, etc.

break·beat (-bēt′) *n.* **1** a pattern of usually syncopated drum beats sampled from a funk, jazz, hip hop, etc. song and, typically, repeated to establish a basic rhythm, as in some kinds of popular dance music **2** dance music that features such a pattern

☆**break·bone fever** (-bōn′) DENGUE

☆**break dancing** ⟦< ?⟧ a style of dance engaged in by youths, involving acrobatic movements, spinning about on the head or shoulders, etc.

break·down (-doun′) *n.* **1** an act, instance, or result of breaking down; specif., *a)* a failure to work or function properly [*breakdown* of a machine, of authority, etc.] *b)* a failure of health; physical, mental, or emotional collapse *c)* decomposition *d)* a separation into parts; analysis ☆**2** a lively, shuffling American country dance

break·er[1] (brāk′ər) *n.* **1** a person or thing that breaks; specif., *a)* a device or structure for breaking up rock, coal, etc. *b)* a wave that breaks into foam against a shore or reef **2** CIRCUIT BREAKER —***SYN.*** WAVE

break·er[2] (brāk′ər) *n.* ⟦altered < Sp *barrica,* akin to BARREL⟧ a small water keg, often carried in lifeboats

break-e·ven (brāk′ē′vən) *adj.* designating that point, as in a commercial venture, at which income and expenses are equal

break·fast (brek′fəst) *n.* ⟦BREAK + FAST[2]⟧ the first meal of the day, typically eaten in the morning —*vi.* to eat breakfast —*vt.* to give breakfast to

☆**breakfast food** any prepared cereal for breakfast

break·front (brāk′frunt′) *adj.* having a front with a central section that projects outward from top to bottom beyond the sections on either side —*n.* a breakfront cabinet or bookcase

break-in (brāk′in′) *n.* the act of forcibly entering a building, apartment, etc., esp. in order to rob —*adj.* designating or of the period of first use, intended to prepare something or train someone new

breaking and entering the felonious act of putting aside any obstacle to entry of a house or other structure owned by another, which if left untouched would prevent entrance, followed by entry, with the intention of committing a crime: also called **breaking and entry**

breaking ball (*or* **pitch)** *Baseball* any pitch that breaks; specif., a curve or slider

breaking point 1 the point at which material breaks under strain **2** the point at which one's endurance, self-control, etc. collapses under trial

break·neck (brāk′nek′) *adj.* very fast, reckless, dangerous, etc.: said of speed, pace, etc.

break·out (-out′) *n.* a sudden, forceful escape, as from prison or enemy troop encirclement —*adj.* achieving, resulting in, or characterized by sudden or unexpected success or popularity

break point *Tennis, etc.* **1** a situation in which the next point scored could result in a SERVICE BREAK **2** a point scored that results in a SERVICE BREAK

break·through (-thro͞o′) *n.* **1** the act, result, or place of breaking through against resistance, as in warfare **2** a strikingly important advance or discovery

break·up (-up′) *n.* the act or an instance of breaking up; specif., *a)* a dispersion *b)* a disintegration or decay *c)* a collapse *d)* a stopping or ending

break·wa·ter (-wôt′ər) *n.* a barrier to break the impact of waves, as before a harbor: often **break′wall′** (-wôl′)

bream[1] (brim, brēm) *n., pl.* **bream** or **breams** ⟦ME *breme* < OFr *bresme* < Frank **brahsima*: for IE base see BRAID⟧ **1** a European freshwater cyprinoid fish (*Abramis brama*) **2** any of various porgy fishes (family Sparidae) ☆**3** any of a number of freshwater sunfishes, as the bluegill

bream[2] (brēm) *vt.* ⟦< ? Du *brem,* furze (see BRAMBLE): burning furze was orig. used in process⟧ [Historical] to clean (a ship's bottom) by applying heat and then scraping

breast (brest) *n.* ⟦ME *brest* < OE *breost* < IE base **bhreus-,* to swell, sprout⟧ **1** either of two milk-secreting glands protruding from the upper, front part of a woman's body **2** a corresponding gland in a female primate **3** a corresponding undeveloped gland in the male **4** figuratively, a source of nourishment **5** *a)* the front part of a person's chest *b)* the corresponding part of some animals, as a bird or lamb **6** the part of a garment, etc. that is over the breast **7** the breast regarded as the center of emotions **8** anything likened to the breast [the *breast* of the sea] **9** *Mining* the face that is being worked at the end of an excavation or tunnel —*vt.* **1** to oppose the breast to; face **2** to face or meet firmly; move forward against

—**beat one's breast** to make an exaggerated display of one's feelings of guilt, remorse, etc. —**make a clean breast of** to confess (guilt, etc.) fully

SYN.—**breast** refers to the front part of the human torso from the shoulders to the abdomen, or it designates either of the female mammary glands; **bosom** refers to the entire human breast but, except in euphemistic applications [a big-*bosomed* matron], is now more common in figurative usage, where it implies the human breast as a source of feeling, a protective, loving enclosure, etc. [the *bosom* of his family]; **bust**, as considered here, almost always implies the female breasts and is the conventional term in referring to silhouette, form, etc., as in garment fitting

breast-beat·ing (brest′bēt′iŋ) ⟦< BEAT ONE'S BREAST (see phr. under prec.)⟧ the act or an instance of making an exaggerated display of one's feelings of guilt, remorse, etc.

breast·bone (-bōn′) *n.* STERNUM

-breast·ed (brest′id) *combining form* having a (specified kind of) breast or breasts [big-*breasted*, bare-*breasted*]

breast-feed (brest′fēd′) *vt.* **-fed′** (-fed′), **-feed′ing** to feed (a baby) milk from the breast; suckle; nurse

breast·pin (-pin′) *n.* ☆an ornamental pin or brooch worn at the breast or near the throat

breast·plate (-plāt′) *n.* **1** a piece of armor for the breast **2** in ancient times, an embroidered cloth worn on the breast of the Jewish high priest: it was set with twelve jewels representing the twelve tribes of Israel: also (RSV) **breast′piece′** (-pēs′)

breast stroke *Swimming* **1** a stroke performed face down in which both arms are extended outward and sideways from a position close to the chest, while the legs engage in a frog kick **2** a contest in which each participant uses such a stroke

breast·work (-wʉrk′) *n.* a low wall put up quickly as a defense in battle

breath (breth) *n.* ⟦ME *breth* < OE *brǣth*, odor, exhalation < IE base **bher-*, well up > FERMENT, BARM, BROOD⟧ **1** air taken into the lungs and then let out **2** the act of breathing; respiration **3** the power to breathe easily and naturally [to get one's *breath* back] **4** life or spirit **5** air or vapor given off from anything **6** air carrying fragrance or odor **7** a puff or whiff, as of air; slight breeze **8** moisture produced by a condensing of the breath, as in cold air **9** an utterance, esp. in a low voice; whisper or murmur **10** *a)* a single respiration *b)* the time taken for this; a moment **11** a slight pause or rest **12** a faint hint or indication **13** *Phonet.* a voiceless exhalation of the airstream with relative stillness at the vocal cords, as in pronouncing (s) or (p) —**catch one's breath 1** to gasp **2** to return to normal breathing after exertion **3** [Informal] to rest or pause —**in the same breath** almost simultaneously —**out of breath** breathless, as from exertion —**save one's breath** [Informal] to refrain from talking when talk would be useless —**take someone's breath away** to strike someone with awe; thrill or dumbfound —**under** (or **below**) **one's breath** in a whisper or murmur

☆**Breath·a·lyz·er** (breth′ə lī′zər) ⟦*breath (an)alyzer*⟧ *trademark for* a device that tests exhaled breath to indicate the amount of alcohol in the body or blood —*n.* [**b-**] such a device

breathe (brēth) *vi.* **breathed, breath′ing** ⟦ME *brethen* < *breth*, BREATH⟧ **1** *a)* to take air into the lungs and let it out again; inhale and exhale, esp. easily and naturally *b)* to inhale (in full, **breathe in**) or exhale (in full, **breathe out**) *c)* to carry on respiration **2** to live **3** [Old Poet.] to give out an odor or aroma **4** [Old Poet.] to blow softly **5** to speak or sing softly; whisper, murmur, etc. **6** to take time to breathe; rest **7** to pant, as from exertion **8** to react with the air after being opened or decanted and thus develop further in flavor and bouquet: said of wine **9** to allow the passage of air, moisture, etc. through or as through pores [a cotton fabric that *breathes*] —*vt.* **1** *a)* to take (air) into the lungs and let it out again; inhale and exhale, esp. easily and naturally *b)* to inhale (in full, **breathe in**) or exhale (in full, **breathe out**) **2** to give out or instill by or as if by breathing [to *breathe* a sigh of relief, *breathe* life into a party] **3** [Old Poet.] to blow softly **4** to speak or sing softly; whisper, murmur, etc. **5** to give time to breathe; rest [to *breathe* a horse] **6** to cause to pant, as from exertion —**breathe again** to have a feeling of relief or reassurance —**breathe a word** to say something or anything [if you *breathe a word* of this to anyone, you'll regret it] —**breathe one's last** to die —**breath′a·ble** *adj.*

breathed (bretht; *for 2 usually* brēthd) *adj.* ⟦BREATH + -ED⟧ **1** having a (specified kind of) breath: used in compounds [foul-*breathed*] **2** ⟦pp. of prec.⟧ *Phonet.* voiceless

breath·er (brē′thər) *n.* **1** *a)* one who breathes in a certain way [a mouth *breather*] *b)* [Slang] one who telephones another person and then breathes audibly instead of talking **2** a small vent, as for the release of moisture from an enclosed space **3** [Informal] *a)* a pause as for rest *b)* an easy contest, task, etc. coming between other, more difficult ones

breath·ing (brē′thiŋ) *adj.* that breathes; living; alive —*n.* **1** respiration **2** a single breath or the time taken by this **3** a pause for rest **4** *see* ROUGH BREATHING, SMOOTH BREATHING

breathing space (or **room**) **1** enough space to breathe, move, etc. freely **2** a chance to rest or consider a situation

breath·less (breth′lis) *adj.* **1** without breath **2** [Old Poet.] no longer breathing; dead **3** out of breath; panting or gasping **4** unable to breathe easily because of excitement, fear, etc. **5** of or characteristic of writing having a light, superficial, or dramatic, fast-paced style intended to excite the interest of the reader **6** still and heavy, as the air; stifling —**breath′less·ly** *adv.* —**breath′less·ness** *n.*

breath·tak·ing (-tāk′iŋ) *adj.* **1** that takes a person's breath away **2** very exciting; thrilling —**breath′tak′ing·ly** *adv.*

breath·y (-ē) *adj.* **breath′i·er, breath′i·est** characterized by an excessive and audible emission of breath [a *breathy* voice, speaker, etc.] —**breath′i·ly** *adv.* —**breath′i·ness** *n.*

brec·ci·a (brech′ē ə, bresh′-) *n.* ⟦It, fragments of stone < Fr *brèche*: see BRASH[2]⟧ rock consisting of sharp-cornered bits of fragmented rock, cemented together by sand, clay, or lime

brec·ci·ate (brech′ē āt′, bresh′-) *vt.* **-at′ed, -at′ing** to form (rock fragments) into breccia —**brec′ci·a′tion** *n.*

Brecht (breHt; E brekt), **Ber·tolt** (ber′tôlt) (born *Eugen Berthold Friedrich Brecht*) 1898-1956; Ger. playwright —**Brecht′ian** *adj.*

Breck·in·ridge (brek′in rij′), **John Cab·ell** (kab′əl) 1821-75; vice president of the U.S. (1857-61); Confederate general

Brec·on·shire (brek′ən shir, -shər) former county of SE Wales, now part of Powys county: also called **Breck′nock′shire** (brek′näk′-, -nək-) or **Breck′nock′**

bred (bred) *vt., vi. pt. & pp. of* BREED

Bre·da (brā dä′) city in S Netherlands

brede (brēd) *n.* ⟦var. of BRAID⟧ [Archaic] braiding or embroidery

breech (brēch; *for vt. 1* brich) *n.* ⟦ME *brech* < OE *brec*, pl. of *broc* < IE base **bhreg-*: see BREAK⟧ **1** the buttocks; rump **2** the lower or back part of a thing; specif., *a)* the lower end of a pulley block *b)* the back end of the barrel of a gun Cf. BREECHES —*vt.* **1** to clothe with breeches **2** to provide (a gun) with a breech

breech·block (brēch′bläk′) *n.* the block in a breech-loading gun which when closed receives the force of the combustion of the charge

☆**breech·cloth** (-klôth′) *n.* a cloth worn about the loins; loincloth: also **breech′clout′** (-klout′)

breech delivery the delivery of a baby presenting itself with its breech or feet first

breech·es (brich′iz) *pl.n.* ⟦see BREECH⟧ **1** trousers reaching to or just below the knees and often tapered to fit closely **2** [Informal] any trousers —**too big for one's breeches** [Informal] too forward, presumptuous, etc. for one's position or status

breeches (18th cent.)

breeches buoy a device for rescuing people at sea, consisting of a piece of strong canvas with leg holes suspended from a life preserver that is run along a rope from ship to shore or to another ship

breech·ing (brich′iŋ, brēch′-) *n.* a harness strap around a horse's hindquarters to help in holding back a vehicle on a downgrade

breech·less (brēch′lis) *adj.* without a breech

breech·load·er (brēch′lōd′ər) *n.* any gun loaded at the breech

breech-load·ing (-lōd′iŋ) *adj.* loading at the breech instead of the muzzle, as many guns: also written **breech′load′ing**

breed (brēd) *vt.* **bred, breed′ing** ⟦ME *breden* < OE *bredan* < *brod*, fetus, hatching: see BROOD⟧ **1** to bring forth (offspring) from the womb or hatch (young) from the egg **2** to be the source of; produce [ignorance *breeds* prejudice] **3** *a)* to cause to reproduce; raise, esp. by controlled mating [to *breed* dogs] *b)* to produce (plants) by selective pollination *c)* to mate with *d)* to develop (a stock or certain characteristics in it) by such mating or pollination **4** to bring up, train, or educate [he was *bred* to be a gentleman] **5** to produce (fissile material) in a breeder reactor —*vi.* **1** to be produced; originate [crime *breeds* in slums] **2** to bring forth offspring; reproduce —*n.* **1** a group, or stock, of animals or plants descended from common ancestors and having similar characteristics, esp. such a group cultivated by humans **2** a kind; sort; type [men of the same *breed*]

breed·er (-ər) *n.* **1** an animal or plant that produces offspring **2** a person who breeds animals or plants **3** BREEDER REACTOR

breeder reactor a nuclear reactor generating nuclear energy and creating additional fuel by producing more fissile material than it consumes

breed·ing (-iŋ) *n.* ⟦see BREED⟧ **1** the producing of young **2** the rearing of young; upbringing, education, or training, esp. in manners or social behavior **3** good upbringing or training [tolerance is a sign of *breeding*] **4** the producing of plants and animals, esp. for the purpose of developing new or better types

breeding ground 1 a place where many animals of a specified kind breed [swamps are *breeding grounds* for mosquitoes] **2** a place, condition, etc. that fosters some activity, idea, etc.

breeks (brēks, briks) *pl.n.* [Chiefly Scot.] BREECHES

breeze[1] (brēz) *n.* ⟦16th-c. nautical term *brise*, prob. (? via Du) < EFris *brisen*, to blow fresh and strong⟧ **1** a light current of air; wind, esp. a gentle wind **2** [Brit. Informal] commotion or disturbance ☆**3** [Informal] a thing easy to do **4** *Meteorol.* any wind ranging in speed from 4 to 31 miles per hour: see the Beaufort scale in the Reference Supplement —*vi.* **breezed, breez′ing** ☆[Informal] to move or go quickly, jauntily, easily, etc. —SYN. WIND[2] —☆**in a breeze** [Informal] with little or no effort; easily —☆**shoot** (or **bat**) **the breeze** [Slang] to converse idly about trivial matters

breeze[2] (brēz) *n.* ⟦Fr *braise*, live coals: see BRAISE⟧ **1** a substance left when coke, coal, or charcoal is burned or processed: it is used as a filler for concrete, etc. **2** small pieces of coke or coal with a diameter of 1.27 cm (.5 in) or less

☆**breeze·way** (brēz′wā′) *n.* a covered passageway, as between a house and garage, often enclosed on the sides

breez·y (-ē) *adj.* **breez′i·er, breez′i·est 1** with breezes blowing; slightly windy [*a breezy* day] **2** light and lively; carefree [*breezy* talk] —**breez′i·ly** *adv.* —**breez′i·ness** *n.*

breg·ma (breg′mə) *n., pl.* **breg′ma·ta** (-mə tə) ⟦ModL < Gr: see BRAIN⟧ the point or area of the skull where the frontal bone and the parietal bones come together —**breg·mat′ic** (-mat′ik) *adj.*

Bre·men (brem′ən; *Ger* brā′mən) **1** state of NW Germany, consisting of the cities of Bremen & Bremerhaven: 156 sq mi (404 sq km) **2** capital of this state: port on the Weser River

Bre·mer·ha·ven (brem′ər hä′vən; *Ger* brā′mər häf′ən) seaport at the mouth of the Weser River, in N Germany, forming an exclave of Bremen state

brems·strah·lung (brem′shträ′lʊŋ) *n.* ⟦Ger, lit., braked radiation < *bremse,* a brake + *strahlung,* radiation⟧ the electromagnetic radiation given off by a high-energy particle, as an electron, when suddenly accelerated or retarded by an electric field or by another charged particle, as an atomic nucleus

Bren·da (bren′də) *n.* ⟦prob. fem. of *Brand* < Ger *brand* or ON *brandr,* a sword: see BRAND⟧ a feminine name

Bren (gun) (bren) ⟦after *Br(no),* Czechoslovakia, where first made + *En(field),* England, where manufactured for the Brit army⟧ a light, fast, gas-operated machine gun used by the British army in WWII

Bren·nan (bren′ən), **William J(oseph), Jr.** 1906-97; associate justice, U.S. Supreme Court (1956-90)

Bren·ner Pass (bren′ər) mountain pass across the Alps at the border between Italy & Austria: 4,495 ft (1,370 m) high

brent (brent) *n.* BRANT

Brent (brent) borough of Greater London, England

☆**br'er** (brʉr, brer) *n.* [South] brother: used before a name

bre·sao·la (bre sō′lə, -zō′-) *n.* ⟦It < *brasare,* to braise, cook slowly⟧ salted, air-dried beef, usually served in thin slices with olive oil and lemon juice

Bre·scia (bre′shä) commune in Lombardy, N Italy, at the foot of the Alps

Bres·lau (bres′lou) *Ger. name for* WROCŁAW

Brest (brest) **1** seaport in W France, on the Atlantic **2** city in SW Belarus, on the Bug River: site of the signing of a separate peace treaty (March, 1918) between Russia & the Central Powers: formerly called **Brest-Li·tovsk** (brest′li tôfsk′)

Bre·tagne (brə tän′y′) *Fr. name for* BRITTANY²

breth·ren (breth′rən; *often,* -ərn) *pl.n.* ⟦ME *bretheren,* pl.: see BROTHER⟧ **1** brothers: now chiefly in religious use **2** [B-] members of the CHURCH OF THE BRETHREN or of other Protestant groups similar in origin and practices

Bret·on¹ (bret′'n) *adj.* ⟦Fr, ult. same word as BRITON⟧ of Brittany or its people, language, or culture —*n.* **1** a person born or living in Brittany **2** the Celtic language spoken in Brittany

Bre·ton² (brə tōn′), **An·dré** (än drā′) 1896-1966; Fr. poet & art critic: a founder of surrealism

Bret·ton Woods (bret′'n) ⟦after *Bretton* Hall, Eng countryseat of one of the founders⟧ resort in the White Mountains, N.H.: site of a United Nations monetary conference (1944) at which the International Monetary Fund was established

Breu·er (broi′ər), **Marcel (Lajos)** 1902-81; U.S. architect & designer, born in Hungary

Breuer chair ⟦after prec., its designer⟧ a chair with a frame of continuous chrome tubing, no back legs, and cane seat and back

Breu·ghel (brü′gəl, broi′-) *alt. sp. of* BRUEGEL

breve (brēv, brev) *n.* ⟦It < L *brevis,* BRIEF⟧ **1** a mark (˘) placed over a short vowel or a short or unstressed syllable **2** *Law* a judicial writ **3** *Music* a note written 𝅜 or ⊨ having the combined time value of two whole notes

bre·vet (brə vet′; *chiefly Brit* brev′it) *n.* ⟦ME < OFr, dim. of *bref,* BRIEF⟧ [Historical] *Mil.* a commission nominally promoting an officer to a higher honorary rank without higher pay but, sometimes, with greater authority —*vt.* **-vet′ted** or **-vet′ed, -vet′ting** or **-vet′ing** to give a brevet to

brev·i- (brev′i, -ē, -ə) ⟦< L *brevis,* BRIEF⟧ *combining form* short [*brevirostrate*]

bre·vi·ar·y (brē′vē er′ē, brēv′yə rē′) *n., pl.* **-ar′ies** ⟦ML *breviarium* < L, an abridgment < *breviarius,* abridged < *brevis,* BRIEF⟧ a book containing the Psalms, readings, prayers, etc. of the Divine Office

brev·i·rost·rate (brev′ə räs′trāt′) *adj.* ⟦BREVI- + ROSTRATE⟧ having a short beak or bill: said of a bird

brev·i·ty (brev′ə tē) *n.* ⟦L *brevitas* < *brevis,* BRIEF⟧ **1** the quality of being brief; shortness of time **2** the quality of being concise; terseness

brew (bro͞o) *vt.* ⟦ME *breuen* < OE *breowan:* see BREAD⟧ **1** to make (beer, ale, etc.) from malt and hops by steeping, boiling, and fermenting **2** to make (tea, coffee, etc.) by infusing tea leaves, ground coffee beans, etc. with hot water **3** to plan (mischief, trouble, etc.); plot; scheme —*vi.* **1** to brew beer, ale, etc. **2** to begin to form: said of a storm, trouble, etc. —*n.* **1** a beverage that has been brewed **2** an amount brewed **3** the brewing process ☆**4** [Informal] a drink of beer —**brew′er** *n.*

brew·age (-ij) *n.* **1** anything brewed; esp., malt liquor **2** the process of brewing

brewer's yeast 1 a yeast (*Saccharomyces cerevisiae*) used in brewing beer **2** the byproduct yeast left after brewing, often used in medicine and foods and as a dietary supplement

brew·er·y (bro͞o′ər ē) *n., pl.* **-er·ies** an establishment where beer, ale, etc. are brewed

brew·ing (bro͞o′iŋ) *n.* **1** the preparation of a brew **2** the amount of a brew made at one time

brew·mas·ter (-mas′tər) *n.* the director of the brewing process in a brewery

brew·pub (-pub′) *n.* a bar or restaurant featuring beer that is brewed on-site

brew·ski (bro͞o′skē) *n., pl.* **-skis, -skies** ⟦< BREW (*n.* 4) + *-ski, -sky,* suffix in Slavic surnames, used jocularly⟧ [Slang] a serving of beer

Brew·ster (bro͞o′stər), **William** 1567?-1644; Eng. Pilgrim who helped settle Plymouth Colony

Brey·er (brī′ər), **Stephen (Gerald)** 1938- ; associate justice, U.S. Supreme Court (1994-)

Brezh·nev¹ (brezh′nef, -nev), **Le·o·nid I(lyich)** (lā ô nēd′) 1906-82; general secretary of the Communist Party of the U.S.S.R. (1964-82)

Brezh·nev² (brezh′nef, -nev) *name* (1982-88) *for* NABEREZHNIYE CHELNY

Bri·an (brī′ən) *n.* ⟦Celt, ? strong⟧ a masculine name

Bri·an Bo·ru (brī′ən bə ro͞o′) A.D. 926?-1014; king of Ireland (1002-14): Ir. name **Brian Bo·ramhe** (brēn bô rō′)

bri·ar¹ (brī′ər) *n.* BRIER¹ —**bri′ar·y** *adj.*

bri·ar² (brī′ər) *n.* **1** a tobacco pipe made from the root of BRIER² (sense 1) **2** *occas. sp. of* BRIER² (senses 1 & 2)

bri·ard (brē ärd′) *n.* ⟦Fr < adj., of *Brie:* see BRIE (CHEESE)⟧ any of a breed of large dog with a coarse, bushy coat and erect ears

bri·ar·root (brī′ər ro͞ot′) *n.* BRIERROOT

bri·ar·wood (-wood′) *n.* BRIERWOOD

bribe (brīb) *n.* ⟦ME < OFr, morsel of bread given to beggars < *briber,* to beg⟧ **1** anything, esp. money, given or promised to induce a person to do something illegal or wrong **2** anything given or promised to induce a person to do something against his or her wishes —*vt.* **bribed, brib′ing 1** to offer or give a bribe to **2** to get or influence by bribing —*vi.* to give a bribe or bribes —**brib′a·ble** *adj.* —**brib′er** *n.*

brib·er·y (brīb′ər ē) *n., pl.* **-er·ies** ⟦ME & OFr *briberie,* theft: see prec.⟧ the giving, offering, or taking of bribes

bric-a-brac (brik′ə brak′) *n.* ⟦Fr *bric-à-brac* < phr. *de bric et de brac,* by hook or by crook⟧ **1** small, rare, or artistic objects placed about a room for decoration **2** knickknacks; gimcracks

brick (brik) *n.* ⟦ME *brike* < MDu < *breken,* BREAK (in sense "piece of baked clay") & MFr *brique* < OFr, of same orig.⟧ **1** a substance made from clay molded into oblong blocks and fired in a kiln or baked in the sun, used in building, paving, etc. **2** one of these blocks, of any of various standard sizes **3** bricks collectively **4** anything shaped like a brick **5** [Old Informal] a fine person —*adj.* **1** built or paved with brick **2** like brick [*brick* red] —*vt.* to face, pave, etc. with brick —**brick up (or in)** to close or wall in with brick —☆**hit the bricks** [Slang] to go out on strike

brick·bat (-bat′) *n.* **1** a piece of brick, esp. one used as a missile **2** an unfavorable or critical remark

☆**brick cheese** a ripened, semisoft American cheese shaped like a brick and containing many small holes

brick·lay·er (-lā′ər) *n.* a person whose work is building or paving with bricks —**brick′lay′ing** (-lā′iŋ) *n.*

brick·le (brik′əl) *adj., n.* ⟦ME *brikel,* var. of *brokel,* brittle < base of OE *brecan,* to BREAK⟧ [Dial.] brittle

brick red yellowish or brownish red —**brick′-red′** *adj.*

bricks-and-mor·tar (briks′ən môrt′ər) *adj.* ☆of retail business operations in stores, as distinguished from those strictly using mail or, esp., the internet: also **brick′-and-mor′tar**

brick wall anything or anyone that is impenetrable, unrelenting, unyielding, etc.

brick·work (-wʉrk′) *n.* **1** a thing or part built of bricks **2** the work of laying bricks

☆**brick·yard** (-yärd′) *n.* a place where bricks are made or sold

bri·co·lage (brē′kō läzh′, brik′ō-) *n.* ⟦Fr < *bricoler,* to putter < *bricole,* odd job < a Prov or It *n.* < ?⟧ **1** the process of making or assembling something from materials at hand **2** something, esp. an artistic work, so made

bri·co·leur (-lʉr′) *n.* ⟦Fr, handyman < *bricoler:* see prec.⟧ a person, esp. an artist, who engages in bricolage

brid·al (brīd′'l) *n.* ⟦ME *bridale* < OE *bryd ealu,* bride ale, marriage feast < *bryd,* BRIDE¹ + *ealu,* ALE⟧ [Archaic] a wedding —*adj.* **1** of a bride **2** of a wedding

bridal wreath ☆a cultivated shrub (*Spiraea prunifolia*) of the rose family, bearing numerous small, white double flowers in the spring

bride¹ (brīd) *n.* ⟦ME < OE *bryd,* akin to Ger *braut,* betrothed, fiancée⟧ a woman who has just been married or is about to be married

bride² (brīd) *n.* ⟦Fr < OFr < OHG *bridel,* akin to BRIDLE⟧ in lace making and other needlework, a loop or tie that connects parts of a pattern

Bride (brīd), Saint *alt. name for* Saint BRIDGET² (of Ireland)

bride·groom (brīd′gro͞om′) *n.* ⟦ME *bridegome* < OE *brydguma,* suitor < *bryd,* bride + *guma* (akin to L *homo*), man; altered by folk etym. after GROOM⟧ a man who has just been married or is about to be married

bride price in some cultures, money and property given to a prospective bride's family by the prospective groom and his family: also **bride′-price′** *n.* or **bride·wealth** (brīd′welth′)

brides·maid (brīdz′mād′) *n.* **1** one of the women who attend the bride at a wedding **2** a runner-up in a competition

bridge[1] (brij) ***n.*** ⟦ME *brigge* < OE *brycge* < IE base **bhrū,* log, beam, hence wooden causeway⟧ **1** a structure built over a river, railroad, highway, etc. to provide a way across for vehicles or pedestrians **2** a thing that provides connection, contact, or transition [a common language is a *bridge* between cultures] **3** *a)* the upper, bony part of the nose *b)* the curved bow of a pair of eyeglasses fitting over the nose **4** *a)* a thin arched, usually wooden support on the belly of violins, lutes, guitars, etc. over which the strings are stretched *b)* a similar support for the strings of a piano, harpsichord, etc. **5** an overhead framework across sets of railroad tracks, for carrying signals; gantry **6** a raised structure on a ship, usually in the forward part, from which it is controlled while underway **7** a dividing partition for keeping fuel in place in a furnace or boiler **8** *Billiards a)* a position of the hand when it is functioning as a support and guide for the striking end of the cue *b)* a device consisting of a long handle with a notched transverse piece at one end that functions similarly: used when the cue ball is positioned beyond the shooter's effective reach **9** *Chem.* HYDROGEN BOND **10** *Dentistry* a fixed or removable mounting for a false tooth or teeth, attached to a real tooth or teeth **11** *Elec.* a device used primarily in measuring resistances, frequencies, etc., by comparing the effect of the unknown element with that of known or standard elements in the circuit **12** *Music* a connecting passage between two sections of a composition —***vt.*** **bridged, bridg′ing 1** to build a bridge on or over **2** to provide a bridge, connection, transition, etc. across or between —***adj.*** designating or of products priced between the least expensive and the premium [a *bridge* line] —**burn one's bridges (behind one)** to commit oneself to a course from which there is no retreat —**bridge′a·ble** ***adj.***

bridge[2] (brij) ***n.*** ⟦< earlier (1886) *biritch,* so-called "Russian whist," altered after prec.; game & name ? of Russ orig.⟧ any of various card games, for two pairs of players, that developed from whist; esp., CONTRACT BRIDGE: see also AUCTION BRIDGE

bridge·board (brij′bôrd′) ***n.*** any of the notched boards holding the treads and risers of a staircase; string

bridge·head (-hed′) ***n.*** **1** a fortified place or position established by an attacking force on the enemy's side of a bridge, river, defile, etc. **2** BEACHHEAD (sense 2)

bridge loan 1 a short-term loan that provides interim financing for the purchase of new property until the old property can be sold **2** a short-term loan used to finance a corporate takeover that is often repaid by selling assets of the acquired company

bridge mix ⟦so named from being served orig. at parties where bridge was played⟧ an assortment of bite-size chocolates and, sometimes, other candies, together with nuts, raisins, etc., typically chocolate-covered

Bridge·port (brij′pôrt′) ⟦for the bridge across the Pequonnock River there⟧ seaport in SW Conn., on Long Island Sound

Bridg·es (brij′iz), **Robert (Seymour)** 1844-1930; Eng. poet: poet laureate (1913-30)

Bridg·et[1] (brij′it) ***n.*** ⟦Ir *Brighid,* lit., strong, lofty < IE base **bheregh-,* high > BARROW[2]⟧ a feminine name: equiv. Ger. & Fr. *Brigitte*

Bridg·et[2] (brij′it) **1** Saint (A.D. 452?-523?); Ir. abbess: a patron saint of Ireland: her day is Feb. 1 **2** Saint (1302?-73); Swed. nun: founder of the order of *Bri(d)gittines:* her day is July 23

Bridge·town (brij′toun′) seaport & capital of Barbados

bridge·work (brij′wurk′) ***n.*** a dental bridge or bridges

bridg·ing (-iŋ) ***n.*** braces used between timbers, as of a floor, to hold them in place and distribute the strain

Bridg·man (brij′mən), **Percy Williams** 1882-1961; U.S. physicist

bri·dle (brīd′l) ***n.*** ⟦ME & OE *bridel* < *bregdan,* move quickly: see BRAID⟧ **1** a head harness for guiding a horse: it consists of headstall, bit, and reins **2** anything resembling a horse's bridle **3** anything that controls or restrains **4** FRENUM **5** a connecting metal strip for limiting motion in machinery **6** *Naut.* a cable with the ends fast and another cable attached to it between the ends for applying force, as in towing a ship —***vt.*** **bri′dled, bri′dling 1** to put a bridle on **2** to curb or control with or as with a bridle —***vi.*** **1** to pull one's head back quickly with the chin drawn in as an expression of anger, scorn, pride, etc. **2** to take offense (*at*) —*SYN.* RESTRAIN

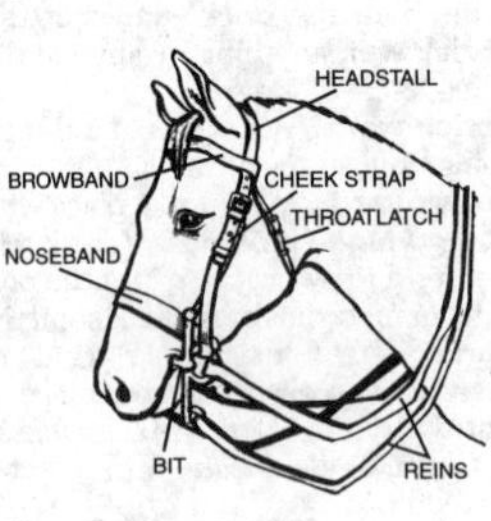

bridle

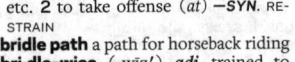

bridle path a path for horseback riding

☆**bri·dle-wise** (-wīz′) ***adj.*** trained to obey the pressure of the reins on the neck instead of the pull on the bit

bri·doon (bri do͞on′) ***n.*** ⟦Fr *bridon* < *bride:* see BRIDE[2]⟧ a kind of light snaffle bit

brie (cheese) (brē) ⟦after *Brie,* region in France, east of Paris, where it is made⟧ a ripened soft, white cheese made in France, or a similar cheese made elsewhere

brief (brēf) ***adj.*** ⟦ME < OFr *bref* < L *brevis* < IE base **mreghu-,* short > MERRY, Gr *brachys*⟧ **1** of short duration or extent **2** short in length **3** using relatively few words; concise **4** curt or abrupt —***n.*** ⟦ME *bref* < OFr < LL *breve* < L, neut. of *brevis:* see ***adj.***⟧ **1** a summary or abstract **2** a concise statement of the main points of a law case, usually filed by counsel for the information of the court **3** [Chiefly Brit.] a set of instructions for the participants in some project, investigation, etc., indicating the scope of their responsibilities: often used fig. **4** *R.C.Ch.* a papal letter less formal than a bull **5** [*pl.*] *a)* closefitting, legless undershorts *b)* women's panties that cover the body from the waist to the leg —***vt.*** **1** to make a summary of **2** to supply with all the pertinent instructions or information [to *brief* pilots before a flight] **3** [Brit.] *a)* to furnish with a legal brief *b)* to hire as counsel —**hold a brief for** to argue for or be in favor of —**in brief** in short; in a few words —**brief′ly** ***adv.*** —**brief′ness** ***n.***

SYN.—**brief** and **short** are opposites of *long* in their application to duration [a *brief* or *short* interval], although **brief** often emphasizes compactness, conciseness, etc. [a *brief* review] and **short** often implies incompleteness or curtailment [a *short* measure, to make *short* work of it]; **short** is usually used where linear extent is referred to [a *short* man] See also **abridgment** —*ANT.* **long**

brief·case (-kās′) ***n.*** a flat, flexible case, usually of leather, for carrying papers, books, etc.

brief·er (-ər) ***n.*** a person who gives a briefing

brief·ing (-iŋ) ***n.*** **1** the act or an instance of supplying pertinent instructions or information **2** the information so supplied

brief·less (-lis) ***adj.*** without clients: said of a lawyer

brief of title ABSTRACT OF TITLE

bri·er[1] (brī′ər) ***n.*** ⟦ME *brere* (with vowel change as in FRIAR < ME *frere*) < OE *brer, brœr*⟧ **1** any prickly or thorny bush, as a bramble or wild rose **2** a growth of such bushes **3** a twig of a brier —**bri′er·y** ***adj.***

bri·er[2] (brī′ər) ***n.*** ⟦Fr *bruyère,* white heath < Gaul **brucus,* heather, broom⟧ **1** an evergreen shrub or tree (*Erica arborea*) of the heath family, native to S Europe, with needlelike leaves and white flowers **2** its root, esp. the root burl, often used to make tobacco pipes **3** *occas. sp. of* BRIAR[2] (sense 1)

bri·er·root (brī′ər ro͞ot′) ***n.*** BRIER[2] (sense 2)

bri·er·wood (-wood′) ***n.*** BRIERROOT

brig[1] (brig) ***n.*** ⟦contr. < BRIGANTINE⟧ a two-masted ship with square-rigged sails

☆**brig**[2] (brig) ***n.*** ⟦< ?⟧ **1** *U.S. Navy* a place where offenders are temporarily confined, as on a warship **2** [Mil. Slang] the guardhouse; prison

bri·gade (bri gād′) ***n.*** ⟦Fr < MFr < OIt *brigata,* troop, company < *brigare,* to contend < *briga,* strife, quarrel⟧ **1** a large unit of soldiers **2** *a)* [Historical] a unit of the U.S. Army comprising two or more regiments *b)* now, a military unit composed of two or more battalions with service and administrative units **3** a group of people organized to function as a unit in some work [a fire *brigade*] —***vt.*** **-gad′ed, -gad′ing** to organize into a brigade

brig·a·dier (brig′ə dir′) ***n.*** ⟦Fr < prec.⟧ **1** [Informal] *short for* BRIGADIER GENERAL **2** a British military officer ranking above a colonel and below a major general

brigadier general *U.S. Mil.* a military officer with an insignia of one star, ranking above a colonel and below a major general

brig·and (brig′ənd) ***n.*** ⟦ME *brigaunt* < OFr < OIt *brigante* < *brigare:* see BRIGADE⟧ a bandit, usually one of a roving band

brig·and·age (-ən dij) ***n.*** ⟦Fr < prec.⟧ plundering by brigands

brig·an·dine (brig′ən dēn′) ***n.*** ⟦LME < MFr < OIt *brigantina* < *brigare:* see BRIGADE⟧ a flexible coat of armor made by fastening small metal scales or rings between two plies of linen, leather, etc.

brig·an·tine (brig′ən tēn′) ***n.*** ⟦earlier *brigandyn* < MFr *brigandin* < OIt *brigantino* < *brigante,* BRIGAND⟧ **1** a two-masted ship like a hermaphrodite brig but with a square-rigged topsail on the mainmast **2** HERMAPHRODITE BRIG

Brig Gen *abbrev.* Brigadier General

bright (brīt) ***adj.*** ⟦ME < OE *bryht,* earlier *beorht* < IE base **bher- eg-,* to gleam, white > BIRCH, Goth *bairhts*⟧ **1** shining with light that is radiated or reflected; full of light **2** clear or brilliant in color or sound; vivid or intense **3** lively; vivacious; cheerful [a *bright* smile] **4** mentally quick; smart, clever, witty, etc. **5** *a)* full of happiness or hope [a *bright* outlook on life] *b)* favorable; auspicious **6** glorious or splendid; illustrious —***adv.*** in a bright manner —***n.*** [*pl.*] [Informal] an automobile's headlights at their brighter, or high-beam, setting —**bright′ly** ***adv.***

SYN.—**bright,** the most general term here, implies the giving forth or reflecting of light, or a being filled with light [a *bright* day, star, shield, etc.]; **radiant** emphasizes the actual or apparent emission of rays of light; **shining** implies a steady, continuous brightness [the *shining* sun]; **brilliant** implies intense or flashing brightness [*brilliant* sunlight, diamonds, etc.]; **luminous** is applied to objects that are full of light or give off reflected or phosphorescent light; **lustrous** is applied to objects whose surfaces gleam by reflected light and emphasizes gloss or sheen [*lustrous* silk] See also **intelligent** —*ANT.* **dull, dim, dark**

Bright (brīt), **John** 1811-89; Eng. statesman, political economist, & orator

bright·en (brīt′'n) ***vt., vi.*** ⟦ME < OE *brihtan* < *beorht,* BRIGHT⟧ **1** to make or become bright or brighter **2** to make or become happy or happier; gladden; cheer up

bright·ness (-nis) ***n.*** **1** the quality or condition of being bright **2** the luminous aspect of a color (as distinct from its hue) by which it is regarded as approaching the maximum luminance of pure white or the lack of luminance of pure black

Brigh·ton (brīt′'n) city in East Sussex, England, on the English Channel: seaside resort

Bright's disease (brīts) ⟦after R. *Bright* (1789-1858), London physician who first diagnosed it⟧ the chronic form of glomerulonephritis: once used for nephritis in general

bright·work (brīt′wurk′) *n.* unpainted metal trim or fittings, as on ships, kept bright by polishing

Brig·id (brij′id), Saint *alt. name for* Saint BRIDGET[2] (of Ireland)

brill (bril) *n., pl.* **brill** or **brills** ⟦< ? Cornish *brilli,* mackerel⟧ an edible European flatfish (*Scophthalmus rhombus*)

Bril·lat-Sa·va·rin (brē yȧ′ sȧ vȧ *ran′*), **An·thelme** (än telm′) 1755-1826; Fr. expert on foods & cooking

bril·liance (bril′yəns) *n.* the fact of being brilliant; great brightness, radiance, intensity, splendor, intelligence, etc.: also **bril′lian·cy** (-yən sē)

bril·liant (-yənt) *adj.* ⟦Fr *brillant,* sparkling, prp. of *briller,* to sparkle, glitter < It *brillare,* sparkle, whirl⟧ **1** shining brightly; sparkling **2** vivid; intense **3** very splendid or distinguished **4** having or showing keen intelligence, great talent or skill, etc. —*n.* a gem, esp. a diamond, cut in a certain way with many facets for maximum brilliance —***SYN.*** BRIGHT —**bril′liant·ly** *adv.*

☆**bril·lian·tine** (bril′yən tēn′) *n.* ⟦< Fr *brillantine:* see prec. & -INE[3]⟧ **1** an oily dressing for grooming the hair **2** a glossy cloth made of mohair and cotton

Bril·lo (bril′ō) *trademark for* a compact pad of steel wool containing soap, used for scouring pots, pans, etc. —*n.* [*also* **b-**] such a pad

☆**Brill's disease** (brilz) ⟦after N. E. *Brill* (1860-1925), U.S. physician⟧ a form of epidemic typhus fever in which the disease recurs years after the original infection: also called **Brill-Zins·ser disease** (bril′zin′sər)

brim (brim) *n.* ⟦ME *brimme,* akin to ON *barmr,* rim: for IE base see BROOM⟧ **1** the topmost edge of a cup, glass, bowl, etc. **2** [Archaic] *a)* a rim or edge around a body of water *b)* the water at such an edge **3** a projecting rim or edge of anything [the *brim* of a hat] —*vi.* **brimmed, brim′ming** to be completely full, often with a resulting overflow [eyes *brimming* with tears] —***SYN.*** BORDER —**brim′less** *adj.*

brim·ful (brim′fool′) *adj.* full to the brim

brim·mer (-ər) *n.* a cup or glass filled to the brim

brim·stone (brim′stōn′) *n.* ⟦ME *brimston* < OE *brynstan:* see BURN[1] & STONE⟧ SULFUR: now chiefly in the phrases **fire and brimstone, hellfire and brimstone,** the torments of damnation to hell

Brin·di·si (brin′də zē; *It* brēn′dē zē) seaport in Apulia, SE Italy, on the Adriatic

brin·dle (brin′dəl) *adj.* ⟦< fol.⟧ BRINDLED —*n.* **1** a brindled color **2** a brindled animal

brin·dled (-dəld) *adj.* ⟦< earlier *brinded,* after *kindled;* prob. < ME *brended* < *brennen,* BURN[1]⟧ having a gray or tawny coat streaked or spotted with a darker color [a *brindled* cow]

brine (brīn) *n.* ⟦ME & OE; prob. < IE **bhrēi-,* to cut (> L *friare,* to crumble) < base **bher-,* to cut; orig. sense "cutting, sharp"⟧ **1** water full of salt; heavily saturated salt solution, as for use in pickling **2** *a)* the water of the sea *b)* the sea; ocean —*vt.* **brined, brin′ing** to soak in or treat with brine

Bri·nell test (bri nel′) ⟦after J. A. *Brinell* (1849-1925), Swed engineer⟧ a test for determining the relative hardness (**Brinell hardness**) of a metal by measuring the diameter of the indentation made when a hardened steel ball is forced into the metal under a given pressure: the measure of hardness (**Brinell number**) is equal to the load in kilograms divided by the surface area of the indentation in square millimeters

brine shrimp any of a genus (*Artemia*) of small fairy shrimp found in salt lakes and marshes and used as living, frozen, or dried food in aquariums

bring (briŋ) *vt.* **brought, bring′ing** ⟦ME *bringen* < OE *bringan* < IE base **bhrenk-,* **bronk-* > Welsh *he-brwng,* to bring, lead⟧ **1** to carry or lead (a person or thing) to the place thought of as "here" or to a place where the speaker will be [*bring* it to my house tomorrow] **2** to cause to be, happen, come, appear, have, etc. [war *brings* death and famine; rest *brings* one health] **3** to lead, persuade, or influence along a course of action or belief **4** to sell for [eggs *bring* a high price today] **5** *Law a)* to present in a law court [to *bring* charges] *b)* to advance (evidence, etc.) —**bring about** to make happen; effect —**bring around (or round) 1** to persuade by arguing, urging, etc. **2** to put or coax into a good humor **3** to bring back to consciousness or health —**bring down 1** to cause to come down or fall **2** to wound or kill —**bring forth 1** *a)* to give birth to *b)* to produce (fruit, flowers, etc.) **2** to make known; disclose —**bring forward 1** to introduce; show **2** *Bookkeeping* to carry over —**bring in 1** to import **2** *a)* to produce (income or revenue) ☆*b)* to cause (an oil well, etc.) to produce **3** to give (a verdict or report) —**bring off** to succeed in doing; accomplish —**bring on** to cause to be, happen, or appear —**bring out 1** to reveal; make clear or clearer **2** to bring (a play, person, etc.) before the public, or to publish (a book, magazine, etc.) **3** to introduce (a girl or young woman) formally to society —**bring over** to convince or persuade —**bring to 1** to revive (an unconscious person) **2** to cause (a ship) to stop —**bring up 1** to take care of during infancy and childhood by educating, nurturing, training, etc.; raise; rear **2** to introduce, as into discussion **3** *a)* to cough up *b)* to vomit **4** to stop abruptly —**bring′er** *n.*

SYN.—**bring** (in strict usage) implies a carrying or conducting to, and **take,** similar action away from, a specified or implied place [*bring* the book to me; I will *take* it back to the library]; **fetch** implies a going after something, getting it, and bringing it back

brink (briŋk) *n.* ⟦ME < MLowG or Dan, shore, bank, grassy edge; prob. < IE **bhreng-,* var. of base **bhren-,* project, edge > L *frons,* FRONT[1]⟧ **1** the edge, esp. at the top of a steep place; verge: often used fig. [at the *brink* of war] **2** the bank, esp. when steep, of a river or other body of water —***SYN.*** BORDER

☆**brink·man·ship** (briŋk′mən ship′) *n.* ⟦prec. + -MANSHIP⟧ the policy of pursuing a hazardous course of action to the brink of catastrophe: also **brinks′man·ship′** (briŋks′-)

brin·y (brīn′ē) *adj.* **brin′i·er, brin′i·est** of or like brine; very salty —**brin′i·ness** *n.*

bri·o (brē′ō) *n.* ⟦It⟧ animation; vivacity; zest

bri·oche (brē ōsh′, -ôsh′; brē′ōsh′, -ôsh′) *n.* ⟦Fr⟧ a light, rich roll made with flour, butter, eggs, and yeast

bri·o·lette (brē′ə let′) *n.* ⟦Fr < ? *brillant,* BRILLIANT⟧ a teardrop diamond cut in triangular facets

bri·o·ny (brī′ə nē) *n., pl.* **-nies** BRYONY

bri·quette or **bri·quet** (bri ket′) *n.* ⟦Fr *briquette,* dim. of *brique,* BRICK⟧ a small block of compressed matter; specif., one made of charcoal, compressed coal dust, sawdust, etc., used for fuel or kindling —*vt.* **-quet′ted, -quet′ting** to form (ore particles, etc.) into briquettes

bris (bris) *n.* ⟦Yiddish < Heb *berit*⟧ BRITH MILAH

bri·sance (bri zäns′) *n.* ⟦Fr, lit., breaking, prp. of *briser,* to break < VL *brisare*⟧ the shattering effect of the sudden release of energy, as in an explosion of nitroglycerin

Bris·bane (briz′bān′, -bən) seaport on the E coast of Australia: capital of Queensland

brisk (brisk) *adj.* ⟦< ? Fr *brusque,* BRUSQUE⟧ **1** quick in manner or movement; energetic [a *brisk* pace] **2** cool, dry, and bracing [*brisk* air] **3** pungent, keen, sharp, etc. [a *brisk* taste, a *brisk* tone of voice] **4** active; busy [*brisk* trading] —***SYN.*** ACTIVE —**brisk′ly** *adv.* —**brisk′ness** *n.*

bris·ket (bris′kit) *n.* ⟦ME *brusket,* akin to Dan *bryske:* for IE base see BREAST⟧ **1** the breast of an animal **2** meat cut from this part

bris·ling (bris′liŋ) *n.* ⟦Norw dial. < older Dan *bretling*⟧ SPRAT

bris·tle (bris′əl) *n.* ⟦ME *bristel,* metathetic < OE *byrst;* akin to Ger *borste,* bristles < IE **bhr̥sti-* < base **bhar-,* point, bristle⟧ **1** any short, stiff, prickly hair of an animal or plant **2** *a)* any of the hairs of a hog or of some other animals, used for brushes *b)* such a hair, or an artificial hair like it, in a brush —*vi.* **-tled, -tling 1** to become stiff and erect, like bristles **2** to have the bristles become erect, as in fear or irritation **3** to show strong anger, irritation, outrage, etc. as by a stiffening of the body **4** to be thickly covered (*with*) [the battlefield *bristled* with guns] —*vt.* **1** to cause to stand up like bristles **2** to put bristles on or in **3** to make bristly

bris·tle·cone pine (bris′əl kōn′) either of two high-elevation pine trees (*Pinus aristata* and *P. longaeva*) of the W U.S., having needles in clusters of five and cones with bristles: they are known for their often twisted, gnarled appearance and extremely long life

bris·tle·tail (-tāl′) *n.* any of a family (Machilidae) of primitive, wingless, thysanuran insects with bristles at the posterior end

bris·tly (bris′lē) *adj.* **-tli·er, -tli·est 1** having bristles; rough with bristles **2** bristlelike; prickly —**bris′tli·ness** *n.*

Bris·tol (bris′təl) seaport in Avon, SW England

Bristol Bay ⟦after Admiral A. J. Hervey (1724-79), 3d Earl of *Bristol*⟧ arm of the Bering Sea between the SW Alas. mainland & the Alaska Peninsula

Bristol board ⟦after BRISTOL⟧ a fine, smooth pasteboard, used by artists, printers, etc.

Bristol Channel arm of the Atlantic, between S Wales & SW England: *c.* 85 mi (137 km) long

brit (brit) *pl.n., sing.* **brit** ⟦Cornish < OCelt *brith,* varicolored; akin to Cornish *bruit,* speckled⟧ **1** the young of the herring and some other fishes **2** small sea animals, esp. certain crustaceans, as copepods, eaten by the baleen whales and many fishes

Brit[1] (brit) [Informal] *adj.* British —*n.* Britisher

Brit[2] *abbrev.* British

Brit·ain (brit′'n) GREAT BRITAIN

Bri·tan·ni·a[1] (bri tan′yə, -tan′ē ə) *n.* ⟦L⟧ **1** [Old Poet.] a female figure symbolizing Great Britain or the British Empire **2** [**b-**] britannia metal

Bri·tan·ni·a[2] (bri tan′yə, -tan′ē ə) **1** *Latin name for* GREAT BRITAIN (the island), esp. the southern part **2** BRITISH EMPIRE

britannia metal [*also* **B- m-**] an alloy consisting chiefly of tin, copper, and antimony, used in making tableware: it resembles pewter but is harder

Bri·tan·nic (bri tan′ik) *adj.* ⟦L *Britannicus* < *Britannia*⟧ of Great Britain; British

britch·es (brich′iz) *pl.n.* [Informal] BREECHES (sense 2)

brith mi·lah (brit mē′lä) ⟦Heb *berit mila,* covenant of circumcision⟧ *Judaism* the rite of circumcision on the eighth day after birth

☆**Brit·i·cism** (brit′ə siz′əm) *n.* a word, phrase, grammatical construction, etc. originating in or peculiar to British English

Brit·ish (brit′ish) *adj.* ⟦ME *Brittish* < OE *Bryttisc* < *Bret,* pl. *Bryttas,* name of the Celt inhabitants of Britain; of Celt orig.⟧ **1** of the ancient Britons **2** of Great Britain or its people, language, or culture **3** of the Commonwealth —*n.* **1** the language of the ancient Britons **2** BRITISH ENGLISH —**the British** the people of Great Britain: sometimes broadly applied to all the people of the Commonwealth

British Antarctic Territory British territory including that part of Antarctica between 20° and 80° west longitude, the South Orkney Islands, & the South Shetland Islands

British Columbia ⟦after the COLUMBIA[1] River⟧ province of SW Canada, on the Pacific: 357,073 sq mi (924,815 sq km); cap. Victoria: abbrev. *BC* or *B.C.*

British Commonwealth (of Nations) *former name for* THE COMMONWEALTH

British Empire [Brit. Historical] the United Kingdom and the British dominions, colonies, etc.

British English the English language as spoken and written in England and as distinguished esp. from AMERICAN ENGLISH

☆**Brit·ish·er** (-ər) *n.* a person born in Great Britain, esp. in England

British Guiana *former name for* GUYANA

British Honduras *former name for* BELIZE

British India the part of India formerly under direct British rule

British Indian Ocean Territory British territory in the Indian Ocean, between Sri Lanka & Mauritius, consisting of the Chagos Archipelago: 23 sq mi (60 sq km)

British Invasion [*sometimes* **B- i-**] the musical movement of the mid-1960s in which Brit. rock-and-roll groups dominated the U.S. pop music industry: the music is characterized variously by catchy melodies, upbeat tempos, etc.

British Isles group of islands consisting of Great Britain, Ireland, & adjacent islands

Brit·ish·ism (-iz′əm) *n.* BRITICISM

British Museum national museum in London, containing antiquities, one of the largest libraries in the world, a department of natural history, etc.

British Somaliland former British protectorate in E Africa: merged with Italian Somaliland (1960) to form Somalia

British thermal unit a unit of heat equal to about 252 calories; quantity of heat required to raise the temperature of one pound of water one degree Fahrenheit: abbrev. *Btu*

British Virgin Islands *see* VIRGIN ISLANDS

British West Indies former British possessions in the West Indies, including Jamaica, Barbados, the Bahamas, Trinidad & Tobago, etc.

Brit·on (brit′'n) *n.* ⟦ME < OFr *Breton* < L *Brito, Britto*; of Celt orig.: see BRITISH⟧ **1** a member of an early Celtic people living in S Britain at the time of the Roman invasion **2** a person born or living in Great Britain, esp. in England

Brit·ta·ny[1] (brit′'n ē) *n.* a feminine name

Brit·ta·ny[2] (brit′'n ē) metropolitan region of NW France, occupying a peninsula between the English Channel & the Bay of Biscay: 10,505 sq mi (27,208 sq km); chief city, Rennes

Brittany spaniel any of a breed of spaniel with long legs, an orange-and-white or liver-and-white coat, and a very short tail or no tail

Brit·ten (brit′'n), **(Edward) Benjamin** Baron Britten of Aldeburgh 1913-76; Eng. composer

brit·tle (brit′'l) *adj.* ⟦ME *britel* < OE *breotan,* to break to pieces; akin to ON *brjota* < IE **bhreu-* < base **bher-,* to cut with a sharp point⟧ **1** easily broken or shattered because hard and inflexible **2** having a sharp, hard quality [*brittle* tones] **3** stiff and unbending in manner; lacking warmth —☆*n.* a brittle, crunchy candy made of sugar, butter, vanilla, etc. and nuts [peanut *brittle*] —**SYN.** FRAGILE —**brit′tle·ly** *adv.*, **brit′tly** —**brit′tle·ness** *n.*

brit·tle·bush (brit′'l boosh′) *n.* a common desert shrub (*Encelia farinosa*) of the composite family, with brittle stems and bright-yellow ray flowers, found in the SW U.S. and NW Mexico

brittle star any of a subclass (Ophiuroidea) of echinoderms having a central disk and five long, narrow, easily breakable arms that can quickly regenerate

Brit·ton·ic (bri tän′ik) *adj.* ⟦< L *Britto,* gen. *Brittonis* (see BRITON) + -IC⟧ BRYTHONIC

britz·ka or **brits·ka** (brits′kə, brich′kä) *n.* ⟦Pol *bryczka,* dim. of *bryka,* freight wagon⟧ a long, spacious carriage with a folding top

Brix scale (briks) ⟦after A. F. *Brix* (1798-1890), Ger chemist⟧ a scale for measuring the density or concentration of sugar in solution

Br·no (bur′nô) city in the SE Czech Republic

bro (brō) *n., pl.* **bros** [Slang] BROTHER; often, specif., a fellow black male: often used as a familiar term of address

Bro or **bro** *abbrev.* brother

broach (brōch) *n.* ⟦ME *broche,* a pin, peg, spit < OFr *broche, broc* < ML *brocca,* a spike, point < L *broccus,* with projecting teeth; of Celt orig.⟧ **1** a sharp-pointed rod used to hold roasting meat; spit **2** a tapered bit on a metal-cutting machine tool that is pulled or pushed through a hole to enlarge or shape the hole **3** a device for tapping casks **4** a hole made by a broach **5** BROOCH —*vt.* **1** to make a hole in so as to let out liquid; tap (a cask) **2** to enlarge or shape (a hole) with a broach **3** to start a discussion of; bring up; introduce [to *broach* a subject] —**SYN.** UTTER[2] —**broach to** *Naut.* to turn or swing so that the beam faces the waves and wind and there is danger of swamping or capsizing —**broach′er** *n.*

broad (brôd) *adj.* ⟦ME *brod* < OE *brad;* akin to Ger *breit*⟧ **1** of large extent from side to side; wide **2** having great extent or expanse; spacious [*broad* prairies] **3** extending all about; clear; open; full [*broad* daylight] **4** easy to understand; not subtle; obvious [a *broad* hint] **5** strongly marked: said of dialects or accents **6** coarse or ribald [a *broad* joke] **7** tolerant; liberal [to take a *broad* view of a matter] **8** wide in range; not limited [a *broad* variety, a *broad* education] **9** main or general; not detailed [in *broad* outline] **10** *Phonet.* pronounced with the tongue held low and flat in the mouth; open, esp. as the (ä) of *father* —*adv.* in a broad manner; widely —*n.* [Slang] a woman: sometimes considered offensive —**broad′ly** *adv.* —**broad′ness** *n.*

SYN.—**broad** and **wide** both are applied to extent from side to side of surfaces having height or length, **wide** being preferred when the distance between limits is stressed [two feet *wide,* a *wide* aperture], and **broad**, when the full extent of surface is considered [*broad* hips, *broad* plains]; **deep**, in this connection, refers to extent backward, as from the front, an opening, etc. [a *deep* lot, a *deep* cave] —**ANT.** **narrow**

broad arrow **1** an arrow with a broad, barbed head **2** an identification mark in the form of a broad arrow that the British government puts on its property, as formerly on prisoners' uniforms

broad·ax or **broad·axe** (brôd′aks′) *n.* an ax with a broad blade, used as a weapon or for hewing timber

broad·band (-band′) *adj.* designating or of cable, communications devices, etc. that can carry a wide range of frequencies or many channels of data allowing large amounts of information to be transmitted at high speeds —*n.* any of several technologies that allow rapid transmission of data, as by using multiple channels simultaneously

broad-based (-bāst′, -bāst′) *adj.* having a foundation or basis that is wide in range; comprehensive or extensive

broad bean a plant (*Vicia faba*) of the pea family, bearing large, broad pods with flat, edible seeds, used for fodder and as a vegetable

broad·bill (-bil′) *n.* any of various birds with a broad bill, as the scaup and shoveler ducks, spoonbill, etc.

broad-brush or **broad·brush** (-brush′) *adj.* ⟦in allusion to the relative width of the brushstrokes in a painting⟧ **1** not specific; general [a *broad-brush* view] **2** sweeping; indiscriminate [*broad-brush* criticism]

broad·cast (-kast′, -käst′) *vt.* **-cast′** or **-cast′ed, -cast′ing** **1** to scatter (seed) over a broad area rather than sow in drills **2** to spread (information, gossip, etc.) widely **3** to transmit, as to a large audience, by radio, television, or the internet —*vi.* to transmit programs by radio, television, or the internet —*adj.* **1** widely scattered **2** of, for, or by radio, television, or internet broadcasting —*n.* **1** the act of broadcasting **2** a program transmitted by radio, television, or the internet —*adv.* far and wide —**broad′cast′er** *n.*

Broad Church a liberal party of the Anglican Church in the late 19th cent. —**Broad′-Church′** *adj.* —**Broad′-Church′man** *n., pl.* **-men**

broad·cloth (-klôth′) *n.* **1** a fine, smooth woolen cloth: so called because it originally was made on wide looms **2** a fine, smooth cotton, rayon, or silk cloth, used for shirts, pajamas, etc.

broad·en (brôd′'n) *vt., vi.* to widen; expand

broad gauge a width, between the rails of a railroad, greater than standard gauge (56.5 in, or 143.5 cm) —**broad′-gauge′** *adj.*, **broad′-gauged′**

broad jump *former name for* LONG JUMP

broad·leaf (-lēf′) *n.* ☆any of various tobaccos with broad leaves used for making cigars —*adj.* BROAD-LEAVED

broad-leaved (-lēvd′) *adj.* **1** having broad leaves: said of many angiosperms **2** having flat rather than needlelike leaves: said of some evergreen shrubs or trees

broad·loom (-lo͞om′) *adj.* woven on a broad, or wide, loom [*broadloom* carpeting]

broad-mind·ed (-mīn′did, -mīn′did) *adj.* tolerant of opinions and behavior that are unconventional or that differ from one's own; not bigoted; liberal —**broad′-mind′ed·ly** *adv.* —**broad′-mind′ed·ness** *n.*

broad seal the public seal of a state or nation

broad·sheet (-shēt′) *n.* **1** BROADSIDE (*n.* 5*a*) **2** the standard newspaper page, about 14 in by 23 in, with columns running down the full sheet: cf. TABLOID (*n.* 1) **3** [Chiefly Brit.] a newspaper using such a page size, generally regarded as having more serious and in-depth content than a tabloid

broad·side (-sīd′) *n.* **1** the entire side of a ship above the waterline **2** the simultaneous firing of all the guns on one side of a warship **3** a vigorous or abusive attack in words, esp. in a newspaper **4** the broad surface of any large object **5** *a)* a large sheet of paper printed on one side, as with a political message *b)* in 17th-cent. England, a popular ballad printed on such a sheet (also **broadside ballad**) *c)* a large sheet of paper printed on both sides, as with advertising, and often folded —*adv.* **1** with the side turned (*to* something) [a boat drifting helplessly, *broadside* to the waves] **2** directly in the side [the train rammed the car *broadside*] **3** indiscriminately [to level charges *broadside*] —*vt.* **-sid′ed, -sid′ing** to hit or attack broadside or with a broadside

broad-spec·trum (-spek′trəm) *adj.* **1** effective against a wide variety of microorganisms [a *broad-spectrum* antibiotic] **2** showing a wide variety [a *broad-spectrum* array]

broad·sword (-sôrd′) *n.* a sword with a broad, double-edged blade, for slashing rather than thrusting

broad·tail (-tāl′) *n.* KARAKUL: see ASTRAKHAN

Broad·way (brôd′wā′) ⟦transl. of Du *Breed Wegh*⟧ **1** street running north and south through New York City, known as the center of the city's main theater and entertainment section **2** the New York commercial theater or entertainment industry

Brob·ding·nag (bräb′diŋ nag′) *n.* in Swift's *Gulliver's Travels,* a land inhabited by giants about 60 feet tall —**Brob′ding·nag′i·an** (-nag′ē ən) *adj., n.*

bro·cade (brō kād′) *n.* ⟦Sp *brocado* < It *broccato,* orig. pp. of *broccare,* to prick, embroider < *brocco:* see BROACH⟧ a rich cloth with a raised design, as of silk, velvet, gold, or silver, woven into it —*vt.* **-cad′ed, -cad′ing** to weave a raised design into (cloth)

bro·cante (brô känt′) *n.* ⟦Fr⟧ in France, a shop or market where second-hand goods are sold

Bro·ca's area (brō′käz) ⟦after P. P. *Broca* (1824-80), Fr surgeon & anthropologist⟧ a region in the left frontal lobe of the brain associated with speech that controls movements of the tongue, lips, and vocal cords

broc·a·telle or **broc·a·tel** (bräk′ə tel′) *n.* ⟦Fr *brocatelle* < It *broccatello,* dim. of *broccato:* see BROCADE⟧ a heavy, figured cloth like brocade, usually of silk and linen

broc·co·li (bräk′ə lē) *n.* ⟦It, pl. of *broccolo,* a sprout, cabbage sprout, dim. of *brocco:* see BROACH⟧ 1 a plant (*Brassica oleracea* var. *italica*) of the crucifer family, related to the cauliflower but bearing tender shoots with greenish buds cooked as a vegetable 2 any of several strains of cauliflower

broccoli raab (*or* rabe) (räb) ⟦prob. < It *broccoli di rapa,* sprouts of the turnip: see prec. & RAPE[2]⟧ a plant (*Brassica rapa ruvo*) of the crucifer family with close clusters of greenish buds and dark-green, somewhat bitter leaves, cooked together as a vegetable

Broch (bräkh), **Her·mann** (her′män) 1886-1951; Austrian novelist, in the U.S. 1940-51

bro·ché (brō shā′) *adj.* ⟦Fr < *brocher,* to stitch, brocade < *broche:* see BROACH⟧ woven with a raised design

bro·chette (brō shet′) *n.* ⟦Fr, dim. of *broche:* see BROACH⟧ a skewer on which small pieces of meat and vegetables are fixed for broiling

bro·chure (brō shoor′) *n.* ⟦Fr < *brocher,* to stitch: see BROACH⟧ a pamphlet, esp. one advertising or promoting something

brock (bräk) *n.* ⟦ME *brok* < OE *brocc* < Brit **brokkos,* sharp, pointed (in reference to its nose); akin to Welsh *brach,* L *broccus:* see BROACH⟧ [Brit. Dial.] a badger

Brock·en (bräk′ən) mountain in the Harz Mountains, central Germany: 3,747 ft (1,142 m): in German folklore, the meeting place of witches on Walpurgis Night

brock·et (bräk′it) *n.* ⟦ME *broket* < Anglo-Norm *broquet,* yearling (of roe deer) < OFr *broc,* a spit, tine of a stag's horn: see BROACH⟧ 1 a two-year-old, male European red deer during its second stage of antler growth 2 any of a genus (*Mazama*) of small South and Central American deer with short, unbranched antlers

bro·de·rie an·glaise (brô drē än glez′; *E* brō′də rē′ än glāz′) ⟦Fr, lit., English embroidery⟧ needlework, used esp. for garment edging, consisting of embroidered eyelets arranged in decorative patterns

Brod·sky (bräd′skē), **Joseph** 1940-96; Russ.-born poet, in the U.S. after 1972

bro·gan (brō′gən) *n.* ⟦Ir, dim. of *brōg:* see BROGUE[2]⟧ a heavy work shoe, fitting high on the ankle

Bro·glie (brô glē′; *Fr* brô′y′) 1 **Achille Charles Léonce Victor** Duc de Broglie 1785-1870; Fr. statesman under Napoleon I & Louis Philippe 2 **Louis Victor** Prince de Broglie 1892-1987; Fr. physicist: brother of Maurice 3 **(Louis César Victor) Maurice** Duc de Broglie 1875-1960; Fr. physicist: great-grandson of Achille

brogue[1] (brōg) *n.* ⟦< ?⟧ the pronunciation peculiar to a dialect, esp. that of English as spoken by the Irish

brogue[2] (brōg) *n.* ⟦Gael & Ir *brōg,* a shoe < ON *broc,* leg covering: for IE base see BREECH⟧ 1 a coarse shoe of untanned leather, formerly worn in Ireland and Scotland 2 a man's heavy oxford shoe, usually with decorative perforations and a wing tip

broi·der (broi′dər) *vt.* ⟦altered (by assoc. with *broid,* obs. var. of BRAID) < obs. *brouder* < MFr *broder* < OFr *brosder* < Frank **brozdon* < Gmc **bruzda,* point (> BRAD) < IE **bhrazdh-* < base **bhar-,* point, bristle⟧ [Archaic] to embroider —**broi′der·y** *n.*

broil[1] (broil) *vt.* ⟦ME *broilen* < OFr *bruillir,* to broil, roast; prob. by confusion of *bruir,* to burn (< Gmc **brojan,* to brew) & *usler* < L *ustulare,* to singe⟧ 1 to cook by exposing to a flame or other direct source of intense heat 2 to expose directly to intense heat —*vi.* 1 to become broiled 2 to become very heated or angry —*n.* 1 the act or state of broiling 2 anything broiled

broil[2] (broil) *n.* ⟦ME *broilen,* to quarrel, concoct lies < OFr *brouillier,* to dirty; prob. ult. < Frank **broth,* mud, froth⟧ a noisy or violent quarrel; brawl —*vi.* to take part in a broil

broil·er (broi′lər) *n.* ☆1 a pan, grill, etc. for broiling 2 the part of a stove designed for broiling 3 a young chicken suitable for broiling

broke (brōk) *vt., vi. pt. of* BREAK —*adj.* [Informal] 1 having little or no ready money 2 bankrupt —**go broke** [Informal] become penniless or bankrupt —**go for broke** [Slang] to risk everything on an uncertain undertaking

bro·ken (brō′kən) *vt., vi.* ⟦ME < OE *brocen,* pp. of *brecan,* BREAK⟧ *pp. of* BREAK —*adj.* 1 split or cracked into pieces; splintered, fractured, burst, etc. 2 not in working condition; out of order [*a broken* watch] 3 not kept or observed; violated [*a broken* promise] 4 disrupted, as by divorce [*a broken* home] 5 sick, weakened, or beaten [*broken* health, *a broken* spirit] 6 bankrupt 7 not even or continuous; interrupted [*broken* terrain, *broken* tones] 8 not complete [*a broken* set of Shakespeare's works] 9 imperfectly spoken, esp. with reference to grammar and syntax [*broken* English] 10 subdued and trained; tamed 11 [Informal] demoted in rank For phrases, see BREAK —**bro′ken·ly** *adv.* —**bro′ken·ness** *n.*

bro·ken-down (brō′kən doun′) *adj.* 1 sick or worn out, as by old age or disease 2 out of order; useless

bro·ken-field (-fēld′) *adj. Football, Rugby* of or having to do with running in which the ball carrier zigzags so as to go past defenders and avoid being tackled by them

bro·ken·heart·ed (-härt′id) *adj.* crushed by sorrow, grief, or disappointment; inconsolable

broken wind *Vet.Med.* HEAVES

bro·ken-wind·ed (-win′did) *adj.* gasping with or as with the heaves

bro·ker (brō′kər) *n.* ⟦ME *brokour* < Anglo-Norm *broceor* < OFr *brokier, brochier,* to BROACH, tap; orig. sense "wine dealer"⟧ 1 a person who acts as an agent or intermediary in negotiating contracts, buying and selling, etc. 2 STOCKBROKER —*vt., vi.* 1 to act as a broker (for) 2 to negotiate or bargain; specif., to influence the outcome of (a political convention) by negotiating, making secret agreements, etc.

bro·ker·age (brō′kər ij) *n.* 1 the business or office of a broker 2 a broker's fee or commission

bro·ker·ing (brō′kər iŋ) *n.* the work of a broker or brokerage: also [Brit.] **bro·king** (brō′kiŋ)

brol·ly (bräl′ē) *n., pl.* **-lies** ⟦altered < (UM)BRELLA⟧ [Brit. Informal] an UMBRELLA (sense 1)

brom- (brōm) *combining form* BROMO-: used before a vowel

bro·mate (brō′māt′) *n.* ⟦BROM(O)- + -ATE[2]⟧ a salt of bromic acid, containing the univalent, negative radical BrO_3 —*vt.* **-mat′ed, -mat′ing** to treat or combine with a bromate or with bromine: see also BROMINATE

brome (brōm) *n.* ⟦< ModL < L *bromos* < Gr, oats, rustling < *bremein,* to rustle < IE base **bherem-,* to rustle, buzz⟧ any of a large genus (*Bromus*) of grasses of the temperate zone, having closed sheaths and spikelets with awns: a few are crop plants but many are weeds: also **brome′grass′**

bro·me·li·ad (brō mē′lē ad′) *n.* ⟦ModL *Bromelia* (after O. *Bromel,* 1639-1705, Swed botanist) + -AD[1]⟧ any member of the pineapple family of plants, usually having stiff, leathery leaves and spikes of bright flowers, as the pineapple and Spanish moss

bro·mic (brō′mik) *adj.* ⟦BROM(O)- + -IC⟧ of or containing pentavalent bromine

bromic acid a toxic acid, $HBrO_3$, that forms bromate salts: it cannot be prepared in the pure state and is stable only in dilute aqueous solutions

bro·mide (brō′mīd′) *n.* ⟦BROM(O)- + -IDE⟧ 1 a compound in which bromine is combined with a certain element, radical, etc., as silver bromide or methyl bromide 2 potassium bromide, KBr, used in medicine as a sedative ☆3 ⟦from association with dullness of mind⟧ a trite saying; platitude —*SYN.* PLATITUDE

☆**bro·mid·ic** (brō mid′ik) *adj.* ⟦see prec.⟧ trite or dull

bro·mi·nate (brō′mə nāt′) *vt.* **-nat′ed, -nat′ing** *Chem.* to treat or combine with bromine —**bro′mi·na′tion** *n.*

bro·mine (brō′mēn′, -min) *n.* ⟦Fr *brome* < Gr *brōmos,* stench + -INE[3]⟧ a chemical element, one of the halogens, usually in the form of a reddish-brown, corrosive liquid, that volatilizes to form a vapor that has an unpleasant odor and is very irritating to mucous membranes: used in making dyes, in photography, and, in the form of certain compounds, in antiknock motor fuel: symbol, Br; at. no. 35: see the periodic table of elements in the Reference Supplement

bro·mism (-miz′əm) *n. Med.* a poisoned condition caused by overuse of bromides: also **bro′min·ism′** (-min iz′əm)

bro·mize (-mīz′) *vt.* **-mized′, -miz′ing** *Chem.* to treat with bromine or a bromide

Brom·ley (bräm′lē) borough of Greater London, England

Bro·mo (brō′mō) *n.* [*also* **b-**] [Informal] *short for* BROMO-SELTZER

bro·mo- (brō′mō) *combining form* bromine [*bromide*]

Bro·mo-Selt·zer (brō′mō selt′sər) *n.* ⟦former trademark < BROMIDE + SELTZER⟧ [*also* **b- s-**] a compound containing a bromide, sodium bicarbonate, etc., used for relief from headaches and upset stomachs, and as a sedative

Bromp·ton mixture (brämp′tən) ⟦after *Brompton* Chest Hospital, London⟧ a mixture of narcotics, tranquilizers, and alcohol, used to kill pain for terminally ill patients: also **Brompton cocktail**

☆**bronc** (bräŋk) *n.* [Informal] BRONCO

bronch- (bräŋk) *combining form* BRONCHO-: used before a vowel

bron·chi (bräŋ′kī′) *n. pl. of* BRONCHUS

bron·chi·al (-kē əl) *adj.* of or pertaining to the bronchi or bronchioles

bronchial tubes the bronchi and the tubes branching from them

bron·chi·ec·ta·sis (bräŋ′kē ek′tə sis) *n.* ⟦ModL < *bronchus,* BRONCHUS + Gr *ektasis,* a stretching out < *ekteinein,* to stretch out < *ek-,* out + *teinein,* to stretch: see TEND[2]⟧ an irreversible, chronic enlargement of certain bronchial tubes

bron·chi·ole (bräŋ′kē ōl′) *n.* ⟦ModL *bronchiolum,* dim. of LL *bronchia,* the bronchi⟧ any of the small subdivisions of the bronchi

bron·chi·ol·i·tis (bräŋ′kē ōl īt′is) *n.* inflammation of the bronchioles, usually caused by a viral infection and commonly found in infants —**bron′chi·ol·it′ic** (-it′ik) *adj.*

bron·chi·tis (bräŋ kīt′is) *n.* ⟦BRONCH(O)- + -ITIS⟧ an inflammation of the mucous lining of the bronchial tubes —**bron·chit′ic** (-kit′ik) *adj.*

bron·cho (bräŋ′kō) *n., pl.* **-chos** *alt. sp. of* BRONCO

bron·cho- (bräŋ′kō, -kə) ⟦< Gr *bronchos,* windpipe⟧ *combining form* the bronchi [*bronchoscope*]

bron·cho·di·la·tor (bräŋ′kō dī′lāt′ər) *n.* any of various drugs, as epinephrine or theophylline, that open bronchial air passages by relaxing the tightened muscles that surround the bronchial tubes, used to treat asthma, bronchitis, emphysema, etc. —**bron′cho·di·la′tion** (-lā′shən) *n.*

bron·cho·pneu·mo·nia (bräŋ′kō noo mō′nyə, -nyoo-) *n.* inflammation of the bronchi accompanied by inflamed patches in the nearby lobules of the lungs

bron·cho·scope (bräŋ′kō skōp′, -kə-) *n.* ⟦BRONCHO- + -SCOPE⟧ a slender, tubular instrument with a small electric light, for examining or treating the inside of the windpipe or the bronchi, or for removing foreign bodies from them —**bron′cho·scop′ic** (-skäp′ik) *adj.* —**bron′cho·scop′i·cal·ly** *adv.* —**bron′chos′co·py** (-käs′kə pē) *n.*

bron·cho·spasm (bräŋ′kō spaz′əm) *n.* spasmodic contraction of the muscular walls of the bronchial air passages to the lungs, as in asthma, which makes breathing difficult —**bron′cho·spas′tic** (-spas′tik) ***adj.***

bron·chus (bräŋ′kəs) ***n.***, *pl.* **-chi′** (-kī′) ⟦ModL < Gr *bronchos,* windpipe⟧ any of the major air passageways of the lungs; esp., either of the two main branches of the trachea, or windpipe

☆**bron·co** (bräŋ′kō) ***n.***, *pl.* **-cos** ⟦MexSp < Sp, rough < VL **bruncus,* a block⟧ a wild or only partially tamed horse or pony of the W U.S. plains

☆**bron·co·bust·er** (-bus′tər) ***n.*** [Chiefly West] a person who breaks, or tames, broncos —**bron′co·bust′ing** ***n.***

Bron·të (brän′tē) **1 Anne** (pseud. *Acton Bell*) 1820-49; Eng. novelist: sister of Charlotte **2 Charlotte** (Mrs. *Arthur Bell Nicholls;* pseud. *Currer Bell*) 1816-55; Eng. novelist: author of *Jane Eyre* **3 Emily (Jane)** (pseud. *Ellis Bell*) 1818-48; Eng. novelist & poet: author of *Wuthering Heights*: sister of Charlotte

☆**bron·to·saur** (brän′tō sôr′, -tə-) ***n.*** ⟦ModL *Brontosaurus,* genus name < Gr *brontē,* thunder (for IE base see BROME) + *sauros,* lizard: so named by O. C. Marsh (see APATOSAURUS), from the volume of the sound it must have made as it walked⟧ APATOSAURUS: also **bron′to·saur′us** (-əs) —**bron′to·saur′i·an** (-ē ən) ***adj.***

Bronx (bräŋks) ⟦after Jonas *Bronck,* early N.Y. settler⟧ northernmost borough of New York City, between the Harlem River & Long Island Sound: usually called **the Bronx**

☆**Bronx cheer** [Slang] RASPBERRY (sense 3)

bronze (bränz) ***n.*** ⟦Fr < It *bronzo* & ML *bronzium;* assoc. with L *Brundisium,* BRINDISI, but prob. ult. < Pers *biriṅ̌,* copper⟧ **1** *a)* an alloy consisting chiefly of copper and tin *b)* any of certain other alloys with a copper base **2** an article, esp. a sculpture, made of bronze **3** a reddish-brown color **4** *short for* BRONZE MEDAL —***adj.*** of or like bronze —***vt.*** **bronzed, bronz′ing** ⟦Fr *bronzer* < the n.⟧ to give a bronze color or coat to —**bronz′y** ***adj.***

Bronze Age a phase of some human cultures, usually after a Stone Age and before an Iron Age, characterized by bronze tools and weapons, specif. such a phase in the Old World *c.* 3500-1000 B.C.

bronze medal a medal, typically bronze in color or composition, given as an award to the person coming in third in a competition, race, etc.

bronz·er (brän′zər) ***n.*** a cosmetic applied to the face to give the appearance of a suntan

Bronze Star Medal a U.S. military decoration awarded for heroic or meritorious achievement or service in combat not involving aerial flight

brooch (brōch, bro͞och) ***n.*** ⟦ME *broche*: see BROACH⟧ a large ornamental pin with a clasp, worn by women, usually at the neck

brood (bro͞od) ***n.*** ⟦ME & OE *brod,* akin to Ger *brut,* a hatching: for IE base see BREATH⟧ **1** the offspring, or a family of offspring, of animals; esp., a group of birds or fowl hatched at one time and cared for together **2** all the children in a family **3** a group of a particular breed or kind *[*the new *brood* of poets*]* —***vt.*** **1** to sit on and hatch (eggs) **2** to hover over or protect (offspring, etc.) with or as with wings **3** to ponder in a troubled or morbid way *[*to *brood* revenge*]* —***vi.*** **1** to brood eggs or offspring **2** to keep thinking about something in a distressed or troubled way; worry: often with *on, over,* or *about* **3** to hover or loom; hang low —***adj.*** kept for breeding *[*a *brood* hen*]*

brood·er (bro͞od′ər) ***n.*** **1** a person or animal that broods ☆**2** a heated shelter for raising young fowl

brood·mare (-mer′) ***n.*** a mare kept for breeding

brood parasitism a type of parasitism in which a bird (**brood parasite**), as a cowbird or European cuckoo, lays and abandons its eggs in the nest of another species

brood·y (-ē) ***adj.*** **brood′i·er, brood′i·est** **1** ready to brood, as poultry **2** inclined to brood, or dwell moodily on one's own thoughts —**brood′i·ly** ***adv.*** —**brood′i·ness** ***n.***

brook[1] (bro͝ok) ***n.*** ⟦ME *brok* < OE *broc;* akin to OHG *bruoh,* moor, swamp < ?⟧ a small stream, usually not so large as a river

brook[2] (bro͝ok) ***vt.*** ⟦ME *brouken,* to use, enjoy < OE *brucan;* akin to Ger *brauchen*: for IE base see FRUIT⟧ to put up with; endure: usually in the negative *[*I will *brook* no interference*]* —**SYN.** BEAR[1]

Brooke (bro͝ok), **Rupert** 1887-1915; Eng. poet

Brook Farm ⟦descriptive name⟧ a farm near West Roxbury (now part of Boston), Mass., where a group of U.S. writers & scholars set up an experimental community (1841-47) based on cooperative living

brook·ite (bro͝ok′īt′) ***n.*** ⟦after H. J. *Brooke* (1771-1857), Eng mineralogist⟧ the hard, orthorhombic form of titanium dioxide, TiO_2, ranging in color from yellow or brown to black

brook·let (-lit) ***n.*** a little brook

Brook·lyn (bro͝ok′lən) ⟦after *Breukelen,* village in the Netherlands⟧ borough of New York City, on W Long Island —**Brook′lyn·ite′** (-lə nīt′) ***n.***

Brooks (bro͝oks) **1 Gwen·do·lyn (Elizabeth)** (gwen′də lən) 1917-2000; U.S. poet **2 Phillips** 1835-93; U.S. clergyman & writer **3 Van Wyck** (wīk) 1886-1963; U.S. critic & biographer

Brooks Range ⟦after A. H. *Brooks* (1871-1924), U.S. geologist⟧ mountain range extending across N Alas.: highest peak, 9,239 ft (2,816 m)

☆**brook trout** a mottled stream trout (*Salvelinus fontinalis*) of North America

broom (bro͞om, bro͝om) ***n.*** ⟦ME & OE *brom,* brushwood < IE base **bh(e)rem-,* to project, a point > BERM, BRAMBLE⟧ **1** any of a group of flowering shrubs (esp. genera *Cytisus, Genista,* and *Spartium*) of the pea family, often grown for their abundant, usually yellow, flowers **2** any of various tools used for sweeping, consisting of a bundle of stiff fibers, or a brush with stiff bristles, attached to a long handle —***vt.*** to sweep as with a broom

☆**broom·corn** (bro͞om′kôrn′) ***n.*** a cultivated variety of sorghum (*Sorghum bicolor*), the panicles of which are used in making brooms and brushes

broom·rape (-rāp′) ***n.*** ⟦BROOM + RAPE[2], used as transl. of ML *rapum genistae,* lit., broom tuber⟧ any of a genus (*Orobanche*) of the broomrape family of leafless, fleshy, parasitic plants growing on the roots of other plants —***adj.*** designating a family (Orobanchaceae, order Scrophulariales) of dicotyledonous leafless plants, including beechdrops, parasitic on the roots of other plants

broom·stick (-stik′) ***n.*** the long handle of a broom

Bros or **bros** *abbrev.* brothers

brose (brōz) ***n.*** ⟦Scot, altered < ME *broues,* beef broth⟧ a dish made by stirring boiling water or milk into oatmeal

broth (brôth, bräth) ***n.*** ⟦ME & OE; akin to OHG *brod*: for IE base see BREAD⟧ a clear, thin soup made by boiling meat, or sometimes cereals or vegetables, in water

broth·el (bräth′əl, brôth′-) ***n.*** ⟦ME, wretched person < OE *brothen,* pp. of *broethan,* to waste away, go to ruin; confused with BORDEL⟧ a place where prostitutes may be engaged for hire

broth·er (bruth′ər) ***n.***, *pl.* **broth′ers**; chiefly religious, **breth′ren** ⟦ME < OE *brothor* < IE base **bhrāter* > Goth *brothar,* L *frater,* OIr *brāthir,* Sans *bhrātar,* Gr *phratēr*⟧ **1** a man or boy as he is related to the other children of his parents: sometimes also used of animals **2** a man or boy related to one by having a parent in common; half brother **3** a stepbrother **4** a foster brother **5** a close male friend who is like a brother **6** a fellow human being **7** *a)* a male fellow member of the same race, church, profession, organization, etc. *[*fraternity *brother]* ☆*b)* [Slang] a fellow black who is male ☆*c)* [Slang] a black man or boy **8** [*often* **B-**] a lay member of a men's religious order **9** [Informal] any man: often used as a familiar term of address —***interj.*** [Slang] used to provide emphasis, often at the beginning of one's remarks

broth·er·hood (-ho͝od′) ***n.*** ⟦ME *brotherhod, brotherhede*: see prec. & -HOOD⟧ **1** the state of being a brother or brothers **2** an association of men united in a common interest, work, creed, etc., as a fraternity, religious order, or labor union **3** a belief in, or feeling of, unity and cooperation among men or among all people

broth·er-in-law (-in lô′) ***n.***, *pl.* **broth′ers-in-law′** **1** the brother of one's husband or wife **2** the husband of one's sibling **3** the husband of a sibling of one's wife or husband

Brother Jonathan ⟦apparently first applied to New England militia besieging Boston by Brit soldiers evacuating the city (March, 1776)⟧ [Historical] the United States or its people personified: predecessor of Uncle Sam

broth·er·ly (-lē) ***adj.*** **1** of a brother or brothers **2** having traits considered typical of brothers; friendly, kind, helpful, etc. —***adv.*** [Archaic] as a brother —**broth′er·li·ness** ***n.***

brougham (bro͞om, brōm; bro͞o′əm, brō′-) ***n.*** ⟦after Lord *Brougham* (1778-1868), Brit political leader⟧ **1** a closed, four-wheeled carriage with the driver's seat outside **2** any of certain early types of automobile; esp., *a)* an electrically powered automobile similar to a coupe *b)* a limousine with the driver's seat unenclosed

brougham

brought (brôt) ***vt.*** ⟦OE *broht,* pt., *(ge)broht,* pp.⟧ *pt. & pp. of* BRING

brou·ha·ha (bro͞o′hä hä′) ***n.*** ⟦Fr; orig., in medieval theater, cry of devil disguised as clergy: said to be < Heb *bārūkh hab-ba,* blessed be he who comes, formula used by Levites to welcome to the Temple⟧ a noisy stir or wrangle; hubbub; uproar; commotion

brow (brou) ***n.*** ⟦ME *broue* < OE *bru* < IE base **bhru-,* eyebrow > Sans *bhrū-h,* ON *brūn*⟧ **1** the eyebrow **2** the forehead **3** [Literary] a facial expression *[*her troubled *brow]* **4** the projecting top edge of a steep hill or cliff

bro·wal·li·a (brō wal′ē ə, -wal′yə) ***n.*** ⟦after J. *Browall* (1707-55), Swed botanist⟧ any of a genus (*Browallia*) of plants of the nightshade family with ornamental blue or white flowers

brow·band (brou′band′) ***n.*** the part of a bridle across the animal's forehead, in front of the ears, that holds the bridle in place

brow·beat (-bēt′) ***vt.*** **-beat′, -beat′en, -beat′ing** to intimidate with harsh, stern looks and talk; bully

brown (broun) ***adj.*** ⟦ME *broun* < OE *brun* < IE base **bhrou-no-* < **bher-,* brown: see BEAR[2]⟧ **1** having the color of chocolate or coffee, a combination of red, black, and yellow **2** having a naturally dark or tanned skin; dark-skinned —***n.*** **1** brown color **2** brown pigment or dye — ***vt., vi.*** to make or become brown, esp. by exposure to sunlight, as in tanning, or to heat, as in cooking —**be browned off** [Slang] to be angry, disgusted, etc. —☆**do up brown** [Slang] to do completely or perfectly —**brown′ish** ***adj.*** —**brown′ness** ***n.***

Brown (broun) **1 Capability** (born *Lancelot Brown*) 1715?-83; Eng. landscape artist **2 Charles Brock·den** (bräk′dən) 1771-1810; U.S. novelist **3 Herbert Charles** 1912-2004; U.S. organic chemist, born in Great Britain **4 John** 1800-59; U.S. abolitionist: as part of a plan for an uprising among slaves, he led a raid on an arsenal at Harpers Ferry: hanged for treason

brown algae any of a class (Phaeophyceae, division Chromophycota) of large, photosynthetic, marine thallophytic algae, including kelp and fucus, having a brown pigment that obscures the green color of chlorophyll

☆**brown-bag** (-bag′) *vt., vi.* **-bagged′**, **-bag′ging** **1** to carry (one's lunch) to work or school, as in a brown paper bag **2** to bring (one's own liquor) into a restaurant, nightclub, etc. which is not permitted to sell liquor but may furnish setups

brown bear any of various tan to dark-brown bears (*Ursus arctos*), found in Europe, North America, etc., including the grizzly bear and Kodiak bear

brown belt a brown-colored belt or sash awarded to a skilled practitioner in many of the martial arts, esp. in judo or karate, in which it is an award just below highest: see also BLACK BELT

☆**brown bet·ty** (bet′ē) [*also* **b- B-**] a baked apple pudding made with butter, spices, sugar, and bread crumbs

brown bread **1** bread made of dark flour **2** BOSTON BROWN BREAD

brown coal LIGNITE

brown dwarf *pl.* **brown dwarfs** or occas. **brown dwarves** a celestial object consisting of a body of gas that gives off a small amount of radiation but lacks sufficient mass to initiate the nuclear fusion that characterizes true stars

Browne (broun) **1 Charles Far·rar** (far′ər) *see* WARD, Artemus **2 Sir Thomas** 1605-82; Eng. physician & writer

brown fat a brownish tissue, rich in unsaturated fats, stored in certain areas of the body by a hibernating animal: it prevents freezing and may help to warm the animal as it awakens

brown·field (broun′fēld′) *n.* ⟦from connotative use of BROWN to contrast with the original "greenness" of the land⟧ real estate, esp. the land, that is heavily contaminated with industrial pollutants, as an abandoned industrial site in a large city

☆**brown goods** ⟦so called with reference to the wooden cabinets of early TVs, radios, etc.⟧ video and audio devices, as TV sets, tape recorders, etc.: cf. WHITE GOODS (sense 2)

Brown·i·an movement (brou′nē ən) ⟦after R. *Brown* (1773-1858), Brit botanist who described it⟧ the constant, random, zigzag movement of small particles dispersed in a fluid medium, caused by collision with molecules of the fluid: also **Brownian motion**

brown·ie (brou′nē) *n.* **1** *Folklore* a small brown elf or goblin that does helpful tasks for people at night **2** [**B-**] a member of the division of the Girl Scouts for girls six to eight years of age: in full **Brownie Girl Scout** ☆**3** a kind of cookie that is a small bar or square of flat, dense, rich chocolate cake, often containing nuts

☆**Brownie point** ⟦< ? the notion that merit points are awarded to Brownie Girl Scouts⟧ [*also* **b- p-**] approval, facetiously regarded as a unit of credit, that is gained, as from a superior, for a relatively unimportant act

Brown·ing (brou′niŋ) **1 Elizabeth Barrett** 1806-61; Eng. poet: wife of Robert **2 John Moses** 1855-1926; U.S. inventor of firearms **3 Robert** 1812-89; Eng. poet

brown lung (disease) a chronic disease of the lungs caused by inhalation of fine textile fibers, esp. cotton; byssinosis

☆**brown-nose** (broun′nōz′) [Slang] *vt., vi.* **-nosed′**, **-nos′ing** ⟦from the image of currying favor by kissing someone's buttocks⟧ to seek favor or approval from (someone) by obsequious behavior; fawn (on) —*n.* one who brown-noses: also **brown′-nos′er** *n.*

brown·out (-out′) *n.* a dimming or partial elimination of lights in a city, as during an electric power shortage

brown rat a common, omnivorous large rat (*Rattus norvegicus*) that swims and dives well, usually lives in underground burrows, and spreads various diseases: the mutant form, a white rat, is used for medical experiments

brown recluse spider ⟦so named from its color and its habit of staying in dark corners of buildings or under rocks⟧ a very poisonous, medium-sized spider (*Loxosceles reclusa*), common in the U.S., having a violin-shaped mark on its cephalothorax and only six eyes

brown rice rice that retains its brown outer coating

brown rot a disease of some fruits, caused by a fungus (*Monilinia fructicola*) and marked by blight, rotting, etc.

brown·shirt (-shurt′) *n.* ⟦so named from the *brown shirt* that was part of the uniform of a storm trooper⟧ **1** [*often* **B-**] a storm trooper in Nazi Germany **2** any Nazi; Hitlerite

brown·stone (-stōn′) *n.* **1** a reddish-brown sandstone, used for building **2** a house with a facade of brownstone

brown study ⟦orig., somber thought < early sense of BROWN, somber, gloomy⟧ a condition of being deep in thought; reverie

brown sugar soft sugar prepared in such a way that the crystals retain a thin, brown coating of dark syrup

Browns·ville (brounz′vil) ⟦after Fort *Brown*, named for Maj. J. *Brown* (1789-1846), killed in defending it⟧ city & port in S Tex., on the Rio Grande

Brown Swiss a hardy breed of large, brown dairy cattle, first raised in Switzerland

brown-tail moth (broun′tāl′) ⟦so named from the *brown* coloration of the end of its abdomen⟧ a white moth (*Euproctis chrysorrhoea*) whose larvae are harmful to trees and cause an irritating skin rash: also written **browntail moth**

brown trout a golden-brown European trout (*Salmo trutta*), widely stocked in North America as a game fish

browse (brouz) *n.* ⟦OFr *brouz*, pl. of *broust*, a bud or shoot < OS *brustian*, to sprout: for IE base see BREAST⟧ **1** leaves, twigs, and young shoots of trees or shrubs, which animals feed on **2** the act of browsing —*vt.* **browsed**, **brows′ing** ⟦ME *brousen* < OFr *brouster* < the n.⟧ **1** to nibble at (leaves, twigs, etc.) **2** to graze on **3** to examine casually; skim **4** *Comput.* to look through information on (the internet, a website, etc.), as with a browser —*vi.* **1** to nibble at leaves, twigs, etc. **2** *a)* to look through a book or books casually, reading passages here and there *b)* to look casually over articles for sale **3** to view or look over casually any collection or gathering, as in searching for items of interest **4** *Comput.* to look through information on the internet, as with a browser —**brows′a·ble** *adj.*

brows·er (brou′zər) *n.* **1** a person or thing that browses **2** *Comput.* software designed to enable a user to access and display data that is on the World Wide Web

brrr or **brr** (bur) *interj.* ⟦echoic: suggestive of shivering⟧ used to signify that one feels cold

Bru·beck (bro͞o′bek), **Dave** (born *David Warren Brubeck*) 1920-2012; U.S. jazz pianist & composer

Bruce[1] (bro͞os) *n.* ⟦Scot, after Fr *Brieuse*, locality in France⟧ a masculine name

Bruce[2] (bro͞os) **1 Len·ny** (len′ē) (born *Leonard Alfred Schneider*) 1925-66; U.S. comedian **2 Robert (the)** 1274-1329; king of Scotland (as *Robert I*, 1306-29): won independence of Scotland from England

bru·cel·lo·sis (bro͞o′sə lō′sis) *n.* ⟦< ModL, after Sir David *Bruce* (1855-1931), Scot physician + -OSIS⟧ a disease, esp. in humans and cattle, caused by bacteria (genus *Brucella*): see UNDULANT FEVER

Bruch (bro͝okh), **Max** 1838-1920; Ger. composer

bru·cine (bro͞o′sēn′, -sin) *n.* ⟦after J. *Bruce* (1730-94), Scot explorer⟧ a bitter, poisonous alkaloid, $C_{23}H_{26}N_2O_4$, found in seeds of nux vomica and other related plants: used as a lubricant additive and, in medicine, as a local anesthetic

Bruck·ner (bro͝ok′nər), **An·ton** (an′tän) 1824-96; Austrian composer

Brue·gel or **Brue·ghel** (brü′gəl, broi′-) **1 Jan** (yän) 1568-1625; Fl. painter: son of Pieter **2 Pie·ter** (pē′tər) 1525?-69; Fl. painter of peasant life

Brug·ge (bro͝og′ə) city in NW Belgium: Fr. name **Bruges** (brüzh)

Bru·in (bro͞o′in) *n.* ⟦Du, brown⟧ **1** the bear in the medieval beast epic *Reynard the Fox* **2** [*also* **b-**] a name for any bear in fable and folklore

bruise (bro͞oz) *vt.* **bruised**, **bruis′ing** ⟦ME *bruisen* < OE *brysan*, to crush, pound < IE base **bhreus-*, to smash, crush; ME form & meaning infl. by OFr *bruisier*, to break, shatter < Gaul **brus-* < same IE base⟧ **1** to injure (tissue), as by a blow, without breaking the skin but causing discoloration **2** to injure the surface or outside of, causing spoilage, denting, etc. [*bruised* peaches, a *bruised* auto fender] **3** to crush with or as with mortar and pestle **4** to hurt (the feelings, spirit, etc.) —*vi.* **1** to bruise tissue, a surface, etc. **2** to be or become bruised —*n.* **1** a bruised area of tissue, of a surface, etc. **2** an injury to one's feelings, spirit, etc.

bruis·er (bro͞o′zər) *n.* [Informal] a strong, pugnacious man

bruit (bro͞ot) *n.* ⟦ME < OFr, noise, uproar, rumor < *bruire*, to rumble, prob. < L *rugire*, to roar; ? infl. by VL **bragire*, to bray⟧ [Archaic] **1** clamor **2** rumor —*vt.* to spread a report of; rumor: often with *about*

Bru·maire (brü mer′) *n.* ⟦Fr < *brume*, fog, mist < L *bruma*: see fol.⟧ the second month (Oct. 22-Nov. 20) of the FRENCH REVOLUTIONARY CALENDAR

bru·mal (bro͞o′məl) *adj.* ⟦L *brumalis* < *bruma*, winter, shortest day of the year < **brevima* < *brevissima*, superl. of *brevis*, BRIEF⟧ [Archaic] of winter; wintry

brume (bro͞om) *n.* ⟦Fr < L *bruma*: see prec.⟧ [Rare] mist; fog; vapor —**bru·mous** (bro͞o′məs) *adj.*

brum·ma·gem (brum′ə jəm) *adj.* ⟦dial. pronun. of BIRMINGHAM (in ME, *Bremingeham*), with ref. to counterfeit coins & cheap jewelry once made there⟧ [Informal] cheap and gaudy —*n.* [Informal] anything cheap and gaudy, esp. jewelry not made of gems and precious metals

Brummell, **George Bryan** *see* BEAU BRUMMELL[2]

brunch (brunch) *n.* ⟦BR(EAKFAST) + (L)UNCH⟧ a late first meal of the day that takes the place of both breakfast and lunch —*vi.* to eat brunch —**brunch′er** *n.*

Brun·dis·i·um (brən diz′ē əm) *Latin name for* BRINDISI

Bru·nei (bro͞o nī′) independent sultanate on the N coast of Borneo, consisting of two enclaves in the Malaysian state of Sarawak: under British protection from 1888 to 1983; member of the Commonwealth: 2,228 sq mi (5,770 sq km); cap. Bandar Seri Begawan

Bru·nel (bro͞o nel′, bro͞o-), Sir **Marc Is·am·bard** (iz′əm bärd′) 1769-1849; Eng. engineer, born in France

Bru·nel·les·chi (bro͞o′nel les′kē), **Fi·lip·po** (fē lēp′pô) 1377-1446; Florentine architect

bru·net (bro͞o net′) *adj.* ⟦Fr < OFr, dim. of *brun*, brown < OHG, BROWN⟧ **1** having black or dark-brown hair, often along with dark eyes and a dark complexion **2** having a dark color: said of hair, eyes, or skin —*n.* a brunet person

bru·nette (-net′) *adj.* ⟦Fr, fem. of prec.⟧ BRUNET —*n.* a brunette woman or girl

Brun·hild (bro͞on′hilt′, -hild′) *n.* ⟦MHG *Brünhild* < OHG *brunna*, armor + *hilti* (or OS *hild*), fight; hence, fighter in armor⟧ in the *Nibelungenlied*, a queen of Iceland whom Gunther, king of Burgundy, gets as his bride with the help of Siegfried's magic: cf. BRYNHILD

☆**bru·ni·zem** (bro͞o′nə zem′) *n.* ⟦coined (1938) by F. F. Riecken and G. Smith, U.S. agronomists < *bruni-*, brown (suggested by Fr *brun*: see BRUNET) + Russ *černozem*, black earth: see CHERNOZEM⟧ any of several dark-brown prairie soils

Bru·no¹ (bro͞o′nō) *n.* ⟦OHG < *brun,* BROWN⟧ a masculine name
Bru·no² (bro͞o′nō) 1 Saint (1030?-1101); Ger. monk: founder of the Carthusians: his day is Oct. 6: also **Saint Bruno of Cologne** 2 **Gior·da·no** (jôr dä′nô) 1548-1600; It. philosopher: burned at the stake by the Inquisition
Bruns·wick (brunz′wik) 1 former duchy (13th-19th cent.) in NC Europe: now part of the German state of Lower Saxony 2 city in NC Germany, in the state of Lower Saxony
Brunswick stew ⟦after *Brunswick* County, Va., where first made⟧ a stew originally made with squirrel and onions, and now usually with rabbit or chicken and corn, okra, onions, tomatoes, lima beans, etc.
brunt (brunt) *n.* ⟦ME *bront* < ? ON *bruna,* to rush⟧ 1 the shock (of an attack) or impact (of a blow) 2 the heaviest or hardest part *[to bear the brunt of the blame]*
bru·schet·ta (bro͞o sket′ə, -shet′ə) *n.* ⟦It < pp. of *bruscare,* to burn, toast⟧ toasted bread rubbed with garlic and drizzled with olive oil, often topped as with chopped tomatoes and herbs
brush¹ (brush) *n.* ⟦ME *brushe* < OFr *broce, brosse,* bush, brushwood < VL **bruscia* < Gmc **bruskaz,* underbrush: for IE base see BREAST⟧ 1 BRUSHWOOD ☆2 sparsely settled country, covered with wild scrub growth 3 *a)* a device having bristles, hairs, or wires fastened into a hard back, with or without a handle attached: brushes are used for cleaning, polishing, painting, smoothing the hair, etc. *b)* a device of wires attached in a fanlike spread to a handle, used as on drums or cymbals for a swishing or muted effect 4 the act of brushing 5 a light, grazing stroke *[a brush of the hand]* 6 BRUSHWORK 7 a bushy tail, esp. that of a fox ☆8 [Slang] BRUSHOFF 9 *Elec. a)* a piece, plate, rod, or bundle of carbon, copper, etc. used as a conductor between an external circuit and a revolving part, as in a motor *b)* BRUSH DISCHARGE —*vt.* 1 to use a brush on; clean, polish, paint, smooth, etc. with a brush 2 to apply, spread, remove, etc. with a stroke or strokes as of a brush 3 to go over lightly, as with a brush 4 to touch or graze in passing —*vi.* to move so as to push lightly aside, skim, or graze past something —**brush aside** (or **away**) 1 to sweep out of the way 2 to dismiss from consideration —☆**brush off** [Slang] to dismiss or get rid of abruptly or rudely —**brush up** 1 to make neat or presentable 2 to refresh one's memory or skill: often with *on [to brush up on one's French]*
brush² (brush) *vi.* ⟦ME *bruschen,* rush < ? OFr *brosser,* to travel (? through woods), beat underbrush for game: see prec.⟧ to hurry —*n.* a short, quick fight, skirmish, etc. *[a brush with the law]*
brush·back pitch (brush′bak′) *Baseball* a fast ball deliberately thrown at or too near a batter's head
brush cut ⟦descriptive⟧ CREW CUT
brush discharge a luminous electric discharge, weaker than a spark, characterized by a crackling sound and glowing fine lines with a brushlike appearance, as in the air surrounding a pointed conductor at high potential
brushed (brusht) *adj.* processed by brushing so as to raise the nap: said of some fabrics or types of leather
☆**brush fire** 1 a fire in brushwood 2 a sudden flare-up, as of a military nature, that threatens to spread or intensify unless brought under control
brush·less (brush′lis) *adj.* not using or requiring a brush or brushes *[a brushless car wash, brushless shaving cream]*
☆**brush·off** (-ôf′) *n.* [Slang] an abrupt or rude dismissal, esp. in the phrase **give** (or **get**) **the brushoff**
brush·stroke (-strōk′) *n.* a mark left on a surface as a result of the application of paint with a paintbrush, often with respect to its distinctive texture, thickness, etc.
brush·wood (-wood′) *n.* 1 chopped-off or broken-off tree branches 2 a thick growth of small trees and shrubs; underbrush; brush
brush·work (-wurk′) *n.* 1 work done with a brush; painting 2 a characteristic way of putting on paint with a brush *[Renoir's brushwork]*
brush·y (-ē) *adj.* **brush′i·er, brush′i·est** 1 bristly; brushlike; bushy 2 covered with brushwood or underbrush —**brush′i·ness** *n.*
brusque (brusk; *chiefly Brit* bro͝osk, bro͝osk) *adj.* ⟦Fr < It *brusco* < ML *bruscus,* brushwood; prob. akin to BRUSH¹, but infl. by It *rusco* < L *ruscum,* butcher's-broom⟧ rough and abrupt in manner or speech; curt: also **brusk** —*SYN.* BLUNT —**brusque′ly** *adv.* —**brusque′ness** *n.*
brus·que·rie (brüs kə rē′) *n.* ⟦Fr < *brusque:* see prec.⟧ brusqueness; curtness
Brus·sels (brus′əlz) capital of Belgium, in the central part: headquarters of the European Union: Fl. name **Brus·sel** (brö′səl)
Brussels carpet ⟦after prec., where it was made⟧ a patterned carpeting made of small loops of colored woolen yarn in a linen warp
Brussels lace ⟦after BRUSSELS, where orig. made⟧ 1 [Historical] a bobbin or needlepoint lace with a raised design 2 a machine-made lace with an appliquéd design
Brussels sprout (brus′əl) ⟦after BRUSSELS: prob. first cultivated in quantity there⟧ 1 *[often pl., with sing. or pl. v.]* a plant (*Brassica oleracea* var. *gemmifera*) of the crucifer family that bears miniature cabbagelike heads along an erect stem 2 one of these edible heads
brut (brüt; *E* bro͞ot) ⟦Fr: see BRUTE⟧ *adj.* very dry: said esp. of champagne to which the minimum amount of sugar has been added

Brussels sprout

bru·tal (bro͞ot′'l) *adj.* ⟦ME & OFr < ML *brutalis*⟧ 1 [Obs.] of or belonging to beasts; animal 2 like a brute; cruel and unfeeling; savage, violent, ruthless, etc. 3 very harsh or rigorous *[a brutal winter]* 4 plain and direct, although distressing in effect *[brutal facts]* —*SYN.* CRUEL —**bru′tal·ly** *adv.*
Bru·tal·ism (bro͞ot′'l iz′əm) [*also* **b-**] a style of architecture that originated in England in the 1950s, characterized by stark, massive forms having repetitive angular features and by coarsely textured exposed concrete —**Bru′tal·ist** *n., adj.* —**Bru′tal·is′tic** *adj.*
bru·tal·i·ty (bro͞o tal′ə tē) *n.* 1 the condition or quality of being brutal 2 *pl.* **-ties** a brutal or savage act, treatment, etc.
bru·tal·ize (bro͞ot′'l īz′) *vt.* **-ized′, -iz′ing** 1 to make brutal 2 to treat in a brutal way —*vi.* to become brutal —**bru′tal·i·za′tion** *n.*
brute (bro͞ot) *adj.* ⟦ME & OFr *brut* < L *brutus,* heavy, dull, irrational, via Osco-Umb < IE base **gwer-,* heavy > Gr *barys,* L *gravis*⟧ 1 lacking the ability to reason *[a brute beast]* 2 having no consciousness or feelings; insensate *[the brute force of nature]* 3 of or like an animal; specif., brutal, cruel, gross, sensual, stupid, etc. —*n.* 1 an animal 2 a person who is brutal or very stupid, gross, sensual, etc.
brut·ish (bro͞ot′ish) *adj.* of or like a brute; savage, gross, stupid, sensual, irrational, etc. —**brut′ish·ly** *adv.* —**brut′ish·ness** *n.*
Bru·tus (bro͞ot′əs), **(Marcus Junius)** 85?-42 B.C.; Rom. statesman & general: one of the conspirators who murdered Julius Caesar
Bru·xelles (brü sel′) *Fr. name for* BRUSSELS
brux·ism (bruk′siz′əm) *n.* ⟦< Gr *ebryxa,* aorist root of *brykein,* to gnash the teeth + -ISM⟧ the habit of unconsciously grinding one's teeth, usually while asleep
Bry·an¹ (brī′ən) *n.* a masculine name: see BRIAN
Bry·an² (brī′ən), **William Jen·nings** (jen′iŋz) 1860-1925; U.S. politician & orator
Bry·ansk (brē änsk′; *Russ* bryänsk) city in W European Russia
Bry·ant (brī′ənt), **William Cul·len** (kul′ən) 1794-1878; U.S. poet & journalist
Bryce (brīs), Viscount **James** 1838-1922; Eng. jurist, statesman, & historian, born in Ireland
Bryn·hild (brin′hild′) *n.* ⟦ON *Brynhildr* < *brynja,* armor + *hildr,* fight⟧ *Norse Myth.* a Valkyrie awakened from an enchanted sleep by Sigurd: deceived by him into marrying Gunnar, she brings about Sigurd's death and then kills herself: cf. BRUNHILD
bry·ol·o·gy (brī äl′ə jē) *n.* ⟦< Gr *bryon,* moss, lichen (< *bryein,* to sprout) + -LOGY⟧ the branch of botany dealing with bryophytes —**bry′o·log′i·cal** (-ə läj′i kəl) *adj.* —**bry·ol′o·gist** *n.*
bry·o·ny (brī′ə nē) *n., pl.* **-nies** ⟦L *bryonia* < Gr *bryōnia* < *bryein:* see prec.⟧ any of a genus (*Bryonia*) of perennial vines of the gourd family with large fleshy roots and greenish flowers
bry·o·phyte (brī′ō fīt′, brī′ə-) *n.* ⟦< ModL < Gr *bryon,* moss + -PHYTE⟧ any of a division (Bryophyta) of plants consisting of the mosses and liverworts —**bry′o·phyt′ic** (-fit′ik) *adj.*
bry·o·zo·an (brī′ō zō′ən, brī′ə-) *n.* ⟦< ModL < Gr *bryon,* moss + -ZO(A) + -AN⟧ any of a phylum (Bryozoa) of minute water animals that form branching, mosslike colonies and reproduce by budding
Bryth·on (brith′ən) *n.* ⟦Welsh < Celt base of L *Brito, Britto:* see BRITON⟧ 1 a member of an early Celtic people living in Britain 2 a speaker of a Brythonic language
Bry·thon·ic (bri thän′ik) *n.* the subdivision of the Celtic branch of Indo-European that includes Cornish, Welsh, and Breton —*adj.* designating or of these languages or the peoples that speak them
bs *abbrev.* 1 balance sheet 2 bill of sale 3 [Slang] bullshit
BS *abbrev.* 1 Bachelor of Science: also **B.S.** 2 [Slang] bullshit
BSA *abbrev.* 1 Bachelor of Science in Agriculture: also **B.S.A.** 2 Boy Scouts of America
BSc or **B.Sc.** *abbrev.* ⟦L *Baccalaureus Scientiae*⟧ Bachelor of Science
BScEd or **B.Sc.Ed.** *abbrev.* Bachelor of Science in Education
☆**B-school** (bē′sko͞ol′) *n.* [Informal] a business school or business college
BSE (bē′es′ē′) *n.* ⟦*b(ovine) s(pongiform) e(ncephalopathy)*, technical term for the disease⟧ MAD COW DISEASE
B side 1 *a)* the side of a phonograph SINGLE (*n.* 1d) opposite the side containing the featured performance; flip side *b)* the recording contained on this side 2 an extra recording released along with a featured performance, as on a CD
bskt *abbrev.* basket
bsmt *abbrev.* basement
B.S.N. or **BSN** *abbrev.* Bachelor of Science in Nursing
BST *abbrev.* bovine somatotropin: see BOVINE GROWTH HORMONE
Bt¹ (bē′tē′) *n.* ⟦*B(acillus) t(huringiensis)*⟧ 1 a Gram-positive, rod-shaped soil bacterium (*Bacillus thuringiensis*) having spores that produce a toxic protein that kills only specific insect larvae as they are feeding 2 this toxic protein, used as an insecticide and in genetic engineering to produce insect-resistant crops
Bt² *abbrev.* Baronet
BTh or **B.Th.** *abbrev.* ⟦L *Baccalaureus Theologiae*⟧ Bachelor of Theology
btry *abbrev.* battery (of artillery)
Btu *abbrev.* British thermal unit(s): also **BTU** or **btu**
BTW *abbrev.* by the way: also **btw**
B2B *abbrev.* ⟦informal sp., where *2* represents homophone *to*⟧ business-to-business

bu *abbrev.* 1 bureau 2 bushel(s)

☆**bub** (bub) *n.* ⟦< Ger *bube,* boy⟧ [Slang] brother; boy; buddy: used in direct address

bu·bal or **bu·bale** (byōō′bəl) *n.* ⟦< ModL *Bubalis* < Gr *boubalis:* see fol.⟧ a rare, N African subspecies of the large, reddish hartebeest (*Alcelaphus buselaphus*): also **bu′ba·lis′** (-bə lis′)

bu·ba·line (byōō′bə līn′, -lin) *adj.* ⟦L *bubalinus* < *bubalus* < Gr *boubalos:* see BUFFALO⟧ 1 of the bubal or other similar hartebeest 2 of or like a buffalo

Bub·ba (bub′ə) *n.* [*also* **b-**] [Chiefly South] [Slang] 1 brother: sometimes used as a familiar term of address 2 close friend 3 a man of the Southern U.S., variously characterized as easygoing, companionable, assertively masculine, uneducated, bigoted, violent, etc.

☆**bub·be** (bub′ē, boob′-; -ə) *n.* ⟦< Yiddish *bube*⟧ [*also in italics*] [Informal] a grandmother or a grandmotherly old woman: also **bub′bie**

bub·ble (bub′əl) *n.* ⟦ME *bobel,* of echoic orig., as in MDu *bubbel*⟧ 1 a very thin film of liquid forming a ball around air or gas [*soap bubbles*] 2 a tiny ball of air or gas in a liquid or solid, as in carbonated water, glass, etc. 3 anything shaped like a bubble, sphere, or hemisphere, as a plastic or glass dome 4 *a)* anything that is ephemeral or insubstantial *b)* any idea, scheme, etc. that seems plausible at first but quickly shows itself to be worthless or misleading 5 a condition or period of extreme overvaluation, as in the market for stocks or real estate, resulting from wildly speculative buying 6 the act, process, or sound of bubbling —*vi.* **-bled, -bling** ⟦ME *bobelen*⟧ 1 to make bubbles; rise in bubbles; boil; foam; effervesce 2 to make a boiling or gurgling sound —*vt.* 1 to form bubbles in; make bubble ☆2 [Informal] to cause (a baby) to burp —**bubble over** 1 to overflow, as boiling liquid 2 to be unrestrained in expressing one's enthusiasm, zest, etc. —☆**on the bubble** [Informal] in a situation in which the outcome is uncertain but already in the process of being determined or decided

bubble and squeak ⟦so named in allusion to the sounds of cooking and frying⟧ [Brit.] a dish consisting of cooked cabbage and potatoes, and sometimes meat, fried together

☆**bubble bath** 1 a bath perfumed by a solution, powder, etc. that forms surface bubbles 2 such a solution, powder, etc.

☆**bubble chamber** a container filled with a superheated, transparent liquid in which charged atomic particles and their collisions can be studied by photographing the bubbles and violent boiling that occur along their paths

☆**bubble gum** 1 a kind of chewing gum for blowing large bubbles 2 a kind of rock music with simple lyrics and melodies that is directed at teenage and younger audiences and variously regarded as insipid, unimaginative, unsophisticated, etc.: also written **bub′ble·gum′** *n.*

bub·ble·head (bub′əl hed′) *n.* [Slang] a person who is silly, frivolous, ignorant, etc. —**bub′ble·head′ed** *adj.*

☆**bubble memory** ⟦from the appearance of these areas under a microscope⟧ a solid-state computer memory device that stores bits of data by means of microscopic magnetized areas (*magnetic bubbles*) in sheets of a semiconductor

bub·bler (bub′lər) *n.* ☆a drinking fountain in which water is forced up in a small arc from a nozzle

☆**bub·ble-top** (bub′əl täp′) *n.* a bulletproof, transparent dome, as over the rear section of an automobile

Bubble Wrap *trademark for* a packaging material made of clear plastic sheets with small bubbles of air to absorb shock — [**b- w-**] any packaging material like this

bub·bly (bub′lē) *adj.* **-bli·er, -bli·est** 1 full of, giving off, or like bubbles 2 lively and high-spirited; vivacious —*n.* [Slang] champagne

☆**bub·by** (bub′ē, boob′-) *n.* [Informal] *var. of* BUBBE

Bu·ber (bōō′bər), **Martin** 1878-1965; Israeli Jewish theologian & philosopher, born in Austria

bub·kes (bub′kəs, boob′-) *n.* [Slang] BUPKIS: also sp. **bub′kis**

bu·bo (byōō′bō′) *n., pl.* **-boes′** ⟦ME < ML < Gr *boubōn,* groin, swollen gland⟧ an inflamed swelling of a lymph node, esp. in the armpit or groin —**bu·bon′ic** (-bän′ik) *adj.*

bubonic plague a contagious disease, the most common form of plague, caused by a bacterium (*Yersinia pestis*) transmitted by fleas from infected rats, and characterized by buboes, fever, prostration, and delirium: see BLACK DEATH

bu·bon·o·cele (byōō bän′ə sēl′) *n.* ⟦Gr *boubōn,* groin + -O- + -CELE⟧ an incomplete or partial hernia forming a swelling in the groin

Bu·ca·ra·man·ga (bōō′kä rä mäŋ′gä) city in NC Colombia

buc·cal (buk′əl) *adj.* ⟦L *bucca,* cheek, mouth cavity (for IE base see BIG) + -AL⟧ 1 of or near the cheek 2 of or in the mouth

buc·ca·neer (buk′ə nir′) *n.* ⟦Fr *boucanier,* user of a *boucan,* native Brazilian grill for roasting meat; orig. applied to Fr hunters of wild oxen in Haiti⟧ a pirate, or sea robber, esp. one who raided along the Spanish coasts of America in the 17th cent.

buc·ci·na·tor (buk′sə nāt′ər) *n.* ⟦L, trumpeter < pp. of *buccinare,* to blow a trumpet < *buccina,* a trumpet < **boucana* < *bos,* ox, COW¹ + *canere,* to sing: see CHANT⟧ the flat muscle of the cheek, which compresses it and retracts the corners of the mouth

Bu·ceph·a·lus (byōō sef′ə ləs) *n.* ⟦L, lit., ox-headed < Gr *bous,* ox, COW¹ + *kephalē,* head: see CEPHALIC⟧ the war horse of Alexander the Great

Bu·chan·an (byōō kan′ən), **James** 1791-1868; 15th president of the U.S. (1857-61)

Bu·cha·rest (bōō′kə rest′, byōō′-) capital of Romania, in the S part

bûche de No·ël (büsh də nô el′) ⟦Fr, lit., log of Christmas⟧ a French Christmas cake made from a thin layer of spongecake that is rolled up and frosted so as to resemble a decorative Yule log

Buch·en·wald (bōō′kən wôld′; *Ger* bookh′ən vält′) village in central Germany, near Weimar, in the state of Thuringia: site (1937-45) of a Nazi concentration camp

Büch·ner (bookh′nər) 1 **E·du·ard** (ā′dōō ärt′) 1860-1917; Ger. biochemist 2 **Ge·org** (gā ôrk′) 1813-37; Ger. poet & dramatist

buck¹ (buk) *n.* ⟦ME *bukke* < OE *bucca,* male goat < IE base **bhugo-* > Ger *bock,* Du *bok,* Ir *boc*⟧ 1 *pl.* **bucks** or **buck** a male deer, antelope, goat, rabbit, etc.: see DOE ☆2 the act of bucking 3 *a)* BUCKSKIN *b)* [*pl.*] casual oxford shoes, originally of buckskin, now usually of light-colored suede, nubuck, etc. 4 [Informal] a young man, esp. one who is bold, lively, vigorous, etc.: sometimes a contemptuous or patronizing term as applied to a young black or North American Indian man 5 [Archaic] a fop or dandy —*vi.* ☆1 to rear upward quickly and descend with the back arched and forelegs stiff, as in an attempt to throw off a rider: said of a horse, mule, etc. 2 to plunge forward with lowered head, as a goat ☆3 [Informal] to resist something as if plunging against it ☆4 [Informal] to move jerkily: said as of a car —*vt.* ☆1 to dislodge or throw by bucking ☆2 [Informal] to resist stubbornly —*adj.* 1 male ☆2 of the lowest military rating [*buck* private, *buck* sergeant] —☆**buck for** [Slang] to work eagerly or too eagerly for (a promotion, etc.) —☆**buck up** [Informal] to cheer up —**buck′er** *n.*

buck² (buk) *n.* ⟦< SAWBUCK⟧ 1 [Now Rare] a sawbuck; sawhorse 2 a small gymnastics horse used especially for training

☆**buck³** (buk) *n.* ⟦< ? BUCKSKIN, used as a medium of exchange⟧ 1 [Historical] *Poker* a counter placed before a player as a reminder to deal next, etc. 2 [Slang] a dollar —**pass the buck** [Informal] to evade blame or responsibility by trying to pass it to someone else —☆**the buck stops here (or with someone)** ⟦coined by President Harry TRUMAN in allusion to the phrase PASS THE BUCK (see above)⟧ the responsibility cannot be shifted to someone else or evaded (by someone)

☆**buck⁴** (buk) *adv.* ⟦orig. uncert.⟧ completely; stark [*buck* naked]

Buck (buk), **Pearl** (born *Pearl Sydenstricker*) 1892-1973; U.S. novelist

☆**buck and wing** a complicated, fast tap dance

☆**buck·a·roo** (buk′ə rōō′, buk′ə rōō′) *n., pl.* **-roos′** ⟦prob. < Sp *vaquero,* cowboy (< *vaca,* cow < L *vacca*); infl. by BUCK¹, *n.* 4⟧ a cowboy

buck·bean (buk′bēn′) *n.* ⟦transl. of Du *boksboon,* lit., goat's bean⟧ a bog plant (*Menyanthes trifoliata*) of the gentian family, with glossy leaves of three leaflets and white flowers; bogbean

☆**buck·board** (buk′bôrd′) *n.* ⟦BUCK¹, *vi.* + BOARD⟧ a four-wheeled, open carriage with the seat or seats carried on a flooring of long, flexible boards whose ends rest directly on the axles

buckboard

buck·brush (-brush′) *n.* ⟦BUCK¹ + BRUSH¹⟧ [Chiefly West] any of various shrubby plants, esp. of the honeysuckle family, fed on by deer

buck·et (buk′it) *n.* ⟦ME *boket* < Anglo-Fr *buket,* dim. of OE *buc,* pitcher, bulging vessel, orig., belly < IE **bhou-,* var. of base **bheu-:* see BIG⟧ 1 a deep, round container with a flat bottom and a curved handle, used to hold or carry water, coal, etc.; pail 2 the amount held by a bucket: also **buck′et·ful′** *pl.* **-fuls′** 3 a thing like a bucket, as a scoop on a power shovel, any of the cups on a water wheel, or any of the curved vanes in the rotor of a turbine 4 [Slang] the rump; buttocks —*vt., vi.* 1 to carry, draw, or lift (water, etc.) in a bucket or buckets 2 to speculate (with) dishonestly as in a bucket shop 3 [Brit.] *a)* to ride (a horse) at a fast pace *b)* to move or drive rapidly or recklessly —**kick the bucket** ⟦< ? obs. *bucket,* beam on which a slaughtered pig was hung⟧ [Slang] to die

bucket brigade a line of persons passing buckets of water along in trying to put out a fire

bucket seat ⟦from the orig. concave shape⟧ a contoured seat for one person, as in an automobile

☆**bucket shop** 1 a business involved in selling, chiefly by telephone solicitation, that uses high-pressure sales tactics, fraudulent claims, etc. 2 [Brit.] an unlicensed travel agency which sells discounted airline tickets

☆**buck·eye** (buk′ī′) *n.* ⟦BUCK¹ + EYE: from the appearance of the seed⟧ 1 any of various trees (genus *Aesculus*) of the horse-chestnut family with large capsules enclosing shiny brown seeds 2 the seed 3 [**B-**] [Informal] a person born or living in Ohio, called the **Buckeye State**

☆**buck fever** [Informal] nervous excitement of novice hunters when they first see game

Buck·ing·ham (buk′iŋ əm) 1 1st Duke of (born *George Villiers*) 1592-1628; Eng. statesman 2 2d Duke of (born *George Villiers*) 1628-87; Eng. statesman & writer: son of 1st Duke

Buckingham Palace the official residence in London of British sovereigns

Buck·ing·ham·shire (-shir′, -shər) county in SC England: 725 sq mi (1,877 sq km): also called **Buck′ing·ham**

buck·le¹ (buk′əl) *n.* ⟦ME *bokel,* a buckle, boss of a shield < OFr *bocle* < LL *bucula,* beaver, shield < L *buccula,* cheek strap of a helmet, dim. of *bucca,* cheek: see BUCCAL⟧ 1 a clasp on one end of a strap or belt for fastening the other end in place 2 a clasplike ornament, as for shoes 3 a clasp on a strap that fits into a matching part on a post, another strap, etc. thereby securing the strap —*vt.* **-led, -ling** to fasten or join with a buckle —*vi.* 1 to be fastened or joined by a buckle 2 [Obs.] to engage in a struggle; grapple —☆**buckle down** to apply oneself energetically; set to work with effort

buck·le² (buk′əl) *vt.* **-led, -ling** ⟦ME *bokelen,* to arch the body < *bokel,* buckle; prob. infl. by OFr *bocler,* to bulge < *bocle*: see prec.⟧ to bend or warp, as by means of pressure or intense heat —*vi.* 1 to bend, warp, or crumple, as under pressure or in intense heat 2 to yield reluctantly to pressure; submit; give in: usually with *under* —*n.* a distortion caused by buckling; bend, bulge, kink, etc.

buck·ler (buk′lər) *n.* ⟦ME *bokeler* < OFr *bocler*: see BUCKLE¹⟧ 1 a small, round shield held by a handle or worn on the arm 2 any protection or defense —*vt.* to protect by shielding; defend

buck·min·ster·ful·ler·ene (buk′min stər fo͝ol′ə rēn′) *n.* ⟦after R. *Buckminster* FULLER⟧ a round, pure-carbon fullerene, C_{60}, with a structure similar to that of a geodesic dome

buck·o (buk′ō′) *n., pl.* **-oes′** ⟦< BUCK¹⟧ 1 [Old Naut. Slang] a blustering or swaggering fellow; bully 2 a young man; fellow: an Irishism often used in familiar address

☆**buck-pass·er** (buk′pas′ər) *n.* ⟦see phr. PASS THE BUCK under BUCK³⟧ [Informal] a person who regularly seeks to shift blame or responsibility to someone else —**buck′-pass′ing** *n.*

☆**buck·ra** (buk′rə) *n.* ⟦< Ibibio & Efik (in Nigeria) *mbākara,* lit., he who surrounds or governs⟧ a white man or boss: term used chiefly in the SE U.S. by blacks

buck·ram (buk′rəm) *n.* ⟦ME *bokeram* < OFr *bouquerant;* prob. after *Bukhara,* city in Uzbekistan⟧ 1 a coarse cotton or linen cloth stiffened with glue or other size, for use in bookbinding, for lining or stiffening clothes, etc. 2 [Archaic] stiffness or formality —*adj.* 1 of or like buckram 2 [Now Rare] stiff; formal —*vt.* to stiffen with buckram

☆**buck·saw** (buk′sô′) *n.* ⟦BUCK² + SAW¹⟧ a saw consisting of a toothed blade set in a frame, held on one side with both hands in cutting wood on a sawbuck

buck·shee (buk′shē′) *adj.* ⟦< BAKSHEESH⟧ [Brit. Slang] free; gratis

☆**buck·shot** (buk′shät′) *n.* large lead shot for shooting deer and other large game

buck·skin (buk′skin′) *n.* 1 the skin of a buck 2 a soft, usually napped, yellowish-gray leather made from the skins of deer or sheep ☆3 a yellowish-gray horse 4 [*pl.*] clothes or shoes made of buckskin ☆5 [*often* **B-**] an American backwoodsman of earlier times —*adj.* made of buckskin

buck·thorn (buk′thôrn′) *n.* ⟦BUCK¹ + THORN⟧ 1 any of a genus (*Rhamnus*) of thorny trees or shrubs of the buckthorn family, bearing small greenish flowers and purple berries 2 any of a genus (*Bumelia*) of trees of the sapodilla family, native to the S U.S. —*adj.* designating a family (Rhamnaceae, order Rhamnales) of dicotyledonous shrubs and trees, including the cascara, jujube, and redroot

buck·tooth (-to͞oth′) *n., pl.* **-teeth′** ⟦BUCK¹ + TOOTH⟧ a projecting front tooth —**buck′toothed′** (-to͞otht′) *adj.*

buck·wheat (buk′hwēt′, -wēt′) *n.* ⟦< ME *bok-* (< OE *boc-*), BEECH + WHEAT, transl. of MDu *boecweit* or MLowG *bokwete*: from the resemblance of the seeds to beechnuts⟧ 1 any of several plants (genus *Fagopyrum*) of the buckwheat family, grown for their black, triangular grains 2 the grain of this plant, from which a dark flour is made ☆3 this flour —*adj.* designating a family (Polygonaceae, order Polygonales) of dicotyledonous plants, including rhubarb, dock, and sorrel

buck·y·ball (buk′ē bôl′) *n.* [Informal] BUCKMINSTERFULLERENE: also **bucky ball**

bu·col·ic (byo͞o käl′ik) *adj.* ⟦L *bucolicus* < Gr *boukolikos* < *boukolos,* herdsman < *bous,* ox (see COW¹) + *-kolos* < ? IE base **kel-,* to drive > HOLD¹, L *celer,* swift⟧ 1 of shepherds; pastoral 2 of country life or farms; rustic —*n.* 1 a pastoral poem 2 a rustic; countrified person —***SYN.*** RURAL —**bu·col′i·cal·ly** *adv.*

Bu·co·vi·na (bo͞o′kə vē′nə) *alt. sp. of* BUKOVINA

Bu·cu·reşti (bo͞o ko͞o resht′) *Romanian name for* BUCHAREST

bud¹ (bud) *n.* ⟦ME *budde,* bud, seedpod < IE base **bheu-*: see BIG⟧ 1 *a)* a small swelling or projection on a plant, from which a shoot, cluster of leaves, or flower develops *b)* a partly opened flower 2 any undeveloped or immature person or thing 3 an asexually produced swelling or growth on the body of a sponge, fungus, etc. that develops into a new individual —*vi.* **bud′ded, bud′ding** ⟦< the *n.*⟧ 1 to put forth buds 2 to begin to develop 3 to be young, promising, etc. —*vt.* 1 to put forth as a bud or buds 2 to cause to bud 3 to insert (a bud of a plant) into the bark of another plant —**in (the) bud** 1 in the time of budding 2 in a budding condition —**nip in the bud** to put an end to at the earliest stage —**bud′der** *n.* —**bud′like′** *adj.*

☆**bud²** (bud) *n.* [Slang] *short for* BUDDY (*n.* 1): usually used in addressing a man or boy

Bu·da·pest (bo͞o′də pest′) ⟦formed by union (1873) of 3 adjacent cities, *Buda, Pest,* & *Óbuda* (Old Buda)⟧ capital of Hungary, in the NC part, on the Danube

Bud·dha¹ (bo͞o′də, bo͝od′ə) *n.* a statue or image of Buddha

Bud·dha² (bo͞o′də, bo͝od′ə) ⟦Sans, the enlightened one; pp. of *budh,* to awake, know < IE base **bheudh-*: see BID¹⟧ Siddhartha Gautama, religious philosopher and teacher who lived in India 563?-483? B.C. and was the founder of Buddhism: the name is a title applied by Buddhists to someone regarded as embodying divine wisdom and virtue

Bud·dhism (bo͞o′diz′əm, bo͝od′iz′əm) *n.* a religion and philosophic system of central and eastern Asia, founded in India in the 6th cent. B.C. by Buddha: it teaches that right thinking and self-denial will enable the soul to reach nirvana, a divine state of release from misdirected desire —**Bud′dhist** *n., adj.* —**Bud′dhis′tic** *adj.*

bud·ding (bud′iŋ) *n.* ⟦see BUD¹, *n.* 3⟧ a type of asexual reproduction in which a new individual or branch develops from an outgrowth on the body of a plant or certain lower animals

bud·dle (bud′'l, bo͝od′-) *n.* ⟦< ?⟧ *Mining* a shallow, inclined trough used to wash or sluice crushed ore

bud·dle·ia (bəd lē′ə, bud′lē ə) *n.* ⟦ModL, after A. *Buddle,* 17th-c. Eng botanist⟧ any of a genus (*Buddleia*) of shrubs and trees of the logania family, native to the tropics but commonly grown in temperate regions for their blossoms of purple, yellow, etc.

☆**bud·dy** (bud′ē) *n., pl.* **-dies** ⟦< ?⟧ [Informal] 1 a close friend; companion; comrade; esp., a comrade in arms 2 either of two persons paired off in a partnership arrangement (**buddy system**) for mutual help and protection, as in combat or in children's camp activities —*vi.* **-died, -dy·ing** [Informal] to associate as a buddy or buddies

☆**bud·dy-bud·dy** (bud′ē bud′ē) *adj.* ⟦redupl.⟧ [Slang] friendly or chummy, often in an effusive or insincere way

budge¹ (buj) *vt., vi.* **budged, budg′ing** ⟦Fr < OFr *bouger,* to move < VL **bullicare,* to boil < L *bullire,* BOIL¹⟧ 1 to move even a little [unable to *budge* the boulder] 2 to yield or cause to yield

budge² (buj) *n.* ⟦ME, a bag, bulge < OFr *bouge,* a bag < L *bulga,* leather bag < Gaul⟧ lambskin dressed so that the wool is worn outward, esp. as a trimming on academic gowns of the past —*adj.* [Archaic] solemn or pompous

budg·er·i·gar (buj′ər i gär′) *n.* ⟦native name⟧ an Australian parakeet (*Melopsittacus undulatus*) having a greenish-yellow body, marked with bright blue on the cheeks and tail feathers, and wings striped with brown

budg·et (buj′it) *n.* ⟦ME *bougette* < OFr, dim. of *bouge*: see BUDGE²⟧ 1 [Obs.] a bag, pouch, or purse, or its contents 2 a collection of items; stock 3 a plan or schedule adjusting expenses during a certain period to the estimated or fixed income for that period 4 the cost or estimated cost of living, operating, etc. 5 the amount of money needed or allotted for a specific use —*vt.* 1 to put on or in a budget; provide for in a budget 2 to plan (expenditures or activities) according to a budget 3 to plan in detail; schedule [*budget* your time] —*vi.* to make a budget —**budg·et·ar·y** (buj′ə ter′ē) *adj.* —**budg′et·er** *n.*

budg·et·eer (buj′ə tir′) *n.* 1 a person who draws up a budget; budgeter 2 a person who adheres to a budget

budg·ie (buj′ē) *n.* [Informal] BUDGERIGAR

bud scale any of the thin, papery or leathery structures covering certain plant buds in winter

bud vase a relatively tall, slender vase, usually footed, for holding a single, stemmed flower, usually a rosebud

Bud·weis (bo͞ot′vīs) *Ger. name for* ČESKÉ BUDĚJOVICE

bud·worm (bud′wurm′) *n.* a caterpillar that feeds on plant buds

bue·nas no·ches (bwe′näs nô′ches) ⟦Sp, lit., good nights⟧ good night

Bue·na·ven·tu·ra (bwe′nä ven to͞o′rä) seaport in W Colombia, on an island in a Pacific inlet

Bue·na Vis·ta (bwā′nə vis′tə, byo͞o′nə) site of a battle (1847) of the Mexican War, near Saltillo, Mexico, in which Santa Ana's army withdrew after a stalemated engagement with U.S. forces under Zachary Taylor, giving Taylor control of N Mexico

Bue·nos Ai·res (bwā′nəs er′ēz, -ī′rēz; bō′nəs; *Sp* bwe′nôs ī′res) 1 seaport & capital of Argentina, on the Río de la Plata within a federal district: 77 sq mi (199 sq km) 2 province of E Argentina, on the Atlantic: 118,754 sq mi (307,572 sq km); cap. La Plata 3 **Lake** lake in the S Andes, on the Chilean-Argentine border: 865 sq mi (2,240 sq km)

bue·nos dí·as (bwe′nôs dē′äs) ⟦Sp, lit., good days⟧ good day; good morning

buff¹ (buf) *n.* ⟦earlier *buffe,* buffalo < Fr *buffle* < It *bufalo,* BUFFALO⟧ 1 a heavy, soft, brownish-yellow leather made from the skin of the buffalo or from other animal hides 2 [Historical] a military coat made of this leather 3 *a)* a stick or small block covered with leather or cloth, used for cleaning or shining *b)* BUFFING WHEEL 4 a dull brownish-yellow color ☆5 [Informal] a devotee or enthusiast, as of a particular area of interest [a jazz *buff*] —*adj.* 1 made of buff 2 of the color buff 3 [Slang] physically, often sexually attractive, as by being pleasingly fit and muscular or having a sexually desirable figure: also **buffed** —*vt.* 1 to clean or shine with a buff or treated cloth 2 to make smooth or soft like buff —***SYN.*** POLISH —**in the buff** naked; nude

buff² (buf) *n.* ⟦ME & OFr *buffe*: see BUFFET¹⟧ a blow: now only in BLINDMAN'S BUFF —*vt.* to lessen the force of —*vi.* to be a buffer

buf·fa·lo (buf′ə lō′) *n., pl.* **-loes′, -lo′, -los′** ⟦It *bufalo* < LL *bufalus,* var. of *bubalus,* wild ox < Gr *boubalos,* buffalo, antelope < *bous,* ox, COW¹⟧ 1 any of various wild oxen, sometimes domesticated, as the water buffalo of India or Cape buffalo of Africa ☆2 popularly, the American bison ☆3 a robe made of buffalo skin ☆4 BUFFALO FISH —☆*vt.* **-loed′, -lo′ing** [Slang] to baffle, bewilder, bluff, or overawe

Buf·fa·lo¹ (buf′ə lō′) *adj.* ☆of, for, or prepared in the manner of BUFFALO WINGS

Buf·fa·lo² (buf′ə lō′) ⟦transl. of the name of a Seneca Indian who lived there⟧ city in W N.Y., on Lake Erie & the Niagara River —**Buf′fa·lo′ni·an** *n.*

water buffalo

☆**buffalo beetle** the hairy larva of a carpet beetle (*Anthrenus scrophulariae*), harmful to furs and woolens

☆**buffalo berry** **1** a shrub (genus *Shepherdia*) of the oleaster family, native to W North America, with silvery leaves **2** its red, fleshy, edible berry

Buffalo Bill *name for* William F. CODY

☆**buffalo bug** CARPET BEETLE

☆**buffalo fish** any of a genus (*Ictiobus*) of large, humpbacked, freshwater sucker fishes found in North America

buffalo grass a low, creeping range grass (*Buchloë dactyloides*) native to the Great Plains and used for forage

☆**buffalo robe** a carriage robe or rug made of the skin of the bison, dressed with the hair on

☆**buffalo soldier** ⟦orig. uncert.⟧ [*also* **B- S-**] [Historical] an African-American soldier, esp. one who served in any of the all-black cavalry units of the U.S. Army in the American West in the second half of the 19th cent.

☆**Buffalo wings** ⟦after BUFFALO[2], New York, where the dish originated⟧ [*also* **b- w-**] spicy fried segments of chicken wings, typically served with a sauce

buff·er[1] (buf′ər) ***n.*** ⟦BUFF[1], *vt.* + -ER⟧ **1** a person who buffs or polishes **2** a buffing wheel, stick, block, or cloth

buff·er[2] (buf′ər) ***n.*** ⟦BUFF[2], v. + -ER⟧ **1** a device using padding, springs, hydraulic pressure, etc. to lessen or absorb the shock of collision or impact **2** any person or thing that serves to lessen shock or prevent sharp impact, as between antagonistic forces **3** any substance in a solution that tends to stabilize the hydrogen ion concentration by neutralizing any added acid or alkali **4** a computer storage area that temporarily holds data being transferred from one device to another, as to compensate for the different processing rates of the devices —***vt.*** **1** to protect against shock or impact; cushion or insulate **2** *Chem.* to add a buffer to (a solution)

buff·er[3] (buf′ər) ***n.*** [Brit. Informal] an elderly man variously regarded as old-fashioned, stodgy, ineffectual, etc.: usually used with *old*

buffer state a small country located between two large, antagonistic powers and regarded as lessening the possibility of conflict between them

buf·fet[1] (buf′it) ***n.*** ⟦ME < OFr, dim. of *buffe*, a blow: prob. echoic⟧ **1** a blow with the hand or fist **2** any blow or shock [*the buffets of fate*] —***vt.*** **1** to hit with the hand or fist; punch; slap **2** to beat back as by repeated blows [*the waves buffeted the boat*] **3** to struggle against —***vi.*** to struggle or force a way by struggling

buf·fet[2] (bə fā′, bo͞o-; *Brit* buf′it) ***n.*** ⟦Fr < OFr, bench (> ME, stool)⟧ **1** a piece of furniture with drawers and cupboards for dishes, table linen, silver, etc.; sideboard **2** *a)* a counter or table where refreshments are served *b)* a restaurant with such a counter or table **3** a meal at which guests serve themselves from a buffet or table

buff·ing wheel (buf′iŋ) a wheel covered with leather, cloth, etc., for buffing, or polishing, metal

☆**buf·fle·head** (buf′əl hed′) ***n.*** ⟦obs. *buffle*, buffalo, fool < Fr (see BUFF[1]) + HEAD⟧ a small North American duck (*Bucephala albeola*), black on top and white underneath

buf·fo (bo͞of′fô; *E* bo͞o′fō) ***n.***, *pl.* **-fi** (-fē) ⟦It, comic: see BUFFOON⟧ an opera singer, generally a bass, who plays a comic role

Buf·fon (bü fōn′), Comte **de** (born *Georges Louis Leclerc*) 1707-88; Fr. naturalist

buf·foon (bə fo͞on′) ***n.*** ⟦Fr *bouffon* < It *buffone*, jester < *buffare*, to jest, puff: of echoic orig.⟧ a person who is always clowning and trying to be funny; clown —**buf·foon′er·y** ***n.*** —**buf·foon′ish** ***adj.***

bu·fo·ten·ine (byo͞o′fə ten′ēn′, -in) ***n.*** ⟦< ModL *Bufo*, genus name (< L, toad) + *-ten-* (< ?) + -INE[3]⟧ a poisonous hallucinogenic alkaloid, $C_{12}H_{16}N_2O$, extracted from toadstools and the skin glands of toads (genus *Bufo*) or made synthetically

bug[1] (bug) ***n.*** ⟦prob. < fol.⟧ **1** any of an order (Hemiptera) of insects with sucking mouthparts and with forewings thickened toward the base, as a water bug or squash bug: also called **true bug** **2** any small arthropod, esp. if regarded as a pest, as a louse, cockroach, or centipede ☆**3** a defect or imperfection, as in a machine or computer program: somewhat informal when used outside of a computer context **4** [Informal] any microscopic organism, esp. one causing disease; germ or virus ☆**5** [Informal] a tiny microphone hidden to record conversation secretly ☆**6** [Slang] *a)* an enthusiast or devotee (often used in comb.) [*a shutterbug pursues photography as a hobby*] *b)* a particular enthusiasm or obsession ☆**7** [Slang] a small, compact automobile **8** ⟦from the asterisk (thought to resemble a *bug*) placed beside the apprentice jockey's name on a racing program⟧ [Slang] the weight allowance (5 pounds, or 2.3 kg) granted to an apprentice jockey for one year after the riding of five winners —☆***vt.*** **bugged**, **bug′ging** **1** [Informal] to hide a microphone in (a room, etc.), as for recording a conversation secretly **2** [Slang] *a)* to annoy, bother, anger, etc. *b)* to confuse or puzzle —***vi.*** [Slang] to bulge or open wide, as in amazement: said of the eyes —☆**bug off** [Slang] to stop annoying someone and leave: also [Brit.] **bugger off** —☆**bug out** [Slang] to run away; desert

bug[2] (bug) ***n.*** ⟦ME *bugge*, akin to Norw dial. *bugge*: see BIG⟧ [Obs.] a bugbear; hobgoblin

Bug (bo͞og) **1** river in S Ukraine, flowing southeastward into the Black Sea: 530 mi (853 km): also called **Southern Bug** **2** river in W Ukraine, flowing northwestward into the Vistula near Warsaw and forming part of the border with Poland: 500 mi (805 km): also called **Western Bug**

bug·a·boo (bug′ə bo͞o′) ***n.***, *pl.* **-boos′** ⟦BUG[2] + BOO[1]⟧ a bugbear

bug·bane (bug′bān′) ***n.*** any of a genus (*Cimicifuga*) of perennial plants of the buttercup family, with long spikes of small white flowers whose offensive odor is supposed to repel insects

bug·bear (bug′ber′) ***n.*** ⟦BUG[2] + BEAR[2]⟧ **1** an imaginary hobgoblin or terror used to frighten children into good conduct **2** anything causing seemingly needless or excessive fear or anxiety

☆**bug-eyed** (-īd′) ***adj.*** [Slang] with bulging eyes

bug·ger (bug′ər) ***n.*** ⟦ME *bougre* < OFr < ML *Bulgarus*, lit., a Bulgarian; orig., 11th-c. Bulgarian heretic⟧ **1** a sodomite **2** a contemptible person **3** a fellow; chap; also, a rascal or scamp: often used humorously or affectionately —***vt.*** to commit sodomy with —**bugger off** [Slang, Chiefly Brit.] to leave; depart: often used in the imperative

bug·ger·y (-ē) ***n.*** SODOMY

bug·gy[1] (bug′ē) ***n.***, *pl.* **-gies** ⟦18th c.; < ?⟧ **1** a light carriage with four (or, in England, two) wheels and a single seat, usually drawn by one horse ☆**2** BABY CARRIAGE **3** [Old Slang] an automobile, esp. an old one

buggy

bug·gy[2] (bug′ē) ***adj.*** **-gi·er**, **-gi·est** **1** swarming or infested with bugs **2** [Informal] characterized by the presence of computer bugs [*buggy software*] ☆**3** ⟦see fol.⟧ [Slang] mentally ill; insane

☆**bug·house** (-hous′) ***n.*** ⟦BUG[1] (*n.* 6a) in extended use, crazy person + HOUSE⟧ [Slang] an insane asylum —***adj.*** [Slang] insane

bu·gle[1] (byo͞o′gəl) ***n.*** ⟦ME, wild ox, drinking horn, hunting horn < OFr < L *buculus*, heifer, young ox, dim. of *bos*, ox, COW[1]⟧ a brass instrument like a trumpet but smaller, and usually without keys or valves: used chiefly for military calls and signals — ***vi., vt.*** **-gled**, **-gling** to call or signal by or as by blowing a bugle —**bu′gler** ***n.***

bu·gle[2] (byo͞o′gəl) ***n.*** ⟦< ? prec. (from the appearance)⟧ a long, tubular glass or plastic bead for trimming dresses, etc. —***adj.*** trimmed with bugles: also **bu′gled**

bu·gle[3] (byo͞o′gəl) ***n.*** ⟦ME & OFr < LL *bugula*, for L *bugillo*, prob. this plant⟧ any of a genus (*Ajuga*) of plants of the mint family, having spikes of white, pink, or blue flowers and often used for ground cover; ajuga

bu·gle·weed (byo͞o′gəl wēd′) ***n.*** **1** BUGLE[3] ☆**2** any of a genus (*Lycopus*) of plants of the mint family, with tiny white or pale blue flowers

bu·gloss (byo͞o′glôs′, -gläs′) ***n.*** ⟦ME & OFr *buglosse* < L *buglossa* < Gr *bouglōssos*, oxtongue < *bous*, ox, COW[1] + *glōssa*, tongue⟧ any of several genera (esp. *Anchusa*) of the borage family of bristly plants with bluish flowers

bug·seed (bug′sēd′) ***n.*** ⟦from appearance of the seeds⟧ a branching, annual weed (*Corispermum hyssopifolium*) of the goosefoot family, with sprays of oval, flat seeds

buhl (bo͞ol) ***n.*** *alt. sp. of* BOULLE

buhr·stone (bur′stōn′) ***n.*** ⟦*buhr*, var. of BURR[3] + STONE⟧ **1** a hard, siliceous rock used to make millstones **2** a millstone cut from such a rock

build (bild) ***vt.*** **built** or [Archaic] **build′ed**, **build′ing** ⟦ME *bilden* < OE *byldan*, to build < base of *bold*, a house, akin to ON *bua*: see BONDAGE⟧ **1** *a)* to make by putting together materials, parts, etc.; construct; erect *b)* to order, plan, or direct the construction of **2** to make a basis for; establish [*to build a theory on facts*] **3** to cause to be or grow; create or develop: often with *up* [*to build good will, to build up a business*] —***vi.*** **1** *a)* to put up a building *b)* to have a house, etc. built **2** to be in the business of building houses, etc. **3** to increase in amount, force, etc.; grow or intensify: often with *up* **4** to depend or be based (*on*) [*this theory builds on others*] —***n.*** the way a thing is built or shaped; form or figure [*a stocky build*] —**build up** **1** to make more desirable, attractive, healthy, etc. [*to build up a product by advertising*] **2** to erect many buildings in (an area)

☆**build-down** (bild′doun′) ***n.*** [Informal] a gradual decrease in nuclear weapons, armed forces, etc., esp. by an agreement in which a smaller number of newer weapons would replace older ones

build·er (bil′dər) ***n.*** **1** a person or animal that builds **2** a person in the business of constructing buildings **3** an ingredient added to a soap or a detergent to increase its effectiveness

builder's knot CLOVE HITCH

build·ing (-diŋ) ***n.*** **1** anything that is built with walls and a roof, as a house or factory; structure **2** the act, process, work, or business of constructing houses, ships, etc.

SYN.—**building** is the general term applied to a fixed structure in which people dwell, work, etc.; **edifice** implies a large or stately building and is sometimes used figuratively [*the edifice of democracy*]; **structure** also suggests an imposing building, but has special application when the material of construction is being stressed [*a steel structure*]; **pile** is applied in poetry and lofty prose to a very large building or mass of buildings

building block ⟦by analogy with a block as of cement used as a unit in the construction of a building, barrier, etc.⟧ a fundamental element, fact, idea, etc. upon which something is built, developed, maintained, etc.: *usually used in pl.*

☆**build·up** or **build-up** (bild′up′) ***n.*** [Informal] **1** praise or favorable publicity, esp. when systematic and intended to make something popular, well-known, etc. 2 a gradual increase in amount, power, influence, etc.; expansion [a military *buildup*]

built (bilt) *vt., vi. pt. & pp. of* BUILD —*adj.* [Informal] having a well-formed, physically attractive body: said usually of a woman

☆**built-in** (bilt′in′) *adj.* **1** made as part of the structure; not detachable [*built-in* cabinets] **2** intrinsic; inherent

built-up (-up′) *adj.* **1** made higher, stronger, larger, etc. by the addition of parts [*built-up* heels] **2** having many buildings on it [a *built-up* suburb]

Bu·jum·bu·ra (bo͞o′jo͝om bo͝or′ə) capital of Burundi: port at the N end of Lake Tanganyika

Bu·ka·vu (bo͞o käv′o͞o) city in the E Democratic Republic of the Congo, on Lake Kivu

Bu·kha·rin (bo͝o khä′rin), **Ni·ko·lai (Ivanovich)** (nē′kô lī′) 1888-1938; Russ. Communist leader & editor

Bu·ko·vi·na (bo͞o′kə vē′nə) region in central Europe, partly in N Romania & partly in SW Ukraine: an Austrian crown land from 1775 to 1918

bul *abbrev.* bulletin

Bu·la·wa·yo (bo͞o′lə wä′yō) city in SW Zimbabwe

bulb (bulb) *n.* ⟦ME < L *bulbus* < Gr *bolbos*⟧ **1** an underground bud that sends down roots and consists of a very short stem covered with leafy scales or layers, as in a lily, onion, or hyacinth **2** a corm, tuber, or tuberous root resembling a bulb, as in a crocus, dahlia, or cyclamen **3** any plant that grows from a bulb **4** anything shaped like a bulb; rounded thing or enlarged part; specif., a LIGHTBULB [the *bulb* of a syringe] **5** *Anat. a)* an enlargement on some tissues, organs, or tubes, as at the root of a hair *b)* [Obs.] MEDULLA OBLONGATA

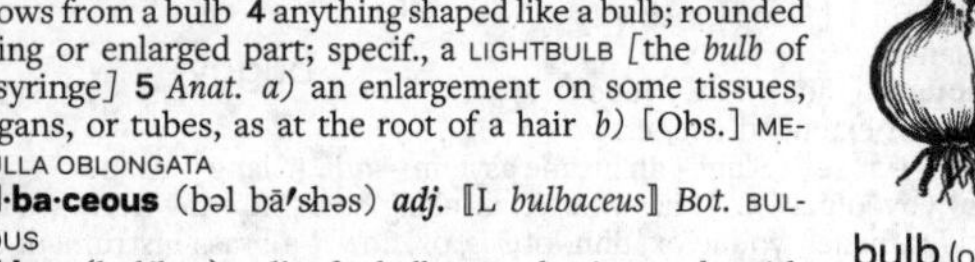

bulb (onion)

bul·ba·ceous (bəl bā′shəs) *adj.* ⟦L *bulbaceus*⟧ *Bot.* BULBOUS

bul·bar (bul′bər) *adj.* of a bulb; esp., having to do with the medulla oblongata

bulbed (bulbd) *adj.* having a bulb or bulbs

bul·bif·er·ous (bul bif′ər əs) *adj.* ⟦< ModL *bulbifer* (< L *bulbus*, BULB + *-fer*, producing: see -FER) + -OUS⟧ of a plant having tiny bulbs, esp. if they replace the buds on the stem, as certain onions

bul·bil (bul′bil′) *n.* ⟦ModL *bulbillus*, dim. of L *bulbus*, BULB⟧ a small bulb or fleshy bud on a flower stalk, as in some onions, or in the axil of a leaf, as in a tiger lily

bul·bo·u·re·thral gland (bul′bə yo͞o rē′thrəl) ⟦< L *bulbus*, BULB + -O- + URETHRAL⟧ COWPER'S GLAND

bul·bous (bul′bəs) *adj.* ⟦L *bulbosus*⟧ **1** of, shaped like, or having a bulb or bulbs **2** growing from a bulb

bul·bul (bo͝ol′bo͝ol′) *n.* ⟦Pers: prob. echoic⟧ **1** a songbird referred to in Persian poetry, perhaps a nightingale **2** any of a family (Pycnonotidae) of small, dull-colored passerine birds of Asia and Africa

Bul·finch (bo͝ol′finch′) **1 Charles** 1763-1844; U.S. architect **2 Thomas** 1796-1867; U.S. writer & mythologist: son of Charles

Bulg *abbrev.* **1** Bulgaria **2** Bulgarian

Bul·ga·kov (bo͝ol gä′kôf), **Mi·kha·il (Afanasyevich)** (mē′khä ēl′) 1891-1940; Russ. novelist & playwright

Bul·gar (bul′gär′, bo͝ol′-) *n., adj.* BULGARIAN

Bul·gar·i·a (bəl ger′ē ə, bo͝ol-) country in the SE Balkan Peninsula, on the Black Sea: founded in the 7th cent. & under Turkish rule from the late 14th cent. until 1878; gained full independence in 1908: 42,823 sq mi (110,910 sq km); cap. Sofia

Bul·gar·i·an (-ē ən) *adj.* of Bulgaria or its people, language, or culture —*n.* **1** a person born or living in Bulgaria **2** the South Slavic language spoken in Bulgaria

bulge (bulj) *n.* ⟦ME < OFr *bouge*: see BUDGE[2]⟧ **1** an outward swelling; protuberance **2** a projecting part, as a military salient ☆**3** [Informal] a sudden increase in size, value, etc. ☆**4** [Informal] advantage or margin of advantage — *vi., vt.* **bulged, bulg′ing** to swell or bend outward; protrude or project —*SYN.* PROJECTION

bul·gur (wheat) (bo͝ol′gər, bul′-) ⟦Turk⟧ wheat that has been cooked, dried, and coarsely ground: used to make tabbouleh or, sometimes, pilaf or couscous

bulg·y (bul′jē) *adj.* **bulg′i·er, bulg′i·est** having a bulge or bulges —**bulg′i·ness** *n.*

bu·li·ma·rex·i·a (byo͞o′li mə rek′sē ə) *n.* ⟦fol. + *-a-* + (ANO)REXIA⟧ BULIMIA (sense 2)

bu·lim·i·a (byo͞o lē′mē ə, -lim′ē ə; bo͞o-) *n.* ⟦ModL < Gr *boulimia* < *bous*, ox, COW[1] + *limos*, hunger < ? IE base **lei-*, to diminish, meager > LITTLE⟧ **1** *Med.* a continuous, abnormal hunger **2** an eating disorder, chiefly in young women, characterized by the gorging of large quantities of food followed by purging, as through self-induced vomiting: cf. ANOREXIA: in full **bulimia ner·vo·sa** (nər vō′sə) —**bu·lim′ic** *adj.*

bulk[1] (bulk) *n.* ⟦ME, heap, cargo < ON *bulki*, a heap, ship's cargo; prob. < IE base **bhel-*: see BALL[1]⟧ **1** size, mass, or volume, esp. if great **2** the main mass or body of something; largest part or portion [the *bulk* of one's fortune] **3** soft, bulky matter of a kind that passes through the intestines without being absorbed and aids in elimination —*vi.* **1** to form into a mass **2** to increase in size, importance, etc. **3** to have size or importance [to *bulk* large in the mind] —*vt.* **1** to make (something) form into a mass **2** to make bulge; stuff **3** to give greater bulk, or size, to —*adj.* **1** total; aggregate **2** not put up in individual packages **3** designating or of mail comprising presorted, identical items mailed in quantity, as catalogs —**in bulk 1** not put up in individual packages **2** in large amounts; in great volume

SYN.—**bulk, mass,** and **volume** all refer to a quantity of matter or collection of units forming a body or whole, **bulk** implying a body of great size, weight, or numbers [the lumbering *bulk* of a hippopotamus, the *bulk* of humanity], **mass**, an aggregate, multitude, or expanse forming a cohesive, unified, or solid body [an egg-shaped *mass*, a *mass* of color, the *mass* of workers], and **volume**, a moving or flowing mass, often of a fluctuating nature [*volumes* of smoke, the *volume* of production]

bulk[2] (bulk) *n.* ⟦ME *balk* < ON *balkr*, partition, wall; akin to BALK⟧ [Archaic] a projecting framework or stall built as the front of a shop

bulk·head (bulk′hed′) *n.* ⟦prec. + HEAD⟧ **1** any of the upright partitions separating parts of a ship, airplane, etc. as for protection against fire or leakage **2** a wall or embankment for holding back earth, fire, water, etc. ☆**3** a boxlike structure built over an opening, as at the head of a staircase, elevator shaft, etc.

bulk·y (bul′kē) *adj.* **bulk′i·er, bulk′i·est 1** *a)* having great bulk; large; massive *b)* relatively large for its weight **2** awkwardly large; big and clumsy —**bulk′i·ly** *adv.* —**bulk′i·ness** *n.*

bull[1] (bo͝ol) *n.* ⟦ME *bole* < OE *bula*, a steer; akin to ON *boli*, Ger *bulle* < IE base **bhel-*: see BALL[1]⟧ **1** the adult male of any bovine animal, as the ox, buffalo, etc. **2** the adult male of certain other large animals, as the elephant, elk, moose, walrus, whale, etc. **3** an investor who buys stocks, commodities, etc. in the belief their price will rise: opposed to BEAR[2] (sense 3) **4** a person regarded as like a bull in size, strength, etc. **5** a bulldog ☆**6** [Slang] a policeman or detective ☆**7** [Slang] *short for* BULLSHIT —*vt.* ☆**1** to make (one's way) with driving force ☆**2** [Slang] to bluff, as with insincere talk —*vi.* [Slang] to talk foolishly, insincerely, etc. —*adj.* **1** male **2** like a bull in size, strength, etc. **3** rising in price [a *bull* market] —☆**shoot the bull** [Slang] to talk idly —**take the bull by the horns** to deal boldly with a danger or difficulty —**the Bull** Taurus, the constellation and second sign of the zodiac

bull[2] (bo͝ol) *n.* ⟦ME & OFr *bulle* < LL *bulla*, a seal < L, anything round, knob, bubble: for IE base see BIG⟧ **1** BULLA (sense 1) **2** an official document, edict, or decree, esp. one from the pope

bull[3] (bo͝ol) *n.* ⟦< ? ME *bul*, trickery, lie⟧ a ludicrously illogical or incongruous mistake in statement (Ex.: I'm glad I hate onions because if I liked onions, I'd eat them, and I can't stand onions)

bull[4] *abbrev.* bulletin

bull- (bo͝ol) ⟦< BULL[1]⟧ *combining form* **1** of a bull or bulls [*bullfight*] **2** like a bull or bull's [*bullhead*] **3** large or male [*bullfrog*]

bul·la (bo͝ol′ə, bul′ə) *n., pl.* **-lae** (-ē) ⟦ML < L: see BULL[2]⟧ **1** a round lead seal attached to an official document from the pope **2** ⟦ModL < L: see BULL[2]⟧ *Med.* a large blister or vesicle —**bul′lous** *adj.*

bul·lace (bo͝ol′is) *n.* ⟦ME *bolas* < OFr *beloce* < ML **bulluca*, small plum⟧ **1** DAMSON (sense 1) ☆**2** MUSCADINE

bul·late (bo͝ol′it, -āt′; bul′-) *adj.* ⟦L *bullatus* < *bulla*, a bubble: see BULL[2]⟧ **1** having blisters **2** blistered or puckered in appearance, as some leaves **3** inflated like a blister

bull-bait·ing (bo͝ol′bāt′iŋ) *n.* the setting of dogs on a chained or confined bull, formerly a popular pastime in England

☆**bull·bat** (-bat′) *n.* ⟦BULL- + BAT[2]⟧ the common nighthawk

☆**bull·bri·er** (-brī′ər) *n.* any of several species of greenbrier common in the forests of the S U.S.

bull·dog (-dôg′) *n.* ⟦so named because orig. raised for use in *bull-baiting*⟧ **1** a short-haired, square-jawed, heavily built dog noted for its strong stubborn grip **2** a short-barreled revolver of large caliber **3** [Brit.] at Oxford and Cambridge universities, a proctor's assistant —*adj.* like or characteristic of a bulldog; stubborn, unrelenting, etc. —☆*vt.* **-dogged′, -dog′ging** to throw (a steer) by taking hold of its horns and twisting its neck

bulldog

☆**bulldog edition** the early edition of a morning newspaper, chiefly for out-of-town distribution

☆**bull·doze** (bo͝ol′dōz′) *vt.* **-dozed′, -doz′ing** ⟦< n. *bulldose*, a severe beating < *bull* (Botany Bay slang), a flogging of 75 lashes + DOSE⟧ **1** [Informal] to force or frighten by threatening; intimidate; bully **2** to move, make level, dig out, etc. with a bulldozer

☆**bull·doz·er** (-dō′zər) *n.* **1** a person who bulldozes **2** a tractor with a large, shovel-like blade on the front, for pushing or moving earth, debris, etc.

☆**bull·dyke** (bo͝ol′dīk′) *n.* [Slang] a lesbian having characteristics traditionally thought of as belonging to men, as an aggressive manner or a masculine appearance: an offensive term of contempt and hostility

bul·let (bo͝ol′it) *n.* ⟦Fr *boulette*, dim. of *boule*, a ball < L *bulla*: see BULL[2]⟧ **1** a small ball or cone-shaped missile of lead, metal alloy, etc., to be shot from a firearm **2** loosely, a bullet in its casing; cartridge **3** anything like a bullet in shape, action, etc. **4** a solid dot used as at the beginning of a line for emphasis ☆**5** a bullet-shaped symbol used to indicate a rapid increase in sales and airplay of musical recordings, videos, etc. —**bite the bullet** [Informal] to confront a painful situation with fortitude or stoicism: from an earlier practice of having the patient bite down on a bullet during battlefield surgery when no anesthetic was available

bul·le·tin (bo͝ol′ə tin) ***n.*** ⟦Fr < It *bulletino,* dim. of LL *bulla:* see BULL[2]⟧ **1** a brief official statement about a matter of public concern **2** a brief statement of the latest news, as in a newspaper or on radio or TV **3** a regular publication, as for the members of some society —***vt.*** to announce or publish in a bulletin

☆**bulletin board** **1** a board or wall area on which bulletins, notices, or displays are put up **2** a computer system accessible by modem, set up to allow users, esp. of microcomputers, to exchange messages, software, etc., usually in a particular field of interest

bul·let·proof (bo͝ol′it pro͞of′) ***adj.*** that bullets cannot pierce —***vt.*** to make bulletproof

bullet train ⟦so named from its aerodynamic shape and great speed, likened to those of a BULLET in motion⟧ **1** a high-speed train, or the rail system in which it runs, in Japan **2** any such high-speed train

☆**bull fiddle** [Informal] DOUBLE BASS

bull·fight (bo͝ol′fīt′) ***n.*** a public show that is popular in Spain, Mexico, and some other countries, in which a matador challenges a bull with a sword in an enclosed arena: in most countries, the bull is usually killed —**bull′fight′er** ***n.*** —**bull′fight′ing** ***n.***

bull·finch (-finch′) ***n.*** ⟦BULL- + FINCH⟧ any of various finches of Europe, Asia, and North America; esp., a European species (*Pyrrhula pyrrhula*) with a black head and white rump

☆**bull·frog** (-frôg′) ***n.*** ⟦BULL- + FROG⟧ a large North American ranid frog (*Rana catesbeiana*) that has a deep, loud croak

bull·head (-hed′) ***n.*** ⟦see BULL-⟧ ☆**1** any of a family (Ictaluridae) of North American freshwater catfishes **2** SCULPIN (sense 1)

bull·head·ed (-hed′id) ***adj.*** blindly stubborn; headstrong —**bull′head′ed·ly** ***adv.*** —**bull′head′ed·ness** ***n.***

☆**bull·horn** (-hôrn′) ***n.*** ⟦BULL- + HORN⟧ a portable electronic voice amplifier

bul·lion[1] (bo͝ol′yən) ***n.*** ⟦ME (? via Du *bulioen*) < OFr *billon,* small coin, alloy of copper with silver < *bille,* a stick, bar: see BILLET[2]⟧ **1** gold and silver regarded as raw material **2** gold or silver in the form of ingots, bars, or sometimes coins

bul·lion[2] (bo͝ol′yən) ***n.*** ⟦infl. by prec., but prob. < Fr *bouillon* < *bouille,* a seal on silk goods < Sp *bolla,* duty on silk < L *bulla:* see BULL[2]⟧ a heavy fringe or lace of twisted gold or silver thread

bull·ish (bo͝ol′ish) ***adj.*** **1** of or like a bull **2** *a)* of, causing, or resulting from expectations of higher prices for stocks, bonds, etc. *b)* optimistic —**bull′ish·ly** ***adv.*** —**bull′ish·ness** ***n.***

bull mastiff a very strong, active breed of dog produced by crossing mastiffs and bulldogs

Bull Moose ⟦so called from the symbol of the party⟧ a member of the Progressive Party led by Theodore Roosevelt in the presidential campaign of 1912

bull-necked (-nekt′) ***adj.*** having a short, thick neck

bull nose a contagious disease of pigs, caused by a bacillus (*Fusobacterium necrophorum*) and characterized by destructive swellings of the snout and mouth

bull·ock (bo͝ol′ək) ***n.*** ⟦ME *bulloke* < OE *bulluc,* dim. of *bula:* see BULL[1]⟧ **1** [Obs.] a young bull **2** a castrated bull; steer

☆**bull·pen** (-pen′) ***n.*** **1** a fenced enclosure for bulls **2** [Informal] a large room or enclosure for a number of people; specif., a barred enclosure in a jail, where prisoners are kept together temporarily, as between their arrest and the placing of charges **3** *Baseball* *a)* an area near the playing field, where relief pitchers practice and warm up *b)* the relief pitchers of one team

☆**bull·pout** (-pout′) ***n.*** the common bullhead or horned pout of the E U.S.

bull·ring (-riŋ′) ***n.*** **1** an arena for bullfighting **2** the circular floor of this arena, on which the spectacle takes place

bull·roar·er (-rôr′ər) ***n.*** a device consisting of a flat piece of wood at the end of a string, which makes a roaring noise when whirled: used in religious ceremonies of the Australian Aborigines

Bull Run ⟦< ?⟧ small stream in NE Va.: site of two Civil War battles (1861 & 1862) in which Union forces were defeated

☆**bull session** ⟦see BULL[1], ***n.*** 7⟧ [Informal] an informal discussion or conversation among a small group

bull's-eye (bo͝olz′ī′) ***n.*** ⟦as in Fr *oeil de boeuf,* Dan *koöie,* cow eye, Sw *oxoga,* ox eye, all applied to small, round windows⟧ **1** a thick, circular glass in a roof, ship's deck, etc., for admitting light **2** any circular opening for light or air **3** *a)* the circular central mark of a target *b)* a shot that hits this *c)* a direct hit *d)* the exact achievement of a goal aimed at **4** *a)* a convex lens for concentrating light *b)* a lantern with such a lens **5** a hard, round candy

bull·shit (bo͝ol′shit′) [Slang] ***n.*** **1** foolish, insincere, exaggerated, or boastful talk **2** anything of little or no value; nonsense —***vt.*** **-shit′** or **-shit′ted, -shit′ting** to deceive, confuse, etc. with bullshit —***vi.*** to engage in conversation, esp. small talk —***interj.*** nonsense Somewhat vulgar —**bull′shit′ter** ***n.***

☆**bull·shot** (bo͝ol′shät′) ***n.*** ⟦*bull-* (< pronun. of BOUILLON) + SHOT[1] (***n.*** 15): prob. jocularly, after prec.⟧ a cocktail made of vodka and bouillon

☆**bull·snake** (-snāk′) ***n.*** any of a genus (*Pituophis*) of large, brownish, nonpoisonous North American colubrid snakes feeding mainly on rodents

bull terrier any of a breed of strong, active dog with a white coat, developed by crossing the bulldog and the terrier

☆**bull tongue** ⟦so called from its shape⟧ a simple, detachable plowshare, used esp. for breaking hard virgin soil

☆**bull·whip** (bo͝ol′hwip′, -wip′) ***n.*** ⟦BULL- + WHIP⟧ a long, heavy whip, formerly used by cattle drivers and teamsters —***vt.*** **-whipped′, -whip′ping** to whip with a bullwhip

bul·ly[1] (bo͝ol′ē) ***n., pl.*** **-lies** ⟦orig., sweetheart < Du *boel,* lover, brother < MHG *buole* (Ger *buhle*), lover, prob. orig. dim. of *bruder,* BROTHER; later infl. by BULL[1]⟧ **1** a person who hurts, frightens, or tyrannizes over those who are smaller or weaker **2** [Brit. Dial.] a companion or comrade **3** [Archaic] a pimp **4** [Archaic] a hired cutthroat or thug **5** [Archaic] a fine fellow —***vt.*** **-lied, -ly·ing** to hurt, frighten, or tyrannize over, as a bully does; browbeat —***vi.*** to behave like a bully —***adj.*** **1** dashing, hearty, or jolly [*my bully lad*] ☆**2** [Informal] fine; very good —☆***interj.*** [Informal] good; well done

bul·ly[2] (bo͝ol′ē) ***n.*** ⟦Fr *bouilli,* boiled beef < pp. of *bouillir,* BOIL[1]⟧ canned or corned beef: also **bully beef**

☆**bully boy** a violent, bullying man; esp., a hired ruffian

bully pulpit ⟦< phrase attributed by G. Putnam (1926) to Theodore ROOSEVELT[2], referring to the presidency as offering "such a bully [= fine] pulpit" for preaching⟧ a position of power and influence used to aggressively promote one's own cause

bul·ly·rag (-rag′) ***vt.*** **-ragged′, -rag′ging** ⟦see BULLY[1], ***vt.*** & RAG[2], ***vt.***⟧ [Informal or Dial.] to bully, intimidate, or browbeat

bully tree ⟦altered < BALATA tree⟧ any of several tropical American trees of the sapodilla family that yield balata

Bü·low (bü′lô), Prince **Bern·hard von** (bern′härt fôn) 1849-1929; Ger. statesman: chancellor (1900-09)

bul·rush (bo͝ol′rush′) ***n.*** ⟦ME *bulryshe* < *bol,* stem (see BOLE[1]) + *rusche,* RUSH[2]⟧ **1** any of a number of marsh plants (genus *Scirpus*) of the sedge family, having slender, round or triangular, solid stems tipped with brown spikelets of minute flowers **2** [Brit.] the cattail **3** popularly, any aquatic plant resembling a bulrush, as the papyrus

Bult·mann (bo͝olt′män), **Rudolf (Karl)** 1884-1976; Ger. Protestant New Testament scholar & theologian

bul·wark (bo͝ol′wərk, bul′-) ***n.*** ⟦ME *bulwerk* < MDu *bolwerc:* see BOLE[1] & WORK⟧ **1** an earthwork or defensive wall; fortified rampart **2** BREAKWATER **3** a person or thing serving as a strong defense or protection **4** [*usually pl.*] the part of a ship's side above the deck —***vt.*** **1** to provide bulwarks for **2** to be a bulwark to

Bul·wer-Lyt·ton (bo͝ol′wər lit′'n) **1 Edward George Earle Lytton** 1st Baron Lytton of Knebworth 1803-73; Eng. novelist & playwright: father of Edward Robert Bulwer-Lytton **2 Edward Robert** *see* MEREDITH[2], Owen

☆**bum**[1] (bum) ***n.*** ⟦< *bummer,* prob. < Ger *bummler,* loafer, habitually tardy person < *bummeln,* to go slowly, waste time⟧ [Informal] **1** a vagrant, hobo, tramp, or beggar; specif., a shabby, often drunken derelict **2** any shiftless or irresponsible person, loafer, idler, etc. **3** a devotee, as of golf or skiing, who devotes so much time to the sport as to disrupt family life, career, etc. **4** an incompetent person, esp. an athlete —***vi.*** **bummed, bum′ming** [Informal] **1** to live as a bum or vagrant **2** to live by begging or by sponging off people —***vt.*** [Slang] to get by begging or sponging; cadge [*to bum a cigarette*] —***adj.*** **bum′mer, bum′mest** [Slang] **1** poor in quality [*bum cooking*] **2** false, erroneous, or invalid [*a bum steer, a bum rap*] **3** lame or ailing [*a bum leg*] —***SYN.*** VAGRANT —**bum someone out** [Slang] to upset, distress, annoy, depress, bore, etc. someone —**give (or get) the bum's rush** [Slang] to eject (or be ejected) forcibly —**on the bum** [Informal] **1** living as a vagrant **2** out of repair; broken

bum[2] (bum) ***n.*** ⟦ME *bom* < ? *botem,* bottom, as Du dial. *boem* < *bodem,* & obs. E *bummery* for bottomry⟧ [Brit. Slang] the buttocks

bum·bail·iff (bum′bāl′if) ***n.*** ⟦prec. + BAILIFF: ? because the officer was often close behind⟧ [Brit.] a bailiff or sheriff's officer: a contemptuous usage

☆**bum·ber·shoot** (bum′bər sho͞ot′) ***n.*** ⟦jocular alteration and merging of UMBR(ELLA) & (PARA)CHUTE⟧ [Slang] an umbrella

bum·ble (bum′bəl) ***vi.*** **-bled, -bling** ⟦? altered < BUNGLE; or ? echoic, suggestive of confused mumbling⟧ **1** to blunder **2** to stumble —***vt.*** to bungle or botch —**bum′bler** ***n.***

bum·ble·bee (bum′bəl bē′) ***n.*** ⟦altered (by assoc. with ME *bomblen,* var. of *bomben,* to boom, buzz, of echoic orig.) < ME *humbul-be* < *humbil,* bumblebee (akin to Ger *hummel* < IE base **kem-,* to hum, of echoic orig.) + *be,* BEE[1]⟧ any of a number of related large, hairy, yellow-and-black social bees (esp. genus *Bombus*)

bum·boat (bum′bōt′) ***n.*** ⟦BUM[2] + BOAT; orig. (17th c.), sailors' slang for garbage boat⟧ a small boat used in a port or anchorage to peddle goods to ships' crews

bumf or **bumph** (bumf) ***n.*** ⟦contr. < *bumfodder,* lit., toilet paper < BUM[2] + FODDER⟧ [Brit. Slang] official documents, regarded disparagingly

bummed (bumd) ***adj.*** ⟦< BUM[1]⟧ [Slang] depressed, upset, distressed, annoyed, etc.: usually with *out*

☆**bum·mer** (bum′ər) ***n.*** ⟦< BUM[1] + -ER⟧ **1** [Old Slang] one who lives by bumming **2** [Slang] any unpleasant or unsatisfactory thing or experience: orig., an unpleasant drug experience

bump (bump) ***vt.*** ⟦echoic⟧ **1** to hit or knock against with a jolt; collide lightly with ☆**2** [Slang] to displace, as from a job or plane reservation ☆**3** [Slang] to raise (a price, a bet in poker, etc.) —***vi.*** **1** to collide with a jolt **2** to move with jerks or jolts —***n.*** **1** a light blow or jolt **2** a swelling or lump, esp. one caused by a blow **3** in phrenology, any of the protuberances of the skull as interpreted with reference to one's mental faculties ☆**4** [Slang] a thrusting movement forward of the lower part of the torso, as in striptease dancing: see also GRIND (***n.*** 5) —☆**bump into** [Informal] to meet unexpectedly —☆**bump off** [Slang] to murder

bump·er[1] (bum′pər) ***n.*** ☆a device for absorbing some of the shock of a collision; specif., either of two bars for this purpose, at the front and rear of a motor vehicle

bump·er[2] (bum′pər) *n.* ⟦prob. < obs. *bombard,* liquor jug, altered after BUMP⟧ 1 a cup or glass filled to the brim 2 [Informal] anything unusually large of its kind —*adj.* unusually large or abundant

bumper car a small electric car with thick rubber bumpers, used in DODGEM

☆**bumper sticker** a gummed paper with a printed slogan, witticism, etc., for sticking on a vehicle's bumper

bump·er-to-bump·er (-tə bum′pər) *adj.* 1 of or having a long line of cars very close together on a road and, often, moving slowly 2 of or pertaining to virtually the entire automobile [a *bumper-to-bumper* warranty, *bumper-to-bumper* inspection]

bump·kin[1] (bump′kin) *n.* ⟦prob. < MDu *bommekijn,* small cask < *bomme,* a cask + *-kijn,* dim. suffix⟧ an awkward or simple person from the country

bump·kin[2] (bump′kin) *n.* ⟦prob. < Du *boomkin,* short tree, dim. of *boom,* tree⟧ a short boom projecting from a sailing ship, used as in securing a stay or brace

bump·tious (bump′shəs) *adj.* ⟦prob. < BUMP, by analogy with FRACTIOUS⟧ disagreeably conceited, arrogant, or forward —**bump′tious·ly** *adv.* —**bump′tious·ness** *n.*

bump·y (bum′pē) *adj.* **bump′i·er, bump′i·est** full of bumps; rough; jolting —**bump′i·ly** *adv.* —**bump′i·ness** *n.*

bum-rush (bum′rush′) *vt.* ⟦prob. related to *the bum's rush,* as in GIVE (or GET) THE BUM'S RUSH (see phr. under BUM[1])⟧ [Informal] to approach, enter, etc. eagerly or forcibly

bun[1] (bun) *n.* ⟦ME *bunne,* wheat cake, bun, prob. < OFr *buigne,* a boil, swelling (> Fr *beigne,* fruit fritter) < Gaul **bunia*⟧ 1 a small roll made of bread dough, sometimes sweetened or spiced or containing raisins, etc. 2 hair worn in a roll or knot

☆**bun**[2] (bun) *n.* ⟦prob. contr. < informal (Scot) *bung,* drunk (short for *bung-full,* filled to the bung)⟧ [Slang] a drunken spree —**get a bun on** [Slang] to become drunk

bu·na (bo͞o′nə, byo͞o′-) *n.* ⟦Ger⟧ a synthetic rubber made by polymerizing butadiene

bunch (bunch) *n.* ⟦ME *bonche,* bundle, hump < OFr (Walloon) *bouge* < Fl *boudje,* dim. of *boud,* bundle⟧ 1 a cluster or tuft of things growing together [a *bunch* of grapes] 2 a collection of things of the same kind fastened or grouped together, or regarded as belonging together [a *bunch* of keys] 3 [Informal] a group of people, esp. of the same kind 4 [Obs.] a hump or protuberance — *vt., vi.* 1 to form or collect into a bunch or bunches; gather together in a mass: often with *up* 2 to gather into loose folds or wads, as a dress, skirt, etc. —**bunch′i·ness** *n.* —**bunch′y** *adj.*

bunch·ber·ry (-ber′ē, -bər ē) *n., pl.* **-ries** ☆a North American dwarf plant (*Cornus canadensis*) of the dogwood family, having minute flowers surrounded by four large, white bracts and, in the fall, bearing bunches of bright-red berries

Bunche (bunch), **Ralph Johnson** 1904-71; U.S. statesman & educator

☆**bunch·flow·er** (bunch′flou′ər) *n.* a tall plant (*Melanthium virginicum*) of the lily family, growing in the E U.S. and having large clusters of white or greenish flowers

☆**bunch grass** any of various grasses that grow in tufts

☆**bun·co** (buŋ′kō) *n., pl.* **-cos** ⟦c. 1875 < Sp *banca,* card game < It, BANK[1]⟧ [Informal] a swindle, esp. at a card game or lottery; confidence game —*vt.* **-coed, -co·ing** [Informal] to swindle; cheat

☆**bun·combe** (buŋ′kəm) *n.* ⟦after *Buncombe* county, N.C.: the representative to Congress (1819-21) from the district including this county felt bound to "make a speech for Buncombe"⟧ BUNKUM

bund[1] or **Bund** (bo͝ont, bo͝ond) *n., pl.* **bunds, Bün′de** (bün′də) ⟦Ger < root of *binden,* BIND⟧ 1 a league or confederation 2 a political organization; specif., the German-American Bund, a former pro-Nazi organization in the U.S. —**bund′ist** *n.*

bund[2] (bund) *n.* ⟦Anglo-Ind < Hindi *band,* embankment, dike < Pers *bändär,* harbor⟧ in India and the Far East, an embankment or quay, or an embanked road along a waterfront

Bun·des·bank (bo͝on′dəs bäŋk′, -baŋk′) *n.* ⟦Ger < *bundes,* gen. of *bund,* BUND[1] + *bank,* BANK[1]⟧ the central bank of Germany

Bun·des·rat or **Bun·des·rath** (bo͝on′dəs rät′) *n.* ⟦Ger < gen. of *bund,* BUND[1] + *rat, rath,* council⟧ 1 a legislative chamber in Germany or Austria that is a federal council acting primarily in an advisory capacity 2 a cabinet-like federal council in Switzerland

Bun·des·tag (bo͝on′dəs täk′, -täg′) *n.* ⟦Ger < gen. of *bund,* BUND[1] + *tag,* meeting: see REICHSTAG⟧ the federal assembly of Germany whose members are elected directly

bun·dle (bun′dəl) *n.* ⟦ME *bundel,* prob. < MDu *bondel,* dim. < *bond* < *binden,* BIND⟧ 1 a number of things tied, wrapped, or otherwise held together 2 a package or parcel 3 a bunch, collection, or group 4 [Slang] a large amount of money 5 *Biol. a)* any of the strands of specialized cells that conduct fluids or add strength in higher plants (in full **vascular bundle**) *b)* an anatomical unit consisting of a number of separate nerve fibers, muscles, etc. closely banded together —*vt.* **-dled, -dling** 1 to make into a bundle; wrap or tie together 2 to offer together with a related product or service for sale at a package price [to *bundle* an internet browser with a PC] 3 to send hastily or without ceremony; hustle (*away, off, out,* or *into*) —*vi.* 1 to move or go hastily; bustle 2 to lie in the same bed with one's sweetheart without undressing: an old courting custom now practiced only by some Amish ☆3 *Politics* to collect a number of campaign contributions from individual donors and deliver them as a single, large contribution —**bundle up** to put on plenty of warm clothing —**bun′dler** *n.* —**bund′ling** *n.*

SYN.—**bundle** refers to a number of things bound together for convenience in carrying, storing, etc. and does not in itself carry connotations as to size, compactness, etc. [a *bundle* of discarded clothing]; **bale** implies a standardized or uniform quantity of goods, as raw cotton, hay, etc. compressed into a rectangular mass and tightly bound; **parcel** and **package** are applied to something wrapped or boxed for transportation, sale, etc. and imply moderateness of size and a compact or orderly arrangement; **pack** is applied to a package of a standard amount [a *pack* of cigarettes] or to a compact bundle carried on the back

Bundt (bunt, bo͝ont) ⟦arbitrary coinage⟧ *trademark for* a type of tube pan with fluted sides —*adj.* [*often* **b-**] 1 designating such a pan or a similarly shaped mold 2 baked in such a pan [a *Bundt* cake]

bung (buŋ) *n.* ⟦ME *bunge* < MDu *bonge*⟧ 1 a cork or other stopper for the hole in a barrel, cask, or keg 2 a bunghole —*vt.* 1 to close (a bunghole) with a stopper 2 to close as with a bung; stop up 3 ⟦prob. infl. by BANG[1]⟧ [Slang] to bruise or damage, as in a fight: with *up* 4 [Brit. Slang] to toss; fling; throw

bun·ga·low (buŋ′gə lō′) *n.* ⟦Anglo-Ind < Gujarati *bangalo* < Hindi *bānglā,* thatched house, lit., Bengalese⟧ 1 in India, a low, one-storied house, usually with a wide, sweeping porch 2 a small house or cottage, usually of one story and an attic

bun·gee cord (bun′jē) ⟦< ?⟧ elasticized cord used to hold objects in place, as luggage on carts or racks, or attached to persons leaping for sport (**bungee jumping**) from great heights so as to allow them to come close to the ground without hitting it

bung·hole (buŋ′hōl′) *n.* a hole in a barrel or keg through which liquid can be poured in or drawn out

bun·gle (buŋ′gəl) *vt.* **-gled, -gling** ⟦< ? Swed *bangla,* to work ineffectually⟧ to spoil by clumsy work or action; botch —*vi.* to do or make things badly or clumsily —*n.* 1 a bungling, or clumsy, act 2 a bungled piece of work —**bun′gler** *n.* —**bun′gling·ly** *adv.*

Bu·nin (bo͞o′nyin), **I·van A·lek·se·ye·vich** (ē vän′ ä′lyik sā′yi vich) 1870-1953; Russ. novelist & poet, in France after 1920

bun·ion (bun′yən) *n.* ⟦< dial. (E Anglian) *bunny* < ME *boni,* swelling < OFr *buigne:* see BUN[1]⟧ an inflammation and swelling of the bursa at the base of the big toe, with a thickening of the skin

bunk[1] (buŋk) *n.* ⟦prob. < Scand cognate of BENCH⟧ 1 a shelflike bed or berth built into or against a wall, as in a ship 2 [Informal] any sleeping place; esp., a narrow cot —☆*vi.* 1 to sleep in a bunk 2 [Informal] to use a makeshift sleeping place —☆*vt.* to provide a sleeping place for

☆**bunk**[2] (buŋk) *n.* [Slang] *short for* BUNKUM

bunk[3] (buŋk) [Brit. Slang] *vi.* to leave in haste; flee —*n.* a hasty departure, as to evade detection: chiefly in the phrase **do a bunk**

bunk bed any of two or three single beds joined one above the other and often provided with a ladder

bunk·er (buŋ′kər) *n.* ⟦Scot < ?⟧ 1 a large bin or tank, as for a ship's fuel 2 an underground fortification of steel and concrete containing a bomb shelter, weapon emplacement, etc., that is often part of a system 3 a sand trap or other barren area serving as a hazard on a golf course —*vt.* 1 to supply (a ship) with fuel 2 *Golf* to hit (a ball) into a bunker

Bun·ker Hill (buŋ′kər) ⟦prob. after G. *Bunker,* early resident of Charlestown⟧ hill in Boston, Mass.: in a battle (1775) of the American Revolution, chiefly at nearby Breed's Hill, colonial forces besieging Boston were dislodged by British troops, but the victory failed to break the siege

bunker mentality a suspicious or defensive state of mind, as of someone who is besieged by complaints or criticism, likened to the mentality of a person who is trapped in a bunker that is under attack

bunk·house (buŋk′hous′) *n.* a kind of barracks for ranch hands, migratory farm workers, etc.

☆**bunk·mate** (-māt′) *n.* a person who sleeps in an adjoining bunk or in the same bunkhouse

☆**bun·ko** (buŋ′kō) *n., pl.* **-kos** BUNCO — *vt.* **-koed, -ko·ing**

☆**bun·kum** (buŋ′kəm) *n.* ⟦phonetic respelling of BUNCOMBE⟧ [Informal] talk that is empty, insincere, or merely for effect; humbug

bun·ny (bun′ē) *n., pl.* **-nies** ⟦dim. of dial. *bun,* rabbit⟧ 1 a rabbit: pet name used by children ☆2 [Slang] a sexually attractive young woman: often used in comb. [ski *bunny,* beach *bunny*]

☆**Bun·ra·ku** (bo͝on rä′ko͞o) *n.* ⟦Jpn, after U. *Bunrakuken,* 19th-c. reviver of the traditional puppet show⟧ [*also* **b-**] a form of puppet show in Japan with nearly life-size puppets, each operated by two or three on-stage puppeteers, while dialogue and narration are spoken by performers just offstage

buns (bunz) *pl.n.* [Slang] the human buttocks

Bun·sen (bun′sən; *Ger* bo͝on′zən), **Robert Wilhelm** 1811-99; Ger. chemist: inventor of the spectroscope

Bun·sen burner (bun′sən) ⟦after prec.⟧ a small gas burner that produces a hot, blue flame, used in chemistry laboratories, etc.: it consists of a hollow metal tube with holes at the bottom for admitting air to be mixed with the gas

bunt[1] (bunt) *vt.* ⟦< ? ME *bounten,* to return⟧ 1 [Brit. Dial.] to strike or butt with or as with horns ☆2 *Baseball* to bat (a pitched ball) lightly without swinging, so that the ball rolls slowly into the infield, usually in attempting to advance a base runner: see DRAG BUNT, SACRIFICE BUNT —*n.* 1 a butt or shove ☆2 *Baseball a)* the act of bunting *b)* a bunted ball

bunt[2] (bunt) *n.* ⟦< earlier dial., a puffball⟧ a disease that destroys the grain of wheat and other grasses, caused by various fungi (genus *Tilletia*)

bunt[3] (bunt) ***n.*** ⟦< ? MLowG & MDu, a binding, bundle; akin to BIND⟧ **1** the sagging part of a fish net **2** the bellying part of a square sail

bun·ting[1] (bun′tiŋ) ***n.*** ⟦< ? ME *bonting,* ger. of *bonten,* to sift: hence, cloth used for sifting⟧ **1** a thin cloth used in making flags, streamers, etc. **2** flags, or strips of cloth in the colors of the flag, used as holiday decorations ☆**3** a baby's garment of soft, warm cloth made into a hooded blanket that exposes only the face

bun·ting[2] (bun′tiŋ) ***n.*** ⟦ME < ?⟧ any of a family (Emberizidae, esp. genera *Passerina* and *Emberiza*) of small, brightly colored passerine birds with short, stout bills

bunt·line (bunt′lin, -līn′) ***n.*** ⟦BUNT[3] + LINE[1]⟧ one of the ropes attached to the foot of a square sail for use in hoisting the sail to the yard for furling

Bu·ñu·el (bo͞o′nyo͞o el′), **Lu·is** (lo͞o ēs′) 1900-83; Sp. film director

bun·ya-bun·ya (bun′yə bun′yə) ***n.*** ⟦< native name⟧ an Australian coniferous tree (*Araucaria bidwillii*) of the araucaria family, with thick, flat, lanceolate needles and large, edible seeds

Bun·yan (bun′yən) **1 John** 1628-88; Eng. writer & preacher: wrote *Pilgrim's Progress* **2 Paul** *see* PAUL BUNYAN

Bun·yan·esque (bun′yən esk′) ***adj.*** ☆**1** of or like the giant lumberjack PAUL BUNYAN or his feats; colossal, prodigious, etc. ☆**2** like or suggestive of the humorously exaggerated tall tales about him

Buo·na·par·te (bwô′nä pär′te) ***n.*** *It. var. of* BONAPARTE[1]

Buo·nar·ro·ti (bwô′när rô′tē), **Michelangelo** *see* MICHELANGELO

buon gior·no (bwôn jyôr′nô) ⟦It⟧ good day; hello

buoy (bo͞o′ē; *also, and for v. 3 usually,* boi) ***n.*** ⟦ME < (? via MDu *boeie*) OFr *buie,* chain < L *boia,* fetter (see BOY): prob. first applied to the chain anchoring the float⟧ **1** *a)* a floating object anchored in a lake, river, etc. to mark a channel, warn of a hazard, etc., variously shaped and colored, and often equipped with a bell or light *b)* a similar but larger and heavier object, usually with a ring on top, to which a ship can be moored (in full **mooring buoy**) **2** LIFE BUOY **—*vt.*** ⟦< Sp *boyar,* to float⟧ **1** to mark or provide with a buoy **2** to keep afloat: usually with *up* **3** to lift up or keep up in spirits; encourage: usually with *up*

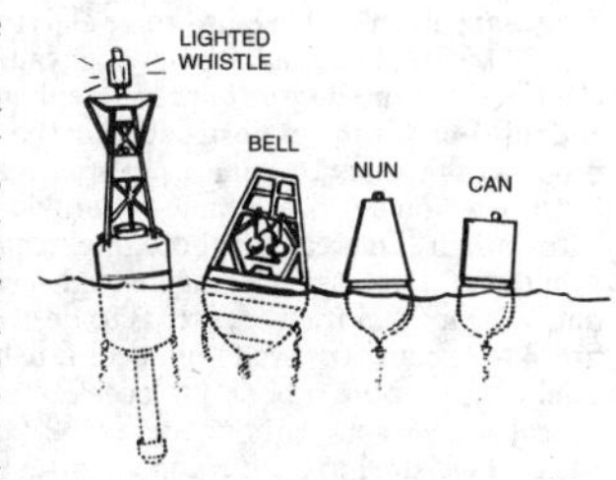

kinds of buoys

buoy·an·cy (boi′ən sē; *also* bo͞o′yən-) ***n.*** ⟦< fol.⟧ **1** the ability or tendency to float or rise in liquid or air **2** the power to keep something afloat; upward pressure on a floating object **3** lightness or resilience of spirit; cheerfulness

buoy·ant (boi′ənt; *also* bo͞o′yənt) ***adj.*** ⟦< ? Sp *boyante* < *boyar,* to float⟧ having or showing buoyancy **—buoy′ant·ly *adv.***

☆**bup·kis** (bup′kəs, bo͝op′-) ***n.*** ⟦< Yiddish *bobkes,* goat droppings⟧ [Slang] **1** nothing [we searched everywhere, but found *bupkis*] **2** even the smallest amount [doesn't know *bupkis* about it] Also sp. **bup′kus, bup′kiss,** or **bup′kes**

☆**bup·pie** (bup′ē) ***n.*** ⟦B(LACK) (*adj.* 2b) + (Y)UPPIE⟧ [Informal] an African-American yuppie

bu·pres·tid (byo͞o pres′tid) ***n.*** ⟦< ModL < L *buprestis* < Gr *bouprēstis,* poisonous beetle which when eaten with fodder caused cattle to swell up and die < *bous,* ox, COW[1] + *prēthein,* to swell up⟧ any of a family (Buprestidae) of beetles with a long, flat, metallic-colored body: the larvae are harmful to woody plants

bur[1] (bur) ***n.*** ⟦ME *burre* < Scand; akin to Dan *burre,* Swed *borre* < IE **bhors-*: for base see BRISTLE⟧ **1** the rough, prickly seedcase or fruit of certain plants, as the sticktight, cocklebur, etc. **2** a weed or other plant with burs **3** anything that clings like a bur **4** *Dentistry* a cutting or drilling bit **5** BURR[1] & BURR[2] **—*vt.* burred, bur′ring 1** to remove burs from **2** to burr

bur[2] *abbrev.* bureau

Bur *abbrev.* **1** Bureau **2** Burma **3** Burmese

bu·ran (bo͞o rän′) ***n.*** ⟦Russ < Turk⟧ a strong NE windstorm of the steppes of Russia and Siberia, bringing blizzards in the winter and hot dust in the summer

Bur·bage (bur′bij), **Richard** 1567?-1619; Eng. actor: associate of Shakespeare

Bur·bank[1] (bur′baŋk), **Luther** 1849-1926; U.S. horticulturist: bred numerous varieties of fruits, vegetables, & flowers

Bur·bank[2] (bur′baŋk) ⟦after Dr. D. *Burbank,* one of the city planners⟧ city in SW Calif.: suburb of Los Angeles

bur·ble (bur′bəl) ***vi.* -bled, -bling** ⟦ME *burbelen,* to bubble; of echoic orig.⟧ **1** to make a gurgling or bubbling sound **2** to babble as a child does **—*n. Aeron.*** the separation and breakup of the streamline flow of air, esp. over the surface of a wing at too great an angle of attack, resulting in a loss of lift and an increase of drag

bur·bot (bur′bət) ***n., pl.* -bot** or **-bots** ⟦ME < OFr *borbote,* altered (infl. by *bourbe,* mud, mire) < earlier *barbote* < *barbe* < L *barba,* a beard⟧ a freshwater gadoid fish (*Lota lota*) with a broad, flat head and barbels on the nose and chin: widely distributed in Europe, Asia, and North America

burbs (burbz) ***pl.n.*** [Informal] *short for* suburbs: see SUBURB (sense 2)

Burck·hardt (bo͝ork′härt), **Jacob** 1818-97; Swiss art historian & critic

bur·den[1] (burd′'n) ***n.*** ⟦ME *birthen* < OE *byrthen,* akin to ON *byrthr,* a load: for IE base see BEAR[1]⟧ **1** anything that is carried; load **2** anything one has to bear or put up with; heavy load, as of work, duty, responsibility, or sorrow **3** the carrying of loads [a beast of *burden*] **4** the carrying capacity of a ship **—*vt.*** to put a burden on; load; weigh down; oppress

bur·den[2] (burd′'n) ***n.*** ⟦ME *burdoun,* bass in music, refrain < OFr *bourdon,* a humming, buzzing < ML *burdo,* wind instrument, bumblebee; of echoic orig.⟧ **1** [Archaic] a bass accompaniment in music **2** a chorus or refrain of a song **3** the drone of a bagpipe **4** a repeated, central idea; theme [the *burden* of a speech]

bur·dened (burd′'nd) ***adj. Naut.*** designating the vessel responsible for taking action to avoid colliding with another vessel: see PRIVILEGED (sense 4)

burden of proof the obligation to prove what is asserted and in dispute

bur·den·some (burd′'n səm) ***adj.*** hard to bear; heavy; oppressive **—*SYN.*** ONEROUS **—bur′den·some·ly *adv.***

bur·dock (bur′däk′) ***n.*** ⟦BUR[1] + DOCK[3]⟧ any of several plants (genus *Arctium*) of the composite family, with large basal leaves and purple-flowered heads covered with hooked prickles

bu·reau (byo͝or′ō) ***n., pl.* -reaus** or **-reaux** (-ōz) ⟦Fr, writing table or desk, office < OFr *burel,* coarse cloth (as table cover) < VL **bura* < LL *burra,* wool, shaggy garment⟧ **1** a writing table or desk, with drawers for papers ☆**2** a chest of drawers, with or without a mirror, as for clothing **3** *a)* an agency for collecting and giving information or performing other services [a credit *bureau,* a travel *bureau*] *b)* a local office of such an agency ☆**4** a government department, or a subdivision of a government department

bu·reauc·ra·cy (byo͝o räk′rə sē, byo͞o-) ***n., pl.* -cies** ⟦Fr *bureaucratie* < prec. + *-cratie,* -CRACY⟧ **1** the administration of government through departments and subdivisions managed by sets of appointed officials following an inflexible routine **2** the officials collectively **3** governmental officialism or inflexible routine: see also RED TAPE **4** the concentration of authority in a complex structure of administrative bureaus

bu·reau·crat (byo͝or′ə krat′) ***n.*** an official in a bureaucracy, esp. one who follows a routine in a mechanical, unimaginative way, insisting on proper forms, petty rules, etc. **—bu′reau·crat′ic *adj.* —bu′reau·crat′i·cal·ly *adv.***

bu·reau·cra·tese (byo͝or′ə kra tēz′, -tēs′; byo͝o rä′krə tēz′) ***n.*** indirect, jargon-laden language of a kind typically found in directives, memos, etc. issued by bureaucrats

bu·reauc·ra·tize (byo͝o rä′krə tīz′, byo͞o-) ***vt., vi.* -tized′, -tiz′ing** to develop into a bureaucracy; make or become bureaucratic **—bu·reauc′ra·ti·za′tion *n.***

bu·rette or **bu·ret** (byo͞o ret′) ***n.*** ⟦Fr < OFr *buirette,* dim. of *buire,* flagon, var. of *buie,* jug < Frank **buk-* < IE **bhōu-,* to swell⟧ a graduated glass tube with a stopcock at the bottom, used as by chemists for measuring small quantities of liquid or gas

burg (burg) ***n.*** **1** [Obs.] a fortified or walled town ☆**2** [Informal] a city, town, or village, esp. one regarded as quiet, unexciting, etc.

-burg (burg) *suffix* burg or borough

bur·gage (bur′gij) ***n.*** ⟦ME < OFr *bourgage* < ML *burgagium* < LL *burgus,* castle, fortress < Gmc **burgs*: see BOROUGH⟧ a former system of land or property tenure in towns, specif., in England, from an overlord for a yearly rental and, in Scotland, from the crown for watching and warding

Bur·gas (bo͝or gäs′) seaport in SE Bulgaria, on the Black Sea

bur·gee (bur′jē) ***n.*** ⟦< ? *burgee's flag,* owner's flag < Fr dial. *bourgeais,* var. of OFr *borjois, burgeis,* master, BOURGEOIS⟧ a swallow-tailed or triangular flag or pennant used on ships for signaling or identification

bur·geon (bur′jən) ***vi.*** ⟦ME *burjounen* < OFr *burjoner* < *burjon,* a bud < VL **burrio,* a bud < LL *burra,* wool, shaggy garment⟧ **1** to put forth buds, shoots, etc.; sprout **2** to grow or develop rapidly; expand; proliferate; flourish [the *burgeoning* suburbs]

☆**bur·ger** (bur′gər) ***n.*** [Informal] *short for* HAMBURGER, CHEESEBURGER, etc.

Bur·ger (bur′gər), **Warren Earl** 1907-95; U.S. jurist: chief justice of the U.S. (1969-86)

☆**-bur·ger** (bur′gər) ⟦< (HAM)BURGER⟧ *combining form* **1** sandwich of a patty of ground meat, fish, etc. [*turkeyburger*] **2** hamburger and [*cheeseburger*]

bur·gess (bur′jis) ***n.*** ⟦ME & OFr *burgeis*: see BOURGEOIS⟧ **1** [Now Rare] a citizen or freeman of a British borough **2** [Brit. Historical] a member of the British Parliament representing a borough, corporate town, or university **3** an elected member of the colonial legislature of Md. or Va.

Bur·gess (bur′jəs), **(Frank) Ge·lett** (jə let′) 1866-1951; U.S. humorist & illustrator

burgh (burg; *Scot* bu′rə) ***n.*** ⟦ME: Scot var. of BOROUGH⟧ **1** [Brit.] a borough **2** in Scotland, an incorporated or chartered town

-burgh (burg) *suffix* -BURG

burgh·er (bur′gər) ***n.*** ⟦ME < *burgh,* BOROUGH; in ModE assimilated < Ger *bürger* or Du *burger*⟧ an inhabitant of a borough or town: now used chiefly to suggest a conservative middle-class citizen

Burgh·ley (bur′lē), 1st Baron (born *William Cecil*) 1520-98; Eng. statesman: advisor to Elizabeth I

bur·glar (bur′glər) ***n.*** ⟦Anglo-L *burglator,* altered by assoc. with L *latro,* thief (orig., hired servant < Gr *latris*: see -LATRY) < OFr *burgeor,* burglar; ult. < LL *burgus*: see BOURGEOIS⟧ a person who commits burglary

bur·glar·i·ous (bər gler′ē əs) ***adj.*** of, constituting, or inclined to burglary **—bur·glar′i·ous·ly *adv.***

☆**bur·glar·ize** (bur′glər īz′) ***vt.* -ized′, -iz′ing** to commit burglary in or upon

bur·gla·ry (bur′glə rē) ***n., pl.* -ries** ⟦BURGLAR + -Y[4]⟧ the act of breaking into a building to commit theft or some other crime **—*SYN.*** THEFT

bur·gle (bʉr′gəl) *vt., vi.* **-gled, -gling** ⟦back-form. < BURGLAR⟧ [Informal] to burglarize or commit burglary

bur·go·mas·ter (bʉr′gō mas′tər, -gə-) *n.* ⟦ME *burghmaster* < MDu *burgemeester* < *burg* (see BOROUGH) + *meester,* MASTER⟧ the mayor or head magistrate of a city or town in the Netherlands, Flanders, Austria, or Germany

bur·go·net (bʉr′gə net′) *n.* ⟦Fr *bourguignotte,* orig., fem. of *Bourguignot,* Burgundian, after *Bourgogne,* Burgundy⟧ a lightweight helmet or steel cap, worn in the 16th cent.

bur·goo (bʉr′go͞o, bər go͞o′) *n.* ⟦18th-c. nautical slang < ? Ar *burghul* < Pers, lit., crushed grain⟧ **1** a thick oatmeal porridge ☆**2** [Dial.] *a)* a highly seasoned soup or stew made of meats and vegetables *b)* a barbecue, picnic, etc. at which this is served

Bur·gos (bo͝or′gôs) city in NC Spain

Bur·goyne (bər goin′, bʉr′goin), **John** 1722-92; Brit. general in the American Revolution: defeated by colonial forces under Gates at Saratoga (1777)

Bur·gun·dy[1] (bʉr′gən dē) *n., pl.* **-dies** [*often* **b-**] **1** *a)* any of the red or white wines, typically dry, made in Burgundy *b)* a red wine of similar type made elsewhere *c)* loosely, any dry red table wine **2** a purplish red

Bur·gun·dy[2] (bʉr′gən dē) **1** historical region in E France of varying extent **2** metropolitan region in E France: 12,194 sq mi (31,582 sq km); chief town, Dijon —**Bur·gun·di·an** (bər gun′dē ən) *adj., n.*

Burgundy

bur·i·al (ber′ē əl) *n.* ⟦ME *biriel,* false sing. of *berieles* < OE *byrgels,* tomb < *byrgan,* BURY⟧ **1** the act of burying; esp., the burying of a dead body; interment **2** *Archaeol. a)* a grave or tomb *b)* the contents of a grave or tomb —*adj.* of or connected with burial

burial ground a cemetery; graveyard

bur·i·er (-ər) *n.* a person or thing that buries

bu·rin (byo͝or′in) *n.* ⟦Fr < OFr < OIt *burino, borino* < Langobardic *boro,* borer; akin to OE *bor:* see BORE[1]⟧ **1** a short, pointed cutting tool with a round handle, used by engravers **2** *Archaeol.* a Stone Age chisel: see AURIGNACIAN

bur·ka (bʉr′kə) *n. alt. sp. of* BURQA

burke (bʉrk) *vt.* **burked, burk′ing** ⟦after William *Burke* (1792-1829), executed for the act, in Edinburgh⟧ **1** [Obs.] to murder by suffocating so as to leave the body unmarked and fit to be sold for dissection **2** to get rid of quietly; evade or suppress, as a parliamentary bill, discussion, etc.

Burke (bʉrk), **Edmund** 1729-97; Brit. statesman, orator, & writer, born in Ireland —**Burk·e·an** (bʉr′kē ən) *adj., n.*

Bur·ki·na Fa·so (bo͝or kē′nə fä′sō) country in W Africa, north of Ghana: under French control from 1895, it became independent (as *Upper Volta*) in 1960: 105,869 sq mi (274,200 sq km); cap. Ouagadougou

Bur·kitt's lymphoma (bʉr′kits) ⟦after D. P. *Burkitt* (1911-93), Brit surgeon in Uganda who first described it (1958)⟧ a cancer characterized by tumors containing lymphoid cells, occurring esp. in children, in the jaw, eyes, and internal organs: it is associated with the Epstein-Barr virus

burl (bʉrl) *n.* ⟦ME *burle* < OFr *bourle,* flocks or ends of threads < VL **burrula,* small flock of wool < LL *burra,* wool⟧ **1** a knot in wool, thread, yarn, etc. that gives a nubby appearance to cloth **2** a kind of knot on some tree trunks or woody roots **3** veneer made from wood with burls in it —*adj.* having a finish or veneer of or like burl —*vt.* to finish (cloth) by taking out the burls, loose threads, etc. —**burled** *adj.*

bur·lap (bʉr′lap′) *n.* ⟦17th-c. *borelappe(s)* < ? ME *borel,* coarse cloth (< OFr *burel:* see BUREAU) + *lappa,* hanging part of a garment, LAP[1] (akin to Ger *lappen,* Du *lap,* rag)⟧ a coarse cloth made of jute or hemp, used for making sacks, in upholstering furniture, as a backing for carpets, etc.

Bur·leigh (bʉr′lē) *alt. sp. of* 1st Baron BURGHLEY

bur·lesque (bər lesk′) *n.* ⟦Fr < It *burlesco* < *burla,* a jest, mockery⟧ **1** any broadly comic or satirical imitation, as of a writing, play, etc.; derisive caricature; parody ☆**2** a sort of vaudeville characterized by low comedy, striptease acts, etc. —*adj.* **1** derisively or comically imitating ☆**2** of or connected with burlesque (vaudeville) — *vt., vi.* **-lesqued′, -lesqu′ing** to imitate derisively or comically; parody —*SYN.* CARICATURE

☆**bur·ley** (bʉr′lē) *n.* ⟦after ? a proper name⟧ [*also* **B-**] a thin-leaved, light-colored tobacco grown in Kentucky and surrounding states, usually containing less nicotine than the dark-colored tobaccos

Bur·ling·ton (bʉr′liŋ tən) ⟦after local pronun. of *Bridlington,* port in NE England⟧ city in SE Ontario, Canada, on Lake Ontario

bur·ly (bʉr′lē) *adj.* **-li·er, -li·est** ⟦ME *borlich,* excellent, noble, handsome, altered (? by assoc. with *bour,* BOWER[1]) < OE *borlice,* very, excellently⟧ **1** big and strong; heavy and muscular **2** rough and hearty in manner; bluff —**bur′li·ness** *n.*

Bur·ma (bʉr′mə) *former name for* MYANMAR: name still in popular use

☆**bur marigold** any of a genus (*Bidens*) of weedy plants of the composite family, having yellow-rayed flowers and barbed fruits

Bur·mese (bər mēz′, -mēs′) *adj.* of Burma (Myanmar) or its people, language, or culture —*n., pl.* **-mese′ 1** a person born or living in Burma (Myanmar) **2** the Tibeto-Burman language of the Burmese **3** any of a breed of domestic cat, originating in Burma, with a short, glossy, dark brown coat and round, yellow eyes: coats of several other colors are found in European varieties Also, for *adj.* & *n.* 1 & 2, **Bur′man** (-mən)

burn[1] (bʉrn) *vt.* **burned** or **burnt, burn′ing** ⟦ME *brennen, bernen, burnen* < ON & OE: ON *brenna,* to burn, light; OE *bærnan,* to kindle (akin to Goth *brannjan,* to cause to burn) & *beornan,* to be on fire, metathetic < Gmc **brinnan* < IE **bhre-n-u-* < base **bhereu-,* to boil forth, well up > BOURN[1], BREAD, L *fervere,* Welsh *brydis,* to boil⟧ **1** to set on fire or subject to combustion, as in order to produce heat, light, or power **2** to destroy by fire **3** to put to death by fire **4** to injure or damage by fire or something with the effect of fire, as intense heat, friction, or acid; scorch, singe, scald, etc. **5** to consume as fuel [*to burn* much gasoline] **6** to transform (body fat, etc.) into energy by metabolism **7** to sunburn **8** to brand **9** to cauterize **10** to harden or glaze (bricks, pottery, etc.) by fire; fire **11** to cause by fire, heat, etc. [*to burn* a hole in a coat] **12** to cause a sensation of heat in [the horseradish *burns* the throat] **13** to use (candles, lights, heaters, etc.) ☆**14** [Slang] to electrocute **15** [Slang] *a)* to cheat, swindle, or rob *b)* to cause to suffer through misplaced trust or confidence: often used in the passive **16** *Comput., Electronics* to copy (data, audio or video files, etc.) onto (a CD, DVD, etc.) by means of a laser —*vi.* **1** to be on fire; flame; blaze **2** to undergo combustion **3** to give out light or heat; shine; glow **4** to be destroyed by fire or heat **5** to be injured or damaged by or as by fire or heat; become scorched, singed, etc. **6** to die by fire **7** to feel hot **8** to be excited or inflamed, as with desire, anger, etc. ☆**9** [Slang] to be electrocuted —*n.* **1** an injury or damage caused by fire, heat, radiation, wind, caustics, etc.: in medicine, burns are classified as **first-degree burn,** reddening, **second-degree burn,** blistering, and **third-degree burn,** destruction of the skin and the tissues under it **2** the process or result of burning, as in brick making ☆**3** a single firing of a rocket or thruster on a space vehicle —**burn down** to burn to the ground —**burn in** to darken (an area of a photographic print) by exposing it to more light —**burn out 1** to cease burning through lack of fuel **2** to disintegrate or wear out by heat from friction, etc. **3** to destroy the home, business, etc. of by fire **4** to exhaust (oneself) or become exhausted from overwork, stress, or dissipation —**burn rubber 1** to accelerate a vehicle so rapidly that the tires squeal as they spin without traction **2** [Informal] to move rapidly; hurry; rush —**burn up 1** to burn completely ☆**2** [Slang] to make or become angry —☆**to burn** [Informal] in excess [money *to burn*]

SYN.—**burn** is the broadest term in this comparison, denoting injury to any extent by fire, intense heat, friction, acid, etc. [a *burnt* log, *sunburned, windburned*]; **scorch** and **singe** both imply superficial burning, **scorch** emphasizing discoloration or damaging of texture [*to scorch* a shirt in ironing], and **singe,** the burning off, often intentional, of bristles, feathers, the ends of hair, etc.; **sear** implies the burning of animal tissue and is applied specifically to the quick browning of the outside, as of roasts, in cooking to seal in the juices; **char** implies a reduction by burning to charcoal or carbon. All of these terms have figurative applications [a *burning* desire, a *scorching* tirade, a *singed* reputation, a soul-*searing* experience, *charred* hopes]

burn[2] (bʉrn) *n.* ⟦ME *burne,* BOURN[1]⟧ [Scot.] a brook

burn·a·ble (bʉr′nə bəl) *adj.* that can be burned —*n.* something, especially refuse, that can be burned

Bur·na·by (bʉr′nə bē) city in SW British Columbia, Canada, east of Vancouver

Burne-Jones (bʉrn′jōnz′), Sir **Edward Co·ley** (kō′lē) 1833-98; Eng. painter & designer

burn·er (bʉr′nər) *n.* **1** the part of a stove, furnace, etc. from which the flame or heat comes **2** an apparatus for burning fuel or trash; furnace, incinerator, etc. **3** ⟦< BURN[1] (*vt.* 16)⟧ a device for copying digital data onto a CD, DVD, etc.

bur·net (bʉr′nit) *n.* ⟦ME < OFr *burnet, brunet:* see BRUNET⟧ any of a genus (*Sanguisorba*) of plants of the rose family, with white, red, purple, or greenish, apetalous flowers in thimble-shaped heads; esp., an herb (*S. minor* or more recently *Poterium sanguisorba*) with leaves that are used as in salads, seasonings, and herbal teas

Bur·nett (bər net′), **Frances (Eliza) Hodg·son** (häj′sən) 1849-1924; U.S. writer, esp. of children's books, born in England

Bur·ney (bʉr′nē), **Fanny** (born *Frances Burney;* married name *Madame d'Arblay*) 1752-1840; Eng. novelist & diarist

burn·ing (bʉr′niŋ) *adj.* **1** that burns **2** of the utmost seriousness or importance [a *burning* issue]

burning bush ⟦after the biblical burning bush: Ex. 3:2⟧ ☆**1** any of several American shrubs (genus *Euonymus*) of the staff-tree family, having brilliant red fruits or leaves **2** GAS PLANT

burning glass a convex lens for focusing the sun's rays so as to produce heat or set fire to something

bur·nish (bʉr′nish) *vt., vi.* ⟦ME *burnishen* < OFr *burniss-,* extended stem of *brunir,* to make brown < *brun:* see BRUNET⟧ to make or become shiny by rubbing; polish —*n.* a gloss or polish —*SYN.* POLISH —**bur′nish·er** *n.*

bur·noose or **bur·nous** (bər no͞os′, bʉr′no͞os′) *n.* ⟦Fr *burnous* < Ar *burnus,* prob. < Gr *birros,* a cloak⟧ a long cloak with a hood, worn by Arabs and Moors

burn·out (bʉrn′out′) *n.* **1** the point at which a rocket's fuel or oxidizer is completely burned up and the rocket enters its free-flight phase or is jettisoned 2 damage caused by overheating ☆3 *a)* a state of emotional exhaustion caused by the stresses of one's work or responsibilities *b)* [Slang] a person in a state of mental or physical exhaustion, as from dissipation or overwork, and therefore fatigued, unmotivated, etc.

Burns (burnz), **Robert** 1759-96; Scot. poet

Burn·side (burn′sīd′), **Ambrose Everett** 1824-81; Union general in the Civil War

☆**burn·sides** (burn′sīdz′) *pl.n.* ⟦after prec.⟧ a style of beard with full side whiskers and mustache, but with the chin cleanshaven

burnt (burnt) *vt., vi. alt. pt. & pp. of* BURN[1] —*adj.* that has been burned

burnt offering an animal, food, etc. burned at an altar as an offering or sacrifice to a god

burnt orange a reddish orange

burnt sienna 1 an orange-red pigment made by calcining raw sienna 2 an orange red

burnt umber 1 a reddish-brown pigment made by calcining raw umber 2 a reddish brown

☆**bur oak** a North American white oak (*Quercus macrocarpa*) having large acorns with fringed cups; mossy-cup oak

☆**burp** (burp) *n.* ⟦echoic⟧ BELCH (*n.* 1) —*vi.* to expel gas through the mouth from the stomach; belch —*vt.* to cause (a baby) to relieve itself of stomach gas, as by patting its back

☆**burp gun** ⟦echoic of the rapid bursts of fire⟧ [Mil. Slang] an automatic pistol or submachine gun

bur·qa (bur′kə) *n.* ⟦Urdu *burqa′* < Ar *burqu′*⟧ a long, loose outer garment that covers the entire body with only a small opening for the eyes, worn outside the home by women in some Muslim countries

burr[1] (bur) *n.* ⟦var. of BUR[1]⟧ 1 a rough edge or ridge left on metal or other material by cutting or drilling 2 a washer on the small end of a rivet 3 BUR[1] (senses 1, 2, & 3) —*vt.* 1 to form a rough edge on 2 to remove burrs from (metal)

burr[2] (bur) *n.* ⟦prob. echoic⟧ 1 the trilling of *r*, with uvula or tongue, as in the dialectal speech of N England and Scotland 2 a whirring sound —*vi.* 1 to speak with a burr 2 to make a whir —*vt.* to pronounce with a burr

burr[3] (bur) *n.* BUHRSTONE

Burr (bur), **Aaron** 1756-1836; U.S. political leader: vice president of the U.S. (1801-05): killed Alexander Hamilton in a duel (1804)

bur reed ⟦descriptive⟧ any of a genus (*Sparganium*) of the bur-reed family, having grasslike leaves and hard, dry, prickly fruits

bur-reed (-rēd′) *adj.* designating a family (Sparganiaceae, order Typhales) of monocotyledonous marsh or water plants

☆**bur·ri·to** (bə rē′tō) *n., pl.* **-tos** ⟦MexSp < Sp, little burro⟧ a Mexican dish consisting of a flour tortilla wrapped around a filling of meat, cheese, fried beans, etc.

bur·ro (bur′ō, boor′ō) *n., pl.* **-ros** ⟦Sp < *burrico* < LL *burricus*, small horse⟧ a donkey, esp. one used as a pack animal in the SW U.S.

Bur·roughs (bur′ōz) 1 **Edgar Rice** 1875-1950; U.S. writer of popular fiction: known for his *Tarzan* stories 2 **John** 1837-1921; U.S. naturalist & writer 3 **William S(eward)** 1914-97; U.S. novelist

bur·row (bur′ō) *n.* ⟦ME *burgh* (see BOROUGH), infl. by *bergh*, hill, *berwen*, to defend, take refuge⟧ 1 a hole or tunnel dug in the ground by an animal 2 any similar passage or hole for shelter, refuge, etc. —*vi.* 1 to make a burrow; dig (*in, into, under*, etc.) 2 to live or hide in or as in a burrow 3 to delve or search, as if by digging —*vt.* 1 to make burrows in (the ground) 2 to make by burrowing 3 to hide or shelter in or as in a burrow

☆**burrowing owl** a ground owl (*Athene cunicularia*) of the prairie regions of North and South America having long legs and a small head: it makes its nest in abandoned burrows

burr·stone (bur′stōn′) *n.* BUHRSTONE

bur·ry[1] (bur′ē) *adj.* **-ri·er, -ri·est** 1 full of burs 2 like a bur; prickly

bur·ry[2] (bur′ē) *adj.* **-ri·er, -ri·est** having a burr: said of speech

bur·sa (bur′sə) *n., pl.* **-sae** (-sē) or **-sas** ⟦ModL < ML, a purse, bag: see PURSE⟧ *Anat.* a sac or pouchlike cavity, esp. one containing a fluid that reduces friction, as between a tendon and bone —**bur′sal** *adj.*

Bur·sa (boor sä′) city in NW Turkey: capital of the Ottoman Empire in the 14th cent.

bur·sar (bur′sər) *n.* ⟦ML *bursarius*, treasurer < *bursa*: see PURSE⟧ 1 a treasurer, as of a college or similar institution 2 in Scotland, a university student who has a scholarship

bur·sa·ry (bur′sə rē) *n., pl.* **-ries** ⟦ML *bursaria* < *bursarius*: see prec.⟧ 1 a treasury, esp. of a college 2 in Scotland and Canada, a university scholarship

burse (burs) *n.* ⟦Fr *bourse*: see BOURSE⟧ 1 a purse 2 BURSARY (sense 2) 3 *R.C.Ch.* a flat, square, silk case for carrying the folded corporal to and from the altar

bur·se·ra (bur′sə rə) *adj.* ⟦< ModL n., after J. *Burser* (1583-1639), Ger botanist⟧ designating a family (Burseraceae, order Sapindales) of dicotyledonous, resinous shrubs and trees, including balm of Gilead, bdellium, and myrrh

bur·si·form (bur′sə fôrm′) *adj.* ⟦< ML *bursa* (see PURSE) + -FORM⟧ *Anat., Zool.* shaped like a bursa, or sac; pouchlike

bur·si·tis (bər sīt′is) *n.* ⟦ModL < BURSA + -ITIS⟧ inflammation of a bursa, as near the shoulder or hip

burst (burst) *vi.* **burst, burst′ing** ⟦ME *bresten, bersten* < OE *berstan* & ON *bresta*, both < IE base *bhres-, to burst, break, crack⟧ 1 to come apart suddenly and violently, as from internal pressure; fly into pieces; break open or out; explode 2 to give sudden expression to some feeling; break (*into* tears, laughter, a tirade, etc.) 3 to go, come, start, appear, etc. suddenly and with force [*he burst into the room*] 4 *a)* to be as full, crowded, or packed as possible *b)* to be filled (*with* anger, pride, energy, etc.) —*vt.* 1 to cause to burst; make explode 2 to fill or cause to swell to the bursting point —*n.* ⟦ME *burst, brist*, a damage, defect, injury < OE *byrst*, loss⟧ 1 the act of bursting; explosion, as of an artillery shell 2 the result of a bursting; break; rupture 3 a sudden, violent display of feeling 4 a sudden, forceful action; spurt [*a burst of speed*] 5 a volley of shots, or a single series of shots from an automatic firearm

bur·then (bur′thən) *n., vt.* [Archaic] BURDEN[1]

bur·ton (burt′'n) *n.* ⟦? altered < BRETON[1]⟧ a kind of tackle consisting of single or double pulley blocks and used as for tightening rigging or moving heavy articles

Bur·ton (burt′'n) 1 Sir **Richard Francis** 1821-90; Eng. writer & explorer 2 **Robert** (pseud. *Democritus Junior*) 1577-1640; Eng. writer & clergyman: author of *The Anatomy of Melancholy*

Bu·ru (boo͞′roo͞) island of Indonesia, in the Molucca group: 3,670 sq mi (9,505 sq km)

Bu·run·di (bə roon′dē, -roo͞n′-) country in EC Africa, east of the Democratic Republic of the Congo: 10,745 sq mi (27,830 sq km); cap. Bujumbura: see RUANDA-URUNDI —**Bu·run′di·an** *adj., n.*

bur·weed (bur′wēd′) *n.* any of various plants with burs, as the burdock, bur marigold, cocklebur, etc.

bur·y (ber′ē) *vt.* **bur′ied, bur′y·ing** ⟦ME *birien* < OE *byrgan*, akin to *beorgan*, to shelter < IE base *bhergh-, protect, preserve > Ger *bergen*, protect, Pol *bróg*, barn⟧ 1 to put (a dead body) into the earth, a tomb, or the sea, usually in a ceremonial manner; inter 2 *a)* to hide (something) in the ground *b)* to cover up so as to conceal [*she buried her face in the pillow*] 3 to put away, as from one's life, mind, etc. [*to bury a feud*] 4 to put (oneself) deeply into; plunge; immerse [*to bury oneself in one's work*] —*SYN.* HIDE[1]

Bur·y (ber′ē) city in Greater Manchester, NW England

bus (bus) *n., pl.* **bus′es** or **bus′ses** ⟦< (OMNI)BUS⟧ 1 a large, long motor vehicle designed to carry many passengers, usually along a regular route; omnibus 2 [Slang] an automobile 3 *Comput.* a communications pathway, as of wires, in a computer or computer system, that transmits and directs data, used for connecting internal components, networks, peripherals, etc. 4 *Elec.* a heavy copper bar, strap, or other similar conductor that is not insulated, usually carries a large current, and connects many electrical circuits: also called **bus bar** —*vt.* **bused** or **bussed, bus′ing** or **bus′sing** 1 to transport by bus; specif., to transport (children) by busing ☆2 in a restaurant, cafeteria, etc., to clear dirty dishes from [*to bus tables*] —*vi.* 1 to go by bus ☆2 to do the work of a busboy —**throw someone under the bus** [Informal] to sacrifice or abandon (a comrade, associate, etc.) as to protect or benefit oneself

Bus or **bus** *abbrev.* business

Bu·san (boo͞′sän′) seaport in SE South Korea, on the Korea Strait

☆**bus·boy** (bus′boi′) *n.* a worker in a restaurant who sets and clears tables

bus·by (buz′bē) *n., pl.* **-bies** ⟦18th c., a large wig; prob. after the name *Busby*⟧ a tall fur hat worn as part of a full-dress uniform by hussars, guardsmen in the British army, etc.

busby

bush[1] (boosh) *n.* ⟦ME < OE *busc* (in place names) < WGmc *busk-; ME *busk, bosk* < ML *boscus* < Frank *busk*, of same WGmc orig.⟧ 1 a woody plant having many stems branching out low instead of one main stem or trunk; shrub 2 a thicket of shrubs 3 anything resembling a bush; esp., *a)* a thickly furred tail *b)* [Slang] a beard *c)* [Slang] a woman's pubic hair (somewhat vulgar) ☆4 ⟦< Colonial Du *bosch*, bush⟧ shrubby woodland or uncleared country, esp. wild or unsettled frontier country: usually with *the* 5 *a)* a branch of ivy as a symbol for wine, formerly used on tavern signboards *b)* [Obs.] a tavern —*vi.* to grow thickly or spread out like a bush —*vt.* to decorate, cover, or surround with bushes —*adj.* ☆⟦see BUSH LEAGUE⟧ [Slang] unprofessional, cheap, petty, etc. —**beat around the bush** to talk around a subject without getting to the point —☆**the bushes** [Slang] rural or small-town districts

bush[2] (boosh) [Brit.] *n.* ⟦MDu *busse*, box < ML *buxis*: see BOX[1]⟧ BUSHING —*vt.* to fit with a bushing

Bush (boosh) 1 **George H(erbert) W(alker)** 1924- ; 41st president of the U.S. (1989-93) 2 **George W(alker)** 1946- ; 43d president of the U.S. (2001-09): son of George 3 **Van·ne·var** (və nē′vär) 1890-1974; U.S. electrical engineer & administrator

bush baby any of a family (Galagidae) of nocturnal prosimian primates of tropical African forests, with a long, bushy tail and large eyes

☆**bush bean** any of various low, erect, bushy forms of the common garden bean (*Phaseolus vulgaris*): see POLE BEAN

bush·buck (-buk′) *n., pl.* **-buck′** or **-bucks′** a small African antelope (*Tragelaphus scriptus*)

bushed (boosht) *adj.* 1 [Chiefly Austral. & N.Z.] bewildered, as by being lost in the bush ☆2 [Informal] very tired; exhausted

bush·el[1] (boosh′əl) *n.* ⟦ME *busshel* < OFr *boissel* < *boisse*, grain measure < Gaul *bostia, handful < *bosta, palm of the hand⟧ 1 a unit of dry measure for grain, fruit, etc., equal to 32 dry quarts or 4 pecks (35.2384 dry liters or 1.2445 cubic feet): abbrev. *bu* **2** a container holding one bushel **3** a weight taken as the equivalent of one bushel **4** [Informal] a large amount Abbrev. *bu*

☆**bush·el**[2] (boosh′əl) ***vt., vi.*** **-eled** or **-elled**, **-el·ing** or **-el·ling** ⟦< ? Ger *bosseln,* to patch up, repair⟧ to repair, renovate, or alter (esp. garments) —**bush′el·er** ***n.***, **bush′el·ler**

bush·el·bas·ket (boosh′əl bas′kit) ***n.*** a rounded basket with a capacity of one bushel

☆**bush·ham·mer** (boosh′ham′ər) ***n.*** ⟦prob. < Ger *bosshammer* < *bossen,* to beat, dress (stone) + *hammer,* HAMMER⟧ a kind of hammer, now usually power-driven, whose face has projecting points, used to dress stone

Bu·shi·do (boo͞′shē dō′) ***n.*** ⟦Jpn, way of the warrior⟧ [*also* **b-**] the chivalric code of the samurai of feudal Japan, emphasizing loyalty, courage, and the preference of death to dishonor

bush·i·ness (boosh′ē nis) ***n.*** a bushy quality or state

bush·ing (boosh′iŋ) ***n.*** ⟦< BUSH[2]⟧ **1** a removable, cylindrical lining or sleeve used in a machine to reduce the effect of friction on moving parts, decrease the diameter of an opening, etc. **2** *Elec.* a similar insulating lining or part

☆**bush jacket** a belted, hip-length jacket with buttoned patch pockets: also **bush coat**

☆**bush league** [Slang] **1** MINOR LEAGUE **2** any small or second-rate sphere of activity, etc. —**bush′-league′** ***adj.***

☆**bush leaguer** [Slang] **1** a baseball player in a bush league **2** an unimportant or second-rate performer in any sphere of activity

bush lot [Cdn.] a tract of timberland

bush·man (boosh′mən) ***n.,*** *pl.* **-men** (-mən) **1** a person who lives in the Australian bush **2** a backwoodsman **3** [**B-**] *a)* a member of a nomadic people living in the region of the Kalahari Desert in S Africa *b)* the Khoisan language of this people: term now considered disparaging by some

bush·mas·ter (-mas′tər) ***n.*** a pit viper (*Lachesis muta*) of Central and South America: the largest venomous snake in the New World

bush pig any of a genus (*Potamochoerus*) of wild African pigs that live in forested regions

bush·rang·er (-rān′jər) ***n.*** ⟦< BUSH[1] (sense 4) + RANGER⟧ **1** a person who lives in the bush; backwoodsman **2** in Australia, an outlaw living in the bush

bush·tit (boosh′tit′) ***n.*** a small, grayish, long-tailed tit (*Psaltriparus minimus*) of a passerine family (Aegithalidae) of birds, found in W North America

☆**bush·wa** (boosh′wä, boozh′-) ***n.*** ⟦prob. altered < BULLSHIT⟧ [Slang] nonsense

☆**bush·whack** (boosh′hwak′, -wak′) ***vi.*** ⟦prob. < BUSH[1] + WHACK⟧ **1** to beat or cut one's way through bushes **2** to move a boat along a stream by pulling at the bushes on the bank **3** to engage in guerrilla fighting, attacking from ambush —*vt.* to ambush —**bush′whack′er** ***n.*** —**bush′whack′ing** ***n.***

bush·y (boosh′ē) ***adj.*** **bush′i·er**, **bush′i·est** **1** covered or overgrown with bushes **2** thick and spreading out like a bush [*a bushy tail*]

bush·y-tailed (-tāld′) ***adj.*** *in figurative use, mainly in the phrase* **bright-eyed and bushy-tailed**, fresh, alert, eager, and lively

bus·i·ly (biz′ə lē) ***adv.*** in a busy manner

busi·ness (biz′nis) ***n.*** ⟦ME *bisinesse* < OE *bisignes:* see BUSY & -NESS⟧ **1** one's work, occupation, or profession **2** a special task, duty, or function **3** rightful concern or responsibility: often used in such phrases as **mind your own business** and **none of your business** **4** a matter, affair, activity, etc. [*the business of packing for a trip*] **5** the buying and selling of commodities and services; commerce; trade **6** a commercial or industrial establishment; store, factory, etc. **7** the trade or patronage of customers **8** commercial practice or policy **9** a bit of action in a drama, as pouring a drink, intended to establish character, take up a pause in dialogue, etc. —***adj.*** **1** of or for business **2** designating or of premium or just-below premium accommodations, as on an aircraft **3** *Bridge* designating a double intended to penalize one's opponents: cf. TAKEOUT (*adj.* 2) —**do business with** **1** to engage in commerce with **2** to have dealings with —**do one's (or its) business** [Slang] to defecate: said esp. of pets —☆**give (or get) the business** [Slang] to subject (or be subjected) to rough treatment, practical joking, etc. —**like nobody's business** [Slang] to a very high degree; with great energy, intensity, etc. —**mean business** [Informal] to be in earnest

SYN.—**business**, in this comparison, refers generally to the buying and selling of commodities and services and connotes a profit motive; **commerce** and **trade** both refer to the distribution or exchange of commodities, esp. as this involves their transportation, but **commerce** generally implies such activity on a large scale between cities, countries, etc.; **industry** refers chiefly to the large-scale manufacture of commodities

business administration a program of studies at a college or university covering finance, management of personnel, etc., designed to prepare a person for a career in business

business agent a representative of a labor union local, who investigates working conditions, negotiates contracts, etc.

business card a small card identifying a person in connection with his or her business, given to a client, potential customer, etc.

☆**business college** a postsecondary school offering courses in word processing, bookkeeping, etc. to prepare students for office work

business cycle the regular alternation of periods of expansion and contraction that occur in an industry or economy

business end [Informal] the end or part of a tool, weapon, etc. most directly involved in carrying out the device's function

business envelope an envelope into which standard-size (8½″ × 11″) letterhead stationery can be put with only two folds: also called **business-size envelope**

busi·ness·like (-līk′) ***adj.*** having the qualities needed in business; efficient, methodical, etc.

busi·ness·man (-man′) ***n.,*** *pl.* **-men′** (-men′) a man in business, esp. as an owner or executive

☆**business office** the office where the financial transactions, bookkeeping, etc. for a firm or institution are carried on

busi·ness·per·son (-pur′sən) ***n.*** a person in business: often used to avoid the gender-specific terms *businessman* and *businesswoman*

☆**business school** a school offering courses, esp. at the graduate level, in economics, management, accounting, etc.

☆**busi·ness·wom·an** (-woom′ən) ***n.,*** *pl.* **-wom′en** (-wim′in) a woman in business, esp. as an owner or executive

bus·ing or **bus·sing** (bus′iŋ) ***n.*** ☆the transporting of children by buses to schools outside their neighborhoods as a result of a federal court's order to desegregate the school system

busk (busk) ***vi.*** ⟦< earlier sense, to seek < MFr *busquer* < Sp *buscar,* to seek (? orig. sense, "to gather wood") < Goth **buska,* a stick, log, akin to MHG *bosch,* a club⟧ [Brit.] to perform for money as a singer or strolling entertainer in public places —**busk′er** ***n.***

bus·kin (bus′kin) ***n.*** ⟦< ? OFr *broissequin* < MDu *brosekin,* small leather boot⟧ **1** a boot reaching to the calf or knee, worn in earlier times; esp., the high, thick-soled, laced boot worn by actors in ancient Greek and Roman tragedy **2** tragic drama; tragedy —**bus′kined** (-kind) ***adj.***

bus·man (bus′mən) ***n.,*** *pl.* **-men** (-mən) the operator of a bus

busman's holiday ⟦from the idea of a bus driver taking a vacation during which he does the driving himself⟧ a holiday or vacation in which one does as recreation what one usually does as one's work

Bu·so·ni (boo͞ zô′nē), **Fer·ruc·cio Ben·ve·nu·to** (fer ro͞ot′chô ben′ve noo͞′tô) 1866-1924; It. composer

buss (bus) ***n., vt., vi.*** ⟦prob., like Ger dial. *bus,* Welsh & Gael *bus,* kiss, lip, of echoic orig.⟧ [Now Chiefly Dial.] kiss, esp. in an unrestrained or playful manner

bus·ses (bus′iz) ***n.*** *alt. pl. of* BUS

bust[1] (bust) ***n.*** ⟦Fr *buste* < It *busto*⟧ **1** a piece of sculpture representing the head, shoulders, and upper chest of a human body **2** a woman's bosom, including her breasts **3** the circumference of a woman's chest, measured at its fullest point —*SYN.* BREAST

bust[2] (bust) ***vt.*** ⟦orig., dial. var. of BURST⟧ [Informal] **1** to burst or break **2** to make penniless or bankrupt ☆**3** to demote in rank ☆**4** to tame (esp. broncos) ☆**5** to hit ☆**6** to arrest **7** to make a RAID (*n.* 2) on —***vi.*** [Informal] **1** to burst or break **2** to become penniless or bankrupt —***n.*** [Informal] ☆**1** a person or thing that is a total failure ☆**2** a financial collapse; economic crash ☆**3** a punch ☆**4** a spree ☆**5** an arrest —**bust one's tail** (or **butt** or **hump**) [Slang] to make great efforts; try very hard: also **bust one's ass** (a somewhat vulgar variant) —**bust′ed** ***adj.***

bus·tard (bus′tərd) ***n.*** ⟦ME < OFr *bistarde* (< OIt *bistarda*) & *ostarde,* both < L *avis tarda,* lit., slow bird, prob. folk etym. for name of Iberian orig.⟧ any of a family (Otididae) of large, heavy, long-legged gruiform birds of Europe, Asia, and Africa

bust·er (bus′tər) ***n.*** ⟦BUST[2] + -ER⟧ ☆**1** *short for* BRONCOBUSTER, TRUSTBUSTER, etc. ☆**2** [*also* **B-**] boy; man; fellow: a mildly contemptuous or jocular term of direct address

-bust·er (bus′tər) ⟦? var. of *burster* (< BURST, *vt.* + -ER), or < BUST[2] + -ER⟧ *combining form* a person or thing that breaks, destroys, or incapacitates (a specified person or thing): used to form slangy compounds [*budgetbuster*]

☆**bus·tic** (bus′tik) ***n.*** ⟦< ?⟧ a tropical tree (*Dipholis salicifolia*) of the sapodilla family, native to S Fla. and the West Indies, with hard, dark wood used in making cabinets

bus·tier (boo͞s tyā′) ***n.*** ⟦Fr < *buste,* bosom: see BUST[1]⟧ **1** a woman's waist-length, tightfitting, often strapless undergarment, somewhat like a corset **2** a woman's outer garment or dress bodice resembling this

bus·tle[1] (bus′əl) ***vi., vt.*** **-tled**, **-tling** ⟦for earlier *buskle* < ME *busken,* to prepare, adorn < ON *buask,* to make onself ready < *bua,* to prepare (*see* BONDAGE) + *sik,* refl. pron.⟧ to hurry busily or with much fuss and bother —***n.*** busy and noisy activity; commotion —**bus′tling·ly** ***adv.***

bus·tle[2] (bus′əl) ***n.*** ⟦< ?⟧ a framework or padding formerly worn at the back by women to puff out the skirt

bust·line (bust′līn′) ***n.*** **1** BUST[1] (sense 3) **2** the size or contour of a woman's breasts

☆**bust·y** (bus′tē) ***adj.*** **bust′i·er**, **bust′i·est** having a large bust, or bosom

bus·y (biz′ē) ***adj.*** **bus′i·er**, **bus′i·est** ⟦ME *busi* < OE *bisig,* occupied, diligent; akin to Du *bezig:* seen only in LowG & E⟧ **1** occupied in some activity; at work; not idle **2** full of activity; characterized by much action or motion **3** *a)* in use at the moment, as a telephone line *b)* indicating such use [*the busy signal*] **4** meddlesome **5** having so much detail, variety of color, etc. as to create a confusing, displeasing effect —***vt.*** **bus′ied**, **bus′y·ing** ⟦ME *busien* < OE *bisgian,* to occupy, employ < *bisgu,* occupation, labor⟧ to make or keep busy: often used reflexively —**bus′y·ness** ***n.***

bustle

SYN.—busy suggests active employment in some task or activity, either temporarily or habitually [I'm *busy* just now]; **industrious** suggests habitual devotion to one's work or activity [an *industrious* salesclerk]; **diligent** implies unremitting attention, usually to a particular task, and connotes enjoyment in the task itself [a *diligent* student of music]; **assiduous** suggests painstaking, persevering preoccupation with some task [*assiduous* study]; **sedulous** implies unremitting devotion to a task until the goal is reached [a *sedulous* investigation of the crime] **—ANT. idle, lazy**

bus·y·bod·y (-bäd′ē) ***n.,*** *pl.* **-bod′ies** a person who mixes into other people's affairs; meddler or gossip

☆**bus·y·work** or **bus·y-work** (-wurk′) ***n.*** an activity, often as assigned to a class in school, that has little purpose beyond keeping one occupied for a time

but[1] (but; *unstressed* bət) ***prep.*** ⟦ME < OE *butan, buton,* without, outside; WGmc comp. < **be-, *bi-,* BY + **utana,* from without: see OUT⟧ **1** with the exception of; excepting; save [nobody came *but* me]: earlier, and still sometimes, regarded as a conjunction and followed by the nominative case [nobody came *but* I (came)] **2** except; other than: used with an infinitive as the object [we cannot choose *but* (to) stay] **—*conj.*** **1** and in spite of this; and even so; yet [he is a villain, *but* he has some virtues] **2** and on the contrary [I am old, *but* you are young] **3** unless; except that [it never rains *but* it pours] **4** that [I don't question *but* you're correct] **5** that . . . not [it's not so high *but* we can jump it] **—*adv.*** **1** only [if I had *but* known] **2** merely; no more than; not otherwise than [he is *but* a child] **3** just [I heard it *but* now] **4** on the other hand; yet: used to introduce a sentence **5** [Slang] absolutely; positively [he did it, *but* good] **—*pron.*** who . . . not; which . . . not [not a man *but* felt it] **—but for** if it were not for **—but that 1** about the fact that [I've no doubt *but that* he'll come] **2** that there is not some chance that [we can't be sure *but that* he's right] Also [Informal] **but what**

but[2] (but) ***n.*** ⟦akin to prec.⟧ [Scot.] the outer room, esp. the kitchen, of a cottage **—but and ben** [Scot.] the whole dwelling: originally, the outer and inner rooms of a two-room cottage

bu·ta·caine sulfate (byo͞ot′ə kān′) ⟦< *butacaine* < BUTA(NE) + (CO)CAINE⟧ a colorless, crystalline substance, $(C_{18}H_{30}N_2O_2)_2{\cdot}H_2SO_4$, used as a local anesthetic, esp. on mucous membranes

bu·ta·di·ene (byo͞ot′ə dī′ēn, -dī ēn′) ***n.*** ⟦< fol. + DI-[1] + -ENE⟧ a highly reactive hydrocarbon, $H_2C{:}CHHC{:}CH_2$, obtained from petroleum and used to make synthetic rubbers and resins

bu·tane (byo͞o′tān′, byo͞o tān′) ***n.*** ⟦BUT(YL) + -ANE⟧ either of two alkanes (**normal butane** and **isobutane**) having the same formula, C_4H_{10}, but different structures and used esp. as a fuel

bu·ta·nol (byo͞o′tə nôl′, -nōl′) ***n.*** ⟦< prec. + -OL[1]⟧ BUTYL ALCOHOL

bu·ta·none (byo͞o′tə nōn′) ***n.*** ⟦BUTAN(E) + -ONE⟧ METHYL ETHYL KETONE

butch (bo͝och) ***adj.*** ⟦prob. after *Butch,* nickname for a boy, contr. < ? fol.⟧ ☆[Slang] masculine in appearance, manner, etc.: sometimes used specif. of a lesbian **—*n.*** ☆**1** [Slang] a tough or rugged man or boy: used chiefly in direct address **2** [Slang] a woman, esp. a lesbian, whose appearance, manner, etc. is that which is traditionally regarded as masculine **3** [Informal] BUZZ CUT

butch·er (bo͝och′ər) ***n.*** ⟦ME *bocher* < OFr *bochier, bouchier,* one who kills and sells he-goats < *bouc,* he-goat < Frank **bukk,* akin to OE *bucca*: see BUCK[1]⟧ **1** a person whose work is killing animals or dressing their carcasses for meat **2** a person who cuts up meat for sale **3** anyone who kills as if slaughtering animals ☆**4** [Old Informal] a person who sells candy, drinks, etc. in theaters, trains, circuses, etc. **—*vt.*** **1** to kill or dress (animals) for meat **2** to kill (people, game, etc.) brutally, senselessly, or in large numbers; slaughter **3** to mess up; botch **—butch′er·er *n.* —butch′er·ly *adj.***

butch·er·bird (-burd′) ***n.*** any of various shrikes which, after killing prey, impale it on thorns: also **butcher bird**

butcher block ⟦because made like a butcher's chopping block⟧ designating or of a thick slab made by gluing together strips of hardwood, as maple or oak, used for counter and table tops, etc.: also **butch′er-block′ *adj.***

butch·er's-broom (bo͝och′ərz bro͞om′) ***n.*** ⟦? because formerly used to sweep butchers' shops⟧ a shrubby plant (*Ruscus aculeatus*) of the lily family, with leathery, leaflike, flattened branches, clusters of small, white flowers, and large, red berries

butch·er·y (bo͝och′ər ē) ***n.,*** *pl.* **-er·ies** ⟦ME *bocherie* < OFr *boucherie:* see BUTCHER⟧ **1** [Now Chiefly Brit.] a place where animals are killed for meat; slaughterhouse **2** the work or business of a butcher **3** brutal bloodshed or slaughter **4** the act or result of botching **—*SYN.*** SLAUGHTER

Bute (byo͞ot) **1** island of Scotland, in the Firth of Clyde: 46 sq mi (119 sq km) **2** former county of SW Scotland, which included this island: also **Bute′shire** (-shir)

bu·tene (byo͞o′tēn′) ***n.*** BUTYLENE

bu·te·o (byo͞ot′ē ō′) ***n.*** ⟦ModL < L: see BUZZARD⟧ any of a genus (*Buteo*) of large, broad-winged, soaring hawks that prey mainly on rodents

but·le (but′'l) ***vi.*** **-led, -ling** ⟦< fol.⟧ [Informal] to serve as a butler: a humorous usage

but·ler (but′lər) ***n.*** ⟦ME *boteler* < OFr *bouteillier,* cupbearer < *bouteille,* BOTTLE[1]⟧ a manservant, now usually the head servant of a household, in charge of wines, pantry, table silver, etc.

But·ler (but′lər) **1 Benjamin Franklin** 1818-93; U.S. politician & Union general in the Civil War **2 Joseph** 1692-1752; Eng. theologian & bishop **3 Samuel** 1612-80; Eng. satirical poet **4 Samuel** 1835-1902; Eng. novelist

butler's pantry a serving pantry between the kitchen and the dining room

butt[1] (but) ***n.*** ⟦< several bases, variously confused in E or Fr: ME *but, butte,* thick end, ? akin to ON *būtr,* block of wood, Du *bot,* stumpy, stocky, or ? < OFr *bout,* end < *buter* (see fol.); ME *but,* target, boundary < MFr *bout,* aim, goal, < *abuter,* to aim < *à,* at (< L *ad*) + *but,* goal (< ?)⟧ **1** the thick end of anything, as of a whip handle, rifle stock, etc. **2** the remaining end of anything; stub; stump; specif., the stub of a smoked cigarette or cigar **3** *a)* ⟦? infl. by Fr *butte,* mound < OFr *buter*⟧ a mound of earth, bales of straw, etc. behind a target, for receiving fired rounds or shot arrows *b)* a target *c)* [*pl.*] a target range **4** a hole in the ground used as a blind by hunters of fowl **5** an object of ridicule or criticism **6** [Slang] a cigarette **7** [Informal] the buttocks **8** [Obs.] *a)* a limit *b)* a goal **9** *Tanning* the part of a hide or pelt that covered the animal's backside **—*vt., vi.*** to join end to end

butt[2] (but) ***vt.*** ⟦ME *butten,* to drive, thrust < OFr *buter* (< Frank **botan*), to thrust against: for IE base see BEAT⟧ **1** to strike or push with the head or horns; ram with the head **2** to strike or bump against **3** to abut on **4** to make abut: (*on, upon,* or *against*) **—*vi.*** **1** to make a butting motion **2** to move or drive headfirst **3** to stick out; project **4** to abut **—*n.*** ⟦ME; prob. < OFr *buter,* or < the v.⟧ **1** a thrust with the head or horns **2** a thrust in fencing **—**☆**butt in (or into)** [Informal] to mix into (another's business, a conversation, etc.) **—butt out!** [Slang] stop meddling! mind your own business!

butt[3] (but) ***n.*** ⟦ME *butte* < OFr *botte* < ML *butta* < LL *buttis,* cask⟧ **1** a large barrel or cask, as for wine or beer **2** a measure of liquid capacity equal to *a)* for wine, 126 gallons (2 hogsheads) or *c.* 104.9 imperial gallons (*c.* 476.9 liters) *b)* for ale or beer, 108 gallons or *c.* 89.9 imperial gallons (*c.* 408.8 liters)

butt[4] (but) ***n.*** ⟦ME *butte, but;* prob. < MLowG *butte* (> Swed *butta,* Du *bot,* Ger *butte*) < adj. *butte,* lumpy: akin to BUTT[2]⟧ any of various flatfishes, as the halibut or turbot

butte (byo͞ot) ***n.*** ⟦Fr, mound < OFr *buter*: see BUTT[2]⟧ a steep, flat-topped hill surrounded by a plain, esp. in the W U.S.; a remnant of a mesa; small mesa

but·ter (but′ər) ***n.*** ⟦ME *butere* < OE < L *butyrum* < Gr *boutyron* < *bous,* ox, COW[1] + *tyros,* cheese; akin to Avestan *tū'ri,* curds⟧ **1** the solid, yellowish, edible fat that results from churning cream or whole milk, used as a spread, in cooking, etc. **2** any of various substances somewhat like butter; specif., *a)* any of certain other spreads for bread [apple *butter,* peanut *butter*] *b)* any of certain vegetables oils having a solid consistency at ordinary temperatures [cocoa *butter*] *c) former term for* any of certain metallic chlorides [*butter* of antimony] **3** [Informal] flattery **—*vt.*** **1** to spread with butter **2** [Informal] to flatter so as to ingratiate oneself: often with *up* **—look as if butter would not melt in one's mouth** to look innocent or demure

but·ter-and-eggs (-ən egz′) ***n.*** a common, weedy plant (*Linaria vulgaris*) of the figwort family, with spurred orange and yellow flowers

☆**but·ter·ball** (-bôl′) ***n.*** **1** BUFFLEHEAD **2** [Informal] a fat person

butter bean any of various light-colored beans, as a lima bean or wax bean

but·ter·bur (-bur′) ***n.*** any of several plants (genus *Petasites*) of the composite family, esp. a European plant (*P. hybridus*), with large, kidney-shaped leaves

☆**butter clam** any of a genus (*Saxidomus*) of large, edible clams found along the Pacific coast of North America

but·ter·cream (-krēm′) ***n.*** a frosting made with butter or shortening mixed with powdered sugar

but·ter·cup (-kup′) ***adj.*** designating a large, widespread family (Ranunculaceae, order Ranunculales) of dicotyledonous flowering plants, including peonies, aconites, and anemones **—*n.*** any of a genus (*Ranunculus*) of normally yellow-flowered plants of the buttercup family, common in meadows and wet places

but·ter·fat (-fat′) ***n.*** the fatty part of milk, from which butter is made: it consists mainly of the glycerides of oleic, stearic, palmitic, and butyric acids

but·ter·fin·gers (-fiŋ′gərz) ***n.*** [Informal] a person who habitually fumbles or drops things, as if because of buttery fingers **—but′ter·fin′gered *adj.***

but·ter·fish (-fish′) ***n.,*** *pl.* **-fish′** or **-fish′es** (see FISH) any of various fishes (esp. family Stromateidae) with a slippery, protective covering of mucus, as a gunnel

but·ter·fly (-flī′) ***n.,*** *pl.* **-flies′** ⟦ME *buterflie* < OE *buttorfleoge* (see BUTTER & FLY[2]): in folklore, it is thought to steal milk or butter⟧ **1** any of various families of lepidopteran insects active in the daytime, having a sucking mouthpart, slender body, ropelike, knobbed antennae, and four broad, usually brightly colored, membranous wings **2** a person, esp. a woman, thought of as flitting about like a butterfly and being frivolous, fickle, etc. **3** *a) short for* BUTTERFLY STROKE *b)* a contest in which each contestant uses a butterfly stroke **4** [*pl.*] an uneasy feeling, as in the abdomen, caused esp. by nervous anticipation: also **butterflies in one's stomach —*adj.*** resembling a butterfly, esp. in having parts that are spread out like wings [*butterfly* chair, *butterfly* table] **—*vt.*** **-flied′, -fly′ing** ⟦from the resemblance of the cut and flattened piece to the outline of the insect⟧ to slice (a pork chop, shrimp, etc.) most of the way through and spread open before cooking

butterfly bandage a butterfly-shaped strip of adhesive medical tape used, when stitches are not required, to keep a deep cut or incision tightly closed while it heals

butterfly bush BUDDLEIA

☆**butterfly chair** ⟦see BUTTERFLY, *adj.*⟧ a lightweight chair consisting of a piece of canvas, leather, etc. slung from a framework of metal bars

but·ter·fly·fish (-fish′) ***n.,*** *pl.* **-fish′** or **-fish′es** (see FISH) any of a percoid family (Chaetodontidae) of small, brightly colored, usually yellow, tropical reef fishes: also written **butterfly fish**

butterfly orchid an orchid (*Oncidium papilio*) with reddish flowers, native to South America

butterfly stroke *Swimming* a stroke performed face down, in which both arms are thrust out at the sides at the same time, brought forward out of the water and then down through the water in a circular motion, while using an up-and-down leg movement

butterfly valve a disk-shaped valve turning on an axis along its diameter, serving esp. as a damper in a pipe or as a choke or throttle in a carburetor

☆**butterfly weed** a North American wildflower (*Asclepias tuberosa*) of the milkweed family, with orange flowers

but·ter·head lettuce (-hed′) ⟦so named from the soft, *buttery* texture of its leaves⟧ a major group of lettuce varieties having soft, pliable leaves and small, loose heads, including bibb and Boston lettuce

butter knife a small, dull-edged knife for cutting or spreading butter

but·ter·milk (but′ər milk′) *n.* **1** the liquid left after butter has been churned from milk **2** a commercially prepared milk drink made by adding bacteria to sweet skim milk

☆**but·ter·nut** (-nut′) *n.* **1** the white walnut tree (*Juglans cinerea*) of E North America, with compound leaves and hard-shell nuts **2** its wood, often used in place of the heavier black walnut **3** *a)* its oily edible nut *b)* the souari nut **4** ⟦from the soldiers' homespun clothing, dyed brown with *butternut* bark dye⟧ [Old Slang] a soldier or supporter of the Confederacy

☆**butternut squash** a small, bell-shaped, smooth winter squash, with yellowish flesh

but·ter·scotch (-skäch′) *n.* **1** a hard, sticky candy made with brown sugar, butter, etc. **2** the flavor of this candy **3** a brown syrup with this flavor —*adj.* made of, or having the flavor of, butterscotch

butter tree any of several trees, as the shea, whose fatty seeds yield a butterlike substance

☆**but·ter·weed** (-wēd′) *n.* any wild plant with yellow flowers or soft leaves, as groundsel or horseweed

but·ter·wort (-wurt′) *n.* any of a genus (*Pinguicula*) of the bladderwort family of small, stemless plants with flat, sticky leaves on which insects are trapped

but·ter·y[1] (but′ər ē, but′rē) *n., pl.* **-ter·ies** ⟦ME *boterie,* ale cellar, pantry < OFr, storage room for casks < ML *buteria:* see BUTT[3]⟧ **1** a storeroom for wine and liquor **2** [Dial.] a LARDER (sense 1) **3** a room in some English colleges where provisions are available to students

but·ter·y[2] (but′ər ē) *adj.* **1** like butter, as in consistency **2** containing or spread with butter **3** inclined to flattery; adulatory

butt hinge a hinge with rectangular parts which are fastened to surfaces that close on each other, as the narrow edge of a door and the jamb

butt·in·sky or **butt·in·ski** (but ins′kē) *n.* ⟦< BUTT IN (see phr. under BUTT[2]) + *-sky, -ski,* suffix in Slavic surnames, used jocularly⟧ [Slang] a person who is constantly butting in or meddling in the affairs of other people

butt joint any joint made by fastening two pieces of wood or metal together end to end or at right angles without overlapping: it is sometimes strengthened with an added part or parts

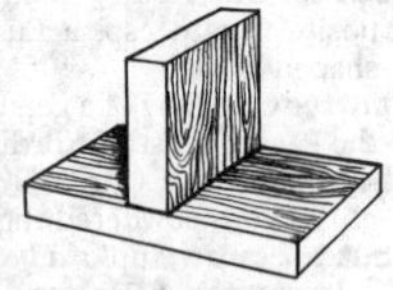
butt joint

but·tock (but′ək) *n.* ⟦ME *buttok* < OE *buttuc,* end, short piece of land: see BUTT[1] & -OCK⟧ **1** either of the two fleshy, rounded parts at the back of the hips; either half of the rump **2** [*pl.*] the rump

but·ton (but′'n) *n.* ⟦ME *botoun* < OFr *boton,* a button, bud < *buter:* see BUTT[2]⟧ **1** any small disk, knob, etc. used as a fastening or ornament, as one put through a buttonhole on a garment **2** anything small and shaped like a button; specif., *a)* a small emblem of membership, distinction, etc., generally worn in the lapel *b)* a small knoblike part, as a bud on a plant or the end of a rattlesnake's rattles *c)* a small knoblike part that is pushed or turned to operate a doorbell, electric lamp, etc. or to select or activate a function on an electronic device *d)* a guard on the tip of a fencing foil *e)* a small, immature mushroom **3** *Comput.* on a computer screen, a stylized figure resembling a button or knob, that is clicked or touched so as to select an option or activate a function ☆**4** [Slang] the point of the chin — *vt., vi.* **1** to fasten with or as with a button or buttons **2** to provide or be provided with a button or buttons —**button up (one's lip)** [Slang] to refrain from talking; esp., to keep a secret —☆**on the button** [Slang] exactly at the desired point, time, objective, etc. —**push someone's button (or buttons)** ⟦see *n.* 2c⟧ to arouse, often in a manipulative way, someone's interest, anger, sympathy, etc. [*advertising that pushes our buttons and makes us want to buy*] —**but′ton·er** *n.*

☆**but·ton·ball** (-bôl′) *n.* **1** PLANE[1] **2** BUTTONBUSH

☆**but·ton·bush** (-boosh′) *n.* a common North American shrub (*Cephalanthus occidentalis*) of the madder family having dense, round clusters of small white flowers

☆**but·ton-down** (-doun′) *adj.* **1** designating a collar, as on a shirt, having points fastened by small buttons to the front of the garment **2** conservative, conventional, etc. [*a button-down mind*]: also **but′toned-down′** —*n.* a shirt with a button-down collar

but·ton·hole (-hōl′) *n.* a slit or loop through which a button can be fastened —*vt.* **-holed′, -hol′ing 1** to make buttonholes in **2** to make with a buttonhole stitch **3** to make (a person) listen to one, as if by grasping his or her coat by a buttonhole —**but′ton·hol′er** *n.*

buttonhole stitch a closely worked loop stitch making a reinforced edge, as around a buttonhole

but·ton·hook (-hook′) *n.* a small hook for pulling buttons through buttonholes, as formerly in some shoes

button man [Slang] SOLDIER (*n.* 2b)

but·ton·mold (-mōld′) *n.* a small disk of wood, metal, etc., which is covered as with cloth or leather to form a button

button quail any of a family (Turnicidae) of small gruiform birds that resemble quail and live in the warm regions of the Old World

but·tons (but′'nz) *n.* [Informal, Chiefly Brit.] a bellhop, hotel page, etc.

☆**button snakeroot 1** BLAZING STAR (sense 1) **2** any of a genus (*Eryngium*) of the umbel family of perennial, thistlelike plants with white or green flowers

☆**button tree 1** any of a genus (*Conocarpus*) of dicotyledonous West Indian trees with buttonlike fruit **2** PLANE[1]

☆**but·ton·wood** (-wood′) *n.* PLANE[1]

but·tress (bu′tris) *n.* ⟦ME *boteras* < OFr *bouterez,* pl. of *bouteret,* flying buttress < *buter:* see BUTT[2]⟧ **1** a projecting structure, generally of brick or stone, built against a wall to support or reinforce it **2** anything like a buttress; support or prop —*vt.* **1** to support or reinforce with a buttress **2** to prop up; bolster

butt shaft a blunt arrow without a barb

butt weld a welded butt joint —**butt′-weld′** *vt.*

Bu·tu·an (bə too′än) city on the NE coast of Mindanao, the Philippines

Bu·tung (boo′tooŋ) island of Indonesia, southeast of Sulawesi: 1,620 sq mi (4,196 sq km)

bu·tut (boo toot′) *n., pl.* **-tut′** ⟦< Wolof adj., small⟧ a monetary unit of Gambia, equal to 1/100 of a dalasi

bu·tyl (byoot′'l) *n.* ⟦< L *butyrum,* BUTTER + -YL⟧ **1** any of the four monovalent organic radicals (**normal butyl, secondary butyl, tertiary butyl, isobutyl**) having the same formula, C_4H_9, but differing in properties and structure ☆**2** BUTYL RUBBER

butyl alcohol any of four isomeric alcohols, C_4H_9OH, obtained from petroleum products: used as solvents and in organic synthesis

butyl aldehyde BUTYRALDEHYDE

bu·tyl·ene (byoot′'l ēn′) *n.* ⟦BUTYL + -ENE⟧ any of four alkenes, including isobutylene, having the same formula, C_4H_8, but differing in properties and structure

☆**butyl rubber** any of a group of synthetic rubbers that are basically copolymers of butylene and isoprene and that are especially impermeable to gases and resistant to abrasion, tearing, etc.

bu·tyr·a·ceous (byoot′ər ā′shəs) *adj.* ⟦L *butyrum* (see BUTTER) + -ACEOUS⟧ of, like, or producing butter

bu·tyr·al·de·hyde (byoot′ər al′də hīd′) *n.* ⟦< L *butyrum,* BUTTER + ALDEHYDE⟧ a clear liquid, $CH_3(CH_2)_2CHO$, with a characteristic aldehyde odor, used in making solvents, synthetic resins, etc.

bu·tyr·ate (byoot′ər āt′) *n.* a salt or ester of butyric acid

bu·tyr·ic (byoo tir′ik) *adj.* ⟦L *butyrum,* BUTTER + -IC⟧ **1** of or obtained from butter **2** of or pertaining to butyric acid

butyric acid a colorless, strong-smelling isomeric fatty acid, $CH_3CH_2CH_2COOH$, found in rancid butter, perspiration, etc. and used to produce fragrances and flavors

bu·tyr·in (byoot′ər in) *n.* ⟦BUTYR(IC) + -IN[1]⟧ a glyceryl ester, $C_3H_5(C_4H_7O_2)_3$, of butyric acid

bux·om (buk′səm) *adj.* ⟦ME, humble, obedient < base of *bouen,* BOW[1] + *-som,* -SOME[1]⟧ **1** [Obs.] *a)* obedient *b)* flexible; pliant **2** [Archaic] healthy, comely, plump, jolly, etc. **3** having a full-bosomed figure: said of a woman —**bux′om·ness** *n.*

Bux·te·hu·de (book′stə hoo′də), **Did·er·ik** (dē′dər ik) 1637-1707; Dan. (perhaps born in Sweden) organist & composer, later in Germany: also Ger. **Diet·rich** (dēt′riH)

bux·us (buk′səs) *n.* ⟦L < Gr *pyxos*⟧ any of a genus (*Buxus*) of evergreen shrubs or small trees with small, leathery leaves: often used as a hedge

buy (bī) *vt.* **bought, buy′ing** ⟦ME *bien* < OE *bycgan* < ? IE base of BOW[1]⟧ **1** to get by paying or agreeing to pay money or some equivalent; purchase **2** to get as by an exchange [*buy* victory with human lives] **3** to be the means of purchasing [all that money can *buy*] **4** to bribe or hire as by bribing ☆**5** [Slang] to accept as true, valid, practical, etc. [I can't *buy* this excuse] **6** [Archaic] *Theol.* to redeem —*vi.* **1** to buy something **2** to buy merchandise as a buyer —*n.* **1** the act of buying; a purchase **2** anything bought or buyable, esp. with reference to its worth as a bargain [a good (or bad) *buy*] ☆**3** [Informal] something worth the price; bargain —**buy in 1** to buy a share of or shares in **2** to buy back (an item) at an auction by a final, high bid when the other bids are much too low: said as of the orig. owner **3** [Slang] to pay money so as to become a participant, member, etc. —**buy into 1** BUY IN (senses 1 & 3) (see phrase above) ☆**2** [Slang] BUY (*vt.* 5) —**buy it** [Slang] to die; specif., to be killed —**buy off** to bribe —**buy out** to buy all the stock, business rights, etc. of —**buy time** GAIN TIME (sense 2) (at TIME) —**buy up** to buy all of or all that is available of —**buy′a·ble** *adj.*

☆**buy·back** (bī′bak′) *n.* **1** an agreement to buy something in return, as by a supplier to buy its customer's product **2** a sale whereby something sold is repurchased from the buyer by the seller or original owner **3** *Finance* the buying by a corporation of its own stock in the open market in order to reduce the number of outstanding shares

buy·er (-ər) *n.* **1** one who buys; consumer **2** a person whose work is to buy merchandise for a retail store

buyer's market a market favorable to buyers, with wide selection, low prices, etc.

buy·out (-out′) *n.* **1** the act of buying out a business or an owner of a business; specif., the gaining of control of a corporation through the acquisition of shares of its stock **2** a compensation package offered to employees to induce them to retire early

Bu·zău (bə zou′) city in Walachia, SE Romania
buzz (buz) *vi.* ⟦echoic⟧ **1** to make a sound like that of a prolonged *z*; hum like a bee **2** to talk excitedly or incessantly, esp. in low tones **3** to gossip **4** to move with a buzzing sound **5** to be filled with noisy activity or talk —*vt.* **1** to utter or tell (gossip, rumors, etc.) in a buzzing manner **2** to make (wings, etc.) buzz **3** to fly an airplane low over (a building, etc.), often as a signal **4** to signal (someone) with a buzzer **5** [Informal] to telephone —*n.* **1** a sound like that of a prolonged *z* or a bee's hum; buzzing **2** a confused sound, as of many excited voices **3** noisy activity; stir; agitation **4** a signal on a buzzer **5** [Informal] BUZZ CUT **6** [Informal] a telephone call **7** [Informal] *a)* rumor or speculation circulating about some person, event, etc. *b)* talk and comment, attention or excitement, etc. about a phenomenon, person, activity, etc. **8** [Slang] a condition of euphoria induced as by drugs —**buzz about** (or **around**) to scurry about —**buzz off** [Slang] go away; depart: often used in the imperative
buz·zard (buz′ərd) *n.* ⟦ME *busard* < OFr *busart* < *buson, buison* (< L *buteo,* kind of hawk) + *-art,* -ARD⟧ **1** any of various Old World hawks (esp. certain species of the genus *Buteo*) that are slow and heavy in flight ☆**2** TURKEY VULTURE **3** a person regarded as mean, grasping, etc.
Buzzards Bay arm of the Atlantic, on the SE coast of Mass., at the base of Cape Cod peninsula
buzz bomb [Informal] a robot bomb, esp. as used against England by Germany in WWII
buzz cut [Informal] a closely cropped haircut
buzzed (buzd) *adj.* ☆[Slang] drunk or intoxicated
buzz·er (buz′ər) *n.* an electrical device that makes a buzzing sound as a signal
buzz·kill (buz′kil′) *n.* ⟦BUZZ (*n.* 8) + KILL[1]⟧ [Slang] something or someone that spoils a good mood or the enjoyment of others: also written **buzz kill**
☆**buzz saw** a saw with teeth spaced around the edge of a disk, esp. one with a large disk affixed to a motor-driven shaft, for use as in a sawmill
buzz·word (-wurd′) *n.* a word or phrase used by members of some in-group, having little or imprecise meaning but sounding impressive to outsiders
BVDs (bē′vē′dēz′) *pl.n.* ⟦< *B.V.D.,* trademark < *Bradley, Voorhees & Day,* manufacturers⟧ [Informal] men's underwear; specif., esp. formerly, men's one-piece long underwear
BVM *abbrev.* ⟦L *Beata Virgo Maria*⟧ Blessed Virgin Mary: also **BV Mary**
Bvt *abbrev.* brevet
B/W or **BW** *abbrev.* black and white
bwa·na (bwä′nə) *n.* ⟦Swahili < Ar *abūna,* our father < *abū,* father⟧ [*often* **B-**] [Historical] master; sir: respectful term of address used in parts of Africa
BWI *abbrev.* British West Indies
bx *abbrev.* box
BX *abbrev.* Base Exchange
by (bī) *prep.* ⟦ME *by, bi, be* < OE *be* (unstressed), *bi* (stressed) < Gmc **bi,* around, about, akin to Gr *amphi,* L *ambi:* see BY-, BE; orig. adv. of place, meaning "beside, near," but already highly specialized prep. in OE⟧ **1** near in space; beside; at [*stand by the wall*] **2** *a)* in or during the time of [*travel by night*] *b)* not later than [*be back by ten o'clock*] **3** *a)* via; through, along, or over [*driving home by the dirt road*] *b)* past; beyond [*to march by the reviewing stand*] *c)* to or within a distance of [*missed the putt by a foot*] **4** toward [*north by northwest*] **5** in behalf of [*he did well by his friends*] **6** with respect to (a given category) [*a lawyer by profession*] **7** *a)* through the means, work, or operations of [*a trip by train, a pact reached by negotiation, made by craftsmen, poems (written) by Poe*] *b)* through the activity or effort of (used before gerunds) [*he won by practicing daily*] **8** produced with (the other parent) [*a son by my first husband*] **9** following in series [*marching two by two*] **10** *a)* with the authority or sanction of [*by your leave*] *b)* according to; in a manner consistent with [*playing by the rules*] *c)* in the name of (used in oaths) [*by all that's holy*] *d)* [Informal] in the opinion of; with [*the plans are OK by me*] **11** *a)* in the amount of, or to the extent or degree of [*apples by the peck*] *b)* at the rate or pace of [*growing dark by degrees, paid by the hour*] *c)* and in another dimension [*two feet by four feet*] **12** using (the given number) as multiplier or divisor —*adv.* **1** close at hand; near [*stand by*] **2** away; aside [*we have put money by*] **3** close in passing; past [*the car sped by*] ☆**4** at the place specified or understood [*stop by on your way home*] — *adj., n. alt. sp. of* BYE[1] —**by and by 1** [Obs.] immediately **2** after a short while; soon **3** sooner or later; eventually —**by and large** ☆on the whole; considering everything —**by oneself 1** alone; solitary **2** unaided —**by the by** incidentally
by- (bī) ⟦< prec.⟧ *prefix* **1** close by; near [*bystander*] **2** side [*bystreet*] **3** on the side; secondary; incidental to the main [*byproduct*]
bya *abbrev.* billion years ago: sometimes written **BYA**
by-and-by (bī′ən bī′) *n.* an unspecified future time
by-blow (bī′blō′) *n.* an indirect blow or hit
Byd·goszcz (bid′gôshch) city in NC Poland
bye[1] (bī) *n.* ⟦var. of BY⟧ **1** something incidental or secondary **2** *a)* the privilege, granted a contestant in a tournament, of automatically advancing to the next round without playing *b)* a situation in which a team, esp. a football team, is not scheduled to play when other teams in its league are scheduled **3** *Cricket* a run made on a bowled ball that the batsman does not touch —*adj.* of secondary importance —**by the bye** incidentally; by the by
bye[2] (bī) *interj.* [Informal] *short for* GOODBYE
bye-bye (bī′bī′, bī′bī′) *n., interj.* [Informal] goodbye —**go bye-bye** to depart; leave: a child's term
by-e·lec·tion (bī′i lek′shən) *n.* a special election held in the interval between regular elections, esp. one held to fill a vacancy in the British House of Commons
Bye·lo·rus·sian Soviet Socialist Republic (bye′lō rush′ən) BELORUSSIAN SOVIET SOCIALIST REPUBLIC: also **Bye′lo·rus′sia** —**Bye′lo·rus′sian** *adj., n.*
by·gone (bī′gôn′) *adj.* that has or have gone by; past; former —*n.* anything that is gone or past —**let bygones be bygones** to let past offenses or disagreements be forgotten
by·law (bī′lô′) *n.* ⟦ME *bi-laue* < *bi,* village (< ON *bȳr* < *būa,* to dwell: see BONDAGE) + *laue,* LAW: meaning infl. by BY⟧ any of a set of rules adopted by an organization or assembly for governing its own meetings or affairs
☆**by·line** (-līn′) *n.* a line identifying the writer of a newspaper or magazine article —*vt.* **by′lined′, by′lin′ing** to supply a byline to (an article)
by·lin·er (-ər) *n.* a person who writes articles with bylines
by·name (-nām′) *n.* **1** a surname **2** a nickname
BYO *abbrev.* bring your own (alcoholic beverages)
BYOB *abbrev.* bring your own bottle (of whiskey, rum, etc.)
by·pass (bī′pas′) *n.* **1** a way, path, etc. between two points that avoids or is auxiliary to the main way; specif., an alternative highway route, as for skirting an urban area **2** a pipe or channel providing an auxiliary passage for gas or liquid, as that leading to the pilot light in a gas stove **3** *Elec.* SHUNT (*n.* 3) **4** *a)* a surgical operation to provide passage for a fluid, as blood, around a diseased or blocked part or organ (in full **bypass operation**) *b)* such a passage —*vt.* **1** to go around instead of through; use a bypass to avoid **2** to furnish with a bypass **3** to ignore, fail to consult, etc.
bypass capacitor *Radio* a capacitor which provides a low-impedance path for alternating current while not passing any direct current
by·past (-past′) *adj.* [Obs.] past; bygone
by·path or **by-path** (-path′) *n.* a secluded path not used very much; byway
by·play (-plā′) *n.* action, gestures, etc. going on aside from the main action or conversation, as in a play
by·prod·uct or **by-prod·uct** (-präd′əkt) *n.* anything produced in the course of making another thing; secondary or incidental product or result
Byrd (burd) **1 Richard Evelyn** 1888-1957; U.S. naval officer & polar explorer **2 William** 1543?-1623; Eng. composer
byre (bīr) *n.* ⟦ME & OE, hut; akin to BOWER[1]⟧ [Brit.] a cow barn
by·road (bī′rōd′) *n.* a road that is not a main road
By·ron[1] (bī′rən) *n.* ⟦< Fr *Biron,* orig. a surname, after *Biron,* district in Périgord, France⟧ a masculine name
By·ron[2] (bī′rən), **George Gordon** 6th Baron Byron 1788-1824; Eng. poet
By·ron·ic (bī rän′ik) *adj.* of, like, or characteristic of Byron or his writings; Romantic, passionate, cynical, ironic, etc. —**By·ron′i·cal·ly** *adv.*
bys·si·no·sis (bis′ə nō′sis) *n.* ⟦ModL < L *byssinus,* made of byssus (see fol.) + -OSIS⟧ BROWN LUNG (DISEASE)
bys·sus (bis′əs) *n., pl.* **bys′sus·es** or **bys′si** (-ī) ⟦L < Gr *byssos,* fine linen or cotton < Sem: cf. Akkadian *būṣ,* Heb *buts*⟧ **1** a fine fabric, esp. a linen cloth, used by the ancients, as in Egypt for mummy wrapping **2** *Zool.* a tuft of filaments, chemically similar to silk, secreted by various marine bivalves, esp. the mussels, and used to attach the mollusk to the substratum
by·stand·er (bī′stan′dər) *n.* a person who stands near but does not participate; mere onlooker
by·street (-strēt′) *n.* a side street off a main street
☆**byte** (bīt) *n.* ⟦arbitrary formation⟧ **1** a string of binary digits (*bits*), usually eight, operated on as a basic unit by a digital computer **2** the basic unit of storage capacity in a computer system
By·tom (bi′tôm) city in SW Poland
by·way (bī′wā′) *n.* **1** a road or path other than the main one, esp. one not used very much; side road; bypath **2** a subsidiary activity, line of study, etc.
by·word (-wurd′) *n.* ⟦ME & OE *biword* < *bi* (see BY) + WORD: formed after L *proverbium* (*pro* + *verbum*), PROVERB⟧ **1** a familiar saying; proverb **2** a person or thing proverbial for some quality **3** an object of scorn or ridicule **4** a favorite or pet word or phrase
Byz·an·tine (biz′ən tēn′, -tīn′; bi zan′tin) *adj.* ⟦L *Byzantinus*⟧ **1** of Byzantium or the Byzantine Empire, or its people or culture **2** of or pertaining to the Eastern Orthodox Church **3** [*occas.* **b-**] resembling the government or politics of the Byzantine Empire in structure, spirit, etc.; specif., characterized by complexity, deviousness, intrigue, etc. **4** *Archit.* designating or of a style developed in Byzantium and E Europe between the 4th and 15th cent., characterized by domes over square areas, round arches, elaborate mosaics, etc. **5** *Art* designating or of the decorative style of the mosaics, frescoes, etc. of the Byzantine Empire, characterized by lack of perspective, use of rich colors, esp. gold, and emphasis on religious symbolism —*n.* a person born or living in Byzantium
Byzantine Empire empire (A.D. 395-1453) in SE Europe & SW Asia, formed by the division of the Roman Empire: cap. Constantinople: see also EASTERN ROMAN EMPIRE
By·zan·ti·um (bi zan′shē əm, -tē əm) ancient city (founded 600? B.C.) on the site of modern ISTANBUL: name changed to CONSTANTINOPLE, A.D. 330

Byzantine Empire (12th cent.)

c[1] or **C** (sē) ***n.***, *pl.* **c's, C's** **1** the third letter of the English alphabet: from the Greek *gamma*, a borrowing from the Phoenician **2** any of the speech sounds that this letter represents, as, in English, the (s) of *cell* or (k) of *call* **3** a type or impression of *c* or *C* **4** the third in a sequence or group **5** an object shaped like C —***adj.*** **1** of *c* or *C* **2** third in a sequence or group **3** shaped like C

c[2] *abbrev.* **1** circa **2** centi-

c[3] *Physics symbol* the speed of light in a vacuum: cf. LIGHT[1] (***n.*** *1a*)

C[1] (sē) ***n.*** **1** the Roman numeral for 100: with a superior bar ($\overline{C}$), 100,000: when C is placed before a greater Roman numeral, it expresses a number 100 less than that numeral (e.g., CM = 900) ☆**2** *Educ.* a grade indicating average work [*a C in biology*] **3** *Music* *a)* the first tone or note in the scale of C major *b)* a key, string, etc. producing this tone *c)* the scale having this tone as the keynote *d)* the sign for 4/4 time **4** a high-level computer programming language —***adj.*** average in quality

C[2] *abbrev.* **1** candle **2** *Elec.* capacitance **3** Cape **4** carat(s) **5** *Baseball* catcher **6** cathode **7** Catholic **8** Celsius (or centigrade) **9** cent(s) **10** centavo(s) **11** *Sports* center **12** centesimo(s) **13** centime(s) **14** centimeter(s) **15** centimo(s) **16** Central **17** century **18** chapter **19** child; children **20** circa **21** cold (on water faucets) **22** College **23** Congress **24** Conservative **25** *Math.* constant **26** contralto **27** copyright **28** coulomb **29** cup(s) **30** curie **31** cycle(s) **32** cytosine **33** ⟦L < earlier *Caius*⟧ *Rom. History* Gaius (the praenomen) **34** *Physics* heat capacity **35** ⟦L *centum*⟧ hundredweight Also, for 1, 4-6, 9-15, 17-20, 25-27, 29-31, 35, **c**

C[3] *Chem. symbol for* carbon

c̄ or **c** *symbol* ⟦L *cum*⟧ *Pharmacy* with

C- (sē) *prefix* cargo transport: used in designations for aircraft [*C*-130, *C*-5A]

ca *abbrev.* **1** *Law* case(s) **2** cathode **3** circa

Ca[1] *abbrev.* **1** *Bible* Canticles **2** cathode

Ca[2] *Chem. symbol for* calcium

CA *abbrev.* **1** California **2** Central America **3** [Brit.] chartered accountant **4** chief accountant **5** chronological age **6** commercial agent **7** Confederate Army **8** controller of accounts Also, for 3-6, 8, **ca**

ca' (kä, kô) ***vt.*** [Scot.] to call, as in driving cattle

.ca *abbrev. Comput.* Canada: a domain name

Caa·ba (kä′bə) *alt. sp. of* KAABA

cab[1] (kab) ***n.*** ⟦< CABRIOLET⟧ **1** a horse-drawn carriage, esp. one for public hire **2** TAXICAB **3** the part of a locomotive, motor truck, crane, etc. in which the operator sits —***vi.*** **cabbed, cab′bing** [Informal] **1** to take a taxicab **2** to drive a taxicab

cab[2] (kab) ***n.*** ⟦Heb (2 Kings 6:25) *qab*, hollow vessel < *qābab*, to hollow out⟧ an ancient Hebrew unit of dry measure, equal to about two quarts

cab[3] (kab) ***n.*** *short for* CABERNET SAUVIGNON

CAB *abbrev.* Civil Aeronautics Board

ca·bal (kə bäl′, -bal′) ***n.*** ⟦Fr, intrigue, society (popularized in England from the initials of the ministers of Charles II) < ML *cabbala*, fol.⟧ **1** a small group of persons joined in a secret, often political, intrigue; junta **2** the intrigues of such a group; plot —***vi.*** **-balled′, -bal′ling** to join in a cabal; plot —**SYN.** PLOT

cab·a·la (kə bä′lə, kab′ə lə) ***n.*** ⟦ML *cabbala* < Heb *kabala*, received lore, tradition < *qbl*, to receive, take⟧ **1** *var. of* KABBALAH **2** any esoteric or secret doctrine; occultism

ca·ba·let·ta (kä′bä let′tä) ***n.***, *pl.* **-let′te** (-let′tā) or Eng. **-tas** ⟦It, dim. (? altered after *caballo*, horse) of *cobbola*, refrain < Prov *cobla*, couplet < L *copula*, COPULA⟧ the bravura section of an aria or duet

cab·a·lism (kab′ə liz′əm) ***n.*** **1** a mystical philosophical doctrine based on the doctrines of the cabala **2** any occult doctrine —**cab′a·list** ***n.*** —**cab′a·lis′tic** (-lis′tik) ***adj.*** —**cab′a·lis′ti·cal·ly** ***adv.***

ca·bal·le·ro (kab′ə ler′ō, -əl yer′ō; *Sp* kä′bä lye′rô) ***n.***, *pl.* **-ros** (-ōz; -rôs) ⟦Sp < LL *caballarius*, CAVALIER < L *caballus*, horse⟧ **1** a Spanish gentleman, cavalier, or knight ☆**2** [Southwest] *a)* a horseman *b)* a lady's escort

☆**ca·ban·a** (kə ban′ə, -yə; -bä′nə, -bän′yə) ***n.*** ⟦Sp *cabaña* < LL *capanna*, hut⟧ **1** a cabin or hut **2** a small shelter used as a bathhouse at a beach or pool

Ca·ba·na·tuan (kä′bə nə twän′) city in SC Luzon, in the Philippines

cab·a·ret (kab′ə rā′, kab′ə rā′) ***n.*** ⟦Fr, tavern < MDu *cabret* < *cambret* < OFr dial. *camberete*, dim. of *cambre*, CHAMBER⟧ **1** a restaurant or cafe with dancing, singing, skits, etc. as entertainment **2** this kind of entertainment

cab·bage[1] (kab′ij) ***n.*** ⟦ME & OFr *caboche*, earlier *caboce* < ?⟧ **1** a common vegetable (*Brassica oleracea* var. *capitata*) of the crucifer family, with thick leaves formed into a round, compact head on a short, thick stalk: cultivated as early as 2000 B.C. **2** an edible bud at the end of the branch on some palm trees **3** [Slang] paper money

cab·bage[2] (kab′ij) ***vt., vi.*** **-baged, -bag·ing** ⟦prob. < Fr *cabasser*, to put into a basket, steal < *cabas*, basket < VL **capacium*, reed basket⟧ [Old Brit. Slang] to steal —***n.*** ⟦prob. < the v.⟧ [Archaic] cloth snippets appropriated by a tailor when cutting out clothes

☆**cabbage bug** HARLEQUIN BUG

cabbage butterfly a common white butterfly (*Pieris rapae*) whose green larvae feed upon cabbage and related plants

cabbage palm any of several palms, as the palmetto, with terminal buds used as a vegetable: also **cabbage tree**

☆**cabbage palmetto** PALMETTO

cabbage rose ⟦in allusion to its large, full flower with many petals, likened to the many leaves of a head of CABBAGE[1]⟧ an ancient cultivated rose (*Rosa centifolia*) from the Caucasus, ancestor of many modern roses

cab·bage·worm (-wurm′) ***n.*** the larval stage of any insect that feeds on cabbage, as the caterpillar of the cabbage butterfly

cab·ba·la (kə bä′lə, kab′ə lə) ***n.*** *var. of* KABBALAH —**cab′ba·list** ***n.*** —**cab′ba·lis′tic** ***adj.***

cab·driv·er (kab′drī′vər) ***n.*** a person who drives a cab: also [Informal] **cab′by** (-ē) or **cab′bie**, *pl.* **-bies**

ca·ber (kā′bər) ***n.*** ⟦Gael *cabar*⟧ a long, heavy pole thrown end over end in a Scottish Highland game to test muscular strength

ca·ber·net (kab′ər nā′; *Fr* kȧ ber ne′) ***n.*** [*also* **C-**] **1** any of several related grapes grown esp. in Bordeaux and Calif. **2** a dry red wine made from these grapes; esp., CABERNET SAUVIGNON

cabernet sau·vi·gnon (sō vē nyōn′; *Fr.*, -nyôn′) [*also* **C- S-**] **1** the most highly prized cabernet grape **2** a fragrant, dry red wine made from this grape, blended into many Bordeaux wines and often bottled as a varietal elsewhere

Ca·be·za de Va·ca (kä be′thä *the* vä′kä), **Ál·var Nú·ñez** (äl′vär no͞o′nyeth) 1490?-1557?; Sp. explorer in the Americas

☆**cab·e·zon** (kab′ə zän′) ***n.*** ⟦Sp *cabezón*, lit., big-headed < *cabeza*, head < L *capitium*, covering for the head < *caput*, HEAD⟧ the largest fish (*Scorpaenichthys marmoratus*) of the sculpin family, found in shallow waters along the Pacific coast of North America

cab·in (kab′in) ***n.*** ⟦ME *caban* < OFr *cabane* < OProv *cabana* < LL *capanna*, hut⟧ **1** a small, one-story house built simply or crudely, as of logs ☆**2** any simple, small structure designed for a brief stay, as for overnight [*tourist cabins*] **3** a private room on a ship, as a bedroom or office **4** a roofed section of a small boat, as a pleasure cruiser, for the passengers or crew **5** the enclosed section of an aircraft, where the passengers sit; also, the section housing the crew or used for cargo —***vt.*** to confine in or as in a cabin; cramp

cabin boy a boy whose work is to serve and run errands for the officers and passengers aboard a ship

cabin class a class of accommodations on a passenger ship, below first class and above tourist class

☆**cabin cruiser** a powerboat with a cabin and the necessary equipment for living on board

Ca·bin·da (kə bin′də) exclave of Angola, on the W coast of Africa, separated from the rest of Angola by 12 sq mi (31 sq km) of the Democratic Republic of the Congo: 2,807 sq mi (7,270 sq km)

cab·i·net (kab′ə nit) ***n.*** ⟦Fr, prob. < It *gabbinetto*, dim. of *gabbia* < L *cavea*, CAGE⟧ **1** a case or cupboard with drawers or shelves for holding or storing things [*a china cabinet, a medicine cabinet*] **2** *a)* a boxlike container, usually decorated, that houses all the assembled components of a record player, radio or television, etc. *b)* a boxlike container for a SPEAKER (sense 2a) **3** [Archaic] *a)* a private council room *b)* a meeting held there ☆**4** [*often* **C-**] a body of official advisors to a president, king, governor, etc.: in the U.S., composed of the heads of the various governmental departments **5** [Archaic] a small, private room —***adj.*** **1** of a kind usually displayed in cabinets [*cabinet curios*] **2** of or made by a cabinetmaker **3** of a political cabinet

cab·i·net·mak·er (-mā′kər) ***n.*** a person who makes fine furniture, decorative moldings, etc. —**cab′i·net·mak′ing** ***n.***

☆**cab·i·net·work** (kab′ə nit wurk′) ***n.*** **1** articles made by a cabinetmaker **2** the work or art of a cabinetmaker Also **cab′i·net·ry** (-ni trē)

☆**cabin fever** a condition of increased anxiety, tension, boredom, etc. caused by living for some time in a confined space or an isolated area, esp. in winter

ca·ble (kā′bəl) ***n.*** ⟦ME & OFr < LL *capulum*, a cable, rope < L *capere*, to take hold: see HAVE⟧ **1** a thick, heavy rope, now often of wire strands **2** the strong, heavy chain attached to a ship's anchor: anchor cables were formerly of rope **3** CABLE LENGTH **4** a bundle of insulated wires through which an electric current can be passed: telegraph or telephone cables are often laid under the ground or on the ocean floor ☆**5** a cablegram **6** CABLE TV —***vt.*** **-bled**, **-bling** **1** to fasten or furnish with a cable or cables **2** to transmit by undersea cable **3** to send a cablegram to —***vi.*** to send a cablegram

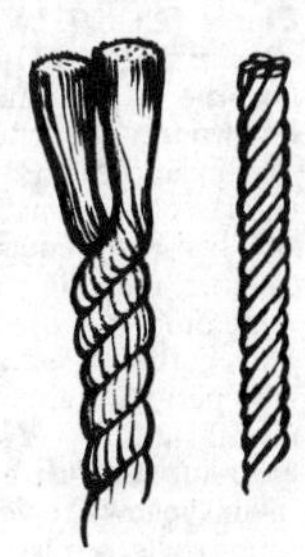
cable

Ca·ble (kā′bəl), **George Washington** 1844-1925; U.S. novelist

☆**cable car** a car drawn by a moving cable, as across a canyon, up a steeply inclined street, etc.

ca·ble·cast (kā′bəl kast′) ***vt.*** **-cast′**, **-cast′ing** ⟦CABLE + (TELE)CAST⟧ *TV* to transmit directly to receivers by means of coaxial cable —***n.*** a program that is cablecast —**ca′ble·cast′er** ***n.***

☆**ca·ble·gram** (-gram′) ***n.*** a message sent by undersea cable

ca·ble-laid (kā′bəl lād′) ***adj.*** made of three or four plain-laid ropes twisted together from right to left

cable length a unit of length used to measure nautical distances or depths, in the U.S. equal to 120 fathoms or 720 ft (219.456 m): in Britain equal to 101.26 fathoms or 607.56 ft (185.184 m) or about one tenth of a nautical mile

☆**cable railway** a street railway on which the cars are pulled by a continuously moving underground cable

cable stitch a type of raised stitch used in knitting: a series of such stitches forms a pattern resembling ropes twisted together

☆**cable TV** a television system in which a high antenna and one or more dish antennas receive signals from distant and local stations, electronic satellite relays, etc. and transmit them by direct cable to the receivers of persons subscribing to the system

cab·man (kab′mən) ***n.***, *pl.* **-men** (-mən) CABDRIVER

cab·o·chon (kab′ə shän′; *Fr* kȧ bô shōn′) ***n.*** ⟦Fr < *caboche*, head⟧ **1** any precious stone cut in convex shape, polished but not faceted **2** the style of cutting such a stone

ca·bom·ba (kə bäm′bə) ***n.*** ⟦ModL < Sp⟧ any of a genus (*Cabomba*) of waterlilies (family Cabombaceae), esp. a species (*C. caroliniana*) with submerged, needlelike leaves and rounded, floating ones: used in aquariums, garden pools, etc.

☆**ca·bood·le** (kə bo͞od′'l) ***n.*** ⟦*ca-*, colloq. intens. prefix (< ? Ger *ge-*) + BOODLE⟧ [Informal] lot; group [*the whole caboodle*]

ca·boose (kə bo͞os′) ***n.*** ⟦MDu *kabuys, kambuis* (< ?), ship's galley⟧ **1** [Brit.] *Naut.* a ship's kitchen; galley ☆**2** the trainmen's car on a freight train, usually at the rear ☆**3** [Slang] the buttocks

Cab·ot (kab′ət) **1 John** (It. name *Giovanni Caboto*) 1450?-98?; It. explorer in the service of England: discovered coast of North America (1497) **2 Sebastian** 1476?-1557?; Eng. cartographer & explorer: son of John

cab·o·tage (kab′ə tij, -täzh′) ***n.*** ⟦Fr < *caboter*, to sail along the coast < MFr *cabo*, cape < Sp < L *caput*, HEAD⟧ **1** coastal navigation and trade, esp. between ports within a country **2** air transport within a country **3** the right to engage in cabotage, esp. as granted to foreign carriers

ca·bret·ta (kə bret′ə) ***adj.*** ⟦< Sp *cabra*, goat (< L *capra*, fem. of *caper*: see CAPRIOLE) + It fem. dim. suffix *-etta*⟧ designating or of a soft leather made from a special kind of sheepskin

ca·bril·la (kə bril′ə, -brē′yə) ***n.*** ⟦Sp, prawn, dim. of *cabra*, goat: see prec.⟧ any of various edible, percoid fishes (family Serranidae) found off Florida, the West Indies, etc.

Ca·bri·ni (kə brē′nē), Saint **Frances Xavier** (1850-1917); U.S. nun, born in Italy: first U.S. citizen canonized: her day is Dec. 22: called *Mother Cabrini*

cab·ri·ole (kab′rē ōl′) ***n.*** ⟦Fr: see fol.⟧ **1** a leg of a table, chair, etc. that curves outward and then tapers inward down to the foot, often clawlike and grasping a ball **2** *Ballet* a leap in which one leg is thrown upward and then both legs are beaten together

cab·ri·o·let (kab′rē ə lā′) ***n.*** ⟦Fr, dim. of *cabriole*, a leap, caper < It *capriola*, CAPRIOLE⟧ **1** a light two-wheeled carriage, usually with a hood that folds, drawn by one horse **2** CONVERTIBLE (***n.*** 2)

cabriolet

ca·bri·to (kä brē′tō) ***n.***, *pl.* **-tos** (-tōs) ⟦Sp⟧ the flesh of a young goat, used as food

cab·stand (kab′stand′) ***n.*** a place where cabs are stationed for hire

cac- (kak) *combining form* CACO-: used before a vowel

ca·ca or **ca-ca** (kä′kä′) ***n.*** [Slang] excrement; feces: chiefly a child's term

ca' canny *see* CANNY

ca·ca·o (kə kä′ō, -kā′-) ***n.***, *pl.* **-os′** (-ōz′) ⟦Sp < Nahuatl *kakawaƛ*, cacao seed⟧ **1** a tropical American tree (*Theobroma cacao*) of the sterculia family, bearing large, elliptical seedpods **2** the nutritious seeds (**cacao beans**) of this tree, from which cocoa and chocolate are made

cacao butter COCOA BUTTER

cac·cia·to·re (kä′chə tôr′ē) ***adj.*** ⟦It, in the manner of hunters; lit., hunter < pp. of *cacciare*, to hunt, chase < VL **captiare*, to CATCH⟧ cooked in a casserole with olive oil and tomatoes, onions, spices, wine, etc. [*chicken cacciatore*]

cach·a·lot (kash′ə lät′, -lō′) ***n.*** ⟦Fr < Sp *cachalote* < colloq. Port *cachola*, head⟧ SPERM WHALE

cache (kash) ***n.*** ⟦Fr < *cacher*, conceal < VL **coacticare*, store up, collect, compress < L *coactare*, constrain < *coactus*, pp. of *cogere*, to collect: see COGENT⟧ **1** a place in which stores of food, supplies, etc. are hidden, as by explorers or trappers **2** a safe place for hiding or storing things **3** anything stored or hidden in such a place **4** *Comput.* a storage area or portion of memory variously designed to store program instructions, copies of recently or frequently accessed Web pages, etc. for faster retrieval —***vt.*** **cached**, **cach′ing** to hide or store in a cache —*SYN.* HIDE[1]

cache·pot (kash′pät′, -pō′) ***n.*** ⟦Fr < *cacher*, to hide (see prec.) + *pot*, POT[1]⟧ a decorative pot, jar, etc., used esp. for holding potted houseplants: also **cache pot**

cache-sexe (kȧsh′seks′) ***n.*** ⟦Fr < *cacher*, to hide (see CACHE) + *sexe*, sex⟧ a small cloth or band worn, as by an otherwise nude dancer, to conceal the genitals

ca·chet (ka shā′, kash′ā) ***n.*** ⟦Fr < *cacher*: see CACHE⟧ **1** a seal or stamp on an official letter or document: see also LETTRE DE CACHET **2** any sign of official approval **3** *a)* a mark or sign showing something is genuine, authentic, or of superior quality *b)* distinction; prestige **4** *Philately* a commemorative design on an envelope that marks some historical or philatelic event **5** a little, round wafer enclosing a bad-tasting medicine —***vt.*** *Philately* to print a cachet on (an envelope)

ca·chex·i·a (kə kek′sē ə) ***n.*** ⟦ModL < Gr *kachexia*, bad habit of body < *kakos*, bad + *hexis*, habit < *echein*, to have < IE base **seĝh-*, to hold fast, conquer > SCHEME⟧ a generally weakened, emaciated condition of the body, esp. as associated with a chronic illness: also **ca·chex′y** (-sē) —**ca·chec′tic** (-kek′tik) ***adj.***, **ca·chex′ic** (-kek′sik)

cach·in·nate (kak′ə nāt′) ***vi.*** **-nat′ed**, **-nat′ing** ⟦< L *cachinnatus*, pp. of *cachinnare*: ult. of echoic orig.⟧ to laugh loudly or too much —**cach′in·na′tion** ***n.***

ca·chou (ka sho͞o′) ***n.*** ⟦Fr < Port *cachu* < Malayalam *kāccu*, akin to Tamil *kācu*⟧ **1** CATECHU **2** a lozenge for sweetening the breath

ca·chu·cha (kə cho͞o′chə) ***n.*** ⟦Sp⟧ **1** an Andalusian dance in 3/4 time, like the bolero **2** music for this

ca·cique (kə sēk′) ***n.*** ⟦Sp < Arawak word meaning "prince," "lord"⟧ **1** *a)* in Spanish America, an Indian chief *b)* in Spanish America and Spain, a local political boss **2** any of various tropical American blackbirds (family Icteridae) with conical bills

cack·hand·ed (kak′han′did) ***adj.*** ⟦prob. < dial. *cack*, excrement⟧ **1** [Brit. Informal] left-handed **2** clumsy; awkward

cack·le (kak′əl) ***vi.*** **-led**, **-ling** ⟦ME *cakelen*; akin to Du *kokkelen*, LowG *kakkeln* < IE base **kak-*: of echoic orig.⟧ **1** to make the shrill, broken vocal sounds of a hen **2** to laugh or chatter with similar sounds —***vt.*** to utter in a cackling manner —***n.*** **1** the act or sound of cackling **2** cackling laughter **3** idle or silly chatter —**cut the cackle** [Brit. Informal] to stop talking and settle down to serious efforts

cac·o- (kak′ō, -ə) ⟦< Gr *kakos*, bad, evil⟧ *combining form* bad, poor, harsh [*cacography*]

cac·o·de·mon or **cac·o·dae·mon** (kak′ō dē′mən) ***n.*** ⟦Gr *kakodaimōn*: see prec. & DEMON⟧ an evil spirit or devil

cac·o·dyl (kak′ō dil′, kak′ə-) ***n.*** ⟦< Gr *kakōdēs*, bad-smelling < *kakos*, bad + *-ōdēs* (< IE base **od-*, to smell > ODOR, OZONE) + -YL⟧ *Chem.* **1** the radical $As(CH_3)_2$, composed of arsenic and methyl: its compounds are poisonous and foul-smelling **2** a poisonous, colorless liquid, $As_2(CH_3)_4$, with an offensive odor: it is a polymer of this radical —**cac′o·dyl′ic** (-dil′ik) ***adj.***

ca·co·e·thes (kak′ō ē′thēz′) ***n.*** ⟦L < Gr *kakoēthēs* < *kakos*, bad + *ēthos*, habit: see ETHICAL⟧ a hankering (to do something); mania

ca·cog·ra·phy (kə käg′rə fē) ***n.*** ⟦CACO- + -GRAPHY⟧ **1** bad handwriting **2** incorrect spelling —**cac·o·graph·ic** (kak′ə graf′ik) ***adj.***, **cac′o·graph′i·cal**

☆**cac·o·mis·tle** (kak′ə mis′əl) ***n.*** ⟦AmSp *cacomixtle* < Nahuatl *ƛa'komisƛi* < *ƛa'ko*, half + *mis-ƛi*, cougar⟧ **1** a slender, long-tailed, raccoonlike carnivore (*Bassariscus astutus*) of the SW U.S. and Mexico **2** its fur Also **cac′o·mix′le** (-mis′əl, -mik′səl)

ca·coph·o·ny (kə käf′ə nē) ***n.***, *pl.* **-nies** ⟦prob. via Fr *cacophonie* < ML *cacophonia* < Gr *kakophōnia* < *kakophōnos*, harsh-sounding < *kakos*, bad, evil + *phōnē*, voice: see PHONO-⟧ harsh, jarring sound; dissonance —**ca·coph′o·nous** (-nəs) ***adj.*** —**ca·coph′o·nous·ly** ***adv.***

cac·tus (kak′təs) ***n.***, *pl.* **-tus·es** or **-ti′** (-tī′) ⟦ModL < Gr *kaktos*, kind of thistle, cardoon⟧ any desert plant of the cactus family, native to the New World, with fleshy stems, reduced or spinelike leaves, and often showy flowers —***adj.*** designating a family (Cactaceae) of dicotyledonous plants (order Caryophyllales), including the prickly pear, saguaro, and cereus

ca·cu·mi·nal (kə kyo͞o′mə nəl) ***adj.*** ⟦< L *cacumen* (gen. *cacuminis*), top (< redupl. of IE base **keu-*: see HIGH) + -AL⟧ *Phonet.* pronounced with the tip of the tongue turned backward and upward against or toward the hard palate —***n.*** a cacuminal sound

cad (kad) ***n.*** ⟦< CADDIE & CADET: orig. applied to servants, then to town boys, by students at British universities and public schools⟧ a man or boy whose behavior is not gentlemanly

CAD[1] (kad) ***n.*** computer-aided design: see CAD/CAM

CAD[2] *abbrev.* coronary artery disease
ca·das·tre or **ca·das·ter** (kə das′tər) *n.* ⟦Fr < It *catastro* < dial. (Venetian) *catastico* < LGr *katastichon*, register, list (lit., line by line): see CATA- & STICH⟧ public record of the extent, value, and ownership of land within a district for purposes of taxation —**ca·das′tral** (-trəl) *adj.*
ca·dav·er (kə dav′ər) *n.* ⟦L, prob. < *cadere*, to fall: see CASE[1]⟧ a dead body, esp. of a person; corpse, as for dissection —*SYN.* BODY —**ca·dav′er·ic** *adj.*
ca·dav·er·ine (-ər ēn′, -ər in) *n.* ⟦prec. + -INE[3]⟧ a colorless, putrid-smelling, liquid ptomaine, $NH_2(CH_2)_5NH_2$, produced by the action of microorganisms on proteins, as in decaying flesh
ca·dav·er·ous (-ər əs) *adj.* ⟦L *cadaverosus*⟧ of or like a cadaver; esp., pale, ghastly, or gaunt and haggard —**ca·dav′er·ous·ly** *adv.* —**ca·dav′er·ous·ness** *n.*
CAD/CAM (kad′kam′) *n.* ⟦*C(omputer-)A(ided) D(esign)/C(omputer-) A(ided) M(anufacturing)*⟧ design and manufacturing by means of a computer system, as in the creation of complex wiring diagrams, the design of coordinated machine parts, etc.
cad·dice (kad′is) *n.* **1** CADDIS[1] **2** CADDIS[2]
cad·die (kad′ē) *n.* ⟦Scot form of Fr *cadet*: see CADET⟧ **1** [Obs.] an errand boy **2** a person who attends a golfer, carrying the clubs, finding the balls, etc. **3** a small, two-wheeled cart, as for carrying golf bags —*vi.* **-died, -dy·ing** to act as a caddie
cad·dis[1] (kad′is) *n.* ⟦ME & OFr *cadas*, floss silk; confused with Fr *cadis*, coarse serge, after CADIZ (? where made)⟧ **1** a coarse woolen material; worsted yarn **2** a worsted ribbon
cad·dis[2] (kad′is) *n.* CADDIS WORM
caddis fly any of an order (Trichoptera) of small, mothlike insects with a soft body, long antennae and legs, and two pairs of hairy, membranous wings
cad·dish (kad′ish) *adj.* like or characteristic of a cad; ungentlemanly —**cad′dish·ly** *adv.* —**cad′dish·ness** *n.*
caddis worm ⟦< OFr *cadas*, floss silk (with reference to the case)⟧ the wormlike larva of the caddis fly that usually lives in fresh water in an elongated case made of twigs, grains of sand, etc. cemented together with silk that it secretes: commonly used as bait by anglers
Cad·do (kad′ō) *n., pl.* **-dos** or **-do** ⟦Louisiana Fr *Cadaux*, shortened < Sp *Cadojodacho* < Caddo *kaduhdáču′*, name of a major group of the Caddo confederacy⟧ **1** a member of any of a group of North American Indian peoples formerly living in Louisiana, Arkansas, and E Texas, now living mainly in Oklahoma **2** the Caddoan language of these peoples
Cad·do·an (-ən) *n.* ⟦coined (1891) by J. W. Powell < prec. + -AN⟧ a family of North American Indian languages, including Caddo, Pawnee, and Arikara
cad·dy[1] (kad′ē) *n., pl.* **-dies** ⟦< earlier CATTY[2] < Malay *kātī*, weight equivalent to a little more than a pound⟧ **1** a small container used for tea **2** any of various devices for holding or storing certain articles, as phonograph records
cad·dy[2] (kad′ē) *n., vi.* CADDIE
cade[1] (kād) *adj.* ⟦LME, a pet⟧ untended by its mother and brought up by a human being, often as a pet [*a cade* lamb]
cade[2] (kād) *n.* ⟦Fr < Prov < LL *catanus*, prob. < Gaul⟧ a bushy Mediterranean juniper (*Juniperus oxycedrus*) whose tarlike oil distilled from the wood is used in the treatment of skin disorders
-cade (kād) ⟦< (CAVAL)CADE⟧ *suffix* procession, parade [*motorcade*]
ca·delle (kə del′) *n.* ⟦Fr < Prov *cadello* < L *catella*, fem. of *catellus*, puppy, whelp < IE base *kat-, to bear young > ON *hathna*, young goat⟧ the larva or adult of a small, shiny, black beetle (*Tenebroides mauritanicus*) harmful to grain
ca·dence (kād′ns) *n.* ⟦ME < OFr < OIt *cadenza* or ML *cadentia* < L *cadens*, prp. of *cadere*, to fall: see CASE[1]⟧ **1** fall of the voice in speaking **2** inflection or modulation in tone **3** any rhythmic flow of sound **4** measured movement, as in dancing or marching, or the beat of such movement **5** *Music* a series of notes or chords at the end of a phrase, section, or composition which indicates a partial or complete conclusion Also **ca′den·cy** (-'n sē) —**ca′denced** (-'nst) *adj.*, **ca·den·tial** (kə den′shəl)
ca·dent (-'nt) *adj.* **1** [Archaic] falling **2** having cadence
ca·den·za (kə den′zə) *n.* ⟦It: see CADENCE⟧ **1** an elaborate, often improvised musical passage played unaccompanied by the solo instrument in a concerto, usually near the end of the first or the final movement **2** any brilliant flourish in an aria or solo passage
ca·det (kə det′) *n.* ⟦Fr, younger son < Gascon *capdet*, captain, chief < Prov *capdel* < LL *capitellum*, dim. of L *caput*, HEAD⟧ **1** [Now Rare] a younger son or brother **2** [Historical] a younger son who became a gentleman volunteer in the army to offset his lack of patrimony **3** a student in training at an armed forces academy **4** a student at a military school ☆**5** any trainee, as a practice teacher or a junior business associate ☆**6** [Old Slang] a pimp —**ca·det′ship** *n.*
☆**Ca·dette** (kə det′) *n.* ⟦prec. + -ETTE⟧ a member of the division of the Girl Scouts for girls twelve to fourteen years of age: in full **Cadette Girl Scout**
cadge (kaj) *vt., vi.* **cadged, cadg′ing** ⟦< ?⟧ [Informal, Chiefly Brit.] to beg or get by begging; sponge —**cadg′er** *n.*
ca·di (kä′dē, kā′-) *n.* ⟦Ar *qāḍī*⟧ a minor Muslim magistrate
Ca·dil·lac[1] (kad′'l ak′) *n.* ⟦< *Cadillac*, trademark for a luxury automobile, after fol.⟧ [Informal] something that is the most luxurious or highest quality of its kind
Ca·dil·lac[2] (kà dē yàk′; *E* kad′'l ak′), Sieur **An·toine de la Mothe** (än twàn də là mōt′) 1658?-1730; Fr. explorer in America
Ca·diz (kə diz′, kā′diz) **1** seaport in SW Spain, on the Atlantic: Sp. name **Cá·diz** (kä′thēth′) **2** city in N Negros, in the Philippines
Cad·me·an (kad mē′ən) *adj.* of or like Cadmus
cad·mi·um (kad′mē əm) *n.* ⟦ModL < L *cadmia*, zinc ore < Gr *kadmeia (gē)*, Cadmean (earth) (so called because found near Thebes, home of CADMUS) + -IUM: so named (1817) by F. Strohmeyer (1776-1835), Ger chemist, because frequently found assoc. with zinc⟧ a silver-white, malleable, ductile, metallic chemical element occurring as a sulfide or carbonate in zinc ores: it is used in some low-melting alloys, electroplating, rechargeable batteries, etc.: highly toxic dust or fumes: symbol, Cd; at. no. 48: see the periodic table of elements in the Reference Supplement —**cad′mic** (-mik) *adj.*
cadmium sulfide a toxic pigment, CdS, varying from lemon yellow (**cadmium yellow**) to yellowish orange (**cadmium orange**) and used in paints, photocells, semiconductors, etc.
Cad·mus (kad′məs) *n.* ⟦Gr *Kadmos*⟧ *Class. Legend* a Phoenician prince and founder of Thebes: he kills a dragon and sows its teeth, from which many armed men rise, fighting each other, until only five are left to help him build the city
ca·dre (ka′drē, kä′-; -drā) *n.* ⟦Fr, a frame < It *quadro* < L *quadrum*, a square: see QUADRATE⟧ **1** basic structure or framework **2** an operational unit, as of staff officers or other key personnel, around which an expanded organization can be built **3** a small, unified group organized to instruct or lead a larger group; nucleus **4** a member of a political, esp. Communist, cadre
ca·du·ce·us (kə do͞o′sē əs, -dyo͞o′-) *n., pl.* **-ce·i′** (-sē ī′) ⟦L, ? via Etr < Gr(Doric) *karykeion*, for Gr *kērykeion* < *kēryx*, herald < IE base *kar-, to praise > OHG *hruom*, Ger *ruhm*⟧ **1** the staff of an ancient herald; esp., the winged staff with two serpents coiled about it, carried by Mercury **2** an emblematic staff like this with either one or two serpents, used as a symbol of the medical profession —**ca·du′ce·an** *adj.*

caduceus

ca·du·ci·ty (kə do͞o′sə tē, -dyo͞o′-) *n.* ⟦Fr *caducité* < LL *caducitas* < L *caducus*: see fol.⟧ **1** the quality or state of being perishable **2** senility
ca·du·cous (-kəs) *adj.* ⟦L *caducus*, falling < *cadere*, to fall: see CASE[1]⟧ *Bot.* falling off early, as some leaves
cae·cil·i·an (sē sil′ē ən, -sil′yən) *n.* ⟦< ModL < L *caecilia*, kind of lizard < *caecus*: see CECUM⟧ any of an order (Gymnophiona) of legless tropical amphibians resembling worms
cae·cum (sē′kəm) *n., pl.* **-ca** (-kə) CECUM —**cae′cal** (-kəl) *adj.*
Caed·mon (kad′mən) fl. late 7th cent. A.D.; first Eng. poet whose name is known
Cae·li·an (sē′lē ən, sēl′yən) ⟦after L *Caelius Mons*, Caelian hill, named after the Tuscan *Caeles Vibenna*⟧ *see* SEVEN HILLS OF ROME
Cae·lum (sē′ləm) *n.* ⟦L, a chisel⟧ a small S constellation between Columba and Eridanus
Caen (kän) chief city of Basse-Normandie, NW France
Caer·nar·von·shire (kär när′vən shir′, -shər) former county of NW Wales, now part of Gwynedd: also **Caer·nar′von**
caes·al·pin·i·a (sez′al pin′ē ə, sēs′-) *adj.* ⟦after A. *Cesalpino* (1519-1603), It botanist & physician⟧ designating a family (Caesalpiniaceae) of leguminous trees and shrubs, including the Kentucky coffee tree
Cae·sar[1] (sē′zər) *n.* ⟦after fol.⟧ **1** the title of the emperor of Rome from Augustus to Hadrian, or of the emperor of the Holy Roman Empire **2** any of the Roman emperors **3** [*often* **c-**] any emperor or dictator
Cae·sar[2] (sē′zər), **(Gaius) Julius** ⟦L *Caesar*, said to be < *caesus*, pp. of *caedere*, to cut down (see -CIDE), but prob. of Etr orig.⟧ 100?-44 B.C.; Rom. general & statesman; dictator (49-44) of the Roman Empire
Caes·a·re·a (ses′ə rē′ə, sez′-, sē′zə-) **1** seaport in ancient Palestine, on the Mediterranean, south of Haifa, Israel: Roman capital of Palestine **2** city in ancient Palestine, near Mt. Hermon: also **Caesarea Philippi** **3** *ancient name for* KAYSERI
Cae·sar·e·an or **Cae·sar·i·an** (sə zer′ē ən) *adj.* of Julius Caesar or the Caesars —*n.* [*also* **c-**] *short for* CAESAREAN SECTION
Caesarean section [*also* **c- s-**] CESAREAN (SECTION)
Cae·sar·ism (sē′zər iz′əm) *n.* [*also* **c-**] absolutism in government; autocracy —**Cae′sar·ist** *adj., n.*
☆**Caesar salad** ⟦so named in honor of Julius CAESAR[2] by Giacomo Junia, Italian-American chef in Chicago, who invented it *c.* 1903⟧ a salad of greens, grated cheese, croutons, anchovies, etc. with a dressing of olive oil, lemon juice, garlic, and raw or coddled eggs
cae·si·um (sē′zē əm) *n.* CESIUM
caes·pi·tose (ses′pə tōs′) *adj.* CESPITOSE
cae·su·ra (si zyoor′ə, -zhoor′ə) *n., pl.* **-ras** or **-rae** (-ē) ⟦L, a cutting < pp. of *caedere*, to cut down: see -CIDE⟧ **1** a break or pause in a line of verse: in Greek and Latin verse, the caesura falls within the metrical foot; in English verse, it is usually about the middle of the line and is shown in scanning by the sign ‖ **2** *Music* a break or pause in the meter of a composition —**cae·su′ral** *adj.*
CAF or **caf** *abbrev.* cost and freight
ca·fard (kà fàr′) *n.* ⟦Fr, low spirits, cockroach, orig., hypocrite, altered

(with pejorative *-ard*) < MFr *caphars* < Ar *kāfir*, hypocrite, lit., infidel: see KAFFIR⟧ melancholy, boredom, listlessness, etc.

ca·fe or **ca·fé** (ka fā′, kə-) ***n.*** ⟦Fr, coffee, coffeehouse < It *caffè*, COFFEE⟧ **1** a coffeehouse **2** a small restaurant, esp. one serving alcoholic drinks and sometimes providing entertainment **3** a barroom

CAFE (ka fā′) *abbrev.* Corporate Average Fuel Economy

ca·fé au lait (ka fā′ō lā′) ⟦Fr, lit., coffee with milk⟧ **1** a drink made by mixing coffee with an equal amount of hot or scalded milk **2** pale brown

café con le·che (kä fā′ kän lā′chā) ⟦Sp, lit., coffee with milk⟧ a drink made by mixing strong coffee with hot or scalded milk

café coronary ⟦< CORONARY (*n.*)⟧ a fatal choking condition brought on when food, dentures, etc. lodge in a person's throat while he or she is eating: it is often misinterpreted as a heart attack

cafe curtains short, straight curtains, esp. for covering the lower part of a window, hung from a rod by means of sliding rings

ca·fé fil·tre (kȧ fā fēl′tr′) ⟦Fr⟧ coffee made by pouring boiling water through ground coffee beans in a filtering device that fits over a cup or pot

☆**cafe society** a social set of people who frequent fashionable restaurants and nightclubs, the theater, etc.

☆**caf·e·te·ri·a** (kaf′ə tir′ē ə) ***n.*** ⟦AmSp, coffee store⟧ a self-service restaurant in which food is displayed on counters —***adj.*** allowing a choice from among several options: used chiefly to designate company benefit or insurance plans that allow each employee to select benefits or coverage best suited to his or her needs

caf·e·to·ri·um (kaf′ə tôr′ē əm) ***n.*** a room or building that is used alternately as a cafeteria and an auditorium, as in a school

caff (kaf) ***n.*** [Brit. Slang] a small, inexpensive restaurant or coffeehouse; cafe

caf·fein·at·ed (kaf′ə nāt′id, kaf′ē ə nāt′id) ***adj.*** containing caffeine

caf·feine (ka fēn′, kaf′ēn′) ***n.*** ⟦Ger *kaffein* (now *coffeïn*, after ModL *coffea*, coffee); coined by F. F. Runge (1795-1867), Ger chemist < *kaffee*, coffee (< Fr *café* < It *caffè*, COFFEE) + *-in*, -INE[3]⟧ a bitter, crystalline alkaloid, $C_8H_{10}N_4O_2$, present in coffee, tea, kola nuts, etc.: it prolongs the stimulating effects of cyclic AMP on the heart and central nervous system: also sp. **caf·fein′**

caf·fè lat·te (ka′fā lä′tā) ⟦It, lit., coffee (with) milk⟧ LATTE

caf·tan (kaf′tan, -tan′; käf tän′) ***n.*** ⟦Turk *qaftān*⟧ **1** a long-sleeved robe with a sash, worn in E Mediterranean countries **2** a long, loose dress, usually with wide sleeves, worn, esp. by women, in the West

Ca·ga·yan de O·ro (kä′gə yän′ dā ôr′ō) city in E Mindanao, in the Philippines

cage (kāj) ***n.*** ⟦ME & OFr < L *cavea*, hollow place, cage < *cavus*, hollow: see CAVE⟧ **1** a box or enclosed structure made of wires, bars, etc., for confining birds or animals **2** a fenced-in area as for confining prisoners of war **3** any openwork structure or frame, as some elevator cars **4** [Archaic] a jail **5** *Baseball* BATTING CAGE **6** *Hockey* the network frame that is the goal —***vt.* caged, cag′ing** to put or confine, as in a cage

Cage (kāj), **John** 1912-92; U.S. composer

cage·ling (kāj′liŋ) ***n.*** a bird kept in a cage

cage match a typically brutal competition, combining elements of wrestling and boxing but with relatively few rules, taking place in a cage or similar confining area

caftan

cag·er (kāj′ər) ***n.*** ⟦< CAGE (in older sense, "a basketball goal") + -ER⟧ ☆[Slang] a basketball player

☆**ca·gey** or **ca·gy** (kā′jē) ***adj.* ca′gi·er, ca′gi·est** ⟦< ?⟧ [Informal] **1** sly; tricky; cunning **2** careful not to get caught or fooled —**ca′gi·ly *adv.*** —**ca′gi·ness *n.***

Ca·glia·ri[1] (käl′yä rē′), **Paolo** *see* VERONESE, Paolo

Ca·glia·ri[2] (käl′yä rē′) seaport & capital of Sardinia, on the S coast

Ca·glio·stro (käl yôs′trō), Count **A·les·san·dro di** (ä′les sän′drô dē) (born *Giuseppe Balsamo*) 1743-95; Sicilian alchemist & charlatan

Cag·ney (kag′nē), **James** 1899-1987; U.S. film actor

Ca·guas (kä′gwäs′) city in EC Puerto Rico

ca·hier (kä yā′) ***n.*** ⟦Fr < OFr *quaer*: see QUIRE[2]⟧ **1** a notebook **2** a report on policy or procedure

Cahn (kän), **Sam·my** (sam′ē) (born *Samuel Cohen*) 1913-93; U.S. composer of popular songs

☆**ca·hoots** (kə ho͞ots′) ***pl.n.*** ⟦< ?⟧ [Slang] partnership; league: chiefly in phrase **in cahoots (with)**, in league (with): usually applied to questionable dealing or to conspiracy

ca·how (kə hou′) ***n.*** ⟦echoic of its cry⟧ a nearly extinct, dark-colored petrel (*Pterodroma cahow*) of Bermuda

CAI *abbrev.* computer-assisted (or -aided) instruction

Cai·a·phas (kā′ə fəs, kī′-) ***n.*** ⟦Gr *Kaiaphas*⟧ *Bible* the high priest who presided at the trial that led to the condemnation of Jesus: Matt. 26:57-66

Cai·cos Islands (kāk′əs) *see* TURKS AND CAICOS ISLANDS

cai·man (kā′mən) ***n.*** ⟦ModL < Sp < Carib *acayuman*⟧ any of a genus (*Caiman*) of Central and South American crocodilian reptiles similar to alligators

Cain (kān) ***n.*** ⟦Heb *qayin*, lit., one created⟧ **1** *Bible* the oldest son of Adam and Eve, who killed his brother Abel: Gen. 4 **2** any murderer, esp. of a brother —☆**raise Cain** [Slang] **1** to create a great commotion **2** to cause much trouble

cai·pi·ri·nha (kī′pi rē′nyə) ***n.*** ⟦BrazPort < *caipira*, farmer, rustic⟧ an iced cocktail, originating in Brazil, made of crushed limes, sugar, and a special Brazilian sugar-cane liquor

ca·ique or **ca·ïque** (kä ēk′) ***n.*** ⟦Fr < It *caicco* < Turk *qayiq*⟧ **1** a light rowboat used on the Bosporus **2** a kind of sailboat used esp. in the E Mediterranean

caird (kerd, kärd) ***n.*** ⟦< Gael *ceard*, a tinker < IE base **kerd-*, skillful, clever > Gr *kerdos*, profit, L *cerdo*, handicraftsman, ON *horskr*, wise⟧ [Scot.] a wandering tinker, vagrant, gypsy, etc.

Cai·rene (kī′rēn) ***n.*** a person born or living in Cairo, Egypt —***adj.*** of Cairo, Egypt, or its people or culture

cairn (kern) ***n.*** ⟦Scot < Gael *carn*, an elevation < IE base **ker-n-*, highest part of the body, horn, hence tip, peak > L *cornu*, HORN, extremity, summit⟧ a conical heap of stones built as a monument or landmark —**cairned *adj.***

cairn·gorm (kern′gôrm′) ***n.*** ⟦after *Cairngorm* mountain and range in NE Scotland, where orig. found < Gael *carngorm* < prec. + *gorm*, blue, azure⟧ a yellow or brown variety of quartz, used as a gem

cairn terrier ⟦said to be so named from its burrowing in *cairns*⟧ a small, shaggy Scottish terrier

Cai·ro (kī′rō; *for 2* ker′ō) **1** capital of Egypt, at the head of the Nile delta **2** ⟦after the capital of Egypt⟧ city in S Ill., at the confluence of the Ohio & Mississippi rivers

cais·son (kā′sən, -sän′) ***n.*** ⟦Fr < It *cassone* < *cassa*, a chest < L *capsa*, a box, CASE[2]⟧ **1** a chest for holding ammunition **2** a two-wheeled wagon for transporting ammunition **3** a watertight enclosure inside which underwater construction work can be done **4** a watertight box for raising sunken ships: after the box is sunk and attached, the water is forced out of it so that it floats **5** a hollow, boat-shaped box, used as a floodgate at a dock or basin

☆**caisson disease** DECOMPRESSION SICKNESS

Caith·ness (kāth′nes′, kāth nes′) former county & former district of NE Scotland

cai·tiff (kāt′if) ***n.*** ⟦ME < OFr *caitif*, a captive, wretched man < L *captivus*, CAPTIVE⟧ a mean, evil, or cowardly person —***adj.*** evil, mean, or cowardly

caj·e·put (kaj′ə pət) ***n.*** *alt. sp. of* CAJUPUT

ca·jole (kə jōl′) ***vt., vi.* -joled′, -jol′ing** ⟦Fr *cajoler*, orig. to chatter like a jay in a cage; ? blend of OFr *cage* (see CAGE) & *jaole*, JAIL⟧ to coax with flattery and insincere talk; wheedle —**SYN.** COAX[1] —**ca·jol′er·y *n.*, ca·jole′ment** —**ca·jol′er *n.*** —**ca·jol′ing·ly *adv.***

☆**Ca·jun** (kā′jən) ***n.*** ⟦< ACADIAN⟧ **1** a native of Louisiana originally descended from Acadian French immigrants **2** the dialect of French spoken by the Cajuns —***adj.*** **1** of the Cajuns or their dialect or culture **2** of or in the style of cooking of the Cajuns, characterized as by the use of pungent spices, sweet and hot peppers, and a well-browned roux to thicken and flavor sauces Often sp. **Ca′jan**

caj·u·put (kaj′ə pət) ***n.*** ⟦Malay *kāyūputīh* < *kāyū*, tree + *putīh*, white⟧ an Australian tree (*Melaleuca leucadendra*) of the myrtle family, with whitish flowers and thick bark, often grown in the extreme S U.S.: its aromatic oil is used in medicine

cake (kāk) ***n.*** ⟦ME < ON *kaka* < IE base **gag-*, **gog-*, something round, lump of something (orig. < baby talk) > Ger *kuchen*: not connected with COOK & L *coquere*⟧ **1** a small, flat mass of dough or batter, or of some hashed food, that is baked or fried **2** a mixture of flour, eggs, milk, sugar, etc. baked as in a loaf and often covered with icing **3** a solid, shaped mass, as of soap or ice **4** a hard crust or deposit — ***vt., vi.* caked, cak′ing** to form into a hard mass or a crust; solidify or encrust —**take the cake** ⟦< the practice of awarding a *cake* as a prize⟧ [Informal] to be the prime example of a type, quality, etc.: usually used ironically as to convey mild disapproval —**cak′y *adj.*** or **cak′ey, cak′i·er, cak′i·est**

cakes and ale the good things of life; worldly pleasures

☆**cake·walk** (kāk′wôk′) ***n.*** **1** an elaborate step or walk formerly performed by blacks in the South competing for the prize of a cake **2** a strutting dance developed from this **3** something easily accomplished, won, etc. —***vi.*** to do a cakewalk —**cake′walk′er *n.***

cal *abbrev.* **1** caliber **2** calorie(s) **3** small calorie(s)

Cal *abbrev.* **1** California **2** large calorie(s)

Cal·a·bar (kal′ə bär′, kal′ə bär′) seaport in SE Nigeria

Calabar bean ⟦after prec., and the *Calabar River*, on which it is situated⟧ the large, brown, poisonous seed of a woody, leguminous tropical African vine (*Physostigma venenosum*) used in medicine as a source of physostigmine

cal·a·bash (kal′ə bash′) ***n.*** ⟦Fr *calebasse* < Sp *calabaza*; prob. < Ar *qar'a yābisa*, dry gourd⟧ **1** a tropical American tree (*Crescentia cujete*) of the bignonia family, or its large, gourdlike fruit **2** *a)* an Old World tropical vine (*Lagenaria siceraria*) of the gourd family, or its bottle-shaped, gourdlike fruit *b)* a large smoking pipe made from the neck of this gourd **3** the dried, hollow shell of a gourd or calabash, used as a bowl, cup, etc. **4** any of various gourds

☆**cal·a·boose** (kal′ə bo͞os′) ***n.*** ⟦Sp *calabozo*⟧ [Dial. or Old Slang] a prison; jail

Ca·la·bri·a (kə lā′brē ə; *It* kä lä′bryä) **1** region occupying the southernmost part of the peninsula of Italy, opposite Sicily: 5,822 sq mi (15,079 sq km) **2** former region (until 11th cent.) constituting what is now S Apulia, in SE Italy —**Ca·la′bri·an *adj.*, *n.***

calabash

ca·la·di·um (kə lā′dē əm) *n.* ⟦ModL < Malay *kélādy*, kind of plant⟧ any of a genus (*Caladium*, esp. *C. bicolor*) of tropical American plants of the arum family, grown for ornament because of their brilliantly colored, variegated leaves

Ca·lais (ka lā′, kal′ā′; *Brit also* kal′i; *Fr* kȧ le′) **1** seaport in N France, on the Strait of Dover **2 Pas de Calais** (pät kȧ le′) *Fr. name for* Strait of DOVER

cal·a·man·co (kal′ə maŋ′kō) *n., pl.* **-coes** or **-cos** ⟦Sp *calamaco, calamanco*⟧ a former kind of woolen cloth woven with a glossy, patterned face

cal·a·man·der (kal′ə man′dər) *n.* ⟦after ? COROMANDEL (COAST)⟧ the hard, heavy, black wood of various East Indian trees (genus *Diospyros*) of the ebony family, used in furniture

ca·la·ma·ri (kä′lə mä′rē, kal′ə mer′ē) *n.* ⟦It < L *calamarius*: see fol.⟧ squid cooked as food, esp. as an Italian dish

cal·a·mar·y (kal′ə mer′ē) *n., pl.* **-mar′ies** ⟦< L *calamarius*, of a writing reed < *calamus*, a reed, pen (see CALAMUS): so named from its pen-shaped skeleton⟧ a squid

cal·a·mine (kal′ə mīn′, -min, -mēn′) *n.* ⟦Fr < ML *calamina* < L *cadmia*, calamine, zinc ore: see CADMIUM⟧ **1** HEMIMORPHITE **2** a pink powder consisting of zinc oxide mixed with a small amount of ferric oxide, used in lotions and ointments for skin disease **3** [Brit.] SMITHSONITE

cal·a·mint (kal′ə mint′) *n.* ⟦ME *calaminte* < OFr *calamente* < ML *calamentum* < L *calaminthe* < Gr *kalaminthē*⟧ any of a genus (*Satureja*) of plants of the mint family, esp. an aromatic species of savory (formerly *S. calamintha* and now *Calamintha nepeta*)

cal·a·mite (kal′ə mīt′) *n.* ⟦< ModL < Gr *kalamitēs*, reedlike: see CALAMUS⟧ an extinct paleozoic plant (order Calamitales) related to modern horsetails but growing to the size of a tree

ca·lam·i·tous (kə lam′ə təs) *adj.* ⟦MFr *calamiteux* < L *calamitosus*⟧ causing or bringing calamity —**ca·lam′i·tous·ly** *adv.*

ca·lam·i·ty (-tē) *n., pl.* **-ties** ⟦MFr *calamité* < L *calamitas*: see CLASTIC⟧ **1** deep trouble or misery **2** any extreme misfortune bringing great loss and sorrow; disaster —*SYN.* DISASTER

Calamity Jane (name for *Martha Jane Burk* or *Burke* or *Martha Jane Canary*) 1852-1903; U.S. frontier figure

cal·a·mon·din (kal′ə män′din) *n.* ⟦Tag *kalamunding*⟧ a spicy orange (*Citrus mitis*) of the Philippines

cal·a·mus (kal′ə məs) *n., pl.* **-mi′** (-mī′) ⟦ME < L < Gr *kalamos*, a stalk, reed, stubble < IE base **kolem-*, stalk, reed > Ger *halm*, L *culmus*⟧ **1** SWEET FLAG **2** any of a genus (*Calamus*) of climbing palms of the Old World that yield rattan **3** the quill of a feather

ca·lan·do (kə län′dō) *adj., adv.* ⟦It < ger. of *calare*, to decrease < L < Gr *chalan*, to slacken⟧ *Musical Direction* with gradually decreasing speed and volume; fading away

ca·lash (kə lash′) *n.* ⟦Fr *calèche* < Ger *kalesche* < Czech *kolésa*, prob. < *kolo*, a WHEEL: for IE base see CYCLE⟧ **1** a four-wheeled carriage with facing double seats and a folding top; barouche **2** such a folding top **3** a folding hood or bonnet worn by women in the 18th cent.

☆**cal·a·ver·ite** (kal′ə ver′īt′) *n.* ⟦after *Calaveras* County, Calif., where first discovered + -ITE[1]⟧ a yellow to silver-white, monoclinic mineral, $AuTe_2$: an ore of gold, it contains a trace of silver

cal·ca·ne·us (kal kā′nē əs) *n., pl.* **-ne·i′** (-nē ī′) ⟦LL < L *calcaneum* < *calx*, the heel: see fol.⟧ **1** the large tarsal bone that forms the heel in humans; heel bone **2** a homologous bone in other tetrapod vertebrates: also **cal·ca′ne·um** (-əm), *pl.* **-ne·a** (-ə) —**cal·ca′ne·al** *adj.*

cal·car (kal′kär′) *n., pl.* **cal·car′i·a** (-ker′ē ə) ⟦L, a spur < *calx* (gen. *calcis*), the heel: for IE base see SCOLEX⟧ **1** *Bot.* a hollow projection or nectar spur, as at the base of a corolla **2** *Ornithology* a spur on a bird's wing or leg —**cal′ca·rate′** (-kə rāt′) *adj.*

cal·car·e·ous (kal ker′ē əs) *adj.* ⟦L *calcarius* < *calx*: see CALCIUM⟧ of, like, or containing calcium carbonate, calcium, or lime

calcareous tufa TUFA

cal·ce·i·form (kal′sē ə fôrm′, kal sē′-) *adj.* ⟦< L *calceus*, a shoe (< *calx*: see CALCAR) + -FORM⟧ CALCEOLATE

cal·ce·o·la·ri·a (kal′sē ə ler′ē ə) *n.* ⟦ModL < L *calceolarius*, shoemaker < *calceolus*, dim. of *calceus*: see prec.⟧ any of a large genus (*Calceolaria*) of South American plants of the figwort family, bearing colorful, slipper-shaped flowers

cal·ce·o·late (kal′sē ə lāt′) *adj.* ⟦< L *calceolus* (see prec.) + -ATE[1]⟧ *Bot.* shaped like a slipper, as the large, middle petal of an orchid

cal·ces (kal′sēz′) *n. alt. pl. of* CALX

cal·ci- (kal′si, -sə) ⟦< L *calx*: see CALCIUM⟧ *combining form* calcareous [*calciferous, calcify*]: also **calc-** (kalk)

cal·cic (kal′sik) *adj.* of or containing calcium or lime

cal·ci·cole (kal′si kōl′) *n.* ⟦orig. adj. < Fr < *calci-*, CALCI- + *-cole*, -COLOUS < L *colere*, to till: see CULT⟧ a plant that grows in calcium-rich soils —**cal·cic·o·lous** (kal sik′ə ləs) *adj.*

cal·cif·er·ol (kal sif′ər ôl′, -ōl′) *n.* ⟦< fol. + *-ol*, as in ERGOSTEROL⟧ ERGOCALCIFEROL

cal·cif·er·ous (-ər əs) *adj.* ⟦CALCI- + -FEROUS⟧ producing or containing calcium, calcium carbonate, or calcite

cal·cif·ic (kal sif′ik) *adj.* resulting from or undergoing calcification

cal·ci·fi·ca·tion (kal′sə fi kā′shən) *n.* **1** a calcifying; specif., the deposition of calcium salts in bodily tissues **2** a calcified substance or structure

cal·ci·fuge (kal′sə fyo͞oj′) *n.* ⟦orig. adj., not growing in limy soil < Fr: see CALCI- & -FUGE⟧ a plant that grows in soils low in calcareous matter —**cal·cif·u·gous** (kal sif′yo͞o gəs) *adj.*

cal·ci·fy (kal′sə fī′) *vt., vi.* **-fied′**, **-fy′ing** ⟦CALCI- + -FY⟧ to change into a hard, stony substance by the deposit of lime or calcium salts

cal·ci·mine (-mīn′, -min) *n.* ⟦< L *calx*: see CALCIUM⟧ a white or tinted liquid of whiting or zinc white, glue, and water, used as a wash chiefly for plastered surfaces —*vt.* **-mined′**, **-min′ing** to coat with calcimine

cal·cine (kal′sīn′, kal sīn′; kal′sin) *vt., vi.* **-cined′**, **-cin′ing** ⟦ME *calcinen* < OFr *calciner* < ML *calcinare* (an alchemists' term) < L *calx*: see CALCIUM⟧ **1** to change to calx or powder by heating to a high temperature, but below the melting point **2** to burn to ashes or powder **3** to oxidize at high temperature See DESTRUCTIVE DISTILLATION, PYROLYSIS, ROAST (sense 4), SMELT[1] —**cal·ci·na·tion** (kal′sə nā′shən) *n.*

cal·cite (kal′sīt′) *n.* ⟦< L *calx* (see CALCIUM) + -ITE[1]⟧ a soft, rhombohedral form of calcium carbonate, $CaCO_3$, found in marble, limestone, and chalk: see MOHS SCALE

cal·ci·to·nin (kal′si tō′nin) *n.* ⟦CALCI- + TON(IC) + -IN[1]⟧ a polypeptide hormone regulating the balance of calcium and phosphate in the blood by direct action on bone and kidney: in mammals, secreted by the thyroid

cal·ci·um (kal′sē əm) *n.* ⟦ModL < L *calx* (gen. *calcis*), lime < or akin to Gr *chalix*, pebble + -IUM: so named (1808) by Sir Humphry DAVY⟧ a soft, silver-white, metallic chemical element, one of the alkaline-earth metals, found in limestone, marble, chalk, etc., always in combination: it is used as a reducing agent and in fertilizer, and is the essential part of bones, shells, and teeth: symbol, Ca; at. no. 20: see the periodic table of elements in the Reference Supplement

calcium arsenate a toxic, white powder, $Ca_3(AsO_4)_2$, used as an insecticide in the form of a spray or dust

calcium carbide a dark-gray, crystalline compound, CaC_2, used to produce acetylene and calcium cyanamide

calcium carbonate a white powder or colorless, crystalline compound, $CaCO_3$, found mainly in limestone, marble, and chalk, as calcite, aragonite, etc., and in bones, teeth, shells, and plant ash: it is used in making lime, paints, plastics, etc.

calcium channel blocker any of a class of drugs, including nifedipine, diltiazem, and verapamil, that relax vascular and other smooth muscle tissue by preventing calcium ions from entering their cells, used to treat headaches, high blood pressure, angina pectoris, heart failure, etc.: sometimes written **cal′ci·um-chan′nel blocker**

calcium chloride a white, crystalline compound, $CaCl_2$, used as a de-icer, dehydrating agent, etc.

calcium cyanamide a white, crystalline compound, $CaCN_2$, used as a fertilizer, weed killer, etc.

calcium hydroxide slaked lime, $Ca(OH)_2$, a white, crystalline compound prepared by the action of water on calcium oxide, used in making plaster, mortar, alkalies, bleaching powder, etc.

calcium light LIMELIGHT (sense 1)

calcium oxide a white, soft, caustic solid, CaO, prepared by heating calcium carbonate; lime: used in making mortar and plaster, in ceramics, etc.

calcium phosphate any of a number of phosphates of calcium found in bones, teeth, etc. and used in medicine and in the manufacture of enamels, glass, cleaning agents, etc.

calc-sin·ter (kalk′sin′tər) *n.* ⟦Ger *kalksinter* < *kalk*, lime + *sinter*, slag⟧ TRAVERTINE

calc·spar (-spär′) *n.* ⟦transl. of Ger *kalkspar* < *kalk*, lime + *spar*, SPAR[1]⟧ CALCITE

cal·cu·la·ble (kal′kyo͞o lə bəl, -kyə-) *adj.* **1** that can be calculated **2** reliable; dependable —**cal′cu·la·bil′i·ty** *n.* —**cal′cu·la·bly** *adv.*

cal·cu·late (kal′kyo͞o lāt′, -kyə-) *vt.* **-lat′ed**, **-lat′ing** ⟦< L *calculatus*, pp. of *calculare*, to reckon < *calculus*, pebble, stone used in doing arithmetic, dim. of *calx*, limestone: see CALCIUM⟧ **1** to determine by using mathematics; compute **2** to reckon or determine by reasoning, evaluating, etc.; estimate; judge **3** to plan or intend for a purpose [a tale *calculated* to mislead us] **4** [Dial.] to think, suppose, guess, etc. ☆**5** [Dial.] to have in mind (*to* go, do, etc.); intend —*vi.* **1** to make a computation **2** to rely or depend (*on*)

SYN.—**calculate** refers to the mathematical determination of a quantity, amount, etc. and implies the use of higher mathematics [to *calculate* distances in astronomy]; **compute** suggests simpler mathematics and implies a determinable, hence precise, result [to *compute* the volume of a cylinder]; **estimate** implies the judging, usually in advance, of a quantity, cost, etc. and connotes an approximate result [to *estimate* the cost of building a house]; **reckon**, an informal substitute for **compute**, suggests the use of simple arithmetic such as can be performed mentally [to *reckon* the days before elections]

cal·cu·lat·ed (-lāt′id) *adj.* **1** done by mathematical calculation **2** undertaken or accepted after the probable results have been estimated [a *calculated* risk] **3** deliberately planned or intended [*calculated* cruelty] **4** apt or likely —**cal′cu·lat′ed·ly** *adv.*

cal·cu·lat·ing (-lāt′iŋ) *adj.* **1** shrewd or cunning, esp. in a selfish way; scheming **2** performing calculations

calculating machine CALCULATOR (sense 3)

cal·cu·la·tion (kal′kyo͞o lā′shən, -kyə-) *n.* **1** the act or process of calculating **2** something deduced by calculating; estimate; plan **3** careful planning or forethought, esp. with selfish motives —**cal′cu·la′tive** (-lāt′iv) *adj.*

cal·cu·la·tor (kal′kyo͞o lāt′ər, -kyə-) *n.* **1** a person who calculates **2** a book of tables for calculating **3** a mechanical or electronic device for the automatic performance of mathematical operations

cal·cu·lous (kal′kyo͞o ləs, -kyə-) ***adj.*** ⟦L *calculosus*⟧ *Med.* caused by or having a calculus or calculi
cal·cu·lus (kal′kyo͞o ləs, -kyə-) ***n.***, *pl.* **-li′** (-lī′) or **-lus·es** ⟦L: see CALCULATE⟧ **1** any abnormal stony mass or deposit formed in the body, as in a kidney or gallbladder or on teeth: see TARTAR (sense 2) **2** *Math. a)* any system of calculation using special symbolic notations *b)* INFINITESIMAL CALCULUS **3** any method or system of calculating, reasoning, or evaluating
calculus of finite differences the branch of mathematics concerned with changes in a dependent variable due to discrete changes in the independent variable
calculus of variations the branch of mathematics that tries to determine a function so as to satisfy specified conditions and to maximize (or minimize) a quantity which depends on the function
Cal·cut·ta (kal kut′ə) *former name for* KOLKATA: name still in popular use
cal·dar·i·um (kal der′ē əm) ***n.***, *pl.* **-i·a** (-ə) ⟦L < *caldarius*, pertaining to warming < *calidus*, warm, hot; akin to *calor*, heat: see CALORIE⟧ in ancient Roman baths, a room for taking hot baths
Cal·de·cott (kôl′də kät′), **Randolph** 1846-86; Eng. artist & illustrator: illustrated many books for children
Cal·der (kôl′dər) **1 Alexander** 1898-1976; U.S. abstract sculptor, esp. of mobiles and stabiles **2 Alexander Stir·ling** (stʉr′liŋ) 1870-1945; U.S. sculptor: father of Alexander
cal·de·ra (kal der′ə) ***n.*** ⟦Sp < LL *caldaria*, a pot for boiling, akin to L *caldarius*: see CALDARIUM⟧ a broad, craterlike basin of a volcano, formed by an explosion or by collapse of the cone
Cal·de·rón (de la Bar·ca) (käl *the* rôn′ *the* lä bär′kä), **Pe·dro** (pe′thrô) 1600-81; Sp. playwright
cal·dron (kôl′drən) ***n.*** *alt. sp. of* CAULDRON
Cald·well (kôld′wel′), **Er·skine** (ʉr′skən) 1903-87; U.S. novelist
Ca·leb (kā′ləb) ***n.*** ⟦Heb *kālēb*, lit., dog: hence, faithful⟧ **1** a masculine name **2** *Bible* a leader of the Israelites who, with Joshua, was permitted by God to enter the Promised Land: Num. 26:65; Deut. 1:36
ca·lèche or **ca·leche** (kə lesh′) ***n.*** ⟦Fr *calèche*: see CALASH⟧ CALASH
Cal·e·do·ni·a (kal′ə dōn′yə, -dō′nē ə) ⟦L, Roman name for part of N Britain, later applied to all of Scotland⟧ *old poet. name for* SCOTLAND —**Cal′e·do′ni·an** ***adj., n.***
Caledonian Canal canal in N Scotland, extending northeastward from the Atlantic to Moray Firth: *c.* 60 mi (97 km)
cal·e·fa·cient (kal′ə fā′shənt) ***adj.*** ⟦L *calefaciens*, prp. of *calefacere* < *calere*, to be warm (see CALORIE) + *facere*, to make, DO[1]⟧ making warm; heating —***n.*** *Med.* a substance applied to the body to give a sensation of heat
cal·e·fac·tion (kal′ə fak′shən) ***n.*** ⟦L *calefactio* < *calefacere*: see prec.⟧ **1** the act of heating **2** the state of being made warm
cal·e·fac·to·ry (kal′ə fak′tə rē) ***adj.*** ⟦LL *calefactorius*: see prec.⟧ producing heat —***n.***, *pl.* **-ries** ⟦ML *calefactorium*⟧ a heated common room in a monastery
cal·en·dar (kal′ən dər) ***n.*** ⟦ME *calender* < L *kalendarium*, account book < *kalendae*, CALENDS⟧ **1** a system of determining the beginning, length, and divisions of a year and for arranging the year into days, weeks, and months **2** a table, chart, register, etc. that shows such an arrangement, usually for a single year **3** a list or schedule, as of pending court cases, bills coming before a legislature, planned social events, etc. —***adj.*** such as that appearing on certain popular, conventional calendars [*calendar* art, a *calendar* girl] —***vt.*** to enter in a calendar; specif., to schedule —**ca·len·dri·cal** (kə len′dri kəl) ***adj.***, **ca·len′dric′** (-drik′)
calendar year the period of time from Jan. 1 through Dec. 31: distinguished from FISCAL YEAR
cal·en·der[1] (kal′ən dər) ***n.*** ⟦Fr *calendre* < ML *calendra* < L *cylindrus*, CYLINDER⟧ a machine with rollers between which paper, cloth, etc. is run, as to give it a smooth or glossy finish —***vt.*** ⟦Fr *calendrer* < the n.⟧ to process (paper, cloth, etc.) in a calender —**cal′en·der·er** ***n.***
cal·en·der[2] (kal′ən dər) ***n.*** ⟦Pers *qalandar*⟧ a member of an order of wandering dervishes among the Sufis
cal·ends (kal′əndz) ***pl.n.*** ⟦ME *calendes* < OE *calend*, beginning of a month < L *kalendae*, the first of the month < *calare*, to announce solemnly, call out < IE base **kel-* > LOW[2], CLAMOR⟧ [*often with sing. v.*] [*sometimes* **C-**] the first day of each month in the ancient Roman calendar
ca·len·du·la (kə len′jə lə, -dyo͞o lə) ***n.*** ⟦ModL < L *kalendae*, calends: prob. because the plants flower in most months⟧ any of a genus (*Calendula*) of plants of the composite family, with yellow or orange flowers, esp. the pot marigold
cal·en·ture (kal′ən chər, -cho͝or′) ***n.*** ⟦Fr < Sp *calentura* < *calentar*, to heat < L *calens*, prp. of *calere*, to be warm: see CALORIE⟧ any fever caused, as in the tropics, by exposure to great heat
ca·les·cent (kə les′ənt) ***adj.*** ⟦L *calescens*, prp. of *calescere*, to grow warm < *calere*, to be warm: see CALORIE⟧ increasing in warmth; getting hot —**ca·les′cence** ***n.***
calf[1] (kaf, käf) ***n.***, *pl.* **calves** or, esp. for 4, **calfs** ⟦ME < OE *cealf* & ON *kalfr* < IE **geleb(h)-* < base **gel-*, to swell, form a ball (hence swelling, fetus, offspring) > CLUB, L *globus*⟧ **1** a young cow or bull **2** the young of some other large animals, as the elephant, whale, hippopotamus, seal, etc. **3** a large piece of ice broken off from an iceberg or coast glacier **4** leather from the hide of a calf; calfskin **5** [Informal] an awkward, callow, or silly youth —**kill the fatted calf** to make a feast of celebration or welcome: Luke 15:23
calf[2] (kaf, käf) ***n.***, *pl.* **calves** ⟦ME < ON *kalfi*; akin to *kalfr*, prec.⟧ the fleshy back part of the leg below the knee
calf love [Informal] immature love between a boy and girl; puppy love
calf's-foot jelly (kafs′fo͝ot′) an edible gelatin made by boiling calves' feet
calf·skin (kaf′skin′) ***n.*** **1** the skin of a calf **2** soft, flexible leather made from this
Cal·ga·ry (kal′gə rē) ⟦after a location on the Isle of Mull, Scotland⟧ city in S Alberta, Canada
Cal·houn (kal ho͞on′), **John Caldwell** 1782-1850; U.S. statesman: vice president (1825-32)
Ca·li (kä′lē) city in SW Colombia
Cal·i·ban (kal′i ban′, -bən) ***n.*** ⟦form of *canibal*, CANNIBAL, with interchanged *n* & *l*; *canibal* occurs in Hakluyt's *Voyages* (1598)⟧ a deformed, brutish creature, the slave of Prospero, in Shakespeare's *The Tempest*
cal·i·ber (kal′ə bər) ***n.*** ⟦Fr & Sp, ult. < Ar *qālib*, a mold, last < Aram < Gr *kalopodion*, shoemaker's last, lit., little wooden foot < *kalon*, wood + *pous* (gen. *podos*), FOOT⟧ **1** the size of a bullet or shell as measured by its diameter **2** the diameter of the bore of a gun, usually measured in hundredths of inches or in millimeters **3** the diameter of a cylindrical body or of its hollowed interior **4** degree of worth or value of a person or thing; quality or ability Also, esp. Brit., **cal′i·bre**
cal·i·brate (kal′ə brāt′) ***vt.*** **-brat′ed**, **-brat′ing** **1** to determine the caliber of **2** to fix, check, or correct the graduations of (a measuring instrument, as a thermometer) —**cal′i·bra′tion** ***n.*** —**cal′i·bra′tor** ***n.***
ca·li·ces (kā′lə sēz′, kal′ə-) ***n.*** *pl. of* CALIX
ca·li·che (kə lē′chē, -chə) ***n.*** ⟦AmSp < Sp *cal*, lime < L *calx*: see CALCIUM⟧ **1** a hardened conglomeration of gravel, rock, and soil that contains sodium nitrate, potassium nitrate, etc., found mainly in arid regions of Chile and Argentina **2** a type of hardpan found in arid regions, as in the SW U.S., containing calcareous deposits, esp. of calcium carbonate
cal·i·cle (kal′i kəl) ***n.*** CALYCULUS
cal·i·co (kal′i kō′) ***n.***, *pl.* **-coes′** or **-cos′** ⟦after CALICUT, where it was first obtained⟧ **1** [Archaic] a kind of cotton cloth from India **2** *a)* a printed cotton fabric *b)* [Brit.] a heavy, white cotton cloth **3** a cat with a mottled coat of black, brown, yellow or orange, etc.: also **calico cat** —***adj.*** **1** of calico **2** spotted like some calico cloth
☆**cal·i·co·back** (-bak′) ***n.*** HARLEQUIN BUG
☆**calico bass** CRAPPIE
☆**calico bush** MOUNTAIN LAUREL
Cal·i·cut (kal′ə kut′) seaport in SW India, on the Arabian Sea
ca·lif (kā′lif; *also*, kal′if) ***n.*** CALIPH —**ca·lif·ate** (kā′lə fət, kal′ə fāt′) ***n.***
Calif *abbrev.* California
Cal·i·for·ni·a (kal′ə fôr′nyə, -nē ə) ⟦Sp, orig. name of a fabled island⟧ **1** state of the SW U.S., on the Pacific coast: admitted 1850: 155,959 sq mi (403,933 sq km); cap. Sacramento: abbrev. *CA*, *Cal*, or *Calif* **2 Gulf of** arm of the Pacific, between Baja California and the Mexican mainland
☆**California laurel** a Pacific coast shrub or tree (*Umbellularia californica*) of the laurel family, having aromatic evergreen leaves and hard wood; Oregon myrtle: a source of bay leaves
Cal·i·for·ni·an (-nyən, -nē ən) ***adj.*** of California: usually used in the predicate —***n.*** a person born or living in California
☆**California poppy** a plant (*Eschscholzia californica*) of the poppy family, with yellow to orange flowers
☆**California rosebay** a Pacific coast shrub or tree (*Rhododendron californicum*) of the heath family, with rosy or purplish flowers
☆**cal·i·for·ni·um** (kal′ə fôr′nē əm) ***n.*** ⟦ModL < CALIFORNIA + -IUM: so named (1950) by the discoverers, G. T. SEABORG and associates, at the University of California⟧ a radioactive, metallic chemical element, one of the actinides, produced by intense neutron bombardment of plutonium or curium: symbol, Cf; at. no. 98: an isotope (**californium-252**) with a half-life of 2.65 years is used as a neutron source in mining, medicine, etc.: see the periodic table of elements in the Reference Supplement
ca·lig·i·nous (kə lij′ə nəs) ***adj.*** ⟦L *caliginosus* < *caligo*, darkness, gloom: for IE base see COLUMBARIUM⟧ [Archaic] dark; obscure
Ca·lig·u·la (kə lig′yo͞o lə) (born *Gaius Caesar*) A.D. 12-41; Rom. emperor (A.D. 37-41): noted for his cruelty
cal·i·pash (kal′ə pash′, kal′ə pash′) ***n.*** ⟦WInd < ? Sp *carapacho*, CARAPACE⟧ a greenish, jellylike, edible substance under the upper shell of a turtle
cal·i·pee (kal′ə pē′, kal′ə pē′) ***n.*** ⟦var. of prec.⟧ a yellowish, jellylike, edible substance inside the lower shell of a turtle
cal·i·per (kal′ə pər) ***n.*** ⟦var. of CALIBER⟧ **1** [*usually pl.*] an instrument consisting of a pair of movable, curved legs fastened together at one end, used to measure the thickness or diameter of something: there are **inside calipers** and **outside calipers** **2** CALIPER RULE **3** thickness, as of paper or cardboard, expressed in mils **4** *a)* the part pressed against the spinning wheel in a hand-operated bicycle braking system *b)* the automotive disc brake housing containing the friction pads — ***vt., vi.*** to measure with calipers
caliper rule a graduated rule with one sliding jaw and one that is stationary
ca·liph (kā′lif, kal′if; kə lēf′) ***n.*** ⟦ME & OFr *calife* < Ar *khalīfa*, caliph, successor < *khalafa*, succeed⟧ supreme ruler: the title taken by Muhammad's successors as secular and religious heads of Islam
ca·liph·ate (kā′lə fət, kal′ə fāt′) ***n.*** **1** the rank or reign of a caliph **2** the land ruled by a caliph
cal·i·sa·ya bark (kal′ə sā′ə) ⟦AmSp < ? Quechua⟧ the bark of the yellow cinchona tree (*Cinchona calisaya*), which yields quinine
cal·is·then·ics (kal′is then′iks) ***pl.n.*** ⟦< Gr *kallos*, beauty + *sthenos*, strength + -ICS⟧ exercises, such as push-ups and sit-ups, to develop a strong, trim body; simple gymnastics —***n.*** the art of developing bodily strength and gracefulness by such exercises —**cal′is·then′ic** ***adj.***, **cal′is·then′i·cal**

ca·lix (kā′liks′, kal′iks′) ***n.***, *pl.* **ca·li·ces** (kā′lə sēz′, kal′ə-) ⟦L < IE base **kel(k)-*, cup > Gr *kylix, kalyx*, Sans *kalá́śa-h* (jug)⟧ a cup; chalice

calk[1] (kôk) ***vt., n.*** CAULK —**calk′er** ***n.***

calk[2] (kôk) ***n.*** ⟦< ? L *calcar*, spur: see CALCAR⟧ **1** a part of a horseshoe that projects downward to prevent slipping ☆**2** a metal plate with spurs, fastened to the sole of a shoe to prevent slipping —***vt.*** **1** to fasten calks on **2** to cut (its leg) accidentally with a calk: said of a horse

call (kôl) ***vt.*** ⟦ME *callen* < Late OE *ceallian* & (or <) ON *kalla* < IE base **gal-*, to scream, shriek > Brythonic *galw*, call, Ger *klage* & (?) MIr *gall*, swan⟧ **1** to say or read in a loud tone; shout; announce [to *call* the names of stations] **2** to command or ask to come; summon [*call* him to supper] **3** to summon to a specific duty, profession, etc. [the army *called* him] **4** to convoke judicially or officially [to *call* a meeting] **5** *a)* to give or apply a name to [*call* the baby Ann] *b)* to designate [they *called* her a cheat] **6** to consider or describe as specified [I *call* it silly] **7** to direct (attention) to **8** to awaken [*call* me at six] **9** to communicate with by telephone **10** to give orders for [to *call* a strike] ☆**11** to stop or halt [game *called* because of rain] **12** to demand or order payment of (a loan or bond issue) **13** to utter or chant directions for (a square dance) ☆**14** to imitate the sounds of in order to attract (a bird or animal) **15** *a)* in pool, to describe (the shot one plans to make) *b)* to predict ☆**16** *a) Poker* to equal (the preceding bet) or to equal the bet of (the preceding bettor) *b)* to challenge on, or force to account for, something said or done *c)* to expose (someone's bluff) by such action ☆**17** *Sports a)* to declare officially to be [the umpire *called* him out] *b)* to invoke (a penalty) against (a player or team) —***vi.*** **1** to speak in a loud tone; shout **2** to utter its characteristic cry, as a bird or animal **3** to visit for a short while: with *on* or *upon* **4** to ask that a person do something, esp. speak, as at a meeting: with *on* or *upon* **5** to telephone ☆**6** *Poker* to equal the preceding bet —***n.*** **1** an act or instance of calling **2** a loud utterance; shout **3** *a)* the distinctive cry of an animal or bird *b)* a sound made in imitation of such a cry to attract an animal or bird *c)* a device that makes such a sound **4** *a)* a summons to a meeting, rehearsal, etc. *b)* the calling up of a quota of men for military service **5** a signal on a bugle, drum, etc. **6** an act or instance of telephoning **7** an economic demand, as for a product **8** a request [a *call* for aid] **9** an inner urging toward a certain action or profession, esp. a religious vocation regarded as divinely inspired **10** an invitation to accept a position as a minister, teacher, etc. **11** power to attract or allure [the *call* of the wild] **12** need; obligation; occasion [no *call* for tears] **13** an order or demand for payment **14** a brief visit, esp. a formal or professional visit **15** a direction given by a caller of square dances **16** ROLL CALL **17** an option to buy a given quantity of a stock, commodity, etc. at a specified price and within a specified time: calls are purchased in expectation of a rise in price: cf. PUT (***n.*** 2) **18** *Bridge* a pass, bid, double, or redouble **19** *a) Sports* an official's decision or ruling [a good *call* by the umpire] *b)* a decision ["What do you want to do?" "I don't care— it's your *call*."] —**call back 1** to ask or command to come back **2** to telephone again or in return **3** to ask purchasers to return (an imperfect or dangerous product), often so that a manufacturing defect can be corrected; recall —**call down 1** to invoke ☆**2** [Informal] to scold sharply; rebuke —**called to the bar** [Brit.] admitted to the practice of law as a barrister —**call for 1** to demand; require [an emergency that *calls for* extreme measures] **2** to come and get; stop for **3** to predict [the forecast *calls for* snow flurries tonight] —**call forth** to bring into action or existence —**call in 1** to summon for help or consultation **2** to take out of circulation, as coin or bonds **3** to demand payment of —**call into question** to raise a question or doubt about —**call off 1** to order away; divert **2** to read aloud in order from a list **3** to cancel (a scheduled event) —**call out 1** to speak aloud; shout **2** to summon into action **3** to summon (workers) to strike **4** to challenge to a duel or to a contest, debate, etc. —**call time** *Sports* to suspend play temporarily —**call up 1** to make someone remember; recall [the aroma of freshly baked bread *calls up* fond memories] **2** to summon, esp. for military duty **3** to telephone **4** to retrieve (data) or access (a file, menu, etc.) and display on a computer screen —**on call 1** available when called for or summoned **2** payable on demand —**within call** close enough to hear if called

SYN.—**call**, in this comparison, is the basic word signifying to request the presence of someone at some place [he *called* the waiter over]; **summon**, the more formal term, implies authority or peremptoriness in the request [to *summon* a witness]; **convoke** and **convene** refer to the summoning of a group to assemble as for deliberation or legislation, but **convoke** implies greater authority or formality [to *convene* a class, to *convoke* a congress]; **invite** suggests a courteous request for someone's presence, esp. as a guest or participant, and usually suggests that the decision to come rests with the invited

cal·la (kal′ə) ***n.*** ⟦ModL < L *calla, calsa*, a plant (of uncert. kind): so named by LINNAEUS⟧ **1** any of several plants (genus *Zantedeschia*) of the arum family, with a conspicuous white, yellow, or pink spathe surrounding a club-shaped, yellow spadix; specif., a plant (*Z. aethiopica*), having a large, showy, white spathe enclosing a yellow spadix: also **calla lily 2** the wild calla (*Calla palustris*), a bog plant of the arum family, having greenish-white spathes and bearing bright-red berries

call·a·ble (kôl′ə bəl) ***adj.*** that can be called; specif., *a)* that must be paid upon demand (said as of a loan) *b)* that must be presented for payment upon notice (said as of a bond)

cal·la·loo (ka′lə lo͞o′, ka′lə lo͞o′) ***n.*** **1** the leaves of the taro, or, sometimes, other plants, cooked and eaten as a vegetable **2** a West Indian stew or soup made with this vegetable and, typically, crabmeat, okra, pork, and coconut milk

call and response 1 a kind of preaching or declaiming that elicits recurring cries of affirmation from the congregation or audience **2** *Music* a pattern of alternating parts, either vocal or instrumental, with the second responding to or repeating the first, such as occurs in gospel music sung by a lead singer and an antiphonal choir —**call′-and-re·sponse′** ***adj.***

cal·lant (käl′ənt) ***n.*** ⟦Du *kalant*, fellow, customer < Fr dial *calant*, for Fr *chalant*, customer < OFr *chaloir*, to be interested < L *calere*, to be warm, desire: see CALORIE⟧ [Scot.] a young fellow; boy; lad: also **cal′lan** (-ən)

Cal·la·o (kə yä′ō) seaport in W Peru

Cal·las (kal′əs, kä′läs), **Maria** (born *Maria Anna Sofia Cecilia Kalogeropaulos*) 1923-77; U.S. operatic soprano

call·back (kôl′bak′) ***n.*** **1** an additional audition as for a theatrical role **2** a return telephone call

☆**call·board** (kôl′bôrd′) ***n.*** *Theater* a bulletin board backstage for posting instructions, rehearsal times, etc.

call box 1 [Brit.] TELEPHONE BOOTH **2** a box, as on a post beside a highway, that holds a telephone for making emergency calls

call·boy (-boi′) ***n.*** **1** a boy who calls actors when it is time for them to go on the stage **2** a bellboy

call center a facility for handling telephone calls from the public, as to a large corporation or institution, with staffers who, variously, answer inquiries, process orders, provide customer service or technical support, etc.

call·er[1] (kôl′ər) ***n.*** **1** a person or thing that calls **2** a person who makes a short visit —***SYN.*** VISITOR

cal·ler[2] (kal′ər, käl′lər) ***adj.*** ⟦MScot, var. of ME *caloure, calver*, fresh (of fish) < ?⟧ [Scot.] **1** fresh: said of food **2** fresh and cool, as a breeze

caller ID a telephone service that identifies the origin of an incoming call by displaying, as on a cell phone screen, the telephone number or name of the caller

call forwarding a telephone service that allows incoming calls to be transferred automatically to another number or extension

☆**call girl** a female prostitute who is called by telephone to her assignations

cal·lig·ra·phy (kə lig′rə fē) ***n.*** ⟦Gr *kalligraphia* < *kalligraphos*, a good penman < *kallos*, beauty + *graphein*, to write: see GRAPHIC⟧ **1** beautiful handwriting, esp. as an art **2** handwriting; penmanship —**cal·lig′ra·pher** ***n.***, **cal·lig′ra·phist** —**cal·li·graph·ic** (kal′ə graf′ik) ***adj.***

Calligraphy

call-in (kôl′in′) ***adj.*** of or having to do with a radio or TV program during which members of the audience call in by telephone to comment on subjects under discussion, ask questions of guests, etc. [a *call-in* show]

call·ing (kôl′iŋ) ***n.*** **1** the action of one that calls **2** one's occupation, profession, or trade **3** an inner urging toward some profession or activity; vocation

☆**calling card 1** a small card with one's name, and sometimes one's address, on it, used in making visits **2** [Informal] an identifying mark or characteristic **3** a form of credit card used for making long-distance telephone calls, by means of which the charges may be either applied to a home or business account or (often *phone card*) deducted from a prepaid amount

Cal·li·o·pe (kə lī′ə pē′; *for 2, often* kal′ē ōp′) ***n.*** ⟦L < Gr *Kalliopē*, the beautiful-voiced < *kallos*, beauty + *ops*, VOICE⟧ **1** *Gr. Myth.* the Muse of eloquence and epic poetry ☆**2** [**c-**] a keyboard instrument like an organ, having a series of steam whistles

cal·li·op·sis (kal′ē äp′sis) ***n.*** ⟦ModL < Gr *kallos*, beauty + *opsis*, appearance < *ōps*, EYE⟧ COREOPSIS

cal·li·per (kal′ə pər) ***n., vt., vi.*** CALIPER

cal·li·pyg·i·an (kal′ə pij′ē ən) ***adj.*** ⟦Gr *kallipygos* < *kallos*, beauty + *pygē*, buttocks⟧ having shapely buttocks: also sp. **cal′li·pyg′e·an**

cal·lis·then·ics (kal′is then′iks) ***pl.n., n.*** CALISTHENICS —**cal′lis·then′ic** ***adj.***

Cal·lis·to (kə lis′tō) ***n.*** ⟦L < Gr *Kallistō*⟧ **1** *Class. Myth.* a nymph loved by Zeus and changed into a bear by Hera **2** the second largest satellite of Jupiter: discovered in 1610 by Galileo

call letters the letters, and sometimes the numbers, that identify a radio or TV transmitting station

☆**call loan 1** a loan that must be repaid on demand **2** a loan to a broker that is secured by shares of stock purchased with the borrowed money and which may be called if the shares decline in value: also **call money**

☆**call number** a group of numbers and letters placed on a book to indicate its location in a library

call of nature ⟦euphemism⟧ a need to defecate or urinate

cal·lose (kal′ōs′) ***n.*** ⟦< L *callosus*, CALLOUS⟧ a carbohydrate in plant cells that plugs the sieve pores when the sieve tubes stop functioning

cal·los·i·ty (kə läs′ə tē) ***n.*** ⟦ME & OFr *calosite* < L *callositas*⟧ **1** the quality or state of being callous, hardened, or unfeeling **2** *pl.* **-ties** a hardened, thickened place on skin or bark; callus

cal·lous (kal′əs) ***adj.*** ⟦ME < L *callosus* < *callum*, hard skin⟧ **1** *a)* having calluses *b)* thick and hardened: usually **cal′loused 2** lacking, or showing a lack of, pity, mercy, etc.; unfeeling — ***vt., vi.*** to make or become callous —***n.*** CALLUS (sense 1) —**cal′lous·ly** ***adv.*** —**cal′lous·ness** ***n.***

cal·low (kal′ō) *adj.* ⟦ME *calwe* < OE *calu*, bare, bald < IE base **gal-*, bald, naked > L *calvus*, bald, Czech *holý*, naked, Ger *kahl*, bald⟧ **1** still lacking the feathers needed for flying; unfledged **2** young and inexperienced; immature —**cal′low·ness** *n.*

☆**call rate** the rate of interest on call loans

call sign the letters or, often, numbers and letters assigned to a licensed broadcasting station, amateur radio operator, etc. as identification, as for sending messages

☆**call slip** a form on which a library patron lists the title and call number of a desired book

call to quarters *Mil.* a bugle call shortly before taps, notifying soldiers to retire to their quarters

call-up (kôl′up′) *n. Mil.* an order, as to those in the reserves, to report for active duty

cal·lus (kal′əs) *n., pl.* **-lus·es** ⟦L, var. of *callum*, hard skin⟧ **1** a hardened, thickened place on the skin **2** the hard substance that forms at the break in a fractured bone and serves to reunite the parts **3** a disorganized mass of cells that develops over cuts or wounds on plants, as at the ends of stem or leaf cuttings — *vi., vt.* to develop or cause to develop a callus

call waiting a telephone service that allows a person already talking on the telephone to be alerted to an incoming call by a faint beep or click and to take that call by putting the first call on hold

calm (käm, kôm; kälm, kôlm) *n.* ⟦ME & OFr *calme* < OIt *calma* < LL (Vulg.: Job 30:30) *cauma*, heat, heat of the day (hence, in It, time to rest, quiet: see SIESTA) < Gr *kauma*, heat, esp. of the sun < *kaiein*, to burn; It sp. infl. by L *calere*, to be hot⟧ **1** lack of wind or motion; stillness **2** lack of agitation or excitement; tranquillity; serenity **3** *Meteorol.* a condition in which the air movement is less than one mile per hour: see the Beaufort scale in the Reference Supplement —*adj.* **1** without wind or motion; still; quiet **2** not agitated or excited; tranquil — *vt., vi.* to make or become calm: often with *down* —**calm′ly** *adv.* —**calm′ness** *n.*

SYN.—**calm** suggests a total absence of agitation or disturbance [*a calm* sea, mind, answer]; **tranquil** implies a more intrinsic or permanent peace and quiet than **calm** [they lead a *tranquil* life]; **serene** suggests an exalted tranquillity [he died with a *serene* smile on his lips]; **placid** implies an undisturbed or unruffled calm and is sometimes used in jocular disparagement to suggest dull equanimity [the townsfolk were as *placid* as cows]; **peaceful** suggests a lack of turbulence or disorder [a *peaceful* gathering] —*ANT.* **stormy, agitated, excited**

calm·a·tive (käm′ə tiv; *esp. for n.*, kal′mə-) *adj.* calming; soothing; sedative —*n.* a sedative medicine

cal·mod·u·lin (kal mäj′o͞o lin′, -jə-) *n.* ⟦CAL(CIUM) + MODUL(ATE) + -IN[1]⟧ a protein in nearly all cells that binds to calcium and regulates many important cell functions, as nerve impulse transmissions and muscle action

cal·o·mel (kal′ə mel′, -məl) *n.* ⟦ModL *calomel*, *calomeles* < Gr *kalos*, beautiful + *melas*, black: see MELANO-⟧ mercurous chloride, HgCl, a white, tasteless powder that darkens on exposure to light: used in standard electrode cells and as a fungicide, insecticide, etc.

ca·lor·ic (kə lôr′ik) *n.* ⟦Fr *calorique* < L *calor*: see fol.⟧ **1** an imagined substance to which the phenomena of burning and oxidation were formerly attributed **2** [Archaic] heat —*adj.* **1** of heat **2** of or pertaining to calories —**ca·lor′i·cal·ly** *adv.*

cal·o·rie (kal′ə rē) *n.* ⟦Fr < L *calor*, heat; akin to *calere*, to be warm < IE base **kel-*, warm > OE *hlēowe*, warm⟧ **1** the amount of heat needed to raise the temperature of one gram of water one degree celsius; gram calorie; small calorie **2** [*occas.* **C-**] the amount of heat needed to raise the temperature of one kilogram of water one degree celsius; great calorie; kilocalorie; 1,000 calories; large calorie **3** *a)* a unit equal to the large calorie, used for measuring the energy produced by food when oxidized in the body *b)* an amount of food able to produce one large calorie of energy

cal·o·rif·ic (kal′ə rif′ik) *adj.* ⟦Fr *calorifique* < L *calorificus* < *calor*, heat (see prec.) + *-ficus*, -FIC⟧ producing heat

cal·o·rim·e·ter (kal′ə rim′ət ər) *n.* ⟦< L *calor* (see prec.) + -METER⟧ an apparatus for measuring amounts of heat, as in chemical combination, friction, etc.

cal·o·rim·e·try (kal′ə rim′ə trē) *n.* ⟦< L *calor* (see CALORIE) + -METRY⟧ measurement of the quantity of heat —**cal·o·ri·met·ric** (kal′ə ri me′trik, kə lôr′ə-) *adj.*, **cal′o·ri·met′ri·cal**

cal·o·rize (kal′ə rīz′) *vt.* **-rized′**, **-riz′ing** ⟦L *calor* (see CALORIE) + -IZE⟧ *Metallurgy* to coat (steel) with aluminum by heating in a closed retort containing aluminum powder: the aluminum alloys with the steel surface and forms a protective coating against oxidation

cal·o·ry (kal′ə rē) *n., pl.* **-ries** CALORIE

ca·lotte (kə lät′) *n.* ⟦Fr < It *calotta* < ? Gr *kalyptra*: see CALYPTRA⟧ **1** a small, brimless cap **2** ZUCCHETTO

cal·o·type (kal′ə tīp′) *n.* ⟦< Gr *kalos*, beautiful + -TYPE⟧ **1** a negative image produced on specially prepared paper by means of an early photographic process (**calotype process**) **2** a print made from such a negative

cal·o·yer (kal′ə yər, kə loi′ər) *n.* ⟦Fr < It *caloiero* < MGr(Ec) *kalogēros*, monk < *kalos*, beautiful + *gēros*, *gēras*, old age: see CORN[1]⟧ a monk of the Eastern Orthodox Church

cal·pac or **cal·pack** (kal′pak′) *n.* ⟦Turk *qālpāk*⟧ a large cap made of felt or sheepskin, worn in some parts of the Near East

Cal·pe (käl′pā) *ancient name for* the Rock of Gibraltar: see also PILLARS OF HERCULES

calque (kalk) *n.* ⟦Fr, an imitation, tracing < *calquer*, to trace < It *calcare*, to press, trample < L, to tread: see CAULK⟧ a borrowing by which a specialized meaning of a word or phrase in one language is transferred to another language by a literal translation of each of the individual elements (Ex.: *masterpiece*, from German *meisterstück*)

cal·trop (kal′trəp, -träp′) *n.* ⟦ME *calketrappe* < OE *calcatrippe*, star thistle & OFr *chaucetrape*, both < ML *calcatrippa* < L *calcare*, to tread upon (< *calx*, heel: see CALCAR) + Gmc **trippon*, TRIP⟧ **1** an iron device with four spikes, placed on the ground so that one spike sticks up to hinder enemy cavalry **2** a similar device used to puncture pneumatic tires **3** any of a number of plants with spiny flowering parts or fruits; specif., *a)* various plants (esp. *Tribulus terrestris*) of the caltrop family *b)* various plants of other families, as star thistle and water chestnut —*adj.* designating a family (Zygophyllaceae) of dicotyledonous plants, shrubs, or trees (order Sapindales), including guaiacum, creosote bush, and bean caper Also **cal′trap** or **cal′throp** (-thrəp)

cal·u·met (kal′yə met′, -mit; kal′yə met′) *n.* ⟦CdnFr < Fr dial., for Fr *chalumeau* < OFr *chalemel* < LL *calamellus*, dim. of L *calamus*, a reed: see CALAMUS⟧ a long-stemmed ceremonial pipe smoked by North American Indians as a token of peace, at sacrifices, etc.

ca·lum·ni·ate (kə lum′nē āt′) *vt., vi.* **-at′ed**, **-at′ing** ⟦< L *calumniatus*, pp. of *calumniari*, to slander < *calumnia*: see CALUMNY⟧ to spread false and harmful statements about; slander —**ca·lum′ni·a′tion** *n.* —**ca·lum′ni·a′tor** *n.*

ca·lum·ni·ous (kə lum′nē əs) *adj.* ⟦L *calumniosus*, full of tricks, swindling⟧ full of calumnies; slanderous —**ca·lum′ni·ous·ly** *adv.*

cal·um·ny (kal′əm nē) *n., pl.* **-nies** ⟦Fr *calomnie* < L *calumnia*, trickery, slander < IE base **kēl-*, **kol-*, to deceive, confuse > OE *hol*, slander⟧ **1** a false and malicious statement meant to hurt someone's reputation **2** the uttering of such a statement; slander

☆**cal·u·tron** (kal′yə trän′) *n.* ⟦< CAL(IFORNIA) + U(NIVERSITY) (for University of Calif., where developed) + -TRON⟧ a large, electromagnetic mass spectrometer used for separating isotopes in quantity

Cal·va·dos (kal′və dōs′, kal′və dōs′) *n.* ⟦after *Calvados*, department in NW France, where chiefly distilled⟧ [*sometimes* **c-**] a French brandy distilled from apple cider

cal·var·i·um (kal ver′ē əm) *n., pl.* **-var′i·a** (-ə) ⟦ModL < L *calvaria*, skull < *calva*, skull⟧ the upper, domed part of the skull: also **cal·var′i·a** —**cal·var′i·al** *adj.*, **cal·var′i·an**

Cal·va·ry (kal′və rē) *n., pl.* **-ries** ⟦LL(Ec) *Calvaria* < L, skull (see prec.): used to translate Gr *kranion*, skull (see CRANIUM) & by the Evangelists to transl. Aram *gūlgūlthā*, GOLGOTHA⟧ **1** *Bible* the place near Jerusalem where the crucifixion of Jesus took place: Luke 23:33, Matt. 27:33 **2** [**c-**] an outdoor representation of the crucifixion of Jesus **3** [**c-**] any experience involving intense pain or anguish

calve (kav, käv) *vi., vt.* **calved**, **calv′ing** ⟦ME *calven* < OE *cealfian* < *cealf*, CALF[1]⟧ **1** to give birth to (a calf) **2** to release (a mass of ice): said of a glacier or an iceberg

Cal·vert (kal′vərt), **George** *see* BALTIMORE[1], Lord

calves (kavz, kävz) *n.* **1** *alt. pl. of* CALF[1] **2** *pl. of* CALF[2]

Cal·vin[1] (kal′vin) *n.* ⟦ModL *Calvinus* < Fr *Cauvin*, *Chauvin*, prob. < L *calvus*, bald: see CALLOW⟧ a masculine name

Cal·vin[2] (kal′vin) **1 John** (born *Jean Caulvin*, *Cauvin*, or *Chauvin*) 1509-64; Fr. Protestant reformer **2 Melvin** 1911-97; U.S. chemist & educator

calv·ing (kav′iŋ) *n.* the period when calves are born on a farm, ranch, etc.

Cal·vin·ism (-iz′əm) *n.* **1** *Christian Theol.* the doctrines of John Calvin and his followers, esp. the doctrine that the elect are predestined to salvation **2** a set of religious practices and beliefs based on Calvin's teachings, often associated with a stern moral code —**Cal′vin·ist** *n., adj.* —**Cal′vin·is′tic** *adj.*, **Cal′vin·is′ti·cal** —**Cal′vin·is′ti·cal·ly** *adv.*

Cal·vi·no (käl vē′nō), **I·tal·o** (ē täl′ō) 1923-85; It. writer

cal·vi·ti·es (kal vish′i ēz′) *n.* ⟦L < *calvus*, bald: see CALLOW⟧ a loss of hair, esp. on top of the head

calx (kalks) *n., pl.* **calx′es** or **cal·ces** (kal′sēz′) ⟦L, small stone, lime: see CALCIUM⟧ **1** the ashy powder left after a metal or mineral has been calcined **2** the heel of the foot

ca·ly·ces (kā′lə sēz′, kal′ə-) *n. alt. pl. of* CALYX

ca·ly·cine (kā′lə sin, -sīn′; kal′ə-) *adj.* of or like a calyx: also **ca·lyc·i·nal** (kə lis′ə nəl)

ca·ly·cle (kā′li kəl) *n.* ⟦see fol.⟧ EPICALYX

ca·lyc·u·lus (kə lik′yo͞o ləs) *n., pl.* **-li′** (-lī′) ⟦ModL < L, dim. of *calyx*, CALYX⟧ *Anat., Zool.* a small, cuplike part, as a taste bud, or a cuplike depression, as in a coral skeleton

Cal·y·don (kal′ə dän′) ancient city in S Aetolia, central Greece —**Cal′y·do′ni·an** (-dō′nē ən, -dōn′yən) *adj.*

Calydonian boar *Gr. Myth.* a boar sent by Artemis to scourge the fields of Calydon and killed by Meleager

ca·lyp·so (kə lip′sō) *adj.* ⟦altered < ? Trinidad patois *kaiso*, town crier, who gave news in rhythm and doggerel⟧ designating or of songs improvised and sung as originally by the native people of Trinidad: they are satirical ballads, usually topical, characterized by wrenched syllabic stress and syncopated rhythms —*n., pl.* **-sos** a calypso song or calypso music

Ca·lyp·so (kə lip′sō) *n.* ⟦L < Gr *Kalypsō* < *kalyptein*: see fol.⟧ **1** in Homer's *Odyssey*, a sea nymph who keeps Odysseus on her island for seven years **2** *pl.* **-sos** [**c-**] an orchid (*Calypso bulbosa*) growing in boggy regions of the Northern Hemisphere: its solitary pink flower has purple or yellow markings

ca·lyp·tra (kə lip′trə) ***n.*** ⟦ModL < Gr *kalyptra*, covering for the head, veil < *kalyptein*, to conceal, cover: for IE base see CONCEAL⟧ **1** the remains of the female sex organ, or archegonium, of a moss, forming the protective caplike covering of the spore case **2** any similar protective hood, cap, or covering of a fruit, flower, or root —**ca·lyp′trate′** (-trāt′) ***adj.***

ca·lyp·tro·gen (kə lip′trə jən) ***n.*** ⟦< prec. + -GEN⟧ the layer of actively dividing cells at the tip of a root in many plants, as grasses, that produces the root cap

ca·lyx (kā′liks′; *also*, kal′iks′) ***n., pl.*** **ca′lyx′es** or **ca·ly·ces** (kā′lə sēz′; *also* kal′ə sēz′) ⟦L, outer covering, pod < Gr *kalyx*: for IE base see CALIX⟧ **1** the outer whorl of protective leaves (sepals) of a flower, usually green **2** *Zool.* a cuplike part or cavity

cal·zo·ne (kal zōn′, -zō′nē) ***n.*** ⟦It, fig. use of *calzone*, pant leg, sing. of *calzoni*, pants⟧ a kind of Italian turnover filled variously with cheese, meat, and vegetables

cam[1] (kam) ***n.*** ⟦Du *cam*, orig., COMB[1]⟧ a moving piece of machinery, as a wheel or projection on a wheel, that gives an eccentric rotation or a reciprocating motion to another wheel, a roller, a shaft, etc., or that receives such motion from it

cam[2] (kam) ***n.*** *short for* CAMERA (sense 3): often used in compounds [*weather cam*]

PLUNGER SHAFT CAM PLUNGER SHAFT CAM

cam

Cam[1] (kam) river in EC England, flowing through Cambridge: 40 mi (64 km)

Cam[2] *abbrev.* **1** Cambodia **2** Cameroon

CAm *abbrev.* Central America

CAM (kam) ***n.*** computer-aided manufacturing: see CAD/CAM

Ca·ma·güey (kä′mä gwā′) city in EC Cuba

ca·ma·ra·de·rie (kam′ə räd′ə rē, käm′-) ***n.*** ⟦Fr < *camarade*, COMRADE⟧ loyalty and warm, friendly feeling among comrades; comradeship

cam·a·ril·la (kam′ə ril′ə; *Sp* kä′mä rēl′yä) ***n.*** ⟦Sp, dim. of *cámara*, chamber < L *camera*, CAMERA⟧ **1** a small meeting room **2** a group of secret or confidential, esp. unofficial, advisers; cabal

☆**cam·ass** or **cam·as** (kam′əs) ***n.*** ⟦AmInd (Chinook) < *chamas*, sweet⟧ any of a genus (*Camassia*) of North American plants of the lily family, with sweet, edible bulbs and racemes of drooping, bluish flowers: see also DEATHCAMAS

Camb *abbrev.* Cambodia

cam·ber (kam′bər) ***n.*** ⟦OFr *cambre*, dial. var. of *chambre*, bent < L *camur*, crooked, arched: for IE base see CAMERA⟧ **1** a slight convex curve of a surface, as of a road, a ship's deck, or a beam **2** in automotive wheel alignment, a slight tilt given to each of a pair of wheels on an axle: positive camber indicates that the bottoms are closer together than the tops, and negative camber indicates the opposite situation: see TOE-IN **3** *Aeron.* the arching curve of an airfoil from the leading edge to the trailing edge — ***vt., vi.*** ⟦Fr *cambrer*⟧ to arch slightly; curve convexly

cam·bist (kam′bist) ***n.*** ⟦Fr *cambiste* < It *cambista* < *cambiare*, to exchange < LL *cambiare* < L *cambire*: see CHANGE⟧ [Now Rare] an expert in trading currencies; foreign-exchange dealer

cam·bi·um (kam′bē əm) ***n.*** ⟦ModL < ML < LL *cambiare*: see CHANGE⟧ a layer of formative cells between the wood and bark in dicotyledonous plants: these cells cause the girth of the stem to increase by dividing and differentiating to form new xylem and phloem tissue, which will eventually become wood and bark —**cam′bi·al** ***adj.***

Cam·bo·di·a (kam bō′dē ə) country in the S Indochinese Peninsula: a French protectorate from 1863 until independence, 1954: 69,900 sq mi (181,040 sq km); cap. Phnom Penh: also, formerly, sometimes known as *Kampuchea* —**Cam·bo′di·an** ***adj., n.***

Cam·bri·a (kam′brē ə) ⟦ML, var. of *Cumbria* < base of OCelt *Combroges*, lit., co-landers > Celt *Cymry*, Welshmen⟧ *old poet. name for* WALES

Cam·bri·an (kam′brēən, kām′-) ***adj.*** **1** of Cambria; Welsh **2** designating or of the first geologic period of the Paleozoic Era, characterized by the development of warm, shallow seas and the first hard-shelled marine animals, esp. trilobites and brachiopods —***n.*** a person born or living in Cambria; Welshman —**the Cambrian** the Cambrian Period or its rocks: see the geologic time chart in the Reference Supplement

Cambrian Mountains mountain system of central Wales: highest point, 2,970 ft (905 m)

cam·bric (kām′brik) ***n.*** ⟦after *Kamerijk*, Fl name of *Cambrai*, city in N France, where orig. made < L *Camaracum*⟧ **1** a very fine, thin linen **2** a cotton cloth that is like this

☆**cambric tea** a hot drink of milk, sugar, and water or, often, weak tea

Cam·bridge (kām′brij′) ⟦ME *Caumbrigge* < OE *Grantanbrycge*, lit., bridge over the Granta (now called the Cam) River⟧ **1** city in EC England: county seat of Cambridgeshire; site of Cambridge University **2** CAMBRIDGESHIRE **3** ⟦after the English city⟧ city in SE Ontario, Canada **4** ⟦after the English city⟧ city in E Mass., across the Charles River from Boston

Cam·bridge·shire (-brij shir′) county in EC England: 1,313 sq mi (3,401 sq km)

Cam·by·ses (II) (kam bī′sēz′) died 522 B.C.; king of Persia (529-522): son of Cyrus the Great

☆**cam·cord·er** (kam′kôr′dər) ***n.*** ⟦CAM(ERA) + (RE)CORDER (*n.* 3)⟧ a handheld device for recording visual images and sound as on a videocassette

Cam·den (kam′dən) borough of N Greater London, England

came[1] (kām) ***vi.*** *pt. of* COME

came[2] (kām) ***n.*** ⟦< ? MDu *kaam*, lit., COMB[1]⟧ a lead strip used to fasten together panes of glass, as in stained-glass windows

cam·el (kam′əl) ***n.*** ⟦ME < OE or OFr < L *camelus* < Gr *kamēlos* < Heb or Phoen *gāmāl*; ult. < ? Bab⟧ **1** either of two species of large, domesticated ruminants (genus *Camelus*) with a humped back, long neck, and large, cushioned feet: capable of storing water in its bodily tissue, the camel is the common beast of burden in Asian and African deserts: see BACTRIAN CAMEL and ARABIAN CAMEL **2** a watertight cylinder used to raise sunken ships, wrecks, etc.: see CAISSON (sense 4) **3** *Naut.* a float, usually consisting of a log or logs, placed alongside a wharf, pier, etc. to protect docking ships —***adj.*** of the tan color of camel's hair

cam·el·back (-bak′) ***adj.*** designating a style of sofa, chair, etc. characterized by a convex curve, suggesting a camel's hump, in the top rail of the back

cam·el·eer (kam′əl ir′) ***n.*** a camel driver

ca·mel·li·a (kə mēl′yə, -mē′lē ə) ***n.*** ⟦ModL, after *Camelli*, It form of the name of G. J. *Kamel* (1661-1706), Moravian Jesuit missionary to the Far East⟧ **1** any of a genus (*Camellia*) of Asian evergreen trees and shrubs of the tea family, with glossy leaves and waxy, roselike flowers **2** the flower

ca·mel·o·pard (kə mel′ə pärd′) ***n.*** ⟦LL *camelopardus* < L *camelopardalus* < Gr *kamēlopardalis* < *kamēlos*, CAMEL + *pardalis*, pard, leopard: so called from neck (like a camel's) and spots (like a pard's)⟧ *former name for* GIRAFFE

Ca·mel·o·par·da·lis (kə mel′ə pär′də lis) ***n.*** ⟦L, giraffe: see prec.⟧ a N constellation between Ursa Major and Cassiopeia; the Giraffe: also called **Ca·mel′o·par′dus** (-pär′dəs)

Cam·e·lot (kam′ə lät′) ***n.*** **1** *Arthurian Legend* the English town where King Arthur has his court and Round Table ☆**2** ⟦from application of the name to the administration of John F. KENNEDY[1]⟧ any time, place, etc. idealized as having excitement, purpose, a high level of culture, etc.

camel's hair **1** the hair of the camel **2** cloth made of this hair, sometimes mixed with wool, etc.: it is usually light tan and very soft —**cam′el's-hair′** ***adj.***, **cam′el-hair′**

camel's-hair brush an artist's small brush, made of hair from a squirrel's tail

Cam·em·bert (cheese) (kam′əm ber′, -bərt) ⟦after *Camembert*, village in Normandy, where first made⟧ a soft, rich, creamy, partly ripened cheese

Ca·me·nae (kə mē′nē) ***pl.n.*** *Rom. Myth.* nymphs with prophetic powers who inhabit springs and fountains: later identified with the Greek Muses

cam·e·o (kam′ē ō′) ***n., pl.*** **-os′** ⟦It *cammeo* < ML *camaeus, camahutus*; ult. < ? Pers *chumāhān*, agate⟧ **1** a carving as on certain stratified gems (sardonyx, agate, etc.) or shells, in which the raised design is in a layer of different color from its background: opposed to INTAGLIO **2** a piece of jewelry so carved, traditionally depicting a head in profile **3** *a)* a minor but well-defined role in a play, film, etc., esp. when performed by a notable actor *b)* a fine bit of descriptive writing —***vi.*** **-oed′**, **-o′ing** to appear in a cameo role

cam·er·a (kam′ər ə, kam′rə) ***n., pl.*** **cam′er·as**; also for 1, **-er·ae′** (-ər ē′) ⟦L *camera*, vault < Gr *kamara*, vaulted chamber < IE base **kam-*, to arch⟧ **1** a chamber: now only in IN CAMERA (see phrase below) **2** *short for* CAMERA OBSCURA **3** ⟦< CAMERA OBSCURA⟧ any of various devices for recording or transmitting images or sequences of images, consisting essentially of a closed case with a lens that focuses incoming light on a sensitive material, as film, or on an electronic receptor —**in camera** **1** in a judge's private office rather than in open court **2** in privacy or secrecy —☆**on (or off) camera** *Film, TV* so positioned as to be within (or out of) the camera's field of view

cam·er·al (-ər əl) ***adj.*** ⟦Ger *kameral* < ML *cameralis*: see prec.⟧ of the chamber of a judge, legislature, etc.

camera lu·ci·da (lo͞o′si də) ⟦ModL, lit., light chamber < L: see CAMERA & LUCID⟧ an optical instrument, containing a prism or an arrangement of mirrors, that appears to project the image of an object being viewed through it onto a surface, thereby allowing its outline to be traced: often used with a microscope

cam·er·a·man (-man′, -mən) ***n., pl.*** **-men′** (-men′, -mən) **1** an operator of a camera, esp. of a film or TV camera **2** CINEMATOGRAPHER

camera ob·scu·ra (əb skyo͝or′ə) ⟦ModL, lit., dark chamber < L: see CAMERA & OBSCURE⟧ a dark chamber with a lens or opening through which an image is projected in natural colors onto an opposite surface

cam·er·a·per·son (kam′ər ə pur′sən) ***n.*** a cameraman or a camerawoman

cam·er·a-read·y (-red′ē) ***adj.*** *Printing* designating or of copy, artwork, etc. that is ready to be photographed for making into a plate for printing

cam·er·a-shy (-shī′) ***adj.*** unwilling to be photographed

cam·e·ra·ta (käm′ə rät′ə, kam′-) ***n.*** ⟦It, lit., comrades, ult. < L *camera*: see CAMERA⟧ a group that performs chamber music

cam·er·a·wom·an (-wo͝om′ən) ***n., pl.*** **-wom′en** (-wim′in) **1** a female operator of a camera, esp. of a film or TV camera **2** a female cinematographer

cam·er·a·work (-wurk′) ***n.*** **1** the work of a cameraperson **2** CINEMATOGRAPHY

cam·er·len·go (kam′ər leŋ′gō) ***n.*** ⟦It *camarlingo*, chamberlain < Gmc *kamerlinc*: see CHAMBERLAIN⟧ *R.C.Ch.* a cardinal in charge of the papal treasury and accounts: also **cam′er·lin′go** (-liŋ′-)

Cam·er·on (kam′ər ən) **1 David (William Donald)** 1966- ; Brit. politician: prime minister (2010-) **2 Richard** 1648?-80; Scot. minister & Covenanter whose followers formed the Reformed Presbyterian Church (1743)

Cam·e·roon (kam′ə ro͞on′) **1** country in WC Africa, on the Gulf of Guinea: formerly a German protectorate, most of the area was under French administration from 1919 until independence in 1960; member of the

Commonwealth: 183,568 sq mi (475,440 sq km); cap. Yaoundé: cf. CAMEROONS **2 Mount** mountain in W Cameroon: 13,350 ft (4,069 m) —**Cam'e·roon'i·an** *adj., n.*

Cam·e·roons (-ro͞onz') former region in W Africa consisting of two trust territories, **French Cameroons** (in 1960 forming the republic of CAMEROON) and **British Cameroons** (in 1961 divided between Cameroon and Nigeria)

Ca·me·roun (kam'ə ro͞on'; *Fr* kȧm ro͞on') *Fr. name for* CAMEROON

cam gear a gear not centered on the shaft, used where discontinuous action is required

cam·i (kam'ē) *n. short for* CAMISOLE

Ca·mille (kə mēl'; *Fr* kȧ mē'y') *n.* ⟦Fr < L *Camilla,* virgin warrior in the *Aeneid*⟧ a feminine name: also **Ca·mil·la** (kə mil'ə)

cam·i·on (kam'ē ən; *Fr* kȧ myôn') *n.* ⟦Fr < MFr *chamion* < ?⟧ a motor truck or heavy dray wagon

cam·i·sa·do (kam'i sä'dō) *n.* ⟦Sp *camisada* < *camisa* < LL *camisia:* see CHEMISE⟧ [Archaic] an attack at night, orig. one in which shirts were worn over armor for identification: also **cam'i·sade'** (-sād')

ca·mise (kə mēs') *n.* ⟦Ar *qamis* < LL *camisia:* see CHEMISE⟧ a loosefitting shirt, smock, or gown

cam·i·sole (kam'i sōl') *n.* ⟦Fr < Sp *camisola,* dim. of *camisa* < LL *camisia:* see CHEMISE⟧ **1** a woman's sleeveless, often lace-trimmed undergarment for the upper body, worn as under a sheer blouse **2** a woman's short negligee

cam·let (kam'lit) *n.* ⟦ME *chamelet* < OFr *chamelot;* prob. < Ar *khamlat* < *khaml,* pile, plush⟧ **1** a medieval fabric of camel's hair or Angora wool **2** a satiny fabric of silk and wool or goat's hair **3** a garment made of either of these fabrics

☆**cam·o** (kam'ō) *n.* **1** [Slang] *short for* CAMOUFLAGE **2** a garment, hat, etc. made of fabric having patterns of or like the mottled brown or green and brown colors of military camouflage

Ca·mões (kə moinsh'), **Lu·iz Vaz de** (lo͞o ēsh' vȧzh də) 1524?-80; Port. epic poet: Eng. name **Cam·o·ëns** (kam'ō enz')

cam·o·mile (kam'ə mīl', -mēl') *n.* ⟦ME *camomille* < OFr *camemile* < L *chamomilla* < Gr *chamaimēlon,* earth apple < *chamai,* on the ground (see CHAMELEON) + *mēlon,* apple (see MELON)⟧ any plant of either of two genera (*Anthemis* and *Matricaria*) of the composite family, with strong-smelling foliage; esp., a plant (*A. nobilis*) whose dried, daisylike flower heads are used as a medicine and in making tea

Ca·mor·ra (kə môr'ə) *n.* ⟦It < ? Sp, quarrel, dispute < ?⟧ **1** a secret society organized in Naples, Italy, *c.* 1820, which became notorious for terror, blackmail, and violence **2** [**c-**] any secret society like this —**Ca·mor'rist** *n.,* **ca·mor'rist**

cam·ou·flage (kam'ə fläzh', -fläj') *n.* ⟦Fr < *camoufler,* to disguise; prob. altered (infl. by *camouflet,* puff of smoke) < It *camuffare,* to disguise⟧ **1** the disguising of troops, ships, guns, etc. to conceal them from the enemy, as by the use of paint, nets, or leaves in patterns merging with the background **2** a disguise or concealment of this kind **3** any device or action used to conceal or mislead; deception — ***vt., vi.*** **-flaged', -flag'ing** to disguise (a thing or person) in order to conceal —**cam'ou·flag'er** *n.*

camp (kamp) *n.* ⟦Fr < OProv < L *campus,* a field: see CAMPUS⟧ **1** *a)* a place where tents, huts, barracks, or other more or less temporary structures have been put up, as for soldiers in training or in bivouac *b)* military life **2** *a)* a group of people who support or advance a common opinion, cause, etc. *b)* the position taken by such a group **3** a tent, cabin, etc., or a group of these, used for temporary vacationers' lodging, as by hunters or fishermen **4** a place in the country for vacationers, esp. children, with outdoor recreation, often organized and supervised **5** the people living in a camp ☆**6** ⟦orig., homosexual jargon⟧ [Slang] *a)* banality, mediocrity, artifice, ostentation, etc. so extreme as to amuse or have a perversely sophisticated appeal *b)* exaggerated effeminate mannerisms, usually affected for amusement —☆***adj.*** [Slang] characterized by CAMP (*n.* 6) —***vi.*** **1** to set up a camp; encamp **2** to live or stay in or as if in a camp: often with *out* —***vt.*** **1** to put into a camp **2** to provide with accommodations —**break camp** to dismantle a camp; pack up camping equipment and go away —☆**camp it up** [Slang] to behave in a camp way

Camp (kamp), **Walter (Chauncey)** 1859-1925; U.S. football authority and coach

Cam·pa·gna di Ro·ma (käm pä'nyä dē rô'mä) low-lying plain in central Italy, around Rome: *c.* 800 sq mi (2,072 sq km)

cam·paign (kam pān') *n.* ⟦Fr *campagne,* open country suited to military maneuvers; hence, military expedition < It *campagna* < LL *campania,* level country < L *campus,* a field: see CAMPUS⟧ **1** a series of military operations with a particular objective in a war **2** a series of organized, planned actions for a particular purpose, as for electing a candidate —***adj.*** designating or of a style of simple, portable furniture, with rectilinear lines, recessed hardware, etc., originally used on military campaigns —***vi.*** to participate in, or go on, a campaign —***SYN.*** BATTLE[1] —**cam·paign'er** *n.*

Cam·pa·ni·a (kam pā'nē ə; *It* käm pä'nyä) ⟦L, lit., plain: see prec.⟧ region in S Italy, on the Tyrrhenian Sea: 5,249 sq mi (13,595 sq km); chief city, Naples —**Cam·pa'ni·an** *adj., n.*

cam·pa·ni·le (kam'pə nē'lē) *n., pl.* **-les** or **-li** (-lē) ⟦It < LL *campana,* a bell, steelyard, after prec.⟧ a bell tower, esp. one that stands apart from any other building

cam·pa·nol·o·gy (kam'pə näl'ə jē) *n.* ⟦ModL *campanologie* < LL *campana* (see prec.) + L *-logia,* -LOGY⟧ **1** the study of bells **2** the art of bell ringing —**cam'pa·nol'o·gist** *n.*

cam·pan·u·la (kam pan'yo͞o lə) *n.* ⟦ModL < LL, dim. of *campana:* see CAMPANILE⟧ any of a genus (*Campanula*) of plants of the bellflower family, as the Canterbury bell, harebell, etc.

cam·pan·u·late (kam pan'yo͞o lit, -lāt') ***adj.*** ⟦< prec. + -ATE[1]⟧ shaped like a bell: said esp. of a flower

Cam·pa·ri (käm pä'rē) *n.* ⟦< name of It manufacturer, after G. *Campari* (1828-82), its founder, who invented the aperitif (1860)⟧ a bitter Italian aperitif, often served mixed with soda water

Camp·bell (kam'bəl) **1 Alexander** 1788-1866; U.S. clergyman, born in Ireland: founder of the Disciples of Christ **2 Joseph (John)** 1904-87; U.S. scholar & writer, esp. on mythology & comparative religion **3 Mrs. Patrick** (born *Beatrice Stella Tanner*) 1865-1940; Eng. actress **4 Thomas** 1777-1844; Scot. poet

Camp·bell-Ban·ner·man (ban'ər mən), Sir **Henry** 1836-1908; Brit. statesman: prime minister (1905-08)

camp chair a lightweight folding chair

camp·craft (kamp'kraft') *n.* the art or practice of camping outdoors

Camp David ⟦renamed by Pres. EISENHOWER after his grandson, *David* Eisenhower⟧ official retreat of the President of the U.S., in N Md., *c.* 70 mi (113 km) northwest of Washington, D.C.

cam·pea·chy wood (kam pē'chē) ⟦after fol., where it was obtained⟧ LOGWOOD (sense 1)

Cam·pe·che (kam pē'chē; *Sp* käm pe'che) **1** state of SE Mexico, in the W Yucatán Peninsula: 20,013 sq mi (51,833 sq km) **2** capital of this state, a port on the Gulf of Campeche **3 Gulf (**or **Bay) of** arm of the Gulf of Mexico, west of the Yucatán Peninsula

camp·er (kam'pər) *n.* **1** a person who vacations at a camp ☆**2** any of various motor vehicles or trailers equipped for camping out

cam·pe·si·no (käm'pe sē'nô) *n., pl.* **-nos** (-nôs) ⟦Sp < *campo,* country < L *campus:* see CAMPUS⟧ a peasant or farm worker in Latin America

cam·pes·tral (kam pes'trəl) ***adj.*** ⟦< L *campester* (gen. *campestris*), of a level field < *campus,* field (see CAMPUS) + -AL⟧ [Rare] of or having to do with fields or the countryside

camp·fire (kamp'fīr') *n.* **1** an outdoor fire at a campsite **2** a social gathering around such a fire

☆**Camp Fire Girl** a girl who is a member of Camp Fire, Inc., an organization for girls founded in 1910, and since 1975 also including boys, to promote character-building activities

camp follower 1 a civilian who goes along with an army, esp. as a vendor of goods or services or as a prostitute **2** a nonmember who is associated with a certain group

☆**camp·ground** (-ground') *n.* **1** a place where a camp is set up **2** a place where a camp meeting or religious revival is held

cam·phene (kam'fēn', kam fēn') *n.* ⟦CAMPH(OR) + -ENE⟧ a toxic, colorless, crystalline terpene, $C_{10}H_{16}$, prepared synthetically from pinene and used like camphor

cam·phire (kam'fīr') *n.* ⟦var. of CAMPHOR: used in KJV (S. of Sol. 1:14) to transl. Heb *kōpher,* henna plant⟧ HENNA

cam·phol (kam'fôl', -fōl') *n.* ⟦< fol. + -OL[1]⟧ BORNEOL

cam·phor (kam'fər) *n.* ⟦ME *camfre* < OFr *camphre* < ML *camfora* < Ar *kāfūr* < Sans *karpuraḥ,* camphor tree⟧ **1** a volatile, crystalline ketone, $C_{10}H_{16}O$, with a strong characteristic odor, derived from the wood of the camphor tree or synthetically from pinene: used to protect fabrics from moths, in manufacturing cellulose plastics, and in medicine as an irritant and stimulant **2** any of several derivatives of terpenes —**cam·phor'ic** (-fôr'ik) ***adj.***

cam·phor·ate (kam'fə rāt') ***vt.*** **-at'ed, -at'ing** to put camphor in or on —*n.* a salt derived from camphor

camphorated oil a solution of camphor in any of various oils, used as a liniment

camphor ball MOTHBALL

☆**camphor ice** an ointment made of white wax, camphor, spermaceti, and castor oil, used for dry, chapped skin

camphor tree an evergreen tree (*Cinnamomum camphora*) of the laurel family, native to Japan and China: it is the source of camphor

Cam·pi·na Gran·de (käm pē'nə grän'də) city in NE Brazil, in E Paraíba state

Cam·pi·nas (käm pē'nəs) city in SE Brazil, near São Paulo

cam·pi·on (kam'pē ən) *n.* ⟦prob. use of obs. *campion* < OFr, lit., CHAMPION (because used for garlands)⟧ any of various flowering plants (genera *Lychnis* and *Silene*) of the pink family, with white, red, or pink flowers

Cam·pi·on (kam'pē ən), **Thomas** 1567-1620; Eng. poet & composer of songs

☆**camp meeting** a religious gathering held outdoors or in a tent, etc., usually lasting several days

cam·po (kam'pō, käm'-) *n., pl.* **-pos** ⟦Port or Sp < L *campus,* field: see CAMPUS⟧ a level, grassy plain in South America, often with scattered plants and small trees

Cam·po·bel·lo (kam'pō bel'ō) island of New Brunswick, Canada, in the Bay of Fundy

Cam·po Gran·de (käm'pō grän'də) city in SW Brazil: capital of Mato Grosso do Sul

☆**camp·o·ree** (kam'pə rē') *n.* ⟦CAMP + (JAMB)OREE⟧ a gathering or assembly of Boy Scouts on the regional or district level: distinguished from JAMBOREE

Cam·pos (käm'pəs) city in SE Brazil, in Rio de Janeiro state

☆**cam·po san·to** (kam'pō san'tō, käm'pō sän'tō) ⟦Sp, lit., holy field⟧ [Southwest] a cemetery

camp robber CANADA JAY

camp shirt a lightweight, short-sleeved shirt with a notched collar and buttoned front: occas. written **camp′shirt′** *n.*

☆**camp·site** (kamp′sīt′) *n.* **1** any site for a temporary camp **2** a public or private park area set aside for camping, often equipped with water, toilets, cooking grills, etc.

camp·stool (-sto͞ol′) *n.* a lightweight folding stool

☆**cam·pus** (kam′pəs) *n., pl.* **-pus·es** ⟦L, a field < IE **kampos*, a corner, cove < base **kamp-*, to bend > Gr *kampē*, bend, curve, Lith *kam̃pas*, corner, area⟧ **1** the grounds, sometimes including the buildings, of a school or college **2** the grounds, sometimes including the buildings, of a commercial or industrial firm, a hospital, etc. —*adj.* **1** on or of the campus **2** of a school or college *[campus* politics*]* —*vt.* **-pused, -pus·ing** to restrict (a student) to campus or dormitory, usually because of an infraction of the rules

☆**camp·y** (kam′pē) *adj.* **camp′i·er, camp′i·est** [Slang] characterized by CAMP (*n.* 6)

cam·py·lot·ro·pous (kam′pi lä′trə pəs) *adj.* ⟦< Gr *kampylos*, curved (akin to *kampē*, a bend: see CAMPUS) & -TROPOUS⟧ having a flower ovule with a structure that is partially inverted, with the stalk attachment at the bottom and the opening near the bottom

cam·shaft (kam′shaft′) *n.* a shaft of which a cam is an essential part, or to which a cam is fastened

Ca·mus (ka mo͞o′; *Fr* kȧ mü′), **Albert** 1913-60; Fr. writer, born in Algeria

can[1] (kan; *unstressed,* kən) *v.aux. pt.* **could** ⟦ME < OE, 1st & 3d pers. sing., pres. indic., of *cunnan*, know, have power to, be able; common Gmc < IE base **gen-*, **gno-* > L *gnoscere*, KNOW; orig. meaning "to be able mentally or spiritually," as distinguished from *may*, "to be able physically"⟧ **1** know or knows how to **2** am, are, or is able to **3** am, are, or is likely or at all likely to *[can* that be true?*]* **4** have or has the moral or legal right to **5** [Informal] am, are, or is permitted to; may As a modal auxiliary, *can* is followed by an infinitive without *to* —*vi.* **1** know or knows how **2** am, are, or is able *[*yes I *can]* **3** am, are, or is likely or at all likely **4** have or has the moral or legal right **5** [Informal] am, are, or is permitted; may —*vt.* [Obs.] know(s) —**can but** can only

USAGE—traditional grammar makes a clear distinction between **can** (for ability) and **may** (for permission), the classic example being the retort, "Yes, you *can* go, but you *may* not"; in everyday speech and writing, however, **can** is generally accepted for both meanings, with **may** being used only when the notion of permission is important to the sense of an utterance and there is a possibility of ambiguity

can[2] (kan) *n.* ⟦ME & OE *canne*, a cup, container < Gmc **kanna* (> LL *canna*, a vessel); prob. < IE base **gan(dh)*, container > MIr *gann*, ON *kani*⟧ **1** any of various containers usually or traditionally cylindrical, made of metal, and with a separate cover *[*a milk *can*, a garbage *can*, a *can* of shoe polish*]* ☆**2** a container made of tinned iron or other metal, in which foods or other perishable products are sealed for preservation ☆**3** the amount that a can holds ☆**4** [Slang] *a)* a prison *b)* the buttocks *c)* a toilet *d) short for* TIN CAN (sense 2) —☆*vt.* **canned, can′ning 1** to put up in airtight cans or jars for preservation **2** [Slang] *a)* to dismiss; discharge *b)* to put an end to; stop —**in the can** recorded, filmed, taped, etc. but not yet released for sale, exhibition, broadcast, viewing, etc.

Can *abbrev.* **1** Canada **2** Canadian **3** Canon

Ca·na (kā′nə) village in Galilee, N Israel: scene of Jesus' first two public miracles: John 2:1-9; 4:46-54

Ca·naan (kā′nən) ⟦LL (Vulg, Gen. 10, fol.) *Chanaan* < Gr *Chanan* < Heb *kena'an*⟧ ancient region at the SE end of the Mediterranean, extending eastward to the Jordan River; the Biblical Promised Land: Gen. 17:8

Ca·naan·ite (-īt′) *n.* **1** a member of the people originally inhabiting Canaan **2** the Semitic language of this people **3** a group of ancient Semitic languages including Phoenician, Punic, and Hebrew —**Ca′naan·it′ish** (-īt′ish) *adj.*, **Ca′naan·it′ic** (-it′ik)

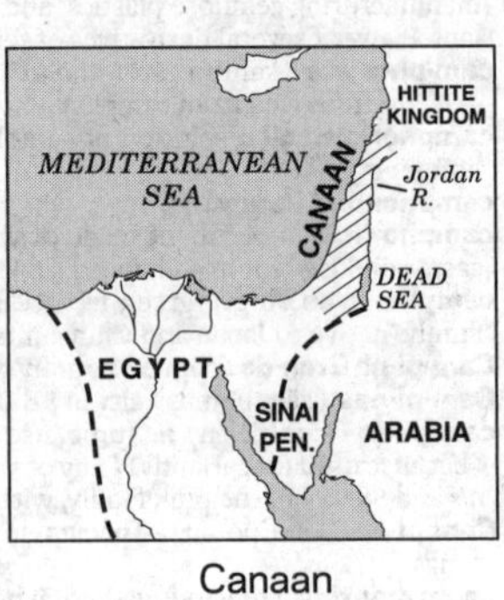

Canaan

Canad *abbrev.* Canadian

Can·a·da (kan′ə də) ⟦Fr < a word for "village" in an extinct (before 1600) Iroquoian language of the lower St. Lawrence River valley⟧ country in N North America: complete British control achieved, 1763; dominion established, 1867; complete autonomy, 1931: member of the Commonwealth: 3,481,753 sq mi (9,017,699 sq km); cap. Ottawa

Canada balsam a thick, yellow, resinous fluid from the balsam fir, used as a transparent cement in microscopy and in lacquers, flavorings, etc.

Canada Day July 1, the Canadian national holiday commemorating the anniversary of the proclamation in 1867 of the establishment of the Dominion of Canada

Canada goose the largest wild goose (*Branta canadensis*) of Canada and the U.S.: it is brownish-gray, with black head and neck and a white patch on each side of the face

Canada jay GRAY JAY

☆**Canada lily** a wild North American lily (*Lilium canadense*) with small, funnel-shaped, orange-yellow or reddish flowers

☆**Canada lynx** a North American lynx (*Lynx lynx canadensis*) with tufted ears and a stubby tail

Canada mayflower a small wildflower (*Maianthemum canadense*) of the lily family, with white flowers and red, beadlike berries, found in the N U.S. and in Canada; bead-ruby

☆**Canada thistle** a prickly European weed (*Cirsium arvense*) of the composite family, with heads of purplish flowers and wavy leaves: now common as a fast-spreading, injurious weed throughout the N U.S.

Ca·na·di·an[1] (kə nā′dē ən) *adj.* of Canada or its people or culture —*n.* a person born or living in Canada

Ca·na·di·an[2] (kə nā′dē ən) river flowing eastward from N N.Mex., across NW Tex., to the Arkansas River in E Okla.: 906 mi (1,458 km)

☆**Canadian bacon** cured, smoked pork taken from the loin in a boneless strip and having a hamlike flavor

Canadian English the English language as spoken and written in Canada

Canadian football a type of football game played in Canada like U.S. football, except in having a larger playing field, 12 players per team, three downs, different scoring and timing rules, etc.

Canadian French the French language as spoken and written by French Canadians, mainly in Quebec and parts of the Maritime Provinces

Ca·na·di·an·ism (kə nā′dē ən iz′əm) *n.* **1** a custom, characteristic, or belief of or originating in Canada **2** a word, phrase, grammatical construction, or other feature originating in or peculiar to Canadian English

Canadian Shield an area of about 2,000,000 sq mi (5,179,980 sq km) of Precambrian strata, consisting largely of granite, gneiss, marble, and other igneous and metamorphic rocks that occupy most of eastern and central Canada & part of NE U.S.

Canadian soldier [Dial.] a mayfly commonly found in large numbers for brief periods during the spring and summer near fresh water along the N U.S. border

ca·naille (kə nāl′; *Fr* kȧ nä′y′) *n.* ⟦Fr, a mob, pack of dogs < It *canaglia* < L *canis*, dog: see HOUND[1]⟧ the mob; rabble

ca·nal (kə nal′) *n.* ⟦ME, pipe or tube < OFr < L *canalis*, pipe, groove, channel < *canna*, reed: see CANE⟧ **1** an artificial waterway for transportation or irrigation **2** a river artificially improved by locks, levees, etc. to permit navigation **3** any of the long, narrow lines once perceived to be on the surface of the planet Mars as seen through earth telescopes: at one time thought by some to be actual canals but now known to be optical illusions **4** *Anat.* any of various tubular passages or ducts —*vt.* **-nalled′** or **-naled′**, **-nal′ling** or **-nal′ing** to build a canal through or across

ca·nal·boat (-bōt′) *n.* a freight-carrying boat, usually long and narrow, used on canals: also **canal boat**

Ca·na·let·to (kä′nä let′tô), **An·to·nio** (än tô′nyô) (born *Antonio Canal* or *Canale*) 1697-1768; It. painter

can·a·lic·u·late (kan′ə lik′yo͞o lit, -lāt′) *adj.* ⟦L *canaliculatus*: see fol.⟧ *Biol.* having a groove or grooves: also **can′a·lic′u·lat′ed** (-lāt′id) or **can′a·lic′u·lar** (-lər)

can·a·lic·u·lus (-ləs) *n., pl.* **-li′** (-lī′) ⟦L, dim. of *canalis*, groove: see CANAL⟧ *Anat., Biol.* a very small groove, or canal, as in bone

ca·nal·i·za·tion (kə nal′ə zā′shən, kan′ə lə-) *n.* **1** the act of canalizing **2** a system of canals or channels **3** the formation of canals in the bodily tissues, naturally or artificially, as sometimes to drain wounds

ca·nal·ize (kə nal′īz′, kan′ə līz′) *vt.* **-ized′, -iz′ing 1** to make a canal through **2** to change into or make like a canal **3** to provide an outlet for, esp. by directing into a specific channel or channels

canal rays *Physics* rays of positive ions passing through openings in the cathode of a vacuum tube

Canal Zone *former name for* a strip of land that extends 5 mi (8 km) on either side of the Panama Canal: the land was formerly under lease to the U.S., which governed it (1904-79); it was returned to Panama and the name abolished in 1979: see also PANAMA CANAL

ca·na·pé (kan′ə pā′, kan′ə pē) *n.* ⟦Fr: see CANOPY; fig. application of Fr sense "upholstered divan"⟧ a cracker or a small piece of bread or toast spread with spiced meat, fish, cheese, etc., served as an appetizer, often with drinks

ca·nard (kə närd′) *n.* ⟦Fr, a duck, hoax; prob. < *can*, echoic for duck's quack + *-ard*, -ARD; short for *(vendre) un canard (à moitié)*, lit., (to half-sell) a duck, i.e., to cheat⟧ **1** a report, claim, or assertion fabricated to mislead, cause harm, etc. **2** *a)* an airplane whose horizontal stabilizer is located forward of the wing or wings *b)* the horizontal control and stabilizing surfaces in such an aircraft

ca·nar·y (kə ner′ē) *n., pl.* **-nar′ies** ⟦Fr *canarie* < Sp *canario* < L *Canaria (insula)*, Canary (island), lit., island of dogs < *canis* dog (see HOUND[1]): so called from its large dogs⟧ **1** a small, yellow finch (*Serinus canaria*) native to the Canary Islands, Madeira, and the Azores **2** CANARY YELLOW **3** a fortified wine similar to Madeira, made in the Canary Islands **4** a lively 16th-cent. Spanish or French court dance **5** [Slang] a squealer; informer

canary grass an annual European grass (*Phalaris canariensis*) with thimble-shaped heads of seeds (**canary seed**) used as food for cage birds

Canary Islands group of islands in the Atlantic, off NW Africa, forming a region of Spain: 2,808 sq mi (7,273 sq km): also **Ca·nar′ies**: Sp. name **Islas Ca·na·ri·as** (ēz′läs kä nä′rē äs)

canary yellow a light yellow

ca·nas·ta (kə nas′tə) *n.* ⟦Sp, basket < *canasto*, contr. < *canastro* < Gr *kan-*

astron: see CANISTER⟧ a card game, a variation of rummy, usually for two or four players, using a double deck of cards and four jokers

Ca·na·ver·al (kə nav′ər əl), **Cape** ⟦Sp *cañaveral*, canebrake⟧ cape on the E coast of Fla.: U.S. proving ground for missiles and spacecraft: see also KENNEDY[2], Cape

Can·ber·ra (kan′ber′ə, -bə rə) capital of Australia, in the Australian Capital Territory

canc *abbrev.* canceled

can·can (kan′kan′) ***n.*** ⟦Fr < ? child's term for "duck" (see CANARD)⟧ a lively dance with much high kicking done by women entertainers, originally in Paris dance halls in the late 19th cent.

can·cel (kan′səl) ***vt.*** **-celed** or **-celled**, **-cel·ing** or **-cel·ling** ⟦ME *cancellen* < Anglo-Fr *canceler* < LL *cancellare*, to strike out, cancel < L, to make resemble a lattice < *cancelli*, pl. of *cancellus*, lattice, grating, dim. of *cancer*, crossed bars, lattice, dissimilated < *carcer*, prison⟧ **1** *a)* to cross out with lines or other marks, as in deleting written matter or marking a check as used and cleared *b)* to print or stamp marks on (a postage stamp) as by machine or handstamp, to prevent reuse **2** to make invalid; annul **3** to do away with; wipe out; abolish, withdraw, etc. [*to cancel an order or a ticket reservation*] **4** to neutralize or balance in force or influence; offset: often with *out* **5** *Math.* to remove (a common factor from both terms of a fraction, equivalents of opposite sign or on opposite sides of an equation, etc.) **6** *Printing* to delete or omit —***vi.*** to offset or cancel each other: with *out* —***n.*** **1** the deletion or omission of matter in type or in print **2** *a)* the matter omitted or deleted *b)* the replacement for this **3** [Informal] CANCELLATION (sense 3) —**can′cel·a·ble** ***adj.*** —**can′cel·er** ***n.***, **can′cel·ler**

can·cel·la·tion (kan′sə lā′shən) ***n.*** **1** the act of canceling **2** something canceled **3** the mark or marks showing that something is canceled Also sp. **can′cel·a′tion**

can·cel·lous (kan′sə ləs) ***adj.*** ⟦ModL < L *cancelli*: see CANCEL⟧ **1** *Anat.* having a porous or spongelike structure: said of bones **2** *Bot.* having a tiny, netlike structure of veins: said of certain leaves Also **can′cel·late** (-sə lit, -lāt′) or **can′cel·lat′ed** (-lāt′əd)

can·cer (kan′sər) ***n.*** ⟦ME & OE < L, a crab; later, malignant tumor; by dissimilation (? already in IE) < IE **karkar-*, redupl. of base **kar-*, hard > HARD, Gr *karbinos*, crab, Sans *karkara*, rough, hard, *karkata*, crab⟧ **1** [**C-**] a N constellation between Gemini and Leo; the Crab **2** [**C-**] the fourth sign of the zodiac, entered by the sun about June 21: also called *the Crab* **3** [**C-**] a person born under this sign: also **Can·cer′i·an** (-sir′ē ən) **4** *a)* a malignant new growth anywhere in the body of a person or animal; malignant tumor: cancers tend to spread locally and to distant parts of the body *b)* any of various diseases characterized by the uncontrolled growth of cells that disrupt body tissue, metabolism, etc.: see also CARCINOMA, SARCOMA **5** anything bad or harmful that spreads and destroys —**can′cer·ous** ***adj.***

can·cer·pho·bi·a (kan′sər fō′bē ə) ***n.*** **1** an excessive fear of getting cancer **2** the false impression that one has cancer Also **can′cer·o·pho′bi·a** (-sər ō-)

can·croid (kaŋ′kroid′, kan′-) ***adj.*** ⟦< L *cancer* (gen. *cancri*), CANCER + -OID⟧ **1** like a crab **2** like cancer

Can·cún (kan ko͞on′) city in SE Mexico, on the Caribbean Sea: winter resort

can·de·la (kan dē′lə, -del′ə) ***n.*** ⟦L, CANDLE⟧ the basic unit of luminous intensity in the SI system, now defined as the luminous intensity, in a given direction, of a source that emits monochromatic radiation of frequency 540 x 10^{12} hertz and that has a radiant intensity in that direction of $^1/_{683}$ watt per steradian: abbrev. *cd* —***adj.*** ⟦< Sp, CANDLE < L⟧ designating a style of cigar with a greenish wrapper

can·de·la·brum (kan′də lä′brəm, -lā′-; *also*, -la′-) ***n.***, *pl.* **-bra** (-brə) or **-brums** ⟦L: see CHANDELIER⟧ a large branched candlestick or an electric lamp like this: also **can′de·la′bra** *pl.* **-bras**

☆**can·de·lil·la** (kan′də lil′ə, -lē′yə) ***n.*** ⟦AmSp < Sp, dim. of *candela* (< L), CANDLE⟧ either of two shrubs (*Euphorbia antisiphylitica* or *Pedilanthus pavonis*) of the spurge family, native to the SW U.S. and Mexico, which yield a wax used for polishes, varnishes, etc.

can·dent (kan′dənt) ***adj.*** ⟦L *candens*, prp. of *candere*, to shine: see fol.⟧ [Archaic] glowing with heat

can·des·cent (kan des′ənt) ***adj.*** ⟦L *candescens*, prp. of *candescere*, inceptive form of *candere*, to shine < IE base **kand-*, to glow > Sans *candati*, (it) gleams⟧ [Rare] glowing with intense heat; incandescent —**can·des′cence** ***n.***

Can·di·a (kan′dē ə) **1** *former name for* CRETE **2** *former name for* IRAKLION

can·did (kan′did) ***adj.*** ⟦L *candidus*, white, pure, sincere < *candere*: see CANDESCENT⟧ **1** free from prejudice or bias; fair; just; impartial **2** very honest or frank in what one says or writes **3** unposed and informal [*a candid photograph*] **4** [Archaic] *a)* white *b)* pure —***SYN.*** FRANK[1] —**can′did·ly** ***adv.***

can·di·da (kan′di də) ***n.*** CANDIDIASIS —**can′di·dal** ***adj.***

☆**can·di·da·cy** (kan′də də sē) ***n.***, *pl.* **-cies** the fact or state of being a candidate: also [Brit.] **can′di·da·ture** (-chər)

can·di·date (kan′də dāt′, -dət) ***n.*** ⟦L *candidatus*, white-robed < *candidus* (see CANDID): office seekers in ancient Rome wore white gowns⟧ **1** a person who seeks, or who has been proposed for, an office, an award, etc. **2** a person or thing apparently destined for, or likely to come to, a specified end [*he's a good candidate for a heart attack*] **3** a student who is near to completion of the requirements for a degree

candid camera a camera, usually small, with a fast lens, used to take informal pictures, as of unposed subjects

can·di·di·a·sis (kan′də dī′ə sis) ***n.***, *pl.* **-ses′** (-sēz′) ⟦< ModL *Candida* (< L *candidus*, white) + -IASIS⟧ a common fungal infection caused by yeast (genus *Candida*, esp. *C. albicans*) that thrives on any moist, cutaneous area of the body, esp. on mucous membranes, between toes, under diapers, etc.: can develop into serious internal and chronic conditions

can·died (kan′dēd′) ***adj.*** **1** cooked in or with sugar or syrup so as to be glazed, encrusted, or preserved [*candied walnuts, candied violets*] **2** crystallized into or like sugar **3** sugary in expression

Can·di·ot (kan′dē ät′) ***adj.*** of Candia (Crete); Cretan —***n.*** a Cretan Also **Can′di·ote′** (-ōt′)

can·dle (kan′dəl) ***n.*** ⟦ME & OE *candel* < L *candela*, a light, torch < *candere*: see CANDESCENT⟧ **1** a cylindrical mass of tallow or wax with a wick through its center, which gives light when burned **2** anything like a candle in form or use **3** *a) former name for* CANDELA *b)* until 1940, a standard unit of luminous intensity equal to a certain fraction of the candle power of a group of 45 carbon-filament lamps kept at the National Bureau of Standards; international candle —***vt.*** **-dled**, **-dling** to examine (eggs) for freshness, fertilization, etc. by placing in front of a light, originally that of a candle —**burn the candle at both ends** to work or, esp., play too much so that one's energy is dissipated —**not hold a candle to** to be not nearly so good as —**(a game) not worth the candle** ⟦orig., in ref. to a game with stakes too low to pay for the light by which to play it⟧ (a thing) not worth doing —**can′dler** ***n.***

☆**can·dle·ber·ry** (-ber′ē) ***n.***, *pl.* **-ries** ⟦so named from the wax coating of its *berry*, used for making *candles*⟧ **1** BAYBERRY (sense 1) **2** CANDLENUT (senses 1 & 2)

can·dle·fish (-fish′) ***n.***, *pl.* **-fish′** a small, oily, edible smelt fish (*Thaleichthys pacificus*) of the N Pacific: when dried it can be burned as a candle

can·dle-foot (-fo͝ot′) ***n.*** FOOT-CANDLE

can·dle·hold·er (-hōl′dər) ***n.*** a candlestick

can·dle·light (-līt′) ***n.*** **1** subdued light given by or as by candles **2** [Old-fashioned] the time for lighting candles; twilight; evening —***adj.*** CANDLELIT (sense 2)

can·dle·lit or **can·dle-lit** (-lit′) ***adj.*** **1** illuminated by candlelight [*a candlelit hallway*] **2** using lighted candles so as to create a particular mood or effect [*a candlelit dinner*]

Can·dle·mas (-məs) ***n.*** ⟦ME *candelmasse* < OE *candelmæsse*: see CANDLE & MASS[1]⟧ a church feast, Feb. 2, commemorating the ritual purification of the Virgin Mary after the birth of Jesus: candles for sacred uses are blessed on this day: also **Candlemas Day**

can·dle·nut (-nut′) ***n.*** **1** the fruit of a tree (*Aleurites moluccana*) of the spurge family, growing in the Pacific Islands: the fruit is burned as a candle by indigenous peoples and processed commercially for its oil **2** this tree

can·dle·pin (-pin′) ***n.*** ⟦so named prob. from its slender, tapered shape⟧ any of the ten nearly cylindrical pins used with a small ball in a game like bowling —***pl.n.*** this game

can·dle·pow·er (-pou′ər) ***n.*** ⟦so called because orig. based on the light given off by a certain type of *candle*⟧ the luminous intensity of a light source expressed in candelas

can·dle·stick (-stik′) ***n.*** a cupped or spiked holder for a candle or candles

can·dle·wick (-wik′) ***n.*** **1** the wick of a candle **2** a soft cotton embroidery thread or fine yarn **3** CANDLEWICKING —***adj.*** designating thread or fine yarn used for candlewicking

can·dle·wick·ing (-wik′iŋ) ***n.*** a kind of embroidery used for a bedspread, tablecloth, or pillow cover, patterned with French knots of candlewick embroidery thread or yarn —***adj.*** CANDLEWICK

can·dle·wood (-wo͝od′) ***n.*** ⟦so called because it burns with a bright flame⟧ **1** any of a genus (*Fouquieria*) of the ocotillo family of spiny desert shrubs or trees with slender stems and brightly colored flowers **2** the wood of any of these ☆**3** any resinous wood cut for kindling or for torches

can-do (kan′do͞o′) ***adj.*** [Informal] characterized by enthusiasm and confidence in taking on tasks or challenges

can·dor (kan′dər) ***n.*** ⟦L, whiteness, openness < *candere*, to shine: see CANDESCENT⟧ **1** the quality of being fair and unprejudiced; impartiality **2** sharp honesty or frankness in expressing oneself **3** [Obs.] *a)* whiteness *b)* purity; innocence *c)* kindliness Brit. sp. **can′dour**

C & W *abbrev.* country and western (music)

can·dy (kan′dē) ***n.***, *pl.* **-dies** ⟦< *sugar candy* < ME *(sugre) candi* < OFr *(sucre) candi* < OIt *(zucchero) candi* < Ar *qandi* < Pers *qand*, cane sugar; prob. < Sans *khaṇḍa*, piece (of sugar)⟧ **1** crystallized sugar made by boiling and evaporating cane sugar, syrup, etc. **2** *a)* a sweet food, usually in small pieces or bars, made mainly from sugar or syrup, with flavoring, fruit, chocolate, nuts, etc. added *b)* a piece of such food **3** [Informal] someone or something variously regarded as being frivolously or superficially desirable, attractive, pleasing, exciting, etc. [*ear candy*] —***vt.*** **-died**, **-dy·ing** ⟦Fr *candir* < It *candire* < *candi*: see the ***n.***⟧ **1** to cook in or with sugar or syrup so as to glaze, encrust, or preserve **2** to crystallize into or like sugar **3** to sweeten; make pleasant —***vi.*** to become candied: see ***vt.*** 1 & 2

☆**can·dy-ass** (kan′dē as′) ***n.*** [Slang] a weak, hesitant, or ineffectual person; wimp; sissy —**can′dy-assed′** (-ast′) ***adj.***

candy cane a stick of hard peppermint candy with diagonal stripes and a curved end for hanging as a Christmas decoration

can·dy-striped (-strīpt′) ***adj.*** having diagonal, colored stripes like those on a certain kind of candy stick

☆**candy striper** ⟦so called from the red-and-white-striped pinafore commonly worn⟧ a teenage girl who does volunteer work in a hospital

can·dy·tuft (-tuft′) *n.* ⟦< CANDIA + TUFT⟧ any of a genus (*Iberis*) of garden plants of the crucifer family, with clusters of white, pink, or purplish flowers

cane (kān) *n.* ⟦ME & OFr *canne* < It *canna* < L, reed, cane < Gr *kanna*; prob. < Assyr *qanū* (or Heb *qaneh*), tube, reed < Sumerian *gin*⟧ **1** the slender, jointed, usually flexible stem of any of certain plants, as bamboo or rattan **2** any plant with such a stem, as sugar cane or sorghum **3** the woody stem of a small fruiting or flowering plant, as the blackberry or rose **4** any of a genus (*Arundinaria*) of tall grasses of the S U.S. **5** a stick or rod used for flogging **6** *a)* WALKING STICK (sense 1) *b)* an aluminum or wooden rod with a curved handle, used for support in walking **7** a split rattan, used in weaving chair seats, wickerwork, etc. —*vt.* **caned**, **can′ing** **1** to flog with a cane **2** to make or furnish (chairs, etc.) with cane —**can′er** *n.*

☆**cane·brake** (kān′brāk′) *n.* ⟦prec. + BRAKE[3]⟧ **1** a dense growth of cane plants **2** an area overgrown with canes

ca·nel·la (kə nel′ə) *n.* ⟦ModL < ML, dim. of L *canna*: see CANE⟧ the fragrant inner bark of a tropical American tree (*Canella winterana*) of a family (Canellaceae) of dicotyledonous, aromatic trees (order Magnoliales), used as a spice and a tonic

ca·neph·o·ros (kə nef′ə räs′) *n., pl.* **-roe′** (-rē′) ⟦L < Gr *kanēphoros* < *kaneon*, a rush basket (< *kanna*: see CANE) + *pherein*, BEAR[1]⟧ **1** in ancient Greece, any of the maidens who carried on her head a basket holding the sacred things used at feasts **2** *Archit.* a representation of this, sometimes used as a caryatid Also **can·e·phor** (kan′ə fôr′)

ca·nes·cent (kə nes′ənt) *adj.* ⟦L *canescens*, prp. of *canescere*, to become white < *canere*, to be white < *canus*, hoary: see HARE⟧ **1** becoming white or grayish **2** covered with a white or grayish down, as some leaves

cane sugar sugar (*sucrose*) obtained from sugar cane

Ca·nes Ve·nat·i·ci (kā′nēz′ və nat′ə sī′) ⟦L, pl. of *canis venaticus*, hunting dog: see VENATIC⟧ a N constellation between Ursa Major and Boötes

☆**can·field** (kan′fēld′) *n.* ⟦after Richard A. *Canfield* (1885-1914), U.S. gambling house proprietor⟧ a form of solitaire used as a gambling game

cangue (kaŋ) *n.* ⟦Fr < Port *canga*, a yoke < Vietnamese *gong*⟧ in China, a large, wooden yoke formerly fastened about the neck as a punishment for petty crime

Ca·nic·u·la (kə nik′yoo lə) *n.* ⟦L, dim. of *canis*, dog: see HOUND[1]⟧ [Rare] Sirius, the Dog Star

ca·nic·u·lar (-lər) *adj.* ⟦ME *caniculer* < L *canicularis* < prec.⟧ **1** *a)* of the Dog Star (Sirius) *b)* measured by its rising **2** of the DOG DAYS in July and August

can·id (kan′id) *n.* CANINE (sense 1)

ca·nine (kā′nīn′) *adj.* ⟦L *caninus* < *canis*, dog: see HOUND[1]⟧ **1** of or like a dog **2** of the family (Canidae) of carnivores that includes dogs, wolves, jackals, and foxes —*n.* **1** a dog or other canine animal **2** a sharp-pointed tooth on either side of the upper jaw and lower jaw, between the incisors and the bicuspids, having a long single root; a cuspid or (in the upper jaw) eyetooth: in full **canine tooth**

Ca·nis Ma·jor (kā′nis mā′jər) ⟦L, the Greater Dog⟧ a S constellation between Monoceros and Columba, containing the bright star Sirius; the Greater Dog

Canis Mi·nor (mī′nər) ⟦L, the Lesser Dog⟧ a N constellation near Gemini and Cancer, containing the bright star Procyon; the Lesser Dog

can·is·ter (kan′is tər) *n.* ⟦ME < L *canistrum*, wicker basket < Gr *kanastron* < *kanna*, a reed: see CANE⟧ **1** a small box or can for coffee, tea, tobacco, etc. **2** a boxlike vacuum cleaner **3** [Historical] lead or iron shot in a container that scattered its contents when fired: in full **canister shot** **4** the part of a gas mask that contains the substances for filtering the air to be breathed

can·ker (kaŋ′kər) *n.* ⟦ME < OFr *cancre* < L *cancer*: see CANCER⟧ **1** an ulcerlike sore, esp. in the mouth: thought to be an immune reaction: cf. COLD SORE: also **canker sore** **2** *a)* a disease of plants that causes local decay of bark and wood *b)* a diseased area of woody tissues **3** [Obs.] CANKERWORM **4** anything that corrupts or gradually destroys **5** [Now Dial.] the dog rose —*vt.* **1** to attack or infect with canker **2** to infect or debase with corruption —*vi.* to become cankered —**can′ker·ous** *adj.*

can·ker·worm (-wurm′) *n.* ☆any of several larvae of geometrid moths that are harmful to fruit and shade trees, esp. the spring cankerworm (*Paleacrita vernata*) that feeds on fruit and foliage

can·na (kan′ə) *n.* ⟦ModL < L: see CANE⟧ any of a genus (*Canna*) of the canna family of broad-leaved tropical plants, often grown for ornament because of the striking foliage and brilliant flowers —*adj.* designating a family (Cannaceae) of monocotyledonous plants (order Zingiberales)

can·na·bin (kan′ə bin) *n.* a poisonous, greenish-black resin extracted from cannabis

can·nab·i·noid (kə nab′ə noid′, kan′ə bə noid′) *n.* any of a group of natural or synthetic compounds, as cannabinol or tetrahydrocannabinol, found in marijuana plants

can·nab·i·nol (kə nab′ə nôl′) *n.* ⟦see fol. & -OL[1]⟧ a yellow chemical compound, $C_{21}H_{26}O_2$, that is an inactive component of marijuana: see TETRAHYDROCANNABINOL

can·na·bis (kan′ə bis) *n.* ⟦ModL < L, hemp < Gr *kannabis*: see HEMP⟧ **1** HEMP **2** marijuana or any other substance derived from the flowering tops of the hemp

Can·nae (kan′ē) ancient town in SE Italy: site of a battle (216 B.C.) in which the Carthaginians under Hannibal defeated the Romans

☆**canned** (kand) *adj.* **1** preserved in airtight cans or jars **2** [Slang] recorded for reproduction as on radio or TV: said of music, laughter, sound effects, etc.

can·nel (coal) (kan′əl) ⟦< ? *candle coal*⟧ a compact variety of bituminous coal that was formed chiefly from spores and burns with a bright, steady flame

can·nel·li·ni bean (kan′ə lē′nē) *pl.* **cannellini beans** or **cannellini** a large white type of kidney bean, much used in Italian cooking

can·nel·lo·ni (kan′ə lō′nē) *n.* ⟦It, pl. of *cannellone*, a hollow noodle, lit., small tube, aug. of *cannello*, a tube, joint of cane, dim. of *canna*, CANE⟧ **1** pasta in the form of tubular casings of dough filled with ground meat or other filling, boiled, then baked in a sauce **2** *pl.* **-ni** or **-nis** one of these filled casings

☆**can·ner** (kan′ər) *n.* a person who cans food

☆**can·ner·y** (kan′ər ē) *n., pl.* **-ner·ies** a factory where foods are canned

Cannes (kan, kanz; *Fr* kån) city in SE France, on the Riviera

can·ni·bal (kan′ə bəl) *n.* ⟦Sp *canibal*, a savage, cannibal (term used by Columbus) < Arawakan *Caniba*, a cannibal people; akin to Carib *galibi*, lit., strong men⟧ **1** a person who eats human flesh **2** an animal that eats its own kind —*adj.* of, resembling, or having the habits of cannibals —**can′ni·bal·ism′** *n.* —**can′ni·bal·is′tic** *adj.*

☆**can·ni·bal·ize** (-īz′) *vt., vi.* **-ized′**, **-iz′ing** **1** to strip (old or worn equipment) of parts for use in other units to help keep them in service **2** to take any or all personnel or components from (one organization) for use in building up another **3** to swallow up or devour (another of the same kind): used fig. **4** to incorporate (parts of someone else's writing, painting, or music or of one's own earlier work) into one's current efforts —**can′ni·bal·i·za′tion** *n.*

can·ni·kin (kan′i kin) *n.* ⟦< CAN[2] + -KIN⟧ a small can, esp. when used as a cup

can·ni·ly (kan′ə lē) *adv.* in a canny manner

can·ni·ness (kan′ē nis) *n.* the quality of being canny

☆**can·ning** (kan′iŋ) *n.* the act, process, or work of putting foods in cans or jars for preservation

Can·ning (kan′iŋ), **George** 1770-1827; Brit. statesman: prime minister (1827)

can·no·li (kə nō′lē) *n.* ⟦It, pl. of *cannolo*, small tube, dim. of *canna* < L, reed, CANE⟧ **1** Italian pastry formed in tubes, deep-fried, and filled with sweetened ricotta cheese and, variously, chocolate, candied fruit, nuts, or liqueur **2** *pl.* **-li** or **-lis** a piece of this pastry

can·non (kan′ən) *n., pl.* **-nons** or **-non** ⟦ME & OFr *canon* < It *cannone* < *canna*: see CANE; in *n.* 5 & *vt.* 2, *vi.* 2, altered < CAROM⟧ **1** *a)* a large, mounted piece of artillery; sometimes, specif., a large gun with a relatively short barrel, as a howitzer *b)* an automatic gun, mounted on an aircraft **2** a part on a bell by which it is hung **3** CANNON BONE **4** *Mech.* a hollow tube within which a shaft revolves independently of the outer tube **5** [Brit.] *Billiards* CAROM —*vt.* **1** to attack with cannon fire **2** [Brit.] to cause to carom —*vi.* **1** to fire cannons **2** [Brit.] to make a carom

Can·non (kan′ən), **Joseph Gur·ney** (gur′nē) 1836-1926; U.S. congressman

can·non·ade (kan′ən ād′) *n.* ⟦Fr *canonnade* < *canon*, CANNON⟧ a continuous firing of artillery —*vt.* **-ad′ed**, **-ad′ing** to attack or fire at with artillery —*vi.* to fire artillery

can·non·ball (kan′ən bôl′) *n.* **1** a heavy ball, esp. of iron, formerly used as a projectile in cannons **2** [Informal] *a)* a fast express train *b)* a hard, driving serve in tennis **3** a feet-first dive done in a tuck position —*adj.* [Slang] fast; rapid —*vi.* [Slang] to move very fast

cannon bone the bone between hock or knee and fetlock in a four-legged, hoofed animal

can·non·eer (kan′ən ir′) *n.* ⟦Fr *canonnier* < *canon*, CANNON⟧ an artilleryman; gunner

cannon fodder soldiers, sailors, etc. thought of as being expended (i.e., killed or maimed) or expendable in war

can·non·ry (kan′ən rē) *n., pl.* **-ries** **1** cannons collectively; artillery **2** cannon fire

can·not (kan′ät′, kə nät′) *v.aux.* can not —**cannot but** be compelled or obliged to; must

can·nu·la (kan′yoo lə, -yə-) *n., pl.* **-lae′** (-lē′) or **-las** ⟦L, dim. of *canna*: see CANE⟧ a tube, usually with a trocar, for insertion into body cavities or ducts, as for drainage: cf. CATHETER

can·nu·lar (-lər) *adj.* tubular: also **can′nu·late** (-lit, -lāt′)

can·ny (kan′ē) *adj.* **-ni·er**, **-ni·est** ⟦< CAN[1] + -Y[3]⟧ **1** careful and shrewd in one's actions and dealings; clever and cautious **2** careful with money; thrifty **3** [Scot.] careful in action; gentle; easy; quiet **4** [Brit. Dial.] good; nice; fine —*adv.* [Scot.] in a canny or cautious manner —**ca′ canny** (kä-, kô-) **1** [Scot.] call "canny"; hence, go cautiously **2** [Brit.] the tactic, as by a labor union, of intentionally slowing down factory production

ca·noe (kə noo′) *n.* ⟦earlier *canoa* < Sp (used by Columbus in 1493) < Carib⟧ a narrow, light boat with its sides meeting in a sharp edge at each end: it is moved by one or more paddles —☆*vi.* **-noed′**, **-noe′ing** to paddle, or go in, a canoe —*vt.* to transport by canoe —**ca·noe′ist** *n.*

ca·no·la (oil) (kə nō′lə) ⟦< CAN(ADA) + (C)OL(Z)A⟧ an oil derived from the seed of any of several varieties of the rape plant, used in cooking, salad dressings, etc.: it is low in saturated fats

can·on[1] (kan′ən) *n.* ⟦ME < OE & OFr < L, measuring line, rule (hence, in ML(Ec), sacred writings admitted to the catalog according to the rule) < Gr *kanōn*, rule, rod < *kanna*: see CANE⟧ **1** a law or body of laws of a church **2** [Rare] any law or decree **3** *a)* an established or basic rule or principle [the *canons* of good taste] *b)* a standard to judge by; criterion *c)* a body of rules, principles, criteria, etc. **4** *a)* the books of the Bible officially accepted by a church or religious body as divinely inspired *b)* the works ascribed to an author that are accepted as genuine *c)* the complete works, as of an author *d)* those works, authors, etc. accepted as major or essential [the Victorian *canon*] **5** *a)* [*often* **C-**] *Eccles.* the fundamental and essentially unvarying part of the Mass, between the Preface and Communion, that centers on consecration of the bread and wine *b)* a list of recognized saints as in the Roman Catholic Church **6** *Music a)* a contrapuntal device in which a melody introduced in one voice is restated in one or more other voices that overlap the first and successive voices in continuous and strict imitation *b)* a composition so constructed —**SYN.** LAW

can·on[2] (kan′ən) ***n.*** ⟦ME < OE *canonic* & OFr *chanoine* < LL(Ec) *canonicus*, a cleric, one living by the canon: see prec.⟧ **1** a member of a clerical group living according to a canon, or rule **2** a clergyman serving in a cathedral or collegiate church **3** CANON REGULAR

ca·ñon (kan′yən; *Sp* kä nyôn′) ***n.*** *alt. sp. of* CANYON

can·on·ess (kan′ən is) ***n.*** a woman religious following a rule similar to that of a canon regular

ca·non·ic (kə nän′ik) ***adj.*** **1** CANONICAL **2** of, or in the manner of, a musical canon

ca·non·i·cal (kə nän′i kəl) ***adj.*** ⟦ME < ML(Ec) *canonicalis*⟧ **1** of, according to, or ordered by church canon **2** authoritative; accepted **3** belonging to the canon of the Bible **4** of a canon (clergyman) —**ca·non′i·cal·ly** ***adv.***

canonical hour *Christianity* **1** any of seven periods of the day assigned to recitation of the Divine Office: the hours are matins (with lauds), prime, terce, sext, none, vespers, and compline **2** the part of the Divine Office assigned to each of these periods

ca·non·i·cals (-kəlz) ***pl.n.*** the clothes prescribed by canon for a clergyman when conducting services

ca·non·i·cate (-kət, -kāt′) ***n.*** CANONRY (sense 1)

can·on·ic·i·ty (kan′ə nis′ə tē) ***n.*** ⟦L *canonicus*, according to rule: see CANON[1]⟧ the fact or condition of being canonical

can·on·ist (kan′ən ist) ***n.*** an expert in canon law —**can′on·is′tic** ***adj.***

can·on·ize (kan′ən īz′) ***vt.*** **-ized′**, **-iz′ing** ⟦ME *canonizen* < LL(Ec) *canonizare*: see CANON[1] + -IZE⟧ **1** to declare (a deceased person) a saint in formal church procedure **2** to glorify **3** to put in the Biblical canon **4** to give church sanction or authorization to —**can′on·i·za′tion** ***n.***

canon law the laws governing the ecclesiastical affairs of a Christian church

canon regular *pl.* **canons regular** *R.C.Ch.* a clergyman of certain religious communities following a monastic rule

can·on·ry (kan′ən rē) ***n.***, *pl.* **-ries** **1** the benefice or position of a canon **2** canons collectively

☆**ca·noo·dle** (kə no͞od′'l) ***vi.*** **-dled**, **-dling** ⟦Ger *knudeln*, to cuddle < or akin to LowG *knuddel*, a knot, clump, dim. of dial. *knude*; akin to OHG *knodo*, OE *cnotta*, KNOT[1]⟧ [Slang] to embrace, kiss, fondle, etc. in making love; pet; neck

ca·no·pic urn (kə nō′pik) ⟦< L *Canopicus*, of CANOPUS[2]⟧ an urn used in ancient Egypt to hold and preserve the internal organs of the mummified dead: also **canopic jar** (or **vase**)

Ca·no·pus[1] (kə nō′pəs) ***n.*** ⟦L < Gr *Kanōpos*: prob. in allusion to the pilot of the fleet of King MENELAUS⟧ a supergiant, binary, variable star in the constellation Carina, the second brightest star: magnitude, −0.62

Ca·no·pus[2] (kə nō′pəs) seaport in ancient Egypt, near the mouth of the Nile

can·o·py (kan′ə pē) ***n.***, *pl.* **-pies** ⟦ME *canape* < ML *canapeum* < L *conopeum* < Gr *kōnōpeion*, couch with mosquito curtains, dim. of *kōnōps*, gnat⟧ **1** a drapery, awning, or other rooflike covering fastened above a bed, throne, etc., or held on poles over a person or sacred thing **2** a structure of canvas on a framework sheltering an area or forming a sheltered walk to the entrance of a building **3** anything that covers or seems to cover like a canopy, as the sky **4** the transparent hood over an airplane cockpit **5** the part of a parachute that opens up and catches the air **6** a rooflike projection over a door, pulpit, etc. **7** the uppermost leafy level of a forest —***vt.*** **-pied**, **-py·ing** to place or form a canopy over; cover; shelter

ca·no·rous (kə nôr′əs) ***adj.*** ⟦L *canorus* < *canor*, a tune < *canere*, sing: see CHANT⟧ [Rare] pleasing in sound; melodious; musical —**ca·no′rous·ly** ***adv.***

Ca·no·va (kä nô′vä), **An·to·nio** (än tô′nyô) 1757-1822; It. sculptor

canst (kanst) ***vi.***, ***vt.*** *archaic 2d pers. sing., pres. indic., of* CAN[1]: used with *thou*

cant[1] (kant) ***n.*** ⟦< L *cantus*: see CHANT⟧ **1** whining, singsong speech, esp. as used by beggars **2** the secret slang of beggars, thieves, etc.; argot **3** the special words and phrases used by those in a certain sect, occupation, etc.; jargon **4** insincere or almost meaningless talk used merely from convention or habit **5** religious phraseology used hypocritically; insincere, pious talk —***vi.*** ⟦< the ***n.***⟧ to use cant; speak in cant —***adj.*** of, or having the nature of, cant —**SYN.** DIALECT —**cant′er** ***n.***

cant[2] (kant) ***n.*** ⟦ME & OFr *cant*, corner, edge, angle < LL *cantus* < L, iron tire of a wheel < Celt, as in Brythonic *cant*, rim of a wheel, edge < IE base **kantho-*, corner, bend⟧ **1** a corner or outside angle, as of a building **2** a sloping or slanting surface; beveled edge **3** a sudden movement, toss, or pitch that causes tilting, turning, or overturning **4** the tilt, turn, or slant thus caused —***vt.*** **1** to give a sloping edge to; bevel **2** to tilt or overturn **3** to throw off or out by tilting **4** to throw with a jerk; pitch; toss —***vi.*** **1** to tilt or turn over **2** to slant —***adj.*** **1** with canted sides or corners **2** slanting

cant[3] (känt) ***adj.*** ⟦ME, bold, brave; prob. < or akin to MDu *kant*⟧ [Brit. Dial.] lusty; bold; hearty

Cant *abbrev.* **1** Canticles **2** Cantonese

can't (kant, känt) *contraction* cannot

Cantab *abbrev.* Cantabrigian

can·ta·bi·le (kän tä′bē lā′) [*also in italics*] *Music* ***adj.***, ***adv.*** ⟦It < LL *cantabilis*, worthy to be sung < L *cantare*: see CHANT⟧ in an easy, flowing manner; like a song: often used as a musical direction —***n.*** a cantabile movement or passage

Can·ta·bri·a (kan tā′brē ə) region of N Spain, on the Bay of Biscay: 2,042 sq mi (5,289 sq km); cap. Santander

Can·ta·bri·an Mountains (kan tā′brē ən) mountain range in N & NW Spain, parallel to the Bay of Biscay: highest peak, 8,687 ft (2,648 m)

Can·ta·brig·i·an (kan′tə brij′ən, -ē ən) ***adj.*** ⟦after ML *Cantabrigia*, CAMBRIDGE⟧ of Cambridge, England, or esp., of the University of Cambridge —***n.*** **1** a student or graduate of the University of Cambridge **2** a person living in Cambridge, England

can·ta·la (kan′tə lə, kan tä′-) ***n.*** ⟦< ?⟧ a hard fiber derived from the leaves of an agave (*Agave cantala*): used in making twine

can·ta·loupe or **can·ta·loup** (kant′ə lōp′) ***n.*** ⟦Fr < It *cantalupo*, after *Cantalupo*, former papal summer estate, near Rome, where the melon was first grown in Europe⟧ any of various fruits of the muskmelon, esp. that of a variety (*Cucumis melo* var. *reticulatus*) having a hard, rough rind and sweet, juicy, orange-colored flesh

can·tan·ker·ous (kan taŋ′kər əs) ***adj.*** ⟦prob. < ME *contakour*, troublemaker (< Anglo-Fr < *contec*, discord) + -OUS⟧ bad-tempered; quarrelsome —**can·tan′ker·ous·ly** ***adv.*** —**can·tan′ker·ous·ness** ***n.***

can·ta·ta (kän tät′ə, kən-) ***n.*** ⟦It < pp. of *cantare*: see CHANT⟧ a musical composition consisting of vocal solos, choruses, etc., often with instrumental accompaniment, used as a setting for a story to be sung but not acted

can·ta·tri·ce (*It* kän′tä trē′che; *Fr* kän tȧ trēs′) ***n.***, *pl.* It. **-tri′ci** (It, trē′chē); Fr. **-trices′** (*Fr*, -trēs′) ⟦Fr & It < L *cantatrix*, fem. of *cantator*, singer < pp. of *cantare*: see CHANT⟧ a female professional singer

cant dog CANT HOOK

can·teen (kan tēn′) ***n.*** ⟦Fr *cantine* < It *cantina*, wine cellar, vault < ? *canto*, corner: see CANT[2]⟧ **1** POST EXCHANGE **2** a place outside a military camp where refreshments and entertainment are provided for members of the armed forces **3** *a)* a place where refreshments can be obtained, as by employees or visitors *b)* such a place serving as a social center, as for teenagers **4** a place where cooked food is dispensed to people in distress, as in a disaster area **5** a small metal or plastic flask, usually encased in canvas, for carrying drinking water **6** a military kit formerly used to carry cooking equipment

can·ter (kan′tər) ***n.*** ⟦contr. < *Canterbury gallop*: in ref. to the pace at which pilgrims rode to Canterbury⟧ **1** a smooth, easy pace like a moderate gallop **2** the rumbling sound of a cantering horse — ***vi.***, ***vt.*** to ride or move at a canter

Can·ter·bur·y (kan′tər ber′ē, -bər ē) city in Kent, SE England; seat of the primate of the Church of England

Canterbury bells a cultivated bellflower (*Campanula medium*) with white, pink, or blue cuplike flowers

Canterbury Tales an unfinished literary work by Chaucer, largely in verse, consisting of stories told as by pilgrims on their way to the shrine of St. Thomas à Becket at Canterbury

can·thar·i·des (kan thar′ə dēz′) ***pl.n.*** ⟦ME *cantarides* < L *cantharides*, pl. of *cantharis*, kind of beetle, Spanish fly < Gr *kantharis*, blister beetle⟧ **1** *pl. of* CANTHARIS **2** [*with sing. or pl. v.*] a dangerous, sometimes fatal, preparation of powdered, dried Spanish flies, formerly used internally as a diuretic and aphrodisiac and externally as a skin irritant

can·tha·ris (kan′thə ris) ***n.***, *pl.* **can·thar·i·des** (kan thar′ə dēz′) ⟦see prec.⟧ SPANISH FLY (sense 1)

cant hook ⟦see CANT[2]⟧ a heavy wooden lever with a blunt tip and a hinged hook near the end: used by lumbermen in handling logs: cf. PEAVEY

cant hook

can·thus (kan′thəs) ***n.***, *pl.* **-thi′** (-thī′) ⟦ModL < Gr *kanthos*: for IE base see CANT[2]⟧ either corner of the eye, where the eyelids meet

can·ti·cle (kan′ti kəl) ***n.*** ⟦ME < L *canticulum*, dim. of *canticum*, song < *cantus*: see CHANT⟧ **1** a song or chant **2** a hymn whose words are taken from the Bible, used in certain church services **3** any of the three main sections of Dante's *Divine Comedy*

Can·ti·cles (kan′ti kəlz) ***n.*** SONG OF SOLOMON: abbrev. *Ca*: also, in the Douay Bible, **Canticle of Canticles**

can·ti·le·na (kan′tə lē′nə) ***n.*** ⟦It < L, song < *cantare*, sing: see CHANT⟧ a smooth, flowing, lyrical passage of vocal, or sometimes instrumental, music

can·ti·le·ver (kant′'l ē′vər, -ev′ər) ***n.*** ⟦as if < CANT[2] + -I- + LEVER, but < ?⟧ **1** a large bracket or block projecting from a wall to support a balcony, cornice, etc. **2** a projecting beam or structure supported at only one end, that is anchored as to a pier or wall —***vt.*** to support by means of cantilevers —**can′ti·le′vered** ***adj.***

cantilever bridge a bridge whose span is formed by two cantilevers projecting toward each other, sometimes with an extra section between them

can·til·la·tion (kant′'l ā′shən) ***n.*** ⟦< *cantillate*, chant (< L *cantillatus*, pp. of *cantillare*, hum, sing low < *cantare*: see CHANT) & -ION]] in Jewish liturgy, a chanting or reciting with certain prescribed musical phrases indicated by notations —**can′til·late′** (-āt′) *vt., vi.* **-lat′ed, -lat′ing**

☆**can·ti·na** (kan tē′nə) *n.* [[Sp < It: see CANTEEN]] [Southwest] a saloon or barroom

can·tle (kant′'l) *n.* [[ME *cantel*, a corner, rim, piece < OFr < ML *cantellus*, dim. of LL *cantus*: see CANT²]] the upward-curving rear part of a saddle

can·to (kan′tō) *n., pl.* **-tos** [[It < L *cantus*, song: see CHANT]] any of the main divisions of certain long poems, corresponding to the chapters of a book

can·ton (kan′tən, -tän′; kan tän′; *for vt. 2* kan tän′, -tōn′ & *Brit*, kən to͞on′) *n.* [[Fr < It *cantone* < LL *cantus*: see CANT²]] 1 any of the political divisions of certain countries or territories; specif., *a)* any of the main divisions of Switzerland *b)* a division of an arrondissement in France 2 *a) Heraldry* a small, square section of a shield, usually in the upper dexter corner *b)* a rectangular section in a flag, in the upper corner nearest the staff —*vt.* 1 to divide into cantons 2 to assign quarters to (troops, etc.); quarter —**can′ton·al** *adj.*

Can·ton (kan tän′) *a former transliteration of* GUANGZHOU

Can·ton crepe (kant′'n, kan′tän′) [[after prec.]] a soft, crinkled silk or rayon fabric, like crepe de Chine but heavier

Can·ton·ese (kan′tə nēz′, -nēs′) *adj.* 1 of Canton (China) or its people, language, or culture 2 designating or of a tradition of Chinese cuisine originating in the Guangdong province —*n.* 1 *pl.* **-ese′** a person born or living in Canton, China 2 the variety of Chinese spoken in Canton

Can·ton flannel (kant′'n, kan′tän′) COTTON FLANNEL

can·ton·ment (kan tän′mənt, -tōn′-; *Brit* kən to͞on′-) *n.* [[Fr *cantonnement*: see CANTON]] 1 the assignment of troops to temporary quarters 2 the quarters assigned

can·tor (kan′tər) *n.* [[L, singer, poet, actor (in LL(Ec), precentor) < *canere*: see CHANT]] 1 a church choir leader; precentor 2 a singer of liturgical solos in a synagogue, who leads the congregation in prayer; hazan —**can·to′ri·al** (-tôr′ē əl) *adj.*

Can·tor (kän′tôr′), **Ge·org (Ferdinand Ludwig Philipp)** (gā′ôrk′) 1845-1918; Ger. mathematician, born in Russia

can·trip (kan′trip′) *n.* [[< ?]] [Chiefly Scot.] 1 a magic spell 2 a prank

can·tus (kant′əs) *n., pl.* **can′tus** [[L: see CANTO]] a melody, esp., the principal part of a polyphonic work

cantus fir·mus (fur′məs) *pl.* **-mi′** (-mī′) [[ML, lit., fixed song]] an existing melody used as the basis for a new polyphonic composition

cant·y (kan′tē) *adj.* [[CANT³ + -Y³]] [Scot. or North Eng.] lively; cheerful

☆**Ca·nuck** (kə nuk′) [Informal] *n.* [[earlier *Kanuck* < ? Haw *kanaka*, man]] a Canadian; sometimes, specif., a French Canadian —*adj.* Canadian; sometimes, specif., French Canadian

USAGE—sometimes a disparaging term

Ca·nute (kə no͞ot′, -nyo͞ot′) [[< Dan *Knut*]] A.D. 994?-1035; 1st Dan. king of England (1017-35) & king of Denmark (1018-35) & of Norway (1028-35): also called **Canute the Great**

can·vas (kan′vəs) *n.* [[ME & OFr *canevas* < It *canavaccio* < VL **cannapaceum*, hempen cloth < L *cannabis*, HEMP]] 1 a closely woven, coarse cloth of hemp, cotton, or linen, often unbleached, used for tents, sails, etc. 2 a sail or set of sails 3 *a)* a specially prepared piece of canvas on which an oil painting is made *b)* such a painting 4 a tent or group of tents, as of a circus 5 any coarse cloth of open mesh weave on which embroidery or tapestry is done —**the canvas** the canvas-covered floor of a boxing ring —**under canvas** 1 in tents 2 with sails unfurled 3 by means of sails

☆**can·vas·back** (-bak′) *n., pl.* **-backs′** or **-back′** [[< the grayish, canvaslike appearance of the back]] a large, North American wild duck (*Aythya valisneria*) with a brownish-red head, dark breast, and light-gray back, hunted as a game bird

can·vass (kan′vəs) *vt.* [[< CANVAS < ? use of canvas for sifting]] 1 to examine or discuss in detail; look over carefully 2 to go through (places) or among (people) asking for (votes, opinions, orders, etc.) —*vi.* to try to get votes, orders, etc.; solicit —*n.* the act of canvassing, esp. in an attempt to estimate the outcome of an election, sales campaign, etc. —**can′vass·er** *n.*

☆**can·yon** (kan′yən) *n.* [[AmSp *cañón* < Sp, a pipe, tube, gorge < *caño*, a tube < L *canna*, a reed: see CANE]] a long, narrow valley between high cliffs, often with a stream flowing through it

can·yon·eer·ing (kan′yə nir′iŋ) *n.* the practice or sport of following a stream, river, etc. through a canyon by walking, swimming, rafting, climbing, rappelling, etc.: also called **can′yon·ing**

can·zo·ne (kän tsô′ne) *n., pl.* **-ni** (-nē) [[It < L *cantio*, song < *canere*: see CHANT]] 1 a lyric poem of Provençal or early Italian troubadours 2 a musical setting for this Also **can·zo′na′** (-nä′)

can·zo·net or **can·zo·nette** (kan′zə net′) *n.* [[It *canzonetta*, dim. of prec.]] a short, sprightly song

caou·tchouc (kou cho͝ok′; kou′cho͝ok′, -cho͞ok′) *n.* [[Fr < obs. Sp *cauchuc* < Quechua]] rubber; esp. India rubber, or crude, natural rubber, obtained from latex

cap¹ (kap) *n.* [[ME *cappe* < OE *cæppe* & ML *cappa* < LL *cappa*, a cape, hooded cloak]] 1 any closefitting head covering, brimless or with only a front visor, and made of wool, cotton, etc., as a baseball cap or overseas cap, or of muslin or lace, as a nurse's or baby's cap 2 *a)* a special covering for the head, worn as a mark of occupation, rank, academic degree, etc. [*a cardinal's cap, fool's cap*] *b)* MORTARBOARD (sense 2) 3 a caplike part or thing; cover or top, as the cap-shaped part of a mushroom, a small metal cover for a bottle, the cover over a camera lens or other projecting or end part, a kneecap, an artificial crown for a tooth, a mountain top, or the capital of a column 4 PERCUSSION CAP 5 a little paper percussion cap for toy guns (**cap guns**) 6 an upper limit set on a budget, cost, etc.; ceiling —*vt.* **capped, cap′ping** 1 to put a cap on 2 to present ceremonially with a special cap, as at a graduation [to *cap* a nurse] 3 to cover the top or end of; form a cap [snow *capped* the hills] 4 *a)* to do as well as or better than; equal or excel *b)* to follow with another that is equivalent or better than; match [to *cap* a quotation] 5 *a)* to bring to a high point or climax *b)* to put a finishing touch on; embellish (often with *off*) [to *cap* off a lovely evening with a late dessert] 6 to set a cap, or upper limit, for —**cap in hand** in a humble or servile manner —☆**cap the climax** to be or do more than could be expected or believed —**set one's cap for** to try to win (someone) as a husband or lover

cap² *abbrev.* 1 capacity 2 capital 3 *a)* capitalization *b)* capitalize *c)* capitalized 4 [[L *capsula*]] *Pharmacy* a capsule 5 [[L *capitulum*]] chapter 6 [[L *capiat*]] *Pharmacy* take

CAP *abbrev.* Civil Air Patrol

Cap·a (kap′ə), **Robert** (born *Endre Ernö Friedman*) 1913-54; U.S. photojournalist, born in Hungary

ca·pa·bil·i·ty (kā′pə bil′ə tē) *n., pl.* **-ties** 1 the quality of being capable; practical ability 2 a capacity for being used or developed 3 [*pl.*] abilities, features, etc. not yet developed or utilized

Ca·pa·blan·ca (kä′pə bläŋ′kə), **Jo·sé Ra·ul** (hô se′ rä o͞ol′) 1888-1942; Cuban chess master: called *Capa* or *the Chess Machine*

ca·pa·ble (kā′pə bəl) *adj.* [[Fr < LL *capabilis* < L *capere*, to take: see HAVE]] having ability; able to do things well; skilled; competent —*SYN.* ABLE —**capable of** 1 susceptible of; admitting of; open to 2 having the ability or qualities necessary for 3 having the temperament or disposition for [*capable of* telling a lie] —**ca′pa·ble·ness** *n.* —**ca′pa·bly** *adv.*

ca·pa·cious (kə pā′shəs) *adj.* [[< L *capax* (gen. *capacis*), large < *capere*, to take (see HAVE) + -OUS]] able to contain or hold much; roomy; spacious —**ca·pa′cious·ly** *adv.* —**ca·pa′cious·ness** *n.*

ca·pac·i·tance (kə pas′i təns) *n.* [[CAPACIT(Y) + -ANCE]] *Elec.* that property of a capacitor which determines how much charge can be stored in it for a given potential difference between its terminals, equal to the ratio of the charge stored to the potential difference and measured in farads: abbrev. *C*

ca·pac·i·tate (-tāt′) *vt.* **-tat′ed, -tat′ing** [[CAPACIT(Y) + -ATE¹]] [Rare] to prepare, fit, or qualify

ca·pac·i·tive (-tiv) *adj.* of electrical capacitance

ca·pac·i·tor (-tər) *n. Elec.* a device consisting of two or more conducting plates separated from one another by a dielectric nonconductor, as glass, mica, plastic, or dry air, used for storing an electric charge; condenser

ca·pac·i·ty (kə pas′i tē) *n., pl.* **-ties** [[ME & OFr *capacite* < L *capacitas* < *capax*: see CAPACIOUS]] 1 the ability to contain, absorb, or receive and hold 2 *a)* the amount of space that can be filled; room for holding; content or volume [a tank with a *capacity* of 21 gallons] *b)* the point at which no more can be contained [filled to *capacity*] 3 the power of receiving and holding knowledge, impressions, etc.; mental ability 4 the ability or qualifications (*for*, or *to* do, something); aptitude 5 maximum output or producing ability [operating at *capacity*] 6 the quality of being adapted (*for* something) or susceptible (*of* something); capability; potentiality 7 a condition of being qualified or authorized; position, function, status, etc. [acting in the *capacity* of an advisor] 8 *Elec.* CAPACITANCE 9 *Law* legal authority or competence —*SYN.* FUNCTION

cap and bells a FOOL'S CAP with little bells on it

cap and gown traditional academic garb featuring a MORTARBOARD (sense 2) and a long robe, worn at some ceremonies, as commencement, and often used to symbolize the academic life

cap and trade a system for reducing atmospheric pollution from carbon emissions, in which emission limits are imposed typically by the government upon individual companies: companies that have reduced emissions below their limits may sell the unused portion of their allotment to companies that have exceeded their limits —**cap′-and-trade′** *adj.*

cap-a-pie or **cap-à-pie** (kap′ə pē′) *adv.* [[OFr *de cap a pie* < *cap*, head (< L *caput*) + *pié*, foot (< L *pes*)]] from head to foot; entirely

ca·par·i·son (kə par′i sən, -zən) *n.* [[Fr *caparaçon* < OProv *caparasso*, large hooded cloak < *capa*: see fol.]] 1 an ornamented covering for a horse; trappings 2 clothing, equipment, and ornaments; outfit —*vt.* 1 to cover (a horse) with trappings 2 to adorn with rich clothing; deck out

cape¹ (kāp) *n.* [[Fr < OProv *capa* < LL *cappa*, cape, hooded cloak]] a sleeveless outer garment hanging over the back and shoulders and often fastening at the neck

cape² (kāp) *n.* [[ME & OFr < ML *caput*, headland < L, HEAD]] a piece of land projecting into a body of water; promontory; headland: for *Cape Cod, Cape Charles, Cape Hatteras*, etc., see COD, CHARLES³, HATTERAS, etc. —**the Cape** 1 Cape of Good Hope 2 Cape of Good Hope Province 3 Cape Cod

Cape Breton Island [[prob. after *Canbreton*, coastal town in France]] island constituting the NE part of Nova Scotia, Canada: 3,981 sq mi (10,311 sq km)

Cape buffalo [[after the *Cape* of GOOD HOPE]] a large, black, nearly hairless, very fierce buffalo (*Syncerus caffer*) of South Africa, with horns joined at the bases to form a helmetlike structure

☆**Cape Cod (cottage)** [[after *Cape* COD]] a rectangular house one or one-and-one-half stories high, with a gable roof

Cape Colony *former name for* CAPE PROVINCE

Cape Coral [[< ?]] city in SW Fla.

Ča·pek (chä′pek′), **Ka·rel** (kär′əl) 1890-1938; Czech playwright and novelist

cape·let (kāp′lit) ***n.*** a very short cape

cap·e·lin (kap′ə lin′) ***n., pl.*** **-lin′** or **-lins′** ⟦CdnFr < Fr *capelan*, codfish: jocular use of OProv *capelan*, chaplain⟧ a small, slender smelt fish (*Mallotus villosus*) of northern seas, used as food and esp. as bait

Ca·pel·la (kə pel′ə) ***n.*** ⟦L, dim. of *capra*, she-goat, fem. of *caper* (see CAPRIOLE): so named because it marks the goat held by AURIGA in ancient diagrams of the constellation⟧ a giant, yellow, binary, variable star, the brightest star in the constellation Auriga: magnitude, 0.08

ca·pel·li·ni (kä′pə lē′nē, kap′ə-) ***n.*** ANGEL-HAIR PASTA

Cape Province former province of South Africa: in full **Cape of Good Hope Province**

ca·per[1] (kā′pər) ***vi.*** ⟦prob. < CAPRIOLE⟧ to skip or jump about in a playful manner; frisk; gambol —***n.*** **1** a playful jump or leap **2** a wild, foolish action or prank ☆**3** [Slang] a criminal plan or act, esp. a robbery —**cut a caper** or **cut capers** to caper

ca·per[2] (kā′pər) ***n.*** ⟦ME *capar, capres* < L *capparis* < Gr *kapparis*⟧ **1** *a)* any of a genus (*Capparis*) of trees and shrubs of the caper family, esp. a prickly, trailing Mediterranean bush (*C. spinosa*) whose tiny, green flower buds are pickled and used to flavor sauces, etc. *b)* BEAN CAPER **2** any of these buds —***adj.*** designating a family (Capparaceae) of dicotyledonous plants (order Capparales), including the bee plant and cleome

cap·er·cail·lie (kap′ər kāl′yē) ***n.*** ⟦< Gael *capull coille*, lit., horse of the woods < *capull*, horse (< L *caballus*: see CAVALIER) + *coille*, forest⟧ the largest species of European grouse (*Tetrao urogallus*): also **cap′er·cail′zie** (-yē, -zē)

Ca·per·na·um (kə pur′nē əm) city in ancient Palestine, on the Sea of Galilee: cf. Matt. 4:12-13; John 2:12

cape·skin (kāp′skin′) ***n.*** ⟦orig. made from the skin of goats from the *Cape* of Good Hope⟧ fine leather, made from sheepskin, used esp. for gloves

Ca·pet (kā′pit, kap′it; *Fr* kȧ pe′), **Hugh** A.D. 938?-996; king of France (987-996)

Ca·pe·tian (kə pē′shən) ***adj.*** designating or of the French dynasty (A.D. 987-1328) founded by Hugh Capet —***n.*** a member of the Capetian dynasty

Cape Town legislative capital of South Africa: seaport & capital of Western Cape province

Cape Verde country on a group of islands in the Atlantic, *c.* 300 mi (483 km) west of Cape VERDE: the islands were under Portuguese control from 1587 until the granting of independence, 1975: 1,557 sq mi (4,033 sq km); cap. Praia

Cape York Peninsula large peninsula in NE Australia, part of Queensland, between the Gulf of Carpentaria & the Coral Sea

cap·ful (kap′fool′) ***n., pl.*** **-fuls′** as much as the cap of the bottle can hold

caph (käf) ***n.*** KAF

Cap Hai·ti·en (kap′ hāt′ē en′, -hā′sē-; -hā′shən) seaport on the N coast of Haiti: Fr. name **Cap-Ha·ï·ti·en** (kȧ pȧ ē tyan′, -syan′)

ca·pi·as (kā′pē əs, kap′ē-) ***n.*** ⟦ME < ML < L, 2d pers. sing., pres. subj., of *capere*, to take⟧ *Law* a writ issued by a court directing an officer to arrest the person named

cap·il·la·ceous (kap′ə lā′shəs) ***adj.*** ⟦L *capillaceus*, hairlike < *capillus*, hair + *-aceus*, -ACEOUS⟧ **1** having hairlike filaments **2** like a hair or thread

cap·il·lar·i·ty (kap′ə ler′i tē) ***n.*** ⟦Fr *capillarité* < L *capillaris*: see fol.⟧ **1** the state of being capillary **2** the property of exerting or having capillary attraction **3** CAPILLARY ATTRACTION

cap·il·lar·y (kap′ə ler′ē; *Brit* kə pil′ə rē) ***adj.*** ⟦L *capillaris* < *capillus*, hair⟧ **1** of or like a hair, esp. in being very slender **2** having a very small bore **3** in or of capillaries —***n., pl.*** **-lar′ies** **1** a tube with a very small bore: also **capillary tube** **2** any of the tiny blood vessels normally connecting the smallest arteries (*arterioles*) with the smallest veins (*venules*)

capillary attraction a force that is the resultant of adhesion, cohesion, and surface tension in liquids which are in contact with solids, as in a capillary tube: when the cohesive force is greater, the surface of the liquid tends to rise in the tube, as with mercury; when the adhesive force is greater, the surface tends to be depressed, as with water: also **capillary action**

cap·i·tal[1] (kap′ət ′l) ***adj.*** ⟦ME & OFr < L *capitalis*, of the head < *caput*, HEAD⟧ **1** punishable by or involving execution (originally by decapitation) [a *capital* offense] **2** most important or most serious; principal; chief [a *capital* virtue] **3** of most political importance, as being the seat of government [a *capital* city] **4** of or having to do with capital, or wealth **5** first-rate; excellent [a *capital* idea] See also CAPITAL LETTER —***n.*** **1** CAPITAL LETTER **2** a city or town that is the official seat of government of a state, nation, etc. **3** a city where a certain industry, activity, etc. is centered [the rubber *capital*] **4** wealth (money or property) owned or used in business by a person, corporation, etc. **5** an accumulated stock of such wealth or its value **6** wealth, in whatever form, used or capable of being used to produce more wealth **7** any source of benefit or assistance **8** [*often* **C-**] capitalists collectively: distinguished from LABOR **9** *Accounting a)* the net worth of a business; amount by which the assets exceed the liabilities *b)* the face value of all the stock issued or authorized by a corporation —**SYN.** CHIEF —**make capital of** to make the most of; exploit

cap·i·tal[2] (kap′ət ′l) ***n.*** ⟦ME < OFr *chapitel* < L *capitellum*, dim. of *caput*, HEAD⟧ the top part of a column or pilaster

capital account **1** an account of the total capital invested in fixed assets by the owners of a business, including real estate, machinery, etc., but excluding current or operating expenses **2** *Accounting* the summed difference between the assets and liabilities of a business on any given date

capital assets any assets, tangible or intangible, that are held for long-term investment

capital expenditure money spent for replacing and improving business facilities, not for operating expenses

☆**capital gain** a profit realized on the sale of a capital asset, as a house, a stock, etc.: *usually used in pl.*

capital goods commodities for use in production, as raw materials, machinery, buildings, etc.; producer goods as distinguished from consumer goods

cap·i·tal-in·ten·sive (-in ten′siv) ***adj.*** requiring a large investment in capital goods and a relatively small labor force [a *capital-intensive* industry or plant]

cap·i·tal·ism (kap′ət ′l iz′əm) ***n.*** **1** an economic system in which all or most of the means of production and distribution, as land, factories, communications, and transportation systems, are privately owned and operated in a relatively competitive environment through the investment of capital to produce profits: it has been characterized by a tendency toward the concentration of wealth, the growth of large corporations, etc. that has led to economic inequality, which has been dealt with usually by increased government action and control **2** the principles, methods, interests, power, influence, etc. of capitalists, especially of those with large holdings

cap·i·tal·ist (-ist) ***n.*** **1** a person who has capital; owner of wealth used in business **2** an upholder of capitalism **3** loosely, a wealthy person —***adj.*** capitalistic

☆**cap·i·tal·is·tic** (kap′ət ′l is′tik) ***adj.*** **1** of or characteristic of capitalists or capitalism **2** upholding, preferring, or practicing capitalism —**cap′i·tal·is′ti·cal·ly** ***adv.***

cap·i·tal·i·za·tion (-ət ′l ə zā′shən) ***n.*** **1** *a)* the act or process of converting something into capital *b)* the amount or sum resulting from this **2** the total capital funds of a corporation, represented by stocks, bonds, undivided profit, surplus, etc. **3** the total par or stated value of the stocks and bonds outstanding of a corporation **4** *a)* the total invested in a business by the owner or owners *b)* the total corporate liability ☆**5** the act or system of using capital letters in writing and printing

cap·i·tal·ize (kap′ət ′l īz′) ***vt.*** **-ized′**, **-iz′ing** **1** to use as capital; convert into capital **2** to calculate the present value of (a periodical payment, annuity, income, etc.); convert (an income, etc.) into one payment or sum equivalent to the computed present value **3** to establish the capital stock of (a business firm) at a certain figure **4** to convert (floating debt) into stock or shares ☆**5** to supply capital to or for (an enterprise) ☆**6** to print or write (a word or words) in capital letters ☆**7** to begin (a word) with a capital letter **8** *Accounting* to set up (expenditures) as assets —**capitalize on something** to use something to one's own advantage or profit

capital letter the form of an alphabetical letter used to begin a sentence or proper name (Ex.: A, B, C, etc. are capital letters; a, b, c, etc. are small letters)

capital levy a tax on accumulated capital, or wealth, esp. a one-time tax levied to retire the public debt

cap·i·tal·ly (kap′ət ′l ē) ***adv.*** in an excellent or admirable manner; very well

capital punishment the penalty of death for a crime

capital ship [Historical] an armored surface vessel of war, other than an aircraft carrier, carrying guns of a caliber greater than eight inches

capital stock **1** the capital of a corporation, divided into negotiable shares **2** the total par or stated value of the authorized and issued shares of stock

capital surplus **1** any surplus of a business firm not derived from direct earnings or profits **2** the excess of the amount of money received by a corporation for a stock issue over the stock's par or stated value

cap·i·tate (kap′i tāt′) ***adj.*** ⟦L *capitatus*, having a head < *caput*, HEAD⟧ **1** enlarged at the head or tip **2** head-shaped, as some flowers

cap·i·tat·ed (kap′i tāt′əd) ***adj.*** ⟦back-form. < fol.⟧ designating or of a healthcare plan that pays providers of medical services a fixed prepayment for each person enrolled, rather than reimbursing fees for actual services rendered

cap·i·ta·tion (kap′i tā′shən) ***n.*** ⟦LL *capitatio* < L *caput*, HEAD⟧ **1** a tax or fee of so much per head; payment per capita: see also POLL TAX **2** *a)* the practice of prepaying doctors, etc. in a capitated healthcare plan *b)* the amount of the prepayment in such a plan

Cap·i·tol[1] (kap′ət ′l) ***n.*** ⟦ME & OFr *capitolie* < L *Capitolium*, temple of Jupiter in Rome; < ? (but possibly related to *caput*, HEAD)⟧ **1** the temple of Jupiter on the Capitoline Hill in ancient Rome ☆**2** the building in which the U.S. Congress meets in Washington, D.C. ☆**3** [*usually* **c-**] the building in which a state legislature meets

Cap·i·tol[2] (kap′ət ′l) CAPITOLINE[2]

Capitol Hill the hill in Washington, D.C. on which stands the Capitol building: often used fig. of the legislative branch of the U.S. government

Cap·i·to·line[1] (kap′ət ′l īn′, -ēn′) ***adj.*** **1** of or having to do with the Capitoline Hill **2** of the temple of Jupiter which stood there

Cap·i·to·line[2] (kap′ət ′l īn′, -ēn′) one of the SEVEN HILLS OF ROME

ca·pit·u·lar (kə pich′oo lər, -pich′ə lər) ***adj.*** ⟦ME *capituler* < ML(Ec) *capitularis* < LL(Ec) *capitulum*, section of a book, chapter < L, heading, dim. of *caput*, HEAD⟧ of a chapter, esp. that of a religious order

ca·pit·u·lar·y (-ler′ē) ***n., pl.*** **-lar′ies** ⟦ML *capitularius* < prec.⟧ an ordinance or a collection of ordinances, esp. as made formerly by Frankish kings

ca·pit·u·late (kə pich′oo lāt′, -pich′ə lāt′) ***vi.*** **-lat′ed**, **-lat′ing** ⟦< LL *capitulatus*, pp. of *capitulare*, to draw up in heads or chapters, arrange conditions

< *capitulum*: see CAPITULAR⟧ **1** to give up (*to* an enemy) on prearranged conditions; surrender conditionally **2** to give up; stop resisting —***SYN.*** YIELD

ca·pit·u·la·tion (kə pich′yoo lā′shən, -pich′ə lā′-) ***n.*** ⟦Fr < ML *capitulatio*: see prec.⟧ **1** a statement of the main parts of a subject **2** the act of capitulating; conditional surrender **3** a document containing terms of surrender, articles of concession, etc.; treaty; covenant

ca·pit·u·lum (kə pich′yoo ləm, -pich′ə ləm) ***n., pl.*** **-la** (-lə) ⟦ModL < L, dim. of *caput*, HEAD⟧ **1** *Anat., Zool.* a knoblike part, as at the end of a bone in a joint **2** *Bot.* HEAD (***n.*** *17a*)

Ca·piz shell (kə pēz′) whitish, translucent shell found primarily in the coastal waters of the Philippines, used in making lamp shades, decorative articles, etc.

cap·let (kap′lit) ***n.*** ⟦< trademark *Caplets* for such tablets, prob. < CAP(SULE) + (TAB)LET⟧ a solid, elongated medicine tablet, coated for easy swallowing

cap'n (kap′'n) ***n.*** [Informal or Dial.] *phonetic sp. of* CAPTAIN

ca·po[1] (kä′pō) ***n., pl.*** **-pos** ⟦short for *capotasto* < It, lit., chief key < *capo*, chief, head (< L *caput*, HEAD) + *tasto*, key < *tastare*, to touch < VL: see TASTE⟧ a device clamped across the fingerboard as of a guitar to raise the pitch of the strings uniformly and thereby facilitate playing in a different key

ca·po[2] (kä′pō, kap′ō) ***n., pl.*** **-pos** ⟦< It, lit., head, chief⟧ a chieftain in a criminal organization such as the Mafia

cap·o·ei·ra (kap′ə wā′rə, kä′pə-) ***n.*** ⟦BrazPort⟧ a sport combining rhythmic dance, martial-arts, and acrobatic movements that originated in 16th-cent. Brazil among African slaves who practiced it as a form of self-defense disguised as dance

ca·pon (kā′pän′, -pən) ***n.*** ⟦ME *capoun* < OE *capun* & OFr *chapon* < L *capo* < IE base *(*s*)*kep-*, to cut > SHAFT⟧ a castrated rooster, esp. one fattened for eating —**ca′pon·ize′** (-pə nīz′) ***vt.*** **-ized′**, **-iz′ing**

ca·po·na·ta (kä′pə nät′ə) ***n.*** ⟦It < dial. (Sicilian) name for the dish⟧ a relish made of chopped eggplant, olives, onions, celery, and herbs in olive oil, usually served as an antipasto

Ca·pone (kə pōn′), **Al(phonse)** 1899-1947; U.S. gangster

cap·o·ral[1] (kap′ə rəl, kap′ə ral′) ***n.*** ⟦Fr < *tabac du caporal*, lit., corporal's tobacco (a better grade than *tabac du soldat*, soldier's tobacco) < It *caporale*, CORPORAL[1]⟧ a kind of tobacco

☆**cap·o·ral**[2] (kap′ə ral′, kä′pō räl′) ***n.*** ⟦AmSp < Sp, foreman < It *caporale*, leader, CORPORAL[1]⟧ [Southwest] the boss or an assistant boss of a ranch

Cap·o·ret·to (kap′ə ret′ō) Italian village (now in Slovenia): scene of a battle of WWI in which the Italian army was defeated by Austro-German forces (1917): Slovenian name KOBARID

ca·pote (kə pōt′) ***n.*** ⟦Fr, dim. of *cape*, CAPE[1]⟧ a long cloak, usually with a hood

Ca·po·te (kə pōt′ē), **Truman** (born *Truman Streckfus Persons*) 1924-84; U.S. writer

Cap·pa·do·cia (kap′ə dō′shē ə, -shə) ancient kingdom, later a Roman province, in E Asia Minor: fl. 3d cent. B.C.–1st cent. A.D.

cap·pel·let·ti (kä′pə let′ē, kap′ə-) ***n.*** ⟦It, pl. of *cappelletto*, dim. of *cappello*, cap⟧ pasta in the form of dumplings filled with meat or cheese, usually served with a sauce or in broth

cap·per (kap′ər) ***n.*** **1** a person or device that caps something or makes caps **2** [Informal] something that follows and is better than an earlier achievement, condition, etc.

cap·puc·ci·no (kä′pə chē′nō, kap′ə-) ***n.*** ⟦It, lit., CAPUCHIN (in allusion to the brown habit worn by the friars)⟧ espresso coffee mixed with steamed milk and sometimes sprinkled with cinnamon or powdered chocolate

Cap·ra (kap′rə), **Frank** (born *Francesco Rosario Capra*) 1897-1991; U.S. film director, born in Italy

cap·re·o·late (kap′rē ə lāt′, kə prē′ə lit) ***adj.*** ⟦< L *capreolus*, tendril, wild goat (see CAPRIOLE: fig. meaning in L from hornlike appearance of tendrils) + -ATE[1]⟧ *Bot.* having tendrils

Ca·pri (kä prē′, kə-; kä′prē′) island near the entrance to the Bay of Naples: 4 sq mi (10.4 sq km)

cap·ric acid (kap′rik) ⟦< L *caper*, goat (see CAPRIOLE) + -IC: named from its goatlike smell⟧ a crystalline fatty acid, $CH_3(CH_2)_8COOH$, occurring as a glyceride in natural fats and oils, used in making artificial fruit flavors, perfumes, etc.

ca·pric·cio (kə prē′chō′) ***n., pl.*** **-cios′** or **-ci** (-chē) ⟦It: see fol.⟧ **1** a prank; whim; caprice **2** a musical composition in various forms, usually lively and whimsical in spirit

ca·price (kə prēs′) ***n.*** ⟦Fr < It *capriccio*, a shivering, whim < *capo* (< L *caput*, HEAD) + *riccio*, curl, frizzled, lit., hedgehog (< L *ericius*: see URCHIN); hence, orig., head with bristling hair, horripilation; meaning infl. by assoc. with It *capriola* (see CAPRIOLE) & *capra* < L *capra*, she-goat⟧ **1** a sudden, impulsive change in the way one thinks or acts; freakish notion; whim **2** a capricious quality or nature **3** *Music* a capriccio

SYN.—**caprice** refers to a sudden, impulsive, apparently unmotivated turn of mind or emotion [*discharged at the caprice of a foreman*]; **whim** and **whimsy** both refer to an idle, quaint, or curious notion, but **whim** more often suggests willfulness and **whimsy** fancifulness [*pursuing a whim, he wrote a poem full of whimsy*]; **vagary** suggests a highly unusual or extravagant notion [*the vagaries in fashion in women's clothes*]; **crotchet** implies great eccentricity and connotes stubbornness in opposition to prevailing thought, usually on some insignificant point [*his crotchets concerning diet*]

ca·pri·cious (kə prish′əs, -prē′shəs) ***adj.*** ⟦Fr *capricieux* < It *capriccioso*: see prec.⟧ **1** subject to caprices; tending to change abruptly and without apparent reason; erratic; flighty **2** [Obs.] showing wit or fancifulness —***SYN.*** INCONSTANT —**ca·pri′cious·ly** ***adv.*** —**ca·pri′cious·ness** ***n.***

Cap·ri·corn (kap′ri kôrn′) ***n.*** ⟦ME < OFr < L *capricornus* < *caper*, goat (see CAPRIOLE) + *cornu*, HORN⟧ **1** Capricornus **2** the tenth sign of the zodiac, entered by the sun about Dec. 22: also called *the Goat* **3** a person born under this sign

Cap·ri·cor·nus (kap′ri kôr′nəs) ***n.*** ⟦L: see prec.⟧ a S constellation between Aquarius and Sagittarius; the Goat

cap·ri·fi·ca·tion (kap′rə fi kā′shən) ***n.*** ⟦L *caprificatio*, fertilization of figs by the pollination of the gall wasp < *caprificare*, to fertilize figs (by this process) < *caprificus*: see fol.⟧ the pollination of certain cultivated figs through the transfer to them of pollen from the caprifig by a fig wasp

cap·ri·fig (kap′rə fig′) ***n.*** ⟦< L *caprificus*, wild fig < *caper* (see fol.) + *ficus*, fig⟧ the wild fig (*Ficus carica* var. *sylvestris*) growing mainly in S Europe and the Near East and used in caprification

cap·ri·ole (kap′rē ōl′) ***n.*** ⟦Fr < It *capriola* < *capriolare*, to leap like a goat < *capriolo*, roe deer < L *capreolus*, wild goat < *caper* (gen. *capri*), he-goat < IE **kapro-* > ON *hafr*, OIr *gabor*⟧ **1** a caper; leap **2** a type of competitive jump in which a trained horse leaps upward but not forward and kicks its hind legs so that they are nearly parallel to the ground —***vi.*** **-oled′**, **-ol′ing** to make a capriole

☆**ca·pri pants** (ka prē′) ⟦after CAPRI⟧ [*often* **C- p-**] light-weight women's pants ending just below the knee or calf: also **ca·pris′** ***pl.n.***

Ca·pri·vi Strip (kə prē′vē) narrow strip of land, *c.* 50 mi (80 km) wide, of NE Namibia, extending eastward to the Zambezi River: *c.* 300 mi (483 km) long

cap rock a relatively impervious rock layer immediately overlying a deposit of oil, gas, salt, etc.

ca·pro·ic acid (kə prō′ik) ⟦*capro-* (for L *caper*, goat: see CAPRIOLE) + -IC: so named from its smell⟧ a colorless, liquid fatty acid, $CH_3(CH_2)_4COOH$, found in butter and other animal fats and used in the manufacture of esters

cap·ro·lac·tam (kap′rō lak′tam′) ***n.*** a white, petroleum-derived substance, $C_6H_{11}NO$, used as a monomer to make synthetic fibers, plastics, etc.

ca·pryl·ic acid (kə pril′ik) ⟦CAPR(IC ACID) + -YL + -IC⟧ a fatty acid, $(CH_3)(CH_2)_6COOH$, with a rancid taste: used in the synthesis of dyes, drugs, perfumes, etc.

caps *abbrev.* capitals

cap·sa·i·cin (kap sā′ə sin) ***n.*** ⟦altered < *capsicine*, another substance, formerly thought to be the source of the sharp taste of CAPSICUM (***n.*** 1): see -INE[3]⟧ an alkaloid, $C_{18}H_{27}NO_3$, with a burning taste, extracted from capsicum

cap screw a kind of bolt used in a tapped hole, usually without a nut, as for fastening cylinder covers, etc.

Cap·si·an (kap′sē ən) ***adj.*** ⟦Fr *capsien*, after L *Capsa*, ancient name of *Gafsa*, city in central Tunisia, near which artifacts were found⟧ designating or of a Mesolithic culture of N Africa characterized by small hand tools

cap·si·cum (kap′si kəm) ***n.*** ⟦ModL < L *capsa*, a box (see CASE[2]), from the shape of the seedpods⟧ **1** *a)* the variously shaped, fleshy, podlike fruit of any of certain cultivated plants (genus *Capsicum*) of the nightshade family, eaten as a vegetable or used as flavoring, and ranging in taste from sweet, as the green or red bell pepper, to hot, as the chili, cayenne, or Tabasco pepper *b)* a plant bearing this fruit **2** any of various preparations derived from these fruits, used as a condiment or, in medicine, as a gastric stimulant

cap·sid (kap′sid) ***n.*** ⟦< Fr *capside* < L *capsa*, a box (see CASE[2]) + Fr *-ide*, -ID⟧ the outer coat of a virus, usually composed of layers of various proteins

cap·size (kap′sīz′, kap sīz′) ***vt., vi.*** **-sized′**, **-siz′ing** ⟦18th-c. naut. slang; ? altered (infl. by dial. *cap*, to overtop + *side*) < Sp *cabezar*, lit., to sink by the head (< *cabo, cabeza*, head)⟧ to overturn or upset: said esp. of a boat —***SYN.*** UPSET

cap sleeve a very short sleeve on a woman's dress, blouse, etc., fashioned by lengthening only the outer shoulder area of the garment to form a caplike extension

cap·so·mere (kap′sə mir′) ***n.*** ⟦Fr *capsomère* < *capside*, CAPSID + *-o-*, -O- + *-mère* < Gr *meros*, a part: see MERIT⟧ a protein that combines with other similar proteins to form the capsid of a virus: sometimes **cap′so·mer** (-mər)

cap·stan (kap′stən) ***n.*** ⟦ME < OProv *cabestan* < ? L *capistrum*, halter, muzzle < *capere*, to take: see HAVE⟧ **1** an apparatus, mainly on ships, around which cables or hawsers are wound for hoisting anchors, lifting weights, etc.: it consists of an upright, spool-shaped cylinder that is turned on an inner shafting by machinery or by hand **2** a rotating spindle in a tape recorder mechanism that regulates the speed at which the tape is driven past the head

capstan bar any of the poles inserted in a capstan and used as levers in turning it by hand

cap·stone (kap′stōn′) ***n.*** **1** *a)* the uppermost stone of a structure *b)* any of the stones in a coping **2** the highest point, as of achievement

cap·su·lar (kap′sə lər, -syoo-) ***adj.*** **1** having the nature of a capsule **2** of or in a capsule

cap·su·late (-lāt′, -lit) ***adj.*** contained in or formed into a capsule: also **cap′su·lat′ed**

cap·sule (kap′səl, -syool) ***n.*** ⟦Fr < L *capsula*, dim. of *capsa*, box: see CASE[2]⟧ **1** [Obs.] a small case or sheath ☆**2** *a)* a small, soluble gelatin container for encasing a dose of medicine, etc. *b)* a dose of medicine, vitamin supplement, etc. so encased ☆**3** *a)* an ejectable airplane cockpit *b)* a detachable, closed compartment designed to hold and protect people, instruments, etc. in a rocket (see SPACECRAFT) (in full **space capsule**) 4 *Anat.* *a)* any sac or membrane enclosing an organ or part *b)* either of two layers of cerebral white matter 5 a case or pod, containing seeds, spores, or carpels; esp., a dry dehiscent fruit 6 *Chem. former name for* any shallow dish or tray for evaporating liquids —*adj.* ☆in a concise or condensed form [*a capsule* biography] —*vt.* **-suled**, **-sul·ing** to condense

cap·sul·ize (-īz′) *vt.* **-ized′**, **-iz′ing** ☆1 to enclose in a capsule 2 to express in a concise form; condense

Capt *abbrev.* Captain

cap·tain (kap′tən) *n.* ⟦ME *capitain* < OFr *capitaine* < LL *capitaneus*, chief < L *caput*, HEAD⟧ 1 *a)* a chief or leader [*captains* of industry] *b)* an important military leader 2 the head of a group or division; specif., *a) U.S. Mil.* an officer ranking above a first lieutenant and below a major *b) U.S. Navy* an officer ranking above a commander and below a rear admiral *c)* the person in command of a ship *d)* the pilot of an airplane *e)* the spokesman for a team in certain sports ☆*f)* a precinct commander in a police or fire department ☆*g)* a district leader of a political party ☆*h)* HEADWAITER ☆*i)* BELL CAPTAIN —*vt.* to be captain of; lead —**cap′tain·cy** (-sē) *n., pl.* **-cies** —**cap′tain·ship′** *n.*

captain's chair 1 a hardwood armchair having a low, curved back, formed of a single rail supported by spindles, and a saddle seat 2 a bucket seat with a high back that includes a headrest, as in some vans, light trucks, etc.

captain's walk WIDOW'S WALK

cap·tan (kap′tan′, -tən) *n.* ⟦< MERCAPTAN⟧ a white powder, $C_9H_8Cl_3NO_2S$, used as a fungicide on fruits, flowers, etc.

cap·tion (kap′shən) *n.* ⟦ME *capcioun* < OFr *capcion* < L *captio* < pp. of *capere*, take: see HAVE⟧ 1 [Archaic] seizure 2 *Law* *a)* a part of a legal instrument, such as an indictment, showing where, when, and by what authority it was executed *b)* a heading showing the names of the parties, court, and docket number in a pleading or deposition ☆3 *a)* a heading or title, as of an article *b)* a descriptive title, or legend, as under an illustration 4 *Film, TV* a subtitle —*vt.* to supply a caption for

cap·tious (-shəs) *adj.* ⟦ME *capcious* < L *captiosus* < prec.⟧ 1 made only for the sake of argument or faultfinding [*captious* criticism] 2 fond of catching others in mistakes; quick to find fault; quibbling; carping —**SYN.** CRITICAL —**cap′tious·ly** *adv.* —**cap′tious·ness** *n.*

cap·ti·vate (kap′tə vāt′) *vt.* **-vat′ed**, **-vat′ing** ⟦< LL(Ec) *captivatus*, pp. of *captivare*, to take captive < L *captivus*: see fol.⟧ 1 [Obs.] to take or hold captive 2 to capture the attention or affection of, as by beauty, excellence, etc.; fascinate; charm —**SYN.** ATTRACT —**cap′ti·vat′ing·ly** *adv.* —**cap′ti·va′tion** *n.* —**cap′ti·va′tor** *n.*

cap·tive (kap′tiv) *n.* ⟦L *captivus* < *captus*, pp. of *capere*, to take: see HAVE⟧ 1 a person caught and held prisoner, as in war 2 a person who is captivated, as by beauty or love —*adj.* 1 *a)* taken prisoner or held by force *b)* not able to act independently [*a captive* nation] ☆*c)* obliged or forced to listen, whether wanting to or not [*a captive* audience] 2 captivated 3 of captivity

cap·tiv·i·ty (kap tiv′i tē) *n., pl.* **-ties** the condition or time of being captive; imprisonment; bondage

cap·to·pril (kap′tō pril′, -tə-) *n.* a white, crystalline oral drug, $C_9H_{15}NO_3S$, that inhibits angiotensin, used to lower high blood pressure and treat heart failure

cap·tor (kap′tər) *n.* ⟦L⟧ a person who captures (someone or something) or holds captive

cap·ture (-chər) *n.* ⟦Fr < L *captura* < *captus*: see CAPTIVE⟧ 1 a taking or being taken by force, surprise, or skill, as enemy troops, an opponent's piece in chess, etc. 2 that which is thus taken or seized; specif., a prize or booty in war 3 the absorption of a particle by an atomic nucleus; esp., the absorption of a neutron or an orbital electron that often results in the immediate emission of radiation —*vt.* **-tured**, **-tur·ing** 1 to take or seize by force, surprise, or skill 2 to represent (something transient, immaterial, etc.) in more or less permanent form [to *capture* her charm on canvas] 3 to effect the capture of (a subatomic particle) 4 to record in the form of stored data [to *capture* a secretarial staff's keystrokes; the security camera *captured* images of the robbery] —**SYN.** CATCH

Cap·u·a (kap′yoo͞ ə) town in S Italy, near Naples: ancient city of Capua (destroyed A.D. 841) was on a nearby site

ca·puche (kə po͞och′, -po͞osh′) *n.* ⟦Fr < It *cappuccio*, cowl < ML *caputium* < LL *cappa*, CAPE[1]⟧ a long, pointed hood, as that worn by the Capuchins

Cap·u·chin (kap′yoo͞ shin′, -chin′; kə pyoo͞′-) *n.* ⟦Fr, monk who wears a cowl < It *cappuccino*, dim. of prec.⟧ 1 a member of a branch (**Friars Minor Capuchin**) of the Franciscan order that adheres strictly to the original rule 2 [**c-**] a woman's cloak with a hood 3 [**c-**] any of a genus (*Cebus*) of New World monkeys with a nearly bare face and a hoodlike crown of hair

Cap·u·let (kap′yə lit, -let′) *n.* the family name of Juliet in Shakespeare's *Romeo and Juliet*

cap·y·bar·a (kap′i bar′ə, -bä′rə) *n.* ⟦Port *capibara* < Tupí *kapigwara*, lit., one who eats grass⟧ any of a family (Hydrochoeridae) of tailless, partially web-footed, South American rodents found in and around lakes and streams: the largest extant rodent, reaching a length of over 1.2 m (*c.* 4 ft)

car[1] (kär) *n.* ⟦ME & NormFr *carre* < L *carrum*, *carrus*, orig., two-wheeled Celtic war chariot < Gaul *carros* (OIr *carr*) < IE **k̑rsos* < base **kers-*, to run > L *currere*, to run, *cursus*, COURSE⟧ 1 any vehicle on wheels 2 [Old Poet.] a chariot ☆3 a vehicle that moves on rails, as a streetcar 4 an automobile ☆5 ELEVATOR (*n.* 2) 6 the part of a balloon or airship for carrying people and equipment

car[2] *abbrev.* carat(s)

ca·ra·ba·o (kä′rə bä′ō) *n., pl.* **-ba′os** or **-ba′o** ⟦Sp < Malay *karbau*⟧ WATER BUFFALO

car·a·bid (kar′ə bid′) *n.* ⟦< ModL < Gr *karabos*, a horned beetle⟧ GROUND BEETLE

car·a·bi·neer or **car·a·bi·nier** (kar′ə bə nir′) *n.* ⟦Fr *carabinier* < *carabine*, CARBINE⟧ a soldier armed with a carbine

car·a·bi·ner (kar′ə bē′nər) *n.* 1 in mountain climbing, an oval metal ring with a snap link used to fasten a rope to the piton 2 a similar coupling device, as for keychains, luggage tags, etc.

ca·ra·bi·nie·re (kä′rä bē nye′re) *n., pl.* **-nie′ri** (-nye′rē) ⟦It < Fr *carabinier*: see CARABINEER⟧ a member of the Italian police

car·a·cal (kar′ə kal′) *n.* ⟦Fr < Sp < Turk *qarah-qulaq* < *qara*, black + *qulaq*, ear⟧ 1 a reddish-brown wildcat (*Caracal caracal*) of SW Asia and E Africa, with black-tipped ears 2 its fur

Car·a·cal·la (kar′ə kal′ə) (born *Marcus Aurelius Antoninus*) A.D. 188-217; Rom. emperor (211-217)

ca·ra·ca·ra (kä′rə kä′rə) *n.* ⟦Sp < Tupí, of echoic orig.⟧ any of various large New World birds of prey (family Falconidae) that feed mostly on carrion

Ca·ra·cas (kə räk′əs, -rak′-; *Sp* kä rä′käs) capital of Venezuela, in the NC part

car·a·cole (kar′ə kōl′) *n.* ⟦Fr < Walloon *caracoll*, lit., snail shell < Sp *caracol* < Catalan *caragol* < Fr *escargot*, snail⟧ a half turn to the right or left made by a horse with a rider —*vi.* **-coled′**, **-col′ing** ⟦Fr *caracoler* < the n.⟧ to make a caracole or caracoles

car·a·cul (kar′ə kul′, -kəl) *n. alt. sp. of* KARAKUL (esp. sense 2)

ca·rafe (kə raf′, -räf′) *n.* ⟦Fr < It *caraffa*; prob. < Ar *gharrâf*, drinking cup < *gharafa*, to draw water⟧ a glass bottle for serving wine, water, or coffee

ca·ra·ga·na (kar′ə gā′nə, -gä′-) *n.* ⟦ModL < Kirghiz *karaghan*, the Siberian pea shrub⟧ any of a genus (*Caragana*) of hardy leguminous shrubs grown for their showy, golden flowers and often as windbreaks in dry climates

car·a·geen (kar′ə gēn′) *n. alt. sp. of* CARRAGEEN

☆**ca·ram·ba** (kä räm′bä; kə räm′bə, -rum′-) *interj.* ⟦AmSp < Sp, euphemism for *carajo*, penis < VL **caraculum*, small arrow⟧ [Chiefly Southwest] used to express surprise, dismay, etc.

car·am·bo·la (kar′əm bō′lə) *n.* ⟦Port, prob. < Marathi *karambal*⟧ 1 a small, tropical shrub or tree (*Averrhoa carambola*, family Oxalidaceae) cultivated for its fruit 2 its glossy, yellow, fleshy, oval fruit with prominent ridges and a star-shaped cross section; star fruit

car·a·mel (kär′məl; kar′ə məl, -mel′) *n.* ⟦Fr < OFr *calamele* < ML *calamella*, var. of *canamella*, sugar cane < L *canna mellis* < *canna* (see CANE) + *mellis*, honey: see MILDEW⟧ 1 burnt sugar, used to color or flavor food or beverages 2 a chewy candy made from a mixture of sugar, milk, butter, etc.

caramel corn a snack consisting of POPCORN (sense 2) covered with caramel

car·a·mel·ize (kär′mə līz′, kar′ə mə-) *vt., vi.* **-ized′**, **-iz′ing** 1 to turn into CARAMEL (sense 1) 2 to brown and sweeten with heat: said of meat, onions, etc.

ca·ran·gid (kə ran′jid′) *n.* ⟦< ModL < Sp *caranga*, horse mackerel, shad⟧ JACK (sense 10*a*) —**ca·ran′goid′** (-raŋ′goid′) *adj.*

car·a·pace (kar′ə pās′) *n.* ⟦Fr < Sp *carapacho*⟧ the horny, protective covering over all or part of the back of certain animals, as the upper shell of the turtle, armadillo, crab, etc.

car·at (kar′ət) *n.* ⟦Fr < It *carato* < Ar *qīrāt*, pod, husk, weight of 4 grains < Gr *keration*, little horn, carob seed, carat, dim. of *keras*, HORN⟧ 1 a unit of weight for precious stones and pearls, equal to 3.0864 grains (200 milligrams): abbrev. *C* 2 KARAT

Ca·ra·vag·gio (kä′rə väj′ō), **Mi·chel·an·ge·lo da** (mē′ke län′je lô dä) (born *Michelangelo Merisi*) 1573-1610; It. painter —**Car′a·vag·gesque′** (-və jesk′) *adj.*

car·a·van (kar′ə van′) *n.* ⟦Fr *caravane* < OFr *carouan* < Pers *kārwān*, caravan⟧ 1 a company of travelers, esp. of merchants or pilgrims traveling together for safety, as through a desert 2 a number of vehicles traveling together 3 a large covered vehicle for passengers, circus animals, gypsies, etc.; van 4 [Brit.] a mobile home or trailer —**car′a·van′er** *n.*

car·a·van·sa·ry (kar′ə van′sə rē) *n., pl.* **-ries** ⟦Fr *caravansérai* < Pers *kārwānsarāī* < *kārwān*, caravan + *sarāī*, palace, mansion, inn⟧ in the Near and Middle East, a kind of inn with a large central court, where caravans stop for the night: also **car′a·van′se·rai′** (-sə rī′, -sə rā′)

car·a·vel (kar′ə vel′) *n.* ⟦MFr < Port *caravela*, dim. of *caravo*, small vessel < LL *carabus*, small wicker boat covered with leather < L, kind of crab < Gr *karabos*⟧ any of several kinds of fast, small sailing ships, esp. one with a narrow, high poop and lateen sails, used by the Spaniards and Portuguese in the 15th and 16th cent.

caravel

car·a·way (kar′ə wā′) *n.* ⟦ME *carawai* < (? via ML *carvi*) OSp *alcarahueya* < Ar *al-karawiyā* < ? Gr *karon*, caraway⟧ 1 a white-flowered biennial herb (*Carum carvi*) of the umbel family, with spicy, strong-smelling seeds 2 the seeds, used as a flavoring for bread, cakes, cheese, etc., and as a carminative

carb (kärb) *n.* [Informal] *short for:* 1 CARBURETOR 2 CARBOHYDRATE

carb- (kärb) *combining form* CARBO-: used before a vowel [*carboxyl*]

car·ba·mate (kär′bə māt′; *also,* kär bam′āt′) ***n.*** a salt or ester of carbamic acid

car·bam·ic acid (kär′bam′ik, -bə mik′; *also,* kär bam′ik) ⟦CARB- + AM(IDO) + -IC⟧ an acid, NH_2COOH, known only by a number of salts and esters including the urethanes

car·ban·i·on (kär ban′ī än′, -ī′ən) ***n.*** ⟦CARB- + ANION⟧ a transient, negatively charged organic ion, as H_3C^-,R_3C^-, that has one more electron than the corresponding free radical

car·ba·ryl (kär′bə ril′) ***n.*** ⟦CARBA(MATE) + ARYL⟧ a white, crystalline, neurotoxic carbamate, $C_{12}H_{11}NO_2$, used as an insecticide, as Sevin, that is highly toxic when first applied but that breaks down quickly and becomes harmless

car·ba·zole (kär′bə zōl′) ***n.*** ⟦CARB- + AZ- + -OLE⟧ a white, crystalline substance, $(C_6H_4)_2NH$, occurring in crude anthracene: it is used in the manufacture of dyes, explosives, insecticides, etc.

car·bide (kär′bīd′) ***n.*** ⟦CARB- + -IDE⟧ a solid compound of an element, usually a metal, with carbon; esp., calcium carbide

car·bine (kär′bīn′, -bēn′) ***n.*** ⟦Fr *carabine* < *carabin,* mounted rifleman < OFr *escarrabin,* corpse bearer during the plague (lit., prob. "carrion beetle," used as epithet for archers from Flanders) < *scarabée:* see SCARAB⟧ **1** a rifle with a short barrel, orig. for use by cavalry ☆**2** a light, semiautomatic or automatic rifle of relatively limited range

car·bi·neer (kär′bə nir′) ***n.*** CARABINEER

car·bi·nol (kär′bə nôl′, -nōl′) ***n.*** ⟦Ger < *carbin* (name used by A. Kolbe, 19th-c. Ger chemist, for the methyl radical) + -OL[1]⟧ **1** METHANOL **2** any alcohol bearing a homologous relation to methanol, as diethyl carbinol

car·bo (kär′bō) ***n.,*** *pl.* **-bos** or **-boes** [Informal] *short for* CARBOHYDRATE

car·bo- (kär′bō, -bə) *combining form* carbon [*carbohydrate*]

car·bo·cy·clic (kär′bō sīk′lik) ***adj.*** ⟦prec. + CYCLIC⟧ designating an organic ring compound in which all the members of the ring are carbon atoms, as benzene or naphthalene: see also ALIPHATIC

car·bo·hy·drate (kär′bō hī′drāt, -bə-) ***n.*** ⟦CARBO- + HYDRATE⟧ any of certain organic compounds, including the sugars, starches, and celluloses, which usually have the general formula $C_x(H_2O)_y$: carbohydrates are subdivided into monosaccharides, disaccharides, etc., and form an important class of foods in animal nutrition, supplying energy to the body

car·bo·lat·ed (kär′bə lāt′id) ***adj.*** containing or treated with carbolic acid

car·bol·ic acid (kär bäl′ik) ⟦CARB(O)- + -OL[1] + -IC⟧ *see* PHENOL (sense 1)

car·bo·lize (kar′bə līz′) ***vt.*** **-lized′, -liz′ing** to treat or sterilize with phenol

car bomb an explosive device concealed within a car and detonated as by remote control, esp. as a weapon of terrorism or means of assassination

car·bon (kär′bən) ***n.*** ⟦Fr *carbone* < L *carbo* (gen. *carbonis*), coal < IE base **ker-,* to burn > HEARTH⟧ **1** a nonmetallic chemical element found in many inorganic compounds and all organic compounds: diamond and graphite are pure carbon; carbon is the basic element in coal, coke, charcoal, soot, etc.: symbol, C; at. no. 6: a radioactive isotope (**carbon-14**) is used as a tracer in chemical and biochemical research, and, because of its half-life of 5,730 years and its presence in all carbon-containing matter, it is a means of dating archaeological specimens, fossils, etc.: see the periodic table of elements in the Reference Supplement **2** a sheet of carbon paper **3** CARBON COPY **4** a stick of carbon used in an arc lamp **5** a carbon plate or rod used in a battery —***adj.*** of, like, or treated with carbon

car·bo·na·ceous (kär′bə nā′shəs) ***adj.*** of, consisting of, or containing carbon

car·bo·na·do (kär′bə nā′dō, -nä′-) ***n.,*** *pl.* **-does** or **-dos** ⟦Sp *carbonada* < *carbón,* charcoal < L *carbo:* see CARBON⟧ **1** [Archaic] a piece of meat, often fish or fowl, scored and broiled **2** ⟦Port, carbonized⟧ a type of tough industrial diamond consisting of a dark, opaque mass of diamond particles, used for drilling and as a semiconductor —***vt.*** **-doed, -do·ing** [Archaic] **1** to score and broil (meat) **2** to cut gashes in; slash; hack

car·bo·na·ra (kär′bō nä′rə) ***adj.*** ⟦It < *alla carbonara,* in the manner of a charcoal maker (dial. form)⟧ designating pasta that is mixed, just after boiling, with a sauce of sautéed bacon, Parmesan cheese, pepper, and beaten eggs, formed as the eggs are cooked slightly by the hot pasta [fettuccine *carbonara*]: in full **al·la carbonara** (ä′lä)

Car·bo·na·ri (kär′bô nä′rē) ***pl.n.,*** *sing.* **-na′ro** (-rô) ⟦It, pl. of *carbonaro,* charcoal burner (< L *carbonarius* < *carbo:* see CARBON): said to be so named from meeting among the charcoal burners and using their jargon⟧ an Italian revolutionary group organized about 1811 to unify Italy and found a republic

car·bon·ate (kär′bə nit; *also, and for v. always,* -nāt′) ***n.*** ⟦Fr: see CARBON & -ATE[2]⟧ **1** a salt of carbonic acid containing the divalent, negative radical CO_3 **2** an uncharged ester of this acid —***vt.*** **-at′ed, -at′ing 1** [Obs.] to burn to carbon; carbonize **2** to charge with carbon dioxide [*carbonated* drinks] **3** to form into a carbonate

car·bon·a·tion (kär′bə nā′shən) ***n.*** **1** saturation with carbon dioxide, as in the manufacture of soda water: also **car′bon·a·ta′tion** (-bən ə tā′shən) **2** the removal of lime, as in sugar refining, by precipitating it with carbon dioxide

carbon bisulfide CARBON DISULFIDE

carbon black finely divided carbon produced by the incomplete burning of oil or gas: used in making rubber, ink, etc.

carbon copy 1 a copy, as of a letter, made with carbon paper **2** any person or thing very much like another

carbon credit in a CAP-AND-TRADE system, an allotted credit based upon the imposed limit of atmospheric carbon emissions: any unused portion of the credit may be sold

carbon cycle 1 the cycle by which plants through photosynthesis use atmospheric carbon dioxide to produce carbohydrates, which are in turn metabolized by animals to decomposition products that return carbon dioxide to the atmosphere **2** a cyclic series of thermonuclear reactions in the interior of some stars, involving carbon as a catalyst and producing large quantities of energy by the transformation of hydrogen into helium: also called **car′bon-ni′tro·gen cycle**

car·bon-date (kär′bən dāt′) ***vt.*** **-dat′ed, -dat′ing** to establish the age of (carbonaceous material) by means of carbon dating

carbon dating a method of establishing the approximate age of carbonaceous materials, such as fossil remains or archaeological specimens, by measuring the amount of radioactive carbon-14 remaining in them: also **carbon-14 dating**

carbon dioxide a colorless, odorless, incombustible gas, CO_2, somewhat heavier than air, that is a product of respiration and combustion: produced commercially and used widely in fire extinguishers, carbonated beverages, etc.: in photosynthesis, carbon dioxide and water are absorbed by plants, which synthesize certain carbohydrates and release oxygen into the air

carbon disulfide a heavy, volatile, colorless liquid, CS_2, highly flammable and poisonous, used as a solvent, insecticide, etc.

carbon fiber ⟦so named because it is produced by the stretching and heating of textile fibers to produce nearly pure *carbon*⟧ a very strong, lightweight synthetic fiber used in protective clothing, spacecraft components, racing shells, etc.

carbon footprint the amount of atmospheric carbon emissions variously produced in a given period of time, as by a particular industry, business, or household

car·bon-14 (-fôr tēn′) ***n.*** *see* CARBON (***n.*** 1)

car·bon·ic (kär bän′ik) ***adj.*** of, containing, or obtained from carbon or carbon dioxide

carbonic acid a weak, colorless acid, H_2CO_3, formed by the solution of carbon dioxide in water and existing only in solution

car·bon·ic-ac·id gas (kär bän′ik as′id) CARBON DIOXIDE: also written **carbonic acid gas**

car·bon·if·er·ous (kär′bə nif′ər əs) ***adj.*** ⟦CARBON + -I- + -FEROUS⟧ **1** producing or containing carbon or coal **2** [*usually* **C-**] designating or of the fifth geologic period of the Paleozoic Era, subdivided into the Pennsylvanian (**the Upper Carboniferous**) and the Mississippian (**the Lower Carboniferous**) and characterized by warm, moist climate and vast swamps which eventually formed into extensive coal deposits —**the Carboniferous** the Carboniferous Period or its rocks: see the geologic time chart in the Reference Supplement

car·bo·ni·um (kär bō′nē əm) ***n.*** ⟦CARB(O)- + (AMM)ONIUM⟧ a transient, positively charged organic ion, as H_3C^+,R_3^+, that has one less electron than the corresponding free radical

car·bon·ize (kär′bə nīz′) ***vt.*** **-ized′, -iz′ing 1** to change into carbon, as by partial burning **2** to treat, cover, or combine with carbon —***vi.*** to become carbonized —**car′bon·i·za′tion *n.***

carbon monoxide a colorless, odorless, highly poisonous gas, CO, produced by the incomplete combustion of carbonaceous material: it burns with a pale-blue flame

carbon neutral functioning in a way that compensates completely for one's atmospheric carbon emissions, as through CARBON OFFSET

carbon offset 1 the process of, or a system for, compensating for carbon emissions from factories, households, motor vehicles, etc., as through reduction of emissions, CAP AND TRADE, investment in renewable energy, etc. **2** such a reduction, investment, etc. made to compensate for carbon emissions

carbon paper 1 very thin paper coated on one side with a waxy, dark-colored preparation, as of carbon: it is placed between two sheets of paper so that the pressure of typing or writing on the upper sheet makes a copy on the lower **2** paper used in the carbon process

carbon process a photographic printing process that uses paper coated with sensitized, pigmented gelatin that becomes progressively hardened and insoluble the more it is exposed to light

carbon tax a tax on carbon emissions, intended to discourage the use of fossil fuels and encourage investment in renewable energy sources

carbon tetrachloride a nonflammable, colorless, poisonous liquid, CCl_4, used in making refrigerants, as a solvent for fats and oils, etc.

car·bon·yl (kär′bə nil′) ***n.*** ⟦CARBON + -YL⟧ **1** the chemical group CO **2** any of a wide variety of compounds containing this group, esp. certain metal compounds —**car′bon·yl′ic** (-nil′ik) ***adj.***

carbonyl chloride PHOSGENE

☆**Car·bo·run·dum** (kär′bə run′dəm) ⟦CARB(ON) + (C)ORUNDUM⟧ *trademark for* very hard abrasives and refractories, esp. silicon carbide, used in grindstones, powders, etc. —***n.*** [**c-**] such substances

car·box·y·he·mo·glo·bin (kär bäk′sə hē′mə glō′bin, -hem′ə-) ***n.*** a compound formed in the blood when carbon monoxide occupies the positions on the hemoglobin molecule normally taken by oxygen, resulting in cellular oxygen starvation

car·box·yl (kär bäk′səl) ***n.*** ⟦CARB(O)- + OX(YGEN) + -YL⟧ the group COOH, characteristic of organic acids, including fatty acids and amino acids —**car′box·yl′ic** (-sil′ik) ***adj.***

car·box·yl·ase (kär bäk′sə lās′) ***n.*** ⟦prec. + -ASE⟧ an enzyme that is capable of removing carbon dioxide from certain organic acids to produce aldehydes, as in the formation of acetaldehyde from pyruvic acid

car·box·yl·ate (kär bäk′sə lāt′) *n.* a salt or ester of a carboxylic acid —*vt.* **-at′ed, -at′ing** to form a carboxylic acid by introducing a carboxyl group into (a compound) —**car·box′yl·a′tion** *n.*

car·boy (kär′boi′) *n.* ⟦< Pers *qarābah*, large leather milk bottle⟧ a large glass or plastic bottle enclosed for protection in basketwork or in a wooden crate: used esp. as a container for corrosive liquids

car·bun·cle (kär′buŋ′kəl) *n.* ⟦ME < OFr < L *carbunculus*, a little coal, gem < *carbo*: see CARBON⟧ 1 *a)* [Archaic] any of certain deep-red gems *b)* a smooth, convex, deep-red garnet 2 a painful bacterial infection (esp. *Staphylococcus aureus*) deep beneath the skin, having a network of pus-filled boils —**car·bun′cu·lar** (-kyo͞o lər) *adj.*

car·bu·ret (kär′byo͞o rāt′, -ret′; -bə-) *vt.* **-ret′ed** or **-ret′ted, -ret′ing** or **-ret′ting** ⟦CARB(O)- + -URET⟧ 1 to combine chemically with carbon 2 to mix or charge (a gas or air) with volatile compounds of carbon in order to increase the potential heat energy —**car′bu·re′tion** (-rā′shən) *n.*

car·bu·ret·ant (-rāt′′nt, -ret′-) *n.* a substance, as gasoline or benzene, added to air or gas to carburet it

car·bu·ret·or (kär′bə rāt′ər, -byo͞o-) *n.* an apparatus for carbureting air or a gas; esp., a device in which air is mixed with gasoline spray to make an explosive mixture in an internal-combustion engine: Brit. **car·bu·ret·tor** (kär′byo͞o ret′ər)

car·bu·rize (kär′byo͞o rīz′, -bə-) *vt.* **-rized′, -riz′ing** ⟦< Fr *carbure*, carbide, hydrocarbon + -IZE⟧ 1 CARBURET (sense 2) 2 to treat or combine with carbon; esp., to treat (iron) by heating in contact with carbon in making case-hardened steel —**car′bu·ri·za′tion** *n.*

car·byl·a·mine (kär′bil′ə mēn′, kär bil′ə mēn′) *n.* ⟦CARB(O)- + -YL + AMINE⟧ any of a group of organic cyanides containing the radical NC

☆**car·ca·jou** (kär′kə jo͞o′, -zho͞o′) *n.* ⟦Fr < Montagnais *kwaahkwaacheew*⟧ WOLVERINE

car·ca·net (kär′kə net′) *n.* ⟦dim. of Fr *carcan*, iron collar, as on pillories < ML *carcannum* < Frank **querkbann* < or akin to ON *kverkband*, neck band⟧ [Archaic] an ornamental collar, band, or necklace, usually of gold and often jeweled

car·cass (kär′kəs) *n.* ⟦ME *carcais* < OFr *carcois* < ?: sp. < Fr *carcasse*⟧ 1 the dead body of an animal, often specif. of a slaughtered animal dressed as meat 2 the human body, living or dead: scornful or humorous usage 3 the worthless remains of something, esp. its outer shell 4 the framework or base structure, as of a ship, tire, etc. Brit. sp. **car′case** (-kəs) —*SYN.* BODY

Car·cas·sonne (kär′kə sän′; *Fr* kȧr kȧ sôn′) city in S France: site of a restored medieval walled city

car·cer·al (kär′sər əl) *adj.* ⟦< L *carceralis* < *carcer*, prison⟧ having to do with, suitable for, or suggestive of a prison [*a carceral* architectural style]

car·cin·o·em·bry·on·ic antigen (kär′sə nō em brē än′ik) ⟦< *carcinoembryonic*, relating to or found in both carcinomatous and embryonic tissues < *carcino-* (< Gr *karkinōma*, cancer: see CARCINOMA) + EMBRYONIC⟧ a glycoprotein, found in serum, urine, etc., that is associated with various types of tumors: monitoring its levels is useful in treating cancer patients

car·cin·o·gen (kär sin′ə jən, -jen′; kär′sə nə-) *n.* ⟦< fol. + -GEN⟧ any substance that produces cancer —**car·ci·no·gen·ic** (kär′sə nō jen′ik) *adj.* —**car′ci·no·gen′e·sis** (-jen′ə sis) *n.*, **car′ci·no′ge·nic′i·ty** (-jə nis′ə tē)

car·ci·no·ma (kär′sə nō′mə) *n., pl.* **-mas** or **-ma·ta** (-mə tə) ⟦L < Gr *karkinōma*, cancer < *karkinoun*, affect with a cancer < *karkinos*, crab: see CANCER⟧ any of several kinds of cancerous growths deriving from epithelial cells: see SARCOMA —**car′ci·nom′a·tous** (-näm′ə təs, -nō′mə-) *adj.*

car·ci·no·ma·to·sis (kär′sə nō′mə tō′sis) *n.* ⟦ModL: see prec. & -OSIS⟧ a condition in which a carcinoma has spread extensively throughout the body

☆**car coat** a short overcoat, usually extending only to about the middle of the thigh

card[1] (kärd) *n.* ⟦ME *carde* < OFr *carte* < ML *carta*, card, paper < L *charta*, leaf of paper, tablet < Gr *chartēs*, layer of papyrus; prob. < Egypt⟧ 1 a flat, stiff piece of thick paper or thin pasteboard, usually rectangular, as *a)* any of a pack of small, specially marked cards used in playing various games; specif., any of a pack of PLAYING CARDS (see also CARDS) *b)* COMPASS CARD ☆*c)* a pasteboard with a number of small articles attached for sale [*a card* of thumbtacks] *d)* POSTCARD *e)* CALLING CARD *f)* a card identifying a person as an agent, member, patron, etc. *g)* CREDIT CARD *h)* an illustrated or decorated card, typically folded and bearing a message or greeting for some occasion; greeting card [*a birthday card*] *i)* a card to advertise or announce an event, product, etc. [*a window card*] *j)* any of a series of cards on which information is recorded [*file card, index card, trading card*] ☆*k)* SCORE CARD (sense 1) ☆2 a series of contests making up a program, esp. in boxing 3 an event or attraction as described in a printed program [*drawing card*] 4 *Electronics a)* a PUNCH CARD or a card with a strip encoded magnetically *b)* a printed circuit board that plugs into a main circuit board 5 [Informal] a witty, comical, or clowning person 6 [Informal] *a)* a force or resource that can be employed to help achieve a goal *b)* a diplomatic or strategic maneuver, esp. one regarded as insincerely or cynically exploiting a (given) issue [*a politician known for playing the race card*] —*vt.* 1 to provide with a card 2 to put on a card 3 to list on cards for filing, cataloging, etc. 4 to make as a score in golf 5 [Slang] to ask (a young person) for identification, as an ID card, as to establish proof of legal age to drink alcohol —*adj.* of or involving PLAYING CARDS [*a card trick*] —**card up one's sleeve** a plan or resource kept secret or held in reserve —☆**in the cards** [Informal] likely or seemingly destined to happen: from the use of cards in fortunetelling: also [Brit.] **on the cards** —**put (or lay) one's cards on the table** to reveal frankly one's intentions, schemes, resources, etc.

card[2] (kärd) *n.* ⟦ME & OFr *carde* < OProv *carda* < *cardar*, to card < VL **caritare* < L *carrere*, to card < IE base **kars-*, to scrape; sp. infl. by assoc. with ML *cardus*, a card, thistle < L *carduus*, thistle, of same orig.⟧ 1 a wire brush for raising the nap on cloth 2 a machine with rollers covered with metal spikes, used to brush, clean, and disentangle the short fibers of wool, cotton, flax, etc. 3 a hand-held implement for this, with short, fine spikes set in leather with a stiff backing —*vt.* to use a card on (fibers) in preparation for spinning —**card′er** *n.* —**card′ing** *n., adj.*

car·da·mom (kär′də məm, -mäm′) *n.* ⟦L *cardamomum* < Gr *kardamōmon* < *kardamon*, cress + *amōmon*, an Indian spice plant⟧ 1 an Asian herb (*Elettaria cardamomum*) of the ginger family 2 its seed capsule or seed, used in medicine and as a spice 3 any of various related plants which produce similar aromatic compounds Also **car′da·mon** (-mən, -män′)

card·board (kärd′bôrd′) *n.* a material made of paper pulp but thicker and stiffer than paper; pasteboard: used for making cards, boxes, etc. —*adj.* 1 of or like cardboard 2 *a)* insubstantial or flimsy [*a cardboard* empire] *b)* superficial or shallow [*cardboard* characters in a play]

card-car·ry·ing (-kar′ē iŋ) *adj.* 1 owning a membership card in a specified organization 2 [Informal] thorough, genuine, etc. [*a card-carrying* pacifist]

☆**card file** a collection of cards containing data or records, arranged systematically, as in alphabetical order, in boxes or drawers: also **card catalog**

card·hold·er (-hōl′dər) *n.* a person having a card, often, specif., a credit card, entitling him or her to certain privileges, services, benefits, etc.

car·di- (kär′dē, -di, -də) *combining form* CARDIO-: used before a vowel

car·di·ac (kär′dē ak′) *adj.* ⟦Fr *cardiaque* < L *cardiacus* < Gr *kardiakos* < *kardia*, HEART⟧ 1 of, near, or affecting the heart 2 relating to the part of the stomach connected with the esophagus —*n.* 1 a medicine that stimulates cardiac action 2 a person with a heart disorder

cardiac arrest the complete failure of the heart to pump blood

cardiac massage a rhythmic compressing of the heart, using the hands to force blood through the blood vessels: an emergency medical procedure for treating heart failure

car·di·al·gi·a (kär′dē al′jē ə, -jə) *n.* ⟦ModL < Gr *kardialgia* < *kardia*, HEART + *algos*, pain: so named because mistakenly thought to be located in the heart⟧ 1 a feeling of pain or discomfort in the region of the heart 2 HEARTBURN

Car·diff (kär′dif) seaport in SE Wales, on the Bristol Channel: capital of Wales & county seat of South Glamorgan

car·di·gan (kär′di gən) *n.* ⟦after 7th Earl of *Cardigan* (1797-1868), Brit general⟧ a sweater or jacket, usually knitted, that opens down the front and is usually collarless and long-sleeved: also **cardigan sweater** (or **jacket**)

cardigan

Car·di·gan (kär′di gən) *n.* the Cardigan Welsh corgi: see WELSH CORGI

Cardigan Bay inlet of St. George's Channel, on the W coast of Wales

Car·di·gan·shire (-shir′, -shər) former county of W Wales, now part of Dyfed: also **Car′di·gan**

car·di·nal (kärd′′n əl) *adj.* ⟦ME < OFr < L *cardinalis*, principal, chief < *cardo*, that on which something turns or depends, orig., door hinge: see SCHERZO⟧ 1 of main importance; principal; chief 2 bright-red, like the robe of a cardinal —*n.* ⟦ME < LL(Ec) *cardinalis*, chief presbyter, cardinal < the L adj.⟧ 1 one of the Roman Catholic officials appointed by the pope to his council (COLLEGE OF CARDINALS) 2 bright red 3 a woman's short cloak, originally red and usually hooded, fashionable in the 18th cent. ☆4 ⟦so named because colored like a cardinal's robe⟧ any of various passerine birds (family Emberizidae); esp., a bright-red, crested American species (*Cardinalis cardinalis*) with a red bill 5 CARDINAL NUMBER —**car′di·nal·ly** *adv.* —**car′di·nal·ship′** *n.*

car·di·nal·ate (-it, -āt′) *n.* 1 the position, dignity, or rank of a cardinal 2 the pope's council of cardinals

☆**cardinal flower** 1 the bright-red flower of a North American plant (*Lobelia cardinalis*) of the bellflower family, that grows in damp places or in shallow water 2 this plant

cardinal number any number used in counting or in showing how many (e.g., two, forty, 627, etc.): distinguished from ORDINAL NUMBER

cardinal points the four principal points of the compass; north, south, east, and west

cardinal virtues the basic virtues of ancient Greek philosophy; justice, prudence, fortitude, and temperance: see also THEOLOGICAL VIRTUES

☆**card index** CARD FILE

car·di·o- (kär′dē ō′, -ə) ⟦< Gr *kardia*, HEART⟧ *combining form* of the heart [*cardiology*]

car·di·o·gram (kär′dē ə gram′) *n.* ELECTROCARDIOGRAM —**car′di·o·graph′** (-graf′) *n.* —**car′di·og′ra·phy** (-äg′rə fē) *n.*

car·di·oid (kär′dē oid′) *n.* ⟦Gr *kardioeidēs*, heart-shaped < *kardia*, HEART + *-oeidēs*, -OID⟧ *Math.* a curve more or less in the shape of a heart, traced by a point on the circumference of a circle that rolls around the circumference of another equal circle

car·di·ol·o·gy (kär′dē äl′ə jē) ***n.*** ⟦CARDIO- + -LOGY⟧ the branch of medicine dealing with the heart, its functions, and its diseases —**car′di·ol′o·gist** ***n.***

car·di·o·my·op·a·thy (kär′dē ō mī äp′ə thē) ***n.,*** *pl.* **-thies′** (-thēz′) any of various diseases of the heart muscle

car·di·o·pul·mo·nar·y (kär′dē ō pool′mə ner′ē, -pul′-) ***adj.*** of or involving the heart and lungs as they function interdependently [*cardiopulmonary* resuscitation]

cardiopulmonary resuscitation an emergency medical procedure which combines cardiac massage with mouth-to-mouth resuscitation; CPR

car·di·o·res·pi·ra·to·ry (-res′pər ə tôr′ē) ***adj.*** CARDIOPULMONARY

car·di·o·ta·chom·e·ter (kär′dē ō tə käm′ət ər) ***n.*** a device for counting heartbeats, usually displaying the number of beats per minute

car·di·o·tho·rac·ic (kär′dē ō thə ras′ik) ***adj.*** of or involving the heart and thorax [a *cardiothoracic* surgeon]

car·di·o·vas·cu·lar (-vas′kyə lər) ***adj.*** of the heart and the blood vessels as a unified bodily system

car·di·tis (kär dīt′is) ***n.*** ⟦ModL < Gr *kardia,* HEART + -ITIS⟧ inflammation of the heart

car·doon (kär do͞on′) ***n.*** ⟦Fr *cardon* < Prov < LL *cardo* < L *carduus:* see CARD[2]⟧ a thistlelike Mediterranean plant (*Cynara cardunculus*) of the composite family, closely related to the artichoke: leaves and roots are edible when blanched

Car·do·zo (kär dō′zō), **Benjamin Nathan** 1870-1938; associate justice, U.S. Supreme Court (1932-38)

card·play·er (kärd′plā′ər) ***n.*** a person who plays cards

cards (kärds) ***pl.n.*** **1** a game or games played with a deck of cards, as bridge, rummy, poker, or pinochle **2** the playing of such games; card playing

☆**cards and spades** ⟦from the scoring, as in casino, of both cards and spades⟧ a generous handicap

☆**card shark** [Informal] **1** an expert card player **2** CARDSHARP

☆**card·sharp** (kärd′shärp′) ***n.*** [Informal] a professional cheater at cards: also **card′sharp′er**

card table a table at which card games are played, esp. a small, square table with folding legs

care (ker) ***n.*** ⟦ME < OE *caru,* sorrow < IE base **ĝar-,* cry out, scream > L *garrulus,* garrulous, Goth *kara,* care, Ger *kar-,* in *karfreitag,* Good Friday⟧ **1** *a)* a troubled or burdened state of mind; worry; concern *b)* a cause of such a mental state **2** close attention or careful heed [to drive with *care*] **3** a liking or regard (*for*) [to show no *care* for others] **4** charge; protection; custody [left in a friend's *care*] **5** something to watch over or attend to; a responsibility **6** services offered by a medical staff, hospital, nursing home, etc. to a patient —***vi.*** **cared, car′ing 1** to have objection, worry, regret, etc.; mind [do you *care* if I go?] **2** to feel concern or interest [to *care* about others] **3** to feel love or a liking (*for*) **4** to take charge of; look after; provide (*for*) **5** to wish (*for*); want [do you *care* for more pie?] —***vt.*** **1** to feel concern about or interest in [I don't *care* what you did] **2** to wish or desire [do you *care* to eat now?] —**could care less** ⟦corruption of phr. *couldn't care less*⟧ [Informal] feel(s) no interest, sympathy, etc. about something —**have a care** to be careful: also **take care** —☆**(in) care of** at the address of —☆**take care of 1** to have charge of or be responsible for; look after; attend to **2** to provide for; protect against trouble, want, etc.

SYN.—**care** suggests a weighing down of the mind, as by dread, apprehension, or great responsibility [worn out by the *cares* of the day]; **concern** suggests mental uneasiness over someone or something in which one has an affectionate interest [I feel *concern* for their welfare]; **solicitude** implies thoughtfulness, often excessive apprehension, for the welfare, safety, or comfort of another [she stroked his head with great *solicitude*]; **worry** suggests mental distress or agitation over some problem [his chief *worry* was that he might fail]; **anxiety** suggests an apprehensive or uneasy feeling with less mental activity than **worry,** often over some indefinite but anticipated evil [he viewed the world situation with *anxiety*] —*ANT.* **unconcern, indifference**

☆**CARE** (ker) *abbrev.* Cooperative for American Relief Everywhere, Inc.

ca·reen (kə rēn′) ***vt.*** ⟦Fr *carener,* careen < OFr *carène, carine* < OIt *carena* < L *carina,* keel of a ship, orig., nutshell: see HARD⟧ **1** to cause (a ship) to lean or lie on one side, as on a beach, for cleaning, repairs, etc. **2** to caulk, clean, or repair (a ship in this position) **3** to cause to lean sideways; tip; tilt —***vi.*** **1** to lean sideways, as a sailing ship before a high wind **2** to lurch from side to side, esp. while moving rapidly —***n.*** the act or position of careening

ca·reer (kə rir′) ***n.*** ⟦Fr *carrière,* road, racecourse < It *carriera* < VL *carraria (via),* carriage (road) < L *carrus,* CAR[1]⟧ **1** [Obs.] a racing course **2** [Archaic] a swift course, as of the sun through the sky **3** one's progress through life or in one's work **4** a profession or occupation which one trains for and pursues as a lifework —☆***adj.*** pursuing a normally temporary activity as a lifework [a *career* soldier] —***vi.*** to move at full speed; rush wildly —**in full career** at full speed

ca·reer·ist (-ist) ***n.*** a person interested chiefly in succeeding in a career, to the neglect of other things —**ca·reer′ism′** ***n.***

☆**career woman** a woman who follows a professional or business career

care·free (ker′frē′) ***adj.*** free from troubles or worry

care·ful (ker′fəl) ***adj.*** ⟦ME & OE: see CARE & -FUL⟧ **1** acting or working in a thoughtful, painstaking way **2** cautious, wary, or guarded [a *careful* reply] **3** accurately or thoroughly done or made; painstaking [a *careful* analysis] **4** [Archaic] feeling or causing sorrow, worry, etc.; anxious —**care′ful·ly** ***adv.*** —**care′ful·ness** ***n.***

SYN.—**careful** implies close attention to or great concern for whatever is one's work or responsibility, and usually connotes thoroughness, a guarding against error or injury, etc.; **meticulous** implies extreme, sometimes finicky, carefulness about details; **scrupulous** implies a conscientious adherence to what is considered right, true, accurate, etc.; **circumspect** implies a careful consideration of all circumstances to avoid error or unfavorable consequences; **cautious** implies a careful guarding against possible dangers or risks; **prudent** implies the exercise of both caution and circumspection, suggesting careful management in economic and practical matters; **discreet** implies the exercise of discernment and judgment in the guidance of one's speech and action and suggests careful restraint; **wary** implies a cautiousness that is prompted by suspicion —*ANT.* **careless, negligent, lax**

care·giv·er (ker′giv′ər) ***n.*** a person who takes care of someone requiring close attention, as a young child or an invalid —**care′giv′ing** ***n.***

care·less (ker′lis) ***adj.*** ⟦ME *careles* < OE *carleas:* see CARE & -LESS⟧ **1** without worry; carefree; untroubled **2** not paying enough attention; not thinking before one acts or speaks; neglectful; heedless; inconsiderate **3** done or made without enough attention, precision, etc.; not painstaking or thorough **4** artless; unstudied [a *careless* grace] —**careless of** indifferent to; untroubled by —**care′less·ly** ***adv.*** —**care′less·ness** ***n.***

ca·ress (kə res′) ***vt.*** ⟦Fr *caresser* < It *carezzare;* ult. < L *carus,* dear: see CHARITY⟧ to touch or stroke lovingly or gently: often used fig., as of a voice or music —***n.*** a gentle or affectionate touch —**ca·ress′er** ***n.*** —**ca·ress′ing·ly** ***adv.*** —**ca·res′sive** ***adj.*** —**ca·res′sive·ly** ***adv.***

SYN.—**caress** refers to a display of affection by gentle stroking or patting; **fondle** implies a more demonstrative show of love or affection, as by hugging or kissing; **pet,** as applied generally, implies treatment with special affection and indulgence, including patting, fondling, etc., but informally it refers to indulgence, esp. by young couples, in hugging, kissing, and amorous caresses; **cuddle** implies affectionate handling, as of a small child by its mother, by pressing or drawing close within the arms; **dandle** implies the showing of playful affection toward a child by moving him or her up and down lightly on the knee

car·et (kar′it, ker′-) ***n.*** ⟦L, there is lacking, 3d pers. sing. of *carere,* to lack⟧ a mark (‸) used in writing or in correcting proof, to show where something is to be inserted

care·tak·er (ker′tāk′ər) ***n.*** **1** a person hired to take care of something or someone, esp. of a house, estate, etc. for an owner who is not always in residence; custodian **2** a person temporarily carrying out the duties as of an office **3** a person who takes care of someone else; often, specif., CAREGIVER —***adj.*** holding power temporarily; interim [a *caretaker* government]

Ca·rew (kə ro͞o′, ker′ē), **Thomas** 1595?-1639?; Eng. poet

care·worn (ker′wôrn′) ***adj.*** worn out by, or showing the effects of, troubles and worry; haggard

☆**car·fare** (kär′fer′) ***n.*** the price of a ride on a subway, bus, etc.

☆**car·ful** (kär′fo͝ol′) ***n.*** as much or as many as a car will hold [a *carful* of kids]

car·go (kär′gō) ***n.,*** *pl.* **-goes** or **-gos** ⟦Sp, burden < *cargar,* to load, impose taxes < VL *carricare:* see CHARGE⟧ the load of commodities carried by a ship, airplane, truck, etc.; freight

cargo cult ⟦< *cargo,* as on ships⟧ a quasi-religious cult among some South Sea islanders, inspired by their limited understanding of modern cargo shipments and characterized by a belief that the spirits of their ancestors will return with supplies of modern goods, thus inaugurating a golden age of prosperity and independence

cargo pants loosefitting, casual pants having a number of cargo pockets, some typically on the side of the upper leg

cargo pocket a capacious pocket sewn onto the outside of a garment or bag, often having a flap and side pleats

☆**car·hop** (kär′häp′) ***n.*** ⟦CAR[1] + (BELL)HOP⟧ a waiter or, esp., a waitress who serves food to customers in cars at a drive-in restaurant

Car·i·a (ker′ē ə) ancient region in SW Asia Minor: fl. 4th-2d cent. B.C.

Car·ib (kar′ib) ***n.*** ⟦AmSp < Sp *caribe, caribal,* altered < *canibal:* see CANNIBAL⟧ **1** a member of an Indian people that formerly inhabited the S West Indies and the N coast of South America, where some members of this people still remain **2** the family of languages of the Caribs —**Car′ib·an** ***adj., n.***

Car·ib·be·an[1] (kar′ə bē′ən, kə rib′ē ən) ***adj.*** **1** of the Caribs or their language or culture **2** of the Caribbean Sea, its islands, etc. —***n.*** CARIB (sense 1)

Car·ib·be·an[2] (kar′ə bē′ən, kə rib′ē ən) CARIBBEAN SEA

Caribbean Sea part of the Atlantic, bounded by the West Indies, Central America, and the N coast of South America: 971,400 sq mi (2,515,916 sq km)

ca·ri·be (kə rē′bā) ***n.,*** *pl.* **-bes** or **-be** ⟦AmSp, lit., Carib (see CANNIBAL): so named from its voracity⟧ PIRANHA

☆**car·i·bou** (kar′ə bo͞o′) ***n.,*** *pl.* **-bous′** or **-bou′** ⟦CdnFr < Algonquian⟧ any of several large North American reindeer

car·i·ca·ture (kar′i kə chər, -cho͝or′) ***n.*** ⟦Fr < It *caricatura,* satirical picture, lit., an overloading < *caricare,* to load, exaggerate < VL *carricare:* see CHARGE⟧ **1** a picture or imitation of a person, literary style, etc. in which certain features or mannerisms are exaggerated for satirical effect **2** the act or art of making such caricatures **3** a likeness or imitation that is so distorted or inferior as to seem ludicrous —***vt.*** **-tured, -tur·ing** to depict in or as in a caricature —**car′i·ca·tur′al** (-chur′əl, -choor′əl) *adj.* —**car′i·ca·tur·ist** *n.*

SYN.—caricature refers to an imitation or representation of a person or thing, in drawing, writing, or performance, that ludicrously exaggerates its distinguishing features; **burlesque** implies the handling of a serious subject lightly or flippantly, or of a trifling subject with mock seriousness; a **parody** ridicules a written work or writer by imitating the style closely, esp. so as to point up its peculiarities or affectations, and by distorting the content nonsensically or changing it to something absurdly incongruous; **travesty**, in contrast, implies that the subject matter is retained, but that the style and language are changed so as to give a grotesquely absurd effect; **satire** refers to a literary composition in which follies, vices, stupidities, and abuses in life are held up to ridicule and contempt; **lampoon** refers to a piece of strongly satirical writing that uses broad humor in attacking and ridiculing the faults and weaknesses of an individual

CARICOM (kar′i käm′) *abbrev.* Caribbean Community

car·i·es (ker′ēz′, -ē ēz′) *n.* ⟦L, decay < IE base *ker-*, to injure > Gr *kēr*, death, destruction, Sans *śṛṇāti*, (he) breaks, crushes⟧ decay of bones or, esp., of teeth

car·il·lon (kar′ə län′; *occas.*, kə ril′yən) *n.* ⟦Fr, chime of bells (orig. composed of four) < OFr *carrignon* < LL *quaternio*: see QUATERNARY⟧ **1** a set of stationary bells, each producing a different musical tone, now usually sounded by means of a keyboard **2** a musical instrument that produces such tones electronically **3** a composition for the carillon **4** an organ stop producing a carillonlike sound

car·il·lon·neur (kar′ə lə nur′) *n.* ⟦Fr⟧ a carillon player

ca·ri·na (kə rī′nə, -rē′-) *n., pl.* **-nas** or **-nae** (-nē) ⟦ModL < L, keel: see CAREEN⟧ *Biol.* a structure or part resembling a keel or ridge, as the projection on the breastbone of a bird —**ca·ri′nal** *adj.*

Ca·ri·na (kə rī′nə, -rē′-) *n.* ⟦L, ship's keel: see CAREEN⟧ a S constellation between Vela and Pictor, containing the bright star Canopus: see ARGO (sense 2)

car·i·nate (kar′ə nāt′, -nit) *adj.* ⟦ModL < L *carinatus* < *carina*: see CARINA⟧ *Biol.* having a ridge down the middle; keel-shaped: also **car′i·nat′ed**

Ca·rin·thi·a (kə rin′thē ə) **1** region of central Europe, bordering Italy and Slovenia: divided between Austria and Yugoslavia (1918) **2** state of S Austria, consisting of a portion of this region

Car·i·o·ca (kar′ē ō′kə) *n.* ⟦BrazPort < Tupí, lit., white house⟧ a person born or living in Rio de Janeiro

car·i·ole (kar′ē ōl′) *n.* ⟦Fr *carriole* < It *carriuolo*, dim. of *carro* < LL *carrum*: see CAR[1]⟧ **1** a small carriage or sleigh drawn by one horse **2** a kind of enclosed sled used formerly by fur traders in the Canadian Northwest

car·i·ous (kər′ē əs) *adj.* ⟦L *cariosus*⟧ having caries; decayed

ca·ri·tas (kär′ē täs′) *n.* ⟦L(Ec)⟧ love for all people

car·jack·ing (kär′jak′iŋ) *n.* ⟦blend of CAR[1] & *hijacking* (n.) < HIJACK⟧ the taking of an occupied automobile by force —**car′jack′** *vt.* —**car′jack′er** *n.*

cark (kärk) [Archaic] *vt., vi.* ⟦ME *carken* < NormFr *carkier*, var. of OFr *chargier*: see CHARGE⟧ to worry or be worried —*n.* distress; anxiety

carl or **carle** (kärl) *n.* ⟦ME & OE *carl* < ON *karl*, a man, CHURL⟧ **1** [Obs.] a peasant, bondman, or villein **2** [Now Chiefly Scot.] an ill-bred fellow; churl **3** [Scot.] a sturdy fellow

Carl (kärl) *n.* a masculine name: see CHARLES[1]

car·line or **car·lin** (kär′lin, ker′-) *n.* ⟦ON *kerling*, wife, old woman < *karl*, a man + fem. suffix⟧ [Scot.] **1** a woman, esp. an old woman **2** a hag; witch

car·ling (kär′liŋ) *n.* ⟦Fr *carlingue* < ON *kerling*, lit., old woman: see prec.⟧ any of the short, wooden or metal pieces running fore and aft beneath the deck of a ship to provide additional support, as under masts, winches, etc.

Car·lisle (kär līl′, kär′līl′) city in NW England; county seat of Cumbria

Car·list (kär′list) *n.* ⟦CARL(OS) + -IST[1]⟧ a supporter of Don Carlos or of his heirs: see CARLOS, Don —**Car′lism′** *n.*

☆**car·load** (kär′lōd′) *n.* **1** a load that fills a car, esp. a freight car **2** the minimum weight of a specific commodity qualifying as a carload of that commodity in railroad shipping rates

☆**car·load·ings** (-iŋz) *pl.n.* the number of railroad carloads shipped in or out within a given period

☆**carload rate** a special low rate for shipment by carloads

Car·los (kär′lōs, -ləs), **Don** (born *Carlos Maria Isidro de Borbón*) 1788-1855; Sp. pretender to the throne

Car·lo·ta (kär lô′tä; *E* kär lät′ə) (born *Marie Charlotte Amélie Augustine Victoire Clémentine Léopoldine*) 1840-1927; empress of Mexico (1864-67): wife of Maximilian

Car·lot·ta (kär lät′ə) *n.* a feminine name: see CHARLOTTE[1]

Car·lo·vin·gi·an (kär′lə vin′jē ən) *adj., n.* CAROLINGIAN

Car·low (kär′lō) county in Leinster province, SE Ireland: 346 sq mi (896 sq km)

Carls·bad (kärlz′bad′) city in SW Calif.

Carls·bad Caverns (kärlz′bad′) system of caves in SE N.Mex., within a national park

Car·lyle (kär līl′, kär′līl′), **Thomas** 1795-1881; Brit. writer, born in Scotland

car·ma·gnole (kär′mə nyōl′) *n.* ⟦Fr, altered (after *Carmagnola*, town in Piedmont, occupied by revolutionaries in 1792) < older *carmignole*, kind of cap (dial. *carmignola*, jacket); prob. ult. < L *carminare*, to card wool < *carmen*, a card < *carrere*: see CARD[2]⟧ **1** the short jacket with wide lapels, or the costume consisting of this jacket, black trousers, a red cap, and tricolored girdle, worn by French Revolutionaries (1792) **2** a lively song and street dance popular during the French Revolution

car·mak·er (kär′māk′ər) *n.* a manufacturer of automobiles

car·man (kär′mən) *n., pl.* **-men** (-mən) a streetcar conductor or motorman

Car·mar·then·shire (kär mär′*th*ən shir′, -shər) former county of SW Wales, now part of Dyfed

car·mel (kär′məl) *n. disputed var. of* CARAMEL —**car′mel·ize′** (-mə līz′) *vt., vi.* **-ized′**, **-iz′ing**

Car·mel (kar′məl), **Mount** mountain ridge in NW Israel, extending as a promontory into the Mediterranean: highest point, *c.* 1,800 ft (549 m)

Car·mel·ite (kär′mə līt′) *n.* ⟦Fr < ML *Carmelita* < LL(Ec) *Carmelites*, inhabitant of prec.⟧ **1** a mendicant friar of the order of Our Lady of Mount Carmel, founded in Syria about 1160 **2** a nun of this order —*adj.* of this order

car·min·a·tive (kär min′ə tiv, kär′mə nāt′iv) *adj.* ⟦ModL *carminativus* < L *carminatus*, pp. of *carminare*, cleanse < *carrere*, CARD[2]⟧ causing gas to be expelled from the stomach and intestines —*n.* a carminative medicine

car·mine (kär′min, -mīn′) *n.* ⟦Fr *carmin* < ML *carminium* < Ar *qirmiz*, crimson (< Sans *kṛimiğā*, insect-produced < *kṛmi*, worm, insect: the dye comes from crushed insects: see COCHINEAL); form infl. by L *minium*, cinnabar red⟧ **1** a red or purplish-red pigment obtained mainly from cochineal **2** its color —*adj.* red or purplish-red; crimson

car·nage (kär′nij) *n.* ⟦Fr < OIt *carnaggio*, ult. < L *caro*: fol.⟧ **1** bloody and extensive slaughter, esp. in battle; bloodshed **2** ⟦Fr < Prov *carnatge*, flesh < *carn* < L *caro*⟧ [Obs.] dead bodies, esp. on a battlefield —*SYN.* SLAUGHTER

car·nal (kär′nəl) *adj.* ⟦ME & OFr < LL(Ec) *carnalis*, fleshly (in contrast to *spiritalis*, SPIRITUAL) < L *caro* (gen. *carnis*), flesh: for IE base see HARVEST⟧ **1** in or of the flesh; bodily; material or worldly, not spiritual **2** having to do with or preoccupied with bodily or sexual pleasures; sensual or sexual —**have carnal knowledge of** [Now Rare] *Law* to have had sexual intercourse with —**car·nal·i·ty** (kär nal′ə tē) *n., pl.* **-ties** —**car′nal·ly** *adv.*

SYN.—carnal implies relation to the body or flesh as the seat of basic physical appetites, now esp. sexual appetites, and usually stresses absence of intellectual or moral influence [*carnal* lust]; **fleshly**, expressing less censure, stresses these appetites and their gratification as natural to the flesh [*fleshly* frailty]; **sensual** stresses relation to or preoccupation with gratifying the bodily senses and usually implies grossness or lewdness [*sensual* lips]; **animal** is applied to the physical nature of humankind as distinguished from intellectual and spiritual nature, and now rarely carries a derogatory implication [*animal* spirits]

car·nall·ite (kär′nəl īt′) *n.* ⟦after Rudolf von *Carnall* (1804-74), Ger mineralogist + -ITE[1]⟧ a hydrous chloride of magnesium and potassium, $MgCl_2 \cdot KCl \cdot 6H_2O$: a valuable source of potassium

Car·nap (kär′nap), **Rudolf** 1891-1970; U.S. logician & positivist philosopher, born in Germany

car·nas·si·al (kär nas′ē əl) *adj.* ⟦< Fr *carnassier*, carnivorous < Prov *carnasa*, bad flesh (+ pejorative *-acea*) < *carn*, flesh < L *caro*: see CARNAGE⟧ designating or of teeth of a flesh-eating animal specialized for slicing or shearing rather than tearing, esp. the last premolars of the upper jaw and the first molars of the lower jaw —*n.* a carnassial tooth

Car·nat·ic (kär nat′ik) region in SE India, between the Coromandel Coast and the Eastern Ghats

car·na·tion (kär nā′shən) *n.* ⟦MFr < L *caro*, flesh (see CARNAL), after OFr *incarnation*, INCARNATION; sense infl. by OIt *carnagione*, flesh-colored < *carnaggio*⟧ **1** *a)* a popular garden and greenhouse plant (*Dianthus caryophyllus*) of the pink family, usually with white, pink, or red double flowers that smell like cloves *b)* the flower of this plant **2** [*often pl.*] a flesh-colored tint formerly used in painting **3** moderate to deep red

car·na·u·ba (kär′nô′bə, -nou′-, -nōō′-) *n.* ⟦BrazPort < Tupí⟧ a Brazilian palm tree (*Copernicia cerifera*) that yields a hard wax used in making polishes, lipsticks, carbon paper, etc.

Car·ne·gie (kär nā′gē, -neg′ē; kär′nə gē′), **Andrew** 1835-1919; U.S. industrialist & philanthropist, born in Scotland

car·nel·ian (kär nēl′yən) *n.* ⟦altered, after L *caro*, flesh (because of its color) < CORNELIAN⟧ a red variety of chalcedony, used in jewelry

car·net (kår ne′) *n.* ⟦Fr⟧ **1** an official certificate; esp., any of various customs documents required of motorists crossing certain national borders **2** a book of tickets for a bus, subway, etc.

car·ney or **car·nie** (kär′nē) *n., pl.* **-nies** [Slang] *alt. sp. of* CARNY

car·ni·fy (kär′nə fī′) *vt., vi.* **-fied′**, **-fy′ing** ⟦L *carnificare*, execute < *caro* (see CARNAGE) + -FY⟧ to form into flesh or fleshlike tissue —**car′ni·fi·ca′tion** *n.*

car·ni·val (kär′nə vəl) *n.* ⟦< Fr *carnaval* (or It *carnevale*) < ML *carnelevarium* < **carnem levare*, to remove meat (see HARVEST & LEVER); assoc. by folk etym. with ML *carne vale*, "Flesh, farewell!" < L *caro*, flesh + *vale*: see VALEDICTION⟧ **1** the period of feasting and revelry just before Lent **2** *a)* a reveling or time of revelry; festivity; merrymaking *b)* a time or place of excess, vitality, chaos, etc. **3** a traveling commercial entertainment with sideshows, rides, games, etc. **4** an organized program of festivities, contests, etc. [a winter sports *carnival*]

car·ni·val·esque (kar′nə vəl esk′) *adj.* like a carnival, as in being excessive, disordered, chaotic, surreal, vital, etc.

car·ni·vore (kär′nə vôr′) *n.* ⟦Fr: see fol.⟧ **1** any of an order (Carnivora) of fanged, flesh-eating mammals, including the dog, bear, cat, and seal **2** any animal that consumes other animals: cf. HERBIVORE, OMNIVORE **3** a plant that ingests small animals, esp. insects

car·niv·o·rous (kär niv′ə rəs) ***adj.*** ⟦L *carnivorus* < *caro*, flesh (see HARVEST) + *vorare*, to devour (see VORACIOUS)⟧ **1** *a)* flesh-eating (opposed to HERBIVOROUS) *b)* insect-eating, as certain plants **2** of the carnivores —**car·niv′o·rous·ly** ***adv.*** —**car·niv′o·rous·ness** ***n.***

Car·not (kȧr nō′) **1 La·zare (Nicolas Marguerite)** (lȧ zȧr′) 1753-1823; Fr. soldier & statesman **2 Ni·co·las Lé·o·nard Sa·di** (nē kô lä′ lā ô nȧr′ sȧ dē′) 1796-1832; Fr. physicist: son of Lazare **3 (Marie François) Sadi** 1837-94; Fr. statesman: president of France (1887-94): grandson of Lazare

car·no·tite (kär′nə tīt′) ***n.*** ⟦after A. *Carnot* (died 1920), Fr mine inspector + -ITE[1]⟧ a yellow, very soft, radioactive, monoclinic mineral, $K_2(UO_2)_2(VO_4)_2 \cdot 3H_2O$, that is a source of uranium, radium, and vanadium

car·ny (kär′nē) ***n., pl.*** **-nies** [Slang] **1** CARNIVAL (sense 3) **2** a person who works in such a carnival

car·ob (kar′əb) ***n.*** ⟦Fr *caroube* < ML *carrubia* < Ar *kharrub*, bean pod < Aram *khārūbā* < Assyr *kharūbu*⟧ **1** a leguminous tree (*Ceratonia siliqua*) of the E Mediterranean, bearing long, flat, leathery, brown pods with a sweet pulp **2** such a pod, used for fodder or in making a nutritious, chocolatelike drink or candy

ca·roche (kə rōch′, -rōsh′) ***n.*** ⟦Fr < It *carroccio* < OIt *carro* < LL *carrum*: see CAR[1]⟧ a coach or carriage used for state occasions in the 17th cent.

car·ol (kar′əl) ***n.*** ⟦ME *carole* < OFr, kind of dance, Christmas song < ML *choraula*, a dance to the flute < L *choraules* < Gr *choraulēs*, flute player who accompanied the choral dance < *choros*, CHORUS + *aulein*, to play the flute < *aulos*, flute⟧ **1** [Obs.] a kind of circle dance **2** a song of joy or praise; esp., a Christmas song —***vi.*** **-oled** or **-olled**, **-ol·ing** or **-ol·ling 1** to sing, esp. in joy; warble **2** to sing carols, esp. Christmas carols, in chorus with others —***vt.*** **1** to sing (a tune, etc.) **2** to praise in song —**car′ol·er *n.*, car′ol·ler**

Car·ol (kar′əl) ***n.*** **1** a feminine name: see CAROLINE **2** ⟦ML *Carolus*: see CHARLES[1]⟧ a masculine name

Car·o·li·na[1] (kar′ə lī′nə) ⟦ModL, fem. of *Carolus* < ML, CHARLES[1]⟧ English colony (1663-1729) including what is now N.C., S.C., Ga., and N Fla. —**the Carolinas** North Carolina and South Carolina

Ca·ro·li·na[2] (kär′ə lē′nə) ⟦after Doña *Carolina* Andino, donor of the town site⟧ city in NE Puerto Rico, near San Juan

☆**Car·o·li·na allspice** (kar′ə lī′nə) any of a genus (*Calycanthus*) of hardy shrubs (family Calycanthaceae) of a dicotyledonous order (Laurales) of plants, bearing reddish-brown, sweet-smelling flowers

Car·o·line (kar′ə lin; *also, and for adj., usually*, -līn′) ***n.*** ⟦Ger & Fr < It *Carolina*, fem. < ML *Carolus*, CHARLES[1]⟧ a feminine name: dim. *Carol, Carrie*; var. *Carolyn* —***adj.*** of Charles I or Charles II of England, or the period in which they lived: also **Car′o·le′an** (-lē′ən)

Car·o·line Islands (kar′ə līn′, -lin) archipelago in the W Pacific: in 1979, four of its five districts gained internal self-government as the *Federated States of Micronesia*, but remained a part of the PACIFIC ISLANDS until 1990

Car·o·lin·gi·an (kar′ə lin′jē ən) ***adj.*** ⟦ML *Carolingi*, pl. of *Carolingus* < *Carolus*, CHARLES[1] + Gmc *-ing*, patronymic suffix + -IAN⟧ designating or of the second Frankish dynasty, founded (A.D. 751) by Pepin the Short, son of Charles Martel —***n.*** a member of this dynasty

Car·o·lin·i·an (kar′ə lin′ē ən) ***adj.*** ⟦after ML *Carolus*, CHARLES[1] + -IAN⟧ **1** of Charlemagne or his period **2** CAROLINE **3** ⟦< *Carolina*⟧ of North Carolina or South Carolina —***n.*** a person born or living in North Carolina or South Carolina

Car·o·lyn (kar′ə lin) ***n.*** a feminine name: see CAROLINE

car·om (kar′əm) ***n.*** ⟦< Fr *carambole* < Sp *carambola*; orig., kind of fruit < Malay *karambil*⟧ **1** *Billiards* any shot in which the cue ball bounces off a cushion or an object ball; specif., such a shot that successively hits the two object balls, giving the shooter a score in most games ☆**2** a striking against a surface and rebounding at an angle —☆***vi.*** **1** to make a carom **2** to strike against a surface and rebound at an angle

car·o·tene (kar′ə tēn′) ***n.*** ⟦< L *carota*, CARROT + -ENE⟧ any of several red or orange isomeric hydrocarbons, $C_{40}H_{56}$, found in butter and in carrots and certain other vegetables, and changed into vitamin A in the liver: sometimes called **car′o·tin** (-tin)

ca·rot·e·noid or **ca·rot·i·noid** (kə rät′'n oid′) ***n.*** any of several red and yellow plant and animal pigments related to and including carotene —***adj.*** **1** of or like carotene **2** of the carotenoids

Ca·roth·ers (kə ruth′ərz), **Wallace Hume** 1896-1937; U.S. chemist

ca·rot·id (kə rät′id) ***adj.*** ⟦Gr *karōtis*, pl. *karōtides*, the two great arteries of the neck < *karoun*, to plunge into sleep or stupor: so called because compression of these was believed to cause unconsciousness⟧ designating, of, or near either of the two principal arteries, one on each side of the neck, which convey the blood from the aorta to the head —***n.*** a carotid artery

ca·rous·al (kə rou′zəl) ***n.*** CAROUSE (*n.* 1)

ca·rouse (kə rouz′) ***vi.*** **-roused′**, **-rous′ing** ⟦obs. Fr *carousse*, carousal < Ger *gar aus*, quite out < *gar austrinken*, to drink up entirely⟧ to drink much alcoholic liquor, esp. along with others having a noisy, merry time —***n.*** **1** a noisy, merry drinking party **2** [Obs.] a glassful drunk all at once, esp. as a toast —**ca·rous′er *n.***

car·ou·sel (kar′ə sel′, kar′ə sel′) ***n.*** ⟦Fr *carrousel* < It dial. (Naples) *carusiello*, tournament in which players threw reed lances or balls of chalk at opponents, orig. lit., chalk ball < *caruso*, shaved head; form infl. by It *carrozza*, stately carriage, prob. < *carro* < L *carrum*: see CAR[1]⟧ ☆**1** a merry-go-round ☆**2** something that revolves like a merry-go-round ☆**3** a circular baggage conveyor in an airport from which passengers pick up their luggage — [**C-**] *trademark for* a revolving tray from which slides are fed one at a time into a projector

carp[1] (kärp) ***n., pl.*** **carp** or **carps** ⟦ME & OFr *carpe* < VL *carpa* < Goth **karpa*⟧ any of various often edible, freshwater cyprinoid fishes found all over the world, including the goldfish: a carp (*Cyprinus carpio*) is harvested for food in Europe and Asia

carp[2] (kärp) ***vi.*** ⟦ME *carpen* < ON *karpa*, to brag; meaning infl. by L *carpere*, to pluck: see EXCERPT⟧ to complain or find fault in a petty or nagging way —**carp′er *n.***

-carp (kärp) ⟦ModL < Gr *karpos*: see HARVEST⟧ *combining form forming nouns* fruit [*endocarp*]

car·pac·cio (kär pä′chō′, -chē ō′) ***n.*** ⟦after fol.: from his use of a red resembling the color of raw beef⟧ an appetizer consisting of very thin slices of raw beef served with a vinaigrette or a mustard sauce: now made also with veal, tuna, etc.

Car·pac·ci·o (kär pä′chô), **Vit·to·re** (vēt tô′re) 1460?-1525?; It. painter

car·pal (kär′pəl) ***adj.*** ⟦ModL *carpalis*⟧ of the carpus —***n.*** a bone of the carpus

car·pa·le (kär pā′lē) ***n., pl.*** **-li·a** (-ə) ⟦ModL, neut. of *carpalis*⟧ CARPAL

carpal tunnel syndrome a medical condition that is characterized by pain, numbness, etc. in the wrist, palm, fingers, and thumb, usually caused by repetitive hand movement, as in typing or knitting, which swells the tissue surrounding the nerve in a tunnel-like passage (**carpal tunnel**) in the wrist

car park [Brit.] PARKING LOT

Car·pa·thi·an Mountains (kär pā′thē ən) mountain system in central Europe, extending southeast from S Poland through the Czech Republic and Ukraine into NE Romania: highest peak, 8,737 ft (2,663 m): also **Carpathians**

car·pe di·em (kär′pā dē′əm) ⟦L, seize the day⟧ make the most of present opportunities

car·pel (kär′pəl) ***n.*** ⟦ModL dim. < Gr *karpos*, fruit: see HARVEST⟧ **1** a simple pistil, regarded as a single ovule-bearing leaf or modified leaflike structure **2** any of the segments of a compound pistil, usually having a single stigma —**car′pel·lar′y** (-pə ler′ē) ***adj.*** —**car′pel·late′** (-pə lāt′) ***adj.***

Car·pen·tar·i·a (kär′pən ter′ē ə), **Gulf of** arm of the Arafura Sea, indenting the N coast of Australia: *c.* 480 mi (772 km) long; 400 mi (644 km) wide

car·pen·ter (kär′pən tər) ***n.*** ⟦ME & Anglo-Fr < LL *carpentarius*, carpenter, wagon maker < L *carpentum*, two-wheeled carriage, cart < Gaul⟧ a workman who builds and repairs wooden things, esp. the wooden parts of buildings, ships, etc. —***vi.*** to do a carpenter's work —***vt.*** to make or repair by or as if by carpentry

carpenter ant any of a genus (*Camponotus*) of large ants that build nests in wooden buildings, tree trunks, etc. by gnawing out a complicated series of chambers

carpenter bee any of certain solitary bees (family Anthophoridae) that bore tunnels in timber, where the females lay eggs

car·pen·try (kär′pən trē) ***n.*** ⟦ME & OFr *carpenterie*⟧ the work or trade of a carpenter

car·pet (kär′pət) ***n.*** ⟦ME < OFr *carpite*, carpet, kind of cloth < ML *carpita*, thick woolen cloth < pp. of L *carpere*, to card, pluck: see EXCERPT⟧ **1** a thick, heavy fabric of wool, cotton, or synthetic fibers for covering a floor, stairs, etc.: it is woven, usually with a pile, or felted **2** a strip, or several joined strips, of such fabric **3** anything like a carpet [*a carpet of snow*] —***vt.*** to cover with or as with a carpet —**on the carpet 1** under consideration **2** before someone in authority, in order to be reprimanded

car·pet·bag (-bag′) ***n.*** a type of traveling bag made of carpeting, with, typically, handles and a clasp at the top —☆***adj.*** of or having to do with carpetbaggers —☆***vi.*** **-bagged′**, **-bag′ging** to act as a carpetbagger

☆**car·pet·bag·ger** (-bag′ər) ***n.*** **1** any of the Northern politicians or adventurers who went South to take advantage of unsettled conditions after the Civil War: contemptuous term with reference to the luggage they used in traveling light **2** any politician, promoter, etc. from the outside whose influence is resented

carpet beetle (*or* bug) any of a number of small beetles (family Dermestidae, esp. genus *Anthrenus*) whose larvae feed on furs and woolens, esp. carpets

car·pet-bomb (kär′pət bäm′) ***vt.*** ⟦from the idea of covering an area evenly⟧ to drop many bombs on (an area) to prepare for advancing ground forces —**car′pet-bomb′ing *n.***

car·pet·ing (kär′pət iŋ) ***n.*** carpets or carpet fabric

☆**carpet sweeper** a hand-operated device with a revolving brush to sweep up dirt from carpets and rugs

☆**car·pet·weed** (kär′pət wēd′) ***n.*** a North American annual weed (*Mollugo verticillata*) of the carpetweed family, that grows close to the ground, forming a mat —***adj.*** designating a family (Aizoaceae) of dicotyledonous plants (order Caryophyllales) growing chiefly on deserts and seashores in warm regions, including the fig marigolds, the mesembryanthemums, and the ice plant

car phone a kind of CELLULAR PHONE that is installed in an automotive vehicle

car·pi (kär′pī′) ***n. pl.*** of CARPUS

-car·pic (kär′pik) *combining form* -CARPOUS [*monocarpic*]

carp·ing (kärp′iŋ) ***adj.*** tending to carp, or find fault; captious —**SYN.** CRITICAL —**carp′ing·ly *adv.***

car·po- (kär′pō, -pə) *combining form* **1** ⟦ModL < Gr *karpos*: see HARVEST⟧ fruit, seeds [*carpology*] **2** ⟦< Gr *karpos*: see CARPUS⟧ carpal or carpus Also, before a vowel, **carp-**

car·po·go·ni·um (kär′pə gō′nē əm) ***n.***, *pl.* **-ni·a** (-ə) ⟦ModL: see prec. & -GONIUM⟧ the female reproductive organ in red algae

car·pol·o·gy (kär päl′ə jē) ***n.*** ⟦CARPO- (sense 1) + -LOGY⟧ the study of the structure of fruits and seeds

car·pool (kär′po͞ol′) ***vi., vt.*** to participate in or transport by participating in a car pool: also **car′-pool′**

☆**car pool** **1** an arrangement by which several people reduce their traveling expenses by commuting in a single automobile **2** a group of people participating in such an arrangement

car·poph·a·gous (kär päf′ə gəs) ***adj.*** ⟦Gr *karpophagos* < *karpos* (see HARVEST) + *phagein* (see -PHAGOUS)⟧ fruit-eating

car·po·phore (kär′pō fôr′, -pə-) ***n.*** ⟦CARPO- (sense 1) + -PHORE⟧ *Bot.* **1** the lengthened receptacle to which the carpels are attached **2** any fruiting body or fruiting structure of a fungus

☆**car·port** (kär′pôrt′) ***n.*** a shelter for an automobile, consisting of a roof extended from the side of a building, sometimes with an additional wall

car·po·spore (kär′pō spôr′, -pə-) ***n.*** a spore developed from the fertilized carpogonium in the red algae

-car·pous (kär′pəs) ⟦ModL *-carpus* < Gr *karpos*: see HARVEST⟧ *combining form forming adjectives* fruited; having a certain number of fruits or a certain kind of fruit [*apocarpous*]

car·pus (kär′pəs) ***n.***, *pl.* **-pi′** (-pī′) ⟦ModL < Gr *karpos*, wrist < IE base **kwerp-*, to turn > OE *hweorfan*⟧ *Anat.* the wrist, or the wrist bones

car·rack (kar′ək) ***n.*** ⟦ME *carrack* < OFr *caraque* < OSp *carraca* < Ar *qarāqīr*, pl. of *qurqūr*, merchant ship: < ? Gr *kerkouros*, a light vessel < *kerkos*, tail + *oura*, tail, stern (see URO-[2])⟧ GALLEON

car·ra·geen or **car·ra·gheen** (kar′ə gēn′) ***n.*** ⟦after *Carragheen*, Ireland⟧ **1** a purplish, edible red algae (*Chondrus crispus*) found on rocky shores of N Europe and North America; Irish moss: used in jellies, lotions, medicines, etc. **2** any of several similar red algae (genus *Gigartina*)

car·ra·geen·an (kar′ə gē′nən) ***n.*** a mixture of polysaccharides extracted from carrageen, used in various foods, cosmetics, etc. as a thickening agent and natural emulsifier: occas. sp. **car′ra·geen′in**

Car·ra·ra (kə rär′ə) commune in Tuscany, NW Italy: a fine white marble (**Carrara marble**) is quarried nearby

car·re·four (kar′ə fo͝or′, kar′ə fo͝or′) ***n.*** ⟦altered (infl. by Fr) < LME *quarefour* < MFr *quarrefour* < VL **quadrifurcum*, orig. neut. of **quadrifurcus*, lit., four-forked, hence, where four roads meet < L *quadri-* (see QUADRI-) + *furca*, FORK⟧ **1** a crossroads or intersection **2** a public square or plaza

car·rel or **car·rell** (kar′əl) ***n.*** ⟦ME *caroll* < ML *carula*, small study in a cloister⟧ a small cubicle, typically in a library, designed to provide privacy for a person studying, reading, using a computer, etc.

Car·rel (kar′əl, kə rel′), **Alexis** 1873-1944; Fr. surgeon & biologist in the U.S. (1905-39)

car·riage (kar′ij; *for 2, usually* kar′ē ij′) ***n.*** ⟦ME *cariage*, baggage, transport < Anglo-Fr, cart, carriage < *carier*, CARRY⟧ **1** the act of carrying; transportation **2** the cost of carrying; transportation charge **3** [Archaic] *a)* management or handling *b)* conduct; behavior **4** a manner of carrying the head and body; posture; bearing **5** *a)* any of various horse-drawn passenger vehicles, esp. an elegant four-wheeled one with an elevated seat for the driver *b) short for* BABY CARRIAGE **6** [Brit.] a railroad passenger car **7** a wheeled frame or support for something heavy [a gun *carriage*] **8** a moving part (of a machine) for supporting and shifting something [the *carriage* of a typewriter] —***SYN.*** BEARING

carriage dog DALMATIAN (*n.* 3)

carriage house an outbuilding for storing a carriage, etc., now, specif., one converted into a dwelling, office, etc.

☆**carriage trade** the wealthy patrons, as of a theater or store, who formerly arrived in private carriages

car·rick bend (kar′ik) a kind of knot used for joining two ropes

carrick bitt *Naut.* either of the two posts supporting a windlass

Car·rie (kar′ē) ***n.*** a feminine name: see CAROLINE

car·ri·er (kar′ē ər) ***n.*** ⟦ME *carier* < *carien*, CARRY⟧ **1** a person or thing that carries, as one who delivers mail or newspapers, or a train, bus, airplane, etc. **2** *a)* a person or company in the business of transporting goods or passengers *b)* a company in the business of providing telephone or data services **3** a messenger or porter **4** a container, support, or course in or on which something is carried or conducted, as a mechanical part or device or a water conduit **5** any of various contrivances for carrying a baby or small pet, specif., *a)* a portable, basketlike seat for a baby, with a handle *b)* a sling worn around the upper body of an adult and designed to hold a baby against the adult's torso *c)* a plastic cage or basket, a nylon bag, etc., designed for transporting a pet **6** a company that insures a certain person, organization, etc. **7** AIRCRAFT CARRIER **8** a person or animal that carries and transmits disease germs or recessive genes, esp. a person who does not seem to be affected by them **9** *Chem.* *a)* a catalytic agent that causes an element or radical to be transferred from one compound to another *b)* a body which supports the catalyst deposited in or on it *c)* a relatively large quantity of a stable substance that is combined with a minute quantity of an isotope, esp. one that is a radioactive tracer, to facilitate its handling **10** *Electronics* an electron, ion, hole, etc. whose movement constitutes a flow of electric current **11** *Radio, TV* the steady transmitted wave whose amplitude, frequency, or phase is modulated by the signal

carrier pigeon **1** *former name for* HOMING PIGEON **2** any of a breed of large show pigeons with big wattles

car·ri·ole (kar′ē ōl′) ***n.*** *alt. sp. of* CARIOLE

car·ri·on (kar′ē ən) ***n.*** ⟦ME *carioun* < Anglo-Fr *carogne* < VL **caronia*, carcass < L *caro*: see HARVEST⟧ **1** the decaying flesh of a dead body, esp. when regarded as food for scavenging animals **2** anything very disgusting or repulsive —***adj.*** **1** of or like carrion **2** feeding on carrion

carrion crow a common crow (*Corvus corone*) of Europe

carrion flower **1** a perennial vine (*Smilax herbacea*) of the lily family, with greenish, foul-smelling flowers **2** *nontechnical name for* STAPELIA

Car·roll (kar′əl) **1 Charles** 1737-1832; Am. Revolutionary leader **2 Lewis** (pseud. of *Charles Lutwidge Dodgson*) 1832-98; Eng. writer and mathematician: author of *Alice's Adventures in Wonderland*

Car·roll·ton (kar′əl tən) ⟦after *Carrollton*, Ill. (the home of the founders), named for Charles CARROLL⟧ city in NE Tex.: suburb of Dallas

car·rom (kar′əm) ***n., vi.*** *alt. sp. of* CAROM

car·ron·ade (kar′ə nād′) ***n.*** ⟦after *Carron*, Scotland, where it was first made⟧ an obsolete type of short, light cannon with a large bore, used at close range

car·rot (kar′ət) ***n.*** ⟦MFr *carotte* < L *carota* < Gr *karōton*, carrot; akin to *kara*, head: see HORN⟧ **1** a biennial plant (*Daucus carota*) of the umbel family, with fernlike leaves and compound umbels of white flowers, usually with one red flower in the center: only the cultivated variety is edible **2** the fleshy, orange-red root of the cultivated strain of this plant (var. *sativa*), eaten as a vegetable **3** something offered as an inducement, like a carrot dangled before a donkey's nose —**carrot and stick** pleasant inducements or promised rewards coupled with threats

☆**car·rot·top** or **car·rot-top** (kar′ət täp′) [Slang] ***n.*** a redheaded person —***adj.*** having red hair: also **car′rot-topped′**

car·rot·y (kar′ət ē) ***adj.*** orange-red, like carrots [*carroty* hair]

car·rou·sel (kar′ə sel′, kar′ə sel′) ***n.*** *alt. sp. of* CAROUSEL

car·ry (kar′ē) ***vt.*** **-ried**, **-ry·ing** ⟦ME *carien* < Anglo-Fr *carier* < NormFr *carre*, CAR[1]⟧ **1** to hold or support while moving [to *carry* a package] **2** to take from one place to another; transport, as in a vehicle [to *carry* the mail] **3** to hold, and direct the motion of; be a channel for; convey [a pipe *carrying* water] **4** to cause to go; lead or impel [his ambition *carried* him to the top] **5** to be a medium for the transmission of [air *carries* sounds; a disease *carried* by mosquitoes] **6** to transfer or extend [to *carry* a wall along a precipice] **7** to transfer (a figure, entry, account, etc.) from one column, page, time, etc. to the next in order **8** *a)* to bear the weight of [the balusters *carry* a railing] *b)* to support or sustain [when others were injured, Jones *carried* the team] **9** to be pregnant with **10** *a)* to bear as a mark *b)* to have as a quality, characteristic, consequence, etc.; involve; imply [to *carry* a guarantee] **11** to have on one's person or keep with one [to *carry* a watch, to *carry* memories] **12** to hold or poise (oneself, one's weight, etc.) in a specified way **13** to conduct (oneself) in a specified way ☆**14** to include as part of its contents or program schedule: said of a newspaper, radio or TV station, etc. **15** to have or keep on a list or register [to be *carried* on the tax list] **16** ☆*a)* to support financially *b)* to bear the cost of [to *carry* insurance on a car] **17** to enable (an opponent, a subordinate, etc.) to continue through one's own efforts, generosity, etc. **18** to capture (a fortress, etc.) **19** to win over, lead, or influence (a group) **20** *a)* to gain support or victory for (a cause, point, etc.) *b)* to win (an election, argument, etc.) *c)* to gain a majority of the votes in (a district, state, etc.) **21** to drink (liquor) without showing the effects **22** [South] to accompany; escort ☆**23** *Commerce* *a)* to keep in stock; deal in [to *carry* leather goods] *b)* to keep on one's account books, etc. **24** *Agric.* *a)* to bear as a crop; produce *b)* to support (livestock) **25** *Golf* to go past or beyond (an object or expanse) or cover (a distance) with one stroke **26** *Hunting* to keep and follow (a scent) **27** *Music* to sing the notes of (a melody or part) accurately —***vi.*** **1** to act as a bearer, conductor, etc. **2** *a)* to have or cover a range [the shot *carried* to the next hill] *b)* to move easily through the air (said of a propelled object) **3** to have the intended effect upon those watching or listening **4** to hold the head, etc. in a specified way: said of a horse **5** to win approval [the motion *carried*] —***n.***, *pl.* **-ries** **1** the range of, or distance covered by, a gun, golf ball, projectile, etc. ☆**2** a portage between two navigable bodies of water **3** the act or manner of carrying —**be** (or **get**) **carried away** to be moved to great or unreasoning emotion or enthusiasm —**carry forward** **1** to proceed or progress with **2** *Bookkeeping* to transfer from one column, page, book, or account to another —**carry off** **1** to kill [the disease *carried off* thousands] **2** to win (a prize, honors, etc.) **3** to handle (a delicate situation), esp. with success —**carry on** **1** to engage in; conduct **2** to go on (*with*); continue as before, esp. in the face of difficulties **3** [Informal] to behave in a wild, extravagant, or childish way **4** [Informal] to engage in an illicit love affair —**carry out** **1** to put (plans, instructions, etc.) into practice **2** to get done; bring to completion; accomplish —**carry over** **1** to have or be remaining **2** to transfer or hold over **3** to postpone or allow to postpone; continue —**carry through** **1** to get done; accomplish **2** to keep (a person) going; sustain

SYN.—**carry** means to take something from one place to another and implies a person as the agent or the use of a vehicle or other medium; **bear** emphasizes the support of the weight or the importance of that which is carried [to be *borne* on a sedan chair, to *bear* good tidings]; **convey**, often simply a formal equivalent of **carry**, is preferred where continuous movement is involved [the boxes are *conveyed* on a moving belt] or where passage by means of an agent or medium is implied [words *convey* ideas]; **transport** is applied to the movement of goods or people from one place to another, esp. over long distances; **transmit** stresses causal agency in the sending or conducting of things [the telegrapher *transmitted* the message]

☆**car·ry·all**[1] (kar′ē ôl′) *n.* ⟦< Fr *carriole* (see CARIOLE); sp. as if < prec. + ALL⟧ **1** a light, covered carriage drawn by one horse and having seats for several people **2** a moderately large, enclosed, trucklike vehicle with removable seats

☆**car·ry·all**[2] (kar′ē ôl′) *n.* a large bag, basket, etc.

car·ry-cot (kar′ē kät′) *n.* [Brit.] CARRIER (sense 5)

car·ry·for·ward (kar′ē fôr′wərd) *n.* a loss, as from the sale of a stock, that may be used in subsequent tax periods to offset taxable capital gains

☆**carrying charge** **1** interest or other extra charge paid on the balance owed in installment buying **2** the costs associated with property ownership, as taxes, upkeep, etc.

car·ry·ings-on (kar′ē iŋz än′) *pl.n.* [Informal] wild, extravagant, or immoral behavior

car·ry-on (kar′ē än′) *adj.* designating lightweight luggage designed to be carried onto an airplane by a passenger, esp. if small enough to fit under an airplane seat or in an overhead compartment —*n.* such a piece of luggage

☆**car·ry·out** (kar′ē out′) *adj.* designating or of prepared food sold as by a restaurant to be eaten away from the premises: also written **car·ry-out**

car·ry-o·ver (kar′ē ō′vər) *n.* **1** the act of carrying over **2** something carried or left over

carry trade a speculative transaction in which a trader buys the currency of a country with a high rate of interest and sells the currency of a country with a low rate of interest

car seat a seat in an automobile; specif., a portable seat that fastens onto a car's built-in seat and is used for securing a small child

car·sick (kär′sik′) *adj.* nauseated from riding in an automobile, bus, etc. —**car′sick′ness** *n.*

Car·son (kär′sən) **1 Kit** (born *Christopher Carson*) 1809-68; U.S. frontiersman **2 Rachel (Louise)** 1907-64; U.S. biologist & science writer

Carson City ⟦after Kit CARSON⟧ capital of Nev., near Lake Tahoe

Car·stensz (kär′stənz), **Mount** *former name for* DJAJA PEAK

cart (kärt) *n.* ⟦ME < ON *kartr* (akin to OE *cræt*; orig., body of a cart made of wickerwork, hamper): for IE base see CRADLE⟧ **1** any of various small, strong, two-wheeled vehicles drawn by a horse, ox, pony, etc. **2** a light, uncovered wagon or carriage **3** a small, wheeled vehicle, drawn or pushed by hand —*vt.* **1** to carry or deliver in or as in a cart, truck, etc.; transport **2** to remove (someone or something) forcefully [*she was carted off to jail*] —**put the cart before the horse** to deal with matters in reverse order, as because of illogical reasoning —**cart′er** *n.*

cart·age (kärt′ij) *n.* **1** the act or work of carting **2** the charge made for carting

Car·ta·ge·na (kär′tə hā′nə, -tə jē′-) **1** seaport in NW Colombia, on the Caribbean **2** seaport in Murcia, SE Spain, on the Mediterranean

Carte (kärt), **Richard D'Oy·ly** (doi′lē) 1844-1901; Eng. producer of Gilbert & Sullivan operas

carte blanche (kärt′ blänsh′) ⟦Fr, lit., white card, i.e., paper bearing only a person's signature, allowing the bearer to fill in conditions⟧ **1** full authority **2** freedom to do as one wishes

carte du jour (kärt′ do͞o zho͞or′; *Fr* kȧrt dü zho͞or′) *pl.* **cartes du jour** (kärts; *Fr* kȧrt) ⟦Fr, lit., card of the day⟧ bill of fare; menu: also **carte** *n.*

car·tel (kär tel′) *n.* ⟦MFr < It *cartello*, dim. of *carta*, CARD[1]⟧ **1** a written agreement between nations at war, esp. as to the exchange of prisoners **2** ⟦Ger *kartell* < Fr *cartel*⟧ an association of industrialists, business firms, etc. for establishing a national or international monopoly by price fixing, ownership of controlling stock, etc.; trust **3** [*often* **C-**] a political bloc in certain European countries —*SYN.* MONOPOLY

car·tel·ize (kär′tel īz′) *vt.* **-ized′**, **-iz′ing** to control or regulate (an industry, the price or supply of a commodity, etc.) by forming a cartel

Car·ter (kärt′ər) **1 Elliott (Cook, Jr.)** 1908-2012; U.S. composer **2 Howard** 1874-1939; Eng. archaeologist: discovered the tomb of Tutankhamen **3 Jim·my** (jim′ē) (legal name *James Earl Carter, Jr.*) 1924- ; 39th president of the U.S. (1977-81)

Car·ter·et (kär′tər it), **John** 1st Earl Granville 1690-1763; Brit. statesman & diplomat

Car·te·sian (kär tē′zhən) *adj.* ⟦after *Cartesius*, L form of DESCARTES⟧ of Descartes or his philosophical or mathematical ideas —*n.* a follower of Descartes' ideas or methods —**Car·te′sian·ism′** *n.*

Cartesian coordinates *Geom.* **1** a pair of numbers that locate a point in a plane by its distances from two fixed, intersecting, usually perpendicular lines in the same plane: see ABSCISSA, ORDINATE **2** a triad of numbers which locate a point in space by its distance from three fixed planes that intersect one another at right angles

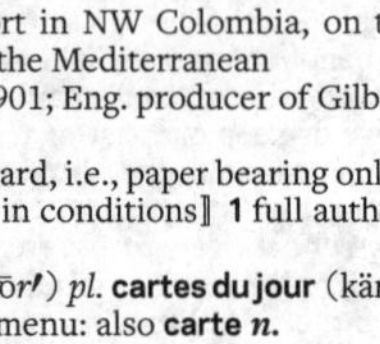

Cartesian coordinates
(x, the abscissa of P; y, the ordinate of P)

Car·thage (kär′thij) ancient city-state in N Africa, founded (9th cent. B.C.) by the Phoenicians near the site of modern Tunis and destroyed by the Romans in 146 B.C. (see PUNIC WARS): rebuilt by the Romans (44 B.C.) & destroyed by the Arabs (A.D. 698) —**Car′tha·gin′i·an** (-thə jin′ē ən) *adj., n.*

Car·thu·sian (kär tho͞o′zhən, -thyo͞o′-) *n.* ⟦ML *Cartusianus*, after *Cartusia, Catorissium*, L name for *Chartreuse*, town in Dauphiné, location of the order's first monastery⟧ a monk or nun of a very strict order founded at Chartreuse, France, in 1084, by Saint Bruno —*adj.* of or connected with the Carthusians

Car·ti·er (kär tē ā′, -tyā′), **Jacques** (zhäk) 1491-1557; Fr. explorer: discovered the St. Lawrence River

Car·tier-Bres·son (kȧr tyā bre sōn′), **Hen·ri** (än rē′) 1908-2004; Fr. photographer

car·ti·lage (kärt′'l ij) *n.* ⟦ME & OFr < L *cartilago*: for IE base see HURDLE⟧ **1** tough, elastic, whitish animal tissue; gristle: the skeletons of embryos and young animals are composed largely of cartilage, most of which later turns to bone **2** a part or structure consisting of cartilage

car·ti·lag·i·nous (kart′'l aj′ə nəs) *adj.* **1** of or like cartilage; gristly **2** having a skeleton made up mainly of cartilage, as any of a class (Chondrichthyes) of fishes (**cartilaginous fish**), including sharks, rays, and skates

cart·load (kärt′lōd′) *n.* as much as a cart holds

car·to·gram (kärt′ə gram′) *n.* ⟦Fr *cartogramme*: see CARD[1] & -GRAM⟧ a map giving statistical data by means of lines, dots, shaded areas, etc.

car·tog·ra·pher (kär täg′rə fər) *n.* ⟦see fol.⟧ a person whose work is making maps or charts

car·tog·ra·phy (kär täg′rə fē) *n.* ⟦< ML *carta* (see CARD[1]) + -GRAPHY⟧ the art or work of making maps or charts —**car·to·graph·ic** (kärt′ə graf′ik) *adj.*, **car′to·graph′i·cal**

car·ton (kärt′'n) *n.* ⟦Fr < It *cartone* < *carta*, paper: see CARD[1]⟧ **1** a cardboard box, esp. a large one, as for shipping merchandise **2** a boxlike container, as of light, waxed cardboard, for liquids **3** a full carton or its contents —*vt.* to put into a carton as for storage or shipment

car·toon (kär to͞on′) *n.* ⟦Fr *carton* < It *cartone*, both in sense 2: see prec.⟧ **1** a drawing, as in a newspaper, caricaturing or symbolizing, often satirically, some event, situation, or person of topical interest **2** a full-size preliminary sketch of a design or picture to be copied in a fresco, tapestry, etc. **3** *a)* a humorous drawing, often with a caption ☆*b)* COMIC STRIP ☆**4** ANIMATED CARTOON —☆*vt.* to draw a cartoon of —☆*vi.* to draw cartoons —**car·toon′ish** *adj.*, **car·toon′y** —**car·toon′ist** *n.*

car·touche or **car·touch** (kär to͞osh′) *n.* ⟦Fr < It *cartoccio*, cartridge, roll of paper < *carta*, paper: see CARD[1]⟧ **1** a scroll-like ornament or tablet, esp. as an architectural feature **2** on Egyptian monuments, an oval or oblong figure containing the hieroglyphs of the name of a ruler or deity **3** [Obs.] a paper cartridge for a firearm

car·tridge (kär′trij) *n.* ⟦altered < prec.⟧ **1** a cylindrical case of cardboard, metal, etc. containing the charge and primer, and usually the projectile, for a firearm **2** any of various small containers, holding a supply of material for a larger device into which it is inserted [*an ink cartridge for a pen, a toner cartridge for a desktop printer*] **3** a protected roll of camera film **4** a replaceable unit in the pickup of an electric phonograph, containing the stylus, or needle

cartridge clip a metal container for cartridges, inserted in certain types of firearms

car·tu·lar·y (kär′chə ler′ē) *n.*, *pl.* **-lar′ies** ⟦ML *chartularium* < L *chartula*: see CHARTER⟧ a collection or register of charters, deeds, etc.

cart·wheel (kärt′hwēl′, -wēl′) *n.* **1** a kind of handspring performed sideways, with the arms and legs extended: often an optional exercise in gymnastic competition ☆**2** [Slang] a large coin, esp. a silver dollar —*vi.* to perform cartwheels

Cart·wright (kärt′rīt) **1 Edmund** 1743-1823; Eng. inventor, esp. of the power loom **2 John** 1740-1824; Eng. political reformer: brother of Edmund

car·un·cle (kar′uŋ′kəl, kə ruŋ′kəl) *n.* ⟦obs. Fr *caruncle* < L *caruncula*, dim. of *caro*: see HARVEST⟧ **1** an outgrowth of flesh, as the comb and wattles of a fowl **2** an outgrowth of an outer seed coat at or near the hilum —**ca·run·cu·lar** (kə ruŋ′kyo͞o lər, -kyə-) *adj.*, **ca·run′cu·lous** (-ləs), or **ca·run′cu·late** (-lit, -lāt′)

Ca·ru·so (kə ro͞o′sō; *It* kä ro͞o′zô), **En·ri·co** (en rē′kô) 1873-1921; It. operatic tenor

car·va·crol (kär′və krôl′, -krōl′) *n.* ⟦< Fr *carvi*, caraway (< MFr < ML: see CARAWAY) + L *acer*, sharp (see ACRID) + -OL[1]⟧ a thick, oily substance, $(CH_3)_2CHC_6H_3(CH_3)(OH)$, extracted from various essential oils and used as a fungicide, disinfectant, etc.

carve (kärv) *vt.* **carved**, **carv′ing** ⟦ME *kerven* < OE *ceorfan* < IE base **gerebh-*, to scratch: see GRAPHIC⟧ **1** to make or shape by or as by cutting, chipping, hewing, etc. [*carve a statue out of wood, carve out a career for oneself*] **2** to decorate the surface of with cut figures or designs **3** to divide by cutting; slice [*to carve meat*] **4** to divide into portions, as land: with *up* —*vi.* **1** to carve statues or designs **2** to carve meat —**carv′er** *n.*

car·vel (kär′vəl) *n.* *var. of* CARAVEL

car·vel-built (kär′vəl bilt′) *adj.* built with the planks of the hull laid edge to edge to form a smooth surface: said of a boat: distinguished from CLINKER-BUILT

carv·en (kär′vən) *vt.*, *vi.* *archaic pp. of* CARVE —*adj.* [Archaic] carved

Car·ver (kär′vər) **1 George Washington** 1864-1943; U.S. botanist & chemist **2 John** 1576?-1621; Pilgrim leader: 1st governor of Plymouth Colony

carv·ing (kär′viŋ) *n.* **1** the work or art of a person who carves **2** a carved figure or design

carving fork a large, two-tined fork with a metal guard to protect the hand, used to hold meat in place as it is being carved

carving knife a large knife for carving meat

☆**car·wash** (kär′wôsh′) *n.* **1** an establishment in the business of washing automobiles **2** a fundraising event in which automobiles are washed for a fee Also sp. **car wash**

Car·y[1] (ker′ē), **(Arthur) Joyce (Lunel)** 1888-1957; Brit. novelist, born in Ireland

Car·y[2] (ker′ē) town in central N.C.: suburb of Raleigh

car·y·at·id (kar′ē at′id, kə rī′ə tid′) ***n.***, *pl.* **car′y·at′ids** (-idz) or **car′y·at′i·des′** (-at′ə dēz′) ⟦< L pl. *caryatides* < Gr *karyatides,* priestesses of the temple of Diana at *Karyai,* Macedonia⟧ a supporting column that has the form of a draped female figure

car·y·o- (kar′ē ō, -ə) *combining form* KARYO-

car·y·op·sis (kar′ē äp′sis) ***n.***, *pl.* **-op′ses′** (-sēz′) or **-op′si·des′** (-sə dēz′) ⟦ModL: see prec. & -OPSIS⟧ a small, dry, one-seeded fruit in which the ovary wall remains joined with the seed in a single grain, as in barley, wheat, corn, rice, etc.

ca·sa (kä′sə) ***n.*** ⟦Sp & It⟧ a house; home: sometimes used in the names of restaurants

ca·sa·ba (kə sä′bə) ***n.*** ⟦after *Kasaba,* former name of Turgutlu, Turkey, place from which the melon orig. was exported⟧ a type of winter melon with a hard, yellow rind and sweet, usually white flesh

Ca·sa·blan·ca (kas′ə blaŋ′kə, kä′sə bläŋ′kə) seaport in NW Morocco, on the Atlantic

Ca·sa Gran·de (kä′sə grän′dā, kas′ə gran′dē) ⟦Sp, large house⟧ the massive, prehistoric structure within Indian ruins in S Ariz., now constituting a national monument

caryatid

Ca·sals (kə säls′, -salz′; *Sp* kä säls′), **Pa·blo** (pä′blō′) (born *Pau Carlos Salvador Defillo de Casals*) 1876-1973; Sp. cellist & composer

Ca·sa·no·va[1] (kaz′ə nō′və, kas′ə-) ***n.*** ⟦see fol.⟧ a man who is very fond of women and has many love affairs

Ca·sa·no·va[2] (kaz′ə nō′və, kas′ə-; *It* kä′zä nô′vä), **Gio·van·ni Gia·co·mo** (jô vän′nē yä′kô mô) 1725-98; It. adventurer, noted for his *Memoirs,* which include accounts of his many love affairs

Ca·sau·bon (kȧ zō bōn′; *E* kə sô′bən), **I·sa·ac** (ē zȧ ȧk′) 1559-1614; Fr. scholar & theologian, born in Switzerland

cas·bah (käz′bä′, kaz′-) ***n.*** ⟦Fr < Ar dial. *qaṣba,* for *qaṣaba,* citadel⟧ **1** in N Africa, a fortress **2** the old, crowded quarter of a N African city

Cas·bah (käz′bä′, kaz′-) the crowded quarter of Algiers, Algeria

cas·ca·bel (kas′kə bel′) ***n.*** ⟦Sp, a small bell, rattle⟧ a projecting part behind the breech of a muzzle-loading cannon

cas·cade (kas kād′) ***n.*** ⟦Fr < It *cascata* < *cascare,* to fall < VL **casicare* < pp. of L *cadere:* see CASE[1]⟧ **1** a small, steep waterfall, esp. one of a series **2** anything suggesting this, as a shower of sparks or an arrangement of lace in rippling folds **3** a connected series, as of amplifiers for an increase in output — ***vt., vi.*** **-cad′ed, -cad′ing 1** to fall or drop in a cascade **2** to connect in a series

Cascade Range ⟦for the *cascades* on the Columbia River⟧ mountain range extending from N Calif., through W Oreg. and Wash., into S British Columbia: highest peak, Mt. Rainier: also called **Cascades**

☆**cas·car·a** (kas ker′ə) ***n.*** ⟦Sp *cáscara,* bark; prob. < *casca,* husk, shell < *cascar:* see CASK⟧ **1** a small tree (*Rhamnus purshiana*) of the buckthorn family, growing on the Pacific coast of the U.S. and furnishing cascara sagrada **2** CASCARA SAGRADA

☆**cascara sa·gra·da** (sə grā′də, -grä′-) ⟦Sp *cáscara sagrada,* lit., sacred bark: see prec.⟧ **1** a laxative made from cascara bark **2** the bark

cas·ca·ril·la (kas′kə ril′ə) ***n.*** ⟦Sp, dim. of *cáscara:* see CASCARA⟧ **1** a West Indian shrubby croton (*Croton eluteria*) **2** its aromatic bark, used as a tonic or as a flavor for tobacco

Cas·co Bay (kas′kō) ⟦< Algonquian, muddy: for the mud flats in the bay⟧ bay on the SW coast of Maine, on which Portland is located

case[1] (kās) ***n.*** ⟦ME & OFr *cas,* an event < L *casus,* a chance, lit., falling, pp. of *cadere,* to fall < IE base **k̑ad-,* to fall > Sans *śad-,* to fall off⟧ **1** an example, instance, or occurrence [a *case* of carelessness, a *case* of measles] **2** a person being treated or helped, as by a doctor or social worker **3** any individual or matter requiring or undergoing official or formal observation, study, investigation, etc. **4** a statement of the facts or circumstances, as in a law court, esp. the argument of one side [the *case* for the defendant] **5** supporting or convincing arguments or evidence; proper grounds for a statement or action [he has no *case*] **6** a matter or issue decided by a judge or in a court of law, specif. one studied or cited as a precedent ☆**7** [Informal] a peculiar or eccentric person ☆**8** [Informal] an infatuation; crush **9** ⟦so named because L cases were thought of as "falling away" from the nom.: see ACCIDENCE⟧ *Gram. a)* the syntactic relationship shown in highly inflected languages such as German and Latin by changes in the form of nouns, pronouns, and adjectives *b)* the form that a noun, pronoun, or adjective takes to show such relationship *c)* any of the sets of such forms [the accusative *case*] *d)* in Modern English and other languages with relatively few inflections, such a relationship, whether expressed by word order or by inflected forms; also, any of these forms or sets of forms, esp. the Modern English subjective, objective, and possessive forms of pronouns and possessive form of nouns —***vt.*** **cased, cas′ing** ☆[Slang] to look over carefully, esp. in preparation for an intended robbery —***SYN.*** INSTANCE —☆**get on (***or* **off) someone's case** to start (or stop) intruding in another's affairs —**in any case** no matter what else may be true; anyhow —**in case** in the event that; if —**in case of** in the event of; if there should happen to be —**in no case** by no means; not under any circumstances; never

case[2] (kās) ***n.*** ⟦ME < OFr dial. *casse* (OFr *chasse*) < L *capsa,* box < *capere,* to take, hold: see HAVE⟧ **1** a container, as a box, crate, chest, sheath, or folder **2** a protective cover or covering part [a leather *case, seedcase*] **3** a full box or its contents [a *case* of beer] **4** a set or pair [a *case* of pistols] **5** a frame as for a window or door **6** a shallow compartmented tray in which printing type is kept —***vt.*** **cased, cas′ing 1** to put into a container **2** to cover or enclose

ca·se·ase (kā′sē ās′) ***n.*** ⟦CASE(IN) + -ASE⟧ an enzyme made from bacterial cultures, that dissolves casein and albumin: used in the process of ripening cheese

ca·se·ate (-āt′) ***vt.*** **-at′ed, -at′ing** *Med.* to undergo caseation

ca·se·a·tion (kā′sē ā′shən) ***n.*** ⟦< L *caseatus,* mixed with cheese < *caseus,* CHEESE[1] + -ATION⟧ **1** the precipitation of casein to form cheese **2** *Med.* a degenerative process in which tissue changes into a dry, cheeselike substance, characteristically associated with tuberculosis

case·book (kās′bo͝ok′) ***n.*** a book containing a selection of source materials on a certain subject, used as a reference work or in teaching methods of research

ca·se·fy (kā′sə fī′) ***vt., vi.*** **-fied′, -fy′ing** ⟦< L *caseus,* CHEESE[1] + -FY⟧ to make or become cheeselike

case·hard·en (kās′härd′'n) ***vt.*** **1** *Metallurgy* to form a hard, thin surface on (an iron alloy) **2** to make callous or unfeeling —**case′hard′ened** ***adj.***

case history (*or* **study)** collected information about an individual or group, for use esp. in sociological, medical, or psychiatric studies

ca·se·in (kā′sē in, kā′sēn′) ***n.*** ⟦< L *caseus,* CHEESE[1] + -IN[1]⟧ a phosphoprotein that is one of the chief constituents of milk and the basis of cheese: used in plastics, glues, etc.

ca·se·in·o·gen (kā′sē in′ō jən) ***n.*** ⟦prec. + -O- + -GEN⟧ [Brit.] the casein in fresh milk before it reacts with rennin

case knife 1 SHEATH KNIFE **2** a table knife

case law law based on previous judicial decisions, or precedents: distinguished from STATUTE LAW

case·load (kās′lōd′) ***n.*** the number of cases being handled as by a court, social agency, or welfare department, or by a caseworker, probation officer, etc.

case·mate (kās′māt′) ***n.*** ⟦Fr < It *casamatta* < Gr *chasmata,* pl. of *chasma,* opening, CHASM; altered by assoc. with It *casa,* house + *matto,* dim, dark⟧ a shellproof or armored enclosure with openings for guns, as in a fortress wall or on a warship —**case′mat′ed** ***adj.***

case·ment (kās′mənt) ***n.*** ⟦ME aphetic for OFr dial **encassement* (OFr *enchassement*) < *en-,* EN-[1] + *casse,* CASE[2] + *-ment,* -MENT⟧ **1** a window frame that opens on hinges along the side: a **casement window** often has two such frames, opening like French doors **2** a casing; covering —**case′ment·ed** ***adj.***

Case·ment (kās′mənt), Sir **Roger David** 1864-1916; Ir. nationalist: hanged by the British as a traitor in WWI

ca·se·ose (kā′sē ōs′) ***n.*** ⟦CASE(IN) + -OSE[2]⟧ a soluble protein derivative formed during the digestion of casein

ca·se·ous (-əs) ***adj.*** ⟦< L *caseus,* CHEESE[1] + -OUS⟧ of or like cheese

ca·sern or **ca·serne** (kə zʉrn′) ***n.*** ⟦Fr *caserne* < Prov *cazerna,* small hut; orig., small room in fortress for a military night watch < L *quaterni:* see QUATERNARY⟧ a military barracks in a fortified town

case shot a quantity of small projectiles enclosed in a single case, as a shrapnel shell, for firing from a gun

☆**case system** a method of legal training by which students analyze and discuss selected cases and decisions rather than systematically study textbooks on law

case·work (kās′wʉrk′) ***n.*** social work in which the worker investigates a case of personal or family difficulty and gives advice and guidance —**case′work′er** ***n.***

case·worm (-wʉrm′) ***n.*** any of various insect larvae that build protective cases about their bodies

cash[1] (kash) ***n.*** ⟦MFr *casse* < OFr < OIt *cassa* < L *capsa:* see CASE[2]⟧ **1** money that a person actually has, including money on deposit; esp., ready money **2** bills and coins; currency **3** money or its equivalent, as a check or money order, paid at the time of purchase, as opposed to credit —***vt.*** **1** to give or get cash for [to *cash* a check] **2** *Bridge* to lead and take a trick with (the highest remaining card in a suit, often, specif., an established suit) —***adj.*** of, for, requiring, or made with cash [a *cash* sale] —☆**cash in 1** to exchange for cash **2** [Slang] to die —☆**cash in on** to get profit or profitable use from —**cash out 1** CASH IN (sense 1) **2** to sell a stock, bond, property, etc. and convert the value into cash

cash[2] (kash) ***n.***, *pl.* **cash** ⟦Port *caixa* < Tamil *kasu* < Sans *karṣa*⟧ any of several Chinese or Indian coins of small value; esp., a Chinese coin with a square hole in the center

Cash (kash), **Johnny** 1932-2003; U.S. country music singer & composer

☆**cash-and-car·ry** (kash′ən kar′ē) ***adj.*** **1** with cash payments and no deliveries **2** operated on a cash-and-carry system

☆**ca·shaw** (kə shô′) ***n.*** *alt. sp. of* CUSHAW

cash bar a bar as at a banquet, club luncheon, or reception, where guests pay for alcoholic drinks

cash·book (kash′bo͝ok′) ***n.*** a book in which all receipts and payments of money are entered

cash cow [Slang] *Business* a profitable asset or resource, as a subsidiary company, producing excess funds that are used to finance investment in other areas, support unprofitable ventures, etc.

cash crop a crop grown by a farmer primarily for sale to others rather than for his or her own use

cash discount a discount from the purchase price allowed a purchaser paying within a specified period

cash·ew (kash′o͞o; *also,* kə sho͞o′) ***n.*** ⟦aphetic < Fr *acajou* < Port *acajú* < Tupí⟧ **1** a tropical evergreen tree (*Anacardium occidentale*) of the cashew family, with kidney-shaped nuts, each at the end of an edible, pear-shaped receptacle (**cashew apple**): the nut yields a vegetable oil and the shell yields an oil used to make resins, plastics, etc. **2** the nut, edible after being roasted: also **cashew nut** —***adj.*** designating a family (Anacardiaceae) of dicotyledonous trees, shrubs, and vines (order Sapindales), including the pistachio, mango, and sumac

cash flow the pattern of receipts and expenditures of a company, government, etc., resulting in the availability or nonavailability of cash

cash·ier[1] (ka shir′) ***n.*** ⟦< MDu or MFr; MDu *cassier* < MFr *caissier* < *caisse*⟧ **1** a person hired to collect and keep a record of customers' payments, as in a store **2** an officer in a bank or company responsible for receipts and disbursements

cash·ier[2] (ka shir′) ***vt.*** ⟦MDu *casseren*, to disband soldiers < MFr *casser*, to break < LL *cassare*, to nullify, destroy < L *cassus*, empty, futile (see QUASH[1]) & *quassare*, to shake, shatter (see QUASH[2])⟧ **1** to dismiss, esp. in dishonor, from a position of command, trust, etc. **2** to discard or reject

☆**cashier's check** a check drawn by a bank on its own funds and signed by the cashier

cash·less (kash′lis) ***adj.*** designating or of financial transactions handled as by means of credit cards, bank transfers, and checks, with no bills or coins handed from person to person [some say we are headed toward a *cashless* society]

cash machine ATM[1]

cash·mere (kash′mir′, kazh′-) ***n.*** ⟦after *Cashmere* (old sp. of KASHMIR)⟧ **1** a fine carded wool obtained from goats of Kashmir and Tibet **2** a soft, twilled cloth made of this or similar wool **3** a cashmere shawl, sweater, coat, etc.

cash on delivery **1** cash payment when a purchase or shipment is delivered **2** with cash paid or due at time of delivery

☆**cash register** a business machine, usually with a money drawer, used to register visibly the amount of each sale: receipts may be recorded and totaled on tapes

cas·i·mere or **cas·i·mire** (kas′ə mir′) ***n.*** *alt. sp. of* CASSIMERE

cas·ing (kās′iŋ) ***n.*** **1** the act of encasing **2** a protective covering; specif., ☆*a)* a cleaned intestine as of cattle, a plastic membrane, etc., used to encase processed meats ☆*b)* the supporting framework of a pneumatic rubber tire exclusive of an inner tube and tread; carcass ☆*c)* a piece of heavy steel pipe used to line a borehole or well, esp. an oil or gas well ☆**3** a frame, as for a window or door opening

ca·si·no (kə sē′nō) ***n., pl.*** **-nos**; for 1, also, **-ni** (-nē) ⟦It, dim. of *casa*, house < L, hut, shed; orig. ? of plaited material < IE base **kat-*, to twist, plait > OE *heathor*, pen, Sans *kōt*, small stable⟧ **1** in Italy, a small country house **2** a public room or building for entertainments, dancing, or, now specif., gambling **3** a card game for two to four players in which the object is to use cards in the hand to take cards or combinations of cards exposed on the table

ca·si·ta (kä sēt′ə) ***n.*** ⟦Sp, dim. of *casa*, house < L: see prec.⟧ in Mexico and the Southwest, a small house

cask (kask, käsk) ***n.*** ⟦ME *caske* < Fr *casque* < Sp *casco*, potsherd, cask, helmet < *cascar*, to break < VL **quassicare*, to break, freq. of L *quassare*, to shake, shatter: see QUASH[2]⟧ **1** a barrel of any size made of staves, esp. one for liquids **2** the contents of a full cask

cas·ket (kas′kit, käs′-) ***n.*** ⟦ME, prob. < NormFr *cassette*, dim. of *casse*, CASE[2]; *-k* by analogy with prec.⟧ **1** a small box or chest, as for valuables ☆**2** a coffin, esp. a costly one —***vt.*** to put into a casket

Cas·lon (kaz′lən), **William** 1692-1766; Eng. type designer

Cas·pi·an Sea (kas′pē ən) inland salt sea between Asia and extreme SE Europe, north of Iran: 143,244 sq mi (371,000 sq km) —**Cas′pi·an** ***adj.***

casque (kask) ***n.*** ⟦Fr: see CASK⟧ **1** a helmet **2** *Anat., Zool.* a helmetlike process or part —**casqued** ***adj.***

Cass (kas), **Lewis** 1782-1866; U.S. statesman

cas·sa·ba (kə sä′bə) ***n.*** *alt. sp. of* CASABA

Cas·san·dra (kə san′drə) ***n.*** ⟦L < Gr *Kassandra*⟧ **1** *Gr. Myth.* a daughter of Priam and Hecuba: to win her love, Apollo gives her prophetic power, but when thwarted, decrees that no one will believe her prophecies **2** a person whose warnings of misfortune are disregarded **3** a feminine name

cas·sa·ta (kə sät′ə) ***n.*** ⟦It⟧ an Italian ice cream combining at least three flavors, chopped nuts, and candied fruits

cas·sa·tion (ka sā′shən) ***n.*** ⟦Fr < MFr *casser*: see CASHIER[2]⟧ *Law* in France, abrogation or annulment, as of a court decision, by a higher court

Cas·satt (kə sat′), **Mary** 1845-1926; U.S. painter in France

cas·sa·va (kə sä′və) ***n.*** ⟦Fr *cassave* < Sp *cazabe* < Taino *casávi, cazábbi*⟧ **1** any of several tropical American plants, shrubs, and trees (genus *Manihot*, esp. *M. esculenta*) of the spurge family, having edible, starchy roots **2** this root or a starch extracted from it, used in making bread and tapioca

Cas·se·grain (kas′ə grān′) ***adj.*** ⟦after L. *Cassegrain* (1629-93), Fr priest & physicist who proposed a design for such a telescope in 1672⟧ of an arrangement of mirrors, lenses, etc. used in reflecting telescopes and microwave antennas, having its focus or transmission point near or behind the center of the main mirror —**Cas′se·grain′i·an** ***adj.***

cas·se·role (kas′ə rōl′) ***n.*** ⟦Fr, dim. of *casse*, bowl, basin < Prov *cassa*, melting pan < VL *cattia* < Gr *kyathion*, dim. of *kyathos*, bowl, cup⟧ **1** an earthenware or glass baking dish, usually with a cover, in which food can be cooked and then served **2** the food baked and served in such a dish, typically rice, potatoes, or macaroni together with meat or fish and vegetables **3** *Chem.* a deep porcelain dish with a handle, used for heating or evaporating a substance

cas·sette (kə set′, ka-) ***n.*** ⟦Fr, dim. of NormFr *casse*, CASE[2]⟧ **1** a case with roll film in it, for loading a camera quickly and easily **2** a similar case with magnetic tape, for use in a tape recorder, VCR, etc.

cas·si·a (kash′ə, kas′ē ə) ***n.*** ⟦ME < L < Gr *kasia*, kind of cinnamon < Heb *qeṣī'āh*, lit., something scraped off⟧ **1** *a)* the bark of a tree (*Cinnamomum cassia*) of the laurel family, native to Southeast Asia: used as the source of a coarse variety of cinnamon (in full **cassia bark**) *b)* this tree **2** *a)* any of a genus (*Cassia*) of herbs, shrubs, and trees of the caesalpinia family, common in tropical countries: the pods of some of these plants have a mildly laxative pulp: from the leaves of others the cathartic drug senna is prepared *b)* cassia pods *c)* cassia pulp

cas·si·mere (kas′ə mir′) ***n.*** ⟦var. of CASHMERE⟧ a woolen cloth, twilled or plain, used for men's suits

Cas·si·ni division (ka sē′nē) ⟦after G. D. *Cassini* (1625-1712), Fr astronomer, born in Italy⟧ the gap or dark region between the two main outer rings of Saturn: it has a width of about 4,700 km (2,920 mi): also **Cassini's division**

cas·si·no (kə sē′nō) ***n.*** *alt. sp. of* CASINO (sense 3)

Cas·si·o·pe·ia (kas′ē ō pē′ə, -pē′yə) ***n.*** ⟦L < Gr *Kassiopeia*⟧ **1** *Gr. Myth.* the wife of Cepheus and mother of Andromeda **2** a N constellation between Andromeda and Cepheus

Cassiopeia's Chair the five brightest stars in the constellation Cassiopeia that seem to form the shape of a W or M

Cas·si·rer (kə sē′rər), **Ernst** (ernst) 1874-1945; Ger. philosopher in Great Britain, Denmark, & the U.S. after 1933

cas·sis (ka sēs′) ***n.*** ⟦Fr, orig., black currant < L *cassia*, CASSIA: the black currant was used as a substitute for cassia in medieval times⟧ **1** *a)* *short for* CRÈME DE CASSIS *b)* a drink made with this liqueur [vermouth *cassis*] **2** a syrup made from black currants

cas·sit·er·ite (kə sit′ər īt′) ***n.*** ⟦< Gr *kassiteros*, tin + -ITE[1]⟧ a very hard and heavy, brown or black mineral, tin dioxide, SnO_2, the chief ore of tin

Cas·si·us (Longinus) (kash′əs, kas′ē əs), **(Gaius)** died 42 B.C.; Rom. general & conspirator against Caesar

cas·sock (kas′ək) ***n.*** ⟦Fr *casaque*; prob. < Turk *qazaq*, nomad, adventurer (> Russ *kozak*, COSSACK); in allusion to their usual riding coat⟧ a long, closefitting vestment, generally black, worn as an outer garment or under the surplice by members of the clergy, choristers, etc.

cas·sou·let (kas′o͝o lā′) ***n.*** ⟦Fr; orig., dial. dim. of *cassolo*, stoneware bowl, dim. of *casso* < Prov *cassa*: see CASSEROLE⟧ a traditional casserole of SW France, consisting of beans slowly baked with various kinds of meat and, often, a leg of confit of duck or goose

cas·so·war·y (kas′ə wer′ē) ***n., pl.*** **-war′ies** ⟦Malay *kasuārī*⟧ any of a family (Casuariidae) of large, flightless birds of Australia and New Guinea with a brightly colored, featherless neck and head: with the larger emus, they form a unique order (Casuariiformes) distinct from rheas and ostriches

cast (kast, käst) ***vt.*** **cast, cast′ing** ⟦ME *casten* < ON *kasta*, to throw⟧ **1** *a)* to put, deposit, or throw with force or violence; fling; hurl *b)* to give vent to as if by throwing [to *cast* aspersions] **2** to deposit (a ballot); register (a vote) **3** *a)* to cause to fall or turn; direct [to *cast* one's eyes or attention on a thing] *b)* to give forth; project [to *cast* light, a shadow, etc.] **4** to throw out or drop (a net, anchor, etc.) at the end of a rope or cable **5** to throw out (a fly, bait, lure, etc.) at the end of a fishing line **6** to draw (lots) or throw (dice) **7** to bring forth (young), esp. prematurely **8** *a)* to throw off or away *b)* to shed; slough [the snake *casts* its skin] **9** to add up (accounts, a sum, etc.); calculate by arithmetic **10** to calculate (a horoscope, tides, etc.) **11** to arrange in some form or system; formulate **12** *a)* to form (molten metal, plastic, etc.) into a particular shape by pouring or pressing into a mold *b)* to make by such a method **13** *a)* to choose and assign actors for (a play, film, etc.) *b)* to select (an actor) for (a role or part) **14** to twist; turn; warp **15** *Naut.* to direct the bow of (a ship) to port or starboard in getting under way —***vi.*** **1** to throw dice **2** to throw out a fly, etc. at the end of a fishing line **3** [Brit. Dial.] to vomit **4** to turn; warp **5** to add up figures; calculate **6** to calculate horoscopes, tides, etc. **7** to be formed in a mold **8** [Obs.] *a)* to make a forecast; conjecture *b)* to deliberate; plan **9** *Hunting* to search for game, a trail, or a lost scent **10** *Naut.* *a)* to cast a ship *b)* to veer —***n.*** **1** the act of casting; a throw; also, a way of casting or distance thrown; specif., *a)* a throw of dice *b)* a stroke of fortune *c)* a turn of the eye; glance; look *d)* a throw of a fishing line, net, etc. *e)* an adding up; calculation *f)* a conjecture; forecast **2** a quantity or thing cast in a certain way; specif., *a)* something thrown up, off, or out, as bait on a line, a pair of hawks in falconry, the dirt thrown up by worms, the shed skin of an insect, etc. *b)* the amount of metal cast at one time *c)* something formed in or as in a mold, as a bronze or plaster reproduction of a statue modeled in clay; also, the mold *d)* a mold or impression taken of an object or of printing type *e)* a plaster form for immobilizing a broken arm, leg, etc. *f)* the set of actors in a play or movie **3** the form or direction in which a thing is cast; specif., *a)* an arrangement *b)* an appearance or stamp, as of features *c)* kind; quality [of an aristocratic *cast*] *d)* a tinge; shade [a reddish *cast*] *e)* a trace or suggestion *f)* a turn or twist to one side; tendency; bent *g)* a slight turning in or out of the eye **4** *Hunting* a scattering of the hounds to find a lost scent **5** *Med.* a substance formed and molded in the cavities of some diseased organs [renal *casts*] —**SYN.** THROW —**cast about 1** to search; look (*for*) **2** to make plans; devise —**cast aside** (or **away**) to discard; abandon —**cast back 1** to refer to something past **2** to resemble some distant ancestor —**cast down 1** to turn downward **2** to sadden; depress; discourage —**cast off 1** to discard; abandon; disown **2** to set free **3** to release or disengage the line or lines holding a vessel in place beside a dock, quay, etc. **4** *Knitting* to make the last row of stitches **5** *Printing* to estimate how many lines or pages of type will be set from (a given amount of copy) —**cast on** *Knitting* to make the first row of stitches —**cast out** to force to get out or go away; expel —**cast up 1** to throw up; vomit **2** to turn upward **3** to add up; total **4** to construct by digging [to *cast up* earthworks]

-cast (kast) ⟦< (BROAD)CAST⟧ *combining form* broadcast [*telecast, podcast*]

Cas·ta·li·a (kas tā′lē ə) ⟦L < Gr *Kastalia*⟧ spring on Mount Parnassus, Greece: in ancient times it was sacred to the Muses and was considered a source of poetic inspiration for those who bathed in it —**Cas·ta′li·an** *adj.*

cas·ta·nets (kas′tə nets′) *pl.n.* ⟦Fr *castagnettes* < Sp *castañetas* (pl.) < dim. of *castaña*, chestnut < L *castanea* (see CHESTNUT): so named from their shape⟧ a pair of small, hollowed pieces of hard wood, ivory, etc., held in the hand by a connecting cord and clicked together with the fingers to beat time to music, esp. in Spanish dances

castanets

cast·a·way (kas′tə wā′) *n.* **1** a person or thing cast out or off, esp. an outcast **2** a shipwrecked person —*adj.* **1** thrown away; discarded **2** cast adrift or stranded, as by shipwreck

caste (kast, käst) *n.* ⟦Fr < Port *casta*, breed, race, caste < L *castus*, pure, chaste, orig., cut off, separated, pp. of *carere*, to be cut off from < IE base **k̑es-*, to cut > MIr *cess*, spear⟧ **1** any of the distinct, hereditary Hindu social classes, each traditionally, but no longer officially, excluded from social dealings with the others **2** any exclusive and restrictive social or occupational class or group **3** rigid class distinction based on birth, wealth, etc., operating as a social system or principle **4** any of the differentiated types of individuals in a colony of social insects —**lose caste** to lose social status or position

cas·tel·lan (kas′tə lən) *n.* ⟦ME & Anglo-Fr *castellain* < ML *castellanus*, keeper of a castle (L, of a castle) < L *castellum*, CASTLE⟧ the warden or governor of a castle

cas·tel·la·ny (-lā′nē, -lə nē) *n., pl.* **-nies 1** the office or position of a castellan **2** all the lands of a castle

cas·tel·lat·ed (-lāt′id) *adj.* ⟦ML *castellatus* < L *castellum*, CASTLE⟧ **1** built with turrets and battlements, like a castle **2** having many castles —**cas′tel·la′tion** *n.*

Cas·te·llón (käs′tel yôn′) seaport in E Spain, on the Mediterranean: in full **Castellón de la Pla′na** (-dā′ lä plä′nä′)

cast·er (kas′tər, käs′-) *n.* **1** a person or thing that casts **2** *a)* a small bottle or other container for serving vinegar, mustard, salt, etc. at the table ☆*b)* a stand for holding several such containers **3** a small wheel or freely rolling ball set in a swiveled frame and attached to each leg, bottom corner, etc. of a piece of furniture or other heavy object so that it can be moved easily

cas·ti·gate (kas′ti gāt′) *vt.* **-gat′ed, -gat′ing** ⟦< L *castigatus*, pp. of *castigare*, to purify, chastise < *castus*, pure (see CASTE) + *agere*: see ACT[1]⟧ to punish or rebuke severely, esp. by harsh public criticism —**SYN.** PUNISH —**cas′ti·ga′tion** *n.* —**cas′ti·ga′tor** *n.* —**cas′ti·ga·to′ry** (-gə tôr′ē) *adj.*

Cas·ti·glio·ne (käs′tē lyô′ne), Conte **Bal·das·sa·re** (bäl′dä sä′re) 1478-1529; It. writer & diplomat

Cas·tile (kas tēl′) region & former kingdom in N and central Spain: gained autonomy in 10th cent. & united with León, & later with Aragon (15th cent.), & became the nucleus of the Spanish monarchy: traditionally divided between Old Castile, to the north (now the region of **Cas·ti·lla-Le·ón**, 36,350 sq mi or 94,147 sq km; cap. Burgos) and New Castile, to the south (now the region of **Cas·ti·lla-La Mancha**, 30,589 sq mi or 79,225 sq km; cap. Toledo): Sp. name **Cas·ti·lla** (käs tē′lyä)

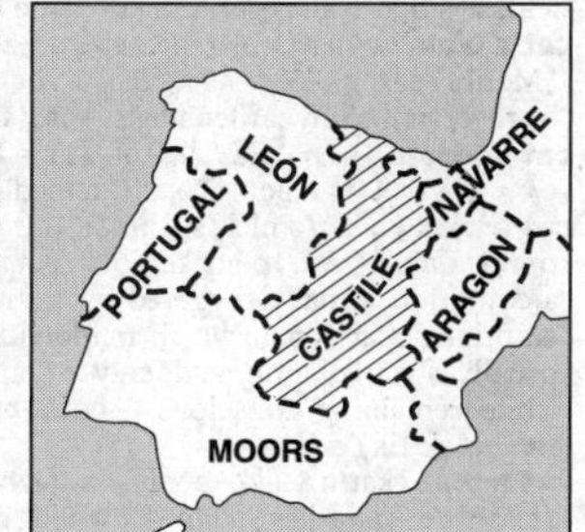

Castile (c. 12th cent.)

Castile soap ⟦ME *Castell sope*, after prec., where first made⟧ [*also* **c- s-**] a fine, mild, hard soap prepared from olive oil and sodium hydroxide

Cas·til·ian (kas til′yən) *adj.* of Castile or its people, language, or culture —*n.* **1** a person born or living in Castile **2** the variety of Spanish spoken in Castile, now the standard form of the language in Spain

cast·ing (kas′tiŋ, käs′-) *n.* **1** the action of a person or thing that casts (in various senses) **2** anything, esp. a metal piece, that has been cast in a mold **3** anything thrown off or ejected **4** [*usually pl.*] *Zool.* the excrement of earthworms

☆**casting couch** the practice of demanding sexual favors in return for casting a performer in a film, TV program, etc.: in allusion to the office couch of a casting director

casting vote (*or* **voice**) the deciding vote cast by the presiding officer when the voting on both sides is equal

cast iron a hard, unmalleable alloy of iron used for casting: it contains a high proportion of carbon and silicon, has low tensile strength, and is very fluid and fusible when molten

cast-i·ron (kast′ī′ərn) *adj.* **1** made of cast iron **2** very hard, rigid, strong, healthy, etc.

cas·tle (kas′əl, käs′-) *n.* ⟦ME < OE & Anglo-Fr *castel* < L *castellum*, dim. of *castrum*, fort⟧ **1** a large building or group of buildings fortified with thick walls, battlements, and often a moat; castles were the strongholds of noblemen in the Middle Ages **2** any massive dwelling somewhat like this **3** a safe, secure place; refuge **4** *Chess* ROOK[2] —*vt.* **-tled, -tling 1** to put into, or furnish with, a castle **2** *Chess* to move (a king) two squares to either side and then, in the same move, set the castle in the square skipped by the king: permitted only when neither piece has been moved before and the spaces between them are not occupied —*vi. Chess* to castle a king

cas·tled (-əld) *adj.* CASTELLATED

castle in the air an imaginary scheme not likely to be realized; daydream: also **castle in Spain**

Cas·tle·reagh (kas′əl rā′, käs′-), Viscount (*Robert Stewart*) 2d Marquis of Londonderry 1769-1822; Brit. statesman, born in Ireland

cast·off (kast′ôf′) *adj.* thrown away; discarded; abandoned —*n.* **1** a person or thing cast off **2** *Printing* an estimate of the lines or pages of type to be set from a given amount of copy

cas·tor[1] (kas′tər) *n.* ⟦Fr < L < Gr *kastōr*, beaver, after CASTOR: with ref. to Castor as protector of women from disease; substance was used for treating women's diseases⟧ **1** [Rare] a beaver **2** a sexual gland of the beaver containing a strong-smelling, oily substance used as a scent in trapping and in making perfumes: also **cas·to·re·um** (kas tôr′ē əm) **3** a hat of beaver or rabbit fur

cas·tor[2] (kas′tər) *n.* CASTER (senses 2 & 3)

Cas·tor (kas′tər) *n.* ⟦L < Gr *Kastōr*⟧ **1** *Class. Myth.* the mortal twin of Pollux: see DIOSCURI **2** a multiple star, actually the second brightest star in the constellation Gemini although it is considered the twin of Pollux: magnitude, 1.58

☆**castor bean** ⟦prob. < past use of oil to replace CASTOR[1]⟧ **1** the large, highly poisonous, beanlike seed of the castor-oil plant **2** the plant itself

castor oil a colorless or yellowish oil from castor beans, used as a cathartic, lubricant, etc.

cas·tor-oil plant (kas′tər oil′) a tropical plant (*Ricinus communis*) of the spurge family, with seeds (castor beans) from which castor oil is extracted

cas·trate (kas′trāt′) *vt.* **-trat′ed, -trat′ing** ⟦< L *castratus*, pp. of *castrare*, to castrate, prune: for IE base see CASTE⟧ **1** *a)* to remove the testicles of; emasculate; geld *b)* [Rare] to remove the ovaries of; spay **2** to deprive of essential virility, vigor, or significance by mutilating, expurgating, subjugating, etc.; emasculate —**cas·tra′tion** *n.*

cas·tra·to (käs trät′ō) *n., pl.* **-ti** (-ē) ⟦It < L *castratus*: see prec.⟧ a singer castrated as a boy to preserve the soprano or contralto range of his voice, esp. in 16th-18th cent. Italy

Cas·tries (kas trēz′, kas′trēz) seaport & capital of St. Lucia, on the NW coast

Cas·tro (kas′trō; *Sp* käs′trô), **Fi·del** (fē del′) 1926- ; Cuban revolutionary leader; prime minister (1959-76) & president (1976-2008): in full **Fidel Castro Ruz** (ro͞os) —**Cas′tro·ism′** *n.*

cast steel steel formed by casting, as distinguished from rolling or forging —**cast′-steel′** *adj.*

cas·u·al (kazh′o͞o əl) *adj.* ⟦ME & OFr *casuel* < LL *casualis*, by chance < L *casus*, chance, event: see CASE[1]⟧ **1** happening by chance; not planned; incidental [a *casual* visit] **2** happening, active, etc. at irregular intervals; occasional [a *casual* worker] **3** slight or superficial [a *casual* acquaintance] **4** *a)* careless or cursory [far too *casual* in his methods] *b)* nonchalant; dispassionate [affecting *casual* unconcern] **5** *a)* informal or relaxed [a *casual* atmosphere] *b)* designed for informal occasions or use [*casual* clothes] —*n.* **1** one who does something only occasionally or temporarily, esp. a casual worker **2** [*pl.*] shoes, clothes, etc. designed for informal occasions **3** *Mil.* a person temporarily attached to a unit, awaiting a permanent assignment or transportation —**SYN.** ACCIDENTAL, RANDOM —**cas′u·al·ly** *adv.* —**cas′u·al·ness** *n.*

cas·u·al·ty (kazh′o͞o əl tē, kazh′əl tē) *n., pl.* **-ties** ⟦ME & OFr *casuelte* < ML *casualitas*: see prec.⟧ **1** an accident, esp. a fatal one **2** *Mil. a)* a member of the armed forces who is lost to active service through being killed, wounded, captured, interned, sick, or missing *b)* [*pl.*] losses of personnel resulting from death, injury, etc. **3** anyone hurt or killed in an accident **4** anything lost, destroyed, or made useless by some unfortunate or unforeseen happening

cas·u·al·wear (kazh′o͞o əl wer′) *n.* clothing for wear on informal occasions: sometimes written **casual wear**

cas·u·a·ri·na (kazh′o͞o ə rē′nə) *n.* ⟦ModL < Malay *kasuārī*, CASSOWARY: so named because the twigs are similar to the bird's feathers⟧ any of a genus (*Casuarina*) of trees of the casuarina family native chiefly to Australia, esp. a species (*C. equisetifolia*) with jointed, green branchlets that bear whorls of scalelike leaves; beefwood; Australian pine —*adj.* designating a family (Casuarinaceae, order Casuarinales) of dicotyledonous trees and shrubs, having slender, drooping branches

cas·u·ist (kazh′o͞o ist′) ***n.*** ⟦Fr *casuiste* < L *casus*: see CASE[1]⟧ a person expert in, or inclined to resort to, casuistry

cas·u·is·tic (kazh′o͞o is′tik) ***adj.*** 1 of or having to do with casuistry or casuists 2 quibbling; sophistical; specious Also **cas′u·is′ti·cal** —**cas′u·is′ti·cal·ly** ***adv.***

cas·u·ist·ry (kazh′o͞o is trē) ***n.***, *pl.* **-ries** ⟦CASUIST + -RY⟧ 1 the application of general principles of ethics to specific problems of right and wrong in conduct, in order to solve or clarify them 2 subtle but misleading or false reasoning; sophistry, often, specif., about moral issues

ca·sus bel·li (kā′səs bel′ī′, käs′əs bel′ē) ⟦L, an occurrence of war⟧ an event provoking war or used as a pretext for making war

cat[1] (kat) ***n.***, *pl.* **cats** or **cat** ⟦ME & OE, both < a general European root < LL *cattus*; prob. of Afr orig.⟧ 1 any of a family (Felidae) of carnivores, including the lion, tiger, cougar, etc., characterized by a lithe body and, in all species but the cheetah, retractile claws 2 a small, lithe, soft-furred animal (*Felis cattus*) of this family, domesticated since ancient times and often kept as a pet or for killing mice 3 a person regarded as being like a cat in some way, as in temperament; specif., a woman who makes spiteful remarks 4 CAT-O'-NINE-TAILS ☆5 a catfish 6 a catboat 7 TIPCAT ☆8 [C-] CATERPILLAR (tractor) ☆9 [Slang] *a)* a jazz musician or enthusiast *b)* any person, esp. a man 10 *Naut.* a tackle for hoisting an anchor to the cathead —***vt.*** **cat′ted**, **cat′ting** to hoist (an anchor) to the cathead —☆**cat around** [Slang] to search promiscuously for sexual partners; be promiscuous: said of a man —**let the cat out of the bag** to let a secret be found out

cat[2] *abbrev.* 1 catalog 2 catechism

CAT *abbrev.* clear-air turbulence

cat·a- (kat′ə) ⟦Gr *kata-* < *kata*, down⟧ *prefix* 1 down, downward [*catabolism*] 2 away, completely [*catalysis*] 3 against [*catapult*] 4 throughout [*cataphoresis*] 5 backward [*cataplasia*] Also, before a vowel, **cat-**

ca·tab·o·lism (kə tab′ə liz′əm) ***n.*** ⟦< prec. + Gr *bolē*, a throw < *ballein*, to throw (see BALL[2]) + -ISM⟧ the process in a plant or animal by which living tissue is changed into energy and waste products of a simpler chemical composition; destructive metabolism: opposed to ANABOLISM —**cat·a·bol·ic** (kat′ə bäl′ik) ***adj.*** —**cat′a·bol′i·cal·ly** ***adv.***

ca·tab·o·lite (-līt′) ***n.*** a waste product of catabolism

ca·tab·o·lize (-līz′) ***vi., vt.*** **-lized′**, **-liz′ing** to undergo or cause to undergo catabolism

cat·a·chre·sis (kat′ə krē′sis) ***n.***, *pl.* **-ses′** (-sēz′) ⟦L < Gr *katachrēsis*, misuse of a word < *katachrēsthai* < *kata-*, against + *chrēsthai*, to use < *chrē*, it is necessary < ? IE **ĝhrē-*, var. of base **ĝher-*, small, be lacking⟧ incorrect use of a word or words, as by misapplication of terminology or by strained or mixed metaphor —**cat′a·chres′tic** (-kres′tik) ***adj.***, **cat′a·chres′ti·cal** —**cat′a·chres′ti·cal·ly** ***adv.***

cat·a·clas·tic (-klas′tik) ***adj.*** ⟦< Gr *kataklastos*, broken down < *kataklan*, to snap off: see CATA- & CLASTIC⟧ designating or of a rock, esp. a metamorphic rock, that was formed, bent, broken, etc. by extreme mechanical pressure

cat·a·clysm (kat′ə kliz′əm) ***n.*** ⟦L *cataclysmos* < Gr *kataklysmos* < *kataklyzein* < *kata-*, down + *klyzein*, to wash: for IE base see CLOACA⟧ 1 a great flood; deluge 2 any great upheaval, as an earthquake or a war, that causes sudden and violent changes, great destruction, etc. —**SYN.** DISASTER —**cat·a·clys·mic** (kat′ə kliz′mik) ***adj.***, **cat′a·clys′mal**

cat·a·comb (kat′ə kōm′) ***n.*** ⟦ME *catacumb*; ult. LL *catacumba*, pl. *catacumbae*, region between 2d & 3d milestones of the Appian Way, Catacombs; prob. by dissimilation < L *cata tumbas*, at the graves < *cata* (< Gr *kata*, down), by + *tumbas*, acc. pl. of *tumba*, TOMB⟧ any of a series of vaults or galleries in an underground burial place: *usually used in pl.*

cat·a·di·op·tric (kat′ə dī äp′trik) ***adj.*** ⟦altered (infl. by CATA-) < CATOPTRIC + DIOPTRIC⟧ designating an optical system, as in some telescopes or cameras, involving both reflection and refraction

ca·tad·ro·mous (kə tad′rə məs) ***adj.*** ⟦CATA- + -DROMOUS⟧ going back to or toward the sea to spawn: said of certain freshwater fishes: cf. ANADROMOUS

cat·a·falque (kat′ə falk′, -fôlk′) ***n.*** ⟦Fr < It *catafalco*, funeral canopy, stage; prob. < VL **catafalicum*, scaffold < *cata-* (< Gr *kata*, down) + **falicum* < L *fala*, wooden tower⟧ 1 a wooden framework, usually draped, on which the body in a coffin lies in state during an elaborate funeral 2 *R.C.Ch.* a coffinlike structure used to represent the dead at a requiem Mass after the actual burial

Cat·a·lan (kat′ə lan′, -lən) ***adj.*** of Catalonia or its people, language, or culture —***n.*** 1 a person born or living in Catalonia 2 the Romance language spoken mainly in Catalonia, closely related to Provençal: it is spoken also in Valencia, Andorra, the Balearic Islands, W Sardinia, and parts of SW France

cat·a·lase (kat′ə lās′) ***n.*** ⟦CATAL(YSIS) + -ASE⟧ an enzyme, found in blood and tissues, that decomposes hydrogen peroxide into water and free oxygen

cat·a·lec·tic (kat′ə lek′tik) ***adj.*** ⟦LL *catalecticus* < Gr *katalēktikos* < *kata-*, down + *lēgein*, to leave off, cease < IE base **(s)lēg-*, loose > SLACK[1], L *laxus*⟧ *Prosody* lacking a syllable, esp. in the last foot

cat·a·lep·sy (kat′ə lep′sē) ***n.*** ⟦LL *catalepsis* < Gr *katalēpsis*, a seizing, grasping < *katalambanein* < *kata-*, down + *lambanein*, to take, seize: for IE base see LATCH⟧ a condition in which consciousness and feeling seem to be temporarily lost, and the muscles become rigid: it may occur in epilepsy, schizophrenia, etc. —**cat′a·lep′tic** (-tik) ***adj., n.***

Cat·a·li·na (Island) (kat′ə lē′nə) SANTA CATALINA (Island)

☆**cat·a·lo** (kat′ə lō′) ***n.***, *pl.* **-loes′** or **-los′** ⟦CAT(TLE) + (BUFF)ALO⟧ a normally sterile hybrid developed from crossing the American bison with domestic cattle

cat·a·log or **cat·a·logue** (kat′ə lôg′, -läg′) ***n.*** ⟦Fr *catalogue* < LL *catalogus* < Gr *katalogos*, a list, register < *katalegein*, to reckon, list < *kata-*, down, completely + *legein*, to say, count: see LOGIC⟧ a complete or extensive list, esp. ☆*a)* an alphabetical card file, as of the books in a library *b)* a list of articles for sale, school courses offered, items on display, etc., usually with descriptive comments and often with illustrations *c)* a book or pamphlet containing such a list *d)* a long list, as of warriors, rivers, or ships, characteristic of the classical epic — ***vt., vi.*** **-loged′** or **-logued′**, **-log′ing** or **-logu′ing** 1 to enter (something) in a catalog 2 to make a catalog (of) —**SYN.** LIST[1] —**cat′a·log′er** ***n.***, **cat′a·logu′er**, **cat′a·log′ist**, or **cat′a·logu′ist**

ca·ta·logue rai·son·né (kȧ tȧ lôg′ re zô nā′) ⟦Fr, lit., reasoned catalog⟧ a catalog of books (esp. in a bibliography), paintings, etc. arranged by subjects and with explanatory notes

Cat·a·lo·ni·a (kat′ə lō′nē ə) region in NE Spain, on the Mediterranean: 12,328 sq mi (31,929 sq km); cap. Barcelona: Sp. name **Ca·ta·lu·ña** (kä′tä lo͞o′nyä′) —**Cat′a·lo′ni·an** ***adj., n.***

☆**ca·tal·pa** (kə tal′pə) ***n.*** ⟦ModL < Creek *katálpa* ? < *ka-*, combining form of *iká*, head + *tálpa*, wing: ? so called from the shape of the flowers⟧ any of a genus (*Catalpa*) of hardy American and Asian trees of the bignonia family, with large, heart-shaped leaves, showy clusters of trumpet-shaped flowers, and slender beanlike pods

ca·tal·y·sis (kə tal′ə sis) ***n.***, *pl.* **-ses′** (-sēz′) ⟦ModL < Gr *katalysis*, dissolution: see CATA- & -LYSIS⟧ the speeding up or, sometimes, slowing down of the rate of a chemical reaction caused by the addition of some substance that does not undergo a permanent chemical change: see INHIBITOR

cat·a·lyst (kat′ə list) ***n.*** 1 any substance serving as the agent in catalysis 2 a person or thing acting as the stimulus in bringing about or hastening a result —**cat′a·lyt′ic** (-lit′ik) ***adj.*** —**cat′a·lyt′i·cal·ly** ***adv.***

catalytic converter a device in an automotive vehicle, designed to convert certain pollutants in the exhaust into harmless compounds by the action of a metal catalyst, as platinum or palladium

catalytic cracking a method used in the petroleum industry for the cracking of petroleum by catalysis

cat·a·lyze (kat′ə līz′) ***vt.*** **-lyzed′**, **-lyz′ing** to change or bring about as a catalyst —**cat′a·lyz′er** ***n.***

cat·a·ma·ran (kat′ə mə ran′) ***n.*** ⟦Tamil *kaṭṭumaram* < *kaṭṭu*, tie + *maram*, log, tree⟧ 1 a narrow log raft or float propelled by sails or paddles 2 a boat, specif. a racing sailboat, with two parallel hulls, built in the style of such a float 3 [Cdn.] a large sled, as for hauling wood

cat·a·me·ni·a (kat′ə mē′nē ə, -mēn′yə) ***pl.n.*** ⟦Gr *katamēnia*, neut. pl. of *katamēnios*, monthly < *kata-*, according to + *mēn*, month: see MOON⟧ [*also with sing. v.*] menstrual discharge; menstruation —**cat′a·me′ni·al** ***adj.***

cat·a·mite (kat′ə mīt′) ***n.*** ⟦L *Catamitus* < Etr *catmite* < Gr *Ganymēdēs*, Ganymede⟧ a boy used in pederasty

cat·a·mount (kat′ə mount′) ***n.*** ⟦see fol.⟧ any of various wildcats; esp., ☆*a)* the puma; cougar ☆*b)* the lynx

cat·a·moun·tain (kat′ə mount′'n) ***n.*** ⟦CAT[1] + obs. *a*, of + MOUNTAIN⟧ [Archaic] any of several wildcats, esp. the leopard or the European wildcat

cat-and-mouse (kat″n mous′) ***adj.*** [Informal] of or designating behavior like that of a cat toying with a mouse; specif., of or designating a strategy by which one repeatedly challenges an opponent while waiting to strike

Ca·ta·nia (kə tän′yə, -tān′-) seaport on the E coast of Sicily, at the foot of Mt. Etna

Ca·tan·za·ro (kä′tän zä′rō) city in S Italy, southeast of Naples: capital of Calabria

cat·a·pho·re·sis (kat′ə fə rē′sis) ***n.*** ⟦ModL < CATA- + Gr *phorēsis*, a bearing < *pherein*, BEAR[1]⟧ ELECTROPHORESIS

cat·a·phyll (kat′ə fil′) ***n.*** ⟦ModL: see CATA- & -PHYLL⟧ *Bot.* any rudimentary leaf, as a bud scale, preceding the true foliage

cat·a·pla·si·a (kat′ə plā′zhə, -zhē ə, -zē ə) ***n.***, *pl.* **-si·ae′** (-zhē ē′, -zē ē′) ⟦ModL: see CATA- & -PLASIA⟧ *Biol.* a change in cells or tissues, characterized by reversion to an earlier stage —**cat′a·plas′tic** (-plas′tik) ***adj.***

cat·a·plasm (kat′ə plaz′əm) ***n.*** ⟦Fr < LL *cataplasma* < Gr *kataplasma*: see CATA- & PLASMA⟧ a poultice, often medicated

cat·a·plex·y (kat′ə plek′sē) ***n.*** ⟦< Ger *Kataplexie* < Gr *kataplēxis*, stupefaction < *kataplēssein*, to strike down < *kata-*, down + *plēssein*: see APOPLEXY⟧ a condition, usually triggered by a strong emotional reaction, in which an individual, usually a narcoleptic, suddenly collapses while remaining conscious —**cat′a·plec′tic** (-plek′tik) ***adj., n.***

cat·a·pult (kat′ə pult′, -poolt′) ***n.*** ⟦L *catapulta* < Gr *katapeltēs* < *kata-*, down, against + base of *pallein*, to toss, hurl⟧ 1 an ancient military contrivance powered by either torsion or tension used for throwing or shooting stones, spears, etc. 2 [Brit.] a slingshot 3 a type of launcher that provides the force to hurl an airplane, missile, etc. from a deck or ramp to provide an initial high speed 4 a device for ejecting a person from an airplane —***vt.*** to shoot

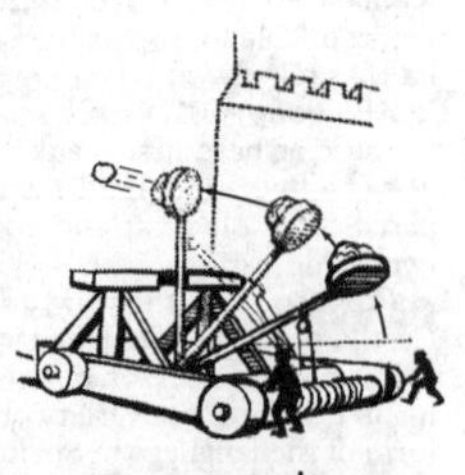
catapult

or launch from or as from a catapult; hurl —*vi.* to be catapulted; move quickly; leap

cat·a·ract (kat′ə rakt′) ***n.*** ⟦ME *cataracte,* floodgate (of heaven), cataract (of the eye) < L *cataracta,* a waterfall, portcullis < Gr *katarhaktēs* < *katarhassein,* to dash down < *kata-,* down + *rhassein,* to strike or ? *arassein,* to smite⟧ **1** a large waterfall **2** any strong flood or rush of water; deluge **3** *a)* [*often pl., with pl. or sing. v.*] an eye disease in which the crystalline lens or its capsule becomes opaque, causing partial or total blindness *b)* the opaque area

ca·tarrh (kə tär′) ***n.*** ⟦ME *catarre* < Fr *catarrhe* < LL *catarrhus* < Gr *katarrhoos* < *katarrhein,* to flow down < *kata-,* down + *rhein,* to flow: see STREAM⟧ inflammation of a mucous membrane, esp. of the nose or throat, causing an increased flow of mucus —**ca·tarrh′al** ***adj.*** —**ca·tarrh′ous** ***adj.***

cat·ar·rhine (kat′ə rīn′, -rin) ***adj.*** ⟦ModL *catarrhinus* < Gr *katarrin,* long-nosed < *kata-* (see CATA-) + *rhis,* nose: see RHINO-⟧ having a nose with the nostrils placed close together and opening to the front —***n.*** a catarrhine animal, as a human, gorilla, or chimpanzee: see PLATYRRHINE

ca·tas·ta·sis (kə tas′tə sis) ***n.,*** *pl.* **-ses′** (-sēz′) ⟦Gr *katastasis,* an arranging, setting forth < *kathistanai* < *kata-,* down + *histanai,* to set up, cause to STAND⟧ the heightened part of the action in ancient drama, leading directly to the catastrophe

ca·tas·tro·phe (kə tas′trə fē) ***n.*** ⟦L *catastropha* < Gr *katastrophē,* an overthrowing < *katastrephein,* to overturn < *kata-,* down + *strephein,* to turn: see STROPHE⟧ **1** the culminating event of a drama, esp. of a tragedy, by which the plot is resolved; denouement **2** a disastrous end, bringing overthrow or ruin **3** any great and sudden calamity, disaster, or misfortune **4** a total or ignominious failure **5** *Geol.* a sudden, violent change, such as an earthquake —**SYN.** DISASTER —**cat·a·stroph·ic** (kat′ə sträf′ik) ***adj.*** —**cat′a·stroph′i·cal·ly** ***adv.***

ca·tas·tro·phism (kə tas′trə fiz′əm) ***n.*** **1** the former theory that geologic changes are caused in general by sudden upheavals rather than gradually: cf. UNIFORMITARIANISM **2** an outlook envisioning imminent catastrophe —**ca·tas′tro·phist** ***n., adj.***

cat·a·to·ni·a (kat′ə tō′nē ə) ***n.*** ⟦ModL CATA- + Gr *tonos,* tension < *teinein:* see TEND[2]⟧ *Psychiatry* a syndrome, esp. of schizophrenia, marked by stupor or catalepsy, often alternating with phases of excitement —**cat′a·ton′ic** (-tän′ik) ***adj., n.***

☆**cat·a·wam·pus** (kat′ə wäm′pəs) ***adj.*** ⟦< ?⟧ [Dial.] askew; awry

Ca·taw·ba (kə tô′bə, -tä′-) ***n.*** ⟦Shawnee *kataapa* < Catawba *(yi*ⁿ*) kátapu,* village name, lit., (people of) the fork⟧ **1** a member of a North American Indian people now living in N South Carolina **2** the Siouan language of this people **3** [*often* **c-**] *a)* a cultivated variety of the fox grape, widely grown in the E U.S. *b)* a wine made from this grape

☆**cat·bird** (kat′burd′) ***n.*** a slate-gray North American passerine bird (*Dumetella carolinensis*) with a black crown and tail: it makes a mewing sound like that of a cat and is in the same family (Mimidae) as the mockingbirds and thrashers

☆**catbird seat** an enviable position, as of power

cat·boat (-bōt′) ***n.*** a catrigged sailboat, usually having a centerboard

☆**cat brier** GREENBRIER, esp. the vine (*Smilax glauca*)

cat burglar ⟦prob. in allusion to the agility and silence of a prowling *cat*⟧ [Slang] a burglar who enters buildings by climbing up to openings in upper stories, roofs, etc.

cat·call (-kôl′) ***n.*** a shrill shout or whistle expressing derision or disapproval, as of a speaker, actor, etc. —***vi.*** to make catcalls

catch (kach, kech) ***vt.* caught, catch′ing** ⟦ME *cacchen* < Anglo-Fr *cachier* < VL **captiare* < L *captare,* to seize < pp. of *capere,* to take hold: see HAVE⟧ **1** to seize and hold, as after a chase; capture **2** to seize or take by or as by a trap, snare, etc. **3** to deceive; ensnare **4** to discover by taking unawares; surprise in some act [*to be caught stealing*] **5** to strike suddenly; hit [*the blow caught him in the arm*] **6** *a)* to overtake [*I caught Tom before he went half a block*] *b)* to get to in time; be in time for [*to catch a train*] **7** to intercept the motion or action of; lay hold of; grab or snatch [*to catch a ball*] **8** *a)* to take or get as by chance or quickly [*to catch someone's attention, to catch a glimpse*] *b)* [Informal] to manage to see, hear, find, etc. [*to catch a radio program*] **9** to take or get passively; incur or contract without intention, as by exposure [*to catch the mumps*] **10** *a)* to take in with one's mind or senses; understand; apprehend *b)* to show an understanding of by depicting [*the statue catches her beauty*] **11** to captivate; charm **12** to cause to be entangled or snagged [*to catch one's heel in a rug*] **13** *Baseball* to act as catcher for (a specified pitcher, a specified game, etc.) —***vi.*** **1** to become held, fastened, or entangled [*her sleeve caught on a nail*] **2** to take hold or spread, as fire **3** to take fire; burn: see also CATCH (ON) FIRE at FIRE **4** to take and keep hold, as a lock **5** to act or serve as a catcher —***n.*** **1** the act of catching **2** a thing that catches or holds **3** the person or thing caught **4** the amount caught **5** a person worth catching, esp. as a husband or wife **6** a snatch, scrap, or fragment [*catches of old tunes*] **7** a break in the voice, caused by emotion ☆**8** an exercise or a simple game consisting of throwing and catching a ball ☆**9** [Informal] a hidden qualification; tricky condition [*a catch in his offer*] **10** *Music* a round for three or more unaccompanied voices **11** *Sports* a catching of a ball in a specified manner **12** *Baseball* the catching of a ball in flight and holding it firmly —***adj.*** **1** designed to trick; tricky [*a catch question on an exam*] **2** attracting or meant to attract attention or interest —**catch as catch can** with any hold, approach, technique, etc.: originally said of a style of wrestling —**catch at** **1** to try to catch **2** to reach for eagerly; seize desperately —**catch it** [Informal] to receive a scolding or other punishment —☆**catch on** **1** to grasp the meaning; understand **2** to become fashionable or popular —**catch oneself** to hold oneself back abruptly from saying or doing something —**catch out** [Chiefly Brit.] to take notice of a person's error, inconsistency, or unacceptable action —**catch up** **1** to take or lift up suddenly; seize; snatch **2** to show to be in error **3** to come up even, as by hurrying or by extra work; overtake **4** to fasten in loops —**catch up on** to engage in more (work, sleep, etc.) so as to compensate for earlier neglect

SYN.—**catch,** the most general term here, refers to a seizing or taking of a person or thing, whether by skill or cunning, and usually implies pursuit; **capture** stresses seizure by force or stratagem [*to capture an outlaw*]; **nab,** an informal word, specifically implies a sudden or quick taking into custody [*the police nabbed the thief*]; **trap** and **snare** both imply the literal or figurative use of a device for catching a person or animal and suggest a situation from which escape is difficult or impossible [*to trap a bear, snared by their false promises*]

☆**catch-all** (kach′ôl′, kech′-) ***n.*** a container or place for holding all sorts of things

catch basin a sievelike device at the entrance to a sewer to stop matter that could block up the sewer

catch crop a supplementary crop grown at a time when the ground would ordinarily lie fallow, as between the plantings of two principal crops: it may be harvested or plowed under to improve the soil

catch·er (-ər) ***n.*** ☆*Baseball* the player stationed behind home plate, who catches pitched balls not hit away by the batter

catch·fly (-flī′) ***n.,*** *pl.* **-flies′** any of various plants (genus *Silene*) of the pink family, with sticky stems that can trap insects

catch·ing (-iŋ) ***adj.*** **1** contagious; infectious **2** attractive

catch·ment (-mənt) ***n.*** **1** the catching or collecting of water, esp. rainfall **2** a reservoir or other basin for catching water **3** the water thus caught

catchment area **1** DRAINAGE BASIN: also called **catchment basin** ☆**2** the geographical area served by a particular government agency, health facility, etc.

catch·pen·ny (-pen′ē) ***adj.*** made merely to sell; cheap and flashy —***n.,*** *pl.* **-nies** a catchpenny commodity

catch·phrase (-frāz′) ***n.*** a phrase that catches or is meant to catch the popular attention: also written **catch phrase**

catch·pole or **catch·poll** (-pōl′) ***n.*** ⟦ME *cacchepol* & Late OE *cæcepol,* tax gatherer < Anglo-Fr *cache-pol,* lit., chicken chaser < ML *cacepollus* < **cacere* (< VL **captiare:* see CATCH) + L *pullus,* fowl: see POULTRY⟧ [Brit. Historical] a sheriff's officer who arrested nonpaying debtors

☆**Catch-22** (-twen′tē to͞o′) ***n.*** ⟦from the title of a novel (1961) by J. Heller (1923-99), U.S. writer⟧ [*often* **catch-22**] a paradox in a law, regulation, or practice that makes one a victim of its provisions no matter what one does

catch·up (-əp) ***n.*** *var. of* KETCHUP

catch-up (-up′) ***adj.*** of or having to do with catching up —☆**play catch-up (ball)** to try to equal or surpass one's opponent in competition, as a ball-game, in which one is behind

catch·weight (-wāt′) ***adj., adv.*** with no restrictions being set on weight [*the jockeys will ride catchweight*]

catch·word (-wurd′) ***n.*** **1** [Historical] the first word of a book page, printed in the lower right-hand corner of the preceding page to catch the binder's eye **2** GUIDE WORD **3** an actor's cue **4** a word or phrase repeated so often that it comes to epitomize a certain group, movement, etc.

catch·y (-ē) ***adj.*** **catch′i·er, catch′i·est** **1** catching attention; arousing interest **2** catching the attention and easily remembered [*a catchy tune*] **3** meant to trick; tricky **4** spasmodic; fitful —**catch′i·ness** ***n.***

cat·claw (kat′klô′) ***n.*** *var. of* CAT'S-CLAW

cate (kāt) ***n.*** ⟦< earlier *acate* ME *achat* < Anglo-Fr *acat,* a purchase, thing bought < *acater:* see CATER⟧ [Archaic] a choice bit; dainty

cat·e·che·sis (kat′ə kē′sis) ***n.,*** *pl.* **-ses′** (-sēz′) ⟦LL(Ec), religious instruction < Gr *katēchēsis,* instruction < *katēchein:* see fol.⟧ oral instruction, esp. of catechumens

cat·e·chet·i·cal (kat′ə ket′i kəl) ***adj.*** ⟦Gr(Ec) *katēchētikos* < Gr *katēchētēs,* instructor < *katēchein,* to instruct by word of mouth (in N.T., instruct in religion) < *kata-,* thoroughly + *ēchein,* to sound: for IE base see ECHO⟧ **1** of, like, or conforming to catechesis or a catechism **2** consisting of, or teaching by the method of, questions and answers Also **cat′e·chet′ic**

cat·e·chin (kat′ə chin′, -kin′) ***n.*** ⟦< CATECH(U) + -IN[1]⟧ a yellow, powdery, acid compound, $C_{15}H_{14}O_6$, used in tanning, textile printing, etc.

cat·e·chism (kat′ə kiz′əm) ***n.*** ⟦LL(Ec) *catechismus* < Gr *katēchismos* < *katēchizein,* to catechize < *katēchein:* see CATECHETICAL⟧ **1** a handbook of questions and answers for teaching the principles of a religion **2** any similar handbook for teaching the fundamentals of a subject **3** a formal series of questions; close questioning **4** [Obs.] catechesis —**cat′e·chis′mal** ***adj.*** —**cat′e·chis′tic** (-kis′tik) ***adj.,*** **cat′e·chis′ti·cal**

cat·e·chist (kat′ə kist′) ***n.*** a person who catechizes, esp. one who instructs catechumens

cat·e·chize (kat′ə kīz′) ***vt.*** **-chized′, -chiz′ing** ⟦ME *catecizen* < LL(Ec) *catechizare* < Gr *katēchizein:* see CATECHETICAL⟧ **1** to teach, esp. in the principles of religion, by the method of questions and answers **2** to question searchingly or fully Also sp. **cat′e·chise′** —**SYN.** ASK —**cat′e·chi·za′tion** (-ki zā′shən) ***n.*** —**cat′e·chiz′er** ***n.***

cat·e·chol (kat′ə chôl, -chōl′, -kôl′, -kōl′) ***n.*** ⟦CATECH(U) + -OL[1]⟧ PYROCATECHOL

cat·e·chol·a·mine (kat′ə chōl′ə mēn′, -min; -kōl′-) ***n.*** ⟦prec. + AMINE⟧ any of various compounds, as norepinephrine and dopamine, that are secretions, or byproducts of secretions, of the medulla of the adrenal gland and that affect the sympathetic nervous system

cat·e·chu (kat′ə cho͞o′, -kyo͞o′) ***n.*** ⟦ModL < Malay *kachu*⟧ a hard, brown substance obtained from an Asian acacia (*Acacia catechu*) and other Asian trees and shrubs: used as an astringent in medicine, and for dyeing, tanning, etc.

cat·e·chu·men (kat′ə kyo͞o′mən) ***n.*** ⟦ME *cathecumine* < LL(Ec) *catechumenus* < Gr *katēchoumenos*, person instructed < *katēchein*: see CATECHETICAL⟧ **1** a person, esp. an adult, receiving instruction in the fundamentals of Christianity before baptism or confirmation **2** a person receiving instruction in the fundamentals of any subject

cat·e·gor·i·cal (kat′ə gôr′i kəl, -gär′-) ***adj.*** ⟦LL *categoricus*: see CATEGORY & -ICAL⟧ **1** without qualifications or conditions; absolute; positive; direct; explicit: said of a statement, theory, etc. **2** of, as, or in a category Also **cat′e·gor′ic** —**cat′e·gor′i·cal·ly** ***adv.***

categorical imperative the Kantian doctrine that one's behavior should be governed by principles which one would have govern the behavior of all people

cat·e·go·rize (kat′ə gə rīz′) ***vt.*** **-rized′**, **-riz′ing** to place in a category; classify —**cat′e·gor′i·za′tion** (-gôr′ə zā′shən) ***n.***

cat·e·go·ry (kat′ə gôr′ē) ***n., pl.*** **-ries** ⟦LL *categoria* < Gr *katēgoria* < *katēgorein*, to accuse, assert, predicate < *kata-*, down, against + *agoreuein*, to declaim, address an assembly < *agora*, AGORA[1]⟧ **1** a class or division in a scheme of classification **2** *Logic* any of the various basic concepts into which all knowledge can be classified

ca·te·na (kə tē′nə) ***n., pl.*** **-nae** (-nē) ⟦L, CHAIN⟧ a linked or connected series, as of excerpted writings

cat·e·nar·y (kat′ə ner′ē; *chiefly Brit*, kə tē′nər ē) ***n., pl.*** **-nar′ies** ⟦L *catenarius* < *catena*, CHAIN⟧ the curve made by a flexible, uniform chain or cord freely suspended between two fixed points —***adj.*** designating or of such a curve: also **cat′e·nar′i·an** (-ner′ē ən)

cat·e·nate (kat′ə nāt′) ***vt.*** **-nat′ed**, **-nat′ing** ⟦< L *catenatus*, pp. of *catenare* < *catena*, CHAIN⟧ to form into a chain or linked series; link —**cat′e·na′tion** ***n.***

ca·ten·u·late (kə ten′yo͞o lit, -lāt′) ***adj.*** ⟦< LL *catenula*, dim. of L *catena*, CHAIN + -ATE[1]⟧ arranged like a chain

ca·ter (kāt′ər) ***vi.*** ⟦< obs. *cater*, buyer < ME *catour*, aphetic for *achatour* < OFr < *achater*, to buy, provide < VL **accaptare* < L *ad-*, to + *captare*, to strive, intens. of *capere*, to take hold: see HAVE⟧ **1** to provide food; serve as a caterer **2** to take special pains in seeking to gratify another's needs or desires: with *to* or, in Brit. usage, *for* —***vt.*** to serve as caterer for (a banquet, wedding, etc.)

cat·er·an (kat′ər ən) ***n.*** ⟦Scot *catherein* < Gael *ceathairne*, common people⟧ a Scottish Highlands brigand

cat·er-cor·nered (kat′ə kôr′nərd, kat′ē-; *esp. formerly*, kat′ər-) ***adj.*** ⟦ME *cater*, four (< OFr *catre* < L *quattuor*, FOUR) + CORNERED⟧ diagonal —***adv.*** diagonally or obliquely Also **cat′er-cor′ner**

ca·ter-cous·in (kāt′ər kuz′ən) ***n.*** ⟦see prec. & COUSIN; orig., fourth-cousin⟧ [Archaic] a close friend

ca·ter·er (kāt′ər ər) ***n.*** one who caters; esp., one whose business is providing food and service as for parties

cat·er·pil·lar (kat′ər pil′ər; kat′ə-) ***n.*** ⟦ME *catirpel* < NormFr *catepilose* (OFr *chatepelose*), lit., hairy cat < L *catta*, CAT[1] + *pilosus* < *pilus*, hair: see PILE[2]⟧ the wormlike larva of various insects, esp. of a butterfly or moth —☆**[C-]** *trademark for* a tractor equipped on each side with a continuous roller belt over cogged wheels, for moving over rough or muddy ground

cat·er·waul (kat′ər wôl′) ***vi.*** ⟦ME *caterwrawen, caterwawen* < *cater* (prob. < MDu *kater*, tomcat) + v. *wrawlen, wawlen*; prob. echoic⟧ to make a shrill, howling sound like that of a cat at rutting time; screech; wail —***n.*** such a sound

cat·fight (kat′fīt′) ***n.*** [Informal] a fight or bitter quarrel, esp. between two women

cat·fish (kat′fish′) ***n., pl.*** **-fish′** or **-fish′es** (see FISH) ☆**1** any of an order (Siluriformes) of bony fishes with barbels, somewhat like a cat's whiskers, about the mouth and usually with a sharp spine in the dorsal and pectoral fins ☆**2** any of certain fishes of this group cooked as food

cat·gut (kat′gut′) ***n.*** ⟦parallel with Du *kattedarm*, but ? altered by assoc. with CAT[1] < *kit gut* < obs. *kit*, fiddle (< ? CITHARA) + GUT⟧ a tough string or thread usually made from the dried intestines of sheep, horses, etc. and used for surgical sutures, for stringing tennis rackets, etc.

cath *abbrev.* **1** cathedral **2** cathode

Cath *abbrev.* **1** Catholic **2** Cathedral

cath- (kath) *prefix* CATA-: formed in combining with initial *h* [*cathepsin*]

ca·thar·sis (kə thär′sis) ***n., pl.*** **-ses′** (-sēz′) ⟦ModL < Gr *katharsis*, purification < *kathairein*, to purify < *katharos*, pure⟧ **1** purgation, esp. of the bowels **2** the purifying of the emotions or relieving of emotional tensions, esp. by art; concept applied originally by Aristotle to the effect of tragic drama on the audience **3** *Psychiatry* the alleviation of fear, problems, and complexes by bringing them to consciousness or giving them expression

ca·thar·tic (-tik) ***adj.*** ⟦Gr *kathartikos*⟧ of or effecting catharsis; purging: also **ca·thar′ti·cal** —***n.*** ⟦LL *catharticum*⟧ a medicine for stimulating evacuation of the bowels; purgative —**SYN.** PHYSIC

Ca·thay (ka thā′, kə-) ⟦ML *Cataya* < Uighur *Khitay*, a Mongol people who ruled in Beijing (936-1122)⟧ *former name for* CHINA

cat·head (kat′hed′) ***n.*** a projecting beam of wood or iron near the bow of a ship, to which an old-fashioned anchor was hoisted

ca·thect (ka thekt′) ***vt.*** ⟦see CATHEXIS⟧ *Psychoanalysis* to concentrate psychic energy on (some particular person, thing, or idea) —**ca·thec′tic** ***adj.***

ca·the·dra (kath′i drə, kə thē′drə) ***n.*** ⟦L, a chair, office of a teacher (in LL(Ec), of a bishop) < Gr *kathedra*, a seat, bench < *kata-*, down + *hedra*, a seat⟧ **1** the throne of a bishop in a cathedral **2** the episcopal see **3** any seat of high authority See also EX CATHEDRA

ca·the·dral (kə thē′drəl) ***n.*** ⟦ME < OFr < LL *cathedralis (ecclesia)*, (church) of a bishop's seat < L *cathedra*: see prec.⟧ **1** the main church of a bishop's see, containing the cathedra **2** loosely, any large, imposing church —***adj.*** **1** of, like, or containing a cathedra **2** official; authoritative **3** of or like a cathedral

cathedral ceiling a high ceiling that slopes upward, following the line of the roof to its peak

ca·thep·sin (kə thep′sin) ***n.*** ⟦< Gr *kathepsein*, boil down, soften < *kata-*, down (see CATA-) + *hepsein*, boil + -IN[1]⟧ any of several intracellular enzymes that act as catalysts in the breakdown of protein

Cath·er (kath′ər), **Wil·la (Sibert)** (wil′ə) 1873-1947; U.S. writer

Cath·er·ine[1] (kath′ə rin, kath′rin) ***n.*** ⟦Fr < L *Catharina, Ecaterina* < Gr *Aikaterinē*; form and meaning infl. by *katharos*, pure, unsullied⟧ a feminine name: dim. *Cathy, Kate, Kathy, Kit, Kitty*; var. *Catharine*; equiv. It. *Caterina*, Ir. *Kathleen*, Russ. *Ekaterina*, Scand. *Karen*, Sp. *Catalina, Catarina*

Cath·er·ine[2] (kath′ə rin, kath′rin) **1** Saint (4th cent. A.D.); Christian martyr of Alexandria: her day is Nov. 25 **2** Saint (1347-80); It. Dominican: her day is April 29: in full **Saint Catherine of Siena** **3** **Catherine I** 1684?-1727; wife of Peter the Great; empress of Russia (1725-27) **4** **Catherine II** 1729-96; German-born empress of Russia (1762-96): called **Catherine the Great**

Catherine de' Medici *see* MEDICI[2]

Catherine of Aragon 1485-1536; 1st wife (1509-33) of Henry VIII of England

Catherine wheel ⟦orig., a spiked wheel symbolizing the instrument of torture involved in the martyrdom of Saint CATHERINE[2] of Alexandria⟧ [*also* **c- w-**] PINWHEEL (sense 2)

cath·e·ter (kath′ət ər) ***n.*** ⟦LL < Gr *kathetēr* < *kathienai*, to let down, thrust in < *kata-*, down + *hienai*, to send: see JET[1]⟧ a slender, hollow tube, as of metal or rubber, inserted into a body passage, vessel, or cavity for passing fluids, making examinations, etc., esp. one for draining urine from the bladder

cath·e·ter·ize (-īz′) ***vt.*** **-ized′**, **-iz′ing** to insert a catheter into —**cath′e·ter·i·za′tion** (-i zā′shən) ***n.***

ca·thex·is (kə theks′is) ***n.*** ⟦ModL < Gr *kathexis*, a holding (< *katechein*, to hold fast < *kata-*, down + *echein*, to hold > OE *sige*, victory): transl. of Ger *besetzung*, as used by Freud⟧ *Psychoanalysis* concentration of psychic energy on some particular person, thing, idea, or aspect of the self

cath·ode (kath′ōd′) ***n.*** ⟦coined by FARADAY < Gr *kathodos*, descent < *kata-*, down + -ODE[1]⟧ **1** in an electroplating cell, the negatively charged electrode, from which current flows **2** in an electron tube, the negatively charged electron emitter **3** in a battery that is a source of electric current, as a dry cell or storage battery, the positive electrode which receives the electrons from the external circuit See ANODE —**ca·thod·ic** (ka thäd′ik) ***adj.***

cathode rays streams of electrons projected from the surface of a cathode: cathode rays produce X-rays when they strike solids

cath·ode-ray tube (-rā′) a vacuum tube in which a stream of electrons is electromagnetically focused on a fluorescent screen, producing lighted dots: such tubes are used as oscilloscopes and picture tubes: abbrev. *CRT*

cath·o·lic (kath′ə lik, kath′lik) ***adj.*** ⟦ME *catholik* < L *catholicus*, universal, general (in LL(Ec) & ML, orthodox, Catholic) < Gr *katholikos* < *kata-*, down, completely + *holos*, whole: see HOLO-⟧ **1** of general scope or value; all-inclusive; universal **2** broad in sympathies, tastes, or understanding; liberal **3** [*often* **C-**] of the Christian church as a whole; specif., of the ancient, undivided Christian church **4** [**C-**] of the Christian church headed by the pope; Roman Catholic **5** [**C-**] of any of the orthodox Christian churches, including the Roman, Greek Orthodox, Anglo-Catholic, etc., as distinguished from the Reformed or Protestant churches —***n.*** **1** [*often* **C-**] a member of the universal Christian church **2** [**C-**] a member of any of the Catholic churches; esp., a Roman Catholic —**ca·thol·i·cal·ly** (kə thäl′i kə lē) ***adv.***

Ca·thol·i·cism (kə thäl′ə siz′əm) ***n.*** the doctrine, faith, practice, and organization of a Catholic church, esp. of the Roman Catholic Church

cath·o·lic·i·ty (kath′ə lis′i tē) ***n.*** **1** the quality or state of being catholic, as in taste, sympathy, or understanding; liberality, as of ideas **2** comprehensive quality; universality **3** [**C-**] Catholicism

ca·thol·i·cize (kə thäl′ə sīz′) ***vt., vi.*** **-cized′**, **-ciz′ing** **1** to make or become catholic **2** [**C-**] to convert or be converted to Catholicism

ca·thol·i·con (-i kän′, -i kən) ***n.*** ⟦ME < ML < Gr *katholikon*, neut. of *katholikos*: see CATHOLIC⟧ [Archaic] a supposed medicine to cure all diseases; panacea

☆**cat·house** (kat′hous′) ***n.*** [Slang] a house of prostitution

Cath·y (kath′ē) ***n.*** a feminine name: see CATHERINE[1]

Cat·i·line (kat′'l īn′) (born *Lucius Sergius Catilina*) 108?-62 B.C.; Rom. politician & conspirator

cat·i·on (kat′ī′ən) ***n.*** ⟦coined by FARADAY < Gr *kation*, thing going down, neut. prp. of *katienai*, to go down < *kata*, down + *ienai*, to go: see VIA⟧ a positively charged ion, esp. one that moves toward the cathode during electrolysis: opposed to ANION —**cat·ionic** (kat′ī än′ik) ***adj.***

cat·kin (kat′kin) ***n.*** ⟦Du *katteken,* dim. of *katte,* CAT[1]: from resemblance to a cat's tail⟧ a drooping, deciduous, scaly spike of unisexual flowers without petals, as on poplars, walnuts, and birches; ament

cat·like (-līk′) ***adj.*** like a cat or cat's; noiseless, stealthy, etc.

Cat·lin (kat′lən), **George** 1796-1872; U.S. ethnologist & artist

cat·mint (-mint′) ***n.*** *Brit. var. of* CATNIP

☆**cat·nap** (-nap′) ***n.*** a short, light sleep; doze —***vi.*** **-napped′**, **-nap′ping** to take a catnap

☆**cat·nip** (-nip′) ***n.*** ⟦CAT[1] + *nip,* dial. for *nep,* catnip < L *nepeta*⟧ an herb (*Nepeta cataria*) of the mint family, with downy leaves and spikes of white or bluish flowers that are used in flavorings and tea: it has somewhat intoxicating effects on some cats

Ca·to (kāt′ō) **1 (Marcus Porcius)** 234-149 B.C.; Rom. statesman: called *the Elder* or *the Censor* **2 (Marcus Porcius)** 95-46 B.C.; Rom. statesman & Stoic philosopher: great-grandson of Cato (*the Elder*): called *the Younger*

cat-o'-moun·tain (kat′ə mount′'n) ***n.*** *alt. sp. of* CATAMOUNTAIN

cat-o'-nine-tails (kat′ə nīn′tālz′) ***n., pl.*** **-tails′** a whip made of nine knotted cords attached to a handle, formerly used for flogging

ca·top·trics (kə täp′triks′) ***pl.n.*** ⟦< Gr *katoptrikos* < *katoptron,* a mirror < *kata-* (see CATA-) + *ōps,* EYE, face⟧ the branch of optics dealing with the reflection of light from mirrors or mirrorlike surfaces —**ca·top′tric′** ***adj.***

cat rig a rig, esp. of a catboat, consisting of a single large sail on a mast well forward in the bow —**cat-rigged** (kat′rigd′) ***adj.***

CAT scan (kat) ⟦*c(omputerized) a(xial) t(omography)*⟧ CT SCAN —**CAT scanner** —**CAT scanning**

cat's-claw (kats′klô′) ***n.*** an acacia shrub (*Acacia greggii*) native to the Southwest and to N Mexico, having spikes of yellow flowers and thorns resembling claws

cat's cradle a children's pastime in which a string looped over the fingers is transferred back and forth on the hands of the players so as to form different designs

cat's cradle

cat-scratch disease (kat′skrach′) an ailment characterized by fever and swollen glands and believed to be caused by bacteria transmitted by the scratch or bite of a cat: also **cat-scratch fever**

cat's-eye (kats′ī′) ***n.*** any gem, stone, or piece of glass that reflects light in a way suggestive of a cat's eye, as a chrysoberyl or chalcedony, a child's marble, or a reflector glass on a road sign

Cats·kill Mountains (kats′kil′) ⟦Du, cat's stream; reason for name unknown⟧ mountain range of the Appalachian system, in SE N.Y.: resort area: highest peak, *c.* 4,200 ft (1,280 m): also **Cats′kills′**

cat's meow, the [Old Informal] a person or thing regarded as wonderful, impressive, very fashionable or stylish, etc.

cat's-paw (kats′pô′) ***n.*** **1** a person used by another to do dangerous, distasteful, or unlawful work; dupe: from the tale of the monkey who used the cat's foot to rake the chestnuts out of the fire **2** a light breeze that ripples the surface of water **3** *Naut.* a hitch in the bight of a rope, used to form two loops through which a hook can be passed

cat·suit (kat′so͞ot′) ***n.*** ⟦? from its accentuating a lithe, sinuous figure, suggestive of the body of a *cat,* similar to garments worn by title character in *Catwoman* comic books (1960s)⟧ a woman's one-piece, tightfitting, typically long-sleeved garment that covers the body from the ankles to the neck

cat·sup (kat′səp) ***n.*** KETCHUP

Catt (kat), **Carrie Chapman** 1859-1947; U.S. leader in the movement for women's suffrage

cat·tail (kat′tāl′) ***n.*** any of a genus (*Typha*) of the cattail family with reedlike leaves and long, brown, fuzzy, cylindrical flower spikes; esp., either of two species (*T. latifolia* and *T. angustifolia*) whose long, flat leaves are used in making baskets and matting —***adj.*** designating a family (Typhaceae, order Typhales) of monocotyledonous, tall marsh plants

☆**cat·ta·lo** (kat′ə lō′) ***n., pl.*** **-loes′** or **-los′** *alt. sp. of* CATALO

Cat·te·gat (kat′i gat′) ***n.*** *alt. sp. of* KATTEGAT

cat·ter·y (kat′ər ē) ***n., pl.*** **-ter·ies** a place where domestic cats are bred or kept

cat·tish (kat′ish) ***adj.*** **1** like a cat; feline **2** CATTY[1] —**cat′tish·ly** ***adv.*** —**cat′tish·ness** ***n.***

cat·tle (kat′'l) ***pl.n.*** ⟦ME & Anglo-Fr *catel* (OFr *chatel*) < ML *captale,* property, stock < L *capitalis,* principal, chief < *caput,* HEAD: orig. sense in var. CHATTEL⟧ **1** [Archaic] farm animals collectively; livestock **2** domesticated oxen collectively; esp., cows, bulls, and steers **3** people in the mass: a contemptuous term

cattle call [Slang] ☆an audition that is open to any interested actor or performer

cattle egret a small, white egret (*Bubulcus ibis*), an Old World bird that has expanded its range to North and South America: it often feeds on insects attracted to cattle and other grazing animals

☆**cat·tle·man** (-mən) ***n., pl.*** **-men** (-mən) a person who tends cattle or raises them for the market

cattle tick fever TEXAS FEVER

catt·le·ya (kat′lē ə) ***n.*** ⟦ModL, after W. *Cattley* (died 1832), Brit horticulturist⟧ any of a genus (*Cattleya*) of tropical American orchids with large, showy blossoms, often grown in greenhouses

Cat·ton (kat′'n), **(Charles) Bruce** 1899-1978; U.S. historian

cat·ty[1] (kat′ē) ***adj.*** **-ti·er**, **-ti·est** **1** of or like a cat **2** spiteful, mean, malicious, etc. —**cat′ti·ly** ***adv.*** —**cat′ti·ness** ***n.***

cat·ty[2] (kat′ē) ***n., pl.*** **-ties** ⟦Malay *kātī*: see CADDY[1]⟧ a unit of weight used in various countries of Southeast Asia: in China it is equal to 500 grams, or 1.102 lb, but elsewhere it is equal to about 1½ lb (680 grams)

cat·ty-cor·nered (kat′ē kôr′nərd, kat′i-) ***adj., adv.*** *var. of* CATER-CORNERED: also **cat′ty-cor′ner**

cat·ty·wam·pus (kat′ə wäm′pəs) ***adj.*** [Dial.] *var. of* CATAWAMPUS

Ca·tul·lus (kə tul′əs), **(Gaius Valerius)** 84?-54? B.C.; Rom. lyric poet

CATV *abbrev.* ⟦*c(ommunity) a(ntenna) t(ele)v(ision)*⟧ cable TV

cat·walk (kat′wôk′) ***n.*** **1** a narrow, elevated walk or platform, as one along the edge of a bridge or over the engine room of a ship **2** a narrow platform extending as from a stage, along which fashion models walk while displaying clothing

cat·whisk·er (-hwis′kər) ***n.*** *Electronics* a sharply pointed, flexible wire used to make contact with a specific point on a semiconductor or a crystal detector

Cau·ca (kou′kä) river in W Colombia, flowing from the Andes northward into the Magdalena River: *c.* 838 mi (1,349 km)

Cau·ca·sia (kô kā′zhə, -shə) the Caucasus

Cau·ca·sian (kô kā′zhən) ***adj.*** **1** of the Caucasus or its peoples or cultures **2** CAUCASOID **3** designating or of the two or more independent families of languages spoken in the Caucasus Also **Cau·cas′ic** (-kas′ik) —***n.*** **1** a person born or living in the Caucasus **2** CAUCASOID

Cau·ca·soid (kô′kə soid′) ***adj.*** ⟦from the erroneous belief that the original home of the hypothetical Indo-Europeans was the fol.⟧ designating or of one of the major geographical varieties of human beings, including peoples of Europe, Africa, the Near East, India, etc., who are generally characterized by tall stature, straight or wavy hair, etc.: loosely called the *white race* although it embraces many peoples of dark skin color: see RACE[2] —***n.*** a member of the Caucasoid population

Cau·ca·sus (kô′kə səs) **1** border region between SE Europe and W Asia, between the Black and Caspian seas: often called **the Caucasus** **2** mountain range in the Caucasus, running northwest to southeast between the Black and Caspian seas: highest peak, Mt. Elbrus: in full **Caucasus Mountains**

☆**cau·cus** (kô′kəs) ***n.*** ⟦prob. after *Caucus* Club, 18th-c. social and political club; ult. < MGr *kaukos,* drinking cup⟧ **1** *a)* a private meeting of leaders or a committee of a political party or faction to decide on policy, pick candidates, etc., esp. prior to a general, open meeting *b)* the group attending such a meeting *c)* a faction or group of politicians [the black Congressional *caucus*] **2** a controlling organization within a British political party —***vi.*** **-cused** or **-cussed**, **-cus·ing** or **-cus·sing** to hold, or take part in, a caucus

cau·dad (kô′dad′) ***adv.*** ⟦< L *cauda,* tail + -AD[2]⟧ *Anat., Zool.* toward the tail or the caudal part of the body; posteriorly: opposed to CEPHALAD

cau·dal (kôd′'l) ***adj.*** ⟦< L *cauda,* tail + -AL⟧ **1** of or like a tail **2** at or near the tail —**cau′dal·ly** ***adv.***

cau·date (kô′dāt′) ***adj.*** ⟦ModL < L *cauda,* tail + -ATE[1]⟧ having a tail or tail-like part: also **cau′dat′ed**

cau·dex (-deks′) ***n., pl.*** **-di·ces′** (-di sēz′) or **-dex′es** ⟦L, tree trunk, log: see HEW⟧ **1** the persistent stem of a perennial plant **2** the stem of a woody plant, esp. of a palm or tree fern

cau·di·llo (kou thē′lyô, -thē′yô) ***n., pl.*** **-llos** (-thē′lyôs, -thē′yôs) ⟦Sp, leader; akin to Prov *capdel,* Gascon *capdet*: see CADET⟧ a leader, esp. a military dictator, of a Spanish-speaking country

cau·dle (kôd′'l) ***n.*** ⟦ME & Anglo-Fr *caudel*; ult. < L *calidus, caldus,* warm < *calere,* to be warm: see CALORIE⟧ a warm drink for invalids, esp. a spiced and sugared gruel with wine or ale added

caught (kôt) ***vt., vi.*** ⟦ME *cahte, cauhte*⟧ *pt. & pp. of* CATCH

caul (kôl) ***n.*** ⟦ME *calle* < OE *cawl,* basket, container, net < ML *cavellum* < L *cavea,* CAGE⟧ **1** the membrane enclosing a fetus; esp., a part of this membrane sometimes enveloping the head of a child at birth: believed by some to bring good luck **2** the part of the peritoneum that extends from the stomach to the large intestine; great omentum

caul·dron (kôl′drən) ***n.*** ⟦ME & Anglo-Fr *caudron* < OFr *chauderon* < L *caldaria*: see CALDARIUM⟧ **1** a large kettle or boiler **2** a violently agitated condition like the boiling contents of a cauldron

cau·les·cent (kô les′ənt) ***adj.*** ⟦< L *caulis,* stem (see HOLE) + -ESCENT⟧ *Bot.* having an obvious stem above the ground

cau·li·cle (kô′li kəl) ***n.*** ⟦L *cauliculus,* dim. of *caulis,* a stem: see HOLE⟧ *Bot.* a small or rudimentary stem, as in an embryo

cau·li·flow·er (kô′lə flou′ər; *often,* kul′ə-) ***n.*** ⟦earlier *cole florye* (altered after COLE) < It *cavolfiore* (< *cavolo,* cabbage + *fiore,* flower) > Fr *chou-fleur*; mod. sp. after L *caulis,* cabbage⟧ **1** a variety of cabbage (*Brassica oleracea* var. *botrytis*) having a dense white mass of fleshy flower stalks that form the head **2** the head of this plant, eaten as a vegetable

☆**cauliflower ear** ⟦descriptive: suggestive of its appearance⟧ an ear permanently deformed as a result of injuries from repeated blows, as in boxing

cau·line (kô′līn′, -lin) ***adj.*** ⟦fol. + -INE[1]⟧ *Bot.* of or growing on a stem, esp. the upper part of a stem

cau·lis (-lis) ***n., pl.*** **-les** (-lēz) ⟦L: see HOLE⟧ the main stem or stalk of a plant

caulk (kôk) *vt.* ⟦ME *cauken,* to tread < OFr *cauquer* < L *calcare* < *calx,* a heel: see CALCAR⟧ **1** to stop up (the cracks, seams, etc.) of (a window frame, boat, etc.) as with a puttylike sealant or oakum **2** to make (a joint of overlapping plates) tight by hammering the edge of one plate into the side of the other —*n.* a soft, resilient, puttylike compound for use in caulking: also **caulking compound** —**caulk′er** *n.*

caus *abbrev.* causative

caus·a·ble (kôz′ə bəl) *adj.* that can be caused

caus·al (-əl) *adj.* ⟦ME *causel* < LL *causalis*⟧ **1** of a cause or causes **2** being or involving a cause **3** relating to cause and effect **4** expressing a cause or reason —*n.* a word expressing a cause, as *since, therefore, for* —**caus′al·ly** *adv.*

cau·sal·gi·a (kô zal′jē ə, -jə) *n.* ⟦ModL < Gr *kausos,* fever, heat (see CAUSTIC) + -ALGIA⟧ a condition of severe burning pain, usually caused by a peripheral nerve injury

cau·sal·i·ty (kô zal′i tē) *n., pl.* **-ties 1** causal quality or agency **2** the interrelation of cause and effect **3** the principle that nothing can exist or happen without a cause

cau·sa·tion (kô zā′shən) *n.* **1** the act of causing **2** a causal agency; anything producing an effect **3** causality

caus·a·tive (kôz′ə tiv′) *adj.* ⟦ME & OFr *causatif* < L *causativus*⟧ **1** producing an effect; causing **2** *Gram.* designating a word or form that expresses causation ["fell" is a *causative* verb meaning "to cause to fall"] —*n.* a causative word or form —**caus′a·tive′ly** *adv.*

cause (kôz) *n.* ⟦ME < OFr < L *causa,* a cause, reason, judicial process, lawsuit: infl. (in senses 4 & 5) by CASE[1]⟧ **1** anything producing an effect or result **2** a person or thing acting voluntarily or involuntarily as the agent that brings about an effect or result [drinking was the *cause* of his downfall] **3** a reason, motive, or ground for some action, feeling, etc.; esp., sufficient reason [*cause* for complaint] **4** any objective or movement that a person or group is interested in and supports, esp. one involving social reform **5** *Law* an action or question to be resolved by a court of law —*vt.* **caused, caus′ing** to be the cause of; bring about; make happen; effect, induce, produce, compel, etc. —**make common cause with** to work together with toward the same objective; join forces with —**cause′less** *adj.* —**caus′er** *n.*

SYN.—**cause,** in its distinctive sense, refers to a situation, event, or agent that produces an effect or result [carelessness is often a *cause* of accident]; **reason** implies the mental activity of a rational being in explaining or justifying some act or thought [she had a *reason* for laughing]; a **motive** is an impulse, emotion, or desire that leads to action [the *motive* for a crime]; an **antecedent** is an event or thing that is the predecessor of, and is responsible for, a later event or thing [war always has its *antecedents*]; a **determinant** is a cause that helps to determine the character of an effect or result [ambition was a *determinant* in his success]

'cause (kôz, kuz) *conj.* [Informal or Dial.] because

cause cé·lè·bre or **cause ce·le·bre** (kôz′ sə leb′, -leb′rə; *Fr* kōz sā le′br′) *pl.* **causes cé·lè·bres** or **causes ce·le·bres** (kôz′ sə leb′, -leb′rə; *Fr* kōz sā le′br′) ⟦Fr, lit., famous case⟧ **1** a celebrated law case, trial, or controversy **2** a person, thing, or incident that has become widely known, often because of controversy

cause of action *Law* the facts alleged in a complaint, upon which is based the plaintiff's right to a legal remedy in a court of law

cau·se·rie (kō′zə rē′) *n.* ⟦Fr < *causer,* to chat < VL *causare,* complain < L *causari,* plead, dispute < *causa*: see CAUSE⟧ **1** an informal talk or discussion **2** a short piece of writing in a conversational style

cause·way (kôz′wā′) *n.* ⟦< fol. + WAY⟧ **1** a raised path or road, as across wet ground or water **2** [Obs.] a paved way or road; highway —*vt.* to furnish with a causeway

cau·sey (kô′zē) *n., pl.* **-seys** ⟦ME *cauce* < Anglo-Fr *caucie* < VL **calciata* < *calciare,* to make a road < L *calx*: see CALCIUM⟧ [Now Brit. Dial.] a causeway

caus·tic (kôs′tik) *adj.* ⟦ME *caustik* < L *causticus* < Gr *kaustikos* < *kaustos,* burning < *kaiein,* to burn⟧ **1** that can burn, eat away, or destroy tissue by chemical action; corrosive **2** cutting or sarcastic in utterance; biting **3** designating or of the curved radial surface, or a plane curve in this surface, formed by the reflection or refraction of rays from a curved solid surface —*n.* ⟦L *causticum* < the adj.⟧ **1** any caustic substance, esp. caustic soda **2** a caustic surface or curve —*SYN.* SARCASTIC —**caus′ti·cal·ly** *adv.* —**caus·tic′i·ty** (-tis′i tē) *n.*

caustic potash POTASSIUM HYDROXIDE

caustic soda SODIUM HYDROXIDE

cau·ter·ant (kôt′ər ənt) *adj.* that cauterizes —*n.* a substance or instrument that cauterizes

cau·ter·ize (kôt′ər īz′) *vt.* **-ized′, -iz′ing** ⟦ME *cauterizen* < LL *cauterizare* < Gr *kautēriazein* < *kautērion, kautēr,* burning or branding iron < *kaiein,* to burn⟧ to burn with a hot needle, a laser, a caustic substance, or an electric current, so as to remove dead or unwanted tissue, prevent the spread of infection, seal blood vessels, etc. —**cau′ter·i·za′tion** *n.*

cau·ter·y (kôt′ər ē) *n., pl.* **-ter·ies** ⟦ME *cauterie* < L *cauterium* < Gr *kautērion*⟧ **1** an instrument or substance for cauterizing **2** the act of cauterizing

cau·tion (kô′shən) *n.* ⟦ME *caucioun* < L *cautio* < *cautus,* pp. of *cavere,* to be on one's guard: see HEAR⟧ **1** a warning; admonition **2** a word, sign, etc. by which warning is given **3** the act or practice of being cautious; wariness ☆**4** [Old Informal] a person or thing provoking notice, comment, attention, etc. —*vt.* to urge to be cautious; warn; admonish —*SYN.* ADVISE

cau·tion·ar·y (-er′ē) *adj.* urging caution or intended to warn; warning; admonishing

cau·tious (kô′shəs) *adj.* full of caution; careful to avoid danger; circumspect; wary —*SYN.* CAREFUL —**cau′tious·ly** *adv.* —**cau′tious·ness** *n.*

Cau·ver·y (kô′vər ē) river in S India, flowing from the Western Ghats southeastward into the Bay of Bengal: *c.* 475 mi (764 km)

cav *abbrev.* cavalry

Ca·va·fy (kə vä′fē), **Constantine** (born *Konstantínos Pétrou Kaváfis*) 1863-1933; Gr. poet, born in Egypt

cav·al·cade (kav′əl kād′, kav′əl kād′) *n.* ⟦Fr < It *cavalcata* < *cavalcare,* to ride < VL **caballicare* < L *caballus*: see fol.⟧ **1** a procession of horsemen or carriages **2** *a)* any procession *b)* a sequence or series, as of events

cav·a·lier (kav′ə lir′) *n.* ⟦Fr < It *cavaliere* < LL *caballarius* < L *caballus,* horse; akin to Gr *kaballēs*; prob. < native name in Asia Minor⟧ **1** an armed horseman; knight **2** a gallant or courteous gentleman, esp. one serving as a lady's escort **3** [C-] a partisan of Charles I of England in his struggles with Parliament (1641-49); Royalist: opposed to ROUNDHEAD —*adj.* **1** [C-] *a)* of the Cavaliers *b)* associated with the court of Charles I of England [*Cavalier poets*] **2** *a)* free and easy *b)* casual or indifferent toward matters of some importance *c)* haughty; arrogant; supercilious —**cav′a·lier′ly** *adv.* —**cav′a·lier′ness** *n.*

ca·val·la (kə val′ə) *n., pl.* **-la** or **-las** ⟦Port < *cavallo,* horse < L *caballa,* fem. of *caballus,* horse (see prec.): sometimes called *horse mackerel* in England⟧ **1** CERO **2** CREVALLE

cav·al·ry (kav′əl rē) *n., pl.* **-ries** ⟦Fr *cavalerie* < It *cavalleria* < *cavaliere*: see CAVALIER⟧ combat troops mounted originally on horses but now often riding in motorized armored vehicles —**cav′al·ry·man** (-mən) *n., pl.* **-men** (-mən)

Cav·an (kav′ən) county in Ulster province, NC Ireland: 730 sq mi (1,891 sq km)

cav·a·tel·li (kav′ə tel′ē, kä′və-) *n.* ⟦It⟧ pasta in various, somewhat tubular, forms, including small shells with rippled edges and short pieces of dough that are curled or rolled before being cooked

cav·a·ti·na (kav′ə tē′nə; *It* kä′vä tē′nä) *n.* ⟦It, dim. of *cavata,* artful production of sound < *cavare,* to dig out, extract < L, to excavate < *cavus*: see fol.⟧ **1** a short, simple solo song or melody that is usually part of a larger composition, such as an opera or oratorio **2** loosely, an instrumental composition of lyric quality

cave (kāv) *n.* ⟦ME & OFr < L *cava,* fem. of *cavus,* hollow < IE base **keu-,* a swelling, arch, cavity⟧ a hollow place inside the earth, usually an opening, as in a hillside, extending back horizontally; cavern —*vt.* **caved, cav′ing** ⟦< the *n.*⟧ to hollow out; make a hollow in —*vi.* **1** to cave in **2** to explore caves —**cave in 1** to fall or sink in or down; collapse **2** to make collapse **3** [Informal] to give way; give in; yield —**cav′er** *n.*

ca·ve·at (kā′vē at′, kav′ē-; kä′vā ät′) *n.* ⟦L, let him beware; 3d pers. sing., pres. subj., of *cavere,* to beware, take heed: see HEAR⟧ **1** *Law* a formal notice that an interested party files with the proper legal authorities, directing them to refrain from an action until the party can be heard **2** a warning

caveat emp·tor (emp′tôr′) ⟦L⟧ let the buyer beware (i.e., one buys at one's own risk)

ca·ve ca·nem (kä′vā kä′nem′) ⟦L⟧ beware of the dog

cave-in (kāv′in′) *n.* **1** an act or instance of caving in **2** a place where the ground, a mine, etc. has caved in

Cav·ell (kav′əl), **Edith Louisa** 1865-1915; Eng. nurse executed by the Germans in WWI

cave man 1 a prehistoric human being of the Stone Age who lived in caves: also **cave dweller 2** a man who is rough and crudely direct, esp. toward women

cav·en·dish (kav′ən dish′) *n.* ⟦prob. after a proper name⟧ leaf tobacco softened, sweetened as with molasses, and pressed into plugs or cakes

Cav·en·dish (kav′ən dish′), **Henry** 1731-1810; Eng. chemist & physicist

cav·ern (kav′ərn) *n.* ⟦ME & OFr *caverne* < L *caverna* < *cavus*: see CAVE⟧ a cave, esp. a large cave —*vt.* **1** to enclose in or as in a cavern **2** to hollow out: often with *out*

cav·ern·ous (kav′ər nəs) *adj.* ⟦ME < L *cavernosus*⟧ **1** full of caverns **2** full of cavities; porous **3** like or characteristic of a cavern; deep-set, hollow, etc. [*a cavernous* voice, *cavernous* cheeks] —**cav′ern·ous·ly** *adv.*

ca·vet·to (kə vet′ō) *n., pl.* **-vet′ti** (-vet′ē) or **-vet′tos** ⟦It, dim. of *cavo,* hollow < L *cavus*⟧ *Archit.* a concave molding with a curve of 90°

cav·i·ar or **cav·i·are** (kav′ē är′, käv′-; kav′ē är′) *n.* ⟦Fr < It *caviale* < Turk *khāvyār* < Pers *khāviyār* < *khāya,* egg + *-dār,* bearing: orig., spawning fish, hence, roe⟧ the salted eggs of sturgeon, salmon, etc. eaten as an appetizer —**caviar to the general** a thing appealing only to a highly cultivated taste: *Hamlet* II, ii

cav·i·corn (kav′i kôrn′) *adj.* ⟦< L *cavus* (see CAVE) + *cornu,* HORN⟧ having hollow horns, as oxen or sheep

cav·il (kav′əl) *vi.* **-iled** or **-illed, -il·ing** or **-il·ling** ⟦OFr *caviller* < L *cavillari* < *cavilla,* jeering < **calvilla* < *calvari,* to deceive; akin to *calumnia,* CALUMNY⟧ to object when there is little reason to do so; resort to trivial faultfinding; carp; quibble (*at* or *about*) —*n.* a trivial objection; quibble —*SYN.* CRITICAL —**cav′il·er** *n.,* **cav′il·ler**

cav·i·ta·tion (kav′i tā′shən) *n.* ⟦< LL *cavitas,* fol. + -ATION⟧ the formation of partial vacuums within a flowing liquid as a result of mechanical force, as with a boat propeller or a pump impeller: when these collapse, pitting or other damage is caused on metal surfaces in contact

cav·i·ty (kav′i tē) *n., pl.* **-ties** ⟦Fr *cavité* < LL *cavitas* < L *cavus,* HOLLOW: see CAVE⟧ **1** a hole or hollow place **2** a natural hollow place within the body [the abdominal *cavity*] 3 a hollow place in a tooth, esp. when caused by decay 4 *Electronics* a space enclosed by metal and with a rodlike projection in the center, used as a resonator, as with a magnetron to produce electromagnetic waves, esp. microwaves: also called **cavity resonator** —**SYN.** HOLE

☆**ca·vort** (kə vôrt′) ***vi.*** ⟦earlier *cavaut*; prob. < *ca-*, colloq. intens. prefix (< ? Ger *ge-*) + VAULT²⟧ 1 to leap about; prance or caper 2 to romp about happily; frolic

Ca·vour (kä vo͝or′), Conte **Ca·mil·lo Ben·so di** (kä mēl′lô ben′sô dē) 1810-61; It. statesman: a leader in the movement to unify Italy

CAVU *abbrev. Aeron.* ceiling and visibility unlimited

ca·vy (kā′vē) ***n.***, *pl.* **-vies** ⟦< ModL *Cavia* < Galibi *cabiai*⟧ any of a family (Caviidae) of short-tailed South American rodents, as the guinea pig

caw (kô) ***n.*** ⟦echoic⟧ the harsh, strident cry of a crow or raven —***vi.*** to make this sound

Cax·ton (kaks′tən), **William** 1422?-91; 1st Eng. printer

cay (kā, kē) ***n.*** ⟦Sp *cayo*⟧ a low island, coral reef, or sandbar

Cay·enne (kī en′, kā-) capital & chief town of French Guiana, on the Atlantic

cay·enne (pepper) (kī en′, kā-) ⟦< Tupí *kynnha*; popularly assoc. with prec.⟧ 1 a very hot, reddish condiment ground from various capsicums 2 a long, conical hot pepper often used to make this condiment 3 the plant (*Capsicum frutescens* var. *longum*) on which these peppers grow

cay·man (kā′mən) ***n.*** *alt. sp. of* CAIMAN

Cay·man Islands (kā′mən, kī män′) British crown colony in the Caribbean, consisting of a group of three islands *c.* 200 mi (322 km) northwest of Jamaica: 100 sq mi (259 sq km): also **Caymans**

Ca·yu·ga (kā yo͞o′gə, kī-) ***n.*** ⟦Cayuga **kayókwe*ⁿ, name of a 17th-c. village: cf. *kayokweⁿhónoⁿ'*, the Cayuga (people)⟧ 1 *pl.* **-gas** or **-ga** a member of a North American Indian people that lived around Cayuga Lake and now lives in N.Y., Okla., and Ontario: see FIVE NATIONS 2 the Iroquoian language of this people

Cayuga Lake ⟦after prec.⟧ lake in WC N.Y., one of the Finger Lakes: 38 mi (61 km) long

Cay·use (kī′yo͞os′, -o͞os′; kī yo͞os′, -o͞os′) ***n.***, *pl.* **-us′es** or **-use′** ⟦< tribal name⟧ 1 a member of a group of North American Indians that lived in the Blue Mountains section of NE Oreg. 2 the language of this people 3 [**c-**] a horse, esp. a small Western horse used by cowboys

Cb *Chem. symbol for* columbium

CB[1] (sē′bē′) ***adj.*** ⟦C(ITIZENS') B(AND)⟧ designating or of shortwave radio that has citizens' band frequencies —***n.***, *pl.* **CB's** a shortwave radio using citizens' band frequencies

CB[2] *abbrev. Football* cornerback: sometimes written **cb**

CBC *service mark* Canadian Broadcasting Corporation

cbd *abbrev.* cash before delivery

CBE *abbrev.* Commander of (the Order of) the British Empire

CBO *abbrev.* Congressional Budget Office

CBOT (*often* sē′bät′) *abbrev.* Chicago Board of Trade

CBS *service mark* Columbia Broadcasting System

CBW *abbrev.* chemical and biological warfare

cc *abbrev.* 1 carbon copy (or copies) 2 cashier's check 3 chapters 4 city council 5 county clerk 6 cubic centimeter(s)

Cc *abbrev.* cirrocumulus

CC *abbrev.* 1 carbon copy (or copies) 2 cashier's check 3 chapters 4 city council 5 closed-captioned 6 Community College 7 county clerk

CCC *abbrev.* 1 Civilian Conservation Corps 2 Commodity Credit Corporation

CCCP ⟦Russ, USSR < *Sojuz Sovetskix Socialističeskix Respublik*; Russ *C*, *P* = English letters *S*, *R*⟧ *abbrev.* Union of Soviet Socialist Republics

CCD (sē′sē′dē′) ***n.*** ⟦*c(harge-)c(oupled) d(evice)*⟧ a light-sensitive electronic detector that converts an image into electronic signals which can be stored, displayed, etc.: used in digital cameras, telescopes, etc.

C-clamp (sē′klamp′) ***n.*** a general-purpose clamp shaped like the letter C

C clef *Music* a sign on a staff indicating that C is the note on the third line (ALTO CLEF) or on the fourth line (TENOR CLEF): distinguished from TREBLE CLEF and BASS CLEF

CCTV *abbrev.* closed circuit television

CCU (sē′sē′yo͞o′) ***n.*** coronary care unit

cd *abbrev.* 1 candela 2 cash discount 3 cord(s)

Cd *Chem. symbol for* cadmium

CD[1] (sē′dē′) ***n.*** 1 the compact-disc format 2 a compact disc or compact-disc player

CD[2] (sē′dē′) ***n.*** CERTIFICATE OF DEPOSIT: also written **C/D**

CD[3] *abbrev.* Civil Defense

CDC *abbrev.* Centers for Disease Control and Prevention

CD4 (sē′dē′fôr′) ***adj.*** designating or of a biochemical receptor found on the surface of various cells, esp. helper T cells: HIV binds to this receptor

Cdn *abbrev.* Canadian

CDO *abbrev.* collateralized debt obligation

CDR or **Cdr** *abbrev.* Commander

CD-R (sē′dē′är′) ***n.*** ⟦CD¹ + *r(ecordable)*⟧ a compact disc, blank when purchased, designed to be recorded on just once by the consumer: cf. CD-RW

CD-ROM (sē′dē′räm′) ***n.*** ⟦*c(ompact) d(isc)* + ROM⟧ a compact disc from which stored data can be accessed

CD-RW (sē′dē′är′dub′əl yo͞o′) ***n.*** ⟦CD¹ + *r(e)w(ritable)*⟧ a compact disc, blank when purchased, designed to be recorded on repeatedly by the consumer: cf. CD-R

CDT *abbrev.* Central Daylight Time

Ce *Chem. symbol for* cerium

CE *abbrev.* 1 of the COMMON ERA: used with dates as an alternative to A.D.: also **C.E.** 2 Civil Engineer

CEA[1] (sē′ē′ā′) ***n.*** CARCINOEMBRYONIC ANTIGEN

CEA[2] *abbrev.* Council of Economic Advisers

ce·a·no·thus (sē′ə nō′thəs) ***n.*** ⟦ModL < Gr *keanōthos*, a type of thistle⟧ any of a genus (*Ceanothus*) of evergreen or deciduous shrubs or small trees of the buckthorn family, native to North America, with clusters of very small, usually blue or white, flowers

Ce·a·rá (se′ä rä′) state on the NE coast of Brazil: 56,505 sq mi (146,347 sq km); cap. Fortaleza

cease (sēs) ***vt.***, ***vi.*** **ceased**, **ceas′ing** ⟦ME *cesen* < OFr *cesser* < L *cessare*, to loiter, be idle < pp. of *cedere*, yield: see CEDE⟧ to bring or come to an end; stop; discontinue —***n.*** ⟦ME & OFr *ces* < v.⟧ a ceasing, as of some activity: chiefly in **without cease** —**SYN.** STOP

cease-and-de·sist order (sēs′ən di zist′, -sist′) an order from a court or government agency demanding cessation of some specified activity

cease-fire (sēs′fīr′) ***n.*** a temporary cessation of warfare by mutual agreement of the participants; truce

cease·less (-lis) ***adj.*** unceasing; continual —**cease′less·ly** ***adv.***

Ce·bu (sā bo͞o′) 1 island in the SC Philippines, between Negros & Leyte: 1,707 sq mi (4,421 sq km) 2 seaport & chief city on this island

Čech·y (chekh′ē) *Czech name for* BOHEMIA²

Ce·cil[1] (sē′səl, ses′əl) ***n.*** ⟦L *Caecilius*, name of a Roman gens; prob. < *caecus* (see CECUM), hence, lit., dim-sighted, blind⟧ a masculine name: fem. *Cecilia, Cecily*

Ce·cil[2] (ses′əl, sē′səl), **William** *see* BURGHLEY

Ce·cile (sə sēl′) ***n.*** a feminine name: see CECILIA¹

Ce·cil·ia[1] (sə sēl′yə) ***n.*** ⟦L *Caecilia*, fem. of *Caecilius*; see CECIL¹⟧ a feminine name: dim. *Cis, Cissie*; var. *Cecile, Cecily, Cicely, Sheila*

Ce·cil·ia[2] (sə sēl′yə), Saint (died A.D. 230?); Christian martyr: patron saint of music: her day is Nov. 22

Cec·i·ly (ses′ə lē) ***n.*** a feminine name: see CECILIA¹

☆**ce·cro·pi·a moth** (si krō′pē ə) ⟦< ModL *Cecropia*, name of a genus of mulberry trees, after fol.⟧ the largest moth (*Hyalophora cecropia*) of the U.S., having wide brown wings, each with a crescent-shaped spot of white edged in red

Ce·crops (sē′kräps′) ***n.*** ⟦Gr *Kekrops*⟧ *Gr. Myth.* the first king of Attica and founder of Athens, represented as half man, half dragon

ce·cum (sē′kəm) ***n.***, *pl.* **-ca** (-kə) ⟦ModL < L *caecum* < *intestinum caecum*, blind intestine < *caecus*, blind < IE base **kai-ka*, one-eyed, squinting > OIr *caech*, one-eyed, blind, Goth *haihs*, one-eyed⟧ 1 the pouch that is the beginning of the large intestine 2 *Zool.* a pouchlike extension from an organ or duct —**ce′cal** ***adj.***

ce·dar (sē′dər) ***n.*** ⟦ME & OFr *cedre* < L *cedrus* < Gr *kedros* < ? IE base **ked-*, to smoke, be sooty⟧ 1 any of a genus (*Cedrus*) of widespreading coniferous trees of the pine family, having clusters of needlelike leaves, cones, and durable wood with a characteristic fragrance, as the **cedar of Lebanon** (*C. libani*) 2 any of various similar trees of other families, as certain kinds of juniper or thuja 3 SPANISH CEDAR 4 the wood of any of these —***adj.*** of cedar

☆**cedar chest** a chest made of cedar, in which woolens, furs, etc. are stored for protection against moths

ce·darn (sē′dərn) ***adj.*** of cedar or cedars

Cedar Rapids ⟦for the rapids of the nearby Cedar River⟧ city in EC Iowa

☆**cedar waxwing** a brownish-gray, crested American waxwing (*Bombycilla cedrorum*), with red, waxlike tips on its secondary wing feathers: sometimes **ce′dar·bird′** ***n.***

cede (sēd) ***vt.*** **ced′ed**, **ced′ing** ⟦Fr *céder* < L *cedere*, to yield, orig., to go, leave < **ce-*, directive particle (< IE **ke-*, this one, HERE) + **sed-*; akin to *sedere*, SIT⟧ 1 to give up one's rights in; surrender formally 2 to transfer the title or ownership of

ce·di (sā′dē) ***n.***, *pl.* **-dis** ⟦< Akan term for cowrie, formerly used as money⟧ the basic monetary unit of Ghana: see the table of monetary units in the Reference Supplement

ce·dil·la (sə dil′ə) ***n.*** ⟦Fr *cédille* < Sp *cedilla*, dim. of *zeda* (< Gr *zēta*, a zeta or *z*): so called because *z* was written after *c* to give the sound of the letter *s*⟧ a hooklike mark put under *c*, as in some French words, to indicate that it is to be sounded as the voiceless palatal fricative (s), as in *façade*

Ced·ric (sed′rik′, sē′drik′) ***n.*** ⟦< ? Celt⟧ a masculine name

cee (sē) ***n.*** the letter C —***adj.*** shaped like C

cef·tri·ax·one (sef′trī′ak′sōn′) ***n.*** ⟦< *cef-*, prob. < CEPHALOSPORIN; remainder of name < ?⟧ a cephalosporin, $C_{18}H_{18}N_8O_7S_3$, administered intravenously and used to treat severe infections

cei·ba (sā′bə; *also, for 2,* sī′bə) ***n.*** ⟦Sp < Arawakan⟧ 1 any of various tropical silk-cotton trees (genus *Ceiba*) 2 KAPOK (sense 1)

ceil (sēl) ***vt.*** ⟦ME *celen* < OFr *celer*, to conceal < L *celare* (see CONCEAL); prob. infl. by L *caelum*, heaven (see CELESTIAL) & OFr *celer* < L *caelare*, to carve⟧ 1 to build a ceiling in or over 2 to cover (the ceiling or walls of a room) with plaster or thin boards

cei·lidh (kā′lē) ***n.*** ⟦< Ir & Gael words meaning "visit," ult. < OIr *céile*, companion⟧ an informal social gathering typically featuring traditional Irish or Scottish folk music, singing, dancing, and storytelling

ceil·ing (sē′liŋ) ***n.*** ⟦< CEIL⟧ 1 the inside top part or covering of a room, opposite the floor 2 any overhanging expanse seen from below 3 an upper limit set on anything, as by official regulation *[a ceiling on prices]* **4** *Aeron. a)* a covering of clouds limiting vertical visibility *b)* the height of the lower surface of such a covering *c)* the maximum height at which an aircraft can fly under normal conditions —☆**hit the ceiling** [Slang] to lose one's temper

☆**ceil·om·e·ter** (sē läm′ət ər) *n.* ⟦< prec. + -O- + -METER⟧ an automatic device used to determine the height of a cloud ceiling, as by means of a reflected light beam

cein·ture (san′chər; *Fr* sen tür′) *n.* ⟦ult. < L *cinctura:* see CINCTURE; out of use after *c.* 1500; reintroduced in 19th c. < Fr *ceinture*⟧ CINCTURE

cel (sel) *n.* ⟦var. of *cell*, shortened < CELLULOID, a material used for the sheets⟧ **1** any of the series of painted images photographed to make an ANIMATED CARTOON **2** a transparent sheet on which a single stage of an animated figure's movement has been painted: it is laid over a painted background to form the completed image

cel·a·don (sel′ə dän′, -dən) *n.* ⟦Fr *céladon*, a delicate green, earlier, a tender lover, after *Céladon*, hero in *Astrée* (romance, early 1600s, by H. d'Urfé, 1567–1625) < L *Celadon*, character in the *Metamorphoses* of OVID < Gr *Keladōn*⟧ a pale grayish-green color

Ce·lan (sə län′), **Paul** (pseud. of *Paul Antschel*) 1920-70; Romanian poet, writing in German

cel·an·dine (sel′ən dīn′, -dēn′, -din) *n.* ⟦ME & OFr *celidoine* < ML *celidonia* < L *chelidonia* < Gr *chelidonion*, swallowwort < *chelidōn*, a swallow < IE echoic base **ghel-* > YELL⟧ **1** a weedy plant (*Chelidonium majus*) of the poppy family, with deeply divided leaves and yellow flowers and juice **2** a perennial plant (*Ranunculus ficaria*) of the buttercup family, with yellow flowers

Ce·la·ya (sə lī′ə) city in Guanajuato state, central Mexico

-cele (sēl) ⟦< Gr *kēlē* < IE base **kaulā* > OE *heala*, hernia, rupture⟧ *combining form* **1** tumor, hernia, or swelling *[cystocele]* **2** -COELE

ce·leb (sə leb′) *n.* [Informal] *short for* CELEBRITY (sense 2)

Cel·e·bes (sel′ə bēz′, sə lē′bēz′) *another name for* SULAWESI

Celebes Sea part of the South Pacific Ocean, north of Sulawesi and south of the Philippines

cel·e·brant (sel′ə brənt) *n.* ⟦< L *celebrans*, prp. of *celebrare:* see fol.⟧ **1** a person who performs a religious rite, as the priest officiating at Mass **2** any person who celebrates; celebrator

cel·e·brate (sel′ə brāt′) *vt.* **-brat′ed, -brat′ing** ⟦ME *celebraten* < L *celebratus*, pp. of *celebrare*, to frequent, go in great numbers, honor < *celeber*, frequented, populous; akin to *celer*, swift: see HOLD[1]⟧ **1** to perform (a ritual, ceremony, etc.) publicly and formally: solemnize **2** to commemorate (an anniversary, holiday, etc.) with ceremony or festivity **3** to honor or praise publicly **4** to mark (a happy occasion) by engaging in some pleasurable activity —*vi.* **1** to observe a holiday, anniversary, etc. with festivities **2** to perform a religious ceremony **3** to mark a happy occasion by engaging in some pleasurable activity —**cel′e·bra′tive** *adj.* —**cel′e·bra′tor** *n.* —**cel′e·bra·to′ry** (-brə tôr′ē) *adj.*

SYN.—**celebrate** means to mark an occasion or event, esp. a joyous one, with ceremony or festivity *[let's celebrate your promotion]*; to **commemorate** is to honor the memory of some person or event as by a ceremony *[to commemorate Lincoln's birthday]*; to **solemnize** is to use a formal, serious ritual *[to solemnize a marriage]*; **observe** and the less formal **keep** mean to mark respectfully a day or occasion in the prescribed and appropriate manner *[to observe, or keep, a religious holiday]*

cel·e·brat·ed (-id) *adj.* much spoken of; famous; renowned —SYN. FAMOUS

cel·e·bra·tion (sel′ə brā′shən) *n.* ⟦L *celebratio*⟧ **1** the act or an instance of celebrating **2** that which is done to celebrate

ce·leb·ri·ty (sə leb′rə tē) *n.* ⟦ME & OFr *celebrite* < L *celebritas*, multitude, fame < *celeber:* see CELEBRATE⟧ **1** wide recognition; fame; renown **2** *pl.* **-ties** a famous or well-publicized person

ce·leb·u·tante (sə leb′yo͞o tänt′) *n.* ⟦prec. + (DEB)UTANTE⟧ [Informal] a young woman from a wealthy background who becomes a celebrity: a humorous and dismissive term

ce·ler·i·ac (sə ler′ē ak′) *n.* ⟦altered < CELERY + ? obs. *ache*, an umbelliferous plant, wild celery, parsley < ME < OFr < L *apium*; prob. < *apis*, bee⟧ a variety of celery (*Apium graveolens* var. *rapaceum*) grown for its edible, fleshy, white root

ce·ler·i·ty (sə ler′i tē) *n.* ⟦Fr *célérité* < L *celeritas* < *celer*, swift: see HOLD[1]⟧ swiftness in acting or moving; speed

cel·er·y (sel′ər ē, sel′rē) *n.* ⟦Fr *céleri* < It *seleri* < L *selinon* < Gr, parsley⟧ a biennial plant (*Apium graveolens* var. *dulce*) of the umbel family, whose long, crisp leafstalks are eaten as a vegetable

celery salt a seasoning made of salt and ground celery seed

celery seed the seeds of celery, or sometimes lovage, used as a seasoning

ce·les·ta (sə les′tə, chə-) *n.* ⟦Fr *célesta* < *céleste*, celestial⟧ a small keyboard instrument with hammers that strike small metal plates to produce bell-like tones: also **ce·leste** (sə lest′, chə-)

Ce·leste (sə lest′) *n.* ⟦Fr *Céleste:* see prec.⟧ a feminine name: var. *Celestine*

ce·les·tial (sə les′chəl) *adj.* ⟦ME & OFr < L *caelestis* < *caelum*, heaven: for IE base see CHINTZ⟧ **1** of or in the sky or universe, as planets or stars **2** *a)* of heaven; divine *[celestial beings]* *b)* highest; perfect *[celestial bliss]* **3** [C-] of the former Chinese Empire —*n.* any being regarded as living in heaven —**ce·les′tial·ly** *adv.*

Celestial Empire ⟦transl. of a former Chin name for China⟧ CHINESE EMPIRE

celestial equator the great circle formed on the celestial sphere by extending the plane of the earth's equator

celestial globe a globe on which the stars, constellations, etc. are depicted in their proper relative positions in the sky

celestial latitude *Astron.* the angular distance of a celestial body from the ecliptic

celestial longitude *Astron.* the arc of the ecliptic measured eastward from the vernal equinox to the point where the ecliptic is intersected by the great circle through the star, planet, etc. and the poles of the ecliptic

celestial mechanics the branch of astronomy that deals with the motion and positions of celestial objects in orbit

celestial navigation navigation based on observation of the sun, moon, stars, or planets to determine position

celestial pole either of two points on the celestial sphere where the extensions of the earth's axis would intersect

celestial sphere an imaginary sphere of infinite extent on which all celestial objects appear to lie: the observer is always at its center

cel·es·tine (sel′əs tin, -tīn′) *n.* ⟦< L *caelestis*, CELESTIAL + -INE[3]: from its blue color⟧ CELESTITE

cel·es·tite (sel′əs tīt′) *n.* ⟦altered (by James Dwight DANA[2]) < prec. + -ITE[1]⟧ a soft, orthorhombic mineral, $SrSO_4$, that is the chief ore of strontium; strontium sulfate

Cel·ia (sēl′yə) *n.* ⟦L *Caelia*, fem. of *Caelius*, name of a Roman gens, of Etr orig., lit., prob. "September"⟧ a feminine name

ce·li·ac (sē′lē ak′) *adj.* ⟦L *coeliacus* < Gr *koiliakos* < *koilia:* see -COELE⟧ of or in the abdominal cavity

celiac disease a chronic nutritional disorder, usually of young children, caused by faulty absorption of gluten in the intestines and characterized by diarrhea and malnutrition

cel·i·ba·cy (sel′ə bə sē) *n.* ⟦< fol. + -CY⟧ **1** the state of being unmarried, esp. that of a person under a vow not to marry **2** complete sexual abstinence

cel·i·bate (sel′ə bət) *n.* ⟦L *caelibatus* < *caelebs*, unmarried (< IE base **kaiwelo-*, alone) + **lib(h)s-*, living (> LIVE[2])⟧ **1** an unmarried person, esp. one under a vow to remain unmarried **2** one who abstains from sexual intercourse —*adj.* of or in a state of celibacy

Cé·line (sā lēn′), **Louis-Fer·di·nand** (lwē fer dē nän′) (born *Louis-Ferdinand Destouches*) 1894-1961; Fr. writer

cell (sel) *n.* ⟦ME < OE < OFr *celle* < L *cella*, small room, hut (LL(Ec), monastic cell) < IE base **kel-*, to conceal > HALL, HELL, HULL[1], Goth *halja*⟧ **1** a small convent or monastery attached to a larger one **2** a hermit's hut **3** a small room or cubicle, as in a convent or prison **4** a very small hollow, cavity, or enclosed space; specif., *a)* any of the compartments in a honeycomb *b)* a small, hollow space in tissue, esp. in bone *c)* the space of an insect's wings enclosed by the veins *d)* any compartment of an ovary; also, a pollen sac or spore sac **5** any of the smallest organizational units of a group or movement, as of a Communist party **6** any of the individual boxes in which words or numerical data may be entered in a TABLE (*n.* 4*b*) or SPREADSHEET: cells read across form *rows*, cells read up or down form *columns* **7** any of the small areas making up a cellular communications system, each having a low-power transmitter and receiver combination **8** [Informal] CELL PHONE **9** *Biol.* a very small, complex unit of protoplasm, usually with a nucleus, cytoplasm, and an enclosing membrane: all plants and animals are made up of one or more cells that usually combine to form various tissues **10** *Elec. a)* an open or sealed container holding electrodes and an electrolyte, used to generate electricity by chemical reactions or to decompose compounds by electrolysis *b)* any compartment of a storage battery *c)* a unit within any device, as a solar battery, that produces voltage by converting radiant energy into electrical energy —*adj. short for* CELLULAR (*adj.* 3) —**celled** *adj.*

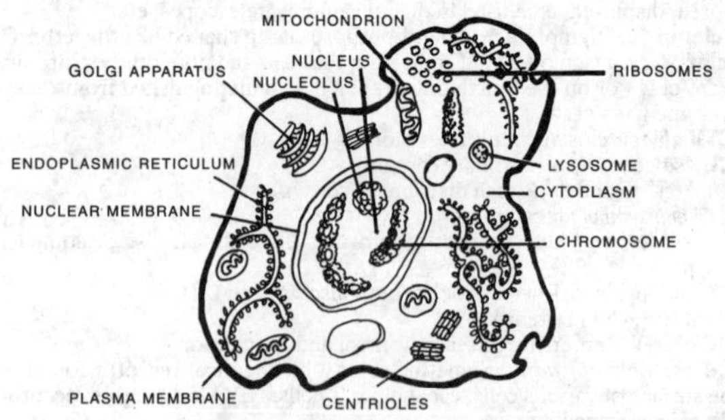

animal cell

cel·la (sel′ə) *n., pl.* **cel′lae** (-ē) ⟦L: see prec.⟧ the inner part of an ancient Greek or Roman temple, housing the statue of a god or goddess

cel·lar (sel′ər) *n.* ⟦ME *celler* < OFr *celier* < L *cellarium*, pantry, storeroom < *cella:* see CELL⟧ **1** a room or group of rooms below the ground level and usually under a building, often used for storing fuel, provisions, or wines **2** a stock of wines kept in such a cellar —*vt.* to store in a cellar —☆**the cellar**

[Informal] the lowest position, as in the relative standing of competing teams

cel·lar·age (-ij) ***n.*** **1** space of or in a cellar **2** cellars collectively **3** the fee for storage in a cellar

cel·lar·er (-ər) ***n.*** a person in charge of a cellar or provisions, as in a monastery

cel·lar·et (sel′ə ret′) ***n.*** ⟦CELLAR + -ET⟧ a cabinet for bottles of wine or liquor, glasses, etc.: also sp. **cel′lar·ette′**

☆**cel·lar·way** (sel′ər wā′) ***n.*** an entrance to a cellar, esp. an outside stairwell leading down to a cellar

cell·block (sel′bläk′) ***n.*** a section of cells in a prison

Cel·li·ni (chə lē′nē), **Ben·ve·nu·to** (ben′və no͞o′tō) 1500-71; It. sculptor & goldsmith: also known for his autobiography

cel·list (chel′ist) ***n.*** a person who plays the cello: also sp. **'cellist**

cell·mate (sel′māt′) ***n.*** a prisoner who shares a cell in a prison or jail with another or others

cell membrane a membrane surrounding a cell or cell part; esp., PLASMA MEMBRANE

cel·lo (chel′ō) ***n.***, *pl.* **-los** or **-li** (-ē) ⟦< VIOLONCELLO⟧ an instrument of the violin family, between the viola and the double bass in size and pitch; violoncello: also sp. **'cello**

cello

cel·loi·din (sə loi′din) ***n.*** ⟦CELL + -OID + -IN[1]⟧ a clear, concentrated, semisolid solution of pyroxylin used in microscopy for embedding specimens that are to be cut into thin cross sections

cel·lo·phane (sel′ə fān′) ***n.*** ⟦< CELL(ULOSE) + -O- + -PHANE⟧ a thin, transparent material made from cellulose, used as a moisture-proof wrapping for foods, tobacco, etc.

cellophane noodles ⟦so called from their fancied resemblance to *cellophane,* because of their transparency and smooth texture when cooked⟧ transparent, stringlike noodles, used esp. in East Asian cooking, made from flour ground from mung beans

cell phone ⟦shortened < CELLULAR PHONE⟧ a kind of mobile radio telephone used in a cellular communications system: also written **cell·phone** (sel′ fōn′) ***n.***

cel·lu·lar (sel′yo͞o lər) ***adj.*** **1** of or like a cell **2** consisting of or containing cells; esp., said of certain porous igneous rock, as pumice **3** of, having to do with, or used in a communications system that has its service area divided into small cells, each having a separate low-power transmitter and receiver combination *[cellular* network*]* **—cel′lu·lar′i·ty** (-lar′ə tē) ***n.***

cellular phone CELL PHONE: also **cellular telephone**

cel·lu·lase (-lās′) ***n.*** ⟦CELLUL(OSE) + -ASE⟧ an enzyme found in some bacteria, fungi, etc. capable of hydrolyzing cellulose into smaller molecules: used in brewing, septic systems, etc.

cel·lule (sel′yo͞ol′) ***n.*** ⟦L *cellula,* dim. of *cella:* see CELL⟧ a very small cell

cel·lu·lite (sel′yo͞o līt′) ***n.*** ⟦Fr, lit., cellulitis, but given new commercial meaning by N. Ronsard, Fr salon owner in New York, and first used in this sense in English in late 1960s⟧ fatty deposits on the hips, thighs, etc., resulting in a lumpy or dimpled appearance of the skin: a nonmedical term

cel·lu·li·tis (sel′yo͞o līt′is) ***n.*** ⟦ModL < CELLULE + -ITIS⟧ an inflammation of connective tissue, esp. of subcutaneous tissue

☆**cel·lu·loid** (sel′yo͞o loid′) ***n.*** ⟦fol. + -OID⟧ **1** a tough, flammable thermoplastic made from pyroxylin and camphor, used, esp. formerly, for toilet articles, novelties, etc. **2** films: from use of celluloid, esp. formerly, for photographic films

cel·lu·lose (sel′yo͞o lōs′) ***n.*** ⟦Fr < L *cellula* (see CELLULE) + Fr *-ose,* -OSE[1]⟧ the chief substance composing the cell walls or fibers of all plant tissue, a polymeric carbohydrate with the general formula $(C_6H_{10}O_5)_x$: it is used in the manufacture of paper, textiles, explosives, etc.

cellulose acetate any of several nonflammable thermoplastics produced by the action of acetic acid or acetic anhydride upon cellulose in the presence of concentrated sulfuric acid: used in making artificial silks, lacquers, photographic films, etc.

cellulose nitrate NITROCELLULOSE

cel·lu·los·ic (sel′yo͞o lō′sik) ***adj.*** of or made from cellulose **—*n.*** a product or material made from cellulose

cel·lu·lous (sel′yo͞o ləs) ***adj.*** [Rare] consisting or full of cells

cell wall *Biol.* the nonliving covering or separating wall of a cell; esp., the relatively rigid covering of a plant cell, containing cellulose, hemicellulose, lignin, etc.

ce·lom (sē′ləm) ***n.*** *alt. sp. of* COELOM

ce·lo·si·a (sə lō′shə, -sē ə) ***n.*** ⟦ModL < Gr *kēleos,* burning: so named because the flowers of some species look as if they had been burned⟧ any of several species (genus *Celosia*) of the amaranth family, of annual garden plants with minute, brilliant red or yellow flowers in large clusters; cockscomb

☆**Cel·o·tex** (sel′ə teks′) ⟦arbitrary formation < ? CEL(LUL)O(SE) + TEX(TURE)⟧ *trademark for* a composition board made of sugar-cane residue, used for insulation in buildings **—*n.*** [*sometimes* **c-**] a sheet or sheets of this material

Cel·si·us (sel′sē əs) ***adj.*** ⟦after A. *Celsius* (1701-44), Swed astronomer, the inventor⟧ designating or of a thermometer on which 0° is the freezing point and 100° is the boiling point of water; centigrade: the formula for converting a Celsius temperature to Fahrenheit is $°F = \frac{9}{5}\,°C + 32$: abbrev. *C* **—*n.*** this thermometer or its scale

celt (selt) ***n.*** ⟦< ML *celtis* < LL **celtis* < Vulg. *vel celte sculpantur in silice* (Job 19:24); prob. ghost word (*certe* in other mss.) adopted as genuine by archaeologists⟧ a prehistoric tool of stone or metal, resembling a chisel or ax head

Celt[1] (kelt; *also* selt) ***n.*** ⟦Fr *Celte,* orig., Breton < L *Celta,* pl. *Celtae* (Gr *Keltoi*), the Gauls⟧ **1** a person who speaks a Celtic language or a descendant of such a person: the Bretons, Irish, Welsh, and Highland Scots are Celts **2** a member of an ancient people in central and W Europe, reputedly including the Gauls and Britons

Celt[2] *abbrev.* Celtic

Celt·ic (kel′tik; *also* sel′tik) ***adj.*** of the Celts or their languages or cultures **—*n.*** a branch of the Indo-European family of languages, divided into Goidelic (Irish, Scottish Gaelic, Manx) and Brythonic (Welsh, Breton, and the extinct Cornish) branches

Celtic cross a Latin cross having a wheel-like circle around the intersection of the bars

Celtic Sea part of the Atlantic south of Ireland, separated from the Irish Sea by St. George's Channel

cem·ba·lo (chem′bə lō′) ***n.***, *pl.* **-li′** (-lē′) or **-los′** ⟦It, harpsichord, cymbal < L *cymbalum,* CYMBAL⟧ HARPSICHORD

ce·ment (sə ment′) ***n.*** ⟦ME & OFr *ciment* < L *caementum,* rough stone, chippings < **caedimentum* < *caedere,* to cut down: see -CIDE⟧ **1** *a)* a powdered substance made of burned lime and clay, mixed with water and sand to make mortar or with water, sand, and gravel to make concrete: the mixture hardens when it dries *b)* CONCRETE (a loose usage) **2** any soft substance that fastens things together firmly when it hardens, as glue **3** anything that joins together or unites; bond **4** CEMENTUM **5** the fine-grained material that binds together the larger constituents in many kinds of sedimentary or clastic rock **6** *Dentistry* a cementlike substance used to fill cavities, set crowns, etc. **7** *Metallurgy* a dust or powder, as of charcoal or sand, or a finely divided metal, used in cementation **—*vt.*** **1** to join or unite with or as with cement **2** to cover with cement **3** to establish firmly or make stronger *[*to *cement* a friendship*]* **—ce·ment′er *n.***

ce·men·ta·tion (sē′men tā′shən) ***n.*** **1** a cementing or being cemented **2** the process by which a solid surrounded by a metallurgical cement is heated intensely and made to combine chemically with the cement to produce a new product

ce·ment·ite (sə men′tīt′) ***n.*** ⟦CEMENT + -ITE[1]⟧ the hard, brittle carbide of iron, Fe_3C, that occurs in and adds strength to steel, cast iron, and most other alloys of iron and carbon

ce·men·tum (sə men′təm) ***n.*** ⟦L *caementum:* see CEMENT⟧ the thin, fairly hard, bony tissue covering the root of a tooth

cem·e·ter·y (sem′ə ter′ē) ***n.***, *pl.* **-ter′ies** ⟦LL(Ec) *coemeterium* < Gr *koimētērion,* sleeping place (in LGr(Ec), cemetery) < *koiman,* to put to sleep; akin to *keimai,* to lie down: see HOME⟧ a place for the burial of the dead; graveyard

cen *abbrev.* central

cen·a·cle (sen′i kəl) ***n.*** ⟦Fr *cénacle* < L *cenaculum,* dining room < *cena,* dinner < OL *cesnas* < IE **(s)kert-* < base **(s)ker-,* to cut > SHEAR, SHORT⟧ **1** [**C-**] the room in which Jesus and his disciples ate the Last Supper **2** a coterie, as of writers

-cene (sēn) ⟦< Gr *kainos,* recent < IE base **ken-,* new > L *recens,* RECENT⟧ *combining form* recent, new, or, esp., designating a (specified) epoch in the Cenozoic Era *[Miocene]*

ce·nes·the·sia (sē′nis thē′zhə, -zhē ə; sen′is-) ***n.*** *Psychol.* the mass of undifferentiated sensations that make one aware of the body and its condition, as in the feeling of well-being or illness: also **ce′nes·the′sis** (-sis) ***n.***

Ce·nis (sə nē′), **Mont** **1** mountain pass between France and Italy in the Graian Alps: 6,830 ft (2,082 m) high **2** nearby railroad tunnel that runs between Italy and France: 8.5 mi (13.7 km) long

ce·no- (sē′nō, -nə; sen′ə) ⟦< Gr *koinos,* common < **komios* < IE base **kom,* with, beside > L *cum*⟧ *combining form* common *[cenospecies]*: also, before a vowel, **cen-**

cen·o·bite (sen′ə bīt′, sē′nə-) ***n.*** ⟦ME < LL(Ec) *coenobita* < *coenobium,* a cloister < Gr *koinobion,* communal life (in LGr(Ec), monastery), neut. of *koinobios* < *koinos,* common + *bios:* see BIO-⟧ a member of a religious order living in a monastery or convent: distinguished from ANCHORITE **—cen′o·bit′ic** (-bit′ik) ***adj.***, **cen′o·bit′i·cal —cen′o·bit′ism′** (-bīt′iz′əm) ***n.***

ce·no·gen·e·sis (sē′nō jen′ə sis, sen′ō-) ***n.*** ⟦*ceno-* (< Gr *kainos:* see -CENE) + -GENESIS⟧ the development of structures in the embryonic or larval stage of an organism that are adaptive and do not appear in the evolutionary history of its group: cf. PALINGENESIS **—ce′no·ge·net′ic** (-jə net′ik) ***adj.***

ce·no·spe·cies (sē′nō spē′shēz, sen′ō-) ***n.*** ⟦CENO- + SPECIES⟧ separate species of organisms that are related through their capability of interbreeding, as dogs and wolves

cen·o·taph (sen′ə taf′) ***n.*** ⟦Fr *cénotaphe* < L *cenotaphium* < Gr *kenotaphion* < *kenos,* empty + *taphos,* tomb⟧ a monument or empty tomb honoring a person or persons whose remains are elsewhere

ce·no·te (sə nōt′ē) ***n.*** ⟦AmSp < Maya *tzonot*⟧ a deep natural well carved out of friable limestone

Ce·no·zo·ic (sē′nə zō′ik, sen′ə-) ***adj.*** ⟦*ceno-* (< Gr *kainos:* see -CENE) + -ZOIC⟧ [*sometimes* **c-**] designating or of the third geologic era of the Phanerozoic Eon, formerly subdivided into the Tertiary and Quaternary periods and now subdivided into the Paleogene, Neogene, and Quartenary periods, characterized by the development of birds and mammals —**the Cenozoic** the Cenozoic Era or its rocks: see the geologic time chart in the Reference Supplement

cense (sens) ***vt.* censed, cens′ing** ⟦ME *censen*, aphetic < *encensen*: see INCENSE[1]⟧ to perfume with incense

cen·ser (sen′sər) ***n.*** ⟦ME < OFr *censier* < *encensier* < *encens*: see INCENSE[1]⟧ an ornamented container in which incense is burned

cen·sor (sen′sər) ***n.*** ⟦L < *censere*, to tax, value, judge < IE base **k̑ens*, speak solemnly, announce > Sans *śáṁsa*, praise, prayer of praise⟧ **1** one of two magistrates in ancient Rome appointed to take the census and, later, to supervise public morals **2** an official with the power to examine publications, films, television programs, etc. and to remove or prohibit anything considered obscene, libelous, politically objectionable, etc. **3** an official in time of war who reads publications, mail, etc. to remove information that might be useful to the enemy **4** in earlier psychoanalytic theory, and still popularly, a part of the unconscious that serves as the agent of censorship —***vt.*** to subject (a book, film, writer, etc.) to the close examination of a censor —**cen·so·ri·al** (sen sôr′ē əl) ***adj.***

cen·so·ri·ous (sen sôr′ē əs) ***adj.*** ⟦L *censorius* < *censere*: see prec.⟧ expressing censure; inclined to find fault; harshly critical —**cen·so′ri·ous·ly *adv.*** —**cen·so′ri·ous·ness *n.***

cen·sor·ship (sen′sər ship′) ***n.*** **1** the act, system, or practice of censoring **2** the office or term of a Roman censor **3** *Psychoanalysis* the agency by which unpleasant ideas, memories, etc. are kept from entering consciousness, except symbolically as in dreams

cen·sur·a·ble (sen′sher ə bəl) ***adj.*** deserving, or liable to, censure; blameworthy —**cen′sur·a·bly *adv.***

cen·sure (sen′shər) ***n.*** ⟦L *censura* < *censor*, CENSOR⟧ **1** a condemning as wrong; strong disapproval **2** a judgment or resolution condemning a person for misconduct; specif., an official expression of disapproval passed by a legislature —***vt.* -sured, -sur·ing** to express strong disapproval of —***SYN.*** CRITICIZE —**cen′sur·er *n.***

cen·sus (sen′səs) ***n.*** ⟦L, orig., pp. of *censere*, to assess: see CENSOR⟧ **1** in ancient Rome, the act of counting the people and evaluating their property for taxation **2** an official, usually periodic, count of population and recording of economic status, age, sex, etc.

cent[1] (sent) ***n.*** ⟦ME & OFr < L *centum*, HUNDRED⟧ ☆**1** *a)* a monetary unit of the U.S., equal to 1/100 of a dollar; penny (symbol, ¢) *b)* a coin of this value, made of an alloy of copper and zinc or tin; penny **2** a monetary unit of various other countries, equal to 1/100 of the basic unit

cent[2] *abbrev.* century; centuries

cen·tal (sent′'l) ***n.*** ⟦CENT(I)- + (QUINT)AL⟧ HUNDREDWEIGHT (sense 1)

cen·tas (sen′täs) ***n.***, *pl.* **-tas** or **-tai** (-tī) ⟦Lith⟧ a monetary unit of Lithuania, equal to 1/100 of a litas

cen·taur (sen′tôr′) ***n.*** ⟦ME < L *Centaurus* < Gr *Kentauros*⟧ *Gr. Myth.* any of a race of monsters with a man's head, trunk, and arms, and a horse's body and legs —**the Centaur** the constellation Centaurus

cen·tau·re·a (sen′tô′rē ə) ***n.*** ⟦ModL < ML *centauria*, CENTAURY⟧ any of a genus (*Centaurea*) of annual and perennial plants of the composite family, having egg-shaped flower heads, including the star thistles and the bachelor's buttons

Cen·tau·rus (sen tô′rəs) ***n.*** ⟦L: see CENTAUR⟧ a S constellation between Hydra and Crux, containing the bright star Alpha Centauri; the Centaur

cen·tau·ry (sen′tô′rē) ***n.***, *pl.* **-ries** ⟦ME *centaurie* < ML *centauria* < L *centaureum* < Gr *kentaureion* < *Kentauros*, centaur: the centaur Chiron was said to have discovered medicinal properties of the plant⟧ any of a genus (*Centaurium*) of small plants of the gentian family, with flat clusters of red or rose flowers

cen·ta·vo (sen tä′vō) ***n.***, *pl.* **-vos** ⟦Sp, a hundredth < L *centum*, HUNDRED⟧ a monetary unit of various countries, equal to 1/100 of the basic unit

cen·te·nar·i·an (sen′tə ner′ē ən) ***adj.*** ⟦< fol.⟧ **1** of 100 years; of a centennial **2** of a centenarian —***n.*** a person at least 100 years old

cen·te·nar·y (sen ten′ər ē, sen′tə ner′ē) ***adj.*** ⟦L *centenarius*, of a hundred < *centeni*, a hundred each < *centum*, HUNDRED⟧ **1** relating to a century; of a period of 100 years **2** of a centennial —***n.***, *pl.* **-nar·ies** CENTENNIAL

cen·ten·ni·al (sen ten′ē əl, -yəl) ***adj.*** ⟦< L *centum*, HUNDRED + *annus*, year (see ANNUAL) + -AL⟧ **1** of 100 years **2** happening once in 100 years **3** lasting 100 years **4** of a 100th anniversary —***n.*** a 100th anniversary or its commemoration —**cen·ten′ni·al·ly *adv.***

Cen·ten·ni·al (sen ten′ē əl, -yəl) city in NC Colo., near Denver

cen·ter (sent′ər) ***n.*** ⟦ME & OFr *centre* < L *centrum*, center, orig., that point of the compass around which the other describes the circle < Gr *kentron*, sharp point, goad < *kentein*, to stitch < IE base **k̑ent-*, to prick > OHG *hantag*, sharp, Goth *handugs*, wise, ON *hannarr*, skillful⟧ **1** a point equally distant from all points on the circumference of a circle or surface of a sphere **2** the point around which anything revolves; pivot **3** *a)* a place at which an activity or complex of activities is carried on [a shopping *center*] *b)* a place from which ideas, influences, etc. emanate [Paris, the fashion *center*] *c)* a place to which many people are attracted [a *center* of interest] **4** the approximate middle point, place, or part of anything **5** a group of nerve cells regulating a particular function [the vasomotor *centers*] **6** *Mech. a)* one of two tapered or conical pins or rods, as on a lathe, for holding a piece of work in position *b)* an indentation in either end of such a piece in which the pin fits **7** *Mil.* that part of an army situated between the flanks **8** [*often* **C-**] *Politics* a position, party, or group between the left (radicals and liberals) and the right (conservatives and reactionaries): so called from the position of the seats occupied in some European legislatures **9** *Sports a)* a player whose position at the start of a contest is at the center of the line or playing area *b) Football* the offensive lineman who passes the ball between the legs to a player in the backfield to start play *c) Baseball* CENTER FIELD —***vt.*** **1** to place in, at, or near the center **2** to draw to one place; gather to a point **3** to furnish with a center **4** *Football* to pass (the ball) to a player in the backfield: said of the center —***vi.*** **1** to be centered; be concentrated or focused: usually with *on* or *in* **2** *Sports* to play the position of center —***SYN.*** MIDDLE —**center around** [Informal] to have as a central point, focus of attention, etc.

center bit a bit with a sharp, projecting center point and cutting wings on either side

☆**cen·ter·board** (-bôrd′) ***n.*** a movable board or metal plate that, when lowered through a slot in the floor of a shallow-draft sailboat, functions like a keel to reduce leeward drift or increase stability, esp. one that moves on a pivot

cen·tered (sent′ərd) ***adj.*** **1** being at the center **2** having (a specified thing) as the focus of interest or activity: used in hyphenated compounds [consumer-*centered*] **3** mentally and emotionally stable; balanced; collected

☆**center field** *Baseball* **1** the middle area of the outfield **2** the defensive position of the outfielder (**center fielder**) who plays there

cen·ter-fire (-fīr′) ***adj.*** designating a cartridge with the primer set in the center of the base: cf. RIMFIRE

☆**cen·ter·fold** (-fōld′) ***n.*** **1** the center facing pages of a magazine, often with one or more extra folds, used for a single photograph or other graphic display **2** the subject of such a display, when it is a young woman or man photographed in the nude

cen·ter·ing (sent′ər iŋ, sen′triŋ′) ***n.*** a temporary frame to support an arch or vault during construction

cen·ter·line (sent′ər līn′) ***n.*** a real or imaginary line passing through the center of something and dividing it into two equal parts

center of gravity that point in a body or system around which its mass or weight is evenly distributed or balanced and through which the force of gravity acts

center of mass the point in a body or system of bodies at which the entire mass may be assumed to be concentrated

cen·ter·piece (sent′ər pēs′) ***n.*** **1** an ornament, bowl of flowers, etc. for the center of a table **2** anything regarded as the most important feature, component, or member

center punch a steel punch for marking a spot where a hole is to be drilled

cen·tes·i·mal (sen tes′ə məl) ***adj.*** ⟦< L *centesimus* (< *centum*, HUNDRED) + -AL⟧ **1** hundredth **2** of or divided into hundredths —**cen·tes′i·mal·ly *adv.***

cen·tes·i·mo (sen tes′ē mō′) ***n.***, *pl.* **-mos′** or **-mi′** (-mē′) ⟦It & Sp < L *centesimus*: see prec.⟧ **1** a money of account of Italy, San Marino, and Vatican City, equal to 1/100 of a lira **2** a monetary unit of Uruguay, equal to 1/100 of a peso **3** a monetary unit of Panama, equal to 1/100 of a balboa

cen·ti- (sen′tə, -ti) ⟦Fr < L < *centum*, HUNDRED⟧ *combining form* **1** one hundred [*centipede*] **2** one hundredth part of; the factor 10^{-2} [*centigram*]

cen·ti·grade (sen′tə grād′) ***adj.*** ⟦Fr: see prec. & GRADE⟧ **1** consisting of or divided into 100 degrees **2** CELSIUS: the preferred term in English until the adoption of *Celsius* in 1948 by an international conference on weights and measures: abbrev. *C*

cen·ti·gram (-gram′) ***n.*** ⟦Fr *centigramme*: see CENTI- & GRAM[1]⟧ one hundredth of a gram (0.154 grain): abbrev. *cg*

cen·ti·li·ter (-lēt′ər) ***n.*** ⟦Fr *centilitre*: see CENTI- & LITER⟧ one hundredth of a liter (0.3376 fluid ounce or 0.6102 cubic inch): abbrev. *cl*: Brit. sp. **cen′ti·li′tre**

cen·time (sän′tēm′, sen′-; *Fr* sän tēm′) ***n.*** ⟦Fr < OFr *centisme*, the hundredth < L *centesimus*: see CENTESIMAL⟧ a monetary unit of various countries, equal to 1/100 of the basic unit

cen·ti·me·ter (sen′tə mēt′ər, sän′-) ***n.*** ⟦Fr *centimètre*: see CENTI- & METER[1]⟧ one hundredth of a meter (0.3937 inch): abbrev. *cm*: Brit. sp. **cen′ti·me′tre**

cen·ti·me·ter-gram-sec·ond (-gram′sek′ənd) ***adj.*** designating or of a system of measurement in which the centimeter, gram, and second are the units of length, mass, and time, respectively: abbrev. *CGS*: see the table of weights and measures in the Reference Supplement

cen·ti·mil·li- (sen′tə mil′i) ⟦CENTI- + MILLI-⟧ *combining form* one hundred-thousandth part of; the factor 10^{-5}

cen·ti·mo (sen′tə mō′) ***n.***, *pl.* **-mos′** ⟦see CENTIME⟧ **1** a monetary unit, equal to 1/100 of the basic unit, of: *a)* Costa Rica *b)* Paraguay *c)* Peru *d)* Venezuela: usually written **céntimo** **2** a monetary unit of São Tomé and Príncipe, equal to 1/100 of a dobra

cen·ti·pede (sen′tə pēd′) ***n.*** ⟦Fr < L *centipeda* < *centi-*, CENTI- + *-peda* < *pes* (gen. *pedis*), FOOT⟧ any of a class (Chilopoda) of elongated, many-segmented, insect-eating arthropods with a pair of legs to each segment, the front pair being modified into poison claws

cen·ti·poise (sen′tə poiz′) ***n.*** ⟦CENTI- + POISE[2]⟧ one hundredth of a poise: the viscosity of water at 15°C equals 1.139 centipoise: abbrev. *cP*

cen·ti·stoke (sen′tə stōk′) ***n.*** one hundredth of a stoke: abbrev. *cSt*

cent·ner (sent′nər) ***n.*** ⟦Ger *centner*, *zentner* < OHG *centenari* < ML *centenarius*, weighing 100 pounds < L: see CENTENARY⟧ in some European countries, a commercial weight approximately equal to the British hundredweight

cen·to (sen′tō) ***n.***, *pl.* **-tos** ⟦L, patchwork blanket < IE base **kentho-*, rags > Sans *kanthā*, patched garment, OHG *hadara*, rag, patch⟧ **1** a literary or musical work made up of passages from other works **2** anything made up of badly matched parts

centr- *combining form* CENTRO-: used before a vowel

cen·tral (sen′trəl) *adj.* ⟦L *centralis*⟧ **1** in, at, or near the center **2** of or forming the center **3** equally distant or accessible from various points **4** most important; main; basic; principal **5** of or having to do with a single source that controls all activity in an organization or system **6** *a)* designating or of that part of a nervous system consisting of the brain and spinal cord or, in many invertebrates, the chief ganglia and their major nerve cords *b)* of the centrum of a vertebra **7** *Phonet.* articulated with the tongue in a position approximately halfway between front and back: said of certain vowels, as (u) in *bud* —☆*n.* a telephone exchange, esp. the main one, or the telephone operator: an early term —**cen′tral·ly** *adv.*

Cen·tral (sen′trəl) former administrative region of SC Scotland, which included the former county of Clackmannan and parts of the former counties of Perth, Stirling, and West Lothian

Central African Republic country in central Africa, north of the Democratic Republic of the Congo & the Republic of the Congo: formerly a French territory, it became independent in 1960: 240,535 sq mi (622,984 sq km); cap. Bangui

Central America part of North America between Mexico and South America; often considered to extend from the Isthmus of Tehuantepec to the Isthmus of Panama —**Central American**

central bank **1** the main, centralized bank of a nation, responsible variously for implementing monetary policy, issuing currency, handling banking transactions for the government and other banks, etc. **2** any of the twelve district banks of the Federal Reserve System —**central banker**

central casting ⟦after *Central Casting Corporation*, founded in 1926 in Hollywood, Cal., to supply extras and bit players to film producers⟧ a studio department or other source that supplies actors to portray roles, often stereotyped roles, in films: usually used metaphorically

central city the principal municipality of a metropolitan area, surrounded by suburbs and smaller towns; esp., the crowded, industrial, often blighted area

Central Intelligence Agency the agency of the federal government concerned with intelligence gathering and other activities involving national security

cen·tral·ism (-iz′əm) *n.* the principle or system of centralizing power or authority, as of a government —**cen′tral·ist** *adj., n.* —**cen′tral·is′tic** *adj.*

cen·tral·i·ty (sen tral′i tē) *n.* **1** the quality, state, or fact of being central; center position **2** the tendency to remain at or near the center

cen·tral·ize (sen′trəl īz′) *vt.* **-ized′**, **-iz′ing** **1** to make central; bring to or focus on a center; gather together **2** to organize under one control; concentrate the power or authority of in a central organization —*vi.* to become centralized —**cen′tral·i·za′tion** *n.* —**cen′tral·iz′er** *n.*

central nervous system *Anat.* the brain and spinal cord of a vertebrate: see AUTONOMIC NERVOUS SYSTEM

Central Powers in WWI, Germany and Austria-Hungary, and their allies, Turkey and Bulgaria

central processing unit the part of a computer that controls its overall activity, as by executing instructions and performing logical operations

☆**Central Standard Time** a standard time used in the zone which includes the central states of the U.S., corresponding to the mean solar time of the 90th meridian west of Greenwich, England: it is six hours behind Greenwich time

☆**Central Time** [*also* **c- t-**] standard time or daylight saving time in the time zone which includes the central states of the U.S.

cen·tre (sent′ər) *n., vt., vi.* **-tred**, **-tring** *Brit. sp. of* CENTER

Cen·tre (sän′tr′) metropolitan region of central France, southwest of Paris: 15,116 sq mi (39,150 sq km); chief city, Orléans

Cen·trex (sen′treks′) *n.* ⟦CENTR(AL) + EX(CHANGE)⟧ a telephone system for businesses, large organizations, etc. in which outside calls can be made directly to, or from, any extension

cen·tri- (sen′tri, -trə) *combining form* CENTRO-

cen·tric (sen′trik′) *adj.* ⟦Gr *kentrikos* < *kentron*: see CENTER⟧ **1** in, at, or near the center; central **2** of or having a center Also **cen′tri·cal** —**cen′tri·cal·ly** *adv.* —**cen·tric′i·ty** (-tris′i tē) *n.*

-cen·tric (sen′trik′) ⟦ME *-centrik* < ML *-centricus* < L *centrum*, CENTER + *-icus*, -IC⟧ *combining form forming adjectives* **1** having a center or centers (of a specified kind or number) [*concentric*] **2** having (a specified thing) as its center [*geocentric*] **3** having (a specified thing) as the focus of attention, efforts, etc. [*Afrocentric*]

cen·trif·u·gal (sen trif′ə gəl, -yə gəl; *chiefly Brit* sen′tri fyo͞o′gəl) *adj.* ⟦< ModL *centrifugus* (coined by NEWTON[2] < CENTRI- + L *fugere*, to flee: see FUGITIVE) + -AL⟧ **1** moving or tending to move away from a center **2** using or acted on by centrifugal force **3** *Bot.* developing from the center outward, as certain flower clusters **4** *Physiol.* conveying away from a center; efferent —☆*n.* a machine that uses or causes centrifugal movement —**cen·trif′u·gal·ly** *adv.*

centrifugal force an inertial force which tends to pull an object outward when it is in orbit or is rotating around a center

cen·trif·u·gal·ize (-īz′) *vt.* **-ized′**, **-iz′ing** to subject to the action of a centrifuge —**cen·trif′u·gal·i·za′tion** *n.*

cen·trif·u·ga·tion (sen trif′yo͞o gā′shən) *n.* a being subjected to centrifugal action, esp. in a centrifuge

cen·tri·fuge (sen′trə fyo͞oj′) *n.* ⟦Fr < ModL *centrifugus*: see CENTRIFUGAL⟧ a machine using centrifugal force to separate particles of varying density, as cream from milk, or to draw off moisture, as in a washing machine —*vt.* **-fuged′**, **-fug′ing** to subject to the action of a centrifuge

cen·tri·ole (sen′trē ōl′) *n.* ⟦partial transl. of Ger *zentriol* < *zentrum* (< L *centrum*), CENTER + *-ol*, dim. suffix < Fr *-ole* < L *-olum*⟧ a small, dense structure in the middle of the centrosome: it doubles before mitosis, and each part forms the center of an aster during mitosis

cen·trip·e·tal (sen trip′ət′l) *adj.* ⟦ModL *centripetus* (coined by NEWTON[2] < CENTRI- + L *petere*, to fall, rush at: see FEATHER + -AL⟧ **1** moving or tending to move toward a center **2** using or acted on by centripetal force **3** *Bot.* developing inward toward the center, as certain flower clusters **4** *Physiol.* conveying toward a center; afferent —**cen·trip′e·tal·ly** *adv.*

centripetal force the force tending to pull a thing toward the center of rotation when it is rotating around a center

-cen·trism (sen′triz′əm) *combining form forming nouns* the state or condition of having (a specified thing) as the center or focus of attention, efforts, etc. [*Eurocentrism*]

cen·trist (sen′trist) *n.* ⟦Fr *centriste*: see CENTER & -IST[1]⟧ a person with moderate political opinions and policies —**cen′trism′** *n.*

-cen·trist (sen′trist) *combining form* **1** *forming nouns* a person having (a specified thing) as the center or focus of attention, efforts, etc. [*Eurocentrist*] **2** *forming adjectives* -CENTRIC (sense 3)

cen·tro- (sen′trō, -trə) ⟦< L *centrum*, CENTER⟧ *combining form* center [*centrosome*]

cen·tro·bar·ic (sen′trō bar′ik) *adj.* ⟦prec. + BAR[2] + -IC⟧ having to do with the center of gravity

cen·troid (sen′troid′) *n.* CENTER OF MASS

cen·tro·mere (sen′trō mir′) *n.* ⟦CENTRO- + -MERE⟧ a small, nonstaining structure, usually near the center of a chromosome to which the spindle fiber attaches during mitosis —**cen′tro·mer′ic** (-mer′ik, -mir′-) *adj.*

cen·tro·some (-trə sōm′) *n.* ⟦CENTRO- + -SOME[3]⟧ a very small body near the nucleus in most animal cells, consisting of a centriole surrounded by a centrosphere: in mitosis it divides, and the two parts move to opposite poles of the dividing cell —**cen′tro·som′ic** (-sōm′ik) *adj.*

cen·tro·sphere (-trō sfir′) *n.* **1** *Biol.* the portion of the centrosome surrounding the centriole; center of an aster **2** *Geol.* the inner part of the earth, beneath the lithosphere and consisting of the mantle and core

cen·trum (sen′trəm) *n., pl.* **-trums** or **-tra** (-trə) ⟦L⟧ **1** a center **2** *Anat.* the part of a vertebra supporting the disks in a spinal column

cen·tum (ken′təm, -to͝om) *adj.* ⟦L, HUNDRED: so named because the initial velar stop of L *centum* illustrates the typical development in this group from the IE palatal stop; i.e., IE *k̂* → centum *k*, satem *š* (sh)⟧ designating or of the group of Indo-European languages, including Germanic, Italic, Hellenic, Celtic, Anatolian, and Tocharian, in which a complicated but systematic development of the Indo-European palatals and labiovelars sets these languages apart from those of the SATEM group

cen·tu·ple (sen′tə pəl; sen to͞o′pəl, -tyo͞o′-) *adj.* ⟦Fr < LL(Ec) *centuplus*: see CENT[1] & DOUBLE⟧ a hundred times as much or as many; hundredfold —*vt.* **-pled**, **-pling** to make centuple; increase a hundredfold

cen·tu·pli·cate (sen to͞o′pli kāt′, -tyo͞o′-; *for adj. & n.*, -kit) *vt.* **-cat′ed**, **-cat′ing** to increase a hundredfold; centuple — *adj., n.* hundredfold

cen·tu·ri·on (sen to͝or′ē ən, -tyo͝or′-) *n.* ⟦ME *centurioun* < L *centurio* (gen. *centurionis*) < *centuria*: see fol.⟧ the commanding officer of an ancient Roman century

cen·tu·ry (sen′chə rē, -shə-) *n., pl.* **-ries** ⟦L *centuria* < *centum*, HUNDRED⟧ **1** any period of 100 years, as from 1620 to 1720 **2** a period of 100 years reckoned from a certain time, esp. from the beginning of the Christian Era (A.D. 1) [A.D. 1 through A.D. 100 is the first *century* A.D.; A.D. 1801 through A.D. 1900 is the 19th *century* A.D.; 400 B.C. through 301 B.C. is the 4th *century* B.C.]: in common usage, a century begins with a year ending in 00 and runs through 99, as 1800-1899 **3** in ancient Rome *a)* a military unit, originally made up of 100 men *b)* a subdivision of the people made for voting purposes **4** a series, group, or amount of a hundred —**cen·tu·ri·al** (sen to͝or′ē əl, -tyo͝or′-) *adj.*

century home a standing house built 100 or more years ago, specif., one so certified: also **century house**

☆**century plant** a tropical American desert agave (*Agave americana*) having fleshy leaves and a tall stalk that bears greenish flowers only once after 10 to 30 years and then dies: mistakenly thought to bloom only once a century

CEO *abbrev.* chief executive officer

ceorl (cherl, cheôrl) *n.* ⟦OE: see CHURL⟧ *Eng. History* a freeman of the lowest class, ranking below a thane

cèpe or **cep** (sep) *n.* ⟦Fr < Gascon dial. *cep*, mushroom < L *cippus*, a stake, post⟧ a large, fleshy, edible boletus mushroom (*Boletus edulis*) with a brown cap and a thick, white stem

ceph·al- (sef′əl) *combining form* CEPHALO-: used before a vowel

ceph·a·lad (sef′ə lad′) *adv.* ⟦CEPHAL(O)- + -AD[2]⟧ *Anat., Zool.* toward the head, or anterior part of the body: opposed to CAUDAD

ce·phal·ic (sə fal′ik) *adj.* ⟦L *cephalicus* < Gr *kephalikos* < *kephalē*, head < IE base **ghebhel-*, head, peak > GABLE, MHG *gebel*, skull⟧ **1** of the head, skull, or cranium **2** in, on, near, or toward the head —**ce·phal′i·cal·ly** *adv.*

-ce·phal·ic (sə fal′ik) *combining form forming adjectives* having a (specified) kind of head or number of heads; -CEPHALOUS [*macrocephalic*]

cephalic index the ratio of the greatest breadth of the human head to its greatest length, from front to back, multiplied by 100; cranial index: see BRACHYCEPHALIC, DOLICHOCEPHALIC, MESOCEPHALIC

ceph·a·lin (sef′ə lin) ***n.*** ⟦CEPHAL(O)- + -IN[1] (modeled on earlier Ger *kephalin*)⟧ a phospholipid, similar to lecithin, found esp. in brain and nerve tissue

ceph·a·li·za·tion (sef′ə li zā′shən) ***n.*** ⟦fol. + -IZATION⟧ the tendency in the evolution of animal life for sensory organs, the nervous system, etc. to become centralized in or near the head

ceph·a·lo- (sef′ə lō, -lə) ⟦see CEPHALIC⟧ *combining form* the head, skull, or brain *[cephalopod]*

ceph·a·lo·chor·date (sef′ə lō kôr′dāt′) ***adj.*** ⟦< ModL *Cephalochordata*: see prec. & CHORDATE⟧ of a subphylum (Cephalochordata) of small, fishlike chordates that have a permanent notochord extending from the anterior to the posterior end —***n.*** any animal of this subphylum; amphioxus; lancelet

ceph·a·lom·e·ter (sef′ə läm′ət ər) ***n.*** an instrument for measuring the head or skull; craniometer —**ceph′a·lom′e·try** (-trē) ***n.***

Ceph·a·lo·ni·a (sef′ə lō′nē ə) largest of the Ionian Islands, off the W coast of Greece: 302 sq mi (782 sq km): Gr. name KEFALLINIA

ceph·a·lo·pod (sef′ə lō päd′) ***n.*** ⟦CEPHALO- + -POD⟧ any of a class (Cephalopoda) of marine mollusks having a distinct head with highly developed eyes, varying numbers of arms, with suckers, attached to the head about the mouth, and a saclike fin-bearing mantle, as an octopus, squid, or cuttlefish

ceph·a·lo·spor·in (sef′ə lō spôr′in) ***n.*** ⟦< ModL *Cephalosporium* + -IN[1]⟧ any of a major group of broad-spectrum antibiotics produced by, or derived from, a fungus (genus *Cephalosporium*): an alternative for people allergic to penicillin

ceph·a·lo·tho·rax (sef′ə lō thôr′aks′) ***n.*** the head and thorax united as a single part, in certain crustaceans and arachnids

ceph·a·lous (sef′ə ləs) ***adj.*** ⟦CEPHAL(O)- + -OUS⟧ having a head

-ceph·a·lous (sef′ə ləs) ⟦see CEPHALIC⟧ *combining form forming adjectives* having a (specified) kind of head or number of heads; -CEPHALIC *[macrocephalous]*

-ceph·a·ly (sef′ə lē) ⟦see CEPHALIC⟧ *combining form forming nouns* a (specified) characteristic or condition of the head *[macrocephaly]*

Ceph·e·id (variable) (sef′ē id, sē′fē-) ⟦after fol. + -ID⟧ *[sometimes* **c-** *(***v-***)]* any of a class of pulsating, yellow, supergiant stars whose brightness varies in regular periods: from the period-luminosity relation, the distance of such a star can be determined

Ce·phe·us (sē′fē əs, -fyo͞os′) ***n.*** ⟦L < Gr *Kēpheus*⟧ **1** *Gr. Myth.* the husband of Cassiopeia and father of Andromeda **2** a N constellation near the celestial pole

cer- (sir, ser) *combining form* CERO-: used before a vowel

ce·ra·ceous (sə rā′shəs) ***adj.*** ⟦< L *cera*, wax < Gr *kēros* + -ACEOUS⟧ waxy; waxlike

Ce·ram (si ram′) one of the Molucca Islands, in Indonesia, west of New Guinea: 6,621 sq mi (17,148 sq km)

ce·ram·al (sə ram′əl, ser′ə mal′) ***n.*** ⟦< fol. + AL(LOY)⟧ CERMET

ce·ram·ic (sə ram′ik) ***adj.*** ⟦Gr *keramikos* < *keramos*, potter's clay, pottery⟧ **1** of or relating to pottery, earthenware, tile, porcelain, etc. **2** of ceramics —***n.*** **1** *[pl., with sing. v.]* the art or work of making objects of baked clay, as pottery, earthenware, etc. **2** an object made of such materials: *often used in pl.* **3** any of various materials formed by baking clay, etc. at a high temperature

ce·ram·ist (ser′ə mist, sə ram′ist) ***n.*** a person who works in ceramics; ceramic artist: also **ce·ram·i·cist** (sə ram′ə sist)

Ceram Sea part of the S Pacific Ocean, within E Indonesia and west of New Guinea

ce·rar·gy·rite (sə rär′jə rīt′) ***n.*** ⟦< Gr *keras*, HORN + *argyros*, silver + -ITE[1]⟧ a soft mineral, AgCl, that is an ore of silver; silver chloride

ce·ras·tes (sə ras′tēz′) ***n.*** ⟦ModL < L < Gr *kerastēs*, horned (serpent) < *keras*, HORN⟧ any of a genus (*Cerastes*) of poisonous African snakes, esp. a viper (*C. cornutus*) with a hornlike spine above each eye; horned viper

ce·rate (sir′āt′, sir′it) ***n.*** ⟦L *ceratus*, pp. of *cerare*, to wax < *cera*, wax < Gr *kēros*⟧ a thick ointment consisting of a fat, as oil or lard, mixed with wax, resin, and other, often medicinal, ingredients

ce·rat·ed (sir′āt′id) ***adj.*** covered with wax; waxed

cer·a·to- (ser′ə tō, -tə) ⟦< Gr *keras* (gen. *keratos*), HORN: see also KERATO-⟧ *combining form* horn, horny *[ceratoid]*: also, before a vowel, **cer·at-**

ce·rat·o·dus (si rat′ə dəs, ser′ə tō′dəs) ***n.*** ⟦ModL < prec. + -ODUS⟧ any of a genus (*Ceratodus*) of extinct lungfishes

cer·a·toid (ser′ə toid′) ***adj.*** ⟦Gr *keratoeidēs*: see CERATO- & -OID⟧ hornlike in shape or hardness; horny

cer·a·top·si·an (ser′ə täp′sē ən) ***n.*** ⟦< ModL *Ceratopsia*: see TRICERATOPS⟧ any of a suborder (Ceratopsia) of horned ornithischian dinosaurs of the Cretaceous with a beaklike snout and a bony crest at the back of the head —***adj.*** of the ceratopsians

Cer·ber·us (sʉr′bər əs) ***n.*** ⟦L < Gr *Kerberos*⟧ *Class. Myth.* the three-headed dog guarding the gate of Hades —**Cer·be·re·an** (sər bir′ē ən) ***adj.***

cer·car·i·a (sər ker′ē ə) ***n.***, *pl.* **-ri·ae′** (-ē ē′) ⟦ModL < Gr *kerkos*, tail⟧ the free-swimming larva of a parasitic trematode worm

cer·cis (sʉr′sis) ***n.*** ⟦ModL < Gr *kerkis*, Judas tree, aspen, lit., weaver's shuttle (orig., prob. staff, rod), dim. of *kerkos*, tail⟧ any of a genus (*Cercis*) of shrubs and small trees of the caesalpinia family, native to North America and Eurasia

cer·cus (sʉr′kəs) ***n.***, *pl.* **cer′ci′** (-sī′) ⟦ModL < Gr *kerkos*, tail⟧ either of a pair of usually jointed, feelerlike appendages at the hind end of the abdomen of many insects

cere (sir) ***n.*** ⟦Fr *cire* < L *cera*, wax < Gr *kēros*⟧ a waxy, often brightly colored, fleshy area at the base of the beak of some birds, as the parrot, eagle, hawk, etc.: it contains the nostrils

ce·re·al (sir′ē əl) ***adj.*** ⟦< L *Cerealis*, of CERES, goddess of agriculture < IE base *k̑er-, *k̑rē-, to grow: see CREATE⟧ of grain or the grasses producing grain —***n.*** **1** any grain used for food, as wheat, oats, or rice **2** any grass producing such grain ☆**3** food made from grain, esp. breakfast food, as oatmeal or cornflakes

cer·e·bel·lum (ser′ə bel′əm) ***n.***, *pl.* **-lums** or **-la** (-ə) ⟦L, dim. of *cerebrum*, brain < IE *k̑eres- < base *k̑er-, top of the head: see HORN⟧ the section of the brain behind and below the cerebrum: it consists of two lateral lobes and a middle lobe, and functions as the coordinating center for muscular movement —**cer′e·bel′lar** ***adj.***

cer·e·br- *combining form* CEREBRO-: used before a vowel

cer·e·bra (ser′ə brə, sə rē′brə) ***n.*** *pl. of* CEREBRUM

cer·e·bral (ser′ə brəl, sə rē′brəl) ***adj.*** ⟦Fr *cérébral* < L *cerebrum*: see CEREBELLUM⟧ **1** of the brain or the cerebrum **2** of, appealing to, or conceived by the intellect rather than the emotions; intellectual **3** *Phonet.* CACUMINAL —***n.*** *Phonet.* a cacuminal sound —**cer′e·bral·ly** ***adv.***

cerebral accident CEREBROVASCULAR ACCIDENT

cerebral cortex the thin layer of gray matter that makes up the outer portion of the cerebrum, responsible for voluntary movement, perception, thinking, speaking, etc.

cerebral hemisphere either of the two lateral halves of the cerebrum

cerebral palsy any of several nonprogressive motor disorders resulting from damage to the central nervous system, esp. before or during birth, and, usually, characterized by spastic paralysis

cer·e·brate (ser′ə brāt′) ***vi.*** **-brat′ed**, **-brat′ing** ⟦< L *cerebrum* (see CEREBELLUM) + -ATE[1]⟧ to use one's brain; think —**cer′e·bra′tion** ***n.***

cer·e·bro- (ser′ə brō′, sə rē′brō) ⟦< L *cerebrum*: see CEREBELLUM⟧ *combining form* brain, cerebrum *[cerebrospinal]*

cer·e·bro·side (ser′ə brō sīd′, sə rē′brō-) ***n.*** ⟦< prec. + -OS(E) + -IDE⟧ a lipid that contains galactose and is found normally in brain and nerve tissue

cer·e·bro·spi·nal (ser′ə brō′spī′nəl, sə rē′brō-) ***adj.*** of or affecting the brain and the spinal cord

cerebrospinal fluid the clear liquid surrounding the brain and spinal cord and filling the cavities of the brain

cerebrospinal meningitis MENINGITIS

cer·e·bro·vas·cu·lar (-vas′kyo͞o lər) ***adj.*** of or pertaining to the blood vessels of the brain

cerebrovascular accident a disturbance of the blood supply to parts of the brain because of blockage or hemorrhage, causing unconsciousness, paralysis, etc.: abbrev. *CVA*: see APOPLEXY

cer·e·brum (ser′ə brəm, sə rē′brəm) ***n.***, *pl.* **-brums** or **-bra** (-brə) ⟦L: see CEREBELLUM⟧ the upper, main part of the brain of vertebrate animals, consisting of left and right hemispheres: in humans it is the largest part of the brain and is believed to control conscious and voluntary processes

cere·cloth (sir′klôth′) ***n.*** ⟦formerly *cered cloth*: see CERE⟧ cloth treated with wax or a similar substance, esp. one used formerly to wrap a dead person for burial

cere·ment (ser′ə mənt, sir′mənt) ***n.*** ⟦Fr *cirement*: see CERE⟧ *[usually pl.]* a cerecloth; shroud

cer·e·mo·ni·al (ser′ə mō′nē əl) ***adj.*** of, for, or consisting of ceremony; ritual; formal —***n.*** **1** an established system of rites or formal actions connected with an occasion, as in religion; ritual **2** a rite or ceremony —**cer′e·mo′ni·al·ism′** ***n.*** —**cer′e·mo′ni·al·ist** ***n.*** —**cer′e·mo′ni·al·ly** ***adv.***

cer·e·mo·ni·ous (-nē əs) ***adj.*** ⟦Fr *cérémonieux*⟧ **1** ceremonial **2** full of ceremony **3** characterized by conventional usages or formality **4** excessively formal or proper —**cer′e·mo′ni·ous·ly** ***adv.*** —**cer′e·mo′ni·ous·ness** ***n.***

cer·e·mo·ny (ser′ə mō′nē; *chiefly Brit*, -mə nē) ***n.***, *pl.* **-nies** ⟦ME *cerimonie* < L *caerimonia*, awe, reverent rite, ceremony; prob. < Etr⟧ **1** a formal act or set of formal acts established by custom or authority as proper to a special occasion, such as a wedding, religious rite, etc. **2** the service or function at which such acts are performed **3** a conventionally courteous or polite act **4** behavior that follows rigid etiquette or a prescribed form **5** *a)* formality or formalities *b)* empty or meaningless formality, or an act suggesting this —**stand on ceremony** to behave with or insist on formality

SYN.—**ceremony** refers to a formal, usually solemn, act established as proper to some religious or state occasion *[the ceremony of launching a ship]*; **rite** refers to the prescribed form for a religious practice *[burial rites]*; **ritual** refers to rites or ceremonies collectively, esp. to the rites of a particular religion *[the ritual of voodooism]*; **formality** suggests a conventional, often meaningless, act or custom, usually one associated with social activity *[the formalities of polite conversation]*

Ce·ren·kov radiation (chə ren′kôf′) ⟦after P. A. *Cerenkov* (1904-90), Russ physicist⟧ radiation emitted when a charged particle travels through a medium at a speed greater than the speed of light through that medium

Ce·res (sir′ēz′) ***n.*** ⟦L: see CEREAL⟧ **1** *Rom. Myth.* the goddess of agriculture, daughter of Ops and Saturn: identified with the Greek Demeter **2** a dwarf planet orbiting the sun in the belt of asteroids between Mars and Jupiter: diameter, 950 km (590 mi)

ce·re·us (sir′ē əs) ***n.*** ⟦ModL < L, wax taper < *cera*, wax: so named from the shape of certain varieties⟧ any of a genus (*Cereus*) of cactus, native to the SW U.S. and Mexico

ce·ri·a (sir′ē ə) ***n.*** ⟦< CERIUM⟧ cerium dioxide, CeO_2, a white compound used as in ceramics

ce·ric (sir′ik, ser′-) *adj.* of or containing tetravalent cerium

ce·rif·er·ous (sə rif′ər əs) *adj.* ⟦< L *cera*, wax + -FEROUS⟧ producing wax

ce·rise (sə rēz′, -rēs′) *n., adj.* ⟦Fr: see CHERRY⟧ cherry red

ce·rite (sir′īt′) *n.* ⟦fol. + -ITE[1]⟧ a rare mineral that is a hydrous silicate of cerium and other metals

ce·ri·um (sir′ē əm) *n.* ⟦ModL < CER(ES) + -IUM: so named (1804) by its discoverers, J. J. BERZELIUS & W. Hisinger (1766-1852), Swed mineralogists, after *Ceres*, which had recently been discovered⟧ a gray chemical element, the most abundant of the rare-earth elements: it is used in alloys, electronic components, and nuclear fuels: symbol, Ce; at. no. 58: see the periodic table of elements in the Reference Supplement

cerium metals a series of closely related metals belonging to the rare-earth elements and having atomic numbers from 57 to 63; lanthanum, cerium, praseodymium, neodymium, promethium, samarium, and europium

cer·met (sʉr′met′) *n.* ⟦CER(AMIC) + MET(AL)⟧ a bonded mixture of ceramic material and a metal, that is tough and heat-resistant: used in gas turbines, nuclear reactor mechanisms, etc.

CERN (sʉrn) *n.* ⟦acronym for Fr *Conseil Européen pour la Recherche Nucléaire*, European Council for Nuclear Research, former name⟧ European Organization for Nuclear Research

cer·nu·ous (sʉr′nyo͞o əs, -no͞o-) *adj.* ⟦L *cernuus*, stooping, head down: for IE base see CEREBELLUM⟧ bending or hanging downward, as a flower or bud

ce·ro (sir′ō) *n., pl.* **-ro** or **-ros** ⟦Sp *sierra* < L *serra*, a saw⟧ a large, marine, food and game scombroid fish (*Scomberomorus regalis*), found in the tropical W Atlantic

ce·ro- (sir′ō, ser′ō; -ə) ⟦< L *cera* < Gr *kēros*, wax⟧ *combining form* wax

ce·ro·plas·tic (sir′ō plas′tik, ser′-) *adj.* ⟦Gr *kēroplastikos* < *kēros*, wax + *plassein*, to form: see PLASTIC⟧ **1** having to do with wax modeling **2** modeled in wax

ce·ro·plas·tics (-tiks) *n.* the art of modeling in wax

ce·rot·ic (sə rät′ik) *adj.* ⟦< L *cerotum*, wax salve < Gr *kērōton* < *kēros*, wax + -IC⟧ designating or of either of two fatty acids, $C_{26}H_{52}O_2$ or $C_{27}H_{54}O_2$, esters of which are found in beeswax and other waxes and oils

ce·rous (sir′əs) *adj.* of or containing trivalent cerium

Cer·ro de Pas·co (ser′ō dā päs′kō) mining town in the mountains of WC Peru: elevation *c.* 14,000 ft (4,267 m)

cert *abbrev.* **1** certificate **2** certified

cer·tain (sʉrt′′n) *adj.* ⟦ME & OFr < VL **certanus* < L *certus*, determined, fixed, orig. pp. of *cernere*, to distinguish, decide, orig., to sift, separate: see HARVEST⟧ **1** fixed, settled, or determined **2** sure (to happen, etc.); inevitable **3** not to be doubted; unquestionable *[certain* evidence*]* **4** not failing; reliable; dependable *[a certain* cure*]* **5** controlled; unerring *[his certain* aim*]* **6** without any doubt; assured; sure; positive *[certain* of his innocence*]* **7** not named or described, though definite and perhaps known *[a certain* person*]* **8** some, but not very much; appreciable *[to a certain* extent*]* —*pron.* *[with pl. v.]* a certain indefinite number; certain ones *(of)* *[certain* of these authors are seldom read*]* —**SYN.** SURE —**for certain** as a certainty; without doubt —**of a certain age** of an unspecified age, but no longer young: usually said of women

cer·tain·ly (-lē) *adv.* **1** beyond a doubt; surely **2** yes

cer·tain·ty (-tē) *n.* ⟦ME *certeinte* < OFr *certaineté*⟧ **1** the quality, state, or fact of being certain **2** *pl.* **-ties** anything certain; definite act —**of a certainty** [Archaic] without a doubt; certainly

SYN.—**certainty** suggests a firm, settled belief or positiveness in the truth of something; **certitude** is sometimes distinguished from the preceding as implying an absence of objective proof, hence suggesting unassailable blind faith; **assurance** suggests confidence, but not necessarily positiveness, usually in something that is yet to happen *[I have assurance* of his continuing support*]*; **conviction** suggests a being convinced because of satisfactory reasons or proof and sometimes implies earlier doubt —**ANT. doubt, skepticism**

cer·tes (sʉr′tēz′) *adv.* ⟦ME & OFr < VL **certas*, for L *certo*, surely < *certus*: see CERTAIN⟧ [Archaic] certainly; verily

cer·ti·fi·a·ble (sʉrt′ə fī′ə bəl, sʉrt′ə fī′ə bəl) *adj.* **1** that can be certified **2** that qualifies for an official declaration of insanity: often a hyperbolic use —**cer′ti·fi′a·bly** (-blē) *adv.*

cer·tif·i·cate (sər tif′i kit; *for v.*, -kāt′) *n.* ⟦ME & OFr *certificat* < ML *certificatum* < LL *certificatus*, pp. of *certificare*, CERTIFY⟧ a written or printed statement by which a fact is formally or officially certified or attested; specif., *a)* a document certifying that one has met specified requirements, as for teaching *b)* a document certifying ownership, a promise to pay, etc. —*vt.* **-cat′ed**, **-cat′ing** to attest or authorize by a certificate; issue a certificate to —**cer·tif′i·ca′tor** *n.* —**cer·tif′i·ca·to′ry** (-kə tôr′ē) *adj.*

certificate of deposit **1** a time deposit paying a specified rate of interest for a specified period of time, with a penalty imposed for premature withdrawal of the deposited funds **2** a certificate acknowledging such a deposit

certificate of incorporation a legal document stating the name and purpose of a proposed corporation, the names of its incorporators, its stock structure, etc.

certificate of origin a certificate submitted by an exporter to those countries requiring it, listing goods to be imported and stating their place of origin

cer·ti·fi·ca·tion (sʉrt′ə fi kā′shən) *n.* ⟦Fr⟧ **1** a certifying or being certified **2** a certified statement

cer·ti·fied (sʉrt′ə fīd′) *adj.* **1** vouched for; guaranteed **2** having, or attested to by, a certificate

☆**certified check** a check for which a bank has guaranteed payment, certifying there is enough money on deposit to cover the check

☆**certified mail** **1** a postal service for recording the mailing and delivery of a piece of first-class mail **2** mail recorded by this service: it is not insurable

☆**certified public accountant** a public accountant certified by a state examining board as having met the requirements of state law

cer·ti·fy (sʉrt′ə fī′) *vt.* **-fied′**, **-fy′ing** ⟦ME *certifien* < OFr *certifier* < LL *certificare* < L *certus*, CERTAIN + -FY⟧ **1** to declare (a thing) true, accurate, certain, etc. by formal statement, often in writing; verify; attest **2** to declare officially insane and committable to a mental institution ☆**3** to guarantee the quality or worth of (a check, document, etc.); vouch for **4** to issue a certificate or license to **5** [Archaic] to assure; make certain —*vi.* to testify *(to)* —**SYN.** APPROVE —**cer′ti·fi′er** *n.*

cer·ti·o·ra·ri (sʉr′shē ə rer′ē) *n.* ⟦ME < LL, lit., to be made more certain: a word in the writ⟧ *Law* a discretionary writ from a higher court to a lower one, or to a board or official with some judicial power, requesting the record of a case for review

cer·ti·tude (sʉrt′ə to͞od′, -tyo͞od′) *n.* ⟦OFr < LL(Ec) *certitudo* < L *certus*, CERTAIN⟧ **1** a feeling of absolute sureness or conviction **2** sureness; inevitability —**SYN.** CERTAINTY

ce·ru·le·an (sə ro͞o′lē ən) *adj.* ⟦L *caeruleus*; prob. < *caelulum*, dim. of *caelum*, heaven: for IE base see CESIUM⟧ sky-blue; azure

ce·ru·men (sə ro͞o′mən) *n.* ⟦< L *cera*, wax; sp. infl. by ALBUMEN⟧ EARWAX —**ce·ru′mi·nous** (-mə nəs) *adj.*

ce·ruse (sir′o͞os′, sə ro͞os′) *n.* ⟦OFr < L *cerussa* < ? Gr **kēroessa*, waxlike < *kēros*, wax⟧ **1** WHITE LEAD **2** a former cosmetic containing white lead

ce·rus·site (sir′ə sīt′, sə rus′īt′) *n.* ⟦< L *cerussa* (see prec.) + -ITE[1]⟧ a soft, heavy, orthorhombic mineral, $PbCO_3$, that is an ore of lead; lead carbonate

Cer·van·tes (ther vän′tes; *E* sər van′tēz, -vän′-), **Mi·guel de** (mē gel′ *the*) 1547-1616; Sp. novelist, poet, & playwright: author of *Don Quixote*: full name **Cervantes Sa·a·ve·dra** (sä′ä ve′thrä; *E* sä′ə vā′drə)

cer·ve·lat (ser və lä′, -lät′) *n.* ⟦Fr⟧ a smoked sausage of beef and pork: also **cer·ve·las′** (-lä′)

cer·ve·za (ser ves′ä) *n.* ⟦Sp⟧ beer

cer·vi·cal (sʉr′vi kəl) *adj.* ⟦< L *cervix* (gen. *cervicis*), the neck + -AL⟧ *Anat.* of the neck or a cervix

cervical cap a plastic or rubber, thimble-shaped contraceptive that is fitted over the cervix to prevent sperm from entering the uterus

cer·vi·ces (sər vī′sēz′, sʉr′və-) *n. alt. pl. of* CERVIX

cer·vi·ci·tis (sʉr′və sīt′is) *n.* ⟦see -ITIS⟧ inflammation of the cervix of the uterus

cer·vi·co- (sʉr′vi kō′, -kə) ⟦< L *cervix*, neck⟧ *combining form* cervical *[cervicitis]*: also, before a vowel, **cer′vic-**

cer·vid (sʉr′vid′) *adj.* ⟦< ModL *Cervidae*, name of the family (< L *cervus*, stag, deer < IE **k̑erewos*, horned, a horned animal < base **k̑er-*, HORN) + -ID⟧ of the deer family

Cer·vin (ser ven′), **Mont** (mōn) *Fr. name for* the MATTERHORN

cer·vine (sʉr′vīn′, -vin) *adj.* ⟦L *cervinus* < *cervus*: see CERVID⟧ of or like a deer

cer·vix (sʉr′viks′) *n., pl.* **cer·vi·ces** (sər vī′sēz′, sʉr′və-) or **-vix′es** ⟦L, the neck⟧ **1** the neck, esp. the back of the neck **2** a necklike part, esp. of the uterus

ce·sar·e·an (section) (sə zer′ē ən) ⟦from the ancient story (by assoc. of the name *Caesar* with L *caedere*, to cut: see CAESAR[2]) that Caesar or an ancestor had been born in this manner⟧ a surgical operation for delivering a baby by cutting through the mother's abdominal and uterine walls: occas. sp. **ce·sar′i·an (section)**

ce·si·um (sē′zē əm) *n.* ⟦ModL, orig. neut. of L *caesius*, bluish-gray (< IE base **(s)kai-*, bright > -HOOD): so named (1860) by R. W. BUNSEN because of the blue line seen in the spectroscope⟧ a soft, silver-white, ductile, metallic chemical element, one of the alkali metals and the most electropositive of all the elements: it ignites in air, reacts vigorously with water, and is used in photoelectric cells: symbol, Cs; at. no. 55: a radioactive isotope (**cesium-137**) with a half-life of 30.17 years is produced by fission and is used in cancer research, radiation therapy, etc.: see the periodic table of elements in the Reference Supplement

Čes·ké Bu·dě·jo·vi·ce (ches′ke bo͞o′de yô′vit sə) city in the SW Czech Republic, on the Vltava River

Čes·ko·slo·ven·sko (ches′kô slô ven′skô) *Czech name for* CZECHOSLOVAKIA

ces·pi·tose (ses′pə tōs′) *adj.* ⟦ModL < L *caespes*, turf, grassy field + -OSE[2]⟧ growing in dense, matlike clumps without creeping stems, as moss, grass, etc.

cess (ses) *n.* ⟦prob. < ASSESS⟧ in Ireland, an assessment; tax: now used only in **bad cess to**, bad luck to

ces·sa·tion (se sā′shən) *n.* ⟦L *cessatio* < pp. of *cessare*, CEASE⟧ a ceasing, or stopping, either forever or for some time

ces·sion (sesh′ən) *n.* ⟦OFr < L *cessio* < *cessus*, pp. of *cedere*, to yield: see CEDE⟧ a ceding or giving up (of rights, property, territory, etc.) to another

ces·sion·ar·y (sesh′ə ner′ē) *n., pl.* **-ar′ies** *Law* ASSIGNEE

cess·pit (ses′pit′) *n.* ⟦< fol. + PIT[2]⟧ a pit for garbage, excrement, etc.

cess·pool (-po͞ol′) *n.* ⟦< ? It *cesso*, privy < L *secessus*, place of retirement (in LL, privy, drain): see SECEDE⟧ **1** a deep hole or pit in the ground, usually covered, to receive drainage or sewage from the sinks, toilets, etc. of a house **2** a center of moral corruption

ces·ta (ses′tə) *n.* ⟦Sp, basket < L *cista*: see CHEST⟧ in jai alai, the narrow, curved, basketlike racket strapped to the forearm, in which the ball is caught and from which it is hurled

c'est la vie (se lȧ vē′) ⟦Fr⟧ that's life; such is life
ces·tode (ses′tōd′) ***n.*** ⟦CEST(US) + -ODE²⟧ any of a class (Cestoda) of parasitic flatworms, with a ribbonlike body and no intestinal canal; tapeworm —***adj.*** of such a worm
ces·toid (-toid′) ***adj.*** ⟦< fol. + -OID⟧ ribbonlike, as a tapeworm
ces·tus¹ (-təs) ***n.*** ⟦L < Gr *kestos*, a girdle; akin to *kentein*, to stitch: see CENTER⟧ in ancient times, a woman's belt or girdle
ces·tus² (-təs) ***n.*** ⟦L *caestus* < *caedere*, to strike, cut down: see -CIDE⟧ a contrivance of leather straps, often weighted with metal, worn on the hand by boxers in ancient Rome

cestus

ce·su·ra (si zyoor′ə, -zhoor′ə) ***n.***, *pl.* **-ras** or **-rae** (-ē) CAESURA
CETA *abbrev.* Comprehensive Employment and Training Act
ce·ta·cean (sə tā′shən) ***n.*** ⟦< ModL < L *cetus*, large sea animal, whale < Gr *kētos* + -ACE(A) + -AN⟧ in some systems of classification, any of an order (Cetacea) of nearly hairless, fishlike water mammals lacking external hind limbs but having paddlelike forelimbs, including whales, porpoises, and dolphins —***adj.*** of the cetaceans: also **ce·ta′ceous** (-shəs)
ce·tane (sē′tān′) ***n.*** ⟦< L *cetus* (see prec.) + -ANE: so named from being related to compounds found in oil from sperm whales⟧ a colorless, liquid alkane, $C_{16}H_{34}$, found in petroleum and, sometimes, in vegetable matter, and used to test fuel oils
cetane number a number that increases with higher quality, representing the ignition properties of diesel engine fuel oils: it is determined by the percentage of cetane that must be mixed with a standard liquid to match the fuel oil's performance in a standard test engine: see OCTANE NUMBER
ce·te·ris pa·ri·bus (set′ər is par′ə bəs, ket′-) ⟦L, other things being equal⟧ all else remaining the same
ce·tol·o·gy (sə täl′ə jē) ***n.*** ⟦< L *cetus*, whale (see CETACEAN) + -OLOGY⟧ the branch of zoology that deals with whales —**ce·to·log·i·cal** (sēt′ə läj′i kəl) ***adj.*** —**ce·tol′o·gist *n.***
Ce·tus (sēt′əs) ***n.*** ⟦L, whale⟧ an equatorial constellation near Pisces
Ceu·ta (syoot′ə; *Sp* thā′oo tä′) Spanish enclave on the coast of Morocco, opposite Gibraltar
Cé·vennes (sā ven′) mountain range in S France, west of the Rhone: highest peak, 5,755 ft (1,754 m)
ce·vi·che (sə vē′chā′, -chē′) ***n.*** ⟦AmSp⟧ a Latin American dish consisting of pieces of raw fish or shellfish marinated in lime juice with chilies, chopped tomatoes, etc., and served chilled as an appetizer
ce·vi·tam·ic acid (sē′vī tam′ik, -vi-) ⟦< C + VITAM(IN) + -IC⟧ ASCORBIC ACID
Cey·lon (sə län′, sā-, sē-) *former name for* SRI LANKA —**Cey·lo·nese** (sel′ə nēz′, sā′lə-) ***adj., n.***, *pl.* **-nese′**
Ceylon moss any of several East Indian species (genus *Gracilaria*) of red algae from which agar is made
Cé·zanne (sā zan′), **Paul** 1839-1906; Fr. painter
cf *abbrev.* **1** *Bookbinding* calf **2** *Baseball a)* center field *b)* center fielder: also **CF 3** ⟦L *confer*⟧ compare **4** cost and freight: also **CF**
Cf *Chem. symbol for* californium
CF *abbrev.* cystic fibrosis
c/f *symbol Bookkeeping* carried forward
CFC *abbrev.* chlorofluorocarbon
CFI or **cfi** *abbrev.* cost, freight, and insurance
CFL *abbrev.* **1** *trademark* Canadian Football League **2** compact fluorescent light (or lamp): also **cfl**
cfm *abbrev.* cubic feet per minute
CFO *abbrev.* chief financial officer
CFP *abbrev.* certified financial planner
cfs *abbrev.* cubic feet per second
CFS *abbrev.* chronic fatigue syndrome
cg or **cgm** *abbrev.* centigram(s)
CG *abbrev.* **1** Coast Guard **2** center of gravity **3** commanding general **4** computer-generated **5** computer graphics Also, for 2 & 3, **cg**
CGI *abbrev.* computer-generated image (or imaging)
CGS or **cgs** *abbrev.* centimeter-gram-second (system): see the table of weights and measures in the Reference Supplement
Ch *abbrev.* **1** chain **2** champion **3** chaplain **4** chapter **5** chief **6** child; children **7** China **8** Chinese **9** *Bible* Chronicles **10** church Also, except for 7-9, **ch**
CH *abbrev.* **1** courthouse **2** customhouse
chab·a·zite (kab′ə zīt′) ***n.*** ⟦Fr *chabazie* < Gr, a misspelling of *chalazie*, voc. of *chalazios*, a gem resembling a hailstone < *chalaza*, hailstone: see CHALAZA⟧ a hard, rhombohedral zeolite, $CaAl_2Si_4O_{12}·6H_2O$, commonly found in basalts
Cha·blis (sha blē′, shə-; *occas.* shab′lē) ***n.*** **1** a dry white Burgundy wine made in or near the town of Chablis, France **2** [*often* **c-**] white wine of similar type made elsewhere
☆**cha-cha** (chä′chä′) ***n.*** ⟦AmSp, of echoic orig.⟧ a modern ballroom dance of Latin American origin, with a basic, repeating pattern of two slow steps and three quick steps —***vi.*** to dance the cha-cha Also **cha′-cha′-cha′**
Cha·co (chä′kô) extensive lowland plain in central South America, stretching across parts of Argentina, Paraguay, and Bolivia: *c.* 300,000 sq mi (776,997 sq km)
cha·conne (sha kän′; *Fr* shȧ kôn′) ***n.*** ⟦Fr < Sp *chacona* < ? Basque *chukun*, pretty⟧ **1** *a)* a slow, solemn dance in 3/4 time, of Spanish or Moorish origin, similar to the passacaglia *b)* later, a popular social dance in France in the 17th and early 18th cent. **2** music for this dance **3** either of two musical forms developed from this music, specif., *a)* a series of variations based on a short harmonic progression *b)* an expanded rondo form
cha·cun à son goût (shȧ kën nȧ sōn goo′) ⟦Fr⟧ everyone to his or her own taste
chad (chad) ***n.*** ⟦< ?⟧ any of the bits of paper that are separated from a PUNCH CARD in the process of punching holes in it
Chad¹ (chad) ***n.*** ⟦< OE *Ceadda*, name of a bishop of Mercia (died A.D. 672), later a saint⟧ a masculine name
Chad² (chad) **1** country in NC Africa, south of Libya: formerly a French territory, it became independent in 1960: 495,755 sq mi (1,284,000 sq km); cap. N'Djamena **2 Lake** lake mostly in Chad, at the juncture of the Chad, Niger, Cameroon, and Nigeria borders: 4,000-10,000 sq mi (10,360-25,900 sq km), reflecting seasonal fluctuation —**Chad′i·an *adj., n.***
Chad·ic (chad′ik) ***n.*** a subfamily of the Afroasiatic family of languages, including Hausa and a large number of other languages of N Nigeria and of Chad —***adj.*** designating or of any or all of these languages
cha·dor or **cha·dar** (chäd′ər, chud′ər) ***n.***, *pl.* **-dors**, **-dars**, or **-dri** (-rē) ⟦Hindi *chadar*⟧ a large, square cloth traditionally worn as a shawl or cloak by Muslim and Hindu women
Chad·wick (chad′wik), Sir **James** 1891-1974; Eng. physicist: discovered the neutron
Chaer·o·ne·a (ker′ə nē′ə) ancient Greek town in Boeotia: site of a battle (338 B.C.) in which the Macedonians defeated the Greeks
chae·ta (kēt′ə) ***n.***, *pl.* **-tae** (-ē) ⟦ModL < Gr *chaitē*, hair < IE base **ghait-*, curly hair > Avestan *gaēsa-*⟧ a bristlelike projection, or seta, esp. on an annelid worm
chae·to- (kēt′ō, -ə) ⟦< Gr *chaitē*, hair: see prec.⟧ *combining form* hair or bristles [*chaetopod*]: see also SETI-: also, before a vowel, **chaet-**
chae·tog·nath (kē′täg nath′) ***n.*** ⟦< ModL: see prec. & -GNATHOUS⟧ ARROWWORM
chae·to·pod (kēt′ə päd′) ***n.*** ⟦CHAETO- + -POD⟧ *Zool.* any of a former class (Chaetopoda) of annelids, including the earthworms and leeches
chafe (chāf) ***vt.*** **chafed**, **chaf′ing** ⟦ME *chaufen* < OFr *chaufer*, to warm < L *calefacere*, to make warm: see CALEFACIENT⟧ **1** to rub so as to stimulate or make warm **2** to wear away by rubbing **3** to irritate or make sore by rubbing **4** to annoy; irritate —***vi.*** **1** to rub (*on* or *against*) **2** to be or become vexed, irritated, or impatient —***n.*** **1** an injury or irritation caused by rubbing **2** [Archaic] a vexed or annoyed state —**chafe at the bit** to be impatient or vexed, as because of delay: originally said of horses
chaf·er (chāf′ər) ***n.*** ⟦ME < OE *ceafor* (orig. sense prob. "devourer") < IE base **ĝebh-*, jaw, mouth, devour > JOWL¹, Ger *kiefer*, jaw, Ir *gob*, mouth⟧ any of various beetles (esp. family Scarabaeidae) that feed on plants, as the cockchafer or rose chafer
chaff (chaf, chäf) ***n.*** ⟦ME *chaf* < OE *ceaf*; akin to MDu *caf*, Ger *kaff*⟧ **1** the husks of wheat or other grain separated in threshing or winnowing **2** finecut hay or straw, used for fodder **3** anything regarded as worthless **4** tiny strips of metal foil used to confuse enemy radar **5** good-natured teasing or joking; banter **6** *Bot.* the bracts that enclose the individual florets on the receptacles of certain composite heads — ***vt., vi.*** to tease or ridicule in a good-natured way
chaf·fer (chaf′ər) ***n.*** ⟦ME *chaffare*, merchandise, trade < OE *ceap*, *cep*, a purchase + *faru*, a journey: see CHEAP & FARE⟧ **1** [Obs.] trade; business **2** [Archaic] a haggling over price or terms; bargaining —***vi.*** **1** [Now Rare] to haggle over price; bargain **2** to chat idly —**chaf′fer·er *n.***
chaf·finch (chaf′inch′) ***n.*** ⟦OE *ceaffinc*: see CHAFF & FINCH: it eats chaff and grain⟧ a small European finch (*Fringilla coelebs*) that has a white patch on each shoulder: often kept in a cage as a pet
chaff·y (chaf′ē) ***adj.*** **chaff′i·er**, **chaff′i·est 1** full of chaff **2** like chaff; worthless
chaf·ing dish (chāf′iŋ) ⟦see CHAFE⟧ a pan with a heating apparatus beneath it, used to cook food at the table or to keep food hot
Cha·gall (shə gäl′), **Marc** (born *Moishe Shagal*) 1889-1985; Russ. painter in France and the U.S.
Cha·gas' disease (shä′gəs) ⟦after Carlos *Chagas*, Brazilian physician who identified it (1909)⟧ a type of trypanosomiasis, common in Central and South America, caused by a parasite (*Trypanosoma cruzi*) that is carried by reduviid insects, and characterized by the eventual invasion and deterioration of cardiac, gastrointestinal, and nervous tissue
Cha·gos Archipelago (chä′gəs) group of islands in the Indian Ocean 1,180 mi (1,899 km) northeast of Mauritius, comprising the British Indian Ocean Territory: chief island, Diego Garcia
Cha·gres (chä′gres) river in Panama, dammed to form Gatun Lake, flowing into the Caribbean
cha·grin (shə grin′; *Brit* shag′rin) ***n.*** ⟦Fr, grief, sorrow, vexation, prob. < Norm *chagreiner*, to become gloomy (said of the weather) < OFr *graignier*, to sorrow < *graim*, sorrowful < Frank **gram*⟧ a feeling of embarrassment or distress because one has failed or been disappointed —***vt.*** **-grined′**, **-grin′ing** ⟦Fr *chagriner*⟧ to cause to feel chagrin; embarrass or distress: usually in the passive voice —**SYN.** ASHAMED

chai (chī) ***n.*** ⟦via an Indian language; ult. < Mandarin *ch'a*, tea⟧ a hot drink of black tea with spices and milk: also **chai tea**

chain (chān) ***n.*** ⟦ME & OFr *chaine* < L *catena* < IE base **kat-*, to twist, twine > prob. OE *heathor*, confinement⟧ **1** a flexible series of joined links, usually of metal, used to pull, confine, etc. or to transmit power **2** TIRE CHAIN **3** [*pl.*] *a)* bonds, shackles, etc. *b)* anything that binds, ties, or restrains [*chains* of love] *c)* captivity; bondage **4** any chainlike ornament, badge, etc. **5** a chainlike measuring instrument, or its measure of length; specif., *a)* a surveyor's (or Gunter's) chain (66 feet or 20.117 meters or 100 links) *b)* an engineer's chain (100 feet or 30.48 meters or 100 links) *c) Football* a chain 10 yards in length, used to measure for a first down (often **the chains**) **6** a series of things connected causally, logically, physically, etc. [*chain* of events, mountain *chain*] ☆**7** a number of stores, restaurants, etc. owned by one company, specif., such a group of franchised businesses having the same name **8** *Chem.* a linkage of atoms in a molecule: see OPEN CHAIN, CLOSED CHAIN, SIDE CHAIN —***vt.*** **1** to fasten or shackle with chains **2** to hold down, restrain, confine, etc. —***SYN.*** SERIES

Chain (chān), **Ernst Boris** 1906-79; Brit. biochemist, born in Germany

chaî·né (she nā′) ***n.*** ⟦Fr < pp. of *chaîner*, to chain⟧ *Ballet* a series of small, quick turns performed as a dancer moves across the stage: also written **chainé**

chain gang a gang of prisoners chained together, as when working outdoors

chain letter a letter to be circulated among many people by being copied, or, sometimes, added to, and then passed to others with a request to do the same

☆**chain lightning** lightning that zigzags across the sky

chain-link (chān′liŋk′) ***adj.*** designating a fence made of galvanized steel links that are continuously interwoven

chain mail flexible armor made of joined metal links

☆**chain·man** (-mən) ***n.***, *pl.* **-men** (-mən) a surveyor's assistant who measures distances with a tape measure or surveyor's chain: chainmen work in pairs

chain of command the hierarchy, in order of rank, of persons having authority in an organization or undertaking, specif. a military one

chain-re·act (-rē akt′) ***vi.*** to be involved in or subjected to a chain reaction

☆**chain-re·act·ing pile** (-rē ak′tiŋ) NUCLEAR REACTOR

chain reaction **1** a self-sustaining series of chemical or nuclear reactions in which the products of the reaction contribute directly to the process: it can be started by light, an electric spark, bombardment with neutrons, etc. **2** any sequence of events, each of which results in, or has an effect on, the following

☆**chain saw** a portable power saw with an endless chain to which the cutting teeth are attached, used as for felling trees, cutting firewood, etc.

chain shot cannon shot consisting of two balls or half balls connected by a chain, formerly used in naval warfare to destroy masts, sails, etc.

chain-smoke (-smōk′) ***vt., vi.*** **-smoked′**, **-smok′ing** to smoke (cigarettes) one right after the other, often, specif., using each to light the next —**chain smoker *n.*, chain′-smok′er**

chain stitch **1** an embroidery stitch in which loops are connected to form a chainlike pattern **2** the basic stitch in crocheting, forming a single chainlike strand of connected loops: the basis of all other stitches —**chain′-stitch′ *vt.***

☆**chain store** any of a chain of retail stores

chain·wheel (-hwēl′) ***n.*** SPROCKET (sense 2)

chair (cher) ***n.*** ⟦ME & OFr *chaire* < L *cathedra*: see CATHEDRA⟧ **1** a piece of furniture for one person to sit on, having a back and, usually, four legs **2** a seat of authority or dignity **3** the position of a player in an instrumental section of a symphony orchestra **4** an important or official position, as a professorship or chairmanship **5** a person who presides over a meeting; chairman [address your remarks to the *chair*] **6** SEDAN CHAIR ☆**7** ELECTRIC CHAIR: used with *the* —***vt.*** **1** to place in a chair; seat **2** to place in authority **3** to preside over as chairman **4** [Brit.] to carry (a person) aloft in public triumph on, or as though on, a chair —**take the chair** to preside as chairman

☆**chair car** a railroad passenger car with pairs of adjustable seats on both sides of the aisle

☆**chair·lift** (-lift′) ***n.*** a conveyor consisting of a number of seats suspended from a power-driven endless cable, used esp. to carry skiers up a mountain slope

chair·man (-mən) ***n.***, *pl.* **-men** (-mən) **1** a person who presides at a meeting or heads a committee, board, etc. **2** a man whose work is to carry or wheel people in a chair —***vt.*** **-maned** or **-manned**, **-man·ing** or **-man·ning** to preside over as chairman —**chair′man·ship′ *n.***

chair·per·son (-pur′sən) ***n.*** CHAIRMAN (*n.* 1): used to avoid the masculine implication of *chairman*

chair·wom·an (-woom′ən) ***n.***, *pl.* **-wom′en** (-wim′in) a female CHAIRMAN (*n.* 1)

chaise (shāz) ***n.*** ⟦Fr, var. of *chaire*, CHAIR⟧ **1** any of various lightweight carriages, esp. one with two wheels and a folding top, for carrying one or two persons **2** POST CHAISE **3** CHAISE LONGUE

chaise longue (shāz′ lôŋ′; *often also* -lounj′ — *see next entry*) *pl.* **chaise longues** or **chaises longues** (shāz′ lôŋz′; -loun′jiz) ⟦Fr, lit., long chair⟧ a couchlike chair with a back support and a seat long enough to support outstretched legs

chaise lounge (lounj) *pl.* **chaise lounges** ⟦by folk etym. < prec.⟧ CHAISE LONGUE

chak·ra (chäk′rə, shäk′-) ***n.*** ⟦Sans *cakra*, wheel: see CHUKKER⟧ in certain forms of yoga, traditional Asian medicine, etc., any of a number of points in the human body, usually seven, that are considered centers of physical or spiritual energy: see CHI[2]

cha·la·za (kə lā′zə) ***n.***, *pl.* **-zae** (-zē) or **-zas** ⟦ModL < Gr, hail < IE base **ghelǝd-*, ice > Pers *žāla*, hail, OSlav *žlědica*, sleet⟧ **1** either of the spiral bands of dense albumen extending from the yolk toward the lining membrane at each end of a bird's egg and serving to keep the yolk suspended near the center of the albumen **2** *Bot.* the basal end of an ovule, opposite the micropyle, where the seed coats and the nucellus join —**cha·la′zal *adj.***

cha·la·zi·on (kə lā′zē ən) ***n.*** ⟦< Gr, dim. of prec.⟧ a chronic sty

chal·can·thite (kal kan′thīt′) ***n.*** ⟦< L *chalcanthum* < Gr *kalkanthon*, vitriol (< *chalkos*, copper + *anthos*, flower: see ANTHO-) + -ITE[1]⟧ a bluish, triclinic mineral, $CuSO_4 \cdot 5H_2O$, that is an ore of copper: hydrous copper sulfate

Chal·ce·don (kal′sə dän′) ancient Greek city on the Bosporus, opposite Byzantium: site of the 4th ecumenical council, A.D. 451 —**Chal′ce·do′ni·an** (-dō′nē ən) ***adj.***

chal·ced·o·ny (kal sed′'n ē, kal′sə dō′nē) ***n.***, *pl.* **-nies** ⟦ME & OFr *calcedoine* < LL (Vulg.) *calcedonius*, used to transl. Gr *chalkēdōn* (only in Rev. 21:19), a precious stone < ?⟧ a type of quartz with a waxy luster and microscopic crystals often forming colorful, parallel bands

chal·cid (kal′sid) ***n.*** ⟦< ModL *Chalcis* (gen. *Chalcidis*), name of the type genus < Gr *chalkos*, copper: so named because of their metallic color⟧ any of a large family (Chalcididae) of very small wasps, either four-winged or wingless, many of whose larvae live as parasites in the eggs, larvae, or pupae of other insects: also **chalcid fly** (or **wasp**) —***adj.*** of these insects

Chal·ci·di·ce (kal sid′ə sē′) peninsula in NE Greece, extending into the Aegean, & terminating in three prongs

chal·co- (kal′kō, -kə) ⟦< Gr *chalkos*, copper, brass⟧ *combining form* copper or brass [*chalcocite*]: also, before a vowel, **chalc-**

chal·co·cite (kal′kə sīt′) ***n.*** ⟦see prec.⟧ a dark-gray, lustrous mineral, Cu_2S, that is an ore of copper; cuprous sulfide

chal·cog·ra·phy (kal käg′rə fē) ***n.*** ⟦ML *chalcographia*, printing: see CHALCO- & -GRAPHY⟧ the art of engraving on copper or brass —**chal·co·graph·ic** (kal′kō graf′ik) ***adj.***

chal·co·py·rite (kal′kō pī′rīt′, -pir′īt′) ***n.*** ⟦CHALCO- + PYRITE⟧ a bright-yellow mineral, $CuFeS_2$, an important ore of copper; copper iron sulfide

Chal·da·ic (kal dā′ik) ***adj., n.*** CHALDEAN

Chal·de·a or **Chal·dae·a** (kal dē′ə) **1** ancient region along the lower courses of the Tigris and Euphrates rivers: S part of Babylonia **2** Babylonia: so called during Chaldean supremacy, *c.* 6th cent. B.C.

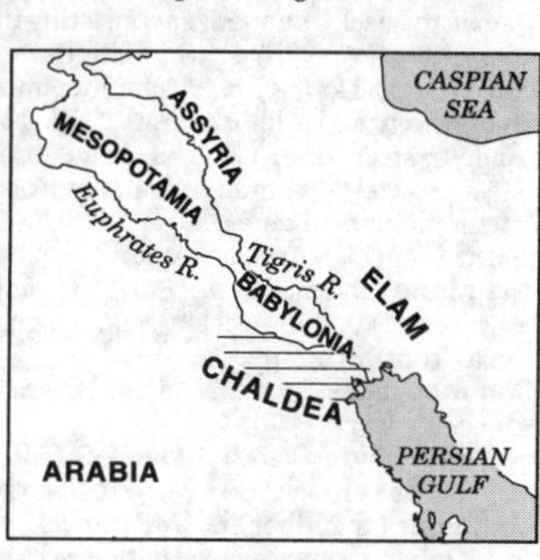

Chaldea

Chal·de·an (-dē′ən) ***adj.*** ⟦L *Chaldaeus* < Gr *Chaldaios*⟧ of Chaldea or its people, language, or culture —***n.*** **1** a person born or living in Chaldea; member of a Semitic people related to the Babylonians **2** the Semitic language of the Chaldeans **3** ⟦from the fact that astrology and magic flourished in Chaldea⟧ [Rare] an astrologer or sorcerer Also **Chal·dae′an**

Chal·dee (kal′dē, kal dē′) ***adj., n.*** CHALDEAN

chal·dron (chôl′drən) ***n.*** ⟦ME < OFr *chauderon*: see CAULDRON⟧ an old unit of dry measure, now used in Great Britain only for measuring coal or coke and equal to 36 bushels

cha·let (sha lā′, sha′lā′) ***n.*** ⟦Swiss-Fr, prob. dim. of OFr *chasel*, farmhouse < VL **casalis*, belonging to a house < L *casa*, a house, cabin⟧ **1** a herdsman's hut or cabin in the Swiss Alps **2** *a)* a type of Swiss house, built of wood with balconies and overhanging eaves *b)* any house, cottage, lodge, etc. built in this style

Cha·lia·pin (shä lyä′pin), **Fyo·dor I·va·no·vich** (fyô′dôr ē vä′nô vich) 1873-1938; Russ. operatic basso

chal·ice (chal′is) ***n.*** ⟦ME & OFr < L *calix*, cup: see CALIX⟧ **1** a cup; goblet **2** the cup for the wine of Holy Communion **3** a cup-shaped flower

chal·iced (-ist) ***adj.*** cup-shaped: said of a flower

chalk (chôk) ***n.*** ⟦ME < OE *cealc* < L *calx*, lime, limestone: see CALCIUM⟧ **1** a white, gray, or yellowish limestone that is soft, porous, and easily pulverized, composed almost entirely of calcite from minute sea shells **2** any substance like chalk in color, texture, etc. **3** a piece of chalk or gypsum, often imbued with a pigment, used for drawing, writing on a blackboard, etc. **4** a mark or line made with chalk **5** [Brit.] a score or tally, as in a game or as of credit given —***adj.*** **1** made or drawn with chalk ☆**2** [Slang] *Horse Racing a)* favored to win, place, or show *b)* betting on favorites only —***vt.*** **1** [Brit.] to treat with chalk; lime or fertilize (soil) **2** to rub or smear with chalk; specif., to rub chalk on the tip of (a billiard cue) **3** to make pale **4** to write, draw, or mark with chalk —***vi.*** to become chalky or powdery, as a painted surface —**chalk out** **1** to mark out as with chalk **2** to outline; plan —**chalk up** [Informal] **1** to score, get, or achieve **2** to attribute or ascribe —**not by a long chalk** [Brit. Informal] not by any means; not at all —**walk a chalk line** [Informal] to behave with strict propriety or obedience

☆**chalk·board** (chôk′bôrd′) ***n.*** BLACKBOARD

chalk·stone (-stōn′) ***n.*** TOPHUS

chalk-stripe (-strīp′) ***n.*** **1** a stripe, as in the fabric of some suits, that is wider and usually more muted than a pinstripe **2** a pattern of such stripes in parallel

☆**chalk talk** a lecture accompanied with diagrams, illustrations, etc. drawn in chalk on a blackboard

chalk·y (-ē) ***adj.*** **chalk′i·er**, **chalk′i·est** **1** of, containing, or covered with chalk **2** like chalk in color; dull white **3** like chalk in texture; gritty, pasty, etc. —**chalk′i·ness** ***n.***

chal·lah (khä′lə) ***n.*** ⟦Yiddish *khale* < Heb *chala,* loaf of bread⟧ the traditional loaf of rich white bread, typically having a braided or twisted form, eaten by Jews on the Sabbath and holidays

chal·lenge (chal′ənj) ***n.*** ⟦ME & OFr *chalenge,* accusation, claim, dispute < L *calumnia,* CALUMNY⟧ **1** a demand for identification *[*a sentry gave the *challenge]* **2** a calling into question; a demanding of proof, explanation, etc. *[*a *challenge* of the premises of an argument*]* **3** a call or dare to take part in a duel, contest, etc. **4** anything, as a demanding task, that calls for special effort or dedication ☆**5** an objection to a vote or to someone's right to vote **6** *Law* a formal objection or exception to a person who has been chosen as a prospective juror —***vt.*** **-lenged**, **-leng·ing** **1** to call to a halt for identification **2** *a)* to call to account *b)* to make objection to; call into question **3** to call or dare to take part in a duel, contest, etc.; defy **4** to call for; make demands on *[*to *challenge* the imagination*]* ☆**5** to object to (a vote) as not valid, or to (a prospective voter) as not qualified to vote **6** to take formal exception to (a prospective juror) —***vi.*** to make, issue, or offer a challenge —**chal′lenge·a·ble** ***adj.*** —**chal′leng·er** ***n.***

chal·lenged (chal′ənjd) ☆***adj.*** disabled or handicapped in a (specified) way *[*mentally *challenged]*

chal·lis (shal′ē) ***n.*** ⟦< ?⟧ a soft, lightweight fabric of wool, cotton, rayon, etc., usually printed with a design

chal·one (kal′ōn′) ***n.*** ⟦Gr *chalōn,* prp. of *chalan,* to slacken⟧ a substance produced within a bodily tissue that inhibits cell division within that tissue

Châ·lons-sur-Marne (shä lōn sür märn′) city in NE France, on the Marne River: scene of defeat (A.D. 451) of Attila by the Romans: also **Châ·lons′**

chal·u·meau (shal′ə mō′) ***n.*** ⟦Fr < OFr *chalemel* < L *calemellus,* dim. of *calamus,* reed: see CALAMUS⟧ **1** an early single-reed wind instrument, forerunner of the clarinet **2** the lowest register of the modern clarinet

☆**cha·lu·pa** (chä lo͞o′pə) ***n.*** ⟦MexSp < Sp, a boat < Fr *chaloupe:* see SHALLOP⟧ a Mexican snack or appetizer consisting of a fried corn tortilla usually in the shape of a boat, with a savory filling

cha·lutz (khä lo͞ots′) ***n.***, *pl.* **cha′lutz·im′** (-lo͞ot tsēm′) HALUTZ

cha·lyb·e·ate (kə lib′ē ət, -āt′) ***adj.*** ⟦ModL *chalybeatus* < L *chalybs* < Gr *chalyps,* steel (after *Chalybes,* name of a people in Pontus noted for their steel) + -ATE[1]⟧ **1** containing salts of iron **2** tasting like iron —***n.*** a chalybeate liquid or medicine

cham (kam) ***n.*** [Archaic] KHAN[1]

cha·made (shə mäd′) ***n.*** ⟦Fr < Port *chamada* < *chamar* < L *clamare,* to cry out: see CLAMOR⟧ [Archaic] *Mil.* a signal for a parley or retreat, sounded on a drum or trumpet

Cha·mae·le·on (kə mē′lē ən) ***n.*** ⟦L: see CHAMELEON⟧ a S constellation near the celestial pole

cham·ae·phyte (kam′i fit′) ***n.*** ⟦< ModL *chamae-,* low, on the ground (< Gr *chamai:* see CHAMELEON) + -PHYTE⟧ any plant with buds near ground level

cham·ber (chām′bər) ***n.*** ⟦ME *chambre* < OFr *chambre, cambre* < LL *camera,* a chamber, room (in L, a vault): see CAMERA⟧ **1** *a)* a room in a house, esp. a bedroom *b)* a reception room in an official residence **2** [*pl.*] [Brit.] a suite of rooms used by one person **3** [*pl.*] a judge's office located near the courtroom **4** an assembly hall **5** a legislative or judicial body or division *[*the *Chamber* of Deputies*]* **6** a council or board *[*a *chamber* of commerce*]* **7** an enclosed space in the body of a plant or animal **8** any enclosed space; compartment; specif., the part of a gun that holds the charge, or any of the compartments for cartridges in the cylinder of a revolver —***vt.*** **1** to provide a chamber or chambers for **2** to put (a cartridge, etc.) into a chamber —***adj.*** of, for, or performing chamber music —**cham′bered** ***adj.***

chamber concert a concert of chamber music

cham·ber·lain (chām′bər lin) ***n.*** ⟦ME *chaumberlein* < OFr *chamberlenc* < OHG *chamarlinc* < *chamara, kamara* (< L *camera*) + dim. suffix *-linc:* see CAMERA & -LING[1]⟧ **1** [Obs.] the bedchamber attendant of a ruler or lord **2** an officer in charge of the household of a ruler or lord; steward **3** a high official in certain royal courts **4** [Brit.] a treasurer, as of a municipality **5** *R.C.Ch.* any of several high officials, as an honorary attendant on the pope

Cham·ber·lain (chām′bər lin) **1 Joseph** 1836-1914; Brit. statesman: father of Neville **2 (Arthur) Neville** 1869-1940; Brit. statesman; prime minister (1937-40): signed MUNICH PACT

Cham·ber·lin (chām′bər lin), **Thomas Chrow·der** (krou′dər) 1843-1928; U.S. geologist

cham·ber·maid (chām′bər mād′) ***n.*** a woman whose work is taking care of bedrooms, as in a hotel

chamber music music for performance by a small group, usually with one player to a part, as in a string quartet, orig. for small audiences

chamber of commerce an association established to further the business interests of its community

chamber orchestra an orchestra much smaller than a symphony orchestra, usually playing compositions suited to it

chamber pot a portable container kept in a bedroom and used for defecating or urinating

☆**cham·bray** (sham′brā′) ***n.*** ⟦var. of CAMBRIC⟧ a smooth fabric of cotton, etc., made by weaving white or unbleached threads across a colored warp: used for dresses, shirts, etc.

cha·me·le·on (kə mē′lē ən, -mēl′yən) ***n.*** ⟦ME *camelioun* < L *chamaeleon* < Gr *chamaileōn* < *chamai,* on the ground (akin to *chthōn,* earth: see HOMAGE) + *leōn,* LION⟧ **1** any of various Old World lizards (family Chamaeleontidae) with an angular head, prehensile tail, eyes that move independently of each other, the ability to change skin color rapidly, and a long, agile tongue for catching prey **2** any of various superficially similar lizards that can change the color of their skin, as the American chameleon **3** a changeable or fickle person —**cha·me·le·on·ic** (kə mē′lē än′ik) ***adj.***

common chameleon

cham·fer (cham′fər) ***n.*** ⟦Fr *chanfrein* < OFr *chanfraindre* < *chant fraindre* < L *cantum frangere:* see CANT[2] & BREAK⟧ a beveled edge or corner, esp. one cut at a 45° angle —***vt.*** **1** to cut a chamfer on; bevel **2** to make a groove or fluting in

cham·fron or **cham·frain** (cham′frən) ***n.*** ⟦Fr *chanfrein* < OFr *chaufrain,* snaffle, chamfron < *chafresner,* to fasten rein or bridle on a horse < L *caput,* HEAD + *frenum,* bridle, reins⟧ the headpiece of the armor worn by war horses in medieval times

cham·ois (sham′ē; *also, esp. for n. 1 & adj. 2,* sham wä′) ***n.***, *pl.* **cham·ois** (sham′ēz; sham wä′) ⟦Fr < LL *camox* < a native Alpine word of IE orig.; akin to Gr *kemas,* young deer: see HIND[2]⟧ **1** a small goat antelope (*Rupicapra rupicapra*) of the mountains of Europe and the Caucasus, having straight horns with the tips bent backward **2** *a)* soft leather made from its skin or from the skin of sheep, deer, goats, etc. *b)* a piece of this leather, used as a polishing cloth: also sp. **cham′my**, *pl.* **-mies** —***adj.*** **1** made of chamois **2** yellowish-brown —***vt.*** **cham·oised** (sham′ēd), **cham·ois·ing** (sham′ē iŋ) to polish with a chamois skin

cham·o·mile (kam′ə mīl′, -mēl′) ***n.*** *alt. sp. of* CAMOMILE

Cha·mo·nix (shȧ mō nē′) valley in E France, north of Mont Blanc: a resort area of the French Alps

Cha·mor·ro (chä môr′ō) ***n.*** **1** *pl.* **-ros** a member of one of the indigenous peoples of Guam and the Northern Mariana Islands **2** the Austronesian language of this people

champ[1] (champ) ***vt.*** ⟦earlier *cham;* prob. echoic⟧ to chew hard and noisily; munch —***n.*** the act of champing —**champ at the bit** **1** to bite upon its bit repeatedly and restlessly: said of a horse **2** to show impatience at restraint; be restless

☆**champ**[2] (champ) ***n.*** [Informal] *short for* CHAMPION (sense 3)

cham·pac or **cham·pak** (cham′pak′, chum′puk′) ***n.*** ⟦Hindi *champak* < Sans *campaka*⟧ an Asian tree (*Michelia champaca*) of the magnolia family, with fragrant, yellow or orange flowers

cham·pagne (sham pān′) ***n.*** **1** [Archaic] any of various wines produced in Champagne, France **2** *a)* now, any effervescent white wine made there or elsewhere: regarded as a symbol of luxurious living *b)* the typical color of such wine; pale, tawny yellow or greenish yellow

Cham·pagne (sham pān′; *Fr* shän pȧn′y′) agricultural and historical region of NE France: now mostly in the metropolitan region of **Champagne-Ardennes**, which also includes part of the Ardennes plateau: 9,887 sq mi (25,607 sq km); chief city, Reims

Champagne

cham·paign (sham pān′) ***n.*** ⟦ME *champain* < OFr *champaigne:* see CAMPAIGN⟧ a broad plain; flat, open country —***adj.*** of or like a champaign

cham·pers (sham′pərz) ***n.*** [Brit. Slang] champagne

cham·per·ty (cham′pər tē) ***n.***, *pl.* **-ties** ⟦ME *champartie* < OFr *champart,* the lord's share in the crop of a tenant's land < L *campi pars* < *campi,* gen. of *campus,* field + *pars,* part: see CAMPUS & PART[2]⟧ *Law* an act or proceeding by which a person who is not concerned in a lawsuit makes a bargain with one of the litigants to help maintain the costs of the suit in return for a share of any proceeds: illegal in most states —**cham′per·tous** (-təs) ***adj.***

cham·pi·gnon (sham pin′yən; *Fr* shän pē nyōn′) ***n.*** ⟦Fr, altered < OFr *champaignuel* < VL **campaniolus* < LL *campania,* field: see CAMPAIGN⟧ any of various edible mushrooms, esp. the meadow mushroom

cham·pi·on (cham′pē ən) ***n.*** ⟦OFr (? via Gmc **kampjo*) < LL *campio,* gladiator < L *campus,* field: see CAMPUS⟧ **1** a valiant fighter **2** a person who fights for another or for a cause; defender; protector; supporter *[*a *champion* of the oppressed] **3** a winner of first place or first prize in a competition —*adj.* winning or capable of winning first place; excelling over all others —*vt.* **1** to fight for; defend; support **2** [Obs.] to challenge to a fight

cham·pi·on·ship (-ship′) *n.* **1** the act of championing; advocacy or defense **2** the position or title of a champion

Cham·plain[1] (sham plān′; *Fr* shän plan′), **Samuel de** 1567-1635; Fr. explorer: founded Quebec (1608)

Cham·plain[2] (sham plān′), **Lake** ⟦after prec., who discovered it⟧ lake on the N section of the border between N.Y. and Vt.: *c.* 125 mi (201 km) long

champ·le·vé (shän lə vā′) *adj.* ⟦Fr < *champ*, field + *levé*, adj. < pp. of *lever*, to raise⟧ designating or of a kind of enamel work in which furrows or hollows cut into a metal surface, usually copper, are filled with vitreous powders and then fired —*n.* a *champlevé* enamel

Cham·pol·lion (shän pô lyōn′), **Jean Fran·çois** (zhän frän swȧ′) 1790-1832; Fr. Egyptologist

Chanc *abbrev.* **1** Chancellor **2** Chancery

chance (chans, chäns) *n.* ⟦ME *chaunce* < OFr *cheance* < VL *cadentia*, that which falls out < L *cadens*, prp. of *cadere*, to fall: see CASE[1]⟧ **1** the happening of events without apparent cause, or the apparent absence of cause or design; fortuity; luck [to leave things to *chance*] **2** an unpredictable event or accidental happening **3** a risk or gamble **4** a ticket in a lottery or raffle **5** an advantageous or opportune time or occasion; opportunity [you'll have a *chance* to go] **6** [*often pl.*] a possibility or probability [there is little *chance* of success; what are their *chances* of winning?] **7** [Archaic] a mishap; mischance ☆**8** *Baseball* an opportunity to field a ball on which a fielder is credited with a putout or assist, or is charged with an error —*adj.* happening by chance; accidental [a *chance* encounter] —*vi.* **chanced, chanc′ing 1** to have the fortune, good or bad [I *chanced* to see them on my walk] **2** to happen by chance [it *chanced* to snow the day we arrived] Followed by an infinitive —*vt.* to leave to chance; risk [let's *chance* it] —*SYN.* HAPPEN, RANDOM —**by chance 1** as it may happen; perchance **2** accidentally —**chance on** (or **upon**) to find or meet by chance —**(the) chances are** the likelihood is [*chances are* she will visit today] —**on the (off) chance** relying on the (remote) possibility; in case —**take one's chances** [Informal] to accept the uncertain outcome as of a course of action

chance·ful (-fəl) *adj.* **1** eventful **2** [Archaic] *a)* dependent on chance *b)* risky

chan·cel (chan′səl) *n.* ⟦ME *chauncel* < OFr *chancel* < LL *cancellus* < L *cancelli*, pl., lattices: see CANCEL⟧ the part of a church around the altar, usually at the east end, reserved for the use of the clergy and the choir: it is sometimes set off by a railing or screen

chan·cel·ler·y (chan′sə lər ē, chans′lər ē) *n., pl.* **-ler·ies** ⟦ME & OFr *chancelerie* < ML *cancellaria*⟧ **1** the rank or position of a chancellor **2** a chancellor's office or the building that houses it **3** the office of an embassy or consulate **4** CHANCERY (sense 6) Also sp. **chan′cel·lor·y**

chan·cel·lor (chan′sə lər) *n.* ⟦ME < *chanceler* < OFr < LL *cancellarius*, secretary, lit., keeper of the barrier: so called from the lattice behind which he worked: see CANCEL⟧ **1** [Obs.] an official secretary to a nobleman or, esp., a king **2** [Rare] the chief secretary of an embassy or consulate **3** [*usually* **C-**] any of several high officials in the British government, sometimes with judicial powers **4** the title of the president or a high executive officer in some universities **5** the prime minister in certain countries ☆**6** a chief judge of a court of chancery or equity in some states of the U.S. **7** *R.C.Ch.* the title of the priest in charge of a diocesan chancery —**chan′cel·lor·ship′** *n.*

Chancellor of the Exchequer the minister of finance in the British government, a member of the Cabinet

Chan·cel·lors·ville (chan′sə lərz vil′) ⟦after a local family name⟧ hamlet in NE Va. (now called *Chancellor*): site of a Civil War battle (May, 1863) won by Confederate forces

chance-med·ley (chans′med′lē) *n.* ⟦lit., mixed chance: see CHANCE & MEDLEY⟧ [Historical] *Law* **1** a sudden fight during which one person kills another, esp. in self-defense **2** such a killing

chanc·er (chan′sər) *n.* ⟦< CHANCE (*vt.*) + -ER⟧ [Brit. Informal] a reckless, improvident, often somewhat unscrupulous opportunist

chan·cer·y (chan′sər ē) *n., pl.* **-cer·ies** ⟦ME *chancerie*, var. of *chancelerie*: see CHANCELLERY⟧ **1** a division of the High Court of Justice in England and Wales, presided over by the Lord High Chancellor of England **2** a court of equity **3** the laws, practice, and proceedings of a court of equity **4** a court of record; office of public archives **5** CHANCELLERY (sense 2) **6** [Brit.] the political department, or its offices, of an embassy or legation **7** *R.C.Ch.* the administrative office of a diocese, under the direction of the bishop —**in chancery 1** in process of litigation in a court of equity **2** in an awkward or helpless situation

chan·cre (shaŋ′kər) *n.* ⟦Fr: see CANCER⟧ the primary lesion, sore, or ulcer of any of various diseases, esp. of syphilis —**chan′crous** (-krəs) *adj.*

chan·croid (-kroid′) *n.* ⟦prec. + -OID⟧ an infectious venereal ulcer, usually on or about the genitals, caused by a bacterium (*Hemophilus ducreyi*); soft chancre

chanc·y (chan′sē, chän′-) *adj.* **chanc′i·er, chanc′i·est 1** risky; uncertain **2** [Scot.] bringing good luck —**chanc′i·ness** *n.*

Chan·dan·na·gar (chun′də nug′ər) port in NE India, near Kolkata: formerly a French dependency, it became part of the republic of India in 1950

chan·de·lier (shan′də lir′) *n.* ⟦Fr < OFr *chandelabre* < L *candelabrum* < *candela*, CANDLE⟧ a lighting fixture hung from a ceiling, with branches for candles, lightbulbs, etc.

chan·delle (shan′del′) *n.* ⟦Fr, lit., CANDLE⟧ a quick, simultaneous climb and turn made by an airplane, in which the momentum of the airplane increases the rate of climb —*vi.* **-delled′, -dell′ing** to make a chandelle

Chan·der·na·gore or **Chan·der·na·gor** (chun′dər nə gôr′) *former var. of* CHANDANNAGAR

Chan·di·garh (chun′dē gər) **1** city in N India; joint capital of the states of Punjab & Hariana **2** territory of India, made up of this city & the surrounding area: 44 sq mi (114 sq km)

chan·dler (chand′lər) *n.* ⟦ME *chandeler* < OFr *chandelier* < *chandoile* (< L *candela*), CANDLE⟧ **1** a maker or seller of candles **2** a retailer of supplies, equipment, etc. of a certain kind

Chan·dler[1] (chand′lər), **Raymond (Thornton)** 1888-1959; U.S. detective-story writer

Chan·dler[2] (chand′lər) ⟦after A. J. *Chandler* (1859-1950), its founder⟧ city in SC Ariz.

Chandler wobble ⟦after S. C. *Chandler* (1846-1913), U.S. astronomer who observed it⟧ a slight, irregular nutation of the earth's rotational axis with a period of *c.* 428 days

chan·dler·y (chand′lər ē) *n., pl.* **-dler·ies 1** a warehouse or storeroom for candles and other small wares **2** the merchandise, business, or warehouse of a chandler

Chan·dra·sekh·ar (chun′drə sā′kər), **Sub·rah·man·yan** (sub′rə män′yən) 1910-95; U.S. astrophysicist, born in India

Cha·nel (shə nel′; *Fr* shȧ nel′), **Co·co** (kō′kō) (born *Gabrielle Chanel*) 1883-1971; Fr. fashion designer & perfumer

Chang (chäŋ) largest river and chief commercial highway of China, flowing from Tibet into the East China Sea near Shanghai: 3,964 mi (6,379 km): former transliteration YANGTZE

Chang·chia·kou (chäŋ′jyä′kō′) *a former transliteration of* ZHANGJIAKOU

Chang·chou (chäŋ′chou′; *Chin* jäŋ′jō′) *a former transliteration of* CHANGZHOU

Chang·chun (chäŋ′choon′) city in NE China; capital of Jilin province

Chang·de (chäŋ′də) city in N Hunan, in SE central China

change (chānj) *vt.* **changed, chang′ing** ⟦ME *changen* < OFr *changier* < LL *cambiare* < L *cambire*, to exchange, barter < Celt (as in OIr *camb*) < IE base **kamb-*, to bend, crook (> Welsh *cam*, Bret *kamm*, crooked)⟧ **1** to put or take (a thing) in place of something else; substitute for, replace with, or transfer to another of a similar kind [to *change* one's clothes, to *change* jobs] **2** to give and receive reciprocally; exchange; switch [let's *change* seats] **3** *a)* to cause to become different; alter; transform; convert [success *changed* him] *b)* to undergo a variation of [leaves *change* color] **4** to give or receive the equivalent of (a coin or bank note) in currency of lower denominations or in foreign money **5** to put a fresh, replacement covering, as a diaper or bedclothes, on —*vi.* **1** *a)* to become different; alter; vary [the scene *changes*] *b)* to undergo alteration or replacement **2** to pass from one phase to another, as the moon **3** to become lower in range: said specif. of the male voice at puberty **4** to leave one train, bus, etc. and board another **5** to put on other clothes **6** to make an exchange —*n.* **1** the act or process of substitution, alteration, or variation **2** absence of monotony; variety **3** something that is or may be substituted; something of the same kind but new or fresh **4** another set of clothes, esp. a fresh set to put on **5** *a)* money returned as the difference between the price of something bought and the bill or coin of larger denomination given in payment *b)* a number of coins or bills whose total value equals a single larger coin or bill *c)* coins of small denomination **6** a place where merchants meet to do business; exchange: also written **'change 7** [*usually pl.*] in bell ringing, any pattern or order in which the bells may be rung —**change off** to take turns —**ring the changes 1** to ring a set of bells with all possible variations **2** to do or say a thing in many and various ways —**the change** [Informal] MENOPAUSE

SYN.—**change** denotes a making or becoming distinctly different and implies either a radical transmutation of character or replacement with something else [I'll *change* my shoes]; **alter** implies a partial change, as in appearance, so that the identity is preserved [to *alter* a garment]; **vary** suggests irregular or intermittent change [to *vary* one's reading]; **modify** implies minor change, often so as to limit or moderate [to *modify* the language of a report]; **transform** implies a change in form and, now, usually, in nature or function [to *transform* matter into energy]; **convert** suggests more strongly change to suit a new function [to *convert* a barn into a house]

change·a·ble (chān′jə bəl) *adj.* ⟦ME⟧ **1** that can change or be changed; likely or tending to change; variable; alterable; fickle **2** having a changing appearance or color, as some silk when looked at from different angles; iridescent —**change′a·bil′i·ty** *n.*, **change′a·ble·ness** —**change′a·bly** *adv.*

change·ful (chānj′fəl) *adj.* full of change; inconstant —**change′ful·ly** *adv.* —**change′ful·ness** *n.*

change·less (-lis) *adj.* unchanging; immutable —**change′less·ly** *adv.* —**change′less·ness** *n.*

change·ling (-liŋ) *n.* **1** *Folklore* a child secretly exchanged for another by fairies **2** [Archaic] a changeable person; turncoat **3** [Archaic] a feeble-minded person

change of life MENOPAUSE

change·o·ver (-ō′vər) *n.* a complete change, as in goods produced, methods of production, or equipment

chang·er (-ər) *n.* **1** a person or thing that changes something **2** *short for*

RECORD CHANGER **3** a device that automatically sets compact discs in position for playing in succession, as from a carousel tray or slotted magazine cartridge

change ringing the act of ringing a series of different changes on a set of bells tuned together

☆**change-up** (-up′) ***n.*** *Baseball* an OFF-SPEED pitch thrown with the same motion as a faster pitch, so as to deceive the batter

Chang·hua (chäŋ′hwä′) city in W Taiwan

Chang·sha (chäŋ′shä′) city in SE China; capital of Hunan province

Chang·teh (chäŋ′də) *a former transliteration of* CHANGDE

Chang·zhou (jäŋ′jō′) city in Jiangsu province, E China, on the Grand Canal

chan·nel[1] (chan′əl) ***n.*** ⟦ME *chanel, canel* < OFr: see CANAL⟧ **1** the bed of a running stream, river, etc. **2** the deeper part of a river, harbor, etc. **3** a body of water joining two larger bodies of water **4** a tubelike passage for liquids **5** *a)* any means of passage *b)* a course through which something moves or is transmitted, conveyed, expressed, etc. **6** [*pl.*] the proper or official course of transmission of communications [to make a request through army *channels*] **7** a long groove or furrow **8** a rolled metal bar whose section is shaped thus ⊔: also **channel iron (**or **bar)** **9** a narrow band of frequencies within which a radio or television transmitting station must keep its signal to prevent interference with other transmitters **10** any path that conducts an electronic signal between two points; specif., a pathway by which data is transmitted between two computers, a mainframe and a terminal, or a computer and a peripheral —***vt.*** **-neled** or **-nelled**, **-nel·ing** or **-nel·ling** **1** to make a channel or channels in **2** to flute (a pillar, column, etc.) **3** to send through a channel **4** to serve as a medium for (a spirit) in channeling

chan·nel[2] (chan′əl) ***n.*** ⟦orig., *chain wale*⟧ [Historical] any of several metal ledges on the sides of a ship used to secure the rigging and keep the ropes free of the gunwales

chan·nel·er or **chan·nel·ler** (chan′əl ər) ***n.*** a person or thing that channels; specif., a medium engaged in channeling

chan·nel·ing or **chan·nel·ling** (chan′əl iŋ) ***n.*** esp. in some New Age beliefs, the process by which a person becomes a conduit for a deceased person, as someone from an ancient culture, who imparts information about a previous life

Channel Islands **1** group of islands in the English Channel, off the coast of Normandy: British crown dependencies with internal self-government: 75 sq mi (194 sq km) **2** SANTA BARBARA ISLANDS

chan·nel·ize (chan′əl īz′) ***vt.*** **-ized′**, **-iz′ing** to provide a channel for —**chan′nel·i·za′tion** ***n.***

chan·nel-surf (chan′əl surf′) ***vi.*** [Informal] to switch TV channels repeatedly using a remote-control device, usually so as to sample brief segments of programs —**chan′nel-surf′ing** ***n.***

Chan·ning (chan′iŋ), **William El·ler·y** (el′ər ē) 1780-1842; U.S. Unitarian leader & social critic

chan·son (shän sôn′) ***n.***, *pl.* **-sons′** (-sôn′) ⟦Fr < L *cantio*: see CANZONE⟧ a song

chanson de geste (də zhest′) ⟦Fr, song of heroic acts⟧ any of the Old French epic poems of the 12th to 14th cent., esp. one connected with the exploits of Charlemagne and his knights, as the *Chanson de Roland (Song of Roland)*

chan·son·nier (shän′sən yā′; *Fr* shän sô nyā′) ***n.*** ⟦Fr < CHANSON⟧ a French cabaret singer and songwriter of topical, often satirical, ballads

chant (chant, chänt) ***n.*** ⟦Fr < L *cantus*, song < the v.⟧ **1** a song; melody **2** *a)* a simple liturgical song in which a string of syllables or words is sung to each tone *b)* words, as of a canticle or psalm, to be sung in this way **3** *a)* a monotonous tone of voice; singsong mode of speaking *b)* a phrase, slogan, or other words that are repeated over and over [the *chant* of the crowd at the stadium] —***vi.*** ⟦ME *chanten* < OFr *chanter, canter* < L *cantare*, freq. of *canere*, to sing < IE base **kan-*, to sing, sound > HEN, Gr *kanachē*, sound, noise, Bret *cana*, sing, Ger *hahn*⟧ **1** to sing a chant; intone **2** to say something monotonously or repetitiously **3** [Old Poet.] to sing; warble —***vt.*** **1** to utter, sing, or recite in the manner of a chant **2** [Old Poet.] to sing or to celebrate in song

chant·er (chan′tər, chän′-) ***n.*** **1** one who chants or sings, esp. as in a choir; chorister **2** a priest who sang Masses in a chantry **3** that pipe of a bagpipe with finger holes on which the melody is played

chan·te·relle (shan′tə rel′, chan′-) ***n.*** ⟦Fr, dim. < L *cantharus*, drinking cup < Gr *kantharos*⟧ any of a genus (*Cantharellus*) of yellow or orange mushrooms with forking, gill-shaped ridges and funnel-shaped caps, esp. an edible species (*C. cibarius*)

chan·teuse (shän to͞oz′, shan-; -to͞os′; *Fr* shän töz′) ***n.*** ⟦Fr: see CHANT⟧ a woman singer of popular ballads, torch songs, etc.

chan·tey (shan′tē, chan′tē) ***n.***, *pl.* **-teys** ⟦< ? Fr *chantez*, imper. of *chanter*: see CHANT⟧ a song formerly sung by sailors in rhythm with their motions while working, as while turning a capstan: also sp. **chan′ty**, *pl.* **-ties**

chan·ti·cleer (chan′ti klir′) ***n.*** ⟦ME *chauntecler* < OFr *chante-cler*, lit., sing loud; name of rooster in the medieval epic "Reynard the Fox": see CHANT & CLEAR⟧ [*often* **C-**] a rooster: used as a proper name

Chan·til·ly (shan til′ē; *Fr* shän tē yē′) town in N France, near Paris: noted for a lace (**Chantilly lace**) first made there

chan·try (chan′trē, chän′-) ***n.***, *pl.* **-tries** ⟦ME *chanterie* < OFr: see CHANT⟧ *R.C.Ch.* **1** an endowment to pay for Masses and prayers for the soul of a specified person, often the endower: an earlier term **2** a chapel or altar endowed, esp. in the Middle Ages, for this

Cha·nu·kah (khä′no͞o kä′) ***n.*** *var. of* HANUKKAH

Chao Phra·ya (chou′ prä yä′, -prī′ə) principal river of Thailand, in the W part, flowing past Bangkok into the Gulf of Thailand: *c.* 160 mi (257 km)

cha·os (kā′äs′) ***n.*** ⟦L < Gr *chaos*, space, CHAOS (sense 1) < IE base **ĝheu-*, **ĝhei-*, to gape: see YAWN⟧ **1** the disorder of formless matter and infinite space, supposed to have existed before the ordered universe **2** extreme confusion or disorder **3** [Archaic] an abyss; chasm ☆**4** ⟦coined (1975) by J. A. Yorke & T.-Y. Li, U.S. mathematicians⟧ *Math.* a pattern or state of order existing within apparent disorder, as in the irregularities of a coastline or a snowflake —**SYN.** CONFUSION

chaos theory the field of mathematics dealing with the unpredictability of complex dynamic systems, as in nature, with respect to CHAOS (sense 4)

cha·ot·ic (kā ät′ik) ***adj.*** **1** in a state of chaos; in a completely confused or disordered condition **2** of or having to do with the theories, dynamics, etc. of mathematical chaos —**cha·ot′i·cal·ly** ***adv.***

chap[1] (chäp, chap) ***n.*** ⟦prob. < ME *cheppe* < ?⟧ CHOP[2]

chap[2] (chap) ***n.*** ⟦< CHAPMAN⟧ [Informal] a man or boy; fellow

chap[3] (chap) ***vt., vi.*** **chapped**, **chap′ping** ⟦ME *chappen*, var. of *choppen*: see CHOP[1]⟧ to crack open; split; roughen, as the skin from exposure to cold —***n.*** a chapped place in the skin

chap[4] *abbrev.* **1** chaplain **2** chapter

☆**cha·pa·re·jos** or **cha·pa·ra·jos** (chap′ə rā′hōs′, shap′-) ***pl.n.*** ⟦MexSp, altered < *chaparreras* (so named because worn to protect from *chaparro*, chaparral)⟧ [Southwest] CHAPS[1]

☆**chap·ar·ral** (shap′ə ral′, chap′-) ***n.*** ⟦AmSp < Sp < *chaparro*, evergreen oak < ? Basque *txapar*⟧ [Southwest] a thicket of shrubs, thorny bushes, etc.

☆**chaparral cock (***or* **bird)** ROADRUNNER

☆**chaparral pea** a thorny, leguminous evergreen shrub (*Pickeringia montana*) growing in chaparrals along the W coast of the U.S.

cha·pa·ti (chə pät′ē) ***n.*** ⟦Hindi *capati* < Sans *carpaṭī*, flat cake < *carpaṭa*, flat⟧ **1** a thin, flat unleavened bread of India, usually of whole-wheat flour, baked in a hot, dry skillet **2** a piece of this Also sp. **cha·pat′ti**

chap·book (chap′bo͝ok′) ***n.*** ⟦CHAP(MAN) + BOOK: chapmen sold such books in the streets⟧ a small book or pamphlet of poems, ballads, religious tracts, etc.

chape (chāp) ***n.*** ⟦ME < OFr, a cape < LL *cappa*: see CAPE[1]⟧ a metal plate or mounting on a scabbard or sheath, esp. a protection for the point

cha·peau (sha pō′) ***n.***, *pl.* **-peaus′** or **-peaux′** (-pōz′) ⟦Fr < OFr *chapel* < VL **cappellus*, dim. of *cappa*: see CAPE[1]⟧ a hat

chap·el (chap′əl) ***n.*** ⟦ME & OFr *chapelle* < ML *cappella*, dim. of *cappa*, cape < LL: orig., sanctuary in which the *cappa* or cope of St. Martin was preserved; then, any sanctuary⟧ **1** a place of Christian worship subordinate to and smaller than a church **2** *a)* a room or building used as a place of worship, as in a hospital, school, or army post *b)* a room in a funeral home for funeral services **3** *a)* a room or recess in a church, set apart for special services and having its own altar *b)* a similar room in some Jewish synagogues **4** a service in a chapel, or any religious service, as at a school **5** the singers of a private chapel, collectively **6** a local chapter of a printers' union **7** in Great Britain, any place of worship for those who are not members of an established church

chap·er·one (shap′ər ōn′, shap′ər ōn′) ***n.*** ⟦Fr < OFr, head covering, hood (hence, protection, protector) < *chape*: see CHAPE⟧ **1** in some cultures, an older or married woman who, as a matter of etiquette, accompanies a girl or young, unmarried woman in public **2** an adult who is present at the parties, dances, etc. of young people, to supervise their behavior — ***vt., vi.*** **-oned′**, **-on′ing** to act as chaperone (to) Also sp. **chap′er·on′** —**SYN.** ACCOMPANY —**chap′er·on′age** ***n.***

chap·fall·en (chäp′fô′lən, chap′-) ***adj.*** ⟦CHAP[1] + FALLEN⟧ **1** having the lower jaw hanging down, as from fatigue **2** disheartened, depressed, or humiliated

chap·i·ter (chap′it ər) ***n.*** ⟦Fr *chapitre*: see CHAPTER⟧ *Archit.* the capital of a column

chap·lain (chap′lən) ***n.*** ⟦ME *chapelain* < OFr < ML *capellanus*, orig., custodian of St. Martin's cloak: see CHAPEL⟧ **1** a clergyman attached to a chapel, as of a royal court **2** a minister, priest, or rabbi serving in a religious capacity with the armed forces, or in a prison, hospital, etc. **3** a member of the clergy, or sometimes a layperson, appointed to perform religious functions in a public institution, club, etc. —**chap′lain·cy** ***n.***, *pl.* **-cies** —**chap′lain·ship′** ***n.***

chap·let (chap′lit) ***n.*** ⟦ME & OFr *chapelet*, dim. of *chapel*: see CHAPEAU⟧ **1** a wreath or garland for the head **2** *a)* a rosary consisting typically of five decades *b)* the prayers said with such beads **3** any string of beads; necklace **4** *Archit.* a small convex molding somewhat resembling a string of beads

chap·let·ed (-id) ***adj.*** wearing a wreath or garland on the head

Chap·lin (chap′lin), Sir **Charles Spencer** (called *Charlie Chaplin*) 1889-1977; Eng. film actor, director, & producer, in the U.S. (1910-52) —**Chap′lin·esque′** ***adj.***

chap·man (chap′mən) ***n.***, *pl.* **-men** (-mən) ⟦ME *chapman* < OE *ceapman*, trader < *ceap*, trade, a bargain (see CHEAP) + MAN⟧ [Archaic] a trader or peddler

Chap·man (chap′mən), **George** 1559?-1634; Eng. poet, playwright, & translator of Homer

chap·pie (chap′ē) ***n.*** [Brit. Informal] CHAP[2]

☆**chaps**[1] (chaps, shaps) ***pl.n.*** ⟦shortened from CHAPAREJOS⟧ leather trousers without a seat, worn over ordinary trousers by cowboys to protect their legs

chaps[2] (chäps, chaps) ***pl.n.*** ⟦see CHAP[1]⟧ CHOPS

chap·ter (chap′tər) ***n.*** ⟦ME & OFr *chapitre, chapitle* < L *capitulum*, head, capital (in LL, division of a writing; in ML, church division), dim. of *caput*, HEAD⟧ **1** any of the main divisions of a book or other writing **2** a thing like a chapter; part; episode [*a chapter* of one's life] **3** *a)* ⟦from meeting at which a *chapter* of monastic rule, etc. was read⟧ a formal meeting of canons headed by a dean, or of the members of a religious order *b)* those assembled at such a meeting ☆**4** a local branch of a club, fraternity, etc. —***vt.*** to divide (a book, etc.) into chapters —**chapter and verse 1** the exact Scriptural reference **2** authority cited (for a statement, belief, etc.) **3** detailed information

chapter book a children's book, typically a work of fiction, of moderate length and complexity, divided into chapters and intended for readers approximately seven to ten years old

☆**chapter 11** (*or* **XI**) ⟦in allusion to *Chapter 11* of the U.S. bankruptcy code⟧ a proceeding under the Federal Bankruptcy Act whereby a company or corporation may, through a court order, remain in business for a time as long as it pays current debts, but must eventually either reorganize and pay its creditors or cease operations

chapter house 1 the place where a chapter, as of monks, meets ☆**2** the house of a fraternity or sorority chapter

Cha·pul·te·pec (chə po͝ol′tə pek′, -pul′-) ⟦Nahuatl, lit., grasshopper hill⟧ a rocky hill in Mexico City: captured (Sept., 1847) in an American assault led by Gen. Winfield Scott in the Mexican War

char[1] (chär) ***vt., vi.*** **charred, char′ring** ⟦back-form. < CHARCOAL⟧ **1** to reduce to charcoal by burning **2** to burn slightly; scorch —***n.*** anything charred; esp., charcoal —***SYN.*** BURN[1]

char[2] (chär) ***n.*** ⟦back-form. < CHARWOMAN⟧ **1** CHARE **2** [Brit. Informal] a charwoman —***vi.*** **charred, char′ring** [Informal, Chiefly Brit.] to work as a charwoman

char[3] (chär) ***n.***, *pl.* **chars** or **char** ⟦< Gael *ceara*, red < *cear*, blood⟧ any of a genus (*Salvelinus*) of trouts with small scales and a red belly

char[4] (chär) ***n.*** ⟦< Chin *ch'a*: see TEA⟧ [Brit. Slang] TEA (***n.*** 3)

char[5] *abbrev.* **1** character **2** charter

char·a·banc or **char-à-banc** (shar′ə baŋ′) ***n.*** ⟦Fr *char-à-banc*, lit., car with bench⟧ [Brit.] a sightseeing bus

char·a·cin (kar′ə sin) ***n.*** ⟦ModL < Gr *charax*, a kind of fish, orig., pointed stake⟧ any of a large family (Characidae, order Cypriniformes) of small, strong-jawed freshwater fishes of South and Central America and Africa

char·ac·ter (kar′ək tər, kar′ik-) ***n.*** ⟦ME *carecter* < OFr *caractère* < L *character*, an engraving instrument < Gr *charaktēr* < *charassein*, to engrave < *charax*, pointed stake⟧ **1** a distinctive mark **2** *a)* any letter, figure, or symbol used in writing and printing *b)* the letters of an alphabet, collectively **3** style of printing or handwriting **4** *a)* a mystic symbol or magical emblem *b)* a code or cipher **5** a distinctive trait, quality, or attribute; characteristic **6** essential quality; nature; kind or sort **7** the pattern of behavior or personality found in an individual or group; moral constitution **8** moral strength; self-discipline, fortitude, etc. **9** *a)* reputation *b)* good reputation [left without a shred of *character*] **10** a statement about the behavior, qualities, etc. of a person, esp. as given by a former employer; reference **11** status; position **12** a personage [great *characters* in history] **13** *a)* a person in a play, story, novel, etc. *b)* a role as portrayed by an actor or actress **14** [Informal] an odd, eccentric, or noteworthy person **15** *Genetics* any attribute, as color, shape, etc., caused in an individual by the action of one or more genes —***vt.*** **1** to write, print, or inscribe **2** to characterize **3** [Archaic] to represent; portray —***SYN.*** DISPOSITION, QUALITY —**in** (or **out of**) **character** consistent with (or inconsistent with) the role or general character

character actor an actor who specializes in supporting roles with certain pronounced or eccentric characteristics

character actress an actress who specializes in supporting roles with certain pronounced or eccentric characteristics

char·ac·ter·is·tic (kar′ək tər is′tik, kar′ik-) ***adj.*** ⟦Gr *charaktēristikos*: see CHARACTER⟧ of or constituting the special character; typical; distinctive [the *characteristic* odor of cabbage] —***n.*** **1** a distinguishing trait, feature, or quality; peculiarity **2** the whole number, or integral part, of a logarithm, as distinguished from the mantissa [4 is the *characteristic* of the logarithm 4.7193] —**char′ac·ter·is′ti·cal·ly** ***adv.***

SYN.—**characteristic** suggests the indication of a quality that is peculiar to, and helps identify, something or someone [the *characteristic* taste of honey]; **individual** and **distinctive** refer to, or suggest the possession of, a quality or qualities that distinguish something from others of its class or kind, **distinctive** often implying excellence [an *individual*, or *distinctive*, literary style]

char·ac·ter·i·za·tion (kar′ək tər ə zā′shən, kar′ik-) ***n.*** **1** the act of characterizing **2** the delineation of character or creation of characters in a play, story, etc.

char·ac·ter·ize (kar′ək tər īz′, kar′ik-) ***vt.*** **-ized′, -iz′ing** ⟦ML *characterizare* < Gr *charaktērizein*: see CHARACTER⟧ **1** to describe or portray the particular qualities, features, or traits of **2** to be the distinctive character of; distinguish [a miser is *characterized* by greed]

char·ac·ter·o·log·i·cal (kar′ək tər ə läj′i kəl, kar′ik-) ***adj.*** of or relating to character or the study of character

character sketch 1 a short piece of writing describing a person, esp. in terms of personality traits and behavior patterns **2** a theatrical portrayal of a highly individualized character or role

char·ac·ter·y (kar′ək tər ē, kar′ik-) ***n.***, *pl.* **-ter·ies** ⟦see CHARACTER & -Y[3]⟧ [Rare] symbols used in expressing thought

cha·rade (shə rād′; *chiefly Brit*, -räd′) ***n.*** ⟦Fr < Prov *charrada* < *charrar*, to gossip, chatter: orig. echoic⟧ **1** a word or phrase acted out or described as in verse, for others to guess **2** [*pl.*] a game in which two teams compete to see which can more quickly guess a group of words or phrases chosen by the other team and acted out in pantomime, often syllable by syllable, by the members of their own **3** a pretense or fiction that can be seen through readily; travesty

cha·ras (chä′rəs) ***n.*** ⟦Hindi⟧ HASHISH

char·broil or **char-broil** (chär′broil′) ***vt.*** ⟦< fol. + BROIL[1]⟧ to broil over a charcoal fire

char·coal (chär′kōl′) ***n.*** ⟦ME *char cole*; prob. < *charren*, to turn (see CHARE) + *cole*, coal (hence, lit., wood turned to coal)⟧ **1** a porous, amorphous form of carbon produced by destructive distillation of wood or other organic matter and used for decolorizing sugar and food, in filters, as a gas absorbent, fuel, etc. **2** a pencil made of this substance **3** a drawing made with such a pencil **4** a very dark gray or brown, almost black —***vt.*** **1** to write or draw with charcoal **2** to charbroil

Char·cot (shär kō′), **Jean Mar·tin** (zhän mär tan′) 1825-93; Fr. neurologist

char·cu·te·rie (shär ko͞ot′ə rē′; *Fr* shär kü trē′) ***n.*** ⟦Fr, pork butcher's shop < *chair*, meat + *cuit*, pp. of *cuire*, to cook⟧ **1** sausage, ham, cold cuts of meat, pâtés, etc. **2** a delicatessen that specializes in charcuterie

chard (chärd) ***n.*** ⟦earlier *card* < Fr *carde* < L *carduus*, thistle, artichoke (see CARD[2]): sp. infl. by Fr *chardon*, artichoke⟧ a kind of beet (*Beta vulgaris* var. *cicla*) whose large leaves and thick stalks are used as food; Swiss chard

Char·din (shär dan′) **1 Jean (Baptiste) Si·mé·on** (zhän sē mā ōn′) 1699-1779; Fr. painter **2 Teilhard de** *see* TEILHARD DE CHARDIN

char·don·nay (shär′də nā′) ***n.*** ⟦Fr⟧ [*also* **C-**] **1** a white grape of Burgundy, used for Chablis, champagne, etc. **2** a dry white wine made from this grape

chare (cher) [Now Rare] ***n.*** ⟦ME *char* < OE *cierr*, a turn, job, piece of work < *cierran*, to turn; akin to Ger *kehren* < IE base **ĝers-*, to turn > Welsh *gyrr*, a driving (of cattle)⟧ a chore, esp. a household chore —***vi.*** **chared, char′ing** to do chores

charge (chärj) ***vt.*** **charged, charg′ing** ⟦ME *chargen* < OFr *chargier* < VL *carricare*, to load a wagon, cart < L *carrus*, wagon, CAR[1]⟧ **I. 1** [Obs.] to put a load on or in **2** to load or fill to capacity or with the usual amount of required material **3** to load (a firearm, cannon, etc.) **4** to saturate (one substance) with another [air *charged* with steam] **5** to add carbon dioxide to (water, etc.) ☆**6** to add an electrical charge to (a battery, etc.) **II. 1** to load a burden on; give as a task, duty, etc. to; make responsible for [a nurse was *charged* with the care of the child] **2** to give instructions to or command authoritatively [to *charge* a jury] **3** to accuse of wrongdoing; censure [he *charged* her with negligence] **4** *a)* to put liability on (a person) *b)* to make liable for (an error, etc.) **5** to ask as a price or fee [to *charge* ten dollars for alterations] **6** *a)* to record as a debt against a person's name or account [to *charge* a purchase] ☆*b)* to make a record of (something borrowed) [to *charge* a library book] *c)* to pay for by using credit, usually by presenting a credit card **III. 1** to bear down on or set upon with force; attack vigorously **2** to bring (a gun or other weapon) to bear on; level; direct **3** *Heraldry* to place a bearing on —***vi.*** **1** to crouch or squat when a command is given: said of dogs **2** to ask payment (*for*) [to *charge* for a service] **3** to attack vigorously or move forward as if attacking — ***n.*** **I. 1** a load or burden **2** the maximum or necessary quantity, as of fuel, that a container or apparatus is built to hold; also, the actual quantity held **3** *a)* the amount of electrical energy stored in a battery, capacitor, etc. *b)* the departure from electrical neutrality at a point, or in a region, as by the accumulation, or deficit, of electrical particles: more electrons than normal produce a negative charge; fewer, a positive charge **4** a cartridge or shell, or the amount of gunpowder needed to discharge a firearm or set off an explosive device ☆**5** [Slang] pleasurable excitement; thrill **II. 1** responsibility or duty (*of*) [to take *charge* of finances] **2** care, custody, or supervision (*of*) **3** a person or thing entrusted to someone's care **4** instruction or command, esp. instruction in points of law given by a judge to a jury **5** accusation or indictment [*charges* of cruelty] **III. 1** the cost or price of an article, service, etc. **2** a liability to pay money; debt; expense **3** ☆*a)* CHARGE ACCOUNT *b)* a debit entered in an account **IV. 1** an attack with great force and speed; onslaught; onset **2** the signal for this **3** *Heraldry* a bearing —***SYN.*** ACCUSE, COMMAND —**charge off 1** to treat or regard as a loss **2** to set down as belonging; ascribe —**in charge** having the responsibility, control, or supervision —**in charge of 1** having the responsibility, control, or supervision of **2** under the control or supervision of; in the custody of: usually **in the charge of**

char·gé (shär zhā′) ***n.*** CHARGÉ D'AFFAIRES

charge·a·ble (chär′jə bəl) ***adj.*** **1** that can be, or is liable to be, charged **2** that may become a public charge

☆**charge account** a business arrangement by which a customer may buy goods or services and pay for them within a specified future period

☆**charge card** a thin plastic card embossed with the owner's name, account number, etc., now typically with a machine-readable strip on which the cardholder's account information is encoded: used when charging purchases

charge-cou·pled device (chärj′kup′əld) *see* CCD

char·gé d'af·faires (shär zhā′ də fer′) *pl.* **char·gés′ d'af·faires′** (-zhāz′-, -zhā′-) ⟦Fr, lit., entrusted with business⟧ **1** a diplomatic official who temporarily takes the place of a minister or ambassador **2** a diplomatic officer of the lowest rank who sometimes heads a low-level mission in a foreign nation

charged particle an atomic particle with a positive or negative charge, as an electron, proton, or helium ion

charg·er[1] (chär′jər) ***n.*** **1** a person or thing that charges **2** a horse ridden in battle or on parade **3** an apparatus used to charge storage batteries

charg·er[2] (chär′jər) ***n.*** ⟦ME *chargeour* < OFr < *chargier*, CHARGE⟧ [Archaic] a large, flat dish; platter

char·grill (chär′gril′) ***vt.*** to grill (meat), esp. over a fire of charcoal or wood

Cha·ri (shä′rē) *alt. sp. of* SHARI

char·i·ly (cher′ə lē) ***adv.*** in a chary manner; cautiously

char·i·ness (-ē nis) ***n.*** the quality of being chary; cautiousness

Cha·ri-Nile (shä′rē nīl′) ***adj.*** designating or of a subfamily of the Nilo-Saharan family of languages, including Sudanic

char·i·ot (char′ē ət) ***n.*** ⟦ME < OFr *charriote* < *char*, car < LL *carrum*: see CAR[1]⟧ **1** a horse-drawn, two-wheeled cart used in ancient times for war, racing, parades, etc. **2** a light, four-wheeled carriage with a coachlike box for several passengers and the driver's seat outside — ***vt., vi.*** to drive or ride in a chariot

Roman racing chariot

char·i·ot·eer (char′ē ə tir′) ***n.*** ⟦ME *charioter* < OFr *charioteur*⟧ a chariot driver —**the Charioteer** the constellation Auriga

cha·ris·ma (kə riz′mə) ***n.*** ⟦Gr(Ec), gift of God's grace < Gr, favor, grace < *charizesthai*, to show favor to < *charis*, grace, beauty, kindness < *chairein*, to rejoice at < IE base **ĝher-*, to desire, like > YEARN⟧ **1** *pl.* **-ma·ta** (-mə tə) *Christian Theol.* a divinely inspired gift, grace, or talent, as for prophesying, healing, etc.: also **char·ism** (kar′iz′əm) **2** a special quality of leadership that captures the popular imagination and inspires allegiance and devotion **3** a special charm or allure that inspires fascination or devotion [the film star's *charisma*]

char·is·mat·ic (kar′iz mat′ik) ***adj.*** **1** of, having, or resulting from charisma **2** designating or of any of various religious groups or movements that stress direct divine inspiration, manifested as in glossolalia or healing powers —***n.*** **1** a member of a charismatic group or movement **2** a person who supposedly has some divinely inspired power, as the ability to prophesy

char·i·ta·ble (char′i tə bəl) ***adj.*** ⟦ME & OFr: see fol.⟧ **1** kind and generous in giving money or other help to those in need **2** of or for charity **3** kind and forgiving in judging others; lenient —***SYN.*** PHILANTHROPIC —**char′i·ta·ble·ness *n.*** —**char′i·ta·bly *adv.***

char·i·ty (char′i tē) ***n., pl.* -ties** ⟦ME & OFr *charite* < L *caritas*, costliness, esteem, affection (in Vulg., often used as transl. of LGr(Ec) *agapē*, AGAPE[2]) < *carus*, dear, valued < IE **karo-* < base **ka-*, to like, desire > WHORE⟧ **1** *Christian Theol.* the love of God for humanity, or a love of one's fellow human beings **2** an act of goodwill or affection **3** the feeling of goodwill; benevolence **4** kindness or leniency in judging others **5** *a)* a voluntary giving of money or other help to those in need *b)* money or help so given *c)* an institution or other recipient of such help **6** a welfare institution, organization, or fund —***SYN.*** MERCY

Char·i·ty (char′i tē) ***n.*** ⟦see prec.⟧ a feminine name

cha·ri·va·ri (shiv′ə rē′, shiv′ə rē′; shə riv′ə rē′) ***n.*** ⟦Fr < LL *caribaria*, headache < Gr *karēbaria*, heaviness in the head < *karē*, var. of *kara*, head (< IE base **ker-*, head, HORN) + *barys*, heavy: see GRAVE[1]⟧ SHIVAREE

char·kha or **char·ka** (chur′kə, chär′-) ***n.*** ⟦Hindi⟧ in India, a spinning wheel used esp. for cotton

char·la·dy (chär′lā′dē) ***n., pl.* -dies** [Brit.] a charwoman

char·la·tan (shär′lə tən) ***n.*** ⟦Fr < It *ciarlatano*, a quack < *cerretano*, one who cries out in the market place < VL *cerretanus*, seller of papal indulgences at *Cerreto*, town in Italy: infl. by It *ciarlare*, to prate⟧ a person who pretends to have expert knowledge or skill that he or she does not have; fake; mountebank —***SYN.*** QUACK[2] —**char′la·tan·ism′ *n.*,** **char′la·tan·ry *pl.* -ries**

Char·le·magne (shär′lə mān′) A.D. 742-814; king of the Franks (768-814): emperor of the Holy Roman Empire (800-814): also called **Charles I** or **Charles the Great**

Char·le·roi (shär′lə roi′; *Fr* shȧr lə rwȧ′) city in SW Belgium, in Hainaut

Charles[1] (chärlz) ***n.*** ⟦Fr < ML *Carolus* or Gmc *Karl*, lit., full-grown; akin to OE *ceorl*, CHURL⟧ a masculine name: dim. *Charley, Charlie, Chuck*; var. *Carl, Karl*; equiv. L. *Carolus*, Ger. *Carl, Karl*, It. *Carlo*, Sp. *Carlos*, Du. *Karel*; fem. *Charlene, Charlotte, Caroline*

Charles[2] (chärlz) **1** Prince (born *Charles Philip Arthur George*) 1948- ; Prince of Wales: son of Elizabeth II **2 Charles I** A.D. 823-877; king of France (843-877) &, as **Charles II**, Holy Roman Emperor (875-877): called *the Bald* **3 Charles I** (born *Charles Stuart*) 1600-49; king of England, Scotland, & Ireland (1625-49): beheaded **4 Charles I** (born *Charles Francis Joseph*) 1887-1922; emperor of Austria &, as **Charles IV**, king of Hungary (1916-18): forced to abdicate **5 Charles I** CHARLEMAGNE **6 Charles II** 1630-85; king of England, Scotland, & Ireland (1660-85) **7 Charles IV** 1294-1328; king of France (1322-28): called *the Fair* **8 Charles IV** 1748-1819; king of Spain (1788-1808): forced to abdicate by Napoleon I **9 Charles V** 1337-80; king of France (1364-80): called *the Wise* **10 Charles V** 1500-58; Holy Roman Emperor (1519-56) &, as **Charles I**, king of Spain (1516-56): abdicated **11 Charles VI** 1368-1422: king of France (1380-1422): called *the Well-Beloved* **12 Charles VII** 1403-61; king of France (1422-61): called *the Victorious* **13 Charles VIII** (born *Charles Albert*) 1697-1745; Holy Roman Emperor (1742-45) **14 Charles XIV (John)** *see* BERNADOTTE, Jean Baptiste Jules **15 Ray** (born *Ray Charles Robinson*) 1930-2004; U.S. rhythm-and-blues musician, singer, & composer

Charles[3] (chärlz) ⟦after CHARLES I of England: see prec.⟧ **1** river in E Mass., flowing into Boston Bay: *c.* 60 mi (97 km) **2 Cape** cape in SE Va., at the mouth of Chesapeake Bay, forming the tip of Delmarva Peninsula

Charles·bourg (shärl′boorg; *Fr* shȧrl bōōr′) borough of Quebec City

Charles Edward Stuart *see* STUART[2]

Charles Martel *see* MARTEL

Charles's law (chärl′ziz) ⟦after J. *Charles* (1746-1823), Fr physicist⟧ the statement that for a body of ideal gas at constant pressure the volume is directly proportional to the absolute temperature

Charles's Wain [Brit.] the BIG DIPPER

Charles·ton[1] (chärl′stən) ***n.*** ⟦after fol., S.C.: see fol.⟧ a lively dance in 4/4 time, popular during the 1920s

Charles·ton[2] (chärl′stən) **1** ⟦after CHARLES II of England: see CHARLES[2]⟧ seaport in S.C. **2** ⟦after the founder's father, *Charles*⟧ capital of W.Va., in the W part

Charles·town (chärlz′toun′) ⟦after CHARLES I of England: see CHARLES[2]⟧ oldest part of Boston, at the mouth of the Charles River: site of the battle of Bunker Hill

☆**char·ley horse** (chär′lē) ⟦ballplayers' slang, *c.* 1888; prob. with reference to a lame racehorse⟧ [Informal] a cramp or soreness in a muscle, specif. of the thigh, caused by strain

char·lock (chär′lək) ***n.*** ⟦ME *cherlok* < OE *cerlic*⟧ a weed (*Brassica kaber*) of the crucifer family, with yellow flowers

char·lotte (shär′lət) ***n.*** ⟦after Queen CHARLOTTE[2]⟧ a molded dessert consisting of an outer layer of strips of bread, cake, etc. and a filling as of custard or cooked fruit

Char·lotte[1] (shär′lət) ***n.*** ⟦Fr, fem. of *Charlot*, dim., of *Charles*⟧ a feminine name: dim. *Lotta, Lottie, Lotty*; equiv. It. *Carlotta*

Char·lotte[2] (shär′lət) ⟦after Queen *Charlotte*, wife of GEORGE III: see GEORGE[2]⟧ city in S N.C.

Charlotte A·ma·lie (ə mäl′yə, ə mäl′ē) ⟦after Queen *Charlotte Amalie*, wife of Christian V of Denmark, to which the islands formerly belonged⟧ capital of the Virgin Islands of the U.S., on St. Thomas

charlotte russe (rōōs) ⟦Fr, lit., Russian charlotte: prob. dedicated to Czar ALEXANDER I⟧ a charlotte filled with Bavarian cream and made in a mold lined with ladyfingers or spongecake

Char·lottes·ville (shär′ləts vil′) ⟦see CHARLOTTE[2]⟧ city in central Va.

Char·lotte·town (shär′lət toun′) ⟦see CHARLOTTE[2]⟧ capital of Prince Edward Island, Canada

charm (chärm) ***n.*** ⟦ME *charme* < OFr < L *carmen*, song, verse, charm < **canmen* < *canere*, to sing: see CHANT⟧ **1** *a)* a chanted word, phrase, or verse assumed to have magic power to help or hurt; incantation *b)* the chanting of such a word, phrase, or verse **2** any object assumed to have such power, as an amulet or talisman **3** any trinket worn as a decoration on a bracelet, necklace, watch chain, etc. **4** any action or gesture assumed to have magic power **5** a quality or feature in someone or something that attracts or delights people **6** *Particle Physics* an individuating property of quarks and other elementary particles: it is expressed as a quantum number, with +1 used of a particle that has charm (**charmed particle**) and 0 used of one that does not —***vt.*** **1** to act on as though by magic; seemingly cast a spell on **2** to protect from harm as though by magic **3** to attract or please greatly; enchant; allure; fascinate; delight —***vi.*** **1** to practice magic **2** to be charming; please greatly —***SYN.*** ATTRACT

charmed quark *Particle Physics* a type of quark with a mass of *c.* 1.0 to 1.6 GeV/c^2, a positive charge that is ⅔ the charge of an electron, +1 charm, and zero strangeness: see FLAVOR (sense 5)

charm·er (-ər) ***n.*** ⟦see CHARM⟧ **1** a delightful, fascinating, or attractive person **2** a person who seemingly casts a spell; enchanter [a snake *charmer*]

char·meuse (shär mōōz′, -mōōs′) ***n.*** ⟦Fr < fem. of *charmeur*, enchanter < *charmer*, to bewitch⟧ a smooth fabric of silk or polyester, like satin in appearance but softer and having less body

charm·ing (chärm′iŋ) ***adj.*** attractive; fascinating; delightful —**charm′ing·ly *adv.***

charm quark *Particle Physics* CHARMED QUARK

char·nel (chär′nəl) ***n.*** ⟦OFr < LL *carnale*, graveyard; neut. of LL(Ec) *carnalis*, CARNAL⟧ **1** [Obs.] a cemetery **2** a building or place where corpses or bones are deposited: in full **charnel house** —***adj.*** of, like, or fit for a charnel

Cha·ro·lais (shä′rə lā′) ***n., pl.* -lais′** (-lāz′, -lā′) ⟦after *Charolais*, region in E France where originated⟧ any of a breed of white beef cattle used in crossbreeding

Cha·ron (ker′ən) ***n.*** ⟦L < Gr *Charōn*⟧ **1** *Gr. Myth.* the boatman who ferries souls of the dead across the river Styx to Hades **2** a satellite of Pluto: it has an orbital period equal to Pluto's rotational period

cha·ro·set (khä rō′set) ***n.*** ⟦Heb < or akin to *cheres*, clay⟧ *Judaism* a mixture of apples, nuts, wine, cinnamon, etc. served as part of the seder at Passover and symbolizing the mortar used by Jewish slaves in Egypt: also **cha·ro′ses** (-sis)

char·poy (chär′poi′) ***n.*** ⟦Hindi *cārpāī* < Pers *čahār-pāī* < *čahār*, FOUR + *pāī* < IE base **pĕd-*, FOOT⟧ a light bed or cot used in India

char·qui (chär′kē) ***n.*** ⟦Sp *charquí, charqué* < Quechua *ch'arki*, dried meat⟧ jerked or dried beef

charr (chär) ***n.*** *alt. sp. of* CHAR[3]

char·ro (chä′rô) ***n., pl.*** **-ros** (-rôs) ⟦MexSp < Sp, ill-bred person < Basque *txar*, bad⟧ a skilled Mexican horseman dressed in an elaborate, traditional costume

chart (chärt) ***n.*** ⟦OFr < ML *carta*: see CARD[1]⟧ **1** a map, esp. one prepared for use in marine or air navigation **2** an outline map on which special information, as on weather conditions or economic resources, is plotted geographically **3** *a)* a group of facts about something, set up in the form of a diagram, table, graph, etc. *b)* such a diagram or graph *c)* a sheet with such diagrams, graphs, etc. ☆**4** [Informal] *a)* an arrangement of a musical composition, as for a jazz band *b)* a list of the best-selling recordings for a given period (*usually used in pl.*) (usually with *the*) —***vt.*** **1** to make a chart of; map; outline **2** to plot (a course) on, or by reference to, a chart or charts **3** to plan (a course of action) **4** to show by, on, or as by a chart —**off the charts** [Informal] in excess of normal standards or expectations

char·ter (chärt′ər) ***n.*** ⟦ME *chartre* < OFr < L *chartula*, dim. of *charta*: see CARD[1]⟧ **1** a franchise or written grant of specified rights made by a government or ruler to a person, corporation, etc. **2** *a)* a document setting forth the aims and principles of a united group, as of nations *b)* the constitution of a city, setting forth its governmental organization and powers *c)* [**C-**] the Charter of the United Nations **3** a document by which a society authorizes the organization of a local chapter or lodge **4** a special privilege or exemption **5** *a)* the hire or lease of a ship, bus, airplane, etc. *b)* the agreement governing this **6** *Eng. Law* an instrument, esp. a deed —***vt.*** **1** to grant a charter to **2** to hire or lease by charter **3** to hire for exclusive use —*SYN.* HIRE —**char′ter·er** ***n.***

chartered accountant in Australia, Britain, Canada, etc., the equivalent of a certified public accountant in the U.S.

Char·ter·house (chärt′ər hous′) ***n.*** **1** a boys' school in Surrey, England, moved from its original location in London that was on the site of a Carthusian monastery **2** [Archaic] a Carthusian monastery

☆**charter member** any of the founders or original members of an organization, esp. an organization with a charter

charter school an alternative school that is founded on a charter, or contract, between a sponsoring group and a governmental unit and is funded with public money

Chart·ism (chärt′iz′əm) ***n.*** **1** a movement for democratic social and political reform in England (1838-48) **2** its principles set forth in the People's Charter (1838) —**Chart′ist** ***n., adj.***

chart·ist (chärt′ist) ***n.*** a person who compiles or uses charts, esp. one who consults charts in order to anticipate fluctuations in the stock market

chart·less (chärt′lis) ***adj.*** **1** without a chart; unguided **2** not mapped; uncharted [*a chartless sea*]

Char·tres (shär′tr′; *E* shär′trə, shärt) city in NC France, near Paris: site of a 13th-cent. Gothic cathedral

Char·treuse (shär tro͞oz′, -tro͞os′; *Fr* shär tröz′) ⟦after *La Grande Chartreuse*, Carthusian monastery in France⟧ *trademark for* a yellow, pale-green, or white liqueur made by Carthusian monks —***n.*** **1** [*occas.* **c-**] this liqueur **2** [**c-**] a pale yellowish-green color —***adj.*** [**c-**] of the color chartreuse

char·tu·lar·y (kär′chə ler′ē) ***n., pl.*** **-lar′ies** *alt. sp. of* CARTULARY

char·wom·an (chär′wo͝om′ən) ***n., pl.*** **-wom′en** (-wim′in) ⟦see CHARE, CHORE⟧ a woman who does general cleaning, as in office buildings

char·y (cher′ē, char′ē) ***adj.*** **char′i·er, char′i·est** ⟦ME *chari*, concerned, sorrowful < OE *cearig*, sorrowful < *cearu, caru*, CARE; change of sense by assoc. with *care*⟧ **1** not taking chances; careful; cautious [*to be chary of offending others*] **2** not giving freely; sparing [*chary of his hospitality*]

Cha·ryb·dis (kə rib′dis) ⟦L < Gr⟧ *former name for* a whirlpool off the NE coast of Sicily, in the Strait of Messina; now called *Galofalo*: see SCYLLA

Chas *abbrev.* Charles

chase[1] (chās) ***vt.*** **chased, chas′ing** ⟦ME *chacen, cacchen*: see CATCH⟧ **1** to follow quickly or persistently in order to catch or harm **2** to run after; follow; pursue **3** to seek after **4** to make run away; drive **5** to hunt (game) **6** [Slang] to court aggressively —***vi.*** **1** to go in pursuit [*to chase after him*] **2** [Informal] to go hurriedly; rush [*to chase around town*] —***n.*** **1** the act of chasing; pursuit **2** *a)* the hunting of game for sport (often with *the*) *b)* anything hunted; quarry **3** [Brit.] *a)* an unenclosed game preserve (distinguished from PARK) *b)* a license to hunt over a specified area or to keep animals there as game —**give chase** to chase; pursue

chase[2] (chās) ***n.*** ⟦Fr *chas*, needle's eye < OFr < VL **capsum* < L *capsa*: see CASE[2]⟧ **1** a groove; furrow **2** the bore of a gun barrel **3** a groove or recess in a wall, made to provide space as for a pipe or conduit **4** a rectangular metal frame in which pages or columns of type are locked —***vt.*** **chased, chas′ing** to make a groove in

chase[3] (chās) ***vt.*** **chased, chas′ing** ⟦aphetic for ENCHASE⟧ to ornament (metal) by engraving, embossing, etc.

Chase (chās) **1 Sal·mon P(ortland)** (sal′mən) 1808-73; chief justice of the U.S. (1864-73) **2 Samuel** 1741-1811; Am. Revolutionary leader: associate justice, U.S. Supreme Court (1796-1811)

chas·er[1] (chā′sər) ***n.*** ⟦CHASE[1] + -ER⟧ **1** a person or thing that chases or hunts; pursuer **2** a gun formerly placed on the stern (**stern chaser**) or bow (**bow chaser**) of a ship, used during pursuit by or of another ship ☆**3** a mild drink, as water, ginger ale, or beer, taken after or with whiskey, rum, etc.

chas·er[2] (chā′sər) ***n.*** ⟦CHASE[3] + -ER⟧ **1** one that engraves or embosses metal **2** a tool for threading screws

Chas·i·dim (has′ə dim′, -dēm′, hä sēd′im; *Heb* khä sē′dim) ***pl.n., sing.*** **Cha·sid** (has′id, hä′sid; *Heb* khä′sid) HASIDIM —**Cha·sid·ic** (ha sid′ik, hä sēd′ik) ***adj.*** —**Chas′i·dism′** ***n.***

chasm (kaz′əm) ***n.*** ⟦L & Gr *chasma*, yawning hollow, gulf < Gr *chainein*, to YAWN⟧ **1** a deep crack in the earth's surface; abyss **2** any break or gap **3** a wide divergence of feelings, sentiments, interests, etc.; rift —**chas′mal** (-məl) ***adj.***, **chas′mic** (-mik)

chas·sé (sha sā′) ***n.*** ⟦Fr, lit., a chasing, orig., pp. of *chasser*: see CATCH⟧ a rapid, gliding dance step forward or sideways —***vi.*** **-séd′, -sé′ing** to perform this step

chasse·pot (shas pō′) ***n.*** ⟦after A. A. *Chassepot* (1833-1905), Fr inventor⟧ a breech-loading rifle used by the French army between 1866 and 1874

chas·seur (sha sʉr′) ***n.*** ⟦Fr < *chasser*: see CATCH⟧ **1** a hunter; huntsman **2** a soldier, esp. one of certain French light infantry troops, trained for rapid action **3** a uniformed attendant

chas·sis (chas′ē, shas′ē) ***n., pl.*** **-sis′** (-ēz′) ⟦Fr *châssis*: see CHASE[2]⟧ **1** a frame on which the carriage of a cannon moves back and forth **2** the frame or undercarriage of a motor vehicle, usually including the axles, suspension, etc. and sometimes the engine, drivetrain, etc. **3** LANDING GEAR **4** *Electronics* *a)* the metal frame on which the parts of an electronic device together with the circuits connecting them are mounted *b)* the assembled frame and parts ☆**5** [Slang] the body or figure, esp. of a woman

chaste (chāst) ***adj.*** ⟦OFr < L *castus*, pure, chaste: see CASTE⟧ **1** not indulging in unlawful sexual activity; virtuous **2** sexually abstinent; celibate **3** pure, decent, or modest in nature, behavior, etc. **4** restrained and simple in style; not ornate —**chaste′ly** ***adv.*** —**chaste′ness** ***n.***

SYN.—**chaste** and **virtuous**, in this connection, imply moral excellence manifested by forbearance from acts or thoughts that do not accord with virginity or strict marital fidelity; **pure** implies chastity through innocence and an absence of seductive influences rather than through self-restraint; **modest** and **decent** are both applied to propriety in behavior, dress, bearing, or speech as exhibiting morality or purity —*ANT.* **immoral, lewd, wanton**

chas·ten (chās′ən) ***vt.*** ⟦ME *chastien* < OFr *chastier* < L *castigare*, to punish, chastise: see CASTIGATE⟧ **1** to punish in order to correct or make better; chastise **2** to restrain from excess; subdue **3** to make purer in style; refine —*SYN.* PUNISH —**chas′ten·er** ***n.***

chas·tise (chas tīz′, chas′tīz′) ***vt.*** **-tised′, -tis′ing** ⟦ME *chastisen* < extended stem of OFr *chastier*: see prec.⟧ **1** to punish, esp. by beating **2** to scold or condemn sharply **3** [Archaic] to chasten —*SYN.* PUNISH —**chas·tise·ment** (chas′tiz mənt; chas tīz′-) ***n.*** —**chas·tis′er** ***n.***

chas·ti·ty (chas′tə tē) ***n.*** ⟦ME *chastite* < OFr *chastete* < L *castitas*: see CHASTE⟧ the quality or state of being chaste; specif., *a)* virtuousness *b)* sexual abstinence; celibacy *c)* decency or modesty *d)* simplicity of style

chastity belt a beltlike device of metal, leather, etc. allegedly fastened on a woman in the Middle Ages to prevent sexual intercourse during the absence of her husband

chas·u·ble (chaz′ə bəl, chas′-; -yə-) ***n.*** ⟦OFr < ML *casubla, casula*, hooded garment; prob. < L *casula*, dim. of *casa*, hut, cottage: see CASINO⟧ a sleeveless outer vestment worn over the alb by priests at Mass

chasuble

chat[1] (chat) ***vi.*** **chat′ted, chat′ting** ⟦< CHATTER⟧ **1** to talk or converse in a light, easy, informal manner **2** *Comput.* to hold a real-time electronic conversation by exchanging typed messages —***n.*** **1** small talk; chitchat [*a letter filled with chat about books*] **2** an easy, informal talk or conversation **3** *Comput.* the act or an instance of chatting: see CHAT[1] (***vi.*** 2) **4** any of various passerine birds with a chattering call ☆**5** any of several songbirds of various families characterized by a chattering song; esp., a yellow-breasted wood warbler (*Icteria virens*) of North America —***adj.*** *Comput.* of or having to do with chatting [*a chat group, chat session*]: see CHAT[1] (***vi.*** 2) —**chat up** [Informal, Chiefly Brit.] to chat with, often, specif., in a flirtatious or seductive way

chat[2] (chat) ***n.*** ⟦Fr < LL *cattus*, CAT[1]⟧ **1** an ament or catkin, as of a willow **2** a samara, as of a maple **3** a spike, as of plantain

☆**chatch·ka** or **chatch·ke** (chäch′kə) ***n.*** [Informal] TCHOTCHKE

châ·teau (sha tō′) ***n., pl.*** **-teaux′** (-tōz′, -tō′) or **-teaus′** ⟦Fr < OFr *chastel, castel* < L *castellum*, CASTLE⟧ **1** a French feudal castle **2** a large country house and estate, esp. in France Also sp. **chateau**

cha·teau·bri·and (sha tō′brē än′, sha′tō-) ***n.*** ⟦after fol.⟧ a thick beef fillet cut from the center of the tenderloin, usually grilled and served with a sauce

Cha·teau·bri·and (shȧ tō brē än′), Vicomte **Fran·çois Re·né de** (frän swȧ rə nā′ də) 1768-1848; Fr. statesman & man of letters

Châ·teau·neuf-du-Pape (shȧ tō nëf dü pȧp′) ***n.*** ⟦Fr, lit., new castle of the Pope, in ref. to a local summer palace of the Avignon Popes⟧ any of certain full-bodied, mainly red wines produced from blends of local grape varieties in and around the S French village of Châteauneuf-du-Pape in the region of the S Rhone

Châ·teau-Thier·ry (shȧ tō tye rē′) town in N France, on the Marne: battle site in WWI

château wine any of certain wines made from grapes grown at a particular château in France, esp. in the region of Bordeaux

chat·e·lain (shat′'l ān′) ***n.*** ⟦Fr *châtelain*, CASTELLAN⟧ CASTELLAN
chat·e·laine (-ān′) ***n.*** ⟦Fr *châtelaine*, fem. of prec.⟧ **1** *a)* the mistress of a castle or château *b)* the mistress of any large household **2** a woman's ornamental chain or clasp, esp. one worn at the waist, with keys or a purse, watch, etc. fastened to it
Chat·ham[1] (chat′əm), 1st Earl of (*see* PITT)
Chat·ham[2] (chat′əm) seaport in Kent, SE England
Chatham Islands group of islands of New Zealand, *c.* 500 mi (805 km) east of North Island: 372 sq mi (963 sq km)
Chat·ham-Kent (-kent′) city in SE Ontario, Canada
cha·toy·ant (shə toi′ənt) ***adj.*** ⟦Fr, prp. of *chatoyer*, to change luster like the eye of a cat < *chat*, cat⟧ having a changeable color or luster [*chatoyant* silk] —***n.*** a gem or polished stone, as the cat's-eye, with such luster —**cha·toy′ance *n.*, cha·toy′an·cy**
chat·room (chat′ro͞om′, -ro͝om′) ***n.*** a location, as on the internet, in which various users can CHAT[1] (***vi.*** 2) informally with one another: often written **chat room**
chat show [Brit.] TALK SHOW
Chat·ta·hoo·chee (chat′ə ho͞o′chē) ⟦< AmInd (Creek), lit., pictured rocks (found in the river)⟧ river flowing from N Ga. southward along the Ga.-Ala. border into the Apalachicola: 436 mi (702 km)
Chat·ta·noo·ga (chat′ə no͞o′gə) ⟦< AmInd (Creek or Cherokee); meaning uncert.⟧ city in SE Tenn., on the Tennessee River at the Ga. border
chat·tel (chat′'l) ***n.*** ⟦ME *chatel* < OFr: see CATTLE⟧ **1** *a)* a movable item of personal property, as a piece of furniture, an automobile, or a head of livestock (in full **chattel personal**) *b)* any interest in real estate less than a freehold (in full **chattel real**) **2** a slave
chat·ter (chat′ər) ***vi.*** ⟦ME *chateren*: orig. echoic⟧ **1** to make short, indistinct sounds in rapid succession [birds and squirrels *chatter*] **2** to talk fast, incessantly, and foolishly **3** to click together rapidly, as the teeth do when the lower jaw trembles from fright or cold **4** to rattle or vibrate [an improperly adjusted tool *chatters*] —***vt.*** to utter with a chattering sound —***n.*** **1** the act or sound of chattering **2** rapid, foolish talk **3** communication, such as email and cell-phone calls, among persons who are involved in terrorism or espionage, as monitored by a government agency —**chat′ter·er *n.***
chat·ter·box (-bäks′) ***n.*** [Informal] a person who talks incessantly
chattering classes [Informal] intellectuals, literary and media people, etc. considered as a group: a dismissive term implying variously elitism, effeteness, habitual faultfinding, etc.
chatter mark **1** a mark left by a tool that chatters **2** any mark or scratch on a rock surface caused by a large, heavy mass, esp. a glacier, sliding over it: also written **chat′ter·mark′ *n.***
Chat·ter·ton (chat′ər tən), **Thomas** 1752-70; Eng. poet
chat·ty (chat′ē) ***adj.*** **-ti·er, -ti·est** **1** fond of chatting **2** light and informal [a *chatty* letter] —**chat′ti·ly** (-'l ē) ***adv.*** —**chat′ti·ness *n.***
Chau·cer (chô′sər), **Geoffrey** 1340?-1400; Eng. poet: author of *The Canterbury Tales* —**Chau·ce′ri·an** (-sir′ē ən) ***adj.***
chauf·feur (shō′fər, shō fur′) ***n.*** ⟦Fr, lit., stoker (operator of a steam-driven car) < *chauffer*, to heat: see CHAFE⟧ a person hired to drive a private automobile for someone else — ***vt., vi.*** to act as chauffeur to (someone)
chaul·moo·gra (chôl mo͞o′grə) ***n.*** ⟦Beng *cāulmugrā*, E Ind tree⟧ any of various SE Asian trees (genus *Taraktogenos*, family Bixaceae and genus *Hydnocarpus*, family Flacourtiaceae) whose seeds yield a nonvolatile oil, once commonly used to treat leprosy
Chaun·cey (chôn′sē, chän′-) ***n.*** ⟦orig., a surname; prob. of Fr orig.⟧ a masculine name
chaunt (chänt) ***n., vt., vi.*** *archaic var. of* CHANT
chaus·sure (shō sür′) ***n.***, *pl.* **-sures** (-sür′) ⟦Fr < *chausser*, to shoe < OFr *chaucier* < L *calceare* < *calceus*, shoe < *calx*, the heel: see CALCAR⟧ an article of footwear; shoe, boot, slipper, etc.
chau·tau·qua (shə tô′kwə) ***n.*** ⟦after fol.: so named from the summer schools inaugurated there in 1874⟧ an educational and recreational assembly with lectures, concerts, etc.
☆**Chau·tau·qua** (shə tô′kwə) ⟦< Seneca name; prob., lit., "one has taken out fish there"⟧ **1** lake in SW N.Y.: 18 mi (29 km) long **2** town on this lake: see also CHAUTAUQUA —**Chau·tau′quan *adj., n.***
chau·vin·ism (shō′və niz′əm) ***n.*** ⟦Fr *chauvinisme*, after N. *Chauvin*, soldier of Napoleon I, notorious for his attachment to the lost imperial cause⟧ **1** militant, unreasoning, and boastful devotion to one's country; jingoism **2** unreasoning devotion to one's race (or one's sex, etc.) with contempt for other races (or the opposite sex, etc.) —**chau′vin·ist *n., adj.*** —**chau′vin·is′tic *adj.*** —**chau′vin·is′ti·cal·ly *adv.***
Chavannes, Puvis de *see* PUVIS DE CHAVANNES, Pierre
chaw (chô) ***n., vt., vi.*** [Now Dial.] CHEW
chay (chā, chī) ***n.*** ⟦< Tamil *cāya*⟧ **1** the root of an Indian plant (*Oldenlandia umbellata*) of the madder family, from which a red dye is obtained **2** this plant
☆**cha·yo·te** (chä yō′tē, -tā′) ***n.*** ⟦Sp < Nahuatl *čayo′λi*⟧ a tropical American perennial vine (*Sechium edule*) of the gourd family, grown for its edible, fleshy, pear-shaped, single-seeded fruit
chaz·an or **chaz·zan** (hä′zən; *Heb* khä zän′) ***n.*** *alt. sp. of* HAZAN
CHD *abbrev.* coronary heart disease
ChE *abbrev.* Chemical Engineer
cheap (chēp) ***adj.*** ⟦< *good cheap*, favorable bargain < ME *god chep* (used as transl. of OFr *à bon marché*) < OE *ceap*, a purchase, bargain, akin to Ger *kaufen*, to buy; ult. < L *caupo*, petty tradesman⟧ **1** low in price or cost; not expensive **2** charging low prices [a chain of *cheap* stores] **3** spending or able to spend little [a *cheaper* clientele] **4** worth more than the price **5** costing little labor or trouble; easily gotten [a *cheap* victory] **6** of little value or poor quality; virtually worthless **7** deserving of scorn; contemptible [made *cheap* by their own behavior] **8** [Informal] stingy; niggardly **9** *Econ.* lowered in exchange value or buying power; also, available at low interest rates: said of money —***adv.*** at a low cost; cheaply —***n.*** ⟦OE *ceap*, market; akin to Dan *kjob* (ON *kaup*) as in *Kjöbnhavn* (Copenhagen)⟧ **1** a market: now only in place names [*Cheapside*] **2** [Obs.] a bargain —**on the cheap** at very little cost; cheaply —**cheap′ly *adv.*** —**cheap′ness *n.***

SYN.—**cheap** and **inexpensive** both mean low in cost or price, but **inexpensive** simply suggests value comparable to the price, and **cheap**, in this sense, stresses a bargain; **cheap** may also imply inferior quality or value, tawdriness, contemptibility, etc. [*cheap* jewelry, to feel *cheap*] —*ANT.* **costly, expensive, dear**

cheap·en (chēp′ən) ***vt.*** ⟦ME *chepen* < OE *ceapian*, to trade, buy (pres. meaning < prec.)⟧ **1** to make cheap or cheaper **2** to depreciate, belittle, or bring into contempt **3** [Archaic] to bargain for —***vi.*** to become cheap or cheaper
☆**cheap·ie** (chēp′ē) [Slang] ***adj.*** cheap, inferior, etc. —***n.*** someone or something cheap, inexpensive, inferior, etc.
cheap-jack (chēp′jak′) ***n.*** ⟦CHEAP (***adj.***) + JACK⟧ a peddler of cheap, inferior articles —***adj.*** cheap, inferior, base, etc.
☆**cheap·o** (chēp′ō) ***adj., n.***, *pl.* **cheap′os** [Slang] CHEAPIE
cheap shot [Slang] an unnecessarily rough or mean action or remark against which there is no ready defense
Cheap·side (chēp′sīd′) street and district of London: in the Middle Ages it was a marketplace
☆**cheap·skate** (chēp′skāt′) ***n.*** ⟦CHEAP + SKATE[3]⟧ [Slang] a person unwilling to give or spend money; stingy person
cheat (chēt) ***n.*** ⟦ME *chete* < *eschete*: see ESCHEAT⟧ **1** the act of deceiving or swindling; deception; fraud **2** a person who defrauds, deceives, or tricks others; swindler ☆**3** [Informal] a person who is sexually unfaithful **4** a code entered into a video game by a player, which allows advancement, as to a higher level, more easily: in full **cheat code** **5** ⟦see CHEATGRASS⟧ CHESS[2] —***vt.*** **1** to deal with dishonestly for one's own gain; defraud; swindle **2** to deceive by trickery; fool; mislead **3** to foil or escape by tricks or by good luck [to *cheat* death] **4** to deprive of or destroy the effect of through error or ignorance [using the wrong word *cheated* him of his legacy] —***vi.*** **1** to practice fraud or deception **2** to behave dishonestly, as at games or on an examination ☆**3** [Informal] to be sexually unfaithful: often with *on* —**cheat′er *n.*** —**cheat′ing·ly *adv.***

SYN.—**cheat**, the most general term in this comparison, implies dealing dishonestly or deceptively with someone, to obtain some advantage or gain; **defraud**, chiefly a legal term, stresses the use of deliberate deception in criminally depriving a person of rights or property; **swindle** stresses the winning of a person's confidence in order to cheat or defraud that person of money, etc.; **trick** implies a deluding by means of a ruse, stratagem, etc., but does not always suggest fraudulence or a harmful motive; **dupe** stresses credulity in the person who is tricked or fooled; **hoax** implies a trick skillfully carried off simply to demonstrate the gullibility of the victim

☆**cheat·ers** (chēt′ərz) ***pl.n.*** [Slang] eyeglasses, esp. dark glasses
cheat·grass (-gras′) ***n.*** ⟦so called prob. from similarity to the grain with which it grows⟧ a fast-spreading, weedy, annual brome grass (*Bromus tectorum*) native to Europe, introduced to the W U.S.: often written **cheat grass**
☆**cheat sheet** [Informal] **1** a sheet of notes used dishonestly, as in doing schoolwork **2** any collection of notes that serves as a handy reference
Che·bok·sa·ry (cheb′äk′sär′ē) city in WC Russia, on the Volga west of Kazan
Che·chen (chech′en) ***n.*** ⟦< obs. Russ *čečen* > modern form, *čečenec*⟧ a person born or living in Chechnya —***adj.*** of Chechnya or its people, language, or culture
Chech·ny·a (chech′nē ə, -nyə) ethnic region in the N Caucasus, Russia: since 1991 its status as a political subdivision of the Russian Federation has been disputed by the Chechens: also sp. **Chech′ni·a**, **Cheche′ny·a**, or **Cheche′ni·a** (chech′nē ə, -nyə)
check (chek) ***n.*** ⟦ME *chek* < OFr *eschec*, *eschac*, a check at chess, repulse < ML *scaccus*, *scahus* < Pers *šāh*, king, principal piece in a game of chess (see SHAH[1]); prob. sense development: king in danger → hostile action → restraining action → means of restraint or control⟧ **1** a sudden stop; abrupt halt **2** any restraint or control put upon action **3** a person or thing that restrains or controls **4** a supervision of accuracy, efficiency, etc. **5** *a)* a test, comparison, examination, etc. to determine if something is as it should be *b)* a standard or sample used in making such a determination **6** a mark (✓) to show approval or verification of something, or to call attention to it ☆**7** an identification ticket or other token enabling one to claim an item left in a checkroom, etc. [a hat *check*] ☆**8** one's bill at a restaurant or bar ☆**9** [Now Rare] a gambling chip **10** *a)* a written order to a bank to pay a named payee a stated amount of money, typically from funds deposited in the payer's checking account *b)* a form, typically preprinted with the payer's name, account number, etc., used for such orders **11** *a)* a pattern of small squares like that of a chessboard *b)* one of these squares **12** a fabric with such a pattern **13** a small split, crack, or chink **14** [Obs.] a rebuke; reprimand **15** *Chess* the condition of a king that is in danger of capture on

the opponent's next move: when in such a condition, one's king must, if possible, be protected **16** *Hockey* a blocking or bumping of an opponent —☆*interj.* **1** [Informal] agreed; I understand; right; OK **2** *Chess* used to signify that one's opponent's king is in check —*vt.* **1** to cause to stop suddenly; halt abruptly **2** to hold back; restrain; control **3** to rebuff, repulse, or rebuke **4** to test, measure, verify, or control by investigation, comparison, or examination *[check* the accounts*]* **5** to mark with a check (✓) **6** to mark with a pattern of squares ☆**7** to deposit or receive for deposit temporarily, as in a checkroom ☆**8** to get (esp. luggage) cleared for shipment **9** to add up the prices of (purchases) and collect the total: said of a cashier, as in a supermarket **10** to make chinks or cracks in ☆**11** *Agric.* to plant in checkrows **12** *Chess* to place (an opponent's king) in check **13** *Hockey* to block or bump (an opponent) **14** *Naut.* to reduce the strain on (a line) by letting it out gradually —*vi.* ☆**1** to agree with one another, item for item *[*the accounts *check]* ☆**2** to investigate in order to determine the condition, validity, etc. of something: often with *on* ☆**3** to draw a check on a bank account **4** to crack in small checks *[*cheap paint may *check]* **5** to stop or halt; specif., to pause, as a hunting dog, to pick up the scent **6** *Falconry* to turn from the pursuit of one prey to follow a lesser one (with *at*) ☆**7** *Poker* to decline one's chance to open a round of betting —*adj.* **1** used to check or verify *[*a *check* experiment*]* **2** having a crisscross pattern; checked —*SYN.* RESTRAIN —☆**check in** **1** to register at a hotel, convention, etc. **2** [Informal] to report, as by presenting oneself *[check in* at the office*]* —**check off** to mark as verified, examined, etc. —☆**check out** **1** to settle one's bill and leave a hotel, hospital, etc. **2** to add up the prices of purchases and collect the total: said of a cashier, as in a supermarket **3** *a)* to examine and verify or approve *b)* to prove to be accurate, in sound condition, etc. upon examination **4** to draw (money) from a bank by check **5** to register items to be loaned out, as books from a library **6** [Slang] to die —☆**check up on** to examine the record, character, actions, etc. of; investigate —**in check** in restraint; under control

☆**check·book** (chek′bo͝ok′) *n.* a book containing detachable forms for writing checks on a bank

checkbook journalism the practice by a reporter or news organization of paying someone for granting an interview or providing other exclusive information

checked (chekt) *adj.* **1** having a pattern of squares *[*a *checked* tablecloth*]* **2** *Phonet.* *a)* ending in a consonant (said of a syllable) *b)* sounded in such a syllable (said of a vowel)

check·er[1] (chek′ər) *n.* ⟦ME *cheker,* chessboard, aphetic < *escheker* < OFr *eschekier* < ML *scaccarium:* see CHECK⟧ **1** a small square, as on a chessboard **2** a pattern of such squares **3** *a)* [*pl., with sing. v.*] a game played on a checkerboard by two players, each with twelve round, flat pieces to move (Brit. name, DRAUGHTS) *b)* any of these pieces **4** SERVICE TREE —*vt.* **1** to mark off in squares, or in patches of color **2** to break the uniformity of, as with varied features or events, with changes in fortune, etc.

check·er[2] (chek′ər) *n.* **1** a person who examines or verifies ☆**2** a person who checks hats, luggage, etc. ☆**3** a cashier, as in a supermarket

☆**check·er·ber·ry** (-ber′ē) *n., pl.* **-ries** **1** WINTERGREEN (sense 1*a*) **2** the edible, red, berrylike fruit of the wintergreen

check·er·bloom (-blo͞om′) *n.* a California perennial plant (*Sidalcea malvaeflora*) of the mallow family, with rosy or purple flowers

check·er·board (-bôrd′) *n.* a square board with 64 squares of two alternating colors, used in checkers and chess

check·ered (chek′ərd) *adj.* **1** having a pattern of squares **2** varied by the use of color and shading **3** marked by diversified features or by varied events, some unpleasant *[*a *checkered* career*]*

checkered flag in auto racing, a signal to all the drivers at the finish line, made by waving a black-and-white checkered flag, indicating that the race has ended because the leader has finished

☆**checking account** a bank account against which the depositor can write checks

☆**check·list** (chek′list′) *n.* a list of things, names, etc. to be checked off or referred to for verifying, comparing, ordering, etc.: also **check list**

check·mate (-māt′) *n.* ⟦ME *chek mat* < OFr *eschec mat,* ult. < Pers *šāh māt,* lit., the king is dead < *šāh,* king + *māt,* he is dead⟧ **1** *Chess* *a)* the move that wins the game by checking the opponent's king so that it cannot be protected *b)* the condition of the king after such a move **2** complete defeat, frustration, etc. —*interj.* *Chess* used to signify that one's opponent's king is in checkmate —*vt.* **-mat′ed, -mat′ing** **1** *Chess* to place in checkmate **2** to defeat completely; frustrate; thwart

☆**check·off** (-ôf′) *n.* an arrangement by which dues of labor-union members are withheld from wages and turned over to the union by the employer

☆**check·out** (-out′) *n.* **1** the act or place of checking out purchases, as in a supermarket **2** the act of checking out of a hotel, motel, etc. **3** the time by which one must check out of a hotel, motel, etc. **4** a testing, esp. of a machine, as for accuracy Also written **check-out**

check·point (-point′) *n.* a place on a highway, on a border between countries, etc. where traffic is stopped, as for inspection by authorities

check·rein (-rān′) *n.* a rein usually running from the bit to the saddle, used to keep a horse from lowering its head

☆**check·room** (-ro͞om′) *n.* ⟦see CHECK (*vt.* 7)⟧ a room in which hats, coats, baggage, parcels, etc. may be left in safekeeping until called for

☆**check·row** (-rō′) *n.* any of a series of rows of plants crossing others at right angles to form a check pattern, so that the plants are equally spaced and the soil can be cultivated along any side —*vt.* to plant (corn, etc.) in checkrows

☆**checks and balances** **1** a system by which governmental powers are distributed among the executive, legislative, and judicial branches with each branch having specified procedures for influencing and restraining actions taken by the others: organizational principles for such a system are set forth in the U.S. Constitution **2** any system for balancing power, protecting against fraud or error, etc. in an institution, business, etc.

☆**check·up** (-up′) *n.* an examination or investigation; specif., a general medical examination

ched·dar (cheese) (ched′ər) ⟦after *Cheddar,* in Somerset, England, where orig. made⟧ *[often* **C-**] a variety of hard, smooth cheese, mild to very sharp

che·der (khä′dər) *n., pl.* ***cha·der·im*** (khä′dä rēm′) ⟦Yiddish *kheyder* < Heb **cheder-tora,* lit., room of learning < *cheder,* room < *v.* root *ḥdr,* to penetrate⟧ *alt. sp. of* HEDER

☆**chee·cha·ko** (chē chä′kō, -chak′ō) *n., pl.* **-kos** ⟦Chinook jargon⟧ in N Canada (esp. the Yukon) and Alaska, a newcomer; tenderfoot

cheek (chēk) *n.* ⟦ME *cheke* < OE *ceoke,* jaw, jawbone; akin to Du *kaak,* LowG *kâke,* jaw (only WGmc)⟧ **1** either side of the face between the nose and ear, below the eye **2** either of two sides of a thing, as the sides of a doorjamb or the jaws of a vise: *usually used in pl.* **3** either of the buttocks **4** [Informal] disrespectful boldness; sauciness; effrontery; impudence —*vt.* [Brit. Informal] to speak insolently to —*SYN.* TEMERITY —**cheek by jowl** close together; intimately —**turn the other cheek** ⟦in allusion to Matt. 5:39⟧ to bear an insult or injury humbly and refrain from retaliating

cheek·bone (chēk′bōn′) *n.* the bone across the upper cheek, that forms the outer side of the eye's bony orbit; zygomatic bone; malar

cheek·piece (-pēs′) *n.* either of the side straps of a bridle, connecting the browband with the bit and holding the bit in place

cheek pouch a pouchlike structure in the cheek of certain rodents, monkeys, etc., used for holding food

cheek·y (chēk′ē) *adj.* **cheek′i·er, cheek′i·est** [Informal] saucy; impudent; insolent —**cheek′i·ly** *adv.* —**cheek′i·ness** *n.*

cheep (chēp) *n.* ⟦echoic⟧ the short, faint, shrill sound made by a young bird; peep; chirp — *vt., vi.* to make, or utter with, such a sound —**cheep′er** *n.*

cheer (chir) *n.* ⟦ME *chere,* the face, demeanor, bearing, mood < OFr *chiere* < LL *cara,* head < Gr *kara* < IE base **k̑er-,* head, HORN; modern senses < phr. good cheer (Fr *bonne chère*)⟧ **1** state of mind or of feeling; mood; spirit: now usually in such phrases as **be of good cheer** and **with good cheer** **2** gaiety; gladness; joy **3** festive entertainment, esp. with food and drink **4** anything that comforts or gladdens one; encouragement **5** *a)* a glad, excited shout used to urge on, welcome, approve, etc. *b)* a jingle, rallying cry, etc. shouted in unison in rooting for a team **6** [Archaic] facial expression —*vt.* **1** to fill with joy, good spirits, and hope; gladden; comfort: often with *up* **2** to urge on or encourage by cheers **3** to greet or applaud with cheers —*vi.* **1** to be or become cheerful; feel encouraged: usually with *up* **2** to shout cheers

cheer·ful (chir′fəl) *adj.* **1** full of cheer; joyful **2** filling with cheer; bright and attractive *[*a *cheerful* room*]* **3** willing; ready *[*a *cheerful* helper*]* —*SYN.* HAPPY —**cheer′ful·ly** *adv.* —**cheer′ful·ness** *n.*

cheer·i·o (-ē ō′) *interj.* [Brit. Informal] **1** goodbye **2** good health: used as a toast

cheer·lead (-lēd′) *vi., vt.* ⟦back-form. < fol.⟧ to act as a cheerleader (for) —**cheer′lead′ing** *n.*

☆**cheer·lead·er** (-lēd′ər) *n.* **1** a person, typically one of a group, who leads fans in cheering for a team, as by shouting practiced cheers, performing acrobatic stunts, etc. **2** a person who enthusiastically promotes or supports a cause

cheer·less (-lis) *adj.* not cheerful; dismal; joyless; dreary —**cheer′less·ly** *adv.* —**cheer′less·ness** *n.*

cheer·ly (-lē) *adv.* [Archaic] cheerily; blithely

cheers (chirz) *interj.* good health: used as a toast

cheer·y (chir′ē) *adj.* **cheer′i·er, cheer′i·est** cheerful; lively; bright —**cheer′i·ly** *adv.* —**cheer′i·ness** *n.*

cheese[1] (chēz) *n.* ⟦ME *chese* < OE *cyse* < Gmc **kasjus* < IE base **kwat-,* to ferment, become sour > L *caseus,* cheese, OE *hwatherian,* to foam⟧ **1** a food made from the curds of soured milk pressed together to form a solid that is usually allowed to ripen **2** a shaped mass of this **3** a thing like cheese in shape or consistency —**cheesed off** [Slang] angry —**cut the cheese** ☆[Slang] to expel gas from the bowels —**say cheese!** smile!: a photographer's traditional cue to someone whose picture is about to be taken

☆**cheese**[2] (chēz) *n.* ⟦prob. < Urdu *chīz,* a thing < Pers *čīz*⟧ [Slang] an important person: cf. BIG CHEESE

cheese[3] (chēz) *vi.* **cheesed, chees′ing** ⟦< ?⟧ [Slang] to stop —**cheese it!** [Slang] run away fast!

cheese·burg·er (chēz′bur′gər) *n.* ⟦CHEESE[1] + -BURGER⟧ a hamburger with a slice of cheese melted onto the beef patty

cheese·cake (-kāk′) *n.* **1** a kind of cake made of cottage cheese or cream cheese, eggs, sugar, etc., usually baked with a bottom crust of crumbs ☆**2** [Informal] display of the figure of a scantily clad, pretty young woman, as in a newspaper photograph

cheese·cloth (-klôth′) *n.* ⟦so named from being used for wrapping curds in the production of *cheese*⟧ a thin cotton cloth with a very loose weave

cheese·par·ing (-per′iŋ) *n.* **1** anything as worthless as a paring of cheese rind **2** miserly handling of money or finances —*adj.* stingy; miserly

cheese·steak (-stāk′) *n.* a sandwich made of thinly sliced, sautéed beef, onion, and green pepper and of melted cheese, and served on a long roll: also written **cheese steak**

chees·y (-ē) *adj.* **chees′i·er, chees′i·est 1** like cheese in consistency, smell, etc. ☆**2** [Slang] *a)* inferior; poor *b)* tasteless; tacky —**chees′i·ness** *n.*

chee·tah (chēt′ə) *n.* ⟦Hindi *chītā*, leopard < Sans *chitraka*, spotted < *chitra*, spot: see CHINTZ⟧ a swift, long-legged cat (*Acinonyx jubatus*) of Africa and S Asia, with a small head, nonretractile claws, and a black-spotted coat: it can be trained to hunt

Chee·ver (chē′vər), **John** 1912-82; U.S. writer

chef (shef) *n.* ⟦Fr < *chef de cuisine*, lit., head of the kitchen: see CHIEF⟧ **1** a cook in charge of a kitchen, as of a restaurant; head cook **2** any cook

chef-d'oeu·vre (she dë′vr′) *n., pl.* ***chefs-d'oeu·vre*** (she dë′vr′) ⟦Fr, principal work⟧ a masterpiece, as in art or literature

chef's salad a salad, often served as the main course, consisting typically of mixed greens, thin strips of ham, chicken, and Swiss cheese, and wedges of hard-boiled egg and tomato

chei·lo- (kī′lō, -lə) ⟦< Gr *cheilos*: see CHILO-⟧ *combining form* CHILO-: also, before a vowel, **cheil-**

chei·ro- (kī′rō, -rə) *combining form* CHIRO-

Che·khov (chek′ôf), **An·ton Pav·lo·vich** (än′tôn päv′lə vich) 1860-1904; Russ. dramatist & short-story writer: also sp. **Che′kov**

Che·kiang (che′kyaŋ′; *Chin* jü′jyäŋ′) *a former transliteration of* ZHEJIANG

che·la (kē′lə) *n., pl.* **-lae** (-lē) ⟦ModL < Gr *chēlē*, claw < IE base **ĝhēi*, to YAWN⟧ a pincerlike claw of a crab, lobster, scorpion, etc.

che·late (kē′lāt′) *adj.* resembling or having chelae —*n.* a chemical compound in which the central atom (usually a metal ion) is attached to neighboring atoms by at least two coordinate bonds in such a way as to form a closed chain —*vt.* **-lat′ed, -lat′ing 1** to cause (a metal ion) to react with another molecule to form a chelate **2** *Med.* to extract (a metal) from the blood by using a chelating agent, as in the treatment for lead poisoning —**che·la′tion** *n.* —**che′la′tor** *n.*

che·lic·er·a (kə lis′ər ə) *n., pl.* **-er·ae′** (-ər ē′) ⟦ModL < Gr *chēlē*, claw (see CHELA) + *keras*, HORN⟧ either of the first pair of appendages of spiders and other arachnids, used for grasping and crushing —**che·lic′er·ate′** (-ər āt′, -ər it) *adj.*

che·lif·er·ous (kə lif′ər əs) *adj.* bearing chelae

che·li·form (kē′lə fôrm′) *adj.* having the form of a chela

Chel·le·an (shel′ē ən) *adj.* ⟦Fr *chelléen*, after *Chelles*, suburb of Paris where the tools were found⟧ ABBEVILLIAN

che·loid (kē′loid′) *n. alt. sp. of* KELOID

che·lo·ni·an (kə lō′nē ən) *adj.* ⟦< ModL *Chelonia* < Gr *chelōnē* (< IE base **ghelou-*, turtle) + -AN⟧ of, like, or being a turtle —*n.* a turtle

Chel·sea (chel′sē) former borough of London, now part of the borough of Kensington and Chelsea

Chel·ten·ham (chelt′'n ham′; *Brit* chelt′nəm, -'n əm) city in Gloucestershire, SW England

Chel·ya·binsk (chel yä′binsk) city in SW Russia, in the S Urals

Chel·yus·kin (chel yoos′kin), **Cape** northernmost point of Asia, on the Taimyr Peninsula, Siberia

chem (*often, for 3,* kem) *abbrev.* **1** chemical(s) **2** chemist **3** chemistry

chem·ic (kem′ik) *adj.* **1** [Archaic] of alchemy; alchemic **2** [Old Poet.] chemical

chem·i·cal (kem′i kəl) *adj.* ⟦prec. + -AL⟧ **1** of or having to do with chemistry **2** made by or used in chemistry **3** operated or made by the use of chemicals [*chemical* burns] ☆**4** of or involving the use of a drug, alcoholic liquor, etc. [*chemical* dependency] —*n.* **1** any substance used in or obtained by a chemical process ☆**2** [Slang] a drug, alcoholic beverage, etc. —**chem′i·cal·ly** *adv.*

chemical abuse the habitual use of a mood-altering drug, alcoholic beverage, etc. —**chemical abuser**

chemical engineering the science or profession of applying chemistry to industrial uses —**chemical engineer**

chemical warfare the use of chemical weapons in war

chemical weapon a chemical, such as poisonous gas, or a chemical device, such as a flamethrower or an incendiary bomb, used, or intended for use, as a weapon

chem·i·lu·mi·nes·cence (kem′i lo͞o′mə nes′əns) *n.* visible light produced by chemical action and not accompanied by heat, including bioluminescence —**chem′i·lu′mi·nes′cent** *adj.*

che·min de fer (shə man′ də fer′) ⟦Fr, a railroad, lit., road of iron⟧ a kind of baccarat, a gambling game

che·mise (shə mēz′) *n.* ⟦ME < OFr < LL *camisia*, shirt, tunic, prob. via Gaul < Gmc **chamithja-* (> OE *hemethe*, Ger *hemd*, shirt) < IE base **kem-*, to cover, cloak > HEAVEN⟧ **1** a woman's undergarment somewhat like a loose, short slip **2** SHIFT (*n. 7b*)

chem·i·sette (shem′i zet′) *n.* ⟦Fr, dim. of *chemise*: see prec.⟧ a detachable shirt front formerly worn by women to fill in the neckline of a dress

chem·i·sorb (kem′i sôrb′, -zôrb′) *vt.* ⟦CHEMI(CAL) + (AD)SORB⟧ to bind (a substance) chemically onto the surface layer of an adsorbent —**chem′i·sorp′tion** *n.*

chem·ist (-ist) *n.* ⟦aphetic < ALCHEMIST⟧ **1** an expert or specialist in chemistry **2** [Brit.] a pharmacist **3** [Obs.] an alchemist

chem·is·try (kem′is trē) *n., pl.* **-tries** ⟦prec. + -RY⟧ **1** the science dealing with the composition and properties of substances, and with the reactions by which substances are produced from or converted into other substances **2** the application of this to a specified subject or field of activity **3** the chemical properties, composition, reactions, and uses of a substance **4** any process of synthesis or analysis similar to that used in chemistry [*the chemistry* of wit] **5** [Informal] *a)* the makeup of a person, group, situation, etc. *b)* interaction between people, esp. with respect to emotional or intellectual qualities; rapport *c)* mutual sexual attraction

Chem·nitz (kem′nits′) city in E Germany, in the state of Saxony: see KARL-MARX-STADT

che·mo (kē′mō) *n.* [Informal] a regimen of CHEMOTHERAPY for treating cancer

che·mo- (kē′mō, -mə; kem′ō, -ə) *combining form* of, with, or by chemicals or chemistry [*chemurgy*]: also, before a vowel, **chem-**

che·mo·au·to·tro·phic (kē′mō ôt′ō träf′ik, kem′ō-) *adj.* ⟦prec. + AUTOTROPHIC⟧ producing organic matter by the use of energy obtained by oxidation of certain chemicals with carbon dioxide as the carbon source: said of some bacteria —**che′mo·au′to·tro′phi·cal·ly** *adv.* —**che′mo·au·tot′ro·phy** (-ô tä′trə fē) *n.*

che·mo·kine (kē′mō kīn′) *n.* ⟦CHEMO- + *-kine* (as in CYTOKINE)⟧ any of various small cytokines that attract white blood cells to the site of an infection

che·mo·pro·phy·lax·is (-prō′fə laks′is) *n., pl.* **-lax′es′** (-ēz′) the prevention of disease by the use of chemical drugs —**che′mo·pro′phy·lac′tic** (-lak′tik) *adj.*

che·mo·re·cep·tor (-ri sep′tər) *n.* **1** *Physiol.* a component of a nerve ending, esp. a protein, that binds chemicals that stimulate sensations of taste, smell, etc. **2** *Anat.* a sense organ responsive to chemical stimuli —**che′mo·re·cep′tive** *adj.*

chem·os·mo·sis (kem′äs mō′sis) *n.* chemical action between substances that are separated by a semipermeable membrane —**chem′os·mot′ic** (-mät′ik) *adj.*

chem·o·sphere (kem′ə sfir′, kē′mə-) *n.* an atmospheric zone about 19 to 80 km (11.8 to 49.7 mi) above the earth's surface, in which photochemical reactions take place

chem·o·stat (kem′ō stat′) *n.* ⟦CHEMO- + -STAT⟧ an apparatus designed to grow bacteria indefinitely while keeping the conditions and colony size constant by having a continuous flow of liquid nutrient wash the colony and steadily remove bacteria

che·mo·ster·i·lant (kē′mō ster′ə lənt, kem′ō-) *n.* any process or chemical compound that can produce sterility, used esp. in insect control

che·mo·sur·ger·y (-sur′jər ē) *n.* the removal of diseased tissue or abnormal growths by using chemical substances

che·mo·syn·the·sis (-sin′thə sis) *n.* the synthesis by certain bacteria of organic compounds from carbon dioxide and water by the use of energy obtained by the oxidation of certain chemicals, as hydrogen sulfide or ammonia: see also PHOTOSYNTHESIS —**che′mo·syn·thet′ic** (-sin thet′ik) *adj.* —**che′mo·syn·thet′i·cal·ly** *adv.*

che·mo·tax·is (-taks′is) *n.* ⟦ModL: see CHEMO- & -TAXIS⟧ the positive or negative response of certain living cells and organisms to a chemical —**che′mo·tac′tic** (-tak′tik) *adj.* —**che′mo·tac′ti·cal·ly** *adv.*

che·mo·tax·on·o·my (-taks än′ə mē) *n.* the biological classification of plants and animals using comparative biochemistry, esp. by studying certain proteins

che·mo·ther·a·py (-ther′ə pē) *n.* ⟦Ger *chemotherapie*, coined (*c.* 1907) by Paul EHRLICH: see CHEMO- & THERAPY⟧ the prevention or treatment of disease by the administration of drugs; specif., the treatment of cancer by means of a regimen of cytotoxins or other anti-cancer drugs: often **che′mo·ther′a·peu′tics** (-ther′ə pyo͞ot′iks) —**che′mo·ther′a·peu′tic** *adj.* —**che′mo·ther′a·peu′ti·cal·ly** *adv.* —**che′mo·ther′a·pist** *n.*

che·mot·ro·pism (kə mä′trə piz′əm, kem ä′-; kem′ō trō′-) *n.* ⟦CHEMO- + TROPISM⟧ the tendency of certain plants or other organisms to turn or bend under the influence of chemical substances —**che·mo·trop·ic** (kē′mō träp′ik, kem′ō-) *adj.*

chem·trail (kem′trāl′) *n.* ⟦CHEM(ICAL) + (CON)TRAIL⟧ any of certain contrails believed by some to contain dangerous chemical agents being dispersed as by the government or military

chem·ur·gy (kem′ər jē) *n.* ⟦CHEM(O)- + -URGY⟧ the branch of chemistry dealing with the utilization of organic products, esp. from farms, in the manufacture of new products not classed as food or clothing (e.g., soybeans as a base for plastics or the production of methane from animal waste or garbage) —**che·mur·gic** (ke mur′jik, kem ur′-) *adj.*

Che·nab (chi näb′) river rising in N India, flowing through Jammu and Kashmir and then southwest into the Sutlej River in Pakistan: *c.* 675 mi (1,086 km)

Chen·chi·ang (jen′jē äŋ′) *a former transliteration of* ZHENJIANG

Cheng·chow or **Cheng·chou** (jen′jou′) *a former transliteration of* ZHENGZHOU

Cheng·de (chuŋ′du′) city in NE Hebei province, in NE China, northeast of Beijing: the former summer residence of the Manchu emperors of China

Cheng·du (chuŋ′do͞o′) city in SC China; capital of Sichuan province

Cheng·teh (chuŋ′du′) *a former transliteration of* CHENGDE

Cheng·tu (chuŋ′do͞o′) *a former transliteration of* CHENGDU

che·nille (shə nēl′) *n.* ⟦Fr, lit., hairy caterpillar < L *canicula*, dim. of *canis*, dog (see HOUND[1]): from its hairy pile⟧ **1** a tufted, velvety yarn used for trimming, embroidery, etc. **2** a fabric filled or woven with such yarn, used for rugs, bedspreads, etc.

che·nin blanc (shen′in bläŋk′; *Fr* shə nan blän′) ⟦Fr < OFr *(reisin) chenin*, (grape) of the dog + *blanc*, white⟧ [*also* **C- B-**] **1** a dry to semisweet white wine **2** the white grape from which it is made

Chen·nai (chen′ī′, chə nī′) seaport on the Coromandel Coast, India: capital of Tamil Nadu state

che·no·pod (kē nə päd′, ken′ə-) *n.* ⟦< ModL *Chenopodium*, name of the genus < Gr *chēn* (gen. *chēnos*), goose + -PODIUM⟧ any plant of the goosefoot family, as spinach

che·ong·sam or **che·ong-sam** (che ôŋ′säm′) *n.* ⟦Chin⟧ a high-necked, closefitting dress with the skirt slit partway up the sides, traditionally worn by Chinese women

Che·ops (kē′äps′) *Gr. name for* KHUFU

cheque (chek) *n. Brit. sp. of* CHECK (*n.* 10)

cheq·uer (chek′ər) *n., vt. Brit. sp. of* CHECKER[1]

Cher (sher) river in central France, flowing northwest into the Loire near Tours: *c.* 200 mi (322 km)

cher·chez la femme (sher shā lä fäm′) ⟦Fr⟧ look for the woman: said humorously to suggest that a woman may be the cause of a problem or puzzle

Che·re·po·vets (cher′ə pə vets′) city in NE Russia, on the Rybinsk Reservoir

cher·i·moy·a (cher′ə moi′ə) *n.* ⟦Sp *chirimoya* < ?⟧ **1** a subtropical South American fruit tree (*Annona cherimola*) of the custard-apple family having heart-shaped, edible fruit with a rough skin and white pulp **2** this fruit

cher·ish (cher′ish) *vt.* ⟦ME *cherischen* < extended stem of OFr *cherir* < *cher*, dear < L *carus*: see CHARITY⟧ **1** to hold dear; feel or show love for [to *cherish* one's family] **2** to take good care of; protect; foster [to *cherish* one's rights] **3** to cling to the idea or feeling of [to *cherish* a hope] —*SYN.* APPRECIATE

Cher·kas·sy (chər kas′ē, -käs-) city & port in central Ukraine, on the Dnieper

Cher·ni·gov (cher nē′gəf) city in NC Ukraine

Cher·no·byl (cher nō′bəl) city in NC Ukraine: site of a nuclear power plant where a serious accident occurred in 1986

Cher·nov·tsy (cher nuf tsē′) city in W Ukraine, on the Prut River

cher·no·zem (cher′nə zem′, -zyôm′) *n.* ⟦Russ *černozem* < *černaja*, fem. of *černyj*, black + *zemlja*, earth: for IE base see HOMO[1]⟧ a black topsoil, rich in humus and lime, found in grasslands of central European Russia

Cher·o·kee (cher′ə kē′) *n.* ⟦< extinct dial. form of Cherokee *tsalaki*, a self-designation⟧ **1** *pl.* **-kees′** or **-kee′** a member of a North American Indian people formerly inhabiting a large area of the S Appalachian Mountains, now living in Oklahoma and North Carolina **2** the Iroquoian language of this people

☆**Cherokee rose** an evergreen climbing rose (*Rosa laevigata*), with fragrant, large, white flowers and glossy leaves, native to China but now growing wild in the S U.S.

che·root (shə ro͞ot′) *n.* ⟦< Tamil *churuṭṭu*, a roll⟧ a cigar with both ends cut square

cherries jubilee ⟦< ?⟧ a dessert of dark sweet cherries served in a flaming brandy sauce over vanilla ice cream

cher·ry (cher′ē) *n., pl.* **-ries** ⟦ME *cheri* < Anglo-Fr *cherise* (taken as pl.) < OFr *cerise* < VL **ceresia* < Gr *kerasion*, cherry < *kerasos*, cherry tree < ? IE base **ker-*; derived by the ancients from *Cerasus*, city on the Black Sea: the city's name is itself from the cherries grown in the area⟧ **1** a small, fleshy fruit containing a smooth, hard pit and ranging from yellow to very dark red, including sweet, sour, and duke cherries **2** any of various prunus trees that bear this fruit **3** the wood of such a tree **4** the bright-red color of certain cherries **5** [Slang] ☆*a)* the hymen *b)* virginity: mildly vulgar —*adj.* **1** bright-red **2** made of cherry wood **3** made with cherries **4** having a flavor like that of cherries **5** [Slang] new or like new [a used car in *cherry* condition]

cherry bomb a round, red, powerful firecracker

cherry laurel any of various prunus shrubs having thick, glossy, evergreen leaves

cher·ry-pick (cher′ē pik′) *vt., vi.* [Informal] to select (the best or most desirable, valuable, etc. items) from a number of options, often, specif., before others have an opportunity to do so —**cher′ry-pick′ing** *n.*

☆**cherry picker** [Slang] an elevator tower, or now usually a crane boom, mounted on a truck, with a platform from which spacecraft on launchers, raised electric power lines, etc. can be serviced

cherry plum a small prunus tree (*Prunus cerasifera*), often used in grafting other varieties of plums; myrobalan

☆**cher·ry·stone** (-stōn′) *n.* a small quahog clam: also **cherrystone clam**

cherry tomato a type of tomato that is about the size of a large cherry or a small walnut and is often used in salads

chert (churt) *n.* ⟦< ?⟧ an extremely dense type of quartz, including jasper and flint, having a dull, opaque luster and made up of microscopic crystals —**chert′y** (-ē) *adj.* **chert′i·er**, **chert′i·est**

cher·ub (cher′əb) *n., pl.* **cher′ubs**; for 1, 2, & 3 usually **-u·bim′** (-yo͞o bim′, -ə bim′) or **-u·bims′** ⟦ME < OE *ceruphin* < LL(Ec) *cherub* < Heb *kerūbh* < Akkadian *karūbu*, gracious < *karābu*, to bless⟧ **1** *Bible* one of the winged heavenly beings that support the throne of God or act as guardian spirits: Ezek. 10 **2** *Christian Theol.* any of the second order of angels, usually ranked just below the seraphim **3** a representation of one of the cherubim as, in early art, a winged angel clothed in red or, later, a chubby, rosy-faced child with wings **4** a person, esp. a child, with a sweet, innocent face —**che·ru·bic** (chə ro͞o′bik) *adj.* —**che·ru′bi·cal·ly** *adv.*

Che·ru·bi·ni (ke′ro͞o bē′nē), **(Maria) Lu·i·gi (Carlo Zenobio Salvatore)** (lo͞o ē′jē) 1760-1842; It. composer

cher·vil (chur′vəl) *n.* ⟦ME *chervel* < OE *cerfelle* < L *chaerephyllum* < Gr *chairephyllon* < *chairein*, to rejoice (see CHARISMA) + *phyllon*, leaf: see -PHYLL⟧ **1** an annual herb (*Anthriscus cerefolium*) of the umbel family, whose leaves are used for flavoring salads, soups, etc. **2** a similar plant (*Chaerophyllum bulbosum*) grown for its carrotlike root **3** SWEET CICELY (sense 2)

Cher·yl (sher′əl) *n.* a feminine name: dim. *Cher, Cheri*; var. *Sheryl*

Ches·a·peake (ches′ə pēk′) ⟦after fol.⟧ city in SE Va., at the base of Chesapeake Bay

Chesapeake Bay ⟦< Algonquian, lit., place on a big river⟧ arm of the Atlantic, extending north into Va. and Md.: *c.* 200 mi (320 km) long

Chesh·ire (chesh′ir, -ər) county in W England: 900 sq mi (2,331 sq km)

Cheshire cat a proverbial grinning cat from Cheshire, England, esp. one described in Lewis Carroll's *Alice's Adventures in Wonderland*

Chesh·van (khesh vän′) *n. var. of* HESHVAN

chess[1] (ches) *n.* ⟦ME *ches, chesse* < OFr *esches*, pl. of *eschec*: see CHECK⟧ a game of skill played on a chessboard by two players, each with 16 chessmen limited in movement according to kind, the object being to checkmate the opponent's king

chess[2] (ches) *n.* ⟦< ?⟧ any of several varieties of brome grass, esp. a weedy kind (*Bromus secalinus*) found in fields of grain

chess·board (ches′bôrd′) *n.* a square board with 64 squares of two alternating colors, used in chess and checkers

chess·man (-mən) *n., pl.* **-men** (-mən) ⟦altered (infl. by MAN) < ME *chesmeyne*, lit., chess retinue < *meyne*, household < OFr *mesnie* < VL **mansionata* < L *mansio*: see MANSION⟧ any of the pieces or pawns used in the game of chess: each player has 1 king, 1 queen, 2 rooks (or castles), 2 knights, 2 bishops, and 8 pawns: see PIECE (*n.* 3g)

chess pie ⟦< dial. *chess*, tier, layer (< ?): so named from being carried in tiers or stacks⟧ a dessert made of a custardlike mixture of butter, sugar, eggs, etc., baked in a pie shell

chest (chest) *n.* ⟦ME *chest, chiste* < OE, ON, or L: OE *cist* & ON *kista* < L *cista* < Gr *kistē*, a box, basket < IE **kista*, woven container > OIr *cess*, basket⟧ **1** a box with a lid and, often, a lock, for storing or shipping things **2** [Rare] a place where money or funds are kept; treasury **3** CHEST OF DRAWERS **4** a cabinet, as for holding medical supplies or toiletries **5** *a)* the part of the body enclosed by the ribs, breastbone, and diaphragm; thorax *b)* the outside front part of this —**get something off one's chest** [Informal] to unburden oneself of some trouble, annoyance, etc. by talking about it

chest·ed (ches′tid) *adj.* having a (specified kind of) chest or thorax: used mainly in compounds [hollow-*chested*]

Ches·ter[1] (ches′tər) *n.* ⟦after fol. (the city)⟧ a masculine name: dim. *Chet*

Ches·ter[2] (ches′tər) **1** ⟦OE *Ceastre*, contr. < L *Legacaestir*, for L *legionum castra*, camp of the legions⟧ city in Cheshire, NW England, south of Liverpool **2** *former name for* CHESHIRE

ches·ter·field (ches′tər fēld′) *n.* ⟦after a 19th-c. Earl of *Chesterfield*⟧ **1** a single-breasted topcoat, usually with a fly front and a velvet collar **2** *a)* a kind of sofa, heavily stuffed and with upright ends *b)* [Cdn.] any sofa

Ches·ter·field (-fēld′), 4th Earl of (*Philip Dormer Stanhope*) 1694-1773; Eng. statesman & writer on manners —**Ches′ter·field′i·an** *adj.*

Ches·ter·ton (ches′tər tən), **G(ilbert) K(eith)** 1874-1936; Eng. writer

Chester White ⟦after *Chester* County, Pa., where reputedly first bred⟧ a variety of large, white hog

chest·nut (ches′nut′, chest′-) *n.* ⟦< *chesten-nut* < ME *chesteine* < OFr *chastaigne* < L *castanea* < Gr *kastaneia*⟧ **1** the smooth-shelled, sweet, edible nut of any of a genus (*Castanea*) of trees of the beech family **2** the tree that it grows on **3** the wood of this tree **4** HORSE CHESTNUT **5** reddish brown **6** a reddish-brown horse **7** the hard callus on the inner side of a horse's leg ☆**8** [Informal] *a)* an old, stale joke or phrase; cliché *b)* a very familiar story, piece of music, etc. that is too often repeated —*adj.* reddish-brown —**pull someone's chestnuts out of the fire** ⟦see CAT'S-PAW⟧ to do a dangerous, hard, or unpleasant thing for someone else

☆**chestnut blight** a disease of chestnut trees, caused by a fungus (*Endothia parasitica*), that has virtually destroyed the American chestnut

chest of drawers an article of furniture, as for a bedroom, consisting of a frame containing a set of drawers, as for keeping clothing

☆**chest-on-chest** (chest′än chest′) *n.* a chest of drawers fitted onto another, somewhat larger one

chest register the lower register of the voice, in which the lower range of tones is produced

chest·y (ches′tē) *adj.* **chest′i·er**, **chest′i·est** [Informal] **1** *a)* having a large chest or thorax *b)* bosomy ☆**2** boastful, proud, or conceited

che·tah (chēt′ə) *n. alt. sp. of* CHEETAH

cheth (khet) *n. alt. sp. of* HET

chet·rum (chet′ro͝om) *n.* ⟦Bhutanese⟧ a monetary unit of Bhutan, equal to 1/100 of a ngultrum

Che·tu·mal (chä′to͞o mäl′) city in SE Mexico: capital of Quintana Roo

che·val-de-frise (shə val′ də frēz′) *n., pl.* **che·vaux′-de-frise′** (shə vō′-) ⟦Fr < *cheval*, a horse + *de*, of + *Frise*, FRIESLAND: first used by Frisians, who lacked cavalry, against Spaniards⟧ **1** an obstacle, usually a piece of wood with projecting spikes, formerly used to hinder enemy horsemen **2** a row of spikes or jagged glass set into the masonry on top of a wall to prevent escape or trespassing

che·val glass (shə val′) ⟦Fr *cheval*, horse, hence frame (see SAWHORSE) + GLASS⟧ a full-length mirror mounted on swivels in a frame

chev·a·lier (shev′ə lir′; *for 1 & 3, usually* shə val yā′) *n.* ⟦ME & Anglo-Fr *chevaler* < LL *caballarius*: see CAVALIER⟧ **1** a member of the lowest rank of the French Legion of Honor **2** a chivalrous man; gallant; cavalier **3** [Historical] a French noble of the lowest rank **4** [Archaic] a knight

che·ve·lure (shəv lür′) *n.* ⟦Fr, head of hair < L *capillatura*, the hair, a being hairy < *capillus*, hair: see CAPILLARY⟧ a head of hair; specif., a coiffure

Chev·i·ot (chev′ē ət; *also, and for 2 usually,* shev′ē ət) *n.* ⟦after fol.⟧ **1** any of a breed of sheep with short, dense wool 2 [*usually* **c-**] *a)* a rough wool fabric in a twill weave, formerly made from the wool of this sheep *b)* a cotton cloth resembling this

Chev·i·ot Hills (chē′vē ət, chev′ē ət) range of hills along the border between England & Scotland: highest point, 2,676 ft (816 m)

chè·vre or **chevre** (shev′rə) ***n.*** ⟦< Fr, goat's-milk cheese, she-goat < OFr, she-goat < L *capra,* fem. of *caper,* goat: see CAPRIOLE⟧ any of various usually soft cheeses made from goat's milk and varying widely in texture and strength of flavor

chev·ron (shev′rən) ***n.*** ⟦ME *cheveroun* < OFr *chevron,* orig., rafter < VL **caprione* < L *caper,* goat: see CAPRIOLE⟧ **1** a heraldic device in the shape of an inverted V **2** an insignia consisting of a V-shaped bar or bars, worn on the sleeve as of a military or police uniform to show rank or service

chev·ro·tain (shev′rə tān′, -tin) ***n.*** ⟦Fr *chevrotin,* orig., fawn during first half year < OFr *chevrot,* dim. of *chèvre,* she-goat < L *capra,* fem. of *caper,* goat: see CAPRIOLE⟧ any of a family (Tragulidae) of very small, hornless ruminants of S Asia and W Africa, having a three-chambered stomach; mouse deer

chev·y (chev′ē) ***n., pl.* chev′ies** ⟦< hunting cry *chivy,* in the ballad of *Chevy Chase* < CHEVIOT (HILLS)⟧ [Brit.] CHIVY — ***vt., vi.* chev′ied, chev′y·ing 1** [Brit.] CHIVY **2** to worry; fret

chew (cho͞o) ***vt.*** ⟦ME *chewen* < OE *ceowan,* to bite, chew < IE base **gjeu-,* to chew > Pers *jāvidan,* Ger *kauen*⟧ **1** to bite and grind or crush with the teeth; masticate **2** [Informal] to damage or destroy as by chewing; mangle, hack, etc.: often with *up* —***vi.* 1** to chew something ☆**2** [Informal] to chew tobacco —***n.* 1** the act of chewing **2** something chewed or for chewing; specif., a portion of tobacco for chewing —☆**chew out** [Slang] to rebuke severely; reprimand —**chew over 1** to think over; consider **2** to discuss at length — **chew the fat** (or **rag**) [Slang] to converse idly; chat —**chew the scenery** [Informal] to overact, as in a play or film —**chew′a·ble** ***adj.*** —**chew′er** ***n.***

☆**chewing gum** a gummy substance, such as chicle, flavored and sweetened for chewing

☆**che·wink** (chə wiŋk′) ***n.*** ⟦echoic of one of its calls⟧ any of the various forms of the rufous-sided towhee found in E North America: see TOWHEE

chew·y (cho͞o′ē) ***adj.*** **chew′i·er, chew′i·est** that needs much chewing [*chewy* candy] —**chew′i·ness** ***n.***

Chey·enne[1] (shī an′, -en′) ***n.*** ⟦Fr < Dakota *šahíyena*: meaning unknown⟧ **1** *pl.* **-ennes′** or **-enne′** a member of a North American Indian people that migrated from Minnesota to the headwaters of the Platte River, and into S Colorado and SW Kansas, and now lives in Oklahoma **2** the Algonquian language of this people

Chey·enne[2] (shī an′, -en′) ⟦after prec.⟧ **1** capital of Wyo., in the SE part **2** river in E Wyo. and W S.Dak., flowing northeast into the Missouri: 527 mi (848 km)

Cheyne-Stokes respiration (chān′stōks′) ⟦after J. *Cheyne* (1777-1836), Scot physician, & W. *Stokes* (1804-78), Ir physician⟧ respiration characterized by cycles of deep, rapid breathing and weak, slow breathing, as in cases of heart failure or coma

chez (shā) ***prep.*** ⟦Fr⟧ at the home of; by; at

CHF *abbrev.* congestive heart failure

chg *abbrev.* **1** change **2** charge

chgd *abbrev.* charged

chi[2] (chē) ***n.*** ⟦Chin *qì,* lit., air, breath: also transliterated, variously, *chi, ch'i,* and, via Jpn, *ki*⟧ in certain Asian systems of belief, medicine, martial arts, etc., the universal life energy that flows around and through the body: blockage or imbalance of this energy can result in illness

chi[1] (kī, kē) ***n.*** ⟦Gr⟧ the twenty-second letter of the Greek alphabet (Χ, χ)

☆**chi·a** (chē′ə) ***n.*** ⟦< MexSp < Nahuatl⟧ a type of sage (*Salvia hispanica*) of Mexico and Central America, bearing oily, edible seeds

Chi·an (kī′ən) ***adj.*** of Chios (Khíos) —***n.*** a person born or living in Chios (Khíos)

Chiang Kai-shek (chaŋ′ kī shek′; *Chin* jyäŋ′-) (born *Chiang Chung-chen*) 1888-1975; Chin. statesman & general: head of Nationalist government on Taiwan (1950-75)

Chiang Mai or **Chiang·mai** (jyäŋ′mī′) city in NW Thailand, on a headstream of the Chao Phraya

Chi·an·ti (kē än′tē, -an′-) ***n.*** ⟦It, after this region in Tuscany⟧ [*also* **c-**] **1** a dry red wine produced in a region of Tuscany in Italy **2** a red wine of similar type made elsewhere

Chi·a·pas (chē ä′pəs) state of SE Mexico, on the Guatemalan border & the Gulf of Tehuantepec: 28,528 sq mi (73,887 sq km); cap. Tuxtla Gutiérrez

chi·a·ro·scu·ro (kē är′ə skoor′ō, -skyoor′-) ***n., pl.* -ros** ⟦It, lit., clear dark < L *clarus,* CLEAR + *obscurus,* dark: see OBSCURE⟧ **1** light and shade in a painting, drawing, etc. treated so as to produce the illusion of depth, a dramatic effect, etc. **2** a style of painting, drawing, etc. emphasizing this **3** a painting, drawing, etc. in which chiaroscuro is used —**chi·a′ro·scu′rist** ***n.***

chi·asm (kī′az′əm) ***n.*** **1** CHIASMA (***n.*** 1 & 2) **2** CHIASMUS

chi·as·ma (kī az′mə) ***n., pl.*** **chi·as′ma·ta** (-tə) ⟦ModL < Gr *chiasma,* a crosspiece < *chiasmos,* placing crosswise < *chiazein,* to mark with a *chi* (χ)⟧ **1** a crossing or intersection of the optic nerves in the hypothalamus of the brain **2** a point of contact between chromosomes during meiosis where two chromatids interchange corresponding segments **3** any crosswise function

chi·as·mus (kī az′məs) ***n., pl.* -as′mi′** (-mī′) ⟦ModL < Gr *chiasmos*: see prec.⟧ *Rhetoric* inversion of the second of two parallel phrases, clauses, etc. (Ex.: she went to Paris; to New York went he) —**chi·as′tic** (-as′tik) ***adj.***

chiaus (chous, choush) ***n.*** ⟦Turk *chāush*⟧ a Turkish messenger, emissary, sergeant, etc.

Chi·ba (chē′bä) city on the E coast of Honshu, Japan, on Tokyo Bay, opposite Tokyo

Chib·cha (chib′chə) ***n.*** ⟦AmSp < Chibcha *zipa,* chief, leader⟧ **1** *pl.* **-chas** or **-cha** a member of a South American Indian people that lived in central Colombia and had a highly developed civilization **2** the language of this people, no longer spoken

Chib·chan (-chən) ***adj.*** designating or of various linguistic groups of South and Central American Indians: some of the languages are still spoken today

chi·bouk or **chi·bouque** (chi bo͝ok′, -bo͞ok′) ***n.*** ⟦Fr *chibouque* < Turk *chibūq*⟧ a Turkish tobacco pipe with a very long stem and a clay bowl

chic (shēk) ***n.*** ⟦Fr, orig., subtlety < MLowG *schick,* order, skill or MHG *schicken,* behavior, arrangement⟧ smart elegance of style and manner: said esp. of women or their clothes —☆***adj.*** **chic′er, chic′est** stylish in a smart, pleasing way

chi·ca (chē′kə) ***n.*** ⟦Sp⟧ [*also in italics*] [Slang] a girl or young woman: often a term of affectionate address

Chi·ca·go (shi kä′gō, -kô′-) ⟦< Fr < Algonquian, lit., place of the onion: from the wild onions growing there⟧ city and port in NE Ill., on Lake Michigan —**Chi·ca′go·an** ***n.***

☆**chi·ca·lo·te** (chik′ə lōt′ē, -ā) ***n.*** ⟦AmSp, name used for various thorny plants < Nahuatl *chicalotl* < *chicaloyo,* thorny⟧ the prickly poppy (*Argemone platyceras*) of Mexico and the SW U.S., with large, white flowers

☆**Chi·ca·na** (chi kä′nə) ***n., pl.* -nas** ⟦see CHICANO⟧ a woman or girl of Mexican descent who is a citizen of, or is living in, the U.S. —***adj.*** of Chicanas

chi·cane (shi kān′) ***n.*** ⟦Fr < *chicaner,* to pettifog, quibble < MLowG *schikken,* to arrange, bring about⟧ **1** CHICANERY **2** an S-shaped section of a track or course, as for motor racing or skiing, designed to slow down the racers —***vi.*** **-caned′, -can′ing** to use chicanery —***vt.* 1** to trick **2** to get by chicanery

chi·can·er·y (shi kān′ər ē) ***n.*** ⟦Fr *chicanerie* < prec.⟧ **1** the use of clever but tricky talk or action to deceive, evade, etc., as in legal dealings **2** *pl.* **-er·ies** an instance of this —***SYN.*** DECEPTION

☆**Chi·ca·no** (chi kä′nō) ***n., pl.* -nos** ⟦aphetic for dial. pronun. of AmSp *Mexicano,* Mexican⟧ a citizen of, or a person living in, the U.S. who is of Mexican descent —***adj.*** of Chicanos

Chi·chén It·zá (chē chen′ ēt sä′) ruined Mayan city in Yucatán, SE Mexico: fl. 10th-12th cent.

chi·chi or **chi-chi** (shē′shē) ***adj.*** ⟦Fr⟧ **1** extremely chic; very smart, elegant, or sophisticated **2** affected, showy, effete, etc. —***n.*** a chichi quality, thing, or person

Chi·chi·haerh (chē′chē′här′) *a former transliteration of* QIQIHAR

chick (chik) ***n.*** ⟦ME *chike,* var. of *chiken,* CHICKEN⟧ **1** a young chicken **2** any young bird **3** [Now Rare] a child: term of endearment ☆**4** [Slang] a young woman —***adj.*** ☆[Slang] intended for, or suited to the tastes of, young women: often a disparaging or dismissive term: see also CHICK FLICK, CHICK LIT

☆**chick·a·dee** (chik′ə dē′) ***n.*** ⟦echoic of its call⟧ any of various titmice (genus *Parus*), generally with black, gray, and white feathers

Chick·a·mau·ga (chik′ə mô′gə) ⟦AmInd: meaning uncert.⟧ creek in NW Ga.: site of a Civil War battle (Sept., 1863) in which Confederate forces routed the Union army

☆**chick·a·ree** (chik′ə rē′) ***n.*** ⟦echoic of its cry⟧ a reddish squirrel (*Tamiasciurus douglasi*) of the W U.S.

Chick·a·saw (chik′ə sô′, -sä′) ***n.*** ⟦< Chickasaw *chikashsha,* a self-designation, or a Muskogean cognate of this⟧ **1** *pl.* **-saws′** or **-saw′** a member of a North American Indian people that formerly lived in N Mississippi and Alabama and now lives in Oklahoma **2** the Muskogean language of this people, closely related to Choctaw

☆**chic·kee** (chik′ē, chi kē′) ***n.*** ⟦< ? AmInd (Creek)⟧ a Seminole Indian house built on stilts, with open sides and a thatched roof of palm leaves

chick·en (chik′ən) ***n.*** ⟦ME *chicken* < OE *cycen* < WGmc **kiukina* < **kiuk-*; like COCK[1], of echoic orig.; akin to MLowG *kûken* (Du *kuiken, kieken*)⟧ **1** a common gallinaceous farm bird (*Gallus domesticus*) raised for its edible eggs or flesh; hen or rooster, esp. a young one: classed in a family (Phasianidae) that includes pheasants, quail, and peafowl **2** the flesh of this bird **3** any young bird; chick **4** a young or inexperienced person **5** [Slang] *a)* ⟦used of a person regarded as being timid as a chicken: revival of an old usage first recorded in *Cymbeline,* V, iii, 42 (1611) by SHAKESPEARE⟧ a timid or cowardly person *b)* a young male homosexual **6** ⟦< CHICKENSHIT⟧ [Mil. Slang] petty insistence on rules —***adj.* 1** made of chicken [*chicken* croquettes] **2** small and tender [*a chicken* lobster] **3** [Slang] timid or cowardly ☆**4** ⟦cf. *n.* 6⟧ [Mil. Slang] characterized by unnecessary discipline or pettiness —☆***vi.*** [Slang] to lose courage and abandon a plan or action: usually with *out* —**count one's chickens before they are hatched** to count on something that may not materialize —☆**play chicken 1** to engage in a test of courage in which, typically, two vehicles are driven directly toward one another in order to see which driver will swerve away first **2** [Slang] to engage in mutual challenges or threats, hoping the opponent will withdraw before actual conflict or collision

chick·en-and-egg (-ənd eg′) ***adj.*** ⟦< common expression, "Which came first, the *chicken* or the *egg?*"⟧ of or relating to a paradoxical situation, question, etc. involving two factors, each of which in turn causes or leads to the other

chicken breast PIGEON BREAST

☆**chicken colonel** ⟦from the eagle insignia worn on the shoulders⟧ [Mil. Slang] an officer with the rank of full colonel

chicken divan ⟦after the *Divan Parisien*, NYC restaurant where invented (1930s)⟧ [*sometimes* **c- D-**] a casserole of boned chicken breast, broccoli or asparagus spears, and cheese sauce

☆**chicken feed** [Slang] an insignificant sum of money

☆**chick·en-fried** (-frīd′) ***adj.*** coated with seasoned flour or batter and fried [*chicken-fried* steak]

☆**chicken hawk** **1** any of various hawks, esp. an accipiter, that prey, or are reputed to prey, on barnyard fowl ☆**2** [Slang] an adult male who seeks out boys or young men for sexual activity **3** ⟦CHICKEN (***n.*** *5a* or ***adj.*** 3) + HAWK[1] (***n.*** 2)⟧ [Slang] a person, esp. a politician, who avidly supports his country's military action but has avoided military service himself in the past: term of contempt used to imply hypocrisy or cowardice

chick·en-heart·ed (-härt′id) ***adj.*** cowardly; timid: also ☆**chick′en-liv′ered** (-liv′ərd)

chicken Ki·ev (kē ev′, kē′ev′) boned chicken breasts pounded until thin, wrapped around lumps of herbed butter, breaded, and fried in butter or deep fat, and usually served with kasha or brown rice

Chicken Little ⟦after the chicken in a children's story who, after being struck by a falling object, warns that the sky is falling⟧ [Informal] a person who spreads baseless or exaggerated reports of danger; alarmist

chick·en·pox (-päks′) ***n.*** ⟦prob. so named with ref. to its mildness as compared with smallpox⟧ an acute, contagious viral disease, usually of young children, characterized by fever and eruptions; varicella

chick·en·shit (-shit′) [Slang] ***adj.*** **1** petty or minor **2** cowardly —***n.*** someone or something that is chickenshit Mildly vulgar

☆**chicken snake** RAT SNAKE

☆**chicken wire** light, pliable wire fencing, used esp. for enclosing chicken coops

☆**chick flick** [Informal] a movie regarded as especially suited to the tastes of young women: see note at CHICK (***adj.***)

☆**chick lit** [Informal] fiction regarded as especially suited to the tastes of young women: see note at CHICK (***adj.***) —**chick′-lit′** ***adj.***

chick·pea (chik′pē′) ***n.*** ⟦for *chick pea* < ME & OFr *chiche* < L *cicer*, pea⟧ **1** a bushy annual plant (*Cicer arietinum*) of the pea family, with short, hairy pods containing usually two seeds; garbanzo **2** the edible seed

chick·weed (-wēd′) ***n.*** ⟦< earlier *chickenweed*: so named because eaten by *chickens*⟧ any of several low-growing plants (esp. genera *Cerastium* and *Stellaria*) of the pink family, often found as weeds in lawns and gardens

Chi·cla·yo (chē klä′yō) city in NW Peru

☆**chic·le** (chik′əl) ***n.*** ⟦AmSp < Nahuatl *čikλi*⟧ a gumlike substance made from the milky juice of the sapodilla tree and used in making chewing gum

chic·ly (shēk′lē) ***adv.*** in a chic style or manner; smartly and elegantly

chic·ness (shēk′nəs) ***n.*** the condition of being chic

☆**chi·co** (chē′kō) ***n.***, *pl.* **-cos** ⟦< AmSp *chicalote*, CHICALOTE⟧ GREASEWOOD (sense 1)

chic·o·ry (chik′ə rē) ***n.***, *pl.* **-ries** ⟦ME *cicory* < OFr *cicorée* < L *cichorium* < Gr *kichora, kichoreia*, chicory, endive, succory⟧ **1** a perennial weedy plant (*Cichorium intybus*) of the composite family, usually with blue flowers: the young leaves are used as a salad **2** its root, roasted and ground, as for mixing with coffee

Chi·cou·ti·mi (shi ko͞o′ti mē′) ⟦< Algonquian *shkoutimeou*, end of the deep water⟧ *see* SAGUENAY (sense 1)

Chic·xu·lub (chēk′so͞o′lo͞ob′) town in NW Yucatán, on the Gulf of Mexico: it is located near the center of a very large impact crater (**Chicxulub Crater**) that was formed *c.* 65 million years ago by a meteorite estimated to be *c.* 6 miles (*c.* 10 km) in diameter

chide (chīd) ***vt., vi.*** **chid′ed** or **chid** (chid), **chid′ed, chid,** or **chid·den** (chid′'n), **chid′ing** ⟦ME *chiden* < OE vi. *cidan*; not found outside OE⟧ to scold; now, usually, to reprove mildly —**chid′ing·ly** ***adv.***

chief (chēf) ***n.*** ⟦ME *chef, chief*, leader < OFr < VL **capum* < L *caput*, HEAD⟧ **1** the head or leader of a group, organization, etc.; person of highest title or authority **2** [Archaic] the most valuable or main part of anything **3** *Heraldry* the upper third of a shield **4** [*usually* **C-**] *Naut.* a chief engineer or chief petty officer —***adj.*** **1** highest, as in rank or office; foremost [the *chief* magistrate] **2** most important or significant; main; principal [the *chief* advantages] —***adv.*** [Archaic] chiefly —**in chief** **1** in the chief position; of highest title or authority [editor *in chief*] **2** [Archaic] chiefly —**chief′dom** ***n.***

SYN.—**chief** is applied to the person or thing first in rank, authority, importance, etc., and usually connotes subordination of all others [his *chief* problem was getting a job]; **principal** is applied to the person who directs or controls others [a *principal* clerk] or to the thing or person having precedence over all others by reason of size, position, importance, etc. [the *principal* products of Africa]; **main**, in strict usage, is applied to the thing, often part of a system or an extensive whole, that is preeminent in size, power, importance, etc. [the *main* line of a railroad]; **leading** stresses capacity for guiding, conducting, or drawing others [a *leading* light, question, etc.]; **foremost** suggests a being first by having moved ahead to that position [the *foremost* statesman of our time]; **capital** is applied to that which is ranked at the head of its kind or class because of its importance or its special significance [the *capital* city] —*ANT.* **subordinate, subservient**

☆**Chief Executive** the President of the U.S.

chief executive officer the highest executive officer of a company, organization, etc.

chief justice the presiding judge of a court made up of several judges

Chief Justice of the United States the presiding judge of the U.S. Supreme Court

chief·ly (chēf′lē) ***adv.*** **1** most of all; above all **2** mainly; mostly —***adj.*** of or like a chief [a *chiefly* rank]

☆**chief master sergeant** *U.S. Air Force* a noncommissioned officer of the highest rank

chief of staff **1** the head member of the staff officers of a division or higher unit in the armed forces, or of the Departments of the Army or Air Force **2** the head of any staff; esp., the head of the physicians and surgeons of a hospital

☆**chief petty officer** *U.S. Navy* an enlisted person ranking below a senior chief petty officer and above a petty officer first class

chief·tain (chēf′tən) ***n.*** ⟦ME *chevetaine* < OFr < LL *capitaneus*, chief in size: see CAPTAIN⟧ a chief or leader, esp. of a clan or tribe —**chief′tain·cy** ***n.***, *pl.* **-cies** —**chief′tain·ship′** ***n.***

chief warrant officer *U.S. Armed Forces* a warrant officer in one of the three highest grades

chiel (chēl) ***n.*** [Scot.] a young man: also **chield** (chēld)

chiff·chaff (chif′chaf′) ***n.*** ⟦echoic of its cry⟧ a small, olive-green and brown European warbler (*Phylloscopus collybita*), feeding mainly on insects and spiders

chif·fon (shi fän′; *also*, shif′än′) ***n.*** ⟦Fr, dim. of *chiffe*, a rag, piece of cloth < ? Ar *šiff*, light garment⟧ **1** a sheer, lightweight fabric of silk, nylon, etc. **2** [*pl.*] ribbons, laces, etc. used as accessories to a woman's dress —***adj.*** **1** made of chiffon **2** *Cooking* made light and porous as by the addition of stiffly beaten egg whites [lemon *chiffon* pie]

chif·fo·nade (shif′ə nād′, -näd′) ***n.*** ⟦Fr *chiffonnade*, akin to *chiffon*: see prec.⟧ lettuce, other vegetables, or various herbs cut into shreds or very thin strips, used esp. as a garnish

chif·fo·nier or **chif·fon·nier** (shif′ə nir′) ***n.*** ⟦Fr, chest of drawers, orig., ragpicker < CHIFFON⟧ a narrow, high bureau or chest of drawers, often with a mirror

chif·fo·robe or **chif·fe·robe** (shif′ə rōb′) ***n.*** ⟦prec. + (WARD)ROBE⟧ [Dial.] a wardrobe with drawers or shelves on one side

chig·ger (chig′ər) ***n.*** ⟦of Afr orig., as in Wolof *jiga*, insect⟧ ☆the tiny, red larva of a family (Trombiculidae) of mites, whose bite causes severe itching

chi·gnon (shēn′yän′) ***n.*** ⟦Fr, var. of *chaînon*, link < OFr *chaeignon*, chain, nape (of the neck) < VL **catenio*, dim. < L *catena*, CHAIN⟧ a knot or coil of hair worn at the back of the neck

chig·oe (chig′ō) ***n.***, *pl.* **-oes′** (-ōz′) ⟦< WInd native name⟧ a flea (*Tunga penetrans*) of tropical America and Africa: the female burrows into the skin, causing painful sores

Chi·hua·hua[1] (chi wä′wä) ☆***n.*** ⟦after fol.⟧ [*also* **c-**] any of a Mexican breed of very small dog with large, pointed ears

Chi·hua·hua[2] (chi wä′wä) **1** state of N Mexico, on the U.S. border: 95,401 sq mi (247,088 sq km) **2** capital of this state

Chi·ka·mat·su Mon·za·e·mon (chē′kä mät′so͞o mōn′zä e mōn′) (born *Sugimori Nobumori*) 1653-1724; Jpn. dramatist: called *the Shakespeare of Japan*: often shortened to *Chikamatsu*

chil- (kil) *combining form* CHILO-: used before a vowel

☆**chi·la·qui·les** (chē′lə kē′lās) ***pl.n.*** ⟦MexSp < Nahuatl⟧ a Mexican dish consisting of pieces of fried tortilla cooked in a thick sauce and garnished with cheese

chil·blain (chil′blān′) ***n.*** ⟦CHIL(L) + *blain* < OE *blegen*, a sore < IE **bhlei-* < base **bhel-*, to blow up, swell > BALL[1]⟧ a painful swelling or sore caused by exposure to cold, esp. on the fingers, toes, or ears —**chil′blained′** ***adj.***

child (chīld) ***n.***, *pl.* **chil′dren** ⟦ME, pl. *childre* (now dial. *childer; children* is double pl.) < OE *cild*, pl. *cild, cildru* < IE **gelt-*, a swelling up < base **gel-*, rounded (sense development: swelling → womb → fetus → offspring > Goth *kilthei*, womb, L *globus*, sphere⟧ **1** a human infant; baby **2** an unborn human offspring; fetus **3** a boy or girl in the period before puberty **4** a son or daughter; offspring **5** *a)* a descendant *b)* a member of a tribe, clan, etc. (*often used in pl.*) [*children* of Israel] **6** a person like a child in interests, judgment, etc., or one regarded as immature and childish **7** a person identified with a specified place, time, etc. [a *child* of the Renaissance] **8** a thing that springs from a specified source; product [a *child* of one's imagination] **9** [Archaic] CHILDE **10** [Brit. Dial.] a female infant —**with child** pregnant: said of a person —**child′less** ***adj.*** —**child′less·ness** ***n.***

Child (chīld), **Francis James** 1825-96; U.S. scholar and collector of Eng. & Scot. ballads

child·bear·ing (chīld′ber′iŋ) ***n.*** the act or process of giving birth to children; parturition

child·bed (-bed′) ***n.*** [Archaic] the condition of a woman who is giving birth

child·birth (-burth′) ***n.*** the act of giving birth to a child

child-care (-ker′) ***adj.*** having to do with the care of children, specif., of preschool children whose parents are employed [a *child-care* center]

childe (chīld) ***n.*** ⟦var. of CHILD⟧ [Archaic] a young man of noble birth, esp. a candidate for knighthood

Chil·der·mas (chil′dər məs) ***n.*** ⟦ME *childermasse* < OE *cildramæsse* < *cildra*, of infants (see CHILD) + *mæsse*, MASS[1]⟧ *former name for* HOLY INNOCENTS' DAY

child·hood (chīld′hood′) ***n.*** ⟦ME *childhod* < OE *cildhad*: see CHILD & -HOOD⟧ **1** the state or time of being a child; esp., the period from infancy to puberty **2** an early stage of development

child·ing (chīl′diŋ′) ***adj.*** ⟦ME < *childen,* to bear a child⟧ [Archaic] **1** bearing a child; pregnant **2** bearing a cluster of newer blossoms around an older blossom

child·ish (chīl′dish) ***adj.*** ⟦ME < OE *cildisc:* see CHILD & -ISH⟧ **1** of, like, or characteristic of a child **2** not fit for an adult; immature; silly —***SYN.*** CHILDLIKE —**child′ish·ly** ***adv.*** —**child′ish·ness** ***n.***

child labor the regular, full-time employment of children under a legally defined age in factories, stores, offices, etc.: in the U.S., the minimum legal age under federal law is 16 (in hazardous occupations, 18)

child·like (chīld′līk′) ***adj.*** **1** belonging or suitable to a child **2** like or characteristic of a child; innocent, trusting, etc. —**child′like′ness** ***n.***

SYN.—**childlike** and **childish** are both applied to persons of any age in referring to characteristics or qualities considered typical of a child, **childlike** suggesting the favorable qualities such as innocence, guilelessness, trustfulness, etc. and **childish,** the unfavorable, as immaturity, foolishness, petulance, etc.

child·ly (-lē) ***adj.*** childlike; childish

child·proof (-pro͞of′) ***adj.*** designed or arranged to prevent operation or damage by a child —***vt.*** to make childproof

chil·dren (chil′drən) ***n.*** ⟦see CHILD⟧ *pl. of* CHILD

children of Israel the Jews; Hebrews

child's play any very simple task

child support an allowance that a court orders paid by a person for the care of a child or children no longer in that person's legal custody

☆**chil·e** (chil′ē) ***n., pl.*** **chiles** *alt. sp. of* CHILI

Chi·le (chil′ē; *Sp* chē′le) country on the SW coast of South America, between the Andes and the Pacific: gained independence from Spain in 1818: 292,260 sq mi (756,950 sq km); cap. Santiago —**Chi·le·an** (chi lā′ən, -lē′-; chil′ē ən) ***adj., n.***

☆**chi·le con car·ne** (chil′ē kän kär′nē) CHILI CON CARNE

chi·le re·lle·no (chē′le re yā′nō) *pl.* **chi·les re·lle·nos** (chē′les re yā′nōs) ⟦Mex Sp, stuffed chile⟧ a Mexican dish consisting of a green chili pepper, usually hot, stuffed as with cheese or a meat mixture, then breaded and fried and served usually with a sauce

Chile saltpeter sodium nitrate, esp. as found naturally in Chile and Peru

☆**chil·i** (chil′ē) ***n., pl.*** **chil′ies** or **chil′is** ⟦MexSp < Nahuatl *či:lli*⟧ **1** the dried pod of red pepper, a very hot seasoning **2** the tropical American hot red pepper (*Capsicum frutescens* var. *longum*) bearing this pod: see CAPSICUM (sense 1) **3** any of various other types of peppers, used esp. in Mexican cooking **4** *a)* CHILI CON CARNE *b)* any of various typically milder-flavored dishes like this, often containing other vegetables, pasta, etc. and sometimes meatless

chil·i·ad (kil′ē ad′) ***n.*** ⟦L *chilias* (gen. *chiliadis*) < Gr *chilias* < *chilioi,* a thousand⟧ **1** a thousand; group of 1,000 **2** 1,000 years

chil·i·arch (kil′ē ärk′) ***n.*** ⟦L *chiliarches* < Gr *chiliarchēs* < *chilioi,* a thousand + *archos,* leader⟧ in ancient Greece, the military commander of 1,000 men

chil·i·asm (kil′ē az′əm) ***n.*** ⟦Gr *chiliasmos* < *chilias:* see CHILIAD⟧ belief in the coming of THE MILLENNIUM —**chil′i·ast′** (-ast′) ***n.*** —**chil′i·as′tic** ***adj.***

☆**chil·i con car·ne** (chil′ē kän kär′nē) ⟦< MexSp *chile con carne,* lit., red pepper with meat⟧ a highly seasoned Tex-Mex dish of ground or chopped beef, chilies or chili powder, and other spices, and, often, beans and tomatoes

☆**chili dog** a hot dog served in a bun and covered with chili con carne

chili pepper CHILI (senses 1 & 3)

☆**chili powder** a powder made of dried chili pods, herbs, etc., used as a seasoning

chi·li re·lle·no (chil′ē re yā′nō) *pl.* **chil′is re·lle′nos** or **chil′ies re·lle′nos** CHILE RELLENO

☆**chili sauce** a spiced sauce of chopped tomatoes, green and red sweet peppers, onions, etc.

Chil·koot Pass (chil′ko͞ot′) ⟦after the *Chilkoot* Indians who inhabited the region⟧ mountain pass in the N Rockies, on the Alas.-British Columbia border: *c.* 3,500 ft (1,067 m) high

chill (chil) ***n.*** ⟦ME *chile* < OE *ciele,* coldness < Gmc **kal-,* to be cold < IE base **gel-,* cold > L *gel-* in *gelidus,* icy⟧ **1** a feeling of coldness that makes one shiver; uncomfortable coolness **2** a moderate coldness **3** a damper on enthusiasm; discouraging influence **4** a feeling of sudden fear, apprehension, etc. **5** coolness of manner; unfriendliness **6** *Metallurgy* a cooled iron mold placed in contact with that part of a casting which is to be cooled rapidly and thus hardened on the surface —***adj.*** CHILLY —***vi.*** **1** to become cool or cold **2** to be seized with a chill; shake or shiver, as with cold or fear ☆**3** [Slang] *a)* to rest or relax *b)* to calm down (usually used in the imperative): usually with *out* **4** *Metallurgy* to become hardened on the surface by rapid cooling —***vt.*** **1** to make cool or cold **2** to cause a chill in **3** to check (enthusiasm, etc.) **4** to depress; dispirit **5** *Metallurgy* to harden (metal) on the surface by rapid cooling —**chill′ing·ly** ***adv.*** —**chill′ness** ***n.***

Chi·llán (chē yän′) city in SC Chile

chill·er (chil′ər) ***n.*** **1** a person or thing that chills **2** [Informal] a novel, film, etc. with a frightening, often weird or supernatural, theme, as involving psychopathic murder, vampires, etc.

chill factor WINDCHILL

chil·li (chil′ē) ***n., pl.*** **-lies** *alt. sp. of* CHILI

chil·lum (chil′əm) ***n.*** ⟦Hindi *cilam*⟧ **1** the part of a hookah that contains the substance being smoked **2** the substance itself, as tobacco or marijuana

chill·y (chil′ē) ***adj.*** **chill′i·er, chill′i·est** **1** moderately cold; uncomfortably cool **2** chilling; making cold **3** cool in manner; unfriendly **4** depressing; dispiriting —**chill′i·ly** ***adv.*** —**chill′i·ness** ***n.***

chi·lo- (kī′lō, -lə) ⟦< Gr *cheilos,* lip; ? akin to *chelynē,* lip: see GILL[1]⟧ *combining form* lip

Chi·lo·é (chē′lō ā′) island off SC Chile: 3,241 sq mi (8,394 sq km)

chi·lo·pod (kī′lō päd′, -lə-) ***n.*** ⟦< ModL *Chilopoda:* see CHILO- & -POD⟧ CENTIPEDE

Chil·pan·cin·go (chēl′pän sēŋ′gō) city in SC Mexico: capital of Guerrero

Chil·tern hundreds (chil′tərn) ⟦after the tract of crown lands in SC England containing the *Chiltern* Hills: see HUNDRED (*n.* 2)⟧ [Brit.] a purely nominal office held from the crown; appointment to it avoids application of the rule that members of Parliament wishing to vacate their seats may not resign

Chi·lung (jē′lo͞oŋ′) *var. of* KEELUNG

chi·mae·ra (kī mir′ə, ki-) ***n.*** ⟦ModL < L⟧ **1** *alt. sp. of* CHIMERA **2** any of an order (Chimaeriformes) of cartilaginous fishes with a smooth skin and tapering body

chim·ar (chim′ər, shim′-) ***n.*** *var. of* CHIMERE

chimb (chīm) ***n.*** *alt. sp. of* CHIME[2]

Chim·bo·ra·zo (chim′bə rä′zō) peak of the Andes, in central Ecuador: *c.* 20,500 ft (6,248 m)

Chim·bo·te (chim bō′tā) city in central Peru, on the Pacific coast

chime[1] (chīm) ***n.*** ⟦ME *chimbe, cimble* < OFr < L *cymbalum,* CYMBAL⟧ **1** a contrivance for striking a bell or set of bells **2** [*usually pl.*] *a)* a set of bells tuned to a musical scale *b)* a similar set of metal tubes, hung vertically and struck with a hammer **3** a single bell rung by a hammer, as in a clock **4** [*usually pl.*] the musical sounds or harmony produced by or as by chimes **5** harmony; agreement —***vi.*** **chimed, chim′ing** **1** to ring out when struck; sound as a chime **2** to sound in harmony, as bells **3** to harmonize; agree —***vt.*** **1** to ring, play, or strike (a bell, set of bells, etc.) **2** to make (music or sound) on chimes **3** to give (the time) by striking bells **4** to call, summon, etc. by sounding a chime —**chime in** **1** to join in or interrupt a conversation **2** to agree —**chim′er** ***n.***

chime[2] (chīm) ***n.*** ⟦ME *chimb* < OE *cimb-* (only in compounds); akin to Du *kim,* Ger *kimme,* an edge & ? COMB[1]⟧ the extended rim at each end of a cask or barrel

chi·me·ra (kī mir′ə, ki-) ***n.*** ⟦ME & OFr < L *chimaera* < Gr *chimaira,* fabulous monster, orig., she-goat that has passed one winter < *cheima,* winter: see HIBERNATE⟧ **1** [**C-**] *Gr. Myth.* a fire-breathing monster, usually represented as having a lion's head, a goat's body, and a serpent's tail **2** any similar fabulous monster **3** an impossible or foolish fancy **4** *Biol.* an organism having two or more genetically distinct types of cells due to mutation, grafting, etc.

chi·mere (chi mir′, shi-) ***n.*** ⟦ME < OFr *chamarre* < Sp *zamarra,* prob. < Ar *sammūr,* Siberian weasel⟧ a loose robe, sleeveless or with lawn sleeves attached, sometimes worn by Anglican bishops: also **chim·er** (chim′ər, shim′-)

chi·mer·ic (kī mer′ik, ki-) ***adj.*** **1** CHIMERICAL **2** of or having to do with chimerism [*chimeric* mice, *chimeric* genes]

chi·mer·i·cal (kī mer′i kəl, ki-) ***adj.*** ⟦CHIMER(A) + -ICAL⟧ **1** imaginary; fantastic; unreal **2** absurd; impossible **3** indulging in unrealistic fancies; visionary —**chi·mer′i·cal·ly** ***adv.***

chi·mer·ism (kī′mər iz′əm) ***n.*** the occurrence of genetically distinct cell types in a single organism

☆**chim·i·chan·ga** (chim′ē chäŋ′gə) ***n.*** ⟦MexSp, var. of *chivichanga,* lit., a trifle: named (1950s, in Ariz.) for a similar Mex food⟧ a deep-fried, tightly rolled burrito

Chim·kent (chim kent′) city in SC Kazakhstan, north of Tashkent

chim·ney (chim′nē) ***n., pl.*** **-neys** ⟦ME *chimene,* a fireplace < OFr *cheminée* < LL *caminata,* fireplace < L *caminus,* furnace, flue < Gr *kaminos,* oven, fireplace; ult. < ? IE base **kam,* to arch > CAMERA⟧ **1** the passage through which smoke or fumes from a fire escape; flue **2** a structure containing a flue or flues and extending above the roof of a building **3** a glass tube set around the flame of a candle or lamp **4** something like a chimney; specif., *a)* a narrow column of rock formed by erosion, esp. that caused by waves ☆*b)* a vertical body of ore *c)* the vent of a volcano or cave **5** [Chiefly Brit.] a smokestack **6** [Dial.] a hearth

chimney corner **1** a large recess with seats at the sides of an old-fashioned fireplace **2** a place near the fire

chimney piece **1** MANTELPIECE **2** [Obs.] a decoration over a fireplace

chimney pot a short pipe fitted to the top of a chimney to carry the smoke away and increase the draft

chimney swallow ☆**1** CHIMNEY SWIFT **2** BARN SWALLOW

chimney sweep a person whose work is cleaning the soot from chimneys

☆**chimney swift** a sooty-brown North American swift (*Chaetura pelagica*) that often makes its nest in a chimney

chimp (chimp) ***n.*** [Informal] a chimpanzee

chim·pan·zee (chim′pan zē′, chim pan′zē) ***n.*** ⟦Fr *chimpanzé* < Bantu (Angola) *kampenzi*⟧ any of a genus (*Pan*) of great apes of Africa, with black hair and large, protruding ears: it is smaller than a gorilla and is noted for its intelligence

chin (chin) ***n.*** ⟦ME < OE *cin* < IE base **ĝenu-,* chin, jawbone > Goth *kinnus,* cheek, L *gena,* cheek, Gr *genys,* chin⟧ the part of the face below the lower lip; projecting part of the lower jaw —***vt.*** **chinned, chin′ning** *Gym.* to pull (oneself) up, while hanging by the hands from a horizontal bar, until the chin is just above the level of the bar —☆***vi.*** **1** [Slang] to converse idly; chat, gossip, etc. **2** to chin oneself —**keep one's chin up** to bear up bravely under trying circumstances —☆**take it on the chin** [Slang] to suffer defeat, severe hardship, etc.

Chin *abbrev.* Chinese

chi·na (chī′nə) *n.* ⟦after fol., where first produced⟧ **1** porcelain or any ceramic ware like porcelain: see PORCELAIN **2** dishes, ornaments, etc. made of china **3** any earthenware dishes or crockery —*adj.* made of china

Chi·na (chī′nə) **1** country in E Asia: before 1912, the CHINESE EMPIRE: 3,705,407 sq mi (9,596,960 sq km); cap. Beijing: officially called the **People's Republic of China** since 1949 **2 Republic of China** this country variously from 1912 until the Kuomintang party fled to Taiwan in 1949 **3 Republic of China** *see* TAIWAN

China aster an annual garden flower (*Callistephus chinensis*) of the composite family, with large blooms of various colors: it is native to China and Japan

chi·na bark (kī′nə, kē′-) ⟦altered (after *China*) < Sp *quina*: see QUININE⟧ CINCHONA (sense 2)

☆**chi·na·ber·ry** (chī′nə ber′ē) *n., pl.* **-ries 1** a tropical Asian tree (*Melia azederach*) of the mahogany family, bearing yellow, beadlike fruit: widely grown as a lawn tree throughout the S U.S. **2** SOAPBERRY (sense 1) **3** the fruit of either of these trees

Chi·na·man (chī′nə mən) *n., pl.* **-men** (-mən) a Chinese person: now often regarded as a mildly contemptuous or patronizing term

China rose 1 a cultivated rose (*Rosa chinensis*) of Chinese origin **2** a large hibiscus (*Hibiscus rosa-sinensis*) with showy flowers

China Sea *see* EAST CHINA SEA & SOUTH CHINA SEA

☆**Chi·na·town** (chī′nə toun′) *n.* the Chinese quarter of any city outside of China

☆**China tree** CHINABERRY (sense 1)

chi·na·ware (chī′nə wer′) *n.* china dishes, ornaments, etc.

China wood oil TUNG OIL

☆**chin·ca·pin** (chiŋ′kə pin′) *n. alt. sp. of* CHINQUAPIN

chinch (chinch) *n.* ⟦Sp *chinche* < L *cimex*, bug: see CIMEX⟧ **1** BEDBUG ☆**2** CHINCH BUG

☆**chinch bug** a small, white-winged, black hemipterous bug (*Blissus leucopterus*) that damages grain plants by sucking out the juices

chin·che·rin·chee (chin′chə rin′chē) *n.* ⟦< ?⟧ a poisonous, bulbous South African plant (*Ornithogalum thyrsoides*) of the lily family, with many spikes of white or yellow, long-lasting flowers

chin·chil·la (chin chil′ə) *n.* ⟦Sp, prob. dim. of *chinche*: see CHINCH⟧ **1** a small rodent (*Chinchilla laniger*) found in the Andes, but bred extensively elsewhere for its fur **2** the valuable, soft, pale-gray fur of this animal **3** a variety of Persian cat, typically pure white **4** ⟦prob. after *Chinchilla*, Sp town where first made⟧ a heavy cloth of wool, or wool and cotton, with a tufted, napped surface, used for making overcoats

chinchilla

Chin·chow or **Chin·chou** (jin′jō′) *a former transliteration of* JINZHOU

Chin·dwin (chin′dwin) river in NW Myanmar, flowing southward into the Irrawaddy: *c.* 520 mi (837 km)

chine[1] (chīn) *n.* ⟦ME < OFr *eschine* < Frank **skina*, small bone, shinbone: see SHIN[1]⟧ **1** the backbone; spine **2** a cut of meat containing part of the backbone **3** a ridge of rock **4** the juncture of the bottom and either of the sides of a boat —*vt.* **chined, chin′ing** to cut along or across the backbone of (a carcass of meat)

chine[2] (chīn) *n.* ⟦ME < OE *cine*, fissure; akin to *cinan*, to burst open < IE base **ĝei*, **ĝi-*, to germinate, bloom > Ger *keim*, germ, bad⟧ [Brit. Dial.] a rocky ravine or deep fissure in a cliff

chine[3] (chīn) *n.* CHIME[2]

Chi·nese (chī nēz′, chī nēs′; *for adj., also* chī′nēz′) *n.* ⟦OFr *Chineis* (Fr *Chinois*)⟧ **1** *pl.* **-nese′** a person born or living in China or a descendant of the people of China **2** the standard language of China, based on Beijing speech; Mandarin **3** any of the various Sino-Tibetan languages of China, including, among others, Mandarin and Cantonese **4** the group consisting of these languages **5** [Informal] Chinese food —*adj.* of China or its people, languages, or culture

Chinese boxes a nest of boxes, each of which fits into the next larger box

☆**Chinese cabbage** any of several vegetables (*Brassica pekinensis* and *B. chinensis*) of the crucifer family, having long, narrow leaves in loose, cylindrical heads and tasting somewhat like cabbage

Chinese checkers ⟦prob. so named from the characteristic ornamentation of the board⟧ a game played on a board with holes arranged in the shape of a six-pointed star, by from two to six players, the winner being the one who first moves his or her set of marbles across the board

Chinese chestnut a chestnut (*Castanea mollissima*) with large, sweet nuts, often crossed with other chestnuts because of its resistance to chestnut blight

Chinese crested 1 a breed of toy dogs in a hairless variety with plumes of hair on the head, feet, and tail and a fully coated variety **2** any dog of this breed

Chinese Empire empire in E Asia, from the founding of its first dynasty (*c.* 2200 B.C.) to the revolution of 1911, including China, Manchuria, Mongolia, Tibet, & Turkestan

Chinese gooseberry KIWI (*n.* 2)

Chinese lantern a lantern made of brightly colored paper that can be folded up

Chi·nese-lan·tern plant (chī′nēz lant′ərn) an ornamental, perennial GROUND-CHERRY (*Physalis alkekengi*) with a red or bright-orange calyx surrounding the fruit

Chinese parsley ⟦so called from its appearance and its use in Asian cuisines⟧ coriander leaves used as an herb; cilantro

Chinese puzzle 1 an intricate puzzle **2** anything intricate and hard to solve

Chinese red any of various shades of red, as chrome red or, esp., a brilliant orange-red

Chinese restaurant syndrome the dizziness, headache, etc. experienced by some people as a reaction to monosodium glutamate, often used to intensify the flavor of Chinese food

Chinese Revolution a revolution (1911-12) in which forces led by Sun Yat-sen overthrew the Manchu dynasty and set up a republic in China

Chinese Turkestan the part of Turkestan under Chinese control, now constituting the section of Xinjiang region, China, south of the Tian Shan mountains: also called *Eastern Turkestan*

Chinese wall ⟦after fol.⟧ something erected or established as a barrier; specif., a rule, procedure, etc. established to prevent the flow of information between different parts of an organization

Chinese Wall GREAT WALL OF CHINA

Chinese water torture WATER TORTURE

Chinese white a dense, white pigment made of zinc oxide, used esp. in white inks

Chinese windlass DIFFERENTIAL WINDLASS

Ching or **Ch'ing** (chiŋ) *n.* the Chinese dynasty (1644-1912) established by the Manchu; Manchu dynasty

Ching·hai (chiŋ′hī′) *a former transliteration of* QINGHAI

Ching·tao (chiŋ′dou′) *a former transliteration of* QINGDAO

Chin Hills (chin) mountain range in NW Myanmar, along the Indian border: highest peak, *c.* 10,000 ft (3,050 m)

chink[1] (chiŋk) *n.* ⟦ME *chine*, with unhistoric *-k*: see CHINE[2]⟧ a narrow opening; crack; fissure; slit —*vt.* **1** to close up the chinks in **2** [Obs.] to form chinks in

chink[2] (chiŋk) *n.* ⟦echoic⟧ **1** a sharp, clinking sound, as of coins striking together **2** [Old Slang] coin or cash — *vi., vt.* to make or cause to make a sharp, clinking sound

Chink (chiŋk) *n., adj.* ⟦prob. altered < CHINA OR CHINESE⟧ [*also* **c-**] [Slang] CHINESE: a contemptuous or patronizing term

☆**chin·ka·pin** (chiŋ′kə pin′) *n. alt. sp. of* CHINQUAPIN

chin·less (chin′lis) *adj.* **1** having a chin that is markedly small or receding **2** ⟦from the stereotypical notion that a prominent chin indicates strong character⟧ [Informal] lacking firmness of character; ineffectual, irresolute, etc.

Chin·ling Shan (jē′liŋ′ shän′) *a former transliteration of* QINLING SHAN

☆**chin music** [Slang] **1** trivial, informal talk **2** *Baseball* the use of a brushback pitch in a game

☆**chi·no** (chē′nō, shē′-) *n., pl.* **-nos** ⟦< AmSp, adj., toasted: in ref. to its color⟧ **1** a strong, khaki-colored, twilled-cotton cloth used for work clothes, uniforms, etc. **2** [*pl.*] pants of chino for casual wear

Chi·no- (chī′nō) *combining form* Chinese and [*Chino*-Soviet]

chi·nois (shēn wä′) *n.* ⟦Fr < the adj., Chinese⟧ a conical, fine-mesh strainer, used esp. for puréeing cooked foods

chi·noi·se·rie (shēn wä zə rē′, -wä′zə rē; *Fr*, -wáz rē′) *n.* ⟦Fr < *chinois*, CHINESE + *-erie*, -ERY⟧ **1** an ornate style of decoration of furniture, textiles, ceramics, etc., esp. in 18th-cent. Europe, based on Chinese motifs **2** articles, designs, etc. in this style collectively

Chi·nook (shə nook′, -nōōk′; chə-) *n.* ⟦< *tsi-núk*, a Salish name for the Chinook people⟧ **1** *pl.* **-nooks′** or **-nook′** a member of a North American Indian people of the Columbia River valley and adjacent regions **2** either of two languages spoken by this people, **Lower Chinook**, now extinct, and **Upper Chinook**, still spoken in Oregon and Washington **3** CHINOOK JARGON **4** [*usually* **c-**] the warm, dry wind blowing intermittently down the east side of the Rockies during the winter and early spring, which causes the rapid thawing of snow: in full **chinook wind**

☆**Chi·nook·an** (-ən) *adj.* of the Chinooks or their language or culture —*n.* a family of North American Indian languages spoken in the Pacific northwest

☆**Chinook jargon** a pidgin consisting of extremely simplified Chinook intermixed with words from English, French, and neighboring American Indian languages: formerly used among traders and Indians in the coastal areas of NW North America

☆**chinook salmon** the largest species (*Oncorhynchus tshawytscha*) of Pacific salmon: it is an endangered species

☆**chin·qua·pin** (chiŋ′kə pin′) *n.* ⟦of Algonquian orig.⟧ **1** any of several, usually bushlike, trees (genus *Castanea*) of the beech family, esp. the dwarf chestnut **2** any of various species (genus *Castanopsis*) of evergreen trees of the beech family, found in W U.S. and Asia **3** the edible nut of any of these trees

chintz (chints) *n.* ⟦earlier *chints*, pl. of *chint* < Hindi *chhīnt*, chintz < Sans *chitra*, spot < IE base **(s)kai-*, bright > -HOOD, OE *hador*, bright, L *caelum*, sky⟧ a cotton cloth printed in colors with flower designs or other patterns and usually glazed

chintz·y (chint′sē) *adj.* **chintz′i·er, chintz′i·est** ⟦prec. + -Y[3]: from the sleazy quality of some chintz fabrics⟧ **1** like chintz ☆**2** [Informal] cheap, stingy, mean, petty, etc.

chin-up (chin′up′) *n.* an exercise in which a person chins himself or herself, specif., one in which the bar is gripped with the palms facing the exerciser

chin-wag (chin′wag′) [Informal, Chiefly Brit.] ***vi.*** **-wagged′**, **-wag′ging** to engage in informal or idle conversation; chat or gossip —***n.*** an informal or idle conversation

Chin·wang·tao (chin′wäŋ′dou′) *a former transliteration of* QINHUANGDAO

Chi·os (kī′äs′) *var. of* KHÍOS

chip (chip) ***vt.*** **chipped**, **chip′ping** ⟦ME *chippen* < OE **cippian* < *cipp*, log, plowshare < L *cippus*, post, stake < IE base **keipo-*, sharp post⟧ **1** [Rare] to cut or chop with an ax or other sharp tool **2** *a)* to break or cut a small piece or thin slice from *b)* to break or cut off (a small piece or pieces) **3** to shape by cutting or chopping [to *chip* a hole in the ice] **4** *Tennis* to hit (a ball) in a short, soft shot with backspin —***vi.*** **1** *a)* to break off in small pieces [this paint *chips* easily] *b)* to lose or be inherently subject to losing a small part or parts of itself [the plate will *chip* easily] **2** *Golf* to make a chip shot **3** *Tennis* to hit a short, soft shot with backspin —***n.*** ⟦ME *chippe* < the v.⟧ **1** a small, thin piece of wood, stone, etc., cut or broken off **2** a place where a small piece has been chipped off [a *chip* on the edge of a plate] **3** wood, palm leaf, or straw split and woven into bonnets, hats, etc. ☆**4** a fragment of dried animal dung, sometimes used for fuel ☆**5** a worthless thing **6** one of the small, round disks or counters used in poker and other gambling games as a token for money **7** *a)* a thin slice or small piece of food [a potato *chip*, a chocolate *chip*] *b)* [*pl.*] [Chiefly Brit.] French fried potatoes **8** *Electronics a)* a semiconductor body on which an integrated circuit is formed or is to be formed *b)* INTEGRATED CIRCUIT **9** *Golf* CHIP SHOT **10** *Tennis* a shot that is chipped —☆**cash in one's chips 1** to turn in one's chips for their equivalent in money **2** [Slang] to die —**chip away (at) 1** to accomplish or deal with (something) a little at a time [to *chip away at* a long-term project] **2** to gradually reduce or lessen (something) [competitors *chipped away at* our annual profits] —☆**chip in** [Informal] **1** to share in giving money or help **2** to add one's comments —**chip off the old block** a person much like his or her parent in appearance or characteristics —☆**chip on one's shoulder** [Informal] an inclination to fight or quarrel —☆**in the chips** [Slang] rich; wealthy —**let the chips fall where they may** let the consequences be what they may —☆**when the chips are down** when something is really at stake

☆**CHIP** (chip) *abbrev.* Children's Health Insurance Program

chip·board (chip′bôrd′) ***n.*** a board made by compressing wood pulp, sawdust, and chips with a resin binder

Chip·e·wy·an (chip′ə wī′ən) ***n.*** ⟦Cree *ochiipwayaaniiw*, lit., one who has pointed skins or hides: prob. in allusion to the Chipewyans' style of hunting shirts⟧ **1** a member of a North American Indian people of NW Canada **2** the Athabaskan language of this people

chip·munk (chip′muŋk′) ***n.*** ⟦of Algonquian orig.⟧ any of two genera (*Eutamias* and *Tamias*) of small North American squirrels having striped markings on the head and back and living mainly on the ground

chi·pot·le (chē pōt′lā) ***n.*** ⟦< MexSp *chile chipotle*, name of this chili (pepper), ult. < Nahuatl *xipotli*⟧ a kind of chili, or hot pepper, that is a dried and smoked jalapeño: it is used esp. in Mexican cooking: also **chipotle pepper**

☆**chipped beef** dried or smoked beef sliced into shavings, often served in a cream sauce

Chip·pen·dale (chip′ən dāl′) ***adj.*** ⟦after Thomas *Chippendale* (*c.* 1718-79), Eng cabinetmaker⟧ designating or of an 18th-cent. Eng. style of furniture characterized by graceful lines and, often, rococo ornamentation

chip·per[1] (chip′ər) ***adj.*** ⟦altered < N Brit *kipper*; ? akin to Du *kipp*, quick, lively⟧ [Informal] cheerful and sprightly; in good spirits

chip·per[2] (chip′ər) ***n.*** a person or thing that chips; esp., a tool for chipping

Chip·pe·wa (chip′ə wä′, -wô′) ***n.***, *pl.* **-was′** or **-wa′** *var. of* OJIBWA: also **Chip′pe·way′** (-wā′)

☆**chipping sparrow** ⟦< *chip*, echoic of its cry⟧ a small North American sparrow (*Spizella passerina*), with a reddish-brown crown and white breast

☆**chip·py** or **chip·pie** (chip′ē) ***n.***, *pl.* **-pies 1** CHIPPING SPARROW **2** a chipmunk **3** [Slang] *a)* a promiscuous young woman *b)* a prostitute

chip shot *Golf* a short, lofted shot, made esp. from just off the putting green

chi·ral (kī′rəl) ***adj.*** ⟦CHIR(O)- + -AL: coined by Lord KELVIN[2], as because of the apparent reversal of right and left sides (and hands) of a person looking into a mirror⟧ *Chem.* designating or of an asymmetrical form, as a molecule, that cannot be superimposed on its mirror image —**chi·ral·i·ty** (kī ral′ə tē) ***n.***

Chi·ri·co (kē′rē kô), **Gior·gio de** (jôr′jô de) 1888-1978; It. painter, born in Greece

chirk (churk) ***vt., vi.*** ⟦ME *chirken*, to twitter, var. of *charken* < OE *cearcian*, to creak, gnash⟧ [Informal] to cheer (*up*)

chi·ro- (kī′rō, -rə) ⟦< Gr *cheir*, hand < IE base **ĝhesr-* > Arm *jeřn*, hand⟧ *combining form* hand [*chiromancy*]

chi·rog·ra·phy (kī räg′rə fē) ***n.*** ⟦prec. + -GRAPHY⟧ handwriting; penmanship —**chi·rog′ra·pher** ***n.*** —**chi·ro·graph·ic** (kī′rō graf′ik) ***adj.***, **chi′ro·graph′i·cal**

chi·ro·man·cy (kī′rō man′sē) ***n.*** ⟦CHIRO- + -MANCY⟧ PALMISTRY —**chi′ro·man′cer** ***n.***

Chi·ron (kī′rän′) ***n.*** ⟦L < Gr *Cheirōn*⟧ *Gr. Myth.* the wisest of all centaurs, famous for his knowledge of medicine: he is the teacher of Asclepius, Achilles, and Hercules

chi·rop·o·dy (kī räp′ə dē) ***n.*** ⟦CHIRO- + -POD + -Y[4]⟧ **1** [Archaic] treatment of hand and foot ailments, esp. corns, warts, etc. **2** PODIATRY —**chi·rop′o·dist** ***n.***

☆**chi·ro·prac·tic** (kī′rō prak′tik, kī′rō prak′tik) ***n.*** ⟦< CHIRO- + Gr *praktikos*, practical: see PRACTICE⟧ the science and art of restoring or maintaining health, practiced by a licensed professional, based on the theory that disease is caused by interference with nerve function, and employing manipulation of the body joints, esp. of the spine, to restore normal nerve function —**chi′ro·prac′tor** ***n.***

chi·rop·ter (kī räp′tər) ***n.*** ⟦< CHIRO- + Gr *pteron*, wing: see FEATHER⟧ BAT[2] —**chi·rop′ter·an** ***adj., n.***

chirp (churp) ***vi.*** ⟦ME *chirpen*, echoic var. of *chirken*, CHIRK⟧ **1** to make the short, shrill sound of some birds or insects **2** to speak in a lively, shrill way —***vt.*** to utter in a sharp, shrill tone —***n.*** a short, shrill sound —**chirp′er** ***n.***

chirp·y (churp′pē) ***adj.*** **chirp′i·er**, **chirp′i·est** [Informal] cheerful and lively; merry —**chirp′i·ly** ***adv.*** —**chirp′i·ness** ***n.***

chirr (chur) ***n.*** ⟦echoic⟧ a shrill, trilled sound, as of some insects or birds —***vi.*** to make such a sound

chir·rup (chir′əp, chur′-) ***vi.*** ⟦var. of CHIRP⟧ **1** to chirp repeatedly **2** to make a series of sharp, sucking sounds with the lips, as in urging a horse on —***n.*** a chirruping sound —**chir′rup·y** ***adj.***

chi·ru (chir′o͞o) ***n.*** ⟦prob. < Tibetan⟧ a Tibetan antelope (*Pantholops hodgsonii*) with dense, soft, woolly hair and, in the male, long, sharp horns: it is an endangered species

chi·rur·geon (kī rur′jən) ***n.*** ⟦altered, after L forms < ME *cirurgian* < OFr *cirurgien* < ME & OFr *cirurgie*: see SURGERY⟧ *archaic var. of* SURGEON —**chi·rur′ger·y** (-jər ē) ***n.*** —**chi·rur′gi·cal** (-ji kəl) ***adj.***

chis·el (chiz′əl) ***n.*** ⟦NormFr (OFr *cisel*) < VL **cisellum*, for L **caesellum* < *caesus*, pp. of *caedere*, to cut: see -CIDE⟧ a hand tool with a sharp, often wedge-shaped, blade for cutting or shaping wood, stone, etc., specif., such a tool that is driven with a mallet or hammer — ***vi., vt.*** **-eled** or **-elled**, **-el·ing** or **-el·ling 1** to cut or shape with a chisel **2** [Informal] *a)* to take advantage of by cheating, sponging, etc. *b)* to get (something) in this way —**chisel in** [Informal] to force oneself upon others without being asked or welcomed —**chis′el·er** ***n.***, **chis′el·ler**

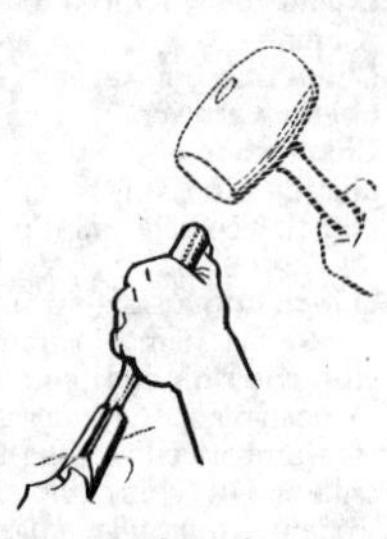
chisel

chis·eled or **chis·elled** (-əld) ***adj.*** **1** cut or shaped with a chisel **2** finely wrought, as if shaped by a chisel

Chis·holm Trail (chiz′əm) ⟦after Jesse *Chisholm* (1806?-68), U.S. frontier scout who established it⟧ cattle trail from San Antonio, Tex., to Abilene, Kans.: important from 1865 until the 1880s

Chi·şi·nau (kē′shē nou′) capital of Moldova, in the central part

chi-square (kī′skwer′) ***n.*** a statistical method used to test whether the classification of data can be ascribed to chance or to some underlying law

chit[1] (chit) ***n.*** ⟦ME *chitte*, prob. var. of *kitte*, for kitten⟧ **1** a child **2** an immature or childish girl

chit[2] (chit) ***n.*** ⟦< *chitty* < Hindi *chiṭṭhi*, letter, note < Sans *chitra*, spot: see CHINTZ⟧ **1** [Chiefly Brit.] a short note or letter; memorandum **2** a voucher of a small sum owed for drink, food, etc.

Chi·ta (chē tä′) city in SE Russia, near the Mongolian border

chit·chat (chit′chat′) [Informal] ***n.*** ⟦redupl. of CHAT[1]⟧ **1** light, familiar, informal talk; chat; small talk **2** gossip —***vi.*** **-chat′ted**, **-chat′ting** to engage in small talk

chi·tin (kī′tin) ***n.*** ⟦Fr *chitine* < Gr *chitōn*: see CHITON⟧ a tough, horny polysaccharide, $(C_8H_{13}NO_5)n$, secreted by the epidermis and forming the main bulk of the outer covering of insects, crustaceans, etc. —**chi′tin·ous** (-əs) ***adj.***

chit·lins or **chit·lings** (chit′linz) ***pl.n.*** *phonetic sp. of* CHITTERLINGS

chi·ton (kī′tən, -tän′) ***n.*** ⟦Gr *chitōn*, garment, tunic, coat of mail: see TUNIC⟧ **1** a loose garment of varying length, similar to a tunic, worn by both men and women in ancient Greece **2** any of a class (Polyplacophora) of mostly small, ovoid marine mollusks, having a dorsal shell consisting of eight articulating calcareous plates and a ventral foot

chi·to·san (kīt′ə san′) ***n.*** a polysaccharide derived from chitin, that absorbs heavy metals while in solution: it is used in industry, esp. to purify waste water

Chit·ta·gong (chit′ə gôŋ′, -gäŋ′) seaport in SE Bangladesh, near the Bay of Bengal

chit·ter (chit′ər) ***vi.*** ⟦ME *chiteren*: orig. echoic⟧ **1** to twitter **2** [Brit. Dial.] to shiver with cold

chit·ter·lings (chit′linz; *occas.* chit′ər liŋz′) ***pl.n.*** ⟦ME *chiterling*, entrails, souse; akin to MLowG *kūt*, soft parts of the body, Ger *kutteln*, chitterlings < IE base **geu-*, to bend > COD[2]⟧ the small intestines of pigs, used for food, usually fried in deep fat

chiv·al·ric (shiv′əl rik′, shi val′rik) ***adj.*** **1** of chivalry **2** chivalrous

chiv·al·rous (shiv′əl rəs) ***adj.*** ⟦ME *chevalrous* < OFr *chevalereus*: see fol.⟧ **1** having the noble qualities of an ideal knight; gallant, courteous, honorable, etc. **2** of chivalry; chivalric —**SYN.** CIVIL —**chiv′al·rous·ly** ***adv.*** —**chiv′al·rous·ness** ***n.***

chiv·al·ry (shiv′əl rē) ***n.*** ⟦ME & OFr *chevalerie* < *chevaler*, knight < *cheval*, horse < L *caballus*: see CAVALRY⟧ **1** a group of knights or gallant gentlemen **2** the medieval system of knighthood **3** the noble qualities a knight was supposed to have, such as courage, honor, and a readiness to help the weak and protect women **4** the demonstration of any of the knightly qualities

chives (chīvz) ***pl.n.*** ⟦ME *cive* < OFr < L *cepa*, onion⟧ [*sometimes with sing.*

v.] a hardy, perennial herb (*Allium schoenoprasum*) of the lily family, with small, slender, hollow leaves having a mild onion aroma and flavor: used in soups, stews, etc.

chiv·y or **chiv·vy** (chiv′ē) ***n.***, *pl.* **chiv′ies** or **chiv′vies** [Brit.] a hunt; chase — ***vt., vi.*** **chiv′ied** or **chiv′vied**, **chiv′y·ing** or **chiv′vy·ing** **1** to fret; harass; nag **2** to manipulate **3** [Brit.] to hunt; chase

chlam·y·date (klam′ə dāt′, -dit) ***adj.*** ⟦L *chlamydatus*, dressed in a military cloak < Gr *chlamyd-*, base of *chlamys*, mantle + -ATE[1]⟧ *Zool.* having a mantle, as certain mollusks

chla·myd·i·a (klə mid′ē ə) ***n.*** ⟦ModL < Gr *chlamys, chlamyd-*, mantle + -IA⟧ a widespread, gonorrhealike sexually transmitted disease caused by a bacterium (*Chlamydia trachomatis*) that also causes trachoma, etc. —**chla·myd′i·al** ***adj.***

chla·myd·o·spore (klə mid′ə spôr′, klam′ə dō′-) ***n.*** ⟦< Gr *chlamyd-* (see CHLAMYDATE) + -O- + SPORE⟧ an enlarged, thick-walled resting spore formed between the vegetative cells of a filamentous fungus or certain protozoans

chla·mys (klā′mis, klam′is) ***n.***, *pl.* **chla′mys·es** or **chlam·y·des** (klam′i dēz′) ⟦L < Gr *chlamys*⟧ a short mantle clasped at the shoulder, worn by men in ancient Greece

chlamys

chlo·as·ma (klō az′mə) ***n.*** ⟦ModL < Gr *chloazein*, to become green < *chloos*, light-green color⟧ a skin discoloration on the face and chest, resulting from pregnancy, disease, malnutrition, etc.

Chlo·e or **Chlo·ë** (klō′ē) ***n.*** ⟦L < Gr *chloē*, blooming, verdant⟧ **1** a feminine name **2** *see* DAPHNIS AND CHLOE

chlor- (klôr) *combining form* CHLORO-: used before a vowel

chlor·ac·ne (klôr ak′nē) ***n.*** an acnelike skin disorder caused by exposure to chlorinated hydrocarbons

chlo·ral (klôr′əl) ***n.*** ⟦CHLOR(O)- + AL(COHOL)⟧ **1** a thin, oily, colorless liquid, CCl_3CHO, with a pungent odor, prepared by the action of chlorine on alcohol: used in the manufacture of DDT **2** *short for* CHLORAL HYDRATE

chloral hydrate a colorless, crystalline compound, $CCl_3 \cdot CH(OH)_2$, used chiefly as a sedative

chlor·a·mine (klôr′ə mēn′, klôr′ə mēn′; klôr am′ēn, -in) ***n.*** ⟦CHLOR(O)- + AMINE⟧ any of various compounds containing chlorine and nitrogen; esp., an unstable, colorless, pungent liquid, NH_2Cl, used to make hydrazine

chlor·am·phen·i·col (klôr′am fen′i kôl′, -kōl′) ***n.*** ⟦CHLOR(O)- + AM(IDE) + PHE(N)- + NI(TRO)- + (GLY)COL⟧ an antibiotic drug, $C_{11}H_{12}Cl_2N_2O_5$, prepared synthetically or isolated from a bacillus (*Streptomyces venezuelae*)

chlo·rate (klôr′āt′, -it) ***n.*** a salt of chloric acid containing the monovalent, negative radical ClO_3

chlor·cy·cli·zine (klôr′sī′klə zēn′) ***n.*** ⟦CHLOR(O)- + CYCLIZINE⟧ an antihistamine, $C_{18}H_{21}ClN_2$, used for treating allergies

☆**chlor·dane** (klôr′dān′) ***n.*** ⟦CHLOR(O)- + *(in)dane*, deriv. of INDENE⟧ a chlorinated, highly poisonous, volatile oil, $C_{10}H_6Cl_8$, formerly used as an insecticide: also **chlor′dan** (-dan)

chlor·di·az·e·pox·ide (klôr′dī az′ə päks′īd′) ***n.*** a tranquilizer, $C_{16}H_{14}ClN_3O$, that relieves anxiety: a hydrochloride derivative of this has similar properties and is the generic name for Librium, etc.

chlo·rel·la (klō rel′ə, klôr el′ə) ***n.*** ⟦ModL < CHLOR(O)- + L *-ella*, fem. dim. suffix⟧ any of a genus (*Chlorella*) of microscopic, unicellular, green algae with spherical cells: several species are rich sources of proteins, carbohydrates, and fats

chlo·ric (klôr′ik) ***adj.*** **1** of or containing pentavalent chlorine **2** designating or of an acid, $HClO_3$, which exists only in solution and whose salts are chlorates

chlo·ride (-īd′) ***n.*** a compound in which chlorine is combined with any of certain other elements or with a radical

chloride of lime a white powder with the approximate formula $CaOCl_2$, obtained by treating slaked lime with chlorine and used for disinfecting and bleaching: also called **chlorinated lime**

chlo·ri·nate (klôr′ə nāt′) ***vt.*** **-nat′ed**, **-nat′ing** to treat or combine (a substance) with chlorine; esp., to pass chlorine into (water or sewage) for purification —**chlo′ri·na′tion** ***n.*** —**chlo′ri·na′tor** ***n.***

chlo·rine (klôr′ēn′, -in) ***n.*** ⟦< Gr *chlōros*, pale green (< IE **ghlō-*, var. of base **ghel-*: see YELLOW) + -INE[3]: so named (1810), from its color, by Sir Humphry DAVY, who proved it to be an element⟧ a greenish-yellow, poisonous, gaseous chemical element, one of the halogens, having a disagreeable odor and obtained by electrolysis of certain chlorides: it is used as a bleaching agent, in water purification, in various industrial processes, etc.: symbol, Cl; at. no. 17: see the periodic table of elements in the Reference Supplement

chlo·rite[1] (-īt′) ***n.*** a salt of chlorous acid containing the monovalent, negative radical ClO_2

chlo·rite[2] (-īt′) ***n.*** ⟦L *chloritis* < Gr *chlōritis* < *chlōros*, pale green⟧ any of a group of usually greenish, soft, monoclinic minerals, $(Mg,Al,Fe)_{12}(Si,Al)_8O_{20}(OH)_{16}$, that break into thin, flexible, micalike sheets and are usually found in metamorphic rocks —**chlo·rit·ic** (klə rit′ik) ***adj.***

chlo·ro- (klôr′ō, -ə) ⟦< Gr *chlōros*, pale green: see CHLORINE⟧ *combining form* **1** green [*chlorophyll, chlorosis*] **2** having chlorine in the molecule [*chloroform*]

chlo·ro·ben·zene (klôr′ō ben′zēn′) ***n.*** a clear flammable liquid, C_6H_5Cl, used as a solvent for paints, lacquers, etc. and in organic synthesis

chlo·ro·fluo·ro·car·bon (klôr′ō flôr′ə kär′bən, -flo͝or′-) ***n.*** any of various nontoxic, nonflammable, inert halocarbon compounds containing carbon, fluorine, chlorine, and hydrogen, used for plastic foam, as a refrigerant, etc.: these compounds are thought to damage the atmosphere

chlo·ro·form (klôr′ə fôrm′) ***n.*** ⟦Fr *chloroforme*: see CHLORO- & FORMYL⟧ a toxic, carcinogenic, colorless, volatile liquid, $CHCl_3$, with a sweet taste, used as a solvent, fumigant, etc. and, formerly, as a general anesthetic —***vt.*** **1** to anesthetize with chloroform **2** to kill with chloroform

chlo·ro·hy·drin (klôr′ō hī′drin′) ***n.*** ⟦CHLORO- + HYDR(O)- + -IN[1]⟧ any organic compound in which a hydroxyl group of a polyhydric alcohol has been replaced by a chlorine atom; esp., a colorless liquid, $ClCH_2CHOHCH_2OH$, prepared by the reaction of hydrochloric acid with glycerol and used in the manufacture of dyes and as a solvent

Chlo·ro·my·ce·tin (klôr′ō mī sēt′′n) ⟦CHLORO- + -MYCETE + -IN[1]⟧ *trademark for* CHLORAMPHENICOL

chlo·ro·phyll or **chlo·ro·phyl** (klôr′ə fil′) ***n.*** ⟦Fr *chlorophylle*: see CHLORO- & -PHYLL⟧ the green pigment found in the chloroplasts of plant cells: it occurs in five forms, esp. (**chlorophyll a**), $C_{55}H_{72}MgN_4O_5$, and (**chlorophyll b**), $C_{55}H_{70}MgN_4O_6$: it is essential to the photosynthetic process and is used as a coloring agent, in topical medicines, etc. —**chlo′ro·phyl′lose′** (-ōs′) ***adj.***, **chlo′ro·phyl′lous** (-əs)

chlo·ro·pic·rin (klôr′ō pik′rin) ***n.*** ⟦CHLORO- + PICR(IC ACID) + -IN[1]⟧ a colorless liquid, CCl_3NO_2, prepared by treating chloroform with concentrated nitric acid, and used in chemical warfare as a poison gas, and in insecticides, fungicides, etc.

chlo·ro·plast (klôr′ə plast′) ***n.*** ⟦CHLORO- + -PLAST⟧ a green, oval plastid containing chlorophyll and carotenoids and found in the cytoplasm of green plants and blue-green algae: see CHROMOPLAST, PHOTOSYNTHESIS

chlo·ro·prene (-prēn′) ***n.*** ⟦CHLORO- + (ISO)PRENE⟧ a colorless liquid, $H_2C:CHCCl:CH_2$, made from acetylene: it can be polymerized to form neoprene

chlo·ro·quine (klôr′ə kwin) ***n.*** ⟦< CHLORO- + QUIN(OLIN)E⟧ a synthetic drug, $C_{18}H_{26}ClN_3$, used in treating malaria, certain kinds of arthritis, etc.

chlo·ro·sis (klə rō′sis) ***n.*** ⟦ModL: see CHLOR(O)- & -OSIS⟧ **1** an abnormal condition of plants in which the green parts lose their color or turn yellow as a result of a lack of chlorophyll production due to disease, lack of light, etc. **2** a form of iron-deficiency anemia sometimes affecting girls at puberty and causing the skin to turn a greenish color —**chlo·rot′ic** (-rät′ik) ***adj.***

chlo·ro·thi·a·zide (klôr′ō thī′ə zīd′) ***n.*** ⟦CHLORO- + THI- + AZ- + -IDE⟧ a synthetic drug, $C_7H_6ClN_3O_4S_2$, used in treating hypertension, heart failure, or various edemas by removing extra salt and water through the kidneys

chlo·rous (klôr′əs) ***adj.*** **1** of or containing trivalent chlorine **2** designating or of an unstable acid, $HClO_2$, a strong oxidizing agent which exists only in solution and whose salts are known as chlorites

chlor·prom·a·zine (klôr präm′ə zēn′) ***n.*** ⟦CHLOR(O)- + *promazine*, $C_{17}H_{20}N_2S$, contr. < *promethazine*, an antihistaminic drug < PRO(PYL) + *(di)meth(ylamine)*, a gaseous compound, $(CH_3)_2NH$ + *(phenothi)azine*, $C_{12}H_9NS$ < PHENO- + THIAZINE⟧ a synthetic drug, $C_{17}H_{19}ClN_2S$, used to treat certain mental disorders and to control nausea and vomiting

☆**chlor·tet·ra·cy·cline** (klôr′te′trə sī′klēn′, -klin) ***n.*** ⟦CHLOR(O)- + TETRACYCLINE⟧ a yellow antibiotic, $C_{22}H_{23}ClN_2O_8$, isolated from a microorganism (*Streptomyces aureofaciens*): it is used against a wide variety of bacterial and rickettsial infections and certain viruses

chm or **chmn** *abbrev.* chairman

Choate (chōt), **Rufus** 1799-1859; U.S. lawyer

chock (chäk) ***n.*** ⟦NormFr *choque*, a block < Gaul **tsukka*, akin to PGmc **stuk-*, a tree trunk, stump: for IE base see STOCK⟧ **1** a block or wedge placed under a wheel, barrel, etc. to keep it from rolling or used to fill in a space **2** *Naut.* a heavy metal fitting fixed to the deck of a ship, through which a line for mooring, towing, etc. is passed —***vt.*** to provide or wedge fast with a chock or chocks —***adv.*** as close or tight as can be

chock

chock·a·block (chäk′ə bläk′) ***adj.*** ⟦see prec. & BLOCK⟧ **1** *Naut. a)* pulled so tight as to have the blocks touching (said of a hoisting tackle) *b)* hoisted all the way up, as a signal flag **2** crowded or jammed —***adv.*** tightly together

chock-full (chäk′fo͝ol′) ***adj.*** ⟦ME *chokkeful, chekefull* < *choke, cheke*, cheek + *-ful*, -FUL; now often assoc. with CHOCK, CHOKE⟧ as full as possible; filled to capacity

choc·o·hol·ic (chôk′ə hôl′ik, chäk′-; -häl′-) ***n.*** ⟦fol. + -HOLIC⟧ [Informal] a person who has an obsessive need to eat chocolate: a humorous, hyperbolic usage

choc·o·late (chôk′lət, chäk′-; chôk′ə lət, chäk′ə-) ***n.*** ⟦? via Fr *chocolat* < Sp *chocolate* < Nahuatl *čokola:λ*⟧ **1** a paste, powder, syrup, or bar made from cacao seeds that have been roasted and ground **2** a drink made of chocolate, hot milk or water, and sugar **3** a candy made of or coated with chocolate **4** the flavor of chocolate **5** reddish brown —***adj.*** **1** made of or flavored with chocolate **2** reddish-brown —**choc′o·lat·y** ***adj.***, **choc′o·lat·ey**

chocolate chip cookie a type of cookie containing bits of solid chocolate and, often, nuts

cho·co·la·tier (chô′kə lə tir′) ***n.*** ⟦Fr < *chocolat*, CHOCOLATE⟧ a maker or seller of chocolate candies, esp. fancy or expensive ones

Choc·taw (chäk′tô′, -tä′) ***n.*** ⟦Choctaw *chahta*, a self-designation⟧ **1** *pl.* **-taws′** or **-taw′** a member of a North American Indian people that lived in S Mississippi, Alabama, Georgia, and Louisiana and now lives in Oklahoma and Mississippi **2** the Muskogean language of this people

choice (chois) ***n.*** ⟦ME & OFr *chois* < *choisir*, to choose < Goth *kausjan*, to taste, test: see CHOOSE⟧ **1** the act of choosing; selection **2** the right, power, or chance to choose; option **3** a person or thing chosen **4** the best or most preferable part **5** a variety from which to choose **6** a supply that is well chosen **7** an alternative —***adj.*** **choic′er**, **choic′est** **1** of special excellence; superior **2** carefully chosen **3** designating or of a grade of government-classified meat between *prime* and *good* —**of choice** that is or are preferred [medically the treatment *of choice*] —**choice′ly** ***adv.*** —**choice′ness** ***n.***

SYN.—**choice** implies the chance, right, or power to choose, usually by the free exercise of one's judgment [a bachelor by *choice*]; **option** suggests the privilege of choosing as granted by a person or group in authority that normally exercises the power [local *option* on liquor sales]; **alternative**, in strict usage, limits a choice to one of two possibilities [the *alternative* of paying a fine or serving 30 days]; **preference** suggests the determining of choice by predisposition or partiality [a *preference* for striped ties]; **selection** implies a wide choice and the exercise of careful discrimination [*selections* from the modern French poets]

choir (kwīr) ***n.*** ⟦< ME *quere* < OFr *cuer* < ML *chorus*, choir < L (see CHORUS); sp. altered under infl. of L⟧ **1** a group of singers organized and trained to sing together, esp. in a church **2** the part of a church they occupy, as a chancel or choir loft ☆**3** an instrumental section of an orchestra [the brass *choir*] **4** any organized group or band, as of dancers **5** *Theol.* any of the nine orders of angels — ***vt., vi.*** [Old Poet.] to sing in chorus

choir·boy (kwīr′boi′) ***n.*** a boy who sings in a choir

choir loft the gallery occupied by the choir in a church

choir·mas·ter (-mas′tər) ***n.*** the director, or conductor, of a choir

choke (chōk) ***vt.*** **choked**, **chok′ing** ⟦ME *choken*, aphetic < OE vt. *aceocian*, to choke, prob. < base of *ceoke*, jaw, CHEEK⟧ **1** to prevent from breathing by blocking the windpipe; suffocate; smother; stifle; often, specif., to prevent from breathing by squeezing the throat of; strangle **2** to block up; obstruct by clogging **3** to hinder the growth or action of; smother; suppress **4** to fill up **5** to cut off some air from the carburetor of (a gasoline engine) in order to make a richer gasoline mixture ☆**6** to hold (a bat, golf club, etc.) away from the end of the handle and closer toward the middle —***vi.*** **1** to be suffocated; have difficulty in breathing **2** to be blocked up; be obstructed **3** to become strained with emotion [a *choked* voice] **4** [Informal] to be unable to perform efficiently, as in a sporting event, because of tension, strong emotion, etc. —***n.*** **1** the act of choking; strangulation **2** a sound of choking **3** the valve that chokes a carburetor **4** a constriction, as in a chokebore —**choke back** to hold back (feelings, sobs, etc.) —**choke down** to swallow with difficulty —**choke off** to bring to an end; end the growth of —**choke up** **1** to block up; clog **2** to fill too full ☆**3** to hold a bat, golf club, etc. away from the end of the handle and closer toward the middle: often with *on* ☆**4** [Informal] to become unable to speak, act efficiently, etc., as because of fear, strong emotion, tension, etc.

☆**choke·ber·ry** (chōk′ber′ē) ***n.***, *pl.* **-ries** **1** the astringent, berrylike fruit of certain North American shrubs (genus *Aronia*) of the rose family **2** such a shrub

choke·bore (-bôr′) ***n.*** **1** a shotgun bore that tapers toward the muzzle to keep the shot closely bunched **2** a gun with such a bore

choke chain a type of CHOKE COLLAR consisting of a metal chain

☆**choke·cher·ry** (-cher′ē) ***n.***, *pl.* **-ries** **1** a North American wild cherry tree (*Prunus virginiana*) **2** its astringent fruit Also written **choke cherry**

choke coil an inductor used to limit or suppress alternating current without stopping direct current

choke collar a training collar for a dog, that tightens when the dog strains at the leash

choke·damp (-damp′) ***n.*** BLACKDAMP

choke·hold (-hōld′) ***n.*** **1** a technique for restraining or subduing a person by locking one's arms around the person's neck **2** firm or absolute control over some activity, process, etc.

chok·er (-ər) ***n.*** **1** a person or thing that chokes **2** a necklace that fits closely around the neck **3** a narrow fur piece worn around the neck **4** [Archaic] a wide neckcloth or stiff collar worn tight around the neck

chok·y (-ē) ***adj.*** **chok′i·er**, **chok′i·est** **1** inclined to choke **2** suffocating; stifling Also sp. **chok′ey**

cho·late (kō′lāt′) ***n.*** a salt or ester of cholic acid

chol·e- (käl′ə, kō′-) ⟦< Gr *cholē*, bile: see CHOLERA⟧ *combining form* bile, gall [*cholesterol, choline*]: also, before a vowel, **chol-**

chol·e·cal·cif·er·ol (käl′ə kal sif′ər ôl′, -ōl′, kō′lə-) ***n.*** a white, crystalline sterol, $C_{27}H_{43}OH$, found esp. in fish-liver oils or produced in the skin by irradiation with sunlight; vitamin D_3: the most common form of vitamin D

chol·e·cyst (käl′ə sist, kō′lə-) ***n.*** ⟦ModL *cholecystis* < Gr *cholē*, bile (see CHOLERA) + *kystis*, bladder⟧ the gallbladder

chol·e·cys·tec·to·my (käl′ə sis tek′tə mē, kō′lə-) ***n.***, *pl.* **-mies** ⟦< prec. + -ECTOMY⟧ the surgical removal of the gallbladder

chol·e·cys·ti·tis (käl′ə sis tīt′is, kō′lə-) ***n.***, *pl.* **-tit′i·des′** (-tit′i dēz′) an infection or inflammation of the gallbladder

chol·e·cys·to·ki·nin (-sis′tə kī′nin) ***n.*** a polypeptide hormone secreted by the upper intestinal lining, that activates the gallbladder and pancreas: its presence in the brain is associated with loss of appetite

cho·lent (chō′lənt, chul′ənt) ***n.*** ⟦Yiddish < ? Fr *chaud*, hot⟧ a stew of beans, potatoes, beef, etc. baked slowly for a long time: a traditional Jewish dish prepared on Friday for eating on the Sabbath

chol·er (käl′ər) ***n.*** ⟦altered (by analogy with L forms) < ME & OFr *colre* < L *cholera*: see fol.⟧ **1** [Obs.] bile: in medieval times yellow bile was considered to be one of the four humors of the body and the source of anger and irritability **2** [Now Rare] anger or ill humor

chol·er·a (käl′ər ə) ***n.*** ⟦L, jaundice < Gr, cholera, nausea < *cholē*, gall, bile < IE base **ĝhel-* > YELLOW⟧ any of various intestinal diseases; specif., an acute, severe, infectious disease (**Asiatic cholera**) common in Asia, caused by bacteria (*Vibrio cholerae*) and characterized by profuse diarrhea, intestinal pain, and dehydration —**chol′e·ra′ic** (-ə rā′ik) ***adj.***

cholera mor·bus (môr′bəs) ⟦L, lit., the disease cholera⟧ *former term for* GASTROENTERITIS

chol·er·ic (käl′ər ik, kə ler′ik) ***adj.*** ⟦ME *colerik*, having choler as the predominant humor, hence of bilious temperament < OFr *colerique* < L *cholericus* < Gr *cholerikos*: see CHOLERA⟧ **1** having or showing a quick temper or irascible nature **2** [Obs.] of or having choler, or bile —*SYN.* IRRITABLE

cho·les·ter·ic (kō′lə ster′ik, kä′lə-; kō les′tər ik) ***adj.*** designating or of a kind of liquid crystal which is characterized by a screwlike structure and great optical activity

cho·les·ter·ol (kə les′tər ôl′, -ōl′) ***n.*** ⟦< CHOLE- + Gr *stereos*, solid, stiff + -OL[1]⟧ a white, crystalline sterol, $C_{27}H_{45}OH$, found esp. in animal fats, blood, nerve tissue, and bile: a precursor of steroidal hormones and, if present in the blood in excessive amounts, a factor in atherosclerosis

cho·les·tyr·a·mine (resin) (kō les′tir ə mēn′, kō les tir′-) a powdery synthetic resin that binds with and prevents the reabsorption of bile acids, used to reduce cholesterol levels, relieve itching associated with jaundice, etc.

cho·lic acid (kō′lik) ⟦< Gr *cholikos* < *cholē*, bile: see CHOLERA⟧ an acid, $C_{24}H_{40}O_5$, found in the bile, generally in combination with amino acids

cho·line (kō′lēn′, -lin) ***n.*** ⟦CHOL(E)- + -INE[3]⟧ a viscous fluid, $(CH_3)_3N(OH)CH_2CH_2OH$, found in many animal and vegetable tissues, that is a precursor of acetylcholine, lecithin, etc.: usually considered a vitamin of the B complex

cho·lin·er·gic (kō′lin ʉr′jik) ***adj.*** ⟦< prec. + Gr *ergon*, WORK + -IC⟧ **1** having the properties of acetylcholine **2** releasing or stimulated by acetylcholine

cho·lin·es·ter·ase (-es′tər ās′) ***n.*** ⟦< CHOLINE + ESTERASE⟧ an enzyme which hydrolyzes a choline ester; esp., acetylcholine, which converts to choline and acetic acid, thus canceling a nerve impulse transmission

☆**chol·la** (chōl′yä, chō′yä) ***n.*** ⟦MexSp < Sp, lit., skull, head⟧ a spiny cactus (genus *Opuntia*) with cylindrical stems, growing in the SW U.S. and Mexico

☆**cho·lo** (chō′lō) ***n.***, *pl.* **-los** PACHUCO

chol·o- (käl′ō, -lə) *combining form* CHOLE-

Cho·lu·la (chō lo͞o′lə) town in central Mexico, near Puebla: site of Toltec and Aztec ruins

chomp (chämp) ***vt., vi.*** ⟦dial. var. of CHAMP[1]⟧ **1** to chew hard and noisily **2** to bite down (*on*), repeatedly and restlessly [to *chomp* on a cigar] —***n.*** the act or sound of chomping —**chomp at the bit** CHAMP AT THE BIT (see phrase under CHAMP[1]) —**chomp′er** ***n.***

Chom·sky (chäm′skē), **(Avram) No·am** (nō′əm) 1928- ; U.S. linguist, educator, & political activist

chon (chun) ***n.***, *pl.* **chon** ⟦Kor⟧ a monetary unit of North Korea, equal to $\frac{1}{100}$ of a won

chon·dri·o·some (kän′drē ə sōm′) ***n.*** ⟦< Gr *chondrion*, dim. of *chondros* (see CHONDRO-) + -SOME[3]⟧ MITOCHONDRION

chon·drite (kän′drīt′) ***n.*** ⟦Ger *chondrit* < Gr *chondros*, granule, grain: see fol.⟧ the type of stony meteorite that contains chondrules —**chon·drit·ic** (kän drit′ik) ***adj.***

chon·dro- (kän′drō, -drə) ⟦< Gr *chondros*, cartilage, grain < IE **ghren-*, extension of base **gher-*, to rub > GRIND⟧ *combining form* cartilage [*chondroma*]: also **chon′dri-** (-drē, -dri, -drə) or, before a vowel, **chon′dr-**

chon·dro·i·tin (kän drō′ə tin, -droit′'n) ***n.*** ⟦< prec. + -ITE[1] (sense 7) + -IN[1]⟧ a highly viscous mucopolysaccharide found in cartilage: it is taken as a food supplement to maintain and repair the elasticity of cartilage: in full **chondroitin sulfate**

chon·dro·ma (kän drō′mə) ***n.***, *pl.* **-mas** or **-ma·ta** (-mə tə) ⟦CHONDRO- + -OMA⟧ a cartilaginous, benign tumor

chon·drule (kän′dro͞ol′) ***n.*** ⟦< ModL *chondrus*, chondrule (< Gr *chondros*: see CHONDRO-) + -ULE⟧ a rounded mass of various minerals, the size of a pea or smaller, in most stony meteorites

Chong·jin (chôŋ′jin′) seaport in NE North Korea, on the Sea of Japan

Chong·qing (cho͝oŋ′chiŋ′) city in Sichuan province, SC China, on the Chang River

choo-choo (cho͞o′cho͞o′) ***n.*** ⟦echoic⟧ a railroad train or locomotive: a child's word

choose (cho͞oz) ***vt.*** **chose**, **cho′sen**, **choos′ing** ⟦ME *chesen*, *cheosen* < OE *ceosan* < IE base **ĝeus-*, to taste, relish > L *gustare*, Goth *kausjan*⟧ **1** to pick out by preference from what is available; take as a choice; select [to *choose* a book at the library] **2** to decide or prefer: with an infinitive object [to *choose* to remain] —***vi.*** **1** to make one's selection **2** to have the desire or wish; please [do as you *choose*] —**cannot choose but** cannot do otherwise than [they *cannot choose but* accede to their host's demands] —☆**choose**

up [Informal] to select (sides), as for an impromptu ballgame, by making alternating choices from a group of available players —**choos′er** *n.*

☆**choos·y** or **choos·ey** (cho͞o′zē) *adj.* **choos′i·er, choos′i·est** [Informal] very careful or fussy in choosing

chop[1] (chäp) *vt.* **chopped, chop′ping** ⟦ME *choppen*, prob. < northern OFr *choper*, for OFr *coper*, to cut off (< VL **cuppare*, to decapitate < **cuppum*, skull < LL *cuppa*, CUP); infl. by *couper*, to strike (< *coup, colp*, a blow: see COUP)⟧ **1** to cut or make by blows with an ax or other sharp tool [*to chop* down a tree; to *chop* a hole] **2** to cut into pieces, often, specif., small pieces: often followed by *up* [*chop* up the onions, *chopped* sirloin] **3** to say in a jerky or abrupt way **4** to hit with a short, sharp downward stroke —*vi.* **1** to make quick, cutting strokes with a sharp tool **2** to do something with a quick, sharp, or jerky motion —*n.* **1** the act of chopping **2** a short, sharp downward blow or stroke **3** a piece chopped off **4** a slice of lamb, pork, etc. cut, along with a piece of bone, from the rib, loin, or shoulder **5** a short, broken movement of waves

chop[2] (chäp) *n.* ⟦var. of CHAP[1]⟧ **1** a jaw **2** a cheek See also CHOPS

chop[3] (chäp) *vi.* **chopped, chop′ping** ⟦LME *choppen*, var. of *chappen*, to barter < OE *ceapian*, to bargain: see CHEAP⟧ to shift or veer suddenly, as the wind; change direction —**chop logic** to argue, esp. in a hairsplitting way

chop[4] (chäp) *n.* ⟦Hindi *chāp*⟧ **1** an official seal, stamp, permit, or license, as orig. in India and China **2** a brand, or trademark **3** [Informal] quality; grade; brand [a writer of the first *chop*]

chop-chop (chäp′chäp′) *adv., interj.* ⟦PidE⟧ [Slang] (do it) quickly; (in a) hurry: used in imagined imitation of the speech of E Asian people

chop·fall·en (-fôl′ən) *adj. var. of* CHAPFALLEN

chop·house (-hous′) *n.* a restaurant serving chops and steaks

Cho·pin (shō′pan, shō pan′), **Fré·dé·ric Fran·çois** (frā dā rēk frän swȧ′) (Pol. name *Fryderyk Franciszek Chopin*) 1810-49; Pol. composer & pianist, in France after 1831

cho·pine (chō pēn′, chäp′in) *n.* ⟦Sp *chapin* < ?⟧ a woman's shoe with a very thick sole, as of cork, worn in the 16th and 17th cent.

chop-logic (chäp′läj′ik) *n.* hairsplitting argumentation or evasive reasoning

chopped liver ⟦Yiddish *gehakteh leber*, traditional dish of chopped, cooked chicken livers, seasonings, etc.; extended use ? from its being a side dish rather than a main course⟧ ☆[Slang] a person or thing regarded as negligible [that suggestion isn't just *chopped liver*]

chop·per (chäp′ər) *n.* **1** a person who chops **2** a tool or machine for chopping, as an ax or cleaver **3** [*pl.*] [Slang] a set of teeth, esp. false teeth ☆**4** [Informal] a helicopter **5** [Informal] a motorcycle **6** *Electronics* a device for interrupting a current, light beam, etc. at regular intervals to make amplification easier, create a pulsating effect, etc.

chopping block a block of hardwood on which meat and vegetables are cut up in food preparation

chop·py[1] (-ē) *adj.* **-pi·er, -pi·est** ⟦< CHOP[3] + -Y[3]⟧ shifting constantly and abruptly, as the wind —**chop′pi·ness** *n.*

chop·py[2] (-ē) *adj.* **-pi·er, -pi·est** ⟦< CHOP[1] + -Y[3]⟧ **1** rough with short, broken waves, as the sea **2** making abrupt starts and stops; jerky; disjointed —**chop′pi·ly** *adv.* —**chop′pi·ness** *n.*

chops (chäps) *pl.n.* ⟦see CHAP[1]⟧ **1** the jaws **2** the mouth and lower cheeks ☆**3** [Slang] technical skill, esp. of a jazz or rock musician

☆**chop shop** [Informal] a place, esp. a garage, where stolen automobiles are dismantled for parts

☆**chop·sock·y** or **chop-sock·y** (chäp′säk′ē) *n.* ⟦coined by *Variety*, a trade magazine, to describe such movies, with a pun on CHOP SUEY⟧ [Slang] a movie featuring martial arts, esp. one made in Southeast Asia in the 1960s or 1970s

chop·sticks (chäp′stiks′) *pl.n.* ⟦PidE for Chin *k'wai-tsze*, the quick ones (see CHOP-CHOP)⟧ **1** a pair of small sticks of wood, ivory, plastic, etc., held together in one hand and used in Asian cuisine as eating and cooking utensils **2** [*occas.* **C-**] a short, choppy traditional melody, usually played on the piano with one finger of each hand

☆**chop su·ey** (chäp′ so͞o′ē) ⟦altered by assoc. with CHOP[1] < Chin *tsa-sui*, lit., various pieces⟧ a Chinese-American dish consisting of meat, bean sprouts, celery, mushrooms, etc. cooked together in a sauce and served with rice

cho·ra·gus (kō rā′gəs, kə-) *n., pl.* **-gi′** (-jī′) ⟦L < Gr *chorēgos* < *choros*, CHORUS + *agein*, to lead: see ACT[1]⟧ **1** the leader of the chorus in an ancient Greek play **2** any leader of a chorus or band —**cho·rag′ic** (-raj′ik) *adj.*

cho·ral (kôr′əl) *adj.* ⟦Fr⟧ of, for, sung by, or recited by a choir or chorus: see also CHORALE —**cho′ral·ly** *adv.*

cho·rale or **cho·ral** (kə ral′, -räl′) *n.* ⟦< Ger *choral (gesang)*, choral (song), hymn⟧ **1** a hymn tune, esp. in the Lutheran service, with a simple melody and rhythm **2** a choral or instrumental composition based on such a tune **3** a group of singers; choir or chorus

choral speaking recitation of poetry, dramatic pieces, etc. by a chorus of speakers

chord[1] (kôrd) *n.* ⟦altered (infl. by L *chorda*) < CORD⟧ **1** [Archaic] the string of a musical instrument **2** a feeling or emotion thought of as being played on like the string of a harp [to strike a sympathetic *chord*] **3** *Aeron.* *a)* an imaginary straight line extending directly through an airfoil from the leading to the trailing edge *b)* the length of such a line **4** *Anat.* CORD (sense 5) **5** *Engineering* a principal horizontal member in a rigid framework, as of a bridge **6** *Geom.* a straight line segment joining any two points on an arc, curve, or circumference: cf. SECANT (sense 1)

chord[2] (kôrd) *n.* ⟦altered (infl. by L *chorda*) < ME *cord*, aphetic < *accord*, ACCORD⟧ *Music* a combination of three or more tones sounded together in harmony — *vi., vt.* **1** to harmonize **2** to play chords on (a piano, guitar, etc.) —**chord′al** *adj.*

chor·date (kôr′dāt′) *n.* ⟦L *chorda* (see CORD) + -ATE[1]⟧ any of a phylum (Chordata) of animals having at some stage of development a notochord, gill slits, and a dorsal tubular nerve cord: the phylum includes the vertebrates, tunicates, and lancelets

chore (chôr) *n.* ⟦ME *cher, cherre*: see CHARE⟧ **1** a small routine task, as of a housekeeper or farmer: *often used in pl.* **2** a hard or unpleasant task —*SYN.* TASK

cho·re·a (kô rē′ə) *n.* ⟦ModL < L, a dance in a ring < Gr *choreia*, choral dance⟧ a disorder of the nervous system characterized by irregular, jerking movements caused by involuntary muscular contractions; Saint Vitus' dance

chor·e·o·graph (kôr′ē ə graf′) *vt., vi.* ⟦back-form. < fol.⟧ **1** to design or plan the movements of (a dance, esp. a ballet) **2** to plan (an event or complex course of action) in careful detail —**chor′e·og′ra·pher** (-äg′rə fər) *n.*

chor·e·og·ra·phy (kôr′ē äg′rə fē) *n.* ⟦Gr *choreia*, dance + -GRAPHY⟧ **1** dancing, esp. ballet dancing **2** the arrangement or the written notation of the movements of a dance, esp. a ballet **3** the art of devising dances, esp. ballets Also [Rare] **cho·reg′ra·phy** (kə reg′-) —**chor′e·o·graph′ic** (-ə graf′ik) *adj.* —**chor′e·o·graph′i·cal·ly** *adv.*

cho·ri·amb (kôr′ē amb′, -am′) *n.* ⟦L *choriambus* < Gr *choriambos* < *choreios*, trochee, lit., pertaining to a chorus + *iambos*, IAMB⟧ a metrical foot consisting, in Greek and Latin verse, of two short syllables between two long ones, or, as in English verse, of two unaccented syllables between two accented ones: also **cho′ri·am′bus** (-am′bəs), *pl.* **-bus·es** —**cho′ri·am′bic** (-am′bik) *adj.*

cho·ric (kôr′ik) *adj.* of, for, or in the manner of a chorus, esp. in an ancient Greek play

☆**cho·rine** (kôr′ēn′) *n.* ⟦CHOR(US) + -INE[2]⟧ [Informal] CHORUS GIRL

cho·ri·o·al·lan·to·is (kôr′ē ō ə lan′tō is) *n.* ⟦ModL: see CHORION & ALLANTOIS⟧ an enveloping vascular fetal membrane formed by the fusion of chorion and allantois in reptiles, birds, and most mammals: that of chicks is used as a culture medium for growing viruses —**cho′ri·o·al′lan·to′ic** (-al′ən tō′ik) *adj.*

cho·ri·o·car·ci·no·ma (kôr′ē ō kär′sə nō′mə) *n., pl.* **-mas** or **-ma·ta** (-tə) ⟦ModL: see CHORION & CARCINOMA⟧ a rare, fast-spreading carcinoma that forms from the trophoblastic cells of a placenta —**cho′ri·o·car′ci·no′ma·tous** *adj.*

cho·ri·oid (kôr′ē oid′) *adj., n.* CHOROID

cho·ri·on (kôr′ē än′) *n.* ⟦ModL < Gr *chorion*, fetal membrane: for IE base see YARN⟧ **1** the outermost of the two membranes that completely envelop a fetus **2** the outer membrane or shell of the eggs of insects and other invertebrates —**cho′ri·on′ic** (-än′ik) *adj.*

chorionic villus sampling a test for detecting genetic abnormalities, determining sex, etc. in a fetus: tissue samples of chorionic villi are removed from the uterus

cho·ri·pet·al·ous (kôr′i pet′'l əs) *n.* ⟦< Gr *chōri*, var. of *chōris*, apart, bereaved (akin to *chōros*: see CHOROGRAPHY) + PETALOUS⟧ POLYPETALOUS

chor·is·ter (kôr′is tər) *n.* ⟦altered (infl. by CHORUS) < ME *querister*, prob. via Anglo-Norm **cueristre* < ML(Ec) *querista* < *chorus*, choir < L: see CHORUS⟧ **1** a member of a choir, esp. a boy singer ☆**2** one who leads the singing in church of a congregation or choir

cho·ri·zo (chō rē′zō, -sō) *n., pl.* **-zos** ⟦Sp⟧ a Spanish or Mexican pork sausage highly seasoned with garlic, paprika, and other spices

C-ho·ri·zon (sē′hə rī′zən) *n.* the third soil zone, consisting of material essentially unaltered by weathering, solution, or the action of plant roots: see ABC SOIL

cho·rog·ra·phy (kō räg′rə fē, kə-) *n.* ⟦L *chorographia*, geography < Gr *chōrographia* < *chōros*, open area (< IE base **ghē-*, to be empty, leave behind > GO[1]) + *graphein*, to write: see GRAPHIC⟧ **1** the art of mapping or describing a region **2** a map or description of a particular region —**cho·ro·graph·ic** (kôr′ə graf′ik) *adj.*

cho·roid (kôr′oid′) *adj.* ⟦Gr *choroeidēs*, contr. < *chorioeidēs* < *chorion*, CHORION + *-eidēs*, -OID⟧ designating or of the chorion or certain other vascular membranes —*n.* the dark, vascular membrane that forms the middle coat of the eye, between the sclera and the retina: see EYE, illus.

chor·tle (chôrt′'l) *vi., vt.* **-tled, -tling** ⟦coined by Lewis CARROLL in *Through the Looking-Glass*, prob. blend of CHUCKLE & SNORT⟧ to make, or utter with, a gleeful chuckling or snorting sound —*n.* such a sound —**chor′tler** *n.*

cho·rus (kôr′əs) *n.* ⟦L, a dance, band of dancers or singers < Gr *choros*⟧ **1** in ancient Greek drama, and drama like it, a company of performers whose singing, dancing, and narration provide explanation and elaboration of the main action **2** in Elizabethan drama, a person who recites the prologue and epilogue **3** a group of dancers and singers performing together in a modern musical show, opera, etc. **4** the part of a drama, song, etc. performed by a chorus **5** a group of people trained to sing or speak something together simultaneously **6** a simultaneous utterance by many [a *chorus* of protest] **7** that which is thus uttered **8** music written for group singing **9** that part of a musical composition in which the company joins the solo singer **10** *a)* the refrain of a song or hymn following each verse *b)* the main tune, as of a jazz piece, following the introduction *c)* *Jazz* a solo, usually an improvised one based on the main tune of a piece — *vt., vi.* to sing, speak, or say in unison —**in chorus** in unison

chorus boy a man singing or dancing in the chorus of a musical show

chorus girl a woman singing or dancing in the chorus of a musical show

Cho·rzów (kô′zho͞of′) city in S Poland

chose[1] (chōz) *vt., vi. pt. & obs. pp. of* CHOOSE

chose[2] (shōz) *n.* ⟦OFr, thing < L *causa,* matter, affair⟧ *Law* a piece of personal property; chattel

cho·sen (chō′zən) *vt., vi. pp. of* CHOOSE —*adj.* 1 picked out by preference; selected 2 *Theol.* elect; favored by God

Cho·sen (chō′sen′) *Jpn. name for* KOREA

chott (shät) *n.* SHOTT

Chou (jō) *n.* third Chinese dynasty (*c.* 1122-256 B.C.)

chou·croute (sho͞o kro͞ot′) *n.* ⟦Fr⟧ 1 sauerkraut 2 a dish consisting of sauerkraut cooked with, variously, pork, ham, or sausages: also ***choucroute garnie*** (gȧr nē′)

Chou En-lai (jō′en′lī′) 1898-1976; Chin. Communist leader: premier (1949-76): Pinyin *Zhou En-lai*

chough (chuf) *n.* ⟦ME < IE base *gou-, to cry, scream > MDu *cauwe,* jackdaw, Ger *kauz,* screech-owl⟧ any of various crowlike birds; esp., a European bird (*Pyrrhocorax pyrrhocorax*) of the crow family, with red legs and beak and glossy, black feathers

chouse[1] (chous) *vt.* **choused, chous′ing** ⟦< CHIAUS: after a Turk interpreter alleged to have swindled London merchants in 1609⟧ [Chiefly Brit.] to cheat; swindle

☆**chouse**[2] (chous) *vt.* ⟦< ?⟧ [West] to herd (cattle) roughly

choux pastry (*or* **paste**) (sho͞o) ⟦< Fr *choux,* cream puffs, pl. of *chou,* lit., cabbage: so named from the pastry's rounded shape⟧ a rich dough made from flour, hot water, melted butter, and eggs, pressed from a pastry bag with a wide tip to form cream puffs, éclairs, etc.

chow (chou) *n.* ⟦< Chin dial. form akin to Cantonese *kaú,* a dog⟧ 1 any of a breed of medium-sized dog, originally from China, with a thick, dark coat and a blue-black tongue: official name **chow chow** ☆2 [Slang] food or mealtime —☆**chow down** [Slang] to eat a meal

chow·chow (chou′chou′) *n.* ⟦PidE < Chin⟧ ☆1 pickled vegetables in a highly seasoned mustard sauce 2 a preserve of orange peel and ginger, originally Chinese

☆**chow·der** (chou′dər) *n.* ⟦Fr *chaudière,* a pot < LL *caldaria:* see CALDRON⟧ a thick soup made variously, but usually containing onions, potatoes, and salt pork, sometimes corn, tomatoes, or other vegetables, and often, specif., clams or fish and milk

chow·der·head (chou′dər hed′) *n.* [Slang] a stupid or ignorant person

☆**chow·hound** (chou′hound′) *n.* [Slang] a person who eats large quantities of food or is fond of eating; glutton or gourmand: also written **chow hound**

☆**chow mein** (chou′ mān′) ⟦Chin *ch'ao,* to fry + *mien,* flour⟧ a Chinese-American dish consisting of a thick stew of meat, celery, bean sprouts, etc., served with fried noodles and, usually, soy sauce

Chr *abbrev.* 1 Christian 2 *Bible* Chronicles

chres·tom·a·thy (kres täm′ə thē) *n., pl.* **-thies** ⟦Gr *chrēstomatheia* < *chrēstos,* useful < *chrē,* it is necessary (see CATACHRESIS) + *mathein,* to learn (akin to *manthanein:* see MATHEMATICAL)⟧ 1 a collection of literary passages, for use in studying a language 2 a collection of passages or pieces from the writings of an author

Chré·tien (*or* **Chres·tien**) **de Troyes** (krā tyan də trwȧ′) fl. 12th cent.; Fr. poet

chrism (kriz′əm) *n.* ⟦ME *crisme* < OE *crisma* < LL(Ec) *chrisma,* an anointing, unction < Gr, oil (in Ec use, anointing) < *chriein,* to rub, anoint: see CHRIST[1]⟧ 1 consecrated oil used in baptism and other sacraments 2 a sacramental anointing with this oil

chris·ma·tion (kriz mā′shən) *n.* ⟦ML *chrismatio,* act of anointing with chrism < *chrismare,* to anoint thus < LL *chrisma,* prec.⟧ *Eastern Orthodox Ch.* the sacrament of anointing with consecrated oil immediately after baptism, analogous in function to CONFIRMATION (*n.* 3a)

chris·ma·to·ry (kriz′mə tôr′ē) *n., pl.* **-ries** ⟦ML(Ec) *chrismatorium*⟧ a container or receptacle for the chrism

chris·om (kriz′əm) *n.* ⟦ME *crisom* (var. of *crisme,* CHRISM), orig., cloth to keep chrism off the face⟧ 1 a white cloth or robe formerly put on a baby at baptism as a symbol of innocence: it was used as a shroud if the child died within a month of birth 2 [Archaic] an innocent baby; infant

Chris·sakes (krī′sāks′) *interj.* [*also* **c-**] [Slang] for Christ's sake: often preceded by *for:* also **Chris′sake′**

Christ[1] (krīst) *n.* ⟦ME & OE *Crist* < LL(Ec) *Christus* < Gr *christos,* the anointed (in N.T., MESSIAH) < *chriein,* to anoint < IE base *ghrēi-, to spread over, smear > GRIME⟧ the Messiah whose appearance is prophesied in the Old Testament

Christ[2] (krīst) Jesus of Nazareth, regarded by Christians as the realization of the Messianic prophecy: originally a title (*Jesus the Christ*), later used as part of the name (*Jesus Christ*): see JESUS[2]: name used interjectionally to express, variously, surprise, wonder, annoyance, etc.

Christ·church (krīst′church′) city on the E coast of South Island, New Zealand

christ·cross (kris′krôs′) *n.* ⟦< ME *Crist cros,* Christ's cross⟧ 1 [Obs.] the figure of a cross (✠) placed before the alphabet in hornbooks 2 [Archaic] the mark of the cross (X) used as a signature by a person who cannot write See CRISSCROSS

chris·ten (kris′ən) *vt.* ⟦ME *cristnen* < OE *cristnian:* see CHRISTIAN⟧ 1 to take into a Christian church by baptism; baptize 2 to give a name to at baptism 3 to give a name to (a ship being launched, etc.) 4 [Informal] to make use of for the first time

Chris·ten·dom (kris′ən dəm) *n.* ⟦ME & OE *cristendom,* Christianity: see CHRISTIAN & -DOM⟧ 1 Christians collectively 2 those parts of the world where most inhabitants profess the Christian faith

chris·ten·ing (kris′ən iŋ) *n.* ⟦ME *cristninge:* see CHRISTEN⟧ the Christian act or ceremony of baptizing and giving a name to an infant; baptism

Christ·er (krīs′tər) *n.* [Slang] a Christian, esp. one actively engaged in proselytizing: a term of contempt or disparagement

Christ·hood (krīst′hood′) *n.* ⟦see -HOOD⟧ the state or fact of being the Christ

Chris·tian (kris′chən, -tyən) *n.* ⟦ME & OE *cristen* < LL(Ec) *Christianus* < Gr *christianos,* a Christian < *christos* (see CHRIST[1]); mod. sp. < L⟧ 1 a person professing belief in Jesus as the Christ, or in the religion based on the teachings of Jesus 2 a masculine name: dim. *Chris;* fem. *Christina, Christine* 3 [Informal] a decent, respectable person —*adj.* 1 *a)* of Jesus Christ or his teachings *b)* of or professing the religion based on these teachings 2 having the qualities demonstrated and taught by Jesus Christ, as love, kindness, humility, etc. 3 of or representing Christians or Christianity 4 [Informal] humane, decent, etc. —**Chris′tian·ly** *adj., adv.*

Christian Brothers a Roman Catholic lay order that undertakes the teaching of youth: in full **Brothers of the Christian Schools**

Christian Era the era beginning with the year 1 according to the modern Gregorian calendar, the year formerly thought to be that of the birth of Jesus Christ (born probably *c.* 8-4 B.C.): A.D. (or the alternative CE) marks dates in this era, and B.C. (or the alternative BCE) marks dates before it: cf. COMMON ERA

Chris·ti·an·i·a[1] (kris′chē an′ē ə, -tē-; -än′-) *n.* [*also* **c-**] CHRISTIE[1]

Chris·ti·an·i·a[2] (kris′chē an′ē ə, -tē-; -än′-) *former name for* OSLO

Chris·ti·an·i·ty (kris′chē an′ə tē, -tē an′-) *n.* ⟦ME *cristianite* < OFr *crestiente* < LL(Ec) *Christianitas* < *Christianus,* CHRISTIAN⟧ 1 Christians collectively 2 the Christian religion, based upon belief in Jesus as the Christ and upon his teachings 3 a particular Christian religious system 4 the state of being a Christian

Chris·tian·ize (kris′chən īz′, -tyən-) *vt.* **-ized′, -iz′ing** ⟦LL(Ec) *christianizare* < Gr(Ec) *christianizein,* to profess Christianity⟧ 1 to convert to Christianity 2 to make Christian in character —**Chris′tian·i·za′tion** *n.* —**Chris′tian·iz′er** *n.*

Christian name the baptismal name or given name, as distinguished from the surname or family name

Christian Science ☆a religion and a system of healing founded by Mary Baker Eddy *c.* 1866, based on an interpretation of the Scriptures asserting that disease, sin, and death may be overcome by understanding and applying the divine principles of Christian teachings —**Christian Scientist**

Christian X (born *Carl Frederick Albert Alexander Vilhelm*) 1870-1947; king of Denmark (1912-47)

Chris·tie[1] (kris′tē) *n., pl.* **-ties** ⟦< CHRISTIANIA[2]⟧ [*occas.* **c-**] *Skiing* any of various high-speed turns to change direction, reduce speed, or stop, made by shifting weight, with the skis parallel when the turn is completed: also sp. **Chris′ty,** *pl.* **-ties**

Chris·tie[2] (kris′tē), Dame **Agatha** (born *Agatha Mary Clarissa Miller*) 1890-1976; Eng. writer of detective stories

Chris·ti·na[1] (kris tē′nə) *n.* ⟦fem. of CHRISTIAN (*n.* 2)⟧ a feminine name: see CHRISTINE

Chris·ti·na[2] (kris tē′nə) 1626-89; queen of Sweden (1632-54)

Chris·tine (kris tēn′) *n.* ⟦fem. of CHRISTIAN (*n.* 2)⟧ a feminine name: dim. *Chris, Chrissie, Tina;* var. *Christina, Christy*

Christ·like (krīst′līk′) *adj.* like Jesus Christ, esp. in character or spirit —**Christ′like′ness** *n.*

Christ·ly (-lē) *adj.* 1 of Jesus Christ 2 Christlike —**Christ′li·ness** *n.*

Christ·mas (kris′məs) *n.* ⟦ME *Cristemas* < OE *Cristesmæsse:* see CHRIST[1] & MASS[1]⟧ 1 a holiday on Dec. 25 celebrating the birth of Jesus Christ: also **Christmas Day** 2 CHRISTMASTIME

Christmas cactus a common houseplant (*Schlumbergera bridgesii*) with flat, jointed, fleshy stems and red flowers that bloom around Christmastime; crab cactus

Christmas Eve the day or, esp., the evening before Christmas Day

Christmas Island 1 island in the Indian Ocean, south of Java: a territory of Australia: 52 sq mi (135 sq km) 2 KIRITIMATI

Christmas stocking a decorative stocking customarily hung, as from a mantlepiece, so as to be filled with small Christmas gifts

Christ·mas·sy or **Christ·mas·y** (kris′mə sē) *adj.* of, like, or suggesting the traditions or feelings associated with the Christmas season

Christ·mas·time (-tīm′) *n.* the Christmas season, traditionally from Christmas Eve through New Year's Day or to Epiphany (Jan. 6): also **Christ′mas·tide′** (-tīd′)

☆**Christmas tree** an evergreen or artificial tree hung with ornaments and lights at Christmastime

Chris·tol·o·gy (kris täl′ə jē) *n.* ⟦< Gr *christos* (see CHRIST[1]) + -OLOGY⟧ the study of the life and work of Jesus Christ and of the literature that relates to him —**Chris′to·log′i·cal** (-tə läj′i kəl) *adj.*

Chris·tophe (krēs tôf′), **Hen·ri** (än rē′) 1767-1820; Haitian revolutionary leader: king of Haiti (1811-20)

Chris·to·pher[1] (kris′tə fər) *n.* ⟦ME *Christofre* < LL(Ec) *Christophorus* < Gr(Ec) *Christophoros,* lit., bearing Christ < *christos* (see CHRIST[1]) + *pherein,* to BEAR[1]⟧ a masculine name: dim. *Chris, Kit, Kris*

Chris·to·pher[2] (kris′tə fər), Saint (3d cent. A.D.); Christian martyr of Asia Minor: patron saint of travelers: his day is July 25

chris·to·phine (kris′tə fēn′) ***n.*** ⟦AmFr⟧ CHAYOTE: also sp. **chris′to·phene′**
Christ's-thorn (krīsts′thôrn′) ***n.*** an Old World spiny shrub (*Paliurus spina-christi*) of the buckthorn family, supposed to have been used for Christ's crown of thorns
Chris·ty[1] (kris′tē) ***n.*** a feminine name: see CHRISTINE
Chris·ty[2] (kris′tē), **Howard Chandler** 1873-1952; U.S. painter & illustrator
chrom- (krōm) *combining form* CHROMO-: used before a vowel
chro·ma (krō′mə) ***n.*** ⟦Gr *chrōma* (gen. *chrōmatos*), color; orig. skin, color of the skin < IE base **ghrēu-*, to rub hard over, crumble > GRITS⟧ SATURATION (sense 2)
chro·mate (krō′māt′) ***n.*** ⟦CHROM(IUM) + -ATE[2]⟧ **1** a salt of chromic acid, containing the divalent, negative radical CrO_4 **2** an uncharged ester of this acid
chro·mat·ic (krō mat′ik) ***adj.*** ⟦LL *chromaticus* < Gr *chrōmatikos*, suited for color: see CHROMA & -ATIC⟧ **1** of color or having color or colors **2** designating or of colors other than black, white, and gray: opposed to ACHROMATIC (sense 1): see also COLOR (***n.*** 3-4) **3** highly colored **4** *Biol.* readily stained **5** *Music a)* using or progressing by semitones *[a chromatic* scale*] b)* producing all the tones of such a scale *[a chromatic* instrument*] c)* using tones not in the key of a work *[chromatic* harmony*]* **—*n.*** *Music* a tone modified by an accidental **—chro·mat′i·cal·ly *adv.* —chro·mat′i·cism′** (-ə siz′əm) ***n.***
chromatic aberration a property of lenses that causes the various colors in a beam of light to be focused at different points, thus causing a margin of colors to appear around the edges of the image
chro·ma·tic·i·ty (krō′mə tis′ə tē) ***n.*** the classification of a color with reference to its hue and its purity, i.e., its departure from white light
chro·mat·ics (krō mat′iks) ***n.*** the scientific study of colors with reference to hue and saturation
chromatic scale a musical scale made up of thirteen tones succeeding by half steps
chro·ma·tid (krō′mə tid′) ***n.*** ⟦CHROMAT(O)- (sense 2) + -ID⟧ any of the structures into which a chromosome divides during mitosis or meiosis
chro·ma·tin (-tin′) ***n.*** ⟦< CHROMA + -IN[1]⟧ a protoplasmic substance in the nucleus of living cells, forming the chromosomes and containing the genes: because it readily takes a deep stain, it is useful in microscopic observation of the cell
chro·ma·tism (-tiz′əm) ***n.*** ⟦Gr *chrōmatismos*: see prec. & -ISM⟧ CHROMATIC ABERRATION
chro·ma·to- (krō′mə tō, krō mat′ə) ⟦< Gr *chrōma* (gen. *chrōmatos*): see CHROMA⟧ *combining form* **1** color or pigmentation *[chromatography]* **2** chromatin *[chromatolysis]* Also, before a vowel, **chro′mat-**
chro·mat·o·gram (krō mat′ə gram′) ***n.*** the arrangement of zones or bands resulting from a chromatographic separation
chro·mat·o·graph (-graf′) ***vt.*** to separate (chemical substances) by chromatography **—*n.*** a display or record of the results of such a separation **—chro·mat′o·graph′ic *adj.* —chro·mat′o·graph′i·cal·ly *adv.***
chro·ma·tog·ra·phy (krō′mə täg′rə fē) ***n.*** ⟦CHROMATO- + -GRAPHY⟧ any of various processes of chemical analysis in which the constituents of a mixture are separated into distinct bands or spots on an adsorbent material: see also GAS CHROMATOGRAPHY
chro·ma·tol·y·sis (-täl′ə sis) ***n.***, *pl.* **-ses′** (-sēz′) ⟦CHROMATO- + -LYSIS⟧ *Med.* the disappearance of certain chromophil granules from nerve cells **—chro·mat·o·lyt·ic** (krō mat′ə lit′ik) ***adj.***
chro·mat·o·phore (krō mat′ə fôr′, krō′mə tə fôr′) ***n.*** ⟦CHROMATO- + -PHORE⟧ **1** a special animal cell, usually dermal, that contains pigment granules: it is often capable of expansion and contraction in such a manner that the skin color changes, as in the chameleon **2** a plastid containing chlorophyll or other pigments
chrome (krōm) ***n.*** ⟦Fr: see CHROMIUM⟧ **1** chromium or chromium alloy, esp. as used for plating **2** any of certain salts of chromium, used in dyeing and tanning **3** a chromium pigment **—*vt.* chromed, chrom′ing 1** to plate with chromium **2** to treat with a salt of chromium, as in dyeing
-chrome (krōm) ⟦< Gr *chrōma*: see CHROMA⟧ *combining form* **1** color or coloring agent *[urochrome]* **2** chromium *[ferrochrome]*
chrome alum an alum of which one of the components is chromium; esp., potassium chromium sulfate, $KCr(SO_4)_2 \cdot 12H_2O$, used in tanning and dyeing
chrome green 1 chromic oxide, Cr_2O_3, used as a green pigment **2** in commercial use, a green pigment made by mixing chrome yellow and Prussian blue
chrome red basic lead chromate, a red, powdery compound, $PbCrO_4 \cdot PbO$, used to make various pigments
chrome steel CHROMIUM STEEL
chrome yellow lead chromate, a yellow, crystalline compound, $PbCrO_4$, used as a yellow pigment
chro·mic (krō′mik) ***adj.*** of or containing trivalent chromium
chromic acid an acid, H_2CrO_4, existing only in solution or known in the form of its salts
chro·mide (krō′mīd′) ***n.*** CICHLID
chro·mi·nance (krō′mə nəns) ***n.*** ⟦CHROM(O)- + (LUM)INANCE⟧ that attribute of light which produces the sensation of color apart from luminance; specif., the color of an object as measured quantitatively in terms of a reference color
chro·mite (krō′mīt′) ***n.*** a hard, black mineral, $FeCr_2O_4$, the chief ore of chromium
chro·mi·um (krō′mē əm) ***n.*** ⟦ModL < Fr *chrome* < Gr *chrōma* (see CHROMA) + -IUM; so named (1797) by N.-L. Vauquelin, Fr chemist, its discoverer, because of its bright-colored compounds⟧ a grayish-white, crystalline, very hard, metallic chemical element with a high resistance to corrosion: used in chromium electroplating, in alloy steel (STAINLESS STEEL), and in alloys containing nickel, copper, manganese, and other metals: symbol, Cr; at. no. 24: see the periodic table of elements in the Reference Supplement
chromium pi·col·i·nate (pi käl′ə nāt′) a chromium salt, $C_{18}H_{12}CrN_3O_6$, used as a nutritional supplement
chromium steel a very hard alloy steel containing chromium
☆**chro·mo** (krō′mō′) ***n.***, *pl.* **-mos** *short for* CHROMOLITHOGRAPH
chro·mo- (krō′mō, -mə) ⟦< Gr *chrōma*: see CHROMA⟧ *combining form* color or pigment *[chromosome, chromolithograph]*
chro·mo·dy·nam·ics (krō′mō dī nam′iks) ***pl.n.*** ⟦prec. (in ref. to fig. notion of "color" as a hypothetical property of quarks: see COLOR, ***n.*** 19) + DYNAMICS⟧ a theory that describes how gluons and their forces bind quarks together to form protons, neutrons, etc. **—chro′mo·dy·nam′ic *adj.***
chro·mo·gen (krō′mə jən) ***n.*** ⟦CHROMO- + -GEN⟧ **1** any substance that can become a pigment or coloring matter, as a substance in organic fluids that forms colored compounds when oxidized, or a compound, not itself a dye, that can become a dye **2** any of certain bacteria that produce a pigment **—chro′mo·gen′ic** (-jen′ik) ***adj.***
chro·mo·lith·o·graph (krō′mō lith′ə graf′) ***n.*** a colored picture printed by the lithographic process from a series of stone or metal plates, the impression from each plate being in a different color **—chro′mo·li·thog′ra·pher** (-li thäg′rə fər) ***n.*** **—chro′mo·lith′o·graph′ic** (-lith′ə graf′ik) ***adj.*** **—chro′mo·li·thog′ra·phy *n.***
chro·mo·mere (krō′mə mir′) ***n.*** ⟦CHROMO- + -MERE⟧ any of the granules of chromatin arranged linearly on a chromosome **—chro′mo·mer′ic** (-mer′ik) ***adj.***
chro·mo·ne·ma (krō′mō nē′mə) ***n.***, *pl.* **-ma·ta** (-tə) ⟦CHROMO- + Gr *nēma*, thread: see NEMATO-⟧ a coiled, twisted, threadlike filament in a chromatid at all stages of mitosis **—chro′mo·ne′mal *adj.***
chro·mo·phil (krō′mə fil) ***adj.*** ⟦CHROMO- + -PHIL⟧ readily stained with dyes **—*n.*** a chromophil cell or cell part
chro·mo·phore (krō′mə fôr′) ***n.*** ⟦CHROMO- + -PHORE⟧ any chemical group, as the azo group, that produces color in a compound and unites with certain other groups to form dyes **—chro′mo·phor′ic** (-fôr′ik) ***adj.***
chro·mo·plast (krō′mə plast′) ***n.*** ⟦CHROMO- + -PLAST⟧ a yellowish to reddish plastid containing carotenoids and found in the cytoplasm of many plant cells: see CHLOROPLAST
chro·mo·pro·tein (krō′mə prō′tēn′) ***n.*** a conjugated protein containing a pigment
chro·mo·some (krō′mə sōm′) ***n.*** ⟦CHROMO- + -SOME[3]⟧ any of the microscopic rod-shaped bodies formed by the incorporation of the chromatin in a cell nucleus during mitosis and meiosis: they carry the genes that convey hereditary characteristics, and are constant in number for each species **—chro′mo·so′mal** (-sō′məl) ***adj.***
chro·mo·sphere (-sfir′) ***n.*** ⟦CHROMO- + -SPHERE⟧ the pinkish, glowing region around a star, esp. the sun, between the hot, dense photosphere and the much hotter, tenuous corona **—chro′mo·spher′ic** (-sfer′ik) ***adj.***
chro·mous (krō′məs) ***adj.*** of or containing divalent chromium
chro·myl (-mil) ***n.*** ⟦CHROM(O)- + -YL⟧ the divalent radical CrO_2
chron *abbrev.* **1** chronicle **2** chronological **3** chronology
Chron *abbrev. Bible* Chronicles
chron- (krän) *combining form* CHRONO-: used before a vowel
chro·nax·ie or **chro·nax·y** (krō′nak′sē) ***n.*** ⟦CHRON(O)- + Gr *axia*, value⟧ the minimum time necessary to excite a tissue, such as that of muscle or nerve cells, with an electric current of twice the rheobase
chron·ic (krän′ik) ***adj.*** ⟦Fr *cronique* < L *chronicus* < Gr *chronikos*, of time < *chronos*, time⟧ **1** lasting a long time or recurring often: said of a disease: distinguished from ACUTE **2** having had an ailment for a long time *[a chronic* patient*]* **3** continuing indefinitely; perpetual; constant *[a chronic* worry*]* **4** by habit, custom, etc.; habitual; inveterate *[a chronic* complainer*]* **—*n.*** a chronic patient **—chron′i·cal·ly *adv.* —chro·nic·i·ty** (krə nis′ə tē) ***n.***

SYN.—**chronic** suggests long duration or frequent recurrence and is used especially of diseases or habits that resist all efforts to eradicate them *[chronic* sinusitis*]*; **inveterate** implies firm establishment as a result of continued indulgence over a long period of time *[*an *inveterate* liar*]*; **confirmed** suggests fixedness in some condition or practice, often from a deep-seated aversion to change *[*a *confirmed* bachelor*]*; **hardened** implies fixed tendencies and a callous indifference to emotional or moral considerations *[*a *hardened* criminal*]*

chronic fatigue syndrome a debilitating medical condition of unknown cause, characterized by prolonged severe fatigue, muscle pain, impaired memory, etc.
chron·i·cle (krän′i kəl) ***n.*** ⟦ME & Anglo-Fr *cronicle* < OFr *chronique* < ML *chronica* < L, pl., pertaining to time, chronicles < Gr *chronika*, annals, pl. of *chronikos*: see CHRONIC⟧ **1** a historical record or register of facts or events arranged in the order in which they happened **2** a narrative; history **—*vt.* -cled, -cling** to tell or write the history of; put into a chronicle **—chron′i·cler** (-klər) ***n.***
Chron·i·cles (krän′i kəlz) ***n.*** *Bible* either of two books of history, 1 & 2 Chronicles: abbrev. *Chron, Chr,* or *Ch*

chron·o- (krän′ō, -ə; krō′nō, -nə) ⟦Gr < *chronos,* time⟧ *combining form* time [*chronograph*]

chron·o·bi·ol·o·gy (krän′ō bī äl′ə jē) ***n.*** the study of biological activity in relation to time, as in various cycles and rhythms —**chron′o·bi′o·log′i·cal** (-ə läj′i kəl) ***adj.*** —**chron′o·bi′o·log′i·cal·ly** ***adv.*** —**chron′o·bi·ol′o·gist** ***n.***

chron·o·gram (krän′ə gram′) ***n.*** ⟦CHRONO- + -GRAM⟧ **1** an inscription in which certain letters, made more prominent, express a date in Roman numerals (Ex.: MerCy MiXed with LoVe In hIm—MCMXLVII = 1947) **2** a record kept by a chronograph

chron·o·graph (-graf′) ***n.*** ⟦CHRONO- + -GRAPH⟧ any of various instruments, as a stopwatch, for measuring and recording brief, precisely spaced intervals of time —**chron′o·graph′ic** ***adj.*** —**chro·nog·ra·phy** (krō näg′rə fē, krə-) ***n.***

chron·o·log·i·cal (krän′ə läj′i kəl) ***adj.*** ⟦< fol. + -ICAL⟧ **1** arranged in the order of occurrence **2** of chronology; esp., containing or relating to an account of events in the order of their occurrence Also **chron′o·log′ic** —**chron′o·log′i·cal·ly** ***adv.***

chro·nol·o·gy (krə näl′ə jē) ***n.,*** *pl.* **-gies** ⟦CHRONO- + -LOGY⟧ **1** the science of measuring time in fixed periods and of dating events and epochs and arranging them in the order of occurrence **2** the arrangement of events, dates, etc. in the order of occurrence **3** a list or table of dates in their proper sequence —**chro·nol′o·gist** ***n.,*** **chro·nol′o·ger**

chro·nom·e·ter (-näm′ət ər) ***n.*** ⟦CHRONO- + -METER⟧ an instrument for measuring time precisely; highly accurate kind of clock or watch, as for scientific use

chron·o·met·ric (krän′ə me′trik) ***adj.*** of a chronometer or chronometry: also **chron′o·met′ri·cal** —**chron′o·met′ri·cal·ly** ***adv.***

chro·nom·e·try (krə näm′ə trē) ***n.*** the scientific measurement of time

chron·o·scope (krän′ə skōp′) ***n.*** ⟦CHRONO- + -SCOPE⟧ an instrument for measuring very small intervals of time

chron·o·ther·a·py (krän′ō ther′ə pē) ***n.*** the strategic use of timing in the administration of a medical treatment, medication, etc. so as to enhance its effectiveness and reduce undesirable side effects: sometimes called **chron′o·ther′a·peu′tics** (-pyo͞ot′iks) —**chron′o·ther′a·peu′tic** ***adj.***

-chro·ous (krō əs) ⟦Gr *-chroos* < *chrōs,* color; akin to *chrōma:* see CHROMA⟧ *combining form forming adjectives* colored [*isochroous*]

chrys·a·lid (kris′ə lid′) ***n.*** CHRYSALIS —***adj.*** of a chrysalis

chrys·a·lis (kris′ə lis) ***n.,*** *pl.* **chry·sal·i·des** (kri sal′ə dēz′) or **chrys′a·lis·es** ⟦L *chrysallis* < Gr, golden-colored chrysalis of a butterfly < *chrysos,* gold: of Sem orig., as in Akkadian *ḫurāṣu,* Heb *hārūz,* gold, Aram *harā,* yellow⟧ **1** the pupa of a butterfly, the form of the insect when between the larval and adult stages and in a case or cocoon **2** the case or cocoon **3** a stage of development when something or someone is still protected

chrys·an·the·mum (kri san′thə məm, -zan′-) ***n.*** ⟦ModL < L < Gr *chrysanthemon,* marigold, lit., golden flower < *chrysos* (see prec.) + *anthemon,* a flower⟧ **1** any of a genus (*Chrysanthemum*) of plants of the composite family, cultivated for their showy flowers which bloom in late summer and fall in a variety of colors, most commonly yellow, white, red, or purple **2** the flower

chrys·a·ro·bin (kris′ə rō′bin) ***n.*** ⟦< Gr *chrysos,* gold (see CHRYSALIS) + (AR)AROB(A) + -IN[1]⟧ a yellow, crystalline substance, $C_{15}H_{12}O_3$, derived from araroba and used in the treatment of various skin disorders

chrys·el·e·phan·tine (kris′el′ə fan′tin, -tīn′) ***adj.*** ⟦Gr *chryselephantinos* < *chrysos* (see CHRYSALIS) + *elephantinos* (see ELEPHANT)⟧ made of, or overlaid with, gold and ivory

chry·so- (kris′ō, -ə) ⟦< Gr *chrysos:* see CHRYSALIS⟧ *combining form* golden, yellow [*chrysoberyl*]: also, before a vowel, **chrys-**

chrys·o·ber·yl (kris′ō ber′il) ***n.*** ⟦prec. + BERYL⟧ a very hard, yellowish or greenish mineral, $BeAl_2O_4$, used as a gem; beryllium aluminum oxide

chrys·o·lite (kris′ə līt′) ***n.*** ⟦ME *crisolite* < OFr < L *chrysolithos* < Gr *chrysolithos,* topaz: see CHRYSO- & -LITE⟧ **1** a yellowish-green gem derived chiefly from varieties of olivine **2** a yellowish-green, reddish, or brownish variety of olivine

chrys·o·prase (-prāz′) ***n.*** ⟦ME & OFr *crisopace* (& Late OE *crisoprassus*) < L *chrysoprasus* < Gr *chrysoprasos* < *chrysos,* gold (see CHRYSALIS) + *prason,* leek (see PRASE): so called from the color⟧ a light-green variety of chalcedony, sometimes used as a semiprecious stone

Chrys·os·tom (kris′əs təm, kri säs′təm), Saint **John** ⟦< Gr *chrysostomos,* golden-mouthed < *chrysos,* gold (see CHRYSALIS) + *stoma,* mouth (see STOMA): epithet earned for eloquence in preaching⟧ (A.D. 347?-407); Gr. church father: archbishop of Constantinople (398-404): his day is Sept. 13

chrys·o·tile (kris′ə til′) ***n.*** ⟦< CHRYSO- + Gr *tilos,* fine hair < *tillein,* to pluck out⟧ a fibrous variety of serpentine, hydrous magnesium silicate, $MG_3SI_2O_5(OH)_4$, that is the principal source of asbestos

chtho·ni·an (thō′nē ən) ***adj.*** ⟦Gr *chthonios,* in the earth < *chthōn,* the earth: see HOMO[1]⟧ designating or of the underworld of the dead and its gods or spirits

chthon·ic (thän′ik) ***adj.*** **1** CHTHONIAN **2** dark, primitive, and mysterious

chub (chub) ***n.,*** *pl.* **chub** or **chubs** ⟦LME *chubbe*⟧ ☆**1** any of several small, freshwater cyprinoid fishes often used as bait **2** any of several freshwater ciscos (genus *Coregonus*) of N regions **3** any of a number of marine fishes with a small mouth; esp., any of a family (Kyphosidae) of percoid fishes

chub·by (chub′ē) ***adj.*** **-bi·er, -bi·est** ⟦< prec.⟧ round and plump; fleshy [a *chubby* baby] —**chub′bi·ness** ***n.***

Chu·chow (jo͞o′jō′) *a former transliteration of* ZHUZHOU

chuck[1] (chuk) ***vt.*** ⟦< ? Fr *choquer,* to shock, strike against < MDu *schokken*⟧ **1** to tap or pat gently, esp. under the chin, as a playful or affectionate gesture **2** to throw with a quick, short movement; pitch; toss **3** [Slang] *a)* to discard; get rid of ☆*b)* to quit (as one's job) —***n.*** **1** a light tap or squeeze under the chin **2** a toss; throw

chuck[2] (chuk) ***n.*** ⟦prob. var. of CHOCK⟧ **1** *a)* a cut of beef including the parts around the neck, the shoulder blade, and the first few ribs *b)* [Chiefly West] food **2** a clamplike device, as on a lathe, by which the tool or work to be turned is held: see DRILL[1], illus. **3** CHOCK

chuck[3] (chuk) ***vi., n.*** ⟦echoic⟧ CLUCK

Chuck (chuk) ***n.*** *nickname for* CHARLES[1]

☆**chuck-a-luck** (chuk′ə luk′) ***n.*** ⟦< CHUCK[1] + LUCK⟧ a gambling game in which players bet on the way three dice, contained in an hourglass-shaped cage, will fall when the cage is pivoted

chuck-full (chuk′fo͝ol′) ***adj.*** *var. of* CHOCK-FULL

☆**chuck·hole** (chuk′hōl′) ***n.*** ⟦< dial. *chock,* a bump in a road, orig., a stump, block (see CHOCK) + HOLE⟧ a rough hole in pavement, made by wear and weathering

chuck·le (chuk′əl) ***vi.*** **-led, -ling** ⟦prob. < CHUCK[3] + freq. suffix *-le*⟧ to laugh softly in a low tone, as in mild amusement —***n.*** a soft, low-toned laugh —SYN. LAUGH —**chuck′ler** ***n.***

chuck·le·head (-hed′) ***n.*** ⟦< ? CHOCK + HEAD⟧ [Informal] a stupid person; dolt —**chuck′le·head′ed** ***adj.***

☆**chuck wagon** ⟦CHUCK[2], *n.* 1*b* + WAGON⟧ a wagon, van, etc. equipped as a kitchen for feeding cowboys or other outdoor workers

☆**chuck·wal·la** (chuk′wäl′ə) ***n.*** ⟦MexSp *chacahuala* < AmInd (Cahuilla) *tcáxxwal*⟧ any of a genus (*Sauromalus*) of large, edible iguanas living in NW Mexico and SW U.S.

☆**chuck-will's-wid·ow** (chuk′wilz′wid′ō) ***n.*** ⟦echoic of its cry⟧ a large nightjar (*Caprimulgus carolinensis*) of the S U.S., often mistaken for the slightly smaller whippoorwill

chud·dar (chud′ər) ***n.*** *var. of* CHADOR

Chud·sko·ye (cho͞ot skoi′yə), **Lake** lake on the Estonian-Russian border: with its S extension, Lake Pskov, *c.* 1,400 sq mi (3,626 sq km)

chuff[1] (chuf) ***n.*** ⟦ME *chuffe*⟧ [Brit. Dial.] a boor; churl

chuff[2] (chuf) ***vi., n.*** ⟦echoic⟧ CHUG

chuffed (chuft) ***adj.*** [Brit. Informal] **1** pleased, delighted, gratified, etc. **2** disgruntled, displeased, unhappy, etc.

chuff·y (chuf′ē) ***adj.*** **chuff′i·er, chuff′i·est** ⟦< obs. *chuff,* a fat cheek + -Y[3]⟧ [Dial.] stocky or plump

☆**chug** (chug) ***n.*** ⟦echoic⟧ any of a series of abrupt, puffing or explosive sounds, as of a steam-powered locomotive —***vi.*** **chugged, chug′ging** to make, or move with, such sounds —***vt.*** [Slang] CHUG-A-LUG

☆**chug-a-lug** (chug′ə lug′) ***vt., vi.*** **-lugged′, -lug′ging** ⟦echoic⟧ [Slang] to drink in continuous gulps or in a single, long gulp; swill

chu·kar (chə kär′) ***n.*** ⟦Hindi *cakor* < Sans *cakōra* < IE echoic base **kāu-,* to scream > HOWL⟧ an Asian and European partridge (*Alectoris chukar*), with red bill and feet, chestnut-colored above and white or gray below: successfully introduced into W U.S.

Chuk·chi or **Chuk·chee** (cho͝ok′chē′) ***n.*** ⟦Russ *čukči* (pl.) < Chukchi name, keepers of the reindeer⟧ **1** a member of a people now living in northernmost Siberia **2** the language of this people

Chukchi Sea part of the Arctic Ocean, north of the Bering Strait

chuk·ka (boot) (chuk′ə) ⟦altered < fol.: from resemblance to boots worn for polo⟧ an ankle-high bootlike shoe, usually with two or three pairs of eyelets

chuk·ker (chuk′ər) ***n.*** ⟦Hindi *chakar* < Sans *cakra,* wheel: for IE base see WHEEL⟧ any of the periods of play, each lasting 7 or 7½ minutes, into which a polo match is divided: also sp. **chuk′kar**

Chu·kot Range (cho͞o kät′) mountain range in NE Siberia: highest peak, *c.* 7,500 ft (2,286 m)

Chu·la Vis·ta (cho͞o′lə vis′tə) ⟦AmSp, lit., beautiful view⟧ city in SW Calif.: suburb of San Diego

chum[1] (chum) [Informal] ***n.*** ⟦late 17th-c. slang; prob. altered sp. of *cham,* clipped form of *chamber (fellow), chamber (mate)*⟧ **1** [Archaic] a roommate **2** a close friend —***vi.*** **chummed, chum′ming** **1** [Archaic] to share the same room **2** to go about together, as close friends do [to *chum* around]

☆**chum[2]** (chum) ***n.*** ⟦< ? Scot *chum,* food⟧ fish blood, fish guts, etc. scattered in the water as to attract game fish —***vi.*** **chummed, chum·ming** to use chum to attract fish

chum[3] (chum) ***n.*** CHUM SALMON

chum·my (chum′ē) ***adj.*** **-mi·er, -mi·est** [Informal] like a chum; intimate; friendly —**chum′mi·ly** ***adv.*** —**chum′mi·ness** ***n.***

chump (chump) ***n.*** ⟦akin to ON *kumba,* block of wood, MHG *kumpf,* dull⟧ **1** a heavy block of wood **2** [Informal] a gullible, foolish, or stupid person; dupe or fool —**off one's chump** [Brit. Slang] insane; crazy

☆**chump change** ⟦< black English⟧ [Slang] an insignificant sum of money

chum salmon (chum) ⟦< Chinook jargon *tsum samun,* spotted salmon⟧ a large salmon (*Oncorhynchus keta*) with pale flesh, found in the N Pacific

Chung·king (cho͝oŋ′kiŋ′) *a former transliteration of* CHONGQING

chunk (chuŋk) ***n.*** ⟦< ? CHUCK[2]⟧ **1** a short, thick piece, as of meat or wood **2** a considerable portion ☆**3** a stocky animal, esp. a horse —☆***vt.*** **1** to form into a chunk or chunks **2** to assmble into a group or groups

☆**chunk·y** (chuŋ′kē) ***adj.*** **chunk′i·er, chunk′i·est** **1** short and thick **2** stocky; thickset **3** containing chunks —**chunk′i·ly** ***adv.*** —**chunk′i·ness** ***n.***

Chun·nel (chun′əl) ⟦< (ENGLISH) CH(ANNEL) + (T)UNNEL⟧ [*also* **c-**] [Informal] railway tunnel that runs beneath the English Channel, between England and France: 31 mi (50 km) long

chun·ter (chun′tər) ***vi.*** ⟦prob. echoic⟧ [Brit.] **1** to mutter or murmur **2** to make a low, rumbling noise

chup·pah (khoo͝p′pə, -pä) ***n., pl.*** **-pahs** or Heb. **-pot** (-pōt, -pōs) ⟦Heb *chupa*⟧ [*also in italics*] the canopy above the bride and groom in a Jewish wedding ceremony: also sp. **chup′pa**

church (church) ***n.*** ⟦ME *chirche, kirke* < OE *cirice* (& ON *kirkja* < OE) < Gmc **kirika* < LGr(Ec) **kyrikē* < Gr *kyriakē (oikia)*, Lord's (house) < *kyriakos*, belonging to the Lord < *kyrios*, ruler < *kyros*, supreme power < IE base **keu-*, a swelling, to be strong, hero > CAVE⟧ **1** a building set apart or consecrated for public worship, esp. one for Christian worship **2** religious service or public worship, esp. among Christians **3** [*usually* **C-**] *a)* all Christians considered as a single body *b)* a particular sect or denomination of Christians **4** the ecclesiastical government of a particular religious group, or its power, as opposed to secular government **5** the profession of the clergy; clerical profession **6** a group of worshipers; congregation —***vt.*** to bring (esp. a woman after childbirth) to church for special services —***adj.*** **1** having to do with organized Christian worship **2** of or connected with a church

Church (church), **Frederic Edwin** 1826-1900; U.S. landscape painter

church·go·er (church′gō′ər) ***n.*** a person who attends church, esp. regularly —**church′go′ing** ***n., adj.***

Church·ill[1] (chur′chil) **1 John** *see* MARLBOROUGH, 1st Duke of **2** Lord **Randolph (Henry Spencer)** 1849-95; Brit. statesman **3** Sir **Winston (Leonard Spencer)** 1874-1965; Brit. statesman & writer: prime minister (1940-45; 1951-55): son of Lord Randolph —**Church·ill·i·an** (chur chil′ē ən) ***adj.***

Church·ill[2] (chur′chil) **1** ⟦after John CHURCHILL[1], Duke of Marlborough, gov. of Hudson's Bay Co. (1685-91)⟧ river in Canada flowing from N Saskatchewan eastward through N Manitoba into Hudson Bay: *c.* 1,000 mi (1,609 km) **2** ⟦after Sir Winston CHURCHILL[1]⟧ river in S Labrador, Canada, flowing east to the Atlantic Ocean: *c.* 600 mi (966 km) long

Churchill Falls ⟦after Sir Winston CHURCHILL[1]⟧ waterfall on the upper Churchill River, SW Labrador: *c.* 245 ft (75 m) high

☆**church key** [Slang] a device for opening cans, esp. originally beer cans, by punching a V-shaped hole in the top

church·ly (church′lē) ***adj.*** **1** of or fit for a church **2** belonging to a church —**church′li·ness** ***n.***

church·man (-mən) ***n., pl.*** **-men** (-mən) **1** a clergyman **2** a member of a church, esp. an active member

Church of Christ, Scientist the Christian denomination embodying the beliefs and practices of CHRISTIAN SCIENCE

Church of England the episcopal church of England; Anglican Church: it is an established church with the sovereign as its head, formed when Henry VIII broke with the papacy in the 16th cent.

Church of Jesus Christ of Latter-day Saints *see* MORMON

Church of Rome the Roman Catholic Church

Church of the Brethren a Protestant denomination, founded in 1708 in Germany and now based in the U.S., that has no creed, baptizes by immersion, practices pacifism, and emphasizes service to others

Church Slavonic or **Church Slavic** OLD CHURCH SLAVONIC

church·war·den (-wôrd′′n) ***n.*** ⟦ME *chirchewardein*: see CHURCH & WARDEN⟧ **1** *Episcopal Ch.* either of two lay officers of a church, who attend to certain secular matters, as care of church property **2** [Brit.] a clay tobacco pipe with a very long stem

church·wom·an (-woom′ən) ***n., pl.*** **-wom′en** (-wim′in) a woman member of a church, esp. an active member

church·y (chur′chē) ***adj.*** [Informal] devoted, often obsessively devoted, to a church and its principles

church·yard (church′yärd′) ***n.*** the yard or ground adjoining a church, often used as a place of burial

churl (churl) ***n.*** ⟦ME *cherl* < OE *ceorl*, peasant, freeman: for IE base see CORN[1]⟧ **1** CEORL **2** a farm laborer; peasant **3** a surly, ill-bred person; boor **4** a selfish or mean person

churl·ish (chur′lish) ***adj.*** **1** of a churl or churls; rustic **2** like a churl; surly; boorish **3** stingy or mean **4** [Now Rare] hard to work or manage —**churl′ish·ly** ***adv.*** —**churl′ish·ness** ***n.***

churn (churn) ***n.*** ⟦ME *chirne* < OE *cyrne*; akin to *cyrnel*, KERNEL: with ref. to grainy appearance of churned cream⟧ **1** a container or contrivance in which milk or cream is beaten, stirred, or shaken to form butter ☆**2** the occurrence, ratio, or amount of turnover of investments, customers, commodities, etc. —***vt.*** ⟦ME *chirnen* < the n.⟧ **1** to stir, beat, or shake (milk or cream) in a churn **2** to make (butter) in a churn **3** to stir up vigorously **4** to produce (foam, etc.) by stirring vigorously ☆**5** to cause a rapid turnover of (a client's investments) so that the broker can claim commissions —***vi.*** **1** to use a churn in making butter **2** to move or stir as if in a churn [*many ideas churning in his brain*] —**churn out** to produce regularly and copiously, esp. in a mechanical or uncreative way

churr (chur) ***n.*** ⟦see CHIRR⟧ a low, trilled or whirring sound made by some birds or insects —***vi.*** to make such a sound

chur·ro (chur′ō) ***n.*** ⟦Sp⟧ a Spanish and Mexican deep-fried pastry somewhat like a long, thin cruller, coated with sugar and often cinnamon

☆**chute**[1] (sho͞ot) ***n.*** ⟦Fr, a fall < OFr *cheute* < *cheoite*, pp. of *cheoir*, to fall < L *cadere*: see CASE[1]⟧ **1** *a)* a waterfall *b)* rapids in a river **2** an inclined or vertical trough or passage down which something may be slid or dropped [*laundry chute*] **3** a steep slide, as for tobogganing

chute[2] (sho͞ot) ***n.*** [Informal] *short for* PARACHUTE —**chut′ist** ***n.***

☆**chute-the-chute** (sho͞ot′ *th*ə sho͞ot′) ***n.*** an amusement-park ride with a steep slide, often into a pool of water

chut·ney (chut′nē) ***n., pl.*** **-neys** ⟦Hindi *chatnī*⟧ a relish made of fruits, as raisins and mangoes, spices, herbs, and sugar, with vinegar or lemon juice: also sp. **chut′nee**

chutz·pah or **chutz·pa** (hoots′pə, khoots′-; -pä) ***n.*** ⟦Yiddish < Heb⟧ [Informal] shameless audacity; impudence; brass

chyle (kīl) ***n.*** ⟦LL *chylus* < Gr *chylos*, juice, humor, chyle < *cheein*, to pour: see FOUND[3]⟧ a milky fluid composed of lymph and emulsified fats: it is formed from chyme in the small intestine, is absorbed by the lacteals, and is passed into the blood through the thoracic duct —**chy·la·ceous** (kī lā′shəs) ***adj.***, **chy·lous** (kī′ləs)

chy·lo·mi·cron (kī′lō mī′krän′) ***n., pl.*** **-cra** (-krə) or **-crons′** ⟦prec. + -o- + MICRON⟧ a micron-sized particle that contains mostly triglycerides with some protein, found in the blood and lymph, esp. after fat is eaten

chyme (kīm) ***n.*** ⟦LL *chymus* < Gr *chymos*, juice < *cheein*: see CHYLE⟧ the thick, semifluid mass resulting from gastric digestion of food: it passes from the stomach into the small intestine, where the chyle is formed from it —**chy·mous** (kī′məs) ***adj.***

chy·mo·pa·pa·in (kī′mō pə pā′in, -pī′in) ***n.*** papain, esp. when injected into a slipped disk to dissolve pain-causing soft cartilage

chy·mo·tryp·sin (kī′mō trip′sin) ***n.*** ⟦< Gr *chymos* (see CHYME) + TRYPSIN⟧ a pancreatic enzyme that is important in the digestion of proteins in the intestines

ci *abbrev.* cubic inch(es)

Ci *abbrev.* **1** cirrus **2** curie(s)

Cia *abbrev.* ⟦Sp *Compañía*⟧ Company

CIA *abbrev.* CENTRAL INTELLIGENCE AGENCY

cia·bat·ta (chə bät′ə) ***n.*** ⟦It, slipper: so named from its shape⟧ an Italian yeast bread made with white flour and olive oil in a long, somewhat flat loaf

ciao (chou) ***interj.*** ⟦It, altered < dial. (Lombard) *schiavo*, lit., slave, used as transl. of Austrian *servus* (for "your obedient servant")⟧ [Informal] **1** hello **2** goodbye

ci·bo·ri·um (sə bôr′ē əm) ***n., pl.*** **-ri·a** (-ə) ⟦ML < L, a cup < Gr *kibōrion*, seed vessel of the Egyptian waterlily, hence, a cup⟧ **1** a canopy of wood, stone, etc. that rests on four columns, esp. one covering an altar; baldachin **2** a covered cup for holding the consecrated wafers of the Eucharist

ci·ca·da (si kā′də, -kä′-) ***n., pl.*** **-das** or **-dae** (-dē) ⟦ME < L⟧ any of a family (Cicadidae) of large, flylike homopteran insects with transparent wings: the male makes a loud, shrill sound by vibrating a special organ on its undersurface

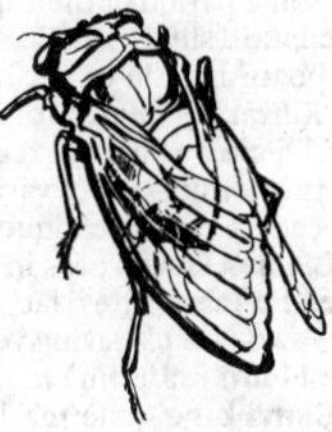

cicada

cic·a·tri·cle (sik′ə trik′əl) ***n.*** ⟦< L *cicatricula*, dim. of *cicatrix*: see fol.⟧ the protoplasmic disc in the yolk of an egg from which the embryo develops; germinal disc

cic·a·trix (sik′ə triks′, si kā′-) ***n., pl.*** **cic·a·tri·ces** (sik′ə trī′sēz′, si kā′trə-) or **cic·a·trix·es** (sik′ə triks′iz, si kā′triks′-) ⟦ME *cicatrice* < OFr < L *cicatrix*, a scar⟧ **1** *Med.* the contracted fibrous tissue at the place where a wound has healed; scar **2** *Bot.* *a)* the scar left on a stem where a branch, leaf, etc. was once attached *b)* the mark left where a wound has healed on a tree or plant *c)* HILUM (sense 2*a*) Also **cic′a·trice′** (-tris′) —**cic′a·tri′cial** (-trish′əl) ***adj.***

cic·a·trize (sik′ə trīz′) ***vt., vi.*** **-trized′**, **-triz′ing** ⟦ME *cicatrizen* < ML *cicatrizare*: see prec.⟧ to heal with the formation of a scar —**cic′a·tri·za′tion** ***n.***

cic·e·ly (sis′ə lē) ***n., pl.*** **-lies** ⟦ME *seseli* < L *seselis* < Gr⟧ SWEET CICELY

Cic·e·ly (sis′ə lē) ***n.*** a feminine name: see CECILIA[1]

Cic·e·ro (sis′ə rō′), **(Marcus Tullius)** 106-43 B.C.; Rom. statesman, orator, & philosopher

cic·e·ro·ne (sis′ə rō′nē; *Brit* chich′ə-) ***n., pl.*** **-nes′** (-nēz′) ⟦It < L *Cicero*, the orator: ? from the usual loquacity of guides⟧ a guide who explains the history and chief features of a place to sightseers

Cic·e·ro·ni·an (sis′ə rō′nē ən) ***adj.*** of or like Cicero or his polished literary style; eloquent

cich·lid (sik′lid′) ***n.*** ⟦< ModL *Cichlidae* < Gr *kichlē*, a sea fish, wrasse⟧ any of a family (Cichlidae) of tropical and subtropical freshwater percoid fishes superficially similar to the American sunfishes —***adj.*** of this family

ci·cis·be·o (chē′chəz bā′ō; *occas.* sə sis′bē ō) ***n., pl.*** **-os** ⟦It⟧ the lover of a married woman: also It. ***ci·cis·be·o*** (chē′chēz bā′ô), *pl.* **-be′i** (-bā′ē)

Cid (sid; *Sp* thēth), **El** (el) or **the** ⟦Sp < Ar *sayyid*, a lord⟧ (born *Rodrigo*, or *Ruy, Díaz de Bivar*) 1040?-99; Sp. soldier & celebrated hero, esp. in Sp. literature

CID *abbrev.* [Brit.] Criminal Investigation Department

-cid·al (sīd′′l) ⟦see fol.⟧ *suffix forming adjectives* **1** of a killer or killing [*homicidal*] **2** that can kill [*fungicidal*]

-cide (sīd) ⟦< Fr or L; Fr *-cide* < L *-cida* < *caedere*, to cut down, kill < IE base **(s)k(h)ai-*, to strike > MDu *heien*⟧ *suffix forming nouns* **1** a killer [*pesticide*] **2** a killing [*genocide*]

ci·der (sī′dər) ***n.*** ⟦ME *cidre, sider* < OFr *sidre, cidere* < LL(Ec) *sicera* < Gr(Ec) *sikera*, an intoxicating drink, of Sem orig., as in Akkadian *šikaru*, barley beer, Heb *shēkār*, strong drink of grain and honey < *shākar*, to become intoxicated⟧ the juice pressed from apples or, formerly, from other fruits, used as a beverage or for making vinegar: **hard cider** is fermented and **sweet cider** is not

cider press a machine that presses the juice out of apples, for making cider

ci·de·vant (sēd vän′, sē də-) *adj.* ⟦Fr, heretofore: applied in the Revolution to former nobles⟧ former; recent

Cie *abbrev.* ⟦Fr *compagnie*⟧ Company

Cien·fue·gos (syen fwā′gōs) seaport on the S coast of Cuba

CIF *abbrev.* cost, insurance, and freight

cig (sig) *n.* [Informal] *short for* CIGARETTE

ci·gar (si gär′) *n.* ⟦Sp *cigarro,* prob. < Maya *sicar,* to smoke rolled tobacco leaves < *sić,* tobacco⟧ a cylindrical roll of cured tobacco for smoking, consisting of cut tobacco wrapped in a tobacco leaf —☆**(close but) no cigar** ⟦< the practice of awarding cigars, as in carnival contests⟧ [Informal] phrase used to describe a situation or outcome in which victory or success is narrowly missed

cig·a·rette (sig′ə ret′, sig′ə ret′) *n.* ⟦Fr dim. of *cigare,* cigar < Sp *cigarro:* see prec.⟧ **1** a thin-paper tube filled with finely cut tobacco for smoking and usually having a filter tip **2** any similar tube for smoking marijuana, tobacco and ground cloves, etc. Also sp. **cig′a·ret′**

cig·a·ril·lo (sig′ə ril′ō) *n., pl.* **-los** ⟦Sp, dim. of *cigarro,* CIGAR⟧ a small, thin cigar

cig·gie or **cig·gy** (sig′ē) *n., pl.* **-gies** [Informal] a cigarette

cig·ua·te·ra (sig′wə ter′ə, -tir′ə) *n.* ⟦AmSp < *cigua,* a marine snail⟧ a type of food poisoning with severe gastrointestinal and neurological symptoms, caused by eating contaminated fish

ci·lan·tro (si lan′trō, -län′-) *n.* ⟦Sp, var. of *culantro* < L *coriandrum,* CORIANDER⟧ coriander leaves used as an herb, esp. in Latin American cooking; Chinese parsley

cil·i·a (sil′ē ə) *pl.n., sing.* **-i·um** (-ē əm) ⟦L, pl. of *cilium,* eyelid; akin to *celare:* see CONCEAL⟧ **1** the eyelashes **2** ⟦ModL⟧ *Bot.* small hairlike processes extending from certain plant cells and forming a fringe, as on the edges of some leaves **3** *Zool.* short, hairlike outgrowths of certain cells, usually capable of rhythmic beating that can produce locomotion and feeding currents, as in protozoans or small worms, or the movement of fluids, as in the ducts of higher forms

cil·i·ar·y (sil′ē er′ē) *adj.* **1** of, like, or having cilia **2** relating to the eyelashes **3** relating to certain fine structures of the eyeball

cil·i·ate (-it, -āt′) *adj.* ⟦ModL < L: see CILIA⟧ *Bot., Zool.* having cilia: usually **cil′i·at′ed** (-āt′id) —*n.* any of a phylum (Ciliophora) of microscopic protozoans characterized by cilia covering the body in whole or in part at some period of their life

cil·ice (sil′is) *n.* ⟦Fr < L *cilicium* (> OE *cilic*), coarse covering of Cilician goats' hair, in LL(Ec), hair shirt < Gr *kilikion,* garment of goats' hair, after *Kilikia,* fol., noted for its goats⟧ HAIR SHIRT

Ci·li·cia (sə lish′ə) region in SE Asia Minor, on the Mediterranean, under the domination of various kingdoms & rulers from the Assyrians in the 7th cent. B.C. until conquered by the Turks in the 15th cent. —**Ci·li′cian** *adj., n.*

Cilician Gates pass in the Taurus Mts., S Turkey

cil·i·o·late (sil′ē ō lāt′, -lit) *adj.* ⟦< ModL *ciliolum,* dim. of *cilium* (see CILIA) + -ATE[1]⟧ *Biol.* having very small cilia

cil·i·um (sil′ē əm) *n. sing. of* CILIA

Ci·ma·bu·e (chē′mä bo͞o′ā), **Gio·van·ni** (jô vän′nē) (born *Bencivieni di Pepo*) 1240?-1302?; Florentine painter

Cim·ar·ron (sim′ə rän′, -rōn′) ⟦AmSp *cimarrón,* wild, unruly (< OSp *cimarra,* thicket): prob. orig. referring to the wild sheep (bighorn) found along its banks⟧ river flowing from NE N.Mex. eastward to the Arkansas River, near Tulsa, Okla.: *c.* 600 mi (966 km)

cim·ba·lom or **cym·ba·lom** (sim′bə ləm) *n.* ⟦Hung *czimbalom* < L *cymbalum,* CYMBAL⟧ a type of large dulcimer associated with Hungarian folk music

Cim·bri (sim′brī′, -brē′) *pl.n.* ⟦L < Gmc (or ? Celt)⟧ the members of a Germanic people, believed to be from Jutland, that invaded N Italy and were defeated by the Romans (101 B.C.) —**Cim′bri·an** (-brē ən) *adj.,* **Cim′bric** (-brik)

ci·met·i·dine (sə met′ə dēn′, -din) *n.* ⟦*ci-* (< CYANO-) + MET(HYL) + (GUAN)IDINE⟧ a drug, $C_{10}H_{16}N_6S$, that blocks the histamine receptors, thus reducing gastric secretion: used in treating certain peptic ulcers

ci·mex (sī′meks′) *n., pl.* **cim·i·ces** (sim′i sēz′) ⟦ModL < L, a bug < IE base **ḱi-,* dark gray > Russ *sinij,* dark blue⟧ any of a genus (*Cimex*) of broad, flat, nearly wingless, bloodsucking, hemipterous bugs, including the common bedbug

Cim·me·ri·an (sə mir′ē ən) *n.* ⟦< L *Cimmerius,* pertaining to the *Cimmerii,* Cimmerians < Gr *Kimmerioi*⟧ any of a mythical people whose land was described by Homer as a region of perpetual mist and darkness —*adj.* extremely dark; gloomy

C in C *abbrev.* Commander in Chief

☆**cinch** (sinch) *n.* ⟦MexSp < Sp *cincha* < L *cingulum,* a girdle < *cingere,* to surround, encircle < IE base **kenk-,* to gird, encircle > Sans *káñcate,* (he) binds, Gr *kakala,* walls⟧ **1** a saddle or pack girth **2** [Informal] a firm grip **3** [Slang] a thing easy to do or sure to happen —*vt.* **1** to fasten (a saddle) on (a horse, burro, etc.) with a cinch **2** to bind firmly **3** [Slang] *a)* to get a firm hold on *b)* to make sure of

cin·cho·na (sin kō′nə) *n.* ⟦ModL: coined by LINNAEUS after the Countess del *Chinchón,* wife of a 17th-c. Peruvian viceroy, who was treated for fever with the bark⟧ **1** any of a genus (*Cinchona*) of tropical South American trees of the madder family, from the bark of which quinine and related medicinal alkaloids are obtained: the trees are widely cultivated in Asia and the East Indies **2** the bitter bark of these trees —**cin·chon′ic** (-kän′ik) *adj.*

cin·chon·i·dine (sin kän′ə dēn′, -din) *n.* an isomeric alkaloid, $C_{19}H_{22}N_2O$, derived from cinchona bark and used for treating malaria and reducing fever

cin·cho·nine (sin′kə nēn′, -nin; siŋ′-) *n.* a stereoisomer of cinchonidine, with the same derivation and use

cin·cho·nism (sin′kə niz′əm, siŋ′-) *n.* a pathological condition resulting from a reaction to or an excessive use of cinchona bark or any of its derivatives, as quinine: it is characterized by headache, ringing in the ears, deafness, etc.

cin·cho·nize (-nīz′) *vt.* **-nized′**, **-niz′ing** to treat with cinchona, quinine, etc.

Cin·cin·nat·i (sin′sə nat′ē, -ə) ⟦from the Society of the *Cincinnati,* formed (1783) by former Revolutionary officers, after fol.⟧ city in SW Ohio, on the Ohio River —**Cin′cin·nat′i·an** (-ē ən) *n.*

Cin·cin·na·tus (sin′sə nāt′əs, -nat′-), **(Lucius Quinctius)** 5th cent. B.C.: Rom. statesman & general: dictator of Rome (458 & 439 B.C.)

☆**Cin·co de Ma·yo** (siŋ′kō də mī′ō) ⟦Sp, fifth (lit., five) of May⟧ May 5, anniversary of the victory of Mexico over French forces at Puebla in 1862: observed by Mexicans and Mexican-Americans

cinc·ture (siŋk′chər) *n.* ⟦L *cinctura,* a girdle < *cingere:* see CINCH⟧ **1** the act of encircling or girding **2** anything that encircles, as a belt or sash for the waist

Cin·cy (sin′sē) *informal name for* CINCINNATI

cin·der (sin′dər) *n.* ⟦ME & OE *sinder,* dross of iron, slag < IE base **sendhro-,* coagulating fluid > Ger *sinter,* dross of iron, stalactite, *sintern,* to trickle, coagulate, Czech *śadra,* gypsum⟧ **1** slag, as from the reduction of metallic ores **2** a rough piece of solid lava from a volcano **3** any matter, as coal or wood, burned out or partly burned, but not reduced to ashes **4** a minute piece of such matter **5** a coal that is still burning but not flaming **6** [*pl.*] ashes from coal or wood —*vt.* **1** [Rare] to burn to cinders **2** to cover with cinders —**cin′der·y** *adj.*

☆**cinder block** a lightweight building block, usually not solid, made of concrete and fine cinders

Cin·der·el·la (sin′dər el′ə) *n.* ⟦CINDER + dim. suffix *-ella:* like Fr *Cendrillon* (dim. < *cendre,* ashes), a partial transl. of Ger *Aschenbrödel,* lit., scullion (< *asche,* ASH[1] + *brodeln,* bubble up, BREW)⟧ **1** the title character of a fairy tale, a household drudge who, with the help of a fairy godmother, marries a prince **2** a person or thing whose merit, value, or beauty is for a time unrecognized —*adj.* resembling Cinderella in being elevated suddenly to a position of honor, glory, etc. [*a Cinderella team in a basketball tournament*]

cinder track a racing track with a surface of fine cinders

cin·e- (sin′ə) ⟦< CINEMA⟧ *combining form* FILM (*n.* 5)

ci·ne·aste (sin′ē ast′) *n.* ⟦Fr *cinéaste* < *ciné(matographe),* film projector + *(enthousi)aste,* ENTHUSIAST⟧ **1** a person involved in film production **2** a devotee of films Also **ci′né·aste′** or **ci′ne·ast′**

cin·e·ma (sin′ə mə) *n.* ⟦short for *cinematograph:* see CINEMATOGRAPHY⟧ [Chiefly Brit.] a film theater —**the cinema** **1** the art or business of making films **2** films collectively —**cin′e·mat′ic** (-mat′ik) *adj.* —**cin′e·mat′i·cal·ly** *adv.*

cin·e·ma·theque (sin′ə mə tek′) *n.* ⟦< Fr *cinémathèque* < *cinéma,* prec. + *(biblio)thèque,* library (< L *bibliotheca:* see BIBLIOTHECA)⟧ a place where films are collected and shown, that may also function as a museum, library, etc.

cin·e·ma·tog·ra·pher (sin′ə mə täg′rə fər) *n.* the chief camera operator of a film crew, who is responsible for camera placement, lighting, etc.

cin·e·ma·tog·ra·phy (-fē) *n.* ⟦< *cinematograph,* film projector < Fr *cinématographe* < Gr *kinēma* (gen. *kinēmatos*), motion + *graphein,* to write⟧ the art, science, and work of photography in making films —**cin′e·mat′o·graph′ic** (-mat′ə graf′ik) *adj.,* **cin′e·mat′o·graph′i·cal** —**cin′e·mat′o·graph′i·cal·ly** *adv.*

ci·né·ma vé·ri·té (sin′ə mə ver′i tā′, -ver′i tā′; *Fr* sē nā mȧ vā rē tā′) ⟦Fr, lit., truth cinema⟧ a form of documentary film in which a small, hand-held camera and unobtrusive techniques are used to record scenes under the most natural conditions possible

cin·e·ole (sin′ē ōl′) *n.* ⟦< ModL *oleum cinae* (oil of wormwood), with transposition of constituents⟧ EUCALYPTOL: also **cin′e·ol′** (-ôl′, -äl′)

cin·e·phile (sin′ə fīl′) *n.* ⟦Fr *cinéphile* < *cinéma,* CINEMA + *-phile,* -PHILE⟧ a devotee of films

Cin·e·plex (sin′ə pleks′) ⟦coined (late 1970s) by N. A. Taylor (1906-2004), Cdn film exhibitor; blend of CINEMA & COMPLEX⟧ *service mark for* MULTIPLEX (*n.*) —*n.* [*usually* **c-**] such a complex

cin·e·rar·i·a (sin′ə rer′ē ə) *n.* ⟦ModL < L *cinerarius,* pertaining to ashes < *cinis* (see fol.): so named from the ashlike grayish down on the leaves⟧ a common hothouse plant (*Senecio cruentus*) of the composite family, with heart-shaped leaves and colorful flowers

cin·e·rar·i·um (-ē əm) *n., pl.* **-rar′i·a** (-ə) ⟦L < *cinis,* ashes: see INCINERATE⟧ a place to keep the ashes of cremated bodies —**cin′e·rar′y** *adj.*

ci·ne·re·ous (sə nir′ē əs) *adj.* ⟦L *cinerosus* < *cinis:* see fol.⟧ **1** of or like ashes **2** of the color of ashes; ash-gray

cin·er·in (sin′ər in′) *n.* ⟦< L *cinis,* ashes (see INCINERATE) + -IN[1]⟧ either of two compounds, $C_{20}H_{28}O_3$ and $C_{21}H_{28}O_5$, in pyrethrum flowers, used in insecticides

cin·gu·lum (siŋ′gyo͞o ləm) *n., pl.* **-la** (-lə) ⟦L, girdle, belt < *cingere,* to encircle: see CINCH⟧ *Zool.* a band or zone, as of color —**cin′gu·late** (-lit, -lāt′) *adj.,* **cin′gu·lat′ed** (-lāt′id)

cin·na·bar (sin′ə bär′) *n.* ⟦ME *cinabare* < L *cinnabaris* < Gr *kinnabari* < ? Ar *zinjafr* < Pers *šangarf,* red lead, cinnabar⟧ **1** mercuric sulfide, HgS, a heavy, bright-red mineral, the principal ore of mercury **2** artificial mercuric sulfide, used as a red pigment **3** brilliant red; vermilion

cin·nam·ic (sə nam′ik) ***adj.*** **1** of or derived from cinnamon **2** designating a white, crystalline, organic acid, C_6H_5·CH:CH·COOH, produced from benzaldehyde: the corresponding aldehyde gives oil of cinnamon its characteristic flavor and odor

cin·na·mon (sin′ə mən) ***n.*** ⟦ME *cinamome* < OFr < L *cinnamomum* < Gr *kinnamōmon* < Heb *qinnāmōn,* cinnamon⟧ **1** the yellowish-brown spice made from the dried inner bark of several trees or shrubs (genus *Cinnamomum*) of the laurel family, native to the East Indies and Southeast Asia **2** this bark **3** any tree or shrub from which this bark is obtained **4** yellowish brown —***adj.*** **1** yellowish-brown **2** made or flavored with cinnamon

cinnamon bear a reddish-brown variety of the American black bear

cinnamon fern a large, New World fern (*Osmunda cinnamomea,* family Osmundaceae) having sterile green fronds and other fronds that bear spores and turn a cinnamon color as the spores mature

cinnamon stone ESSONITE

cin·que·cen·tist (chiŋ′kwə chen′tist) ***n.*** an Italian artist or writer of the cinquecento

cin·que·cen·to (-tō) ***n.*** ⟦It, five hundred, short for *mille cinquecento,* one thousand five hundred⟧ the 16th cent. as a period in Italian art and literature

cinque·foil (siŋk′foil′) ***n.*** ⟦ME *cink foil* < OFr *cinquefoil* < It *cinquefoglie* < L *quinquefolium* < *quinque,* FIVE + *folium,* leaf: see FOLIATE⟧ **1** any of a genus (*Potentilla*) of plants of the rose family, with white, yellow, or red flowers and fruit like a dry strawberry: some species have compound leaves with five leaflets arranged like the fingers on a hand **2** *Archit.* a circular design made up of five converging arcs

cinquefoil

Cinque Ports (siŋk) ⟦sp. used in E from at least the 16th c.: < older *sink pors* < OFr *cink porz,* five ports < L *quinque portus*⟧ group of towns (orig. five: Hastings, Romney, Hythe, Dover, and Sandwich) on the SE coast of England: they formerly (11th-15th cent.) received privileges in return for providing naval defense at a time when England had no navy

CIO *abbrev.* **1** Congress of Industrial Organizations: see AFL-CIO **2** chief information officer

ci·on (sī′ən) ***n.*** SCION (sense 1)

ciop·pi·no (chə pē′nō) ***n.*** ⟦< It dial.; dish originated prob. among It immigrants in San Francisco⟧ a spicy stew of fish and various shellfish, containing tomatoes, onions, green pepper, red wine, garlic, etc.

CIP *abbrev.* Cataloging in Publication

Ci·pan·go (si paŋ′gō) *former name for* a group of islands east of Asia, prob. what is now Japan: name used by Marco Polo & medieval geographers

ci·pher (sī′fər) ***n.*** ⟦ME *cifre* < OFr *cyfre* < ML *cifra* < Ar *ṣifr, ṣefr,* a cipher, nothing < *ṣafara,* to be empty⟧ **1** [Old-fashioned] the symbol 0, indicating a value of zero **2** a person or thing of no importance or value **3** *a)* a system of secret writing based on a key, or set of predetermined rules or symbols *b)* a message in such writing *c)* the key to such a system (see also CODE) **4** an intricate weaving together of letters, as a monogram **5** an Arabic numeral —***vi.*** [Old-fashioned] to solve arithmetic problems —***vt.*** to write with a CIPHER (***n.*** 3*a*); encode

cip·o·lin (sip′ə lin) ***n.*** ⟦Fr < It *cipollino,* lit., little onion (ult. < L *cepa,* onion): from its structure⟧ a variety of Italian marble with alternating layers or streaks of color, esp. of white and green

Cip·ro (sip′rō) *trademark for* CIPROFLOXACIN

cip·ro·flox·a·cin (sip′rō fläk′sə sin) ***n.*** ⟦altered < elements of the chemical name⟧ a synthetic, broad-spectrum antibiotic, $C_{17}H_{18}FN_3O_3$·HCl·H_2O, used in treating urinary tract infections, lung infections, etc.: in full **ciprofloxacin hydrochloride**

cir or **circ** *abbrev.* **1** circa **2** circular

cir·ca (sʉr′kə) ***prep.*** ⟦L⟧ [*also in italics*] about: used before an approximate date or figure [*circa* 1650]

cir·ca·di·an (sər kā′dē ən, sʉr′kə dē′ən) ***adj.*** ⟦coined < L *circa,* about + *diem,* acc. sing. of *dies,* day: see DEITY⟧ *Biol.* designating or of behavioral or physiological rhythms associated with the 24-hour cycles of the earth's rotation, as, in man, the regular metabolic, glandular, and sleep rhythms which may persist through a dislocation of day and night caused by high-speed travel: see also DIURNAL

Cir·cas·sia (sər kash′ə, -kash′ē ə) region in the NW Caucasus, on the Black Sea

Cir·cas·si·an (ser kash′ən, -ē ən) ***n.*** **1** a member of a group of Caucasian peoples of Circassia **2** a person living in Circassia **3** the North Caucasian language spoken in Circassia —***adj.*** of Circassia or its people, language, or culture

Circassian walnut the hard, heavy, brown or purplish wood of the English walnut

Cir·ce (sʉr′sē) ***n.*** ⟦L < Gr *Kirkē*⟧ in Homer's *Odyssey,* an enchantress who turns men into swine —**Cir·ce·an** (sər sē′ən, sʉr′sē ən) ***adj.***

cir·ci·nate (sʉr′sə nāt′) ***adj.*** ⟦L *circinatus,* pp. of *circinare,* to make round < *circinus,* a drawing compass < Gr *kirkinos* < *kirkos:* see CIRCUS⟧ rounded or circular; specif., rolled into a coil on its axis with the apex in the center, as the new fronds of a fern —**cir′ci·nate′ly** ***adv.***

Cir·ci·nus (sʉr′sə nəs) ***n.*** ⟦L, drawing compass: see prec.⟧ a S constellation near Centaurus

cir·cle (sʉr′kəl) ***n.*** ⟦ME *cercle* < OFr < L *circulus,* a circle, dim. of *circus:* see CIRCUS⟧ **1** a plane figure bounded by a single curved line, every point of which is equally distant from the point at the center of the figure: ECCENTRICITY (sense 3) **2** the line bounding such a figure; circumference **3** anything shaped like a circle, as a circular road, a ring, a crown, or a halo **4** [Old Poet.] the orb of a heavenly body **5** the orbit of a heavenly body **6** a balcony or tier of seats as in a theater [the dress *circle*] **7** a complete or recurring series, usually ending as it began; cycle; period **8** a group of people bound together by common interests; coterie **9** [Historical] a territorial division, esp. in Germany **10** range or extent, as of influence or interest; scope **11** *a)* GREAT CIRCLE *b)* a parallel of latitude (see also ARCTIC CIRCLE, ANTARCTIC CIRCLE) **12** an astronomical instrument with a part in the form of a calibrated circle **13** *Logic* a faulty manner of reasoning in which the conclusion that is to be proved is assumed in a premise [guilty of arguing in a *circle*]: see also VICIOUS CIRCLE —***vt.*** **-cled, -cling** **1** to form a circle around; encompass; surround **2** to move around, as in a circle —***vi.*** to go around in a circle; revolve —***SYN.*** COTERIE —☆**circle the wagons** [Informal] to take defensive action; prepare for an attack: from arranging a wagon train in a circular formation —**come full circle** to return to an original position or state after going through a series or cycle —**cir′cler** (-klər) ***n.***

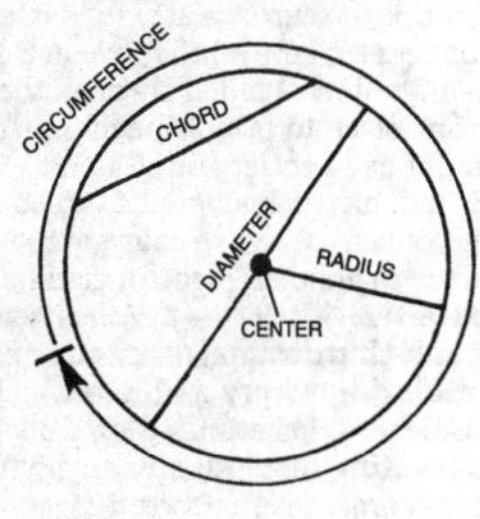

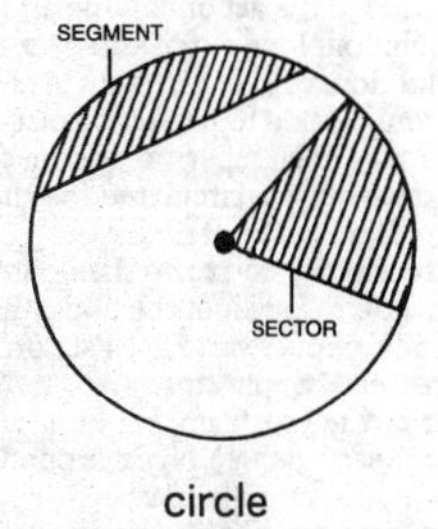

circle

cir·clet (sʉr′klit) ***n.*** ⟦ME *cerclet* < OFr, dim. of *cercle,* prec.⟧ **1** a small circle **2** a ring or circular band worn as an ornament

cir·cuit (sʉr′kit) ***n.*** ⟦ME < OFr < L *circuitus,* a going around, circuit < *circumire* < *circum* (see CIRCUM-) + *ire,* to go: see YEAR⟧ **1** the line or the length of the line forming the boundaries of an area **2** the area bounded **3** the act of going around something; course or journey around [the moon's *circuit* of the earth] **4** *a)* the regular journey of a person performing certain duties, as of an itinerant preacher or a judge holding court at designated places *b)* the district periodically traveled through in the performance of such duties *c)* the route traveled ☆**5** the judicial district of a U.S. Court of Appeals **6** *a)* a number of associated theaters at which plays, movies, etc. are shown in turn *b)* a group of nightclubs, resorts, etc. at which entertainers appear in turn ☆*c)* a sequence of contests or matches held at various places, in which a particular group of athletes compete; also, an association or league of athletic teams [the professional bowlers' *circuit*] **7** *Elec. a)* a complete or partial path over which current may flow *b)* any hookup, wiring, etc. that is connected into this path, as for radio, television, or sound reproduction —***vi.*** to go in a circuit —***vt.*** to make a circuit about —***SYN.*** CIRCUMFERENCE —**cir′cuit·al** (-kit ′l) ***adj.***

circuit board *Electronics* an insulated board or panel on which interconnected circuits and other components are mounted or printed

☆**circuit breaker** a switchlike safety device that automatically interrupts the flow of an electrical current in a circuit when it has become excessive

☆**circuit court** any court that holds sessions in various locations within its judicial district

☆**circuit court of appeals** COURT OF APPEALS (sense 2)

cir·cu·i·tous (sər kyo͞o′ət əs) ***adj.*** ⟦ML *circuitosus* < L *circuitus:* see CIRCUIT⟧ roundabout; indirect; devious —**cir·cu′i·tous·ly** ***adv.*** —**cir·cu′i·tous·ness** ***n.***

☆**circuit rider** a minister who traveled from place to place in an assigned circuit to preach

cir·cuit·ry (sʉr′kə trē) ***n.*** the scheme or system of an electric circuit, or the elements making up such a circuit, as in a computer

cir·cu·i·ty (sər kyo͞o′ə tē) ***n., pl.*** **-ties** ⟦OFr *circuité* < L *circuitus*⟧ the quality or state of being circuitous; devious procedure; indirection

cir·cu·lar (sʉr′kyə lər) ***adj.*** ⟦ME *circulare* < L *circularis*⟧ **1** in the shape of a circle; round **2** relating to a circle **3** moving in a circle or spiral **4** roundabout; circuitous **5** designating or of an invalid argument in which the conclusion that is to be proved is assumed in a premise **6** intended for circulation among a number of people —***n.*** an advertisement, letter, etc., usually prepared in quantities for extensive circulation —***SYN.*** ROUND[1] —**cir′cu·lar′i·ty** (-ler′ə tē) ***n.***, **cir′cu·lar·ness** —**cir′cu·lar·ly** ***adv.***

circular file ⟦in ref. to the circular rim of an office wastebasket⟧ [Informal] a wastebasket: a humorous usage implying that a thing is worth "filing" only in the trash

cir·cu·lar·ize (-lər īz′) ***vt.*** **-ized′, -iz′ing** **1** to make circular; make round **2** to send circulars to **3** to canvass as for opinions or support —**cir′cu·lar·i·za′tion** ***n.*** —**cir′cu·lar·iz′er** ***n.***

circular mil a unit of measurement for the thickness of wires, equal to the area of a circle with a diameter of one mil

circular saw a saw in the form of a disk with a toothed edge, rotated at high speed as by a motor

cir·cu·late (sʉr′kyə lāt′) *vi.* **-lat′ed, -lat′ing** ⟦< L *circulatus,* pp. of *circulari,* to form a CIRCLE⟧ **1** to move in a circle, circuit, or course and return to the same point, as blood through the body **2** to go from person to person or from place to place; specif., *a)* to move about freely, as air *b)* to move about as in society or at a party *c)* to be made widely known, felt, established, distributed, etc. *d)* to be distributed to a circle or mass of readers or collectors —*vt.* to cause to move around freely or go from one person or place to another; place in circulation —**cir′cu·la·to′ry** (-lə tôr′ē) *adj.*, **cir′cu·la′tive** (-lāt′iv) —**cir′cu·la′tor** *n.*

circulating decimal REPEATING DECIMAL

circulating library a library which loans books or other materials for use elsewhere, sometimes for a daily fee

circulating medium any medium of exchange that can be passed in ordinary commerce, as currency

cir·cu·la·tion (sʉr′kyə lā′shən) *n.* ⟦ME *circulacioun* < L *circulatio:* see CIRCULATE⟧ **1** free movement around from place to place, as of air in ventilating **2** the act of moving around in a complete circuit; specif., the movement of blood out of and back to the heart through the arteries and veins **3** the flow of sap in a plant **4** the passing of something, as money or news, from person to person or place to place; dissemination **5** *a)* the distribution of newspapers, magazines, etc. among readers *b)* the extent to which something is circulated, as the average number of copies of a magazine sold in a given period

circulatory system the system responsible for circulating blood and lymph throughout the body, that supplies nutrients and oxygen to the cells and removes various waste products: it consists of the heart, blood, blood vessels, lymph, etc.

cir·cum- (sʉr′kəm, sər kum′) ⟦< L *circum,* around, about, adv. acc. of *circus:* see CIRCUS⟧ *prefix* around, about, surrounding, on all sides [*circumnavigate, circumscribe*]

cir·cum·am·bi·ent (sʉr′kəm am′bē ənt) *adj.* extending all around; surrounding —**cir′cum·am′bi·ence** *n.*, **cir′cum·am′bi·en·cy**

cir·cum·am·bu·late (-am′byoo͞ lāt′) *vt., vi.* **-lat′ed, -lat′ing** ⟦< LL *circumambulatus,* pp. of *circumambulare* < L *circum* (see CIRCUM-) + *ambulare* (see AMBULATE)⟧ to walk around —**cir′cum·am′bu·la′tion** *n.* —**cir′cum·am′bu·la·to′ry** (-lə tôr′ē) *adj.*

cir·cum·bo·re·al (sʉr′kəm bôr′ē əl) *adj.* of or having to do with plants and animals inhabiting boreal regions of North America and Eurasia

cir·cum·cise (sʉr′kəm sīz′) *vt.* **-cised′, -cis′ing** ⟦ME *circumcisen* < OFr *circonciser* < L *circumcisus,* pp. of *circumcidere,* to cut around, in LL(Ec), to circumcise < *circum,* around + *caedere,* to cut: see -CIDE⟧ **1** *a)* to cut off all or part of the foreskin of (a male) *b)* to cut off the labia minora or clitoris of (a female) **2** [Archaic] to cleanse from sin; purify

cir·cum·ci·sion (sʉr′kəm sizh′ən) *n.* ⟦ME *circumcisioun* < LL(Ec) *circumcisio*⟧ **1** a circumcising, or being circumcised, either as a religious rite, as of the Jews or Muslims, or as a hygienic measure **2** [Archaic] a cleansing from sin

cir·cum·fer·ence (sər kum′fər əns, -frəns) *n.* ⟦ME < L *circumferentia* < *circumferens,* prp. of *circumferre* < *circum,* around + *ferre,* to carry, BEAR[1]⟧ **1** the line bounding a circle, a rounded surface, or an area suggesting a circle **2** the distance measured by this line —**cir·cum′fer·en′tial** (-fər en′shəl) *adj.* —**cir·cum′fer·en′tial·ly** *adv.*

SYN.—**circumference** refers to the line bounding a circle or any approximately circular or elliptical area; **perimeter** extends the meaning to a line bounding any area, as a triangle, square, or polygon; **periphery**, in its literal sense identical with **perimeter**, is more frequently used of the edge of a physical object or in an extended metaphoric sense [the *periphery* of understanding]; **circuit** now usually refers to a traveling around a periphery [the moon's *circuit* of the earth]; **compass** refers literally to an area within specific limits but is often used figuratively [the *compass* of the city, the *compass* of freedom]

cir·cum·flex (sʉr′kəm fleks′) *n.* ⟦L *circumflexus,* pp. of *circumflectere* < *circum,* around + *flectere,* to bend⟧ a mark (ˆ or ˜) used over certain vowel letters in the orthography of some languages to indicate a specific sound or quality, or used in certain systems of symbols for representing speech sounds: in modern use, as in French, the form (ˆ) is the most common: also **circumflex accent** —*adj.* **1** of, with, or marked by a circumflex **2** bending around; curved —*vt.* **1** [Now Rare] to bend around; curve **2** to write with a circumflex —**cir′cum·flex′ion** (-flek′shən) *n.*

cir·cum·flu·ent (sər kum′floo͞ ənt) *adj.* ⟦L *circumfluens,* prp. of *circumfluere,* to flow around < *circum,* around + *fluere,* to flow: see FLUENT⟧ flowing around; surrounding; encompassing: also **cir·cum′flu·ous** (-floo͞ əs)

cir·cum·fuse (sʉr′kəm fyoo͞z′) *vt.* **-fused′, -fus′ing** ⟦< L *circumfusus,* pp. of *circumfundere* < *circum,* around + *fundere,* to pour: see FOUND[3]⟧ **1** to pour or spread (a fluid) around; diffuse **2** to surround (*with* a fluid); suffuse (*in*) —**cir′cum·fu′sion** *n.*

cir·cum·lo·cu·tion (-lō kyoo͞′shən) *n.* ⟦ME *circumlocucioun* < L *circumlocutio:* see CIRCUM- & LOCUTION⟧ **1** a roundabout, indirect, or lengthy way of expressing something; periphrasis **2** an instance of this —**cir′cum·loc′u·to′ry** (-läk′yə tôr′ē) *adj.*

cir·cum·nav·i·gate (-nav′ə gāt′) *vt.* **-gat′ed, -gat′ing** ⟦< L *circumnavigatus,* pp. of *circumnavigare:* see CIRCUM- & NAVIGATE⟧ to sail or fly around (the earth, an island, etc.) —**cir′cum·nav′i·ga′tion** *n.* —**cir′cum·nav′i·ga′tor** *n.*

cir·cum·nu·ta·tion (-nyoo͞ tā′shən) *n.* ⟦CIRCUM- + NUTATION⟧ *Bot.* the irregular spiral or elliptical rotation of the apex of a growing stem, root, or shoot, caused by differences in the rate of growth of the opposite sides

cir·cum·po·lar (-pō′lər) *adj.* **1** surrounding or near either pole of the earth **2** *Astron.* moving around either of the celestial poles: said of celestial objects, esp. stars, which never sink below the horizon

cir·cum·ro·tate (-rō′tāt′) *vi.* **-tat′ed, -tat′ing** to turn like a wheel; rotate —**cir′cum·ro·ta′tion** *n.*

cir·cum·scis·sile (-sis′il) *adj.* ⟦CIRCUM- + SCISSILE⟧ *Bot.* opening or splitting by a transverse fissure around the circumference, leaving an upper and lower half: said of certain seed pods or capsules

cir·cum·scribe (sʉr′kəm skrīb′, sʉr′kəm skrīb′) *vt.* **-scribed′, -scrib′ing** ⟦ME *circumscriben* < L *circumscribere:* see CIRCUM- & SCRIBE⟧ **1** to trace a line around; encircle; encompass **2** *a)* to set or mark off the limits of; limit; confine *b)* to restrict the action of; restrain **3** *Geom. a)* to draw a plane figure around (another plane figure) either to intersect each vertex of the inner figure, as a circle around a square, or to have each side of the outer figure tangent to the inner figure, as a square around a circle *b)* to enclose a solid figure within (another solid figure) in a similar manner, as a cube within a sphere or a sphere within a cube —*SYN.* LIMIT —**cir′cum·scrib′a·ble** *adj.* —**cir′cum·scrib′er** *n.*

cir·cum·scrip·tion (sʉr′kəm skrip′shən) *n.* ⟦L *circumscriptio*⟧ **1** a circumscribing or being circumscribed **2** a boundary or outline **3** a limitation or restriction **4** a surrounding substance **5** a circumscribed space or area **6** an inscription, as around a coin or medal —**cir′cum·scrip′tive** *adj.*

cir·cum·spect (sʉr′kəm spekt′) *adj.* ⟦ME < L *circumspectus,* pp. of *circumspicere,* to look about: see CIRCUM- & SPY⟧ careful to consider all related circumstances before acting, judging, or deciding —*SYN.* CAREFUL —**cir′cum·spec′tion** *n.* —**cir′cum·spect′ly** *adv.*

cir·cum·stance (sʉr′kəm stans′, -stəns) *n.* ⟦OFr < L *circumstantia,* a standing around, condition < *circumstare* < *circum,* around + *stare,* STAND⟧ **1** a fact or event accompanying another, either incidentally or as an essential condition or determining factor [*circumstances* alter cases] **2** any happening or fact; event **3** [*pl.*] conditions surrounding and affecting a person, esp. financial conditions [in comfortable *circumstances*] **4** chance; luck [*circumstance* would have it so] **5** ceremony; show [pomp and *circumstance*] **6** *a)* accompanying or surrounding detail *b)* fullness of detail —*vt.* **-stanced′, -stanc′ing** to place in certain circumstances —*SYN.* OCCURRENCE —**under no circumstances** under no conditions; never —**under the circumstances** conditions being what they are or were —**cir′cum·stanced′** *adj.*

cir·cum·stan·tial (sʉr′kəm stan′shəl) *adj.* **1** having to do with, or depending on, circumstances **2** not of primary importance; incidental **3** full or complete in detail **4** full of pomp or display; ceremonial —**cir′cum·stan′tial·ly** *adv.*

circumstantial evidence evidence based on circumstances associated with a matter, from which inferences bearing on that matter can be made, rather than evidence that is straightforward and conclusive; indirect evidence

cir·cum·stan·ti·al·i·ty (-stan′shē al′ə tē) *n.* **1** the quality of being circumstantial **2** *pl.* **-ties** particularity; detail

cir·cum·val·late (-val′āt′) *vt.* **-lat′ed, -lat′ing** ⟦< L *circumvallatus,* pp. of *circumvallare* < *circum,* around + *vallare,* to fortify with a rampart < *vallum,* rampart, WALL⟧ to surround with or as with a wall or trench —*adj.* surrounded by or as by a wall or trench —**cir′cum·val·la′tion** *n.*

cir·cum·vent (sʉr′kəm vent′, sʉr′kəm vent′) *vt.* ⟦< L *circumventus,* pp. of *circumvenire* < *circum,* around + *venire,* COME⟧ **1** to surround or circle around **2** to surround or encircle with evils, enmity, etc.; entrap **3** to get the better of or prevent from happening by craft or ingenuity **4** to avoid or evade —**cir′cum·ven′tion** *n.* —**cir′cum·ven′tive** *adj.*

cir·cum·vo·lu·tion (-və loo͞′shən) *n.* ⟦ME *circumvolucioun* < ML *circumvolutio* < L *circumvolutus,* pp. of *circumvolvere:* see fol.⟧ **1** the act of rolling or turning around a center or axis **2** a fold, twist, or spiral **3** a circuitous course or form

cir·cum·volve (sʉr′kəm välv′) *vt., vi.* **-volved′, -volv′ing** ⟦L *circumvolvere* < *circum,* around + *volvere,* to roll: see WALK⟧ to revolve

cir·cus (sʉr′kəs) *n.* ⟦L, a circle, ring, racecourse < or akin to Gr *kirkos,* a circle < IE **kirk-* < base **(s)ker-,* to turn, bend > Gr *korōnos* & L *curvus,* curved⟧ **1** in ancient Rome, an oval or oblong arena with tiers of seats around it, used as for games or chariot races **2** a similar arena, often enclosed in a tent or building for performances by acrobats, trained animals, clowns, etc. **3** a traveling show of this sort or its personnel, equipment, etc. **4** the performance of such a show **5** [Brit.] a circular open place where many streets come together: used esp. in place names ☆**6** [Informal] anything thought of as being like a circus, as an event, place, or activity that is riotously entertaining, spectacular, frenzied, disorganized, etc. [a media *circus*]

circus catch ⟦so called prob. in comparison to the feats of acrobats in a *circus*⟧ a spectacular or difficult catch, esp. one made by a fielder in baseball or a receiver in football

Circus Max·i·mus (mak′si məs) ⟦L, lit., largest racecourse⟧ a large amphitheater built in Rome *c.* 329 B.C., used as for chariot races and games

ci·ré (sē rā′) *adj.* ⟦Fr, lit., waxed, orig. pp. of *cirer,* to wax < *cire:* see CERE⟧ having a smooth, glossy finish imparted by treatment as with wax —*n.* ciré silk, straw, etc.

Cir·e·na·i·ca (sir′ə nā′i kə; *It* chē′re nä′ē kä) *It. name for* CYRENAICA

cirque (surk) *n.* ⟦Fr < L *circus:* see CIRCUS⟧ **1** a circular space or arrangement **2** [Old Poet.] a circle; ring **3** [Archaic] a circus **4** *Geol.* a steep, hollow excavation high on a mountainside, made by glacial erosion; natural amphitheater

cir·rate (sir′āt′) *adj.* ⟦L *cirratus* < *cirrus,* a curl⟧ *Biol.* having cirri

cir·rho·sis (sə rō′sis) *n., pl.* **-ses′** (-sēz′) ⟦ModL < Gr *kirrhos,* tawny + -OSIS: so named by R. T. H. Laënnec (1781-1826), Fr physician, because of the orange-yellow appearance of the diseased liver⟧ a degenerative disease in an organ of the body, esp. the liver, marked by excess formation of connective tissue and, usually, subsequent painful swelling —**cir·rhot′ic** (-rät′ik) *adj.*

cir·ri (sir′ī′) *n. pl. of* CIRRUS (sense 1)

cir·ri·form (sir′i fôrm′) *adj.* CIRROSE (sense 2)

cir·ri·ped (sir′i ped′) *n.* ⟦< ModL < CIRRI + L *pes* (gen. *pedis*), FOOT⟧ any of a class (Cirripedia) of saltwater crustaceans that are attached or parasitic as adults, including the barnacles and the rhizocephalans

cir·ro- (sir′ō, -ə) *combining form* cirrus [*cirrostratus*]: also **cir′ri-** (-i)

cir·ro·cu·mu·lus (sir′ō kyōō′myə ləs) *n.* the type of white cloud that resembles a small puff, flake, or streak, found at high altitudes and consisting of ice crystals and water droplets: see CLOUD

cir·rose (sir′ōs′) *adj.* ⟦< L *cirrus,* a curl + -OSE[1]⟧ **1** *Biol.* having or resembling cirri **2** of or like cirrus clouds Also **cir′rous** (-əs)

cir·ro·stra·tus (sir′ō strāt′əs, -strat′-) *n.* the type of thin, whitish cloud found at high altitudes and consisting of ice crystals: such clouds often produce halo phenomena: see CLOUD

cir·rus (sir′əs) *n.* ⟦L, a lock, curl, tendril⟧ **1** *pl.* **cir′ri′** (-ī′) *Biol. a)* a plant tendril *b)* a flexible, threadlike tentacle or appendage, as the feelers of certain organisms *c)* a cone-shaped cluster of fused cilia, occurring in many species of infusorians **2** *pl.* **cir′rus** *Meteorol.* the type of white cloud that resembles a wispy filament, found at high altitudes and consisting of ice crystals

cir·soid (sur′soid′) *adj.* ⟦Gr *kirsoeidēs* < *kirsos,* enlargement of a vein + -OID⟧ like a varix, or enlarged blood vessel; varicose

CIS *abbrev.* Commonwealth of Independent States

cis- (sis) ⟦< L *cis,* on this side: see HERE⟧ *prefix* **1** on this side of [*cisalpine*] **2** subsequent to **3** *Chem.* designating an isomer having certain atoms or groups on the same side of a given plane in the molecule: in chemical names, usually printed in italic type and hyphenated and disregarded in alphabetization [*cis*-butene]: see TRANS-

cis·al·pine (sis al′pīn′, -pin) *adj.* ⟦L *cisalpinus:* see prec. & ALPINE⟧ on this (the southern) side of the Alps, from the viewpoint of Rome as the seat of the Roman Empire

☆**cis·at·lan·tic** (-at lan′tik) *adj.* on this (the speaker's) side of the Atlantic

☆**cis·co** (sis′kō) *n., pl.* **-co, -coes, -cos** ⟦< CdnFr *ciscovette* < Algonquian⟧ any of various trouts (esp. genus *Coregonus*) found in the colder lakes of the NE U.S. and of Canada

Cis·kei (sis′kī′) former black homeland in SE South Africa, on the Indian Ocean: granted independence in 1981, it was abolished in 1994

cis·lu·nar (sis lōō′nər) *adj.* ⟦CIS- + LUNAR⟧ on this side of the moon, between the moon and the earth

cis·mon·tane (sis män′tān′, sis′män tān′) *adj.* ⟦L *cismontanus*⟧ on this side of the mountains, esp. of the Alps

cis·plat·in (sis plat′′n) *n.* ⟦CIS- + PLATIN(UM)⟧ a white, powdery drug, $PtCl_2H_6N_2$, containing platinum, used to stop the growth of cancerous tumors, esp. in the ovary, testis, or bladder

cis·soid (sis′oid′) *n.* ⟦Gr *kissoeidēs,* ivylike < *kissos,* ivy + *eidos,* -OID⟧ *Math.* a curve converging into a pointed tip —*adj.* designating the angle formed by the concave sides of two intersecting curves: opposed to SISTROID

cis·sy (sis′ē) *n., pl.* **-sies** *Brit. var. of* SISSY

cist (sist; *also for 1,* kist) *n.* ⟦L *cista* < Gr *kistē* (see CHEST); sense 1 via Welsh *kist faen,* lit., stone coffin⟧ **1** a prehistoric tomb made of stone slabs or hollowed out of rock **2** in ancient times, a box or chest, esp. one containing sacred utensils

Cis·ter·cian (si stur′shən) *adj.* ⟦ME & OFr *Cistercien* < OFr, after ML *Cistercium* (now *Cîteaux,* France), orig. convent (1098) of the order⟧ designating or of a monastic order following a strict interpretation of the Benedictine rule —*n.* a Cistercian monk or nun

cis·tern (sis′tərn) *n.* ⟦ME *cisterne* > OFr < L *cisterna,* reservoir for water < *cista,* CHEST⟧ **1** a large receptacle for storing water; esp., a tank, usually underground, in which rainwater is collected for use **2** *Anat.* a sac or cavity containing a natural bodily fluid

cis·ter·na (si stur′nə) *n., pl.* **-nae** (-nē) ⟦L: see prec.⟧ *Anat.* a cistern; specif., any of the enlarged spaces below the arachnoid —**cis·ter′nal** *adj.*

cis·tron (sis′trän′) *n.* ⟦CIS- + TR(ANS)- + -ON⟧ the smallest sequence of DNA needed to direct the synthesis of a functional polypeptide; a gene

cis·tus (sis′təs) *n.* ⟦ModL < Gr *kistos,* rockrose⟧ any of a genus (*Cistus*) of low shrubs of the rockrose family, with white or purplish flowers resembling single roses: some species yield labdanum

cit *abbrev.* **1** citation **2** cited **3** citizen

cit·a·del (sit′ə del′, -dəl) *n.* ⟦< It *cittadella,* dim. of *cittade,* city < L *civitas,* citizenship: see CITY⟧ **1** a fortress on a commanding height for defense of a city **2** a fortified place; stronghold **3** a place of safety; refuge

ci·ta·tion (sī tā′shən) *n.* ⟦ME *citacion* < OFr *citation* < L *citatio,* a command (in LL, a summoning) < pp. of *citare:* see fol.⟧ **1** a summons to appear before a court of law **2** the act of citing, or quoting **3** a passage cited; quotation **4** a reference as to a legal statute, a previous law case, or a written authority, as precedent or justification ☆**5** *a)* honorable mention in an official report for bravery or meritorious service in the armed forces *b)* a formal statement of the reasons for honoring a person in public with an award or degree —**ci′ta′tor** *n.* —**ci·ta·to·ry** (sīt′ə tôr′ē) *adj.*

cite (sīt) *vt.* **cit′ed, cit′ing** ⟦ME *citen* < OFr *citer,* to summon < L *citare,* to arouse, summon < *ciere,* to put into motion, rouse < IE base **kei-* > Gr *kinein,* to move, OE *hatan,* to command⟧ **1** to summon to appear before a court of law **2** to quote (a passage, book, speech, writer, etc.) **3** to refer to or mention as by way of example, proof, or precedent ☆**4** to mention in a CITATION (sense 5) **5** [Archaic] to stir to action; arouse —*n.* [Informal] CITATION (sense 3) —**cit′a·ble** *adj.,* **cite′a·ble**

cith·a·ra (sith′ə rə) *n.* ⟦L < Gr *kithara*⟧ an ancient musical instrument somewhat resembling a lyre

cith·er (sith′ər) *n.* ⟦Fr *cithare* < prec.⟧ *var. of* CITTERN

cith·ern (sith′ərn) *n. var. of* CITTERN

cit·ied (sit′ēd) *adj.* **1** having a city or cities on it [the *citied* earth] **2** like a city

☆**cit·i·fied** (sit′i fīd′) *adj.* having the manners, dress, etc. attributed to city people

cit·i·zen (sit′ə zən, -sən) *n.* ⟦ME & Anglo-Fr *citizein,* altered (? infl. by *denizen*) < OFr *citeain* < *cité:* see CITY; sense 3 infl. by use of Fr *citoyen* during the Fr Revolution⟧ **1** [Historical] a native or inhabitant, esp. a freeman or burgess, of a town or city **2** a native, inhabitant, or denizen of any place [*citizens* of the deep] **3** a member of a state or nation, esp. one with a republican form of government, who owes allegiance to it by birth or naturalization and is entitled to full civil rights **4** a civilian, as distinguished from a person in military service, from a policeman, etc.

SYN.—**citizen** refers to a member of a state or nation, esp. one with a republican government, who owes it allegiance and is entitled to full civil rights either by birth or naturalization; **subject** is the term used when the government is headed by a monarch or other sovereign; **national** is applied to a person residing away from the country of which he or she is, or once was, a citizen or subject, and is especially used of one another by fellow countrymen living abroad; **native** refers to one who was born in the country under question, and is applied specifically to an original or indigenous inhabitant of the region —*ANT.* **alien**

cit·i·zen·ess (-is) *n.* ⟦orig. transl. of Fr *citoyenne,* fem. of *citoyen* (Fr Revolutionary term)⟧ [Now Rare] a woman citizen: see -ESS

cit·i·zen·ry (-rē) *n.* all citizens as a group

citizen's arrest an arrest made by a citizen who is not a law officer, as allowed under common law or by statute

☆**citizens band** a band of shortwave radio frequencies set aside by the FCC for local use at low power by private persons or businesses: also written **citizens' band, citizen's band**

cit·i·zen·ship (-ship′) *n.* **1** the status or condition of a citizen **2** the duties, rights, and privileges of this status **3** a person's conduct as a citizen

citizenship papers the document stating that a naturalized person has been formally declared a citizen

Cit·lal·te·petl (sē′tläl tā′pet′′l) ORIZABA

cit·ole (sit′ōl′, si tōl′) *n.* ⟦OFr: orig. dim. < L *cithara,* CITHARA⟧ CITTERN

cit·ral (si′trəl) *n.* ⟦CITR(I)- + AL(DEHYDE)⟧ a liquid aldehyde, $C_9H_{15}·CHO$, with a pleasant odor, found in oil of lemon, oil of lime, etc. and used as a flavoring agent and in perfumes

cit·rate (si′trāt′, sī′-) *n.* ⟦CITR(I)- + -ATE[2]⟧ a salt or ester of citric acid

cit·re·ous (si′trē əs) *adj.* ⟦L *citreus:* see CITRUS⟧ of the yellow color of a lemon

cit·ri- (si′tri, -trə) *combining form* **1** citrus, citrus fruits [*citriculture*] **2** citric, citric acid [*citrate*] Also **cit·ro-** (si′trō, -trə) or, before a vowel, **citr-**

cit·ric (-trik) *adj.* ⟦< prec. + -IC⟧ **1** of or from citrus fruits **2** designating or of an acid, $C_6H_8O_7$, obtained from such fruits, used in making flavoring extracts, dyes, citrates, etc.

☆**cit·ri·cul·ture** (si′tri kul′chər) *n.* the cultivation of citrus fruits

cit·rine (-trin, -trēn′, -trīn′) *adj.* ⟦OFr < ML *citrinus* < L *citrus,* CITRUS⟧ of the yellow color of a lemon —*n.* **1** lemon yellow **2** a yellow, semiprecious variety of quartz resembling topaz

cit·ron (-trən) *n.* ⟦Fr, lemon < It *citrone* < L *citrus,* CITRUS⟧ **1** a yellow, thick-skinned fruit resembling a lime or lemon but larger and less acid **2** the semitropical tree (*Citrus medica*) of the rue family bearing this fruit **3** the candied rind of this fruit, used as a confection, in fruitcake, etc. ☆**4** CITRON MELON

cit·ron·el·la (si′trə nel′ə) *n.* ⟦ModL < *citron:* see prec.⟧ **1** a volatile, sharp-smelling oil used in perfume, soap, insect repellents, etc.: also **citronella oil** **2** the S Asian grass (*Cymbopogon nardus*) from which this oil is derived

cit·ron·el·lal (-nel′lal) *n.* ⟦< prec. + -AL⟧ a colorless liquid, $C_{10}H_{18}O$, with a very strong lemon odor, found in lemons and eucalyptus oil, and used in perfumes and soaps

☆**citron melon** a kind of fruit with a hard white flesh, that grows on a variety of watermelon plant (*Citrullus lanatus* var. *citroides*): used only candied or preserved

cit·rus (si′trəs) *n.* ⟦ModL < L, citron tree (> Gr *kitron*), prob. via Etr < base of Gr *kedros,* juniper, CEDAR⟧ **1** any of a genus (*Citrus*) of trees and shrubs of the rue family, that bear oranges, lemons, limes, or other such fruit **2** any such fruit —*adj.* of these trees and shrubs: also sp. **cit′rous** (-trəs)

cit·rus·y (si′trə sē) *adj.* having the flavor or smell of lemons, limes, or oranges; tangy, tart, etc.

Cit·tà del Va·ti·ca·no (chēt tä′ del vä′tē kä′nô) *It. name for* VATICAN CITY

cit·tern (sit′ərn) ***n.*** ⟦< CITHER, prob. infl. by ME *giterne*: see GITTERN⟧ a stringed instrument of the guitar family, pear-shaped with a flat back, popular from the 15th to the 18th cent.

cit·y (sit′ē) ***n.***, *pl.* **cit′ies** ⟦ME *cité, citet* < OFr < L *civitas,* citizenship, community of citizens, hence state, city < *civis,* townsman: see HOME⟧ **1** *a)* a center of population larger or more important than a town or village *b)* the commercial or entertainment district of such a population center **2** in the U.S., an incorporated municipality whose boundaries and powers of self-government are defined by a charter from the state in which it is located **3** in Canada, any of various large urban municipalities within a province **4** in Great Britain, a borough or town with a royal charter, usually a town that has been or is an episcopal see **5** all of the people of a city **6** in ancient Greece, a city-state —***adj.*** of, in, for, or characteristic of a city —**the City** the financial and commercial district of Greater London

☆**city chicken** pieces of pork or veal that are put onto skewers, breaded, and cooked by braising or baking

city editor ☆**1** a newspaper editor who handles local news and distributes assignments to reporters **2** [Brit.] a newspaper editor who handles financial and commercial news

☆**city father** any of the important officials of a city, as a councilman or alderman

☆**city hall** **1** a building which houses the offices of a municipal government **2** a municipal government —**fight city hall** [Informal] to take up the apparently futile fight against petty or impersonal bureaucratic authority

☆**city manager** the chief administrative official of a city or other municipality under a COUNCIL-MANAGER PLAN

city of God heaven: Ps. 46:4

City of Light *name for* PARIS[2]

City of Seven Hills *name for* ROME[2]

city planning the technique, profession, etc. of planning and coordinating the development or rehabilitation of urban areas —**city planner**

☆**cit·y·scape** (sit′ē skāp′) ***n.*** ⟦CITY + -SCAPE⟧ **1** a pictorial view, as a painting or photograph, of a city or section of one **2** a view of a city as from an aircraft or skyscraper, or of city buildings silhouetted against the horizon **3** a city scene with typical elements

☆**city slicker** [Informal] a city dweller regarded, esp. by rural people, as a smooth, tricky person

cit·y-state (-stāt′) ***n.*** a state made up of an independent city and the territory directly controlled by it, as in ancient Greece

cit·y·wide (sit′ē wīd′) ***adj.*** extending throughout a city

Ciu·dad Bo·lí·var (syōō däd′ bō lē′vär′) city in NE Venezuela, on the Orinoco

Ciudad Juá·rez (hwä′res′) city in N Mexico, across the Rio Grande from El Paso, Tex.

Ciudad Ma·de·ro (mä der′ō′) city in Tamaulipas state, EC Mexico: suburb of Tampico

Ciudad Vic·to·ri·a (vik tôr′ē ə, -ē ä′) city in EC Mexico: capital of Tamaulipas

civ (siv) ***n.*** [Informal] *short for* CIVILIZATION [a college course in Western *Civ*]

civ·et (siv′it) ***n.*** ⟦Fr *civette* < It *zibetto* < Ar *zabād*⟧ **1** a yellowish, fatty substance with a musklike scent, secreted by a gland near the genitals of the civet cat and used in making some perfumes **2** the civet cat **3** its fur

civet cat **1** any of several nocturnal, catlike carnivores (family Viverridae) of Africa, India, Malaysia, and S China, with spotted, yellowish fur: valued for its CIVET (sense 1) ☆**2** CACOMISTLE

civ·ic (siv′ik) ***adj.*** ⟦L *civicus,* civil < *civis:* see HOME⟧ of a city, citizens, or citizenship —**civ′i·cal·ly *adv.***

civ·ic-mind·ed (siv′ik mīn′dəd) ***adj.*** having, showing, or actively carrying out one's concern for the condition and affairs of one's community; public-spirited —**civ′ic-mind′ed·ness *n.***

☆**civ·ics** (siv′iks) ***n.*** ⟦< CIVIC: see -ICS⟧ the branch of political science that deals with civic affairs and the duties and rights of citizenship

civ·ies (siv′ēz) ***pl.n.*** [Informal] *alt. sp. of* CIVVIES

civ·il (siv′əl) ***adj.*** ⟦OFr < L *civilis* < *civis:* see HOME⟧ **1** of a citizen or citizens [*civil* rights] **2** of a community of citizens, their government, or their interrelations [*civil* service, *civil* war] **3** polite or courteous, esp. in a merely formal way **4** of citizens in procedures or matters that are not military or religious [*civil* marriage] **5** designating legally recognized divisions of time [a *civil* year] **6** *Law* *a)* [*sometimes* **C-**] of or according to Roman civil law or modern civil law *b)* relating to the private rights of individuals and to legal actions involving these: distinguished from CRIMINAL

SYN.—**civil** implies merely a refraining from rudeness [keep a *civil* tongue in your head]; **polite** suggests a more positive observance of etiquette in social behavior [it is not *polite* to interrupt]; **courteous** suggests a still more positive and sincere consideration of others that springs from an inherent thoughtfulness [always *courteous* to strangers]; **chivalrous** implies disinterested devotion to the cause of the weak, esp. to helping women [quite *chivalrous* in her defense]; **gallant** suggests a dashing display of courtesy, esp. to women [her *gallant* lover] —*ANT.* **rude**

civil death [Historical] *Law* the condition of a person who forfeits or is deprived of all civil rights

civil defense the system for warning and sheltering the civilian population in the event of an attack, esp. a nuclear attack

civil disobedience nonviolent opposition to a government policy or law by refusing to comply with it, on the grounds of conscience: see also NONCOOPERATION, PASSIVE RESISTANCE

civil engineering the branch of engineering dealing with the design and construction of highways, bridges, tunnels, waterworks, harbors, etc. —**civil engineer**

ci·vil·ian (sə vil′yən) ***n.*** ⟦ME < OFr *civilien* < L *civilis,* CIVIL⟧ **1** any person not an active member of the armed forces or of an official force having police power **2** [Archaic] a specialist in civil or Roman law —***adj.*** of or for civilians; nonmilitary

ci·vil·ian·ize (sə vil′yən īz′) ***vt.*** **-ized′, -iz′ing** to staff with civilians or place under civilian control —**ci·vil′ian·i·za′tion *n.***

ci·vil·i·ty (sə vil′ə tē) ***n.***, *pl.* **-ties** ⟦ME *civilite* < OFr < L *civilitas* (< *civilis,* CIVIL), politics, hence politic behavior, politeness⟧ **1** politeness, esp. in a merely formal way **2** a civil, or polite, act or utterance

civ·i·li·za·tion (siv′ə lə zā′shən) ***n.*** ⟦ML *civilizatio*⟧ **1** the process of civilizing or becoming civilized **2** the condition of being civilized; social organization of a high order, marked by the development and use of a written language and by advances in the arts and sciences, government, etc. **3** the total culture of a particular people, nation, period, etc. **4** the countries and peoples considered to have reached a high stage of social and cultural development **5** intellectual and cultural refinement **6** the amenities, esp. creature comforts of civilized life

civ·i·lize (siv′ə līz′) ***vt.*** **-lized′, -liz′ing** ⟦Fr *civiliser* < L *civilis:* see CIVIL & -IZE: lit., to make citified⟧ **1** to bring out of a primitive or savage condition and into a state of civilization **2** to improve in habits or manners; refine —**civ′i·liz′a·ble *adj.*** —**civ′i·lized′ *adj.***

civil law **1** the body of codified law developed from Roman law and still in force in many European and American nations: distinguished from COMMON LAW **2** the body of law that an individual nation or state has established for itself: cf. INTERNATIONAL LAW **3** the body of law having to do with the private rights of individuals

civil liberties liberties guaranteed to all individuals by law, custom, judicial interpretation, etc.; rights, as of speaking or acting as one likes, granted to citizens without governmental interference or restraint except as determined necessary for the public welfare

civ·il·ly (siv′əl ē) ***adv.*** **1** with civility; politely **2** in relation to civil law, civil rights, etc.

civil marriage a marriage performed by a justice of the peace, judge, or similar official, not by a clergyman

civil rights ☆the rights of citizens; specif., those rights guaranteed to the individual by the 13th, 14th, 15th, and 19th Amendments to the Constitution of the United States and by other acts of Congress, esp. the right to vote, exemption from involuntary servitude, and equal treatment of all people with respect to the enjoyment of life, liberty, and property and to the protection of law —☆**the civil rights movement** [*often* **the C- R- M-**] the political movement in the U.S., esp. in the mid-20th cent., supporting civil rights for African-Americans

civil servant a civil-service employee

civil service ⟦orig. applied to the civilian staff of the British East India Company⟧ **1** all those employed in government administration except in the armed forces, legislature, or judiciary **2** any government service in which a position is secured through competitive public examination

civil union a legally recognized marriage-like union of same-sex partners

civil war war between geographical sections or political factions of the same nation —**the Civil War** the war between the North (the Union) and the South (the Confederacy) in the U.S. (1861-65)

civil year CALENDAR YEAR

civ·vies (siv′ēz) ***pl.n.*** [Informal] civilian clothes, as distinguished from a military uniform; mufti

CJ *abbrev.* Chief Justice

CJD *abbrev.* Creutzfeldt-Jakob disease

ck *abbrev.* **1** cask **2** check

cl *abbrev.* **1** carload **2** carload lots **3** center line **4** centiliter(s) **5** civil law **6** claim **7** class **8** clause **9** clearance **10** cloth

Cl *Chem. symbol for* chlorine

clab·ber (klab′ər) [Dial.] ***n.*** ⟦Ir *clabar* < *claba,* thick⟧ thickly curdled sour milk; bonnyclabber — ***vi., vt.*** to curdle

clach·an (klákh′ən) ***n.*** ⟦Gael; prob. < *clach,* stone⟧ [Scot. or Irish] a hamlet

clack (klak) ***vi.*** ⟦ME *clacken,* prob. < ON *klaka,* to chatter; of echoic orig.⟧ **1** to make a sudden, sharp sound, as by striking two hard substances together **2** to talk fast, foolishly, etc.; chatter **3** to cluck or cackle —***vt.*** to cause to make a sudden, sharp sound —***n.*** **1** a sudden, sharp sound **2** a device that makes such sounds **3** chatter

Clack·man·nan·shire (klak man′ən shir′, -shər) administrative division of EC Scotland: formerly a county & district

clack valve a valve, often hinged at one side, which closes with a clacking sound and allows fluid to flow in only one direction

Clac·to·ni·an (klak tō′nē ən) ***adj.*** ⟦after *Clacton*-on-Sea, England, where such tools were found⟧ designating or of a Lower Paleolithic culture, characterized by chopping tools made by flaking

clad (klad) ***vt.*** **clad, clad′ding** **1** *alt. pt. & pp. of* CLOTHE **2** to face the surface of [to *clad* a tower in marble] **3** to bond a layer of another metal to —***adj.*** **1** clothed; dressed **2** having a layer of some other metal or of an alloy bonded to it [*clad* steel, *clad* coins]

clad·ding (-iŋ) ***n.*** ⟦see prec.⟧ **1** a layer of some metal or alloy bonded to another metal **2** the process of bonding such materials

clade (klād) ***n.*** ⟦< Gr *klados,* a branch: see HOLT⟧ a group of living organisms that includes all the descendants sharing specific genetic traits of a common ancestor

clad·ist (klad′ist) ***n.*** a specialist in cladistics

cla·dis·tic (klə dis′tik) ***adj.*** of or pertaining to clades or cladistics

cla·dis·tics (klə dis′tiks) ***n.*** ⟦CLAD(E) + -IST(IC) + -ICS⟧ a method of classifying living organisms, often using computer techniques, based on the relationships between phylogenetic branching patterns from a common ancestor: also **clad·ism** (klad′iz′əm)

cla·doc·er·an (klə däs′ər ən) ***n.*** ⟦ModL < Gr *klados,* a branch, shoot (see HOLT) + Gr *keras,* HORN + -AN⟧ WATER FLEA

clad·ode (klad′ōd′) ***n.*** CLADOPHYLL

clad·o·gram (klad′ə gram′) ***n.*** a branching diagram used in cladistics to illustrate speciation and the relationships between species by showing the development and divergence of clades

clad·o·phyll (klad′ə fil′) ***n.*** ⟦< Gr *klados,* a branch (see HOLT) + *phyllon,* leaf: see -PHYLL⟧ a green, flattened branch arising from the axil of a leaf, with the shape and functions of a foliage leaf

claim (klām) ***vt.*** ⟦ME *claimen* < OFr *claimer,* to call, claim < L *clamare,* to cry out: see CLAMOR⟧ **1** to demand or ask for as rightfully belonging or due to one; assert one's right to (a title, accomplishment, etc. that should be recognized) [to *claim* a record in the high jump] **2** to call for; require; deserve [a problem that *claims* attention] ☆**3** to state as a fact or as one's belief (something that may be called into question); assert —***n.*** **1** a demand for something rightfully or allegedly due **2** a right or title to something [her sole *claim* to fame] **3** something claimed, as *a)* a piece of land staked out by a settler or miner *b)* money demanded for an insurance settlement ☆**4** a statement, as a fact, of something that may be called into question; assertion —***SYN.*** DEMAND —**lay claim to** to assert one's right or title to —**claim′a·ble** ***adj.***

claim·ant (klām′ənt) ***n.*** a person who makes a claim

claim·er (klām′ər) ***n.*** **1** a person who makes a claim; claimant **2** a horse entered in a claiming race

claiming race a horse race in which each horse entered is made available for purchase, or claiming, at a fixed price which a buyer must agree to pay before the race is run

clair·au·di·ence (kler ô′dē əns) ***n.*** ⟦CLAIR(VOYANCE) + AUDIENCE (sense 1)⟧ the occult ability to perceive and understand sounds that cannot be heard

Claire (kler) ***n.*** a feminine name: see CLARA

clair·voy·ance (kler voi′əns) ***n.*** ⟦Fr < fol.⟧ **1** the occult ability to perceive things that are not in sight or that cannot be seen, or that are in the future **2** keen perception or insight

clair·voy·ant (-ənt) ***adj.*** ⟦Fr, lit., seeing clearly < *clair,* clear + *voyant,* seeing, prp. of *voir* < L *videre,* to see: see WISE[1]⟧ **1** of clairvoyance **2** apparently having clairvoyance **3** having great insight; keenly perceptive —***n.*** a clairvoyant person —**clair·voy′ant·ly** ***adv.***

clam (klam) ***n., pl.*** **clams** or **clam** ⟦< obs. *clam,* clamp (< OE *clamm,* bond, fetter: for IE base see CLIMB); with ref. to the action of the shells⟧ **1** any of various hard-shell, usually edible, bivalve mollusks, some of which live in the shallows of the sea, others in fresh water **2** the soft, edible part of such a mollusk **3** [Informal] a reticent or taciturn person ☆**4** CLAMSHELL (sense 2) ☆**5** [Slang] *a)* a dollar *b) Jazz* a misplayed note —***vi.*** **clammed, clam′ming** to dig, or go digging, for clams —☆**clam up** [Informal] to keep silent or refuse to talk —**clam′mer** ***n.***

cla·mant (klā′mənt) ***adj.*** ⟦L *clamans* (gen. *clamantis*), prp. of *clamare:* see CLAMOR⟧ **1** clamorous; noisy **2** demanding attention; urgent —**cla′mant·ly** ***adv.***

☆**clam·bake** (klam′bāk′) ***n.*** **1** a feast or picnic, originally at the seashore, at which clams are steamed or baked with lobster, chicken, corn on the cob, etc., originally on heated stones under a covering of seaweed **2** the food so prepared **3** [Informal] any large, noisy social gathering

clam·ber (klam′bər) ***vi.*** ⟦ME *clambren;* akin to ON *klembra,* Ger *(sich) klammern,* to hook (oneself) on: for IE base see CLIMB⟧ to climb with effort or clumsily, esp. by using the hands as well as the feet —***n.*** a clumsy or hard climb —**clam′ber·er** ***n.***

clam·dig·gers (klam′dig′ərz) ***pl.n.*** casual pants extending to just below the knee or mid-calf

clam·my (klam′ē) ***adj.*** **-mi·er, -mi·est** ⟦ME < *clam,* viscous, muddy, prob. < OE *clam,* mud, clay: for IE base see CLAY⟧ unpleasantly moist, cold, and sticky —**clam′mi·ly** ***adv.*** —**clam′mi·ness** ***n.***

clam·or (klam′ər) ***n.*** ⟦ME *clamour* < OFr < L *clamor* < *clamare,* to cry out < IE **kelā-* < base **kel-,* to call, yell > L *calare,* to call out, *clarus,* clear, Gr *kalein,* to call, name, OE *hlowan,* to LOW[2]⟧ **1** a loud outcry; uproar **2** a vehement, continued expression of the general feeling or of public opinion; loud demand or complaint **3** a loud, sustained noise —***vi.*** to make a clamor; cry out, demand, or complain noisily —***vt.*** to express with, or bring about by, clamor Brit. sp. **clam′our** —***SYN.*** NOISE —**clam′or·er** ***n.***

clam·or·ous (-əs) ***adj.*** ⟦ME < ML *clamorosus:* see prec.⟧ **1** loud and confused; noisy **2** loudly demanding or complaining —***SYN.*** VOCIFEROUS —**clam′or·ous·ly** ***adv.*** —**clam′or·ous·ness** ***n.***

clamp[1] (klamp) ***n.*** ⟦ME < MDu *klampe:* for IE base see CLIMB⟧ any of various devices for clasping or fastening things together, or for bracing parts; esp., an appliance with two parts that can be brought together, usually by a screw, to grip something —***vt.*** **1** to grip, fasten, or brace with or as with a clamp ☆**2** to put in effect forcefully; impose [to *clamp* a curfew on the town] —☆**clamp down (on)** to become more strict (with)

C-clamp

clamp[2] (klamp) ***n.*** ⟦var. of CLUMP⟧ the sound of heavy footsteps —***vi.*** to tread heavily

☆**clamp·down** (-doun′) ***n.*** a clamping down; repression or suppression, as in censoring

clams casino broiled clams topped with garlic butter, bacon, bread crumbs, etc. and served in their bottom shells

clam·shell (klam′shel′) ***n.*** **1** the shell of a clam ☆**2** a dredging bucket, hinged like the shell of a clam —***adj.*** designating or of any of certain manufactured products designed to open and close by a hinge along one edge

clan (klan) ***n.*** ⟦Gael & Ir *clann, cland,* offspring, tribe < L *planta,* offshoot: see PLANT⟧ **1** an early form of social group, as in the Scottish Highlands, composed of several families claiming descent from a common ancestor, bearing the same family name, and following the same chieftain **2** in certain primitive societies, a tribal division, usually exogamous, of matrilineal or patrilineal descent from a common ancestor **3** a group of people with interests in common; clique; set **4** [Informal] FAMILY (sense 3)

clan·des·tine (klan des′tin) ***adj.*** ⟦Fr *clandestin* < L *clandestinus,* secret, hidden < *clam,* secret < base of *celare,* to hide: see CONCEAL⟧ kept secret or hidden, esp. for some illicit purpose; surreptitious; furtive —***SYN.*** SECRET —**clan·des′tine·ly** ***adv.*** —**clan·des′tine·ness** ***n.*** —**clan′des·tin′i·ty** ***n.***

clang (klaŋ) ***vi.*** ⟦echoic, but assoc. with L v. *clangere,* also of echoic orig.⟧ **1** to make, or strike together with, a loud, sharp, ringing sound, as of metal being struck **2** to move with such a sound **3** to make a loud, harsh cry, as esp. the crane does —***vt.*** to cause to make a clanging sound —***n.*** a clanging sound or cry

clang·er (klaŋ′ər) ***n.*** ⟦see prec.⟧ [Brit. Informal] a mistake or blunder

clang·or (klaŋ′ər, -gər) ***n.*** ⟦L < *clangere:* see CLANG⟧ a clanging sound, esp. a continued clanging —***vi.*** to make a clangor Brit. sp. **clang′our** —**clang′or·ous** ***adj.*** —**clang′or·ous·ly** ***adv.***

clank (klaŋk) ***n.*** ⟦like Du *klank,* MHG *klanc,* of echoic orig.⟧ a sharp, metallic sound, not so resonant as a clang and shorter in duration —***vi.*** **1** to make a clank **2** to move with a clank —***vt.*** to cause to clank

clan·nish (klan′ish) ***adj.*** **1** of a clan **2** tending to associate closely with one's own group and to avoid others —**clan′nish·ly** ***adv.*** —**clan′nish·ness** ***n.***

clans·man (klanz′mən) ***n., pl.*** **-men** (-mən) a member of a clan

clans·wom·an (-woom′ən) ***n., pl.*** **-wom′en** (-wim′in) a woman who is a member of a clan

clap[1] (klap) ***vi.*** **clapped, clap′ping** ⟦ME *clappen* < OE *clæppan,* to throb, beat; akin to ON *klapp,* OHG *klapf,* clap, crack: orig. echoic⟧ **1** to make a sudden, explosive sound, as of two flat surfaces being struck together **2** to strike the palms of the hands together, as in applauding —***vt.*** **1** to strike together briskly and loudly **2** [Rare] to applaud by clapping the hands **3** to strike with an open hand, as in hearty greeting or encouragement **4** to put, move, set, etc. swiftly [*clapped* into jail] **5** to put together or contrive hastily [to *clap* together a makeshift stage] —***n.*** **1** a sudden, explosive sound, as of clapping [a *clap* of thunder] **2** the act of striking the hands together, as in applauding **3** a sharp slap, as in hearty greeting —**clap eyes on** [Informal] to catch sight of; see

clap[2] (klap) ***n.*** ⟦< ME *claper,* brothel, orig. rabbit burrow < OFr *clapier*⟧ [Slang] gonorrhea: with *the*

clap·board[1] (klab′ərd, klap′bôrd′) ***n.*** ⟦partial transl. of MDu *klapholt* < *klappen,* to fit + *holt,* wood, board⟧ ☆a long, narrow board with one edge thicker than the other, used as siding —☆***vt.*** to cover with clapboards

clap·board[2] (klap′bôrd′) ***n.*** ⟦prob. < CLAP[1] + BOARD⟧ *Film* a board consisting of a chalk slate (or now LED screen) and two hinged pieces that are struck together at the beginning of a scene, used to identify the take and synchronize sound

clapped-out (klapt′out′) ***adj.*** [Brit. Informal] **1** worn-out, obsolete, etc. [*clapped-out* machinery] **2** exhausted; weary

clap·per (klap′ər) ***n.*** **1** a person who claps **2** anything that makes a clapping sound **3** the moving part inside a bell, that strikes the side of the bell; tongue **4** the tongue of a garrulous person: used facetiously **5** CLAPBOARD[2]

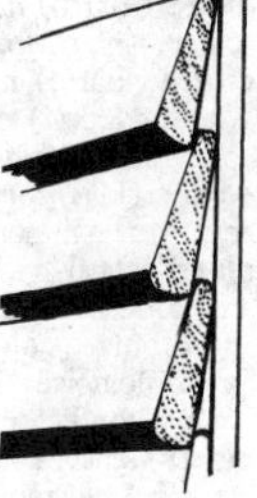
clapboards

clap·per·claw (-klô′) ***vt.*** ⟦prob. < prec. + CLAW⟧ [Now Chiefly Dial.] **1** to claw or scratch with the hand and nails **2** to revile or scold

clapper rail ⟦so named from the sound of its territorial call⟧ a hen-sized, brownish-gray rail (*Rallus longirostris*) with a long, pointed bill

clapt (klapt) ***vi., vt. archaic pt. of*** CLAP[1]

clap·trap (klap′trap′) ***n.*** ⟦CLAP[1] (*n.* 2) + TRAP[1]: orig., a trick intended to elicit applause⟧ absurd, insincere, or empty talk or writing

claque (klak) ***n.*** ⟦Fr < *claquer,* to clap: echoic⟧ **1** a group of people paid to go to a play, opera, etc. and applaud **2** a group of admiring or fawning followers

Clar·a (klar′ə, kler′ə) ***n.*** ⟦< L *clara,* fem. of *clarus,* bright, CLEAR⟧ a feminine name: var. *Clare, Clarice, Clarissa;* equiv. Fr. *Claire*

Clare[1] (kler) ***n.*** **1** a masculine name: see CLARENCE **2** a feminine name: see CLARA
Clare[2] (kler), **John** 1793-1864; Eng. poet
Clare[3] (kler) county in W Ireland, in Munster province: 1,231 sq mi (3,188 sq km)
Clar·ence (klar′əns, kler′əns) ***n.*** **1** ⟦< name of Eng dukedom of *Clarence,* after *Clare,* town in Suffolk⟧ a masculine name: var. *Clare* **2** ⟦after the Duke of *Clarence,* later WILLIAM IV⟧ **[c-]** a closed, four-wheeled carriage with seats for four inside and a seat for the driver outside
Clar·en·don (klar′ən dən), 1st Earl of (*Edward Hyde*) 1609-74; Eng. statesman & historian
clar·et (klar′it) ***n.*** ⟦ME < OFr *(vin) claret,* clear (wine); dim. of *cler,* CLEAR⟧ **1** a dry red wine, esp. red Bordeaux **2** purplish red: also **claret red** ***—adj.*** purplish-red
claret cup an iced drink of claret, lemon juice, brandy, sugar, and soda
Clar·ice (klar′is, klə rēs′) ***n.*** ⟦Fr *Clarisse*⟧ a feminine name: see CLARA
clarified butter butter with the water and milk solids removed, used for cooking at high temperatures without burning
clar·i·fy (klar′ə fī′) ***vt., vi.*** **-fied′, -fy′ing** ⟦ME *clarifien* < OFr *clarifier* < LL(Ec) *clarificare,* to make illustrious < L *clarus,* famous, CLEAR + *facere,* to make, DO[1]⟧ **1** to make or become clear and free from impurities: said esp. of liquids **2** to melt (butter) and remove the water and milk solids **3** to make or become easier to understand [to *clarify* one's meaning] **—clar′i·fi·ca′tion** ***n.*** **—clar′i·fi′er** ***n.***
clar·i·net (klar′ə net′) ***n.*** ⟦Fr *clarinette,* dim. of *clarine,* little bell < ML *clario:* see fol.⟧ a single-reed woodwind instrument with a long wooden or metal tube and a flaring bell, played by means of holes and keys: also [Archaic] **clar′i·o·net′** (-ē ə net′) **—clar′i·net′ist** ***n.,*** **clar′i·net′tist**

clarinet

clar·i·on (klar′ē ən) ***n.*** ⟦ME *clarioun* < OFr *clarion* < ML *clario,* a trumpet < L *clarus,* CLEAR⟧ **1** a trumpet of the Middle Ages producing clear, sharp, shrill tones **2** [Old Poet.] the sound of a clarion, or a sound like this ***—adj.*** clear, sharp, and ringing [a *clarion* call] ***—vt.*** to announce forcefully or loudly
Cla·ris·sa (klə ris′ə) ***n.*** ⟦It⟧ a feminine name: see CLARA
clar·i·ty (klar′ə tē) ***n.*** ⟦ME *clarite* < OFr *clarte* < L *claritas* < *clarus,* CLEAR⟧ the quality or condition of being clear; clearness
Clark[1] (klärk) ***n.*** ⟦< the surname *Clark,* CLERK, a literate or scholarly person⟧ a masculine name
Clark[2] (klärk) **1 George Rogers** 1752-1818; Am. frontiersman & Revolutionary War leader **2 Tom C(ampbell)** 1899-1977; associate justice, U.S. Supreme Court (1949-67) **3 William** 1770-1838; Am. explorer: see LEWIS[2], Meriwether
Clarke (klärk), Sir **Arthur C(harles)** 1917-2008; Eng. writer, esp. of science fiction
Clark Fork ⟦after William CLARK[2]⟧ river flowing from W Mont. northwest into Pend Oreille Lake in N Ida.: *c.* 300 mi (483 km)
☆**clark·i·a** (klärk′ē ə) ***n.*** ⟦ModL, after William CLARK[2]⟧ any of a genus (*Clarkia*) of W American wildflowers of the evening-primrose family, having white, rosy, or purple flowers
☆**Clark's nutcracker** (klärks) ⟦after William CLARK[2]⟧ *see* NUTCRACKER (sense 2)
Clarks·ville (klärks′vil′) ⟦after George Rogers CLARK[2]⟧ city in N Tenn., on the Cumberland River
cla·ro (klär′ō) ***adj.*** ⟦Sp < L *clarus,* CLEAR⟧ light-colored and mild: said of a cigar ***—n., pl.*** **-ros** a claro cigar
clar·y (klar′ē) ***n., pl.*** **-ies** ⟦ME *clare* < ML *sclarea*⟧ any of several plants (genus *Salvia*) of the mint family, esp. a species (*S. sclarea*) grown as an ornamental or herb
-clase (klās) *combining form* ⟦Fr < Gr *klasis,* a breaking < *klan,* to break: see CLASTIC⟧ a mineral having a (specified) type of cleavage
clash (klash) ***vi.*** ⟦echoic⟧ **1** to collide or strike together with a loud, harsh, metallic noise **2** *a)* to come into conflict; disagree sharply *b)* to fail to harmonize [colors that *clash*] ***—vt.*** to strike together with a loud, harsh, metallic noise ***—n.*** **1** a harsh noise, as of a collision **2** *a)* a sharp disagreement; conflict *b)* lack of harmony
clasp (klasp, kläsp) ***n.*** ⟦ME *claspe, clapse;* ? akin to OE *clyppan,* clasp: see CLIP[2]⟧ **1** a fastening, as a hook, buckle, or catch, to hold two things or parts together **2** the act of holding or grasping; embrace **3** a grip of the hand **4** a metal bar attached to the ribbon of a military decoration to show a subsequent award of the same medal or to specify the type or place of service ***—vt.*** ⟦ME *claspen* < the n.⟧ **1** to fasten with or as with a clasp **2** to hold tightly with the arms or hands; grasp firmly; embrace **3** to grip with the hand **4** to entwine about; cling to **—clasp′er** ***n.***
clasp knife a large pocketknife, esp. one with blades which, when open, can be secured by a catch
class[1] (klas, kläs) ***n.*** ⟦Fr *classe* < L *classis,* class or division of the Roman people; akin to *calare,* to call: see CLAMOR⟧ **1** a number of people or things grouped together because of certain likenesses or common traits; kind; sort; category **2** a group of people considered as a unit according to economic, occupational, or social status; esp., a social rank or caste [the working *class,* the middle *class*] **3** high social rank or caste **4** the division of society into ranks or castes ☆**5** *a)* a group of students taught together according to standing, subject, etc. *b)* a meeting of such a group *c)* a group of students graduating together [the *class* of 1988] *d)* any group of persons that share a given year, as those elected to public office or selected for some honor **6** a division or grouping according to grade or quality [as orators, the two councilors were not in the same *class*] **7** conscripted troops, or men liable to conscription, all of whom were born in the same year [called up the *class* of 1952] **8** *Biol.* a major category in the classification of animals, plants, etc., ranking above an order and below a division or phylum: it can include one order or many similar orders: the Latinized class names are capitalized but not italicized (Ex.: Mammalia, mammals) **9** *Gram.* in some languages, the formal classification by which nouns are grouped according to animateness, sex, shape, and other criteria: see GENDER[1] **10** [Informal] excellence, esp. of style or appearance ***—vt.*** to put in a class; classify ***—adj.*** [Slang] **1** first-class; very good **2** elegant; classy
class[2] *abbrev.* classification
class action (suit) a legal action brought by one or more persons on behalf of themselves and a much larger group, all of whom have the same grounds for action
☆**class book** a book published by members of a school or college class, containing pictures of students and teachers, an account of student activities, etc.
class consciousness an awareness of belonging to a class in the social order, with definite economic interests; sense of class solidarity **—class′-con′scious** ***adj.***
clas·sic (klas′ik) ***adj.*** ⟦L *classicus,* relating to the (highest) classes of the Roman people, hence, superior < *classis,* CLASS[1]⟧ **1** of the highest class; being a model of its kind; excellent; standard; authoritative; established [a *classic* example of expressionism] **2** CLASSICAL (senses 2 & 3) **3** of or having a style that is balanced, formal, objective, restrained, regular, simple, etc.: a term variously interpreted and generally opposed to ROMANTIC **4** famous or well-known, esp. as being traditional or typical [a *classic* court case] ☆**5** [Informal] continuing in fashion because of its simple style: said of an article of apparel ***—n.*** **1** a writer, artist, etc. or a literary or artistic work that is generally recognized as excellent, authoritative, etc. **2** [*pl.*] *a)* the works produced by the outstanding authors of ancient Greece and Rome (usually with *the*) *b)* [*with sing. v.*] the field of study dealing with these works and with ancient Greek and Latin [her major is *classics*] ☆**3** any item, event, etc. that is classic, as a traditional sports event or an article of clothing
clas·si·cal (klas′i kəl) ***adj.*** **1** CLASSIC (senses 1 & 3) **2** of the art, literature, and culture of the ancient Greeks and Romans, or their writers, artists, etc. **3** characteristic of or derived from the literary and artistic standards, principles, and methods of the ancient Greeks and Romans **4** well versed in or devoted to Greek and Roman culture, literature, etc. [a *classical* scholar] **5** designating or of a specified area or course of study that is or has been standard and traditionally authoritative, not new, recent, and experimental [*classical* political science] **6** *a)* [*occas.* **C-**] of, characteristic of, or like a style of music marked by an emphasis on formal composition, as in instrumental works in the sonata form, by precise standards of performance appropriate to a symphony orchestra, and by a sense of balance, order, clarity, etc. *b)* [*occas.* **C-**] designating or of the period (*c.* 1750-*c.* 1830) characterized by this style *c)* designating or of art music of the European tradition, including such forms as the symphony, the opera, chamber music, the sonata, etc. (distinguished from folk or popular music or jazz) **—clas′si·cal′i·ty** (-kal′ə tē) ***n.,*** **clas′si·cal·ness —clas′si·cal·ly** ***adv.***
clas·si·cal·ism (-iz′əm) ***n.*** CLASSICISM
classical mechanics [*with sing. v.*] *Physics* the study of mechanics using Newton's laws rather than quantum theory and relativity
clas·si·cism (klas′ə siz′əm) ***n.*** **1** the aesthetic principles or qualities regarded as characteristic of ancient Greece and Rome; objectivity, formality, balance, simplicity, restraint, etc.: generally contrasted with ROMANTICISM **2** adherence to such principles **3** knowledge of the literature, art, and culture of ancient Greece and Rome; classical scholarship **4** a Greek or Latin idiom or expression
clas·si·cist (-sist) ***n.*** **1** an advocate of the principles of classicism **2** a student of or specialist in ancient Greek and Roman literature, art, and culture; a classical scholar **3** one who advocates the teaching of Greek and Latin in the schools
clas·si·cize (-sīz′) ***vt.*** **-cized′, -ciz′ing** to make classic or classical ***—vi.*** to use or affect a classic style or form
clas·si·co (klas′i kō′, kläs′-) ***adj.*** ⟦It, CLASSIC⟧ made from grapes grown in a certain specified area in Italy with a reputation for superior quality [*Chianti* classico]
clas·si·fi·ca·tion (klas′ə fi kā′shən) ***n.*** ⟦Fr⟧ **1** a classifying or being classified; arrangement according to some systematic division into classes or groups **2** *a)* a system of such classes or groups *b)* such a class or group **3** *Biol.* TAXONOMY **—clas·si·fi·ca·to·ry** (klas′ə fik′ə tôr′ē) ***adj.***
clas·si·fied (klas′ə fīd′) ***adj.*** **1** secret or confidential and available only to authorized persons ☆**2** of or pertaining to classified advertising [the *classified* section of a newspaper] ***—n.*** **1** *short for* CLASSIFIED ADVERTISEMENT **2** [*pl.*] a section of classified advertisements, as in a newspaper
☆**classified advertising** advertising compactly arranged, as in newspaper columns, according to subject, under such listings as *help wanted* and *lost and found* **—classified advertisement**
clas·si·fy (klas′ə fī′) ***vt.*** **-fied′, -fy′ing** ⟦< L *classis* (see CLASS[1]) + -FY⟧ **1**

to arrange or group in classes according to some system or principle **2** to place in a class or category **3** to designate (governmental documents, reports, etc.) to be secret or confidential and available only to authorized persons —**clas′si·fi′a·ble** *adj.* —**clas′si·fi′er** *n.*

clas·sis (klas′is) *n., pl.* **clas′ses′** (-ēz′) ⟦L, CLASS[1]⟧ **1** a governing body in certain Reformed churches, consisting of the minister and representative elders from each church in a district **2** such a district

class·ism (klas′iz′əm) *n.* discrimination against people on the basis of social class —**class′ist** *n., adj.*

class·less (klas′lis) *adj.* having no distinct social or economic classes [a *classless* society]

☆**class·mate** (-māt′) *n.* a member of the same class at a school or college

clas·son (klas′än′) *n.* *Particle Physics* either of two stable elementary particles, the photon and the graviton, having no mass or electric charge: a classon is a boson

☆**class·room** (-ro͞om′) *n.* a room in a school or college in which classes are taught

class struggle in Marxism, the constant economic and political struggle held to exist between those social classes regarded as exploiting and those regarded as exploited; specif., in capitalist countries, the struggle between capitalists (bourgeoisie) and workers (proletariat)

class·y (klas′ē) *adj.* **class′i·er, class′i·est** [Informal] first-class, esp. in style or manner; elegant; fine —**class′i·ness** *n.*

clas·tic (klas′tik) *adj.* ⟦< Gr *klastos,* broken < *klan,* to break (< IE **kla-,* var. of base **kel-,* to strike > HOLT, Gr *klēma,* L *calamitas,* calamity) + -IC⟧ **1** designating an anatomical model with removable sections to show internal structure **2** *Geol.* consisting of fragments of older rocks

clath·rate (klath′rāt′) *adj.* ⟦L *clathratus,* pp. of *clathrare,* to furnish with a lattice < L *clathri,* lattice < Gr (Doric) *klaithra,* a bar, fence⟧ **1** *Bot.* resembling latticework; reticulated **2** *Chem.* of or pertaining to a mixture in which the molecules of one substance are completely entrapped in the crystal lattice or cell-like structure of the other

clat·ter (klat′ər) *vi.* ⟦ME *clateren* < OE **clatrian* (akin to MDu *klateren*) < IE base **gal-,* to CALL, cry out⟧ **1** to make, or move with, a rapid succession of loud, sharp noises; rattle **2** to chatter noisily —*vt.* to cause to clatter —*n.* ⟦ME *clater* < the v.⟧ **1** a rapid succession of loud, sharp noises **2** a tumult; hubbub **3** noisy chatter —**clat′ter·er** *n.* —**clat′ter·ing·ly** *adv.*

Claude (klôd) *n.* ⟦Fr < L *Claudius,* name of a Roman gens, prob. < *claudus,* lame⟧ a masculine name: fem. *Claudia*

Clau·del (klō del′), **Paul (Louis Charles)** 1868-1955; Fr. poet, playwright, & diplomat

Claude Lor·rain (klōd lô *ran′*) (born *Claude Gelée*) 1600-82; Fr. painter

Clau·di·a (klô′dē ə) *n.* ⟦L⟧ a feminine name: see CLAUDE

clau·di·ca·tion (klô′di kā′shən) *n.* ⟦L *claudicatio* < *claudicatus,* pp. of *claudicare,* to limp < *claudus,* lame⟧ *Med.* lameness, esp. when caused by an impaired flow of blood to the leg muscles

Clau·di·us (klô′dē əs) **1 Claudius I** (*Tiberius Claudius Drusus Nero Germanicus*) 10 B.C.-A.D. 54; Rom. emperor (41-54) **2 Claudius II** (*Marcus Aurelius Claudius Gothicus*) A.D. 214-270; Rom. emperor (268-270)

claus·al (klôz′əl) *adj.* of or constituting a clause

clause (klôz) *n.* ⟦OFr < ML *clausa,* for L *clausula,* a closing (in legal use, section or clause) < *clausus,* pp. of *claudere,* to CLOSE[2]⟧ **1** *Gram.* a group of words containing a subject and a finite verb, usually forming part of a compound or complex sentence: clauses may be joined by parataxis (The house is secluded; you will like it), by modified parataxis (The house is secluded, and you will like it), and by hypotaxis (Because the house is secluded, you will like it): see DEPENDENT CLAUSE, INDEPENDENT CLAUSE **2** a particular article, stipulation, or provision in a formal or legal document

Clau·se·witz (klou′zə vits′), **Karl von** (kärl fôn) 1780-1831; Prus. army officer & writer on military strategy

claus·tral (klôs′trəl) *adj.* ⟦ME < LL *claustralis* < L *claustrum:* see CLOISTER⟧ **1** of or related to a cloister **2** secluded, isolated, or retired from the world

claus·tro·pho·bi·a (klôs′trə fō′bē ə) *n.* ⟦< L *claustrum* (see CLOISTER) + -PHOBIA⟧ an abnormal fear of being in an enclosed or confined place —**claus′tro·phobe′** *n.* —**claus′tro·pho′bic** *adj., n.*

cla·vate (klā′vāt′) *adj.* ⟦ModL *clavatus* < L *clava,* a club + *-atus,* -ATE[1]⟧ oblong and thicker at one end; club-shaped —**cla′vate′ly** *adv.* —**cla·va′tion** *n.*

clave[1] (klāv) *vt., vi. archaic pt. of* CLEAVE[1] or CLEAVE[2]

cla·ve[2] (klä′vā′) *n.* ⟦AmSp < Sp, keystone < L *clavis,* a key: see CLOSE[2]⟧ **1** either of a pair of cylindrical hardwood sticks that make a hollow sound when struck together, used as a percussion instrument in Latin music: *usually used in pl.* **2** a syncopated rhythm pattern of alternating phrases of three and two beats, used in Latin dance music

cla·ver (klā′vər) [Scot.] *vi.* ⟦Scot, prob. < or akin to Gael *clabaire,* babbler⟧ to indulge in idle talk; gossip —*n.* gossip; chatter

clav·i·chord (klav′i kôrd′) *n.* ⟦ME *clavicord* < ML *clavicordium* < L *clavis,* a key (see CLOSE[2]) + *chorda,* CHORD[1]⟧ a stringed musical instrument with a keyboard, predecessor of the piano: horizontal strings, generally of equal length, are struck at various points from below by metal wedges (*tangents*) at the end of each key, producing soft tones with limited dynamics: cf. HARPSICHORD

clav·i·cle (klav′i kəl) *n.* ⟦Fr *clavicule* < L *clavicula,* dim. of *clavis,* a key: see CLOSE[2]⟧ the bone that connects the scapula with the sternum; collarbone —**cla·vic·u·lar** (kla vik′yo͞o lər) *adj.*

clav·i·corn (klav′i kôrn′) *adj.* ⟦< ModL *Clavicornia* < L *clava,* a club + *cornu,* HORN⟧ of a large group of related beetle families with club-shaped antennae —**clav′i·cor′nate′** (-kôr′nāt′) *adj.*

cla·vi·er (klə vir′; *for 1 & 3, also* klā′vē ər, klav′ē ər) *n.* ⟦Fr, keyboard, orig., a key holder < L *clavis,* a key: see CLOSE[2]; sense 2 via Ger *klavier*⟧ **1** the keyboard of an organ, harpsichord, piano, etc. **2** any stringed instrument that has a keyboard **3** a dummy keyboard used for silent practice

clav·i·form (klav′ə fôrm′) *adj.* ⟦< L *clava,* a club + -FORM⟧ CLAVATE

claw (klô) *n.* ⟦ME *claue* < OE *clawu* < IE **g(e)l-eu-* < base **gel-,* to make round, clench (as a fist) > CLING, CLAMP[1], CLIMB⟧ **1** a sharp, hooked or curved horny structure, or nail, on the foot of a bird and of many reptiles and mammals **2** a foot with such structures at its end **3** the pincers, or chela, of a lobster, crab, scorpion, etc., or on the limb of certain insects **4** anything resembling or regarded as a claw [the *claw* of a hammer] —*vt., vi.* to scratch, clutch, pull, climb, dig, or tear with or as with claws —**claw back** ⟦extended from general sense, "to get something back through great effort"⟧ to recover (money paid out previously), as by means of a claw-back provision —**clawed** *adj.*

claw·back (klô′bak′) *adj.* ⟦< CLAW BACK (see phr. under prec.)⟧ designating or of a provision, as in a law or contract, for recovering money paid out to a payee or grantee who has failed to honor stated conditions —*n.* a recovering of money paid out previously

claw hammer **1** a hammer with one end of the head forked and curved like a claw, used for pulling nails **2** [Informal] a swallow-tailed coat

clay (klā) *n.* ⟦ME *clei* < OE *clæg* < IE base **glei-,* to stick together > CLAMMY, Ger *klei,* mud, L *glus,* GLUE⟧ **1** *a)* a firm, fine-grained earth, plastic when wet, composed chiefly of hydrous aluminum silicate minerals: it is produced by the chemical decomposition of rocks or the deposit of fine rock particles in water and is used in the manufacture of bricks, pottery, and other ceramics *b)* soil composed of mineral particles of very small size **2** *a)* ⟦as in Gen. 2:7⟧ earth, esp. as a symbol of the material of the human body *b)* the human body

Clay (klā), **Henry** 1777-1852; U.S. statesman & orator

clay·bank (-baŋk′) *adj.* of the color of a bank of clay; dull brownish-yellow [a *claybank* horse]

clay·ey (klā′ē) *adj.* **clay′i·er, clay′i·est** **1** of, smeared with, or full of clay **2** like clay: also **clay′ish**

Clay·ma·tion (klā mā′shən) ⟦CLAY + (ANI)MATION⟧ *trademark for* a process of photographing a kind of animated cartoon using three-dimensional clay puppet figures —*n.* any process of film animation like this

clay mineral any of a group of minerals, mainly hydrous aluminum silicates, occurring in very tiny crystals that readily adsorb water

clay·more (klā′môr′) *n.* ⟦Gael *claidheamhmor* < *claidheamh,* sword (< IE **klād-* < base **kel-,* to strike > HOLT) + *mor,* great⟧ **1** a large, two-edged broadsword formerly used by Scottish Highlanders **2** a broadsword with a basket hilt worn by Scottish regiments **3** [*also* **C-**] an antipersonnel mine that scatters shrapnel in a particular, often fan-shaped, area when it explodes: also **claymore mine**

clay·pan (klā′pan′) *n.* a clay layer in the soil that restricts downward movement of water and growth of roots: sometimes written **clay pan**

☆**clay pigeon** a brittle, saucerlike disk as of baked clay, tossed into the air from a trap as a target in skeet and trapshooting

clay·stone (klā′stōn′) *n.* **1** rock consisting of hardened clay **2** a hard concretionary body often found in clay deposits Sometimes written **clay stone**

☆**clay·to·ni·a** (klā tō′nē ə) *n.* ⟦ModL, after J. Clayton (*c.* 1685-1773), Am botanist⟧ any of a genus (*Claytonia*) of small, spring-flowering plants of the purslane family, with white and rose-colored flowers

cld *abbrev.* **1** called **2** cleared

clean (klēn) *adj.* ⟦ME *clene* < OE *clæne,* clean, pure < IE **ĝ(e)lēi-* < base **ĝel-,* to gleam > OIr *gel,* gleaming, white, OHG *kleini,* gleaming, bright, fine (> Ger *klein,* small)⟧ **1** *a)* free from dirt, contamination, impurities, pollutants, etc.; unsoiled; unstained *b)* free from disease, infection, radioactivity, etc. ☆**2** producing little immediate fallout: said of nuclear weapons **3** producing few or no pollutants; non-polluting [*clean* energy] **4** recently laundered; fresh and unused **5** *a)* morally pure; sinless *b)* not obscene or indecent [a *clean* joke] **6** fair; sportsmanlike [a rough but *clean* contest] **7** keeping oneself or one's surroundings clean; neat and tidy **8** *a)* shapely; well-formed [a *clean* profile] *b)* elegantly trim, straight, smooth, etc.; not ornate [*clean* architectural lines] **9** skillful; deft [a *clean* stroke] **10** having no obstructions, flaws, or roughnesses; clear; regular [a *clean* drain] **11** entire; complete; thorough [a *clean* sweep] **12** having few corrections; legible [*clean* copy for the printer] **13** *a)* with nothing in it or on it [*clean* pockets, a *clean* sheet of paper] *b)* having no blemishes, offenses, demerits, etc. [a student's *clean* academic record] ☆**14** [Slang] *a)* not carrying a weapon, illegal drugs, etc. *b)* innocent of an alleged crime *c)* free from the use or presence of, or from addiction to, narcotics or other illicit drugs **15** *Bible a)* free from ceremonial defilement *b)* fit for food (said of certain animals) —*adv.* ⟦OE *clæne*⟧ **1** in a clean manner **2** [Informal] completely; wholly [*clean* forgotten] —*vt.* **1** to make clean **2** to remove (dirt, impurities, etc.) in making clean **3** to empty or clear **4** to prepare (fish, fowl, etc.) for cooking ☆**5** [Slang] to take away or use up the money or possessions of: often with *out* **6** *Weight Lifting* to lift (a barbell) from the floor to the shoulders in one continuous movement: cf. CLEAN AND JERK —*vi.* **1** to be made clean **2** to perform the act of cleaning —**clean out** **1** to empty so as to make clean **2** to empty —**clean up** **1** to make clean, neat, or orderly 2 to make oneself clean and neat; get washed, combed, etc. 3 [Informal] to dispose of completely; finish ☆4 [Slang] to make much money or profit —☆**clean up on** [Slang] to defeat; beat —☆**come clean** [Slang] to confess; tell the truth —**clean′a·ble** *adj.* —**clean′ness** *n.*

SYN.—**clean**, the broader term, denotes generally the removal of dirt or impurities, as by washing or brushing; **cleanse** suggests more specifically the use of chemicals, purgatives, etc., and is often used metaphorically to imply purification [to *cleanse* one's mind of evil thoughts] —*ANT.* **soil, dirty**

clean and jerk *Weight Lifting* a lift in which the barbell is cleaned and then thrust directly overhead so that the arms are completely extended

clean-cut (klēn′kut′) *adj.* 1 with a clear, sharp edge or outline 2 well-formed 3 distinct; clear 4 good-looking, trim, neat, etc.

clean·er (-ər) *n.* a person or thing that cleans; specif., *a)* a person who owns or works in a dry-cleaning establishment *b)* [*usually pl.*] a dry-cleaning establishment *c)* a preparation for removing dirt or grime —☆**take to the cleaners** [Slang] to swindle (someone) of a substantial amount of money

clean·hand·ed (-han′did) *adj.* blameless; innocent

clean·limbed (-limd′) *adj.* having shapely limbs

clean·ly[1] (klen′lē) *adj.* **-li·er, -li·est** ⟦ME *clenli* < OE *clænlice* < *clæne,* CLEAN⟧ 1 keeping oneself or one's surroundings clean 2 always kept clean —**clean′li·ness** *n.*

clean·ly[2] (klēn′lē) *adv.* in a clean manner

☆**clean room** a room, or other enclosed area, designed to create and maintain an atmosphere virtually free of such contaminants as dust, pollen, or bacteria: used in hospitals, laboratories, etc.

cleanse (klenz) *vt.* **cleansed, cleans′ing** ⟦ME *clensen* < OE *clænsian* < *clæne,* CLEAN⟧ to make clean, pure, etc.; clean; purge —*SYN.* CLEAN

cleans·er (klen′zər) *n.* any preparation for cleansing, esp. a powder as for scouring pots and enamel surfaces

clean·shav·en (klēn′shā′vən) *adj.* having all the hairs, esp. the whiskers, shaved off

clean·up (klēn′up′) *n.* 1 the act of cleaning up ☆2 elimination of crime, vice, graft, etc. —☆*adj. Baseball* designating or of the fourth batter in a team's lineup: so positioned because regarded as most likely to drive in runners on base

clear (klir) *adj.* ⟦ME *cler* < OFr < L *clarus,* orig., clear-sounding, hence clear, bright: for IE base see CLAMOR⟧ 1 free from clouds or mist; bright; light [*a clear* day] 2 free from cloudiness, muddiness, etc.; transparent or pure; not turbid [*a clear* crystal, *a clear* red] 3 having no blemishes [*a clear* complexion] 4 not faint or blurred; easily seen or heard; sharply defined; distinct [*a clear* outline, *clear* tones] 5 perceiving acutely; keen or logical [*a clear* eye, *a clear* mind] 6 serene and calm [*a clear* countenance] 7 free from confusion or ambiguity; not obscure; easily understood [the meaning is *clear*] 8 obvious; unmistakable [*a clear* case of neglect] 9 certain; positive [to be *clear* on a point] 10 free from guilt or a charge of guilt; innocent [*a clear* conscience] 11 free from charges or deductions; net [to earn *a clear* $30,000] 12 free from debt or encumbrance [*a clear* title to the house] 13 free from qualification; absolute; complete [*a clear* victory] 14 free from contact; not entangled, confined, hindered, etc. [a style *clear* of cant] 15 free from impediment or obstruction; open [keep the fire lanes *clear*] 16 freed or emptied of freight or cargo —*adv.* 1 in a clear manner; so as to be clear 2 all the way; completely [it sank *clear* to the bottom] —*vt.* 1 to make clear or bright 2 to free from impurities, blemishes, cloudiness, muddiness, etc. 3 *a)* to make intelligible, plain, or lucid; clarify *b)* to decode or decipher 4 to rid of obstructions, entanglements, or obstacles; open [to *clear* a path through snow] 5 to get rid of; remove 6 to empty or unload [to *clear* a freighter of cargo] 7 to free (a person or thing) *of* or *from* something 8 to free from a charge or a suspicion of guilt; prove the innocence of; acquit 9 to pass or leap over, by, etc. 10 to pass without contact [the tug *cleared* the bridge] 11 to discharge (a debt) by paying it 12 to give or get clearance for 13 to be passed or approved by [the plan *cleared* the committee] 14 to go through (a customs office) 15 to handle and deal with (letters, files, etc.) properly 16 to make (a given amount) as profit or earnings not subject to charges or deductions; net 17 to make (the sight) clear or sharp 18 *a)* to rid (the throat) of phlegm by hawking or coughing *b)* to rid (the voice) of hoarseness thus 19 *Banking* to pass (a check, draft, etc.) through a clearinghouse —*vi.* 1 to become clear, unclouded, etc. 2 to pass away; vanish 3 to get clearance, as a ship leaving a port 4 *Banking* to be accepted or received through a clearinghouse, as a check, draft, etc. —*n.* a clear space —*interj.* stand clear!: a command used as in warning others away during defibrillation —**clear away** 1 to take away so as to leave a cleared space 2 to go away; go out of sight —**clear off** 1 to clear away 2 to remove something from in order to make clear —**clear out** 1 to clear by emptying ☆2 [Informal] to go away; depart —**clear the air** (or **atmosphere**) to get rid of emotional tensions, misunderstandings, etc. —**clear up** 1 to make or become clear 2 to make orderly 3 to become unclouded, sunny, etc. after being cloudy or stormy 4 to explain 5 to cure or become cured [this will *clear up* your cold] —**in the clear** 1 free from enclosing or limiting obstructions 2 [Informal] free from suspicion or guilt —**stand clear** to stand, or to move oneself, out of the way: often used as a command —**clear′a·ble** *adj.* —**clear′er** *n.* —**clear′ly** *adv.* —**clear′ness** *n.*

SYN.—**clear** suggests freedom from cloudiness, haziness, muddiness, etc., either literally or figuratively [*a clear* liquid, *clear* logic]; **transparent** suggests such clearness that objects on the other side (or by extension, meanings, etc.) may be seen distinctly [plate glass is *transparent*]; **translucent** implies the admission of light, but so diffused that objects on the other side cannot be clearly distinguished [stained glass is *translucent*]; **pellucid** suggests the sparkling clearness of crystal [a slab of *pellucid* ice, *pellucid* writing] See also **evident** —*ANT.* **opaque, cloudy, turbid**

clear air turbulence turbulent air, not associated with a storm, that affects the flight of aircraft

clear·ance (klir′əns) *n.* 1 an act or instance of clearing 2 the clear space or distance between moving objects or mechanical parts, or between a moving object and that which it passes through, over, under, etc. 3 official, esp. governmental, authorization allowing a person to examine classified documents, participate in confidential projects, etc. 4 *a)* a certificate from the collector of customs authorizing a ship to enter or leave port (also **clearance papers**) *b)* the act or process of meeting the requirements for getting this certificate 5 *Aeron.* permission, usually from a control tower, to take off, land, etc. 6 *Banking* the adjustment of debits and credits, exchange of checks, etc. in a clearinghouse

clearance sale a sale to get rid of old merchandise and make room for new

Cle·ar·chus (klē är′kəs) died 401? B.C.; Spartan general

clear-cut (klir′kut′) *adj.* 1 clearly and sharply outlined 2 distinct; definite; not doubtful; unambiguous 3 having all of its trees cut down —*vt.* to cut down all of the trees in (an area) Also written **clear′cut′** —**clear′-cut′ting** *n., adj.,* **clear′cut′ting**

clear·eyed (-īd′) *adj.* 1 having clear eyes or vision 2 perceptive; thinking clearly

clear·head·ed (-hed′id) *adj.* having or indicating a clear mind; lucid; unconfused —**clear′head′ed·ly** *adv.* —**clear′head′ed·ness** *n.*

clear·ing (klir′iŋ) *n.* 1 a making clear or being cleared ☆2 an area of land cleared of trees 3 *Banking a)* the exchanging of checks, etc. and balancing of accounts between banks *b)* the procedure for doing this *c)* [*pl.*] the amount of the balances thus settled

clear·ing·house (-hous′) *n.* 1 an office maintained by a group of banks as a center for exchanging checks drawn against one another, for balancing accounts, etc. 2 a central office, as for the collection and dissemination of information

clear·sight·ed (klir′sīt′id) *adj.* 1 seeing clearly 2 perceiving, understanding, or thinking clearly —**clear′sight′ed·ly** *adv.* —**clear′sight′ed·ness** *n.*

clear·sto·ry (-stôr′ē) *n., pl.* **-ries** *alt. sp. of* CLERESTORY

Clear·wa·ter (klir′wôt′ər) ⟦descriptive⟧ city in WC Fla., on the Gulf of Mexico: suburb of St. Petersburg

clear·wing (klir′wiŋ′) *n.* any of a family (Aegeriidae) of day-flying, wasplike moths with transparent, scaleless wings

cleat (klēt) *n.* ⟦ME *clete* < OE **cleat* (WGmc **klaut*), a lump < IE **g(e)leu-* < base **gel-*: see CLIMB⟧ 1 a piece of wood, metal, or plastic, often wedge-shaped, fastened to something to strengthen it or give secure footing: cleats are used on gangways, under shelves, on the soles or heels of shoes, etc. 2 *Naut.* a small metal or wood fitting, specif. one with projecting ends, fixed as to the deck of a ship and used to secure a rope —*vt.* to fasten to or with a cleat

cleav·age (klēv′ij) *n.* 1 a cleaving, splitting, or dividing 2 the manner in which a thing splits 3 a cleft; fissure; division 4 the hollow between a woman's breasts, as made visible by a low-cut neckline 5 *Biol. a)* cell division, esp. the series of mitotic cell divisions that transform the fertilized ovum into the earliest embryonic stage *b)* any single division in this series 6 *Mineralogy* the tendency of some minerals to break in definite planes, producing smooth surfaces

cleave[1] (klēv) *vt.* **cleaved** or **cleft** or **clove, cleaved** or **cleft** or **clo′ven, cleav′ing** ⟦ME *cleven* < OE *cleofan*; akin to Ger *klieben* < IE base **gleubh-,* to cut, slice > Gr *glyphein,* carve, L *glubere,* to peel⟧ 1 to divide by a blow, as with an ax; split 2 to pierce 3 to sever; disunite —*vi.* 1 to split; separate; fall apart 2 to make one's way by or as by cutting —**cleav′a·ble** *adj.*

cleave[2] (klēv) *vi.* **cleaved, cleav′ing** ⟦ME *cleven* < OE *cleofian,* to adhere; akin to Ger *kleben* < IE **gleibh-* < base **glei-*: see CLAY⟧ 1 to adhere; cling (*to*) 2 to be faithful (*to*) —*SYN.* STICK

cleav·er (klēv′ər) *n.* ⟦CLEAVE[1] + -ER⟧ a heavy cutting tool with a broad blade, used by butchers

cleav·ers (-ərz) *n., pl.* **-ers** ⟦< CLEAVE[2]⟧ any of various plants (genus *Galium*) of the madder family, esp. a weedy species (*G. aparine*), with stalkless leaves arranged in whorls, clusters of small, white or yellow flowers, and square stems

cleek (klēk) *n.* ⟦Scot < ME *cleke, cleche,* pastoral staff, crosier < *clechen,* to seize, catch < OE **clæcan;* akin to *clyccan:* see CLUTCH[1]⟧ 1 [Chiefly Scot.] a large hook 2 *Golf former term for: a)* the number one iron (see IRON, sense 6) *b)* the number four wood (see WOOD[1], sense 6)

clef (klef) *n.* ⟦Fr < L *clavis,* a key: see CLOSE[2]⟧ a symbol written at the beginning of a musical staff to indicate the pitch of the notes: there are three clefs: G (treble), F (bass), and C (alto or tenor)

clefs

cleft[1] (kleft) *n.* ⟦ME *clift* < OE **clyft* < *cleofan:* see CLEAVE[1]⟧ **1** an opening made by or as by cleaving; crack; crevice **2** a hollow between two parts

cleft[2] (kleft) *vi. alt. pt. & pp. of* CLEAVE[1] *—vt.* **1** *alt. pt. & pp. of* CLEAVE[1] **2** to insert (a scion) into the stock of a plant *—adj.* **1** split; divided **2** *Bot.* divided by one or more narrow spaces extending more than halfway to the midrib: said of leaves, as an oak leaf

cleft lip **1** a congenital lip deformity often accompanying a cleft palate, in which, usually, the upper lip fails to form completely, leaving a vertical cleft in the center **2** such a lip

cleft palate a cleft from front to back along the middle of the palate, or roof, of the mouth, caused by the failure of the two parts of the palate to join in prenatal development

Cleis·the·nes (klīs′thə nēz′) fl. *c.* 500 B.C.; Athenian statesman

cleis·tog·a·mous (klīs täg′ə məs) *adj.* ⟦< Gr *kleistos,* closed (see CLOSE[2]) + -GAMOUS⟧ *Bot.* having small, unopened, self-pollinating flowers, usually in addition to the showier flowers: also **cleis′to·gam′ic** (-tə gam′ik)

cleis·tog·a·my (-mē) *n.* ⟦< Gr *kleistos* (see prec.) + -GAMY⟧ *Bot.* self-pollination of certain unopened flowers

clem·a·tis (klem′ə tis, klə mat′is) *n.* ⟦L < Gr *klēmatis,* brushwood, clematis < *klēma,* vine, cutting: see CLASTIC⟧ any of a genus (*Clematis*) of perennial plants and woody vines of the buttercup family, with bright-colored flowers of varying size and form

Cle·men·ceau (klā män sō′; *E* klem′ən sō′), **Georges (Benjamin Eugène)** (zhôrzh) 1841-1929; Fr. statesman: premier of France (1906-09; 1917-20)

clem·en·cy (klem′ən sē) *n., pl.* **-cies** ⟦ME *clemencie* < L *clementia* < *clemens,* merciful⟧ **1** forbearance, leniency, or mercy, as toward an offender or enemy **2** a merciful or lenient act **3** mildness, as of weather **—SYN.** MERCY

Clem·ens (klem′ənz), **Samuel Lang·horne** (laŋ′hôrn′) (pseud. *Mark Twain*) 1835-1910; U.S. writer & humorist

clem·ent (klem′ənt) *adj.* ⟦L *clemens,* prob. < IE base **k̂lei-,* to bend: see INCLINE⟧ **1** forbearing; lenient; merciful **2** mild, as weather **—clem′ent·ly** *adv.*

Clem·ent[1] (klem′ənt) *n.* ⟦L *Clemens* < *clemens,* mild: see prec.⟧ a masculine name: dim. *Clem;* fem. *Clementine, Clementina*

Clem·ent[2] (klem′ənt) **1** Saint **Clement I** (died A.D. 97); pope (88-97): martyr & Apostolic Father: his day is Nov. 23 **2 Clement VII** (born *Giulio de' Medici*) 1478-1534; pope (1523-34): excommunicated Henry VIII

clem·en·tine (klem′ən tīn′, -tēn′) *n.* ⟦Fr *clémentine*⟧ a small, orange-colored citrus fruit, grown mainly in the W Mediterranean region, that may be a variety or a hybrid of the tangerine

Clem·en·tine (klem′ən tīn′, -tēn′) *n.* ⟦Fr < L *Clemens:* see CLEMENT[1]⟧ a feminine name: also **Clem′en·ti′na** (-tē′nə)

Clement of Alexandria (*Titus Flavius Clemens*) A.D. 150?-215?; Gr. Christian theologian

clench (klench) *vt.* ⟦ME *clenchen* < OE *-clencan* (in *beclencan*), lit., to make cling, caus. of *clingan:* see CLING⟧ **1** CLINCH (*vt.* 1) **2** to bring together tightly; close (the teeth or fist) firmly **3** to grip tightly *—n.* **1** a firm grip **2** a device that clenches **—clench′er** *n.*

cle·o·me (klē ō′mē) *n.* ⟦ModL⟧ any of a large genus (*Cleome*) of mostly tropical plants of the caper family, with white, pink, yellow, green, or purple flowers having stalked petals and long stamens; spider flower: see BEE PLANT

Cle·om·e·nes III (klē äm′ə nēz′) died 219? B.C.; king of Sparta (235?-220? B.C.); sought to institute sweeping social reforms

Cle·on (klē′än′) died 422? B.C.; Athenian demagogue

Cle·o·pa·tra (klē′ō pa′trə, klē′ə-, -pā′-, -pä′-) 69?-30 B.C.; queen of Egypt (51-49; 48-30): paramour of Julius Caesar & Mark Antony

Cleopatra's Needle either of two ancient Egyptian obelisks, one in London, the other in New York City, sent as gifts (1878) by the ruler of Egypt to England & the U.S.

CLEP *abbrev.* College-Level Examination Program

clepe (klēp) *vt.* ⟦ME *clepen* < OE *cleopian, clipian*⟧ **1** [Obs.] to call or address (a person) **2** [Archaic] to call by name; name: generally in the archaic past participle, *yclept, ycleped*

clep·sy·dra (klep′si drə) *n., pl.* **-dras** or **-drae′** (-drē′) ⟦L < Gr *klepsydra,* water clock < *kleptein,* to steal (see KLEPTOMANIA) + *hydōr,* WATER⟧ WATER CLOCK

clep·to·ma·ni·a (klep′tō mā′nē ə, -tə-) *n. alt. sp. of* KLEPTOMANIA

clere·sto·ry (klir′stôr′ē) *n., pl.* **-ries** ⟦ME *clerestorie* < *cler,* CLEAR + *storie,* STORY[2]⟧ the upper part of a wall, specif. of a church, containing windows for lighting the central part of a lofty room or space

cler·gy (klur′jē) *n., pl.* **-gies** ⟦ME *clergie,* office or dignity of a clergyman < OFr < LL(Ec) *clericus:* see CLERK⟧ persons ordained for religious service; ministers, priests, rabbis, etc., collectively

cler·gy·man (-mən) *n., pl.* **-men** (-mən) a member of the clergy; minister, priest, rabbi, etc.

cler·gy·per·son (-pur′sən) *n.* a member of the clergy: used to avoid the masculine implication of *clergyman*

cler·gy·wom·an (-woom′ən) *n., pl.* **-wom′en** (-wim′in) a woman who is a member of the clergy

cler·ic (kler′ik) *n.* ⟦LL(Ec) *clericus:* see CLERK⟧ a member of the clergy *—adj.* relating to the clergy or one of its members

cler·i·cal (kler′i kəl) *adj.* ⟦ME < LL(Ec) *clericalis,* clerical, priestly < *clericus:* see CLERK⟧ **1** relating to the clergy or one of its members **2** relating to office clerks or their work **3** favoring clericalism *—n.* **1** a member of the clergy **2** [*pl.*] clerics' garments **3** a person who favors clericalism **—cler′i·cal·ly** *adv.*

clerical collar a stiff, white collar buttoned at the back, worn by certain members of the clergy

cler·i·cal·ism (-iz′əm) *n.* political influence or power of the clergy, or a policy or principles favoring this: generally a derogatory term **—cler′i·cal·ist** *n.*

cler·i·hew (kler′ə hyoo′) *n.* ⟦after E. *Clerihew* Bentley (1875-1956), Eng author⟧ a humorous, quasi-biographical poem made up of two rhymed couplets with lines of varying length and meter

cler·i·sy (kler′i sē) *n.* ⟦ME *clericia* < LL(Ec) *clericus:* see fol.⟧ educated people as a class

clerk (klurk; *Brit* klärk) *n.* ⟦ME < OFr & OE *clerc,* both < LL(Ec) *clericus,* a priest < Gr(Ec) *klērikos,* a cleric < *klēros,* lot, inheritance (later, from use in LXX, Deut. 18:2, of the Levites, hence the Christian clergy), orig., a shard used in casting lots < IE **klaro-* < base **kel-,* to strike > OIr *clar,* a board, tablet, L *calamitas,* CALAMITY⟧ **1** a layman who has certain minor duties in a church **2** an office worker who keeps records, types letters, does filing, etc. **3** an official in charge of the records, accounts, etc. of a school board, court, town, etc. ☆**4** a hotel employee who keeps the register, assigns guests to rooms, etc. ☆**5** a person who sells in a store; salesclerk **6** a person who handles mail, etc., as in a post office **7** [Archaic] a clergyman **8** [Archaic] a literate person; scholar *—vi.* ☆to work or be employed as a clerk, esp. a salesclerk **—clerk′ship′** *n.*

clerk·ly (-lē) *adj.* **-li·er, -li·est** **1** of or like a clerk **2** [Obs.] scholarly *—adv.* **-li·er, -li·est** in a clerkly manner

Cler·mont-Fer·rand (kler mōn fe rän′) city in central France, in the Auvergne region

cleve·ite (klēv′īt′) *n.* ⟦after P. T. *Cleve* (1840-1905), Swed chemist⟧ a radioactive crystalline variety of uraninite, found in Norway

Cleve·land[1] (klēv′lənd), **(Stephen) Gro·ver** (grō′vər) 1837-1908; 22d and 24th president of the U.S. (1885-89; 1893-97)

Cleve·land[2] (klēv′lənd) **1** ⟦after Moses *Cleaveland* (1754-1806), surveyor of the WESTERN RESERVE⟧ city and port in NE Ohio, on Lake Erie **2** former county in N England, on the North Sea: 231 sq mi (597 sq km)

clev·er (klev′ər) *adj.* ⟦ME *cliver,* prob. < EFris *klüfer* or Norw dial. *klöver,* ready, skillful; ? infl. by OE *clifer,* claw, hand, in the sense, "adroit with the hand": for the latter sense development, see ADROIT, DEXTEROUS⟧ **1** skillful in doing something; adroit; dexterous **2** quick in thinking or learning; intelligent, ingenious, quick-witted, witty, facile, etc. **3** showing ingenuity or quick, sometimes superficial, intelligence [*a clever* book] **4** [Dial.] *a)* amiable; good-natured *b)* handsome, convenient, nice, etc. **—clev′er·ly** *adv.* **—clev′er·ness** *n.*

SYN.—clever, in this comparison, implies quick-wittedness or adroitness, as in contriving the solution to a problem [*a clever* reply]; **cunning** suggests great skill or ingenuity, but often implies deception or craftiness [*cunning* as a fox]; **ingenious** stresses inventive skill, as in origination or fabrication [*an ingenious* explanation]; **shrewd** suggests cleverness accompanied by practicality [*a shrewd* understanding of the situation], sometimes verging on craftiness [*a shrewd* politician] See also **intelligent**

clev·is (klev′is) *n.* ⟦ult. akin to CLEAVE[2]⟧ a U-shaped metal fitting with holes in the ends through which a pin or bolt is passed in order to attach one thing to another

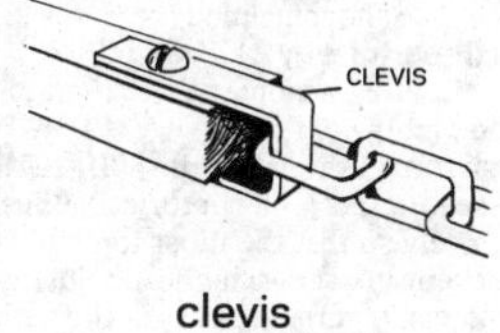

clevis

clew (kloo) *n.* ⟦ME *cleue* < OE *cliwen,* akin to Du *klüwen* & dissimilated Ger *knäuel* < IE base **gel-:* see CLAW⟧ **1** a ball of thread or yarn: in Greek legend, a thread is used by Theseus as a guide out of the labyrinth **2** *archaic sp. of* CLUE **3** *Naut. a)* either of the lower corners of a square sail *b)* the after lower corner of a fore-and-aft sail *c)* [*pl.*] a combination of lines by which a hammock is hung *—vt.* **1** to wind (*up*) into a ball **2** CLUE **—clew down** (or **up**) to lower (or raise) a sail by means of clew lines

clew lines the ropes connecting the clews of a sail with the yard, used in raising or lowering the sail

cli·ché (klē shā′) *n.* ⟦Fr < *clicher,* to stereotype < Ger *klitsch,* clump, claylike mass (hence, orig., to pattern in clay)⟧ **1** [Archaic] a stereotype printing plate **2** an expression or idea that has become trite **—SYN.** PLATITUDE

cli·chéd (klē shād′) *adj.* **1** full of clichés [*a dull, clichéd* style] **2** trite; stereotyped [*a clichéd* theme]

click (klik) *n.* ⟦echoic, but assoc. with ME *clike,* a locking latch (< OFr *clique*) & *cliken,* to chatter (< OFr *cliquer*)⟧ **1** a slight, sharp sound like that of a door latch snapping into place **2** a mechanical device, as a catch or pawl, that clicks into position **3** an instance of clicking [*a click* of a mouse button] **4** [Informal] a flash of insight; epiphany **5** *Phonet.* any of a class of stops, common in some African languages, made by touching the tongue to the roof of the mouth, drawing in the breath, and abruptly withdrawing the tongue from the roof of the mouth [the sound represented in English by the spelling "tsk" is *a click*] *—vi.* **1** to make a click **2** [Informal] *a)* to be suddenly clear or comprehensible *b)* to fit, work, or get along together successfully *c)* to be a success **3** *Comput.* to select or activate an icon, menu item, etc. by positioning the cursor over it and pressing a mouse button: usually with *on* *—vt.* **1** to cause to click **2** *Comput.* to select or activate (an icon, menu item, etc.) using the cursor and mouse **—click′er** *n.*

click beetle any of a family (Elateridae) of beetles that, when on their backs, can usually spring up with a clicking sound
click·e·ty-clack (klik′ə tē klak′) *n.* ⟦echoic⟧ a rhythmic, metallic sound, as that made by the wheels of a moving train —*vi.* to make this sound
cli·ent (klī′ənt) *n.* ⟦OFr < L *cliens,* follower, retainer < IE base **klei-,* to lean, as in L *clinare* (see INCLINE); basic sense, "one leaning on another (for protection)"⟧ 1 [Archaic] a person dependent on another, as for protection or patronage 2 a person or company for whom a lawyer, accountant, advertising agency, etc. is acting 3 a customer 4 a person served by a social agency, psychotherapist, etc. 5 a nation, state, etc. dependent on another politically, economically, etc.: also **client state** 6 *Comput.* a terminal or personal computer that is connected to a SERVER (sense 3) —**cli·en·tal** (klī′ən təl, klī en′təl) *adj.*
cli·en·tele (klī′ən tel′; *also* klē′ən-, -än-) *n.* ⟦Fr *clientèle* < L *clientela,* relation of patron and client, patronage: see prec.⟧ all one's clients or customers, collectively: also **cli·ent·age** (klī′ən tij)
cliff (klif) *n.* ⟦ME & OE *clif* < IE **gleibh-,* to adhere, be attached < base **glei-* (see CLAY): basic sense prob. "slippery, smooth rock"⟧ a high, steep face of rock, esp. one on a coast; precipice —**cliff′y** *adj.*
☆**cliff dweller** 1 a member of an ancient North American Indian people of the Southwest that lived in hollows or caves in cliffs: they were ancestors of the Pueblo Indians 2 [Informal] a person who lives in a large urban apartment house —**cliff′-dwell′ing** *adj.*
☆**cliff·hang·er** or **cliff-hang·er** (-haŋ′ər) *n.* 1 an early type of serialized film in which each episode ended with a suspenseful climax, as the hero hanging from a cliff 2 any highly suspenseful story, situation, etc. —**cliff′hang′ing** *adj.*, **cliff′-hang′ing**
Clif·ford (klif′ərd) *n.* ⟦< the surname or place name *Clifford* < CLIFF + FORD, hence, lit., ford at the cliff⟧ a masculine name: dim. *Cliff*
☆**cliff swallow** a North American swallow (*Petrochelidon pyrrhonota*) that builds its gourdlike nest of mud, grass, etc. against a cliff or under the eaves of a building
Clif·ton (klif′tən) *n.* ⟦< the surname *Clifton* < the place name *Clifton* < CLIFF + *-ton,* town; hence, lit., town at the cliff⟧ a masculine name
cli·mac·ter·ic (klī mak′tər ik, klī′mak ter′ik) *n.* ⟦L *climactericus* < Gr *klimaktērikos* < *klimaktēr,* round of a ladder < *klimax,* ladder: see CLIMAX⟧ 1 a period in the life of a person when an important physiological change occurs; specif., the period of perimenopause 2 any crucial period —*adj.* of or resembling a climacteric; crucial: also **cli′mac·ter′i·cal**
cli·mac·tic (klī mak′tik) *adj.* of, constituting, or in the order of a climax: also **cli·mac′ti·cal** —**cli·mac′ti·cal·ly** *adv.*
cli·mate (klī′mət) *n.* ⟦ME *climat* < OFr < LL *clima* < Gr *klima,* region, zone < base of *klinein,* to slope (see INCLINE): orig., slope of the earth from the equator toward the poles⟧ 1 the prevailing or average weather conditions of a place, as determined by the temperature and meteorological changes over a period of years 2 the prevailing or average indoor temperature, humidity, etc., as of a room or building 3 any prevailing conditions affecting life, activity, etc. *[a favorable climate of opinion]* 4 a region with certain prevailing weather conditions *[to move to a warmer climate]* —**cli·mat·ic** (klī mat′ik) *adj.* —**cli·mat′i·cal·ly** *adv.*
cli·mate-con·trolled (-kən trōld′) *adj.* equipped with an automatic system for controlling its interior temperature, humidity, etc. *[a climate-controlled shopping mall]*
cli·ma·tol·o·gy (klī′mə täl′ə jē) *n.* the science dealing with climate and climatic phenomena —**cli′ma·to·log′i·cal** (-tə läj′i kəl) *adj.* —**cli′ma·tol′o·gist** *n.*
cli·max (klī′maks′) *n.* ⟦LL < Gr *klimax,* ladder < base of *klinein,* to slope: see INCLINE⟧ 1 a rhetorical series of ideas, images, etc. arranged progressively so that the most forceful is last 2 the final, culminating element or event in a series; highest point, as of interest or excitement; specif., *a)* the decisive turning point of the action, as in a drama *b)* an orgasm 3 *Ecol.* a final, self-perpetuating community of plants and animals that develops in a particular climate, soil, etc.: it will persist as long as the same conditions prevail — *vi., vt.* to reach or bring to a climax —**SYN.** SUMMIT
climb (klīm) *vi., vt.* **climbed, climb′ing** ⟦ME *climben* < OE *climban* < IE **glembh-* (> CLAMBER, CLUMP) < base **gel-,* to make round, clench, as the fist: basic sense, "to cling to, grip"⟧ 1 to go up by using the feet and, often, the hands 2 to rise or ascend gradually to a higher point; mount 3 to move (*down, over, along,* etc.), using the hands and feet ☆4 to get (*into* or *out of* clothes or a piece of clothing) hastily, perfunctorily, etc. 5 *Bot.* to grow upward on (a wall, trellis, etc.) by winding around or adhering with tendrils —*n.* 1 an act or instance of climbing; rise; ascent 2 a thing or place to be climbed —**climb down** [Chiefly Brit.] to back down from a position one has taken, as on an issue —**climb′a·ble** *adj.*
climb·down (klīm′doun′) *n.* ⟦< CLIMB DOWN (see under prec.)⟧ [Chiefly Brit.] an act or instance of backing down from a position or claim
climb·er (klīm′ər) *n.* 1 one that climbs up ☆2 a device with sharp spikes fastened to the shoe or strapped to the leg, for use in climbing telephone poles, trees, etc. ☆3 [Informal] a person who tries to advance socially or in business 4 *Bot.* a climbing plant or vine
climbing iron either of a pair of metal frames with spikes that may be strapped over footgear or on the inside of the leg to aid in climbing trees, public utility poles, etc.
climbing perch any of a genus (*Anabas*) of freshwater gouramies of Southeast Asia and Africa that can live out of water briefly and travel short distances over land
clime (klīm) *n.* ⟦LL *clima:* see CLIMATE⟧ [Old Poet.] a region or realm, esp. with reference to its climate
clin- (klīn) *combining form* CLINO-: used before a vowel
clinch (klinch) *vt.* ⟦var. of CLENCH⟧ 1 to secure (a nail, bolt, etc. that has been driven through something) by bending or flattening the projecting end 2 to fasten firmly together by this means 3 *a)* to settle (an argument, bargain, etc.) definitely *b)* to make sure of winning; win conclusively —*vi.* ☆1 *Boxing* to grip the opponent's body with one or both arms so as to hinder punching effectiveness ☆2 [Slang] to embrace —*n.* 1 *a)* a fastening, as with a clinched nail *b)* the bent or flattened part of a clinched nail, bolt, etc. ☆2 *Boxing* an act of clinching ☆3 [Slang] an embrace
clinch·er (klinch′ər) *n.* a person or thing that clinches; specif., a conclusive or decisive point, argument, act, etc.
cline (klīn) *n.* ⟦prob. back-form. < INCLINE⟧ a gradual change in a trait or in the frequency of a trait within a species over a geographical area —**cli′nal** *adj.*
cling (kliŋ) *vi.* **clung, cling′ing** ⟦ME *clingen* < OE *clingan,* to adhere, stick together < IE **gel-g-* < base **gel-:* see CLIMB⟧ 1 to hold fast by or as by embracing, entwining, or sticking; adhere 2 *a)* to be or stay near, as if holding fast *b)* to be emotionally attached —☆*adj., n.* CLINGSTONE —**SYN.** STICK —**cling′er** *n.* —**cling′ing·ly** *adv.* —**cling′y** *adj.* **-i·er, -i·est**
cling·fish (kliŋ′fish′) *n., pl.* **-fish′** or **-fish′es** (see FISH) any of an order (Gobiesociformes) of small, marine bony fishes having a sucking disc on the ventral surface near the head, with which they cling to rocks, etc.
☆**cling·ing vine** (kliŋ′iŋ) a woman regarded as helpless and dependent in her relationship with a man
Cling·mans Dome (kliŋ′mənz) ⟦after U.S. Senator T. L. *Clingman* (1812-97) from N.C.⟧ mountain on the Tenn.-N.C. border; highest peak of the Great Smoky Mountains: 6,642 ft (2,024 m)
☆**cling·stone** (kliŋ′stōn′) *adj.* having pulp that clings to the pit, as some peaches: see FREESTONE —*n.* such a peach
clin·ic (klin′ik) *n.* ⟦Fr *clinique* < Gr *klinikē* (*technē*), (practice) at the sickbed < *klinikos,* of the bed < *klinē,* bed < *klinein,* to recline: see LEAN[1]⟧ 1 the teaching of medicine by examining and treating patients in the presence of students 2 a class so taught 3 a place where patients are studied or treated by specialist physicians practicing as a group 4 a department of a hospital or medical school, where outpatients are treated, sometimes without being charged or for a small fee 5 an organization or institution that offers some kind of advice, treatment, or instruction *[a maternal health clinic]* 6 a brief, intensive session of group instruction in a specific skill, field of knowledge, etc. *[a basketball clinic]*
clin·i·cal (klin′i kəl) *adj.* 1 of or connected with a clinic or a sickbed 2 having to do with the direct treatment and observation of patients, as distinguished from experimental or laboratory study 3 purely scientific; impersonal *[clinical detachment]* 4 austere, antiseptic, etc., like a medical clinic —**clin′i·cal·ly** *adv.*
clinical thermometer a thermometer for measuring body temperature
cli·ni·cian (kli nish′ən, klə-) *n.* an expert in or practitioner of clinical medicine, psychology, etc.
clink (kliŋk) *vi., vt.* ⟦ME *clinken* < MDu *klinken:* orig. echoic⟧ to make or cause to make a slight, sharp sound, as of glasses striking together —*n.* 1 such a sound 2 ⟦< name of an 18th-c. prison in Southwark (London)⟧ [Informal] a jail; prison
clink·er (kliŋk′ər) *n.* ⟦Du *klinker,* vitrified brick that clinks when struck < *klinckaerd* < *klinken,* to ring⟧ 1 [Archaic] a very hard brick 2 a hard mass of fused stony matter formed in a furnace, as from impurities in the coal 3 [Slang] *a)* a mistake or error; often, specif., a misplayed musical note *b)* a total failure —*vi.* to form clinkers in burning
clink·er-built (-bilt′) *adj.* ⟦*clinker* < *clink,* dial. var. of CLENCH⟧ built with the planks of the hull overlapping, as a boat: distinguished from CARVEL-BUILT
clink·stone (kliŋk′stōn′) *n.* ⟦transl of Ger *klingstein* < *klingen,* to ring, clink + *stein,* STONE: so named from the metallic sound produced when it is struck⟧ *former term for* PHONOLITE
cli·no- (klī′nō, -nə) ⟦< Gr *klino-* < *klinein,* to recline: see INCLINE⟧ *combining form* slope *[clinometer]*
cli·nom·e·ter (klī näm′ət ər) *n.* ⟦prec. + -METER⟧ an instrument for measuring angles of slope or inclination —**cli·no·met·ric** (klī′nō me′trik) *adj.*, **cli′no·met′ri·cal** —**cli·nom′e·try** (-ə trē) *n.*
clin·quant (kliŋ′kənt) [Archaic] *adj.* ⟦Fr, prp. of earlier *clinquer,* to clink, glitter < MDu *klinken*⟧ glittering with or as with gold or silver; tinseled —*n.* imitation gold leaf; tinsel
Clin·ton[1] (klint′'n) *n.* ⟦< the surname *Clinton* < the place name *Clinton* < ? ME *clint,* cliff (< ON) + OE *tun,* enclosure, village: see TOWN⟧ a masculine name: dim. *Clint*
Clin·ton[2] (klint′'n) 1 **Bill** (legal name *William Jefferson Clinton;* born *William Jefferson Blythe IV*) 1946- ; 42d president of the U.S. (1993-2001) 2 **De Witt** (də wit′) 1769-1828; U.S. statesman: governor of N.Y. (1817-21; 1825-28) 3 **George** 1739-1812; vice president of the U.S. (1805-12): uncle of De Witt 4 **Sir Henry** 1738-95; Brit. general: commander of Brit. forces in North America (1778-82)
☆**clin·to·ni·a** (klin tō′nē ə) *n.* ⟦ModL, after De Witt CLINTON[2]⟧ any of a genus (*Clintonia*) of hardy plants of the lily family, with white or yellow flowers and blue berries
Cli·o (klī′ō, klē′ō) *n.* ⟦L < Gr *Kleiō* < *kleiein,* to celebrate < *kleos,* fame, glory:

see LOUD] 1 *Gr. Myth.* the Muse of history 2 *pl.* **-os** any of the awards given annually for special achievements in advertising

cli·o·met·rics (klī′ō me′triks′) *n.* ⟦< prec. + Gr *metron,* measure: see METER[1]⟧ in the study of history, the use of statistical methods in the analysis of numerical data, as from business, census, or voting records —**cli′o·met′ric** *adj.* —**cli′o·me·tri′cian** (-mə trish′ən) *n.*

clip[1] (klip) *vt.* **clipped, clip′ping** ⟦ME *clippen* < ON *klippa*⟧ 1 to cut or cut off with shears or scissors 2 to cut (an item) out of (a newspaper, magazine, etc.) 3 *a)* to cut short *b)* to shorten by omitting syllables, letters, etc. 4 to cut the hair of 5 to cut off the edge of (coins) 6 [Informal] to hit or punch with a quick, sharp blow ☆7 [Slang] to cheat or swindle, esp. by overcharging —*vi.* 1 to clip something 2 to move rapidly —*n.* 1 an act or instance of clipping 2 a thing clipped; specif., the amount of wool clipped from sheep at one time or in one season 3 a rapid pace 4 *Film, TV* a sequence of film, videotape, etc., as a short selection taken from a longer feature or a brief piece inserted in a newscast 5 [Informal] a quick, sharp blow 6 CLIPPED FORM —**at a** (or **one**) **clip** [Informal] on one particular occasion; at one particular time

clip[2] (klip) *vi., vt.* **clipped, clip′ping** ⟦ME *clippen* < OE *clyppan,* to embrace < IE **gleb-* < base **gel-*: see CLIMB⟧ 1 to fasten with a clip or clips 2 [Now Chiefly Dial.] to hug; embrace closely ☆3 *Football* to block (an opponent who is not carrying the ball) from behind: an illegal act —*n.* 1 any of various devices that clip or fasten things together, grip or hold something, etc. 2 CARTRIDGE CLIP 3 [Obs.] an embrace ☆4 *Football* an act of clipping

☆**clip·board** (klip′bôrd′) *n.* 1 a portable writing board with a hinged clip at the top to hold papers 2 *Comput.* a portion of memory for temporarily storing data that is to be pasted: see PASTE (*vt.* 3)

clip-clop (klip′kläp′) *n., vi.* CLOP

clip-fed (-fed′) *adj.* automatically loaded from a cartridge clip: said of certain repeating firearms

☆**clip joint** [Slang] a nightclub, restaurant, store, etc. that charges excessive prices

clip-on (-än′) *n., adj.* (something) attached by means of a clip or clips [*clip-on* earrings]

clipped form a shortened form of a word, as *pike* (for *turnpike*) or *fan* (for *fanatic*)

clip·per (klip′ər) *n.* ⟦ME < *clippen,* CLIP[1]; senses 3 & 4 infl. (?) by MDu *klepper,* orig., swift horse < LowG *kleppen,* to sound like hoofbeats (echoic)⟧ 1 a person who cuts, trims, etc. 2 [*usually pl.*] a tool for cutting or trimming [a barber's *clippers*] 3 ⟦for sense, see CUTTER⟧ ☆*a)* a sharp-bowed, narrow-beamed sailing ship (*c.* 1830-54) built for great speed *b)* a modified form of this with less speed and greater cargo capacity 4 something regarded as exceptionally swift 5 *Electronics* a circuit designed to limit the amplitude of an output signal to a preset level

clipper ship

clip·ping (klip′iŋ) *n.* ⟦< CLIP[1]⟧ 1 the act of cutting out or trimming off 2 something cut out or trimmed off [hair *clippings*] ☆3 a news story or other item clipped from a newspaper, magazine, etc.

clique (klik, klēk) *n.* ⟦Fr < OFr *cliquer,* to make a noise: of echoic orig.⟧ a small, exclusive circle of people; snobbish or narrow coterie —*SYN.* COTERIE —**cliqu′ish** (-ish) *adj.,* **cliqu′ey,** or **cliqu′y** (-ē) —**cliqu′ish·ly** *adv.* —**cliqu′ish·ness** *n.*

Clis·the·nes (klis′thə nēz′) *var. of* CLEISTHENES

clit (klit) *n.* [Vulgar Slang] the clitoris

clit·o·ri·dec·to·my (klit′ə ri dek′tə mē, klīt′-) *n., pl.* **-to·mies** (-mēz) ⟦ModL *clitorid-* (< *clitoris,* fol. + -ECTOMY⟧ the removal of part or all of the clitoris, specif. as a ritualistic practice in some cultures

clit·o·ris (klit′ə ris, kli tôr′is) *n., pl.* **clit′o·ris·es** or **cli·tor·i·des** (kli tôr′ə dēz′) ⟦ModL < Gr *kleitoris* < *kleitys,* var. of *klitys,* hill; akin to *klinein,* to slope: see INCLINE⟧ a small, sensitive, erectile organ at the upper end of the vulva —**clit′o·ral** *adj.,* **cli·tor′ic**

Clive[1] (klīv) *n.* ⟦< the surname *Clive*⟧ a masculine name

Clive[2] (klīv), **Robert** Baron Clive of Plassey 1725-74; Brit. soldier & statesman: established Brit. control of India

cli·vi·a (klī′vē ə, kliv′ē ə) *n.* any of a genus (*Clivia*) of South African evergreen plants of the lily family, having orange-to-scarlet, lilylike flowers that bloom in early spring

clk *abbrev.* clerk

clo·a·ca (klō ā′kə) *n., pl.* **-cae′** (-sē′, -kē′) or **-cas** ⟦L < *cluere,* to cleanse < IE base **klū-,* to rinse, clean > Gr *klyzein,* to wash, Ger *lauter,* pure⟧ 1 a sewer or cesspool 2 *Zool. a)* the cavity into which both the intestinal and the genitourinary tracts empty in reptiles, birds, amphibians, and many fishes *b)* in some invertebrates, a similar cavity serving as an excretory, respiratory, and reproductive duct —**clo·a′cal** (-kəl) *adj.*

cloak (klōk) *n.* ⟦ME *cloke,* cloak < OFr < ML *clocca* (see CLOCK[1]), a bell, cloak: so called from its bell-like appearance⟧ 1 a loose outer garment, usually sleeveless and extending to or below the knees 2 something that covers or conceals; disguise —*vt.* 1 to cover with or as with a cloak 2 to conceal; hide

cloak-and-dag·ger (klōk′ən dag′ər) *adj.* of or characteristic of the activities of spies and undercover agents, esp. as extravagantly depicted in popular suspense fiction

cloak·room (-ro͞om′) *n.* a room where hats, coats, umbrellas, etc. can be left temporarily

clob·ber[1] (kläb′ər) *vt.* ⟦< ?⟧ [Slang] 1 *a)* to beat or hit repeatedly; maul *b)* to strike with great force 2 to defeat decisively

clob·ber[2] (kläb′ər) *n.* ⟦< ?⟧ [Brit. Slang] 1 clothing 2 possessions

clo·chard (klô′shär′) *n., pl.* **-chards′** (-shär′) ⟦Fr < *clocher,* to limp (< VL *cloppicare* < L *cloppus,* lame) + *-ard,* -ARD⟧ a tramp or vagrant

cloche (klōsh) *n.* ⟦Fr < ML *clocca,* a bell: see fol.⟧ 1 a transparent covering used to protect or force delicate plants 2 a closefitting, bell-shaped hat for women

clock[1] (kläk) *n.* ⟦ME *clokke,* orig., clock with bells < ML *clocca,* bell < Celt, as in OIr *cloc* (> OE *clugge,* OHG *glocka*), bell < ? IE base **kel-,* to cry out, sound > CLAMOR⟧ 1 a device used for measuring and indicating time, traditionally by means of pointers moving over a dial: clocks, unlike watches, are not meant to be worn or carried about ☆2 *short for* TIME CLOCK 3 a measuring or recording device suggestive of a clock, as a taximeter 4 *short for* BIOLOGICAL CLOCK —*vt.* 1 to measure the speed or record the time of (a race, runner, motorist, etc.) with a stopwatch or other timing device 2 to measure (work done, distance covered, etc.) with a registering device 3 ⟦orig., to punch in the face < n., slang, the human face⟧ [Informal] to hit or punch (someone) violently —**around the clock** day and night without stopping —**clock in** (or **out**) to record the time of one's arrival (or departure) by means of a time clock

clock[2] (kläk) *n.* ⟦< ? prec., because of original bell shape⟧ a woven or embroidered ornament on the side of a sock or stocking, going up from the ankle —**clocked** *adj.*

clock·like (-līk′) *adj.* as precise or regular as a clock

clock·mak·er (-māk′ər) *n.* a maker or repairer of clocks

☆**clock radio** a radio with a built-in clock that can be set to turn the radio on or off at any desired time

clock·wise (-wīz′) *adv., adj.* ⟦CLOCK[1] + -WISE⟧ in the direction in which the hands of a clock rotate

clock·work (-wurk′) *n.* 1 the mechanism of a clock 2 any similar mechanism, consisting of springs and geared wheels, as in some mechanical toys —**like clockwork** very regularly, precisely, and evenly

clod (kläd) *n.* ⟦ME & OE < IE **g(e)leu-* < base **gel-,* to make round > CLIMB⟧ 1 a lump, esp. a lump of earth, clay, loam, etc. 2 earth; soil 3 a dull, stupid person; dolt 4 the part of a neck of beef nearest the shoulder —**clod′dish** *adj.* —**clod′dish·ly** *adv.* —**clod′dish·ness** *n.* —**clod′dy** *adj.*

clod·hop·per (kläd′häp′ər) *n.* ⟦prec. + HOPPER, ? by assoc. with GRASSHOPPER⟧ 1 a plowman 2 a clumsy, stupid person; lout 3 a coarse, heavy shoe, like a plowman's

clod·poll (-pōl′) *n.* ⟦CLOD + POLL⟧ a stupid or foolish person; blockhead: also sp. **clod′pole′**

clo·fi·brate (klō fī′brāt′, -fib′rāt′) *n.* ⟦< ? C(H)LO(RO)- + FIBR(O)- + -ATE[2]⟧ a drug, $C_{12}H_{15}ClO_3$, taken to reduce the level of lipids, esp. cholesterol, in the blood

clog (kläg, klôg) *n.* ⟦ME *clogge,* a lump of wood < ? *clod,* CLOD + *logge,* LOG[1]⟧ 1 a weight fastened to the leg of an animal to hinder motion 2 anything that hinders or obstructs; hindrance 3 a shoe, sandal, etc. with a thick, usually wooden, sole: light clogs are used in clog dancing 4 CLOG DANCE —*vt.* **clogged, clog′ging** 1 to hinder; impede 2 to fill with obstructions or with thick, sticky matter; stop up; jam —*vi.* 1 to become stopped up 2 to become thick or sticky, so as to clog 3 to do a clog dance —**clog′gi·ness** *n.* —**clog′gy** *adj.*

clog dance a dance in which clogs are worn to beat out the rhythm —**clog dancer** —**clog dancing**

cloi·son·né (kloi′zə nā′; *Fr* klwȧ zô nā′) *adj.* ⟦Fr, lit., partitioned < *cloison,* partition < VL **clausio* < L *clausus*: see CLOSE[1]⟧ designating or of a kind of enamel work in which the surface decoration is set in hollows formed by shaped pieces of wire welded to a metal plate —*n.* cloisonné enamel

clois·ter (klois′tər) *n.* ⟦ME < OFr *cloistre* & OE *clauster,* both < ML(Ec) *claustrum,* portion of monastery closed off to the laity < L, a bolt, place shut in < pp. of *claudere,* to CLOSE[2]⟧ 1 a place of religious seclusion: monastery or convent 2 monastic life 3 any place where one may lead a secluded life 4 an arched way or covered walk along the inside wall or walls of a monastery, convent, church, or college building, with a columned opening along one side leading to a courtyard or garden —*vt.* 1 to seclude or confine in or as in a cloister 2 to furnish or surround with a cloister —**clois′tered** *adj.* —**clois′tral** (-trəl) *adj.*

SYN.—**cloister** is the general term for a place of religious seclusion, for either men or women, and emphasizes in connotation retirement from the world; **convent,** once a general term synonymous with **cloister,** is now usually restricted to such a place for women (nuns), formerly called a **nunnery; monastery** usually refers to a cloister for men (monks); an **abbey** is a cloister ruled by an abbot or abbess; a **priory** is a cloister ruled by a prior or prioress and is sometimes a subordinate branch of an abbey

clomb (klōm) *vi., vt. archaic pt. & pp. of* CLIMB

clo·mi·phene (klō′mə fēn′) *n.* ⟦< C(H)LO(RO)- + (A)MI(NE) + PHEN(YL)⟧ a synthetic drug, $C_{26}H_{28}ClNO \cdot C_6H_8O_7$, used primarily to stimulate ovulation: in full **clomiphene citrate**

clomp (klämp) *vi.* ⟦echoic⟧ to walk heavily or noisily; clump

☆**clone** (klōn) ***n.*** ⟦< Gr *klōn*, a twig < *klan*, to break: see CLASTIC⟧ **1** *Biol.* all the descendants derived asexually from a single individual, as by cuttings, bulbs, etc. or by fission, parthenogenesis, etc. **2** an individual produced by means of CLONING **3** [Informal] a person or thing very much like another **4** *Comput.* a hardware or software product, esp. a personal computer, designed to function like an original, typically higher-priced, product from another manufacturer —***vt.*** **cloned**, **clon′ing** **1** to produce by means of CLONING **2** [Informal] to make a copy of; imitate —**clon′al** ***adj.*** —**clon′al·ly** ***adv.***

clon·ic (klän′ik) ***adj.*** of or pertaining to clonus —**clo·nic·i·ty** (klō nis′i tē) ***n.***

clon·i·dine (klän′ə dēn′, -din; klō′nə-) ***n.*** ⟦C(H)LO(RO)- (sense 2) + (A)N(ILINE) + (IM)ID(E) + -INE³⟧ a white, crystalline drug, $C_9H_9Cl_2N_3·HCl$, taken orally, used to lower high blood pressure and, experimentally, to ease withdrawal from narcotics: in full **clonidine hydrochloride**

☆**clon·ing** (klōn′iŋ) ***n.*** ⟦see CLONE⟧ **1** the technique of producing a genetically identical duplicate of an organism by replacing the nucleus of an unfertilized ovum with the nucleus of a tissue cell from the organism **2** any of various techniques for producing genetically identical DNA fragments, stem cells, etc.

clonk (klôŋk, klänk) ***n., vi., vt.*** ⟦echoic⟧ [Informal] CLUNK

clo·nus (klō′nəs) ***n.*** ⟦ModL < Gr *klonos*, turmoil < *kelomai*, to start, impel < IE base **kel-* > HOLD¹, < L *celer*, swift⟧ a series of muscle spasms induced by sudden stretching or certain nervous diseases: see TONUS

clop (kläp) ***n.*** ⟦echoic⟧ a sharp, clattering sound, like hoofbeats on a pavement —***vi.*** **clopped**, **clop′ping** to make, or move with, such a sound

clo·qué (klō kā′) ***n.*** ⟦Fr, lit., blistered, pp. of *cloquer*, to blister < *cloque*, a blister, bubble, dial. var. of *cloche*, a bell: see CLOCHE⟧ a fabric with a raised design: also written **cloque**

close¹ (klōs) ***adj.*** **clos′er**, **clos′est** ⟦ME *clos* < OFr < L *clausus*, pp. of *claudere* (see fol.); senses under II from notion "with spaces or intervals closed up"⟧ **I.** *denoting the fact or state of being closed or confined* **1** shut; not open **2** enclosed or enclosing; shut in **3** confined or confining; narrow [*close* quarters] **4** carefully guarded [*close* custody] **5** shut away from observation; hidden; secluded **6** secretive; reserved; reticent **7** miserly; stingy **8** restricted, as in membership **9** oppressively warm and stuffy: said of the weather, atmosphere, etc. **10** not readily available [credit is *close*] **11** *Phonet.* articulated with the tongue relatively high in the mouth, near the palate: said of certain vowels, as the (ē) in *eat* **II.** *denoting nearness* **1** with little space between; with the intervening space closing or closed up; near together **2** having parts or elements near together; compact; dense [*close* marching order, *close* weave] **3** fitting tightly [a *close* coat] **4** *a)* down or near to the surface on which something grows; very short [a *close* shave] *b)* not far away; nearby [a *close* neighbor] **5** near in interests, affection, etc.; intimate; familiar [a *close* friend] **6** varying little from the original or model [a *close* translation] **7** strict; thorough; careful [a *close* search] **8** compactly expressed; concise [a *close* description] **9** accurate; logical; precise [*close* reasoning] **10** nearly equal or alike [*close* in age] **11** difficult to resolve or uncertain in outcome [a *close* decision] —***adv.*** **clos′er**, **clos′est** in a close manner; very near; closely —**close by** nearby; close at hand —**close to the wind** **1** *Naut.* heading as closely as possible in the direction from which the wind is blowing **2** barely avoiding what is unlawful —**close′ly** ***adv.*** —**close′ness** ***n.***

SYN.—**close** suggests something whose parts or elements are near together with little space between [*close*-order drill]; **dense** suggests such a crowding together of elements or parts as to form an almost impervious mass [a *dense* fog]; **compact** suggests close and firm packing, esp. within a small space, and usually implies neatness and order in the arrangement of parts [a *compact* bundle]; **thick**, in this connection, suggests a great number of parts massed tightly together [*thick* fur] See also **familiar, stingy** —ANT. **open, dispersed**

close² (klōz) ***vt.*** **closed**, **clos′ing** ⟦ME *closen* < OFr *clos-*, stem of *clore* < L *claudere*, to close, block up < IE base **klēu*, **klāu-*, hook, crooked or forked branch, close with a hook or bar > SLOT¹, LOT, Gr *kleistos*, closed, L *clavis*, key, *clavus*, nail, OIr *clo*, nail, Ger *schliessen*, to lock⟧ **1** *a)* to move (a door, lid, etc.) to a position that covers the opening; shut *b)* to shut by so moving its lid, cover, etc. [*close* a jewelry box, one's eyes, etc.] **2** to bar entrance to or exit from [to *close* a street] **3** to fill up or stop (an opening) **4** *a)* to draw the edges of together [to *close* an incision] *b)* to fold up or bring together the parts of [to *close* an umbrella] *c)* to bring together the covers of (a book, magazine, etc.) so that the pages cannot be seen, read, etc. **5** to clench (a fist) **6** to bind together; unite [to *close* forces] **7** to bring to an end; finish **8** to stop or suspend the operation of (a school, business, etc.) **9** to complete or make final (a sale, agreement, etc.) **10** to make stubbornly resistant [to *close* one's mind] —***vi.*** **1** to undergo shutting [the door *closes* quietly] **2** to come to an end **3** *a)* to end or suspend operations [the store *closes* at noon] *b)* in the stock exchange, to show an indicated price level at the day's end [steel *closed* high] **4** to have its edges become joined together [the wound has *closed*] **5** to come together **6** to take hold [her hand *closed* on the package] **7** to throng closely together [his friends *closed* about him] **8** to lessen an intervening distance; gain [*closing* on the lead runner] **9** to make contact or come close, as in order to begin fighting **10** *a)* to conclude a business transaction *b)* to be concluded (said of a business transaction) —***n.*** **1** a closing or being closed **2** the final part or conclusion; end **3** [Archaic] a hand-to-hand encounter —**close down** ☆**1** to shut or stop entirely ☆**2** to settle down (*on*), as darkness or a fog —**close in** **1** to draw near from various directions, as to cut off escape [the wolves *closed in* for the kill] **2** to surround or confine —☆**close out** **1** to dispose of (goods) by sale, as in ending a business **2** to terminate (a position in securities or commodities), as by buying shares in order to cover a short sale of stock —**close round** to encircle; surround —**close up** **1** to draw nearer together **2** to shut or stop up entirely **3** to heal, as a wound does —**clos′a·ble** ***adj.***

SYN.—to **close** is to come or bring to a stop, as if by shutting something regarded as previously open [nominations are now *closed*]; to **end** means to stop some process, whether or not it has been satisfactorily completed [let's *end* this argument]; to **conclude** is to bring or come to a formal termination, often by arriving at some decision [to *conclude* negotiations]; to **finish** is to bring to a desired end that which one has set out to do, esp. by adding perfecting touches [to *finish* a painting]; to **complete**, in its distinctive sense, is to finish by filling in the missing or defective parts [the award will *complete* his happiness]; to **terminate** is to bring or come to an end regarded as a limit or boundary [to *terminate* a privilege] —ANT. **begin, start, commence**

close³ (klōs) ***n.*** ⟦ME *clos* < OFr < L *clausum*, orig., neut. pp. of *claudere*: see prec.⟧ [Chiefly Brit.] **1** an enclosed place, as a farmyard **2** enclosed grounds around or beside a building [a cathedral *close*] **3** a narrow street or passageway; also, a dead-end street

☆**close call** (klōs) [Informal] a narrow escape from danger

close corporation (klōs) a corporation in which a few persons hold all of the stock, which is rarely or never placed on the market: also **closed corporation**

close-cropped (klōs′kräpt′) ***adj.*** **1** clipped very short [*close-cropped* hair] **2** cut or grazed down to, or almost to, ground level [*close-cropped* pasture]

closed (klōzd) ***adj.*** **1** not open; shut [a *closed* door] **2** covered over or enclosed [a *closed* wagon] **3** functioning independently; self-sufficient [a *closed* economic system] **4** not receptive to new or different ideas [a *closed* mind] **5** not open to further analysis or debate [a *closed* question] **6** *a)* restricted to certain individuals; exclusive [a *closed* society] *b)* not open to the public or to nonmembers [a *closed* meeting] **7** *Math.* *a)* of or pertaining to a curve with no end points *b)* of a surface whose plane sections are closed curves *c)* of a set in which an operation on pairs of its elements always produces an element of the set *d)* of a set of points containing all its limit points, as the set of points on and within a circle: complementary to an open set **8** *Phonet.* ending in a consonant sound: said of a syllable **9** *Sports* designating a stance, as of a golfer or of a batter in baseball, in which the front foot is closer than the rear foot to an imaginary straight line, as one joining tee and green or one joining home plate and second base

closed-cap·tioned (klōzd′kap′shənd) ***adj.*** designating or of TV programs featuring captions for the deaf which are made visible only by means of a special decoding device

closed chain any structural arrangement, used in the models and formulas of molecules, consisting of a chain of atoms that forms a closed geometric figure; ring: see OPEN CHAIN, SIDE CHAIN

closed circuit a system for transmitting a telecast over cables, via satellite, etc. to a limited number of receivers connected to a circuit —**closed′-cir′cuit** ***adj.***

closed-door (-dôr′) ***adj.*** characterized by restricted admission or access, specif. as to exclude the public or press [*closed-door* board meetings]

☆**closed-end** (-end′) ***adj.*** of or pertaining to an investment company issuing a fixed number of shares which are traded on an exchange

☆**closed gentian** any of several North American plants (genus *Gentiana*) with dark-blue, closed, tubular flowers

☆**closed primary** *see* DIRECT PRIMARY ELECTION

☆**closed season** any of various annual periods during which it is illegal to kill or capture certain game or fish

☆**closed shop** **1** a factory, business, etc. operating under a contractual arrangement between a labor union and the employer by which only members of the union may be employed **2** this arrangement

close·fist·ed (klōs′fis′tid) ***adj.*** stingy —**close′fist′ed·ness** ***n.***

close·fit·ting (-fit′iŋ) ***adj.*** fitting tightly, esp. in such a way as to show the contours of the body

close·grained (-grānd′) ***adj.*** having a fine, compact grain or texture [*closegrained* wood]: also written **close-grained**

close·hauled (-hôld′) ***adj.*** having the sails adjusted for heading as nearly as possible into the wind

close-knit (klōs′nit′) ***adj.*** closely united or joined together, as by social or family ties

close·mouthed (klōz′mouthd′, -moutht′) ***adj.*** not talking much; telling little; taciturn: also **close′lipped′** (-lipt′)

close order (klōs) an arrangement of troops in compact units at close intervals and distances, as for marching

close·out (klōz′out′) ***n.*** **1** a selling off at discounted prices of the inventory of a business going into liquidation or of particular goods that will no longer be carried **2** something offered at such a sale

close punctuation (klōs) punctuation characterized by the use of many commas and other marks: opposed to OPEN PUNCTUATION

close quarters (klōs) **1** [Historical] an enclosed space on a ship, in which a last stand could be made against boarders **2** space that is narrow or crowded **3** hand-to-hand encounter with an enemy

clos·er (klō′zər) ***n.*** **1** someone or something that closes **2** a person adept at completing a business deal, an assignment, etc. successfully **3** *Baseball* a relief pitcher who specializes in pitching the final innings of a close game

close-run (klōs′run′) ***adj.*** [Chiefly Brit.] decided, achieved, settled, etc. by the narrowest of margins: usually used in the phrase **a close-run thing**

☆**close shave** (klōs) [Informal] a narrow escape from danger

clos·et (kläz′it) ***n.*** ⟦OFr, small enclosure, dim. of *clos*: see CLOSE[1]⟧ **1** a small room or cupboard for clothes, household supplies, linens, etc. **2** a small, private room for reading, meditation, etc. **3** a monarch's private chamber as for prayer or conference **4** WATER CLOSET **5** a state of secrecy, esp. concerning personal homosexual orientation or activity: used with *the* —***adj.*** **1** private, secret, or clandestine *[a closet drinker]* **2** marked by theorizing; speculative *[closet thinking]* —***vt.*** **1** to shut up in a private room for confidential discussion *[to closet oneself with councilors]* **2** to hide (someone or something): often with *away*

closet drama drama written mainly to be read, not staged

clos·et·ed (kläz′it id) ***adj.*** concealing one's identity, esp. one's sexual orientation *[a closeted homosexual]*

☆**close-up** (klōs′up′) ***n.*** **1** a photograph or a film or TV shot taken at very close range or with a telephoto lens **2** a close or personal view or interpretation

clos·trid·i·um (kläs trid′ē əm) ***n.,*** *pl.* **-trid′i·a** (-ə) ⟦ModL < Gr *klōstēr*, a spindle (see CLOTHO) + ModL *-idium*, dim. suffix < Gr *-idion*: so named from its shape⟧ any of a large genus (*Clostridium*) of spore-forming, anaerobic, rod-shaped bacteria, many of which produce toxins, including those causing tetanus and botulism —**clos·trid′i·al** ***adj.***

clo·sure (klō′zhər) ***n.*** ⟦OFr < L *clausura*, a closing < pp. of *claudere*, to CLOSE[2]⟧ **1** a closing or being closed **2** a finish; end; conclusion **3** the feeling that one's prolonged state of emotional distress over some traumatic experience or situation has finally ended **4** anything that closes or shuts **5** CLOTURE **6** *Geol.* the vertical distance between the highest point of an anticlinal structure and the lowest contour that encircles it **7** *Math.* the property of a set in which an operation on pairs of its elements always produces an element of the set **8** *Phonet.* a blocking of the air stream at some point in the oral cavity —***vt.*** **-sured, -sur·ing** CLOTURE

clot (klät) ***n.*** ⟦ME & OE: akin to Du *kloot*, ball, Ger *klotz*, a block: for IE base see CLIMB⟧ **1** a soft lump of earth, clay, etc.; clod **2** a soft, thickened area or lump formed on or within a liquid; specif., a lump produced by the natural thickening of certain proteins in the blood, as at the site of a wound (in full **blood clot**) **3** a thick or jumbled mass or cluster; agglomeration **4** [Brit. Slang] a stupid or silly person; fool — ***vt., vi.*** **clot′ted, clot′ting** to thicken or form into a clot or clots; coagulate

cloth (klôth, kläth) ***n.,*** *pl.* **cloths** (klôthz, kläthz; *also* klôths, kläths *for "kinds of cloth"*) ⟦ME < OE *clath*, cloth, hence garment, akin to *-clithan*, to stick, *clitha*, poultice < IE **gleit-* (> Ger *kleid*, dress) < base **glei-*, to stick > CLAY⟧ **1** a woven, knitted, or pressed fabric of fibrous material, as cotton, wool, silk, hair, or synthetic fibers **2** a piece of such fabric for a specific use *[tablecloth, washcloth, loincloth]* —***adj.*** **1** made of cloth **2** CLOTHBOUND —**the cloth** **1** the usual or identifying dress of a profession, esp. of the clergy **2** the clergy collectively

cloth·bound (-bound′) ***adj.*** having a binding of stiff pasteboard covered with cloth: said of a book

clothe (klōth) ***vt.*** **clothed** or **clad**, **cloth′ing** ⟦ME *clothen* < OE *clathian*: see CLOTH⟧ **1** to put clothes on; dress **2** to provide with clothes **3** to cover over as if with a garment *[hills clothed in snow]*

clothes (klōthz, klōz) ***pl.n.*** ⟦ME < OE *clathas*, clothes, pl. of *clath*, CLOTH⟧ **1** articles, typically of cloth, designed to cover, protect, or adorn the body; garments; attire **2** [Now Rare] BEDCLOTHES

clothes·horse (-hôrs′) ***n.*** **1** a frame on which to hang clothes, etc. for airing or drying **2** [Slang] a person who dresses conspicuously in fashionable clothes

clothes·line (-līn′) ***n.*** a rope or wire on which clothes and linens are hung for drying or airing

clothes moth any of a family (Tineidae) of small moths that lay their eggs in articles of wool, fur, etc. upon which the hatched larvae feed

☆**clothes·pin** (-pin′) ***n.*** a small clip, as a forked peg of wood or plastic, for fastening clothes on a line

☆**clothes·pole** (-pōl′) ***n.*** a pole for supporting a clothesline

clothes·press (-pres′) ***n.*** a closet, wardrobe, or chest in which to keep clothes

☆**clothes tree** an upright pole with branching hooks or pegs near the top to hold coats and hats

cloth·ier (klōth′yər, klō′thē ər) ***n.*** ⟦ME, one who makes or sells cloth⟧ **1** a person who makes or sells clothes **2** a dealer in cloth

cloth·ing (klō′thiŋ) ***n.*** ⟦ME: see CLOTH⟧ **1** wearing apparel; clothes; garments **2** a covering

Clo·tho (klō′thō) ***n.*** ⟦L < Gr *Klōthō* < *klōthein*, to spin < IE base **klo-* > L *colus*, distaff, Gr *klōstēr*, spindle⟧ *Class. Myth.* that one of the three Fates who spins the thread of human life

cloth yard **1** a medieval unit of measure for cloth, fixed at 37 inches by Edward VI of England: also used as a length for longbow arrows **2** now, the standard yard (36 inches), as used in measuring cloth

clo·ture (klō′chər) ***n.*** ⟦Fr *clôture*, a closing, closing of debate < OFr *closture* < ML *clostura* (altered after L *claustrum*: see CLOISTER) < L *clausura*: see CLOSURE⟧ the parliamentary procedure by which debate is closed and the measure under discussion is put to an immediate vote —***vt.*** **-tured, -tur·ing** to apply cloture to (a debate, bill, etc.)

cloud (kloud) ***n.*** ⟦ME *cloude, clude*, orig., mass of rock, hence, mass of cloud < OE *clud*, mass of rock: for IE base see CLIMB⟧ **1** a visible mass of tiny, condensed water droplets or ice crystals suspended in the atmosphere: clouds are commonly classified into four groups: *A* (high clouds above 6,096 m or 20,000 ft): CIRRUS, CIRROSTRATUS, CIRROCUMULUS; *B* (intermediate clouds, 1,981 m to 6,096 m or 6,500 to 20,000 ft): ALTOSTRATUS, ALTOCUMULUS; *C* (low clouds, below 1,981 m or 6,500 ft): STRATUS, STRATOCUMULUS, NIMBOSTRATUS; *D* (clouds of great vertical continuity): CUMULUS, CUMULONIMBUS **2** a mass of smoke, dust, steam, etc. **3** a great number of things close together and in motion *[a cloud of locusts]* **4** an appearance of murkiness or dimness, as in a liquid **5** a dark marking, as in marble **6** anything that darkens, obscures, threatens, or makes gloomy —***vt.*** **1** to cover or make dark as with clouds **2** to make muddy or foggy **3** to darken; obscure; threaten **4** to make gloomy or troubled **5** to cast slurs on; sully (a reputation, etc.) —***vi.*** **1** to become cloudy **2** to become gloomy or troubled —**have one's head in the clouds** **1** to be impractical or fanciful **2** to engage in daydreaming —**the cloud** the internet considered as the medium for CLOUD COMPUTING —**under a cloud** **1** under suspicion of wrongdoing **2** in a depressed or troubled state of mind

types of clouds

cloud·ber·ry (kloud′ber′ē) ***n.,*** *pl.* **-ries** a northern wild raspberry (*Rubus chamaemorus*) with large, orange-colored fruit

☆**cloud·burst** (-burst′) ***n.*** a sudden, very heavy rain

cloud-capped (-kapt′) ***adj.*** having clouds around the top

cloud chamber an enclosed chamber supersaturated with a liquid vapor, for revealing the presence of ionizing particles that cause liquid droplets to form

cloud computing computing in which software and applications are stored on remote servers and accessed via the internet by users from their PCs

cloud-cuck·oo-land (kloud′kōō′kōō land′) ***n.*** ⟦transl. of Gr *nephelokokkygia* < *nephelē*, cloud + *kokkyx*, cuckoo; name of a utopian city between heaven and earth in *The Birds*, comedy by ARISTOPHANES⟧ a place or condition that is fanciful, lacking in reality, impractically utopian, etc.

cloud ear TREE EAR

☆**cloud forest** a forest, usually near coastal mountain peaks in tropical regions, that has an almost constant cloud cover, even during the dry season

cloud·land (kloud′land′) ***n.*** region of dreams, imagination, or impractical speculation; visionary realm

cloud·less (-lis) ***adj.*** free from clouds; clear; bright —**cloud′less·ly** ***adv.*** —**cloud′less·ness** ***n.***

cloud·let (-lit) ***n.*** a small cloud

☆**cloud nine** [Slang] a condition of great joy or bliss; euphoric state

cloud·y (kloud′ē) ***adj.*** **cloud′i·er, cloud′i·est** **1** covered with clouds; overcast **2** of or like clouds **3** variegated or streaked, as marble **4** opaque, muddy, or foggy *[a cloudy liquid]* **5** obscure; vague; not clear *[cloudy ideas]* **6** troubled; gloomy —**cloud′i·ly** ***adv.*** —**cloud′i·ness** ***n.***

Clou·et (klōō e′, -ā′) **1 Fran·çois** (frän swȧ′) 1510?-72?; Fr. portrait painter: son of Jean **2 Jean** (zhän) 1485?-1540?; Fr. portrait painter of Fl. descent

clough (kluf, klou) ***n.*** ⟦ME < OE *cloh-* < **klanh*; akin to Ger *klinge*, narrow gorge⟧ [Rare] a narrow gorge

clout (klout) ***n.*** ⟦ME *cloute* < OE *clut* (akin to MLowG *klūt*, clod of earth), orig., lump of something, hence, piece of cloth, patch: for IE base see CLIMB⟧ **1** [Now Chiefly Dial.] *a)* a piece of cloth or leather for patching *b)* any piece of cloth, esp. one for cleaning; rag **2** a blow, with or as with the hand; rap ☆**3** [Informal] *a)* a hard hit, as in baseball *b)* power or influence; esp., political power **4** *Archery* a form of long-distance shooting in which archers aim at a large target laid out on the ground with a flag in the center —***vt.*** ⟦ME *clutien* < the n.⟧ **1** [Now Chiefly Dial.] to patch or mend coarsely **2** [Informal] to strike, as with the hand **3** [Informal] to hit (a ball) hard

clove[1] (klōv) ***n.*** ⟦ME *clowe* < OFr *clou (de girofle)*, lit., nail (of clove) < L *clavus*, nail (see CLOSE[2]); so called from its shape⟧ **1** the dried flower bud of a tropical evergreen tree (*Eugenia aromatica*) of the myrtle family, originally native to the East Indies: used as a pungent, fragrant spice **2** the tree

clove[2] (klōv) ***n.*** ⟦ME < OE *clufu*, akin to *cleofan*, to split: see CLEAVE[1]⟧ a segment of a bulb, as of garlic

clove[3] (klōv) ***vt., vi.*** *alt. pt. of* CLEAVE[1]

clove hitch a kind of knot used to fasten a rope around a spar, pole, or another rope

clo·ven (klō′vən) ***vt., vi.*** *alt. pp. of* CLEAVE[1] —***adj.*** divided; split

cloven foot (*or* **hoof**) a foot divided by a cleft, as in the ox, deer, and sheep: used as a symbol of the Devil, who is usually pictured with such hoofs —**clo′ven-foot′ed** ***adj.***, **clo′ven-hoofed′** (-hōōft′)

clove pink CARNATION (sense 1)

clo·ver (klō′vər) ***n.*** ⟦ME < OE *clafre*, akin to MLowG *klāver*, Ger *klee* < IE base **glei-*, to stick: see CLAY⟧ **1** any of a genus (*Trifolium*) of low-growing plants of the pea family, usually with leaves of three leaflets and small flowers in dense heads: cf. RED CLOVER, WHITE CLOVER **2** any similar plant of the pea family: cf. SWEET CLOVER **3** a leaf of any of these plants, with a (specified) number of leaflets *[a four-leaf clover]* —**in clover** living a life of ease and luxury, as cattle in good pasture

clo·ver·leaf (-lēf′) ***n.**, pl.* **-leafs′** ☆an interchange which, by means of an overpass with curving ramps that form the outline of a four-leaf clover and other connecting roads, permits traffic to move or turn in any of four directions with little interference —***adj.*** in the shape or pattern of a leaf of clover

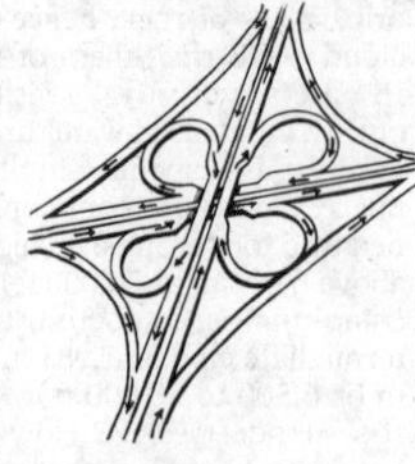
cloverleaf

☆**Clo·vis** (klō′vis) ***adj.*** ⟦after *Clovis,* town in N.Mex., near where such points have been found⟧ of or having to do with a North American culture of the late Pleistocene Epoch characterized by the use of stone and flint points with a hollow base

Clo·vis I (klō′vis) A.D. 466?-511; founder of Frank. monarchy: king of the Franks (481-511)

clown (kloun) ***n.*** ⟦< ? Scand, as in Ice *klunni,* clumsy person⟧ **1** [Obs.] a peasant or farmer; rustic **2** a clumsy, boorish, or incompetent person **3** a performer who entertains, as in a circus, by antics, jokes, tricks, etc.; jester **4** a person who constantly plays the fool, makes jokes, etc.; buffoon —***vi.*** **1** to perform as a clown **2** to play practical jokes, act silly, etc. —**clown′er·y** ***n.*** —**clown′ish** ***adj.*** —**clown′ish·ly** ***adv.*** —**clown′ish·ness** ***n.***

cloy (kloi) ***vt., vi.*** ⟦aphetic < ME *acloien,* to hamper, harm, obstruct < OFr *encloyer,* to fasten with a nail, hinder < *clou,* a nail < L *clavus,* nail: see CLOSE[2]⟧ to make weary or displeased by too much of something, esp. something sweet, rich, etc. —**SYN.** SATIATE

cloy·ing (kloi′iŋ) ***vt., vi.*** *prp. of* CLOY —***adj.*** **1** displeasing or distasteful because of excess *[cloying* sweetness*]* **2** overly sweet, sentimental, etc. *[a cloying* romance novel*]* —**cloy′ing·ly** ***adv.***

clo·za·pine (klō′zə pēn′) ***n.*** ⟦< C(H)LO(RO)- (sense 2) + altered elements of BENZODIAZEPINE⟧ a synthetic antipsychotic drug, $C_{18}H_{19}ClN_4$, used as a sedative and for severe cases of schizophrenia

cloze (klōz) ***adj.*** ⟦shortened & altered < CLOSURE⟧ designating or of a test of comprehension in which blank spaces at regular intervals in a text must be filled in with appropriate words

CLU *abbrev.* Chartered Life Underwriter

club (klub) ***n.*** ⟦ME *clubbe* < ON *klubba,* cudgel < IE **geleb(h)-* < base **gel-,* form a ball > CLIMB, CALF[1]⟧ **1** *a)* a heavy stick, usually thinner at one end, used as a weapon *b)* anything used to threaten or coerce **2** *a)* GOLF CLUB *b)* INDIAN CLUB **3** a group of people associated for a common purpose or mutual advantage, usually in an organization that meets regularly: see also BOOK CLUB **4** the room, building, or facilities used by such a group **5** *a)* an organization that owns, controls, or sponsors an athletic team *b)* the team playing for or representing such an organization **6** a nightclub **7** *a)* any of a suit of playing cards marked with black figures shaped like a leaf of clover (♣) *b) [pl., with sing. or pl. v.]* this suit of cards ☆**8** *short for* CLUB SANDWICH *[a* turkey *club]* —***vt.*** **clubbed, club′bing 1** to beat or strike as with a club **2** to combine or pool (resources, etc.) for a common purpose **3** to unite for a common purpose **4** to use (a rifle or the like) as a club by hitting with the butt end —***vi.*** **1** to unite or combine for a common purpose **2** [Informal] to patronize or frequent nightclubs —**club′ber** ***n.***

club·ba·ble or **club·a·ble** (klub′ə bəl) ***adj.*** ⟦coined (early 1780s) by Samuel JOHNSON⟧ suited to membership in a club; sociable

club·by (klub′ē) ***adj.*** **-bi·er, -bi·est** [Informal] **1** friendly or sociable, esp. in an effusive way **2** restricted, clannish, or exclusive, as some clubs are

☆**club car** LOUNGE CAR

club chair ⟦from use in private clubs⟧ a large, heavily upholstered armchair, usually with a low back

club fighter a mediocre boxer who fights mostly on programs at small sporting clubs

club·foot (klub′foot′) ***n.*** **1** a congenital deformity of the foot, characterized by a misshapen or twisted appearance; talipes **2** *pl.* **-feet′** (-fēt′) a foot so deformed —**club′foot′ed** ***adj.***

club fungus BASIDIOMYCETE

club·hand (-hand′) ***n.*** **1** a congenital deformity of the hand analogous to clubfoot **2** a hand so deformed

club·haul (-hôl′) ***vt.*** ⟦< naut. *club* (to drift with anchor dragging) + HAUL⟧ to tack (a vessel in a precarious situation) by dropping the lee anchor as soon as the wind is out of the sails, then cutting the cable when the ship swings off onto the new tack

club·head (-hed′) ***n.*** the metal or wooden head of a golf club

club·house (-hous′) ***n.*** **1** a building occupied by or used by a club ☆**2** *a)* a locker room used by an athletic team *b) Baseball* such a room with showers and physical-therapy apparatus **3** an enclosed section of the grandstand at a racetrack with a restaurant and a temperature-controlled environment

club·man (-mən, -man′) ***n.**, pl.* **-men** (-mən, -men′) a man who is a member of, or spends much time at, a private club or clubs

club moss LYCOPOD

club·room (-ro͞om′) ***n.*** a room used by a club as a meeting place or for social affairs

club root a disease of plants of the cabbage family, caused by a slime mold (*Plasmodiophora brassicae*) and characterized by swellings of the roots

☆**club sandwich** a sandwich made of three or more slices of toast with layers of chicken, bacon, lettuce, tomatoes, mayonnaise, etc. between them

club soda SODA WATER

☆**club steak** a small beefsteak cut from the loin tip

☆**club·wom·an** (-woom′ən) ***n.**, pl.* **-wom′en** (-wim′in) a woman member of a club or clubs, esp. one who devotes much time to club activities

cluck (kluk) ***vi.*** ⟦ME *clokken* < OE *cloccian*: orig. echoic⟧ to make a low, sharp, clicking sound, as that of a hen calling her chicks —***vt.*** to utter with such a sound *[to cluck* one's disapproval*]* —***n.*** **1** the sound of clucking ☆**2** [Slang] a dull, stupid person; dolt

clue (klo͞o) ***n.*** ⟦var. of CLEW⟧ something that leads out of a perplexity; esp., a fact or object that helps to solve a problem or mystery —***vt.*** **clued, clu′ing 1** to indicate by or as by a clue ☆**2** [Informal] to provide with the necessary information: often with *in*

clue·less (klo͞o′ləs) ***adj.*** **1** lacking clues or information **2** [Informal] *a)* stupid; obtuse *b)* ignorant or uninformed, specif. regarding a certain situation or matter *[clueless* about baseball*]*

Cluj-Na·po·ca (klo͞ozh′nə pō′kə) city in Transylvania, NW Romania

clum·ber (spaniel) (klum′bər) ⟦after *Clumber,* estate of the Duke of Newcastle⟧ *[also* **C- s-***]* a short-legged spaniel with a heavy body and a thick coat of straight, white hair marked with yellow or orange

clump (klump) ***n.*** ⟦< Du *klomp* or LowG *klump*: for IE base see CLUB⟧ **1** a lump; mass **2** a mass of bacteria **3** a cluster, as of shrubs or trees **4** the sound of heavy footsteps —***vi.*** **1** to walk heavily; tramp **2** to form clumps —***vt.*** **1** to plant in a clump; group together in a cluster **2** to cause to form clumps

clump·y (klum′pē) ***adj.*** **clump′i·er, clump′i·est 1** full of or like clumps **2** heavy and clumsy: also **clump′ish**

clum·sy (klum′zē) ***adj.*** **-si·er, -si·est** ⟦ME *clumsid,* numb with cold, pp. of *clumsen,* to benumb < ON base akin to Swed dial *klummsen,* to benumb with the cold; akin to CLAM: for IE base see CLIMB⟧ **1** lacking grace or skill in movement; awkward **2** awkwardly shaped or made; ill-constructed **3** badly contrived; inelegant *[a clumsy* style*]* —**SYN.** AWKWARD —**clum′si·ly** ***adv.*** —**clum′si·ness** ***n.***

clung (kluŋ) ***vi.*** *pt. & pp. of* CLING

clunk (kluŋk) ***n.*** ⟦echoic⟧ **1** a dull, heavy, hollow sound **2** [Informal] a heavy blow **3** [Slang] a dull or stupid person — ***vi., vt.*** to move or strike with a clunk or clunks

☆**clunk·er** (kluŋk′ər) ***n.*** [Slang] **1** an old machine in poor repair; esp., a noisy, dilapidated automobile **2** a mistake or blunder

clunk·y (kluŋk′ē) ***adj.*** **clunk′i·er, clunk′i·est** [Slang] **1** clumsy or awkward **2** not stylish or attractive **3** making a clunking sound

Clu·ny (klo͞o′nē; *Fr* klü nē′) town in EC France: site of a Benedictine monastery (910-1790)

Cluny lace ⟦after prec.⟧ a heavy bobbin lace with an open design, made of silk and cotton thread

clu·pe·id (klo͞o′pē id′) ***n.*** ⟦< ModL *Clupea* (< L *clupea,* kind of small river fish) + -ID⟧ any of a family (Clupeidae, order Clupeiformes) of soft-finned, bony fishes, as herring or sardines —***adj.*** of this family of fishes

clus·ter (klus′tər) ***n.*** ⟦ME < OE *clyster,* cluster; akin to north Ger dial. *kluster,* CLAW, CLOT⟧ **1** a number of things of the same sort gathered together or growing together; bunch **2** a number of persons, animals, or things grouped together **3** *Phonet.* a group of nonsyllabic phonemes, esp. a group of two or more consecutive consonants — ***vi., vt.*** to gather or grow in a cluster or clusters —**clus′ter·y** ***adj.***

cluster bomb an aerial bomb that explodes in midair and scatters smaller bombs across a wide area

cluster headache a type of recurrent headache characterized by sudden onset and intense pain on one side of the face near the eye

clutch[1] (kluch) ***vt.*** ⟦ME *clucchen* < OE *clyccan,* to clench (infl. in meaning by ME *cloke,* a claw) < IE **glek-* (> CLING) < base **gel-*: see CLIMB⟧ **1** to grasp, seize, or snatch with a hand or claw **2** to grasp or hold eagerly or tightly —***vi.*** **1** to snatch or seize (*at*) **2** to engage the clutch of an automobile, etc. ☆**3** [Informal] to become tense with anxiety, fear, etc.: often with *up* —***n.*** ⟦ME *clucche* < the v.⟧ **1** a claw or hand in the act of seizing **2** *[usually pl.]* power; control **3** *a)* the act of clutching *b)* a grasp; grip **4** *a)* any device, mechanical, electromagnetic, or hydraulic, for engaging or disengaging a DRIVE SHAFT *b)* the lever or pedal, as in an automobile, by which this device is operated **5** a device for gripping and holding, as in a crane **6** a woman's small handbag with no handle or strap, held in the hand: also **clutch bag** ☆**7** [Informal] a critical situation or emergency *[dependable in the clutch]* —☆***adj.*** [Informal] **1** designating or done in a critical situation **2** likely to function well or be successful in such a situation —**SYN.** TAKE

clutch[2] (kluch) ***vt.*** ⟦dial. < ME *clekken* (< ON *klekja*), to hatch⟧ [Rare] to hatch (chicks) —***n.*** **1** a nest of eggs **2** a brood of chicks **3** a number of persons, animals, or things gathered together; cluster

clut·ter (klut′ər) ***n.*** ⟦var. of *clotter* < CLOT⟧ **1** a number of things scattered in disorder; jumble **2** ⟦var. of CLATTER⟧ [Dial.] CLATTER **3** the interference on a radarscope caused by hills, buildings, etc. —***vt.*** to put into disorder; jumble: often with *up* —***vi.*** [Dial.] to make a clatter; bustle —**clut′ter·y** ***adj.***

Clw·yd (klo͞o′id) county in N Wales, on the Irish Sea: 938 sq mi (2,429 sq km)

Clyde[1] (klīd) ***n.*** ⟦< Scot surname *Clyde,* after the River fol.⟧ a masculine name

Clyde[2] (klīd) **1** river in S Scotland, flowing northwestward into the Firth of Clyde: 106 mi (171 km) **2 Firth of** estuary of the Clyde, flowing southward into the North Channel: 64 mi (103 km)

Clydes·dale (klīdz′dāl′) ***n.*** ⟦after *Clydesdale*, the valley of the River prec., where the breed originated⟧ any of a breed of large, heavy draft horse, usually bay, brown, or black with areas of white on the face and shanks and with heavily feathered legs

clyp·e·ate (klip′ē āt′, -it) ***adj.*** ⟦< L *clipeatus*, pp. of *clipeare*, to arm with a shield < *clipeus*, a shield⟧ *Biol.* **1** shaped like a round shield **2** having a shieldlike process

clyp·e·us (klip′ē əs) ***n., pl.*** **clyp′e·i′** (-ē ī′) ⟦ModL < L *clipeus, clupeus*, a shield⟧ a median plate or shieldlike process on the anterior portion of the head of certain insects

clys·ter (klis′tər) ***n.*** ⟦ME *clister* < L *clyster* < Gr *klystēr* < *klyzein*, to wash: see CLOACA⟧ an enema

Cly·tem·nes·tra (klī′təm nes′trə) ***n.*** *Gr. Myth.* the wife of Agamemnon: with the aid of her lover Aegisthus she murders her husband and is in turn killed by their son Orestes

cm *abbrev.* **1** centimeter(s) **2** circular mil **3** common meter **4** court-martial

Cm *Chem. symbol for* curium

CM *abbrev.* Commonwealth of the Marianas

cm^2 *abbrev.* square centimeter(s)

cm^3 *abbrev.* cubic centimeter(s)

CMA *abbrev.* **1** census metropolitan area: census term used in Canada **2** certified medical assistant

cmd *abbrev.* command

cmdg *abbrev.* commanding

Cmdr *abbrev.* Commander

CME *abbrev.* Chicago Mercantile Exchange

CMG *abbrev.* Companion of (the Order of) St. Michael and St. George

cml *abbrev.* commercial

c'mon (kə män′) ***interj.*** [Informal] *phonetic sp. of* COME ON! (in informal pronunciation) (see phrase at COME) used to signify *a)* invitation, often to a different location *[c'mon in; c'mon along]* *b)* encouragement, threat, urging to action, etc. *[c'mon, Bill! you can do it!]* *c)* objection, disagreement, refusal to believe, etc. *[c'mon, you can't be serious!]*

CMSgt *abbrev.* Chief Master Sergeant

CMV *abbrev.* cytomegalovirus

Cn[1] *abbrev.* ⟦L < earlier *Cnaeus*⟧ *Rom. History* Gnaeus (the praenomen)

Cn[2] *Chem. symbol for* copernicium

C/N or **CN** *abbrev.* credit note

CNG *abbrev.* compressed natural gas

cni·dar·i·an (ni der′ē ən) ***n.*** ⟦ModL *Cnidaria* < Gr *knidē*, nettle + -ARIA: so called for the creatures' stinging cells⟧ any of a phylum (Cnidaria) of invertebrate animals, mainly marine, including jellyfishes, hydrozoans, and anthozoans, characterized by stinging cells and a saclike body cavity with a single opening for ingesting food and eliminating wastes; coelenterate

Cni·dus (nī′dəs) ancient Dorian city in Caria, SW Asia Minor: taken by Persians (540 B.C.)

CNN *service mark* Cable News Network

CNO *abbrev.* Chief of Naval Operations

Cnos·sus (näs′əs) *alt. sp. of* KNOSSOS

☆**C-note** (sē′nōt′) ***n.*** ⟦for CENTURY-note⟧ [Slang] a one-hundred-dollar bill

CNS *abbrev.* central nervous system

co *abbrev.* **1** care of **2** *Bookkeeping* carried over **3** company **4** county

Co[1] *abbrev.* **1** Company **2** *Bible* Corinthians **3** County

Co[2] *Chem. symbol for* cobalt

CO *abbrev.* **1** Colorado **2** Commanding Officer **3** conscientious objector

co- (kō) ⟦var. of COM-, orig. occurring only before a vowel, *h*, or *gn*⟧ *prefix* **1** together *[coact]* **2** mutually, equally *[coextensive]* **3** joint or jointly *[copilot, coauthor]* **4** *Math.* complement of *[cosine]*

C/O *abbrev.* **1** cash order **2** care of: also **c/o** **3** *Bookkeeping* carried over

co·ac·er·va·tion (kō as′ər vā′shən) ***n.*** ⟦ME *coacervacioun*, a heaping together < L *coacervatio* < *coacervatus*, pp. of *coacervare*, to heap up < *co-* (see COM-) + *acervare*, to form a heap < *acervus*, a heap⟧ a reversible, emulsoid stage existing between the sol and gel formations, in which the addition of a third substance causes the separation of the sol into two immiscible liquid phases: an essential stage in the formation of proteins, antibodies, etc.

coach (kōch) ***n.*** ⟦Fr *coche* < Ger *kutsche* < Hung *kocsi* (*szekér*), (carriage of) *Kócs*, village in Hungary where it was first used⟧ **1** a large, covered, four-wheeled carriage used formerly as a public conveyance, with seats for passengers inside and an open, raised seat in front for the driver ☆**2** a railroad passenger car **3** the lowest-priced class of accommodations on some aircraft **4** a BUS (sense 1) **5** an enclosed automobile, usually a two-door sedan **6** ⟦orig., university slang⟧ a private tutor who prepares a student in a subject or for an examination **7** an instructor or trainer, as of athletes, actors, or singers ☆**8** *Baseball* a member of the team at bat, stationed near first and near third base to signal and direct the base runners and batters **9** *Sports* the person who is in overall charge of a team and the strategy in games: cf., for baseball, MANAGER (sense *c*): often called **head coach** —***adv.*** in or by means of coach accommodations: see ***n.*** 3 —***vt.*** **1** [Rare] to carry in a coach **2** to instruct in a subject, or prepare for an examination, by private tutoring **3** to instruct and train (athletes, actors, etc.) —***vi.*** **1** to ride in a coach **2** to act as a coach —**coach′a·ble** ***adj.***

coach dog DALMATIAN

coach·man (kōch′mən) ***n., pl.*** **-men** (-mən) the driver of a coach

co·act (kō akt′, kō′akt′) ***vi.*** ⟦CO- + ACT[1]⟧ to work or act together —**co·ac′tive** ***adj.***

co·ac·tion[1] (kō ak′shən, kō′ak′-) ***n.*** ⟦ME *coaccioun* < ML *coactio* < L *coactare*, to constrain, force, freq. of *cogere*: see COGENT⟧ [Now Rare] coercion; force —**co·ac′tive** ***adj.***

co·ac·tion[2] (kō ak′shən, kō′ak′-) ***n.*** ⟦CO- + ACTION⟧ **1** cooperative action **2** *Ecol.* any important interaction between two organisms, as in symbiosis or parasitism

co·ad·ju·tant (kō aj′ə tənt) ***adj.*** ⟦fol. + -ANT⟧ helping each other; cooperating —***n.*** an assistant

co·ad·ju·tor (kō aj′ə tər; *also, and for 2 usually*, kō′ə jo͞ot′ər) ***n.*** ⟦ME < OFr *coadjuteur* < LL *coadjutor* < L *co-*, together + *adjutor*, assistant < *adjuvare*: see AID⟧ **1** an assistant; helper **2** a person, often another bishop, appointed to assist a bishop, often becoming the successor

co·ad·u·nate (kō aj′ə nit, -nāt′) ***adj.*** ⟦LL *coadunatus*, pp. of *coadunare*, to unite < L *co-*, together + *adunare*, to join < *ad-*, to + *unare*, to unite < *unus*, ONE⟧ **1** united; joined together **2** *Biol.* grown together —**co·ad′u·na′tion** ***n.***

co·ag·u·la·ble (kō ag′yo͞o lə bəl, -yə-) ***adj.*** ⟦ML *coagulabilis*⟧ that can be coagulated —**co·ag′u·la·bil′i·ty** ***n.***

co·ag·u·lant (-lənt) ***n.*** ⟦L *coagulans*, prp. of *coagulare*: see COAGULATE⟧ a substance that brings about coagulation

co·ag·u·lase (-lās′) ***n.*** ⟦fol. + -ASE⟧ an enzyme produced by certain bacteria, which causes coagulation of blood plasma

co·ag·u·late (-lāt′) ***vt.*** **-lat′ed**, **-lat′ing** ⟦ME *coagulaten* < L *coagulatus*, pp. of *coagulare*, to cause to curdle < *coagulum*: see fol.⟧ to cause (a liquid) to become a soft, semisolid mass; curdle; clot —***vi.*** to become coagulated —**co·ag′u·la′tion** ***n.*** —**co·ag′u·la′tive** ***adj.*** —**co·ag′u·la′tor** ***n.***

co·ag·u·lum (-ləm) ***n., pl.*** **-la** (-lə) ⟦L *coagulum*, means of coagulation, rennet < *cogere*, to curdle, collect: see COGENT⟧ a clot, curd, or coagulated albuminoid substance

Co·a·hui·la (kō′ə wē′lə) state of N Mexico, on the Texas border: 58,522 sq mi (151,571 sq km); cap. Saltillo

coal (kōl) ***n.*** ⟦ME & OE *col*, charcoal, live coal, akin to Ger *kohle*, ON *kol* < IE base **g(e)u-lo-*, live coal > Ir *gual*⟧ **1** a kind of dark-brown to black, combustible, sedimentary rock resulting from the partial decomposition of vegetable matter away from air and under varying degrees of increased temperature and pressure over a period of millions of years: used as a fuel and in the production of coke, coal gas, water gas, and many coal-tar compounds **2** a piece (or collectively, pieces) of this rock **3** a piece of glowing or charred wood, coal, or similar substance; ember **4** charcoal —***vt.*** **1** to reduce (a substance) to charcoal by burning **2** to provide with coal —***vi.*** to take in a supply of coal —**haul (or rake, drag, or call) over the coals** to criticize sharply; censure; scold —**heap coals of fire on someone's head** to cause someone to feel remorse by returning good for evil: Prov. 25:22

☆**coal car** **1** an open railroad car for transporting coal **2** TENDER[3] (sense 3)

coal·er (kōl′ər) ***n.*** **1** a ship, freight car, etc. for transporting coal **2** a large mechanical apparatus for loading coal as into a ship

co·a·lesce (kō′ə les′) ***vi.*** **-lesced′**, **-lesc′ing** ⟦L *coalescere* < *co-*, together + *alescere*, to grow up: see ADOLESCENT⟧ **1** to grow together, as the halves of a broken bone **2** to unite or merge into a single body, group, or mass —***SYN.*** MIX —**co′a·les′cence** (-les′əns) ***n.*** —**co′a·les′cent** ***adj.***

coal·fish (kōl′fish′) ***n., pl.*** **-fish′** or **-fish′es** (see FISH) **1** a dark-colored pollock fish (*Pollachius virens*) **2** any of various other dark-colored fishes

coal gas **1** a gas produced by the destructive distillation of bituminous coal: used for lighting and heating **2** a poisonous gas given off by burning coal

coal·i·fi·ca·tion (kōl′ə fi kā′shən) ***n.*** ⟦COAL + -I- + -FICATION⟧ the process by which vegetable matter is transformed into coal

coaling station a place where ships or trains take on coal

co·a·li·tion (kō′ə lish′ən) ***n.*** ⟦ML *coalitio* < LL *coalitus*, fellowship, orig. pp. of *coalescere*: see COALESCE⟧ **1** a combination; union **2** an alliance of factions, nations, etc., for some specific purpose, as of political parties in times of national emergency —***SYN.*** ALLIANCE —**co′a·li′tion·ist** ***n.***

coal measures **1** coal beds or strata **2** sedimentary Carboniferous rocks that include coal-bearing strata

☆**coal oil** **1** kerosene or any other oil obtained by fractional distillation of petroleum **2** crude petroleum **3** unrefined oil, obtained by destructive distillation of coal: used as a lamp fuel

Coal·sack (kōl′sak′) ***n.*** *Astron.* a prominent dark nebula in the Milky Way near the constellation Crux: usually with *the*: sometimes written **Coal Sack**

coal tar a black, thick, opaque liquid obtained by the destructive distillation of bituminous coal, used in making dyes, medicines, plastics, paints, etc.

coal·y (kōl′ē) ***adj.*** **coal′i·er**, **coal′i·est** **1** full of coal **2** of or like coal; esp., black

coam·ing (kōm′iŋ) ***n.*** ⟦17th c. < ?⟧ a raised border around a hatchway, roof opening, etc., to keep out water

co-an·chor (kō′aŋ′kər, kō aŋ′kər) ***n.*** one of the usually two anchors for a radio or TV newscast — ***vi., vt.*** to act as a co-anchor (of)

co·ap·ta·tion (kō′ap tā′shən) ***n.*** ⟦LL(Ec) *coaptatio*, an accurate joining together < *coaptare*, to fit, adjust < L *co-*, together + *aptare*, to fit, adapt, freq. of *apere*, to fasten (see APT[1]): coined by St. AUGUSTINE[2] of Hippo to transl. Gr *harmonia*: see HARMONY⟧ the joining or adjusting of parts to each other, as of the ends of a broken bone

co·arc·tate (kō ärk′tāt′) ***adj.*** ⟦< L *coarctatus*, pp. of *coarctare*, to press together < *co-*, together + *artare*, to press together < *artus*, fitted, narrow < *artus*, a joint (see ART[1]): sp. infl. by assoc. with *arcere*, to enclose⟧ *Biol.* **1** compressed or constricted **2** rigidly enclosed in the last larval skin: said of certain insect pupae —**co′arc·ta′tion** ***n.***

coarse (kôrs) *adj.* **coars′er, coars′est** ⟦specialized var. of COURSE in sense of "ordinary or usual order," as in *of course*⟧ **1** of inferior or poor quality; common *[coarse* fare*]* **2** consisting of rather large elements or particles *[coarse* sand*]* **3** not fine or delicate in texture, structure, form, etc.; rough; harsh *[coarse* features, *coarse* cloth*]* **4** for rough or crude work or results *[a coarse* file, *coarse* measurements*]* **5** lacking in refinement or good taste; vulgar; crude *[a coarse* joke*]* —**coarse′ly** *adv.* —**coarse′ness** *n.*

SYN.—**coarse**, in this comparison, implies such a lack of refinement in manners or speech as to be offensive to one's aesthetic or moral sense *[coarse* laughter*]*; **gross** suggests a brutish crudeness or roughness *[gross* table manners*]*; **indelicate** suggests a verging on impropriety or immodesty *[an indelicate* remark*]*; **vulgar**, in this connection, emphasizes a lack of proper training, culture, or good taste *[the vulgar* ostentation of her home*]*; **obscene** is used of that which is offensive to decency or modesty and implies lewdness *[obscene* gestures*]*; **ribald** suggests such mild indecency or lewdness as might bring laughter from those who are not too squeamish *[ribald* jokes *]* —ANT. **refined**

coarse fishing 1 [Chiefly Brit.] fishing for any nonsalmonid, freshwater fish (**coarse fish**) **2** fishing for ROUGH FISH

coarse·grained (kôrs′grānd′) *adj.* **1** having a coarse texture **2** lacking in refinement or delicacy; crude Also written **coarse-grained**

coars·en (kôr′sən) *vt., vi.* to make or become coarse

coast (kōst) *n.* ⟦ME *coste*, coast < OFr, a rib, hill, shore, coast < L *costa*, a rib, side⟧ **1** land alongside the sea; seashore **2** [Obs.] frontier; borderland ☆**3** ⟦< CdnFr, hillside, slope⟧ an incline down which a slide is taken ☆**4** a slide or ride, as on a sled going down an incline by the force of gravity —*vi.* **1** to sail near or along a coast, esp. from port to port ☆**2** to go down an incline, as on a sled ☆**3** to continue in motion on momentum or by the force of gravity after propelling power has stopped ☆**4** to continue without serious effort, letting one's past efforts carry one along —*vt.* to sail along or near the coast of —SYN. SHORE[1] —**the Coast** ☆[Informal] in the U.S., the Pacific coast —**the coast is clear** there is no apparent danger of being caught or observed

coast·al (kōs′təl) *adj.* of, at, near, or along a coast

coast·er (kōs′tər) *n.* **1** a person or thing that coasts **2** a ship that carries cargo or passengers from port to port along a coast ☆**3** a sled or wagon for coasting **4** ⟦< obs. sense of *coast*, vi., "to pass close to or around"⟧ a small tray, usually on wheels, as for passing a wine decanter around a table **5** a small tray, mat, or disk placed under a glass or bottle to protect a table or other surface ☆**6** *short for* ROLLER COASTER (sense 1)

☆**coaster brake** a brake in the freewheel mechanism of certain bicycles, operated by reversing pressure on the pedals

coast guard 1 *a)* a governmental force employed to defend a nation's coasts, prevent smuggling, aid vessels in distress, maintain lighthouses, etc. ☆*b)* [**C- G-**] the UNITED STATES COAST GUARD **2** a member of a coast guard —**coast guards·man** (gärdz′mən), *pl.* **-men** (-mən), **coast guard·man** (gärd′mən), *pl.* **-men** (-mən)

coast·land (kōst′land′) *n.* land along a coast

coast·line (-līn′) *n.* the contour or outline of a coast

Coast Mountains mountain range in W British Columbia & S Alas.; N continuation of the Cascade Range: highest peak, 13,260 ft (4,042 m)

Coast Ranges series of mountain ranges along the W coast of North America, extending from Alas. to Baja California: highest peak, Mt. Logan

coast·ward (-wərd) *adj., adv.* toward the coast: also **coast′wards** (-wərdz) *adv.*

coast·wise (-wīz′) *adv., adj.* along and near the coast: also **coast′ways′** (-wāz′) *adv.*

coat (kōt) *n.* ⟦ME *cote*, a coat < OFr < Frank **kotta*, coarse cloth; akin to Ger *kotze*, shaggy overcoat⟧ **1** a sleeved outer garment opening down the front and varying in length, as a suit jacket or a topcoat or overcoat **2** a natural outer covering of an animal, as of fur or wool **3** the outer covering of a plant or animal structure, tissue, etc. *[a seed coat]* **4** a layer of some substance, as paint, over a surface **5** [Dial.] a petticoat or skirt **6** [Obs.] customary garb of a profession or class —*vt.* **1** to provide or cover with a coat **2** to cover with a layer of something —**coat′ed** *adj.*

coat·dress (kōt′dres′) *n.* a coatlike dress having a buttoned front and, usually, lapels and long sleeves

coated paper a paper whose surface has been treated to take halftone impressions or color printing

coat hanger HANGER (*n.* 4*b*)

co·a·ti (kō ät′ē) *n., pl.* **-tis** ⟦Tupí < *cua*, a cincture + *tim*, the nose: so called from appearance of its snout⟧ any of a genus (*Nasua*) of small, tree-dwelling, raccoonlike carnivores with a long, flexible snout, found in Mexico and Central and South America

co·a·ti-mun·di or **co·a·ti-mon·di** (-mun′dē) *n., pl.* **-di** or **-dis** ⟦Tupí < prec. + *mondi*, solitary⟧ COATI

coat·ing (kōt′iŋ) *n.* **1** a coat or layer over a surface *[a coating* of enamel*]* **2** cloth for making coats

coat of arms *pl.* **coats of arms** ⟦transl. of Fr *cotte d'armes*, light garment worn over armor, generally blazoned with heraldic arms⟧ a group of emblems and figures (heraldic bearings) usually arranged on and around a shield and serving as the special insignia of some person, family, or institution

coat of mail *pl.* **coats of mail** ⟦transl. of Fr *cotte de mailles*, lit., coat of meshes⟧ a sleeved protective garment made of interlinked metal rings or overlapping plates

coat rack 1 a rack, often wall-mounted, or upright pole fitted with branching hooks or pegs on which to hang coats, hats, etc. **2** a rack with tubular bars for holding garments on hangers, as in a cloakroom Sometimes written **coat′rack′** *n.*

coat·room (kōt′ro͞om′) *n.* CLOAKROOM

coat·tail (kōt′tāl′) *n.* the back part of a coat below the waist; esp., either half of this part when divided, as on a swallow-tailed coat —☆**ride (**or **hang**, etc.**) on someone's coattails** to have one's success dependent on that of someone else

coat-trail·ing (kōt′trā′liŋ) *n.* ⟦< notion of *trailing one's coat*, daring someone to step on it⟧ [Brit.] provocative or contentious writing, speech, behavior, etc.

Co·at·za·co·al·cos (kō ät′sə kō äl′kōs′) city in EC Mexico, in Veracruz state

co·au·thor (kō′ô′thər, kō ô′thər) *n.* a joint author; collaborator —*vt.* to be a coauthor of

coax[1] (kōks) *vt.* ⟦orig. slang, "to make a *coax* of" < obs. slang *coax, cox, cokes*, a fool, ninny⟧ **1** to induce or try to induce to do something; (seek to) persuade by soothing words, an ingratiating manner, etc.; wheedle **2** to get by coaxing —*vi.* to use gentle persuasion, urging, etc. —**coax′er** *n.* —**coax′ing·ly** *adv.*

SYN.—**coax** suggests repeated attempts to persuade someone to do something and implies the use of soothing words, an ingratiating manner, etc.; **cajole** suggests the use of flattery or other blandishments; **wheedle** implies even more strongly the use of subtle flattery or craftily artful behavior in gaining one's ends

co·ax[2] (kō′aks′) *adj. short for* COAXIAL (sense 3) —*n.* a coaxial cable

co·ax·i·al (kō ak′sē əl) *adj.* ⟦CO- + AXIAL⟧ **1** having a common axis: also **co·ax′al** (-ak′səl) **2** designating a compound speaker consisting of a smaller unit mounted within and connected with a larger one on a common axis: the smaller unit reproduces the higher frequencies, beyond the range of the larger ☆**3** designating a high-frequency transmission line or cable in which a solid or stranded central conductor is surrounded by an insulating medium which, in turn, is surrounded by a solid or braided outside conductor in the form of a cylindrical shell: it is used for sending telephone, telegraph, television, etc. impulses

cob (käb) *n.* ⟦ME, prob. < LowG, as in Du *kobbe* < Gmc base **kubb-*, something rounded⟧ **1** [Brit. Dial.] *a)* a lump or small mass, as of coal *b)* a leader; chief ☆**2** a corncob **3** a male swan **4** a short-legged, thickset riding horse

co·bal·a·min (kō bal′ə min) *n.* vitamin B_{12}

co·balt (kō′bôlt′) *n.* ⟦Ger *kobalt*: so named (*c.* 1730) by Georg Brandt (1694-1768), Swed chemist < Ger *kobold*, lit., goblin; term used for the ore by miners, who regarded it as worthless and as injurious because of its arsenic content⟧ a hard, lustrous, steel-gray, ductile, metallic chemical element, found in various ores: it is used in the preparation of magnetic, wear-resistant, and high-strength alloys: its compounds are used in the production of inks, paints, and varnishes: symbol, Co; at. no. 27: a radioactive isotope (**cobalt-60**) is used in the treatment of cancer, in research, etc.: see the periodic table of elements in the Reference Supplement

cobalt blue 1 a dark-blue pigment consisting of a mixture of cobalt and aluminum oxides **2** dark blue

co·bal·tic (kō bôl′tik) *adj.* **1** of cobalt **2** of or containing trivalent cobalt

co·balt·ite (kō′bôl tīt′) *n.* a hard, silver-white mineral, CoAsS, that is an ore of cobalt; cobalt arsenic sulfide: also called **cobalt glance**

co·bal·tous (kō bôl′təs) *adj.* of or containing divalent cobalt

Cobb (käb), **Ty(rus Raymond)** (tī) 1886-1961; U.S. baseball player

cob·ber (käb′ər) *n.* ⟦prob. < Heb (via Yiddish) *chaver*, comrade⟧ [Austral. Slang] a close companion; comrade

Cob·bett (käb′it), **William** (pseud. *Peter Porcupine*) 1762?-1835; Eng. journalist & political reformer

cob·ble[1] (käb′əl) *vt.* **-bled, -bling** ⟦ME < *cobelere*, COBBLER[2]⟧ **1** to mend or patch (shoes, etc.) **2** to make or compose hastily or clumsily; improvise: often with *up* or *together*

cob·ble[2] (käb′əl) *n.* ⟦prob. < COB⟧ **1** a cobblestone **2** [*pl.*] COB COAL —*vt.* **-bled, -bling** to pave with cobblestones

☆**cob·bler**[1] (käb′lər) *n.* ⟦< ?⟧ **1** an iced drink containing wine, whiskey, or rum with citrus fruit, sugar, etc. **2** a deep-dish fruit pie, usually with a thick top crust of biscuit dough

cob·bler[2] (käb′lər) *n.* ⟦ME *cobelere* < ?⟧ **1** a person whose work is mending shoes or making shoes to order **2** [Archaic] a clumsy, bungling workman

cob·ble·stone (käb′əl stōn′) *n.* ⟦ME *cobel ston*: see COBBLE[2] & STONE⟧ a rounded stone larger than a pebble and smaller than a boulder, formerly much used for paving streets

Cobb salad (käb) ⟦after R. H. *Cobb* (1899-1970), U.S. restaurateur credited with its creation⟧ *[also* **c- s-***]* a salad consisting typically of chopped lettuce, chicken, cheddar, hard-boiled eggs, bacon, and avocado mixed with a vinaigrette dressing and topped with blue cheese

cob coal ⟦see COB⟧ coal in large, rounded lumps

Cob·den (käb′dən), **Richard** 1804-65; Eng. economist & statesman: advocate of free trade

co·bel·lig·er·ent (kō′bə lij′ər ənt) *n.* a nation associated but not formally allied with another or others in waging war

Cob·ham (käb′əm), Lord *see* OLDCASTLE

☆**co·bi·a** (kō′bē ə) *n.* ⟦< ?⟧ a large, voracious percoid game fish (*Rachycen-*

tron canadum) found in warm seas: it has a conspicuous black stripe along each side of the body

co·ble (kō′bəl, käb′əl) ***n.*** ⟦ME *cobel* < OE *cuopel*, prob. < Celt, as in Welsh *ceubal*, Bret *caubal* (> ? L *caupulus*)⟧ **1** a small fishing boat with a lug sail, a deeper draft at the bow than at the stern, and a large rudder, used off the northeast coast of England **2** in Scotland, a short, flat-bottomed rowboat

Co·blenz (kō′blents′) *alt. sp. of* KOBLENZ

cob·nut (käb′nut′) ***n.*** ⟦see COB⟧ FILBERT

COBOL (kō′bôl′) ***n.*** ⟦*co(mmon) b(usiness) o(riented) l(anguage)*⟧ a computer language employing English words, used in business applications: also written **Cobol**

co·bra (kō′brə) ***n.*** ⟦< Port *cobra (de capello)*, serpent (of the hood) < L *colubra*, a snake: see COLON¹⟧ **1** any of several genera (esp. *Naja*) of very poisonous elapine snakes of Asia and Africa, having around the neck loose skin which is expanded into a hood when the snake is excited **2** leather made of the skin of this snake

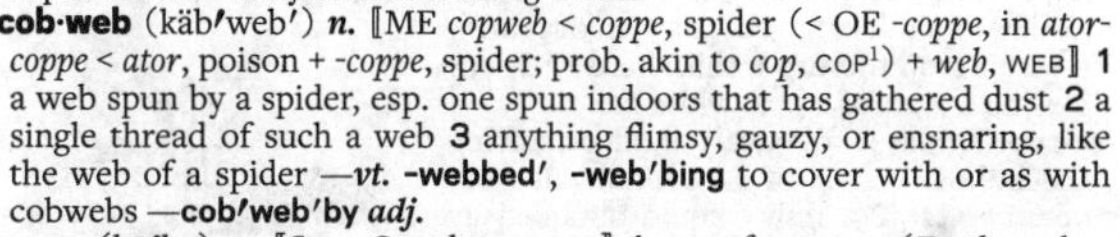
Indian cobra

COBRA (kō′brə) *abbrev.* Consolidated Omnibus Budget Reconciliation Act: the U.S. law that concerns the continuation of group healthcare benefits after termination of employment

cobra de ca·pel·lo (dē kə pel′ō) *pl.* **cobras de capello** ⟦see COBRA⟧ a varicolored cobra (*Naja naja*), esp. of India, with an eyelike marking on the hood

co-brand (kō′brand′) ***vt.*** to market (a product) under two or more brand names

Co·burg (kō′burg′) city in central Germany, in the state of Bavaria: 19th-cent. capital of the duchy of Saxe-Coburg-Gotha

cob·web (käb′web′) ***n.*** ⟦ME *copweb* < *coppe*, spider (< OE *-coppe*, in *atorcoppe* < *ator*, poison + *-coppe*, spider; prob. akin to *cop*, COP¹) + *web*, WEB⟧ **1** a web spun by a spider, esp. one spun indoors that has gathered dust **2** a single thread of such a web **3** anything flimsy, gauzy, or ensnaring, like the web of a spider —***vt.*** **-webbed′**, **-web′bing** to cover with or as with cobwebs —**cob′web′by** ***adj.***

co·ca (kō′kə) ***n.*** ⟦Sp < Quechuan *cuca*⟧ **1** any of a genus (*Erythroxylon*, esp. *E. coca*) of tropical, mostly American shrubs of the coca family, whose dried leaves are the source of cocaine and other alkaloids **2** these dried leaves —***adj.*** designating a family (Erythroxylaceae, order Linales) of dicotyledonous shrubs and trees

co·caine (kō kān′, kō′kān′) ***n.*** ⟦prec. + -INE³⟧ a crystalline alkaloid, $C_{17}H_{21}NO_4$, obtained from dried coca leaves: it was once much used in medicine and dentistry to lessen pain, but it is habit-forming when used as a stimulant

co·cain·ism (kō kān′iz′əm) ***n.*** a diseased condition resulting from excessive or habitual use of cocaine

co·cain·ize (kō kān′īz′) ***vt.*** **-ized′**, **-iz′ing** to anesthetize with cocaine

-coc·cal (käk′əl) *combining form forming adjectives* of or produced by a (specified kind of) coccus [*gonococcal*]: also **-coc′cic′** (-sik′)

coc·ci (käk′sī′) ***n.*** *pl. of* COCCUS

coc·cid (käk′sid′) ***n.*** ⟦< ModL *Coccidae* < Gr *kokkis*, dim. of *kokkos*, berry⟧ any of a family (Coccidae) of scale insects, usually with a soft, waxy outer covering

☆**coc·cid·i·oi·do·my·co·sis** (käk sid′ē oi′dō mī kō′sis) ***n.*** ⟦< ModL *Coccidioides* + MYCOSIS⟧ an infectious disease of people and animals, caused by a fungus (*Coccidioides immitis*) and characterized by respiratory difficulties, fever, and, rarely, skin eruptions

coc·cid·i·o·sis (käk sid′ē ō′sis) ***n.*** ⟦ModL < *coccidium*, little berry + -OSIS⟧ a contagious intestinal disease of domestic and wild animals, birds, and, rarely, people, caused by members of an order (Coccidia) of sporozoans living as parasites in the intestines

-coc·coid (käk′oid′) *combining form forming adjectives* like a (specified kind of) coccus [*staphylococcoid*]

coc·co·lith (käk′ə lith′) ***n.*** ⟦< ModL *coccus* (see fol.) + -LITH⟧ a minute calcareous plate covering the body of certain golden algae (division Chromophycota)

coc·cus (käk′əs) ***n.***, *pl.* **coc·ci** (käk′sī′) ⟦ModL < Gr *kokkos*, a kernel, seed, berry⟧ **1** a bacterium of a spherical shape **2** any of the carpels, containing one seed, into which compound fruits split when ripe —**coc′coid′** ***adj.***

-coc·cus (käk′əs) *combining form forming nouns* coccus: used in names of various bacteria [*gonococcus*]

coc·cyx (käk′siks′) ***n.***, *pl.* **coc·cy·ges** (käk sī′jēz′) ⟦L, cuckoo < Gr *kokkyx* (< *kokku*, echoic of its cry): so called because shaped like a cuckoo's beak⟧ a small, triangular bone at the lower end of the vertebral column, formed by the fusion of four rudimentary vertebrae and articulating with the sacrum —**coc·cyg′e·al** (-sij′ē əl) ***adj.***

coch *abbrev.* ⟦L *cochleare*⟧ *Pharmacy* a spoonful

Co·cha·bam·ba (kō′chə bäm′bə) city in central Bolivia

co-chair (kō cher′; *also, for v.* kō′cher′) ***n.*** a person who chairs a committee, meeting, etc. jointly with another or others —***vt.*** to preside at or over as a co-chair

Co·chin (kō′chin′, käch′in) ***n.*** ⟦after fol., place of orig.⟧ [*also* **c-**] any of an Asian breed of large domestic fowl with black, buff, white, or gray plumage and thickly feathered legs: also called **Cochin China**

Cochin China historic region and former French colony in SE Indochina: the S part of Vietnam

coch·i·neal (käch′ə nēl′, käch′ə nēl′) ***n.*** ⟦Fr *cochenille*, prob. < L *coccinus*, scarlet-colored < *coccum*, a berry, scarlet: see COCCUS⟧ a red dye made from the dried bodies of female cochineal insects: used, esp. formerly, in coloring foods, cosmetics, etc.: see LAKE²

cochineal insect any of a family (Dactylopiidae) of scale insects, esp. one (*Dactylopius coccus*) that has a brilliant-red bodily fluid, feeds on certain cactuses, is found chiefly in Mexico, and was formerly much used as a source of cochineal

Co·chise (kō chēs′) 1815?-74; Apache Indian chief

coch·le·a (käk′lē ə, kōk′lē ə) ***n.***, *pl.* **-le·ae′** (-lē ē′) or **-le·as** ⟦ModL < L < Gr *kochlias*, snail, snail shell < *kochlos*, shellfish; akin to *konchē*: see CONCH⟧ the spiral-shaped part of the inner ear, containing the cochlear nerve endings —**coch′le·ar** (-lē ər) ***adj.***

cochlear implant an electronic device surgically implanted in the cochlea, used to improve the hearing of a hearing-impaired person by converting sound waves into impulses that are sent directly to the auditory nerve

cochlear nerve the branch of the auditory nerve that connects with the cochlea and transmits impulses to the hearing center of the brain

coch·le·ate (-lē āt′, -it) ***adj.*** ⟦ModL < L *cochleatus*, spiral-shaped: see COCHLEA⟧ shaped like the shell of a snail: also **coch′le·at′ed** (-lē āt′əd)

cock¹ (käk) ***n.*** ⟦ME *cok* < OE *coc* & OFr *coq*, like Dan *kok*, ON *kokkr*, of echoic orig.⟧ **1** *a)* the male of the chicken; rooster *b)* the male of certain other birds **2** [Archaic] *a)* the crowing of a rooster, esp. at sunrise *b)* cockcrow **3** a woodcock **4** a weather vane in the shape of a rooster; weathercock **5** a leader or chief, esp. one with some boldness or arrogance **6** a faucet or valve for regulating the flow of a liquid or gas **7** *a)* the hammer of a firearm *b)* the position of such a hammer when set for firing **8** a tilting or turning upward, as of the eye or ear **9** a jaunty, erect position [the *cock* of a hat] **10** [Slang] the penis: considered vulgar by many —***vt.*** **1** to tilt or set (a hat, etc.) jauntily on one side **2** to raise to an erect position [a dog *cocks* his ears] **3** to tilt or turn (the eye or ear) toward something **4** *a)* to set the hammer of (a gun) in firing position *b)* to set (a tripping device, as for the shutter of a camera) ready to be released **5** to draw back (one's fist, arm, etc.) ready to strike —***vi.*** **1** to assume an erect or tilted position **2** [Archaic] to behave in a cocky way; strut

cock² (käk) ***n.*** ⟦ME *cokke*, akin to ON *køkkr*, Dan *kok*, a pile < IE **quqā-* < base **gēu-*: see COG¹⟧ a small, cone-shaped pile, as of hay —***vt.*** to pile in cocks

cock·ade (käk ād′) ***n.*** ⟦Fr *cocarde* < OFr *coq*, a cock: from resemblance to its comb⟧ a rosette, knot of ribbon, etc. worn on the hat as a badge —**cock·ad′ed** ***adj.***

cock-a-doo·dle-doo (käk′ə do͞od′'l do͞o′) ***n.*** ⟦echoic⟧ *a conventionalized term for* the crow of a rooster

cock-a-hoop (käk′ə ho͞op′) ***adj.*** ⟦Fr *coq à huppe*, cock with a crest⟧ [Informal, Chiefly Brit.] **1** in very high spirits; elated; exultant **2** boastful; conceited

Cock·aigne (käk ān′) ***n.*** ⟦ME *cokaygne* < OFr *(pais de) cocaigne*, (land of) sugar cake < MLowG *kokenje*, sugar cake, cookie < *koke*, cake; akin to CAKE, Ger *kuchen*⟧ *Medieval Legend* an imaginary land of luxurious and idle living

cock-a-leek·ie (käk′ə lē′kē) ***n.*** ⟦var. of *cocky-leeky* < *cocky*, dim. of COCK¹ + *leeky*, dim. of LEEK⟧ [Scot.] a soup made by boiling chicken with leeks

cock·a·lo·rum (käk′ə lôr′əm) ***n.*** ⟦pseudo L extension of COCK¹; infl. by Du *kockeloeren*, to crow⟧ **1** a little man with an exaggerated idea of his own importance **2** boastful talk; crowing

☆**cock·a·ma·mie** (käk′ə mā′mē) ***adj.*** ⟦alteration of DECALCOMANIA, prob. infl. by *cock-a-nee-nee*, 19th-c. name in New York for a cheap molasses candy⟧ [Slang] **1** of poor quality; inferior **2** silly; ridiculous

cock-and-bull story (käk′ən bo͝ol′) ⟦for earlier *cockalane* < Fr *(saillir du) coq en l'âne*, lit., (to jump from) the cock to the donkey⟧ an absurd, improbable story

cock·a·poo (käk′ə po͞o′) ***n.***, *pl.* **-poos′** ⟦< COCKER¹ + POODLE⟧ a dog crossbred from a cocker spaniel and a poodle

cock·a·tiel or **cock·a·teel** (käk′ə tēl′, käk′ə tēl′) ***n.*** ⟦Du *kaketielje*, dim. of *kaketoe*: see fol.⟧ a small, crested Australian parrot (*Nymphicus hollandicus*) with a long tail and yellow head

cock·a·too (käk′ə to͞o′, käk′ə to͞o′) ***n.***, *pl.* **-toos′** ⟦Du *kaketoe* < Malay *kakatua*; prob. echoic in orig., but < ? *kakak*, brother, sister + *tua*, old; sp. infl. by COCK¹⟧ any of a number of crested parrots (esp. genus *Cacatua*) of Australia and the East Indies, usually with predominantly white plumage, often tinged with yellow or pink

cock·a·trice (käk′ə tris′) ***n.*** ⟦*cocatrice* < OFr *cocatris*, crocodile < LL *calcatrix*, she who treads < *calcare*, to tread < *calx*, heel: see CALCAR⟧ **1** a mythical serpent hatched from a cock's egg and having power to kill by a look **2** *Bible* (KJV) an unidentified deadly serpent

cock·boat (käk′bōt′) ***n.*** ⟦ME *cokbote* < *cok*, ship's boat (< Anglo-Fr *coque* < Du *kogghe* < VL *cocca* < ? L *concha*: see CONCH) + *bote*, BOAT⟧ [Now Rare] a small boat propelled by oars, esp. one used as a ship's tender

cock·chaf·er (käk′chāf′ər) ***n.*** ⟦COCK¹ (? because of size) + CHAFER⟧ any of several large European scarab beetles whose grubs live in the soil and feed on the roots of plants

Cock·croft (käk′krôft′), Sir **John Douglas** 1897-1967; Eng. nuclear physicist

cock·crow (käk′krō′) *n.* the time when roosters begin to crow; early morning; dawn: also **cock′crow′ing**

cocked hat 1 a three-cornered hat with a turned-up brim 2 a hat pointed in front and in back and with the crown rising to a point —**knock into a cocked hat** [Slang] to damage or spoil completely

cock·er[1] (käk′ər) *n.* 1 COCKER SPANIEL 2 a person who breeds or trains fighting cocks

cock·er[2] (käk′ər) *vt.* ⟦ME *cokeren* < ?⟧ to coddle; pamper

cock·er[3] (käk′ər) *n.* [Slang] a man, esp. an old one: a jocular or derogatory term: often used with *old*

cock·er·el (käk′ər əl) *n.* ⟦dim. of COCK[1]⟧ a young rooster, less than a year old

cocker spaniel ⟦from its use in hunting *(wood)cock*⟧ any of a breed of small spaniels with a compact body, short legs, long, silky hair, and long, drooping ears

cock·eye (käk′ī′) *n.* ⟦COCK[1], *vi.* + EYE⟧ a squinting eye

cock·eyed (-īd′) *adj.* 1 cross-eyed 2 [Slang] *a)* tilted to one side; crooked; awry *b)* silly; ridiculous; foolish *c)* drunk

cock·fight (käk′fīt′) *n.* a fight between gamecocks, usually wearing metal spurs on the legs, with informal betting on the outcome and with prize money awarded to the owner of the winner: cockfights are illegal in the U.S. —**cock′fight′ing** *n.*

cock·horse (käk′hôrs′, käk′hôrs′) *n.* ⟦16th c., toy horse⟧ 1 ROCKING HORSE 2 HOBBYHORSE (sense 2)

cock·i·ly (käk′ə lē) *adv.* [Informal] in a cocky manner

cock·i·ness (käk′ē nis) *n.* [Informal] the quality of being cocky

cock·le[1] (käk′əl) *n.* ⟦ME *cokel* < OFr *coquille*, a blister, shell, cockle, altered (infl. by *coq*, COCK[1]) < L *conchylium* < Gr *konchylion*, shellfish < *konchē*: see CONCH⟧ 1 any of a family (Cardiidae) of edible, marine bivalve mollusks with two heart-shaped, radially ridged shells 2 a cockleshell 3 a wrinkle; pucker — *vi., vt.* **-led**, **-ling** ⟦Fr *coquiller* < the n.⟧ to wrinkle; pucker —**warm the cockles of someone's heart** ⟦prob. < L *cochlea*, winding cavity, lit., snail: see COCHLEA⟧ to make someone feel pleased or cheerful

cock·le[2] (käk′əl) *n.* ⟦ME *cokkel* < OE *coccel*, darnel, tares⟧ any of various weeds that grow in grainfields, as the corn cockle

☆**cock·le·bur** (-bur′) *n.* any of a genus (*Xanthium*) of coarse plants of the composite family, bearing closed burs and growing commonly as a weed

cock·le·shell (-shel′) *n.* 1 the shell of a cockle 2 loosely, any bivalve shell of a marine mollusk 3 any small, usually fragile, lightweight boat

cock·loft (käk′lôft′) *n.* ⟦orig., lit. or fig., a loft where cocks roost⟧ a small loft, attic, or garret

cock·ney (käk′nē) [*often* **C-**] *n., pl.* **-neys** ⟦ME *cokenei*, spoiled child, milksop; understood as *coken-ey*, lit., cock's egg < *coken* (OE *cocena*, gen. pl.), of cocks + *ey* (OE *æg*), egg; ? infl. by Fr *acoquiné*, idle, spoiled (< *coquin*, rascal)⟧ 1 a person born in the East End of London, England, traditionally one born within the sound of "Bow Bells" (i.e., the bells of St. Mary-le-Bow) and speaking a characteristic dialect 2 this dialect, characterized by extreme diphthongization, loss of the initial (h) sound, and use of an intrusive (r) 3 loosely, any person born or living in London: a humorous or disparaging usage —*adj.* of or like cockneys or their dialect —**cock′ney·ish** *adj.*

cock·ney·fy (käk′nē fī′, -ni-) *vt.* **-fied′**, **-fy′ing** to give a cockney quality to (one's speech, manner, etc.)

cock·ney·ism (käk′nē iz′əm) *n.* an idiom, pronunciation, quality, etc. characteristic of cockneys

cock of the walk a dominating person, esp. an overbearing one, in any group

cock·pit (käk′pit′) *n.* 1 an enclosed circular area for cockfights 2 a place where there have been many battles 3 a sunken space in the deck of a boat, usually toward the stern and for use by the helmsman 4 the space in a small airplane for the pilot and, sometimes, passengers, or in a large airplane for the pilot and copilot or crew 5 the driver's seat in a racing car 6 [Historical] the quarters of junior officers on a sailing warship, used for the treatment of the wounded during a battle 7 [Obs.] the pit of a theater

cock·roach (käk′rōch′) *n.* ⟦Sp *cucaracha*, wood louse, cockroach, altered by assoc. with COCK[1] + ROACH[1]⟧ any of an order (Blattaria) of insects with long antennae and a flat, soft body: some species are common household pests

cocks·comb (käks′kōm′) *n.* 1 the red, fleshy growth on the head of a rooster 2 *alt. sp. of* COXCOMB 3 an ornamental plant (*Celosia cristata*) of the amaranth family, with red or yellow flower heads somewhat suggestive of a rooster's crest

cock·shut (käk′shut′) *n.* ⟦COCK[1] + SHUT: prob. in ref. to the time when poultry are shut in for the night⟧ [Now Brit. Dial.] evening twilight

cock·shy (käk′shī′) *n., pl.* **-shies′** ⟦COCK[1] + SHY[2]⟧ 1 a throw at a mark 2 the mark aimed at

☆**cocks·man** (käks′mən) *n., pl.* **-men** (-mən) [Slang] a man with a reputation for great sexual virility and for his many successes as a seducer: somewhat vulgar

cock·spur (käk′spur′) *n.* 1 the spur of a rooster 2 a hawthorn (*Crataegus crusgalli*) having long thorns

cock·suck·er (käk′suk′ər) *n.* [Vulgar Slang] 1 one who performs fellatio 2 a person regarded as despicable, disgusting, etc.

cock·sure (käk′shoor′) *adj.* ⟦COCK[1] + SURE⟧ 1 absolutely sure or certain 2 sure or self-confident in a stubborn or overbearing way —**cock′sure′ness** *n.*

cock·swain (käk′sən, -swān′) *n. alt. sp. of* COXSWAIN

cock·tail[1] (käk′tāl′) *n.* ⟦< ?⟧ ☆1 any of various alcoholic drinks made of a distilled liquor mixed as with wine, fruit juice, or soda water and usually iced ☆2 an appetizer served at the beginning of a meal, as fruit juice, tomato juice, diced fruits, or seafood with a sharp sauce 3 any combination or collection of ingredients, esp. one of ingredients regarded as incompatible or markedly different 4 *Med.* a medication, typically liquid, consisting of a mixture of various substances

cock·tail[2] (käk′tāl′) *n.* ⟦< COCK[1] *vi.* + TAIL[1]⟧ [Archaic] 1 a horse with a docked tail 2 a horse of impure breed

cocktail dress a dress of short to medium length esp. for semiformal occasions

☆**cocktail lounge** a room in a restaurant, hotel, etc. where alcoholic drinks are served

☆**cocktail table** a low table as for serving refreshments, esp. one in a living room

cock-teas·er or **cock·teas·er** (käk′tē′zər) *n.* [Slang] a woman who behaves in a way calculated to arouse men sexually but who has no intention of having sexual intercourse with them: somewhat vulgar

cock-up (käk′up′) *n.* [Brit. Slang] a state or instance of confusion; mix-up

cock·y (käk′ē) *adj.* **cock′i·er**, **cock′i·est** ⟦< COCK[1] + -Y[2]⟧ [Informal] jauntily conceited or overbearing; self-confident in an aggressive or swaggering way

co·co (kō′kō′) *n., pl.* **-cos′** ⟦Sp & Port < L *coccum*, a seed, kernel < Gr *kokkos*, a berry⟧ 1 the coconut palm tree 2 its fruit; coconut —*adj.* made of the fiber from coconut husks

co·coa (kō′kō′) *n.* ⟦< Sp *cacao*, CACAO⟧ 1 powder made from cacao seeds that have been roasted and ground, with much of the fat (see COCOA BUTTER) removed; pulverized chocolate 2 a drink made by adding sugar and hot milk or hot water to this powder 3 a reddish-yellow brown

cocoa butter a yellowish-white fat prepared from cacao seeds: used in pharmacy and in making cosmetics and chocolate candies

co·co·nut or **co·coa·nut** (kō′kə nut′) *n.* the fruit of the coconut palm, consisting of a thick, fibrous, brown, oval husk under which there is a thin, hard shell enclosing a layer of edible white meat

coconut and coconut palm

coconut milk 1 the sweet fluid occupying the hollow center of a coconut: also **coconut water** 2 a milky liquid obtained by pressing coconut flesh

coconut oil oil obtained from the dried meat of coconuts, used for making soap, as an edible fat, etc.

coconut palm (or tree) a tall palm tree (*Cocus nucifera*) that bears coconuts and grows throughout the tropics: also **coco palm**

co·coon (kə ko͞on′) *n.* ⟦Fr *cocon* < Prov *coucoun*, egg shell, dim. of *coca*, shell-like container < ML *coco*, shell, hull⟧ 1 the silky or fibrous case which the larvae of certain insects spin about themselves for shelter during the pupa stage 2 any protective cover like this, as the egg capsule of certain spiders, leeches, etc. 3 any cover used to waterproof or protect something, esp. military equipment for transport or storage —*vt.* 1 to enclose protectively, as in a cocoon 2 to isolate (oneself)

Co·cos Islands (kō′kōs) group of small coral islands in the Indian Ocean, south of Sumatra: a territory of Australia: 5.5 sq mi (14.2 sq km)

co·cotte[1] (kō kät′) *n.* ⟦Fr, orig., hen < *coc*, cock < OFr *coq*⟧ a woman who is sexually promiscuous

co·cotte[2] (kō kät′) *n.* ⟦Fr < MFr *cocasse*, cooking pot, ult. < L *cucuma*⟧ a small casserole for a single portion of food

co·co·zel·le (kō′kə zel′ē) *n.* ⟦< It dial. dim. of *cocuzza*, squash, gourd < LL *cucutia*⟧ a variety of summer squash similar to the zucchini

Coc·teau (kôk tō′), **Jean** (zhän) 1889-1963; Fr. poet, novelist, playwright, and film writer and director

Co·cy·tus (kō sīt′əs) *n.* ⟦L < Gr *Kōkytos*, lit., a shrieking, wailing < *kōkyein*, to wail, redupl. of IE base **kau-*, HOWL⟧ *Gr. Myth.* the river of wailing, a tributary of the Acheron in Hades

cod[1] (käd) *n., pl.* **cod** or **cods** ⟦ME < ? fol., in reference to shape⟧ any of various gadoid fishes of northern seas, important as a source of cod-liver oil and food, esp. any of a genus (*Gadus*) with firm flesh and soft fins, found off the coast of Newfoundland and Norway

cod[2] (käd) *n.* ⟦ME < OE *codd*, akin to ON *koddi*, cushion < IE **geut-* < base **geu-*, to bend, arch > COT[2], L *guttur*, throat⟧ 1 [Archaic] a bag 2 [Dial.] a pod; husk 3 [Obs.] the scrotum

cod[3] (käd) [Brit. Slang] *n.* 1 a hoax; trick 2 a parody or satire —*adj.* 1 mock; sham 2 parodic or satirical —*vt.* 1 to fool, hoax, trick, etc. 2 to tease

Cod (käd), **Cape** ⟦< fish name⟧ hook-shaped peninsula in E Mass. from Buzzards Bay to Provincetown: 64 mi (103 km) long

COD[1] (käd) *n.* ⟦*c(hemical) o(xyen) d(emand)*⟧ 1 the amount of oxidizing agent needed to oxidize the organic and oxidizable inorganic matter in waste water 2 this matter in the waste water See BOD

☆**COD**[2] or **cod** *abbrev.* cash (or collect) on delivery

co·da (kō′də) *n.* ⟦It < L *cauda*, a tail⟧ 1 *Music* a more or less independent passage added to the end of a section or composition so as to reinforce the sense of conclusion 2 something coming after or at the end

cod·dle (käd′l) *vt.* **-dled, -dling** ⟦prob. < CAUDLE⟧ **1** to cook (esp. eggs in the shell) gently by heating in water not quite at boiling temperature **2** to treat (someone) with more care or concern than is required or regarded as appropriate; be overindulgent toward; cosset; pamper

code (kōd) *n.* ⟦OFr < L *codex* (earlier *caudex*), wooden tablet for writing (hence, book: in LL(Ec), code of laws), orig., tree trunk, wood split into tablets, prob. < *cudere, *caudere,* to strike < IE base **kāu-* > HEW⟧ **1** a body of laws, as of a nation or city, organized for easy reference **2** any set of principles or rules of conduct [a moral *code*] **3** a set of signals representing letters or numerals, used to send messages, as by telegraph or flags **4** *a)* a system of symbols used as in secret writing or information processing, in which letters, figures, etc. are arbitrarily given certain meanings *b)* the symbols in such a system **5** a sequence of biochemical molecular units that combine in certain specific ways, as in the genetic code **6** *a)* a binary system for converting information, data, etc. into a form for use in computers, telecommunications, etc. *b)* a string of characters in such a system, constituting data, programming, etc. —*vt.* **cod′ed, cod′ing 1** to put in the form or symbols of a code **2** to put in a binary form, as for computer use —*vi.* to write or modify a computer program —**cod′er** *n.*

co·dec (kō′dek′) *n.* ⟦blend of *coder* (see prec.) & DECODER⟧ **1** an integrated circuit that converts analog data into digital and vice versa, used as to transmit images or sounds **2** a software program that encodes data or a signal for later decoding to view or listen to, used as to transmit or store images or sounds

co·dec·li·na·tion (kō′dek′lə nā′shən) *n.* the astronomical coordinate complementary to the declination: see POLAR DISTANCE

co·de·fend·ant (kō′di fen′dənt) *n.* a joint defendant

co·deine (kō′dēn′) *n.* ⟦< Gr *kōdeia,* poppy head + -INE[3]⟧ a narcotic alkaloid, $C_{18}H_{21}NO_3{\cdot}H_2O$, derived from opium and resembling morphine, but less habit-forming: used in cough medicines and to relieve pain

code name a name applied to a person, project, etc. that is being kept secret or that is otherwise unidentified ["Manhattan Project" was the *code name* for the secret project to develop the atomic bomb] —**code′-name′** *vt.* **-named′, -nam′ing**

Code Na·po·lé·on (kōd nȧ pô lā ōn′) ⟦Fr⟧ the Napoleonic Code, the body of French civil law enacted in 1804: the model for the civil codes of many nations

co·de·pend·ent or **co-de·pend·ent** (kō′dē pen′dənt, -di-) *adj.* ⟦CO- + DEPENDENT⟧ **1** *a)* psychologically influenced or controlled by, reliant on, or needing another person who is addicted to alcohol, drugs, etc. *b)* of or having to do with this kind of relationship **2** mutually dependent —*n.* a person who is codependent —**co′de·pend′en·cy** *n.*, **co′-de·pend′en·cy** (-dən sē), *pl.* **-cies** —**co′de·pend′ence** *n.*, **co′-de·pend′ence** (-dəns)

co·de·ter·mi·na·tion (kō′dē tur′mə nā′shən, -di-) *n.* a system of industrial management in which workers share responsibility for the operation of a company, as through elected representation on a corporate supervisory board

☆**code word 1** a word or phrase with a secret meaning, often, specif., one used to convey an idea or attitude that cannot be openly divulged because it is socially or politically unacceptable **2** a euphemistic word or phrase

co·dex (kō′deks′) *n., pl.* **co·di·ces** (kō′də sēz′, käd′ə-) ⟦L: see CODE⟧ **1** [Obs.] a code, or body of laws **2** a manuscript volume, esp. of the Scriptures or of a classic text

Codex Ju·ris Ca·no·ni·ci (jo͝or′is kə nän′ə sī′) ⟦L, Code of Canon Law⟧ official body of laws governing the Roman Catholic Church since 1918, now revised: replaced the CORPUS JURIS CANONICI

cod·fish (käd′fish′) *n., pl.* **-fish′** or **-fish′es** (see FISH) COD[1]

codg·er (käj′ər) *n.* ⟦prob. var. of CADGER⟧ [Informal] an elderly fellow, sometimes one who is eccentric: a term used in good humor

cod·i·cil (käd′i səl, -sil′) *n.* ⟦ME < L *codicillus,* dim. of *codex*: see CODE⟧ **1** *Law* an addition to a will, that changes, explains, revokes, or adds provisions **2** an appendix or supplement —**cod′i·cil′la·ry** (-sil′ər ē) *adj.*

co·di·col·o·gy (kō′də kä′lə jē, käd′ə-) *n.* ⟦Fr *codicologie* < L *codic-* < *codex*: see CODE⟧ [Chiefly Brit.] the study of manuscripts as artifacts in their cultural context

cod·i·fy (käd′ə fī′, kō′də-) *vt.* **-fied′, -fy′ing** ⟦CODE + -I- + -FY⟧ to arrange (laws, rules, etc.) systematically —**cod′i·fi·ca′tion** (-fi kā′shən) *n.* —**cod′i·fi′er** (-fī′ər) *n.*

cod·ling[1] (käd′liŋ) *n., pl.* **-ling** or **-lings 1** a young cod **2** HAKE

cod·ling[2] (käd′liŋ) *n.* ⟦earlier *querdling,* altered (infl. by suffix -LING[1]) < Anglo-Fr *querdelyon,* lit., heart of lion⟧ **1** a variety of elongated apple **2** a small, unripe apple Also **cod′lin** (-lin)

codling moth a nearly cosmopolitan small moth (*Cydia pomenella*) whose larva bores into and destroys apples, pears, quinces, etc.: also **codlin moth**

cod-liv·er oil (käd′liv′ər) oil from the liver of the cod and related fishes, rich in vitamins A & D and used in vitamin supplements

☆**co·don** (kō′dän′) *n.* ⟦CODE + *-on,* as in PROTON⟧ a small group of chemical units, consisting of a sequence of three nucleotides, that codes the incorporation of a specific small group of amino acids into a protein molecule during the synthesis of the protein; codons are present in DNA and RNA

cod·piece (käd′pēs′) *n.* ⟦COD[2] + PIECE⟧ a bag or flap fastened over the front opening in the tight breeches worn by men in the 15th and 16th cent.

cods·wal·lop (kädz′wäl′əp) *n.* ⟦< ?⟧ [Brit. Slang] nonsense; specif., talk or writing that is foolish and insincere

Co·dy (kō′dē), **William F(rederick)** 1846-1917; U.S. plainsman, frontier scout, & showman: called *Buffalo Bill*

☆**co·ed**[1] or **co-ed** (kō′ed′) [Informal] *n.* a young woman attending a coeducational college or university —*adj.* **1** coeducational **2** of or having to do with a coed **3** involving, used by, or open to people of both sexes [*coed* teams, *coed* clothing styles]

coed[2] *abbrev.* coeducational

☆**co·ed·u·ca·tion** (kō′ej′ə kā′shən) *n.* an educational system in which students of both sexes attend classes together —**co′ed′u·ca′tion·al** *adj.* —**co′ed′u·ca′tion·al·ly** *adv.*

coef *abbrev.* coefficient

co·ef·fi·cient (kō′ə fish′ənt) *n.* ⟦CO- + EFFICIENT: orig. an adj. meaning "cooperating"⟧ **1** a factor that contributes to produce a result **2** *Math.* a number or algebraic symbol prefixed as a multiplier to a variable or unknown quantity (Ex.: *x* in $x(y+z)$, *6* in *6ab*) **3** *Physics* a number, constant for a given substance, used as a multiplier in measuring the change in some property of the substance under given conditions [the *coefficient* of expansion]

coe·la·canth (sē′lə kanth′) *n.* ⟦< ModL *Coelacanthus* < Gr *koilos* (see fol.) + *akantha,* thorn (see ACANTHO-)⟧ any of an order (Coelacanthiformes) of lobefin fishes, now extinct except for the latimeria

-coele (sēl) ⟦< Gr *koilia,* body cavity < *koilos,* hollow: for IE base see CAVE⟧ *combining form* cavity, chamber of the body or of an organ [*blastocoele*]: also **-coel**

coe·len·ter·ate (si len′tər it, -āt′) *n.* ⟦< ModL *Coelenterata* < *coelenteron*: see fol.⟧ CNIDARIAN

coe·len·ter·on (-tər än′, -tər ən) *n., pl.* **-ter·a** (-rə) ⟦ModL < Gr *koilos* (see -COELE) + *enteron,* intestine: see ENTERO-⟧ the internal body cavity of coelenterates, flatworms, etc.

coe·li·ac (sē′lē ak′) *adj.* ⟦L *coeliacus* < Gr *koiliakos* < *koilia*: see -COELE⟧ *alt. sp. of* CELIAC

coe·lom (sē′ləm) *n.* ⟦Gr *koiloma* < *koilos*: see -COELE⟧ the main body cavity of most higher multicellular animals, in which the visceral organs are suspended —**coe·lom·ic** (si läm′ik, -lō′mik) *adj.*

coe·lo·stat (sē′lə stat′) *n.* ⟦< L *caelum,* sky, heavens + -STAT⟧ an optical system, used with a fixed telescope, consisting of two mirrors with a moving mirror mounted on an axis parallel to the earth's axis of rotation and driven by clockwork so as to reflect the same portion of the sky continuously or to track the sun

coe·nes·the·sia (sē′nis thē′zhə, -zhē ə; sen′is-) *n.* ⟦ModL < Gr *koinos* (see CENO-) + *aisthēsis,* feeling⟧ *alt. sp. of* CENESTHESIA

coe·no- (sē′nō, -nə; sen′ō, -ə) *combining form* CENO-: also, before a vowel, **coen-**

coe·no·bite (sen′ə bīt′, sē′nə-) *n. alt. sp. of* CENOBITE

coe·no·cyte (sē′nə sīt′, sen′ə-) *n.* ⟦COENO- + -CYTE⟧ **1** SYNCYTIUM **2** *a)* a mass of protoplasm containing several nuclei formed from an original cell with one nucleus *b)* an organism of such a mass

coe·no·sarc (-särk′) *n.* ⟦COENO- + Gr *sarx,* flesh: see SARCASM⟧ the fleshy portion of the stalks and stolons of hydroids, that secretes the perisarc

coe·nu·rus (si no͝or′əs, -nyo͝or′-) *n., pl.* **-ri′** (-ī′) ⟦ModL, lit., common tail < COEN(O)- + Gr *oura,* tail: so called in allusion to the single body with many heads⟧ the compound larva of any of certain tapeworms causing any of various diseases, as the staggers

☆**co·en·zyme** (kō en′zīm′) *n.* an organic nonprotein compound of low molecular weight that can unite with an apoenzyme to form an active enzyme complex (*holoenzyme*)

co·e·qual (kō ē′kwəl) *adj., n.* equal —**co′e·qual′i·ty** (-ē kwäl′ə tē) *n.*

co·erce (kō urs′) *vt.* **-erced′, -erc′ing** ⟦ME *cohercen* < OFr *cohercier* < L *coercere,* to surround, restrain < *co-,* together + *arcere,* to confine: see EXERCISE⟧ **1** to restrain or constrain by force, esp. by legal authority; curb **2** to force or compel, as by threats, to do something **3** to bring about by using force; enforce —**SYN.** FORCE —**co·er′ci·ble** *adj.* —**co·er′ci·bly** *adv.*

co·er·cion (kō ur′shən, -zhən) *n.* ⟦L *coercio*⟧ **1** the act or power of coercing **2** government by force

co·er·cive (-siv) *adj.* of coercion or tending to coerce —**co·er′cive·ly** *adv.* —**co·er′cive·ness** *n.*

co·er·civ·i·ty (kō′ər siv′ə tē) *n.* the magnetic intensity, usually measured in oersteds, needed to completely demagnetize a substance that has been fully magnetized

☆**coes·ite** (kō′zīt′, -sīt′) *n.* ⟦after Loring *Coes,* Jr. (1915-78), U.S. chemist + -ITE[1]⟧ a very hard, monoclinic form of silica, SiO_2, produced under very great pressure and found in the sandstone of large meteor craters

co·es·sen·tial (kō′i sen′shəl) *adj.* having one and the same essence or nature —**co′es·sen′tial·ly** *adv.*

co·e·ta·ne·ous (kō′ē tā′nē əs) *adj.* ⟦L *coaetaneus* < *co-,* with + *aetas,* AGE⟧ contemporary; coeval

co·e·ter·nal (kō′ē tur′nəl) *adj.* existing together eternally —**co′e·ter′ni·ty** (-nə tē) *n.* —**co′e·ter′nal·ly** *adv.*

co·e·val (kō ē′vəl) *adj.* ⟦< LL(Ec) *coævus* < L *co-,* together + *aevum,* an AGE + -AL⟧ of the same age or period; contemporary —*n.* a contemporary —**SYN.** CONTEMPORARY —**co′e′val·ly** *adv.*

co·ev·o·lu·tion (kō′ev′ə lo͞o′shən) *n.* the interdependent evolution of two or more species, in which genetic changes in one result in adaptive changes in the other or others [the *coevolution* of insect pollinators and the plants they pollinate] —**co′ev′o·lu′tion·ar·y** *adj.*

co·ex·ec·u·tor (kō′ig zek′yo͞o tər) *n.* a person acting as executor jointly with another

co·ex·ist (kō′ig zist′) *vi.* **1** to exist together at the same time or in the same place **2** to live together without hostility or conflict despite differences —**co′ex·ist′ence** *n.* —**co′ex·ist′ent** *adj.*

co·ex·tend (kō′ik stend′) *vt., vi.* to extend equally in space or time —**co′ex·ten′sion** (-ik sten′shən) *n.*

co·ex·ten·sive (kō′ik sten′siv) *adj.* having the same extent in time or space —**co′ex·ten′sive·ly** *adv.*

co·fac·tor (kō′fak′tər) *n.* **1** any one of two or more factors, the combined effects of which may cause a certain result or condition, esp. a disease: also written **co-factor** **2** *Biochem.* an accessory substance, esp. a coenzyme, that must be present for a particular biological reaction to occur

C of C *abbrev.* Chamber of Commerce

C of E *abbrev.* Church of England

cof·fee (kôf′ē, käf′-) *n.* ⟦It *caffè* < Turk *qahwe* < Ar *qahwa*, coffee, said to be after *Kaffa*, area in Ethiopia, home of the plant⟧ **1** a dark-brown, aromatic drink made by brewing in water the roasted and ground beanlike seeds of a tall tropical shrub (genus *Coffea*) of the madder family **2** these seeds, found in the red berries of the shrub: also **coffee beans** **3** the shrub itself **4** the color of coffee to which milk or cream has been added; light brown **5** a reception or social gathering at which coffee, tea, etc. are served, esp. one held for the purpose of promoting a cause or introducing a political candidate —*adj.* flavored with coffee [*coffee* ice cream]

☆**coffee break** a brief respite from work when coffee or other refreshment is typically taken

☆**cof·fee·cake** (-kāk′) *n.* a kind of cake or roll, often containing nuts, raisins, etc. or coated with sugar or icing, to be eaten with coffee or the like

cof·fee·house (-hous′) *n.* a place where coffee and other refreshments are served and people gather for conversation, entertainment, etc.

☆**coffee klatch** (*or* **klatsch**) KAFFEEKLATSCH

coffee maker a utensil, as an electrical appliance, for brewing coffee

coffee mill a machine for grinding roasted coffee beans

cof·fee·pot (-pät′) *n.* a container with a lid and a spout, in which coffee is made or served

coffee shop an informal restaurant, as in a hotel, where light refreshments or meals are served

☆**coffee table** a low table, usually in front of a sofa

cof·fee-ta·ble book (kôf′ē tā′bəl) a large, lavishly produced book with many illustrations and, often, an inferior text, esp. one regarded as being for ostentatious display, as on a coffee table

coffee tree **1** any tree or shrub that produces coffee beans ☆**2** KENTUCKY COFFEE TREE

cof·fer (kôf′ər, käf′-) *n.* ⟦ME < OFr *cofre*, a chest < L *cophinus:* see COFFIN⟧ **1** a chest or strongbox for keeping money or valuables **2** [*pl.*] a treasury; funds **3** a decorative sunken panel as in a vault, dome, etc. **4** a cofferdam **5** a lock in a canal —*vt.* **1** to enclose in a coffer or chest **2** to furnish with decorative sunken panels

cof·fer·dam (-dam′) *n.* ⟦prec. + DAM[1]⟧ **1** a watertight temporary structure in a river, lake, etc., for keeping the water from an enclosed area that has been pumped dry so that a bridge foundation, dam, or pier may be constructed **2** a watertight box or chamber attached to the side of a ship so that repairs can be made below the waterline **3** an empty space serving as a protective barrier, as between two compartments of a ship

cof·fin (kôf′in, käf′-) *n.* ⟦ME & OFr *cofin*, basket, coffer < L *cophinus* < Gr *kophinos*, a basket⟧ **1** the case or box in which a dead body is buried **2** the horny part of a horse's hoof —*vt.* to put into or as if into a coffin

coffin bone the foot bone inside the hoof of a horse

☆**coffin corner** ⟦radio slang, prob. with reference to the grave of the defending team's hopes⟧ any of the corners of a football field formed by a goal line and side line: punts are sometimes directed to a coffin corner so that the ball will go out of bounds near the opponent's goal line

☆**coffin nail** [Old Slang] a cigarette

cof·fle (kôf′əl, käf′-) *n.* ⟦Ar *qāfila*, caravan⟧ a group of animals or slaves fastened together in a line, or driven along together —☆*vt.* **-fled**, **-fling** to fasten together in or as in a coffle

cog[1] (käg, kôg) *n.* ⟦ME *cog, cogge* < ? Scand, as in Norw *kug*, Swed *kugge*, a cog, tooth < IE **gugā* a hump, ball < base **gēu-*, to bend, arch > OE *cycgel*, CUDGEL⟧ **1** *a)* any of a series of teeth on the rim of a wheel, for transmitting or receiving motion by fitting between the teeth of another wheel; gear tooth *b)* a cogwheel ☆**2** a person or thing regarded as a minor but necessary part of the structure of an activity or organization —**cogged** *adj.*

cog[2] (käg, kôg) *n.* ⟦altered (infl. by prec.) < earlier *cock*, to secure, prob. ult. < It *cocca*, a notch⟧ a projection on a beam that fits into a corresponding groove or notch in another beam, making a joint — *vt., vi.* **cogged**, **cog′ging** to join by a cog or cogs

cog[3] (käg, kôg) *vt.* **cogged**, **cog′ging** ⟦prob. slang extension of COG[1]⟧ to manipulate (dice) in a fraudulent manner —*vi.* [Obs.] to cheat; swindle —*n.* [Obs.] a deception; trick

cog[4] or **cogn** *abbrev.* cognate

co·gen·cy (kō′jən sē) *n.* ⟦ML *cogencia*⟧ the quality or condition of being cogent; power to convince

co·gen·er·a·tion (kō′jen′ər ā′shən) *n.* the process of generating electricity and useful heat jointly, as by utilizing waste steam for heating —**co′gen′er·a′tor** *n.*

co·gent (kō′jənt) *adj.* ⟦L *cogens*, prp. of *cogere*, to collect < *co-*, together + *agere*, to drive: see ACT[1]⟧ forceful and to the point, as a reason or argument; compelling; convincing —**SYN.** VALID —**co′gent·ly** *adv.*

cog·i·tate (käj′ə tāt′) *vi., vt.* **-tat′ed**, **-tat′ing** ⟦< L *cogitatus*, pp. of *cogitare* < **coagitare*: see CO- & AGITATE⟧ to think seriously and deeply (about); ponder; meditate; consider —**SYN.** THINK[1] —**cog′i·ta·ble** (-tə bəl) *adj.* —**cog′i·ta′tion** *n.* —**cog′i·ta′tor** *n.*

cog·i·ta·tive (käj′ə tāt′iv) *adj.* ⟦ME *cogitatif* < LL *cogitativus*⟧ **1** capable of cogitating **2** tending to cogitate; thoughtful; meditative

co·gi·to er·go sum (käj′ə tō′ ur′gō so͞om′, kō′jə tō′-, kō′gi tō′-; -er′gō so͝om′) ⟦L⟧ I think, therefore I exist: the fundamental tenet of the philosophy of Descartes

co·gnac (kōn′yak′, kôn′-) *n.* ⟦Fr⟧ **1** a French brandy distilled from wine in the area of Cognac, France **2** loosely, any French brandy or any brandy

cog·nate (käg′nāt′) *adj.* ⟦L *cognatus*, related by birth < *co-*, together + *gnatus*, pp. of *gnasci*, older form of *nasci*, to be born: see GENUS⟧ **1** related by family; having the same ancestor **2** having the same nature or quality **3** *Linguis.* related through the same source; derived from a common original form [English "apple" and German "apfel" are *cognate* words; French and Spanish are *cognate* languages] —*n.* **1** *a)* a person related to another through common ancestry *b)* a relative on the mother's side **2** a cognate word, language, or thing —**SYN.** RELATED

cog·na·tion (käg nā′shən) *n.* ⟦ME *cognacioun* < L *cognatio*: see prec.⟧ relationship by descent from the same ancestor or source

cog·ni·tion (käg nish′ən) *n.* ⟦ME *cognicioun* < L *cognitio*, knowledge < *cognitus*, pp. of *cognoscere*, to know < *co-*, together + *gnoscere*, KNOW⟧ **1** the process of knowing in the broadest sense, including perception, memory, and judgment **2** the result of such a process; perception, conception, etc. —**cog·ni′tion·al** *adj.* —**cog′ni·tive** (-nə tiv) *adj.*

☆**cognitive dissonance** ⟦coined by L. Festinger (1919-89), U.S. social psychologist⟧ the confused mental condition that results from holding incongruous, often mutually contradictory, beliefs simultaneously

cognitive science the study of cognition, involving the disciplines of psychology, linguistics, artificial intelligence, etc.

cog·ni·za·ble (käg′ni zə bəl, käg nī′-; *occas.* kän′ə zə bəl) *adj.* ⟦COGNIZ(E) + -ABLE⟧ **1** that can be known or perceived **2** *Law* *a)* within the jurisdiction of a court *b)* within the jurisdiction of the judicial system

cog·ni·zance (käg′nə zəns; *occas.* kän′ə-) *n.* ⟦ME *cognisaunce* < OFr *conoissance*, knowledge < *conoissant*, prp. of *conoistre*, to know < L *cognoscere:* see COGNITION⟧ **1** perception or knowledge; esp., the range of knowledge possible through observation **2** official observation of or authority over something **3** *Heraldry* a distinguishing badge or device **4** *Law* *a)* the hearing of a case in court *b)* the right or power of dealing with a matter judicially; jurisdiction —**take cognizance of** to notice or recognize

cog·ni·zant (-zənt) *adj.* having cognizance; aware or informed (*of* something) —**SYN.** AWARE

cog·nize (käg′nīz′, käg nīz′) *vt.* **-nized′**, **-niz′ing** ⟦back-form. < COGNIZANCE⟧ to take cognizance of; notice

cog·no·men (käg nō′mən) *n., pl.* **-no′mens** or **-nom′i·na** (-näm′i nə) ⟦L < *co-*, with + *nomen*, NAME: sp. infl. by assoc. with **gnomen* < Gr *gnōma*, mark, token: akin to L *gnoscere*, KNOW⟧ **1** the third or family name of an ancient Roman (Ex.: Marcus Tullius *Cicero*) **2** any family name; surname; last name **3** any name; esp., a nickname —**cog·nom′i·nal** (-näm′i nəl) *adj.*

co·gno·scen·te (käg′nə shen′tē, kôg′nə-, kän′yə-) *n., pl.* **-ti** (-tē) ⟦It, orig. prp. of *conoscere*, to know < L *cognoscere*: see COGNITION⟧ a person with special knowledge in some field, esp. in the fine arts

cog·nos·ci·ble (käg näs′ə bəl) *adj.* ⟦LL *cognoscibilis* < L *cognoscere*: see COGNITION⟧ [Rare] that can be known or perceived; cognizable

cog·no·vit (käg nō′vit) *n.* ⟦short for L *cognovit actionem*, lit., he has acknowledged the action⟧ *Law* a written acknowledgment of a debt, esp. as contained in a note (**cognovit note**), by which the debtor authorizes that judgment be entered for the creditor without a trial if the debt is not paid when it becomes due

co·gon (kō gōn′) *n.* ⟦Sp *cogón* < Tagalog name⟧ any of several tall, coarse grasses (genus *Imperata*), esp. a grass (*I. cylindrica*) of the Philippines, used for forage and thatching

cog railway a railway for a very steep grade with traction supplied by a central cogged rail that meshes with a cogwheel on the engine

cog·wheel (käg′hwēl′, -wēl′) *n.* a wheel with a rim notched into teeth, which mesh with those of another wheel or of a rack to transmit or receive motion

co·hab·it (kō hab′it) *vi.* ⟦LL(Ec) *cohabitare* < L *co-*, together + *habitare*, to dwell < *habitus*: see HABIT⟧ **1** to live together as husband and wife, esp. when not legally married **2** to live or exist together; share the same place —**co·hab′i·ta′tion** *n.*

co·hab·it·ant (kō hab′i tənt) *n.* ⟦< LL *cohabitans*, prp. of prec.⟧ a person living together with another or others

Co·han (kō′han′), **George M(ichael)** 1878-1942; U.S. actor, playwright, theatrical producer, & writer of popular songs

co·heir (kō′er′, kō er′) *n.* a person who inherits jointly with another or others

co·heir·ess (kō′er′is, kō er′is) *n.* a female coheir

co·here (kō hir′) *vi.* **-hered′**, **-her′ing** ⟦L *cohaerere* < *co-*, together + *haerere*, to stick⟧ **1** *a)* to stick together, as parts of a mass *b)* to be united as by molecular cohesion **2** to be connected naturally or logically, as by a common principle; be consistent **3** to become or stay united in action; be in accord —**SYN.** STICK

co·her·ence (kō hir′əns, -her′-) *n.* ⟦Fr < L *cohaerentia* < *cohaerens*, prp. of prec.⟧ **1** the act or condition of cohering; cohesion **2** the quality of being logically integrated, consistent, and intelligible; congruity [*his story lacked coherence*] **3** *Physics* that property of a set of waves or sources of waves in which the oscillations maintain a fixed relationship to each other Also **co·her′en·cy**

co·her·ent (kō hir′ənt, -her′-) ***adj.*** ⟦Fr < L *cohaerens,* prp.: see COHERE⟧ **1** sticking together; having cohesion **2** having coherence; logically connected; consistent; clearly articulated **3** capable of logical, intelligible speech, thought, etc. **4** *Physics* exhibiting coherence —**co·her′ent·ly** ***adv.***

co·he·sion (kō hē′zhən) ***n.*** ⟦Fr < L *cohaesus,* pp. of *cohaerere:* see COHERE⟧ **1** the act or condition of cohering; tendency to stick together **2** *Bot.* the union of like flower parts **3** *Physics* the force by which the molecules of a substance are held together: distinguished from ADHESION

co·he·sive (-hēs′iv) ***adj.*** sticking together; causing or characterized by cohesion —**co·he′sive·ly** ***adv.*** —**co·he′sive·ness** ***n.***

Cohn (kōn), **Ferdinand Julius** 1828-98; Ger. botanist and early bacteriologist

co·ho (kō′hō′) ***n.,*** *pl.* **-ho′** or **-hos′** ⟦earlier *co-hue,* prob. < Salish (Chilliwack dial.) *kwúhw-uth*⟧ a comparatively small salmon (*Oncorhynchus kisutch*), native to the N Pacific Ocean and now widely introduced as a game fish into fresh waters of the N U.S.: also **coho salmon**

co·ho·bate (kō′hō bāt′) ***vt.*** **-bat′ed, -bat′ing** ⟦< pp. of ModL *cohobare,* orig. to give a darker color to (a distilled liquid) < Ar *qohba,* brownish color⟧ to redistill (a distillate) one or more times

co·hort (kō′hôrt′) ***n.*** ⟦ME < L *cohors,* enclosure, enclosed company, hence, retinue, crowd < *co-,* CO- + IE **ĝhr̥tis,* a gathering < base **ĝher-,* to grasp, enclose > YARD[2]⟧ **1** an ancient Roman military unit of 300-600 men, constituting one tenth of a legion **2** a band of soldiers **3** any group or band **4** an associate, colleague, or supporter [*one of the mayor's cohorts*] **5** a conspirator or accomplice **6** a subgroup sharing a common factor in a statistical survey, as age or income level

☆**co·hosh** (kō′häsh′, kō häsh′) ***n.*** ⟦< Algonquian name⟧ **1** any of several American herbs, as bugbane and baneberry **2** a North American herb (*Caulophyllum thalictroides*) of the barberry family, formerly used medicinally by the Indians

co·hune (kō ho͞on′) ***n.*** ⟦< Central AmInd name *cóhun*⟧ a Central American palm tree (*Orbignya cohune*) with featherlike leaves and large nuts that yield an edible oil used to make soap

coif (koif; *for n. 5 & vt. 2 usually* kwäf) ***n.*** ⟦ME & OFr *coife* < LL *cofea,* a cap, hood < ?⟧ **1** a cap that fits the head closely **2** a white cap formerly worn by English lawyers, esp. by serjeants-at-law **3** the rank of serjeant-at-law **4** a thick skullcap formerly worn under a hood of mail **5** ⟦back-form. < COIFFURE⟧ a style of arranging the hair —***vt.*** **coifed, coif′ing;** also, and for 2 usually, **coiffed, coif′fing 1** to cover with or as with a coif **2** *a)* to style (the hair) *b)* to give a coiffure to

coif·feur (kwä fʉr′) ***n.*** ⟦Fr < *coiffer,* to dress hair < prec.⟧ a male hairdresser

coif·feuse (kwä fʉz′; -fyo͞oz′, -fo͞oz′) ***n.*** a female hairdresser

coif·fure (kwä fyoor′) ***n.*** ⟦Fr < OFr *coife,* COIF⟧ **1** a headdress **2** a style of arranging the hair —***vt.*** **-fured′, -fur′ing** to COIF (sense 2)

coign of vantage (koin) ⟦*coign,* archaic var. of *coin* (QUOIN)⟧ an advantageous position for observation or action

coil[1] (koil) ***vt.*** ⟦ME *coilen,* to select, cull < OFr *coillir,* to gather, pick < L *colligere,* to gather together: see COLLECT[2]⟧ to wind or gather (rope, a hose, etc.) into a circular or spiral form —***vi.*** **1** to wind around and around **2** to move in a winding course —***n.*** **1** anything wound or gathered into a series of rings or a spiral **2** such a series of rings or a spiral **3** a single turn of a coiled figure **4** a series of connected pipes in rows or coils **5** a roll of postage stamps for use in a dispenser or vending machine; also, a stamp from such a roll **6** *Elec.* a spiral or loop of wire or other conducting element used as an inductor, heating element, etc.

coil[2] (koil) ***n.*** ⟦Early ModE < ?⟧ [Archaic] commotion; turmoil

Coim·ba·tore (koim′bə tôr′) city in S India, in the state of Tamil Nadu

coin (koin) ***n.*** ⟦ME < OFr *coin, coigne,* a wedge, stamp, corner < L *cuneus,* a wedge < IE base **kū-,* pointed > OIr *cuil,* L *culex,* gnat, Avestan *sū-kā,* needle⟧ **1** *archaic var. of* QUOIN **2** *a)* a usually round piece of metal with a distinctive stamp, and of a fixed value and weight, issued by a government as money *b)* such pieces collectively **3** [Slang] money —***adj.*** requiring, or containing machines requiring, one or more coins for operation [*a coin laundry*] —***vt.*** **1** *a)* to make (coins) by stamping metal *b)* to make (metal) into coins **2** to make up; devise; invent (a new word or phrase) —***vi.*** **1** to make coins **2** [Brit.] to make counterfeit money —**coin money** [Informal] to earn or accumulate wealth rapidly —**pay a person back in the same coin** to treat a person in the same way the person treated oneself —**coin′er** ***n.***

coin·age (koin′ij) ***n.*** ⟦ME < OFr *coignaige*⟧ **1** the act or process of coining **2** metal money; coins **3** a system of money or metal currency **4** an invented word or expression [*"laser" is a recent coinage*]

co·in·cide (kō′in sīd′) ***vi.*** **-cid′ed, -cid′ing** ⟦Fr *coincider* < ML *coincidere* < L *co-,* together + *incidere,* to fall upon: see INCIDENT⟧ **1** to take up the same place in space; be exactly alike in shape, position, and area **2** to occur at the same time; take up the same period of time **3** to hold equivalent positions, as on a scale **4** to be identical; correspond exactly [*our interests coincide*] **5** to be in accord; agree —**SYN.** AGREE

co·in·ci·dence (kō in′sə dəns) ***n.*** ⟦Fr < ML *coincidentia*⟧ **1** the fact or condition of coinciding **2** an accidental and remarkable occurrence of events or ideas at the same time, suggesting but lacking a causal relationship

co·in·ci·dent (-dənt) ***adj.*** ⟦Fr < ML *coincidens,* prp.⟧ **1** occurring at the same time **2** taking up the same position in space at the same time **3** in agreement; similar or identical [*where desire and need are coincident*] —**co·in′ci·dent·ly** ***adv.***

co·in·ci·den·tal (kō in′sə dent′'l) ***adj.*** characterized by coincidence —**co·in′ci·den′tal·ly** ***adv.***

coin-op (koin′äp′) ***adj.*** [Informal] coin-operated

coin-op·er·at·ed (koin′äp′ə rāt′id) ***adj.*** started or operated by inserting a coin or coins in a slot

co·in·sur·ance (kō′in shoor′əns) ***n.*** **1** a form of property insurance in which the insured shares in losses proportionately to the extent that the amount of insurance falls short of a specified percentage of the value of the insured property **2** joint insurance by two or more insurers

☆**co·in·sure** (-in shoor′) ***vt., vi.*** **-sured′, -sur′ing 1** to insure with coinsurance **2** to insure jointly with another or others —**co′in·sur′er** ***n.***

Coin·treau (kwän trō′) ⟦named (1875) by its Fr creator, É. Cointreau (1849-1923), for the distillery founded by his father and uncle in Angers⟧ *trademark for* a sweet, colorless, orange-flavored liqueur —***n.*** [*sometimes* **c-**] this liqueur

coir (koir) ***n.*** ⟦Port *cairo* < Malayalam *kāyar,* a rope, cord < Tamil *kāyaru,* to be twisted⟧ the prepared fiber of the husks of coconuts, used to make matting and rope

cois·trel or **cois·tril** (kois′trəl) ***n.*** ⟦prob. < ME *custrel,* a soldier (armed with a *custille,* two-edged dagger) < OFr *coustellier*⟧ [Archaic] **1** a groom in charge of a knight's horses **2** a knave; varlet; scoundrel

co·i·tion (kō ish′ən) ***n.*** ⟦L *coitio* < *coitus,* pp. of *coire* < *co-,* CO- + *ire,* to go: see EXIT⟧ sexual intercourse

co·i·tus (kō′it əs, koi′təs; *also* kō ēt′əs) ***n.*** ⟦L: see prec.⟧ sexual intercourse —**co′i·tal** ***adj.***

coitus in·ter·rup·tus (in′tə rup′təs) ⟦ModL, interrupted coitus⟧ sexual intercourse in which the penis is withdrawn before ejaculation in an effort to avoid the deposit of semen in the vagina

co·jo·nes (kô hô′nes) ***pl.n.*** ⟦Sp⟧ [Informal] **1** the testicles **2** [*with sing. v.*] courage; guts Sometimes considered vulgar

coke[1] (kōk) ***n.*** ⟦< ME *colke,* core, charcoal (the unconsumed "core" of burned wood) < IE **gel-ĝ-,* rounded < base **gel-:* see CLAW⟧ **1** coal from which most of the gases have been removed by heating: it burns with intense heat and little smoke, and is used as an industrial fuel **2** a solid residue left after the distillation of petroleum or other liquid hydrocarbons — ***vt., vi.*** **coked, cok′ing** to change into coke

☆**coke**[2] (kōk) [Slang] ***n.*** ⟦short for COCAINE⟧ cocaine —***vi.*** **coked, cok′ing** to use cocaine, often to excess: with *out* or *up*

Coke[1] (kōk) ⟦shortened < *Coca-Cola,* trademark for original brand of this drink (1886) < COCA, original source of the caffeine + COLA[1], source of the flavoring⟧ *trademark for* a kind of cola drink —***n.*** [*occas.* **c-**] any cola drink

Coke[2] (ko͝ok), Sir **Edward** 1552-1634; Eng. jurist

☆**Coke-bot·tle** (kōk′bät′'l) ***adj.*** ⟦< COKE[1]: by analogy with the bottoms of original glass Coca-Cola bottles⟧ [Slang] designating eyeglasses with very thick lenses

coke·head (kōk′hed′) ***n.*** [Slang] a habitual user of cocaine

coke oven an oven in which COKE[1] is made

col[1] (käl) ***n.*** ⟦Fr < L *collum,* the neck: see COLLAR⟧ **1** a gap between peaks in a mountain range, used as a pass **2** *Meteorol.* the point of lowest pressure between two anticyclones or the point of highest pressure between two cyclones

col[2] *abbrev.* **1** collateral **2** collected **3** collector **4** college **5** colony **6** color **7** column

Col *abbrev.* **1** Colombia **2** Colonel **3** *Bible* Colossians

COL *abbrev.* **1** Colonel **2** cost of living

col- (käl, kəl) *prefix* COM-: used before *l* [*collinear*]

co·la[1] (kō′lə) ***n.*** ⟦L form of WAfr name⟧ **1** an African tree (*Cola acuminata*) of the sterculia family whose seeds, or nuts, contain caffeine and yield an extract used in soft drinks and medicines **2** a sweet, carbonated soft drink flavored with this extract

co·la[2] (kō′lə) ***n.*** **1** *pl. of* COLON[1] (sense 2) **2** *alt. pl. of* COLON[2]

☆**COLA** (kō′lə) ***n.*** ⟦*c(ost-)o(f-)l(iving) a(djustment)*⟧ a regular adjustment as of wages or social-security payments, based on fluctuations in the cost of living

col·an·der (kul′ən dər, käl′-) ***n.*** ⟦prob. altered < ML *colator,* ult. < L *colare,* to strain < *colum,* strainer⟧ a perforated pan, usually bowl-shaped, for draining off liquids, as in washing vegetables

co·lat·i·tude (kō lat′ə to͞od′, -tyo͞od′) ***n.*** *Astron.* the complement of the latitude

Col·bert (kôl ber′), **Jean Bap·tiste** (zhän bȧ tēst′) 1619-83; Fr. statesman: minister of finance (1661-83)

Col·by (cheese) (kōl′bē) ⟦after *Colby,* Wis., where first produced⟧ a variety of cheese similar to cheddar but softer, moister, and more porous

col·can·non (kəl kan′ən, kôl′kan′-) ***n.*** ⟦Ir *cāl ceannan* < *cāl,* cabbage (< L *caulis*) + *ceannan,* white-headed < *ceann,* white⟧ an Irish dish made of potatoes and greens, esp. cabbage, boiled together and mashed

Col·ches·ter (kōl′chis tər, -ches-) city in SE England, in Essex

col·chi·cine (käl′chi sēn′, -sin′; käl′ki-) ***n.*** ⟦< fol. + -INE[3]⟧ a poisonous, yellow alkaloid, $C_{22}H_{25}NO_6$, extracted from the seeds or corms of a species of colchicum (*Colchicum autumnale*): used in the treatment of gout, in genetic engineering, and to produce chromosome doubling in plants for greater growth and fertile hybrids

col·chi·cum (käl′chi kəm, käl′ki-) ***n.*** ⟦ModL < Gr *kolchikon,* plant with a poisonous root, after *Kolchis*, fol., home of MEDEA⟧ **1** any of a genus (*Colchicum*) of plants of the lily family, with crocuslike flowers usually blooming in the fall; autumn crocus **2** its dried seeds or corm: see COLCHICINE

Col·chis (käl′kis) ancient country south of the Caucasus Mountains, on the Black Sea, in what is now Georgia —**Col·chi·an** (käl′kē ən) *adj., n.*

col·co·thar (käl′kō thər, -kə-) *n.* ⟦Sp *colcotar* < Ar *qulquṭār* < Gr *chalkanthos*, solution of blue vitriol (copper sulfate) < *chalkos*, copper + *anthos*, flower⟧ a brownish-red oxide of iron, obtained by heating ferrous sulfate: it is used as a pigment, polishing agent, etc.

cold (kōld) *adj.* ⟦ME < OE (Anglian) *cald* < IE base **gel-*, cold > COOL, Ger *kalt*, L *gelidus*⟧ **1** of a temperature significantly or noticeably lower than average, normal, expected, or comfortable; very chilly; frigid [*a cold* wind] **2** *a)* without the proper heat or warmth [this soup is *cold*] *b)* without the proper heat, warmth, or warm-up period (said of tires, engines, etc.) **3** dead **4** feeling chilled **5** without warmth of feeling; unfeeling; indifferent [a *cold* personality] **6** not cordial or kind; unfriendly [a *cold* reception] **7** sexually frigid **8** depressing or saddening; gloomy [to realize the *cold* truth] **9** not involving one's feelings; detached; objective [*cold* logic] **10** designating or having colors that suggest cold, as tones of blue, green, or gray **11** still far from what is being sought: said of the seeker **12** not strong or fresh; faint or stale [dogs tracking a *cold* scent] **13** no longer providing new or useful information, clues, etc. [following a *cold* paper trail] ☆**14** [Informal] unconscious [the boxer was knocked *cold*] **15** [Informal] unlucky or ineffective [a *cold* streak in baseball] —*adv.* [Informal] ☆**1** absolutely; completely [she was stopped *cold*] ☆**2** with complete mastery [the actor had the lines down *cold*] **3** with little or no preparation [to enter a game *cold*] —*n.* **1** *a)* absence of heat; lack of warmth: often thought of as an active force *b)* a low temperature; esp., one below freezing **2** the sensation produced by a loss or absence of heat **3** cold weather **4** a contagious, viral infection of the respiratory passages, esp. of the nose and throat, characterized by an acute inflammation of the mucous membranes, nasal discharge, malaise, etc. —**catch** (or **take**) **cold** to become ill with a cold —**cold comfort** little or no comfort at all —**come in from the cold** to come out of exile, isolation, etc.; resume an active role —**leave someone cold** to fail to arouse someone's interest —**have** (or **get**) **cold feet** ☆[Informal] to lose courage or resolve as the time of a planned action or event approaches —**in the cold** ignored; neglected —**throw cold water on** to be unenthusiastic about or toward; discourage —**cold′ly** *adv.* —**cold′ness** *n.*

cold·blood·ed (kōld′blud′id) *adj.* **1** having a body temperature that fluctuates, approximating that of the surrounding air, land, or water [fish and reptiles are *coldblooded* animals] **2** easily affected by cold **3** lacking kindness and pity; cruel —**cold′blood′ed·ly** *adv.* —**cold′blood′ed·ness** *n.*

cold call a telephone call or visit made to a prospective customer without a referral, without information sent in advance, etc.: also **cold′-call′** *n.* —**cold′-call′** *vt., vi.*

cold case ⟦see COLD, *adj.* 13⟧ an unsolved criminal case that is or was no longer being investigated

☆**cold cash** money paid in full at the time of a business transaction

cold chisel a hardened and tempered steel chisel without a handle, for cutting or chipping cold metal

☆**cold-cock** (-käk′) *vt.* ⟦< ? COLD + COCK[1] (penis)⟧ [Slang] to strike so as to make unconscious

cold comfort ineffective or insufficient consolation

cold cream a creamy, soothing preparation of emulsified oil for softening and cleansing the skin

cold cuts slices of cold meats and, usually, cheeses

cold duck ⟦transl. of Ger *kalte ente* < ?⟧ a drink made from equal parts of sparkling burgundy and champagne

cold-eyed (kōld′īd′) *adj.* **1** lacking kindness and compassion; coldblooded; unfeeling **2** calm and impartial; dispassionate; objective [a *cold-eyed* evaluation of the facts]

cold frame an unheated, boxlike, glass-covered structure for protecting young plants outdoors

cold front *Meteorol.* the forward edge of a cold air mass advancing under a warmer air mass

☆**cold fusion** a hypothetical process of producing NUCLEAR FUSION at or near room temperature, with a much higher energy yield than that produced by traditional fusion

cold·heart·ed (-härt′id) *adj.* lacking sympathy; unfeeling

cold light light not accompanied by the heat of combustion or incandescence, as phosphorescent light

cold pack **1** cold, wet blankets or sheets wrapped around a patient's body as a means of treatment **2** a process of canning foodstuffs in which the raw products are placed in jars first and then subjected to heat **3** a quickly activated, disposable chemical ice pack used in first aid, esp. for athletic injuries —**cold′-pack′** *vt.*

☆**cold rubber** a synthetic rubber formed by polymerizing and curing the starting materials, as butadiene-styrene, at a temperature of 5°C (41°F) or lower: used in automobile tires because of its special resistance to abrasion

cold shoulder [Informal] deliberate indifference or coldness; a slight, rebuff, or snub: often used with *the* —**cold′-shoul′der** *vt.*

☆**cold snap** a sudden, brief spell of cold weather

cold sore a sore, caused by a viral infection, consisting of little blisters that form in or around the mouth during a cold or fever; herpes simplex

cold storage storage of perishable foods, furs, etc. in a very cold place, esp. in a refrigerating chamber

cold sweat perspiration accompanied by a cold, clammy feeling

☆**cold turkey** ⟦< ?⟧ [Slang] **1** abruptly and totally: said of withdrawal from an addiction to drugs, tobacco, etc. **2** in a frank, blunt, or matter-of-fact way [to talk *cold turkey* about our chances] **3** without preparation or preliminaries —**cold′-tur′key** *adj.*

cold type **1** typesetting done by a method other than the casting of molten type **2** text set by photocomposition

cold war a conflict between nations that act with hostility toward one another but do not engage in direct warfare —**the Cold War** the protracted cold war (1945-91) between the non-Communist and Communist countries, esp. between the U.S. and the Soviet Union, in which each side attempted to check the global power and influence of the other: the Cold War was characterized by a buildup of large military forces and nuclear arsenals, military interventions as in Asia and Africa, the use of propaganda and espionage, etc.

cold warrior [*also* **C- W-**] a person in government, the military, etc. who was involved in the Cold War

cold-wa·ter (kōld′wôt′ər, -wät′-) *adj.* designating a room, apartment, etc. that is not provided with hot water or, sometimes, a bathroom [a *cold-water* flat]

☆**cold wave** **1** a period of weather colder than normal **2** a permanent in which the hair is set with a liquid chemical preparation

cole (kōl) *n.* ⟦ME *col* < OE *cal* < L *caulis, colis*, a cabbage, stem: see HOLE⟧ any of a genus (*Brassica*) of plants of the crucifer family; esp., rape

Cole (kōl), **Thomas** 1801-48; U.S. landscape painter

co·lec·to·my (kō lek′tə mē, kə-) *n., pl.* **-mies** ⟦COL(ON) + -ECTOMY⟧ the surgical removal of all or part of the colon

☆**cole·man·ite** (kōl′mən īt′) *n.* ⟦after W. T. *Coleman* (1824-93), U.S. manufacturer of borax⟧ a white or colorless, monoclinic mineral, $Ca_2B_6O_{11} \cdot 5H_2O$, that is an ore of boron; hydrous calcium borate

Coleman lantern (*or* **lamp)** ⟦< *Coleman*, a trademark for such a lantern⟧ a gasoline lantern that gives a bright light, used by campers

Coleman stove ⟦< *Coleman*, a trademark for such a stove⟧ a portable kerosene camp stove

co·le·op·ter·an (kō′lē äp′tər ən, käl′ē-) *n.* ⟦< ModL *Coleoptera* (< Gr *koleopteros*, sheath-winged < *koleos*, sheath + *pteron*, wing: see FEATHER) + -AN⟧ BEETLE[1] (sense 1) —**co′le·op′ter·ous** *adj.*

co·le·op·tile (kō′lē äp′til, käl′ē-) *n.* ⟦ModL *coleoptilum* < Gr *koleos*, sheath + *ptilon*, feather, prob. < IE **pti-*, var. of base **pet-*: see FEATHER⟧ the tubular protective sheath which surrounds the young shoot in the germinating grass seed

co·le·o·rhi·za (kō′lē ō rī′zə, käl′ē-) *n., pl.* **-zae′** (-zē′) ⟦ModL < Gr *koleos*, sheath + *rhiza*, root⟧ a protective root sheath of grass seedlings through which the primary root emerges

Cole·ridge (kōl′rij, kō′lər ij), **Samuel Taylor** 1772-1834; Eng. poet & critic

☆**cole·slaw** (kōl′slô′) *n.* ⟦< Du *kool*, cabbage (akin to COLE) + *sla*, for *salade*, salad⟧ a salad made of shredded raw cabbage, mayonnaise or other dressing, seasonings, etc.: also **cole slaw**

Col·et (käl′it), **John** 1467?-1519; Eng. theologian & classical scholar

Co·lette (kô let′), **(Sidonie Gabrielle Claudine)** 1873-1954; Fr. novelist

co·le·us (kō′lē əs) *n.* ⟦ModL < Gr *koleos*, a sheath: so named because of the way in which the stamens are joined⟧ any of a genus (*Coleus*) of plants of the mint family, native to Africa and the East Indies, grown for their bright-colored leaves

cole·wort (kōl′wurt′) *n.* ⟦ME: see COLE & WORT[2]⟧ **1** COLE **2** any kind of cabbage, as kale, whose leaves do not form a compact head

col·ic (käl′ik) *n.* ⟦ME *colik* < OFr *colique* < LL *colicus*, pertaining to colic, sick with colic < Gr *kōlikos* < *kōlon*, incorrect form for *kolon*, colon: from being seated in the colon and parts adjacent⟧ **1** acute abdominal pain caused by various abnormal conditions in the bowels **2** a condition of infants characterized by frequent crying due to various discomforts —*adj.* **1** of colic **2** of or near the colon —**col′ick·y** (-ik ē) *adj.*

☆**col·ic·root** (-ro͞ot′) *n.* **1** ⟦so called because it was believed to cure *colic*⟧ a North American bitter herb (*Aletris farinosa*) of the lily family, with white or yellow flowers **2** any of certain other plants, as butterfly weed, supposed to cure colic

☆**col·ic·weed** (-wēd′) *n.* any of several North American plants, as the Dutchman's-breeches

co·li·form (kō′lə fôrm′, käl′ə-) *adj.* ⟦COL(ON) + -I- + -FORM⟧ designating, of, or like the aerobic bacillus normally found in the colon: a coliform count is often used as an indicator of fecal contamination of water supplies

Co·li·gny (kô lē nyē′), **Gas·pard de** (gás pár′ də) 1519-72; Fr. admiral & Huguenot leader

Co·li·ma (kə lē′mə) **1** state of SW Mexico, on the Pacific: 2,106 sq mi (5,455 sq km) **2** its capital **3** inactive volcano in Jalisco state, near the Colima border: *c.* 14,000 ft (4,267 m): in full **Ne·va·do de Colima** (nə väd′ō de) **4** active volcano on the Jalisco-Colima border: *c.* 12,750 ft (3,886 m)

☆**col·in** (käl′in) *n.* ⟦AmSp < Nahuatl⟧ the bobwhite or similar bird

Co·lin (käl′in, kōl′-) *n.* ⟦prob. after Saint COLUMBA[2] (< L *columba*, dove), patron saint of Cornish parishes⟧ a masculine name

Col·i·se·um (käl′ə sē′əm) *n.* ⟦ModL < L *colosseum*⟧ **1** COLOSSEUM (sense 1) **2** [**c-**] a large building or stadium for sports events, exhibitions, etc.

co·li·tis (kō līt′is, kə-) *n.* ⟦ModL < Gr *kolon*, colon, large intestine + -ITIS⟧ inflammation of the large intestine

coll *abbrev.* 1 collateral 2 colleague 3 collect 4 collection 5 collective 6 collector 7 college 8 colloquial

col·lab (kə lab′) *n.* [Informal] a collaboration, specif., an amateur video consisting of portions shot or created by different people

col·lab·o·rate (kə lab′ə rāt′) *vi.* **-rat′ed, -rat′ing** ⟦< LL(Ec) *collaboratus,* pp. of *collaborare,* to work together < L *com-,* with + *laborare,* to work: see LABOR⟧ 1 to work together, esp. in some literary, artistic, or scientific undertaking 2 to cooperate with an enemy invader —**col·lab′o·ra′tion** *n.* —**col·lab′o·ra′tive** (-rāt′iv, -rə tiv) *adj.* —**col·lab′o·ra′tor** *n.*

col·lab·o·ra·tion·ist (kə lab′ə rā′shən ist) *n.* a person who cooperates with an enemy invader

col·lage (kə läzh′) *n.* ⟦Fr, a pasting < *colle,* paste < Gr *kolla,* glue⟧ 1 an art form in which, variously, small objects, bits of newspaper, cloth, pressed flowers, etc. are pasted together on a surface in incongruous relationship for their symbolic or suggestive effect 2 a composition so made 3 any collection of seemingly unrelated bits and parts, as in a photomontage —*vt.* **-laged′, -lag′ing** to arrange (material) in a collage —**col·lag′ist** *n.*

col·la·gen (käl′ə jən) *n.* ⟦< Gr *kolla,* glue + -GEN⟧ a fibrous protein found in connective tissue, bone, and cartilage —**col′la·gen′ic** (-jen′ik) *adj.* —**col·lag·e·nous** (kə laj′ə nəs) *adj.*

col·lag·e·nase (kə laj′ə nās′, käl′ə jə nās′) *n.* ⟦see -ASE⟧ any enzyme that breaks down collagen

col·lapse (kə laps′) *vi.* **-lapsed′, -laps′ing** ⟦< L *collapsus,* pp. of *collabi* < *com-,* together + *labi,* to fall: see LAP[1]⟧ 1 to fall down or fall to pieces, as when supports or sides fail to hold; cave in; shrink together suddenly 2 to break down suddenly; fail; give way [the enemy's defense *collapsed*] 3 *a)* to break down or fail suddenly in health or physical strength *b)* to fall down, as from a blow or exhaustion *c)* to fall or drop drastically, as in value or force 4 to fold or come together compactly —*vt.* to cause to collapse —*n.* the act of collapsing; a falling in or together; failure or breakdown, as in business or health —**col·laps′i·bil′i·ty** *n.* —**col·laps′i·ble** *adj.*

col·lar (käl′ər) *n.* ⟦ME *coler* < OFr *colier* < L *collare,* band or chain for the neck < *collum,* the neck < IE base **kwel-,* to turn > WHEEL, Ger *hals,* neck⟧ 1 the part of a garment that encircles the neck 2 a cloth band or folded-over piece attached to the neck of a garment 3 an ornamental band, chain, or circlet worn around the neck 4 a band of leather or metal for the neck of a dog, cat, etc. 5 the part of a harness that fits around the base of the neck of a horse or other draft animal and against which the animal exerts pressure in pulling a load 6 a ring or flange, as on rods or pipes, to prevent sideward motion, connect parts, etc. 7 a distinctive band, as of a different color or texture, around the neck of an animal, bird, etc. 8 the foam that forms on the top of a glass of beer ☆9 [Slang] an arrest or capture —*vt.* 1 to put a collar on 2 to seize by the collar 3 [Informal] *a)* to take hold or control of; seize or capture *b)* to stop and delay by talking to —**go for the collar** *Baseball* to go without a hit in a game —**col·lar·less** *adj.*

col·lar·bone (-bōn′) *n.* CLAVICLE

col·lard (käl′ərd) *n.* ⟦contr. < COLEWORT⟧ 1 a kind of kale with coarse leaves borne in tufts 2 [*pl.*] the leaves of this plant, used as a vegetable: also called **collard greens**

collat *abbrev.* collateral

col·late (kō′lāt′, kä′-; kə lāt′) *vt.* **-lat′ed, -lat′ing** ⟦< L *collatus,* pp. of *conferre,* to bring together < *com-,* together + *ferre,* to BEAR[1]⟧ 1 to compare (texts, data, etc.) critically in order to consolidate, note similarities and differences, etc. 2 *a)* to gather (the sections of a book, pages of a document, etc.) together in proper order *b)* to examine (such material) to see that all pages, plates, etc. are in proper order, as for binding 3 to examine (a book) to see whether all pages and plates are present 4 to appoint (a clergyman) to a benefice —*SYN.* COMPARE —**col′la′tor** *n.*

col·lat·er·al (kə lat′ər əl) *adj.* ⟦ME < ML *collateralis* < L *com-,* together + *lateralis,* LATERAL⟧ 1 side by side; parallel 2 parallel in time, rank, importance, etc.; corresponding 3 accompanying or existing in a subordinate, corroborative, or indirect relationship 4 descended from the same ancestors but in a different line [a cousin is a *collateral* relative] 5 *a)* designating or of security given as a pledge for the fulfillment of an obligation *b)* secured or guaranteed by property, as stocks or bonds [a *collateral* loan] —*n.* 1 a collateral relative ☆2 anything, such as stocks or bonds, that secures or guarantees the discharge of an obligation —**col·lat′er·al·ly** *adv.*

collateral damage 1 *euphemism for* the unintended killing of civilians and destruction of untargeted buildings, land, etc. during a military operation 2 the unintended detrimental consequences of any action or decision

col·lat·er·al·ize (-īz′) *vt.* **-ized′, -iz′ing** 1 to give collateral as security for (a loan) 2 to use as collateral —**col·lat′er·al·i·za′tion** *n.*

col·la·tion (kō lā′shən, kä-, kə-) *n.* ⟦ME *collacioun* < OFr *collacion,* discourse < L *collatio:* see COLLATE⟧ 1 the act, process, or result of collating 2 a conference or gathering, as of monks at the close of the day to listen to a reading from a religious book and to discuss it 3 a light meal: originally such a meal was served in a monastery during the COLLATION (sense 2) 4 *Library Science* the physical description of a book, including the trim size, number of pages and illustrations, etc.

col·league (käl′ēg′) *n.* ⟦Fr *collègue* < L *collega,* one chosen along with another < *com-,* with + *legare,* to appoint as deputy: see LEGATE⟧ a fellow worker in the same profession; associate —*SYN.* ASSOCIATE

col·lect[1] (kə lekt′) *vt.* ⟦ME *collecten* < OFr *collecter* < L *collectus:* see fol.⟧ 1 to gather together; assemble 2 to gather (stamps, books, etc.) as a hobby 3 to call for and receive (money) for (rent, a fund, taxes, bills, etc.) 4 to regain control of (oneself or one's wits); summon up (one's faculties or powers) ☆5 [Now Chiefly Brit.] to pick up; fetch —*vi.* 1 to gather; assemble [a crowd *collected*] 2 to accumulate [water *collects* in the basement] 3 to collect payments, contributions, etc. — *adj., adv.* ☆with payment to be made by the receiver [to telephone *collect*] —*SYN.* GATHER

col·lect[2] (käl′ekt′) *n.* ⟦ME & OFr *collecte* < LL *collecta,* a gathering together of ideas from the day's reading < L, a gathering, contribution of money < *collectus,* pp. of *colligere* < *com-,* together + *legere,* to gather < IE base **leĝ-,* to collect > LEECH[1]⟧ [*also* **C-**] a short prayer suitable to the time or occasion, used in certain church services, as before the Epistle at Mass

col·lect·ed (kə lek′tid) *adj.* 1 gathered together; assembled [the *collected* works of Poe] 2 in control of oneself; calm and self-possessed —*SYN.* COOL —**col·lect′ed·ly** *adv.* —**col·lect′ed·ness** *n.*

col·lect·i·ble or **col·lect·a·ble** (kə lek′tə bəl) *adj.* 1 that can be collected 2 suitable or desirable for collecting, as by a hobbyist —*n.* any of a class of things that people collect as a hobby, typically a thing of no great intrinsic value

col·lec·tion (kə lek′shən) *n.* ⟦ME *collecioun* < L *collectio*⟧ 1 the act or process of collecting 2 things collected, specif., as in a hobby [a *collection* of stamps] 3 a mass or pile; accumulation 4 money collected, as during a church service

col·lec·tive (kə lek′tiv) *adj.* ⟦ME & OFr *collectif* < L *collectivus*⟧ 1 formed by collecting; gathered into a whole 2 of, as, or characteristic of a group; of or by all or many of the individuals in a group acting together [the *collective* effort of the students] 3 designating or of any enterprise in which people work together as a group, esp. under a system of collectivism [a *collective* farm] 4 *Gram. a)* designating a noun which is singular in form but denotes a collection of individuals (e.g., *army, orchestra, crowd*): it is treated as singular when the collection is thought of as a whole and as plural when the individual members are thought of as acting separately *b)* designating a prefix which denotes a collecting or a collection —*n.* 1 any collective enterprise; specif., a collective farm 2 the people working in such an enterprise 3 *Gram.* a collective noun —**col·lec′tive·ly** *adv.*

collective bargaining negotiation between organized workers and their employer or employers for reaching an agreement on wages, fringe benefits, hours, and working conditions

collective fruit MULTIPLE FRUIT

collective security a system of international security in which the participating nations agree to take joint action against a nation that attacks any one of them

collective unconscious in the theory of C. G. Jung, the part of the unconscious mind that each human being inherits along with all other human beings: it contains certain patterns, or archetypes, observable in all cultures

col·lec·tiv·ism (kə lek′tə viz′əm) *n.* ⟦Fr *collectivisme* (*c.* 1880): see COLLECTIVE & -ISM⟧ the ownership and control of the means of production and distribution by the people collectively; socialism —**col·lec′tiv·ist** *n., adj.* —**col·lec′tiv·is′tic** *adj.*

col·lec·tiv·i·ty (käl′ek tiv′ə tē) *n., pl.* **-ties** 1 the quality or state of being collective 2 a collective whole 3 the people as a whole

col·lec·tiv·ize (kə lek′tə vīz′) *vt.* **-ized′, -iz′ing** to organize under a system of collectivism —**col·lec′ti·vi·za′tion** *n.*

☆**collect on delivery** payment in cash when a purchase or shipment is delivered

col·lec·tor (kə lek′tər) *n.* ⟦ME *collectour* < ML *collector*⟧ a person or thing that collects; specif., *a)* a person whose work is collecting taxes, overdue bills, etc. *b)* a person who collects stamps, books, etc. as a hobby *c)* in some transistors, the region or layer of semiconductor material, acting as an electrode, that receives the electric current from the base

col·leen (kä lēn′, kä′lēn′) *n.* ⟦Ir *cailin,* dim. of *caile,* girl⟧ [Irish] a girl

Col·leen (kä lēn′, kä′lēn′) *n.* ⟦Ir: see prec.⟧ a feminine name

col·lege (käl′ij) *n.* ⟦ME & OFr < L *collegium,* community, society, guild, fraternity < *collega:* see COLLEAGUE⟧ 1 an association of individuals having certain powers and duties, and engaged in some common pursuit [the electoral *college*] 2 ⟦orig. with ref. to the university communities of Oxford & Cambridge⟧ an institution of higher education that grants degrees, as a bachelor's degree after a four-year course or an associate degree after a two-year course: it is sometimes the undergraduate division of a university 3 any of the schools of a university offering instruction and granting degrees in any of several specialized courses of study, esp. graduate study, as in liberal arts, architecture, law, or medicine 4 a school offering specialized instruction in some profession or occupation [a secretarial *college*] 5 [Brit.] a private secondary school [Eton *College*] 6 the students, faculty, or administrators of a college 7 a clerical group that has been given the legal status of an ecclesiastical corporation 8 the building or buildings of a college

College of Arms HERALDS' COLLEGE

College of Cardinals the cardinals of the Roman Catholic Church, serving as a privy council to the pope and electing his successor

college try ⟦< phr. (*give it the old*) *college try,* to make one's best effort for one's team, school, etc.⟧ [Informal] an enthusiastic attempt that utilizes all one's energy and resources

col·le·gi·al (kə lē′jəl, -jē əl) *adj.* ⟦ME < L *collegialis*⟧ 1 with authority or power shared equally among colleagues 2 COLLEGIATE 3 characterized by mutual consideration and respect among colleagues

col·le·gi·al·i·ty (kə lē′jē al′ə tē) *n.* 1 the sharing of authority among colleagues 2 *R.C.Ch.* the principle that authority is shared by the pope and the bishops 3 considerate and respectful conduct among colleagues or an atmosphere, relationship, etc. characterized by this

col·le·gian (kə lē′jən, -jē ən) ***n.*** ⟦ME, member of a college < ML *collegianus*⟧ a college student

col·le·giate (kə lē′jit, -jē it) ***adj.*** ⟦ME *collegiat* < LL *collegiatus,* member of a college⟧ **1** of or like a college **2** of, like, or for college students **3** of or like a collegiate church

collegiate church 1 a church served by resident canons **2** in Scotland, a church with two or more ministers serving jointly ☆**3** in the U.S., *a)* a church associated with others under a joint body of pastors *b)* such an association of churches

col·le·gi·um (kə lē′jē əm, kə leg′ē əm) ***n.,*** *pl.* **-gi·a** (-ə) or **-gi·ums** ⟦L: see COLLEGE⟧ **1** an amateur musical ensemble, as of early music, esp. one associated with a college or university: in full **col·le′gi·um mu′si·cum** (-myōō′zi kum), *pl.* **col·le·gi·a mu·si·ca** (kə lē′jē ə myōō′zi kə, kə leg′ē ə-) **2** a group of individuals with equal power or authority; esp., an administrative board for a Soviet commissariat

col·lem·bo·lan (kə lem′bō lən) ***n.*** ⟦< ModL *Collembola* (< Gr *kolla,* glue + *embolon,* a peg, akin to *embolos,* a wedge: see EMBOLUS) + -AN⟧ SPRINGTAIL

col·len·chy·ma (kə leŋ′ki mə) ***n.*** ⟦< Gr *kolla,* glue + *enchyma,* a steeping, infusion < *enchein,* to pour in < *en-,* in + *cheein,* to pour: see FOUND[3]⟧ plant tissue consisting of elongated cells thickened at the corners, often found between the epidermis and the cortex of young stems —**col·len·chym·a·tous** (käl′ən kim′ə təs) ***adj.***

col·let (käl′it) ***n.*** ⟦Fr, dim. of *col,* the neck < L *collum:* see COLLAR⟧ **1** a metal band or ring, such as is used in a watch to hold the end of a balance spring **2** a small metal band used in ring settings **3** a chuck with a conical or tapered end, for gripping circular pieces to be turned on a lathe —***vt.*** to set in, or furnish with, a collet

col·lide (kə līd′) ***vi.*** **-lid′ed, -lid′ing** ⟦L *collidere* < *com-,* together + *laedere,* to strike, injure⟧ **1** to come into violent contact; strike violently against each other; crash **2** to come into conflict; clash

col·lid·er (kə līd′ər) ***n.*** *Nuclear Physics* a type of particle accelerator in which two beams of high-energy charged particles moving in opposite directions are made to collide head-on

col·lie (käl′ē) ***n.*** ⟦said to be < *coaly,* coal-black, from the color of some of the breed⟧ any of a breed of large, long-haired dog with a long, narrow head: first bred in Scotland for herding sheep

collie

col·lier (käl′yər) ***n.*** ⟦ME *colyer:* see COAL & -IER⟧ [Chiefly Brit.] **1** a coal miner **2** a ship for carrying coal

col·lier·y (-ē) ***n.,*** *pl.* **-lier·ies** ⟦prec. + -Y[4]⟧ [Chiefly Brit.] a coal mine and its buildings, equipment, etc.

col·li·gate (käl′ə gāt′) ***vt.*** **-gat′ed, -gat′ing** ⟦< L *colligatus,* pp. of *colligare,* to bind together < *com-,* together + *ligare,* to bind (see LIGATURE)⟧ **1** to bind together **2** to relate (isolated facts) by some reasonable explanation, esp. so as to evolve a general principle —**col′li·ga′tion** ***n.***

col·li·mate (käl′ə māt′) ***vt.*** **-mat′ed, -mat′ing** ⟦< ModL *collimare,* false reading of L *collineare,* to direct in a straight line < *com-,* with + *lineare,* to make straight < *linea,* a LINE[2]⟧ **1** to make (light rays, etc.) parallel **2** to adjust the line of sight of (a telescope, surveyor's level, etc.) —**col′li·ma′tion** ***n.***

col·li·ma·tor (-māt′ər) ***n.*** ⟦see prec.⟧ **1** a small telescope with crosshairs at its focus, fixed to another telescope, surveying instrument, etc. for adjusting the line of sight **2** a device that causes a beam of radiation, as light, to move as parallel rays

col·lin·e·ar (kə lin′ē ər) ***adj.*** ⟦COL- (var. of COM-) + LINEAR⟧ in, or sharing, the same straight line, as two points or planes

Col·lins[1] (käl′inz) ***n.*** ⟦supposedly after its inventor, a bartender named Tom Collins⟧ ☆[*also* **c-**] an iced drink made with gin (*Tom Collins*), or vodka, rum, whiskey, etc., mixed with soda water, lime or lemon juice, and sugar

Col·lins[2] (käl′inz) **1 Michael** 1890-1922; Ir. revolutionary leader **2 (William) Wil·kie** (wil′kē) 1824-89; Eng. novelist **3 William** 1721-59; Eng. poet

☆**col·lin·si·a** (kə lin′sē ə, -zē ə) ***n.*** ⟦ModL, after Z. *Collins* (1764-1831), Am botanist⟧ any of a genus (*Collinsia*) of hardy, low-growing plants of the figwort family, with flowers arranged in whorls

col·li·sion (kə lizh′ən) ***n.*** ⟦ME < LL *collisio* < pp. of L *collidere:* see COLLIDE⟧ **1** the act of colliding, or coming together with sudden, violent force **2** a clash or conflict of opinions, interests, etc.

col·lo·cate (käl′ə kāt′) ***vt.*** **-cat′ed, -cat′ing** ⟦< L *collocatus,* pp. of *collocare,* to place together < *com-,* together + *locare:* see LOCATE⟧ to arrange; esp., to set side by side

col·lo·ca·tion (käl′ə kā′shən) ***n.*** ⟦L *collocatio*⟧ a collocating or being collocated; specif., an arrangement, as of words in a sentence

☆**col·lo·di·on** (kə lō′dē ən) ***n.*** ⟦< Gr *kollōdēs,* gluelike < *kolla,* glue + *eidos,* form⟧ a highly flammable, colorless or pale-yellow, viscous solution of pyroxylin in a mixture of alcohol and ether: it dries quickly, forming a tough, elastic film, and is used as a protective coating for wounds, in cements, etc.

col·logue (kə lōg′) ***vi.*** **-logued′, -logu′ing** ⟦< Fr *colloque,* conference < L *colloquium* (see COLLOQUY); sp. altered by assoc. with obs. *colleague,* to conspire⟧ **1** [Archaic] to confer or converse privately **2** [Dial.] to intrigue or conspire

col·loid (käl′oid′) ***n.*** ⟦< Gr *kolla,* glue + -OID; coined by T. Graham (1805-69), Scot chemist⟧ **1** *a)* a solid, liquid, or gaseous substance made up of very small, insoluble particles (as single large molecules or masses of smaller molecules) that remain in suspension in a surrounding solid, liquid, or gaseous medium of different matter *b)* a state of matter consisting of such a substance dispersed in a surrounding medium: all living matter contains colloidal material, and a colloid has only a negligible effect on the freezing point, boiling point, or vapor pressure of the surrounding medium **2** the iodine-containing, gelatinous protein stored in the thyroid

col·loi·dal (kə loid′'l) ***adj.*** **1** of, like, or containing a colloid **2** of the nature, or in the form, of a colloid

col·lop (käl′əp) ***n.*** ⟦ME *colhoppe,* a dish of fried or roasted meat, a morsel < Scand, as in Swed *kollops,* OSwed *kolhuppadher,* cooked on coal < *kol,* COAL + ? *huppa,* to leap⟧ **1** a portion or piece; esp., a small slice of meat **2** [Archaic] a fold of fatty flesh on the body

colloq *abbrev.* **1** colloquial **2** colloquialism

col·lo·qui·al (kə lō′kwē əl) ***adj.*** ⟦< L *colloquium* (see COLLOQUY) + -AL⟧ **1** having to do with or like conversation; conversational **2** INFORMAL (sense *e*) —**col·lo′qui·al·ly** ***adv.***

col·lo·qui·al·ism (-iz′əm) ***n.*** **1** colloquial quality, style, or usage **2** a colloquial word or expression **3** loosely, a localism, or regionalism

col·lo·quist (käl′ə kwist) ***n.*** a participant in a colloquy

col·lo·qui·um (kə lō′kwē əm) ***n.,*** *pl.* **-qui·a** (-ə) or **-qui·ums** ⟦L: see fol.⟧ an organized conference or seminar on some subject, involving a number of scholars or experts

col·lo·quy (käl′ə kwē) ***n.,*** *pl.* **-quies** ⟦L *colloquium,* conversation < *com-,* together + *loqui,* speak⟧ a conversation, esp. a formal discussion; conference

col·lo·type (käl′ə tīp′) ***n.*** ⟦< Gr *kolla,* glue + -TYPE⟧ **1** a photomechanical process by which inked reproductions are transferred to paper directly from an image formed on a sheet of hardened gelatin **2** the printed reproduction

col·lude (kə lōōd′) ***vi.*** **-lud′ed, -lud′ing** ⟦L *colludere* < *com-,* with + *ludere,* to play: see LUDICROUS⟧ to act in collusion or conspire, esp. for a fraudulent purpose

col·lu·sion (kə lōō′zhən) ***n.*** ⟦ME < L *collusio* < *collusus,* pp. of *colludere:* see prec.⟧ a secret agreement for fraudulent or illegal purpose; conspiracy —**col·lu′sive** (-siv) ***adj.*** —**col·lu′sive·ly** ***adv.***

col·lu·vi·um (kə lōō′vē əm) ***n.,*** *pl.* **-vi·a** (-ə) or **-vi·ums** ⟦ML, altered < L *colluvies,* dregs, sweepings < *colluere,* to wash out < *col-,* var. of *com-,* COM- + *luere,* var. of *lavare,* to LAVE⟧ rock fragments, sand, etc. that accumulate on steep slopes or at the foot of cliffs

col·lyr·i·um (kə lir′ē əm) ***n.,*** *pl.* **-i·a** (-ə) or **-i·ums** ⟦L < Gr *kollyrion,* eye salve (in the form of a tablet) < *kollyra,* loaf of coarse bread, loaf-shaped tablet⟧ any medicated preparation for the eyes; eyewash

col·ly·wob·bles (käl′ē wäb′əlz) ***pl.n.*** ⟦prob. < COLIC + WOBBLE⟧ [Informal] pain in the abdomen; bellyache: usually with *the*

Colo *abbrev.* Colorado

col·o·bus (käl′ə bəs) ***n.*** ⟦ModL < Gr *kolobos,* curtailed, docked (akin to *kolos,* maimed: for IE base see HOLT): prob. so named because of the absent or rudimentary thumbs⟧ any of a genus (*Colobus*) of thumbless, long-haired, black and white African monkeys: also **colobus monkey**

col·o·cynth (käl′ə sinth′) ***n.*** ⟦L *colocynthis* < Gr *kolokynthis*⟧ **1** an African and Asian perennial vine (*Citrullus colocynthis*) of the gourd family, whose small, dried fruits are used in making a strong cathartic **2** this fruit, or the cathartic prepared from it; bitter apple

co·logne (kə lōn′) ***n.*** a perfumed toilet water made of alcohol and aromatic oils; eau de Cologne

Co·logne (kə lōn′) ⟦Fr, after L *Colonia (Agrippina),* the colony (of Agrippina)⟧ city in W Germany, on the Rhine, in the state of North Rhine-Westphalia: Ger. name KÖLN

col·om·bard (käl′əm bärd′, kul′-) ***n.*** ⟦Fr⟧ **1** a white grape, originally of France, widely grown in California **2** a slightly dry white wine made from this grape In full **French colombard**

Co·lom·bi·a (kə lum′bē ə; *Sp* kô lôm′byä) country in NW South America, on the Pacific Ocean & the Caribbean Sea: gained independence from Spain in 1819: 439,736 sq mi (1,138,910 sq km); cap. Bogotá —**Co·lom′bi·an** ***adj., n.***

Co·lom·bo (kə lum′bō) capital of Sri Lanka: seaport on the W coast

co·lon[1] (kō′lən) ***n.*** ⟦L < Gr *kōlon,* part of a verse, member, limb < IE base *(*s*)*kel-,* to bend, crooked > L *coluber,* snake, *calx,* heel⟧ **1** a mark of punctuation (:) used before an extended quotation, explanation, example, series, etc. and after the salutation of a formal letter **2** *pl.* **co′la** (-lə) in Greek prosody, a section of a prosodic period, consisting of a group of two to six feet forming a rhythmic unit with a principal accent

co·lon[2] (kō′lən) ***n.,*** *pl.* **-lons** or **-la** (-lə) ⟦L < Gr *kolon*⟧ that part of the large intestine extending from the cecum to the rectum

co·lon[3] (kô lôn′; *E* kə lōn′) ***n.*** ⟦Fr⟧ a colonist, esp. one who owns a plantation

co·lón (kə lōn′) ***n.*** ⟦AmSp, after Sp *Colón,* COLUMBUS[1]⟧ the basic monetary unit of Costa Rica and, formerly, El Salvador: see the table of monetary units in the Reference Supplement: also Sp. **co·lón** (kô lôn′), *pl.* **-lon′es** (-lô′nes)

Co·lón[1] (kə lōn′) ⟦see prec.⟧ seaport in Panama, at the Caribbean end of the Panama Canal

Co·lón[2] (kô lôn′), **Ar·chi·pié·la·go de** (är′chē pyā′lä gô *the*) *Sp. name for* GALÁPAGOS ISLANDS

colo·nel (kur′nəl) ***n.*** ⟦earlier *coronel* < Fr *colonel, coronel* (*-r-* by dissimilation) < It *colonello* < *colonna,* (military) column < L *columna,* COLUMN; Fr & E sp. modified after L & It, but older pronun. kept in E⟧ 1 a military officer ranking above a lieutenant colonel and below a brigadier general, and corresponding to a captain in the navy ☆2 an honorary, nonmilitary title in some Southern or Western U.S. states —**colo′nel·cy** (-sē) *n., pl.* **-cies**

co·lo·nia (kə lôn′yə; *Sp* kô lô′nyä) *n., pl.* **-nias** ⟦MexSp⟧ 1 in Mexico, a neighborhood, district, or suburb of a city 2 in the SW U.S., a rural settlement or part of a city whose residents are mainly Mexican and Mexican-American

co·lo·ni·al (kə lō′nē əl) *adj.* 1 of or living in a colony or colonies 2 [*often* **C-**] of the thirteen British colonies that became the U.S., or characteristic of the styles of their period 3 made up of or having colonies 4 characteristic of or having to do with colonialism —*n.* 1 an inhabitant of a colony 2 [*also* **C-**] a house built in any of various styles of the colonial period, typically a square or rectangular dwelling having two stories, a highly symmetrical exterior, and, often, a central hall from which all downstairs rooms extend —**co·lo′ni·al·ly** *adv.*

colonial animal COMPOUND ANIMAL

co·lo·ni·al·ism (-iz′əm) *n.* the system or policy by which a country maintains foreign colonies, esp. in order to exploit them economically —**co·lo′ni·al·ist** *n., adj.*

co·lon·ic (kə län′ik) *adj.* of or having to do with the intestinal colon [*colonic* irrigation] —*n.* ENEMA

☆**col·o·nist** (käl′ə nist) *n.* 1 any of the original settlers or founders of a colony 2 an inhabitant of a colony

col·o·nize (käl′ə nīz′) *vt.* **-nized′**, **-niz′ing** 1 to found or establish a colony or colonies in 2 to settle (persons) in a colony ☆3 to place (voters) illegally in (a district) so as to influence an election —*vi.* 1 to found or establish a colony or colonies 2 to settle in a colony —**col′o·ni·za′tion** *n.* —**col′o·niz′er** *n.*

col·on·nade (käl′ə nād′) *n.* ⟦Fr < It *colonnato* < *colonna* < L *columna,* COLUMN⟧ *Archit.* a series of columns set at regular intervals, usually supporting a roof or series of arches —**col′on·nad′ed** *adj.*

co·lon·o·scope (kə län′ə skōp′) *n.* a fiber-optic endoscope used to examine the inside of the colon and, often, to take tissue samples —**co·lon′o·scop′ic** (-skäp′ik) *adj.* —**co·lon·os·co·py** (kō′lən äs′kə pē) *n.*

col·o·ny (käl′ə nē) *n., pl.* **-nies** ⟦ME *colonie* < L *colonia* < *colonus,* farmer < *colere,* to cultivate: see CULT⟧ 1 *a)* a group of people who settle in a distant land but remain under the political jurisdiction of their native land *b)* the region thus settled 2 a territory distant from the state having jurisdiction or control over it 3 [**C-**] [*pl.*] the thirteen British colonies in North America that won their independence in the Revolutionary War and became the U.S.: they were Va., N.Y., Mass., Conn., R.I., N.H., Md., N.J., N.C., S.C., Pa., Del., and Ga. 4 *a)* a community of people of the same nationality or pursuits concentrated in a particular district or place [the Hungarian *colony* of Cleveland, an artists' *colony*] *b)* such a district or place 5 *Bacteriology* a group of cells that are derived from a single initial cell, growing separately on a solid culture medium 6 *Biol.* a group of similar plants or animals living or growing together 7 *Zool.* a compound organism consisting of several to many incompletely separated individuals, as in corals and hydroids

col·o·phon (käl′ə fən, -fän′) *n.* ⟦LL < Gr *kolophōn,* summit, top, end: see COLUMN⟧ 1 a notation often placed in a book, at the end, giving facts about its production ☆2 the distinctive emblem of the publisher, as on the title page or cover of a book

col·o·pho·ny (käl′ə fō′nē, kə läf′ə nē) *n.* ⟦ME *colofonie* < L *colophonia (resina)* < Gr *kolophōnia (rhētinē),* lit., Colophonian (resin), after *Kolophōn,* Colophon, ancient Ionian city: see prec.⟧ ROSIN

col·or (kul′ər) *n.* ⟦ME & OFr *colour* < L *color* < OL *colos,* orig., a covering < IE base **kel-,* to conceal, hide > HULL[1], HALL⟧ 1 the sensation resulting from stimulation of the retina of the eye by light waves of certain lengths 2 the property of reflecting light of a particular wavelength: the distinct colors of the spectrum are red, orange, yellow, green, blue, indigo, and violet, each of these shading into the next; the *primary colors* of the spectrum are red, green, and blue, the light beams of which variously combined can produce any of the colors 3 any coloring matter; dye; pigment; paint: the *primary colors* of paints, pigments, etc. are red, yellow, and blue, which, when mixed in various ways, produce the *secondary colors* (green, orange, purple, etc.): black, white, and gray are often called colors (*achromatic colors*), although black is caused by the complete absorption of light rays, white by the reflection of all the rays that produce color, and gray by an imperfect absorption of all these rays 4 any color other than black, white, or gray; chromatic color: color is distinguished by the qualities of *hue* (as red, brown, yellow, etc.), *lightness* (for pigmented surfaces) or *brightness* (for light itself), and *saturation* (the degree of intensity of a hue) 5 color of the face; esp., a healthy rosiness or a blush 6 the color of a person's skin 7 skin pigmentation of a particular people or racial group, esp. when non-Caucasoid 8 [*pl.*] a colored badge, ribbon, costume, etc. that identifies the wearer's rank, group, etc. 9 [*pl.*] *a)* a flag or banner of a country, regiment, etc. *b)* the armed forces of a country, symbolized by the flag [to serve with the *colors*] 10 [*pl.*] the side that a person is on; position or opinion [stick to your *colors*] 11 outward appearance or semblance; plausibility 12 appearance of truth, likelihood, validity, or right; justification [the circumstances gave *color* to his contention] 13 general nature; character [the *color* of his mind] 14 vivid quality or character, as in a personality, literary work, etc.: see also LOCAL COLOR 15 *Art* the way of using color, esp. to gain a total effect 16 *Law* an apparent or prima-facie right ☆17 *Mining* a trace of gold found in panning 18 *Music a)* timbre, as of a voice or instrument; tone color *b)* elaborate ornamentation 19 *Particle Physics* a unique force or charge on each type of quark that controls how quarks combine to form hadrons: although called red, green, and blue, they are not related to visual colors 20 *Photog., TV, etc.* reproduction of images in chromatic colors rather than in black, white, and gray 21 *Radio, TV* colorful details, background data, etc. supplied by a sports commentator between play-by-play descriptions of the action —*adj. Radio, TV* designating or of a sports commentator who supplies COLOR (*n.* 21) —*vt.* ⟦L *colorare*⟧ 1 to give color to; impregnate or cover with color, as with paint, stain, or dye 2 to change the color of 3 to give a pleasing, convincing, or reasonable appearance to; make plausible 4 to alter or influence to some degree, as by distortion or exaggeration [prejudice *colored* his views] —*vi.* 1 to become colored 2 to change color, as ripening fruit 3 to blush or flush 4 to engage in the child's pastime of drawing or coloring pictures with wax crayons, etc. —**call to the colors** 1 call or order to serve in the armed forces 2 *Mil.* a bugle call for the daily flag-raising and flag-lowering ceremonies —**change color** 1 to become pale 2 to blush or flush —**lose color** to become pale —**of color** who is nonwhite; now esp., who is black [a woman *of color*] —**show one's (true) colors** 1 to reveal one's true self 2 to make one's opinions, position, etc. known —**under color of** under the pretext or guise of —**col′or·er** *n.*

SYN.—**color** is the general term, for which see the definition above; **shade** refers to any of the gradations of a color with reference to its degree of darkness [a light *shade* of green]; **hue**, often equivalent to **color**, is used specifically to indicate a modification of a basic color [orange or a reddish *hue*]; **tint** refers to a gradation of a color with reference to its degree of whiteness and suggests a paleness or delicacy of color [pastel *tints*]; **tinge** suggests the presence of a small amount of color, usually diffused throughout [white with a *tinge* of blue]

col·or·a·ble (kul′ər ə bəl) *adj.* ⟦LL *colorabilis*⟧ 1 capable of being colored 2 apparently valid, but actually specious —**col′or·a·bly** *adv.*

Col·o·rad·an (käl′ə rad′ən, -rä′dən) *adj.* of Colorado: usually used in the predicate —*n.* a person born or living in Colorado

col·o·ra·do (käl′ə rä′dō, kul′ə rad′ō) *adj.* ⟦Sp, red, lit., colored, pp. of *colorar* < L *colorare* < *color*: see COLOR⟧ of medium strength and color: said of cigars

Col·o·rad·o (käl′ə rad′ō, -rä′dō) ⟦< Sp name of the river, *Río Colorado,* lit., reddish-brown river⟧ 1 Mountain State of the W U.S.: admitted 1876; 103,718 sq mi (268,627 sq km); cap. Denver: abbrev. *CO* or *Colo* 2 river in SW U.S., flowing from the Rocky Mts. of N Colo. southwest through Utah & along the Arizona-Nevada & Arizona-California borders into the Gulf of California: 1,450 mi (2,333 km) 3 river in Tex., flowing from the NW part southeast into the Gulf of Mexico: 840 mi (1,352 km)

☆**Colorado beetle** a widely distributed black-and-yellowish beetle (*Leptinotarsa decemlineata*) that is a destructive pest of potatoes and other plants

Colorado Desert desert in SE Calif., west of the Colorado River: *c.* 2,000 sq mi (5,180 sq km)

Colorado Springs ⟦for the mineral springs in the area⟧ city in central Colo.: site of the U.S. Air Force Academy

☆**col·or·ant** (kul′ər ənt) *n.* ⟦Fr < prp. of *colorer,* to color⟧ a pigment, dye, etc. used to give color to something

col·or·a·tion (kul′ər ā′shən) *n.* 1 the condition of being colored 2 the way a thing is colored 3 the technique of using colors, as in painting

col·o·ra·tu·ra (kul′ə rə toor′ə, -tyoor′-) *n.* ⟦It < L *coloratus,* pp. of *colorare,* to COLOR⟧ 1 brilliant runs, trills, etc., used to display a singer's skill 2 music containing such ornamentation 3 a soprano who sings such music: in full **coloratura soprano**

color bar COLOR LINE

col·or-bear·er (kul′ər ber′ər) *n.* the person assigned to carry the colors, or flag, as in a parade or ceremony

col·or·blind (-blīnd′) *adj.* 1 unable to perceive colors or to distinguish between certain colors, as red and green ☆2 not influenced by considerations of race —**col′or·blind′ness** *n.*

col·or·cast (-kast′) *n.* ⟦COLOR + (TELE)CAST⟧ a television broadcast in color —*vt., vi.* **-cast′** or **-cast′ed**, **-cast′ing** to televise in color

col·or-code (-kōd′) *vt.* **-cod′ed**, **-cod′ing** to use specific colors, according to a code, for wires, switches, cards, files, etc.

co·lo·rec·tal (kō′lə rek′təl) *adj.* of or having to do with the colon and rectum [a *colorectal* exam]

col·ored (kul′ərd) *adj.* 1 having color 2 of a (specified) color 3 of a group other than the Caucasoid 4 [Old-fashioned] BLACK (*adj.* 2*b*) 5 [**C-**] in South Africa, of racially mixed parentage: in this sense, usually sp. **Coloured** 6 altered, influenced, distorted, or exaggerated to some degree [remarks *colored* by prejudice]

col·or·fast (kul′ər fast′) *adj.* that will keep its original color without fading or running —**col′or·fast′ness** *n.*

☆**col·or-field** (kul′ər fēld′) *adj.* designating or of a style of abstract painting in which colors are applied to a canvas, often in large patches, with little variation in tone and little emphasis on form

color filter colored glass, dyed gelatin, etc., used to produce certain color or light effects, as in photography

col·or·ful (kul′ər fəl) *adj.* 1 full of color or of vivid colors 2 full of interest or variety; vivid —**col′or·ful·ly** *adv.* —**col′or·ful·ness** *n.*

☆**color guard** the persons carrying and escorting the colors, or flag, in a parade, ceremony, etc.

col·or·if·ic (kul′ər if′ik) *adj.* ⟦Fr *colorifique:* see COLOR & -FIC⟧ **1** producing or imparting color **2** of color

col·or·im·e·ter (kul′ər im′ət ər) *n.* ⟦COLOR + -I- + -METER⟧ an instrument for determining the intensity and hue of a color, as of a solution in chemical analysis, by comparing it with standard colors

col·or·im·e·try (-im′ə trē) *n.* the analysis or measurement of color by means of a colorimeter —**col·or·i·met·ric** (kul′ər ə me′trik) *adj.* —**col′or·i·met′ri·cal·ly** *adv.*

col·or·ing (kul′ər iŋ) *n.* **1** the act or art of applying colors **2** anything applied to impart color; pigment, dye, stain, etc. **3** *a)* the way a thing is naturally colored; coloration *b)* the effect created by a particular use of color **4** the color of the skin **5** specious or false appearance **6** alteration or influence

coloring book a book of black-and-white line drawings intended to be colored as by children with crayons, watercolors, etc.

col·or·ist (kul′ər ist) *n.* **1** a person who uses colors **2** an artist skillful in using colors **3** a beautician who specializes in dyeing hair

col·or·is·tic (kul′ər is′tik) *adj.* **1** having to do with color or the use of color **2** *Music* of or characterized by an emphasis on timbre or tonal effects —**col′or·is′ti·cal·ly** *adv.*

col·or·ize (kul′ər īz′) *vt.* **-ized′**, **-iz′ing** to prepare a video version of (a black-and-white film) in which color tones have been added by means of a computer program —**col′or·i·za′tion** *n.*

col·or·less (kul′ər lis) *adj.* **1** without color **2** dull in color; gray or pallid **3** lacking variety or interest; dull —**col′or·less·ly** *adv.* —**col′or·less·ness** *n.*

☆**color line** the barrier of social, political, and economic restrictions imposed on blacks or other nonwhites —**cross (or draw) the color line** to flout (or impose or honor) the color line

color phase **1** a variant, atypical coloration of fur, feathers, skin, etc. occurring in an individual or an animal group **2** a seasonal change in the coat or coloration of certain animals

col·or·point shorthair (kul′ər point′) any of a breed of domestic cat, bred by crossing a Siamese and an American shorthair, with blue, almond-shaped eyes and a short, glossy, white coat shading to a darker color at the face, ears, feet, and tail

Co·los·sae (kə läs′ē) city in ancient Phrygia, SW Asia Minor (fl. 5th cent. B.C.): cf. COLOSSIANS —**Co·los′sian** (-läsh′ən) *adj., n.*

co·los·sal (kə läs′əl) *adj.* **1** like a colossus in size; huge; gigantic **2** astonishingly great; extraordinary [*a colossal fool*] —**SYN.** ENORMOUS —**co·los′sal·ly** *adv.*

Col·os·se·um (käl′ə sē′əm) *n.* ⟦L, orig., neut. of *colosseus,* gigantic < *colossus,* COLOSSUS⟧ **1** an amphitheater in Rome, built *c.* A.D. 75-80: much of it is still standing **2** [**c-**] COLISEUM (sense 2)

Co·los·sians (kə läsh′ənz) *n.* a book of the New Testament from the Apostle Paul to the Christians of Colossae: abbrev. *Col*

co·los·sus (kə läs′əs) *n., pl.* **-los′si′** (-ī′) or **-los′sus·es** ⟦ME < L < Gr *kolossos*⟧ **1** a gigantic statue **2** [**C-**] the gigantic statue of Apollo set at the entrance to the harbor of Rhodes *c.* 280 B.C. and included among the Seven Wonders of the World **3** any huge or important person or thing

co·los·to·my (kə läs′tə mē) *n., pl.* **-mies** ⟦COLO(N) + -STOMY⟧ **1** the surgical operation of forming an artificial opening in the abdominal wall from the colon **2** such an opening

co·los·trum (kə läs′trəm) *n.* ⟦L, beestings⟧ the first fluid, rich in protein, secreted by the mother's mammary glands for several days just after giving birth

col·our (kul′ər) *n., adj., vt., vi. Brit. sp. of* COLOR

-co·lous (kə ləs) ⟦< base of L *colere,* to cultivate (see CULT) + -OUS⟧ *combining form* growing (or living) in or among [*arenicolous*]

col·pi·tis (käl pīt′is) *n.* ⟦< Gr *kolpos,* womb (see GULF) + -ITIS⟧ inflammation of the vagina; vaginitis

col·por·teur (käl′pôrt′ər) *n.* ⟦Fr, peddler; altered by assoc. with *col,* neck < OFr *comporter:* see COMPORT⟧ a traveling distributor or seller of Bibles, religious tracts, etc. —**col′por′tage** (-ij) *n.*

col·po·scope (käl′pə skōp′) *n.* ⟦< Gr *kolpos* (see COLPITIS) + -O- + -SCOPE⟧ a magnifying instrument used in a medical examination of the vagina and cervix, esp. for detecting cancer —**col·po·scop·ic** (käl′pə skäp′ik) *adj.* —**col·pos·co·py** (käl päs′kə pē) *n.*

colt (kōlt) *n.* ⟦ME & OE < ? IE **gel-d* < base **gel-,* to form a ball > CLAW⟧ **1** a young male horse, donkey, etc.; specif., a Thoroughbred four years of age or under or a Standardbred three years of age **2** a young, inexperienced person

Colt (kōlt), **Samuel** 1814-62; U.S. inventor of a type of revolver

col·ter (kōl′tər) *n.* ⟦ME *culter* < OFr *coltre* or OE *culter,* both < L *culter,* plowshare < IE base **(s)kel-,* to cut > HALF⟧ a blade or disk on a plow, for forming the vertical wall of the furrow

colt·ish (kōl′tish) *adj.* of or like a colt; esp., frisky, frolicsome, etc. —**colt′ish·ly** *adv.*

Col·trane (kōl′trān′), **John (William)** 1926-67; U.S. jazz saxophonist & composer

colts·foot (kōlts′foot′) *n., pl.* **-foots′** a plant (*Tussilago farfara*) of the composite family, with heads of small, yellow flowers and large leaves whose shape suggests a colt's footprint

col·u·brid (käl′yoo brid′) *n.* ⟦< ModL *Colubridae* < L *coluber:* see fol.⟧ any of a large, worldwide family (Colubridae) of generally nonpoisonous snakes, including garter snakes, racers, and kingsnakes —*adj.* of or having to do with this family

col·u·brine (käl′yoo brīn′, -brin) *adj.* ⟦L *colubrinus* < *coluber,* serpent: see COLON[1]⟧ **1** of, characteristic of, or like a snake **2** COLUBRID

co·lu·go (kə lōō′gō) *n.* FLYING LEMUR

Col·um (käl′əm), **Pad·raic** (pô′thrig) 1881-1972; Ir. poet and playwright, in the U.S.

Co·lum·ba[1] (kə lum′bə) *n.* ⟦L, a dove: see COLUMBARIUM⟧ a S constellation near Canis Major

Co·lum·ba[2] (kə lum′bə), Saint (A.D. 521-597); Ir. missionary: converted Scotland to Christianity: his day is June 9

col·um·bar·i·um (käl′əm ber′ē əm) *n., pl.* **-i·a** (-ə) ⟦L, lit., dovecote < *columba,* dove, orig., gray bird < IE base **kel-, *kāl-,* grayish color > Gr *chelainos,* black⟧ ☆**1** a vault with niches for urns containing the ashes of cremated bodies **2** such a niche

☆**Co·lum·bi·a**[1] (kə lum′bē ə, -byə) *n.* ⟦after Christopher COLUMBUS[1]⟧ [Old Poet.] the U.S. personified as a woman

Co·lum·bi·a[2] (kə lum′bē ə, -byə) **1** ⟦after prec.⟧ capital of S.C., on the Congaree River **2** city in central Mo. **3** ⟦after the *Columbia,* captained by R. Gray, which sailed into it in 1792⟧ river rising in SE British Columbia and flowing south & west through Wash., & along the Wash.-Oreg. border into the Pacific: 1,210 mi (1,947 km)

Co·lum·bi·an (kə lum′bē ən) *adj.* **1** of Columbia **2** of Christopher Columbus

col·um·bine (käl′əm bīn′, -bin′) *n.* ⟦ME & OFr < ML *columbina* < L *columbinus,* dovelike (see COLUMBARIUM): the flower is thought to resemble a flock of doves⟧ any of a genus (*Aquilegia*) of plants of the buttercup family, with dainty, spurred flowers of various colors —*adj.* [Rare] of or like a dove

Col·um·bine (käl′əm bīn′) *n.* ⟦It *Colombina* < L *columbina,* fem. of *columbinus,* dovelike: see COLUMBARIUM⟧ daughter of Pantaloon and sweetheart of Harlequin: a stock character in early pantomime

co·lum·bite (kə lum′bīt′) *n.* ⟦fol. + -ITE[1]⟧ a black, orthorhombic mineral, $(Fe,Mn)(Nb,Ta)_2O_6$, that is an ore of niobium and tantalum

co·lum·bi·um (kə lum′bē əm) *n.* ⟦ModL: so named (1801) by C. Hatchett (1765-1847), Brit chemist < COLUMBIA[1] + -IUM, because the ore had been brought to London from Massachusetts⟧ *former name for* NIOBIUM

Co·lum·bus[1] (kə lum′bəs), **Christopher** (It. name *Cristoforo Colombo;* Sp. name *Cristóbal Colón*) 1451?-1506; It. explorer in the service of Spain: discovered America (1492)

Co·lum·bus[2] (kə lum′bəs) ⟦after prec.⟧ **1** capital of Ohio, in the central part **2** city in W Ga., on the Chattahoochee River

Columbus Day a legal holiday in the U.S. commemorating the discovery of America by Columbus (Oct. 12, 1492), observed in most states on the second Monday in October

col·u·mel·la (käl′yoo mel′ə, -yə-) *n., pl.* **-mel′lae** (-ē) ⟦ModL < L, dim. of *columen:* see fol.⟧ any of a number of columnlike structures in plants and animals, as a small bone in the middle ear of amphibians, reptiles, etc. —**col′u·mel′lar** *adj.* —**col′u·mel′late′** (-āt′, -it) *adj.*

col·umn (käl′əm) *n.* ⟦ME & OFr *colomne* < L *columna,* collateral form of *columen,* column, pillar < IE base **kel-,* to project > HILL, HOLM[1], Gr *kolophōn*⟧ **1** a slender upright structure, generally consisting of a cylindrical shaft, a base, and a capital; pillar: it is usually a supporting or ornamental member in a building **2** anything like a column in shape or function [*a column of smoke, the spinal column*] **3** a formation of troops, ships, etc. in a file or adjacent files **4** *a)* any of the vertical sections of words or data that are displayed side by side, as on a newspaper page, separated by a rule or blank space *b)* in a TABLE (*n.* 4b), any of the parallel series of cells running up and down **5** *a)* any of a series of feature articles appearing regularly in a newspaper or magazine, by a particular writer or about a certain subject *b)* such a series —**co·lum·nar** (kə lum′nər) *adj.* —**col′umned** (-əmd) *adj.*

CAPITAL
SHAFT
BASE
PLINTH

column

co·lum·ni·a·tion (kə lum′nē ā′shən) *n.* the architectural use or arrangement of columns

☆**col·um·nist** (käl′əm nist′) *n.* a person who writes or prepares a column, as in a newspaper or magazine

co·lure (kō loor′, kə-; kō′loor′) *n.* ⟦< L *coluri* < Gr *kolouroi,* the colures, lit., dock-tailed (ones), pl. of *kolouros* < *kolos,* docked (see HOLT) + *oura,* tail (see URO-[2]): the "tail" (i.e., the lower part) is cut off from view by the horizon⟧ either of two great circles of the celestial sphere intersecting each other at right angles at the celestial poles: one passes through the solstices (**solstitial colure**), the other through the equinoxes (**equinoctial colure**)

co·ly (kō′lē) *n., pl.* **co′lies** ⟦ModL *colius* < Gr *kolios,* green woodpecker⟧ any of an order (Coliiformes) of small African birds with a long tail and a crested head, that creeps about on tree branches

col·za (käl′zə) *n.* ⟦Fr < Du *koolzaad* < *kool,* a cabbage (akin to COLE) + *zaad,* SEED⟧ **1** any of several plants (genus *Brassica*) of the crucifer family, esp. rape, whose seeds yield an oil used in lubricants, salad dressings, etc. **2** this oil: in full **colza oil**

com *abbrev.* **1** comedy **2** comma **3** commerce **4** commercial **5** common **6** communication

Com *abbrev.* **1** Commander **2** Commission **3** Commissioner **4** Committee

COM (käm) ***n.*** computer-output microfilm

.com (dät′käm′) *abbrev. Comput.* commercial: a widely used domain name

com- (käm, kəm) ⟦L *com-* < OL *com* (L *cum*), with < IE **kom,* closely along, next to, with > Gr *koinos,* common⟧ *prefix* with, together: also used as an intensifier *[common; command]* It becomes *col-* before *l*; *cor-* before *r*; *con-* before *c, d, g, j, n, q, s, t,* or *v*, or, sometimes, *f*; and *co-* before *h* or a vowel

co·ma[1] (kō′mə) ***n.*** ⟦ModL < Gr *kōma* (gen. *kōmatos*), deep sleep < IE base **keme-,* to grow tired > Sans *śamītē,* to work, prepare, Gr *kamatos,* fatigue, effort⟧ **1** a state of deep, prolonged unconsciousness caused by injury or disease **2** a condition of stupor or lethargy

co·ma[2] (kō′mə) ***n., pl.* -mae** (-mē) ⟦L, hair of the head, foliage < Gr *komē,* hair⟧ **1** *Astron.* a comet's gaseous cloud surrounding the solid nucleus and forming, with the nucleus, the comet's head **2** *a)* a bunch of branches, as on the top of some palm trees *b)* a terminal cluster of bracts on a flowering stem, as in pineapples *c)* a tuft of hairs at the end of certain seeds **3** *Photog.* a blur caused by the spherical aberration of oblique rays of light passing through a lens

Co·ma Ber·e·ni·ces (kō′mə ber′ə nī′sēz′) ⟦L, Berenice's Hair: see prec.⟧ a N constellation between Virgo and Canes Venatici, containing the north galactic pole; Berenice's Hair

co·make (kō′māk′, kō′māk′) ***vt.* -made′, -mak′ing** COSIGN **—co′mak′er *n.***

Co·man·che (kə man′chē) ***n., pl.* -ches** or **-che** ⟦MexSp < Ute *komanchi,* stranger⟧ **1** a member of a North American Indian people that formerly ranged from the Platte River to the Mexican border and now lives in Oklahoma **2** the Shoshone dialect of this people

co·mate (kō′māt′) ***adj.*** ⟦L *comatus,* hairy < *coma:* see COMA[2]⟧ *Bot.* hairy or tufted

co·ma·tose (kō′mə tōs′, käm′ə-) ***adj.*** ⟦see COMA[1] & -OSE[2]⟧ **1** of, like, or in a coma or stupor **2** as if in a coma; lethargic; torpid

co·mat·u·lid (kō mach′o͞o lid′) ***n.*** ⟦< ModL *Comatulidae,* name of the family (< L *comatulus,* having hair neatly curled, dim. of *comatus,* COMATE) + -ID⟧ FEATHER STAR: also **co·mat′u·la** (-lə), *pl.* **-lae′** (-lē′)

comb[1] (kōm) ***n.*** ⟦ME < OE *camb,* comb, lit., toothed object < IE **ĝombhos* (> Sans *jámbah,* Gr *gomphos,* tooth) < base **ĝembh-, *ĝombh-,* to bite, tooth⟧ **1** a thin strip of hard rubber, plastic, metal, etc. with teeth, passed through the hair to arrange, untangle, or clean it, or set in the hair to hold it in place or as an ornament **2** anything like a comb in form, function, or location; specif., *a)* a currycomb *b)* a fine-toothed implement or machine used to clean and straighten long fibers of wool, cotton, flax, etc. *c)* a red, fleshy outgrowth on the top of the head, as of a rooster *d)* a thing like a rooster's comb in position or appearance, as the crest of a helmet **3** a honeycomb **—*vt.* 1** to clean, straighten out, or arrange with a comb **2** to remove with or as with a comb; separate: often with *out* ☆**3** to search thoroughly; look everywhere in *[to comb a house for a missing book]* **—☆*vi.*** to roll over; break: said of waves

comb[2] (ko͞om, kōm) ***n.*** COOMB

comb[3] *abbrev.* **1** combination **2** combining

com·bat (kəm bat′, käm′bat′; kum′bat′; *for n. & adj.,* käm′bat′) ***vi.* -bat′ed** or **-bat′ted, -bat′ing** or **-bat′ting** ⟦Fr *combattre* < VL **combattere* < L *com-,* with + *battuere,* to beat, fight: see BATTER[1]⟧ to fight, contend, or struggle **—*vt.*** to fight or struggle against; oppose, resist, or seek to get rid of **—*n.*** ⟦Fr < the v.⟧ **1** armed fighting; battle **2** any struggle or conflict; strife **—*adj. Mil.*** of or for combat **—SYN.** BATTLE[1]

com·bat·ant (kəm bat′'nt; *also, and esp. Brit,* käm′bə tənt) ***adj.*** ⟦ME < OFr, prp. of *combattre:* see prec.⟧ **1** fighting **2** ready or prepared to fight **—*n.*** a person who engages in combat; fighter

combat fatigue [Old-fashioned] POST-TRAUMATIC STRESS DISORDER occurring as after prolonged combat in warfare

com·bat·ive (kəm bat′iv; *also, and esp. Brit,* käm′bə tiv′) ***adj.*** fond of fighting or struggling; ready or eager to fight; pugnacious **—com·bat′ive·ly *adv.* —com·bat′ive·ness *n.***

combe[1] (ko͞om, kōm) ***n.*** *var. of* COOMB

comb·er (kōm′ər) ***n.*** **1** a person or thing that combs, as wool, flax, etc. ☆**2** a large wave that rolls over or breaks on a beach, reef, etc.

com·bi·na·tion (käm′bə nā′shən) ***n.*** ⟦ME *combinacioun* < LL *combinatio,* a joining two by two⟧ **1** a combining or being combined **2** a thing formed by combining **3** an association of persons, firms, political parties, etc. for a common purpose **4** *a)* the series of numbers or letters used in opening a combination lock *b)* the mechanism operating such a lock **5** a one-piece undergarment combining an undershirt and drawers **6** *Chem.* a uniting of substances to form a compound **7** *Math.* any of the various groupings, or subsets, into which a number, or set, of units may be arranged without regard to order: dual combinations of A, B, C, and D are AB, AC, AD, BC, BD, CD: cf. PERMUTATION **8** *Pool* a shot in which an object ball is pocketed as a result of being struck by another object ball: in full **combination shot —com′bi·na′tion·al *adj.***

☆**combination lock** a lock operated by a dial or other mechanism that is turned to a set series of numbers or letters to work the mechanism that opens it

com·bi·na·tive (käm′bə nāt′iv, -bə nə tiv′; kəm bī′nə tiv′) ***adj.*** **1** of or characterized by combination **2** having the ability to combine **3** resulting from combination

com·bi·na·to·ri·al (käm′bə nə tôr′ē əl, kəm bī′nə-) ***adj.*** of or involving combination, esp. mathematical combination

com·bi·na·to·rics (käm′bə nə tôr′iks) ***n.*** ⟦< fol. + -ICS⟧ a branch of mathematics dealing with combinations and permutations

com·bi·na·to·ry (kəm bī′nə tôr′ē) ***adj.*** combinative

com·bine (kəm bīn′; *for n. & v. 3,* käm′bīn′) ***vt., vi.* -bined′, -bin′ing** ⟦ME *combinen* < OFr *combiner* < LL *combinare,* to unite < L *com-,* together + *bini,* two by two < base of *bis:* see BI-[1]⟧ **1** to come or bring into union; act or mix together; unite; join **2** to unite to form a chemical compound ☆**3** ⟦< *n.* 1⟧ to harvest and thresh with a combine **—*n.*** ☆**1** a machine for harvesting and threshing grain **2** an association of persons, corporations, etc. for commercial or political, sometimes unethical, purposes **—SYN.** JOIN **—com·bin′a·ble *adj.* —com·bin′er *n.***

comb·ings (kō′miŋz) ***pl.n.*** loose hair, wool, etc. removed in combing

combining form a word form that occurs only in compounds or derivatives, and that can combine with other such forms or with affixes to form a word (Ex.: *bio-* and *-lysis* in *biolysis*)

comb jelly (kōm) CTENOPHORE

com·bo (käm′bō′) ***n., pl.* -bos′** **1** [Informal] a combination **2** a small jazz ensemble composed usually of from three to six instrumentalists

comb-o·ver (kōm′ō′vər) ***n.*** a man's hairstyle in which, in an attempt to conceal baldness, the hair is combed up from the sides or back of the head and across the scalp

com·bust (kəm bust′) ***vt., vi.*** ⟦ME < L *combustus,* pp. of *comburere,* to burn up: see COMBUSTION⟧ to undergo or cause to undergo combustion; burn

com·bus·ti·ble (kəm bus′tə bəl) ***adj.*** ⟦Fr < ML *combustibilis:* see fol.⟧ **1** that catches fire and burns easily; flammable **2** easily aroused; excitable; fiery **—*n.*** a flammable substance **—com·bus′ti·bil′i·ty *n.* —com·bus′ti·bly *adv.***

com·bus·tion (kəm bus′chən) ***n.*** ⟦ME < OFr < LL *combustio* < L *combustus,* pp. of *comburere* (for **com-urere*), to burn < *com-,* intens. + **burere* (by faulty separation of *amburere,* to burn around < *ambi-,* AMBI- + *urere,* to burn, singe): see EMBER[1]⟧ **1** the act or process of burning **2** rapid oxidation accompanied by heat and, usually, light, as with magnesium **3** slow oxidation accompanied by relatively little heat and no light, as with a carbohydrate **4** violent excitement or agitation; tumult **—com·bus′tive** (-tiv) ***adj.***

combustion chamber **1** the chamber in a reciprocating engine between the cylinder head and the piston, in which combustion occurs **2** the chamber inside a jet engine or rocket engine in which fuel and air, or an oxidizer, are mixed and burned: see COMBUSTOR

combustion furnace a furnace used in the laboratory to carry out elemental analysis of organic compounds

combustion tube a tube of heat-resistant glass, silica, or ceramic, in which a substance can be reduced, as in a combustion furnace

☆**com·bus·tor** (kəm bus′tər) ***n.*** the chamber and related assembly in a jet engine, gas turbine, etc., in which combustion occurs

comd *abbrev.* command

comdg *abbrev.* commanding

Comdr *abbrev.* Commander

Comdt *abbrev.* Commandant

come (kum) ***vi.* came, come, com′ing** ⟦ME *comen* < OE *cuman,* akin to Goth *qiman,* Ger *kommen* < IE base **gwem-, *gwā-,* to go, come > L *venire,* to come, Gr *bainein,* to go⟧ **1** to move from a place thought of as "there" to or into a place thought of as "here": *a)* in the second person, with relation to the speaker *[come to me, will you come to the dance tonight?]* *b)* in the first person, with relation to the person addressed *[I will come to see you]* *c)* in the third person, with relation to the person or thing approached *[he came into the room]* **2** to approach or reach by or as by moving toward **3** to arrive or appear *[help will come]* **4** to extend; reach *[the bus line comes near the hotel]* **5** to happen; take place *[success came to him early in life]* **6** to take form in the mind, as through recollection *[her name finally came to him]* **7** to occur in a certain place or order *[after 9 comes 10]* **8** *a)* to become actual; evolve; develop *[peace will come in time]* *b)* to proceed; progress; get (*along*) *[how's your new book coming (along)?]* **9** *a)* to be derived *[milk comes from cows]* *b)* to be descended *[he comes from an old family]* *c)* to be a native, resident, or former resident (with *from*) **10** to be caused; result *[illness may come from a poor diet]* ☆**11** to be due or owed (*to*): used in the participle *[to get what is coming to one]* **12** to pass by or as by inheritance *[the house came to him on the death of his father]* **13** to enter into a certain state or condition *[this word has come into use]* **14** to get to be; become *[my shoe came loose]* **15** to be obtainable or available *[this dress comes in four sizes]* **16** to amount; add up (*to*) **17** [Informal] to have a sexual orgasm: somewhat vulgar ➥*Come* is often used in the subjunctive, with the subject inverted, to mean "when (a specified time or event) occurs" *[come autumn, we can harvest the crop]* **—*n.*** [Slang] SEMEN: somewhat vulgar **—*interj.*** used to express irritation, impatience, remonstrance, etc. *[oh come! it's not that bad]* **—as good** (or **tough** or **strong,** etc.) **as they come** among the best (or toughest, strongest, etc.) **—come about** **1** to happen; occur **2** to turn about **3** *Naut.* to change course so that the sail or sails shift from one side of the vessel to the other, esp. to do so as by turning the bow into and across the wind; tack **—come across** **1** to meet by accident; find by chance **2** [Informal] to be effective, readily understood, etc. ☆**3** [Slang] to give, do, or say what is wanted; provide (*with* what is needed) **—come across (as)** [Informal] to seem or appear (to be) *[he comes across as a shy person]* **—come again?** [Informal] what did you say? please repeat that! **—come alive** **1** to become excited, enthusiastic, etc. **2** to become exciting, interesting, etc. *[new curtains made the room come alive]* **—come along** **1** to appear or arrive **2** to proceed or succeed **—come and get it!** [Informal] the meal is ready!: a summons to eat **—come around** (or **round**) **1** to revive; recover **2** to make a turn or change in direction **3** to concede or yield, as to a demand **4** [Informal] to come to visit **—come at** **1** to reach; attain **2**

to approach angrily or swiftly, as in attacking —**come back** 1 to return ☆2 [Informal] to make a comeback —**come between** to cause estrangement between; divide —**come by** 1 to get; acquire; gain ☆2 to pay a visit —**come down** 1 to suffer loss in status, wealth, etc. 2 [Slang] to take place; happen —**come down on** (or **upon**) to scold; criticize harshly —☆**come down with** to contract (a cold, flu, etc.) —**come forward** to offer one's services, testimony, etc.; volunteer —**come in** 1 to enter 2 to arrive 3 to begin to be used; come into fashion ☆4 to start producing, as an oil well 5 to finish in a competitive event [he *came in* fifth] 6 *Golf see phrase under* IN[1] 7 *a) Radio* to answer a call or signal *b) Radio, TV, etc.* to be received —**come in for** [Informal] to get or become eligible to get —**come into** 1 to enter into; join 2 to inherit —**come of age** to reach the age when one has full legal rights: often used fig. for any arrival at maturity, one's prime, etc. [baseball *came of age* in the 1920s]: see also OF AGE under AGE —**come off** 1 to become unfastened or detached 2 to happen; occur 3 to end up; emerge, as from a contest ☆4 [Informal] to prove effective, successful, etc. [humor that didn't *come off*] —☆**come off it!** [Slang] stop acting or talking in that way! —**come on** 1 to make progress 2 to meet by accident; find 3 to appear, begin to work, make an entrance, etc. —**come on!** [Informal] used to signify *a)* invitation, often to a different place *b)* encouragement, urgency, etc. [*come on!* you can do it] *c)* objection, disagreement, refusal to believe, etc. [*come on!* you can't be serious] Often used as a cajoling expression equivalent to *please* —**come on to** [Slang] to make sexual advances toward —**come out** 1 to be disclosed; become evident 2 to be offered for public inspection, sale, etc. 3 to be formally introduced to society; make a debut 4 to end up; turn out [how did the election *come out?*] ☆5 to become actively homosexual or reveal that one is homosexual —**come out for** to announce one's approval of; endorse —**come out with** 1 to disclose 2 to say; utter; publish 3 to offer for public inspection, sale, etc. —**come over** to happen to; occur to; seize [a strange feeling *came over* me] —**come through** 1 to wear through ☆2 to complete or endure something successfully ☆3 [Informal] to do what is wanted; provide (*with* what is needed) —**come to** 1 to recover consciousness 2 *Naut. a)* to bring the ship's head nearer the wind *b)* to stop moving; also, to anchor —**come up** 1 to arise; begin [a light breeze *came up*] 2 to be mentioned, as in a discussion 3 to rise or improve, as in status 4 to be put forward, as for a vote 5 [Brit.] to enter a university —**come upon** 1 to meet or encounter by accident 2 to attack —**come up to** 1 to reach or extend to 2 to equal —**come up with** to propose, produce, find, suggest, etc.

come·back (kum′bak′) ***n.*** 1 a return to a previous state or position, as of success ☆2 a witty reply ☆3 ground for complaint

Com·e·con (käm′i kän′) ***n.*** Council for Mutual Economic Assistance: a trade organization of Communist countries during the Cold War

co·me·di·an (kə mē′dē ən) ***n.*** ⟦Fr *comédien:* see COMEDY⟧ 1 an actor who plays comic parts 2 an entertainer who tells jokes, sings comic songs, etc. 3 a person who amuses others by behaving in a comic way 4 [Rare] a writer of comedy

co·me·dic (kə mē′dik) ***adj.*** of or having to do with comedy

co·me·di·enne (kə mē′dē en′) ***n.*** ⟦Fr *comédienne, fem.*⟧ a woman comedian

com·e·do (käm′ə dō′) ***n., pl.* com′e·do′nes′** (-dō′nēz′) or **com′e·dos′** ⟦L, glutton < *comedere,* to eat up: see COMESTIBLE⟧ a plug of dirt and fatty matter in a skin duct; blackhead

☆**come·down** (kum′doun′) ***n.*** a fall to a low or lower status or position, as of power or wealth

com·e·dy (käm′ə dē) ***n., pl.* -dies** ⟦ME & OFr *comedie* < L *comoedia* < Gr *kōmōidia* < *kōmos,* revel, carousal + *aeidein,* to sing: see ODE⟧ 1 [Obs.] a drama or narrative with a happy ending or nontragic theme [Dante's *Divine Comedy*] 2 *a)* any of various types of play or film with a more or less humorous treatment of characters and situation and a happy ending (see also COMEDY OF MANNERS, FARCE, HIGH COMEDY, LOW COMEDY) *b)* such plays or films collectively *c)* the branch of drama having to do with such plays *d)* the writing, acting, or theoretical principles of this kind of drama 3 a novel or any narrative having a comic theme, tone, etc. 4 the comic element in a literary work, or in life 5 an amusing or comic event or sequence of events

comedy of manners a type of comedy depicting and satirizing the manners and customs of fashionable society: see also HIGH COMEDY

come-hith·er (kum′hith′ər) ***adj.*** [Informal] flirtatious or sexually inviting [a *come-hither* look]

come·ly (kum′lē) ***adj.* -li·er, -li·est** ⟦ME *comli* < OE *cymlic* < *cyme,* lovely, delicate, orig., feeble; akin to MHG *kume,* weak (Ger *kaum,* scarcely) < IE base **gou-,* to cry out > Gr *goaein,* to groan, bewail⟧ 1 pleasant to look at; attractive; fair 2 [Archaic] seemly; decorous; proper —***SYN.*** BEAUTIFUL —**come′li·ness *n.***

Co·me·ni·us (kō mē′nē əs), **John Amos** (born *Jan Amos Komensky*) 1592-1670; Moravian educational reformer & theologian

☆**come-on** (kum′än′) ***n.*** [Slang] 1 an inviting look or gesture 2 something offered as an inducement 3 a swindler, esp. a shill

com·er (kum′ər) ***n.*** 1 a person who arrives or shows up [a contest open to all *comers*] ☆2 [Informal] a person or thing that shows promise of being a success

co·mes·ti·ble (kə mes′tə bəl) ***adj.*** ⟦Fr < L *comestus, comesus,* pp. of *comedere,* to eat < *com-,* intens. + *edere,* to EAT⟧ [Rare] eatable; edible —***n.*** [*usually pl.*] food

com·et (käm′it) ***n.*** ⟦ME *comete* < OE *cometa* & OFr *comete,* both < L *cometa* < Gr *komētēs,* lit., long-haired (star) < *komē,* lit., hair of the head⟧ a small, frozen mass of water, gas, rocks, and dust revolving around the sun in a parabolic or elliptical orbit: as it nears the sun it vaporizes, forming a coma and, usually, a long tail of ions that points away from the sun —**com′et·ar′y** (-ə ter′ē) ***adj.,* co·met·ic** (kō met′ik)

☆**come·up·pance** (kum′up′əns) ***n.*** ⟦< COME + UP[1] + -ANCE⟧ [Informal] deserved punishment; retribution

com·fit (kum′fit, käm′-) ***n.*** ⟦ME & OFr *confit,* orig., pp. of *confire,* to preserve < L *conficere:* see CONFECT⟧ a candy or sweetmeat; esp., a candied fruit, nut, etc.

com·fort (kum′fərt) ***vt.*** ⟦ME *comforten* < OFr *conforter,* to comfort < LL (esp. in Vulg. of O.T.) *confortare,* to strengthen much < L *com-,* intens. + *fortis,* strong: see FORT[1]⟧ 1 to soothe in distress or sorrow; ease the misery or grief of; bring consolation or hope to 2 to give a sense of ease to 3 *Law* to help; aid —***n.*** 1 aid; encouragement: now only in **aid and comfort** 2 relief from distress, grief, etc.; consolation 3 a person or thing that comforts 4 a state of ease and quiet enjoyment, free from worry, pain, or trouble 5 anything that makes life easy or comfortable ☆6 a quilted bed covering; comforter —**com′fort·ing *adj.*** —**com′fort·less *adj.***

SYN.—**comfort** suggests the lessening of misery or grief by cheering, calming, or inspiring with hope; **console** suggests less positive relief but implies a moderation of the sense of loss or disappointment [to *console* someone on the death of a parent]; **solace** suggests the relieving of melancholy, boredom, or loneliness [he *solaced* himself with music]; **relieve** suggests the mitigation, often temporary, of misery or discomfort so as to make it bearable [to *relieve* the poor]; **soothe** implies the calming or allaying of pain or distress [to *soothe* a fretful child] —***ANT.*** **afflict, distress**

com·fort·a·ble (kumf′tər bəl, kum′fər tə bəl) ***adj.*** ⟦ME < ML *confortabilis*⟧ 1 providing comfort or ease 2 in a state of comfort; at ease in body or mind; contented 3 [Informal] sufficient to satisfy; adequate [a *comfortable* salary] —☆***n.*** a quilted bed covering; comforter —**com′fort·a·ble·ness *n.*** —**com′fort·a·bly *adv.***

SYN.—**comfortable** implies the absence of disturbing, painful, or distressing features and, in a positive sense, stresses ease, contentment, and freedom from care [a *comfortable* climate]; **cozy** suggests such comfort as might be derived from shelter against storm or cold [a *cozy* nook by the fire]; **snug** is used of something that is small and compact, but just large enough to provide ease and comfort, and often also carries connotations of coziness [a *snug* apartment]; **restful** is applied to that which promotes relaxation and freedom from stress [*restful* music] —***ANT.*** **miserable**

com·fort·er (kum′fər tər) ***n.*** ⟦ME *comfortour* < OFr *conforteor*⟧ 1 a person or thing that comforts ☆2 a quilted bed covering 3 a long woolen scarf —**the Comforter** *Bible* the Holy Spirit: John 14:26

comfort food [Informal] any food eaten not only for its pleasing taste but also for a sense of contentment, nostalgia, etc. that it provides

☆**comfort station** a public toilet or restroom

comfort zone [Informal] a situation or range of conditions or options that someone finds acceptable, familiar, easy, etc. [risky investments are outside of my *comfort zone*]

com·frey (kum′frē) ***n., pl.* -freys** ⟦ME & OFr *confirie* < VL **confervia,* comfrey, for L *conferva,* a water plant < *confervere,* to heal, grow together, orig., to seethe, boil together < *com-,* with + *fervere,* to boil (see FERVENT): from its use in medicine to coagulate blood at a wound⟧ any of a genus (*Symphytum*) of European plants of the borage family, with rough, hairy leaves and small blue, purplish, or yellow flowers, sometimes used for forage or ornament

com·fy (kum′fē) ***adj.* -fi·er, -fi·est** [Informal] comfortable

com·ic (käm′ik) ***adj.*** ⟦ME *comice* < L *comicus* < Gr *kōmikos* < *kōmos,* revel⟧ 1 of, like, or having to do with comedy 2 amusing or intended to be amusing; humorous; funny 3 of comic strips or cartoons —***n.*** 1 a comedian 2 the humorous element in art or life ☆3 *a)* COMIC STRIP or COMIC BOOK *b)* [*pl.*] a section of comic strips, as in a newspaper (often with *the*) —***SYN.*** FUNNY

com·i·cal (käm′i kəl) ***adj.*** 1 causing amusement; humorous; funny; droll 2 [Obs.] of or fit for comedy —***SYN.*** FUNNY —**com′i·cal′i·ty** (-kal′ə tē) ***n.*** —**com′i·cal·ly *adv.***

☆**comic book** a paper booklet of extended comic strips

Co·mice (kō mēs′) ***n.*** ⟦Fr⟧ a very sweet, yellow-green winter pear: also **Comice pear**

comic opera opera with humorous situations, a story that ends happily, and, usually, some spoken dialogue

☆**comic strip** 1 a sequence of several related cartoon drawings typically arranged in a horizontal strip 2 a series of such strips, typically about a set of recurring characters, regularly published as in the comics section of a newspaper

Co·mines (kô mēn′), **Phi·lippe de** (fē lēp′ də) 1447?-1511?; Fr. historian & diplomat

Com·in·form (käm′in fôrm′) ***n.*** ⟦< *Com(munist) Inform(ation)*⟧ the Communist Information Bureau, an association of various European Communist parties (1947-56) that functioned to spread Soviet propaganda

com·ing (kum′iŋ) ***adj.*** 1 approaching; immediately next [this *coming* Tuesday] 2 showing promise of being successful, popular, or important [a *coming* young actor, the *coming* thing] —***n.*** an arrival or approach —☆**have (something) coming to one** to deserve or merit (something) —**where someone is coming from** ☆[Informal] someone's perspective or point of view

co-min·gle (kə miŋ′gəl, kō-) ***vt., vi.* -gled, -gling** *alt. sp. of* COMMINGLE

com·ing-of-age (kum′iŋ əv āj′) ***n.*** the act or an instance of reaching maturity: often used attributively

Com·in·tern (käm′in turn′) ***n.*** ⟦< *Com(munist) Intern(ational)*⟧ the international organization (*Third International*) of Communist parties (1919-43) formed by Lenin originally to promote revolution throughout Europe

co·mi·ti·a (kō mish′ē ə, -mish′ə) ***n.*** ⟦L, pl. of *comitium,* meeting place < *com-,* together + pp. stem of *ire,* to go: see EXIT⟧ in ancient Rome, an assembly of citizens for electing officials, passing laws, etc. —**co·mi′ti·al** ***adj.***

com·i·ty (käm′ə tē) ***n., pl.*** **-ties** ⟦ME *comite,* association < L *comitas* < *comis,* polite, kind; earlier *cosmis,* prob. < *co-* (see COM-), with + **smi-s* < IE base **smei-,* to SMILE⟧ **1** courteous behavior; politeness; civility **2** COMITY OF NATIONS **3** agreement among cooperating Christian denominations to avoid duplication of churches, missions, etc. in specific areas **4** *Law* the principle by which the courts of one jurisdiction may give effect to the laws and decisions of another, or may stay their own proceedings in deference to those in another jurisdiction

comity of nations **1** the courtesy and respect of peaceful nations for each other's laws and institutions **2** loosely, the nations showing such courtesy and respect

☆**com·ix** (käm′iks) ***pl.n.*** comic books printed by an underground press

comm *abbrev.* **1** commander **2** commentary **3** commerce **4** commission **5** committee **6** commonwealth **7** communication

com·ma (käm′ə) ***n.*** ⟦L < Gr *komma,* clause in a sentence, that which is cut off < *koptein,* to cut off < IE base **(s)kep-,* to cut, split > CAPON, SHAFT⟧ **1** a mark of punctuation (,) used to indicate a slight separation of sentence elements, as in setting off nonrestrictive or parenthetical elements, items in a series, etc. **2** a slight pause

comma bacillus the bacillus (*Vibrio cholerae,* formerly, *V. comma*) causing Asiatic cholera

com·mand (kə mand′, -mänd′) ***vt.*** ⟦ME *commanden* < OFr *comander* < VL **commandare* < L *com-,* intens. + *mandare,* to commit, entrust: see MANDATE⟧ **1** to give an order or orders to; direct with authority **2** to have authority or jurisdiction over; control **3** to have ready for use [to *command* a large vocabulary] **4** to deserve and get; require as due, proper, or becoming [to *command* respect] **5** to control or overlook from a higher position [the fort *commands* the entire valley] **6** [Obs.] to demand authoritatively —***vi.*** **1** to exercise power or authority; be in control; act as a commander **2** to overlook, as from a height —***n.*** **1** the act of commanding **2** an order; direction; mandate **3** authority to command **4** power to control or dominate by position **5** range of view **6** ability to have and use; mastery [a good *command* of the English language] **7** *a)* a military or naval force, organization, or district, under a specified authority or jurisdiction *b)* AIR COMMAND **8** the post where the person in command is stationed **9** *Comput. a)* a request entered by means of a keyboard, mouse, etc. to have a particular function performed *b)* INSTRUCTION (sense 3c) —**at someone's command** available or ready for someone to direct or make use of at will

SYN.—**command,** when it refers to a giving of orders, implies the formal exercise of absolute authority, as by a sovereign or military leader; **order** often stresses peremptoriness, sometimes suggesting an arbitrary exercise of authority [I *ordered* him out of the house]; **direct** and **instruct** are both used in connection with supervision, as in business relations, **instruct** perhaps more often stressing explicitness of details in the directions given; **enjoin** suggests a directing with urgent admonition [he *enjoined* them to secrecy] and sometimes implies a legal prohibition; **charge** implies the imposition of a task as a duty, trust, or responsibility See also **power**

com·man·dant (käm′ən dant′, -dänt′) ***n.*** ⟦Fr, orig. prp. of OFr *comander:* see prec.⟧ **1** a commanding officer, specif. one in charge of a fort or military school **2** [**C-**] *U.S. Marine Corps* the commanding officer of the Corps

command economy a highly regulated economy in which decisions regarding the type and quantity of goods produced, the level of prices and wages, etc. are mandated by a central authority

com·man·deer (käm′ən dir′) ***vt.*** ⟦Du *kommandeeren,* to command, (esp. Afrik) to commandeer < OFr *comander,* COMMAND⟧ **1** to force into military service **2** to seize (property) for military or government use **3** [Informal] to take forcibly

com·mand·er (kə man′dər, -män′-) ***n.*** ⟦ME *comaundour* < OFr *comandeor*⟧ **1** a person who commands; leader; specif., *a)* the chief officer of a unit in certain societies and fraternal orders *b)* COMMANDING OFFICER **2** a high-ranking member of an order of knighthood **3** *U.S. Navy* an officer ranking above a lieutenant commander and below a captain —**com·mand′er·ship′** ***n.***

commander in chief *pl.* **commanders in chief** **1** the supreme commander of the armed forces of a nation, as, in the U.S., the President **2** an officer in command of all armed forces in a certain theater of war

com·mand·er·y (-ē) ***n., pl.*** **-er·ies** ⟦ME *comaundrie* < OFr *comanderie* < ML *commendaria* (< *commenda,* commendation, an entrusting < L *commendare,* COMMEND), benefice entrusted to someone: sp. infl. by assoc. with COMMAND⟧ **1** the estate administered by a commander of an order of knights ☆**2** a branch or lodge in certain societies and fraternal orders

com·mand·ing (kə man′diŋ, -män′-) ***vt., vi. prp. of*** COMMAND —***adj.*** **1** having authority; controlling or dominating **2** impressive, esp. in a dignified or imperial way **3** controlling or dominating by position [a *commanding* hilltop] **4** very large [a *commanding* lead]

commanding officer the officer in command of any of certain units or installations in the armed forces

com·mand·ment (kə mand′mənt, -mänd′-) ***n.*** ⟦ME & OFr *comandement*⟧ an authoritative command or order; mandate; precept; specif., any of the TEN COMMANDMENTS

command module the component of a spacecraft used to house the crew members, communication equipment, etc. on the trip to and from lunar orbit

com·man·do (kə man′dō, -män′-) ***n., pl.*** **-dos** or **-does** ⟦Afrik < Port, lit., party commanded < *commandar,* to govern, command < VL **commandare,* COMMAND⟧ **1** [Historical] *a)* in South Africa, a force of Boer troops *b)* a raid or expedition made by such troops **2** *a)* a small raiding force trained to operate inside territory held by the enemy *b)* a member of such a group

command performance a performance, as of a play, put on as for a ruler by command or request

command post the field headquarters of a military unit, from which the commander directs operations

com·meas·ure (kəm mezh′ər, kə-) ***vt.*** **-ured, -ur·ing** to equal in measure or extent —**com·meas′ur·a·ble** ***adj.***

comme ci, comme ça (kôm sē′ kôm sä′) ⟦Fr⟧ SO-SO

com·me·dia dell'ar·te (kə mā′dē ə del är′te) ⟦It, lit., comedy of art⟧ a type of Italian comedy developed in the 16th through 18th cent. and employing a stereotyped plot, improvised dialogue, and stock characters such as Pantaloon, Harlequin, and Columbine

comme il faut (kô mēl fō′) ⟦Fr⟧ as it should be; proper; fitting

com·mem·o·rate (kə mem′ə rāt′) ***vt.*** **-rat′ed, -rat′ing** ⟦< L *commemoratus,* pp. of *commemorare,* to call to mind < *com-,* intens. + *memorare,* to remind: see MEMORY⟧ **1** to honor the memory of, as by a ceremony **2** to keep alive the memory of; serve as a memorial to —***SYN.*** CELEBRATE —**com·mem′o·ra′tor** ***n.***

com·mem·o·ra·tion (kə mem′ə rā′shən) ***n.*** **1** the act of commemorating **2** a celebration in memory of someone or something —**in commemoration of** in honor of the memory of

com·mem·o·ra·tive (kə mem′ə rə tiv′, -rāt′iv) ***adj.*** serving to commemorate: sometimes **com·mem′o·ra·to′ry** (-tôr′ē) —***n.*** anything that commemorates, as a stamp or coin that marks an event or honors a person, issued in limited quantities and for a limited time —**com·mem′o·ra′tive·ly** ***adv.***

com·mence (kə mens′) ***vi., vt.*** **-menced′, -menc′ing** ⟦ME *commencen* < OFr *comencier* < VL **cominitiare,* orig., to initiate as priest, consecrate < L *com-,* together + *initiare,* to INITIATE⟧ to begin; start; originate —***SYN.*** BEGIN —**com·menc′er** ***n.***

com·mence·ment (-mənt) ***n.*** **1** the act or time of commencing; beginning; start **2** *a)* the ceremonies at which degrees or diplomas are conferred at a school or college *b)* the day when this takes place

com·mend (kə mend′) ***vt.*** ⟦ME *commenden* < L *commendare,* to entrust to, commend < *com-,* intens. + *mandare,* to commit to one's charge: see MANDATE⟧ **1** to put in the care of another; entrust **2** to mention as worthy of attention; recommend **3** to express approval of; praise **4** [Archaic] to transmit the kind regards of —**com·mend′a·ble** ***adj.*** —**com·mend′a·bly** ***adv.***

com·men·dam (kə men′dam′) ***n.*** ⟦< ML *dare in commendam,* to give in trust: see COMMANDERY⟧ [Historical] **1** the temporary holding of a benefice, with the right to its revenues, by a cleric or layman in the absence of a proper incumbent: one was said to hold the benefice *in commendam* **2** a benefice held in this way

com·men·da·tion (käm′ən dā′shən) ***n.*** ⟦ME *commendacion* < L *commendatio*⟧ **1** the act or an instance of commending; esp., formal recommendation or praise **2** [*pl.*] [Archaic] greetings or regards, as to a friend

☆**Commendation Medal** a U.S. military decoration awarded for meritorious achievement or service

com·mend·a·to·ry (kə men′də tôr′ē) ***adj.*** ⟦LL *commendatorius* < L *commendator,* one who commends⟧ **1** serving to commend; expressing praise or approval **2** recommending

com·men·sal (kə men′səl) ***n.*** ⟦ME < ML *commensalis* < L *com-,* with + *mensa,* table: see MENSAL⟧ **1** a companion at meals **2** *Biol.* either of the organisms living in commensalism —***adj.*** designating, of, or like a commensal —**com·men′sal·ly** ***adv.***

com·men·sal·ism (-iz′əm) ***n.*** *Biol.* a close association or union between two kinds of organisms, in which one is benefited by the relationship and the other is neither benefited nor harmed

com·men·su·ra·ble (kə men′shoor ə bəl, -sər-) ***adj.*** ⟦LL *commensurabilis* < L *com-,* together + *mensurare,* to measure < *mensura,* MEASURE⟧ **1** measurable by the same standard or measure; specif., designating two quantities having a common measure which is contained an integral number of times in each **2** properly proportioned; proportionate —***SYN.*** PROPORTIONATE —**com·men′su·ra·bil′i·ty** ***n.*** —**com·men′su·ra·bly** ***adv.***

com·men·su·rate (-shoor it, -sər-) ***adj.*** ⟦LL *commensuratus* < *com-,* with + *mensuratus,* pp. of *mensurare:* see prec.⟧ **1** equal in measure or size; coextensive **2** corresponding in extent or degree; proportionate **3** COMMENSURABLE (sense 1) —***SYN.*** PROPORTIONATE —**com·men′su·rate·ly** ***adv.*** —**com·men′su·ra′tion** (-ā′shən) ***n.***

com·ment (käm′ent′) ***n.*** ⟦ME & OFr < L *commentum,* invention < *commentus,* pp. of *comminisci,* to contrive; devise < *com-,* intens. + base of *meminisse,* to remember; akin to *mens,* MIND⟧ **1** *a)* a note in explanation, criticism, or illustration of something written or said; annotation *b)* such notes collectively **2** a remark or observation made in criticism or as an expression of opinion **3** talk; chatter; gossip —***vi.*** ⟦ME *commenten* < OFr *commenter* < L *commentari,* to consider thoroughly⟧ to make a comment or comments (*on* or *upon*); make remarks —***vt.*** [Rare] to make comments on; annotate —*SYN.* REMARK —**no comment!** I have nothing to say!: often used in lieu of an incriminating or undiplomatic reply

com·men·tar·y (käm′ən ter′ē) *n., pl.* **-tar′ies** ⟦L *commentarius,* notebook, annotation < *commentari:* see prec.⟧ **1** a series of explanatory notes or annotations, often forming a treatise on a text **2** a series of remarks or observations, usually connected in a loose narrative **3** something having the force of a comment, remark, or illustration **4** [*usually pl.*] a historical narrative based on personal experience [Caesar's *Commentaries*] —*SYN.* REMARK —**com′men·tar′i·al** *adj.*

com·men·tate (käm′ən tāt′) *vt.* **-tat′ed, -tat′ing** ⟦back-form. < fol.⟧ to write or deliver a commentary on —*vi.* to perform as a COMMENTATOR (sense 2)

com·men·ta·tor (käm′ən tāt′ər) *n.* ⟦L, inventor, contriver (in LL, interpreter): see COMMENT⟧ **1** a person who writes or delivers a commentary **2** a person who reports, analyzes, and evaluates news events and trends on radio or television

com·merce (käm′ərs; *for v.,* kə murs′) *n.* ⟦Fr < L *commercium* < *com-,* together + *merx,* merchandise: see MARKET⟧ **1** the buying and selling of goods, esp. when done on a large scale between cities, states, or countries; trade **2** social intercourse **3** [Rare] sexual intercourse —*vi.* **-merced′, -merc′ing** [Archaic] to have personal dealings (*with*) —*SYN.* BUSINESS

com·mer·cial (kə mur′shəl) *adj.* **1** of or connected with commerce or trade **2** of or having to do with stores, office buildings, etc. [*commercial* property] **3** of a lower grade, or for use in large quantities in industry [*commercial* sulfuric acid] **4** *a)* made, done, or operating primarily for profit *b)* designed to have wide popular appeal **5** offering training in business skills, methods, etc. **6** *Radio, TV* paid for by sponsors —*n. Radio, TV* a paid advertisement —**com·mer′cial·ly** *adv.*

commercial bank a bank primarily concerned with accepting demand deposits, used as checking accounts

com·mer·cial·ism (-iz′əm) *n.* the practices and spirit of commerce or business, often, specif., as showing an undue regard for profit —**com·mer′cial·ist** *n.* —**com·mer′cial·is′tic** *adj.*

com·mer·cial·ize (-īz′) *vt.* **-ized′, -iz′ing 1** to run as a business; apply commercial methods to **2** to engage in or make use of mainly for profit, esp. at a sacrifice of other values **3** to cause to be affected by commercialism —**com·mer′cial·i·za′tion** *n.*

☆**commercial paper 1** negotiable instruments, as bills of exchange, used regularly in the course of business **2** *Finance* short-term promissory notes issued by large corporations and sold to investors either directly by the issuer or through dealers

commercial traveler a traveling salesman

Com·mie (käm′ē) *adj., n.* [*sometimes* **c-**] [Informal] Communist: a derogatory usage

com·mi·na·tion (käm′ə nā′shən) *n.* ⟦ME *comminacioun* < L *comminatio* < *comminatus,* pp. of *comminari,* to threaten < *com-,* intens. + *minari,* to MENACE⟧ a threat or denunciation —**com·mi·na·to·ry** (käm′i nə tôr′ē, kə min′ə-) *adj.*

Com·mines (kô mēn′), **Philippe de** *alt. sp. of* COMINES, Philippe de

com·min·gle (kə miŋ′gəl, kä-) *vt., vi.* **-gled, -gling** to mingle together; intermix; blend

com·mi·nute (käm′ə no͞ot′, -nyo͞ot′) *vt.* **-nut′ed, -nut′ing** ⟦< L *comminutus,* pp. of *comminuere,* to make small < *com-,* intens. + *minuere,* to make small: see MINUTE[2]⟧ to reduce to small, fine particles; make into powder; pulverize; triturate —**com′mi·nu′tion** *n.*

com·mis (kô mē′) *n., pl.* **-mis′** (-mē′) ⟦Fr, lit., a deputy < adj. < pp. of *commettre,* to commit, appoint⟧ an apprentice in an entry-level position in a restaurant kitchen

com·mis·er·a·ble (kə miz′ər ə bəl) *adj.* worthy of commiseration; pitiable

com·mis·er·ate (kə miz′ər āt′) *vt.* **-at′ed, -at′ing** ⟦< L *commiseratus,* pp. of *commiserari,* to pity < *com-,* intens. + *miserari,* to pity: see MISERY⟧ to feel or show sorrow or pity for —*vi.* to condole or sympathize (*with*) —*SYN.* PITY —**com·mis′er·a′tion** *n.* —**com·mis′er·a′tive** (-ər āt′iv, -ər ə tiv) *adj.* —**com·mis′er·a′tive·ly** *adv.*

com·mish (kə mish′) *n.* ☆[Informal] *short for* COMMISSIONER

com·mis·sar (käm′ə sär′) *n.* ⟦Russ *komissar* < ML *commissarius:* see COMMISSARY⟧ **1** the head of any of the former commissariats in the U.S.S.R.: in 1946, title changed to *minister* **2** a representative of the government or communist party in the U.S.S.R., responsible for political orientation, esp. in a military unit

com·mis·sar·i·at (käm′ə ser′ē ət) *n.* ⟦Fr < *commissaire,* commissary < ML *commissarius:* see fol.⟧ **1** the branch of an army which provides food and supplies for the troops **2** food supplies **3** ⟦Russ *komissariat*⟧ any of the government departments in the U.S.S.R.: since 1946, called *ministry*

com·mis·sar·y (käm′ə ser′ē) *n., pl.* **-sar′ies** ⟦ME *commissarie* < ML *commissarius* < L *commissus,* pp. of *committere:* see COMMIT⟧ **1** a person to whom some duty is given by authority; deputy; specif., *a)* in France, a police official *b)* a person representing a bishop in a part of his diocese **2** [Obs.] an army officer in charge of providing soldiers with food and other supplies **3** food supplies ☆**4** a store, as in a lumber camp or army camp, where food and supplies can be obtained ☆**5** a restaurant in a film or television studio —**com′mis·sar′i·al** *adj.*

com·mis·sion (kə mish′ən) *n.* ⟦ME & OFr < ML *commissio,* delegation of business (in L, a bringing together in a contest) < L *commissus,* pp. of *committere:* see COMMIT⟧ **1** *a)* an authorization to perform certain duties or tasks, or to take on certain powers *b)* a document giving such authorization **2** authority to act in behalf of another **3** that which a person is authorized to do for another **4** the state of being authorized to perform certain duties or tasks **5** an entrusting, as of power and authority, to a person or body **6** the act of committing or doing; perpetration, as of a crime **7** *a)* a group of people officially appointed to perform specified duties *b)* an administrative agency of the government with quasi-judicial and quasi-legislative powers *c)* a type of municipal governing body (see COMMISSION PLAN) **8** a fee or a percentage of the proceeds paid to a salesperson, broker, etc., either in addition to, or in lieu of, wages or salary **9** *Mil.* *a)* an official certificate conferring rank; specif., a document issued by the government, making one a commissioned officer in the U.S. armed forces *b)* the rank or authority conferred —*vt.* **1** to give a commission to **2** to give power or authority to; authorize **3** to give an order for (a thing to be made or done) **4** *Naut.* to put (a vessel) into service —*SYN.* AUTHORIZE —**in commission 1** entrusted to commissioners **2** in use **3** in fit condition for use —**out of commission 1** not in use **2** not in fit condition for use

com·mis·sion·aire (kə mish′ə ner′) *n.* ⟦Fr⟧ [Brit.] a person, esp. any of a group of pensioned service personnel, employed to do errands or small tasks, as a uniformed doorkeeper or a messenger

commissioned officer an officer in the armed forces holding rank by a commission: the lowest rank in the U.S. Army, Air Force, and Marine Corps is second lieutenant; in the Navy and Coast Guard, ensign

com·mis·sion·er (kə mish′ə nər) *n.* **1** a person authorized to do certain things by a commission or warrant **2** a member of a COMMISSION (sense 7) **3** an official in charge of a certain government bureau, commission, departmental office, etc. **4** an official appointed to administer a territory, province, etc. ☆**5** a person selected to regulate and control a professional sport or an association of amateur athletic teams —**com·mis′sion·er·ship′** *n.*

☆**commission house** a brokerage firm that buys and sells for customers on a commission basis

commission merchant a person who buys or sells goods for others on a commission basis

☆**commission plan** a form of municipal government in which all legislative and administrative powers are in the hands of an elected commission (usually five or six heads of various municipal departments)

com·mis·sure (käm′ə sho͝or′) *n.* ⟦ME & OFr < L *commissura* < *commissus,* pp. of *committere:* see fol.⟧ **1** a line where two parts join or unite; joint; seam **2** *Anat.* the area where symmetrical parts join, as of the lips or of the brain's hemispheres —**com·mis·su·ral** (kə mish′ər əl, käm′ə sho͝or′əl) *adj.*

com·mit (kə mit′) *vt.* **-mit′ted, -mit′ting** ⟦ME *committen* < L *committere,* to bring together, commit < *com-,* together + *mittere,* to send: see MISSION⟧ **1** to give in charge or trust; deliver for safekeeping; entrust; consign [we *commit* his fame to posterity] **2** to put officially in custody or confinement [*committed* to prison] **3** to hand over or set apart to be disposed of or put to some purpose [to *commit* something to the trash heap] **4** to do or perpetrate (an offense or crime) **5** to bind as by a promise; pledge; engage [*committed* to the struggle] **6** to make known the opinions or views of [to *commit* oneself on an issue] **7** to refer (a bill, etc.) to a committee to be considered —*vi.* [Informal] to make a pledge or promise: often with *to* —**commit to memory** to learn by heart; memorize —**commit to paper (**or **writing)** to write down; record —**com·mit′ta·ble** *adj.*

SYN.—**commit**, the basic term here, implies the delivery of a person or thing into the charge or keeping of another; **entrust** implies committal based on trust and confidence; **confide** stresses the private nature of information entrusted to another and usually connotes intimacy of relationship; **consign** suggests formal action in transferring something to another's possession or control; **relegate** implies a consigning to a specific class, sphere, place, etc., esp. one of inferiority, and usually suggests the literal or figurative removal of something undesirable

com·mit·ment (-mənt) *n.* **1** a committing or being committed **2** official consignment by court order of a person as to prison or a mental hospital **3** a pledge or promise to do something **4** dedication to a long-term course of action; engagement; involvement **5** a financial liability undertaken, as an agreement to buy or sell securities **6** the act of sending proposed legislation to a committee

com·mit·tal (kə mit′'l) *n.* the act of committing; commitment

com·mit·tee (kə mit′ē) *n.* ⟦ME *committe,* a representative < Anglo-Fr *commité,* pp. (for Fr *commis*) of *commettre,* to commit < L *committere:* see COMMIT⟧ **1** a group of people chosen, as from the members of a legislature or club, to consider, investigate, and report or act on some matter or on matters of a certain kind **2** a group of people organized to support some cause **3** [Archaic] someone into whose charge someone or something is committed —**in committee** under consideration by a committee, as a resolution or bill

com·mit·tee·man (-mən) *n., pl.* **-men** (-mən) **1** a member of a committee ☆**2** a ward or precinct leader for a political party

☆**committee of the whole** a committee comprising all the members of a legislative body, etc. under more informal rules than those used in a regular session

com·mit·tee·wom·an (-wo͝om′ən) *n., pl.* **-wom′en** (-wim′in) a female member of a committee

com·mix (kə miks′) *vt., vi.* ⟦back-form. < ME *commixt,* mixed together < L *commixtus:* see fol.⟧ [Archaic] to mix together; blend

com·mix·ture (-chər) *n.* ⟦L *commixtura* < *commixtus,* pp. of *commiscere,* to mix together < *com-,* together + *miscere,* to MIX⟧ a mixture

com·mode (kə mōd′) *n.* ⟦Fr, chest of drawers, orig., convenient, suitable < L *commodus,* suitable: see COM- & MODE⟧ **1** a high headdress worn by women around 1700 **2** a chest of drawers **3** a small, low table with drawers or cabinet space: also **commode table** **4** a movable washstand **5** a kind of chair enclosing a chamber pot **6** TOILET (*n.* 4*b*)

com·mod·i·fy (kə mäd′ə fī′) *vt.* **-fied′**, **-fy′ing** **1** COMMODITIZE **2** to treat as or make into a mere commodity to be bought and sold or to be used in selling something else [an automobile ad campaign that *commodifies* the American dream] —**com·mod′i·fi·ca′tion** (-fi kā′shən) *n.*

com·mo·di·ous (kə mō′dē əs) *adj.* ⟦ME, convenient < ML *commodiosus* < L *commodus:* see COMMODE⟧ offering plenty of room; spacious; roomy —**com·mo′di·ous·ly** *adv.* —**com·mo′di·ous·ness** *n.*

com·mod·i·tize (kə mäd′ə tīz′) *vt.* **-tized′**, **-tiz′ing** to make (a product or service) a COMMODITY (sense 4) —**com·mod′i·ti·za′tion** (-ti zā′shən) *n.*

com·mod·i·ty (kə mäd′ə tē) *n., pl.* **-ties** ⟦ME & OFr *commodite,* benefit, profit < L *commoditas,* fitness, adaptation < *commodus:* see COMMODE⟧ **1** any useful thing **2** anything bought and sold; any article of commerce **3** [*pl.*] basic items or staple products, as of agriculture or mining **4** a product or service that has become so standardized that buyers stop distinguishing between competing brands and typically seek the lowest price **5** [Archaic] personal advantage

com·mo·dore (käm′ə dôr′) *n.* ⟦earlier *commadore, commandore,* prob. via Du *kommandeur* < Fr *commandeur* < OFr *comandeor* < *comander:* see COMMAND⟧ **1** *U.S. Navy a)* [Historical] an officer ranking above a captain and below a rear admiral: the rank was abolished in 1899 but temporarily restored in WWII *b)* an officer, with the rank of captain, commanding two or more small ships, as destroyers **2** the president of a yacht club **3** the senior captain of a merchant fleet

Com·mo·dus (käm′ə dəs), **Lucius Ae·li·us Au·re·li·us** (ē′lē əs ô rē′lē əs) A.D. 161-192; emperor of Rome (180-192)

com·mon (käm′ən) *adj.* ⟦ME *commun* < OFr *comun* < L *communis* (OL *comoinis*), shared by all or many < IE **kom-moini-*, common (< **kom-*, COM- + **moini-*, achievement < base **mei-*, to exchange, barter) > OE *gemœne,* public, general, Ger *gemein:* see MEAN[2]⟧ **1** belonging equally to, or shared by, two or more or by all [the *common* interests of a group] **2** belonging or relating to the community at large; public [*common* carriers] **3** widely existing; general; prevalent [*common* knowledge] **4** widely but unfavorably known [a *common* criminal] **5** *a)* met with or occurring frequently; familiar; usual [a *common* sight] *b)* basic; simple; rudimentary [*common* courtesy] **6** not of the upper classes; of the masses [the *common* man] **7** having no rank [a *common* soldier] **8** below ordinary; inferior [*common* ware] **9** not refined; vulgar; low; coarse **10** *Anat.* formed of or dividing into branches **11** *Gram. a)* designating a noun that refers to any of a group or class ["book," "apple," and "street" are *common* nouns] (opposed to PROPER) *b)* designating gender that can be either masculine or feminine [the word "child" is of *common* gender] **12** *Math.* belonging equally to two or more quantities [a *common* denominator] —*n.* ☆**1** [*often pl., with pl. or sing. v.*] land owned or used by all the inhabitants of a place; tract of open public land, esp. as a park in a city or town **2** [*often* **C-**] *Eccles. a)* the office or service suitable for any of a class of festivals *b)* the ordinary of the Mass **3** *Law* the right that a person has, in common with the owner or others, in the land or waters of another ➡See also COMMONS —**in common** equally with, or shared by, another or all concerned —**com′mon·ness** *n.*

SYN.—**common** refers to that which is met with most frequently or is shared by all or most individuals in a group, body, etc., and may imply prevalence, usualness, or, in a depreciatory sense, inferiority [a *common* belief, a *common* hussy]; **general** implies connection with all or nearly all of a kind, class, or group and stresses extensiveness [*general* unrest among the people]; **ordinary** implies accordance with the regular or customary pattern, stressing commonplaceness and lack of special distinction [an *ordinary* workday]; **familiar** applies to that which is widely known and readily recognized [a *familiar* feeling]; **popular** and, in this connection, **vulgar** imply widespread currency, acceptance, or favor among the general public or the common people [a *popular* song, *Vulgar* Latin] See also **mutual** —**ANT.** **unusual, exceptional**

com·mon·a·ble (-ə bəl) *adj.* ⟦see prec.⟧ **1** allowed to pasture on land owned by the village, town, etc. **2** held in common: said of land

com·mon·age (-ij) *n.* ⟦see COMMON, *n.* 1 & -AGE⟧ **1** the right to pasture on land owned by the village, town, etc. **2** the state of being held in common **3** public or common land **4** the common people; commonalty

com·mon·al·i·ty (käm′ən al′ə tē) *n.* ⟦ME *communaltie* < OFr *communalté:* see COMMUNAL & -TY[1]⟧ **1** the common people; commonalty **2** a sharing as of common features or characteristics

com·mon·al·ty (käm′ən əl tē) *n., pl.* **-ties** ⟦ME & OFr *communalte:* see COMMUNAL⟧ **1** the common people; people not of the upper classes **2** a general body or group **3** a corporation or its membership

common carrier a person or company in the business of transporting passengers or goods for a fee, at uniform rates available to all persons

common cold COLD (*n.* 4)

common denominator **1** a common multiple of the denominators of two or more fractions [10 is a *common denominator* of ½ and ⅗] **2** a characteristic, element, etc. held in common

common difference the positive or negative constant added to each term in an arithmetic progression

com·mon·er (-ər) *n.* ⟦ME *communer* < *commun,* COMMON⟧ **1** a person not of the nobility; member of the commonalty **2** [Brit.] at some universities, a student who does not have a scholarship and therefore pays for food (called *commons*) and other expenses

Common Era the era beginning with the year 1 according to the modern Gregorian calendar: term used as an alternative to CHRISTIAN ERA, esp. by scholars and non-Christians: CE marks dates in this era, BCE marks dates before it

common fraction a fraction whose numerator and denominator are both whole numbers: cf. COMPLEX FRACTION, DECIMAL

common law the law of a country or state based on custom, usage, and the decisions and opinions of law courts: it is now largely codified by legislative definition: distinguished from STATUTE LAW

com·mon-law marriage (käm′ən lô′) *Law* a marriage not solemnized by religious or civil ceremony but effected by cohabitation as husband and wife

common logarithm *Math.* a logarithm having 10 for its base

com·mon·ly (käm′ən lē) *adv.* **1** in a common manner **2** in the usual course of events; ordinarily

common market **1** an association of countries formed to effect a closer economic union, esp. by means of mutual tariff concessions **2** [**C- M-**] the European Economic Community

common measure *Music* COMMON TIME

common multiple *Math.* a number or quantity evenly divisible by each element of a given set [12 is a *common multiple* of the set 2, 3, 4, 6]

com·mon·place (-plās′) *n.* ⟦lit. transl. of L *locus communis,* Gr *koinos topos,* general topic⟧ **1** [Obs.] a passage marked for reference or included in a COMMONPLACE BOOK **2** a trite or obvious remark; truism; platitude **3** anything common or ordinary —*adj.* neither new nor interesting; obvious or ordinary —**SYN.** PLATITUDE, TRITE

commonplace book a book in which extracts, poems, aphorisms, etc. are copied down for future reference, often together with one's ideas and reflections

common pleas *Law* ☆**1** in some U.S. states, a court having general and original jurisdiction over civil and criminal trials **2** in England, a former superior court with jurisdiction over civil suits

common room [Brit.] a room at a college used by faculty members or students for socializing, relaxation, etc.

com·mons (käm′ənz) *pl.n.* ⟦see COMMON⟧ **1** the common people; commonalty **2** [*often with sing. v.*] *a)* the body politic that is made up of commoners *b)* [**C-**] HOUSE OF COMMONS **3** [*often with sing. v.*] *a)* food provided for meals in common for all members of a group *b)* a room, building, table, or tables where such food is served, as at a college *c)* an allowance or ration of food **4** *see* COMMON (*n.* 1)

☆**common school** a public elementary school

common sense ordinary good sense or sound practical judgment —**com′mon·sense′** *adj.*, **com′mon·sen′si·cal** (-sen′sə kəl)

☆**com·mon-si·tus picketing** (käm′ən sīt′əs) the picketing of an entire construction site by a union striking against a particular contractor or subcontractor working on only one section

☆**common stock** ordinary capital stock in a company without a definite dividend rate or the privileges of preferred stock, but usually giving its owner a vote at shareholders' meetings in proportion to the owner's holdings

common time *Music* a meter of four beats to the measure; 4/4 time

com·mon·weal (käm′en wēl′) *n.* ⟦ME *commun wele:* see COMMON & WEAL[2]⟧ **1** the public good **2** [Archaic] a commonwealth

com·mon·wealth (-welth′) *n.* ⟦ME *commun welthe:* see COMMON & WEALTH⟧ **1** the people of a nation or state; body politic **2** *a)* a nation or state in which there is self-government; democracy or republic *b)* a federation of states [the *Commonwealth* of Australia] ☆**3** *a)* loosely, any state of the U.S. *b)* officially, Ky., Mass., Pa., or Va., which were so designated in their first constitutions: *Commonwealth* is also the official designation of Puerto Rico, in its special status under the U.S. government **4** a group of people united by common interests **5** [Obs.] the general welfare; commonweal —**the Commonwealth** **1** the government in England under the Cromwells and Parliament from 1649 to 1660: see also PROTECTORATE **2** association of independent nations, mostly former components of the British Empire, united for purposes of consultation and mutual assistance: all members acknowledge the British sovereign as symbolic head of the association: in full **the Commonwealth of Nations**

Commonwealth Day a holiday in honor of THE COMMONWEALTH (sense 2), celebrated on the second Monday of March

Commonwealth of Independent States a loose confederation of countries that were part of the U.S.S.R.: it includes Armenia, Azerbaijan, Belarus, Georgia, Kazakhstan, Kyrgyzstan, Moldova, Russia, Tajikistan, Turkmenistan, Ukraine, and Uzbekistan: abbrev. *CIS*

com·mo·tion (kə mō′shən) *n.* ⟦L *commotio* < *commotus,* pp. of *commovere,* to move, disturb < *com-*, together + *movere,* to MOVE⟧ **1** violent motion; turbulence **2** a noisy rushing about; confusion; bustle **3** [Archaic] a civil uprising **4** [Archaic] mental agitation

com·move (kə mo͞ov′) *vt.* **-moved′**, **-mov′ing** ⟦ME *commoeven* < OFr *commoveir* < L *commovere:* see prec.⟧ to move strongly; agitate; disturb; excite

com·mu·nal (kə myo͞on′əl, käm′yə nəl) *adj.* ⟦ME & OFr < LL *communalis*⟧ **1** of a commune or communes **2** of or belonging to the community; shared, or participated in, by all; public **3** designating or of social or economic organization in which there is common ownership of property —**com·mu·nal·i·ty** (käm′yo͞o nal′ə tē) *n.* —**com·mu′nal·ly** *adv.*

com·mu·nal·ism (-iz′əm) ***n.*** ⟦Fr *communalisme*⟧ **1** a theory or system of government in which communes or local communities, sometimes on an ethnic or religious basis, have virtual autonomy within a federated state **2** the conflicting allegiance resulting from this **3** communal organization —**com·mu′nal·ist** ***n., adj.***

com·mu·nal·ize (-īz′) ***vt.*** **-ized′**, **-iz′ing** to make communal; make public property of —**com′mu·nal·i·za′tion** ***n.***

Com·mu·nard (käm′yoo närd′) ***n.*** ⟦Fr⟧ **1** a person who supported or took part in the Commune of Paris (1871) **2** [**c-**] a resident or member of a COMMUNE[2] (sense 5)

com·mune[1] (kə myo͞on′; *for n.* käm′yo͞on′) ***vi.*** **-muned′**, **-mun′ing** ⟦ME *communen* < OFr *comuner,* to make common, share < *comun* (see COMMON); also < OFr *communier,* to administer the sacrament < L *communicare,* to share (LL(Ec), to receive the sacrament): see COMMUNICATE⟧ **1** *a)* to talk together intimately *b)* to be in close spiritual harmony *with* [to *commune* with nature] **2** [Archaic] to receive Holy Communion —***n.*** [Old Poet.] intimate conversation —**commune with oneself** to think; ponder

com·mune[2] (käm′yo͞on′) ***n.*** ⟦ME & OFr < ML *communia,* orig. pl. of L *commune,* lit., that which is common < *communis,* COMMON⟧ **1** [Archaic] the common people **2** a community; specif., *a)* a local body for self-government, esp. in medieval towns *b)* [Historical] MIR **3** the smallest administrative district of local government in France, Belgium, and some other countries in Europe **4** a strictly organized collective farm, as in China ☆**5** a small group of people living communally and sharing in work, earnings, etc. —**the Commune 1** the revolutionary government of Paris from 1792 to 1794 **2** the revolutionary government established in Paris from March 18 to May 28, 1871

com·mu·ni·ca·ble (kə myo͞o′ni kə bəl) ***adj.*** ⟦ME < LL *communicabilis*⟧ **1** that can be communicated, as an idea **2** that can be transmitted, as a disease **3** [Archaic] talkative —**com·mu′ni·ca·bil′i·ty** ***n.*** —**com·mu′ni·ca·bly** ***adv.***

com·mu·ni·cant (kə myo͞o′ni kənt) ***n.*** ⟦< L *communicans,* prp.: see fol.⟧ **1** a person who receives Holy Communion or belongs to a church that celebrates this sacrament **2** [Rare] a person who communicates information; informant —***adj.*** [Rare] communicating

com·mu·ni·cate (kə myo͞o′ni kāt′) ***vt.*** **-cat′ed**, **-cat′ing** ⟦< L *communicatus,* pp. of *communicare,* to impart, share, lit., to make common < *communis,* COMMON⟧ **1** to pass along; impart; transmit (as heat, motion, or a disease) **2** to make known; give (information, signals, or messages) —***vi.*** **1** to receive Holy Communion **2** *a)* to give or exchange information, signals, or messages in any way, as by talk, gestures, or writing *b)* to have a sympathetic or meaningful relationship **3** to be connected [the living room *communicates* with the dining room] —**com·mu′ni·ca′tor** ***n.***

com·mu·ni·ca·tion (kə myo͞o′ni kā′shən) ***n.*** **1** the act of transmitting **2** *a)* a giving or exchanging of information, signals, or messages as by talk, gestures, or writing *b)* the information, signals, or message **3** close, sympathetic relationship **4** a means of communicating; specif., *a)* [*pl.*] a system for sending and receiving messages, as by telephone, telegraph, radio, etc. *b)* [*pl.*] a system as of routes for moving troops and materiel *c)* a passage or way for getting from one place to another **5** [*often pl., with sing. v.*] *a)* the art of expressing ideas, esp. in speech and writing *b)* the science of transmitting information, esp. in symbols

com·mu·ni·ca·tive (kə myo͞o′ni kāt′iv, -ni kə tiv) ***adj.*** **1** giving information readily; forthcoming **2** of communication —**com·mu′ni·ca′tive·ly** ***adv.*** —**com·mu′ni·ca′tive·ness** ***n.***

com·mun·ion (kə myo͞on′yən) ***n.*** ⟦ME *communioun* < OFr *communion* < L *communio,* a sharing (in LL(Ec), the sacrament of communion) < *communis,* COMMON⟧ **1** the act of sharing; possession in common; participation [a *communion* of interest] **2** the act of sharing one's thoughts and emotions with another or others; intimate converse **3** an intimate relationship with deep understanding **4** a group of Christians professing the same faith and practicing the same rites; denomination **5** [**C-**] *a)* a sharing in, or celebrating of, the Eucharist, or Holy Communion *b)* the consecrated bread or wine of the Eucharist; Holy Communion

com·mu·ni·qué (kə myo͞o′ni kā′, kə myo͞o′ni kā′) ***n.*** ⟦Fr, orig. pp. of *communiquer,* to communicate < L *communicare*⟧ an official communication or bulletin

com·mu·nism (käm′yoo niz′əm, -yə-) ***n.*** ⟦Fr *communisme* < *commun* (< OFr *comun*) + *isme*: see COMMON & -ISM⟧ **1** any theory or system of government characterized by the ownership or sharing of all property by the community as a whole **2** [*often* **C-**] *a)* as envisioned by Marx, a future condition of mankind achieved after the revolutionary overthrow of capitalism and a transitional stage of socialism, and characterized by a largely self-regulating society whose members have renounced private property and personal wealth, national identity, social-class differences, etc. *b)* a political system that advances revolutionary principles for achieving this condition, either as formulated by Marx or as modified by Lenin, Stalin, Mao Tse-tung, etc., characterized by a single ruling party, centralized economic planning, the curtailment of individual liberties, etc. **3** loosely, leftist or socialist ideas, activity, etc.

com·mu·nist (-nist) ***n.*** ⟦Fr *communiste*⟧ **1** an advocate or supporter of communism **2** [**C-**] a member of a Communist Party **3** loosely, anyone advocating ideas thought of as being leftist or subversive —***adj.*** **1** of, characteristic of, or like communism or communists **2** advocating or supporting communism **3** [**C-**] of or having to do with a Communist Party —**com′mu·nis′tic** ***adj.*** —**com′mu·nis′ti·cal·ly** ***adv.***

Communist Party 1 a political party that advances the revolutionary principles of communism; specif., the dictatorial ruling party in the Soviet Union, the People's Republic of China, etc. **2** any of various parties that espouse Marxist or socialist principles, as in France, Italy, etc.

com·mu·ni·tar·i·an (kə myo͞o′nə ter′ē ən) ***n.*** a member or advocate of a communistic or communalist community —**com·mu′ni·tar′i·an·ism′** ***n.***

com·mu·ni·ty (kə myo͞o′nə tē) ***n., pl.*** **-ties** ⟦ME & OFr *communite* < L *communitas,* community, fellowship < *communis,* COMMON⟧ **1** *a)* all the people living in a particular district, city, etc. *b)* the district, city, etc. where they live **2** a group of people forming a smaller social unit within a larger one, and sharing common interests, work, identity, location, etc. [a college *community,* the labor *community*] **3** a group of nations loosely or closely associated because of common traditions or for political or economic advantage **4** society in general; the public **5** ownership or participation in common [*community* of goods] **6** similarity; likeness [*community* of tastes] **7** *a)* the condition of living with others *b)* friendly association; fellowship **8** *Ecol.* BIOCENOSIS

☆**community center** a meeting place, often a complex of buildings, where the people of a community may carry on cultural, recreational, or social activities

☆**community chest (*or* fund)** a fund collected annually in many cities and towns through private contributions and used to support certain local agencies and institutions engaged in social service

☆**community college** a junior college established to serve a certain community and sometimes supported in part by it, often emphasizing career, rather than academic, programs

☆**community property** in certain states of the U.S., property acquired by a husband or wife, or by both, during marriage and consequently owned in common by both

community service unpaid work which benefits the community; specif., such work imposed on a convicted person as a sentence

com·mu·nize (käm′yə nīz′) ***vt.*** **-nized′**, **-niz′ing** **1** to subject to communal ownership and control **2** to cause to become communistic —**com′mu·ni·za′tion** ***n.***

com·mut·a·ble (kə myo͞ot′ə bəl) ***adj.*** that can be commuted —**com·mut′a·bil′i·ty** ***n.***

com·mu·tate (käm′yə tāt′) ***vt.*** **-tat′ed**, **-tat′ing** ⟦back-form. < fol.⟧ to repeatedly reverse the direction of (an electric current), esp. in a motor that uses direct current as its power source or in a generator that produces direct current

com·mu·ta·tion (käm′yə tā′shən) ***n.*** ⟦ME & OFr *commutacion* < L *commutatio,* a changing < *commutatus,* pp. of *commutare,* COMMUTE⟧ **1** an exchange; substitution **2** *a)* the substitution of one kind of payment for another *b)* the payment made ☆**3** the act of traveling as a commuter, esp. by using a commutation ticket **4** *Elec.* the repeated reversal of the direction of a current by a commutator **5** *Law* a change of a sentence or punishment to one that is less severe

☆**commutation ticket** a ticket entitling the holder to travel over the same route, as on a railroad, a specified number of times at a reduced rate

com·mu·ta·tive (kə myo͞ot′ə tiv, käm′yə tāt′iv) ***adj.*** **1** of commutation; involving exchange or replacement **2** *Math.* of or pertaining to an operation in which the order of the elements does not affect the result, as, in addition, $3 + 2 = 2 + 3$ and, in multiplication, $2 \times 3 = 3 \times 2$

com·mu·ta·tor (käm′yə tāt′ər) ***n.*** ⟦< L *commutatus* (pp. of *commutare,* fol.) + -OR⟧ a device that commutates an electric current, esp. a split-ring metallic conductor that spins rapidly with the armature of a DC motor or generator while in contact with the fixed brushes

com·mute (kə myo͞ot′) ***vt.*** **-mut′ed**, **-mut′ing** ⟦ME *commuten* < L *commutare,* to change < *com-,* intens. + *mutare,* to change: see MISS[1]⟧ **1** to change (one thing) *for* or *into* another; exchange; substitute **2** to change (an obligation, punishment, etc.) to one that is less severe **3** to substitute (payment in a lump sum) for payment in installments —***vi.*** **1** *a)* to be a substitute *b)* to make up; compensate ☆**2** to travel as a commuter —☆***n.*** the trip of a commuter

☆**com·mut·er** (-ər) ***n.*** a person who travels regularly, esp. by automobile, bus, train, etc., between two points at some distance from each other, esp. between a residence and a place of employment —***adj.*** of or for commuters or commuting [a *commuter* airline]

Com·ne·nus (käm nē′nəs) ***n., pl.*** **-ne′ni** (-nī) name of a ruling family of the Byzantine Empire (1057-59; 1081-1185) and of the empire of Trebizond (1204-1461)

Co·mo (kō′mō), **Lake** lake in Lombardy, N Italy: 56 sq mi (145 sq km)

Com·o·rin (käm′ə rin), **Cape** cape at the southernmost tip of India

Com·o·ros (käm′ə rōz) country on a group of islands (**Comoro Islands**) in the Indian Ocean, at the head of the Mozambique Channel: formerly a French territory, it became independent in 1975: 838 sq mi (2,170 sq km); cap. Moroni

co·mose (kō′mōs′) ***adj.*** ⟦L *comosus* < *coma,* hair < Gr *komē*⟧ *Bot.* having a tuft of hairs; hairy

☆**comp**[1] (kämp) ***vi.*** ⟦< ACCOMPANY⟧ *Jazz* to play an accompaniment, usually, specif., one consisting primarily of chords played in a syncopated rhythm: said of a pianist, guitarist, etc.

comp[2] (kämp) [Slang] ***n.*** ⟦< COMPLIMENTARY⟧ a free theater ticket, book, etc. given usually for promotional purposes —***vt.*** **1** to give as a comp **2** to give a comp to

comp[3] (kämp) ***n.*** *short for* comprehensive examination (see COMPREHENSIVE, ***n.***): *usually used in pl.*

comp[4] *abbrev.* 1 comparative 2 compare 3 compensation 4 compilation 5 compiled (by) 6 compiler 7 complete 8 composer 9 composition 10 compound

com·pact (kəm pakt′, käm′pakt′; *for n., always* käm′pakt′) *adj.* ⟦ME < L *compactus,* concentrated, pp. of *compingere,* to fasten together < *com-,* with, together + *pangere,* to fix, fasten: see PEACE⟧ 1 closely and firmly packed or put together; dense; solid 2 taking little space; arranged neatly in a small space 3 not diffuse or wordy; terse 4 [Archaic] made up or composed (*of*) ☆5 designating or of a relatively small, light, economical model of automobile —*vt.* 1 to pack or join firmly together 2 to make by joining or putting together 3 to make more dense; compress; condense —*n.* 1 ⟦< the *adj.,* 2⟧ a small cosmetic case, usually containing face powder and mirror ☆2 a compact automobile 3 ⟦< L pp. of *compacisci,* to agree together < same base as *compingere*⟧ an agreement between two or more individuals, states, etc.; covenant —*SYN.* CLOSE[1] —**com·pact′ly** *adv.* —**com·pact′ness** *n.*

com·pact disc (*or* **disk)** (käm′pakt′) a small, plastic OPTICAL DISC for storing digital data, recording sounds digitally, etc.

com·pac·tion (kəm pak′shən) *n.* a compacting or being compacted; compression

☆**com·pac·tor** (kəm pak′tər, käm′pak′tər) *n.* a device that compresses trash into small bundles for easy disposal

☆**com·pa·dre** (kəm pä′drā′) *n.* ⟦Sp, friend, lit., godfather < ML(Ec) *compater:* see COMPÈRE⟧ [Southwest] a close friend; buddy

com·pan·ion[1] (kəm pan′yən) *n.* ⟦ME *compainoun* < OFr *compagnon* < VL **companio,* lit., bread fellow, messmate (calque of Goth *gahlaiba,* one who eats of the same bread < *ga-,* with + *hlaifs,* bread, LOAF[1]) < L *com-,* with + *panis,* bread⟧ 1 a person who associates with or accompanies another or others; associate; comrade 2 a person employed to live or travel with another 3 either of two persons not married to each other but otherwise in an intimate, spouse-like relationship: often, specif., used when the persons are of the same sex 4 [C-] a member of the lowest rank in an order of knighthood 5 a thing that matches another in sort, color, etc.; one of a pair or set 6 a handbook on a specific subject [a *companion* to French literature] 7 a pet, esp. one toward which one feels companionship: often **animal companion** 8 [Obs.] a scoundrel —*vt.* to accompany —*SYN.* ASSOCIATE

com·pan·ion[2] (kəm pan′yən) *n.* ⟦Du *kampanje,* quarterdeck < OFr *compagne,* steward's room in a galley < It *(camera della) compagna,* (room of the) company, crew < VL *compania:* see COMPANY⟧ *Naut.* 1 the covering at the head of a companionway 2 COMPANIONWAY

com·pan·ion·a·ble (-ə bəl) *adj.* having the qualities of a good companion; sociable —**com·pan′ion·a·bly** *adv.*

com·pan·ion·ate (-it) *adj.* of or like companions

☆**companionate marriage** a proposed system of trial marriage in which the couple would postpone having children and could be divorced by mutual consent, until a final decision to stay married is reached

com·pan·ion·ship (-ship′) *n.* ⟦COMPANION[1] + -SHIP⟧ the relationship of companions; fellowship

com·pan·ion·way (-wā′) *n.* ⟦COMPANION[2] + WAY⟧ a stairway leading from one deck of a ship to another

com·pa·ny (kum′pə nē) *n., pl.* **-nies** ⟦ME & OFr *compaignie* < VL *compania,* lit., group sharing bread: see COMPANION[1]⟧ 1 companionship; society [to enjoy another's *company*] 2 a group of people; specif., *a)* a group gathered for social purposes *b)* a group associated for some purpose, as to form a commercial or industrial firm [a theatrical *company,* a manufacturing *company*] 3 a trade guild in the Middle Ages 4 the partners whose names are not given in the title of a firm [John Smith and *Company*] 5 a guest or guests; visitor or visitors 6 a habitual associate or associates [people are judged by the *company* they keep] 7 *Mil.* a body of troops; specif., the lowest administrative unit, as of infantry, normally composed of two or more platoons and a headquarters 8 all of a ship's personnel, including the officers: in full **ship's company** —*vt.* **-nied, -ny·ing** [Archaic] to accompany —*vi.* [Archaic] to associate (*with*) —*SYN.* TROOP —**keep company** 1 to associate (*with*) 2 to go together; associate habitually: said esp. of a couple intending to marry —**keep (a person) company** to stay with (a person) so as to provide companionship —**part company** 1 to stop associating (*with*) 2 to separate and go in different directions

☆**company union** an organization of workers in a single company, not affiliated with any group of labor unions: the term generally implies control by the employers

compar *abbrev.* comparative

com·pa·ra·ble (käm′pə rə bəl, kəm par′ə bəl) *adj.* ⟦ME & OFr < L *comparabilis*⟧ 1 that can be compared 2 worthy of comparison —**com′pa·ra·bil′i·ty** *n.,* **com′pa·ra·ble·ness** —**com′pa·ra·bly** *adv.*

com·par·a·tist (kəm par′ə tist) *n.* ⟦fol. + -IST[1]⟧ a person who uses a comparative method; often, specif., a specialist in comparative literature: also **com·par′a·tiv·ist** (-tiv ist)

com·par·a·tive (kəm par′ə tiv) *adj.* ⟦ME < L *comparativus*⟧ 1 that compares; involving comparison as a method, esp. in a branch of study [*comparative* linguistics] 2 estimated by comparison with something else; relative [a *comparative* success] 3 *Gram.* designating or of the second degree of comparison of adjectives and adverbs; expressing a greater degree of a quality or attribute than that expressed in the positive degree: usually indicated by the suffix -ER (*harder*) or by the use of *more* with the positive form (*more honest*) —*n.* 1 [Obs.] a rival 2 *Gram. a)* the comparative degree *b)* a word or form in this degree —**com·par′a·tive·ness** *n.*

comparative literature the comparative study of works of literature of different languages or from different nations or historical periods

com·par·a·tive·ly (-lē) *adv.* 1 in a comparative manner 2 by comparison; relatively

com·pa·ra·tor (käm′pə rāt′ər, kəm par′ət ər) *n.* any of various instruments, esp. in electronics, for comparing some measurement, as of length, brightness, or voltage, with a fixed standard

com·pare (kəm per′) *vt.* **-pared′, -par′ing** ⟦ME *comparen* < OFr *comparer* < L *comparare* < *com-,* with + *parare,* to make equal < *par:* see PAR[1]⟧ 1 to regard as similar; liken *to* [to *compare* life to a river] 2 to examine in order to observe or discover similarities or differences: often followed by *with* [*compare* their voting records] 3 *Gram.* to form the comparative and superlative degrees of (an adjective or adverb) —*vi.* 1 *a)* to be worthy of comparison (*with*) *b)* to be regarded as similar or equal 2 to make comparisons 3 to stand in comparison; measure up [how does my car *compare* with his?] —*n.* [Old Poet.] comparison —**beyond (or past or without) compare** without equal; incomparably good, bad, great, etc.

SYN.—**compare** refers to a literal or figurative putting together in order to note points of resemblance and difference, and implies the weighing of parallel features for relative values [to *compare* Shakespeare with Schiller]; **contrast** implies a comparing for the purpose of emphasizing differences [to *contrast* farm life with city life]; **collate** implies detailed, critical comparison, specif., of different versions of the same text

com·par·i·son (kəm par′ə sən) *n.* ⟦ME < OFr *comparaison* < L *comparatio* < pp. of prec.⟧ 1 a comparing or being compared; estimation of similarities and differences 2 sufficient likeness to make meaningful comparison possible; possibility of comparison; similarity [there is no *comparison* between the two singers] 3 *Gram.* the modification of an adjective or adverb in its positive degree to show the comparative and superlative degrees (Ex.: *long, longer, longest; good, better, best; slowly, more slowly, most slowly*) —**by comparison** when compared (to something already mentioned) [after a frigid January, February felt downright balmy *by comparison*] —**in comparison with (or to)** compared with (or to)

comparison shop to compare the prices of a product or service from among various brands or sellers, so as to find the best bargain —**comparison shopper**

com·part (kəm pärt′) *vt.* ⟦< OFr *compartir* or LL *compartiri* < *com-,* intens. + *partiri, partire:* see PART[1], *vt.*⟧ to divide into parts; subdivide; partition

com·part·ment (kəm pärt′mənt; *for v.,* -ment′, -mənt) *n.* ⟦Fr *compartiment* < It *compartimento* < *compartire,* prec.⟧ 1 any of the divisions into which a space is partitioned off 2 a separate section, part, division, or category —*vt.* COMPARTMENTALIZE —**com·part·men·tal** (käm′pärt′men′təl) *adj.* —**com·part′ment′ed** *adj.*

com·part·men·tal·ize (käm′pärt ment′′l īz′) *vt.* **-ized′, -iz′ing** to put or separate into detached compartments, divisions, or categories —**com′part·men′tal·i·za′tion** *n.*

com·pass (kum′pəs; *also* käm′-) *vt.* ⟦ME *compassen* < OFr *compasser,* to go around < VL **compassare* < L *com-,* together + *passus,* a step: see PACE[1]⟧ 1 [Archaic] to go around; make a circuit of 2 ENCOMPASS (sense 1) 3 to grasp mentally; understand; comprehend 4 to reach successfully; achieve; accomplish [to *compass* one's ends] 5 to plot or contrive (something harmful) —*n.* ⟦ME & OFr *compas,* a circle, prob. < the v.⟧ 1 [*sometimes pl.*] an adjustable instrument consisting of two arms connected at one end by a hinge, with typically one arm having a pencil or pen attached to its other end and the other arm ending in a point: used for drawing arcs and circles, measuring distances on a map, etc.: also **pair of compasses** 2 a boundary line; circumference 3 an enclosed area 4 full extent or range; reach; scope; specif., range of tones, as of a voice 5 any of various instruments for showing geographical direction, esp. one consisting of a magnetic needle swinging freely on a pivot and pointing to the magnetic north 6 [Archaic] a circuit; course —*adj.* round; circular or semicircular —*SYN.* RANGE —**com′pass·a·ble** *adj.*

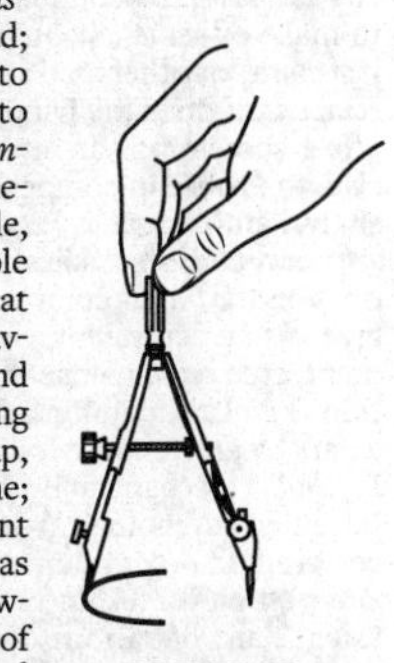

compass
(*n.* sense 1)

compass card the circular card mounted on a free pivot inside a compass and marked with the points of direction and, often, the degrees of the circle

com·pas·sion (kəm pash′ən) *n.* ⟦ME & OFr < LL(Ec) *compassio,* sympathy < *compassus,* pp. of *compati,* to feel pity < L *com-,* together + *pati,* to suffer: see PASSION⟧ sorrow for the sufferings or trouble of another or others, accompanied by an urge to help; deep sympathy; pity —*SYN.* PITY

com·pas·sion·ate (-it; *for v.,* -āt′) *adj.* feeling or showing compassion; sympathizing deeply; pitying —*vt.* **-at′ed, -at′ing** to pity —*SYN.* TENDER[1] —**com·pas′sion·ate·ly** *adv.*

☆**compass plant** 1 a coarse plant (*Silphium laciniatum*) of the composite family, with large, bristly leaves and heads of yellow flowers, found on the prairies of the central U.S.: the leaves reputedly point in a north-and-south direction 2 any of various other plants whose leaves supposedly point to the north and south

compass saw ⟦see COMPASS (*adj.*)⟧ a handsaw with a narrow, tapering blade for cutting small circles, curves, etc.

com·pat·i·ble (kəm pat′ə bəl) ***adj.*** ⟦ME & ML *compatibilis* < LL(Ec) *compati*: see COMPASSION⟧ **1** *a)* capable of living together harmoniously or getting along well together (*with*) *b)* in agreement; congruent (*with*) **2** *a)* that can work well together, get along well together, combine well, etc. [a *compatible* couple, *compatible* colors] *b)* that can function or be used together without change or alteration **3** that can be mixed without reacting chemically or interfering with one another's action or state: said of drugs, insecticides, etc. **4** *Bot.* that can be cross-fertilized or grafted readily **5** *Comput.* designating or of *a)* computer components, software, etc. that can be used with a specified computer or computer system (often in hyphenated compounds) *b)* computers or computer systems that can use the same components, software, etc. —***n.*** a computer component, software, etc. that is COMPATIBLE (sense 5*a*) —**com·pat′i·bil′i·ty** ***n.***, **com·pat′i·ble·ness** —**com·pat′i·bly** ***adv.***

com·pa·tri·ot (kəm pā′trē ət) ***n.*** ⟦Fr *compatriote* < LL *compatriota*: see COM- & PATRIOT⟧ **1** a fellow countryman **2** a colleague —**com·pa′tri·ot·ism′** ***n.***

Com·pa·zine (käm′pə zēn′) *trademark for* a drug, $C_{28}H_{32}ClN_3O_8S$, used to control serious nausea or vomiting and to reduce anxiety

compd *abbrev.* compound

com·peer (käm′pir′, käm pir′) ***n.*** ⟦ME & OFr *compair* < L *compar*: see COM- & PAR[1]⟧ **1** a person of the same rank or status; equal; peer **2** a companion; comrade

com·pel (kəm pel′) ***vt.*** **-pelled′**, **-pel′ling** ⟦ME *compellen* < OFr *compellir* < L *compellere* < *com-*, together + *pellere*, to drive: see FELT[1]⟧ **1** to force or constrain, as to do something **2** to get or bring about by force **3** [Archaic] to gather or drive together by force, as a flock —***SYN.*** FORCE —**com·pel′la·ble** ***adj.*** —**com·pel′ler** ***n.***

com·pel·la·tion (käm′pə lā′shən) ***n.*** ⟦L *compellatio* < *compellare*, to accost, address < L *compellere*: see prec.⟧ [Now Rare] APPELLATION

com·pel·ling (kəm pel′iŋ) ***adj.*** **1** that compels **2** irresistibly or keenly interesting, attractive, etc.; captivating [a *compelling* drama] —**com·pel′ling·ly** ***adv.***

com·pend (käm′pend′) ***n.*** COMPENDIUM

com·pen·di·ous (kəm pen′dē əs) ***adj.*** ⟦ME < L *compendiosus*, short: see fol.⟧ **1** containing all the essentials in a brief form; concise **2** comprehensive; inclusive —**com·pen′di·ous·ly** ***adv.*** —**com·pen′di·ous·ness** ***n.***

com·pen·di·um (kəm pen′dē əm) ***n.***, *pl.* **-di·ums** or **-di·a** (-ə) ⟦L, a weighing together, abridgment < *compendere*, to weigh together < *com-*, together + *pendere*, to weigh⟧ a summary or abstract containing the essential information in a brief form; concise but comprehensive treatise

com·pen·sa·ble (kəm pen′sə bəl) ***adj.*** ⟦< ME *compensen*, fol. + -ABLE⟧ entitling to compensation

com·pen·sate (käm′pən sāt′) ***vt.*** **-sat′ed**, **-sat′ing** ⟦< L *compensatus*, pp. of *compensare*, to weigh one thing against another < *com-*, with + *pensare*, freq. of *pendere*, to weigh: see PENDANT⟧ **1** [Now Rare] to make up for; be a counterbalance to in weight, force, etc. **2** to make equivalent or suitable return to; recompense; pay [to *compensate* an owner for land taken by a city] **3** *Mech.* to counteract or make allowance for (a variation) —***vi.*** **1** to make or serve as compensation or amends (*for*) **2** *a)* to make an adjustment, or otherwise act, so as to balance or offset something [a golfer *compensating* for the wind by altering her swing] *b)* to serve to balance or offset something [an altered swing that *compensates* for the wind] **3** *Psychol.* to engage in compensation —***SYN.*** PAY[1] —**com·pen·sa·tive** (kəm pen′sə tiv, käm′pən sāt′iv) ***adj.*** —**com·pen·sa·to·ry** (kəm pen′sə tôr′ē) ***adj.***

com·pen·sa·tion (käm′pən sā′shən) ***n.*** ⟦ME *compensacioun* < L *compensatio*⟧ **1** a compensating or being compensated **2** *a)* anything given as an equivalent, or to make amends for a loss, damage, unemployment, etc.; recompense *b)* payment for services; esp., wages or remuneration **3** *Biol.* the counterbalancing of a defect in the structure or function of a part by greater activity in or development of one or more other parts **4** *Psychol.* a mechanism by which an individual seeks to make up for a real or imagined psychological defect by developing or exaggerating a psychological strength —**com′pen·sa′tion·al** ***adj.***

com·pen·sa·tor (käm′pən sāt′ər) ***n.*** **1** a person or thing that compensates **2** any of various devices or circuits used to correct or offset some disturbing action, as speed deviations in a moving system or excessive current in a circuit

com·père (käm′per′) ***n.*** ⟦Fr, lit., godfather < ML(Ec) *compater*, orig., joint father (of the faithful) < L *com-*, with + *pater*, FATHER⟧ [Chiefly Brit.] a MASTER OF CEREMONIES (sense 2)

com·pete (kəm pēt′) ***vi.*** **-pet′ed**, **-pet′ing** ⟦L *competere*, to strive together for, be qualified < *com-*, together + *petere*, to rush at, desire: see FEATHER⟧ to enter into, or be in, rivalry; contend; vie

com·pe·tence (käm′pə təns) ***n.*** ⟦Fr *compétence* < L *competentia*, a meeting, agreement < *competens*, prp. of *competere*: see prec.⟧ **1** sufficient means for one's needs **2** condition or quality of being competent; ability; fitness; specif., legal capability, power, or jurisdiction Also **com′pe·ten·cy** (-tən sē)

com·pe·tent (-tənt) ***adj.*** ⟦ME < OFr < L *competens*, prp. of *competere*: see COMPETE⟧ **1** well qualified; capable; fit [a *competent* doctor] **2** sufficient; adequate [a *competent* understanding of law] **3** permissible or properly belonging: with *to* **4** *Law* legally qualified, authorized, or fit —***SYN.*** ABLE —**com′pe·tent·ly** ***adv.***

com·pe·ti·tion (käm′pə tish′ən) ***n.*** ⟦L *competitio*⟧ **1** the act of competing; rivalry **2** a contest, or match **3** official participation in organized sport **4** opposition, or effective opposition, in a contest or match **5** rivalry in business, as for customers or markets **6** the person or persons against whom one competes **7** *Ecol.* the struggle among individual organisms for food, water, space, etc. when the available supply is limited

SYN.—**competition** denotes a striving for the same object, position, prize, etc., usually in accordance with certain fixed rules; **rivalry** implies keen competition between opponents more or less evenly matched, and, unqualified, it often suggests unfriendliness or even hostility; **emulation** implies endeavor to equal or surpass in achievement, character, etc. another, usually one greatly admired

com·pet·i·tive (kəm pet′ə tiv) ***adj.*** **1** of, involving, or based on competition **2** likely to succeed in competition [a *competitive* team] —**com·pet′i·tive·ly** ***adv.*** —**com·pet′i·tive·ness** ***n.***

com·pet·i·tor (kəm pet′ət ər) ***n.*** ⟦L⟧ **1** a person who competes; rival **2** a rival business, team, etc.

Com·piègne (kōn pyen′y′) town in N France, on the Oise River: the armistices between the Allies & Germany (1918) & between Germany & France (1940) were signed near here

com·pi·la·tion (käm′pə lā′shən) ***n.*** ⟦ME *compilacioun* < L *compilatio*, a pillaging, hence collection of documents < *compilatus*, pp. of fol.⟧ **1** the act of compiling **2** something compiled, as a report

com·pile (kəm pīl′) ***vt.*** **-piled′**, **-pil′ing** ⟦ME *compilen* < OFr *compiler* < L *compilare*, to snatch together, plunder < *com-*, together + *pilare*, to compress, ram down⟧ **1** to gather and put together (statistics, facts, etc.) in an orderly form **2** to compose (a book, etc.) of materials gathered from various sources **3** to translate (a computer program, instruction, etc. in a high-level language) into machine language: said of a compiler program

com·pil·er (-pīl′ər) ***n.*** a person or thing that compiles; specif., a computer program that translates instructions, other programs, etc. in a high-level language into machine language

com·pla·cen·cy (kəm plā′sən sē) ***n.*** ⟦LL *complacentia* < L *complacens*: see fol.⟧ quiet satisfaction; contentment; often, specif., self-satisfaction, or smugness: also **com·pla′cence** (-səns)

com·pla·cent (kəm plā′sənt) ***adj.*** ⟦L *complacens*, prp. of *complacere*, to be very pleasing < *com-*, intens. + *placere*, to PLEASE⟧ **1** satisfied; esp., self-satisfied, or smug **2** affable; complaisant —**com·pla′cent·ly** ***adv.***

com·plain (kəm plān′) ***vi.*** ⟦ME *compleinen* < OFr *complaindre* < VL **complangere*, orig., to beat the breast < L *com-*, intens. + *plangere*, to strike: see PLAINT⟧ **1** to claim or express pain, displeasure, etc. **2** to find fault; declare annoyance **3** to make an accusation; bring a formal charge —**com·plain′er** ***n.*** —**com·plain′ing·ly** ***adv.***

com·plain·ant (kəm plān′ənt) ***n.*** ⟦ME *compleinaunt* < prp. of OFr *complaindre*: see prec.⟧ *Law* a person who files a charge or makes the complaint in court; plaintiff

com·plaint (kəm plānt′) ***n.*** ⟦ME *complainte* < OFr < *complaindre*⟧ **1** the act of complaining; utterance of pain, displeasure, annoyance, etc. **2** a subject or cause for complaining; grievance **3** an illness; ailment **4** *Law* a pleading setting forth the plaintiff's case or cause of action; formal charge or accusation

com·plai·sance (kəm plā′zəns, -səns; *also* käm′plə zans′) ***n.*** ⟦Fr < fol.⟧ **1** willingness to please; disposition to be obliging and agreeable; affability **2** an act or instance of this

com·plai·sant (kəm plā′zənt, -sənt; *also* käm′plə zant′) ***adj.*** ⟦Fr, prp. of *complaire*, to please, humor < L *complacere*: see COMPLACENT⟧ willing to please; affably agreeable; obliging —**com·plai′sant·ly** ***adv.***

com·pleat (kəm plēt′) ***adj.*** *archaic sp. of* COMPLETE

☆**com·plect·ed** (kəm plek′tid) ***adj.*** ⟦altered < COMPLEXIONED⟧ COMPLEXIONED

com·ple·ment (käm′plə mənt; *for v.*, -ment′) ***n.*** ⟦ME < L *complementum*, that which fills up or completes < *complere*: see COMPLETE⟧ **1** something that completes or enhances something else [the wine was a fine *complement* to the meal] **2** the amount or number needed to fill or complete **3** a complete set; entirety **4** something added to complete a whole; either of two parts that complete each other **5** *Gram.* a word or group of words that, with the verb, completes the meaning and syntactic structure of the predicate (Ex.: *foreman* in "make him foreman," *paid* in "he expects to get paid") **6** *Immunology* a complex series of proteins in the blood plasma that acts with specific antibodies to destroy corresponding antigens, as bacteria or foreign proteins **7** *Math.* *a)* the number of degrees that must be added to a given angle or arc to make it equal 90 degrees *b)* the subset which must be added to any given subset to yield the original set **8** *Music* the difference between a given interval and the complete octave **9** *Naut.* all of a ship's personnel, including the officers, required to operate a ship —***vt.*** to be a complement to [a colorful scarf will *complement* the black dress]

com·ple·men·tar·i·ty (käm′plə men ter′ə tē) ***n.*** the state or fact of being complementary; necessary interrelationship or correspondence

com·ple·men·ta·ry (käm′plə men′tə rē) ***adj.*** **1** acting as a complement; completing **2** making up what is lacking in one another Also **com′ple·men′tal** (-men′təl)

complementary angle either of two angles that together form a 90° angle

complementary colors any two colors of the spectrum that, combined in the right intensities, produce white or nearly white light

complement fixation *Immunology* the fixing of complement into the product of an antigen-antibody reaction: used as an infection indicator in certain serologic tests that measure the presence or absence of free, active complement

com·plete (kəm plēt′) ***adj.*** ⟦ME & OFr *complet* < L *completus*, pp. of *com-*

plere, to fill up, complete < *com-,* intens. + *plere,* to fill: see FULL[1]⟧ **1** lacking no component part; full; whole; entire **2** brought to a conclusion; ended; finished **3** thorough; absolute [to have *complete* confidence in someone] **4** accomplished; skilled; consummate ☆**5** *Football* successfully executed: said of a forward pass —***vt.*** **-plet′ed, -plet′ing 1** to end; finish; conclude **2** to make whole, full, or perfect **3** to successfully execute or effect [to *complete* a telephone call, *complete* a forward pass] —**complete with** including; along with: said of an additional feature, piece, etc. [the new house comes *complete with* a built-in pool] —**com·plete′ly** ***adv.*** —**com·plete′ness** ***n.***

SYN.—complete implies inclusion of all that is needed for the integrity, perfection, or fulfillment of something [a *complete* set, *complete* control]; **full** implies the inclusion of all that is needed [a *full* dozen] or all that can be held, achieved, etc. [in *full* bloom]; **total** implies an adding together of everything without exception [*total* number] and is, in general applications, equivalent to **complete** [*total* abstinence]; **whole** and **entire** imply unbroken unity, stressing that not a single part, individual, instance, etc. has been omitted or diminished [the *whole* student body, one's *entire* attention]; **intact** is applied to that which remains whole after passing through an experience that might have impaired it [the tornado left the barn *intact*] See also **close** —***ANT.*** **partial, defective**

complete metamorphosis physical changes in the development of certain insects that include egg, larva, pupa, and adult stages, as in beetles, moths, or bees

com·ple·tion (kəm plē′shən) ***n.*** ⟦ME < L *completio*⟧ **1** the act of completing, or finishing **2** the state of being completed **3** *Football* a successful forward pass

com·plet·ist (-plēt′ist) ***n.*** a collector who aims to gather as a hobby one example of every item in a particular set or category

com·plex (kăm pleks′, kăm′pleks′; kəm pleks′; *for n. always* kăm′pleks′) ***adj.*** ⟦< L *complexus,* pp. of *complecti,* to encircle, embrace < *com-,* with + *plectere,* to weave: see FLAX⟧ **1** consisting of two or more related parts **2** not simple; involved or complicated —***n.*** **1** a group of interrelated ideas, activities, etc. that form, or are viewed as forming, a single whole **2** an assemblage of units, as buildings or roadways, that together form a single, comprehensive group **3** *Psychoanalysis a)* an integration of impulses, ideas, and emotions related to a particular object, activity, etc., largely unconscious, but strongly influencing the individual's attitudes and behavior *b)* popularly, an exaggerated dislike or fear —**com·plex′ly** ***adv.***

SYN.—complex refers to that which is made up of many elaborately interrelated or interconnected parts, so that much study or knowledge is needed to understand or operate it [a *complex* mechanism]; **complicated** is applied to that which is highly complex and hence very difficult to analyze, solve, or understand [a *complicated* problem]; **intricate** specifically suggests a perplexingly elaborate interweaving of parts that is difficult to follow [an *intricate* maze]; **involved,** in this connection, is applied to situations, ideas, etc. whose parts are thought of as intertwining in complicated, often disordered, fashion [an *involved* argument] —***ANT.*** **simple**

complex fraction a fraction with a fraction in its numerator or denominator, or in both

com·plex·ion (kəm plek′shən) ***n.*** ⟦ME *complexioun* < OFr *complexion,* combination of humors, hence temperament < L *complexio,* combination < *complexus:* see COMPLEX⟧ **1** *a)* [Historical] the combination of the qualities of cold, heat, dryness, and moisture, or of the four humors, in certain proportions believed to determine the temperament and constitution of the body *b)* [Obs.] the temperament or constitution of the body **2** the color, texture, and general appearance of the skin, esp. of the face **3** general appearance or nature; character; aspect —**com·plex′ion·al** ***adj.***

com·plex·ioned (-shənd) ***adj.*** having a (specified) complexion [light-*complexioned*]

com·plex·i·ty (kəm plek′sə tē) ***n.*** **1** the condition or quality of being complex **2** *pl.* **-ties** anything complex or intricate; complication

complex number any number expressed as $a + bi$, where a and b are real numbers and i is the imaginary unit, $\sqrt{-1}$: if b is zero the expression is a real number, but if b is not zero the expression is an imaginary number

complex sentence *Gram.* a sentence consisting of an independent clause and one or more dependent clauses (Ex.: He eats fish when he goes to a restaurant)

com·pli·a·ble (kəm plī′ə bəl) ***adj.*** [Archaic] COMPLIANT

com·pli·ance (kəm plī′əns) ***n.*** **1** a complying with or giving in to a request, wish, or demand; acquiescence **2** a tendency to give in readily to others Also **com·pli′an·cy** —**in compliance with** in accordance with

com·pli·ant (-ənt) ***adj.*** complying or tending to comply; yielding; submissive —***SYN.*** OBEDIENT —**com·pli′ant·ly** ***adv.***

com·pli·ca·cy (kăm′pli kə sē) ***n.*** **1** the condition or quality of being complicated **2** *pl.* **-cies** anything complicated; complication

com·pli·cate (kăm′pli kāt′; *for adj.,* -kit, -kāt′) ***vt., vi.*** **-cat′ed, -cat′ing** ⟦< L *complicatus,* pp. of *complicare,* to fold together < *com-,* together + *plicare,* to fold, weave: see FLAX⟧ to make or become intricate, difficult, or involved —***adj.*** **1** [Archaic] COMPLICATED **2** *Biol.* folded lengthwise, as some leaves or insects' wings

com·pli·cat·ed (-kāt′id) ***adj.*** made up of parts intricately involved; hard to untangle, solve, understand, analyze, etc. —***SYN.*** COMPLEX —**com′pli·cat′ed·ly** ***adv.***

com·pli·ca·tion (kăm′pli kā′shən) ***n.*** **1** the act of complicating, or making involved **2** a complicated condition or structure; complex, involved, or confused relationship of parts **3** a complicating factor or occurrence as in the plot of a story or in the unfolding of events **4** *Med.* a second disease or abnormal condition occurring during the course of a primary disease

com·plice (kăm′plis) ***n.*** ⟦ME & OFr < LL *complex,* a participant, confederate < L *complicare:* see COMPLICATE⟧ [Archaic] an accomplice or associate

com·plic·it (kəm plis′it) ***adj.*** having or showing complicity; implicated: sometimes **com·plic′i·tous** (-plis′ə təs)

com·plic·i·ty (kəm plis′ə tē) ***n., pl.*** **-ties** ⟦Fr *complicité* < L *complex* (gen. *complicis*): see COMPLICE⟧ the fact or state of being an accomplice; partnership in wrongdoing

com·pli·er (kəm plī′ər) ***n.*** a person who complies

com·pli·ment (kăm′plə mənt; *for v.,* -ment′) ***n.*** ⟦Fr < It *complimento* < Sp *cumplimiento* < *cumplir,* to fill up < VL **complire,* for L *complere,* to COMPLETE⟧ **1** a formal act or expression of courtesy or respect **2** [*often pl.*] something said in admiration, praise, or flattery **3** [*pl.*] courteous greetings; respects [send it with our *compliments*] **4** [Now Chiefly Dial.] a gift given for services; tip —***vt.*** **1** to pay a compliment to; congratulate **2** to present something to (a person) as an act of politeness or respect

com·pli·men·ta·ry (kăm′plə men′tə rē) ***adj.*** **1** paying or containing a compliment; expressing courtesy, respect, admiration, or praise **2** given free as a courtesy [a *complimentary* ticket] —**com′pli·men′ta·ri·ly** (-men′te rə lē) ***adv.***

com·pline or **com·plin** (kăm′plən) ***n.*** ⟦ME *compli(n)* < OFr *complie* < ML(Ec) *completa (hora),* completed (hour) < L *completus:* see COMPLETE⟧ [*often* **C-**] the last of the seven canonical hours; night prayer: also **com′plines** or **com′plins** (-plənz)

com·plot (kăm′plăt; *for v.* kəm plăt′) [Archaic] ***n.*** ⟦Fr < OFr *complote,* agreement (earlier, a crowd) < ? **compeloter,* to form into a ball < *com-,* together + *pelote,* a ball, ult. < L *pila,* a ball⟧ a plotting together; conspiracy — ***vt., vi.*** **-plot′ted, -plot′ting** to plot together; conspire

com·ply (kəm plī′) ***vi.*** **-plied′, -ply′ing** ⟦ME *complien* < OFr *complir* < L *complere:* see COMPLETE⟧ to act in accordance (*with* a request, order, rule, etc.)

com·po (kăm′pō′) ***n., pl.*** **-pos′** ⟦< COMPOSITION⟧ a composite substance, as mortar or plaster

com·po·nent (kəm pō′nənt) ***adj.*** ⟦L *componens,* prp. of *componere:* see COMPOSITE⟧ serving as one of the parts of a whole; constituent —***n.*** **1** *a)* an element or ingredient *b)* any of the main constituent parts, as of a high-fidelity sound system **2** any of the elements into which a vector quantity, as force or velocity, may be resolved: any vector is the sum of its components —***SYN.*** ELEMENT

com·port (kəm pôrt′) ***vt.*** ⟦ME *comporten* < OFr *comporter,* to allow, admit of < L *comportare,* to bring together < *com-,* together + *portare,* carry: see FARE⟧ to behave or conduct (oneself) in a specified manner —***vi.*** to agree or accord (*with*) —***SYN.*** BEHAVE

com·port·ment (-mənt) ***n.*** ⟦Fr *comportement:* see prec.⟧ behavior or bearing; deportment

com·pose (kəm pōz′) ***vt.*** **-posed′, -pos′ing** ⟦ME *composen* < OFr *composer* < *com-,* with + *poser,* to place; meaning infl. by L *componere:* see COMPOSITE⟧ **1** to form in combination; make up; constitute [mortar is *composed* of lime, sand, and water] **2** to put together; put in proper order or form **3** to create (a musical or literary work) **4** to adjust or settle; reconcile [to *compose* differences] **5** to put (oneself, one's mind, etc.) in a state of tranquillity or repose; calm **6** *Printing a)* to set (type) *b)* to produce (printed matter) as by computer, photocomposition, etc. —***vi.*** **1** to create musical or literary works **2** *Printing* to set type

com·posed (-pōzd′) ***adj.*** calm; tranquil; self-possessed —***SYN.*** COOL —**com·pos′ed·ly** (-pō′zid lē) ***adv.*** —**com·pos′ed·ness** (-pō′zid nis) ***n.***

com·pos·er (-pō′zər) ***n.*** a person who composes, esp. one who composes music

composing room a room in which typesetting is done

composing stick a hand-held adjustable metal tray in which a compositor sets type into words

com·pos·ite (kəm păz′it) ***adj.*** ⟦L *compositus,* pp. of *componere,* to put together < *com-,* together + *ponere,* to place: see POSITION⟧ **1** formed of distinct parts; compound **2** [**C-**] designating or of a classical Roman order of architecture, in which the scroll-like ornaments of the Ionic capital are combined with the acanthus design of the Corinthian **3** *Bot.* designating the largest family (Asteraceae, order Asterales) of dicotyledonous plants, including the daisy, thistle, artichoke, and chrysanthemum, characterized by flower heads composed of dense clusters of small flowers surrounded by a ring of small leaves or bracts —***n.*** **1** a thing of distinct parts; compound; esp., any of a class of high-strength, lightweight engineering materials consisting of various combinations of alloys, plastics, and ceramics **2** *Bot.* a composite plant —**com·pos′ite·ly** ***adv.***

composite number an integer that can be evenly divided by some whole number other than itself or 1: distinguished from PRIME NUMBER

composite photograph a photograph made by combining photographs, as by superimposing one on another

composite school [Cdn.] a secondary school offering commercial and industrial as well as academic courses

com·po·si·tion (kăm′pə zish′ən) ***n.*** ⟦ME *composicioun* < L *compositio,* a putting together < *compositus:* see COMPOSITE⟧ **1** the act of composing, or putting together a whole by combining parts; specif., *a)* the putting together of words, esp. in a correct and effective way; art of writing *b)* the creation of musical works 2 the makeup of a thing or person; aggregate of ingredients or qualities and manner of their combination; constitution 3 that which is composed; specif., *a)* a mixture of several parts or ingredients *b)* a musical work [Mozart's *compositions* for string quartet] *c)* an exercise in writing done as schoolwork *d)* a painting, sculpture, etc. with respect to the aesthetic arrangement of its elements or features 4 an arrangement of the parts of a work of art so as to form a unified, harmonious whole 5 an agreement, or settlement, often by compromise, as by the creditors of a potential bankrupt 6 the state or quality of being composite 7 *Linguis.* the device or process of forming compounds from two or more base morphemes: distinguished from AFFIXATION 8 *Printing* the work or skill of setting matter for printing —**com′po·si′tion·al** *adj.*

composition of forces *Mech.* the process of finding a force (the *resultant*) whose effect will equal that of two or more given forces (the *components*)

com·pos·i·tor (kəm päz′ət ər) *n.* ⟦L, arranger, disposer: see COMPOSITE⟧ a person, esp. a typesetter, who sets matter for printing

com·pos men·tis (käm′pəs men′tis) ⟦L⟧ *Law* of sound mind; sane

com·post (käm′pōst′) *n.* ⟦ME < OFr *composte,* condiment (> Fr *compote*) < VL **composita* < L *compositus:* see COMPOSITE⟧ 1 a mixture; compound 2 decayed organic matter used as a soil fertilizer and made variously from grass clippings, leaves, kitchen scraps, manure, etc. that are combined and allowed to decompose in a pile (**compost heap**) or bin —*vt.* to convert (grass clippings, etc.) into compost —*vi.* to make or use compost —**com′post′a·ble** *adj.* —**com′post′er** *n.*

com·po·sure (kəm pō′zhər) *n.* ⟦COMPOS(E) + -URE⟧ calmness of mind or manner; tranquillity; self-possession —*SYN.* EQUANIMITY

com·pote (käm′pōt′) *n.* ⟦Fr: see COMPOST⟧ 1 a dish of fruits stewed in a syrup ☆2 a long-stemmed dish for serving candy, fruit, nuts, etc.

com·pound[1] (käm pound′, käm′pound′; kəm pound′; *for adj. usually & for n. always,* käm′pound′) *vt.* ⟦ME *compounen* < OFr *compon(d)re,* to arrange, direct < L *componere,* to put together: see COMPOSITE⟧ 1 to mix or combine 2 to make by combining parts or elements 3 to settle by mutual agreement; specif., to settle (a debt) by a compromise payment of less than the total claim 4 to compute (interest) on the sum of the principal and the accumulated interest which has accrued at regular intervals [interest *compounded* semiannually] 5 to increase or intensify by adding new elements [to *compound* a problem] —*vi.* 1 to agree 2 to compromise with a creditor 3 to combine and form a compound —*adj.* made of two or more separate parts or elements —*n.* 1 a thing formed by the mixture or combination of two or more parts or elements 2 a substance containing two or more elements chemically combined in fixed proportions: distinguished from MIXTURE in that the constituents of a compound lose their individual characteristics and the compound has new characteristics 3 a word composed of two or more base morphemes, whether hyphenated or not: English compounds are usually distinguished from phrases by reduced stress on one of the elements and by changes in meaning (Ex.: *black′bird′, black′ bird′; grand′aunt′, grand′ aunt′*) —**compound a felony** (or **crime**) ⟦< *vt.* 3⟧ to agree, for a bribe or repayment, not to inform about or prosecute for a felony (or crime): it is an illegal act

com·pound[2] (käm′pound′) *n.* ⟦Anglo-Ind < Malay *kampong,* enclosure⟧ 1 KAMPONG 2 an enclosed space with a building or group of buildings within it

compound animal any animal, such as most hydroids, corals, and bryozoans, composed of a number of individuals produced by budding from a single parent and usually so fused together that no demarcation is clearly distinguishable

compound engine an engine in which the steam is expanded under progressively lower pressures from cylinder to cylinder, to avoid excessive loss of steam by condensation

compound eye an eye made up of numerous simple eyes functioning collectively, as in insects

compound fraction COMPLEX FRACTION

compound fracture a bone fracture in which broken ends of bone have pierced the skin

compound interest interest computed on the sum of the principal and the accrued interest: cf. SIMPLE INTEREST

compound leaf a leaf divided into two or more leaflets with a common leafstalk

compound meter *Music* any time signature in which the upper figure is a multiple of 3, as 6/8, 9/8, 12/8, etc.

compound microscope a microscope having an objective lens for forming an intermediate image and an eyepiece for viewing that image

compound number a quantity expressed in two or more sorts of related units (Ex.: 4 ft, 7 in; 1 lb, 3 oz)

compound sentence *Gram.* a sentence consisting of two or more independent, coordinate clauses (Ex.: She drinks coffee, but he prefers tea)

compound time *Brit. var. of* COMPOUND METER

com·pra·dor or **com·pra·dore** (käm′prə dôr′) *n.* ⟦Port, buyer < LL *comparator* < L *comparare,* to procure, buy < *com-,* with + *parare,* to make ready, PREPARE⟧ [Historical] in China, a native agent for a foreign business, who had charge over the native workers

com·pre·hend (käm′prē hend′, -pri-) *vt.* ⟦ME *comprehenden* < L *comprehendere* < *com-,* with + *prehendere,* to catch hold of, seize: see PREHENSILE⟧ 1 to grasp mentally; understand 2 to include; take in; comprise —*SYN.* INCLUDE, UNDERSTAND —**com′pre·hend′i·ble** *adj.* —**com′pre·hend′ing·ly** *adv.*

com·pre·hen·si·ble (-hen′sə bəl) *adj.* ⟦L *comprehensibilis*⟧ that can be comprehended; intelligible —**com′pre·hen′si·bil′i·ty** *n.* —**com′pre·hen′si·bly** *adv.*

com·pre·hen·sion (-hen′shen) *n.* ⟦ME *comprehensioun* < L *comprehensio* < *comprehensus,* pp. of *comprehendere:* see COMPREHEND⟧ 1 the fact of including or comprising; inclusiveness 2 *a)* the act of grasping with the mind *b)* understanding or knowledge that results from this 3 the capacity for understanding ideas, facts, etc.

com·pre·hen·sive (-hen′siv) *adj.* ⟦LL *comprehensivus*⟧ 1 dealing with all or many of the relevant details; including much; inclusive [a *comprehensive* survey] 2 able to comprehend fully [a *comprehensive* mind] 3 of or designating property insurance that covers a number of risks in the same policy —*n.* [*usually pl.*] an examination in a major field of study that a graduate, or sometimes undergraduate, student must pass to receive a degree: in full **comprehensive examination** —**com′pre·hen′sive·ly** *adv.* —**com′pre·hen′sive·ness** *n.*

com·press (kəm pres′; *for n.* käm′pres′) *vt.* ⟦ME *compressen* < OFr *compresser* < LL *compressare* < L *compressus,* pp. of *comprimere,* to squeeze < *com-,* together + *premere,* to PRESS[1]⟧ 1 to press together; make more compact by or as by pressure 2 to encode (digital data) so that it can be stored or transmitted in significantly fewer bits —*n.* 1 a pad of folded cloth, sometimes medicated or moistened, for applying pressure, heat, cold, etc. to some part of the body ☆2 a machine for compressing cotton bales —*SYN.* CONTRACT —**com·press′i·bil′i·ty** *n.* —**com·press′i·ble** *adj.*

com·pressed (kəm prest′) *adj.* 1 pressed together; made more compact by pressure 2 *Bot.* flattened lengthwise, as the stalk of an aspen leaf 3 *Zool.* flattened into a thin, convex, streamlined shape, as the body of the flounder or other flatfish

compressed air air held under pressure in a container: the force generated when the air is released is used to operate machines, tools, etc.

com·pres·sion (kəm presh′ən) *n.* ⟦ME < OFr < L *compressio*⟧ 1 a compressing or being compressed 2 *Mech.* the compressing of the air-fuel mixture in an internal-combustion engine just before ignition

compression ratio in an internal-combustion engine, the ratio of the largest volume to the smallest volume of a cylinder, measured before and after the compressing action of the piston

com·pres·sive (-pres′iv) *adj.* compressing or tending to compress —**com·pres′sive·ly** *adv.*

com·pres·sor (-pres′ər) *n.* 1 a person or thing that compresses 2 a muscle that compresses a part 3 a machine, esp. a pump, for compressing air, gas, etc.

com·pri·ma·ri·o (kôm′prē mä′rē ô) *n., pl.* **-ma′ri** (-rē) ⟦It < *com-,* with (see COM-) + *primario,* first (< L *primarius,* PRIMARY)⟧ a singer of a secondary role in an opera: also Eng. **com·pri·ma·ri·o** (käm′prə mär′ē ō), *pl.* **-ri·os**

com·prise (kəm prīz′) *vt.* **-prised′, -pris′ing** ⟦ME *comprisen* < OFr *compris,* pp. of *comprendre* < L *comprehendere,* COMPREHEND⟧ 1 to include; contain 2 to consist of; be composed of [a nation *comprising* thirteen states] 3 to make up; form; constitute: in this sense still regarded by some as a loose usage [a nation *comprised* of thirteen states] —*SYN.* INCLUDE —**com·pris′a·ble** *adj.* —**com·pris′al** *n.*

com·pro·mise (käm′prə mīz′) *n.* ⟦ME & OFr *compromis* < LL *compromissum,* a compromise, mutual promise < L *compromissus,* pp. of *compromittere,* to make a mutual promise to abide by an arbiter's decision < *com-,* together + *promittere,* to PROMISE⟧ 1 a settlement in which each side gives up some demands or makes concessions 2 *a)* an adjustment of opposing principles, systems, etc. by modifying some aspects of each *b)* the result of such an adjustment 3 something midway between two other things in quality, effect, etc. 4 *a)* exposure, as of one's reputation, to danger, suspicion, or disrepute *b)* a weakening, as of one's principles —*vt.* **-mised′, -mis′ing** 1 to settle or adjust by concessions on both sides 2 to lay open to danger, suspicion, or disrepute 3 to weaken or give up (one's principles, ideals, etc.) as for reasons of expediency 4 *Med.* to weaken or otherwise impair [drugs that *compromised* his immune system] —*vi.* to make a compromise or compromises —**com′pro·mis′er** *n.*

comp time (kämp) ⟦< *comp(ensatory) time*⟧ paid time off from work, given to an employee in lieu of overtime pay

Comp·ton (kämp′tən) 1 **Arthur Hol·ly** (häl′ē) 1892-1962; U.S. physicist 2 **Karl Taylor** 1887-1954; U.S. physicist; brother of Arthur

comp·trol·ler (kən trō′lər; *also,* kəmp-, kämp′trō′lər) *n.* ⟦altered (infl. by Fr *compte,* an account) < CONTROLLER⟧ CONTROLLER (sense 1, esp. in government usage) —**comp·trol′ler·ship′** *n.*

com·pul·sion (kəm pul′shən) *n.* ⟦ME & LL *compulsio* < L *compulsus,* pp. of *compellere:* see COMPEL⟧ 1 a compelling or being compelled; coercion; constraint 2 that which compels; driving force 3 *Psychol.* an irresistible, repeated, irrational impulse to perform some act

com·pul·sive (-siv) *adj.* ⟦ML *compulsivus*⟧ of, having to do with, or resulting from compulsion —**com·pul′sive·ly** *adv.*

com·pul·so·ry (-sə rē) *adj.* ⟦ML *compulsorius* < LL *compulsor,* one who compels⟧ 1 that must be done, undergone, etc.; obligatory; required 2 compelling; coercive —**com·pul′so·ri·ly** *adv.* —**com·pul′so·ri·ness** *n.*

com·punc·tion (kəm puŋk′shən) *n.* ⟦ME *compunccion* < OFr *compunction* < LL *compunctio,* a pricking (in LL(Ec), the pricking of conscience) < L *compunctus,* pp. of *compungere,* to prick, sting < *com-,* intens. + *pungere,* to prick: see POINT⟧ 1 a sharp feeling of uneasiness brought on by a sense of guilt; remorse 2 a feeling of slight regret for something done —*SYN.* PENITENCE, QUALM —**com·punc′tious** *adj.* —**com·punc′tious·ly** *adv.*

com·pur·ga·tion (käm′pər gā′shən) *n.* ⟦LL *compurgatio,* a purifying < L *compurgatus,* pp. of *compurgare,* to purge, purify < *com-,* intens. + *purgare,* to PURGE⟧ the former practice of clearing an accused person by the oaths of others testifying to that person's innocence

com·pur·ga·tor (käm′pər gāt′ər) ***n.*** ⟦ML: see prec.⟧ one who testified in a compurgation

com·pu·ta·tion (käm′pyoo tā′shən) ***n.*** ⟦ME *computacioun* < L *computatio*⟧ **1** the act of computing; calculation **2** a method of computing **3** a result obtained in computing; computed amount —**com′pu·ta′tion·al** ***adj.***

com·pute (kəm pyoot′) ***vt.*** **-put′ed, -put′ing** ⟦L *computare* < *com-,* with + *putare,* to reckon, orig., to prune: see PURE⟧ **1** to determine (a number, amount, etc.) by arithmetic; calculate **2** to determine or calculate by using a computer —***vi.*** **1** to determine a number, amount, etc. **2** to use a computer **3** [Informal] to make sense; seem reasonable; add up [an explanation that does not *compute*] —***n.*** computation: chiefly in the phrase **beyond compute** —***SYN.*** CALCULATE —**com·put′a·bil′i·ty** ***n.*** —**com·put′a·ble** ***adj.***

com·put·er (kəm pyoot′ər) ***n.*** **1** a person who computes **2** a device used for computing and otherwise processing information; specif., an electronic machine which, by means of stored instructions, is used to perform rapid, often complex calculations, compile and correlate data, download and play audio and video communications, access the Web, send and receive email, etc.; now, esp., DIGITAL COMPUTER: see also ANALOG COMPUTER

☆**com·put·er·ese** (kəm pyoot′ər ēz′) ***n.*** the jargon used in computer technology: see -ESE

computer graphics the technology dealing with the generation of pictures, designs, etc. on a computer: see also GRAPHIC (*n.*)

com·put·er·ize (kəm pyoot′ər īz′) ***vt.*** **-ized′, -iz′ing** **1** to equip with electronic computers so as to facilitate or automate procedures **2** to operate, produce, etc. by means of an electronic computer —**com·put′er·i·za′tion** ***n.***

computer science the science dealing with computer technology, including hardware, peripherals, and programming

Comr *abbrev.* Commissioner

com·rade (käm′rad′, -rəd) ***n.*** ⟦Fr *camarade* < Sp *camarada,* chamber mate < L *camera:* see CAMERA⟧ **1** a friend; close companion **2** a person who shares interests and activities in common with others; partner; associate: used as a form of address, as in a Communist party **3** [**C-**] [Informal] a Communist; esp., a fellow Communist —***SYN.*** ASSOCIATE —**com′rade·ly** (-rəd lē) ***adj.*** —**com′rade·ship′** ***n.***

comrade in arms a fellow soldier

☆**com·rade·ry** (käm′rad rē) ***n.*** ⟦altered (after COMRADE) < CAMARADERIE⟧ *var. of* CAMARADERIE

Com·sat (käm′sat′) ⟦< COM(MUNICATION) + SAT(ELLITE)⟧ *trademark for* any of various communications satellites for relaying microwave transmissions, as of telephone and television signals

Com·stock·er·y (käm′stäk′ər ē, kum′-) ***n.*** ⟦after A. *Comstock* (1844-1915), U.S. self-appointed censor: prob. coined by George Bernard SHAW⟧ [*often* **c-**] ruthless suppression of plays, books, etc. alleged to be offensive or dangerous to public morals

Com·stock Lode (käm′stäk′, kum′-) ⟦after H. T. *Comstock* (1820-70), who held first claim to it⟧ a rich deposit of silver & gold discovered in 1859 in W Nev.: virtually depleted by 1890

comte (kōnt) ***n.*** ⟦Fr⟧ COUNT[2]

Comte (kōnt; *E* kōnt, kônt), **(Isidore) Au·guste (Marie François Xavier)** (ô güst′) 1798-1857; Fr. philosopher: founder of positivism —**Com·ti·an** ***adj.,*** **Com·te·an** (käm′tē ən, kōm′-)

com·tesse (kōn tes′) ***n.*** ⟦Fr⟧ COUNTESS

Co·mus (kō′məs) ***n.*** ⟦L < Gr *kōmos,* festival⟧ *Class. Myth.* a young god of festivity and revelry

con[1] (kän) ***adv.*** ⟦contr. < L *contra,* against⟧ against; in opposition [to argue a matter pro and *con*] —***n.*** a reason, vote, position, etc. in opposition

con[2] (kän) ***vt.*** **conned, con′ning** ⟦ME *connen,* to be able < OE *cunnan:* see CAN[1]⟧ to peruse carefully; study; fix in the memory

con[3] (kän) ***vt., n.*** **conned, con′ning** *alt. sp. of* CONN

☆**con**[4] (kän) [Informal] ***adj.*** CONFIDENCE [a *con* man] —***vt.*** **conned, con′ning** **1** to swindle (a victim) by first gaining the person's confidence **2** to trick or fool, esp. by glib persuasion —***n.*** the act or an instance of conning; swindle; trick

☆**con**[5] (kän) ***n.*** [Slang] *short for* CONVICT

con[6] (kän) ***n.*** [Informal] *short for* CONVENTION (sense 3): often used in convention names

con[7] *abbrev.* **1** consolidated **2** consul **3** continued

con- (kän, kən) *prefix* COM-: used before *c, d, g, j, n, q, s, t, v,* and sometimes *f* [*condominium, confrere*]

Co·na·kry (kän′ə krē′; *Fr* kô nȧ krē′) seaport & capital of Guinea, on the Atlantic Ocean

con a·mo·re (kän′ə môr′ē; *It* kôn′ ä mô′re) ⟦It, lit., with love⟧ **1** *Musical Direction* tenderly **2** [*also in roman type*] with enthusiasm or devotion

Conan Doyle, Sir **Arthur** *see* DOYLE, Sir Arthur Conan

Co·nant (kō′nənt), **James Bryant** 1893-1978; U.S. chemist & educator

☆**con artist** [Informal] CONFIDENCE MAN

co·na·tion (kō nā′shən) ***n.*** ⟦L *conatio,* an attempt < pp. of *conari,* to undertake, attempt < IE base **ken-,* to strive⟧ *Psychol.* any inclination, drive, or desire to do something —**co·na′tion·al** (-nā′shə nəl) ***adj.***

con·a·tive (kän′ə tiv, kōn′-) ***adj.*** **1** having to do with conation **2** *Linguis.* expressing endeavor or effort: said of an aspect of certain verbs

co·na·tus (kō nāt′əs) ***n., pl.*** **co·na′tus** ⟦L < *conari:* see CONATION⟧ a directed effort; natural tendency or striving

con bri·o (kän′brē′ō, kôn′-) ⟦It⟧ *Musical Direction* with spirit or vigor; spiritedly

conc *abbrev.* **1** concentrate **2** concentration **3** concrete

con·ca·nav·a·lin A (kän′kə nav′ə lən ā′) ⟦CON- + *canavalin,* substance with which it occurs in the jack bean < ModL *Canavalia,* genus name of the bean⟧ a lectin isolated from jack bean that agglutinates red blood cells, human cancer cells, etc. and causes resting cells to divide: used to stimulate or test the activity of certain cells, as T cells

con·cat·e·nate (kən kat′'n āt′, kän-) ***adj.*** ⟦LL *concatenatus,* pp. of *concatenare,* to link together < L *com-,* together + *catenare,* to chain < *catena,* a CHAIN⟧ linked together; connected —***vt.*** **-nat′ed, -nat′ing** to link together or join, as in a chain

con·cat·e·na·tion (kən kat′'n ā′shən, kän-) ***n.*** ⟦LL *concatenatio:* see prec.⟧ **1** a linking together or being linked together in a series **2** a series of things or events regarded as causally or dependently connected

con·cave (kän kāv′; *also, & for n. usually,* kän′kāv′) ***adj.*** ⟦ME & OFr < L *concavus,* hollow < *com-,* intens. + *cavus,* hollow: see CAVE⟧ having a surface that is curved like the inside of a bowl —***n.*** a concave surface, object, etc. —***vt.*** **-caved′, -cav′ing** to make concave —**con·cave′ly** ***adv.*** —**con·cave′ness** ***n.***

con·cav·i·ty (kän kav′ə tē, kən-) ***n.*** ⟦ME & OFr *concavite* < LL *concavitas*⟧ **1** the quality or condition of being concave **2** *pl.* **-ties** a concave surface, line, etc.

con·ca·vo-con·cave (kän kā′vō kän kāv′) ***adj.*** concave on both sides, as some lenses

con·ca·vo-con·vex (-kän veks′) ***adj.*** **1** concave on one side and convex on the other **2** *Optics* designating a lens whose concave face has a greater degree of curvature than its convex face, so that the lens is thinnest in the middle

con·ceal (kən sēl′) ***vt.*** ⟦ME *concelen* < OFr *conceler* < L *concelare,* to hide < *com-,* together + *celare,* to hide < IE base **kel,* to hide, conceal > HALL, HULL[1], Gr *kalyptein*⟧ **1** to put out of sight; hide **2** to keep from another's knowledge; keep secret —***SYN.*** HIDE[1] —**con·ceal′a·ble** ***adj.*** —**con·ceal′er** ***n.*** —**con·ceal′ment** ***n.***

con·cede (kən sēd′) ***vt.*** **-ced′ed, -ced′ing** ⟦L *concedere* < *com-,* with + *cedere,* to go, grant, CEDE⟧ **1** to admit as true or valid; acknowledge [to *concede* a point in argument] **2** to acknowledge as certain or proper [a candidate *conceding* defeat on election night] **3** to end (an unfinished match or contest) by declaring that one has been defeated [to *concede* a baseball game if down by ten runs] **4** to grant as a right, privilege, or favor [to *concede* autonomy to local governments, to *concede* a gimme in a golf match] —***vi.*** **1** to make a concession ☆**2** to acknowledge defeat in an election —**con·ced′er** ***n.***

con·ceit (kən sēt′) ***n.*** ⟦ME *conceite* < *conceiven,* CONCEIVE⟧ **1** [Obs.] *a)* an idea; thought; concept *b)* personal opinion **2** an exaggerated opinion of oneself, one's merits, etc.; vanity **3** ⟦< It *concetto,* of same ult. orig.⟧ *a)* a fanciful or witty expression or notion; often, specif., a striking and elaborate metaphor, sometimes one regarded, esp. formerly, as strained and arbitrary *b)* the use of such expressions in writing or speaking **4** a flight of imagination; fancy **5** a small, imaginatively designed item —***vt.*** **1** [Obs.] to think or imagine **2** [Brit. Dial.] to think well of; take a fancy to —***SYN.*** PRIDE

con·ceit·ed (-id) ***adj.*** **1** having an exaggerated opinion of oneself, one's merits, etc.; vain **2** [Obs.] whimsical; fanciful —**con·ceit′ed·ly** ***adv.*** —**con·ceit′ed·ness** ***n.***

con·ceiv·a·ble (kən sēv′ə bəl) ***adj.*** ⟦ME⟧ that can be conceived, understood, imagined, or believed —**con·ceiv′a·bil′i·ty** ***n.*** —**con·ceiv′a·bly** ***adv.***

con·ceive (kən sēv′) ***vt.*** **-ceived′, -ceiv′ing** ⟦ME *conceiven* < OFr *conceveir* < L *concipere* (pp. *conceptus*), to take in, receive < *com-,* together + *capere,* to take: see HAVE⟧ **1** *a)* to become pregnant with *b)* to cause to begin life [the young couple *conceived* their first child] **2** to form or develop in the mind **3** to hold as one's conviction or opinion; think; imagine **4** to understand; apprehend **5** to put in words; couch; express —***vi.*** **1** *a)* to become pregnant *b)* to cause an offspring to begin life [the couple had no trouble *conceiving*] **2** to form a concept or idea (*of*)

con·cel·e·brate (kän sel′ə brāt′, kən-) ***vt.*** **-brat′ed, -brat′ing** ⟦< L *concelebratus,* pp. of *concelebrare,* to celebrate (a solemnity) in large numbers: see CON- & CELEBRATE⟧ to celebrate (the Eucharistic liturgy) jointly, the prayers being said in unison by two or more of the officiating priests —**con′cel·e·bra′tion** ***n.***

con·cent (kən sent′) ***n.*** ⟦L *concentus* < *concinere,* to sing together < *com-,* with + *canere,* to sing: see CHANT⟧ [Archaic] **1** musical harmony or concord **2** agreement; accord

con·cen·ter (kən sen′tər) ***vt., vi.*** ⟦Fr *concentrer* < L *com-,* together + *centrum,* CENTER⟧ to bring or come to a common center; concentrate or converge

con·cen·trate (kän′sən trāt′) ***vt.*** **-trat′ed, -trat′ing** ⟦< prec. + -ATE[1]⟧ **1** to bring to, or direct toward, a common center **2** to collect or focus (one's thoughts, efforts, etc.) **3** to increase the strength, density, or intensity of —***vi.*** **1** to come to or toward a common center **2** to direct one's thoughts or efforts; fix one's attention (*on* or *upon*) **3** to increase in strength, density, or intensity —***n.*** a substance that has been concentrated; specif., a liquid that has been made denser, as by the removal of some of its water [orange-juice *concentrate*] —**con′cen·tra′tor** ***n.***

con·cen·tra·tion (kän′sən trā′shən) ***n.*** ⟦ML *concentratio*⟧ **1** a concentrating or being concentrated **2** close or fixed attention **3** strength or density, as of a solution **4** a concentrated substance

concentration camp a camp in which political dissidents, members of minority ethnic groups, etc. are confined
con·cen·tra·tive (kän′sən trāt′iv, kən sen′trə tiv) *adj.* concentrating or tending to concentrate
con·cen·tric (kən sen′trik) *adj.* ⟦ME *concentrik* < OFr *concentrique* < ML *concentricus* < L *com-*, together + *-centricus*, -CENTRIC⟧ having a center in common [*concentric circles*]: also **con·cen′tri·cal** —**con·cen′tri·cal·ly** *adv.* —**con·cen·tric·i·ty** (kän′sen tris′ə tē) *n.*

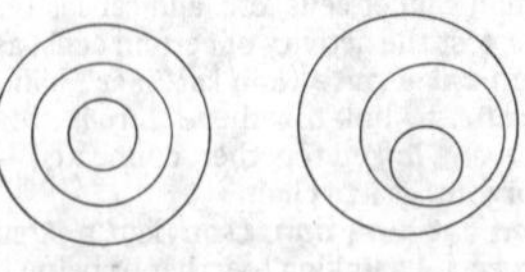
concentric circles eccentric circles

Con·cep·ción (kən sep′sē ōn′; *Sp* kôn sep′syôn′) city in SC Chile
con·cept (kän′sept′) *n.* ⟦L *conceptus*: see CONCEIVE⟧ **1** an idea or thought, esp. a generalized idea of a thing or class of things; abstract notion **2** *a)* an original idea, design, etc.; conception *b)* a central or unifying idea or theme (often used attributively) [*a concept restaurant with a Victorian decor and menu*] —***SYN.*** IDEA
con·cep·ta·cle (kən sep′tə kəl) *n.* ⟦L *conceptaculum*, receptacle < pp. of *concipere*: see CONCEIVE⟧ *Bot.* a sac opening outward and containing reproductive cells, found in some brown algae
con·cep·tion (kən sep′shən) *n.* ⟦ME *concepcioun* < OFr *conception* < L *conceptio*, a comprehending, conception < *conceptus*: see CONCEIVE⟧ **1** a conceiving or being conceived; specif., the conceiving of an embryo **2** that which is conceived; specif., an embryo or fetus **3** the beginning of some process, chain of events, etc. **4** the act, process, or power of conceiving mentally; formulation of ideas, esp. of abstractions **5** a mental impression; general notion; concept **6** an original idea, design, plan, etc. —***SYN.*** IDEA —**con·cep′tion·al** *adj.*
con·cep·tive (-tiv) *adj.* ⟦L *conceptivus*⟧ having the power of mental conception
con·cep·tu·al (kən sep′cho͞o əl) *adj.* ⟦ML *conceptualis*⟧ of or having to do with a concept or concepts —**con·cep′tu·al·ly** *adv.*
conceptual art a type of art in which the artist's idea, or concept, of a work of art and of the means of executing that idea have primary importance while the artwork itself, which may or may not be produced, is regarded as secondary —**conceptual artist**
con·cep·tu·al·ism (-iz′əm) *n.* **1** the doctrine, intermediate between nominalism and realism, that universals exist explicitly in the mind as concepts, and implicitly in things as shared qualities **2** [*usually* **C-**] the conceptual-art movement of the 20th cent. or its theories, methods, etc. —**con·cep′tu·al·ist** *adj., n.* —**con·cep′tu·al·is′tic** *adj.*
con·cep·tu·al·ize (-īz′) *vt.* **-ized′**, **-iz′ing** to form a concept or idea of; conceive —**con·cep′tu·al·i·za′tion** *n.*
con·cep·tus (kən sep′təs) *n., pl.* **-tus·es** ⟦L, that which is conceived < pp. of *concipere*: see CONCEIVE⟧ the entire product of conception until birth, including the sac, cord, and placenta
con·cern (kən surn′) *vt.* ⟦ME *concernen* < ML *concernere*, to perceive, have regard to, fig. use of LL *concernere*, to sift, mix, as in a sieve < L *com-*, with + *cernere*, to sift, hence perceive, comprehend: see CRISIS⟧ **1** to have a relation to or bearing on; deal with **2** to draw in; engage or involve; be a proper affair of [*that doesn't concern you*] **3** to cause to feel uneasy or anxious —*n.* **1** a matter of interest or importance to one; that which relates to or affects one; affair; matter; business **2** interest in or regard for a person or thing **3** relation; reference **4** worry; anxiety [*to feel concern over one's health*] **5** a business establishment; company; firm —***SYN.*** CARE —**as concerns** in regard to; with reference to; about —**concern oneself 1** to busy oneself (*with, about, over, in* something); take an interest **2** to be worried, anxious, or uneasy
con·cerned (kən surnd′) *adj.* **1** involved or interested: often with *in* **2** uneasy or anxious
con·cern·ing (-surn′iŋ) *prep.* relating to or having to do with; in regard to; about
con·cern·ment (-surn′mənt) *n.* [Rare] concern; specif., *a)* an affair; matter *b)* importance *c)* worry; anxiety
con·cert (kən surt′; *for n. & adj.* kän′sərt) *vt., vi.* ⟦Fr *concerter* < It *concertare* < L, to contend, contest < *com-*, with + *certare*, to contend, strive: meanings infl. by CONSORT & L *conserere*, to join together⟧ to arrange or settle by mutual understanding; contrive or plan together; devise —*n.* ⟦Fr < It *concerto*, agreement, union < the v.⟧ **1** mutual agreement; concord; harmony of action **2** musical consonance **3** a program of vocal or instrumental music, usually one in which a number of musicians perform together —*adj.* of or for concerts —**in concert 1** in unison; in agreement; together **2** performing in a concert
con·cert·ed (kən surt′id) *adj.* **1** mutually arranged or agreed upon; made or done together; combined **2** *Music* arranged in parts **3** characterized by striving and determination [*a student's concerted effort*] —**con·cert′ed·ly** *adv.*
con·cert·go·er (kän′sərt gō′ər) *n.* a person who attends a concert, esp. one who goes to concerts regularly
concert grand (piano) the largest size of grand piano, for concert performance
con·cer·ti·na (kän′sər tē′nə) *n.* ⟦CONCERT + -INA: coined (1829) by C. Wheatstone: see WHEATSTONE BRIDGE⟧ a musical instrument similar to an accordion but smaller and with buttons instead of a keyboard

concertina

concertina wire ⟦so called because coils of the wire can be stretched or compressed, much like the bellows of a CONCERTINA⟧ RAZOR WIRE
con·cer·ti·no (kän′cher tē′nō, kôn′-) *n.* ⟦It dim.⟧ **1** a brief concerto, usually in a single movement **2** the solo group in a concerto grosso
con·cert·ize (kän′sər tīz′) *vi.* **-ized′**, **-iz′ing** to perform as a soloist in concerts; esp., to make concert tours
con·cert·mas·ter (kän′sərt mas′tər) *n.* ⟦transl. of Ger *konzertmeister*⟧ the leader of the first violin section of a symphony orchestra, who plays the solo passages and often serves as assistant to the conductor: also **con′cert·meis′ter** (-mīs′tər)
con·cer·to (kən cher′tō) *n., pl.* **-tos** or **-ti** (-tē) ⟦It: see CONCERT, *n.*⟧ a musical composition for one or more solo instruments and an orchestra, traditionally in three symphonic movements
concerto gros·so (grō′sō) *pl.* **concerti gros′si** (-sē) ⟦It, lit., big concerto⟧ a composition for a small group of solo instruments, as a trio, contrasted with and accompanied by a full orchestra
concert pitch *Music* **1** a pitch, slightly higher than the usual pitch, to which concert instruments are sometimes tuned to achieve an increased brilliance of quality **2** the standard pitch to which instruments are tuned and voices are pitched so as to be compatible in performance: it is currently designated as A above middle C, with a frequency of 440 vibrations per second **3** the actual sound of a note written for a transposing instrument, as the trumpet
con·ces·sion (kən sesh′ən) *n.* ⟦ME & OFr < L *concessio* < *concessus*, pp. of *concedere*⟧ **1** an act or instance of conceding, granting, or yielding **2** a thing conceded or granted; acknowledgment, as of an argument or claim **3** a privilege granted by a government, company, etc.; esp., *a)* the right to use land, as for a specific purpose *b)* [Cdn.] a government grant of land forming a subdivision of a township ☆*c)* the right or a lease to engage in a certain activity for profit on the lessor's premises [*a refreshment or parking concession*] ☆*d)* the land, space, etc. so granted or leased
con·ces·sion·aire (kən sesh′ə ner′) *n.* ⟦Fr *concessionnaire*⟧ the holder of a concession granted by a government, company, etc.; specif., the holder of a concession to sell refreshments, etc., as at a carnival: often ☆**con·ces′sion·er**
con·ces·sion·ar·y (kən sesh′ə ner′ē) *adj.* of a concession —*n., pl.* **-ar′ies** a concessionaire
concession road [Cdn.] any of the parallel roads of a township, about a mile apart, following closely the original survey lines
con·ces·sive (kən ses′iv) *adj.* ⟦LL *concessivus*⟧ **1** having the character of concession; conceding or tending to concede **2** expressing concession [*"though" is a concessive conjunction*]
conch (käŋk, känch) *n., pl.* **conchs** (käŋks) or **conch·es** (kän′chiz) ⟦ME *conke* < L *concha* < Gr *konchē*, mussel, shell < IE base **konkho-* > Sans *śankhá-*, mussel⟧ **1** *a)* the large, spiral, univalve shell of any of various marine mollusks *b)* such a mollusk, often edible **2** *Rom. Myth.* such a shell used as a trumpet by the Tritons **3** CONCHA (sense 1) ☆**4** [*often* **C-**] [Informal] a longtime resident of the Florida Keys, specif. of Key West
con·cha (käŋ′kə) *n., pl.* **-chae** (-kē) ⟦L: see prec.⟧ **1** *Anat.* any of several structures resembling a shell in form, as a thin, bony projection inside the nasal cavity, the hollow of the external ear, or the whole external ear **2** *Archit.* the half dome covering an apse
con·chie or **con·chy** (kän′chē, -shē) *n., pl.* **-chies** ⟦short for CONSCIENTIOUS⟧ [Slang] a conscientious objector
con·chif·er·ous (käŋ kif′ər əs) *adj.* ⟦< CONCHA + -FEROUS⟧ having or bearing a shell
con·chi·o·lin (käŋ kī′ə lin) *n.* ⟦< L *concha*, a mussel (see CONCH) + -OL[2] + -IN[1]⟧ an albuminoid protein of mollusks, forming the main portion of the organic matrix of the shell
con·choid (käŋ′koid′) *n.* ⟦< Gr *konchoeidēs (grammē)*, conchoid (line), lit., mussel-like: see CONCH & -OID⟧ a curve traced by an end point of a segment of constant length located on a straight line that rotates about a fixed point, while the other end point moves along a straight line that does not go through the fixed point
con·choi·dal (käŋ koid′'l) *adj.* ⟦< Gr *konchoeidēs* (see prec.) + -AL⟧ *Mineralogy* producing smooth convexities or concavities, like those of a clamshell, when fractured: said of a brittle substance
con·chol·o·gy (-käl′ə jē) *n.* ⟦see CONCH & -LOGY⟧ the branch of natural history that deals with the shells of mollusks —**con·chol′o·gist** *n.*
con·ci·erge (kōn syerzh′, kän-, -sē erzh′; *Fr* kōn syerzh′) *n.* ⟦Fr, prob. ult. < VL **conservius* < L *conservus*, fellow slave < *com-*, with + *servus*, slave⟧ **1** a doorkeeper **2** a custodian or head porter, as of an apartment house **3** a hotel employee who assists guests as by booking theater reservations or arranging for transportation
con·cil·i·ar (kən sil′ē ər) *adj.* ⟦< L *concilium*, COUNCIL + -AR⟧ of, from, or by means of a council

con·cil·i·ate (kən sil′ē āt′) *vt.* **-at′ed, -at′ing** ⟦< L *conciliatus,* pp. of *conciliare,* to bring together, win over < *concilium,* COUNCIL⟧ **1** to win over; soothe the anger of; make friendly; placate **2** to gain (regard, good will, etc.) by friendly acts **3** [Archaic] to reconcile; make consistent —*SYN.* PACIFY —**con·cil′i·a·ble** *adj.* —**con·cil′i·a′tion** *n.* —**con·cil′i·a′tor** *n.*

con·cil·i·a·to·ry (-ə tôr′ē) *adj.* tending to conciliate or reconcile: also **con·cil′i·a′tive** (-āt′iv)

con·cin·ni·ty (kən sin′ə tē) *n., pl.* **-ties** ⟦L *concinnitas* < *concinnus,* skillfully joined, beautiful < **con-cid-nos,* cut together (so as to fit) < *com-,* with + base of *caedere,* to cut: see -CIDE⟧ a skillful arrangement of parts; harmony; elegance, esp. of literary style

con·cise (kən sīs′) *adj.* ⟦L *concisus,* cut off, brief, pp. of *concidere,* to cut off < *com-,* intens. + *caedere,* to cut: see -CIDE⟧ brief and to the point; short and clear —**con·cise′ly** *adv.* —**con·cise′ness** *n.*

SYN.—**concise** implies the stating of much in few words, by removing all superfluous or expanded details [a *concise* summary]; **terse** adds to this the connotation of polished smoothness [a *terse* style], but may also suggest brevity to the point of rudeness [a rather *terse* response]; **laconic** suggests brevity to the point of curtness or ambiguity ["You'll see," was his *laconic* reply]; **succinct** implies clarity but compactness in the fewest words possible [she spoke in *succinct* phrases]; **pithy** suggests forcefulness and wit resulting from compactness [*pithy* axioms] —*ANT.* **redundant, prolix**

con·ci·sion (kən sizh′ən) *n.* ⟦L *concisio*⟧ **1** [Obs.] a cutting off; division **2** concise quality; conciseness

con·clave (kän′klāv′) *n.* ⟦ME & OFr < L, a room which may be locked < *com-,* with + *clavis,* a key: see CLOSE[2]⟧ **1** *R.C.Ch.* *a)* the private meeting of the cardinals to elect a pope *b)* the cardinals collectively **2** any private or secret meeting **3** any large conference or convention

con·clude (kən klo͞od′) *vt.* **-clud′ed, -clud′ing** ⟦ME *concluden,* to conclude < L *concludere,* to shut up, enclose < *com-,* together + *claudere,* to shut, CLOSE[2]⟧ **1** to bring to a close; end; finish **2** to decide by reasoning; infer; deduce **3** to decide; determine **4** to arrange or settle; come to an agreement about [to *conclude* a pact] —*vi.* **1** to come to a close; end; finish **2** to come to an agreement —*SYN.* CLOSE[2], DECIDE, INFER

con·clu·sion (kən klo͞o′zhən) *n.* ⟦ME & OFr < L *conclusio,* a closing, conclusion < pp. of prec.⟧ **1** the end or last part; specif., *a)* the last division of a discourse, often containing a summary of what went before *b)* the last step in a reasoning process; judgment, decision, or opinion formed after investigation or thought *c)* the third and last part of a syllogism *d)* the last of a chain of events; outcome **2** an act or instance of concluding; final arrangement (*of* a pact, treaty, etc.) **3** *Law* *a)* the findings of a court as to the existence of an alleged fact or the application of a particular law *b)* the closing of a plea or address to a court or jury —**in conclusion** lastly; in closing —**try conclusions with** [Old-fashioned] to engage in an argument or contest with

con·clu·sive (-siv) *adj.* ⟦LL *conclusivus* < pp. of L *concludere,* CONCLUDE⟧ that settles a question; final; decisive —**con·clu′sive·ly** *adv.* —**con·clu′sive·ness** *n.*

con·clu·so·ry (-sə rē) *adj.* **1** coming to a conclusion or decision; conclusive **2** *Law* asserted as a conclusion without supporting facts

con·coct (kən käkt′) *vt.* ⟦< L *concoctus,* pp. of *concoquere,* to boil together, prepare < *com-,* together + *coquere,* COOK⟧ **1** to make by combining various ingredients; compound **2** to devise, invent, or plan —**con·coct′er** *n.* —**con·coc′tion** *n.* —**con·coc′tive** *adj.*

con·com·i·tance (kən käm′ə təns) *n.* ⟦ML *concomitantia* < LL *concomitans,* prp. of *concomitari,* to attend < L *com-,* together + *comitari,* to accompany < *comes,* companion: see COUNT[2]⟧ the fact of being concomitant; accompaniment; existence in association: also **con·com′i·tan·cy**

con·com·i·tant (-käm′ə tənt) *adj.* ⟦< LL *concomitans:* see prec.⟧ accompanying; attendant —*n.* an accompanying or attendant condition, circumstance, or thing —**con·com′i·tant·ly** *adv.*

con·cord (kän′kôrd′, käŋ′-) *n.* ⟦ME & OFr *concorde* < L *concordia,* agreement, union < *concors* (gen. *concordis*), of the same mind < *com-,* together + *cor,* HEART⟧ **1** agreement; harmony **2** *a)* friendly and peaceful relations, as between nations *b)* a treaty establishing this **3** *Gram.* AGREEMENT **4** *Music* a combination of simultaneous and harmonious tones; consonance

Con·cord[1] (käŋ′kərd) *n.* ⟦after fol., Mass., where the grape originated⟧ ☆**1** a large, dark-blue, cultivated variety of fox grape, used esp. for making juice and jelly: in full **Concord grape** ☆**2** a wine made from this grape

Con·cord[2] (kän′kôrd; *for 2 & 3* käŋ′kərd) ⟦prob. alluding to the amity hoped for among the inhabitants and their neighbors⟧ **1** city in W Calif., near Oakland **2** capital of N.H., on the Merrimack River **3** town in E Mass., near Boston: with Lexington, site of the first battles of the Revolutionary War (April 19, 1775)

con·cord·ance (kən kôrd′ns) *n.* ⟦ME *concordaunce* < OFr *concordance* < ML *concordantia* < L *concordans,* prp. of *concordare,* to agree < *concors:* see CONCORD⟧ **1** agreement; harmony **2** an alphabetical list of the chief words used in a book or by a writer, with the passages in which they occur identified or cited

con·cord·ant (-kôrd′'nt) *adj.* ⟦Fr < L *concordans:* see prec.⟧ agreeing; consonant; harmonious —**con·cord′ant·ly** *adv.*

con·cor·dat (kən kôr′dat′) *n.* ⟦Fr < ML *concordatum,* agreement < L *concordatus,* pp. of *concordare:* see CONCORDANCE⟧ **1** a compact; formal agreement; covenant **2** an agreement between a pope and a government concerning the regulation of church affairs

☆**Concord coach** ⟦after CONCORD[2], N.H., where the coaches were made⟧ a type of stagecoach used by early settlers of the W U.S.

con·course (kän′kôrs′) *n.* ⟦ME & OFr *concours* < L *concursus,* a running together < *concurrere:* see CONCUR⟧ **1** a coming or flowing together **2** a crowd; throng; gathering ☆**3** a large open area or hall where crowds gather, as in a park or railroad station **4** a broad thoroughfare

con·cres·cence (kən kres′əns) *n.* ⟦L *concrescentia* < *concrescere,* to grow together < *com-,* together + *crescere,* to grow: see CRESCENT⟧ *Biol.* a growing together of parts or cells, as of the lips of the blastopore of the embryo during gastrulation

con·crete (kän′krēt′; *also, and for vt. 1 & vi. usually,* kän krēt′) *adj.* ⟦ME *concret* < L *concretus,* pp. of *concrescere:* see prec.⟧ **1** formed into a solid mass; coalesced **2** having a material, perceptible existence; of, belonging to, or characterized by things or events that can be perceived by the senses; real; actual **3** referring to a particular; specific, not general or abstract **4** made of concrete **5** *Gram.* designating a thing or class of things that can be perceived by the senses [a *concrete* noun]: opposed to ABSTRACT —*n.* **1** a concrete thing, condition, idea, etc. **2** a hard, compact building material formed when a mixture of cement, sand, gravel, and water dries: used in making bridges, road surfaces, etc. —*vt.* **-cret′ed, -cret′ing** **1** to form into a mass; solidify **2** to make of, or cover with, concrete —*vi.* to solidify —**con·crete′ly** *adv.* —**con·crete′ness** *n.*

concrete music MUSIQUE CONCRÈTE

☆**concrete poetry** an art form combining elements of poetry and typography, in which words, word fragments, etc. are variously arranged to produce a composition with visual, as well as poetic, meaning

con·cre·tion (kən krē′shən) *n.* ⟦L *concretio:* see CONCRETE⟧ **1** a solidifying or being solidified **2** an act or instance of concretizing **3** a solidified mass; specif., *a)* *Geol.* an inclusion in sedimentary rock, usually rounded and harder than the surrounding rock, resulting from the formation of succeeding layers of mineral matter about some nucleus, as a grain of sand *b)* *Med.* a solidified mass, usually inorganic, deposited in the body; calculus —**con·cre′tion·ar′y** *adj.*

con·cret·ism (kän krēt′iz′əm) *n.* the practice of seeking to give definite form to abstract things or ideas

con·cret·ize (kän′krē tīz′, kän krēt′īz′) *vt.* **-ized′, -iz′ing** to make (something) concrete; make specific; give definite form to —**con′cret·iz′a·ble** *adj.*

con·cu·bi·nage (kən kyo͞o′bə nij) *n.* ⟦ME & OFr⟧ **1** *Law* cohabitation without a legal marriage **2** the state of being a concubine

con·cu·bine (kän′kyo͞o bīn′, käŋ′-) *n.* ⟦ME < OFr *concubin(e)* < L *concubina* (masc. *concubinus*) < *concumbere,* to lie with < *com-,* with + *cubare,* to lie down: see CUBE[1]⟧ **1** *Law* a woman who cohabits with a man although not legally married to him **2** in certain polygamous societies, a secondary wife, of inferior social and legal status

con·cu·pis·cence (kən kyo͞op′ə səns) *n.* ⟦ME & OFr < LL(Ec) *concupiscentia* < L *concupiscens,* prp. of *concupiscere,* to desire eagerly < *com-,* intens. + *cupiscere,* to wish, desire < *cupere,* to desire: see CUPID⟧ strong desire or appetite, esp. sexual desire; lust —**con·cu′pis·cent** *adj.*

con·cur (kən kur′) *vi.* **-curred′, -cur′ring** ⟦ME *concurren* < L *concurrere,* to run together < *com-,* together + *currere,* to run: see CURRENT⟧ **1** to occur at the same time; happen together; coincide **2** to combine in having an effect; act together [several events *concurred* to bring about this result] **3** to agree (*with*); be in accord (*in* an opinion, etc.) —*SYN.* CONSENT

con·cur·rence (-əns) *n.* ⟦ME < ML *concurrentia* < L *concurrens:* see fol.⟧ **1** a coming or happening together in time or place **2** a combining to produce or bring about something **3** agreement; accord **4** *Geom.* *a)* the point where three or more lines or planes meet *b)* the junction of lines or surfaces Also **con·cur′ren·cy**

con·cur·rent (-ənt) *adj.* ⟦ME < L *concurrens:* prp. of *concurrere,* CONCUR⟧ **1** occurring at the same time; existing together **2** meeting in or going toward the same point; converging **3** acting together; cooperating **4** in agreement; harmonious **5** exercised equally over the same area [*concurrent* jurisdiction] —*n.* a concurrent circumstance, cause, etc. —**con·cur′rent·ly** *adv.*

☆**concurrent resolution** a resolution passed by one branch of a legislature and concurred in by the other, indicating the opinion of the legislature but not having the force of law: cf. JOINT RESOLUTION

concurring opinion *Law* an opinion issued by one or more judges which agrees with the decision reached by the majority of the court, but offers additional or different reasons for reaching that decision

con·cuss (kən kus′) *vt.* ⟦< L *concussus,* pp. of *concutere:* see fol.⟧ to cause to have a concussion

con·cus·sion (kən kush′ən) *n.* ⟦ME *concussioun* < L *concussio* < pp. of *concutere,* shake violently < *com-,* together + *quatere,* to shake: see QUASH[2]⟧ **1** a violent shaking; agitation; shock, as from impact **2** *Med.* a condition of impaired functioning of some organ, esp. the brain, as a result of a violent blow or impact —**con·cus′sive** (-kus′iv) *adj.*

cond *abbrev.* conductivity

Con·dé (kōn dā′), Prince **de** (*Louis II de Bourbon, Duc d'Enghien*) 1621-86; Fr. general: called *the Great Condé*

con·demn (kən dem′) *vt.* ⟦ME *condempnen* < OFr *condemner* < L *condemnare* < *com-,* intens. + *damnare,* to harm, condemn: see DAMN⟧ **1** to pass an adverse judgment on; disapprove of strongly; censure **2** *a)* to declare to be guilty of wrongdoing; convict *b)* to pass judicial sentence on; inflict a penalty upon *c)* to doom ☆**3** to take (private property) for public use by the power of eminent domain; expropriate **4** to declare unfit for use or service [to *condemn* a slum tenement] —*SYN.* CRITICIZE —**con·dem′na·ble** (-dem′nə bəl, -ə bəl) *adj.* —**con·demn′er** *n.*

con·dem·na·tion (kän′dem nā′shən, -dəm-) *n.* ⟦ME *condempnacioun* < L *condemnatio*⟧ **1** a condemning or being condemned **2** a cause for condemning

con·dem·na·to·ry (kən dem′nə tôr′ē) *adj.* ⟦< L *condemnatus,* pp. of *condemnare* (see CONDEMN) + -ORY⟧ condemning; expressing condemnation, explicitly or implicitly

con·den·sate (kän′dən sāt′, kən den′sāt′) *n.* a product of condensation

con·den·sa·tion (kän′dən sā′shən) *n.* ⟦LL *condensatio*⟧ **1** the act of condensing, as the reduction of a gas to a liquid or the abridgment of a piece of writing **2** the product of such an act [to read a *condensation* of a novel] **3** the condition of being condensed

con·dense (kən dens′) *vt.* **-densed′, -dens′ing** ⟦Fr *condenser* < L *condensare* < *condensus,* very dense < *com-,* intens. + *densus,* DENSE⟧ **1** to make more dense or compact; reduce the volume of; compress **2** to express in fewer words; make concise; abridge **3** to change (a substance) to a denser form, as from a gas to a liquid **4** *Chem.* to cause molecules of (the same or different substances) to combine to form a more complex compound, often with elimination of a simple molecule, as water: see POLYMERIZATION —*vi.* to become condensed —*SYN.* CONTRACT —**con·dens′a·ble** *adj.,* **con·dens′i·ble** —**con·dens′a·bil′i·ty** *n.,* **con·dens′i·bil′i·ty**

☆**condensed milk** cow's milk made very thick by evaporation, sweetened with sugar, and then canned and sterilized: cf. EVAPORATED MILK

condensed type *Printing* a typeface narrower than the standard type for the series

con·dens·er (kən den′sər) *n.* a person or thing that condenses; specif., *a)* an apparatus for converting gases or vapors to a liquid state *b)* a lens or series of lenses for concentrating light rays on an object or area *c) Elec.* CAPACITOR

con·de·scend (kän′di send′) *vi.* ⟦ME *condescenden* < OFr *condescendre* < LL(Ec) *condescendere,* to let oneself down, condescend < L *com-,* together + *descendere,* DESCEND⟧ **1** to descend voluntarily to the level, regarded as lower, of the person one is dealing with; be graciously willing to do something regarded as beneath one's dignity; deign **2** to deal with others in a proud or haughty way **3** [Obs.] to make concessions; agree; assent —*SYN.* STOOP[1]

con·de·scend·ence (-sen′dəns) *n.* ⟦ML *condescentia*⟧ **1** condescension **2** [Scot.] a listing of particulars

con·de·scend·ing (-sen′diŋ) *adj.* showing condescension; esp., patronizing —**con′de·scend′ing·ly** *adv.*

con·de·scen·sion (-sen′shən) *n.* ⟦LL(Ec) *condescensio* < pp. of *condescendere*⟧ **1** act or instance of condescending **2** a patronizing manner or behavior

con·dign (kən dīn′, kän′dīn′) *adj.* ⟦ME & OFr *condigne* < L *condignus,* very worthy < *com-,* intens. + *dignus,* worthy: see DIGNITY⟧ deserved; suitable: said esp. of punishment for wrongdoing —**con·dign′ly** *adv.*

Con·dil·lac (kōn dē yȧk′), **É·tienne Bon·not de** (ā tyen′ bô nō′ də) 1715-80; Fr. philosopher

con·di·ment (kän′də mənt) *n.* ⟦ME & OFr < L *condimentum* < *condire,* to pickle, var. of *condere,* to put together < *com-,* together + *-dere,* to put, DO[1]⟧ **1** a seasoning or relish for food **2** anything added to a prepared food, often, specif., to a sandwich, to add flavor, as ketchup, mustard, mayonnaise, onions, pickles, etc.

con·di·tion (kən dish′ən) *n.* ⟦ME & OFr *condicion* < L *condicio,* agreement, situation < *condicere,* to speak with, agree < *com-,* together + *dicere,* to speak: see DICTION⟧ **1** anything called for as a requirement before the performance or completion of something else; provision; stipulation [to impose *conditions* by contract] **2** anything essential to the existence or occurrence of something else; prerequisite [hard work is a *condition* of success] **3** anything that modifies or restricts the nature, existence, or occurrence of something else; external circumstance or factor [*conditions* were favorable for business] **4** manner or state of being **5** *a)* state of health [what's the patient's *condition?*] *b)* an illness; ailment [a lung *condition*] **6** a proper or healthy state [athletes train to be in *condition*] **7** social position; rank; station **8** [Obs.] *a)* disposition of mind; character *b)* characteristic; trait ☆**9** *Educ. a)* the requirement that a student make up deficiencies in a certain subject in order to pass it *b)* the grade stating this requirement **10** *Gram.* a clause expressing a condition, as one beginning with *if* **11** *Law* a clause in a contract, will, etc. that revokes, suspends, or modifies one or more of its stipulations upon the happening of an uncertain future event **12** *Logic* a proposition on which the truth of another proposition depends —*vi.* **1** [Archaic] to make conditions; bargain (*with*) **2** to apply a conditioner to the hair, etc. —*vt.* **1** to set as a condition or requirement; stipulate **2** to impose a condition or conditions on **3** to be a condition of; determine **4** to affect, modify, or influence **5** to bring into a proper or desired condition **6** to apply a conditioner to ☆**7** *Educ.* to give a grade of CONDITION (*n.* 9*b*) to **8** *a) Psychol.* to develop a conditioned response or behavior pattern in (a person or animal) *b)* to cause to become accustomed (*to* something) (usually in the pp.) [we have been *conditioned* to accept long lines at the bank] —*SYN.* STATE —**on condition that** provided that; if

con·di·tion·al (kən dish′ən əl) *adj.* **1** *a)* containing, implying, or dependent on a condition or conditions; qualified; not absolute [a *conditional* award] *b) Logic* designating or including a compound proposition that has the form "if p, then q," in which *p* and *q* are two different propositions **2** expressing a condition [a *conditional* clause] —*n. Gram.* a word, clause, mood, or tense expressing a condition —**con·di′tion·al′i·ty** (-al′ə tē) *n.* —**con·di′tion·al·ly** *adv.*

con·di·tioned (kən dish′ənd) *adj.* **1** in a (specified) condition **2** subject to conditions; depending on certain conditions **3** in a proper or desired condition **4** having developed a conditioned response or behavior pattern

conditioned response a reflex in which the response (e.g., secretion of saliva in a dog) is occasioned by a secondary stimulus (e.g., the ringing of a bell) repeatedly associated with the primary stimulus (e.g., the sight of meat): also **conditioned reflex**

con·di·tion·er (kən dish′ə nər) *n.* something or someone that conditions; specif., a product or ingredient intended to add fullness and body to the hair

con·di·tion·ing (kən dish′ən iŋ) *n.* **1** the act or an instance of bringing into a desired condition, often, specif., of athletic fitness **2** an application of conditioner to the hair, etc. **3** *Psychol.* the act or an instance of instilling a conditioned response or behavior pattern

☆**con·do** (kän′dō′) *n., pl.* **-dos′** or **-does′** *short for* CONDOMINIUM (sense 2)

con·dole (kən dōl′) *vi.* **-doled′, -dol′ing** ⟦LL(Ec) *condolere,* to suffer with < L *com-,* with + *dolere,* to grieve: see DOLEFUL⟧ to express sympathy; mourn in sympathy; commiserate —*vt.* [Archaic] to show grief for —**con·do′la·to′ry** (-dō′lə tôr′ē) *adj.* —**con·dol′er** *n.*

con·do·lence (kən dō′ləns) *n.* ⟦< LL(Ec) *condolens:* see prec.⟧ [*often pl.*] expression of sympathy with another in grief: also **con·dole′ment** —*SYN.* PITY

con do·lo·re (kôn dô lô′re) ⟦It⟧ *Musical Direction* with grief; sadly

con·dom (kän′dəm, kun′-) *n.* ⟦earlier *condam, quondam* < It *guantone* < *guanto,* a glove < Frank **want,* glove, mitten (> Fr *gant*)⟧ **1** a thin protective sheath for the penis, generally of latex, used to prevent venereal infection or as a contraceptive **2** a thin, lubricated polyurethane sheath placed in the vagina to prevent venereal infection or as a contraceptive: in full **female condom**

con·do·min·i·um (kän′də min′ē əm) *n., pl.* **-i·ums** ⟦ModL: see COM- & DOMINIUM⟧ **1** *a)* joint rule by two or more states *b)* the territory so ruled **2** *a)* a form of real property ownership in which the purchaser of each unit of an apartment building or in a complex of multiunit dwellings acquires full title to the unit and an undivided interest in the common elements (the land, roof, elevator, etc.) *b)* such a unit, or such a building or complex

Con·don (kän′dən), **Edward U(hler)** 1902-74; U.S. physicist

con·do·na·tion (kän′də nā′shən) *n.* ⟦L *condonatio* < pp. of fol.⟧ the act of condoning, esp. of implying forgiveness by overlooking an offense

con·done (kən dōn′) *vt.* **-doned′, -don′ing** ⟦L *condonare* < *com-,* intens. + *donare,* to give: see DONATION⟧ to forgive, pardon, or overlook (an offense) —**con·don′a·ble** *adj.* —**con·don′er** *n.*

con·dor (kän′dər, -dôr; *for 3, Sp* kôn′dôr′) *n.* ⟦Sp *cóndor* < Quechuan *cuntur*⟧ **1** a very large vulture (*Vultur gryphus*) of the South American Andes, with black plumage, bare head and neck, and a ruff of downy white feathers at the base of the neck **2** a similar vulture (*Gymnogyps californianus*) of the mountains of S Calif.: an endangered species **3** *pl.* **con·do·res** (kôn dô′res) any of various South American coins stamped with the figure of a condor

California condor

Con·dor·cet (kōn dôr sā′), **Marquis de** (born *Marie Jean Antoine Nicolas de Caritat*) 1743-94; Fr. social philosopher, mathematician, and political leader

con·dot·tie·re (kän′dô tyer′ā; *It* kôn′dôt tye′re) *n., pl.* **-ri** (-ē; *It,* -rē) ⟦It < *condotto,* one hired < L *conductus,* mercenary soldier < pp. of *conducere,* to hire, lead together (see fol.); infl. in It by *condotta,* leadership < same L source⟧ in Europe from the 14th to the 16th cent., a captain of a band of mercenaries

con·duce (kən do͞os′, -dyo͞os′) *vi.* **-duced′, -duc′ing** ⟦ME *conducen* < L *conducere* < *com-,* together + *ducere,* to lead: see DUCT⟧ to tend or lead (*to* an effect); contribute

con·du·cive (-do͞o′siv, -dyo͞o′-) *adj.* that conduces or contributes; tending or leading (*to*) —**con·du′cive·ness** *n.*

con·duct (kän′dukt′, -dəkt; *for v.* kən dukt′) *n.* ⟦< L *conductus,* pp. of *conducere:* see CONDUCE⟧ **1** [Rare] the act of leading; guidance **2** the process or way of managing or directing; management; handling **3** the way that one acts; behavior; deportment **4** [Obs.] an escort; convoy —*vt.* **1** to show the way to; lead; guide; escort **2** to manage, control, or direct **3** to be the leader of; direct (an orchestra, choir, etc.) **4** to behave or direct (oneself) in a specified way **5** to be able to transmit or carry; convey [iron *conducts* electricity] —*vi.* **1** to be or mark the way; lead **2** to act as a conductor —**con·duct′i·ble** *adj.* —**con·duct′i·bil′i·ty** *n.*

SYN.—**conduct,** in this comparison, implies a supervising by using one's executive skill, knowledge, and wisdom [to *conduct* a sales campaign]; **direct** implies less supervision of actual details, but stresses the issuance of general orders or instructions [to *direct* the construction of a dam]; **manage** implies supervision that involves the personal handling of all details [to *manage* a department]; **control** implies firm direction by regulation or restraint and often connotes complete domination [the school board *controls* the system] See also **behave**

con·duct·ance (kən duk′təns) ***n.*** the ability of a component to conduct electricity, measured in siemens and equal to the ratio of the current to the voltage: it is the reciprocal of resistance: symbol, G: see ADMITTANCE (sense 3)

con·duc·tion (kən duk′shən) ***n.*** ⟦L *conductio*: see CONDUCT⟧ **1** a conveying, as of liquid through a channel, esp. in plants **2** *Physics a)* transmission of electricity, heat, etc. through a material *b)* CONDUCTIVITY (see also CONVECTION, RADIATION) **3** *Physiol.* the transmission of nerve impulses

con·duc·tive (-tiv) ***adj.*** **1** having conductivity **2** having to do with conduction

con·duc·tiv·i·ty (kän′duk tiv′ə tē) ***n.*** **1** the property of conducting or transmitting heat, electricity, etc. **2** *Elec.* conductance per unit of area or volume, measured in siemens per meter: the reciprocal of resistivity

con·duc·tor (kən duk′tər) ***n.*** **1** a person who conducts; leader; guide; manager **2** the director of an orchestra, choir, etc. ☆**3** the person who has charge of the passengers and collects fares on a train, streetcar, or bus **4** a substance or thing that conducts electricity, heat, sound, etc. —**con·duc·tor·i·al** (kän′duk tôr′ē əl) ***adj.*** —**con·duc′tor·ship′** ***n.***

con·duc·tress (kən duk′trəs) ***n.*** a female conductor: see -ESS

con·du·it (kän′do͞o it, -dit) ***n.*** ⟦ME & OFr < L *conductus*: see CONDUCE⟧ **1** a pipe or channel for conveying fluids **2** a tube, pipe, or protected trough for electric wires **3** any channel, or means, whereby something is passed on **4** [Archaic] a fountain

con·du·pli·cate (kän do͞o′pli kit, -dyo͞o′-) ***adj.*** ⟦L *conduplicatus*, pp. of *conduplicare* < *com-*, with + *duplicare*: see DUPLICATE⟧ folded lengthwise along the middle, as certain leaves and petals in the bud

con·dyle (kän′dil, -dīl′) ***n.*** ⟦Fr < L *condylus* < Gr *kondylos*, knuckle, orig., hard lump or knob⟧ a rounded process at the end of a bone, forming a ball-and-socket joint with the hollow part of another bone —**con′dy·lar** (-də lər) ***adj.***

con·dy·loid (-də loid′) ***adj.*** of or like a condyle

con·dy·lo·ma (kän′də lō′mə) ***n., pl.*** **-ma·ta** (-mə tə) ⟦L < Gr *kondylōma* < *kondylos*: see CONDYLE⟧ a wartlike, inflammatory growth on the skin, usually occurring near the anus or genital organs

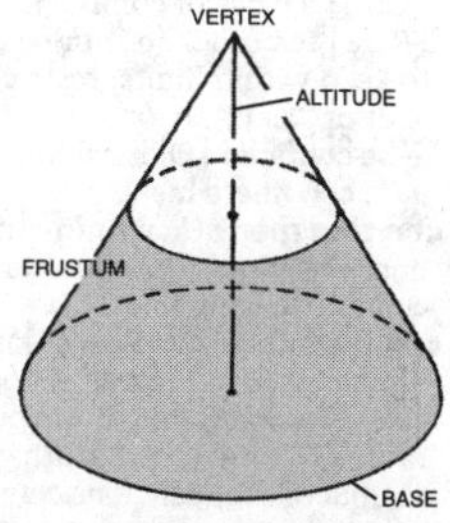

parts of a cone
(sense 1*a*)

cone (kōn) ***n.*** ⟦ME < L *conus* < Gr *kōnos*, a wedge, peak, cone < IE base *kō(n)-*, to sharpen > HONE[1], L *cos*⟧ **1** *a)* a flat-based, single-pointed solid formed by a rotating straight line that traces out a closed-curved base from a fixed vertex point that is not in the same plane as the base; esp., one (**right circular cone**) formed by tracing a circle from a vertex perpendicular to the center of the base (also formed by rotating a right triangle 360° with either leg as the axis, or by rotating an isosceles triangle 360° with the altitude as the axis) *b)* the surface of such a solid *c)* a similar unbounded surface extending outward in both directions from a point: it is formed by rotating in an elliptical or circular pattern a straight line that always passes through this point **2** any object or mass shaped like a cone; specif., *a)* a crisp shell of pastry for holding a scoop of ice cream *b)* the peak of a volcano *c)* any of various machine parts *d)* any of the brightly colored plastic objects used as a barrier to divert traffic from roadwork, from a chuckhole, etc. (in full **traffic cone**) **3** *Bot. a)* a reproductive structure of certain nonflowering plants, consisting of an elongated central axis upon which are borne, usually in a spiral fashion, overlapping scales, bracts, sporophylls, etc.: cones produce pollen, spores, and ovules and are found in cycads, conifers, club mosses, horsetails, etc. *b)* any similar structure, as the catkin of hops **4** *Zool. a)* any of the flask-shaped cells in the retina of most vertebrates, sensitive to bright light and color *b)* CONE SHELL **5** the DIAPHRAGM (sense 5) of a speaker, usually cone-shaped —***vt.*** **coned, con′ing** to shape like a cone or a conical segment

cones of conifers

☆**cone·flow·er** (kōn′flou′ər) ***n.*** any of several genera (esp. *Rudbeckia, Ratibida,* and *Echinacea*) of showy plants of the composite family, having cone-shaped receptacles, as the black-eyed Susan

☆**CON·EL·RAD** (kän′əl rad′) ***n.*** ⟦*con(trol of) el(ectromagnetic) rad(iation)*⟧ a former system (from 1951 to 1963) of shifting broadcasting frequencies of AM stations to prevent possible use of their radio beams by enemy aircraft as a navigational aid

☆**cone·nose** (kōn′nōz′) ***n.*** any of certain hemipteran insects (family Reduviidae) with a conelike base on the sucking beak, esp. a bloodsucking genus (*Triatoma*) that sometimes transmits parasites: found in the S U.S. and tropical America

cone shell any of a family (Conidae) of tropical marine snails, most species of which can inflict a very poisonous bite

☆**Con·es·to·ga wagon** (kän′ə stō′gə) ⟦after *Conestoga* Valley, Lancaster County, Pa., where the wagons were made⟧ a broad-wheeled covered wagon used for hauling freight in colonial America: cf. PRAIRIE SCHOONER

co·ney (kō′nē) ***n., pl.*** **-neys** or **-nies** ⟦ME *coni* (taken as sing. of OFr *conis*) < OFr *conin, conil* (pl. *conis*) < L *cuniculus*, rabbit⟧ **1** a kind of rabbit or a pika: early term no longer in scientific use **2** rabbit fur **3** a small animal mentioned in the Bible, probably the hyrax **4** any of several marine fishes; esp., a grouper (*Epinephelus fulvus*) of the tropical W Atlantic **5** [Obs.] a gullible person; dupe

Co·ney Island (kō′nē) ⟦< Du *Konynen Eyland*, rabbit island⟧ beach & amusement park in Brooklyn, N.Y., on a peninsula, formerly an island, at the SW end of Long Island

conf *abbrev.* **1** ⟦L *confer*⟧ compare **2** conference

con·fab (kän′fab′; *for v. also* kən fab′) [Informal] ***n.*** **1** a confabulation; chat **2** a discussion, conference meeting, etc. —***vi.*** **-fabbed′, -fab′bing** to engage in a confab

con·fab·u·late (kən fab′yə lāt′) ***vi.*** **-lat′ed, -lat′ing** ⟦< pp. of L *confabulari*, to talk together < *com-*, together + *fabulari*, to converse: see FABLE⟧ **1** to talk together in an informal way; chat **2** *Psychol.* to fill in gaps in the memory with detailed accounts of fictitious events believed true by the narrator —**con·fab′u·la′tion** ***n.*** —**con·fab′u·la·to′ry** (-lə tôr′ē) ***adj.***

con·far·re·a·tion (kän far′ē ā′shən) ***n.*** ⟦L *confarreatio* < *confarreare*, to marry < *farreum*, spelt cake < *farreus*, spelt < *far*, kind of grain: see FARINA⟧ in ancient Rome, the most solemn form of marriage, marked by the offering of a cake of spelt as a sacrifice to Jupiter

con·fect (kən fekt′) ***vt.*** ⟦< L *confectus*, pp. of *conficere*, to prepare < *com-*, with + *facere*, to make, DO[1]⟧ to prepare or make, esp. by mixing or combining

con·fec·tion (kən fek′shən) ***n.*** ⟦ME *confeccioun* < OFr *confeccion* < L *confectio*⟧ **1** the act or process of confecting **2** any kind of candy or other sweet preparation, such as ice cream or preserves **3** a sweetened mixture of drugs; electuary **4** a product or work having a frivolous, whimsical, or contrived effect **5** a fancy, stylish article of women's clothing —***vt.*** [Archaic] to prepare as a confection

con·fec·tion·ar·y (-er′ē) ***adj.*** **1** of or like a confection **2** of confectioners or their work —***n., pl.*** **-ar′ies** ☆**1** CONFECTIONERY (sense 3) **2** a confection

con·fec·tion·er (-ər) ***n.*** a person whose work or business is making or selling confectionery

☆**confectioners' sugar** sugar ground into a very fine powder, finer than powdered sugar

con·fec·tion·er·y (-er′ē) ***n., pl.*** **-er′ies** **1** confections or candy, collectively **2** the business or work of a confectioner ☆**3** a confectioner's shop; candy store

Confed *abbrev.* Confederate

con·fed·er·a·cy (kən fed′ər ə sē) ***n., pl.*** **-cies** ⟦ME & OFr *confederacie* < LL *confoederatus*: see CONFEDERATE⟧ **1** people, groups, nations, or states united for some common purpose **2** a league or alliance formed by such a union; federation or confederation **3** people united for an unlawful purpose; conspiracy —***SYN.*** ALLIANCE —☆**the Confederacy** the league of Southern states that seceded from the U.S. in 1860 & 1861; Ala., Ark., Fla., Ga., La., Miss., N.C., S.C., Tenn., Tex., & Va.: official name **Confederate States of America**

con·fed·er·al (kən fed′ər əl) ***adj.*** ⟦< CONFEDERATION, after FEDERAL⟧ being or of a confederation of independent nations or states [progress toward a *confederal* Europe]

con·fed·er·ate (kən fed′ər it; *for v.,* -āt′) ***adj.*** ⟦ME *confederat* < LL *confoederatus*, pp. of *confoederare*, to unite by a league < *foedus*, a league: see FAITH⟧ **1** united in a confederacy or league ☆**2** [**C-**] of the Confederacy —***n.*** **1** a person, group, nation, or state united with another or others for a common purpose; ally; associate **2** an associate in an unlawful act or plot; accomplice ☆**3** [**C-**] any Southern supporter of the Confederacy — ***vt., vi.*** **-at′ed, -at′ing** to unite in a confederacy; ally —***SYN.*** ASSOCIATE

Confederate Memorial Day *see* MEMORIAL DAY

con·fed·er·a·tion (kən fed′ər ā′shən) ***n.*** ⟦ME *confederacion* < LL *confoederatio*: see CONFEDERATE⟧ **1** a uniting or being united in a league or alliance **2** a league or alliance; specif., independent nations or states joined in a league or confederacy whose central authority is usually confined to common defense and limited political cooperation —***SYN.*** ALLIANCE —☆**the Confederation** **1** the United States of America (1781-89) under the Articles of Confederation **2** the union of Ontario, Quebec, Nova Scotia, and New Brunswick in 1867 to form the Dominion of Canada

con·fed·er·a·tive (kən fed′ər āt′iv, -ər ə tiv′) ***adj.*** of confederates or a confederation

con·fer (kən fur′) ***vt.*** **-ferred′, -fer′ring** ⟦L *conferre*, to bring together, compare, confer < *com-*, together + *ferre*, to BEAR[1]⟧ **1** to give, grant, or bestow **2** [Obs.] to compare —***vi.*** to have a conference or talk; meet for discussion; converse —***SYN.*** GIVE —**con·fer′ra·ble** ***adj.*** —**con·fer′rer** ***n.***

☆**con·fer·ee** (kän′fər ē′) ***n.*** **1** a participant in a conference **2** a person on whom an honor, degree, or favor is conferred

con·fer·ence (kän′fər əns, -frəns; *for n. 6* kən fur′əns) ***n.*** ⟦Fr *conférence* < ML *conferentia* < L *conferens*, prp. of *conferre*: see CONFER⟧ **1** the act of conversing or consulting on a serious matter **2** a formal meeting of a number of people for discussion or consultation **3** a meeting of committees from both branches of a legislature to reconcile the differences between bills passed by both branches **4** [*often* **C-**] *a)* a national or district governing body of the Methodist Church *b)* a national or district association of Mennonite or certain other Protestant churches *c)* a district governed or represented by a conference **5** a national or regional association, as of colleges or their athletic teams **6** a conferral; bestowal: also sp. **con·fer′rence** —*vi.* **-enced, -enc·ing 1** to participate in or hold a conference **2** to confer, usually over some distance, by means of an electronic communications system or computer network —**con′fer·enc·ing** *n.* —**con·fer·en·tial** (kän′fər en′shəl) *adj.*

conference call a conversation or meeting participated in by three or more persons and conducted by means of telephones, computers, etc.

conference table a large table, often rectangular, around which a number of people may be seated, as when holding a conference

con·fer·ral (kən fur′əl) *n.* a conferring of an honor, degree, or favor; bestowal: also **con·fer′ment** (-mənt)

con·fer·va (kən fur′və) *n., pl.* **-vae** (-vē) or **-vas** ⟦L: see COMFREY⟧ *Bot. a former name for* any of various threadlike green algae, esp. a genus (*Tribonema*) found chiefly in fresh water —**con·fer′val** *adj., n.,* **con·fer′void′**

con·fess (kən fes′) *vt.* ⟦ME *confessen* < OFr *confesser* < ML(Ec) **confessare* < L *confessus,* pp. of *confiteri,* to acknowledge, confess < *com-,* together + *fateri,* to acknowledge; akin to *fari,* to speak: see FAME⟧ **1** *a)* to admit (a fault or crime) *b)* to acknowledge (an opinion or view) **2** to declare one's faith in **3** [Old Poet.] to be evidence of; reveal; manifest **4** *Eccles. a)* to tell (one's sins) to God, esp. in public worship service or in private *b)* to hear the confession of (a person) (said of a priest) —*vi.* **1** to admit a fault or crime; acknowledge one's guilt **2** *Eccles. a)* to take part in public confession or make one's confession to a priest *b)* to hear confessions (said of a priest) —*SYN.* ACKNOWLEDGE —**confess to** to admit or admit having; acknowledge —**stand confessed as** to be revealed or admitted as

con·fess·ed·ly (-id lē) *adv.* by confession; admittedly

con·fes·sion (kən fesh′ən) *n.* **1** the act of confessing; acknowledgment; specif., *a)* an admission of guilt, esp. formally in writing, as by a person charged with a crime *b)* the confessing of sins to a priest in the sacrament of penance *c)* a general acknowledgment of sin, or a form expressing this used in public worship **2** something confessed **3** *a)* a statement of religious beliefs, esp. as held by a Christian church, usually longer than a creed (in full **confession of faith**) *b)* a church having such a confession: communion **4** the tomb or shrine of a martyr or confessor **5** [*sometimes pl.*] a story of or as of one's life experiences, revealing faults and confidential personal details

con·fes·sion·al (-ə nəl) *n.* ⟦Fr, orig. *(chaire) confessionale,* (chair) for confession⟧ **1** a small, enclosed place in a church, where a priest hears confessions **2** confession to a priest —*adj.* of, characterized by, or for a confession or confessions

con·fes·sor (kən fes′ər) *n.* **1** a person who confesses **2** *a)* a Christian who suffered for his or her faith *b) R.C.Ch.* a male saint who was not a martyr **3** a priest authorized to hear confessions

con·fet·ti (kən fet′ē) *pl.n.* ⟦It, pl. of *confetto,* sweetmeat < ML *confectum* < L *confectus*: see CONFECT⟧ **1** [Historical] candies, or plaster imitations of candies, scattered about at carnivals or other celebrations **2** [*with sing. v.*] bits of colored paper now used in this way

con·fi·dant (kän′fə dant′, -dänt′; kän′fə dant′, -dänt′) *n.* ⟦Fr *confident* (fem. *confidente*) < L *confidens,* prp. of *confidere,* CONFIDE⟧ a close, trusted friend, to whom one confides intimate matters or secrets

con·fi·dante (-dant′, -dänt′) *n.* a woman or girl confidant

con·fide (kən fīd′) *vi.* **-fid′ed, -fid′ing** ⟦L *confidere* < *com-,* intens. + *fidere,* to trust: see FAITH⟧ to trust (*in* someone), esp. by sharing secrets or discussing private affairs —*vt.* **1** to tell or talk about as a secret [to *confide* one's troubles to a friend] **2** to entrust (as a duty, object, or person) *to* someone —*SYN.* COMMIT —**con·fid′er** *n.*

con·fi·dence (kän′fə dəns) *n.* ⟦ME < L *confidentia* < *confidens,* prp. of prec.⟧ **1** firm belief; trust; reliance **2** the fact of being or feeling certain; assurance **3** belief in one's own abilities; self-confidence **4** a relationship as confidant [take me into your *confidence*] **5** the belief that another will keep a secret; assurance of secrecy [told in strict *confidence*] **6** something told as a secret **7** *Bible* object of trust: Prov. 3:26 —☆*adj.* swindling or used to swindle

SYN.—**confidence,** in this comparison, implies belief in one's own abilities, or, esp. in the form **self-confidence,** reliance on one's own powers [he has *confidence* he will win]; **assurance,** in this connection, suggests an even stronger belief in one's ability, but in an unfavorable sense, it may connote (as may **confidence**) conceited or arrogant self-sufficiency; **self-possession** suggests that presence of mind which results from the ability to control one's feelings and behavior; **aplomb** refers, usually in a favorable sense, to an evident assurance of manner manifesting self-possession [he stood his ground with admirable *aplomb*] See also **belief** —*ANT.* **diffidence, shyness**

☆**confidence game** a swindle effected by gaining the confidence of the victim

☆**confidence man** a swindler who tries to gain the confidence of the victim in order to defraud

con·fi·dent (kän′fə dənt) *adj.* **1** full of confidence; specif., *a)* assured; certain [*confident* of victory] *b)* sure of oneself; self-confident; bold [a *confident* manner] **2** [Obs.] trustful; confiding —*n.* CONFIDANT —*SYN.* SURE —**con′fi·dent·ly** *adv.*

con·fi·den·tial (kän′fə den′shəl) *adj.* **1** told in confidence; imparted in secret **2** of or showing trust in another; confiding **3** not publicly or generally known; secret **4** entrusted with private or secret matters [a *confidential* agent] —*SYN.* FAMILIAR —**con′fi·den′ti·al′i·ty** (-shē al′ə tē) *n.,* **con′fi·den′tial·ness** —**con′fi·den′tial·ly** *adv.*

con·fid·ing (kən fīd′iŋ) *adj.* trustful or inclined to trust —**con·fid′ing·ly** *adv.*

con·fig·u·ra·tion (kən fig′yə rā′shən) *n.* ⟦L *configuratio* < *configurare,* to form after < *com-,* together + *figurare*: see FIGURE⟧ **1** *a)* arrangement of parts *b)* form or figure as determined by the arrangement of parts; contour; outline **2** *Chem.* the structure of a compound, esp. in the spatial relation of atoms in the molecule **3** GESTALT **4** *Comput.* the way in which a computer and peripheral equipment are interconnected and programmed to operate as a system —*SYN.* FORM —**con·fig′u·ra′tion·al** *adj.* —**con·fig′u·ra′tive** *adj.*

con·fig·u·ra·tion·ism (-iz′əm) *n.* GESTALT PSYCHOLOGY

con·fig·ure (kən fig′yər) *vt.* **-ured, -ur·ing** ⟦< L *configurare,* to form according to a pattern < *com-,* together + *figurare*: see FIGURATIVE⟧ **1** to construct or arrange in a certain way **2** *Comput.* to arrange or design the CONFIGURATION (sense 4) of —**con·fig′ur·a·ble** *adj.*

con·fine (kən fīn′; *for n. 1* kän′fīn′) *n.* ⟦ME *confinies,* pl. < OFr *confins,* pl., a border, boundary < L *confinium* (pl. *confinia*), boundary, limit < *confinis,* bordering on < *com-,* with + *finis,* an end: see FINISH⟧ **1** [*usually pl.*] a boundary or bounded region; border; limit **2** [Old Poet.] confinement **3** [Obs.] a place of confinement —*vi.* **-fined′, -fin′ing** ⟦Fr *confiner* < the n.⟧ [Rare] to border (*on*) or be contiguous (*with* or *to* another region) —*vt.* **1** to keep within limits; restrict [to *confine* a talk to ten minutes] **2** to keep shut up, as in prison, in bed because of illness, indoors, etc. —*SYN.* LIMIT —**be confined** [Old-fashioned] to be giving birth to a child —**con·fin′a·ble** *adj.,* **con·fine′a·ble**

con·fine·ment (kən fīn′mənt) *n.* a confining or being confined; specif., *a)* imprisonment *b)* limitation; restriction; restraint *c)* [Old-fashioned] childbirth; lying-in

con·firm (kən furm′) *vt.* ⟦ME *confermen* < OFr *confermer* < L *confirmare* < *com-,* intens. + *firmare,* to strengthen < *firmus,* FIRM[1]⟧ **1** to make firm; strengthen; establish; encourage **2** to make valid by formal approval; ratify **3** to prove the truth, validity, or authenticity of; verify **4** to cause to undergo the religious ceremony of confirmation —**con·firm′a·ble** *adj.*

SYN.—to **confirm** is to establish as true that which was doubtful or uncertain [to *confirm* a rumor]; **substantiate** suggests the producing of evidence that proves or tends to prove the validity of a previous assertion or claim [the census figures *substantiate* his charge]; **corroborate** suggests the strengthening of one statement or testimony by another [the witnesses *corroborated* her version of the event]; to **verify** is to prove to be true or correct by investigation, comparison with a standard, or reference to ascertainable facts [to *verify* an account]; **authenticate** implies proof of genuineness by an authority or expert [to *authenticate* a painting]; **validate** implies official confirmation of the validity of something [to *validate* a will] —*ANT.* **contradict, disprove**

con·fir·mand (kän′fər mand′, kän′fər mand′) *n.* ⟦< L *confirmandus,* fit to be confirmed < *confirmare,* prec.⟧ a person who is to be confirmed in a religious ceremony

con·fir·ma·tion (kän′fər mā′shən) *n.* ⟦ME & OFr *confirmacion* < L *confirmatio* < pp. of *confirmare*⟧ **1** a confirming or being confirmed; corroboration; ratification; verification **2** something that confirms or proves **3** *a)* a Christian ceremony variously viewed as a sacrament conferring spiritual strength of the Holy Spirit or as a nonsacramental rite admitting to full church membership ☆*b)* a Jewish ceremony in which young people reaffirm their belief in the basic spiritual and ethical concepts of Judaism

con·firm·a·to·ry (kən fur′mə tôr′ē) *adj.* confirming or tending to confirm: also **con·firm′a·tive**

con·firmed (kən furmd′) *adj.* **1** firmly established, as in a habit or condition; habitual [a *confirmed* bachelor] **2** chronic, as a disease **3** corroborated; proved **4** *a)* having received Christian confirmation *b)* having reaffirmed belief through Jewish confirmation —*SYN.* CHRONIC —**con·firm′ed·ly** *adv.*

con·fis·ca·ble (kən fis′kə bəl) *adj.* liable to be confiscated: also **con·fis·cat·a·ble** (kän′fə skāt′ə bəl)

con·fis·cate (kän′fis kāt′) *vt.* **-cat′ed, -cat′ing** ⟦< L *confiscatus,* pp. of *confiscare,* to lay up in a chest < *com-,* together + *fiscus,* money basket, public treasury: see FISCAL⟧ **1** to seize (private property) for the public treasury, usually as a penalty **2** to seize by or as by authority; appropriate —**con′fis·ca′tion** *n.* —**con′fis·ca′tor** *n.*

con·fis·ca·to·ry (kən fis′kə tôr′ē) *adj.* of, effecting, or virtually amounting to confiscation [a *confiscatory* tax]

con·fit (kōn fē′) *n.* ⟦Fr < OFr, something preserved: see COMFIT⟧ meat or poultry, esp. duck or goose, cooked immersed in its own fat with herbs and other seasonings and then preserved within the solidified fat

con·fit·e·or (kən fit′ē ər, -fē′tē-) *n.* ⟦ME < LL(Ec), I confess: see CONFESS⟧ [*also* C-] a formal prayer, as at the beginning of a Mass, in which sins are confessed: term used esp. in ref. to the traditional Latin Mass

con·fi·ture (kän′fə choor′) *n.* ⟦Late OFr < *confit,* COMFIT⟧ a confection, sweetmeat, or preserve

con·fla·grant (kən flā′grənt) *adj.* ⟦L *conflagrans,* prp. of *conflagrare*: see fol.⟧ burning; ablaze

con·fla·gra·tion (kän′flə grā′shən) *n.* ⟦L *conflagratio* < pp. of *conflagrare,* to burn < *com-*, intens. + *flagrare*, to burn: see BLACK⟧ a big, destructive fire

con·flate (kən flāt′) ***vt.*** **-flat′ed, -flat′ing** ⟦< L *conflare*: see fol.⟧ to combine or mix (two variant readings into a single text, etc.)

con·fla·tion (kən flā′shən) ***n.*** ⟦ME *conflacioun* < LL *conflatio* < L *conflare*, to blow together < *com-*, together + *flare*, to BLOW[1]⟧ a combining, as of two variant readings of a text into a composite reading

con·flict (kən flikt′; *for n.* kän′flikt′) ***vi.*** ⟦ME *conflicten* < L *conflictus*, pp. of *confligere*, to strike together < *com-*, together + *fligere*, to strike: see INFLICT⟧ **1** [Obs.] to fight; battle; contend **2** to be antagonistic, incompatible, or contradictory; be in opposition; clash [ideas that *conflict*] **—*n.*** **1** a fight or struggle, esp. a protracted one; war **2** sharp disagreement or opposition, as of interests or ideas; clash **3** emotional disturbance resulting from a clash of opposing impulses or from an inability to reconcile impulses with realistic or moral considerations **4** [Rare] collision of moving bodies **—con·flic′tion *n.*** **—con·flic′tive *adj.***

SYN.—**conflict** refers to a sharp disagreement or collision as in interests or ideas and emphasizes the process rather than the end [the *conflict* over slavery]; **fight**, a rather general word for any contest, struggle, or quarrel, stresses physical or hand-to-hand combat; **struggle** implies great effort or violent exertion, physical or otherwise [the *struggle* for existence]; **contention** most frequently applies to heated verbal strife, or dispute [religious *contention* broke out]; **contest** refers to a struggle, either friendly or hostile, for supremacy in some matter [athletic *contests*, a *contest* of wits] **—*ANT.* accord, harmony**

con·flict·ed (kən flikt′ed) ***adj.*** in a state or condition of emotional conflict

conflict of interest a conflict between one's obligation to the public good and one's self-interest, as in the case of a public officeholder who owns stock in a company seeking government contracts

con·flic·tu·al (kən flik′cho͞o əl) ***adj.*** characterized by or having to do with conflict

con·flu·ence (kän′flo͞o əns) ***n.*** ⟦OFr < LL *confluentia* < L *confluens*, prp. of *confluere* < *com-*, together + *fluere*, to flow: see FLUCTUATE⟧ **1** a flowing together, esp. of two or more streams **2** the place where they join, or a stream formed in this way **3** a coming together as of people; crowd; throng

con·flu·ent (-ənt) ***adj.*** ⟦ME & L *confluens*: see prec.⟧ **1** flowing or running together so as to form one [*confluent* streams] **2** *Med.* running together so as to form a merged mass, as sores, pimples, etc. **—*n.*** a stream uniting with another; loosely, a tributary

con·flux (kän′fluks′) ***n.*** ⟦< L *confluxus*, pp. of *confluere*: see CONFLUENCE⟧ CONFLUENCE

con·fo·cal (kän fō′kəl) ***adj.*** *Math.* having the same focus or focuses

con·form (kən fôrm′) ***vt.*** ⟦ME *conformen* < OFr *conformer* < L *conformare*, to fashion, form < *com-*, together + *formare*, to FORM⟧ **1** to make the same or similar [to *conform* one's idea to another's] **2** to bring into harmony or agreement; adapt: often used reflexively **—*vi.*** **1** to be or become the same or similar **2** to be in accord or agreement [the house *conforms* to specifications] **3** to behave in a conventional way, esp. in accepting without question customs, traditions, prevailing opinion, etc. **4** *Eng. History* to adhere to the practices of the Anglican Church **—*SYN.*** ADAPT, AGREE **—con·form′er *n.***

con·form·a·ble (kən fôr′mə bəl) ***adj.*** ⟦ME⟧ **1** that conforms; specif., *a)* similar *b)* in harmony or agreement *c)* adapted; suited **2** quick to conform; obedient; compliant **3** *Geol.* uninterruptedly parallel: said of sedimentary strata that show no disturbance at the time of deposition **—con·form′a·bil′i·ty *n.*** **—con·form′a·bly *adv.***

con·form·al (-fôr′məl) ***adj.*** ⟦< LL(Ec) *conformalis*, conformable, similar < L *conformare*: see CONFORM⟧ **1** *Math.* of a transformation in which corresponding angles are equal **2** designating or of a map projection in which shapes at any point are true, but areas become increasingly exaggerated

con·form·ance (-fôr′məns) ***n.*** CONFORMITY

con·for·ma·tion (kän′fôr mā′shən, -fər-) ***n.*** ⟦L *conformatio* < pp. of *conformare*⟧ **1** [Rare] a conforming or being conformed; adaptation **2** *a)* a completed or symmetrical formation and arrangement of the parts of a thing *b)* the structure or form of a thing as determined by such arrangements; specif., the shape or outline, as of an animal

con·form·ist (kən fôr′mist) ***n.*** a person who tends to CONFORM (*vi.* 3) **—*adj.*** characterized by the tendency to CONFORM (*vi.* 3) **—con·form′ism′ *n.***

con·form·i·ty (kən fôr′mə tē) ***n.***, *pl.* **-ties** ⟦ME *conformite* < OFr < ML **conformitas* < L *conformare*: see CONFORM⟧ **1** the condition or fact of being in harmony or agreement; correspondence; congruity; similarity **2** action in accordance with customs, rules, prevailing opinion, etc.; conventional behavior **3** *Eng. History* adherence to the practices of the Anglican Church

con·found (kən found′; *for 3, usually* kän′-) ***vt.*** ⟦ME *confounden* < OFr *confondre* < L *confundere*, to pour together, confuse < *com-*, together + *fundere*, to pour: see FOUND[3]⟧ **1** to mix up or lump together indiscriminately; confuse **2** to make feel confused; bewilder **3** to damn: used as a mild oath **4** [Archaic] to defeat or destroy **5** [Archaic] to abash **—*SYN.*** PUZZLE

con·found·ed (kən foun′did) ***adj.*** **1** confused; bewildered **2** damned: a mild oath **—con·found′ed·ly *adv.***

con·fra·ter·ni·ty (kän′frə tʉr′nə tē) ***n.***, *pl.* **-ties** ⟦ME *confraternite* < ML *confraternitas*: see COM- & FRATERNITY⟧ **1** fraternal bond; brotherhood **2** a group of men (or, sometimes, men and women) associated for some purpose or in a profession; esp., a religious society, usually of laymen, with a devotional or charitable purpose

con·frere (kän′frer′, kän frer′) ***n.*** ⟦ME & OFr: see COM- & FRÈRE⟧ a fellow member or worker; colleague or associate, as in a profession

con·front (kən frunt′) ***vt.*** ⟦Fr *confronter* < ML *confrontare* < L *com-*, together + *frons*, forehead: see FRONT[1]⟧ **1** to face; stand or meet face to face **2** to face or oppose boldly, defiantly, or antagonistically **3** to bring face to face (*with*) [to *confront* someone with the facts] **4** to set side by side to compare

con·fron·ta·tion (kän′frən tā′shən) ***n.*** the act or an instance of confronting boldly, defiantly, or antagonistically **—con′fron·ta′tion·al *adj.*** **—con′fron·ta′tion·ist *n., adj.***

Con·fu·cian·ism (kən fyo͞o′shən iz′əm) ***n.*** the ethical teachings formulated by Confucius and introduced into Chinese religion, emphasizing devotion to parents, family, and friends, cultivation of the mind, self-control, and just social activity **—Con·fu′cian·ist *n., adj.***

Con·fu·cius (kən fyo͞o′shəs) (L. name of *K'ung Fu-tzu*) 551?-479? B.C.; Chin. philosopher & teacher **—Con·fu′cian** (-shən) ***adj., n.***

con·fuse (kən fyo͞oz′) ***vt.*** **-fused′, -fus′ing** ⟦ME *confusen* < *confus*, perplexed < OFr < L *confusus*, pp. of *confundere*: see CONFOUND⟧ **1** to mix up; jumble together; put into disorder **2** to mix up mentally; specif., *a)* to bewilder; perplex *b)* to embarrass; disconcert; abash *c)* to fail to distinguish between; mistake the identity of **—*SYN.*** PUZZLE **—con·fus′ed·ly** (-fyo͞oz′ id lē) ***adv.*** **—con·fus′ed·ness *n.*** **—con·fus′ing *adj.*** **—con·fus′ing·ly *adv.***

con·fu·sion (kən fyo͞o′zhən) ***n.*** ⟦ME & OFr < L *confusio*⟧ a confusing or being confused; specif., *a)* state of disorder *b)* bewilderment; distraction *c)* embarrassment *d)* failure to distinguish between things **—covered with confusion** greatly embarrassed **—con·fu′sion·al *adj.***

SYN.—**confusion** suggests an indiscriminate mixing or putting together of things so that it is difficult to distinguish the individual elements or parts [the hall was a *confusion* of languages]; **disorder** and **disarray** imply a disturbance of the proper order or arrangement of parts [the room was in *disorder*, her clothes were in *disarray*]; **chaos** implies total and apparently irremediable lack of organization [the troops are in a state of *chaos*]; **jumble** suggests a confused mixture of dissimilar things [his drawer was a *jumble* of clothing and books]; **muddle** implies a snarled confusion resulting from mismanagement or incompetence [they've made a *muddle* of the negotiations] **—*ANT.* order, system**

con·fu·ta·tion (kän′fyo͞o tā′shən) ***n.*** ⟦L *confutatio* < pp. of *confutare*: see fol.⟧ **1** the act of confuting **2** an argument, evidence, etc. that confutes **—con·fu·ta·tive** (kən fyo͞ot′ə tiv) ***adj.***

con·fute (kən fyo͞ot′) ***vt.*** **-fut′ed, -fut′ing** ⟦L *confutare* < *com-*, intens. + **futare* < IE base **bhau-t*, **bhu-t*, to strike, BEAT⟧ **1** to prove (a person, statement, etc.) to be in error or false; overcome by argument or proof **2** [Obs.] to make useless **—*SYN.*** DISPROVE

cong *abbrev. Pharmacy* congius

Cong *abbrev.* **1** Congregational **2** Congress **3** Congressional

con·ga (käŋ′gə) ***n.*** ⟦AmSp *(danza) Conga*, Congo (dance) < Sp *Congo*, CONGO: from the assumed Afr orig. of the dance⟧ **1** a Latin American dance of African origin with a repeated pattern of three steps followed by a kick: the dancers typically form a winding line **2** syncopated music for this dance, in 2/4 time **3** an elongated bass drum played with the hands **—*vi.*** to dance the conga

Con·ga·ree (käŋ′gər ē) ⟦AmInd: meaning unknown⟧ river in S.C., joining the Wateree to form the Santee River: 52 mi (84 km)

con·gé (kän′zhā′, -jā′; *Fr* kōn zhā′) ***n.*** ⟦Fr, leave, departure < OFr *congie* < L *commeatus*, a going to and fro < *commeare*, to come and go < *com-*, intens. + *meare*, to go: see PERMEATE⟧ **1** a curt dismissal **2** permission to leave **3** a formal farewell **4** a bow, esp. at leave-taking **5** *Archit.* a concave molding

con·geal (kən jēl′) ***vt., vi.*** ⟦ME *congelen* < OFr *congeler* < L *congelare* < *com-*, together + *gelare*, to freeze: see GELATIN⟧ **1** to solidify or thicken by cooling or freezing **2** to thicken; coagulate; jell **—con·geal′a·ble *adj.*** **—con·geal′ment *n.***

con·gee[1] (kän′jē) ***n.*** ⟦ME *conge* < OFr *congie*⟧ [Now Rare] CONGÉ **—*vi.*** **-geed, -gee·ing** [Now Rare] to take formal leave; esp., to bow in leaving

con·gee[2] (kän′jē) ***n.*** ⟦< ? Tamil⟧ in Asian cooking, a thin gruel of rice and water

con·ge·la·tion (kän′jə lā′shən) ***n.*** ⟦ME *congelacioun* < OFr *congelation* < L *congelatio* < pp. of *congelare*⟧ **1** a congealing or being congealed **2** something congealed

con·ge·ner (kän′jə nər) ***n.*** ⟦L, of the same race or kind < *com-*, together + *genus* (gen. *generis*), race, GENUS⟧ **1** a person or thing of the same kind, class, race, or genus **2** a substance, formed in an alcoholic beverage during fermentation or distillation, that gives the beverage its characteristic flavor, color, etc. **—con′ge·ner′ic** (-ner′ik) ***adj.***, **con·gen·er·ous** (kən jen′ər əs)

con·gen·ial (kən jēn′yəl) ***adj.*** ⟦see COM- & GENIAL[1]⟧ **1** kindred; compatible [*congenial* tastes] **2** having the same tastes and temperament; friendly; sympathetic [*congenial* friends] **3** suited to one's needs or disposition; agreeable [*congenial* work] **—con·ge·ni·al·i·ty** (kən jē′nē al′ə tē) ***n.*** **—con·ge′nial·ly *adv.***

con·gen·i·tal (kən jen′ə təl) ***adj.*** ⟦< L *congenitus*, born together with < *com-*, together + *genitus*: see GENITAL⟧ **1** existing as such at birth [a *congenital* disease] **2** existing as if inborn; inherent [a *congenital* cheerfulness] **—*SYN.*** INNATE **—con·gen′i·tal·ly *adv.***

con·ger (eel) (käŋ′gər) ⟦ME < OFr *congre* < LL *congrus*, for L *conger* < Gr *gongros*, conger, prob. < IE base **geng-*, **gong-*, a lump, rounded object⟧

any of a family (Congridae, order Anguilliformes) of large saltwater eels, with a long dorsal fin, sharp teeth, and powerful jaws; esp., any of an edible genus (*Conger*) of eels

con·ge·ries (kän′jə rēz′, kän jir′ēz) ***n.***, *pl.* **-ri·es** ⟦L < *congerere*: see fol.⟧ a collection of things or parts massed together; heap; pile

con·gest (kən jest′) ***vt.*** ⟦< L *congestus*, pp. of *congerere*, to bring together, pile up < *com-*, together + *gerere*, to carry, perform⟧ **1** *a)* to cause too much blood, mucus, etc. to accumulate in the vessels of (a part of the body) *b)* to clog with mucus or other bodily fluid [*congested* sinuses] **2** to fill to excess; overcrowd [*a congested* highway] —***vi.*** to become congested —**con·ges′tion** (-jes′chən) ***n.*** —**con·ges′tive** (-jes′tiv) ***adj.***

congestive heart failure heart failure characterized by weakness, breathlessness, and abnormal congestion in the circulatory system, esp. in the lungs or lower legs

con·gi·us (kän′jē əs) ***n.***, *pl.* **-gi·i′** (-ī′) ⟦ME < L < Gr *konchos*, a measure, orig., CONCH⟧ an ancient Roman unit of liquid measure equal to a little less than seven pints

con·glo·bate (kən glō′bāt′, kän′glō bāt′) ***vt., vi.*** **-bat′ed, -bat′ing** ⟦L *conglobatus*, pp. of *conglobare* < *com-*, with + *globare*, to make into a globe < *globus*, GLOBE⟧ to form or collect into a ball or rounded mass: also **con·globe** (kən glōb′) —***adj.*** formed into a ball or rounded mass —**con′glo·ba′tion *n.***

con·glom·er·ate (kən gläm′ər āt′; *for adj. & n.*, -ər it) ***vt., vi.*** **-at′ed, -at′ing** ⟦< L *conglomeratus*, pp. of *conglomerare*, to roll together < *com-*, together + *glomerare*, to gather into a ball < *glomus*, a ball < IE **glem-* < base **gel-*: see CLIMB⟧ to form or collect into a rounded or compact mass —***adj.*** **1** formed or collected into a rounded or compact mass; clustered **2** made up of separate parts or substances collected together into a single mass **3** *Geol.* made up of rock fragments or pebbles cemented together by clay, silica, etc. Also **con·glom′er·at′ic** (-ər at′ik) or **con·glom′er·it′ic** (-ər it′ik) —***n.*** **1** a conglomerate mass; cluster ☆**2** a large corporation formed by the merger or acquisition of a number of companies in unrelated, widely diversified industries **3** *Geol.* a conglomerate rock

con·glom·er·a·teur (kən gläm′ər ə tʊr′) ***n.*** ⟦< prec. + *-eur*, as in ENTREPRENEUR⟧ a person who forms a business conglomerate

con·glom·er·a·tion (kən gläm′ər ā′shən) ***n.*** ⟦LL *conglomeratio*⟧ **1** a conglomerating or being conglomerated **2** a collection, mixture, or mass of miscellaneous things

con·glom·er·a·tor (kən gläm′ər āt′ər) ***n.*** CONGLOMERATEUR

con·glu·ti·nant (kən glo͞ot′′n ənt) ***adj.*** ⟦< L *conglutinans*, prp. of *conglutinare*: see fol.⟧ **1** conglutinating **2** *Med.* promoting healing or uniting, as of the edges of a wound

con·glu·ti·nate (kən glo͞ot′′n āt′) ***adj.*** ⟦ME *conglutinaten* < L *conglutinatus*, pp. of *conglutinare*, to glue together < *com-*, together + *glutinare*, to glue < *gluten*, GLUE⟧ glued or stuck together; adhering — ***vt., vi.*** **-nat′ed, -nat′ing** to stick together; unite by or as by adhesion —**con·glu′ti·na′tion *n.*** —**con·glu′ti·na′tive *adj.***

con·go (käŋ′gō) ***n.*** CONGOU

Con·go (käŋ′gō) **1** river in central Africa, flowing through the Democratic Republic of the Congo into the Atlantic: 2,718 mi (4,374 km) **2 Democratic Republic of the Congo** country in central Africa, on the equator: 905,568 sq mi (2,345,410 sq km); cap. Kinshasa: formerly *Belgian Congo* (1908-60); *Congo* (1960-71); *Zaire* (1971-97) **3 Republic of the Congo** country in WC Africa, west of the Democratic Republic of the Congo: 132,047 sq mi (342,000 sq km); cap. Brazzaville: formerly *People's Republic of the Congo* (1970-90) —**Con·go·lese** (käŋ′gə lēz′) ***adj., n.***

Congo dye (*or* **color**) any of certain azo dyes, derived mainly from benzidine

☆**congo eel** an eel-like salamander (*Amphiuma means*) with two pairs of very small, weak legs, found in the swamps of the SE U.S.: also called **congo snake**

Con·go-Kor·do·fan·i·an (-kôr′də fan′ē ən) ***adj.*** NIGER-KORDOFANIAN

Congo red a sodium salt, $C_{32}H_{22}O_6N_6S_2Na_2$, used for dyeing wool and cotton and as an acid-base indicator: it becomes blue in an acid solution and remains red in an alkaline or neutral solution

con·gou (käŋ′go͞o′) ***n.*** ⟦Amoy Chin *kong-hu*, labor: because the tea has been processed with care⟧ a variety of black Chinese tea

con·grat·u·late (kən grach′ə lāt′, -graj′-) ***vt.*** **-lat′ed, -lat′ing** ⟦< L *congratulatus*, pp. of *congratulari* < *com*,- together + *gratulari*, to wish joy < *gratus*, agreeable: see GRACE⟧ **1** to express to (a person) one's pleasure at good fortune or success; felicitate [*congratulate* the winner] **2** [Obs.] to rejoice at; celebrate **3** [Obs.] to greet; hail —**congratulate oneself** to take pride (in one's accomplishment, etc.) —**con·grat′u·la′tor *n.*** —**con·grat′u·la·to′ry** (-lə tôr′ē) ***adj.***

con·grat·u·la·tion (kən grach′ə lā′shən, -graj′-) ***n.*** ⟦< L *congratulatio*⟧ the act of congratulating

con·grat·u·la·tions (kən grach′ə lā′shənz, -graj′-) ***pl.n.*** expressions of pleasure and best wishes on the occasion of another's good fortune or success —***interj.*** I congratulate you Also [Slang] **con·grats′** (-grats′)

con·gre·gant (käŋ′grə gənt, kän′-) ***n.*** **1** one who congregates **2** a member of a congregation, specif. of a church, synagogue, etc.

con·gre·gate (käŋ′grə gāt′, kän′-; *for adj.*, -git) ***vt., vi.*** **-gat′ed, -gat′ing** ⟦< L *congregatus*, pp. of *congregare*, to congregate < *com-*, together + *gregare*, to collect into a flock, gather < *grex*, a flock: see GREGARIOUS⟧ to gather into a mass or crowd; collect; assemble —***adj.*** **1** assembled; collected **2** collective —**con′gre·ga′tive *adj.*** —**con′gre·ga′tor *n.***

con·gre·ga·tion (käŋ′grə gā′shən, kän′-) ***n.*** ⟦ME *congregacioun* < OFr *congregation* or L *congregatio*, an assembling (in ML(Ec), religious community)⟧ **1** a congregating or being congregated **2** a gathering of people or things; assemblage **3** an assembly of people for religious worship or teaching **4** the members of a particular place of worship ☆**5** a settlement, town, or parish in the colonies of early New England where Congregationalism was established **6** *Bible* the whole body or assembly of Israelites **7** *R.C.Ch.* *a)* any of certain religious communities following a common rule *b)* a division of an order, made up of a group of monasteries *c)* a committee, as of cardinals, in charge of some department of church affairs

con·gre·ga·tion·al (-shə nəl) ***adj.*** **1** of or like a congregation **2** [**C-**] of Congregationalism or Congregationalists

con·gre·ga·tion·al·ism (-shə nəl iz′əm) ***n.*** **1** a form of church organization in which each local congregation is self-governing **2** [**C-**] the beliefs and practices of a Protestant denomination in which each member church is self-governing: prominent in early New England and later marked by union with other Protestant denominations —**Con′gre·ga′tion·al·ist *n., adj.***

con·gress (käŋ′grəs, kän′-) ***n.*** ⟦ME *congresse* < L *congressus*, a meeting, hostile encounter, pp. of *congredi*, to come together < *com-*, together + *gradi*, to walk < *gradus*, a step: see GRADE⟧ **1** a coming together; meeting **2** sexual intercourse **3** social interaction **4** an association or society **5** an assembly or conference; specif., a formal assembly of representatives, as from various nations or churches, to discuss problems **6** any of various legislatures, esp. the national legislature of a republic ☆**7** [**C-**] *a)* the legislature of the U.S., consisting of the Senate and the House of Representatives *b)* a session of this legislature *c)* the body of Senators and Representatives during any of the two-year terms of Representatives

☆**congress boot** [*often* **C- b-**] a high shoe with an elastic insert in each side: also called **congress gaiter** (*or* **shoe**)

☆**con·gres·sion·al** (kən gresh′ə nəl) ***adj.*** ⟦< L *congressio*, a coming together < *congressus* (see CONGRESS) + -AL⟧ **1** of a congress **2** [**C-**] of Congress —**con·gres′sion·al·ly *adv.***

☆**Congressional district** any of the districts into which a state is divided for electing congressmen: each district elects a member of the House of Representatives

Congressional Medal *see* MEDAL OF HONOR

☆**Congressional Record** a daily publication of the proceedings of Congress, including a complete stenographic report of all remarks and debate

☆**con·gress·man** (käŋ′gris mən, kän′-) ***n.***, *pl.* **-men** (-mən) [*often* **C-**] a member of Congress, esp. of the House of Representatives

☆**Congress of Industrial Organizations** a group of affiliated labor unions in the U.S. and Canada, founded in 1938 and merged with the American Federation of Labor in 1955 to form the AFL-CIO

con·gress·per·son (-pʉr′sən) ***n.*** [*often* **C-**] CONGRESSMAN: used to avoid the masculine implication of *congressman*

con·gress·wom·an (-wo͝om′ən) ***n.***, *pl.* **-wom′en** (-wim′in) [*often* **C-**] a woman member of Congress, esp. of the House of Representatives

Con·greve (kän′grēv, käŋ′-), **William** 1670-1729; Eng. Restoration playwright

con·gru·ence (käŋ′gro͞o əns, kän′-; kən gro͞o′əns) ***n.*** ⟦ME < L *congruentia*: see fol.⟧ **1** the state or quality of being in agreement; correspondence; harmony **2** *Geom.* *a)* the property of a plane or solid figure whereby it coincides with another plane or solid figure as after being moved, rotated, or flipped over *b)* the property of having the same measure (said as of two lines or two angles) **3** *Math.* the relation between two integers each of which, when divided by a third (called the *modulus*), leaves the same remainder Also **con′gru·en·cy**

con·gru·ent (-ənt) ***adj.*** ⟦ME < L *congruens*, prp. of *congruere*, to come together, correspond, agree < *com-*, with + **gruere*, *ruere*, to fall: see RUIN⟧ **1** in agreement; corresponding; harmonious **2** *Geom.* *a)* of figures, having identical shape and size *b)* having the same measure (said as of two lines or two angles) **3** *Math.* in congruence [*congruent* numbers] —**con′gru·ent·ly *adv.***

con·gru·i·ty (kän gro͞o′ə tē, kən-) ***n.***, *pl.* **-ties** ⟦ME *congruite* < OFr < ML *congruitas*⟧ **1** the condition or fact of being congruous or congruent; specif., *a)* agreement; harmony *b)* fitness; appropriateness *c)* *Geom.* exact coincidence (of two or more figures) **2** an instance of agreement

con·gru·ous (käŋ′gro͞o əs, kän′-) ***adj.*** ⟦L *congruus*⟧ **1** congruent **2** corresponding to what is right, proper, or reasonable; fitting; suitable; appropriate —**con′gru·ous·ly *adv.*** —**con′gru·ous·ness *n.***

con·ic (kän′ik) ***adj.*** ⟦ModL *conicus* < Gr *kōnikos* < *kōnos*, a peak, CONE⟧ conical —***n.*** CONIC SECTION

con·i·cal (kän′i kəl) ***adj.*** **1** of a cone **2** resembling or shaped like a cone —**con′i·cal·ly *adv.***

conic projection a type of map projection made by projecting and reproducing an image of the earth's surface on the surface of a cone and unrolling this to a plane surface on which the parallels of latitude are then concentric circles and the meridians equally spaced radii

conic section **1** a curve, either an ellipse, circle, parabola, or hyperbola, produced by the intersection of a plane with a right circular cone **2** [*pl.*, *with sing. v.*] the branch of geometry dealing with ellipses, circles, parabolas, and hyperbolas: also **con′ics *n.***

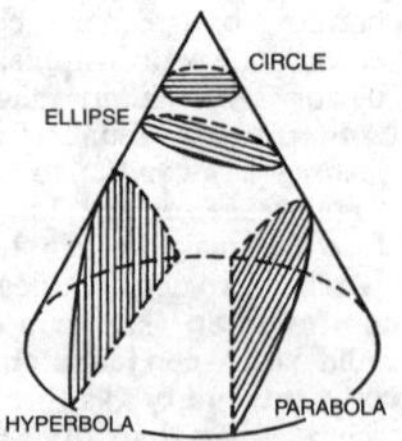

conic sections

co·nid·i·al (kō nid′ē əl, kə-) ***adj.*** 1 of or like conidia 2 producing conidia Also **co·nid′i·an**

co·nid·i·o·phore (kō nid′ē ə fôr′, kə-) ***n.*** ⟦< fol. + -PHORE⟧ a specialized branch of the hypha, in certain fungi, that bears conidia

co·nid·i·um (kō nid′ē əm, kə-) ***n., pl.*** **-i·a** (-ə) ⟦ModL < Gr *konis,* dust (see INCINERATE) + -IUM⟧ a small asexual spore abstricted from the tip of a conidiophore in certain fungi

con·i·fer (kän′ə fər, kō′nə-) ***n.*** ⟦L, cone-bearing: see CONE & -FER⟧ any of a class (Pinatae) of cone-bearing, gymnospermous trees and shrubs, mostly evergreens, including the pine, spruce, fir, cedar, yew, and cypress

co·nif·er·ous (kō nif′ər əs, kə-) ***adj.*** 1 bearing cones 2 of conifers

co·ni·ine (kō′nē ēn′, -in; kō′nēn′) ***n.*** ⟦< fol. + -INE[3]⟧ a very poisonous, oily alkaloid, $C_8H_{17}N$, extracted from the poison hemlock: also **co·nine** (kō′nēn, kō′nin)

co·ni·um (kō′nē əm, kō nī′əm) ***n.*** ⟦ModL < Gr *kōneion,* hemlock; prob. akin to *kōnos,* CONE⟧ any of a small genus (*Conium*) of poisonous biennial herbs of the umbel family, with carrotlike leaves and rounded fruits, as the poison hemlock

conj *abbrev.* 1 conjugation 2 conjunction

con·jec·tur·al (kən jek′chər əl) ***adj.*** 1 based on or involving conjecture 2 inclined to make conjectures —**con·jec′tur·al·ly** ***adv.***

con·jec·ture (kən jek′chər) ***n.*** ⟦ME < L *conjectura,* a putting together, guess, inference < *conjectus,* pp. of *conjicere,* to throw together, guess < *com-,* together + *jacere,* to throw: see JET[1]⟧ 1 an inferring, theorizing, or predicting from incomplete or uncertain evidence; guesswork [an editorial full of *conjecture*] 2 an inference, theory, or prediction based on guesswork; guess 3 [Obs.] occult divination —***vt.*** **-tured, -tur·ing** to arrive at or propose by conjecture; guess —***vi.*** to make a conjecture —**SYN.** GUESS —**con·jec′tur·a·ble** ***adj.***

con·join (kən join′) ***vt., vi.*** ⟦ME *conjoinen* < OFr *conjoindre* < L *conjungere* < *com-,* together + *jungere,* JOIN⟧ to join together; unite; combine

con·joint (-joint′) ***adj.*** ⟦OFr < L *conjunctus,* pp. of *conjungere*: see prec.⟧ 1 joined together; united; combined; associated 2 of or involving two or more in association; joint —**con·joint′ly** ***adv.***

con·ju·gal (kän′jə gəl) ***adj.*** ⟦L *conjugalis* < *conjunx, conjux,* husband or wife < *com-,* together + base akin to L *jugum,* YOKE, *jungere,* JOIN⟧ of marriage or the relation between husband and wife; matrimonial; specif., of or accommodating the sexual relations between spouses [*conjugal* visits to a spouse in prison] —**con′ju·gal′i·ty** (-jə gal′ə tē) ***n.*** —**con′ju·gal·ly** ***adv.***

con·ju·gant (kän′jə gənt) ***n.*** either of a pair of one-celled organisms, or of gametes, in the process of conjugation

con·ju·gate (kän′jə gət; *also, and for v. always,* -gāt′) ***adj.*** ⟦ME *conjugat* < L *conjugatus,* pp. of *conjugare,* to join together < *com-,* together + *jugare,* to join < *jugum,* YOKE⟧ 1 joined together, esp. in a pair; coupled 2 *Bot.* BIJUGATE 3 *Chem. a)* related to each other by the difference of a proton: said of acids and bases *b)* of or pertaining to the alternation of single and double bonds in organic compounds 4 *Gram.* derived from the same base and, usually, related in meaning: said of words 5 *Math.* specially related or having the same or similar properties, as two points, lines, or quantities —***n.*** 1 a conjugate word 2 a conjugate point, line, quantity, etc. 3 a chemically conjugated substance —***vt.*** **-gat′ed, -gat′ing** 1 [Archaic] to join together; unite; couple 2 *Biochem.* to join (compounds) so that the resulting substance can be readily removed, as a toxic product in the body 3 *Gram.* to inflect (a verb) systematically, giving its different forms according to voice, mood, tense, number, and person —***vi.*** 1 *Biol.* to unite in conjugation 2 *Gram. a)* to conjugate a verb *b)* to be conjugated —**con′ju·ga′tor** ***n.***

conjugated protein a combination of a protein with a nonprotein molecule, as in hemoglobin

con·ju·ga·tion (kän′jə gā′shən) ***n.*** ⟦ME *conjugacion* < L *conjugatio*⟧ 1 a conjugating or being conjugated; union 2 *Biol.* any of various types of sexual reproduction in which certain algae, fungi, etc. exchange genetic material 3 *Gram. a)* a methodical presentation or arrangement of the inflectional forms of a verb; paradigm *b)* the act or process of producing such an arrangement or paradigm *c)* a class of verbs with similar inflectional forms —**con′ju·ga′tion·al** ***adj.*** —**con′ju·ga′tion·al·ly** ***adv.*** —**con′ju·ga′tive** ***adj.***

con·junct (kən juŋkt′; *also, and for n. always,* kän′juŋkt′) ***adj.*** ⟦ML < L *conjunctus,* pp. of *conjungere*: see CONJOIN⟧ 1 joined together; joint; associated 2 *Music* pertaining to progression by successive degrees of a scale —***n.*** a person or thing joined or associated with another

con·junc·tion (kən juŋk′shən) ***n.*** ⟦ME *conjunccion* < OFr *conjunction* < L *conjunctio* < pp. of *conjungere:* see CONJOIN⟧ 1 a joining together or being joined together; union; association; combination 2 an occurring together; coincidence [the *conjunction* of events] 3 *Astrol., Astron.* the condition of two or more celestial bodies, esp. a planet with the sun, located along the same celestial longitude when observed from the earth 4 *Gram.* an uninflected word used to connect words, phrases, clauses, or sentences; connective: conjunctions may be coordinating (Ex.: *and, but, or*), subordinating (Ex.: *if, when, as, because, though*), or correlative (Ex.: *either . . . or, both . . . and*) —**con·junc′tion·al** ***adj.*** —**con·junc′tion·al·ly** ***adv.***

con·junc·ti·va (kän′jəŋk tī′və) ***n., pl.*** **-vas** or **-vae** (-vē) ⟦ME < ML (*membrana*) *conjunctiva,* connecting (membrane): see fol.⟧ the mucous membrane lining the inner surface of the eyelids and covering the front part of the eyeball —**con′junc·ti′val** ***adj.***

con·junc·tive (kən juŋk′tiv) ***adj.*** ⟦ME *conjunctif* < L *conjunctivus,* connective (in LL, subjunc. mood) < *conjunctus:* see CONJOINT⟧ 1 serving to join together; connective 2 united; combined; joint 3 *Gram. a)* used as a conjunction [the *conjunctive* adverb "consequently"] *b)* connecting both the meaning and the construction of sentence elements ["and" and "moreover" are *conjunctive*] *c)* always used in conjunction with the verb: said of unstressed forms of personal, reflexive, or reciprocal pronouns in some Romance languages (Ex.: *me* in French *il me faut*) —***n.*** *Gram.* a conjunctive word; esp., a conjunction —**con·junc′tive·ly** ***adv.***

con·junc·ti·vi·tis (kən juŋk′tə vīt′is) ***n.*** ⟦ModL: see CONJUNCTIVA & -ITIS⟧ inflammation of the conjunctiva

con·junc·ture (kən juŋk′chər) ***n.*** ⟦ML *conjunctura:* see CONJOIN⟧ 1 [Rare] a joining together or being joined together 2 a combination of events or circumstances, esp. one creating a critical situation; crisis

con·jun·to (kän khōōn′tō) ***n.*** ⟦Sp⟧ 1 a lively Latin American dance music of Cuban and Mexican origin, influenced by European polkas, Mexican ballads, etc. 2 *pl.* **-tos** a band, featuring male vocalists, an accordion, trumpets, a large 12-string guitar, percussion, etc., that plays this music

con·ju·ra·tion (kän′jə rā′shən) ***n.*** ⟦ME *conjuracioun* < L *conjuratio*⟧ 1 the act of conjuring; invocation 2 a magic spell; incantation 3 magic; sorcery 4 [Archaic] a solemn entreaty; adjuration

con·jure (kun′jər, kän′-; *for vi. 1 & vt. 1* kən joor′) ***vi.*** **-jured, -jur·ing** ⟦ME *conjuren* < OFr *conjurer* < L *conjurare,* to swear together, conspire < *com-,* together + *jurare,* to swear: see JURY[1]⟧ 1 [Obs.] to be sworn in a conspiracy 2 to summon a demon or spirit as by a magic spell 3 to practice magic or legerdemain —***vt.*** 1 to call upon or entreat solemnly, esp. by some oath 2 to summon (a demon or spirit) as by a magic spell 3 to bring about by conjuration —**conjure up** 1 to cause to be or appear as by magic or legerdemain 2 to call to mind [the music *conjured up* memories]

con·jur·er or **con·ju·ror** (kun′jər ər, kän′-; *for 1* kən joor′ər) ***n.*** ⟦ME *conjurour*: see prec.⟧ 1 a person who solemnly entreats or appeals to someone 2 a magician; sorcerer 3 a person skilled in legerdemain

conk[1] (käŋk, kôŋk) [Slang] ***n.*** ⟦< CONCH⟧ 1 [Brit.] the nose 2 the head 3 a blow on the head —***vt.*** to hit on the head —**conk out** 1 to stop suddenly to operate or function 2 to become very tired and fall asleep 3 to die

conk[2] (käŋk, kôŋk) ***n.*** ⟦altered < ? CONCH⟧ ☆a shelflike growth of fungus found on various trees, usually on the trunk

☆**conk**[3] (käŋk, kôŋk) ***n.*** ⟦< ? name of a kind of copal, used for straightening hair⟧ a hair style, as worn by some blacks, in which the hair is straightened, as with lye, and smoothed down —***vt.*** to straighten and arrange hair thus

conk·er (käŋ′kər) ***n.*** ⟦Brit dial., orig., a snail shell (< CONCH + -ER): the game was orig. played with shells⟧ [Brit.] 1 [*pl., with sing. v.*] a child's game played with horse chestnuts tied to strings 2 a horse chestnut

☆**con man** [Informal] CONFIDENCE MAN

con mo·to (kän mō′tō; *It* kôn mô′tô) ⟦It, with motion⟧ *Musical Direction* with animated movement

conn (kän) ***vt.*** **conned, conn′ing** ⟦earlier *cond* < ME *conduen,* to conduct < OFr *conduire* < L *conducere*: see CONDUCE⟧ *Naut.* to direct the movements of (a ship), specif. by giving directions to the helmsman —***n.*** *Naut.* 1 the station of a person who conns 2 the act of or responsibility for conning a ship

Conn *abbrev.* Connecticut

Con·nacht (kän′ôt, -əkht) province of NW Ireland: 6,609 sq mi (17,117 sq km)

con·nate (kə nāt′, kän′āt′) ***adj.*** ⟦LL *connatus,* pp. of *connasci,* to be born at the same time < L *com-,* together + *nasci,* to be born: see NATURE⟧ 1 inborn; innate 2 coexisting since birth or the beginning 3 having the same origin or nature; related; cognate —**con′nate·ly** ***adv.***

con·nat·u·ral (kän′nach′ər əl, kən-) ***adj.*** ⟦ML *connaturalis:* see prec.⟧ 1 innate; natural 2 related in nature; cognate —**con′nat′u·ral·ly** ***adv.*** —**con·nat′u·ral·ness** ***n.***

Con·naught (kän′ôt) *var. of* CONNACHT

con·nect (kə nekt′) ***vt.*** ⟦ME *connecten* < L *connectere,* to bind together < *com-,* together + *nectere,* to fasten⟧ 1 to join or fasten (two things together, or one thing *with* or *to* another); link; couple 2 to show or think of as related; associate [to *connect* germs with disease] 3 to provide with a circuit for communicating by telephone 4 to plug into an electrical circuit —***vi.*** 1 to join or be joined ☆2 to meet so that passengers can transfer promptly: said of trains, buses, etc. 3 to be related in some way or in a proper or logical way 4 [Informal] *a)* to reach the thing aimed at *b)* to establish a rapport (*with*) *c)* *Sports* to hit a ball, target, etc. solidly *d)* *Sports* to be successful [*connected* on eighty percent of his shots] —**SYN.** JOIN —**con·nec′tor** ***n.***, **con·nect′er**

con·nect·ed (-nek′tid) ***adj.*** 1 linked together; united 2 linked together coherently or logically [expressing *connected* ideas on a subject] 3 related by blood 4 having social or professional relationships, or connections: usually in the phrase **well-connected** —**con·nect′ed·ly** ***adv.*** —**con·nect′ed·ness** ***n.***

Con·nect·i·cut (kə net′ə kət) ⟦< Algonquin (Mahican), lit., place of the long river⟧ 1 New England state of the U.S.: one of the 13 original states; 4,845 sq mi (12,548 sq km); cap. Hartford: abbrev. *CT* or *Conn* 2 river in NE U.S., flowing from N N.H. across Mass. & Conn. into Long Island Sound: 407 mi (655 km)

Con·nect·i·cut·er (-kət ər) ***n.*** a person born or living in Connecticut

connecting rod a reciprocating rod connecting two or more moving parts of a machine, as the crankshaft and a piston of an automobile

con·nec·tion (kə nek′shən) ***n.*** ⟦ME *conneccioun* < L *connexio* < *connexus,* pp. of *connectere:* see CONNECT⟧ 1 a joining or being joined; coupling; union 2 a part or thing that joins; means of joining **3** a relationship; association; specif., *a)* the relation between things that depend on, involve, or follow each other; causal relationship *b)* the logical linking together of words or ideas; coherence *c)* the relationship of a word or statement to the context, as it affects the meaning [in that *connection*, let me say this] *d)* affinity as by family ties, business, or common interests **4** *a)* a relative, as by distant kinship or marriage *b)* a business associate or acquaintance, esp. an influential one through whom one can get special favors: *usually used in pl.* ☆**5** [*often pl.*] the act or a means of transferring from one train, bus, etc. to another in the course of a journey **6** a group of people associated together as in politics, business, or worship **7** a religious sect or denomination **8** a telephone or telegraph line between points ☆**9** [Slang] *a)* a person who sells narcotics illicitly to addicts *b)* a narcotics sale or purchase **10** *Elec.* a circuit —**in connection with 1** together with; in conjunction with **2** with reference to —**con·nec′tion·al** *adj.*

con·nec·tive (kə nek′tiv) *adj.* connecting or serving to connect —*n.* **1** something that connects; esp., a word that connects phrases, clauses, or other words, as a conjunction or relative pronoun **2** *Bot.* an anther's lobe-connecting tissue that splits open, allowing the pollen to escape —**con·nec′tive·ly** *adv.* —**con·nec·tiv·i·ty** (kän′ek tiv′ə tē, kə nek′-) *n.*

connective tissue tissue found throughout the body, serving to bind together and support other tissues and organs: it includes various kinds of fibrous tissue, fat, bone, and cartilage

con·nex·ion (kə nek′shən) *n. Brit. sp. of* CONNECTION

conning tower ⟦prp. of CONN⟧ **1** a heavily armored pilothouse on a warship, for use in battle **2** a low observation tower on a submarine, serving also as an entrance to the interior

☆**con·nip·tion** (kə nip′shən) *n.* ⟦arbitrary pseudo-Latin coinage⟧ [*often pl.*] [Informal] a fit of anger, hysteria, etc.; tantrum: also **conniption fit**

con·niv·ance (kə nī′vəns) *n.* ⟦Fr *connivence* < L *coniventia*, < prp. of *conivere*: see fol.⟧ **1** the act of conniving **2** passive cooperation, as by consent or pretended ignorance, esp. in wrongdoing

con·nive (kə nīv′) *vi.* **-nived′**, **-niv′ing** ⟦< L *conivere*, to wink, connive < *com-*, intens. + base akin to *nictare*, to wink < IE base **knei-gwh-*, to bend > Goth *hneiwan*, to bend, bow, OE *hnigian*, to bow (the head)⟧ **1** to pretend not to see or look (*at* something wrong or evil), thus giving tacit consent or cooperation; feign ignorance of another's wrongdoing **2** *a)* to cooperate secretly (*with* someone), esp. in wrongdoing; conspire *b)* to scheme in an underhanded way —**con·niv′er** *n.*

con·niv·ent (-nī′vənt) *adj.* ⟦L *conivens*, prp. of *conivere*: see prec.⟧ *Biol.* with the ends inclined toward each other, as wings or anthers

con·nois·seur (kän′ə sʉr′, -soor′) *n.* ⟦Fr (now *connaisseur*) < OFr *conoisseor*, a judge, one well versed < *conoistre* < L *cognoscere*, to know: see COGNITION⟧ a person who has expert knowledge and keen discrimination in some field, esp. in the fine arts or in matters of taste —**SYN.** AESTHETE —**con′nois·seur′ship** *n.*

con·no·ta·tion (kän′ə tā′shən) *n.* ⟦ME *connotacion* < ML *connotatio*⟧ **1** the act or process of connoting **2** something connoted; idea or notion suggested by or associated with a word, phrase, etc. in addition to its explicit meaning, or denotation ["politician" has different *connotations* from "statesman"] **3** *Logic* the properties possessed by all the objects in a term's extension; intension: cf. DENOTATION (sense 5) —**con·no·ta·tive** (kän′ə tāt′iv, kə nōt′ə tiv) *adj.*, **con′no·ta′tion·al** —**con′no·ta′tive·ly** *adv.*

con·note (kə nōt′) *vt.* **-not′ed**, **-not′ing** ⟦ML *connotare* < L *com-*, together + *notare*, to mark: see NOTE⟧ **1** to suggest or convey (associations, overtones, etc.) in addition to the explicit, or denoted, meaning [the word "mother" means "female parent," but it generally *connotes* love, care, tenderness, etc.] **2** to imply or involve as a result, accompaniment, etc.

con·nu·bi·al (kə noo′bē əl, -nyoo′-) *adj.* ⟦L *conubialis* < *conubium*, marriage < *com-*, together + *nubere*, to marry: see NUBILE⟧ of marriage or the state of being married; conjugal —**con·nu′bi·al′i·ty** (-bē al′ə tē) *n.* —**con·nu′bi·al·ly** *adv.*

co·no·dont (kō′nə dänt′, kän′ə-) *n.* ⟦Ger *konodont* < Gr *kōnos*, a wedge, CONE + *odous* (gen. *odontos*), TOOTH⟧ a very small fossil of the Paleozoic and Mesozoic eras, prob. a tooth from an extinct, eel-like vertebrate

co·noid (kō′noid′) *adj.* ⟦Gr *kōnoeidēs*: see CONE & -OID⟧ cone-shaped: also **co·noi′dal** —*n.* **1** a cone-shaped thing **2** *Geom.* a solid described by a conic section revolving about its axis

con·quer (käŋ′kər, kän′-) *vt.* ⟦ME *conqueren* < OFr *conquerre* < VL **conquaerere* (for L *conquirere*), to search for, procure < L *com-*, intens. + *quaerere*, to seek, acquire⟧ **1** to get possession or control of by or as by winning a war **2** to overcome by physical, mental, or moral force; get the better of; defeat —*vi.* to make conquests; win —**con′quer·a·ble** *adj.* —**con′quer·or** *n.*

SYN.—**conquer** implies gaining mastery over someone or something by physical, mental, or moral force [to *conquer* bad habits]; **vanquish** implies a thorough overpowering or frustrating, often in a single conflict or battle [a *vanquished* army]; to **defeat** is to get the better of, often only for the time being [the *defeated* troops rallied and counterattacked]; **overcome** implies the overpowering of an antagonist or the surmounting of difficulties; to **subdue** is to defeat so as to break the spirit of resistance; to **subjugate** is to bring under complete subjection; **overthrow** implies a victory in which a prevailing power is dislodged by force; to **rout** is to defeat so overwhelmingly that the enemy is put to disorderly flight

con·quest (käŋ′kwest′, kän′-) *n.* ⟦ME *conqueste* < OFr < ML *conquestus* < L *conquisitus*, pp. of *conquirere*⟧ **1** the act or process of conquering **2** something conquered, esp. land taken in war **3** *a)* a winning of someone's affection or favor *b)* a person whose affection or favor has been won —**SYN.** VICTORY —**the (Norman) Conquest** the conquering of England by the Normans under William the Conqueror in 1066

con·quis·ta·dor (kän kēs′tə dôr′, -kwis′-) *n.*, *pl.* **con·quis′ta·dors′** or **con·quis′ta·dor′es′** (-dôr′ēz′, -ās′) ⟦Sp, conqueror < *conquistar*, to conquer, defeat < pp. of VL **conquaerere*: see CONQUER⟧ any of the Spanish conquerors of Mexico, Peru, or other parts of America in the 16th cent.

Con·rad[1] (kän′rad) *n.* ⟦Ger *Konrad* or Fr *Conrade*; both < OHG *Kuonrat*, *Chuonrat*, lit., bold or wise counselor < *kuon*, bold, wise (akin to KEEN[1]) + *rat*, counsel < *ratan*, to advise (akin to READ[1])⟧ a masculine name

Con·rad[2] (kän′rad), **Joseph** (born *Józef Teodor Konrad Nalecz Korzeniowski*) 1857-1924; Eng. novelist, born in Poland

cons *abbrev.* **1** consecrated **2** consolidated **3** consonant **4** constable **5** constitutional **6** construction **7** consul

Cons *abbrev.* **1** constable **2** Constitution **3** consul

con·san·guin·e·ous (kän′saŋ gwin′ē əs, -san-) *adj.* ⟦L *consanguineus*, of the same blood: see COM- & SANGUINE⟧ having the same ancestor; closely related: also **con·san′guine** (-saŋ′gwin) —**con′san·guin′e·ous·ly** *adv.*

con·san·guin·i·ty (kän′saŋ gwin′ə tē, -san-) *n.* ⟦ME & OFr *consanguinite* < L *consanguinitas*: see prec.⟧ **1** relationship by descent from the same ancestor; blood relationship: distinguished from AFFINITY **2** close association; connection

con·science (kän′shəns) *n.* ⟦OFr < L *conscientia*, consciousness, moral sense < prp. of *conscire* < *com-*, with + *scire*, to know (see SCIENCE): replacing ME *inwit*, knowledge within⟧ **1** a knowledge or sense of right and wrong, with an urge to do right; moral judgment that opposes the violation of a previously recognized ethical principle and that leads to feelings of guilt if one violates such a principle **2** [Obs.] *a)* consciousness *b)* inner thoughts or feelings —**in (all) conscience** in fairness; on any reasonable ground —**on one's conscience** causing one to feel guilty —**con′science·less** *adj.*

conscience clause a clause in a law exempting those whose religious or moral principles forbid compliance

conscience money money one pays to relieve one's conscience, as in compensation for some former dishonesty

con·science-strick·en (-strik′ən) *adj.* feeling guilty or remorseful because of having done some wrong

con·sci·en·tious (kän′shē en′shəs) *adj.* ⟦Fr *conscientieux* < ML *conscientiosus*: see CONSCIENCE & -OUS⟧ **1** governed by, or made or done according to, what one knows is right; scrupulous; honest **2** showing care and precision; painstaking —**con′sci·en′tious·ly** *adv.* —**con′sci·en′tious·ness** *n.*

conscientious objector ☆a person who for reasons of conscience refuses to take part in warfare

con·scion·a·ble (kän′shə nə bəl) *adj.* ⟦< CONSCIENCE + -ABLE⟧ [Obs.] CONSCIENTIOUS (sense 1) —**con′scion·a·bly** *adv.*

con·scious (kän′shəs) *adj.* ⟦L *conscius*, knowing, aware < *conscire*: see CONSCIENCE⟧ **1** having a feeling or knowledge (*of* one's own sensations, feelings, etc. or *of* external things); knowing or feeling (*that* something is or was happening or existing); aware; cognizant **2** able to feel and think; in the normal waking state **3** aware of oneself as a thinking being; knowing what one is doing and why **4** SELF-CONSCIOUS **5** accompanied by an awareness of what one is thinking, feeling, and doing; intentional [*conscious* humor] **6** known to or felt by oneself [*conscious* guilt] —**SYN.** AWARE —**the conscious** *Psychol.* that part of one's mental activity of which one is fully aware at any given time: see also UNCONSCIOUS, PRECONSCIOUS —**con′scious·ly** *adv.*

-con·scious (kän′shəs) *combining form* aware of and attaching importance to [status-*conscious*]

con·scious·ness (kän′shəs nis) *n.* **1** the state of being conscious; awareness of one's own feelings, what is happening around one, etc. **2** the totality of one's thoughts, feelings, and impressions; conscious mind

☆**con·scious·ness-rais·ing** (-rā′ziŋ) *n.* the process of making a person aware of, or informed about, a social issue so as to elicit an appropriate or desired response

con·script (kən skript′; *for adj. & n.* kän′skript′) ☆*vt.* ⟦< the *adj.*⟧ **1** to enroll for compulsory service in the armed forces; draft **2** to force (labor, capital, etc.) into service for the government —*adj.* ⟦L *conscriptus*, pp. of *conscribere*, to enroll < *com-*, with + *scribere*, to write⟧ conscripted —*n.* a conscripted person; draftee —**con·scrip′tion** *n.*

con·se·crate (kän′si krāt′) *vt.* **-crat′ed**, **-crat′ing** ⟦ME *consecraten* < L *consecratus*, pp. of *consecrare* < *com-*, together + *sacrare*: see SACRED⟧ **1** *a)* to set apart as holy; make or declare sacred for religious use *b)* to make (someone) a bishop, ruler, etc. by a religious ceremony **2** to devote entirely; dedicate [to *consecrate* one's life to art] **3** to cause to be revered or honored; hallow [ground *consecrated* by their martyrdom] —*adj.* [Archaic] consecrated —**SYN.** DEVOTE —**con′se·cra′tor** *n.* —**con′se·cra·to′ry** (-kre tôr′ē) *adj.*

con·se·cra·tion (kän′si krā′shən) *n.* **1** a consecrating or being consecrated **2** a ceremony for this **3** [*often* **C-**] the act or an instance of consecrating the bread and wine in the Mass or in a Communion service

con·se·cu·tion (kän′si kyoo′shən) *n.* ⟦ME *consecucioun* < L *consecutio*: see fol.⟧ **1** logical sequence; chain of reasoning **2** sequence; succession

con·sec·u·tive (kən sek′yoo tiv, -yə-) *adj.* ⟦Fr *consécutif* < ML *consecutivus* < pp. of L *consequi*: see CONSEQUENCE⟧ **1** following in order, without interruption; successive [for four *consecutive* days] **2** proceeding from one part or idea to the next in logical order, as a story, reasoning, etc. —**con·sec′u·tive·ly** *adv.* —**con·sec′u·tive·ness** *n.*

con·sen·su·al (kən sen′sho͞o əl) *adj.* ⟦< fol. + -AL⟧ 1 involving consent, esp. mutual consent 2 *Rom. Law* of contracts, existing by the mere consent of the parties 3 *Physiol.* of or caused by reflex action that occurs either with voluntary action or because of stimulation to a corresponding part: said as of the reaction of both pupils when only one is stimulated —**con·sen′su·al·ly** *adv.*

con·sen·sus (kən sen′səs) *n.* ⟦L < pp. of *consentire:* see fol.⟧ 1 an opinion held by all or most 2 general agreement, esp. in opinion

con·sent (kən sent′) *vi.* ⟦ME *consenten* < OFr *consentir* < L *consentire* < *com-*, with + *sentire,* to feel: see SENSE⟧ 1 *a)* to agree (*to* do something) *b)* to willingly engage in a sexual act (often in the phrase **consenting adult**) *c)* to give permission, approval, or assent (*to* something proposed or requested) in opinion 2 [Obs.] to agree —*n.* 1 permission, approval, or assent; specif., INFORMED CONSENT 2 agreement in opinion or sentiment *[*by common *consent]* —**con·sent′er** *n.*

SYN.—**consent** implies compliance with something proposed or requested, stressing this as an act of the will; to **assent** is to express acceptance of or adherence to an opinion or proposition; **agree** implies accord reached by settling differences of opinion or overcoming resistance; **concur** implies agreement arrived at formally on a specific matter, often with regard to a line of action; to **accede** is to yield one's assent to a proposal; **acquiesce** implies tacit agreement or restraint of opposition in accepting something about which one has reservations —*ANT.* **dissent, refuse, deny**

con·sen·ta·ne·ous (kän′sen tā′nē əs) *adj.* ⟦L *consentaneus:* see prec.⟧ [Rare] 1 agreeing; suited (*to*); consistent (*with*) 2 unanimous —**con′sen·ta′ne·ous·ly** *adv.*

consent decree a negotiated agreement of the parties to a lawsuit which resolves the disputed issues and is sanctioned by the court; often, specif., such an agreement by which the defendant agrees to cease an activity or practice asserted by the government to be illegal: also **consent judgment** (or **agreement**)

con·sen·tient (kən sen′shənt) *adj.* ⟦L *consentiens,* prp. of *consentire:* see CONSENT⟧ united in opinion; agreeing

con·se·quence (kän′si kwens′, -kwəns) *n.* ⟦OFr < L *consequentia* < *consequens,* prp. of *consequi,* to follow after < *com-*, with + *sequi,* to follow: see SEQUENT⟧ 1 a result of an action, process, etc.; outcome or effect, often, specif., an adverse one 2 a logical result or conclusion; inference 3 the relation of effect to cause 4 importance as a cause or influence *[*a matter of slight *consequence]* 5 importance in rank; influence *[*a person of *consequence]* —*SYN.* EFFECT, IMPORTANCE —**in consequence (of)** as a result (of) —**take the consequences** to accept the adverse results of one's actions

con·se·quent (-kwent′, -kwənt) *adj.* ⟦OFr < L *consequens:* see prec.⟧ 1 following as a result; resulting 2 proceeding in logical sequence —*n.* 1 anything that follows 2 *Logic a)* the second term of a conditional proposition *b)* an inference 3 *Math.* the second term, denominator, or divisor of a ratio: distinguished from ANTECEDENT —**consequent on (or upon)** 1 following as a result of 2 inferred from

con·se·quen·tial (kän′si kwen′shəl) *adj.* ⟦< L *consequentia* (see CONSEQUENCE) + -AL⟧ 1 following as an effect or inference 2 important 3 [Rare] acting important; pompous —**con′se·quen′ti·al′i·ty** (-shē al′ə tē) *n.*, **con′se·quen′tial·ness** —**con′se·quen′tial·ly** *adv.*

con·se·quent·ly (kän′si kwent′lē, -kwənt-) *adv.* ⟦ME⟧ as a result; by logical inference; therefore

con·serv·an·cy (kən sʉr′vən sē) *n.* 1 conservation of natural resources 2 [Brit.] a commission authorized to supervise a forest, river, or port 3 an organization dedicated to the protection of natural resources, historical buildings, etc.

con·ser·va·tion (kän′sər vā′shən) *n.* ⟦ME *conservacioun* < OFr *conservation* < L *conservatio*⟧ 1 the act or practice of conserving; protection from loss, waste, etc.; preservation 2 the official care, protection, or management of natural resources 3 the preservation, reconditioning, and restoration of works of art —**con′ser·va′tion·al** *adj.*

con·ser·va·tion·ist (-ist) *n.* a person who advocates the conservation of natural resources

conservation of energy the principle that the total energy in an isolated physical system does not increase or diminish but only changes form

conservation of matter the principle that matter is neither created nor destroyed during any physical or chemical change: also **conservation of mass**

con·serv·a·tism (kən sʉr′və tiz′əm) *n.* the principles and practices of a conservative person or party; tendency to oppose change in institutions and methods

con·serv·a·tive (kən sʉr′və tiv) *adj.* ⟦OFr *conservatif* < LL *conservativus*⟧ 1 conserving or tending to conserve; preservative 2 of or characteristic of a conservative; tending to preserve established ways or institutions and to resist or oppose radical change; specif., *a)* of a political tendency or movement in recent times variously promoting laissez-faire capitalism and more decentralized government and opposing gun control, legalized abortion, etc. *b)* [**C-**] designating or of the major political party of Great Britain or the similar one in Canada that is characterized by conservative positions on social and economic issues ☆3 moderate; cautious; safe *[*a *conservative* estimate*]* 4 [**C-**] *Judaism* designating or of a movement that accepts traditional forms and religious ritual that have been adapted to modern life with moderation and flexibility —*n.* 1 [Archaic] a preservative 2 a conservative person 3 [**C-**] a member of the Conservative Party of Great Britain or of the Conservative Party of Canada —**con·serv′a·tive·ly** *adv.* —**con·serv′a·tive·ness** *n.*

con·serv·a·tize (-tīz′) *vt.* **-tized′**, **-tiz′ing** to make politically or socially conservative

con·ser·va·toire (kən sʉr′və twär′, -sʉr′və twär′) *n.* ⟦Fr < It *conservatorio*⟧ CONSERVATORY (*n.* 2)

con·ser·va·tor (kən sʉr′və tôr′, -vət ər; *also* kän′sər vāt′ər) *n.* ⟦ME *conservatour* < L *conservator* < pp. of *conservare:* see CONSERVE⟧ 1 a protector, guardian, or custodian 2 a person whose work is the preservation, reconditioning, and restoration of works of art —**con·ser′va·tor·ship′** *n.*

con·serv·a·to·ry (kən sʉr′və tôr′ē) *adj.* ⟦< ModL & It: ModL *conservatorium,* a greenhouse < ML, a preserver < LL, neut. of *conservatorius,* preserving < *conservatus,* pp. of *conservare;* It *conservatorio,* a refuge, academy, conservatory < *conservare* < L: see fol.⟧ [Rare] that preserves —*n., pl.* **-ries** 1 a room enclosed in glass, for growing and showing plants; noncommercial greenhouse 2 a school, or academy, of the fine arts, specif. of music

con·serve (kən sʉrv′; *for n., usually* kän′sʉrv′) *vt.* **-served′**, **-serv′ing** ⟦ME *conserven* < OFr *conserver* < L *conservare,* to keep, preserve < *com-*, with + *servare:* see OBSERVE⟧ 1 to keep from being damaged, lost, or wasted; save 2 to make (fruit) into preserves —*n.* [*often pl.*] a kind of jam made of two or more fruits, often with nuts or raisins added —**con·serv′a·ble** *adj.* —**con·serv′er** *n.*

con·sid·er (kən sid′ər) *vt.* ⟦ME *consideren* < OFr *considerer* < L *considerare,* to look at closely, observe < *com-*, with + *sidus,* a star: see SIDEREAL⟧ 1 [Archaic] to look at carefully; examine 2 to think about in order to understand or decide; ponder *[*to *consider* a problem*]* 3 to keep in mind; take into account *[*her health is good if you *consider* her age*]* 4 to be thoughtful of (others, their feelings, etc.); show consideration for 5 to regard as; think to be *[*I *consider* him an expert*]* 6 to believe or conclude after thought *[*we *consider* that the defendant is not guilty*]* —*vi.* to think carefully or seriously; reflect

SYN.—**consider** basically denotes a directing of the mind to something in order to understand it or to make a decision about it; **study** implies more intense concentration of the mind and methodical attention to details; **contemplate** implies a deep, continued mental viewing of a thing, sometimes suggesting the use of intuitive powers in envisioning something or dwelling upon it; **weigh** suggests a balancing of contradictory information, conflicting opinions, or possible eventualities in reaching a decision; **reflect**, suggesting a turning of one's thoughts back to something, implies quiet, earnest consideration

con·sid·er·a·ble (kən sid′er ə bəl) *adj.* ⟦ME⟧ 1 worth considering; important; noteworthy 2 much or large *[considerable* success*]* —*n.* ☆[Chiefly Dial.] a large amount or number; much —**con·sid′er·a·bly** *adv.*

con·sid·er·ate (kən sid′er it) *adj.* ⟦ME *considerat* < L *consideratus,* pp. of *considerare:* see CONSIDER⟧ 1 having or showing regard for others and their feelings; thoughtful 2 [Obs.] well-considered; deliberate —*SYN.* THOUGHTFUL —**con·sid′er·ate·ly** *adv.* —**con·sid′er·ate·ness** *n.*

con·sid·er·a·tion (kən sid′ər ā′shən) *n.* ⟦ME *consideracioun* < L *consideratio*⟧ 1 the act of considering; careful thought or attention; deliberation 2 thoughtful or sympathetic regard for others 3 something that is, or should be, considered, as in making a decision 4 a thought or opinion produced by considering 5 regard; esteem; importance 6 a recompense, as for a service rendered; fee; compensation 7 *Law* something of value given or done in exchange for something of value given or done by another, in order to make a binding contract; inducement for a contract —**in consideration of** 1 because of 2 in return for —**on no consideration** not for any reason; never —**take into consideration** to keep in mind; take into account; make allowance for —**under consideration** being thought over or discussed

con·sid·ered (kən sid′ərd) *adj.* 1 arrived at after careful thought; thought out 2 highly regarded; respected

con·sid·er·ing (kən sid′ər iŋ) *prep.* in view of; taking into account —*adv.* [Informal] taking all circumstances into account; all things considered

con·si·glie·re (kôn′sē lye′re) *n., pl.* **-ri** (-rē) ⟦It, counselor, advisor < *consiglio,* advice < L *consilium,* COUNSEL⟧ the chief advisor or aide to a Mafia leader: often humorously or ironically applied to any high-ranking aide

con·sign (kən sīn′) *vt.* ⟦L *consignare,* to seal, register < *com-*, together + *signare,* to sign, mark < *signum,* SIGN⟧ 1 to hand over; give up or deliver *[consigned* to jail*]* 2 to put in the care of another; entrust *[consign* the orphan to her uncle's care*]* 3 to assign to an undesirable position or place; relegate *[consigned* to oblivion*]* 4 to send or deliver, as goods to be sold —*vi.* [Obs.] to agree or submit —*SYN.* COMMIT —**con·sign′a·ble** *adj.* —**con·sig·na·tion** (kän′sig nā′shən) *n.*

con·sign·ee (kän′sīn ē′, kən sīn′ē) *n.* a person or dealer to whom something, esp. goods, is consigned

con·sign·ment (kən sīn′mənt) *n.* 1 a consigning or being consigned 2 something consigned; esp., a shipment of goods sent to a dealer for sale or safekeeping —**on consignment** shipped or turned over to a dealer for sale, with payment to the owner to follow the sale

con·sign·or (kän′sīn ôr′; kən sīn′ôr′, -ər) *n.* a person or firm that consigns goods to a dealer: also **con·sign·er** (kən sīn′ər)

con·sist (kən sist′) *vi.* ⟦L *consistere,* to stand together < *com-*, together + *sistere,* to place, caus. of *stare,* to STAND⟧ 1 to be formed or composed (*of*) *[*water *consists* of hydrogen and oxygen*]* 2 to be contained or inherent (*in* something) as a cause, effect, or characteristic *[*wisdom does not *consist* only in knowing facts] **3** to exist in harmony (*with*); be consistent (*with*) **4** to be characterized (by something); have its existence (*in*) [her "culture" *consists* merely in watching television] **5** [Archaic] to hold together or be held together; exist (usually *by* some means or agent)

con·sis·ten·cy (kən sis′tən sē) ***n.***, *pl.* **-cies** ⟦ML *consistentia:* see fol.⟧ **1** *a)* the condition of holding together; firmness or thickness, as of a liquid *b)* amount or degree of this [oil of the wrong *consistency*] **2** agreement; harmony; logical connection [arguments lacking *consistency*] **3** agreement with what has already been done or expressed; conformity with previous practice Also **con·sis′tence**

con·sis·tent (kən sis′tənt) ***adj.*** ⟦L *consistens,* prp. of *consistere:* see CONSIST⟧ **1** [Rare] holding together; firm; solid [*consistent* soil] **2** in agreement or harmony; in accord; compatible [deeds not *consistent* with his words] **3** holding always to the same principles or practice [*consistent* behavior] —**con·sis′tent·ly** ***adv.***

con·sis·to·ry (kən sis′tə rē) ***n.***, *pl.* **-ries** ⟦ME *consistorie* < OFr < L *consistorium,* place of assembly, council < *consistere:* see CONSIST⟧ **1** *a)* [Obs.] a meeting place for a council or court *b)* the meeting of a council **2** *a)* a church council or court, as the papal senate or a council of deacons *b)* a session of such a body —**con·sis·to·ri·al** (kän′sis tôr′ē əl) ***adj.***

con·so·ci·ate (kən sō′shē āt′; *also, for n.,* -it) ***n.*** ⟦ME *consociat* < L *consociatus,* pp. of *consociare,* to share with, join < *com-,* with + *sociare,* to join: see SOCIABLE⟧ [Rare] an associate — ***vt., vi.*** **-at′ed**, **-at′ing** to join together; unite in association —**con·so′ci·a′tion** ***n.***

con·sol (kän′säl′, kən säl′) ***n. sing. of*** CONSOLS

con·so·la·tion (kän′sə lā′shən) ***n.*** ⟦ME *consolacioun* < OFr *consolation* < L *consolatio*⟧ **1** a consoling or being consoled; comfort; solace **2** a person or thing that consoles

consolation prize a prize given to a contestant who does well but does not win, or who wins in a match for those previously defeated

con·sol·a·to·ry (kən säl′ə tôr′ē, -sōl′-) ***adj.*** ⟦ME *consolatorie* < L *consolatorius* < pp. of *consolari*⟧ consoling or tending to console; comforting

con·sole[1] (kən sōl′) ***vt.*** **-soled′**, **-sol′ing** ⟦Fr *consoler* < L *consolari* < *com-,* with + *solari,* to comfort, SOLACE⟧ to make feel less sad or disappointed; comfort —***SYN.*** COMFORT —**con·sol′a·ble** ***adj.*** —**con·sol′ing·ly** ***adv.***

con·sole[2] (kän′sōl′) ***n.*** ⟦Fr, prob. contr. < *consolateur,* lit., one who consoles (see prec.); name for carved figures supporting cornices or as rails in choir stalls (sense development analogous to that of MISERICORD, ***n.*** 1)⟧ **1** an ornamental bracket for supporting a shelf, bust, cornice, etc. **2** CONSOLE TABLE **3** the desklike frame containing the keys, stops, pedals, and other controls of an organ **4** a radio, television, or phonograph cabinet designed to stand on the floor ☆**5** an instrument panel or unit, containing gauges and the controls for operating aircraft, automobiles, computers, and other electrical or electronic systems **6** a raised portion between bucket seats in an automobile, containing storage compartments, switches and controls, a gearshift, etc.

con·sole table (kän′sōl′) **1** a table supported by ornamental consoles **2** a small table with legs curved or carved to resemble consoles, placed against a wall

con·sol·i·date (kən säl′ə dāt′) ***vt., vi.*** **-dat′ed**, **-dat′ing** ⟦< L *consolidatus,* pp. of *consolidare* < *com-,* together + *solidare,* to make solid < *solidus,* solid: see HOLO-⟧ **1** to combine into a single whole; merge; unite **2** to make or become strong, stable, firmly established, etc. [the troops *consolidated* their position] **3** to make or become solid or compact —***SYN.*** JOIN —**con·sol′i·da′tor** ***n.***

☆**consolidated school** a public school attended by pupils from several adjoining, esp. rural, districts

con·sol·i·da·tion (kən säl′ə dā′shən) ***n.*** a consolidating or being consolidated; specif., *a)* a merger; union *b)* a stabilization; strengthening *c)* a solidification

con·sols (kän′sälz′, kən sälz′) ***pl.n.*** ⟦< *consolidated annuities*⟧ British government securities, esp. those established in 1751 by the consolidation of nine loans

con·som·mé (kän′sə mā′, kän′sə mā′) ***n.*** ⟦Fr, orig. pp. of *consommer,* to CONSUMMATE; confused with *consumer,* to CONSUME⟧ a clear soup made by boiling meat, and sometimes vegetables, in water and straining: it is served hot or as a cold jelly

con·so·nance (kän′sə nəns) ***n.*** ⟦ME & OFr < L *consonantia* < *consonans,* prp. of *consonare,* to sound together with < *com-,* with + *sonare* < *sonus,* SOUND[1]⟧ **1** harmony or agreement of elements or parts; accord **2** a pleasing combination of simultaneous musical sounds; harmony of tones **3** *Prosody* repetition of a consonant sound in stressed syllables in the middle or at the end of words (Ex.: sta*r*/doo*r,* con*ceive*/be*hoove*)

con·so·nan·cy (-nən sē) ***n.*** CONSONANCE (sense 1)

con·so·nant (-nənt) ***adj.*** ⟦OFr < L *consonans:* see CONSONANCE⟧ **1** in harmony or agreement; in accord **2** harmonious in tone: opposed to DISSONANT **3** *Prosody* having consonance **4** consonantal —***n.*** **1** any speech sound in the production of which the speaker completely stops and then releases the air stream, as in (p, t, k, b, d, g), stops it at one point while it escapes at another, as in (m, n, ŋ, l, r), forces it through a loosely closed or very narrow passage, as in (f, v, s, z, sh, zh, th, *th,* H, kh, h, w, y), or uses a combination of these means, as in (ch, j): cf. VOWEL **2** a letter or symbol representing such a sound **3** *Linguis.* any phoneme, esp. one produced as described above, that does not form the peak of a syllable —**con′so·nant·ly** ***adv.***

con·so·nan·tal (kän′sə nant′'l) ***adj.*** **1** having the nature or function of a consonant **2** of or having a consonant or consonants

consonant shift a sound change or series of connected sound changes in the consonants of a language or family of languages, as a series of changes in the Indo-European stops that set Germanic apart from other Indo-European languages, or of changes in the Germanic stops that set High German apart from other Germanic languages

con·sort (kän′sôrt′; *for v.* kən sôrt′) ***n.*** ⟦OFr < L *consors* (gen. *consortis*), partner, neighbor < *com-,* with + *sors,* a share, lot: see SORT⟧ **1** [Obs.] a partner; companion **2** a wife or husband; spouse, esp. of a reigning king or queen **3** a ship that travels along with another **4** [Rare] *a)* ⟦OFr *consorte* < L *consortium,* community of goods < *consors*⟧ association; fellowship; company *b)* agreement; accord **5** *a)* a 16th-17th-cent. English chamber music ensemble, sometimes including vocalists (term now used in the name of certain chamber ensembles, esp. those specializing in music of the Renaissance) *b)* the music composed for such an ensemble —***vi.*** **1** to keep company or associate (*with* someone, esp. someone considered objectionable, undesirable, etc.) [*consorting* with thieves] **2** to be in harmony or agreement; be in accord —***vt.*** [Obs.] **1** to associate; join: usually reflexive **2** to accompany or escort

con·sor·ti·um (kən sôr′tē əm; -sôr′shē əm, -shəm) ***n.***, *pl.* **-ti·a** (-ə) ⟦L, community of goods: see prec.⟧ **1** a partnership or association; specif., *a)* a temporary alliance of two or more business firms in a common venture *b)* an international banking agreement or association **2** *Law* the companionship and support provided by marriage, including the right of each spouse to receive this from the other

con·spe·cif·ic (kän′spə sif′ik) ***adj.*** ⟦< *conspecies,* fellow species (see CON- & SPECIES), modeled on SPECIFIC⟧ belonging to the same species

con·spec·tus (kən spek′təs) ***n.*** ⟦L, a view, range of sight, pp. of *conspicere:* see fol.⟧ **1** a general view; survey **2** a summary; outline; synopsis; digest

con·spic·u·ous (kən spik′yo͞o əs) ***adj.*** ⟦L *conspicuus,* open to view < *conspicere,* to look at, observe < *com-,* intens. + *specere,* see: see SPY⟧ **1** easy to see or perceive; obvious [a *conspicuous* billboard] **2** attracting attention by being unexpected, unusual, outstanding, or egregious; striking [*conspicuous* bravery, *conspicuous* folly] —***SYN.*** NOTICEABLE —**con·spic′u·ous·ly** ***adv.*** —**con·spic′u·ous·ness** ***n.***

☆**conspicuous consumption** ⟦coined by T. VEBLEN in *The Theory of the Leisure Class* (1899)⟧ showy extravagance in buying or using goods or services, meant to impress others with one's wealth, status, etc.

con·spir·a·cy (kən spir′ə sē) ***n.***, *pl.* **-cies** ⟦ME *conspiracie,* prob. via ML *conspirancia* < L *conspirare:* see CONSPIRE⟧ **1** a planning and acting together secretly, esp. for an unlawful or harmful purpose, such as murder or treason **2** the plan agreed on; plot **3** the group taking part in such a plan **4** a combining or working together [the *conspiracy* of events] —***SYN.*** PLOT

conspiracy theory any theory that purports to explain something by ascribing it to collusion among powerful conspirators: a usually dismissive term implying that the theory is far-fetched, paranoid, etc. —**conspiracy theorist**

con·spir·a·tor (kən spir′ət ər) ***n.*** ⟦ME *conspiratour* < OFr < ML *conspirator* < pp. of L *conspirare:* see CONSPIRE⟧ a person who takes part in a conspiracy

con·spir·a·to·ri·al (kən spir′ə tôr′ē əl) ***adj.*** **1** of or characteristic of a conspirator or conspiracy **2** conspiring or fond of conspiracy —**con·spir′a·to′ri·al·ly** ***adv.***

con·spire (kən spīr′) ***vi.*** **-spired′**, **-spir′ing** ⟦ME *conspiren* < OFr *conspirer* < L *conspirare,* to breathe together, agree, unite < *com-,* together + *spirare,* to breathe: see SPIRIT⟧ **1** to plan and act together secretly, esp. in order to commit a crime **2** to combine or work together for any purpose or toward any effect [events *conspired* to ruin him] —***vt.*** [Rare] to plan or plot

con spi·ri·to (kän spir′i tō′) ⟦It⟧ *Musical Direction* with spirit; with vigor

const or **Const** *abbrev.* **1** constable **2** constant **3** constitution **4** constitutional **5** construction

con·sta·ble (kän′stə bəl; *Brit* kun′-) ***n.*** ⟦ME < OFr *conestable* < LL *comes stabuli,* lit., count of the stable, hence chief groom < L *comes,* companion, fellow (see COUNT[2]) + *stabulum,* STABLE[2]⟧ **1** in the Middle Ages, the highest-ranking official of a royal household, court, etc. **2** the warden or keeper of a royal fortress or castle **3** a peace officer in a town or village, with powers and jurisdiction somewhat more limited than those of a sheriff **4** [Chiefly Brit.] a police officer

Con·sta·ble (kun′stə bəl, kän′-), **John** 1776-1837; Eng. landscape painter

con·stab·u·lar·y (kən stab′yə ler′ē) ***n.***, *pl.* **-lar′ies** ⟦ML *constabularia*⟧ **1** the territory under the jurisdiction of a constable **2** constables, collectively, as of a district **3** a police force characterized by a military organization but distinct from the regular army —***adj.*** of constables or a constabulary: also **con·stab′u·lar** (-lər)

Con·stance[1] (kän′stəns) ***n.*** ⟦Fr < L *Constantia,* lit., constancy: see CONSTANCY⟧ a feminine name: dim. *Connie*

Con·stance[2] (kän′stəns), **Lake (of)** lake bounded by Switzerland, Germany, & Austria: 208 sq mi (539 sq km); *c.* 46 mi (74 km) long: Ger. name BODENSEE

con·stan·cy (kän′stən sē) ***n.*** ⟦L *constantia* < *constans,* prp. of *constare* < *com-,* together + *stare,* to STAND⟧ the state or quality of being unchanging; specif., *a)* firmness of mind or purpose; resoluteness *b)* steadiness of affections or loyalties; faithfulness *c)* freedom from variation or change; regularity; stability

con·stant (kän′stənt) ***adj.*** ⟦ME & OFr *constaunt* < L *constans:* see prec.⟧ **1** not changing; remaining the same; specif., *a)* remaining firm in purpose; resolute *b)* remaining steady in affections or loyalties; faithful *c)* remaining free from variation or change; regular; stable **2** going on all the time;

continual; persistent [*constant* interruptions] —*n.* **1** anything that does not change or vary **2** *Math., Physics a)* a quantity that always has the same value (in full **absolute constant**) *b)* a quantity, vector, etc. assumed to have one value throughout a particular discussion or investigation (in full **arbitrary constant**): opposed to VARIABLE —**SYN.** CONTINUAL, FAITHFUL —**con′stant·ly** *adv.*

Con·stant (kōn stän′), **Benjamin** (*Henri Benjamin Constant de Rebecque*) 1767-1830; Fr. writer & politician, born in Switzerland

Con·stan·ţa (kôn stän′tsä) seaport in SE Romania, on the Black Sea

con·stant·an (kän′stən tan′) *n.* ⟦so named from its *constant*-temperature coefficient of resistance: see CONSTANT⟧ an alloy of copper (*c.* 55%) and nickel (*c.* 45%), used in pyrometers and thermocouples

Con·stan·tine[1] (kän′stən tēn′, -tīn′) *n.* ⟦L *Constantinus* < *constans:* see CONSTANCY⟧ a masculine name

Con·stan·tine[2] (kän′stən tēn′; *Fr* kōn stän tēn′) city in NE Algeria

Con·stan·tine I (kän′stən tēn′, -tīn′) (*Flavius Valerius Aurelius Constantinus*) A.D. 280?-337; emperor of Rome (306-337): converted to Christianity: called *the Great*

Con·stan·ti·no·ple (kän′stan tə nō′pəl) *former name* (A.D. 330-1930) *for* ISTANBUL: name still used within the Eastern Orthodox Church in some contexts

con·stel·late (kän′stə lāt′) *vi., vt.* **-lat′ed, -lat′ing** ⟦< LL *constellatus:* see fol.⟧ to unite in or as in a constellation; cluster

con·stel·la·tion (kän′stə lā′shən) *n.* ⟦ME *constellacion* < OFr < LL *constellatio* < *constellatus,* set with stars < L *com-,* with + pp. of *stellare,* to shine < *stella,* STAR⟧ **1** *a)* an apparent grouping of stars in the sky, traditionally named for some object, animal, or mythological being that its outline is thought to suggest *b)* the area of the sky assigned to such a grouping of stars: currently the sky is considered to have 88 constellations **2** any cluster, gathering, or collection **3** *Astrol.* the grouping of celestial bodies at any particular time, esp. at a person's birth **4** *Psychol.* a group of related thoughts or feelings regarded as clustered about one central idea —**con·stel·la·to·ry** (kən stel′ə tôr′ē) *adj.*

con·ster·nate (kän′stər nāt′) *vt.* **-nat′ed, -nat′ing** ⟦L *consternatus,* pp. of *consternare:* see fol.⟧ to overcome with consternation; unnerve; dismay

con·ster·na·tion (kän′stər nā′shən) *n.* ⟦L *consternatio* < *consternare,* to terrify < *com-,* intens. + base akin to L *sternax,* headstrong, restive < IE base **ster-,* rigid, stiff > STARE, STRENUOUS⟧ a feeling of confusion, helplessness, shock, or dismay

con·sti·pate (kän′stə pāt′) *vt.* **-pat′ed, -pat′ing** ⟦< L *constipatus,* pp. of *constipare,* to press or crowd together < *com-,* together + *stipare,* to cram, pack: see STIFF⟧ to cause constipation in —**con′sti·pat′ed** *adj.*

con·sti·pa·tion (kän′stə pā′shən) *n.* ⟦ME *constipacioun* < OFr *constipation* < L *constipatio:* see prec.⟧ a condition in which the feces are hard and elimination from the bowels is infrequent and difficult: also used fig. to suggest stagnation, constraint, obstinacy, etc.

con·stit·u·en·cy (kən stich′o͞o ən sē) *n., pl.* **-cies** ⟦< fol. + -CY⟧ **1** all the people, esp. voters, served by a particular elected official, esp. a legislator **2** the district of such a group of voters, etc. **3** a group of clients, supporters, etc.

con·stit·u·ent (kən stich′o͞o ənt) *adj.* ⟦< L *constituens,* prp. of *constituere:* see fol.⟧ **1** necessary in forming or making up a whole; component [a *constituent* part] **2** that can or does appoint or vote for a representative **3** authorized to make or revise a political constitution or establish a government [a *constituent* assembly] —*n.* **1** a person who appoints another to act as agent or representative **2** a member of a constituency, esp. any of the voters represented by a particular official **3** a necessary part or element; component **4** an element of a word or construction (Ex.: in "they painted signs" the main elements *they* and *painted signs* are called *immediate constituents*; the further morphologically indivisible elements *they, paint, -ed, sign,* and *-s* are called *ultimate constituents*) —**SYN.** ELEMENT —**con·stit′u·ent·ly** *adv.*

con·sti·tute (kän′stə to͞ot′, -tyo͞ot′) *vt.* **-tut′ed, -tut′ing** ⟦ME *constituten* < L *constitutus,* pp. of *constituere,* to set up, establish < *com-,* together + *statuere,* to set: see STATUE⟧ **1** to set up (a law, government, institution, etc.); establish **2** to set up (an assembly, proceedings, etc.) in a legal or official form **3** to give a certain office or function to; appoint [our officially *constituted* spokesperson] **4** to make up; be the components or elements of; form; compose [twelve people *constitute* a jury] **5** to be actually as designated; meet the definition of or be tantamount to [such action *constitutes* a felony]

con·sti·tu·tion (kän′stə to͞o′shən, -tyo͞o′-) *n.* ⟦ME *constitucioun* < OFr *constitution* < L *constitutio:* see prec.⟧ **1** the act of setting up or making up; establishment, appointment, or formation **2** the way in which a thing is made up; structure; organization; makeup **3** the physical, or rarely mental, makeup of a person [a man of strong *constitution*] **4** the way in which a government, state, society, etc. is organized **5** a decree, regulation, or custom **6** *a)* the system of fundamental laws and principles of a government, state, society, corporation, etc., written or unwritten *b)* a document or set of documents in which these laws and principles are written down —**the Constitution** the document containing the fundamental laws of the United States: it consists of the seven original articles, adopted in 1789, and twenty-seven amendments

con·sti·tu·tion·al (-shə nəl) *adj.* **1** of or in the constitution of a person or thing; basic; essential **2** for improving a person's constitution; good for one's health **3** of, in, authorized by, subject to, dependent on, dealing with, or in accordance with the constitution of a nation, state, or society [*constitutional* rights, a *constitutional* monarchy] **4** upholding the constitution —*n.* a walk taken for one's health

con·sti·tu·tion·al·ism (-shə nəl iz′əm) *n.* **1** government according to a constitution **2** adherence to constitutional principles or government —**con′sti·tu′tion·al·ist** *n.*

con·sti·tu·tion·al·i·ty (kän′stə to͞o′shə nal′ə tē, -tyo͞o′-) *n.* the quality or condition of being constitutional; esp., accordance with the constitution of a nation or state

con·sti·tu·tion·al·ize (kän′stə to͞o′shə nəl īz′, -tyo͞o′-) *vt.* **-ized′, -iz′ing** to bring under the authority of a CONSTITUTION (sense 6*b*) [to *constitutionalize* the funding of public schools] —**con′sti·tu′tion·al·i·za′tion** *n.*

con·sti·tu·tion·al·ly (kän′stə to͞o′shən əl ē, -tyo͞o′-) *adv.* **1** in composition or physique [*constitutionally* frail] **2** by nature or temperament [*constitutionally* incapable of lying] **3** in accordance with the (or a) constitution

con·sti·tu·tive (kän′stə to͞ot′iv, -tyo͞ot′-; kən stich′o͞o tiv′) *adj.* ⟦LL *constitutivus:* see CONSTITUTE⟧ **1** having power to establish, appoint, or enact **2** making a thing what it is; basic **3** forming a part (*of*); constituent; component —**con′sti·tu′tive·ly** *adv.*

constr *abbrev.* construction

con·strain (kən strān′) *vt.* ⟦ME *constreinen* < OFr *constreindre* < L *constringere,* to bind together, draw together < *com-,* together + *stringere,* to draw tight: see STRICT⟧ **1** to force into, or hold in, close bounds; confine **2** to hold back by force; restrain **3** to force; compel; oblige [he was *constrained* to agree] —**SYN.** FORCE

con·strained (kən strānd′) *adj.* **1** compelled; forced; obliged **2** forced and unnatural [a *constrained* laugh] —**con·strain′ed·ly** (-strān′id lē) *adv.*

con·straint (kən strānt′) *n.* ⟦ME *constreinte* < OFr: see CONSTRAIN⟧ **1** a constraining or being constrained; specif., *a)* confinement or restriction *b)* compulsion or coercion **2** *a)* repression of natural feelings or behavior *b)* forced, unnatural manner; awkwardness **3** something that constrains

con·strict (kən strikt′) *vt.* ⟦< L *constrictus,* pp. of *constringere:* see CONSTRAIN⟧ **1** to make smaller or narrower, esp. at one place, by binding, squeezing, or shrinking; contract **2** to hold in; limit; restrict —**con·stric′tive** *adj.*

con·stric·tion (-strik′shən) *n.* ⟦ME *constriccioun* < L *constrictio*⟧ **1** a constricting or being constricted; contraction or restriction **2** a feeling of tightness or pressure, as in the chest **3** something that constricts **4** a constricted part

con·stric·tor (-strik′tər) *n.* ⟦ModL⟧ something that constricts; specif., *a)* a muscle that contracts a cavity or opening, or compresses an organ *b)* a snake that kills by coiling around its prey and squeezing, thereby making breathing impossible

con·stringe (kən strinj′) *vt.* **-stringed′, -string′ing** ⟦L *constringere:* see CONSTRAIN⟧ [Rare] to cause to contract, constrict, or shrink —**con·strin′gent** *adj.*

con·stru·a·ble (kən stro͞o′ə bəl) *adj.* that can be construed

con·struct (kən strukt′; *for n.* kän′strukt′) *vt.* ⟦< L *constructus,* pp. of *construere* < *com-,* together + *struere,* to pile up, build: see STREW⟧ **1** to build, form, or devise by fitting parts or elements together systematically **2** *Geom.* to draw (a figure) so as to meet the specified requirements —*n.* **1** something built or put together systematically **2** *a)* an idea or perception resulting from a synthesis of sense impressions, etc. *b)* a concept or theory devised to integrate in an orderly way the diverse data on a phenomenon (also **logical construct**) —**SYN.** MAKE[1] —**con·struc′tor** *n.,* **con·struct′er**

con·struc·tion (kən struk′shən) *n.* ⟦ME *construccioun* < OFr *construction* < L *constructio*⟧ **1** the act or process of constructing **2** the way in which something is constructed; manner or method of building **3** something constructed; structure; building **4** an explanation or interpretation [to put the wrong *construction* on a statement] **5** *Linguis.* a grammatical pattern consisting of two or more immediate constituents **6** a three-dimensional work of art, usually nonrepresentational and constructed of more than one material —**con·struc′tion·al** *adj.* —**con·struc′tion·al·ly** *adv.*

con·struc·tion·ist (-ist) *n.* ⟦see prec.⟧ a person who interprets, or believes in interpreting, a law, document, etc., specif., the U.S. Constitution, in a specified way: see also STRICT CONSTRUCTION

construction paper heavy, colored paper used, as by children in school, for crayon and ink drawings, watercolors, cutouts, etc.

con·struc·tive (kən struk′tiv) *adj.* ⟦ML *constructivus*⟧ **1** leading to improvements or advances; formative; positive [*constructive* criticism] **2** of construction or structure **3** inferred or implied by legal or judicial interpretation [*constructive* fraud] —**con·struc′tive·ly** *adv.* —**con·struc′tive·ness** *n.*

con·struc·tiv·ism (-iz′əm) *n.* an early 20th-cent. movement in sculpture, painting, architecture, etc., originating in the Soviet Union, characterized by abstract and geometric design, man-made materials, and massive structural form —**con·struc′tiv·ist** *adj., n.*

con·strue (kən stro͞o′) *vt.* **-strued′, -stru′ing** ⟦ME *construen* < L *construere:* see CONSTRUCT⟧ **1** to analyze (a sentence, clause, etc.) so as to show its syntactic construction and its meaning **2** loosely, to translate (a passage) orally **3** to explain or deduce the meaning of; interpret [her silence was *construed* as agreement] **4** to infer or deduce **5** *Gram.* to combine in syntax [the verb "let," unlike "permit," is *construed* with an infinitive omitting the "to"] —*vi.* **1** to analyze sentence structure, esp. in translating **2** to be able to be construed, as a sentence —**SYN.** EXPLAIN

con·sub·stan·tial (kän′səb stan′shəl) ***adj.*** ⟦ME *consubstancial* < LL(Ec) *consubstantialis:* see COM- & SUBSTANTIAL⟧ *Christian Theol.* having the same substance: said esp. of the persons of the Trinity —**con′sub·stan′ti·al′i·ty** (-shē al′ə tē) ***n.***

con·sub·stan·ti·ate (-stan′shē āt′) ***vt., vi.*** **-at′ed, -at′ing** ⟦< LL(Ec) *consubstantiatus,* pp. of *consubstantiare* < L *com-,* with + *substantia:* see SUBSTANCE⟧ to unite in one common substance or nature

con·sub·stan·ti·a·tion (-stan′shē ā′shən) ***n.*** ⟦ML(Ec) *consubstantiatio* < LL(Ec) *consubstantiare* (see prec.), modeled on *transubstantio:* see TRANSUBSTANTIATION⟧ *Theol.* the doctrine that the substance of the bread and wine of the Eucharist exists, after consecration, side by side with the substance of the body and blood of Christ but is not changed into it

con·sue·tude (kän′swi to͞od′, -tyo͞od′) ***n.*** ⟦OFr < L *consuetudo:* see CUSTOM⟧ established custom or usage —**con′sue·tu′di·nar′y** (-to͞od′′n er′ ē, -tyo͞od′′n er′ē) ***adj.***

con·sul (kän′səl) ***n.*** ⟦OFr < L *consulere,* to deliberate, take counsel: see CONSULT⟧ **1** either of the two chief magistrates of the ancient Roman republic **2** one of the three highest officials of the French republic from 1799 to 1804 **3** a person appointed by a government to aid and serve its citizens and business interests in a foreign city —**con′sul·ar** (-ər) ***adj.*** —**con′sul·ship′** ***n.***

consular agent an official serving as a CONSUL (sense 3) at a place of little commercial importance

con·sul·ate (-it) ***n.*** ⟦ME *consulat* < L *consulatus*⟧ **1** the position, powers, and functions of a consul **2** the office or residence of a consul **3** the term of office of a consul; consulship **4** a government by consuls —**the Consulate** ⟦Fr *Consulat*⟧ the consular government of France from 1799 to 1804

consul general *pl.* **consuls general** or **consul generals** a CONSUL (sense 3) stationed in a principal commercial city, who supervises other consuls within his district

con·sult (kən sult′; *also, for n.,* kän′sult′) ***vi.*** ⟦L *consultare* < pp. of *consulere,* to deliberate, consider, orig., prob., to call together, as in *consulere senatum,* to gather the senate, hence ask (it) for advice < *com-,* with + IE base **sel-,* to take, seize > SELL, Gr *helein,* to take⟧ to talk things over in order to decide or plan something; confer —***vt.*** **1** *a)* to seek an opinion from; ask the advice of [to *consult* a lawyer] *b)* to refer to or turn to, esp. for information [to *consult* a map] **2** to keep in mind while acting or deciding; show regard for; consider [*consult* your own wishes in the matter] **3** [Obs.] *a)* to confer about *b)* to plan for —***n.*** a consultation —**con·sult′er** ***n.***

con·sult·an·cy (kən sult′′n sē) ***n., pl.*** **-cies 1** the act or business of providing professional or technical advice **2** [Chiefly Brit.] a consulting firm **3** the position of a consultant

con·sult·ant (kən sult′′nt) ***n.*** ⟦< L *consultans,* prp. of *consultare*⟧ **1** [Obs.] a person who consults an oracle **2** an expert who is called on for professional or technical advice or opinions

con·sul·ta·tion (kän′səl tā′shən) ***n.*** ⟦L *consultatio*⟧ **1** the act of consulting **2** a meeting to discuss, decide, or plan something, as a meeting of several doctors to discuss the diagnosis and treatment of a patient

con·sult·a·tive (kən sult′ə tiv′, kän′səl tā′-) ***adj.*** of or relating to consultation; advisory [a *consultative* body]: also **con·sult′a·to′ry** (-tôr′ē)

con·sult·ing (kən sult′iŋ) ***adj.*** consulted for professional or technical advice; advisory [a *consulting* engineer]

con·sul·tor (kən sult′ər) ***n.*** **1** a counselor or advisor **2** *R.C.Ch.* one of a group of priests appointed to advise and assist a bishop

con·sum·a·ble (kən so͞om′ə bəl, -syo͞om′-) ***adj.*** able or intended to be consumed —***n.*** a resource, commercial product, etc. that is consumed: *usually used in pl.*

con·sume (kən so͞om′, -syo͞om′) ***vt.*** **-sumed′, -sum′ing** ⟦ME *consumen* < OFr *consumer* < L *consumere,* to use up, eat, waste < *com-,* together + *sumere,* to take < *sub-,* under + *emere,* to buy, take: see REDEEM⟧ **1** to destroy, as by fire; do away with **2** *a)* to use up *b)* to spend wastefully; squander (time, energy, money, etc.) **3** to eat or drink up; devour **4** to absorb completely; engross or obsess [*consumed* with envy, a *consuming* interest] **5** to buy for one's personal needs —***vi.*** **1** [Now Rare] to waste away; perish **2** to buy consumer goods or services for one's personal needs

con·sum·ed·ly (-id lē) ***adv.*** extremely or excessively

con·sum·er (kən so͞om′ər) ***n.*** a person or thing that consumes; specif., a person who buys goods or services for personal needs and not for resale: opposed to PRODUCER

☆**consumer credit** credit extended for buying goods and services for one's personal use through installment plans, charge accounts, short-term loans, etc.

consumer goods goods, such as food, clothing, etc., for satisfying people's needs rather than for producing other goods or services: also **consumers' goods**

con·sum·er·ism (-iz′əm) ***n.*** **1** the practice and policies of protecting the consumer by publicizing defective and unsafe products, misleading business practices, etc. **2** the consumption of goods and services **3** a theory that a continual increase in the consumption of goods is sound economically

☆**con·sum·er·ist** (-ist) ***n.*** **1** an advocate of consumerism **2** [Informal] one who wants to have the latest consumer products

con·sum·er·i·za·tion (kən so͞om′ər i zā′shən) ***n.*** the practice by a business or industry of adopting technological innovations, esp. computer and communciations innovations, that have originated in the general consumer market

con·sum·mate (kän′sə mit, kən sum′it; *for v.* kän′sə māt′) ***adj.*** ⟦L *consummatus,* pp. of *consummare,* to sum up, finish < *com-,* together + *summa,* SUM[1]⟧ **1** complete or perfect in every way; supreme [*consummate* happiness] **2** very skillful; highly expert [a *consummate* liar] —***vt.*** **-mat′ed, -mat′ing** ⟦ME *consummaten*⟧ **1** to bring to completion or fulfillment; finish; accomplish **2** to make (a marriage) actual by sexual intercourse —**con′sum·mate·ly** ***adv.*** —**con·sum·ma·tive** (kän′sə māt′iv, kən sum′ə tiv′) ***adj.,*** **con′sum·ma·to′ry** (-ə tôr′ē) —**con′sum·ma′tor** ***n.***

con·sum·ma·tion (kän′sə mā′shən) ***n.*** ⟦ME *consummacioun* < OFr *consumation* < L *consummatio*⟧ **1** a consummating or being consummated; completion; fulfillment **2** an end; conclusion; outcome

con·sump·tion (kən sump′shən) ***n.*** ⟦ME *consumpcioun* < OFr *consomption* < L *consumptio* < *consumptus,* pp. of *consumere*⟧ **1** *a)* a consuming or being consumed *b) Econ.* the using up of goods or services, either by consumers or in the production of other goods *c)* the amount consumed **2** [Old-fashioned] *a)* a wasting away of the body *b)* a disease causing this; esp., tuberculosis of the lungs

con·sump·tive (kən sump′tiv) ***adj.*** ⟦ME *consumpt* < L *consumptus* (see prec.) + -IVE⟧ **1** consuming or tending to consume in a wasteful or destructive way **2** [Old-fashioned] of, having, or relating to tuberculosis of the lungs —***n.*** [Old-fashioned] a person who has tuberculosis of the lungs —**con·sump′tive·ly** ***adv.***

cont *abbrev.* **1** containing **2** contents **3** continent **4** continue **5** continued **6** contract **7** control

Cont *abbrev.* Continental

con·tact (kän′takt′; *for v., occas.* kən takt′) ***n.*** ⟦L *contactus,* pp. of *contingere,* to touch, seize < *com-,* together + *tangere,* to touch: see TACT⟧ **1** the act or state of touching or meeting [two surfaces in *contact*] **2** the state or fact of being in touch, communication, or association (*with*) [to come into *contact* with new ideas] ☆**3** *a)* an acquaintance, esp. one who is influential *b)* a connection with such a person [his *contacts* at city hall] **4** *Elec. a)* a connection or point of connection between two conductors in a circuit *b)* a device for opening and closing such a connection **5** *Med.* a person who may have caught a disease from an infected person **6** *short for* CONTACT LENS: *usually used in pl.* —***vt.*** **1** to place in contact **2** to come into contact with ☆**3** to get in touch or communication with —***vi.*** to be in or come into contact —***adj.*** of, involving, or relating to contact —***adv.*** by means of contact flying

contact dermatitis dermatitis caused by direct contact with an irritating substance, as an allergen or chemical

☆**contact flying** flying an airplane in conditions of good visibility so that the course and altitude can be determined by observing points or objects on the ground; VFR: distinguished from INSTRUMENT FLYING: also **contact flight**

contact lens a tiny, thin corrective lens worn directly over the cornea of the eye: the lens floats on a film of tears

con·tac·tor (kän′tak′tər, kän tak′-) ***n.*** *Elec.* a heavy-duty switching device, esp. a relay, used to open and close a circuit

contact paper a type of reinforced paper with an adhesive backing, used to cover the surface of a shelf, countertop, etc.

contact print a photographic print made with the negative pressed against a photosensitive surface

contact sport a sport, as boxing or football, that necessarily involves bodily contact between opponents

con·ta·gion (kən tā′jən) ***n.*** ⟦ME *contagioun* < L *contagio,* a touching < *contingere:* see CONTACT⟧ **1** the spreading of disease from one individual to another by direct or indirect contact **2** any disease thus spread; contagious disease **3** the causative agent of a communicable disease; bacteria or virus **4** contagious quality **5** *a)* the spreading of an emotion, idea, custom, etc. from person to person until many are affected [the *contagion* of mirth] *b)* the emotion, idea, etc. so spread **6** a bad influence that tends to spread; corruption

con·ta·gious (-jəs) ***adj.*** ⟦OFr *contagieus* < LL *contagiosus*⟧ **1** spread by direct or indirect contact; communicable: said of diseases **2** carrying, or liable to transmit, the causative agent of a contagious disease **3** for the care of contagious patients **4** spreading or tending to spread from person to person [*contagious* laughter] —**con·ta′gious·ly** ***adv.*** —**con·ta′gious·ness** ***n.***

con·ta·gi·um (kən tā′jəm, -jē əm) ***n., pl.*** **-gi·a** (-jē ə) ⟦L, a touching, var. of *contagio:* see CONTAGION⟧ [Obs.] CONTAGION (sense 3)

con·tain (kən tān′) ***vt.*** ⟦ME *conteinen* < OFr *contenir* < L *continere,* to hold < *com-,* together + *tenere,* to hold: see THIN⟧ **1** to have in it; hold, enclose, or include [the can *contains* tea; the list *contains* 50 items] **2** to have the capacity for holding **3** to be equivalent to [a gallon *contains* four quarts] **4** to hold back or within fixed limits; specif., *a)* to restrain (one's feeling, oneself, etc.) *b)* to check the power, expansion, or influence of **5** to be divisible by, esp. without a remainder [10 *contains* 5 and 2] —***vi.*** [Archaic] to restrain one's feelings —**con·tain′a·ble** ***adj.***

SYN.—**contain,** in strict usage, signifies an enclosing within or including as a component, part, or fraction, and **hold,** the capacity for containing [the bottle *contains* two ounces of liquid, but it *holds* a pint]; to **accommodate** is to hold comfortably without crowding [an elevator built to *accommodate* twelve people]

con·tain·er (kən tān′ər) ***n.*** **1** a thing that contains or can contain something; box, crate, can, jar, etc. **2** a huge, standardized metal container for use in containerization

con·tain·er·board (kən tān′ər bôrd′) ***n.*** sturdy cardboard used as in making containers and typically consisting of a corrugated layer sandwiched between smooth facing layers

con·tain·er·ize (kən tān′ər īz′) ***vt.*** **-ized′**, **-iz′ing** to pack (general cargo) into huge, standardized containers for more efficient shipment, as in transferring from one mode of transportation to another —**con·tain′er·i·za′tion** ***n.***

con·tain·er·ship (kən tān′ər ship′) ***n.*** a large ship for transporting containerized cargo: also written **container ship**

con·tain·ment (kən tān′mənt) ***n.*** a containing or being contained; specif., *a)* the policy of attempting to prevent the influence of an opposing nation or political system from spreading *b)* prevention of the spread or escape of something toxic or otherwise harmful *c)* the steel and concrete shell used in a nuclear power plant (in full **containment structure**)

con·tam·i·nant (kən tam′ə nənt) ***n.*** a substance that contaminates another substance, the air, water, etc.

con·tam·i·nate (kən tam′ə nāt′) ***vt.*** **-nat′ed**, **-nat′ing** ⟦ME *contaminaten* < L *contaminatus*, pp. of *contaminare*, to defile < *contamen*, contact, contagion < *com-*, together + base of *tangere*, to touch: see TACT⟧ to make impure, infected, corrupt, radioactive, etc. by contact with something or by the addition of something; pollute; defile; sully; taint —**con·tam′i·na′tive** ***adj.*** —**con·tam′i·na′tor** ***n.***

SYN.—**contaminate** means to make impure, unclean, or unfit for use through contact or addition [fumes were *contaminating* the air]; **taint** emphasizes effect over cause and implies that some measure of decay or corruption has taken place [*tainted* food]; **pollute** implies complete befoulment, decay, or corruption through contamination; **defile** implies pollution or desecration of that which should be held sacred

con·tam·i·na·tion (kən tam′ə nā′shən) ***n.*** ⟦ME *contaminacioun* < L *contaminatio*⟧ **1** a contaminating or being contaminated **2** something that contaminates

contd *abbrev.* continued

conte[1] (kōnt; *Fr* kōnt) ***n.***, *pl.* **contes** (kōnts; *Fr* kōnt) ⟦Fr < *conter*: see COUNT[1]⟧ **1** a medieval tale of adventure **2** esp. in France, *a)* a highly fanciful tale or story *b)* a concise and literary short story

con·te[2] (kôn′te) ***n.***, *pl.* **con′ti** (-tē) ⟦It⟧ COUNT[2]

con·té (kän′tā, -tē) ***n.*** ⟦< *Conté*, a trademark for such a crayon⟧ a hard crayon made of clay and graphite, usually black, gray, or brown: also called **conté crayon**

con·temn (kən tem′) ***vt.*** ⟦ME *contempnen* < OFr *contemner* < L *contemnere* < *com-*, intens. + *temnere*, to scorn⟧ [Chiefly Literary] to treat or think of with contempt; scorn —***SYN.*** DESPISE —**con·temn′er** ***n.***, **con·tem′nor** (-tem′ər, -tem′nər)

con·tem·plate (kän′təm plāt′) ***vt.*** **-plat′ed**, **-plat′ing** ⟦< L *contemplatus*, pp. of *contemplari*, to gaze attentively, observe (orig., in augury, to mark out space for observation) < *com-*, intens. + *templum*, TEMPLE[1]⟧ **1** to look at intently; gaze at **2** to think about intently; study carefully **3** to have in mind as a possibility or plan; intend —***vi.*** to meditate or muse, sometimes specif. in a religious or mystical way —***SYN.*** CONSIDER —**con′tem·pla′tor** ***n.***

con·tem·pla·tion (kän′təm plā′shən) ***n.*** ⟦ME *contemplacion* < OFr < L *contemplatio*⟧ **1** thoughtful inspection, study, etc. **2** religious or mystical meditation **3** expectation or intention

con·tem·pla·tive (kən tem′plə tiv′, kän′təm plāt′iv) ***adj.*** ⟦ME *contemplatif* < OFr < L *contemplativus*⟧ of or inclined to contemplation; thoughtful; meditative —***n.*** one who is dedicated to religious meditation, esp. in a religious order —***SYN.*** PENSIVE —**con·tem′pla·tive·ly** ***adv.*** —**con·tem′pla·tive·ness** ***n.***

con·tem·po·ra·ne·ous (kən tem′pə rā′nē əs) ***adj.*** ⟦L *contemporaneus* < *com-*, with + *tempus*: see fol.⟧ existing or happening in the same period of time —***SYN.*** CONTEMPORARY —**con·tem′po·ra·ne′i·ty** (-pə rə nē′ə tē; -nā′-) ***n.***, **con·tem′po·ra′ne·ous·ness** —**con·tem′po·ra′ne·ous·ly** ***adv.***

con·tem·po·rar·y (kən tem′pə rer′ē) ***adj.*** ⟦< L *com-*, with + *temporarius*, of time < *tempus*, time: see TEMPER⟧ **1** living or happening in the same period of time **2** of about the same age **3** [*often* **C-**] of or in the style of the present or recent times; modern: see MODERN —***n.***, *pl.* **-rar′ies** **1** a person living in the same period as another or others **2** a person or thing of about the same age or date of origin as another

SYN.—**contemporary** and **contemporaneous** both mean existing or happening at the same period of time, **contemporary** (often applied to the present) referring more often to persons or their works, and **contemporaneous**, to events; **coeval** implies extension over the same period of time when a remote time or very long duration is involved; **synchronous** implies exact correspondence in time of occurrence or rate of movement; **simultaneous** implies occurrence in the same brief interval of time

con·tem·po·rize (kən tem′pə rīz′) ***vt.***, ***vi.*** **-rized′**, **-riz′ing** to make or be contemporary

con·tempt (kən tempt′) ***n.*** ⟦OFr < L *contemptus*, scorn, pp. of *contemnere*: see CONTEMN⟧ **1** the feeling or attitude of one who looks down on somebody or something as being low, mean, or unworthy; scorn **2** the condition of being despised or scorned **3** the punishable act of showing disrespect for the authority or dignity of a court (or legislature), as by disobedience, unruliness, etc.: in full **contempt of court** (or **congress**, etc.) —**beneath contempt** unworthy even to be despised: a hyperbolic use

con·tempt·i·ble (kən temp′tə bəl) ***adj.*** ⟦ME < L *contemptibilis*⟧ **1** deserving of contempt or scorn; worthless; despicable **2** [Obs.] contemptuous —**con·tempt′i·bil′i·ty** ***n.***, **con·tempt′i·ble·ness** —**con·tempt′i·bly** ***adv.***

con·temp·tu·ous (kən temp′choo͞ əs) ***adj.*** ⟦ML *contemptuosus*⟧ full of contempt; scornful; disdainful —**con·temp′tu·ous·ly** ***adv.*** —**con·temp′tu·ous·ness** ***n.***

con·temp·tus mun·di (kən temp′təs moon′dē) ⟦L⟧ contempt for the world, esp. the material world

con·tend (kən tend′) ***vi.*** ⟦ME *contenden*, to compete < L *contendere*, to stretch out, strive after < *com-*, together + *tendere*, to stretch: see TENSE[1]⟧ **1** to strive in combat; fight **2** to strive in competition; vie [*contend* for a prize] **3** to strive in debate or controversy; dispute —***vt.*** to hold to be a fact; assert [we *contend* that he is guilty]

con·tend·er (kən ten′dər) ***n.*** **1** one who contends **2** a person, team, etc. having or regarded as having a good chance to win a contest or competition [their team is just not a legitimate *contender* this year]

con·tent[1] (kən tent′) ***adj.*** ⟦OFr < L *contentus*, pp. of *continere*: see CONTAIN⟧ **1** happy enough with what one has or is; not desiring something more or different; satisfied **2** willing: used in the British House of Lords as an affirmative vote **3** [Archaic] pleased —***vt.*** to make content; satisfy: often used reflexively —***n.*** contentment —***SYN.*** SATISFY

con·tent[2] (kän′tent′) ***n.*** ⟦ME < ML *contentum* (pl. *contenta*), orig. neut. pp. of L *continere*: see CONTAIN⟧ **1** [*usually pl.*] *a)* all that is contained in something; everything inside [the *contents* of a jar, trunk, etc.] *b)* all that is contained or dealt with in a written work or a speech [a table of *contents*] **2** *a)* all that is dealt with in a course or area of study, work of art, discussion, etc. *b)* essential meaning; substance [the *content* of a poem as distinguished from its form] **3** [Rare] *a)* a holding power; capacity *b)* volume or area **4** the amount (of a specified substance) contained [iron with a high carbon *content*] **5** *a) Business* written matter, pictorial images, movies, videos, recorded music, etc. regarded collectively as the source material for merchandise in various, esp. electronic, formats or media *b) Comput.* such material made available on the World Wide Web

con·tent·ed (kən tent′id) ***adj.*** having or showing no desire for something more or different; satisfied [a *contented* look] —**con·tent′ed·ly** ***adv.*** —**con·tent′ed·ness** ***n.***

con·ten·tion (kən ten′shən) ***n.*** ⟦ME *contencioun* < OFr *contention* < L *contentio* < pp. of *contendere*: see CONTEND⟧ **1** the act of contending; strife, struggle, controversy, dispute, quarrel, etc. **2** a statement or point that one argues for as true or valid —***SYN.*** CONFLICT, DISCORD —**in** (or **out of**) **contention** having a (or no) chance to win

con·ten·tious (kən ten′shəs) ***adj.*** ⟦ME *contencios* < L *contentiosus*: see prec.⟧ **1** always ready to argue; quarrelsome **2** of or marked by contention **3** provoking or likely to provoke controversy [a *contentious* proposal] —***SYN.*** BELLIGERENT —**con·ten′tious·ly** ***adv.*** —**con·ten′tious·ness** ***n.***

con·tent·ment (kən tent′mənt) ***n.*** ⟦ME *contentement* < OFr⟧ **1** the state, quality, or fact of being contented **2** [Archaic] a satisfying or being satisfied

con·ter·mi·nous (kən tur′mə nəs, kän-) ***adj.*** ⟦L *conterminus*, bordering upon < *com-*, together + *terminus*, an end: see TERM[2]⟧ **1** having a common boundary; contiguous **2** contained within the same boundaries or limits [the *conterminous* U.S. includes all the states but Alaska and Hawaii] —**con·ter′mi·nous·ly** ***adv.***

con·tes·sa (kôn tes′sä; *E* kän tes′ə) ***n.***, *pl.* **con·tes·se** (kôn tes′se) or Eng. **con·tes·sas** (kän tes′əz) ⟦It⟧ [*also in roman type*] COUNTESS

con·test (kən test′; *for n.* kän′test′) ***vt.*** ⟦Fr *contester* < L *contestari*, to call to witness, bring action < *com-*, together + *testari*, to bear witness < *testis*, a witness: see TESTIFY⟧ **1** to try to disprove or invalidate (something) as by argument or legal action; dispute [to *contest* a will] **2** to fight for (ground, a military position, etc.); struggle to win or keep —***vi.*** to contend; struggle (*with* or *against*) —***n.*** **1** a fight, struggle, conflict, or controversy **2** any race, game, debate, etc. in which individuals or teams compete with one another to determine the winner —***SYN.*** CONFLICT —**no contest** **1** *Law* NOLO CONTENDERE **2** a match or competition in which one side easily dominates —**con·test′a·ble** ***adj.*** —**con·test′er** ***n.***

con·test·ant (kən test′ənt) ***n.*** ⟦Fr⟧ **1** one that competes in a contest **2** a person who contests a claim, decision, etc.

con·tes·ta·tion (kän′tes tā′shən) ***n.*** ⟦Fr < L *contestatio* < *contestari*⟧ the act of contesting; conflict

con·text (kän′tekst′) ***n.*** ⟦ME < L *contextus*, a joining together, orig., pp. of *contexere*, to weave together < *com-*, together + *texere*, to weave: see TECHNIC⟧ **1** the parts of a sentence, paragraph, discourse, etc. immediately next to or surrounding a specified word or passage and determining its exact meaning [to quote a remark out of *context*] **2** the whole situation, background, or environment relevant to a particular event, personality, creation, etc.

con·tex·tu·al (kən teks′choo͞ əl) ***adj.*** of, depending on, or belonging to the context —**con·tex′tu·al·ly** ***adv.***

con·tex·tu·al·ize (kən teks′choo͞ əl īz′) ***vt.*** **-ized′**, **-iz′ing** to place (a word, event, etc.) into a particular or appropriate context for the purpose of interpretation or analysis —**con·tex′tu·al·i·za′tion** ***n.***

con·tex·ture (kən teks′chər) ***n.*** ⟦Fr < L *contextus*: see CONTEXT⟧ **1** a weaving together; fabrication **2** an interwoven mass; fabric **3** the way in which a thing is put together; structure; composition **4** [Rare] CONTEXT

contg *abbrev.* containing

con·ti·gu·i·ty (kän′tə gyoo͞′ə tē) ***n.***, *pl.* **-ties** ⟦Fr *contiguité* < ML *contiguitas*: see fol.⟧ the state of being contiguous; nearness or contact

con·tig·u·ous (kən tig′yoo͞ əs) ***adj.*** ⟦L *contiguus*, bordering upon < base of *contingere*, to touch upon: see CONTACT⟧ **1** in physical contact; touching along all or most of one side 2 near, next, or adjacent —*SYN.* ADJACENT —**con·tig′u·ous·ly** *adv.* —**con·tig′u·ous·ness** *n.*

con·ti·nence (känt′'n əns) *n.* ⟦OFr < L *continentia* < prp. of *continere*: see CONTAIN⟧ 1 self-restraint; moderation 2 self-restraint in, esp. total abstinence from, sexual activity

con·ti·nent (känt′'n ənt) *adj.* ⟦OFr < L *continens*, prp. of *continere*: see CONTAIN⟧ 1 self-restrained; temperate 2 characterized by self-restraint in, esp. by total abstinence from, sexual activity 3 [Obs.] restrictive —*n.* 1 [Rare] a thing that retains or contains something 2 the mainland: now rare except in **the Continent**, all of Europe except the British Isles 3 any of the main large land areas of the earth, conventionally regarded (with or without outlying islands) as units; Africa, Asia, Australia, Europe, North America, South America, and, usually, Antarctica —**con′ti·nent·ly** *adv.*

con·ti·nen·tal (känt′'n ent′'l) *adj.* 1 of a continent 2 [*sometimes* **C-**] of or characteristic of the continent of Europe, excluding the British Isles ☆3 [**C-**] of the American colonies at the time of the American Revolution, or of the states just after this [the *Continental* Army] 4 [*often* **C-**] designating that portion of the U.S. landmass south of Canada 5 *Meteorol.* of the relatively dry air or climate associated with large land masses: see AIR MASS —*n.* 1 [*usually* **C-**] a person living on the continent of Europe, excluding the British Isles ☆2 [**C-**] a soldier of the American army during the Revolution ☆3 a piece of paper money issued by the Continental Congress: it became almost worthless before the end of the war, hence the phrases **not care (**or **give) a continental** and **not worth a continental** —**con′ti·nen′tal·ly** *adv.*

continental breakfast [*also* **C- b-**] a light breakfast, usually of rolls and coffee or tea, such as is typically eaten in some countries on the Continent

continental code MORSE[1]

Continental Congress either of two assemblies of representatives from the American colonies during the Revolutionary period: the first was held in 1774 to express grievances against British colonial policy; the second convened in 1775, created the Continental army, issued the Declaration of Independence (1776), and operated temporarily as the legislative body of the U.S.

Continental Divide ridge of the Rocky Mountains forming a North American watershed that separates rivers flowing in an easterly direction from those flowing in a westerly direction

continental drift the theory that continents slowly shift their positions as a result of plate tectonics, currents in the molten rocks of the earth's mantle, etc.

continental shelf a submerged shelf of land that begins at a continental shoreline, slopes downward gradually at an angle of about 0.1° for a variable distance, and ends at the top of a much steeper downward slope (**continental slope**) at an angle of about 3° to 6° until it reaches the ocean floor: at the outer edge of the shelf the depth of the ocean is usually between about 90 m (300 ft) and 180 m (600 ft)

con·tin·gence (kən tin′jəns) *n.* ⟦OFr < ML *contingentia* < L *contingens*, CONTINGENT⟧ 1 CONTINGENCY 2 the act or state of touching; tangency; contact

con·tin·gen·cy (-jən sē) *n., pl.* **-cies** ⟦see prec.⟧ 1 the quality or condition of being contingent; esp., dependence on chance or uncertain conditions 2 something whose occurrence depends on chance or uncertain conditions; a possible, unforeseen, or accidental occurrence [be prepared for any *contingency*] 3 some thing or event which depends on or is incidental to another [the *contingencies* of war] —*SYN.* EMERGENCY

con·tin·gent (kən tin′jənt) *adj.* ⟦L *contingens*, prp. of *contingere*, to touch: see CONTACT⟧ 1 [Obs.] touching; tangential 2 that may or may not happen; possible 3 happening by chance; accidental; fortuitous 4 unpredictable because dependent on chance 5 dependent (*on* or *upon* something uncertain); conditional 6 *Logic* true only under certain conditions or in certain contexts; not always or necessarily true 7 *Philos.* not subject to determinism; free —*n.* 1 [Now Rare] an accidental or chance happening 2 a share or quota, as of troops, laborers, delegates, etc. 3 a group forming part of a larger group —**con·tin′gent·ly** *adv.*

con·tin·u·al (kən tin′yo͞o əl) *adj.* ⟦ME *continuel* < OFr < L *continuus*: see CONTINUE⟧ 1 happening over and over again; repeated often; going on in rapid succession 2 going on uninterruptedly; continuous —**con·tin′u·al·ly** *adv.*

SYN.—**continual** applies to that which recurs repeatedly or goes on unceasingly over a long period of time [*continual* arguments]; **continuous** applies to that which extends without interruption in either space or time [a *continuous* expanse]; **constant** stresses uniformity, steadiness, or regularity in occurrence or recurrence [the *constant* beat of the heart]; **incessant** implies unceasing or uninterrupted activity [*incessant* chatter]; **perpetual** applies to that which lasts or persists for an indefinitely long time [a *perpetual* nuisance]; **eternal** stresses endlessness or timelessness [the *eternal* verities] —*ANT.* **intermittent, interrupted**

con·tin·u·ance (kən tin′yo͞o əns) *n.* ⟦OFr: see CONTINUE⟧ 1 the act or process of continuing, or lasting 2 the time during which an action, process, or state lasts; duration 3 the fact of remaining (*in* a place or condition); stay 4 [Rare] continuation; sequel 5 *Law* a postponement or adjournment to a later date

con·tin·u·ant (kən tin′yo͞o ənt) *n.* ⟦ME < L *continuans*, prp.: see CONTINUE⟧ *Phonet.* a speech sound that can be prolonged as long as the breath lasts, with no significant change in the quality of the sound: continuants include *fricatives* (s, f, th, etc.), *nasals* (m, n, ŋ), *liquids* (l, r), and *vowels*: distinguished from STOP

con·tin·u·a·tion (kən tin′yo͞o ā′shən) *n.* ⟦ME *continuacioun* < OFr *continuation* < L *continuatio* < pp. of *continuere*: see CONTINUE⟧ 1 a keeping up or going on without interruption; continued and unbroken existence or action 2 a taking up or beginning again after an interruption; resumption 3 a part or thing added to make something reach further or last longer; extension, supplement, sequel, etc.

con·tin·u·a·tive (kən tin′yo͞o āt′iv, -yo͞o ə tiv′) *adj.* ⟦LL *continuativus*⟧ 1 continuing something 2 *Gram.* expressing continuation [a *continuative* clause]

con·tin·u·a·tor (-yo͞o āt′ər) *n.* a person who continues something, as work begun by another

con·tin·ue (kən tin′yo͞o) *vi.* **-ued, -u·ing** ⟦ME *continuen* < OFr *continuer* < L *continuare*, to join, make continuous < *continuus*, continuous < *continere*: see CONTAIN⟧ 1 to remain in existence or effect; last; endure [the war *continued* for five years] 2 to go on in a specified course of action or condition; persist [to *continue* to mourn, soldiers *continuing* east to the sea] 3 to go on or extend; stretch [the road *continues* to the highway] 4 to remain in the same place or position; stay [to *continue* in office for another year] 5 to go on again after an interruption; resume —*vt.* 1 to go on with; carry on; keep up; persist in 2 to carry farther; extend 3 to go on with (an activity, story, etc.) again after an interruption; resume 4 to cause to remain; keep; retain [to *continue* someone in office] 5 *Law* to postpone or adjourn to a later date —**con·tin′u·a·ble** *adj.* —**con·tin′u·er** *n.*

SYN.—**continue** implies a going on in a specified course or condition and stresses uninterrupted existence rather than duration; **last** stresses duration, either for the specified time, or if unqualified, for a time beyond that which is usual; **endure** implies continued resistance to destructive influences or forces; **abide** is applied to that which remains stable and steadfast, esp. in contrast to that which is changing and transitory; **persist** implies continued existence beyond the expected or normal time —*ANT.* **stop, cease**

continued fraction a fraction whose denominator consists of a whole number plus a fraction whose denominator consists of a whole number plus a fraction, and so forth

continued proportion GEOMETRIC PROGRESSION

continuing education a program of classes for adult students offered by a college, university, etc. on a part-time basis, as for updating knowledge and skills in some professional field

con·ti·nu·i·ty (kän′tə no͞o′ə tē, -nyo͞o′-) *n., pl.* **-ties** ⟦OFr *continuite* < L *continuitas*⟧ 1 the state or quality of being continuous; connectedness; coherence 2 a continuous flow, series, or succession; unbroken, coherent whole 3 continuous duration ☆4 *a)* the practice of creating and maintaining a smooth and continuous plan or record of the physical details of a film, TV program, etc. *b)* a script that contains such details: see also SHOOTING SCRIPT 5 a series of comments or announcements connecting the parts of a radio or TV program 6 the script or story of a comic strip 7 *Film* smooth and matching transitions from one shot or sequence to the next

con·tin·u·o (kən tin′yo͞o ō′) *n.* ⟦It, orig., continuous < L *continuus*: see CONTINUE⟧ a continuous bass accompaniment, indicated by a shorthand method in notation, and played as on a harpsichord or organ, esp. in baroque music

con·tin·u·ous (kən tin′yo͞o əs) *adj.* ⟦L *continuus*: see CONTINUE⟧ 1 going on or extending without interruption or break; unbroken; connected 2 *Math.* designating a function whose value at each point is closely approached by its values at neighboring points —*SYN.* CONTINUAL —**con·tin′u·ous·ly** *adv.* —**con·tin′u·ous·ness** *n.*

continuous wave *Electronics* an electromagnetic wave, esp. a radio wave, with a constant amplitude and frequency

con·tin·u·um (kən tin′yo͞o əm) *n., pl.* **-u·a** (-yo͞o ə) or **-u·ums** ⟦L, neut. of *continuus*⟧ 1 a continuous whole, quantity, or series; thing whose parts cannot be separated or separately discerned 2 *Math.* the set of all real numbers See also SPACE-TIME (*n.* 1)

con·to (kän′tō) *n., pl.* **-tos** ⟦Port, lit., account, count < L *computus*: see COUNT[1]⟧ a money of account of Portugal and Cape Verde, equal to 1,000 escudos

con·tort (kən tôrt′) *vt., vi.* ⟦< L *contortus*, pp. of *contorquere*, to whirl, twist < *com-*, together + *torquere*, to twist: see TORT⟧ to twist or wrench out of its usual form into one that is grotesque; distort violently [a face *contorted* with pain] —*SYN.* DEFORM

con·tor·tion (kən tôr′shən) *n.* ⟦ME *contorsioun*⟧ 1 a contorting or being contorted, esp. of the face or body 2 a contorted condition or position —**con·tor′tive** *adj.*

con·tor·tion·ist (-ist) *n.* a person, as a circus acrobat, who can contort his or her body into unnatural positions

con·tour (kän′to͝or′) *n.* ⟦Fr < It *contorno* < LL *contornare*, to go around < L *com-*, intens. + *tornare*, to turn in a lathe: see TURN⟧ [*often pl.*] 1 the general shape or form of a figure, configuration, etc. [the rounded *contours* of the foothills] 2 the outline of such a shape —*vt.* 1 to make a contour or outline of 2 to mark contour lines on 3 to shape or mold to conform to the contour of something [a chair *contoured* to fit the body] 4 to construct (a road, etc.) in accordance with natural contours —*adj.* 1 made so as to conform to the shape or outline of something [*contour* sheets for a bed] 2 characterized by the making of furrows along the natural contour lines so as to avoid erosion, as on a hillside [*contour* farming] —*SYN.* OUTLINE

contour feathers feathers, including the wing and tail feathers, that form the surface plumage of a bird and determine the outer contour

contour interval the difference in value between adjacent contour lines on a map or chart

contour line a line on a map or chart connecting all points of the same elevation (or depth) in a particular area

contour map a map showing contour lines

contr *abbrev.* **1** contract **2** contraction **3** contralto **4** contrary **5** control **6** controller

con·tra[1] (kän′trə) ***prep.*** ⟦L⟧ against

con·tra[2] (kän′trə, kōn′-) ***n.*** ⟦AmSp, short for *contrarrevolucionario,* a counterrevolutionary⟧ [*also* **C-**] a member of any of the groups which sought to overthrow the Sandinista government in Nicaragua

con·tra- (kän′trə) ⟦< L *contra,* against < OL **com-tro-* (< *com-,* COM- + **-tero-,* compar. suffix); designating assoc. of two (opposites)⟧ *prefix* **1** against, opposite, opposed to, contrary [*contradict, contraceptive*] **2** lower in musical pitch or register [*contrabassoon*]

con·tra·band (kän′trə band′) ***n.*** ⟦Sp *contrabanda,* a smuggling < It *contrabando* < *contra-,* against + *bando* < ML *bannum* < Frank **ban,* a command; akin to OE *ban*: see BAN[1]⟧ **1** unlawful or prohibited trade **2** goods forbidden by law to be imported or exported; smuggled merchandise **3** CONTRABAND OF WAR ☆**4** during the Civil War, a black slave who fled to, or was smuggled or found behind, the Union lines —***adj.*** forbidden by law to be imported or exported

con·tra·band·ist (-ist) ***n.*** a person who trades in contraband goods; smuggler

contraband of war war materiel, as ammunition or weapons, which, by international law, may rightfully be intercepted and seized by either belligerent when shipped to the other one by a neutral country

con·tra·bass (kän′trə bās′) ***adj.*** ⟦see CONTRA- & BASS[1]⟧ pitched an octave lower than the normal bass —***n.*** DOUBLE BASS —**con′tra·bass′ist** ***n.***

con·tra·bas·soon (kän′trə bə so͞on′) ***n.*** the double bassoon, larger than the bassoon and an octave lower in pitch

con·tra·cep·tion (kän′trə sep′shən) ***n.*** ⟦CONTRA- + (CON)CEPTION⟧ the intentional prevention of fertilization of an ovum, as by special devices, drugs, etc.

con·tra·cep·tive (kän′trə sep′tiv) ***adj.*** of or used for contraception —***n.*** any contraceptive device or agent

con·tract (kän′trakt′ *for n. & usually for vt. 1 & vi. 1;* kən trakt′ *for v. generally*) ***n.*** ⟦OFr < L *contractus,* pp. of *contrahere,* to draw together, make a bargain < *com-,* together + *trahere,* to DRAW⟧ **1** an agreement between two or more people to do something, esp. one formally set forth in writing and enforceable by law; compact; covenant **2** a formal agreement of marriage or betrothal **3** a document containing the terms of a contract **4** the branch of law having to do with contracts ☆**5** [Informal] an assignment to murder someone for pay **6** *Bridge a)* the highest bid in an auction *b)* the number of tricks, and the suit or no-trump preference, stated in such a bid *c)* CONTRACT BRIDGE —***vt.*** **1** *a)* to enter upon, or undertake, by contract *b)* to hire (a person, business, etc.) to perform under contract [we *contracted* him to fix the roof] **2** to get, acquire, or incur [to *contract* a disease, a debt, etc.] **3** *a)* to reduce in size; draw together; narrow; shrink; shorten [cold *contracts* metals] *b)* to draw (the brow or brows) together; knit **4** to narrow in scope; restrict **5** [Rare] to betroth **6** *Gram.* to shorten (a word or phrase) by the omission of a letter or sound, as in *I'm, e'er, can't* —***vi.*** **1** to make a contract; agree formally [to *contract* for a new car] **2** to become reduced in size or bulk; draw together; shrink; narrow; shorten —**contract out 1** to assign (a job) by contract; specif., to subcontract **2** [Chiefly Brit.] to withdraw from a contract or agreement —**con·tract′i·bil′i·ty** ***n.*** —**con·tract′i·ble** ***adj.***

SYN.—**contract** implies a drawing together of surface or parts and a resultant decrease in size, bulk, or extent; to **shrink** is to contract so as to be short of the normal or required length, amount, extent, etc. [those shirts have *shrunk*]; **condense** suggests reduction of something into a more compact or more dense form without loss of essential content [*condensed* milk; to **compress** is to press or squeeze into a more compact, orderly form [a lifetime's work *compressed* into one volume]; **deflate** implies a reduction in size or bulk by the removal of air, gas, or in extended use, anything insubstantial [to *deflate* a balloon, one's ego, etc.] —***ANT.*** **expand, inflate**

con·tract bridge (kän′trakt′) a form of bridge, developed from auction bridge, in which only the number of tricks named in the contract may be counted toward a game, additional tricks being counted as a bonus score

con·trac·tile (kən trak′til) ***adj.*** ⟦CONTRACT (*vt.* 3) + -ILE⟧ **1** having the power of contracting **2** producing contraction —**con·trac·til·i·ty** (kän′trak til′ə tē) ***n.***

con·trac·tion (kən trak′shən) ***n.*** ⟦ME *contraccioun* < OFr *contraction* < L *contractio*⟧ **1** a contracting or being contracted **2** the shortening and thickening of a muscle fiber or a muscle in action, esp. of the uterus during labor **3** *Gram. a)* the shortening of a word or phrase by the omission of one or more sounds or letters *b)* a word form resulting from this (Ex.: *she's* for *she is, aren't* for *are not*) **4** *Econ.* a period of decrease in business activity —**con·trac′tion·al** ***adj.***

con·trac·tive (kən trak′tiv) ***adj.*** ⟦ML *contractivus*⟧ **1** having the power of contracting **2** producing or tending to produce contraction **3** of contraction

con·trac·tor (kän′trak′tər; *also, and for 3 usually,* kən trak′tər) ***n.*** **1** one of the parties to a contract **2** a person who contracts to supply certain materials or do certain work for a stipulated sum, esp. one who does so in any of the building trades; often, specif., a GENERAL CONTRACTOR **3** a thing that contracts, narrows, or shortens; esp., a muscle that contracts

con·trac·tu·al (kən trak′cho͞o əl) ***adj.*** of, or having the nature of, a contract —**con·trac′tu·al·ly** ***adv.***

con·trac·ture (kən trak′chər) ***n.*** a condition of abnormal shortening or shrinkage of a muscle, tendon, etc., often with persistent flexion or distortion at a joint

con·tra·dance (kän′trə dans′) ***n.*** CONTREDANSE

con·tra·dict (kän′trə dikt′) ***vt.*** ⟦< L *contradictus,* pp. of *contradicere* < *contra-,* CONTRA- + *dicere,* to speak: see DICTION⟧ **1** *a)* to assert the opposite of (what someone else has said) *b)* to deny the statement of (a person) **2** to declare (a statement, report, etc.) to be false or incorrect **3** to be contrary or opposed to; go against [the facts *contradict* his theory] —***vi.*** to speak in denial; oppose verbally —***SYN.*** DENY —**con′tra·dict′a·ble** ***adj.*** —**con′tra·dic′tor** ***n.*,** **con′tra·dict′er**

con·tra·dic·tion (kän′trə dik′shən) ***n.*** ⟦ME *contradiccioun* < OFr *contradiction* < L *contradictio*⟧ **1** a contradicting or being contradicted **2** a statement in opposition to another; denial **3** a condition in which things tend to be contrary to each other; inconsistency; discrepancy **4** a person, thing, or statement having contradictory elements or qualities

con·tra·dic·tious (-dik′shəs) ***adj.*** **1** inclined to contradict; contentious **2** [Archaic] CONTRADICTORY (sense 1)

con·tra·dic·to·ry (kän′trə dik′tə rē) ***adj.*** ⟦ME *contradictorie* < LL *contradictorius*⟧ **1** involving a contradiction; inconsistent: also **con′tra·dic′tive** **2** inclined to contradict or deny —***n.*,** *pl.* **-ries** **1** something that contradicts; an opposite **2** *Logic* either of two proportions so related that only one can be true and, likewise, only one can be false: see CONTRARY (*n.* 2) —**con′tra·dic′to·ri·ly** (-rə lē) ***adv.*** —**con′tra·dic′to·ri·ness** (-rē nis) ***n.***

con·tra·dis·tinc·tion (kän′trə dis tiŋk′shən) ***n.*** distinction by contrast [tolerance in *contradistinction* to love] —**con′tra·dis·tinc′tive** (-tiv) ***adj.*** —**con′tra·dis·tinc′tive·ly** ***adv.***

con·tra·dis·tin·guish (-dis tiŋ′gwish′) ***vt.*** to distinguish (one thing from another) by contrasting

☆**con·trail** (kän′trāl′) ***n.*** ⟦CON(DENSATION) + TRAIL⟧ a white trail of condensed water vapor that sometimes forms in the wake of an aircraft; vapor trail

con·tra·in·di·cate (kän′trə in′di kāt′) ***vt.*** **-cat′ed, -cat′ing** to make (the indicated, or expected, procedure or treatment) inadvisable —**con′tra·in′di·ca′tion** ***n.*** —**con′tra·in·dic′a·tive** (-in dik′ə tiv) ***adj.***

con·tral·to (kən tral′tō) ***n.*,** *pl.* **-tos** or **-ti** (-tē) ⟦It: see CONTRA- & ALTO⟧ **1** the range of a low female voice between mezzo-soprano and tenor, usually from about the first F below middle C to the second F above; alto **2** *a)* a voice or singer with such a range *b)* a part for such a voice —***adj.*** of, for, or having the range of a contralto

con·tra·po·si·tion (kän′trə pə zish′ən) ***n.*** a placing opposite or over against; antithesis; contrast

con·tra·pos·i·tive (-päz′ə tiv′) ***n.*** *Logic* a proposition obtained by negating and transposing the terms of a given proposition [the *contrapositive* of "All A is B" is "All not-B is not-A"]

con·trap·tion (kən trap′shən) ***n.*** ⟦< ? CON(TRIVE) + TRAP[1], *n.* 2 + -TION⟧ a device or machine regarded as strange, incomprehensible, makeshift, etc.; contrivance or gadget

con·tra·pun·tal (kän′trə punt′'l) ***adj.*** ⟦It *contrappunto* (see COUNTERPOINT + -AL⟧ **1** of or characterized by counterpoint **2** according to the principles of counterpoint —**con′tra·pun′tal·ly** ***adv.***

con·tra·pun·tist (-punt′ist) ***n.*** an expert in the principles and art of counterpoint

con·trar·i·an (kän trer′ē ən) ***n.*** a person who typically acts or thinks in a way contrary to popular or accepted opinion; specif., an investor who seeks to make a profit by acting in opposition to majority opinion, prevailing wisdom, etc., as by buying a company's stock when it is out of favor with the majority of investors —***adj.*** of, by, or being a contrarian

con·tra·ri·e·ty (kän′trə rī′ə tē) ***n.*** ⟦ME *contrarieté* < OFr < LL *contrarietas* < L *contrarius*⟧ **1** the condition or quality of being contrary **2** *pl.* **-ties** anything that is contrary; inconsistency or discrepancy

con·trar·i·ous (kən trer′ē əs) ***adj.*** ⟦ME < ML *contrariosus* < L *contrarius*⟧ [Now Chiefly Dial.] contrary; esp., perverse

con·trar·i·wise (kän′trer′ē wīz′; *for 3, often* kən trer′ē wīz′) ***adv.*** ⟦ME < fol. + -WISE⟧ **1** on the contrary; from the opposite point of view **2** in the opposite way; in a reversed order, direction, etc. **3** perversely

con·trar·y (kän′trer′ē; *for adj. 4, often* kən trer′ē) ***adj.*** ⟦ME *contrarie* < OFr *contraire* < L *contrarius,* opposite, opposed < *contra,* against⟧ **1** opposed; in opposition [*contrary* to the rules] **2** opposite in nature, order, direction, etc.; altogether different **3** unfavorable [*contrary* winds] **4** inclined to oppose or disagree stubbornly; perverse —***n.*,** *pl.* **-trar′ies** **1** the opposite; thing that is the opposite of another **2** *Logic* either of two propositions so related that only one can be true but both may be false: see CONTRADICTORY (*n.* 2) —***adv.*** in a contrary way; contrariwise —**by contraries** [Archaic] contrary to what is expected —**on the contrary** as opposed to what has been said —**to the contrary** to the opposite effect; in reversal of what is stated —**con·trar·i·ly** (kän′trer′ə lē, kən trer′-) ***adv.*** —**con′trar′i·ness** ***n.***

SYN.—**contrary,** in this comparison, implies a habitual disinclination to accept orders, advice, etc.; **perverse** implies an unreasonable obstinacy in deviating from what is considered right or acceptable; **restive** is applied to persons who are impatient under restraint or discipline and hence are hard to control or keep in order; **balky** implies a stopping short and stubbornly refusing to go on See also **opposite**

con·trast (kən trast′; *for n.* kän′trast′) *vt.* ⟦Fr *contraster* < It & VL **contrastare*, to withstand < L *contra*, against + *stare*, to STAND⟧ to compare so as to point out the differences; set off against one another —*vi.* to show differences when compared; form a contrast —*n.* **1** a contrasting or being contrasted **2** a difference, esp. a striking difference, between things being compared **3** a person or thing showing differences when compared with another **4** the effect of a striking difference, as in color or tone, of adjacent parts of a painting, photograph, video-screen image, etc. —**SYN.** COMPARE —**con·trast′a·ble** *adj.* —**con·trast′ing·ly** *adv.* —**con·trast′ive** *adj.*

con·trast·y (kän′tras′tē, kən tras′tē) *adj. Photog.* showing sharp contrasts of tone, as between light and dark areas

con·tra·val·la·tion (kän′trə və lā′shən) *n.* ⟦Fr *contrevallation* < L *contra*, counter + *vallatio*, entrenchment < *vallum*, WALL⟧ a fortification set up to protect a besieging force from attack by the defenders of the besieged place or by a relieving force from the outside

con·tra·vene (kän′trə vēn′) *vt.* **-vened′**, **-ven′ing** ⟦Fr *contrevenir* < LL *contravenire* < L *contra*, against + *venire*, to COME⟧ **1** to go against; oppose; conflict with; violate [practices *contravening* an ethical code] **2** to disagree with in argument; contradict —**con′tra·ven′tion** (-ven′shən) *n.*

con·tre·coup (kän′trə ko͞o′) *n.* ⟦Fr < *contre* (L *contra*), against + *coup*, a blow, COUP⟧ an injury, as to the brain, resulting from a blow but produced in a part opposite to the part that received the blow, resulting from the impact of the organ against an unyielding surface

con·tre·danse (kän′trə dans′) *n.* ⟦Fr, altered (infl. by *contre*, opposite) < COUNTRY-DANCE⟧ **1** a folk dance in which the partners form two facing lines; country-dance **2** music for this dance

con·tre·temps (kän′trə tän′) *n., pl.* **-temps′** (-tän′, -tänz′) ⟦Fr, altered (infl. by *contre*, opposite & *temps*, time) < OFr *contrestant*, prp. of *contrester* < VL **contrastare*, CONTRAST⟧ **1** an inopportune happening causing confusion or embarrassment; awkward mishap **2** a brief or minor argument or quarrel

contrib *abbrev.* **1** contribution **2** contributor

con·trib·ute (kən trib′yo͞ot) *vt., vi.* **-ut·ed**, **-ut·ing** ⟦< L *contributus*, pp. of *contribuere*: see COM- & TRIBUTE⟧ **1** to give or provide jointly with others; give to a common fund **2** to write and give or sell (an article, story, poem, etc.) to a magazine, newspaper, or other publication **3** to give or furnish (knowledge, ideas, etc.) —**contribute to** to have a share in bringing about (a result); be partly responsible for [fatigue *contributed* to his defeat] —**con·trib′u·tive** *adj.* —**con·trib′u·tor** *n.*

con·tri·bu·tion (kän′trə byo͞o′shən) *n.* ⟦ME *contribucioun* < OFr *contribution* < L *contributio*⟧ **1** the act of contributing **2** something contributed, as money to a charity or a poem to a magazine **3** *a)* a special levy or tax *b)* [Archaic] a levy for supporting an army in the field

con·trib·u·to·ry (kən trib′yo͞o tôr′ē) *adj.* ⟦ME *contributorie* < ML *contributorius*⟧ **1** contributing, as to a common fund **2** having a share in bringing about a result [*contributory* negligence] **3** involving, or having the nature of, a contribution —*n., pl.* **-ries** a person or thing that contributes

con·trite (kən trīt′, kän′trīt′) *adj.* ⟦ME *contrit* < OFr < LL(Ec) *contritus*, lit., worn out, ground to pieces, pp. of L *conterere*, to grind < *com-*, together + *terere*, to rub: see THROW⟧ **1** feeling contrition; repentant **2** showing or resulting from contrition —**con·trite′ly** *adv.* —**con·trite′ness** *n.*

con·tri·tion (kən trish′ən) *n.* ⟦ME *contricioun* < OFr *contrition* < LL(Ec) *contritio*, grief: see prec.⟧ **1** remorse for having done wrong **2** *Theol.* sorrow for having offended God: **perfect contrition** is such sorrow arising out of pure love of God —**SYN.** PENITENCE

con·triv·ance (kən trī′vəns) *n.* **1** the act, way, or power of contriving **2** something contrived, as an invention, mechanical device, or ingenious plan

con·trive (kən trīv′) *vt.* **-trived′**, **-triv′ing** ⟦ME *contreven* < OFr *controver*, to find out, contrive, imagine < VL *contropare*, to compare < *com*, COM- + *tropus*, TROPE⟧ **1** to think up; devise; scheme; plan [to *contrive* a way to help] **2** to construct skillfully or ingeniously; fabricate **3** to bring about, as by a scheme; manage [he *contrived* to get in] **4** to scheme for evil purposes —*vi.* to form plans; scheme —**con·triv′a·ble** *adj.* —**con·triv′er** *n.*

con·trived (-trīvd′) *adj.* too obviously the result of forethought and planning; forced; artificial

con·trol (kən trōl′) *vt.* **-trolled′**, **-trol′ling** ⟦ME *countrollen* < Anglo-Fr *contreroller* < Fr *contrerole* < ML *contrarotulus*, a counter, register < L *contra*, against + *rotulus*: see ROLL⟧ **1** [Obs.] to check or verify (payments, accounts, etc.) by comparison with a duplicate register **2** to regulate (financial affairs) **3** to verify (an experiment) by comparison with a standard or by other experiments **4** to exercise authority over; direct; command **5** to operate or regulate [this knob *controls* the volume of sound] **6** to hold back; curb; restrain [*control* your grief] —*n.* **1** the act or fact of controlling; power to direct or regulate; ability to use effectively [her *control* over her passions, the violinist's *control* of his vibrato] **2** the condition of being directed or restrained; restraint [the car went out of *control*] **3** a means of controlling; check [wage and price *controls*] **4** a standard of comparison for verifying or checking the findings of an experiment; specif., such a standard obtained by withholding the substance, treatment, drug, etc. being tested **5** *a)* an instrument or apparatus to regulate a mechanism (*usually used in pl.*) *b)* a device used to adjust or control [the volume *control* on an amplifier] **6** a spirit supposed to direct the actions and speech of a spiritualistic medium —**SYN.** CONDUCT, POWER —**con·trol′la·bil′i·ty** *n.* —**con·trol′la·ble** *adj.*

control experiment an experiment in which the variable factors are controlled so as to make it possible to observe the results of varying one factor at a time

control freak [Informal] a person characterized by the obsessive need to control or manipulate small details, the actions of others, etc.

control group a group that serves as the CONTROL (*n.* 4) in a scientific experiment; specif., such a group that does not receive the substance, drug, treatment, etc. being tested

☆**controlled substance** a drug regulated by the Federal Controlled Substances Acts, including opiates, depressants, stimulants, and hallucinogens

con·trol·ler (kən trōl′ər) *n.* ⟦ME *countrollour* < Anglo-Fr *contrerollour* < OFr *contreroller*: see CONTROL⟧ **1** the chief accounting officer with responsibility for internal auditing, as in a business, government (usually sp. *comptroller*), or institution **2** a person or device that controls —**con·trol′ler·ship′** *n.*

con·trol·ling (kən trōl′iŋ) *adj.* characterized by the obsessive need to control the actions of others

controlling interest the ownership or control of sufficient shares in a company to allow for an exercise of control over that company

control rod an adjustable rod or bar containing a neutron-absorbing material or, in a fast reactor, fuel used to regulate the fission chain reaction inside a nuclear reactor core

control tower a tower at an airport with radar, etc. from which air traffic is directed, chiefly by radio

con·tro·ver·sial (kän′trə vur′shəl, -sē əl) *adj.* ⟦LL *controversialis*⟧ **1** of, subject to, or stirring up controversy; debatable **2** [Rare] liking to take part in controversy; disputatious —**con′tro·ver′sial·ly** *adv.*

con·tro·ver·sial·ist (-ist) *n.* a person who takes part in controversy or likes to do so

con·tro·ver·sy (kän′trə vur′sē) *n., pl.* **-sies** ⟦ME *controversie* < L *controversia* < *controversus*, turned in an opposite direction < *contra*, against + *versus*: see VERSE⟧ **1** a lengthy discussion of an important question in which opposing opinions clash; debate; disputation **2** a quarrel or dispute —**SYN.** ARGUMENT

con·tro·vert (kän′trə vurt′, kän′trə vurt′) *vt.* ⟦back-form. < prec., modeled on words ending in *-vert* (e.g., DIVERT, REVERT)⟧ **1** to argue or reason against; contradict; deny; dispute **2** to argue about; debate; discuss —**SYN.** DISPROVE —**con′tro·vert′i·ble** *adj.* —**con′tro·vert′i·bly** *adv.*

con·tu·ma·cious (kän′tyo͞o mā′shəs, -tə-) *adj.* ⟦< fol. + -OUS⟧ obstinately resisting authority; insubordinate; disobedient —**con′tu·ma′cious·ly** *adv.*

con·tu·ma·cy (kän′tyo͞o mə sē, -tə-) *n., pl.* **-cies** ⟦ME *contumacie* < L *contumacia* < *contumax*, haughty, stubborn < *com-*, intens. + *tumere*, to swell up: see TUMOR⟧ stubborn refusal to submit to authority, esp. that of a law court; insubordination; disobedience

con·tu·me·li·ous (kän′tyo͞o mē′lē əs, -to͞o-) *adj.* ⟦ME < OFr *contumelieus* < L *contumeliosus* < *contumelia*: see fol.⟧ rude in a contemptuous way; insulting and humiliating —**con′tu·me′li·ous·ly** *adv.*

con·tu·me·ly (kän′to͞o mə lē, -tyo͞o-; kän′to͞om lē, -tyo͞om-; kən to͞o′mə lē, -tyo͞o′-) *n., pl.* **-lies** ⟦ME *contumelie* < OFr < L *contumelia*, a reproach, abuse; prob. akin to CONTUMACY⟧ **1** haughty and contemptuous rudeness; insulting and humiliating treatment or language **2** an instance of this; scornful insult

con·tuse (kən to͞oz′, -to͞oz′) *vt.* **-tused′**, **-tus′ing** ⟦ME *contusen* < L *contusus*, pp. of *contundere*, to beat, break to pieces < *com-*, intens. + *tundere*, to beat: see STEEP[1]⟧ to injure without breaking the skin; bruise

con·tu·sion (kən tyo͞o′zhən, -to͞o-) *n.* ⟦ME *contusioun* < L *contusio*: see prec.⟧ **1** a bruising or being bruised **2** a bruise; injury in which the skin is not broken

co·nun·drum (kə nun′drəm) *n.* ⟦16th-c. Oxford University L slang for pedant, whim, etc.; early sp. *quonundrum*⟧ **1** a riddle whose answer contains a pun (Ex.: What's the difference between a jeweler and a jailer? One sells watches and the other watches cells.) **2** any puzzling question or problem —**SYN.** MYSTERY[1]

con·ur·ba·tion (kän′ər bā′shən) *n.* ⟦< CON- + L *urbs*, city + -ATION⟧ an extremely large, densely populated urban area, usually a complex of suburbs and smaller towns together with the large city at their center

con·va·lesce (kän′və les′) *vi.* **-lesced′**, **-lesc′ing** ⟦L *convalescere*, to begin to grow strong < *com-*, intens. + *valescere*, to grow strong, inchoative of *valere*, to be strong: see VALUE⟧ to recover gradually from illness; regain strength and health

con·va·les·cence (-ləs′əns) *n.* ⟦Fr < L *convalescens*, prp. of prec.⟧ **1** gradual recovery after illness **2** the period of such recovery

con·va·les·cent (-les′ənt) *adj.* ⟦< L *convalescens*⟧ **1** gradually recovering health after illness **2** of or having to do with convalescence [a *convalescent* diet] —*n.* a person who is convalescing

con·vec·tion (kən vek′shən) *n.* ⟦L *convectio* < pp. of *convehere*, to bring together < *com-*, together + *vehere*, to carry, bear⟧ **1** a transmitting or conveying **2** *a)* the mass movement of portions of a fluid within the fluid, caused by differences in density *b)* the transfer of heat by its absorption by a fluid at one point, followed by motion of the fluid and rejection of the heat at another point —*adj.* designating or of an oven, grill, etc. that circulates the hot air continuously, by means of a fan, for faster, more even cooking —**con·vec′tion·al** *adj.* —**con·vec′tive** *adj.* —**con·vec′tive·ly** *adv.* —**con·vec′tor** *n.*

con·ve·nance (kän′və nəns, -näns′; *Fr* kōnv näns′) ***n.***, *pl.* **-nan·ces** (-nən siz, -nän′siz; *Fr*, -näns′) ⟦Fr, fitness, propriety < *convenir*, to be in accord, fit < L *convenire*, fol.⟧ conventional social usage

con·vene (kən vēn′) ***vi.*** **-vened′**, **-ven′ing** ⟦ME *convenen* < OFr *convenir* < L *convenire* < *com-*, together + *venire*, to COME⟧ to meet together; assemble, esp. for a common purpose —***vt.*** **1** to cause to assemble, or meet together [to *convene* members of the committee] **2** to cause (a meeting, etc.) to take place, as by calling its participants **3** to summon before a court of law —***SYN.*** CALL

con·ven·er or **con·ve·nor** (kən vēn′ər) ***n.*** a person responsible for calling participants to a meeting, specif. a committee meeting

con·ven·ience (kən vēn′yəns) ***n.*** ⟦ME < L *convenientia* < *convenire*, CONVENE⟧ **1** the quality of being convenient; fitness or serviceability **2** personal well-being; comfort **3** a condition personally favorable or suitable; advantage **4** anything that adds to one's comfort or saves work; useful, handy, or helpful device, article, service, etc. **5** [Brit.] a LAVATORY (sense 2), esp. one for the public Also [Archaic] **con·ven′ien·cy** (-yən sē), *pl.* **-cies** —**at someone's convenience** at a time, or in a place or manner, suitable to someone

☆**convenience food** a food that is easy to prepare and serve, as a frozen dinner or packaged mix

☆**convenience store** a small store, often franchised, offering a limited selection of food and household products and staying open for longer hours at a convenient location

con·ven·ient (-yənt) ***adj.*** ⟦ME < L *conveniens*, prp. of *convenire*, CONVENE⟧ **1** adding to one's comfort; easy to do, use, or get to; causing little trouble or work; handy **2** easily accessible (*to*); near (*to*) **3** [Obs.] appropriate; suitable —**con·ven′ient·ly** ***adv.***

con·vent (kän′vənt, -vent′) ***n.*** ⟦OFr < L *conventus*, assembly (in ML(Ec), religious house, convent), orig. pp. of *convenire*, CONVENE⟧ **1** a community of nuns or, sometimes, monks, living under strict religious vows **2** the building or buildings occupied by such a community —***SYN.*** CLOISTER

con·ven·ti·cle (kən ven′ti kəl) ***n.*** ⟦ME < OFr *conventicule* < L *conventiculum*, dim. of prec.⟧ **1** a religious assembly held illegally and secretly by certain Protestant sects that disputed the authority of the Church of England in the 16th and 17th cent. **2** the meeting place of such an assembly

con·ven·tion (kən ven′shən) ***n.*** ⟦ME *convencioun* < L *conventio* < pp. of *convenire*, CONVENE⟧ **1** [Rare] a convening or being convened **2** *a)* an assembly, often periodical, of members or delegates, as of a political, social, professional, or religious group *b)* the members or delegates at such an assembly *c)* in the U.S., an official gathering of delegates of a political party to select candidates for office, formulate party policies, etc. **3** a large, organized public exhibition centered around a particular industry or activity and typically featuring speakers, vendors, etc. [a sportsmen's *convention*, comic book *convention*] **4** *a)* an agreement between persons, nations, etc. [a copyright *convention*, the Geneva *Convention*] *b)* general agreement on the usages and practices of social life [bohemian revolt against *convention*] **5** *a)* a customary practice, rule, method, etc.; usage [the soliloquy was an Elizabethan dramatic *convention*] *b) Card Games* a bid or play understood by partners to have a special meaning when made by either of them

con·ven·tion·al (kən ven′shə nəl) ***adj.*** ⟦LL *conventionalis*⟧ **1** having to do with a convention or assembly **2** of, sanctioned by, or growing out of custom or usage; customary **3** *a)* depending on or conforming to formal or accepted standards or rules rather than nature; not natural, original, or spontaneous [*conventional* behavior] *b)* not unusual or extreme; ordinary **4** stylized; conventionalized **5** nonnuclear [*conventional* weapons] **6** *Law* based on an agreement between parties; contractual —**con·ven′tion·al·ism′** ***n.*** —**con·ven′tion·al·ist** ***n.*** —**con·ven′tion·al·ly** ***adv.***

con·ven·tion·al·i·ty (kən ven′shə nal′ə tē) ***n.***, *pl.* **-ties** **1** the quality, fact, or condition of being conventional **2** conventional behavior or act **3** a conventional form, usage, or rule

con·ven·tion·al·ize (kən ven′shən əl īz′) ***vt.*** **-ized′**, **-iz′ing** **1** to make conventional **2** *Art* to treat in an abstract or simplified manner; stylize —**con·ven′tion·al·i·za′tion** ***n.***

☆**conventional wisdom** the generally accepted belief with regard to some matter, or the set of beliefs held by most people

☆**con·ven·tion·eer** (kən ven′shən ir′) ***n.*** a delegate or member attending a convention

con·ven·tu·al (kən ven′choo͞ əl) ***adj.*** ⟦ME < ML *conventualis*⟧ of, like, or characteristic of a convent —***n.*** **1** a member of a convent **2** [**C-**] a member of a branch (**Friars Minor Conventual**) of the Franciscan order under a modified rule that permits the holding of property in common

con·verge (kən vurj′) ***vi.*** **-verged′**, **-verg′ing** ⟦LL *convergere* < L *com-*, together + *vergere*, to bend: see VERGE[2]⟧ **1** to come together or tend to come together at a point **2** to move or be directed toward each other or toward the same place, purpose, or result **3** to approach a definite limit, as the sum of certain infinite series of numbers (Ex: $1 + \frac{1}{2} + \frac{1}{4} + \frac{1}{8} + \frac{1}{16} + \frac{1}{32} \ldots = 2$) —***vt.*** to cause to converge

con·ver·gence (kən vur′jəns) ***n.*** ⟦< CONVERGENT⟧ **1** the act, fact, or condition of converging **2** the point at which things converge **3** *Biol.* the development of similarities in unrelated organisms living in similar environments Also **con·ver′gen·cy**, *pl.* **-cies** —**con·ver′gent** ***adj.***

con·vers·a·ble (kən vur′sə bəl) ***adj.*** ⟦Fr < ML *conversabilis*⟧ **1** *a)* easy to talk to; affable *b)* liking to talk **2** [Archaic] of or fit for conversation

con·ver·sant (kən vur′sənt, kän′vər-) ***adj.*** ⟦ME *conversaunt* < OFr *conversant* < L *conversans*, prp. of *conversari*: see CONVERSE[1]⟧ familiar or acquainted (*with*), esp. as a result of study or experience; versed (*in*) —**con·ver′sance** ***n.***, **con·ver′san·cy** —**con·ver′sant·ly** ***adv.***

con·ver·sa·tion (kän′vər sā′shən) ***n.*** ⟦ME *conversacioun* < OFr *conversation* < L *conversatio* < pp. of *conversari*: see CONVERSE[1]⟧ **1** the act or an instance of talking together; specif., *a)* familiar talk; verbal exchange of ideas, opinions, etc. *b)* an informal conference on a problem or area of interest by representatives of governments, factions, etc. **2** sexual intercourse: now only in the legal phrase *criminal conversation*, i.e., adultery as grounds for divorce or other action **3** [Archaic] manner of living; behavior **4** [Obs.] social intercourse **5** [Obs.] familiarity based on study or use —**make conversation** [Informal] to engage in light, informal conversation, often, specif., out of mere politeness

con·ver·sa·tion·al (-shə nəl) ***adj.*** **1** of, like, or for conversation **2** fond of or given to conversation; liking to converse **3** *Comput.* INTERACTIVE (sense 3) —**con′ver·sa′tion·al·ly** ***adv.***

con·ver·sa·tion·al·ist (-shə nəl ist) ***n.*** a person who converses; esp., one who enjoys and is skilled at conversation: also **con′ver·sa′tion·ist** (-shə nist)

conversation piece **1** a type of genre painting, popular in the 18th cent., which shows a group of people in an appropriate setting **2** something, as an unusual article of furniture, that attracts attention or invites comment

con·ver·sa·zi·o·ne (kôn′ver sä tsyô′ne) ***n.***, *pl.* **-ni** (-nē) ⟦It, lit., conversation⟧ a social gathering for conversation about literature, the arts, etc.: also Eng. **con·ver·sa·zio·ne** (kän′vər sät′sē ō′nē), *pl.* **-nes** (-nēz)

con·verse[1] (kən vurs′; *for n.* kän′vurs′) ***vi.*** **-versed′**, **-vers′ing** ⟦ME *conversen* < OFr *converser* < L *conversari*, to live with, keep company with, freq. of *convertere*: see CONVERT⟧ **1** to hold a conversation; talk **2** [Obs.] to consort; interact socially —***n.*** **1** informal talk; conversation **2** [Obs.] social interaction —***SYN.*** SPEAK —**con·vers′er** ***n.***

con·verse[2] (kän′vurs; *also, for adj.*, kən vurs′) ***adj.*** ⟦L *conversus*, pp. of *convertere*: see CONVERT⟧ reversed in position, order, action, etc.; opposite; contrary; turned about —***n.*** **1** a thing related in a converse way; the opposite **2** *Logic* a proposition obtained by conversion —**con·verse′ly** ***adv.***

con·ver·sion (kən vur′zhən, -shən) ***n.*** ⟦ME *conversioun* < OFr *conversion* < L *conversio* < pp. of *convertere*: see CONVERT⟧ **1** a converting or being converted; specif., *a)* a change from lack of faith to religious belief; adoption of a religion *b)* a change from one belief, religion, doctrine, opinion, etc. to another **2** *Finance a)* an exchange of one kind or class or security for another *b)* an exchange of a currency for an equivalent amount of another currency or precious metal ☆**3** *Football a)* an additional scoring opportunity of a point or two, as by kicking, passing, or running with the ball, awarded to a team after it scores a touchdown *b)* the score so made **4** *Rugby* a somewhat similar play as in football that scores two points after a try **5** *Law a)* unlawful appropriation or use of another's property, resulting in a deprivation of ownership rights *b)* an exchange of property from real to personal, or the reverse, as for settling the terms of a will (in full **equitable conversion**) **6** *Logic* the interchanging of the terms of a proposition (Ex.: "All of A is B" becomes "All of B is A") **7** *Math.* a change in the form of a quantity, a unit, or an expression without a change in the value **8** *Psychiatry* a mechanism by which emotional conflict is transformed into an apparent physical disability affecting the sensory or voluntary motor systems and having symbolic meaning: also **conversion reaction** and [Archaic] **conversion hysteria** —**con·ver′sion·al** ***adj.***, **con·ver′sion·ar′y** (-er′ē)

conversion van a van for utility use that has been customized with a luxury interior

con·ver·so (kən ver′sō; *Sp* kôn ver′sô) ***n.***, *pl.* **-sos** (-sōz; *Sp*, -sôs) ⟦Sp, a convert⟧ a Jew living in Spain or Portugal during the Spanish Inquisition who converted to Christianity under threat of persecution: cf. MARRANO

con·vert (kən vurt′; *for n.* kän′vurt′) ***vt.*** ⟦ME *converten* < OFr *convertir* < L *convertere* < *com-*, together + *vertere*, to turn: see VERSE⟧ **1** to change from one form or use to another; transform [*convert* grain into flour] **2** to cause to change as from one religion, doctrine, or course to another **3** to exchange for something equal in value **4** *Finance a)* to exchange (preferred stock, bonds, etc.) for another kind or class of security, esp. common stock *b)* to exchange (a currency) for an equivalent amount of another currency or precious metal **5** *Football, Rugby* to make (the extra point or points of a conversion) after a touchdown or try **6** *Law a)* to appropriate or use (another's property) by CONVERSION (sense 5*a*) *b)* to change (property) from real to personal, or the reverse **7** *Logic* to change (a proposition) by conversion —***vi.*** **1** to be converted ☆**2** *Bowling* to knock down all of the standing pins on the second bowl, scoring a spare ☆**3** *Football, Rugby* to make a conversion —***n.*** a person converted, as to a religion —***SYN.*** CHANGE, TRANSFORM

con·vert·er (kən vur′tər) ***n.*** a person or thing that converts; specif., *a)* a furnace for converting pig iron into steel in the Bessemer process *b)* an electrical device for converting alternating current into direct current (cf. INVERTER) *c)* the part of a radio receiver that changes modulated high frequencies to lower frequencies *d)* any device for adapting a radio or television receiver to added frequencies or modulations *e)* CATALYTIC CONVERTER

converter reactor a nuclear reactor that produces less fissionable material than it consumes, or one that produces a different fissionable material than it consumes

con·vert·i·ble (kən vurt′ə bəl) ***adj.*** ⟦OFr < LL(Ec) *convertibilis*⟧ that can be converted —***n.*** **1** a thing that can be converted ☆**2** an automobile with a top, as of canvas, that can be folded back or removed **3** *Finance* a bond or preferred stock that can be converted into common stock at the holder's option —**con·vert′i·bil′i·ty** *n.* —**con·vert′i·bly** *adv.*

☆**con·vert·i·plane** (kən vʉrt′ə plān′) *n.* ⟦prec. + (AIR)PLANE⟧ an aircraft designed to take off and land vertically like a helicopter but to fly forward in level flight like a conventional airplane

con·ver·tor (kən vʉr′tər) *n. alt. sp. of* CONVERTER

con·vex (kän veks′, kən-; *also, & for n. usually,* kän′veks′) *adj.* ⟦L *convexus,* vaulted, arched, pp. of *convehere,* to bring together < *com-,* together + *vehere,* to bring: see WAY⟧ curving outward like the surface of a sphere —*n.* a convex surface, line, object, etc. —**con·vex′ly** *adv.* —**con·vex′ness** *n.*

con·vex·i·ty (kän vek′sə tē, kən-) *n.* ⟦L *convexitas*⟧ 1 the quality or condition of being convex 2 *pl.* **-ties** a convex surface, line, etc.

con·vex·o-con·cave (kän vek′sō kän kāv′, kən-) *adj.* 1 convex on one side and concave on the other 2 *Optics* designating a lens whose convex face has a greater degree of curvature than its concave face, so that the lens is thickest in the middle

con·vex·o-con·vex (-kän veks′) *adj.* convex on both sides, as some lenses

con·vex·o-plane (-plān′) *adj.* PLANO-CONVEX

con·vey (kən vā′) *vt.* ⟦ME *conveien* < Anglo-Fr *conveier* (OFr *convoier*), to escort, convoy < VL **conviare,* to accompany on the way < L *com-,* together + *via,* way: see VIA⟧ 1 to take from one place to another; transport; carry [a chimney *conveys* smoke to the outside] 2 to serve as a channel or medium for; transmit 3 to make known; communicate in words, actions, appearance, etc. 4 to transfer, as property or title to property, from one person to another 5 [Obs.] *a)* to take away secretly *b)* to steal —**SYN.** CARRY —**con·vey′a·ble** *adj.*

con·vey·ance (kən vā′əns) *n.* ⟦ME *conveiaunce*⟧ 1 the act of conveying 2 a means of conveying; carrying device, esp. a vehicle 3 *a)* the transfer of the ownership of real property from one person to another *b)* the document by which this is effected; deed

con·vey·anc·ing (-ən siŋ) *n.* ⟦< prec. + -ING⟧ the act or work of drawing up documents for transferring the ownership of real property —**con·vey′anc·er** *n.*

con·vey·or or **con·vey·er** (kən vā′ər) *n.* one that conveys; esp., a CONVEYOR BELT

conveyor (*or* **conveyer) belt** a mechanical contrivance for conveying something by means of an endless chain or belt

con·vict (kən vikt′; *for n.* kän′vikt′) *vt.* ⟦ME *convicten* < L *convictus,* pp. of *convincere:* see CONVINCE⟧ 1 to prove (a person) guilty [*convicted* by the evidence] 2 to judge and find guilty of an offense charged [the jury *convicted* him of theft] 3 to bring to a realization of one's guilt [*convicted* by his own conscience] —*n.* 1 a person found guilty of a crime and sentenced by a court 2 a person serving a sentence in prison

con·vic·tion (kən vik′shən) *n.* ⟦ME < LL(Ec) *convictio,* proof, demonstration⟧ 1 a convicting or being convicted 2 [Rare] the act of convincing 3 the state or appearance of being convinced, as of the truth of a belief [to speak with *conviction*] 4 a strong belief —**SYN.** CERTAINTY, OPINION

con·vic·tive (kən vik′tiv) *adj.* having power to convince or convict —**con·vic′tive·ly** *adv.*

con·vince (kən vins′) *vt.* **-vinced′**, **-vinc′ing** ⟦L *convincere,* to overcome, convict of error < *com-,* intens. + *vincere,* to conquer: see VICTOR⟧ 1 [Obs.] to overcome, confute, or convict 2 to persuade to believe, by argument or evidence; make feel sure [*convinced* of the validity of her argument] 3 to persuade *to* do something: a usage still objected to by some [we *convinced* him to see a doctor] —**con·vinc′er** *n.* —**con·vin′ci·ble** *adj.*

con·vinced (-vinst′) *adj.* persuaded, or otherwise feeling certainty [*convinced* of the child's goodness]

con·vinc·ing (-vin′siŋ) *adj.* causing one to feel sure or to believe or agree; persuading as by evidence; cogent —**SYN.** VALID —**con·vinc′ing·ly** *adv.*

con·viv·i·al (kən viv′ē əl) *adj.* ⟦L *convivialis* < *convivium,* a feast < *convivere,* to carouse together < *com-,* together + *vivere,* to live: see QUICK⟧ 1 having to do with a feast or festive activity 2 fond of eating, drinking, and good company; sociable; jovial —**con·viv′i·al·ist** *n.* —**con·viv′i·al′i·ty** (-al′ə tē) *n.* —**con·viv′i·al·ly** *adv.*

con·vo·ca·tion (kän′vō kā′shən, -və-) *n.* ⟦ME *convocacioun* < L *convocatio*⟧ 1 the act of convoking 2 a group that has been convoked; esp., an ecclesiastical or academic assembly —**con′vo·ca′tion·al** *adj.*

con·voke (kən vōk′) *vt.* **-voked′**, **-vok′ing** ⟦Fr *convoquer* < L *convocare,* to call together < *com-,* together + *vocare,* to call < *vox,* VOICE⟧ to call together for a meeting; summon to assemble; convene —**SYN.** CALL

con·vo·lute (kän′və lo͞ot′) *adj.* ⟦L *convolutus,* pp. of *convolvere:* see CONVOLVE⟧ rolled up in the form of a spiral with the coils falling one upon the other, as in leaves or shells; coiled — *vt., vi.* **-lut′ed**, **-lut′ing** to wind around; coil —**con′vo·lute′ly** *adv.*

con·vo·lut·ed (-id) *adj.* 1 having convolutions, as in the kidney's tubules; coiled; spiraled 2 extremely involved; intricate; complicated [a *convoluted* style]

con·vo·lu·tion (kän′və lo͞o′shən) *n.* ⟦ML *convolutio* < L *convolutus,* pp. of *convolvere:* see fol.⟧ 1 a twisting, coiling, or winding together 2 a convoluted condition 3 a fold, twist, or coil of something convoluted; specif., any of the irregular folds or ridges on the surface of the brain

con·volve (kən välv′) *vt., vi.* **-volved′**, **-volv′ing** ⟦L *convolvere,* to roll together < *com-,* together + *volvere,* to roll: see WALK⟧ to roll, coil, or twist together

con·vol·vu·lus (kən väl′vyo͞o ləs, -vyə-) *n., pl.* **-lus·es** or **-li′** (-lī′) ⟦ModL < L, bindweed < *convolvere:* see prec.⟧ any of a genus (*Convolvulus*) of trailing, twining, or erect plants of the morning-glory family, with funnel-shaped flowers and triangular leaves

con·voy (kän′voi′; *also, for v.,* kən voi′) *vt.* ⟦ME *convoien* < OFr *convoier:* see CONVEY⟧ to go along with as an escort, esp. in order to protect; escort —*n.* 1 the act of convoying 2 a protecting escort, as for ships or troops 3 a group as of ships or vehicles traveling together for mutual protection or convenience —**SYN.** ACCOMPANY

con·vulse (kən vuls′) *vt.* **-vulsed′**, **-vuls′ing** ⟦< L *convulsus,* pp. of *convellere,* to tear loose < *com-,* together + *vellere,* to pluck: see REVULSION⟧ 1 to shake or disturb violently; agitate 2 to cause convulsions, or spasms, in 3 to cause to shake as with laughter, rage, or grief

con·vul·sion (kən vul′shən) *n.* ⟦L *convulsio* < *convulsus:* see prec.⟧ 1 a violent, involuntary contraction or spasm of the muscles: *often used in pl.* 2 [*usually pl.*] a violent fit of laughter 3 any violent disturbance, as a social upheaval or an earthquake —**con·vul′sion·ar′y** *adj.*

con·vul·sive (-siv) *adj.* 1 having the nature of a convulsion 2 having, producing, or marked by convulsions —**con·vul′sive·ly** *adv.* —**con·vul′sive·ness** *n.*

co·ny (kō′nē) *n., pl.* **-nies** *alt. sp. of* CONEY

coo[1] (ko͞o) *vi.* ⟦echoic⟧ 1 to make the soft, murmuring sound of pigeons or doves, or a sound like this 2 to speak gently and lovingly: see BILL[2] (*vi.* 2) —*vt.* to express gently and lovingly; utter with a coo —*n.* the sound made in cooing —**coo′ing·ly** *adv.*

coo[2] (ko͞o) *interj.* [Brit. Slang] used variously to express surprise, doubt, delight, etc.

COO *abbrev.* chief operating officer

coo·coo (ko͞o′ko͞o′; *also* ko͝ok′o͞o) *adj.* [Slang] *alt. sp. of* CUCKOO (*adj.*)

cook (ko͝ok) *n.* ⟦ME *cok* < OE *coc* < VL *cocus* < L *coquus* < *coquere,* to cook < IE base **pekw-,* to cook > Gr *peptein,* Sans *pácate,* (he) cooks, OE *afigen,* fried⟧ a person who prepares food for eating —*vt.* ⟦ME *coken* < the n.⟧ 1 to prepare (food) for eating by subjecting to heat, as by boiling, baking, frying, etc. 2 to subject to heat or to some treatment suggestive of a heating process 3 [Informal] to tamper with; falsify 4 [Slang] to spoil; ruin —*vi.* 1 to act or serve as a cook 2 to undergo the process of being cooked 3 *Jazz* to play, esp. to improvise, in an inspired and rhythmically exciting way —**cook up** [Informal] to concoct; devise; invent [to *cook up* an alibi] —☆**what's cooking?** [Slang] what's happening?

Cook[1] (ko͝ok), **James** 1728-79; Eng. naval officer & explorer: explored Australia, New Zealand, Antarctica, etc.

Cook[2] (ko͝ok), **Mount** mountain of the Southern Alps, New Zealand: highest peak in New Zealand: 12,349 ft (3,764 m)

☆**cook·book** (ko͝ok′bo͝ok′) *n.* a book containing recipes and other information for the preparation of food

cook·er (ko͝ok′ər) *n.* 1 an apparatus or utensil for cooking 2 [Brit.] a stove for cooking

cook·er·y (ko͝ok′ər ē) *n.* ⟦ME *cokerie*⟧ [Chiefly Brit.] the art, practice, or work of cooking

cook·house (ko͝ok′hous′) *n.* a place for cooking, as an outdoor kitchen or a ship's galley

cook·ie (ko͝ok′ē) *n.* ⟦prob. Du *koekje,* dim. of *koek,* a cake; akin to CAKE⟧ ☆1 a small, sweet cake, variously shaped, filled, etc., but usually flat and either crisp or chewy 2 [Scot.] a bun ☆3 [Slang] *a)* a person, esp. one qualified as *tough, smart, shrewd,* etc. *b)* an attractive young woman ☆4 *Comput.* a small file placed automatically by a website or an online service onto the hard disk of someone accessing that website or service, for the purpose of storing information about and later recognizing that user —☆**toss one's cookies** [Slang] to vomit; throw up: a humorous euphemism

cookie cutter a piece of metal or plastic shaped in the outline of an animal, geometric figure, etc., used for cutting cookies from dough rolled out in a thin sheet

☆**cook·ie-cut·ter** (-kut′ər) *adj.* [Informal] of or designating something regarded as indistinguishable from, or monotonously similar to, others of its kind

☆**cookie jar** a jar for storing cookies —**(with) a (**or **one's) hand in the cookie jar** [Informal] (in) the act of stealing something

cookie sheet a flat metal pan on which cookies are baked

Cook Inlet arm of the Gulf of Alaska, in S Alas.

Cook Islands group of islands in the South Pacific, west of the Society Islands: a self-governing territory associated with New Zealand: 91 sq mi (235 sq km)

☆**cook-off** (ko͝ok′ôf′) *n.* a cooking contest in which participants prepare their own recipes, as for chili or barbecued spare ribs, held as a public event, usually outdoors, with the food for sale to the public

☆**cook·out** (ko͝ok′out′) *n.* 1 a party or gathering at which a meal is prepared at an outdoor grill or fireplace and eaten outdoors 2 the meal so prepared

Cook's tour (ko͝oks) ⟦after Thomas Cook & Son, Brit travel agents⟧ any guided sightseeing or inspection tour: a humorous usage

☆**cook·stove** (ko͝ok′stōv′) *n.* a stove for cooking

Cook Strait strait between North Island & South Island, New Zealand: narrowest point, 16 mi (26 km)

cook·top (ko͝ok′täp′) *n.* 1 the upper surface of a kitchen stove, containing the burners or heating elements 2 such a surface or unit with heating elements installed separately, as on a kitchen counter

☆**cook·ware** (ko͝ok′wer′) *n.* cooking utensils; pots, pans, etc.

cook·y (ko͝ok′ē) *n., pl.* **cook′ies** *alt. sp. of* COOKIE

cool (ko͞ol) *adj.* ⟦ME & OE *col* < IE base **gel-,* cold, to freeze > CHILL, COLD,

L *gelu*⟧ 1 moderately cold; neither warm nor very cold 2 tending to reduce discomfort in warm or hot weather [*cool* clothes] 3 *a)* not excited; calm; composed [*cool* in an emergency] ☆*b)* marked by control of the emotions; restrained [*cool* jazz] *c)* [Informal] emotionally uninvolved; uncommitted; dispassionate 4 showing dislike or indifference; not cordial [a *cool* manner] 5 calmly impudent or bold 6 not suggesting warmth: said of colors in the blue-green end of the spectrum ☆7 [Slang] very good, pleasing, etc.; excellent ☆8 [Slang] in agreement or accord ➥Also used informally, emphasizing the magnitude of some number or amount [the lottery winner won a *cool* million dollars] —*adv.* in a cool manner —*n.* 1 a cool place, time, thing, part, etc. [the *cool* of the evening] ☆2 [Slang] cool, dispassionate attitude or manner —*vi.* ⟦ME *colien* < OE *colian,* to cool⟧ to become cool or colder —*vt.* to make cool or colder —**cool down** 1 to lower the body temperature, pulse, etc. after vigorous exercise 2 to become less heated, passionate, agitated, angry, etc. —☆**cool it** [Slang] to calm down —**cool off** 1 to calm down 2 to lose enthusiasm, interest, etc. —☆**cool out** [Slang] to make or become relaxed, calm, mollified, etc. [soothing words *cooled* him *out*] —☆**play it cool** [Informal] to exercise strict control over one's emotions; stay aloof, unenthusiastic, or uncommitted —**cool′ish** *adj.* —**cool′ly** *adv.* —**cool′ness** *n.*

SYN.—**cool**, in this comparison, implies freedom from the heat of emotion or excitement, suggesting a calm, dispassionate attitude or a controlled alertness in difficult circumstances; **composed** suggests readiness to meet a trying situation through self-possession or the disciplining of one's emotions; **collected** stresses a being in full command of one's faculties or emotions in a distracting situation; **unruffled** suggests the maintenance of poise or composure in the face of something that might agitate or embarrass one; **nonchalant** stresses a cool lack of concern or casual indifference —*ANT.* **excited, agitated**

cool·ant (ko͞ol′ənt) *n.* a substance, usually a fluid, used to remove heat, as from a nuclear reactor, an internal-combustion engine, molten metal, etc.: cf. REFRIGERANT

cool-down (ko͞ol′doun′) *n.* the act or an instance of gradually slowing or cooling down after vigorous exercise

cool·er (ko͞ol′ər) *n.* 1 a device, container, or room for cooling things or keeping them cool 2 anything that cools 3 a cold, refreshing drink, sometimes containing wine or other alcohol ☆4 [Slang] jail: with *the*

Coo·ley's anemia (ko͞o′lēz) ⟦after Thomas *Cooley* (1871-1945), U.S. pediatrician⟧ a form of thalassemia characterized by severe anemia, growth retardation, etc. and usually resulting in death at an early age: the genes causing this condition are inherited from both parents

cool·head·ed (ko͞ol′hed′id) *adj.* not easily flustered; calm

Coo·lidge (ko͞o′lij), **(John) Calvin** 1872-1933; 30th president of the U.S. (1923-29)

coo·lie (ko͞o′lē) *n.* ⟦Hindi *qulī,* hired servant, prob. < *kolī,* name of a tribe or caste of Gujarat⟧ 1 in India, China, etc., an unskilled native laborer: chiefly historical 2 [Informal] any person doing hard or menial work for little pay

cool·ing-off period (ko͞ol′iŋ ôf′) a period of time for the cooling of anger, tension, etc., as to allow for negotiation or reconciliation

coolth (ko͞olth) *n.* ⟦< COOL, modeled on WARMTH⟧ coolness: now chiefly a humorous usage

coomb (ko͞om) *n.* ⟦ME < OE *cumb* (in place names) < Celt base **kumbos* < IE **kumb-,* var. of base **keu-,* bend > CUP, HIVE⟧ [Brit.] a deep, narrow valley; ravine: also sp. **coombe**

☆**coon** (ko͞on) *n.* 1 *short for* RACCOON 2 [Slang] a black person: a term of contempt or derision

☆**coon·can** (ko͞on′kan′) *n.* ⟦< earlier *conquian* < MexSp *conquain* < *conquian* < Sp *con quién,* with whom⟧ an early form of the card game rummy

☆**coon cat** CACOMISTLE

coon·hound (ko͞on′hound′) *n.* any of several breeds of muscular, medium-sized hound that track game by scent, with a short, dense coat and long, drooping ears: originally bred in the U.S. to track and tree raccoons

☆**coon's age** ⟦fanciful & emphatic < RACCOON⟧ [Informal] an indefinitely long time

☆**coon·skin** (ko͞on′skin′) *n.* the skin of a raccoon, used as a fur —*adj.* made of coonskin

☆**coon·tie** (ko͞on′tē) *n.* ⟦Seminole *kunti,* coontie flour, starch⟧ a tropical Floridian cycad (*Zamia floridana*) with underground trunks that yield a starch

coop (ko͞op) *n.* ⟦ME *coupe,* akin to MDu, MLowG *kupe,* OHG *kuofa* < L *cupa,* tub, cask < IE **keup-,* hollow, mound: for IE base see COOMB⟧ 1 a small cage, pen, or building as for poultry 2 *a)* any place of confinement *b)* [Slang] a jail —*vt.* to confine as in a coop: usually with *up* —☆**fly the coop** [Slang] to escape, as from a jail

co-op[1] (kō′äp′, kō äp′) *n.* [Informal] a cooperative

co-op[2] or **coop** *abbrev.* cooperative

coo·per (ko͞o′pər) *n.* ⟦ME *couper* < MDu *cuper* < LL *cuparius* < L *cupa,* a cask: see COOP⟧ a person whose work is making or repairing barrels and casks —*vt., vi.* to make or repair (barrels and casks)

Coo·per (ko͞o′pər) 1 **Gary** (born *Frank James Cooper*) 1901-61; U.S. film actor 2 **James Fen·i·more** (fen′ə môr′) 1789-1851; U.S. novelist 3 **Peter** 1791-1883; U.S. inventor, industrialist, & philanthropist

coo·per·age (ko͞o′pər ij) *n.* 1 the workshop of a cooper 2 *a)* the work of a cooper *b)* the price charged for such work

co·op·er·ate or **co-op·er·ate** (kō äp′ər āt′) *vi.* **-at′ed, -at′ing** ⟦< LL *cooperatus,* pp. of *cooperari,* to work together < L *co-,* with + *operari,* to work < *opus* (gen. *operis*), work: see OPUS⟧ 1 to act or work together with another or others for a common purpose 2 to combine so as to produce an effect 3 to engage in economic cooperation Sometimes **co·öp′er·ate′** —**co·op′er·a′tor** *n.*, **co-op′er·a′tor**

co·op·er·a·tion or **co-op·er·a·tion** (kō äp′ər ā′shən) *n.* ⟦LL *cooperatio*⟧ 1 the act of cooperating; joint effort or operation 2 the association of a number of people in an enterprise for mutual benefits or profits 3 *Ecol.* an interaction between organisms that is largely beneficial to all those participating Sometimes **co·öp′er·a′tion** —**co·op′er·a′tion·ist** *n.*, **co-op′er·a′tion·ist**

co·op·er·a·tive or **co-op·er·a·tive** (kō äp′ər ə tiv, -ər āt′iv) *adj.* 1 cooperating or inclined to cooperate 2 designating or of an organization (as for the production or marketing of goods), an apartment house, store, etc. owned by and operated for the benefit of members who use its facilities or services —*n.* a cooperative society, store, etc. Sometimes **co·öp′er·a·tive** —**co·op′er·a·tive·ly** *adv.*, **co-op′er·a·tive·ly** —**co·op′er·a·tive·ness** *n.*, **co-op′er·a·tive·ness**

☆**Coo·per's hawk** ⟦after W. *Cooper,* 19th-c. U.S. ornithologist⟧ a medium-sized hawk (*Accipiter cooperii*) with a long, rounded tail and short, rounded wings

Coo·pers·town (ko͞o′pərz toun′) ⟦founded by Judge William *Cooper,* father of James Fenimore COOPER, around 1790⟧ village in central N.Y., near the source of the Susquehanna River: home of the National Baseball Hall of Fame and Museum

coo·per·y (ko͞o′pər ē) *n., pl.* **-per·ies** ⟦COOPER + -Y[3]⟧ the work, shop, or product of a cooper

co-opt (kō äpt′, kō′äpt′) *vt.* ⟦L *cooptare,* to choose, elect < *co-* (var. of *com-*), with + *optare,* to choose: see OPTION⟧ 1 to add (a person or persons) to a group by vote of those already members 2 to appoint as an associate 3 to persuade or lure (an opponent) to join one's own system, party, etc. 4 to make use of for one's own purposes; take over or adopt Sometimes **co-öpt′** —**co′-op·ta′tion** *n.*, **co-op′tion** —**co-op′ta·tive** (-tə tiv) *adj.*, **co-op′tive**

co·or·di·nate or **co-or·di·nate** (kō ôrd′'n it, -āt′; *for v.,* -āt′) *adj.* ⟦ML *coordinatus,* pp. of *coordinare,* to set in order, arrange < L *co-* (var. of *com-*), with + *ordinare,* to arrange < *ordo,* ORDER⟧ 1 of the same order or importance; equal in rank 2 of or involving coordination or coordinates 3 *Gram.* being of equal structural rank [*coordinate* clauses] —*n.* 1 a coordinate person or thing ☆2 [*pl.*] articles of clothing, luggage, etc. designed to form a pleasing ensemble when worn or used together 3 *Math.* any of a set of numbers in a reference system that locates the position of a point —*vt.* **-nat′ed, -nat′ing** 1 to place in the same order, rank, etc.; make coordinate 2 to bring into proper order or relation; adjust (various parts) so as to have harmonious action; harmonize ☆3 to design as coordinates [to *coordinate* pieces of designer luggage] —*vi.* to become coordinate; function harmoniously Sometimes **co·ör′di·nate** —**co·or′di·nate·ly** *adv.*, **co-or′di·nate·ly** —**co·or′di·na·tive** *adj.*, **co-or′di·na·tive** (-nə tiv, -nāt′iv) —**co·or′di·na′tor** *n.*, **co-or′di·na′tor**

coordinate bond the type of covalent bond in which the shared pair of electrons is supplied by only one of the atoms; dative bond

co·or·di·nat·ed or **co-or·di·nat·ed** (kō ôrd′'n āt′id) *adj.* showing or having coordination; specif., ☆*a)* having good muscular coordination and reflexes *b)* gathered together or designed so as to match or harmonize [*coordinated* furnishings] Sometimes **co·ör′di·nat′ed**

Coordinated Universal Time UNIVERSAL TIME as periodically adjusted to coordinate with atomic clocks: it serves as the official international basis for STANDARD TIME: abbrev. *UTC*

coordinating conjunction a conjunction that connects coordinate words, phrases, or clauses (Ex.: *and, but, for, or, nor, yet, so*)

co·or·di·na·tion or **co-or·di·na·tion** (kō ôrd′'n ā′shən) *n.* ⟦LL *coordinatio*⟧ 1 a coordinating or being coordinated 2 the state or relation of being coordinate; harmonious adjustment or action; specif., the harmonious action of muscles in producing complex movements and tasks Sometimes **co·ör′di·na′tion**

coordination complex one of a number of complex compounds in which an atom or group of atoms is bound to the central atom by a shared pair of electrons supplied by the coordinated group and not by the central atom: also called **coordinate valence**

Coos (ko͞os) *n.* ⟦prob. < AmInd⟧ 1 *pl.* **Coos** a member of a North American Indian people living in SW Oregon 2 the language of this people, of uncertain relationship

coot (ko͞ot) *n., pl.* **coots** or **coot** ⟦ME *cote* < ? MDu *koet*⟧ 1 any of a genus (*Fulica*) of ducklike, freshwater birds of the rail family, with long-lobed toes ☆2 SCOTER 3 [Informal] an amusing or eccentric old fellow

coot·er (ko͞ot′ər) *n.* ⟦orig. uncert.; possibly ult. < an Afr language⟧ [Chiefly South] any of various large freshwater terrapins (esp. *Pseudemys concinna*) of the S U.S. and N Mexico

coot·ie (ko͞ot′ē) *n.* ⟦Brit WWI army slang, earlier a seaman's term < Malay *kutu,* dog tick⟧ [Slang] LOUSE (sense 1*a*): now chiefly a child's term

co-own (kō′ōn′, kō′ōn′) *vt., vi.* to own (something) jointly —**co′-own′er** *n.* —**co′-own′er·ship′** *n.*

cop[1] (käp) *n.* ⟦ME & OE *cop,* prob. akin to Ger *kopf* & Du *kop,* head < LL *cuppa:* see CUP⟧ 1 [Now Dial.] the top or crest, as of a hill 2 a cone-shaped roll of thread or yarn coiled round a spindle

cop[2] (käp) [Slang] *vt.* **copped, cop′ping** ⟦< north Brit dial. form of obs.

cap, to seize; prob. < OFr *caper* < L *capere,* to take: see HAVE⟧ 1 to seize, capture, take, win, steal, etc. 2 to buy (drugs) —☆*n.* ⟦prob. < COPPER²⟧ a policeman —☆**cop a plea** to plead guilty to a criminal charge, esp. so as to get a lighter sentence —☆**cop out** 1 to confess to the police, often implicating another 2 *a)* to go back (*on* a promise, commitment, etc.); back down; renege *b)* to give up; quit; surrender —☆**cop to** to admit or acknowledge

cop³ *abbrev.* copyright

☆**co·pa·cet·ic** or **co·pa·set·ic** (kō′pə set′ik) *adj.* ⟦< ?⟧ [Old Slang] good, excellent, fine, etc.

co·pai·ba (kō pā′bə, -pī′-) *n.* ⟦Sp & Port < Tupí *cupaíba*⟧ 1 an aromatic resin obtained from certain South American trees (genus *Copaifera*) of the caesalpinia family: formerly used in medicine, now used in varnishes, etc. 2 any of these trees

co·pal (kō′pəl, -pal′) *n.* ⟦Sp < Nahuatl *copalli,* resin⟧ fossil resin and other hard resins from tropical trees, used in varnishes and lacquers

☆**co·palm** (kō′päm′) *n.* ⟦< MexSp *copalme*⟧ 1 a brownish, aromatic resin obtained from the sweet gum tree 2 the tree

Co·pán (kō pän′) ruined Mayan city in W Honduras: fl. *c.* 7th-8th cent. A.D.

co·par·ce·nar·y (kō pär′sə ner′ē) *n., pl.* **-nar′ies** ⟦CO- + PARCENARY⟧ 1 *Law* joint heirship; partnership in inheritance 2 joint partnership or ownership

co·par·ce·ner (-sə nər) *n.* ⟦CO- + PARCENER⟧ *Law* a person who shares jointly with others in an inheritance

co·part·ner (kō pärt′nər, kō′pärt′-) *n.* a partner, or associate —**co·part′ner·ship′** *n.*

co·pay (kō′pā′) *n. short for* CO-PAYMENT: also written **co′pay′**

co-pay·ment (kō′pā′mənt) *n.* payment required of an insured person for that portion of medical expenses not paid by the insurance company; specif., a fixed fee required for each prescription, visit to a doctor, etc.: also written **co′pay′ment**

COPD *abbrev.* chronic obstructive pulmonary disease

cope¹ (kōp) *vi.* **coped, cop′ing** ⟦ME *coupen* < OFr *coper, colper,* to strike < *colp,* COUP⟧ 1 to fight or contend (*with*) successfully or on equal terms 2 to deal with problems, troubles, etc. 3 [Archaic] to meet, encounter, or have to do (*with*) —*vt.* 1 [Archaic] to meet, as in a contest; encounter 2 [Obs.] to match equally

cope² (kōp) *n.* ⟦ME < ML *capa,* var. of LL *cappa:* see CAP¹⟧ 1 a large, capelike vestment worn by priests at certain ceremonies 2 anything regarded as covering like a cope, as a vault or the sky 3 COPING —*vt.* **coped, cop′ing** to cover or provide with a cope or coping

cope³ (kōp) *vt.* **coped, cop′ing** [back-form. < COPING] to cut or shape (a part used in building) so that it will fit over or against another part, as a coping or molding

co·peck (kō′pek′) *n. alt. sp. of* KOPECK

Co·pen·hag·en (kō′pən hā′gən, -hä′-; kō′pən hā′gən, -hä′-) capital of Denmark; seaport on the E coast of Zealand: Dan. name KØBENHAVN

co·pe·pod (kō′pə päd′) *n.* ⟦< Gr *kōpē,* oar < *kaptein,* to gulp down (see HAVE) + -POD⟧ any of a class (Copepoda) of small, sometimes parasitic, crustaceans living in either salt or fresh water

Copernican system the theory of Copernicus that the planets revolve around the sun and that the turning of the earth on its axis from west to east accounts for the apparent rising and setting of the stars: basis of modern astronomy

co·per·ni·ci·um (kō′pər nē′sē əm; -nish′ē əm, -nis′-) *n.* ⟦ModL, after fol. + -IUM⟧ a radioactive chemical element with a very short half-life: a transactinide produced by bombarding lead with zinc ions: symbol, Cn; at. no. 112: see the periodic table of elements in the Reference Supplement

Co·per·ni·cus (kō pʉr′ni kəs), **Nic·o·la·us** (nik′ə lā′əs) (L. form of *Mikolaj Kopernik*) 1473-1543; Pol. astronomer —**Co·per′ni·can** *adj., n.*

cope·stone (kōp′stōn′) *n.* 1 *a)* the uppermost stone in a structure *b)* any of the stones in a coping 2 the highest point, as of achievement

cop·i·er (käp′ē ər) *n.* 1 a person who copies; specif., *a)* an imitator *b)* a transcriber 2 a duplicating machine: specif., a photocopier

co·pi·lot (kō′pī′lət) *n.* the assistant pilot of an airplane, who aids or relieves the pilot

cop·ing (kō′piŋ) *n.* ⟦< fig. use of COPE²⟧ the top layer of a masonry wall, usually sloped to carry off water

coping saw a handsaw with a narrow blade set in a U-shaped frame, used esp. for cutting curved outlines

co·pi·ous (kō′pē əs) *adj.* ⟦ME < L *copiosus* < *copia,* abundance < *co-,* together + *ops,* riches, power: see OPUS⟧ 1 very plentiful; abundant 2 wordy; profuse or diffuse in language 3 full of information —*SYN.* PLENTIFUL —**co′pi·ous·ly** *adv.* —**co′pi·ous·ness** *n.*

co·pla·nar (kō plā′nər) *adj. Math.* in the same plane: said of figures, points, etc.

Cop·land (kōp′lənd), **Aaron** 1900-90; U.S. composer

Cop·ley (käp′lē), **John Sin·gle·ton** (siŋ′gəl tən) 1738-1815; Am. painter, in England after 1775

co·pol·y·mer (kō päl′ə mər) *n. Chem.* a compound produced by copolymerization —**co·pol′y·mer′ic** (-mer′ik) *adj.*

co·po·lym·er·i·za·tion (kō′pə lim′ər ə zā′shən, kō päl′ə mʉr′ə-) *n.* a process resembling polymerization, in which unlike molecules unite in alternate or random sequences in a chain —**co′po·lym′er·ize′** (-ər īz′) *vt., vi.* **-ized′, -iz′ing**

☆**cop-out** (käp′out′) *n.* [Slang] 1 the act or an instance of copping out, as by confessing, reneging, quitting, etc. 2 one who cops out 3 an excuse for inaction or failure

cop·per¹ (käp′ər) *n., pl.* **-per** or **-pers** ⟦ME & OE *coper* < LL *cuprum,* contr. < *Cyprium* (*aes*), Cyprian (brass), copper, after Gr *Kyprios,* CYPRUS, noted for its copper mines⟧ 1 a reddish-brown, malleable, ductile, metallic element that is corrosion-resistant and an excellent conductor of electricity and heat: symbol, Cu; at. no. 29: see the periodic table of elements in the Reference Supplement 2 [Now Chiefly Brit.] *a)* a coin of copper or bronze, as a penny *b)* a large metal container or boiler, orig. of copper 3 the color of copper; reddish brown 4 any of various small, copper-colored butterflies (family Lycaenidae) found in temperate regions —*adj.* 1 of copper 2 copper-colored; reddish-brown —*vt.* 1 to cover or coat with copper ☆2 ⟦from use of a copper coin to indicate such a bet in faro⟧ [Slang] to bet against (another's bet) —**cop′per·y** *adj.*

cop·per² (käp′ər) *n.* ⟦prob. < COP², *v.*⟧ [Slang] a policeman

Copper Age a phase in some human cultures between a Stone Age and a Bronze Age, characterized by the introduction and development of copper tools and weapons

cop·per·as (käp′ər əs) *n.* ⟦ME & OFr *coperose* < ML *coperosium,* prob. < *(*aqua*) *cuprosa,* lit., copper (water) < L *cupreus,* of copper⟧ FERROUS SULFATE

☆**cop·per·head** (käp′ər hed′) *n.* 1 a poisonous North American pit viper (*Agkistrodon contortrix*) with a copper-colored head and dark-brown cross bands 2 [C-] [Old Informal] a Northerner who sympathized with the South at the time of the Civil War: so called in the North

Cop·per·mine (käp′ər mīn′) ⟦for the *copper* in the region⟧ river in Nunavut & Northwest Territories, Canada, flowing northwest into the Arctic Ocean: 525 mi (845 km)

cop·per·plate (käp′ər plāt′) *n.* 1 a flat piece of copper etched or engraved for printing 2 a print made from this 3 a printing or engraving process using copperplate 4 in calligraphy, a graceful style of handwriting, patterned after copperplate etchings

copper pyrites CHALCOPYRITE

cop·per·smith (käp′ər smith′) *n.* a person whose work is making utensils and other things out of copper

copper sulfate a blue, crystalline substance, $CuSO_4 \cdot 5H_2O$, that effloresces and turns white when heated; blue vitriol: used in making pigments, germicides, batteries, etc.

cop·pice (käp′is) *n.* ⟦ME *copis* < OFr *copeis* < *coper, colper,* to strike: see COUP⟧ COPSE

co·pra (kä′prə, kō′-) *n.* ⟦Port < Malayalam *koppara* < Hindi *khoprā*⟧ dried coconut meat, the source of coconut oil

cop·ro- (käp′rō, -rə) ⟦< Gr *kopros,* dung⟧ *combining form* dung, excrement, feces [*coprolite*]: also, before a vowel, **copr-**

co·pro·cess·or (kō′prä′səs ər) *n. Comput.* an auxiliary processing unit designated for a particular operation

cop·ro·lite (käp′rō līt′, -rə-) *n.* ⟦COPRO- + -LITE⟧ fossilized excrement —**cop′ro·lit′ic** (-lit′ik) *adj.*

cop·rol·o·gy (kə präl′ə jē) *n.* ⟦COPRO- + -LOGY⟧ the treatment of scatological or pornographic subjects in art and literature

cop·roph·a·gous (kə präf′ə gəs) *adj.* ⟦COPRO- + -PHAGOUS⟧ feeding on dung, as some beetles —**cop·roph′a·gy** (-jē) *n.*

cop·ro·phil·i·a (käp′rō fil′ē ə, -rə-) *n.* ⟦COPRO- + -PHILIA⟧ *Psychol.* an abnormal interest in feces

copse (käps) *n.* ⟦< COPPICE⟧ a thicket of small trees or shrubs

Copt (käpt) *n.* ⟦ModL *Coptus:* see COPTIC⟧ 1 an Egyptian who is a descendant of Egypt's ancient inhabitants 2 a member of the Coptic Church

☆**cop·ter** (käp′tər) *n. short for* HELICOPTER

Cop·tic (käp′tik) *n.* ⟦ModL *Coptus,* earlier *Cophtus* < Ar *Quft, Qift,* the Copts < Coptic *Gyptios* < Gr *Aigyptios,* Egyptian⟧ the Afroasiatic language of the Copts, derived from ancient Egyptian and attested from the 3d cent. A.D.: now used only in the ritual of the Coptic Church —*adj.* 1 of the Copts or their language or culture 2 of the Coptic Church

Coptic Church the native Christian church of Egypt and of Ethiopia, Monophysitic in doctrine

cop·u·la (käp′yoo lə, -yə-) *n., pl.* **-las** ⟦L, a band, link (earlier *co-apula*) < *co-,* together + *apere,* to join: see APT¹⟧ something that connects or links together; specif., *a)* *Gram.* LINKING VERB *b)* *Logic* the connecting link between the subject and predicate of a proposition —**cop′u·lar** *adj.*

cop·u·late (käp′yoo lāt′, -yə-) *vi.* **-lat′ed, -lat′ing** ⟦ME *copulaten* < L *copulatus,* pp. of *copulare,* to unite, couple < *copula:* see prec.⟧ to have sexual intercourse —**cop′u·la′tion** *n.* —**cop′u·la·to′ry** (-lə tôr′ē) *adj.*

cop·u·la·tive (-lāt′iv, -lə tiv) *adj.* ⟦ME *copulatif* < LL *copulativus* < L *copulatus:* see prec.⟧ 1 joining together; coupling 2 *Gram.* *a)* connecting coordinate words, phrases, or clauses [*a copulative* conjunction] *b)* involving connected words or clauses *c)* having the nature of a copula [*a copulative* verb] 3 of or for copulating —*n. Gram.* a copulative word

cop·y (käp′ē) *n., pl.* **cop′ies** ⟦ME *copie,* abundance, full transcript < OFr < ML *copia,* copious transcript < L *copia,* plenty: see COPIOUS⟧ 1 a thing made just like another; imitation of an original; full reproduction or transcription 2 [Now Rare] a model or pattern, as of penmanship, to be imitated or reproduced 3 any of a number of books, magazines, engravings, etc. printed from the same plates or having the same printed matter 4 matter to be set in type or put on a printing plate 5 subject matter for a journalist, novelist, etc. [a trip that made good *copy*] 6 the words of an advertisement, as distinct from the layout, pictures, music, etc. —*vt., vi.* **cop′ied, cop′y·ing** 1 to make a copy or copies of (a piece of writing, a computer file, etc.); reproduce, transcribe, etc. 2 to make or do something in imitation of (some thing or person); imitate 3 to hear and understand: used as in radio communication 4 [Informal] to provide (someone) with a copy of a specified document, text, etc. [*copy* all staff members with the annual report] 5 *Comput.* to place (a copy of a file) onto a disk or other storage device: often with *to*

SYN.—**copy**, the broadest of these terms, refers to any imitation, often only approximate, of an original [a carbon *copy*]; **reproduction** implies a close imitation of the original, often, however, with differences, as of material, size, or quality [a *reproduction* of a painting]; a **facsimile** is an exact reproduction in appearance, sometimes, however, differing in scale [a photostated *facsimile* of a document]; a **duplicate** is a double, or counterpart, of something, serving all the purposes of the original [all the books of a single printing are *duplicates*]; a **replica** is an exact reproduction of a work of art, in strict usage, one made by the original artist See also **imitate**

cop·y·book (-book′) *n.* a book containing models of handwriting, formerly used in teaching penmanship —*adj.* ordinary; trite; commonplace [*copybook* maxims]

☆**copy boy** [Now Rare] an employee who runs errands in a newspaper office: now often **copy aide**

☆**cop·y·cat** (-kat′) [Informal] *n.* a person who imitates or mimics another's behavior, actions, ideas, etc.: originally a child's term —*adj.* designating an action, behavior, an idea, etc. that closely imitates that of another [a case of arson that inspires *copycat* crimes] —*vt.* **-cat′ted, -cat′ting** to imitate or mimic —*vi.* to act as a copycat

☆**copy desk** the desk in a newspaper office where copy is edited and headlines are written

☆**copy editor** a person whose work is editing and correcting the grammar, punctuation, etc. of articles or manuscripts, as in a newspaper office or publishing house —**cop·y-ed·it** (käp′ē ed′it) *vt.*

cop·y·hold (-hōld′) *n. Eng. Law* tenure of property less than a freehold, proved by a written transcript or record in the rolls of a manorial court

cop·y·hold·er (-hōl′dər) *n.* ☆1 a person who reads copy aloud to a proofreader 2 a device for holding copy, as for a typesetter 3 *Eng. Law* a person who holds land by copyhold

cop·y·ist (-ist) *n.* 1 a person who makes written copies; transcriber 2 a person who imitates; copier

☆**cop·y·read·er** (-rēd′ər) *n.* COPY EDITOR —**cop′y·read′** *vt.* **-read′** (-red′), **-read′ing**

cop·y·right (-rīt′) *n.* ⟦COPY + RIGHT⟧ the exclusive right to the publication, production, or sale of the rights to a literary, dramatic, musical, or artistic work, or to the use of a commercial print or label, granted by law for a specified period of time to an author, composer, artist, distributor, etc.: symbol, © —*vt.* to protect (a book, song, print, etc.) by copyright —*adj.* 1 protected by copyright 2 of or pertaining to copyright —**cop′y·right′a·ble** *adj.* —**cop′y·right′er** *n.*

copy-text (-tekst′) *n.* a manuscript or earlier published version of a text, used as the basis for an emended, scholarly edition

cop·y·writ·er (-rīt′ər) *n.* a writer of copy for advertisements or promotional material

coq au vin (kōk′ ō van′, -van′) ⟦Fr, lit., rooster in (the) wine⟧ chicken sautéed and then stewed in red wine with onions, mushrooms, and seasonings

coque·li·cot (kōk′li kō′) *n.* ⟦Fr, equiv. of COCK-A-DOODLE-DOO, echoic: applied to the poppy because of similarity of color to that of a cockscomb⟧ CORN POPPY

Co·que·lin (kô klan′), **Be·noit Cons·tant** (bə nwá′ kōn stän′) 1841-1909; Fr. actor

co·quet (kō ket′) *vi.* **-quet′ted, -quet′ting** ⟦Fr *coqueter,* to flirt, lit., to strut like a rooster < *coquet,* dim. of *coq,* a rooster: see COCK[1]⟧ 1 to behave as a coquette; flirt 2 to trifle or dally (*with* an idea, offer, etc.) —*adj.* coquettish —*SYN.* TRIFLE

co·quet·ry (kō′kə trē, kō ke′trē) *n., pl.* **-ries** ⟦Fr *coqueterie* < *coqueter:* see prec.⟧ 1 the behavior or act of a coquette; flirting 2 the act of trifling or dallying

co·quette (kō ket′) *n.* ⟦Fr *coquette,* fem.: see COQUET⟧ a girl or woman who merely out of vanity tries to get men's attention and admiration; flirt —*vi.* **-quet′ted, -quet′ting** to behave as a coquette; flirt —**co·quet′tish** *adj.* —**co·quet′tish·ly** *adv.* —**co·quet′tish·ness** *n.*

co·quil·la nut (kō kēl′yə, -kē-) ⟦Sp *coquillo* or Port *coquilho,* dim. of *coco,* coconut⟧ the fruit of a piassava palm (*Attalea funifera*) of Brazil: it yields palm oil and has a very hard, brown, ivorylike shell used in cabinetwork and by carvers

co·quille (kō kēl′; *Fr* kô kē′y′) *n.* ⟦Fr, a shell < OFr: see COCKLE[1]⟧ 1 a scallop shell or shell-shaped dish in which minced seafood is baked and served 2 any food so served

☆**co·qui·na** (kō kē′nə) *n.* ⟦Sp, shellfish, dim. < dial. form of L *concha:* see CONCH⟧ 1 a soft, whitish limestone made up of broken sea shells and corals: used as a building material 2 any of a genus (*Donax*) of small, delicately colored saltwater clams

Co·quit·lam (kə kwit′ləm) ⟦< a word in a Salish language⟧ city in SW British Columbia, Canada

co·qui·to (kō kēt′ō) *n., pl.* **-tos** ⟦Sp, dim. of *coco,* coco palm⟧ a wine palm (*Jubaea spectabilis*) of Chile whose sweet sap and nuts are used for food

cor[1] (kôr) *n.* ⟦Heb⟧ an ancient Hebrew unit of liquid, and sometimes dry, measure equal to about 58 gallons: it was equivalent to the HOMER[1]

cor[2] (kôr) *interj.* ⟦earlier *Gor* < **Gord,* altered < GOD⟧ [Brit.] used to express surprise, admiration, irritation, etc.

cor[3] *abbrev.* 1 corner 2 cornet 3 coroner 4 corpus 5 correction 6 correlative 7 correspondence 8 correspondent 9 corresponding

Cor *abbrev.* 1 *Bible* Corinthians 2 Coroner

cor- (kôr) *prefix* COM-: used before *r* [*correlation*]

Cor·a (kôr′ə) *n.* ⟦L < Gr *Korē,* lit., maiden, name of Proserpina < IE base **k̂er-,* to grow > CERES, CREATE⟧ a feminine name

cor·a·ci·i·form (kôr′ə sī′ə fôrm′) *adj.* ⟦< ModL *Coracii,* name of the suborder < Gr *korax,* RAVEN[1] + -FORM⟧ of or belonging to an order (Coraciiformes) of birds with a strong, sharp bill, fused front toes, and usually bright coloration, as the kingfishers, bee eaters, and hornbills

cor·a·cle (kôr′ə kəl) *n.* ⟦< Welsh *corwgl* < *corwg,* orig., leather-covered boat; akin to L *corium,* hide: see CORIUM⟧ a short, roundish boat made as of animal skins or canvas waterproofed and stretched over a wicker or wooden frame

cor·a·coid (kôr′ə koid′) *adj.* ⟦ModL *coracoides* < Gr *korakoeidēs,* like a raven < *korax,* RAVEN[1] + *eidos,* -OID⟧ designating or of a rudimentary bony process on the shoulder blade in mammals, or a bone in monotremes and certain fossil reptiles that extends from the shoulder blade to the breastbone —*n.* this bony process or bone

cor·al (kôr′əl, kär′-) *n.* ⟦OFr < L *coralium* < Gr *korallion* < ? Heb *gōrāl,* pebble or Ar *garal,* small stone⟧ 1 the hard, stony skeleton secreted by certain marine polyps (class Anthozoa) and often deposited in extensive masses forming reefs and atolls in tropical seas 2 any such polyp (esp. order Scleractinia) living singly or in large colonies 3 a piece of coral, esp. the red kind used in jewelry 4 the mature ovaries of the lobster 5 a yellowish red or yellowish pink: also called **coral red** or **coral pink** —*adj.* 1 made of coral 2 yellowish-red or yellowish-pink

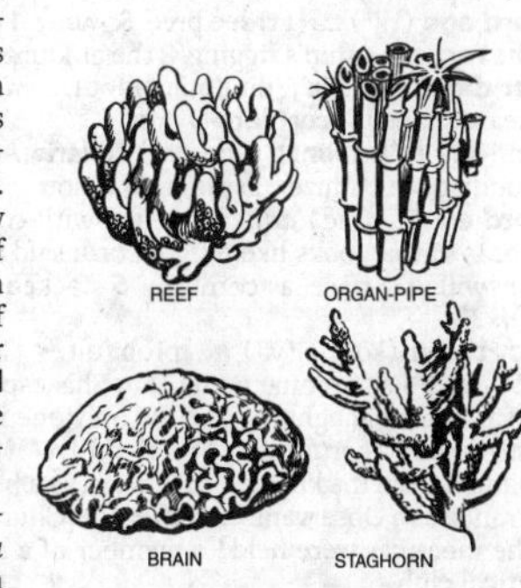

types of coral

☆**coral bells** a perennial, ornamental alumroot (*Heuchera sanguinea*) native to SW North America, with racemes of drooping pink or white flowers: also written **cor′al-bells′** *n.*

☆**cor·al·ber·ry** (-ber′ē) *n., pl.* **-ries** a small North American shrub (*Symphoricarpos orbiculatus*) of the honeysuckle family, with variously colored flowers and pink or purple berries

cor·al·line (kôr′ə līn′, -lin) *n.* ⟦ModL *corallina* < the adj.⟧ 1 any animal related to or resembling the corals 2 any of a family (Corallinaceae) of red algae that produce limestone —*adj.* ⟦LL *corallinus,* coral-red⟧ 1 consisting of coral or corallines 2 resembling coral, esp. in color

cor·al·loid (-loid′) *adj.* resembling coral in appearance and form: also **cor·al·li·form** (kôr əl′ə fôm′) or **cor′al·loi′dal**

coral reef a reef in relatively shallow, tropical seas composed chiefly of the skeletons of coral

cor·al·root (kôr′əl ro͞ot′) *n.* any of a genus (*Corallorhiza*) of saprophytic, brownish orchids with branched, coral-colored roots and no leaves

Coral Sea part of the S Pacific, northeast of Australia & south of the Solomon Islands

coral snake ☆any of several small, poisonous, burrowing elapine snakes (genera *Micrurus* and *Micruroides*), found in the S U.S. and subtropical America, with coral-red, yellow, and black bands around its body

Coral Springs ⟦after the company (*Coral* Ridge Properties) that once owned the land, and the natural *springs* found there⟧ city in SE Fla.

cor an·glais (kôr′ äŋ glā′) *pl.* **cors anglais** (kôr′-) ⟦Fr⟧ ENGLISH HORN

co·ran·to (kō ran′tō, -rän′-) *n.* ⟦altered < COURANTE, modeled on It & Sp words ending in *-o*⟧ COURANTE

cor·beil (kôr′bel′, -bəl) *n.* ⟦Fr *corbeille* < LL *corbicula,* dim. of L *corbis,* basket < IE *(*s*)*kerb(h)-,* to twist > base *(*s*)*ker-,* to turn > SHRIMP⟧ a sculptured basket of fruit, flowers, etc., used in architectural design

cor·bel (kôr′bəl, -bel′) *n.* ⟦OFr, dim. of *corb* < L *corvus,* RAVEN[1]: so called from its beaked shape⟧ 1 a piece of stone, wood, or metal, often in the form of a bracket, projecting from the side of a wall and serving to support a cornice, the spring of an arch, etc. 2 a short timber placed lengthwise under a beam or girder —*vt.* **-beled** or **-belled, -bel·ing** or **-bel·ling** to provide or support with a corbel or corbels

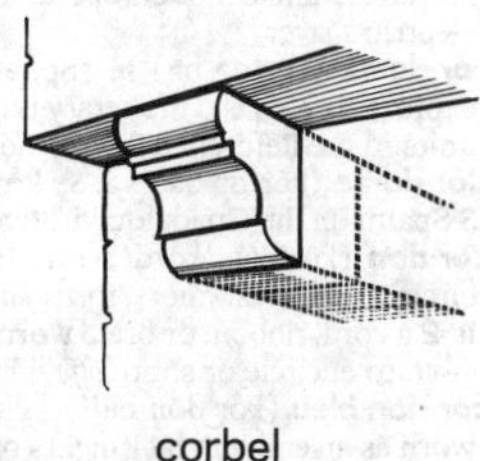
corbel

cor·bel·ing (-bəl iŋ) *n.* 1 the fashioning of corbels 2 courses of masonry, like steps in reverse

cor·bie (kôr′bē) *n., pl.* **-bies** ⟦ME *corbe* < OFr *corb:* see CORBEL⟧ [Scot.] a crow or raven

corbie gable a gable with corbiesteps

cor·bie·step (-step′) *n.* ⟦CORBIE + STEP⟧ one of a series of steps at the upper end wall of some gables

☆**cor·bi·na** (kôr bē′nə) *n.* CORVINA

Corbusier, Le *see* LE CORBUSIER

Cor·co·va·do (kôr′kô vä′thoo) mountain in SE Brazil, near Rio de Janeiro: 2,310 ft (704 m): there is a gigantic (98.5 ft; 30m) statue of Christ on its top

Cor·cy·ra (kôr sī′rə) *former name for* CORFU

cord (kôrd) *n.* ⟦ME & OFr *corde* < L *chorda* < Gr *chordē*, catgut, chord, cord < IE base **gher-*, intestine > YARN⟧ **1** a thick string or thin rope **2** any force acting as a tie or bond **3** ⟦from use of a cord in measuring⟧ a measure of wood cut for fuel, equal to 128 cubic feet (3.6 m^3), as arranged in a pile 8 feet (2.4 m) long, 4 feet (1.2 m) high, and 4 feet (1.2 m) wide: see also FACE CORD **4** *a)* a rib on the surface of a fabric *b)* cloth with a ribbed surface; corduroy *c)* [*pl.*] corduroy trousers **5** *Anat.* any part resembling a cord [the spinal *cord*, vocal *cords*, umbilical *cord*] **6** *Elec.* a slender, flexible, insulated electrical cable, as one fitted at one end with an electrical plug to connect a lamp to an outlet —*vt.* **1** to fasten, connect, or provide with a cord or cords **2** to stack (wood) in cords —**cut the cord** ⟦with ref. to the umbilical *cord*⟧ [Informal] to cease being overdependent, as upon one's parents

cord·age (-ij′) *n.* ⟦Fr: see prec. & -AGE⟧ **1** cords and ropes collectively, esp. the ropes in a ship's rigging **2** the amount of wood, in cords, in a given area

cor·date (kôr′dāt′, -dit) *adj.* ⟦ModL *cordatus* < L *cor* (gen. *cordis*), HEART⟧ heart-shaped —**cor′date·ly** *adv.*

Cor·day (d'Armont) (kôr dā′), **(Marie Anne) Charlotte** 1768-93; Fr. Girondist sympathizer: assassin of Marat

cord·ed (kôr′did) *adj.* **1** fastened with cords **2** made of or provided with cords **3** that looks like a tight cord: said as of a muscle **4** having a ribbed or twilled surface, as corduroy **5** stacked in cords: said of wood: see CORD (*n.* 3)

Cor·del·ia (kôr dēl′yə) *n.* ⟦prob. ult. < Celt *Creiryddlydd*, lit., daughter of the sea⟧ **1** a feminine name **2** in Shakespeare's *King Lear*, the youngest of Lear's three daughters, and the only one faithful to him

Cor·de·lier (kôr′də lir′; *Fr* kôr də lyā′) *n.* ⟦OFr < *cordelle* (see fol.): so named from the knotted cord worn as a belt⟧ **1** in France, a member of the Franciscan Observants **2** ⟦after the Church of the *Cordeliers*, Paris, where the meetings were held⟧ a member of a radical French Revolutionary political club

☆**cor·delle** (kôr del′, kôr′del′) *n.* ⟦Fr, dim. of OFr *corde*, rope: see CORD⟧ a towrope, esp. as formerly used on Mississippi flatboats and keelboats —*vt.* **-delled′**, **-dell′ing** to tow with or as with a cordelle

cord·grass (kôrd′gras′) *n.* any of a genus (*Spartina*) of marsh grasses: some may reach a height of 3 m (9.8 ft) in tidal mud flats

cor·dial (kôr′jəl; *chiefly Brit* kôr′dē əl) *adj.* ⟦ME < ML *cordialis* < L *cor* (gen. *cordis*), HEART⟧ **1** [Rare] stimulating the heart; invigorating; reviving **2** *a)* warm and friendly; hearty [a *cordial* hello] *b)* sincere; deeply felt [a *cordial* distaste for formality] —*n.* **1** [Rare] a medicine, food, or drink that stimulates the heart **2** an aromatic, syrupy alcoholic drink; liqueur —**SYN.** AMIABLE —**cor′dial·ly** *adv.* —**cor′dial·ness** *n.*

cor·di·al·i·ty (kôr′jē al′ə tē, kôr jal′-; *chiefly Brit* kôr′dē al′-) *n.* **1** cordial quality; warm, friendly feeling **2** *pl.* **-ties** a warm, friendly act or remark

cor·di·er·ite (kôr′dē ər īt′) *n.* ⟦after P. L. A. *Cordier* (1777-1861), Fr geologist + -ITE[1]⟧ a bluish, very hard, pleochroic, crystalline mineral, magnesium aluminum silicate, $(Mg,Fe)_2Al_4Si_5O_{18}$, used sometimes as a gem

cor·di·form (kôr′də fôrm′) *adj.* ⟦< L *cor* (gen. *cordis*), HEART + -FORM⟧ heart-shaped

cor·dil·le·ra (kôr′dil yer′ə, -də ler′ə) *n.* ⟦Sp < *cordilla*, dim. of *cuerda*, rope, cord < L *chorda*: see CORD⟧ a mountain range or a series of parallel mountain ranges that are usually the principal mountain system of a continent —**cor′dil·le′ran** *adj.*

Cor·dil·le·ras (kôr′dil yer′əz) **1** mountain system of W North America, including all mountains between the E Rockies & the Pacific coast **2** mountain system of W South America; Andes

cord·ing (kôr′diŋ) *n.* the ribbed surface of corded cloth

cord·ite (kôr′dīt′) *n.* ⟦CORD + -ITE[1]: so called from its stringy appearance⟧ a smokeless explosive containing nitroglycerin, guncotton, petroleum jelly, and acetone

☆**cord·less** (kôrd′lis) *adj.* **1** lacking a cord **2** operated only or optionally by batteries, unlike models operated only by current from an outlet [a *cordless* electric shaver]

cór·do·ba (kôr′də bə) *n.* ⟦Sp, after F. Fernández de *Córdoba*, 16th-c. Sp explorer⟧ the basic monetary unit of Nicaragua: see the table of monetary units in the Reference Supplement

Cór·do·ba (kôr′də bə, -və; *Sp* kôr′thô bä) **1** city in NC Argentina **2** city in S Spain, on the Guadalquivir River **3** city in EC Mexico, in Veracruz state

cor·don (kôr′dən, kôrd′'n) *n.* ⟦OFr, dim. of *corde*: see CORD⟧ **1** a line or circle of police, soldiers, forts, ships, etc. stationed around an area to guard it **2** a cord, ribbon, or braid worn as a decoration or badge **3** STRINGCOURSE —*vt.* to encircle or shut (*off*) with a cordon

cor·don bleu (kôr dōn blö′) ⟦Fr, blue ribbon⟧ **1** the blue ribbon formerly worn as an emblem by Knights of the Order of the Holy Ghost, the highest order of knighthood in France under the Bourbon monarchy **2** any very high distinction **3** a person entitled to wear the *cordon bleu* **4** any person highly distinguished in a certain field; specif., a very skilled chef **5** stuffed with ham and Gruyère cheese, breaded, and sautéed [veal *cordon bleu*]

cordon sa·ni·taire (sä nē ter′) ⟦Fr, lit., sanitary cordon⟧ **1** a barrier restraining free movement of people or goods, so as to keep a disease, infection, etc. from spreading from one locality into another **2** a belt of countries serving to isolate another country and check its aggressiveness or lessen its influence

Cor·do·va (kôr′də və) *Eng. name for* CÓRDOBA

Cor·do·van (kôr′də vən) *adj.* ⟦< Sp *cordobán*, after CÓRDOBA⟧ **1** of Córdoba **2** [**c-**] made of cordovan —*n.* **1** a person born or living in Córdoba **2** [**c-**] a fine-grained, colored leather, usually of split horsehide, but orig. made of goatskin at Córdoba, Spain **3** [**c-**] [*pl.*] shoes made of this leather

cor·du·roy (kôr′də roi′) *n.* ⟦prob. < *cord* + obs. *duroy*, a coarse fabric formerly produced in England: hence, corded duroy⟧ **1** a heavy cotton fabric with a piled, velvety surface, ribbed vertically **2** [*pl.*] trousers made of this fabric —*adj.* **1** made of, or ribbed like, corduroy ☆**2** made of logs laid crosswise [a *corduroy* road]

cord·wain (kôrd′wān′) *n.* ⟦ME & OFr *cordewan* < Prov *cordoan* < Port < Sp *cordobán*: see CORDOVAN⟧ [Archaic] cordovan leather

cord·wain·er (-wān′ər) *n.* ⟦ME *cordwaner* < OFr *cordoanier*: see prec.⟧ [Archaic] a shoemaker, orig. one who worked in cordovan leather

cord·wood (kôrd′wood′) *n.* wood stacked or sold in cords

core (kôr) *n.* ⟦ME < OFr *cor*, prob. < L *cor*, HEART⟧ **1** the hard, central part of an apple, pear, etc., that contains the seeds **2** the central or innermost part of anything **3** the most important part, as of a matter, discussion, etc.; essence; pith **4** in foundry work, that part of a mold which forms the interior of a hollow casting **5** a cylindrical sample of earth strata, as of rock, soil, snow, or ice, that is removed from the ground or ocean floor by boring with a long hollow drill and used to study the various layers of material that were deposited over a long period of geologic time **6** the central region of a nuclear reactor that contains the fissile fuel and, usually, control rods, moderator, etc. **7** the wood center to which outer layers of veneer are attached **8** *Anat.* the main muscles of the human trunk, including those of the back, sides, abdomen, and, sometimes, pelvis **9** *Chem.* the nucleus together with the closed electron shells of an atom; kernel **10** *Elec.* a mass of magnetic material placed inside a wire coil, serving to channel and increase the strength of the magnetic field resulting from current in the coil **11** *Geol.* the central zone inside the earth that begins at a depth of *c.* 2,900 km (*c.* 1,800 mi): it is extremely hot and has a liquid outer part and a solid inner part that are thought to be composed of iron and nickel —*vt.* **cored**, **cor′ing** to remove the core of —*adj.* central, basic, or most important; main [*core* values, *core* knowledge]

CORE (kôr) *abbrev.* Congress of Racial Equality

core curriculum a set of school or college courses in subjects considered essential to a suitable education, as in providing necessary skills or common cultural knowledge

co·re·la·tion (kō′ri lā′shən) *n.* CORRELATION —**co′-rel′a·tive** (-rel′ə tiv) *adj.* —**co′-rel′a·tive·ly** *adv.*

co·re·li·gion·ist (kō′ri lij′ə nist) *n.* a person of the same religion or religious denomination

Co·rel·li (kô rel′ē; *It* kô rel′lē), **Arc·an·ge·lo** (är kän′je lô) 1653-1713; It. composer & violinist

core memory CORE STORAGE

☆**co·re·op·sis** (kō′rē äp′sis, kôr′ē-) *n.* ⟦ModL < Gr *koris*, bug (< IE base *(*s*)*ker-*, to cut > SHEAR) + *opsis*, appearance (see -OPSIS): so named from the shape of the fruit⟧ any of a genus (*Coreopsis*) of plants of the composite family, having showy heads with yellow, crimson, or maroon ray flowers

cor·er (kôr′ər) *n.* a cutting or piercing instrument for removing the cores of apples, pears, etc.

co·re·spond·ent (kō′ri spän′dənt) *n.* ⟦CO- + RESPONDENT⟧ *Law* a person charged with or named as having committed adultery with the wife or husband from whom a divorce is being sought —**co′re·spond′en·cy** *n.*

core storage a kind of computer memory consisting of storage units made of ferromagnetic rings

corf (kôrf) *n., pl.* **corves** ⟦ME < MDu & MLowG < L *corbis*, a basket: see CORBEIL⟧ [Brit.] a basket or small cart, as for carrying coal, ore, etc. in mines

Cor·fu (kôr′foo; kôr foo′, -fyoo′) one of the Ionian Islands, off the W coast of Greece: 247 sq mi (640 sq km)

cor·gi (kôr′gē) *n.* WELSH CORGI

co·ri·a·ceous (kō′rē ā′shəs, kôr′ē-) *adj.* ⟦LL *coriaceus* < L *corium*, hide: see CORIUM⟧ of or like leather

co·ri·an·der (kôr′ē an′dər, kôr′ē an′dər) *n.* ⟦ME & OFr *coriandre* < L *coriandrum* < Gr *koriandron, koriannon*⟧ **1** a European annual herb (*Coriandrum sativum*) of the umbel family **2** its strong-smelling, seedlike fruit, used in flavoring food and liqueurs, and, formerly, in medicines **3** the leaf of this plant, used as an herb in cooking; cilantro

Co·rinne (kō rin′, -rēn′; kô-, kə-) *n.* ⟦Fr < L *Corinna* < Gr *Korinna*, ? dim. of *Korē*: see CORA⟧ a feminine name

Cor·inth (kôr′inth, kär′-) **1** ancient city in the NE Peloponnesus, at the head of the Gulf of Corinth, noted for its luxury: fl. 7th-2d cent. B.C. **2** modern city near the site of ancient Corinth: Gr. name KORINTHOS **3 Gulf of** arm of the Ionian Sea, between the Peloponnesus & central Greece: *c.* 80 mi (129 km) long **4 Isthmus of** land strip joining the Peloponnesus with central Greece: *c.* 4-8 mi (6.4-13 km) wide & 20 mi (32 km) long

Co·rin·thi·an (kə rin′thē ən) *adj.* **1** of Corinth or its people or culture **2** dissolute and loving luxury, as the people of Corinth were said to be **3** in the style of the art of Corinth; gracefully elaborate **4** designating or of a classical (Greek or Roman) order of architecture, distinguished by a slender, fluted column and a bell-shaped capital decorated with a design of acanthus leaves —*n.* **1** a person born or living in Corinth **2** a lover of elegantly luxurious living; sybarite **3** a wealthy man about town

Co·rin·thi·ans (-ənz) *n.* either of two books of the New Testament that were letters from the Apostle Paul to the Christians of Corinth: abbrev. *Cor* or *Co*

Cor·i·o·la·nus (kôr′ē ə lā′nəs) *n.* a tragedy (*c.* 1608) by Shakespeare, based on the story of Gaius Marcius Coriolanus, a legendary Roman general of the 5th cent. B.C.

Cor·i·o·lis effect (kôr′ē ō′lis) ⟦see fol.⟧ the apparent deflection of a moving mass of water, air, etc. to the right in the Northern Hemisphere and to the left in the Southern Hemisphere

Coriolis force ⟦after G. G. de *Coriolis* (1792-1843), Fr mathematician⟧ an apparent deflective force acting on a moving object, as an airplane, that is being observed from a rotating system, as the surface of the earth: it is proportional to the speed of the object and is in a direction perpendicular to its direction of motion

co·ri·um (kôr′ē əm) *n., pl.* **-ri·a** (-ə) ⟦L, skin, hide < IE base *(*s*)*ker-*, to cut > SHEAR, L *cortex*⟧ **1** DERMIS **2** the elongated middle portion of the forewing of a hemipteran insect

cork (kôrk) *n.* ⟦ME < Sp *corcho,* cork, ult. (via ? Ar *al-qurq*) < L *quercus,* oak: see FIR[1]⟧ **1** the light, thick, elastic outer bark of an oak tree, the **cork oak** (*Quercus suber*) of the beech family, that grows in the Mediterranean area: used for floats, stoppers, linoleum, insulation, etc. **2** *a)* a piece of cork or something made of cork; esp., a stopper for a bottle, cask, etc. *b)* a similar stopper made of rubber, glass, etc. **3** *Bot.* the dead, waterproof outer bark of the stems of woody plants —*adj.* made of cork —*vt.* **1** to stop or seal with a cork **2** to hold back; check **3** to blacken with burnt cork **4** *Baseball* to modify (a bat) by drilling a hole in the large end and filling it with cork or rubber: this practice is believed to give the batter an unfair advantage and is illegal —☆**blow one's cork** [Slang] to lose one's temper; become enraged

Cork (kôrk) **1** county on the S coast of Ireland, in Munster province: 2,880 sq mi (7,459 sq km) **2** its county seat, a seaport

cork·age (kôr′kij) *n.* ⟦CORK + -AGE⟧ a charge made, as at a restaurant, for opening and serving each bottle of wine or liquor bought elsewhere and brought in by a patron, or, occas., for every bottle opened and served, regardless of source

cork·board (kôrk′bôrd′) *n.* **1** cardboard made with granulated cork, used esp. for insulation **2** a bulletin board made of this material

cork cambium *Bot.* a layer of formative cells between the cork and the cortex, from which the cork is formed

cork elm any of several tall elms (genus *Ulmus*) of the E U.S., with corky ridges

cork·er (kôr′kər) *n.* ⟦slang senses < CORK in sense "stopper"⟧ **1** a worker or device that corks bottles **2** [Slang] *a)* a remarkable person or thing *b)* an argument, statement, etc. that appears conclusive *c)* a preposterous lie

cork·ing (kôr′kiŋ) *adj., adv., interj.* ⟦< CORK⟧ [Informal] very good or very well; excellent(ly)

cork·screw (kôrk′skro͞o′) *n.* a device for pulling corks out of bottles, usually a spiral-shaped piece of steel with a point at one end and a handle at the other —*adj.* shaped like a corkscrew; spiral — *vi., vt.* to move in a spiral; twist

corkscrew

cork·wood (-wo͝od′) *n.* **1** any of several trees whose wood is very light; specif., ☆*a)* the only species (*Leitneria floridana*) of a family (Leitneriaceae, order Leitneriales) of dicotyledonous shrubs or small trees found in swampy regions of the SE U.S. ☆*b)* the balsa **2** the wood of any of these trees

cork·y (kôr′kē) *adj.* **cork′i·er, cork′i·est 1** of or like cork **2** having its taste and smell affected by a cork stopper that is rotten or broken: said esp. of wine

corm (kôrm) *n.* ⟦ModL < Gr *kormos,* trunk of a tree with branches lopped off < *keirein,* to cut off < IE base *(*s*)*ker-* > HARVEST⟧ a fleshy, thickened, vertical, underground stem, usually having annual segments with a bud at the tip, thin external scale leaves, and roots at the base, as in the gladiolus: corms differ from bulbs in having much more stem tissue and fewer scale leaves

Cor·mack (kôr′mak), **Allan (MacLeod)** 1924-98; U.S. physicist, born in South Africa

cor·mel (kôr′məl) *n.* ⟦CORM + *-el,* dim. suffix < ME < OFr < L *-ellus*⟧ a new, small corm arising from a mature corm

cor·mo·rant (kôr′mə rənt) *n.* ⟦ME *cormoraunt* < OFr *cormareng* < *corp marenc* < L *corvus marinus* < *corvus,* RAVEN[1] + *marinus,* MARINE⟧ **1** any of a family (Phalacrocoracidae) of large, voracious, pelecaniform diving birds with webbed toes and a hooked beak **2** a greedy person

corn[1] (kôrn) *n.* ⟦ME & OE < IE base **ger-,* to ripen, mature, grow old > GRAIN, CHURN, Gr *gerōn,* old man⟧ **1** [Now Dial.] a tiny, hard particle, as of salt or sand; granule; grain **2** a small, hard seed or seedlike fruit, esp. a seed or grain of a cereal grass; kernel: now chiefly in compounds [*peppercorn, barleycorn*] ☆**3** *a)* a cultivated American cereal plant (*Zea mays*) of the grass family, with the grain borne on cobs enclosed in husks; maize *b)* the ears or kernels of this cereal plant **4** [Brit.] *a)* the seeds of all cereal grasses, as wheat, rye, barley, etc.; grain *b)* any plant or plants producing grain **5** the leading cereal crop in a particular place, as wheat in England or oats in Scotland and Ireland **6** [Informal] corn whiskey ☆**7** ⟦see CORNY[1] (*adj.* 2)⟧ [Informal] ideas, humor, music, etc. regarded as old-fashioned, trite, banal, or sentimental —*vt.* **1** to form into granules **2** to preserve or pickle with salt granules or in brine **3** to feed grain to (animals)

corn[2] (kôrn) *n.* ⟦ME & OFr *corne* < L *cornu,* HORN⟧ a hard, thick, painful growth of skin, esp. on a toe, caused by pressure or friction

☆**corn·ball** (kôrn′bôl′) [Slang] *adj.* ⟦CORN[1] (*n.* 7) + (SCREW)BALL⟧ unsophisticated, old-fashioned, banal, sentimental, etc.; corny —*n.* a cornball person or thing

☆**Corn Belt** region in the NC plains area of the Midwest where much corn and cornfed livestock are raised: it extends from W Ohio to E Nebr. and NE Kans.

☆**corn borer** the larva of a European moth (*Ostrinia nubilalis*), now a destructive pest in the U.S., feeding on corn and other plants

☆**corn bread** a baked or fried flat bread made with cornmeal and, variously, milk or water, flour, eggs, sugar, etc.: also written **corn′bread′** *n.*

☆**corn·cake** (kôrn′kāk′) *n.* JOHNNYCAKE

☆**corn·cob** (-käb′) *n.* **1** the woody core of an ear of corn, on which the kernels grow in rows **2** a corncob pipe

☆**corncob pipe** a tobacco pipe with a bowl made of a hollowed piece of dried corncob

corn cockle a tall annual weed (*Agrostemma githago*) of the pink family, with flat, pinkish flowers and poisonous seeds, often found in grainfields

corn·crake (-krāk′) *n.* ⟦see CRAKE⟧ a brown, short-billed N European rail (*Crex crex*), often found in grainfields

☆**corn·crib** (-krib′) *n.* a ventilated structure, with or without a roof, for storing ears of corn

☆**corn·dodg·er** (-däj′ər) *n.* [Dial.] a small cake of cornmeal, baked or fried hard: also written **corn dodger**

☆**corn dog** a wiener covered with cornmeal batter and deep-fried

cor·ne·a (kôr′nē ə) *n.* ⟦ME < ML < L *cornea* (*tela*), horny (web, tissue), fem. sing. of *corneus* < *cornu,* HORN⟧ the transparent tissue over the front of the eyeball, covering the iris and pupil —**cor′ne·al** *adj.*

☆**corn ear·worm** (ir′wurm′) the larva of a noctuid moth (*Heliothis zea*), that feeds on corn ears and other crops

corned (kôrnd) *vt. pt. & pp. of* CORN[1] —*adj.* preserved with salt or brine [*corned* beef]

Cor·neille (kôr nā′y′; *E* kôr nā′, -nāl′), **Pierre** (pyer) 1606-84; Fr. dramatist

cor·nel (kôr′nəl) *n.* ⟦ME & OFr *corneille* < VL **cornea* < L *cornus;* akin to Gr *kranos,* cornel tree, prob. akin to *kerasos,* cherry tree: see CHERRY⟧ DOGWOOD (sense 1), esp. bunchberry

Cor·nel·ia[1] (kôr nēl′yə) *n.* ⟦L, fem. of *Cornelius*⟧ a feminine name

Cor·nel·ia[2] (kôr nēl′yə) 2d cent. B.C.; mother of Gaius & Tiberius Gracchus

cor·nel·ian (kôr nēl′yən) *n.* ⟦ME & OFr *corneline,* dim. < OFr *corneola,* prob. (because of similarity of color) < VL **cornea:* see CORNEL⟧ CARNELIAN

Cor·nel·ius (kôr nēl′yəs) *n.* ⟦L, name of a Roman gens⟧ a masculine name: fem. *Cornelia*

Cor·nell (kôr nel′) **1 Ezra** 1807-74; U.S. capitalist & philanthropist **2 Katharine** 1898-1974; U.S. actress

cor·ne·ous (kôr′nē əs) *adj.* ⟦L *corneus* < *cornu,* HORN⟧ horny; hornlike

cor·ner (kôr′nər) *n.* ⟦ME < OFr *corniere* < ML *cornerium* < L *cornu,* projecting point, HORN⟧ **1** the point or place where lines or surfaces join and form an angle **2** the area or space within the angle formed at the joining of lines or surfaces [the *corner* of a room] **3** the area at the tip of any of the angles formed at a street intersection **4** something used to form, mark, protect, or decorate a corner **5** a remote, secret, or secluded place [look in every nook and *corner*] **6** region; quarter; part [every *corner* of America] **7** an awkward position from which escape is difficult [driven into a *corner*] ☆**8** a monopoly acquired on a stock or a commodity so as to be able to control the price **9** *Boxing* any of the four areas in the ring where the ropes meet to form 90° angles, esp., either of two such areas at opposite ends of the ring, used by the boxers between rounds for rest and medical attention ☆**10** *Football short for* CORNERBACK —*vt.* ☆**1** to drive or force into a corner or awkward position, so that escape is difficult ☆**2** to get a monopoly on (a stock or commodity) —*vi.* **1** to meet at or abut (*on*) a corner: said of land, buildings, etc. **2** to turn corners: said of a vehicle [a car that *corners* easily] —*adj.* **1** at or on a corner [a *corner* store] **2** used in a corner [a *corner* table] —**SYN.** MONOPOLY —**around the corner** in the immediate vicinity or future —☆**cut corners 1** to take a direct route by going across corners **2** to cut down expenses, time, labor, etc. —**in someone's corner** ⟦in ref. to CORNER (*n.* 9), the place where a boxer's seconds wait just outside the ring⟧ allied with or supporting someone —**out of the corner of one's eye** by means of one's peripheral vision —**the (four) corners of the earth** the farthest parts of the earth —**turn the corner** to get safely past the critical point

cor·ner·back (-bak′) ☆*n. Football* either of two defensive backs who are positioned outside of the linebackers and are primarily responsible for covering pass receivers

cor·nered (kôr′nərd) *adj.* having (a specified number or type of) corners [a three-*cornered* hat]

corner kick *Soccer* a FREE KICK by which an offensive player puts the ball in play from the corner of the field (**corner area**): awarded after a defensive player has sent the ball across any portion of his or her own goal line not lying between the goal posts

cor·ner·man (kôr′nər man′) *n., pl.* **-men′** (-men′) **1** ⟦see IN SOMEONE'S CORNER (phr. under CORNER)⟧ *Boxing* a second, esp. a trainer skilled in first aid **2** *Sports* a player positioned near a corner of the field, court, etc.

corner office ⟦because an office at the corner of a floor is typically more spacious⟧ the room or rooms assigned to the highest managerial position within a corporation, branch, etc.: often used fig. for the position itself

cor·ner·stone (-stōn′) *n.* ⟦ME⟧ **1** a stone that forms part of the corner of a building; esp., a foundation stone of this kind, often inscribed, laid at a ceremony that marks the beginning of building **2** the basic, essential, or most important part; foundation

cor·ner·wise (-wīz′) *adv.* **1** with the corner to the front **2** from one corner to an opposite corner; diagonally Also **cor′ner·ways′** (-wāz′)

cor·net (kôr net′; *Brit* kôr′nit) *n.* ⟦ME & OFr, dim. of *corn,* a horn < L *cornu,* HORN⟧ **1** a brass instrument similar to the trumpet in pitch and construction but more compact and with a deeper mouthpiece **2** *a)* a piece of paper twisted like a cone, for holding sugar, candy, etc. *b)* a cone-shaped piece of pastry, often filled as with whipped cream **3** the spreading, white headdress of a Sister of Charity

cor·net-à-pis·tons (kôr net′ə pis′tənz; *Fr* kôr nā à pēs tōn′) *n., pl.* **cor·nets′-à-pis′tons** (-nets′ə-; *Fr.,* -nā zà-) CORNET (sense 1)

☆**cor·net·ist** or **cor·net·tist** (kôr net′ist) *n.* a cornet player

☆**corn·fed** (kôrn′fed′) *adj.* **1** fed on corn **2** [Informal] rustically robust and simple, unsophisticated, etc.

corn·field (-fēld′) *n.* a field in which corn is grown

☆**corn·flakes** (-flāks′) *pl.n.* a breakfast cereal of crisp flakes made from hulled corn and served cold, as with milk: also **corn flakes**

☆**corn flour** **1** flour made from corn **2** [Brit.] cornstarch

corn·flow·er (-flou′ər) *n.* an annual plant (*Centaurea cyanus*) of the composite family, with tiny, raylike, white, pink, or blue flowers forming a round head at the top of the stem

☆**corn·hole**[1] (-hōl′) [Slang] *n.* the anus, esp. as the site of anal intercourse —*vt.* **-holed′**, **-hol′ing** to penetrate in an act of anal intercourse Considered vulgar by many

☆**corn·hole**[2] (-hōl′) *n.* ⟦from the use of dried kernels of *corn* in the bags⟧ a game in which players toss small bags similar to beanbags at or into a hole in the top of a box

☆**corn·husk·er** (-hus′kər) *n.* **1** a person or machine that husks corn **2** [C-] [Informal] a person born or living in Nebraska, called the **Cornhusker State**

☆**corn·husk·ing** (-hus′kiŋ) *n.* **1** the husking of corn **2** a gathering of friends and neighbors for husking corn; husking bee: it is generally a festive event, followed by dancing, etc.

cor·nice (kôr′nis) *n.* ⟦Fr < It < L *coronis,* curved line, flourish in writing < Gr *korōnis,* curved object: see CROWN⟧ **1** a horizontal molding projecting along the top of a wall, building, etc. **2** the top part of an entablature **3** a projecting, decorative strip above a window, designed to keep a curtain rod from showing —*vt.* **-niced**, **-nic·ing** to top as with a cornice

cor·niche (kôr nēsh′) *n.* ⟦Fr, lit., prec.⟧ a roadway that winds along a cliff or steep slope

cor·ni·chon (kôr′nē shōn′) *n.* ⟦Fr⟧ a small sour pickle

cor·nic·u·late (kôr nik′yoo͞ lit, -lāt′) *adj.* ⟦L *corniculatus* < *corniculus,* dim. of *cornu,* HORN⟧ having horns or hornlike projections; horned

cor·ni·fy (kôr′nə fī′) *vt.* **-fied′**, **-fy′ing** KERATINIZE —**cor′ni·fi·ca′tion** *n.* —**cor′ni·fied′** *adj.*

Cor·nish (kôr′nish) *adj.* of Cornwall or its people, language, or culture —*n.* **1** the Celtic language spoken in Cornwall until *c.* 1800, closely related to Breton and Welsh **2** *pl.* **Cor′nish** *a)* any of a Brit. breed of chicken with meat of a particularly good quality *b)* any of a breed of miniature chicken crossbred from a Cornish chicken and a Plymouth Rock chicken (popularly called **Cornish hen**)

Cor·nish·man (-mən) *n., pl.* **-men** (-mən) a person born or living in Cornwall

Corn Laws in England, certain laws imposing heavy duties on the importation of grain, repealed in 1846

corn·meal (kôrn′mēl′) *n.* ☆**1** meal made from corn (maize) **2** meal made from some other grain, as, in Scotland, oats: see CORN[1]

corn on the cob one or more ears of corn, boiled or roasted and served with the kernels intact

☆**corn·pone** (-pōn′) *adj.* ⟦< fol.: see CORNY[1] (*adj.* 2)⟧ [Informal] depicting rural, esp. Southern, life or people in a stereotyped or sentimental way *[cornpone comedy]*

☆**corn pone** [Chiefly South] a kind of corn bread baked in small oval loaves, or pones

corn poppy a species of poppy (*Papaver rhoeas*), often found in grainfields of Europe and Asia

☆**corn·row** (kôrn′rō′) *n.* **1** a hairstyle in which the hair is arranged in an intricate pattern of tight, parallel braids close to the scalp **2** any one of a number of such braids so arranged: *usually used in pl.* —*vt.* to arrange in cornrows

corn salad a European herb (*Valerianella locusta*) of the valerian family, often found in cornfields, with rose, blue, or white flowers and leaves that are used in salads

☆**corn silk** the long, silky fibers that are the styles of an ear of corn: the longer fibers hang out of the husk in a tuft which catches pollen

☆**corn smut** a disease of corn caused by a smut fungus (*Ustilago maydis*), forming large black swellings

☆**corn snow** snow that has melted and refrozen, as in the spring, to form coarse granules

☆**corn·stalk** (-stôk′) *n.* a stalk of corn (maize)

☆**corn·starch** (-stärch′) *n.* a fine, granular or powdery starch made from corn: used in cooking and to make corn sugar, corn syrup, etc.

☆**corn sugar** a dextrose made from cornstarch

☆**corn syrup** a syrup made from cornstarch: it is a mixture of dextrose, maltose, and dextrins

cor·nu (kôr′nyoo͞, -noo͞) *n., pl.* **-nu·a** (-ə) ⟦L, HORN⟧ *Anat.* any horn-shaped structure —**cor′nu·al** (-nyoo͞ əl) *adj.*

cor·nu·co·pi·a (kôr′nə kō′pē ə, -nyoo͞-) *n.* ⟦L *cornu copiae,* horn of plenty: see HORN & COPIOUS⟧ **1** *Gr. Myth.* a horn of the goat that suckled Zeus: it becomes full of whatever its owner wants **2** *a)* a representation in painting, sculpture, etc. of a horn overflowing with fruits, flowers, and grain; horn of plenty *b)* any container shaped like a cone or horn, as for displaying in this fashion as a centerpiece **3** an overflowing fullness; abundance

cornucopia

cor·nut·ed (kôr noo͞t′id, -noo͞t′-) *adj.* ⟦< L *cornutus,* horned < *cornu,* HORN⟧ **1** having horns **2** horn-shaped **3** [Archaic] cuckolded

cor·nu·to (kôr noo͞t′ō) *n., pl.* **-tos** ⟦It: see prec.⟧ a cuckold

Corn·wall (kôrn′wôl′; *chiefly Brit,* -wəl) county at the SW tip of England: 1,363 sq mi (3,530 sq km): in full **Cornwall and Isles of Scilly**

Corn·wal·lis (kôrn wôl′is, -wäl′-), **Charles** 1st Marquis Cornwallis 1738-1805; Eng. general & statesman: commanded Brit. forces during American Revolution

☆**corn whiskey** a whiskey distilled from a fermented mash of not less than 80 percent corn grain

corn·y[1] (kôr′nē) *adj.* **corn′i·er**, **corn′i·est** ⟦CORN[1] + -Y[2]⟧ **1** of or producing corn ☆**2** ⟦from stereotypical attributon of such qualities and sentiments to farmers and country people⟧ [Informal] unsophisticated, old-fashioned, trite, sentimental, etc.

corn·y[2] (kôr′nē) *adj.* **corn′i·er**, **corn′i·est** ⟦CORN[2] + -Y[2]⟧ having or relating to corns on the feet

co·rol·la (kə rōl′ə, -räl′ə) *n.* ⟦ModL < L, dim. of *corona,* CROWN⟧ the petals, or inner floral leaves, of a flower —**cor·ol·late** (kôr′ə lāt′) *adj.*, **cor′ol·lat′ed**

cor·ol·lar·y (kôr′ə ler′ē, kär′-; *Brit & often Cdn,* kə räl′ər ē) *n., pl.* **-lar′ies** ⟦ME *corolarie* < LL *corollarium,* a deduction < L, orig., money paid for a garland, hence gift, gratuity < *corolla:* see prec.⟧ **1** a proposition that follows from another that has been proved **2** an inference or deduction **3** anything that follows as a normal result

cor·o·man·del (kôr′ə man′dəl) *n.* ⟦after fol.⟧ **1** CALAMANDER **2** a form of decorative lacquer, developed in China and used esp. on screens, depicting figures, scenes, etc. through the use of intaglio

Cor·o·man·del Coast (kôr′ə man′dəl) coastal region of SE India, on the Bay of Bengal: has a low shoreline with no good harbors

co·ro·na (kə rō′nə) *n., pl.* **-nas** or **-nae** (-nē) ⟦L, CROWN⟧ **1** a crown or something resembling a crown **2** a circular chandelier hanging from a church ceiling **3** a long cigar with straight sides and blunt ends **4** *Anat. a)* a crownlike part *b)* the crown of a tooth, of a skull, etc. **5** *Archit.* the top projection of a cornice **6** *Astron. a)* the layer of ionized gas surrounding the sun, characterized by an extremely low density, an extremely high temperature, and a constantly changing shape extending great distances from the sun: clearly visible during a total solar eclipse *b)* a ring of colored light seen around a luminous body, as the sun or moon, formed by the diffraction of light caused by mist, dust, etc. **7** *Bot.* an extra whorl of flower parts between the corolla and the stamens, as in the daffodil, forming a crownlike or cuplike part **8** *Elec.* a luminous discharge that may occur around a high-voltage conductor due to ionization of the surrounding air

Co·ro·na (kə rō′nə) ⟦Sp & L, wreath, CROWN: so named for the circular boulevard around the city⟧ city in S Calif.

Corona Aus·tra·lis (ô strā′lis) ⟦L, Southern Crown⟧ a S constellation near Sagittarius; the Southern Crown

Corona Bo·re·al·is (bôr′ē al′is, -ā′lis) ⟦L, Northern Crown⟧ a N constellation between Hercules and Boötes; the Northern Crown

cor·o·nach (kôr′ə nəkh) *n.* ⟦Ir *coranach* & Gael *corranach* < *comh-,* together + *ranach,* outcry < *ran,* to weep⟧ **1** [Scot.] a dirge, sung or played on bagpipes **2** [Irish] a wailing lament for the dead

Co·ro·na·do (kôr′ə nä′dō; *Sp* kô′rô nä′thô), **Fran·cis·co Vás·quez de** (frän thēs′kô väs′keth the) 1510?-54?; Sp. explorer of what is now the Southwest in the U.S.

co·ro·na·graph (kə rō′nə graf′) *n.* ⟦< earlier *coronograph* < CORON(A) + -O- + -GRAPH⟧ a telescope designed for observing the corona of the sun by means of devices that obstruct the light of the sun's disk

cor·o·nal (kôr′ə nəl, kär′-; *for adj., also* kə rōn′əl) *n.* ⟦ME & LL *coronalis* < L *corona,* CROWN⟧ **1** a circlet for the head; diadem; crown; coronet **2** a wreath; garland —*adj.* **1** of a crown, coronet, or halo **2** *Anat. a)* of the corona of the skull *b)* designating, of, or lying in the direction of the coronal suture

coronal suture *Anat.* a suture that extends across the skull between the frontal and parietal bones

cor·o·nar·y (kôr′ə ner′ē, kär′-) *adj.* ⟦L *coronarius:* see CROWN⟧ 1 of, or in the form of, a crown 2 *Anat. a)* like a crown; encircling *b)* designating or relating to either of two arteries, or their branches, coming from the aorta and supplying blood directly to the heart muscle —☆*n., pl.* **-nar′ies** loosely, a heart attack

coronary care unit the facility in a hospital specializing in the intensive care and monitoring of patients having serious heart problems

coronary heart disease a type of cardiovascular disease caused by the accumulation of plaque in the coronary arteries and characterized by angina pectoris, heart attack, etc.: also called **coronary artery disease**

coronary insufficiency an inability of the coronary arteries to deliver an adequate blood supply to the myocardium, resulting in angina pectoris and heart failure

☆**coronary thrombosis** ⟦coined (1912) by J. B. Herrick (1861-1954), U.S. physician⟧ the formation of a clot in a branch of either of the coronary arteries, resulting in obstruction of that artery: also called **coronary occlusion**

cor·o·na·tion (kôr′ə nā′shən, kär′-) *n.* ⟦ME & OFr *coronacion* < L *coronatus,* pp. of *coronare,* to crown < *corona,* CROWN⟧ the act or ceremony of crowning a sovereign

co·ro·na·vi·rus (kə rō′nə vī′rəs) *n.* ⟦ModL < L *corona,* CROWN + VIRUS: so named from the shape of its outer shell⟧ any of a family (Coronaviridae) of large RNA viruses that cause upper respiratory tract infections and gastrointestinal diseases in humans and animals —**co·ro′na·vi′ral** *adj.*

cor·o·ner (kôr′ə nər, kär′-) *n.* ⟦ME, officer of the crown < Anglo-Fr *corouner* < *coroune, corone,* a crown < L *corona,* CROWN⟧ a public officer who determines by inquest, sometimes with a jury, the causes of any deaths not obviously due to natural causes

cor·o·net (kôr′ə net′, kär′-; kôr′ə net′, kär′-) *n.* ⟦ME *corounet* < OFr *coronete,* dim. of *corone* < L *corona,* CROWN⟧ 1 a small crown worn by princes and others of high rank 2 an ornamental band of precious metal, jewels, flowers, etc., worn around the head 3 the part of a horse's foot just above the hoof —**cor′o·net′ed** *adj.*

Co·rot (kə rō′; *Fr* kô rō′), **Jean Bap·tiste Ca·mille** (zhän bȧ tēst′ kȧ mē′y′) 1796-1875; Fr. painter

Corp *abbrev.* 1 Corporal 2 Corporation: also **corp** or [Brit.] **corpn**

cor·po·ra (kôr′pə rə) *n. pl. of* CORPUS

corpora cal·lo·sa (kə lō′sə) *pl. of* CORPUS CALLOSUM

cor·po·ral¹ (kôr′pə rəl, -prəl) *n.* ⟦< Fr *caporal* < It *caporale,* a corporal < *capo,* chief, head < L *caput,* HEAD: sp. infl. by assoc. with *corps* or fol.⟧ the lowest-ranking noncommissioned officer, just below a sergeant; specif., an enlisted person in the fourth grade in the U.S. Army and Marine Corps —**cor′po·ral·cy** *n., pl.* **-cies** —**cor′po·ral·ship′** *n.*

cor·po·ral² (kôr′pə rəl, -prəl) *adj.* ⟦L *corporalis* < *corpus* (gen. *corporis*), body: see CORPUS⟧ 1 of the body; bodily 2 [Now Rare] personal 3 [Obs.] CORPOREAL (sense 2) —*SYN.* BODILY —**cor′po·ral·ly** *adv.*

cor·po·ral³ (kôr′pə rəl) *n.* ⟦OFr < ML *corporale* < *corporalis (palla),* body (cloth): see prec.⟧ *Eccles.* a small linen cloth put on the center of the altar, on which the bread and chalice are placed for the Eucharist

cor·po·ral·i·ty (kôr′pə ral′ə tē) *n.* ⟦LL(Ec) *corporalitas:* see CORPORAL²⟧ the state or quality of being material or having a body; bodily existence or substance

corporal punishment punishment inflicted directly on the body, as flogging: now usually distinguished from capital punishment, imprisonment, etc.

☆**corporal's guard** 1 a squad commanded by a corporal 2 any small group of people, sometimes a bare minimum for a given purpose

corpora lu·te·a (lo͞ot′ē ə) *pl. of* CORPUS LUTEUM

corpora stri·a·ta (strī āt′ə) *pl. of* CORPUS STRIATUM

cor·po·rate (kôr′pə rit, -prit) *adj.* ⟦ME *corporat* < L *corporatus,* pp. of *corporare,* to make into a body < *corpus,* body: see CORPUS⟧ 1 [Archaic] united; combined 2 having the nature of, or acting by means of, a corporation; incorporated 3 of a corporation or corporations; specif., of, suitable for, or characteristic of large business corporations 4 shared by all members of a unified group; common; joint [*corporate* responsibility] 5 CORPORATIVE (sense 2) —**cor′po·rate·ly** *adv.*

cor·po·ra·tion (kôr′pə rā′shən) *n.* ⟦ME *corporacioun* < LL(Ec) *corporatio,* assumption of a body, incarnation < pp. of L *corporare:* see prec.⟧ 1 a legal entity that exists independently of the person or persons who have been granted the charter creating it and that is invested with many of the rights given to individuals: a corporation may enter into contracts, buy and sell property, etc. 2 a group of people, as the mayor and aldermen of an incorporated town, legally authorized to act as an individual 3 any of the political and economic bodies forming a corporative state, each being composed of the employers and employees in a certain industry, profession, etc. 4 ⟦prob. from assoc. with CORPULENT, etc.⟧ [Informal] a large, prominent belly

cor·po·rat·ist (kôr′pə rə tist′) *adj.* of or characteristic of a corporative state —**cor′po·rat·ism′** *n.*

cor·po·ra·tive (kôr′pə rā′tiv, -rə tiv′) *adj.* ⟦LL *corporativus*⟧ 1 of or connected with a corporation 2 designating or of a state, as theoretically Italy under Fascism (1924-1943), in which political and economic power is vested in an organization of corporations: see CORPORATION (sense 3)

cor·po·ra·tize (kôr′pə rə tīz′) *vt.* 1 to make resemble in some fashion a large business corporation 2 to bring under the control of a business corporation —**cor′po·ra·ti·za′tion** *n.*

cor·po·ra·tor (kôr′pə rāt′ər) *n.* a member of a corporation

cor·po·re·al (kôr pôr′ē əl) *adj.* ⟦< L *corporeus* < *corpus:* see CORPUS⟧ 1 of, for, or having the nature of, the body; physical; bodily; not spiritual 2 of a material nature; perceptible by the senses; tangible —*SYN.* BODILY, MATERIAL —**cor·po′re·al·ly** *adv.*

cor·po·re·al·i·ty (kôr pôr′ē al′ə tē) *n.* the state or quality of being corporeal; bodily existence

cor·po·re·i·ty (kôr′pə rē′ə tē) *n.* ⟦ML *corporeitas* < L *corporeus*⟧ 1 CORPOREALITY 2 material or bodily substance

cor·po·sant (kôr′pə sant′, -zant′) *n.* ⟦Port *corpo santo,* holy body < L *corpus sanctum,* holy body⟧ SAINT ELMO'S FIRE

corps (kôr) *n., pl.* **corps** (kôrz) ⟦ME < OFr *corps, cors,* body < L *corpus,* body: see CORPUS⟧ 1 a body of people associated in some work, organization, etc. under common direction [a diplomatic *corps*] 2 *Mil. a)* a branch of the armed forces having some specialized function [the Signal *Corps,* the Marine *Corps*] *b)* a tactical subdivision of an army, normally composed of two or more divisions, plus auxiliary service troops

corps de bal·let (kôr′ də ba lā′) ⟦Fr⟧ the ensemble of a ballet company; esp., the ensemble apart from the featured dancers

corpse (kôrps) *n.* ⟦var. of CORPS⟧ 1 a dead body, esp. of a person 2 something once vigorous but now lifeless and of no use 3 [Obs.] a living body —*SYN.* BODY

corps·man (kôr′mən) *n., pl.* **-men** (-mən) 1 a member of a paramedical unit 2 a member of a military medical corps

cor·pu·lence (kôr′pyo͞o ləns, -pyə-) *n.* ⟦< L *corpulentia:* see fol.⟧ fatness or stoutness of body; obesity: also **cor′pu·len·cy**

cor·pu·lent (-lənt) *adj.* ⟦< L *corpulentus* < fol.⟧ fat and fleshy; stout; obese —**cor′pu·lent·ly** *adv.*

cor·pus (kôr′pəs) *n., pl.* **cor′po·ra** (-pə rə) ⟦L, body < IE base **krep-,* **krp-,* body, form > (MID)RIFF, OHG *href,* belly, womb, Sans *kṛpā,* form⟧ 1 a human or animal body, esp. a dead one: now mainly a facetious usage 2 a complete or comprehensive collection, as of laws or writings of a specified type [the *corpus* of civil law] 3 the main body or substance of anything 4 the principal, as distinguished from the interest or income, of an estate, fund, etc. 5 *Anat.* the main part of an organ; also, a mass of tissue with a specialized function

corpus cal·lo·sum (kə lō′səm) *pl.* **corpora cal·lo′sa** (-sə) ⟦ModL, lit., callous body⟧ a mass of white, transverse fibers connecting the cerebral hemispheres in human beings and in other higher mammals

Corpus Chris·ti¹ (kris′tē) ⟦L, Body of Christ⟧ a festival celebrated on the Thursday or Sunday after Trinity Sunday, in honor of the Eucharist

Corpus Chris·ti² (kris′tē) ⟦after *Corpus Christi* Bay (on which it lies): bay so named by Sp explorers entering it (1519) on prec.⟧ city in SE Tex., on the Gulf of Mexico

cor·pus·cle (kôr′pus′əl, -pə səl) *n.* ⟦L *corpusculum,* dim. of *corpus:* see CORPUS⟧ 1 a very small particle 2 *Anat.* a protoplasmic particle or cell with a special function; esp., any of the erythrocytes (*red corpuscles*) or leukocytes (*white corpuscles*) that float in the blood, lymph, etc. of vertebrates Also **cor·pus·cule** (kôr pus′kyo͞ol′) —**cor·pus·cu·lar** (kôr pus′kyo͞o lər, -kyə-) *adj.*

corpus de·lic·ti (də lik′tī′, -tē′) ⟦ModL, lit., body of the crime⟧ 1 the facts constituting or proving a crime; material substance or foundation of a crime: the corpus delicti in a murder case is not just the body of the victim, but the fact that the victim has been murdered 2 loosely, the body of the victim in a murder case

corpus ju·ris (jo͝or′is) ⟦L, body of law⟧ a collection of all the laws of a nation or district

Corpus Juris Ca·no·ni·ci (kə nän′ə sī′) ⟦ML, body of canon law⟧ the body of laws governing the Roman Catholic Church up to 1918: superseded by the CODEX JURIS CANONICI

Corpus Juris Ci·vi·lis (si vī′lis) ⟦L, body of civil law⟧ the body of civil, or Roman, law, compiled and issued during the reign of Justinian: it has been the basis of most European law

corpus lu·te·um (lo͞ot′ē əm) *pl.* **corpora lu′te·a** (-ə) ⟦ModL, lit., luteous body⟧ 1 *Anat.* a mass of yellow tissue formed in the ovary by a ruptured graafian follicle that has discharged its ovum: if the ovum is fertilized, this tissue secretes the hormone progesterone, needed to maintain pregnancy 2 a preparation containing this hormone, used in ovarian therapy; progesterone

corpus stri·a·tum (strī āt′əm) *pl.* **corpora stri·a′ta** (-ə) ⟦ModL, lit., striated body⟧ *Anat.* either of two striated ganglia in front of the thalamus in each half of the brain

corr *abbrev.* 1 corrected 2 correction 3 correspondence 4 corresponding

cor·rade (kə rād′) *vt., vi.* **-rad′ed, -rad′ing** ⟦< L *corradere,* to scrape together < *com-,* together + *radere,* to scrape: see RAT⟧ to erode by the abrasive action of running water, wind, glacial ice, etc. containing sand, pebbles, and other debris —**cor·ra′sion** (-rā′zhən) *n.* —**cor·ra′sive** (-rā′siv) *adj.*

☆**cor·ral** (kə ral′) *n.* ⟦Sp < *corro,* a circle, ring < L *currere,* to run: see CURRENT⟧ 1 an enclosure for holding or capturing horses, cattle, or other animals; pen 2 a defensive area made by drawing up covered wagons to form an enclosing circle —*vt.* **-ralled′, -ral′ling** 1 to drive into or confine within a corral 2 to surround or capture; round up 3 to arrange (wagons) in the form of a corral 4 [Slang] to take possession of; lay hold of

cor·rect (kə rekt′) *vt.* ⟦ME *correcten* < L *correctus,* pp. of *corrigere* < *com-,* together + *regere,* to lead straight, rule: see RECKON⟧ 1 to make right; change from wrong to right; remove errors from 2 to point out or mark the errors or faults of **3** to make conform to a standard **4** to scold or punish so as to cause to rectify faults **5** to cure, remove, or counteract (a fault, disease, etc.) —*vi.* to make corrections; specif., to make an adjustment so as to compensate (*for* an error, counteracting force, etc.) —*adj.* **1** conforming or adhering to an established standard; proper [*correct* behavior] **2** conforming to fact or logic; true, accurate, right, or free from errors **3** equal to the required or established amount, number, price, etc. —**cor·rect′a·ble** *adj.* —**cor·rect′ly** *adv.* —**cor·rect′ness** *n.* —**cor·rec′tor** *n.*

SYN.—**correct** connotes little more than absence of error [*a correct* answer] or adherence to conventionality [*correct* behavior]; **accurate** implies a positive exercise of care to obtain conformity with fact or truth [an *accurate* account of the events]; **exact** stresses perfect conformity to fact, truth, or some standard [the *exact* time, an *exact* quotation]; **precise** suggests minute accuracy of detail and often connotes a finicky or overly fastidious attitude [*precise* in all his habits] See also **punish** —*ANT.* **wrong, false**

correcting lens (*or* plate) a thin lens used to correct spherical aberration introduced by the spherical mirror in certain optical systems

cor·rec·tion (kə rek′shən) *n.* ⟦ME *correccion* < OFr *correction* < L *correctio*⟧ **1** a correcting or being corrected **2** a change that corrects a mistake; change from wrong to right, or from abnormal to normal; emendation; rectification **3** the amount of change made in correcting **4** *a)* punishment or scolding to correct faults *b)* [*usually pl.*] punishment and rehabilitation within a prison system **5** *Finance* a sudden, usually short-term decline, as in the stock market, following a rapid or dramatic rise in prices —**cor·rec′tion·al** (-əl) *adj.*

correction fluid WHITE-OUT

corrections facility a prison, detention home, etc.: also **correctional facility**

cor·rect·i·tude (kə rek′tə to͞od′, -tyo͞od′) *n.* ⟦< CORRECT, after RECTITUDE⟧ the quality of being correct, esp. in conduct; propriety

cor·rec·tive (kə rek′tiv) *adj.* ⟦Fr *correctif* < LL *correctivus*⟧ tending or meant to correct or improve; remedial —*n.* something corrective; remedy —**cor·rec′tive·ly** *adv.*

Cor·reg·gio (kə rej′ō), **(Antonio Allegri da)** 1494?-1534; It. painter

Cor·reg·i·dor (kə reg′ə dôr′) small fortified island in the Philippines, at the entrance to Manila Bay: in WWII, American-Filipino troops fought on for a month after the fall of Bataan; finally invaded & its garrison forced to surrender (May, 1942); recaptured (Feb., 1945)

cor·re·late (kôr′ə lāt′, kär′-) *n.* ⟦back-form. < fol.⟧ either of two interrelated things, esp. if one implies the other —*adj.* closely and naturally related —*vi.* **-lat′ed, -lat′ing** to be mutually related (*to* or *with*) —*vt.* to bring (a thing) into mutual relation (*with* another thing); calculate or show the reciprocal relation between; specif., to bring (one of two related or interdependent quantities, sets of statistics, etc.) into contrast (*with* the other)

cor·re·la·tion (kôr′ə lā′shən, kär′-) *n.* ⟦ML *correlatio*: see COM- & RELATION⟧ **1** mutual relationship or connection **2** the degree of relative correspondence, as between two sets of data [*a correlation* of 75%] **3** a correlating or being correlated —**cor′re·la′tion·al** *adj.*

correlation coefficient *Statistics* any of several measures of concomitant variation in two or more variables

cor·rel·a·tive (kə rel′ə tiv) *adj.* ⟦ML *correlativus*⟧ **1** having or involving a mutual relationship; reciprocally dependent [*correlative* rights and duties] **2** *Gram.* expressing mutual relation and used in pairs [in "Neither Tom nor I can go," "neither" and "nor" are *correlative* conjunctions] —*n.* **1** a thing closely related to something else **2** a correlative word —**cor·rel′a·tive·ly** *adv.* —**cor·rel′a·tiv′i·ty** *n.*

cor·re·spond (kôr′ə spänd′, kär′-) *vi.* ⟦MFr *correspondre* < ML *correspondere* < L *com-*, together + *respondere*, to RESPOND⟧ **1** to be in agreement (*with* something); conform (*to* something); tally; harmonize **2** to be similar, analogous, or equal (*to* something) **3** to communicate (*with* someone) by exchanging letters, esp. regularly —*SYN.* AGREE —**cor′re·spond′ing·ly** *adv.*

cor·re·spond·ence (-spän′dəns) *n.* ⟦ME < ML *correspondentia* < prp. of *correspondere*: see prec.⟧ **1** agreement with something else or with one another; conformity **2** similarity; analogy **3** *a)* communication by exchange of letters *b)* the letters received or written **4** *Math.* a clearly defined relationship between two members of a set, or different sets, as one-to-one correspondence

☆**correspondence school** a school that gives courses of instruction (**correspondence courses**) by mail, sending lessons and examinations to a student periodically, and correcting and grading the returned answers

cor·re·spond·en·cy (-spän′dən sē) *n., pl.* **-cies** *var. of* CORRESPONDENCE (senses 1 & 2)

cor·re·spond·ent (-spän′dənt) *adj.* ⟦ME < ML *correspondens*, prp. of *correspondere*, CORRESPOND⟧ corresponding; agreeing; matching; analogous —*n.* **1** a thing that corresponds; correlate **2** *a)* a person who exchanges letters with another *b)* a person who writes to a magazine or newspaper, expressing an opinion, as on public affairs **3** a person hired by a newspaper, radio or television network, etc. to furnish news, articles, newscast segments, etc. of a certain type or from a distant place **4** a person or firm acting for, or having regular business relations with, another at a distance

corresponding angles *Geom.* a pair of nonadjacent angles, one interior and one exterior, on the same side of a transversal: these paired angles are equal if the lines cut by the transversal are parallel

cor·re·spon·sive (-spän′siv) *adj.* [Archaic] corresponding

co·rri·da (kô rē′thä; E kə rēd′ə) *n., pl.* **-das** ⟦Sp *corrida (de toros)*, (bull-) baiting, lit., a running, race < fem. pp. of *correr*, to run < L *currere*: see CURRENT⟧ a public program in which a series of bullfights, usually six, are held

cor·ri·dor (kôr′ə dər, kär′-; -dôr′) *n.* ⟦Fr < It *corridore*, a gallery, corridor, runner < *correre*, to run < L *currere*: see CURRENT⟧ **1** a long passageway or hall, esp. one onto which several rooms open **2** a strip of land, or an air-space, forming a passageway through foreign-held land, as from a country to its seaport

cor·rie (kôr′ē, kär′ē) *n.* ⟦< Gael *coire*, cauldron < IE base **kwer-*, pot > OE *hwer*, kettle⟧ [Scot.] a round hollow in a hillside

Cor·rie·dale (kôr′ē dāl′, kär′-) *n.* ⟦after *Corriedale*, New Zealand⟧ a breed of rather large, white-faced sheep, developed in New Zealand for their wool and meat

Cor·rien·tes (kôr ryen′tes) city in N Argentina, on the Paraná River

cor·ri·gen·dum (kôr′ə jen′dəm, kär′-) *n., pl.* **-da** (-də) ⟦L, ger. of *corrigere*: see CORRECT⟧ **1** an error to be corrected, esp. one in a printed work **2** [*pl.*] a list of such errors with their corrections, inserted in the published work

cor·ri·gi·ble (kôr′ə jə bəl, kär′-) *adj.* ⟦ME < OFr < ML *corrigibilis* < L *corrigere*: see CORRECT⟧ capable of being corrected, improved, or reformed —**cor′ri·gi·bil′i·ty** (-bil′ə tē) *n.* —**cor′ri·gi·bly** *adv.*

cor·rob·o·rant (kə räb′ə rənt) *adj.* ⟦L *corroborans*, prp. of *corroborare*: see fol.⟧ **1** corroborating **2** [Obs.] strengthening: said of a medicine or tonic —*n.* [Obs.] a tonic

cor·rob·o·rate (kə räb′ə rāt′) *vt.* **-rat′ed, -rat′ing** ⟦< L *corroboratus*, pp. of *corroborare*, to strengthen < *com-*, intens. + *roborare* < *robur*, strength: see ROBUST⟧ **1** [Obs.] to strengthen **2** to make more certain the validity of; confirm; bolster; support [evidence to *corroborate* his testimony] —*SYN.* CONFIRM —**cor·rob′o·ra′tion** *n.* —**cor·rob′o·ra′tor** *n.*

cor·rob·o·ra·tive (kə räb′ə rāt′iv, -ər ə tiv′) *adj.* corroborating or tending to corroborate; confirmatory: also **cor·rob′o·ra·to′ry** (-ər ə tôr′ē)

cor·rob·o·ree (kə räb′ə rē′) *n.* ⟦Austral dial. < native *korobra*, dance⟧ **1** a dance festival held at night by Austral. Aborigines to celebrate tribal victories and similar events **2** in Australia, *a)* a large or noisy festivity *b)* an uproar; tumult

cor·rode (kə rōd′) *vt.* **-rod′ed, -rod′ing** ⟦ME *corroden* < OFr *corroder* < L *corrodere*, to gnaw to pieces < *com-*, intens. + *rodere*, to gnaw: see RAT⟧ **1** to eat into or wear away gradually, as by rusting or by the action of chemicals **2** to work upon insidiously and cause to deteriorate [a heart corroded by *bitterness*] —*vi.* to become corroded —**cor·rod′i·ble** *adj.*

cor·ro·sion (kə rō′zhən) *n.* ⟦ME *corrosioun* < OFr *corrosion* < LL *corrosio* < pp. of L *corrodere*: see prec.⟧ **1** a corroding or being corroded **2** a substance, as rust, formed by corroding

cor·ro·sive (kə rō′siv) *adj.* ⟦OFr *corrosif* < ML *corrosivus*⟧ **1** corroding or causing corrosion **2** bitingly sarcastic; cutting; acid —*n.* something causing corrosion —**cor·ro′sive·ly** *adv.* —**cor·ro′sive·ness** *n.*

corrosive sublimate MERCURIC CHLORIDE

cor·ru·gate (kôr′ə gāt′, kär′-) *vt., vi.* **-gat′ed, -gat′ing** ⟦< L *corrugatus*, pp. of *corrugare*, to wrinkle < *com-*, intens. + *rugare*, to wrinkle⟧ to shape or contract into parallel grooves and ridges; make wrinkles in; furrow

corrugated cardboard (*or* paper) cardboard or paper corrugated so as to be resilient, used for wrapping or packing

corrugated iron sheet iron or steel, usually galvanized, corrugated to give it added strength in construction

cor·ru·ga·tion (kôr′ə gā′shən, kär′-) *n.* ⟦ML *corrugatio*⟧ **1** a corrugating or being corrugated **2** any of the parallel ridges or grooves of a corrugated surface

cor·rupt (kə rupt′) *adj.* ⟦ME < L *corruptus*, pp. of *corrumpere*, to destroy, spoil, bribe < *com-*, together + *rumpere*, to break: see RUPTURE⟧ **1** [Obs.] changed from a sound condition to an unsound one; spoiled; contaminated; rotten **2** deteriorated from the normal or standard; specif., *a)* morally unsound or debased; perverted; evil; depraved *b)* taking bribes; venal *c)* containing alterations, errors, or admixtures of foreignisms (said of texts, languages, etc.) — *vt., vi.* to make or become corrupt —*SYN.* DEBASE —**cor·rupt′er** *n.*, **cor·rup′tor** —**cor·rupt′ly** *adv.* —**cor·rupt′ness** *n.*

cor·rupt·i·ble (kə rup′tə bəl) *adj.* ⟦ME < LL(Ec) *corruptibilis*⟧ that can be corrupted, esp. morally —**cor·rupt′i·bil′i·ty** (-tə bil′ə tē) *n.* —**cor·rupt′i·bly** *adv.*

cor·rup·tion (kə rup′shən) *n.* ⟦ME *corrupcion* < OFr *corruption* < L *corruptio* < *corruptus*, CORRUPT⟧ **1** the act or fact of making, becoming, or being corrupt **2** evil or wicked behavior; depravity **3** bribery or similar dishonest dealings **4** decay; putridity; rottenness **5** something corrupted, as an improperly altered word or text **6** [Rare] a corrupting influence

cor·rup·tion·ist (-ist) *n.* a person who engages in or upholds corrupt practices, esp. in public life

cor·rup·tive (kə rup′tiv) *adj.* ⟦ME *corruptif* < LL(Ec) *corruptivus*⟧ tending to corrupt or produce corruption —**cor·rup′tive·ly** *adv.*

corrupt practices acts laws limiting contributions to and expenditures in election campaigns, making illegal certain methods of influencing voters, etc.

cor·sage (kôr säzh′, -säj′) *n.* ⟦Fr < OFr *cors*: see CORPS & -AGE⟧ **1** the bodice of a dress ☆**2** a small bouquet for a woman to wear, as at the waist or shoulder

cor·sair (kôr′ser′, kôr ser′) *n.* ⟦Fr *corsaire* < Prov *corsar* < It *corsaro* < ML *cursarius*, pirate, orig. swift < L *cursus*, COURSE⟧ **1** a privateer, esp. of Barbary **2** a pirate **3** a pirate ship

corse (kôrs) *n.* [Archaic] a dead body; corpse

Corse (kôrs) *Fr. name for* CORSICA

corse·let (kôrs′lit; *for 2,* kôr′sə let′) *n.* ⟦Fr < OFr, dim. of *cors:* see CORPS⟧ **1** a piece of armor formerly worn to protect the trunk: also sp. **cors′let 2** a woman's undergarment combining a lightweight corset, usually without stays, or a girdle, and a bra: also sp. **cor′se·lette′**

cor·set (kôr′sit) *n.* ⟦OFr, dim. of *cors:* see CORPS⟧ **1** a closefitting undergarment, often tightened with laces and reinforced with stays, worn, chiefly by women, to give support or a desired figure to the body from the hips to or including the breast **2** *a)* a medieval, closefitting outer jacket; jerkin *b)* [Archaic] BODICE (sense 2) —*vt.* to dress in, fit with, or enclose as in a corset

cor·se·tiere (kôr′sə tir′, -tyer′) *n.* ⟦Fr *corsetière,* fem. of *corsetier,* corset maker < *corset,* prec. + *-ier,* -ER⟧ **1** a person who fits clients for the correct size and type of corset, bra, etc. **2** a manufacturer of or dealer in foundation garments

cor·set·ry (kôr′sə trē) *n.* **1** the work or trade of making, selling, or fitting corsets, girdles, etc. **2** corsets, girdles, etc., collectively

Cor·si·ca (kôr′si kə) political unit of France, an island in the Mediterranean north of Sardinia: 3,351 sq mi (8,680 sq km); chief city, Ajaccio —**Cor′si·can** *adj., n.*

Cor·tá·zar (kôr tə zär′; *Sp* kôr tä′zər), **Ju·li·o** (hoo′lē ō) 1914-84; Argentine writer

cor·tege or **cor·tège** (kôr tezh′, -tāzh′) *n.* ⟦Fr *cortège* < It *corteggio,* retinue < *corte* < L *cohors:* see COURT⟧ **1** the group of attendants accompanying a person; retinue **2** a ceremonial procession, as at a funeral

Cor·tes (kôr′tez′; *Sp* kôr′tes) *n.* ⟦Sp, pl. of *corte* < L *cohors:* see COURT⟧ the legislature of Spain

Cor·tés (kôr tez′; *Sp* kôr tes′), **Her·nan·do** (hər nan′dō) or **Her·nán** (er nän′) 1485-1547; Sp. soldier & explorer: conqueror of Mexico: also sp. **Cor·tez′**

cor·tex (kôr′teks′) *n., pl.* **-ti·ces′** (-tə sēz′) ⟦L, bark of a tree: see CORIUM⟧ **1** *a)* the outer part or external layers of an internal organ, as of the kidney or the adrenal glands *b)* the outer layer of gray matter over most of the brain **2** *Bot. a)* a layer of tissue in the roots and stems of dicotyledonous plants, located between the stele and epidermis *b)* loosely, any layer of stem tissue external to the xylem *c)* an outer layer of tissue in certain algae, lichens, and fungi **3** *Pharmacy* the bark or rind of a plant

cor·ti·cal (kôr′ti kəl) *adj.* ⟦ModL *corticalis* < L *cortex* (gen. *corticis*), bark of a tree⟧ **1** of a cortex **2** consisting of cortex **3** involving, or in some way caused by, the brain cortex —**cor′ti·cal·ly** *adv.*

cor·ti·cate (-kit, -kāt′) *adj.* ⟦L *corticatus* < *cortex*⟧ **1** having a cortex **2** covered with bark or a barklike substance Also **cor′ti·cat′ed** (-kāt′id) or **cor′ti·cose′** (-kōs′)

cor·ti·co- (kôr′ti kō′) ⟦< L *cortex* (gen. *corticis*), bark⟧ *combining form* cortex *[corticosteroid]:* also, before a vowel, **cortic-**

cor·ti·coid (kôr′ti koid′) *n.* CORTICOSTEROID

cor·ti·co·ster·oid (kôr′ti kō′stir′oid′, -käs′tə roid′) *n.* ⟦CORTICO- + STEROID⟧ any of the steroidal hormones secreted by the adrenal cortex, or any compound derived from these or prepared synthetically and having a similar structure

cor·ti·co·ster·one (kôr′ti kō′stir′ōn′, -käs′tə rōn′) *n.* ⟦CORTICO- + STER(OL) + -ONE⟧ a corticosteroid, $C_{21}H_{30}O_4$, that aids muscle efficiency, carbohydrate metabolism, etc.

cor·ti·co·tro·pin (kôr′ti kō′trō′pin) *n.* ⟦CORTICO- + -TROP(IC) + -IN[1]⟧ ACTH: also **cor′ti·co′tro′phin** (-fin)

cor·tin (kôr′tin) *n.* ⟦CORT(EX) + -IN[1]⟧ a mixture of hormones from the adrenal cortex

cor·ti·na (kôr tē′nə, -tī′-) *n.* ⟦ModL < LL(Ec), CURTAIN⟧ in some mushrooms with gills, a veil-like membrane extending downward from the outer edge of the cap

cor·ti·sol (kôrt′ə sôl′, -sōl′) *n.* ⟦fol. + -OL[1]⟧ HYDROCORTISONE

☆**cor·ti·sone** (kôrt′ə sōn′, -zōn′) *n.* ⟦contr. < CORTICOSTERONE: so named by Edward C. Kendall (1886-1972), U.S. physician⟧ a corticosteroid, $C_{21}H_{28}O_5$, used as a replacement in adrenal insufficiency and in the treatment of various inflammatory, allergic, and neoplastic diseases

Cort·land (kôrt′lənd) *n.* a variety of large, dark-red apple

Coruña, La *see* LA CORUÑA

co·run·dum (kə run′dəm) *n.* ⟦Tamil *kurundam* < Sans *kuruvinda,* ruby⟧ a very hard mineral, aluminum oxide, Al_2O_3: a dark, coarse variety *(emery)* is used for grinding and polishing; clear, transparent varieties *(ruby, sapphire)* are used as gems: see MOHS SCALE

Co·run·na (kə run′ə) *Eng. name for* LA CORUÑA

cor·us·cate (kôr′ə skāt′, kär′-) *vi.* **-cat′ed, -cat′ing** ⟦< L *coruscatus,* pp. of *coruscare,* to move quickly, glitter < *coruscus,* vibrating, shimmering⟧ to give off flashes of light; glitter; sparkle —**co·rus·cant** (kə rus′kənt) *adj.*

cor·us·ca·tion (kôr′ə skā′shən, kär′-) *n.* ⟦L *coruscatio*⟧ **1** a coruscating; sparkling **2** a flash or gleam of light **3** a sudden brilliant display, as of wit

cor·vée (kôr vā′) *n.* ⟦Fr < OFr *corovee* < ML *corrogata (opera),* required (work) < pp. of L *corrogare,* to bring together (by entreaty) < *com-,* intens. + *rogare,* to ask: see ROGATION⟧ **1** the enforced and unpaid labor of a peasant for his feudal lord **2** forced labor exacted by a government, as for the construction of public works

corves (kôrvz) *n. pl. of* CORF

cor·vette (kôr vet′) *n.* ⟦Fr, prob. < MDu *korver,* pursuit ship < MLG *korf,* kind of boat, basket < L *corbis,* basket: see CORBEIL⟧ **1** a former sailing warship larger than a sloop and smaller than a frigate, usually with one tier of guns **2** a fast warship smaller than a destroyer and used chiefly for convoy duty

cor·vid (kôr′vid) *n.* ⟦< ModL *Corvidae* < L *corvus,* RAVEN[1]⟧ any of a family (Corvidae) of passerine birds typically having a stout bill, strong legs, omnivorous eating-habits, and open nests and displaying aggressive behavior, including the crows, jays, and magpies

☆**cor·vi·na** (kôr vē′nə) *n.* ⟦Sp, orig. fem. of *corvino,* ravenlike (< L *corvinus* < *corvus,* RAVEN[1]): so named because of its color⟧ **1** a gray, marine drum fish *(Menticirrhus undulatus)* found in the surf along the California coast **2** any of several marine fishes valued for food and sport, as certain drum fish (genus *Cynoscion*)

cor·vine (kôr′vīn′, -vin) *adj.* ⟦L *corvinus* < *corvus,* RAVEN[1]⟧ of or like a crow or raven

Cor·vus (kôr′vəs) *n.* ⟦L, RAVEN[1]⟧ a small S constellation near Virgo; the Crow

Cor·y·bant (kôr′ə bant′) *n., pl.* **-bants′** or **Cor′y·ban′tes′** (-ban′tēz′) **1** *a)* any of the attendants who follow the Phrygian goddess Cybele with dancing and frenzied orgies *b)* a priest in the worship of Cybele **2** [**c-**] a reveler —**Cor′y·ban′tic** (-ban′tik) *adj.,* **Cor′y·ban′tian** (-ban′shən)

co·ryd·a·lis (kō rid′'l is, kə-) *n.* ⟦ModL < Gr *korydallis,* crested lark < *korys,* helmet < IE **kereu-* < base **ker-,* HORN⟧ any of a genus *(Corydalis)* of plants of the fumitory family, with spurred yellow, rose, blue, or purple flowers

cor·ymb (kôr′im, -imb) *n.* ⟦Fr *corymbe* < L *corymbus,* cluster of fruit or flowers < Gr *korymbos;* akin to *korys:* see prec.⟧ a broad, flat-topped cluster of flowers in which the outer flower stalks are long and those toward the center progressively shorter, as in the candytuft —**cor·ym·bose** (kôr′im bōs′, kə rim′bōs′) *adj.,* **co·rym·bous** (kə rim′bəs) —**cor′ym·bose′ly** *adv.*

cor·y·phae·us (kôr′ə fē′əs) *n., pl.* **-phae′i′** (-ī′) ⟦L < Gr *koryphaios* < *koryphē,* head, top; akin to *korys:* see CORYDALIS⟧ **1** the leader of the chorus in ancient Greek drama **2** a leader, as of a sect or movement

co·ry·phée (kō′ri fā′, kôr′ə-) *n.* ⟦Fr: see prec.⟧ a ballet dancer ranking just above the corps de ballet and below the soloists

co·ry·za (kə rī′zə) *n.* ⟦ModL < LL < Gr *koryza,* catarrh⟧ *Med.* a cold in the head; acute nasal congestion

cos[1] (käs, kôs) *n.* ⟦after Cos[1], whence orig. imported⟧ ROMAINE: also **cos lettuce**

cos[2] *abbrev.* **1** cash on shipment **2** companies **3** *Trigonometry* cosine **4** counties

Cos[1] (käs, kôs) *Latin name for* KOS

Cos[2] *abbrev.* **1** companies **2** counties

COS *abbrev.* cash on shipment

Co·sa Nos·tra (kō′sə nō′strə) ⟦It, our thing, our affair⟧ **1** *name for* MAFIA, esp. the Mafia in the U.S. **2** [**c- n-**] any exclusive, dominating organization or group

cosec *abbrev. Trigonometry* cosecant

co·se·cant (kō sē′kənt, -kant′) *n.* ⟦Fr *cosécante,* for ModL *co. secans,* short for *complementi secans,* lit., secant of the complement⟧ *Trigonometry* the reciprocal of the sine; specif. *a)* the ratio of the hypotenuse to the opposite side of a given acute angle in a right triangle *b)* an equivalent, positive or negative ratio for certain related angles (Ex.: the cosecant of 57° or 123° is 1.1923, of 237° or 303° is −1.1923) or real numbers representing radians (Ex.: the cosecant of .9948 radians (57°) is 1.1923)

co·seis·mal (kō sīz′məl, -sīs′-) *adj.* ⟦CO- + SEISM(IC) -AL⟧ of or designating points, or lines connecting such points, simultaneously affected by an earthquake shock: also **co·seis′mic** (-mik) —*n.* a coseismal line

Co·sen·za (kō zent′sə) city in S Italy, southeast of Naples

co·sey or **co·sie** (kō′zē) *adj., n. alt. sp. of* COZY

cosh (käsh) [Informal, Chiefly Brit.] *n.* ⟦Brit slang < Romani, contr. < *koshter,* a skewer, stick⟧ a blackjack, bludgeon, or similar weapon —*vt.* to strike with a cosh

cosh·er (käsh′ər) *vi.* ⟦< Ir *coisir,* a feast < ? IE base **kois-,* to be concerned > L *cura,* care⟧ to be feasted, as at the dwelling of a vassal, tenant, etc. —*vt.* to pamper: sometimes with *up*

co·sign (kō′sīn′, kō′sīn′) *vt., vi.* **1** to sign (a promissory note) in addition to the maker, thus becoming responsible for the obligation if the maker should default **2** to sign jointly —**co′sign′er** *n.*

co·sig·na·to·ry (kō sig′nə tôr′ē) *adj.* signing jointly —*n., pl.* **-ries** one of two or more joint signers, as of a treaty

co·sine (kō′sīn′) *n.* ⟦ModL < *co. sinus,* short for *complementi sinus,* lit., sine of the complement⟧ *Trigonometry* the reciprocal of the secant; specif. *a)* the ratio of the adjacent side of a given acute angle in a right triangle to the hypotenuse *b)* an equivalent, positive or negative ratio for certain related angles (Ex.: the cosine of 57° or 303° is .5446, of 123° or 237° is −.5446) or real numbers representing radians (Ex.: cosine of .9948 radians (57°) is .5446)

cos·me·ceu·ti·cal (käz′mə sōōt′i kəl, -syōōt′-) *n.* ⟦fol. + (PHARMA)CEUTICAL⟧ a cosmetic preparation marketed as having medicinal properties but not requiring a prescription

cos·met·ic (käz met′ik) *adj.* ⟦Gr *kosmētikos,* skilled in arranging < *kosmein,* to arrange, adorn < *kosmos,* order⟧ **1** beautifying or designed to beautify the complexion, hair, etc. **2** for improving the appearance by the removal or correction of blemishes or deformities, esp. of the face **3** of or for improving the appearance without making any basic changes, as to conceal defects, make more acceptable, etc.; also, superficial —*n.* **1** any cosmetic preparation for the skin, hair, etc., as blush or powder **2** anything cosmetic: *often used in pl.* —**cos·met′i·cal·ly** *adv.*

☆**cos·me·ti·cian** (käz′mə tish′ən) ***n.*** a person whose work is making, selling, or applying cosmetics

cos·met·i·cize (käz met′ə sīz′) ***vt.*** **-cized′**, **-ciz′ing** to make cosmetic; improve the appearance of: also **cos′me·tize′ -tized′**, **-tiz′ing**

cosmetic surgery plastic surgery performed primarily for cosmetic rather than for medical reasons —**cosmetic surgeon**

☆**cos·me·tol·o·gy** (käz′mə täl′ə jē) ***n.*** the skill or work of hairstyling, applying cosmetics, etc., as in a beauty salon —**cos′me·tol′o·gist *n.***

cos·mic (käz′mik) ***adj.*** ⟦Gr *kosmikos* < *kosmos,* universe, order⟧ **1** of the cosmos; relating to the universe as a whole **2** of the universe exclusive of the earth [*cosmic* dust] **3** vast; grandiose —**cos′mi·cal·ly *adv.***

cosmic dust minute, meteoric grains distributed throughout space and often forming interplanetary or interstellar clouds that reflect and absorb light

cosmic microwave background BACKGROUND RADIATION (sense 1)

☆**cosmic noise** interference caused by radio waves originating in sources beyond the earth

☆**cosmic rays** ⟦coined (1925) by R. A. Millikan (1868-1953), U.S. physicist⟧ streams of high-energy charged particles from outer space, composed of protons, alpha particles, and a few heavier nuclei, which bombard the atoms in the upper atmosphere and produce various secondary nuclear particles that shower the earth

cosmic string any of a class of hypothetical, threadlike concentrations of invisible matter: cosmic strings are immensely long and extremely massive

cos·mo- (käz′mō, -mə) ⟦< Gr *kosmos,* universe, world, order⟧ *combining form* world, universe [*cosmology*]

cos·mog·o·ny (käz mäg′ə nē) ***n.*** ⟦Gr *kosmogonia,* creation of the world < *kosmogonos* < *kosmos,* universe + *-gonos,* -GONY⟧ **1** the study of the origin of the universe **2** *pl.* **-nies** a theory or account of this [an ancient Greek *cosmogony*] —**cos·mo·gon·ic** (käz′mə gän′ik) ***adj.***, **cos′mo·gon′i·cal** —**cos·mog′o·nist *n.***

cos·mog·ra·phy (käz mäg′rə fē) ***n.*** ⟦ME *cosmographie* < LL *cosmographia* < Gr *kosmographia,* description of the world: see COSMO- & -GRAPHY⟧ **1** a general description of the world **2** the science dealing with the structure of the universe as a whole and of its related parts: geology, geography, and astronomy are branches of cosmography —**cos·mog′ra·pher *n.*** —**cos·mo·graph·ic** (käz′mə graf′ik) ***adj.***, **cos′mo·graph′i·cal** —**cos′mo·graph′i·cal·ly *adv.***

☆**Cos·mo·line** (käz′mə lēn′) ⟦COSM(ETIC) + -OL[2] + -INE[3]⟧ *trademark for* petrolatum of a heavy grade, used esp. as a protective coating for firearms, metals, etc. —***n.*** [**c-**] this substance —***vt.*** **-lined′**, **-lin′ing** [**c-**] to coat with this substance

cosmological constant a constant devised originally by Einstein in the general theory of relativity to represent a hypothetical repulsive force that offsets gravity

cos·mol·o·gy (käz mäl′ə jē) ***n.*** ⟦ML *cosmologia:* see COSMO- & -LOGY⟧ **1** the scientific study of the form, content, organization, and evolution of the universe **2** the branch of metaphysics dealing with the origin and structure of the universe —**cos·mo·log·i·cal** (käz′mə läj′ə kəl) ***adj.*** —**cos′mo·log′i·cal·ly *adv.*** —**cos·mol′o·gist *n.***

cos·mo·naut (käz′mə nôt′, -nät′) ***n.*** ⟦Russ *kosmonavt* < *kosmos,* cosmos (< Gr) + *-navt* < Gr *nautēs,* sailor: see NAUTICAL⟧ a Soviet or Russian astronaut

☆**cos·mop·o·lis** (käz mäp′ə lis) ***n.*** ⟦fol. + (METRO)POLIS⟧ a large city inhabited by people from many different nations

cos·mo·pol·i·tan (käz′mə päl′ə tən) ***adj.*** ⟦< fol. + -AN⟧ **1** common to or representative of all or many parts of the world; not national or local **2** not bound by local or national habits or prejudices; at home in all countries or places **3** characterized by worldly sophistication; fashionable, urbane, etc. **4** having a worldwide distribution, as some plants or animals —***n.*** **1** a cosmopolitan person or thing; cosmopolite **2** [*also* **C-**] a cocktail made of vodka, cranberry and lime juices, and orange liqueur, served in a martini glass —**cos′mo·pol′i·tan·ism′ *n.***

cos·mop·o·lite (käz mäp′ə līt′) ***n.*** ⟦Gr *kosmopolitēs* < *kosmos,* world + *politēs,* citizen < *polis,* POLIS⟧ **1** a cosmopolitan person **2** a plant or animal found in most parts of the world —**cos·mop′o·lit′ism′ *n.***

cos·mos (käz′məs; *for 1-3, also,* -mōs′, -mäs′) ***n.*** ⟦ME < Gr *kosmos,* universe, harmony⟧ **1** the universe considered as a harmonious and orderly system **2** [Rare] harmony; order **3** any complete and orderly system **4** *pl.* **cos′mos** any of a genus (*Cosmos*) of tropical American plants of the composite family, with featherlike leaves and heads of white, pink, or purple flowers

☆**cos·mo·tron** (käz′mə trän′) ***n.*** ⟦COSM(IC RAYS) + (CYCL)OTRON⟧ a high-energy proton accelerator

cos·play (käs′plā′) ***n.*** ⟦COS(TUME) + PLAY⟧ a social activity in which fans dress up like characters from manga, anime, video games, etc. —**cos′play′er *n.***

co·spon·sor (kō′spän′sər, kō′spän′sər) ***n.*** a joint sponsor, as of a proposed piece of legislation —***vt.*** to be a cosponsor of —**co′spon′sor·ship′ *n.***

Cos·sack (käs′ak′, -ək) ***n.*** ⟦Russ *kozak* < Turk *qazaq,* adventurer, guerrilla⟧ a member of any of several groups of peasants, chiefly of Russian and Polish descent, that lived in autonomous communal settlements, esp. in the Ukraine, until the late 19th cent: in return for special privileges, they served in the cavalry under the czars —***adj.*** [*often* **c-**] of or characteristic of the Cossacks or their culture

cos·set (käs′it) ***n.*** ⟦< ? OE *cot-sæta,* cot dweller; similar in sense to It *casiccio* (< *casa,* house), pet lamb⟧ [Now Rare] a pet lamb or any small pet —***vt.*** to show excessive care or concern in dealing with or caring for (someone); coddle; pamper

cost (kôst, käst) ***vt.*** **cost**, **cost′ing** ⟦ME *costen* < OFr *coster* < ML *costare* < L *constare,* to stand together, stand at, cost < *com-,* together + *stare,* to STAND⟧ **1** *a)* to be obtained or obtainable for (a certain price); be priced at *b)* to cause or require the expenditure, loss, or experience of [victory *cost* him his health]: orig. construed as a *vi.* with the apparent object an adverbial adjunct, and still felt as a *vi.* when used with an adverb [it *cost* him dearly] **2** **cost′ed**, **cost′ing** *Business* to estimate the cost of making, producing, carrying out, etc.: said as of a product or program: often with *out* —***vi.*** [Informal] to be expensive —***n.*** **1** *a)* the amount of money, etc. asked or paid for a thing; price *b)* the amount spent in producing or manufacturing a commodity *c)* the amount paid for something by a dealer, contractor, etc.: a markup is usually added to arrive at a selling price [stoves sold at *cost* in a special sale] **2** *a)* the amount of money, time, effort, etc. required to achieve an end *b)* loss, sacrifice; detriment [to smoke at the *cost* of one's health] **3** [*pl.*] *Law* the expenses of a lawsuit, esp. those assessed by the court against the losing party —**at all costs** regardless of the cost or difficulty involved; by any means required: also **at any cost**

cos·ta (käs′tə, kôs′-) ***n.***, *pl.* **-tae** (-tē) ⟦ModL < L, a rib (> COAST)⟧ **1** *Anat.* a rib **2** a riblike part, as the thickened fore edge of an insect's wing or the central vein of a leaf

Cos·ta Bra·va (käs′tə brä′vä, kôs′-) ⟦Sp, wild coast: so named for the rugged terrain⟧ coast of Catalonia, Spain, northeast of Barcelona: site of many resorts

cost accounting *Accounting* **1** a system for recording, analyzing, and allocating production and distribution costs **2** the keeping of such records —**cost accountant**

Cos·ta del Sol (käs′tə *th*el sôl, kôs′-) ⟦Sp, coast of the sun⟧ coast region of S Spain, on the Mediterranean, east of Gibraltar: site of many resorts

cos·tal (käs′təl, kôs′-) ***adj.*** ⟦Fr < ModL *costalis* < L *costa,* a rib⟧ of or near a rib or the ribs

Cos·ta Me·sa (kōs′tə mā′sə) ⟦Sp *costa mesa,* coast plateau⟧ city in SW Calif., near Long Beach

co·star (kō′stär′; *for v., usually* kō′stär′) ***n.*** ⟦CO- + STAR⟧ any featured actor or actress given equal prominence with another or others in a film, play, etc. —***vt., vi.*** **-starred′**, **-star′ring** to present as or be a costar

cos·tard (käs′tərd) ***n.*** ⟦ME, ribbed apple < OFr *coste,* a rib + *-ard,* -ARD⟧ **1** a variety of large apple, native to England **2** [Archaic] a person's head: humorous or contemptuous usage

Cos·ta Ri·ca (käs′tə rē′kə, kôs′-, kōs′-) ⟦Sp, rich coast⟧ country in Central America, northwest of Panama: revolted against Spain in 1821; became an independent republic in 1848: 19,730 sq mi (51,100 sq km); cap. San José —**Cos′ta Ri′can**

cos·tate (käs′tāt′, kôs′-) ***adj.*** ⟦ModL *costatus* < L < *costa,* a rib⟧ having ribs or riblike ridges

cost-ben·e·fit (kôst′ben′ə fit) ***adj.*** designating or of an analysis that evaluates the cost-effectiveness of a project or policy

cost-ef·fec·tive (kôst′ə fek′tiv) ***adj.*** producing good results for the amount of money spent; economical or efficient —**cost′-ef·fec′tive·ness *n.***

cost-ef·fi·cient (-ə fish′ənt) ***adj.*** COST-EFFECTIVE —**cost′-ef·fi′cien·cy *n.***

cos·ter·mon·ger (käs′tər muŋ′gər, kôs′-) ***n.*** ⟦Early ModE *costardmonger,* apple dealer: see COSTARD & MONGER⟧ [Brit.] a person who sells fruit or vegetables from a cart or street stand: also **cos′ter**

cos·tive (käs′tiv, kôs′-) ***adj.*** ⟦ME < OFr *costeve,* pp. of *costever* < L *constipare:* see CONSTIPATE⟧ constipated or constipating: used fig. to mean uncommunicative, stingy, etc. —**cos′tive·ly *adv.*** —**cos′tive·ness *n.***

cost·ly (kôst′lē, käst′-) ***adj.*** **-li·er**, **-li·est** ⟦ME: see COST & -LY[1]⟧ **1** *a)* costing much; expensive; dear *b)* at the cost of great effort, damage, sacrifice, etc. [a *costly* victory] **2** magnificent; sumptuous **3** [Archaic] lavish; extravagant —**cost′li·ness *n.***

SYN.—**costly** refers to something that costs much and usually implies richness, magnificence, rareness, etc. [*costly* gems]: it is often applied to that which it would cost much in money or effort to correct or replace [a *costly* error]; **expensive** implies a price in excess of the article's worth or of the purchaser's ability to pay [an *expensive* hat]; **dear**, now chiefly a Brit. usage, implies an exorbitant price or one considerably beyond the normal or fair price [veal is so *dear* these days]; **valuable**, in this connection, implies such great value as to bring a high price [a *valuable* collection]; **invaluable** suggests value so great that it cannot be appraised in monetary terms [*invaluable* aid] —***ANT.*** **cheap**

cost·mar·y (käst′mer′ē, kôst′-) ***n.*** ⟦ME *costmarye* < *cost* (< OE < L *costum* < Gr *kostos,* name of an aromatic plant) + *Marie,* (St.) Mary⟧ an herb (*Chrysanthemum balsamita*) of the composite family, with many small flower heads, having sweet-smelling leaves that are used in flavoring

cost of living the average cost of the necessities of life for a particular period of time, including such things as food, shelter, clothes, and medical expenses

☆**cost-plus** (kôst′plus′) ***adj.*** with the price for goods or services set at the cost of materials, labor, etc. plus a specified percentage or amount of profit, as in some government contracts with industry

cos·trel (käs′trəl) ***n.*** ⟦ME < OFr *costerel,* dim. of *costier,* something at the side < L *costa,* a rib⟧ [Now Chiefly Dial.] a large bottle or flask with loops by which it can be hung

cos·tume (käs′to͞om′, -tyo͞om′) ***n.*** ⟦18th-c. art term < Fr < It < L *consuetudo,* CUSTOM⟧ **1** *a)* the style of dress, including accessories, typical of a certain country, period, profession, etc. *b)* a set of outer clothes in such a style, as worn in a play or at a masquerade **2** a set of outer clothes for some purpose or occasion, esp. one worn by a woman —***vt.*** **-tumed′, -tum′ing** to provide with a costume; put a costume on; dress —**cos′tume·ry** ***n.***

☆**costume jewelry** jewelry made of relatively inexpensive materials or set with imitation gems

☆**cos·tum·er** (käs′to͞om′ər, -tyo͞om′-) ***n.*** **1** a person who makes, sells, or rents costumes **2** a clothes rack or hat tree

cos·tum·i·er (käs to͞om′ē ər, -tyo͞om′-; *Fr* kôs tü myā′) ***n.*** ⟦Fr⟧ COSTUMER (sense 1)

co·sy (kō′zē) ***adj.*** **-si·er, -si·est,** ***n., pl.*** **-sies** *chiefly Brit. sp. of* COZY —**co′si·ly** ***adv.*** —**co′si·ness** ***n.***

cot[1] (kät) ***n.*** ⟦Anglo-Ind < Hindi *khāṭ* < Sans *khaṭvā*⟧ **1** a narrow, collapsible bed, as one made of canvas or plastic sheeting on a frame that can be folded up **2** [Brit.] a baby's crib

cot[2] (kät) ***n.*** ⟦ME & OE, cottage, hut, lit., covered place; akin to MDu *kote,* ON *kot* < IE base **geu-,* to curve, bend > COD[2]⟧ **1** [Old Poet.] a cottage; small house **2** a small shelter; cote **3** a covering or sheath, as for a hurt finger

cot[3] *abbrev. Trigonometry* cotangent

co·tan·gent (kō tan′jənt, kō′tan′-) ***n.*** ⟦ModL *cotangens* < *co. tangens,* short for *complementi tangens,* lit., tangent of the complement⟧ *Trigonometry* the reciprocal of the tangent; specif. *a)* the ratio of the adjacent side of a given acute angle in a right triangle to the opposite side *b)* an equivalent, positive or negative ratio for certain related angles (Ex.: the cotangent of 57° or 237° is .6494, of 123° or 303° is –.6494) or real numbers representing radians (Ex.: the cotangent of .9948 radians (57°) is .6494)

cote[1] (kōt) ***n.*** ⟦ME, COT[2]⟧ **1** a small shelter or shed for fowl, sheep, doves, etc. **2** [Now Brit. Dial.] a cottage

cote[2] (kōt) ***vt.*** **cot′ed, cot′ing** ⟦< ? MFr *cotoyer,* to go by the side of, coast along < OFr *costeier* < *coste,* COAST⟧ [Obs.] to pass by the side of; go around

Côte d'A·zur (kōt dȧ zür′) ⟦Fr, lit., coast of azure: in allusion to the clear blue of the Mediterranean Sea and the sky⟧ the part of the Riviera that is in France

Côte d'I·voire (kōt dē vwär′) *official name for* IVORY COAST

co·tem·po·rar·y (kō tem′pə rer′ē) ***adj., n.*** *archaic var. of* CONTEMPORARY

co·ten·ant (kō ten′ənt, kō′ten′-) ***n.*** one of two or more persons who own a piece of property, each having an undivided right of possession —**co·ten′an·cy** ***n.***

co·te·rie (kōt′ə rē) ***n.*** ⟦Fr, orig., organization of peasants holding land from a feudal lord < OFr *cotier,* COTTER[1]⟧ a close circle of friends who share a common interest or background; clique

SYN.—**coterie** is a small, intimate, somewhat select group of people associated for social or other reasons [a literary *coterie*]; **circle** suggests any group of people having in common some particular interest or pursuit [jazz *circles*]; **set** refers to a group, usually larger and, hence, less exclusive than a **coterie**, having a common background, interests, etc. [the sporting *set*]; **clique** refers to a small, highly exclusive group, often within a larger one, and implies snobbery, selfishness, or, sometimes, intrigue [a *clique* of obscurantist poets]

co·ter·mi·nous (kō tʉr′mə nəs) ***adj.*** CONTERMINOUS: also **co·ter′mi·nal** —**co·ter′mi·nous·ly** ***adv.***

co·thur·nus (kō thʉr′nəs) ***n., pl.*** **-ni′** (-nī′) ⟦L < Gr *kothornos*⟧ **1** a high, thick-soled boot or buskin worn by actors in ancient Greek and Roman tragedies **2** tragedy or a lofty, tragic style in drama Also **co·thurn** (kō′thʉrn′)

co·tid·al (kō tīd′'l) ***adj.*** indicating the coincidence in time or extent of tides [*cotidal* lines on a map]

☆**co·ti·ja** (kō′tē′hä) ***n.*** ⟦after the town of *Cotija* in the Mexican state of Michoacán⟧ a hard, white Mexican cheese made from cow's milk

co·til·lion (kō til′yən) ***n.*** ⟦Fr *cotillon,* orig., petticoat < OFr *cote:* see COAT⟧ **1** *a)* a brisk, lively dance characterized by many intricate figures and the continual changing of partners *b)* music for such a dance **2** a formal ball, esp. one at which debutantes are presented Also sp. **co·til′lon**

co·ti·nus (kō tī′nəs) ***n.*** ⟦L < Gr *kotinos,* wild olive tree⟧ SMOKE TREE

Cot·man (kät′mən), **John Sell** 1782-1842; Eng. painter

co·to·ne·as·ter (kə tō′nē as′tər) ***n.*** ⟦ModL < L *cotonea,* QUINCE + -ASTER[2]⟧ any of a genus (*Cotoneaster*) of shrubs of the rose family, grown for their attractive leaves, red or white flowers, and small, red or black fruits

Co·to·nou (kô tô no͞o′) seaport & administrative capital of Benin, on the Gulf of Guinea

Co·to·pax·i (kō′tə pak′sē; *Sp* kô′tô pä′hē) volcano in the Andes, in N Ecuador: 19,344 ft (5,896 m)

cot·quean (kät′kwēn′) ***n.*** ⟦COT[2] + QUEAN⟧ [Archaic] **1** a vulgar, scolding woman **2** a man who does housework or other work regarded as women's

Cots·wold (käts′wōld, -wəld) ***n.*** any of a breed of sheep with long wool, orig. from the Cotswold Hills

Cotswold Hills range of hills in SW central England, mostly in Gloucestershire: also **Cotswolds**

cot·ta (kät′ə) ***n.*** ⟦ML *cota, cotta* < Frank **kotta:* see COAT⟧ a short surplice

cot·tage (kät′ij) ***n.*** ⟦ME *cotage* < ML *cotagium* < OFr *cote* or ME *cot,* COT[2]⟧ **1** a small, usually one-storied house, often one that is the dwelling of a peasant or a farm laborer ☆**2** a house at a resort or in the country, used for vacations or as a summer home ☆**3** any of several separate dwelling units, as of an institution or camp, in which residents are housed in small groups

☆**cottage cheese** a soft, white cheese made by straining and salting the curds of slightly soured milk and, often, adding cream

cottage fries potatoes that have been thinly sliced and then fried

cottage industry **1** a manufacturing activity carried on, as in the early part of the Industrial Revolution, by farming out work to be done in the workers' homes **2** any relatively small-scale business operation carried on as from the home **3** any limited pursuit or activity involving an unusually large number of independent participants [James Joyce scholarship is a *cottage industry* among U.S. academics]

☆**cottage pudding** plain cake covered with a sweet sauce

cot·tag·er (-ər) ***n.*** **1** a person who lives or vacations in a cottage **2** [Brit.] a farm laborer **3** [Cdn.] a summer resident

Cott·bus (kät′bəs, -bo͝os′) city in E Germany, on the Spree River, in the state of Brandenburg

cot·ter[1] (kät′ər) ***n.*** ⟦ME < OFr *cotier* < *cote,* cottage < OE *cot* (or MDu *kote*), COT[2]⟧ a cottager; specif., *a)* [Scot.] a tenant farmer *b)* [Irish] a cottier Also sp. **cot′tar**

cot·ter[2] (kät′ər) ***n.*** ⟦ME *coter* < ?⟧ **1** a bolt or wedge put through a slot to hold together parts of machinery **2** COTTER PIN

cotter pin a metal fastener consisting of a pin bent back on itself so as to form a head opposite the two ends: it is designed to be slipped through a slot and its ends then spread apart to hold it in place

Cot·ti·an Alps (kät′ē ən) division of the W Alps, between France & Italy: highest peak, *c.* 12,600 ft (3,840 m)

cot·ti·er (kät′ē ər) ***n.*** ⟦ME & OFr *cotier,* COTTER[1]⟧ **1** in Great Britain and Ireland, a farmer who lives in a cottage **2** [Historical] in Ireland, a peasant renting a small piece of land under a system (called **cottier tenure**) of renting land to the highest bidder

cot·ton (kät′'n) ***n.*** ⟦ME *cotoun* < OFr *coton* < (? via It *cotone*) Ar *quṭun* < ? Egypt⟧ **1** the soft, white seed hairs filling the seedpods of various shrubby plants (genus *Gossypium*) of the mallow family, originally native to the tropics **2** a plant or plants producing this material **3** the crop of such plants **4** thread or cloth made of cotton **5** a downy, cottonlike substance growing on other plants —***adj.*** of cotton —**cotton on (to)** [Brit. Informal] to begin to comprehend (something) —**cotton to** ⟦< ? notion of cotton mixing well with wool, etc.⟧ [Informal] to become drawn to; take a liking to —**cotton up to** [Informal] to try to ingratiate oneself, or make friends, with

Cot·ton (kät′'n), **John** 1584-1652; Am. Puritan clergyman, born in England: grandfather of Cotton Mather

cotton ball a small ball of soft, absorbent cotton, often used to remove cosmetics, to appy medication to the skin, etc.

☆**cotton batting** thin, pressed layers of fluffy, absorbent cotton, used for surgical dressing, quilting, etc.

☆**Cotton Belt** region in S and SE U.S., extending from Texas to the Carolinas, where much cotton is grown

☆**cotton candy** a cottony candy consisting of threadlike fibers of melted sugar spun into a fluffy mass around a paper cone

cotton flannel a soft cotton cloth with a napped surface, resembling woolen flannel

☆**cotton gin** ⟦see GIN[2]⟧ a machine for separating cotton fibers from the seeds

cotton grass any of a genus (*Eriophorum*) of grasslike plants of the sedge family, with flower heads resembling tufts of cotton, common in northern bogs

☆**cotton gum** a tall tupelo (*Nyssa aquatica*) with cottony leaves, found in swamps of the SE U.S.

☆**cot·ton·mouth** (-mouth′) ***n.*** ⟦from the whitish interior of its mouth⟧ WATER MOCCASIN

☆**cot·ton-pick·ing** (-pik′ən, -pik′iŋ) ***adj.*** [Slang] worthless, damned, hateful, etc.: used as a general intensive of opprobrium

cot·ton·seed (-sēd′) ***n.*** the seed of the cotton plant, from which an oil (**cottonseed oil**) is pressed for use in margarine, cooking oil, soap, etc.

☆**cottonseed meal** hulled cottonseed ground up after the oil has been removed, used as fertilizer and fodder

☆**cotton stainer** any of a genus (*Dysdercus*) of small, red hemipteran insects that puncture cotton bolls and stain the fibers

☆**cot·ton·tail** (-tāl′) ***n.*** any of several common American rabbits (genus *Sylvilagus*) with a short, fluffy tail that is white underneath

cot·ton·weed (-wēd′) ***n.*** any of various wild plants with a cottony appearance, as the cudweed

☆**cot·ton·wood** (-wood′) ***n.*** any of several poplars that have seeds thickly covered with cottony or silky hairs, esp. a rapidly growing lowland tree (*Populus deltoides*) of the E and central U.S.

cotton wool **1** raw cotton ☆**2** COTTON BATTING

cot·ton·y (kät′'n ē) ***adj.*** **1** of or like cotton; downy; fluffy **2** covered with cottonlike hairs or fibers

cot·y·le·don (kät′ə lēd′'n) ***n.*** ⟦ModL < L, name of a plant < Gr *kotylēdōn* < *kotylē,* a hollow, cavity⟧ the first single leaf or one of the first pair of leaves produced by the embryo of a flowering plant, or any of various similar structures found in conifers: see MONOCOTYLEDON, DICOTYLEDON —**cot′y·le′don·ous** ***adj.,*** **cot′y·le′don·al**

couch (kouch) ***n.*** ⟦ME & OFr *couche,* a bed, lair: see the ***vt.***⟧ **1** an article of furniture on which one may sit or lie down; sofa; divan **2** any resting place **3** in brewing, a layer of grain spread to germinate **4** [Old Poet.] a place for sleeping; bed **5** [Obs.] an animal's lair or den **6** *Fine Arts* a priming layer or coat, as of paint or varnish —*vt.* ⟦ME *couchen* < OFr *coucher,* to lie down < L *collocare,* to lay < *com-,* together + *locare,* to place: see LOCAL⟧ **1** to lay or put on or as on a couch, as to sleep: now usually used reflexively or in the passive voice **2** to lower or bring down; esp., to lower (a spear, lance, etc.) to an attacking position **3** to put in specific or particular words; phrase; express *[*the speech was *couched* in flowery language*]* **4** to embroider with thread laid flat and fastened down with fine stitches **5** in brewing, to spread (grain) in a thin layer to germinate **6** [Archaic] to put in a layer **7** [Obs.] to hide **8** *Surgery* to remove (a cataract) by using a needle to push down the crystalline lens of the eye —*vi.* **1** to lie down on a bed **2** to lie in hiding or in ambush **3** to lie in a pile, as decomposing leaves —☆**on the couch** [Informal] undergoing psychotherapy

couch·ant (kou′chənt) *adj.* ⟦Fr *couchant,* prp. of *coucher:* see prec.⟧ **1** lying down: said esp. of animals **2** *Heraldry* lying down or crouching, but keeping the head up *[*a lion *couchant]*

cou·chette (ko͞o shet′) *n.* ⟦Fr, dim. of *couche,* COUCH⟧ an inexpensive berth on a European train, consisting of a shelflike bed that folds down to allow passengers to sleep in their clothes: there are usually four couchettes in a first-class compartment and six in a second-class compartment

couch grass ⟦< *couch,* var. of QUITCH⟧ a European perennial grass (*Agropyron repens*) that spreads rapidly by its underground stems and is a troublesome weed in North America; quack grass

☆**couch potato** [Slang] a chronic television viewer, esp. one regarded as lazy, out of shape, etc.

cou·dé (ko͞o dā′) *adj.* ⟦< Fr, bent, angled < pp. of *couder* < *coude,* the elbow < L *cubitum:* see CUBIT⟧ of a reflecting telescope system of mirrors, lenses, cameras, etc. in which the light is reflected through an opening in the side and then to a distant observation room

cou·gar (ko͞o′gər, -gär′) *n., pl.* **-gars** or **-gar** ⟦Fr *couguar,* contr. (by the Comte de BUFFON) < *cuguacuara,* faulty transcription of Port *çuçuarana,* for Tupí *susuarana,* lit., false deer < *suusú,* deer + *rana,* false: so named from its color⟧ **1** a large, powerful, tawny cat (*Puma concolor*) with a long, slender body and a long tail; puma; mountain lion: it was once found widely from Canada to Patagonia but is now an endangered species **2** [Slang] an older, typically middle-aged, woman who dates or aggressively pursues much younger men

cough (kôf) *vi.* ⟦ME *coughen,* akin to MDu *cuchen,* to cough, Ger *keuchen,* to gasp⟧ **1** to expel air suddenly and noisily from the lungs through the glottis, to clear the air passages or as the result of an involuntary muscle spasm in the throat **2** to make a sound like this —*vt.* **1** to expel by coughing **2** to express or utter by coughing —*n.* **1** the act or sound of coughing **2** a condition, as of the lungs or throat, causing frequent coughing —**cough up 1** to bring up or eject (phlegm, food, etc.) by coughing ☆**2** [Slang] to hand over (money or the like) —**cough′er** *n.*

☆**cough drop** a small medicated tablet, often sweetened and flavored, for the relief of coughs, hoarseness, etc.

could (kood) *v.aux.* ⟦altered (infl. by WOULD, SHOULD) < ME *coud* < OE *cuthe* (akin to Goth *kuntha,* OHG *konda,* ON *kunna*), pt. of *cunnan,* to be able: see CAN[1]⟧ **1** *pt. of* CAN[1] *[*he gave what he *could* give*]* **2** used as a modal auxiliary in verbal phrases with present or future time reference, generally equivalent to CAN[1] in meaning and use, with the following functions: *a)* expressing esp. a shade of doubt or a lesser degree of ability or possibility *[*it *could* be so*]* *b)* expressing a lesser degree of permission *[could* I go?*]* *c)* forming the present conditional *[*it would help if he *could* wait*]* *d)* forming the past conditional *[*he would have left if he *could]* *e)* expressing or suggesting politely less certainty than CAN[1] *[could* you wait?*]* ➥As a modal auxiliary, *could* is followed by an infinitive without *to* —*vi. pt. of* CAN[1] *[*he gave what he *could]* —*vt.* [Obs.] *pt. of* CAN[1]

could·n't (kood′'nt) *contraction* could not

couldst (koodst) *v. archaic 2d pers. sing. pt. of* CAN[1]: used with *thou:* also **could·est** (kood′ist)

could've (kood′əv) *contraction* could have

cou·lee (ko͞o′lē) *n.* ⟦Fr *coulée* < *couler,* to flow < L *colare,* to strain: see COLANDER⟧ **1** a stream of molten lava or a sheet of solidified lava ☆**2** [Northwest] a deep gulch or ravine, usually dry in summer

cou·li·biac (ko͞o lē byäk′) *n.* ⟦Fr < Russ *kulebjaka* < ?⟧ a Russian dish of rich pastry with a filling of salmon or other fish and mushrooms, onions, egg, buckwheat, dill, etc.

cou·lis (ko͞o lē′, ko͞o′lē) *n., pl.* **-lis′** ⟦Fr, orig., meat juices < *couler,* to flow: see COULEE⟧ a purée of fruit or vegetables used as a light sauce

cou·lisse (ko͞o lēs′) *n.* ⟦Fr < *couler:* see COULEE⟧ **1** a grooved timber in which a sluice gate, etc. slides **2** *a)* any of the side flats of a theater stage *b)* the space between two such flats

cou·loir (ko͞ol wär′) *n.* ⟦Fr < *couler:* see COULEE⟧ a deep mountain gorge or gully

cou·lomb (ko͞o′läm′, -lōm′) *n.* ⟦after C. A. de *Coulomb* (1736-1806), Fr physicist⟧ the basic unit of electric charge in the SI and MKS systems, equal to the charge of 6.281×10^{18} electrons; the charge carried by a current of one ampere in one second: *abbrev. C*

Cou·lomb's law (ko͞o lämz′, ko͞o′lämz′) ⟦see prec.⟧ *Physics* the statement that the electrostatic force between two charged bodies acts along the line between them, is directly proportional to the product of their magnitudes, and is inversely proportional to the square of the distance between them: similarly charged bodies repel one another, while oppositely charged bodies attract one another

coul·ter (kōl′tər) *n. alt. sp. of* COLTER

Cou·ma·din (ko͞o′mə din) *trademark for* the sodium form of the anticoagulant warfarin

cou·ma·rin (ko͞o′mə rin′) *n.* ⟦Fr *coumarine* < *coumarou,* tonka bean < Port < Tupí *cumaru*⟧ a toxic, white crystalline substance, $C_9H_6O_2$, with the odor of vanilla, obtained from the tonka bean and certain other plants or made synthetically: used in perfumes, soaps, etc.

cou·ma·rone (ko͞o′mə rōn′) *n.* ⟦Ger *kumaron* < *kumarin* (< Fr *coumarine,* prec.) + *-on,* -one < Gr *-ōnē:* see -ONE⟧ a colorless liquid, C_8H_6O, derived from coal tar and combined with indene to produce synthetic resins used in paints, adhesives, etc.

coun·cil (koun′səl) *n.* ⟦ME *counceil* < OFr *concile* < L *concilium,* group of people, meeting < *com-,* together + *calere,* to call (see CLAMOR); confused in form and meaning in ME with COUNSEL⟧ **1** a group of people called together for consultation, discussion, advice, etc. **2** a group of people chosen as an administrative, advisory, or legislative assembly **3** *a)* the legislative body of a city or other municipality *b)* [Brit.] the administrative body of a county, town, city, district, etc. **4** an assembly of church officials to discuss points of doctrine, etc. **5** *a)* a body of delegates from local units of a union, confederation, etc. *b)* an organization or society, or one of its levels of governing bodies **6** the discussion or deliberation in a council —*adj.* [Brit.] designating or of dwelling units built or provided by a local COUNCIL (*n.* 3b) *[council* houses*]*

coun·cil·man (-mən) *n., pl.* **-men** (-mən) a member of a council, esp. of the governing body of a city or town: also **coun′cil·per′son** (-pur′sən) —**coun′cil·man′ic** (-man′ik) *adj.*

coun·cil-man·a·ger plan (-man′ə jər) a form of municipal government in which an elected, usually nonpartisan, council sets policy, passes ordinances, and appoints a city manager, who administers the day-to-day operations of the municipality under the council's supervision

council of ministers the highest administrative body of a nation, usually advisors to the chief executive

coun·ci·lor (koun′sə lər) *n.* ⟦< COUNSELOR, by confusion with COUNCIL⟧ a member of a council: also [Chiefly Brit.] **coun′cil·lor** —**coun′ci·lor·ship′** *n.*

coun·cil·wom·an (koun′səl woom′ən) *n., pl.* **-wom′en** (-wim′in) a woman who is a member of a council

coun·sel (koun′səl) *n.* ⟦ME & OFr *counseil* < L *consilium* (for base see CONSULT); confused in ME with COUNCIL⟧ **1** a mutual exchange of ideas, opinions, etc.; discussion and deliberation **2** *a)* advice resulting from such an exchange *b)* any advice **3** *a)* a lawyer or group of lawyers giving advice about legal matters and representing clients in court *b)* anyone whose advice is sought; consultant **4** [Archaic] intention or resolution; purpose **5** [Archaic] wisdom or judgment **6** [Obs.] a confidential idea, plan, etc.; secret —*vt.* **-seled** or **-selled**, **-sel·ing** or **-sel·ling 1** to give advice to; advise **2** to urge the acceptance of (an action, plan, etc.); recommend —*vi.* to give or take advice —*SYN.* ADVISE, LAWYER —**keep one's own counsel** to keep one's thoughts, plans, etc. to oneself —**take counsel** to discuss and deliberate; exchange advice, opinions, etc.

coun·sel·ee (koun′sə lē′) *n.* a person who is being professionally counseled

coun·sel·ing or **coun·sel·ling** (koun′sə liŋ) *n.* **1** the providing of expert guidance or advice **2** assistance provided by a psychotherapist in dealing with emotional or psychological problems —**in counseling** regularly consulting a psychotherapist

coun·se·lor or **coun·sel·lor** (koun′sə lər) *n.* ⟦ME *counseilere* < OFr *consellier* < L *consiliator*⟧ **1** a person who counsels; advisor; specif., one who advises students or clients regarding educational and occupational alternatives, personal problems, etc. **2** a legal advisor, as of an embassy or legation **3** a lawyer, esp. one who conducts cases in court: in full **counselor-at-law 4** a person in charge of a group of children at a camp **5** *Mormon Ch.* one of the advisors to a presiding officer —*SYN.* LAWYER —**coun′se·lor·ship′** *n.*, **coun′sel·lor·ship′**

count[1] (kount) *vt.* ⟦ME *counten* < OFr *conter* < L *computare,* COMPUTE⟧ **1** to name numbers in regular order to (a certain number) *[*to *count* five*]* **2** to add up, one by one, by units or groups, so as to get a total *[count* the money*]* **3** to check by numbering off; inventory **4** to take account of; include *[*six, *counting* me*]* **5** to believe or take to be; consider *[*to *count* oneself fortunate*]* —*vi.* **1** to name numbers or add up items in order **2** to be taken into account; have importance, value, etc. *[*his opinions don't *count]* **3** to have a specified value: often with *for [*a touchdown *counts* for six points*]* **4** to rely or depend (*on* or *upon*) **5** *Music* to keep time by counting the beats —*n.* **1** the act of counting; adding or numbering **2** the number reached by counting; total number or quantity **3** a reckoning or accounting **4** [Archaic] regard; notice; account **5** *Baseball* the number of balls and strikes that have been pitched to the batter **6** *Bowling* the number of pins knocked down by the first ball in a frame following a frame in which a spare or strike is scored: added to the score of the spare or strike of the preceding frame **7** *Boxing* the counting of seconds up to ten, during which a boxer who has been knocked down must rise or lose the match **8** *Law* any of the charges in an indictment, each of which gives a reason and is sufficient for prosecution —*SYN.* RELY —**and counting** so far, but with more expected *[*four straight rainy days, *and counting]* —☆**count in** to include —**count off** to separate into equal divisions by counting —**count out** ☆**1** to disregard; omit **2** *Boxing* to declare (a boxer) defeated when he has remained down for a count of ten —**count′a·ble** *adj.*

count[2] (kount) *n.* ⟦ME *counte* < OFr *conte* < L *comes* (gen. *comitis*), companion < *com-*, with + *ire*, to go: see EXIT⟧ a nobleman in European countries, having a rank equivalent to that of an English earl

☆**count·down** (kount′doun′) ***n.*** ⟦so called from the reverse *counting* of units of time from the highest number *down* to zero⟧ the schedule of operations just before the firing of a rocket, the detonation of an explosive device, etc.; also, the counting off, in reverse order, of units of time in such a schedule

coun·te·nance (kount′'n əns) ***n.*** ⟦ME & OFr *contenance*, bearing, conduct < L *continentia*, lit., way one holds oneself, restraint < *continere*: see CONTAIN⟧ **1** the look on a person's face that shows one's nature or feelings **2** the face; facial features; visage **3** *a)* a look of approval on the face *b)* approval; support; sanction **4** calm control; composure **5** [Obs.] *a)* the way a thing looks; appearance *b)* false appearance —***vt.*** **-nanced**, **-nanc·ing** to give support or sanction to; approve or tolerate —**SYN.** FACE —**in countenance** calm; composed —**put (or stare) out of countenance** to cause to lose composure; embarrass; disconcert

count·er[1] (kount′ər) ***n.*** ⟦ME *countour*: in senses 1 & 2 < OFr *conteor* < L *computator* < *computare*; in senses 3, 4, 5 < OFr *contouer*, counting room, table of a bank < ML *computatorium* < L *computare*, COMPUTE⟧ **1** *a)* a person or thing that counts; computer *b)* any of various complex devices for detecting and counting ionizing particles, including Geiger and scintillation counters **2** an indicator on a machine, for keeping count of turns, strokes, etc. of the machine or its parts **3** a small object used in some games, as for keeping score **4** an imitation coin or token **5** a long table, board, cabinet top, etc., as in a store, lunchroom, or kitchen, for the display and sale of goods, the serving or preparing of food, etc. —**over the counter 1** in direct trading between buyers and sellers: said of sales of stock not conducted through a stock exchange **2** without a prescription [a drug that can be purchased *over the counter*] —**under the counter** in a surreptitious manner: said of sales, payments, etc. made illegally or unethically

coun·ter[2] (kount′ər) ***adv.*** ⟦ME *countre* < OFr *contre* < L *contra*, against, CONTRA-⟧ in a contrary direction, manner, etc.; in opposition; opposite —***adj.*** that acts in opposition, tends in an opposite direction, or is opposite or contrary; opposed or opposing —***n.*** **1** the opposite; contrary **2** an opposing or checking force or action **3** [Obs.] the breast of a horse **4** a stiff leather piece around the heel of a shoe or boot **5** the curved, overhanging part of the stern of some ships **6** a depression between the raised parts of a typeface **7** *Boxing* COUNTERPUNCH **8** *Fencing* a parry made with a circular motion of the blade in an attempt to divert the opponent's blade from whichever angle it is thrust **9** *Football* a play in which most blockers move in one direction while the running back with the ball moves in the opposite direction: in full **counter play** —***vt., vi.*** **1** to act, do, move, etc. counter to (a person or thing); oppose or check **2** to say or do (something) in reply, defense, or retaliation **3** *Boxing* to strike one's opponent while receiving or parrying (a blow)

coun·ter- (kount′ər) ⟦ME *countre-* < OFr *contre-* < L *contra-*, CONTRA-⟧ *combining form* **1** opposite, contrary to [*counterclockwise*] **2** in retaliation or return [*counterplot*] **3** complementary [*counterpart*] **4** competing, contending [*counterbid*]

coun·ter·act (kount′ər akt′) ***vt.*** to act directly against; check, neutralize, or undo the effect of with opposing action —**coun′ter·ac′tion** ***n.*** —**coun′ter·ac′tive** ***adj., n.***

coun·ter·ar·gu·ment (kount′ər är′gyo͞o mənt) ***n.*** an argument, or a reason or line of reasoning, given in opposition to another argument

coun·ter·at·tack (kount′ər ə tak′; *for v., also* kount′ər ə tak′) ***n.*** an attack made in opposition to, or in reprisal for, another attack —***vt., vi.*** to attack in reprisal, or so as to offset the enemy's attack

coun·ter·bal·ance (kount′ər bal′əns; *for v., also* kount′ər bal′əns) ***n.*** **1** a weight used to balance another weight; counterpoise **2** any force or influence that balances or offsets another —***vt.*** **-anced**, **-anc·ing** to be a counterbalance to; offset

coun·ter·blow (kount′ər blō′) ***n.*** a blow given in return

coun·ter·change (kount′ər chānj′) ***vt.*** **-changed′**, **-chang′ing 1** to transpose; interchange **2** to checker; variegate

coun·ter·charge (kount′ər chärj′; *for v., also* kount′ər chärj′) ***n.*** **1** a charge in answer to another charge or against the accuser **2** an attack in return —***vt.*** **-charged′**, **-charg′ing 1** to attack in return **2** to accuse in return

coun·ter·check (kount′ər chek′; *for v., also* kount′ər chek′) ***n.*** **1** anything that checks, restrains, etc. **2** a check upon a check; double check —***vt.*** **1** to check or restrain by a counteraction **2** to check again; confirm by a second check

☆**counter check** a check available at a bank for the use of depositors in making withdrawals: so called because such checks were originally kept on a counter

coun·ter·claim (kount′ər klām′; *for v., also* kount′ər klām′) ***n.*** an opposing claim, esp. one by a defendant against a plaintiff's claim in a lawsuit —***vt., vi.*** to present as, or make, a counterclaim —**coun′ter·claim′ant** ***n.***

coun·ter·clock·wise (kount′ər kläk′wīz′) ***adj., adv.*** in a direction opposite to that in which the hands of a clock move

coun·ter·cul·ture (kount′ər kul′chər) ***n.*** a culture, as that of many young people of the 1960s and 1970s, manifested by a lifestyle that is opposed to the prevailing culture —**coun′ter·cul′tur·al** ***adj.*** —**coun′ter·cul′tur·ist** ***n.***, **coun′ter·cul′tur·al·ist**

coun·ter·cy·cli·cal (kount′ər sik′li kəl) ***adj.*** designating or of fiscal policy that attempts to minimize extreme fluctuations in the business cycle, as by increasing spending and reducing taxes during periods of decline

coun·ter·es·pi·o·nage (kount′ər es′pē ə näzh′, -näj′) ***n.*** actions to prevent or thwart enemy espionage

coun·ter·ex·am·ple (kount′ər eg zam′pəl) ***n.*** an example used to support an argument or claim that is in opposition to another argument or claim

coun·ter·fac·tu·al (kount′ər fak′cho͞o əl) ***adj.*** contrary to the facts of an event, situation, etc. —***n.*** a counterfactual idea, assumption, or argument

coun·ter·feit (kount′ər fit′) ***adj.*** ⟦ME *countrefete* < OFr *contrefait*, pp. of *contrefaire*, to make in opposition, imitate < *contre-*, counter- + *faire* < L *facere*, to make, DO[1]⟧ **1** made in imitation of something genuine so as to deceive or defraud; forged [*counterfeit* money] **2** pretended; sham; feigned [*counterfeit* sorrow] —***n.*** **1** *a)* an imitation made to deceive; forgery *b)* something that so closely resembles something else as to mislead **2** [Obs.] an impostor; cheat —***vt., vi.*** **1** to make an imitation of (money, pictures, etc.), usually in order to deceive or defraud **2** to pretend; feign **3** to resemble (something) closely —**SYN.** ARTIFICIAL, FALSE —**coun′ter·feit′er** ***n.***

coun·ter·foil (-foil′) ***n.*** ⟦COUNTER- + FOIL[2]⟧ the stub of a check, postal money order, receipt, etc. kept by the issuer as a record of the transaction

coun·ter·force (-fôrs′) ***n.*** a force, action, etc. that counters or checks another; specif., the use of strategic air and missile nuclear forces to destroy the nuclear striking power of the enemy, esp. as an opening action in hostilities

coun·ter·in·sur·gen·cy (kount′ər in sur′jən sē) ***n.*** military and political action carried on to defeat an insurgency

coun·ter·in·tel·li·gence (-in tel′ə jəns) ***n.*** **1** actions to counter enemy intelligence, espionage, sabotage, etc. **2** the persons or agency engaged in such actions

coun·ter·in·tu·i·tive (-in to͞o′i tiv, -tyo͞o′-) ***adj.*** contrary to an intuitive belief or to commonsense expectations

coun·ter·ir·ri·tant (-ir′ə tənt) ***n.*** anything used to produce a slight irritation, as of an area of the skin, in order to relieve more serious inflammation elsewhere

count·er·man (kount′ər man′, -mən) ***n.***, *pl.* **-men′** (-men′, -mən) a man whose work is serving customers at a counter, as of a lunchroom or cafeteria

coun·ter·mand (kount′ər mand′; *also, and for n. always,* kount′ər mand′) ***vt.*** ⟦ME *contremaunden* < OFr *contremander* < L *contra*, against + *mandare*: see MANDATE⟧ **1** to cancel or revoke (a command or order) **2** to call back or order back by a contrary order —***n.*** a command or order canceling another

coun·ter·march (kount′ər märch′; *for v., also* kount′ər märch′) ***n.*** **1** a march back or in the opposite direction **2** a marching movement in which a file or column reverses its direction, the individuals remaining in the same order and position —***vi., vt.*** to perform, or cause to perform, a countermarch

coun·ter·meas·ure (kount′ər mezh′ər) ***n.*** an action taken in opposition or retaliation

coun·ter·mel·o·dy (kount′ər mel′ə dē) ***n.*** in a musical composition, a melody subordinate to but distinct from the principal melody

coun·ter·mine (kount′ər mīn′; *for v., also* kount′ər mīn′) ***n.*** ⟦ME *countremine*: see COUNTER- & MINE[1]⟧ **1** a military mine for intercepting or destroying an enemy mine **2** COUNTERPLOT —***vi., vt.*** **-mined′**, **-min′ing 1** to intercept (an enemy mine) with a countermine **2** COUNTERPLOT

coun·ter·move (kount′ər mo͞ov′; *for v., also* kount′ər mo͞ov′) ***n.*** a move made in opposition or retaliation —***vi., vt.*** **-moved′**, **-mov′ing** to move in opposition or retaliation

coun·ter·of·fen·sive (kount′ər ə fen′siv, kount′ər ə fen′siv) ***n.*** an attack by troops who have been defending a position

coun·ter·of·fer (kount′ər ôf′ər) ***n.*** an offer proposed in response to one that is unsatisfactory

coun·ter·pane (kount′ər pān′) ***n.*** ⟦altered (after PANE) < ME *countrepoint*, coverlet < OFr *contre pointe*, earlier *cuilte pointe* < L *culcita puncta*, lit., pricked (i.e., embroidered) quilt < *culcita* (see QUILT) + *puncta* (see POINT)⟧ a bedspread; coverlet

coun·ter·part (-pärt′) ***n.*** ⟦ME *countrepart*: see COUNTER- & PART[2]⟧ **1** a person or thing that corresponds to or closely resembles another, as in form or function **2** a thing which, when added to another, completes or complements it **3** a copy or duplicate, as of a lease

coun·ter·par·ty (kount′ər pärt′ē) ***n.*** either of the parties to a derivative contract; specif., a financial firm whose business involves being such a party, as in contracts with individual investors

coun·ter·plot (kount′ər plät′; *for v., also* kount′ər plät′) ***n.*** a plot to defeat another plot —***vt., vi.*** **-plot′ted**, **-plot′ting** to plot against (a plot); defeat (a plot) with another

coun·ter·point (kount′ər point′) ***n.*** ⟦ME *countrepoint* < MFr *contrepoint* < It *contrappunto*, lit., pointed against: see COUNTER- & POINT, ***n.***⟧ **1** *a)* the technique of combining two or more distinct lines of music that sound simultaneously, esp. with an emphasis on melodic, as opposed to harmonic, progression *b)* this kind of composition **2** any melody played or sung against a basic melody **3** a thing set up in contrast or interaction with another —***vt.*** **1** to provide musical counterpoint to (a melody, etc.) **2** to provide, or serve as, contrast to (another)

coun·ter·poise (kount′ər poiz′; *for v., also* kount′ər poiz′) ***n.*** ⟦NormFr *countrepeis* (OFr *contrepois*): see COUNTER[2] & POISE[1]⟧ **1** a weight that balances another **2** a force, influence, or power that balances or neutralizes another **3** a state of balance or equilibrium —***vt.*** **-poised′**, **-pois′ing** COUNTERBALANCE

coun·ter·pose (kount′ər pōz′) ***vt.*** **-posed′**, **-pos′ing** to put or present in contrast to or as a counterbalance to —**coun′ter·po·si′tion** (-pə zish′ən) ***n.***

coun·ter·pro·duc·tive (kount′ər prə duk′tiv) ***adj.*** bringing about effects or results regarded as contrary to those intended

coun·ter·pro·gram·ming (kount′ər prō′gram′iŋ) ***n.*** *TV* the practice of scheduling a program opposite another program, esp. a popular one, that appeals to a different kind of audience —**coun′ter·pro′gram′** ***vt., vi.*** **-grammed′**, **-gram′ming**

coun·ter·pro·po·sal (kount′ər prə pō′zəl) ***n.*** a proposal made in opposition to another proposal

coun·ter·punch (-punch′) ***n.*** *Boxing* a punch delivered while receiving or parrying an opponent's blow —***vi.*** to strike with a counterpunch

coun·ter·ref·or·ma·tion (kount′ər ref′ər mā′shən) ***n.*** a reform movement to oppose a previous one

Counter-Reformation (kount′ər ref′ər mā′shən) ***n.*** the reform movement in the Roman Catholic Church in the 16th cent., following the Protestant Reformation and in response to it

coun·ter·rev·o·lu·tion (-rev′ə lo͞o′shən) ***n.*** **1** a political movement or revolution against a government or social system set up by a previous revolution **2** a movement to combat revolutionary tendencies —**coun′ter·rev′o·lu′tion·ar′y** ***n., adj., pl.*** **-ar′ies** —**coun′ter·rev′o·lu′tion·ist** ***n.***

coun·ter·scarp (kount′ər skärp′) ***n.*** ⟦Fr *contrescarpe:* see COUNTER- & SCARP⟧ the outer slope or wall of a ditch or moat in a fortification

coun·ter·shaft (-shaft′) ***n.*** an intermediate shaft that transmits motion from the main shaft of a machine to a working part

coun·ter·sign (kount′ər sīn′; *for v., also* kount′ər sīn′) ***n.*** **1** a signature added to a document previously signed by another, for authentication or confirmation **2** a secret sign or signal in answer to another, as in a secret society **3** *Mil.* a secret word or signal which must be given to a guard or sentry by someone wishing to pass; password —***vt.*** to authenticate (a previously signed document) by adding one's own signature —**coun′ter·sig′na·ture** (-sig′nə chər) ***n.***

coun·ter·sink (kount′ər siŋk′) ***vt.*** **-sunk′**, **-sink′ing** **1** to enlarge the top part of (a hole in metal, wood, etc.) so that the head of a bolt, screw, etc. will fit flush with or below the surface **2** to sink the head of (a bolt, screw, etc.) into such a hole —***n.*** **1** a bit for countersinking holes **2** a countersunk hole

coun·ter·spy (kount′ər spī′) ***n., pl.*** **-spies** a spy used in counterespionage

coun·ter·sue (kount′ər so͞o′) ***vi., vt.*** **-sued′**, **-su′ing** **1** to bring a countersuit (against) **2** to counterclaim

coun·ter·suit (kount′ər so͞ot′) ***n.*** an opposing lawsuit asserting a counterclaim, brought by a defendant against a plaintiff in the original suit

coun·ter·ten·or (kount′ər ten′ər) ***n.*** ⟦ME *countretenour* < OFr *contreteneur:* see COUNTER- & TENOR⟧ **1** an adult male voice, usually in falsetto, with a range similar to the contralto and sometimes reaching the soprano **2** a voice or singer with such a range; a male alto **3** a part for such a voice —***adj.*** of, for, or having the range of a countertenor

coun·ter·top (kount′ər täp′) ***n.*** the upper surface of a COUNTER[1] (sense 5)

coun·ter·trans·fer·ence (kount′ər trans fur′əns, -trans′fər əns) ***n.*** in psychotherapy, transference in which the psychoanalyst or other psychotherapist substitutes the client for the original object of his or her own repressed impulses

coun·ter·type (kount′ər tīp′) ***n.*** **1** an opposite type **2** a parallel, or corresponding, type

coun·ter·vail (kount′ər vāl′, kount′ər vāl′) ***vt.*** ⟦ME *countrevailen* < OFr *contrevaloir* < *contre* (see COUNTER[2]) + *valoir,* to avail < L *valere,* to be strong: see VALUE⟧ **1** to make up for; compensate **2** to counteract; be successful, useful, etc. against; avail against **3** [Archaic] to match or equal —***vi.*** to avail (*against*)

coun·ter·weigh (kount′ər wā′, kount′ər wā′) ***vt.*** COUNTERBALANCE

coun·ter·weight (kount′ər wāt′) ***n.*** a weight equal to another; counterbalance

counter word any word freely used as a general term of approval or disapproval without reference to its more exact meaning, as *nice, terrible, lousy, terrific*

coun·ter·work (kount′ər wurk′) ***n.*** anything made in opposition, as a fortification to oppose an enemy fortification

count·ess (kount′is) ***n.*** ⟦ME *countesse* < OFr *contesse* < ML *cometissa:* see COUNT[2] & -ESS⟧ **1** the wife or widow of a count or earl **2** a noblewoman whose rank is equal to that of a count or earl

coun·ti·an (kount′ē ən) ***n.*** a native or inhabitant of a certain county

count·ing·house (kount′iŋ hous′) ***n.*** [Now Rare] a building or office in which a firm keeps records, handles correspondence, etc.: also called **counting room**

counting number NATURAL NUMBER

count·less (kount′lis) ***adj.*** too many to count; innumerable; myriad

☆**count noun** a noun denoting something that is countable: it can form a plural and be preceded by *a* or *an* or a numeral (Ex.: *dog, tree, idea*): cf. MASS NOUN

count palatine [Historical] **1** in Germany, a count granted certain powers from the emperor in his own territory **2** in England, an earl with supreme power in his county: also **earl palatine**

coun·tri·fied (kun′trə fīd′) ***adj.*** ⟦< fol. + -FY + -ED⟧ **1** rural; rustic **2** having the appearance, characteristics, or actions attributed to country people

coun·try (kun′trē) ***n., pl.*** **-tries** ⟦ME *contre* < OFr *contrée* < VL **(regio) contrata,* region lying opposite < L *contra:* see CONTRA-⟧ **1** an area of land; region [wooded *country*] **2** the whole land or territory of a nation or state **3** the people of a nation or state **4** the land of a person's birth or citizenship **5** land with farms and small towns; rural region, as distinguished from a city or town **6** *short for* COUNTRY MUSIC —***adj.*** **1** of, in, or from a rural district **2** characteristic of or like that of the country; rustic **3** [Now Dial.] of one's own country; native

country and western COUNTRY MUSIC

☆**country club** a social club, usually in the outskirts of a city, with a clubhouse, golf course, and other facilities

country cousin a rural visitor to a large city who is bewildered or excited by it: a humorously patronizing term

coun·try-dance (-dans′) ***n.*** an English folk dance, esp. one in which partners form two facing lines

coun·try·fied (kun′trə fīd′) ***adj.*** *alt. sp. of* COUNTRIFIED

country gentleman a man of some wealth who lives on a country estate

coun·try·man (kun′trē mən) ***n., pl.*** **-men** (-mən) **1** a man who lives in the country **2** a person of one's own country; compatriot

☆**country mile** [Informal] a very long way or extent

country music a form of popular music which derives from the rural folk music of the SE and SW U.S., traditionally characterized by string-band instrumentation

country rock **1** rock surrounding a mineral deposit or containing intrusive igneous rock **2** a form of popular music combining features of rock and country music

coun·try·seat (kun′trē sēt′) ***n.*** a rural mansion or estate

coun·try·side (-sīd′) ***n.*** a rural region or its inhabitants

country western COUNTRY MUSIC

coun·try·wide (kun′trē wīd′, -wīd′) ***adj., adv.*** by or throughout the whole land or nation

coun·try·wom·an (-wo͝om′ən) ***n., pl.*** **-wom′en** (-wim′in) **1** a woman who lives in the country **2** a woman of one's own country; compatriot

coun·ty (kount′ē) ***n., pl.*** **-ties** ⟦ME *counte* < OFr *conté* < ML *comitatus,* jurisdiction of a count or earl < L *comes:* see COUNT[2]⟧ **1** a small administrative district of a country; esp., ☆*a)* the largest local administrative subdivision of most states of the U.S. *b)* any of the chief administrative districts into which England, Wales, Northern Ireland, and Ireland are divided *c)* an administrative district in certain Canadian provinces *d)* an electoral district in rural New Zealand **2** the people living in a county **3** [Obs.] the region governed by a count or earl —***adj.*** of, in, for, or characteristic of a county

☆**county agent** a government-employed specialist assigned in rural, suburban, and urban areas to offer informal education and assistance in improved agricultural practices, natural resources management, home economics, etc.

county borough **1** a former unit of local government in England and Wales **2** any of four units of local government in Ireland

☆**county commissioner** a member of an elected governing board in the counties of certain states of the U.S.

county palatine the land held by a count palatine

☆**county seat** a town or city that is the seat or center of government of a county: also [Brit.] **county town**

coup (ko͞o) ***n., pl.*** **coups** (ko͞oz; *Fr* ko͞o) ⟦ME *coupe* & Fr *coup,* both < OFr *colp* < ML *colpus* < VL *colapus* < L *colaphus,* a cuff, box on the ear < Gr *kolaphos*⟧ **1** literally, a blow **2** a sudden, successful move or action; brilliant stroke **3** COUP D'ÉTAT

coup de fou·dre (ko͞ot fo͞o′drʼ) ⟦Fr, lit., bolt of thunder⟧ **1** a thunderbolt **2** a sudden, intense feeling of love

coup de grâce (ko͞o′də gräs′) ⟦Fr, lit., stroke of mercy⟧ **1** the blow, shot, etc. that brings death to a sufferer; death blow **2** any effort or maneuver that clinches victory or success, as by finishing an opponent

coup de main (ko͞od man′) ⟦Fr, lit., stroke of hand⟧ a surprise attack or movement, as in war

coup de maî·tre (ko͞od me′trʼ) ⟦Fr, lit., stroke of a master⟧ a masterstroke; stroke of genius

coup d'é·tat (ko͞o′dā tä′) ⟦Fr, lit., stroke of state⟧ the sudden, forcible overthrow of a ruler, government, etc., sometimes with violence, by a small group of people already having some political or military authority

coup de thé·â·tre (ko͞ot tā ä′trʼ) ⟦Fr, lit., stroke of theater⟧ **1** a surprising or startling turn in a drama **2** an action for sensational effect; theatrical action

coup d'oeil (ko͞o dë′y′) ⟦Fr, lit., stroke of eye⟧ a rapid glance

coupe (ko͞op; *orig., now rarely,* ko͞o pā′) ***n.*** ⟦< fol.⟧ a closed, two-door automobile with a body smaller than that of a sedan

cou·pé (ko͞o pā′) ***n.*** ⟦Fr, orig. pp. of *couper,* to cut, strike < *coup,* COUP⟧ **1** a closed carriage seating two passengers, with a seat outside for the driver **2** in British railway cars, a half-compartment at the end, with seats on only one side **3** COUPE

Cou·perin (ko͞o pran′), **Fran·çois** (frän swȧ′) 1668-1733; Fr. composer & organist

cou·ple (kup′əl) ***n.*** ⟦ME < OFr *cople* < L *copula,* a band, link: see COPULA⟧ **1** anything joining two things together; bond; link **2** two things or persons of the same sort that are somehow associated **3** two people, esp. a man and woman, who are engaged, married, or joined as partners, as in a dance or game **4** [Informal] an indefinite small number; a few [a *couple* of ideas]: now often used with adjectival force, omitting the *of* [a *couple* cups of coffee] **5** *Elec.* two dissimilar metals or alloys placed in electrical contact with each other to create a galvanic or thermoelectric current; voltaic couple **6** *Mech.* two equal forces producing rotation by moving in parallel but opposite directions —***vt.*** **-pled**, **-pling** ⟦ME *couplen* < OFr *copler* < L *copulare*

< *copula*] 1 to join together by fastening or by association; link; connect 2 [Archaic] to join in marriage 3 *Elec.* to join (two or more circuits) by a common magnetic or electric field or by direct connection —*vi.* 1 to come together; unite 2 to unite in sexual intercourse; copulate —**SYN.** PAIR

cou·pler (kup′lər) *n.* a person or thing that couples; specif., *a)* a device for coupling two railroad cars *b)* a device on an organ connecting two keyboards or keys an octave apart so that they can be played together

cou·plet (kup′lit) *n.* ⟦Fr, dim. of *couple,* COUPLE⟧ 1 two successive lines of poetry, esp. two of the same length that rhyme 2 [Rare] a couple; pair

cou·pling (kup′liŋ) *n.* 1 the act of joining together, pairing, copulating, etc. 2 a flexible or rigid mechanical device or part for joining parts together, as two shafts 3 COUPLER (sense *a)* 4 the part of the body, as of a dog or horse, between the hipbones and the ribs; loin 5 a method or device for joining two electric circuits for the transference of energy from one to the other

railroad coupling

cou·pon (ko͞o′pän′, kyo͞o′-) *n.* ⟦Fr, remnant, coupon < *couper,* to cut: see COUP⟧ 1 a detachable printed statement on a bond, specifying the interest due at a given time: each coupon on a bond is presented for payment at the proper time 2 a certificate or ticket entitling the holder to a specified right, as redemption for cash or gifts, reduced purchase price, etc. 3 a part of a printed advertisement as for use in ordering goods, samples, or literature

cour·age (kur′ij) *n.* ⟦ME & OFr *corage,* heart, spirit < L *cor,* HEART⟧ 1 the attitude of facing and dealing with anything recognized as dangerous, difficult, or painful, instead of withdrawing from it; quality of being fearless or brave; valor 2 [Obs.] mind; purpose; spirit —**the courage of one's convictions** the courage to do what one thinks is right

cou·ra·geous (kə rā′jəs) *adj.* having or showing courage; brave —**SYN.** BRAVE —**cou·ra′geous·ly** *adv.* —**cou·ra′geous·ness** *n.*

cou·rante (ko͞o ränt′) *n.* ⟦Fr < *courant,* prp. of *courir,* to run, glide < L *currere,* to run: see CURRENT⟧ 1 an old, lively French dance with running steps, or the music for this 2 a stylized dance of this type used as a movement in a classical suite Also **cou·rant′** (-ränt′)

Cour·bet (ko͝or be′), **Gus·tave** (güs tàv′) 1819-77; Fr. painter

cou·reur de bois (ko͞o rër də bwä′) *pl.* ***cou·reurs de bois*** (ko͞o rër) ⟦Fr, lit., runner of the woods⟧ an unlicensed French or French-Indian fur trader or trapper roving the early frontiers of Canada

cour·gette (ko͝or zhet′) *n.* ⟦Fr, dim. of *courge,* gourd⟧ [Chiefly Brit.] a zucchini

cou·ri·er (ko͝or′ē ər, kur′-) *n.* ⟦ME *corour* (< OFr *coreor* < LL *curritor*) & *courier* (< OFr *courrier* < It *corriere*), both ult. < L *currere,* to run: see CURRENT⟧ 1 a messenger sent in haste or on a regular schedule with messages, parcels, etc.; specif., *a)* a member of the diplomatic corps charged with carrying messages *b)* a spy carrying secret information 2 a person hired to take care of hotel accommodations and luggage and to act as guide for a traveler

cour·lan (ko͝or′lən) *n.* ⟦Fr < Galibi *kurlíri,* echoic of the cry⟧ LIMPKIN

Cour·land (ko͝or′lənd) *alt. sp. of* KURLAND

course (kôrs) *n.* ⟦ME *cours* & Fr *course,* both < OFr *cours* < L *cursus,* pp. of *currere,* to run: see CURRENT⟧ 1 an onward movement; going on from one point to the next; progress 2 the progress or duration of time [in the *course* of a week] 3 a way, path, or channel of movement; specif., *a)* the path to be followed by participants in a race *b)* GOLF COURSE 4 the direction taken, esp. that taken or to be taken by a ship or plane, expressed in degrees measured clockwise from north or by points of the compass 5 *a)* a regular manner of procedure [the law must take its *course*] *b)* a way of behaving; mode of conduct [our wisest *course*] 6 *a)* a series of like things in some regular order *b)* a particular succession of events or actions 7 regular or natural order or development [the *course* of true love] 8 a part of a meal served at one time [the main *course* was roast beef] 9 an encounter of knights contesting in a tournament 10 a horizontal row or layer, as of bricks in a wall or shingles on a roof 11 *Educ. a)* a complete series of studies leading to graduation or a degree *b)* any of the separate units of instruction in a subject, made up of recitations, lectures, etc. 12 *Naut.* a sail on any of the lowest yards of a square-rigged ship —*vt.* **coursed, cours′ing** 1 to run or chase after; pursue 2 to cause (esp. hunting hounds) to chase 3 to run through or over; traverse —*vi.* to move swiftly; run or race —**in due course** in the usual or proper sequence (of events) —**in the course of** in the progress or process of; during —**of course** 1 as is or was to be expected; naturally 2 certainly; without doubt —**on** (or **off**) **course** moving (or not moving) in the intended direction

cours·er[1] (kôr′sər) *n.* ⟦ME < OFr *corsier* < *cours,* COURSE⟧ 1 a graceful, spirited, or swift horse 2 a war horse; charger

cours·er[2] (kôr′sər) *n.* ⟦< ModL *Cursorius,* name of the genus < LL, lit., pertaining to running: see CURSORY⟧ any of various Asian and African swift-running shorebirds (family Glareolidae) that live in sandy, semidesert areas

cours·er[3] (kôr′sər) *n.* 1 a person or thing that courses 2 a dog for coursing

course·ware (kôrs′wer′) *n.* ⟦COURSE + -WARE⟧ computer software designed to provide instruction or training

course·work (kôrs′wurk′) *n.* the various assignments, exercises, examinations, etc. completed by a student to fulfill the requirements for passing a particular class or course of study

cours·ing (kôr′siŋ) *n.* 1 the action of a person or thing that courses 2 hunting with hounds trained to follow game by sight rather than scent

court (kôrt) *n.* ⟦OFr < VL *curtis* < L *cohors* (gen. *cohortis*), enclosed place: see COHORT⟧ 1 *a)* an uncovered space wholly or partly surrounded by buildings or walls; courtyard *b)* a special section or area of a building, as a museum, somewhat like such a space but roofed, as with a skylight 2 a short street, often closed at one end 3 *a)* a specially prepared space, usually quadrangular and often enclosed and roofed, for playing any of several games, as basketball, handball, tennis, or squash *b)* any of the divisions of such a space 4 a mansion or manor with a large, uncovered entrance area: now used only in proper names [Hampton *Court*] ☆5 a motel: in full **motor court** 6 *a)* the palace of a sovereign *b)* the family, advisors, and attendants of a sovereign, considered as a group *c)* a sovereign together with councilors, ministers, etc. as a governing body *d)* any formal gathering, reception, etc. held by a sovereign 7 respectful or flattering attention paid to someone in order to get something 8 courtship; wooing 9 [Brit.] the board of directors of a corporation 10 *a)* a person or persons appointed to try law cases, make investigations, etc.; judge or judges; law court *b)* a building or hall where trials are held, official investigations made, etc. *c)* a judicial assembly, whether civil, ecclesiastical, or military; also, a regular session of such an assembly —*vt.* 1 to pay respectful or flattering attention to (a person) in order to get something 2 to try to get the love of in order to marry; woo 3 to try to get; seek [to *court* success] 4 to make oneself open or liable to [to *court* insults] 5 *Zool.* to engage in the instinctive behavior necessary to attracting (another) as a mate —*vi.* to carry on a courtship —*adj.* of or fit for a court [a *court* jester] —**(the ball is) in someone's court** ⟦< use in tennis⟧ (a problem is) awaiting action or a decision by someone —**out of court** 1 without a trial in a law court 2 not important enough for consideration or examination —**pay court to** to court, as for favor or love —**court′er** *n.*

court bouillon (ko͝or′bo͞o yän′, -bo͞ol-; *Fr* ko͞or bo͞o yōn′) ⟦Fr, lit., short BOUILLON⟧ an aromatic liquid used esp. for poaching fish and made by cooking together white wine, water, onions, celery, carrots, and herbs

court card ⟦altered < *coat card* by assoc. with COURT⟧ [Brit.] FACE CARD

cour·te·ous (kurt′ē əs) *adj.* ⟦ME *courteis* < OFr *corteis* < *court:* see COURT & -EOUS⟧ polite and gracious; considerate toward others; well-mannered —**SYN.** CIVIL —**cour′te·ous·ly** *adv.* —**cour′te·ous·ness** *n.*

cour·te·san (kôrt′ə zən, kôrt′ə zan′; *also, esp. formerly,* kurt′-) *n.* ⟦Fr *courtisane* < It *cortigiana,* a prostitute, orig., court lady < *corte,* court < VL *curtis:* see COURT⟧ 1 [Archaic] a prostitute, esp. one catering to men of wealth or nobility 2 [Historical] a MISTRESS (sense 4*a*) of a king or of a man of wealth or nobility Sometimes sp. **cour′te·zan**

cour·te·sy (kurt′ə sē; *for* 4, kurt′sē) *n., pl.* **-sies** ⟦ME *courteisie* < OFr *curteisie:* see COURTEOUS⟧ 1 courteous behavior; gracious politeness 2 a polite, helpful, or considerate act or remark 3 an act or usage intended to honor or compliment [a former legislator addressed as "Senator" by *courtesy*] 4 [Obs.] a curtsy —*adj.* 1 of or having to do with courtesy or a courtesy 2 provided free as a courtesy; complimentary —**courtesy of** without charge, as a gesture of goodwill

☆**courtesy card** a card entitling the bearer to special privileges, as at a hotel, bank, or store

court hand a kind of handwriting formerly used in English legal documents; Gothic handwriting

court·house (kôrt′hous′) *n.* 1 a building in which law courts are held ☆2 a building that houses the offices of a county government ☆3 a county seat: used in names of towns or cities

cour·ti·er (kôrt′ē ər, -yər) *n.* ⟦ME *curteour* < OFr *cortoier,* to frequent the court < *court, cort,* COURT⟧ 1 an attendant at a royal court 2 a person who uses flattery to get something or to win favor

court·ly (kôrt′lē) *adj.* **-li·er, -li·est** ⟦ME⟧ 1 suitable for a king's court; dignified, polite, elegant, etc. [*courtly* manners] 2 flattering, esp. in an obsequious way —*adv.* **-li·er, -li·est** in a courtly manner —**court′li·ness** *n.*

court-mar·tial (kôrt′mär′shəl) *n., pl.* **courts′-mar′tial**; for 2, also **court′-mar′tials** 1 a court of personnel in the armed forces for the trial of persons accused of breaking military law: see SUMMARY COURT-MARTIAL, SPECIAL COURT-MARTIAL, GENERAL COURT-MARTIAL 2 a trial by a court-martial 3 a conviction by a court-martial —*vt.* **-tialed** or **-tialled, -tial·ing** or **-tial·ling** 1 to try by a court-martial 2 to convict by a court-martial

Court·ney (kôrt′nē) *n.* ⟦< Brit surname *Courtney,* after *Courtenay,* town in France⟧ a feminine and masculine name

☆**court of appeals** [*often* **C- of A-**] 1 a state court to which appeals are taken from the trial courts: usually it is an intermediate appellate court, but in several states it is the final appellate court 2 any of the federal appellate courts, one in each of eleven judicial circuits, intermediate between the U.S. district courts and the Supreme Court

court of record a court which has a permanent record of its proceedings maintained

Court of St. James ⟦after ST. JAMES'S PALACE⟧ the British royal court

court plaster ⟦so called from former use as beauty spots by court ladies⟧ cloth covered with isinglass or some other adhesive material, formerly used for protecting minor cuts and scratches in the skin

court reporter a person whose job is to produce a verbatim record of the oral remarks and statements, esp. testimony, presented at a court trial, deposition, etc.

court·room (kôrt′ro͞om′) ***n.*** a room in which a law court is held
court·ship (-ship′) ***n.*** the activity or period of courting or wooing
court shoe [Brit.] PUMP[2]
court·side (-sīd′) ***n.*** *Sports* the area immediately around a court, esp. a basketball or tennis court [interviews from *courtside*] — ***adj., adv.*** at, in, or from this area
court tennis *see* TENNIS
court·yard (-yärd′) ***n.*** an outdoor space enclosed by walls, adjoining or within a castle or other large building
cous·cous (ko͞os′ko͞os′, ko͞os ko͞os′) ***n.*** ⟦Fr < Berber *kuskus* < Ar < *kaskasa,* to grind, pound⟧ a N African dish made with crushed grain, often semolina, usually steamed and served as with lamb or chicken in a spicy sauce
cous·in (kuz′ən) ***n.*** ⟦ME *cosin* < OFr < L *consobrinus,* orig., child of a mother's sister, also cousin, relation < *com-,* with + *sobrinus,* cousin on the mother's side < base of *soror,* SISTER⟧ **1** [Obs.] a collateral relative more distant than a brother or sister, descended from a common ancestor **2** the son or daughter of one's uncle or aunt: also called *first cousin, full cousin,* or *cousin-german:* one's *second cousin* is a child of one's parent's first cousin; one's *first cousin once removed* is a child of one's first cousin (or, conversely, a first cousin of one's parent) **3** loosely, any relative by blood or marriage **4** a person or thing thought of as somehow related to another [our Mexican *cousins*] **5** a title of address used by one sovereign to another sovereign or to a nobleman —**cous′in·ly** ***adj., adv.*** —**cous′in·ship′** ***n.***
cous·in·age (kuz′ən ij) ***n.*** **1** the state or condition of being a cousin; the relationship between cousins; kinship **2** a group of cousins or of relatives
cous·in-ger·man (kuz′ən jur′mən) ***n., pl.*** **cous′ins-ger′man** ⟦Fr *cousin germain:* see COUSIN & GERMAN⟧ a first cousin; child of one's uncle or aunt
cous·in·ry (kuz′ən rē) ***n., pl.*** **-ries** cousins or other relatives, collectively
Cous·teau (ko͞o stō′), **Jacques (Yves)** 1910-97; Fr. marine explorer, writer, & television producer
couth (ko͞oth) ***adj.*** ⟦ME *cuthe* < OE *cuth* (see UNCOUTH); current use also back-form. < UNCOUTH⟧ **1** refined; polished; civilized: a humorous usage **2** [Archaic] known; familiar —***n.*** refinement; cultivation
cou·ture (ko͞o to͝or′, -tyo͝or′; *Fr* ko͞o tür′) ***n.*** ⟦Fr, sewing, seam < VL **consutura,* seam < L *consutus,* pp. of *consuere,* to sew, stitch, join < *con-,* together (see COM-) + *suere,* to SEW⟧ the work or business of designing new fashions in women's clothes; also, women's clothes in new or specially designed fashions
cou·tu·ri·er (ko͞o tü ryā′; *E* ko͞o′to͝or ē ā′, -tyo͝or-) ***n.*** ⟦Fr, akin to prec.⟧ a designer of fashionable clothing for women, esp. one in the business of making and selling such clothes
cou·tu·ri·ère (*-ryer′*; E, -ē er′) ***n.*** ⟦Fr⟧ a woman couturier
cou·vade (ko͞o väd′) ***n.*** ⟦Fr < *couver,* to hatch < OFr *cover:* see COVEY⟧ a custom of some societies, as the Carib Indians, in which the father of a child just born engages in certain rites, such as resting in bed, as if he had borne the child
co·va·lence (kō′vā′ləns, ko′vā′-) ***n.*** **1** the number of pairs of electrons that an atom can share with its neighboring atoms **2** COVALENT BOND —**co′va′lent** ***adj.***
covalent bond the chemical bond formed between two atoms when they share electrons in pairs, so that each atom provides half the electrons: see IONIC BOND, COORDINATE BOND
co·var·i·ance (kō′ver′ē əns, kō′ver′-) ***n.*** *Statistics* a measure of the relationship between two variables whose values are observed at the same time; specif., the average value of the product of the two variables diminished by the product of their average values
cove[1] (kōv) ***n.*** ⟦ME < OE *cofa,* cave, cell < IE **gupā,* den < base **geu-,* to bend, arch > COD[2], COOMB⟧ **1** a sheltered nook or recess, as in cliffs **2** a small bay or inlet ☆**3** a small valley or pass ☆**4** a strip of open land extending into the woods **5** *Archit. a)* a concave molding, esp. one where the wall meets the ceiling or floor *b)* a trough for concealed light fixtures on a wall near a ceiling *c)* a concave arch or vault — ***vt., vi.*** **coved, cov′ing** to form in a cove; curve concavely
cove[2] (kōv) ***n.*** ⟦Romany *covo,* that man⟧ [Brit. Slang] a boy or man; chap; fellow
cov·en (kuv′ən) ***n.*** ⟦ME *covin,* a group of confederates, agreement, secret plan < OFr *covin* or ML *covina:* both < ML *convenium* < VL **convenium,* an agreement < L *convenire:* see CONVENE⟧ a gathering or meeting, esp. of witches
cov·e·nant (kuv′ə nənt) ***n.*** ⟦OFr, agreement, orig., prp. of *covenir* < L *convenire:* see CONVENE⟧ **1** a binding and solemn agreement to do or keep from doing a specified thing; compact **2** an agreement among members of a church to defend and maintain its doctrines, polity, and faith **3** [**C-**] an agreement of Presbyterians in Scotland in 1638 to oppose episcopacy: also called **National Covenant** **4** [**C-**] an agreement between the parliaments of Scotland and England in 1643 to extend and preserve Presbyterianism: also called **Solemn League and Covenant** **5** *Law a)* a formal, sealed contract *b)* a clause of such a contract *c)* a suit for damages for violation of such a contract **6** *Theol.* the promise made by God to humanity and the relationship it established, as described in the Bible —***vt.*** to promise by a covenant —***vi.*** to make a covenant —**cov′e·nan′tal** (-nant′'l) ***adj.***
cov·e·nan·tee (kuv′ə nən tē′) ***n.*** the party to whom the promises set down in a covenant are made
cov·e·nant·er (kuv′ə nən tər; *for 2, also* kuv′ə nan′tər) ***n.*** **1** a person who enters into a covenant **2** [**C-**] a person who supported either of the Scottish Presbyterian Covenants
cov·e·nan·tor (kuv′ə nən tər) ***n.*** the party that has made the promises set down in a covenant
Cov·en·try (kuv′ən trē, käv′-) city in central England, in West Midlands —**send someone to Coventry** ⟦prob. 17th-c. Cavalier use, in that the town was strongly Roundhead⟧ to ostracize or banish someone
cov·er (kuv′ər) ***vt.*** ⟦ME *coveren* < OFr *covrir* < L *cooperire* < *co-,* intens. + *operire,* to hide < IE **op-wer-,* to cover < **op(i)-,* back, against + **wer,* to cover, protect > WARN⟧ **1** to place something on, over, or in front of, so as to conceal, protect, or close **2** to extend over; overlay; blanket [snow *covered* the highway] **3** to copulate with (the female): said chiefly of a stallion **4** to clothe **5** to coat, sprinkle, etc. thickly [*covered* with mud] **6** to sit on (eggs); brood; incubate **7** to conceal by hiding or screening **8** to keep from harm or injury by shielding; protect by screening **9** to include and provide for; take into account [the law *covers* such cases] **10** *a)* to protect against financial loss or liability, as by insurance or reserve funds *b)* to make up for (a loss, injury, etc.) by insurance, reserve funds, etc. *c)* to be sufficient for payment of (expenses, a debt, etc.) **11** to accept (a bet); stake the equivalent of (an opponent's stake) in a wager **12** to travel over; go the length of [to *cover* a distance] **13** to work in or be responsible for (a particular area or range of activity) [to *cover* a territory as a salesman] **14** to deal with; treat of [to *cover* a subject] **15** to bring upon (oneself) by one's actions [to *cover* oneself with glory] **16** to point a firearm or similar weapon at; put or keep within the range and in the aim of a gun or the like ☆**17** to record or perform a COVER (***n.*** 9) of **18** *Card Games* to put a higher card on (a previously played card) ☆**19** *Finance* to buy stock to replace (shares borrowed from a broker to effect a short sale) ☆**20** *Journalism* to have the assignment of gathering and reporting the details of (a news story) **21** *Mil.* to keep (a person or group) within sight or contact so as to protect from enemy action **22** *Sports a)* to watch, guard, defend, or defend against *b) Baseball* to be ready to receive a throw to (a particular base) *c) Football* to attempt to prevent (a pass receiver) from catching the ball or prevent (a punted ball) from being returned —***vi.*** **1** to spread over a surface, as a liquid does **2** to put on a cap, hat, etc. ☆**3** to provide an alibi, excuse, or subterfuge (*for* another) —***n.*** **1** anything that covers, as a bookbinding, the front part of the binding of a magazine, a jar lid, a box top, etc. **2** a shelter for protection, as from gunfire **3** a hiding place for game, as a thicket, underbrush, etc. **4** ⟦modeled on Fr *couvert*⟧ a tablecloth and setting for a meal, esp. for one person **5** [*pl.*] bedclothes used to cover a person in bed ☆**6** COVER CHARGE **7** something used for hiding one's real actions, intentions, etc. **8** *a)* an envelope or wrapper for mail *b)* an envelope or postal card with a stamp, postmark, and cachet of historical or philatelic significance ☆**9** a version of a song, esp. one that has become popular in a particular recording, as performed or recorded in imitation of the original or with a fresh interpretation —**break cover** to come out of protective shelter —**cover up** **1** to cover entirely; envelop; wrap **2** to keep blunders, crimes, etc. from being known —**take cover** to seek protective shelter —**under cover** in secrecy or concealment —**cov′er·er** ***n.***
☆**cov·er·age** (kuv′ər ij) ***n.*** **1** the amount, extent, etc. covered by something **2** *Football* the defensive tactics of a defender or a defensive team against a passing play **3** *Insurance* all the risks covered by an insurance policy **4** *Journalism* the extent to which a news story is covered
cov·er·all (-ôl′) ***n.*** [*usually pl.*] a one-piece, loosefitting, outer garment with sleeves and legs, worn, often over regular clothing, as to protect against dirt
☆**cover band** ⟦see COVER, ***vt.*** 17 & ***n.*** 9⟧ a BAND[2] that specializes in performing covers
☆**cover charge** ⟦see COVER, ***n.*** 4⟧ a fixed charge added to the cost of food and drink at a nightclub or restaurant
cover crop a quick-growing crop, as vetch or clover, used for a short time to protect soil from erosion and then plowed under as fertilizer
Cov·er·dale (kuv′ər dāl′), **Miles** (mīlz) 1488-1568; Eng. clergyman & translator of the Bible (1535)
☆**covered wagon** a large wagon with an arched cover of canvas, used by American pioneers
☆**cover girl** a young woman model whose picture appears on magazine covers
cov·er·ing (kuv′ər iŋ) ***n.*** anything that covers
cov·er·let (kuv′ər lit) ***n.*** ⟦ME *coverlite* < Anglo-Fr *covre-let* < OFr *covrir,* COVER + *lit,* bed < L *lectus:* see LIE[1]⟧ **1** a bed covering; bedspread **2** any covering
cover letter a letter sent along with, and serving to explain, an enclosure, package, etc.: also **covering letter**
cov·er·lid (-lid) ***n.*** *archaic or dial. var. of* COVERLET
co·versed sine (kō′vərst) ⟦*co-* (as in COSINE) + VERSED SINE⟧ *Trigonometry* one minus the sine of a given angle
cover story the article in a magazine that deals with the subject depicted on the cover
co·vert (kō′vərt, kuv′ərt) ***adj.*** ⟦OFr, pp. of *covrir,* COVER⟧ **1** concealed, hidden, disguised, or surreptitious [a *covert* threat] **2** [Archaic] sheltered; protected **3** *Law* protected by a husband: said of a married woman —***n.*** **1** a covered or protected place; shelter **2** a hiding place for game, as underbrush or a thicket **3** COVERT CLOTH **4** *Ornithology* any of the small feathers covering a particular area of a bird, as the bases of the larger feathers of a wing or tail —**SYN.** SECRET —**cov′ert·ly** ***adv.*** —**cov′ert·ness** ***n.***
covert cloth (kuv′ərt, kō′vərt) a smooth, twilled, lightweight cloth, usually of wool, used for suits and topcoats

cov·er·ture (kuv′ər chər) *n.* ⟦OFr < LL **coopertura* < L: see COVER⟧ **1** a covering **2** a refuge **3** a concealment or disguise **4** *Law* the status of a married woman

cov·er-up (kuv′ər up′) *n.* **1** an attempt to keep blunders, crimes, etc. from being disclosed ☆**2** an outer garment, esp. for wearing over a swimsuit

cov·et (kuv′it) *vt., vi.* ⟦ME *coveiten* < OFr *coveitier* < LL **cupiditare* < L *cupiditas:* see CUPIDITY⟧ to want ardently (esp., something that another person has); long for with envy —*SYN.* ENVY —**cov′et·er** *n.*

cov·et·ous (kuv′ət əs) *adj.* ⟦ME *coveitous* < OFr⟧ tending to covet; greedy; avaricious —*SYN.* GREEDY —**cov′et·ous·ly** *adv.* —**cov′et·ous·ness** *n.*

cov·ey (kuv′ē) *n., pl.* **-eys** ⟦ME < OFr *covée,* a brood < *cover,* to sit on, hatch < L *cubare,* to lie down: see CUBE[1]⟧ **1** a small flock or brood of birds, esp. partridges or quail **2** a small group of people or, sometimes, things —*SYN.* GROUP

cov·in (kuv′in) *n.* ⟦ME: see COVEN⟧ **1** [Archaic] treachery or fraud, or a group engaged in this **2** *Law* a conspiracy of two or more people to defraud or injure another or others

cov·ing (kōv′iŋ) *n.* a concave molding or arch; cove

cow[1] (kou) *n.* ⟦ME *cou,* cow, pl. *kye* (southern doubled pl. *kyn*) < OE *cū,* pl. *cy* < IE base **gwou-,* cow, ox > Sans *gauḥ,* Gr *bous,* L *bos,* OIr *bo,* Ger *kuh*⟧ **1** the mature female of domestic cattle (genus *Bos*), valued for its milk **2** the mature female of certain other mammals, as the buffalo, elephant, moose, whale, etc.: the male of such animals is called a *bull* ☆**3** [Informal or West] a domestic bovine animal, whether a steer, bull, cow, or calf: *usually used in pl.* —☆**have a cow** [Slang] to become very agitated or angry

cow[2] (kou) *vt.* ⟦< ON *kūga,* to subdue; meaning infl. by prec., COWARD⟧ to make timid and submissive by filling with fear or awe; intimidate

cow·age (kou′ij) *n. alt. sp. of* COWHAGE

cow·ard (kou′ərd) *n.* ⟦ME & OFr *couard,* coward, lit., with tail between the legs < OFr *coue, coe,* tail < L *cauda,* tail⟧ a person who lacks courage, esp. one who is shamefully unable to control fear and so shrinks from danger or trouble —*adj.* [Archaic] cowardly

Cow·ard (kou′ərd), Sir **Noel (Pierce)** 1899-1973; Eng. playwright, actor, and songwriter

cow·ard·ice (kou′ər dis′) *n.* ⟦ME & OFr *couardise* < *couard:* see COWARD⟧ lack of courage; esp., shamefully excessive fear of danger, difficulty, or suffering

cow·ard·ly (kou′ərd lē) *adj.* of or typical of a coward; shamefully fearful —*adv.* in the manner of a coward —**cow′ard·li·ness** *n.*

SYN.—**cowardly**, the general term, suggests a reprehensible lack of courage in the face of danger or pain [a *cowardly* deserter]; **craven** implies abject or fainthearted fear [a *craven* fear for one's life]; **pusillanimous** implies an ignoble, contemptible lack of courage or endurance [*pusillanimous* submission]; **dastardly** connotes a sneaking, malicious cowardice that is manifested in a despicable act [a *dastardly* informer] —*ANT.* **brave**

cow·bane (kou′bān′) *n.* ⟦COW[1] + BANE⟧ **1** any of several water hemlocks with intensely poisonous roots and clusters of small white flowers **2** any other plant that is poisonous to cattle, as locoweed

cow·bell (-bel′) *n.* **1** a bell hung from a cow's neck to clank when she moves and thus indicate where she is **2** such a bell without the clapper, mounted on the bass drum and used in playing popular music and jazz

cow·ber·ry (-ber′ē) *n., pl.* **-ries** **1** a low creeping shrub (*Vaccinium vitis-idaea*) of the heath family, with white or pink flowers and dark-red, acid berries **2** its berry

cow·bind (-bīnd′) *n.* either of two poisonous, climbing bryonies (*Bryonia alba* or *B. dioica*) with black or red berries and fleshy roots formerly used in medicine as a cathartic

☆**cow·bird** (-burd′) *n.* any of a number of small American blackbirds (esp. *Molothrus ater*) often seen near cattle: cowbirds lay eggs in other birds' nests

cow·boy (kou′boi′) *n.* ☆**1** a ranch worker who rides horseback much of the time on his job of herding and tending cattle ☆**2** a performer in a rodeo or Wild West show ☆**3** a conventionalized character in novels, motion pictures, etc., typically an adventurer of the Old West who rides horseback and carries pistols ☆**4** [Informal] a man regarded variously as being bold, daring, independent, etc. or brash, reckless, out of control, etc.

cowboy boot a boot having a thick, angled heel of medium height and, usually, a pointed toe and ornamental stitching, tooling, etc.: traditionally worn by American cowboys

cowboy hat a wide-brimmed hat, usually of felt, with a soft, high crown, traditionally worn by American cowboys

☆**cow·catch·er** (-kach′ər) *n.* PILOT (*n.* 5)

☆**cow college** [Informal] **1** an agricultural college **2** a small, not well-known college in a rural area

Cow·ell (kou′əl), **Henry (Dixon)** 1897-1965; U.S. composer

cow·er (kou′ər) *vi.* ⟦ME *couren,* prob. < ON base seen in Dan *kūre,* Sw *kura,* to squat; akin to Ger *kauern* < IE base **geu-,* to curve, bend > COD[2], CHICKEN⟧ **1** to crouch or huddle up, as from fear or cold **2** to shrink and tremble, as from someone's anger, threats, or blows; cringe

cow·fish (kou′fish′) *n., pl.* **-fish′** or **-fish′es** (see FISH) **1** a marine dolphin (*Tursiops gilli*) of the Pacific Ocean **2** any of the smaller marine whales, as the grampus **3** any of several trunkfishes with hornlike processes on the head **4** [Rare] a dugong or manatee

cow·flop (kou′fläp′) *n.* [Slang] COWPAT: also **cow′flap′** (-flap′)

☆**cow·girl** (kou′gurl′) *n.* a female COWBOY (senses 1-3)

cow·hage (kou′ij) *n.* ⟦altered by assoc. with cow[1] < Hindi *kawānch*⟧ a tropical, leguminous vine (*Mucuna pruriens*) bearing pods covered with fine barbed hairs that easily penetrate animal or human skin, causing intense itching: some strains are grown for forage

☆**cow·hand** (kou′hand′) *n.* COWBOY (sense 1)

cow·herb (-urb′) *n.* a pink-flowered annual plant (*Saponaria vaccaria*) of the pink family, growing as a weed in North America

cow·herd (-hurd′) *n.* a person who tends grazing cattle

cow·hide (-hīd′) *n.* **1** *a)* the hide of a cow or, often, that of any bovine animal *b)* leather made from such hide ☆**2** a whip made of rawhide or braided leather —☆*vt.* **-hid′ed, -hid′ing** to flog with a cowhide

☆**cow killer** a large velvet ant (*Dasymutilla occidentalis*) of the S and E U.S.: the wingless female has a powerful sting

cowl[1] (koul) *n.* ⟦ME *coule* < OE *cugle* < LL(Ec) *cuculla* < L *cucullus,* cap, hood < ? IE base **(s)keu-,* to cover > SKY⟧ **1** *a)* a monk's hood *b)* a monk's cloak with a hood **2** something shaped like a cowl; esp., *a)* a hood-shaped metal cover for the top of a chimney, used to increase the draft *b)* the part of an automobile body to which the windshield and dashboard are fastened *c)* a cowling —*vt.* to put a cowl on; cover with or as with a cowl

cowl[2] (kōl, ko͞ol) *n.* ⟦ME *covel* < OFr *cuvele* or OE *cufel, cyfl,* both < LL *cupella,* dim. of L *cupa,* vat, tub: see CUP⟧ [Archaic] a large, two-handled tub for carrying water, usually borne on a pole

cowled (kould) *adj.* **1** wearing or having a cowl **2** hood-shaped; hooded; cucullate

Cow·ley (kou′lē), **Abraham** 1618-67; Eng. poet & essayist

cow·lick (kou′lik′) *n.* ⟦from the notion that the hair looks as if it had been licked by a cow⟧ a tuft of hair on the head that cannot easily be combed flat

cowl·ing (koul′iŋ) *n.* ⟦see COWL[1]⟧ a contoured housing as around the engine of an airplane, racing car, outboard motor, etc., usually having ducts or vents that allow air to pass through

cowl·staff (kōl′staf′, ko͞ol′-) *n.* ⟦COWL[2] + STAFF[1]⟧ [Archaic] a pole run through the handles of a large tub so that it can be carried between two persons

☆**cow·man** (kou′mən) *n., pl.* **-men** (-mən) **1** a man who owns or operates a cattle ranch **2** a man who tends cattle

co·work·er or **co-work·er** (kō′wur′kər) *n.* a person with whom one works in the same workplace —**co′work′ing** *n., adj.,* **co′-work′ing**

cow parsley a tall, biennial weed (*Anthriscus sylvestris*) of the umbel family, with tiny white flowers and parsleylike leaves, native to temperate areas of the Old World

cow parsnip any of several perennial plants (genus *Heracleum*) of the umbel family, with flattened clusters of white or purple flowers and thick, tubular stems

cow·pat (kou′pat′) *n.* ⟦< PAT[2] (*n.* 4)⟧ a piece or pile of cow manure: also [Informal] **cow′pie′** (-pī′) or **cow′plop′** (-pläp′)

☆**cow·pea** (kou′pē′) *n.* **1** a viny annual plant (*Vigna unguiculata*) of the pea family, bearing seeds in slender pods: grown in S U.S. for forage, green manure, etc. **2** the edible seed of this plant, cooked as a vegetable; black-eyed pea

Cow·per (ko͞o′pər; *also* kou′-), **William** 1731-1800; Eng. poet

Cow·per's gland (kou′pərz, ko͞o′-) ⟦after William *Cowper* (1666-1709), Eng anatomist⟧ either of two small glands with ducts opening into the male urethra: during sexual excitement they secrete a mucous substance: see BARTHOLIN'S GLAND

cow pilot SERGEANT MAJOR (sense 3)

☆**cow·poke** (kou′pōk′) *n.* ⟦see COWPUNCHER⟧ [Informal] COWBOY

☆**cow pony** any horse used by a cowboy in herding cattle

cow·pox (kou′päks′) *n.* a contagious viral disease of cows that causes pustules on the udders: see also VARIOLA

COWPS *abbrev.* Council on Wage and Price Stability

☆**cow·punch·er** (-pun′chər) *n.* ⟦< *punching,* term for herding cattle, in ref. to the prod used in driving them⟧ [Informal] COWBOY

cow·rie or **cow·ry** (kou′rē) *n., pl.* **-ries** ⟦Hindi *kauṛī* < Sans *kaparda*⟧ **1** any of a number of gastropods (family Cypraeidae) having brightly colored, glossy shells and found in warm seas **2** the shell of any of these mollusks, esp. the shell of the **money cowrie** (*Cypraea moneta*), formerly used as currency in parts of Africa and S Asia

cow shark any of a family (Hexanchidae, order Hexanchiformes) of primitive sharks, having six or seven gill slits

cow·shed (kou′shed′) *n.* a shelter for cows

cow·slip (-slip′) *n.* ⟦ME *couslippe* < OE *cuslyppe,* lit., cow dung < *cu,* cow + *slyppe,* paste: see SLIP[3]⟧ **1** a European primrose (*Primula veris*) with yellow or purple flowers ☆**2** MARSH MARIGOLD ☆**3** SHOOTING STAR (sense 2) ☆**4** VIRGINIA COWSLIP

☆**cow town** **1** a town in a cattle-ranching region, esp. one with stockyards, slaughterhouses, etc. **2** [Informal] any town or city regarded as being dull, unsophisticated, etc.

cox (käks) *n., pl.* **cox′es** COXSWAIN (sense 2) —*vt., vi.* to be a coxswain for (a boat or crew, esp. a racing shell or its crew)

cox·a (käk′sə) *n., pl.* **cox′ae** (-sē) ⟦L, hip, angle < IE base **koksā* > Ger *hachse,* Achilles' tendon, OIr *coss,* foot⟧ **1** the hip or hip joint **2** the segment of the leg that attaches to the body of an insect or other arthropod —**cox′al** *adj.*

cox·al·gi·a (käks al′jē ə, -jə) *n.* ⟦ModL: see prec. & -ALGIA⟧ a pain in, or disease of, the hip or hip joint: also **cox′al′gy** (-jē) —**cox·al′gic** *adj.*

cox·comb (käks′kōm′) *n.* ⟦for *cock's comb*⟧ **1** a cap topped with a notched strip of red cloth like a cock's comb, formerly worn by jesters 2 a silly, vain, foppish fellow; dandy —**cox·comb·i·cal** (käks käm′i kəl, -kōm′-) *adj.*

cox·comb·ry (-kōm′rē) *n., pl.* **-ries** ⟦see prec.⟧ 1 silly conceit or foppery 2 an instance of this

☆**cox·sack·ie·vi·rus** (ko͝ok säk′ē vī′rəs) *n.* ⟦so named because first found in a patient from *Coxsackie,* N.Y.⟧ any of a group of enteroviruses that cause several diseases, as viral meningitis: also written **Coxsackie virus**

cox·swain (käk′sən, -swān′) *n.* ⟦< COCK(BOAT) + SWAIN⟧ 1 a sailor in charge of a ship's boat and usually acting as its helmsman 2 *Rowing* the person who steers a racing shell and calls out the rowing rhythm for the crew

COX-2 inhibitor (käks′to͞o′) ⟦< C(YCLO)OX(YGENASE) + 2⟧ a nonsteroidal anti-inflammatory drug that suppresses a specific type of cyclooxygenase that triggers pain and inflammation, used to treat arthritis, chronic pain, etc.: also written **Cox-2 inhibitor**

coy (koi) *adj.* ⟦ME, still, quiet < OFr *coi,* earlier *quei* < LL **quetus* < L *quietus:* see QUIET⟧ 1 [Obs.] quiet; silent 2 [Archaic] *a)* shrinking from contact or familiarity with others; bashful; shy *b)* primly reserved; demure 3 affecting innocence or shyness, esp. in a playful or coquettish manner 4 reticent or evasive, as in making a commitment 5 [Archaic] inaccessible; secluded 6 [Obs.] disdainfully aloof —*vi.* [Archaic] to behave in a coy way —*vt.* [Obs.] to pet or caress —**coy′ly** *adv.* —**coy′ness** *n.*

coy·dog (kī′dôg′, -däg′; koi′-) *n.* the hybrid offspring of a coyote and wild dog

☆**coy·o·te** (kī ōt′ē, kī′ōt′) *n., pl.* **coy·o′tes** or **coy·o′te** ⟦AmSp < Nahuatl *koyo:λ*⟧ 1 a wild animal (*Canis latrans*) of the dog family, native to the North American plains: it resembles a small wolf 2 [Slang] a smuggler of illegal aliens from Mexico into the U.S.

☆**co·yo·til·lo** (kō′yə til′ō, koi′ə-) *n., pl.* **-los** ⟦AmSp, dim. of prec.⟧ a thorny shrub (*Karwinskia humboldtiana*) of the buckthorn family, found in Mexico and the SW U.S.: it has toxic berries

coy·pu (koi′po͞o′) *n., pl.* **-pus′** or **-pu′** ⟦AmSp *coipu* < Araucanian *coypu*⟧ NUTRIA

coz (kuz) *n.* [Informal] cousin

coz·en (kuz′ən) *vt., vi.* ⟦< ME *cosin,* fraud, trickery < ? OFr *cosson,* horse-trader < L *cocio, coctio,* a broker, dealer⟧ 1 to cheat; defraud 2 to deceive —**coz′en·age** *n.*

Co·zu·mel (kō′zə mel′, kä′-) island of Mexico, near the E coast of Yucatán: winter resort and site of ancient Maya ruins: 34 mi (*c.* 55 km) long

co·zy (kō′zē) *adj.* **-zi·er, -zi·est** ⟦Scot; prob. < Scand, as in Norw *kose sig,* to make oneself comfortable, *koselig,* snug⟧ warm and comfortable; snug —*n., pl.* **-zies** a knitted or padded cover placed over a teapot to keep the contents hot —**SYN.** COMFORTABLE —☆**cozy up to** [Informal] to try to ingratiate oneself, or make friends, with —☆**play it cozy** [Slang] to act cautiously so as to avoid risk —**co′zi·ly** *adv.* —**co′zi·ness** *n.*

cp *abbrev.* 1 candlepower 2 chemically pure 3 compare

cP *abbrev.* centipoise(s)

CP *abbrev.* 1 Command Post 2 Common Pleas 3 Common Prayer 4 Communist Party

CPA (sē′pē′ā′) *n., pl.* **CPAs** CERTIFIED PUBLIC ACCOUNTANT

CPB *trademark* Corporation for Public Broadcasting

cpd *abbrev.* compound

cpi *abbrev. Comput., Typography* characters per inch

CPI *abbrev.* Consumer Price Index

Cpl *abbrev.* Corporal

cpm *abbrev.* cycles per minute

CPM *abbrev.* ⟦L *mille,* thousand⟧ cost per thousand

CPO *abbrev.* Chief Petty Officer

CPR *abbrev.* cardiopulmonary resuscitation

cps *abbrev.* 1 cycle(s) per second 2 *Comput.* characters per second

CPS *abbrev.* Certified Professional Secretary

Cpt *abbrev.* Captain

CPU (sē′pē′yo͞o′) *n.* central processing unit: also **cpu**

CQ[1] (sē′kyo͞o′) *n.* signal given by radio amateurs, inviting others to enter into communication

CQ[2] *abbrev. Mil.* charge of quarters

cr *abbrev.* 1 credit 2 creditor

Cr[1] *abbrev.* cruzado

Cr[2] *Chem. symbol for* chromium

CR *abbrev.* Costa Rica

crab[1] (krab) *n.* ⟦ME *crabbe* < OE *crabba* < IE base **grebh-,* **gerebh-,* to scratch: see GRAPHIC⟧ 1 any of various decapods with four pairs of legs, one pair of pincers, a flattish shell, and a short, broad abdomen folded under its thorax 2 any of other similar arthropods, as the horseshoe crab 3 the edible part of a crab 4 *a)* CRAB LOUSE *b)* [*pl.*] [Informal] infestation by crab lice (often with *the*) 5 any of various machines for hoisting heavy weights 6 *Aeron.* the apparent sideways motion of an aircraft with respect to the ground when headed into a crosswind —*vi.* **crabbed, crab′bing** to fish for crabs; catch crabs —*vt. Aeron.* to head (an aircraft) into a crosswind in order to counteract drift, thus causing apparent sideways motion with respect to the ground —**catch a crab** *Rowing* to fail to clear the water on the recovery stroke accidentally, thereby unbalancing the boat or impeding its movement —**the Crab** Cancer, the constellation and fourth sign of the zodiac —**crab′ber** *n.*

blue crab

crab[2] (krab) *n.* ⟦ME *crabbe,* akin ? to Scot *scrabbe,* Swed dial. *scrabba,* wild apple⟧ 1 CRAB APPLE 2 a person who has a sour temper or is always complaining —*adj.* of a crab apple or the tree that it grows on —*vt.* **crabbed, crab′bing** 1 [Obs.] *a)* to irritate; vex *b)* to sour; embitter 2 [Rare] to find fault with; criticize —*vi.* [Informal] to complain peevishly; grumble —☆**crab one's act (the deal,** etc.) to ruin or frustrate one's scheme (the deal, etc.) —**crab′ber** *n.*

crab apple 1 any of several species of small, very sour apples (genus *Malus*), growing wild or cultivated and used for making jellies and preserves 2 a tree bearing crab apples: also **crab tree**

Crabbe (krab), **George** 1754-1832; Eng. poet

crab·bed (krab′id) *adj.* ⟦< CRAB[1], infl. by CRAB[2]⟧ 1 peevish; morose; cross 2 hard to understand because intricate or complicated 3 hard to read or make out because cramped or irregular [*crabbed* handwriting] —**crab′bed·ly** *adv.* —**crab′bed·ness** *n.*

crab·by (krab′ē) *adj.* **-bi·er, -bi·est** ⟦see prec.⟧ cross and complaining; peevish; ill-tempered —**crab′bi·ly** *adv.* —**crab′bi·ness** *n.*

☆**crab cactus** CHRISTMAS CACTUS

crab·grass (krab′gras′) *n.* ⟦CRAB[1] + GRASS: so named from fancied resemblance of the creeping stems to the legs of a crab⟧ ☆any of several weedy annual grasses (genus *Digitaria*) which spread rapidly because of their freely rooting stems, becoming a pest in lawns and gardens: also written **crab grass**

crab louse a crab-shaped human louse (*Phthirus pubis*) that infests the pubic regions, armpits, etc.

crab·meat (krab′mēt′) *n.* CRAB[1] (*n.* 3): also written **crab meat**

Crab nebula a crab-shaped, rapidly expanding cloud of gas in the constellation Taurus, containing a neutron-star pulsar: believed to be the remnants of the supernova of A.D. 1054

crab spider any of a family (Thomisidae) of spiders that move sideways like crabs

crab·stick (krab′stik′) *n.* 1 a stick, cane, or club made of the wood of the crab apple tree or some other wood 2 [Archaic] an ill-tempered person

crab·wise (krab′wīz′) *adv.* ⟦CRAB[1] + -WISE: in allusion to the sideways movements of crabs⟧ toward one side; sideways; laterally

crack[1] (krak) *vi.* ⟦ME *craken* < OE *cracian,* to resound, akin to Ger *krachen* < IE base **ger-*: see CROW[1]⟧ 1 to make a sudden, sharp noise, as of something breaking 2 to break or split, usually without complete separation of parts 3 *a)* to become harsh or rasping, as the voice when hoarse *b)* to change suddenly from one register to another, as the voice of a boy in adolescence 4 [Informal] to move with speed: now chiefly in phrase **get cracking,** to start moving with dispatch 5 [Informal] to break down [to *crack* under a strain] —*vt.* 1 to cause to make a sharp, sudden noise 2 to cause to break or split, as by a sharp blow or by heavy pressure, intense heat, etc. 3 to destroy or impair [to *crack* all opposition] 4 to cause (the voice) to crack ☆5 to subject (as petroleum) to the process of cracking: see CRACKING[2] 6 to hit or strike with a sudden, sharp blow or impact 7 to break through the difficulties of; manage to solve [to *crack* a secret code] 8 [Informal] to manage to gain entrance or acceptance in 9 [Informal] *a)* to break open or into; force open [to *crack* a safe] *b)* to open and consume the contents [to *crack* a bottle] *c)* to open and read or study [to *crack* a book] *d)* to open slightly (a door, window, etc.) 10 [Slang] to make (a joke) —*n.* 1 a sudden, sharp noise, as of something breaking [the *crack* of a whip] 2 *a)* a break, usually without complete separation of parts; fracture *b)* a slight defect; flaw [*cracks* in his composure] ☆3 a narrow opening, as between boards; chink; fissure; crevice 4 an abrupt, erratic shift of vocal tone, as from emotion or in adolescence 5 a moment; instant [at the *crack* of dawn] 6 a sudden, sharp blow or impact ☆7 [Informal] an attempt or try [to take a *crack* at working a puzzle] ☆8 [Slang] a joke, gibe, or sharp remark 9 [Old Slang] a burglar or burglary —*adj.* [Informal] excelling in skill or performance; first-rate [a *crack* shot, *crack* troops] —**SYN.** BREAK —**crack a smile** [Slang] to smile, esp. when not inclined to do so —☆**crack down (on)** to become strict or stricter (with) —☆**cracked up to be** [Informal] alleged or believed to be —**crack up** 1 to crash, as (in) an airplane 2 [Informal] *a)* to break down physically or mentally *b)* to break into a fit of laughter or tears —☆**crack wise** [Old Slang] to joke or gibe —**fall between (or through) the cracks** [Informal] to be unfairly overlooked or omitted, as because of exceptional circumstances

crack[2] (krak) *n.* ⟦so called prob. from *cracking* the baked substance into pieces, or from the *cracking* or *crackling* sound it makes when smoked⟧ ☆[Slang] hard, pebblelike pieces of highly purified cocaine prepared for smoking: a highly potent and addictive form of cocaine —*adj.* ☆designating or of cocaine in this form

☆**crack·a·jack** (krak′ə jak′) *adj., n.* [Slang] CRACKERJACK

crack baby [Slang] an infant, typically born prematurely, with a condition caused by the excessive consumption of crack cocaine by the mother during pregnancy and characterized by malformations and learning disabilities

crack·back (block) (krak′bak′) *Football* a block in which a player, usually a wide receiver, angles back sharply toward the middle of the field and blocks a defensive player from the side

crack·brain (krak′brān′) *n.* a crackbrained person

crack·brained (-brānd′) *adj.* so senseless or unreasonable as to seem insane; crazy

☆**crack·down** (krak′doun′) ***n.*** a resorting to strict or stricter measures of discipline or punishment

cracked (krakt) ***adj.*** **1** broken or fractured, usually without complete separation of parts; having a crack or cracks **2** harsh or strident [a *cracked* voice] **3** [Informal] mentally unbalanced

cracked wheat coarsely milled wheat particles

crack·er (krak′ər) ***n.*** ⟦< CRACK[1], ***vi.***; sense 5 < earlier sense "braggart, boaster"⟧ **1** a person or device that cracks **2** a firecracker **3** a little paper roll used as a favor at parties: it contains a trinket or candy, and bursts with a popping noise when the ends are pulled **4** a thin, crisp wafer or biscuit ☆**5** POOR WHITE: contemptuous term **6** [*usually* **C-**] [Informal] a person born or living in Florida or Georgia: a humorous usage **7** [Slang] *Comput.* HACKER[2] (sense 2)

crack·er-bar·rel (-bar′əl) ***adj.*** ⟦< the large barrel of soda crackers formerly found in general stores⟧ [Informal] designating or typical of the informal discussions on all subjects by persons gathered at a country store [a *cracker-barrel* philosopher]

☆**crack·er·jack** (krak′ər jak′) ***adj.*** ⟦late 19th-c. slang: extension of CRACK[1], ***adj.*** + JACK (nickname)⟧ [Slang] outstanding, as in skill or ability; excellent —***n.*** **1** [Slang] a person or thing of recognized excellence **2** [*also* **C-**] [*occas. pl.*] CRACKER JACK

☆**Cracker Jack** *trademark for* a confection of sweet, glazed popcorn and peanuts

crack·ers (krak′ərz) ***adj.*** ⟦altered (infl. by CRACKER) < CRACKED⟧ [Slang, Chiefly Brit.] crazy; insane

crack·head (krak′hed′) ***n.*** [Slang] a habitual user of crack cocaine

crack·ing[1] (krak′iŋ) ***adj.*** excellent; fine —***adv.*** [Informal] very

crack·ing[2] (krak′iŋ) ***n.*** ☆the process of breaking down heavier hydrocarbons by heat and pressure or by catalysts into lighter hydrocarbons of lower molecular weight, as in producing gasoline from petroleum

crack·le (krak′əl) ***vi.*** **-led, -ling** ⟦ME *crakelen,* freq. of *craken,* CRACK[1]⟧ **1** to make a succession of slight, sharp, popping sounds, as of dry wood burning **2** to be bursting with energy and vivacity **3** to develop a finely cracked surface —***vt.*** **1** to crush or break with cracking sounds **2** to produce a finely cracked surface on —***n.*** **1** a succession of cracking sounds **2** vivacity; animation **3** *a)* the fine, irregular surface cracks on some pottery, porcelain, etc. *b)* CRAQUELURE (sense 1) **4** CRACKLEWARE

crack·le·ware (-wer′) ***n.*** pottery, porcelain, etc. with a finely cracked surface

crack·ling (krak′liŋ; *for 2, usually,* -lin) ***n.*** **1** the producing of a succession of slight, sharp popping sounds **2** *a)* the browned, crisp rind of roast pork *b)* [*pl.*] the crisp part remaining after hog fat or poultry fat has been rendered

crack·ly (-lē) ***adj.*** crackling or tending to crackle

crack·nel (krak′nəl) ***n.*** ⟦ME *crakenelle,* altered < OFr *craquelin* < MDu *krakeling* < *kraken;* akin to CRACK[1]⟧ **1** a variety of hard, crisp biscuit **2** [*pl.*] small pieces of crisply fried fat pork **3** [*pl.*] cracklings

crack of doom ⟦phr. in *Macbeth,* IV, i⟧ the signal for the beginning of Judgment Day

crack·pot (krak′pät′) [Informal] ***n.*** ⟦< *cracked pot* < CRACK[1] + POT[1] in obs. sense, "cranium, brainpan"⟧ a mentally unbalanced or eccentric person; often, specif., a person who holds or is a proponent of a highly unorthodox or eccentric belief —***adj.*** by or characteristic of a crackpot [*crackpot* conspiracy theories]

cracks·man (kraks′mən) ***n.***, *pl.* **-men** (-mən) ⟦< CRACK[1] (***vt.*** *9a*) + MAN⟧ [Old Slang] a burglar or safecracker

crack·up (krak′up′) ***n.*** a cracking up; specif., *a)* a crash, as of an airplane *b)* [Informal] a mental or physical breakdown; collapse

☆**crack·y** (krak′ē) ***interj.*** [Archaic] used to express surprise or provide emphasis: now only in the interjectional phrase **by cracky**

Cra·cow (kra′kou, krā′-; -kō) *var. of* KRAKÓW

-cra·cy (krə sē) ⟦Fr *-cracie* < ML *-cratia* < Gr *-kratia,* rule < *kratos,* rule, strength: see HARD⟧ *combining form* a (specified) type of government; rule by [*autocracy, theocracy*]

cra·dle (krād′'l) ***n.*** ⟦ME *cradel* < OE *cradol* < **kradula,* little basket; akin to OHG *kratto,* basket < IE base **ger-,* to twist, turn > CRANK[1], CRAMP[1], CREEK⟧ **1** a baby's small bed, usually on rockers **2** the earliest period of one's life; infancy **3** the place of a thing's beginning or early development [the *cradle* of civilization] **4** [Old Poet.] a place of rest [rocked in the *cradle* of the deep] **5** anything resembling a cradle or used somewhat like a cradle, as for holding or rocking; specif., *a)* wooden or metal framework to support or lift a boat, ship, aircraft, etc. that is being built or repaired ☆*b)* CREEPER (sense 7) *c)* the support on which the handset of a telephone (**cradle telephone**) rests when not in use *d) Agric.* a frame fastened to a scythe (**cradle scythe**) so that the grain can be laid evenly as it is cut *e) Med.* a frame for keeping bedclothes from touching an injured limb, etc. ☆*f) Mining* a boxlike device on rockers, for washing the gold out of gold-bearing sand —***vt.*** **-dled, -dling** **1** to place, rock, or hold in or as in a cradle **2** to take care of in infancy; nurture **3** to cut (grain) with a cradle scythe ☆**4** *Mining* to wash (gold-bearing sand) in a cradle —***vi.*** [Obs.] to lie in or as in a cradle —***adj.*** from birth or by way of upbringing [a *cradle* Catholic, one's *cradle* language] —**rob the cradle** to take as one's sweetheart or one's spouse a person much younger than oneself

cradle cap [Informal] a skin condition in infants characterized by a yellowish, greasy crust on the scalp, usually caused by an excessive flow of sebum

cra·dle·song (-sôŋ′) ***n.*** a lullaby

craft (kraft, kräft) ***n.*** ⟦ME < OE *cræft,* strength, power; akin to Ger *kraft,* strength, force (sense "skill" only in E) < IE **grep-* < base **ger-,* to twist, turn (see CRADLE): basic sense "cramping of muscles during exertion of strength"⟧ **1** a special skill, art, or dexterity **2** *a)* any occupation or avocation requiring special skills, especially manual ones, including carpentry, sewing, pottery, etc. *b)* any of various hobbies in which things are made by hand, including painting, origami, scrapbooking, etc. **3** an article or articles made by a process using manual skills **4** the members of a skilled trade **5** skill in deceiving or underhanded planning; guile; slyness **6** *pl.* **craft** ⟦prob. < phr. *vessels of small craft,* lit., of small power⟧ a boat, ship, or aircraft —***vt.*** to make with skill, artistry, or precision: usually in pp. —***adj.*** **1** of, for, or having to do with a CRAFT (sense 2) [*craft* paper, a *craft* store] **2** designating or of beer or ale produced by a microbrewery —***SYN.*** ART[1]

-craft (kraft, kräft) ⟦< prec.⟧ *combining form* the work, skill, or practice of

crafts·man (krafts′mən, kräfts′-) ***n.***, *pl.* **-men** (-mən) **1** a worker in a skilled trade; artisan **2** any highly skilled, painstaking, technically dexterous worker, specif. in the manual arts —**crafts′man·ship′** ***n.***

crafts·per·son (-pur′sən) ***n.***, *pl.* **-per′sons** or **-peo′ple** (-pē′pəl) CRAFTSMAN: used to avoid the masculine implication of *craftsman*

crafts·wom·an (krafts′woom′ən) ***n.***, *pl.* **-wom′en** (-wim′in) a woman who works in a skilled trade or a craft; artisan

craft union a labor union to which only workers in a certain trade, craft, or occupation can belong: distinguished from INDUSTRIAL UNION

craft·y (kraf′tē, kräf′-) ***adj.*** **craft′i·er, craft′i·est** ⟦ME *crafti,* powerful, sly: see CRAFT & -Y[2]⟧ subtly deceitful; sly; cunning; artful [a *crafty* rascal] —***SYN.*** SLY —**craft′i·ly** ***adv.*** —**craft′i·ness** ***n.***

crag[1] (krag) ***n.*** ⟦ME < Celt, as in Welsh *craig,* Ir *carraig,* Gael *creag* < IE base **kar-,* HARD⟧ a steep, rugged rock that rises above others or projects from a rock mass

crag[2] (krag) ***n.*** ⟦ME *cragge* < MDu *crage:* for IE base see CRAW⟧ [Chiefly Scot.] the neck, throat, or craw

crag·gy (krag′ē) ***adj.*** **-gi·er, -gi·est** having many crags; steep and rugged: also **crag′ged** (-id) —**crag′gi·ness** ***n.***

crags·man (kragz′mən) ***n.***, *pl.* **-men** (-mən) an expert climber of crags

Craig[1] (krāg) ***n.*** a masculine name

Craig[2] (krāg), **Edward (Henry) Gordon** 1872-1966; Brit. theatrical designer & director

Crai·gie (krā′gē), Sir **William Alexander** 1867-1957; Eng. lexicographer, born in Scotland

Cra·io·va (krä yô′və) city in SW Romania

crake (krāk) ***n.***, *pl.* **crakes** or **crake** ⟦ME *crak* < ON *kraka,* CROW[1]⟧ any of several rails with long legs and a short bill; esp., the corncrake

cram (kram) ***vt.*** **crammed, cram′ming** ⟦ME *crammen* < OE *crammian,* to squeeze in, stuff; akin to MHG *krammen,* grip with claws < IE **grem-,* to press, compress (> L *gremium,* lap, bosom) < base **ger-,* to hold, seize⟧ **1** to fill (a space) beyond normal capacity by pressing or squeezing; pack full or too full **2** to stuff; force [to *cram* papers into a drawer] **3** to feed to excess; stuff with food **4** to prepare (a student) or review (a subject) for an examination in a hurried, intensive way —***vi.*** **1** to eat too much or too quickly **2** to study or review a subject in a hurried, intensive way, as in preparation for an examination —***n.*** **1** a crowded condition; crush **2** the act of cramming for an examination —**cram′mer** ***n.***

Cram (kram), **Ralph Adams** 1863-1942; U.S. architect & writer

cram·bo (kram′bō′) ***n.*** ⟦< ? L *crambe,* cabbage (as in *crambe repetita,* lit., cabbage repeatedly served, hence repeated story, old tale) < Gr *krambē*⟧ an old game in which players find rhymes for words or lines of verse given by each other

cram·oi·sy or **cram·oi·sie** (kram′oi zē′, kram′ə zē) [Archaic] ***adj.*** ⟦Fr *cramoisi* < It *cremesi* < Ar *qirmizī,* scarlet-hued: see CARMINE⟧ crimson —***n.*** crimson cloth

cramp[1] (kramp) ***n.*** ⟦ME *crampe* < OFr, bent, twisted < Frank **kramp;* akin to MDu & MLowG *krampe:* for IE base see CRADLE⟧ **1** a sudden, painful, involuntary contraction of a muscle or muscles from chill, strain, etc. **2** partial local paralysis, as from excessive use of muscles **3** [*usually pl.*] abdominal or uterine spasms and pain —***vt.*** to cause a cramp or cramps in: often in the passive

cramp[2] (kramp) ***n.*** ⟦MDu *krampe,* lit., bent in, hence anything bent in; akin to prec.⟧ **1** a metal bar bent to form a right angle at each end, for holding together blocks of stone, timbers, etc.: also called **cramp iron** **2** a device for clasping or fastening things together; a clamp **3** anything that confines or hampers **4** a cramped condition or part —***vt.*** **1** to fasten with or as with a cramp **2** to confine; hamper; restrain **3** to turn (the front wheels of an automobile, etc.) sharply —***adj.*** CRAMPED —**cramp someone's style** [Slang] to hamper someone's usual skill or confidence in doing something

cramped (krampt) ***adj.*** **1** confined or restricted [*cramped* quarters] **2** irregular and crowded, as some handwriting

cramp·fish (-fish′) ***n.***, *pl.* **-fish′** or **-fish′es** (see FISH) ELECTRIC RAY

cram·pon (kram′pən, -pän′) ***n.*** ⟦Fr < Frank **krampo,* iron hook; akin to CRAMP[2]⟧ **1** either of a pair of iron hooks for raising heavy weights **2** either of a pair of spiked iron plates fastened on shoes to prevent slipping Also **cram·poon** (kram po͞on′)

Cra·nach (krä′näkh, kran′ək), **Lu·cas** (lo͞o′käs) 1472-1553; Ger. painter & engraver

☆**cran·ber·ry** (kran′ber′ē, -bər ē) ***n.***, *pl.* **-ries** ⟦< Du *kranebere,* LowG *kraan-*

bere, lit., crane berry: name used by early settlers in U.S., replacing earlier Brit *fen berry*⟧ **1** a firm, sour, edible, red berry, the fruit of any of several trailing evergreen shrubs (genus *Vaccinium*) of the heath family **2** any of these shrubs

whooping crane

☆**cranberry bush** (*or* **tree**) a North American viburnum (*Viburnum trilobum*) bearing clusters of white flowers and juicy, red fruit, often used for preserves

crane (krān) *n.* ⟦ME < OE *cran:* akin to Du *kraan,* Ger *kranich* < IE **gr-on* < base **ger-*: see CROW[1]⟧ **1** *pl.* **cranes** or **crane** *a)* any of a family (Gruidae) of usually large gruiform wading birds with very long legs and neck, and a long, straight bill *b)* popularly, any of various unrelated birds, as herons and storks **2** any of various machines for lifting or moving heavy weights by means of a movable projecting arm or a horizontal beam traveling on an overhead support **3** any device with a swinging arm fixed on a vertical axis [a fireplace *crane* is used for holding a kettle] — *vt., vi.* **craned, cran′ing 1** to raise or move with a crane **2** to stretch (the neck) as a crane does, as in straining to see over something

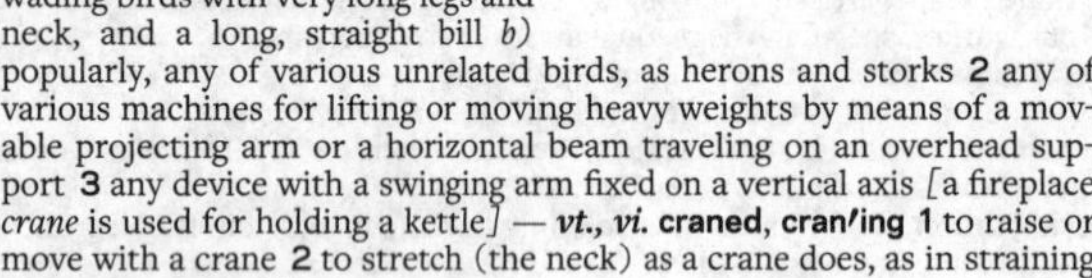

Crane (krān) **1 (Harold) Hart** 1899-1932; U.S. poet **2 Stephen** 1871-1900; U.S. novelist & short-story writer

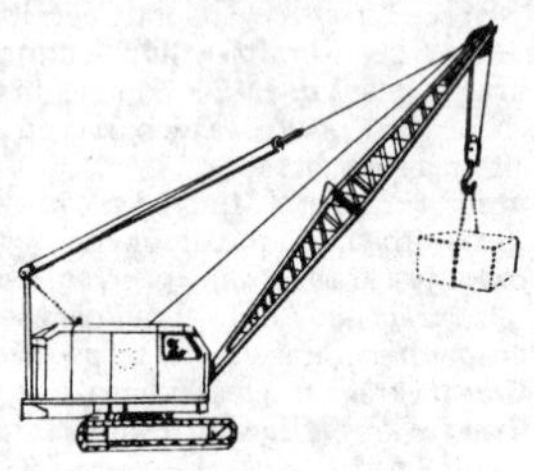

crawler crane

crane fly any of a family (Tipulidae) of slender, mosquitolike dipterous flies with long legs

cranes·bill or **crane's-bill** (krānz′ bil′) *n.* GERANIUM (sense 1)

cra·ni·al (krā′nē əl) *adj.* of or from the cranium —**cra′ni·al·ly** *adv.*

cranial index CEPHALIC INDEX: see BRACHYCRANIAL, MESOCRANIAL

cranial nerve a peripheral nerve coming from the brainstem: many animals, including humans, have twelve pairs of such nerves, including the olfactory, optic, trigeminal, facial, and auditory nerves

cra·ni·ate (krā′nē it, -āt′) *adj.* having a skull or cranium, as fishes, reptiles, birds, and mammals —*n.* a craniate animal

cra·ni·o- (krā′nē ō, -ə) ⟦Gr *kranio-* < *kranion:* see CRANIUM⟧ *combining form* cranium, cranium and [*craniology*]

cra·ni·o·fa·cial (krā′nē ō fā′shəl) *adj.* of or having to do with both the cranium and the face

cra·ni·ol·o·gy (krā′nē äl′ə jē) *n.* the scientific study of skulls, esp. human skulls, and their characteristics, including differences in size, shape, etc.

cra·ni·om·e·ter (-äm′ət ər) *n.* an instrument for measuring skulls

cra·ni·om·e·try (-äm′ə trē) *n.* the science of measuring skulls; cranial measurement

cra·ni·o·sa·cral (krā′nē ō sā′krəl) *adj.* **1** of the cranium and sacrum **2** PARASYMPATHETIC

cra·ni·ot·o·my (krā′nē ät′ə mē) *n., pl.* **-mies** the surgical operation of opening the skull

cra·ni·um (krā′nē əm) *n., pl.* **-ni·ums** or **-ni·a** (-ə) ⟦ML < Gr *kranion* < IE base **ker-* > HORN, L *cerebrum,* Ger *hirn,* brain⟧ **1** the skull **2** the bones forming the enclosure of the brain; brainpan **3** the skull, excluding the lower jaw

crank[1] (kraŋk) *n.* ⟦ME < OE *cranc-,* as in *crancstæf,* yarn comb, CRINGE, CRINKLE: basic sense "something twisted": for IE base see CRADLE⟧ **1** a handle or arm bent at right angles and connected to a shaft of a machine, used to transmit motion or to change rotary motion into reciprocating motion, or vice versa **2** [Informal] *a)* a person who has odd, stubborn notions about something; eccentric *b)* an irritable, complaining person; cranky person **3** [Archaic] a bend or turn **4** [Rare] *a)* a fanciful or unusual turn of speech or thought; conceit *b)* a strange or fantastic action or idea; whim; caprice —*vt.* **1** to form into the shape of a crank **2** to start or operate by means of a crank **3** [Rare] to provide with a crank —*vi.* **1** to turn a crank, as in starting an engine or operating a device **2** [Obs.] to wind and twist; zigzag —☆**crank out** [Informal] to produce at a steady and prolific rate: used to suggest automatic or machinelike production [an author who *cranks out* bestsellers] —**crank up** [Informal] **1** to get started ☆**2** to increase, esp. to a high level, the loudness, speed, etc. of [to *crank up* the volume on a stereo]

crank[2] (kraŋk) *adj.* ⟦earlier *crank sided* < Du or Fris *krengd,* laid over (< *krengan,* to push over, lit., make cringe; akin to CRINGE): assimilated in form to prec.⟧ **1** *Naut.* CRANKY (sense 5) **2** loose and shaky: said of machinery

crank[3] (kraŋk) *adj.* ⟦LME *cranke* < ?⟧ **1** [Now Dial.] high-spirited; lively **2** self-confident in a swaggering way

crank·case (kraŋk′kās′) *n.* the metal casing that encloses the crankshaft of an internal-combustion engine: see OIL PAN

cran·kle (kraŋ′kəl) *n., vi., vt.* **-kled, -kling** ⟦freq. of CRANK[1]⟧ [Archaic] bend, twist, or crinkle

crank·ous (krȧŋ′kəs) *adj.* [Scot.] cranky; ill-tempered; irritable

crank·pin (kraŋk′pin′) *n.* the offset part, often a cylindrical bar or pin, of a crank or crankshaft to which a connecting rod is attached: also written **crank pin**

crank·shaft (-shaft′) *n.* a shaft having one or more cranks for transmitting motion: see CONNECTING ROD

crank·y (kraŋ′kē) *adj.* **crank′i·er, crank′i·est 1** in poor condition; apt to operate poorly **2** irritable; cross **3** odd; eccentric **4** [Rare] full of turns; crooked **5** *Naut.* liable to lurch or capsize; unstable —*SYN.* IRRITABLE —**crank′i·ly** *adv.* —**crank′i·ness** *n.*

Cran·mer (kran′mər), **Thomas** 1489-1556; Eng. churchman: archbishop of Canterbury (1533-56)

cran·nied (kran′ēd) *adj.* full of crannies or chinks

cran·nog (kran′əg) *n.* ⟦Ir < *crann,* a tree, mast, beam⟧ an ancient Irish or Scottish lake dwelling, built on an artificial island or shallows

cran·ny (kran′ē) *n., pl.* **-nies** ⟦ME *crani* < OFr *cran, cren,* a notch < OIt *crena,* a groove < VL, a notch: see CRENATE⟧ a small, narrow opening; crack, as in a wall

☆**crap**[1] (krap) *n.* ⟦see CRAPS⟧ **1** CRAPS (sense 1) **2** a losing first throw at craps —**crap out 1** to lose at craps by throwing a two, three, or twelve on the first throw or a seven after one's point has been established **2** [Slang] to fail, withdraw, give up, etc. because of exhaustion, cowardice, etc.

crap[2] (krap) [Slang] *n.* ⟦ME, chaff, siftings < OFr *crape,* scale, ordure or ML *crappa,* chaff, prob. < Gmc **krappa,* a hook, scale⟧ **1** excrement: somewhat vulgar ☆**2** nonsense, falseness, insincerity, etc. ☆**3** something useless, inferior, or worthless; trash; junk —*vi.* **crapped, crap′ping** to defecate: somewhat vulgar —☆*interj.* used to express anger, disgust, surprise, etc.: somewhat vulgar —**crap′py** *adj.* **-pi·er, -pi·est**

crape (krāp) *n.* ⟦Fr *crêpe:* see CREPE⟧ **1** CREPE (sense 1) **2** a piece of black crepe as a sign of mourning, often worn as a band around the arm —*vt.* **craped, crap′ing** [Rare] to cover with black crepe

☆**crape·hang·er** (-haŋ′ər) *n.* [Slang] a pessimist or killjoy

☆**crape myrtle** ⟦so named because of its crinkled, crepelike flowers⟧ an ornamental shrub (*Lagerstroemia indica*) of the loosestrife family, widely grown in the S U.S., with usually pinkish flowers

crap·per (krap′ər) *n.* ⟦< CRAP[2]⟧ [Slang] TOILET (*n.* 4): somewhat vulgar

☆**crap·pie** (krap′ē) *n., pl.* **-pies** or **-pie** ⟦< ?⟧ any of a genus (*Pomoxis*) of small North American sunfishes found in sluggish streams and ponds throughout E and central U.S.; specif., the black crappie or white crappie

☆**craps** (kraps) *pl.n.* ⟦Fr *crabs, craps* < obs. E *crabs,* lowest throw at hazard, two aces⟧ **1** a gambling game played with two dice: a first throw of seven or eleven wins, and a first throw of two, three, or twelve loses, while any other first throw, to win, must be repeated before a seven is thrown **2** CRAP[1] (sense 2)

☆**crap·shoot** (krap′sho͞ot′) *n.* [Informal] a situation or undertaking whose outcome involves a high probability of failure or loss; gamble

☆**crap·shoot·er** (krap′sho͞ot′ər) *n.* a gambler at craps

crap·u·lence (krap′yo͞o ləns) *n.* ⟦< CRAPULENT < LL *crapulentus* < L *crapula:* see fol.⟧ **1** sickness caused by excess in drinking or eating **2** gross intemperance, esp. in drinking —**crap′u·lent** *adj.*

crap·u·lous (-ləs) *adj.* ⟦LL *crapulosus* < L *crapula,* drunkenness < Gr *kraipalē,* drunken headache < ?⟧ **1** characterized by intemperance, esp. in drinking; debauched **2** sick from such intemperance

craque·lure (krak lo͝or′) *n.* ⟦Fr < *craqueler,* CRACKLE (*vt.* 2)⟧ **1** the network of fine cracks found on the surface of some oil paintings, caused primarily by the shrinkage of aging paint, varnish, and ground **2** CRACKLE (*n.* 3*a*)

crash[1] (krash) *vi.* ⟦ME *crashen,* prob. echoic var. of *craken* (see CRACK[1]); akin to Dan *krase,* to crackle, Ger *krach,* crash, disaster < *krachen,* to crack⟧ **1** to fall, collide, or break with force and with a loud, smashing noise **2** *a)* to make a sudden, loud noise, as of something falling and shattering *b)* to move or go with such a noise **3** to fall or land violently out of control so as to be damaged or smashed: said of aircraft **4** to come to sudden ruin; collapse; fail [their business *crashed*] ☆**5** [Slang] *a)* to sleep *b)* to get a place to sleep temporarily ☆**6** [Slang] to come down swiftly from the euphoria induced by a drug ☆**7** *Comput.* to become inoperable because of a malfunction in the equipment or an error in the program —*vt.* **1** to break or dash into pieces; smash; shatter **2** to cause (a car, airplane, etc.) to crash **3** to cause to make a crashing sound **4** to force or impel with or as with a crashing noise: with *in, out, through,* etc. ☆**5** [Informal] to get into (a party, theater, etc.) without an invitation, ticket, etc. —*n.* **1** a loud, sudden noise, as of something falling and shattering **2** a breaking or smashing into pieces **3** a crashing, as of a car or an airplane **4** a sudden fall, collapse, or ruin, esp. of business or a business enterprise —*adj.* [Informal] designed for urgent, concentrated implementation and speedy results [a *crash* diet, a *crash* course in Greek] —*SYN.* BREAK

crash[2] (krash) *n.* ⟦earlier *crasko, crasho,* "Russian linen," prob. contr. < Russ *krašenina,* colored linen < *krasit',* to color < *krasa,* beauty⟧ a coarse cotton or linen cloth with a plain, loose weave, used for towels, curtains, clothes, etc. and in bookbinding

Crash·aw (krash′ô), **Richard** 1613?-49; Eng. religious poet

crash dive a sudden emergency dive by a submarine to escape from attack —**crash′-dive′** *vi.* **-dived′, -div′ing**

crash helmet a thickly padded, protective helmet worn by racing-car drivers, motorcyclists, aviators, etc.

crash·ing (krash′iŋ) *adj.* [Informal] thorough; complete [*a crashing* bore]

crash-land (krash′land′) *vt., vi.* to bring (an airplane) down in a forced landing, esp. without use of the landing gear, so that some damage results —**crash landing**

crash pad ☆[Slang] a place to live or sleep temporarily

crash·wor·thy (krash′wur′thē) *adj.* able to protect its passengers from the effects of a crash or collision: said of a vehicle —**crash′wor′thi·ness** *n.*

crass (kras) *adj.* ⟦L *crassus,* thick, gross, fat, akin to *cratis:* see CRATE⟧ **1** grossly stupid, dull, or obtuse **2** tasteless, insensitive, and coarse **3** money-grubbing; blatantly materialistic —**crass′ly** *adv.* —**crass′ness** *n.,* **cras′si·tude′** (-ə to͞od′, -ə tyo͞od′)

Cras·sus (kras′əs), **(Marcus Licinius)** 115?-53 B.C.; Rom. statesman & general

-crat (krat) ⟦Fr *-crate* < Gr *kratēs* < *kratos,* rule, strength: see HARD⟧ *combining form* participant in or supporter of (a specified kind of) government or ruling body [*democrat, aristocrat*]

cratch (krach) *n.* ⟦ME *crecche* < OFr *grecha,* crib: see CRÈCHE⟧ [Brit. Dial.] a bin or rack for fodder

crate (krāt) *n.* ⟦L *cratis,* wickerwork, hurdle < IE base **kert-,* to weave > HURDLE⟧ **1** *a)* a large basket or hamper of wickerwork, or a box or case made of slats of wood, for packing things to be shipped or stored *b)* a box or case with wire or slatted sides, as for confining an animal **2** [Slang] an old, decrepit automobile or airplane —☆*vt.* **crat′ed, crat′ing** to pack or enclose in a crate

cra·ter (krāt′ər) *n.* ⟦L, mixing bowl (for wine), mouth of a volcano < Gr *kratēr* < *kerannynai,* to mix: see IDIOSYNCRASY⟧ **1** in ancient Greece or Rome, a kind of large bowl or jar shaped like an amphora **2** a bowl-shaped cavity, as at the mouth of a volcano or geyser **3** a pit resembling this, specif. one caused by a bomb or by the impact of a meteorite, as on the moon **4** ⟦L, bowl, vessel for liquids⟧ [**C-**] *Astron.* a S constellation between Hydra and Corvus —*vt.* to make craters in —*vi.* **1** to form craters **2** [Slang] to fail completely

cra·ter·ing (-iŋ) *n.* **1** the process in which many craters are formed on a surface, as on a moon **2** the resulting craters

Crater Mound huge, circular depression in central Ariz., believed to have been made by a meteorite: depth, 600 ft (183 m); diameter, 0.75 mi (1.2 km)

☆**C ration** ⟦< C(OMBAT)⟧ a canned ration used in the field in WWII and later

cra·ton (krā′tän) *n.* ⟦ult. < Gr *kratos,* strength: see HARD⟧ a stable, broad, horizontal rock formation of the earth's crust, that is the principal part of a continent and its continental shelf —**cra·ton·ic** (krə tän′ik) *adj.*

craunch (krănch, krônch) *vt., vi., n.* ⟦earlier form of CRUNCH: orig. echoic⟧ *dial. var. of* CRUNCH

cra·vat (krə vat′) *n.* ⟦Fr *cravate* < *Cravate,* Croat, Croatian < Ger *Krawat,* dial. form of *Kroat* < Croatian *Hrvat:* so applied in Fr in reference to scarves worn by Croatian soldiers⟧ **1** a neckerchief or scarf **2** a necktie

crave (krāv) *vt.* **craved, crav′ing** ⟦ME *craven* < OE *crafian,* lit., to demand as right < base of *cræft,* strength, might: see CRAFT⟧ **1** to ask for earnestly; beg **2** to long for eagerly; desire strongly **3** to be in great need of —*vi.* to have a strong desire (*for*) —*SYN.* DESIRE —**crav′er** *n.*

cra·ven (krā′vən) *adj.* ⟦ME *cravant* < OFr < *cravanté,* pp. of *cravanter,* to break < VL **crepantare,* to cause to burst < L *crepare,* to rattle, creak < IE **krep-* < base **ker-* > RAVEN[1]⟧ very cowardly; abjectly afraid —*n.* a thorough coward —*SYN.* COWARDLY —**cra′ven·ly** *adv.* —**cra′ven·ness** *n.*

crav·ing (krā′viŋ) *n.* an intense and prolonged desire; yearning or appetite, as for affection or a food or drug

craw (krô) *n.* ⟦ME *craue* < OE **craga,* akin to MLowG *krage,* MDu *kraghe,* Ger *kragen,* collar, orig., neck < IE base **gwer-,* to swallow > L *vorare,* to devour⟧ **1** the crop of a bird or insect **2** the stomach of any animal —**to stick in the** (or **someone's**) **craw** to be unacceptable or displeasing to someone

☆**craw·dad** (krô′dad′) *n.* ⟦fanciful alteration of fol.⟧ [Dial.] CRAYFISH

craw·fish (-fish′) *n., pl.* **-fish′** or **-fish′es** (see FISH) CRAYFISH —*vi.* [Informal] to withdraw from a position; back down

crawl[1] (krôl) *vi.* ⟦ME *craulen* < ON *krafla* < Gmc base **krab-,* **kreb-,* to scratch (> Ger *krabbeln*): for IE base see CRAB[1]⟧ **1** *a)* to move slowly by dragging the body along the ground, as a worm does *b)* to move slowly by dragging the body along the ground, as by pulling with the hands, as a very young baby does **2** to go on hands and knees; creep **3** to move or go slowly or feebly **4** to move or act in an abjectly servile manner **5** to swarm or teem (*with* crawling things) —*n.* **1** the act of crawling; slow movement **2** *Swimming* a stroke in which one lies prone, with the face in the water except when turned briefly sideward for breathing, and uses alternate overarm strokes and a flutter kick **3** a bulletin, explanation, or credits run up or across a TV screen **4** [Brit. Slang] PUB-CRAWL —**make someone's flesh** (or **skin**) **crawl** to give someone a feeling of fear or repugnance, as if insects were crawling on his or her skin —**crawl′er** *n.*

SYN.—**crawl,** in its strict usage, suggests movement by dragging the prone body along the ground [*a snake crawls*] and, figuratively, connotes abjectness or servility; **creep** suggests movement, often furtive, on all fours [*a baby creeps*] and, figuratively, connotes slow, stealthy, or insinuating progress

crawl[2] (krôl) *n.* ⟦WIndDu *kraal* < Sp *corral:* see CORRAL⟧ an enclosure in shallow water for confining fish, turtles, etc.

☆**crawler tractor** a tractor with a continuous roller belt over cogged wheels on each side, for moving over rough or muddy ground

☆**crawl space** an unfinished space of limited height, as under a roof or floor, allowing access to wiring, plumbing, etc.

crawl·y (krôl′ē) *adj.* **crawl′i·er, crawl′i·est** CREEPY

cray·fish (krā′fish′) *n., pl.* **-fish′** or **-fish′es** (see FISH) ⟦altered, by assoc. with FISH < ME *crevise* < OFr *crevice* < OHG *krebiz:* see CRAB[1]⟧ ☆**1** any of various families of small, usually freshwater decapods somewhat resembling little lobsters **2** SPINY LOBSTER **3** the flesh of a crayfish used as food, esp. in Cajun and Creole cooking

cray·on (krā′ən, -än′) *n.* ⟦Fr, pencil < *craie,* chalk < L *creta,* chalk, white earth, prob. < (*terra*) *creta,* sifted (earth) < pp. of *cernere,* to sift: see CRISIS⟧ **1** a small stick of chalk, charcoal, or colored wax, used for drawing, coloring, or writing **2** a drawing made with crayons — *vt., vi.* to draw or color with crayons —**cray′on·ist** *n.*

craze (krāz) *vt.* **crazed, craz′ing** ⟦ME *crasen,* to crack, break < Scand, as in Dan *krase,* to crackle, Swed *krasa,* to break up⟧ **1** [Obs.] to break or shatter **2** to cause to become mentally ill; make insane **3** to produce a crackled surface or small cracks in the glaze of (pottery, porcelain, etc.) —*vi.* **1** to become mentally ill **2** [Now Rare] to break, shatter, crack, etc. **3** to become finely cracked, as the glaze of pottery —*n.* **1** an exaggerated enthusiasm; mania **2** something that is currently the fashion; fad **3** a crack in glaze or enamel, as of pottery —*SYN.* FASHION

cra·zy (krā′zē) *adj.* **-zi·er, -zi·est** ⟦< prec.⟧ **1** *a)* having flaws or cracks *b)* shaky or rickety; unsound **2** [Informal] *a)* unsound of mind; mentally unbalanced or deranged; psychopathic; insane *b)* of or for an insane person: now usually regarded as a demeaning or offensive use **3** temporarily unbalanced, as with great excitement or rage **4** [Informal] foolish, wild, fantastic, etc.; not sensible [*a crazy* idea] **5** [Informal] very enthusiastic or eager [*crazy* about the movies] —☆*interj.* [Slang] used to express approval, pleasure, wonder, etc.: now rare —☆*n., pl.* **-zies** [Slang] an eccentric or mentally unbalanced person —☆**like crazy** [Informal] with great energy, intensity, etc.; without restraint —**cra′zi·ly** *adv.* —**cra′zi·ness** *n.*

☆**crazy bone** FUNNY BONE

Crazy Horse (Dakota name *Ta-sunko-witko*) 1842?-77; Dakota Indian chief

☆**crazy quilt** **1** a quilt made of pieces of cloth of various colors, patterns, shapes, and sizes **2** anything formed of incongruous or miscellaneous parts; patchwork; hodgepodge

☆**cra·zy·weed** (-wēd′) *n.* LOCOWEED

C-re·ac·tive protein (sē′rē ak′tiv) ⟦< *C-(polysaccharide) reactive*⟧ **1** a globulin in the blood produced by the liver in response to inflammation **2** a blood test for detecting the presence of this globulin so as to measure the level of inflammation, as in estimating the likelihood of a heart attack

creak (krēk) *vi.* ⟦ME *creken,* to make a sound like geese, crows, etc.; echoic var. of *croken:* see CROAK⟧ **1** to make a harsh, shrill, grating, or squeaking sound, as rusted hinges do **2** to move slowly with or as with such a sound —*n.* such a sound

creak·y (krēk′ē) *adj.* **creak′i·er, creak′i·est** creaking or apt to creak —**creak′i·ly** *adv.* —**creak′i·ness** *n.*

cream (krēm) *n.* ⟦ME *creme* < OFr *craime, cresme,* prob. blend of LL(Ec) *chrisma* (see CHRISM) & VL *crama* < Celt base (as in Bret *crammen,* skin, surface), ult. < IE base **(s)ker-,* to cut > L *corium,* hide⟧ **1** the oily, yellowish part of milk, which rises to the top and which may be separated: commercial cream contains 18% or more butterfat **2** any of various foods or confections made of cream or having a creamy consistency [*ice cream*] **3** a cosmetic or emulsion with a creamy consistency **4** the best or finest part **5** the color of cream; yellowish white —*adj.* **1** containing cream; made of cream **2** having the consistency of cream; creamy **3** cream-colored —*vi.* **1** to form into cream or a foamy substance **2** to form cream or a creamy foam on top —*vt.* **1** to remove the cream from **2** *a)* to remove, use, etc. the best part of *b)* to remove, use, etc. (the best or most desirable items) (usually with *off*) **3** to add cream to **4** to cook with cream or a cream sauce **5** to beat into a creamy consistency; make into a creamy mixture **6** to let (milk) form cream **7** to separate as cream ☆**8** [Slang] *a)* to beat, thrash, or defeat soundly *b)* to hurt, damage, etc., as by striking with great force —**cream of** creamed purée of [*cream of* tomato soup] —**cream of the crop** the best of a group

cream cheese a soft, white, unripened cheese made of cream or of milk enriched with cream and not ripened

cream-col·ored (-kul′ərd) *adj.* yellowish-white

☆**cream·cups** (-kups′) *n., pl.* **-cups′** an annual plant (*Platystemon californicus*) of the poppy family, with small, cream-colored flowers, native to the SW U.S.: also written **cream cups**

cream·er (krēm′ər) *n.* ☆**1** a small pitcher for cream **2** a device for separating cream from milk **3** a nondairy substance that is used in place of cream, as in coffee

☆**cream·er·y** (-ər ē) *n., pl.* **-er·ies** ⟦Fr *crèmerie:* see CREAM & -ERY⟧ **1** a place where milk and cream are pasteurized, separated, and bottled, and butter and cheese are made **2** a shop where dairy products are sold

cream of tartar a white, acid, crystalline substance, $KC_4H_5O_6$, used in baking powder, medicine, etc.; potassium hydrogen tartrate

☆**cream puff** **1** a hollow pastry filled with custard or whipped cream **2** [Informal] something, esp. something for sale, that is old or secondhand but in excellent condition: said as of an automobile or house: also **cream′puff′** *n.* **3** [Slang] a weak or ineffective person; a sissy

cream sauce a sauce made of butter and flour cooked together with milk or cream

cream sherry a dark, sweet sherry that is made by sweetening oloroso

☆**cream soda** soda pop, usually colorless, that is flavored with vanilla

cream·ware (krēm′wer′) *n.* cream-colored, glazed earthenware popular in the 18th and 19th cent.

cream·y (krēm′ē) *adj.* **cream′i·er, cream′i·est 1** full of cream **2** *a)* like cream in consistency; oily, smooth, etc. *b)* of the color of cream; yellowish-white —**cream′i·ness** *n.*

crease[1] (krēs) *n.* ⟦earlier *creaste,* lit., ridge < ME *creste, crece,* CREST⟧ **1** a line, mark, or ridge made by folding and pressing cloth, paper, etc. *[*the *crease* in trousers*]* **2** a fold or wrinkle *[creases* in a jowl*]* **3** *Cricket* any of the lines that mark off the station of the batsman or of the bowler **4** *Hockey, Lacrosse* an area marked off by lines in front of or around the goal cage, which cannot be entered by players on the offense except under certain conditions —*vt.* **creased, creas′ing 1** to fold and make a crease in **2** to wrinkle; muss ☆**3** to graze and injure slightly with a bullet —*vi.* to become creased —**creas′er** *n.* —**creas′y** *adj.*

crease[2] (krēs) *n. alt. sp. of* KRIS

cre·ate (krē āt′; *often* krē′āt′) *vt.* **-at′ed, -at′ing** ⟦ME *createn* < L *creatus,* pp. of *creare,* to create < IE **krē-,* var. of base **ker-,* to grow, cause to grow > CEREAL⟧ **1** to cause to come into existence; bring into being; make; originate; esp., to make or design (something requiring art, skill, invention, etc.) **2** to bring about; give rise to; cause *[*new industries *create* new jobs*]* **3** to invest with a new rank, function, etc. **4** to be the first to portray (a particular role in a play) —*adj.* [Archaic] created

cre·a·tine (krē′ə tēn′, -tin) *n.* ⟦< Gr *kreas,* flesh (see CRUDE) + -INE[3]⟧ a crystalline substance, $C_4H_9N_3O_2$, present in muscle tissue, usually in the form of phosphocreatine

cre·at·i·nine (krē at′ə nēn′, -nin) *n.* ⟦Ger *kreatinin* < *kreatin* (see prec.) + -INE[3]⟧ the anhydride of creatine, $C_4H_7N_3O$, found in blood, muscle, and esp. urine, where measurement of its excretion is used to evaluate kidney function

cre·a·tion (krē ā′shən) *n.* ⟦ME *creacion* < L *creatio*⟧ **1** a creating or being created **2** the universe and everything in it; all the world **3** anything created; esp., something original created by the imagination; invention, design, etc. —**the Creation** *Theol.* God's creating of the world

cre·a·tion·ism (-iz′əm) *n. Theol.* **1** the doctrine that God creates a new soul for every human being born: opposed to TRADUCIANISM **2** a doctrine that ascribes the origin of matter, species, etc. to acts of creation by God, often, specif., such a doctrine that rejects Darwinian evolution and upholds the description of Creation in the Book of Genesis —**cre·a′tion·ist** *n.*

creation science teaching and research based upon the belief that the biblical account of the creation of the world is scientific fact

cre·a·tive (krē āt′iv) *adj.* ⟦ML *creativus*⟧ **1** creating or able to create **2** having or showing imagination and artistic or intellectual inventiveness *[creative* writing*]* **3** stimulating the imagination and inventive powers *[creative* toys*]* **4** imaginatively or inventively deceptive *[creative* accounting*]* —**cre·a′tive·ly** *adv.* —**cre·a′tive·ness** *n.*

cre·a·tiv·i·ty (krē′ā tiv′ə tē) *n.* creative ability; artistic or intellectual inventiveness

cre·a·tor (krē āt′ər) *n.* ⟦ME *creatour* < L *creator*⟧ one who creates —**the Creator** God; the Supreme Being

crea·ture (krē′chər) *n.* ⟦OFr < L *creatura*⟧ **1** anything created, animate or inanimate **2** an animate or living being; esp., ☆*a)* [Chiefly Dial.] a domestic animal, specif. a horse *b)* a human being (often used in a patronizing, contemptuous, commiserating, or endearing sense) *c)* a strange or imaginary being **3** one completely dominated by another or dependent on another —**the creature** whiskey or other intoxicating liquor: humorous usage —**crea′tur·al** *adj.*, **crea′ture·ly**

creature comfort anything providing bodily comfort, as food, clothing, or shelter

crèche (kresh, krāsh) *n.* ⟦Fr < OFr *greche* < Frank **kripja,* CRIB⟧ **1** a display, typically in miniature, of a stable with figures, as at Christmas, representing a scene at the birth of Jesus **2** an institution for foundlings **3** [Chiefly Brit.] a day nursery

Cré·cy (krā sē′; *E* kres′ē) village in N France: scene of an English victory (1346) over the French in the HUNDRED YEARS' WAR: also **Cré·cy-en-Pon·thieu** (-än pōn tyë′)

cred (kred) *n.* ⟦prob. shortened < STREET CRED⟧ [Slang] credibility and acceptance, as in a particular field: see also STREET CRED

cre·dal (krēd′'l) *adj.* of a creed or creeds; creedal

cre·dence (krēd′'ns) *n.* ⟦OFr < ML *credentia* < L *credens,* prp. of *credere*: see CREED⟧ **1** belief, esp. in the reports or testimony of another *[*to give *credence* to rumors*]* **2** credentials: now only in the phrase LETTERS OF CREDENCE **3** *Eccles.* a small table at the side of the altar for the bread, wine, etc. used in the Eucharistic service —*SYN.* BELIEF

cre·den·da (kri den′də) *pl.n., sing.* **-den′dum** (-dəm) ⟦L, pl. of ger. of *credere:* see CREED⟧ doctrines to be believed; matters of faith

cre·dent (krēd′'nt) *adj.* **1** [Rare] giving credence; believing **2** [Obs.] credible

cre·den·tial (kri den′shəl) *adj.* ⟦ME *credencial* < ML *credentialis:* see CREDENCE⟧ [Rare] entitling to credit, confidence, etc.; accrediting —*n.* [*usually pl.*] **1** anything giving evidence that someone is entitled to or deserving of credit, confidence, etc. **2** a document that serves as official proof of a person's position, authority, etc.; specif., LETTERS OF CREDENCE —*vt.* **-tialed** or **-tialled, -tial·ing** or **-tial·ling** to furnish with credentials

cre·den·tial·ism (kri den′shəl iz′əm) *n.* reliance, often excessive reliance, on a person's credentials, specif. academic degrees, as indicators of his or her abilities or potential for success as an employee

cre·den·za (kri den′zə) *n.* ⟦It, buffet holding foods to be tasted before serving, orig., faith, confidence (in *fare la credenza,* to make confidence, to taste) < ML *credentia,* CREDENCE⟧ **1** a type of buffet or sideboard **2** a low cabinet for use as in an office

☆**credibility gap 1** an apparent disparity between what is said and the actual facts **2** the inability to have one's statements accepted as factual or one's professed motives accepted as the true ones

cred·i·ble (kred′ə bəl) *adj.* ⟦ME < L *credibilis* < *credere:* see CREED⟧ that can be believed; believable; reliable —*SYN.* PLAUSIBLE —**cred′i·bil′i·ty** *n.*, **cred′i·ble·ness** —**cred′i·bly** *adv.*

cred·it (kred′it) *n.* ⟦Fr *crédit* < It *credito* < L *creditus,* pp. of *credere:* see CREED⟧ **1** belief or trust; confidence; faith **2** [Rare] the quality of being credible or trustworthy **3** *a)* the favorable estimate of a person's character; reputation; good name *b)* one's influence based on one's reputation **4** praise or approval to which one is entitled; commendation *[*to deserve *credit* for trying*]* **5** a person or thing bringing approval or honor *[*a *credit* to the team*]* **6** *a)* acknowledgment of work done or assistance given *b)* [*pl.*] a list of such acknowledgments in a film, television program, book, etc. **7** *a)* the amount of money remaining in a bank account, etc. *b)* a sum of money made available by a bank, on which a specified person or firm may draw *c)* such sums collectively **8** *Accounting a)* the acknowledgment of payment on a debt by entry of the amount in an account *b)* the right-hand side of an account, where such amounts are entered *c)* an entry on this side *d)* the sum of such entries *e)* sum deducted (from an amount owed) or added (as to a bank account) in making an adjustment **9** *Business a)* trust in one's integrity in money matters and one's ability to meet payments when due *b)* one's financial reputation or status *c)* the time allowed for payment *d)* permission to pay later for goods or services, or a system for doing so *[*a store that extends *credit* to its best customers*]* ☆**10** *Educ. a)* the certification of a student's successful completion of a unit or course of study *b)* a unit of work so certified —*vt.* **1** to believe in the truth, reliability, etc. of; trust **2** to give credit to or deserved commendation for **3** to give credit in a bank account, charge account, etc. **4** [Rare] to bring honor to **5** *Accounting* to enter on the credit side ☆**6** *Educ.* to enter a credit or credits on the record of (a student) —*SYN.* ASCRIBE —**credit someone with** to believe that someone has or is responsible for; ascribe to someone —**do credit to** to bring approval or honor to —**give credit to 1** to have confidence or trust in; believe **2** to commend —**give one credit for 1** to commend one for **2** to believe or recognize that one has —**on credit** with the agreement that payment will be made at a future date —**to one's credit** bringing approval or honor to one

cred·it·a·ble (kred′i tə bəl) *adj.* **1** deserving some credit or praise **2** ascribable (*to*) **3** [Obs.] credible **4** [Obs.] having good financial credit —**cred′it·a·bil′i·ty** *n.* —**cred′it·a·bly** *adv.*

☆**credit bureau** an agency that is a clearinghouse for information on the credit rating of individuals or firms

☆**credit card** a thin, plastic, machine-readable card with which the cardholder can charge purchases, obtain cash loans at an ATM, etc.

cred·it-de·fault swap (kred′it dē fôlt′, -di fôlt′) *Finance* a contract stipulating that the parties exchange the exposure to loss should a creditor default

credit hour a unit of academic credit: see HOUR (*n.* 7)

☆**credit line 1** a printed acknowledgment of work done or assistance given, as on a newspaper article or film **2** LINE OF CREDIT

cred·i·tor (kred′it ər) *n.* ⟦ME *creditour* < L *creditor:* see CREDIT⟧ a person who extends credit or to whom money is owed

☆**credit rating** the rating given to an individual or business firm as a credit risk, based on past records of debt repayment, financial status, etc.

☆**credit union** a cooperative association for pooling savings of members and making loans to them at a low rate of interest

cred·it·wor·thy (kred′it wur′thē) *adj.* considered sufficiently sound financially to be granted credit: also sp. **credit-worthy** —**cred′it·wor′thi·ness** *n.*

cre·do (krē′dō′, krā′-) *n., pl.* **-dos′** ⟦ME < L, I believe: see CREED⟧ **1** CREED **2** [*usually* **C-**] *a)* the Apostles' Creed or the Nicene Creed, both of which (in Latin) begin with *credo b)* a musical setting for either of these

cre·du·li·ty (krə do͞o′lə tē, -dyo͞o′-) *n.* ⟦ME *credulite* < OFr < L *credulitas* < *credulus*: see fol.⟧ a tendency to believe too readily, esp. with little or no proof; lack of skepticism

cred·u·lous (krej′oo ləs, -ə ləs) *adj.* ⟦L *credulus* < *credere:* see CREED⟧ **1** tending to believe too readily; easily convinced **2** resulting from or indicating credulity —**cred′u·lous·ly** *adv.* —**cred′u·lous·ness** *n.*

Cree (krē) *n.* ⟦Fr *Cri,* shortened < earlier *Cristinaux* < 17th-c. Algonquin *kirishtinoo,* name of a band of Cree Indians⟧ **1** *pl.* **Crees** or **Cree** a member of a North American Indian people living mainly in the Canadian Prairie Provinces **2** the Algonquian language of this people

creed (krēd) *n.* ⟦ME *crede* < OE *creda* < L *credo,* lit., I believe (< *credere,* to trust, believe < IE **kred-dhē-,* to attribute magic power to, believe < base **kred-,* magic power of a thing + **dhē-,* to place, DO[1]⟧ **1** a brief statement of religious belief; confession of faith **2** a specific statement of this kind, accepted by a church **3** any set of beliefs or principles **4** a religious affiliation —**the Creed** the Apostles' Creed —**creed′al** *adj.*

creek (krēk, krik) *n.* ⟦ME (rare) *creke* (> mod. pronun. krēk), ME (common) *crike* (> pronun. krik) < ON *kriki,* a bend, winding, hence winding inlet, akin to OFris *kreke,* MDu *creke*: for IE base see CRADLE⟧ **1** [Now Chiefly Brit.] a narrow inlet or bay ☆**2** a small stream, somewhat larger than a brook 3 [Obs.] a narrow or winding passage —☆**up the** (or **a**) **creek (without a paddle)** [Slang] in trouble

Creek (krēk, krik) ***n.*** ⟦shortened < earlier *Ochese Creek Indians,* 17th-c. name for the Indians of the upper Ocmulgee River in Georgia⟧ **1** *pl.* **Creeks** or **Creek** a member of a cultural and political grouping (the **Creek Confederacy**) of North American Indian peoples, mainly Muskogean, formerly of Georgia and Alabama, now living in Oklahoma and Florida: see SEMINOLE **2** the Muskogean language used as a lingua franca in the Creek Confederacy; Muskogee

creel (krēl) ***n.*** ⟦ME *crel* < OFr *grail:* see GRIDDLE⟧ **1** a wicker basket, canvas bag, etc. for holding fish, often worn over the shoulder by a person who fishes **2** a basketlike cage for trapping fish, shellfish, etc. **3** a frame or rack for holding the bobbins or spools in spinning or weaving

creep (krēp) ***vi.*** **crept, creep′ing** ⟦ME *crepen* < OE *creopan,* to creep, lit., go bent down; akin to Swed *krypa* < IE base **ger-:* see CRADLE⟧ **1** to move along with the body close to the ground, as on hands and knees, in the way that a baby does **2** to move slowly, stealthily, timidly, or furtively **3** to come on gradually and almost unnoticed: often with *up* **4** to cringe; fawn **5** to grow along the ground or a wall, as some plants **6** to slip slightly out of position ☆**7** to change in shape as the result of constant stress, temperature, etc.: said of materials, metals, etc. —***n.*** **1** the act of creeping **2** a creeping movement **3** the gradual deformation of a material, esp. a metal or alloy, due to constant stress, high temperature, etc. ☆**4** [Slang] a person regarded as very annoying, disgusting, etc. **5** *Geol.* the slow, almost imperceptible movement of soil and loose rock down a slope —**SYN.** CRAWL[1] —**creep out** *pt. & pp.* **creeped** [Slang] to make frightened or disgusted —**make one's flesh** (or **skin**) **creep** to give one a feeling of fear, repugnance, etc. —**the creeps** [Informal] a feeling of fear, repugnance, etc.

creep·age (krē′pij′) ***n.*** a gradual creeping movement

creep·er (-pər) ***n.*** **1** a person, animal, or thing that creeps **2** any plant whose stem puts out tendrils or rootlets by which it can creep along a surface as it grows *[the Virginia creeper]* **3** any of various small passerine birds (esp. family Certhiidae) that creep on trees, bushes, or walls looking for insects, larvae, etc. to eat, including the wall creeper, certain wood warblers, etc. **4** a device with metal hooks for dragging the bottom of a lake, pond, etc.; grapnel ☆**5** [*usually pl.*] a metal plate with spikes, fastened to a shoe to prevent slipping **6** any device for carrying material to or from a machine, or from one part of a machine to another ☆**7** a low frame or platform on wheels or casters, for a mechanic to lie on when working under an automobile **8** a very low gear as on a truck, for dragging heavy loads, climbing steep inclines, etc.: in full **creeper gear** ☆**9** [*pl.*] a baby's one-piece garment, combining pants and shirt

creeping bent grass a type of bent grass (*Agrostis stolonifera* var. *palustris*) grown in moist places and often used for golf greens

creeping eruption a skin eruption with intense itching, caused by the burrowing of various larvae under the skin

creep·y (krē′pē) ***adj.*** **creep′i·er, creep′i·est** **1** creeping; moving slowly **2** having or causing a feeling of fear or disgust, as if insects were creeping on one's skin —**creep′i·ly** ***adv.*** —**creep′i·ness** ***n.***

creep·y-crawl·y (krē′pē krôl′ē) ***n.***, *pl.* **-ies** ⟦redupl. based on CREEP + CRAWL[1]⟧ [Slang] something, as a crawling insect or spider, regarded as frightening and repugnant

creese (krēs) ***n.*** *alt. sp. of* KRIS

cre·mains (krē mānz′) ***pl.n.*** ⟦blend of fol. & REMAINS⟧ the ashes remaining after a body has been cremated

cre·mate (krē′māt′, kri māt′) ***vt.*** **-mat′ed, -mat′ing** ⟦< L *crematus,* pp. of *cremare,* to burn < IE base **ker-,* to burn > HEARTH, L *carbo,* coal⟧ to burn up, esp. to burn (a dead body) to ashes —**cre·ma′tion** ***n.*** —**cre′ma′tor** ***n.***

cre·ma·to·ry (krē′mə tôr′ē, krem′ə-) ***n.*** ⟦ModL *crematorium*⟧ **1** a furnace for cremating dead bodies **2** a building with such a furnace in it Also **cre′ma·to′ri·um** (-ē əm), *pl.* **-ri·ums, -ri·a** (-ē ə), or **-ries** —***adj.*** of or for cremation: also **cre′ma·to′ri·al**

creme (krēm) ***n.*** CREAM (*n.* 2 & 3) *[creme-filled tortes]* —***adj.*** CREAM (*adj.* 1 & 2) *[creme rinses for dry hair]*

crème (krem, krēm; *Fr* krem) ***n.*** ⟦Fr⟧ **1** cream **2** a thick liqueur

crème an·glaise (krem′ äŋ glāz′; *Fr* krem än glez′) ⟦Fr, lit., English cream⟧ [*sometimes in italics*] a custardlike cream sauce, often flavored with vanilla, served with fresh fruit, rich chocolate desserts, etc.

crème brû·lée (krem′bro͞o lā′; *Fr* krem brü lā′) ⟦Fr, lit., burnt cream⟧ a rich custard covered with a crust formed of caramelized sugar

crème de ca·ca·o (krem′ də kō′kō′; -kə kā′ō, -kā′-) ⟦Fr, lit., cream of CACAO (*n.* 2)⟧ a sweet liqueur, brown or colorless, with a chocolate flavor

crème de cas·sis (krem də ka sēs′) ⟦Fr, lit., cream of black currant⟧ a sweet, purplish-red liqueur flavored with black currants

crème de la crème (krem′də lä krem′) ⟦Fr, lit., cream of the cream⟧ the very best

crème de menthe (krem′ də mänt′, menth′, mint′) ⟦Fr, lit., cream of mint⟧ a sweet liqueur, green or colorless, flavored with mint

crème fraîche (krem′ fresh′; *Fr* krem fresh′) ⟦Fr, lit., fresh cream; prob. orig. as distinct from buttermilk, butter, etc.⟧ slightly fermented high-fat cream, milder than sour cream, served with fresh fruit or other desserts and used in sauces

cre·mi·ni (mushroom) (kri mē′nē) ⟦< It, pl. of *cremino* < *crema,* cream⟧ a brown mushroom having a somewhat firmer texture and stronger flavor than the more common white edible mushroom

Cre·mo·na (kri mō′nə; *It* kre mô′nä) commune in Lombardy, N Italy, on the Po River: famous (fl. 16th-17th cent.) for making Amati, Guarnerius, & Stradivarius violins —**Crem·o·nese** (krem′ə nēz′, -nēs′) ***adj.***

cre·nate (krē′nāt′) ⟦ModL *crenatus* < VL *crena,* a notch, groove < IE **(s)krei-,* to separate: see CRISIS⟧ ***adj.*** having a notched or scalloped edge, as certain leaves: also **cre′nat′ed** —**cre′nate′ly** ***adv.***

cre·na·tion (kri nā′shən) ***n.*** **1** the condition of being crenate **2** a crenate formation; specif., *a)* a CRENATURE (sense 1) *b)* the shrunken, notched appearance of a red blood cell, as when exposed to extremely salty solutions

cren·a·ture (kren′ə chər, krē′nə-) ***n.*** ⟦CRENAT(E) + -URE⟧ **1** a rounded projection, as on the margin of a leaf, etc. **2** a notch between such projections

cren·el (kren′əl) ***n.*** ⟦OFr, dim. < VL *crena,* a notch: see CRENATE⟧ any of the indentations or loopholes in the top of a battlement or wall; embrasure: also **cre·nelle** (kri nel′) —***vt.*** **-eled** or **-elled, -el·ing** or **-el·ling** to crenelate

cren·el·ate or **cren·el·late** (kren′əl āt′) ***vt.*** **-el·at′ed** or **-el·lat′ed, -el·at′ing** or **-el·lat′ing** ⟦Fr *créneler* (< OFr *crenel:* see prec.) + -ATE[1]⟧ to furnish with battlements or crenels, or with squared notches —**cren′el·a′tion** ***n.***, **cren′el·la′tion**

cren·shaw melon (kren′shô′) ⟦< ?⟧ a large winter melon with greenish-yellow skin and sweet, salmon-colored flesh

cren·u·late (kren′yo͞o lit, -lāt′) ***adj.*** ⟦ModL *crenulatus* < *crenula,* dim. < VL *crena,* a notch, groove⟧ having tiny notches or scallops, as some leaves or shells: also **cren′u·lat′ed** (-lāt′id)

cren·u·la·tion (kren′yo͞o lā′shən) ***n.*** ⟦see prec.⟧ **1** a tiny notch or scallop **2** the condition of having tiny notches or scallops

cre·o·dont (krē′ə dänt′) ***n.*** ⟦< ModL *Creodonta,* pl. < Gr *kreas,* flesh (see CRUDE) + *odous,* TOOTH⟧ any of a former suborder (Creodonta) of small, primitive, extinct carnivores with small brains

Cre·ole (krē′ōl′) ***n.*** ⟦Fr *créole* < Sp *criollo* < Port *crioulo,* native to the region, born at home < *criar,* to rear, nourish < L *creare,* CREATE⟧ **1** a person of European parentage born in the West Indies, Central America, tropical South America, or the Gulf States **2** a descendant of such persons; specif., ☆*a)* a person descended from the original French settlers of Louisiana, esp. of the New Orleans area ☆*b)* a person descended from the original Spanish settlers in the Gulf States, esp. Texas ☆*c)* a person of mixed Creole and black descent **3** French as spoken by Creoles, esp. in the New Orleans area: distinguished from CAJUN ☆**4** loosely, anyone from Louisiana **5** [**c-**] the form of language (e.g., Gullah) that develops when speakers of mutually unintelligible languages remain in persistent and long-lasting contact with each other, with one of the contributing languages typically dominant —***adj.*** **1** of or characteristic of the Creoles **2** designating or of the languages of the Creoles ☆**3** [*usually* **c-**] prepared with sautéed tomatoes, green peppers, onions, etc. and spices *[creole sauce]*

cre·ol·ize (krē′ə līz′) ***vt.*** **-ized′, -iz′ing** to cause (a pidgin) to develop into a CREOLE (*n.* 5) —***vi.*** to develop into a CREOLE (*n.* 5) —**cre′ol·i·za′tion** ***n.***

Cre·on (krē′än′) ***n.*** ⟦Gr *Kreōn*⟧ *Gr. Legend* a king of Thebes who has his niece Antigone entombed alive because she defies him: see ANTIGONE

cre·o·sol (krē′ə sôl′, -sōl′) ***n.*** ⟦< fol. + -OL[1]⟧ a colorless, pungent, oily liquid, $CH_3OC_6H_3(CH_3)OH$, obtained from beechwood tar and the resin guaiac: it is used as an antiseptic and is an active part of creosote

cre·o·sote (krē′ə sōt′) ***n.*** ⟦Ger *kreosot* < Gr *kreas* (gen. *kreōs*), flesh (see CRUDE) + *sōtēr,* savior < *sōzein,* to save, preserve < IE base **teu-,* to swell (> TUMOR); so named (1832) by K. v. Reichenbach (1788-1869), Ger scientist⟧ **1** a transparent, oily liquid with a pungent odor, obtained by the distillation of wood tar and used as an antiseptic **2** a black, oily liquid with a pungent odor, obtained by the distillation of coal tar and used as a wood preservative —***vt.*** **-sot′ed, -sot′ing** to treat (wood, etc.) with creosote

☆**creosote bush** an evergreen shrub (*Larrea divaricata*) of the caltrop family with a pungent odor like that of creosote, found in N Mexico and the SW U.S.

crepe or **crêpe** (krāp; *for 3, also* krep) ***n.*** ⟦Fr *crêpe* < L *crispus:* see CRISP⟧ **1** a thin, crinkled cloth of silk, rayon, cotton, wool, etc.; crape **2** *a)* CRAPE (sense 2) *b)* CREPE RUBBER **3** a very thin pancake, generally served rolled up or folded with a filling: usually sp. *crêpe*

crepe de Chine (krāp′ də shēn′) ⟦Fr *crêpe de Chine,* lit., crepe of China⟧ [*also* **c- de c-**] a soft, rather thin crepe, usually of silk, used for blouses, lingerie, etc.

crepe myrtle CRAPE MYRTLE

crepe paper thin paper crinkled like crepe

crepe rubber soft rubber in sheets with a wrinkled surface, used for shoe soles

crêpes su·zette (krāp′ so͞o zet′; *Fr* krep sü zet′) ⟦Fr < pl. of *crêpe,* CREPE + *Suzette,* dim. of *Suzanne*⟧ crêpes that are rolled or folded and heated in an orange-flavored sauce and usually served in flaming brandy

cre·pey (krāp′ē) ***adj.*** wrinkled like crepe cloth or paper

crep·i·tate (krep′ə tāt′) ***vi.*** **-tat′ed, -tat′ing** ⟦< pp. of L *crepitare,* freq. of *crepare:* see CRAVEN⟧ to make slight, sharp, repeated crackling sounds; crackle —**crep′i·tant** ***adj.*** —**crep′i·ta′tion** ***n.***

crept (krept) ***vi.*** *pt. & pp. of* CREEP

cre·pus·cu·lar (kri pus′kyo͞o lər) ***adj.*** ⟦see fol.⟧ **1** of or like twilight; dim **2** active at twilight or just before sunrise *[crepuscular insects]*

cre·pus·cule (kri pus′kyo͞ol′) ***n.*** ⟦Fr *crépuscule* < L *crepusculum,* dim. < *creper,* dark⟧ twilight; dusk: also **cre·pus′cle** (-pus′əl)

cre·scen·do (kri shen′dō′) ***adj., adv.*** ⟦It, prp. of *crescere,* to grow < L: see fol.⟧ [*also in italics*] *Music* with a gradual increase in loudness: often used as a musical direction, indicated by the sign < —***n.***, *pl.* **-dos′** **1** [*also in italics*] *Music* *a)* a gradual increase in loudness *b)* a crescendo passage **2** any gradual increase in force, intensity, etc. **3** loosely, a state of great loudness, intensity, etc. —*vi.* **-doed′**, **-do′ing** to increase gradually in loudness or intensity

cres·cent (kres′ənt) *n.* ⟦altered (infl. by L) < ME *cressaunt* < OFr *creissant,* prp. of *creistre,* to increase < L *crescere,* to come forth, grow, inchoative of *creare:* see CREATE⟧ **1** a phase of a planet or a moon, when it appears to have one concave edge and one convex edge, esp., of the moon just after new moon (**waxing crescent**) or just before new moon (**waning crescent**) **2** a figure of or like the moon in either of these phases **3** anything shaped more or less like this, specif., *a)* a curved roll or bun *b)* a residential street or part of a street **4** ⟦in allusion to the crescent emblem of Turkey⟧ [*also* **C-**] *a)* Turkish or Muslim power *b)* a figure or symbol shaped like a crescent, that represents Turkey or Islam —*adj.* **1** [Old Poet.] increasing; growing **2** shaped like a crescent —**cres·cen·tic** (kri sen′tik) *adj.*

crescent wrench ⟦< *Crescent,* a trademark for this kind of wrench⟧ a wrench with a head shaped like a crescent, having one movable jaw adjusted by a screw to allow the head to fit various sizes of nuts, bolts, etc.: see WRENCH, illus.

cres·cive (kres′iv) *adj.* ⟦< L *crescere* (see CRESCENT) + -IVE⟧ [Rare] growing; increasing

cre·sol (krē′sôl′, -sōl′) *n.* ⟦< CREOSOTE + -OL¹⟧ any of three isomeric, colorless, oily liquids or solids with the formula $CH_3C_6H_4OH$, prepared by the fractional distillation of coal tar and used in the preparation of disinfectants, fumigating compounds, and dyestuffs

cress (kres) *n.* ⟦ME *cresse* < OE *cressa;* akin to Ger *kresse,* cress⟧ any of various plants of the crucifer family, as watercress, the pungent leaves of which are used in salads and as garnishes

cres·set (kres′it) *n.* ⟦ME < OFr *craisset* < *craisse:* see GREASE⟧ a metal container for burning oil, wood, etc., fastened as to a pole or wall and used as a torch or lantern

Cres·si·da (kres′i də) *n. Medieval Legend* a Trojan woman who is unfaithful to her lover, TROILUS

crest (krest) *n.* ⟦ME *creste* < OFr < L *crista,* prob. < IE base *(*s*)*kreis-,* to shake > MIr *cressaim,* I shake, ON *hrista,* to shake⟧ **1** any process or growth on the head of an animal, as a comb or feathered tuft on certain birds **2** a plume or emblem, formerly worn on a helmet **3** a helmet or its apex **4** a heraldic device placed above the shield in a coat of arms, or used separately on seals, silverware, note paper, etc. **5** the top of anything, or the line or surface along the top; summit; ridge [the *crest* of a wave, a mountain *crest*] **6** the highest point, level, degree, etc. **7** *a)* the ridge of the neck of a horse, lion, etc. *b)* the mane growing on this **8** CRESTING **9** a projecting ridge, as along a bone —*vt.* **1** to provide or decorate with a crest **2** to lie at the top of; crown **3** to reach the crest of —*vi.* **1** to form a crest, as a wave **2** to reach its highest level [the flooding river *crested* at 30 feet]

crest·ed (kres′tid) *adj.* having a crest

☆**crested flycatcher** any of various tyrant flycatchers (esp. genus *Myiarchus*) with a prominent crest

crest·fall·en (krest′fôl′ən) *adj.* **1** with drooping crest or bowed head **2** dejected, disheartened, or humbled

crest·ing (kres′tiŋ) *n.* an ornamental ridging on a wall, roof, etc.

cre·syl·ic (kri sil′ik) *adj.* ⟦CRES(OL) + -YL + -IC⟧ **1** of or from cresol or creosote **2** of various acids composed of different mixtures of phenols and used in making plastics, disinfectants, etc.

cre·ta·ceous (kri tā′shəs, krē-) *adj.* ⟦L *cretaceus* < *creta:* see CRAYON⟧ **1** [Now Rare] containing, composed of, or having the nature of, chalk **2** [*usually* **C-**] designating or of the third and last geologic period of the Mesozoic Era, characterized by the formation of huge oil and chalk deposits, the development of the first flowering plants and placental mammals, and the extinction of toothed birds, ammonites, and dinosaurs —**the Cretaceous** the Cretaceous Period or its rocks: see the geologic time chart in the Reference Supplement

Crete (krēt) **1** Greek island in the E Mediterranean: 3,219 sq mi (8,336 sq km); cap. Iraklion: ancient Gr. name KRETE; modern Gr. name KRÍTI **2 Sea of** S section of the Aegean Sea, between Crete and the Cyclades —**Cre·tan** (krēt′'n) *adj., n.*

cre·tin (krēt′'n; *Brit* kre′tin) *n.* ⟦Fr *crétin,* dial. form of *chrétien;* lit., Christian, hence human being (in contrast to brutes) < LL(Ec) *Christianus,* CHRISTIAN: sense development as in SILLY⟧ **1** [Archaic] a person suffering from cretinism **2** a very stupid or foolish person: in this sense, considered offensive by some —**cre′tin·ous** *adj.*

cre·tin·ism (-iz′əm) *n.* ⟦Fr *crétinisme:* see prec.⟧ a congenital deficiency of thyroid secretion with resulting deformity and mental deficiency

cre·tonne (krē tän′, krē′tän′) *n.* ⟦Fr, after *Creton,* village in Normandy, noted for its cloth since the 16th c.⟧ a heavy, unglazed, printed cotton or linen cloth, used for curtains, slipcovers, etc.

Cre·ü·sa (krē yo͞o′sə) *n. Class. Myth.* **1** the bride of Jason, killed by the sorcery of the jealous Medea **2** the wife of Aeneas and daughter of Priam

Creutz·feldt-Ja·kob disease (kroits′felt yä′kōb, -kôp) ⟦after H. *Creutzfeldt* (1885-1964) & A. *Jakob* (1884-1931), Ger neurologists⟧ an incurable degenerative disease of the nervous system, caused by a prion and characterized by neurological impairment, dementia, etc.

cre·val·le (krə val′ē, -ə) *n.* ⟦altered < CAVALLA⟧ JACK (sense 10*a*); esp., the **crevalle jack** (*Caranx hippos*) of the tropical Atlantic

cre·vasse (krə vas′) *n.* ⟦Fr < OFr *crevace,* CREVICE⟧ **1** a deep crack or fissure, esp. in a glacier ☆**2** a break in the levee of a river, dike, etc. —*vt.* **-vassed′**, **-vass′ing** to make a crevasse or crevasses in

Crève·coeur (krev ko͝or′; *Fr* krev kër′), **Mi·chel Guil·laume Jean de** (mē shel′ gē yōm′ zhän də) (pseud. *J. Hector St. John*) 1735-1813; Am. essayist & agriculturist, born in France

crev·ice (krev′is) *n.* ⟦ME *crevace* < OFr < VL **crepacia,* a crack < L *crepare:* see CRAVEN⟧ a narrow opening caused by a crack or split; fissure; cleft; chink —**crev′iced** *adj.*

crew¹ (kro͞o) *n.* ⟦ME *creue,* increase, growth < OFr < pp. of *creistre,* to grow < L *crescere:* see CRESCENT⟧ **1** a group of people associating or classed together; company, set, gang, etc. **2** a group of people working together, usually under the direction of a foreman or leader [a road *crew,* gun *crew*] **3** *a)* all of a ship's personnel, usually excepting the officers *b)* on a small sailboat, the person or persons who assist the helmsman, as by handling the sails **4** AIRCREW: see also GROUND CREW **5** *a)* a rowing team for a racing shell, usually of two, four, six, or eight oarsmen with or without a coxswain *b)* the sport of rowing racing shells **6** [Archaic] an organized band of armed men — *vt., vi.* to serve (on) as the crew or a crew member —**crew′man** *n., pl.* **-men**

crew² (kro͞o) *vi.* [Chiefly Brit.] *alt. pt. of* CROW² (sense 1)

☆**crew cut** a style of man's or boy's haircut in which the hair is cropped close to the head, but left bristly on top to look like a brush

crew·el (kro͞o′əl) *n.* ⟦LME *crule* < ?⟧ **1** a fine, less tightly twisted kind of worsted yarn used in embroidery **2** CREWELWORK

crew·el·work (-wurk′) *n.* embroidery done with crewel

☆**crew neck** a round neckline, as on a sweater, fitting close around the base of the neck

crew sock any of various socks that cover some or all of the ankle, but do not extend over the calf

crib (krib) *n.* ⟦ME & OE, ox stall, couch, akin to Ger *krippe,* Frank **kripja:* basic sense "what is woven or plaited, basket" < IE **grebh-* < base **ger-,* to wind, turn, weave; senses of "steal," etc. < thieves' slang < orig. sense "to put in a basket"; *n.* 4 from biblical application of sense 1⟧ **1** a rack, trough, or box for fodder; manger **2** a stall for cattle, oxen, etc. **3** a small house or room **4** a small bed with high sides, for a baby **5** a framework of wooden or metal bars for support or strengthening, as in a mine **6** a framework or enclosure as for storing grain ☆**7** a structure secured under water, serving as a pier, a water intake, etc. **8** [Informal] *a)* a petty theft *b)* a plagiarism *c)* notes, a translation of a foreign writing, or other aids used, often dishonestly, in doing schoolwork **9** [Slang] the house, apartment, etc. where a person lives **10** *Cribbage* the cards discarded by the players and forming an extra hand for the dealer, counted for points but not played —*vt.* **cribbed, crib′bing 1** to shut up in or as in a crib; confine **2** to furnish with a crib or cribs **3** [Informal] *a)* to steal *b)* to plagiarize —*vi.* **1** to have the habit of CRIB BITING **2** [Informal] to do schoolwork dishonestly, as by using a CRIB (*n.* 8*c*) —**crib′ber** *n.*

crib·bage (krib′ij′) *n.* ⟦< prec. + -AGE⟧ a card game for two players that can be played by three or four, in which the object is to form various combinations that count for points: the score is traditionally kept by moving pegs on a small board (**cribbage board**)

crib·bing (krib′iŋ) *n.* **1** the action of one that cribs **2** something cribbed **3** a timber framework lining a mine shaft **4** CRIB BITING

crib biting a habit that some horses have of biting wood, as the stall door or feeding trough, and at the same time swallowing air —**crib′-bite′** *vi.* **-bit′**, **-bit′ten** or **-bit′**, **-bit′ing**

crib death SUDDEN INFANT DEATH SYNDROME

crib·ri·form (krib′ri fôrm′) *adj.* ⟦< L *cribrum,* sieve, akin to *cervere,* to separate (see CRISIS) + -FORM⟧ perforated like a sieve

crib·work (krib′wurk′) *n.* a supporting framework of beams, logs, etc. built in layers, each layer having its unit at right angles to those of the layer below

cri·ce·tid (krī sēt′id, -set′-) *n.* ⟦< ModL *Cricetidae* < Slav, as in Russ *krysa,* rat or Czech *křeček,* hamster⟧ any of a family (Cricetidae) of rodents, including hamsters and New World rats and mice

crick¹ (krik) *n.* ⟦LME *crykke* < ON *kriki,* bend: see CREEK⟧ a painful muscle spasm or cramp in the neck, back, etc. —*vt.* to cause a crick in

crick² (krik) *n.* ☆*dial. var. of* CREEK (sense 2)

Crick (krik), **Francis H(arry) C(ompton)** 1916-2004; Eng. scientist: helped determine the structure of DNA

crick·et¹ (krik′it) *n.* ⟦ME *criket* < OFr *criquet* < *criquer,* to creak, of echoic orig.⟧ **1** any of various families (esp. Gryllidae) of generally dark-colored, leaping, orthopteran insects usually having long antennae: the males produce a characteristic chirping noise by rubbing parts of the forewings together **2** a small metal toy or signaling device that makes a clicking sound when pressed

crick·et² (krik′it) *n.* ⟦OFr *criquet,* a stake or bat in a ball game; prob. dim. of MDu *cricke,* a stick; akin to CRUTCH⟧ **1** a game played with a red leather ball and a flat wooden bat by two teams of eleven players each on a large field: the teams bat and bowl alternately, the batting team attempting to score runs: the team scoring the most runs wins the game: popular in England and other parts of the Commonwealth **2** [Informal] fair play; sportsmanship —*vi.* to play cricket —**crick′et·er** *n.*

crick·et³ (krik′it) *n.* ⟦< ?⟧ a wooden footstool

cri·coid (krī′koid′) *adj.* ⟦Gr *krikoeidēs,* ring-shaped < *krikos,* ring (akin to *kirkos:* see CIRCUS) + *-eidēs,* -OID⟧ designating or of the ring-shaped cartilage forming the lower part of the larynx

cri de coeur (krēt kër′) ⟦Fr, lit., cry from the heart⟧ an impassioned protest, complaint, etc.

cried (krīd) *vi., vt. pt. & pp. of* CRY

cri·er (krī′ər) *n.* **1** a person who cries **2** *a)* an official who shouts out announcements, as in a court *b)* TOWN CRIER **3** a person who shouts out announcements about his or her wares; huckster

cri·key (krī′kē) *interj.* ⟦euphemism for CHRIST[2]⟧ [Brit. Slang] used to express surprise, wonder, etc.

Crile (krīl), **George Washington** 1864-1943; U.S. surgeon

crim *abbrev.* criminal

crim con *abbrev.* criminal conversation

crime (krīm) *n.* ⟦OFr < L *crimen*, verdict, object of reproach, offense, prob. < IE *(s)krei-* (> SCREAM), extension of base *ker-*: see RAVEN[1]⟧ **1** an act committed in violation of a law prohibiting it, or omitted in violation of a law ordering it; often, specif., such an act of a serious nature, as a felony: crimes are variously punishable by death, imprisonment, or the imposition of certain fines or restrictions: the range of crime includes felonies and misdemeanors, but not petty violations of local ordinances **2** an offense against morality; sin **3** criminal acts, collectively **4** [Informal] something regrettable or deplorable; shame [it's a *crime* you didn't finish school]

Cri·me·a (krī mē′ə, krə-) **1** peninsula south of the mainland of Ukraine, extending into the Black Sea: *c.* 10,000 sq mi (25,900 sq km): formerly with *the*: Russ. name KRIM **2** autonomous republic of Ukraine, coextensive with this peninsula: cap. Simferopol —**Cri·me′an** *adj.*

crime against humanity a mass killing or other atrocity committed in furtherance of a program of genocide

Crimean War a war (1853-56) over the domination of SE Europe, in which Great Britain, France, Turkey, and Sardinia defeated Russia

crime pas·si·on·nel (krēm pä sē ə nel′) *pl.* ***crimes pas·si·on·nels*** (krēm pä′ sē ə nel′) ⟦Fr, lit., a crime pertaining to the passions⟧ a sexually motivated crime; specif., the murder of a spouse, lover, etc., motivated by jealousy: also sp. ***crime pas′si·on·el′***

crim·i·nal (krim′ə nəl) *adj.* ⟦ME < OFr *criminel* < L *criminalis* < *crimen*: see CRIME⟧ **1** having the nature of crime; being a crime **2** *a)* involving or relating to crime *b)* dealing with law cases involving crime (distinguished from CIVIL) **3** guilty of crime **4** [Informal] regrettable or deplorable —*n.* a person guilty of, or legally convicted of, a crime —**crim′i·nal·ly** *adv.*

criminal conversation CONVERSATION (sense 2)

crim·i·nal·ist (krim′ə nəl ist) *n.* ⟦< L *criminalis*, CRIMINAL + -IST[1]: orig., a person or writer learned in criminal law⟧ an expert in the use of scientific methods to investigate crimes, specif. by collecting and analyzing physical evidence; forensic investigator

crim·i·nal·i·ty (krim′ə nal′ə tē) *n.* **1** the quality, state, or fact of being criminal **2** *pl.* **-ties** a criminal action

crim·i·nal·ize (krim′ə nəl īz′) *vt.* **-ized′**, **-iz′ing** to make criminal —**crim′i·nal·i·za′tion** *n.*

criminal law that area of law which deals in any way with crimes and their punishments

criminal lawyer a lawyer whose practice is largely devoted to the defense of those accused of crime

crim·i·nate (krim′ə nāt′) *vt.* **-nat′ed**, **-nat′ing** ⟦< L *criminatus*, pp. of *criminari* < *crimen*: see CRIME⟧ **1** to accuse of a crime or crimes **2** to give proof of the guilt of; incriminate **3** to condemn; censure —**crim′i·na′tion** *n.* —**crim′i·na′tive** *adj.*, **crim′i·na·to′ry** (-nə tôr′ē) —**crim′i·na′tor** *n.*

cri·mi·ni (mushroom) (kri mē′nē) CREMINI MUSHROOM

crim·i·nol·o·gy (krim′ə näl′ə jē) *n.* ⟦< L *crimen*, gen. *criminis* (see CRIME) + -LOGY⟧ the scientific study and investigation of crime and criminals —**crim′i·no·log′i·cal** (-nə läj′i kəl) *adj.* —**crim′i·no·log′i·cal·ly** *adv.* —**crim′i·nol′o·gist** *n.*

crim·i·nous (krim′ə nəs) *adj.* ⟦< OFr *crimineux*, of the nature of a crime < L *criminosus* < *crimen*: see CRIME⟧ [Now Rare] CRIMINAL (senses 2 & 3)

crim·i·ny or **crim·i·ne** (krim′ə nē, krī′mə-) *interj.* ⟦? euphemism for CHRIST[2]⟧ [Slang] used to express surprise, anger, etc.

crim·mer (krim′ər) *n. alt. sp. of* KRIMMER

crimp[1] (krimp) *vt.* ⟦< MDu *crimpen*, to draw together, wrinkle; akin to CRAMP[1]⟧ **1** to press into narrow, regular folds; pleat or corrugate **2** to make (hair, etc.) wavy or curly **3** to gash (the flesh of a fish, etc.) so as to make the muscles contract and stay firm in cooking **4** to mold or bend (leather for shoe uppers, etc.) into shape **5** to pinch together or fold the edge of (one part) tightly over another ☆**6** [Informal] to obstruct or hamper —*n.* **1** the act of crimping **2** a crimped pleat, fold, or part ☆**3** [*usually pl.*] crimped hair ☆**4** wavy condition; esp., the natural waviness of wool fiber —☆**put a crimp in** [Informal] to obstruct; hinder —**crimp′er** *n.*

crimp[2] (krimp) [Historical] *n.* ⟦< prec., prob. in sense of "press, impress"⟧ a person who got men by force or trickery to serve as sailors or soldiers —*vt.* to trick or force (men) into service as sailors or soldiers

crim·ple (krim′pəl) *vt., vi.* **-pled**, **-pling** ⟦ME *crimplen*, freq. of *crimpen*, CRIMP[1]⟧ to wrinkle, crinkle, or crumple

crimp·y (krim′pē) *adj.* **crimp′i·er**, **crimp′i·est** ⟦< CRIMP[1]⟧ having small folds or waves; curly [*crimpy* hair] —**crimp′i·ness** *n.*

crim·son (krim′zən; -sən) *n.* ⟦ME *cremesin* < ML *cremesinum*, ult. < Ar *qirmiz*: see CARMINE⟧ **1** deep red **2** deep-red coloring matter —*adj.* **1** deep-red **2** bloody — *vt., vi.* to make or become crimson

crimson clover an annual clover (*Trifolium incarnatum*) with elongated heads of deep-red flowers, often grown in the S U.S. as a cover or green-manure crop

cringe (krinj) *vi.* **cringed**, **cring′ing** ⟦ME *crengen* (with nasalized vowel as in HINGE), caus. < OE *cringan*, to fall (in battle): for IE base see CRADLE⟧ **1** to draw back, bend, crouch, etc., as when afraid; shrink from something dangerous or painful **2** to act in a timid, servile manner; fawn —*n.* the act of cringing —**cring′er** *n.*

crin·gle (kriŋ′gəl) *n.* ⟦ME < ON *kringla*, circle, or MDu *kringel*, ring, both ult. < IE base *ger-*: see CRADLE⟧ a small loop or ring of rope or metal on the edge of a sail, through which a line may be run for fastening the sail

cri·nite (krī′nīt′) *adj.* ⟦L *crinitus*, pp. of *crinire*, to provide with hair < *crinis*, hair; akin to L *crista*: see CREST⟧ **1** hairy **2** *Bot.* having hairy tufts

crin·kle (kriŋ′kəl) *vi., vt.* **-kled**, **-kling** ⟦ME *crenklen*, freq. < OE *crincan*, var. of *cringan*: see CRINGE⟧ **1** to be or cause to be full of wrinkles, twists, or ripples **2** to rustle or crackle, as paper when crushed —*n.* **1** a wrinkle, twist, or ripple **2** a rustling or crackling sound —**crin′kly** *adj.* **-kli·er**, **-kli·est**

☆**crin·kle·root** (-ro͞ot′) *n.* a toothwort (*Dentaria diphylla*) with small, white or lilac-colored flowers and a white, tuberous, pungent rhizome

crin·kum-cran·kum (kriŋ′kəm kraŋ′kəm) *n.* ⟦redupl. of CRANK[1]⟧ [Archaic] anything full of twists and turns

cri·noid (krī′noid′, krin′oid′) *adj.* ⟦Gr *krinoeidēs*, lilylike < *krinon*, lily + *-eidēs*, -OID⟧ **1** lily-shaped **2** designating or of a class (Crinoidea) of echinoderms, some of which are flowerlike in form and are anchored by a stalk, others of which are free-swimming —*n.* an animal of this class, as a sea lily or feather star

crin·o·line (krin′ə lin, -lēn′) *n.* ⟦Fr < It *crinolino* < *crino*, horsehair (< L *crinis*: see CRINITE) + *lino*, linen < L *linum*: see LINE[2]⟧ **1** a coarse, stiff, heavily sized cloth used as a lining for stiffening garments: orig. made of horsehair and linen **2** a petticoat of this cloth, worn under a skirt to make it puff out **3** HOOP SKIRT

cri·num (krī′nəm) *n.* ⟦ModL < Gr *krinon*, lily⟧ any of a large genus (*Crinum*) of tropical bulbous plants of the lily family, with thick, straplike leaves and large, tubular flowers of white, pink, or red

cri·o·lla (krē ô′yä) *n., pl.* **-llas** (-yäs) ⟦Sp⟧ a woman or girl of Spanish descent born in Spanish America

cri·o·llo (krē ô′yô) *n., pl.* **-llos** (-yôs) ⟦Sp: see CREOLE⟧ **1** a person of Spanish descent born in Spanish America: see also CREOLE **2** any of various domestic animals bred in Latin America —*adj.* designating or of a criollo or criollos

cripes (krīps) *interj.* ⟦euphemism for *Christ*⟧ [Slang] used to express surprise, annoyance, disgust, etc.: also **cripe**

crip·ple (krip′əl) *n.* ⟦ME *cripel* < OE *crypel* (akin to Ger *krüppel*) < base of *creopan*: see CREEP⟧ **1** a person or animal that is lame or otherwise disabled in a way that prevents normal motion of the limbs or body: now somewhat offensive when used to refer to a person ☆**2** [Dial.] thicketed, swampy or low, wet land —*vt.* **-pled**, **-pling** **1** to make cripple of; lame **2** to make unable or unfit to act, function effectively, etc.; disable —**SYN.** MAIM —**crip′pler** *n.*

Cri·sey·de (kri sā′də) *n. var.* (in Chaucer) *of* CRESSIDA

cri·sis (krī′sis) *n., pl.* **-ses′** (-sēz′) ⟦L < Gr *krisis* < *krinein*, to separate, discern < IE *(s)krei-*, to sift, separate < base *(s)ker-*, to cut > SHEAR, L *cernere*, to separate, Ger *rein*, pure⟧ **1** *a)* the turning point of a disease for better or worse, esp. a sudden recovery (see LYSIS) *b)* an intensely painful attack of a disease; paroxysm **2** a turning point in the course of anything; decisive or crucial time, stage, or event **3** a time of, or a state of affairs involving, great danger or trouble, often one which threatens to result in unpleasant consequences [an economic *crisis*] —**SYN.** EMERGENCY

crisp (krisp) *adj.* ⟦ME & OE < L *crispus*, curly, waving < IE base *(s)kreisp-*, to shake > CREST⟧ **1** stiff and brittle; easily broken, snapped, or crumbled [*crisp* bacon, cookies, etc.] **2** fresh and firm [*crisp* celery] **3** fresh and tidy [a *crisp* uniform] **4** sharp and clear [a *crisp* analysis] **5** lively; animated [*crisp* dialogue] **6** fresh and invigorating; bracing [*crisp* air] **7** sharply and squarely hit [a *crisp* tennis shot] **8** closely curled and wiry [*crisp* hair] **9** rippled; wavy; wrinkled —*n.* **1** something crisp; now, specif., *a)* a piece of food, esp. a cookie, that is thin and crisp or contains a crunchy ingredient *b)* something made crisp, as by overcooking (chiefly in the phrase **to a crisp**) [dinner burned *to a crisp*] *c)* a dessert consisting of fruit baked with a crumbly topping as of flour, sugar, and butter [apple *crisp*] **2** [Brit.] POTATO CHIP — *vt., vi.* to make or become crisp —**SYN.** FRAGILE —**crisp′ly** *adv.* —**crisp′ness** *n.*

cris·pa·tion (kris pā′shən) *n.* ⟦< L *crispare* (see prec.) + -ATION⟧ **1** a curling or being curled **2** a slight, involuntary contraction of the muscles or skin

crisp·er (kris′pər) *n.* something that makes or keeps things crisp; specif., the compartment for storing vegetables in a refrigerator

Cris·pin[1] (kris′pin) *n.* ⟦< L *Crispinus* < *crispus*, curled (see CRISP), hence, lit., curly⟧ a masculine name

Cris·pin[2] (kris′pin), Saint (3d cent. A.D.); Rom. Christian martyr: patron saint of shoemakers: his day is Oct. 25

crisp·y (kris′pē) *adj.* **crisp′ier**, **crisp′i·est** CRISP (chiefly senses 1 & 2) —**crisp′i·ness** *n.*

cris·sakes (krī′sāks′) *interj.* [*often* **C-**] [Slang] for Christ's sake: often preceded by *for*: also **cris′sake′**

criss·cross (kris′krôs′) *n.* ⟦ME *Christcros*, Christ's cross, the cross at the head of an alphabet, for the symbol X (Gr χ), abbrev. of Christ (*Christos*)⟧ **1** a mark made of two crossed lines (X), often used as a signature by people who cannot write their names **2** a pattern made of crossed lines **3** a being confused or at cross-purposes —*adj.* marked with or moving in crossing lines —*vt.* **1** to mark or cover with crossing lines **2** to move to and fro across —*vi.* to move crosswise —*adv.* **1** crosswise **2** awry

cris·sum (kris′əm) *n., pl.* **-sa** (-ə) ⟦ModL < L *crissare*, for *crisare*, to move the haunches < IE *(s)kreit- < base *(s)ker-, to turn > L *curvus*: see CURVE⟧ 1 the area under the tail of a bird, around the cloacal opening 2 the feathers covering this

cris·ta (kris′tə) ***n.***, *pl.* **-tae** (-tē) ⟦L, a crest, comb: see CREST⟧ *Anat., Zool.* any of various crestlike structures, as a saclike projection extending inward from the inner membrane of mitochondria

cris·tate (kris′tāt′) ***adj.*** ⟦L *cristatus* < *crista*: see CREST⟧ crested, as some birds: also **cris′tat′ed**

Cris·tó·bal (kris tō′bəl) seaport in Panama, at the Caribbean entrance to the Panama Canal: part of the city of Colón

crit (krit) ***n.*** [Informal] *short for:* 1 CRITICISM (sense 1) 2 CRITIC

cri·te·ri·on (krī tir′ē ən) ***n.***, *pl.* **-ri·a** (-ē ə) or **-ri·ons** ⟦< Gr *kritērion*, means of judging < *kritēs*, judge; akin to *kritikos*: see fol.⟧ a standard, rule, or test by which something can be judged; measure of value —***SYN.*** STANDARD

USAGE—the use of *criteria* as a singular form is becoming more widespread, but is still objected to by many

crit·ic (krit′ik) ***n.*** ⟦L *criticus* < Gr *kritikos*, a critic, orig., critical, able to discern < *krinein*: see CRISIS⟧ 1 *a)* a person who forms and expresses judgments of people or things according to certain standards or values *b)* such a person whose profession is to write or broadcast such judgments of books, music, paintings, sculpture, plays, films, television, etc., as for a newspaper 2 a person who indulges in faultfinding and censure

crit·i·cal (krit′i kəl) ***adj.*** 1 tending to find fault; censorious 2 characterized by careful analysis and judgment [a sound *critical* estimate of the problem] 3 of professional or scholarly critics or criticism; specif., *a)* consisting of or incorporating criticism [a *critical* biography of Wordsworth] *b)* characterized by criticism regarded as emphasizing faults and shortcomings [a highly *critical* movie review] 4 *a)* of or forming a crisis or turning point; decisive [a *critical* moment in history] *b)* necessary; essential [a designated *critical* habitat for an endangered species] 5 dangerous or risky; causing anxiety [a *critical* situation in international relations] 6 of the crisis of a disease 7 designating or of important products or raw materials subject to increased production and restricted distribution under strict control, as in wartime 8 *a)* designating or of a point at which a change in character, property, or condition is effected *b)* designating or of the point at which a nuclear chain reaction becomes self-sustaining: see also CRITICAL POINT 9 designating or of a medical condition in which the patient is at high risk of dying and thus requires special treatment, monitoring, nursing care, etc. —**crit′i·cal′i·ty** (-kal′ə tē) ***n.***, **crit′i·cal·ness** —**crit′i·cal·ly** ***adv.***

SYN.—**critical**, in its strictest use, implies an attempt at objective judging so as to determine both merits and faults [a *critical* review], but it often (and **hypercritical**, always) connotes emphasis on the faults or shortcomings; **faultfinding** implies a habitual or unreasonable emphasis on faults or defects; **captious** suggests a characteristic tendency to find fault with, or argue about, even the pettiest details [a *captious* critic]; **caviling** stresses the raising of quibbling objections on the most trivial points [a *caviling* grammarian]; **carping** suggests peevishness, perversity, or censoriousness in seeking out faults See also **acute**

critical angle 1 *Optics* the smallest possible angle of incidence at which light rays are totally reflected 2 *Aeron.* that angle of attack at which the flow of air around an airfoil suddenly changes, with an abrupt reduction in lift and an increase of drag: see STALL[1] (*n.* 6)

critical constants constant values related to the critical point of a substance, specif. the critical temperature, pressure, density, and volume

critical density the density of a substance measured when it is at its critical temperature and pressure

critical mass 1 the minimum amount of fissile material that can sustain a nuclear chain reaction under a given set of conditions 2 the minimum amount or number required for something to happen, begin, etc.

critical point the physical condition, specified by pressure or density, at which a substance at its critical temperature can exist as a liquid and vapor in equilibrium

critical pressure the minimum pressure necessary to liquefy a gas at its critical temperature

critical temperature that temperature above which a given gas cannot be liquefied, regardless of the pressure applied

critical volume the volume of a unit mass (usually one mole) of a substance measured when it is at its critical temperature and pressure

crit·ic·as·ter (krit′ik as′tər) ***n.*** ⟦CRITIC + -ASTER[2]⟧ an incompetent, inferior critic

crit·i·cise (krit′ə sīz′) ***vi., vt.*** **-cised′**, **-cis′ing** *alt. Brit. sp. of* CRITICIZE

crit·i·cism (krit′ə siz′əm) ***n.*** 1 the act of making judgments; analysis of qualities and evaluation of comparative worth; esp., the critical consideration and judgment of literary or artistic work 2 a comment, review, article, etc. expressing such analysis and judgment 3 the act of finding fault; censure; disapproval 4 the art, principles, or methods of a critic or critics 5 the scientific or scholarly investigation of texts or documents to discover their origin, history, or original form

crit·i·cize (krit′ə sīz′) ***vi., vt.*** **-cized′**, **-ciz′ing** 1 to analyze and judge as a critic 2 to judge disapprovingly; find fault (with); censure —**crit′i·ciz′a·ble** ***adj.*** —**crit′i·ciz′er** ***n.***

SYN.—**criticize**, in this comparison, is the general term for finding fault with or disapproving of a person or thing; **reprehend** suggests sharp or severe disapproval, generally of faults, errors, etc. rather than of persons; **blame** stresses the fixing of responsibility for an error, fault, etc.; **censure** implies the expression of severe criticism or disapproval by a person in authority or in a position to pass judgment; **condemn** and **denounce** both imply an emphatic pronouncement of blame or guilt, **condemn** suggesting the rendering of a judicial decision, and **denounce**, public accusation against persons or their acts —***ANT.*** **praise**

cri·tique (kri tēk′) ***n.*** ⟦Fr < Gr *kritikē (technē)*, critical (art) < *kritikos*: see CRITIC⟧ 1 a critical analysis or evaluation of a subject, situation, literary work, etc. 2 the act or art of criticizing; criticism — ***vt., vi.*** **-tiqued′**, **-tiqu′ing** to analyze and evaluate (a subject, literary work, etc.); criticize

crit·ter (krit′ər) ***n.*** *dial. var. of* CREATURE (esp. sense 2): often sp. **crit′tur**

croak (krōk) ***vi.*** ⟦ME *croken* < OE **cracian* < *cræcettan*, to make sounds like a raven < IE base **ger-* (> CRAKE, CRANE, CROW[2]), of echoic orig.⟧ 1 to make a deep, hoarse sound, as that of a frog or raven 2 to speak in deep, hoarse tones 3 to talk dismally; foretell evil or misfortune; grumble 4 [Slang] to die —***vt.*** 1 to utter in deep, hoarse tones 2 [Slang] to kill —***n.*** a croaking sound —**croak′y** (-ē) ***adj.*** **croak′i·er**, **croak′i·est**

croak·er (-ər) ***n.*** 1 an animal that croaks 2 any of various drum fishes that make croaking or grunting sounds 3 a person who talks dismally or foretells evil 4 [Slang] a doctor

Cro·at (krō′at, -ət; krōt) ***n.*** 1 a person born or living in Croatia 2 CROATIAN (*n.* 2) —***adj.*** CROATIAN

Cro·a·tia (krō ā′shə) country in the NW Balkan Peninsula: at one time part of Austria-Hungary, it was a constituent republic of Yugoslavia (1946-91): 21,831 sq mi (56,542 sq km); cap. Zagreb

Cro·a·tian (krō ā′shən) ***adj.*** of Croatia or its people, language, or culture —***n.*** 1 a Croat 2 the western variety of Serbo-Croatian, written in the Latin alphabet

croc (kräk) ***n.*** [Informal] *short for* CROCODILE

Cro·ce (krô′che; *E* krō′chē), **Be·ne·det·to** (be′ne det′tô) 1866-1952; It. philosopher & critic

cro·chet (krō shā′) ***n.*** ⟦Fr, small hook: see CROTCHET⟧ a kind of needlework in which loops of a thread or yarn are interconnected by means of a single hooked needle (**crochet hook**) — ***vi., vt.*** **-cheted′** (-shād′), **-chet′ing** to do crochet or make by crochet —**cro·chet′er** (-shā′ər) ***n.***

cro·cid·o·lite (krō sid′′l īt′) ***n.*** ⟦< Gr *krokis* (gen. *krokidos*), var. of *krokys*, nap on woolen cloth (akin to *krekein*, to weave: see REEL[3]) + -LITE⟧ a bluish, fibrous amphibole, $Na_2(Fe,Mg)_5Si_8O_{22}(OH)_2$, that is a type of asbestos

crock[1] (kräk) ***n.*** ⟦ME *crokke* < OE *crocca*, akin to Ger *krug* < ? IE base **ger-*, to turn, twist > CRIB⟧ 1 an earthenware pot or jar 2 a broken piece of earthenware ☆3 ⟦clip of *a crock of shit*⟧ [Slang] something that is absurd, insincere, exaggerated, etc.; nonsense

crock[2] (kräk) ***n.*** ⟦Brit dial. < ?⟧ 1 [Dial.] soot; smut 2 coloring matter rubbed off from dyed fabric —***vt.*** [Dial.] to soil with soot or smut —***vi.*** to give off coloring matter: said of dyed fabric

crock[3] (kräk) ***n.*** ⟦< ON *kraki*, a weak, crippled person, orig., a bent object: for IE base see CROCK[1]⟧ 1 an old broken-down horse 2 [Slang] anyone or anything worthless, useless, or worn-out, as from old age 3 [Slang] a medical patient who complains chronically about minor or imaginary illnesses — ***vi., vt.*** [Informal] to make or become disabled; break down; collapse: often with *up*

crocked (kräkt) ***adj.*** ⟦pp. of *crock*, to disable, injure, prob. < or akin to prec.⟧ ☆[Slang] drunk; intoxicated

crock·er·y (kräk′ər ē) ***n.*** ⟦CROCK[1] + -ERY⟧ earthenware pots, jars, dishes, etc.

crock·et (kräk′it) ***n.*** ⟦ME *croket* < NormFr *croquet* (OFr *crochet*): see CROTCHET⟧ a carved ornament, as of curved leaves or flowers, decorating the angles of roofs, gables, etc., esp. in Gothic architecture

Crock·ett (kräk′it), **Da·vy** (dā′vē) (born *David Crockett*) 1786-1836; U.S. frontiersman & politician

crock·pot (kräk′pät′) ***n.*** ⟦< fol.⟧ an electric cooker like a Crock-Pot: also written **crock pot**

Crock-Pot (kräk′pät′) *trademark for* an electric cooker consisting of an earthenware pot inside a container with a heating element that maintains a steady low temperature, used as for simmering stews for several hours

croc·o·dile (kräk′ə dīl′) ***n.*** ⟦ME *cocodril* < OFr *cocodrille* < ML *cocodrillus*, altered < L *crocodilus* < Gr *krokodilos*, lizard (hence, "lizard of the Nile," crocodile) < **krokodrilos* < *krokē*, pebble, gravel (? akin to Sans *śárkarā*, SUGAR) + *drilos*, worm⟧ 1 any of a subfamily (Crocodylinae) of large, flesh-eating, lizardlike crocodilian reptiles living in or around tropical streams and having thick, horny skin composed of scales and plates, a long tail, and a long, narrow, triangular head with massive jaws: it has on each side of the lower jaw a large tooth that protrudes upward from its closed mouth 2 leather made from a crocodile's hide 3 [Brit.] a long line of persons, esp. school children, moving in file, as when out for a walk

Crocodile *another name for* LIMPOPO

crocodile bird a small African courser (*Pluvianus aegyptius*) which feeds on insects that are often parasites on the crocodile

crocodile tears insincere tears or a hypocritical show of grief: from an old belief that crocodiles shed tears while eating their prey

croc·o·dil·i·an (kräk′ə dil′ē ən) ***adj.*** 1 of or like a crocodile 2 of an order (Crocodylia) of reptiles including the crocodile, alligator, caiman, and gavial —***n.*** any reptile of this order

cro·co·ite (krō′kō īt′) ***n.*** ⟦< Gr *krokos*, saffron (see fol.) + -ITE[1]⟧ a reddish, monoclinic mineral, $PbCrO_4$; lead chromate: also **cro·co·i·site** (krō kō′ə sīt′, kräk′wə sīt′)

cro·cus (krō′kəs) ***n.*** ⟦ME < L < Gr *krokos*, saffron, via Sem (as in Heb *karkōm*, Ar *kurkum*, Aram *kūrkāmā*, saffron, crocus), ult. < Sans *kuṅkumam*⟧ **1** *pl.* **cro′cus·es** or **cro′ci′** (-sī′) any of a large genus (*Crocus*) of spring-blooming plants of the iris family, with fleshy corms and a yellow, purple, or white flower **2** an orange-yellow color; saffron **3** powdered iron oxide used for polishing

Croe·sus[1] (krē′səs) ***n.*** ⟦after fol.⟧ a very rich man

Croe·sus[2] (krē′səs) fl. 6th cent. B.C.; last king of Lydia (560-546), noted for his great wealth

croft (krôft) ***n.*** ⟦ME < OE, akin to MDu *krocht*, hill, field among dunes < Gmc **krufta*, lit., that which bends < IE base **ger-*: see CRADLE⟧ [Brit.] **1** a small, enclosed field **2** a small farm, esp. one worked by a renter —**croft′er *n.***

Crohn's disease (krōnz) ⟦after B. B. *Crohn* (1884-1983), U.S. physician, coauthor of an article about the disease (1932)⟧ chronic inflammation of the digestive tract, esp. of the lower small intestine and colon, which may develop thick scars

crois·sant (krə sänt′; *Fr* krwȧ sän′) ***n., pl.*** **-sants′** (-sänts′, *Fr*, -sän′) ⟦Fr, lit., CRESCENT: used in 19th c. to translate Ger *hörnchen* (lit., little horn); such rolls or cakes, shaped like the emblem of Turkey, were originated in Vienna to celebrate defeat of the Turks in 1689⟧ a rich, flaky bread roll made in the shape of a crescent

Croix de Guerre (krwȧd ger′) ⟦Fr, cross of war⟧ a French military decoration for bravery in action

Cro-Mag·non (krō mag′nən, -man′yən) ***adj.*** ⟦after the *Cro-Magnon* cave, Dordogne department, SW France, where remains were discovered⟧ belonging to a prehistoric, Caucasoid type of human who lived on the European continent, distinguished by tallness and erect stature, and by the use of stone and bone implements, principally of Aurignacian culture —***n.*** a member of this group

crom·lech (kräm′lek′) ***n.*** ⟦Welsh < *crom*, bent, crooked + *llech*, flat stone⟧ **1** DOLMEN **2** a Neolithic monument of megaliths, arranged in a circle and surrounding a mound or dolmen

Cromp·ton (krämp′tən), **Samuel** 1753-1827; Eng. inventor of the spinning mule (1779)

Crom·well (kräm′wel, -wəl; krum′-) **1 Oliver** 1599-1658; Eng. revolutionary leader & head (Lord Protector) of the Commonwealth (1653-58) **2 Richard** 1626-1712; Lord Protector of the Commonwealth (1658-59): son of Oliver **3 Thomas** Earl of Essex 1485?-1540; Eng. statesman

Cromwell current ⟦after T. *Cromwell* (1922-58), U.S. oceanographer⟧ a strong, equatorial, subsurface current flowing east across the Pacific Ocean under the weaker, western-flowing equatorial surface currents

crone (krōn) ***n.*** ⟦ME term of abuse: beast, hag (revived by Sir Walter SCOTT[2] in mod. sense) < Anglo-Fr *carogne* (see CARRION) either directly or via MDu *kronje* in sense "old ewe"⟧ an ugly, withered old woman; hag

Cro·nus (krō′nəs) ***n.*** ⟦L < Gr *Kronos*⟧ *Gr. Myth.* a Titan who overthrows his father, Uranus, to become ruler of the universe and is himself overthrown by his son Zeus: identified with the Roman Saturn

cro·ny (krō′nē) ***n., pl.*** **-nies** ⟦Brit university slang < ? Gr *chronios*, long-continued (hence taken as "old friend") < *chronos*, time⟧ a companion or associate: now usually a humorous or disapproving usage [the mayor's political *cronies*]

☆**cro·ny·ism** (-nē iz′əm) ***n.*** favoritism shown to close friends, esp. in political appointments to office

crook (krook) ***n.*** ⟦ME *crok* < ON *krókr*, var. of *krākr*, a bending, hook, bay: for IE base see CRADLE⟧ **1** a hooked, bent, or curved thing or part; hook **2** *a)* a shepherd's staff, with a hook at one end *b)* a bishop's staff resembling this; crosier **3** a bending or being bent **4** a bend or curve ☆**5** [Informal] a person who steals or cheats; swindler or thief —***vt.*** **crooked** (krookt), **crook′ing 1** to bend or curve **2** [Slang] to steal —***vi.*** to bend or curve

crook·back (-bak′) ***n.*** [Rare] a hunchback —**crook′backed′ *adj.***

crook·ed (krookt; *for 2 & 3* krook′id) ***adj.*** **1** having a crook or hook **2** not straight; bent; curved; askew ☆**3** not straightforward; dishonest; swindling —**crook′ed·ly *adv.*** —**crook′ed·ness *n.***

Crookes (krooks), Sir **William** 1832-1919; Eng. chemist & physicist

Crookes tube ⟦after prec.⟧ an early cathode-ray tube with a cathode, anode, and some low-pressure gas

☆**crook·neck** (krook′nek′) ***n.*** any of several varieties of squash with a long, tapering, curved neck

croon (krōōn) ***vi., vt.*** ⟦ME & MDu *cronen*, akin to MLowG *kronen*, to growl < IE base **ger-*: see CROW[1]⟧ **1** to sing or hum in a low, gentle tone ☆**2** to sing (popular songs) in a soft, sentimental manner —***n.*** a low, gentle singing or humming —**croon′er *n.***

crop (kräp) ***n.*** ⟦ME *croppe* < OE *croppa*, a cluster, flower, crop of bird, hence kidney, pebble; akin to Frank **kruppa*, Ger *kropf*, a swelling, crop of bird (basic sense "something swelling out or swollen") < IE **gr-eu-b-*, curving out < base **ger-*: see CRADLE⟧ **1** a saclike enlargement of a bird's gullet or of a part of the digestive tract of earthworms and some insects, in which food is stored before digestion; craw **2** any agricultural product, growing or harvested, or collected, as wheat, cotton, fruit, honey, etc. **3** the yield of any product in one season or place **4** a group or collection appearing together [a new *crop* of students] **5** the entire tanned hide of an animal **6** the handle or butt of a whip **7** a stick with a handle at one end and a thong or tab at the other, used to direct a horse in horseback riding: in full **riding crop 8** ⟦< the v.⟧ the act or result of cropping, esp. *a)* hair cut close to the head *b)* this style of haircut *c)* an earmark on an animal, made by clipping —***vt.*** **cropped, crop′ping 1** to cut off or bite off the tops or ends of [sheep *crop* grass] **2** to grow or harvest as a crop **3** to cause crops to grow on or in **4** to cut (hair, the ears, etc.) short **5** to cut short the ears, hair, etc. of **6** to remove sections, as along the edges, of (a photographic image) so as to improve the composition of the finished print —***vi.*** **1** to bear a crop or crops ☆**2** to plant or grow a crop **3** to feed by cropping grass, etc.; graze —***adj.*** cut or designed to be shorter than usual at the bottom: said esp. of items of women's casual apparel [*crop* tops expose the midriff; *crop* pants extend only to the calves]: also **cropped** —**crop out** (or **up**) **1** to appear unexpectedly **2** to appear at the surface, as a rock formation at the earth's surface; outcrop

crop circle any large, usually circular, pattern formed typically on farmland by the bending or crushing of upright crops and variously attributed to geological forces, alien spacecraft, hoaxers, etc.

crop-dust·ing (-dust′iŋ) ***n.*** the process of spraying growing crops with pesticides from an airplane —**crop′-dust′ *vi., vt.*** —**crop′-dust′er *n.***

crop-eared (-ird′) ***adj.*** having the ears cropped

crop·land (-land′) ***n.*** land used to grow and harvest crops

crop·per (-ər) ***n.*** **1** a person or thing that crops **2** a machine or workman that cuts or shears leather, nap from cloth, etc. **3** a sharecropper **4** a plant that yields a crop **5** ⟦< ? phr. *neck and crop*⟧ a precipitate fall: now chiefly in COME A CROPPER (see phr. below) —**come a cropper** [Informal] **1** to fall heavily or headlong **2** to come to ruin; fail

☆**crop·pie** (kräp′ē) ***n., pl.*** **-pies** or **-pie** CRAPPIE

crop rotation a system or the practice of rotating in a fixed order the kinds of crops, as grain or grass, grown in the same field, as to maintain soil fertility

cro·quem·bouche (krōk′əm bōōsh′; *Fr* krôk än bōōsh′) ***n.*** ⟦Fr, lit., crunch in the mouth (in ref. to the sugar glaze) < *croquer* (see CROQUIS) + *bouche*, the mouth⟧ a French dessert consisting of a cone-shaped mound of small cream puffs glazed with caramelized sugar

croque-mon·sieur (krōk′mə syʉr′; *Fr* krôk mə syö′) ***n., pl.*** **-sieur′, -sieurs′** ⟦Fr, lit., crunch-sir: see CROQUIS & MONSIEUR; reason for name uncert.⟧ a sandwich filled with ham and cheese, either dipped in egg batter or buttered on the outside, and toasted or grilled: also written **croque monsieur**

cro·quet (krō kā′) ***n.*** ⟦Fr, dial. form of *crochet*: see CROTCHET⟧ **1** an outdoor game in which the players use mallets to drive a wooden ball through a series of hoops placed in the ground **2** the act of croqueting — ***vt., vi.*** **-queted′** (-kād′), **-quet′ing** in croquet, to drive away (an opponent's ball) by hitting one's own which has been placed in contact with it

cro·quette (krō ket′) ***n.*** ⟦Fr < *croquer*, to crunch: see fol.⟧ a small, rounded or cone-shaped mass of chopped, cooked meat, fish, or vegetables, coated with egg and crumbs and fried in deep fat

cro·quis (krō′kē) ***n., pl.*** **cro′quis** (-kē, -kēz) ⟦Fr < *croquer*, to sketch, draw hastily, earlier to know slightly, nibble, crunch < *croc*, a crackling noise, of echoic orig.⟧ a rough sketch, esp. one made by a designer of women's fashions

crore (krōr) ***n., pl.*** **crores** or **crore** ⟦< Hindi *karoṛ*⟧ in India and Pakistan, one hundred lakhs, or the sum of ten million: said specif. of rupees

Cros·by (krôz′bē, kräz′-), **Bing** (biŋ) (born *Harry Lillis Crosby*) 1903-77; U.S. popular singer & film actor

cro·sier (krō′zhər) ***n.*** ⟦ME *crocer* < OFr *crocier*, bearer of a staff < *croce*, bishop's staff < ML *crocia* < Frank **krukja* (akin to CRUTCH); prob. infl. by assoc. with OFr *croc*, hook, hooked staff (< ON *krókr*: see CROOK)⟧ **1** a staff with a crook at the top, carried by or before a bishop or abbot as a symbol of pastoral function **2** *Bot.* FIDDLEHEAD (sense 2)

cross (krôs, kräs) ***n.*** ⟦< ME *cros* & *crois*; *cros* < OE *cros* & ON *kross*, both < OIr *cros* < L *crux* (gen. *crucis*), a cross < IE **kreuk-*, extension of base **(s)ker-*, to turn, bend > L *curvus*; ME *crois* < OFr < L *crux*⟧ **1** an upright post with a bar across it near the top, to which the ancient Romans fastened convicted persons to die **2** a representation or figure of a cross, used as a badge, decoration, etc.; also, such a badge, decoration, etc. [the Distinguished Service *Cross*] **3** a monument in the form of a cross, or with a cross on it, marking a crossroad, boundary, grave, etc. **4** a staff with a cross at the top, carried before an archbishop as a sign of his authority **5** *a)* a representation of a cross, in any of various recognized forms, as a symbol of the crucifixion of Jesus, hence of the Christian religion *b)* a crucifix **6** *a)* the act of crossing, as from one side of a stage to the other *b)* the act of crossing oneself **7** any trouble or affliction that one has to bear; also,

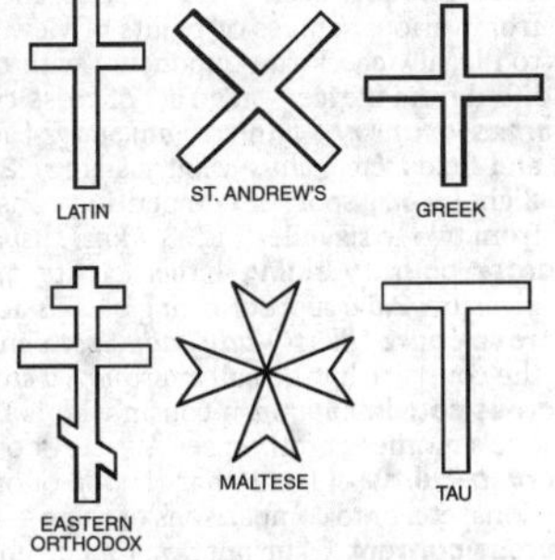

kinds of crosses

anything that thwarts or frustrates **8** any design, mark, or object made by two lines or surfaces that intersect one another **9** a mark (X) made as a signature, as by a person who cannot write **10** *a)* a crossing, or mixing, of varieties or breeds; hybridization *b)* the result of such mixing; hybrid **11** something that combines the qualities of two different things or types **12** [Slang] a dishonest action, fixed contest or match, etc. **13** *Boxing* a blow delivered over and across the opponent's lead **14** [**C-**] the Northern Cross **15** [**C-**] the Southern Cross —*vt.* **1** to make the sign of the cross over or upon **2** to place across or crosswise [*cross* your fingers] **3** to lie or cut across; intersect [where two streets *cross* one another] **4** to draw or put a line or lines across [*cross* your t's] **5** to pass over; go from one side to the other of; go across [to *cross* the ocean] **6** to carry or lead across **7** to extend or reach across [the bridge *crosses* a river] **8** to meet and pass (each other) **9** to bring into contact, causing electrical interference [the wires were *crossed*] **10** to go counter to; thwart; oppose **11** to interbreed (animals or plants); breed (an individual of one type) with one of another; hybridize; cross-fertilize —*vi.* **1** to lie across; intersect **2** to go or extend from one side to the other: often with *over* **3** to pass each other while moving in opposite directions **4** to interbreed; hybridize; cross-fertilize —*adj.* **1** lying or passing across or through; transverse; crossing or crossed [*cross* street, *cross* ventilation] **2** going counter; contrary; opposed [at *cross* purposes] **3** irritated or irritable; ill-tempered **4** involving reciprocal actions, etc. **5** of mixed variety or breed; hybrid; crossbred **6** [Archaic] causing harm; unfavorable —*adv.* crosswise —**SYN.** IRRITABLE —**cross off** (or **out**) to cancel by or as by drawing lines across —**cross oneself** to outline the form of a cross as a Christian religious act by moving the hand from the forehead to the breast and then from one shoulder to the other —**cross one's fingers** to cross one finger over another of the same hand: superstitiously believed to bring good luck or mitigate the wrong of telling a half-truth —**cross one's heart** to make an outline of an X, by a movement of the hand or fingers, over one's heart as a token that one is telling the truth —**cross someone's mind** to come suddenly or briefly to someone's mind —**cross someone's palm** ⟦from the old practice of making a cross on a fortuneteller's hand with a coin when paying the fee⟧ to pay someone money, esp. as a bribe —**cross someone's path** to meet or encounter someone —**cross up 1** to confuse or disorder **2** to deceive, or double-cross —**the Cross 1** the cross on which Jesus was put to death **2** the suffering and death or Atonement of Jesus **3** Christianity or Christendom **4** *a)* the constellation Crux *b)* the constellation Cygnus —**cross′a·ble** *adj.* —**cross′ly** *adv.* —**cross′ness** *n.*

cross- (krôs, kräs) *combining form* cross (in various senses) or across [*crossbow, crossbreed, crosswise*]

cross·bar (krôs′bär′) *n.* a bar, line, or stripe placed crosswise, as the horizontal bar of a football goal post —*vt.* **-barred′**, **-bar′ring** to furnish or mark with crossbars

cross·beam (-bēm′) *n.* any transverse beam in a structure

cross·bed·ded (-bed′id) *adj. Geol.* having layers of rock oblique or transverse to the main beds of stratified rock

cross·bill (-bil′) *n.* any of a genus (*Loxia*) of finches having a bill with curving points that cross

cross·bones (-bōnz′) *n.* a representation of two thigh bones, placed across each other to form an X, as a symbol of danger: see also SKULL AND CROSSBONES

cross·bow (-bō′) *n.* a weapon consisting of a bow set transversely on a wooden stock: the stock is grooved to direct a short, heavy arrow (*bolt*) or stone and notched to hold the bowstring, which is released by a trigger —**cross′bow′man** *n., pl.* **-men**

crossbow

cross·bred (-bred′) *adj.* produced by the interbreeding of different varieties or breeds —*n.* a crossbred plant or animal; hybrid; mongrel

cross·breed (-brēd′) *vt., vi.* **-bred′** (-bred′), **-breed′ing** HYBRIDIZE —*n.* HYBRID (sense 1)

cross-check (-chek′) *vt., vi.* **1** to check or verify from various sources or points of view **2** *Ice Hockey* to illegally check (an opponent) with one's stick held in both hands and lifted from the ice —*n.* an act of cross-checking

cross-coun·try (-kun′trē) *adj., adv.* **1** across open country through woods and fields, etc. [*cross-country* skiing] **2** across a country [a *cross-country* flight] —*n.* a sport or competition consisting of a cross-country footrace, from two to six miles (1.2-3.7 km), usually between teams of contestants

cross-country skiing 1 the activity of skiing across open country for pleasure **2** the sport of racing on skis across open country

cross·court (-kôrt′) *adv., adj. Sports* into, toward, or in the other side of the court [to hit the ball *crosscourt*, a *crosscourt* pass]

cross cousin *Anthrop.* a cousin who is the child of one's father's sister or one's mother's brother: see PARALLEL COUSIN

cross-cul·tur·al (-kul′chər əl) *adj.* of or relating to different cultures, nations, etc. or to comparisons of them —**cross′-cul′tur·al·ly** *adv.*

cross·cur·rent (-kur′ənt) *n.* **1** a current flowing at an angle to the main current **2** an opposing opinion, influence, or tendency

cross·cut (-kut′) *adj.* **1** made or used for cutting across **2** cut across —*n.* **1** a cut across **2** something that cuts across **3** *Film a)* the alternation of (shots in a scene, scenes in a sequence, etc.) as to suggest opposition, parallel action, etc. (also **cross′cut′ting**) *b)* such shots, scenes, etc. **4** *Mining a)* a passageway, air shaft, etc. cut to connect two shafts or tunnels that are roughly parallel *b)* a connection from a shaft or tunnel through or to a vein of ore —*vt., vi.* **-cut′**, **-cut′ting 1** to cut across **2** *Film* to alternate (shots, scenes, etc.) using a crosscut

crosscut saw a saw with a blade designed to cut across the grain of wood

cross-dress·ing (-dres′iŋ) *n.* the wearing of clothing typically worn by the opposite sex —**cross′-dress′er** *n.*

crosse (krôs) *n.* ⟦Fr < OFr *crois*: see CROSS⟧ a long-handled stick with a net at one end, used in playing lacrosse to catch, carry, or throw the ball

cross-ex·am·ine (krôs′ig zam′in) *vt., vi.* **-ined**, **-in·ing 1** to question closely **2** *Law* to question (a witness produced by the opposing side) as in order to challenge previous testimony —**cross′-ex·am′i·na′tion** (-ə nā′shən) *n.* —**cross′-ex·am′in·er** *n.*

cross-eye (krôs′ī′) *n.* an abnormal condition in which the eyes are turned toward each other; convergent strabismus; esotropia —**cross′-eyed′** (-īd′) *adj.*

cross-fade (krôs′fād′) *Film, Radio, TV vi.* **-fad′ed**, **-fad′ing** to fade out a scene or sound while fading in another —*n.* a transition, as in a film or broadcast, produced by cross-fading

cross-fer·tile (-furt′'l) *adj.* capable of cross-fertilization or of being cross-fertilized

cross-fer·ti·lize (krôs′furt′'l īz′) *vt., vi.* **-lized′**, **-liz′ing 1** to fertilize or be fertilized by pollen with different genes **2** *a)* to fertilize or be fertilized by a male gamete from another animal, as in the mutual exchange of sperm between individuals in a hermaphroditic species *b)* to fuse a male and female gamete derived from different varieties or species —**cross′-fer′ti·li·za′tion** (-furt′'l ə zā′shən) *n.*

cross-file (krôs′fīl′, kräs′-) *vi., vt.* **-filed′**, **-fil′ing** to register as a candidate in more than one party's primary election

cross·fire (-fīr′) *n.* **1** *Mil.* fire directed at an objective from two or more positions so that the lines of fire cross **2** any energetic exchange, as of opposing opinions Also written **cross fire**

cross-grained (-grānd′) *adj.* **1** having a grain that is irregular or that runs across the longitudinal axis: said of timber **2** cantankerous; contrary; perverse

cross·hair (-her′) *n.* a line or, typically, one of a pair of crossed lines, as of fine wire or hair, mounted in the eyepiece of a telescopic gun sight, surveyor's level, etc. to assist in precise aiming or centering of the instrument: also sp. **cross hair** —**in the** (or **someone's**) **crosshairs** targeted (by someone) for hostile or critical action or scrutiny

cross·hatch (-hach′) *vt., vi.* to shade (a drawing) with two sets of parallel lines that cross each other

cross·head (-hed′) *n.* a sliding bar or block joining a connecting rod and a piston rod: converts reciprocating motion into rotary motion, as in the steam engine

cross-in·dex (-in′deks′) *vt., vi.* to provide (a reference book, index, etc.) with systematic cross-references

cross·ing (krôs′iŋ) *n.* ⟦see CROSS⟧ **1** the act of passing across, thwarting, interbreeding, etc. **2** an intersection, as of railroad lines or streets **3** a place where a railroad line, street, river, etc. may be crossed

crossing guard SCHOOL (CROSSING) GUARD

cross·ing-o·ver (-ō′vər) *n.* an exchange of equivalent genetic material between homologous chromatids during meiosis

cross-leg·ged (-leg′id, -legd′; -lā′gid, -lāgd′) *adj., adv.* **1** with the ankles crossed and the knees spread apart **2** with one leg crossed over the other Said usually of a seated person

cross·let (-lit) *n.* ⟦ME *crosselet* < Anglo-Fr *croiselete*, dim. of OFr *crois*: see CROSS⟧ *Heraldry* a small cross

cross-link (-liŋk′) *n.* a crosswise connecting part; specif., an atom or group connecting parallel chains in a complex molecule —*vt.* to join crosswise

cros·sop·te·ryg·i·an (krə säp′tə rij′ē ən, krä-) *n.* ⟦< ModL *Crossopterygii*, name of the group (< Gr *krossoi*, fringe + *pteryx*, fin, wing: see PTERYGOID) + -AN⟧ any coelacanth: thought to be the precursors of amphibians

cross·o·ver (-ō′vər) *n.* **1** the act, means, or place of crossing over from one part or side, to another ☆**2** a track by which a railroad train can be switched from one line to another ☆**3** a person who votes for a candidate of a political party other than the party he or she usually supports ☆**4** a CROSSOVER (*adj.* 3) musical style **5** a motor vehicle with a body like that of a station wagon or sport utility vehicle, built on an automobile, rather than a truck, frame: it is often lower than a sport utility vehicle and operates more like a car **6** *Biol. a)* CROSSING-OVER *b)* a character resulting from crossing-over —*adj.* **1** designating or of a circuit, network, etc. that divides amplified sound into frequency bands and distributes them to the proper component of a speaker system, as to a woofer or tweeter **2** designating or by voters who are crossovers [the *crossover* vote] **3** designating or of a form of popular music in which elements of musical genres that appeal to a limited audience are combined with more widely accepted forms to gain a larger audience [*crossover* jazz] **4** made up of elements appealing to more specialized tastes that have been combined to gain broader acceptance

cross-own·er·ship (krôs′ōn′ər ship′) *n.* ownership of two or more companies in a single industry or market; often, specif., ownership of two media outlets, as a newspaper and radio station, in a single market

cross·patch (-pach′) *n.* ⟦CROSS- + dial. *patch*, fool, childish person⟧ [Informal] a cross, bad-tempered person

cross·piece (-pēs′) *n.* a piece lying across another

cross-pol·li·nate (krôs′päl′ə nāt′) *vt., vi.* **-nat′ed**, **-nat′ing** to subject or be subjected to cross-pollination

cross-pol·li·na·tion (-päl′ə nā′shən) *n.* the transfer of pollen from the anther of one flower to the stigma of another with a different genetic composition, as by insects, or deliberately by a botanist

cross-pur·pose (krôs′pur′pəs) *n.* a contrary or conflicting purpose: usually in the phrase **at cross purposes**, acting, often unintentionally, according to conflicting goals

cross-ques·tion (-kwes′chən) *vt.* to cross-examine —*n.* a question asked in cross-examination

cross-re·fer (-ri fur′) *vt.* **-ferred′**, **-fer′ring** to refer from one part (of a book, index, etc.) to another —*vi.* to make a cross-reference

cross-ref·er·ence (-ref′ər əns) *n.* a reference from one part of a book, catalog, index, etc. to another part, for additional information —*vt.* **-enced**, **-enc·ing** **1** to provide (an index, reference book, etc.) with systematic cross-references **2** CROSS-REFER

cross relation *Music* the simultaneous or successive occurrence of a note and its chromatic alteration, as C and C♯, in different voices; false relation

cross-rhythm (krôs′rith′əm) *n.* in jazz and popular music, a rhythm played simultaneously with one or more contrasting rhythms

cross·road (krôs′rōd′) *n.* **1** a road that crosses another road **2** a road that connects two or more main roads **3** [*usually pl., with sing. v.*] *a)* the place where two or more roads intersect, often the site of a rural settlement *b)* any center of congregation, activity, etc. for a widespread area *c)* a time in which important changes occur or major decisions must be made

cross·ruff (-ruf′) *n.* ⟦CROSS- + RUFF[2]⟧ *Card Games* a sequence of plays in which a card is led from the hand of each of two partners in turn, which the other trumps

cross section **1** *a)* a cutting through something, esp. at a right angle *b)* the plane surface so exposed *c)* a drawing or photograph of a plane surface exposed by or as if by such a cutting *d)* a piece, slice, or SECTION (*n. 2b*) prepared in this manner **2** a sample that has enough of each kind in it to show what the whole is like **3** *Nuclear Physics* a measure of the probability that a nuclear reaction will take place, under specified conditions, between two particles or a particle and another target: usually expressed in terms of the effective area a single target presents to the incoming particle: see BARN **4** *Surveying* a vertical section of the ground surface taken at right angles to a survey line —**cross′-sec′tion** *vt.* —**cross′-sec′tion·al** *adj.*

cross-sell (krôs′sel′) *vt.* **-sold′**, **-sell′ing** to sell (additional, usually related, products or services) to a customer

cross-stitch (-stich′) *n.* **1** a stitch, as in embroidery or for sewing a patch, formed from two stitches crossed in an X **2** needlework made with this stitch — *vt., vi.* to sew or embroider with this stitch

cross-talk (-tôk′) *n.* **1** interference in one communications channel from another or others **2** incidental conversation, as in a moderated discussion **3** repartee or banter, as before an audience

cross·tie (-tī′) *n.* **1** a beam, post, rod, etc. placed crosswise to give support ☆**2** any of the transverse timbers supporting the rails of a railroad track

☆**cross·town** (-toun′) *adj.* **1** running or extending across the main avenues or transportation lines of a town or city [*a crosstown bus*] **2** located on the other side of a town or city [*the school's crosstown rival*]

cross-train·i·ng (krôs′trān′iŋ) *n.* the act or an instance of training or competing in several different sports at the same time —*adj.* of or having to do with cross-training [*cross-training shoes*]

cross·trees (-trēz′) *pl.n.* two short bars across a ship's masthead, to spread the rigging that supports the mast

☆**cross·walk** (-wôk′) *n.* a crossing lane marked off for pedestrians

cross·way (-wā′) *n.* CROSSROAD (esp. sense 3)

cross·wind (-wind′) *n.* a wind blowing at any angle across the intended line of flight of an aircraft, the course of a ship, etc.

cross·wise (-wīz′) *adv.* **1** [Archaic] in the form of a cross **2** so as to cross; across —*adj.* that lies or extends across; crossing; transverse Also **cross′ways′** (-wāz′)

☆**cross·word puzzle** (-wurd′) an arrangement of numbered squares to be filled in with words, a letter to each square, so that a letter appearing in a word placed horizontally is usually also part of a word placed vertically: numbered synonyms and definitions are given as clues for the words

cros·ti·ni (krôs tē′nē) *pl.n.* ⟦It, pl. of *crostino*, lit., crouton, ult. < L *crusta*, CRUST⟧ [*sometimes with sing. v.*] small pieces of toast with a savory topping, as of pâté, shrimp, cheese, or mushrooms

crotch (kräch) *n.* ⟦ME *croche*, var. of *crucche*, CRUTCH⟧ **1** a pole forked on top **2** a forked place, as where a tree trunk divides into two branches **3** the place where the legs fork from the human body **4** the seam or place where the legs of a pair of pants meet —**crotched** *adj.*

crotch·et (kräch′it) *n.* ⟦ME & OFr *crochet*, dim. < *croc*, hook: see CROSIER⟧ **1** [Archaic] *a)* a small hook *b)* a hooklike part or device **2** ⟦< sense "hooked, twisted"⟧ a peculiar whim or stubborn notion **3** [Chiefly Brit.] QUARTER NOTE —***SYN.*** CAPRICE

crotch·et·y (-ē) *adj.* cantankerous or eccentric —**crotch′et·i·ness** *n.*

cro·ton (krōt′'n) *n.* ⟦ModL < Gr *krotōn*, a tick, castor-oil plant or (in pl.) its ticklike seeds⟧ **1** any of a large, mostly tropical genus (*Croton*) of shrubs, trees, and herbs of the spurge family: certain species yield croton oil and cascarilla, formerly used in medicine, and others are poisonous range weeds in the SW U.S. **2** any of a genus (*Codiaeum*) of shrubs of the spurge family, grown for their ornamental, leathery leaves

☆**Croton bug** (krot′'n) ⟦after *Croton* Aqueduct (of the water-supply system of New York City): so named from becoming numerous in the city after the opening of the aqueduct⟧ a small, winged cockroach (*Blattella germanica*); German cockroach

cro·ton·ic acid (krō tän′ik) ⟦CROTON + -IC⟧ a colorless crystalline compound, $CH_3CH{:}CHCOOH$, existing in two isomeric forms: used in organic synthesis, the manufacture of resins, etc.

croton oil a thick, bitter oil obtained from croton seeds: it is used as a counterirritant and, rarely, as a strong cathartic

crouch (krouch) *vi.* ⟦ME *crouchen* < OFr *crochir*, to be bent < *croc*, a hook: see CROSIER⟧ **1** to stoop or bend low with the limbs drawn close to the body, as an animal ready to spring or cowering in fear **2** to cringe or bow in a servile manner —*vt.* [Archaic] to cause to bend low —*n.* the act or position of crouching

croup[1] (kro͞op) *n.* ⟦< obs. or dial. *croup*, to speak hoarsely, of echoic orig.⟧ a condition resulting from any obstruction of the larynx, esp. an inflammation of the respiratory passages, with labored breathing, sharp and abrupt coughing, and laryngeal spasm —**croup′y** *adj.*

croup[2] (kro͞op) *n.* ⟦ME *croupe* < OFr < Frank **kruppa*: see CROP⟧ the top of the rump of a horse, dog, etc., just behind the loin

crou·pi·er (kro͞o′pē ā′, -ər) *n.* ⟦Fr, orig., one who rides on the croup, hence an inferior assistant: see prec.⟧ a person in charge of a gambling table, who rakes in and pays out the money

crouse (kro͞os) *adj.* ⟦ME *crous*, fierce, grim, prob. < or akin to MLowG *krus* (Ger *kraus*), curly, tangled⟧ [Scot.] lively; pert; brisk

crou·stade (kro͞o städ′) *n.* ⟦Fr < OFr *crouste* (Fr *croûte*), CRUST⟧ a shell, as of pastry or toasted bread, with a savory filling, as of mushrooms

crou·ton (kro͞o′tän′, kro͞o tän′) *n.* ⟦Fr *croûton* < *croûte*, a crust < OFr *crouste* < L *crusta*: see CRUST⟧ any of the small, crisp pieces of toasted or fried bread often served in soup or salads

crow[1] (krō) *n.* ⟦ME *crowe* < OE *crawa*, akin to Ger *krähe*, ON *kraka* < IE base **ger-*, echoic of hoarse cry > CRAKE, CRANE, CRACK[1]⟧ **1** *a)* any of a genus (*Corvus*) of large, nonmigratory corvids with glossy black plumage and a typical harsh call, including the raven, rook, and jackdaw *b)* certain other unrelated birds, as the turkey vulture **2** [Rare] a crowbar —**as the crow flies** in a straight, direct line —☆**eat crow** [Informal] to undergo the humiliation as of having to retract a statement or admit an error —**the Crow** the constellation Corvus

crow[2] (krō) *vi.* **crowed** or, for 1, [Chiefly Brit.] **crew** (kro͞o), **crowed**, **crow′ing** ⟦ME *crouen* < OE *crawan*: for IE base see prec.⟧ **1** to make the shrill cry of a rooster **2** to boast in triumph; exult [*to crow over a victory*] **3** to make a sound expressive of well-being or pleasure, as a baby does —*n.* a crowing sound —***SYN.*** BOAST[2]

Crow (krō) *n.* ⟦< Fr *gens de corbeaux*, lit., raven people, transl. of Crow *apsáaloke*, crow people⟧ **1** *pl.* **Crows** or **Crow** a member of a North American Indian people living in the upper basins of the Yellowstone and Bighorn rivers **2** the Siouan language of this people

crow·bar (krō′bär′) *n.* ⟦from the pointed end's resemblance to a crow's beak⟧ a long metal bar, usually with a bent, often forked, wedge-shaped end, used as a lever for prying, etc.

crow·ber·ry (-ber′ē) *adj.* ⟦prob. transl. of Ger *krähenbeere*⟧ designating a family (Empetraceae, order Ericales) of dicotyledonous shrubby evergreens —*n., pl.* **-ries** **1** any of several hardy, low, evergreen shrubs (genus *Empetrum*) of the crowberry family, found in N regions **2** the black, edible berry of any of these shrubs

crowd[1] (kroud) *vi.* ⟦ME *crouden* < OE *crudan*, to press, drive, akin to MHG *kroten*, to oppress < IE base **greut-*, to compel, press > CURD, Ir *gruth*, curdled milk⟧ **1** to press, push, or squeeze **2** to push one's way (*forward, into, through*, etc.) **3** to come together in a large group; throng —*vt.* **1** to press, push, or shove **2** to press or force closely together; cram **3** to fill too full; occupy to excess, as by pressing or thronging **4** *a)* to be or press very near to ☆*b) Baseball* to stand very close to (the plate) in batting **5** [Informal] to put (a person) under pressure or stress, as by dunning or harassing —*n.* **1** a large number of people or things gathered closely together **2** the common people; the masses ☆**3** [Informal] a group of people having something in common; set; clique —**crowd (on) sail** to put up an unusually large number of sails in order to increase the ship's speed —**crowd out** to force (someone or something) out of a limited space by arriving or appearing there —**crowd′ed** *adj.*

SYN.—**crowd** is applied to an assembly of persons or things in close proximity or densely packed together and may suggest lack of order, loss of personal identity, etc. [*crowds lined the street*]; **throng** specifically suggests a moving crowd of people pushing one another [*throngs of celebrators at Times Square*]; **multitude** stresses greatness of number in referring to persons or things assembled or considered together [*a multitude arrayed against him*]; **swarm** suggests a large, continuously moving group [*a swarm of sightseers*]; **mob**, properly applied to a disorderly or lawless crowd, is an abusive term when used to describe the masses or any specific group of people; **host** specifically suggests a large organized body marshaled together but may be used generally of any sizable group considered collectively [*he has a host of friends*]; **horde** specifically refers to any large predatory band [*a horde of office seekers*]

crowd[2] (kroud) *n.* ⟦ME *croud* < Welsh *crwth* < IE **krut-*, arch, breast, belly < base **(s)kreu-*, round > MIr *cruind*, round⟧ **1** CRWTH **2** [Brit. Dial.] a violin

crowd-pleas·er (kroud′plēz′ər) *n.* [Informal] something or someone widely or dependably popular —**crowd′-pleas′ing** *adj.*

crow·foot (krō′foot′) *n., pl.* **-foots′** or **-feet′** **1** any of a number of plants of the buttercup family, characterized by simple or variously lobed leaves somewhat resembling a crow's foot, esp. any of a genus (*Ranunculus*) of chiefly yellow-flowered plants **2** CALTROP (sense 1) **3** *Naut.* an arrangement of cords run through a block pulley to suspend an awning, etc.

crown (kroun) *n.* ⟦ME *coroune* < OFr *corone* < L *corona*, a garland, crown < Gr *korōnē*, curved object, wreath < IE base **(s)ker-*, to turn, bend > L *curvus, crux*⟧ **1** a garland or wreath worn on the head as a sign of honor, victory, etc. **2** a reward or honor given for merit; specif., the position or title of a champion in a sport **3** a circlet or headdress, often of gold and jewels, worn by a monarch as an emblem of sovereignty **4** [*usually* **C-**] *a)* the position, power, or dominion of a monarch *b)* the monarch as head of the state *c)* the government of a nation having a monarch or of a constitutional monarchy: usually with *the* **5** anything serving to adorn or honor like a crown **6** the figure of a crown or a thing like a crown as in shape or position **7** *a)* a coin bearing the figure of a crown *b)* a British coin equal to 25 (new) pence: no longer coined *c)* any of various coins or monetary units whose name means *crown* (see KORUNA, KRONA, KRONE[1]) **8** the top part of the skull or head **9** the top part of a hat **10** the summit or highest point, as of a mountain or arch **11** the highest quality, point of development, state, etc. of anything **12** *a)* the enamel-covered part of a tooth, projecting beyond the gum line *b)* an artificial substitute for this, usually of porcelain or gold **13** the lowest point of an anchor, between the arms **14** *Bot. a)* CORONA (sense 7) *b)* the point at or just below the surface of the ground where the stem and the root join, esp. in perennial herbs *c)* the leafy head of a tree —*vt.* **1** *a)* to put a crown on the head of *b)* to make (a person) a monarch; enthrone **2** to honor or reward as with a crown **3** to be at the top of; surmount **4** to be the crown, highest part, or chief ornament of **5** to complete successfully; put the finishing touch on **6** to cover (a tooth) with an artificial crown **7** [Slang] to hit on the head **8** *Checkers* to place a piece of the same color on (an opponent's piece that has crossed the board and reached the end row), thus making it a king —*vi. Med.* to appear at the vaginal opening during labor: said of the top of a baby's head —**crown′er** *n.*

☆**crown cap** a metal bottle cap whose edges are crimped over the mouth

crown colony a British colony directly under the control of the home government in London

crown·er (kroun′ər, kro͞on′-) *n.* [Now Dial., Chiefly Brit.] CORONER

crown glass **1** window glass made in flat, circular plates by blowing and whirling, with a small knot in the center left by the blower's rod **2** a very clear optical glass with a low index of refraction

crown jewels **1** the jewelry and the emblems of office, such as the crown and scepter, that are worn or carried by the sovereign of a country on state occasions **2** [*sing.*] the best or most valuable part of a whole or member of a group

crown land **1** land owned by the Crown, the income from which (or, in Britain, a fixed payment by Parliament in place of it) goes to the reigning monarch **2** land under control of the government in certain countries and colonies of the Commonwealth

crown lens a lens made of crown glass; specif., the convex member of an achromatic lens

crown molding ⟦so named from its position along the top⟧ a horizontal molding projecting along the top of a wall and typically shaped to function as a decorative feature

crown of thorns ⟦descriptive of appearance; in allusion to the *crown of thorns* placed on the head of Jesus: see, e.g., Matt. 27:29⟧ **1** a coral-eating starfish (*Acanthaster planci*) of the tropical Pacific region, having arms covered with long spines: also **crown-of-thorns (starfish)** **2** a shrub (*Euphorbia milii*) of the spurge family, having long spines and bright red or yellow bracts

Crown Point ⟦mistransl. of Fr name *Pointe à la Chevelure*, scalping point⟧ town in NE N.Y., on Lake Champlain: site of a fort important in the French and Indian & the Revolutionary wars

crown prince the male heir apparent to a throne

crown princess **1** the wife of a crown prince **2** a female heir presumptive to a throne

crown roast a rib roast tied in a circle like a crown and served with the ribs sticking up and paper frills on each one

crown saw HOLE SAW

crown vetch a European plant (*Coronilla varia*) of the pea family, with pink and white flowers: sometimes cultivated in the U.S. as a ground cover, esp. along highways

crown wheel (*or* **gear**) a gearwheel with teeth set in the rim perpendicularly to its plane

crow's-foot (krōz′fo͝ot′) *n., pl.* **-feet′** ⟦so called from seeming resemblance to the imprint of a *crow's foot*⟧ **1** any of the wrinkles that often develop at the outer corners of the eyes of adults: *usually used in pl.* **2** a three-pointed, stitched design put on a garment **3** *Aeron.* a way of rigging one rope to several ropes in order to distribute pull in handling balloons and airships Also **crows′foot′**

crow's-nest (-nest′) *n.* **1** a small, partly enclosed platform near the top of a ship's mast, for the lookout **2** any platform like this

Croy·don (kroid′'n) borough of S Greater London, England

croze (krōz) *n.* ⟦prob. < Fr *creux* < OFr *crues*, a hollow, groove, prob. < Gaul⟧ a groove at either end inside a cask, in which the head is fixed

cro·zier (krō′zhər) *n. alt. sp. of* CROSIER

crs *abbrev.* **1** creditors **2** credits

CRT (sē′är′tē′) *n.* CATHODE-RAY TUBE

cru (kro͞o; *Fr* krü) *n.* ⟦Fr, lit., growth, production < *crû* < OFr *creue*: see CREW[1]⟧ **1** *Winemaking* a group of vineyards producing wine of comparable quality and character **2** loosely, a specified quality of wine [*grand cru*]

cru·ces (kro͞o′sēz′) *n. alt. pl. of* CRUX

cru·cial (kro͞o′shəl) *adj.* ⟦Fr < L *crux*, CROSS⟧ **1** of supreme importance; decisive; critical [*a crucial* decision] **2** *Med.* having the form of a cross [*a crucial* incision] —*SYN.* ACUTE —**cru′cial·ly** *adv.*

cru·ci·ate (kro͞o′shē it, -āt′) *adj.* ⟦< ModL *cruciatus* (in L, pp. of *cruciare*, to crucify) < L *crux*, CROSS⟧ **1** cross-shaped **2** *Bot.* having leaves or petals arranged in the form of a cross **3** *Zool.* crossing: said of wings

cru·ci·ble (kro͞o′sə bəl) *n.* ⟦ML *crucibulum*, lamp, crucible, prob. < Gmc, as in OE *cruce*, pot, jug, MHG *kruse*, earthen pot (see CRUSE) + L suffix *-ibulum* (as in *thuribulum*, censer), but assoc. by folk etym. with L *crux*, CROSS, as if in ref. to a lamp burning before a cross⟧ **1** a container made of a substance that can resist great heat, for melting, fusing, or calcining ores, metals, etc. **2** the hollow at the bottom of an ore furnace, where the molten metal collects **3** a severe test or trial

crucible steel a high-grade steel made by melting special steel mixes in a crucible furnace or by fusing flux, wrought iron, and carbon: used for making knives, tools, etc.

cru·ci·fer (kro͞o′sə fər) *n.* ⟦LL(Ec) < L *crux*, CROSS + *ferre*, to BEAR[1]; sense 2 < arrangement of flower petals in the form of a cross⟧ **1** a person who carries a cross, as in a church procession **2** *Bot.* any plant of the crucifer family —*adj.* designating a family (Brassicaceae, order Capparales) of dicotyledonous plants with cross-shaped flowers, pointed pods, and strong, cabbagelike odors, including cabbage, turnip, broccoli, radish, horseradish, and alyssum —**cru·cif′er·ous** (-sif′ər əs) *adj.*

cru·ci·fix (kro͞o′sə fiks′) *n.* ⟦ME < OFr or ML; OFr *crucefix* < ML(Ec) *crucifixus*, orig. pp. of LL(Ec) *crucifigere*: see CRUCIFY⟧ a cross with the figure of the crucified Jesus Christ on it

cru·ci·fix·ion (kro͞o′sə fik′shən) *n.* **1** a crucifying or being crucified **2** [**C-**] a representation of the Crucifixion as in painting or statuary —**the Crucifixion** the crucifying of Jesus

cru·ci·form (kro͞o′sə fôrm′) *adj.* ⟦< L *crux*, CROSS + -FORM⟧ cross-shaped —**cru′ci·form′ly** *adv.*

cru·ci·fy (kro͞o′sə fī′) *vt.* **-fied′**, **-fy′ing** ⟦ME *crucifien* < OFr *crucifier* < VL **crucificare* < LL(Ec) *crucifigere* < L *crux*, CROSS + *figere*: see FIX⟧ **1** to put to death by nailing or binding to a cross and leaving to die of exposure **2** to mortify (the flesh) as by asceticism **3** to be very cruel to; torment —**cru′ci·fi′er** *n.*

crud[1] (krud) *vt., vi.* **crud′ded**, **crud′ding** ⟦ME *crudden* < *crud*: see CURD⟧ [Dial.] to curdle —*n.* **1** [Dial.] a curd **2** [Slang] any coagulated substance, caked deposit, dregs, filth, etc. **3** [Slang] a worthless, disgusting, or contemptible person or thing —**crud′dy** *adj.* **-di·er**, **-di·est**

crud[2] (krud) *n.* ⟦< ? Welsh *cryd*, fever, plague⟧ [Slang] an imaginary or vaguely identified disease or ailment: with *the*

crude (kro͞od) *adj.* **crud′er**, **crud′est** ⟦ME < L *crudus*, bleeding, raw, rough < IE base **kreu-*, congealed (blood) > RAW, Gr *kryos*, frost & *kreas*, flesh, L *crusta*, *cruor*, MIr *cru*, blood⟧ **1** in a raw or natural condition, before being prepared for use; not refined or processed **2** lacking finish, grace, tact, or taste; uncultured [*crude* remark] **3** not carefully made or done; rough [*crude* woodwork] **4** stark and bare; undisguised or unadorned [*crude* reality] **5** [Archaic] not ripe; immature **6** *Statistics* untreated as by analysis, differentiation into groups, etc. —☆*n.* an unrefined or unprocessed substance; specif., crude petroleum —**crude′ly** *adv.* —**crude′ness** *n.*

cru·di·tés (kro͞o′də tā′; *Fr* krü dē tā′) *pl.n.* ⟦Fr, lit., raw things: see fol.⟧ raw vegetables cut up and served as an hors d'oeuvre, usually with a dip or with sauces

cru·di·ty (kro͞o′də tē) *n.* ⟦ME *crudite* < OFr < L *cruditas*⟧ **1** the condition or quality of being crude **2** *pl.* **-ties** a crude action, remark, etc.

cru·el (kro͞o′əl) *adj.* ⟦OFr < L *crudelis* < *crudus*: see CRUDE⟧ **1** deliberately seeking to inflict pain and suffering; enjoying others' suffering; without mercy or pity **2** causing, or of a kind to cause, pain, distress, etc. —**cru′el·ly** *adv.* —**cru′el·ness** *n.*

SYN.—**cruel** implies indifference to the suffering of others or a disposition to inflict it on others [*cruel* fate]; **brutal** implies an animal-like or savage cruelty that is altogether unfeeling [*a brutal* prison guard]; **inhuman** stresses the complete absence of those qualities expected of a civilized human being, such as compassion, mercy, or benevolence; **pitiless** implies a callous refusal to be moved or influenced by the suffering of those one has wronged; **ruthless** implies a cruel and relentless disregard for the rights or welfare of others, while in pursuit of a goal —*ANT.* **humane, kind**

cru·el·ty (-tē) *n.* ⟦ME *cruelte* < OFr < L *crudelitas* < prec.⟧ **1** the quality or condition of being cruel; inhumanity; hardheartedness **2** *pl.* **-ties** a cruel action, remark, etc. **3** *Law* willful infliction of physical pain or suffering upon a person or animal, or of mental distress upon a person

cru·et (kro͞o′it) *n.* ⟦ME < Anglo-Fr, dim. of OFr *crue*, earthen pot < Gmc **kruka* (Ger *krug*): see CROCK[1]⟧ a small glass bottle, as for serving vinegar or oil at the table

Cruik·shank (kro͝ok′shaŋk), **George** 1792-1878; Eng. caricaturist & illustrator

cruise (kro͞oz) *vi.* **cruised**, **cruis′ing** ⟦< Du *kruisen*, to cross, cruise < *kruis*, cross < L *crux*, CROSS⟧ **1** to sail from place to place, as for pleasure or in search of something **2** to ride about in a similar manner [*a taxi cruises* to pick up passengers] ☆**3** to go over a wooded area to estimate its lumber yield 4 *a)* to move at the most efficient speed for sustained travel (said of an aircraft) *b)* to operate at a predetermined speed by use of a regulating mechanism (CRUISE CONTROL) (said of an automobile) ☆5 [Slang] to go about looking for a sex partner —*vt.* 1 to sail, journey, or move over or about ☆2 to make a cruising trip over (a wooded area) ☆3 [Slang] to approach (a person) or visit (a place) in seeking a sex partner 4 [Informal] to browse or sample a succession of channels on (a TV), of Web pages on (the internet), etc. —*n.* the action of cruising; esp., a cruising voyage by ship, often, specif., one taken for pleasure on a cruise ship

cruise control a device for keeping the speed of a motor vehicle constant for a period of time, as when driving on a turnpike

☆**cruise missile** a long-range, jet-propelled guided missile designed to fly at low altitude and launched as from an airplane, submarine, or ship

cruis·er (kro͞o′zər) *n.* 1 one that cruises, as a powerboat, airplane, or squad car 2 any of several types of fast and maneuverable warship smaller than a battleship and having less armor and firepower 3 CABIN CRUISER

cruis·er·weight (kro͞o′zər wāt′) *n.* ⟦< prec.: from their being the second-heaviest weight class and the second-heaviest type of warship⟧ a boxer between a light heavyweight and a heavyweight, with a maximum weight of 200 pounds (90.7 kg)

cruise ship a ship used to carry groups of tourists from port to port on a designated route and usually equipped to entertain them lavishly along the way

cruising radius the greatest distance that an aircraft or ship can cruise, away from and back to a certain point without refueling

☆**crul·ler** (krul′ər) *n.* ⟦Du *kruller* < *krullen,* to CURL⟧ 1 a kind of doughnut characterized by a ridged or twisted appearance and a rich dough 2 [Now Dial.] any friedcake or doughnut

crumb (krum) *n.* ⟦ME *crome* < OE *cruma,* lit., scraping from bread crust, akin to Ger *krume* < IE **gr-eu,* to scratch, scrape (> Ger *krauen,* to scratch) < base **ger-,* to turn, twist⟧ 1 a very small piece broken off something; small particle or bit, esp. of bread, cake, etc. 2 any bit or scrap [*crumbs* of knowledge] 3 the soft part of bread within the crust ☆4 [Slang] a worthless, disgusting, or despicable person: also **crum·bum** (krum′bum′) —*vt. Cooking* to cover or thicken with crumbs

crum·ble (krum′bəl) *vt.* **-bled, -bling** ⟦freq. of CRUMB⟧ to break into crumbs or small pieces —*vi.* to fall to pieces; disintegrate —*n.* 1 a baked dessert of fruit topped with a crumbly pastry mixture 2 [Rare] a crumb or crumbling substance

crum·bly (-blē) *adj.* **-bli·er, -bli·est** 1 apt to crumble; easily crumbled 2 crumblike; consisting of crumbs or small particles —**crum′bli·ness** *n.*

crumb·y (krum′ē) *adj.* **-i·er, -i·est** 1 full of crumbs ☆2 [Slang] CRUMMY —**crumb′i·ness** *n.*

crum·horn (krum′hôrn′) *n.* ⟦< Ger *krummhorn* < *krumm,* crooked + *horn,* HORN⟧ an early double-reed musical instrument with a curve at the end of the tube

crum·my (krum′ē) *adj.* **-mi·er, -mi·est** ⟦< CRUM(B), with basic notion "brittle, friable, hence worthless" + -Y[2]⟧ [Slang] 1 dirty, cheap, shabby, disgusting, etc. 2 inferior, worthless, contemptible, etc. —**crum′mi·ness** *n.*

crump (krump) [Chiefly Brit.] *vt., vi.* ⟦echoic⟧ to strike or explode with a heavy thud —*n.* 1 the act or sound of crumping 2 an exploding shell or bomb

crum·pet (krum′pit) *n.* ⟦prob. < ME *crompid (cake)* < OE *crompeht,* flat cake, lit., full of crumples, wrinkled < *crump,* twisted: for IE base see CRUMB⟧ a small, unsweetened batter cake baked on a griddle: it is usually toasted before serving

crum·ple (krum′pəl) *vt.* **-pled, -pling** ⟦ME *crumplen,* var. of *crimplen,* to wrinkle, freq. of *crimpen,* CRIMP[1]⟧ 1 to crush together into creases or wrinkles 2 to cause to collapse —*vi.* 1 to become crumpled 2 to fall or break down; collapse —*n.* a crease or wrinkle

crum·ply (-plē) *adj.* **-pli·er, -pli·est** easily crumpled

crunch (krunch) *vi., vt.* ⟦earlier *craunch,* of echoic orig.⟧ 1 to bite or chew with a noisy, crackling sound 2 to press, grind, tread, fall, etc. with a noisy, crushing sound 3 [Informal] to process (a vast quantity of numbers or other data) rapidly [using a computer to *crunch* population statistics] —*n.* 1 the act or sound of crunching 2 an exercise much like a SIT-UP, except that the upper body is raised only slightly off the floor rather than to an upright position ☆3 [Informal] a tight situation; specif., an economic squeeze ☆4 [Slang] a showdown

crunch·time (krunch′tīm′) *n.* [Slang] the tense, critical phase of an activity: often written **crunch time**

crunch·y (-ē) *adj.* **crunch′i·er, crunch′i·est** making a crunching sound, as when chewed —**crunch′i·ness** *n.*

cru·or (kro͞o′ôr′) *n.* ⟦L, blood (which flows from a wound): see CRUDE⟧ coagulated blood; gore

crup·per (krup′ər, kroop′-) *n.* ⟦ME *crouper* < OFr *cropiere* < *crope,* rump < Frank **kruppa:* see CROP⟧ 1 a padded leather strap passed around the base of a horse's tail and attached to the saddle or harness to keep it from moving forward 2 the croup of a horse 3 [Informal] the buttocks

cru·ral (kroor′əl, kro͞o′rəl) *adj.* ⟦L *cruralis* < *crus* (gen. *cruris*): see fol.⟧ *Anat.* of or pertaining to the leg or thigh, or a leglike structure

crus (krus, kro͞os) *n., pl.* **cru·ra** (kro͞o′rə, kroor′ə) ⟦L, leg, shank⟧ 1 the part of a leg or hind limb between the knee and the ankle; shank 2 any anatomical structure resembling a leg or (in the plural) a pair of legs, as the cerebral peduncles

cru·sade (kro͞o sād′) *n.* ⟦< Sp *cruzada,* altered after Fr *croisade,* both < ML *cruciata* < pp. of *cruciare,* to mark with a cross < L *crux,* CROSS⟧ 1 [*sometimes* **C-**] any of the separate military expeditions undertaken as part of THE CRUSADES (see phrase below) 2 a vigorous, concerted action for some cause or idea, or against some abuse —*vi.* **-sad′ed, -sad′ing** to engage in a crusade —**the Crusades** a series of military expeditions undertaken chiefly by European Christians from the 11th to the end of the 13th cent. to recover the Holy Land from the Muslims —**cru·sad′er** *n.*

cru·sa·do (kro͞o zä′do͞o) *n., pl.* **-does** or **-dos** ⟦Port *cruzado,* orig., pp. of *cruzar* < ML *cruciare:* see prec.⟧ an obsolete Portuguese coin with the figure of a cross on it

cruse (kro͞os, kro͞oz) *n.* ⟦ME *crouse* < OE *cruse,* akin to MDu *cruyse,* ON *krus,* Ger *krause,* pot with lid⟧ a small container for liquids such as water, oil, honey, or wine

crush (krush) *vt.* ⟦ME *crushen* < OFr *croisir,* to gnash (teeth), crash, break < Frank **krostjan,* to gnash; akin to OSwed *krysta,* Goth *kriustan*⟧ 1 to press between two opposing forces so as to break or injure; put out of shape or condition by pressure; squeeze together; crumple 2 to press, grind, or pound into small particles or into powder 3 to subdue or suppress by or as by force; overwhelm 4 to oppress harshly 5 to force out or extract by pressing or squeezing —*vi.* 1 to be or become crushed 2 to press forward; crowd (*into, against,* etc.) —*n.* 1 a crushing; severe pressure 2 a crowded mass, esp. of people ☆3 [Informal] an infatuation: often in the phrase **have a crush on,** to be infatuated with —**SYN.** BREAK —**crush′a·ble** *adj.* —**crush′er** *n.*

crush·ing (-iŋ) *adj.* 1 overwhelming or decisive [a *crushing* defeat] 2 hurtful or demoralizing [*crushing* remarks] —**crush′ing·ly** *adv.*

Cru·soe (kro͞o′sō), **Robinson** *see* ROBINSON CRUSOE

crust (krust) *n.* ⟦ME *cruste* < OFr or L: OFr *crouste* < L *crusta:* for IE base see CRUDE⟧ 1 *a)* the hard, crisp outer part of bread *b)* a piece of this *c)* any dry, hard piece of bread 2 the pastry shell of a pie 3 any hard surface layer, as of snow or soil 4 a hard deposit formed by wine on the inside surface of a bottle 5 [Slang] audacity; insolence; gall 6 *Geol.* the solid, rocky outer portion or shell of the earth; lithosphere 7 *Med.* a dry, hard outer layer of blood, pus, or other bodily secretion — *vt., vi.* 1 to cover or become covered with a crust 2 to form or harden into a crust

crus·ta·cean (krus tā′shən) *n.* ⟦ModL *Crustacea* < *crustaceus,* having a crust or shell < L *crusta,* prec.⟧ any of a subphylum (Crustacea) of arthropods, including shrimps, crabs, barnacles, and lobsters, that usually live in the water and breathe through gills: they have a hard outer shell and jointed appendages —*adj.* of crustaceans

crus·ta·ceous (-shəs) *adj.* ⟦ModL *crustaceus:* see prec.⟧ 1 of or like a crust 2 having a hard crust or shell 3 *Zool.* CRUSTACEAN

crust·al (krus′təl) *adj.* of a crust, esp. the earth's crust

crust·y (krus′tē) *adj.* **crust′i·er, crust′i·est** ⟦ME⟧ 1 having, forming, or resembling a crust 2 rough and outspoken; not patient, kindly, or refined —**crust′i·ly** *adv.* —**crust′i·ness** *n.*

crutch (kruch) *n.* ⟦ME *crucche* < OE *crycce,* staff, akin to Ger *krücke* < IE base **ger-:* see CRADLE⟧ 1 any of various devices used, often in pairs, by lame people as an aid in walking; typically, a staff with a hand grip and a padded crosspiece on top that fits under the armpit 2 anything one leans or relies on for support, help, etc.; prop 3 any device that resembles a crutch 4 [Archaic] the crotch of the human body 5 *Naut.* a forked support for a spar when the sail is furled —*vt.* to support with or as with a crutch or crutches; prop up

crux (kruks; *also* krooks) *n., pl.* for 1, 2, & 3 **crux′es** or **cru·ces** (kro͞o′sēz′) ⟦L, CROSS⟧ 1 *Heraldry* a cross 2 a difficult problem; puzzling thing 3 the essential or deciding point 4 [**C-**] a small S constellation near the celestial pole, containing the Coalsack; the Southern Cross; the Cross

crux an·sa·ta (kruks′an sāt′ə) ⟦L, cross with a handle < *crux,* CROSS + fem. of *ansatus* < *ansa,* a handle⟧ the ankh, an ancient Egyptian symbol

cru·za·do (kro͞o zä′dō, -sä-) *n., pl.* **-dos** ⟦Port: see CRUSADO⟧ the former basic monetary unit of Brazil

crwth (kro͞oth) *n.* ⟦Welsh: see CROWD[2]⟧ an ancient Celtic musical instrument, somewhat like a violin, but with a broad, shallow body

cry (krī) *vi.* **cried, cry′ing** ⟦ME *crien* < OFr *crier* < L *quiritare,* to wail, shriek (var. of *quirritare,* to squeal like a pig < **quis,* echoic of a squeal); assoc. in ancient folk etym. with L *Quirites,* Roman citizens (as if meaning "to call the *Quirites,*" implore their help)⟧ 1 to make a loud vocal sound or utterance; call out, as for help; shout 2 to sob and shed tears, in expressing sorrow, pain, grief, etc.; weep 3 *a)* to plead or clamor (*for*) *b)* to show or suggest a great need (*for*) [problems *crying* for solution] 4 to utter its characteristic call: said of an animal —*vt.* 1 to plead or beg for [to *cry* quarter] 2 to utter loudly; shout; exclaim 3 to call out (wares for sale, services offered, etc.); announce publicly 4 to bring into a specified condition by crying [to *cry* oneself asleep] —*n., pl.* **cries** ⟦ME & OFr *cri* < the v.⟧ 1 a loud vocal sound expressing pain, anger, fright, joy, etc. 2 any loud utterance; shout 3 an announcement or advertisement called out publicly 4 an urgent appeal; plea 5 popular report; rumor; rallying call or battle cry; watchword 6 the current opinion or fashion 7 clamor of the people; public outcry 8 a slogan 9 a sobbing and shedding of tears; fit of weeping 10 the characteristic vocal sound of an animal 11 *a)* the baying of hounds in the chase *b)* a pack of hounds —**a far cry** 1 a great distance; long way 2 a thing much different —**cry down** to belittle; disparage —**cry in one's beer** [Informal] to lament or complain in a maudlin manner —**cry off** to withdraw from an agreement or undertaking —**cry one's eyes out** to weep much and bitterly —**cry out** 1 to shout; yell 2 to complain loudly —**cry up** to shout praise of; praise highly —**in full cry** in eager pursuit: said of a pack of hounds

SYN.—**cry** implies the expression of grief, sorrow, pain, or distress by making mournful, convulsive sounds and shedding tears; **weep** more specifically stresses the shedding of tears; to **sob** is to weep aloud with a catch in the voice and short, gasping breaths; **wail** implies the uttering of loud, prolonged, mournful cries in unsuppressed lamentation; **keen**, specifically an Irish term, signifies a wailing in lamentation for the dead; to **whimper** is to cry with subdued, whining, broken sounds, as a fretful or frightened child does; **moan** suggests the expression of sorrow or pain in a low, prolonged, mournful sound or sounds; **blubber**, a derisive term used chiefly of children, implies a contorting or swelling of the face with weeping, and broken, inarticulate speech

☆**cry·ba·by** (-bā′bē) *n., pl.* **-bies** [Informal] 1 a person, esp. a child, who cries often or with little cause 2 a person who complains when he or she fails to win or get his or her own way

cry·ing (-iŋ) *adj.* 1 that cries 2 demanding immediate notice or remedy [a *crying* need] —**for crying out loud!** [Slang] an exclamation of annoyance or surprise

cry·o- (krī ō, -ə) ⟦< Gr *kryos*, cold, frost: see CRUDE⟧ *combining form* cold or freezing [*cryogen*]

cry·o·bi·ol·o·gy (krī′ō bī äl′ə jē) *n.* ⟦prec. + BIOLOGY⟧ the science that studies organisms, esp. warmblooded animals, at low temperatures —**cry′o·bi·ol′o·gist** *n.*

cry·o·gen (krī′ō jən, -ə-) *n.* ⟦CRYO- + -GEN⟧ a refrigerant

cry·o·gen·ics (krī′ō jen′iks, -ə-) *Biochem., Med. n.* ⟦prec. + -ICS⟧ 1 the science that deals with the production of very low temperatures and their effect on the properties of matter 2 loosely, CRYONICS —**cry′o·gen′ic** *adj.*

cryogenic surgery CRYOSURGERY

cry·o·hy·drate (-hī′drāt′) *n.* ⟦CRYO- + HYDRATE⟧ a crystalline solid containing water of crystallization only at low temperatures, as salt mixed with ice

cry·o·lite (krī′ō līt′, -ə-) *n.* ⟦CRYO- + -LITE: with reference to its icy appearance⟧ a fluoride of sodium and aluminum, Na_3AlF_6, found in Greenland or produced synthetically and used in the molten state in the electrolytic production of aluminum

cry·om·e·ter (krī äm′ət ər) *n.* ⟦CRYO- + -METER⟧ a thermometer, usually filled with alcohol, for measuring lower temperatures than a mercury thermometer will register

☆**cry·on·ics** (krī än′iks) *n.* ⟦CRYO- + *-n-* + -ICS⟧ the practice of freezing the body of a person who has just died in order to preserve it for possible resuscitation in the future, as when a cure for the disease that caused death has been found —**cry·on′ic** *adj.*

cry·o·phyte (krī′ō fīt′, -ə-) *n.* ⟦CRYO- + -PHYTE⟧ a plant, esp. any of various algae and fungi, that grows on ice or snow

cry·o·pre·serve (krī′ō pri zurv′) *vt.* **-served′**, **-serv′ing** ⟦CRYO- + PRESERVE⟧ to preserve (biological material, food, etc.) using very low temperatures —**cry′o·pres′er·va′tion** *n.* —**cry′o·pre·served′** *adj.*

cry·o·probe (krī′ə prōb′) *n.* a surgical instrument for conducting intense cold to small areas of tissue, as to treat tumors or remove skin blemishes

cry·os·co·py (krī äs′kə pē) *n.* ⟦CRYO- + -SCOPY⟧ the science that studies the freezing points of liquids

cry·o·stat (krī′ō stat′, -ə-) *n.* ⟦CRYO- + -STAT⟧ a regulator for maintaining a constant, low temperature

cry·o·sur·ger·y (krī′ō sur′jər ē) *n.* ⟦CRYO- + SURGERY⟧ surgery involving the selective destruction of tissues by freezing them, as with liquid nitrogen —**cry′o·sur′gi·cal** *adj.*

cry·o·ther·a·py (krī′ō ther′ə pē) *n. Med.* treatment by the use of cold, as by the application of ice packs or by lowering the body temperature

crypt (kript) *n.* ⟦ME *cript* < L *crypta* < Gr *kryptē* < *kryptos*, hidden < *kryptein*, to hide < IE **krubh-* < base **kru-*, to pile up, cover > OIr *cráu*, hut⟧ 1 an underground chamber or vault, as one under the main floor of a church, often, esp. formerly, serving as a burial place 2 *Anat.* any of various recesses, glandular cavities, or follicles in the body —**crypt·al** (krip′təl) *adj.*

crypt- (kript) *combining form* CRYPTO-: used before a vowel

☆**crypt·a·nal·y·sis** (kript′ə nal′ə sis) *n.* ⟦CRYPT(OGRAM) + ANALYSIS⟧ the act or science of deciphering a code or coded message without a prior knowledge of the key —**crypt·an′a·lyst′** (-an′ə list′) *n.* —**crypt′an′a·lyt′ic** (-an′ə lit′ik) *adj.*

cryp·tic (krip′tik) *adj.* ⟦LL *crypticus* < Gr *kryptikos* < *kryptos*: see CRYPT⟧ 1 *a)* having a hidden or ambiguous meaning; mysterious; baffling [a *cryptic* comment] *b)* obscure and curt in expression 2 *Zool.* serving to conceal, as the form or coloration of certain animals Also **cryp′ti·cal** —*SYN.* OBSCURE —**cryp′ti·cal·ly** *adv.*

cryp·to- (krip′tō, -tə) ⟦< Gr *kryptos*: see CRYPT⟧ *combining form* 1 secret or hidden [*cryptogram*] 2 being such secretly and not by public avowal [a *crypto*-Fascist]

cryp·to·bi·o·sis (krip′tō bī ō′sis, -tə-) *n.* ANABIOSIS —**cryp′to·bi·ot′ic** (-bī ät′ik) *adj.*

cryp·to·clas·tic (krip′tō klas′tik, -tə-) *adj.* ⟦CRYPTO- + CLASTIC⟧ *Mineralogy* consisting of microscopic grains

cryp·to·coc·cal (krip′tō käk′əl, -tə-) *adj.* of or having to do with cryptococcosis [*cryptococcal* meningitis]

cryp·to·coc·co·sis (krip′tō kä kō′sis, -tə-) *n., pl.* **-ses′** (-sēz′) ⟦< ModL *Cryptococcus* + -OSIS⟧ a systemic, opportunistic infection caused by a yeastlike imperfect fungus (*Cryptococcus neoformans*, family Torulopsidaceae) and characterized by nodules in the lungs, skin, brain, etc.

cryp·to·crys·tal·line (-kris′təl in) *adj. Mineralogy* having a crystalline structure of submicroscopic crystals

cryp·to·gam (krip′tə gam′) *n.* ⟦Fr *cryptogame* < Gr *kryptos* (see CRYPT) + *gamos*, marriage (see GAMO-)⟧ a plant that bears no flowers or seeds but propagates by means of spores, as algae, mosses, ferns, etc. —**cryp′to·gam′ic** *adj.*, **cryp·tog′a·mous** (-täg′ə məs)

cryp·to·gen·ic (krip′tə jen′ik) *adj.* ⟦CRYPTO- + -GENIC⟧ IDIOPATHIC

cryp·to·gram (krip′tə gram′) *n.* ⟦CRYPTO- + -GRAM⟧ something written in code or cipher —**cryp′to·gram′mic** *adj.*

cryp·to·graph (krip′tə graf′) *n.* 1 CRYPTOGRAM 2 a device for writing or solving cryptograms

cryp·tog·ra·phy (krip täg′rə fē) *n.* ⟦CRYPTO- + -GRAPHY⟧ 1 the art of writing or deciphering messages in code 2 the system used in a code or cipher —**cryp·tog′ra·pher** *n.*, **cryp·tog′ra·phist** —**cryp·to·graph·ic** (krip′tə graf′ik) *adj.* —**cryp′to·graph′i·cal·ly** *adv.*

cryp·tol·o·gy (krip täl′ə jē) *n.* the study of secret codes or ciphers and the devices used to create and decipher them —**cryp·to·lo·gic** (krip′tə läj′ik) *adj.*, **cryp′to·log′i·cal** *adj.* —**cryp·tol′o·gist** *n.*

cryp·to·me·ri·a (krip′tō mir′ē ə, -tə-) *n.* ⟦ModL < Gr *kryptos*, hidden (see CRYPT) + *meros*, a part (see MERIT) + ModL *-ia* (see -IA): so named because the seeds are "hidden" within the scales of the cones⟧ a tall, cone-bearing East Asian tree (*Cryptomeria japonica*) of the baldcypress family

cryp·to·nym (krip′tə nim′) *n.* ⟦CRYPT(O)- + -ONYM⟧ CODE NAME

cryp·to·pine (krip′tō pēn′, -pin; -tə-) *n.* ⟦CRYPT(O)- + OP(IUM) + -INE[3]⟧ a poisonous alkaloid, $C_{21}H_{23}NO_5$, found in opium

cryp·tor·chi·dism (krip tôr′ki diz′əm) *n.* a congenital condition in which one or both testicles fail to descend into the scrotum: also **cryp·tor′chism′** (-kiz′əm) —**cryp·tor′chid** (-kid) *n., adj.*

cryp·to·spo·rid·i·o·sis (krip′tō spə rid′ē ō′sis) *n., pl.* **-ses′** (-sēz′) ⟦< fol. + -OSIS⟧ an intestinal disease that is transmitted by contaminated food or water, caused by cryptosporidia and characterized by diarrhea, cramps, etc., which may be severe for an individual with a weakened immune system

cryp·to·spo·rid·i·um (krip′tō spə rid′ē əm) *n., pl.* **-i·a** (-ə) ⟦ModL < CRYPTO- + *spora* (see SPORE) + *-idium*, dim. suffix < Gr *-idion*⟧ a sporozoan (*Cryptosporidium parvum*, family Cryptosporidiidae) that causes cryptosporidiosis

cryp·to·xan·thin (krip′tō zan′thin, -tə-) *n.* ⟦CRYPTO- + XANTH(O)- + -IN[1]⟧ a carotenoid pigment, $C_{40}H_{56}O$, in butter, eggs, and various plants, that can be converted into vitamin A in the body

cryp·to·zo·ic (krip′tō zō′ik, -tə-) *adj.* ⟦< CRYPTO- + Gr *zōē*, life + -IC⟧ relating to animals that live in hidden locations, as in crevices or under leaves, rocks, etc.

cryp·to·zo·ol·o·gy (krip′tō zō äl′ə jē) *n.* the branch of zoology dealing with attempts to verify the existence or survival of animals generally regarded as legendary or extinct, as the Abominable Snowman —**cryp′to·zo′o·log′i·cal** (-ə läj′i kəl) *adj.* —**cryp′to·zo·ol′o·gist** (-jist) *n.*

cryst *abbrev.* 1 crystalline 2 crystallography

crys·tal (kris′təl) *n.* ⟦altered (modeled on L) < ME & OFr *cristal*, OE *cristalla* < L *crystallum*, crystal, ice < Gr *krystallos* < *kryos*: see CRUDE⟧ 1 *a)* a clear, transparent mineral; esp., pure quartz *b)* a piece of such quartz cut in the form of an ornament 2 *a)* a very clear, brilliant glass *b)* articles made of this glass, such as goblets, bowls, or other ware ☆3 the transparent protective covering over the face of a watch 4 anything clear and transparent like crystal 5 a solidified form of a substance in which the atoms or molecules are arranged in a definite pattern that is repeated regularly in three dimensions: crystals tend to develop forms bounded by definitely oriented plane surfaces that are harmonious with their internal structures: see CRYSTAL SYSTEM 6 *Elec., Radio a)* a piezoelectric body or plate, as of quartz, used to control the frequency of an oscillator or as a circuit element in a crystal filter *b)* a piezoelectric body used in a transducer, as in a crystal pickup or microphone —*adj.* 1 of or composed of crystal 2 like crystal; clear or transparent 3 *Radio* of or using a crystal

Crys·tal (kris′təl) *n.* ⟦see prec.⟧ a feminine name

crystal detector *Radio* a semiconductor rectifier used for demodulation

crystal gazing divination with the aid of a ball (**crystal ball**) of rock crystal or, commonly, glass, into which one stares in seeking certain images, esp. of future events —**crystal gazer**

crys·tall- (kris′təl) *combining form* CRYSTALLO-: used before a vowel

crystal lattice the regular spaced pattern resulting when atoms, molecules, or ions are arranged to form a crystal

crys·tal·lif·er·ous (kris′təl if′ər əs) *adj.* ⟦CRYSTALL(O)- + -I- + -FEROUS⟧ producing or containing crystals

crys·tal·line (kris′təl in, -īn′, -ēn′) *adj.* ⟦ME < OFr & L; OFr *crystalin* < L *crystallinus* < Gr *krystallinos*: see CRYSTAL⟧ 1 consisting or made of crystal or crystals 2 like crystal; clear or transparent 3 having the structure of a crystal

crystalline lens LENS (sense 3)

crys·tal·lite (kris′təl īt′) *n.* ⟦CRYSTALL(O)- + -ITE[1]⟧ 1 a tiny, embryonic crystal, too small to be identified with any mineral species 2 a rock consisting mainly of such tiny crystals —**crys·tal·lit·ic** (kris′təl it′ik) *adj.*

crys·tal·lize (kris′təl īz′) *vt.* **-lized′**, **-liz′ing** 1 to cause to form crystals or take on a crystalline structure 2 to give a definite form to 3 to coat with sugar —*vi.* 1 to become crystalline in form 2 to take on a definite form [their customs *crystallized* into law] —**crys′tal·liz′a·ble** *adj.* —**crys′tal·li·za′tion** *n.*

crys·tal·lo- (kris′tə lō, -lə) ⟦< Gr *krystallos*, CRYSTAL⟧ *combining form* crystal *[crystallography]*

crys·tal·log·ra·phy (kris′tə läg′rə fē) ***n.*** ⟦prec. + -GRAPHY⟧ the science of the form, structure, properties, and classification of crystals —**crys·tal·lo·graph·ic** (kris′tə lō graf′ik) ***adj.***, **crys′tal·lo·graph′i·cal**

crys·tal·loid (kris′təl oid′) ***adj.*** ⟦CRYSTALL(O)- + -OID⟧ **1** like a crystal **2** having the nature of a crystalloid —***n.*** **1** a substance, usually crystallizable, which, when in solution, readily passes through vegetable and animal membranes: compare COLLOID **2** a small crystalloid grain of protein found in some cells, seeds, etc. —**crys′tal·loi′dal** ***adj.***

crystal meth [Slang] large, hard crystals of highly purified methamphetamine: a more potent, addictive form of methamphetamine

crystal pickup a piezoelectric vibration pickup or detector, as used on electric phonographs: cf. MAGNETIC PICKUP

crystal pleat one of a series of fine, permanently pressed pleats of varying widths, usually in a sheer fabric

crystal set a primitive type of radio receiver with a crystal detector instead of an electron tube detector

crystal system any of the seven groups (cubic, hexagonal, rhombohedral, tetragonal, orthorhombic, monoclinic, and triclinic) of crystals classified on the basis of the relationships of their crystallographic axes (imaginary lines of reference used to describe the crystal planes)

crystal violet a rosaniline dye, $C_{25}H_{30}ClN_3$, used as an antiseptic, an indicator, and a bacterial stain in Gram's method: cf. GENTIAN VIOLET

crys·tal·ware (kris′təl wer′) ***n.*** glassware made of lead crystal

cs *abbrev.* **1** capital stock **2** case(s) **3** civil service

Cs[1] *abbrev. Meteorol.* cirrostratus

Cs[2] *Chem. symbol for* cesium

CS *abbrev.* **1** capital stock **2** Christian Science **3** Christian Scientist **4** civil service

CSA *abbrev.* Confederate States of America

csc *abbrev. Trigonometry* cosecant

CSC *abbrev.* **1** Civil Service Commission **2** ⟦L *Congregatio a Sancta Cruce*⟧ Congregation of the Holy Cross

C-sec·tion (sē′sek′shən) ***n.*** [Informal] CESAREAN (SECTION): also written **c-section**

CS (gas) (sē′es′) ⟦after B. *C(orson)* (1896-1987) & R. *S(toughton)* (1906-57), U.S. chemists who discovered the compound⟧ a powerful tear gas in the form of an aerosol, $C_{10}H_5ClN_2$, with the odor of pepper, used by police and the military, esp. to control riots

CSM *abbrev.* Command Sergeant Major

CSP *abbrev.* ⟦L *Congregatio Sancti Pauli*⟧ Congregation of Saint Paul

C-SPAN (sē′span′) *service mark* Cable Satellite Public Affairs Network

CST *abbrev.* Central Standard Time

ct *abbrev.* **1** cent **2** county **3** court

Ct *abbrev.* **1** carat(s) **2** Connecticut **3** Court

CT *abbrev.* **1** Central Time **2** computed (or computerized) tomography **3** Connecticut

CTE *abbrev.* chronic traumatic encephalopathy

cten·o- (ten′ō, tē′nō, ten′ə, tē′nə) ⟦< Gr *kteis* (gen. *ktenos*) < **pktenos*; akin to L *pecten*, comb: see PECTEN⟧ *combining form* ctenoid scales, teeth, etc. *[ctenophore]*: also, before a vowel, **cten-**

cte·noid (ten′oid′, tē′noid′) ***adj.*** ⟦< prec. + -OID⟧ having an edge with projections like the teeth of a comb, as the posterior margin of the scales of certain fishes

cte·noph·o·ran (tə näf′ō rən, -ə-) ***adj.*** of a ctenophore —***n.*** CTENOPHORE

cten·o·phore (ten′ə fôr′, tē′nə-) ***n.*** ⟦CTENO- + -PHORE⟧ any of a phylum (Ctenophora) of sea animals with an oval, transparent, jellylike body bearing eight rows of comblike plates that aid in swimming

Ctes·i·phon (tes′ə fän′) ancient ruined city on the Tigris, near Baghdad, in present-day Iraq (fl. 1st cent. B.C.–5th cent. A.D.)

ctn *abbrev.* **1** carton **2** *Trigonometry* cotangent

ctr *abbrev.* center

Ctrl *abbrev.* control: a key on a standard computer keyboard: also **ctrl**

CT scan ⟦*c(omputerized) t(omography)*⟧ **1** a noninvasive method of diagnosing disorders of the body, esp. of the soft tissues, including the brain: it uses a computerized combination of many tomograms to form an image **2** the image so formed —**CT scanner** —**CT scanning**

cu *abbrev.* cubic

Cu[1] *abbrev. Meteorol.* cumulus

Cu[2] ⟦L *cuprum*⟧ *Chem. symbol for* copper

cua·dri·lla (kwä drēl′yä, -drē′-) ***n.***, *pl.* **-llas** ⟦Sp, dim. of *cuadro*, a square⟧ **1** in bullfighting, a matador's team of assistants **2** any group of associates or attendants

cub (kub) ***n.*** ⟦Early ModE *cubbe*, young fox < ? OIr *cuib*, whelp⟧ **1** a young fox, wolf, bear, lion, tiger, whale, etc. **2** an inexperienced, awkward youth **3** [Old-fashioned] a novice newspaper reporter **4** [**C-**] CUB SCOUT —**cub′bish** ***adj.***

Cu·ba (kyoo͞′bə; *Sp* koo͞′bä) **1** island in the West Indies, south of Fla. **2** country comprising this island & several small nearby islands: gained independence from Spain in 1898: 42,803 sq mi (110,860 sq km); cap. Havana —**Cu′ban** ***adj., n.***

cub·age (kyoo͞′bij) ***n.*** ⟦CUB(E) + -AGE⟧ cubic content or volume

Cu·ba li·bre (kyoo͞′bə lē′brə, koo͞′-; -brā′) ⟦Sp, lit., free (adj.) Cuba⟧ [*also* **c- l-**] an iced cocktail made of rum, lime juice, and cola

Cuban heel a type of shoe heel of medium height and width

cu·ba·ture (kyoo͞′bə chər) ***n.*** ⟦< L *cubus*, CUBE[1], after QUADRATURE⟧ **1** the determination of cubic content **2** cubic content

cub·by·hole (kub′ē hōl′) ***n.*** ⟦dim. < Brit dial. *cub*, little shed (akin to MHG *kobe*, cage, stall: for IE base see COVE[1]) + HOLE⟧ **1** a small, enclosed space or room that confines snugly or uncomfortably **2** a small, open compartment as in a desk; pigeonhole Also **cub′by**, *pl.* **-bies**

cube[1] (kyoo͞b) ***n.*** ⟦Fr < L *cubus* < Gr *kybos*, a cube, die, vertebra < IE base **keu(b)-*, to bend, turn > HIP[1], HIVE, L *cubare*, to lie down⟧ **1** a solid with six equal, square sides **2** anything having more or less this shape *[an ice cube]* **3** the product obtained by multiplying a given number or quantity by its square; third power *[the cube of 3 is 27 (3 × 3 × 3)]* —***vt.*** **cubed, cub′ing 1** to raise to the third power; obtain the cube of (a number or quantity) **2** to cut or shape into cubes; dice *[cube the vegetables]* **3** to score (meat) in a crisscross pattern in order to tenderize it **4** to measure the cubic content of —**cub′er** ***n.***

☆**cu·be**[2] (kyoo͞′bā, koo͞′-) ***n.*** ⟦< Sp *quibey* < native name⟧ any tropical American plant of a genus (*Lonchocarpus*) of the pea family, whose roots yield rotenone

cu·beb (kyoo͞′beb′) ***n.*** ⟦ME *quibibe* < OFr *cubebe* < ML *cubeba* < Ar *kubāba*, var. of *kabāba*⟧ **1** *a)* a tropical vine (*Piper cubeba*) of the pepper family *b)* the small, spicy berry of this vine, used as a spice, flavoring, etc. ☆**2** a cigarette made from the crushed dried berries, formerly smoked to relieve catarrh

cube root the number or quantity of which a given number or quantity is the cube *[the cube root of 8 is 2]*

cube steak a thin slice of beef that has been tenderized by being cubed

cu·bic (kyoo͞′bik) ***adj.*** ⟦ME *cubik* < OFr *cubique* < L *cubicus* < Gr *kybikos*: see CUBE[1]⟧ **1** having the shape of a cube **2** having three dimensions, or having the volume of a cube whose length, width, and depth (or height) each measure the given unit *[a cubic foot]* **3** designating or of a crystal system having three axes of equal length, each of which intersects at right angles with the others: see CRYSTAL SYSTEM **4** *Math.* of the third power or degree; relating to the cubes of numbers or quantities

cu·bi·cal (-bi kəl) ***adj.*** cubic; esp., cube-shaped —**cu′bi·cal·ly** ***adv.***

cu·bi·cle (kyoo͞′bi kəl) ***n.*** ⟦L *cubiculum* < *cubare*, to lie down: see CUBE[1]⟧ **1** a small sleeping compartment, as in a dormitory **2** any small compartment, as for study; often, specif., a WORKSTATION (sense 1) set off by partitions, typically one of several in an office

cubic measure a system of measuring volume in cubic units, in which 1,728 cubic inches = 1 cubic foot, and 1,000 cubic millimeters = 1 cubic centimeter: see the table of weights and measures in the Reference Supplement

cu·bic·u·lum (kyoo͞ bik′yoo͞ ləm) ***n.***, *pl.* **-u·la** (-lə) ⟦L: see CUBICLE⟧ a burial chamber, as in a catacomb

cubic zirconia a synthetic crystalline compound of zirconium oxide, fashioned to resemble diamonds, etc.: also **cubic zirconium**

cu·bi·form (kyoo͞′bə fôrm′) ***adj.*** cube-shaped

cub·ism (kyoo͞b′iz′əm) ***n.*** [*often* **C-**] a movement in art, esp. of the early 20th cent., characterized by a breakdown of the subject into cubes and other geometric forms in abstract arrangements rather than by a realistic representation —**cub′ist** (-ist) ***n., adj.*** —**cu·bis′tic** ***adj.***

cu·bit (kyoo͞′bit) ***n.*** ⟦ME & OE < L *cubitum*, the elbow, cubit: for IE base see CUBE[1]⟧ an ancient unit of linear measure, about 18-22 inches (45.4-55.5 cm): originally the length of a man's arm from the end of the middle finger to the elbow

cu·boid (kyoo͞′boid′) ***adj.*** ⟦Gr *kyboeidēs*: see CUBE[1] & -OID⟧ **1** shaped like a cube **2** designating a cubelike tarsal bone on the outside of the foot between the metatarsals and the calcaneus —***n.*** **1** a six-sided figure each face of which is a rectangle **2** the cuboid bone —**cu·boi′dal** ***adj.***

Cub Scout a member of a division of the Boy Scouts of America for boys eight to ten years of age

cu·ca·ra·cha (koo͞′kä rä′chä) ***n.***, *pl.* **-chas** ⟦Sp⟧ a cockroach

☆**cu·chi·fri·to** (koo͞′chē frē′tō) ***n.***, *pl.* **-tos** ⟦AmSp < *cuchí*, pig + *frito*, fried⟧ a small piece of pork, pig's stomach, etc. dipped in batter and deep-fried

Cu·chul·ain or **Cu·chul·lin** (koo͞ kul′in) ***n.*** ⟦Ir⟧ *Celt. Legend* a heroic warrior who single-handedly defends his country against invaders

cu·ci·na (koo͞ chē′nä) ***n.***, *pl.* **-ne** (-nā) ⟦It, kitchen, cuisine⟧ style of cooking; cuisine

cuck·ing stool (kuk′iŋ) ⟦ME *coking-stole*, lit., toilet seat < ME *coken* < OIce *kuka*, to defecate: the instrument was orig. made like a toilet seat to heighten the indignity⟧ [Historical] a chair to which a person was fastened and exposed to public ridicule, or sometimes ducked in water, as a punishment

cuck·old (kuk′əld) ***n.*** ⟦ME *cokewold* < OFr *cucuault* < *cucu* (see fol.): said to be in allusion to the female bird's habit of changing mates⟧ a man whose wife has committed adultery —***vt.*** to make a cuckold of —**cuck′old·ry** (-rē) ***n.***

cuck·oo (koo͞′koo͞′; *also* ko͝ok′oo͞) ***n.*** ⟦ME < OFr *coucou*, *cucu*, echoic of the bird's cry⟧ **1** any of a family (*Cuculidae*, order Cuculiformes) of birds with a long, slender body, grayish-brown on top and white below: many, including the European species (*Cuculus canorus*), lay eggs in the nests of other birds, but the American species hatch and rear their own young **2** *a)* the call of a cuckoo, which sounds somewhat like its name *b)* an imitation of this call **3** [Slang] a crazy or foolish person —***vi.*** to utter or imitate the call of a cuckoo —***vt.*** to repeat continually, as the cuckoo does its call —***adj.*** [Slang] crazy; foolish; silly

cuckoo clock a clock with a small toy figure of a cuckoo in it, which pops out at regular intervals, usually on the hour, to the accompaniment of a sound imitating the bird's call

cuck·oo·flow·er (-flou′ər) ***n.*** **1** a bitter cress (*Cardamine pratensis*) bearing white or rose flowers; lady's-smock **2** RAGGED ROBIN Also written **cuckoo-flower**

cuck·oo·pint (-pint′) ***n.*** a European wildflower (*Arum maculatum*) of the arum family, with large, sagittate leaves and a spadix and spathe similar to those of the jack-in-the-pulpit

cuckoo spit (*or* spittle) **1** a frothy substance produced on plants by the nymphs of spittlebugs to envelop their larvae **2** such an insect

cu·cul·late (kyo͞o kul′āt′, -it; kyo͞o′kə lāt′, -lit) ***adj.*** ⟦LL(Ec) *cuculatus* < *cucullа*, for L *cucullus*, hood: see COWL[1]⟧ shaped like a hood; cowled, as the leaves of violets: also **cu·cul′lat′ed**

cu·cum·ber (kyo͞o′kum′bər; *occas.*, -kəm-) ***n.*** ⟦ME *cucomer* < OFr or L; OFr *cocombre* < L *cucumis* (gen. *cucumeris*)⟧ **1** a trailing annual vine (*Cucumis sativus*) of the gourd family, grown for its edible fruit **2** the long fruit, with a green rind and firm, white flesh, gathered before fully mature and used in salads or preserved as pickles —**cool as a cucumber** **1** comfortably cool **2** calm and self-possessed

☆**cucumber tree** an American magnolia tree (*Magnolia acuminata*) with large, greenish flowers and fruit resembling a small cucumber

cu·cur·bit (kyo͞o kur′bit) ***n.*** ⟦L *cucurbita*⟧ **1** any plant of the gourd family **2** ⟦Fr *cucurbite* < L *cucurbita*: so called in allusion to its shape⟧ a large, gourd-shaped flask with a wide mouth, formerly used in distillation

Cú·cu·ta (ko͞o′ko͞o tä) city in N Colombia

cud (kud) ***n.*** ⟦ME < OE *cudu, cwudu*, ball of cud, lit., what is rounded < IE base **gwet-*, resin, gum > Ger *kitt*, cement, glue⟧ a mouthful of previously swallowed food regurgitated from the first two chambers of the stomach of cattle and other ruminants back to the mouth, where it is chewed slowly a second time —**chew the cud** to recall and think over something; ruminate; ponder

cud·bear (kud′ber′) ***n.*** ⟦coined < CUTHBERT[1] by Dr. *Cuthbert* Gordon, 18th-c. Brit physician, who developed the dye⟧ **1** a purple dye prepared from lichens **2** ORCHIL

cud·dle (kud′'l) ***vt.*** **-dled, -dling** ⟦Early ModE, to make comfortable, prob. < ME (northern dial.) **cudelen* for **couthelen* (for *-d*, see FIDDLE) < *couth*, known, hence acquainted with, comfortable with (see UNCOUTH) + *-le*, freq. suffix⟧ to hold lovingly and gently in one's arms; embrace and fondle —***vi.*** to lie close and snug; nestle —***n.*** **1** a cuddling **2** an embrace; hug —**SYN.** CARESS

cud·dle·some (-səm) ***adj.*** CUDDLY (sense 1)

cud·dly (kud′lē) ***adj.*** **-dli·er, -dli·est** **1** having a quality or nature which invites cuddling **2** fond of cuddling

cud·dy[1] (kud′ē) ***n.***, *pl.* **-dies** ⟦17th-c.: < ? MLowG *kaiüte* < NormFr *cahutte*, ult. < MHG *hütte*, HUT⟧ [Rare] **1** *a)* a small cabin on a ship *b)* the cook's galley on a small ship **2** any small room, cupboard, or closet

cud·dy[2] (kud′ē, ko͝od′ē) ***n.***, *pl.* **-dies** ⟦< ? *Cuddy*, dim. of CUTHBERT[1]⟧ [Chiefly Scot.] **1** a donkey **2** a fool

cudg·el (kuj′əl) ***n.*** ⟦ME (SW dial.) *kuggel* < OE *cycgel*, lit., club with rounded head, akin to Ger *kugel*, ball < IE base **geu-*, to curve, bend > COD[2]⟧ a short, thick stick or club —***vt.*** **-eled** or **-elled, -el·ing** or **-el·ling** to beat with a cudgel —**take up the cudgels (for)** to come to the defense (of)

cud·weed (kud′wēd′) ***n.*** ⟦prob. CUD + WEED[1]: of uncertain allusion⟧ any of several small plants (genus *Gnaphalium*) of the composite family, with cottony or woolly leaves

cue[1] (kyo͞o) ***n.*** ⟦< *q*, Q, used in plays in the 16th & 17th c. to indicate actors' entrances; prob. abbrev. of some L word (as *quando*, when, or *qualis*, in what manner)⟧ **1** a bit of dialogue, action, or music that is a signal for an actor's entrance or speech, or for the working of curtains, lights, sound effects, etc. **2** *Music* a gesture or written device used to signal the entry of one or more instrumentalists or vocalists **3** anything serving as a signal to do something **4** an indirect suggestion; hint **5** [Now Rare] *a)* the role that one is assigned to play *b)* a necessary course of action **6** [Archaic] frame of mind; mood; temperament **7** *Psychol.* a secondary stimulus that guides behavior, often without entering consciousness —***vt.*** **cued, cu′ing** or **cue′ing** **1** to give a cue to **2** to ready (a recording) to play back from a certain point: often with *up* —☆**cue in** to add (dialogue, music, etc.) at a particular point in a script —**on cue** **1** in response to a CUE[1] (*n.* 1) **2** at a fitting or opportune moment —**take one's cue from** to follow the advice, example, etc. of

cue[2] (kyo͞o) ***n.*** ⟦var. of QUEUE⟧ **1** QUEUE (*n.* 1) **2** a long, tapering, tipped rod used in billiards and pool to strike the cue ball: also called **cue stick** **3** a long, shovel-like stick used in shuffleboard to push the disks —***vt.*** **cued, cu′ing** or **cue′ing** **1** to braid (hair) **2** to strike (a cue ball) with a cue

cue ball in billiards or pool, the white or yellowish ball that a player strikes directly with the cue

cue card a card, unseen by the audience, carrying dialogue, lyrics, etc. as an aid to a television performer

Cuen·ca (kweŋ′kä) city in SC Ecuador

Cuer·na·va·ca (kwer′nə vä′kə) city in SC Mexico: capital of Morelos

☆**cues·ta** (kwes′tə) ***n.*** ⟦Sp < L *costa*, side, rib⟧ [Southwest] a ridge or hill characterized by a steep incline on one side and a gentle slope on the other

cuff[1] (kuf) ***n.*** ⟦by sense extension < ME *cuffe, coffe*, hand covering, glove < ? ML *cuffia*, head covering, parallel with OFr *coife*: see COIF⟧ **1** a band or fold at the end of a sleeve, either sewn in or detachable **2** a turned-up fold at the bottom of a trouser leg **3** the part of a glove covering the wrist or forearm **4** a handcuff: *usually used in pl.* **5** any of various bandlike or folded parts, as of a shoe or golf bag: esp., the inflatable arm wrap of a sphygmomanometer —***vt.*** to put a cuff or cuffs on —☆**off the cuff** ⟦in ref. to impromptu notes made on one's *cuff*⟧ [Informal] in an offhand manner; extemporaneously —☆**on the cuff** ⟦in ref. to a note made on the creditor's *cuff*⟧ [Slang] on credit —**shoot one's cuffs** to flex the elbow or wrist so as to expose one's shirt cuffs beyond the coat sleeves

cuff[2] (kuf) ***vt.*** ⟦Early ModE < ? prec. (in orig. sense, "a glove")⟧ to strike, esp. with the open hand; slap —***vi.*** to fight or scuffle —***n.*** a slap or blow

cuff link a stud or similar device inserted into prepared holes in a shirt cuff to keep it closed

Cu·fic (ko͞o′fik, kyo͞o′-) ***adj.*** *alt. sp. of* KUFIC

Cu·ia·bá (ko͞o′yä bä′) city in WC Brazil; capital of Mato Grosso state

cui bo·no (kwē bō′nō′) ⟦L, lit., to whom for a good⟧ **1** for whose benefit? i.e., who stands to gain from this? **2** to what purpose? i.e., of what utility is this?

cui·rass (kwi ras′) ***n.*** ⟦Fr *cuirasse* < It *corazza* < VL **coracea*, for L (*vestis*) *coriacea*, leather (clothing) < *corium*, leather, hide: see CORIUM⟧ **1** a piece of closefitting armor for protecting the breast and back, orig. made of leather **2** the breastplate of such armor **3** *Zool.* a protective structure of bony plates —***vt.*** to cover with or as with a cuirass

cui·ras·sier (kwē′rə sir′) ***n.*** ⟦Fr⟧ a cavalryman wearing a cuirass

Cuis·i·nart (kwē′zən ärt′) ⟦ult. < Fr *cuisine*, kitchen: see fol.⟧ *trademark for* a kind of food processor —***n.*** [*often* **c-**] a food processor like this

cui·sine (kwē zēn′, kwi-) ***n.*** ⟦Fr < LL *cocina*, earlier *coquina*, kitchen < L *coquere*, to COOK⟧ **1** [Archaic] the kitchen **2** style of cooking; manner of preparing food **3** the food prepared, as at a restaurant

cuisse (kwis) ***n.*** ⟦ME *cuissues* < OFr *cuisseaux*, pl. of *cuissel* < *cuisse*, thigh < L *coxa*, hip: see COXA⟧ a piece of armor to protect the thigh: also **cuish** (kwish)

cuke (kyo͞ok) ***n.*** [Informal] *short for* CUCUMBER (sense 2)

culch (kulch) ***n.*** *alt. sp. of* CULTCH

cul-de-sac (kul′də sak′, ko͝ol′-) ***n.***, *pl.* **cul′-de-sacs′** or **culs′-de-sac′** ⟦Fr, lit., bottom of a sack⟧ **1** a passage or position with only one outlet; blind alley; specif., a dead-end street with a turnaround at the closed end **2** a situation from which there is no escape **3** *Anat.* a blind pouch, as the cecum

cul·do·scope (kul′də skōp′) ***n.*** ⟦< prec. + -SCOPE⟧ an endoscope used in a medical examination of the ovary, uterus, etc., inserted through the upper vaginal wall into the pelvic cavity —**cul·dos·co·py** (kul däs′kə pē) ***n.***

-cule (kyo͞ol, kyo͝ol, kyəl) ⟦< Fr or L; Fr *-cule* < L *-culus, -cula, -culum*⟧ *suffix forming nouns* small [*animalcule*]: added to nouns

cu·let (kyo͞o′lit, -let′) ***n.*** ⟦OFr, dim. of *cul*, posterior, bottom < L *culus*, anus < IE base *(*s*)*keu-*, to cover < SKY, HIDE[1]⟧ the small facet at the base of a gem whose face is cut as a brilliant

cu·lex (kyo͞o′leks′) ***n.*** ⟦ModL < L, a gnat < IE base **k̑ū-*, sharp, pointed > OIr *cuil*, gnat, Sans *śula-*, spear⟧ any of a large genus (*Culex*) of mosquitoes, including many of the most common species found in North America and Europe —**cu·li·cine** (kyo͞o′lə sin, -sīn′) ***adj., n.***

Cu·lia·cán (ko͞ol′yə kän′) city in NW Mexico: capital of Sinaloa: in full **Culiacán Ro·sa·les** (rō zäl′äz, -säl′äs)

cu·lic·id (kyo͞o′lə sid′) ***adj.*** ⟦< ModL *Culicidae*, name of the family < L *culex* (gen. *culicis*): see CULEX⟧ of the mosquito family —***n.*** a mosquito

cu·li·nar·y (kyo͞o′lə ner′ē, kul′ə-) ***adj.*** ⟦LL *culinarius* < L *culina*, kitchen < base of *coquere*, COOK⟧ **1** of the kitchen **2** of cooking **3** suitable for or used in cooking

cull (kul) ***vt.*** ⟦ME *cullen* < OFr *coillir* < L *colligere*: see COLLECT[2]⟧ **1** *a)* to pick out; select [*to cull facts from an encyclopedia*] *b)* to pick out in order to discard or destroy [*a librarian culled unneeded books*] **2** *a)* to select and gather (flowers or fruit); pick ☆*b)* *Forestry* to select trees to be felled for timber **3** to examine (a collection or group) in order to select desired parts or, esp., to discard or destroy unwanted parts [*to cull a herd*] —***n.*** something picked out; esp., something rejected as not being up to standard

Cul·len (kul′ən), **Coun·tee** (koun′tē) 1903-46; U.S. poet

cul·len·der (kul′ən dər) ***n.*** *var. of* COLANDER

cul·let (kul′it) ***n.*** ⟦< Fr *collet*, dim. of *col*, neck, with reference to glass debris at the neck of a bottle in blowing⟧ scraps of waste glass that can be remelted

cul·lion (kul′yən) ***n.*** ⟦ME *coillon*, wretch, lit., testicle < OFr *coillon* < VL **coleone*, eunuch < **colea*, scrotum < L *coleus* < ? *colum*, a strainer⟧ [Obs.] a low, contemptible fellow

cul·lis (kul′is) ***n.*** ⟦Fr *coulisse*: see COULISSE⟧ *Archit.* a gutter or groove

cul·ly (kul′ē) [Old Slang] ***n.***, *pl.* **-lies** ⟦17th-c. thieves' slang, prob. contr. of CULLION⟧ **1** a dupe **2** a fellow; companion; mate —***vt.*** **-lied, -ly·ing** to trick; deceive; cheat

culm[1] (kulm) ***n.*** ⟦northern Brit dial. < ME *colme, culme* < ? OE *col*, COAL + ? suffix as in *fæthm*, FATHOM⟧ **1** waste material from coal screenings or washings **2** fine pieces of anthracite coal

culm[2] (kulm) ***n.*** ⟦L *culmus*, a stalk, stem < IE **kolemos* > Gr *kalamos*, reed, Ger *halm*, blade (of grass)⟧ the jointed stem of various grasses, usually hollow —***vi.*** to grow or develop into a culm

cul·mi·nant (kul′mə nənt) ***adj.*** ⟦ML *culminans*, prp. of *culminare*: see fol.⟧ **1** at the highest point or altitude **2** culminating

cul·mi·nate (kul′mə nāt′) ***vi.*** **-nat′ed, -nat′ing** ⟦< ML *culminatus*, pp. of *culminare* < L *culmen* (gen. *culminis*), peak, summit, contr. of *columen*: see COLUMN⟧ **1** to reach its highest or lowest altitude: said of a celestial body **2**

to reach its highest point or climax; result (*in*) —*vt.* to bring to its climax; cap
cul·mi·na·tion (kul′mə nā′shən) *n.* **1** a culminating; reaching of the highest or lowest altitude or point **2** the highest point; zenith; climax
cu·lottes (ko͞o′läts′, kyo͞o′-) *pl.n.* ⟦Fr < *cul*, posterior: see CULET⟧ [*occas. sing.*] women's or girls' pants made full in the legs to resemble a skirt and extending to just below the knee or to mid-calf
cul·pa (ko͝ol′pə, kul′-) *n.* ⟦L⟧ **1** fault; guilt **2** *Law* neglect or fault; negligence
cul·pa·ble (kul′pə bəl) *adj.* ⟦altered, modeled on L < ME *coupable* < OFr < L *culpabilis* < *culpa*, crime, fault, blame⟧ deserving blame; blameworthy —**cul′pa·bil′i·ty** (-bil′ə tē) *n.* —**cul′pa·bly** (-blē) *adv.*
cul·prit (kul′prit) *n.* ⟦< Anglo-Fr *cul. prit*, contr. for phr. *culpable, prit (a averer nostre bille)*, lit., guilty, ready (to prove our case): words used by prosecutor in opening case < *culpable* (see prec.) + *prit*, for OFr *prest* < LL *praestus*, ready⟧ **1** a person guilty of a crime or offense; offender **2** [Archaic] a person accused of a crime, esp. by arraignment before a law court **3** anything or anyone regarded as the cause of some problem, misfortune, etc.
cult (kult) *n.* ⟦< L *cultus*, care, cultivation, orig. pp. of *colere*, to till: see WHEEL⟧ **1** *a)* a system of religious worship or ritual *b)* a quasi-religious group, often living in a colony and typically with a charismatic leader who indoctrinates members with beliefs regarded as unorthodox or extremist **2** *a)* devoted attachment to, or extravagant admiration for, a person, principle, or lifestyle, esp. when regarded as a fad [the *cult* of nudism] *b)* the object of such attachment **3** a group of followers; sect —**cult′ic** *adj.* —**cult′ism′** *n.* —**cult′ist** *n.*
cultch (kulch) *n.* ⟦< ? OFr *culche, couche*, layer, deposit: see COUCH⟧ **1** old shells, stones, etc., forming a spawning bed for oysters **2** [Dial.] rubbish
cul·ti·gen (kul′ti jən) *n.* ⟦CULTI(VATED) + -GEN⟧ a cultivated plant not known in a wild form and presumably originated in cultivation
cul·ti·va·ble (kul′tə və bəl) *adj.* ⟦ML *cultivabilis*⟧ that can be cultivated: also **cul′ti·vat′a·ble** (-vāt′ə bəl) —**cul′ti·va·bil′i·ty** (-və bil′ə tē) *n.*
☆**cul·ti·var** (kul′ti vär′, -vər) *n.* ⟦*culti(vated) var(iety)*⟧ a variety of a plant species originating and continuing in cultivation and given a name in a modern language
cul·ti·vate (kul′tə vāt′) *vt.* **-vat′ed, -vat′ing** ⟦< ML *cultivatus*, pp. of *cultivare* < LL *cultivus*, tilled < L *cultus*: see CULT⟧ **1** to prepare and use (soil or land) for growing crops; till **2** to break up the surface soil around (plants) in order to destroy weeds, prevent crusting, and preserve moisture **3** to grow (plants, crops, etc.) **4** to improve or develop (plants) by various horticultural techniques **5** to improve by care, training, or study; refine [to *cultivate* one's mind] **6** to promote the development or growth of; acquire and develop [to *cultivate* a taste for music] **7** to seek to develop familiarity with; give one's attention to; pursue
cul·ti·vat·ed (-id) *adj.* **1** prepared and used for growing crops; tilled [*cultivated* land] **2** grown by cultivation: opposed to WILD (sense 1) **3** trained and developed; refined; cultured
cultivated mushroom an edible mushroom (*Agaricus bisporus*) with a pale cap and stalk: the most common food mushroom
cul·ti·va·tion (kul′tə vā′shən) *n.* **1** the act of cultivating (in various senses) **2** refinement, or culture
cul·ti·va·tor (kul′tə vāt′ər) *n.* **1** a person who cultivates **2** an implement or machine for loosening the earth and destroying weeds around growing plants
cul·trate (kul′trāt′) *adj.* ⟦L *cultratus*, knifelike < *culter*, a knife: see COLTER⟧ sharp-edged and pointed
cul·tur·al (kul′chər əl) *adj.* **1** of or pertaining to culture; specif., of the training and refinement of the intellect, interests, taste, skills, and arts **2** of or having to do with a particular culture **3** obtained by breeding or cultivation —**cul′tur·al·ly** *adv.*
cultural anthropology a major division of anthropology that deals with all aspects of past and present human cultures, including language, customs, and behavior
cultural (*or* culture) lag the failure of one aspect of a cultural complex to keep pace with the changes in some other related aspect, as the failure of social institutions to keep pace with the rapid advances in technology
Cultural Revolution the period of social upheaval (1966-76) in the People's Republic of China initiated by MAO TSE-TUNG in an attempt to consolidate power and eliminate Western cultural influence: it came to be characterized by civil disorder, economic crisis, and brutal repression
cul·tur·a·ti (kul′chər ät′ē) *pl.n.* ⟦fol. + (LITER)ATI⟧ [Informal] people who take a great interest in culture and the arts: often dismissive
cul·ture (kul′chər) *n.* ⟦ME < L *cultura* < *colere*: see CULT⟧ **1** cultivation of the soil **2** production, development, or improvement of a particular plant, animal, commodity, etc. **3** *a)* the growth of bacteria, microorganisms, or other plant and animal cells in a specially prepared nourishing fluid or solid *b)* a colony of microorganisms or cells thus grown **4** *a)* development, improvement, or refinement of the intellect, emotions, interests, manners, and taste *b)* the result of this; refined ways of thinking, talking, and acting **5** development or improvement of physical qualities by special training or care [body *culture*, voice *culture*] **6** *a)* the ideas, customs, skills, arts, etc. of a people or group, that are transferred, communicated, or passed along, as in or to succeeding generations *b)* such ideas, customs, etc. of a particular people or group in a particular period; civilization *c)* the particular people or group having such ideas, customs, etc. **7** the values and goals of a particular business, esp. a large corporation, as reflected in its management style, employee morale, levels of productivity and efficiency, etc. —*vt.* **-tured, -tur·ing** **1** to cultivate **2** to grow (microorganisms or cells) in a specially prepared medium
cul·tured (-chərd) *adj.* **1** produced or obtained by cultivation **2** *Biol.* grown in a specially prepared medium: said of microorganisms or cells **3** refined in speech, behavior, etc.
cultured pearl a pearl grown within a mollusk by controlled stimulation, as by insertion of a bead of mother-of-pearl
culture medium a nutrient substance sterilized and prepared for the controlled growth of microorganisms or cells
☆**culture shock** the alienation, confusion, surprise, etc. that may be experienced by someone encountering unfamiliar surroundings, a strange city or community, a different culture, etc.
☆**culture vulture** [Slang] a person who professes great interest in culture and the arts: a jocular or derisive term
cul·tur·ist (kul′chər ist) *n.* **1** a person engaged in the culture of plants or animals **2** one who advocates, or is devoted to, general cultural advancement
cul·tus (kul′təs) *n.* ⟦L⟧ a cult, esp. a religious cult
cul·ver (kul′vər) *n.* ⟦ME < OE *culfer, culufre* < VL **columbra*, for L *columbula*, dim. of *columba*: see COLUMBARIUM⟧ [Archaic] a dove or pigeon
cul·ver·in (kul′vər in) *n.* ⟦Fr *coulevrine* < *couleuvre*, adder < VL **culobra*, for L *colubra*, a serpent, snake < IE base **(s)kel-*, to bend: see COLON[1]⟧ **1** a kind of medieval musket **2** a long, heavy cannon of the 15th-17th cent.
cul·vert (kul′vərt) *n.* ⟦late 18th-c. < ?⟧ a conduit, esp. a drain, as a pipelike construction of stone, concrete, or metal, that passes under a road, railroad track, footpath, etc. or through an embankment

culvert

cum[1] (kum, ko͝om) *prep.* ⟦L⟧ with: used, chiefly in hyphenated compounds, with the general meaning "combined with," "plus" [vaudeville-*cum*-burlesque]
cum[2] (kum) *n.* [Slang] *phonetic sp. of* COME (*n.*): somewhat vulgar
cum. *abbrev.* cumulative
Cu·mae (kyo͞o′mē) ancient Greek city in Campania, SW Italy, near Naples: thought to have been the first Greek colony in Italy, founded 9th or 8th cent. B.C.
Cu·mae·an (kyo͞o mē′ən) *adj.* **1** of Cumae **2** of or relating to a famous sibyl of Cumae: cf. SIBYLLINE BOOKS
Cu·ma·ná (ko͞o′mə nä′) seaport of NE Venezuela, on the Caribbean
cum·ber (kum′bər) *vt.* ⟦ME *combren*, aphetic < *acombren* < OFr *encombrer* < *en-* (see EN-[1]) + *combre*, obstruction, barrier < VL **comboros*, something brought together, ult. (? via Gaul) < IE **kom* (see COM-) + base **bher-*, BEAR[1]⟧ **1** to hinder by obstruction or interference; hamper **2** to burden in a troublesome way **3** [Obs.] to perplex or distress —*n.* anything that cumbers
Cum·ber·land (kum′bər lənd) **1** former county of NW England, now part of Cumbria county **2** ⟦after William Augustus, Duke of *Cumberland* (1721-65), Brit general, son of George II⟧ river in S Ky. & N Tenn., flowing west into the Ohio at the S Ill. border: 687 mi (1,106 km)
Cumberland Gap pass in the Cumberland Plateau, at the juncture of the Virginia, Kentucky, & Tennessee borders: *c.* 1,700 ft (518 m) high
Cumberland Plateau (*or* Mountains) ⟦after William Augustus, Duke of *Cumberland*: see CUMBERLAND (the river)⟧ division of the W Appalachians, extending from S W.Va. to N Ala.
cum·ber·some (kum′bər səm) *adj.* hard to handle or deal with as because of size, weight, or complexity; burdensome; unwieldy; clumsy —**SYN.** HEAVY —**cum′ber·some·ly** *adv.* —**cum′ber·some·ness** *n.*
☆**cum·bi·a** (ko͝om′bē ə) *n.* ⟦AmSp, prob. < Sp *cumbé*, traditional dance of African origin⟧ **1** a Latin American dance, orig. of Colombia, involving short, gliding steps **2** music for this dance, similar to salsa
cum·brance (kum′brəns) *n.* a troublesome burden
Cum·bri·a (kum′brē ə) county in NW England, on the Scottish border: 2,632 sq mi (6,817 sq km) —**Cum′bri·an** *adj., n.*
cum·brous (kum′brəs) *adj.* CUMBERSOME —**cum′brous·ly** *adv.* —**cum′brous·ness** *n.*
cum gra·no sa·lis (ko͝om grä′nō sä′lis) ⟦ModL, with a grain of salt⟧ not too literally; with some reservations
cum·in (kum′in; ko͞o′min, kyo͞o′-, ko͝o′-) *n.* ⟦ME < OFr *cumin* < L *cuminum* < Gr *kyminon* < Sem, as in Heb *kammōn*, Ar *kammūn*⟧ **1** a small herb (*Cuminum cyminum*) of the umbel family, bearing umbels of small, white or rose flowers **2** its aromatic fruits, used for flavoring pickles, soups, etc. Also sp. **cum′min**
cum lau·de (ko͝om lou′de, kum lô′dē) ⟦L, lit., with praise⟧ phrase signifying above-average academic distinction upon graduating from a college or university: see also MAGNA CUM LAUDE, SUMMA CUM LAUDE
cum·mer (kum′ər) *n.* ⟦ME *commare* < OFr *commere* < LL(Ec) *commater* < L *com-*, with + *mater*, MOTHER[1]⟧ [Scot.] **1** a godmother **2** a woman companion **3** a woman or girl
cum·mer·bund (kum′ər bund′) *n.* ⟦Hindi *kamarband* < Pers, loin band < *kamar*, loins + *band*, a band⟧ a broad waistband for wear with a tuxedo and other men's formal dress or as a woman's accessory
Cum·mings (kum′iŋz), **E(dward) E(stlin)** 1894-1962; U.S. poet: also written **e e cummings**
cum·quat (kum′kwät′) *n. alt. sp. of* KUMQUAT

cum·shaw (kum′shô′) ***n.*** ⟦< dial. form of Chin *kan hsieh*, grateful thanks⟧ a tip or gratuity

cu·mu·late (kyo͞o′myə lāt′; *for adj.*, -lit, -lāt′) ***vt., vi.*** **-lat′ed, -lat′ing** ⟦< L *cumulatus*, pp. of *cumulare*, to heap up, amass < *cumulus*: see CUMULUS⟧ to gather into a heap; accumulate —***adj.*** gathered into a heap —**cu′mu·la′tion *n.***

cu·mu·la·tive (kyo͞o′myə lə tiv′; *occas.*, -lāt′iv) ***adj.*** ⟦see prec.⟧ **1** increasing in effect, size, quantity, etc. by successive additions; accumulated *[cumulative interest]* **2** taking successive additions into account *[a cumulative average]* **3** designating or of preferred stock that pays regular dividends which, if not paid on the scheduled date, accumulate and take priority over dividend payments to other classes of the company's stock **4** *Law* designating additional evidence that gives support to earlier evidence —**cu′mu·la·tive′ly *adv.***

cumulative voting a system of voting, as in some corporate and legislative elections, in which each voter is allowed as many votes as there are offices to be filled and may freely allocate them among the candidates, even by giving all the votes to one candidate

cu·mu·li·form (kyo͞o′myə lə fôrm′) ***adj.*** ⟦L *cumuli*, pl. of *cumulus* + -FORM⟧ designating, or having the form of, a cumulus, or esp. any cloud with lofty vertical development: cf. STRATIFORM

cu·mu·lo·nim·bus (kyo͞o′myə lō′nim′bəs) ***n.*** the type of dense cloud that develops vertically through all cloud levels, consisting of water droplets, ice crystals, and sometimes hail, and associated with thunder, lightning, and heavy showers: see CLOUD

cu·mu·lous (kyo͞o′myə ləs) ***adj.*** of, or having the form of, a cumulus, esp. the cloud

cu·mu·lus (kyo͞o′myə ləs) ***n., pl.*** **-li′** (-lī′) ⟦L, a heap < IE **k̂u-melos*, a swelling, increase < base **k̂eu-*, a swelling > CAVE⟧ **1** a heap; mass; pile **2** the type of bright, billowy cloud with a dark, flat base, that develops vertically through all cloud levels and consists mostly of water droplets

Cu·nax·a (kyo͞o nak′sə) ancient town in Babylonia, near the Euphrates: site of a battle (401 B.C.) in which Cyrus the Younger was killed

cunc·ta·tion (kuŋk tā′shən) ***n.*** ⟦L *cunctatio* < *cunctari*, to hesitate, linger < IE base **k̂ouk-, *k̂enk-*: see HANG⟧ [Rare] a delaying or delay —**cunc·ta·tive** (kuŋk′tāt′iv, -tə tiv) ***adj.***

cu·ne·al (kyo͞o′nē əl) ***adj.*** ⟦< L *cuneus*, a wedge: for IE base, see CULEX⟧ wedge-shaped; esp., cuneiform

cu·ne·ate (kyo͞o′nē it, -āt′) ***adj.*** ⟦L *cuneatus* < prec.⟧ *Bot.* wedge-shaped; tapering, as some leaves: also **cu′ne·at′ed** (-āt′id) —**cu′ne·ate·ly *adv.***

cu·ne·i·form (kyo͞o nē′ə fôrm′, kyo͞o′nē ə-) ***adj.*** ⟦< L *cuneus* (see CUNEAL) + -FORM⟧ **1** wedge-shaped **2** designating the characters in ancient Akkadian, Assyrian, Babylonian, and Persian inscriptions, or the inscriptions themselves —***n.*** cuneiform characters or inscriptions

cuneiform characters
(Assyrian, c. 700 B.C.)

cun·ner (kun′ər) ***n.*** ⟦Brit var. *conner* < ? CONN, in sense "directing fishing boats to herring shoals"⟧ a small, edible, brownish-blue wrasse fish (*Tautogolabrus adspersus*) found along the Atlantic coast of North America

cun·ni·lin·gus (kun′ə liŋ′gəs) ***n.*** ⟦ModL < L, lit., vulva-licker < *cunnus*, vulva + *lingere*, to LICK⟧ a sexual activity involving oral contact with the female genitals

cun·ning (kun′iŋ) ***adj.*** ⟦ME, having skill, knowing < prp. of *cunnen*, to know: see CAN[1]⟧ **1** [Now Rare] skillful or clever **2** skillful in deception; sly; crafty **3** made or done with skill or ingenuity ☆**4** attractive or pretty in a delicate way; cute —***n.*** **1** [Now Rare] clever proficiency; skill **2** skill in deception; slyness; craftiness —**SYN.** CLEVER, SLY —**cun′ning·ly *adv.*** —**cun′ning·ness *n.***

Cun·ning·ham (kun′iŋ ham, -əm), **Merce** (murs) 1919-2009; U.S. dancer & choreographer

cunt (kunt) ***n.*** ⟦ME *cunte*, female genitals, akin to ON *kunta* < Gmc **kuntōn* < ?⟧ [Vulgar Slang] **1** the vulva or vagina **2** sexual intercourse with a woman **3** *a)* a woman (a term of hostility and contempt) *b)* any unpleasant or contemptible person

cup (kup) ***n.*** ⟦ME & OE *cuppe* < LL *cuppa*, altered < L *cupa*, tub < IE **keup-*, a hollow < base **keu-*, to bend, arch > COOMB, HUMP⟧ **1** a small, open container for beverages, usually bowl-shaped and with a handle **2** the bowl part of a drinking vessel **3** a cup and its contents **4** the amount a cup holds; cupful: a standard measuring cup holds 8 fluid ounces (*c.* 237 milliliters) or 16 tablespoons: abbrev. *C* **5** anything shaped like a cup or bowl **6** an ornamental, usually metal, cup with a stem and base, given as a prize **7** *a)* the chalice containing the wine at Communion *b)* the wine **8** one's portion, share, or allotment *[his cup of happiness was full]* **9** something served as in a cup: see CLARET CUP, FRUIT CUP **10** either of two sections of a bra, each of which supports a breast **11** a padded, hard-plastic protective device worn over the genitals by a male athlete **12** *Biol.* any cuplike organ or structure **13** *Golf* the container set in the hole sunk into the green, into which the ball drops **14** *Med.* a small glass bowl or similar object used in cupping —***vt.*** **cupped, cup′ping 1** to curve or shape into a rounded, cuplike form *[to cup one's hands]* **2** to hold by or as by enclosing with the hand or hands **3** *Med.* to treat with or subject to cupping —**in one's cups** drunk; intoxicated —**cup′like′ *adj.***

cup·bear·er (-ber′ər) ***n.*** a person who fills and serves the wine cups, as in a king's palace

cup·board (kub′ərd) ***n.*** ⟦ME *cuppebord*: see CUP & BOARD⟧ a closet or cabinet with shelves for holding cups, plates, food, and the like

☆**cup·cake** (kup′kāk′) ***n.*** **1** a little cake for one person, baked in a small, cup-shaped mold and often iced **2** [Slang] an attractive young woman: often a patronizing or dismissive term

cu·pel (kyo͞o′pəl, kyo͞o pel′) ***n.*** ⟦Fr *coupelle* < ML *cupella*, dim. < L *cupa*: see CUP⟧ **1** a small, shallow, porous cup used in assaying gold, silver, etc. **2** a hearth for refining metals —***vt.*** **-peled** or **-pelled, -pel·ing** or **-pel·ling** to assay or refine in a cupel —**cu′pel·la′tion** (-pə lā′shən) ***n.***

cup·fer·ron (kyo͞op′fər än′, ko͞op′-) ***n.*** ⟦CUP(RIC) + FERR(O)- + -ON⟧ a white crystalline material, $C_6H_5N(NO)ONH_4$, soluble in water or alcohol: used as a precipitating reagent for copper, iron, aluminum, etc.

cup·ful (kup′fo͝ol′) ***n.*** ***pl.*** **cup′fuls′** or **cups′ful′** as much as a cup will hold: see CUP (*n.* 4)

Cu·pid (kyo͞o′pid) ***n.*** ⟦ME & OFr *Cupide* < L *Cupido* < *cupido*, desire, passion < *cupidus*, eager, passionate < *cupere*, to desire < IE base **kup-*, to boil, smoke, be disturbed > Gr *kapnos*, smoke⟧ **1** *Rom. Myth.* the god of love, son of Venus: usually represented as a winged boy with bow and arrow and identified with the Greek Eros **2** [**c-**] a representation of Cupid as a naked, winged cherub, as on a valentine

cu·pid·i·ty (kyo͞o pid′ə tē) ***n.*** ⟦ME & Anglo-Fr *cupidite* < L *cupiditas* < *cupidus*: see prec.⟧ excessive desire for something, esp. for wealth; avarice; greed

cu·pid's-bow (kyo͞o′pidz bō′) ***adj.*** in the shape of the bow that Cupid is usually pictured as carrying *[a cupid's-bow mouth]*

cup of tea [Informal] **1** a favorite or well-suited thing, activity, etc. *[golf isn't his cup of tea]* **2** a thing to be taken into consideration or account; matter: used esp. in the phrase **a different cup of tea**

cu·po·la (kyo͞o′pə lə) ***n.*** ⟦It < L *cupula*, dim. of *cupa*: see CUP⟧ **1** a rounded roof or ceiling **2** a small, domelike structure on a roof **3** a small furnace for melting metals **4** any of various dome-shaped structures —**cu′po·laed** (-ləd) ***adj.***

cup·pa (kup′ə) ***n.*** [Brit. Informal] a cup of tea

cupped (kupt) ***adj.*** shaped like a cup; hollowed

cup·ping (kup′iŋ) ***n.*** the application to the skin of glass cups from which the air has been exhausted, in order to draw the blood to the surface: used, esp. formerly, to treat a variety of illnesses —**cup′per *n.***

cup·py (kup′ē) ***adj.*** designating or of a track for horse races that lacks resilience and is marked with many shallow depressions

cupola

cupr- *combining form* copper

cu·pre·ous (kyo͞o′prē əs, ko͞o′-) ***adj.*** ⟦LL *cupreus* < *cuprum*: see COPPER[1]⟧ **1** of or containing copper **2** copper-colored

cu·pri- (kyo͞o′pri, ko͞o′-) ⟦see CUPRO-⟧ *combining form* containing copper with a valence of two; cupric

cu·pric (kyo͞o′prik, ko͞o′-) ***adj.*** ⟦CUPR(O)- + -IC⟧ of or containing divalent copper

cu·prif·er·ous (kyo͞o prif′ər əs, ko͞o-) ***adj.*** ⟦CUPRI- + -FEROUS⟧ containing copper

cu·prite (kyo͞o′prīt′, ko͞o′-) ***n.*** a reddish mineral, Cu_2O, that is an ore of copper; cuprous oxide

cu·pro- (kyo͞o′prō, ko͞o′-) ⟦< L *cuprum*: see COPPER[1]⟧ *combining form* containing copper with a valence of one; cuprous

cu·pro·nick·el (kyo͞o′prō nik′əl, ko͞o′-) ***n.*** an alloy of copper and nickel, used in the manufacture of hardware and in some coins

cu·prous (kyo͞o′prəs, ko͞o′-) ***adj.*** ⟦CUPR(O)- + -OUS⟧ of or containing monovalent copper

cu·pu·late (kyo͞o′pyo͞o lāt′, -lit; -pyə-) ***adj.*** ⟦< fol. + -ATE[1]⟧ **1** shaped like a cupule or cup **2** having a cupule

cu·pule (kyo͞o′pyo͞ol) ***n.*** ⟦ME < L *cupula*: see CUPOLA⟧ *Biol.* a cuplike structure, as the part of an acorn that holds the nut

cur[1] (kur) ***n.*** ⟦ME *curre*, earlier *kurdogge*, prob. < ON or MLowG, as in Swed dial. *kurre*, MLowG *korre*, dog: basic sense "snarling, growling" < ON *kurra* or MLowG *korren*, to growl⟧ **1** a dog of mixed breed; mongrel **2** a mean, contemptible person

cur[2] *abbrev.* **1** currency **2** current

cur·a·ble (kyo͝or′ə bəl) ***adj.*** that can be cured —**cur′a·bil′i·ty** (-bil′ə tē) ***n.***

cu·ra·çao (kyo͝or′ə sō′, ko͝or′ə sou′) ***n.*** ⟦after the island of fol., where orig. made⟧ [*also* **C-**] a liqueur made by flavoring distilled spirits with the dried peel of bitter oranges: also **cu′ra·çoa′** (-sō′)

Cu·ra·çao (kyo͝or′ə sō′, ko͝or′ə sou′) **1** island nation associated with the Kingdom of the Netherlands, just north of the coast of Venezuela: 171 sq mi (443 sq km); cap. Willemstad **2** *former name for* NETHERLANDS ANTILLES

cu·ra·cy (kyo͝or′ə sē) ***n., pl.*** **-cies** the position, office, or work of a curate

☆**cu·ran·de·ra** (ko͞o′rän de′rä) ***n.*** ⟦AmSp, fem. of fol.⟧ a female curandero

☆**cu·ran·de·ro** (-de′rō) ***n.*** ⟦AmSp < Sp, healer < *curar*, to heal < L *curare*: see CURATIVE⟧ a Hispanic healer who makes use of folk medicine, rituals, etc.

cu·ra·re or **cu·ra·ri** (kyo͞o rä′rē, ko͞o-) ***n.*** ⟦Port *curare*, *curari* or Sp *curaré*, *urarí* < native (Tupí) name⟧ **1** a black, resinous substance prepared from the juices of certain South American plants and used by some Indians for poisoning arrows: it causes motor paralysis when introduced into the bloodstream and is used as a muscle relaxant **2** any of certain plants (esp. *Chondrodendron tomentosum* of the moonseed family) from which curare is prepared

cu·ra·rine (kyo͞o rä′rēn′, -rin; ko͞o-) ***n.*** any of a group of alkaloids derived from curare

cu·ra·rize (kyo͞o rä′rīz′, ko͞o-) ***vt.*** **-rized, -riz·ing** to treat with curare —**cu·ra·ri·za·tion** (kyo͞o rä′ri zā′shən) ***n.***

cu·ras·sow (kyo͞o′rə sō′, kyo͞o ras′ō′) ***n.*** ⟦< CURAÇAO⟧ any of several dark, crested, gallinaceous game birds (family Cracidae, esp. genera *Crax* and *Mitu*) of South and Central America, which usually nest in trees

cu·rate (kyoor′it; *for v.*, -āt′) ***n.*** ⟦ME *curat* < ML *curatus*, one responsible for the care of souls < L *curatus*: see CURATIVE⟧ **1** [Archaic] any clergyman **2** a clergyman who assists a vicar or rector —***vt.*** **-rat′ed, -rat′ing** to act as a curator for (an exhibition, museum department, etc.) —**cu·ra′tion** ***n.***

curate's egg ⟦based on a joke in an 1895 issue of the English magazine *Punch:* when served a stale egg at his bishop's home, a timid curate says that parts of it are excellent⟧ [Brit.] something that has both good and bad characteristics or parts

cu·ra·tive (kyoor′ət iv) ***adj.*** ⟦ME < OFr *curatif* < ML *curativus* < L *curatus*, pp. of *curare*, to take care of < *cura*: see CURE⟧ **1** of or for the curing of disease **2** curing, tending to cure, or having the power to cure —***n.*** a thing that cures; remedy

cu·ra·tor (kyo͞o rāt′ər, kyoor′āt′ər; kyoor′ət ər) ***n.*** ⟦ME *curatour* < L *curator* < *curare*: see prec.⟧ **1** a person in charge of a formal collection or exhibition, as at a museum or zoo **2** *Civil Law* a guardian, as of a minor —**cu·ra·to·ri·al** (kyoor′ə tôr′ē əl) ***adj.*** —**cu·ra′tor·ship′** ***n.***

curb (kurb) ***n.*** ⟦ME & OFr *courbe*, curve, curb, orig., adj., curved, bent < L *curvus*: see CURVE⟧ **1** *a)* a chain or strap passed around a horse's lower jaw and attached to the bit: the curb checks the horse by causing it to lower its head when the reins are pulled *b)* a type of bit having such a chain or strap (also **curb bit**) **2** anything that checks, restrains, or subdues **3** an enclosing framework **4** a raised margin around or along an edge, to strengthen or confine **5** the stone or concrete edging forming a gutter along a street **6** a market dealing in stocks and bonds not listed on the stock exchange: so called from the fact that early markets conducted their business on the street —***vt.*** **1** to restrain; check; control [*to curb an impulse*] **2** to lead (a dog being walked) to the curb or some other place where it may pass its waste matter **3** to provide with a curb —***SYN.*** RESTRAIN

curb appeal pleasing, inviting quality that interests prospective buyers: said of the exterior of a house for sale

curb·ing (-iŋ) ***n.*** **1** material for a curb **2** CURB (sense 5)

curb roof **1** MANSARD (ROOF) **2** GAMBREL ROOF

☆**curb service** service offered to customers who wish to remain in their cars, as at a drive-in restaurant

curb·side (kurb′sīd′) ***adj., adv.*** at the curb or on the sidewalk adjacent to the street —***n.*** CURB (sense 5)

curb·stone (kurb′stōn′) ***n.*** **1** any of the stones, or a row of stones, making up a curb **2** CURB (sense 5)

curch (kurch) ***n.*** ⟦sing. formed < *curches* < OFr *couvrechés*, pl. of *couvrechef*: see KERCHIEF⟧ [Scot.] a woman's kerchief for the head

cur·cu·li·o (kər kyo͞o′lē ō′) ***n.***, *pl.* **-li·os′** ⟦ModL < L, grain worm, weevil; akin to *circulus*: see CIRCLE⟧ any of a family (Curculionidae) of weevils: see WEEVIL

cur·cu·ma (kur′kyo͞o mə) ***n.*** ⟦ModL < Ar *kurkum*: see CROCUS⟧ any of a genus (*Curcuma*) of tropical plants of the ginger family, with thick, tuberous rootstocks that yield starch, including the turmeric

curd (kurd) ***n.*** ⟦15th-c. form, by metathesis < ME *crud*, orig., any coagulated substance < IE base **greut-*, to press, coagulate > CROWD[1]⟧ [*often pl.*] the coagulated part of milk, from which cheese is made: it is formed when milk sours and is distinguished from whey, the watery part — ***vt., vi.*** to form into curd; curdle

cur·dle (kurd′'l) ***vt., vi.*** **-dled, -dling** ⟦prec. + -LE, sense 1⟧ to form into curd; coagulate; congeal —**curdle someone's blood** to horrify or terrify someone

curd·y (kurd′ē) ***adj.*** **1** full of curd **2** like curd

cure (kyoor) ***n.*** ⟦OFr < L *cura*, care, concern, trouble < OL **coira* < IE base **kois-*, be concerned⟧ **1** a healing or being healed; restoration to health or a sound condition **2** a medicine or treatment for restoring health; remedy **3** a system, method, or course of treating a disease, ailment, etc. **4** spiritual charge of persons in a particular district; care of souls **5** the work or position of a curate; curacy **6** a process for curing meat, fish, tobacco, etc. —***vt.*** **cured, cur′ing** **1** to restore to health or a sound condition; make well; heal **2** to get rid of or counteract (an ailment, evil, bad habit, etc.) **3** to get rid of a harmful or undesirable condition in: with *of* [*cured him of lying*] **4** *a)* to preserve (meat, fish, etc.), as by salting or smoking *b)* to process (tobacco, leather, etc.), as by drying or aging **5** to encourage the proper hardening of (concrete or mortar) by regulating humidity and temperature —***vi.*** **1** to bring about a cure **2** to undergo curing, preserving, or processing [*tobacco cures in the sun*] —**cure′less** ***adj.*** —**cur′er** ***n.***

SYN.—**cure** and **heal** both imply a restoring to health or soundness, **cure** specifically suggesting the elimination of disease, distress, evil, etc., and **heal**, the making or becoming whole of a wound, sore, etc. or, figuratively, the mending of a breach; **remedy** stresses the use of medication or a specific corrective treatment in relieving disease, injury, distress, etc.

cu·ré (kyo͞o rā′, kyoor′ā′; *Fr* kü rā′) ***n.*** ⟦Fr < ML *curatus*: see CURATE⟧ in France, a parish priest

cure-all (kyoor′ôl′) ***n.*** ☆something supposed to cure all ailments or evils; panacea

cu·ret or **cu·rette** (kyo͞o ret′, kyoor et′) ***n.*** ⟦Fr < *curer*, to cleanse < L *curare* < *cura*: see CURE⟧ a spoon-shaped surgical instrument for the removal of tissue from the walls of body cavities —***vt.*** **-ret′ted, -ret′ting** to clean or scrape with a curet

cu·ret·tage (kyo͞o ret′ij′, kyoor et′-; kyo͞o′rə täzh′, kyoor′ə-) ***n.*** ⟦Fr: see prec.⟧ the process of curetting

cur·few (kur′fyo͞o′) ***n.*** ⟦ME *curfeu* < OFr *covrefeu*, lit., cover fire < *covrir* (see COVER) + *feu*, fire < L *focus*, fireplace: see FOCUS⟧ **1** *a)* in the Middle Ages, the ringing of a bell every evening as a signal for people to cover fires, put out lights, and retire *b)* the bell *c)* the time at which it was rung **2** *a)* a time, generally in the evening, set as a deadline beyond which inhabitants of occupied cities in wartime, children under a specified age, etc. may not appear on the streets or in public places *b)* the regulation establishing this time

cu·ri·a (kyoor′ē ə) ***n.***, *pl.* **-ri·ae′** (-ē′) ⟦L (in ML, court) < OL **co-viria*, assembly of men < *co-*, together + **viro-*, man: see VIRILE⟧ **1** in ancient Rome, *a)* any of the ten political subdivisions into which the Latin, Sabine, and Etruscan tribes were each divided *b)* its meeting place *c)* the senate house at Rome **2** a medieval judicial council or court held in the king's name **3** [**C-**] the administrative body of the Roman Catholic Church, consisting of various departments, courts, officials, etc., functioning under the authority of the pope: in full **Curia Ro·ma·na** (rō mä′nə, -mā′-) —**cu′ri·al** ***adj.***

cu·rie (kyo͞o′rē′, kyo͞o rē′) ***n.*** ⟦after Marie CURIE⟧ a basic unit of radioactivity, equal to a rate of decay of 3.7×10^{10} disintegrations per second (3.7037×10^{10} becquerels): abbrev. *Ci*

Cu·rie (kyoo rē′, kyoor′ē; *Fr* kü rē′) **1 Marie** (born *Marie Skłodowska*) 1867-1934; Pol. chemist & physicist in France: discovered polonium & radium (1898) in collaboration with her husband **2 Pierre** 1859-1906; Fr. physicist: husband of Marie

Curie point ⟦after Pierre CURIE⟧ the temperature at which the magnetic properties of a substance change from ferromagnetic to paramagnetic, usually lower than the substance's melting point: also **Curie temperature**

Curie's law ⟦after Pierre CURIE⟧ the law that the ratio of the magnetization of a paramagnetic substance to the magnetizing force is in inverse proportion to the absolute temperature

cu·ri·o (kyoor′ē ō′) ***n.***, *pl.* **-os′** ⟦contr. of CURIOSITY⟧ any unusual or rare article

cu·ri·o·sa (kyoor′ē ō′sə) ***pl.n.*** ⟦L, lit., curious objects⟧ curiosities; specif., books, etc. dealing with strange, often erotic, subjects

cu·ri·os·i·ty (kyoor′ē äs′ə tē) ***n.***, *pl.* **-ties** ⟦ME *curiousite* < OFr *curiosité* < L *curiositas* < *curiosus*: see fol.⟧ **1** a desire to learn or know **2** a desire to learn about things that do not properly concern one; inquisitiveness **3** anything curious, strange, rare, or novel **4** [Obs.] the quality of being careful, scrupulous, or fastidious

cu·ri·ous (kyoor′ē əs) ***adj.*** sometimes compar. **cu′ri·ous·er**: often in allusion to Lewis Carroll's *Alice's Adventures in Wonderland* ⟦ME < OFr *curios* < L *curiosus*, careful, diligent, curious; akin to *cura*, care: see CURE⟧ **1** eager to learn or know **2** unnecessarily inquisitive; prying **3** arousing attention or interest because unusual or strange; odd **4** [Rare] highly detailed, as in workmanship; elaborate **5** [Obs.] fastidious —**cu′ri·ous·ly** ***adv.*** —**cu′ri·ous·ness** ***n.***

SYN.—**curious**, in this comparison, implies eagerness or anxiousness to find out things and may suggest a wholesome desire to be informed; **inquisitive** implies a habitual tendency to be curious, esp. about matters that do not concern one, and an attempt to gain information by persistent questioning; **meddlesome** suggests unwelcome intrusion into the affairs of others; **prying** suggests an officious inquisitiveness and meddlesomeness that persists against resistance

Cu·ri·ti·ba (ko͞o′rē tē′bə) city in S Brazil; capital of Paraná state

☆**cu·ri·um** (kyo͞o′rē əm, kyoor′ē-) ***n.*** ⟦ModL, after Pierre & Marie CURIE + -IUM: so named in their honor (1946) by G. T. SEABORG, its discoverer, by analogy with the corresponding rare earth GADOLINIUM⟧ an extremely radioactive, metallic chemical element, one of the actinides, generally produced by neutron bombardment of plutonium or americium: symbol, Cm; at. no. 96: see the periodic table of elements in the Reference Supplement

curl (kurl) ***vt.*** ⟦ME *curlen*, by metathesis < *crullen*, to curl, bend, twist < *crul*, curly, akin to Du *krul* < Gmc **kruzla* < IE **greu-s* < base **ger-*: see CRADLE⟧ **1** to wind or twist (esp. hair) into ringlets or coils **2** to cause to roll over or bend around **3** to raise the upper corner of (the lip), as in showing contempt or scorn —***vi.*** **1** to form curls; become curled **2** to assume a spiral or curved shape **3** to move in a spiral or curved course **4** to play the game of curling —***n.*** **1** a little coil of hair; ringlet **2** anything with a spiral or curled shape; any coil **3** a curling or being curled **4** any of various diseases of plants in which the leaves curl up **5** an exercise, typically done with weights, in which an extended arm is flexed, bringing the hand back toward the shoulder, or an extended leg is flexed, bringing the foot back toward the buttock —**curl up** **1** to gather into spirals or curls; roll up **2** to sit or lie with the legs drawn up **3** [Informal] to collapse; break down —**in curl** curled

curl·er (kur′lər) ***n.*** a person or thing that curls; specif., *a)* any of various rollers, clasps, etc. on which a strand of hair is wound for curling *b)* a person who plays the game of curling

cur·lew (kur′lo͞o′, kurl′yo͞o′) ***n.***, *pl.* **-lews′** or **-lew′** ⟦ME *curleu* < OFr *corlieu*, of echoic orig., but infl. by assoc. with *corlieu*, messenger, courier⟧ any of a genus (*Numenius*, family Scolopacidae) of large, brownish shorebirds with long legs and a long, down-curved bill

curl·i·cue (kʉr′li kyo͞o′) ***n.*** ⟦< CURLY + CUE[2]⟧ a fancy curve, flourish, etc. as in a design or in handwriting

curl·ing (kʉr′liŋ) ***n.*** ⟦so named from the curving path of the stone when slid⟧ a game played on ice by two teams of four players each, in which a heavy, thick disk of stone or iron (**curling stone**) is slid toward a target circle at the other end of the rink: players may sweep the ice before the moving disk to remove ice particles and control the course and speed of the disk

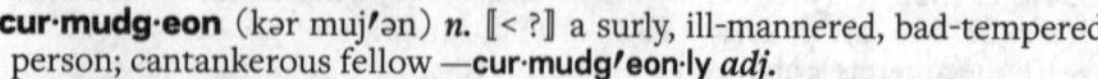

curling

curling iron (*or* **irons**) an instrument for curling or waving the hair, generally a metal rod around which, after it is heated, a tress of hair is rolled into a ringlet

curl·pa·per (kʉrl′pā′pər) ***n.*** a piece of paper around which a tress of hair may be wrapped to make it curl

curl·y (kʉr′lē) ***adj.*** **curl′i·er, curl′i·est 1** curling or tending to curl **2** having curls **3** having an undulating grain, as certain woods do —**curl′i·ness *n.***

cur·mudg·eon (kər muj′ən) ***n.*** ⟦< ?⟧ a surly, ill-mannered, bad-tempered person; cantankerous fellow —**cur·mudg′eon·ly *adj.***

cur·rach or **cur·ragh** (kʉr′ək, kʉr′ə) ***n.*** ⟦Ir & Gael *curach*, akin to Welsh *corwg*, skin boat⟧ [Scot. or Irish] CORACLE

cur·ra·jong (kʉr′ə jôŋ′) ***n.*** *alt. sp. of* KURRAJONG

cur·rant (kʉr′ənt) ***n.*** ⟦ME *corauns* < *(reisins of) Coraunce* < Anglo-Fr *(raisins de) Corauntz*, (raisins of) Corinth: orig. imported from Corinth⟧ **1** the raisin of a small, seedless grape (a cultivar of *Vitis vinifera*) grown in the Mediterranean region, used in cooking **2** *a)* the small, sour, red, white, or black berry of several species of hardy shrubs (genus *Ribes*) of the saxifrage family, used for jellies and jams *b)* a shrub bearing this fruit

cur·ren·cy (kʉr′ən sē) ***n., pl.*** **-cies** ⟦ML *currentia*, a current < L *currens*: see fol.⟧ **1** a continual passing from hand to hand, as of a medium of exchange; circulation ☆**2** the money in circulation in any country; often, specif., paper money **3** common acceptance; general use; prevalence *[the currency of a pronunciation]* **4** [Rare] the time during which anything is current

cur·rent (kʉr′ənt) ***adj.*** ⟦altered (infl. by L) < ME *curraunt* < OFr *curant*, prp. of *courre* < L *currere*, to run < IE base **kers-*, to run, wagon > Gaul *carros*⟧ **1** [Obs.] running or flowing **2** *a)* now going on; now in progress *[the current month, his current job]* *b)* at the present time; contemporary *[current fashions]* *c)* of most recent date *[the current edition]* **3** passing from person to person; circulating *[current money, current rumors]* **4** commonly used, known, or accepted; prevalent *[a current term]* **5** *Accounting a)* designating any asset that would normally be converted into cash within one year *b)* designating any liability that must be paid within one year —***n.*** **1** a flow of water or air, esp. when strong or swift, in a definite direction; specif., such a flow within a larger body of water or mass of air **2** a general tendency or drift; course **3** *Elec.* the flow or rate of flow of electrons, ions, or holes in a conductor or medium between two points having a difference in potential, measured in amperes and equal to the ratio of the voltage to the resistance: symbol, I —***SYN.*** PREVAILING, TENDENCY —**cur′rent·ly *adv.***

current density the amount of electric current passing through a cross-sectional area (perpendicular to the direction of current) of a conductor in a given unit of time: commonly expressed in amperes per square centimeter or amperes per square inch

cur·ri·cle (kʉr′i kəl) ***n.*** ⟦L *curriculum*: see fol.⟧ a light, two-wheeled carriage drawn by two horses side by side

cur·ric·u·lum (kə rik′yo͞o ləm, -yə-) ***n., pl.*** **-u·la** (-lə) or **-u·lums** ⟦L, lit., a running, course, race, career < *currere*, to run: see CURRENT⟧ **1** a fixed series of studies required, as in a college, for graduation, qualification in a major field of study, etc. **2** all of the courses, collectively, offered in a school, college, etc., or in a particular subject —**cur·ric′u·lar *adj.***

curriculum vi·tae (vīt′ē, vēt′ī) *pl.* **curricula vitae** ⟦L, course of life⟧ a summary of one's personal history and professional qualifications, as that submitted by a job applicant; résumé

cur·ri·er (kʉr′ē ər) ***n.*** ⟦ME *curriour* < OFr *corier* < L *coriarius* < *corium*, hide (see CORIUM): infl. by assoc. with CURRY[1]⟧ a person who curries tanned leather

☆**Cur·ri·er and Ives** (kʉr′ē ər ənd īvz′) ⟦after N. *Currier* (1813-88) & J. M. *Ives* (1824-95), U.S. founders of the lithographing firm that published the prints⟧ any of a 19th-cent. series of prints showing the manners, people, and events of the times

cur·rish (kʉr′ish) ***adj.*** of or resembling a cur; bad-tempered; mean; ill-bred —**cur′rish·ly *adv.***

cur·ry[1] (kʉr′ē) ***vt.*** **-ried, -ry·ing** ⟦ME *curraien* < OFr *correier, conreder*, to put in order < VL **corredare* < L *com-*, with + *-red-*, base appearing in **arredare*: for IE base see RIDE⟧ **1** to use a currycomb on **2** to prepare (tanned leather) by soaking, scraping, cleaning, beating, etc. **3** to beat or flog —**curry favor** ⟦altered (by assoc. with FAVOR) < ME *curraien favel*, to flatter, lit., curry the chestnut horse; OFr *favel*, chestnut horse (taken as symbol of duplicity) < dial. form of OHG *falo*, pale, akin to OE *fealu*; see FALLOW[2]⟧ to try to win favor by flattery, fawning, etc.

cur·ry[2] (kʉr′ē) ***n., pl.*** **-ries** ⟦Tamil *kari*, sauce⟧ **1** CURRY POWDER **2** a dish, as a kind of stew or a sauce, prepared with curry powder —***vt.*** **-ried, -ry·ing** to prepare with curry powder

cur·ry·comb (kʉr′ē kōm′) ***n.*** ⟦CURRY[1] + COMB[1]⟧ a circular comb with rows of teeth or ridges, for rubbing down, grooming, and cleaning a horse's coat —***vt.*** CURRY[1]

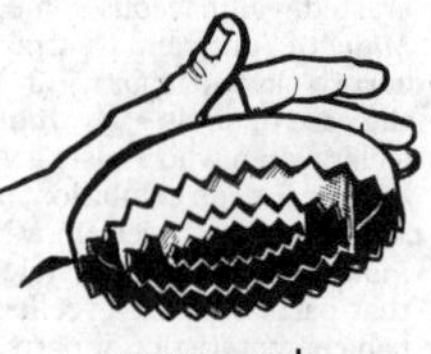

currycomb

curry powder a powder prepared from turmeric and various other spices, as coriander, cumin, ginger, and cayenne pepper, used as a seasoning, originally in India

curse (kʉrs) ***n.*** ⟦ME & Late OE n. *curs*, v. *cursian*: prob. < L *cursus* (see COURSE), used of the course of daily liturgical prayers and of the set of imprecations in the formal recital of offenses entailing excommunication; hence, consignment to an evil fate⟧ **1** a calling on God or the gods to send evil or injury down on some person or thing **2** a profane, obscene, or blasphemous oath, imprecation, etc. expressing hatred, anger, vexation, etc. **3** evil or injury that seems to come in answer to a curse **4** any cause of evil or injury —***vt.*** **cursed** or [Archaic] **curst, curs′ing 1** to call evil or injury down on; damn **2** to swear at; use profane, blasphemous, or obscene language against **3** to bring evil or injury on; afflict —***vi.*** to utter a curse or curses; swear; blaspheme —**be cursed with** to be afflicted with; suffer from —**the curse** [Old Slang] menstruation, or a menstrual period

SYN.—**curse** is the general word for calling down evil or injury on someone or something; **damn** carries the same general meaning but, in strict usage, implies the use of the word "damn" in the curse *[he damned his enemies = he said, "Damn my enemies!"]*; **execrate** suggests cursing prompted by great anger or abhorrence; **anathematize** strictly refers to the formal utterance of solemn condemnation by ecclesiastical authority See also **blasphemy** —***ANT.*** **bless**

curs·ed (kʉr′sid, kʉrst) ***adj.*** **1** under a curse **2** deserving to be cursed; specif., *a)* evil; wicked *b)* detestable; hateful *[this cursed cold]* **3** [Archaic] malevolent; quarrelsome: usually sp. **curst**

cur·sive (kʉr′siv) ***adj.*** ⟦ML *cursivus* < L *cursus*: see COURSE⟧ flowing; not disconnected; specif., designating writing in which the strokes of the letters are joined in each word —***n.*** **1** a cursive character **2** a manuscript in cursive writing **3** *Printing* a typeface that looks like handwriting, but with unconnected letters

cur·sor (kʉr′sər) ***n.*** ⟦L, runner < *cursus*: see COURSE⟧ on a computer screen, a movable indicator, such as an underline, a stylized figure, or a spot of highlighting, that indicates one's current interactive position within the display, as where in text a typed keystroke would appear, which icon would be affected by a click of the mouse, etc.

cur·so·ri·al (kər sôr′ē əl) ***adj.*** ⟦< fol. + -AL⟧ *Zool.* having legs or structural parts adapted for running

cur·so·ry (kʉr′sə rē) ***adj.*** ⟦LL *cursorius* < *cursor*, runner < *cursus*: see COURSE⟧ hastily, often superficially, done; performed rapidly with little attention to detail —***SYN.*** SUPERFICIAL —**cur′so·ri·ly *adv.*** —**cur′so·ri·ness *n.***

curt (kʉrt) ***adj.*** ⟦L *curtus*: see SHORT⟧ **1** [Archaic] short or shortened **2** brief, esp. to the point of rudeness; terse or brusque *[a curt reply]* —***SYN.*** BLUNT —**curt′ly *adv.*** —**curt′ness *n.***

cur·tail (kər tāl′) ***vt.*** ⟦ME *curtailen*, altered (by assoc. with *taillen* < OFr *taillier*: see TAILOR) < OFr *curtald*, CURTAL⟧ to cut short; reduce; abridge —***SYN.*** SHORTEN —**cur·tail′ment *n.***

cur·tain (kʉrt′'n) ***n.*** ⟦ME & OFr *cortine* < LL(Ec) *cortina*, lit. a cauldron, enclosing circle of a theater, curtain (< IE base **(s)ker-*, to CURVE); used in Vulg. instead of L *cors, cohors* (see COURT) to translate Gr *aulaia*, curtain (esp. in a theater) < *aulē*, open court, taken as if the same word as L *aula*, pot: for IE base see OVEN⟧ **1** a piece of cloth or other material, sometimes arranged so that it can be drawn up or sideways: it may be hung for decoration, as at a window, or used to cover, conceal, or shut off something **2** anything that covers, conceals, separates, or shuts off *[a curtain of fog]* **3** that part of a wall between two bastions, gates, etc. **4** *Archit.* an enclosing wall that does not support a roof **5** *Theater a)* the large drape or hanging screen at the front of the stage, which is drawn up or aside to reveal the stage *b)* the opening of the curtain at the beginning, or its closing at the end, of a play, act, or scene *c)* an effect, line, or situation in a play just before the curtain closes *d)* CURTAIN CALL ☆**6** [*pl.*] [Slang] death; the end —***vt.*** **1** to provide or decorate with a curtain **2** to cover, conceal, or shut off as with a curtain —**bring down** (or **draw** or **drop**) **the curtain on 1** to end **2** to conceal —**lift** (or **raise**) **the curtain on 1** to begin **2** to reveal

curtain call 1 a call, usually by continued applause, for the performers to return to the stage at the end of a play, act, etc. **2** such a return, acknowledging the applause

curtain lecture ⟦in ref. to bed curtains⟧ a private reprimand given by a wife to her husband, as in bed

curtain raiser 1 a short play or skit presented before a longer production **2** any brief preliminary event, entertainment, etc.

curtain speech a speech delivered from in front of the curtain typically at the end of a theatrical performance

curtain wall an independently supported outer wall that carries only its own weight and is freely removable

cur·tal (kʉrt′'l) [Obs.] ***adj.*** ⟦OFr *curtald* < *court*, short < L *curtus*, SHORT⟧ shortened; curtailed —***n.*** a horse with a docked tail

curtal ax ⟦altered < CUTLASS⟧ [Archaic] a cutlass

cur·tate (kʉr′tāt′) ***adj.*** ⟦L *curtatus*, pp. of *curtare*, to shorten < *curtus*, SHORT⟧ shortened; abbreviated

cur·te·sy (kʉrt′ə sē) ***n.***, *pl.* **-sies** ⟦var. of COURTESY⟧ the life interest which a husband acquires in the lands of his wife upon her death, provided they have children capable of inheriting: curtesy has been altered or abolished by statute in many U.S. states and in England

cur·ti·lage (kʉrt′'l ij) ***n.*** ⟦ME < OFr *cortillage* < *cortil*, dim. < LL *cortis*, COURT⟧ *Law* the fenced-in ground and buildings immediately surrounding a house or dwelling

Cur·tis (kʉrt′is) ***n.*** ⟦< NormFr *curteis* (OFr *corteis*): see COURTEOUS⟧ a masculine name: dim. *Curt*

Cur·tiss (kʉrt′is), **Glenn (Hammond)** 1878-1930; U.S. aviator & pioneer in aircraft construction

curt·sy (kʉrt′sē) ***n.***, *pl.* **-sies** ⟦var. of COURTESY⟧ a gesture of greeting, respect, etc. made, esp. formerly, by girls and women and characterized by a bending of the knees and a slight lowering of the body —***vi.*** **-sied**, **-sy·ing** to make a curtsy Also sp. **curt′sey**

cu·rule (kyo͞o′ro͞ol′) ***adj.*** ⟦L *curulis* < *currus*, chariot; akin to *currere*, to run: see CURRENT⟧ **1** designating a chair like an upholstered campstool with heavy curved legs, in which only the highest civil officers of Rome were privileged to sit **2** privileged to sit in a curule chair; of the highest rank

cur·va·ceous (kər vā′shəs) ***adj.*** ⟦CURV(E) + -ACEOUS⟧ having a full, shapely figure: said of a woman

cur·va·ture (kʉr′və chər) ***n.*** ⟦ME < L *curvatura* < *curvare*: see fol.⟧ **1** a curving or being curved **2** a curve; curved part of anything **3** *Geom.* the rate of deviation of a curve or curved surface from a straight line or plane surface tangent to it **4** *Med.* an abnormal curving of a part [*curvature* of the spine]

curve (kʉrv) ***adj.*** ⟦L *curvus*, bent: see CROWN⟧ [Archaic] curved —***n.*** **1** a line having no straight part; bend having no angular part **2** a thing or part having the shape of a curve **3** the act of curving, or the extent of this **4** [*pl.*] the pronounced curving outline of a shapely female figure ☆**5** *Baseball* a ball thrown by a right-handed pitcher that curves to the pitcher's left, or one thrown by a left-handed pitcher that curves to the pitcher's right **6** *a)* a curved line or similar graphic representation showing variations occurring or expected to occur in prices, business conditions, group achievements, etc. *b)* the statistical distribution of a group according to such variations; specif., a statistical distribution of student test scores, etc. within a class, used as a tool in assigning grades **7** FRENCH CURVE **8** *Math.* a one-dimensional continuum of points in a space of two or more dimensions, such as a parabola in a plane or a helix in three-dimensional space: a straight line or line segment is a type of curve — ***vt., vi.*** **curved**, **curv′ing 1** to form a curve by bending **2** to move in a curved path **3** to employ a CURVE (*n.* 6*b*) on (test scores, etc.) —**ahead of (or behind) the curve** anticipating (or not keeping up with) current trends, developments, etc. —**on a curve** according to a CURVE (*n.* 6*b*)

SYN.—curve suggests a swerving or deflection in a line that follows or approximates the arc of a circle [he *curved* the next pitch]; **bend** refers to the curving of something that is normally straight but that yields to pressure or tension [to *bend* a wire]; **twist**, in this connection, implies greater resistance in the object to be bent and often connotes a wrenching out of the normal line [to *twist* one's arm]; **turn**, in this comparison often interchangeable with **bend**, is used specifically where the object is curved back upon itself [to *turn* a bed sheet]

curve·ball (kʉrv′bôl′) ***n.*** *Baseball* CURVE (sense 5)

cur·vet (kʉr′vet; *for v., usually* kər vet′) ***n.*** ⟦It *corvetta*, dim. < *corvo* < L *curvus*: see CROWN⟧ in equestrian exhibitions, a movement in which a horse rears, then leaps forward, raising the hind legs just before the forelegs come down —***vi.*** **-vet′ted** or **-vet′ed**, **-vet′ting** or **-vet′ing** to make a curvet —***vt.*** to cause to curvet

cur·vi- (kʉr′və) ⟦< L *curvus*, curved: see CROWN⟧ *combining form* curved or bent [*curvilinear*]

cur·vi·lin·e·ar (kʉr′və lin′ē ər) ***adj.*** consisting of or enclosed by a curved line or lines: also **cur′vi·lin′e·al** —**cur′vi·lin′e·ar·ly** ***adv.***

curv·y (kʉr′vē) ***adj.*** **curv′i·er**, **curv′i·est 1** having curves or a curve [a *curvy* road] **2** [Informal] curvaceous

Cur·zon (kʉr′zən), **George Nathaniel** 1st Marquis Curzon of Kedleston 1859-1925; Eng. statesman: viceroy of India (1899-1905)

Cus·co (ko͞os′kō) *alt. sp. of* CUZCO

cus·cus (kus′kəs) ***n.*** ⟦ModL < native name in New Guinea⟧ any of a genus (*Phalanger*, family Phalangeridae) of sluggish, tree-dwelling phalangers native to NE Australia and nearby islands, mostly herbivorous with foxlike ears and a prehensile tail

cu·sec (kyo͞o′sek′) ***n.*** ⟦CU(BIC) + SEC(OND)⟧ a unit for measuring volume of flow, equal to one cubic foot per second

Cush (ko͝osh, kush) ***n.*** *Bible* **1** the oldest of Ham's sons **2** the land inhabited by his descendants, thought to be on the W shore of the Red Sea: Gen. 10:8; 1 Chron. 1:10 —**Cush′ite′** ***adj., n.***

cush·at (kush′ət, ko͝osh′-) ***n.*** ⟦N Brit dial. < ME *coushote* < OE *cushote* as if < *cu-*, COO[1] + base of *sceotan*, to dart, SHOOT[1]; in sense "cooing darter"⟧ a wood pigeon (*Columba palumbus*)

☆**cu·shaw** (kə shô′) ***n.*** ⟦< AmInd (Algonquian)⟧ a variety of crookneck squash (*Cucurbita moschata*) similar to the pumpkin

Cush·ing (ko͝osh′iŋ) **1 Caleb** 1800-79; U.S. diplomat: negotiated treaty (1845) opening Chin. ports to U.S. trade **2 Harvey (Williams)** 1869-1939; U.S. neurosurgeon

Cush·ing's disease ⟦after Harvey CUSHING⟧ a disorder of the adrenal cortex caused by a tumor in the pituitary, characterized by obesity, hypertension, diabetes mellitus, etc.

Cushing's syndrome ⟦after Harvey CUSHING⟧ a medical condition characterized by obesity, hypertension, excessive hair growth, etc., caused by an overactive adrenal gland or large doses of corticosteroids

cush·ion (ko͝osh′ən) ***n.*** ⟦ME *cuisshin* < OFr *coissin* < ML *coxinum*, altered (after L *coxa*, hip) < Gallo-Roman **culcinum*, for L *culcita*, cushion, QUILT⟧ **1** a pillow or soft pad for sitting or kneeling upon, or reclining against; specif., a removable one forming part of a sofa, chair, etc. **2** a thing like a cushion in shape, softness, or use, as a small pillow used in lace-making, padding of various sorts, etc. **3** a fatty or fibrous padlike part of the body **4** anything serving to absorb shock, as air or steam in some machines, the elastic inner rim of a billiard table, or a soft, padded insole **5** anything that moderates an adverse effect, relieves a distressing condition, provides comfort, etc. —***vt.*** **1** to provide with a cushion or cushions **2** *a)* to seat or set on a cushion *b)* to prop up with a cushion or cushions **3** to hide or suppress, as if under a cushion **4** to absorb (shock or noise) **5** to act as a cushion, as in protecting from shock or injury, moderating ill effects, relieving distress, etc. [the bush *cushioned* his fall] —**cush′ion·y** ***adj.***

Cush·it·ic (ko͝osh it′ik, kush-) ***adj.*** ⟦CUSH + -IT(E) + -IC⟧ designating or of a group of languages spoken in Ethiopia and E Africa, constituting a subfamily of the Afroasiatic family of languages —***n.*** this group of languages

cush·y (ko͝osh′ē) ***adj.*** **cush′i·er**, **cush′i·est** ⟦orig. Brit army slang < Hindi *khush*, pleasant < Pers *khūsh*⟧ [Slang] easy, comfortable, etc. [a *cushy* job, *cushy* sofa] —**cush′i·ness** ***n.***

cusk (kusk) ***n.***, *pl.* **cusk** or **cusks** ⟦Brit local name < ?⟧ **1** a large, edible gadoid fish (*Brosme brosme*) found in the N Atlantic ☆**2** BURBOT

cusp (kusp) ***n.*** ⟦L *cuspis* (gen. *cuspidis*), point, pointed end, spear⟧ **1** a point or pointed end; apex; peak **2** *Anat. a)* any of the elevations on the chewing surface of a tooth *b)* any of the triangular flaps of a heart valve **3** *Archit.* a projecting point where two arcs meet, as in the internal curve of an arc **4** *Astrol.* the transitional part of a sign or house **5** *Astron.* either horn of a crescent, as of the moon **6** *Geom.* the tip of a pointed curve —**on the cusp 1** *Astrol.* at or during a CUSP (sense 4) **2** at or during a time of transition, as the moment of or just before a major change or event

cus·pate (kus′pit, -pāt′) ***adj.*** CUSPIDATE: also **cus′pat′ed** (-pāt′id) or **cusped** (kuspt)

cus·pid (kus′pid) ***n.*** ⟦L *cuspis*: see CUSP⟧ a tooth with one cusp; canine tooth —***adj.*** CUSPIDATE

cus·pi·date (kus′pə dāt′, -dit) ***adj.*** ⟦L *cuspidatus*, pp. of *cuspidare*, to make pointed < *cuspis*⟧ **1** having a cusp or cusps **2** having a short, abrupt point, as some leaves Also **cus′pi·dat′ed**

cus·pi·da·tion (kus′pə dā′shən) ***n.*** the use of cusps for decoration, as in architecture

☆**cus·pi·dor** (kus′pə dôr′) ***n.*** ⟦Port *cuspideira* < *cuspir*, to spit < L *conspuere* < *com-*, intens. + *spuere*, to spit out, SPEW⟧ SPITTOON

cuss (kus) [Informal] ***n.*** ⟦< CURSE⟧ **1** a curse ☆**2** ⟦< ? CUSTOMER⟧ a person, esp. one regarded as bad-tempered, annoying, etc.: used humorously or contemptuously — ***vt., vi.*** to curse; swear (at): often with *out* —**cuss′er** ***n.***

cuss·ed (kus′id) ***adj.*** ⟦< prec. or CURSED⟧ [Informal] **1** cursed **2** perverse; stubborn —**cuss′ed·ly** ***adv.*** —**cuss′ed·ness** ***n.***

cuss·word (-wʉrd′) ***n.*** [Informal] SWEARWORD

cus·tard (kus′tərd) ***n.*** ⟦ME, altered < *crustade*, any dish baked in a crust, ult. (? via Prov *crostado*) < L *crusta*, CRUST⟧ **1** a mixture of eggs, milk, flavoring, and, often, sugar, either boiled or baked **2** *short for* FROZEN CUSTARD

cus·tard-ap·ple (kus′tərd ap′əl) ***adj.*** ⟦< prec., with references to the flavor and color⟧ designating a family (Annonaceae, order Magnoliales) of dicotyledonous tropical trees and shrubs including the papaw, sweetsop, and soursop —***n.*** **1** any of a genus (esp. *Annona reticulata*) of small trees of this family, grown for their large, edible, heart-shaped fruits: also **custard apple 2** the fruit

Cus·ter (kus′tər), **George Armstrong** 1839-76; U.S. army officer: killed in a battle with Dakota Indians on the LITTLE BIGHORN River

cus·to·di·al (kəs tō′dē əl) ***adj.*** of custody or custodians

cus·to·di·an (kəs tō′dē ən) ***n.*** ⟦< fol.⟧ **1** a person who has the custody or care of something, as of a private library; caretaker; keeper **2** a person or firm having a legal duty to protect and, often, manage specified assets of an individual or group **3** a person responsible for the care and maintenance of a building; janitor —**cus·to′di·an·ship′** ***n.***

cus·to·dy (kus′tə dē) ***n.***, *pl.* **-dies** ⟦ME *custodie* < L *custodia* < *custos*, a guard, keeper < IE **(s)keudh-* < base **(s)keus-*, to cover > SKY⟧ **1** a guarding or keeping safe; care; protection; guardianship **2** the right of having one's children in one's immediate care, awarded under various arrangements to one or both of the parents by a court as a result of a divorce or separation —**in custody** in the keeping of the police; under arrest —**take into custody** to arrest

cus·tom (kus′təm) ***n.*** ⟦ME < OFr *costume* < L *consuetudo* < *consuescere*, to accustom < *com-*, intens. + *suescere*, to become accustomed < *suere*, to be accustomed, akin to *suus*, one's own: for IE base see SUICIDE⟧ **1** a usual practice or habitual way of behaving; habit **2** *a)* a social convention carried on by tradition and enforced by social disapproval of any violation *b)* such practices, collectively **3** under feudalism, a service, rent, etc. regularly paid to a lord **4** [*pl.*] *a)* duties or taxes imposed by a government on imported and, occasionally, exported goods *b)* [*with sing. v.*] the government agency in charge of collecting these duties, or any of its offices **5** *a)* the regular support or patronage of a business establishment *b)* customers as a group **6** *Law* such usage as by common consent and long-established, uniform practice has taken on the force of law —*adj.* **1** made or done to order or, sometimes, made extra fine, as if to order **2** making things to order, or dealing in things made to order [a *custom* tailor] —**SYN.** HABIT

cus·tom·ar·i·ly (kus′tə mer′ə lē) *adv.* according to custom; usually

cus·tom·ar·y (kus′tə mer′ē) *adj.* ⟦ML *customarius*: see CUSTOM⟧ **1** in keeping with custom, or usage; usual; habitual **2** *Law* holding or held by custom —*n., pl.* **-ar′ies** a collection of the laws established by custom for a manor, region, etc. —**SYN.** USUAL —**cus′tom·ar′i·ness** *n.*

☆**cus·tom-built** (kus′təm bilt′) *adj.* built to order, according to the customer's specifications

cus·tom·er (kus′tə mər) *n.* ⟦ME < OFr *coustumier*: see CUSTOM⟧ **1** a person who buys, esp. one who buys from, or patronizes, an establishment regularly **2** [Informal] any person with whom one has dealings [a rough *customer*]

cus·tom·house (kus′təm hous′) *n.* a building or office where customs or duties are paid and ships are cleared for entering or leaving: also **cus′toms·house′**

☆**cus·tom·ize** (kus′tə mīz′) *vt.* **-ized′**, **-iz′ing** ⟦CUSTOM + -IZE⟧ to make, build, or modify according to personal or individual specifications —**cus′tom·iz′a·ble** *adj.* —**cus′tom·i·za′tion** (-mə zā′shən, -mī′-) *n.* —**cus′tom·iz′er** *n.*

☆**cus·tom-made** (-mād′) *adj.* made to order, according to the customer's specifications

customs union a union of nations that agree to eliminate customs restrictions among members and to follow a common tariff policy toward all other nations

cut (kut) *vt.* **cut**, **cut′ting** ⟦ME *cutten, kytten* < Late OE **cyttan* < Scand base seen in Swed dial., Ice *kuta*, to cut with a knife: the word replaced OE *ceorfan* (see CARVE), *snithan, scieran* (see SHEAR) as used in its basic senses⟧ **I.** *denoting penetration or incision* **1** to make an opening in as with a sharp-edged instrument; pierce; incise; gash **2** to pierce, hit sharply, constrict, etc. so as to hurt **3** to hurt the feelings of **4** to grow (a new tooth making its way through the gum) **II.** *denoting separation, removal, or division* **1** to remove or divide into parts with a sharp-edged instrument; sever **2** to carve (meat) **3** to cause to fall by severing; fell; hew **4** to mow or reap with a scythe, sickle, etc. **5** to pass through or across; intersect; divide [the path *cuts* the meadow diagonally] **6** *a)* to divide (a pack of cards) at random so as to rearrange the pack after the dealer has shuffled or so as to show a card to determine the dealer, partners, etc. *b)* to select (a card) at random from a pack, as by cutting the deck **7** to castrate; geld **8** [Informal] to pretend not to see or know (a person); snub **9** [Informal] to stay away from (a school class, etc.) without being excused **10** [Informal] to cause to stop operating [*cut* the engine] ☆**11** [Slang] to stop; discontinue [*cut* the noise] ☆**12** [Informal] to discharge from a job, release from a sports team, etc. **III.** *denoting reduction* **1** *a)* to make less by or as by severing a part or parts; reduce, abridge, curtail, etc. [to *cut* salaries, *cut* a speech by ten minutes] *b)* to remove as in an effort to make something shorter [to *cut* two scenes from a play] **2** to make shorter by severing the ends of (hair, branches, fingernails, etc.); trim; shear; pare ☆**3** to dilute (alcohol, etc.) **4** to dissolve or break up the fat globules of [lye *cuts* grease] **IV.** *denoting performance by incision, etc.* to make, do, form, or decorate by or as by cutting; specif., *a)* to make (an opening, clearing, channel, etc.) by incising, drilling, hacking, or excavating *b)* to engrave; inscribe *c)* to type or otherwise mark (a stencil) for mimeographing *d)* to trim cloth so as to form the parts for (a garment) ☆*e)* to edit (film) by deleting some scenes and assembling others into a desired sequence *f)* to hit, drive, or throw (a ball) so that it spins *g)* to cause (a wheel) to turn sharply ☆*h)* to make a recording of (a speech, music, etc.) on (a phonograph record) *i)* to shape (a diamond), as by sawing or grinding *j)* [Informal] to fill out (said of a bank check) —*vi.* **1** to do the work of a sharp-edged instrument; pierce, sever, gash, etc. **2** to do cutting; work as a cutter **3** to take cutting; be severed, etc. [pine *cuts* easily] **4** to use an instrument that cuts **5** to cause pain by or as by sharp, piercing, or lashing strokes [the wind *cut* through his thin clothes] **6** [Informal] to swing a bat, club, etc. at a ball **7** to change direction suddenly, as while running **8** to move swiftly **9** *Film, TV, etc. a)* to make a sudden change, as from one scene or character to another *b)* to end the filming or taping of a scene, as by shouting a command (*cut!*) or giving a sign —*adj.* **1** that has been cut **2** made, formed, or decorated by cutting **3** reduced; lessened **4** castrated **5** [Slang] having a trim, athletic physique with well-defined muscles **6** *Bot.* having an indented edge; incised, as some leaves or petals —*n.* **1** a cutting or being cut **2** a stroke or blow with a sharp-edged instrument, whip, etc. **3** *a)* [Informal] a swing taken at a ball *b)* spin imparted to a ball, as by hitting the lower side of it **4** an opening, incision, wound, etc. made by a sharp-edged instrument **5** *a)* the omission of a part *b)* the part omitted **6** a piece or part cut off or out; specif., *a)* any of the segments of the carcass of a meat animal *b)* a slice from such a segment **7** the edge or outline of something cut ☆**8** *a)* the amount cut, as of timber *b)* a reduction; lessening; decrease **9** SHORTCUT **10** a passage or channel cut or dug out or worn away **11** the style in which a thing is cut; fashion; form [a stylish *cut*] **12** an act, remark, etc. that hurts one's feelings **13** *a)* a block or plate engraved for printing, or the impression made from it *b)* a printed picture, as in a newspaper, book, etc. **14** ⟦< ? Welsh *cwt*, lot⟧ one of the bits of straw, stick, paper, etc. used in drawing lots to decide something **15** [Informal] the act of snubbing or ignoring ☆**16** [Informal] an unauthorized absence from school, etc. ☆**17** [Informal] a share, as of profits or loot ☆**18** [Informal] a BAND[1] (*n.* 7) on a phonograph record **19** *Film a)* a sudden change from one image to another *b)* an assembled version of a movie [a rough *cut*, final *cut*, etc.] —**a cut above** [Informal] somewhat better than —**cut across** to take a shorter course by going straight across as in a diagonal direction —☆**cut a deal** [Slang] to reach an agreement; make a bargain —**cut a figure 1** to attract attention **2** to make a (specified kind of) showing or impression —**cut and dried 1** prepared or arranged beforehand; routine **2** lifeless; dull; boring —**cut and run** ⟦from the earlier naval phrase meaning "to cut the anchor cable and set sail immediately"⟧ [Informal] to flee a difficult situation —**cut back 1** to make shorter by cutting off the end **2** to reduce, decrease, or discontinue (production, personnel, etc.) ☆**3** to go back to earlier narrative events, as in a novel or film ☆**4** to change direction suddenly, as in football —**cut dead** [Informal] to snub completely —**cut down 1** to cause to fall by cutting; fell **2** to kill, as by shooting **3** to reduce; lessen **4** [Informal] to humiliate, humble, etc. by criticizing sharply —**cut down to size** [Informal] to reduce the prestige or importance of —**cut in 1** *a)* to move in suddenly, as into a small opening in a lane of traffic *b)* to move into another's place [don't *cut in* line] (also **cut into**) **2** to join in suddenly; break in on; interrupt ☆**3** to interrupt a couple dancing in order to dance with one of them **4** to blend (shortening) into flour, etc. as with a knife **5** to put or bring in; introduce **6** to make a connection, as into an electrical circuit **7** [Informal] to give a share to —**cut it** [Informal] to do or perform satisfactorily or successfully —**cut it fine** [Informal] **1** to make exact calculations **2** to make exact distinctions —**cut it out** [Informal] to stop doing what one is doing —**cut loose** ☆[Informal] to act or speak without self-control —☆**cut no ice** [Informal] to make no impression —**cut off 1** to separate from other parts by cutting; sever **2** to stop abruptly **3** to shut off **4** to break in on; interrupt **5** to intercept **6** to disinherit —**cut out 1** to remove by cutting **2** to leave or take out; remove; omit; eliminate **3** [Informal] to eliminate and take the place of (a rival) **4** to make or form by or as by cutting **5** [Informal] to stop running: said of an engine ☆**6** [Informal] to discontinue; stop **7** [Informal] fit or suited by nature [not *cut out* for academia] **8** [Slang] to leave abruptly —**cut short** to stop abruptly before the end —**cut one's teeth on** to learn or use at an early age —**cut through 1** to penetrate or go through by cutting **2** to go straight through —☆**cut to the chase** ⟦< CUT, *vi.* 9*a*, with reference to a scene involving a *chase*, as in a crime film⟧ [Informal] to go directly to the essential element, without further preliminaries, delay, etc. —**cut up 1** to cut into pieces **2** to inflict cuts or lacerations on **3** [Informal] *a)* to criticize harshly *b)* to cause to be dejected or distressed ☆**4** [Slang] to clown, joke, etc. to attract attention —☆**make the cut** [Informal] to be among those remaining after others have been eliminated, as in a golf tournament

cut-and-paste (kut′'n pāst′) *adj.* [Informal] made or composed by piecing together parts that already exist, often in a way that suggests haste or lack of inspiration

cut-and-thrust (-thrust′) *n.* ⟦< techniques employed in swordplay⟧ a lively, aggressive manner [the *cut-and-thrust* of partisan politics]: also **cut and thrust**

cu·ta·ne·ous (kyo͞o tā′nē əs) *adj.* ⟦ModL *cutaneus* < ML < L *cutis*: see CUTICLE⟧ of, on, or affecting the skin

cut·a·way (kut′ə wā′) *n.* a coat with the front of the skirt cut so as to curve back to the tails, worn by men for formal daytime occasions: also **cutaway coat** —*adj.* designating or of a diagram or model showing, in cross section, or with walls, etc. cut away, the parts or workings, as of a structure or machine

cut·back (kut′bak′) *n.* the act or result of cutting back; specif., *a)* a reduction or discontinuance, as of production, personnel, etc. ☆*b)* a sequence of earlier events introduced at a later point in a novel, film, etc.

☆**cut·bank** (-baŋk′) *n.* an eroded, concave bank formed at a bend of a river or stream by the flow of water around the bend

cutch (kuch) *n. var. of* CATECHU

Cutch (kuch) *alt. sp. of* KUTCH

cut·down (kut′doun′) *n.* a medical procedure of cutting into a body cavity or vessel, esp. a vein, to attach a catheter for drainage, examination, etc.

cutaway

☆**cute** (kyo͞ot) *adj.* **cut′er**, **cut′est** ⟦aphetic < ACUTE⟧ **1** [Informal] *a)* clever; crafty *b)* insolent; impertinent **2** pretty or attractive, esp. in a lively, wholesome, or dainty way **3** [Informal] straining for effect; artificial —**meet cute** *Film* to meet for the first time, often in a contrived or unusual way: said of the main characters in their first scene together —**the cutes** [Informal] cute mannerisms, ploys, devices, etc. designed to charm or attract others —**cute′ly** *adv.* —**cute′ness** *n.*

cute·sy or **cute·sie** (kyo͞ot′sē) *adj.* **-si·er**, **-si·est** [Informal] cute in a forced or exaggerated way: also [Slang] **cute′sy-poo′** (-po͞o′)

☆**cut·ey** (kyo͞ot′ē) *n.* [Slang] *alt. sp. of* CUTIE

cut glass glass, esp. flint glass, shaped or ornamented by grinding and polishing
cut-grass (kut′gras′) *n.* any grass (esp. *Leersia oryzoides*) having tiny hooks along the edges of the blades that cause scratches on the human skin
Cuth·bert (kuth′bərt), Saint (A.D. 635?-687?); Eng. bishop: his day is March 20
cut·i·cle (kyoo͞t′i kəl) *n.* ⟦L *cuticula*, skin, dim. < *cutis*, skin < IE base *(*s*)*keu-t-*, to cover > HIDE²⟧ **1** the outer layer of the skin; epidermis **2** hardened skin, such as accumulates at the base and sides of a fingernail **3** *Bot.* a delicate, waxy layer over the outer surface of the epidermis of plants: it contains cutin and protects against water loss and parasitic infections **4** *Zool.* the nonliving, thick or thin, tough outer structure secreted by the epidermis in many invertebrate organisms, as insects, crustaceans, earthworms, etc. —**cu·tic·u·lar** (kyoo tik′yə lər) *adj.*
cu·tic·u·la (kyoo͞ tik′yoo͞ lə, -yə-) *n., pl.* **-lae′** (-lē′) ⟦L⟧ CUTICLE (esp. sense 4)
cu·tie (kyoo͞t′ē) ☆*n.* ⟦CUT(E) + -IE⟧ [Slang] a cute person, esp. a pretty girl or young woman: also **cu′tie-pie′** (-pī′)
cu·tin (kyoo͞t′'n, kyoo͞′tin) *n.* ⟦< L *cutis* (see CUTICLE) + -IN¹⟧ *Bot.* a varnishlike material covering the epidermis of land plants and containing waxes, resins, fatty acids, etc.
☆**cut-in** (kut′in′) *n.* something that is cut in, as a close-up of some object inserted into a film sequence
cu·tin·i·za·tion (kyoo͞′tə nə zā′shən, kyoo͞t′'n ə-) *n. Bot.* a process in which the outermost plant cells become thickened and covered with cutin, making them waterproof —**cu′tin·ize′** (-īz′) *vi., vt.* **-ized′**, **-iz′ing**
cu·tis (kyoo͞t′is) *n., pl.* **-tes** (-ēz) or **-tis·es** ⟦L: see CUTICLE⟧ **1** the vertebrate skin, including both of its layers, the dermis and the epidermis **2** the dermis only; corium
cut·lass (kut′ləs) *n.* ⟦Fr *coutelas*, via ? Prov or It *coltellaccio* < L *cultellus*, dim. of *culter*: see COLTER⟧ a short, thick, curving sword with a single cutting edge, formerly used esp. by sailors
cut·lass·fish (-fish′) *n., pl.* **-fish′** or **-fish′es** (see FISH) any of a family (Trichiuridae) of very long, thin percoid fishes with a wide mouth and sharp, pointed teeth, found near the surface in tropical seas: also written **cutlass fish**
cut·ler (kut′lər) *n.* ⟦ME & Anglo-Fr *cuteler* < OFr *coutelier* < ML *cultellarius*, one who makes knives < L *cultellus*: see CUTLASS⟧ a person who makes, sells, or repairs knives and other cutting tools
cut·ler·y (kut′lər ē) *n.* ⟦ME *cutellerie* < OFr *coutellerie*: see prec.⟧ **1** the work or business of a cutler **2** cutting implements, such as knives and scissors **3** knives, spoons, and other implements used in preparing and eating food
cut·let (kut′lit) *n.* ⟦altered (infl. by CUT) < Fr *côtelette*, dim. of OFr *costel*, dim. of *coste*, rib < L *costa*: see COAST⟧ **1** a small slice of meat from the ribs or leg, for frying or broiling, often served breaded **2** a small, flat croquette of chopped meat or fish
cut·line (-līn′) *n.* CAPTION (sense 3*b*)
cut·man (-man′) *n., pl.* **-men′** (-men′) *Boxing* a person who specializes in administering first aid to a boxer between rounds
cut·off (kut′ôf′) *n.* **1** the act of cutting off; esp., the limit or ending set for a process, activity, etc. **2** a road or passage that cuts across, shortening the distance ☆**3** *a)* a new and shorter channel cut by a river across a bend, or dug out to straighten it *b)* the water thus cut off **4** the act of stopping steam, etc. from entering the cylinder of an engine **5** any device for cutting off a connection, the flow of a fluid, etc. ☆**6** [*pl.*] jeans with the legs cut off at or above the knees, or shorts made to look like this —*adj.* **1** of an arbitrary ending or limit [*cutoff* date] **2** *Baseball* having to do with a fielder who is in a position to relay a throw from an outfielder to an infielder in an attempt to put out a base runner
cutoff frequency *Electronics* a frequency level above or below which a device fails to respond or operate efficiently
cut·out (-out′) *n.* **1** a device, as a circuit breaker or an emergency switch, for breaking an electric circuit **2** a device for letting exhaust gases from an internal-combustion engine pass directly into the air instead of through a muffler **3** a design cut out of something, or to be cut out **4** ⟦from the practice of notching album jackets to indicate this⟧ a discontinued recording deleted from the catalog, for sale at a reduced price
☆**cut·o·ver** (-ō′vər) *adj.* cleared of trees —*n.* land cleared of trees
cut·purse (-purs′) *n.* ⟦orig., a thief who stole *purses* by *cutting* them from the belts to which they were attached⟧ [Archaic] a pickpocket
☆**cut-rate** (-rāt′) *adj.* **1** available at a lower price or rate; cheap **2** offering cut-rate goods or services
Cut·tack (kut′ək) city in E India
cut·ter (kut′ər) *n.* **1** a device, tool, or machine for cutting **2** a person who cuts or whose work is cutting; specif., a person whose work is cutting to patterns the sections that form a garment **3** *a)* a boat carried, esp. formerly, aboard large ships to transport personnel or supplies *b)* an armed sailing vessel, formerly used by revenue authorities, as to pursue smugglers (also **revenue cutter**) *c)* a small, armed, engine-powered ship, used by the Coast Guard as for patrol duty (also **Coast Guard cutter**) *d)* a single-masted yacht or sailboat carrying two headsails under normal wind conditions ☆**4** a small, light sleigh, usually drawn by one horse
cut·throat (kut′thrōt′) *n.* a violent criminal, esp. one who murders —*adj.* **1** murderous **2** merciless; ruthless ☆**3** played by persons competing as individuals rather than with partners, as some forms of bridge or pinochle
cutthroat trout ⟦so named from the reddish patch⟧ a game fish (*Salmo clarki*) with a reddish patch under the jaw, usually found in high mountain streams near the NW North American coast
cut time ALLA BREVE (sense 2)
cut·ting (kut′iŋ) *n.* **1** the act of one that cuts **2** a piece cut off **3** [Brit.] a clipping, as from a newspaper **4** [Brit.] a passage for trains, cars, etc. cut through a hill or high ground; cut **5** *Hort.* a slip or shoot cut away from a plant for rooting or grafting —*adj.* **1** that cuts or for cutting [*a cutting* tool, *cutting* board] **2** chilling or piercing **3** wounding the feelings; sarcastic —*SYN.* INCISIVE —**cut′ting·ly** *adv.*
cutting edge **1** the effective or decisive element **2** the leading or most important position; forefront; vanguard **3** the most advanced or innovative position; the avant-garde —**cut′ting-edge′** *adj.*
cut·tle·bone (kut′'l bōn′) *n.* the internal shell of cuttlefish, used as a food supplement for caged birds or as a polishing agent
cut·tle·fish (-fish′) *n., pl.* **-fish′** or **-fish′es** (see FISH) ⟦ME *codel* < OE *cudele*, akin to Norw dial. *kaule* (**kodle*), OLowG *cudele*, older Du *kuttlevisch*: sense "pouch fish": for IE base see COD²⟧ any of a family (Sepiidae) of cephalopods that have suckers on their eight arms and two tentacles, a hard internal shell, large complex eyes, and a water-ejecting jetlike siphon for locomotion: when in danger, most cuttlefishes eject a dark-brown, inklike fluid: also **cut′tle**
cut·ty (kut′ē) [Scot. or North Eng.] *adj.* ⟦< CUT⟧ short —*n. pl.* **-ties** a short spoon or tobacco pipe
cutty stool ⟦orig., a short seat: see prec.⟧ [Scot. Historical] a seat in a church, in which offenders sat and were publicly rebuked by the minister
☆**cut·up** (kut′up′) *n.* ⟦< CUT UP (sense 4) (see phr. under CUT)⟧ [Informal] a person who clowns, plays practical jokes, etc. to attract attention
cut·wa·ter (-wôt′ər) *n.* **1** the forward edge of a ship's stem at and below the waterline **2** the angular edge of the pier of a bridge, facing upstream
cut·work (-wurk′) *n.* openwork embroidery in which part of the cloth is cut away from the design
cut·worm (-wurm′) *n.* any of a number of soil-dwelling caterpillars (family Noctuidae) that feed on young plants of cabbage, corn, etc., cutting them off at ground level
CUV *abbrev.* crossover utility vehicle
cu·vée (kü vā′) *n.* ⟦Fr, a vat's contents, VINTAGE (*n.* 1*b*) < *cuve*, vat: see fol.⟧ a blend of wine, generally the result of combining wines from several batches to achieve a characteristic flavor
cu·vette (kyoo͞ vet′) *n.* ⟦Fr, basin, dim. of *cuve*, vat < L *cupa*, tub: see CUP⟧ a small glass tube used in spectrometry and photometry
Cu·vier (kü vyā′; *E* koo͞′vē ā′), Baron **Georges (Léopold Chrétien Frédéric Dagobert)** (zhôrzh) 1769-1832; Fr. naturalist
Cuyp (koip), **Ael·bert** or **Aal·bert** (äl′bert) 1620-91; Du. painter
Cuz·co (koo͞s′kō) city in S Peru: capital of the Inca empire, 12th-16th cent.
CV or **cv** *abbrev.* curriculum vitae
CVA *abbrev.* cerebrovascular accident
CVD *abbrev.* cardiovascular disease
CVS *abbrev.* chorionic villus sampling
CWA *abbrev.* Communications Workers of America
cwm (koo͞m) *n.* ⟦Welsh *cwmm*, COOMB⟧ *Geol.* CIRQUE
CWO *abbrev.* **1** cash with order: also **cwo** **2** Chief Warrant Officer
cwt *abbrev.* ⟦L *c*(*entum*), HUNDRED + *w*(*eigh*)*t*⟧ hundredweight
-cy (sē, si) ⟦< ME & OFr *-cie*, L *-cia*, *-tia*, Gr *-kia*, *-keia*, *-tia*, *-teia*⟧ *suffix* **1** quality, condition, state, or fact of being [*idiocy*] **2** position, rank, or office of [*captaincy, curacy*]
cy·an (sī′an, -ən) *n.* ⟦< Gr *kyanos*: see CYANO-⟧ a greenish-blue color —*adj.* greenish-blue in color
cy·an- (sī′ən) *combining form* CYANO-: used before a vowel
cy·an·a·mide (sī an′ə mīd′, -mid) *n.* ⟦CYAN(O)- + AMIDE⟧ **1** a caustic, white, crystalline compound, $H_2N{\cdot}CN$, usually prepared by the reaction of carbon dioxide with calcium cyanamide in water and used to make other chemicals, as thiourea: also **cy·an′a·mid** (-mid) **2** CALCIUM CYANAMIDE
cy·a·nate (sī′ə nāt′) *n.* **1** a salt of cyanic acid containing the monovalent, negative radical CNO **2** an uncharged ester of this acid
cy·an·ic (sī an′ik) *adj.* ⟦CYAN(O)- + -IC⟧ **1** of or containing cyanogen **2** blue
cyanic acid a colorless, poisonous, unstable acid, N:COH, prepared by heating cyanuric acid
cy·a·nide (sī′ə nīd′) *n.* ⟦CYAN(O)- + -IDE⟧ a substance composed of a cyanogen group in combination with some element or radical; esp., potassium cyanide, KCN, or sodium cyanide, NaCN, extremely poisonous, white, crystalline compounds with an odor of bitter almonds: used in electroplating, extracting gold from low-grade ores, etc. —*vt.* **-nid′ed**, **-nid′ing** to treat with cyanide
cyanide process a process of extracting gold or silver from low-grade ores by treating them with a solution of sodium cyanide or potassium cyanide
cy·a·nine (sī′ə nēn′, -nin) *n.* ⟦CYAN(O)- + -INE³⟧ a soluble, crystalline, blue dye, $C_{29}H_{35}N_2I$, derived from quinoline and used as a sensitizer in photography
cy·a·nite (-nīt′) *n.* ⟦fol. + -ITE¹⟧ KYANITE
cy·a·no- (sī′ə nō′, -nə; sī an′ō, -ə) ⟦ModL < Gr *kyanos*, the color blue < or akin to Hittite *kuwanna*(*n*)-, copper (blue)⟧ *combining form* **1** dark-blue **2** *Chem.* of or containing the cyanogen group
cy·a·no·bac·te·ri·a (sī′ə nō bak tir′ē ə) *pl.n., sing.* **-ri·um** (-əm) BLUE-GREEN ALGAE
cy·a·no·co·ba·la·min (-kō bal′ə min) *n.* an active form of vitamin B_{12}: also **cy′a·no·co·ba′la·mine′** (-mēn′)

cy·an·o·gen (sī an′ə jən) ***n.*** ⟦CYANO- + -GEN⟧ **1** a colorless, poisonous, flammable gas, N:C·C:N **2** the radical CN, occurring in cyanides

cy·a·no·hy·drin (sī′ə nō hī′drin) ***n.*** ⟦CYANO- + HYDR(O)- + -IN[1]⟧ any of a class of organic chemical compounds containing the CN and OH radicals

cy·a·no·sis (sī′ə nō′sis) ***n.***, *pl.* **-ses′** (-sēz′) ⟦ModL < Gr *kyanōsis*, dark-blue color: see CYANO- & -OSIS⟧ a bluish coloration of the skin or mucous membranes, caused by lack of oxygen or by abnormal hemoglobin in the blood —**cy′a·not′ic** (-nät′ik) ***adj.***

cy·a·nu·rate (sī′ə nyoor′āt′, -it) ***n.*** ⟦< fol. + -ATE[2]⟧ a salt or ester of cyanuric acid

cy·a·nu·ric acid (-ik) ⟦CYAN(O)- + URIC⟧ a white, crystalline acid, $C_3N_3(OH)_3$, made by heating urea and used in making melamine, bleaches, etc.

Cyb·e·le (sib′ə lē′) ***n.*** ⟦L < Gr *Kybelē*⟧ *Myth.* a nature goddess of ancient Asia Minor: identified with the Greek Rhea

cy·ber (sī′bər) ***adj.*** ⟦see fol.⟧ **1** of or relating to computers or computing [*cyber* security] **2** of, utilizing, or taking place on the internet [*cyber* shopping, a *cyber* tour of London]

cy·ber- (sī′bər) ⟦< CYBERNETIC OR CYBERNETICS⟧ *combining form* computers, computing, internet [*cybercrime, cybernaut*]

cy·ber·at·tack (sī′bər ə tak′) ***n.*** an attack, as on a government, military, or financial network, executed from cyberspace

cy·ber·bul·ly (sī′bər bool′ē) ***n.*** a person who bullies another or others by means of texting, social media, etc.

cy·ber·ca·fe (sī′bər ka fā′) ***n.*** a coffee shop, cafe, etc. that provides its customers with computer terminals for access to the internet, usually for a fee

☆**cy·ber·nate** (sī′bər nāt′) ***vt.*** **-nat′ed, -nat′ing** ⟦back-form. < fol.⟧ to subject to cybernation

☆**cy·ber·na·tion** (sī′bər nā′shən) ***n.*** ⟦CYBERN(ETICS) + -ATION: coined (*c.* 1961) by D. N. Michael (1923-2000), U.S. sociologist⟧ the use of computers to control and carry out operations, as in manufacturing

cy·ber·naut (sī′bər nôt′, -nät′) ***n.*** ⟦CYBER- + (ASTRO)NAUT⟧ a person who uses the internet regularly and with great competence

☆**cy·ber·net·ics** (sī′bər net′iks) ***n.*** ⟦coined (1948) by Norbert WIENER < Gr *kybernētēs*, helmsman (< *kybernan*, to steer, GOVERN) + -ICS⟧ the science dealing with the comparative study of human control systems, as the brain and nervous system, and complex electronic systems —**cy′ber·net′ic** ***adj.***

☆**cy·ber·punk** (sī′bər puŋk′) ***n.*** ⟦CYBER- + PUNK[2] (*n.* 3b)⟧ **1** a type of science fiction typically describing a violent, urban future in which computers and drugs predominate **2** [Slang] HACKER[2]

cy·ber·sex (sī′bər seks′) ***n.*** sexual activity or arousal by means of text messaging, online pornography, etc.

☆**cy·ber·space** (sī′bər spās′) ***n.*** ⟦CYBER(NETIC) + SPACE: coined by William Gibson, U.S.-Canadian writer, in his novel *Neuromancer* (1984)⟧ the internet together with connected computers, etc., thought of as being a boundless environment providing access to information, interactive communication, and, in science fiction, a form of VIRTUAL REALITY

cy·ber·war (sī′bər wôr′) ***n.*** strategic warfare waged by means of cyberattacks —**cy′ber·war′rior** (-wôr′yər, -wôr′ē ər) ***n.***

☆**cy·borg** (sī′bôrg′) ***n.*** ⟦*cyb(ernetic) org(anism)*⟧ in science fiction, a human being modified for life in a hostile or alien environment by the substitution of artificial organs and other body parts

cyc *abbrev.* **1** cyclopedia **2** cycle

cy·cad (sī′kad′) ***n.*** ⟦ModL *Cycas* (gen. *Cycadis*) < Gr *kykas*, erroneous sp. for *koïkas*, acc. pl. of *koïx*, doum palm⟧ any of a class (Cycadatae) of gymnospermous tropical shrubs and trees resembling thick-stemmed palms, with crowns of leathery, fernlike leaves and large cones containing fleshy seeds

cy·cas (sī′kas′) ***n.*** ⟦see prec.⟧ any of a genus (*Cycas*) of cycads with leathery, dark-green leaves and short, thick trunks, grown for ornament

cycl- *combining form* CYCLO-: used before a vowel

Cyc·la·des (sik′lə dēz′) group of islands of Greece, on the S Aegean: 993 sq mi (2,572 sq km) —**Cy·clad·ic** (si klad′ik, sī-) ***adj.***

cy·cla·mate (sī′klə māt′, sik′lə-) ***n.*** ⟦*cycl(ohexylsulph)amate* < *cyclohexyl*, C_6H_{11}, a monovalent radical + *sulfamate*, ester of *sulfamic* acid (HSO_3NH_2)⟧ a synthetic salt derived from an organic acid, $C_6H_{11}NHSO_3H$, esp. the sodium or calcium salt, with an extremely sweet taste: used as a sweetener

cy·cla·men (sī′klə mən, sik′lə-) ***n.***, *pl.* **-mens** ⟦ModL < L *cyclaminos* < Gr *kyklaminos* < *kyklos*, a circle (? with reference to the form of the roots): see WHEEL⟧ any of a genus (*Cyclamen*) of plants of the primrose family, having heart-shaped leaves and white, pink, or red flowers with reflexed petals

cy·cla·zo·cine (sī′klə zō′sēn′, -sin) ***n.*** ⟦CYCL(O)- + (PENT)AZOCINE⟧ a pain-killing, nonaddictive, synthetic drug, $C_{18}H_{25}NO$, that blocks the effects of heroin or morphine

cy·cle (sī′kəl) ***n.*** ⟦ME *cicle* < LL *cyclus* < Gr *kyklos*, a circle, cycle: see WHEEL⟧ **1** a recurring period of a definite number of years, used as a measure of time **2** a period of time within which a round of regularly recurring events is completed [the business *cycle*] **3** a complete set of events or phenomena recurring in the same sequence **4** a very long period of time; an age **5** all of the traditional or legendary poems, songs, etc. connected with a hero or an event [the Charlemagne *cycle*] **6** a series of poems or songs on the same theme **7** a bicycle, tricycle, or motorcycle **8** [Archaic] *Astron.* the orbit of a celestial body **9** *Biol.* a recurring series of functional changes or events **10** *Elec.* one complete period of the reversal of an alternating current from positive to negative and back again —***vi.*** **-cled, -cling 1** to occur or recur in cycles; pass through a cycle **2** to ride a bicycle, tricycle, or motorcycle —☆**hit (or go) for the cycle** *Baseball* to hit (or try to hit) a single, double, triple, and home run in one game: said of a player

cy·clic (sik′lik, sī′klik) ***adj.*** **1** of, or having the nature of, a cycle; moving or occurring in cycles **2** *Chem.* of or relating to a major group of organic compounds, structured in closed chains, including aromatic, alicyclic, and heterocyclic compounds: compare ALIPHATIC —**cy′cli·cal·ly** ***adv.***

cy·cli·cal (sik′li kəl; *for sense 1 also* sīk′-) ***adj.*** **1** CYCLIC **2** tending to rise and fall in line with the fluctuations of the business cycle [*cyclical* stocks]

cy·clist (sīk′list, -əl ist) ***n.*** a person who rides a bicycle, motorcycle, etc.

cy·cli·zine (sī′klə zēn′, -zin) ***n.*** ⟦CYCL(O)- + -I- + (PIPERA)ZINE⟧ an antihistamine, $C_{18}H_{22}N_2$, used for treating nausea and motion sickness

cy·clo (sē′klō, sī′-) ***n.***, *pl.* **-clos** ⟦Fr < ? *cycle*, a bicycle, tricycle, etc., or *cyclo-* (< *cyclomoteur*, a moped)⟧ a three-wheeled passenger vehicle, as of Southeast Asia, that is propelled like a bicycle by pedaling or by a motor

cy·clo- (sī′klō, -klə; sik′-, -lə) ⟦< Gr *kyklos*, a circle: see WHEEL⟧ *combining form* **1** of a circle or wheel, circular [*cyclotron*] **2** CYCLIC (sense 2) [*cycloparaffin*]

cy·clo·hex·ane (sī′klō hek′sān′) ***n.*** ⟦prec. + HEXANE⟧ one of the cycloparaffins, C_6H_{12}, present in petroleum: used as a solvent, paint remover, etc.

cy·cloid (sī′kloid′) ***n.*** ⟦Gr *kykloeidēs*, circular < *kyklos* (see WHEEL) + *-eidēs*, -OID⟧ *Geom.* a curve traced by any point on a radius, or an extension of the radius, of a circle which rolls without slipping through one complete revolution along a straight line in a single plane; trochoid —***adj.*** **1** circular **2** designating or having fish scales that are roundish in form with smooth edges **3** designating or of a cyclothymic person —**cy·cloi·dal** (sī kloid′'l) ***adj.***

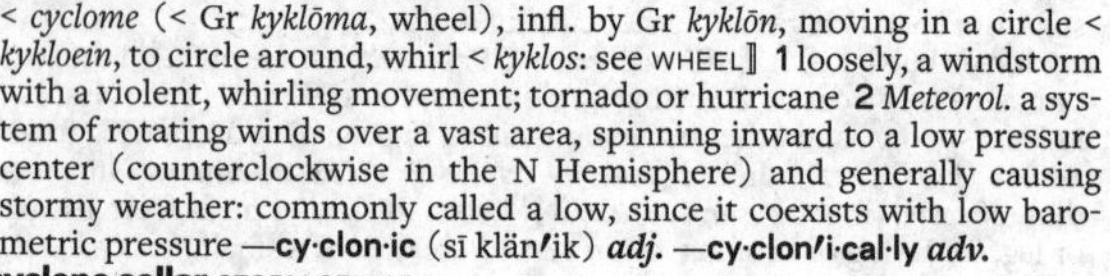

cycloids

cy·clom·e·ter (sī kläm′ət ər) ***n.*** ⟦CYCLO- + -METER⟧ **1** an instrument for measuring the arcs of circles **2** an instrument for recording the revolutions of a wheel, used to measure the distance, speed, etc. traveled by a bicycle

cy·clone (sī′klōn′) ***n.*** ⟦altered < *cyclome* (< Gr *kyklōma*, wheel), infl. by Gr *kyklōn*, moving in a circle < *kykloein*, to circle around, whirl < *kyklos*: see WHEEL⟧ **1** loosely, a windstorm with a violent, whirling movement; tornado or hurricane **2** *Meteorol.* a system of rotating winds over a vast area, spinning inward to a low pressure center (counterclockwise in the N Hemisphere) and generally causing stormy weather: commonly called a low, since it coexists with low barometric pressure —**cy·clon·ic** (sī klän′ik) ***adj.*** —**cy·clon′i·cal·ly** ***adv.***

☆**cyclone cellar** STORM CELLAR

☆**cyclone fence** ⟦< *Cyclone*, former trademark for such a fence⟧ a heavy-duty chain-link fence

cy·clo·nite (sī′klə nīt′) ***n.*** ⟦contr. < *cyclo(-trimethylene-tri)nit(ramin)e*: intended to suggest CYCLONE & -ITE[1]⟧ an insoluble, crystalline compound, $C_3H_6N_6O_6$, used as a powerful explosive or a rat poison

cy·clo·ox·y·gen·ase (sī′klō äk′sə jə nās′) ***n.*** ⟦CYCLO- + *oxygenase*, an enzyme < OXYGEN + -ASE⟧ any of a group of enzymes that regulate the production of prostaglandins: one type promotes the health of the stomach and kidneys, another triggers pain and inflammation

cy·clo·par·af·fin (sī′klō par′ə fin) ***n.*** ⟦CYCLO- + PARAFFIN⟧ any of a series of saturated alicyclic hydrocarbons of the general formula C_nH_{2n}, having a closed chain of three or more carbon atoms, as cyclohexane

Cy·clo·pe·an (sī′klō pe′ən, -klə-; sī klō′pē ən) ***adj.*** ⟦< L *Cyclopeus* < Gr *Kyklōpeios* < *Kyklōps*, CYCLOPS + -AN⟧ **1** of the Cyclopes **2** [**c-**] huge; gigantic; enormous; massive

cy·clo·pe·di·a or **cy·clo·pae·di·a** (sī′klə pē′dē ə) ***n.*** *former term for* ENCYCLOPEDIA —**cy′clo·pe′dic** ***adj.***, **cy′clo·pae′dic**

cy·clo·pen·tane (sī′klō pen′tān′) ***n.*** ⟦CYCLO- + PENTANE⟧ a colorless liquid cycloparaffin, C_5H_{10}, derived from certain petroleums

cy·clo·phos·pha·mide (sī′klō fäs′fə mīd′) ***n.*** ⟦CYCLO- + PHOSPH(ORIC) + AMIDE⟧ a white, crystalline compound, $C_7H_{15}Cl_2N_2O_2P$, used in treating certain malignancies, esp. lymphomas

cy·clo·ple·gi·a (-plē′jē ə, -jə) ***n.*** ⟦ModL < CYCLO- + -PLEGIA⟧ paralysis of those muscles of the eye responsible for visual accommodation —**cy′clo·ple′gic** (-jik) ***adj.***

cy·clo·pro·pane (-prō′pān′) ***n.*** ⟦CYCLO- + PROPANE⟧ a colorless, flammable, gaseous cycloparaffin, C_3H_6, used as a general anesthetic

Cy·clops (sī′kläps′) ***n.***, *pl.* **Cy·clo·pes** (sī klō′pēz′) or **-clops′** ⟦L < Gr *Kyklōps*, lit., round-eyed < *kyklos* (see WHEEL) + *ōps*, EYE⟧ *Gr. Myth.* any of a race of giants who have only one eye, in the middle of the forehead

cy·clo·ram·a (sī′klə ram′ə, -rä′mə) ***n.*** ⟦< CYCLO- + Gr *horama*, a view < *horan*, to see < IE base **wer-*, to heed > WARN⟧ **1** a series of large pictures, as of a landscape, put on the wall of a circular room so as to appear in natural perspective to a spectator standing in the center **2** a large, curved curtain or screen used as a background for stage settings —**cy′clo·ram′ic** ***adj.***

cy·clo·sis (sī klō′sis) ***n.*** ⟦ModL < Gr *kyklōsis*, an enveloping, surrounding < *kykloun*, to encircle < *kyklos*, a circle: see WHEEL⟧ a regular cyclic movement of protoplasm within a cell

cy·clo·spo·ra (sī′klō spôr′ə) ***n.*** ⟦ModL < CYCLO- + *spora* (see SPORE)⟧ any of a genus (*Cyclospora*) of sporozoa, esp. one (*Cyclospora cayetanensis*) that causes an intestinal disease similar to cryptosporidiosis

cy·clo·spor·ine (sī′klō spôr′in, -ēn′) ***n.*** a drug, produced by a fungus (*Tolypocladium inflatum*), that suppresses the T cells that reject foreign tissue after an organ transplant without suppressing other cells that fight infections and cancer: also **cy′clo·spor′in A** (-in)

cy·clos·to·mate (sī kläs′tə māt′) ***adj.*** **1** having a round mouth **2** of a cyclostome or the cyclostomes Also **cy·clo·stom·a·tous** (sī′klə stäm′ə təs, -stōm′-)

cy·clo·stome (sī′klə stōm′) ***n.*** ⟦CYCLO- + -STOME⟧ JAWLESS FISH

cy·clo·style (sī′klə stīl′) ***n.*** a kind of duplicating process using stencils formed by a pen with a small, toothed wheel —***vt.*** **-styled′**, **-styl′ing** to make copies by using cyclostyle

cy·clo·thy·mi·a (sī′klə thī′mē ə) ***n.*** ⟦ModL < CYCLO- + Gr *thymos*, spirit: see DULL⟧ an emotional condition characterized by alternate periods of elation and depression: considered by some to be a mild form of BIPOLAR (AFFECTIVE) DISORDER —**cy′clo·thy′mic** ***adj., n.***

☆**cy·clo·tron** (sī′klə trän′) ***n.*** ⟦CYCLO- + -TRON⟧ a circular particle accelerator for positively charged ions (usually protons, deuterons, and alpha particles), normally used to initiate nuclear transformations upon collision with a suitable target: through the combined action of a constant magnetic field with an oscillating electrostatic field across two D-shaped, hollow electrodes, it causes a particle to move in an increasingly large spiral path inside the electrodes with increasing kinetic energy and velocity

cy·der (sī′dər) ***n.*** ***Brit. var. of*** CIDER

cyg·net (sig′net, -nit) ***n.*** ⟦ME *cignet*, dim. < Fr *cygne*, swan < VL *cicinus* < L *cycnus* or *cygnus* < Gr *kyknos*, swan, prob. echoic of swan's cry⟧ a young swan

Cyg·nus (sig′nəs) ***n.*** ⟦L < *cygnus* or *cycnus*, swan < Gr *kyknos*: see prec.⟧ **1** *Gr. Myth.* a king of the Ligurians who is changed into a swan **2** a N constellation in the Milky Way near Lyra, containing the bright star Deneb; the Northern Cross; the Cross; the Swan

cyl *abbrev.* cylinder

cyl·in·der (sil′ən dər) ***n.*** ⟦Fr *cylindre* < L *cylindrus* < Gr *kylindros* < *kylindein*, to roll < IE base *(*s*)*kel-*, to bend > CALCAR, COLON[1]⟧ **1** *Geom.* *a)* a solid figure consisting of two parallel bases in the form of congruent, closed curves joined by a smooth, continuous, closed surface; specif., such a figure (**right circular cylinder**) having circular bases and a surface perpendicular to the bases *b)* the surface of such a solid **2** anything having the shape of a cylinder, whether hollow or solid; specif., *a)* the turning part of a revolver, containing chambers for cartridges *b)* the chamber in which the piston moves in a reciprocating engine *c)* the barrel of a pump *d)* on a printing press, a roller carrying the printing plates or the part receiving the impression *e)* a large, hollow, cylindrical clay object with cuneiform inscriptions, or a similar small stone worn on the wrist in ancient times in the Middle East

cylinder head the closed end, usually detachable, of a cylinder in an internal-combustion engine

cy·lin·dri·cal (sə lin′dri kəl) ***adj.*** of or having the shape of a cylinder: also **cy·lin′dric** —**cy·lin′dri·cal′i·ty** (-kal′ə tē) ***n.*** —**cy·lin′dri·cal·ly** ***adv.***

cyl·in·droid (sil′in droid′) ***n.*** ⟦Gr *kylindroeidēs*: see CYLINDER & -OID⟧ a type of cylinder with elliptical bases —***adj.*** resembling a cylinder

cy·lix (sī′liks, sil′iks) ***n., pl.*** **cyl′i·ces′** ***var. of*** KYLIX

cy·ma (sī′mə) ***n., pl.*** **-mae** (-mē) ⟦ModL < Gr *kyma*: see CYME⟧ *Archit.* a molding of a cornice, whose profile is a line partly convex and partly concave

cy·ma·ti·um (si mā′shē əm) ***n., pl.*** **-ti·a** (-ə) ⟦L < Gr *kymation*, dim. of *kyma*, wave: see CYME⟧ *Archit.* a cyma, esp. one topping an entablature

cym·bal (sim′bəl) ***n.*** ⟦ME < OFr *cymble* & OE *cymbal*, both < L *cymbalum* < Gr *kymbalon* < *kymbē*, hollow of a vessel < IE **kumb-* < base **keu-*, bend, arch > COOMB, HUMP⟧ a circular, slightly concave brass plate used as a percussion instrument producing a variety of metallic sounds: it is struck with a drumstick, brush, etc. or used in pairs which are struck together to produce a crashing, ringing sound —**cym′bal·ist** ***n.***

cym·ba·lom (sim′bə ləm) ***n.*** ***alt. sp. of*** CIMBALOM

cym·bid·i·um (sim bid′ē əm) ***n.*** ⟦ModL < L *cymba*, a boat, skiff (< Gr *kymbē*, boat, hollow of a vessel: see CYMBAL) + ModL *-idium*, dim. suffix (< Gr *-idion*)⟧ any of a genus (*Cymbidium*) of tropical Asian orchids, producing sprays of moderate-sized flowers in shades of white, pink, cream, yellow, or maroon

cyme (sīm) ***n.*** ⟦L *cyma*, young cabbage sprout < Gr *kyma*, something swollen, a billow, a wave, young cabbage sprout < *kyein*, to be pregnant < IE base **keu-*, to swell > L *cavus*, HOLLOW⟧ a flat-topped inflorescence formed by a growth pattern in which the initial stem and all subsequent emerging lateral stems terminate with a blossom

cy·mene (sī′mēn′) ***n.*** ⟦< Gr *kyminon*: see CUMIN⟧ a colorless hydrocarbon, $CH_3C_6H_4CH(CH_3)_2$, occurring in three isomeric forms (*orthocymene*, *metacymene*, and *paracymene*), derived from toluene: the most common form, paracymene, is found in the oil of certain plants, as cumin and wild thyme, and is used in paints and solvents

cy·mo- (sī′mō, -mə) ⟦Gr *kymo-* < *kyma*: see CYME⟧ *combining form* wave [*cymophane*]

cy·mo·graph (sī′mə graf′) ***n.*** ⟦CYMO- + -GRAPH⟧ KYMOGRAPH

cy·moid (sī′moid′) ***adj.*** resembling a cyma or cyme

cy·mo·phane (sī′mə fān′) ***n.*** ⟦CYMO- + -PHANE⟧ an opalescent variety of chrysoberyl

cy·mose (sī′mōs′, sī mōs′) ***adj.*** ⟦L *cymosus* < *cyma*: see CYME⟧ **1** of or like a cyme; determinate **2** bearing a cyme or cymes Also **cy′mous** (-məs)

Cym·ric (kim′rik, sim′-) ***adj.*** ⟦< *Cymri*, western Britons, Welsh < Welsh *Cymry*, pl. of *Cymro* < *Cymru*, Wales: see CAMBRIA⟧ of the Celtic people of Wales or their language or culture —***n.*** Brythonic, the group of Celtic languages that includes Welsh, Breton, and extinct Cornish

Cym·ry (-rē) ***pl.n.*** the Cymric Celts; the Welsh

cyn·ic (sin′ik) ***n.*** ⟦L *Cynicus* < Gr *kynikos*, lit., doglike, as if < *kyōn*, dog (see HOUND[1]), nickname of Diogenes, but prob. in allusion to the *Kynosarges*, a gymnasium where the Cynics taught (< *kyōn* + *argos*, lit., white dog, so named after an animal in a myth concerning Hercules, to whom the gymnasium was sacred)⟧ **1** [**C-**] a member of a school of ancient Greek philosophers who held virtue to be the only good and stressed independence from worldly needs and pleasures: they became critical of the rest of society and its material interests **2** a cynical person —***adj.*** [**C-**] of or like the Cynics or their doctrines

cyn·i·cal (sin′i kəl) ***adj.*** ⟦< L *cynicus*, of the Cynics: see prec.⟧ **1** believing that people are motivated in all their actions only by selfishness; denying the sincerity of people's motives and actions, or the value of living **2** sarcastic, sneering, etc. **3** [**C-**] Cynic —**cyn′i·cal·ly** ***adv.***

SYN.—**cynical** implies a contemptuous disbelief in human goodness and sincerity [*cynical* about anybody returning one's lost wallet]; **misanthropic** suggests a deep-seated hatred or distrust of people in general [*a misanthropic* hermit]; **pessimistic** implies an attitude, often habitual, of expecting the worst to happen [*pessimistic* about one's chances to win] —***ANT.*** **optimistic**

cyn·i·cism (sin′ə siz′əm) ***n.*** **1** [**C-**] the philosophy of the Cynics **2** the attitudes or beliefs of a cynical person **3** a cynical remark, idea, or action

cy·no·sure (sī′nə shoor′, sin′ə-) ***n.*** ⟦L < Gr *kynosoura*, dog's tail, constellation of Ursa Minor < *kyōn* (see HOUND[1]) + *oura*, tail: see URO-[2]⟧ **1** [**C-**] *former name for* the constellation Ursa Minor, or the North Star which is in this constellation **2** any person or thing that is a center of attention

Cyn·thi·a (sin′thē ə) ***n.*** ⟦L < Gr *Kynthia*, epithet of Artemis, orig. fem. of *Kynthios*, lit., of or from *Kynthos*, Cynthus, mountain in Delos, celebrated as the birthplace of Apollo and Artemis⟧ **1** a feminine name: dim. *Cindy* **2** ARTEMIS **3** the moon personified

CYO *abbrev.* Catholic Youth Organization

cy·pher (sī′fər) ***n., vt., vi.*** ***Brit. sp. of*** CIPHER

cy-pres (sē′prā′, sī′-) ***adj., adv.*** ⟦Late Anglo-Fr < OFr *si pres*, so nearly < L *sic*, so + *presse*, adv. of *pressus*, pp. of *premere*, PRESS[1]⟧ *Law* as near(ly) as possible: designating or according to an equitable doctrine for the interpretation of legal instruments having specific terms which cannot be carried out literally, whereby the court attempts to reform the instrument in accordance with the general intent of the settlor, testator, etc. rather than allow it to fail —***n.*** the cy-pres doctrine Also written **cy pres**

cy·press[1] (sī′prəs) ***adj.*** ⟦ME *cipres* < OFr < LL(Ec) *cypressus*, for L *cupressus* < Gr *kyparissos*⟧ designating a family (Cupressaceae) of conifers including the junipers —***n.*** **1** any of a genus (*Cupressus*) of evergreen, cone-bearing trees of the cypress family, native to North America, Europe, and Asia, with dark foliage and a distinctive symmetrical form **2** any of a number of related trees, including the baldcypress and white cedar **3** the wood of any of these trees **4** the branches or sprigs of the cypress, used as a symbol of mourning

cy·press[2] (sī′prəs) ***n.*** ⟦ME *cipres*, after OFr *Cipre*, CYPRUS⟧ any of various textile fabrics, originally made in Cyprus; specif., a fine, gauzelike lawn or silk: in black, it was often worn for mourning

☆**cypress vine** a tropical American, annual twining vine (*Ipomoea quamoclit*) of the morning-glory family, with showy, trumpet-shaped, scarlet or white flowers and finely divided pinnate leaves

Cyp·ri·an[1] (sip′rē ən) ***adj.*** ⟦< L *Cyprius* < Gr *Kyprios*, after *Kypros*, CYPRUS + -AN⟧ **1** CYPRIOT (***adj.***) **2** [Archaic] wanton; licentious: in reference to the worship of Aphrodite in Cyprus in ancient times —***n.*** **1** CYPRIOT (***n.*** 1) **2** [*also* **c-**] [Archaic] a prostitute

Cyp·ri·an[2] (sip′rē ən), Saint (born *Thascius Caecilius Cyprianus*) A.D. 200?-258; Christian martyr: bishop of Carthage (248-258): his day is Sept. 16

cyp·ri·noid (si′prə noid′) ***n.*** ⟦< Gr *kyprinos*, carp + -OID⟧ any of a family (Cyprinidae, order Cypriniformes) of freshwater bony fishes, including the carps, minnows, and dace —***adj.*** of or like such fishes Also **cyp′ri·nid** (-nid)

Cyp·ri·ot (sip′rē ət) ***adj.*** of Cyprus or its peoples, languages, or cultures —***n.*** **1** a person born or living in Cyprus **2** the variety of Greek spoken in Cyprus Also **Cyp′ri·ote′** (-ōt′)

cyp·ri·pe·di·um (sip′rə pē′dē əm) ***n., pl.*** **-di·ums** or **-di·a** (-ə) ⟦ModL, ladyslipper < Gr *Kypris*, Venus (lit., the Cyprian goddess) + *podion*, slipper, dim. < *pous* (gen. *podis*), FOOT⟧ **1** any of a genus (*Cypripedium*) of soil-rooted orchids of the North Temperate Zone, with flat leaves and white, yellow, or rosy-purple flowers, each having a pouchlike lip petal; ladyslipper **2** any of various cultivated species (genus *Paphiopedilum*) of tropical orchids with fleshy, folded leaves and green, yellow, or brown-purple flowers of waxy texture

Cy·prus (sī′prəs) country on an island at the E end of the Mediterranean, south of Turkey: colonized by Phoenicians and ancient Greeks; at various times ruled by Persian, Roman, Ptolemaic, Byzantine, & Ottoman Empires: formerly a British territory, it became independent in 1960 & a member of the Commonwealth in 1961: 3,571 sq mi (9,250 sq km); cap. Nicosia

cyp·se·la (sip′sə lə) ***n., pl.*** **-lae′** (-lē′) ⟦ModL < Gr *kypselē*, a hollow vessel; akin to *kybos*, CUBE[1]⟧ an achene derived from an inferior ovary, as in plants of the composite family

Cy·ra·no de Ber·ge·rac (sir′ə nō′də bʉr′zhə rak′; *Fr* sē rȧ nō′də ber zhȧ rȧk′), **Sa·vi·nien de** (sav′in yen′də; *Fr* sȧ vē nyan də) 1619-55; Fr. writer & soldier, famous for his large nose: title character of a poetic drama by Edmond Rostand (1897)

Cyr·e·na·ic (sir′ə nā′ik, sī′rə-) *adj.* **1** of Cyrenaica or Cyrene **2** of the Greek school of philosophy founded by Aristippus of Cyrene, who considered immediate, sensual pleasure the greatest good —*n.* a philosopher of the Cyrenaic school

Cyr·e·na·i·ca (sir′ə nā′i kə, sī′rə-) **1** region of E Libya **2** ancient Greek kingdom (7th-4th cent. B.C.) in the same general region, dominated by the city of Cyrene

Cy·re·ne (sī rē′nē) ancient Greek city in N Africa, on the Mediterranean: capital of Cyrenaica

Cy·ril[1] (sir′əl) *n.* ⟦LL *Cyrillus* < Gr *Kyrillos*, lit., lordly < *kyrios*, a lord: see CHURCH⟧ a masculine name

Cy·ril[2] (sir′əl) **1** Saint (A.D. 376?-444); Christian theologian: archbishop of Alexandria (412-444): his day is June 27 **2** Saint (born *Constantine*) (A.D. 827?-869); Gr. prelate & missionary; apostle to the Slavs: his day is Feb. 14

Cy·ril·lic (sə ril′ik) *adj.* designating or of the Slavic alphabet traditionally attributed to Saint Cyril, 9th cent. apostle to the Slavs: in modified form, it is still used in Russia, Bulgaria, and other Slavic countries

Cy·rus[1] (sī′rəs) *n.* ⟦L < Gr *Kyros* < OPers *Kūrush*⟧ a masculine name: dim. *Cy*

Cy·rus[2] (sī′rəs) **1** 424?-401 B.C.; Pers. prince: called *the Younger*: see CUNAXA **2 Cyrus II** died 529? B.C.; king of the Medes & Persians: founder of the Persian Empire: called *the Great*

cyst (sist) *n.* ⟦ModL *cystis* < Gr *kystis*, sac, bladder < ? IE base **kus-*, var. of **kwes-*, to WHEEZE, blow⟧ **1** any of certain saclike structures in plants or animals **2** such a structure or pocket in the body when abnormal and filled with fluid or diseased matter **3** a spherical, usually thick membrane, resistant to freezing, drying, etc., with which certain organisms are surrounded when in a resting stage

cyst- (sist) CYSTO-: used before a vowel

-cyst (sist) ⟦< Gr *kystis*: see CYST⟧ *combining form* sac, pouch, bladder *[blastocyst]*

cys·tec·to·my (sis tek′tə mē) *n., pl.* **-mies** ⟦CYST(O)- + -ECTOMY⟧ **1** the surgical removal of a cyst **2** the surgical removal of the gallbladder or of part of the urinary bladder

cys·te·ine (sis′tē in, -tē ēn′) *n.* a nonessential amino acid, $HSCH_2CH(NH_2)COOH$, derived from cystine: see AMINO ACID

cys·ti- (sis′tē, -ti, -tə) *combining form* CYSTO-

cyst·ic (sis′tik) *adj.* ⟦ModL *cysticus*⟧ **1** of or like a cyst **2** having or containing a cyst or cysts **3** enclosed in a cyst **4** *Anat.* of the gallbladder or the urinary bladder

cys·ti·cer·coid (sis′tə sʉr′koid′) *adj.* of or like a cysticercus —*n.* the larva of certain tapeworms, similar to a cysticercus but having a much smaller bladder

cys·ti·cer·cus (-kəs) *n., pl.* **-cer′ci′** (-sī′) ⟦ModL < CYSTI- (var. of CYSTO-) + Gr *kerkos*, tail⟧ the larva of certain tapeworms, parasitic in an intermediate host, in which the head and neck are partly enclosed in a bladderlike cyst; bladderworm

cystic fibrosis a congenital disease, usually of children, characterized by fibrosis and malfunctioning of the pancreas, and by frequent respiratory infections

cys·tine (sis′tēn, -tin) *n.* ⟦CYST(O)- + -INE[3]: so named from having been found first in urinary calculi⟧ a nonessential amino acid, $C_4H_6(NH_2)_2S_2(COOH)_2$: see AMINO ACID

cys·ti·tis (sis tīt′is) *n.* ⟦fol. + -ITIS⟧ an inflammation of the urinary bladder

cys·to- (-tō, -tə) ⟦< Gr *kystis*, bladder, sac: see CYST⟧ *combining form* bladder, sac *[cystocele]*

cys·to·cele (-sēl′) *n.* ⟦CYSTO- + -CELE⟧ a hernia of the urinary bladder into the vagina

cys·toid (sis′toid′) *adj.* like a cyst or bladder —*n.* a cystlike formation

cys·to·lith (sis′tō lith′, -tə-) *n.* ⟦CYSTO- + -LITH⟧ *Bot.* a crystalline deposit of calcium carbonate occurring as a knob on the end of a stalk within a plant cell

cys·to·scope (sis′tə skōp′) *n.* ⟦CYSTO- + -SCOPE⟧ an instrument for visually examining the interior of the urinary bladder —*vt.* **-scoped′**, **-scop′ing** to examine with a cystoscope —**cys′to·scop′ic** (-skäp′ik) *adj.*

cys·tos·co·py (sis täs′kə pē) *n., pl.* **-pies** examination of the urinary bladder or tract with the aid of a cystoscope

cys·tot·o·my (sis tät′ə mē) *n., pl.* **-mies** ⟦CYSTO- + -TOMY⟧ the surgical operation of making an incision into the urinary bladder or gallbladder

-cyte (sīt) ⟦< Gr *kytos*, a hollow; akin to L *cutis*: see CUTICLE⟧ *combining form* cell *[lymphocyte]*

Cy·the·ra (si thir′ə) ⟦L < Gr *Kythera*⟧ Greek island just south of the Peloponnesus, near which Aphrodite is fabled to have arisen from the sea

Cyth·er·e·a (sith′ər ē′ə) *n.* ⟦L < Gr *Kythereia* < *Kythera*: see prec.⟧ APHRODITE —**Cyth′e·re′an** *adj.*

cy·ti·dine (sit′ə dēn′, sīt′-) *n.* ⟦CYTOSINE + *-idine* < -IDE + -INE[3]⟧ a white, crystalline nucleoside, $C_9H_{13}N_3O_5$, condensed from cytosine and ribose: it is a major component of RNA

cy·to- (sīt′ō, -ə) ⟦< Gr *kytos*, a hollow: see -CYTE⟧ *combining form* cell or cells *[cytology, cytoplasm]*

cy·to·chem·is·try (sīt′ō kem′is trē) *n.* the study of the chemical constituents of cells by selective staining of cell parts and by analysis of cellular extracts

cy·to·chrome (sīt′ə krōm′) *n.* ⟦CYTO- + -CHROME⟧ any of several iron-containing enzymes found in almost all animal and plant cells, very important in cell respiration

cy·to·ge·net·ics (sīt′ō jə net′iks) *n.* the science correlating cytology and genetics as they relate to the behavior of chromosomes and genes in cells with regard to heredity and variation —**cy′to·ge·net′ic** *adj.*, **cy′to·ge·net′i·cal** —**cy′to·ge·net′i·cist** (-ə sist) *n.*

cy·to·kine (sīt′ō kīn′) *n.* ⟦< CYTO- + Gr *kinein*, to move: see CITE⟧ any of a group of molecules, including interferon, interleukin, and tumor necrosis factor, secreted by certain cells of the immune system, which modulate certain cell functions associated with immune response

cy·to·ki·ne·sis (-ki nē′sis) *n.* ⟦CYTO- + Gr *kinēsis*, motion: see KINESIOLOGY⟧ cytoplasmic changes occurring in a cell during mitosis, meiosis, and fertilization —**cy′to·ki·net′ic** (-net′ik) *adj.*

☆**cy·to·ki·nin** (sīt′ō kī′nin) *n.* ⟦CYTO- + KININ⟧ any of a group of organic compounds which behave like hormones in plants, promoting cell division and cell differentiation into roots and shoots, inhibiting aging, etc.

cy·tol·o·gy (sī täl′ə jē) *n.* ⟦CYTO- + -LOGY⟧ the branch of biology dealing with the structure, function, pathology, and life history of cells —**cy·to·log·ic** (sī′tō läj′ik) *adj.*, **cy′to·log′i·cal** —**cy′to·log′i·cal·ly** *adv.* —**cy·tol′o·gist** *n.*

cy·tol·y·sin (-ə sin) *n.* a substance or antibody that produces cytolysis

cy·tol·y·sis (-ə sis) *n.* ⟦CYTO- + -LYSIS⟧ *Biol.* the disintegration or dissolution of cells —**cy·to·lyt·ic** (sī′tə lit′ik) *adj.*

cy·to·meg·a·lo·vi·rus (sīt′ō meg′ə lō vī′rəs) *n.* ⟦CYTO- + MEGALO- + VIRUS⟧ any of a group of herpesviruses that cause enlargement of the epithelial cells, esp. of the salivary glands: associated with pneumonia and with abnormalities in newborn infants

cy·to·plasm (sīt′ō plaz′əm) *n.* ⟦CYTO- + -PLASM⟧ the protoplasm of a cell, outside the nucleus —**cy′to·plas′mic** *adj.*

cy·to·plast (-plast′) *n.* CYTOPLASM

cy·to·sine (sīt′ō sēn′) *n.* ⟦Ger *zytosin* < *zyt-*, CYTO- + *-os*, -OSE[2] + *-in*, -INE[3]⟧ a pyrimidine base, $C_4H_5N_3O$, contained in the nucleic acids of all tissue: it links with guanine in the DNA structure

cy·to·skel·e·ton (sīt′ō skel′ə tən) *n.* a flexible network of various kinds of protein filaments, as microtubules, in the cytoplasm of eukaryotic cells, providing structure for the cell and helping with normal cell activity, esp. with movement and cellular division —**cy′to·skel′etal** (-təl) *adj.*

cy·to·tax·on·o·my (sīt′ō tak sän′ə mē) *n.* the branch of taxonomy that uses cytologic structures, esp. the chromosomes, as an aid in classifying organisms —**cy′to·tax′o·nom′ic** (-sə näm′ik) *adj.*

cy·to·tox·ic (sīt′ō täks′ik) *adj.* **1** that harms or destroys living cells *[cytotoxic drug therapy]* **2** of or relating to cytotoxins, their effects, etc. —**cy′to·tox·ic′i·ty** (-is′ə tē) *n.*

cytotoxic T cell a killer T cell: see KILLER CELL

cy·to·tox·in (sīt′ō täks′in) *n.* a chemical substance that destroys, or impairs the function of, specific living cells

cy·to·troph·o·blast (sīt′ō träf′ō blast′) *n.* ⟦CYTO- + TROPHOBLAST⟧ the thickened, inner part of the mammalian placenta nearest to the fetus, covering the chorion during early pregnancy

Cyz·i·cus (siz′i kəs) ancient Greek city in NW Asia Minor, on the S shore of the Sea of Marmara

CZ *abbrev.* **1** cubic zirconia **2** Canal Zone

czar (zär) *n.* ⟦Russ *tsar′*, contr. of *tsesar* < OSlav *cěsarĭ*; prob. via Goth *kaisar* < L *Caesar*: see CAESAR[2]⟧ **1** an emperor: title of any of the former emperors of Russia and, at various times, the sovereigns of other Slavic nations ☆**2** any person having great or unlimited power; autocrat **3** a person given broad administrative powers to make government policy *[the President's energy czar]* —**czar′dom** *n.*

czar·das (chär′däsh′) *n.* ⟦Hung *csárdás*⟧ **1** a Hungarian dance consisting of a slow section followed by a fast one **2** music for this

czar·e·vitch (zär′ə vich′) *n.* ⟦Russ *tsarevich*, son of a czar⟧ the eldest son of a czar of Russia

cza·rev·na (zä rev′nə) *n.* the daughter of a czar of Russia

cza·ri·na (zä rē′nə) *n.* ⟦Ger *zarin, czarin*, fem. of *zar, czar* < Russ *tsaritsa*⟧ the wife of a czar; empress of Russia: also **cza·rit′za** (-rēt′sə)

czar·ism (zär′iz′əm) *n.* **1** the Russian government under the czars **2** absolute rule; despotism —**czar′ist** *adj., n.*

Czech[1] (chek) *n.* **1** a Bohemian or Moravian Slav, or a Silesian Slav of the Czech Republic **2** the West Slavic language of the Czechs **3** loosely, a person born or living in Czechoslovakia **4** a person born or living in the Czech Republic —*adj.* of the Czechs or their language or culture: often **Czech′ish**

Czech[2] *abbrev.* Czechoslovakia

Czech·o·slo·vak (chek′ə slō′väk′, -vak′) *adj.* of Czechoslovakia or its peoples or cultures —*n.* a person born or living in Czechoslovakia Also **Czech′o·slo·vak′i·an** (-slō vä′kē ən, -vak′ē ən)

Czech·o·slo·va·ki·a (chek′ə slō vä′kē ə) former country in central Europe, south of Poland and east of Germany: formed (1918) by the merger of Bohemia, Moravia, and parts of Silesia and Slovakia, in 1993 it was divided into the Czech Republic and Slovakia: Czech name ČESKOSLOVENSKO

Czech Republic country in central Europe: formerly the W constituent republic of Czechoslovakia: 30,450 sq mi (78,866 sq km); cap. Prague

Czer·ny (cher′nē), **Karl** 1791-1857; Austrian composer

Czę·sto·cho·wa (chan′stô Hô′vä) city in S Poland, on the Warta River

D

d[1] or **D** (dē) ***n., pl.*** **d's, D's 1** the fourth letter of the English alphabet: from the Greek *delta*, a borrowing from the Phoenician **2** any of the speech sounds that this letter represents, as, in English, the (d) of *dog* **3** a type or impression for *d* or *D* **4** the fourth in a sequence or group **5** an object shaped like D —***adj.*** **1** of *d* or *D* **2** fourth in a sequence or group **3** shaped like D

d[2] *abbrev.* **1** dam (in pedigrees) **2** date **3** daughter **4** day(s) **5** dead **6** deci- **7** degree **8** *Physics* density **9** departs **10** departure **11** diameter **12** died **13** *Physics* distance **14** division **15** dollar **16** dorsal **17** dose **18** dyne(s) **19** ⟦L *da*⟧ *Pharmacy* give **20** ⟦L *denarius*, pl. *denarii*⟧ PENNY (***n.*** 1*b*); pence

D[1] (dē) ***n.*** **1** a Roman numeral for 500; with a superior bar ($\bar{D}$), 500,000 or, less often, 5,000 ☆**2** *Educ.* a grade indicating below-average work, or merely passing **3** *Music a)* the second tone or note in the ascending scale of C major *b)* a key, string, etc. producing this tone *c)* the scale having this tone as the keynote —***adj.*** below average in quality

D[2] *abbrev.* **1** dairy: an abbrev. indicating that something has been prepared according to kosher laws **2** December **3** *Sports* defense **4** Democrat **5** Democratic **6** *Chem.* deuterium **7** digital **8** divorced **9** Doctor **10** Don **11** drive (on automotive automatic-shift indicators) **12** Duchess **13** Duke **14** Dutch **15** ⟦L *Dominus*⟧ Lord

d- (dē) *prefix Chem.* dextrorotatory: usually printed in italic type [*d*-limonene] or symbolized by a plus sign (+)

D- (dē) *prefix Chem.* having an asymmetrical, right-handed spatial arrangement of atoms: usually printed as a small capital [D-glucose]

d'- *prefix* [Informal] do [*d'you* know the story?]

-'d[1] *suffix* **1** had [*I'd* seen it before] **2** would or should [we said *we'd* help] **3** did [*how'd* you get here?]

-'d[2] *suffix var. of* -ED used *a)* esp. in old poetry, to indicate a nonsyllabic ending [*foster'd*] *b)* to spell the inflected forms of some words, esp. initialisms [*mascara'd, OD'd*]

da[1] (dä) *adv., interj.* ⟦Russ⟧ yes

da[2] *abbrev.* **1** daughter **2** day(s) **3** deca-; deka-

Da *abbrev. Bible* Daniel

DA[1] or **D.A.** (dē′ā′) ***n.*** ⟦< *d*(*uck's*) *a*(*ss*)⟧ [Slang] DUCKTAIL

DA[2] *abbrev.* **1** District Attorney **2** Doctor of Arts Also **D.A.**

dab[1] (dab) ***vt., vi.*** **dabbed, dab′bing** ⟦ME *dabben*, to strike, akin to MDu *dabben* & Norw *dabba* < ? IE base **dhabh-*, to strike⟧ **1** to touch or stroke lightly and quickly **2** to pat with something soft or moist **3** to put on (paint, etc.) with light, quick strokes —***n.*** **1** a light, quick stroke; tap; pat **2** a small, soft or moist bit of something [a *dab* of lip gloss] —**dab′ber *n.***

dab[2] (dab) ***n.*** ⟦ME *dabbe* < ?⟧ **1** any of several flounders (esp. *Limanda proboscidea*) of coastal waters **2** any small flatfish

dab[3] (dab) ***n.*** [Brit. Informal] an expert; dab hand

DAB *abbrev.* Dictionary of American Biography

dab·ble (dab′əl) ***vt.*** **-bled, -bling** ⟦Du *dabbelen*, freq. of MDu *dabben*, to strike, DAB[1]⟧ **1** to dip lightly in and out of a liquid **2** to wet by dipping, splashing, or sprinkling —***vi.*** **1** to play in water, as with the hands **2** to feed by reaching with the bill into shallow water: said of certain ducks and other water birds **3** to do something superficially, not seriously: with *in* or *at* [to *dabble* in painting] —**dab′bler *n.***

dab·chick (dab′chik′) ***n.*** ⟦DAB[1] + CHICK: from the manner of diving⟧ **1** the smallest European grebe (*Podiceps ruficollis*) ☆**2** PIED-BILLED GREBE

dab hand ⟦< ? DAB[1], *vt., vi.* 3⟧ [Brit. Informal] an expert

dabs (dabz) ***pl.n.*** ⟦so called prob. from putting a DAB[1] of ink from each finger into the spaces on a suspect's police record⟧ [Brit. Slang] fingerprints

dab·ster (dab′stər) ***n.*** ⟦DAB[1] + -STER⟧ **1** [Brit. Informal] an expert **2** [Informal] an amateurish worker; dabbler

da ca·po (dä kä′pô) ⟦It, from (the) head⟧ *Musical Direction* from the beginning: a note to the performer to repeat the passage

Dac·ca (dä′kä, dak′ə) *former sp. of* DHAKA

dace (dās) ***n., pl.*** **dace** or **dac′es** ⟦ME, dial. form (with *-r-* loss as in BASS[2]) of *dars* < OFr *dars* < VL *darsus*, of Gaul orig.⟧ any of various small, freshwater cyprinoid fishes (esp. genera *Phoxinus* and *Rhinichthys*)

da·cha (dä′chä) ***n.*** ⟦Russ *dača*, orig., a giving, gift < *dat'*, to give < IE base **do-*, to give > Sans *dāti-*, Gr *dosis*, gift⟧ in Russia, a country house or cottage used as a vacation retreat

Da·chau (dä′kou′; *Ger.*, -khou′) city in S Germany, near Munich, in the state of Bavaria: site (1933-45) of a Nazi concentration camp

dachs·hund (däks′hoont′) ***n.*** ⟦Ger < *dachs*, badger (prob. < IE base **tegu-*, THICK) + *hund*, dog: see HOUND[1]⟧ any of a breed of small dog with a long body, short legs, and drooping ears, of three varieties — smooth (or short-haired), long-haired, and wire-haired

dachshund

Da·cia (dā′shə) ancient region in SE Europe, inhabited by a Thracian people; later, a Roman province (2d-3d cent.): it corresponded approximately to modern Romania —**Da′cian *adj., n.***

da·coit (də koit′) ***n.*** ⟦Hindi *ḍakāit*, robber < *ḍākā*, attack by robbers⟧ a member of a gang of robbers in India or Burma (Myanmar)

da·coit·y (-ē) ***n., pl.*** **-coit′ies** ⟦Hindi *ḍakāitī*: see prec.⟧ robbery by dacoits

dac·quoise (da kwäz′) ***n.*** ⟦Fr < fem. of *dacquois*, of *Dax*, town in SW France⟧ a layered dessert of meringue with nuts, with a buttery chocolate or mocha filling

☆**Da·cron** (dā′krän′, dak′rän′) ⟦arbitrary formation, with *-on* as in NYLON, RAYON⟧ *trademark for* a synthetic polyester fiber or a washable, wrinkle-resistant fabric made from it —***n.*** [*also* **d-**] this fiber or fabric

dac·ry·o- (dak′rē ō, -ə) ⟦< Gr *dakryon*, TEAR[2]⟧ *combining form* **1** tear or tears **2** the lacrimal apparatus Also, before a vowel, **dac′ry-**

dac·tyl (dak′təl) ***n.*** ⟦ME *dactil* < L *dactylus* < Gr *daktylos*, a finger or (by analogy with the three joints of a finger) a dactyl⟧ **1** a metrical foot consisting, in Greek and Latin verse, of one long syllable followed by two short ones, or, as in English verse, of one accented syllable followed by two unaccented ones (Ex.: "táke hĕr ŭp | téndĕrlȳ̆") **2** *Zool.* a finger or toe

dac·tyl·ic (dak til′ik) ***adj.*** of or made up of dactyls —***n.*** a dactylic line of poetry

dac·tyl·o- (dak′tə lō′, dak til′ə) ⟦< Gr *daktylos*, a finger⟧ *combining form meaning* **1** finger, toe, digit [*dactylology*] ☆**2** fingerprint [*dactylography*] Also, before a vowel, **dac′tyl-**

dac·tyl·o·gram (dak til′ə gram′) ***n.*** ⟦prec. + -GRAM⟧ a fingerprint

dac·ty·log·ra·phy (dak′tə läg′rə fē) ***n.*** ⟦DACTYLO- + -GRAPHY⟧ the study of fingerprints as a means of identification

dac·ty·lol·o·gy (-läl′ə jē) ***n.*** ⟦DACTYLO- + -LOGY⟧ the use of a finger alphabet, as among people who are deaf

-dac·ty·lous (dak′tə ləs) ⟦see fol.⟧ *combining form forming adjectives* having fingers, toes, etc. of a (specified) kind or number

-dac·ty·ly (dak′tə lē) ⟦< Gr *daktylos*, a finger⟧ *combining form forming nouns* a (specified) condition of the fingers, toes, etc.: also **-dac·tyl·i·a** (dak til′ē ə)

dad (dad) ***n.*** ⟦< child's cry *dada*⟧ [Informal] FATHER

da·da (dä′dä′, -də) ***n.*** ⟦Fr, lit., hobbyhorse (< baby talk, altered < ? *dia dia*, giddap), selected by Tristan Tzara, Romanian artist & leader of the movement, because of its resemblance to meaningless babble, as symbolic of the movement⟧ [*also* **D-**] a movement (1916-22) in painting, sculpture, and literature characterized by fantastic, abstract, or incongruous creations, by rejection of all accepted conventions, and by nihilistic satire: also **da′da·ism′** —**da′da·ist *adj., n.*** —**da′da·is′tic *adj.***

dad·dy (dad′ē) ***n., pl.*** **-dies** ⟦see DAD⟧ [Informal] **1** father; dad: often a child's term of affectionate address **2** GRANDDADDY (sense 2)

daddy long·legs (lôŋ′legz′, -lägz′) *pl.* **-legs′** **1** HARVESTMAN (sense 2) **2** CRANE FLY

da·do (dā′dō) ***n., pl.*** **-does** ⟦It, a die, die-shaped part of pedestal, hence pedestal < L *datum*, a die, lit., what is given: see DATE[1]⟧ **1** the part of a pedestal between the cap and the base **2** the lower part of the wall of a room if decorated differently from the upper part, as with panels or an ornamental border **3** *a)* a rectangular groove cut in the side of one board so that another board may be fitted into it usually at right angles *b)* the joint thus made (in full, **dado joint**) —***vt.*** **-doed, -do·ing** **1** to furnish with a dado **2** to fit into a dado groove

Da·dra and Na·gar Ha·vel·i (də drä′ and nə gur′ hä′vel ē) territory of India (formerly two territories) consisting of an enclave on the S coast of Gujarat state: 190 sq mi (492 sq km)

DAE *abbrev.* Dictionary of American English

dae·dal (dēd′'l) ***adj.*** ⟦L *daedalus* < Gr *daidalos* < *daidallein*, to work artfully < IE base **del-*, to split, carve > L *dolere*, to feel pain⟧ [Chiefly Literary] **1** skillfully made **2** highly wrought

Dae·da·li·an or **Dae·da·le·an** (dē dāl′ē ən, -yən) ***adj.*** **1** of Daedalus **2** [**d-**] DAEDAL

Daed·a·lus (ded′'l əs, dēd′-) ***n.*** ⟦L < Gr *Daidalos*, lit., the artful craftsman

< *daidalos:* see DAEDAL] *Gr. Myth.* the skillful artist and builder of the Labyrinth in Crete, from which, by means of wings he made, he and his son Icarus escaped

dae·mon (dē′mən) *n.* [L, a spirit (in LL(Ec), evil spirit, demon) < Gr *daimōn*, divine power, fate, god, in LGr(Ec), evil spirit < IE base **dā(i)-*, to part, divide, tear apart > TIME, TATTER] **1** *Gr. Myth.* any of the secondary divinities ranking between the gods and men **2** a guardian spirit; inspiring or inner spirit **3** DEMON (sense 2) —**dae·mon·ic** (di män′ik) *adj.*

daff[1] (daf) *vi.* [< ME *daffe*, fool < *dafte*, DAFT] [Scot.] to act the part of a fool; behave playfully

daff[2] (daf) *vt.* [var. of DOFF] **1** [Archaic] to turn or thrust aside **2** [Obs.] to take off (clothes); doff

daf·fa·down·dil·ly or **daf·fy·down·dil·ly** (daf′ə doun′dil′ē) *n., pl.* **-lies** [Old Poet.] a daffodil: also **daf′fo·dil′ly** or **daf′fa·dil′ly**

daf·fo·dil (daf′ə dil′) *n.* [ME *affodille* < ML *affodillus* < LL *asphodelus* < Gr *asphodelos*: initial *d-* < ?] **1** any of various plants (genus *Narcissus*) of the lily family with a typically yellow flower having a large, trumpetlike corona **2** the flower

daf·fy (daf′ē) *adj.* **-fi·er, -fi·est** [DAFF[1] + -Y[2]] [Informal] **1** crazy; foolish; silly **2** frolicsome in a giddy way —**daf′fi·ness** *n.*

daft (daft) *adj.* [ME *dafte* < OE *(ge)dæfte*, mild, gentle (for the sense development, see CRETIN, SILLY) < IE base **dhabh-*, to fit > L *faber*, a joiner, artisan] **1** silly; foolish **2** insane; crazy **3** [Scot.] merry or frolicsome in a giddy way —**daft′ly** *adv.* —**daft′ness** *n.*

dag[1] (dag) *n.* [ME *dagge*] **1** DAGLOCK **2** [Obs.] a hanging, usually pointed, end

dag[2] *abbrev.* dekagram(s)

da Gam·a (də gä′mə, də gam′ə), **Vas·co** (väs′kō, vas′-) 1460-1524; Port. navigator: discovered the sea route around Africa to India

Dag·en·ham (dag′ən əm) former municipal borough of SE England: see BARKING

Dag·e·stan (dag′ə stän′, däg′-) autonomous republic of Russia, between Georgia & the Caspian Sea: 19,420 sq mi (50,300 sq km); cap. Makhachkala: also sp. **Dagh′e·stan′**

dag·ga (dag′ə) *n.* [Afrik, hemp, prob. < Hottentot *daga-b*] MARIJUANA

dag·ger (dag′ər) *n.* [ME *daggere* < OFr *dague* < OProv *daga*] **1** a weapon with a short, pointed blade, used for stabbing **2** a symbol (†) used as a reference mark or to indicate that a person listed has died: cf. DOUBLE DAGGER —*vt.* **1** to stab with a dagger **2** to mark with a dagger —**stare (**or **look) daggers at** to look at with anger or hatred

dag·ger·board (-bôrd′) *n.* [so named because it is placed into the water with a thrusting motion] *Naut.* a centerboard, specif. one that is thrust directly into the water rather than being swung down on a pivot

dag·gle (dag′əl) *vt., vi.* **-gled, -gling** [< dial. *dag*, to besprinkle, make muddy, prob. < ON *dǫggva*, to bedew, besprinkle < *dǫgg* (gen. *dǫggvar*), dew + -LE] [Chiefly Dial.] to soil by trailing through mud

dag·lock (dag′läk′) *n.* [< ME *dagge*, a loose, hanging end (< ?) + LOCK[2]] a lock of wool matted with dirt, dung, etc.

Dag·mar (dag′mär′) *n.* [Dan < Gmc **dag-*, DAY, brightness + **-mar*, akin to OE *mære*, splendid] a feminine name

da·go (dā′gō) *n., pl.* **-gos** or **-goes** [prob. altered < earlier *diego* < Sp *Diego*, James] [*also* **D-**] [Slang] a person, often dark-skinned, of Spanish, Portuguese, or, now esp., Italian descent: a term of hostility and contempt

Da·gon (dā′gän′) *n.* [ME < LL(Ec) < LGr(Ec) < Heb < ? *dāgān*, grain (hence ? god of agriculture)] *Myth.* the chief god of the ancient Philistines and later of the Phoenicians, sometimes represented as half man and half fish

☆**da·guerre·o·type** (də ger′ō tīp′, -ē ō-) *n.* [after Louis J. M. *Daguerre* (1789-1851), Fr painter who developed the method] **1** a photograph made by an early method on a plate of chemically treated metal **2** this method —*vt.* **-typed′, -typ′ing** to photograph by this method —**da·guerre′o·typ′y** *n.*

☆**Dag·wood (sandwich)** (dag′wood′) [after comic-strip character *Dagwood* Bumstead (created by U.S. cartoonist Chic Young, 1901-73), who made such sandwiches for himself] a thick sandwich with a variety of fillings, often of foods regarded as incompatible

dah (dä) *n.* [echoic of the sound of this character as produced by an old-fashioned telegraph] the dash character in Morse code

da·ha·be·ah, da·ha·bee·yah, *or* **da·ha·bi·ah** (dä′hə bē′ə) *n.* [Ar *dhahabīya*, lit., golden one (fem.) < *dhabab*, golden] a large passenger boat used on the Nile, orig. equipped with lateen sails, now generally powered by an engine

Da Hing·gan Ling (dä′ hiŋ′gän′ liŋ′) mountain range in NE China along the E border of Mongolia: highest peak, 5,670 ft (1,728 m): cf. XIAO HINGGAN LING

dahl (däl) *n. alt. sp. of* DAL[1]

Dahl (däl), **Ro·ald** (rō′äl) 1916-90; Brit. writer, esp. of children's books

dahl·ia (dal′yə, däl′-; *chiefly Brit* dāl′-) *n.* [ModL, after A. *Dahl*, 18th-c. Swed botanist] **1** any of a genus (*Dahlia*) of perennial plants of the composite family, with tuberous roots and large, showy flower heads in various bright colors, native to Mexico and Central America **2** the flower of this plant

Da·ho·mey (də hō′mē) *former name for* BENIN

☆**da·hoon** (də ho͞on′) *n.* [< ?] an evergreen tree or shrub (*Ilex cassine*) of the holly family, native to the S U.S. and used for hedges

dai·kon (dī′kən, -kän) *n.* [Jpn < *dai*, big + *kon*, root] a Japanese radish (*Raphanus sativus* var. *longipinnatus*) having a long, white root that is eaten raw or cooked

dai·li·ness (dā′lē nəs, -li-) *n.* [see fol.] the ordinary quality or merely routine aspects of some condition, way of life, etc. [a romantic dreamer who could not endure the *dailiness* of marriage]

dai·ly (dā′lē) *adj.* [ME *dayly* < OE *dæglic* < *dæg*, DAY] **1** done, happening, published, etc. every day or every weekday **2** calculated by the day [*daily* rate] —☆*n., pl.* **-lies 1** a daily newspaper **2** [*usually pl.*] RUSH[1] (*n.* 8) —*adv.* every day; day after day

daily double a betting procedure or bet, in which winning depends on choosing both winners in two specified horse or dog races on the same program

☆**daily dozen** [Informal] gymnastic setting-up exercises (originally twelve) done daily

dai·mon (dī′mōn′) *n. var. of* DAEMON —**dai·mon′ic** (-män′ik) *adj.*

dai·myo (dī′myō′) *n., pl.* **-myo′** or **-myos′** [Jpn < Chin *dai*, great + *mio*, name] a hereditary feudal nobleman of Japan: also sp. **dai′mio′**

dain·ty (dān′tē) *n., pl.* **-ties** [ME *deinte*, excellent, fine, orig., feeling of esteem < Anglo-Fr *deinté* < OFr *deinté* < L *dignitas*, worth, DIGNITY] a choice food; delicacy —*adj.* **-ti·er, -ti·est 1** delicious and choice [a *dainty* morsel] **2** delicately pretty or lovely **3** *a)* of or showing delicate and refined taste; fastidious *b)* overly or affectedly fastidious; squeamish —**dain′ti·ly** *adv.* —**dain′ti·ness** *n.*

SYN.—**dainty**, in this comparison, suggests delicate taste and implies a tendency to reject that which does not fully accord with one's refined sensibilities [a *dainty* appetite]; **nice** suggests fine or subtle discriminative powers, esp. in intellectual matters [a *nice* distinction in definition]; **particular** implies dissatisfaction with anything that fails to conform in detail with one's standards [*particular* in one's choice of friends]; **fastidious** implies adherence to such high standards as to be disdainfully critical of even minor nonconformities [a *fastidious* taste in literature]; **squeamish** suggests such extreme sensitiveness to what is unpleasant, or such prudishness, as to result in disgust or nausea [not too *squeamish* in his business dealings] See also **delicate**

☆**dai·qui·ri** (dak′ə rē) *n.* [after *Daiquirí*, village in E Cuba, source of the rum first used in this drink] a cocktail made of rum, sugar, and lime or lemon juice

dair·y (der′ē) *n., pl.* **-ies** [ME *daierie* < *daie*, dairymaid < OE *dæge*, (female) bread maker < *dag*, DOUGH + *-erie*, -ERY] **1** a building or room where milk and cream are kept and butter and cheese are made **2** DAIRY FARM **3** *a)* a commercial establishment that processes and distributes milk and milk products *b)* a retail store where these are sold **4** milk and the foods made from it, considered as a group or category —*adj.* of milk, cream, butter, cheese, etc.

dairy cattle cows raised mainly for their milk

dairy farm a farm in the business of producing milk and milk products —**dairy farmer** —**dairy farming**

dair·y·ing (-iŋ) *n.* the business of producing, making, or selling dairy products

dair·y·maid (-mād′) *n.* [Now Rare] a girl or woman who milks cows or works in a dairy

dair·y·man (-mən) *n., pl.* **-men** (-mən) a man who works in or for a dairy or who owns or manages a dairy

da·is (dā′is; *often* dī′-) *n., pl.* **da′is·es** [ME & OFr *deis*, high table in a hall < ML *discus*, table < L, quoit, DISCUS] a platform raised above the floor at one end of a hall or room, as for a throne, seats of honor, a speaker's stand, etc.

dai·shi·ki (dä shē′kē, də-) *n. alt. sp. of* DASHIKI

dai·sy (dā′zē) *n., pl.* **-sies** [ME *daies ie* < OE *dæges eage*, lit., day's eye < *dæges*, gen. of *dæg*, DAY + *eage*, EYE] ☆**1** a common plant (*Chrysanthemum leucanthemum*) of the composite family, bearing flowers with white rays around a yellow disk; oxeye daisy **2** any similar member of the composite family; esp., the ENGLISH DAISY **3** the flower of any of these plants **4** [Old Slang] something excellent —**push up (the) daisies** [Slang] to be dead and buried

daisy (sense 1)

Dai·sy (dā′zē) *n.* [< prec.] a feminine name

daisy chain 1 a garland or string of interlinked daisies ☆**2** any interlinked series

daisy wheel [descriptive of its shape] a flat, circular printing element of a word-processing printer or of an electric typewriter

Da·kar (də kär′, dăk′är) seaport & capital of Senegal, on the W coast

☆**Da·kin's solution** (dā′kinz) [after H. D. *Dakin* (1880-1952), Eng chemist in America] a weak, mildly alkaline solution of sodium hypochlorite, used as an antiseptic in the treatment of wounds

Da·ko·ta[1] (də kōt′ə) *n.* [< Dakota *dakóta*, allies < *da*, to think of as + *koda*, friend] **1** *pl.* **-tas** or **-ta** a member of any of a group of North American Indian peoples (also called *Sioux*) of the plains of the N U.S. and adjacent S Canada **2** the Siouan language of this group —*adj.* **1** of the Dakota Indians or their language or culture **2** of North Dakota, South Dakota, or both —**the Dakotas** North Dakota and South Dakota —**Da·ko′tan** *adj., n.*

Da·ko·ta[2] (də kōt′ə) [< prec.] former U.S. territory (1861-89), orig. including an area that is present-day N.Dak., S.Dak., and much of what is now Wyo. & Mont.

dal[1] (däl) *n.* [Hindi *dāl*] **1** any of various kinds of pulse used as food in In-

dia **2** a dish of India made by simmering this in water with spices, herbs, oil, onions, etc. to a thick, mushy consistency and served as with chapatis or rice
dal[2] (däl) *abbrev.* dekaliter(s)
Da·lai La·ma (dä′lī lä′mə) ⟦Mongolian *dalai*, ocean + *blama*: see LAMA⟧ the traditional high priest of Lamaism
da·la·si (dä′lə sē′, dä lä′sē′) *n., pl.* **-si′** ⟦Mandingo, lit., complete: short for *dalasi fano*, a complete pane (of the cloth formerly used for money)⟧ the basic monetary unit of Gambia: see the table of monetary units in the Reference Supplement
Dalcroze, Émile Jaques *see* JAQUES-DALCROZE
dale (dāl) *n.* ⟦ME < OE *dæl* (pl. *dalu*), infl. by ON *dalr* < IE base **dhel-*, a hollow > DELL, Gr *thalamos*, inner chamber⟧ a valley
Dale[1] (dāl) *n.* ⟦< the surname *Dale*, orig., a person living in or near a prec.⟧ a masculine and feminine name
Dale[2] (dāl) **1** Sir **Henry Hallet** 1875-1968: Brit. physiologist **2** Sir **Thomas** died 1619; Eng. colonial governor of Va. (1611; 1614-16)
d'A·lem·bert (dȧ län ber′), **Jean le Rond** (zhän lə rōn′) 1717-83; Fr. philosopher & encyclopedist
dales·man (dālz′mən) *n., pl.* **-men** (dālz′mən) a person living in a dale, specif. in N England
da·leth (däl′et, däl′əd) *n.* ⟦Heb, door⟧ the fourth letter of the Hebrew alphabet (ד)
Dal·hou·sie (dal ho͞o′zē, -hou′-) **1** Earl of (*George Ramsay*) 1770-1838; Brit. general, born in Scotland; governor of the British colonies in Canada (1819-28) **2** Marquis of (*James Andrew Broun-Ramsay*) 1812-60; Brit. statesman, born in Scotland; governor general of India (1847-59): son of the Earl of Dalhousie
Da·lí (dä′lē), **Sal·va·dor** (sal′və dôr′) (born *Salvador Felipe Jacinto Dalí i Domènech*) 1904-89; Sp. surrealist painter
Da·lian (dä′lyen′) seaport in Liaoning province, NE China: see LÜDA
Da·lit (dul′it, däl′-) *n.* a member of the Scheduled Castes: see also UNTOUCHABLE (sense 2)
Dal·las (dal′əs) ⟦after G. M. *Dallas* (1792-1864), U.S. vice president (1845-49)⟧ city in NE Tex.
☆**dalles** (dalz) *pl.n.* ⟦Fr *dalle*, water trough, conduit, ult. < ON *dœla*, drain gutter (on a ship's deck); akin to *dalr*: see DALE⟧ the rapids of a river between the steep, rocky walls of a narrow canyon
dal·liance (dal′yəns, -ē əns) *n.* ⟦ME *daliaunce* < *dalien*⟧ the act of dallying; flirting, toying, or trifling
☆**Dal·lis grass** (dal′is) ⟦< ?⟧ a tall, succulent, forage grass (*Paspalum dilatatum*), with hairy spikelets, much grown in the S U.S.: also **Dallas grass**
Dall sheep (dôl) ⟦after W. H. *Dall* (1845-1927), U.S. naturalist⟧ a wild sheep (*Ovis dalli*) with white hair and long spiral horns, living in the mountains of NW North America: also **Dall's sheep**
dal·ly (dal′ē) *vi.* **-lied**, **-ly·ing** ⟦ME *dalien* < OFr *dalier*, to converse, trifle⟧ **1** to flirt; play at love **2** to deal lightly or carelessly (*with*); trifle; toy **3** to waste time; loiter —*SYN.* LOITER, TRIFLE —**dal′li·er** (-ē ər, -yər) *n.*
Dal·mane (dal′mān) *trademark for* a yellow, crystalline hypnotic drug, $C_{21}H_{25}Cl_3FN_3O$, prescribed for insomnia
Dal·ma·tia (dal mā′shə) region along the Adriatic coast, mostly in Croatia
Dal·ma·tian (dal mā′shən) *adj.* of Dalmatia or its people —*n.* **1** a person born or living in Dalmatia, esp. a Slavic-speaking one **2** a Romance language formerly spoken in Dalmatia **3** any of a breed of large, short-haired dog with black or liver-colored spots on a white coat

Dalmatian

dal·mat·ic (dal mat′ik) *n.* ⟦ME *dalmatik* < OFr *dalmatique* < LL(Ec) *dalmatica (vestis)*, Dalmatian (garment), after *Dalmatia*: orig. made of Dalmatian wool⟧ **1** a loose outer garment with short, wide sleeves and open sides, worn by a deacon, or by a cardinal, bishop, or abbot **2** a similar robe worn by an English king at his coronation
dal se·gno (däl se′nyô) ⟦It⟧ *Musical Direction* from the sign: a note to the performer to return and repeat from the sign 𝄋
dal·ton (dôlt′'n) *n.* ⟦after fol.⟧ ATOMIC MASS UNIT
Dal·ton (dôlt′'n), **John** 1766-1844; Eng. chemist & physicist —**Dal·to·ni·an** (dôl tō′nē ən) *adj.*
Dal·ton·ism (dôlt′'n iz′əm) *n.* ⟦after prec., who had colorblindness and investigated it scientifically⟧ colorblindness, esp. red-green blindness
Da·ly (dā′lē), **(John) Au·gus·tin** (ô gus′tin) 1838-99; U.S. playwright & theatrical manager
dam[1] (dam) *n.* ⟦ME < Gmc base seen in MLowG, MDu *dam*, ON *dammr*, MHG *tam*, Goth *faur-dammjan*, to stop up < IE base **dhē-*, to set, put in place > DO[1], L *facere*⟧ **1** a barrier built to hold back flowing water **2** the water thus kept back **3** any barrier like a dam, as a rubber sheet used in dentistry to keep a tooth dry —*vt.* **dammed**, **dam′ming 1** to build a dam in **2** to keep back or confine by or as by a dam: usually with *up*
dam[2] (dam) *n.* ⟦ME, var. of *dame*, DAME⟧ **1** the female parent of any four-legged, esp. domestic, animal **2** [Archaic] a mother
dam·age (dam′ij) *n.* ⟦ME < OFr < *dam* < L *damnum*, loss, injury: see DAMN⟧ **1** injury or harm to a person or thing, resulting in a loss in soundness or value **2** [*pl.*] *Law* money claimed by, or ordered paid to, a person to compensate for injury or loss caused by the wrong of the opposite party or parties **3** [Informal] cost or expense —*vt.* **-aged**, **-ag·ing** to do damage to —*vi.* to incur damage —*SYN.* INJURE —**dam′age·a·ble** *adj.*
dam·an (dam′ən) *n.* ⟦< Ar (prob. dial.) *daman Isrā'īl*, sheep of Israel⟧ HYRAX
Da·man (də män′) small region on the coast of NW India: part of the territory of Daman and Diu
Daman and Diu territory of India, consisting of Daman region & Diu island: formerly part of a territory that included Goa: 43 sq mi (112 sq km)
Da·man·hûr (dä′män ho͞or′) city in N Egypt, in the Nile delta
dam·ar (dam′ər) *n. alt. sp. of* DAMMAR
Dam·a·scene (dam′ə sēn′, dam′ə sēn′) *adj.* ⟦L *Damascenus*, of Damascus⟧ **1** of Damascus or its people or culture **2** [**d-**] of damascening or damask —*n.* **1** a person born or living in Damascus **2** [**d-**] damascened work **3** [**d-**] a small plum: see DAMSON —*vt.* [**d-**] **-scened′**, **-scen′ing** to decorate (iron, steel, etc.) with wavy markings or with inlaid patterns of gold or silver
Da·mas·cus (də mas′kəs) capital of Syria, in the SW part: an ancient city dating to *c.* 2,000 B.C.
Damascus steel 1 a hard, flexible steel decorated with wavy lines, orig. made in Damascus and used for sword blades **2** any steel like this
dam·ask (dam′əsk) *n.* ⟦It *damasco*, after L *Damascus* (the city)⟧ **1** a durable, lustrous, reversible fabric as of silk or linen, in figured weave, used for table linen, upholstery, etc. **2** *a)* DAMASCUS STEEL *b)* the wavy markings of such steel **3** deep pink or rose —*adj.* **1** [Obs.] of or from Damascus **2** made of damask **3** like damask **4** deep-pink or rose —*vt.* **1** to ornament with flowered designs or wavy lines **2** to make deep-pink or rose
damask rose a very fragrant cultivated rose (*Rosa damascena*), with clusters of white to red flowers, important as a source of attar of roses: an ancestor of hybrid roses
damask steel DAMASCUS STEEL
Da·ma·vand (dä′mə vänd′, dam′ə vand′) highest peak of the Elburz Mountains, N Iran: 18,934 ft (5,771 m)
dame (dām) *n.* ⟦ME < OFr < L *domina*, lady, fem. of *dominus*, a lord: see DOMINATE⟧ **1** [**D-**] [Archaic] a title given to a woman in authority or the mistress of a household: now only in personifications [*Dame* Care] **2** an elderly or matronly woman **3** [**D-**] in Great Britain *a)* the legal title of the wife of a knight or baronet *b)* the title of a woman who has received an order of knighthood (used always with the given name) **4** [Slang] a woman or girl
dame's violet ⟦transl. of ModL *viola matronalis*⟧ an old-fashioned garden flower (*Hesperis matronalis*) of the crucifer family, with white or purple fragrant flowers in spring and early summer: also **dame's rocket**
Da·mi·en (dā′mē ən; *Fr* dȧ myan′), Father (born *Joseph de Veuster*) 1840-89; Belgian Roman Catholic priest & missionary to the leper colony on Molokai
Dam·i·et·ta (dam′ē et′ə) seaport in N Egypt, in the E Nile delta
dam·mar or **dam·mer** (dam′ər) *n.* ⟦Malay *dāmar*⟧ **1** any of various resins from evergreen trees (genus *Agathis*) of Australia, New Zealand, and East Indies, used in making varnish, lacquers, etc. **2** any of various natural resins from trees (esp. genera *Shorea* and *Balanocarpus*) native to Southeast Asia and the East Indies, used in varnishes and paints requiring high resistance to wear
damn (dam) *vt.* **damned**, **damn′ing** ⟦ME *damnen* < OFr *damner* < L *damnare*, to condemn, fine < *damnum*, loss, injury, akin to Gr *dapanē*, cost < IE **depno-*, sacrificial feast < base **dā(i)-*, to part, divide > TIME, TATTER⟧ **1** *a)* [Obs.] to condemn as guilty *b)* to condemn to an unhappy fate; doom *c)* *Theol.* to condemn to endless punishment **2** to condemn as bad or inferior: often used in the imperative as a curse **3** to criticize adversely **4** to cause the ruin of; make fail **5** to swear at by saying "damn" —*vi.* to swear or curse; say "damn," etc. —*n.* the saying of "damn" as a curse — *adj., adv.* [Informal] *short for* DAMNED —*interj.* used to express anger, annoyance, disappointment, etc. —*SYN.* CURSE —**damn with faint praise** to praise with so little enthusiasm as, in effect, to disparage or condemn —**not give** (or **care**) **a damn** [Informal] not care at all —**not worth a damn** [Informal] worthless
dam·na·ble (dam′nə bəl) *adj.* ⟦ME < OFr < LL *damnabilis* < L *damnare*: see prec.⟧ **1** deserving damnation **2** deserving to be sworn at; outrageous; execrable —**dam′na·bly** *adv.*
dam·na·tion (dam nā′shən) *n.* ⟦ME *damnacioun* < OFr *damnation* < LL(Ec) *damnatio*, the displeasure of God < L, condemnation⟧ a damning or being damned —*interj.* used to express anger
dam·na·to·ry (dam′nə tôr′ē) *adj.* ⟦L *damnatorius*⟧ **1** threatening with damnation; damning **2** condemning [*damnatory* evidence]
damned (damd; *also, as in oratory*, dam′nid) *adj.* **1** condemned or deserving condemnation **2** [Informal] deserving cursing; outrageous: now often a mere intensive [*a damned* shame] —*adv.* [Informal] very [*a damned* good job] —**do** (or **try**) **one's damnedest** (or **damndest**) [Informal] to do or try one's utmost —**the damned** *Theol.* souls doomed to eternal punishment
dam·ni·fy (dam′nə fī′) *vt.* **-fied′**, **-fy′ing** ⟦Early ModE < OFr *damnifier* < LL(Ec) *damnificare*, to harm < L *damnum* (see DAMN) + *facere*, to make, DO[1]⟧ *Law* to cause injury, damage, or loss to
Dam·o·cles (dam′ə klēz′) *n.* ⟦L < Gr *Damoklēs*⟧ *Class. Legend* a courtier of ancient Syracuse who was given a lesson in the perils to a ruler's life when the king seated him at a feast under a sword hanging by a single hair —**sword of Damocles** any imminent danger

dam·oi·selle, dam·o·sel, *or* **dam·o·zel** (dam′ə zel′) ***n.*** [Archaic] a damsel

Da·mon and Pyth·i·as (dā′mən ənd pith′ē əs) *Class. Legend* friends so devoted to each other that when Pythias, who has been condemned to death, wants time to arrange his affairs, Damon pledges his life that his friend will return: Pythias returns and both are pardoned

damp (damp) ***n.*** ⟦MDu, vapor, steam, akin to OHG, MHG, Ger *dampf* < IE base **dhem-*, to smoke, mist > DANK⟧ **1** a slight wetness; moisture **2** a harmful gas sometimes found in mines; firedamp; blackdamp **3** [Archaic] a dejected or depressed state —***adj.*** **1** somewhat moist or wet; humid **2** dejected; depressed —***vt.*** **1** to make damp; moisten **2** to slow the combustion of (a fire) by cutting off most of the air supply; bank: usually with *down* **3** to check or reduce (energy or action) **4** to check or deaden the vibration of (a piano string, drum membrane, etc.) **5** to reduce the amplitude of (oscillations, waves, etc.) —**SYN.** WET —**damp off** to wither and die because of mildew, as seedlings, plant shoots, etc. —**damp′ish** ***adj.*** —**damp′ly** ***adv.*** —**damp′ness** ***n.***

☆**damp-dry** (-drī′) ***vt.*** **-dried′**, **-dry′ing** to dry (laundry) so that some moisture is retained —***adj.*** designating or of laundry so treated

damp·en (dam′pən) ***vt.*** **1** to make damp; moisten **2** to deaden, depress, reduce, or lessen —***vi.*** to become damp —**damp′en·er** ***n.***

damp·er (dam′pər) ***n.*** ⟦see DAMP⟧ **1** anything that deadens or depresses **2** a movable plate or valve in the flue of a stove or furnace, for controlling the draft **3** a device to check vibration in the strings of a stringed keyboard instrument **4** a device for lessening the oscillation of a magnetic needle, a moving coil, etc. —**put a damper on** to depress, inhibit, lessen, etc.; dampen [the worsening economy has *put a damper on* new construction]

damper (sense 2)

Dam·pier (dam′pyer, -pē ər, -pir), **William** 1652-1715; Eng. explorer & pirate

damp·ing-off (dam′piŋ ôf′) ***n.*** a fungal disease of plants that causes young seedlings to decay and wither

Dam·rosch (dam′räsh), **Walter (Johannes)** 1862-1950; U.S. conductor & composer, born in Germany

dam·sel (dam′zəl) ***n.*** ⟦*damesele* < OFr *dameisele* < VL **dominicella*, dim. of L *domina*: see DAME⟧ [Now Literary] a girl; maiden

dam·sel·fish (-fish′) ***n., pl.*** **-fish′** or **-fish′es** (see FISH) any of a percoid family (Pomacentridae) of small, rough-scaled, brightly colored tropical reef fishes

dam·sel·fly (-flī′) ***n., pl.*** **-flies′** any of a suborder (Zygoptera) of slow-flying, usually brightly colored dragonflies with long wings held vertically when at rest

dam·son (dam′zən, -sən) ***n.*** ⟦ME *damasin* < OFr *damascene*, plum of Damascus < L *Damascenus*, lit., of Damascus⟧ **1** a variety of small, purple plum; bullace **2** the prunus tree (*Prunus domestica* var. *insititia*) on which it grows

Dan[1] (dan) ***n.*** ⟦ME < OFr < L *dominus*, master, lord > DON[1]: see DOMINATE⟧ [Archaic] master; sir: a title [*Dan Cupid*]

Dan[2] (dan) ***n.*** ⟦Heb *dān*, a judge⟧ *Bible* **1** Jacob's fifth son, whose mother was Bilhah: Gen. 30:1-6 **2** the tribe of Israel descended from him, which settled in N Palestine: Num. 1:38

Dan[3] (dan) village in NE Israel: site of an ancient town at the northernmost extremity of Israelite territory: cf. BEERSHEBA —**from Dan to Beersheba** **1** *Bible* from one end of Israel to the other: Judg. 20:1 **2** from end to end; throughout; everywhere

Dan[4] *abbrev.* **1** *Bible* Daniel **2** Danish

Da·na[1] (dā′nə) ***n.*** a masculine and feminine name

Da·na[2] (dā′nə) **1 Charles Anderson** 1819-97; U.S. newspaper editor **2 James Dwight** 1813-95; U.S. geologist & mineralogist **3 Richard Henry** 1815-82; U.S. writer & lawyer

Dan·a·e or **Dan·a·ë** (dan′ā ē′) ***n.*** ⟦Gr *Danaē*⟧ *Gr. Myth.* the mother of Perseus by Zeus, who visits her in the form of a shower of gold

Da·na·i·des or **Da·na·ï·des** (də nā′ə dēz′) ***pl.n.***, *sing.* **Dan′a·id′** *Gr. Myth.* the fifty daughters of Danaus, a king of Argos: forty-nine murder their husbands at their father's command and are condemned in Hades to draw water forever with a sieve

Da Nang (də naŋ′, də näŋ′) seaport in central Vietnam, on the South China Sea

Dan·a·us (dan′ā əs) ***n.*** *see* DANAIDES

dance (dans, däns) ***vi.*** **danced**, **danc′ing** ⟦ME *dauncen* < OFr *danser* < ? Frank **dintjan*, to tremble, move back and forth⟧ **1** to move the body and feet in rhythm, ordinarily to music **2** to take part in or perform a dance **3** to move lightly and gaily; caper **4** to bob up and down **5** to be stirred into rapid movement, as leaves in a wind —***vt.*** **1** to take part in or perform (a dance) **2** *a)* to cause to dance *b)* to cause to move lightly, bob up and down, etc. —***n.*** **1** rhythmic movement of the body and feet, ordinarily to music **2** a particular kind of dance, as the waltz, tango, etc. **3** the art of dancing, esp. as performed in ballet or modern dance **4** *a)* a party to which people come to dance *b)* one round of dancing at such a party **5** a piece of music for dancing **6** rapid, lively movement **7** any elaborate or ritualized sequence of actions, specif., an instinctive one performed by two animals as a part of courting or mating —**dance around** [Informal] to avoid or evade (a question, concern, etc.); sidestep; dodge —**dance attendance on** to be always near so as to wait on, lavish attention on, etc. —**dance to another tune** to alter one's actions or opinions as a result of changed conditions —**dance′a·ble** ***adj.*** —**danc′er** ***n.***

dance band a BAND[2] (***n.*** 2) that plays for dancing, esp. as distinguished from one that plays for listening; specif., such a band that plays popular music of the 1930s and 1940s

dance hall a large, usually public, hall for dancing

dance of death a symbolic portrayal, esp. in medieval art, of Death whirling persons away in dance as each dies

D and C ⟦D(ILATION) & C(URETTAGE)⟧ a minor surgical procedure in which the cervix is dilated and the lining of the uterus is scraped, usually to obtain a tissue sample, remove polyps, or terminate a pregnancy

dan·de·li·on (dan′də lī′ən; *also*, dan′dē līn′) ***n.*** ⟦ME *dentdelyon* < OFr *dent de lion*, lit., tooth of the lion < L *dens* (gen. *dentis*), TOOTH + *de*, of + *leo*, lion: so called from the jagged leaves⟧ any of several plants (genus *Taraxacum*) of the composite family, common weeds with yellow flowers and jagged leaves often used as greens

dan·der (dan′dər) ***n.*** ⟦< ?⟧ **1** tiny particles, as from feathers, skin, or hair, that may cause allergies ☆**2** [Informal] anger or temper —**have one's** (or **get someone's**) **dander up** [Informal] to be (or cause someone to become) angry

dan·di·a·cal (dan dī′ə kəl) ***adj.*** [Literary] dandyish

Dan·die Din·mont terrier (dan′dē din′mänt′, -mənt) ⟦after *Dandie* (Andrew) *Dinmont*, character in Scott's novel *Guy Mannering* (1815)⟧ any of a breed of small terrier with short legs, drooping ears, and a generally rough coat with a mass of silky hair on top of the head

dan·di·fy (dan′də fī′) ***vt.*** **-fied′**, **-fy′ing** to make look like a dandy; dress up —**dan′di·fi·ca′tion** ***n.***

dan·dle (dan′dəl) ***vt.*** **-dled**, **-dling** ⟦< ? or akin to OIt *dandolare*, (later) *dondolare*, to swing up and down, dally, trifle⟧ **1** to dance (a small child) up and down on the knee or in the arms **2** to pamper; indulge —**SYN.** CARESS

Dan·dong (dän′dooŋ′) seaport in Liaoning province, NE China, at the mouth of the Yalu River

dan·druff (dan′drəf) ***n.*** ⟦< earlier *dandro, dander* (< ?) + dial. *hurf*, scab < ON *hrufa*: see GRAUPEL⟧ **1** little scales or flakes of dead skin formed on the scalp **2** a condition of the scalp in which such scales are formed —**dan′druff·y** ***adj.***

dan·dy (dan′dē) ***n., pl.*** **-dies** ⟦< ? playful Scot form of *Andy* < *Andrew*: see MERRY-ANDREW⟧ **1** *a)* a man who pays too much attention to his clothes and appearance; fop *b)* a meticulously well-dressed man **2** a kind of British yawl or ketch **3** [Informal] something very good or first-rate —***adj.*** **-di·er**, **-di·est** **1** [Rare] of or for a dandy; foppish ☆**2** [Informal] very good; first-rate —**dan′dy·ish** ***adj.*** —**dan′dy·ism′** ***n.***

dandy roll ⟦< ?⟧ *Papermaking* a cylinder covered with wire gauze that puts on the watermark

Dane (dān) ***n.*** ⟦ME *Dan* < ON *Danir* (pl.) the Danes, akin to OE *Dene* (prob. "lowlanders" < IE base **dhen-*, level lowland > DEN); orig., name of a continental Anglian people⟧ a person born or living in Denmark

Dane·geld (-geld′) ***n.*** ⟦ME < ON **Danagiald* < *Dana*, gen. pl. of *Danr*, Dane + *gjald*, payment, penalty, akin to OE *gieldan*: see YIELD⟧ an Anglo-Saxon tax first levied to support forces resisting the Danes invading England and later continued as a land tax

Dane·law or **Dane·lagh** (-lô′) ***n.*** ⟦ME *Denelawe* < OE *Dena lagu*, Danes' law⟧ **1** the code of laws established in E and N England by Danish invaders and settlers in the 9th and 10th cent. A.D. **2** the E and N section of England that was under this code

dang (daŋ) ***vt., adj., adv., interj.*** [Informal] *euphemism for* DAMN (the curse) —**danged** ***adj., adv.***

dan·ger (dān′jər) ***n.*** ⟦ME *daunger*, power, domination, arrogance < OFr *danger*, absolute power of an overlord < VL **dominarium* < L *dominium*, lordship < *dominus*, a master: see DOMINATE⟧ **1** liability to injury, damage, loss, or pain; peril [to live in constant *danger*] **2** a thing that may cause injury, pain, etc. **3** [Obs.] power of a lord, esp. to harm

SYN.—**danger** is the general term for liability to injury or evil, of whatever degree or likelihood of occurrence [the *danger* of falling on icy walks]; **peril** suggests great and imminent danger [in *peril* of death]; **jeopardy** emphasizes exposure to extreme danger [liberty is in *jeopardy* under tyrants]; **hazard** implies a foreseeable but uncontrollable possibility of danger, but stresses the element of chance [the *hazards* of hunting big game]; **risk** implies the voluntary taking of a dangerous chance —**ANT. safety, security**

dan·ger·ous (-əs) ***adj.*** ⟦ME < OFr *dangereus*⟧ full of danger; likely to cause injury, pain, etc.; unsafe; perilous —**dan′ger·ous·ly** ***adv.*** —**dan′ger·ous·ness** ***n.***

dan·gle (daŋ′gəl) ***vi.*** **-gled**, **-gling** ⟦< Scand, as in Dan *dangle*, Ice *dingla*, to dangle⟧ **1** to hang loosely so as to swing back and forth [a long tail *dangled* from the kite] **2** to be a hanger-on; follow (*after*) **3** to refer to an implied, rather than stated, word in the sentence in which it occurs: said of a modifier [in "After marrying him, the house seemed more cheerful," "marrying" is a *dangling* participle] —***vt.*** **1** to hold (something) so that it hangs and swings loosely [the child *dangled* the doll by its arm] **2** to offer in a tempting or teasing way as an inducement —**dan′gler** ***n.***

☆**dan·gle·ber·ry** (-ber′ē) ***n., pl.*** **-ries** ⟦prec. + BERRY⟧ a blue huckleberry (*Gaylussacia frondosa*), native to E North America

Dan·iel[1] (dan′yəl) *n.* ⟦Heb *dānī'ēl*, lit., God is my judge⟧ **1** a masculine name: dim. *Dan, Danny*; fem. *Danielle* **2** *Bible a)* a Hebrew prophet whose faith saved him in the lions' den: Dan. 6:16-23 *b)* the book containing his stories and prophecies (abbrev. *Dan, Da,* or *Dn*)
Dan·iel[2] (dan′yəl), **Samuel** 1562-1619; Eng. poet
Dan·ielle (dan yel′) *n.* ⟦Fr, fem. of *Daniel*, DANIEL[1]⟧ a feminine name: see DANIEL[1]
Dan·iels (dan′yelz), **Josephus** 1862-1948; U.S. statesman & journalist: secretary of the navy (1913-21)
da·ni·o (dā′nē ō′) *n., pl.* **-os′** ⟦ModL, old name of a genus < E Ind native name⟧ any of several brightly colored, tropical, Asian cyprinoid aquarium fish
Dan·ish (dān′ish) *adj.* ⟦ME < OE *Denisc*: see DANE⟧ of Denmark or its people, language, or culture —*n.* **1** the N Germanic language spoken in Denmark **2** [*also* **d-**] *short for* DANISH PASTRY
Danish pastry [*also* **d- p-**] (a) rich, flaky pastry of raised dough filled with fruit, cheese, etc. and usually topped with icing
Danish West Indies those islands of the Virgin Islands occupied by Denmark from the 17th cent. to 1917: now *Virgin Islands of the United States*
Dan·ite (dan′īt′) *adj.* of the Hebrew tribe of Dan —*n.* **1** a member of this tribe ☆**2** a member of an alleged secret Mormon organization, supposed to have been formed about 1838
D'An·jou pear (dan′jo͞o; *Fr* dän zho͞o′) ANJOU PEAR
dank (daŋk) *adj.* ⟦ME, akin to ON *dǫkk*, marshy area, Swed dial. *dunken*, moist < IE **dhengwo-* < base **dhem*: see DAMP⟧ disagreeably damp; moist and chilly —*SYN.* WET —**dank′ly** *adv.* —**dank′ness** *n.*
Danl *abbrev.* Daniel
Dan·mark (dan′märk) *Dan. name for* DENMARK
d'An·nun·zio (dä no͞on′tsyô), **Ga·bri·e·le** (gä′brē e′le) 1863-1938; It. poet, writer, & political adventurer
danse du ven·tre (däns dü vän′tr') ⟦Fr⟧ BELLY DANCE
danse ma·ca·bre (däns má kä′br') ⟦Fr⟧ DANCE OF DEATH
dan·seur (dän sʉr′; *Fr* dän sër′) *n.* ⟦Fr, dancer⟧ a male ballet dancer
dan·seur no·ble (dän sër nô′bl') ⟦Fr, lit., noble dancer⟧ [*also in roman type*] *Ballet* a male dancer suited for certain heroic, or noble, roles by virtue of his exceptional grace, technique, and strength
dan·seuse (dän so͞oz′; *Fr* dän söz′) *n., pl.* **-seuses′** (-so͞oz′; *Fr*, -söz′) ⟦Fr, fem. of *danseur*, dancer⟧ a female ballet dancer
Dan·te (Alighieri) (dän′tā, dan′tē) (born *Durante Alighieri*) 1265-1321; It. poet: wrote *The Divine Comedy* —**Dan′te·an** *adj., n.* —**Dan·tesque′** (-tesk′) *adj.*
Dan·ton (dän tōn′), **Georges Jacques** (zhôrzh zhäk) 1759-94; Fr. Revolutionary leader
Dan·ube (dan′yo͞ob) ⟦Celt *Dānuvius* < IE **dānu-*, stream < base **dā-*, liquid, flow⟧ river in S Europe, flowing from the Black Forest in S Germany eastward into the Black Sea: *c.* 1,770 mi (2,850 km): Bulg. name DUNAV, Czech name DUNAJ, Ger. name DONAU, Hung. name DUNA, Romanian name DUNĂREA, Russ. name DUNAI —**Da·nu·bi·an** (də nyo͞o′bē ən) *adj.*
Dan·zig (dant′sig; *Ger* dän′tsiH) *Ger. name for* GDAŃSK
Dao·ism (dou′iz′əm) *n. var. of* TAOISM —**Dao′ist** *n., adj.*
dap (dap) *vi.* **dapped, dap′ping** ⟦var. of DAB[1], ? infl. by DIP⟧ **1** to fish by dropping the bait gently onto the surface of the water **2** to dip lightly into water, as a bird **3** to bounce or skip
Daph·ne (daf′nē) *n.* ⟦L < Gr *daphnē*, the laurel or bay tree⟧ **1** a feminine name **2** *Gr. Myth.* a nymph who is changed by her father into a laurel tree so that she may escape Apollo's advances **3** [**d-**] any of a genus (*Daphne*) of small evergreen shrubs of the mezereum family, with fragrant flowers
Daph·nis and Chlo·e (*or* **Chlo·ë**) (daf′nis ənd klō′ē) two lovers in an old Greek pastoral romance of the same name, attributed to Longus (*c.* 3d cent. A.D.)
dap·per (dap′ər) *adj.* ⟦ME *daper*, agile, trim < MDu *dapper*, nimble, powerful, akin to Ger *tapfer*, brave, ON *dapr*, heavy < IE base **dheb-*, thick, solid, stocky: the sense development is from "heavy, powerful" to "nimble" to "trim, neat"⟧ **1** small and active **2** trim, neat, or smart in dress or appearance —**dap′per·ly** *adv.* —**dap′per·ness** *n.*
dap·ple (dap′əl) *adj.* ⟦ME in comp. *dappel-grai*, dapple-gray < ON *depill*, a spot, dot, splash of water < *dapi*, a pool⟧ marked or variegated with spots; mottled: also **dap′pled** —*n.* **1** a spotted condition **2** an animal whose skin is spotted — *vt., vi.* **-pled, -pling** to cover or become covered with spots, as of a different color [daisies *dappled* the meadow]
dap·ple-gray (-grā′) *adj.* gray spotted with darker gray —*n.* a dapple-gray horse
dap·sone (dap′sōn′) *n.* a white, crystalline powder, $(C_6H_4NH_2)_2SO_2$, used in the treatment of leprosy and of a dermatitis somewhat resembling herpes
DAR *abbrev.* Daughters of the American Revolution
☆**darb** (därb) *n.* ⟦prob. contr. < obs. slang *darby*, ready money, orig., a strict usurer's bond, short for *Father Darby's bonds* < surname *Darby* or *Derby*⟧ [Old Slang] a person or thing regarded as remarkable or excellent
d'Ar·blay (där′blā), Madame *see* BURNEY, Fanny
Dar·by and Jo·an (där′bē ənd jō an′, -jōn′) ⟦< an 18th-c. song⟧ any old married couple much devoted to each other
d'Arc (dårk), **Jeanne** (zhån) *Fr. name for* JOAN OF ARC
Dar·da·nelles (där′də nelz′) strait joining the Sea of Marmara and the Aegean Sea, between European & Asiatic Turkey: *c.* 40 mi (64 km) long; 1-4 mi (1.6-6.4 km) wide

Dardanelles

Dar·da·ni·an (där dā′nē ən) *adj., n.* ⟦L *Dardanius* < Gr *Dardanios*, after *Dardanos*, son of Zeus, pl. *Dardanoi*, a people allied with the Trojans in the Trojan War, later identified with them⟧ TROJAN: also **Dar′dan** (-dən)
Dar·dic (där′dik) *n.* a group of Indo-European languages spoken in NE Afghanistan, NW Pakistan, and Kashmir: also **Dard** (därd)
dare (der, dar) *vi.* **dared, dar′ing**; 3d pers. sing., pres. indic., **dare** or **dares** ⟦ME *dar, der* < OE *dear, dearr*, 1st pers. sing., pres. indic. of *durran*, to dare < IE base **dhers-*, to dare > Gr *tharsein*, to be bold⟧ to have enough courage or audacity for some act; be fearless; venture —*vt.* **1** to have courage for; venture upon [he will *dare* any danger] **2** to oppose and defy; face [he *dared* the wrath of the tyrant] **3** to challenge (someone) to do something hard, dangerous, or rash, esp. as a test of courage —*n.* a challenge to do a hard, dangerous, or rash thing, esp. as a test of courage —**dare say** to think likely; suppose [I *dare say* you're right] —**dar′er** *n.*
Dare (der), **Virginia** born 1587; 1st child born in America of Eng. parents
DARE (der) *abbrev.* Dictionary of American Regional English
dare·dev·il (-dev′əl) *adj.* bold and reckless —*n.* **1** a bold, reckless person **2** one who performs dangerous stunts professionally —**dare′dev′il·ry** (-rē) *n.*, **dare′dev′il·try** (-trē)
daren't (dernt, darnt) *contraction* dare(s) not; do not or does not dare
dare·say (der′sā′, der′sā′) *v.* DARE SAY (see phrase at DARE): used in the 1st pers., pres. tense
Dar es Sa·laam (där′ es sə läm′) seaport in Tanzania, on the Indian Ocean
Dar·fur (där foor′) region of W Sudan: a sultanate in the early 19th cent.
Da·rien (dar′ē en′, der′-; *also* där yen′) **1 Gulf of** wedge-shaped extension of the Caribbean, between N Colombia & E Panama **2 Isthmus of** *former name for* Isthmus of PANAMA[2]
dar·ing (der′iŋ) *adj.* having, showing, or requiring a bold willingness to take risks or violate conventions; fearless [a *daring* book, a *daring* enterprise] —*n.* bold courage —**dar′ing·ly** *adv.*
Da·ri·us I (də rī′əs) 550?-486? B.C.; king of Persia (522-486): called *the Great*: also **Darius Hys·tas·pes** (his tas′pəs)
Dar·jee·ling (där jē′liŋ) *n.* ⟦after *Darjeeling*, district in NE India⟧ a fine variety of tea grown in the mountains around Darjeeling
dark (därk) *adj.* ⟦ME *derk* < OE *deorc*, gloomy, cheerless < IE **dherg-* < base **dher-*, dirty, somber > DREGS⟧ **1** *a)* entirely or partly without light *b)* neither giving nor receiving light ☆**2** giving no performance; closed [this theater is *dark* tonight] **3** *a)* almost black *b)* not light in color; deep in shade **4** not fair in complexion; brunet or swarthy **5** hidden; secret **6** not easily understood; hard to make clear; obscure **7** gloomy; hopeless; dismal **8** angry or sullen [responding to criticism with *dark* looks] **9** evil; sinister **10** ignorant; unenlightened **11** deep and rich, with a melancholy sound **12** *Phonet.* back: said of vowels —*n.* **1** the state of being dark **2** night; nightfall **3** a dark color or shade — *vt., vi.* [Obs.] to darken —**in the dark 1** in a place with no light **2** uninformed; ignorant —**keep dark** to keep secret or hidden —**dark′ish** *adj.* —**dark′ly** *adv.* —**dark′ness** *n.*

SYN.—**dark**, the general word in this comparison, denotes a partial or complete absence of light [a *dark* night]; **dim** implies so little light that objects can be seen only indistinctly; **dusky** suggests the grayish, shadowy light of twilight [a *dusky* winter evening]; **murky** now usually suggests the thick, heavy darkness of fog or smoke-filled air [the *murky* ruins of a temple]; **gloomy** suggests a dismal or cheerless darkness [a *gloomy* forest] —*ANT.* **light, bright**

dark adaptation adaptation of the eye to vision in the dark by dilation of the pupil, increased sensitivity of the retina, etc. —**dark′-a·dapt′ed** *adj.*
Dark Ages the Middle Ages, esp. the earlier part from about A.D. 476 to about the end of the 10th cent.: so called from the idea that this period in Europe was characterized by intellectual stagnation, widespread ignorance and poverty, and cultural decline
Dark Continent *former name for* Africa, esp. before the late 19th cent., when little was known of it
dark·en (där′kən) *vi.* to become dark or darker —*vt.* **1** to make dark or darker **2** to make blind —**not darken someone's door** (or **doorway**) not come to someone's home —**dark′en·er** *n.*
dark energy energy whose existence is postulated by astrophysicists to account for the perceived acceleration of the expansion of the universe: see also DARK MATTER
dark-field illumination (därk′fēld′) the illumination of the field of a microscope by directing a beam of light from the side so that the specimen is seen against a dark background
dark-field microscope ULTRAMICROSCOPE
dark horse 1 an unexpected winner in a horse race, thought beforehand to have very little chance **2** an almost unknown contestant regarded by few

as a likely winner ☆3 *Politics* a person who gets or may get the nomination unexpectedly, often by a compromise

dark lantern a lantern with a shutter that can hide the light

dar·kle (där′kəl) *vi.* **-kled, -kling** ⟦< DARKLING⟧ [Literary] **1** to appear dark or unclear **2** to grow dark and gloomy

dark·ling (därk′liŋ) [Old Poet.] *adv.* ⟦ME *derkeling*: see DARK & -LING[2]⟧ in the dark —*adj.* **1** in or happening in darkness **2** dark, dim, or obscure

darkling beetle any of a family (Tenebrionidae) of sluggish, dark beetles that feed on plants at night

dark matter invisible matter whose existence is postulated by astrophysicists to account for the large amount of observed gravitation that cannot be accounted for by visible matter: see also DARK ENERGY

dark reaction the second phase of photosynthesis, that does not require the presence of light, during which ATP releases stored energy that is used to convert carbon dioxide molecules into sugars and other nutrients: cf. LIGHT REACTION

dark·room (därk′ro͞om′) *n.* a room from which all actinic rays are excluded, so that photographs can be developed in it

dark·some (-səm) *adj.* [Old Poet.] **1** dark; darkish **2** dismal

dark·y or **dark·ie** (där′kē) *n., pl.* **-ies** ☆[Old Informal] a Negro: a derogatory or contemptuous term: also sp. **dark′ey**, *pl.* **-ies** or **-eys**

dar·ling (där′liŋ) *n.* ⟦ME *dereling* < OE *deorling*, dim. of *deore*, DEAR⟧ **1** a person much loved by another: often a term of affectionate address **2** a favorite **3** a sweet, lovable, or gracious person —*adj.* **1** very dear; beloved **2** [Informal] cute; attractive [*a darling* dress]

Dar·ling (där′liŋ) river in SE Australia, flowing southwest into the Murray River: *c.* 1,700 mi (2,736 km)

Darm·stadt (därm′stat; *Ger* därm′shtät) city in SW Germany, in the state of Hesse

darm·stadt·i·um (därm stat′ē əm) *n.* ⟦after prec., site of laboratory where discovered⟧ a radioactive chemical element with a very short half-life: it is a transactinide usually produced by bombarding lead with high-energy nuclear particles: symbol, Ds; at. no. 110: see the periodic table of elements in the Reference Supplement

darn[1] (därn) *vt., vi.* ⟦< MFr dial. *darner*, to piece together, mend < Bret *darn*, a piece < IE base **der-*, to pull off, split apart > TEAR[1]⟧ to mend (cloth) or repair (a hole or tear in cloth) by sewing a network of stitches across the gap —*n.* a darned place in fabric —**SYN.** MEND —**darn′er** *n.*

darn[2] (därn) *vt., vi., n., adj., adv., interj.* [Informal] *euphemism for* DAMN (the curse) —**darned** *adj., adv.*

dar·nel (där′nəl) *n.* ⟦ME < Fr dial. (Wal) *darnelle*, prob. < OFr dial. *darnu*, stupefied (< Frank **darn*) + *niella* < VL *nigella*, black caraway < L *niger*, black: so called from its supposed stupefying qualities⟧ a weedy rye grass (*Lolium temulentum*) with poisonous seeds, often found in grainfields

darn·ing (där′niŋ) *n.* **1** a mending with interlaced stitches **2** things to be darned

darning needle **1** a large needle for darning **2** DRAGONFLY

Darn·ley (därn′lē), Lord (*Henry Stewart* or *Stuart*) 1545-67; 2d husband of Mary, Queen of Scots: father of James I

Dar·row (dar′ō), **Clarence (Seward)** 1857-1938; U.S. lawyer

dar·shan (där′shən, dʉr′-) *n.* ⟦Hindi *darśan* < Sans *darśana*, a seeing, akin to *dṛś*, sight < IE base **derk-*, to see > Gr *derkomai*, I see, OE *torht*, bright⟧ *Hinduism* the uplift, blessing, etc. which one gets in the presence of a deity or holy person

dart (därt) *n.* ⟦ME < OFr < Frank **darod* (akin to OE *daroth*), spear⟧ **1** a small, pointed missile, usually with the rear end feathered, used as for throwing at a target in games or for shooting from a blowgun **2** anything resembling this **3** a sudden, quick movement **4** a short, stitched fold that tapers to a point, used to shape a garment **5** [*pl., with sing. v.*] a game in which darts (see sense 1) are thrown at a target (**dart′board′**) — *vt., vi.* **1** to throw, shoot, or send out suddenly and fast **2** to move suddenly and fast

darts and dartboard

dart·er (-ər) *n.* **1** a thing or animal that darts **2** ANHINGA ☆**3** any of various small, brightly colored freshwater perches of North America

Dart·moor (därt′moor, -môr) a prison in Devon, SW England

Dart·mouth (därt′məth) ⟦named in honor of Sir W. Legge, 2d Earl of *Dartmouth* (1672-1750)⟧ former city in S Nova Scotia, Canada, now part of Halifax

☆**Dar·von** (där′vän′) *trademark for* PROPOXYPHENE HYDROCHLORIDE

Dar·win[1] (där′win) **1 Charles (Robert)** 1809-82; Eng. naturalist: originated theory of evolution by natural selection **2 Erasmus** 1731-1802; Eng. naturalist, physician, & poet: grandfather of Charles

Dar·win[2] (där′win) capital of Northern Territory, Australia: seaport on the Timor Sea

Dar·win·i·an (där win′ē ən) *adj.* **1** of or having to do with Charles Darwin or his methods **2** of, having to do with, or suggestive of Darwinism —*n.* an adherent of Darwinism

Darwinian theory Charles Darwin's theory of evolution, which holds that all species of plants and animals developed from earlier forms by hereditary transmission of slight variations in successive generations, and that NATURAL SELECTION determines which forms will survive

Dar·win·ism (där′win iz′əm) *n.* **1** the Darwinian theory **2** adherence to the Darwinian theory —**Dar′win·ist** *adj., n.* —**Dar′win·is′tic** *adj.*

dash[1] (dash) *vt.* ⟦ME *dashen*, to strike, rush < Scand, as in Swed *daska*, Dan *daske*, slap; prob. of echoic orig.⟧ **1** to throw so as to break; smash **2** to strike with violence **3** to throw, knock, or thrust: with *away*, *down*, *against*, etc. **4** to splash or spatter (liquid) on (someone or something) **5** to mix with a little of another substance **6** to destroy; frustrate [to *dash* someone's hopes] **7** to depress; discourage **8** to put to shame; abash **9** ⟦euphemism for DAMN⟧ [Old Informal] to damn: usually in the imperative as a mild curse —*vi.* **1** to strike violently (*against* or *on*) **2** to move swiftly or impetuously; rush —*n.* **1** the effect or sound of smashing or splashing **2** a small quantity of something added [a *dash* of salt] **3** a sudden, swift movement; rush ☆**4** a short, fast run or race **5** spirited quality; vigor; verve **6** striking or showy appearance or display **7** *short for* DASHBOARD (sense 2) **8** a hasty stroke with pen or brush **9** either of two marks (— or –), used in printing and writing to indicate a break in sentence structure or a parenthetical element, or to connect numbers showing a range of dates, times, etc.: see also EM DASH, EN DASH **10** *Telegraphy* a long sound or signal, as in Morse code: cf. DOT[1] —**cut a dash** [Informal] to make a striking appearance or impression —**dash off** **1** to do or write hastily **2** to rush away

dash[2] (dash) *n.* in W Africa, *a)* a gift or tip offered to get better service *b)* a bribe *c)* bribery

dash·board (dash′bôrd′) *n.* **1** [Historical] a screen at the front or side of a carriage, boat, etc. for protection against splashing **2** a panel below the windshield, as in an automobile, containing the instrument panel

da·sheen (da shēn′) *n.* ⟦< ?⟧ TARO

dash·er (dash′ər) *n.* **1** a person or thing that dashes **2** a device for agitating milk or cream in a churn or ice-cream freezer **3** [Informal] a person full of dash or spirit

☆**da·shi·ki** (dä shē′kē, də-) *n.* ⟦said to be of Yoruba orig., but prob. coined (1967) by J. Benning, its U.S. manufacturer⟧ a loosefitting, usually brightly colored, robe or tunic modeled after an African tribal garment

dash·ing (dash′iŋ) *adj.* **1** full of dash or spirit; bold and lively **2** showy; striking; stylish —**dash′ing·ly** *adv.*

Dasht-e-Ka·vir (däsh′tē kə vir′) large salt-desert plateau in NC Iran: *c.* 18,000 sq mi (46,620 sq km)

Dasht-e-Lut (däsh′tē lo͞ot′) vast desert region of central and SE Iran, extending southward from the Dasht-e-Kavir

☆**dasn't** (das′′nt) *contraction* [Dial.] dare not

das·sie (das′ē, däs′ē) *n.* ⟦Afrik⟧ HYRAX

das·tard (das′tərd) *n.* ⟦ME, a craven, prob. < Scand base, as in ON *dasast*, to become exhausted (see DAZE) + ME *-ard*, -ARD⟧ a sneaky, cowardly evildoer

das·tard·ly (-lē) *adj.* of or like a dastard; mean and cowardly —**SYN.** COWARDLY —**das′tard·li·ness** *n.*

da·sym·e·ter (də sim′ə tər, da-) *n.* ⟦< Gr *dasys*, dense (? akin to L *densus*, DENSE) + -METER⟧ a device for measuring the density of gases

das·y·ure (das′ē yoor′) *n.* ⟦ModL *dasyurus* < Gr *dasys*, thick, hairy + *oura*, tail: see URO-[2]⟧ any of a family (Dasyuridae) of small, mostly Australian marsupials that feed on flesh or insects

dat *abbrev.* dative

DAT (dat) *n.* DIGITAL AUDIO TAPE: also treated as an abbreviation

da·ta (dāt′ə, dat′ə; *Brit also* dä′tə) *pl.n.* ⟦pl. of DATUM: still often so used by scientists⟧ [*now usually with sing. v.*] **1** facts or figures to be processed; evidence, records, statistics, etc. from which conclusions can be inferred; information **2** information in a form suitable for storing and processing by a computer

da·ta·base (-bās′) *n.* **1** a large collection of data in a computer, organized so that it can be expanded, updated, and retrieved rapidly for various uses **2** any large or extensive collection of information Also **data base** or **da′ta·bank′** (-baŋk′)

data mining comparative analysis of existing databases for the purpose of discovering new information

data processing the rapid recording and handling of large amounts of information, as business data, by means of mechanical or, esp., computer equipment

data processor a machine, esp. a computer, that performs data processing

da·ta·ry (dāt′ər ē) *n., pl.* **-ries** ⟦ML *datarius*, official of the Roman chancery < L, to be given away < *datus*: see fol.⟧ *R.C.Ch.* a former office of the Curia, in charge of papal benefices

date[1] (dāt) *n.* ⟦ME < OFr < L *data*, fem. of *datus*, pp. of *dare*, to give (the first word in Roman letters, giving the place and time of writing, as *data Romae*, lit., given at Rome) < IE base **dō-*, to give > Gr *dōron*, gift, *didonai*, to give, Russ *dat'*, to give⟧ **1** a statement, as on a document or coin, specifying when it was made **2** the time at which a thing happens or is done **3** the time that anything lasts or goes on **4** [*pl.*] a person's birth and death dates, usually expressed in years **5** the day of the month ☆**6** *a)* an appointment for a set time, esp. one for a social engagement with a person with whom one is having or considering having a romantic or sexual relationship *b)* such an engagement *c)* a person with whom one has such an engagement

—*vt.* **dat′ed, dat′ing 1** to mark (a letter, etc.) with a date **2** to find out, determine, set, or record the date of **3** to assign a date to **4** *a)* to show or reveal as typical of a certain period or age *b)* to make seem old-fashioned or out-of-date **5** to reckon by dates **6** to have a date or dates with —*vi.* **1** to belong to, or have origin in, a definite period in the past: usually with *from* **2** to be or seem outdated or old-fashioned ☆**3** to have dates (see *n.* 6*b* above) [I seldom *dated* while attending college] —**to date** until now; as yet —**up to date** in or into agreement with the latest facts, ideas, styles, etc. —**dat′a·ble** *adj.*, **date′a·ble** —**dat′er** *n.*

date² (dāt) *n.* ⟦ME < OFr < L *dactylus* < Gr *daktylos*, a date, prob. < Sem, as in Ar *dáqal*, date palm⟧ **1** the sweet, fleshy fruit of the date palm, having a large, hard seed **2** DATE PALM

date·book (dāt′bo͝ok′) *n.* a notebook for entering upcoming social or business appointments, birthdays and anniversaries, etc.

dat·ed (dāt′id) *adj.* **1** marked with a date [contains *dated* material] **2** out-of-date or old-fashioned

date·less (dāt′lis) *adj.* **1** without a date **2** without limit or end **3** too old for its date to be fixed **4** still good or interesting though old

date·line (-līn′) *n.* ☆**1** the date and place of writing or issue, as given in a line in a letter, a newspaper, a dispatch, etc. **2** INTERNATIONAL DATE LINE —☆*vt.* **-lined′, -lin′ing** to furnish with a dateline

date line INTERNATIONAL DATE LINE

date palm a cultivated desert palm tree (*Phoenix dactylifera*) that has a stout trunk and large leaves and bears dates

☆**date rape** rape committed by a person known to the victim, usually during a date or other social interaction —**date′-rape′** *adj.*

date-rape drug a stupefying or sleep-inducing drug given surreptitiously to a woman so as to render her unable to fend off a sexual assault

da·tive (dāt′iv) *adj.* ⟦ME < L *dativus*, relating to giving < *datus* (see DATE¹); its grammatical use in LL (*casus*) *dativus*, dat. (case), translates Gr *dotikē*⟧ *Gram.* designating, of, or in the case of the indirect object of a finite verb —*n.* **1** the dative case: in English this case may be expressed analytically by *to* or by word order (Ex.: I gave the book *to Jack*, I gave *him* the book) **2** a word or phrase in this case —**da′tive·ly** *adv.*

dative bond COORDINATE BOND

da·to or **dat·to** (dä′tō) *n., pl.* **-tos** ⟦Sp < Tag *dato*; akin to Malay *datóq*⟧ the chief of a Muslim Moro tribe in the Philippine Islands

da·tum (dāt′əm, dat′-; *Brit also* dä′təm) *n., pl.* **da′ta** (-ə) or **da′tums** ⟦L, what is given, neut. of *datus*: see DATE¹⟧ **1** something known or assumed; information from which conclusions can be inferred: see also DATA **2** a real or assumed thing, used as a basis for calculations or measurements, as a level (also **datum plane**) from which elevations and depths are measured in surveying

da·tu·ra (də to͝or′ə, -tyo͝or′ə) *n.* ⟦ModL < Hindi *dhatūrā* < Sans *dhattūra*⟧ **1** any of a genus (*Datura*) of herbs, shrubs, or trees of the nightshade family, which are poisonous and have an unpleasant odor **2** the flower of any of these

dau *abbrev.* daughter

daub (dôb, däb) *vt., vi.* ⟦ME *dauben* < OFr *dauber*, to whiten, whitewash < L *dealbare*, to whiten, whitewash < *de-*, intens. + *albus*, white: see ALBUM⟧ **1** to cover or smear with sticky, soft matter, such as plaster or grease **2** to smear (plaster, grease, etc.) on **3** to paint coarsely or unskillfully —*n.* **1** anything daubed on **2** a daubing stroke or splash **3** a poorly painted picture —**daub′er** *n.*

daube (dōb) *n.* ⟦Fr⟧ a stew of meat, usually beef, braised with red wine, vegetables, and herbs

Dau·bi·gny (dō bē nyē′), **Charles Fran·çois** (shȧrl frän swȧ′) 1817-78 Fr. landscape painter

Dau·det (dō dā′) **1 Al·phonse** (ȧl fōns′) 1840-97; Fr. novelist **2 Lé·on** (lā ōn′) 1867-1942; Fr. politician & journalist: son of Alphonse

Dau·gav·pils (dou′guv pils) city in SE Latvia, on the Western Dvina (Daugava) River

daugh·ter (dôt′ər) *n.* ⟦ME *doughter* < OE *dohtor*, akin to Goth *dauhtar*, Ger *tochter* < IE base **dhugheter* > Sans *duhitár*, Gr *thugatēr*⟧ **1** a girl or woman as she is related to either or both parents: sometimes also used of animals **2** a female descendant **3** *a)* a stepdaughter *b)* an adopted daughter *c)* a daughter-in-law **4** a female thought of as having been formed by some influence, as a child is by a parent [a *daughter* of the French Revolution] **5** anything thought of as like a daughter in relation to its source or origin [colonies are *daughters* of the mother country] **6** *Physics* an element that results immediately from the disintegration of a radioactive element

daughter cell *Biol.* either of the two cells that result from the division of a cell, as in mitosis

daugh·ter-in-law (-in lô′) *n., pl.* **daugh′ters-in-law′** the wife of one's son or, now sometimes, of one's daughter

daugh·ter·ly (-lē) *adj.* of, like, or proper to a daughter —**daugh′ter·li·ness** *n.*

Dau·mier (dō myā′), **Ho·no·ré** (ô nô rā′) 1808-79; Fr. painter, lithographer, & caricaturist

daunt (dônt, dänt) *vt.* ⟦ME *daunten* < OFr *danter, donter* < L *domitare*, to tame, freq. of *domare*, TAME⟧ to make discouraged; intimidate; dishearten —*SYN.* DISMAY

daunt·less (-lis) *adj.* that cannot be daunted or intimidated; fearless —**daunt′less·ly** *adv.* —**daunt′less·ness** *n.*

dau·phin (dô′fin, dō′-; *Fr* dō fan′) *n.* ⟦Fr, lit., DOLPHIN: used as a proper name by the lords of DAUPHINÉ, and hence as a title by the oldest son of the king after the province of DAUPHINÉ was ceded to the crown⟧ the heir to the French throne, usually the eldest son of the king: a title used from 1349 to 1830

dau·phine (dô′fēn′, dō′-; *Fr* dō fēn′) *n.* ⟦fem. of Fr *dauphin*: see prec.⟧ the wife of a dauphin: also **dau·phin·ess** (dô′fin is, dō′-)

Dau·phi·né (dō fē nā′) historic region of SE France, on the Italian border, north of Provence

daut (dôt, dät) *vt.* [Scot.] to fondle; pet; caress

Da·vao (dä vou′) seaport in the Philippines, on the SE coast of Mindanao

da·ven (dä′vən) *vi.* ⟦Yiddish *davnen*, to pray⟧ *Judaism* to recite the prayers of the liturgy, traditionally with a back-and-forth swaying motion

D'Av·e·nant or **Dav·e·nant** (dav′ə nənt), Sir **William** 1606-68; Eng. poet & playwright

dav·en·port (dav′ən pôrt′) *n.* ⟦< ?⟧ ☆**1** a large couch or sofa, sometimes convertible into a bed **2** [Brit.] a small writing desk with a hinged lid

Dav·en·port (dav′ən pôrt′) ⟦after Col. G. *Davenport* (1783-1845), fur trader⟧ city in E Iowa, on the Mississippi

Da·vid¹ (dā′vid) *n.* ⟦Heb *Dāwīdh*, lit., beloved⟧ **1** a masculine name: dim. *Dave, Davey, Davy*; fem. *Davida, Vida* **2** (died 970? B.C.) the second king of Israel and Judah (*c.* 1000-*c.* 970), succeeding Saul: as a youth he killed GOLIATH, and he is the reputed writer of many Psalms

Da·vid² (dā′vid; *for 3* dȧ vēd′) **1** Saint (6th cent. A.D.); Welsh bishop: patron saint of Wales: his day is March 1 **2 David I** 1084-1153; king of Scotland (1124-53) **3 Jacques Louis** (zhȧk lwē) 1748-1825; Fr. neoclassical painter

Da·vid d'An·gers (dȧ vēd′ dän zhā′) (born *Pierre Jean David*) 1788?-1856; Fr. sculptor

Da·vid·son (dā′vid sən), **Jo(seph)** 1883-1952; U.S. sculptor

da Vin·ci (də vin′chē; *It* dä vēn′chē), **Le·o·nar·do** (lē′ə när′dō; *It* le′ô när′dô) 1452-1519; It. painter, sculptor, architect, engineer, & scientist

Da·vis (dā′vis) **1 Bet·te** (bet′ē) (born *Ruth Elizabeth Davis*) 1908-89; U.S. film actress **2 Jefferson** 1808-89; U.S. statesman: president of the Confederacy (1861-65) **3 Miles** 1926-91; U.S. jazz trumpeter & composer **4 Richard Harding** 1864-1916; U.S. journalist, novelist, & editor

Davis Strait arm of the Atlantic between Baffin Island, Canada, and W Greenland: *c.* 200-400 mi (322-644 km) wide

da·vit (dā′vit; *also* dav′it) *n.* ⟦ME & OFr *daviot*, dim. of *David*, prob. with reference to the slaying of Goliath⟧ **1** either of a pair of uprights that can be swung out over the side of a ship for lowering or raising a small boat **2** a crane in a ship's bow, formerly used to raise or lower the anchor

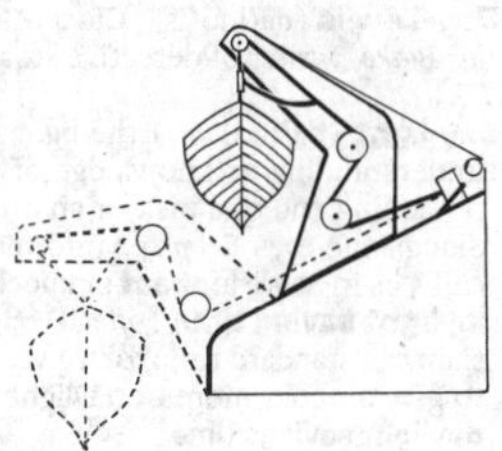
davit (sense 1)

Da·vy (dā′vē), Sir **Hum·phry** (hum′frē) 1778-1829; Eng. chemist

Da·vy Jones (dā′vē jōnz′) *Folklore* the spirit of the sea or the sea personified: term used chiefly by sailors of the 18th-19th cent.

Davy Jones's locker (jōn′ziz) the bottom of the sea thought of as the grave of those drowned at sea or buried there: also **Davy Jones' locker**

Davy lamp ⟦after Sir Humphry DAVY, its inventor⟧ an early safety lamp for miners, in which the flame was enclosed by wire gauze as a protection against firedamp

daw¹ (dô) *n.* ⟦ME *dawe*, akin to OHG *taha*, Ger *dohle* < PGmc **dhakw-*, echoic of its cry⟧ JACKDAW

daw² (dô) *vi.* [Scot.] to dawn

daw·dle (dôd′'l) *vi., vt.* **-dled, -dling** ⟦< ? or akin to ME *dadel(ing)*, chattering (of birds), *dadelar*, glib talker, prob. of echoic orig.⟧ to waste (time) in trifling or by being slow; idle: often with *away* —*SYN.* LOITER —**daw′dler** *n.*

dawn (dôn, dän) *vi.* ⟦ME *daunen*, back-form. < *dauninge*, earlier *dauinge*, daybreak, prob. altered (infl. by ON *dagan*, dawn) < OE *dagung* < *dagian*, to become day < *dæg*, DAY⟧ **1** to begin to be day; grow light **2** to begin to appear or develop; come forth **3** to begin to be understood or felt: usually with *on* or *upon* [the meaning suddenly *dawned* on me] —*n.* **1** the beginning of daylight in the morning; daybreak **2** the beginning (*of* something) [the *dawn* of the Space Age]

Dawn (dôn) *n.* ⟦see prec.⟧ a feminine name

dawn redwood a coniferous Chinese tree (*Metasequoia glyptostroboides*) of the baldcypress family, resembling the redwood of California but having deciduous twigs and needles: it is now propagated in the U.S.

Daw·son¹ (dô′sən), Sir **John William** 1820-99; Cdn. geologist, naturalist, & educator

Daw·son² (dô′sən) ⟦after G. M. *Dawson* (1849-1901), Cdn geologist⟧ city in W Yukon Territory, Canada, on the Yukon River: former gold-mining center

Dawson Creek city in E British Columbia, Canada: S terminus of the Alaska Highway

day (dā) *n.* ⟦ME *dai* < OE *dæg* (pl. *dagas*), akin to ON *dagr*, Goth *dags*, OHG *tag* < PGmc **dagwaz*, prob. < IE base **aghes*, day, with *d-* by assoc. with base **dhegwh-*, to burn⟧ **1** *a)* the period of light between sunrise and sunset *b)* daylight *c)* sunshine **2** *a)* the 24-hour period (**mean solar day**) that it takes the earth to rotate once on its axis with respect to the sun: the civil or legal day is from midnight to midnight, the astronomical day from noon to noon (see SIDEREAL DAY) *b) Astron.* the time that it takes any celestial body to revolve once on its axis 3 [*often* **D-**] a particular or specified day [Memorial *Day*] 4 [*also pl.*] a period or time; era; age [the best writer of her *day*, in *days* of old] 5 a time of flourishing, power, glory, success, etc. [he has had his *day*] 6 the struggle or contest occurring on a certain day or in a certain period of time [they won the *day*] 7 the time one works each day [an eight-hour *day*] 8 an unspecified past or future time [one of these *days*] 9 [*pl.*] one's lifetime; life [to spend one's *days* in study] —**back in the day** [Informal] at some time in the past —**call it a day** [Informal] to stop whatever one is engaged in, as work —**day after day** every day or for many successive days —**day by day** each day —**day in, day out** every day —**from day to day** 1 from one day to the next 2 without particular concern about the future

Day·ak (dī′ak′) *n. alt. sp. of* DYAK

day·bed (dā′bed′) *n.* a couch that can also be used as a bed

day·book (-bo͝ok′) *n.* 1 a diary or journal 2 *Bookkeeping* a book for recording in order each day's transactions

day·break (-brāk′) *n.* the time in the morning when daylight first appears; dawn

day care daytime care given to preschool children or to school children after school or during vacation, as at a day-care center, or to the elderly, as at a social agency: also written **day′care′** *n.*

day·dream (-drēm′) *n.* 1 a pleasant, dreamlike thinking or wishing; reverie 2 a pleasing but visionary notion or scheme —*vi.* to have daydreams —**day′dream′er** *n.*

☆**day·flow·er** (-flou′ər) *n.* 1 any of a genus (*Commelina*) of plants of the spiderwort family, with creeping stems, pointed leaves, and usually blue flowers 2 the flower

day·fly (-flī′) *n., pl.* **-flies′** the adult mayfly

☆**Day-Glo** (dā′glō′) *trademark for* a coloring agent added to pigments, dyes, etc. to produce any of a variety of fluorescent colors —*adj.* [*also* **day-glo**] designating, of, or like such a color or colors

☆**day in court** an opportunity to present one's side of a matter, in or as in a court of law

day job ⟦from the usual hours of such a job⟧ a regular, full-time job, esp. as distinct from some other pursuit that is less remunerative and more uncertain

day laborer an unskilled worker paid by the day

Day-Lew·is (dā′lo͞o′is), **C(ecil)** 1904-72; Brit. poet & (under pseud. *Nicholas Blake*) writer of detective stories, born in Ireland: poet laureate (1968-72)

day·light (dā′līt′) *n.* 1 the light of day; sunlight 2 dawn; daybreak 3 full understanding or knowledge of something hidden or obscure 4 the approaching end of a task or an ordeal [to see *daylight* ahead] 5 [*pl.*] [Old Slang] the eyes 6 [*pl.*] [Informal] consciousness: often used hyperbolically, as in **scare** (or **beat** or **knock**, etc.) **the daylights out of**

daylight saving time [*often* **D- S- T-**] standard time that is one hour later than the standard time for a given zone based on mean solar time: it is used to give an hour more of daylight at the end of the usual working day: also **daylight savings time**

day lily 1 any of a genus (*Hemerocallis*) of plants of the lily family, with showy, trumpet-shaped flowers, usually opening for a single day 2 PLANTAIN LILY

day·long (dā′lôŋ′) *adj., adv.* through the entire day; all day

day-neu·tral (-no͞o′trəl) *adj.* maturing and blooming whether exposed to long or short periods of darkness

☆**day nursery** a nursery school for the daytime care and training of preschool children, as of working parents

Day of Atonement YOM KIPPUR

Day of Judgment JUDGMENT DAY

Day One [*also* **d- o-**] [Informal] the beginning of some period

day·pack (dā′pak′) *n.* a kind of knapsack for carrying a day's supplies, as while hiking or sightseeing

day room a room for recreation, reading, or writing, as in a barracks, institution, or the like

days (dāz) *adv.* ⟦OE *dæges* < *dæg*, DAY + adv. gen. *-es, -s*⟧ during every day or most days

day school 1 a school that has classes only in the daytime 2 a private school whose students live at home and attend classes daily: cf. BOARDING SCHOOL

days·man (dāz′mən) *n., pl.* **-men** (-mən) [Archaic] an arbiter

days of grace GRACE PERIOD

day·spring (dā′spriŋ′) *n.* ⟦ME *daies spring* (*daies*, gen. of *dai*): see DAY & SPRING⟧ [Old Poet.] the dawn

day·star (dā′stär′) *n.* ⟦ME *daisterre*: see DAY & STAR⟧ 1 MORNING STAR 2 [Old Poet.] the sun

day student a student at a college or secondary school who does not reside in a facility provided by the school

day·time (-tīm′) *n.* the time between dawn and dusk; also, the time between sunrise and sunset

day-to-day (dā′tə dā′) *adj.* 1 everyday; daily; routine 2 very short-term and hence requiring daily reevaluation [the ballplayer's injury was listed as *day-to-day*]

Day·ton (dāt′'n) ⟦after Gen. Elias *Dayton* (1737-1807)⟧ city in SW Ohio

Day·to·na Beach (dā tō′nə) ⟦after M. *Day*, the founder⟧ resort city in NE Fla., on the Atlantic

day trading rapid buying and selling of stocks on the internet in seeking to profit from momentary price fluctuations, with all positions typically closed out by the end of each day's trading —**day trader**

☆**day-trip·per** (dā′trip′ər) *n.* [Chiefly Brit.] a person who takes a pleasure trip, returning home the same day

day·work (dā′wurk′) *n.* work done, esp. by a domestic worker, and paid for on a daily basis

daze (dāz) *vt.* **dazed, daz′ing** ⟦ME *dasen* < ON *dasa-*, refl. *dasast*, to become weary < *dasi*, lazy, tired < IE base **dhē-*, to wear away > L *fames*, hunger⟧ 1 to stupefy, stun, or bewilder, as by a shock or blow 2 to dazzle —*n.* a dazed condition —**daz′ed·ly** *adv.*

daz·zle (daz′əl) *vt.* **daz′zled, daz′zling** ⟦freq. of prec.⟧ 1 to overpower or dim the vision of with very bright light or moving lights 2 to confuse, surprise, or overpower as by a brilliant display or exceptional qualities —*vi.* 1 to be overpowered by glare 2 to arouse admiration by a brilliant display —*n.* 1 the act of dazzling 2 something that dazzles —**daz′zle·ment** *n.* —**daz′zling·ly** *adv.*

db *abbrev.* decibel(s): also **dB**

Db *Chem. symbol for* dubnium

DB *abbrev.* 1 database 2 *Football* defensive back: sometimes written **db**

dba *abbrev.* doing business as: also **d/b/a**

DBA or **D.B.A.** *abbrev.* Doctor of Business Administration

DBCP *abbrev.* a pesticide, $CH_2BrCHBrCH_2Cl$, thought to cause sterility

DBE *abbrev.* Dame Commander of the Order of the British Empire

dbh *abbrev. Forestry* diameter at breast height

dbl *abbrev.* double

DBMS *abbrev.* database management system

DBS *abbrev.* direct broadcast satellite

dbx ⟦< *db*, abbrev. for DECIBEL + *(e)x(pander)*⟧ *trademark* an electronic system for reducing unwanted noise, used in tape recording, broadcasting, etc.

DC *abbrev.* 1 DA CAPO 2 direct current: also **dc** 3 District of Columbia: also D.C. 4 Doctor of Chiropractic

DCL or **D.C.L.** *abbrev.* [Brit.] Doctor of Civil Law

dd *abbrev.* delivered

DD or **D.D.** *abbrev.* ⟦L *Divinitatis Doctor*⟧ Doctor of Divinity

D/D or **d/d** *abbrev. Banking* demand draft

D-day or **D-Day** (dē′dā′) *n.* ⟦< D[1] (first letter of DAY)⟧ the day on which a military attack or other important event is to take place; specif., June 6, 1944, the day of the invasion of W Europe by Allied forces in WWII

☆**DDD** (dē′dē′dē′) *n.* ⟦*d(ichloro)d(iphenyl)d(ichloroethane)*⟧ a colorless, crystalline insecticide, $(ClC_6H_4)_2CHCHCl_2$, closely related to DDT but considered to be less toxic to animals; TDE

DDE (dē′dē′ē′) *n.* ⟦*d(ichloro)d(iphenyldichloro)e(thylene)*⟧ a toxic residue of DDT often found in animal tissue: it inhibits calcium production, causing many birds to produce extremely thin eggshells that break on contact with the brooder

DDS or **D.D.S.** *abbrev.* Doctor of Dental Surgery

DDT (dē′dē′tē′) *n.* ⟦*d(ichloro)d(iphenyl)t(richloroethane)*⟧ a powerful insecticide $(ClC_6H_4)_2CHCCl_3$, effective upon contact: its use is restricted by law due to damaging environmental effects

de (də, dē) *prep.* ⟦Fr < L *de*: see DE-⟧ of or from: used in French or Spanish family names, originally indicating place of origin: also, esp. in French names, **De**

DE *abbrev.* 1 *Football* defensive end: sometimes written **de** 2 Delaware

de- (dē, di, də) ⟦L, a prefix signifying separation, cessation, intensification, or contraction; also < Fr *dé-* (< L *de*) or OFr *des-* (< L *dis-*): see DIS-⟧ *prefix* 1 away from, off [*debar, derail*] 2 down [*degrade, decline*] 3 wholly, entirely [*defunct*] 4 reverse the action of; undo [*defrost, decode*]

DEA *abbrev.* Drug Enforcement Administration

☆**de·ac·ces·sion** (dē′ak sesh′ən) *vt.* ⟦DE- + ACCESSION⟧ to remove (an item) from a museum or library collection preparatory to selling it

dea·con (dē′kən) *n.* ⟦ME *deken* < OE *deacon* < LL(Ec) *diaconus*, a servant of the church, deacon < Gr *diakonos*, servant, messenger (in N.T., deacon) < *dia-* (see DIA-) + *-konein*, to strive < IE base **ken-* > L *conari*, to try, Welsh *digon*, can⟧ 1 a cleric ranking just below a priest in the Roman Catholic and Anglican churches 2 in some Protestant churches, *a)* a person in training to be a minister *b)* an officer who helps the minister in matters not having to do with worship —*vt.* ☆1 [Old Informal] to read (a verse) aloud before it is sung by the congregation: usually with *off* ☆2 [Old Slang] *a)* to pack (produce) so that only the best shows *b)* to deal with deceptively

dea·con·ess (dē′kən is) *n.* ⟦ME *dekenesse* < LL(Ec) *diaconissa*, fem. of *diaconus*: see prec. & -ESS⟧ in some Protestant denominations, a woman consecrated or commissioned to serve in a church-related agency or hospital

de·ac·ti·vate (dē ak′tə vāt′) *vt.* **-vat′ed, -vat′ing** 1 to make (something, as an explosive, chemical, or mechanism) inactive or inoperative 2 *Mil.* to place (a military unit) on a nonactive status; demobilize —**de·ac′ti·va′tion** *n.*

dead (ded) *adj.* ⟦ME *ded* < OE *dēad*, akin to ON *dauthr*, OHG *tōt*, Goth *dauths*: orig. pp. of an old v. base appearing in ON *deyja*, OS *dojan*, OHG *touwen*, all < IE base **dheu-*, DIE[1]⟧ 1 no longer living; having died 2 naturally without life; inanimate [*dead* stones] 3 such as to suggest death; deathlike [a *dead* faint] 4 lacking positive qualities, as of warmth, vitality, interest, brightness, brilliance, etc. [a *dead* handshake, a *dead* party, a *dead* white color] 5 wholly indifferent; insensible [*dead* to love] 6 without feeling, motion, or power [his arm hung *dead* at his side] 7 *a)* not burning; extinguished [*dead* coals] *b)* extinct [a *dead* volcano] **8** characterized by little or no movement or activity; slack, stagnant, etc. [*dead* water] **9** designating an axle that supports but does not drive a wheel **10** having lost resilience or elasticity [a *dead* tennis ball] **11** no longer used or significant; obsolete [*dead* languages, *dead* laws] **12** *a)* not fertile; barren [*dead* soil] *b)* not yielding a return; unproductive [*dead* capital] **13** certain as death; unerring; sure [a *dead* shot] **14** exact; precise [*dead* center] **15** complete; total; absolute [a *dead* stop] **16** unvarying; undeviating [*dead* level] **17** [Informal] very tired; exhausted **18** *Elec.* *a)* having no current passing through [a *dead* wire] *b)* having lost its charge [a *dead* battery] **19** *Printing* set, but no longer needed for use [*dead* type] **20** *Sports* *a)* no longer in play [a *dead* ball] *b)* suspended or canceled [a play that was whistled *dead*] —*n.* the time of greatest darkness, most intense cold, etc. [the *dead* of night, the *dead* of winter] —*adv.* **1** completely; absolutely [*dead* wrong, *dead* set against the idea] **2** directly [*dead* ahead] —**dead in the water** [Informal] **1** at a standstill from the loss of power, momentum, vigor, etc. **2** destined for certain failure or ruin; doomed —☆**dead to rights** [Informal] in an undeniably incriminating situation; red-handed —**dead to someone** [Informal] dismissed from someone's consideration, affections, etc. [because he betrayed the family, he is *dead to me*] —**dead to the world** [Informal] sound asleep —**the dead** those who have died —**dead′ness** *n.*

SYN.—**dead** is the general word for someone or something that was alive but is no longer so; **deceased** and **departed** are both euphemistic, esp. for one who has recently died, but the former is largely a legal, and the latter a religious, usage; **late** always precedes the name or title of one who has recently died [the *late* Mr. Green] or of one who preceded the incumbent in some office or function [his *late* employer]; **extinct** is applied to a species, race, etc. that has no living member; **inanimate** refers to that which has never had life [*inanimate* rocks]; **lifeless** is equivalent to either **dead** or **inanimate** [her *lifeless* body, *lifeless* blocks]

dead·beat (-bēt′) *adj.* **1** making a beat without recoil [a *deadbeat* clock escapement] **2** not oscillating: said of an indicator on a meter, etc. ☆**3** [Informal] designating a parent who fails to make court-ordered payments for the support of a child —☆*n.* [Slang] **1** a person who tries to evade paying debts **2** a lazy, idle person

dead·bolt (-bōlt′) *n.* ⟦so named prob. because the bolt cannot move by itself: see DEAD (*adj.* 6)⟧ a lock for a door, with a square-headed bolt that can be moved only by turning the key or a knob: it has no spring: also written **dead bolt**

dead-cat bounce (ded′kat′) ⟦from the notion that even a *dead cat* would *bounce* a little if it were dropped from a great height⟧ a brief, unsustainable rally, esp. in the stock market, after a steep decline

dead center **1** the position of maximum (**top dead center**) or minimum (**bottom dead center**) extension of a crank and a connecting rod, in which both are in the same straight line **2** a nonrevolving center, as of a lathe spindle **3** the exact center

dead drop ⟦see DROP (*n.* 11)⟧ a prearranged place where a spy leaves documents, etc. for later retrieval by a confederate

dead duck (*or* **pigeon)** ☆[Slang] a person or thing that is ruined or certain to suffer ruin, failure, or death; goner

dead·en (ded′'n) *vt.* ⟦DEAD + -EN, replacing ME *deden*⟧ **1** to lessen the vigor, intensity, or liveliness of; dull **2** to take away the sensitivity of; make numb **3** to treat (a wall, floor, or ceiling) so as to keep sounds from going through; make soundproof —*vi.* to become as if dead; lose vigor, intensity, etc.

dead end **1** an end of a street, alley, etc. that has no regular exit **2** a situation from which there seems no way to escape, move forward, etc.; an impasse

dead-end (ded′end′; *for vi.* ded′end′) *adj.* **1** having only one exit or outlet [a *dead-end* street] **2** giving no opportunity for progress or advancement [a *dead-end* job] ☆**3** ⟦after *Dead End,* a play (1935) by Sidney Kingsley about New York slum life⟧ [Informal] of or characteristic of slums or slum life —*vi.* **1** to terminate in a dead end: said as of a street **2** to reach or come to a dead end [to *dead-end* in a middle management position]

dead·en·ing (ded′'n iŋ) *n.* material used to make rooms soundproof

dead·eye (-ī′) *n.* **1** a round, flat block of wood with three holes in it for a lanyard, used in pairs on a sailing ship to hold the shrouds and stays taut **2** [Slang] an accurate marksman

dead·fall (-fôl′) *n.* **1** a trap arranged so that a heavy weight is dropped on the prey, killing or disabling it ☆**2** a tangled mass of fallen trees and brush

dead hand MORTMAIN

dead·head (-hed′) *n.* ☆**1** [Informal] a person using a free ticket to get into a show, ride a train, etc. ☆**2** a vehicle traveling, as to a terminal, without cargo or passengers ☆**3** a log floating on end, sometimes fully submerged ☆**4** [Slang] a stupid or boring person —☆*vt.* **1** to drive (a vehicle) as a deadhead **2** to remove withered flowers from (a plant), as to encourage further blooming —☆*vi.* to make a trip without passengers or cargo

dead heat a race in which two or more contestants reach the finish line at exactly the same time; tie

dead letter **1** a law, practice, etc. no longer enforced or operative but not formally done away with **2** a letter that cannot be delivered or returned, as because of incorrect address and lack of return address

dead-let·ter office (ded′let′ər) the postal department to which dead letters are sent to be opened and returned, or destroyed

dead lift **1** a direct lifting without any mechanical assistance, as of a dead weight **2** [Archaic] a difficult task requiring all one's power **3** *Weight Lifting* a type of exercise in which a person lifts a barbell off the floor, stands up straight, and holds the weight hanging downward at arm's length

dead·light (ded′līt′) *n.* **1** a round metal cover placed over a ship's porthole in stormy weather **2** a window of heavy glass set in the deck or side of a ship **3** a skylight made so as not to be opened

dead·line (-līn′) *n.* ☆**1** [Historical] a line around a prison beyond which a prisoner could go only at the risk of being shot by a guard ☆**2** a boundary which it is forbidden to cross ☆**3** the latest time by which something must be done or completed [a *deadline* for payment, publication, etc.]

dead load *Engineering* the uniform, constant pressure or weight inherent in any structure: opposed to LIVE LOAD

dead·lock (-läk′) *n.* **1** a standstill resulting from the action of equal and opposed forces; stalemate **2** a tie between opponents in the course of a contest **3** DEADBOLT —*vt., vi.* to bring or come to a deadlock

dead·ly (ded′lē) *adj.* **-li·er, -li·est** ⟦ME *dedlich* < OE *deadlic:* see DEAD & -LY[1]⟧ **1** causing death or likely to cause death [a *deadly* poison] **2** to the death; mortal or implacable [*deadly* combat, *deadly* enemies] **3** typical of death [*deadly* pallor] **4** very harmful; destructive **5** *a)* extreme or excessive [*deadly* silence] *b)* out-and-out; utter [with *deadly* gravity] **6** oppressively tiresome [a *deadly* bore] **7** perfectly accurate [*deadly* aim] **8** *Theol.* causing spiritual death [the seven *deadly* sins] —*adv.* **-li·er, -li·est** **1** in a way suggestive of death [to lie *deadly* still] **2** extremely or excessively [*deadly* serious] —*SYN.* FATAL —**dead′li·ness** *n.*

deadly nightshade BELLADONNA (sense 1)

deadly sins ⟦see DEADLY, sense 8⟧ the seven capital sins (pride, covetousness, lust, anger, gluttony, envy, and sloth)

dead march solemn funeral music in slow march tempo; esp., a military funeral march

dead-on (ded′än′) *adj.* [Informal] completely accurate; exact; on target [a *dead-on* impersonation of the president]

☆**dead·pan** (ded′pan′) *n.* ⟦see PAN[1] (*n.* 8)⟧ **1** an expressionless face **2** a person, as an actor, who has or assumes such a face — *adj., adv.* without expression or show of emotion; blank(ly) — *vt., vi.* **-panned′, -pan′ning** to do or say (something) in a deadpan manner

dead point DEAD CENTER

dead reckoning ⟦< *ded. reckoning,* abbrev. of *deduced reckoning*⟧ the finding of a ship's position by an estimate based on data recorded in the log, as speed and the time spent on a certain course, rather than by more precise means, as astronomical observations or Loran

Dead Sea ⟦transl. of L *Mare Mortuum,* transl. of Gr *Nekra Thalassa:* because high salinity makes it virtually devoid of living things⟧ inland body of salt water on the Israeli-Jordanian border: *c.* 390 sq mi (1,010 sq km); surface, *c.* 1,349 ft (411 m) below sea level (the lowest known point on earth)

Dead Sea Scrolls a number of scrolls dating from about 100 B.C. to about A.D. 70 discovered at various times since 1947 in caves near the Dead Sea: they contain Jewish Scriptural writings and religious writings of an Essene community

dead set the motionless stance of a hunting dog in pointing game

☆**dead soldier** [Slang] an empty beer, wine, or whiskey bottle

dead-stick (ded′stik′) *adj.* designating a landing made by an aircraft or spacecraft without using power

dead weight **1** the weight of an inert person or thing **2** a heavy or oppressive burden **3** the weight of a vehicle without a load **4** DEAD LOAD

dead·wood (ded′wood′) *n.* **1** dead wood on trees ☆**2** a useless or burdensome person or thing **3** heavy timbers at the bow or, esp., the stern of a wooden ship, just above the keel

dead zone *Ecol.* a large area within a body of water, where levels of oxygen are too low to support aquatic life, typically resulting from polluted runoff

deaf (def) *adj.* ⟦ME *def* < OE *deaf,* akin to Ger *taub,* Goth **daufs* < IE **dheubh-,* misty, obscured < base **dheu-:* see DULL⟧ **1** physiologically unable to hear, totally or partially **2** unwilling to hear or listen [*deaf* to her pleas] —**the deaf** **1** people who are deaf **2** [**the D-**] the community of deaf people who communicate primarily in ASL —**deaf′ly** *adv.* —**deaf′ness** *n.*

deaf-and-dumb (-'n dum′) *adj.* of, for, or being a person unable to hear or speak

USAGE—because *dumb* can mean either "mute" or "stupid", this term is now regarded as offensive and is seldom used

deaf·en (def′ən) *vt.* **1** to make deaf **2** to overwhelm with noise **3** [Archaic] to drown out (a sound) with a louder sound —**deaf′en·ing** *adj., n.* —**deaf′en·ing·ly** *adv.*

deaf-mute (def′myoo͞t′) *n.* a person who is deaf, esp. from birth, and therefore unable to speak: most deaf-mutes, having the necessary vocal organs, can learn to speak —*adj.* of or being a deaf-mute

USAGE—now regarded as somewhat offensive or insulting

deal[1] (dēl) *vt.* **dealt, deal′ing** ⟦ME *delen* < OE *dǣlan,* to divide, share, akin to Ger *teilen:* see fol.⟧ **1** to portion out or distribute **2** to give; administer [to *deal* someone a blow] **3** [Informal] to trade or sell ☆**4** [Slang] to sell (illegal drugs) —*vi.* **1** to have to do (*with*); concern oneself or itself [science *deals* with facts] **2** to act or conduct oneself: followed by *with* [*deal* fairly with others] **3** to consider or attend to; handle; cope (*with*) [to *deal* with a problem] **4** to do business; trade (*with* or *in*) [to *deal* with the corner grocer, to *deal* in cutlery] **5** to distribute playing cards to the players ☆**6** [Slang] to sell illegal drugs —*n.* **1** *a)* the act of distributing playing cards *b)* cards dealt *c)* a player's turn or right to deal *d)* a round of play **2** *a)* a business transaction *b)* [Informal] an advantageous transaction; bargain ☆3 a bargain or agreement, esp. when secret or underhanded ☆4 *a)* [Informal] a particular kind of behavior or conduct toward another; treatment [a square *deal*] *b)* a particular plan, policy, or administration, usually involving some sort of distribution [the New *Deal*] —**big deal** [Informal] ☆1 a very important or impressive person or thing ☆2 an exclamation of mock wonderment, admiration, joy, etc. —**do a deal** [Informal] to arrange, settle, or conclude a transaction —☆**make a big deal out of** [Informal] to attach extreme importance to; make a big fuss about —☆**the real deal** [Slang] someone or something regarded as genuine, valid, of superior quality, etc.

deal² (dēl) ***n.*** ⟦ME *del* < OE *dǣl*, a part, share, akin to Goth *dails*⟧ an indefinite, but considerable, amount or degree: now usually preceded by *good* or *great* [a great *deal* of trouble]

deal³ (dēl) ***n.*** ⟦ME & MDu *dele* < PGmc **thela-* < IE base **telo-*, flat surface, board > Gr *tēlia*, baker's board, gambling table⟧ 1 a fir or pine board of any of several sizes 2 fir or pine wood —***adj.*** made of deal

de·a·late (dē ā′lāt′) ***adj.*** ⟦DE- + ALATE⟧ having lost its wings: said of ants and other insects whose wings are shed after the mating flight: also **de·a′lat′ed** —**de′a·la′tion** ***n.***

deal·er (dē′lər) ***n.*** 1 a person who deals; specif., *a)* one who distributes cards in a card game *b)* a buyer and seller; person engaged in trading [a *dealer* in furs] ☆*c)* [Slang] one who sells illegal drugs 2 a person who acts in a specified way [a plain *dealer*]

☆**deal·er·ship** (-ship′) ***n.*** a franchise to market a product in a specified area, or a distributor holding such a franchise

deal·fish (dēl′fish′) ***n.***, *pl.* **-fish′** or **-fish′es** (see FISH) RIBBONFISH

deal·ing (dē′liŋ) ***n.*** 1 the act of one who deals; distribution 2 way of acting toward others 3 [*usually pl.*] transactions or relations, usually of business

dealt (delt) ***vt., vi.*** *pt. and pp. of* DEAL¹

de·am·i·nate (dē am′ə nāt′) ***vt.*** **-nat′ed**, **-nat′ing** to remove the amino group, NH_2, from (a molecule), usually by hydrolysis, oxidation, or reduction, with the accompanying formation of ammonia —**de′am·i·na′tion** ***n.***

de·am·i·nize (-nīz′) ***vt.*** **-nized′**, **-niz′ing** DEAMINATE —**de·am′i·ni·za′tion** ***n.***

dean (dēn) ***n.*** ⟦ME *den* < OFr *deien*, dean < LL(Ec) *decanus*, chief of ten monks < LL(Ec), leader of ten < L *decem*, TEN⟧ 1 *a)* the presiding official of a cathedral or collegiate church *b)* *R.C.Ch.* a priest chosen by his bishop to supervise a number of parishes within the diocese ☆2 an official of a school, college, or university, esp. one in charge of students, faculty, or a division of studies 3 *a)* the senior member of a particular group *b)* an experienced and preeminent member of a group [the *dean* of American poets] —**dean′ship′** ***n.***

Dean¹ (dēn) ***n.*** a masculine name

Dean² (dēn), **James (Byron)** 1931-55; U.S. film actor

Deane (dēn), **Silas** 1737-89; Am. Revolutionary patriot & diplomat

dean·er·y (dēn′ər ē) ***n.***, *pl.* **-er·ies** 1 the position, authority, or jurisdiction of a dean 2 the official residence of a dean

☆**dean's list** a list of students achieving the highest grades, periodically issued at certain colleges

dear (dir) ***adj.*** ⟦ME *dere* < OE *deore*, precious, costly, beloved, akin to Du *duur*, Ger *teuer*⟧ 1 much loved; beloved 2 much valued; highly thought of; esteemed: used with a title or name as a polite form of address, as in writing letters [*Dear* Sir] 3 [Now Chiefly Brit.] high-priced; costly 4 earnest; fervent [our *dearest* wish] —***adv.*** 1 with deep affection 2 at a high cost —***n.*** 1 a loved person; darling: often a term of affectionate address 2 an endearing person; one who arouses gentle affection, tenderness, or gratitude —***interj.*** used to express distress, surprise, pity, etc., usually in phrases [oh, *dear! dear* me! *dear* God!] —*SYN.* COSTLY —**dear′ly** ***adv.*** —**dear′ness** ***n.***

Dear·born (dir′bərn, -bôrn′) ⟦after Gen. Henry *Dearborn*, U.S. Secretary of War (1801-09)⟧ city in SE Mich.: suburb of Detroit

dear·ie or **dear·y** (dir′ē) ***n.***, *pl.* **-ies** [Informal] dear; darling: now often ironic or humorous

☆**Dear John (letter)** [Informal] a letter from one's fiancée or girlfriend breaking off an engagement or love affair, or from one's wife asking for a divorce

dearth (durth) ***n.*** ⟦ME *derth* < *dere*: see DEAR & -TH¹⟧ 1 [Obs.] costliness; dearness 2 scarcity of food 3 any scarcity or lack

death (deth) ***n.*** ⟦ME *deth* < OE *dēath*, akin to OS *dōth*, OHG *tōd*, ON *dauthi*: see DEAD⟧ 1 the act or fact of dying; permanent ending of all life in a person, animal, or plant 2 [D-] the personification of death, usually pictured as a skeleton in a black robe, holding a scythe 3 the state of being dead 4 any ending resembling dying; total destruction [the *death* of our hopes] 5 any condition or experience thought of as like dying or being dead 6 the cause of death [smoking will be the *death* of him] 7 murder or bloodshed 8 [Obs.] pestilence [the Black *Death*] —**at death's door** nearly dead —**be death on** to deal with in a devastating manner —**do to death** 1 [Archaic] to kill 2 to use, perform, etc. so often that it becomes tiresome; overdo —**in at the death** 1 present at the killing of the quarry by the hounds 2 present at the end or culmination —**put to death** to kill or cause to be killed; execute —**to death** to the extreme; very much [he worries me *to death*] —**to the death** 1 to the very end (of a struggle, quarrel, etc.) 2 to the end of life; always —**death′like′** ***adj.***

death·bed (-bed′) ***n.*** the bed on which a person dies —***adj.*** done or made in the last hours of one's life, as one is dying [a *deathbed* will] —**on one's deathbed** during or in the last hours of one's life, as one is dying

death bell a bell tolled to announce a death

death·blow (-blō′) ***n.*** 1 a blow that causes death 2 a thing or event that is destructive or fatal (*to* something)

☆**death·cam·as** (-kam′əs) ***n.*** any of various plants (genus *Zigadenus*) of the lily family, with grasslike basal leaves and clusters of greenish or white flowers: often poisonous to sheep: also sp. **death camass**

death camp a concentration camp in which large numbers of prisoners die, as by execution or starvation

death cap a deadly amanita (*Amanita phalloides*) with a white, scaly cap and a cuplike structure enveloping the base of the stalk of the mushroom: also **death cup**

death chamber 1 a room in which someone has died 2 a room in which condemned prisoners are executed

death duty [Brit.] INHERITANCE TAX

death·ful (deth′fəl) ***adj.*** 1 deathlike; deathly 2 [Archaic] deadly; murderous 3 [Archaic] subject to death; mortal

☆**death house** the section of a prison containing an execution chamber and the cells in which persons condemned to die are housed in the days just before their execution

death instinct *Psychoanalysis* the destructive or aggressive instinct, based on a compulsion to return to an earlier harmonious state and, ultimately, to nonexistence

death·less (deth′lis) ***adj.*** that cannot die; living forever; immortal —**death′less·ly** ***adv.*** —**death′less·ness** ***n.***

death·ly (-lē) ***adj.*** ⟦ME *dethlich* < OE *dēathlic*: see DEATH⟧ 1 [Archaic] causing death; deadly 2 like or characteristic of death —***adv.*** 1 in a deathlike way; to a deadly degree 2 extremely [*deathly* ill]

death mask a cast of a person's face taken soon after death

death penalty, the 1 a sentence of death by execution: also **death sentence** 2 CAPITAL PUNISHMENT

death rate the number of deaths per year per thousand of population in a given community, area, or group: sometimes other units of time or population are used

death rattle a sound that sometimes comes from the throat of a dying person, caused by breath passing through mucus

☆**death row** [*sometimes* **D- R-**] the section of a prison housing persons condemned to death

death's-head (deths′hed′) ***n.*** a human skull or a representation of it, symbolizing death

death's-head moth a large, dark-colored European hawk moth (*Acherontia atropos*) with markings on its back that resemble a human skull

deaths·man (deths′mən) ***n.***, *pl.* **-men** (-mən) [Archaic] an executioner

death squad 1 FIRING SQUAD (sense 1) 2 a group whose function is to kill political enemies, members of rival criminal or ethnic groups, etc.

death tax any tax on, or arising from, a deceased person's estate, as an estate tax or inheritance tax

☆**death·trap** (deth′trap′) ***n.*** 1 an unsafe building, vehicle, etc. 2 any very dangerous place or situation

Death Valley dry, hot desert basin in E Calif. & S Nev.: contains lowest point in Western Hemisphere, 282 ft (86 m) below sea level

death warrant 1 an official order to put a person to death 2 anything that makes inevitable the destruction or end of a person or thing

death·watch (deth′wäch′) ***n.*** 1 a vigil kept beside a dead or dying person 2 a guard set over a person soon to be executed 3 any of various insects, esp. any of a family (Anobiidae) of wood-burrowing beetles whose heads make a tapping sound superstitiously regarded as an omen of death

death wish *Psychiatry* a conscious or unconscious desire for the death of another or for one's own death

Deau·ville (dō′vil; *Fr* dō vēl′) resort town in NW France, on the English Channel

☆**deb¹** (deb) ***n.*** [Informal] *short for* DEBUTANTE

deb² *abbrev.* debenture

de·ba·cle (di bä′kəl, -bak′əl; dā-) ***n.*** ⟦Fr *débâcle*, breakup, overthrow < *débâcler*, to break up < *dé-*, DE-, + *bâcler*, to bar, prob. < VL **bacculare* < **bacculum*, var. of L *baculum*, staff: see BACILLUS⟧ 1 a breaking up of ice in a river, etc. 2 a rush of debris-filled waters 3 an overwhelming defeat or rout 4 a total, often ludicrous, collapse or failure

de·bag (dē bag′) ***vt.*** **-bagged′**, **-bag′ging** ⟦see BAG (*n.* 9)⟧ [Brit. Slang] to remove the trousers from (someone) by force, usually as a prank

de·bar (dē bär′) ***vt.*** **-barred′**, **-bar′ring** ⟦ME *debarren* < Anglo-Fr *debarrer*: see DE- & BAR¹⟧ 1 to keep (a person) *from* some right or privilege; exclude; bar 2 to prevent, hinder, or prohibit —*SYN.* EXCLUDE —**de·bar′ment** ***n.***

de·bark (dē bärk′) ***vt., vi.*** ⟦Fr *débarquer*: see DE- & BARK³⟧ to unload from or leave a ship or aircraft —**de·bar·ka·tion** (dē′bär kā′shən) ***n.***

de·base (dē bās′, di-) ***vt.*** **-based′**, **-bas′ing** ⟦DE- + *base*, aphetic < ABASE⟧ to make lower in value, quality, character, dignity, etc.; cheapen —**de·base′ment** ***n.*** —**de·bas′er** ***n.***

SYN.—**debase** implies generally a lowering in quality, value, dignity, etc. [greed had *debased* his character]; **deprave** suggests gross degeneration, esp. with reference to morals [a mind *depraved* by crime]; **corrupt** implies a deterioration or loss of soundness by some destructive or contaminating influence [a government *corrupted* by bribery]; **debauch** implies a loss of moral purity or integrity as through dissipation or intemperate indulgence [*debauched* young profligates]; **pervert** suggests a distorting of or departure from what is considered right, natural, or true [a *perverted* sense of humor] See also **degrade** —*ANT.* **elevate, improve**

de·bat·a·ble (dē bāt′ə bəl, di-) ***adj.*** **1** lending itself to formal debate; having strong points on both sides **2** that can be questioned or disputed **3** in dispute, as land claimed by two countries

de·bate (dē bāt′, di-) ***vi.*** **-bat′ed, -bat′ing** ⟦ME *debaten* < OFr *debatre*, to fight, contend, debate: see DE- & BATTER[1]⟧ **1** to discuss opposing reasons; argue **2** to take part in a formal discussion or a contest in which opposing sides of a question are argued **3** to deliberate (*with* oneself or *in* one's own mind) **4** [Obs.] to fight or quarrel —***vt.*** **1** to dispute about, esp. in a meeting or legislature **2** to argue (a question) or argue with (a person) formally **3** to consider reasons for and against; deliberate on —***n.*** ⟦ME & OFr *debat* < the v.⟧ **1** discussion or consideration of opposing reasons; argument about or deliberation on a question **2** a formal contest of skill in reasoned argument, with two teams taking opposite sides of a specified question **3** the art or study of formal debate —***SYN.*** DISCUSS —**de·bat′er** ***n.***

de·bauch (dē bôch′, di-) ***vt.*** ⟦Fr *débaucher* < OFr *desbaucher*, to seduce, orig., to separate (branches from trunk) < *des-*, away from + *bauch*, beam, tree trunk < Frank **balko*, beam: for IE base see BALK⟧ to lead astray morally; corrupt; deprave —***n.*** ⟦Fr *débauche* < the v.⟧ **1** DEBAUCHERY (sense 1) **2** an orgy —***SYN.*** DEBASE —**de·bauch′ed·ly** (-id lē) ***adv.*** —**de·bauch′er** ***n.*** —**de·bauch′ment** ***n.***

deb·au·chee (deb′ô shē′; di bôch′ē′, -bôch′ē′) ***n.*** ⟦Fr *débauché*, pp. of *débaucher*: see prec.⟧ a person who indulges in debauchery; dissipated person

de·bauch·er·y (dē bôch′ər ē, di-) ***n.***, *pl.* **-er·ies** **1** extreme indulgence of one's appetites, esp. for sensual pleasure; dissipation **2** [*pl.*] orgies **3** [Archaic] a leading astray morally

de·ben·ture (di ben′chər) ***n.*** ⟦ME *debentur* < ML < L, 3d pers. pl., pres. pass. indic., of *debere*: see DEBT: so called from receipts beginning with the Latin words *debentur mihi*, there are owing to me⟧ **1** a voucher or certificate acknowledging that a debt is owed by the signer **2** a customhouse order for payment of a drawback, as to an importer **3** an interest-bearing bond issued against the general credit of a corporation or governmental unit, with no specific pledge of assets

de Bergerac, Cyrano *see* CYRANO DE BERGERAC, Savinien de

de·bil·i·tate (dē bil′ə tāt′, di-) ***vt.*** **-tat′ed, -tat′ing** ⟦< L *debilitatus*, pp. of *debilitare*, to weaken < *debilis*, weak, not strong < *de-* (see DE-) + deriv. of IE base **bel-*, strong > Gr *belteros*, better⟧ to make weak or feeble; enervate —***SYN.*** WEAKEN —**de·bil′i·ta′tion** ***n.***

de·bil·i·ty (də bil′ə tē) ***n.***, *pl.* **-ties** ⟦ME *debilite* < OFr *débilité* < L *debilitas*, weakness < *debilis*: see prec.⟧ weakness or feebleness, esp. of the body

deb·it (deb′it) ***n.*** ⟦LME & OFr *debite* < L *debitum*, what is owing, debt; neut. pp. of *debere*: see DEBT⟧ **1** *Accounting a)* the left-hand side of an account, where entries are made showing an increase in assets, a decrease in liabilities, etc. *b)* such an entry *c)* the sum of such entries *d)* a sum deducted from one's bank account, as for a check **2** a disadvantage or shortcoming —***vt.*** to enter as a debit or debits; enter on the left-hand side of an account

debit card a kind of bank card that allows the cost of purchases to be automatically debited, or deducted, from the cardholder's bank account

deb·o·nair (deb′ə ner′) ***adj.*** ⟦ME *debonaire* < OFr < *de bon aire*, lit., of good breed or race: see AERIE⟧ **1** [Archaic] pleasant and friendly in a cheerful way; genial **2** easy and carefree in manner; jaunty; sprightly **3** elegant and gracious; urbane Also sp. **deb′o·naire′** —**deb′o·nair′ly** ***adv.***

de·bone (dē bōn′, di-) ***vt.*** **-boned′, -bon′ing** BONE (sense 1)

Deb·o·rah (deb′ə rə, deb′rə) ***n.*** ⟦Heb *debōrāh*, lit., a bee⟧ **1** a feminine name: dim. *Debbie, Debby*; var. *Debra* **2** *Bible* a prophetess and one of the judges of Israel: Judg. 4 & 5

de·bouch (dē bo͞osh′, di-) ***vi.*** ⟦Fr *déboucher*, to emerge from < *dé-* (see DE-) + *bouche*, mouth, opening < L *bucca*, cheek: see BUCCAL⟧ **1** *Mil.* to come forth from a narrow or shut-in place into open country **2** to come forth; emerge —***n.*** a *débouché*

dé·bou·ché (dā bo͞o shā′) ***n.*** ⟦Fr, pp.: see prec.⟧ an outlet, as for troops to debouch through

de·bouch·ment (dē bo͞osh′mənt, di-) ***n.*** ⟦Fr *débouchement*⟧ **1** the act of debouching **2** a mouth, as of a river; outlet: also **de·bou·chure** (dā′bo͞o sho͝or′, di bo͞o′-)

Deb·ra (deb′rə) ***n.*** a feminine name: dim. *Debbie, Debby*: see DEBORAH

De·bre·cen (deb′rət sen′) city in E Hungary

de·bride·ment (di brēd′mənt) ***n.*** ⟦< Fr *débridement* < *débrider*, to cut away tissue, lit., to unbridle < *de-* (see DE-) + *bride*, bridle < MHG *bridel*, akin to ME⟧ *Surgery* the cutting away of dead or contaminated tissue or foreign material from a wound to prevent infection —**de·bride′** ***vt.*** **-brid′ed, -brid′ing**

de·brief (dē brēf′) ***vt.*** ⟦DE- + BRIEF⟧ to question (someone) for the purpose of obtaining information, as in an official investigation; specif., to question (a pilot, emissary, etc.) concerning a flight or mission just completed and, often, to instruct as to restrictions in making this information public —**de·brief′ing** ***n.***

de·bris or **dé·bris** (də brē′; *also* dā′brē′, dā′brē′; *chiefly Brit* deb′rē) ***n.*** ⟦Fr *débris* < OFr *desbrisier*, to break apart: see DE- & BRUISE⟧ **1** rough, broken bits and pieces of stone, wood, glass, etc., as after destruction; rubble **2** bits and pieces of rubbish; litter **3** *pl.* **-bris′** (-brēz′) a heap of rock fragments, as that deposited by a glacier

dé·brouil·lard (dā bro͞o yär′) ***adj., n.*** ⟦Fr⟧ (one who is) skilled or resourceful at handling any difficulty

Debs (debz), **Eugene V(ictor)** 1855-1926; U.S. labor leader & Socialist candidate for president

debt (det) ***n.*** ⟦altered (after L) < ME & OFr *dette* < L *debitum*, neut. pp. of *debere*, to owe < *de-*, from + *habere*, to have: see HABIT⟧ **1** something owed by one person to another or others **2** an obligation or liability to pay or return something **3** the condition of owing [to be in *debt* a thousand dollars] **4** *Theol.* a sin —**be in someone's debt** to be indebted, obligated, or beholden to someone

debt of honor [Now Rare] a gambling debt that is not legally enforceable

debt·or (det′ər) ***n.*** ⟦altered (after L) < ME *dettur* < OFr *detor* < L *debitor* < *debitus*, pp. of *debere*: see DEBT⟧ a person, company, nation, etc. that owes something to another or others

de·bug (dē bug′) ***vt.*** **-bugged′, -bug′ging** ⟦DE- + BUG[1]⟧ **1** to remove insects from **2** to find and correct the defects, errors, malfunctioning parts, etc. in **3** [Informal] to find and remove hidden electronic listening devices from (a place)

☆**de·bunk** (dē buŋk′) ***vt.*** ⟦DE- + BUNK[2]⟧ to expose the false or exaggerated claims, pretensions, glamour, etc. of

De·bus·sy (də bü sē′; *E* deb′yo͞o sē′), **(Achille-)Claude** (klōd; *E* klôd) 1862-1918; Fr. composer

de·but (dā byo͞o′, də-; dā′byo͞o′; *Brit also* deb′yo͞o′) ***n.*** ⟦Fr *début* < *débuter*, to play first, lead off < *(jouer) de but*, (to play) for the mark: see DE- & BUTT[1]⟧ **1** a first appearance before the public, as of an actor **2** the formal introduction of a young woman into upper-class society **3** the beginning of a career, course, etc. —***vi.*** **-buted′** (-byo͞od′), **-but′ing** to make a debut —***vt.*** to present for the first time Often sp. **début**

deb·u·tant (deb′yo͞o tänt′, -tant′; *also* deb′yo͞o tänt′, -tant′) ***n.*** ⟦Fr *débutant*, prp. of *débuter*: see prec.⟧ a person making a debut

deb·u·tante (deb′yo͞o tänt′, -tant′; *also* deb′yo͞o tänt′, -tant′) ***n.*** ⟦< Fr, fem. of prec.⟧ a girl or woman, typically 16-18 years of age, making a debut, esp. into upper-class society

De·bye (də bī′), **Peter J(oseph) W(illiam)** 1884-1966; U.S. physicist & chemist, born in the Netherlands

dec *abbrev.* **1** deceased **2** declaration **3** declination **4** decrease

Dec *abbrev.* **1** December **2** declination

dec·a- (dek′ə) ⟦< Gr *deka*, TEN⟧ *combining form* ten; the factor 10^1 [*decane*]: also, before a vowel, **dec-**

dec·ade (dek′ād′; *also, and for 3 usually*, dek′əd, -id; *Brit also* di kād′, də-) ***n.*** ⟦LME < OFr < LL *decas* (gen. *decadis*) < Gr *dekas* < *deka*, TEN⟧ **1** a group of ten **2** a period of ten years; esp., in the Gregorian calendar *a)* officially, a ten-year period beginning with the year 1, as 1921-1930, 1931-1940, etc. *b)* in common usage, a ten-year period beginning with a year 0, as 1920-1929, 1930-1939, etc. **3** a division of the rosary consisting of one large bead and ten small beads

dec·a·dence (dek′ə dəns) ***n.*** ⟦Fr *décadence*, a falling away < ML *decadentia* < prp. of VL **decadere*, to fall away < L *de-*, from + *cadere*, to fall: see CASE[1]⟧ **1** a process, condition, or period of decline, as in morals, art, literature, etc.; deterioration; decay **2** lavish or sensual self-indulgence Also **dec′a·den·cy** (-dən sē)

dec·a·dent (dek′ə dənt) ***adj.*** ⟦Fr *décadent*: see prec.⟧ **1** in a state of decline; characterized by decadence **2** lavishly or sensually self-indulgent —***n.*** **1** a decadent person, esp. a writer or artist active in a period of decadence **2** [*often* **D-**] any of a group of late-19th-cent., chiefly French writers characterized by a highly mannered style and an emphasis on the morbid and perverse —**dec′a·dent·ly** ***adv.***

de·caf (dē′kaf′) [Informal] ***n.*** decaffeinated coffee —***adj.*** decaffeinated

de·caf·fein·at·ed (dē kaf′ə nāt′əd, di-) ***adj.*** ⟦pp. of *decaffeinate* < DE- + CAFFEINE + -ATE[1]⟧ having all or most of its caffeine removed [*decaffeinated coffee*]

dec·a·gon (dek′ə gän′) ***n.*** ⟦ML *decagonum*: see DECA- & -GON⟧ a polygon with ten sides and ten angles —**dec·ag·o·nal** (dek ag′ə nəl) ***adj.***

dec·a·gram (-gram′) ***n.*** ⟦Fr *décagramme*: see DECA- & GRAM[1]⟧ DEKAGRAM

dec·a·he·dron (dek′ə hē′drən) ***n.***, *pl.* **-drons** or **-dra** (-drə) ⟦ModL: see DECA- & -HEDRON⟧ a solid figure with ten plane surfaces —**dec′a·he′dral** (-drəl) ***adj.***

de·cal (dē′kal, di kal′) ***n.*** ⟦< DECAL(COMANIA)⟧ a decorative picture or design printed on specially prepared paper for transferring to glass, wood, etc.

de·cal·ci·fy (dē kal′sə fī′) ***vt.*** **-fied′, -fy′ing** to remove calcium or calcium compounds from (bones, soil, etc.) —**de·cal′ci·fi·ca′tion** ***n.*** —**de·cal′ci·fi′er** ***n.***

de·cal·co·ma·ni·a (dē kal′kō mā′nē ə, -kal′kə-) ***n.*** ⟦Fr *décalcomanie* < *décalquer*, to trace, copy (< *dé-*, DE- + *calquer*, to copy < It *calcare*, to press, trample < L *calcare*: see CAULK) + *manie* < Gr *mania*, madness⟧ **1** the process of transferring decals to glass, wood, etc. **2** DECAL

de·ca·les·cence (dē′kə les′əns) ***n.*** ⟦< L *decalescens*, prp. of *decalescere*, to become warm: see DE- & CALESCENT⟧ a sudden decrease in the rate of temperature rise of heated metal after a certain temperature has been reached (795°C for iron) due to greater absorption of heat —**de′ca·les′cent** ***adj.***

dec·a·li·ter (dek′ə lēt′ər) ***n.*** ⟦Fr *décalitre*: see DECA- & LITER⟧ *alt. sp. of* DEKALITER

Dec·a·logue or **Dec·a·log** (dek′ə lôg′) ***n.*** ⟦ME *decaloge* < LL(Ec) *decalogus* < Gr(Ec) *dekalogos*: see DECA- & -LOGUE⟧ [*sometimes* **d-**] TEN COMMANDMENTS

dec·a·me·ter (dek′ə mēt′ər) ***n.*** ⟦Fr *décamètre*: see DECA- & METER[1]⟧ *alt. sp. of* DEKAMETER

de·camp (dē kamp′, di-) ***vi.*** ⟦Fr *décamper*, to break camp: see DE- & CAMP⟧ **1** to break or leave camp **2** to go away suddenly and secretly; run away —**de·camp′ment** ***n.***

dec·a·nal (dek′ə nəl, di kān′əl) ***adj.*** ⟦< LL(Ec) *decanus* (see DEAN) + -AL⟧ of a dean or deanery

dec·ane (dek′ān′) *n.* ⟦DEC(A)- + -ANE⟧ any of the isomeric alkanes with the formula $C_{10}H_{22}$ that are present in petroleum or in certain petroleum products, such as kerosene

de·cant (dē kant′, di-) *vt.* ⟦Fr *décanter* < ML *decanthare* < L *de-*, from + *cant(h)us*: see CANT²⟧ **1** to pour off (a liquid, as wine) gently without stirring up the sediment **2** to pour from one container into another —**de·can·ta·tion** (dē′kan tā′shən) *n.*

de·cant·er (dē kant′ər, di-) *n.* a decorative glass bottle, generally with a stopper, from which wine, etc. is served after being decanted

decanter

de·cap·i·tate (dē kap′ə tāt′, di-) *vt.* **-tat′ed**, **-tat′ing** ⟦Fr *décapiter* < ML *decapitatus*, pp. of *decapitare* < L *de-*, off + *caput*, HEAD⟧ **1** to cut off the head of; behead **2** to remove or destroy that part regarded as essential to the operation of [to *decapitate* a terrorist cell] —**de·cap′i·ta′tion** *n.* —**de·cap′i·ta′tor** *n.*

dec·a·pod (dek′ə päd′) *adj.* ⟦< ModL *Decapoda*, name of the order: see DECA- & -POD⟧ ten-legged —*n.* **1** any of an order (Decapoda) of crustaceans having ten legs, as a lobster, shrimp, or crab **2** a squid —**de·cap·o·dal** (di kap′ə dəl) *adj.*, **de·cap′o·dous** (-dəs) —**de·cap′o·dan** (-dən) *adj., n.*

De·cap·o·lis (di kap′ə lis) ancient region of NE Palestine, mostly east of the Jordan, occupied by a confederation (formed *c.* 65 B.C.) of ten Greek cities

de·car·bon·ate (dē kär′bə nāt′) *vt.* **-at′ed**, **-at′ing** to remove carbon dioxide or carbonic acid from

de·car·bon·ize (-nīz′) *vt.* **-ized′**, **-iz′ing** to remove carbon from —**de·car′bon·i·za′tion** *n.*

de·car·box·y·la·tion (dē′kär′bäk′si lā′shən) *n.* ⟦DE- + CARBOXYL + -ATION⟧ the removal or loss of a carboxyl group from an organic compound, as amino acid, usually resulting in the formation of carbon dioxide —**de′car·box′y·late′** *vt., vi.* **-lat′ed**, **-lat′ing**

de·car·bu·rize (dē kär′bə rīz′, -byoo-) *vt.* **-rized′**, **-riz′ing** DECARBONIZE —**de·car′bu·ri·za′tion** *n.*

dec·a·syl·la·ble (dek′ə sil′ə bəl) *n.* a word or line of verse having ten syllables —**dec′a·syl·lab′ic** (-si lab′ik) *adj., n.*

de·cath·lete (di kath′lēt′) *n.* ⟦blend of fol. & ATHLETE⟧ a participant in a decathlon

de·cath·lon (di kath′län′, -lən) *n.* ⟦DEC(A)- + Gr *athlon*: see ATHLETE⟧ an athletic contest in which each contestant takes part in ten events (100-meter dash, 400-meter dash, long jump, 16-pound shot-put, high jump, 110-meter hurdles, discus throw, pole vault, javelin throw, and 1500-meter run): the winner is the contestant receiving the highest total of points

De·ca·tur (di kāt′ər), **Stephen** 1779-1820; U.S. naval officer

de·cay (dē kā′, di-) *vi.* ⟦ME *decaien* < Anglo-Fr & OFr *decäir* < VL **decadere*: see DECADENCE⟧ **1** to lose strength, soundness, health, beauty, prosperity, etc. gradually; waste away; deteriorate **2** to rot or decompose **3** to undergo radioactive disintegration spontaneously —*vt.* to cause to decay —*n.* **1** a gradual decline; deterioration **2** a wasting away **3** a rotting or decomposing, as of vegetable matter **4** *a)* rottenness *b)* decayed or rotted matter **5** *a)* the spontaneous disintegration of radioactive atoms with a resulting decrease in their number (see HALF-LIFE) *b)* the spontaneous disintegration of a particle or nucleus, as a meson, baryon, etc., as it changes into a more stable state (see RADIOACTIVE SERIES)

SYN.—**decay** implies gradual, often natural, deterioration from a normal or sound condition [his teeth have begun to *decay*]; **rot** refers to the decay of organic, esp. vegetable, matter, caused by bacteria, fungi, etc. [*rotting* apples]; **putrefy** suggests the offensive, foul-smelling rotting of animal matter [bodies *putrefying* in the fields]; **spoil** is the common informal word for the decay of foods [fish *spoils* quickly in summer]; **molder** suggest a slow, progressive, crumbling decay [old buildings *molder* away]; **disintegrate** implies the breaking up of something into parts or fragments so that the wholeness of the original is destroyed [the *disintegration* of rocks]; **decompose** suggests the breaking up or separation of something into its component elements [a *decomposing* chemical compound]: it is also a somewhat euphemistic substitute for **rot** and **putrefy**

Dec·can Plateau (dek′ən) triangular tableland occupying most of the peninsula of India, between the Eastern Ghats & Western Ghats & south of the Narbada River: also called **the Deccan**

decd *abbrev.* deceased

de·cease (dē sēs′, di-) *n.* ⟦ME & OFr *deces* < L *decessus*, lit., departure, pp. of *decedere*, to depart, go away < *de-*, from + *cedere*, to go: see CEDE⟧ death —*vi.* **-ceased′**, **-ceas′ing** [Archaic] to die —*SYN.* DIE¹

de·ceased (dē sēst′, di-) *adj.* dead —*SYN.* DEAD —**the deceased** the dead person or persons

de·ce·dent (dē sēd′'nt, di-) *n.* ⟦L *decedens*, prp. of *decedere*: see DECEASE⟧ *Law* a deceased person

de·ceit (dē sēt′, di-) *n.* ⟦ME < OFr *deceite* < pp. of *deceveir*: see DECEIVE⟧ **1** the act of representing as true what is known to be false; a deceiving or lying **2** a dishonest action or trick; fraud or lie **3** the quality of being deceitful

de·ceit·ful (dē sēt′fəl, di-) *adj.* **1** tending to deceive; apt to lie or cheat **2** intended to deceive; deceptive; false —*SYN.* DISHONEST —**de·ceit′ful·ly** *adv.* —**de·ceit′ful·ness** *n.*

de·ceive (dē sēv′, di-) *vt.* **-ceived′**, **-ceiv′ing** ⟦ME *deceiven* < OFr *deceveir* < L *decipere*, to ensnare, deceive < *de-*, from + *capere*, to take: see HAVE⟧ **1** to make (a person) believe what is not true; delude; mislead **2** [Archaic] to be false to; betray **3** [Archaic] to while away (time) —*vi.* to use deceit; lie —**de·ceiv′a·ble** *adj.* —**de·ceiv′er** *n.* —**de·ceiv′ing·ly** *adv.*

SYN.—to **deceive** is to deliberately misrepresent facts by words, actions, etc., generally to further one's ends [a broker *deceiving* a client into buying unprofitable stocks]; to **mislead** is to cause to follow the wrong course or to err in conduct or action, although not always by deliberate deception [*misled* by the sign into going to the wrong floor]; to **beguile** is to use wiles and enticing prospects in deceiving or misleading [*beguiled* by promises of a fortune]; to **delude** is to fool someone so completely that what is false is accepted as being true; to **betray** is to break faith while appearing to be loyal

de·cel·er·ate (dē sel′ər āt′) *vt., vi.* **-at′ed**, **-at′ing** ⟦DE- + (AC)CELERATE⟧ to reduce the speed (of); slow down —**de·cel′er·a′tion** *n.* —**de·cel′er·a′tor** *n.*

de·cel·er·on (dē sel′ər än′) *n.* ⟦< prec. + (AILER)ON⟧ an aileron used to slow down an aircraft in flight; speed brake

De·cem·ber (dē sem′bər, di-) *n.* ⟦ME & OFr *Decembre* < L *December* < *decem*, TEN (+ *-ber* < ?): so named as the tenth month of the ancient Roman year, which began with March⟧ the twelfth and last month of the year, having 31 days: abbrev. *Dec.* or *D.*

De·cem·brist (-brist) *n.* any of the conspirators against Czar Nicholas I of Russia, in December, 1825

de·cem·vir (dē sem′vir) *n.*, *pl.* **-virs** or **-vir·i′** (-vi rī′) ⟦L, sing. of *decemviri* < *decem*, TEN + *vir*, a man: for IE base: see WEREWOLF⟧ **1** a member of a council of ten magistrates in ancient Rome: in 451-450 B.C. this body drew up the first Roman code of laws **2** a member of any authoritative group of ten men —**de·cem′vi·ral** (-vi rəl) *adj.*

de·cem·vi·rate (-və rit, -rāt′) *n.* ⟦see prec. & -ATE²⟧ **1** a body of decemvirs **2** the position or term of such a group

de·cen·cy (dē′sən sē) *n.*, *pl.* **-cies** ⟦L *decentia* < *decens*: see DECENT⟧ **1** the quality or condition of being decent; propriety of conduct and speech; proper behavior, modesty, courtesy, etc. **2** [*pl.*] socially proper actions; the proprieties **3** [*pl.*] things needed for a proper or comfortable standard of living —*SYN.* DECORUM

de·cen·na·ry (dē sen′ə rē) *n.*, *pl.* **-ries** ⟦< L *decennis*, lasting ten years < *decem*, TEN + *annus*, year (see ANNUAL) + -ARY⟧ DECADE (sense 2) —*adj.* ten-year; decennial

de·cen·ni·al (dē sen′ē əl) *adj.* ⟦< L *decennium* (see fol.) + -AL⟧ **1** happening every ten years **2** lasting ten years —☆*n.* a tenth anniversary or its commemoration —**de·cen′ni·al·ly** *adv.*

de·cen·ni·um (-ē əm) *n.*, *pl.* **-ni·ums** or **-ni·a** (-ə) ⟦L < *decennis*: see DECENNARY⟧ DECADE (sense 2)

de·cent (dē′sənt) *adj.* ⟦MFr *décent* < L *decens* (gen *decentis*), prp. of *decere*, to befit < IE base **dek-*, to receive, greet, be suitable, teach > Sans *dákṣati*, (he) is helpful, L *docere*, to teach, Gr *dokein*, to think, seem⟧ **1** proper and fitting [a *decent* burial] **2** not immodest; not obscene; chaste [*decent* language] **3** conforming to approved social standards; respectable [*decent* apparel] **4** reasonably good; adequate [*decent* wages] **5** fair and kind [*decent* treatment] **6** [Informal] adequately clothed for propriety —*SYN.* CHASTE —**de′cent·ly** *adv.*

de·cen·ter (dē sent′ər) *vt.* to cause to undergo a shift away from what has been its traditional center, focus, orientation, or emphasis [a *decentered* view of history]

de·cen·tral·ize (dē sen′trə līz′) *vt.* **-ized′**, **-iz′ing** to break up a concentration of (governmental authority, industry, population, etc.) in a main center and distribute more widely —**de·cen′tral·i·za′tion** *n.*

de·cep·tion (dē sep′shən, di-) *n.* ⟦ME *decepcioun* < OFr *deception* < L *deceptio* < pp. of *decipere*: see DECEIVE⟧ **1** the act or practice of deceiving **2** the fact or condition of being deceived **3** something that deceives, as an illusion, or is meant to deceive, as a fraud

SYN.—**deception** is applied to anything that deceives, whether by design or illusion; **fraud** suggests deliberate deception in dishonestly depriving a person of property, rights, etc.; **subterfuge** suggests an artifice or stratagem used to deceive others and to evade something or gain some end; **trickery** implies the use of tricks or ruses in deceiving others; **chicanery** implies the use of petty trickery and subterfuge, esp. in legal actions

de·cep·tive (dē sep′tiv, di-) *adj.* ⟦Fr *déceptif* < LL *deceptivus*: see DECEIVE & -IVE⟧ deceiving or intended to deceive —**de·cep′tive·ness** *n.*

de·cep·tive·ly (-lē) *adv.* **1** in a deceitful manner **2** in a misleading manner [a *deceptively* spacious bungalow is one having more interior room than one might suppose]

de·cer·e·brate (dē ser′ə brāt′) *adj.* of or having to do with an animal or person lacking cerebral functions, as in consequence of an experiment or an illness —*n.* a decerebrate animal or person —*vt.* **-brat′ed**, **-brat′ing** to eliminate cerebral functions of (an animal), as by surgical removal of the cerebrum or by severing the brain stem —**de·cer′e·bra′tion** *n.*

de·cer·ti·fy (dē sur′tə fī′) *vt.* **-fied′**, **-fy′ing** to disqualify by invalidating a previously granted certificate or license —**de′cer′ti·fi·ca′tion** *n.*

dec·i- (des′i, -ə) ⟦Fr *deci-* < L *decimus*, tenth < *decem*, TEN⟧ *combining form* one tenth part of; the factor 10^{-1} [*decigram*]

dec·i·bel (des′ə bəl, -bel′) *n.* ⟦prec. + BEL⟧ **1** *Acoustics* a numerical expression of the relative loudness of a sound: the difference in decibels between two sounds is ten times the common logarithm of the ratio of their power levels **2** *Electronics, Radio* a numerical expression of the relative differences in power levels of electrical signals equal to ten times the common logarithm of the ratio of the two signal powers Sometimes an absolute reference is used in the power ratio (10^{-16} watt per sq cm in acoustics, one milliwatt in electronics and radio)

de·cide (di sīd′, dē-) ***vt.* -cid′ed, -cid′ing** ⟦ME *deciden* < L *decidere,* to cut off, decide < *de-,* off, from + *caedere,* to cut: see -CIDE⟧ **1** to end (a contest, dispute, etc.) by giving one side the victory or by passing judgment **2** to make up one's mind, or reach a decision, about; determine [*to decide* what to do] **3** to cause to reach a decision —***vi.*** to arrive at a judgment, choice, or decision —**de·cid′a·ble *adj.*** —**de·cid′er *n.***

SYN.—**decide** implies the bringing to an end of vacillation, doubt, dispute, etc. by making up one's mind as to an action, course, or judgment; **determine** in addition suggests that the form, character, function, scope, etc. of something are precisely fixed [the club *decided* on a lecture series and appointed a committee to *determine* the speakers, the dates, etc.]; **settle** stresses finality in a decision, often one arrived at by arbitration, and implies the termination of all doubt or controversy; to **conclude** is to decide after careful investigation or reasoning; **resolve** implies firmness of intention to carry through a decision [he *resolved* to lose 10 pounds]

de·cid·ed (di sīd′id, dē-) ***adj.*** **1** definite and unmistakable; clear-cut [a *decided* change] **2** unhesitating; determined —**de·cid′ed·ly *adv.***

de·cid·u·a (di sij′o͞o ə) ***n., pl.*** **-ae** (-ē) or **-as** ⟦ModL *(membrana) decidua,* deciduous (membrane), orig. fem. of L *deciduus:* see fol.⟧ a mucous membrane lining the uterus during pregnancy, cast off at childbirth —**de·cid′u·al *adj.***

de·cid·u·ous (di sij′o͞o əs) ***adj.*** ⟦L *deciduus* < *decidere,* to fall off < *de-,* off, down + *cadere,* to fall: see CASE[1]⟧ **1** falling off or out at a certain season or stage of growth, as some leaves, antlers, insect wings, or milk teeth **2** shedding leaves annually: opposed to EVERGREEN **3** short-lived; temporary —**de·cid′u·ous·ly *adv.*** —**de·cid′u·ous·ness *n.***

dec·i·gram (des′ə gram′) ***n.*** ⟦Fr: see DECI- & GRAM[1]⟧ one tenth of a gram (1.5432 grains or 0.003527 ounce): abbrev. *dg*

dec·ile (des′īl′, -il) ***n.*** ⟦DEC(A)- + -ILE⟧ *Statistics* any of the values which divide a frequency distribution into ten groups of equal frequency; also, any of these groups

dec·i·li·ter (des′ə lēt′ər) ***n.*** ⟦Fr *décilitre:* see DECI- & LITER⟧ one tenth of a liter (3.376 fluid ounces or 6.1024 cubic inches): abbrev. *dl:* Brit. sp. **dec′i·li′tre**

de·cil·lion (di sil′yən) ***n.*** ⟦< L *dec(em),* TEN + (M)ILLION⟧ **1** the number represented by 1 followed by 33 zeros **2** [Brit.] the number represented by 1 followed by 60 zeros —***adj.*** amounting to one decillion in number

dec·i·mal (des′ə məl; *also* des′məl) ***adj.*** ⟦OFr < ML *decimalis* < L *decimus,* tenth < *decem,* TEN⟧ of or based on the number 10; progressing by tens —***n.*** **1** a fraction with an unwritten denominator of 10 or some power of 10, indicated by a point (**decimal point**) before the numerator (Ex.: .5 = $^5/_{10}$): in full **decimal fraction** **2** any number written using a decimal point: in full **decimal number**

☆**decimal classification** *Library Science* a system of classifying books by the use of numbers with decimals

dec·i·mal·ize (des′ə məl īz′) ***vt.*** **-ized′, -iz′ing** to adopt a decimal system for (currency, measurements, etc.) —**dec′i·mal·i·za′tion *n.***

dec·i·mal·ly (-məl ē) ***adv.*** **1** by tens **2** in decimals

decimal system **1** a system of computation based on the number ten ☆**2** DECIMAL CLASSIFICATION

dec·i·mate (des′ə māt′) ***vt.*** **-mat′ed, -mat′ing** ⟦< L *decimatus,* pp. of *decimare* < *decem,* TEN⟧ **1** [Obs.] to select by lot and kill every tenth one of **2** to destroy or kill a large part of [famine *decimated* the population] **3** [Obs.] to take a tenth part of; tithe —**dec′i·ma′tion *n.*** —**dec′i·ma′tor *n.***

dec·i·me·ter (des′ə mēt′ər) ***n.*** ⟦Fr *décimètre:* see DECI- & METER[1]⟧ one tenth of a meter (3.937 inches): abbrev. *dm:* Brit. sp. **dec′i·me′tre**

de·ci·pher (di sī′fər, dē-) ***vt.*** ⟦DE- + CIPHER⟧ **1** to translate (a message in cipher or code) into ordinary, understandable language; decode **2** to make out the meaning of (ancient inscriptions, illegible writing, etc.) —**de·ci′pher·a·ble *adj.*** —**de·ci′pher·ment *n.***

de·ci·sion (di sizh′ən, dē-) ***n.*** ⟦ME *decisioun* < OFr *decision* < L *decisio,* a cutting short, decision < *decisus,* pp. of *decidere,* DECIDE⟧ **1** the act of deciding or settling a dispute or question by giving a judgment **2** the act of making up one's mind **3** a judgment or conclusion reached or given **4** determination; firmness of mind [a man of *decision*] **5** *Baseball* a win or loss recorded by a pitcher **6** *Boxing* a victory on points instead of by a knockout —**de·ci′sion·al *adj.***

de·ci·sive (di sī′siv, dē-) ***adj.*** ⟦ML *decisivus* < L *decisus:* see prec.⟧ **1** that settles or can settle a dispute, question, etc.; conclusive [*decisive* evidence] **2** determining or closely affecting what comes next; critically important; crucial [a *decisive* moment in his career] **3** having the quality of decision; showing determination or firmness [a *decisive* tone of voice] —**de·ci′sive·ly *adv.*** —**de·ci′sive·ness *n.***

deck[1] (dek) ***n.*** ⟦prob. aphetic < MLowG *verdeck* (< *ver-,* FOR- + *decken,* to cover: see THATCH), transl. of It *coperta,* cover⟧ **1** any extended horizontal structure in a ship or boat serving as a floor and structural support, and covering, partially or fully, the portion of the vessel that is lower than it is **2** any platform, floor, shelf, etc. suggestive of a ship's deck; specif., *a)* an outdoor wooden platform enclosed by a low railing, typically, such a platform adjoining a house *b)* a platform used for viewing [an observation *deck*] **3** a section of tiered seating at a stadium [the upper *deck*] **4** a set of playing cards; pack ☆**5** [Slang] a packet containing a narcotic, as heroin **6** TAPE DECK —***vt.*** ☆[Slang] to knock down; floor —**below decks** below the main deck —**clear the decks** **1** to remove unnecessary things from the decks of a ship, as for combat **2** to get ready for action —☆**hit the deck** [Slang] **1** to get out of bed; get up **2** to get ready for action **3** to throw oneself to the floor, ground, etc., as to avoid injury **4** to be knocked down —☆**on deck** [Informal] **1** ready; on hand **2** waiting to take one's turn, as at batting in baseball —☆**play with a full deck** ⟦with ref. to playing cards⟧ to be mentally competent: usually in negative constructions

deck[2] (dek) ***vt.*** ⟦MDu *decken,* to cover: see THATCH⟧ **1** *a)* to clothe with finery [*decked* out in his best suit] *b)* to cover with ornaments; adorn; trim [*deck* the halls with boughs of holly]: often followed by *out* **2** to furnish (a ship, etc.) with a deck **3** [Archaic] to cover

deck chair a lightweight folding chair, usually with arms and a leg rest, used on ship decks, etc.

Deck·er (dek′ər), **Thomas** *alt. sp. of* Thomas DEKKER

-deck·er (dek′ər) *combining form* **1** *forming nouns* something having (a specified number of) decks, layers, etc. [double-*decker*] **2** *forming adjectives* having (a specified number of) decks, layers, etc.

☆**deck·hand** (dek′hand′) ***n.*** a common sailor most of whose duties are performed on the main deck

deck·house (-hous′) ***n.*** a small cabinlike structure located topside on a ship

deck·le (dek′əl) ***n.*** ⟦Ger *deckel,* dim. of *decke,* a cover < *decken:* see THATCH⟧ **1** a removable wooden frame used as an edging for the four sides of a sheet mold in making paper by hand **2** either of the two edgings used to control the width of a sheet of paper in a papermaking machine **3** the outermost layer of meat and fat on a roast or steak

deckle edge **1** the rough, irregular edge of a sheet of paper after it leaves the deckle and before it is trimmed: such edges are often favored as decorative **2** an imitation of such an edge produced on trimmed paper, as by tearing —**deck·le-edged** (dek′əl ejd′) ***adj.***

deck tennis a game somewhat like tennis, in which a small ring of rope, etc. is tossed back and forth over a net: so called because often played on passenger liners

de·claim (di klām′, dē-) ***vi.*** ⟦ME *declamen* < L *declamare* < *de-,* intens. + *clamare,* to cry, shout: see CLAMOR⟧ **1** to recite a speech, poem, etc. with studied or artificial eloquence **2** *a)* to speak in a dramatic, pompous, or blustering way *b)* to make an impassioned verbal attack; deliver a tirade —***vt.*** **1** to recite (a poem, speech, etc.) **2** to utter with feeling, pomposity, etc. —**de·claim′er *n.***

dec·la·ma·tion (dek′lə mā′shən) ***n.*** ⟦ME *declamacioun* < L *declamatio* < pp. of prec.⟧ **1** the act or art of declaiming **2** a speech, poem, etc. that is or can be declaimed

de·clam·a·to·ry (di klam′ə tôr′ē, dē-) ***adj.*** ⟦L *declamatorius*⟧ **1** of, or characterized by, declaiming **2** marked by passion or pomposity; bombastic

de·clar·a·ble (di kler′ə bəl, dē-) ***adj.*** that can be or must be declared for taxation

dec·la·ra·tion (dek′lə rā′shən) ***n.*** ⟦ME *declaracioun* < OFr *declaration* < L *declaratio*⟧ **1** the act of declaring; announcement **2** a thing declared **3** a formal statement; proclamation **4** a statement of taxable goods [a *declaration* at the customs office] **5** *Card Games a)* MELD[1] *b)* a bid in bridge, esp. the winning bid **6** *Law a)* a statement of the plaintiff's cause for complaint in a court action *b)* an unsworn statement, made out of court, which may be admissible in evidence under certain circumstances

Declaration of Independence the formal statement, written by Thomas Jefferson and adopted July 4, 1776, by the Second Continental Congress, declaring the thirteen American colonies free and independent of Great Britain: there were fifty-six signers

de·clar·a·tive (di kler′ə tiv, dē-) ***adj.*** ⟦LL *declarativus:* see DECLARE⟧ making a statement or assertion [a *declarative* sentence] —**de·clar′a·tive·ly *adv.***

de·clar·a·to·ry (-ə tôr′ē) ***adj.*** ⟦ME *declaratorie* < ML *declaratorius*⟧ DECLARATIVE

de·clare (di kler′, dē-) ***vt.*** **-clared′, -clar′ing** ⟦ME *declaren* < OFr *declarer* < L *declarare* < *de-,* intens. + *clarare,* to make clear < *clarus,* CLEAR⟧ **1** to make clearly known; state or announce openly, formally, etc. **2** to show or reveal **3** to say positively or emphatically **4** to make a statement, or account, of (taxable goods), as at customs **5** to authorize the payment or distribution of (a dividend, etc.) **6** *Card Games* to meld —***vi.*** **1** to make a declaration **2** to state openly a choice, opinion, etc. (*for* or *against*) —**declare oneself** **1** to state strongly one's opinion **2** to reveal one's true character, identity, etc. —**I (do) declare!** I am surprised, startled, etc.

SYN.—**declare** implies a making known openly by an explicit or clear statement, often one expressed formally [he *declared* his intention to run for office]; to **announce** is to make something of interest known publicly or officially, esp. something of the nature of news [to *announce* a sale]; to **publish** is to make known through a medium that reaches the general public, now esp. the medium of printing; **proclaim** implies official, formal announcement, made with the greatest possible publicity, of something of great moment or significance [“*Proclaim* liberty throughout all the land . . .”] See also **assert**

de·clar·ed·ly (-id lē) ***adv.*** openly or admittedly

de·clar·er (-ər) ***n.*** **1** one who declares **2** *Bridge* the member of the partnership which made the winning bid who plays both his or her own and the dummy's hand as a result of having been the first to bid the trump suit or no-trump

dé·clas·sé (dā′klä sā′) *adj.* ⟦Fr, pp. of *déclasser*, to cause to lose class: see DE- & CLASS[1]⟧ **1** having lost class; lowered in social status **2** vulgar, unseemly, gauche, etc.

de·clas·si·fy (dē klas′ə fī′) *vt.* **-fied′**, **-fy′ing** ☆to remove (governmental documents, reports, etc.) from secret or restricted classifications —**de·clas′si·fi·ca′tion** *n.*

de·claw (dē klô′) *vt.* to remove the claws of (esp. a domestic cat)

de·clen·sion (di klen′shən, dē-) *n.* ⟦ME *declenson* < OFr *declinaison* < L *declinatio*, a bending aside, inflection (< pp. of *declinare*: see DECLINE): ME form infl. by assoc. with L *descensio*, a descending: see DESCEND⟧ **1** a bending or sloping downward; slope; descent **2** a falling off or away; decline; deterioration **3** ⟦from the concept of cases as "declining" from the nominative: cf. CASE[1], *n.* 9⟧ *Gram. a)* a class of nouns, pronouns, or adjectives having the same or a similar system of inflections to show case *b)* the inflection of nouns, pronouns, or adjectives

de·clen·sion·al (-əl) *adj. Gram.* of declension

de·clin·a·ble (di klīn′ə bəl, dē-) *adj. Gram.* that can be declined; having case inflections

dec·li·na·tion (dek′lə nā′shən) *n.* ⟦ME *declinacioun* < L *declinatio*: see DECLENSION⟧ **1** a bending or sloping downward; deviation from the horizontal or vertical **2** an oblique variation from some definite direction **3** the angle formed by a magnetic needle with the line pointing to the geographical North Pole **4** a polite declining or refusal **5** [Archaic] decline; deterioration; decay **6** *Astron.* the angular distance of a celestial body north or south from the celestial equator: it is used with RIGHT ASCENSION to find an exact position in the sky: abbrev. *Dec, dec*

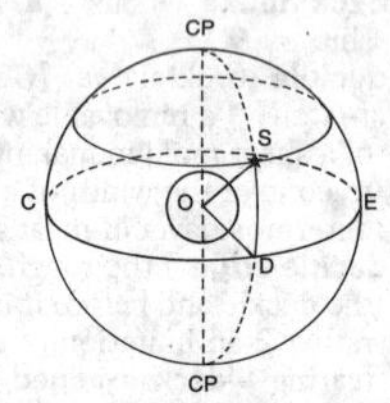

declination
CP, celestial poles; CE, celestial equator; O, observer or center of earth; DS, or angle DOS, declination of star S

de·cline (di klīn′, dē-) *vi.* **-clined′**, **-clin′ing** ⟦ME *declinen* < OFr *decliner*, to bend, turn aside < L *declinare*, to bend from, inflect < *de-*, from (see DE-) + *clinare*, to bend: see LEAN[1]⟧ **1** to bend, turn, or slope downward or aside **2** *a)* to sink, as the setting sun *b)* to approach the end; wane [the day is *declining*] **3** to lessen in force, health, value, etc.; deteriorate; decay **4** to descend to behavior that is base or immoral **5** to refuse to accept or do something, esp. in a way that is formally polite —*vt.* **1** to cause to bend or slope downward or aside **2** to refuse, esp. in a formally polite way [I must *decline* your offer] **3** *Gram.* to inflect (a noun, pronoun, or adjective) systematically, giving its different forms according to case, number, and gender —*n.* **1** a declining or becoming less, smaller, etc.; decay **2** a failing of health, etc. **3** a period of decline **4** the last part [the *decline* of life] **5** [Archaic] a wasting disease **6** a downward slope —**de·clin′er** *n.*

SYN.—**decline** implies courtesy in expressing one's nonacceptance of an invitation, proposal, etc. [he *declined* the nomination]; **refuse** is a more direct, sometimes even blunt term, implying an emphatic denial of a request, demand, etc. [to *refuse* a person money]; **reject** stresses a negative or antagonistic attitude and implies positive refusal to accept, use, believe, etc. [they *rejected* the damaged goods]; **repudiate** implies the disowning, disavowal, or casting off with condemnation of a person or thing as having no authority, worth, validity, truth, etc. [to *repudiate* the claims of faith healers]; to **spurn** is to refuse or reject with contempt or disdain [she *spurned* his attentions] —*ANT.* **accept**

de·cliv·i·tous (di kliv′ə təs, dē-) *adj.* ⟦L *declivitas* (see fol.) + -OUS⟧ fairly steep

de·cliv·i·ty (di kliv′ə tē, dē-) *n., pl.* **-ties** ⟦L *declivitas* < *declivis*, a sloping downward < *de-*, down + *clivus*, a slope < IE **kloiwos* < base **klei-*, LEAN[1]⟧ a downward slope or sloping, as of a hill: opposed to ACCLIVITY

dec·o (dek′ō, dā′kō) *adj.* [*also* **D-**] of or having to do with art deco

de·coct (dē käkt′) *vt.* ⟦ME *decocten* < pp. of L *decoquere*, to boil down < *de-*, down + *coquere*, COOK⟧ to extract the essence, flavor, etc. of by boiling

de·coc·tion (dē käk′shən) *n.* **1** a decocting or being decocted **2** an extract produced by decocting

de·code (dē kōd′) *vt.* **-cod′ed**, **-cod′ing** **1** to translate (a coded message) into ordinary language **2** to convert (data) by removing or reversing previously applied electronic code

de·cod·er (dē kōd′ər) *n.* **1** a person who decodes messages **2** a device that decodes scrambled messages sent by telephone **3** in an electronic digital computer, a circuit device that determines the content of a given instruction or performs digital-to-analog conversion **4** an electronic device that converts a digitized signal, as of a cable TV channel, to its original form

de·col·late (dē käl′āt′) *vt.* **-lat′ed**, **-lat′ing** ⟦< L *decollatus*, pp. of *decollare*, to behead < *de-*, from + *collum*, neck: see COLLAR⟧ to behead —**de·col·la·tion** (dē′kä lā′shən) *n.*

dé·col·le·tage (dā käl′ə täzh′; *Fr* dā kôl tȧzh′) *n.* ⟦Fr < *décolleter*: see fol.⟧ **1** *a)* the neckline or top of a dress cut low so as to bare the neck, shoulders, and cleavage *b)* the flesh revealed in this type of dress **2** a décolleté dress, etc.

dé·col·le·té (dā käl′ə tā′; *Fr* dā kôl tā′) *adj.* ⟦Fr, pp. of *décolleter*, to bare the neck and shoulders < *dé-* (L *de-*), from + *collet*, dim. of *col* (< L *collum*), neck: see COLLAR⟧ **1** cut low so as to bare the neck and shoulders, as some dresses **2** wearing a décolleté dress, etc.

de·col·o·ni·za·tion (dē käl′ə nə zā′shən) *n.* the act or process of eliminating colonialism or freeing from colonial status: also **de·co·lo·ni·al·i·za·tion** (dē′kə lō′nē əl ə zā′shən) —**de·col′o·nize′** (-ə nīz′) *vt., vi.* **-nized′**, **-niz′ing**

de·col·or·ize (dē kul′ər īz′) *vt.* **-ized′**, **-iz′ing** to take the color out of, as by bleaching —**de·col′or·i·za′tion** *n.*

de·com·mis·sion (dē′kə mish′ən) *vt.* **1** to end or revoke the commission of **2** to take (a ship, nuclear power plant, etc.) out of service

de·com·pen·sa·tion (dē käm′pən sā′shən) *n.* **1** failure of the heart muscle to compensate for a valvular or myocardial defect; heart failure **2** *Psychiatry* failure of defense mechanisms in response to stress, resulting in a mental disorder

de·com·pose (dē′kəm pōz′) *vt., vi.* **-posed′**, **-pos′ing** ⟦Fr *décomposer*: see DE- & COMPOSE⟧ **1** to break up or separate into basic components or parts **2** to rot —*SYN.* DECAY —**de′com·pos′a·ble** *adj.* —**de·com·po·si·tion** (dē′käm pə zish′ən) *n.*

de·com·pound (dē′kəm pound′; *also, and for n., usually,* dē käm′pound′) *vt.* **1** [Obs.] to compound (things already compounded) **2** to break up (a compound) into its parts; decompose —*adj.* **1** compounded of substances already compounded **2** *Bot.* made up of parts that are themselves compound, as bipinnate leaves —*n.* a compound containing some other compound or compounds

de·com·press (dē′kəm pres′) *vt.* **1** to free from pressure **2** to free (a deep-sea diver, tunnel worker, etc.) from compression or air pressure by means of an air lock **3** *Comput.* to restore (compressed data) to its original state: see COMPRESS (*vt.* 2) —*vi.* [Informal] to become relaxed, less tense, etc.; unwind

de·com·pres·sion (-presh′ən) *n.* **1** a decompressing or being decompressed **2** a surgical operation to relieve excessive pressure, as in the cranium, a body cavity, etc.

☆**decompression sickness** a condition caused by the formation of nitrogen bubbles in the blood or other tissues as the result of a sudden lowering of atmospheric pressure, as in deep-sea divers, astronauts, and pilots ascending too quickly: it is characterized by tightness in the chest, by pains in the joints, and by convulsions and collapse in severe cases

de·con·gest·ant (-jes′tənt) *n.* a medication or treatment that relieves congestion, as in the nasal passages

de·con·se·crate (dē kän′si krāt′) *vt.* **-crat′ed**, **-crat′ing** to revoke or annul the consecrated status of (a church building)

de·con·struct (dē′kən strukt′) *vt.* ⟦back-form. < fol.⟧ **1** to analyze (a text) by using deconstruction **2** to subject to rigorous analysis, as to reveal weakness or error **3** to take apart; disassemble

de·con·struc·tion (-struk′shən) *n.* ⟦Fr *déconstruction*⟧ an analytic method, esp. of literary criticism, originated in France in the mid-20th cent. and based on a theory that, by the very nature of language and usage, no text can have a fixed, coherent meaning —**de′con·struc′tion·ist** *n., adj.*

de·con·tam·i·nate (-tam′ə nāt′) *vt.* **-nat′ed**, **-nat′ing** to rid of a polluting or harmful substance, as poison gas, radioactive products, etc. —**de′con·tam′i·na′tion** *n.*

de·con·trol (-trōl′) *vt.* **-trolled′**, **-trol′ling** to free from controls —*n.* withdrawal of controls

de·cor or **dé·cor** (dā kôr′, di-; *also* dā′kôr′) *n.* ⟦Fr < L *decor*, beauty, elegance < *decere*: see fol.⟧ **1** decoration **2** the decorative scheme of a room, stage set, etc.

dec·o·rate (dek′ə rāt′) *vt.* **-rat′ed**, **-rat′ing** ⟦< L *decoratus*, pp. of *decorare*, to decorate < *decus*, an ornament < IE base **deḱ*, to receive, be suitable > DECENT⟧ **1** to add something to so as to make more attractive; adorn; ornament **2** to plan and arrange the colors, furnishings, etc. of **3** to paint or wallpaper [to *decorate* a room] **4** to give a medal or similar token of honor to —*vi.* to plan or implement the interior decoration of a house, room, office, etc. —*SYN.* ADORN

dec·o·ra·tion (dek′ə rā′shən) *n.* ⟦ME *decoracioun* < OFr *decoration* < ML *decoratio*⟧ **1** the act of decorating **2** anything used for decorating; ornament **3** a medal, badge, or similar token of honor

☆**Decoration Day** *another name for* MEMORIAL DAY

dec·o·ra·tive (dek′ə rə tiv, -ə rāt′iv) *adj.* that serves to decorate; ornamental —**dec′o·ra·tive·ly** *adv.* —**dec′o·ra·tive·ness** *n.*

dec·o·ra·tor (dek′ə rāt′ər) *n.* a person who decorates; specif., a specialist in interior decoration

dec·o·rous (dek′ə rəs; *also* di kôr′əs) *adj.* ⟦L *decorus*, becoming < *decor*: see DECOR⟧ characterized by or showing decorum, propriety, good taste, etc. —**dec′o·rous·ly** *adv.* —**dec′o·rous·ness** *n.*

de·cor·ti·cate (dē kôr′ti kāt′) *vt.* **-cat′ed**, **-cat′ing** ⟦< L *decorticatus*, pp. of *decorticare* < *de-*, from + *cortex*, bark: see CORTEX⟧ to remove the bark, husk, or peel from —**de·cor′ti·ca′tion** *n.* —**de·cor′ti·ca·tor** *n.*

de·co·rum (di kôr′əm) *n.* ⟦L, neut. of *decorus*, fit, proper < *decor*: see DECOR⟧ **1** propriety and good taste in behavior, dress, etc. **2** an act or requirement of polite behavior: *often used in pl.*

SYN.—**decorum** implies stiffness or formality in rules of conduct or behavior established as suitable to the circumstances [levity not in keeping with *decorum*]; **decency** implies observance of the requirements of modesty, good taste, etc. [have the *decency* to thank her]; **propriety** suggests conformity with conventional standards of proper or correct behavior, manners, etc. [his offensive language oversteps the bounds of *propriety*]; **dignity**, in this connection, implies conduct in keeping with one's position or one's self-respect; **etiquette** refers to the forms established by convention or prescribed social arbiters for behavior in polite society

de·cou·page or **dé·cou·page** (dā′ko͞o päzh′) ***n.*** ⟦Fr *découpage* < *découper*, to cut out < *dé-*, DE- + *couper*, to cut < *coup*: see COUP⟧ **1** the art of cutting out designs or illustrations from paper, foil, etc., mounting them decoratively on a surface, and applying several coats of varnish or lacquer **2** work done by decoupage —***vt.*** **-paged′, -pag′ing** to decorate by using decoupage

de·cou·ple (dē kup′′l) ***vt.*** **-pled, -pling** **1** to take apart; separate **2** to disconnect (devices, systems, etc.) [to *decouple* electric circuits]

de·coy (dē koi′, di-; *for n., usually* dē′koi′) ***n.*** ⟦< Du *de kooi*, the cage < *de*, def. art. (akin to THE) + *kooi*, cage < WGmc **kawia* < L *cavea*, CAGE⟧ **1** a place into which wild ducks, etc. are lured for capture **2** an artificial bird or animal, or sometimes a trained live one, used to lure game to a place where it can be shot **3** a thing or person used to lure or tempt into danger or a trap [a police *decoy*] — ***vt., vi.*** to lure or be lured into a trap, danger, etc. —***SYN.*** LURE

de·crease (di krēs′, dē-; *also, & for n. usually*, dē′krēs′) ***vi., vt.*** **-creased′, -creas′ing** ⟦ME *decresen* < OFr *decreistre* < L *decrescere* < *de-*, from, away + *crescere*, grow: see CRESCENT⟧ to become or cause to become less, smaller, etc.; diminish —***n.*** ⟦ME *decres*⟧ **1** a decreasing; lessening; diminution **2** amount of decreasing —**on the decrease** decreasing —**de·creas′ing·ly** ***adv.***

SYN.—**decrease** and **dwindle** suggest a growing gradually smaller in bulk, size, volume, or number, but **dwindle** emphasizes a wasting away to the point of disappearance [his hopes *decreased* as his fortune *dwindled* away to nothing]; **lessen** is equivalent to **decrease**, except that it does not imply any particular rate of decline [his influence *lessened* overnight]; **diminish** emphasizes subtraction from the whole by some external agent [disease had *diminished* their ranks]; **reduce** implies a lowering, or bringing down [to *reduce* prices] —***ANT.*** **increase**

de·cree (di krē′, dē krē′) ***n.*** ⟦ME *decre* < OFr *decret* < L *decretum*, neut. of *decretus*, pp. of *decernere*, to decree < *de-*, from + *cernere*, to sift, judge: see CERTAIN⟧ **1** an official order, edict, or decision, as of a church, government, court, etc. **2** something that is or seems to be foreordained —***vt.*** **-creed′, -cree′ing** to order, decide, or appoint by decree or officially —***vi.*** to issue a decree; ordain

dec·re·ment (dek′rə mənt) ***n.*** ⟦L *decrementum* < *decrescere*, DECREASE⟧ **1** a decreasing or decrease; loss; waste **2** amount lost by decrease or waste **3** *Math.* the quantity by which a variable decreases or is decreased: a negative decrement results in an increase

de·crep·it (di krep′it, dē-) ***adj.*** ⟦ME & OFr < L *decrepitus* < *de-*, intens. + *crepitus*, pp. of *crepare*, to creak, rattle (in LL, to burst, die): see CRAVEN⟧ broken down or worn out by old age, illness, or long use —***SYN.*** WEAK —**de·crep′it·ly** ***adv.***

de·crep·i·tate (di krep′ə tāt′, dē-) ***vt.*** **-tat′ed, -tat′ing** ⟦< ModL **decrepitatus*, pp. of **decrepitare* < L *de-*, intens. + *crepitare*, to crackle, rattle < *crepare*: see prec.⟧ to roast or calcine (salts, minerals, etc.) until a crackling sound is caused or until this sound stops —***vi.*** to crackle when exposed to heat —**de·crep′i·ta′tion** ***n.***

de·crep·i·tude (-to͞od′, -tyo͞od′) ***n.*** ⟦Fr *décrépitude*⟧ the condition of being decrepit; feebleness or infirmity

de·cre·scen·do (dā′krə shen′dō, dē′-) [*also in italics*] *Music* ***adj., adv.*** ⟦It, prp. of *decrescere* < L, DECREASE⟧ with a gradual decrease in loudness; diminuendo: often used as a musical direction, indicated by the sign > —***n.,*** *pl.* **-dos** **1** a gradual decrease in loudness **2** a decrescendo passage

de·cres·cent (di kres′ənt, dē-) ***adj.*** ⟦L *decrescens*, prp. of *decrescere*, DECREASE⟧ decreasing; lessening; waning: said esp. of the moon in its final quarter

de·cre·tal (di krēt′′l, dē-) ***adj.*** ⟦ME < LL *decretalis*⟧ of or containing a decree —***n.*** **1** a decree **2** *R.C.Ch.* *a)* a decree issued by the pope on some matter of ecclesiastical discipline *b)* [*usually pl.*] any collection of such decrees, formerly a part of canon law

dec·re·to·ry (dek′rə tôr′ē, di krēt′ə rē) ***adj.*** ⟦L *decretorius*⟧ **1** settled by a decree **2** having the nature or force of a decree: also **de·cre·tive** (di krēt′iv)

☆**de·crim·i·nal·ize** (dē krim′ə nəl īz′) ***vt.*** **-ized′, -iz′ing** to eliminate or reduce the legal penalties for (a specified crime) —**de·crim′i·nal·i·za′tion** ***n.***

de·cry (di krī′, dē-) ***vt.*** **-cried′, -cry′ing** ⟦Fr *décrier* < OFr *descrier*: see DE- & CRY⟧ **1** to speak out against strongly and openly; denounce [to *decry* religious intolerance] **2** to depreciate (money, etc.) officially —***SYN.*** DISPARAGE —**de·cri′al** (-krī′əl) ***n.***

☆**de·crypt** (dē kript′) ***vt.*** ⟦DE- + *crypt*, as in CRYPTOGRAM⟧ to decode or decipher

de·cu·bi·tus ulcer (di kyo͞o′bi təs) ⟦< ModL *decubitus*, reclining position < L *decumbere*, to lie down: see fol.⟧ BEDSORE

de·cum·bent (dē kum′bənt) ***adj.*** ⟦L *decumbens*, prp. of *decumbere*, to lie down < *de-*, down + *-cumbere* < *cubare*, to recline, lie down: see CUBE[1]⟧ **1** lying down **2** *Bot.* trailing on the ground and rising at the tip, as some stems —**de·cum′ben·cy** (-bən sē) ***n.***

dec·u·ple (dek′yo͞o pəl) ***adj.*** ⟦ME < L *decuplus* < *decem*, TEN + *-plus*, -FOLD⟧ **1** consisting of or including ten **2** ten times as much or as many; tenfold —***n.*** an amount ten times as much or as many —***vt.*** **-pled, -pling** to make ten times as much or as many; multiply by ten

de·cu·ri·on (dē kyo͝or′ē ən) ***n.*** ⟦ME *decurioun* < L *decurio* < *decuria*, company of ten men < *decem*, TEN⟧ *Rom. History* **1** an officer having charge of ten men **2** a member of a municipal or colonial senate

de·cur·rent (dē kur′ənt) ***adj.*** ⟦L *decurrens*, prp. of *decurrere* < *de-*, down + *currere*, to run: see CURRENT⟧ *Bot.* extending down along the stem, as the base of some leaves

de·curved (dē kurvd′) ***adj.*** ⟦transl. of LL *decurvatus* < L *de-*, DE- + *curvatus*, pp. of *curvare*, to CURVE⟧ *Zool.* curved or bent downward

de·cus·sate (dē kus′āt′, dek′ə sāt′; *for adj., usually* di kus′it) ***vt., vi.*** **-sat′ed, -sat′ing** ⟦< L *decussatus*, pp. of *decussare*, to cross in the form of an X < *decussis*, the figure ten (X) < *decem*, TEN⟧ to cross or cut so as to form an X; intersect —***adj.*** **1** forming an X; decussated **2** *Bot.* arranged in pairs growing at right angles to those above and below: said of leaves or branches —**de·cus′sate·ly** ***adv.***

de·cus·sa·tion (dē′kə sā′shən, dek′ə-) ***n.*** ⟦L *decussatio*⟧ **1** a decussating or being decussated **2** an intersection forming an X **3** *Anat.* a crossing of bands of nerve fibers in the brain or spinal cord

de·dans (də dän′; *Fr*, -dän′) ***n.***, *pl.* **de·dans′** (-dänz′; *Fr*, -dän′) ⟦Fr, lit, the interior < OFr *dedenz* < *de-*, from + LL *deintus*, from within < L *de-*, from + *intus*, within < IE **entos*, within < base **en-*, IN[1]⟧ *Court Tennis* **1** a gallery for spectators in the end wall of a court **2** the spectators at a match in court tennis

ded·i·cate (ded′i kit; *for v.*, -kāt′) ***adj.*** ⟦ME *dedicat* < L *dedicatus*, pp. of *dedicare*, to consecrate, declare < *de-*, intens. + *dicare*, to proclaim < *dicere*, to say: see DICTION⟧ [Archaic] dedicated —***vt.*** **-cat′ed, -cat′ing** ⟦ME *dedicaten* < the adj.⟧ **1** to set apart for worship of a deity or devote to a sacred purpose **2** to set apart seriously for a special purpose; devote to some work, duty, etc. [she *dedicated* her life to serving the poor] **3** to address or inscribe (a book, artistic performance, etc.) to someone or something as a sign of honor or affection ☆**4** to open formally (a public building, fair, etc.) **5** *Law* to devote to public use —***SYN.*** DEVOTE —**ded′i·ca′tor** ***n.***

ded·i·cat·ed (ded′i kāt′əd) ***vt. pt. & pp. of*** DEDICATE —***adj.*** **1** devoted or faithful **2** designating a device, piece of electronic equipment, computer program, etc. made to be used for a particular purpose or task

ded·i·ca·tion (ded′i kā′shən) ***n.*** ⟦ME *dedicacioun* < L *dedicatio*⟧ **1** a dedicating or being dedicated **2** an inscription, as in a book, dedicating it to a person, cause, etc. **3** wholehearted devotion

ded·i·ca·to·ry (ded′i kə tôr′ē) ***adj.*** of or as a dedication: also **ded′i·ca′tive** (-kāt′iv, -kə tiv)

de·dif·fer·en·ti·a·tion (dē dif′ər en′shē ā′shən) ***n.*** a reversal of cell development, esp. in plants, so that the differentiation that had occurred previously is lost and the cell becomes more generalized in structure

de·duce (di do͞os′, -dyo͞os′; dē-) ***vt.*** **-duced′, -duc′ing** ⟦ME *deducen* < L *deducere*, to lead down, bring away < *de-*, down + *ducere*, to lead: see DUCT⟧ **1** to trace the course or derivation of **2** to infer by logical reasoning; reason out or conclude from known facts or general principles —***SYN.*** INFER —**de·duc′i·ble** ***adj.***

de·duct (di dukt′, dē-) ***vt.*** ⟦ME *deducten* < L *deductus*, pp. of *deducere*: see prec.⟧ to take away or subtract (a quantity)

de·duct·i·ble (-ə bəl) ***adj.*** **1** that can be deducted **2** that is allowed as a deduction in computing income tax [*deductible* expenses] —***n.*** **1** a clause in an insurance policy stating that the insurer will pay that portion of a loss, damage, etc. remaining after a stipulated amount, to be paid by the insured party, is deducted **2** the amount stipulated —**de·duct′i·bil′i·ty** ***n.***

de·duc·tion (di duk′shən, dē-) ***n.*** ⟦ME *deduccioun* < L *deductio*⟧ **1** a deducting or being deducted; subtraction **2** *a)* a sum or amount deducted or allowed to be deducted as, specif., from taxable income *b)* something for which such an amount may be deducted from taxable income **3** *Logic* the act or process of deducing; reasoning from the general to the specific, or from premises to a logically valid conclusion; also, a conclusion reached by such reasoning: distinguished from INDUCTION —**de·duc′tive** ***adj.*** —**de·duc′tive·ly** ***adv.***

Dee[1] (dē), **John** 1527-1608; Eng. alchemist, astrologer, and mathematician (called *Dr. Dee*)

Dee[2] (dē) **1** river in NE Scotland, flowing east into the North Sea: 90 mi (145 km) **2** river in N Wales and W England, flowing northeast into the Irish Sea: 70 mi (113 km)

deed (dēd) ***n.*** ⟦ME *dede* < OE *ded, dæd*, akin to Ger *tat*, ODu *dede*, ON *dath*, Goth *deds*: for IE base see DO[1]⟧ **1** a thing done; act **2** a feat of courage, skill, etc. **3** action; actual performance [honest in word and *deed*] **4** *Law* a document by which a conveyance of real property is effected —☆***vt.*** to convey (property) by such a document

deed poll ⟦so named because the edge of a legal document made by one person was *polled*, or trimmed evenly (see POLL, *vt.* 1): edges of documents between two parties had matching notches (see INDENTURE, *n.* 2)⟧ [Brit.] a legal document by which a person changes his or her name

☆**dee·jay** (dē′jā′) ***n.*** ⟦D(ISC) J(OCKEY)⟧ DJ

deem (dēm) ***vt., vi.*** ⟦ME *deman* < OE *deman*, to judge, decree < base of *dom*, DOOM[1]⟧ to think, believe, or judge

de-em·pha·size (dē em′fə sīz′) ***vt.*** **-sized′, -siz′ing** to remove emphasis from; lessen the importance or prominence of —**de-em′pha·sis** (-sis) ***n.***

deep (dēp) ***adj.*** ⟦ME *dep* < OE *deop*, akin to Ger *tief*, Goth *diups* < IE base **dheub-*, deep, hollow > DIP, DUMP[1]⟧ **1** extending far downward from the top or top edges, inward from the surface, or backward from the front [a *deep* cut, a *deep* lake, a *deep* drawer] **2** extending down, inward, etc. a specified length or distance [water eight feet *deep*] **3** *a)* located far down or back [*deep* in the outfield] *b)* coming from or going far down or back [a *deep* breath] **4** far off in time or space [the *deep* past] **5** hard to understand; abstruse [a *deep* book] **6** extremely grave or serious [in *deep* trouble] **7** strongly felt [*deep* love] **8** intellectually profound [a *deep* discussion] **9** *a)* tricky and sly; devious [*deep* dealings] *b)* carefully guarded [a *deep* secret] **10** dark and rich [a *deep* red] **11** sunk in or absorbed by: with *in* [*deep* in thought] **12** *a)* great in degree; intense [*deep* joy] *b)* heavy and unbroken [a *deep* sleep] **13** much involved [*deep* in debt] **14** of low pitch or range [a *deep* voice] **15** large; big [*deep* cuts in the budget] **16** *Sports* having many good players in reserve [a team *deep* in pitching] —*n.* ⟦ME *dep* < OE *deop*⟧ **1** a deep place or any of the deepest parts, as in water or earth **2** the extent of encompassing space or time, of the unknown, etc. **3** the middle part; part that is darkest, most silent, etc. [in the *deep* of night] **4** *Naut.* any of the unmarked fathom points between those marked on a lead line —*adv.* ⟦ME *depe* < OE *deope*⟧ in a deep way or to a deep extent; far down, far in, far back, etc. [to dig *deep*] —***SYN.*** BROAD —**go off the deep end** ⟦in ref. to a swimming pool with both a deep end and a shallow end⟧ [Informal] **1** to behave in a rash or reckless manner **2** to go insane —**in deep water** in trouble or difficulty —**the deep** [Old Poet.] the sea or ocean —**deep′ly** *adv.* —**deep′ness** *n.*

deep-chest·ed (-ches′tid) *adj.* having, or coming as from, a thick chest [a *deep-chested* roar]

deep-dish (dēp′dish′) *adj.* prepared and served in a deep pan or dish [*deep-dish* pizza]

☆**deep-dish pie** a pie, usually of fruit, baked in a deep dish and having only a top crust

deep-dyed (-dīd′) *adj.* **1** stained throughout **2** thoroughgoing; unmitigated [a *deep-dyed* villain]

deep·en (dē′pən) *vt., vi.* to make or become deep or deeper

deep fat cooking oil or fat that is deep enough in the pan to cover food that is to be deep-fried

deep focus the technique of producing filmed or photographed images having a depth of field in which both objects in the foreground and objects in the background are in focus —**deep′-fo′cus** *adj.*

☆**deep·freeze** (dēp′frēz′) *n.* ⟦< *Deepfreeze*, a trademark for a deep freezer⟧ **1** a deep freezer **2** storage in or as in a deep freezer **3** a condition of suspended activity, dealings, etc. —*vt.* **-froze′**, **-fro′zen**, **-freez′ing** **1** to subject (foods) to sudden freezing so as to preserve and store **2** to store in a deep freezer

☆**deep freezer** any freezer for quick-freezing and storing food

deep-fry (-frī′) *vt.* **-fried′**, **-fry′ing** to fry in a deep pan of boiling fat or oil

deep-laid (-lād′) *adj.* carefully worked out and kept secret [*deep-laid* plans]

deep pocket [*usually pl.*] [Informal] extensive financial resources; great wealth —**deep′-pock′et** *adj.*, **deep′-pock′et·ed**

deep-root·ed (-ro͞ot′id, -root′id) *adj.* **1** having deep roots **2** firmly fixed or established; ingrained [*deep-rooted* bias]

deep scattering layer any of the stratified zones in the ocean which reflect sound during echo sounding, usually composed of marine organisms which migrate vertically from *c.* 250 to 800 m (*c.* 820 to 2,625 ft)

deep-sea (-sē′) *adj.* in or of the deeper parts of the sea [*deep-sea* fishing]

deep-seat·ed (-sēt′id) *adj.* **1** placed or originating far beneath the surface **2** DEEP-ROOTED (sense 2)

deep-set (-set′) *adj.* **1** deeply set **2** firmly fixed

deep-six (-siks′) [Slang] *n.* ⟦prob. orig. in ref. to the customary minimum depth, as measured by a lead line, for burial at sea⟧ **1** [Archaic] burial at sea **2** a discarding or disposing of something —*vt.* to get rid of, as by throwing overboard

☆**deep South** [*also* **D- S-**] that area of the U.S. regarded as most typically Southern and conservative, especially the southernmost parts of Ga., Ala., Miss., and La.

deep space OUTER SPACE

☆**deep structure** in transformational grammar, the abstract syntactic pattern underlying the construction in the surface structure of a sentence

deep throat ⟦< *Deep Throat*, journalists' code name for the anonymous informant in the WATERGATE scandal, taken < title of a pornographic film (1972) depicting fellatio⟧ [*also* **D- T-**] an anonymous informant who secretly provides inside information to a journalist

deep·wa·ter (dēp′wôt′ər, -wät′-) *adj.* of or relating to the deepest zones of ocean water, esp. with regard to drilling, shipping, etc.

deer (dir) *n., pl.* **deer** or **deers** ⟦ME *der* < OE *deor*, wild animal, akin to Ger *tier*, ON *dȳr* < IE base **dhewes*, **dheus-*, to stir up, blow, breathe (> DUSK, DOZE[1], FURY): for sense development cf. ANIMAL⟧ **1** any of a family (Cervidae) of ruminants, including the elk, moose, and reindeer; esp., the smaller species, as the white-tailed deer and mule deer: in most species, usually only the males grow and shed bony antlers annually **2** [Obs.] any animal; beast

☆**deer·fly** (dir′flī′) *n., pl.* **-flies′** any of certain bloodsucking, dipterous flies, esp. any of a genus (*Chrysops*) of a family (Tabanidae) of insects that includes the horseflies

deer·hound (-hound′) *n.* SCOTTISH DEERHOUND

☆**deer mouse** a mostly North American, white-footed mouse (genus *Peromyscus*)

deer·skin (dir′skin′) *n.* **1** the hide of a deer **2** leather or a garment made from this —*adj.* made of deerskin

deer·stalk·er (-stôk′ər) *n.* **1** a hunter who stalks deer **2** a hunter's cap with a visor in front and in back

deer tick a tick that is parasitic on deer; esp., any of a genus (*Ixodes*) of ticks that transmit the spirochete causing Lyme disease

☆**de-es·ca·late** (dē es′kə lāt′) *vi., vt.* **-lat′ed**, **-lat′ing** to reverse the effect of escalation on (something); reduce or lessen in scope, magnitude, etc. —**de-es′ca·la′tion** *n.*

DEET (dēt) *n.* ⟦< *diethyltoluamide*, chemical name⟧ an oily, liquid neurotoxin, $C_{12}H_{17}NO$, used in insect and tick repellents: sometimes written **deet**

def[1] (def) *adj.* [Slang] excellent; first-rate

def[2] *abbrev.* **1** defendant **2** defense **3** defensive **4** deferred **5** defined **6** definition

de·face (dē fās′, di-) *vt.* **-faced′**, **-fac′ing** ⟦ME *defacen* < OFr *desfacier*: see DE- & FACE⟧ **1** to spoil the appearance of; disfigure; mar **2** to make illegible by injuring the surface of —**de·face′ment** *n.* —**de·fac′er** *n.*

de fac·to (dē fak′tō, dā-, də-) ⟦L⟧ existing or being such in actual fact or for all practical purposes, though not by legal establishment, official recognition, etc. [a *de facto* government]: cf. DE JURE

de·fal·cate (dē fal′kāt′, -fôl′-, di-) *vi.* **-cat′ed**, **-cat′ing** ⟦< ML *defalcatus*, pp. of *defalcare*, to cut off: see DE- & FALCATE⟧ to steal or misuse funds entrusted to one's care; embezzle —**de·fal′ca′tor** *n.*

de·fal·ca·tion (dē′fal kā′shən, -fôl-) *n.* ⟦ML *defalcatio*: see prec.⟧ **1** embezzlement **2** the amount embezzled

def·a·ma·tion (def′ə mā′shən) *n.* ⟦ME *defamacioun* < OFr *difamacion* < LL *diffamatio*⟧ a defaming or being defamed; detraction, slander, or libel

de·fam·a·to·ry (dē fam′ə tôr′ē, di-) *adj.* ⟦ML *diffamatorius*⟧ defaming or tending to defame; slanderous

de·fame (dē fām′, di-) *vt.* **-famed′**, **-fam′ing** ⟦ME *defamen*, *diffamen* < OFr *diffamer* or ML *defamere*, both < L *diffamare* < *dis-*, from + *fama*: see FAME⟧ **1** to attack or injure the reputation or honor of by false and malicious statements; malign, slander, or libel **2** [Archaic] to bring infamy on; disgrace **3** [Obs.] to accuse —**de·fam′er** *n.*

de·fa·mil·i·ar·ize (dē fə mil′yər īz′, -mil′ē ər-) *vt.* **-ized′**, **-iz′ing** to make (something well-known or well-established) seem unfamiliar, strange, disconcerting, etc., as in order to reinterpret or subvert it [to *defamiliarize* accepted truths]

de·fang (dē faŋ′) *vt.* **1** to remove the fangs of [to *defang* a snake] **2** to render harmless [to *defang* an opposing candidate] —**de·fanged′** *adj.*

def art *abbrev.* definite article

de·fat (dē fat′) *vt.* **-fat′ted**, **-fat′ting** to remove all or most of the fat or fat content from (esp. food)

de·fault (dē fôlt′, di-; *also* dē′fôlt) *n.* ⟦ME < OFr *defaute* < VL **defallita*, pp. of **defallere*, to lack < L *de-*, away + *fallere*, to FAIL⟧ **1** failure to do something or be somewhere when required or expected; specif., *a)* failure to pay money due *b)* failure to appear in court to defend or prosecute a case *c)* failure to take part in or finish a contest **2** *Comput.* a preset choice, setting, etc. for automatic use as by a program when no other is specified by a user **3** any choice or option that someone naturally or routinely falls back on or resorts to **4** [Obs.] a fault, lack, or want —*adj.* **1** *Comput.* designating a choice, setting, etc. that is the DEFAULT (*n.* 2) [a *default* printer] **2** being the choice or option regarded as routine, automatic, etc. [the Administration's *default* position on tax cuts] —*vi.* ⟦ME *defauten* < OFr *defauter*⟧ **1** to fail to do something or be somewhere when required or expected; specif., *a)* to fail to make payment when due *b)* to fail to appear in court when required *c)* to fail to take part in or finish a contest **2** to lose a contest by default **3** to turn or proceed *to* a particular choice or option automatically or routinely: informal except in technical uses —*vt.* **1** to fail to do, pay, finish, etc. (something) when required **2** to lose (a contest, etc.) by default; forfeit —**in default of** in the absence of; through lack of —**de·fault′er** *n.*

de·fea·sance (dē fē′zəns, di-) *n.* ⟦ME & Anglo-Fr *defesaunce* < OFr *defesance* < *defesant*, prp. of *defaire, desfaire*: see DEFEAT⟧ **1** the annulment of a contract or deed **2** a clause stating a condition the fulfillment of which makes the deed, contract, etc. void in whole or in part

de·fea·si·ble (dē fē′zə bəl, di-) *adj.* ⟦see prec. & -IBLE⟧ that can be undone or made void

de·feat (dē fēt′, di-) *vt.* ⟦ME *defeten* < *defet*, disfigured, null and void < OFr *desfait*, pp. of *desfaire*, to undo < ML *disfacere*, to deface, ruin < L *dis-*, from + *facere*, to DO[1]⟧ **1** to win victory over; overcome; beat **2** to bring to nothing; frustrate [*defeating* our plans] **3** to make null and void **4** [Obs.] to undo; destroy —*n.* ⟦ME *defet*⟧ **1** the act of defeating, or gaining victory **2** the fact of being defeated **3** frustration **4** nullification —***SYN.*** CONQUER

de·feat·ist (-ist) *n.* ⟦Fr *défaitiste*⟧ a person who too readily accepts or expects defeat —*adj.* of or characteristic of a defeatist —**de·feat′ism′** *n.*

de·fea·ture (dē fē′chər) *n.* ⟦altered (after DE- & FEATURE) < ME *defaitor* < OFr *desfaiture* < *desfaire*: see DEFEAT⟧ **1** [Archaic] disfigurement **2** [Obs.] defeat

def·e·cate (def′ə kāt′) *vt.* **-cat′ed**, **-cat′ing** ⟦< L *defaecatus*, pp. of *defaecare*, to cleanse from dregs, strain < *de-*, from + *faex* (gen. *faecis*), grounds, dregs⟧ to remove impurities from; refine (sugar, wine, etc.) —*vi.* **1** to become free from impurities **2** to excrete waste matter from the bowels —**def′e·ca′tion** *n.* —**def′e·ca′tor** *n.*

de·fect (dē′fekt′; *also, and for v. always,* dē fekt′, di-) *n.* ⟦ME < L *defectus* < *deficere*, to undo, fail < *de-*, from + *facere*, to DO[1]⟧ **1** lack of something necessary for completeness; deficiency; shortcoming **2** an imperfection or weakness; fault; flaw; blemish —*vi.* 1 to forsake a party or cause, esp. so as to join the opposition 2 to leave one's country because of disapproval of its political policies and settle in another that opposes such policies —**de·fec′tor** *n.*

SYN.—defect implies a lack of something essential to completeness or perfection [a *defect* in vision]; an **imperfection** is any faulty detail that detracts from perfection [minor *imperfections* of style]; a **blemish** is a superficial or surface imperfection that mars the appearance [skin *blemishes*]; a **flaw** is an imperfection in structure or substance, such as a crack or gap, that mars the wholeness or continuity [a *flaw* in a metal bar]

de·fec·tion (dē fek′shən, di-) *n.* ⟦L *defectio* < *defectus*: see prec.⟧ 1 abandonment of loyalty, duty, or principle; desertion 2 the act of defecting from one's country 3 a failing or failure

de·fec·tive (dē fek′tiv, di-) *adj.* ⟦ME & OFr *defectif* < LL *defectivus*⟧ 1 having a defect or defects; imperfect; faulty 2 *Gram.* lacking some of the usual forms of inflection ["ought" is a *defective* verb] 3 having a physical or mental defect; subnormal —*n.* ☆1 a person with some physical or mental defect 2 *Gram.* a defective word —**de·fec′tive·ly** *adv.* —**de·fec′tive·ness** *n.*

de·fem·i·nize (dē fem′ə nīz′) *vt.* **-nized′**, **-niz′ing** to divest of feminine attributes or physical characteristics —**de·fem′i·ni·za′tion** *n.*

de·fence (dē fens′, di-) *n. Brit. sp. of* DEFENSE

de·fend (dē fend′, di-) *vt.* ⟦ME *defenden* < OFr *defendre* < L *defendere*, to ward off, repel < *de-*, away, from + *fendere*, to strike < IE base **gwhen-*, to strike > Gr *theinein*, to kill, strike, OE *guth*, combat⟧ 1 *a)* to guard from attack; keep from harm or danger; protect *b)* to protect (a goal, etc.) against scoring by an opponent 2 to support, maintain, or justify [*defend* one's conduct] 3 *Law a)* to oppose (an action) *b)* to plead (one's cause) in defense *c)* to act as lawyer for (an accused) —*vi.* to make a defense —**de·fend′a·ble** *adj.* —**de·fend′er** *n.*

de·fend·ant (dē fen′dənt, di-; *often, in legal use*, -dant′) *adj.* ⟦ME *defendaunt* < OFr *defendant*, prp. of *defendre*⟧ defending —*n. Law* the defending party; person sued or accused: opposed to PLAINTIFF

Defender of the Faith a title used by English sovereigns, originally conferred upon Henry VIII by Pope Leo X

de·fen·es·tra·tion (dē fen′ə strā′shən) *n.* ⟦ModL *defenestratio* < L *de-* + *fenestra*, window⟧ a throwing out through a window —**de·fen′es·trate′** *vt.* **-trat′ed**, **-trat′ing**

de·fense (dē fens′, di-; *also, and for n. 6 usually*, dē′fens′) *n.* ⟦ME < OFr < LL *defensa* < fem. of L *defensus*, pp. of *defendere*⟧ 1 the act or power of defending, or guarding against attack, harm, or danger 2 the fact or state of being defended 3 *a)* something that defends; means of or resources for protection *b)* a plan or system for defending 4 justification or support by speech or writing; vindication 5 self-protection, as by boxing 6 *Sports a)* a team when it is attempting to prevent scoring by an opponent in any contest *b)* the ability to prevent an opposing team from scoring *c)* the strategy, plays, etc. used to prevent an opposing team from scoring 7 *a)* the arguments in behalf of the defendant in a law case ☆*b)* the defendant and his or her lawyer or lawyers, collectively —*vt.* **-fensed′**, **-fens′ing** [Informal] to plan or execute a defense against (esp. an offensive maneuver) in a game or sport —**on defense** *Sports* engaged in an attempt to prevent an opposing team from scoring

de·fense·less (-lis) *adj.* lacking defense; unable to defend oneself; open to attack; helpless; unprotected —**de·fense′less·ly** *adv.* —**de·fense′less·ness** *n.*

de·fense·man (-mən) *n., pl.* **-men** (-mən) *Ice Hockey, Lacrosse* either of two players positioned close to their own goal to prevent scoring and to gain possession of the puck

defense mechanism 1 any self-protective physiological system or reaction of an organism 2 *Psychiatry* any thought process, as repression, introjection, denial, displacement, or sublimation, unconsciously used by an individual as a defense against feelings of guilt, anxiety, shame, etc.

de·fen·si·ble (dē fen′sə bəl, di-) *adj.* ⟦ME & OFr *defensable* < L *defensabilis* < *defensare*, intens. < *defendere*: see DEFEND⟧ that can be defended, protected, or justified —**de·fen′si·bil′i·ty** *n.* —**de·fen′si·bly** *adv.*

de·fen·sive (dē fen′siv, di-) *adj.* ⟦ME & OFr *defensif* < ML *defensivus* < L *defensus*: see DEFENSE⟧ 1 defending 2 of or for defense 3 designating or of the side that defends a goal, basket, etc. in a contest 4 constantly feeling under attack and hence quick to justify one's actions —*n.* 1 [Obs.] something that defends 2 a position of defense: chiefly in the phrase **on the defensive**, in a condition of resisting or being ready to resist attack or danger —**de·fen′sive·ly** *adv.* —**de·fen′sive·ness** *n.*

de·fer[1] (dē fur′, di-) *vt., vi.* **-ferred′**, **-fer′ring** ⟦ME *differren* < OFr *differer*: see DIFFER⟧ 1 to put off to a future time; postpone; delay 2 to postpone the induction of (a person) into compulsory military service —**SYN.** YIELD —**de·fer′ra·ble** *adj.* —**de·fer′rer** *n.*

de·fer[2] (dē fur′, di-) *vi.* **-ferred′**, **-fer′ring** ⟦ME *deferen* < OFr *deferer*, to yield, pay deference to < L *deferre*, to bring down < *de-*, down + *ferre*, to BEAR[1]⟧ to give in to the wish or judgment of another, as in showing respect; yield with courtesy (*to*)

def·er·ence (def′ər əns, def′rəns) *n.* ⟦Fr *déférence* < L *deferens*, prp. of *deferre*: see prec.⟧ 1 a yielding in opinion, judgment, or wishes 2 courteous regard or respect —**SYN.** HONOR —**in deference to** out of regard or respect for (a person or the person's position or wishes)

def·er·ent[1] (def′ər ənt) *adj.* DEFERENTIAL

def·er·ent[2] (def′ər ənt) *adj.* ⟦Fr *déférent* < L *deferens*, prp. of *deferre*: see DEFER[2]⟧ 1 carrying down or out 2 *Anat.* of or relating to the vas deferens

def·er·en·tial (def′ər en′shəl) *adj.* showing deference; very respectful —**def′er·en′tial·ly** *adv.*

de·fer·ment (dē fur′mənt, di-) *n.* a deferring or being deferred; postponement: also **de·fer′ral** (-fur′əl)

de·ferred (dē furd′, di-) *adj.* ⟦pp. of DEFER[1]⟧ 1 postponed 2 having the rights, interest, or payment withheld until a certain date [a *deferred* annuity]

de·fer·ves·cence (dē′fər ves′əns, def′ər-) *n.* ⟦Ger *defervescenz* (first used by K. A. Wunderlich, 1815-77, Ger physician) < L *defervescens*, prp. of *defervescere*, to cool off, orig. stop boiling < *de-*, down, DE- + *fervescere*, to grow hot: see EFFERVESCE⟧ the abating or disappearance of a fever

de·fi·ance (dē fī′əns, di-) *n.* ⟦ME *defiaunce* < OFr *defiance* < *defier*, DEFY⟧ 1 the act of defying; open, bold resistance to authority or opposition 2 a challenge —**in defiance of** 1 defying 2 in spite of

de·fi·ant (-ənt) *adj.* ⟦Fr *défiant*, prp. of *défier*⟧ full of defiance; openly and boldly resisting —**de·fi′ant·ly** *adv.*

de·fib·ril·late (dē fib′rə lāt′, -fī′brə-) *vt.* **-lat′ed**, **-lat′ing** to stop fibrillation of (the heart), as by the use of electric current —**de·fib′ril·la′tion** *n.* —**de·fib′ril·la′tor** *n.*

de·fi·cien·cy (dē fish′ən sē, di-) *n.* ⟦ME *deficience* < LL *deficientia* < L *deficiens*, prp. of *deficere* to lack, fail < *de-*, from + *facere*, to DO[1]⟧ 1 the quality or state of being deficient; absence of something essential; incompleteness 2 *pl.* **-cies** *a)* a shortage *b)* the amount of shortage; deficit

deficiency disease a disease, as rickets or pellagra, caused by a dietary lack of vitamins, minerals, etc. or by an inability to metabolize them

deficiency judgment *Law* a judgment in favor of a mortgagee for the remainder of a debt not completely cleared by foreclosure and sale of the mortgaged property

de·fi·cient (dē fish′ənt, di-) *adj.* ⟦L *deficiens*: see DEFICIENCY⟧ 1 lacking in some essential; incomplete; defective 2 inadequate in amount, quality, or degree; not sufficient —*n.* a deficient person or thing —**de·fi′cient·ly** *adv.*

def·i·cit (def′ə sit) *n.* ⟦L, there is lacking, 3d pers. sing., pres. indic., of *deficere* (see DEFICIENCY): from use as first word in inventory clauses⟧ the amount by which a sum of money is less than the required or desired amount; specif., an excess of liabilities over assets, of losses over profits, or of expenditure over income

deficit financing the practice of seeking to stimulate a nation's economy by increasing government expenditures beyond revenue

deficit spending government expenditures that exceed revenue

de fi·de (dā fē′dā) ⟦L⟧ *R.C.Ch.* of faith: used to designate doctrines held to be revealed by God and so requiring the unconditional assent of faith by all

de·fi·er (dē fī′ər, di-) *n.* a person who defies

def·i·lade (def′ə lād′, def′ə lād′) *vt., vi.* **-lad′ed**, **-lad′ing** ⟦< Fr *défilade*, a filing off, succession < *défiler*: see DEFILE[2]⟧ to arrange (troops and fortifications) so that the terrain will protect them, esp. from gunfire against either flank —*n.* 1 the act of defilading 2 the protection afforded by defilading

de·file[1] (dē fīl′, di-) *vt.* **-filed′**, **-fil′ing** ⟦ME *defilen*, altered (by assoc. with *filen*, to make foul < OE *fylan* < *ful*, FOUL) < *defoulen* < OFr *defouler*, to tread underfoot, insult < *de-*, intens. + *fouler* < ML *fullare*, to tread, FULL[2]⟧ 1 to make filthy or dirty; pollute 2 to make ceremonially unclean 3 to corrupt 4 to profane or sully [*defiled* his good name] 5 to violate the chastity of; deflower: now an old-fashioned or literary use —**SYN.** CONTAMINATE —**de·file′ment** *n.* —**de·fil′er** *n.*

de·file[2] (dē fīl′, di-; dē′fīl′) *vi.* **-filed′**, **-fil′ing** ⟦Fr *défiler*, to file off, unravel < *dé-* (L *de*), from + *filer*, to form a line < *fil*, thread: see FILE[1]⟧ to march in single file or by files —*n.* ⟦Fr *défilé* < the v.⟧ 1 a narrow passage through which troops must defile 2 any narrow valley or mountain pass 3 a march in single file or by files

de·fine (dē fīn′, di-) *vt.* **-fined′**, **-fin′ing** ⟦ME *diffinen* < OFr *definer* & ML *diffinire*, both < L *definire*, to limit, define < *de-*, from + *finire*, to set a limit to, bound: see FINISH⟧ 1 *a)* to determine or set down the boundaries of *b)* to trace the precise outlines of; delineate 2 to determine or state the extent and nature of; describe exactly [*define* your duties] 3 *a)* to give the distinguishing characteristics of *b)* to constitute the distinction of; differentiate [reason *defines* man] 4 to state the meaning or meanings of (as a word) —*vi.* to prepare definitions, as of words —**de·fin′a·ble** *adj.* —**de·fin′er** *n.*

def·i·nite (def′ə nit) *adj.* ⟦L *definitus*, pp. of *definire*: see prec.⟧ 1 having exact limits 2 precise and clear in meaning; explicit 3 certain; positive [it's *definite* that he'll go] 4 *Bot.* having a constant number of stamens, etc., fewer than 20 but always a multiple of the number of petals 5 *Gram.* limiting or specifying; referring to a specific or previously identified person, thing, etc. ["the" is the *definite* article] —**SYN.** EXPLICIT —**def′i·nite·ness** *n.*

definite integral *Math.* an integral in which the range of integration is specified: its value equals the area on a graph bounded by a curve, the x-axis, and two given ordinates

def·i·nite·ly (-lē) *adv.* 1 in a precise, distinct, or determined manner 2 beyond a doubt; certainly: now the prevailing meaning

def·i·ni·tion (def′ə nish′ən) *n.* ⟦ME *diffinicioun* < OFr *definicion* & ML *diffinitio*, both < L *definitio*⟧ 1 a defining or being defined 2 a statement of what a thing is 3 a statement of the meaning as of a word or phrase 4 *a)* a putting or being in clear, sharp outline *b)* a making or being definite, explicit, and clear 5 the power of a lens to show (an object) in clear, sharp outline 6 the degree of distinctness of a photograph, etc. 7 the clearness with which recorded or broadcast sounds or televised images are reproduced; absence of fuzziness —**by definition** as consistent with its very meaning, nature, or purpose [a teacher *by definition* faces the everyday challenges of the classroom] —**def′i·ni′tion·al** *adj.*

de·fin·i·tive (dē fin′ə tiv, di-) *adj.* ⟦ME *diffinitif* < OFr *definitif* < L *definitivus* < pp. of *definire*, DEFINE⟧ **1** that decides or settles in a final way; decisive; conclusive [a *definitive* answer] **2** most nearly complete and accurate; authoritative [a *definitive* biography] **3** serving to define; limiting or distinguishing precisely [*definitive* details] **4** designating or of a postage stamp for regular use, issued for an unlimited period —*n.* a definitive postage stamp: distinguished from COMMEMORATIVE —**de·fin′i·tive·ly** *adv.* —**de·fin′i·tive·ness** *n.*

definitive host the organism on or in which a parasite lives in the adult stage

de·fin·i·tude (dē fin′ə to͞od′, -tyo͞od′) *n.* ⟦< L *definitus* (see DEFINITE), after FINITUDE⟧ [Rare] the quality of being definite; precision

def·la·grate (def′lə grāt′) *vt., vi.* **-grat′ed, -grat′ing** ⟦< L *deflagratus*, pp. of *deflagrare*, to burn, consume < *de-*, intens. + *flagrare*, to burn: see FLAGRANT⟧ to burn rapidly, with intense heat and dazzling light —**def′la·gra′tion** *n.*

de·flate (dē flāt′, di-) *vt., vi.* **-flat′ed, -flat′ing** ⟦DE- + (IN)FLATE⟧ **1** to collapse by letting out air or gas [to *deflate* a tire] **2** to make or become smaller or less important **3** to cause deflation of (currency, prices, etc.) Opposed to INFLATE —*SYN.* CONTRACT —**de·fla′tor** *n.*

de·fla·tion (dē flā′shən, di-) *n.* **1** a deflating or being deflated **2** a reduction in the general level of prices as a result of a severe decline in economic activity **3** *Geol.* erosion by the wind See INFLATION —**de·fla′tion·ar′y** *adj.*

de·flect (dē flekt′, di-) *vt., vi.* ⟦L *deflectere* < *de-*, from + *flectere*, to bend⟧ to turn or make go to one side —**de·flec′tive** *adj.* —**de·flec′tor** *n.*

de·flec·tion (dē flek′shən, di-) *n.* ⟦LL *deflexio* < L *deflexus*, pp. of prec.⟧ **1** *a)* a deflecting or being deflected; a turning aside, bending, or deviation *b)* the amount of this **2** the deviation from the zero mark of the needle or pointer of a measuring instrument

de·flexed (dē flekst′) *adj.* ⟦earlier *deflex* (< L *deflexus*, pp. of *deflectere*, DEFLECT) + -ED⟧ bent downward, as branches, leaves, or hairs

de·flex·ion (dē flek′shən, di-) *n. Brit. sp. of* DEFLECTION

def·lo·ra·tion (def′lə rā′shən) *n.* ⟦ME *defloracioun* < OFr *desfloracion* < LL *defloratio*⟧ the act of deflowering

de·flow·er (dē flou′ər) *vt.* ⟦ME *deflouren* < OFr *desflorer* < L *deflorare* < *de-*, from + *flos* (gen. *floris*), FLOWER⟧ **1** to take the virginity from (a woman) by having sexual intercourse with her **2** to ravage or spoil **3** to remove flowers from (a plant)

De·foe (di fō′), **Daniel** 1660-1731; Eng. writer

de·fog·ger (dē fôg′ər, -fäg′-; di-) *n.* an apparatus for clearing condensed moisture, as from a car window —**de·fog′** *vt.* **-fogged′, -fog′ging**

☆**de·fo·li·ant** (dē fō′lē ənt) *n.* a chemical substance that causes leaves to fall from growing plants

de·fo·li·ate (-āt′) *vt.* **-at′ed, -at′ing** ⟦< LL *defoliatus*, pp. of *defoliare* < *de-*, from + *folium*, a leaf: see FOLIATE⟧ **1** to strip (trees, etc.) of leaves ☆**2** to use a defoliant on —**de·fo′li·a′tion** *n.* —**de·fo′li·a′tor** *n.*

de·force (dē fôrs′) *vt.* **-forced′, -forc′ing** ⟦ME *deforcen* < Anglo-Fr *deforcier* < OFr *de-*, from + *forcier*, to force < VL **fortiare* < LL *forcia, fortia*: see FORCE⟧ *Law* **1** to keep (property) from the rightful owner by force **2** to keep (a person) from rightful possession by force —**de·force′ment** *n.*

de·for·ciant (-fôr′shənt) *n.* ⟦ME *deforciaunt*⟧ *Law* a person who deforces another or another's property

de·for·est (dē fôr′ist) *vt.* to clear (land) of forests or trees —☆**de·for′est·a′tion** *n.*

De For·est (di fôr′ist, di fär′-), **Lee** 1873-1961; U.S. inventor of telegraphic, telephonic, & radio apparatus

de·form (dē fôrm′, di-) *vt.* ⟦ME *deformen* < OFr *deformer* < L *deformare* < *de-*, from + *forma*, FORM⟧ **1** to impair the form or shape of **2** to make ugly; disfigure **3** *Physics* to change the shape of by pressure or stress —*vi.* to become deformed

SYN.—**deform** implies a marring of form, appearance, or character, as if by pressure or stress [a body *deformed* by disease]; **distort** implies a twisting or wrenching out of the normal or proper shape or form [a mind *distorted* by fear]; **contort** suggests an even more violent wrenching out of shape so as to produce a grotesque or unpleasant result [a face *contorted* by pain]; **warp** implies a bending out of shape, as of wood in drying, and, hence, suggests a turning aside from the true or right course [judgment *warped* by prejudice]

de·for·ma·tion (dē′fôr mā′shən, def′ər-) *n.* ⟦ME *deformacioun* < L *deformatio*⟧ **1** a deforming or being deformed **2** the result of deforming; disfigurement **3** a change in form for the worse **4** *Physics a)* the changing of form or shape, as by stress *b)* the changed form that results

de·formed (dē fôrmd′, di-) *adj.* changed as in form or shape, esp., changed to such an extent as to be misshapen, disfigured, or ugly

de·form·i·ty (dē fôr′mə tē, di-) *n., pl.* **-ties** ⟦ME *deformite* < OFr *deformité* < L *deformitas* < *deformis*, misshapen < *de-*, from + *forma*, FORM⟧ **1** the condition of being deformed **2** *a)* abnormal bodily formation *b)* a deformed or disfigured part of the body **3** ugliness or depravity **4** anything deformed or disfigured

de·frag (dē frag′, di-) *vt.* **-fragged′, -frag′ging** [Informal] DEFRAGMENT

de·frag·ment (dē frag′mənt, di-) *vt.* ⟦DE- + FRAGMENT (v.)⟧ to reorganize the contents of (a hard disk) so that dispersed fragments of each file are stored in contiguous sectors, as for faster retrieval —**de·frag′men·ta′tion** *n.*

de·fraud (dē frôd′, di-) *vt.* ⟦ME *defrauden* < OFr *defrauder* < L *defraudare* < *de-*, from + *fraudare*, to cheat < *fraus*, FRAUD⟧ to take away or hold back property, rights, etc. from by fraud; cheat —*SYN.* CHEAT —**de·frau·da·tion** (dē′frô dā′shən) *n.* —**de·fraud′er** *n.*

de·fray (dē frā′, di-) *vt.* ⟦Fr *défrayer* < OFr *defraier* < *de-* (L *de*), from, off + **frai* (Fr *frais*, pl.), expense, cost, "damages," prob. < L *fractum*, neut. pp. of *frangere*, to BREAK⟧ to pay or furnish the money for (the cost or expenses) —**de·fray′a·ble** *adj.* —**de·fray′al** *n.*, **de·fray′ment**

de·frock (dē fräk′) *vt.* to revoke the rank or function of (a priest or minister)

de·frost (dē frôst′, di-) *vt.* **1** to remove frost or ice from by thawing **2** to cause (frozen foods) to become unfrozen —*vi.* to become defrosted

de·frost·er (-ər) *n.* any device for melting ice and frost or preventing their formation, as on a windshield

deft (deft) *adj.* ⟦ME *defte, dafte*: see DAFT⟧ skillful in a quick, sure, and easy way; dexterous —*SYN.* DEXTEROUS —**deft′ly** *adv.* —**deft′ness** *n.*

de·funct (dē fuŋkt′, di-) *adj.* ⟦L *defunctus*, pp. of *defungi*, to do, finish, die < *de-*, from, off + *fungi*, to perform: see DE- & FUNCTION⟧ **1** [Now Rare] no longer living; deceased **2** no longer existing or functioning, as because of failure [a *defunct* government]

de·fund (dē fund′, di-) *vt.* to stop providing funds, esp. government funds, for (a program, group, etc.)

de·fuse (dē fyo͞oz′, di-) *vt.* **-fused′, -fus′ing 1** to remove the fuse or fuze from (a bomb or other explosive device) **2** to render harmless **3** to make less tense, as by diplomacy

de·fy (dē fī′, di-; *also, for n.*, dē′fī′) *vt.* **-fied′, -fy′ing** ⟦ME *defien* < OFr *defier*, to distrust, repudiate, defy < LL **disfidare* < *dis-*, from + **fidare*, to trust < *fidus*, faithful: see FAITH⟧ **1** to resist or oppose boldly or openly **2** to resist completely in a baffling way [the puzzle *defied* solution] **3** to dare (someone) to do or prove something **4** [Archaic] to challenge (someone) to fight —*n., pl.* **-fies′** a defiance or challenge

deg *abbrev.* degree(s)

dé·ga·gé (dā′gä zhā′) *adj.* ⟦Fr, pp. of *dégager*, to disengage⟧ **1** free and easy or unconstrained in manner or attitude **2** uncommitted, uninvolved, detached, etc. **3** *Ballet* with leg extended and arched foot pointing

de·gas (dē gas′) *vt.* **-gassed′, -gas′sing** to remove gas from (an area, substance, or product) —**de·gas′i·fi·ca′tion** *n.*

De·gas (də gä′, dā-), **(Hilaire Germain) Ed·gar** (ed gȧr′) 1834-1917; Fr. painter

de Gaulle (də gôl′), **Charles (André Joseph Marie)** 1890-1970; Fr. general & statesman: president of France (1959-69)

de·gauss (dē gous′) *vt.* ⟦DE- + GAUSS⟧ to demagnetize (as a ship for protection against magnetic mines) by passing an electric current through a coil or coils along or around the edge in order to neutralize the surrounding magnetic field —**de·gauss′er** *n.*

de·gen·er·a·cy (di jen′ər ə sē) *n.* **1** the state of being degenerate **2** the process of degenerating **3** *pl.* **-cies** a degenerate action

de·gen·er·ate (dē jen′ər it, di-; *for v.*, -āt′) *adj.* ⟦L *degeneratus*, pp. of *degenerare*, to become unlike one's race, degenerate < *degener*, not genuine, base < *de-*, from + *genus*, race: see GENUS⟧ **1** having sunk below a former or normal condition, character, etc.; deteriorated **2** morally corrupt; depraved —*n.* a degenerate person, esp. one who is morally depraved or sexually perverted —*vi.* **-at′ed, -at′ing 1** to lose former normal or higher qualities **2** to decline or become debased morally, culturally, etc. **3** *Biol.* to undergo degeneration; deteriorate —**de·gen′er·ate·ly** *adv.* —**de·gen′er·ate·ness** *n.*

de·gen·er·a·tion (dē jen′ər ā′shən; di-) *n.* ⟦LL *degeneratio*⟧ **1** the process of degenerating **2** a degenerate condition **3** *Biol.* deterioration or loss of a function or structure in the course of evolution, as in the vestigial eyes of many cave animals **4** *Med.* deterioration in structure or function of cells, tissues, or organs, as in disease or aging

de·gen·er·a·tive (dē jen′ər ə tiv, di-; -āt′iv) *adj.* **1** of, showing, or causing degeneration **2** tending to degenerate —**de·gen′er·a·tive·ly** *adv.*

degenerative joint disease OSTEOARTHRITIS

de·glam·or·ize (dē glam′ər īz′) *vt.* **-ized′, -iz′ing** to make less glamorous or attractive —**de·glam′or·i·za′tion** *n.*

de·glaze (dē glāz′) *vt.* **-glazed′, -glaz′ing 1** to remove the glaze from **2** to remove the bits of sautéed or roasted meat and the juices from (a pan) by adding wine, stock, water, etc. and scraping: usually, the resulting liquid is used in or as a sauce

de·glu·ti·nate (dē glo͞ot′'n āt′) *vt.* **-nat′ed, -nat′ing** ⟦< L *deglutinatus*, pp. of *deglutinare*, to unglue < *de-*, from + *glutinare*, to glue < *gluten*, GLUE⟧ to extract gluten from (wheat, etc.) —**de·glu′ti·na′tion** *n.*

de·glu·ti·tion (dē′glo͞o tish′ən) *n.* ⟦Fr *déglutition* < pp. of LL *deglutire*, to swallow down < L *de-*, from, down + *glutire*, to swallow: see GLUTTON⟧ the act, process, or power of swallowing

de·grad·a·ble (dē grād′ə bəl, di-) *adj.* capable of being degraded or degrading; esp., capable of being readily decomposed by chemical action, as some plastics: distinguished from BIODEGRADABLE —**de·grad′a·bil′i·ty** *n.*

deg·ra·da·tion (deg′rə dā′shən) *n.* ⟦Fr *dégradation* < LL *degradatio* < *degradare*: see fol.⟧ **1** a degrading or being degraded in rank, status, or condition **2** a degraded condition **3** *Geol.* the lowering of land surfaces by erosion **4** *R.C.Ch.* laicization of a cleric, imposed as a penalty

de·grade (dē grād′, di-) *vt.* **-grad′ed, -grad′ing** ⟦ME *degraden* < OFr *degrader* < LL *degradare*, to reduce in rank < L *de-*, down + *gradus*: see DE- & GRADE⟧ **1** to lower in rank or status, as in punishing; demote **2** to lower or corrupt in quality, moral character, or value; debase **3** to bring into dishonor or contempt **4** *Chem.* to convert (an organic compound) into a simpler compound by removal of one or more parts of the molecule; decompose **5** *Geol.* to lower (a land surface) by erosion —*vi.* **1** [Rare] to sink to a lower grade or type **2** to be converted into a simpler compound or compounds; decompose —**de·grad′er** *n.*

SYN.—**degrade** literally means to lower in grade or rank, but it commonly implies a lowering or corrupting of moral character and self-respect; **abase** suggests a loss, often merely temporary and self-imposed, of dignity and respect [he *abased* himself before his employer]; **debase** implies a decline in value, quality, or character [a *debased* mind]; to **humble** is to lower the pride or increase the humility, esp. of another, and, unqualified, suggests that such lowering is deserved [*humbled* by the frightening experience]; to **humiliate** is to humble or shame another painfully and in public [*humiliated* by their laughter]

de·grad·ed (-id) *adj.* disgraced, debased, depraved, etc.

de·grad·ing (-iŋ) *adj.* that degrades; debasing —SYN. BASE² —**de·grad′ing·ly** *adv.*

de·grease (dē grēs′, -grēz′) *vt.* **-greased′**, **-greas′ing** to remove grease or a greasy substance from —**de·greas′er** *n.*

de·gree (di grē′) *n.* ⟦ME *degre* < OFr *degré*, degree, step, rank < VL **degradus* < *degradare*: see DEGRADE⟧ **1** any of the successive steps or stages in a process or series **2** a step in the direct line of descent [a cousin in the second *degree*] **3** social or official rank, position, or class [a man of low *degree*] **4** relative condition; manner, respect, or relation [each contributing to victory in his *degree*] **5** extent, amount, or relative intensity [hungry to a slight *degree*, burns of the third *degree*] **6** *Algebra* rank as determined by the sum of a term's exponents [the terms a^3c^2 and x^5 are of the fifth *degree*] **7** *Educ.* a rank given by a college or university to a student who has completed a required course of study, or to a distinguished person as an honor **8** *Gram.* a grade of comparison of adjectives and adverbs [the positive *degree* is "good," the comparative *degree* is "better," and the superlative *degree* is "best"] ☆**9** *Law* the seriousness of a crime [murder in the first *degree*] **10** *Astron., Geog., Math., etc.* a unit of measure for angles or arcs, one 360th part of the circumference of a circle: the measure of an angle is the number of degrees between its sides considered as radii of a circle: symbol, ° [a right angle has 90 *degrees*] **11** *Music* the relative position of a note within a given scale [B is the second *degree* in the scale of A] **12** *Physics a)* a unit of measure on a scale, as for temperature *b)* a line marking a degree, as on a thermometer —**by degrees** step by step; gradually —**to a degree 1** [Old-fashioned, Chiefly Brit.] to a great extent **2** somewhat: also **to some degree**

de·greed (di grēd′) *adj.* having been awarded a college or university degree [a *degreed* engineer]

de·gree-day (di grē′dā′) *n.* a unit which represents one degree of variation from a standard average daily temperature, used as in determining fuel requirements

degrees of freedom *Statistics* the number of independent variables entering into a statistical measure or frequency distribution

de·gres·sion (di gresh′ən) *n.* ⟦ML *degressio* < L *degressus*, pp. of *degredi*, to go down < *de*, down + *gradi*, to step: see GRADE⟧ a going down; descent or decrease; specif., a gradual decrease in the rate of taxation on sums below a specified amount —**de·gres′sive** *adj.*

de·gus·ta·tion or **dé·gus·ta·tion** (dē′gəs tā′shən, dā′-) *n.* [*also in italics*] **1** the act of sampling a wide variety of foods, wines, etc. **2** an assortment, as of foods or wines, provided for sampling

de gus·ti·bus non dis·pu·tan·dum (est) (dā go͝os′tē bo͝os′ nôn dēs′po͞o tän′do͝om est) ⟦L⟧ there is no arguing about tastes

de haut en bas (də ō′ tän bä′) ⟦Fr, lit., from high to low⟧ with haughtiness; condescending(ly)

de·hisce (dē his′) *vi.* **-hisced′**, **-hisc′ing** ⟦L *dehiscere* < *de-*, off + *hiscere*, to gape, inchoative of *hiare*: see HIATUS⟧ to split open along definite structural lines, as the seedpods of legumes, lilies, etc. do

de·his·cence (-his′əns) *n.* ⟦L *dehiscens*, prp. of *dehiscere*: see prec.⟧ a splitting open, as of a pod or anther, along definite structural lines —**de·his′cent** *adj.*

☆**de·horn** (dē hôrn′) *vt.* to remove the horns from (an animal)

Deh·ra Dun (der′ə do͞on′) city in N Uttar Pradesh, N India

de·hu·man·ize (dē hyo͞o′mə nīz′) *vt.* **-ized′**, **-iz′ing** to deprive of such human qualities as pity, kindness, individuality, or creativity; make inhuman or machinelike —**de·hu′man·i·za′tion** *n.*

de·hu·mid·i·fi·er (dē′hyo͞o mid′ə fī′ər, -yo͞o-) *n.* a device or appliance for dehumidifying indoor air

de·hu·mid·i·fy (dē′hyo͞o mid′ə fī′) *vt.* **-fied′**, **-fy′ing** to remove moisture from (the air, etc.) —**de′hu·mid′i·fi·ca′tion** *n.*

de·hy·drate (dē hī′drāt′) *vt.* **-drat′ed**, **-drat′ing** ⟦< DE- + Gr *hydōr*, water + -ATE¹⟧ to remove water from (a compound, substance, bodily tissues, etc.); dry [foods are *dehydrated* to preserve them for future use] —*vi.* to lose water; become dry —**de′hy·dra′tion** *n.* —**de·hy′dra′tor** *n.*

☆**de·hy·dro·gen·ase** (dē hī′drə jə nās′, dē′hī dräj′ə nās′) *n.* ⟦DE- + HYDROGEN + -ASE⟧ any oxidoreductase enzyme that acts as a catalyst, in chemical reactions involving oxidation, by the removal of hydrogen

de·hy·dro·gen·ate (dē hī′drə jə nāt′, dē′hī dräj′ə nāt′) *vt.* **-at′ed**, **-at′ing** to remove hydrogen from: also **de·hy′dro·gen·ize′** (-nīz′) **-ized′**, **-iz′ing** —**de′hy·dro·gen·a′tion** *n.*

de·hyp·no·tize (dē hip′nə tīz′) *vt.* **-tized′**, **-tiz′ing** to arouse from a hypnotic trance

de-ice (dē īs′) *vt.* **-iced′**, **-ic′ing** to melt ice from or keep free of ice —**de-ic′er** *n.*

de·i·cide (dē′ə sīd′) *n.* **1** ⟦LL(Ec) *deicida* < L *deus*, god + *caedere*, to kill: see -CIDE⟧ the killer of a god **2** ⟦< L *deus*, god + -CIDE⟧ the killing of a god

deic·tic (dīk′tik) *adj.* ⟦Gr *deiktikos* < *deiktos*, capable of proof < *deiknynai*, to prove; akin to L *dicere*: see DICTION⟧ **1** [Rare] directly pointing out or proving **2** *Linguis.* having the function of pointing out or specifying, and having its reference determined by its context [the words "this," "there," and "you" are *deictic*]

de·if·ic (dē if′ik) *adj.* ⟦LL *deificus*⟧ **1** deifying or making divine **2** godlike; divine

de·i·fi·ca·tion (dē′ə fi kā′shən) *n.* ⟦ME *deificacioun* < LL(Ec) *deificatio*⟧ **1** the act of deifying **2** the state of being deified **3** a deified embodiment

de·i·fy (dē′ə fī′) *vt.* **-fied′**, **-fy′ing** ⟦ME *deifien* < OFr *deifier* < LL(Ec) *deificare*, to make divine < L *deus*, god + *facere*, to make, DO¹⟧ **1** to make a god of; rank among the gods **2** to look upon or worship as a god **3** to glorify, exalt, or adore in an extreme way; idolize

deign (dān) *vi.* ⟦ME *deignen* < OFr *deignier* < L *dignare, dignari*, to deem worthy < *dignus*, worthy: see DIGNITY⟧ to condescend to do something thought to be slightly beneath one's dignity [the duchess *deigned* to shake my hand] —*vt.* to condescend to give [to *deign* no answer] —SYN. STOOP¹

deil (dēl) *n.* ⟦ME *deile*, var. of *devel*, DEVIL⟧ [Scot.] **1** the devil **2** a mischievous person

Dei·mos (dī′məs, dā′-) *n.* ⟦Gr *deimos*, lit., panic, personified as an attendant of Ares: see DIRE⟧ ☆the smaller of the two satellites of Mars: cf. PHOBOS

de·in·dus·tri·al·i·za·tion (dē′in dus′trē əl ə zā′shən) *n.* a decline or reduction in the number of heavy industries and in the importance of industrialism, as in a country or region

de·in·sti·tu·tion·al·ize (dē′in stə to͞o′shən ə līz′, -tyo͞o′-) *vt.* **-ized′**, **-iz′ing** to discharge (a patient) as from a mental hospital —**de′in·sti·tu′tion·al·i·za′tion** *n.*

de·i·on·ize (dē ī′ə nīz′) *vt.* **-ized′**, **-iz′ing** **1** to remove ions from (water) by the use of cation and anion exchangers **2** to restore (ionized gas) to its former condition

Deir·dre (dir′drə) *n.* ⟦OIr *Derdriu*, prob. akin to MIr *der*, young girl⟧ **1** a feminine name **2** *Celt. Legend* an Irish heroine who elopes to Scotland with her lover to avoid marrying the king: when the lover is treacherously killed, she commits suicide

de·ism (dē′iz′əm) *n.* ⟦Fr *déisme* < L *deus*, god⟧ belief in the existence of a God on purely rational grounds without reliance on revelation or authority; esp., the 17th- and 18th-cent. doctrine that God created the world and its natural laws, but takes no further part in its functioning

de·ist (dē′ist) *n.* ⟦Fr *déiste*⟧ a believer in deism —SYN. ATHEIST —**de·is′tic** *adj.*, **de·is′ti·cal** —**de·is′ti·cal·ly** *adv.*

de·i·ty (dē′ə tē) *n.* ⟦ME *deite* < OFr *deité* < LL(Ec) *deitas*, divinity (after L *divinitas*) < L *deus*, god < IE **deiwos*, god < base **dei-*, to gleam, shine > Sans *deva*, god, L *dies*, day, *divus*, god⟧ **1** the state of being a god; divine nature; godhood **2** *pl.* **-ties** a god or goddess —**the Deity** God

dé·jà vu (dā′zhə vo͞o′) ⟦Fr, already seen⟧ an uncanny feeling that one has been in this same place or had this same, specific experience before, although it is actually new to one

de·ject (dē jekt′, di-) *vt.* ⟦ME *dejecten* < L *dejectus*, pp. of *dejicere* < *de-*, down + *jacere*, to throw: see JET¹⟧ to cast down in spirit; dishearten; depress —*adj.* [Archaic] dejected

de·jec·ta (dē jek′tə) *pl.n.* ⟦ModL, neut. pl. of L *dejectus*: see prec.⟧ feces; excrement

de·ject·ed (dē jek′tid, di-) *adj.* in low spirits; depressed; disheartened —SYN. SAD —**de·ject′ed·ly** *adv.* —**de·ject′ed·ness** *n.*

de·jec·tion (dē jek′shən, di-) *n.* ⟦ME *dejeccioun* < L *dejectio*: see DEJECT⟧ **1** lowness of spirits; depression **2** *Med. a)* defecation *b)* feces; excrement

dé·jeu·ner (dā zhë nā′) *n.* ⟦Fr < OFr *desjeuner* < VL **disjejunare*: see DINE⟧ lunch

de ju·re (dē jo͝or′ē, dā-, di-) ⟦L⟧ by right or legal establishment [*de jure* government]: cf. DE FACTO

dek·a- (dek′ə) *combining form* ten; the factor 10^1: also, before a vowel, **dek-**

dek·a·gram (dek′ə gram′) *n.* ten grams, or one tenth of a hectogram (0.3527 ounce): abbrev. *dag*

De Kalb (də kalb′; *Ger* kälp′), **Jo·hann** (yō′hän′) (born *Johann Kalb*) 1721-80; Fr. general, born in Germany, who served in the Am. Revolutionary army: called *Baron de Kalb*

dek·a·li·ter (dek′ə lēt′ər) *n.* ten liters, or one tenth of a hectoliter (2.6418 gallons liquid measure or 1.135 pecks dry measure): abbrev. *dal*: Brit. sp. **dek′a·li′tre**

dek·a·me·ter (-mēt′ər) *n.* ten meters, or one tenth of a hectometer (32.808 feet): abbrev. *dam*: Brit. sp. **dek′a·me′tre**

deke (dēk) [Slang] *Sports n.* ⟦< DEC(OY) (*vt., vi.*)⟧ a quick, deceptive movement made so as to elude an opponent —*vi., vt.* **deked**, **dek′ing** or **deke′ing** to make such a movement against (an opponent)

Dek·ker (dek′ər), **Thomas** 1572?-1632?; Eng. playwright

dek·ko (dek′ō) *n.* ⟦Hindi *dekho*, pl. imper. of *dekhnā*, to see, akin to Sans *dṛś*, sight: see DARSHAN⟧ [Brit. Informal] a look; glance

de Koon·ing (də ko͞o′niŋ), **Wil·lem** (wil′əm) 1904-97; U.S. painter, born in the Netherlands

del *abbrev.* **1** delegate; delegation **2** delete **3** deliver

Del *abbrev.* Delaware

del. *abbrev.* ⟦L *delineavit*⟧ he (or she) drew it: formerly used after the artist's signature on a painting

De·la·croix (də lȧ krwȧ′), **(Ferdinand Victor) Eu·gène** (ö zhen′) 1798-1863; Fr. painter

Del·a·go·a Bay (del′ə gō′ə) inlet of the Indian Ocean, on the SE coast of Mozambique

de la Mare (del′ə mer′, -mar′), **Walter (John)** 1873-1956; Eng. poet & novelist

de·lam·i·nate (dē lam′ə nāt′) *vt., vi.* **-nat′ed, -nat′ing** to separate into layers

de·lam·i·na·tion (dē lam′ə nā′shən) *n.* **1** separation into layers **2** *Embryology* the formation of endoderm by the splitting of the blastoderm into two layers of cells

De·la·ney clause (*or* **amendment)** (də lā′nē) ⟦after U.S. Congressman J. J. *Delaney* (1901-87), its author⟧ an amendment to a 1958 Federal law, prohibiting the use of any food additive found to cause cancer in people or animals

De·la·roche (də lȧ rôsh′), **(Hippolyte) Paul** 1797-1856; Fr. painter

de·late (dē lāt′) *vt.* **-lat′ed, -lat′ing** ⟦< L *delatus*, pp. of *deferre*: see DEFER[2]⟧ **1** [Chiefly Scot.] to accuse or inform against **2** [Archaic] to announce; make public —**de·la′tion** *n.* —**de·la′tor** *n.*

De·lau·nay (də lō nā′), **Ro·bert** (rô ber′) 1885-1941; Fr. painter

De·la·vigne (də lȧ vēn′y′), **(Jean François) Cas·i·mir** (kȧ zē mir′) 1793-1843; Fr. poet & playwright

Del·a·ware[1] (del′ə wer′, -war′) *n.* ⟦after the DELAWARE[2] River⟧ **1** *pl.* **-wares′** or **-ware′** a member of any of a group of North American Indian peoples that lived in the Delaware River valley, now living mainly in Oklahoma and Ontario **2** the Algonquian language of these peoples **3** a small, sweet, reddish American grape

Del·a·ware[2] (del′ə wer′, -war′) ⟦after DE LA WARR, Baron⟧ **1** state of the E U.S., on the Atlantic: one of the 13 original states; 1,954 sq mi (5,060 sq km); cap. Dover: abbrev. *DE* or *Del* **2** river flowing from the Pennsylvania-New York and Pennsylvania-New Jersey borders into Delaware Bay: *c.* 280 mi (451 km)

Del·a·war·e·an (-wer′ē ən, -war′-) *adj.* of the state of Delaware: usually used in the predicate —*n.* a person born or living in Delaware

Delaware Bay ⟦after fol.⟧ estuary of the Delaware River, & an inlet of the Atlantic, between SW N.J. and E Del.: *c.* 55 mi (89 km) long

De La Warr (del′ə wer′, -war′), Baron (*Thomas West*) 1577-1618; 1st Eng. colonial governor of Va. (1610-11): called *Lord Delaware*

de·lay (dē lā′, di-) *vt.* ⟦ME *delaien* < OFr *delaier* < *de-*, intens. + *laier*, to leave, let, altered (? after conjugation of *faire*) < *laissier* < L *laxare*: see RELAX⟧ **1** to put off to a future time; postpone **2** to make late; slow up; detain —*vi.* to stop for a while; linger —*n.* **1** a delaying or being delayed **2** the period of time for which something is delayed —**de·lay′er** *n.*

delayed neutron a neutron emitted from short half-life products formed as a result of nuclear fission: important in the control of nuclear reactors

delaying action maneuvers to cover a retreat, gain time, etc.

de·le (dē′lē) *vt.* **-led, -le·ing** ⟦L, imper. sing. of *delere*: see DELETE⟧ *Printing* to take out (a letter, word, etc.); delete: usually in the imperative and expressed by the mark (♆), indicating the matter to be deleted —*n.* this mark

de·lec·ta·ble (di lek′tə bəl) *adj.* ⟦ME & OFr < L *delectabilis* < *delectare*: see DELIGHT⟧ very pleasing; delightful; now, esp., pleasing to the taste; delicious; luscious —**de·lec′ta·bil′i·ty** *n.* —**de·lec′ta·bly** *adv.*

de·lec·ta·tion (dē′lek tā′shən, di lek′-, del′ək-) *n.* ⟦ME *delectacioun* < OFr *delectation* < L *delectatio* < *delectare*: see DELIGHT⟧ delight; enjoyment; entertainment

del·e·ga·cy (del′ə gə sē) *n.* **1** a delegating or being delegated **2** *pl.* **-cies** a delegation

del·e·gate (del′ə git; *for v.*, -gāt′) *n.* ⟦ME *delegat* < ML *delegatus* < pp. of L *delegare*, to send from one place to another, appoint, assign < *de-*, from + *legare*, to send: see LEGATE⟧ **1** a person authorized or sent to speak and act for others; representative, as at a convention ☆**2** [Historical] a representative of a U.S. Territory in the House of Representatives, with the right to speak but not to vote ☆**3** a member of a House of Delegates —*vt.* **-gat′ed, -gat′ing 1** to send or appoint as a representative or deputy **2** to entrust (authority, power, etc.) to a person acting as one's agent or representative

del·e·ga·tion (del′ə gā′shən) *n.* ⟦L *delegatio*⟧ **1** a delegating or being delegated **2** a body of delegates

de·le·git·i·mize (dē lə jit′ə mīz′) *vt.* **-mized′, -miz′ing** to diminish or undermine the legitimacy or authority of; discredit, devalue, etc. —**de·le·git′i·mi·za′tion** (-mə zā′shən, -mī′-) *n.*

de·lete (dē lēt′, di-) *vt.* **-let′ed, -let′ing** ⟦< L *deletus*, pp. of *delere*, to blot out, destroy < *de-*, from + base of *linere*, to daub, rub over (writing on a wax table with the blunt end of the style) < IE base **lei-*, viscous, smooth > LIME[1]⟧ to take out (a printed or written letter, word, etc.); cross out —*SYN.* ERASE

del·e·te·ri·ous (del′ə tir′ē əs) *adj.* ⟦Gr *dēlētērios* < *dēlētēr*, a destroyer < *dēleisthai*, to injure < IE base **del-*, to split⟧ harmful to health or well-being; injurious —*SYN.* PERNICIOUS —**del′e·te′ri·ous·ly** *adv.* —**del′e·te′ri·ous·ness** *n.*

de·le·tion (dē lē′shən, di-) *n.* ⟦L *deletio*⟧ **1** a deleting or being deleted **2** a deleted word, passage, etc. **3** *Genetics* the absence of some normal portion of a chromosome

de·lev·er·age (dē lev′ər ij, -lev′rij) *vi., vt.* **-aged, -ag·ing** *Finance* **1** to reduce (the amount of one's debt) **2** to reduce the amount leveraged on (an asset, etc.)

Delft (delft) city in W Netherlands

delft·ware (delft′wer′) *n.* **1** glazed earthenware, usually blue and white, which originated in Delft **2** any similar ware Also **delft** or **delf** (delf)

Del·hi (del′ē) **1** territory in N India, including the cities of Delhi & New Delhi: 573 sq mi (1,483 sq km) **2** city in this territory, on the Jumna River: see also NEW DELHI

☆**del·i** (del′ē) *n. short for* DELICATESSEN

Del·ia (dēl′yə) *n.* ⟦L, fem of *Delius*, of Delos⟧ a feminine name

De·li·an (dē′lē ən) *adj.* of Delos

de·lib·er·ate (di lib′ər it; *for v.*, -āt′) *adj.* ⟦ME < L *deliberatus*, pp. of *deliberare*, to consider, weigh well < *de-*, intens. + *librare*, to weigh < *libra*, a scales⟧ **1** carefully thought out and formed, or done on purpose; premeditated **2** careful in considering, judging, or deciding; not rash or hasty **3** unhurried and methodical [take *deliberate* aim] —*vi.* **-at′ed, -at′ing** to think or consider carefully and fully; esp., to consider reasons for and against a thing in order to make up one's mind [a jury *deliberates*] —*vt.* to consider carefully —*SYN.* THINK[1], VOLUNTARY —**de·lib′er·ate·ly** *adv.* —**de·lib′er·ate·ness** *n.* —**de·lib′er·a′tor** *n.*

de·lib·er·a·tion (di lib′ər ā′shən) *n.* ⟦ME *deliberacioun* < OFr *deliberation* < L *deliberatio*⟧ **1** a deliberating, or considering carefully **2** [*often pl.*] consideration and discussion of alternatives before reaching a decision [the *deliberations* of statesmen] **3** the quality of being deliberate; carefulness; slowness

de·lib·er·a·tive (di lib′ər āt′iv, -ər ə tiv) *adj.* ⟦L *deliberativus*⟧ **1** of or for deliberating [a *deliberative* assembly] **2** characterized by or resulting from deliberation —**de·lib′er·a′tive·ly** *adv.*

De·libes (də lēb′), **(Clément Philibert) Lé·o** (lā ō′) 1836-91; Fr. composer

del·i·ca·cy (del′i kə sē) *n.* ⟦ME *delicacie* < ML *delicacia* < L *delicatus*: see fol.⟧ **1** the quality of being delicate as in taste, odor, or texture **2** fragile beauty or graceful slightness, softness, etc.; fineness [the *delicacy* of a petal, of spun glass, or of a child's face] **3** weakness of constitution or health; frailty **4** the quality or condition of needing careful and deft handling [negotiations of great *delicacy*] **5** fineness of feeling, observation, or appreciation [*delicacy* of musical taste] **6** sensitiveness of response [the *delicacy* of a compass] **7** fineness of touch, skill, etc. **8** a fine regard for the feelings of others **9** a sensitive or, sometimes, finicky distaste for what is considered improper or offensive **10** *pl.* **-cies** a choice food [caviar and other *delicacies*] **11** [Obs.] luxuriousness

del·i·cate (del′i kit) *adj.* ⟦ME *delicat* < L *delicatus*, giving pleasure, delightful < **delicare*, for OL *delicere*, to allure, entice < *de-*, intens. + *lacere*: see DELIGHT⟧ **1** pleasing in its lightness, mildness, subtlety, etc. [a *delicate* flavor, odor, or color] **2** beautifully fine in texture, quality, or workmanship [*delicate* linen, *delicate* skin] **3** slight and subtle [a *delicate* difference] **4** easily damaged, spoiled, or disordered [a *delicate* vase, a *delicate* stomach] **5** frail in health [a *delicate* child] **6** *a)* needing careful handling, tact, etc. [a *delicate* situation] *b)* showing tact, consideration, etc. **7** finely sensitive in feeling, understanding, discriminating, or responding [a *delicate* ear for music, a *delicate* gauge] **8** finely skilled **9** having or showing a sensitive or, sometimes, finicky distaste for what is considered offensive or improper —*n.* [Archaic] a delicacy; dainty —**del′i·cate·ly** *adv.* —**del′i·cate·ness** *n.*

SYN.—**delicate** and **dainty** are both used to describe things that are pleasing to highly refined tastes or sensibilities, **delicate** implying fragility, subtlety, or fineness, and **dainty**, smallness, fastidiousness, or gracefulness; **exquisite** is applied to something so delicately wrought or subtly refined as to be appreciated by only the most keenly discriminating or fastidious —*ANT.* **gross, crude, coarse**

☆**del·i·ca·tes·sen** (del′i kə tes′ən) *n.* ⟦Ger *delikatessen*, derived by folk etym. < *delikat* (< Fr *délicat*) + *essen*, food, but actually pl. of *delikatesse* < Fr *délicatesse*, delicacy (< *délicat*: see prec.) assoc. with It *delicatezza*, ult. of same orig.⟧ **1** prepared cooked meats, smoked fish, cheeses, salads, relishes, etc., collectively **2** a shop where such foods are sold

de·li·cious (di lish′əs) *adj.* ⟦ME < OFr *delicieus* < L *deliciosus* < *deliciae*, delight < OL *delicere*: see DELICATE⟧ **1** very enjoyable; delightful [a *delicious* bit of gossip] **2** very pleasing to the senses, esp. to taste or smell —☆*n.* [**D-**] a variety of sweet, chiefly red or yellow winter apple —**de·li′cious·ly** *adv.* —**de·li′cious·ness** *n.*

de·lict (di likt′) *n.* ⟦L *delictum*, a fault < pp. of *delinquere*: see DELINQUENCY⟧ *Law* an offense; wrong or injury

de·light (di līt′) *vt.* ⟦ME *deliten* < OFr *delitier* < L *delectare*, to delight, freq. of OL *delicere* < *de-*, from + *lacere*, to entice, lit., to ensnare < IE base **lek-*, twig, snare > OE *læl*, whip: sp. infl. by LIGHT[2]⟧ to give great joy or pleasure to —*vi.* **1** to give great joy or pleasure **2** to be highly pleased; rejoice: usually with *in* or an infinitive —*n.* ⟦ME & OFr *delit* < the v.⟧ **1** great joy or pleasure **2** something giving great joy or pleasure **3** [Old Poet.] the power of pleasing —*SYN.* PLEASURE

de·light·ed (-id) *adj.* **1** highly pleased; happy **2** [Obs.] delightful —**de·light′ed·ly** *adv.*

de·light·ful (-fəl) *adj.* giving delight; very pleasing; charming: also [Archaic] **de·light′some** (-səm) —**de·light′ful·ly** *adv.* —**de·light′ful·ness** *n.*

De·li·lah (di lī′lə) *n.* ⟦Heb *delīlāh*, lit., delicate⟧ **1** *Bible* the lover of Samson, who betrayed him to the Philistines: Judg. 16 **2** a seductive, treacherous woman; temptress

de·lim·it (dē lim′it) *vt.* ⟦Fr *délimiter* < L *delimitare* < *de-*, from + *limitare*⟧ to set the limits or boundaries of: also **de·lim′i·tate′** (-ə tāt′) **-tat′ed, -tat′ing** —**de·lim′i·ta′tion** *n.* —**de·lim′i·ta′tive** *adj.*

de·lim·it·er (dē lim′it ər) *n. Comput.* a letter, symbol, etc. used to set off one string of characters or item of data from another

de·lin·e·ate (di lin′ē āt′) *vt.* **-at′ed, -at′ing** ⟦< L *delineatus*, pp. of *delineare*, to mark out, sketch < *de-*, from + *linea*, LINE[2]⟧ **1** to trace the outline of; sketch out **2** to draw; depict **3** to depict in words; describe —**de·lin′e·a′tion** *n.* —**de·lin′e·a′tive** *adj.* —**de·lin′e·a′tor** *n.*

de·lin·quen·cy (di liŋ′kwən sē) *n., pl.* **-cies** ⟦LL *delinquentia* < L *delinquens*, prp. of *delinquere*, to leave undone, commit a fault < *de-*, from + *linquere*, to leave < IE base **leikw-*, to leave > Gr *leipein*, to leave, OE *lœn*, LOAN⟧ **1** failure or neglect to do what duty or law requires ☆**2** an overdue debt, tax, etc. **3** a fault: misdeed ☆**4** behavior, esp. by the young, that is antisocial or in violation of the law: see JUVENILE DELINQUENCY

de·lin·quent (-kwənt) *adj.* ⟦L *delinquens*: see prec.⟧ **1** failing or neglecting to do what duty or law requires ☆**2** past the time for payment; overdue *[delinquent taxes]* —*n.* a delinquent person; esp., a juvenile delinquent —**de·lin′quent·ly** *adv.*

del·i·quesce (del′i kwes′) *vi.* **-quesced′, -quesc′ing** ⟦L *deliquescere* < *de-*, from + *liquescere*, to melt, inchoative of *liquere*, to be LIQUID⟧ **1** to melt away **2** *Biol. a)* to melt away in the course of growth or decay: said of some of the parts of certain fungi *b)* to branch into many fine divisions: said of the veins of many leaves **3** *Chem.* to become liquid by absorbing moisture from the air: cf. HYGROSCOPIC —**del′i·ques′cence** *n.* —**del′i·ques′cent** *adj.*

de·lir·i·ous (di lir′ē əs) *adj.* ⟦L *deliriosus*: see fol. & -OUS⟧ **1** in a state of delirium; raving incoherently **2** of, characteristic of, or caused by delirium **3** wildly excited *[delirious* with joy*]* —**de·lir′i·ous·ly** *adv.* —**de·lir′i·ous·ness** *n.*

de·lir·i·um (di lir′ē əm) *n., pl.* **-i·ums** or **-i·a** (-ə) ⟦L, madness < *delirare*, to rave, lit., to turn the furrow awry in plowing < *de-*, from + *lira*, a line, furrow: see LIST[1]⟧ **1** a temporary state of extreme mental excitement, marked by restlessness, confused speech, and hallucinations: it sometimes occurs during a fever or in some forms of insanity **2** uncontrollably wild excitement or emotion *[a delirium* of joy*]* —***SYN.*** MANIA

delirium tre·mens (trē′mənz, trem′ənz) ⟦ModL (1813), lit., trembling delirium⟧ a violent delirium resulting chiefly from excessive drinking of alcoholic liquor and characterized by sweating, trembling, anxiety, and frightening hallucinations

de·lish (də lish′) *adj.* [Slang] *short for* DELICIOUS

de·list (dē list′) *vt.* to remove (a name or item) from a list, directory, or catalog; specif., to remove (a company's stock) from the register of stocks approved for trading on an exchange

De·li·us (dē′lē əs, dēl′yəs), **Frederick** 1862-1934; Eng. composer

de·liv·er (di liv′ər) *vt.* ⟦ME *delivren* < OFr *délivrer* < VL *deliberare*, to liberate < *de-*, intens. + *liberare*, to LIBERATE⟧ **1** to set free or save from evil, danger, or restraint; liberate *[delivered* from bondage*]* **2** to assist (a female) at the birth of (offspring) *[*to *deliver* a woman of twins, to *deliver* a baby*]* **3** to give forth, or express, in words; make (a speech or pronouncement); utter **4** to give or hand over; transfer **5** to carry to and leave at the proper place or places; distribute *[deliver* the mail*]* **6** to give or send forth; discharge; emit *[*the oil well *delivered* 20 barrels a day*]* **7** to strike (a blow) **8** to throw or toss *[*the pitcher *delivered* a curve*]* ☆**9** [Informal] to cause (votes, a political delegation, etc.) to go to the support of a particular candidate or cause —*vi.* **1** to give birth to a child **2** to make deliveries, as of merchandise ☆**3** to do, give, produce, etc. something expected or promised; come through *[*our new food processor *delivers* on all its promises*]* —***SYN.*** RESCUE —**be delivered of** to give birth to —**deliver oneself of** to express; utter —**de·liv′er·er** *n.*

de·liv·er·a·ble (di liv′ər ə bəl) *adj.* capable of being delivered —*n.* something to be supplied, as to a customer, as part of the process of carrying out a project, developing a product or application, etc.

de·liv·er·ance (di liv′ər əns) *n.* ⟦ME *deliveraunce*: see DELIVER & -ANCE⟧ **1** a setting free; rescue or release **2** the fact or state of being freed **3** an opinion, judgment, etc. formally or publicly expressed

de·liv·er·y (di liv′ər ē) *n., pl.* **-er·ies** ⟦ME *deliveri* < OFr *delivré*, pp. of *délivrer*: see DELIVER⟧ **1** a giving or handing over; transfer **2** a distributing, as of goods or mail **3** a giving birth; childbirth **4** any giving or sending forth **5** the act or manner of giving a speech, striking a blow, throwing a ball, etc. **6** something delivered or to be delivered, as mail, goods, a pitched ball, etc. **7** [Now Rare] a setting free, or rescuing **8** *Law a)* the irrevocable transfer of a deed or other instrument of conveyance *b)* the transfer of goods or interest in goods from one person to another

☆**de·liv·er·y·man** (-man′, -mən) *n., pl.* **-men′** (-men′, -mən) a man whose work is delivering goods to purchasers

dell (del) *n.* ⟦ME & OE *del* < IE base **dhel-*, cavity, hollow > DALE, Welsh *dol*, Du *dal*, Ger *tal*, valley⟧ a small, secluded valley or glen, usually a wooded one

del·la Rob·bia (del′lä rôb′byä; *E* del′ə rō′bē ə), **Lu·ca** (lo͞o′kä) 1400?-82; Florentine sculptor & worker in enameled terra cotta: member of a family of artists

☆**dells** (delz) *pl.n. var. of* DALLES

Del·mar·va Peninsula (del mär′və) ⟦< DEL(AWARE)[2] + MAR(YLAND) + V(IRGINI)A[2]⟧ peninsula in the E U.S., between Chesapeake Bay on the west & Delaware Bay & the Atlantic on the east, consisting of Del. & parts of Md. & Va.: *c.* 180 mi (290 km) long

Del·mon·i·co steak (del män′ə kō) ⟦after the *Delmonico* restaurants in New York City, after L. *Delmonico* (1813-81), U.S. restaurateur⟧ *[also* **d-***]* CLUB STEAK

De·lorme or **de l'Orme** (də lôrm′), **Phi·li·bert** (fē lē ber′) 1515-70; Fr. Renaissance architect

De·los (dē′läs) small island of the Cyclades in the Aegean: legendary birthplace of Artemis and Apollo

de·louse (dē lous′, -louz′) *vt.* **-loused′, -lous′ing** to rid of lice —**de·lous′er** *n.*

Del·phi (del′fī) town in ancient Phocis, on the slopes of Mount Parnassus: seat of the famous ancient oracle of Apollo (**Delphic oracle**)

Del·phic (del′fik) *adj.* **1** of Delphi **2** designating or of the oracle of Apollo at Delphi in ancient times **3** obscure in meaning; ambiguous; oracular Also **Del′phi·an** (-fē ən)

del·phi·nine (del′fə nēn′, -nin) *n.* ⟦fol. + -INE[3]⟧ a poisonous, white, crystalline alkaloid, $C_{33}H_{45}NO_9$, found in the seeds of certain larkspurs

del·phin·i·um (del fin′ē əm) *n.* ⟦ModL < Gr *delphinion*, larkspur < Gr *delphis, delphin*, DOLPHIN: from some resemblance of the nectary to a dolphin⟧ any of a genus (*Delphinium*) of plants of the buttercup family, bearing spikes of spurred, irregular flowers, usually blue, on tall stalks: several species are poisonous

Del·phi·nus (del fī′nəs) *n.* ⟦L, lit., dolphin: see prec.⟧ a small N constellation between Pegasus and Aquila; the Dolphin

Del·sarte system (del särt′) ⟦after François *Delsarte* (1811-71), Fr teacher of singing & dramatics⟧ a system of calisthenics combined with singing, declamation, and dancing to develop bodily grace and poise

del·ta (del′tə) *n.* ⟦L < Gr *delta*, of Sem orig., as in Heb *dāleth*, 4th letter of the alphabet, lit., door⟧ **1** the fourth letter of the Greek alphabet (Δ, δ) **2** something in the shape of a delta (Δ); specif., a tract of flat land, usually triangular, formed by deposits of soil and sand at the mouth of a large river —*adj.* **1** *[usually* **D-***]* of, in, or from THE DELTA (see phrase below) *[Delta* blues*]* **2** *Chem. see* ALPHA —**the Delta** low-lying region in NW Miss., extending eastward from the Mississippi River —**del·ta·ic** (del tā′ik) *adj.*

delta ray high-energy electrons ejected from atoms by primary ionizing particles passing through matter

delta wave any of the slowest electrical brain waves, having frequencies less than four hertz and indicating, in adults, deep sleep or brain disease: also **delta rhythm**

delta wing the triangular structure of certain jet aircraft with sweptback wings —**del′ta-wing′** *adj.*, **del′ta-winged′**

☆**del·ti·ol·o·gy** (del′tē äl′ə jē) *n.* ⟦< Gr *deltion* (dim. of *deltos*, tablet for writing) + -OLOGY⟧ the collection and study of postcards, usually as a hobby —**del′ti·ol′o·gist** *n.*

del·toid (del′toid′) *adj.* ⟦Gr *deltoeidēs*: see DELTA & -OID⟧ **1** shaped like a delta; triangular **2** designating or of a large, triangular muscle which covers the shoulder and raises the arm away from the side —*n.* the deltoid muscle

delts (delts) *pl.n.* [Slang] deltoid muscles, esp. of a bodybuilder or weight lifter

de·lude (di lo͞od′) *vt.* **-lud′ed, -lud′ing** ⟦ME *deluden* < L *deludere* < *de-*, from + *ludere*, to play: see LUDICROUS⟧ **1** to fool, as by false promises or wrong notions; mislead; deceive; trick **2** [Obs.] to elude or frustrate —***SYN.*** DECEIVE

del·uge (del′yo͞oj′) *n.* ⟦ME < OFr < L *diluvium* < *dis*, off, from + *luere*, var. of *lavare*, to LAVE⟧ **1** a great flood **2** a heavy rainfall **3** an overwhelming, floodlike rush of anything *[a deluge* of visitors*]* —*vt.* **-uged′, -ug′ing** **1** to flood; inundate **2** to overwhelm as with a flood —**the Deluge** *Bible* the great flood in Noah's time: Gen. 7

de·lu·sion (di lo͞o′zhən) *n.* ⟦ME *delusioun* < LL *delusio* < *delusus*, pp. of *deludere*⟧ **1** a deluding or being deluded **2** a false belief or opinion **3** *Psychiatry* a false, persistent belief maintained in spite of evidence to the contrary —**de·lu′sion·al** *adj.*

SYN.—**delusion** implies belief in something that is contrary to fact or reality, resulting from deception, a misconception, or a mental disorder *[*to have *delusions* of grandeur*]*; **illusion** suggests the false perception or interpretation of something that has objective existence *[*perspective in drawing gives the *illusion* of depth*]*; **hallucination** implies the apparent perception, in nervous or mental disorder, of something external that is actually not present; **mirage** refers to an optical illusion caused by atmospheric conditions, and, in figurative use, implies an unrealizable hope or aspiration

de·lu·sive (di lo͞os′iv) *adj.* ⟦L *delusus* (see prec.) + -IVE⟧ **1** tending to delude; misleading **2** of or like a delusion; unreal Also **de·lu′so·ry** (-lo͞o′sə rē) —**de·lu′sive·ly** *adv.* —**de·lu′sive·ness** *n.*

de·luxe (di luks′, -lo͝oks′) *adj.* ⟦Fr, lit., of luxury⟧ of extra fine quality; luxurious; sumptuous; elegant —*adv.* in a deluxe manner

delve (delv) *vi.* **delved, delv′ing** ⟦ME *delven* < OE *delfan*, to dig, akin to OHG *(bi)telban*, to bury, Du *delven* < IE base **dhelbh-*, to dig out > Czech *dlubati*, to hollow out⟧ **1** [Now Dial., Chiefly Brit.] to dig with a spade **2** to investigate for information; search (*into* books, the past, etc.) —*vt.* [Now Dial., Chiefly Brit.] to dig or turn up (ground) —*n.* [Obs.] a den or pit dug out —**delv′er** *n.*

Dem *abbrev.* **1** Democrat **2** Democratic

de·mag·net·ize (dē mag′nə tīz′) *vt.* **-ized′, -iz′ing** to reduce or remove magnetism in or the magnetic properties of —**de·mag′net·i·za′tion** *n.* —**de·mag′net·iz′er** *n.*

dem·a·gog·ic (dem′ə gäj′ik, -gäg′ik, -gō′jik) *adj.* ⟦Gr *dēmagōgikos:* see fol.⟧ of, like, or characteristic of a demagogue or demagogy: also **dem′a·gog′i·cal** —**dem′a·gog′i·cal·ly** *adv.*

dem·a·gogue or **dem·a·gog** (dem′ə gäg′, -gôg′) *n.* ⟦< Gr *dēmagōgos*, leader of the people < *dēmos*, the people (see DEMOCRACY) + *agōgos*, leader < *agein*, to lead: see ACT[1]⟧ **1** [Obs.] a leader of the common people **2** a person who tries to stir up the people by appeals to emotion, prejudice, etc. in order to win them over quickly and so gain power —*vi.* **-gogued′** or **-goged′**, **-gogu′ing** or **-gog′ing** to behave as a demagogue —*vt.* to seize upon and use (an issue, event, etc.) in the inflammatory manner of a demagogue so as to sway public opinion

dem·a·gog·y (dem′ə gä′jē, -gäg′ē, -gō′jē) *n.* ⟦Gr *dēmagōgia*, control of the people⟧ the methods or practices of a demagogue: also ☆**dem′a·gogu′er·y** (-gäg′ər ē)

de·mand (di mand′, -mänd′) *vt.* ⟦ME *demaunden* < OFr *demander*, to demand < L *demandare*, to give in charge < *de-*, away, from + *mandare*, to entrust: see MANDATE⟧ **1** to ask for boldly or urgently **2** to ask for as a right or with authority **3** to order to appear; summon **4** to ask to know or be informed of **5** to call for as necessary; require; need *[the work demands patience]* **6** *Law* to ask relief in court for (what is due one) —*vi.* to make a demand —*n.* **1** the act of demanding **2** a thing demanded **3** a strong or authoritative request **4** an urgent requirement or claim **5** [Obs.] a question; query **6** *Econ.* the desire for a commodity together with ability to pay for it; also, the amount people are ready and able to buy at a certain price: opposed to SUPPLY[1] (*n.* 7) **7** *Law* a peremptory claim which presupposes no doubt of the claimant's rights —**in demand** wanted or sought —**on demand** when presented for payment

SYN.—**demand** implies a calling for as due or necessary, connoting a peremptory exercise of authority or an imperative need *[to demand obedience]*; **claim** implies a demanding of something as allegedly belonging to one *[to claim a throne]*; **require** suggests a pressing need, often one inherent in the nature of a thing, or the binding power of rules or laws *[aliens are required to register]*; **exact** implies a demanding and the enforcing of the demand at the same time *[an exacting foreman]*

de·mand·ant (di man′dənt) *n. Law* PLAINTIFF

demand bill a bill payable on demand

☆**demand deposit** a bank deposit from which withdrawals may be made on demand, typically by writing checks

de·mand·ing (di man′diŋ) *adj.* making difficult or irksome demands on a person's resources, patience, energy, etc. —**de·mand′ing·ly** *adv.*

demand loan CALL LOAN (sense 1)

demand note a promissory note payable on demand

de·mand-pull (di mand′pool′) *adj.* designating or having to do with a form of inflation in which prices are driven up by an excess demand for goods and services, relative to their supply

de·man·toid (di man′toid′) *n.* ⟦Ger < *demant*, diamond (< MHG *diemant* < OFr *diamant*, DIAMOND) + *-oid*, -OID⟧ a transparent, green variety of andradite, used as a semiprecious gem

de·mar·cate (dē mär′kāt, di-, dē′mär kāt′) *vt.* **-cat·ed**, **-cat·ing** ⟦backform. < fol.⟧ **1** to set or mark the limits of; delimit **2** to mark the difference between; distinguish; separate Also **de·mark′** (-märk′)

de·mar·ca·tion (dē′mär kā′shən) *n.* ⟦Sp *demarcación* (in *línea de demarcación*, 1493) < *de-* (L *de*), from + *marcar*, to mark boundaries < Gmc **marka*, a boundary, MARK[1]⟧ **1** the act of setting and marking limits or boundaries **2** a limit or boundary **3** a separation or distinction

dé·marche (dā märsh′) *n.* ⟦Fr < *démarcher* < OFr *demarchier*, orig., to trample under foot: see DE- & MARCH[1]⟧ **1** a line of action; move or countermove; maneuver, as a protest or warning, in diplomatic relations **2** a public action in the form of a protest to the government or those in power

de·ma·te·ri·al·ize (dē′mə tir′ē ə līz′) *vi., vt.* **-ized′**, **-iz′ing** to lose or cause to lose material form

Dem·a·vend (dem′ə vend′) *var. of* DAMAVAND

deme (dēm) *n.* ⟦Gr *dēmos*, deme, people, district: see DEMOCRACY⟧ **1** any of the more than 100 districts into which ancient Attica was divided **2** *Biol.* a particular interbreeding population within a species

de·mean[1] (dē mēn′, di-) *vt.* ⟦DE- + MEAN[2], after DEBASE⟧ to lower in status or character; degrade; humble *[to demean oneself by taking a bribe]*

de·mean[2] (dē mēn′, di-) *vt.* ⟦see fol.⟧ to behave, conduct, or comport (oneself) —*SYN.* BEHAVE

de·mean·or (di mēn′ər) *n.* ⟦ME *demenure* < *demenen*, to rule, govern oneself, behave < OFr *demener*, to lead < *de-* (L *de*), from + *mener*, to lead < LL *minare*, to drive (cattle) < L *minari*, to threaten: see MENACE⟧ outward behavior; conduct; deportment: Brit. sp. **de·mean′our** —*SYN.* BEARING

de·ment (dē ment′) *vt.* ⟦< L *dementare* < *demens* (gen. *dementis*), mad, out of one's mind < *de-*, out from + *mens*, MIND⟧ [Archaic] to make insane

de·ment·ed (dē ment′id, di-) *adj.* ⟦pp. of prec.⟧ mentally deranged; insane; mad —**de·ment′ed·ly** *adv.*

de·men·tia (di men′shə) *n.* ⟦L, insanity < *demens*: see DEMENT⟧ **1** [Obs.] insanity; madness **2** *Psychiatry* a disorder of the mind affecting perception, memory, and judgment, characterized by reduced ability to remember, control muscular movements, recognize familiar objects and sounds, etc. —*SYN.* INSANITY

dementia prae·cox (prē′käks′) ⟦ModL: see PRECOCIOUS & prec.⟧ *a former term for* SCHIZOPHRENIA

Dem·e·rar·a (sugar) (dem′ə rar′ə, -rer′ə) ⟦after *Demerara*, region of Guyana, original source of this type of sugar⟧ [*also* **d- s-**] [Brit.] a coarse, light-brown cane sugar

de·mer·it (dē mer′it, di-) *n.* ⟦ME & OFr *demerite* < ML *demeritum*, fault < pp. of *demerere*, to forfeit, not merit, with meaning altered (*de-* taken in negative sense) < L, to merit < *de-*, intens. + *merere*, to deserve⟧ **1** a quality deserving blame; fault; defect **2** lack of merit ☆**3** a mark recorded against a student, trainee, etc. for poor conduct or work

☆**Dem·e·rol** (dem′ər ôl′, -ōl′) *trademark for* MEPERIDINE

de·mer·sal (dē mur′səl) *adj.* ⟦< L *demersus*, pp. of *demergere*, to submerge < *de-*, DE- + *mergere*, to sink (see MERGE) + -AL⟧ found on or near the bottom of a sea, lake, etc.; benthic

de·mesne (di mān′; *also*, -mēn′) *n.* ⟦ME & OFr *demeine* < L *dominium* (see DOMAIN); sp. altered by assoc. with OFr *mesnee*, household < L *mansio*: see MANSION⟧ **1** *Law* possession (of real estate) in one's own right **2** [Historical] the land or estate belonging to a lord and not rented or let but kept in his hands **3** the land around a mansion; lands of an estate **4** a region or domain: also used fig.

De·me·ter (di mēt′ər) *n.* ⟦Gr *Dēmētēr* < Gr(Doric) *Damatēr* < *da-* (? name for the earth) + *matēr*, MOTHER[1]⟧ *Gr. Myth.* the goddess of agriculture and fertility: identified with the Roman Ceres

dem·i- (dem′i, -ə, -ē) ⟦ME & OFr < *demi*, half < L *dimidius*, half, back-form. < *dimidiatus*, halved, ult. < *dis-*, apart + *medius*, middle⟧ *prefix* **1** half *[demivolt]* **2** less than usual in size, power, etc. *[demigod]*

dem·i-glace (dem′ē glas′, -gläs′) *n.* ⟦Fr, lit., half-glaze⟧ a rich brown sauce made from beef stock that is cooked slowly with wine until reduced to half its original volume: it is served with meat or used as a base for other sauces

dem·i·god (dem′i gäd′) *n.* **1** *Myth.* *a)* a lesser god; minor deity *b)* the offspring of a human being and a god or goddess **2** a godlike person

dem·i·john (-jän′) *n.* ⟦Fr *dame-jeanne*, demijohn, lit., Dame Jeanne: prob. orig. a fanciful name for the bottle⟧ a large bottle of glass or earthenware, with a narrow neck and a wicker casing

de·mil·i·ta·rize (dē mil′ə tə rīz′) *vt.* **-rized′**, **-riz′ing** **1** to free from organized military control **2** to take away the military power or character of —**de·mil′i·ta·ri·za′tion** *n.*

De Mille (də mil′) **1 Agnes (George)** 1905-93; U.S. dancer & choreographer: niece of Cecil **2 Cecil B(lount)** 1881-1959; U.S. film producer & director

dem·i·mon·daine (dem′i män dān′) *n.* ⟦Fr⟧ a woman of the demimonde

dem·i·monde (dem′i mänd′) *n.* ⟦Fr < *demi-* (see DEMI-) + *monde*, world, society < L *mundus*, world⟧ **1** the class of women who have lost social standing because of sexual promiscuity **2** a demimondaine **3** prostitutes as a group **4** any group whose activities are ethically questionable

de·min·er·al·ize (dē min′ər ə līz′) *vt.* **-ized′**, **-iz′ing** **1** to cause the loss of minerals from (bones or teeth) **2** to remove minerals, as salt, from (water) —**de·min′er·al·i·za′tion** *n.*

dem·i·rep (dem′i rep′) *n.* ⟦DEMI- + REP(UTATION)⟧ a woman of poor reputation, suspected of sexual promiscuity

de·mise (dē mīz′, di-) *n.* ⟦Fr *démise*, fem. pp. of OFr *démettre*, to dismiss, put away < L *demittere*: see DEMIT⟧ **1** *Law* a transfer of an estate by lease, esp. for a fixed period **2** the transfer of sovereignty by death or abdication **3** a ceasing to exist; death —*vt.* **-mised′**, **-mis′ing** **1** to grant or transfer (an estate) by lease, esp. for a fixed period **2** to transfer (sovereignty) by death or abdication

dem·i·sem·i·qua·ver (dem′i sem′i kwā′vər) *n.* [Chiefly Brit.] THIRTY-SECOND NOTE

de·mit (dē mit′, di-) *vt.* **-mit′ted**, **-mit′ting** ⟦L *demittere*, to send down, let fall < *de-*, down + *mittere*, to send: see MISSION⟧ **1** to resign (a position or office) **2** [Archaic] to dismiss —*vi.* to resign —**de·mis′sion** (-mish′ən) *n.*

dem·i·tasse (dem′i täs′, -tas′, dem′ē-) *n.* ⟦Fr < *demi-* (see DEMI-) + *tasse*, a cup (see TASS)⟧ a small cup of or for black coffee served following dinner

dem·i·urge (dem′ē urj′) *n.* ⟦Gr *dēmiourgos*, one who works for the people, skilled workman, creator < *dēmios*, belonging to the people < *demos*, the people: see DEMOCRACY) + *-ergos*, worker (see WORK)⟧ **1** [*often* **D-**] *a)* in Platonism, a deity or creative force that shaped the material world *b)* in Gnosticism, a deity subordinate to the supreme deity, sometimes considered the creator of evil **2** a ruling force or creative power —**dem′i·ur′gic** (-ur′jik) *adj.*, **dem′i·ur′gi·cal**

dem·i·volt (dem′i vōlt′) *n.* ⟦Fr *demi-volte* < *demi-* (see DEMI-) + *volte*, a leap < *volter* < OIt *voltare* (see VAULT[2])⟧ in exhibition riding, a half turn with the forelegs of the horse raised: also sp. **dem′i·volte′**

dem·o (dem′ō) *n., pl.* **-os** **1** a phonograph or tape recording made to demonstrate the talent of a performer, quality of a song, etc. **2** *short for:* *a)* DEMONSTRATION (sense 3) *b)* [Chiefly Brit.] DEMONSTRATION (sense 5) ☆*c)* DEMONSTRATOR (sense 2)

de·mob (dē mäb′) *vt.* **-mobbed′**, **-mob′bing** [Brit. Informal] to demobilize —*n.* [Brit. Informal] demobilization

de·mo·bi·lize (dē mō′bə līz′) *vt.* **-lized′**, **-liz′ing** **1** to disband (troops) **2** to discharge (a person) from the armed forces —**de·mo′bi·li·za′tion** *n.*

de·moc·ra·cy (di mäk′rə sē) *n., pl.* **-cies** ⟦Fr *démocratie* < ML *democratia* < Gr *dēmokratia* < *dēmos*, the people (< IE **damos*, a division of the people < base **da-*, to cut, divide > TIDE[1]) + *kratein*, to rule < *kratos*, strength: see HARD⟧ **1** government in which the people hold the ruling power either directly or through elected representatives; rule by the ruled **2** a country, state, etc. with such government **3** majority rule **4** the principle of equality of rights, opportunity, and treatment, or the practice of this principle **5** the common people, esp. as the wielders of political power

dem·o·crat (dem′ə krat′) *n.* ⟦Fr *démocrate* < *démocratie*: see prec.⟧ **1** a person who believes in and upholds government by the people; advocate of rule by the majority **2** a person who believes in and practices the principle of equality of rights, opportunity, and treatment **3** [**D-**] a member of the Democratic Party

dem·o·crat·ic (dem′ə krat′ik) *adj.* ⟦Fr *démocratique* < ML *democraticus* < Gr *dēmokratikos*⟧ **1** of, belonging to, or upholding democracy or a democracy **2** of, for, or popular with all or most people [*a democratic art form*] **3** treating persons of all classes in the same way; not snobbish **4** [**D-**] of, belonging to, or characteristic of the Democratic Party —**dem′o·crat′i·cal·ly** *adv.*

☆**Democratic Party** one of the two major political parties in the U.S.: it emerged in the late 1820s from a split in the Democratic-Republican Party, which had, in turn, developed from the Republican Party led by Thomas Jefferson

Democratic Republic of the Congo *see* CONGO

de·moc·ra·tize (di mäk′rə tīz′) *vt., vi.* **-tized′**, **-tiz′ing** ⟦Fr *démocratiser* < ML *democratizare* < Gr *dēmokratizein*⟧ to make or become democratic —**de·moc′ra·ti·za′tion** *n.*

De·moc·ri·tus (di mäk′rə təs) 460?-370? B.C.; Gr. philosopher: exponent of atomism

dé·mo·dé (dā mô dā′) *adj.* ⟦Fr⟧ out-of-date; old-fashioned

de·mod·u·late (dē mäj′ə lāt′) *vt.* **-lat′ed**, **-lat′ing** to cause to undergo demodulation

de·mod·u·la·tion (dē mäj′ə lā′shən) *n. Radio* the process of recovering at the receiver a signal that has been modulated on a carrier wave; detection

de·mod·u·la·tor (dē mäj′ə lāt′ər) *n. Radio* a device used in demodulation

De·mo·gor·gon (dē′mō gôr′gən, dem′ō-) *n.* ⟦LL: prob. of Asian orig., but infl. by L *daemon* (see DAEMON) + *Gorgo* (see GORGON)⟧ a terrifying and mysterious god or demon of the underworld: believed by medieval and Renaissance scholars to have been a figure in ancient mythology

dem·o·graph·ic (dem′ə graf′ik, dē′mə-) *adj.* of or having to do with demography, demographics, or a demographic —*n.* **1** any of the classification factors or characteristics used in demography, as a certain age range **2** a group of people falling within a particular DEMOGRAPHIC (sense 1) or set of demographics —**dem′o·graph′i·cal·ly** *adv.*

dem·o·graph·ics (dem′ə graf′iks, dē′mə-) *pl.n.* the demographic characteristics of a population, esp. as classified by age, sex, income, etc., for market research, sociological analysis, etc.

de·mog·ra·phy (di mäg′rə fē) *n.* ⟦< Gr *dēmos*, the people (see DEMOCRACY) + -GRAPHY⟧ the statistical science dealing with the distribution, density, vital statistics, etc. of human populations —**de·mog′ra·pher** *n.*

dem·oi·selle (dem′wä zel′) *n.* ⟦Fr < OFr *dameisele*: see DAMSEL⟧ **1** a damsel **2** a small crane (*Anthropoides virgo*) of Africa, Asia, and Europe **3** DAMSELFLY ☆**4** DAMSELFISH

de·mol·ish (di mäl′ish) *vt.* ⟦< extended stem of Fr *démolir* < L *demoliri*, to pull down, destroy < *de-*, down + *moliri*, to build, construct < *moles*, a mass: see MOLE[3]⟧ **1** to pull down, tear down, or smash to pieces (a building, etc.) **2** to destroy; ruin; bring to naught —*SYN.* DESTROY —**de·mol′ish·er** *n.* —**de·mol′ish·ment** *n.*

dem·o·li·tion (dem′ə lish′ən, dē′mə-) *n.* ⟦Fr *démolition* < L *demolitio*⟧ a demolishing or being demolished; often specif., destruction by explosives

☆**demolition derby** a public show in which old automobiles are driven into one another repeatedly until only one is still moving

de·mon (dē′mən) *n.* ⟦ME < L: see DAEMON⟧ **1** DAEMON (senses 1 & 2) **2** a devil; evil spirit **3** a person or thing regarded as evil, cruel, etc. [*the demon of jealousy*] **4** *a)* a person who has great energy or skill [*a demon at golf*] *b)* an enthusiast or devotee, or one who indulges to excess [*a speed demon on the highway*] —**de·mon·ic** (di män′ik) *adj.* —**de·mon′i·cal·ly** *adv.*

de·mon·e·tize (dē män′ə tīz′) *vt.* **-tized′**, **-tiz′ing** **1** to deprive (esp. currency) of its standard value **2** to stop using (silver or gold) as a monetary standard —**de·mon′e·ti·za′tion** *n.*

de·mo·ni·ac (dē mō′nē ak′, di-) *adj.* ⟦ME *demoniak* < LL(Ec) *daemoniacus* < Gr *daimoniakos*⟧ **1** possessed or influenced by a demon **2** of a demon or demons **3** like or characteristic of a demon; fiendish; frenzied Also **de·mo·ni·a·cal** (dē′mə nī′ə kəl) —*n.* a person supposedly possessed by a demon —**de′mo·ni′a·cal·ly** *adv.*

de·mon·ism (dē′mən iz′əm) *n.* **1** belief in the existence and powers of demons **2** DEMONOLATRY —**de′mon·ist** *n.*

de·mon·ize (-īz′) *vt.* **-ized′**, **-iz′ing** **1** *a)* to make into a demon *b)* to characterize or conceive of as evil, cruel, inhuman, etc. [*to demonize a political opponent*] **2** to bring under the influence of demons —**de′mon·i·za′tion** *n.*

de·mon·o- (dē′mən ō) ⟦Gr *daimono-* < *daimōn*: see DAEMON⟧ *combining form* demon [*demonolatry*]: also, before a vowel, **de·mon-** (dē′mən)

de·mon·ol·a·try (dē′mən äl′ə trē) *n.* ⟦prec. + -LATRY⟧ the worship of demons —**de′mon·ol′a·ter** *n.*

de·mon·ol·o·gy (-äl′ə jē) *n.* the study of demons or of beliefs about them —**de′mon·ol′o·gist** *n.*

de·mon·stra·ble (di män′strə bəl, dem′ən-) *adj.* ⟦ME & OFr < L *demonstrabilis*⟧ that can be demonstrated, or proved —**de·mon′stra·bil′i·ty** *n.*, **de·mon′stra·ble·ness** —**de·mon′stra·bly** *adv.*

dem·on·strate (dem′ən strāt′) *vt.* **-strat′ed**, **-strat′ing** ⟦< L *demonstratus*, pp. of *demonstrare*, to point out, show < *de-*, out, from + *monstrare*, to show: see MUSTER⟧ **1** to show by reasoning; prove **2** to explain or make clear by using examples, experiments, etc. **3** to show the operation or working of; specif., to show (a product) in use in an effort to sell it **4** to show (feelings) plainly —*vi.* **1** to show one's feelings or views by taking part in a mass meeting, parade, etc. **2** to show military power or preparedness

dem·on·stra·tion (dem′ən strā′shən) *n.* ⟦ME *demonstracion* < L *demonstratio* < *demonstrare*: see prec.⟧ **1** the act, process, or means of making evident or proving **2** an explanation by example, experiment, etc. **3** a practical showing of how something works or is used; specif., such a showing of a product in an effort to sell it **4** a display or outward show [*a demonstration of grief*] **5** a public show of feeling or opinion, as by a mass meeting or parade **6** a show of military force or preparedness **7** a logical proof in which a certain conclusion is shown to follow from certain premises

de·mon·stra·tive (di män′strə tiv; *also* dem′ən strāt′iv) *adj.* ⟦ME & OFr *demonstratif* < L *demonstrativus*: see DEMONSTRATE⟧ **1** that demonstrates or shows; illustrative **2** giving convincing evidence or conclusive proof: usually with *of* **3** having to do with demonstration **4** showing feelings openly and frankly **5** *Gram.* pointing out; specifying ["this" is a *demonstrative* pronoun] —*n. Gram.* a demonstrative pronoun or adjective —**de·mon′stra·tive·ly** *adv.* —**de·mon′stra·tive·ness** *n.*

dem·on·stra·tor (dem′ən strāt′ər) *n.* **1** one that demonstrates; specif. a person who takes part in a public demonstration ☆**2** a product, as an automobile, used in demonstrations

☆**de·mor·al·ize** (dē môr′ə līz′, di-) *vt.* **-ized′**, **-iz′ing** ⟦coined (1793) by Noah WEBSTER[3] < DE- + MORAL + -IZE⟧ **1** [Now Rare] to corrupt the morals of; deprave **2** to lower the morale of; weaken the spirit, courage, discipline, or staying power of **3** to throw into confusion —**de·mor′al·i·za′tion** *n.* —**de·mor′al·iz′er** *n.*

de mor·tu·is nil ni·si bo·num (dā môr′tōō is nil′ nē′sē bō′nōōm, -nəm) ⟦L⟧ (say) nothing but good of the dead

de·mos (dē′mäs′) *n.* ⟦Gr *dēmos*: see DEMOCRACY⟧ **1** the people or commonalty of an ancient Greek state **2** the common people; the people; the masses

De·mos·the·nes (di mäs′thə nēz′) 384-322 B.C.; Athenian orator & statesman

☆**de·mote** (dē mōt′, di-) *vt.* **-mot′ed**, **-mot′ing** ⟦DE- + (PRO)MOTE⟧ to reduce to a lower grade; lower in rank: opposed to PROMOTE —**de·mo′tion** *n.*

de·mot·ic (dē mät′ik) *adj.* ⟦ML *demoticus* < Gr *dēmotikos* < *dēmotes*, one of the people < *dēmos*: see DEMOCRACY⟧ **1** *a)* of the people; popular; specif., VERNACULAR (sense 2) *b)* in or of idiomatic, colloquial, everyday language [*a novelist with a good ear for demotic dialogue*] **2** designating or of a simplified system of ancient Egyptian writing: distinguished from HIERATIC —*n.* **1** [**D-**] ROMAIC **2** everyday language; the way real people speak

de·mount (dē mount′) *vt.* to remove from a mounting [*to demount a motor*] —**de·mount′a·ble** *adj.*

Demp·sey (demp′sē), **Jack** (born *William Harrison Dempsey*) 1895-1983; U.S. professional boxer

de·mul·cent (dē mul′sənt, di-) *adj.* ⟦L *demulcens*, prp. of *demulcere*, to stroke down, soften < *de-*, down + *mulcere*, to stroke < IE **melk-*, var. of base **melg-* to stroke > MILK⟧ soothing —*n.* a medicine or ointment that soothes an irritated or inflamed mucous membrane

de·mur (dē mur′, di-) *vi.* **-murred′**, **-mur′ring** ⟦ME *demuren* < OFr *demorer* < L *demorari*, to delay < *de-*, from + *morari*, to delay < *mora*, a delay < IE base **(s)mer-*, to remember > MEMORY⟧ **1** to hesitate because of one's doubts or objections; have scruples; object **2** *Law* to enter a demurrer —*n.* **1** an act or instance of demurring **2** an objection raised or exception taken Also, for *n.*, **de·mur′ral** —*SYN.* OBJECT

de·mure (di myoor′) *adj.* ⟦ME *demur* < *de-* (prob. intens.) + *mur* < OFr *meür*, ripe, mature < L *maturus*, MATURE⟧ **1** decorous; modest; reserved **2** affectedly modest or shy; coy —*SYN.* SHY[1] —**de·mure′ly** *adv.* —**de·mure′ness** *n.*

de·mur·rage (di mur′ij) *n.* ⟦OFr *demorage*, a delay < *demorer*: see DEMUR⟧ **1** the compensation payable to a carrier of freight whose vehicle or vessel is delayed, as by failure to load or unload the freight within the time allowed **2** the delay itself

de·mur·rer (di mur′ər) *n.* ⟦OFr *demorer*, to DEMUR: inf. used as n.⟧ **1** a plea for the dismissal of a lawsuit on the grounds that even if the statements of the opposing party are true, they do not sustain the claim because they are insufficient or otherwise legally defective **2** an objection; demur **3** a person who demurs

de·my (dē mī′) *n., pl.* **-mies′** ⟦ME: see DEMI-⟧ any of several sizes of writing and printing paper, between 15½ by 20 and 18 by 23 inches

de·my·e·lin·ate (dē mī′ə lin āt′) *vt.* **-at′ed**, **-at′ing** to destroy or damage the myelin sheath of (nerves) —**de·my′e·li·na′tion** *n.*

de·mys·ti·fy (dē mis′tə fī′) *vt.* **-fied′**, **-fy′ing** to remove the mystery or mystique from; make rational or comprehensible; clarify —**de·mys′ti·fi·ca′tion** *n.*

de·my·thol·o·gize (dē′mi thäl′ə jīz′) *vt.* **-gized′**, **-giz′ing** *Theol.* to eliminate elements viewed as mythological from (the Bible, a belief, etc.)

den (den) *n.* ⟦ME < OE *denn*, lair, pasture, akin to MLowG, place where grass is trodden down, lair < IE base **dhen-*, level place⟧ **1** the cave or other lair of a wild animal **2** a retreat or headquarters, as of thieves; haunt **3** a small, squalid room **4** a small, cozy room in a house, where a person can be alone to read, work, etc. **5** a small, localized unit of Cub Scouts —*vi.* **denned**, **den′ning** to live or hide in or as in a den

Den *abbrev.* Denmark

De·na·li (di nä′lē) ⟦lit., the great one, the high one, in an Athabaskan language⟧ mountain of the Alaska Range, SC Alas: highest peak in North America: 20,310 ft (6,190 m): former name *Mount McKinley*

de·nar (dē′när) *n.* ⟦Macedonian⟧ the basic monetary unit of Macedonia: see the table of monetary units in the Reference Supplement

de·nar·i·us (di nar′ē əs) *n., pl.* **-nar′i·i′** (-ē ī′) ⟦ME < L, orig., adj., containing ten < *deni*, by tens < *decem*, TEN⟧ 1 an ancient Roman silver coin, the penny of the New Testament 2 an ancient Roman gold coin, worth 25 silver denarii

den·a·ry (den′ə rē, dē′nə-) *adj.* ⟦see prec.⟧ having to do with the number ten; tenfold; decimal

de·na·tion·al·ize (dē nash′ə nə līz′) *vt.* **-ized′, -iz′ing** ⟦Fr *dénationaliser*: see DE- & NATIONALIZE⟧ 1 to deprive of national rights or status 2 to place (an industry owned or controlled by the government) under private ownership —**de·na′tion·al·i·za′tion** *n.*

de·nat·u·ral·ize (dē nach′ə rə līz′) *vt.* **-ized′, -iz′ing** 1 to make unnatural 2 to take citizenship from —**de·nat′u·ral·i·za′tion** *n.*

de·na·ture (dē nā′chər) *vt.* **-tured, -tur·ing** ⟦ML *denaturare*: see DE- & NATURE⟧ 1 to change the nature of; take natural qualities away from 2 to make (alcohol, etc.) unfit for human consumption without spoiling for other uses 3 to change the structure of (a protein) by heat, acids, alkalies, etc., so that the original properties are greatly changed or eliminated 4 to add a nonfissionable isotope to (a fissionable isotope) so that the mixture cannot be used in nuclear bombs but can still be used as fuel material —**de·na′tur·ant** *n.* —**de·na′tur·a′tion** *n.*

de·na·zi·fy (dē nät′sə fī′) *vt.* **-fied′, -fy′ing** to rid of Nazi elements or influences —**de·na′zi·fi·ca′tion** *n.*

Den·bigh·shire (den′bi shir′, -shər; -bē-) former county of N Wales, now part of Clwyd and Gwynedd counties: also **Den′bigh** (-bi, -bē)

dendr- *combining form* DENDRO-: used before a vowel

den·dri- (den′dri, -drə) *combining form* DENDRO-

den·dri·form (-fôrm′) *adj.* shaped like a tree

den·drite (den′drīt′) *n.* ⟦< Gr *dendritēs*, of a tree < *dendron*, a tree: see fol.⟧ 1 a branching, treelike mark made by one mineral crystallizing in another 2 a stone or mineral with such a mark 3 the branched part of a nerve cell that carries impulses toward the cell body 4 [*pl.*] the protoplasmic filaments of a nerve cell —**den·drit·ic** (den drit′ik) *adj.*, **den·drit′i·cal** —**den·drit′i·cal·ly** *adv.*

den·dro- (den′drō, -drə) ⟦< Gr *dendron*, earlier *dendreon*, a tree, redupl. < IE base *drewo-, TREE⟧ *combining form* tree [*dendrochronology*]

☆**den·dro·chro·nol·o·gy** (-krə näl′ə jē) *n.* the science of dating past events or climatic changes by a comparative study of growth rings in tree trunks —**den′dro·chron′o·log′i·cal** (-krän′ə läj′i kəl) *adj.*

den·droid (den′droid′) *adj.* ⟦Gr *dendroeidēs*: see DENDRO- & -OID⟧ treelike in form

den·drol·o·gy (den dräl′ə jē) *n.* ⟦DENDRO- + -LOGY⟧ the scientific study of trees and woody plants, esp. their taxonomy —**den′dro·log′ic** (-drə läj′ik) *adj.*, **den′dro·log′i·cal** —**den·drol′o·gist** *n.*

-den·dron (den′drən, -drän′) ⟦< Gr *dendron*, a tree: see DENDRO-⟧ *combining form* tree or treelike structure [*rhododendron*]

dene (dēn) *n.* ⟦ME; prob. akin to DUNE⟧ [Brit.] a low dune or sandy tract near a seashore

De·ne (den′ē, -ā) *n., pl.* **Dene** or **Denes** ⟦Fr *déné* < Athabaskan, a self-designation, lit., people⟧ 1 a member of any of the Athabaskan peoples of the Northwest Territories, Canada 2 the group of languages spoken by these peoples —*adj.* of these peoples or their cultures

Den·eb (den′eb′) *n.* ⟦Ar *dhanab (aldajāja)*, tail (of the hen)⟧ a supergiant, variable star, the brightest star in the constellation Cygnus: magnitude, 1.25: see also SUMMER TRIANGLE

den·e·ga·tion (den′ə gā′shən) *n.* ⟦Fr *dénégation* < L *denegatio* < *denegare*: see DENY⟧ a denying or a denial

☆**den·gue** (deŋ′gā, -gē) *n.* ⟦WIndSp < Swahili *dinga*, cramplike attack, confused with Sp *dengue*, fastidiousness⟧ an infectious tropical disease transmitted by mosquitoes and characterized by severe pains in the joints and back, fever, and rash

Deng Xiao·ping (duŋ′ shou′piŋ′) 1904-97; Chin. Communist leader; member of the Central Committee of the Communist Party (resigned 1987); held various official titles (1967-89), including deputy prime minister; China's de facto ruler (*c.* 1981-97)

den·i (den′ē) *n., pl.* **den′i** ⟦Macedonian⟧ a monetary unit of Macedonia, equal to $\frac{1}{100}$ of a denar

de·ni·a·bil·i·ty (dē nī′ə bil′ə tē, di-) *n.* ☆the ability to deny an accusation as by claiming to have no knowledge of the actions or events involved

de·ni·a·ble (dē nī′ə bəl, di-) *adj.* that can be denied —**de·ni′a·bly** *adv.*

de·ni·al (dē nī′əl, di-) *n.* 1 the act of denying; a saying "no" (to a request, demand, etc.) 2 a statement in opposition to another; contradiction [the *denial* of a rumor] 3 the act of disowning; repudiation [the *denial* of one's family] 4 a refusal to believe or accept (a doctrine, etc.) 5 *Psychol.* an unconscious thought process whereby one allays anxiety by refusing to acknowledge certain unpleasant facts, feelings, etc.: now often in the phrase **in denial** 6 SELF-DENIAL 7 *Law* the opposing by a defendant of a claim or charge against him or her

de·nic·o·tin·ize (dē nik′ə tin īz′) *vt.* **-ized′, -iz′ing** ⟦DE- + NICOTIN(E) + -IZE⟧ to remove nicotine from (tobacco)

de·nier[1] (də nir′; *for 2*, den′yər; *Fr* də nyā′) *n.* ⟦ME *dener* < OFr *denier* < L *denarius*, DENARIUS⟧ 1 a small, obsolete French coin of little value 2 a unit of weight for measuring the fineness of threads of silk, rayon, nylon, etc., equal to .05 gram per 450 meters

de·ni·er[2] (dē nī′ər, di-) *n.* a person who denies

den·i·grate (den′ə grāt′) *vt.* **-grat′ed, -grat′ing** ⟦< L *denigratus*, pp. of *denigrare*, to blacken < *de-*, intens. + *nigrare*, to blacken < *niger*, black: see -ATE[1]⟧ 1 [Archaic] to blacken 2 to disparage the character or reputation of; defame —**den′i·gra′tion** *n.* —**den′i·gra′tor** *n.* —**den·i·gra·to·ry** (den′ə grə tôr′ē, də nig′rə-) *adj.*

den·im (den′əm) *n.* ⟦< Fr *(serge) de Nîmes*, (serge) of Nîmes, where first made⟧ 1 a coarse, sturdy twilled cotton cloth used as for jeans, overalls, and uniforms 2 [*pl.*] garments, as pants or shirts, made of this material, usually blue

Den·is[1] (den′is; *Fr* də nē′) *n.* a masculine name: see DENNIS

De·nis[2] (də nē′), Saint (3d cent. A.D.); patron saint of France: his day is Oct. 9

De·nise (də nēs′) *n.* ⟦Fr, fem. of *Denis*, DENNIS⟧ a feminine name: see DENNIS

de·ni·trate (dē nī′trāt′) *vt.* **-trat′ed, -trat′ing** to remove nitric acid, the nitrate radical, the nitro group, or nitrogen oxide from —**de′ni·tra′tion** *n.*

de·ni·tri·fy (dē nī′trə fī′) *vt.* **-fied′, -fy′ing** 1 to remove nitrogen or its compounds from 2 to reduce (nitro groups, nitrates, or nitrites) to compounds of lower oxidation —**de·ni′tri·fi·ca′tion** *n.*

den·i·zen (den′ə zən) *n.* ⟦ME *denisein* < Anglo-Fr *deinzein* < OFr, native inhabitant < *denz*, within < LL *de-intus* < L *de intus*, from within⟧ 1 *a)* an inhabitant or occupant *b)* a frequenter of a particular place 2 [Brit.] an alien granted specified rights of citizenship 3 an animal, plant, foreign word, etc. that has become naturalized —*vt.* [Brit.] to naturalize

De·niz·li (den′əz lē′) city in SW Turkey, near ancient Laodicea

Den·mark (den′märk′) ⟦ME *Denemarche* < OE *Denemearce*: see DANE & MARK[1]⟧ country in Europe, occupying most of the peninsula of Jutland and several nearby islands in the North and Baltic seas: 16,639 sq mi (43,094 sq km); cap. Copenhagen

Denmark Strait arm of the N Atlantic between SE Greenland & Iceland: *c.* 130 mi (209 km) wide

☆**den mother** a woman who supervises meetings of a den of Cub Scouts

Den·nis (den′is) *n.* ⟦Fr *Denis* < L *Dionysius*⟧ a masculine name: var. *Denis*; fem. *Denise*

de·nom·i·nate (dē näm′ə nāt′, di-; *for adj., usually*, -nit) *vt.* **-nat′ed, -nat′ing** ⟦< L *denominatus*, pp. of *denominare*, to name < *de-*, intens. + *nominare*: see NOMINATE⟧ to give a specified name to; call —*adj.* being used to quantify a unit of measure ["15" in "15 feet" is a *denominate* number]

de·nom·i·na·tion (dē näm′ə nā′shən, di-) *n.* ⟦ME *denominacioun* < OFr < L *denominatio*: see prec.⟧ 1 the act of denominating 2 a name; esp., the name of a class of things 3 a class or kind (esp. of units in a system) having a specific name or value [coins or stamps of different *denominations*] 4 a particular religious body, with a specific name, organization, etc.

de·nom·i·na·tion·al (-nā′shən əl) *adj.* of, sponsored by, or under the control of a religious denomination; sectarian —**de·nom′i·na′tion·al·ly** *adv.*

de·nom·i·na·tion·al·ism (-nā′shən əl iz′əm) *n.* 1 denominational principles 2 a denominational system 3 acceptance or support of such principles or system 4 division into denominations

de·nom·i·na·tive (dē näm′ə nāt′iv, -nə tiv; di-) *adj.* ⟦LL *denominativus*⟧ 1 denominating; naming 2 *Gram.* formed from a noun or adjective ["to eye" is a *denominative* verb] —*n.* a denominative word, esp. a verb

de·nom·i·na·tor (dē näm′ə nāt′ər, di-) *n.* 1 [Now Rare] a person or thing that denominates 2 a shared characteristic 3 the usual level; standard 4 *Math.* the term below or to the right of the line in a fraction [4 is the *denominator* of $\frac{3}{4}$]: see NUMERATOR

de·no·ta·tion (dē′nō tā′shən) *n.* ⟦LL *denotatio*⟧ 1 the act of denoting 2 the direct, explicit meaning or reference of a word or term: cf. CONNOTATION 3 an indication or sign 4 [Rare] a distinguishing name; designation 5 *Logic* the class of all the particular objects to which a term refers; extension: cf. CONNOTATION (sense 3)

de·no·ta·tive (dē′nō tāt′iv, di nōt′ə tiv) *adj.* 1 denoting; indicative 2 of denotation —**de′no·ta′tive·ly** *adv.*

de·note (dē nōt′, di-) *vt.* **-not′ed, -not′ing** ⟦Fr *dénoter* < MFr < L *denotare*, to mark out, denote < *de-*, down + *notare*, to mark < *nota*, NOTE⟧ 1 to be a sign of; indicate [dark clouds *denote* rain] 2 to signify or refer to explicitly; stand for; mean: said of words, signs, or symbols: distinguished from CONNOTE 3 *Logic* to be the name for (individuals or instances of a class) —**de·not′a·ble** *adj.*

de·noue·ment or **dé·noue·ment** (dā′no͞o män′) *n.* ⟦Fr < *dénouer*, to untie < *dé-* (L *dis-*), from, out + *nouer*, to tie < L *nodare*, to knot < *nodus*, a knot: see NODE⟧ 1 the outcome, solution, unraveling, or clarification of a plot in a drama, story, etc. 2 the point in the plot where this occurs 3 any final revelation or outcome

de·nounce (dē nouns′, di-) *vt.* **-nounced′, -nounc′ing** ⟦ME *denouncen* < OFr *denoncier* < L *denuntiare*: see DENUNCIATION⟧ 1 to accuse publicly; inform against [to *denounce* an accomplice in crime] 2 to condemn strongly as evil 3 to give formal notice of the ending of (a treaty, armistice, etc.) 4 [Obs.] to announce, esp. in a menacing way —***SYN.*** CRITICIZE —**de·nounce′ment** *n.* —**de·nounc′er** *n.*

de no·vo (di nō′vō, dē-, dā-) ⟦L, lit., from new⟧ once more; anew; again

Den·pa·sar (dən päs′är) seaport in S Bali, Indonesia

dense (dens) *adj.* **dens′er, dens′est** ⟦ME < L *densus*, compact < IE base *dens-, thick > Gr *dasys*, thick (used of hair), Hittite *dassuš*, strong⟧ 1 having the parts crowded together; packed tightly together; compact 2 difficult to get through, penetrate, etc. [a *dense* fog, *dense* ignorance] 3 slow to understand; stupid 4 *Photog.* opaque due to a heavy concentration of metallic silver: said of an overexposed or overdeveloped negative —***SYN.*** CLOSE[1], STUPID —**dense′ly** *adv.* —**dense′ness** *n.*

den·sim·e·ter (den sim′ət ər) *n.* ⟦< L *densus,* prec. + -METER⟧ any instrument for measuring density or specific gravity

den·si·tom·e·ter (den′sə täm′ət ər) *n.* ⟦< fol. + -METER⟧ **1** a device for measuring optical density, as of a photographic negative **2** DENSIMETER

den·si·ty (den′sə tē) *n., pl.* **-ties** ⟦Fr *densité* < L *densitas*⟧ **1** the quality or condition of being dense; specif., *a)* thickness; compactness *b)* stupidity *c) Photog.* degree of opacity of a negative **2** quantity or number per unit, as of area **3** CURRENT DENSITY **4** *Physics* ratio of the mass of an object to its volume

dent[1] (dent) *n.* ⟦ME, var. of DINT⟧ **1** a slight hollow made in a surface by a blow or pressure **2** an appreciable effect, often a lessening or adverse effect —*vt.* to make a dent in —*vi.* to become dented

dent[2] (dent) *n.* ⟦Fr < L *dens,* TOOTH⟧ a toothlike projection as in a gearwheel, lock, etc.

dent[3] *abbrev.* **1** dentist **2** dentistry

dent- (dent) *combining form* DENTI-: used before a vowel

den·tal (dent′'l) *adj.* ⟦ModL *dentalis* < L *dens* (gen. *dentis*), TOOTH⟧ **1** of or for the teeth or dentistry **2** *Phonet.* articulated with the tip of the tongue against or near the front teeth: said as of (th) and (*th*) —*n.* a dental consonant —**den′tal·ly** *adv.*

☆**dental floss** thin, strong thread for removing food particles from between the teeth or plaque from unexposed tooth surfaces

dental hygiene the study and practice of procedures designed to maintain oral health, specif. those concerned with polishing teeth and removing tartar

☆**dental hygienist** a licensed specialist who cleans teeth, takes dental X-rays, etc. under the supervision of a dentist

den·ta·li·um (den tā′lē əm) *n., pl.* **-li·a** (-ə) ⟦ModL < L *dentalis,* DENTAL + -IUM⟧ any of a genus (*Dentalium*) of marine mollusks

den·tate (den′tāt′) *adj.* ⟦ME *dentat* < L *dentatus* < *dens,* TOOTH⟧ **1** having teeth or toothlike projections; toothed or notched **2** *Bot.* having a toothed margin: said of some leaves —**den′tate′ly** *adv.*

den·ta·tion (den tā′shən) *n.* **1** the quality or state of being dentate **2** a toothlike projection, as on a leaf

☆**dent corn** a strain of Indian corn (*Zea mays* var. *indentata*) in which the mature kernel develops a slight depression at the tip

den·ti- (den′ti, -tə) ⟦< L *dens,* TOOTH⟧ *combining form* **1** tooth or teeth [*dentiform*] **2** dental, dental and

den·ti·cle (den′ti kəl) *n.* ⟦L *denticulus,* dim. of *dens,* TOOTH⟧ a small tooth or toothlike projection

den·tic·u·late (den tik′yo͞o lit, -lāt′) *adj.* ⟦L *denticulatus*⟧ **1** having denticles **2** having dentils **3** *Bot.* finely dentate Also **den·tic′u·lat′ed** —**den·tic′u·late·ly** *adv.*

den·tic·u·la·tion (den tik′yo͞o lā′shən) *n.* **1** the quality or condition of being denticulate **2** a denticle

den·ti·form (den′tə fôrm′) *adj.* tooth-shaped

den·ti·frice (den′tə fris) *n.* ⟦ME *dentifricie* < L *dentifricium,* tooth powder < *dens,* TOOTH + *fricare,* to rub: see FRIABLE⟧ any preparation for cleaning teeth, as a powder, paste, or liquid

den·tig·er·ous (den tij′ər əs) *adj.* bearing teeth

den·til (den′til) *n.* ⟦MFr *dentille,* dim. of *dent* < L *dens,* TOOTH⟧ *Archit.* any of a series of small rectangular blocks projecting like teeth, as from under a cornice

den·tin (den′tin) *n.* ⟦< L *dens,* TOOTH + -INE[3]⟧ the hard, dense, calcareous tissue forming the body of a tooth, under the enamel and surrounding the pulp canal: see TOOTH, illus.: also **den′tine′** (-tēn′, -tin)

den·tist (den′tist) *n.* ⟦Fr *dentiste* < ML *dentista* < L *dens,* TOOTH⟧ a person whose profession is the care of teeth and the surrounding soft tissues, including the prevention and elimination of decay, the replacement of missing teeth with artificial ones, the correction of malocclusion, etc.

den·tist·ry (den′ti strē) *n.* the profession or work of a dentist

den·ti·tion (den tish′ən) *n.* ⟦L *dentitio,* a teething < *dentire,* to cut teeth < *dens,* TOOTH⟧ **1** the teething process **2** the number and kind of teeth and their arrangement in the mouth

den·to- (den′tō, -tə) *combining form* DENTI- [*dentosurgical*]

den·toid (den′toid′) *adj.* ⟦DENT(I)- + -OID⟧ tooth-shaped

Den·ton (dent′'n) ⟦after Rev. John B. *Denton,* a pioneer⟧ city in NE Tex.

den·to·sur·gi·cal (den′tō sur′ji kəl) *adj.* relating to or used in both dentistry and surgery

D'En·tre·cas·teaux Islands (dän′trə kas′tō) group of islands off SE New Guinea: part of the country of Papua New Guinea: *c.* 1,200 sq mi (3,108 sq km)

den·ture (den′chər) *n.* ⟦Fr < *dent,* tooth < L *dens,* TOOTH⟧ **1** a set of teeth **2** [*often pl.*] a fitting for the mouth, with artificial teeth, often a full set

den·tur·ist (den′chər ist) *n.* a person who makes, repairs, and sells dentures directly to the public

de·nu·cle·ar·ize (dē no͞o′klē ər īz′, -nyo͞o′-) *vt.* **-ized′**, **-iz′ing** **1** to ban or prevent the possession or construction of nuclear weapons in (a country, region, etc.) **2** to remove or dismantle the nuclear weapons of —**de·nu′cle·ar·i·za′tion** *n.*

de·nu·date (dē no͞o′dāt′, -nyo͞o′-, di-; den′yo͞o dāt′) *vt.* **-dat′ed**, **-dat′ing** ⟦< L *denudatus,* pp. of *denudare,* to strip off < *de-,* off + *nudare,* strip: see NUDE⟧ DENUDE —**de·nu·da·tion** (dē′no͞o dā′shən, -nyo͞o-; den′yo͞o-) *n.*

de·nude (dē no͞od′, -nyo͞od′; di-) *vt.* **-nud′ed**, **-nud′ing** ⟦L *denudare*: see prec.⟧ to make bare or naked; strip; specif., *a)* to destroy all plant and animal life in (an area) *b) Geol.* to expose (layers of rock) by erosion, weathering, etc. —*SYN.* STRIP[1]

de·nu·mer·a·ble (dē no͞o′mər ə bəl, -nyo͞o′-) *adj.* ⟦DE- + NUMERABLE⟧ countable: said of a set, either finite or infinite, whose elements can be put in one-to-one correspondence with the natural integers

de·nun·ci·a·tion (dē nun′sē ā′shən, di-) *n.* ⟦ME *denunciacioun* < L *denuntiatio* < *denuntiatus,* pp. of *denuntiare,* to announce, denounce < *de-,* intens. + *nuntiare,* ANNOUNCE⟧ the act of denouncing —**de·nun′ci·a·to′ry** (-ə tôr′ē) *adj.,* **de·nun′ci·a′tive** (-āt′iv)

Den·ver (den′vər) ⟦after J. W. *Denver* (1817-92), governor of Kans.⟧ capital of Colo., in the NC part

Denver boot ⟦after prec.⟧ a large metal clamp locked to a wheel of a motor vehicle by the police to immobilize the vehicle: used primarily to force people to pay their parking tickets

de·ny (dē nī′, di-) *vt.* **-nied′**, **-ny′ing** ⟦ME *denien* < OFr *denier* < L *denegare* < *de-,* intens. + *negare,* to deny: see NEGATION⟧ **1** to declare (a statement) untrue; contradict **2** to refuse to accept as true or right; reject as unfounded, unreal, etc. **3** to refuse to acknowledge as one's own; disown; repudiate **4** to refuse the use of or access to **5** to refuse to grant or give **6** to refuse the request of (a person) **7** [Obs.] to forbid —**deny oneself** **1** to do without desired things **2** to abstain from

SYN.—**deny** implies a refusal to accept as true, real, valid, existent, or tenable [*he denied the charge*]; to **gainsay** is to dispute what a person says or to challenge the person saying it [*facts that cannot be gainsaid*]; **contradict** not only implies emphatic denial, but, in addition, often suggests belief or evidence that the opposite or contrary is true; **impugn** implies a direct, forceful attack against that which one calls into question [*she impugned his motives*]

De·nys (də nē′), Saint *see* DENIS[2], Saint

de·o·dand (dē′ō dand′) *n.* ⟦Anglo-Fr *deodande* < ML(Ec) *deodandum* < *Deo dandum,* lit., to be given to God < L *Deo,* dat. of *Deus,* God + *dandum,* ger. of *dare,* to give: see DATE[1]⟧ [Historical] *Eng. Law* an item of personal property, as an animal, that causes a person's death and is consequently forfeited to the crown to be used for some pious purpose

de·o·dar (dē′ō där′) *n.* ⟦Hindi *deodār* < Sans *dēvadāru,* lit., tree of the gods < *dēva-ḥ,* god (akin to L *deus*) + *daru,* wood: see TREE⟧ **1** a tall Himalayan cedar (*Cedrus deodara*) with drooping branches and fragrant, durable, light-red wood **2** the wood

de·o·dor·ant (dē ō′dər ənt) *adj.* ⟦< DE- + L *odorans,* prp. of *odorare,* to smell < *odor,* ODOR⟧ having the power of preventing, destroying, or masking undesired odors —*n.* any deodorant preparation; esp., a liquid or semisolid substance used on the body

de·o·dor·ize (dē ō′də rīz′) *vt.* **-ized′**, **-iz′ing** to remove or mask the odor of or in —**de·o′dor·i·za′tion** *n.*

de·o·dor·iz·er (-rīz′ər) *n.* any substance or device used in deodorizing something; esp., a spray or the like used to mask odors, as in a room

de·on·tic (dē än′tik) *adj.* ⟦< Gr *deon* (gen. *deontos*) (see fol.) + -IC⟧ of, relating to, or based on some binding ethical rule; deontological

de·on·tol·o·gy (dē′än täl′ə jē) *n.* ⟦< Gr *deon* (gen. *deontos*), that which is binding, necessity < *dein,* to bind (see DIADEM) + -LOGY⟧ the ethical doctrine which holds that the worth of an action is determined as by its conformity to some binding rule rather than by its consequences —**de·on·to·log·i·cal** (dē än′tə läj′i kəl) *adj.*

De·o vo·len·te (dā′ō vō len′tā) ⟦LL(Ec)⟧ God being willing

de·ox·i·dize (dē äks′ə dīz′) *vt.* **-dized′**, **-diz′ing** to remove oxygen from (a compound)

de·oxy- (dē äks′ī, -ə) *combining form* containing less oxygen than its parent compound [*deoxyribose*]

de·oxy·cor·ti·cos·ter·one (dē äks′i kôr′ti käs′tər ōn′) *n.* a corticosteroid, $C_{21}H_{30}O_3$, that causes the retention of water and salt in the kidney

de·oxy·gen·ate (dē äks′ə jə nāt′) *vt.* **-at′ed**, **-at′ing** to remove oxygen, esp. free oxygen, from (water, air, blood, etc.)

de·oxy·ri·bo·nu·cle·ic acid (dē äks′ə rī′bō no͞o klē′ik, -nyo͞o-; -klā′-) ⟦< fol. + NUCLEIC ACID⟧ DNA

de·oxy·ri·bose (dē äks′ē rī′bōs) *n.* ⟦DEOXY- + RIBOSE⟧ the sugar component, $C_5H_{10}O_4$, of DNA

dep *abbrev.* **1** department **2** departs **3** departure **4** deposed **5** deposit **6** deputy

de·part (dē pärt′, di-) *vi.* ⟦ME *departen* < OFr *departir* < VL *departire,* to divide, separate, for L *dispartire* < *dis-,* apart + *partire,* to divide < *pars* (see PART[2]): orig. *vt.,* to divide⟧ **1** to go away (*from*); leave **2** to set out; start **3** to die **4** to turn aside (*from*) [*to depart from custom*] —*vt.* to leave [*flight 10 departs Chicago at 2 P.M.*] —*n.* [Obs.] a departure —**depart this life** to die

de·part·ed (-id) *adj.* **1** gone away; past; bygone **2** dead —*SYN.* DEAD —**the departed** the dead person or dead persons

de·part·ee (dē′pär tē′) *n.* one who has departed, as from a place, a position, or a country

de·part·ment (dē pärt′mənt, di-) *n.* ⟦ME & OFr *departement* < *departir*: see DEPART⟧ **1** a separate part, division, or branch, as of a government, business, or school [*the police department, the accounting department, the history department*] **2** a field of knowledge or activity [*rewriting is his department*] ☆**3** a specialized column or section appearing regularly in a periodical **4** an administrative district in France, Greece, or certain Latin American countries

de·part·men·tal (dē′pärt ment′'l, di pärt′-) *adj.* 1 having to do with a department or departments 2 arranged into departments —**de′part·men′tal·ly** *adv.*

de·part·men·tal·ism (-iz′əm) *n.* strict or excessive adherence to departmental organization and rules

de·part·men·tal·ize (-īz′) *vt.* **-ized′**, **-iz′ing** to organize into departments; subdivide —**de′part·men′tal·i·za′tion** *n.*

☆**department store** a large retail store for the sale of many kinds of goods arranged in departments

de·par·ture (dē pär′chər, di-) *n.* ⟦ME < OFr *departeure*⟧ 1 a departing, or going away 2 a starting out, as on a trip or new course of action 3 a deviation or turning aside (*from*) 4 [Archaic] death 5 *Naut.* the distance due east or west from the meridian of its starting point covered by a ship on a given course

de·pend (dē pend′, di-) *vi.* ⟦ME *dependen* < OFr *dependre* < L *dependere*, to hang down from < *de-*, down + *pendere*, to hang: see PENDANT⟧ 1 to be influenced or determined by something else; be contingent (*on*) 2 to have trust; rely (*on*) 3 to rely (*on*) for support or aid 4 [Rare] to hang down 5 *Law* to be undecided or pending —**SYN.** RELY

de·pend·a·ble (dē pen′də bəl, di-) *adj.* that can be depended on; trustworthy; reliable —**SYN.** RELIABLE —**de·pend′a·bil′i·ty** *n.*, **de·pend′a·ble·ness** —**de·pend′a·bly** *adv.*

de·pend·ence (dē pen′dəns, di-) *n.* ⟦ME *dependaunce* < OFr *dependance* or ML *dependentia* < L *dependens*: see DEPENDENT⟧ 1 the condition or fact of being dependent; specif., *a)* a being contingent upon or influenced, controlled, or determined by something else *b)* reliance (*on* another) for support or aid *c)* subordination 2 reliance; trust 3 DEPENDENCY (sense 4) Also sp. **de·pend′ance**

de·pend·en·cy (dē pen′dən sē, di-) *n., pl.* **-cies** 1 dependence 2 something dependent or subordinate 3 a land or territory geographically distinct from the country governing it, and held in trust or as a possession, etc. in a subordinate status 4 addiction to alcohol or drugs 5 any emotional need or reliance regarded as excessive, unhealthy, etc. Also sp. **de·pend′an·cy**

de·pend·ent (dē pen′dənt, di-) *adj.* ⟦ME < OFr *dependant* < L *dependens*, prp. of *dependere*: see DEPEND⟧ 1 hanging down 2 influenced, controlled, or determined by something else; contingent 3 relying (*on* another) for support or aid 4 subordinate 5 addicted —*n.* 1 a person who depends on someone else for existence, support, etc. 2 [Obs.] a subordinate part Also, esp. for n., **de·pend′ant** —**de·pend′ent·ly** *adv.*

dependent clause *Gram.* a clause that cannot function syntactically as a complete sentence by itself but has a nominal, adjectival, or adverbial function within a larger sentence; subordinate clause (Ex.: She will visit us *if she can.*): distinguished from INDEPENDENT CLAUSE

dependent variable a variable whose value is determined by the value of another variable, as *y* in y = 5x

de·per·son·al·ize (dē pur′sən əl īz′) *vt.* **-ized′**, **-iz′ing** 1 to deprive of individuality; treat in an impersonal way 2 to cause to lose one's sense of personal identity —**de·per′son·al·i·za′tion** *n.*

de·pict (dē pikt′, di-) *vt.* ⟦ME *depicten* < L *depictus*, pp. of *depingere* < *de-*, intens. + *pingere*, to PAINT⟧ 1 to represent in a drawing, painting, sculpture, etc.; portray; picture 2 to picture in words; describe —**de·pic′tion** *n.* —**de·pic′tor** *n.*

de·pig·men·ta·tion (dē′pig mən tā′shən) *n.* loss of, or deficiency in, pigmentation

dep·i·late (dep′ə lāt′) *vt.* **-lat′ed**, **-lat′ing** ⟦< L *depilatus*, pp. of *depilare*, to deprive of hair < *de-*, from + *pilus*, hair⟧ to remove hair from (a part of the body) —**dep′i·la′tion** *n.* —**dep′i·la′tor** *n.*

de·pil·a·to·ry (di pil′ə tôr′ē) *adj.* serving to remove unwanted hair —*n., pl.* **-ries** a depilatory cream or other substance or device

de·plane (dē plān′) *vi.* **-planed′**, **-plan′ing** to get out of an airplane after it lands

de·plete (dē plēt′, di-) *vt.* **-plet′ed**, **-plet′ing** ⟦< L *depletus*, pp. of *deplere*, to empty < *de-*, from + *plere*, to fill: see FULL[1]⟧ 1 *a)* to make less by gradually using up (resources, funds, strength, etc.) *b)* to use up gradually the resources, strength, etc. of 2 to empty wholly or partly —**de·ple′tive** *adj.*

de·ple·tion (dē plē′shən, di-) *n.* 1 a depleting or being depleted 2 the gradual using up or destruction of capital assets, esp. of natural resources

de·plor·a·ble (dē plôr′ə bəl, di-) *adj.* that can or should be deplored; regrettable, wretched, very bad, etc. —**de·plor′a·bly** *adv.*

de·plore (dē plôr′, di-) *vt.* **-plored′**, **-plor′ing** ⟦Fr *déplorer* < L *deplorare* < *de-*, intens. + *plorare*, to weep⟧ 1 to be regretful or sorry about; lament 2 to regard as unfortunate or wretched 3 to condemn as wrong; disapprove of —**de·plor′er** *n.*

de·ploy (dē ploi′, di-) *vt.* ⟦Fr *déployer*, to unfold, display < OFr *desployer*, to unfold < L *displicare*, to scatter (in ML, to unfold): see DISPLAY⟧ 1 *Mil.* *a)* to spread out (troops, etc.) so as to form a wider front *b)* to station or place (forces, equipment, etc.) in accordance with a plan 2 to spread out or bring into position, lit. or fig., for use, action, etc. —*vi.* to be deployed —**de·ploy′ment** *n.*

de·plume (dē plo͞om′) *vt.* **-plumed′**, **-plum′ing** ⟦ME *deplumen* < ML *deplumare*: see DE- & PLUME⟧ 1 to pull or pluck the feathers from 2 to strip of honor, riches, etc. —**de′plu·ma′tion** *n.*

de·po·lar·ize (dē pō′lər īz′) *vt.* **-ized′**, **-iz′ing** to destroy or counteract the polarity or polarization of —**de·po′lar·i·za′tion** *n.* —**de·po′lar·iz′er** *n.*

de·po·lit·i·cize (dē′pə lit′ə sīz′) *vt.* **-cized′**, **-ciz′ing** to remove from political influence —**de·po·lit′i·ci·za′tion** *n.*

de·pone (dē pōn′) *vt., vi.* **-poned′**, **-pon′ing** ⟦L *deponere*, to put down (in ML, testify): see DEPOSE⟧ [Archaic] to declare under oath, esp. in writing; testify

de·pon·ent (dē pō′nənt, di-) *adj.* ⟦L *deponens*, prp. of *deponere*, to lay down, set down: see DEPOSE⟧ *Gram.* designating any of those verbs in classical Latin and Greek having passive or middle voice forms and an active meaning —*n.* 1 *Gram.* a deponent verb 2 *Law* *a)* a person who testifies under oath, esp., one who makes a deposition *b)* AFFIANT

Dep·o-Pro·ve·ra (dep′ō prə ver′ə) *trademark for* a synthetic progestin, $C_{24}H_{34}O_4$, used to treat uterine or kidney cancer, to prevent conception for long periods, etc.

de·pop·u·late (dē päp′yə lāt′) *vt.* **-lat′ed**, **-lat′ing** ⟦< L *depopulatus*, pp. of *depopulari*, to lay waste < *de-*, from + *populari*, to ravage, ruin < *populus*, PEOPLE⟧ to reduce the population of, esp. by violence, disease, etc. —**de·pop′u·la′tion** *n.* —**de·pop′u·la′tor** *n.*

de·port (dē pôrt′, di-) *vt.* ⟦OFr *deporter* < *de-* (L *de*), intens. + *porter* < L *portare*, to carry, bear: see PORT[2]⟧ 1 to behave or conduct (oneself) in a specified way 2 ⟦Fr *déporter* < L *deportare*, to carry away, banish < *de-*, from + *portare*⟧ to carry or send away; specif., to force (an alien) to leave a country by official order; expel —**SYN.** BANISH, BEHAVE

de·port·a·ble (-ə bel) *adj.* 1 liable to deportation 2 punishable by deportation

de·por·ta·tion (dē′pôr tā′shən) *n.* ⟦Fr *déportation* < L *deportatio*⟧ a deporting or being deported; expulsion, as of an undesirable alien, from a country

de·port·ee (dē′pôr tē′) *n.* ⟦DEPORT + -EE[1]⟧ a deported person or one sentenced to deportation

de·port·ment (dē pôrt′mənt, di-) *n.* ⟦OFr *deportement*: see DEPORT⟧ the manner of conducting or bearing oneself; behavior; demeanor —**SYN.** BEARING

de·pos·al (dē pō′zəl) *n.* the act of deposing from office; deposition

de·pose (dē pōz′, di-) *vt.* **-posed′**, **-pos′ing** ⟦ME *deposen*, to deprive of office, testify < OFr *deposer*, to set down < *de-* (L *de*), from, away + *poser* (see POSE[1]), to cease, lie down; confused in sense and form with L *deponere* (pp. *depositus*), to lay down, lay aside (in ML, testify): see fol.⟧ 1 to remove from office or a position of power, esp. from a throne; oust 2 [Archaic] to lay down 3 *Law* *a)* to state or testify under oath but out of court *b)* to take the deposition of (a witness) —*vi.* to bear witness —**de·pos′a·ble** *adj.*

de·pos·it (dē päz′it, di-) *vt.* ⟦< L *depositus*, pp. of *deponere*, to put down < *de-*, down + *ponere*, to put: see POSITION⟧ 1 to place or entrust for safekeeping 2 to put (money) in a bank, as for safekeeping or to earn interest 3 to put down as a pledge or partial payment 4 to put, lay, or set down 5 to cause (sand, sediment, etc.) to settle or form by a natural process —*n.* ⟦L *depositum* < *depositus*: see the *vt.*⟧ 1 something placed or entrusted for safekeeping; specif., money put in a bank 2 *a)* a pledge or partial payment *b)* a sum of money paid as security on something rented, or for a returnable bottle, etc. 3 the act of depositing 4 a depository 5 *a)* something deposited or left lying *b)* *Geol., Mining* sand, clay, mineral masses, etc. deposited by the action of wind, water, volcanic eruption, or ice —**on deposit** placed or entrusted for safekeeping

de·pos·i·tar·y (dē päz′ə ter′ē, di-) *n., pl.* **-tar′ies** ⟦LL *depositarius* < L *depositum*: see prec.⟧ 1 a person, firm, etc. entrusted with something for safekeeping; trustee 2 a storehouse; depository

dep·o·si·tion (dep′ə zish′ən, dē′pə-) *n.* ⟦ME & OFr < L *depositio*, a laying or putting down < L *depositus*: see DEPOSIT⟧ 1 a deposing or being deposed; removal from office or position of power 2 the act of testifying 3 a depositing or being deposited 4 something deposited or left lying 5 *Law* the testimony of a witness made under oath, but not in open court, and written down to be used when the case comes to trial

de·pos·i·tor (dē päz′ət ər, di-) *n.* a person who deposits something, esp. money in a bank

de·pos·i·to·ry (dē päz′ə tôr′ē, di-) *n., pl.* **-ries** ⟦LL *depositorium*: see DEPOSIT⟧ 1 a place where things are put for safekeeping; storehouse 2 a trustee; depositary

de·pot (dē′pō; *military & Brit* dep′ō) *n.* ⟦Fr *dépôt*, a deposit, storehouse < L *depositum*: see DEPOSIT⟧ 1 a storehouse; warehouse ☆2 a railroad or bus station: originally used of a freight station 3 *Mil.* *a)* a storage place for supplies *b)* a station for assembling either recruits for training or combat replacements for assignment to a unit

de·prave (dē prāv′, di-) *vt.* **-praved′**, **-prav′ing** ⟦ME *depraven* < OFr *depraver* < L *depravare*, to make crooked < *de-*, intens. + *pravus*, crooked < IE base **pra-*, to bend > MIr *rāth*, bulwark⟧ 1 to lead into bad habits; make morally bad; corrupt; pervert 2 [Obs.] to defame or slander —**SYN.** DEBASE —**dep·ra·va·tion** (dep′rə vā′shən) *n.* —**de·prav′er** *n.*

de·praved (-prāvd′) *adj.* morally bad; corrupt; perverted —**de·prav′ed·ly** (-prā′vid lē) *adv.*

de·prav·i·ty (dē prav′ə tē, di-) *n.* ⟦altered (after DEPRAVE) < obs. *pravity* < L *pravitas*, crookedness⟧ 1 a depraved condition; corruption; wickedness 2 *pl.* **-ties** a depraved act or practice

dep·re·cate (dep′rə kāt′) *vt.* **-cat′ed**, **-cat′ing** ⟦< L *deprecatus*, pp. of *deprecari*, to ward off by intercession < *de-*, off, from + *precari*, PRAY⟧ 1 to feel and express disapproval of; plead against 2 to depreciate; belittle 3 [Archaic] to try to avert by prayer —**dep′re·cat′ing·ly** *adv.* —**dep′re·ca′tion** *n.* —**dep′re·ca′tor** *n.*

dep·re·ca·to·ry (dep′rə kə tôr′ē) *adj.* ⟦LL(Ec) *deprecatorius*⟧ 1 deprecating 2 apologetic or belittling Also **dep′re·ca′tive** (-kāt′iv)

de·pre·ci·a·ble (dē prē′shē ə bəl, -shə bəl) *adj.* that can be depreciated, or lessened in value

de·pre·ci·ate (dē prē′shē āt′, di-) *vt.* **-at′ed, -at′ing** ⟦ME *depreciaten* < LL *depretiatus,* pp. of *depretiare,* to lower the price of (in LL(Ec), to make light of) < L *de-,* from + *pretiare,* to value < *pretium,* PRICE⟧ **1** to reduce in value or price **2** to make seem less important; belittle; disparage —☆*vi.* to drop in value or price —***SYN.*** DISPARAGE —**de·pre′ci·a′tor** *n.* —**de·pre′ci·a·to′ry** (-shē ə tôr′ē, -shə tôr′ē-) *adj.,* **de·pre′ci·a′tive** (-shē āt′iv, -shə tiv)

de·pre·ci·a·tion (dē prē′shē ā′shən, di-) *n.* ⟦see prec.⟧ ☆**1** *a)* a decrease in value of property through wear, deterioration, or obsolescence *b)* the allowance made for this in bookkeeping, accounting, etc. ☆**2** a decrease in the purchasing power of money **3** a making seem less important; disparagement

dep·re·date (dep′rə dāt′) *vt., vi.* **-dat′ed, -dat′ing** ⟦LL *depraedatus,* pp. of *depraedari* < L *de-,* intens. + *praedari,* to plunder < *praeda,* booty, PREY⟧ [Rare] to plunder —**dep′re·da′tor** *n.* —**dep·re·da·to·ry** (dep′rə də tôr′ē, -dāt′ər ē; di pred′ə tôr′ē) *adj.*

dep·re·da·tion (dep′rə dā′shən) *n.* ⟦LL *depraedatio:* see prec.⟧ the act or an instance of robbing, plundering, or laying waste

de·press (dē pres′, di-) *vt.* ⟦ME *depressen* < OFr *depresser* < L *depressus,* pp. of *deprimere,* to press down, sink < *de-,* down + *premere,* to PRESS[1]⟧ **1** to press down; push or pull down; lower **2** to lower in spirits; make gloomy; discourage; sadden **3** to decrease the force or activity of; weaken **4** to lower in value, price, or amount **5** [Obs.] to suppress **6** *Music* to lower the pitch of —**de·press′ing** *adj.* —**de·press′ing·ly** *adv.*

de·pres·sant (dē pres′ənt, di-) *adj.* ⟦prec. + -ANT⟧ lowering the rate of muscular or nervous activity —*n.* a depressant medicine, drug, etc.; sedative

de·pressed (dē prest′, di-) *adj.* **1** pressed down **2** lowered in position, intensity, amount, or degree **3** flattened or hollowed, as if pressed down **4** gloomy; dejected; sad **5** suffering from psychological depression **6** characterized by widespread unemployment, poverty, lack of opportunity, etc.; impoverished [*a depressed* area] **7** *Bot.* flattened, as if from downward pressure **8** *Zool.* having the horizontal diameter longer than the vertical; broad —***SYN.*** SAD

de·press·i·ble (dē pres′ə bəl, di-) *adj.* that can be depressed

de·pres·sion (dē presh′ən, di-) *n.* ⟦ME *depressioun* < OFr *depression* < L *depressio:* see DEPRESS⟧ **1** a depressing or being depressed **2** a depressed part or place; hollow or low place on a surface **3** low spirits; gloominess; dejection; sadness **4** a decrease in force, activity, amount, etc. **5** *Astron.* the angular distance of a celestial body below the horizon ☆**6** *Econ.* a period or condition marked by slackening of business activity, widespread unemployment, falling prices and wages, etc. **7** *Med.* a decrease in functional activity **8** *Meteorol. a)* a lowering of the atmospheric pressure indicated by the fall of mercury in a barometer *b)* an area of relatively low barometric pressure; low **9** *Psychol.* an emotional condition, either neurotic or psychotic, characterized by feelings of hopelessness, inadequacy, etc. **10** *Surveying* the angular distance of an object below the horizontal plane —**the (Great) Depression** the period of economic depression which began in 1929 and lasted through most of the 1930s

Depression glass cheap glassware mass-produced during the Depression of the 1930s, usually molded in patterns in pale colors, and collectible since the early 1970s

de·pres·sive (dē pres′iv, di-) *adj.* **1** tending to depress **2** characterized by psychological depression —*n.* a person suffering from psychological depression —**de·pres′sive·ly** *adv.*

de·pres·so·mo·tor (di pres′ō mōt′ər) *adj.* slowing down or decreasing motor activity —*n.* a depressomotor drug, etc.

de·pres·sor (dē pres′ər, di-) *n.* **1** a person or thing that depresses **2** any of various muscles that draw down a part of the body **3** a nerve which when stimulated decreases the activity of a part of the body **4** an instrument that presses a protruding part out of the way during a medical examination or operation [a tongue *depressor*]

de·pres·sur·ize (dē presh′ər īz′) *vt.* **-ized′, -iz′ing** to reduce pressure in or eliminate pressure from —**de·pres′sur·i·za′tion** *n.*

dep·ri·va·tion (dep′rə vā′shən; *also* dē′prī vā′-) *n.* ⟦ME *deprivacioun*⟧ **1** a depriving or being deprived **2** a loss Also [Rare] **de·priv·al** (dē prī′vəl, di-) —**dep′ri·va′tion·al** *adj.*

de·prive (dē prīv′, di-) *vt.* **-prived′, -priv′ing** ⟦ME *depriven* < ML(Ec) *deprivare* < L *de-,* intens. + *privare,* to deprive, separate: see PRIVATE⟧ **1** to take something away from forcibly; dispossess [to *deprive* someone of his property] **2** to keep from having, using, or enjoying [to be *deprived* of one's rights] **3** to remove from office, esp. ecclesiastical office

de·prived (-prīvd′) *adj.* that has undergone deprivation; specif., of or from a poor or depressed area; underprivileged

De Pro·fun·dis (dā′ prō fo͝on′dis) ⟦LL(Ec), out of the depths⟧ *name for* Psalm 130 (in the Douay version, Psalm 129): from the first words of the Latin version

☆**de·pro·gram** (dē prō′gram′, -grəm) *vt.* **-grammed′** or **-gramed′, -gram′ming** or **-gram′ing** to cause to abandon a rigid commitment to certain beliefs, values, etc., as those of a religious cult, by undoing the effects of indoctrination —**de·pro′gram′mer** *n.*

dep·side (dep′sīd′, -sid) *n.* ⟦Ger *depsid* < Gr *depsein,* to tan + *-id,* -IDE⟧ any of a class of anhydrides, similar to esters, formed from phenol carboxylic acids by the combination of a carboxyl group with a phenol group

dept *abbrev.* **1** department **2** deputy

depth (depth) *n.* ⟦ME *depthe* < *dep:* see DEEP & -TH[1]⟧ **1** *a)* the distance from the top downward, from the surface inward, or from front to back *b)* perspective, as in a painting **2** the quality or condition of being deep; deepness; specif., *a)* intensity, as of colors, silence, or emotion *b)* profundity of thought *c)* lowness of pitch **3** the middle part [the *depth* of winter] **4** [*usually pl.*] the far inner or inmost part [the *depths* of a wood] **5** [*usually pl.*] the deep or deepest part, as of the sea **6** [*usually pl.*] *a)* the most extreme degree, as of despair *b)* a low state or condition [shocked that their principles had fallen to such *depths*] **7** reserve strength, as of suitable substitute players for a team —**in depth** in a thorough and comprehensive way [analysis *in depth*] —**out of** (or **beyond**) **one's depth** **1** in water too deep for one **2** past one's ability or understanding

depth charge (*or* **bomb**) a powerful explosive charge that is dropped from a ship or airplane and explodes under water: used esp. against submarines

depth of field the range of distances from a lens within which photographed or filmed objects are in focus: reducing the aperture of a lens increases the depth of field

depth perception ability to see objects in perspective

depth psychology any system of psychology, as psychoanalysis, dealing with the processes of the unconscious

dep·u·rate (dep′yo͞o rāt′) *vt.* **-rat′ed, -rat′ing** ⟦< ML *depuratus,* pp. of *depurare,* to purify < L *de-,* intens. + *purare,* to purify < *purus,* PURE⟧ to purify

dep·u·ta·tion (dep′yo͞o tā′shən, -yə-) *n.* ⟦ME *deputacioun* < LL *deputatio*⟧ **1** a deputing or being deputed **2** a group of persons, or one person, appointed to represent others

de·pute (dē pyo͞ot′, di-) *vt.* **-put′ed, -put′ing** ⟦ME *deputen* < OFr *deputer* < L *deputare,* to cut off, detach, hence depute < *de-,* from + *putare,* lit., to cleanse, lop off: see PURE⟧ **1** to give (authority, functions, etc.) to someone else as deputy **2** to appoint as one's substitute, agent, etc.

dep·u·tize (dep′yo͞o tīz′, -yə-) *vt.* **-tized′, -tiz′ing** to appoint as deputy, esp. as temporary deputy —*vi.* to act as deputy, esp. as temporary deputy —**dep′u·ti·za′tion** *n.*

dep·u·ty (dep′yo͞o tē, -yə-) *n., pl.* **-ties** ⟦ME *depute* < Anglo-Fr *deputé,* pp. of OFr *deputer:* see DEPUTE⟧ **1** a person appointed to act as a substitute for, or as an assistant to, another, specif., a SHERIFF (sense 2) **2** a member of any of certain national legislatures or their lower houses, as in France, Italy, or Albania —*adj.* acting as deputy —***SYN.*** AGENT

De Quin·cey (də kwin′sē), **Thomas** 1785-1859; Eng. essayist & critic

de·rac·i·nate (dē ras′ə nāt′, di-) *vt.* **-nat′ed, -nat′ing** ⟦Fr *déraciner* < *dé-* (L *dis-*), from + *racine,* a root < LL *radicina* < L *radix* (gen. *radicis*), ROOT[1]⟧ **1** to pull up by or as by the roots; uproot; eradicate **2** to separate from one's roots or ties, esp. ethnic or national ones —**de·rac′i·na′tion** *n.* —**de·rac′i·nat′ed** *adj.*

de·rail (dē rāl′) *vt.* ⟦Fr *dérailler* < *dé-,* from (see DE-) + *rail* < OFr *reille:* see RAIL[1]⟧ to cause (a train, etc.) to go off the rails —*vi.* to go off the rails —**de·rail′ment** *n.*

de·rail·leur (di rā′lər) *n.* ⟦Fr *dérailleur,* derailer, with reference to the "derailing" of the chain from the sprocket⟧ a mechanism for shifting gears on a bicycle, that moves the chain from one to another of the different-sized sprocket wheels

De·rain (də ran′), **An·dré** (än drā′) 1880-1954; Fr. painter

de·range (dē rānj′, di-) *vt.* **-ranged′, -rang′ing** ⟦Fr *déranger* < OFr *desrengier* < *des-* (L *dis-*), apart + *rengier:* see RANGE⟧ **1** to upset the arrangement, order, or operation of; unsettle; disorder **2** to make insane —**de·ranged′** *adj.* —**de·range′ment** *n.*

de·rate (dē rāt′) *vt.* **-rat′ed, -rat′ing** to reduce the electrical power rating of (a nuclear power plant, furnace, electrical component, etc.) to improve safety, reliability, or efficiency

Der·by[1] (dur′bē; *chiefly Brit,* där′bē) *n., pl.* **-bies** **1** ⟦after the twelfth Earl of fol., who founded the race in 1780⟧ a race for three-year-old horses, run annually at Epsom Downs in Surrey **2** any similar horse race; esp., the Kentucky Derby ☆**3** [**d-**] any of various contests or races, open to anyone who wishes to enter [a fishing *derby,* demolition *derby*] ☆**4** [**d-**] a stiff felt hat with a round crown and curved brim; bowler

Der·by[2] (dur′bē; *chiefly Brit,* där′bē) **1** city in Derbyshire, central England **2** DERBYSHIRE

Der·by·shire (dur′bi shir, -shər; *chiefly Brit,* där′-) county in central England: 1,015 sq mi (2,629 sq km)

☆**de·re·al·i·za·tion** (dē rē′əl i zā′shən) *n.* a loss or lessening of one's sense of the reality of things, as in the reaction to certain drugs

☆**de·re·cho** (de rā′chō) *n.* ⟦Sp, adj., straight, direct⟧ an extensive, fast-moving band of severe thunderstorms characterized by straight-line winds

de·rec·og·nized (dē rek′əg nīzd′) *adj.* having had official or legal recognition revoked

☆**de·reg·u·late** (dē reg′yə lāt′) *vt.* **-lat′ed, -lat′ing** to remove regulations governing [to *deregulate* the price of natural gas] —**de·reg′u·la′tion** *n.*

Der·ek (der′ik) *n.* a masculine name: var. *Derrick;* equiv. Du. *Dirk*

der·e·lict (der′ə likt′) *adj.* ⟦L *derelictus,* pp. of *derelinquere,* to forsake utterly, abandon < *de-,* intens. + *relinquere:* see RELINQUISH⟧ **1** deserted by the owner; abandoned; forsaken ☆**2** neglectful of duty; remiss; negligent —*n.* **1** a property abandoned by the owner; esp., an abandoned ship on the open sea **2** a destitute person, without a home or regular job and rejected by society **3** land exposed by the receding of water —***SYN.*** REMISS

der·e·lic·tion (der′ə lik′shən) *n.* ⟦L *derelictio:* see prec.⟧ **1** [Now Rare] an abandoning or forsaking **2** [Now Rare] the state of being abandoned or forsaken **3** a neglect of, or failure in, duty; a being remiss **4** *Law* the gaining of land from water by the gradual retreat of the sea below the usual watermark

de·ride (di rīd′) *vt.* **-rid′ed, -rid′ing** ⟦L *deridere* < *de-*, pejorative + *ridere*, to laugh: see RIDICULE⟧ to laugh at in contempt or scorn; make fun of; ridicule —*SYN.* RIDICULE —**de·rid′er** *n.* —**de·rid′ing·ly** *adv.*

de ri·gueur (dā′ri gʉr′, də-) ⟦Fr, lit., of strictness⟧ **1** required by etiquette; according to good form; proper **2** required by fashion; fashionable

de·ri·sion (di rizh′ən) *n.* ⟦ME < LL *derisio* < *derisus*, pp. of *deridere*⟧ **1** a deriding or being derided; contempt or ridicule **2** [Rare] a person or thing derided

de·ri·sive (di rī′siv, -ziv) *adj.* ⟦ML *derisivus*: see prec. & -IVE⟧ **1** showing derision; ridiculing **2** provoking derision; ridiculous Also **de·ri′so·ry** (-sə rē, -zə-) —**de·ri′sive·ly** *adv.* —**de·ri′sive·ness** *n.*

deriv *abbrev.* **1** derivation **2** derived

der·i·va·tion (der′ə vā′shən) *n.* ⟦ME *derivacioun* < L *derivatio* < pp. of *derivare*: see DERIVE⟧ **1** a deriving or being derived **2** descent or origination **3** something derived; a derivative **4** the source or origin of something **5** the origin and development of a word; etymology **6** *a)* *Gram.* the process of forming words from bases by the addition of affixes other than inflectional morphemes, or by internal phonetic change [the *derivation* of "warmth" from "warm"] *b)* *Linguis.* in generative grammar, the process of forming sentences —**der′i·va′tion·al** *adj.*

de·riv·a·tive (də riv′ə tiv) *adj.* ⟦ME *derivatif* < LL *derivativus* < L *derivatus*, pp. of *derivare*: see fol.⟧ **1** derived **2** using or taken from other sources; not original **3** of derivation —*n.* **1** something derived **2** *Chem.* a substance derived from, or of such composition and properties that it may be considered as derived from, another substance by chemical change, esp. by the substitution of one or more elements or radicals **3** *Finance* a contract, as an option or futures contract, whose value depends on the value of the securities, commodities, etc. that form the basis of the contract **4** *Linguis.* a word formed from another or others by derivation **5** *Math.* the limiting value of a rate of change of a function with respect to a variable; the instantaneous rate of change, or slope, of a function (Ex.: the derivative of *y* with respect to *x*, often written dy/dx, is 3 when y = 3x) —**de·riv′a·tive·ly** *adv.*

de·rive (di rīv′) *vt.* **-rived′, -riv′ing** ⟦ME *deriven* < OFr *deriver* < L *derivare*, to divert, orig., to turn a stream from its channel < *de-*, from + *rivus*, a stream: see RIVAL⟧ **1** to get or receive (something) *from* a source **2** to get by reasoning; deduce or infer **3** to trace from or to a source; show the derivation of **4** *Chem.* to obtain or produce (a compound) from another compound by replacing one element with one or more other elements —*vi.* to come (*from*); be derived; originate —*SYN.* RISE —**de·riv′a·ble** *adj.* —**de·riv′er** *n.*

derm- (dʉrm) *combining form* DERMATO-: used before a vowel

-derm (dʉrm) ⟦see fol.⟧ *combining form* skin or covering [*blastoderm, endoderm*]

der·ma[1] (dʉr′mə) *n.* ⟦ModL < Gr *derma*, skin < IE base **der-*, to skin, flay > TEAR[1]⟧ DERMIS

der·ma[2] (dʉr′mə) *n.* ⟦Yiddish *derme*, pl. of *darm*, gut < MHG < OHG *daram* < IE **tormo-s*, hole < base **ter-*, to rub, bore > THROW, Gr *tormos*, hole⟧ KISHKE

☆**der·ma·bra·sion** (dʉr′mə brā′zhən) *n.* ⟦DERM(IS) + ABRASION⟧ the surgical procedure of scraping off upper layers of the epidermis with an abrasive device, as in seeking to repair acne scars, blemishes, etc.

der·mal (dʉr′məl) *adj.* of the skin or the dermis

der·map·ter·an (dər map′tər ən) *n.* ⟦< ModL *Dermaptera* (see DERMA[1] & PTERO-) + -AN⟧ EARWIG

der·ma·ti·tis (dʉr′mə tīt′is) *n.* ⟦fol. + -ITIS⟧ inflammation of the skin: see also CONTACT DERMATITIS

der·ma·to- (dʉr′mə tō; dər mat′ō, -ə) ⟦Gr *dermato-* < *derma* (gen. *dermatos*), skin: see DERMA[1]⟧ *combining form* skin or hide [*dermatology*]: also, before a vowel, **dermat-**

der·ma·to·gen (dʉr′mə tə jən, dər mat′ə-) *n.* ⟦prec. + -GEN⟧ *Bot.* a layer of dividing cells from which the epidermis is formed

☆**der·ma·to·glyph·ics** (dʉr′mə tō glif′iks) *pl.n.* ⟦< DERMATO- + Gr *glyphein*, to carve (see GLYPH) + -IC + -S⟧ the patterns of skin ridges on the lower surface of the hand or foot —*n.* ⟦see -ICS⟧ the study of these, as in medical diagnosis —**der′ma·to·glyph′ic** *adj.*

der·ma·tol·o·gy (dʉr′mə täl′ə jē) *n.* ⟦DERMATO- + -LOGY⟧ the branch of medicine dealing with the skin, hair, and nails —**der′ma·to·log′ic** (-tə läj′ik) *adj.*, **der′ma·to·log′i·cal** (-läj′i kəl) —**der′ma·tol′o·gist** *n.*

der·ma·tome (dʉr′mə tōm′) *n.* ⟦DERMA[1] + -TOME⟧ any of the segmentally arranged mesodermal masses in a vertebrate embryo, destined to form dermis

der·ma·to·phyte (dʉr′mə tō fīt′, dər mat′ə-) *n.* any plant parasitic on the skin, as the fungus that causes ringworm

der·ma·to·plas·ty (-plas′tē) *n.* ⟦DERMATO- + -PLASTY⟧ plastic surgery of the skin, as by skin grafts

der·ma·to·sis (dʉr′mə tō′sis) *n.*, *pl.* **-to′ses′** (-sēz′) ⟦DERMAT(O)- + -OSIS⟧ any disorder of the skin: see DERMATITIS

der·mes·tid (dər mes′tid) *n.* ⟦< ModL *Dermestidae* < Gr *dermēstēs*, a leather-eating worm < *derma*, skin (see DERMA[1]) + *esthiein*, to eat < *esthi*, imper. of *edmenai*, EAT⟧ any of a family (Dermestidae) of small, drab-colored beetles whose larvae and adults are destructive to hides, furs, woolens, cereals, etc.

der·mic (dʉr′mik) *adj.* DERMAL

der·mis (dʉr′mis) *n.* ⟦ModL, back-form. < LL *epidermis*, EPIDERMIS⟧ the layer of skin just below the epidermis

der·mo- (dʉr′mō, -mə) ⟦< Gr *derma*: see DERMA[1]⟧ *combining form* DERMATO-

der·moid (dʉr′moid′) *adj.* ⟦prec. + -OID⟧ **1** consisting of tissues of ectodermal origin, such as skin, hair, and teeth, as found in certain benign, congenital tumors **2** skinlike

der·mop·ter·an (dər mäp′tər′ən) *n.* ⟦< ModL *Dermoptera* < *dermo-*, DERMO- + *-ptera* (see PTERO-) + -AN⟧ FLYING LEMUR

der·nier cri (der nyā krē′) ⟦Fr, lit., the latest cry⟧ the latest fashion; last word

der·o·gate (der′ə gāt′) *vt.* **-gat′ed, -gat′ing** ⟦ME *derogaten* < L *derogatus*, pp. of *derogare*, to repeal part of (a law), detract from < *de-*, from + *rogare*, to ask: see ROGATION⟧ **1** [Archaic] to take (a part or quality) away *from* something so as to impair it **2** [Rare] to lower in esteem; disparage —*vi.* **1** to take something desirable away; detract (*from*) **2** to lower oneself; lose face

der·o·ga·tion (der′ə gā′shən) *n.* ⟦ME *derogacioun* < OFr *derogation* < L *derogatio*: see prec.⟧ **1** a lessening or weakening (*of* power, authority, position, etc.) **2** disparagement; detraction **3** a lowering of oneself; loss of rank

de·rog·a·to·ry (di räg′ə tôr′ē) *adj.* ⟦L *derogatorius*: see DEROGATE⟧ **1** [Archaic] tending to lessen or impair; detracting **2** disparaging; belittling Also **de·rog′a·tive** —**de·rog′a·to′ri·ly** *adv.*

der·rick (der′ik) *n.* ⟦after Thos. *Derrick*, London hangman of the early 17th c.: first applied to a gallows⟧ **1** a large apparatus for lifting and moving heavy objects: it consists of a long beam pivoted at the base of a vertical, stationary beam and moved by ropes running on pulleys ☆**2** a tall, tapering framework, as over an oil well, to support drilling machinery, etc.

derrick
(sense 2)

Der·ri·da (de rē dä′), **Jacques** (zhäk) 1930-2004; Fr. philosopher, born in Algeria

der·ri·ère (der′ē er′) *n.* ⟦Fr, back part, rear, orig. *adv.*, behind < LL *deretro* < L *de retro* < *de*, from + *retro*, back: see RETRO-⟧ the buttocks

der·ring-do (der′iŋ do͞o′) *n.* ⟦ME *derrynge do*, *durring don*, lit., daring to do; misunderstood as abstract n. by Edmund SPENSER[2] and thence popularized by Sir Walter SCOTT[2] in his novel *Ivanhoe* (1819)⟧ daring action; reckless courage

☆**der·rin·ger** (der′in jər) *n.* ⟦after Henry *Deringer* 1786-1868, U.S. gunsmith⟧ a small, short-barreled pistol

der·ris (der′is) *n.* ⟦ModL < Gr, hide < IE base **der-*: see DERMA[1]⟧ any of a genus (*Derris*) of woody East Indian plants of the pea family, from whose roots rotenone is extracted

Der·ry (der′ē) *another name for* LONDONDERRY (the district & seaport)

der·vish (dʉr′vish) *n.* ⟦Turk *dervish* < Pers *darvēsh*, beggar⟧ a member of any of various Muslim religious groups dedicated to a life of poverty and chastity: some dervishes practice whirling, chanting, etc. as religious acts

DES *abbrev.* diethylstilbestrol

de·sa·cral·ize (dē sā′krə līz′) *vt.* **-ized′, -iz′ing** to deprive of sacred qualities or hallowed status; make nonsacred or less sacred —**de·sa′cral·i·za′tion** *n.*

de·sal·i·na·tion (dē sal′ə nā′shən) *n.* ⟦DE- + SALIN(E) + -ATION⟧ the removal of salt, esp. from sea water to make it drinkable —**de·sal′i·nate′** (-sal′ə nāt′) *vt.* **-nat′ed, -nat′ing**

de·sa·li·ni·za·tion (dē sā′lə nə zā′shən, dē sal′ə-) *n.* ⟦DE- + SALIN(E) + -IZATION⟧ the removal of salt, esp. from sea water to make it drinkable —**de·sa′lin·ize′** (-sā′lə nīz′, -sal′ə-) *vt.* **-ized′, -iz′ing**

☆**de·salt** (dē sôlt′) *vt.* to remove salt from (esp. sea water)

des·cant (des′kant′; *for v., also* des kant′) *n.* ⟦ME < Anglo-Fr *deschaunt* & ML *discantus* < L *dis-*, from, apart + *cantus*, song: see CHANT⟧ **1** in medieval music, *a)* two-part singing in which there is a fixed, known melody and an additional but subordinate melody that is higher in pitch *b)* this added upper melody *c)* the highest voice in polyphonic singing, as the treble or soprano: in these senses, many musicologists prefer DISCANT **2** a varied song or melody **3** ⟦< the v.⟧ a comment; criticism; discourse —*vi.* ⟦ME *discanten* < the n.⟧ **1** to talk or write at length; comment expansively; discourse (*on* or *upon*) **2** to sing or play a descant to the main melody **3** to sing

Des·cartes (dā kärt′), **Re·né** (rə nā′) 1596-1650; Fr. philosopher & mathematician

de·scend (dē send′, di-) *vi.* ⟦ME *descenden* < OFr *descendre* < L *descendere*, to climb down, fall < *de-*, down + *scandere*, to climb < ? IE base **skend-*, **skand-*, to leap > Gr *skandalon* (> SCANDAL), Sans *skandati*, (he) leaps⟧ **1** to move from a higher to a lower place; come down or go down **2** to pass from an earlier to a later time, from greater to less, from general to particular, etc. **3** to slope or extend downward **4** to come down (*from* a source, as from an ancestor): usually with auxiliary *be* [he is *descended* from pioneers] **5** to pass by inheritance or heredity [the estate *descended* to the nephew] **6** to lower oneself or stoop (*to* some act) **7** to make a sudden attack, raid, or visit (*on* or *upon*) **8** *Astron.* to move toward the horizon **9** *Music* to move down the scale —*vt.* to move, step, or pass down or down along —**de·scend′i·ble** *adj.*

de·scend·ant (dē sen′dənt, di-) *adj.* ⟦ME *descendaunt* < OFr *descendant* < L *descendens*, prp. of *descendere*: see prec.⟧ descending: also **de·scend′ent** —*n.* **1** a person who is an offspring, however remote, of a certain ancestor, family, group, etc. **2** something that derives from an earlier form

de·scend·er (dē sen′dər, di-) *n.* **1** a person or thing that descends **2** *Typography* *a)* the extension or downward stroke of any of certain lowercase letters such as *g*, *j*, or *p* *b)* any such letter

de·scent (dē sent′, di-) *n.* ⟦ME *descent* < OFr *descente* < *descendre*: see

DESCEND] 1 a descending; coming down or going down 2 lineage; ancestry 3 one generation (in a specified lineage) 4 a downward slope 5 a way down or downward 6 a sudden attack, raid, or invasion (*on* or *upon*) 7 a decline; fall 8 a stooping (*to* an act) 9 *Law* transference (of property) to heirs or offspring by inheritance

Des·chutes (dā sho͞ot′) [< Fr *rivière des chutes*, river of the falls] river in central and N Oreg., flowing from the Cascade Range north into the Columbia River: *c.* 250 mi (402 km)

☆**de·scram·ble** (dē skram′bəl) *vt.* **-bled**, **-bling** to make (incoming scrambled signals) intelligible, as by the use of special electronic equipment; unscramble —**de·scram′bler** *n.*

de·scribe (di skrīb′) *vt.* **-scribed′**, **-scrib′ing** [ME *descriven* < OFr *descrivre* < L *describere*, to copy down, transcribe < *de-*, from + *scribere*, to write: see SCRIBE] 1 to tell or write about; give a detailed account of 2 to picture in words 3 to move through space in such a way as to represent or conform to (the outline of a given shape) [the gymnast's rotating arm *described* an arc] 4 [Obs.] to descry: so used through confusion —**de·scrib′a·ble** *adj.* —**de·scrib′er** *n.*

de·scrip·tion (di skrip′shən) *n.* [ME *descripcioun* < OFr *description* < L *descriptio*, a marking out, delineation < pp. of *describere*: see prec.] 1 the act, process, art, or technique of describing or picturing in words 2 a statement or passage that describes 3 sort, kind, or variety [books of every *description*] 4 the act of tracing or outlining [the *description* of a circle]

de·scrip·tive (di skrip′tiv) *adj.* describing; of or characterized by description; specif., *a)* designating or of a branch of a science in which its data or materials are described and classified [*descriptive* anatomy] *b) Gram.* designating an adjective that indicates a quality or condition of the person or thing named by the word it modifies ["big" in "big barn" is a *descriptive* adjective] —**de·scrip′tive·ly** *adv.* —**de·scrip′tive·ness** *n.*

descriptive geometry the system of geometry that uses plane projections and perspective drawings of solid figures, usually in order to describe and analyze their properties for engineering and manufacturing purposes

descriptive linguistics the branch of linguistics that describes the structure of a language as it exists, without reference to its history or to comparison with other languages

de·scrip·tor (di skrip′tər) *n.* [L, describer < pp. of *describere*, DESCRIBE] 1 a word or phrase used as a label to describe or classify 2 *Comput.* a term used to identify or locate a file or specific data

de·scry (di skrī′) *vt.* **-scried′**, **-scry′ing** [ME *descrien* < OFr *descrier*, to proclaim < *des-*, from + *crier*: see CRY] 1 to catch sight of; discern (distant or obscure objects) 2 to look for and discover; detect —**SYN.** SEE[1]

Des·de·mo·na (dez′də mō′nə) *n. see* OTHELLO

des·e·crate (des′i krāt′) *vt.* **-crat′ed**, **-crat′ing** [DE- (sense 4) + (CON)SECRATE] to take away the sacredness of; treat as not sacred; profane —**des′e·crat′er** *n.*, **des′e·cra′tor**

des·e·cra·tion (des′i krā′shən) *n.* a desecrating or being desecrated —**SYN.** SACRILEGE

de·seg·re·gate (dē seg′rə gāt′) *vt.*, *vi.* **-gat′ed**, **-gat′ing** to abolish the segregation of races in (public schools, etc.) —**de·seg′re·ga′tion** *n.*

de·sen·si·tize (dē sen′sə tīz′) *vt.* **-tized′**, **-tiz′ing** 1 to take away the sensitivity of; make less sensitive 2 to make (a photographic plate or film) less sensitive to light 3 *Med.* to make (a person, animal, or tissue) nonreactive or nonallergic to a substance by removing the antibodies from sensitized cells —**de·sen′si·ti·za′tion** *n.* —**de·sen′si·tiz′er** *n.*

de·sert[1] (di zʉrt′) *vt.* [Fr *déserter* < LL *desertare* < *desertus*, pp. of L *deserere*, to desert, lit., to disjoin < *de-*, from + *serere*, to join < IE base **ser-*, to join, place in a row > Gr *eirein*, to fasten in rows, L *series*] 1 to forsake (someone or something that one ought not to leave); abandon 2 to leave (one's post, military service, etc.) without permission 3 to fail (someone) when most needed —*vi.* to leave one's post, military duty, etc. without permission and with no intent to return, or, in war, in order to avoid hazardous duty —**SYN.** ABANDON —**de·sert′er** *n.*

des·ert[2] (dez′ərt) *n.* [ME < OFr < LL(Ec) *desertum*, a desert, for L *deserta* < *desertus*: see prec.] 1 an uncultivated region without inhabitants; wilderness 2 a dry, barren, sandy region, often extremely hot —*adj.* 1 of a desert or deserts 2 wild and uninhabited [a *desert* island] —**SYN.** WASTE

de·sert[3] (di zʉrt′) *n.* [ME & OFr *deserte* < *deservir*: see DESERVE] 1 the fact of deserving reward or punishment 2 [*often pl.*] deserved reward or punishment [to get one's just *deserts*] 3 the quality of deserving reward; merit

de·sert·i·fi·ca·tion (di zʉrt′ə fi kā′shən) *n.* [DESERT[2] + -I- + -FICATION] the change of arable land into a desert either from natural causes or as a result of human activity

de·ser·tion (di zʉr′shən) *n.* [ME *desercioun* < OFr *desertion* < L *desertio*] 1 a deserting or being deserted 2 *Law* the willful abandonment of one's spouse, children, etc.

Desert Storm the principal military operation carried out by UN forces in the Gulf War

de·serve (di zʉrv′) *vt.* **-served′**, **-serv′ing** [ME *deserven* < OFr *deservir*, to deserve < L *deservire*, to serve diligently < *de-*, intens. + *servire*, SERVE] to have a right to because of acts or qualities; be worthy of (reward, punishment, etc.); merit —*vi.* to be worthy

de·served (di zʉrvd′) *adj.* rightfully earned or merited; just —**de·serv′ed·ly** (-zʉr′vid lē) *adv.*

de·serv·ing (di zʉr′viŋ) *adj.* 1 having merit; worthy of aid, a reward, etc. [a *deserving* student] 2 worthy (of) [a subject most *deserving* of attention] —*n.* [Now Rare] desert; merit or demerit

de Se·ver·sky (də sə ver′skē), **Alexander P(rocofieff)** 1894-1974; U.S. aeronautical engineer, born in Russia

de·sex (dē seks′) *vt.* 1 to remove the sex organs of 2 to suppress or lessen the sexual characteristics of

de·sex·u·al·ize (dē sek′sho͞o əl īz′) *vt.* **-ized′**, **-iz′ing** DESEX —**de·sex′u·al·i·za′tion** *n.*

des·ha·bille (des′ə bēl′) *n. var. of* DISHABILLE

De Si·ca (də sē′kə), **Vit·to·ri·o** (vi tôr′ē ō) 1901-74; It. film actor & director

des·ic·cant (des′i kənt) *adj.* [L *desiccans*, prp. of *desiccare*: see fol.] drying —*n.* a substance having a great affinity for water and used as a drying agent

des·ic·cate (des′i kāt′) *vt.* **-cat′ed**, **-cat′ing** [< L *desiccatus*, pp. of *desiccare*, to dry up completely < *de-*, intens. + *siccare*, to dry < *siccus*, dry < IE base **seikw-*, to drip, pour out > OE *seon*, to trickle, *sic*, small stream] 1 to dry completely 2 to preserve (food) by drying —*vi.* to become completely dry —**des′ic·ca′tion** *n.* —**des·ic·ca·tive** (des′i kāt′iv, də sik′ət iv) *adj.*, *n.*

des·ic·ca·tor (-ər) *n.* 1 an apparatus for drying foods, etc., esp. by heat 2 a chemist's device containing a water-absorbing material, used to dry or store substances

de·sid·er·ate (di zid′ər āt′) *vt.* **-at′ed**, **-at′ing** [< L *desideratus*, pp. of *desiderare*: see DESIRE] to want; miss; need —**de·sid′er·a′tion** *n.* —**de·sid·er·a·tive** (di zid′ər āt′iv, -ər ə tiv) *adj.*

de·sid·er·a·tum (di sid′ə rät′əm, -zid′-; -rāt′-) *n.*, *pl.* **-ta** (-ə) [L, neut. of *desideratus*: see prec.] something needed and wanted

de·sign (di zīn′) *vt.* [ME *designen* < L *designare*, to mark out, define < *de-*, out, from + *signare*, to mark < *signum*, a mark, SIGN] 1 to make preliminary sketches of; sketch a pattern or outline for; plan 2 to plan and carry out, esp. by artistic arrangement or in a skillful way 3 to form (plans, etc.) in the mind; contrive 4 to plan to do; purpose; intend 5 to intend or set apart for some purpose —*vi.* 1 to make designs 2 to make original plans, sketches, patterns, etc.; work as a designer —*n.* [Fr *dessein* < It *disegno* < *disignare* < L *designare*] 1 a plan; scheme; project 2 purpose; intention; aim 3 a thing planned for or outcome aimed at 4 development according to a plan [to find a *design* in history] 5 [*pl.*] a secret, usually dishonest or selfish scheme: often with *on* or *upon* [to have *designs* on another's property] 6 a plan or sketch to work from; pattern [a *design* for a house] 7 the art of making designs or patterns 8 the arrangement of parts, details, form, color, etc. so as to produce an artistic unit; artistic invention [the *design* of a rug] 9 a finished artistic work or decoration —**SYN.** INTEND, PLAN —**by design** deliberately; purposely

des·ig·nate (dez′ig nāt′; *for adj.*, -nit, -nāt′) *adj.* [ME < L *designatus*, pp. of *designare*: see prec.] named for an office, etc. but not yet in it [ambassador *designate*] —*vt.* **-nat′ed**, **-nat′ing** 1 to point out; mark out; indicate; specify 2 to refer to by a distinguishing name, title, etc.; name 3 to name for an office or duty; appoint —**des′ig·na′tive** *adj.* —**des′ig·na′tor** *n.*

designated driver the person in a group who has been designated as the one who will abstain from alcoholic beverages so as to be able to safely drive the others in a motor vehicle

☆**designated hitter** *Baseball* a player in the regular batting order who does not play a defensive position, but has been designated to bat in place of the pitcher

des·ig·na·tion (dez′ig nā′shən) *n.* [ME *designacioun* < L *designatio*: see DESIGNATE] 1 a pointing out; indication 2 a naming for an office, post, or duty 3 a distinguishing name, title, etc.

des·ig·nee (dez′ig nē′, dez′ig nē′) *n.* a person designated

de·sign·er (di zīn′ər) *n.* a person who designs; specif., one who makes original sketches, patterns, etc. [a scene *designer*] —*adj.* 1 designating or of products, esp. fashionable clothing, styled by and often named after a noted designer [*designer* jeans] 2 designating any fashionable brand name 3 artificially altered, as chemically or genetically, to effect or maximize some desirable quality or benefit, usually while also minimizing undesirable ones [*designer* crops]

☆**designer drug** a drug that has been developed by changing slightly the chemical structure of an existing drug, as to evade legal prohibition or to produce certain desired effects

de·sign·ing (di zīn′iŋ) *adj.* 1 that designs, or makes plans, patterns, etc. 2 scheming; crafty; artful —*n.* the art or work of creating designs, patterns, etc.

de·sir·a·ble (di zīr′ə bəl) *adj.* [ME < OFr: see fol. & -ABLE] 1 worth wanting or having; worthwhile, beneficial, expedient, etc. 2 arousing desire; pleasing, attractive, etc. —*n.* a desirable person or thing —**de·sir′a·bil′i·ty** *n.*, **de·sir′a·ble·ness** —**de·sir′a·bly** *adv.*

de·sire (di zīr′) *vt.* **-sired′**, **-sir′ing** [ME *desiren* < OFr *desirer* < L *desiderare*, orig., prob., to await from the stars < *de-*, from + *sidus*, star: see SIDEREAL] 1 to wish or long for; crave; covet 2 to ask for; request 3 to want sexually —*vi.* to have or feel a desire —*n.* 1 a strong wish or craving 2 sexual appetite; lust 3 an asking for something; request 4 a thing or person desired

SYN.—**desire**, generally interchangeable with the other words here in the sense of 'to long for,' stresses intensity or ardor [to *desire* success]; **wish** is not so strong a term as **desire** and has special application when an unrealizable longing is meant [he *wished* summer were here]; **want**, specifically suggesting a longing for something lacking or needed, generally is a more informal equivalent of **wish** [she *wants*, or *wishes*, to go with us]; **crave** suggests desire to gratify a physical appetite or an urgent need [to *crave* affection]

de·sir·ous (di zīr′əs) *adj.* [ME < OFr *desireus* < LL *desiderosus* < L *desiderare*: see prec.] desiring; having or characterized by desire

de·sist (di zist′, -sist′) ***vi.*** ⟦LME *desisten* < OFr *desister* < L *desistere* < *de-*, from + *sistere*, to cause to stand < *stare*, to STAND⟧ to cease (*from* an action); stop; abstain [*desist* from fighting] —**SYN.** STOP —**de·sist′ance** ***n.***

desk (desk) ***n.*** ⟦ME *deske* < ML *desca*, a table, ult. < L *discus*: see DISCUS⟧ **1** a piece of furniture equipped with drawers, compartments, etc., and a flat or sloping top for writing, drawing, or reading **2** a lectern **3** *a)* the post of a clerk, official, etc. in a department or office *b)* the place in a hotel where guests are registered, mail is picked up, etc. *c)* a division of a newspaper or other office, carrying out some specialized function [the city *desk*; the trading *desk*] **4** a musician's stand in an orchestra —***adj.*** **1** of, for, or on a desk **2** done at a desk [a *desk* job]

☆**desk·man** (-man′) ***n.***, *pl.* **-men′** (-men′) a person who works at a desk, esp. one who edits copy in a newspaper office

desk·top (-täp′) ***n.*** **1** the top, or working surface, of a desk **2** the background to the icons of a GUI screen display: cf. WALLPAPER (sense 2) **3** a desktop microcomputer —***adj.*** designating or of a piece of equipment, as a microcomputer, designed to be used on a desk or table

desktop publishing a system or process for designing, editing, and producing camera-ready documents, as newsletters, brochures, or magazines, using a microcomputer, special software, and a printer

des·man (des′mən) ***n.*** ⟦< Swed *desman-råtta* < *desman*, musk + *råtta*, rat⟧ a molelike, aquatic, insectivorous mammal (family Talpidae) with webbed feet and a long, flexible snout: one species (*Desmana moschata*), trapped for its fur, is found in Russia and the other (*Galemys pyrenaicus*) in the Pyrenees

des·mid (-mid) ***n.*** ⟦ModL *desmidium*, dim. < Gr *desmos*, a chain; akin to *dein*, to bind: see DIADEM⟧ any of a group of microscopic, freshwater green algae having single cells composed of two identical half-cells with the nucleus located between them

des·moid (-moid′) ***adj.*** ⟦< Gr *desmos* (see prec.) + -OID⟧ **1** like a ligament **2** of fibrous texture: said of certain tumors

Des Moines (də moin′) ⟦Fr, lit., of the monks⟧ **1** river in Iowa, flowing southeast into the Mississippi: *c.* 325 mi (523 km) **2** capital of Iowa, in the central part

des·mo·some (dez′mə sōm′) ***n.*** ⟦< Gr *desmos*, a bond, chain (see DESMID) + -SOME[3]⟧ *Cytology* a beltlike or buttonlike structure in or on the surface of a cell, that helps to hold adjacent cells together

Des·mou·lins (dā mo͞o lan′), **(Lucie Simplice) Ca·mille (Benoît)** (kȧ mē′y′) 1760-94; Fr. Revolutionary journalist & pamphleteer

des·o·late (des′ə lit; *for v.*, -lāt′) ***adj.*** ⟦ME *desolat* < L *desolatus*, pp. of *desolare*, to leave alone, forsake, strip of inhabitants < *de-*, intens. + *solare*, to make lonely < *solus*, SOLE[2]⟧ **1** left alone; lonely; solitary **2** uninhabited; deserted **3** made uninhabitable; laid waste; in a ruinous state **4** forlorn; wretched —***vt.*** **-lat′ed**, **-lat′ing** ⟦ME *desolaten* < the adj.⟧ **1** to make desolate; rid of inhabitants **2** to make uninhabitable; lay waste; devastate **3** to forsake; abandon **4** to make forlorn, wretched, etc. —**des′o·late·ly** ***adv.*** —**des′o·late·ness** ***n.*** —**des′o·la′tor** ***n.***, **des′o·lat′er**

des·o·la·tion (des′ə lā′shən) ***n.*** ⟦ME *desolacioun* < OFr *desolation* < LL(Ec) *desolatio*⟧ **1** a making desolate; laying waste **2** a desolate condition **3** lonely grief; misery **4** loneliness **5** a desolate place

de·sorb (dē sôrb′, dē′-) ***vt.*** ⟦DE- + (AB)SORB⟧ to remove (an adsorbed or absorbed material) by a chemical or physical process —**de·sorp′tion** (-sôrp′shən) ***n.***

De So·to or **de So·to** (di sōt′ō), **Her·nan·do** (hər nan′dō) 1500?-42; Sp. explorer in America: discovered the Mississippi River (1541)

de·spair (di sper′) ***vi.*** ⟦ME *despeiren* < OFr *desperer* < L *desperare*, to be without hope < *de-*, without + *sperare*, to hope < *spes*, hope < IE base **spēi*, to prosper, expand: see SPEED⟧ to lose hope; be without hope: usually with *of* —***vt.*** [Archaic] to give up hope of —***n.*** **1** loss of hope **2** a person or thing causing despair

de·spair·ing (-iŋ) ***adj.*** feeling or showing despair; hopeless —**SYN.** HOPELESS —**de·spair′ing·ly** ***adv.***

des·patch (di spach′) ***vt.***, ***n.*** *var. of* DISPATCH

des·per·a·do (des′pər ä′dō, -ā′-) ***n.***, *pl.* **-does** or **-dos** ⟦OSp pp. of *desperar* < L *desperare*: see DESPAIR⟧ a dangerous, reckless criminal; bold outlaw

des·per·ate (des′pər it) ***adj.*** ⟦ME *desperat* < L *desperatus*, pp. of *desperare*: see DESPAIR⟧ **1** *a)* driven to or resulting from loss of hope; rash or violent because of despair [a *desperate* criminal] *b)* having a very great desire, need, etc. [*desperate* for affection] **2** offering so little chance, as for improvement, as to cause despair; extremely dangerous or serious [a *desperate* illness] **3** extreme; drastic [in *desperate* need] **4** [Archaic] despairing; without hope —**SYN.** HOPELESS —**des′per·ate·ly** ***adv.*** —**des′per·ate·ness** ***n.***

des·per·a·tion (des′pər ā′shən) ***n.*** ⟦ME *desperacioun* < L *desperatio*⟧ **1** the state of being desperate **2** recklessness resulting from despair

des·pi·ca·ble (di spik′ə bəl, des′pi kə bəl) ***adj.*** ⟦LL *despicabilis*: see fol.⟧ deserving to be despised; contemptible —**des·pi′ca·ble·ness** ***n.*** —**des·pi′ca·bly** ***adv.***

de·spise (di spīz′) ***vt.*** **-spised′**, **-spis′ing** ⟦ME *despisen* < OFr *despis-*, stem of *despirer* < L *despicere*, to look down upon, despise < *de*, down, from + *specere*, to look at: see SPECTACLE⟧ **1** to look down on with contempt and scorn **2** to regard with dislike or repugnance

SYN.—**despise** implies a strong emotional response toward that which one looks down upon with contempt or aversion [to *despise* a hypocrite]; to **scorn** is to feel indignation toward or deep contempt for [to *scorn* the offer of a bribe]; **disdain** implies a haughty or arrogant contempt for what one considers beneath one's dignity [to *disdain* flattery]; **contemn**, chiefly a literary word, implies a vehement disapproval of a person or thing as base, vile, or despicable See also **hate**

de·spite (di spīt′) ***n.*** ⟦ME & OFr *despit* < L *despectus*, a looking down upon, despising < *despicere*: see prec.⟧ **1** a contemptuous act; insult; injury **2** malice; spite **3** [Archaic] contempt; scorn —***prep.*** in spite of; notwithstanding —***vt.*** **-spit′ed**, **-spit′ing** [Archaic] to scorn —**in despite of** **1** in defiance of **2** in spite of

de·spite·ful (-fəl) ***adj.*** ⟦ME *despitful*: see prec. & -FUL⟧ [Archaic] spiteful; malicious —**de·spite′ful·ly** ***adv.***

de·spoil (dē spoil′, di-) ***vt.*** ⟦ME *despoilen* < OFr *despoiller* < L *despoliare* < *de-*, intens. + *spoliare*, to strip, rob: see SPOIL⟧ to deprive of something of value by or as by force; rob; plunder —**SYN.** RAVAGE —**de·spoil′er** ***n.*** —**de·spoil′ment** ***n.***

de·spo·li·a·tion (di spō′lē ā′shən) ***n.*** ⟦LL *despoliatio*: see prec.⟧ a despoiling or being despoiled; pillage

de·spond (di spänd′) ***vi.*** ⟦L *despondere*, to lose courage, yield < *de-*, from + *spondere*, to promise: see SPONSOR⟧ to lose courage or hope; become disheartened; be depressed —***n.*** despondency: now chiefly in **slough of despond** (see SLOUGH[2], ***n.*** 2)

de·spond·en·cy (di spän′dən sē) ***n.*** ⟦see fol.⟧ loss of courage or hope; dejection: also **de·spond′ence** (-dəns)

de·spond·ent (di spän′dənt) ***adj.*** ⟦L *despondens*, prp. of *despondere*: see DESPOND⟧ filled with despondency; dejected —**SYN.** HOPELESS —**de·spond′ent·ly** ***adv.***

des·pot (des′pət) ***n.*** ⟦OFr *despote* < Gr *despotēs*, a master, lord < IE **dems-potis*, lit., house master < **dem-*, house (> TIMBER, L *domus*) + **potis*, master, husband (> L *potis*, POTENT, Goth *-faths*, husband)⟧ **1** [Historical] a title applied to certain classes of rulers, as Byzantine emperors or bishops of the Eastern Church **2** an absolute ruler; king with unlimited powers; autocrat **3** anyone in charge who acts like a tyrant

des·pot·ic (des pät′ik) ***adj.*** ⟦Fr *despotique* < Gr *despotikos*⟧ of or like a despot; autocratic; tyrannical: also **des·pot′i·cal** —**des·pot′i·cal·ly** ***adv.***

des·pot·ism (des′pə tiz′əm) ***n.*** ⟦Fr *despotisme*⟧ **1** rule or domination by a despot; autocracy **2** the methods or acts of a despot; tyranny **3** a political system, state, etc. dominated by a despot

de·spu·mate (di spyo͞o′māt′, des′pyo͞o māt′) ***vt.*** **-mat′ed**, **-mat′ing** ⟦< L *despumatus*, pp. of *despumare*, to skim off < *de-*, off, from + *spumare*, to foam < *spuma*, FOAM⟧ **1** to take the scum off; skim **2** to throw off as froth —***vi.*** to become rid of scum —**des′pu·ma′tion** ***n.***

des·qua·mate (des′kwə māt′, di skwā′-) ***vi.*** **-mat′ed**, **-mat′ing** ⟦< L *desquamatus*, pp. of *desquamare*, to scale off < *de-*, off + *squama*, a scale, SQUAMA⟧ to fall off in scales; peel off: said esp. of the top layer of skin or mucous membrane —**des′qua·ma′tion** ***n.***

des·sert (di zʉrt′) ***n.*** ⟦ME < OFr < *desservir*, to clear the table < *des-* (L *de*), from + *servir* (L *servire*), SERVE⟧ ☆**1** a usually sweet course, as of pie, cake, or ice cream, served at the end of a meal **2** [Brit.] uncooked fruit served after, or in place of, the sweet course

des·sert·spoon (-spo͞on′) ***n.*** a spoon between a teaspoon and tablespoon in size, used in eating dessert

dessert wine any sweet wine suitable for serving with desserts

des·sia·tine (des′yə tēn′) ***n.*** ⟦Russ *desjatina*, lit., tithe < *desjat′*, ten < IE **dekm̥t-* < base **dekm̥* > TEN⟧ a Russian unit of land measure equal to about 2.7 acres

de·sta·bi·lize (dē stā′bə līz′) ***vt.*** **-lized′**, **-liz′ing** to upset the stability or equilibrium of; unbalance

de Staël, Madame *see* STAËL

de·stain (dē stān′) ***vt.*** to remove stain from (a specimen or part of a specimen) to facilitate microscopic study

de-Stal·i·ni·za·tion (dē stäl′i nə zā′shən) ***n.*** in the Soviet Union, the official denunciation of Stalin after his death and the eradication of monuments, etc. commemorating him

de·ster·i·lize (dē ster′ə līz′) ***vt.*** **-lized′**, **-liz′ing** to bring back from a sterile state; specif., to release (gold) from a neutralized position into an active position in the monetary system where it can support credit and monetary issues

de Stijl (də stīl′, -stāl′) ⟦Du, lit., the style, name of a journal founded (1917) by the Dutch painters Piet MONDRIAN and T. van Doesburg (1883-1931)⟧ an abstract art movement marked by the use of rectangular forms and by emphasis on primary colors or grays and blacks

des·ti·na·tion (des′tə nā′shən) ***n.*** ⟦ME *destinacioun* < L *destinatio*, settlement, appointment < *destinare*: see fol.⟧ **1** [Rare] a destining or being destined **2** the end for which something or someone is destined **3** the place toward which someone or something is going or sent —***adj.*** designating or of a place that draws visitors or tourists [a *destination* resort, spa, etc.]

des·tine (des′tin) ***vt.*** **-tined**, **-tin·ing** ⟦ME *destinen* < OFr *destiner* < L *destinare*, to fasten down, secure < *de-*, intens. + **stanare* < base of *stare*, STAND⟧ **1** to predetermine, as by fate: usually in the passive **2** to set apart for a certain purpose; intend —**destined for** **1** headed for; bound for **2** intended for [*destined for* leadership]

des·ti·ny (des′tə nē) ***n.***, *pl.* **-nies** ⟦ME *destine* < OFr *destinee*, fem. pp. of *destiner*: see prec.⟧ **1** the seemingly inevitable or necessary succession of events **2** what will necessarily happen to any person or thing; (one's) fate **3** that which determines events: said of either a supernatural agency or necessity —**SYN.** FATE

des·ti·tute (des′tə to͞ot′, -tyo͞ot′) ***adj.*** ⟦ME < L *destitutus*, pp. of *destituere*, to forsake, abandon < *de-*, down, away + *statuere*, to set, place: see STATUTE⟧ **1** not having; being without; lacking (with *of*) [*destitute* of trees] **2** lacking the necessities of life; living in complete poverty **3** [Obs.] abandoned; forsaken —***SYN.*** POOR

des·ti·tu·tion (des′tə to͞o′shən, -tyo͞o′-) ***n.*** ⟦ME *destitucioun* < L *destitutio*⟧ the state of being destitute; esp., abject poverty —***SYN.*** POVERTY

des·tri·er (des′trē ər, des trir′) ***n.*** ⟦ME *destrer* < OFr *destrier* < ML *dextrarius* < VL **dextrare*, to lead (by the right hand) < *dextra*, right hand: see DEXTER⟧ [Archaic] a war horse; charger

de·stroy (di stroi′) ***vt.*** ⟦ME *destroien* < OFr *destruire* < L *destruere* < *de-*, down + *struere*, to build: see STRUCTURE⟧ **1** to tear down; demolish **2** to break up or spoil completely; ruin **3** to bring to total defeat; crush **4** to put an end to; do away with **5** to kill **6** to neutralize the effect of **7** to make useless —***vi.*** to bring about destruction

SYN.—**destroy** implies a tearing down or bringing to an end by wrecking, ruining, killing, eradicating, etc. and is the term of broadest application here [to *destroy* a city, one's influence, etc.]; **demolish** implies such destructive force as to completely smash to pieces [the bombs *demolished* the factories]; **raze** means to level to the ground, either destructively or by systematic wrecking with a salvaging of useful parts; to **annihilate** is to destroy so completely as to blot out of existence [rights that cannot be *annihilated*]

de·stroy·er (di stroi′ər) ***n.*** **1** a person or thing that destroys **2** ⟦orig. *torpedo-boat destroyer*⟧ a small, fast, highly maneuverable warship armed with 3-inch or 5-inch guns, depth charges, torpedoes, etc.

☆**destroyer escort** a warship smaller and slower than a destroyer, used mainly to escort merchant ships

destroying angel either of two species (*Amanita verna* or *A. virosa*) of large, deadly, white amanita mushrooms found during warm weather in moist forests

☆**de·struct** (di strukt′, dē′strukt′) ***n.*** ⟦back-form. < DESTRUCTION⟧ the deliberate destruction of a malfunctioning missile, rocket, etc. after its launch —***vi.*** to be automatically destroyed —***vt.*** to destroy (a rocket, etc.) deliberately by remote control

de·struct·i·ble (di struk′tə bəl) ***adj.*** ⟦LL *destructibilis*⟧ that can be destroyed; subject to destruction —**de·struct′i·bil′i·ty** ***n.***

de·struc·tion (di struk′shən) ***n.*** ⟦ME *destruccioun* < OFr *destruction* < L *destructio* < *destructus*, pp. of *destruere*: see DESTROY⟧ **1** the act or process of destroying; demolition or slaughter **2** the fact or state of being destroyed **3** the cause or means of destroying —***SYN.*** RUIN

de·struc·tion·ist (-ist) ***n.*** a person who believes in or favors destruction, as of an existing social order

de·struc·tive (di struk′tiv) ***adj.*** ⟦OFr *destructif* < LL *destructivus*⟧ **1** tending or likely to cause destruction **2** causing or producing destruction; destroying **3** merely negative; not helpful [*destructive* criticism] —**de·struc′tive·ly** ***adv.*** —**de·struc′tive·ness** ***n.***, **de·struc·tiv·i·ty** (dē′struk′tiv′ə tē, di-)

destructive distillation the decomposition of a material, as coal, wood, etc., by heat in the absence of air, followed by the recovery of volatile products of the decomposition by condensation or other means: a type of calcination: see PYROLYSIS

de·struc·tor (di struk′tər) ***n.*** ⟦LL < *destructus*: see DESTRUCTION⟧ **1** [Brit.] an incinerator for rubbish ☆**2** an explosive device for bringing about a destruct

des·ue·tude (des′wi to͞od′, -tyo͞od′) ***n.*** ⟦ME < L *desuetudo* < *desuetus*, pp. of *desuescere*, to disuse < *de-*, from + *suescere*, to be accustomed: see CUSTOM⟧ the condition of not being used or practiced any more; disuse [laws fallen into *desuetude*]

de·sul·fur·ize (dē sul′fər īz′) ***vt.*** **-ized′**, **-iz′ing** to remove sulfur from: also **de·sul′fur** —**de·sul′fur·i·za′tion** ***n.*** —**de·sul′fur·iz′er** ***n.***

des·ul·to·ry (des′əl tôr′ē; *also* dez′-) ***adj.*** ⟦L *desultorius* < *desultor*, vaulter < *desultus*, pp. of *desilire*, to leap down < *de-*, down, from + *salire*, to leap: see SALIENT⟧ **1** passing from one thing to another in an aimless way; disconnected; not methodical [a *desultory* conversation] **2** lacking direct relevance; random; incidental [a *desultory* observation] —***SYN.*** RANDOM —**des′ul·to′ri·ly** ***adv.*** —**des′ul·to′ri·ness** ***n.***

det *abbrev.* **1** detachment **2** detail

de·tach (dē tach′, di-) ***vt.*** ⟦Fr *détacher* < OFr *detachier, destachier* < *de-*, DE- + *estachier*, to ATTACH⟧ **1** to unfasten or separate and remove; disconnect; disengage **2** to send (troops, ships, etc.) on a special mission —**de·tach′a·bil′i·ty** ***n.*** —**de·tach′a·ble** ***adj.***

de·tached (dē tacht′, di-) ***adj.*** **1** not connected; separate **2** not involved by emotion, interests, etc.; aloof; impartial —***SYN.*** INDIFFERENT —**de·tach′ed·ly** ***adv.*** —**de·tach′ed·ness** ***n.***

de·tach·ment (dē tach′mənt, di-) ***n.*** ⟦Fr *détachement*⟧ **1** a detaching; separation **2** *a)* the sending of troops or ships on special service *b)* a unit of troops separated from a larger unit for special duty *c)* a small permanent unit organized for special service **3** the state of being disinterested, impartial, or aloof

de·tail (di tāl′, dē′tāl′) ***n.*** ⟦Fr *détail* < the v.⟧ **1** the act of dealing with things item by item [the *detail* of business] **2** an account that gives the particulars [to go into *detail*] **3** any of the small parts that go to make up something; item; particular [the *details* of a plan] **4** *a)* any small secondary or accessory part or parts of a picture, statue, building, etc. *b)* a small segment as of a painting, reproduced separately for detailed study **5** *a)* one or more soldiers, sailors, etc. chosen for a particular task *b)* the task itself —***vt.*** ⟦Fr *détailler*, to cut up, tell in particulars < *dé-* (L *de*), from + *tailler*, to cut: see TAILOR⟧ **1** to give the particulars of; tell, item by item **2** to choose for a particular task [*detail* a man for sentry duty] **3** to provide DETAILING for ☆**4** to clean (an automotive vehicle) inside and outside, with meticulous attention to details, usually for a fee —**in detail** item by item; with particulars

detail drawing a separate drawing of a small part or section, as of a machine, showing the details

de·tailed (dē′tāld′, di tāld′) ***adj.*** marked by careful attention to detail [a *detailed* plan]

de·tail·ing (dē′tāl′iŋ, di tāl′iŋ) ***n.*** small, typically decorative, features as in a painting or on a garment, building, or automobile

☆**detail man** a salesman for a pharmaceutical firm who visits doctors, dentists, etc. in a certain district to promote new drugs

de·tain (dē tān′, di-) ***vt.*** ⟦ME *deteinen* < OFr *detenir* < L *detinere*, to hold down or off, keep back, detain < *de-*, off, from + *tenere*, to hold: see TENANT⟧ **1** to keep in custody; confine **2** to keep from going on; hold back **3** [Obs.] to withhold —**de·tain′ment** ***n.***

de·tain·ee (dē′tān ē′) ***n.*** a person held in custody, usually for political reasons

de·tain·er (dē tān′ər, di-) ***n.*** **1** a person or thing that detains **2** ⟦Anglo-Fr *detener*, inf. used as n. < OFr *detenir*: see DETAIN⟧ *Law a)* the unlawful withholding of land or goods from the rightful owner *b)* the detention of a person without the person's consent *c)* a writ for continuing to hold a person already in custody

de·tas·sel (dē tas′əl) ***vt.*** **-seled** or **-selled**, **-sel·ing** or **-sel·ling** to remove tassels from (corn) so as to assure cross-pollination for the production of hybrid corn seed

de·tect (dē tekt′, di-) ***vt.*** ⟦ME *detecten* < L *detectus*, pp. of *detegere*, to uncover < *de-*, from + *tegere*, to cover: see THATCH⟧ **1** to catch or discover, as in a misdeed **2** to discover or manage to perceive (something hidden or not easily noticed) [to *detect* a flaw in an argument] **3** *Radio a)* RECTIFY (sense 4) *b)* DEMODULATE **4** [Obs.] to uncover; reveal —**de·tect′a·ble** ***adj.***, **de·tect′i·ble**

☆**de·tec·ta·phone** (dē tek′tə fōn′, di-) ***n.*** ⟦prec. + *-a-* + (TELE)PHONE⟧ a device for listening secretly to others' telephone conversations

de·tec·tion (dē tek′shən, di-) ***n.*** ⟦ME < LL *detectio*: see DETECT⟧ **1** a finding out or being found out: said esp. of what tends to elude notice **2** DEMODULATION

de·tec·tive (dē tek′tiv, di-) ***adj.*** **1** of or for detection **2** of detectives and their work —***n.*** **1** ⟦short for *detective policeman*⟧ a person on a police force, whose work is investigating and trying to solve crimes **2** ⟦short for *private detective*⟧ a person working privately to investigate crimes, gather information, etc.

detective story a MYSTERY[1] (sense 2*b*) involving a crime and the gradual discovery of who committed it, esp. a highly formalized one in which a detective, often a private detective, solves a crime, usually a murder, by means of careful observation and logical reasoning

de·tec·tor (dē tek′tər, di-; *also, esp. for 2 & 3,* dē′tek′-) ***n.*** **1** a person or thing that detects **2** an apparatus or device for indicating the presence of something, as electric waves **3** DEMODULATOR

de·tent (dē′tent′; *also* di tent′) ***n.*** ⟦Fr *détente* < *détendre*, to relax, unbend < *dé-* (L *dis-*), from + *tendre*, to stretch: see TEND[2]⟧ *Mech.* a part that stops or releases a movement, as a catch for controlling the striking of a clock

dé·tente or **de·tente** (dā tänt′; *also* dā′tänt′) ***n.*** ⟦Fr: see prec.⟧ a lessening of tension or hostility, esp. between nations, as through treaties, trade agreements, etc.

de·ten·tion (dē ten′shən, di-) ***n.*** ⟦ME *detencioun* < OFr *detention* < L *detentio* < *detentus*, pp. of *detinere*: see DETAIN⟧ **1** a detaining or being detained; specif., *a)* a keeping in custody; confinement *b)* an enforced delay **2** a form of punishment in which a student is required to stay after school

☆**detention home** a place where juvenile offenders or delinquents are held in custody, esp. temporarily pending disposition of their cases by the juvenile court

de·ter (dē tʉr′, di-) ***vt.*** **-terred′**, **-ter′ring** ⟦L *deterrere* < *de-*, from + *terrere*, to frighten: see TERROR⟧ to keep or discourage (a person, group, or nation) from doing something by instilling fear, anxiety, doubt, etc. —**de·ter′ment** ***n.***

de·terge (dē tʉrj′, di-) ***vt.*** **-terged′**, **-terg′ing** ⟦L *detergere*, to wipe off < *de-*, off, from + *tergere*, to wipe, cleanse < IE **terg-* < base **ter-*: see THROW⟧ to cleanse (a wound, etc.)

de·ter·gen·cy (dē tʉr′jən sē) ***n.*** the quality or power of cleansing: also **de·ter′gence** (-jəns)

de·ter·gent (dē tʉr′jənt, di-) ***adj.*** ⟦L *detergens*, prp. of *detergere*: see DETERGE⟧ cleansing —***n.*** a cleansing substance; specif., a surface-active chemical preparation, as, now esp., a linear alkyl sulfonate, that is capable of emulsifying dirt or oil: compare SOAP

de·te·ri·o·rate (dē tir′ē ə rāt′, di-) ***vt., vi.*** **-rat′ed**, **-rat′ing** ⟦< LL *deterioratus*, pp. of *deteriorare*, to make worse < L *deterior*, worse, inferior < **deter*, below < de-, from + *-ter*, compar. suffix⟧ to make or become worse; lower in quality or value; depreciate —**de·te′ri·o·ra′tion** ***n.***

de·te·ri·o·ra·tive (-rāt′iv) ***adj.*** tending to deteriorate

de·ter·mi·na·ble (dē tʉr′mi nə bəl, di-) ***adj.*** ⟦ME < OFr < LL *determinabilis*⟧ **1** that can be determined **2** that can be ended; terminable —**de·ter′mi·na·bil′i·ty** ***n.*** —**de·ter′mi·na·bly** ***adv.***

de·ter·mi·na·cy (dē tʉr′mi nə sē, di-) ***n.*** **1** the state or quality of being determinate **2** the condition of being determined, as in being caused or in having predictable results

de·ter·mi·nant (dē tʉr′mi nənt, di-) ***adj.*** ⟦L *determinans*, prp. of *determinare*⟧ determining —***n.*** **1** a thing or factor that determines **2** *Math.* the sum of the products formed from a square matrix in accordance with certain laws —***SYN.*** CAUSE

de·ter·mi·nate (dē tʉr′mi nit, di-) ***adj.*** ⟦ME < L *determinatus*, pp. of *determinare*: see DETERMINE⟧ **1** having exact limits; definite; distinct; fixed **2** settled or decided; conclusive **3** *Bot.* having a flower at the end of the primary axis and of each secondary axis; cymose —**de·ter′mi·nate·ly** ***adv.*** —**de·ter′mi·nate·ness** ***n.***

determinate cleavage cell division in a fertilized or unfertilized egg resulting in daughter cells that are no longer able to produce a complete embryo by themselves

☆**determinate growth** **1** growth of a plant stem that is terminated early by the formation of a bud **2** naturally self-limited growth, resulting in a plant of a definite maximum size

de·ter·mi·na·tion (dē tʉr′mi nā′shən, di-) ***n.*** ⟦L *determinatio*⟧ **1** a determining or being determined (in all senses of the verb) **2** a decision arrived at by thought and investigation; conclusion **3** a firm intention **4** the quality of being resolute; firmness of purpose **5** *Law* the ending of an estate or of an interest or right in property

de·ter·mi·na·tive (dē tʉr′mi nāt′iv, -nə tiv; di-) ***adj.*** ⟦Fr *déterminatif*⟧ determining or serving to determine —***n.*** a thing or factor that determines —**de·ter′mi·na′tive·ly** ***adv.***

de·ter·mi·na·tor (dē tʉr′mi nāt′ər, di-) ***n.*** DETERMINER

de·ter·mine (dē tʉr′mən, di-) ***vt.*** **-mined, -min·ing** ⟦ME *determinen* < OFr *determiner* < L *determinare*, to bound, limit < *de-*, from + *terminare*, to set bounds < *terminus*, an end: see TERM[2]⟧ **1** to set limits to; bound; define **2** to settle (a dispute, question, etc.) conclusively; decide **3** to reach a decision about after thought and investigation; decide upon **4** to establish or affect the nature, kind, or quality of; fix [genes *determine* heredity] **5** to find out exactly; calculate precisely; ascertain [to *determine* a ship's position] **6** to give direction to; shape or affect **7** *Law* to end; terminate —***vi.*** **1** to decide; resolve **2** *Law* to come to an end —***SYN.*** DECIDE, LEARN

de·ter·mined (-mənd) ***adj.*** **1** having one's mind made up; decided; resolved **2** resolute; unwavering —**de·ter′mined·ly** ***adv.*** —**de·ter′mined·ness** ***n.***

de·ter·min·er (dē tʉr′mi nər, di-) ***n.*** **1** anything that determines **2** *Gram.* a word, such as *a, the, this, each, some, either, or my*, that determines the use of a noun without essentially modifying it and is placed before a descriptive adjective

de·ter·min·ism (dē tʉr′mi niz′əm, di-) ***n.*** the doctrine that everything, including one's choice of action, is the necessary result of a sequence of causes —**de·ter′min·ist** ***n., adj.*** —**de·ter′min·is′tic** ***adj.*** —**de·ter′min·is′ti·cal·ly** ***adv.***

de·ter·rence (dē tʉr′əns, di-; *also, chiefly Brit & Cdn*, -ter′-) ***n.*** **1** the act of deterring **2** the policy or practice of stockpiling nuclear weapons to deter another nation from making a nuclear attack

de·ter·rent (-ənt) ***adj.*** ⟦L *deterrens*, prp. of *deterrere*: see DETER⟧ deterring or tending to deter —***n.*** a thing or factor that deters; hindrance

de·ter·sive (dē tʉr′siv, di-) ***adj., n.*** ⟦Fr *détersif* < L *detersus*, pp. of *detergere*: see DETERGE⟧ detergent

de·test (dē test′, di-) ***vt.*** ⟦Fr *détester* < L *detestari*, to curse by calling the gods to witness, execrate, detest < *de-*, down + *testari*, to witness < *testis*, a witness: see TESTIFY⟧ to dislike intensely; hate; abhor —***SYN.*** HATE —**de·test′er** ***n.***

de·test·a·ble (dē tes′tə bəl, di-) ***adj.*** ⟦ME & OFr < L *detestabilis*⟧ that is or should be detested; hateful; execrable; odious —***SYN.*** HATEFUL —**de·test′a·bil′i·ty** ***n.***, **de·test′a·ble·ness** —**de·test′a·bly** ***adv.***

de·tes·ta·tion (dē′tes tā′shən) ***n.*** ⟦ME *detestacioun* < OFr *detestation* < L *detestatio*: see DETEST⟧ **1** intense dislike or hatred; loathing **2** a detested person or thing

de·thatch (dē thach′) ***vt.*** to remove the accumulated thatch from (a lawn); thatch

de·throne (dē thrōn′) ***vt.*** **-throned′, -thron′ing** **1** to remove from a throne; depose **2** to oust from any high position —**de·throne′ment** ***n.*** —**de·thron′er** ***n.***

det·i·nue (det′'n yo͞o′, -'n o͞o′) ***n.*** ⟦ME < OFr, fem. pp. of *detenir*: see DETAIN⟧ *Law* **1** the unlawful detention of personal property which originally was rightfully acquired **2** an action or writ for the recovery of property unlawfully detained, as in a pawnshop

det·o·nate (det′'n āt′) ***vi.*** **-nat′ed, -nat′ing** ⟦< L *detonatus*, pp. of *detonare*, to thunder < *de-*, intens. + *tonare*, to THUNDER⟧ to explode violently and noisily —***vt.*** to cause (a bomb, dynamite, etc.) to explode —**det′o·na′tion** ***n.***

det·o·na·tor (det′'n āt′ər) ***n.*** **1** a fuse, percussion cap, etc. for setting off explosives **2** an explosive

de·tour (dē′toor′; *also* dē toor′, di-) ***n.*** ⟦Fr *détour*, a turning, evasion < *détourner*, to turn aside < OFr *destourner* < *des-* (L *dis-*), away + *tourner*: see TURN⟧ **1** a roundabout way; deviation from a direct way **2** a route used when the direct or regular route is closed to traffic —***vi.*** to go by way of a detour —***vt.*** ☆**1** to cause to go by way of a detour **2** to go around or avoid by using a detour; bypass

de·tox (dē täks′; *also, and for n. always,* dē′täks′) [Informal] ***vt., vi.*** *short for* DETOXIFY —***n.*** **1** *short for* DETOXIFICATION **2** a section of a hospital or clinic for drug or alcohol detoxification

de·tox·i·cate (dē täk′si kāt′) ***vt.*** **-cat′ed, -cat′ing** DETOXIFY —**de·tox′i·ca′tion** ***n.***

de·tox·i·fy (dē täk′si fī′) ***vt., vi.*** **-fied′, -fy′ing** ⟦DE- + TOXI(N) + -FY⟧ **1** to remove a poison or poisonous effect from (something) **2** to undergo or cause to undergo withdrawal from drug or alcohol addiction, usually by means of a specific program of treatment —**de·tox′i·fi·ca′tion** ***n.***

de·tract (dē trakt′, di-) ***vt.*** ⟦ME *detracten* < L *detractare*, to decline, depreciate < *detractus*, pp. of *detrahere*, to draw away < *de-*, from + *trahere*, to DRAW⟧ **1** to take or draw away **2** [Now Rare] to belittle; disparage —***vi.*** to take something desirable away (*from*) [frowning *detracts* from her beauty]

de·trac·tion (dē trak′shən, di-) ***n.*** ⟦ME *detraccioun*⟧ **1** a taking away; detracting **2** a malicious discrediting of someone's character, accomplishments, etc., as by revealing hidden faults or by slander —**de·trac′tive** ***adj.***

de·trac·tor (-trak′tər) ***n.*** a person or thing that detracts; specif., a person who belittles or disparages

de·train (dē trān′) ***vi., vt.*** to get off or remove from a railroad train —**de·train′ment** ***n.***

de·trib·al·ize (dē trī′bəl īz′) ***vi., vt.*** **-ized′, -iz′ing** ⟦DE- + TRIBAL + -IZE⟧ to abandon or cause to abandon tribal organization —**de·trib′al·i·za′tion** ***n.***

det·ri·ment (de′trə mənt) ***n.*** ⟦ME & OFr < L *detrimentum*, a rubbing off, damage < *detritus*, pp. of *deterere*, to rub off, wear away < *de-*, off, from + *terere*, to rub: see THROW⟧ **1** damage; injury; harm **2** anything that causes damage or injury

det·ri·men·tal (de′trə ment′'l) ***adj.*** ⟦see prec.⟧ causing detriment; harmful —***SYN.*** PERNICIOUS —**det′ri·men′tal·ly** ***adv.***

de·tri·tion (dē trish′ən) ***n.*** ⟦ML *detritio*: see DETRIMENT + -ION⟧ a wearing away or down by friction

de·tri·tus (di trīt′əs) ***n.*** ⟦L, a rubbing away: see DETRIMENT⟧ **1** fragments of rock produced by disintegration, abrasion, etc. **2** any debris —**de·tri′tal** ***adj.***

De·troit (di troit′) **1** ⟦< Fr *détroit*, a strait: so named because it connects the lakes⟧ river flowing south from Lake St. Clair into Lake Erie: *c.* 31 mi (50 km) **2** ⟦after the river⟧ city in SE Mich., on the Detroit River

de trop (də trō′) ⟦Fr⟧ **1** too much; too many **2** unwanted; superfluous; in the way

de·trude (dē tro͞od′) ***vt.*** **-trud′ed, -trud′ing** ⟦L *detrudere* < *de-*, down + *trudere*, THRUST⟧ **1** to press down with force **2** to thrust away or out —**de·tru′sion** ***n.***

de·trun·cate (dē truŋ′kāt′) ***vt.*** **-cat′ed, -cat′ing** ⟦< L *detruncatus*, pp. of *detruncare*: see DE- & TRUNCATE⟧ to cut off a part of; truncate

de·tu·mes·cence (dē′to͞o mes′əns, -tyo͞o-) ***n.*** ⟦< L *detumescens*, prp. of *detumescere*, to stop swelling, subside: see DE- & TUMESCENCE⟧ a gradual shrinking of a swelling, specif., of an erection of the penis —**de′tu·mes′cent** ***adj.***

Deu·ca·li·on (do͞o kāl′ē ən, dyo͞o-) ***n.*** ⟦L < Gr *Deukaliōn*⟧ *Gr. Myth.* a son of Prometheus: he and his wife, Pyrrha, were the only survivors of a great flood sent by Zeus

deuce[1] (do͞os, dyo͞os) ***n.*** ⟦ME *deus, dewes* < OFr *deus* < L *duos*, acc. of *duo*, TWO⟧ **1** a playing card with two spots **2** the side of a die bearing two spots, or a throw of the dice totaling two **3** ⟦< Fr *à deux de jeu*⟧ *Tennis, etc.* a tie score (in tennis, 40 each, or any tie score beyond this), after which one player or side must score two successive points to win the game

deuce[2] (do͞os, dyo͞os) ***n.*** ⟦ME *dewes*, two in dice or cards, confused with *dewes*, God < OFr *dieu* & L *deus* (see DEITY): meaning in reference to low score at dice⟧ [Old Brit. Slang] devil; dickens: used, with *the*, only in interjectional phrases, as a mild oath or exclamation of annoyance, surprise, or frustration [what the *deuce* is he doing?]

deu·ced (do͞o′sid, dyo͞o′-; do͞ost, dyo͞ost) ***adj.*** ⟦see prec.⟧ **1** devilish; confounded **2** extreme: used in mild oaths or exclamations —***adv.*** extremely; very: also **deu′ced·ly** (-sid lē)

de·us ex ma·chi·na (dā′əs eks mä′kē nə, dē′-; -mak′ē-) ⟦L, god from a machine⟧ **1** in ancient Greek and Roman plays, a deity brought in by stage machinery to intervene in the action **2** any unconvincing character or event brought artificially into a plot to settle an involved situation

Deut *abbrev. Bible* Deuteronomy

deut- (do͞ot, dyo͞ot) *combining form* DEUTO-: used before a vowel

deuter- (do͞ot′ər, dyo͞ot′ər) *combining form* DEUTERO-: used before a vowel

deu·ter·ag·o·nist (do͞ot′ər ag′ə nist, dyo͞ot′-) ***n.*** ⟦Gr *deuteragōnistēs*: see DEUTERO- & AGONIZE & -IST[1]⟧ in classical Greek drama, the character second in importance to the protagonist

deu·ter·an·ope (do͞ot′ər ə nōp′, dyo͞ot′-) ***n.*** a person who has deuteranopia

deu·ter·an·o·pi·a (do͞ot′ər ə nō′pē ə, dyo͞ot′-) ***n.*** ⟦DEUTER(O)- + AN-[1] + -OPIA⟧ a type of color blindness characterized by the loss of green vision and a distortion of vision in the red-yellow-green part of the spectrum

deu·ter·at·ed (do͞ot′ər āt′id, dyo͞ot′-) ***adj.*** **1** designating or of a substance, compound, or organism in which part or all of the normal hydrogen atoms are replaced with deuterium **2** containing deuterium

☆**deu·ter·ide** (do͞ot′ər īd′, dyo͞ot′-) ***n.*** ⟦< fol. + -IDE⟧ a compound analogous to a hydride, in which ordinary hydrogen is replaced by deuterium

☆**deu·te·ri·um** (do͞o tir′ē əm, dyo͞o-) ***n.*** ⟦ModL: see fol. & -IUM⟧ a hydrogen isotope used in nuclear reactors, accelerators, etc.: symbol, D; at. wt. 2.0141: see HEAVY WATER

deu·ter·o- (do͞ot′ər ō, dyo͞ot′-) ⟦< Gr *deuteros*, second, orig., farther from, a compar. form < base of *deuein*, dial. var of *dein*, to lack, be far from < IE base *deu-, to move away, distance > Sans *dūráh*, remote, L *durare*, to last⟧ *combining form* second, secondary [*deuterogamy*]

deu·ter·o·ca·non·i·cal (do͞ot′ər ō′kə nän′i kəl, dyo͞ot′-) ***adj.*** ⟦prec. + CANONICAL⟧ of or constituting a second or subsequent canon; specif., designating certain Biblical books accepted as canonical in the Roman Catholic Church, but held by Protestants to be apocryphal

deu·ter·og·a·my (do͞ot′ər äg′ə mē, dyo͞ot′-) ***n.*** ⟦ML *deuterogamia* < Gr: see DEUTERO- & -GAMY⟧ a marriage after the death or divorce of the first spouse

☆**deu·ter·on** (do͞ot′ər än′, dyo͞ot′-) ***n.*** ⟦ModL: see DEUTERIUM⟧ the nucleus of an atom of deuterium, containing one proton and one neutron

Deu·ter·on·o·mist (do͞ot′ər än′ə mist, dyo͞ot′-) the otherwise unidentified writer or writers of source material for the Book of Deuteronomy and certain other portions of the Old Testament

Deu·ter·on·o·my (do͞ot′ər än′ə mē, dyo͞ot′-) ***n.*** ⟦LL(Ec) *Deuteronomium* < Gr *Deuteronomion*: see DEUTERO- & -NOMY⟧ the fifth book of the Pentateuch in the Bible, in which the law of Moses is set down in full for the second time: abbrev. *Deut* or *Dt*

deu·to- (do͞ot′ō, dyo͞ot′ō; -ə) *combining form* DEUTERO-

deu·to·plasm (-plaz′əm) ***n.*** ⟦prec. + -PLASM⟧ the yolky substance in eggs or ova that provides food for the developing embryo —**deu′to·plas′mic** (-plaz′mik) ***adj.***

deutsche mark (doich′märk′) ⟦Ger, German MARK[2]⟧ [*also* **D- m-**] the former basic monetary unit of Germany, superseded in 2002 by the EURO: abbrev. *DM*: also written **deutsche′mark′** ***n.***

Deutsch·land (doich′länt′) ⟦Ger < *Deutsch*, German (< OHG *diutisc*, of the people < OHG *thioda*, akin to OE *theod* & OIr *tuoth*, people < IE **teutā-*, crowd < base **tēu-*, to swell > THUMB, THOUSAND < L *tumere*, to swell) + OHG *-isc*, -ISH + Ger *land*, LAND⟧ *Ger. name for* GERMANY

deut·zi·a (do͞ot′sē ə, dyo͞ot′-, doit′-) ***n.*** ⟦ModL, after Jean *Deutz*, 18th-c. Du flower fancier⟧ any of a genus (*Deutzia*) of small shrubs of the saxifrage family, bearing many white flowers in the spring

dev *abbrev. Statistics* deviation

de·va (dā′və) ***n.*** ⟦Sans *deva*, god: see DEITY⟧ *Hindu Myth.* a god or good spirit

De Va·ler·a (dev′ə ler′ə, -lir′-), **Ea·mon** (ā′mən) 1882-1975; Ir. statesman, born in U.S.: prime minister of Ireland (1937-48; 1951-54; 1957-59): president (1959-73)

de·val·u·a·tion (dē val′yo͞o ā′shən) ***n.*** **1** *a)* a reduction in the amount or fineness of a metal, esp. gold, officially designated as the standard of value of a monetary unit *b)* an official lowering of the exchange value of a currency with reference to other currencies **2** a lessening in value, importance, etc.

de·val·ue (dē val′yo͞o) ***vt.*** **-ued**, **-u·ing** **1** to lessen or, sometimes, annul the value, importance, etc. of **2** to subject (a monetary unit or a currency) to devaluation Also **de·val·u·ate** (dē val′yo͞o āt′) **-at′ed**, **-at′ing**

De·va·na·ga·ri (dā′və nä′gə rē) ***n.*** ⟦Sans *devanāgarī*, city (writing) of the gods < *deva*, god (see DEITY) + *nāgara*, city⟧ the alphabet in which Sanskrit and most of the modern languages of N India are written

dev·as·tate (dev′ə stāt′) ***vt.*** **-tat′ed**, **-tat′ing** ⟦< L *devastatus*, pp. of *devastare*, to lay waste < *de-*, intens. + *vastare*, to make empty < *vastus*, empty: see VAST⟧ **1** to lay waste; make desolate; ravage; destroy **2** to make helpless; overwhelm [the teacher's criticism *devastated* him] —SYN. RAVAGE —**dev′as·tat′ing** ***adj.*** —**dev′as·tat′ing·ly** ***adv.*** —**dev′as·ta′tor** ***n.***

dev·as·ta·tion (dev′ə stā′shən) ***n.*** a devastating or being devastated; destruction; desolation

de·vein (dē vān′) ***vt.*** to remove the veinlike intestine from shrimp or other shellfish

de·vel·op (di vel′əp) ***vt.*** ⟦Fr *développer* < OFr *desveloper* < *des-* (L *dis-*), apart + *voloper*, to wrap, prob. OIt *viluppo*, a bundle < ? *faluppa*, bundle of straw; infl. by L *volvere*, to roll⟧ **I.** *to cause to grow gradually in some way* **1** to build up or expand (a business, industry, etc.) **2** to make stronger or more effective; strengthen (muscles) **3** to bring (something latent or hypothetical) into activity or reality **4** to cause (one's personality, a bud, etc.) to unfold or evolve gradually **5** to make (housing, highways, etc.) more available or extensive **6** *Chess* to position (chessmen or a chessman) strategically in the early stages of a game **7** *Music* to elaborate (a theme) as by rhythmic or melodic changes **8** *Photog.* *a)* to immerse (an exposed film, plate, or printing paper) in various chemical solutions in order to make the picture visible *b)* to make (a picture) visible by doing this **II.** *to show or work out by degrees* **1** to make (a theme or plot) known gradually **2** to explain more clearly; enlarge upon **3** *Geom.* to change the form of (a surface); esp., to flatten out (a curved surface) **4** *Math.* to work out in detail or expand (a function or expression) —***vi.*** **1** to come into being or activity; occur or happen **2** to become larger, fuller, better, etc.; grow or evolve, esp. by natural processes ☆**3** to become known or apparent; be disclosed **4** to progress economically, socially, and politically from an underdeveloped condition [the *developing* nations] —**de·vel′op·a·ble** ***adj.***

de·vel·op·er (di vel′əp ər) ***n.*** a person or thing that develops; specif., *a)* a person or company that develops real estate on a speculative basis *b)* *Comput.* a person or company that develops software, applications, etc. *c)* *Photog.* a chemical used to develop film, plates, etc.

de·vel·op·ment (di vel′əp mənt) ***n.*** ⟦Fr *développement*⟧ **1** a developing or being developed **2** a step or stage in growth, advancement, etc. **3** an event or happening **4** a thing that is developed; specif., a number of structures on a large tract of land, built by a real-estate developer —**de·vel′op·men′tal** (-ment′′l) ***adj.*** —**de·vel′op·men′tal·ly** ***adv.***

developmental biology the study of the development of multicellular organisms, including the study of the earliest stages of embryonic structure and tissue differentiation

developmentally disabled having a condition such as INTELLECTUAL DISABILITY, autism, etc. that impedes normal childhood development

dé·ve·lop·pé (dā′və lə pā′; *Fr* dā vlô pā′) ***n.*** ⟦Fr < pp. of *développer*, to stretch out, open out, DEVELOP⟧ *Ballet* a movement in which the leg is slowly unfolded into the air

De·ven·ter (dā′vən tər) city in E Netherlands: medieval commercial & educational center

de·verb·a·tive (dē vur′bə tiv, di-) ***adj.*** ⟦DE- + VERB + -ATIVE⟧ **1** formed from a verb [the noun "thinker," derived from "think," is *deverbative*] **2** used in the formation of a word from a verb [the *deverbative* suffix "-er"] —***n.*** a deverbative word

Dev·e·reux (dev′ə ro͞o′, -ro͝oks′), **Robert** *see* ESSEX[1], 2d Earl of

de·vest (dē vest′, di-) ***vt.*** ⟦OFr *devester* < L *devestire*, to undress < *dis-*, from + *vestire*, to dress < *vestis*, a dress: see VEST⟧ **1** [Obs.] to undress; strip **2** *Law* *a)* to take away (a right, property, etc.) *b)* [Archaic] to strip *of* a title, etc.

De·vi (dā′vē) ***n.*** ⟦Sans, fem. of *deva*, god: see DEITY⟧ a Hindu goddess, the consort of Siva

de·vi·ant (dē′vē ənt) ***adj.*** ⟦< LL *devians*, prp. of *deviare*: see fol.⟧ deviating, esp. from what is considered normal in a group or for a society —***n.*** a person whose behavior is deviant —**de′vi·ance** (-əns) ***n.***, **de′vi·an·cy** (-ən sē)

de·vi·ate (dē′vē āt′; *for adj. & n.*, -it) ***vi.*** **-at′ed**, **-at′ing** ⟦< LL *deviatus*, pp. of *deviare*, to turn aside < *de-*, from + *via*, road: see VIA⟧ to turn aside (*from* a course, direction, standard, doctrine, etc.); diverge; digress —***vt.*** to cause to deviate —***adj.*** DEVIANT —***n.*** a deviant; esp., one whose sexual behavior is deviant —**de′vi·a′tor** ***n.***

SYN.—**deviate** suggests a turning aside, often to only a slight degree, from the correct or prescribed course, standard, doctrine, etc. [to *deviate* from the truth]; **swerve** implies a sudden or sharp turning from a path, course, etc. [the car *swerved* to avoid hitting us]; **veer**, originally used of ships and wind, suggests a turning or series of turnings so as to change direction; **diverge** suggests the branching off of a single path or course into two courses constantly leading away from each other [the sides of an angle *diverge* from a single point]; **digress** suggests a wandering, often deliberate and temporary, from the main topic in speaking or writing

de·vi·a·tion (dē′vē ā′shən) ***n.*** ⟦ME *deviacion* < LL *deviatio*⟧ the act or an instance of deviating; specif., *a)* sharp divergence from normal behavior *b)* divergence from the official ideology or policies of a political party, esp. a Communist party *c)* the deflection of a magnetic compass needle due to magnetic influences; specif., on a ship, such deflection caused by the ship's own magnetic properties *d)* *Statistics* the amount by which a number differs from an average or other comparable value (see MEAN DEVIATION, STANDARD DEVIATION)

de·vi·a·tion·ism (-iz′əm) ***n.*** the practice or advocacy of deviation in politics, esp. from Communism —**de′vi·a′tion·ist** ***adj.***, ***n.***

de·vice (di vīs′) ***n.*** ⟦ME & OFr *devis*, division, will < OFr *deviser*: see DEVISE⟧ **1** a thing devised; plan; scheme, esp. a sly or underhanded scheme; trick **2** a contrivance, esp. a mechanical one, for some specific purpose **3** something used to gain an artistic effect [rhetorical *devices*] **4** an ornamental figure or design **5** a design, often with a motto, on a coat of arms; heraldic emblem **6** any motto or emblem **7** [Archaic] the act or power of devising —**leave someone to his** (or **her**) **own devices** to allow someone to act independently or as he (or she) wishes

dev·il (dev′əl) ***n.*** ⟦ME *devel* < OE *deofol* < LL(Ec) *diabolus* < Gr *diabolos*, slanderous (in LXX, Satan; in N.T., devil) < *diaballein*, to slander, lit., throw across < *dia-*, across + *ballein*, to throw: see BALL[2]⟧ **1** *Theol.* *a)* [*often* **D-**] the chief evil spirit, a supernatural being subordinate to, and the foe of, God, and the tempter of human beings; Satan: typically depicted as a man with horns, a tail, and cloven feet (with *the*) *b)* any evil spirit; demon **2** a very wicked or malevolent person **3** a person who is mischievous, energetic, reckless, etc. **4** an unlucky, unhappy person [that poor *devil*] **5** anything that is difficult or is hard to operate, control, understand, etc. **6** [Old-fashioned] PRINTER'S DEVIL **7** any of various machines for tearing things, as paper or rags, to bits —***vt.*** **-iled** or **-illed**, **-il·ing** or **-il·ling** **1** ⟦from the notion of heat⟧ to prepare (food, often chopped food) with hot seasoning [*deviled* ham] **2** to tear up (rags, etc.) with a special machine ☆**3** to annoy; torment; tease —**a devil of a** an extreme example of a —**between the devil and the deep (blue) sea** between equally unpleasant alternatives —**give the devil his due** to acknowledge the ability or success of even a wicked or unpleasant person —**go to the devil** **1** to fall into bad habits; degenerate morally **2** go to hell!: used in the imperative as an expression of anger or annoyance at someone —**play the devil with** [Informal] to cause to go awry; upset —**raise the devil** **1** to conjure up the devil **2** [Informal] to make a commotion or have a boisterous good time —**the devil!** [Informal] an exclamation of anger, surprise, negation, etc.: often in such phrases as **the devil you did!**, meaning "did you really?" —**the devil to pay** trouble as a consequence

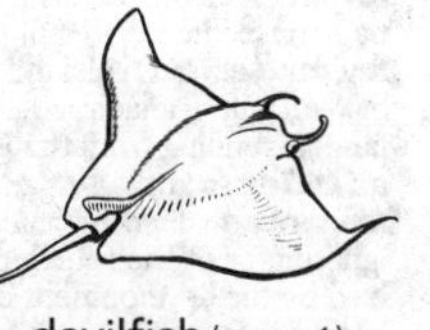
devilfish (sense 1)

dev·il·fish (dev′əl fish′) ***n.***, *pl.* **-fish′** or

-fish'es (see FISH) 1 any manta: so called because its pectoral fins, located near the eyes, resemble horns 2 any large cephalopod, esp. the octopus

dev·il·ish (dev′'l ish) *adj.* ⟦ME *develish*⟧ 1 of or like a devil; wicked; cruel; diabolic 2 mischievous; energetic; reckless 3 [Informal] *a)* extremely bad *b)* very great; extreme —*adv.* [Informal] extremely; excessively —**dev′il·ish·ly** *adv.* —**dev′il·ish·ness** *n.*

dev·il-may-care (dev′əl mā ker′) *adj.* reckless or careless; happy-go-lucky

dev·il·ment (dev′əl mənt) *n.* mischief or mischievous action

dev·il·ry (dev′əl rē) *n., pl.* **-ries** ⟦ME *develri*⟧ [Chiefly Brit.] 1 black magic; witchcraft 2 evil or diabolic behavior; great wickedness or cruelty 3 DEVILTRY (sense 1)

devil's advocate ⟦transl. of ML *advocatus diaboli*⟧ 1 *R.C.Ch.* an official selected to examine the facts critically and raise objections in the case of a dead person named for beatification or canonization 2 a person who upholds what is regarded as the wrong side or an indefensible cause, perversely or for argument's sake

dev·il's-darn·ing-nee·dle (dev′əlz därn′iŋ nēd′'l) *n.* DRAGONFLY

☆**dev·il's-food cake** (dev′əlz fo͞od′) a rich cake made with chocolate or cocoa and baking soda

Devil's Island one of a group of French islands off the coast of French Guiana: site of a former penal colony

☆**devil's paintbrush** a perennial European hawkweed (*Hieracium aurantiacum*) with leafless flower stalks bearing a cluster of orange-red heads: now a common weed in N U.S. and Canada

devil's tattoo a rapid or nervous drumming with the fingers or feet

devil's walking-stick ☆HERCULES'-CLUB (sense 1)

dev·il·try (dev′əl trē) *n., pl.* **-tries** ⟦altered < DEVILRY⟧ 1 reckless mischief, fun, etc. 2 DEVILRY (senses 1 & 2)

☆**dev·il·wood** (dev′əl wood′) *n.* a small evergreen tree (*Osmanthus americanus*) of the olive family, with whitish bark, glossy leaves, greenish flowers, and hard wood, found in SE U.S.

de·vi·ous (dē′vē əs) *adj.* ⟦L *devius* < *de-*, off, from + *via*, road: see VIA⟧ 1 not in a straight path; roundabout; winding 2 deviating from the proper or usual course; going astray 3 not straightforward or frank; deceiving —**de′vi·ous·ly** *adv.* —**de′vi·ous·ness** *n.*

de·vis·al (di vī′zəl) *n.* the act of devising

de·vise (di vīz′) *vt., vi.* **-vised′**, **-vis′ing** ⟦ME *devisen* < OFr *deviser*, to distribute, direct, regulate, talk < VL **divisare* < L *divisus*, pp. of *dividere*: see DIVIDE⟧ 1 to work out or create (something) by thinking; contrive; plan; invent 2 *Law* to bequeath (real property) by a will 3 [Archaic] to make secret plans for; plot 4 [Obs.] to guess or imagine —*n. Law* 1 a gift of real property by a will 2 a will, or clause in a will, granting such a gift 3 the property so granted —**de·vis′a·ble** *adj.* —**de·vis′er** *n.*

dev·i·see (dev′ə zē′, di vī′zē) *n.* ⟦< prec. + -EE[1]⟧ *Law* the person to whom real property has been devised

de·vi·sor (dev′ə zôr′, di vī′zôr′) *n.* ⟦Anglo-Fr *devisour*⟧ *Law* a person who devises property; testator

de·vi·tal·ize (dē vīt′'l īz′) *vt.* **-ized′**, **-iz′ing** to make listless or ineffective; lower the vitality of; weaken —**de·vi′tal·i·za′tion** *n.*

de·vit·ri·fy (dē vi′trə fī′) *vt.* **-fied′**, **-fy′ing** ⟦Fr *dévitrifier*: see DE- & VITRIFY⟧ 1 to take away or destroy the glassy qualities of 2 to make (glass, etc.) opaque, hard, and crystalline, as by prolonged heating —**de·vit′ri·fi·ca′tion** *n.*

de·voice (dē vois′) *vt.* **-voiced′**, **-voic′ing** UNVOICE: also **de·vo·cal·ize** (dē vō′kəl īz′) **-ized′**, **-iz′ing**

de·void (di void′) *adj.* ⟦ME, orig. pp. of *devoiden*, to put away < OFr *desvuidier* < *des-* (L *dis-*), from + *vuidier*: see VOID⟧ completely without; empty or destitute (*of*)

de·voir (də vwär′, dev′wär′) *n.* ⟦ME < OFr, to owe < L *debere*, to owe: see DEBT⟧ 1 duty 2 [*pl.*] acts or expressions of due respect or courtesy, as in greeting

dev·o·lu·tion (dev′ə lo͞o′shən, dē′və-) *n.* ⟦ML *devolutio*, a rolling back < L *devolutus*, pp. of *devolvere*: see fol.⟧ 1 [Obs.] a rolling down or falling 2 a passing down from stage to stage 3 the passing (of property, rights, authority, etc.) from one person to another 4 a delegating (of duties) to a substitute or subordinate 5 a delegating (of power or authority) by a central government to local governing units 6 *Biol.* evolution in function or structure toward greater simplicity or to the point of disappearance; DEGENERATION —**dev′o·lu′tion·ar′y** *adj.* —**dev′o·lu′tion·ist** *n.*

de·volve (di välv′, -vôlv′) *vt.* **-volved′**, **-volv′ing** ⟦ME *devolven* < L *devolvere*, to roll down < *de-*, down + *volvere*, to roll: see WALK⟧ to transfer or pass on (duties, responsibilities, etc.) to another or others —*vi.* 1 to pass or be transferred to another or others 2 to change gradually for the worse; decline; deteriorate; degenerate —**de·volve′ment** *n.*

Dev·on[1] (dev′ən) *n.* any of a breed of medium-sized, red beef cattle, originally raised in the area of Devon, England

Dev·on[2] (dev′ən) 1 island of the Arctic Archipelago, north of Baffin region of Nunavut, Canada: 20,861 sq mi (54,030 sq km) 2 county in SW England, extending from the Bristol Channel to the English Channel: 2,588 sq mi (6,703 sq km)

De·vo·ni·an (di vō′nē ən) *adj.* 1 of Devon, England 2 [*sometimes* **d-**] designating or of the fourth geologic period of the Paleozoic Era, characterized by the development of the first ferns, mosses, gymnosperms, sharks, bony fishes, amphibians, and wingless insects: so called because rocks of the Devonian Period were first studied in Devon, England —**the Devonian** the Devonian Period or its rocks: see the geologic time chart in the Reference Supplement

Dev·on·shire (dev′ən shir′, -shər) DEVON[2] (the county)

de·vote (di vōt′) *vt.* **-vot′ed**, **-vot′ing** ⟦< L *devotus*, pp. of *devovere*, to dedicate by vow < *de-*, from + *vovere*, to vow: see VOTE⟧ 1 to set apart for a special use or service; dedicate 2 to give up (oneself or one's time, energy, etc.) to some purpose, activity, or person 3 [Obs.] to curse or doom —**de·vote′ment** *n.*

SYN.—to **devote** is to give up or apply oneself or something with the seriousness or earnestness evoked by a formal vow [to *devote* one's life to a cause]; to **dedicate** is to set apart or assign (something), as in a formal rite, to some serious, often sacred, purpose [to *dedicate* a temple]; to **consecrate** is to set apart for some religious or holy use [to *consecrate* ground for a church]; **hallow**, a stronger word, suggests an intrinsic holiness in the thing set apart [to *hallow* the Sabbath]

de·vot·ed (-id) *adj.* 1 characterized by devotion or zeal; dedicated 2 very loving, loyal, or faithful [a *devoted* husband] 3 [Obs.] doomed —**de·vot′ed·ly** *adv.* —**de·vot′ed·ness** *n.*

dev·o·tee (dev′ō tē′, -tā′) *n.* 1 a person strongly devoted to something or someone [a *devotee* of the ballet] 2 a person extremely devoted to religion; zealot

de·vo·tion (di vō′shən) *n.* ⟦ME *devociun* < OFr *devotion* < L *devotio*⟧ 1 the fact, quality, or state of being devoted 2 piety; devoutness 3 religious worship 4 [*often pl.*] one or more prayers or other religious practices, specif. of a private or nonofficial kind 5 loyalty or deep affection 6 the act of devoting

de·vo·tion·al (-shə nəl) *adj.* of or characterized by devotion —☆*n.* a brief worship service —**de·vo′tion·al·ly** *adv.*

de·vour (di vour′) *vt.* ⟦ME *devouren* < OFr *devorer* < L *devorare* < *de-*, intens. + *vorare*, to swallow whole: see VORACIOUS⟧ 1 to eat or eat up hungrily, greedily, or voraciously 2 to consume or destroy with devastating force 3 to take in greedily with the eyes, ears, or mind [the child *devours* fairy tales] 4 to absorb completely; engross [*devoured* by curiosity] 5 to swallow up; engulf —**de·vour′er** *n.*

de·vout (di vout′) *adj.* ⟦ME < OFr *devot* < L *devotus*, devoted (in LL(Ec), devout): see DEVOTE⟧ 1 very religious; pious 2 showing reverence 3 earnest; sincere; heartfelt —**de·vout′ly** *adv.* —**de·vout′ness** *n.*

SYN.—**devout** implies sincere, worshipful devotion to one's faith or religion; **pious** suggests scrupulous adherence to the forms of one's religion but may, in derogatory usage, connote hypocrisy [the *pious* burghers who defraud their tenants]; **religious** stresses faith in a particular religion and constant adherence to its tenets [to lead a *religious* life]; **sanctimonious** in current usage implies a hypocritical pretense of piety or devoutness and often connotes smugness or haughtiness [his *sanctimonious* disapproval of dancing]

De Vries (də vrēs′), **Hugo** 1848-1935; Du. botanist

dew (do͞o, dyo͞o) *n.* ⟦ME < OE *deaw*, akin to Ger *tau* < IE base **dheu-*, to run > Sans *dhāvati*, a spring, brook⟧ 1 the condensation formed, usually during the night, on lawns, cars, etc. as a result of relatively warm air contacting a cool surface 2 anything regarded as refreshing, gently falling, pure, etc., like dew 3 any moisture in small drops, as perspiration —*vt.* [Old Poet.] to wet with or as with dewdrops; bedew

de·wan (dē wän′) *n.* ⟦Hindi *dīwān* < Pers: see DIVAN⟧ in India, any of various high officials

Dew·ar (flask) (do͞o′ər, dyo͞o′ər) ⟦after Sir James *Dewar* (1848-1923), Scot chemist & physicist⟧ [*also* **d- (flask)**] a double-walled flask with a vacuum between the walls, which are silvered on the inside, used esp. for storage of liquefied gases

de·wa·ter (dē wôt′ər) *vt.* to remove water from, esp. in large-scale processing of sewage, chemicals, etc.

dew·ber·ry (do͞o′ber′ē, dyo͞o′-) *n., pl.* **-ries** 1 any of various trailing blackberry plants (genus *Rubus*) 2 the fruit of any of these plants

dew·claw (-klô′) *n.* ⟦prob. so called because it does not touch the ground, but only the dew on the surface⟧ 1 a functionless digit on the foot of some animals, as on the inner side of a dog's leg or above the true hoof in cattle, deer, etc. 2 the claw or hoof at the end of such a digit

dew·drop (-dräp′) *n.* a drop of dew

Dew·ey (do͞o′ē, dyo͞o′-) 1 **George** 1837-1917; U.S. admiral in the Spanish-American War 2 **John** 1859-1952; U.S. philosopher & educator: exponent of pragmatism 3 **Mel·vil** (mel′vil) (born *Melville Louis Kossuth Dewey*) 1851-1931; U.S. librarian & educator: originator of a system (**Dewey Decimal System**) for book classification in libraries, using three-digit numbers, further extended beyond a decimal point for subclasses

dew·fall (-fôl′) *n.* 1 the formation of dew 2 the time of the evening when this begins

dew·lap (-lap′) *n.* ⟦ME *dewlappe*: see DEW & LAP[1]⟧ a loose fold of skin hanging from the throat of cattle and certain other animals, or a similar loose fold under the chin of a person —**dew′lapped′** (-lapt′) *adj.*

☆**DEW line** (do͞o, dyo͞o) ⟦*D*(*istant*) *E*(*arly*) *W*(*arning*)⟧ a line of radar stations near the 70th parallel in North America, maintained by Canada and the United States, intended to give warning of hostile aircraft or missiles

de·worm (dē wurm′) *vt.* WORM (*vt.* 4)

dew point the temperature at which a condensable component of a gas (as, esp., water vapor in the air) starts to condense into liquid

dew-point spread (do͞o′point′, dyo͞o′-) the degrees of difference between the air temperature and the dew point: also called **dew-point deficit** or **dew-point depression**

dew worm NIGHT CRAWLER

dew·y (do͞o′ē, dyo͞o′ē) *adj.* **dew′i·er, dew′i·est** ⟦ME *deui* < OE *deawig*⟧ **1** wet or damp with dew **2** of dew **3** [Old Poet.] dewlike; refreshing, gentle, etc. —**dew′i·ly** *adv.* —**dew′i·ness** *n.*

dew·y-eyed (-īd′) *adj.* ☆trustful, innocent, optimistic, etc.; not cynical or suspicious

☆**Dex·e·drine** (dek′sə drēn′, -drin) ⟦DEX(TRO)- + (EPH)EDRINE⟧ *trademark for* DEXTROAMPHETAMINE

☆**dex·ie** (dek′sē) *n.* [Slang] a pill containing dextroamphetamine: also sp. **dex′y**, *pl.* **dex′ies**

dex·i·o·trop·ic (dek′sē ō träp′ik, -sē ə-) *adj.* ⟦< Gr *dexios*, on or toward the right (for IE base see fol.) + -TROPIC⟧ spiraling to the right if viewed from the side: said as of the dextral whorls in most gastropod shells: opposed to LAEOTROPIC

dex·ter (deks′tər) *adj.* ⟦L *dexter*, right, to the right < IE **deks-* < base **dek̑-*, to take: see DECENT⟧ **1** of or on the right-hand side **2** [Obs.] auspicious because seen on the right **3** *Heraldry* on the right-hand side of a shield (the left as seen by the viewer): opposed to SINISTER

dex·ter·i·ty (deks ter′ə tē) *n.* ⟦L *dexteritas*, skillfulness, handiness < *dexter*: see prec.⟧ **1** skill in using one's hands or body; adroitness **2** skill in using one's mind; cleverness

dex·ter·ous (deks′tər əs, -trəs) *adj.* ⟦DEXTER + -OUS⟧ **1** having or showing skill in the use of the hands or body **2** having or showing mental skill —**dex′ter·ous·ly** *adv.* —**dex′ter·ous·ness** *n.*

SYN.—**dexterous** implies an expertness, natural or acquired, demonstrated in the ability to do things with skill and precision [*a dexterous mechanic*]; **adroit** adds to this a connotation of cleverness and resourcefulness and is now generally used of mental facility [*an adroit evasion*]; **deft** suggests a nimbleness and sureness of touch [*a deft seamstress*]; **handy** suggests skill, usually without training, at a variety of small tasks [*a handy man around the house*] —*ANT.* **clumsy, awkward, inept**

dextr- *combining form* DEXTRO-: used before a vowel

dex·tral (deks′trəl) *adj.* ⟦< L *dextra*, right-hand side (see DEXTER) + -AL⟧ **1** on the right-hand side; right **2** right-handed **3** having whorls that rise to the apex in counterclockwise spirals from the opening at the lower right: said of the shells of most gastropods Opposed to SINISTRAL —**dex·tral′i·ty** (-tral′ə tē) *n.* —**dex′tral·ly** *adv.*

dex·tran (deks′tran′, -trən) *n.* ⟦DEXTR- + -AN⟧ a chainlike polymer of glucose produced by certain strains of bacteria acting on sucrose, as in sugar-refinery tanks, in various fermentation processes, or in the formation of dental plaque: it is used as a substitute or expander for blood plasma, in confections, etc.

dex·trin (deks′trin) *n.* ⟦Fr *dextrine* (see DEXTER & -IN[1]): so called because it rotates the plane of polarization to the right⟧ any of a number of water-soluble, gummy, dextrorotatory polysaccharides obtained from the breakdown of starch and used as adhesives, as sizes, in certain foods, etc.: also **dex′trine** (-trēn′, -trin)

dex·tro (deks′trō) *adj. Chem.* DEXTROROTATORY

dex·tro- (deks′trō, deks′trə) ⟦< L *dexter*: see DEXTER⟧ *combining form* **1** toward or on the right-hand side [*dextrorotatory*] **2** *Chem.* dextrorotatory [*dextrose*]

dex·tro·am·phet·a·mine (deks′trō am fet′ə mēn′) ⟦prec. + AMPHETAMINE⟧ *n.* a potentially habit-forming drug used as a central-nervous-system stimulant and appetite depressant

dex·tro·glu·cose (-glo͞o′kōs′) *n.* DEXTROSE

dex·tro·ro·ta·tion (-rō tā′shən) *n.* dextrorotatory direction or movement

dex·tro·ro·ta·to·ry (-rōt′ə tôr′ē) *adj.* **1** turning or circling to the right, in a clockwise direction **2** that turns the plane of polarized light to the right or clockwise: said of certain compounds, etc. Also **dex′tro·ro′ta·ry** (-rōt′ə rē)

dex·trorse (deks′trôrs′, deks trôrs′) *adj.* ⟦L *dextrorsus*, toward the right < *dexter* (see DEXTER) + *versus*, turning: see VERSE⟧ *Bot.* twining upward to the right, as the stems of some vines do: opposed to SINISTRORSE —**dex′trorse′ly** *adv.*

dex·trose (deks′trōs′) *n.* ⟦DEXTR- + -OSE[2]⟧ a right-handed form of glucose found in plants and animals and in human blood, and made by the hydrolysis of starch with acids or enzymes

dex·trous (deks′trəs) *adj.* DEXTEROUS

dey (dā) *n.* ⟦Fr *dey* < Turk *dāi*, maternal uncle: orig., friendly title given to an older person⟧ **1** the former title of the governor of Algiers **2** a pasha in the former Barbary States of Tunis and Tripoli

Dez·ful (dez fo͞ol′) city in W Iran

Dezh·nev (dyezh′nyev), **Cape** cape at the northeasternmost point of Asia, in Russia, projecting into Bering Strait: also **Cape Dezh′nev·a** (-nye və)

DF *abbrev.* **1** *Radio* direction finder: also **D/F** **2** ⟦Sp *Distrito Federal*⟧ Federal District (in Mexico)

DFA or **D.F.A.** *abbrev.* Doctor of Fine Arts

DFC *abbrev.* Distinguished Flying Cross

dg *abbrev.* decigram(s)

dh *abbrev. Baseball* designated hitter: also **DH**

Dhak·a (dä′kə, dak′ə) capital of Bangladesh, in the WC part

dhal (däl) *n. alt. sp. of* DAL[1]

Dhan·bad (dän′bäd) city in E Bihar, NE India

dhar·ma (där′mə, dʉr′-) *n.* ⟦Sans, law, custom < IE base **dher-*, to hold, support > L *firmus*, OHG *tarnen*, to conceal⟧ *Buddhism, Hinduism* **1** cosmic order or law, including the natural and moral principles that apply to all beings and things **2** dutiful observance of this law in one's life; right conduct

dhar·na (-nə) *n.* ⟦Hindi *dharnā*, persistence, a holding firm: for IE base see prec.⟧ in India, a method of seeking justice by sitting at the door of one's debtor or wrongdoer and fasting until justice is obtained

Dhau·la·gi·ri (dou′lə gir′ē) mountain of the Himalayas, in NC Nepal: 26,810 ft (8,172 m)

DHEA (dē′āch′ē′ā′) *n.* ⟦< *d(e)h(ydro)e(pi)a(ndrosterone)*, chemical name⟧ a hormone that is a precursor to testosterone and estrogen, secreted mainly by the adrenal cortex, esp. during puberty, and made synthetically for use as a nutritional supplement

dhim·mi (dim′ē) *n.*, *pl.* **-mi** or **-mis** ⟦Ar⟧ a non-Muslim living under sharia

dhim·mi·tude (dim′ə to͞od′, -tyo͞od′) *n.* ⟦prec. + -TUDE⟧ the condition or status of non-Muslims living under sharia

dho·bi (dō′bē) *n.* ⟦Hindi < *dhob*, washing; akin to Sans *dhāvati*, (he) cleans, *dhavala*, shining white < IE base **dheu-*, gleaming⟧ in India, a person who does laundry

dhole (dōl) *n.*, *pl.* **dholes** or **dhole** a red-colored wild dog (*Cuon alpinus*) of central and E Asia, which hunts in packs, attacking even large game

D-ho·ri·zon (dē′hə rī′zən) *n.* a stratum, as of rock, sometimes underlying the C-horizon

dho·ti (dō′tē) *n.* ⟦Hindi *dhotī*⟧ a loincloth worn by Hindu men in India, or the cloth used for it: also **dhoo′ti** (do͞o′-)

dhow (dou) *n.* ⟦< Ar *dāwa*⟧ a ship with a lateen sail or sails and a raised deck at the stern, used along the coasts of the Indian Ocean

DHS *abbrev.* Department of Homeland Security

dhur·rie (dʉr′ē, du′rē) *n.* a coarse cotton or wool rug woven in India in a flat weave and in various designs: in full **dhurrie rug**

di or **dia** *abbrev.* diameter

Di *Chem. symbol for* didymium

DI *abbrev.* drill instructor

di-[1] (dī) ⟦Gr *di-* < *dis-*, twice < IE **dwis* (> L *bis*, MHG *zwis*) < base **dwo*, TWO⟧ *prefix* **1** twice, double, twofold [*dichroism, dicotyledon*] **2** *Chem.* having two atoms, molecules, radicals, etc. [*diacid*]: see BI-[1] (sense 8) Also **dis-** (dis)

di-[2] (di, dī) *prefix* DIS-: used before *b, d, g, l, m, n, r*, or *v*

di-[3] (dī) *prefix* DIA-

di·a- (dī′ə) ⟦ME < OFr < L < Gr *dia*, through, across < **disa*, in two, apart < IE **dis-* < base **dwo*, TWO⟧ *prefix* **1** through, throughout, across [*diachronic, diagram*] **2** apart, between [*dialect, diacritical*]

di·a·base (-bās′) *n.* ⟦Fr < Gr *diabasis*, a crossing over < *dia-* (see prec.) + *bainein*, to go, COME⟧ **1** *former term for* DIORITE **2** a finely crystalline, intrusive basaltic rock made up mainly of labradorite and pyroxene **3** [Brit.] altered dolerite —**di′a·bas′ic** (-bās′ik) *adj.*

di·a·be·tes (dī′ə bēt′ēz′, -is) *n.* ⟦ME *diabete* < L *diabetes*, a siphon (in LL, diabetes) < Gr *diabētēs* < *diabainein*, to pass through < *dia* (see DIA-) + *bainein*, to go, COME⟧ any of various diseases characterized by an excessive discharge of urine; esp., DIABETES MELLITUS

diabetes in·sip·i·dus (in sip′i dəs) ⟦ModL, lit., insipid diabetes⟧ a disorder caused by a pituitary deficiency and characterized by the heavy discharge of urine and intense thirst

diabetes mel·li·tus (mə līt′əs) ⟦ModL, lit., honey diabetes < L *mellitus*, of honey, honeyed < *mel*, honey: see MILDEW⟧ a chronic form of diabetes involving an insulin deficiency and characterized by an excess of sugar in the blood and urine, and by hunger, thirst, and gradual loss of weight: see also TYPE 1 DIABETES and TYPE 2 DIABETES

di·a·bet·ic (dī′ə bet′ik) *adj.* of or having diabetes —*n.* a person who has diabetes

di·a·ble·rie (dē ä′blə rē, dē ä′blə rē′) *n.* ⟦Fr < OFr < *diable*, devil < LL(Ec) *diabolus*: see DEVIL⟧ **1** a dealing with devils, as by sorcery or witchcraft **2** lore about devils, diabolism, etc. **3** deviltry; mischief

di·a·bol·ic (dī′ə bäl′ik) *adj.* ⟦Fr *diabolique* < LL(Ec) *diabolicus* < *diabolus*: see DEVIL⟧ **1** of the Devil or devils **2** very wicked or cruel **3** extremely or ingeniously difficult, vexatious, etc.; fiendish Also, and for senses 2 & 3 usually, **di′a·bol′i·cal** —**di′a·bol′i·cal·ly** *adv.*

di·ab·o·lism (dī ab′ə liz′əm) *n.* ⟦< LL(Ec) *diabolus* (see DEVIL) + -ISM⟧ **1** dealings with the Devil or devils, as by sorcery or witchcraft **2** belief in or worship of the Devil or devils **3** diabolic action or behavior **4** the character or condition of the Devil or a devil —**di·ab′o·list** (-list) *n.*

di·ab·o·lize (-līz′) *vt.* **-lized′**, **-liz′ing** **1** to make diabolic **2** to portray as diabolic

di·a·chron·ic (dī′ə krän′ik) *adj.* ⟦DIA- + CHRONIC⟧ of or concerned with the study of changes occurring over a period of time, as in language, mores, etc.: cf. SYNCHRONIC (sense 2) —**di′a·chron′i·cal·ly** *adv.*

di·ac·id (dī as′id, dī′as′id) *adj.* **1** containing in each molecule two atoms of hydrogen replaceable by basic atoms or radicals: usually said of acids and acid salts **2** capable of forming a salt or ester by reacting with one molecule of a diacid, or two of a monoacid: usually said of bases and alcohols —*n.* an acid having in each molecule two hydrogen atoms which can be replaced by a metal or react with basic substances

di·ac·o·nal (dī ak′ə nəl; *also* dē-) *adj.* ⟦LL(Ec) *diaconalis*⟧ of a deacon or deacons

di·ac·o·nate (dī ak′ə nit, -nāt′; *also* -, dē-) *n.* ⟦LL(Ec) *diaconatus*⟧ **1** the rank, office, or tenure of a deacon **2** a group or board of deacons

di·a·crit·ic (dī′ə krit′ik) *adj.* ⟦Gr *diakritikos* < *diakrinein*, to distinguish < *dia-*, across + *krinein*, to discern: see CRISIS⟧ DIACRITICAL —*n.* a diacritical mark

di·a·crit·i·cal (-i kəl) *adj.* **1** serving to distinguish; distinguishing **2** able to distinguish —**di′a·crit′i·cal·ly** *adv.*

diacritical mark any of various marks, as a macron or cedilla, added to a letter or symbol to indicate its pronunciation or to distinguish it in some way

di·ac·tin·ic (dī′ak tin′ik) *adj.* capable of transmitting actinic rays of light —**di·ac′tin·ism′** *n.*

di·a·del·phous (dī′ə del′fəs) *adj.* ⟦< DI-[1] + Gr *adelphos*, brother (see MONADELPHOUS) + -OUS⟧ **1** arranged in two bundles or sets by the fusion of the filaments: said of stamens **2** having the stamens so arranged, as in the sweet pea

di·a·dem (dī′ə dem′, -dəm) *n.* ⟦ME & OFr *diademe* < L *diadema* < Gr *diadēma*, a band, fillet < *dia-*, through + IE **demn*, a band < base **de-*, to bind > Gr *dein*⟧ **1** a crown **2** an ornamental cloth headband worn as a crown **3** royal power, authority, or dignity —*vt.* to put a diadem on; crown

di·ad·ro·mous (dī ad′rə məs) *adj.* ⟦DIA- + -DROMOUS⟧ **1** *Bot.* with leaf veins radiating in a fanlike arrangement **2** *Zool.* migrating between fresh and salt water: said of certain fishes

di·aer·e·sis (dī er′ə sis) *n. alt. sp. of* DIERESIS

diag *abbrev.* **1** diagonal **2** diagram

di·a·gen·e·sis (dī′ə jen′ə sis) *n.* ⟦ModL: see DIA- & -GENESIS⟧ *Geol.* the physical, chemical, and biological changes in sediment from the time it is deposited until it is consolidated into sedimentary rock

di·a·ge·ot·ro·pism (dī′ə jē ä′trə piz′əm) *n.* ⟦DIA- + GEOTROPISM⟧ the tendency of the stems, branches, rhizomes, etc. of certain plants to grow in a direction horizontal to the surface of the earth —**di′a·ge′o·trop′ic** (-jē′ō träp′ik) *adj.*

Dia·ghi·lev (dē äg′ə lef), **Ser·gei (Pavlovich)** (ser′gā) 1872-1929; Russ. ballet producer

di·ag·nose (dī′əg nōs′, -nōz′; dī′əg nōs′, -nōz′) *vt., vi.* **-nosed′**, **-nos′ing** ⟦back-form. < fol.⟧ **1** to make a diagnosis of (a disease, a problem, etc.) **2** to identify a disease, condition, etc. in (a patient) [they *diagnosed* him as having mumps] —**di′ag·nos′a·ble** *adj.*

di·ag·no·sis (dī′əg nō′sis) *n., pl.* **-ses′** (-sēz′) ⟦ModL < Gr *diagnōsis*, a distinguishing < *diagignōskein*, to distinguish: see DIA- & -GNOSIS⟧ **1** the act or process of discovering or identifying a diseased condition by means of a medical examination, laboratory test, etc. **2** a careful examination and analysis of the facts in an attempt to understand or explain something [a *diagnosis* of the economy] **3** a decision or opinion based on such examination **4** *Taxonomy* a short scientific description for classification

di·ag·nos·tic (dī′əg näs′tik) *adj.* ⟦ML *diagnosticus* < Gr *diagnōstikos*⟧ **1** of or constituting a diagnosis **2** of value for a diagnosis; specif., characteristic **3** *Comput.* of or having to do with the use of computer diagnostics —*n.* **1** [*usually pl., with sing. v.*] the art, science, or method of diagnosis, esp. medical diagnosis **2** a distinguishing sign or symptom; characteristic **3** *Comput.* a routine for testing a piece of hardware or for locating an error in a program —**di′ag·nos′ti·cal·ly** *adv.*

di·ag·nos·ti·cian (dī′əg näs tish′ən) *n.* a person who makes diagnoses; specif., a specialist in diagnostics

di·ag·o·nal (dī ag′ə nəl, -ag′nəl) *adj.* ⟦L *diagonalis* < Gr *diagōnios* < *dia-*, through + *gōnia*, an angle, corner: see KNEE⟧ **1** extending between the vertices of any two nonadjacent angles in a polygonal figure or between any two vertices not in the same face in a polyhedral figure **2** moving or extending obliquely, esp. at a 45° angle; slanting **3** having slanting markings, lines, etc. —*n.* **1** *a)* a diagonal line or plane *b)* VIRGULE **2** any diagonal course, row, order, or part **3** cloth woven with diagonal lines; twill —**di·ag′o·nal·ly** *adv.*

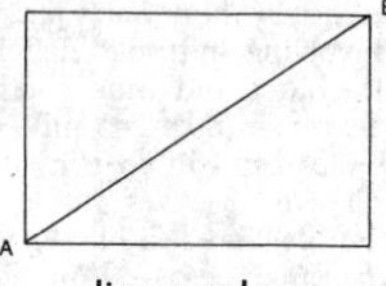

diagonal (AB)

di·a·gram (dī′ə gram′) *n.* ⟦Gr *diagramma* < *diagraphein*, to mark out by lines, draw < *dia-* (see DIA-) + *graphein*, to write (see GRAPHIC)⟧ **1** a geometric figure, used to illustrate a mathematical statement, proof, etc. **2** a sketch, drawing, or plan that explains a thing by outlining its parts and their relationships, workings, etc. **3** a chart or graph explaining or illustrating ideas, statistics, etc. —*vt.* **-gramed′** or **-grammed′**, **-gram′ing** or **-gram′ming** to show or represent by a diagram; make a diagram of —**di′a·gram·mat′ic** (-grə mat′ik) *adj.*, **di′a·gram·mat′i·cal** —**di′a·gram·mat′i·cal·ly** *adv.*

di·a·ki·ne·sis (dī′ə ki nē′sis, -kī-) *n.* ⟦ModL < DIA- + Gr *kinēsis*, motion < *kinein*, to move: see CITE⟧ in the first meiotic division of germ cells, a late prophase stage in which the maternal and paternal chromosomes have paired within the nucleus —**di′a·ki·net′ic** (-net′ik) *adj.*

di·al[1] (dī′əl) *n.* ⟦ME < ML *dialis*, daily < L *dies*, day: see DEITY⟧ **1** a sundial **2** the face of a watch or clock **3** *a)* the face of a meter, gauge, compass, etc. on which a pointer or the like indicates an amount, degree, direction, etc. *b)* an illuminated strip on a radio, marked with frequency numbers and equipped with a pointer, for indicating the station selected **4** a usually graduated disk or knob for controlling some function, as the selection of a TV channel or the temperature of an oven **5** *a)* a rotating disk on a telephone, used in making connections automatically *b)* loosely, an arrangement of numbered push buttons on a telephone, used for this purpose —*vt., vi.* **-aled** or **-alled**, **-al·ing** or **-al·ling** **1** to measure (something) with or as with a dial **2** to tune in (a radio station, television channel, program, etc.) ☆**3** to call (a person, telephone number, etc.) on a telephone by using a dial, keypad, etc. —**di′al·er** *n.*, **di′al·ler**

dial[2] *abbrev.* **1** dialect(al) **2** dialectic(al)

di·al-a- (dī′əl ə) ⟦prob. < *Dial-a-Prayer*, an early telephone service of this kind⟧ *combining form forming nouns* naming a service or product that can be accessed or ordered by telephone

di·a·lect (dī′ə lekt′) *n.* ⟦L *dialectus* < Gr *dialektos*, discourse, discussion, dialect < *dialegesthai*, to discourse, talk < *dia*, between (see DIA-) + *legein*, to choose, talk (see LOGIC)⟧ **1** the sum total of local characteristics of speech **2** [Rare] the sum total of an individual's characteristics of speech; idiolect **3** popularly, any form of speech considered as deviating from a real or imaginary standard speech **4** *Linguis.* *a)* a form or variety of a spoken language, including the standard form, peculiar to a region, community, social group, occupational group, etc.: in this sense, *dialects* are regarded as being, to some degree, mutually intelligible while *languages* are not mutually intelligible *b)* any language as a member of a group or family of languages [English is a West Germanic *dialect*] —*adj.* of or in a dialect [*dialect* ballads] —**di′a·lec′tal** *adj.* —**di′a·lec′tal·ly** *adv.*

SYN.—**dialect**, in this comparison, refers to a form of a language peculiar to a locality or group and differing from the standard language in matters of pronunciation, syntax, etc.; **vernacular** today commonly refers to the informal or colloquial variety of a language as distinguished from the formal or literary variety; **cant**, in this connection, refers to the distinctive stock words and phrases used by a particular sect, class, etc. [clergymen's *cant*]; **jargon** is used of the special vocabulary and idioms of a particular class, occupational group, etc., esp. by one who is unfamiliar with these; **argot** refers esp. to the secret jargon of thieves and tramps; **lingo** is a humorous or mildly contemptuous term applied to any language, dialect, or jargon by one to whom it is unintelligible

☆**dialect atlas** LINGUISTIC ATLAS

dialect geography LINGUISTIC GEOGRAPHY

di·a·lec·tic (dī′ə lek′tik) *n.* ⟦ME *dialetik* < OFr *dialetique* < L *dialectica* (*ars*) < Gr *dialektikē* (*technē*), the dialectic (art) < *dialektikos*: see DIALECT⟧ **1** [*often pl.*] the art or practice of examining opinions or ideas logically, often by the method of question and answer, so as to determine their validity **2** logical argumentation **3** [*often pl.*] *a)* the method of logic used by Hegel and adapted by Marx to observable social and economic processes: it is based on the principle that an idea or event (*thesis*) generates its opposite (*antithesis*), leading to a reconciliation of opposites (*synthesis*) *b)* the general application of this principle in analysis, criticism, exposition, etc. —*adj.* DIALECTICAL

di·a·lec·ti·cal (-ti kəl) *adj.* **1** of or using dialectic **2** of or characteristic of a dialect; dialectal —**di′a·lec′ti·cal·ly** *adv.*

dialectical materialism the philosophy stemming from the writings of Marx and Engels which applies Hegel's dialectical method to observable social processes and to nature

di·a·lec·ti·cian (dī′ə lek tish′ən) *n.* ⟦Fr *dialecticien*⟧ [Now Rare] an expert in dialectic; logician

di·a·lec·tol·o·gy (-täl′ə jē) *n.* the scientific study of dialects —**di′a·lec·tol′o·gist** *n.* —**di′a·lec′to·log′i·cal** (-tə läj′i kəl) *adj.* —**di′a·lec′to·log′i·cal·ly** *adv.*

di·al·lage (dī′ə lij′) *n.* ⟦Fr < Gr *diallagē*, change, interchange < *diallassein*, to interchange < *dia*, through (see DIA-) + *allassein*, to alter < *allos*, other (see ELSE): so named from having unlike fracture planes⟧ a greenish mineral that is a laminated variety of monoclinic pyroxene

di·a·log (dī′ə lôg′, -läg′) *n., vi., vt. alt. sp. of* DIALOGUE

di·a·log·i·cal (dī′ə läj′i kəl) *adj.* of or marked by dialogue: also **di′a·log′ic** —**di′a·log′i·cal·ly** *adv.*

di·al·o·gist (dī al′ə jist, dī′ə lôg′ist) *n.* **1** a writer of dialogues **2** a person who takes part in a dialogue —**di·a·lo·gis·tic** (dī′ə lə jis′tik, dī al′ə-; dī′ə lôg′is′-) *adj.*

di·a·logue (dī′ə lôg′, -läg′) *n.* ⟦ME *dialog* < OFr *dialogue* < L *dialogus* < Gr *dialogos* < *dialegesthai*: see DIALECT⟧ **1** a talking together; conversation **2** interchange and discussion of ideas, esp. when open and frank, as in seeking mutual understanding or harmony **3** a literary work in the form of a conversation on a single topic **4** the passages of talk in a play, story, etc. —*vi.* **-logued′**, **-logu′ing** to hold a conversation —*vt.* to express in dialogue

☆**dial tone** a buzzing or humming sound indicating to the user of a telephone that the line is open and a number may be dialed

di·al-up (dī′əl up′) *adj. Comput.* of or having to do with the use of standard telephone lines [*dial-up* access to the internet]: often written **dialup**

di·al·y·sis (dī al′ə sis) *n., pl.* **-ses′** (-sēz′) ⟦L < Gr, separation, dissolution < *dialyein*, to separate, dissolve < *dia-*, apart + *lyein*, to loose: see LOSE⟧ **1** *Chem.* any process in which the smaller dissolved molecules in a solution separate from the larger molecules by diffusing through a semipermeable membrane **2** *Med.* any of various procedures, usually performed on a regular basis on patients who have impaired kidney function, in which chemical dialysis is used to remove toxic waste, chemicals, etc. from the blood —**di·a·lyt·ic** (dī′ə lit′ik) *adj.* —**di′a·lyt′i·cal·ly** *adv.*

di·a·lyze (dī′ə līz′) *vt.* **-lyzed′**, **-lyz′ing** to apply dialysis to or separate by dialysis —*vi.* to undergo dialysis

di·a·lyz·er (-lī′zər) *n.* an apparatus for dialyzing, esp. one used as an artificial kidney

diam *abbrev.* diameter

di·a·mag·net·ic (dī′ə mag net′ik) ***adj.*** having or relating to diamagnetism —***n.*** a diamagnetic substance, as bismuth or zinc: also **di′a·mag′net** (-nət)

di·a·mag·net·ism (-mag′nə tiz′əm) ***n.*** **1** the property that certain substances have of being weakly repelled by both poles of a magnet **2** diamagnetic force **3** diamagnetic phenomena **4** the science that deals with such phenomena and substances

di·a·man·té (dē′ə män′tā, -män tā′) ***adj.*** ⟦Fr < pp. of *diamanter*, to tinsel, lit., set with diamonds < *diamant*, DIAMOND⟧ decorated with rhinestones or with other brightly glittering bits of material *[diamanté* sandals*]* —***n.*** glittering ornamentation

di·am·e·ter (dī am′ət ər) ***n.*** ⟦ME & OFr *diametre* < ML *diametra* < L *diametrus* < Gr *diametros* < *dia-*, through + *metron*, a measure: see METER[1]⟧ **1** a line segment passing through the center of a circle, sphere, etc. from one side to the other **2** the length of such a segment; width or thickness of a circular or spherical figure or object **3** *Optics* the unit of measure of the magnifying power of a lens

di·a·met·ri·cal (dī′ə me′tri kəl) ***adj.*** **1** of or along a diameter: also **di·am·e·tral** (dī am′ə trəl) **2** designating an opposite, a contrary, a difference, etc. that is wholly so; complete *[diametrical* opposites*]*: also **di′a·met′ric** —**di′a·met′ri·cal·ly** ***adv.***

di·a·mine (dī′ə mēn′, dī′ə mēn′; dī am′ēn′, -in) ***n.*** any of a group of chemical compounds containing two NH_2 radicals; double amine

di·a·mond (dī′mənd, dī′ə mənd) ***n.*** ⟦ME *diamaunt* < OFr *diamant* < ML *diamas* (gen. *diamantis*), for L *adamas* < Gr, ADAMANT, diamond⟧ **1** a usually colorless, crystalline mineral consisting of pure carbon, with nearly perfect cleavage and the greatest hardness of any substance: unflawed, transparent stones are cut into gems of great brilliance, and less perfect forms are used for cutting tools, abrasives, etc. **2** a gem or other piece cut from this mineral **3** *a)* a lozenge-shaped plane figure (◇) *b)* any of a suit of playing cards marked with such figures in red *c)* [*pl., with sing. or pl. v.*] this suit of cards *d)* any rhombus, including a square, oriented with one point at the top and one at the bottom *[*a baseball *diamond]* ☆**4** *Baseball a)* the infield *b)* the whole playing field —***adj.*** **1** of, like, or set with a diamond or diamonds **2** marking or celebrating the 60th, or sometimes 75th, year *[*a *diamond* jubilee*]* —***vt.*** to adorn with or as with diamonds —**diamond in the rough** **1** a diamond in its natural state **2** a person or thing of fine quality but lacking polish

di·a·mond·back (-bak′) ***adj.*** having diamond-shaped markings on the back —***n.*** ☆**1** a large, poisonous rattlesnake (*Crotalus adamanteus*) with diamond-shaped markings on its back, native to the S U.S. ☆**2** an edible turtle (*Malaclemys terrapin*) with diamond-shaped markings on its shell, found in coastal salt marshes from Cape Cod to Mexico: in full **diamondback terrapin** **3** a small, brown-and-white cosmopolitan moth (*Plutella xylostella*) whose wings, when folded, form a diamond

Diamond Head promontory in SE Oahu, Hawaii, near Honolulu, consisting of the rim of an extinct volcanic crater

diamond wedding a 60th, or sometimes 75th, wedding anniversary

Di·an·a (dī an′ə) ***n.*** ⟦ML < L < **Diviana* < *divus, dius*, divine: see DEITY⟧ **1** a feminine name: dim. *Di*; Fr. *Diane* **2** *Rom. Myth.* the virgin goddess of the moon and of hunting: identified with the Greek Artemis

di·an·drous (dī an′drəs) ***adj.*** ⟦DI-[1] + -ANDROUS⟧ having two stamens

Di·ane (dī an′) ***n.*** a feminine name: dim. *Di*; var. *Dianne*: see DIANA

di·an·thus (dī an′thəs) ***n.*** ⟦ModL < Gr *dios*, divine (see DEITY) + *anthos*, a flower⟧ any of a genus (*Dianthus*) of plants of the pink family, including the carnation and sweet william

di·a·pa·son (dī′ə pā′zən, -sən) ***n.*** ⟦ME *diapasoun* < L *diapason* < Gr *diapasōn*, contr. < *hē dia pasōn chordōn symphōnia*, concord through all of the notes < *dia*, through + *pasōn*, gen. pl. of *pas*, all⟧ **1** *a)* the entire range of a musical instrument or voice *b)* the entire range of some activity, emotion, etc. **2** one of the principal stops of an organ, covering the instrument's complete range and producing its characteristic tone quality **3** a swelling burst of harmony **4** a standard of musical pitch **5** a tuning fork **6** [Obs.] the interval of an octave **7** [Obs.] complete harmony

☆**di·a·pause** (dī′ə pôz′) ***n.*** ⟦Gr *diapausis*, a pause < *diapauein*, to bring to an end, pause: see DIA- & PAUSE⟧ a period of delayed development or growth accompanied by reduced metabolism and inactivity, esp. in certain insects, snails, etc.

di·a·pe·de·sis (dī′ə pə dē′sis) ***n.***, *pl.* **-ses′** (-sēz′) ⟦ModL < Gr *diapēdēsis*, lit., a leaping through < *dia-*, through + *pēdan*, to leap < IE base **pēd-*, FOOT⟧ the migration of blood cells, esp. erythrocytes, through intact capillary walls into the tissues —**di′a·pe·det′ic** (-det′ik) ***adj.***

di·a·per (dī′pər, dī′ə pər) ***n.*** ⟦ME < OFr *diapre, diaspre*, kind of ornamented cloth < ML *diasprum*, flowered cloth, altered (after *dia-*, DIA-, because of ML pronun. of initial *j-*) < *jaspis* < L *iaspis*, JASPER⟧ **1** *a)* [Archaic] cloth or fabric with a woven pattern of repeated small figures, such as diamonds *b)* a napkin, towel, etc. of such cloth *c)* such a pattern, as in art **2** *a)* a soft, absorbent cloth folded and arranged between the legs and around the waist of a baby to absorb and contain excretions *b)* a piece of absorbent material with a waterproof outer layer, having the same function but intended to be discarded after a single use (in full **disposable diaper**) —***vt.*** **1** to give a diaper design to **2** to put a fresh diaper on (a baby)

diaper rash an irritation of the skin of infants in the area covered by a diaper, usually caused by prolonged contact with urine

di·aph·a·nous (dī af′ə nəs) ***adj.*** ⟦ML *diaphanus* < Gr *diaphanēs*, transparent < *diaphainein*, to shine through < *dia-*, through + *phainein*, to show: see FANTASY⟧ **1** so fine or gauzy in texture as to be transparent or translucent *[diaphanous* cloth*]* **2** vague or indistinct; airy —**di·aph′a·nous·ly** ***adv.*** —**di·aph′a·nous·ness** ***n.***

di·a·phone (dī′ə fōn′) ***n.*** ⟦DIA- + -PHONE⟧ a group of speech sounds consisting of all the variants of a given phoneme in all the utterances of all the speakers of a given language

di·a·pho·re·sis (dī′ə fə rē′sis) ***n.*** ⟦LL < Gr *diaphorēsis*, a carrying away, perspiration < *diaphorein* < *dia-*, through + *pherein*, BEAR[1]⟧ perspiration, esp. when profuse

di·a·pho·ret·ic (-ret′ik) ***adj.*** ⟦ME *diaforetic* < LL *diaphoreticus*: see prec.⟧ producing or increasing perspiration —***n.*** a diaphoretic medicine, treatment, etc.

di·a·phragm (dī′ə fram′) ***n.*** ⟦ME *diafragma* < LL *diaphragma* < Gr < *dia-*, through + *phragma*, a fence < *phrassein*, to enclose⟧ **1** the partition of muscles and tendons that separates the chest cavity from the abdominal cavity; midriff **2** *a)* any membrane or partition that separates one thing from another *b)* a dividing wall at the node of a plant stem **3** a device to regulate the amount of light entering the lens of a camera, microscope, etc. ☆**4** a small, flexible contraceptive device of rubber or plastic that fits over the cervix of the uterus **5** a thin, flexible disk or cone that vibrates in response to sound waves to produce electrical signals, as in a microphone, or that vibrates in response to electrical signals to produce sound waves, as in a speaker —**di′a·phrag·mat′ic** (-frag mat′ik) ***adj.*** —**di′a·phrag·mat′i·cal·ly** ***adv.***

di·aph·y·sis (dī af′ə sis) ***n.***, *pl.* **-ses′** (-sēz′) ⟦ModL < Gr, line of separation, spinous process of the tibia < *diaphyein*, to grow through < *dia-*, through + *phyein*, to bring forth: see PHYSIC⟧ the shaft of a long bone, as distinguished from the growing ends —**di·a·phys·e·al** ***adj.***, **di·a·phys·i·al** (dī′ə fiz′ē əl)

di·a·pir (dī′ə pir′) ***n.*** ⟦< Gr *diapeirainein*, to pierce through⟧ *Geol.* a dome formation in which the rigid top layers have been split open by pressure from an underlying plastic core —**di·a·pir·ic** (dī′ə pir′ik) ***adj.***

di·a·poph·y·sis (dī′ə päf′ə sis) ***n.***, *pl.* **-ses′** (-sēz′) ⟦ModL: see DIA- & APOPHYSIS⟧ the transverse process of a vertebra —**di·ap·o·phys·i·al** (dī′ap′ e fiz′ē əl) ***adj.***

di·a·pos·i·tive (dī′ə päz′ə tiv) ***n.*** ⟦DIA- (sense 1) + POSITIVE (***n.***, sense *d*)⟧ a positive photographic image on a transparent material, as a photographic slide or lantern slide

di·ar·chy (dī′är′kē) ***n.***, *pl.* **-chies** ⟦DI-[1] + -ARCHY⟧ government shared by two rulers, powers, etc.

di·a·rist (dī′ə rist) ***n.*** a person who keeps a diary

di·a·ris·tic (dī′ə ris′tik) ***adj.*** having the nature of, or in the style of, a diary

di·ar·rhe·a (dī′ə rē′ə) ***n.*** ⟦ME *diarea* < OFr *diarrie* & LL *diarrhoea* < Gr *diarrhoia* < *dia-*, through + *rhein*, to flow: see STREAM⟧ excessive frequency and looseness of bowel movements: chiefly Brit. sp. **di·ar·rhoe′a** —**di′ar·rhe′al** ***adj.***, **di′ar·rhe′ic**, or **di′ar·rhet′ic** (-ret′ik)

di·ar·thro·sis (dī′är thrō′sis) ***n.***, *pl.* **-ses′** (-sēz′) ⟦ModL < Gr *diarthrōsis* < *diarthroun*, to divide by joints, articulate < *dia-*, through + *arthroun*, to connect by a joint < *arthron*, a joint: see ARTHRO-⟧ *Anat.* any articulation, as of the hip, permitting free movement in any direction

di·a·ry (dī′ə rē) ***n.***, *pl.* **-ries** ⟦L *diarium*, daily allowance (of food or pay); hence, record of this < *dies*, day: see DEITY⟧ **1** a daily written record, esp. of the writer's own experiences, thoughts, etc. **2** a book for keeping such a record

Di·as (dē′əsh; *E* dē′əs), **Bar·tho·lo·me·u** (bär′too loo me′oo) 1450?-1500; Port. navigator & explorer: 1st European to round Cape of Good Hope (1486)

Di·as·po·ra (dī as′pə rə) ***n.*** ⟦Gr *diaspora*, a scattering < *diasperein*, to scatter < *dia-*, across + *speirein*, to sow: see SPORE⟧ **1** *a)* the dispersion of the Jews after the Babylonian Exile *b)* the Jews thus dispersed *c)* the places where they settled **2** [**d-**] any scattering of people with a common origin, background, beliefs, etc.

di·a·spore (dī′ə spôr′) ***n.*** ⟦< Gr *diaspora*: see prec.⟧ a native hydrate of aluminum, $Al_2O_3{\cdot}H_2O$, which crackles and disperses when heated

di·a·stase (dī′ə stās′) ***n.*** ⟦Fr < Gr *diastasis*, a separation < *dia*, apart + *histanai*, STAND⟧ a vegetable amylase enzyme, occurring in the seed of grains and malt, that is capable of changing starches into maltose and later into dextrose —**di·a·stat·ic** (dī′ə stat′ik) ***adj.***

di·a·stem (dī′ə stem′) ***n.*** ⟦LL *diastema* < Gr *diastēma*, an interval < *diistanai*, to set apart < *dia-*, apart + *histanai*, STAND⟧ a minor interruption in the deposition of sedimentary material

di·a·ste·ma (dī′ə stē′mə) ***n.***, *pl.* **-ste′ma·ta** (-tə) ⟦Gr *diastēma*: see prec.⟧ a natural space in the body; specif., the gap between two teeth, esp. of the upper jaw —**di′a·ste·mat′ic** (-sti mat′ik) ***adj.***

di·as·ter (dī as′tər) ***n.*** ⟦DI-[1] + -ASTER[1]⟧ AMPHIASTER —**di·as′tral** ***adj.***

di·as·to·le (dī as′tə lē′) ***n.*** ⟦LL < Gr *diastolē*, expansion, dilatation < *diastellein*, to separate, dilate < *dia-*, apart + *stellein*, to put: see LOCAL⟧ the usual rhythmic dilatation of the heart, esp. of the ventricles, following each contraction (*systole*), during which the heart muscle relaxes and the chambers fill with blood —**di·a·stol·ic** (dī′ə stäl′ik) ***adj.***

di·as·tro·phism (dī as′trə fiz′əm) ***n.*** ⟦< Gr *diastrophē*, distortion < *diastrephein*, to turn aside, distort < *dia-*, aside + *strephein*, to turn (see STROPHE) + -ISM⟧ **1** the process by which the earth's surface is reshaped through rock movements and displacements **2** formations so made —**di·a·stroph·ic** (dī′ə sträf′ik) ***adj.***

di·a·tes·sa·ron (dī′ə tes′ə rän′) ***n.*** ⟦L(Ec) < Gr(Ec) (*Evangelion*) *dia tessarōn*, lit., (Gospel) through four, title of Tatian's harmony of four Gospels (2d c.) < Gr *dia*, through + *tessarōn*, gen. of *tessares*, four < IE base **kwetwer-*, FOUR⟧ the four Gospels combined into a single account

di·a·ther·man·cy (dī′ə thur′mən sē) *n.* ⟦Fr *diathermansie* < Gr *dia-*, through + *thermansis*, a heating⟧ the property of transmitting infrared or heat rays —**di′a·ther′ma·nous** *adj.*

di·a·ther·mic (-mik) *adj.* ⟦Fr *diathermique*⟧ **1** relating to diathermy **2** letting heat rays pass through freely

di·a·ther·my (dī′ə thur′mē) *n.* ⟦ModL *diathermia* < Gr *dia-*, through + *thermē*, heat: see WARM⟧ medical treatment in which heat is produced beneath the skin by a high-frequency electric current, radiation, etc., to warm or destroy tissue

di·ath·e·sis (dī ath′ə sis) *n., pl.* **-ses′** (-sēz′) ⟦ModL < Gr *diathesis*, arrangement < *diatithenai*, to arrange < *dia-*, apart + *tithenai*, to put⟧ a predisposition to certain diseases —**di·a·thet·ic** (dī′ə thet′ik) *adj.*

di·a·tom (dī′e täm′, -təm) *n.* ⟦ModL *diatoma* < Gr *diatomos*, cut in two < *diatemnein*, to cut through < *dia-*, through + *temnein*, to cut: see -TOMY⟧ any of a class (Bacillariophyceae) of microscopic algae (division Chromophycota), one-celled or in colonies, whose cell walls consist of interlocking parts and valves and contain silica: diatoms are a source of food for all kinds of marine life —**di·a·to·ma·ceous** (dī′ə tə mā′shəs, dī at′ə-) *adj.*

di·a·tom·ic (dī′ə täm′ik) *adj.* ⟦DI-[1] + ATOMIC⟧ **1** having two atoms in the molecule **2** having two replaceable atoms or radicals in the molecule

di·at·o·mite (dī at′ə mīt′) *n.* a light-colored, soft sedimentary rock formed mainly of the siliceous shells of diatoms and used in a finely pulverized state as an abrasive, absorbent, filter, etc.: also called **diatomaceous earth**

di·a·ton·ic (dī′ə tän′ik) *adj.* ⟦Fr *diatonique* < LL *diatonicus* < Gr *diatonikos*, stretched through (the notes) < *dia-*, through + *teinein*, to stretch: see TEND[2]⟧ *Music* designating, of, or using a scale of eight tones that is either a MAJOR SCALE or a MINOR SCALE: cf. CHROMATIC SCALE —**di′a·ton′i·cal·ly** *adv.* —**di′a·ton′i·cism′** (-ə siz′əm) *n.*

di·a·tribe (dī′ə trīb′) *n.* ⟦Fr < L *diatriba*, learned discussion < Gr *diatribē*, a wearing away < *diatribein* < *dia-*, through + *tribein*, to rub, akin to L *terere*, to rub: see THROW⟧ a bitter, abusive criticism or denunciation

di·at·ro·pism (dī a′trə piz′əm) *n.* ⟦DIA- + TROPISM⟧ *Bot.* the tendency of some plant parts to place themselves crosswise to the line of force of a stimulus —**di·a·trop·ic** (dī ə träp′ik) *adj.*

Dí·az (dē′äs), **(José de la Cruz) Por·fi·ri·o** (pôr fē′rē ô) 1830-1915; Mex. general & statesman: president of Mexico (1877-80; 1884-1911)

Dí·az del Cas·ti·llo (dē′äth del kä stē′lyô), **Ber·nal** (ber näl′) 1492?-1581?; Sp. historian & soldier with Cortés

di·az·e·pam (dī az′ə pam′) *n.* ⟦(BENZO)DIAZEP(INE) + *-am* (< ?)⟧ a tranquilizer, $C_{16}H_{13}ClN_2O$, that relaxes muscles and prevents or inhibits convulsions

di·a·zine (dī′ə zēn′; dī az′ēn′, dī az′in) *n.* ⟦DI-[1] + AZINE⟧ any chemical compound with a molecular structure consisting of four atoms of carbon and two of nitrogen, arranged in a ring; esp., any of the three isomeric compounds having the formula $C_4H_4N_2$

di·az·i·non (dī az′ə nän′) *n.* ⟦prec. + -ON(E)⟧ a colorless liquid, $C_{12}H_{21}N_2O_3PS$, used as an insecticide, especially against flies

di·az·o (dī az′ō, -ā′zō) *adj.* ⟦DI-[1] + AZO⟧ having a group of two nitrogen atoms combined directly with one organic radical

di·az·o- (dī az′ō, -ā′zō) *combining form* diazo: also, before a vowel, **di·az-** (dī az′, -āz′)

di·az·o·a·mi·no (dī az′ō ə mē′nō, dī ā′zō-; -am′ə nō′) *adj.* denoting or of a diazo compound containing the group N:N·NH

di·a·zole (dī′ə zōl′, dī az′ōl′) *n.* ⟦DIAZ(O)- + -OLE⟧ **1** any of a group of chemical compounds with a 5-membered ring containing three atoms of carbon and two of nitrogen **2** a derivative of such a compound

di·a·zo·ni·um (dī′ə zō′nē əm) *adj.* ⟦DIAZ(O)- + (AMM)ONIUM⟧ designating or containing the organic radical N⋮N, which occurs in a series of aromatic compounds

di·az·o·tize (dī az′ə tīz′) *vt.* **-tized′**, **-tiz′ing** ⟦< Fr *diazoter* (see DI-[1] & AZOTE) + -IZE⟧ to convert chemically into a diazo compound

dib (dib) *vi.* **dibbed**, **dib′bing** ⟦ME *dibben*, to dip; prob. akin to DIP⟧ DIBBLE (*vi.* 2)

di·ba·sic (dī bā′sik) *adj.* **1** denoting or of an acid with two hydrogen atoms either or both of which may be replaced by basic radicals or atoms to form a salt **2** having two atoms of a monovalent metal —**di·ba·sic·i·ty** (dī′bā sis′ə tē) *n.*

dib·ble (dib′əl) *n.* ⟦ME *dibbel*, prob. < *dibben*: see DIB⟧ a pointed tool used to make holes in the soil for seeds, bulbs, or young plants: also called **dib′ber** (-ər) —*vt.* **-bled**, **-bling** **1** to make a hole in (the soil) with a dibble **2** to plant with a dibble —*vi.* **1** to use a dibble **2** to dip bait gently into the water

dibble

dib·buk (dib′ək) *n. alt. sp. of* DYBBUK

d'I·ber·ville (dē ber vēl′), Sieur (born *Pierre Le Moyne*) 1661-1706; Fr. explorer in North America

di·bran·chi·ate (dī braŋ′kē it, -āt′) *adj.* ⟦< ModL *Dibranchia* < Gr *di-*, two + *branchia*, gills of fish⟧ having one pair of gills: said of most cephalopods, including the squids and octopuses: opposed to TETRABRANCHIATE

dibs (dibz) *n.* ⟦contr. < *dibstone*, a jack or a sheep knucklebone in a children's game < *dib* (< ?) + STONE⟧ ☆[Slang] a claim to a share of, or rights in, something wanted [I've got first *dibs* on that candy bar] —☆*interj.* used to announce such a claim

di·cast (dī′kast′, dik′ast′) *n.* ⟦Gr *dikastēs* < *dikazein*, to pass judgment < *dikē*, right, law, justice, akin to L *dicere*: see DICTION⟧ in ancient Athens, any of a large group of citizens chosen annually to serve as a court hearing cases

dice (dīs) *pl.n., sing.* **die** or **dice** ⟦ME *dis*, pl.: see DIE[2]⟧ **1** small cubes of bone, plastic, etc. marked on each side with a different number of spots (from one to six) and used, usually in pairs, in games of chance **2** [*with sing. v.*] a gambling game played with dice **3** any small cubes, as of food —*vi.* **diced**, **dic′ing** to play or gamble with dice —*vt.* **1** [Archaic] to lose by gambling with dice: often with *away* **2** to cut (vegetables, etc.) into small cubes **3** to mark with a pattern of cubes or squares; checker —**no dice** ⟦from a call in craps disallowing a throw⟧ [Informal] **1** no: used in refusing a request **2** no success, luck, etc. —**dic′er** *n.*

di·cen·tra (dī sen′trə) *n.* ⟦ModL < DI-[1] + Gr *kentron*, a spur: see CENTER⟧ any of a genus (*Dicentra*) of plants of the fumitory family with deeply cut leaflets and heart-shaped flowers of white, rose, etc., as Dutchman's-breeches; bleeding heart

di·ceph·a·lous (dī sef′ə ləs) *adj.* ⟦Gr *dikephalos* < *di-* (see DI-[1])⟧ having two heads, as certain fetal monsters

dic·ey (dī′sē) *adj.* **dic′i·er**, **dic′i·est** ⟦DICE + -Y[3]⟧ [Informal] hazardous; risky; chancy

di·cha·si·um (dī kā′zē əm, -zhē-) *n., pl.* **-si·a** (-ə) ⟦ModL < Gr *dichasis*, a division < *dichazein*, to divide into two < *dicha*: see DICHO-⟧ *Bot.* a cyme in which two opposite branches arise below each terminal flower: also **di·cha′sial cyme**

di·chlo·ride (dī klôr′īd) *n.* BICHLORIDE

di·chlo·ro·phe·nox·y·a·ce·tic acid (dī klôr′ō fi näk′sē ə sēt′ik) a chloride derivative of phenol and acetic acid, $C_6H_3Cl_2OCH_2COOH$, used to destroy broad-leaved weeds without injuring grass; 2,4-D

di·cho- (dī′kō, -kə) ⟦Gr *dicho-* < *dicha*, in two, asunder, akin to *dis*: see DI-[1]⟧ *combining form* in two, asunder [*dichotomy*]: also, before a vowel, **dich-**

di·chog·a·my (dī käg′ə mē) *n.* ⟦prec. + -GAMY⟧ the maturing of pistils and stamens at different times, preventing self-pollination —**di·chog′a·mous** *adj.*, **di·cho·gam·ic** (dī′kō gam′ik)

di·chon·dra (dī kän′drə) *n.* ⟦ModL < *di-* (see DI-[1]) + Gr *chondros*, grain (see CHONDRO-)⟧ any of a genus (*Dichondra*) of creeping vines of the morning-glory family, sometimes cultivated in warm climates as ground cover

di·chot·o·mize (dī kät′ə mīz′) *vt.* **-mized′**, **-miz′ing** ⟦see fol. & -IZE⟧ to divide or separate into two parts —*vi.* to undergo or exhibit dichotomy —**di·chot′o·mist** (-mist) *n.* —**di·chot′o·mi·za′tion** (-mə zā′shən, -mī′-) *n.*

di·chot·o·my (-mē) *n., pl.* **-mies** ⟦Gr *dichotomia*: see DICHO- & -TOMY⟧ **1** division into two parts, groups, or classes, esp. when these are sharply distinguished or opposed **2** *Astron.* the appearance of the moon or of a planet when half of the surface facing the earth is illuminated **3** *Biol.* a dividing or branching into two equal parts, esp. when repeated —**di·chot′o·mous** (-məs) *adj.* —**di·chot′o·mous·ly** *adv.*

di·chro·ic (dī krō′ik) *adj.* having or showing dichroism or dichromatism: also **di′chro·it′ic** (-it′ik)

di·chro·ism (dī′krō iz′əm) *n.* ⟦< Gr *dichroos*, of two colors < *di-*, two + *chrōs*, skin, complexion, color (for IE base see CHROMA) + -ISM⟧ **1** the property that doubly refracting crystals have of transmitting light of different colors when looked at from different angles **2** the property of a substance of transmitting light of different colors depending on its thickness or on its concentration in solution **3** the property of a substance of having one color when it reflects light and another when it transmits light

di·chro·mate (dī krō′māt′, dī′krō-) *adj.* ⟦< DI-[1] + CHROMATE⟧ a salt of dichromic acid containing the divalent, negative radical Cr_2O_7

di·chro·mat·ic (dī′krō mat′ik) *adj.* ⟦DI-[1] + CHROMATIC⟧ **1** having two colors **2** of or characterized by dichromatism **3** *Biol.* having two seasonal varieties of coloration that are independent of sex or age, as certain species of insects, owls, or parrots

di·chro·ma·tism (dī krō′mə tiz′əm) *n.* **1** the quality or condition of being dichromatic **2** color blindness in which a person can see only two of the three primary colors (red, green, and blue) **3** DICHROISM

di·chro·mic (dī krō′mik) *adj.* **1** DICHROMATIC **2** *Chem. a)* having two atoms of chromium per molecule *b)* designating an acid, $H_2Cr_2O_7$, that exists only in solution, which forms dichromates

di·chro·scope (dī′krə skōp′) *n.* ⟦< Gr *dichroos* (see DICHROISM)⟧ an optical instrument used to study dichroic crystals, solutions, etc.

dick[1] (dik) [Slang] *n.* ⟦< DICK, the nickname⟧ **1** the penis: considered vulgar by some **2** a man who is regarded as obnoxious, stupid, etc.: mildly vulgar —*vt.* **1** to have sexual intercourse with: considered vulgar by some **2** *a)* to cheat, deceive, trick, etc. *b)* to vacillate or equivocate thereby causing distress or trouble to: often with *around:* mildly vulgar —**dick around** **1** to spend time wastefully or unprofitably **2** to be busy in a desultory way Mildly vulgar

dick[2] (dik) *n.* ⟦shortened & altered < DETECTIVE⟧ [Slang] a detective

Dick (dik) *n. nickname for* RICHARD[1]

☆**dick·cis·sel** (dik sis′əl) *n.* ⟦echoic of its cry⟧ a bunting (*Spiza americana*) with a black throat and yellow breast, living in prairie regions of Canada and the U.S. and migrating to N South America

dick·ens (dik′ənz) *n.* ⟦prob. < *Dickon*, nickname for RICHARD[1]⟧ [Old Brit. Slang] devil; deuce: used, with *the*, only in interjectional phrases, as a mild oath or exclamation of annoyance, surprise, or frustration [*what the dickens* is that about?]

Dick·ens (dik′ənz), **Charles (John Huffam)** (pseud. *Boz*) 1812-70; Eng. novelist

Dick·en·si·an (di ken′zē ən) *adj.* of, characteristic of, or like the writings of Dickens, specif. in their emphasis on eccentric or broadly comic characters, a teeming, often squalid, metropolis, etc.

☆**dick·er** (dik′ər) *vi.* ⟦< *dicker*, ten, ten hides (as a unit of barter) < ME *dycer*, akin to Du *daker*, Ger *decher*, Dan *deger*, ult. < L *decuria*, a division of ten < *decem*, TEN⟧ to trade by bargaining, esp. on a small or petty scale; barter or haggle —*n.* ⟦< the *vi.*⟧ the act of bargaining or haggling

dick·ey[1] (dik′ē) *n., pl.* **-eys** ⟦< the nickname DICK⟧ **1** a brief garment worn beneath a jacket, dress, etc. and designed to resemble the collar and front of a shirt, blouse, or sweater **2** a child's bib or pinafore **3** a small bird: also **dickey bird** **4** *a)* the driver's seat in a carriage (also **dickey box**) *b)* a seat at the back of a carriage, as for servants

dick·ey[2] (dik′ē) *adj.* [Brit.] *alt. sp. of* DICKY[2]

dick·head (dik′hed′) *n.* ⟦see DICK[1], *n.* 1-2⟧ [Slang] a man who is regarded as obnoxious, stupid, etc.: mildly vulgar

dick·ie (dik′ē) *n. alt. sp. of* DICKEY[1] (senses 1, 2, & 4)

Dick·in·son (dik′in sən) **1 Emily (Elizabeth)** 1830-86; U.S. poet **2 John** 1732-1808; Am. statesman

☆**Dick test** ⟦after George F. *Dick* (1881-1967) & his wife, Gladys *Dick* (1881-1963), U.S. physicians⟧ a skin test formerly used for determining susceptibility or immunity to scarlet fever

dick·y[1] (dik′ē) *n., pl.* **dick′ies** *alt. sp. of* DICKEY[1]

dick·y[2] (dik′ē) *adj.* **dick′i·er, dick′i·est** ⟦late 18th-c. Brit slang < ?⟧ [Brit. Informal] diseased; unsound [*a dicky* heart]

di·cli·nous (dī′kli nəs, dī klī′nəs) *adj.* ⟦< DI-[1] + Gr *klinē*, bed + -OUS⟧ *Bot.* having the stamens and pistils in separate flowers —**di·cli·nism** (dī′kli niz′ əm) *n.*, **di′cli·ny** (-nē)

di·cot·y·le·don (dī′kät′ə lēd′'n) *n. Bot.* any of a class (Magnoliopsida) of angiosperms, as oak trees, legumes, and cactuses, with an embryo containing two cotyledons (seed leaves), characterized by net-veined leaves, flower parts in fours or fives, and the presence of cambium: often clipped to **di′cot′** —**di′cot′y·le′don·ous** *adj.*

di·crot·ic (dī krät′ik) *adj.* ⟦< Gr *dikrotos*, double-beating (< *di-*, DI-[1] + *krotos*, rattling noise) + -IC⟧ of or having a double pulse beat with each heart beat [*a dicrotic* artery] —**di′cro·tism′** (-krə tiz′əm) *n.*

dict *abbrev.* dictionary

dic·ta (dik′tə) *n. alt. pl. of* DICTUM

☆**Dic·ta·phone** (dik′tə fōn′) ⟦fol. + -PHONE⟧ *trademark for* a machine that records spoken words so that they can be played back later for typed transcripts, etc. —*n.* [*sometimes* **d-**] any such machine

dic·tate (dik′tāt′; *also, for v.* dik tāt′) *vt., vi.* **-tat′ed, -tat′ing** ⟦< L *dictatus*, pp. of *dictare*, freq. of *dicere*, to speak: see DICTION⟧ **1** to speak or read (something) aloud for someone else to write down **2** to prescribe or command forcefully **3** to impose or give (orders) with or as with authority **4** to give (orders or instructions) arbitrarily —*n.* **1** an authoritative command **2** a guiding principle or requirement [the *dictates* of conscience]

dictating machine a device that records spoken words, as on audiocassettes, for playing back later to prepare a transcript: also **dictating/transcribing machine**

dic·ta·tion (dik tā′shən) *n.* ⟦LL *dictatio*: see DICTATE⟧ **1** the dictating of words for another to write down **2** the words so spoken or read **3** the giving of authoritative orders or commands

dic·ta·tor (dik′tāt′ər, dik tāt′ər) *n.* ⟦ME *dictatour* < L *dictator*: see DICTATE⟧ **1** in ancient Rome, a magistrate with supreme authority, appointed in times of emergency **2** a ruler with absolute power and authority, esp. one who exercises it tyrannically **3** a person who orders others about domineeringly, or one whose pronouncements on some subject are meant to be taken as the final word **4** a person who dictates words for another to write down

dic·ta·to·ri·al (dik′tə tôr′ē əl) *adj.* of, like, or characteristic of a dictator; tyrannical; domineering —**dic′ta·to′ri·al·ly** *adv.*

SYN.—**dictatorial** implies the domineering, autocratic methods or manner of a dictator [the *dictatorial* enunciation of his opinions]; **arbitrary** suggests the unreasoned, unpredictable use of one's power or authority in accord only with one's own will or desire [an *arbitrary* decision]; **dogmatic** suggests the attitude of a religious teacher in asserting certain doctrines as absolute truths not open to dispute [the scientific method is not *dogmatic*]; **doctrinaire** implies a rigid adherence to abstract doctrines or theories, without regard to their practical application

dic·ta·tor·ship (dik′tāt′ər ship′, dik tāt′-) *n.* **1** the position or office of a dictator **2** the time during which a dictator rules **3** a state ruled by a dictator **4** absolute power or authority

dictatorship of the proletariat absolute control of economic and political power in a country by a government of the working class (proletariat): regarded in Communist theory as a means of effecting the transition from capitalism to communism

dic·tion (dik′shən) *n.* ⟦L *dictio*, a speaking (in LL, word) < pp. of *dicere*, to say, orig., point out in words < IE base **deik-*, to point out > Gr *deiknynai*, to prove, Ger *zeigen*, to show, OE *teon*, to accuse, *tæcan*, TEACH⟧ **1** manner of expression in words; choice of words; wording **2** manner of speaking or singing; enunciation

dic·tion·ar·y (dik′shə ner′ē) *n., pl.* **-ar′ies** ⟦ML *dictionarium* < LL *dictio*: see prec.⟧ **1** a book of alphabetically listed words in a language, with definitions, etymologies, pronunciations, and other information; lexicon **2** a book of alphabetically listed words in a language with their equivalents in another language [a Spanish-English *dictionary*] **3** any alphabetically arranged list of words or articles relating to a special subject [a medical *dictionary*]

☆**Dic·to·graph** (dik′tə graf′) ⟦< L *dictus*, pp. of *dicere*, to speak (see DICTION) + -GRAPH⟧ *trademark for* a telephonic instrument used for secretly listening to or recording conversations —*n.* [*sometimes* **d-**] such an instrument

dic·tum (dik′təm) *n., pl.* **-tums** or **-ta** (-tə) ⟦L, something said, word, neut. of *dictus*, pp. of *dicere*: see DICTION⟧ **1** a statement or saying, esp. a formal statement, specif. *a)* of fact, opinion, principle, etc. *b)* of one's will or judgment **2** *Law* a judge's remark or observation on some point of law which is not essential to the case in question, hence not binding as a legal precedent

☆**dic·ty** (dik′tē) *adj.* [Slang] **1** high-class **2** stylish; fashionable **3** snobbish Originally and chiefly used by African-Americans

☆**di·cu·ma·rol** (dī ko͞o′mə rôl′, -rōl′; -kyo͞o′-) *n.* ⟦< *dicoumarin*, earlier name for this substance (DI-[1] + *(bishydroxy)coumarin*) + -OL[1]⟧ a white, crystalline powder, $C_{19}H_{12}O_6$, originally extracted from spoiled sweet clover, used to retard blood clots

did (did) ⟦ME *dide* < OE *dyde*: see DO[1]⟧ *vt., vi., v.aux. pt. of* DO[1]

Did·a·che (did′ə kē′) *n.* ⟦Gr *didachē (tōn dōdeka apostolōn)*, the teaching (of the twelve apostles)⟧ an anonymous, early 2d-cent. Christian treatise on morality and church practice

☆**di·dact** (dī′dakt′) *n.* ⟦back-form. < fol.⟧ a didactic person

di·dac·tic (dī dak′tik; *also* di-) *adj.* ⟦Gr *didaktikos*, apt at teaching < *didaskein*, to teach, prob. redupl. < IE base **dens-*, wisdom, to teach, learn > Avestan *dīdainghē*, I am taught⟧ **1** used or intended for teaching or instruction **2** morally instructive, or intended to be so **3** too much inclined to teach others; boringly pedantic or moralistic —**di·dac′ti·cal·ly** *adv.* —**di·dac′ti·cism′** (-tə siz′əm) *n.*

di·dac·tics (-tiks) *pl.n.* PEDAGOGY

di·dap·per (dī′dap′ər) *n.* ⟦ME *didopper* < OE *dufedoppa* < *dufan*, to dive + *-doppa* < base of *dyppan*: see DIP⟧ DABCHICK

did·dle[1] (did′'l) *vt.* **-dled, -dling** ⟦dial. *duddle, diddle*, to totter, akin to DODDER[1]⟧ **1** [Informal] to move back and forth in a jerky or rapid manner; jiggle **2** [Slang] *a)* to have sexual intercourse with *b)* to masturbate —*vi.* to move back and forth jerkily or rapidly —**did′dler** *n.*

did·dle[2] (did′'l) [Informal] *vt.* **-dled, -dling** ⟦? after Jeremy *Diddler*, character in the play *Raising the Wind* (1803), by James Kenney: name prob. < dial. *duddle*, to trick, ult. < OE *dyderian*, to fool⟧ **1** to cheat, swindle, or victimize **2** to waste (time) in trifling: often followed by *away* —*vi.* to waste time; dawdle —**did′dler** *n.*

☆**did·dly** (did′lē) [Slang] *n.* anything at all or of any consequence [doesn't know *diddly* about computers] —*adj.* trivial, unimportant, etc. Also sp. **did′dley**

☆**diddly squat** [Slang] DIDDLY (*n.*) —**did′dly-squat′** *adj.*

Di·de·rot (dē′də rō′; *Fr* dē drō′), **Denis** 1713-84; Fr. encyclopedist & philosopher

did·ger·i·doo (dij′ə rē do͞o′, dij′ə rē do͞o′) *n., pl.* **-doos′** ⟦name in a language of N Australia⟧ a wind instrument made from a long, hollowed branch that is blown on one end to produce a drone of low-pitched, resonant tones: it originated among Aborigines of N Australia: also sp. **did′jer·i·du′** or **did′jer·i·doo′**

did·n't (did′'nt) *contraction* did not

☆**di·do** (dī′dō) [Informal] *n., pl.* **-does** or **-dos** ⟦< ? fol., from the story that Dido, on purchasing as much land as might be covered with the hide of a bull, ordered the hide cut into thin strips, with which she surrounded a large area⟧ a mischievous or foolish action —**cut (up) didoes** to behave in a mischievous or silly way

Di·do (dī′dō) *n.* ⟦L < Gr *Didō*⟧ *Rom. Myth.* founder and queen of Carthage: in the *Aeneid* she falls in love with Aeneas and kills herself when he leaves her

Did·rik·son (did′rik sen), **Mildred** (Mrs. *George Zaharias*) 1913-56; U.S. athlete in many sports: called *Babe Didrikson (Zaharias)*

didst (didst) *vt., vi., v.aux. archaic 2d pers. sing., past indic., of* DO[1]: used with *thou*

☆**di·dy** (dī′dē) *n., pl.* **-dies** ⟦baby-talk alteration of DIAPER⟧ [Informal or Dial.] DIAPER (sense 2): also sp. **di′die**

di·dym·i·um (dī dim′ē əm) *n.* ⟦ModL: so named (1841) by C. G. Mosander (see ERBIUM) < Gr *didymos*, twin (because assoc. with lanthanum) + -IUM⟧ **1** a rare metal, formerly considered an element but later found to be a mixture of rare-earth elements neodymium and praseodymium: symbol, Di: the name is still used for naming oxides and salts **2** any commercial mixture of rare-earth elements found in monazite sand

did·y·mous (did′ə məs) *adj.* ⟦< Gr *didymos*, twin, double < *dyo*, TWO⟧ *Biol.* growing in pairs; twin

Did·y·mus (did′ə məs) *n.* ⟦L < Gr *Didymos*: see prec.⟧ *see* THOMAS[1] (the Apostle)

di·dyn·a·mous (dī din′ə məs) *adj.* ⟦< ModL *didynamia*, coined (1735) by LINNAEUS < Gr *di-* (see DI-[1]) + *dynamis*, power (see DYNAMIC), for a former class of plants, in reference to the two stamens of greater length + -OUS⟧ of or having four stamens occurring in pairs of unequal length

die[1] (dī) *vi.* **died, dy′ing** ⟦ME *dien* < ON *deyja* < IE base **dheu-*, to pass away, become senseless > OS *doian*, to die, OE *dead*, OHG *tot*, dead⟧ **1** to stop living; become dead **2** to suffer the agony of death or an agony regarded as like it **3** *a)* to cease existing; end *b)* to stop functioning **4** to lose force or activity; become weak, faint, unimportant, etc. **5** to fade or wither away **6**

to become alien or indifferent (*to*), as if dead **7** to pine away, as with desire **8** [Informal] to wish with extreme intensity; yearn [she's *dying* to learn the secret] **9** *Theol.* to suffer spiritual death —**die away** to become weaker and cease gradually: also **die down** —**die back** to wither to the roots or woody part: also **die down** —**die hard** to cling to life, a cause, etc.; resist to the last —**die off** to die one by one until all are gone —**die out** to go out of existence —**to die for** [Informal] overwhelmingly excellent and satisfying: a hyperbolic phrase used postpositively [a chocolate parfait *to die for*]

SYN.—**die** is the basic, simple, direct word meaning to stop living or to become dead; **decease**, **expire**, and **pass away** (see PASS[2], *vi.* 7) are all euphemisms, **decease** being also the legal term, **expire** meaning literally to breathe one's last breath, and **pass away** suggesting a coming to an end; **perish** implies death by a violent means or under difficult circumstances

die[2] (dī) *n., pl.* for 1 & 2, **dice** (dīs); for 3 & 4, **dies** (dīz) ⟦ME *de* (pl. *dis*) < OFr *de* < VL **datum*, orig. neut of L *datus*: see DATE[1]⟧ **1** a small, marked cube used in games of chance: see also DICE **2** any small cube resembling this **3** *Archit.* a dado of a pedestal **4** *Mech.* any of various tools or devices, originally cubical in form, for molding, stamping, cutting, or shaping; specif., *a)* a piece of engraved metal used for stamping money, medals, etc. *b)* the stationary part of a machine for shaping or punching holes in sheet metal, etc.; matrix (distinguished from PUNCH[1]) *c)* the punch and matrix as a unit *d)* a tool used for cutting threads, as of screws or bolts *e)* a piece of metal with a hole through it, used in drawing wire, extruding rods, etc. —*vt.* **died**, **die′ing** to mold, stamp, cut, or shape with a die —**the die is cast** ⟦transl. of L *jacta est alea*, ascribed to Caesar at the Rubicon⟧ the irrevocable decision has been made

☆**die·back** (dī′bak′) *n.* a disease of vascular plants characterized by a dying backward from the tip of twigs and branches and caused by parasites, insufficient moisture, etc.

die casting **1** the process of making a casting by forcing molten metal into a metallic mold, or die, under great pressure **2** a casting so made —**die caster**

di·e·cious (dī ē′shəs) *adj. alt. sp. of* DIOECIOUS

dief·fen·bach·i·a (dēf′ən bak′ē ə) *n.* ⟦ModL, after Ernst *Dieffenbach* (1811-55), 19th-c. Ger botanist + *-ia*, -IA⟧ any of a genus (*Dieffenbachia*) of tropical plants of the arum family, with thick, fleshy jointed stems and large leaves, dark green and often splashed with white: grown as houseplants, though poisonous

Di·e·go Gar·ci·a (dē ā′gō gär sē′ə) chief island of the Chagos Archipelago, British Indian Ocean Territory: 17 sq mi (44 sq km)

die-hard or **die·hard** (dī′härd′) *adj.* stubbornly resistant to change or unwaveringly loyal even in spite of inevitable defeat, failure, etc. [a *die-hard* conservative, a *die-hard* fan of the losers] —*n.* a person who displays such resistance or loyalty

☆**diel·drin** (dēl′drin) *n.* ⟦*Diel(s-Al)d(e)r (reaction)* + -IN[1]⟧ a highly toxic, long-lasting insecticide, $C_{12}H_8OCl_6$, restricted by law to nonagricultural use

di·e·lec·tric (dī′i lek′trik) *n.* ⟦DI(A)- + ELECTRIC: so called because it permits the passage of the lines of force of an electrostatic field but does not conduct the current⟧ a material, as rubber, glass, etc., or a medium, as a vacuum, gas, etc., that does not conduct electricity but can sustain an electric field: dielectrics are used in capacitors, between adjacent wires in a cable, etc. —*adj.* having the properties or function of a dielectric

dielectric constant the ratio of the capacitance of a capacitor in which a particular insulating material is the dielectric, to its capacitance in which a vacuum is the dielectric

☆**dielectric heating** the heating of dielectric materials by subjecting them to a high-frequency, alternating electric field, used in the bonding, drying, etc. of materials, as plastics and plywoods

Diels (dēlz; *Ger* dēls), **Otto (Paul Hermann)** 1876-1954; Ger. organic chemist

Dien Bien Phu (dyen′ byen′ fo͞o′) village in NW Vietnam: besieged & captured by Vietminh forces (1954), marking the end of French occupation of Indochina

di·en·ceph·a·lon (dī′ən sef′ə län′, -lən) *n.* ⟦ModL < DIA- + ENCEPHALON⟧ the posterior end of the forebrain, including the thalami and hypothalamus —**di′en·ce′phal′ic** (-sə′fal′ik) *adj.*

die-off (dī′ôf′) *n.* a biological phenomenon in which a great number of similar algae, plants, or animals die suddenly due to some natural cause, as a significant change in local living conditions or a fast-spreading disease

Di·eppe (dē ep′) city in N France, on the English Channel

di·er·e·sis (dī er′ə sis) *n., pl.* **-ses′** (-sēz′) ⟦LL *diaeresis* < Gr *diairesis*, division < *diairein*, to divide, separate < *dia-*, apart + *hairein*, to take: see HERESY⟧ **1** the separation of two consecutive vowels, esp. of a diphthong, into two syllables **2** a mark (¨) placed over the second of two consecutive vowels to show that it is pronounced in a separate syllable: the dieresis is now usually replaced by a hyphen (*reënter*, *re-enter*) or simply omitted (*cooperate*, *naive*): the mark is also used, as in this dictionary, to show a certain pronunciation of a vowel (ä, ë, ö, ü): cf. UMLAUT **3** *Prosody* a slight break or pause in a line of verse, resulting when the end of a metric foot coincides with the end of a word —**di·e·ret·ic** (dī′ə ret′ik) *adj.*

die·sel (dē′zəl, -səl) *n.* ⟦after R. *Diesel* (1858-1913), Ger inventor⟧ [*occas.* **D-**] **1** a type of internal-combustion engine that burns fuel oil: the ignition is brought about by heat resulting from air compression, instead of by an electric spark as in a gasoline engine: also **diesel engine** (or **motor**) **2** a locomotive, truck, etc. powered by such an engine **3** a petroleum distillate used in diesel engines —*adj.* of, for, or having a diesel engine [*diesel* fuel] —*vi.* to continue to run after the ignition is turned off: said of an internal-combustion engine

die·sink·er (dī′siŋk′ər) *n.* a person or machine that makes dies used in stamping or shaping —**die′sink′ing** *n.*

Di·es I·rae (dē′äs ē′rā, dē′äz ir′ā) ⟦L, Day of Wrath⟧ a medieval Latin hymn about Judgment Day, beginning *Dies Irae*: it was formerly sung at the Mass for the dead

di·e·sis (dī′ə sis) *n., pl.* **-ses′** (-sēz′) ⟦L < Gr < *diienai*, to send through < *dia-*, through + *hienai*, to send: see JET[1]⟧ DOUBLE DAGGER

di·es non (dī′ēz′ nän′, dē′äs nōn′) ⟦L *dies non (juridicus)*, not a (court) day⟧ *Law* a day on which courts are not in session, as a legal holiday

die·stock (dī′stäk′) *n.* a frame to hold dies for cutting threads on water pipes, screws, bolts, etc.

di·es·trus (dī es′trəs) *n.* ⟦ModL < DIA- + ESTRUS⟧ the interval between periods of sexual heat in female mammals —**di·es′trous** (-trəs) *adj.*

di·et[1] (dī′ət) *n.* ⟦ME *diete* < OFr < ML *dieta*, diet, daily food allowance (meaning infl. by fol.) < L *diaeta* < Gr *diaita*, way of life, regimen < *dia-*, through + root of *aisa*, fate < IE **aito-*, share < base **ai-*, to give, allot⟧ **1** *a)* what a person or animal usually eats and drinks; daily fare *b)* figuratively, what a person regularly reads, listens to, does, etc. **2** *a)* a program or plan consisting of a special or limited selection of food and drink and designed to promote health or a gain or loss of weight; specif., such a program or plan designed to promote weight loss *b)* the food and drink such a plan prescribes — *vi., vt.* ⟦ME *dieten* < ML *dietare*⟧ to eat or cause to eat special or limited food, esp. for losing weight —*adj.* **1** of or for a diet, esp. one designed for weight loss [*diet* pills] **2** containing fewer calories and hence not promoting weight gain [*diet* cola] —**di′et·er** *n.*

di·et[2] (dī′ət) *n.* ⟦ME *diete* < OFr < ML *dieta* < L *dies*, day: see DEITY⟧ **1** [Scot.] a day's session of an assembly **2** a formal assembly, as formerly of princes, electors, etc. of the Holy Roman Empire **3** in some countries, a national or local legislative assembly

di·e·tar·y (dī′ə ter′ē) *n., pl.* **-ies** ⟦ME *dietarie* < ML *dietarium*⟧ **1** a system of diet **2** daily food allowance or ration —*adj.* **1** of diet **2** of a dietary

di·e·tet·ic (dī′ə tet′ik) *adj.* ⟦L *diaeteticus* < Gr *diaitētikos*⟧ of, relating to, or designed for a particular diet of food and drink: also **di′e·tet′i·cal** —**di′e·tet′i·cal·ly** *adv.*

di·e·tet·ics (-iks) *n.* the study of the kinds and quantities of food needed for health

di·eth·yl·bar·bi·tu·ric acid (dī eth′əl bär′bə tyoor′ik, -toor′-) BARBITAL

di·eth·yl carbinol (dī eth′əl) a colorless, liquid isomer of amyl alcohol, $(CH_3CH_2)_2CHOH$, used in drugs and as a solvent

di·eth·yl ether ETHER (sense 4)

di·eth·yl·stil·bes·trol (-stil bes′trôl′, -trōl′) *n.* ⟦*diethyl-* (< DI-[1] + ETHYL) + STILBESTROL⟧ a synthetic estrogen, $C_{18}H_{20}O_2$, used as a substitute for natural estrogens: a probable carcinogen now banned by the FDA as a food supplement for fattening cattle: abbrev. *DES*

☆**di·e·ti·tian** (dī′ə tish′ən) *n.* an expert in dietetics; specialist in planning meals or diets: also [Now Rare] **di′e·ti′cian**

Die·trich (dē′trik), **Mar·le·ne** (mär lā′nə, -lē′nə) (born *Marie Magdalene Dietrich*) 1901?-92; U.S. film actress, born in Germany

Dieu et mon droit (dyö ā mōn drwå′) ⟦Fr⟧ God and my right: motto of British royalty

dif- (dif) *prefix* DIS-: used before *f*

diff or **dif** (dif) *n.* [Slang] *short for* DIFFERENCE [what's the *diff?*]

dif·fer (dif′ər) *vi.* ⟦ME *differen* < OFr *differer* < L *differre*, to carry apart, differ < *dis-*, apart + *ferre*, to bring, BEAR[1]⟧ **1** to be unlike; be not the same: often with *from* **2** to be of opposite or unlike opinions; disagree **3** [Archaic] to quarrel (*with*)

dif·fer·ence (dif′ər əns, dif′rəns) *n.* ⟦ME < OFr < L *differentia* < *differens*, prp. of *differre*: see prec.⟧ **1** condition, quality, fact, or instance of being different **2** the way in which people or things are different; esp., a determining point or factor that makes for a distinct change or contrast **3** *a)* the state of holding a differing opinion; disagreement *b)* the point at issue; point of disagreement **4** a dispute; quarrel **5** a discrimination or distinction in preference **6** a significant effect on or change in a situation **7** *Math.* the amount by which one quantity differs from another; remainder left after subtraction —*vt.* **-enced**, **-enc·ing** [Rare] to distinguish as or make different —**(it's the) same difference** [Slang] there is no difference —**make a difference** **1** to have an effect; matter **2** to change the outlook or situation —**make no difference** to have no effect; not matter —**split the difference** **1** to share the remainder equally **2** to make a compromise —**what's the difference?** [Informal] what does it matter?

dif·fer·ent (dif′ər ənt, dif′rənt) *adj.* ⟦ME < OFr < L *differens*: see prec.⟧ **1** not alike; dissimilar: with *from*, or, esp. informally, *than*, and, in Brit. usage, *to* **2** not the same; distinct; separate; other **3** various **4** unlike most others; unusual —**dif′fer·ent·ly** *adv.* —**dif′fer·ent·ness** *n.*

SYN.—**different**, applied to things that are not alike, implies individuality [three *different* doctors] or contrast [the twins wore *different* hats]; **diverse** more emphatically sets apart the things referred to, suggesting a conspicuous difference [*diverse* interests]; **divergent** suggests a branching off in different directions with an ever-widening distance between, and stresses irreconcilability [*divergent* schools of thought]; **distinct**, as applied to two or more things, stresses that each has a different identity and is unmistakably separate from the others, whether or not they are similar in kind, class, etc. [charged with two *distinct* offenses]; **dissimilar** stresses absence of similarity in appearance, properties, or nature [*dissimilar* techniques]; **disparate** implies essential or thoroughgoing difference, often stressing an absence of any relationship between things [*disparate* concepts]; **various** emphasizes the number and diversity of kinds, types, etc. [*various* gifts] —**ANT. alike, similar**

dif·fer·en·ti·a (dif′ər en′shē ə, -shə) ***n.***, *pl.* **-ti·ae′** (-shi ē′) *Logic* a distinguishing characteristic, esp. one that distinguishes one species from another of the same genus

dif·fer·en·ti·a·ble (-shē ə bəl, -shə bəl) ***adj.*** **1** open to differentiation **2** *Math.* designating or of a function which has a derivative at the point in question

dif·fer·en·tial (dif′ər en′shəl) ***adj.*** ⟦ML *differentialis* < L *differentia*: see DIFFERENCE⟧ **1** of, showing, or depending on a difference or differences [*differential* rates] **2** constituting or making a specific difference; distinguishing [*differential* qualities] **3** producing differing effects or results, as by the use of differing components [a *differential* gear] **4** *Math.* of or involving differentials —***n.*** **1** a differentiating amount, degree, factor, etc. [*differentials* in salary] **2** *Math.* *a)* an infinitesimal difference between two consecutive values of a variable quantity *b)* the derivative of a function multiplied by a small increment of the independent variable **3** *Mech.* a differential gear —**dif′fer·en′tial·ly** ***adv.***

differential calculus *Math.* the branch of mathematics dealing with derivatives and their applications: cf. INTEGRAL CALCULUS

differential coefficient DERIVATIVE (*n.* 5)

differential equation *Math.* any equation containing a derivative: such an equation is called an **ordinary differential equation** if it has only one independent variable and a **partial differential equation** if it has more than one independent variable

differential gear (*or* **gearing**) a certain arrangement of gears (*epicyclic train*) connecting two axles in the same line and dividing the driving force between them, but allowing one axle to turn faster than the other: it is used in the driving axles of automobiles to permit a difference in axle speeds when making turns

differential windlass a windlass with two drums of different diameters providing a MECHANICAL ADVANTAGE

dif·fer·en·ti·ate (dif′ər en′shē āt′) ***vt.*** **-at′ed, -at′ing** ⟦< ML *differentiatus*, pp. of *differentiare* < L *differentia*: see DIFFERENCE⟧ **1** to constitute a difference in or between **2** to make unlike; develop specialized differences in **3** to perceive or express the difference in; distinguish between; discriminate **4** *Math.* to work out the differential or derivative of (a function) —***vi.*** **1** to become different or differentiated; develop new characteristics **2** to perceive or express a difference **3** *Biol.* to undergo differentiation —**SYN.** DISTINGUISH

differential windlass

dif·fer·en·ti·a·tion (-en′shē ā′shən) ***n.*** **1** a differentiating or being differentiated **2** *Biol.* the modification of an organ, tissue, etc. in structure or function during development into a more specialized state **3** *Math.* the working out of the differential or derivative

dif·fi·cile (dif′ə sēl′, dē′fē-) ***adj.*** ⟦MFr < L *difficilis*, difficult: reintroduced < Fr⟧ hard or difficult; esp., hard to deal with, please, etc.

dif·fi·cult (dif′i kult′, -kəlt) ***adj.*** ⟦ME, back-form. < fol.⟧ **1** *a)* hard to do, make, manage, understand, etc.; requiring extra effort, skill, or thought *b)* having or characterized by difficulties or troubles [stocks holding up despite a *difficult* economy] **2** hard to satisfy, persuade, please, etc. —**SYN.** HARD —**dif′fi·cult′ly** ***adv.***

dif·fi·cul·ty (dif′i kul′tē, -kəl′-) ***n.***, *pl.* **-ties** ⟦ME & OFr *difficulte* < L *difficultas* < *difficilis*, difficult < *dis-*, not + *facilis*, easy: see FACILE⟧ **1** the condition or fact of being difficult **2** something that is difficult, as a hard problem or an obstacle or objection **3** trouble, distress, etc., or a cause of this **4** a disagreement or quarrel —**in difficulties** in distress, esp. financially

SYN.—difficulty is applied to anything hard to contend with, without restriction as to nature, intensity, etc. [a slight *difficulty*, great *difficulty*]; **hardship**, stronger in connotation, suggests suffering, privation, or trouble that is extremely hard to bear [the *hardships* of poverty]; **rigor** suggests severe hardship but further connotes that it is imposed by external, impersonal circumstances beyond one's control [the *rigors* of winter]; **vicissitude**, a bookish word, suggests a difficulty that is likely to occur in the course of something, often one inherent in a situation [the *vicissitudes* of political life]

dif·fi·dence (dif′ə dəns) ***n.*** ⟦ME < L *diffidentia* < *diffidens*, prp. of *diffidere*, to distrust < *dis-*, not + *fidere*, to trust: see FAITH⟧ lack of confidence in oneself, marked by hesitation in asserting oneself; shyness

dif·fi·dent (-dənt) ***adj.*** ⟦L *diffidens*: see prec.⟧ full of diffidence; lacking self-confidence; timid; shy —**SYN.** SHY[1] —**dif′fi·dent·ly** ***adv.***

dif·fract (di frakt′) ***vt.*** ⟦< L *diffractus*, pp. of *diffringere*, to break in pieces < *dis-*, apart + *frangere*, BREAK⟧ to subject to diffraction

dif·frac·tion (di frak′shən) ***n.*** ⟦ML *diffractio* < L *diffractus*: see prec.⟧ **1** the breaking up of a ray of light into dark and light bands or into the colors of the spectrum, caused by the interference of one part of a beam with another, as when the ray is deflected at the edge of an opaque object or passes through a narrow slit **2** a similar breaking up of other waves, as of sound or electricity —**dif·frac′tive** (-tiv) ***adj.*** —**dif·frac′tive·ly** ***adv.***

diffraction grating *Optics* a plate of glass or polished metal ruled with a series of very close, equidistant, parallel lines, used to produce a spectrum by the diffraction of reflected or transmitted light

dif·fuse (di fyo͞os′; *for v.*, -fyo͞oz′) ***adj.*** ⟦ME < L *diffusus*, pp. of *diffundere*, to pour in different directions < *dis-*, apart + *fundere*, to pour: see FOUND[2]⟧ **1** spread out or dispersed; not concentrated **2** using more words than are needed; long-winded; wordy — ***vt., vi.*** **-fused′, -fus′ing** **1** to pour, spread out, or disperse in every direction; spread or scatter widely **2** *Physics* to mix by diffusion, as gases, liquids, etc. —**SYN.** WORDY —**dif·fuse′ly** ***adv.*** —**dif·fuse′ness** ***n.***

dif·fus·er or **dif·fu·sor** (di fyo͞o′zər) ***n.*** a person or thing that diffuses, as a device for distributing light evenly

dif·fus·i·ble (di fyo͞o′zə bəl) ***adj.*** that can be diffused —**dif·fus′i·bil′i·ty** ***n.***

dif·fu·sion (di fyo͞o′zhən) ***n.*** ⟦ME *diffusioun* < L *diffusio*⟧ **1** a diffusing or being diffused; specif., *a)* a dissemination, as of news *b)* a scattering of light rays, as by reflection; also, the dispersion and softening of light, as by passage through frosted glass *c)* an intermingling of the molecules of liquids, gases, etc. **2** wordiness; diffuseness **3** *Anthrop.* the spread of a cultural or technological practice or innovation from one region or people to another, as by trade or conquest

dif·fu·sion·ism (-iz′əm) ***n.*** *Anthrop.* the theory that certain similar practices, inventions, etc. that exist among different cultures or peoples are solely or primarily the result of diffusion as opposed to independent discovery or development —**dif·fu′sion·ist** ***adj., n.***

dif·fu·sive (di fyo͞o′siv) ***adj.*** ⟦ML *diffusivus*⟧ **1** tending to diffuse **2** characterized by diffusion **3** diffuse —**dif·fu′sive·ly** ***adv.*** —**dif·fu′sive·ness** ***n.***

dig[1] (dig) ***vt.*** **dug, dig′ging** ⟦ME *diggen* < Anglo-Fr **diguer* < OFr *digue*, dike < Du *dijk*: see DIKE[1]⟧ **1** to break and turn up or remove (ground, etc.) with a spade or other tool, or with hands, claws, snout, etc. **2** to make (a hole, cellar, one's way, etc.) by or as by doing this **3** to uncover and get from the ground or another surface in this way [to *dig* potatoes, to *dig* a nail out of a board] ☆**4** to find out, as by careful study or investigation; unearth: usually with *up* or *out* [to *dig* out the truth] **5** to thrust, jab, or prod [to *dig* an elbow into someone's ribs] ☆**6** [Slang] *a)* to understand *b)* to approve of or like *c)* to notice; look at [*dig* that shirt!] —***vi.*** **1** to dig the ground or any surface **2** to make a way by or as by digging (*through, into, under*) ☆**3** [Informal] to work or study hard —***n.*** **1** the act of digging **2** [Informal] a thrust, poke, nudge, etc. **3** [Informal] a sarcastic comment; taunt; gibe **4** an archaeological excavation or its site **5** ⟦short for DIGGINGS, used specif. to refer to the place where a farmer digs, or works the land, usually living in the same area⟧ [*pl.*] [Informal, Chiefly Brit.] living quarters; lodgings —**dig in** **1** to dig trenches or foxholes for cover **2** to entrench oneself **3** [Informal] *a)* to begin to work intensively *b)* to begin eating —**dig in one's heels** [Informal] to refuse to give up or modify one's opinion, policy, attitude, etc., esp. when faced with opposition —**dig into** **1** to penetrate by or as by digging **2** [Informal] to work hard at

dig[2] *abbrev.* digest

di·gam·ma (dī gam′ə) ***n.*** ⟦Gr < *di-*, two + *gamma*: so called because it resembles two gammas (Γ) in form⟧ the sixth letter (ϝ) of the early Greek alphabet, derived from the Semitic *vav* and having the sound of the English *w*: it was replaced in the Latin alphabet by F

di·gas·tric (dī gas′trik) ***adj.*** ⟦ModL *digastricus* < Gr *di-*, two + *gastēr*, belly: see GASTRO-⟧ designating or of a muscle that bellies out from both sides of its tendon, esp. such a muscle in the neck that helps to lower the jaw and indirectly moves the tongue

di·gen·e·sis (dī jen′ə sis) ***n.*** ⟦ModL: see DI-[1] & GENESIS⟧ *Biol.* successive reproduction by two processes, sexual in one generation and asexual in the next —**di·ge·net·ic** (dī jə net′ik) ***adj.***

di·gest (dī′jest′; *for v.* di jest′, dī-) ***n.*** ⟦ME < L *digesta* (in LL, a collection of writings), orig. pl. of *digestus*, pp. of *digerere*, to separate, explain < *di-*, apart + *gerere*, to bear, carry⟧ **1** a condensed but comprehensive account of a body of information; summary or synopsis, as of scientific, legal, or literary material **2** a book, periodical, etc. consisting chiefly of such summaries or synopses or of articles condensed from other publications **3** [**D-**] [*often pl.*] *Rom. Law* the Pandects of the Emperor Justinian —***vt.*** ⟦ME *digesten* < L *digestus*: see the ***n.***⟧ **1** *a)* to arrange or classify systematically, usually in condensed form *b)* to condense (a piece of writing) by briefly summarizing its contents **2** to change (food), esp. in the mouth, stomach, and intestines by the action of gastric and intestinal juices, enzymes, and bacteria, into a form that can be absorbed by the body **3** to aid the digestion of (food) **4** to think over and absorb **5** to soften, disintegrate, etc. by the use of heat, usually together with water or other liquid —***vi.*** **1** to be digested **2** to digest food —**SYN.** ABRIDGMENT

di·gest·er (di jes′tər, dī-) ***n.*** **1** a person who makes a digest **2** a heavy metal container in which substances are heated or cooked to soften them or extract soluble elements from them **3** AUTOCLAVE

di·gest·i·ble (-tə bəl) ***adj.*** ⟦ME < OFr < LL *digestibilis*⟧ that can be digested —**di·gest′i·bil′i·ty** ***n.*** —**di·gest′i·bly** ***adv.***

di·ges·tif (dē zhes tēf′) ***n.*** ⟦Fr, a digestive aid⟧ an after-dinner drink, as brandy or a liqueur

di·ges·tion (di jes′chən, dī-) ***n.*** ⟦ME *digestioun* < OFr *digestion* < L *digestio*⟧ **1** the act or process of digesting food **2** the ability to digest food **3** the absorption of ideas **4** decomposition of sewage by bacteria

di·ges·tive (-tiv) ***adj.*** ⟦ME & OFr *digestif* < L *digestivus*⟧ of, for, or aiding digestion ***—n.*** any substance or drink that aids digestion **—di·ges′tive·ly** ***adv.*** **—di·ges′tive·ness** ***n.***

digged (digd) ***vt., vi.*** *archaic pt. & pp. of* DIG[2]

dig·ger (dig′ər) ***n.*** **1** a person or thing that digs; specif., any tool or machine for digging ☆**2** [**D-**] a member of any of several North American Indian peoples of the SW U.S. that dug roots for food: often a disparaging term, esp. in historical contexts **3** DIGGER WASP **4** [**D-**] [Slang] an Australian or New Zealander, esp. one who is a soldier

digger wasp any of various wasps from several families, that lay eggs on caterpillars, spiders, etc. that they have paralyzed and buried in nests dug in the ground

dig·gings (dig′iŋz, -inz) ***pl.n.*** **1** materials dug out **2** [*often with sing. v.*] a place where digging or mining, esp. gold mining, is done **3** [Slang] *a)* place, or locality *b)* one's lodging or quarters

dight (dīt) ***vt.*** **dight** or **dight′ed**, **dight′ing** ⟦ME *dihten* < OE *dihtan*, to arrange, dispose, make < L *dictare*, to say: see DICTATE⟧ [Archaic] **1** to adorn **2** to equip

dig·it (dij′it) ***n.*** ⟦ME < L *digitus*, a finger, toe, inch < IE base **deik-*, to show, point > L *dicere*, to say: see DICTION⟧ **1** a finger or toe **2** a unit of linear measure equal to ¾ inch, based on the breadth of a finger **3** any numeral from 0 to 9: so called because originally counted on the fingers

dig·i·tal (dij′it′l) ***adj.*** ⟦ME < L *digitalis*⟧ **1** of, like, or constituting a digit, esp. a finger **2** having digits **3** performed with a finger **4** using numbers that are digits to represent all the variables involved in calculation **5** using a row of digits, rather than numbers on a dial, to provide numerical information [*a digital* watch, a *digital* thermometer]: cf. ANALOG (sense 4) **6** *a)* designating or of data, images, sounds, etc. that are stored, transmitted, manipulated, or reproduced by a process using groups of electronic bits represented as 1 or 0 *b)* of or by means of such a process, as one using a digital computer **7** *a)* designating or of a recording technique in which sounds or images are converted into groups of electronic bits and stored on a magnetic or optical medium: the groups of bits are read electronically, as by a laser beam, for reproduction *b)* designating or of a type of radio or TV transmission and reception in which data, sounds, or images are sent or received as groups of electronic bits ***—n.*** **1** a finger **2** a key played with a finger, as on the piano **—dig′i·tal·ly** ***adv.***

digital audio tape an audio cassette tape recorded using digital techniques, resulting in sound that is virtually free of distortion

digital camera a camera that records images in digital form: digitized images can be viewed on a screen, printed on paper, transmitted electronically, etc.

☆**digital computer** a computer for processing data represented by discrete, localized physical signals, as the presence or absence of an electric current: the most commonly used kind of computer: cf. ANALOG COMPUTER

dig·i·tal·in (dij′i tal′in; *also*, -tā′lin) ***n.*** ⟦< fol. + -IN[1]⟧ a poisonous, crystalline glycoside, $C_{36}H_{56}O_{14}$, obtained from the seed of the digitalis

dig·i·tal·is (dij′i tal′is; *also*, -tā′lis) ***n.*** ⟦ModL, foxglove < L *digitalis*, belonging to the finger < *digitus*, a finger, DIGIT: so named (1542) by L. Fuchs (see FUCHSIA), from its thimblelike flowers, after the Ger name *fingerhut*, thimble⟧ **1** any of a genus (*Digitalis*) of plants of the figwort family, with long spikes of thimblelike flowers; foxglove **2** the dried leaves of a common digitalis plant (*Digitalis purpurea*) that usually has purple flowers **3** a medicine made from these leaves, used as a heart stimulant

☆**dig·i·tal·ize**[1] (dij′it′l īz′) ***vt.*** **-ized′**, **-iz′ing** to treat with sufficient digitalis drugs to achieve the desired therapeutic effect **—dig′i·tal·i·za′tion** ***n.***

dig·i·tal·ize[2] (dij′it′l īz′) ***vt.*** DIGITIZE

digital satellite system DIRECT BROADCAST SATELLITE

digital video recorder a device for recording, storing, and replaying, in digital form, video received from a television signal

dig·i·tate (dij′i tāt′) ***adj.*** ⟦L *digitatus*: see DIGIT⟧ **1** having separate fingers or toes **2** like a digit; fingerlike **3** *Bot.* having fingerlike divisions, as some compound leaves Also **dig′i·tat′ed** **—dig′i·tate′ly** ***adv.*** **—dig′i·ta′tion** ***n.***

dig·i·ti- (dij′i ti, -tə) ⟦Fr < L *digitus*, DIGIT⟧ *combining form* of the fingers or toes [*digitigrade*]

dig·i·ti·form (dij′i tə fôrm′) ***adj.*** shaped like a finger

dig·i·ti·grade (-grād′) ***adj.*** ⟦Fr: see DIGITI- & -GRADE⟧ walking on the toes with the heels not touching the ground, as cats, dogs, or horses ***—n.*** any animal that walks in this manner

dig·i·tize (dij′i tīz′) ***vt.*** **-tized′**, **-tiz′ing** to convert (text, a photograph, sound, etc.) into a digital format **—dig′i·ti·za′tion** ***n.*** **—dig′i·tiz′er** ***n.***

dig·i·tox·in (dij′i täk′sin) ***n.*** ⟦DIGI(TALIS) + TOXIN⟧ a glycoside, $C_{41}H_{64}O_{13}$, extracted from digitalis leaves: like digitalis in physiological action, but more potent

di·glos·si·a (dī gläs′ē ə, -glôs′-) ***n.*** ⟦ModL < Fr *diglossie* < Gr *diglōssos*, speaking two languages < *di-*, DI-[1] + *glōssa*, language: see GLOSS[2]⟧ *Linguis.* within a speech community, the use of two varieties of a language having different degrees of prestige, with speakers regularly using each in its appropriate social contexts

di·glot (dī′glät′) ***adj.*** ⟦Gr *diglōttos*, speaking two languages < *di-*, two + *glōtta*, *glossa*, the tongue: see GLOSS[2]⟧ bilingual ***—n.*** a bilingual edition of a book

dig·ni·fied (dig′nə fīd′) ***adj.*** having or showing dignity or stateliness **—dig′ni·fied′ly** (-fīd′lē, -fī′əd lē) ***adv.***

dig·ni·fy (dig′nə fī′) ***vt.*** **-fied′**, **-fy′ing** ⟦ME *dignifien* < OFr *dignifier* < ML *dignificare* < L *dignus*, worthy + *-ficare* < *facere*, to make, DO[1]⟧ **1** to give dignity to; make worthy of esteem; honor, exalt, or ennoble **2** to make seem worthy or noble, as by giving a high-sounding name to [*to dignify* cowardice by calling it prudence]

dig·ni·tar·y (dig′nə ter′ē) ***n.***, *pl.* **-tar′ies** ⟦< L *dignitas*, dignity + -ARY⟧ a person holding a high, dignified position or office ***—adj.*** of or like a dignitary

dig·ni·ty (dig′nə tē) ***n.***, *pl.* **-ties** ⟦ME & OFr *dignite* < L *dignitas*, worth, merit < *dignus*, worthy < IE base **dek-*, to receive, be fitting > DECOR, DOCILE⟧ **1** the quality of being worthy of esteem or honor; worthiness **2** high repute; honor **3** the degree of worth, repute, or honor **4** a high position, rank, or title **5** loftiness of appearance or manner; stateliness **6** proper pride and self-respect **7** [Archaic] a dignitary **—SYN.** DECORUM

dig·ox·in (dij äks′ən) ***n.*** ⟦DIG(ITALIS) + (T)OXIN⟧ a white, crystalline, purified form of digitalis, $C_{41}H_{64}O_{14}$, used to improve the heart's pumping action

di·graph (dī′graf′) ***n.*** ⟦DI-[1] + -GRAPH⟧ a combination of two letters functioning as a unit to represent one sound (Ex.: *re*a*d*, *bre*a*d*, *ch*in, *graph*ic) **—di·graph′ic** ***adj.*** **—di·graph′i·cal·ly** ***adv.***

di·gress (di gres′, dī-) ***vi.*** ⟦< L *digressus*, pp. of *digredi*, to go apart < *dis-*, apart + *gradi*, to go, step: see GRADE⟧ to turn aside; esp., to depart temporarily from the main subject in talking or writing **—SYN.** DEVIATE

di·gres·sion (-gresh′ən) ***n.*** ⟦ME < L *digressio*⟧ an act or instance of digressing; a wandering from the main subject in talking or writing **—di·gres′sion·al** ***adj.***

di·gres·sive (-gres′iv) ***adj.*** digressing or given to digression **—di·gres′sive·ly** ***adv.*** **—di·gres′sive·ness** ***n.***

di·he·dral (dī hē′drəl) ***adj.*** ⟦< DI-[1] + Gr *hedra*, a seat, base + -AL⟧ **1** having or formed by two intersecting plane faces [*a dihedral* angle] **2** *a)* having wings that form a dihedral angle with each other, as some airplanes *b)* being inclined to each other at a dihedral angle (said of airplane wing pairs) ***—n.*** **1** a dihedral angle **2** the acute angle, normally upward, between the wings of certain airplanes, designed to improve lateral stability

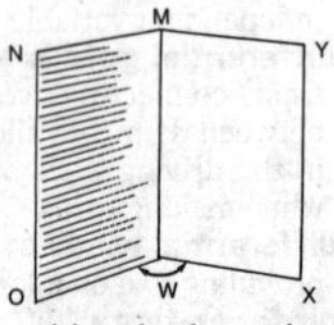

M N Y O W X

dihedral angle
(angle formed by planes MWON and MWXY)

di·hy·brid (dī hī′brid) ***n.*** ⟦DI-[1] + HYBRID⟧ *Genetics* an offspring of parents differing from one another in two pairs of alleles

Di·jon (dē zhōn′) city in EC France

Di·jon mustard (dē zhän′, dē′zhän′) ⟦after prec., where orig. made⟧ a seasoning of mild mustard paste, usually blended with white wine

dik-dik (dik′dik′) ***n.*** ⟦< name in a language of eastern Africa: prob. echoic of its cry⟧ any of several very small antelopes (genus *Madoqua*) found in E Africa

dike[1] (dīk) ***n.*** ⟦ME < OE *dic* & ON *diki*, akin to DITCH, Du *dijk*, Ger *deich* < IE base **dhēigw-*, **dhīgw-*, to pierce, fasten > L *figere*, FIX⟧ **1** [Now Brit. Dial.] *a)* a ditch or watercourse *b)* the bank of earth thrown up in digging a ditch **2** an embankment or dam made to prevent flooding by the sea or by a river **3** a protective barrier or obstacle **4** [Scot.] a low dividing wall of earth or stone **5** [Archaic] a raised causeway **6** *Geol.* igneous rock that solidified as a tabular body in a more or less vertical fissure ***—vt.*** **diked**, **dik′ing** **1** to provide, protect, or enclose with a dike or dikes **2** to drain by a ditch

dike[2] (dīk) ***n.*** *alt. sp. of* DYKE[2] **—dik′ey** ***adj.***

dik·tat (dik tät′, dik′tät′) ***n.*** ⟦Ger, a dictate⟧ an authoritarian decree, order, or policy

dil. *abbrev.* ⟦L *dilue*⟧ *Pharmacy* dilute; dissolve

☆**Di·lan·tin** (dī lan′tin, di-) ⟦< *di(pheny)l(hyd)ant(o)in*⟧ *trademark for* PHENYTOIN

di·lap·i·date (də lap′ə dāt′) ***vi., vt.*** **-dat′ed**, **-dat′ing** ⟦< L *dilapidatus*, pp. of *dilapidare*, to squander, demolish < *dis-*, apart + *lapidare*, to throw stones at < *lapis*, a stone: see LAPIDARY⟧ to become or cause to become partially ruined and in need of repairs, as through neglect

di·lap·i·dat·ed (-id) ***adj.*** falling to pieces or into disrepair; broken down; shabby and neglected

di·lap·i·da·tion (də lap′ə dā′shən) ***n.*** ⟦ME *dilapidacioun* < LL *dilapidatio*⟧ **1** a dilapidating or becoming dilapidated **2** a dilapidated condition **—SYN.** RUIN

di·lat·ant (dī lāt′′nt, də-) ***adj.*** ⟦L *dilatans*, prp. of *dilatare*: see DILATE⟧ **1** dilating or tending to dilate **2** expanding in bulk when the shape is changed: said of masses of certain granular substances **3** becoming solid, or setting, under pressure, as certain colloidal solutions: the inverse of THIXOTROPY ***—n.*** a thing that can dilate **—di·lat′an·cy** ***n.***

dil·a·ta·tion (dil′ə tā′shən, dīl′ə-) ***n.*** ⟦ME *dilatacioun* < OFr *dilatation* < LL *dilatatio*⟧ **1** DILATION **2** *Med.* the state of enlargement of an organ, cavity, duct, or opening of the body beyond normal size: cf. DILATION **—dil′a·ta′tion·al** ***adj.***

di·late (dī′lāt′; dī lāt′, də-) ***vt.*** **-lat′ed**, **-lat′ing** ⟦ME *dilaten* < L *dilatare* < *dis-*, apart + *latus*, wide: see LATERAL⟧ to make wider or larger; cause to expand or swell; stretch ***—vi.*** **1** to become wider or larger; swell **2** to speak or write in detail (*on* or *upon* a subject) **—SYN.** EXPAND **—di·lat′a·bil′i·ty** ***n.*** **—di·lat′a·ble** ***adj.*** **—di·lat′ive** ***adj.***

di·la·tion (dī lā′shən, di-) ***n.*** **1** a dilating or being dilated, as of the pupil of an eye, a blood vessel, or the cervix during childbirth: cf. DILATATION **2** a dilated part

dil·a·tom·e·ter (dil′ə täm′ət ər) ***n.*** an instrument for measuring volume changes in order to determine the transition points between phases

di·la·tor (dī′lāt′ər; dī lāt′-, də-) ***n.*** a person or thing that dilates; specif., *a)* any muscle that dilates a part of the body *b)* a surgical instrument for dilating an opening, wound, etc.

dil·a·to·ry (dil′ə tôr′ē) ***adj.*** ⟦ME *dilatorie* < LL *dilatorius* < L *dilator*, dilatory person < *dilatus*, pp. of *differre*, DEFER[1]⟧ **1** causing or tending to cause delay; meant to gain time, defer action, etc. **2** inclined to delay; slow or late in doing things —**dil′a·to′ri·ly** ***adv.*** —**dil′a·to′ri·ness** ***n.***

Di·laud·id (dī lôd′əd, di-; -lô′did) *trademark for* an addictive, narcotic painkiller, $C_{17}H_{20}ClNO_3$, that is stronger than morphine

dil·do (dil′dō) ***n.***, *pl.* **-dos** or **-does** ⟦< ? It *diletto*, delight⟧ a device shaped like an erect penis and used for sexual stimulation: also sp. **dil′doe**

di·lem·ma (də lem′ə, dī-) ***n.*** ⟦LL < LGr(Ec) *dilēmma* < *di-*, two + *lēmma*, proposition: see LEMMA[1]⟧ **1** an argument necessitating a choice between equally unfavorable or disagreeable alternatives **2** any situation in which one must choose between unpleasant alternatives **3** any serious problem —***SYN.*** PREDICAMENT —**dil·em·mat·ic** (dil′ə mat′ik) ***adj.***

dil·et·tante (dil′ə tänt′) ***n.***, *pl.* **dil′et·tantes′** or **dil′et·tan′ti** (-tän′tē) ⟦It < prp. of *dilettare*, to delight < L *delectare*, to charm, DELIGHT⟧ **1** [Now Rare] a person who loves the fine arts **2** a person who follows an art or science only for amusement and in a superficial way; dabbler —***adj.*** of or characteristic of a dilettante —***SYN.*** AESTHETE, AMATEUR —**dil′et·tant′ish** ***adj.*** —**dil′et·tant′ism′** ***n.***

Di·li (dil′ē) capital of East Timor, in the N part: before 1975, capital of Portuguese Timor

dil·i·gence[1] (dil′ə jəns) ***n.*** ⟦ME < OFr < L *diligentia* < *diligens*, prp. of *diligere*, to esteem highly, select < *di-*, apart + *legere*, to choose, collect: see LOGIC⟧ **1** the quality of being diligent; constant, careful effort; perseverance **2** [Obs.] speed; haste **3** *Law* the degree of attention or care expected of a person in a given situation

dil·i·gence[2] (dil′ə jəns; *Fr* dē lē zhäns′) ***n.*** ⟦Fr < *carrosse de diligence*, lit., coach of diligence, i.e., fast coach < *faire diligence*, to hurry⟧ a public stagecoach, esp. as formerly used in France

dil·i·gent (dil′ə jənt) ***adj.*** ⟦ME < OFr < L *diligens*: see DILIGENCE[1]⟧ **1** persevering and careful in work; industrious **2** done with careful, steady effort; painstaking —***SYN.*** BUSY —**dil′i·gent·ly** ***adv.***

dill (dil) ***n.*** ⟦ME & OE *dile*, akin to OS *dille*, OHG *tilli*⟧ **1** any of a genus (*Anethum*) of plants of the umbel family, esp. a European herb (*A. graveolens*) with bitter seeds and aromatic leaves, used to flavor pickles, soups, etc. **2** the seeds or leaves **3** DILL PICKLE

☆**dill pickle** a cucumber pickle flavored with dill

☆**dil·ly** (dil′ē) ***n.***, *pl.* **-lies** ⟦orig. adj., prob. altered & contr. < DEL(IGHTFUL) + -Y[2]⟧ [Slang] a surprising or remarkable person, thing, event, etc.

dil·ly·dal·ly (dil′ē dal′ē) ***vi.*** **-lied, -ly·ing** ⟦redupl. of DALLY⟧ to waste time in hesitation or vacillation; loiter or dawdle

Dil·they (dil′tā), **Wilhelm** 1833-1911; Ger. philosopher

dil·ti·a·zem (dil tī′ə zəm) ***n.*** a bitter, white, crystalline powder, $C_{22}H_{27}ClN_2O_4S$, that dilates blood vessels, used in treating angina pectoris, hypertension, etc.: in full **diltiazem hydrochloride**

dil·u·ent (dil′yoo ənt) ***adj.*** ⟦L *diluens*, prp. of *diluere*⟧ diluting —***n.*** a diluting substance

di·lute (di lo͞ot′, dī-) ***vt.*** **-lut′ed, -lut′ing** ⟦< L *dilutus*, pp. of *diluere*, to wash away < *dis-*, off, from + *luere*, var. of *lavare*, to LAVE⟧ **1** to thin down or weaken as by mixing with water or other liquid **2** to change or weaken (in brilliance, force, effect, etc.) by mixing with something else —***vi.*** to become diluted —***adj.*** diluted —**di·lute′ness** ***n.*** —**di·lut′er** ***n.***, **di·lu′tor**

di·lu·tion (-lo͞o′shən) ***n.*** **1** a diluting or being diluted **2** something diluted

di·lu·vi·al (di lo͞o′vē əl) ***adj.*** ⟦LL *diluvialis* < L *diluvium*: see fol.⟧ **1** of or caused by a flood, esp. the Deluge **2** of debris left by a flood or glacier Also **di·lu′vi·an**

di·lu·vi·um (-əm) ***n.***, *pl.* **-vi·ums** or **-vi·a** (-ə) ⟦L, a deluge < *diluere*: see DILUTE⟧ *Geol. former term for* glacial DRIFT (***n.*** 10): it was originally thought to have been caused by a great flood, esp. the Deluge

dim[1] (dim) ***adj.*** **dim′mer, dim′mest** ⟦ME < OE, akin to ON *dimmr*, dark < IE base **dhem-*, to be dusty, misty > DAMP, Ger *dunkel*, dark⟧ **1** not bright; somewhat dark **2** not clear or distinct in character; lacking definition, distinction, strength, etc. **3** without luster; dull **4** not clearly seen, heard, perceived, or understood; vague **5** not clearly seeing, hearing, understanding, etc. **6** not likely to turn out well *[dim* prospects*]* **7** [Informal] lacking intelligence; stupid —***vt.*** **dimmed, dim′ming** **1** to make dim **2** to make seem dim, as by comparison **3** to turn (headlights) down by switching from high to low beam —***vi.*** to grow dim —***n.*** **1** [Archaic] dim light; dimness; dusk **2** [*pl.*] headlights on a low-beam setting —***SYN.*** DARK —**take a dim view of** to view skeptically, pessimistically, etc. —**dim′ly** ***adv.*** —**dim′ness** ***n.***

dim[2] *abbrev.* **1** dimension **2** diminutive

Di·Mag·gi·o (də mä′jē ō′, -maj′ē ō′), **Joe** (born *Joseph Paul DiMaggio*) 1914-99; U.S. baseball player

Di·mashq (dē mäshk′) *Ar. name for* DAMASCUS

dim bulb ⟦because not very *bright*: pun based on BRIGHT, ***adj.*** 1 & 4⟧ [Informal] a slow-witted person; dimwit —**dim′-bulb′** ***adj.***

dime (dīm) ***n.*** ⟦ME < OFr *disme*, tithe, tenth < L *decima (pars)*, tenth (part), fem. of *decimus* < *decem*, TEN⟧ ☆a U.S. or Canadian coin equal to ten cents; tenth of a dollar: the U.S. dime is made of cupronickel —***adj.*** ☆*Football* designating or of a defense using six defensive backs to defend against an expected pass play —☆**a dime a dozen** [Informal] abundant and easily obtained; cheap —☆**on a dime** [Informal] at an exact point or within very narrow limits

di·men·hy·dri·nate (dī′men hī′drə nāt′) ***n.*** ⟦< *dime(thyl)* + *(diphe)nhydr(am)in(e)* + -ATE[2]⟧ a crystalline solid, $C_{24}H_{28}ClN_5O_3$, used to control nausea and vomiting, as in motion sickness

☆**dime novel** a hack paperback novel of a type popular in the later 19th and early 20th cent., usually sensational or melodramatic and originally costing a dime

di·men·sion (də men′shən; *also* dī-) ***n.*** ⟦ME *dimensioun* < L *dimensio*, a measuring < *dimensus*, pp. of *dimetiri*, to measure off < *dis-*, off, from + *metiri*, to MEASURE⟧ **1** *a)* a measurable extent, as length, width, or depth *b)* a hypothetical extension or continuum beyond these, in any of various physical or abstract systems *[*a theory involving higher *dimensions]*: see also FOURTH DIMENSION **2** [*pl.*] measurements in length and width, and often depth **3** [*often pl.*] *a)* extent, size, or degree *b)* scope or importance **4** the nature and relationship of the units entering into some physical quantity *[*the *dimension* for speed is length divided by time*]* **5** [*often pl.*] [Obs.] bodily form **6** *Math.* a number, usually an integer, representing the geometric dimensions of some physical or abstract system —***adj.*** designating lumber, stone, etc. cut to specified dimensions —***vt.*** to shape to or mark with specified dimensions: usually in past participle —**di·men′sion·less** ***adj.***

di·men·sion·al (-shə nəl) ***adj.*** **1** of dimension or dimensions **2** having (a specified number of) dimensions *[*a three-*dimensional* figure*]* —**di·men′sion·al′i·ty** (-nal′ə tē) ***n.*** —**di·men′sion·al·ly** ***adv.***

di·mer (dī′mər) ***n.*** ⟦DI-[1] + (POLY)MER⟧ a compound formed by the combination of two identical molecules or monomers —**di·mer′ic** (-mer′ik) ***adj.***

dim·er·ous (dim′ər əs) ***adj.*** ⟦ModL *dimerus*: see DI-[1] & -MEROUS⟧ having two parts; specif., *a)* having two members in each whorl (said of flowers) *b)* having two-jointed tarsi (said of insects)

☆**dime store** FIVE-AND-TEN-CENT STORE

dim·e·ter (dim′ə tər) ***n.*** ⟦LL < Gr *dimetros* < *di-*, two + *metron*, a MEASURE⟧ **1** a line of verse containing two metrical feet **2** verse consisting of dimeters —***adj.*** having two metrical feet

di·meth·yl (dī meth′əl) ***adj.*** containing two methyl radicals

dimethyl sulf·ox·ide (sulf äk′sīd) DMSO

di·met·ric projection (dī me′trik) ⟦ult. < Gr *di-*, twice (see DI-[1]) + *metron*, MEASURE (***n.***)⟧ a type of AXONOMETRIC PROJECTION in which the object is shown with two of its three principal axes tilted equally from the plane of viewing

di·mid·i·ate (di mid′ē āt′, dī-) ***adj.*** ⟦< L *dimidiatus*, pp. of *dimidiare*, to divide into halves < *dimidium*, a half < *dis-*, apart, from + *medius*, MID[1]⟧ **1** halved **2** *Biol.* having only one half developed **3** *Bot.* split on one side, as the calyptra of mosses —***vt.*** **-at′ed, -at′ing** [Archaic] to halve

dimin *abbrev.* diminutive

di·min·ish (də min′ish) ***vt.*** ⟦ME *diminishen*, a blend of *diminuen*, to reduce (< OFr *diminuer* < L *diminuere*, var. of *deminuere* < *de-*, from + *minuere*, to lessen < *minus*, small) & *minishen*, to make smaller < OFr *menusier* < VL **minutiare* < L *minutus*, MINUTE[2]⟧ **1** to make, or make seem, smaller; reduce in size, degree, importance, etc.; lessen **2** *Archit.* to cause to taper **3** *Music* to reduce (a perfect or a minor interval) by a half step —***vi.*** **1** to become smaller or less **2** *Archit.* to taper —***SYN.*** DECREASE —**di·min′ish·a·ble** ***adj.***

di·min·ished (-isht) ***adj.*** **1** made smaller; lessened; reduced **2** *Music* lessened by a half step: said of intervals or of chords formed with such an interval

di·min·ish·ing returns (-ish iŋ) *Econ.* the proportionately smaller increase in productivity observed after a certain point in the increase of capital, labor, etc.

di·min·u·en·do (də min′yo͞o en′dō) ***adj., adv., n.***, *pl.* **-dos** ⟦It, diminishing, prp. of *diminuere* < L: see DIMINISH⟧ [*also in italics*] *Musical Direction* DECRESCENDO

dim·i·nu·tion (dim′ə no͞o′shən, -nyo͞o′-) ***n.*** ⟦ME < OFr < L *deminutio*⟧ **1** a diminishing or being diminished; lessening; decrease **2** *Music* variation of a theme by shortening, usually halving, the time value of the notes: cf. AUGMENTATION

di·min·u·tive (də min′yo͞o tiv, -yə-) ***adj.*** ⟦ME & OFr *diminutif* < LL *diminutivus* < pp. of L *deminuere*, DIMINISH⟧ **1** much smaller than ordinary or average; very small; tiny **2** *Gram.* expressing smallness or diminution *[*a *diminutive* suffix or name*]* —***n.*** **1** a very small person or thing **2** *a)* a word or name formed from another by the addition of a suffix expressing smallness in size or, sometimes, endearment or condescension, as *ringlet (ring + -let)*, *Jackie (Jack + -ie)*, *lambkin (lamb + -kin)* *b)* such a suffix —***SYN.*** SMALL —**di·min′u·tive·ly** ***adv.*** —**di·min′u·tive·ness** ***n.***

dim·i·ty (dim′ə tē) ***n.***, *pl.* **-ties** ⟦ME *demit* < ML *dimitum* < MGr *dimitos*, double-threaded < *dis-*, TWO + *mitos*, a thread: cf. TWILL⟧ a thin, corded or patterned cotton cloth

dim·mer (dim′ər) ***n.*** a device, as a rheostat, for dimming an electric light or set of lights

di·mor·phism (dī môr′fiz′əm) ***n.*** ⟦< Gr *dimorphos*, having two forms (< *di-*, two + *morphē*, form) + -ISM⟧ **1** *Bot.* the state of having two different kinds of leaves, flowers, stamens, etc. on the same plant or in the same species **2** *Mineralogy* the property of crystallizing in two forms **3** *Zool.* the occurrence of two types of individuals in the same species, distinct in coloring, size, etc. —**di·mor′phic** (-fik) ***adj.***, **di·mor′phous** (-fəs)

dim·out (dim′out′) ***n.*** a dimming or reduction of the night lighting, as in a city, to make it less easily visible, as to enemy aircraft

dim·ple (dim′pəl) ***n.*** ⟦ME *dimpel*, akin to MHG *tumpfel*, Ger *tümpel*, deep hole in water < nasalized var. of Gmc **dup-*, to be deep < IE base **dheub-*, **dheup-*, hollow, deep > DEEP, DIP⟧ **1** a small, natural hollow on the surface of the body, as on the cheek or chin **2** any little hollow, as on water ***—vt.*** **-pled, -pling** to make dimples in ***—vi.*** to show or form dimples **—dim′ply** (-plē) ***adj.***

dim sum (dim′ sum′, -so͝om′) ⟦Chin dial. (Cantonese) *tim sam* < *tim*, dot + *sam*, heart⟧ **1** a small dumpling filled variously with minced meat, vegetables, etc. and steamed or fried **2** a variety of such dumplings and other foods served as a light meal

☆**dim·wit** (dim′wit′) ***n.*** [Slang] a stupid person; simpleton **—dim′wit′ted** ***adj.* —dim′wit′ted·ly *adv.* —dim′wit′ted·ness *n.***

din (din) ***n.*** ⟦ME *dine* < OE *dyne*, akin to ON *dynr* < IE base **dhwen-*, **dhun-*, to sound, boom > Sans *dhvani-*, sound, noise, word⟧ a loud, continuous noise; confused clamor or uproar ***—vt.*** **dinned, din′ning 1** to beset with a din **2** to repeat insistently or noisily *[to din an idea into someone's ears]* ***—vi.*** to make a din **—SYN.** NOISE

DIN (din) ***n.*** ⟦acronym⟧ any of various international technical standards, as for electronic equipment or photographic film, set by the German association Deutsches Institut für Normung

Di·nah (dī′nə) ***n.*** ⟦Heb *dīnāh*, lit., judged⟧ a feminine name

di·nar (di när′) ***n.*** ⟦Ar *dīnār* < LGr *dēnarion* < L *denarius*: see DENARIUS⟧ the basic monetary unit of: *a)* Algeria *b)* Bahrain *c)* Iraq *d)* Jordan *e)* Kuwait *f)* Libya *g)* Serbia *h)* Tunisia: see the table of monetary units in the Reference Supplement

Di·nar·ic Alps (di nar′ik) range of the E Alps, extending from Croatia through Bosnia and Herzegovina, Montenegro, Serbia, Kosovo, & N Albania: highest peak, *c.* 8,800 ft (2,682 m)

din-din (din′din′) ***n.*** ⟦redupl.; orig. a child's term⟧ [Informal] dinner

din·dle (din′dəl, din′əl) ***vt., vi.*** **-dled, -dling** ⟦ME *dindelen*, prob. < *dine* (see DIN), with intrusive *-d-* and freq. suffix⟧ [Scot. or North Eng.] to tingle or vibrate, as with or from a loud sound

d'In·dy (dan dē′), **(Paul Marie Théodore) Vin·cent** (van sän′) 1851-1931; Fr. composer

dine (dīn) ***vi.*** **dined, din′ing** ⟦ME *dinen* < OFr *disner* < VL **disjejunare* < L *dis-*, away + LL *jejunare*, to fast < L *jejunus*, hungry⟧ to eat dinner ***—vt.*** to provide a dinner for, or entertain at dinner ***—n.*** [Obs.] dinner **—dine on** (or **upon**) to eat a meal featuring or consisting of *[to dine on lobster and shrimp]* **—dine out** to eat dinner away from home

din·er (dīn′ər) ***n.*** **1** a person eating dinner ☆**2** DINING CAR ☆**3** a small restaurant built to look like a dining car ☆**4** a small restaurant with a counter along one side and booths on the other

di·ner·ic (dī ner′ik) ***adj.*** ⟦< DI-[1] + < LGr *nēron*, *nēros*, water + -IC⟧ *Physics* constituting, or having to do with, the surface of contact of two immiscible liquids in a container

☆**di·ner·o** (di ner′ō) ***n.*** ⟦Sp < L *denarius*, DENARIUS⟧ [Informal] money

Din·e·sen (dē′nə sən, din′ə-), **I·sak** (ē′säk) (pseud. of *Karen Blixen*, or *Karen von Blixen-Finecke*; born *Karen Christenze Dinesen*) 1885-1962; Dan. writer

☆**di·nette** (dī net′) ***n.*** ⟦see DINE & -ETTE⟧ **1** an alcove or small, partitioned space used as a dining room **2** a set of table and chairs for such a space

ding (diŋ) ***vi.*** ⟦ME *dingen*, to strike, beat < Scand (as in ON *dengja*, to hammer): see DINT⟧ **1** to make a sound like that of a bell; ring **2** [Slang] to strike; hit ***—vt.*** **1** to make ring **2** [Informal] to repeat insistently or tiresomely; din ☆**3** [Informal] *a)* to make a small dent in *b)* to injure slightly *[to be dinged from a fall from a bicycle]* ***—n.*** **1** the sound of a bell ☆**2** [Informal] a small dent **3** [Slang] *short for* DING-A-LING

☆**ding-a-ling** (diŋ′ə liŋ′) ***n.*** ⟦< the ringing in the head of a punch-drunk boxer⟧ [Slang] a crazy, stupid, or eccentric person

Ding an sich (diŋ′ än ziH′) ⟦Ger, lit., thing in itself⟧ *Philos.* NOUMENON

☆**ding·bat** (diŋ′bat′) ***n.*** ⟦< DING, in obs. sense "to fling" + BAT[1]⟧ **1** [Old Informal] a stone, stick, or other object suitable for throwing **2** [Informal] *Printing* any of various decorative marks, as at the beginning of a paragraph **3** [Slang] a foolish or erratic person

ding-dong (diŋ′dôŋ′, -däŋ′) ***n.*** ⟦echoic⟧ **1** the sound of a bell being rung ☆**2** [Slang] DING-A-LING ***—adj.*** [Informal] carried out, as a contest or fight, with continual, successive changes in the lead or advantage; vigorously contested ***—vi.*** to sound with a ding-dong ***—vt.*** to impress by repeating

ding·er (diŋ′gər) ***n.*** [Slang] *Baseball* HOME RUN

din·ghy (diŋ′gē, diŋ′ē) ***n., pl.*** **-ghies** ⟦Hindi *ḍiṅgī*⟧ **1** a rowboat used originally on the rivers of India **2** a small boat carried on a ship **3** a small boat used as a tender as to a yacht **4** a small, single-masted racing boat **5** an inflatable life raft Also sp. **din′gey**

din·gle (diŋ′gəl) ***n.*** ⟦ME *dingel*, abyss, deep hollow, prob. akin to OE *ding*, dungeon: ult. < IE base **dhengh-*, to press, cover: see DUNG⟧ a small, deep, wooded valley; dell

din·go (diŋ′gō) ***n., pl.*** **-goes** ⟦native name⟧ the Australian wild dog (*Canis dingo*), usually tawny in color, with short, pointed ears and a bushy tail

ding·us (diŋ′əs) ***n.*** ⟦Du *dinges* (or Ger *dings*), thingamabob, orig. gen. of *ding*, THING[1]⟧ [Informal] any device; contrivance; gadget: humorous substitute for a name temporarily forgotten or not known

din·gy (din′jē) ***adj.*** **-gi·er, -gi·est** ⟦orig. dial. var. of DUNGY⟧ **1** dirty-colored; not bright or clean; grimy **2** dismal; shabby **—din′gi·ly *adv.* —din′gi·ness *n.***

☆**dining car** a railroad car equipped to serve meals to passengers

dining room a room for eating meals, esp. dinner

di·ni·tro- (dī nī′trō, -trə) *combining form* having two nitro groups per molecule *[dinitrobenzene]*

di·ni·tro·ben·zene (dī nī′trō ben′zēn′) ***n.*** any of three isomeric compounds, $C_6H_4(NO_2)_2$, formed by the reaction of nitric acid and benzene or nitrobenzene: used in dyes, organic synthesis, etc.

dink[1] (diŋk) ***n.*** DROP SHOT (sense 2) ***—adj.*** *Baseball* of a hit made as a result of striking the ball poorly *[a dink double]*

dink[2] (diŋk) ***n.*** [Slang] a fool, jerk, etc.

dink[3] (diŋk) ***n.*** [Slang, Chiefly Mil.] a person born in Southeast Asia, esp. Vietnam, or of Southeast Asian descent: a term of hostility and contempt

DINK (diŋk) ***n.*** ⟦*d(ouble) i(ncome,) n(o) k(ids)*⟧ [Informal] either of two people joined as a married couple who have two incomes and no children: also written **dink**

Din·ka (diŋ′kä, -kə) ***n.*** **1** a member of a group of Sudanic peoples living in S Sudan (the country) **2** the language of these peoples, belonging to the Chari-Nile subfamily of the Nilo-Saharan family of languages

din·key (diŋ′kē) ***n.*** ⟦prob. < DINKY⟧ ☆a small locomotive for hauling cars, shunting, etc. in a railroad yard

din·kum (diŋ′kəm) [Austral. Slang] ***adj.*** ⟦< dial. (Lincolnshire), a fair share of work < ?⟧ honest or genuine ***—adv.*** honestly or genuinely Often in the phrase **fair dinkum**

dink·y (diŋ′kē) ***adj.*** **-i·er, -i·est** ⟦< Scot *dink*, finely dressed, trim⟧ [Informal] small and unimportant; of no consequence —☆***n., pl.*** **din′kies** *alt. sp. of* DINKEY

din·ner (din′ər) ***n.*** ⟦ME *diner* < OFr *disner*, inf. used as n.: see DINE⟧ **1** the main meal of the day, whether eaten in the evening or about noon **2** a banquet in honor of some person or event **3** a complete meal at a set price with no course omitted; table d'hôte

dinner jacket a tuxedo jacket

☆**dinner ring** a woman's ring set with a large stone or group of stones, worn on formal occasions

dinner theater a restaurant at which a play, musical, etc. is presented while or after dinner is served

din·ner·time (din′ər tīm′) ***n.*** the usual time for serving or eating dinner

din·ner·ware (-wer′) ***n.*** plates, cups, saucers, etc., collectively

di·no (dī′nō) ***n.*** [Informal] *short for* DINOSAUR

di·no- (dī′nō, -nə) ⟦< Gr *deinos*, terrible: see DIRE⟧ *combining form* terrible, dreadful *[dinosaur]*

di·no·flag·el·late (dī′nō flaj′ə lit, -lāt′) ***n.*** ⟦< ModL *Dinoflagellata* < Gr *dinos*, rotation (< IE base **deye-*, to swing, whirl > OIr *dīan*, swift) + ModL *flagellum* (see FLAGELLUM) + *-ata*, L, neut. pl. of *-atus*: see -ATE[1]⟧ any of a class (Dinophyceae) of single-celled algae (division Chromophycota), mainly marine and often with a cellulose shell: some species are luminescent, and some cause the red tides that are extremely toxic to marine life: also classified in a class (Dinoflagellata) of protozoans

di·no·saur (dī′nə sôr′) ***n.*** ⟦< ModL *Dinosaurus*, orig. a genus name < Gr *deinos* (see DINO-) + *sauros* (see -SAURUS): coined by Sir R. Owen (1804-92), Brit anatomist & paleontologist⟧ **1** any of various extinct, mostly land-dwelling, four-limbed saurischian or ornithischian reptiles of the Mesozoic Era, including some *c.* 30 m (98.4 ft) long: the flesh-eaters usually walked on their hind limbs, the plant-eaters on all fours **2** loosely, any large, extinct reptile of the Paleozoic or Mesozoic eras **3** someone or something thought of as being old-fashioned, outmoded, resistant to change, etc. **—di′no·sau′ri·an** (-sôr′ē ən) ***adj.***

di·no·there (dī′nō thir′, -nə-) ***n.*** ⟦< DINO- + Gr *thēr*, wild beast: see FIERCE⟧ any of a genus (*Dinotherium*, order Proboscidea) of extinct elephantlike mammals of the Miocene Epoch with tusks curving downward from the lower jaw

dint (dint) ***n.*** ⟦ME < OE *dynt* < IE base **dhen-*, to strike > DING⟧ **1** force; exertion: now chiefly in **by dint of 2** a dent **3** [Archaic] a blow ***—vt.*** **1** to dent **2** to drive in with force

Din·wid·die (din wid′ē, din′wid ē), **Robert** 1693-1770; Brit. lieutenant governor of Va. (1751-58)

dioc *abbrev.* diocesan

di·oc·e·san (dī äs′ə sən) ***adj.*** ⟦ME < ML *diocesanus*⟧ of a diocese ***—n.*** the bishop of a diocese

di·o·cese (dī′ə sis, -sēz′) ***n.*** ⟦ME & OFr *diocise* < L *diocesis*, district, government (in LL(Ec), diocese) < Gr *dioikēsis*, administration < *dioikein*, to keep house < *dia-*, through + *oikos*, a house: see ECO-⟧ the district under a bishop's jurisdiction

Di·o·cle·tian (dī′ə klē′shən) (L. name *Gaius Aurelius Valerius Diocletianus*) A.D. 245-313; Rom. emperor (284-305)

di·ode (dī′ōd′) ***n.*** ⟦DI-[1] + -ODE[1]⟧ an electronic device with two electrodes, as either an electron tube with an anode and a cathode or a transistor with a pn junction, used mainly as a rectifier since it conducts current in only one direction

di·oe·cious (dī ē′shəs) ***adj.*** ⟦< DI-[1] + Gr *oikos*, a house (see ECO-) + -OUS⟧ *Biol.* having the male reproductive organs in one individual and the female organs in another; having separate sexes **—di·oe′cious·ly *adv.* —di·oe′cism′** (-siz′əm) ***n.***

Di·og·e·nes (of Si·no·pe) (dī äj′ə nēz′ əv si nō′pē) 412?-323? B.C.; Gr. philosopher: noted for founding the Cynical school of philosophy

Di·o·mede Islands (dī′ə med′) ⟦so named by Vitus BERING, who discovered them (1728) on St. Diomede's Day (August 16)⟧ two islands in the Bering Strait, between Siberia & Alaska; **Big Diomede**, Russia (Russ. name *Ratmanov*) & **Little Diomede**, U.S.: U.S.-Russia boundary passes between them

Di·o·me·des (dī′ə mē′dēz′) *n. Gr. Legend* a Greek warrior at the siege of Troy, who helps Odysseus steal the statue of Athena: also **Di′o·med′** (-med′) or **Di′o·mede′** (-mēd′)

Di·o·ne (dī ō′nē) *n.* ⟦after *Dione*, a female Titan, mother of Aphrodite⟧ a satellite of Saturn, sharing an orbit with a smaller satellite **(Dione B)**

Di·o·ny·si·a (dī′ə nish′ē ə, -nish′ə; -nis′ē ə, -niz′-) *pl.n.* ⟦L < Gr *Dionysia (hiera)*, (rites) of Dionysus⟧ any of the various Greek festivals in honor of Dionysus, esp. those at Athens from which the Greek drama originated

Di·o·nys·i·ac (-nis′ē ak′, -niz′-) *adj.* ⟦L *Dionysiacus* < Gr *Dionysiakos*⟧ **1** of Dionysus or the Dionysia **2** DIONYSIAN (sense 2)

Di·o·ny·si·an (-nish′ən; -nis′ē ən, -niz′-) *adj.* **1** Dionysiac **2** of the orgiastic nature of the Dionysia; wild, frenzied, and sensuous: distinguished from APOLLONIAN **3** of any of several historical figures named Dionysus

Di·o·ny·si·us (-nish′əs, -nis′ē əs, -nī′sē əs) **1** 430?-367 B.C.; Gr. tyrant of ancient Syracuse (405-367): called *the Elder* **2** 395?-340? B.C.; Gr. tyrant of Syracuse (367-356; 347-343): son of Dionysius the Elder: called *the Younger*

Dionysius Ex·ig·u·us (ig zig′yōō əs, -sig′-) 6th cent. A.D.; Rom. monk & Christian theologian, born in Scythia: believed to have introduced the current system of numbering years on the basis of the Christian Era

Dionysius of Halicarnassus fl. 1st cent. B.C.; Gr. critic & historian in Rome

Di·o·ny·sus or **Di·o·ny·sos** (dī′ə nī′səs) *n.* ⟦L < Gr *Dionysos*⟧ *Gr. Myth.* the god of wine and revelry: identified with the Roman Bacchus

di·op·side (dī äp′sīd′, -sid) *n.* ⟦Fr < *di-* (see DI-[3]) + Gr *opsis*, appearance, sight (< *ōps*, EYE); assoc. in meaning with Gr *diopsis*, transparency < *dia-*, through + *opsis*, sight⟧ a light-colored, hard, crystalline pyroxene, $CaMg(Si_2O_6)$, calcium magnesium silicate, found in some limestones and metamorphic rocks and sometimes used as a gem

di·op·tase (dī äp′tās′) *n.* ⟦Fr < Gr *dia-*, through + *optazein*, to see < *optos*, visible < *ops*, EYE⟧ a hard, green, brittle, crystalline mineral, $Cu_6Si_6O_{18}\cdot 6H_2O$, hydrous copper silicate, used in making jewelry

di·op·ter or **di·op·tre** (dī äp′tər) *n.* ⟦Fr *dioptre* < L *dioptra* < Gr instrument for leveling, etc. < *dia-*, through + base of *opsis*, sight < *ops*, EYE⟧ a unit of measure of the power of a lens, equal to the power of a lens with a focal length of one meter —**di·op′tral** *adj.*

di·op·tom·e·ter (dī′äp täm′ət ər) *n.* ⟦DI-[3] + OPTOMETER⟧ an instrument for testing the refraction of the eye —**di′op·tom′e·try** *n.*

di·op·tric (dī äp′trik) *adj.* ⟦Gr *dioptrikos*, relating to the DIOPTER⟧ **1** of optical lenses or the method of numbering them according to their refractive powers; dioptral **2** of dioptrics; refractive **3** helping the sight by refractive correction Also **di·op′tri·cal**

di·op·trics (-triks′) *n.* ⟦< prec.⟧ [Archaic] the branch of optics dealing with the refraction of light through lenses

Di·or (dē ôr′; *Fr* dē ôr′), **Chris·tian** (kris′chən; *Fr* krēs tyän′) 1905-57; Fr. couturier

di·o·ram·a (dī′ə ram′ə, -rä′mə) *n.* ⟦DI(A)- + (PAN)ORAMA⟧ **1** a picture painted on a set of transparent cloth curtains and looked at through a small opening **2** a miniature scene, wholly or partially three-dimensional, depicting figures in a naturalistic setting **3** a museum display of a preserved or reconstructed specimen, as of wildlife in a simulation of its habitat —**di′o·ram′ic** *adj.*

di·o·rite (dī′ə rīt′) *n.* ⟦Fr < Gr *diorizein*, to divide < *dia-*, through + *horizein*, to separate: see HORIZON⟧ a dark-gray, intrusive igneous rock consisting chiefly of plagioclase and hornblende

Di·os·cu·ri (dī′äs kyoor′ī′) *pl.n.* ⟦Gr *Dioskouroi* < *Dios* (gen. of *Zeus*) + *kouroi*, pl. of *kouros*, boy, son⟧ *Gr. Myth.* Castor and Pollux, twin sons of Leda

di·os·gen·in (dī′əz jen′in; dī äz′jə nin′) *n.* ⟦Ger < ModL *Dios(corea)*, genus name of the yam⟧ a steroid, $C_{27}H_{42}O_3$, found in yams and used to synthesize various hormones, as progesterone

di·ox·ane (dī äk′sān′) *n.* ⟦DI-[1] + OX- + -ANE⟧ a colorless, liquid ether, $C_4H_8O_2$, prepared from ethylene oxide or glycol and used as a solvent for fats, etc. and in cosmetics, deodorants, etc.

di·ox·ide (dī äk′sīd′, -sid) *n.* an oxide containing two atoms of oxygen per molecule

di·ox·in (dī äk′sin) *n.* ⟦DI-[1] + OX(A)- + -IN[1]⟧ any of a family of heterocyclic hydrocarbons; esp., any of a number of isomers of a highly toxic chlorinated teratogen, TCDD, that occurs as an impurity in some herbicides and defoliants, including trichlorophenoxyacetic acid, a component of Agent Orange

dip (dip) *vt.* **dipped** or occas. **dipt**, **dip′ping** ⟦ME *dippen* < OE *dyppan*, to immerse < Gmc **dup-*, to be deep: see DIMPLE⟧ **1** to put into or under liquid for a moment and then quickly take out; immerse **2** to dye in this way **3** to clean (sheep, hog, dogs, etc.) by bathing in disinfectant **4** to make (a candle) by putting a wick repeatedly in melted tallow or wax **5** to coat, plate, or galvanize by immersion **6** to get or take out by, or as if by, scooping up with a container, the hand, etc. **7** to lower and immediately raise again *[dip* the flag in salute*]* ☆**8** to put (snuff) on the gums, as with a snuff stick —*vi.* **1** to plunge into a liquid and quickly come out **2** to sink or seem to sink suddenly *[*the sun *dips* into the ocean*]* **3** to undergo a slight, usually temporary decline *[*sales *dipped* in May*]* **4** to slope down **5** to lower a container, the hand, etc. into liquid, a receptacle, etc., esp. in order to take something out: often used fig. *[*to *dip* into one's savings*]* **6** to read here and there in a book, etc., or inquire into a subject superficially **7** *Aeron.* to drop suddenly before climbing —*n.* **1** a dipping or being dipped **2** *a)* a brief plunge into water or other liquid *b)* a brief swim **3** a liquid into which something is dipped, as for dyeing **4** whatever is removed by or used in dipping **5** a candle made by dipping **6** *a)* a downward slope or inclination *b)* the amount of this **7** a slight hollow **8** a short downward plunge, as of an airplane **9** *a)* a sweet, liquid sauce for desserts ☆*b)* a variously flavored, thick, creamy sauce, in which crackers, etc. are dipped to be eaten as appetizers **10** [Slang] a pickpocket **11** *Geol., Mining* the downward inclination of a stratum or vein, with reference to a horizontal plane **12** *Gym.* the act of lowering oneself between parallel bars by bending the arms until the chin reaches the bar level, and then raising oneself by straightening the arms **13** *Physics a)* the deviation of a dip needle from the horizontal *b)* the amount of such deviation **14** *Surveying* the angular amount by which the horizon is below eye level

Dip *abbrev.* Diploma

di·pet·al·ous (dī pet′'l əs) *adj.* BIPETALOUS

di·phase (dī′fāz′) *adj.* having two phases: also **di·pha′sic** (-fā′zik)

di·phen·hy·dra·mine (dī′fen hī′drə mēn′) *n.* ⟦DI-[1] + PHEN- + *hydramine*, a type of amine < HYDR(O)- + AMINE⟧ a powerful antihistamine, $C_{17}H_{21}NO\cdot HCl$, used to treat a variety of allergic disorders: in full **diphenhydramine hydrochloride**

di·phen·yl (dī fen′əl, -fēn′-) *n.* a crystalline compound, $(C_6H_5)_2$, with a pleasant odor, used to preserve fruit, as a heat-transfer agent, etc.

di·phen·yl- (dī fen′əl, -fēn′-) *combining form* containing two phenyl groups in each molecule

di·phen·yl·a·mine (dī fen′əl ə mēn′, -fēn′-; -am′ēn′, -in) *n.* ⟦DIPHENYL + AMINE⟧ a colorless, crystalline chemical compound, $(C_6H_5)_2NH$, used as a stabilizer of explosives and propellants, as a test for nitric acid, and in making dyes

di·phos·gene (dī fäs′jēn′) *n.* a poisonous, liquid compound, $ClCO_2CCl_3$, related to phosgene and used as a lung-irritant gas in chemical warfare

diph·the·ri·a (dif thir′ē ə, dip-) *n.* ⟦ModL < Fr *diphthérie* (so named (1855) by A. Trousseau (1801-67), Fr physician, replacing earlier *diphthérite*, first used (1821) by P. Bretonneau (1778-1862), Fr physician) < Gr *diphthera*, leather < *dephein*, to tan hides < IE base **deph-*, to knead, stamp > Arm *top'el*, to strike⟧ an acute infectious disease caused by a bacterium (*Corynebacterium diphtheriae*) and characterized by weakness, high fever, the formation in the air passages of a tough, membranelike obstruction to breathing, and the production of a potent neurotoxin —**diph·the′ri·al** *adj.*

diph·the·rit·ic (dif′thə rit′ik) *adj.* ⟦< earlier Fr *diphthérite* (see prec.) + -IC⟧ **1** of, characteristic of, or like diphtheria **2** having diphtheria Also **diph·ther·ic** (dif ther′ik)

diph·thong (dif′thôŋ; *often* dip′-) *n.* ⟦ME *diptonge* < LL *diphthongus* < Gr *diphthongos* < *di-*, two + *phthongos*, voice, sound < *phthengesthai*, to utter⟧ **1** *Phonet.* a complex vowel sound made by gliding continuously from the position for one vowel to that for another within the same syllable, as (ou = ä→ōō) in *down*, (ī = ä→ē) in *ride*, (oi = ô→ē) in *boy* **2** *Printing* either of the ligatures æ or œ, pronounced as diphthongs in classical Latin —**diph·thon′gal** (-thôŋ′gəl, -əl) *adj.*

diph·thong·ize (-gīz′, -īz′) *vt.* **-ized′**, **-iz′ing** to pronounce (a simple vowel) as a diphthong —*vi.* to become a diphthong —**diph′thong′i·za′tion** *n.*

diph·y·cer·cal (dif′i sur′kəl) *adj.* ⟦< Gr *diphyēs*, twofold (< *di-*, DI-[1] + *phyein*, to bear, bring forth: see BE) + *kerkos*, tail + -AL⟧ designating, of, or having a tail fin in which the upper and lower lobes taper symmetrically to a point to which the spinal column extends

di·phy·let·ic (dī′fī let′ik) *adj.* having two ancestral lines of descent

di·phyl·lous (dī fil′əs) *adj.* having two leaves or sepals

diph·y·o·dont (dif′ē ō dänt′) *adj.* ⟦< Gr *diphyēs* (see DIPHYCERCAL) + -ODONT⟧ developing two consecutive sets of teeth, as most mammals do

dipl *abbrev.* diplomatic

di·ple·gi·a (dī plē′jē ə, -jə) *n.* paralysis of similar parts on both sides of the body

di·plex (dī′pleks′) *adj.* ⟦altered (after DI-[1]) < DUPLEX⟧ using a single circuit or transmission link for the simultaneous transmission or reception of two signals

dip·lo- (dip′lō, -lə) ⟦< Gr *diploos* < *di-*, DI-[1] + IE **-plo-*, -fold: see DOUBLE⟧ *combining form* two, double, twin *[diplococcus]*: also, before a vowel, **dipl-**

dip·lo·blas·tic (dip′lō blas′tik, -lə-) *adj. Zool.* of or pertaining to a body with only two cellular layers, the ectoderm and the endoderm

dip·lo·coc·cus (-käk′əs) *n., pl.* **-coc′ci′** (-käk′sī′) any of a group of parasitic, spherical bacteria occurring in pairs, as the pneumococcus that causes lobar pneumonia —**dip′lo·coc′cal** (-käk′əl) *adj.*, **dip′lo·coc′cic** (-käk′sik)

☆**dip·lod·o·cus** (dip läd′ə kəs, -lō′də-) *n.* ⟦ModL < DIPLO- + Gr *dokos*, main supporting beam: coined (1878) by O. C. Marsh: see APATOSAURUS⟧ any of a genus (*Diplodocus*) of huge, plant-eating sauropod dinosaurs of the Jurassic and Cretaceous periods

dip·lo·e (dip′lō ē′) *n.* ⟦ModL < Gr *diploē*, lit., a fold, doubling < *diploos*, DOUBLE⟧ the spongy bone between the two dense inner and outer layers of the skull bones —**di·plo·ic** (di plō′ik) *adj.*

dip·loid (dip′loid′) *adj.* ⟦DIPL(O)- + -OID⟧ **1** twofold or double **2** *Biol.* having twice the number of chromosomes normally occurring in a mature germ cell: most somatic cells are diploid —*n.* a diploid cell —**dip·loi′dy** (-loi′dē) *n.*

di·plo·ma (də plō′mə) *n., pl.* **-mas**; for 1, also, **-ma·ta** (-mə tə) ⟦L, state letter of recommendation < Gr *diplōma*, folded letter < *diploun*, to double < *diploos*, DOUBLE⟧ **1** an official state document or historical document; charter **2** a certificate conferring honors, privileges, etc. **3** a certificate issued to a student by a school, college, or university, indicating graduation or the conferring of a degree

di·plo·ma·cy (də plō′mə sē) ***n.*** ⟦Fr *diplomatie* < *diplomate*: see DIPLOMAT⟧ **1** the conducting of relations between nations, as in building up trade, making treaties, etc. **2** skill in doing this **3** skill in dealing with people; tact —***SYN.*** TACT

☆**diploma mill** [Informal] an unaccredited school or college that grants relatively worthless diplomas, as for a fee

dip·lo·mat (dip′lə mat′) ***n.*** ⟦Fr *diplomate*, back-form. < *diplomatique* (after nouns ending in *-ate*, as *aristocrate*), DIPLOMATIC⟧ **1** a representative of a government who conducts relations with the governments of other nations; person whose career or profession is diplomacy **2** a person skilled in dealing with other people; tactful person Also **di·plo·ma·tist** (də plō′mə tist)

dip·lo·mate (dip′lə māt′) ***n.*** ⟦DIPLOM(A) + -ATE[2]⟧ a doctor who is certified as a specialist by an examining board in a particular branch of medicine

dip·lo·mat·ic (dip′lə mat′ik) ***adj.*** ⟦Fr *diplomatique* < ModL *diplomaticus* < L *diploma* (gen. *diplomatis*), DIPLOMA⟧ **1** *a)* of official or original documents *b)* designating or of a copy or edition exactly reproducing an original document or manuscript **2** of or connected with diplomacy **3** tactful and adroit in dealing with people —***SYN.*** SUAVE —**dip′lo·mat′i·cal·ly** ***adv.***

diplomatic immunity exemption from local taxation, court action, etc. in a foreign country, granted by international law to all members of a diplomatic service, their families, etc.

dip·lont (dip′länt′) ***n.*** ⟦< DIPL(O)- + *-ont*, a cell, organism (< Gr *ontos*: see ONTO-)⟧ an animal or plant whose somatic nuclei are diploid

dip·lo·pi·a (dip lō′pē ə) ***n.*** ⟦ModL < Gr *diploos*, double + *ōps* (gen. *ōpos*); akin to *ops*, EYE⟧ a vision disorder in which a single object appears double; double vision —**dip·lop′ic** (-läp′ik) ***adj.***

dip·lo·pod (dip′lō päd′) ***n.*** ⟦< ModL *Diplopoda*, name of the class: see DIPLO- & -POD⟧ MILLIPEDE

di·plo·sis (di plō′sis, dī-) ***n.*** ⟦ModL < Gr *diplōsis*, a doubling⟧ doubling of the number of chromosomes through the fusion of two haploid sets in the union of gametes, resulting in the formation of the somatic chromosome number

dip needle a freely rotating, magnetized needle used to indicate the direction of the earth's magnetism: it is horizontal at the magnetic equator (*aclinic line*) but vertical at the magnetic poles

dip·no·an (dip′nō ən, dip nō′-) ***adj.*** ⟦< Gr *dipnoos*, double-breathed < DI-[1] + *pnoē*, breath (see PNEUMA) + -AN⟧ of various fishes that can respire by lungs as well as by gills —***n.*** a dipnoan fish

dip·o·dy (dip′ə dē) ***n., pl.*** **-dies** ⟦LL *dipodia* < Gr < *di-*, twice + *pous* (gen. *podos*), FOOT⟧ *Prosody* a metrical unit consisting of two feet —**di·pod·ic** (dī päd′ik) ***adj.***

di·pole (dī′pōl′) ***n.*** **1** *Physics* any system having two equal but opposite electric charges or magnetic poles separated by a very small distance **2** *Chem.* a polar molecule in which the centers of positive and negative charge are separated **3** a radio or television antenna that is a single linear conductor (commonly equal in length to one half the wavelength at the frequency employed) separated at the center as by a transmission line feed: in full **dipole antenna** —**di·po′lar** (-pō′lər) ***adj.***

dip·per (dip′ər) ***n.*** **1** a person whose work is dipping something in liquid ☆**2** a long-handled cup or similar container for dipping **3** any of a family (Cinclidae) of passerine birds living near swift streams in which they wade and dive in search of insects, larvae, etc.; water ouzel **4** [**D-**] *see* BIG DIPPER, LITTLE DIPPER —**dip′per·ful′** ***n., pl.*** **-fuls′**

dip·py (dip′ē) ***adj.*** **-pi·er, -pi·est** [Slang] foolish, eccentric, or crazy

di·pro·pel·lant (dī′prō pel′ənt) ***n.*** BIPROPELLANT

dip·shit (dip′shit′) ***n.*** [Slang] a person thought of as being contemptible, weak, stupid, worthless, etc.; jerk: somewhat vulgar

dip·so (dip′sō) ***n.*** [Slang] a dipsomaniac

dip·so·ma·ni·a (dip′sə mā′nē ə, -mān′yə) ***n.*** ⟦ModL < Gr *dipsa*, thirst + -MANIA⟧ *former technical term for* ALCOHOLISM (sense 1) —**dip′so·ma′ni·ac′** (-ak′) ***n.*** —**dip′so·ma·ni′a·cal** (-mə nī′ə kəl) ***adj.***

dip·stick (dip′stik′) ***n.*** a graduated metal rod for measuring the depth of a substance in its container, as of oil in a crankcase

dipt (dipt) ***vt., vi.*** *occas. pt. & pp. of* DIP

dip·ter·al (dip′tər əl) ***adj.*** *Archit.* surrounded by a double row of columns

dip·ter·an (dip′tər ən) ***n.*** ⟦< ModL *Diptera* < neut. pl. of Gr *dipteros*: see fol.⟧ any of a large order (Diptera) of insects, including the true flies, mosquitoes, and gnats, usually having one pair of functional, membranous wings and a vestigial second pair used as a balancing organ

dip·ter·ous (dip′tər əs) ***adj.*** ⟦ModL *dipterus* < Gr *dipteros*: see DI-[1] & PTERO- & -OUS⟧ **1** having two wings, as some insects, or two winglike appendages, as some seeds **2** of the dipterans

dip·tych (dip′tik′) ***n.*** ⟦LL *diptycha*, writing tablet of two leaves < Gr, neut. pl. of *diptychos*, folded < *di-*, twice + *ptychē*, a fold < *ptyssein*, to fold⟧ **1** an ancient writing tablet made up of a hinged pair of wooden or ivory pieces folding to protect the inner waxed writing surfaces **2** a picture painted or carved on two hinged tablets **3** anything consisting of two parallel or contrasting parts

dir *abbrev.* director

Di·rac (di rak′), **Paul (Adrien Maurice)** 1902-84; Eng. mathematician & nuclear physicist

dir·dum (dir′dəm, dʉr′-) ***n.*** ⟦ME *durdom* < Celt, as in Ir *deardan*, tempest, Welsh *dwrdd*, noise < IE base **dor-d-*, echoic⟧ [Scot. or North Eng.] an uproar, as of censure

dire (dīr) ***adj.*** **dir′er, dir′est** ⟦L *dirus*, fearful < IE base **dwei-*, to fear > Gr *deimos*, panic⟧ **1** arousing terror or causing extreme distress; dreadful; terrible **2** calling for quick action; urgent *[a dire need]* —**dire′ly** ***adv.*** —**dire′ness** ***n.***

di·rect (də rekt′; *also* dī-) ***adj.*** ⟦ME < L *directus*, pp. of *dirigere*, to lay straight, direct < *di-*, apart, from + *regere*, to keep straight, rule: see REGAL⟧ **1** by the shortest way, without turning or stopping; not roundabout; not interrupted; straight *[a direct route]* **2** honest and to the point; straightforward; frank *[a direct answer]* **3** with nothing or no one between; immediate; close, firsthand, or personal *[direct contact, direct knowledge, direct marketing]* **4** in an unbroken line of descent; lineal **5** exact; complete; absolute *[the direct opposite]* **6** in the exact words of the speaker *[a direct quotation]* **7** not needing a mordant: said of certain dyes **8** by or of action of the people through popular vote instead of through representatives or delegates **9** *Astron.* from west to east: opposed to RETROGRADE **10** *Math.* designating or of a relation between variables in which one increases or decreases with the other *[a direct proportion]*: opposed to INVERSE —***vt.*** **1** to manage the affairs, course, or action of; guide; conduct; regulate **2** to order or command with authority **3** to turn or point (a person or thing) toward an object or goal; aim; head **4** to tell (a person) the way to a place **5** to address (words, remarks, etc.) to a specific person or persons, or in a specific direction **6** to write the name and address on (a letter, etc.) **7** *a)* to plan the action and effects of (a play, film, etc.) and to supervise and instruct (the actors and technicians) in the carrying out of such a plan *b)* to rehearse and conduct the performance of (a choir, band, etc.) —***vi.*** **1** to give directions; make a practice of directing **2** to be a director, as of a group of performers —***adv.*** in a direct manner; directly —***SYN.*** COMMAND, CONDUCT —**di·rect′ness** ***n.***

direct action action aimed directly at achieving an objective; esp., the use of strikes, demonstrations, civil disobedience, etc. in disputes or struggles for rights

direct broadcast satellite a system for relaying television or radio broadcasts from geostationary satellites to small dish antennas connected to the receivers of individual customers

direct current an electric current flowing in one direction: abbrev. *DC*: cf. ALTERNATING CURRENT

di·rect·ed (də rek′tid; *also* dī-) ***adj.*** indicated either as being positive or negative, as a number or angle, or as having an assigned direction, as a segment or vector

di·rec·tion (də rek′shən; *also* dī-) ***n.*** ⟦ME *direccioun* < L *directio*⟧ **1** the act of directing; management; supervision **2** [*usually pl.*] instructions for doing, operating, using, preparing, etc. **3** an authoritative order or command **4** the point toward which something faces or the line along which something moves or lies *["north," "up," "forward," and "left" are directions]* **5** an aspect, line of development, way, trend, etc. *[research in new directions]* **6** *Theater a)* the director's plan for achieving certain effects, as of acting, lighting, etc. *b)* the instructions for this to the actors and others **7** *Music a)* a word, phrase, or sign showing how a note, passage, etc. is to be played *b)* the work or art of directing a choir, band, etc.

di·rec·tion·al (-shə nəl) ***adj.*** **1** of, aimed at, or indicating (a specific) direction **2** designed for radiating or receiving radio signals most effectively in one or more particular directions *[a directional antenna]* **3** designed to pick up or send out sound most efficiently in one direction —**di·rec′tion·al′i·ty** (-nal′ə tē) ***n.*** —**di·rec′tion·al·ly** ***adv.***

direction finder a device for finding out the direction from which radio waves or signals are coming, as a loop antenna that can be rotated freely on a vertical axis

di·rec·tive (də rek′tiv; *also* dī-) ***adj.*** **1** directing; tending or intended to direct **2** indicating direction —***n.*** a general instruction or order issued authoritatively

di·rect·ly (də rekt′lē; *also* dī-) ***adv.*** **1** in a direct way or line; straight **2** with nothing or no one between *[directly responsible]* **3** exactly; completely *[directly opposite]* **4** *a)* instantly; right away *b)* fairly soon; shortly —***conj.*** [Chiefly Brit.] as soon as

☆**direct mail** advertisements, solicitations, etc. mailed directly to a large number of individuals

direct marketing marketing by means of direct contact with potential clients or customers, as by direct mail, telephone solicitation, door-to-door selling, etc.

direct object *Gram.* the word or words denoting the thing or person that receives the action of a transitive verb; goal or result of a verbal action (Ex.: *ball* in "he hit the ball")

Di·rec·toire (dē′rek twär′) ***n.*** ⟦Fr < ML *directorium*: see DIRECTORY⟧ an executive body of five men in the First Republic in France, given office Oct. 27, 1795, and ousted Nov. 9, 1799 —***adj.*** designating or of a style of furniture, dress, etc. of the time of the Directoire, characterized by simple neoclassical lines

di·rec·tor (də rek′tər; *also* dī-) ***n.*** ⟦Anglo-Fr *directour* < LL *director*⟧ a person or thing that directs or controls; specif., *a)* the head of a project, bureau, school, etc.; supervisor *b)* a member of a board chosen to direct the affairs of a corporation or institution ☆*c)* a person who directs a play, film, etc. *d)* *Music* a conductor —**di·rec′tor·ship′** ***n.***

di·rec·tor·ate (-it) ***n.*** **1** the position of director **2** a board of directors

di·rec·to·ri·al (dī′rek tôr′ē əl, də rek′-) ***adj.*** **1** of a director or directorate **2** of directing or management

director's chair ⟦from its use on the set by film directors⟧ a lightweight folding armchair, usually a wooden or metal frame with a canvas back and seat

di·rec·to·ry (də rek′tə rē; *also* dī-) *adj.* ⟦LL *directorius*⟧ directing, guiding, or advising —*n., pl.* **-ries** ⟦ML *directorium* < LL *directorius*⟧ **1** a book of directions, as for church service **2** a book listing the names, addresses, etc. of a specific group of persons [*a telephone directory*] **3** *Comput. a)* a grouping of files that are stored on a disk, diskette, etc. *b)* a listing of such files **4** a directorate **5** [**D-**] DIRECTOIRE

☆**direct primary election** a preliminary election at which candidates for public office are chosen by direct vote of the people instead of by delegates at a convention: in a *closed primary,* voters must declare party affiliation and may vote only for candidates of their party

☆**di·rec·tress** (də rek′tris) *n.* a woman who is a director: see -ESS

di·rec·trice (dē rek trēs′; *E* də rek′tris) *n.* ⟦Fr⟧ [*also in roman type*] a woman who directs or controls; specif., the female head of a business, school, etc.

di·rec·trix (də rek′triks; *also* dī-) *n., pl.* **-trix·es** or **-tri·ces′** (-trə sēz′) **1** [Rare] a woman director **2** *Geom. a)* a fixed line associated with a conic section and its focus and eccentricity *b)* the curve that bounds the base of a cone or cylinder

direct tax a tax levied directly on the person by whom it is to be paid, as an income tax or inheritance tax

Di·re Da·wa (dē′rā dou′ə) city in E Ethiopia: also written **Di′re·da′wa**

dire·ful (dīr′fəl) *adj.* dreadful; terrible —**dire′ful·ly** *adv.*

dirge (durj) *n.* ⟦ME < L *dirige,* imper. of *dirigere,* to DIRECT, the first word of an antiphon (Psalm 5:8) in the Office for the Burial of the Dead⟧ **1** a funeral hymn **2** a slow, sad song, poem, or musical composition expressing grief or mourning; lament

dir·ham (dir ham′) *n.* ⟦Ar < L *drachma,* DRACHMA⟧ **1** the basic monetary unit of: *a)* Morocco *b)* the United Arab Emirates: see the table of monetary units in the Reference Supplement **2** a monetary unit of: *a)* Libya, equal to $^1/_{1000}$ of a dinar *b)* Qatar, equal to $^1/_{1000}$ of a riyal

dir·i·gi·ble (dir′ə jə bəl, də rij′ə-) *adj.* ⟦ML *dirigibilis:* see DIRECT & -IBLE⟧ that can be directed or steered —*n.* an airship; esp., a zeppelin

dir·i·gisme (dir′ə zhiz′əm, dir′ə zhiz′əm; *Fr* dē rē zhēs′m′) *n.* ⟦Fr⟧ [*often in italics*] government control or intervention, esp. in business activity or the economy —**dir′i·giste′** (-zhist′, -zhēst′) *adj.*

dir·i·ment (dir′ə mənt) *adj.* ⟦< L *dirimens,* prp. of *dirimere,* to interrupt < *dis-,* apart + *emere,* to take: see REDEEM⟧ invalidating; nullifying: chiefly in *R.C.Ch.* **diriment impediment,** an obstacle to a marriage or a condition that invalidates a marriage

dirk (durk) *n.* ⟦so spelled by Dr. Johnson; earlier *dork, durk* < ?⟧ a long, straight dagger —*vt.* to stab with a dirk

dirl (dirl, durl) *vt., vi.* ⟦var. of Scot *thirl,* to pierce < ME *thirlen, thrillen:* see THRILL⟧ [Scot. or North Eng.] to vibrate or tingle

dirn·dl (durn′dəl) *n.* ⟦Ger *dirndl(kleid),* orig., (peasant) girl's (dress), dial. dim. of *dirne,* maid, girl < OHG *diorna,* servant girl, akin to OE *theow,* servant, slave⟧ **1** a kind of dress with a full skirt, gathered waist, and close-fitting bodice **2** a full skirt with a gathered waist: also **dirndl skirt**

dirt (durt) *n.* ⟦ME, by metathesis < *drit* < ON *drita,* excrement, akin to OE *dritan,* to excrete < IE base **dher-* (see DARK) > L *forire,* defecate⟧ **1** any unclean or soiling matter, as mud, dust, dung, trash, etc.; filth **2** earth or garden soil **3** anything common, filthy, or contemptible **4** dirtiness, nastiness, corruption, etc. ☆**5** obscene writing, speech, etc.; pornography ☆**6** malicious talk or gossip ☆**7** *Mining* the gravel, soil, etc. from which gold is separated by washing or panning —*adj.* ☆having a surface of compacted earth [*a dirt road*] —☆**do someone dirt** [Slang] to do harm to someone, as by deception or malicious gossip —**hit the dirt** [Slang] to drop to the ground

dirt·bag (durt′bag′) *n.* ☆[Slang] a physically or morally disgusting person

☆**dirt bike** an off-road motorbike with special tires, large fenders, etc.

dirt-cheap (-chēp′) *adj., adv.* [Informal] as cheap as dirt; very inexpensive(ly)

☆**dirt farmer** [Informal] a farmer who works his or her own land

☆**dirt-poor** (durt′poor′) *adj.* extremely poor; destitute

dirt·y (durt′ē) *adj.* **dirt′i·er, dirt′i·est** ⟦ME *dritti*⟧ **1** soiled or soiling with dirt; unclean **2** causing one to be soiled with dirt [*a dirty occupation*] **3** lacking luster or brilliance; dull, grayish, etc. [*a dirty green*] **4** obscene; pornographic; lewd [*dirty jokes*] **5** given to lechery or lustful thoughts [*a dirty mind, dirty old man*] **6** disagreeable or contemptible; mean; nasty [*a dirty coward*] **7** unfair; dishonest; unsportsmanlike [*a dirty player*] **8** unkind; malicious or malevolent [*dirty remarks*] ☆**9** producing much fallout: said of nuclear weapons **10** revealing anger or irritation [*a dirty look*] **11** squally; rough [*dirty weather*] ☆**12** [Slang] rasping, reedy, rough, etc. in tone [*a dirty trumpet*] — *vt., vi.* **dirt′ied, dirt′y·ing** to make or become dirty; soil; tarnish; stain —**a dirty shame** a very unfortunate circumstance —**dirt′i·ly** *adv.* —**dirt′i·ness** *n.*

SYN.—**dirty** is applied to that which is covered or filled with any kind of dirt and is the broadest of these terms [*a dirty face, a dirty room*]; **soiled** generally suggests the presence of superficial dirt in an amount sufficient to impair cleanness or freshness [*a soiled shirt*]; **grimy** suggests soot or granular dirt deposited on or ingrained in a surface [*a miner with a grimy face*]; **filthy** is applied to that which is disgustingly dirty [*filthy as a pigpen*]; **foul** implies extreme filth that is grossly offensive or loathsome because of its stench, putridity, or corruption [*foul air*] —**ANT. clean**

dirty bomb a nonnuclear bomb that has been packed with radioactive material so that it will contaminate a wide area when it explodes

dirty linen (*or* **laundry**) secrets or private problems, esp. those that could cause gossip

☆**dirty pool** [Slang] the use of unfair or dishonest tactics

dirty rice ⟦so named from its brownish color, produced by the giblets⟧ a Cajun dish of rice cooked with vegetables, chicken giblets, etc.

☆**dirty tricks** [Informal] unethical or illegal tactics, specif., such tactics used to discredit, harass, etc. one's political opponents

dirty word **1** an obscene or coarse word **2** any word or phrase considered unpleasant or offensive in a specific place or context

☆**dis**[1] (dis) *vt.* **dissed, dis′sing** ⟦DIS(RESPECT)⟧ [Slang] **1** to show disrespect for; insult **2** to express strong disapproval of; condemn

dis[2] *abbrev.* **1** discount **2** distance

Dis (dis) *n.* ⟦L, contr. < *dives,* rich, transl. of Gr *Ploutōn,* PLUTO⟧ **1** the god of the lower world; Pluto **2** the lower world; Hades

dis- (dis; *in some words,* diz) ⟦< ME or OFr or L; OFr *des-* < L *dis-* < IE **dis-* (< **dwis-,* twice, in two < base **dwi-*: see BI-[1]) > OE *te-,* OHG *zi-,* Goth *dis-*⟧ *prefix* **1** *forming verbs a)* away, apart [*dismiss, disperse*] *b)* to deprive of, expel from [*disfrock, disbar*] *c)* to cause to be the opposite of [*disable*] *d)* to fail, cease, refuse to [*dissatisfy, disappear, disallow*] *e)* to do the opposite of [*disjoin, disintegrate*] *f)* more so (used as an intensifier) [*disannul*] **2** *forming adjectives* not, the opposite of, un- [*dishonest, dissatisfied, displeasing*] **3** *forming nouns* opposite of, lack of [*disease, disunion*] In words of Latin origin it becomes *di-* before *b, d, g, l, m, n, r,* or *v;* and *dif-* before *f*

dis·a·bil·i·ty (dis′ə bil′ə tē, dis′-) *n., pl.* **-ties** **1** a disabled condition **2** that which disables, as an illness, injury, or physical handicap **3** a legal disqualification or incapacity **4** something that restricts; limitation; disadvantage

disability clause a clause in an insurance contract entitling a policyholder who becomes permanently disabled to cease premium payments without loss of life insurance, and sometimes to receive a specified indemnity

dis·a·ble (dis ā′bəl, dis′-) *vt.* **-bled, -bling** **1** to make unable, unfit, or ineffective; cripple; incapacitate **2** to make legally incapable; disqualify legally **3** *Comput.* to make (a device, a software function, etc.) inactive: opposed to ENABLE (sense 3) —**SYN.** MAIM —**dis·a′ble·ment** *n.*

dis·a·bled (-bəld) *adj.* **1** not in proper working order; out of commission [*a disabled ship*] **2** having a physical or mental disability —**the disabled** those who are physically or mentally disabled; the handicapped

dis·a·buse (dis′ə byōōz′) *vt.* **-bused′, -bus′ing** to rid (someone) of false ideas

di·sac·cha·ride (dī sak′ə rīd′) *n.* any of a group of sugars with a common formula, $C_{12}H_{22}O_{11}$, as sucrose, maltose, and lactose, which on hydrolysis yield two monosaccharides: see OLIGOSACCHARIDE

dis·ac·cord (dis′ə kôrd′) *vi.* ⟦ME *disacorden* < OFr *desacorder:* see DIS- & ACCORD⟧ to refuse to agree; disagree —*n.* lack of accord; discord; disagreement

dis·ac·cred·it (dis′ə kred′it, dis′-) *vt.* to cause to be no longer accredited or authorized

dis·ac·cus·tom (dis′ə kus′təm, dis′-) *vt.* ⟦OFr *desacostumer:* see DIS- & ACCUSTOM⟧ to cause to be no longer accustomed (*to* something); rid of a habit

dis·ad·van·tage (dis′əd van′tij) *n.* ⟦ME *disavauntage* < OFr *desavantage:* see DIS- & ADVANTAGE⟧ **1** an unfavorable situation or circumstance; drawback; handicap **2** loss or injury, as to reputation or credit; detriment —*vt.* **-taged, -tag·ing** to act to the disadvantage of —**at a disadvantage** in an unfavorable situation (for doing something)

dis·ad·van·taged (-ijd) *adj.* deprived of a decent standard of living, education, etc. by poverty and a lack of opportunity; underprivileged

dis·ad·van·ta·geous (dis′ad′vən tā′jəs) *adj.* causing or characterized by disadvantage; unfavorable; adverse; detrimental —**dis′ad′van·ta′geous·ly** *adv.*

dis·af·fect (dis′ə fekt′) *vt.* **1** [Archaic] to cause to lose affection **2** to make unfriendly, discontented, or disloyal, as toward the government or some other authority: usually in the pp. —**dis′af·fect′ed** *adj.* —**dis′af·fec′tion** *n.*

dis·af·fil·i·ate (dis′ə fil′ē āt′, dis′-) *vt., vi.* **-at′ed, -at′ing** to end an affiliation (with) —**dis′af·fil′i·a′tion** *n.*

dis·af·firm (dis′ə furm′, dis′-) *vt.* **1** to deny or contradict (a former statement) **2** *Law a)* to refuse to abide by (a contract, agreement, etc.); repudiate *b)* to reverse or set aside (a former decision) —**dis′af·firm′ance** *n.,* **dis′af′fir·ma′tion** (-af′ər mā′shən)

dis·af·for·est (dis′ə fôr′ist, dis′e fôr′-) *vt.* ⟦ML *disafforestare:* see DIS- & AFFOREST⟧ *Eng. Law* to reduce from the legal status of a forest to that of ordinary land

dis·ag·gre·gate (dis ag′rə gāt′) *vt.* **-gat′ed, -gat′ing** to break down, or separate into parts, as to classify or analyze [*to disaggregate census data according to household size*] —*vi.* to break up or apart —**dis·ag′gre·ga′tion** (-gā′shən) *n.* —**dis·ag′gre·ga′tive** (-gāt′iv) *adj.*

dis·a·gree (dis′ə grē′) *vi.* **-greed′, -gree′ing** ⟦LME *disagre* < OFr *desagreer:* see DIS- & AGREE⟧ **1** to fail to agree; be different; differ **2** to differ in opinion; often, specif., to quarrel or dispute **3** to be harmful or give distress or discomfort, specif. physical discomfort: followed by *with* [*a damp climate disagrees with me*]

dis·a·gree·a·ble (-ə bəl) *adj.* ⟦ME *disagreable* < OFr *desagreable:* see prec. & -ABLE⟧ **1** not to one's taste; unpleasant; offensive **2** hard to get along with; quarrelsome —**dis′a·gree′a·ble·ness** *n.* —**dis′a·gree′a·bly** *adv.*

dis·a·gree·ment (dis′ə grē′mənt) *n.* **1** refusal to agree or comply **2** failure to agree; difference; incongruity; discrepancy [a *disagreement* between accounts] 3 difference of opinion 4 a quarrel or dispute

dis·al·low (dis′ə lou′) *vt.* ⟦ME *disalouen* < Anglo-Fr *desalouer*, to blame, disapprove of: see DIS- & ALLOW⟧ to refuse to allow; reject as untrue, invalid, or illegal —**dis′al·low′ance** *n.*

dis·am·big·u·ate (dis′am big′yo͞o āt′) *vt.* **-at′ed, -at′ing** to remove the ambiguity from (an ambiguous utterance or form) —**dis′am·big′u·a′tion** *n.*

dis·an·nul (dis′ə nul′) *vt.* to cancel completely; annul

dis·ap·pear (dis′ə pir′) *vi.* ⟦ME *disaperen*: see DIS- & APPEAR⟧ 1 to cease to be seen; go out of sight 2 to cease being; go out of existence, use, etc.; become lost or extinct —*vt.* [Informal] to cause to disappear; specif., to kidnap and execute (persons) in a clandestine program of political terror: informal except in the political sense —*SYN.* VANISH —**dis′ap·pear′ance** *n.*

dis·ap·point (dis′ə point′) *vt.* ⟦ME *disapointen* < OFr *desapointer*: see DIS- & APPOINT⟧ 1 to fail to satisfy the hopes or expectations of; leave unsatisfied 2 to undo or frustrate (a plan, intention, etc.); balk; thwart —*vi.* to cause disappointment [her popular novels never *disappoint*] —**dis′ap·point′ing·ly** *adv.*

dis·ap·point·ment (-mənt) *n.* 1 a disappointing or being disappointed 2 a person or thing that disappoints

dis·ap·pro·ba·tion (dis′ap′rə bā′shən) *n.* disapproval

dis·ap·prov·al (dis′ə pro͞o′vəl) *n.* 1 failure or refusal to approve; rejection 2 unfavorable opinion; condemnation

dis·ap·prove (dis′ə pro͞ov′) *vt.* **-proved′, -prov′ing** 1 to have or express an unfavorable opinion of; consider (something) wrong; condemn 2 to refuse to approve; reject —*vi.* to have or express disapproval (*of*) —**dis′ap·prov′ing·ly** *adv.*

dis·arm (dis ärm′, dis′-) *vt.* ⟦ME *disarmen* < OFr *desarmer*: see DIS- & ARM[2]⟧ 1 to take away weapons or armaments from 2 to deprive of the ability to hurt; make harmless 3 to overcome the hostility of; make friendly —*vi.* 1 to lay down arms 2 to reduce or do away with armed forces and armaments

dis·ar·ma·ment (-är′mə mənt) *n.* 1 the act of disarming 2 the reduction of armed forces and armaments, as to a limitation set by treaty

dis·arm·ing (-ärm′iŋ) *adj.* 1 removing or allaying suspicions, fears, or hostility 2 making friendly or agreeable; ingratiating —**dis·arm′ing·ly** *adv.*

dis·ar·range (dis′ə rānj′, dis′ə rānj′) *vt.* **-ranged′, -rang′ing** to undo the order or arrangement of; make less neat; disorder

dis·ar·ray (dis′ə rā′) *vt.* ⟦ME *disaraien* < OFr *desareer*: see DIS- & ARRAY⟧ 1 to throw into disorder or confusion; upset 2 [Archaic] to undress —*n.* ⟦ME *disarai* < OFr *desarroi*⟧ 1 an untidy condition; disorder; confusion 2 a state of disorderly or insufficient dress —*SYN.* CONFUSION

dis·ar·tic·u·late (dis′är tik′yo͞o lāt′, dis′-) *vt.* **-lat′ed, -lat′ing** to separate at the joints; disjoint —*vi.* to become disjointed —**dis′ar·tic′u·la′tion** *n.*

dis·as·sem·ble (dis′ə sem′bəl, dis′ə sem′-) *vt.* **-bled, -bling** ☆to take apart —☆**dis′as·sem′bly** (-blē) *n.*

dis·as·so·ci·ate (dis′ə sō′shē āt′, -sē-) *vt.* **-at′ed, -at′ing** to sever association with; separate; dissociate —**dis′as·so′ci·a′tion** *n.*

dis·as·ter (di zas′tər) *n.* ⟦OFr *desastre* < It *disastro* < L *dis-*, negative prefix + *astrum*, a star (see ASTRAL): from astrological beliefs: cf. ILL-STARRED⟧ 1 any happening that causes great harm or damage; serious or sudden misfortune; calamity 2 an utter failure [his latest novel is a *disaster*]

SYN.—**disaster** implies great or sudden misfortune that results in loss of life, property, etc. or that is ruinous to an undertaking; **calamity** suggests a grave misfortune that brings deep distress or sorrow to an individual or to the people at large; **catastrophe** is specifically applied to a disastrous end or outcome; **cataclysm** suggests a great upheaval, esp. a political or social one, that causes sudden and violent change with attending distress, suffering, etc.

dis·as·trous (di zas′trəs) *adj.* ⟦Fr *désastreux*⟧ of the nature of a disaster; causing great harm, damage, etc.; calamitous —**dis·as′trous·ly** *adv.*

dis·a·vow (dis′ə vou′) *vt.* ⟦ME *disavouen* < OFr *desavoer*: see DIS- & AVOW⟧ to deny any knowledge or approval of, or responsibility for; disclaim; disown —**dis′a·vow′al** *n.*

dis·band (dis band′) *vt.* ⟦MFr *desbander*: see DIS- & BAND[1]⟧ 1 to break up (an association or organization) 2 to dismiss (a military force) from service —*vi.* to cease to exist or function as an organization; scatter; disperse —**dis·band′ment** *n.*

dis·bar (dis bär′, dis′-) *vt.* **-barred′, -bar′ring** to expel (a lawyer) from the bar; deprive of the right to practice law —*SYN.* EXCLUDE —**dis·bar′ment** *n.*

dis·be·lief (dis′bə lēf′, dis′bə lēf′) *n.* refusal to believe; absence of belief —*SYN.* UNBELIEF

dis·be·lieve (dis′bə lēv′, dis′-) *vt.* **-lieved′, -liev′ing** to refuse to believe; reject as untrue —*vi.* to refuse to believe (*in*) —**dis′be·liev′er** *n.*

dis·bud (dis bud′) *vt.* **-bud′ded, -bud′ding** to remove buds from the stems of (a plant), usually leaving only terminal buds, to ensure growth of large blooms —**dis·bud′ding** *n.*

dis·bur·den (dis burd′′n, dis′-) *vt.* 1 to relieve of a burden or of anything burdensome 2 to get rid of (a burden); unload —*vi.* to get rid of a burden —**dis·bur′den·ment** *n.*

dis·burse (dis burs′) *vt.* **-bursed′, -burs′ing** ⟦OFr *desbourser* < *des-*, DIS- + *bourse, borse*, purse: see DIS- & BOURSE⟧ to pay out; expend —**dis·burs′a·ble** *adj.* —**dis·burs′er** *n.*

dis·burse·ment (-burs′mənt) *n.* 1 the act of disbursing 2 money disbursed; expenditure

disc[1] (disk) *n.* 1 DISK 2 a phonograph record 3 OPTICAL DISC 4 *Biol.* any disk-shaped part or structure

disc[2] *abbrev.* 1 discount 2 discovered

dis·calced (dis kalst′) *adj.* ⟦< L *discalceatus*, unshod < *dis-*, not + *calceatus*, a sandal, shoe < pp. of *calceare*, to provide with shoes < *calceus*, a shoe: see CALCEIFORM⟧ barefooted, as members of certain religious orders

dis·cant (dis′kant′; *for v.* dis′kant′ *or* dis kant′) *n., vi.* DESCANT

dis·card (dis kärd′; *for n.* dis′kärd′) *vt.* ⟦OFr *descarter*, prob. < *des-* + *carte*: see DIS- & CARD[1]⟧ 1 *Card Games a)* to remove (a card or cards) from one's hand *b)* to play (a card not a trump and not in the suit led) when holding no cards in the suit led 2 to throw away, abandon, or get rid of as no longer valuable or useful —*vi. Card Games* to make a discard —*n.* 1 a discarding or being discarded 2 something discarded 3 *Card Games* the card or cards discarded

dis·car·nate (dis kär′nit) *adj.* ⟦< DIS- + L *caro* (gen. *carnis*), flesh: see CARNAL⟧ not having a physical body; disembodied; incorporeal

disc brake a brake, as on an automobile, that functions by causing two friction pads to press on either side of a disc rotating along with the wheel

dis·cern (di surn′, -zurn′) *vt.* ⟦ME *discernen* < OFr *discerner* < L *discernere* < *dis-*, apart + *cernere*, to separate: see HARVEST⟧ 1 to separate (a thing) mentally from another or others; recognize as separate or different 2 to perceive or recognize; make out clearly —*vi.* to perceive or recognize the difference —**dis·cern′i·ble** *adj.* —**dis·cern′i·bly** *adv.*

SYN.—**discern** implies a making out or recognizing of something visually or mentally [to *discern* one's motives]; **perceive** implies recognition by means of any of the senses, and, with reference to mental apprehension, often implies keen understanding or insight [to *perceive* a change in attitude]; **distinguish**, in this connection, implies a perceiving clearly or distinctly by sight, hearing, etc. [he *distinguished* the voices of men down the hall]; **observe** and **notice** both connote some measure of attentiveness and usually suggest use of the sense of sight [to *observe* an eclipse, to *notice* a sign]

dis·cern·ing (-iŋ) *adj.* having or showing good judgment or understanding; astute —**dis·cern′ing·ly** *adv.*

dis·cern·ment (-mənt) *n.* 1 an act or instance of discerning 2 the power of discerning; keen perception or judgment; insight; acumen

dis·charge (dis chärj′; *also, & for n. usually,* dis′chärj′) *vt.* **-charged′, -charg′ing** ⟦ME *dischargen* < OFr *descharger* < VL **discarricare*, to unload < L *dis-*, from + *carrus*, wagon, CAR[1]⟧ 1 to relieve of or release from something that burdens or confines; specif., *a)* to remove the cargo of (a ship); unload *b)* to release the charge of (a gun); fire *c)* to release (a soldier, jury, etc.) from duty *d)* to dismiss (a special committee) after it has reported to the legislature of which it is a part *e)* to dismiss from employment *f)* to release (a prisoner) from jail, (a defendant) from suspicion, (a patient) as cured, (a debtor or bankrupt) from obligations, etc. 2 to release or remove (that by which one is burdened or confined); specif., *a)* to unload (a cargo) *b)* to shoot (a projectile) *c)* to remove (dye) from cloth 3 to relieve oneself or itself of (a burden, load, etc.); specif., *a)* to throw off; send forth; emit [to *discharge* pus] *b)* to get rid of; acquit oneself of; pay (a debt) or perform (a duty) 4 *Archit. a)* to relieve (a wall, etc.) of excess pressure by distribution of weight *b)* to distribute (weight) evenly over a supporting part ☆5 *Elec.* to remove stored energy from (a battery or capacitor) —*vi.* 1 to get rid of a burden, load, etc. 2 to be released or thrown off 3 to fire; go off: said of a gun, etc. 4 to emit waste matter: said of a wound, etc. 5 to run: said of a dye 6 to lose or give off a stored electrical charge —*n.* ⟦OFr *descharge* < the v.⟧ 1 a discharging or being discharged 2 that which discharges, as a legal order for release, a certificate of dismissal from military service, etc. 3 that which is discharged, as pus from a sore 4 a flow of electric current across a gap, as in a spark or arc —*SYN.* FREE —**dis·charge′a·ble** *adj.* —**dis·charg′er** *n.*

discharge lamp *Elec.* a discharge tube, as with neon or mercury vapor, used as a lamp

discharge tube *Elec.* any of various devices in which a gas or metal vapor inside sealed glass is used to conduct current when voltage is applied

☆**disc harrow** *alt. sp. of* DISK HARROW

dis·ci·ple (di sī′pəl) *n.* ⟦ME < OFr *desciple* & OE *discipul*, both < L *discipulus*, learner, in LL(Ec), a disciple of Jesus < **discipere*, to comprehend < *dis-*, apart + *capere*, to hold (see HAVE): infl. by *discere*, to learn⟧ 1 a pupil or follower of any teacher or school of religion, learning, art, etc. 2 an early follower of Jesus, esp. one of the Apostles 3 [D-] a member of the Disciples of Christ —*SYN.* FOLLOWER —**dis·ci′ple·ship′** *n.*

☆**Disciples of Christ** a Protestant denomination, founded *c.* 1809 by Alexander Campbell, that makes the Bible the only basis for faith and practice, and baptizes by immersion

dis·ci·pli·nar·i·an (dis′ə pli ner′ē ən) *n.* a person who believes in or enforces strict discipline

dis·ci·pli·nar·y (dis′ə pli ner′ē; *Brit* dis′i plin′ə ri) *adj.* 1 of or having to do with discipline 2 that enforces discipline by punishing or correcting

dis·ci·pline (dis′ə plin) *n.* ⟦ME < OFr *descepline* < L *disciplina* < *discipulus*: see DISCIPLE⟧ 1 a branch of knowledge or learning 2 *a)* training that develops self-control, character, or orderliness and efficiency *b)* strict control to enforce obedience 3 the result of such training or control; specif., *a)* self-control or orderly conduct *b)* acceptance of or submission to authority and control 4 a system of rules, as for a church or monastic order 5 treatment that corrects or punishes —*vt.* **-plined, -plin·ing** 1 to subject to discipline; train; control **2** to punish —***SYN.*** PUNISH —**dis′ci·plin·a·ble** *adj.* —**dis′ci·plin·al** *adj.* —**dis′ci·plin·er** *n.*

dis·ci·plined (dis′ə plind) *adj.* having or characterized by discipline *[a disciplined* intellect*]*

☆**disc jockey** DJ

dis·claim (dis klām′) *vt.* ⟦ME *disclaimen* < Anglo-Fr *desclamer:* see DIS- & CLAIM⟧ **1** to give up or renounce any claim to or connection with **2** to refuse to acknowledge or admit; deny; repudiate —*vi.* to make a disclaimer

dis·claim·er (-ər) *n.* ⟦Anglo-Fr *desclamer,* inf. used as n.⟧ **1** a disclaiming; denial or renunciation, as of a claim, title, etc. **2** a refusal to accept responsibility; disavowal

dis·cla·ma·tion (dis′klə mā′shən) *n.* an act of disclaiming; renunciation; repudiation

dis·cli·max (dis klī′maks′) *n. Ecol.* a climax community disrupted and changed by continuous disturbance, esp. by humans or domestic animals

dis·close (dis klōz′) *vt.* **-closed′, -clos′ing** ⟦ME *disclosen* < base of OFr *desclore:* see DIS- & CLOSE[2]⟧ **1** to bring into view; uncover **2** to reveal; make known; esp., to expose (something secret or not generally known) **3** to reveal (dental plaque) as by applying a special coloring agent to the teeth —***SYN.*** REVEAL[1] —**dis·clos′er** *n.*

dis·clo·sure (-klō′zhər) *n.* **1** a disclosing or being disclosed **2** a thing disclosed; revelation

☆**dis·co** (dis′kō) *n.* ⟦shortened < DISCOTHÈQUE⟧ **1** *pl.* **-cos** a nightclub or public place for dancing to recorded music played by a disc jockey **2** a kind of dance music popular especially in the 1970s, having elements of soul music and a strong Latin American beat —*adj.* of discos, the music played there, etc. —*vi.* **-coed, -co·ing** to dance at a disco

dis·co- (dis′kō, -kə) ⟦< L *discus,* DISCUS⟧ *combining form* **1** disk-shaped; discoid **2** phonograph record *[discography]*

dis·cog·ra·phy (dis käg′rə fē) *n., pl.* **-phies** ⟦prec. + (BIBLIO)GRAPHY⟧ **1** the systematic cataloging of phonograph records **2** a list of the recordings of a particular performer, composer, composition, etc. —**dis·cog′ra·pher** *n.*

dis·coid (dis′koid′) *adj.* ⟦LL *discoides* < Gr *diskoeidēs,* disk-shaped < *diskos,* a disk + *-eidēs,* -OID⟧ **1** shaped like a disk **2** *Bot.* lacking ray flowers and having only tubular florets, as the inner part of a composite flower head Also **dis·coi′dal** —*n.* anything shaped like a disk

dis·col·or (dis kul′ər) *vt., vi.* ⟦ME *discolouren* < OFr *descolourer* < ML *discolorare* < L *discolor,* of another color: see DIS- & COLOR⟧ to change in color as by fading, streaking, or staining

dis·col·or·a·tion (dis kul′ə rā′shən, dis′kul ər ā′-) *n.* **1** a discoloring or being discolored **2** a discolored spot or mark

dis·col·our (-kul′ər) *vt., vi. Brit. sp. of* DISCOLOR

☆**dis·com·bob·u·late** (dis′kem bäb′yə lāt′) *vt.* **-lat′ed, -lat′ing** ⟦whimsical alteration and extension, prob. of fol.⟧ [Informal] to upset the composure of; disconcert: a usually humorous usage —**dis′com·bob′u·la′tion** *n.*

dis·com·fit (dis kum′fit) *vt.* ⟦ME *discomfiten* < OFr *desconfit,* pp. of *desconfire* < VL **disconficere* < L *dis-* + *conficere:* see CONFECT⟧ **1** [Archaic] to defeat; overthrow **2** to frustrate the plans or expectations of **3** to make uneasy; disconcert —***SYN.*** EMBARRASS

dis·com·fi·ture (-fi chər) *n.* ⟦ME < OFr *desconfiture*⟧ a discomfiting or being discomfited; frustration, confusion, etc.

dis·com·fort (dis kum′fərt) *n.* ⟦ME < OFr *desconfort* < *desconforter,* to discourage: see DIS- & COMFORT⟧ **1** lack of comfort; uneasiness; inconvenience **2** anything causing this —*vt.* to cause discomfort to; distress

dis·com·fort·a·ble (dis kumf′tər bəl, -kum′fər tə bəl) *adj.* ⟦ME < OFr *desconfortable*⟧ [Archaic] causing discomfort

dis·com·mend (dis′kə mend′) *vt.* [Rare] to express disapproval of

dis·com·mode (dis′kə mōd′) *vt.* **-mod′ed, -mod′ing** ⟦< DIS- + L *commodare,* to make suitable: see ACCOMMODATE⟧ to cause bother to; inconvenience

dis·com·mod·i·ty (-mäd′ə tē) *n., pl.* **-ties** [Archaic] inconvenience

dis·com·pose (dis′kəm pōz′) *vt.* **-posed′, -pos′ing 1** to disturb the calm or poise of; fluster; disconcert **2** [Now Rare] to disturb the order of —***SYN.*** DISTURB —**dis′com·po′sure** (-pō′zhər) *n.*

dis·con·cert (dis′kən sʉrt′) *vt.* ⟦OFr *desconcerter:* see DIS- & CONCERT⟧ **1** to frustrate (plans, etc.) **2** to upset the composure of; embarrass; confuse —***SYN.*** EMBARRASS —**dis′con·cert′ing** *adj.* —**dis′con·cert′ing·ly** *adv.*

dis·con·firm (dis′kən fʉrm′) *vt.* to declare (a theory, proposition, etc.) to be invalid —**dis·con′fir·ma′tion** (-kän′fər mā′shən) *n.*

dis·con·form·i·ty (dis′kən fôrm′ə tē, dis′-) *n.* ⟦ML *disconformitas:* see DIS- & CONFORMITY⟧ **1** [Archaic] lack of conformity **2** *Geol.* a type of unconformity with parallel layers of rock strata

dis·con·nect (dis′kə nekt′; *for n., usually* dis′kə nekt′) *vt.* to break or undo the connection of; separate, detach, unplug, etc. —*vi.* to become disconnected —*n.* **1** a disconnection, as in an electrical system **2** [Informal] a lack of communication or compatibility *[a disconnect* between her beliefs and her behavior*]* —**dis′con·nec′tion** *n.*

dis·con·nect·ed (-nek′tid) *adj.* **1** separated, detached, unplugged, etc. **2** broken up into unrelated parts; incoherent —**dis′con·nect′ed·ly** *adv.* —**dis′con·nect′ed·ness** *n.*

dis·con·so·late (dis kän′sə lit) *adj.* ⟦ME < ML *disconsolatus* < L *dis-* + *consolatus,* pp. of *consolari:* see DIS- & CONSOLE[1]⟧ **1** so unhappy that nothing will comfort; inconsolable; dejected **2** causing or suggesting dejection; cheerless —**dis·con′so·late·ly** *adv.* —**dis·con′so·late·ness** *n.,* **dis′con·so·la′tion** (-lā′shən)

dis·con·tent (dis′kən tent′) *adj.* ⟦ME⟧ DISCONTENTED —*n.* **1** lack of contentment; dissatisfaction; restless desire for something more or different: also **dis′con·tent′ment 2** a person who is discontented, esp. with social or political norms or conditions: *often used in pl.* —*vt.* to make discontented

dis·con·tent·ed (dis′kən tent′id) *adj.* not contented; wanting something more or different —**dis′con·tent′ed·ly** *adv.*

dis·con·tin·u·ance (dis′kən tin′yo͞o əns) *n.* ⟦ME < Anglo-Fr: see DISCONTINUE & -ANCE⟧ **1** a stopping or being stopped; cessation or interruption **2** *Law* the stopping of a legal action prior to trial, either voluntarily by the plaintiff or by order of the court

dis·con·tin·u·a·tion (-tin′yo͞o ā′shən) *n.* ⟦Fr < ML *discontinuatio*⟧ DISCONTINUANCE (sense 1)

dis·con·tin·ue (dis′kən tin′yo͞o) *vt.* **-ued, -u·ing** ⟦ME *discontinuen* < OFr *discontinuer* < ML *discontinuare:* see DIS- & CONTINUE⟧ **1** to stop using, doing, etc.; cease; give up **2** *Law* to effect a discontinuance of (a suit) —*vi.* to stop; end —***SYN.*** STOP

dis·con·ti·nu·i·ty (dis′kän tə no͞o′ə tē, -nyo͞o′-) *n., pl.* **-ties** ⟦ML *discontinuitas:* see prec. & -ITY⟧ **1** lack of continuity or logical sequence **2** a gap or break **3** *Math.* a value of the independent variable x of a mathematical function f(x) at which this function is not continuous

dis·con·tin·u·ous (dis′kən tin′yo͞o əs) *adj.* not continuous; broken up by interruptions or gaps; intermittent —**dis′con·tin′u·ous·ly** *adv.*

dis·co·phile (dis′kō fīl′, -kə-) *n.* an expert on, or collector of, phonograph records

dis·cord (dis′kôrd′; *for v., usually* dis kôrd′) *n.* ⟦ME < OFr *descorde* < L *discordia* < *discors* (gen. *discordis*), discordant < *dis-,* apart + *cor,* HEART⟧ **1** lack of concord; disagreement; dissension; conflict **2** a harsh or confused noise, as the sound of battle; clash; din **3** *Music* a lack of harmony in tones sounded together; inharmonious combination of tones; dissonance —*vi.* to disagree; clash

SYN.**—discord** denotes disagreement or lack of concord and may imply quarreling between persons, clashing qualities in things, dissonance in sound, etc.; **strife** stresses the struggle to win out where there is a conflict or disagreement; **contention** suggests verbal strife as expressed in argument, controversy, dispute, etc.; **dissension** implies difference of opinion, usually suggesting contention between opposing groups in a body —***ANT.*** **harmony, agreement**

dis·cord·ant (dis kôrd′'nt) *adj.* ⟦ME *discordaunt* < OFr *descordant,* prp. of *descorder:* see prec.⟧ **1** not in accord; disagreeing; conflicting **2** not in harmony; dissonant; clashing —**dis·cord′ance** *n.,* **dis·cord′an·cy** —**dis·cord′ant·ly** *adv.*

dis·co·thèque (dis′kə tek′) *n.* ⟦Fr < *disque,* disk, record (< L *discus:* see DISCUS) + *(biblio)thèque,* library < L *bibliotheca:* see BIBLIOTHECA⟧ DISCO (*n.* 1)

dis·count (dis′kount′; *for v., also* dis kount′) *n.* ⟦< OFr *desconter,* to count off < ML *discomputare:* see DIS- & COMPUTE⟧ **1** *a)* a reduction from a usual or list price *b)* a deduction from a debt, allowed for paying promptly or in cash **2** the interest deducted in advance by one who buys, or lends money on, a bill of exchange, promissory note, etc. **3** the rate of interest charged for discounting a bill, note, etc. **4** a discounting, as of a bill, note, etc. —*vt.* **1** to pay or receive the present value of (a bill of exchange, promissory note, etc.), minus a deduction to cover interest for the purchaser **2** to deduct an amount or percent from (a bill, price, etc.) **3** to sell at less than the regular price **4** *a)* to take (a story, statement, opinion, etc.) at less than face value, allowing for exaggeration, bias, etc. *b)* to disbelieve or disregard entirely; set aside as inaccurate or irrelevant **5** to lessen the effect of by anticipating; reckon with in advance —*vi.* to lend or sell with discounts —**at a discount 1** below the regular price; below face value **2** worth little; unwanted and easily obtained

dis·coun·te·nance (dis kount′'n əns) *vt.* **-nanced, -nanc·ing** ⟦DIS- + COUNTENANCE⟧ **1** to make ashamed or embarrassed; disconcert **2** to refuse approval or support to; discourage

dis·count·er (dis′koun tər) *n.* one that discounts; specif., DISCOUNT HOUSE

☆**discount house (*or* store)** a retail store that sells its goods for less than the regular or list prices

discount rate 1 DISCOUNT (*n.* 3) **2** the rate at which the Federal Reserve Banks discount or rediscount securities offered by member banks

dis·cour·age (di skʉr′ij) *vt.* **-aged, -ag·ing** ⟦ME *discoragen* < OFr *descoragier:* see DIS- & COURAGE⟧ **1** to deprive of courage, hope, or confidence; dishearten **2** to advise or persuade (a person) to refrain **3** to prevent or try to prevent by disapproving or raising objections or obstacles —*vi.* to become discouraged

dis·cour·age·ment (-mənt) *n.* ⟦OFr *descoragement*⟧ **1** a discouraging **2** the fact, state, or feeling of being discouraged **3** anything that discourages

dis·cour·ag·ing (-iŋ) *adj.* that discourages; disheartening; depressing —**dis·cour′ag·ing·ly** *adv.*

dis·course (dis′kôrs′; *also, & for v. usually,* dis kôrs′) *n.* ⟦ME & OFr *discours* < L *discursus,* discourse < pp. of *discurrere,* to run to and fro < *dis-,* from, apart + *currere,* to run: see CURRENT⟧ **1** communication of ideas, information, etc., esp. by talking; conversation **2** a long and formal treatment of a subject, in speech or writing; lecture; treatise; dissertation **3** [Archaic] ability to reason; rationality —*vi.* **-coursed′, -cours′ing 1** to carry on conversation; talk; confer **2** to speak or write (*on* or *upon* a subject) formally and at some length —*vt.* [Archaic] to utter or tell —***SYN.*** SPEAK —**dis·cours′er** *n.*

dis·cour·te·ous (dis kʉr′tē əs) *adj.* not courteous; impolite; rude; ill-mannered —***SYN.*** RUDE —**dis·cour′te·ous·ly** *adv.* —**dis·cour′te·ous·ness** *n.*

dis·cour·te·sy (dis kurt′ə sē) ***n.*** **1** lack of courtesy; impoliteness; bad manners; rudeness **2** *pl.* **-sies** a rude or impolite act or remark
dis·cov·er (di skuv′ər) ***vt.*** ⟦ME *discoveren* < OFr *descovrir* < LL *discooperire*, to discover, reveal: see DIS- & COVER⟧ **1** to be the first to find out, see, or know about **2** to find out; learn of the existence of; realize **3** to be the first nonnative person to find, come to, or see (a continent, river, etc.) **4** to bring to prominence; make famous **5** *a)* [Now Rare] to reveal; disclose; expose *b)* [Archaic] to uncover —***SYN.*** LEARN —**dis·cov′er·a·ble** ***adj.*** —**dis·cov′er·er** ***n.***
dis·cov·ert (dis kuv′ərt) ***adj.*** ⟦ME < OFr *descovert*, lit., not covered, hence not protected: see DIS- & COVER⟧ *Law* having no husband: said of a spinster, widow, or divorcée —**dis·cov′er·ture** (-ər chər) ***n.***
dis·cov·er·y (di skuv′ər ē, -skuv′rē) ***n.***, *pl.* **-er·ies** **1** the act of discovering **2** anything discovered **3** [Archaic] the act of revealing; disclosure **4** *Law* any pretrial procedures, as the taking of depositions, for compelling the disclosure of pertinent factual information
☆**Discovery Day** COLUMBUS DAY
dis·cred·it (dis kred′it) ***vt.*** **1** to reject as untrue; disbelieve **2** to be a reason for disbelieving or distrusting; cast doubt on [their earlier lies *discredit* anything they may say] **3** to damage the credit or reputation of; disgrace —***n.*** **1** absence or loss of belief or trust; disbelief; doubt **2** damage to one's reputation; loss of respect or status; disgrace; dishonor **3** something that causes disgrace or loss of status
dis·cred·it·a·ble (-ə bəl) ***adj.*** damaging to one's reputation or status; disgraceful —**dis·cred′it·a·bly** ***adv.***
dis·creet (di skrēt′) ***adj.*** ⟦ME & OFr *discret* < L *discretus*, pp. of *discernere*: see DISCERN⟧ careful about what one says or does; prudent; esp., keeping silent or preserving confidences when necessary —***SYN.*** CAREFUL —**dis·creet′ly** ***adv.*** —**dis·creet′ness** ***n.***
dis·crep·an·cy (di skrep′ən sē) ***n.***, *pl.* **-cies** ⟦ME *discrepauns* < OFr *discrepance* < L *discrepantia* < *discrepans*, prp. of *discrepare*, to sound differently < *dis-*, from + *crepare*, to rattle: see CRAVEN⟧ lack of agreement, or an instance of this; difference; inconsistency
dis·crep·ant (di skrep′ənt; *also* dis′krə pənt) ***adj.*** ⟦ME *discrepante* < L *discrepans*⟧ lacking agreement; differing; at variance; inconsistent —**dis·crep′ant·ly** ***adv.***
dis·crete (di skrēt′) ***adj.*** ⟦ME *discret*: see DISCREET⟧ **1** separate and distinct; not attached to others; unrelated **2** made up of distinct parts; discontinuous **3** designating or of an electronic circuit having separate transistors, resistors, etc. —**dis·crete′ly** ***adv.*** —**dis·crete′ness** ***n.***
dis·cre·tion (di skresh′ən) ***n.*** ⟦ME *discrecioun* < OFr *discrecion* < L *discretio*, separation (in LL, discernment) < *discretus*: see DISCREET⟧ **1** the freedom or authority to make decisions and choices; power to judge or act **2** the quality of being discreet, or careful about what one does and says; prudence **3** [Archaic] the action or power of discerning; judgment —**at one's discretion** as one wishes
dis·cre·tion·ar·y (-er′ē) ***adj.*** **1** left to or regulated by one's own discretion or judgment [an appointee with *discretionary* powers]: also **dis·cre′tion·al** **2** administered by a proxy [a *discretionary* investment account]
discretionary income the income a person has available for discretionary use after all mandatory obligations, as taxes, and all basic living costs, as for food and housing, have been paid: cf. DISPOSABLE INCOME
dis·crim·i·na·ble (di skrim′ə nə bəl) ***adj.*** that can be discriminated or distinguished
dis·crim·i·nant (-nənt) ***n.*** *Math.* an expression whose value or sign is used to classify functions
dis·crim·i·nate (di skrim′i nāt′; *for adj.*, -nit) ***vt.*** **-nat′ed**, **-nat′ing** ⟦< L *discriminatus*, pp. of *discriminare*, to divide, distinguish < *discrimen*, division, distinction < *discernere*: see DISCERN⟧ **1** to constitute a difference between; differentiate **2** to recognize the difference between; distinguish —***vi.*** **1** to see the difference (*between* things); distinguish **2** to be discerning **3** to make distinctions in treatment; show partiality (*in favor of*) or prejudice (*against*) —***adj.*** involving discrimination; distinguishing carefully —***SYN.*** DISTINGUISH
dis·crim·i·nat·ing (-nāt′iŋ) ***adj.*** **1** that discriminates; distinguishing **2** able to make or see fine distinctions; discerning **3** DISCRIMINATORY
dis·crim·i·na·tion (di skrim′i nā′shən) ***n.*** ⟦L *discriminatio*⟧ **1** the act of discriminating, or distinguishing differences **2** the ability to make or perceive distinctions; perception; discernment **3** *a)* partiality, or bias, in the treatment of a person or group, which is unfair, illegal, etc. *b)* an act, policy, pattern of behavior, etc. characterized by such partiality
dis·crim·i·na·tive (di skrim′i nāt′iv, -nə tiv) ***adj.*** **1** making fine distinctions; discerning **2** characterized by or showing partiality or prejudice; discriminatory
dis·crim·i·na·tor (-nāt′ər) ***n.*** **1** one that discriminates **2** *Radio* a circuit for demodulating frequency-modulated or phase-modulated carrier waves
dis·crim·i·na·to·ry (-nə tôr′ē) ***adj.*** **1** practicing discrimination, or showing prejudice **2** discriminating, or distinguishing
dis·cur·sive (di skur′siv) ***adj.*** ⟦ML *discursivus* < L *discursus*: see DISCOURSE⟧ **1** wandering from one topic to another; skimming over many apparently unconnected subjects; rambling; desultory; digressive **2** based on the conscious use of reasoning rather than on intuition —**dis·cur′sive·ly** ***adv.*** —**dis·cur′sive·ness** ***n.***
dis·cus (dis′kəs) ***n.***, *pl.* **dis′cus·es** or **dis·ci** (dis′ī′) ⟦L < Gr *diskos* < base of *dikein*, to throw, akin to *deiknynai*, to show, point out: see DICTION⟧ **1** a heavy disk, usually made of metal and wood, that is thrown for distance as a test of strength and skill **2** the throwing of the discus as a field event in track and field meets: in full **discus throw**

discus

dis·cuss (di skus′) ***vt.*** ⟦ME *discussen*, to examine, scatter < L *discussus*, pp. of *discutere*, to strike asunder, scatter < *dis-*, apart + *quatere*, to shake, beat: see QUASH[2]⟧ **1** [Obs.] to disperse; dispel **2** to talk or write about; take up in conversation or in a discourse; consider and argue the pros and cons of —**dis·cuss′a·ble** ***adj.***, **dis·cuss′i·ble** —**dis·cuss′er** ***n.***

SYN.—**discuss** implies a talking about something in a deliberative fashion, with varying opinions offered constructively and usually amicably, so as to settle an issue, decide on a course of action, etc.; **argue** implies the citing of reasons or evidence to support or refute an assertion, belief, proposition, etc.; **debate** implies a formal argument, usually on public questions, in contests between opposing groups; **dispute** implies argument in which there is a clash of opposing opinions, often presented in an angry or heated manner

☆**dis·cuss·ant** (-ənt) ***n.*** a person taking part in an organized discussion
dis·cus·sion (di skush′ən) ***n.*** ⟦ME *discussioun* < LL *discussio*⟧ the act of discussing; talk or writing in which the pros and cons or various aspects of a subject are considered —**under discussion** being discussed
dis·dain (dis dān′) ***vt.*** ⟦ME *disdeinen* < OFr *desdaignier* < VL **disdignare*, for LL *dedignare* < L *dedignari* < *dis-*, DIS- + *dignari*: see DEIGN⟧ to regard or treat as unworthy or beneath one's dignity; specif., to refuse or reject with aloof contempt or scorn —***n.*** the feeling, attitude, or expression of disdaining; aloof contempt or scorn —***SYN.*** DESPISE
dis·dain·ful (-fəl) ***adj.*** feeling or expressing disdain; scornful and aloof —***SYN.*** PROUD —**dis·dain′ful·ly** ***adv.*** —**dis·dain′ful·ness** ***n.***
dis·ease (di zēz′) ***n.*** ⟦ME *disese*, inconvenience, trouble, sickness < OFr *desaise*, discomfort < *des-*, DIS- + *aise*, EASE⟧ **1** any departure from health; illness in general **2** a particular destructive process in an organ or organism, with a specific cause and characteristic symptoms; specif., an illness; ailment **3** any harmful or destructive condition, as of society —***vt.*** **-eased′**, **-eas′ing** ⟦ME *disesen* < OFr *desaaisier* < the n.⟧ to cause disease in; infect or derange: usually in pp. —**dis·eased′** ***adj.***

SYN.—**disease** may apply generally to any deviation of the body from its normal or healthy state, or it may refer to a particular disorder with a specific cause and characteristic symptoms; **malady** usually refers to a deep-seated chronic disease, frequently one that is ultimately fatal; **ailment** refers to a mild, chronic disorder [the minor *ailments* of the aged]

dis·em·bark (dis′im bärk′, dis′im bärk′) ***vt.*** ⟦Fr *désembarquer*: see DIS- & EMBARK⟧ [Now Rare] to unload (passengers or goods) from a ship, aircraft, etc. —***vi.*** to go ashore from a ship or leave an aircraft or other means of transportation —**dis′em·bar·ka′tion** ***n.***
dis·em·bar·rass (dis′im bar′əs) ***vt.*** to rid or relieve of something embarrassing, annoying, entangling, perplexing, or burdensome
dis·em·bod·y (dis′im bäd′ē, dis′im bäd′ē) ***vt.*** **-bod′ied**, **-bod′y·ing** to free from bodily existence; make incorporeal —**dis′em·bod′ied** ***adj.*** —**dis′em·bod′i·ment** ***n.***
dis·em·bogue (dis′im bōg′) ***vt.***, ***vi.*** **-bogued′**, **-bogu′ing** ⟦Sp *desembocar*, to come out of the mouth of a river or haven < *des-* (L *dis-*), apart + *embocar*, to enter by the mouth < L *in*, in + *bucca*, cheek: see BUCCAL⟧ to pour out (its waters) at the mouth; empty (itself): said esp. of a stream, river, etc.
dis·em·bow·el (dis′im bou′əl) ***vt.*** **-eled** or **-elled**, **-el·ing** or **-el·ling** to take out the bowels, or entrails, of; eviscerate —**dis′em·bow′el·ment** ***n.***
dis·em·pow·er (dis′im pou′ər) ***vt.*** to take away or diminish the authority or influence of
dis·en·chant (dis′in chant′) ***vt.*** ⟦Fr *désenchanter*: see DIS- & ENCHANT⟧ **1** to set free from an enchantment or illusion **2** to make no longer pleased with or charmed by someone or something: often in the pp. [*disenchanted* with a once-favorite vacation spot] —**dis′en·chant′ment** ***n.***
dis·en·cum·ber (dis′in kum′bər) ***vt.*** ⟦OFr *desencombrer*: see DIS- & ENCUMBER⟧ to relieve of a burden; free from a hindrance or annoyance
dis·en·dow (dis′in dou′) ***vt.*** to deprive of endowment —**dis′en·dow′ment** ***n.***
dis·en·fran·chise (dis′in fran′chīz′) ***vt.*** **-chised′**, **-chis′ing** **1** to deprive of the rights of citizenship, esp. of the right to vote **2** to deprive of a privilege, right, or power —**dis′en·fran′chise′ment** (-chīz′mənt, -chiz-) ***n.***
dis·en·gage (dis′in gāj′) ***vt.*** **-gaged′**, **-gag′ing** ⟦OFr *desengagier*: see DIS- & ENGAGE⟧ to release or loosen from something that binds, holds, entangles, or interlocks; unfasten; detach; disentangle; free —***vi.*** to release oneself or itself; become disengaged
dis·en·gaged (-in gājd′) ***adj.*** **1** having no engagements; at leisure **2** set loose; detached **3** not in gear
dis·en·gage·ment (-in gāj′mənt) ***n.*** **1** a disengaging or being disengaged **2** freedom from obligation, occupation, etc.; ease; leisure **3** withdrawal from a stated policy, previous involvement or position, etc.; specif., withdrawal of military forces, political influence, etc. from an area
dis·en·tail (dis′in tāl′) ***vt.*** *Law* to free from entail
dis·en·tan·gle (dis′in taŋ′gəl) ***vt.*** **-gled**, **-gling** **1** to free from something

that entangles, confuses, etc.; extricate; disengage **2** to straighten out (anything tangled, confused, etc.); unravel; untangle —*vi.* to get free from a tangle —**dis′en·tan′gle·ment** *n.*

dis·en·thrall or **dis·en·thral** (dis′in thrôl′) *vt.* to free from bondage or slavery; liberate

di·sep·al·ous (dī sep′əl əs) *adj. Bot.* having two sepals

dis·e·quil·i·brate (dis′i kwil′i brāt′) *vt.* **-brat′ed, -brat′ing** to destroy the equilibrium in or of; throw out of balance —**dis′e·quil′i·bra′tion** *n.*

dis·e·qui·lib·ri·um (dis′ē′kwi lib′rē əm) *n., pl.* **-ri·ums** or **-ri·a** (-ə) lack or destruction of equilibrium, esp. in the economy

dis·es·tab·lish (dis′i stab′lish, dis′i stab′-) *vt.* **1** to deprive of the status of being established **2** to deprive (a state church) of official sanction and support by the government —**dis′es·tab′lish·ment** *n.*

dis·es·teem (dis′i stēm′, dis′i stēm′) *vt.* to hold in low esteem; dislike; despise; slight —*n.* lack of esteem; disfavor

di·seur (dē zör′) *n.* ⟦Fr, lit., speaker < base *dis-* of *dire* (L *dicere*), to say, speak⟧ an entertainer who performs monologues, dramatic impersonations, etc.

di·seuse (dē zöz′) *n.* ⟦Fr⟧ a woman *diseur*

dis·fa·vor (dis fā′vər) *n.* **1** an unfavorable opinion; dislike; disapproval **2** the state of being disliked or disapproved of [he fell into *disfavor* with his patron] **3** an unkind or harmful act; disservice —*vt.* to regard or treat unfavorably; slight

dis·fig·ure (dis fig′yər) *vt.* **-ured, -ur·ing** ⟦ME *disfiguren* < OFr *desfigurer* < *des-*, DIS- + *figurer* < L *figurare*, to fashion, form < *figura*, FIGURE⟧ to hurt the appearance or attractiveness of; deform; deface; mar

dis·fig·ure·ment (-mənt) *n.* **1** a disfiguring or being disfigured **2** anything that disfigures; blemish; defect; deformity Also **dis·fig′u·ra′tion** (-yə rā′shən)

dis·fran·chise (dis fran′chīz′) *vt.* **-chised′, -chis′ing** DISENFRANCHISE —**dis·fran′chise′ment** (-chīz′mənt, -chiz-) *n.*

dis·frock (dis fräk′) *vt.* DEFROCK

dis·gorge (dis gôrj′) *vt., vi.* **-gorged′, -gorg′ing** ⟦OFr *desgorger*: see DIS- & GORGE⟧ **1** to force (something swallowed) out through the throat; vomit **2** to give up (something) against one's will **3** to pour forth (its contents) —**dis·gorge′ment** *n.*

dis·grace (dis grās′) *n.* ⟦Fr *disgrâce* < It *disgrazia* < *dis-* (L *dis-*), not + *grazia*, favor < L *gratia*: see GRACE⟧ **1** the state of being in disfavor, as because of bad conduct **2** loss of favor or respect; public dishonor; ignominy; disrepute; shame **3** a person or thing that brings shame, dishonor, or reproach (*to* one, etc.) —*vt.* **-graced′, -grac′ing** ⟦Fr *disgracier* < It *disgraziare* < the n.⟧ **1** to bring shame or dishonor upon; be a discredit to; be unworthy of [to *disgrace* one's family] **2** to dismiss from a position of favor; punish by degrading; humiliate

dis·grace·ful (dis grās′fəl) *adj.* causing or characterized by disgrace; shameful —**dis·grace′ful·ly** *adv.* —**dis·grace′ful·ness** *n.*

dis·grun·tle (dis grunt′'l) *vt.* **-tled, -tling** ⟦DIS- + obs. *gruntle*, freq. of GRUNT⟧ to make peevishly discontented; displease and make sulky —**dis·grun′tle·ment** *n.*

dis·guise (dis gīz′) *vt.* **-guised′, -guis′ing** ⟦ME *disgisen* < OFr *desguiser*, to change costume: see DIS- & GUISE⟧ **1** to make appear, sound, etc. different from usual so as to be unrecognizable [to *disguise* one's voice] **2** to hide or obscure the existence or real nature of [to *disguise* an emotion] **3** [Obs.] to alter or disfigure —*n.* **1** any clothes, equipment, manner, etc. used for disguising **2** the state of being disguised **3** the act or practice of disguising Also [Now Rare] **dis·guise′ment** —**dis·guis′ed·ly** (-gīz′id lē) *adv.* —**dis·guis′er** *n.*

dis·gust (dis gust′) *n.* ⟦MFr *desgoust*, distaste < *des-* (see DIS-) + L *gustus*, a taste, relish: see GUSTO⟧ a sickening distaste or dislike; deep aversion; repugnance —*vt.* ⟦MFr *desgouster* < *des-* (see DIS-) + L *gustare*, to taste⟧ to cause to feel disgust; be sickening, repulsive, or very distasteful to —*vi.* to arouse disgust —**dis·gust′ed** *adj.* —**dis·gust′ed·ly** *adv.* —**dis·gust′ing** *adj.* —**dis·gust′ing·ly** *adv.*

dis·gust·ful (-fəl) *adj.* **1** causing disgust; disgusting **2** full of disgust —**dis·gust′ful·ly** *adv.*

dish (dish) *n.* ⟦ME < OE *disc*, dish, plate < PGmc *diskuz < L *discus*: see DISCUS⟧ **1** *a)* any container, generally rounded, shallow, and concave and of porcelain, earthenware, glass, plastic, etc. for serving or holding food *b)* [*pl.*] plates, bowls, saucers, cups, etc., collectively **2** *a)* the food in a dish *b)* a particular kind of food, or food prepared in a certain way [one's favorite *dish*] **3** a dishful **4** a dish-shaped object **5** *a)* the reflector of a DISH ANTENNA *b)* DISH ANTENNA **6** a dishlike concavity, or the amount of this **7** [Informal] a favorite thing; preference ☆**8** [Slang] a sexually attractive person, esp. a young woman ☆**9** [Slang] gossip, esp. when disparaging or malicious: often with *the* —*vt.* **1** to serve (food) in a dish: usually with *up* or *out* **2** to shape (an object, surface, or hole) like a dish: make concave: usually with *out* ☆**3** [Informal] *Sports* to pass (a ball or puck) to a teammate: often with *off* ☆**4** [Slang] to gossip about, esp. in a disparaging way **5** [Slang, Chiefly Brit.] to cheat, frustrate, ruin, etc. —*vi.* **1** to be or become dish-shaped; cave in ☆**2** [Slang] to gossip, esp. disparagingly —☆**dish it out** [Slang] to subject others to difficulty, criticism, hardship, ridicule, etc.

dis·ha·bille (dis′ə bēl′) *n.* ⟦Fr *déshabillé*, pp. of *déshabiller*, to undress < *dés-* (see DIS-) + *habiller*, to dress, altered (after *habit*: see HABIT) < OFr *abillier*, to prepare, orig., to dress a log < *bille*, log: see BILLET[2]⟧ **1** the state of being dressed only partially or in night clothes **2** [Now Rare] clothing worn in this state

dish antenna an antenna with a dish-shaped, usually concave parabolic, reflector, used to transmit or receive radio and TV signals, as from orbiting satellites

dis·har·mo·nize (dis här′mə nīz′) *vt., vi.* **-nized′, -niz′ing** to put or be out of harmony

dis·har·mo·ny (dis här′mə nē) *n.* absence of harmony; discord —**dis′har·mo′ni·ous** (-här mō′nē əs) *adj.*

dish·cloth (dish′klôth′) *n.* a cloth for use in washing dishes

☆**dishcloth gourd** **1** any of a genus (*Luffa*) of tropical vines of the gourd family, having thin-shelled, large, cylindrical fruits with dense fibrous interior tissues used for dishcloths or filters **2** this fruit

dis·heart·en (dis härt′'n) *vt.* to deprive of courage or enthusiasm; discourage; depress; daunt —**dis·heart′en·ing** *adj.* —**dis·heart′en·ing·ly** *adv.* —**dis·heart′en·ment** *n.*

dished (disht) *adj.* **1** dish-shaped; concave **2** farther apart at the top than at the bottom: said of a pair of wheels having camber

di·shev·el (di shev′əl) *vt.* **-eled** or **-elled, -el·ing** or **-el·ling** ⟦back-form. < fol.⟧ **1** to cause (hair, clothing, etc.) to become disarranged and untidy, as by pulling or loosening, etc.; tousle or rumple **2** to cause the hair or clothes of (a person) to become thus disarranged —**di·shev′el·ment** *n.*

di·shev·eled or **di·shev·elled** (-əld) *adj.* ⟦ME *discheveled* < OFr *deschevelé* (pp. of *descheveler*, to tousle < *des-*, DIS- + *chevel*, hair < L *capillus*) + *-ed*, -ED⟧ **1** disarranged and untidy; tousled; rumpled: said of hair, clothing, etc. **2** having disheveled hair or clothing

dish·ful (dish′fool′) *n., pl.* **-fuls′** as much as a dish holds

dis·hon·est (dis än′ist) *adj.* ⟦ME < OFr *deshoneste*, altered (after *des-*, DIS-) < L *dehonestus*: see DE- & HONEST⟧ not honest; lying, cheating, etc. —**dis·hon′est·ly** *adv.*

SYN.—**dishonest** implies the act or practice of telling a lie, or of cheating, deceiving, stealing, etc. [a *dishonest* official]; **deceitful** implies an intent to make someone believe what is not true, as by giving a false appearance, using fraud, etc. [a *deceitful* advertisement]; **lying** suggests only the act of telling a falsehood [curb your *lying* tongue]; **untruthful** is used as a somewhat softened substitute for lying, esp. with reference to statements, reports, etc. [an *untruthful* account] —*ANT.* **honest**

dis·hon·es·ty (dis än′is tē) *n.* ⟦ME *dishoneste* < OFr *deshonesté*⟧ **1** the quality of being dishonest; dishonest behavior; deceiving, stealing, etc. **2** *pl.* **-ties** a dishonest act or statement; fraud, lie, etc.

dis·hon·or (dis än′ər) *n.* ⟦ME *deshonour* < OFr *deshonor*: see DIS- & HONOR⟧ **1** *a)* loss of honor, respect, or reputation *b)* state of shame; disgrace; ignominy **2** a person, thing, or action that brings dishonor; discredit **3** the act of refusing or failing to pay a check, draft, bill of exchange, etc. —*vt.* **1** to treat disrespectfully; insult **2** to bring shame or discredit upon; disgrace **3** to violate the virginity or chastity of **4** to refuse or fail to pay (a check, draft, bill of exchange, etc.) —**dis·hon′or·er** *n.*

dis·hon·or·a·ble (-ə bəl) *adj.* causing or deserving dishonor; not honorable; shameful; disgraceful —**dis·hon′or·a·ble·ness** *n.* —**dis·hon′or·a·bly** *adv.*

☆**dish·pan** (dish′pan′) *n.* a pan or other shallow container in which dishes, cooking utensils, etc. are washed

☆**dishpan hands** dry, rough, reddened hands, as from washing many dishes

☆**dish·rag** (-rag′) *n.* DISHCLOTH

☆**dish towel** a towel for drying dishes

☆**dish·wash·er** (-wôsh′ər) *n.* **1** a machine for washing dishes, cooking utensils, etc. **2** a person, esp. an employee as of a restaurant, who washes dishes, etc.

dish·wa·ter (-wôt′ər) *n.* water in which dishes, cooking utensils, etc. are, or have been, washed

dish·y (dish′ē) *adj.* **dish′i·er, dish′i·est** [Slang] **1** [Chiefly Brit.] attractive, esp. sexually so ☆**2** full of dish, or gossip; gossipy

dis·il·lu·sion (dis′i lo͞o′zhən) *vt.* **1** to free from illusion or false ideas; disenchant **2** to take away the ideals or idealism of and make disappointed, bitter, etc. —*n.* DISILLUSIONMENT

dis·il·lu·sion·ment (-mənt) *n.* **1** an act of disillusioning **2** the fact or state of being disillusioned

dis·in·cen·tive (dis′in sen′tiv) *n.* a thing or factor that keeps one from doing something; deterrent

dis·in·cli·na·tion (dis′in′klə nā′shən) *n.* a dislike or lack of desire; aversion; reluctance

dis·in·cline (dis′in klīn′) *vt.* **-clined′, -clin′ing** to make unwilling or reluctant

dis·in·clined (-klīnd′) *adj.* unwilling; reluctant —*SYN.* RELUCTANT

dis·in·fect (dis′in fekt′) *vt.* ⟦Fr *désinfecter*: see DIS- & INFECT⟧ to destroy the harmful bacteria, viruses, etc. in or on; sterilize —**dis′in·fec′tion** *n.*

dis·in·fect·ant (dis′in fek′tənt) *adj.* ⟦Fr *désinfectant*⟧ disinfecting —*n.* anything that disinfects; means for destroying harmful bacteria, viruses, etc.

dis·in·fest (dis′in fest′, dis′in fest′) *vt.* to remove insects, small rodents, or other pests from —**dis·in·fes·ta·tion** (dis′in′fes tā′shən) *n.*

dis·in·fla·tion (dis′in flā′shən) *n.* a slowing of an inflationary trend in the general level of prices by means of fiscal or monetary policy; reduction of the rate of inflation —**dis′in·fla′tion·ar′y** *adj.*

dis·in·for·ma·tion (dis′in′fər mā′shən) *n.* false information spread deliberately, specif. by a government, in order to mislead enemies or to mold public opinion

dis·in·gen·u·ous (dis′in jen′yo͞o əs) *adj.* 1 not straightforward; not candid or frank 2 slyly deceptive or misleading, typically by means of a pretense of ignorance or unawareness —**dis′in·gen′u·ous·ly** *adv.* —**dis′in·gen′u·ous·ness** *n.*

dis·in·her·it (dis′in her′it) *vt.* ⟦altered (after INHERIT) < earlier *disherit*⟧ 1 to deprive (esp. an heir) of an inheritance or the right to inherit 2 to deprive of any right or established privilege —**dis′in·her′it·ance** *n.*

dis·in·te·grate (dis in′tə grāt′) *vt., vi.* **-grat′ed**, **-grat′ing** 1 to separate into parts or fragments; break up; disunite 2 to undergo or cause to undergo a nuclear transformation as a result of radioactive decay or a nuclear reaction —*SYN.* DECAY —**dis·in′te·gra′tive** *adj.* —**dis·in′te·gra′tor** *n.*

dis·in·te·gra·tion (dis in′tə grā′shən) *n.* 1 the act or process of disintegrating 2 *Nuclear Physics* any change in a nucleus of an atom, whether spontaneous or induced, in which one or more particles, photons, etc. are emitted

dis·in·ter (dis′in tʉr′) *vt.* **-terred′**, **-ter′ring** ⟦Fr *désenterrer*: see DIS- & INTER⟧ 1 to remove from a grave, tomb, etc.; dig up; exhume 2 to bring (something hidden) to light —**dis′in·ter′ment** *n.*

dis·in·ter·est (dis in′trist; -in′tər est′, -in′trəst) *n.* 1 lack of personal or selfish interest 2 lack of interest or concern; indifference

dis·in·ter·est·ed (dis in′tris tid; -in′tər est′id, -in′trəs tid) *adj.* 1 not influenced by personal interest or selfish motives; impartial; unbiased 2 uninterested; indifferent: this usage, a revival of an obsolete meaning, is objected to by some —*SYN.* INDIFFERENT —**dis·in′ter·est·ed·ly** *adv.* —**dis·in′ter·est·ed·ness** *n.*

☆**dis·in·ter·me·di·a·tion** (dis′in′tər mē′dē ā′shən) *n.* the withdrawal of funds from banks and savings institutions in order to invest them in government securities, commercial paper, etc. paying higher rates of interest

dis·in·vest·ment (dis′in vest′mənt) *n.* a diminution or expenditure of capital investment, as in the failure to replenish inventories or in the sale of a capital item

dis·in·vite (dis′in vīt′) *vt.* **-vit′ed**, **-vit′ing** to withdraw or cancel the invitation of (a person or organization) —**dis′in′vi·ta′tion** *n.*

dis·jec·ta mem·bra (dis jek′tə mem′brə) ⟦L⟧ scattered parts or fragments, as of an author's writings

dis·join (dis join′, dis′join′) *vt.* ⟦ME *disjoinen* < OFr *desjoindre* < L *disjungere*: see DIS- & JOIN⟧ to undo the joining of; separate; detach —*vi.* [Obs.] to become separated

dis·joint (dis joint′, dis′joint′) *adj.* ⟦ME < OFr *desjoint*, pp. of *desjoindre*: see prec.⟧ *Math.* of sets having no members in common —*vt.* to destroy the unity, connections, or orderliness of

dis·joint·ed (-id) *adj.* disconnected; without unity or coherence —**dis·joint′ed·ly** *adv.* —**dis·joint′ed·ness** *n.*

dis·junct (dis juŋkt′, dis′juŋkt′) *adj.* ⟦L *disjunctus*, pp. of *disjungere*: see DISJOIN⟧ 1 disjoined; separated 2 *Music* having to do with progression by intervals greater than a second 3 *Zool.* having the body sharply divided by deep furrows, as in the divisions into head, thorax, and abdomen in most insects

dis·junc·tion (dis juŋk′shən) *n.* ⟦ME *disjunccioun* < L *disjunctio*⟧ 1 a disjoining or being disjoined; separation: also **dis·junc′ture** (-chər) 2 *a)* *Logic* the relation between the alternatives of a disjunctive proposition *b)* a disjunctive proposition

dis·junc·tive (-tiv) *adj.* ⟦ME *disjunctif* < L *disjunctivus*⟧ 1 disjoining; separating or causing to separate 2 having to do with disjunction 3 *Gram.* indicating a contrast or an alternative between words, clauses, etc. [in "John or Bob may go, but their sister may not," "or" and "but" are *disjunctive* conjunctions] 4 *Logic* designating or including a compound proposition consisting of two alternatives joined by *or* —*n. Gram.* a disjunctive conjunction —**dis·junc′tive·ly** *adv.*

disk (disk) *n.* ⟦L *discus*: see DISCUS⟧ 1 a thin, flat, circular thing of any material 2 anything like this in form [the moon's *disk*] 3 any of the sharp, circular blades of a disk harrow 4 *Anat.* a layer of fibrous connective tissue with small masses of cartilage among the fibers, occurring between adjacent vertebrae 5 *Bot. a)* DISK FLOWER *b)* a circular nectary around the center of some flowers 6 a thin, flat, circular plate coated with ferromagnetic particles, on which computer data can be stored 7 DISC[1] 8 [Obs.] DISCUS

disk·ette (di sket′) *n.* FLOPPY DISK

disk flower any of the tubular flowers that make up the central disk of the flower head of a composite plant

☆**disk harrow** a harrow with sharp, revolving circular blades, used to break up soil for sowing

☆**disk jockey** DISC JOCKEY

disk wheel a wheel made solid from rim to hub instead of having spokes

dis·like (dis līk′) *vt.* **-liked′**, **-lik′ing** to have a feeling of not liking; feel aversion to; have objections to —*n.* 1 a feeling of not liking; distaste; aversion; antipathy 2 something disliked —**dis·lik′a·ble** *adj.*, **dis·like′a·ble**

dis·lo·cate (dis′lō kāt′) *vt.* **-cat′ed**, **-cat′ing** ⟦< ML *dislocatus*, pp. of *dislocare*: see DIS- & LOCATE⟧ 1 to put out of place; specif., to displace (a bone) from its proper position at a joint 2 to upset the order of; disarrange; disrupt

dis·lo·ca·tion (dis′lō kā′shən) *n.* 1 a dislocating or being dislocated 2 an imperfection in the atomic structure of a crystal, usually consisting of one or more missing or disordered atoms in the crystal lattice

dis·lodge (dis läj′) *vt.* **-lodged′**, **-lodg′ing** ⟦ME *disloggen* < OFr *deslogier*: see DIS- & LODGE⟧ to force from a position or place where lodged, hiding, etc.; drive out —*vi.* to leave a lodging place —**dis·lodg′ment** *n.*

dis·loy·al (dis loi′əl) *adj.* ⟦OFr *desloial*: see DIS- & LOYAL⟧ not loyal or faithful; faithless —*SYN.* FAITHLESS —**dis·loy′al·ly** *adv.*

dis·loy·al·ty (-tē) *n.* 1 the quality of being disloyal 2 *pl.* **-ties** a disloyal act

dis·mal (diz′məl) *adj.* ⟦ME, orig. n., evil days (of the medieval calendar) < OFr *dis mal* < ML *dies mali*, evil days: see DEITY & MAL-⟧ 1 causing gloom or misery; depressing 2 dark and gloomy; bleak; dreary 3 depressed; miserable —**dis′mal·ly** *adv.*

dismal science ⟦< use by Thomas CARLYLE in essay (1849)⟧ the science of economics: a humorous usage

Dismal Swamp marshy, forested region between Norfolk, Va., & Albemarle Sound, N.C.: *c.* 30 mi (48 km) long; traversed by a canal that is part of the Intracoastal Waterway

dis·man·tle (dis mant′'l) *vt.* **-tled**, **-tling** ⟦OFr *desmanteller*, to take off one's cloak: see DIS- & MANTLE⟧ 1 to strip of covering 2 to strip (a house, ship, etc.) of furniture, equipment, means of defense, etc. 3 to take apart; disassemble —*SYN.* STRIP[1] —**dis·man′tle·ment** *n.* —**dis·man′tler** *n.*

dis·mast (dis mast′) *vt.* to remove or destroy the mast or masts of

dis·may (dis mā′) *vt.* ⟦ME *dismayen* < Anglo-Fr **desmaier* < *des-*, intens. + OFr *esmayer*, to deprive of power < VL **exmagare* < L *ex-*, from + Gmc base **mag*, power: see MAIN⟧ to make apprehensive or discouraged, as by a problem or troublesome prospect —*n.* a feeling of discouragement or consternation, as at the prospect of trouble

SYN.—**dismay** suggests fear or, esp. in modern usage, discouragement at the prospect of some difficulty or problem which one does not quite know how to resolve [*dismayed* at his lack of understanding]; **appall** suggests terror or (now more commonly) dismay at a shocking but apparently unalterable situation [an *appalling* death rate]; **horrify** suggests horror or loathing (or, in a weakened sense, irritation) at that which shocks or offends one [*horrified* at the suggestion]; **daunt** implies a becoming disheartened in the performance of an act that requires some courage [never *daunted* by adversity]

dis·mem·ber (dis mem′bər) *vt.* ⟦ME *dismembren* < OFr *desmembrer*: see DIS- & MEMBER⟧ 1 to remove the limbs of by cutting or tearing 2 to pull or cut to pieces; separate into parts; divide up or mutilate —**dis·mem′ber·ment** *n.*

dis·miss (dis mis′) *vt.* ⟦ME *dismissen* < ML *dismissus*, pp. of *dismittere*, for L *dimittere*, to send away < *dis-*, from + *mittere*, to send: see MISSION⟧ 1 to send away; cause or allow to leave 2 to remove or discharge from a duty, office, position, or employment 3 to put out of one's mind [to *dismiss* one's fears] 4 to remove from consideration or reject as lacking in importance or value [to *dismiss* our suggestions as irrelevant] 5 *Law* to discontinue or reject (a claim or action) —*SYN.* EJECT —**dis·miss′i·ble** *adj.*

dis·miss·al (dis mis′əl) *n.* 1 a dismissing or being dismissed 2 an order for the dismissing of someone Also [Archaic] **dis·mis′sion** (-mish′ən)

dis·mis·sive (-mis′iv) *adj.* 1 [Rare] dismissing or expressing dismissal 2 haughty and contemptuous, condescending, etc. in dismissing from consideration —**dis·mis′sive·ly** *adv.*

dis·mount (dis mount′; *for vt. 1 & 3 often, & for n. usually*, dis′mount′) *vi.* to get off or down, as from a horse, bicycle, etc.; alight —*vt.* 1 to remove (a thing) from its mounting or setting 2 to cause to dismount, as from a horse 3 to take apart; dismantle —*n.* the act of dismounting

Dis·ney (diz′nē), **Walt(er Elias)** 1901-66; U.S. film producer, esp. of animated cartoons

Dis·ney·esque (diz′nē esk′) *adj.* in the manner or style of the animated films, theme parks, etc. of Walt Disney or his successors

Dis·ney·fy (diz′nē fī′) *vt.* **-fied′**, **-fy′ing** to transform (something) so that it has Disneyesque characteristics or qualities: often used negatively to suggest superficiality, kitsch, slick commercialization, etc. —**Dis′ney·fi·ca′tion** *n.*

☆**Dis·ney·land** (diz′nē land′) *n.* ⟦after an amusement center in Anaheim, Calif., created by Walt DISNEY⟧ a place or condition of unreality, fantasy, incongruity, etc.

dis·o·be·di·ence (dis′ō bē′dē əns, -ə bē′-) *n.* ⟦ME < OFr *desobedience*: see DIS- & OBEDIENCE⟧ refusal to obey; failure to follow rules, commands, etc.; insubordination

dis·o·be·di·ent (-ənt) *adj.* ⟦ME < OFr *desobedient*⟧ not obedient; refusing or failing to obey; insubordinate; refractory —**dis′o·be′di·ent·ly** *adv.*

dis·o·bey (dis′ō bā′, -ə bā′) *vt., vi.* ⟦ME *disobeien* < OFr *desobeir*: see DIS- & OBEY⟧ to refuse or fail to obey

dis·o·blige (dis′ə blīj′) *vt.* **-bliged′**, **-blig′ing** ⟦Fr *désobliger*: see DIS- & OBLIGE⟧ 1 to refuse to oblige or do a favor for 2 to slight; offend 3 to inconvenience; incommode —**dis′o·blig′ing** *adj.* —**dis′o·blig′ing·ly** *adv.*

dis·op·er·a·tion (dis′äp ər ā′shən) *n. Ecol.* a coaction that is harmful to the organisms involved

dis·or·der (dis ôr′dər) *n.* ⟦prob. < Fr *désordre*⟧ 1 a lack of order; confusion; jumble 2 a breach of public peace; riot 3 a disregard of system; irregularity 4 an upset of normal function; ailment —*vt.* 1 to throw into disorder; disarrange 2 to upset the normal functions or health of —*SYN.* CONFUSION

dis·or·dered (-dərd) *adj.* 1 put out of order; jumbled 2 not normal in health or function; ill

dis·or·der·ly (dis ôr′dər lē) *adj.* 1 not orderly; untidy; unsystematic 2 causing a disturbance; unruly; riotous 3 *Law* violating public peace, safety, or order —*adv.* [Archaic] in a disorderly manner —**dis·or′der·li·ness** *n.*

disorderly conduct *Law* any petty offense against public peace, safety, or order

disorderly house any establishment where offenses against public peace, safety, or order habitually occur; esp., a house of prostitution

dis·or·gan·ize (dis ôr′gə nīz′) *vt.* **-ized′**, **-iz′ing** ⟦Fr *désorganiser*: see DIS- & ORGANIZE⟧ to disrupt or break up the order, arrangement, or system of; throw into confusion or disorder —**dis·or′gan·i·za′tion** *n.*

dis·o·ri·ent (dis ôr′ē ent′) *vt.* ⟦Fr *désorienter*: see DIS- & ORIENT, *vt.*⟧ **1** to turn away from the east: see ORIENT (*vt.* 1 & 2) **2** to cause to lose one's bearings **3** to confuse mentally, esp. with respect to time, place, and the identity of persons and objects Also **dis·o′ri·en·tate′** (-ən tāt′), **-tat′ed**, **-tat′ing** —**dis·o′ri·en·ta′tion** *n.*

dis·own (dis ōn′) *vt.* to refuse to acknowledge as one's own; repudiate; cast off

dis·par·age (di spar′ij) *vt.* **-aged**, **-ag·ing** ⟦ME *disparagen* < OFr *desparagier*, to marry one of inferior rank < *des-* (see DIS-) + *parage*, rank < *per*, PEER[1]⟧ **1** to lower in esteem; discredit **2** to speak slightingly of; show disrespect for; belittle —**dis·par′ag·ing** *adj.* —**dis·par′ag·ing·ly** *adv.*

SYN.—to **disparage** is to attempt to lower in esteem, as by insinuation, invidious comparison, faint praise, etc.; to **depreciate** is to lessen (something) in value as by implying that it has less worth than is usually attributed to it [he *depreciated* her generosity]; **decry** implies vigorous public denunciation, often from the best of motives [to *decry* corruption in government]; **belittle** is equivalent to **depreciate**, but stresses a contemptuous attitude in the speaker or writer; **minimize** suggests an ascription of the least possible value or importance [don't *minimize* your own efforts] —*ANT.* **extol, praise, magnify**

dis·par·age·ment (-mənt) *n.* **1** a disparaging or being disparaged; detraction **2** anything that discredits

dis·pa·rate (dis′pə rət; *also* di spar′it) *adj.* ⟦L *disparatus*, pp. of *disparare*, to separate < *dis-*, apart, not + *parare*, to make equal < *par*, equal: see PAR[1]⟧ essentially not alike; distinct or different in kind; unequal —*SYN.* DIFFERENT —**dis′pa·rate·ly** *adv.* —**dis′pa·rate·ness** *n.*

dis·par·i·ty (di spar′ə tē) *n.*, *pl.* **-ties** ⟦Fr *disparité* < ML *disparitas* < L *dispar*, unequal: see DIS- & PAR[1]⟧ **1** inequality or difference, as in rank, amount, quality, etc. **2** unlikeness; incongruity

dis·part (dis pärt′) *vt.*, *vi.* ⟦prob. < It *dispartire* < L, to divide < *dis-*, apart, from + *partire*, to part, divide < *pars*, PART[2]⟧ [Archaic] to divide into parts; separate

dis·pas·sion·ate (dis pash′ə nət) *adj.* free from passion, emotion, or bias; calm; impartial —*SYN.* FAIR[1] —**dis·pas′sion** *n.* —**dis·pas′sion·ate·ly** *adv.*

dis·patch (di spach′; *for n., esp. 4-5, also* dis′pach′) *vt.* ⟦Sp *despachar* & It *dispacciare*, to send off, lit., to remove impediments, hence facilitate < OFr *despeechier* < *des-* (see DIS-) + *(em)peechier*, to impede < LL *impedicare*, to entangle < L *in-*, in + *pedica*, a shackle < *pes*, FOOT⟧ **1** to send off or out promptly, usually on a specific errand or official business **2** to put an end to; kill **3** to finish quickly or promptly **4** [Informal] to eat up quickly —*n.* **1** a dispatching; sending out or off **2** an act of killing **3** efficient speed; promptness **4** a message, esp. an official message **5** a news story sent to a newspaper or broadcaster, as by a correspondent —*SYN.* HASTE, KILL[1]

dis·patch·er (di spach′ər; dis′pach′-) *n.* **1** a person who dispatches ☆**2** a transportation worker who sends out trains, buses, trucks, etc., according to a schedule

dis·pel (di spel′) *vt.* **-pelled′**, **-pel′ling** ⟦ME *dispellen* < L *dispellere* < *dis-*, apart + *pellere*, to drive: see FELT⟧ to scatter and drive away; cause to vanish; disperse —*SYN.* SCATTER

dis·pen·sa·ble (di spen′sə bəl) *adj.* ⟦ML(Ec) *dispensabilis*⟧ **1** that can be dispensed, dealt out, or administered **2** that can be dispensed with; not important **3** open to DISPENSATION (sense 6) —**dis·pen′sa·bil′i·ty** *n.*

dis·pen·sa·ry (di spen′sə rē) *n.*, *pl.* **-ries** ⟦< ML *dispensarius*, one who dispenses, steward⟧ a room or place, as in a school, summer camp, or factory, where medicines and first-aid treatment are available

dis·pen·sa·tion (dis′pən sā′shən) *n.* ⟦ME *dispensacioun* < OFr *despensation* < L *dispensatio*, management, charge < pp. of *dispensare*, DISPENSE⟧ **1** a dispensing, or giving out; distribution **2** anything dispensed or distributed **3** the system by which anything is administered; management **4** any release or exemption from an obligation **5** *Law* the suspension of a statute in a specific case for extenuating reasons **6** *R.C.Ch.* an exemption or release from the provisions of a specific church law **7** *Theol.* *a)* the ordering of events under divine authority *b)* any religious system —**dis′pen·sa′tion·al** *adj.*

dis·pen·sa·to·ry (di spen′sə tôr′ē) *n.*, *pl.* **-ries** ⟦ML *dispensatorium* < LL *dispensatorius*, of management or control < L *dispensare*: see fol.⟧ **1** a handbook on the preparation and use of medicines; pharmacopeia **2** [Obs.] a dispensary

dis·pense (di spens′) *vt.* **-pensed′**, **-pens′ing** ⟦ME *dispensen* < OFr *despenser* < L *dispensare*, to pay out < pp. of *dispendere*, to weigh out < *dis-*, out + *pendere*, to weigh: see PENDANT⟧ **1** to give or deal out; distribute **2** to prepare and give out (medicines, prescriptions, etc.) **3** to administer [to *dispense* the law justly] **4** to exempt; excuse —*SYN.* DISTRIBUTE —**dispense with 1** to get rid of; do away with **2** to do without; manage without

dis·pens·er (di spen′sər) *n.* a person or thing that dispenses; specif., a container, machine, etc. designed to dispense its contents in handy units or portions

dis·peo·ple (dis pē′pəl) *vt.* **-pled**, **-pling** [Obs.] DEPOPULATE

di·sper·mous (dī spur′məs) *adj.* ⟦DI-[1] + -SPERMOUS⟧ *Bot.* having two seeds

dis·per·sal (di spur′səl) *n.* a dispersing or being dispersed; distribution

dis·perse (di spurs′) *vt.* **-persed′**, **-pers′ing** ⟦ME *dispersen* < L *dispersus*, pp. of *dispergere*, to scatter abroad < *dis-*, out + *spargere*, to scatter, strew: see SPARK[1]⟧ **1** to break up and scatter in all directions; spread about; distribute widely **2** to dispel (mist, etc.) **3** to break up (light) into its component colored rays —*vi.* to break up and move in different directions; scatter —*SYN.* SCATTER —**dis·pers′er** *n.* —**dis·pers′i·ble** *adj.*

disperse system a two-phase colloidal system consisting of the colloidal particles (**disperse phase**) and the medium in which they are suspended (**disperse medium**)

dispersing agent *Chem.* a surface-active substance added to a suspension, usually a colloid, to improve the separation of particles and to prevent settling or clumping: also **dis·per·sant** (di spurs′ənt) *n.*

dis·per·sion (di spur′zhən, -shən) *n.* ⟦ME *dispersioun* < OFr *dispersion* < L *dispersio*⟧ **1** a dispersing or being dispersed **2** the breaking up of light into component colored rays, as by means of a prism **3** the resolution of a complex electromagnetic radiation into components in accordance with some characteristic, as wavelength or energy **4** the variation or scattering of data around some average or central value **5** a colloidal system with its dispersed particles and the medium in which these are suspended **6** [D-] DIASPORA (sense 1)

dis·per·sive (di spur′siv) *adj.* dispersing or tending to disperse —**dis·per′sive·ly** *adv.*

dis·per·soid (di spur′soid) *n.* ⟦< E *disperse* (adj.), dispersed (ult. < L *dispersus*: see DISPERSE) + -OID⟧ a colloidal system, as an emulsion, in which the colloidal particles are quite small and well suspended in the disperse medium

dis·pir·it (di spir′it) *vt.* to lower the spirits of; make sad, discouraged, or apathetic; depress; deject —**dis·pir′it·ed** *adj.* —**dis·pir′it·ed·ly** *adv.*

dis·pit·e·ous (dis pit′ē əs) *adj.* ⟦ME < OFr *despiteus*: see DESPITE & -OUS⟧ [Archaic] without pity or mercy; ruthless

dis·place (dis plās′, dis′-) *vt.* **-placed′**, **-plac′ing** ⟦OFr *desplacer*: see DIS- & PLACE⟧ **1** to move from its usual or proper place **2** to remove from office; discharge **3** to take the place of; supplant or replace (a person or thing that one is the cause of or occasion for removing, pushing aside, etc.) [a ship *displaces* a certain amount of water, factory workers that have been *displaced* by machines] —*SYN.* REPLACE

displaced person a person forced from his or her country, esp. as a result of war, and left homeless elsewhere

dis·place·ment (dis plās′mənt, dis′-) *n.* **1** a displacing or being displaced **2** *a)* the weight or volume of a fluid displaced by a floating object; specif., the weight of water, in long tons, displaced by a ship *b)* the volume displaced by a stroke of a piston **3** the difference between a later position of a thing and its original position **4** *Geol.* the relative movement of rock strata on the two sides of a fault **5** *Psychiatry* a defense mechanism in which an emotion or idea, usually repressed, is transferred to another, more acceptable object

dis·plant (dis plant′) *vt.* [Obs.] to transplant, dislodge, or displace

dis·play (di splā′) *vt.* ⟦ME *displeien* < OFr *despleier* < L *displicare*, to scatter, unfold < *dis-*, apart + *plicare*, to fold: see PLY[1]⟧ **1** [Obs.] to unfold, spread out, or unfurl **2** to unfold to the eye; put or spread out so as to be seen; exhibit **3** to unfold to the mind; disclose; reveal **4** to print conspicuously, as in large or fancy type —*n.* **1** a displaying; exhibition **2** anything displayed; exhibit **3** showy exhibition; ostentation **4** *a)* a manifestation [a *display* of courage] *b)* a mere show of something that is not genuine [a *display* of sympathy] **5** *Zool.* the act or an instance of displaying [the peacock fans his showy tail feathers as part of a courtship *display*]: see the *vi.* **6** a visual representation of data, as on a computer video screen —*vi.* *Zool.* to engage in an instinctive behavior serving primarily as a signal to others —*adj.* designating printing type in larger sizes, used for headings, advertisements, etc. —*SYN.* SHOW —**dis·play′a·bil′i·ty** *n.* —**dis·play′er** *n.*

dis·please (dis plēz′, dis′-) *vt.*, *vi.* **-pleased′**, **-pleas′ing** ⟦ME *displesen* < OFr *desplaisir* < VL **displacere*, for L *displicere* < *dis-*, not + *placere*: see PLEASE⟧ to fail to please or to be disagreeable (to); annoy; offend; irritate

dis·pleas·ure (-plezh′ər) *n.* ⟦ME *displesir* < OFr *desplaisir*, inf. used as n.: see prec.⟧ **1** the fact or feeling of being displeased; dissatisfaction, disapproval, annoyance, etc. **2** [Archaic] discomfort, sorrow, trouble, etc. —*SYN.* OFFENSE

dis·port (di spôrt′) *vi.* ⟦ME *disporten*, to bear, support < OFr *desporter* < *des-* (see DIS-) + *porter* < L *portare*, to carry: see PORT[3]⟧ to indulge in amusement; play; frolic —*vt.* to amuse or divert (oneself) —*n.* [Archaic] a disporting; amusement; play

dis·pos·a·ble (di spō′zə bəl) *adj.* **1** that can be or is intended to be thrown away after use [*disposable* bottles] **2** that can be disposed of **3** available to use without restriction —*n.* something that can be or is intended to be disposed of, or thrown away, after use: *usually used in pl.*

disposable income the income a person has available for spending, saving, or investing after all taxes and other mandatory obligations have been paid: cf. DISCRETIONARY INCOME

dis·pos·al (di spō′zəl) *n.* **1** the act of disposing; specif., *a)* arrangement in a particular order [the *disposal* of furniture in a room] *b)* a dealing with matters or settling of affairs *c)* a giving away; transfer; bestowal *d)* a getting rid of **2** the power to dispose of **3** a device installed in the drain of a kitchen sink to grind up garbage that is then flushed down the drain —**at one's disposal** available to use as one wishes

dis·pose (di spōz′) *vt.* **-posed′**, **-pos′ing** ⟦ME *disposen* < OFr *disposer*, to put apart, hence arrange < perf. stem of L *disponere*, to arrange: see DIS- & POSITION⟧ **1** to place in a certain order or arrangement **2** to arrange (matters); settle or regulate (affairs) **3** to make willing; incline **4** to make susceptible or liable —*vi.* to have the power to arrange or settle affairs —**dispose of** 1 to deal with conclusively; settle 2 to give away or sell 3 to get rid of; throw away

dis·posed (-spōzd′) *adj.* inclined; having a certain tendency or inclination: often preceded by an adverb [to feel well-*disposed* toward someone]

dis·pos·er (di spō′zər) *n.* 1 a person or thing that disposes 2 DISPOSAL (sense 3)

dis·po·si·tion (dis′pə zish′ən) *n.* ⟦ME *disposicioun* < OFr *disposition* < L *dispositio* < *dispositus*, pp. of *disponere*, to arrange: see DIS- & POSITION⟧ 1 a putting in order or being put in order; arrangement [the *disposition* of the troops] 2 management or settlement of affairs 3 a selling or giving away, as of property 4 a getting rid of something [the *disposition* of wastes] 5 the power or authority to arrange, settle, or manage; control 6 an inclination or tendency [a *disposition* to quarrel] 7 one's customary frame of mind; one's nature or temperament —**dis′po·si′tion·al** *adj.*

SYN.—**disposition** refers to the normal or prevailing aspect of one's nature [a genial *disposition*]; **temperament** refers to the balance of traits that are manifested in one's behavior or thinking [an artistic *temperament*]; **temper** refers to one's basic emotional nature, esp. as regards relative quickness to anger [a hot *temper*, an even *temper*]; **character** is applied to the sum of moral qualities associated with a distinctive individual [a weak *character*] and, unqualified, suggests moral strength, self-discipline, etc. [a man of *character*]; **personality** is applied to the sum of physical, mental, and emotional qualities that distinguish one as a person [a negative *personality*] and, unqualified, suggests attractiveness or charm [a girl with *personality*]

dis·pos·i·tive (dis päz′ə tiv) *adj.* ⟦< L *dispositus*, pp. of *disponere*, to arrange⟧ that disposes of, or settles, a dispute, question, etc.; conclusive; decisive

dis·pos·sess (dis′pə zes′) *vt.* to deprive of the possession of something, esp. land, a house, etc.; oust —**dis′pos·ses′sion** (-zesh′ən) *n.* —**dis′pos·ses′sor** *n.*

dis·po·sure (di spō′zhər) *n.* [Archaic] disposition or disposal (in various senses)

dis·praise (dis prāz′, dis′prāz′) *vt.* **-praised′**, **-prais′ing** ⟦ME *dispreisen* < OFr *despreisier*, to blame: see DIS- & PRAISE⟧ to speak of with disapproval or disparagement; censure —*n.* a dispraising; blame —**dis·prais′ing·ly** *adv.*

dis·prize (dis prīz′, dis′-) *vt.* **-prized′**, **-priz′ing** ⟦ME *disprisen* < OFr *despriser*, var. of *despreisier*: see prec.⟧ [Archaic] to regard as of low value; not prize

dis·proof (dis pro͞of′, dis′-; dis′pro͞of′) *n.* 1 the act of disproving; refutation 2 evidence that disproves

dis·pro·por·tion (dis′prə pôr′shən, dis′-) *n.* a lack of proportion; lack of symmetry; disparity —*vt.* to cause to be disproportionate —**dis′pro·por′tion·al** *adj.* —**dis′pro·por′tion·al·ly** *adv.*

dis·pro·por·tion·ate (-shə nət) *adj.* not proportionate; not in proportion —**dis′pro·por′tion·ate·ly** *adv.*

dis·prove (dis pro͞ov′) *vt.* **-proved′**, **-proved′** or **-prov′en**, **-prov′ing** ⟦ME *disproven* < OFr *desprover*: see DIS- & PROVE⟧ to prove to be false or in error; refute; confute —**dis·prov′a·ble** *adj.*

SYN.—**disprove** implies the presenting of evidence or reasoned arguments that demonstrate an assertion, etc. to be false or erroneous; **refute** implies a more thorough assembly of evidence and a more careful development of argument, hence suggests conclusiveness of proof against; **confute** suggests the overwhelming or silencing of a person by argument or proof; **controvert** implies a disputing or denying of statements, arguments, etc. in an endeavor to refute them; **rebut** stresses formality in refuting an argument, such as is observed in debate, court procedure, etc.

Dis·pur (dis′po͝or′) city in NE India: capital of Assam state

dis·put·a·ble (di spyo͞ot′ə bəl, dis′pyə tə bəl) *adj.* ⟦L *disputabilis*⟧ that can be disputed; debatable —**dis·put′a·bil′i·ty** *n.* —**dis·put′a·bly** *adv.*

dis·pu·tant (di spyo͞ot′'nt, dis′pyə tənt) *adj.* ⟦L *disputans*, prp. of *disputare*⟧ disputing —*n.* a person who disputes or debates

dis·pu·ta·tion (dis′pyo͞o tā′shən) *n.* ⟦ME *disputacioun* < L *disputatio*⟧ 1 the act of disputing; dispute 2 discussion marked by formal debate, often as an exercise

dis·pu·ta·tious (dis′pyo͞o tā′shəs) *adj.* inclined to dispute; fond of arguing; contentious: also **dis·pu·ta·tive** (dis pyo͞ot′ə tiv) —**dis′pu·ta′tious·ly** *adv.* —**dis′pu·ta′tious·ness** *n.*

dis·pute (di spyo͞ot′) *vi.* **-put′ed**, **-put′ing** ⟦ME *disputen* < OFr *desputer* < L *disputare*, lit., to compute, discuss, hence argue about < *dis-*, apart + *putare*, to think: see PUTATIVE⟧ 1 to argue; debate 2 to quarrel —*vt.* 1 to argue or debate (a question); discuss pro and con 2 to question the truth of; doubt 3 to oppose in any way; resist 4 to fight for; contest [to *dispute* every foot of ground] —*n.* 1 a disputing; argument; debate 2 a quarrel 3 [Obs.] a fight —*SYN.* ARGUMENT, DISCUSS —**beyond dispute** 1 not open to dispute or question; settled 2 indisputably —**in dispute** still being argued about; not settled

dis·qual·i·fy (dis kwôl′ə fī′, dis′-) *vt.* **-fied′**, **-fy′ing** 1 to make unfit or unqualified; incapacitate 2 to make or declare ineligible; take a right or privilege away from, as of further participation in a sport, for breaking rules —**dis·qual′i·fi·ca′tion** (-fi kā′shən) *n.*

dis·qui·et (dis kwī′ət, dis′-) *vt.* to make anxious, uneasy, or restless; disturb; fret —*n.* a disturbed or uneasy feeling; anxiety; restlessness —*adj.* [Archaic] restless; uneasy —**dis·qui′et·ing** *adj.* —**dis·qui′et·ing·ly** *adv.*

dis·qui·e·tude (-kwī ə to͞od′, -tyo͞od′) *n.* a disturbed or uneasy condition; restlessness; anxiety

dis·qui·si·tion (dis′kwi zish′ən) *n.* ⟦L *disquisitio* < *disquisitus*, pp. of *disquirere*, to investigate < *dis-*, apart + *quaerere*, to seek⟧ a formal discussion of some subject, often in writing; discourse or treatise

Dis·rae·li (diz rā′lē), **Benjamin** 1st Earl of Beaconsfield 1804-81; Brit. statesman & writer: prime minister (1868; 1874-80)

dis·rate (dis rāt′) *vt.* **-rat′ed**, **-rat′ing** to lower in rating or rank; demote

dis·re·gard (dis′ri gärd′) *vt.* 1 to pay little or no attention to 2 to treat without due respect; slight —*n.* 1 lack of attention; neglect 2 lack of due regard or respect —*SYN.* NEGLECT —**dis′re·gard′ful** *adj.*

dis·rel·ish (dis rel′ish) *n., vt.* dislike

dis·re·mem·ber (dis′ri mem′bər) *vt.* [Dial. or Informal] to forget; be unable to remember

dis·re·pair (dis′ri per′) *n.* the condition of needing repairs; state of neglect; dilapidation

dis·rep·u·ta·ble (dis rep′yo͞o tə bəl) *adj.* 1 not reputable; having or causing a bad reputation; discreditable 2 not fit to be seen; dirty, shabby, etc. —**dis·rep′u·ta·bly** *adv.*

dis·re·pute (dis′ri pyo͞ot′) *n.* lack or loss of repute; bad reputation; disgrace; disfavor

dis·re·spect (dis′ri spekt′, dis′ri spekt′) *n.* lack of respect or esteem; discourtesy —*vt.* to have or show lack of respect for

dis·re·spect·a·ble (-ə bəl) *adj.* not respectable

dis·re·spect·ful (-fəl) *adj.* having or showing lack of respect; discourteous; impolite; rude —**dis′re·spect′ful·ly** *adv.* —**dis′re·spect′ful·ness** *n.*

dis·robe (dis rōb′) *vt., vi.* **-robed′**, **-rob′ing** to undress

dis·rupt (dis rupt′) *vt., vi.* ⟦< L *disruptus*, pp. of *disrumpere*, to break apart < *dis-*, apart (see DIS-) + *rumpere*, to break: see RUPTURE⟧ 1 to break apart; split up; rend asunder 2 to disturb or interrupt the orderly course of (a social affair, meeting, etc.) —**dis·rupt′er** *n.*, **dis·rup′tor** —**dis·rup′tion** *n.*

dis·rup·tive (dis rup′tiv) *adj.* 1 causing disruption 2 produced by disruption —**dis·rup′tive·ly** *adv.*

disruptive discharge a sudden and large increase in electric current through an insulating medium, caused by failure of the medium under stress

☆**diss** (dis) *vt.* [Slang] *alt. sp. of* DIS[1]

dis·sat·is·fac·tion (dis′sat is fak′shən, dis sat′is-) *n.* 1 the condition of being dissatisfied or displeased; discontent 2 anything that dissatisfies

dis·sat·is·fac·to·ry (-tə rē) *adj.* not satisfactory; unsatisfactory

dis·sat·is·fied (dis′sat′is fīd′, dis-) *adj.* 1 not satisfied; displeased 2 showing dissatisfaction

dis·sat·is·fy (-fī′) *vt.* **-fied′**, **-fy′ing** to fail to satisfy; make discontented; displease

dis·seat (dis sēt′, dis′-) *vt.* [Archaic] UNSEAT

dis·sect (di sekt′; *also* dī sekt′, dī′sekt′) *vt.* ⟦< L *dissectus*, pp. of *dissecare*, to cut apart < *dis-*, apart + *secare*, to cut: see SAW[1]⟧ 1 to cut apart piece by piece; separate into parts, as a body for purposes of study; anatomize 2 to examine or analyze closely

dis·sect·ed (-id) *adj.* 1 cut up into parts 2 *Bot.* consisting of many lobes or segments, as some leaves 3 *Geol.* cut by erosion into valleys and hills [a *dissected* plateau]

dis·sec·tion (di sek′shən; *also* dī sek′-, dī′sek′-) *n.* ⟦LL *dissectio*⟧ 1 a dissecting or being dissected 2 anything dissected, as a plant or animal for study 3 analysis part by part; detailed examination

dis·sec·tor (-tər) *n.* 1 a person who dissects 2 an instrument used in dissecting

dis·seize (dis sēz′) *vt.* **-seized′**, **-seiz′ing** ⟦ME *disseisen* < Anglo-Fr *disseisir* < OFr *dessaisir*: see DIS- & SEIZE⟧ *Law* to deprive wrongfully of real property; dispossess unlawfully: also sp. **dis·seise′**

dis·sei·zee or **dis·sei·see** (dis′sē zē′, dis sē′zē′) *n.* *Law* a disseized person

dis·sei·zin or **dis·sei·sin** (dis sē′zin) *n.* ⟦ME *disseisine* < OFr *dessaisine* < *dessaisir*⟧ *Law* a disseizing or being disseized; unlawful dispossession from real property

dis·sei·zor or **dis·sei·sor** (-zər, -zôr′) *n.* ⟦ME *disseisour*⟧ *Law* a person who disseizes

dis·sem·ble (di sem′bəl) *vt.* **-bled**, **-bling** ⟦ME *dissemblen* < OFr *dessembler* < *des-*, DIS- + *sembler* < L *simulare*: see SIMULATE⟧ 1 to conceal under a false appearance; disguise [to *dissemble* fear by smiling] 2 [Obs.] to pretend to be in a state of; simulate; feign [to *dissemble* innocence] 3 [Obs.] to pretend not to notice; ignore —*vi.* to conceal the truth, or one's true feelings, motives, etc., by pretense; behave hypocritically —**dis·sem′blance** *n.* —**dis·sem′bler** *n.*

dis·sem·i·nate (di sem′ə nāt′) *vt.* **-nat′ed**, **-nat′ing** ⟦< L *disseminatus*, pp. of *disseminare*, lit., to scatter seed, hence disseminate < *dis-*, apart + *seminare*, to sow < *semen*, SEED⟧ to scatter far and wide; spread abroad, as if sowing; promulgate widely —**dis·sem′i·na′tion** *n.* —**dis·sem′i·na′tive** *adj.* —**dis·sem′i·na′tor** *n.*

dis·sem·i·nule (di sem′ə nyo͞ol′) *n.* ⟦prec. + -ULE⟧ *Biol.* a detachable plant organ or structure of an organism capable of being dispersed and of propagating, as a seed, resting egg, etc.

dis·sen·sion (di sen′shən) *n.* ⟦ME *dissencion* < OFr *dissension* < L *dissensio* < *dissensus*, pp. of *dissentire*: see DISSENT⟧ a difference of opinion; disagreement or, esp., discord as expressed in intense quarreling or wrangling, as within a group [*dissension* among party members]: often in **dissension in the ranks**, dissatisfaction with those in authority —*SYN.* DISCORD

dis·sen·sus (di sen′səs) ***n.*** ⟦prob. < DIS- + CONSENSUS⟧ lack of consensus; discord

dis·sent (di sent′) ***vi.*** ⟦ME *dissenten* < L *dissentire* < *dis-*, apart + *sentire*, to feel, think: see SEND⟧ **1** [Now Rare] to differ with another's opinion; disagree **2** to openly differ with or reject an official, esp. political, belief, procedure, etc. **3** to reject the doctrines and forms of an established church —***n.*** the act of dissenting; specif., *a)* the rendering of a minority opinion in the decision of a law case *b)* religious nonconformity —**dis·sent′ing** ***adj.*** —**dis·sent′ing·ly** ***adv.***

dis·sent·er (-ər) ***n.*** **1** a person who dissents **2** [*sometimes* **D-**] a British Protestant who does not belong to the Anglican Church; Nonconformist

dis·sen·tient (di sen′shənt) ***adj.*** ⟦L *dissentiens*, prp. of *dissentire*⟧ dissenting, esp. from the majority opinion —***n.*** a person who dissents; dissenter

dis·sen·tious (-shəs) ***adj.*** [Now Rare] of or inclined to dissension; quarrelsome; contentious

dis·sep·i·ment (di sep′ə mənt) ***n.*** ⟦L *dissaepimentum* < *dis-*, from + *saepire*, to fence in: see SEPTUM⟧ *Biol.* a separating membrane or partition, as that between adjacent carpels of a compound ovary

dis·ser·ta·tion (dis′ər tā′shən) ***n.*** ⟦LL *dissertatio* < L *dissertare*, to discuss, argue, freq. of *disserere* < *dis-*, apart + *serere*, to join: see SERIES⟧ a formal and lengthy discourse or treatise on some subject, esp. one based on original research and written in partial fulfillment of requirements for a doctorate: see THESIS

dis·serve (dis surv′, dis′-) ***vt.*** **-served′**, **-serv′ing** [Rare] to do a disservice to; harm

dis·serv·ice (-sur′vis) ***n.*** ⟦DIS- + SERVICE[1]⟧ **1** harmful action; injury **2** a harmful or unkind act

dis·sev·er (di sev′ər) ***vt.*** ⟦ME *disseveren* < OFr *dessevrer* < LL *disseparare* < L *dis-*, intens. + *separare*, to SEPARATE⟧ **1** to cause to part; sever; separate **2** to divide into parts —***vi.*** to separate or part; disunite —**dis·sev′er·ance** ***n.***, **dis·sev′er·ment**

dis·si·dence (dis′ə dəns) ***n.*** ⟦L *dissidentia* < *dissidens*, prp. of *dissidere*, to disagree < *dis-*, apart + *sidere*, SIT⟧ disagreement; dissent

dis·si·dent (-dənt) ***adj.*** ⟦L *dissidens*: see prec.⟧ not agreeing; dissenting —***n.*** a dissident person; dissenter —**dis′si·dent·ly** ***adv.***

dis·sil·i·ent (di sil′ē ənt) ***adj.*** ⟦L *dissiliens*, prp. of *dissilire*, to leap or burst apart < *dis-*, apart + *salire*, to leap: see SALIENT⟧ springing or bursting apart, as some plant capsules or pods

dis·sim·i·lar (di sim′ə lər, dis′-) ***adj.*** not similar or alike; different —**SYN.** DIFFERENT —**dis·sim′i·lar·ly** ***adv.***

dis·sim·i·lar·i·ty (dis′sim′ə lar′ə tē, dis′sim′-) ***n.*** **1** absence of similarity; unlikeness; difference **2** *pl.* **-ties** an instance or point of difference or unlikeness

dis·sim·i·late (di sim′ə lāt′) ***vt.*** **-lat′ed**, **-lat′ing** ⟦DIS- + (AS)SIMILATE⟧ **1** to make dissimilar **2** to cause to undergo dissimilation —***vi.*** to become dissimilar —**dis·sim′i·la′tive** ***adj.***

dis·sim·i·la·tion (di sim′ə lā′shən) ***n.*** **1** a making or becoming dissimilar **2** *Linguis.* a process of linguistic change in which one of two similar or identical phonemes within a word or phrase becomes unlike the other (Ex.: OFr *marbre* becomes Eng *marble*; L *peregrinus* becomes It *pellegrino*)

dis·si·mil·i·tude (dis′si mil′ə to͞od′, -tyo͞od′) ***n.*** ⟦ME < L *dissimilitudo* < *dissimilis*, unlike < *dis-*, not + *similis*, like⟧ dissimilarity; difference

dis·sim·u·late (di sim′yo͞o lāt′) ***vt., vi.*** **-lat′ed**, **-lat′ing** ⟦ME *dissimulaten* < pp. of L *dissimulare*: see DIS- & SIMULATE⟧ to hide (one's feelings, motives, etc.) by pretense; dissemble —**dis·sim′u·la′tion** ***n.*** —**dis·sim′u·la′tor** ***n.***

dis·si·pate (dis′ə pāt′) ***vt.*** **-pat′ed**, **-pat′ing** ⟦ME *dissipaten* < L *dissipatus*, pp. of *dissipare*, to scatter < *dis-*, apart + *supare*, to throw < IE base *swep- > Sans *svapū*, broom, LowG *swabbeln*, to SWAB⟧ **1** to break up and scatter; dispel; disperse **2** to drive completely away; make disappear **3** to waste or squander —***vi.*** **1** to be dissipated; disperse or vanish **2** to spend much time and energy on indulgence in pleasure, esp. drinking, gambling, etc., to the point of harming oneself —**SYN.** SCATTER —**dis′si·pat′er** ***n.***, **dis′si·pa′tor** —**dis′si·pa′tive** ***adj.***

dis·si·pat·ed (-id) ***adj.*** **1** scattered **2** squandered or wasted **3** characterized by, or showing the harmful effects of, dissipation

dis·si·pa·tion (dis′ə pā′shən) ***n.*** ⟦ME *dissipacioun* < L *dissipatio*: see DISSIPATE⟧ **1** a scattering or being scattered; dispersion **2** a wasting or squandering **3** an idle or frivolous amusement or diversion **4** indulgence in pleasure to the point of harming oneself; intemperance; dissoluteness

dis·so·ci·a·ble (di sō′shē ə bəl, -shə-) ***adj.*** ⟦Fr < L *dissociabilis*⟧ that can be dissociated; separable; distinguishable —**dis·so′ci·a·bil′i·ty** ***n.***

dis·so·cial (dis sō′shəl, dis′-) ***adj.*** unsocial or unsociable

dis·so·ci·ate (di sō′shē āt′; *also*, -sē āt′) ***vt.*** **-at′ed**, **-at′ing** ⟦< L *dissociatus*, pp. of *dissociare* < *dis-*, apart + *sociare*, to join < *socius*, companion: see SOCIAL⟧ **1** to break the ties or connection between; sever association with; separate; disunite **2** to cause to undergo dissociation —***vi.*** **1** to part company; stop associating **2** to undergo dissociation —**dissociate oneself from** to deny or repudiate any connection with

dis·so·ci·a·tion (di sō′sē ā′shən, -shē-) ***n.*** ⟦L *dissociatio*⟧ **1** a dissociating or being dissociated; separation **2** *Chem.* the breaking up of a compound into simpler components, as with heat or a solvent, frequently in a reversible manner so that the components may recombine **3** *Psychol. a)* a split in the conscious process in which a group of mental activities breaks away from the main stream of consciousness and functions as a separate unit, as if belonging to another person *b)* the abnormal separation of related ideas, thoughts, or emotions —**dis·so′ci·a′tive** ***adj.***

dissociative identity disorder MULTIPLE PERSONALITY DISORDER

dis·sol·u·ble (di säl′yə bəl) ***adj.*** ⟦L *dissolubilis* < *dissolvere*: see DISSOLVE⟧ that can be dissolved —**dis·sol′u·bil′i·ty** ***n.***

dis·so·lute (dis′ə lo͞ot′) ***adj.*** ⟦L *dissolutus*, loosened, lax, unrestrained; pp. of *dissolvere*: see DISSOLVE⟧ dissipated and immoral; profligate; debauched —**dis′so·lute′ly** ***adv.*** —**dis′so·lute′ness** ***n.***

dis·so·lu·tion (dis′ə lo͞o′shən) ***n.*** ⟦ME *dissolucioun* < L *dissolutio*⟧ a dissolving or being dissolved; specif., *a)* a breaking up or into parts; disintegration *b)* the termination, as of a business, association, or union *c)* the ending of life; death *d)* the dismissal of an assembly or adjournment of a meeting

dis·solve (di zälv′, -zôlv′) ***vt., vi.*** **-solved′**, **-solv′ing** ⟦ME *dissolven* < L *dissolvere*, to loosen < *dis-*, apart + *solvere*, to loosen: see SOLVE⟧ **1** to make or become liquid; liquefy; melt **2** to merge with a liquid; pass or make pass into solution **3** to break up; disunite; decompose; disintegrate **4** to end by or as by breaking up; terminate **5** to disappear or make disappear **6** *Film, TV* to combine or be combined in a lap dissolve —☆***n.*** *Film, TV short for* LAP DISSOLVE —**SYN.** ADJOURN, MELT —**dissolve in** (or **into**) **tears** weep —**dis·solv′a·ble** ***adj.*** —**dis·solv′er** ***n.***

dis·sol·vent (-ənt) ***adj.*** ⟦L *dissolvens*, prp. of *dissolvere*⟧ that can dissolve other substances —***n.*** a dissolvent substance; solvent

dis·so·nance (dis′ə nəns) ***n.*** ⟦ME *dissonaunce* < LL *dissonantia* < L *dissonans*, prp. of *dissonare*, to be discordant < *dis-*, apart + *sonus*, a SOUND[1]⟧ **1** an inharmonious sound or combination of sounds; discord **2** any lack of harmony or agreement; incongruity **3** *Music* a chord that sounds incomplete or unfulfilled until resolved to a harmonious chord

dis·so·nant (-nənt) ***adj.*** **1** characterized by or constituting a dissonance; discordant **2** opposing in opinion, temperament, etc.; incompatible; incongruous —**dis′so·nant·ly** ***adv.***

dis·suade (di swād′) ***vt.*** **-suad′ed**, **-suad′ing** ⟦L *dissuadere* < *dis-*, away, from + *suadere*, to persuade: see SWEET⟧ **1** to turn (a person) aside (*from* a course, etc.) by persuasion or advice **2** [Obs.] to advise against (an action) —**dis·suad′er** ***n.***

dis·sua·sion (di swā′zhən) ***n.*** ⟦ME *dissuasioun* < L *dissuasio*⟧ the act of dissuading

dis·sua·sive (-siv) ***adj.*** trying or meant to dissuade —**dis·sua′sive·ly** ***adv.***

dis·syl·la·ble (dis sil′ə bəl, dis′sil′-) ***n.*** DISYLLABLE —**dis·syl·lab·ic** (dis′si lab′ik) ***adj.***

dis·sym·me·try (dis sim′ə trē) ***n.***, *pl.* **-tries** **1** a lack or deficiency of symmetry **2** symmetry in opposite directions, as of a person's hands —**dis·sym·met·ri·cal** (dis′si me′tri kəl) ***adj.***, **dis′sym·me′tric**

dist *abbrev.* **1** distance **2** distributor **3** district

dis·taff (dis′taf′) ***n.*** ⟦ME *distaf* < OE *distæf* < *dis-*, flax (see DIZEN) + *stæf*, STAFF[1]⟧ **1** a staff on which fibers, as flax or wool, are wound before being spun into thread **2** woman's work or concerns **3** [Archaic] woman, or women in general —***adj.*** female; specif., designating the maternal side of a family

distaff

dis·tain (di stān′) ***vt.*** ⟦ME *disteinen* < OFr *desteindre* < L *dis-*, apart + *tingere*, to wet, TINGE⟧ [Archaic] **1** to discolor; stain **2** to stain the honor of; disgrace

dis·tal (dis′təl) ⟦DIST(ANT) + -AL: formed in contrast to PROXIMAL⟧ ***adj.*** *Anat.* farthest from the center or the point of attachment or origin; terminal: opposed to PROXIMAL —**dis′tal·ly** ***adv.***

dis·tance (dis′təns) ***n.*** ⟦ME *distaunce* < OFr *distance* < L *distantia* < *distans*, prp. of *distare*, to stand apart < *dis-*, apart + *stare*, STAND⟧ **1** the fact or condition of being separated or removed in space or time; remoteness **2** a gap, space, or interval between two points, lines, objects, etc. **3** an interval between two points in time **4** the length of a line between two points [the *distance* between Paris and Rome] **5** a remoteness in relationship; dissimilarity; disparity [the *distance* between wealth and poverty] **6** a remoteness in behavior; coolness of manner; reserve **7** a remote point in space [away in the *distance*] **8** a faraway point of time [at this *distance* we cannot know Neanderthal man] **9** *Painting* the depicting of distance, as in a landscape **10** *Horse Racing* a space that is a certain distance back from the finish line: in order to be qualified for future heats, a horse must have reached this space by the time the winner has completed the course —***adj.*** *Track & Field* that covers a middle distance or a long distance [to train as a *distance* runner] —***vt.*** **-tanced**, **-tanc·ing** **1** to place or hold at some distance **2** *a)* to place (oneself) at an emotional distance *from* something *b)* to cause to be at a mental or emotional distance from an audience, reader, etc. **3** to do better or more than; leave behind; outdo; outdistance —**go the distance** to last through an activity; specif., to pitch an entire baseball game without being replaced —**keep at a distance** to be reserved or cool toward; treat aloofly —**keep one's distance** to be or remain aloof or reserved

distance learning any system of individualized, esp. postsecondary instruction for students at a distance from a campus, utilizing the internet, videoconferencing, preprogrammed courses, etc.

dis·tant (dis′tənt) ***adj.*** ⟦ME *distaunt* < L *distans*: see DISTANCE⟧ **1** having a gap or space between; separated **2** widely separated; far apart or far away in space or time **3** at a measured interval; away [a town 100 miles *distant*] **4** far apart in relationship; remote [a *distant* cousin] **5** cool in manner; aloof; reserved **6** from or at a distance [a *distant* sound] **7** faraway or dreamy [a *distant* look] —***SYN.*** FAR —**dis′tant·ly** ***adv.***

dis·tan·ti·ate (di stan′shē āt′) ***vt.*** **-at′ed, -at′ing** ⟦< L *distantia*, DISTANCE + -ATE[1]⟧ to put or keep at an emotional or intellectual distance —**dis·tan′ti·a′tion** ***n.***

dis·taste (dis tāst′, dis′tāst′) ***n.*** ⟦DIS- + TASTE (***n.***); prob. formed similarly to MFr *desgoust*: see DISGUST⟧ dislike or aversion (*for*) —***vt.*** **-tast′ed, -tast′ing** [Archaic] **1** to have a distaste for; dislike **2** to displease, offend —***vi.*** [Obs.] to be distasteful

dis·taste·ful (-fəl) ***adj.*** **1** unpleasant to taste **2** causing distaste; disagreeable —**dis·taste′ful·ly** ***adv.*** —**dis·taste′ful·ness** ***n.***

Dist Atty *abbrev.* District Attorney

dis·tem·per[1] (dis tem′pər) ***vt.*** ⟦ME *distemperen* < OFr *destemprer* or ML *distemperare*, to disorder (esp. the "tempers," or four humors) < L *dis-*, apart + *temperare*, to mix in proportion: see TEMPER⟧ **1** [Obs.] to make bad-tempered; disturb; ruffle **2** to upset or unbalance the functions of; derange; disorder —***n.*** **1** a mental or physical derangement or disorder; disease **2** any of several infectious diseases of animals, characterized by rhinitis, fever, etc.; specif., *a)* an infectious viral disease of young dogs *b)* strangles, a disease of horses **3** civil disorder or turmoil

dis·tem·per[2] (dis tem′pər) ***vt.*** ⟦OFr *destemprer* < ML *distemperare*, to mix, dilute < L *dis-*, intens. + *temperare*: see prec.⟧ **1** to mix (colors or pigments) with water and glue, size, or some other binding medium **2** to paint with such a mixture —***n.*** **1** a method of painting using distempered pigment, as for wall decoration **2** a painting done in this way **3** distempered paint **4** any of various water-based paints, as whitewash, calcimine, etc.

dis·tem·per·a·ture (dis tem′pər ə chər) ***n.*** ⟦< DISTEMPER[1], after TEMPERATURE⟧ [Archaic] a disordered condition of the body or mind

dis·tend (di stend′) ***vt., vi.*** ⟦ME *distenden* < L *distendere* < *dis-*, apart + *tendere*, to stretch: see TEND[2]⟧ **1** to stretch out **2** to expand; make or become swollen —***SYN.*** EXPAND

dis·ten·si·ble (-sten′sə bəl) ***adj.*** ⟦< LL *distensus* (L *distentus*), pp. of *distendere*⟧ that can be distended

dis·ten·tion or **dis·ten·sion** (-sten′shən) ***n.*** ⟦L *distentio*⟧ a distending or being distended; inflation; expansion

dis·tich (dis′tik′) ***n.*** ⟦L *distichon* < Gr < *distichos*, having two rows < *di-*, two + *stichos*, a row, verse < base of *steichein*, to step: see STILE[1]⟧ two successive lines of verse regarded as a unit; couplet

dis·tich·ous (dis′ti kəs) ***adj.*** ⟦< LL *distichus* < Gr *distichos* (see prec.) + -OUS⟧ *Bot.* arranged in two vertical rows, as leaves on opposite sides of a stem —**dis′tich·ous·ly** ***adv.***

dis·till or **dis·til** (di stil′) ***vi.*** **-tilled′, -till′ing** ⟦ME *distillen* < OFr *distiller* < L *distillare*, for *destillare*, to trickle down < *de-*, down + *stillare*, to drop < *stilla*, a drop: see STONE⟧ **1** to fall in drops; trickle; drip **2** to undergo distillation **3** to be produced as the essence of something —***vt.*** **1** to cause or allow to fall in drops **2** to subject to, or purify or refine by, distillation [to *distill* water] **3** to remove, extract, or produce by distillation [to *distill* whiskey] **4** to purify, refine, or concentrate as if by distillation [to *distill* one's style] **5** to draw out or obtain the part that is essential, pure, etc.

dis·til·late (dis′tə lāt′, -lit; *also* di stil′it) ***n.*** ⟦< L *distillatus*, pp. of *distillare*⟧ **1** a product of distillation; liquid obtained by distilling **2** the essence of anything

dis·til·la·tion (dis′tə lā′shen) ***n.*** **1** a distilling; specif., the process of first heating a mixture to separate the more volatile from the less volatile parts, and then cooling and condensing the resulting vapor so as to produce a more nearly pure or refined substance **2** anything distilled; distillate

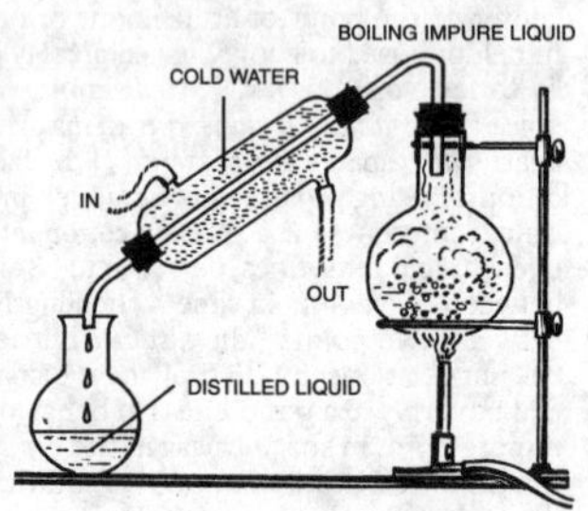

distillation

dis·tilled (di stild′) ***adj.*** produced by distillation

dis·till·er (di stil′ər) ***n.*** **1** a person or apparatus that distills **2** a person, company, etc. in the business of making alcoholic liquors produced by distillation

dis·till·er·y (di stil′ər ē) ***n., pl.*** **-er·ies** a place where distilling is carried on; specif., an establishment where alcoholic liquors are distilled

dis·tinct (di stiŋkt′) ***adj.*** ⟦ME & OFr < L *distinctus*, pp. of *distinguere*: see DISTINGUISH⟧ **1** not alike; different **2** not the same; separate; individual **3** clearly perceived or marked off; clear; plain [a *distinct* image] **4** well-defined; unmistakable; definite [a *distinct* success] **5** [Old Poet.] decorated or variegated —***SYN.*** DIFFERENT —**dis·tinct′ly** ***adv.*** —**dis·tinct′ness** ***n.***

dis·tinc·tion (di stiŋk′shən) ***n.*** ⟦ME *distinccioun* < OFr *distinction* < L *distinctio* < pp. of *distinguere*: see DISTINGUISH⟧ **1** the act of making or keeping distinct; differentiation between or among things **2** the condition of being different; difference **3** that which makes or keeps distinct; quality, mark, or feature that differentiates **4** the state of getting special recognition or honor; fame; eminence [a singer of *distinction*] **5** the quality that makes one seem superior or worthy of special recognition [to serve with *distinction*] **6** a mark or sign of special recognition or honor

dis·tinc·tive (di stiŋk′tiv) ***adj.*** ⟦ME < ML *distinctivus*⟧ making distinct; distinguishing from others; characteristic —***SYN.*** CHARACTERISTIC —**dis·tinc′tive·ly** ***adv.*** —**dis·tinc′tive·ness** ***n.***

dis·tin·gué (dē staŋ gā′) ***adj.*** ⟦Fr⟧ having an air of distinction; distinguished

dis·tin·guish (di stiŋ′gwish) ***vt.*** ⟦< L *distinguere*, to separate, discriminate < *dis-*, apart + *-stinguere*, to prick < IE base **steig-*, to prick, pierce (> STICK, Ger *sticken*, to embroider, Gr *stigma*) + -ISH, sense 2⟧ **1** to separate or mark off by differences; perceive or show the difference in; differentiate **2** to be an essential characteristic of; characterize **3** to perceive clearly; recognize plainly by any of the senses **4** to separate and classify **5** to make famous or eminent; give distinction to [to *distinguish* oneself in battle] —***vi.*** to make a distinction (*between* or *among*) —**dis·tin′guish·a·ble** ***adj.*** —**dis·tin′guish·a·bly** ***adv.***

SYN.—**distinguish** implies a recognizing or marking apart from others by special features or characteristic qualities [to *distinguish* good from evil]; **discriminate**, in this connection, suggests a distinguishing of minute or subtle differences between similar things [to *discriminate* scents]; **differentiate** suggests the noting or ascertaining of specific differences between things by comparing in detail their distinguishing qualities or features See also **discern**

dis·tin·guished (-gwisht) ***adj.*** **1** celebrated; eminent **2** having an air of distinction —***SYN.*** FAMOUS

Distinguished Flying Cross ☆**1** a U.S. military decoration awarded for heroism or extraordinary achievement while participating in aerial flight **2** a British Royal Air Force decoration awarded for gallantry while flying in combat

Distinguished Service Cross ☆**1** a U.S. Army decoration awarded for extraordinary heroism in combat **2** a British Royal Navy decoration awarded for distinguished service against the enemy

Distinguished Service Medal ☆**1** a U.S. military decoration awarded for exceptionally meritorious service to the government in a duty of great responsibility **2** a British Royal Navy or Marines decoration awarded for distinguished service in time of war

Distinguished Service Order a British military decoration awarded in recognition of special services in action

di·stome (dī′stōm′) ***n.*** ⟦< ModL *Distoma*, name of the type genus: see DI-[1] & STOMA⟧ any of various digenetic, parasitic trematode flatworms, with an anterior oral sucker and the posterior sucker located on the ventral surface

dis·tort (di stôrt′) ***vt.*** ⟦< L *distortus*, pp. of *distorquere*, distort < *dis-*, intens. + *torquere*, to twist: see TORT⟧ **1** to twist out of shape; change the usual or normal shape, form, or appearance of **2** to misrepresent; misstate; pervert [to *distort* the facts] **3** to modify (a wave, sound, signal, etc.) so as to produce an unfaithful reproduction —***SYN.*** DEFORM —**dis·tort′er** ***n.***

dis·tor·tion (di stôr′shən) ***n.*** ⟦L *distortio*⟧ **1** a distorting or being distorted **2** anything distorted —**dis·tor′tion·al** ***adj.***

distr *abbrev.* **1** distributed **2** distribution **3** distributor

dis·tract (di strakt′) ***vt.*** ⟦ME *distracten* < L *distractus*, pp. of *distrahere*, to draw apart < *dis-*, apart + *trahere*, DRAW⟧ **1** to draw (the mind, attention, etc.) away in another direction; divert **2** to draw in conflicting directions; create conflict or confusion in **3** [Obs.] to drive insane; craze —**dis·tract′i·ble** ***adj.*** —**dis·tract′ing** ***adj.*** —**dis·tract′ing·ly** ***adv.***

dis·tract·ed (di strakt′id) ***adj.*** unable to give proper attention to or concentrate on, as because of mental disturbance, anxiety, etc. —**dis·tract′ed·ly** ***adv.***

dis·trac·tion (di strak′shən) ***n.*** ⟦ME *distraccioun* < L *distractio*⟧ **1** a distracting or being distracted; confusion **2** anything that distracts; specif., *a)* a mental intrusion or cause of confusion *b)* anything that gives mental relaxation; amusement; diversion **3** great mental disturbance or distress —**dis·trac′tive** ***adj.***

dis·train (di strān′) ***vt., vi.*** ⟦ME *distreinen* < OFr *destreindre* < ML *distringere*, to force by seizure of goods < L, to pull asunder, detain < *dis-*, apart + *stringere*, to draw tight, stretch: see STRICT⟧ *Law* to seize and hold (property) as security or indemnity for a debt —**dis·train′a·ble** ***adj.*** —**dis·train′er** ***n.***, **dis·trai′nor**

dis·train·ee (dis′trān ē′) ***n.*** ⟦prec. + -EE[1]⟧ a person whose property has been distrained

dis·traint (di strānt′) ***n.*** ⟦ME *distreint* < OFr *destreinte*⟧ *Law* the action of distraining; seizure

dis·trait (di strā′) ***adj.*** ⟦ME < OFr *destrait*, pp. of *distraire* < L *distrahere*: see DISTRACT⟧ absent-minded; inattentive —***SYN.*** ABSENT-MINDED

dis·traught (di strôt′) ***adj.*** ⟦ME, var. of prec.⟧ **1** extremely troubled; mentally confused; distracted; harassed **2** driven mad; crazed —***SYN.*** ABSENT-MINDED

dis·tress (di stres′) ***vt.*** ⟦ME *distressen* < OFr *destrecier*, orig., to constrain (to do something) < *destrece*, constraint < ML *destrescia* < L *districtus*, pp. of *distringere*: see DISTRAIN⟧ **1** to cause sorrow, misery, or suffering to; pain **2** to cause discomfort to; trouble **3** to exhaust or weaken with strain of any sort **4** [Archaic] to constrain (to do something) **5** *Law* to distrain —***n.*** **1** the state of being distressed; pain, suffering, discomfort, etc. **2** anything that distresses; affliction **3** a state of danger or trouble; bad straits **4** *Law a)* distraint *b)* the property distrained —**dis·tress′ing** ***adj.*** —**dis·tress′ing·ly** ***adv.***

SYN.—**distress** implies mental or physical strain imposed by pain, trouble, worry, or the like and usually suggests a state or situation that can be relieved [*distress* caused by famine]; **suffering** stresses the actual enduring of pain, distress, or tribulation [the *suffering* of the wounded]; **agony** suggests mental or physical torment so excruciating that the body or mind is convulsed with the force of it [in mortal *agony*]; **anguish** has equal force but is more often applied to acute mental suffering [the *anguish* of despair]

dis·tressed (-strest′) *adj.* **1** full of distress; anxious, suffering, troubled, etc. **2** *a)* given the appearance of being antique, as by having the finish marred [a *distressed* walnut table] *b)* given the appearance of wear, as by being faded or torn [a sale on *distressed* jeans] **3** designating or of an area in which there is widespread unemployment, poverty, etc. **4** designating or of goods, esp. repossessed goods, sold at low prices or at a loss

dis·tress·ful (di stres′fəl) *adj.* **1** causing distress; painful; grievous **2** feeling, expressing, or full of distress

dis·trib·u·tar·y (di strib′yoo ter′ē) *n., pl.* **-tar′ies** ⟦< fol., by analogy with TRIBUTARY⟧ any branch of a river that flows away from the main stream and does not rejoin it

dis·trib·ute (di strib′yoot, -yoot) *vt.* **-ut·ed, -ut·ing** ⟦ME *distributen* < L *distributus*, pp. of *distribuere*, to distribute < *dis-*, apart + *tribuere*, to allot: see TRIBUTE⟧ **1** to divide and give out in shares; allot **2** to scatter or spread out, as over a surface **3** to divide and arrange according to a classification; classify **4** to put (things) in various distinct places **5** [Obs.] to administer, as justice **6** *Printing* to break up (set type) and put the letters back in the proper boxes **7** *Law* to apportion (an intestate's property) to those entitled to it **8** *Logic* to use (a term) in such a way as to refer to all members of its extension —**dis·trib′ut·a·ble** *adj.*

SYN.—**distribute** implies a dealing out of portions or a spreading about of units among a number of recipients [to *distribute* leaflets]; **dispense** suggests the careful measuring out of that which is distributed [to *dispense* drugs]; **divide** suggests separation of a whole into parts to be shared [an inheritance *divided* among five children]; **dole** implies a distributing of money, food, etc. in charity or in a sparing or niggardly manner

distributed processing a system consisting of a network of microcomputers performing certain functions and linked with a main computer used for more complex tasks

☆**dis·trib·u·tee** (di strib′yoo tē′) *n. Law* one of those to whom an intestate's property is to be apportioned

dis·tri·bu·tion (dis′tri byoo′shən) *n.* ⟦ME *distribucioun* < L *distributio*⟧ **1** a distributing or being distributed; specif., *a)* apportionment by law (*of* funds, property, etc.) *b)* the process by which commodities get to final consumers, including storing, selling, shipping, and advertising *c)* frequency of occurrence or extent of existence **2** anything distributed; portion; share **3** the result of distributing; arrangement **4** *Statistics* the relative arrangement of the elements of a statistical population based on some criterion, as frequency, time, or location —**dis′tri·bu′tion·al** *adj.*

distribution class FORM CLASS

distribution ratio *Chem.* the ratio of concentrations of a solute distributed between two immiscible solvents in contact with each other, as iodine in water and chloroform

dis·trib·u·tive (di strib′yoo tiv′, -yoot iv) *adj.* ⟦ME & OFr *distributif* < LL *distributivus*⟧ **1** distributing or tending to distribute **2** relating to distribution **3** *Gram.* referring individually to all members of a group ["each" and "either" are *distributive* words] **4** *Math.* of or having to do with a property, law, or principle in which the relationship between two combined operations, as multiplication and addition or multiplication and subtraction, is such that the results are the same whether the first operation is done on each item of a set and then combined or done once on the items in the set that have already been combined (Ex.: a(b + c) = ab + ac) —*n.* a distributive word or expression —**dis·trib′u·tive·ly** *adv.*

dis·trib·u·tor (di strib′yoot ər) *n.* a person or thing that distributes; specif., ☆*a)* an agent or business firm that distributes goods to consumers or dealers ☆*b)* a device for distributing electric current to the spark plugs of a gasoline engine so that they fire in proper order —**dis·trib′u·tor·less** *adj.* —**dis·trib′u·tor·ship′** *n.*

dis·trict (dis′trikt) *n.* ⟦Fr < ML *districtus*, orig., control; hence in feudal law, a territory within which a lord had jurisdiction < L: see DISTRESS⟧ **1** a geographical or political division made for a specific purpose [a school *district*] **2** any region; part of a country, city, etc. [the business *district*] —☆*vt.* to divide into districts

☆**district attorney** in the U.S., a lawyer serving in a specified judicial district as prosecutor for the state or for the federal government in criminal cases

☆**district court** **1** the federal trial court sitting in each judicial district of the U.S. **2** in some states of the U.S., the court of general jurisdiction in each judicial district

District of Columbia ⟦after Christopher COLUMBUS[1]⟧ federal district of the U.S., on the N bank of the Potomac River: 61 sq mi (159 sq km); coextensive with the city of Washington: abbrev. *DC* or *D.C.*

dis·trust (dis trust′) *n.* a lack of trust, of faith, or of confidence; doubt; suspicion —*vt.* to have no trust, faith, or confidence in; doubt; suspect

dis·trust·ful (-fəl) *adj.* distrusting; doubting —**distrustful of** suspicious of; having no confidence in —**dis·trust′ful·ly** *adv.* —**dis·trust′ful·ness** *n.*

dis·turb (di sturb′) *vt.* ⟦ME *distourben* < OFr *distourber* < L *disturbare*, to drive asunder < *dis-*, intens. + *turbare*, to disorder < *turba*, a crowd, mob: see TURBID⟧ **1** to break up the quiet or serenity of; agitate (what is quiet or still) **2** to upset mentally or emotionally; make uneasy or anxious **3** to break up the settled order or orderly working of [to *disturb* the books on a shelf] **4** to break in on; interrupt **5** to inconvenience [if I call later, will I be *disturbing* you?] —**dis·turb′er** *n.*

SYN.—**disturb** implies the unsettling of normal mental calm or powers of concentration by worry, interruption, etc. [to *disturb* one's train of thought]; **discompose** implies the upsetting of one's self-possession [her sudden outburst *discomposed* him]; to **perturb** is to cause to have a troubled or alarmed feeling [the bad news *perturbed* him]; **agitate** suggests an arousing of intense mental or emotional excitement [he was so *agitated*, he could not answer]

dis·turb·ance (di sturʹbəns) *n.* ⟦ME < OFr *distourbance*⟧ **1** *a)* a disturbing or being disturbed *b)* any departure from normal **2** anything that disturbs **3** the state of being worried, troubled, or anxious **4** commotion; disorder

dis·turbed (di sturbd′) *adj.* mentally or emotionally upset or unbalanced

di·sul·fate (dī sul′fāt′) *n.* **1** PYROSULFATE **2** a chemical compound containing two sulfate radicals per molecule Cf. BISULFATE

di·sul·fide (dī sul′fīd′) *n.* **1** a chemical compound in which two sulfur atoms are united with a single radical or with a single atom of an element; bisulfide **2** an organic compound in which the radical SS is attached to two different carbon atoms

dis·un·ion (dis yoon′yən) *n.* **1** the breaking up or ending of union; separation **2** lack of unity; discord

dis·un·ion·ist (-ist) *n.* **1** a person who advocates or tries to cause disunion ☆**2** a person favoring secession, as in the Civil War; secessionist —**dis·un′ion·ism′** *n.*

dis·u·nite (dis′yoo nīt′) *vt.* **-nit′ed, -nit′ing** to destroy or take away the unity of; divide or separate —*vi.* to become separated or divided

dis·u·ni·ty (dis yoon′ə tē) *n.* lack of unity

dis·use (-yoos′) *n.* the fact or state of being or becoming unused; lack of use

dis·used (-yoozd′) *adj.* no longer used

dis·u·til·i·ty (dis′yoo til′ə tē) *n.* a lack of utility; quality of being harmful, inconvenient, etc.

dis·val·ue (dis val′yoo) *vt.* **-val′ued, -val′u·ing** to regard as of little or no value; depreciate —*n.* negative value

di·syl·la·ble (dī sil′ə bəl, di′sil′-; *also* di sil′-) *n.* ⟦altered (by analogy with SYLLABLE) < Fr *dissyllabe* < L *disyllabus* < Gr *disyllabos*, of two syllables < *di-*, two + *syllabē*, SYLLABLE⟧ a word of two syllables —**di·syl·lab·ic** (dī′si lab′ik, di′-) *adj.*

☆**dit** (dit) *n.* ⟦echoic of the sound of this character as produced by an old-fashioned telegraph⟧ the dot character in Morse code

ditch (dich) *n.* ⟦ME *dich* < OE *dic*, a ditch, drain: see DIKE[1]⟧ a long, narrow channel dug into the earth, as a trough for drainage or irrigation —*vt.* **1** to border with a ditch **2** to make a ditch or ditches in ☆**3** *a)* to cause (a car, wagon, etc.) to go into a ditch *b)* to derail (a train) **4** to set (a disabled aircraft) down on water and abandon it ☆**5** [Slang] *a)* to get rid of *b)* to get away from (an unwanted companion, etc.) —*vi.* **1** to dig a ditch or ditches **2** to ditch a disabled plane

di·the·ism (dī′thē iz′əm) *n.* belief in two supreme gods; dualism

dith·er (dith′ər) *vi.* ⟦ME *dideren*, prob. akin to *daderen*, DODDER[1]⟧ **1** to be nervously excited or confused **2** to be indecisive; vacillate, waver, etc. —*n.* a nervously excited or confused condition —**dith′er·ing** *adj.*, **dith′er·y**

di·thi·on·ic acid (dī′thī än′ik) ⟦DI-[1] + THIONIC⟧ an acid, $H_2S_2O_6$, having two sulfur atoms in each molecule and existing only in salts or solutions

dith·y·ramb (dith′ə ram′; *also*, -ramb′) *n.* ⟦L *dithyrambus* < Gr *dithyrambos*⟧ **1** in ancient Greece, an impassioned choric hymn in honor of Dionysus **2** any extravagantly emotional speech or writing —**dith′y·ram′bic** (-bik) *adj., n.*

☆**dit·sy** (dit′sē) *adj.* **-si·er, -si·est** ⟦? altered < DIZZY⟧ [Slang] silly, flighty, disorganized, eccentric, etc.: also sp. **dit′zy**

dit·ta·ny (dit′'n ē) *n., pl.* **-nies** ⟦ME *ditane* < OFr *ditan* < L *dictamnum* < Gr *diktamnon*, ? after *Diktē*, Mount Dicte, in Crete, where it grew⟧ **1** a creeping, woolly herb (*Origanum dictamnus*) of the mint family, native to Crete **2** GAS PLANT ☆**3** a small perennial herb (*Cunila origanoides*) of the mint family, found in E U.S.

dit·to (dit′ō) *n., pl.* **-tos** ⟦It (Tuscan), var. of *detto*, said < L *dictus*, pp. of *dicere*, to say: see DICTION⟧ **1** the same (as something said or appearing above or before) **2** a duplicate; another of the same **3** DITTO MARK —*adv.* as said above; as before; likewise —*vt.* **-toed, -to·ing** **1** to duplicate or make copies of **2** to indicate repetition of, by using ditto marks **3** to do again; repeat

ditto mark a mark (") used in itemized lists or tables to show that a word, figure, or passage above is to be repeated

dit·ty (dit′ē) *n., pl.* **-ties** ⟦ME *dite* < OFr *dité* < L *dictatum*, thing dictated, neut. pp. of *dictare*: see DICTATE⟧ a short, simple song

ditty bag (or box) ⟦< ? obs. *dutty*, coarse calico, orig. Anglo-Ind, prob. < Hindi *dhōtī*, loincloth⟧ a small bag (or box) used as by sailors for holding sewing equipment, toilet articles, etc.

☆**ditz** (dits) *n.* ⟦back-form. < DITSY⟧ [Slang] a person thought of as being flighty, eccentric, silly, etc.

Di·u (dē′oo) small island just off the coast of Gujarat state, NW India: part of the territory of Daman and Diu

di·u·re·sis (dī′yoo rē′sis) *n., pl.* **-ses′** (-sēz′) ⟦ModL < Gr *diourein* < *dia-*, through + *ourein*, to urinate < *ouron*, URINE⟧ an increased or excessive excretion of urine

di·u·ret·ic (-ret′ik) *adj.* ⟦ME *diuretik* < LL *diureticus* < Gr *diourētikos* < *diourein*: see prec.⟧ increasing the excretion of urine —*n.* a diuretic drug or other substance —**di′u·ret′i·cal·ly** *adv.*

di·ur·nal (dī ʉr′nəl) *adj.* ⟦ME < L *diurnalis* < *diurnus*, daily < *dies*, day: see DEITY⟧ **1** occurring each day; daily **2** of, done, or happening in the daytime: opposed to NOCTURNAL **3** *a)* *Bot.* opening in the daytime and closing at night (said of a flower) *b)* *Zool.* active in the daytime —*n.* **1** [Archaic] a daily newspaper **2** *Eccles.* a service book containing prayers for the daytime canonical hours and for compline —**di·ur′nal·ly** *adv.*

div *abbrev.* **1** dividend **2** division **3** divisor **4** divorced

Div *abbrev.* Division

di·va (dē′və) *n., pl.* **-vas** or **-ve** (-ve) ⟦It < L, goddess, fem. of *divus*, god: see DEITY⟧ **1** a leading woman singer, esp. in grand opera **2** [Informal] a woman, often a celebrity, with a reputation for being haughty, temperamental, hard to please, etc.

di·va·gate (dī′və gāt′; *also* div′ə-) *vi.* **-gat′ed, -gat′ing** ⟦< pp. of LL *divagari*, to wander about < L *dis-*, from + *vagari*, to wander: see VAGABOND⟧ **1** to wander about **2** to stray from the subject; digress —**di′va·ga′tion** *n.*

di·va·lent (dī vā′lənt, dī′vā′lənt) *adj.* *Chem.* **1** having two valences **2** having a valence of two See -VALENT

di·van (di van′; *for 1, also* di vän′; *for 2 & 3, also* dī′van′) *n.* ⟦Turk *dīwān* < Pers, orig., bundle of written sheets, hence accounts, customhouse, council room, appropriate furniture⟧ **1** in the Ottoman Empire, *a)* a council of state or the room in which it was held *b)* the audience chamber of a government office **2** a large, low couch or sofa, usually without armrests or back **3** a coffee room, café, or smoking room

di·var·i·cate (dī var′i kāt′, di-) *vi., vt.* **-cat′ed, -cat′ing** ⟦< L *divaricatus*, pp. of *divaricare*, to spread apart < *dis-*, apart + *varicare*, to straddle: see PREVARICATE⟧ to spread widely apart; separate into diverging parts or branches; fork; branch —*adj.* spreading or branching far apart; widely diverging

di·var·i·ca·tion (dī var′i kā′shən, di-) *n.* **1** a divaricating, or branching **2** a difference of opinion

di·var·i·ca·tor (dī var′i kāt′ər, di-) *n.* the muscle that stretches apart the shells of a brachiopod

dive (dīv) *vi.* **dived** or **dove, dived, div′ing** ⟦ME *diven* < OE *dyfan*, to immerse, caus. of *dufan*, to dive, akin to ON *dȳfa*, to plunge, *dūfa*, a wave < IE base **dheup-*, DEEP⟧ **1** to plunge headfirst into water **2** to go underwater; submerge, as a submarine or skin diver **3** to plunge the hand or body suddenly into something [to *dive* into a foxhole] **4** to bring oneself zestfully or with abandon into something [to *dive* into one's work] **5** to make a steep, sudden descent or take a sudden drop, as an airplane —*vt.* **1** to cause to dive; specif., to send (one's airplane) into a dive **2** [Archaic] to explore or penetrate by or as by diving —*n.* **1** a plunge into water headfirst; esp., any of various formalized plunges performed as in a competition **2** any sudden plunge or submersion **3** a sharp descent or sudden drop, as of an airplane **4** [Informal] a cheap, disreputable saloon, gambling place, etc. **5** *Football* a play in which a running back carries the ball while plunging directly into the line a short distance away —☆**take a dive** [Slang] to lose a prizefight purposely by pretending to get knocked out

dive bomber an airplane designed to release bombs while diving steeply at a target —**dive′bomb′** *vt., vi.*

div·er (dī′vər) *n.* one that dives; specif., *a)* a person who works or explores underwater, usually breathing air supplied through a special mask or helmet *b)* any of several diving water birds, esp. a loon

di·verge (dī vʉrj′; *also* di-) *vi.* **-verged′, -verg′ing** ⟦ML *divergere* (for LL *devergere*) < L *dis-*, apart + *vergere*, to turn: see VERGE[2]⟧ **1** to go or move in different directions from a common point or from each other; branch off [paths that *diverge*] **2** to take on gradually a different form or become a different kind [*diverging* customs] **3** to depart from a given viewpoint, practice, etc.; differ [*diverging* opinions] —*vt.* to make diverge —*SYN.* DEVIATE

di·ver·gence (-vʉr′jəns) *n.* ⟦ML *divergentia*⟧ **1** a diverging, separating, or branching off **2** a becoming different in form or kind **3** departure from a particular viewpoint, practice, etc. **4** difference of opinion; disagreement Also **di·ver′gen·cy**, *pl.* **-cies**

di·ver·gent (-vʉr′jənt) *adj.* ⟦ML *divergens*, prp. of *divergere*⟧ **1** diverging **2** varying from one another or from a norm; deviating; different **3** causing divergence **4** not convergent, as a mathematical sequence —*SYN.* DIFFERENT —**di·ver′gent·ly** *adv.*

di·vers (dī′vərz) *adj.* ⟦ME & OFr *divers(e)*: see fol.⟧ **1** several; various **2** [Archaic] diverse

di·verse (də vʉrs′, dī-; dī′vʉrs′) *adj.* ⟦ME & OFr < L *diversus*, pp. of *divertere*, to turn aside < *dis-*, apart + *vertere*, to turn: see VERSE⟧ **1** different; dissimilar **2** varied; diversified —*SYN.* DIFFERENT —**di·verse′ly** *adv.* —**di·verse′ness** *n.*

di·ver·si·fied (də vʉr′sə fīd′, dī-) *adj.* varied

di·ver·si·fy (də vʉr′sə fī′, dī-) *vt.* **-fied′, -fy′ing** ⟦ME *diversifien* < OFr *diversifier* < ML *diversificare*, to make different < L *diversus* (see DIVERSE) + *facere*, DO[1]⟧ **1** to make diverse; give variety to; vary **2** to divide up (investments, liabilities, etc.) among different companies, securities, etc. **3** to expand (a business, line of products, etc.) by increasing the variety of things produced or of operations undertaken —*vi.* to undertake expansion of a line of products or otherwise multiply business operations —**di·ver′si·fi·ca′tion** *n.*

di·ver·sion (də vʉr′zhən, -shən; dī-) *n.* ⟦ME *diversioun* < ML *diversio* (for LL *deversio*)⟧ **1** a diverting or turning aside [*diversion* of funds from the treasury] **2** distraction of attention [*diversion* of the enemy] **3** anything that diverts or distracts the attention; specif., a pastime or amusement

di·ver·sion·ar·y (-er′ē) *adj.* **1** having the nature of a diversion **2** *Mil.* serving to distract the enemy from the main point of attack [*diversionary* tactics]

di·ver·sion·ist (-ist) *n.* a person engaged in diversionary activity or tactics

di·ver·si·ty (də vʉr′sə tē, dī-) *n., pl.* **-ties** ⟦ME *diversite* < OFr *diverseté*⟧ **1** quality, state, fact, or instance of being diverse; difference **2** variety **3** *a)* a policy of selecting people so as to assemble a group that is diverse, esp. with respect to race and gender *b)* the composition of a group with respect to race, gender, etc.

di·vert (də vʉrt′, dī-) *vt.* ⟦ME *diverten* < OFr *divertir* < L *divertere*: see DIVERSE⟧ **1** to turn (a person or thing) aside from a course, direction, etc. into another; deflect **2** to distract the attention of **3** to amuse; entertain —*SYN.* AMUSE

di·ver·tic·u·li·tis (dī′vər tik′yoo līt′is) *n.* ⟦see -ITIS⟧ inflammation of a diverticulum, specif. one within the intestine

di·ver·tic·u·lo·sis (-lō′sis) *n.* ⟦see -OSIS⟧ the abnormal condition of having a number of diverticula protruding from the wall of the intestinal tract

di·ver·tic·u·lum (dī′vər tik′yoo ləm) *n., pl.* **-la** (-lə) ⟦L *diverticulum*, var. of *deverticulum*, a bypath < *devertere*, to turn aside: see DE- & VERSE⟧ *Anat.* a normal or abnormal pouch or sac opening out from a tubular organ or main cavity

di·ver·ti·men·to (di ver′ti men′tō) *n., pl.* **-ti** (-tē) or **-tos** ⟦It: see DIVERT⟧ any of various light, melodic instrumental compositions in several movements

di·vert·ing (də vʉrt′iŋ, dī-) *adj.* that diverts; esp., amusing or entertaining —**di·vert′ing·ly** *adv.*

di·ver·tisse·ment (di vʉrt′is mənt; *Fr* dē ver tēs män′) *n., pl.* **-ments** (-mənts; *Fr* -män′) ⟦Fr.: see DIVERT⟧ [*also in italics*] **1** a diversion; amusement **2** a short ballet, etc. performed between the acts of a play or opera; entr'acte **3** DIVERTIMENTO

Di·ves (dī′vēz′) *n.* ⟦ME: so named < use of L *dives*, rich, in the parable in the Vulg.⟧ **1** *traditional name for* the rich man in a parable: cf. Luke 16:19-31 **2** any rich man

di·vest (də vest′, dī-) *vt.* ⟦altered < DEVEST⟧ **1** to strip *of* clothing, equipment, etc. **2** to deprive or dispossess *of* rank, rights, etc. **3** to disencumber or rid *of* something unwanted **4** *Law* DEVEST —*vi.* *Business* to sell off an asset or assets —*SYN.* STRIP[1]

di·vest·i·ture (-ə chər) *n.* a divesting or being divested: also **di·vest′ment** or **di·ves′ture**

di·vide (də vīd′) *vt.* **di·vid′ed, di·vid′ing** ⟦ME *dividen* < L *dividere*, to separate, divide, distribute < *di-* (< *dis-*, apart) + base seen in *vidua*, WIDOW < IE base **weidh-*, to separate (prob. < *wi-*, apart + *dhē*, set, DO[1])⟧ **1** to separate into parts; split up; sever **2** to separate into groups; classify **3** to make or keep separate by or as by a boundary or partition **4** to give out in shares; apportion; distribute **5** to cause disagreement between or among; alienate **6** to separate (a parliamentary body) into groups in voting on a question **7** *Math.* *a)* to separate into equal parts by a divisor *b)* to function as a divisor of **8** *Mech.* to mark off the divisions of; graduate; gradate —*vi.* **1** to be or become separate; part **2** to differ in opinion; disagree **3** to separate into groups in voting on a question: said of a parliament, esp. that of the United Kingdom **4** to share **5** *Math.* *a)* to do division *b)* to undergo division; be divisible (*by*) —*n.* **1** the act of dividing ☆**2** a ridge that divides two drainage areas; watershed **3** a division; boundary —*SYN.* DISTRIBUTE, SEPARATE —**di·vid′a·ble** *adj.*

di·vid·ed (-id) *adj.* **1** *a)* separated into parts; parted *b)* having a center strip, as of turf, separating traffic moving in opposite directions [a *divided* highway] *c)* having distinct indentations or notches reaching to the base or midrib, as in certain compound leaves **2** disagreeing or differing in opinion

div·i·dend (div′ə dend′, -dənd) *n.* ⟦< L *dividendum*, that which is to be divided < *dividendus*, ger. of *dividere*⟧ **1** the number or quantity to be divided **2** *a)* a sum or quantity, usually of money, to be divided among stockholders, creditors, members of a cooperative, etc. *b)* an individual's share of such a sum or quantity **3** a gift of something extra; bonus **4** the refund made under some insurance policies to the insured from the year's surplus profit —*SYN.* BONUS

di·vid·er (də vīd′ər) *n.* a person or thing that divides; specif., *a)* [*pl.*] an instrument for dividing lines, measuring or marking off distances, etc.; compasses *b)* a screen, set of shelves, etc. used to separate a room into distinct areas

div·i-div·i (div′ē div′ē) *n.* ⟦Sp < Carib word⟧ **1** a small tropical American tree (*Caesalpinia coriaria*) of the caesalpinia family **2** its curled, astringent pods, which yield tannic acid

div·i·na·tion (div′ə nā′shən) *n.* ⟦ME *divinacioun* < L *divinatio* < *divinatus*, pp. of *divinare*: see fol.⟧ **1** the act or practice of trying to foretell the future or explore the unknown by occult means **2** a prophecy; augury **3** a successful guess or intuitive perception —**di·vin·a·to·ry** (də vin′ə tôr′ē) *adj.*

di·vine (də vīn′) *adj.* ⟦ME & OFr < L *divinus* < *divus*, god, DEITY⟧ **1** of or like God or a god **2** given or inspired by God; holy; sacred **3** devoted to God; religious; sacrosanct **4** having to do with theology **5** supremely great, good, etc. **6** [Informal] very pleasing, attractive, etc. —*n.* **1** a member of the clergy **2** a theologian —*vt.* **-vined′, -vin′ing** ⟦ME *devinen* < OFr *deviner* < L *divinare* < *divinus*⟧ **1** to prophesy **2** to guess; conjecture **3** to find out by intuition —*vi.* **1** to engage in divination **2** to make a conjecture **3** to use a divining rod —***SYN.*** HOLY —**di·vine′ly** *adv.* —**di·vin′er** *n.*

Divine Comedy a long narrative poem in Italian, written (*c.* 1307-21) by Dante Alighieri: it deals with the author's imagined journey through Hell, Purgatory, and Paradise

Divine Liturgy *Eastern Orthodox Ch.* the Eucharistic rite

Divine Office the Psalms, readings, prayers, etc. used at the canonical hours

divine right of kings the former belief that royal authority to rule comes only from God

div·ing bell (dīv′iŋ) a large, hollow, bell-shaped apparatus supplied with air through a hose, in which persons can work underwater

☆**diving board** a flexible board projecting over a swimming pool, lake, etc., for use as a takeoff in diving

diving duck any of various ducks that dive for food or protection, as the redhead

☆**diving suit** a heavy, waterproof garment covering the body, worn by divers working underwater: it has a detachable helmet into which air is pumped through a hose

divining rod a forked branch or stick used by dowsers and others in seeking water or minerals hidden in the earth: it is believed that when the stick dips downward, the location of water or a mineral deposit is indicated

di·vin·i·ty (də vin′ə tē) *n., pl.* **-ties** ⟦ME & OFr *divinite* < L *divinitas* < *divinus*⟧ **1** the quality or condition of being divine **2** a divine being; a god; deity **3** a divine power, virtue, etc. **4** the study of religion; theology ☆**5** a soft, creamy kind of candy —**the Divinity** God

divinity school ⟦see prec.⟧ a Protestant theological seminary

di·vi·nyl·ben·zene (dī vī′nəl ben′zēn′) *n.* ⟦DI-[1] + VINYL + BENZENE⟧ an unsaturated aromatic monomer, $C_6H_4(CH{:}CH_2)_2$, existing in three isomeric forms: used to produce special synthetic rubbers, ion-exchange resins, etc.

di·vis·i·ble (də viz′ə bəl) *adj.* ⟦ME < LL *divisibilis*⟧ that can be divided; dividable, esp. without leaving a remainder —**di·vis′i·bil′i·ty** *n.*

di·vi·sion (də vizh′ən) *n.* ⟦ME *divisioun* < L *divisio* < *divisus*, pp. of *dividere*⟧ **1** a dividing or being divided; separation **2** a sharing or apportioning; distribution **3** a difference of opinion; disagreement **4** a separation into groups in voting **5** anything that divides; partition; boundary **6** anything separated or distinguished from the whole or from the larger unit of which it is a part, as *a)* a particular section of a country, state, etc. divided off as for administration *b)* a particular department of a government, business, school, or other organization *c)* a particular rank or kind, as of students or athletes, based on achievement, age, sex, etc. *d)* a segment, as of the body **7** *Biol.* a major category in the classification of living organisms, esp. plants, ranking above a class and below a kingdom: it can include one class or many similar classes: the Latinized division names are capitalized but not italicized (Ex.: Pinophyta, gymnosperms): cf. PHYLUM (*n.* 1) **8** *Hort.* a form of plant propagation in which new plants are grown from segments detached from the parent plant **9** *Math.* the process of finding how many times a number (the *divisor*) is contained in another number (the *dividend*): the number of times equals the *quotient* **10** *Mil.* a major tactical or administrative unit that can act independently and is under one command; specif., *a)* an army unit larger than a regiment and smaller than a corps, to which various numbers and types of battalions can be attached as required *b)* a tactical subdivision of a naval squadron *c)* an air force unit of two or more combat wings —***SYN.*** PART[1] —**di·vi′sion·al** *adj.*

di·vi·sion·ism (-iz′əm) *n.* ⟦from the juxtaposing of individual dots of color on the canvas, as opposed to mixing colors first on the palette⟧ POINTILLISM —**di·vi′sion·ist** *n., adj.*

division sign the sign (÷) used to indicate that the preceding number or quantity is to be divided by the following number or quantity (Ex.: 8÷4=2 or 2a÷a=2)

di·vi·sive (də vī′siv, -ziv; *also*, -vis′iv) *adj.* ⟦LL *divisivus*⟧ causing division; esp., causing disagreement or dissension —**di·vi′sive·ly** *adv.* —**di·vi′sive·ness** *n.*

di·vi·sor (də vī′zər) *n.* the number or quantity by which the dividend is divided to produce the quotient

di·vorce (də vôrs′) *n.* ⟦ME & OFr < L *divortium* < *divortere*, var. of *divertere*, to turn different ways: see DIVERSE⟧ **1** legal and formal dissolution of a marriage **2** any complete separation or disunion —*vt.* **-vorced′**, **-vorc′ing** **1** to dissolve legally a marriage between; separate by divorce **2** to dissolve the marriage with (one's spouse) **3** to separate; disunite —*vi.* to get a divorce

☆**di·vor·cé** (di vôr′sā′, -sē′; div′ôr sā′, -sē′) *n.* ⟦Fr, orig. pp. of *divorcer*⟧ a divorced man

☆**di·vor·cée** or **di·vor·cee** (di vôr′sā′, -sē′; div′ôr sā′, -sē′) *n.* ⟦Fr, fem. of prec.⟧ a divorced woman

di·vorce·ment (də vôrs′mənt) *n.* divorce

div·ot (div′ət) *n.* ⟦Scot dial. < ?⟧ **1** [Scot.] a thin slice of turf as used for roofing **2** *Golf* a lump of turf dislodged by a player's club in making a stroke

di·vul·gate (də vul′gāt′) *vt.* **-gat′ed**, **-gat′ing** ⟦< L *divulgatus*, pp. of *divulgare*⟧ [Rare] DIVULGE

di·vulge (də vulj′) *vt.* **-vulged′**, **-vulg′ing** ⟦ME *divulgen* < L *divulgare* < *di-* (< *dis-*), apart + *vulgare*, to make public < *vulgus*, the common people: see VULGAR⟧ to make known; disclose; reveal —***SYN.*** REVEAL[1]

di·vul·gence (-vul′jəns) *n.* a divulging or being divulged; disclosure: also **di·vulge′ment** (-vulj′mənt)

di·vul·sion (də vul′shən) *n.* ⟦< L *divulsio* < *divulsus*, pp. of *divellere*, to rend asunder < *di-* (< *dis-*), apart + *vellere*, to pull out, pluck: see REVULSION⟧ a tearing or being torn apart; violent rending or separation

div·vy (div′ē) *vt., vi.* **-vied**, **-vy·ing** ⟦< DIVIDE⟧ [Slang] to share; divide (*up*) —*n.* [Slang] a division

di·wan (dē wän′) *n.* DEWAN

Dix (diks), **Dor·o·the·a (Lynde)** (dôr′ə thē′ə) 1802-87; U.S. social reformer

Dix·ie (dik′sē) ⟦< *Dixie* (earlier, *Dixie's Land*), title of song (1859) by Daniel D. Emmett (1815-1904), U.S. songwriter, after *Dixie*, orig. name of a Negro character in a minstrel play (1850)⟧ the Southern states of the U.S. collectively; Dixieland

☆**Dix·ie·crat** (-krat′) *n.* ⟦prec. + (DEMO)CRAT⟧ a member of a party of Southern Democrats opposed to the civil rights platform of the Democratic Party in 1948

☆**Dixie cup** ⟦< *Dixie*, a trademark for such a cup⟧ [*also* **d- c-**] a small paper drinking cup

Dix·ie·land[1] (-land′) *adj.* in, of, or like a style of small-band, improvised jazz characterized by fast, ragtime tempos and a strict beat, and associated historically with early white New Orleans musicians —*n.* Dixieland jazz

Dix·ie·land[2] (-land′) the South; Dixie: also written **Dixie Land**

DIY (dē′ī′wī′) *n.* DO-IT-YOURSELF

Di·yar·ba·kir (dē yär′bä kir′) city in SE Turkey, on the Tigris

diz·en (dī′zən; *also* diz′ən) *vt.* ⟦MDu *disen*, to put flax on a distaff < LowG *diesse*, bunch of flax, akin to OE *dis-*: see DISTAFF⟧ [Archaic] BEDIZEN

di·zy·got·ic (dī′zī gät′ik) *adj.* developing from two fertilized eggs, as fraternal twins: also **di·zy·gous** (dī zī′gəs)

diz·zy (diz′ē) *adj.* **-zi·er**, **-zi·est** ⟦ME *disi, dusi* < OE *dysig*, foolish < IE base **dhewes-*, to eddy, whirl > DEER⟧ **1** having a whirling, dazed sensation; giddy; lightheaded **2** causing or likely to cause such a sensation **3** confused; bewildered **4** [Informal] silly; foolish; harebrained —*vt.* **-zied**, **-zy·ing** to make dizzy —**diz′zi·ly** *adv.* —**diz′zi·ness** *n.* —**diz′zy·ing·ly** *adv.*

dizzy spell a brief period of dizziness

DJ (dē′jā′) ☆*n.* ⟦D(ISC) J(OCKEY)⟧ **1** a person who conducts a radio program of recorded music, esp. popular music **2** a person who plays recorded music for dancing at a disco, party, etc.

Dja·ja Peak (jä′yə) mountain in the Indonesian province of Papua, W New Guinea: *c.* 16,500 ft (5,029 m)

Dja·kar·ta (jə kärt′ə) *alt. sp. of* JAKARTA

Dja·wa (jä′və) *Indonesian name for* JAVA[2]

djeb·el (jeb′əl) *n.* ⟦Fr < Ar *jebel*⟧ JEBEL

djel·la·ba or **djel·la·bah** (jə lä′bə) *n.* ⟦Ar *jallaba*, contr. < *jallābīya*⟧ a long, loose outer garment worn in Arabic countries

DJIA *abbrev.* Dow Jones Industrial Average

Dji·bou·ti (ji bo͞ot′ē) **1** country in E Africa, on the Gulf of Aden: 8,880 sq mi (23,000 sq km) **2** its capital, a seaport —**Dji·bou′ti·an** *adj., n.*

djinn (jin) *n., pl.* **djinns** or **djinn** *alt. sp. of* JINN

djin·ni (ji nē′, jin′ē) *n., pl.* **djinn** *alt. sp. of* JINNI

dkg *abbrev.* dekagram(s)

dkl *abbrev.* dekaliter(s)

dkm *abbrev.* dekameter(s)

dl *abbrev.* deciliter(s)

DL *abbrev.* **1** *Football* defensive lineman: sometimes written **dl** **2** *Sports* disabled list

D layer the lowest area of the ionosphere, having increased ion density and existing only in the daytime: it begins at an altitude of about 70 km (*c.* 43 mi) and merges with the E layer

DLit, DLitt, D.Lit., *or* **D.Litt.** *abbrev.* ⟦L *Doctor Lit(t)erarum*⟧ Doctor of Letters (or Literature)

DLS or **D.L.S.** *abbrev.* Doctor of Library Science

dm *abbrev.* decimeter(s)

DM *abbrev.* **1** deutsche mark: also **Dm** **2** Doctor of Music: also **D.M., DMus,** or **D.Mus.**

DMA or **D.M.A.** *abbrev.* Doctor of Musical Arts

D-mark (dē′märk′) *n.* DEUTSCHE MARK

DMD or **D.M.D.** *abbrev.* Doctor of Dental Medicine

DMin or **D.Min.** *abbrev.* Doctor of Ministry

DMSO (dē′em′es′ō′) *n.* ⟦*d(i)m(ethyl) s(ulf)o(xide)*⟧ a colorless liquid, $(CH_3)_2SO$, that diffuses very rapidly through the skin: used as a solvent and experimentally in medicine

DMT (dē′em′tē′) *n.* ⟦*d(i)m(ethyl)t(ryptamine)*⟧ a natural, or synthetic, hallucinogenic drug, $C_{12}H_{16}N_2$, similar to LSD in its effects, which are, however, more rapid in onset and shorter in duration

DMV *abbrev.* Department (or Division) of Motor Vehicles

DMZ *abbrev.* demilitarized zone

Dn *abbrev. Bible* Daniel

DNA (dē′en′ā′) *n.* ⟦D(EOXYRIBO)N(UCLEIC) A(CID)⟧ **1** a nucleic acid that is bound in double helical chains by hydrogen bonds between the bases, generally found in the chromosomes of the cell nucleus but also found in the mitochondria: it contains the genetic code and transmits the hereditary pattern **2** figuratively, basic nature or qualities; makeup, constitution, essence, etc.

DNA fingerprinting the identification, as in forensic investigations, of the unique nucleotide sequences in DNA segments of an individual (**DNA fingerprint**) from a group of genetically similar organisms

DNA virus any virus having DNA as its genetic material: see VIRUS (sense 2*a*)

DNB *abbrev.* Dictionary of National Biography

Dnepr (nē′pər, dnē′-; *Russ* dnyepr) *Russ. name for* DNIEPER

Dne·pro·dzer·zhinsk (dnye′prô dzer zhinsk′) city in SC Ukraine, on the Dnieper just west of Dnepropetrovsk

Dne·pro·pe·trovsk (-pye trôfsk′) city in SC Ukraine, on the Dnieper

Dnestr (nēs′tər, dnēs′-; *Russ* dnyestr) *Russ. name for* DNIESTER

Dnie·per (nē′pər, dnē′-) river in W Russia, Belarus, & Ukraine, flowing from the Valdai Hills south and southwest into the Black Sea: 1,420 mi (2,285 km): Ukrainian name **Dni′pro** (dnē′prō)

Dnies·ter (nēs′tər, dnēs′-) river in SW Ukraine & Moldova, flowing from the Carpathian Mountains southeast into the Black Sea: c. 850 mi (1,368 km): Ukrainian name **Dnis′ter** (dnēs′ter)

DNR *abbrev.* do not resuscitate

do[1] (do͞o) *vt.* **did, done, do′ing** ⟦ME & OE *don*, akin to Ger *tun*, OS *duan* < IE base **dhē-*, to put, place, set > Sans *dadhāmi*, Gr *tithenai*, to place, put, L *-dere* (as in *condere*, to set down), *facere*, to do, make⟧ **1** *a)* to execute; effect; perform (an act, action, etc.) *[do* great deeds*]* *b)* to carry out; fulfill *[do* what I tell you*]* **2** to bring about; cause; produce *[*it *does* no harm; who *did* this to you?*]* **3** to exert (efforts, etc.) *[do* your best*]* **4** *a)* to deal with as is required; attend to *[do* the ironing*]* *b)* to attend to cosmetically *[do* one's nails, have one's hair *done]* **5** to have as one's work or occupation; work at or on *[*what does he *do* for a living?*]* **6** to work out; solve *[do* a problem*]* **7** to produce or appear in (a play, etc.) *[*we *did* Hamlet*]* **8** *a)* to play the role of *[*I *did* Polonius*]* *b)* [Informal] to mimic or imitate *[do* Cary Grant*]* **9** to write or publish (a book), compose (a musical score), etc. **10** *a)* to cover (distance) *[*to *do* a mile in four minutes*]* *b)* to move along at a speed of *[*to *do* 60 miles an hour*]* **11** to translate *[*to *do* Horace into English*]* **12** to give; render *[*to *do* honor to the dead*]* **13** to suit; be convenient to *[*this will *do* me very well*]* **14** to decorate or design *[do* a room in earth tones*]* **15** [Informal] to have or take (a meal) *[*let's *do* lunch*]* **16** [Informal] to visit as a sightseer; tour *[*they *did* England in two months*]* **17** [Informal] *a)* to prepare; cook *[*that restaurant *does* ribs really well*]* *b)* to eat *[*let's *do* Mexican tonight*]* **18** [Informal] to cheat; swindle: now chiefly in the phrase **do someone out of** *[*they *did him out of* his rightful share*]* **19** [Informal] to serve (a jail term) **20** [Slang] to take; ingest; use *[*we've never *done* drugs*]* **21** [Slang] to perform a sexual act upon; specif., to have sexual intercourse with **22** [Slang] to kill —*vi.* **1** to act in a specified way; behave or perform *[*he *does* well when treated well*]* **2** to be active; work *[do;* don't merely talk*]* **3** to finish: used in the perfect tense *[*have *done* with dreaming*]* **4** to get along; fare *[*mother and child are *doing* well*]* **5** to be adequate or suitable; serve the purpose *[*the black dress will *do]* **6** to take place; go on *[*anything *doing* tonight?*]* **7** [Informal, Chiefly Brit.] used as a substitute verb after a modal auxiliary or a form of *have* in a perfect tense *[*I haven't seen the film, but she may have *done]* —*v.aux.* **1** used to give emphasis, or as a legal convention *[do* stay a while, *do* hereby enjoin*]* **2** used to ask a question *[did* you write?*]* **3** used to serve as part of a negative command or statement *[do* not go; they *do* not like it*]* **4** used to serve as a substitute verb *[*love me as I *do* (love) you*]* **5** used to form inverted constructions after some adverbs *[*little *did* he realize*]* —*n., pl.* **do's** or **dos 1** [Informal, Chiefly Brit.] a hoax; swindle **2** [Informal, Chiefly Brit.] a party or social event **3** [Slang] excrement; feces *[*dog *do]* —*SYN.* PERFORM —**do down** [Brit. Informal] **1** to criticize, belittle, or demean; disparage **2** to gain advantage over, as by deception —**do in 1** [Slang] to kill **2** [Informal] to tire out; exhaust —**do over** [Informal] to redecorate —**do right (**or **well, wrong,** etc.**) by someone** to act rightly (or well, wrongly, etc.) toward or for someone — **do's (**or **dos) and don'ts** [Informal] the things permitted or required and the things forbidden; rules and regulations —**do up 1** [Informal] to prepare **2** to wrap up; tie up; fasten **3** to arrange (the hair) so that it is off the neck and shoulders —**do up right** [Informal] to do carefully or thoroughly — **do oneself well (**or **proud)** ⟦modeled on Ger *sich gütlich tun*⟧ to achieve success for oneself —**do with 1** to make use of: often with *can* or *could* **2** to find helpful or agreeable: usually with *can* or *could [*I could *do with* a cold drink*]* —**do without** to get along without (something); dispense with (something) —**have to do with 1** to be related to or connected with: also [Brit.] **be to do with 2** to be associated with; deal with

do[2] (dō) *n.* ⟦It (< *dominus*, first word of a Latin hymn): used instead of earlier UT: see GAMUT⟧ *Music* a syllable representing the first or last tone of the diatonic scale: see SOLFEGGIO

do[3] (do͞o) *n.* [Slang] *short for* HAIRDO

Do or **do** *abbrev.* ditto

DO or **D.O.** *abbrev.* Doctor of Osteopathy

DOA *abbrev.* dead on arrival

do·a·ble (do͞o′ə bəl) *adj.* that can be done

DOB *abbrev.* date of birth

☆**dob·ber** (däb′ər) *n.* ⟦< Du *dobber*⟧ [Dial.] the float on a fisherman's line

Dob·bin (däb′in) *n.* ⟦nickname for ROBIN, ROBERT[1]⟧ a traditional name for a draft horse, farm horse, etc., esp. a plodding, patient one: sometimes used informally to refer to the typical workhorse

dob·by weave (däb′ē) ⟦< *Dobbie*, dim. of *Dob, Dobbin*: see prec.⟧ a weave with small, geometric patterns

Do·bell's solution (dō belz′) ⟦after H. B. *Dobell* (1828-1917), Eng physician⟧ a solution of sodium borate, sodium bicarbonate, etc., formerly used as a mouthwash

Do·ber·man pin·scher (dō′bər mən pin′chər, -shər) ⟦Ger *Dobermann pinscher* after L. *Dobermann*, 19th-c. breeder + *pinscher*, terrier, after ? *Pinzgau*, area in N Austria known for breeding of dogs⟧ any of a breed of large dog with erect ears and a short, smooth, usually dark coat with tan markings: traditionally the tail is docked: also called **Doberman** *n.*

Do·bie (dō′bē), **J(ames) Frank** 1888-1964; U.S. writer, esp. on the folklore of the Southwest

Do·bos torte (dō′bōs, -bōsh) ⟦after Jozsef *Dobos* (1847-1924), Hung baker who created it⟧ [*also* **d- t-**] a rich cake having many thin layers of sponge cake with creamy mocha filling and a caramel glaze on top

do·bra (dō′brə) *n.* ⟦after a former Port gold coin < Port, lit., doubloon, orig., fem. of *dobro*, double < L *duplus*, DOUBLE⟧ the basic monetary unit of São Tomé and Príncipe: see the table of monetary units in the Reference Supplement

☆**Do·bro** (dō′brō′) ⟦after *Do(pera) bro(thers)*, who developed it (*c.* 1928); infl. by Czech *dobro*, good⟧ *trademark for* a type of acoustic steel guitar with a circular resonator made of metal, esp. aluminum or tin, built into the guitar's hollow body, used in country music: it is played while held flat, often in the lap —*n.* [*often* **d-**] an instrument of this type

Do·bru·ja (dō′bro͞o jə) region in SE Europe, on the Black Sea: divided, since 1940, between Romania & Bulgaria

☆**dob·son** (däb′sən) *n.* ⟦fisherman's term < ? the name *Dobson*⟧ HELLGRAMMITE

☆**dob·son·fly** (-flī′) *n., pl.* **-flies′** any of a family (Corydalidae) of large neuropteran insects whose larvae live in water: the male, in some species, develops enormous mandibles

Dob·son unit (däb′sən) ⟦after G. M. B. *Dobson* (1889-1976), Brit meteorologist & early ozone researcher⟧ a basic unit used to measure the amount of ozone in a vertical column of the atmosphere above a specific location on earth, equal to 2.69 × 10^{20} ozone molecules per square meter: abbrev. *DU*

☆**doc**[1] (däk) *n.* [Slang] doctor: often used as a general term of address

doc[2] *abbrev.* document

☆**do·cent** (dō′sənt; *also* dō sent′) *n.* ⟦Ger, earlier sp. of *dozent*, teacher, lecturer < L *docens*, prp. of *docere*, to teach: see DECENT⟧ **1** in some American universities, a teacher or lecturer not on the regular faculty **2** a tour guide and lecturer, as at a museum

Do·ce·tism (dō sēt′iz′əm) *n.* ⟦< Gr(Ec) *Dokētai*, name of the sect < *dokein*, to seem, believe (see DOGMA) + -ISM⟧ a belief among some early Christians that Christ merely seemed to have a human body: it came to be considered heretical —**do·ce′tic** (-sēt′ik) *adj.*

doc·ile (däs′əl; *Cdn & Brit, usually* dō′sīl′) *adj.* ⟦Fr < L *docilis*, easily taught < *docere*, to teach: see DECENT⟧ **1** [Now Rare] easy to teach; teachable **2** easy to manage or discipline; submissive —*SYN.* OBEDIENT —**doc′ile·ly** *adv.* —**do·cil·i·ty** (dä sil′ə tē, dō-) *n.*

dock[1] (däk) *n.* ⟦orig., mud channel made by a vessel's bottom at low tide: hence, dock < MDu *docke*, channel < It *doccia*, conduit, canal: see DOUCHE⟧ **1** a large structure or excavated basin for receiving ships, equipped with gates to keep water in or out ☆**2** a landing pier; wharf **3** the area of water between two landing piers ☆**4** a platform at which trucks or freight cars are loaded and unloaded ☆**5** a building, platform, or area for servicing aircraft —*vt.* **1** to bring or pilot (a ship) to or into a dock and moor it ☆**2** to join (vehicles) together in outer space —*vi.* **1** to come to or into a dock and moor ☆**2** to join up with another vehicle in outer space

dock[2] (däk) *n.* ⟦< Fl *docke, dok*, hutch, pen, cage⟧ the place where the accused stands or sits in court

dock[3] (däk) *n.* ⟦ME *dokke* < OE *docce*, akin to MHG *tocke*, bundle, tuft⟧ any of various tall, coarse weeds (genus *Rumex*) of the buckwheat family, with stout taproots, small green or brown flowers, and large leaves: see SORREL[1]

dock[4] (däk) *n.* ⟦ME *dok* < OE *-docca* or ON *dockr*, a short, stumpy tail, akin to prec.⟧ **1** the solid part of an animal's tail, excluding the hair **2** an animal's bobbed tail —*vt.* ⟦ME *dokken* < the n.⟧ **1** to cut off the end of (a tail, etc.); clip or bob **2** to shorten the tail of by cutting **3** to deduct a part from (wages, etc.) **4** to deduct a part from the wages of **5** to remove part of

dock·age[1] (däk′ij) *n.* ⟦DOCK[1] + -AGE⟧ **1** the fee charged for the use of a dock **2** docking accommodations **3** the docking of ships

dock·age[2] (däk′ij) *n.* ⟦DOCK[4] + -AGE⟧ a cutting off or down; curtailment; deduction

dock·er[1] (däk′ər) *n.* [Chiefly Brit.] LONGSHOREMAN

dock·er[2] (däk′ər) *n.* a person or thing that docks

dock·et (däk′it) *n.* ⟦earlier *doggette*, abstract, register < ? It *doghetta*, small heraldic bend⟧ **1** a summary, as of a legal proceeding, or a list of legal decisions ☆**2** a list of cases to be tried by a law court **3** any list or summary of things to be done; agenda **4** a label listing the contents of a package, directions, etc. —*vt.* ☆**1** to enter in a docket **2** to put a docket, or label, on; ticket

dock·land (däk′land′, -lənd) *n.* [*often pl.*] [Brit.] the district around the docks of a port, esp. of the city of London

☆**dock·mack·ie** (-mak′ē) *n.* ⟦? via Du < AmInd (Lenape) *dogekumak*⟧ a shrub (*Viburnum acerifolium*) of the honeysuckle family, with clusters of yellow-white flowers

dock·side (-sīd′) *n.* the area alongside a dock

☆**dock·wal·lop·er** (-wäl′əp ər) *n.* ⟦DOCK[1] + WALLOPER⟧ [Informal] LONGSHOREMAN

dock·work·er (-wur′kər) *n.* LONGSHOREMAN

dock·yard (-yärd′) *n.* **1** SHIPYARD **2** *Brit. term for* NAVY YARD

doc·tor (däk′tər) *n.* ⟦ME *doctour*, teacher, learned man < OFr or < L *doctor*, teacher < pp. of *docere*, to teach: see DECENT⟧ **1** [Archaic] a teacher or learned man **2** a person who holds a doctorate **3** a physician or surgeon **4** a person licensed to practice any of the healing arts, as an osteopath, dentist, veterinarian, etc. **5** [**D-**] a title used in addressing any person who holds a doctorate **6** a witch doctor or medicine man **7** a makeshift device, apparatus, etc., for emergency use **8** a bright-colored artificial fly used in fishing —*vt.* [Informal] **1** to try to heal; apply medicine to **2** to repair; mend **3** to make suitable or improve by altering in a certain way **4** to tamper with or change in order to deceive [to *doctor* accounts] —*vi.* **1** [Informal] to practice medicine ☆**2** [Dial.] to undergo medical treatment, take medicine, etc.

doc·tor·al (-əl) ***adj.*** for or having to do with a doctorate [a *doctoral* dissertation]

doc·tor·ate (-it) ***n.*** ⟦ML *doctoratus*⟧ **1** any degree at the highest level awarded by universities, either as an indication of the successful completion of academic study, as *Doctor of Philosophy*, or as an honorary degree and title, as *Doctor of Laws*: also **doctor's (degree) 2** the status of doctor

Doctor of Philosophy the highest doctorate awarded by a university for original research in any discipline

doc·tri·naire (däk′tri ner′) ***n.*** ⟦Fr < *doctrine*, doctrine⟧ a person who dogmatically seeks to apply theories regardless of the practical problems involved —***adj.*** stubbornly adhering to a doctrine or theory —**SYN.** DICTATORIAL —**doc′tri·nair′ism′ *n.***

doc·trine (däk′trin) ***n.*** ⟦ME < L *doctrina* < *doctor*: see DOCTOR⟧ **1** something taught; teachings **2** something taught as the principles or creed of a religion, political party, etc.; tenet or tenets; belief; dogma **3** a rule, theory, or principle of law ☆**4** an official statement of a nation's policy, esp. toward other nations [the Monroe *Doctrine*] —**doc′tri·nal** (-tri nəl) ***adj.*** —**doc′tri·nal·ly *adv.***

SYN.—doctrine refers to a theory based on carefully worked out principles and taught or advocated by its adherents [scientific or social *doctrines*]; **dogma** refers to a belief or doctrine that is handed down by authority as true and indisputable, and often connotes arbitrariness, arrogance, etc. [religious *dogma*]; **tenet** emphasizes the maintenance or defense, rather than the teaching, of a theory or principle [the *tenets* of a political party]; **precept** refers to an injunction or dogma intended as a rule of action or conduct [to teach by example rather than by *precept*]

doc·u- (däk′yo͞o, -yə) *combining form* documentary [*docudrama*]

☆**doc·u·dra·ma** (däk′yo͞o drä′mə) ***n.*** a fictionalized dramatization for television of an actual event or about real people

doc·u·ment (däk′yo͞o mənt, -yə-; *for v.,* -ment′) ***n.*** ⟦ME & OFr < L *documentum*, lesson, example, proof < *docere*, to teach: see DECENT⟧ **1** something containing information, esp. information in printed or written form, often, specif., something that is relied upon to record or prove something: documents may be on paper, in digital or electronic form, etc. **2** anything serving as proof —*vt.* **1** to provide with a document or documents **2** to provide (a book, pamphlet, etc.) with documents or supporting references **3** to prove, as by reference to documents **4** to gather and report the details of; cover or chronicle —**doc′u·men′tal** (-ment′'l) ***adj.***

doc·u·men·tar·i·an (däk′yo͞o mən ter′ē ən, -yə-) ***n.*** a producer of documentaries: also **doc′u·men′ta·rist** (-ment′ə rist)

doc·u·men·ta·ry (däk′yo͞o ment′ə rē, -yə-) ***adj.*** **1** consisting of, supported by, contained in, or serving as a document or documents **2** designating or of a film, TV program, etc. that dramatically shows or analyzes news events, social conditions, etc., with little or no fictionalization —***n.,*** *pl.* **-ries** a documentary film, TV show, etc.

doc·u·men·ta·tion (-mən tā′shən, -men-) ***n.*** **1** the supplying of documents or supporting references; use of documentary evidence **2** the documents or references thus supplied **3** the collecting, abstracting, and coding of printed or written information for future reference **4** instructions, notes, etc. for using a piece of computer hardware or software

DOD or **DoD** *abbrev.* Department of Defense

dod·der[1] (däd′ər) ***vi.*** ⟦ME *daderen*, akin to OE *dyderian*, to confuse, delude, MDu *doten*, DOTE < IE **dheudh-*, to whirl in confusion, shake (> Gr *thysanos*, fringe) < base **dheu-*; see DULL⟧ **1** to shake or tremble, as from old age **2** to be unsteady; totter

dod·der[2] (däd′ər) ***n.*** ⟦ME *doder* < Late OE *dodder* < same base as prec.: akin to dial. *dodder*, quaking-grass & Ger *dotter*, egg yolk⟧ any of a genus (*Cuscuta*) of parasitic plants of the morning-glory family, lacking leaves, roots, and chlorophyll, but having special suckers for drawing nourishment from the host

dod·dered (däd′ərd) ***adj.*** ⟦prob. < ME *dodden*, to cut off; ? infl. by DODDER[1]⟧ having lost its branches or top because of age, decay, etc.: said of a tree

dod·der·ing (däd′ər iŋ) ***adj.*** ⟦< DODDER[1]⟧ unsteady or unsound, as from old age; shaky, tottering, etc.: also **dod′der·y**

do·dec·a- (dō′dek′ə) ⟦< Gr *dōdeka*, twelve < *dō-*, two < IE **dwō-*, TWO + Gr *deka*, TEN⟧ *combining form* twelve: also, before a vowel, **dodec-**

do·dec·a·gon (dō dek′ə gän′, -gən) ***n.*** ⟦Gr *dōdekagōnon*: see prec. & -GON⟧ a plane figure with twelve angles and twelve sides

do·dec·a·he·dron (dō′dek ə hē′drən) ***n.,*** *pl.* **-drons** or **-dra** (-drə) ⟦Gr *dōdekaedron*: see DODECA- & -HEDRON⟧ a solid figure with twelve plane faces —**do′dec·a·he′dral** (-drəl) ***adj.***

Do·dec·a·nese (dō dek′ə nēz′, -nēs′) group of Greek islands in the Aegean, off the SW coast of Turkey: 1,048 sq mi (2,714 sq km) —**Do·dec′a·ne′sian** (-nē′zhən, -shən) ***adj., n.***

do·dec·a·phon·ic (dō′dek ə fän′ik, dō dek′-) ***adj.*** ⟦DODECA- + -PHON(E) + -IC⟧ TWELVE-TONE —**do·dec′a·pho·nist** (-fə nist, -fōn′ist) ***n.*** —**do·dec′a·pho·ny** (-fə nē, -fōn′ē) ***n.,*** **do·dec′a·pho·nism′** (-fə niz′əm, -fōn′iz′əm)

dodge (däj) ***vi.*** **dodged, dodg′ing** ⟦? akin to Scot *dod*, to jog: for IE base see DODDER[1]⟧ **1** to move or twist quickly aside; shift suddenly, as to avoid a blow **2** to use tricks, deceits, or evasions; be shifty —*vt.* **1** to avoid (a blow, etc.) by moving or shifting quickly aside **2** to evade (a question, charge, etc.) by trickery, cleverness, etc. **3** to avoid meeting **4** *Photog.* to lighten an area on (a print) to achieve a shading effect by blocking light in selected areas during an exposure, as in enlargement —*n.* **1** a dodging **2** a trick used in evading or cheating **3** a clever or resourceful device, plan, etc.

dodge·ball (däj′bôl′) ***n.*** ⟦see DODGE (*vt.* 1)⟧ a game in which players are eliminated if they are unable to keep from being hit by a ball, typically an inflated one, thrown by an opposing player

Dodge City ⟦? after Col. Richard I. *Dodge*, prominent city official⟧ city in SW Kans., on the Arkansas River: famous as a frontier town on the Santa Fe Trail

☆**dodg·em** (däj′əm) ***n.*** ⟦< *Dodgem*, a trademark < DODG(E) + (TH)EM⟧ an amusement-park ride consisting of small electric cars with thick rubber bumpers, whose drivers try to bump their cars into others while trying to avoid being hit themselves

dodg·er (-ər) ***n.*** **1** a person who dodges **2** a tricky, dishonest person; shifty rascal **3** CORNDODGER ☆**4** a small handbill **5** *Photog.* a device for dodging: see DODGE (*vt.* 4)

dodg·er·y (-ər ē) ***n.*** trickery, evasiveness, etc.

Dodg·son (däj′sən), **Charles Lut·widge** (lut′wij) *see* CARROLL, Lewis

dodg·y (däj′ē) ***adj.*** **dodg′i·er, dodg′i·est** [Informal, Chiefly Brit.] **1** tricky or evasive **2** risky or uncertain

do·do (dō′dō) ***n.,*** *pl.* **-dos** or **-does** ⟦Port *doudo*, lit., foolish, stupid⟧ **1** a large extinct bird (*Raphus cucullatus*) that had rudimentary wings useless for flying: formerly found on Mauritius **2** *a)* an old-fashioned person; fogy *b)* [Slang] a stupid person; dullard

Do·do·ma (dō′də mä′, -mə) capital of Tanzania, in the central part

doe (dō) ***n.,*** *pl.* **does** or **doe** ⟦ME *do* < OE *da*, akin to Alemannic *te* < IE base **dome-*, TAME⟧ the female deer, antelope, rabbit, goat, etc.: see BUCK[1]

Doe (dō) ***n.*** a name (*John Doe, Jane Doe*) used in law courts, legal papers, etc. to refer to any person whose name is unknown

DOE *abbrev.* Department of Energy

doe-eyed (dō′īd′) ***adj.*** **1** having large, soft, limpid eyes **2** naive; guileless; childlike

do·er (do͞o′ər) ***n.*** **1** a person who does something or acts in a specified manner [a *doer* of good] **2** a person who gets things done

does (duz) ***vt., vi.*** *3d pers. sing., pres. indic., of* DO[1]

doe·skin (dō′skin′) ***n.*** **1** the skin of a female deer **2** leather made from this or, now usually, from lambskin **3** a fine, soft, smooth woolen cloth with a slight nap, used for suits, sportswear, etc.

does·n't (duz′ənt) *contraction* does not

do·est (do͞o′ist) ***vt., vi.*** *archaic 2d pers. sing., pres. indic., of* DO[1]: used with *thou*

do·eth (-ith) ***vt., vi.*** *archaic 3d pers. sing., pres. indic., of* DO[1]

doff (däf, dôf) ***vt.*** ⟦ME *doffen* < *don of*: see DO[1] & OFF[1]⟧ **1** to take off (clothes, etc.) **2** to remove or lift (one's hat), as in greeting **3** to put aside or discard

dog (dôg, däg) ***n.,*** *pl.* **dogs** or **dog** ⟦ME, generalized in sense < late, rare OE *docga, dogga* (usual *hund*: see HOUND[1]) < ?⟧ **1** *a)* any of a large and varied group of domesticated canines (*Canis familiaris*) often kept as a house pet or used for hunting, guarding people or property, etc. *b)* any of various wild canines **2** the male of a canine **3** a mean, contemptible fellow **4** a prairie dog, dogfish, or other animal thought to resemble a dog **5** ⟦< its orig. shape: cf. Fr *chenet*⟧ an andiron; firedog **6** [Informal] a person [lucky *dog*] ☆**7** [*pl.*] [Slang] feet **8** [Informal] HOT DOG (sense 1) **9** [Slang] *a)* an unattractive or unpopular person ☆*b)* an unsatisfactory thing or unsuccessful venture **10** *Mech.* any of several devices for holding or grappling **11** *Meteorol. a)* a parhelion; sundog *b)* a fogdog —***adj.*** designating a family (Canidae) of meat-eating animals that includes dogs, foxes, wolves, coyotes, and jackals —*vt.* **dogged, dog′ging 1** to follow, hunt, or track down doggedly ☆**2** to hold or secure with a mechanical dog —***adv.*** ⟦< phr. *as ___ as a dog*⟧ very; completely: used in comb. [*dog*-tired] —**a dog's age** [Informal] a long time —**a dog's life** a wretched existence —**dog in the manger** ⟦from the fable of AESOP in which a dog stays in an ox's manger and keeps the ox from eating the hay, even though the dog cannot eat it himself⟧ a person who keeps others from having or enjoying something which that person either has but cannot use and may not want or does want but cannot have —**dog it** [Slang] to fail to exert the maximum or expected effort —**every dog has his day** something good or lucky happens to everyone at one time or another —**go to the dogs** [Informal] to deteriorate; degenerate —**let sleeping dogs lie** to let well enough alone; not disturb things as they are for fear of something worse —☆**put on the dog** [Slang] to make a show of being very elegant, wealthy,

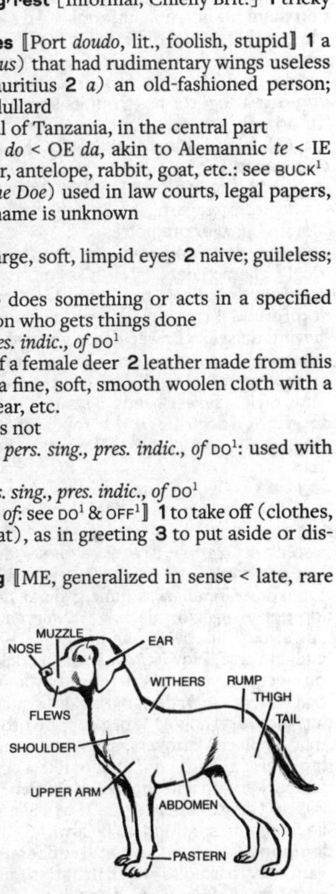

MUZZLE
NOSE
EAR
WITHERS
RUMP
THIGH
TAIL
FLEWS
SHOULDER
UPPER ARM
ABDOMEN
PASTERN

dog (Labrador retriever)

etc. —**teach an old dog new tricks** to induce a person of settled habits to adopt new methods or ideas —**the Greater Dog** the constellation Canis Major: also called **the Big Dog** —**the Lesser Dog** the constellation Canis Minor: also called **the Little Dog**

☆**dog and pony show** [Informal] an elaborate event, presentation, etc. intended to impress or influence people: a dismissive term: also written **dog-and-pony show**

dog·bane (dôg′bān′) *adj.* ⟦so named because said to be poisonous to dogs⟧ designating a family (Apocynaceae, order Gentianales) of dicotyledonous herbs, shrubs, and trees, including frangipani and periwinkle —*n.* any of a genus (*Apocynum*) of sometimes poisonous plants of the dogbane family, with opposite, entire leaves, small white or pink flowers, and milky juice

dog·ber·ry (dôg′ber′ē) *n., pl.* **-ries** 1 the berry or fruit of any of various plants, as the mountain ash and gooseberry 2 any of these plants

dog biscuit 1 a hard biscuit containing ground bones, meat, etc., for feeding dogs ☆2 [Slang] an army field-ration biscuit

dog·cart (dôg′kärt′) *n.* 1 a small, light cart drawn by dogs 2 a small, light, open 19th-cent. carriage, usually with two wheels, having two seats arranged back to back: it originally had a box under the seat for a sportsman's dog

☆**dog·catch·er** (dôg′kach′ər) *n.* a local official whose work is catching and impounding stray or unlicensed animals

dog collar 1 a collar to be worn by a dog 2 [Slang] CLERICAL COLLAR

dog days the hot, uncomfortable days in July and August: so called because during that period the Dog Star (Sirius) rises and sets with the sun

doge (dōj) *n.* ⟦It < L *dux*, leader < *ducere*, to lead: see DUCT⟧ the chief magistrate of either of the former republics of Venice and Genoa

dog-ear (dôg′ir′) *n.* ⟦from its shape⟧ a turned-down corner of the page of a book, magazine, etc. —*vt.* to turn down the corner of (a page or pages) Also written **dogear**

dog-eared (-ird′) *adj.* ⟦see prec.⟧ 1 having a corner turned down: said of a page in a book, magazine, etc. 2 having pages with turned-down corners [*a dog-eared* paperback] 3 shabby, run-down, worn-out, etc. [a *dog-eared* hotel, *dog-eared* prejudices]

dog-eat-dog (dôg′ēt dôg′) *adj.* ⟦from the proverb, "Dog does not eat dog"⟧ characterized by ruthless or savage competition

☆**dog·face** (dôg′fās′) *n.* [Slang] *U.S. Army* an infantryman in WWII

dog fennel 1 an annual weed (*Anthemis cotula*) of the composite family, having daisylike flower heads with white rays and yellow centers, and an offensive smell; mayweed ☆2 a tall, annual weed (*Eupatorium capillifolium*) of the composite family, with finely divided leaves and a terminal cluster of tiny, rayless flower heads 3 HEATH ASTER

dog·fight (dôg′fīt′) *n.* 1 a rough, violent fight between, or as between, dogs 2 *Mil.* an instance of combat as between fighter planes at close quarters

dog·fish (dôg′fish′) *n., pl.* **-fish′** or **-fish′es** (see FISH) 1 any of various small sharks, as a spiny dogfish or the smooth dogfish 2 BOWFIN

dog·ged (dôg′id, däg′-) *adj.* ⟦ME < *dogge*, DOG⟧ not giving in readily; persistent; stubborn —*SYN.* STUBBORN —**dog′ged·ly** *adv.* —**dog′ged·ness** *n.*

Dog·ger Bank (-er) extensive sand bank in the central North Sea, between England & Denmark, submerged at a depth of 60-120 ft (18-37 m)

dog·ger·el (dôg′ər əl) *n.* ⟦ME *dogerel* (Chaucer), prob. < It *doga*, barrel stave, but infl. by *dog* as in DOG LATIN: parallel with Ger *knüttelvers*, lit., cudgel verse, Prov *bastonnet*, little stick, type of verse⟧ 1 trivial, awkward, often comic verse characterized by a monotonous rhythm 2 any trivial or bad poetry —*adj.* designating or of such verse Also **dog·grel** (dôg′rəl)

☆**dog·gie bag** (dôg′ē) a bag supplied to a patron of a restaurant, in which may be placed leftovers, as to take home to a dog or other pet

dog·gish (dôg′ish) *adj.* 1 of or like a dog; esp., snarling or snapping 2 [Informal] stylish and showy —**dog′gish·ly** *adv.* —**dog′gish·ness** *n.*

dog·go (dôg′ō) *adv.* ⟦< DOG + -O⟧ [Slang] out of sight: chiefly in the phrase **lie doggo**, to stay hidden; lie low

dog·gone (dôg′gôn′) *interj.* ⟦euphemism for *God damn*⟧ damn; darn: used variously to express anger, irritation, surprise, pleasure, etc. —*vt.* **-goned′**, **-gon′ing** [Informal] to damn —*n.* [Informal] a damn —*adj.* [Informal] damned: also **dog′goned′**

dog·gy (dôg′ē) *n., pl.* **-gies** 1 a little dog 2 any dog: a child's word Also **dog′gie** —*adj.* **-gi·er**, **-gi·est** 1 of or like a dog ☆2 [Informal] stylish and showy

dog·house (dôg′hous′) *n.* a small, roofed structure for sheltering a dog —☆**in the doghouse** [Slang] in disfavor

☆**do·gie** (dō′gē) *n.* ⟦< ?⟧ [West] a stray or motherless calf

dog Latin ⟦< DOG, used attributively in negative sense, "bad, mongrel"⟧ incorrect or ungrammatical Latin

dog·leg (dôg′leg′, -lāg′) *n.* a sharp angle or bend like that formed by a dog's hind leg, as in a golf fairway —*vi.* **-legged′**, **-leg′ging** to go or lie in one direction and then angle off in another —*adj.* of, or having the form of, a dogleg: also **dog′leg′ged** (-leg′id, -legd′; -lā′gid, -lāgd′)

dog·ma (dôg′mə, däg′-) *n., pl.* **-mas** or **-ma·ta** (-mə tə) ⟦L, an opinion, that which one believes (in LL(Ec), a decree, order) < Gr, opinion, judgment < *dokein*, to seem: see DECENT⟧ 1 a doctrine; tenet; belief 2 doctrines, tenets, or beliefs, collectively 3 a positive, arrogant assertion of opinion 4 *Eccles.* a doctrine or body of doctrines formally and authoritatively affirmed —*SYN.* DOCTRINE

dog·mat·ic (dôg mat′ik) *adj.* ⟦L *dogmaticus* < Gr *dogmatikos*⟧ 1 of or like dogma; doctrinal 2 stating opinion in an assertive or arrogant manner: also **dog·mat′i·cal** —*SYN.* DICTATORIAL —**dog·mat′i·cal·ly** *adv.*

dog·mat·ics (-iks) *n.* ⟦< earlier sing. n. *dogmatic*, having the same meaning: see prec. & -ICS⟧ the study of religious dogmas, esp. those of Christianity

dog·ma·tism (dôg′mə tiz′əm, däg′-) *n.* ⟦Fr *dogmatisme* < ML *dogmatismus* < Gr *dogmatizein*, to lay down a decree: see DOGMA⟧ dogmatic assertion of opinion, usually without reference to evidence —**dog′ma·tist** *n.*

dog·ma·tize (-tīz′) *vi.* **-tized′**, **-tiz′ing** ⟦Fr *dogmatiser* < ML *dogmatizare* < Gr *dogmatizein*⟧ to speak or write dogmatically —*vt.* to formulate or express as dogma —**dog′ma·tiz′er** *n.*

☆**dog·nap** (dôg′nap′) *vt.* **-napped′** or **-naped′**, **-nap′ping** or **-nap′ing** ⟦DOG + (KID)NAP⟧ to steal (a dog), esp. in order to sell it to a medical research laboratory —**dog′nap′per** *n.*, **dog′nap′er**

☆**do-good·er** (dōō′good′ər) *n.* [Informal] an idealistic person who seeks to correct social ills: a dismissive term —**do′-good′** *adj.* —**do′-good′ing** *n.*, **do′-good′ism′**

dog paddle *Swimming* a simple stroke in which the body is kept nearly upright, the arms paddle, and the legs move up and down as in running

☆**dog·rob·ber** (dôg′räb′ər) *n.* ⟦so called because said to be willing even to *rob* a *dog* of its bone to please his superior⟧ [Mil. Slang] an officer's orderly

dog rose ⟦transl. of the taxonomic name⟧ a European wild rose (*Rosa canina*), with pink flowers and hooked spines

☆**dog salmon** CHUM SALMON

dogs·bod·y (dôgz′bäd′ē) *n., pl.* **-bod′ies** ⟦from Brit navy slang: a junior officer; orig., a dish made from dried peas boiled in water⟧ [Brit. Informal] a person appointed or hired to do menial work; drudge

dog's breakfast (*or* dinner) [Informal, Chiefly Brit.] a botched or muddled piece of work

dog sled a sled drawn by dogs: also written **dog′sled′** *n.* —**dog′-sled′** *vi.* **-sled′ded**, **-sled′ding** —**dog′-sled′der** *n.*

dog's-tail (dôgz′tāl′) *n.* any of a genus (*Cynosurus*) of perennial grasses, esp. the **crested dog's-tail** (*C. cristatus*) with a slender spike resembling that of timothy

Dog Star 1 SIRIUS 2 PROCYON: usually called *the Little Dog Star*

dog tag 1 an identification tag or license tag for a dog ☆2 [Slang] a military identification tag worn about the neck

dog-tired (dôg′tīrd′) *adj.* ⟦< phr. (*as*) *tired* (*as a*) *dog*⟧ very tired; exhausted

dog·tooth (dôg′tōōth′) *n., pl.* **-teeth′** 1 a canine tooth; eyetooth 2 an ornamental molding in some medieval buildings, consisting of a series of projections often resembling petals radiating from a raised center 3 HOUNDSTOOTH (CHECK)

dogtooth violet ☆any of a genus (*Erythronium*) of small plants of the lily family, esp. an American, early spring flower (*E. americanum*) with two mottled leaves and a yellow flower, or a European plant (*E. denscanis*) with a purple or rose flower

dog·trot (dôg′trät′) *n.* 1 a slow, easy trot, like a dog's ☆2 [Chiefly South] a covered passageway between two parts of a building

dog·watch (dôg′wäch′) *n.* *Naut.* either of the two duty periods (from 4 to 6 P.M. and from 6 to 8 P.M.) that are half the length of a normal period

dog whistle a WHISTLE (*n.* 1) designed to produce a high pitch that cannot be heard by humans but can be used to train or call dogs

dog·wood (dôg′wood′) *adj.* ⟦shortened < *dogberry wood, dogberry tree*⟧ designating a family (Cornaceae, order Cornales) of dicotyledonous small trees and shrubs —*n.* 1 any of a genus (*Cornus*) of trees and shrubs of the dogwood family, esp. the flowering dogwood 2 its hard, closegrained wood

☆**do·gy** (dō′gē) *n., pl.* **-gies** *alt. sp. of* DOGIE

Do·ha (dō′hə) seaport & capital of Qatar, on the Persian Gulf

Doh·ná·nyi (dô′nän yē; *E* dôk nän′yē, däk-), **Er·nö** (er′në) (Ger. name *Ernst von Dohnanyi*) 1877-1960; Hung. composer & pianist

DOI *abbrev.* Department of the Interior

doi·ly (doi′lē) *n., pl.* **-lies** ⟦after a 17th-c. London draper named *Doily* or *Doyley*⟧ 1 a small napkin 2 a small mat, as of lace or paper, put under a dish, vase, or the like, as a decoration or to protect a surface

do·ing (dōō′iŋ) *vt., vi. pp. of* DO[1] —*n.* 1 something done 2 [*pl.*] *a*) actions, events, etc. *b*) [Dial.] social activities or a social event

doit (doit) *n.* ⟦Du *duit*, akin to ON *thveiti*, a small weight of silver: for IE base see WHITTLE⟧ 1 a small, obsolete Dutch coin of little value 2 anything of trifling value

☆**do-it-your·self** (dōō′it yoor self′) *n.* the practice of constructing, repairing, or redecorating something, as in one's home, by oneself instead of hiring another to do it —*adj.* of, used for, or engaged in do-it-yourself —**do′-it-your·self′er** *n.*

do·jo (dō′jō) *n., pl.* **-jos** ⟦Jpn⟧ a studio or room in which martial arts are taught

do·lab·ri·form (dō lab′ri fôrm′) *adj.* ⟦< L *dolabra*, pickax (< *dolare*, to chip < IE base **del-*, to cut) + -FORM⟧ shaped like the head of an ax, as certain leaves

☆**Dol·by** (dōl′bē) ⟦after R. *Dolby* (1933–2013), U.S. recording engineer⟧ *trademark for* an electronic system used, as in tape recording, to reduce unwanted noise for improved sound quality

dol·ce (dôl′che; *E* dōl′chā) *adj., adv.* ⟦It, sweet⟧ [*also in roman type*] *Musical Direction* sweetly and softly

dolce far nien·te (fär nyen′te) ⟦It, (it is) sweet doing nothing⟧ pleasant idleness or inactivity

dolce vi·ta (vē'tä) ⟦It, (the) sweet life⟧ an easygoing, often dissolute, way of life: usually with *la*

dol·drums (dōl'drəmz, däl'-) *pl.n.* ⟦< ? ME *dul* (see DULL), after TANTRUM⟧ 1 *a)* low spirits; gloomy, listless feeling *b)* sluggishness or complete inactivity; stagnation 2 *a)* equatorial ocean regions noted for dead calms and light fluctuating breezes *b)* such calms and breezes, located between the belts of the NE and SE trade winds (cf. HORSE LATITUDES)

dole¹ (dōl) *n.* ⟦ME *dol* < OE *dal*, a share, parallel to *dæl*: see DEAL²⟧ 1 a giving out of money or food to those in great need; relief 2 that which is thus given out 3 anything given out sparingly 4 [Informal, Chiefly Brit.] a form of government aid to the unemployed, as in England: usually preceded by *the* and often in the phrase **on the dole**, receiving such aid 5 [Archaic] one's destiny or lot —*vt.* **doled, dol'ing** to give sparingly or as a dole: usually with *out* —**SYN.** DISTRIBUTE

dole² (dōl) *n.* ⟦see fol.⟧ [Archaic] sorrow; dolor

dole·ful (dōl'fəl) *adj.* ⟦ME *dolful* < *dol*, grief (< OFr *doel* < VL *dolus*, grief, pain < L *dolere*, to suffer < IE base **del-*, **dol-*, to split, cut) + *-ful*, -FUL⟧ full of or causing sorrow or sadness; mournful; melancholy: also [Rare] **dole'some** (-səm) —**SYN.** SAD —**dole'ful·ly** *adv.* —**dole'ful·ness** *n.*

dol·er·ite (däl'ər īt') *n.* ⟦Fr *dolérite* < Gr *doleros*, deceptive < *dolos*, deceit (for IE base see TALE): from its close resemblance to diorite⟧ DIABASE (sense 2)

dol·i·cho·ce·phal·ic (däl'i kō'sə fal'ik) *adj.* ⟦< Gr *dolichos*, long (akin to Goth *tulgus*, firm) + -CEPHALIC⟧ having a relatively long head; having a head whose width is less than 76 percent of its length from front to back: see also CEPHALIC INDEX: also **dol'i·cho·ceph'a·lous** (-sef'ə ləs) —**dol'i·cho·ceph'a·ly** (-sef'ə lē) *n.*

doll (däl) *n.* ⟦< *Doll*, nickname for DOROTHY⟧ 1 *a)* a child's toy, puppet, marionette, etc. made to resemble a human being; often, specif., a child's toy made to resemble an infant *b)* any similar toy made to resemble a nonhuman character as from television, cartoons, etc. 2 a pretty but frivolous or silly young woman 3 a pretty child 4 [Slang] any girl or young woman 5 [Slang] any attractive or lovable person — *vt., vi.* [Informal] to dress stylishly or showily: with *up*

dol·lar (däl'ər) *n.* ⟦LowG & Fl *daler* < Ger *thaler* (now *taler*), contr. < *Joachimsthaler*, coin made (orig. in 1519) at (St.) *Joachimstal*, Bohemia < (St.) *Joachim* + *thal*, *tal*, valley: see DALE⟧ ☆1 the basic monetary unit of the U.S., equal to 100 cents: symbol, $: certain other countries, as Ecuador, Panama, El Salvador, and the Marshall Islands, have officially adopted this monetary unit 2 any of the standard monetary units of various other countries, as of Australia, Barbados, and Canada: see the table of monetary units in the Reference Supplement 3 the Mexican peso 4 a coin or piece of paper money of the value of a dollar 5 [Obs.] a Spanish coin (piece of eight) used in American Revolutionary times

dollar (cost) averaging see AVERAGE (*vi.* 3)

☆**dollar diplomacy** 1 the policy of using the economic power or influence of a government to promote and protect in other countries the business interests of its private citizens, corporations, etc. 2 the use of economic power by a country to further foreign policy goals

dol·lar·ize (däl'ər īz') *vi.* **-ized'**, **-iz'ing** to adopt the U.S. dollar as an official or unofficial currency —*vt.* to convert (a country's economy or monetary system) to one based on the dollar —**dol'lar·i·za'tion** *n.*

☆**dollar sign** a symbol ($) for dollar or dollars

☆**dollar store** a store that sells a wide variety of inexpensive merchandise typically priced at a dollar

doll·house (däl'hous') *n.* 1 a small-scale model or replica of a house, for use with a child's toy dolls 2 a very small house

dol·lop (däl'əp) *n.* ⟦< ? ON *dolp*, small dangling ball⟧ 1 a soft mass or blob, as of some food 2 a small quantity of liquid; splash, jigger, dash, etc. 3 a measure or amount *[a dollop of wit]* —*vt.* to put or give out in dollops

dol·ly (däl'ē) *n., pl.* **-lies** ⟦dim. of DOLL⟧ 1 a doll: a child's word 2 a tool used to hold a rivet at one end while a head is hammered out of the other end 3 [Dial.] a stick or board for stirring, as in laundering clothes or washing ore ☆4 any of various low, wheeled platforms as for moving heavy objects ☆5 *Film, TV* a low, wheeled platform on which the camera is mounted for moving it about the set —☆*vi.* **-lied**, **-ly·ing** to move a dolly forward (*in*), backward (*out*), etc. in photographing or televising the action —☆*vt.* to move (a camera, load, etc.) on a dolly

dol·ly·bird (däl'ē burd') *n.* ⟦*dolly*, attractive, stylish (< DOLL + -Y²) + BIRD (*n.* 8)⟧ [Brit. Informal] an attractive young woman

Dol·ly Var·den (däl'ē värd'n) ⟦after the character in Dickens' novel *Barnaby Rudge* (1841)⟧ 1 a dress of sheer figured muslin worn over a bright-colored petticoat ☆2 a red-spotted trout (*Salvelinus malma*) found in streams west of the Rocky Mountains and in E Asia

dol·ma (dōl'mə) *n., pl.* **-mas** or **-ma'des** (-mä'thēz) ⟦< ModGr < Turk, something filled or stuffed⟧ a dish consisting of a grape leaf, cabbage leaf, green pepper, etc. stuffed with rice, ground meat, chopped onions, spices, etc. and cooked

dol·man (dōl'mən, däl-) *n., pl.* **-mans** ⟦Fr < Ger < Hung *dolmany* < Turk *dolāmā*, parade attire of the Janizaries⟧ 1 a long Turkish robe 2 a woman's coat or wrap with dolman sleeves

dolman sleeve ⟦< prec.⟧ a kind of sleeve for a coat or a dress, tapering from a wide opening at the armhole to a narrow one at the wrist

dol·men (dōl'mən, däl'-) *n.* ⟦Fr < Bret *taol*, table + *men*, stone⟧ a Neolithic tomb or monument consisting of a large, flat stone laid across upright stones; cromlech

do·lo·mite (dō'lə mīt', däl'ə-) *n.* ⟦after Déodat de *Dolomieu* (1750-1801), Fr geologist⟧ 1 a light-colored, semihard, rhombohedral mineral, calcium magnesium carbonate, $CaMg(CO_3)_2$, with a glassy luster and perfect cleavage, used in making cement, chemicals, etc. 2 a light-colored sedimentary rock consisting mainly of dolomite and calcite, used as a building stone

Do·lo·mites (dō'lə mīts', däl'ə-) division of the E Alps, in N Italy: highest peak, 10,965 ft (3,342 m): also **Dolomite Alps**

do·lor (dō'lər) *n.* ⟦ME & OFr *dolour* < L *dolor* < *dolere*, to suffer: see DOLEFUL⟧ 1 [Old Poet.] sorrow; grief 2 *R.C.Ch.* one of the seven traditional sorrows in the life of the Virgin Mary

Do·lor·es (də lôr'is) *n.* ⟦Sp < *María de los Dolores*, lit., Mary of the Sorrows⟧ a feminine name: dim. *Lolita*

do·lo·ro·so (dô'lô rô'sô; E dō'lə rō'sō) *adj., adv.* ⟦It, painful, sorrowful < LL *dolorosus*: see DOLOR⟧ *Musical Direction* with a sorrowful or plaintive quality

do·lor·ous (dō'lər əs, däl'ər-) *adj.* ⟦OFr *dolerous* < LL *dolorosus*: see DOLOR⟧ 1 very sorrowful or sad; mournful 2 [Archaic] painful —**do'lor·ous·ly** *adv.*

do·lour (dō'lər) *n. Brit. sp. of* DOLOR

dol·phin (däl'fin, dôl'-) *n.* ⟦ME *dolfin* < OFr *dalphin* < VL *dalfinus*, for L *delphinus* < Gr *delphinos*, gen. of *delphis*, akin to *delphys*, womb (< IE base **gwelbh-*): so named from its shape⟧ 1 any of two widespread families (Platanistidae and Delphinidae) of toothed whales having high levels of intelligence and usually a beaklike snout 2 any of a percoid family (Coryphaenidae) of marine game fishes with colors that brighten and change when the fish is taken out of the water 3 *Naut.* a buoy, pile, or, esp., a cluster of piles for mooring a vessel —**the Dolphin** the constellation Delphinus

dolphin striker a small spar under the bowsprit of a sailing vessel, used, together with the martingales, to brace the jib boom or flying jib boom

dolt (dōlt) *n.* ⟦prob. < ME *dolte*, pp. of *dullen*: see DULL, *vt., vi.*⟧ a stupid, slow-witted person; blockhead —**dolt'ish** *adj.* —**dolt'ish·ly** *adv.* —**dolt'ish·ness** *n.*

Dom (däm) *n.* ⟦Port < L *dominus*, a lord, master: see DOMINATE⟧ 1 a title given to certain monks and clerics 2 a title of respect formerly given to gentlemen of Brazil and Portugal: used with the given name

-dom (dəm) ⟦ME & OE *dom*, state, condition, power: see DOOM¹⟧ *suffix* 1 rank, position, or dominion of *[kingdom]* 2 fact or state of being *[martyrdom]* 3 a total of all who are *[officialdom]*

do·main (dō mān', də-) *n.* ⟦ME *domein* < MFr *domaine* < L *dominium*, right of ownership, dominion < *dominus*, a lord: see DOMINATE⟧ 1 territory under one government or ruler; dominion 2 land belonging to one person; estate 3 supreme ownership: see also EMINENT DOMAIN, PUBLIC DOMAIN 4 field or sphere of activity or influence *[the domain of science]* 5 *Biol.* in some taxonomic systems, the highest classification category, ranking above a kingdom 6 *Comput.* DOMAIN NAME 7 *Math.* *a)* the set of those values of an independent variable which exist for a given function *b)* the set of all integers, or a set of elements which can be combined in the same way as the integers 8 *Physics* a region in a ferromagnetic material within which the atoms are magnetically aligned: alignment of these regions results in the material being magnetized

domain name a unique string of keyboard characters serving as the part of an internet or Web address that is legally registered as by a particular organization, email service, etc.

do·mal (dōm'əl) *adj.* CACUMINAL

dome (dōm) *n.* ⟦sense 1 < L *domus*, house (< IE **domu-* < base **dem-*, to build); others < Fr *dôme* < Prov *doma* < LL(Ec), roof, building, cathedral < Gr *dōma*, housetop, house, temple < same IE base: see TIMBER, DOMINATE⟧ 1 [Old Poet.] a mansion or stately building 2 a hemispherical roof or one formed by a series of rounded arches or vaults on a round or many-sided base; cupola 3 any dome-shaped structure or object; specif., a sports stadium covered with a dome 4 [Slang] the head; esp., the rounded top of the head 5 *Geol.* *a)* an anticlinal structure of circular or broadly elliptical form *b)* a type of crystal formation in which two symmetrical faces meet at an angle to form a horizontal ridge —*vt.* **domed, dom'ing** 1 to cover with or as with a dome 2 to form into a dome —*vi.* to swell out like a dome

domes·day (do͞omz'dā, dōmz'-) *n. obs. var. of* DOOMSDAY

Domesday Book ⟦said to be so named because it judged all men without bias, like the Last Judgment⟧ the record of a survey of England made under William the Conqueror in 1086, listing all landowners and showing the value and extent of their holdings

do·mes·tic (dō mes'tik, də-) *adj.* ⟦ME < OFr *domestique* < L *domesticus* < *domus*: see DOME⟧ 1 having to do with the home or housekeeping; of the house or family *[domestic joys]* 2 of one's own country or the country referred to 3 made or produced in the home country; native *[domestic wine]* 4 domesticated; tame: said of animals 5 enjoying and attentive to the home and family life —*n.* 1 a servant for the home, as a maid or cook 2 [*pl.*] native products 3 [*pl.*] sheets, blankets, towels, etc. —**do·mes'ti·cal·ly** *adv.*

do·mes·ti·cate (dō mes'ti kāt', də-) *vt.* **-cat'ed**, **-cat'ing** ⟦< ML *domesticatus*, pp. of *domesticare*, to tame, live in a family < L *domesticus* < *domus*: see DOME⟧ 1 to accustom to home life; make domestic 2 *a)* to tame (wild animals) and breed for human use *b)* to adapt and cultivate (wild plants) for human use *c)* to introduce (foreign animals or plants) into another region or country; naturalize 3 to bring (a foreign custom, word, etc.) into a region or country and make it acceptable —*vi.* [Archaic] to become domestic —**do·mes'ti·ca'tion** *n.*

do·mes·tic·i·ty (dō′mes tis′ə tē) ***n.*** **1** home life; family life **2** devotion to home and family life **3** *pl.* **-ties** [*pl.*] household affairs

domestic partner either PARTNER (*n.* 2) of an unmarried heterosexual or homosexual couple in a relationship (**domestic partnership**) considered as being equivalent to marriage for the purpose of extending certain legal rights and employment benefits

☆**domestic relations court** in some states, a court with jurisdiction over matters involving relations within the family or household, as between husband and wife or parent and child

☆**domestic science** HOME ECONOMICS

domestic violence unlawful, violent behavior within a household, esp. that which involves spouses or domestic partners

do·mi·cal (dōm′i kəl, däm′-) ***adj.*** **1** of or like a dome **2** having a dome, domes, or domelike structure

dom·i·cile (däm′ə sīl′, -sil; *also,* dō′mə-) ***n.*** ⟦ME *domicelle* < OFr *domicile* < L *domicilium,* a dwelling, home < *domus:* see DOME⟧ **1** a customary dwelling place; home; residence **2** *Law* one's fixed place of dwelling, where one intends to reside more or less permanently —***vt.*** **-ciled′**, **-cil′ing** to establish in a domicile —**dom′i·cil′i·ar′y** (-sil′ē er′ē) ***adj.***

dom·i·cil·i·ate (däm′ə sil′ē āt′; *also* dō′mə-) ***vt.*** **-at′ed**, **-at′ing** DOMICILE —**dom′i·cil′i·a′tion** ***n.***

dom·i·nance (däm′ə nəns) ***n.*** a dominating, or being dominant; control; authority: also **dom′i·nan·cy**

dom·i·nant (däm′ə nənt) ***adj.*** ⟦L *dominans,* prp. of *dominari:* see fol.⟧ **1** exercising authority or influence; dominating; ruling; prevailing **2** *Genetics* designating or relating to that one of any pair of allelic hereditary factors which, when both are present in the germ plasm, dominates over the other and appears in the organism: opposed to RECESSIVE **3** *Music* of or based upon the fifth tone of a diatonic scale —***n.*** **1** *Ecol.* that species of plant or animal most numerous in a community or exercising control over the other organisms by its influence upon the environment **2** *Genetics* a dominant character or factor **3** *Music* the fifth note of a diatonic scale —**dom′i·nant·ly** ***adv.***

SYN.—**dominant** refers to that which dominates or controls, or has the greatest effect [*dominant* characteristics in genetics]; **predominant** refers to that which is at the moment uppermost in importance or influence [the *predominant* reason for his refusal]; **paramount** is applied to that which ranks first in importance, authority, etc. [of *paramount* interest to me]; **preeminent** implies prominence because of surpassing excellence [the *preeminent* writer of his time]; **preponderant** implies superiority in amount, weight, power, importance, etc. [the *preponderant* religion of a country]

---

dom·i·nate (däm′ə nāt′) ***vt., vi.*** **-nat′ed**, **-nat′ing** ⟦< L *dominatus,* pp. of *dominari,* to rule < *dominus,* a master < **domonos* < base of *domus:* see DOME⟧ **1** to rule or control by superior power or influence [to *dominate* a group] **2** to tower over (other things); rise high above (the surroundings, etc.) [a building that *dominates* the city] **3** to have foremost place (in something) [to *dominate* a baseball league] —**dom′i·na′tive** (-nāt′iv) ***adj.*** —**dom′i·na′tor** ***n.***

dom·i·na·tion (däm′ə nā′shən) ***n.*** ⟦ME *dominacioun* < OFr *domination* < L *dominatio*⟧ a dominating or being dominated; rule; control; ascendancy

☆**dom·i·na·trix** (däm′i nā′triks) ***n., pl.*** **-trix·es** or **-tri·ces′** (-trə sēz′) a woman who subjects her masochistic sexual partner to bondage, the infliction of ritualistic punishments, etc.; specif., a prostitute who performs such acts for her customers

dom·i·neer (däm′ə nir′) ***vi., vt.*** ⟦Du *domineren* < Fr *dominer* < L *dominari:* see DOMINATE⟧ to rule (*over*) in a harsh or arrogant way; tyrannize; bully

dom·i·neer·ing (-iŋ) ***adj.*** arrogant; overbearing; tyrannical —SYN. MASTERFUL —**dom′i·neer′ing·ly** ***adv.***

Dom·i·nic[1] (däm′ə nik) ***n.*** ⟦ML *Dominicus,* lit., of the Lord: see DOMINICAL⟧ a masculine name: dim. *Dom;* var. *Dominick*

Dom·i·nic[2] (däm′ə nik), Saint (1170-1221); Sp. priest: founder of the Dominican order: his day is Aug. 8

Dom·i·ni·ca (däm′ə nē′kə, də min′i kə) country that is an island of the Windward group in the West Indies: a British-controlled territory from 1783 to 1978, when it became independent; member of the Commonwealth: 291 sq mi (754 sq km); cap. Roseau —**Dom′i·ni′can** ***adj., n.***

do·min·i·cal (dō min′i kəl, də-) ***adj.*** ⟦ME < ML(Ec) *dominicalis,* of the Lord (Jesus) < LL(Ec) *Dominicus,* of the Lord < L, belonging to a master < *dominus,* a master: see DOMINATE⟧ **1** having to do with or originating with Jesus as the Lord **2** having to do with the Lord's Day (Sunday)

dominical letter any of the first seven letters in the alphabet as used in church calendars to indicate Sundays: the letters are assigned to the first seven days of January, and the letter falling to Sunday is the arbitrary symbol for Sunday the rest of the year

Do·min·i·can (dō min′i kən, də-) ***adj.*** **1** of Saint Dominic **2** designating or of a mendicant order founded by him **3** of the Dominican Republic —***n.*** **1** a member of a mendicant order of friars or nuns founded in 1215 by Saint Dominic **2** a person born or living in the Dominican Republic

Dominican Republic country occupying the E part of the island of Hispaniola, in the West Indies: independent since 1844: 18,815 sq mi (48,730 sq km); cap. Santo Domingo

Dom·i·nick (däm′ə nik) ***n.*** **1** a masculine name: see DOMINIC[1] **2** DOMINIQUE

dom·i·nie (däm′ə nē; *for 2, usually* dō′mə-) ***n.*** ⟦< voc. (*domine*) of L *dominus:* see DOMINATE⟧ **1** in Scotland, a schoolmaster **2** [Informal] any pastor or clergyman

do·min·ion (də min′yən, dō-) ***n.*** ⟦ME *dominioun* < ML *dominio* < L *dominus:* see DOMINATE⟧ **1** rule or power to rule; sovereign authority; sovereignty **2** a governed territory or country **3** [**D-**] a name formerly used for certain self-governing nations of THE COMMONWEALTH (sense 2) **4** *Law* ownership; dominium —SYN. POWER

Dominion Day *former name for* CANADA DAY

☆**Dom·i·nique** (däm′ə nēk′) ***n.*** ⟦Fr, DOMINICA⟧ any of a breed of American domestic chicken with yellow legs and gray, barred plumage

do·min·i·um (dō min′ē əm) ***n.*** ⟦L: see DOMAIN⟧ *Law* the right of property and its ownership and control

dom·i·no (däm′ə nō′) ***n., pl.*** **-noes′** or **-nos′** ⟦Fr & It, hooded cloak (worn by cathedral canons) < dat. of L *dominus,* a lord, master⟧ **1** a loose cloak or robe with wide sleeves and hood, worn with a mask at masquerades **2** a small mask, generally black, for covering the area around the eyes; half mask **3** a person dressed in such a cloak or mask **4** ⟦Fr < Sp: in reference to the blackness of the piece⟧ *a)* a small, oblong piece of wood, plastic, etc. marked into halves, each half being blank or having usually from one to six dots marked on it *b)* [*pl., with sing. v.*] a game played with a number of such pieces, usually 28, which the players must match according to the dots on each half

☆**domino theory** the theory that a certain result (**domino effect**) will follow a certain cause like a row of upright dominoes falling if the first is pushed; specif., the theory that if a nation becomes a Communist state, the nations nearby will also

Do·mi·nus (dō′mē no͝os, däm′ē-) ***n.*** ⟦L⟧ the Lord; God

Dominus vo·bis·cum (vō bis′ko͝om) ⟦L⟧ the Lord be with you

Do·mi·tian (də mish′ən) (L. name *Titus Flavius Domitianus Augustus*) A.D. 51-96; Rom. emperor (81-96)

Dom Rep *abbrev.* Dominican Republic

don[1] (dän) ***n.*** ⟦Sp < L *domnus,* contr. < *dominus,* master: see DOMINATE⟧ **1** a distinguished man **2** a head, tutor, or fellow of a Brit. college or university, esp. at Oxford or Cambridge **3** an important Mafia leader

don[2] (dän) ***vt.*** **donned**, **don′ning** ⟦contr. of *do on*⟧ to put on (a garment, etc.); dress in (a certain color or material)

Don[1] (dän; *Sp* dôn) ***n.*** ⟦Sp < L *dominus,* lord, master: see DOMINATE⟧ **1** Sir; Mr.: a Spanish title of respect, used with the given name: abbrev. *D* [*Don Pedro*] **2** [**d-**] a Spanish nobleman or gentleman

Don[2] (dän; *Russ* dôn) river in SC European Russia, flowing southward into the Sea of Azov: *c.* 1,200 mi (1,931 km)

Do·na (dô′nə) ***n., pl.*** **-nas** ⟦Port < L *domina:* see fol.⟧ **1** Lady; Madam: a Portuguese title of respect, used with the given name **2** [**d-**] a Portuguese lady

Do·ña (dô′nyä) ***n., pl.*** **-ñas** ⟦Sp < L *domina,* mistress, lady, fem. of *dominus:* see DOMINATE⟧ **1** Lady; Madam: a Spanish title of respect, used with the given name **2** [**d-**] a Spanish lady

Don·ald (dän′əld) ***n.*** ⟦Ir *Donghal,* lit., brown stranger (or ? Gael *Domhnall,* lit., world ruler)⟧ a masculine name: dim. *Don*

Do·nar (dō′när′) ***n.*** ⟦OHG: see THUNDER⟧ *Gmc. Myth.* the god of thunder: identified with the Norse Thor

☆**do·nate** (dō′nāt′, dō nāt′) ***vt., vi.*** **-nat′ed**, **-nat′ing** ⟦back-form. < DONATION⟧ **1** to give, esp. to some philanthropic or religious cause; contribute **2** to permit the removal of, or to bequeath (one's blood for transfusion, an organ for transplantation, etc.) —SYN. GIVE —**do′na′tor** (-ər) ***n.***

Do·na·tel·lo (dô′nä tel′lô; *E* dän′ə tel′ō) (born *Donato di Niccolò di Betto Bardi*) 1386?-1466; It. sculptor

do·na·tion (dō nā′shən) ***n.*** ⟦ME *donacioun* < L *donatio* < *donatus,* pp. of *donare* < *donum,* gift < IE **donom* < base **do-,* give: see DATE[1]⟧ **1** the act of donating **2** a gift or contribution, as to a charitable organization —SYN. PRESENT

Don·a·tist (dän′ə tist) ***n.*** ⟦ML *Donatista,* after *Donatus,* Bishop of Casae Nigrae, founder of the sect⟧ a member of a North African Christian sect that flourished in the 4th cent., noted for rigorous standards of morality and sanctity, esp. as they applied to the clergy —**Don′a·tism′** ***n.***

don·a·tive (dän′ə tiv, dō′nə-) ***n.*** ⟦ME *donatif* < L *donativum* < *donativus*⟧ a donation or gift

Do·nau (dō′nou) *Ger. name for* the DANUBE

Don·bas or **Don·bass** (dôn bäs′) DONETS BASIN

Don·cas·ter (däŋ′kas tər, -kəs-) city in NC England, in South Yorkshire

Don Cossack a member of the eastern branch of the Cossacks, living along the Don

done (dun) ***vt., vi.*** *pp. of* DO[1] —***adj.*** **1** completed; ended **2** sufficiently cooked **3** socially acceptable because acceptable to arbiters of good taste: usually in a negative construction [it just isn't *done*] —**done (for)** [Informal] **1** dead, ruined, etc. **2** discarded or dismissed as a failure

do·nee (dō nē′) ***n.*** ⟦DON(OR) + -EE[1]⟧ the recipient of a donation

Don·e·gal (dän′ə gôl′; *Ir* dun′ə gôl′) northernmost county of Ireland, in Ulster province: 1,865 sq mi (4,830 sq km)

done·ness (dun′nis) ***n.*** **1** the fact or condition of being cooked thoroughly [test the cake for *doneness*] **2** the degree to which food, esp. red meat, has been cooked [grill the steak to the desired *doneness*]

Do·nets (də nets′; *Russ* dô nyets′) river in SW Russia & Ukraine, flowing southeast into the Don: *c.* 650 mi (1,046 km)

Donets Basin major industrial and coal-producing region in the lower valley of the Donets River

Do·netsk (dô nyetsk′) city in SE Ukraine, in the Donets Basin

dong[1] (dôŋ, däŋ) ***n.*** ⟦echoic⟧ the sound of a large bell

dong² (däŋ) ***n.*** ⟦Vietnamese⟧ the basic monetary unit of Vietnam: see the table of monetary units in the Reference Supplement
dong³ (dôŋ) ***n.*** [Slang] the penis: somewhat vulgar
don·ga (däŋ′gə) ***n.*** ⟦Afrik < Zulu *udonga*⟧ in South Africa, a gully in a veld
Dong·ting Hu (dooŋ′tiŋ′ho͞o′) lake in Hunan province, SE China: *c.* 1,450 sq mi (3,755 sq km); during floods, over 4,000 sq mi (10,360 sq km)
Do·ni·zet·ti (dän′ə zet′ē; *It* dô′nē dzet′tē), **Ga·e·ta·no** (gä′e tä′nô) 1797-1848; It. composer
don·jon (dun′jən, dän′-) ***n.*** ⟦old sp. of DUNGEON⟧ the heavily fortified inner tower or keep of a castle
Don Juan (dän′wän′, -hwän′; *also*, -jo͞o′ən) **1** *Sp. Legend* a dissolute nobleman and seducer of women: he is the hero of many poems, plays, and operas **2** any man who seduces women or has one love affair after another; libertine; philanderer; rake
don·key (däŋ′kē, dôŋ′-, duŋ′-) ***n., pl.*** **-keys** ⟦also earlier *donky*: late slang, rhyming with and patterned after MONKEY: < ? DUNCAN¹ or < ? DUN¹⟧ **1** a domesticated ASS¹ (sense 1) **2** a person regarded as stupid, foolish, or obstinate
donkey engine **1** a small steam engine, esp. one used on a ship as for lifting cargo ☆**2** a small locomotive
donkey jacket [Brit.] a heavy jacket, often having a waterproof panel across the shoulders, worn especially by workingmen
donkey's years [Informal, Chiefly Brit.] a very long time
don·key-work (däŋ′kē wurk′) ***n.*** hard work, esp. if routine or menial
Don·na¹ (dän′ə) ***n.*** ⟦It < L *domina*, fem. of *dominus*: see DOMINATE⟧ a feminine name
Donna² (dô′nä) ***n.*** ⟦It: see prec.⟧ **1** Lady; Madam: an Italian title of respect, used with the given name **2** [**d-**] an Italian lady
Donne (dun), **John** 1572-1631; Eng. poet & clergyman
don·née (dô nā′, də-) ***n.*** ⟦Fr < fem. pp. of *donner*, to give < L *donare*: see DONATION⟧ an incident, idea, etc. that serves as an author's starting point or inspiration for a novel, play, etc.
Don·ner Pass (dän′ər) ⟦after the ill-fated *Donner* party who wintered there 1846-47⟧ mountain pass in E Calif., in the Sierra Nevada: *c.* 7,100 ft (2,164 m) high
don·nish (dän′ish) ***adj.*** of or like a university don; specif., intellectual, bookish, pedantic, etc. —**don′nish·ly** ***adv.*** —**don′nish·ness** ***n.***
don·ny·brook (dän′ē brook′) ***n.*** ⟦< fol.⟧ [Informal] a rough, rowdy fight or free-for-all
Donnybrook Fair a yearly fair formerly held at Donnybrook, near Dublin, Ireland, during which there was much brawling and rowdiness
do·nor (dō′nər, -nôr′) ***n.*** ⟦ME & Anglo-Fr *donour* < L *donator*⟧ **1** a person who donates; giver **2** one from whom blood for transfusion, tissue for grafting, etc. is taken **3** an atom that contributes a pair of electrons to another atom to form a covalent bond with it
do-noth·ing (do͞o′nuth′iŋ) ***n.*** a person without ambition or initiative; idler —***adj.*** showing no ambition or initiative; complacent
Don Qui·xo·te (dän′kē hōt′ē, -ā; *also*, dän′ kwik′sət) **1** a satirical novel by Cervantes, published in two parts (1605, 1615) **2** the hero of this novel, who tries in a chivalrous but unrealistic way to rescue the oppressed and fight evil
don't (dōnt) *contraction* **1** do not **2** does not: generally considered a nonstandard usage
do·nut (dō′nut′) ***n.*** *informal sp. of* DOUGHNUT
☆**doo·bie** (do͞o′bē) ***n.*** ⟦< ?⟧ [Slang] a marijuana cigarette
☆**doo·dad** (do͞o′dad′) ***n.*** ⟦see DOOHICKEY⟧ [Informal] **1** a trinket; bauble **2** any small object or device whose name is not known or is temporarily forgotten
doo·dle (do͞od′'l) ***vi.*** **-dled**, **-dling** ⟦Ger *dudeln*, to play (the bagpipe), hence to trifle, dawdle (< Pol *dudlić* < *dudy*, a bagpipe < Turk *duduk*, a flute); reinforced by echoic TOOTLE & DAWDLE⟧ **1** to move aimlessly or foolishly; dawdle ☆**2** to scribble or draw aimlessly or nervously, esp. when the attention is elsewhere; make doodles ☆**3** [Informal] to play music in a casual, informal way —***n.*** ☆a mark, design, figure, etc. made in doodling —**doo′dler** ***n.***
☆**doo·dle·bug** (-bug′) ***n.*** ⟦prec. + BUG¹⟧ **1** the larva of certain ant lions: see ANT LION **2** [Informal] a divining rod or another similar device used in trying to locate something underground **3** [Informal] BUZZ BOMB
doo-doo (do͞o′do͞o′) ***n.*** **1** [Informal] feces; excrement: originally a child's term **2** [Slang] trouble: usually in the phrase **in deep doo-doo** Also written **doodoo**
doo·dy (do͞o′dē) ***n.*** [Slang] feces; excrement
☆**doo·fus** (do͞o′fəs) ***n.*** ⟦< ?⟧ [Slang] a stupid, foolish, or inept person
☆**doo·hick·ey** (do͞o′hik′ē) ***n.*** ⟦fanciful extension of DO¹, as in DOODAD⟧ [Informal] any small object or device whose name is not known or is temporarily forgotten
☆**doo·lie** (do͞o′lē) ***n.*** ⟦prob. < Gr *doulos*, a slave⟧ [Informal] a freshman at the U.S. Air Force Academy
Doo·lit·tle (do͞o′lit′'l), **Jimmy** (born *James Harold Doolittle*) 1896-1993; U.S. aviator & general
doom¹ (do͞om) ***n.*** ⟦ME & OE *dom*, lit., what is laid down, decree, akin to Goth *doms*, judgment < IE base **dhē-*: see DO¹⟧ **1** [Historical] a statute; decree **2** a judgment; esp., a sentence of condemnation **3** destiny; fate **4** tragic fate; ruin or death **5** Judgment Day —***vt.*** **1** to pronounce judgment on; condemn; sentence **2** to destine to a tragic fate **3** to ordain as a penalty —**SYN.** FATE

doom² (do͞om) ***n.*** *alt. sp. of* DOUM
☆**doom·say·er** (do͞om′sā′ər) ***n.*** a person disposed to predicting catastrophe, disaster, etc.
dooms·day (do͞omz′dā′) ***n.*** ⟦ME *domesdai* < OE *domes dæg* < *domes*, gen. of *dom*, DOOM¹ + DAY⟧ **1** JUDGMENT DAY **2** any day of reckoning **3** any catastrophic day
Doomsday Book DOMESDAY BOOK
doom·y (do͞om′ē) ***adj.*** **doom′i·er**, **doom′i·est** characterized by or filled with a sense of impending doom or disaster [*doomy* shadows, the *doomy* chords] —**doom′i·ly** ***adv.***
Doon (do͞on) river in SW Scotland, flowing north into the Firth of Clyde: *c.* 30 mi (48 km)
door (dôr) ***n.*** ⟦ME *dure*, *dor* < OE *duru* fem. (orig., pair of doors), *dor* neut., akin to Ger *tür*, door, *tor*, gate < IE base **dhwer-*, **dhwor-*, door > L *fores* (pl. of *foris*), two-leaved door, Gr *thyra*, door (in pl., double door)⟧ **1** a movable structure for opening or closing an entrance, as to a building or room, or giving access to a closet, cupboard, etc.: most doors turn on hinges, slide in grooves, or revolve on an axis: term often used fig. **2** the room or building to which a particular door belongs [two *doors* down the hall] **3** any opening with a door in it; doorway **4** DOORWAY (sense 2) —**lay at the door of** to blame (a person) for —**lie at someone's door** to be imputable or chargeable to someone —**out of doors** outside a house, building, etc.; outdoors —**show someone the door** to ask or command someone to leave
door·bell (dôr′bel′) ***n.*** a mechanism, now usually activated by a push button at the entrance of a building or room, that rings, buzzes, etc. to alert the occupants of a visitor
do-or-die (do͞o′ər dī′) ***adj.*** showing or involving a desperate effort or need to succeed
door·jamb (dôr′jam′) ***n.*** ⟦see JAMB⟧ a vertical piece of wood, etc. constituting the side of a doorway
door·keep·er (-kēp′ər) ***n.*** a person guarding the entrance of a house, hotel, etc.; porter
door·knob (-näb′) ***n.*** a small knob or lever on a door, usually for releasing the latch
door·man (-man′, -mən) ***n., pl.*** **-men′** (-men′, -mən) a person whose work is opening the door of a building for those who enter or leave, hailing taxicabs, etc.
door·mat (-mat′) ***n.*** **1** a mat for people to wipe their shoes on before entering a house, room, etc. **2** a person easily mistreated, imposed on, exploited, etc.
door·nail (-nāl′) ***n.*** a large-headed nail used to decorate or strengthen some doors —**dead as a doornail** dead beyond a doubt
door·plate (-plāt′) ***n.*** a plate on an entrance door, bearing the number, occupant's name, etc.
door·post (-pōst′) ***n.*** DOORJAMB
☆**door prize** ⟦so called because lottery tickets were orig. given at the entrance⟧ a prize given by lottery to one or more of those attending some public function
door·sill (-sil′) ***n.*** a length of wood, masonry, etc. along the bottom of a doorway; threshold
door·step (-step′) ***n.*** the step or steps in front of an outside door
door·stop (-stäp′) ***n.*** **1** a device used to hold a door open at a desired position or prevent it from closing too forcibly or slamming against a wall **2** a thin wooden strip affixed to a frame of a doorway, against which the door closes
☆**door-to-door** (-tə dôr′) ***adj., adv.*** (going) from one home to the next, calling on each in turn [a *door-to-door* salesman, selling *door-to-door*]
door·way (-wā′) ***n.*** **1** an opening in a wall that can be closed by a door; portal **2** anything regarded as an opportunity or a means of access
☆**door·yard** (-yärd′) ***n.*** a yard onto which a door of a house opens
☆**doo-wop** (do͞o′wäp′) ***n.*** ⟦< nonsense syllables sung in accompaniment⟧ **1** a singing style for popular music, esp. of the 1950s, featuring a lead singer supported by a chorus and often involving falsetto and a cappella singing **2** music sung in this style Also written **doowop**
☆**doo·zy** or **doo·zie** (do͞o′zē) ***n., pl.*** **-zies** ⟦orig. var. of DAISY, later assoc. with *Duesenberg* (automobile) as standard of excellence⟧ [Slang] anything outstanding of its kind: also **doo′zer** (-zər)
do·pa (dō′pə) ***n.*** ⟦*d(ihydr)o(xy)p(henyl)a(lanine)*⟧ an amino acid, $C_9H_{11}NO_4$, that is converted by an enzyme in the bloodstream into dopamine: its levorotatory isomer (**L-dopa**) is used as a drug in treating Parkinson's disease: often written **DOPA**
☆**do·pa·mine** (dō′pə mēn′, -min) ***n.*** ⟦*d(ihydr)o(xy)p(henyl)* + AMINE⟧ an amine, $C_8H_{11}NO_2$, that is an intermediate biochemical product in the synthesis of norepinephrine, epinephrine, and melanin, and is a neurotransmitter
dop·ant (dōp′ənt) ***n.*** ⟦fol. + -ANT⟧ an impurity added to a pure substance to produce a deliberate change, as with laser crystals and semiconductors: also called **doping agent**
☆**dope** (dōp) ***n.*** ⟦Du *doop*, sauce, dip, baptism < *doopen*, to dip < Gmc **dup-*, to be deep: see DIMPLE⟧ **1** any thick liquid or pasty substance, or other material, used to lubricate or absorb something **2** *a)* a dressing, varnish, or filler, as for protecting the cloth covering of airplane wings, surfaces, etc. *b)* any additive, as a food preservative **3** a drug used to stimulate or hinder a racehorse's performance **4** [Informal] any drug or narcotic, or such drugs collectively **5** [Informal] a slow-witted, stupid, or lethargic person **6** [Slang] *a)* advance information on a racehorse's condition *b)*

any information, esp. as used for prediction 7 [Slang, Chiefly South] a carbonated drink, usually cola 8 *Photog.* a developer —*vt.* **doped, dop′ing** 1 to give dope to; treat with dope 2 to drug or stupefy 3 to introduce an adulterant, additive, or impurity into (another substance) in order to produce a deliberate change —**dope out** [Slang] to figure out or work out; solve

☆**dope fiend** [Slang] a drug addict

dop·er (dōp′ər) *n.* [Slang] a drug addict

☆**dope-sheet** (dōp′shēt′) *n.* 1 a RACING FORM, esp. one dealing with a program of races at one track 2 [Informal] a printed source of information

☆**dope·ster** (dōp′stər) *n.* ⟦DOPE (OUT) + -STER⟧ [Informal] one who analyzes or predicts trends as in politics or sports

dop·ey or **dop·y** (dō′pē) *adj.* **-i·er, -i·est** [Informal] ☆1 under the influence of a narcotic 2 mentally slow or confused; lethargic or stupid 3 silly, ridiculous, etc. —**dop′i·ness** *n.*

dop·pel·gäng·er (däp′əl geŋ′ər; -gäŋ′ər, -gaŋ′-) *n.* ⟦Ger < *doppel,* double + *gänger,* goer: see GANG²⟧ *Folklore* a ghostly double or wraith of a living person

Dop·pler effect (däp′lər) ⟦after C. *Doppler* (1803-53), Austrian mathematician and physicist⟧ the apparent change of frequency of sound waves or light waves, varying with the relative velocity of the source and the observer: if the source and observer are drawing closer together, the observed frequency is higher than the emitted frequency

Doppler radar a type of radar that uses the Doppler shift to measure the speed and direction of a target, as a moving object, storm, or tornado

Doppler shift the shift in frequency, usually measured in hertz, due to the Doppler effect

Dor·a (dôr′ə) *n.* a feminine name: see DOROTHY, THEODORA

do·ra·do (dō rä′dō, də-) *n.* ⟦Sp < adj., lit., gilded, pp. of *dorar* < LL *deaurare*: see DORY²⟧ 1 DOLPHIN (sense 2) 2 [**D-**] a S constellation between Pictor and Reticulum, containing part of the Larger Magellanic Cloud

☆**do-rag** (do͞o′rag′) *n.* ⟦< DO³⟧ [Slang] a cloth tied around the head to keep a process hairstyle in place; also, any bandanna worn around the head

dor·bee·tle (dôr′bēt″l) *n.* ⟦< ME *dore* (< OE *dora,* a beetle < IE base **dher-,* to buzz > Gr *thrylein,* to murmur, babble) + BEETLE¹⟧ 1 any of several European dung beetles 2 any beetle that flies with a buzzing sound Also **dor**

Dor·cas (dôr′kəs) *n.* ⟦L < Gr *Dorkas,* lit., gazelle⟧ *Bible* a woman who spent her life making clothes for the poor: Acts 9:36-41

Dor·dogne (dôr dôn′y′) river in SW France, flowing southwest to unite with the Garonne and form the Gironde estuary: *c.* 300 mi (483 km)

Dor·drecht (dôr′dreHt) city in SW Netherlands, on the Maas (Meuse) delta

do·ré (dô rā′) *adj.* ⟦Fr: see DORY²⟧ coated with gold or a gold color; gilded [bronze *doré*]

Do·ré (dô rā′), **(Paul) Gus·tave** (güs tȧv′) 1832-83; Fr. book illustrator & painter

dor·hawk (dôr′hôk′) *n.* ⟦*dor,* a buzzing insect (see DORBEETLE) + HAWK¹: so named from eating such insects⟧ NIGHTJAR

Do·ri·an (dôr′ē ən) *adj.* ⟦< L *Dorius* < Gr *Dōrios* < *Dōris*⟧ DORIC —*n.* a native of Doris; member of one of the four main peoples of ancient Greece

Dor·ic (dôr′ik, där′-) *adj.* ⟦L *Doricus* < Gr *Dōrikos*⟧ 1 of Doris or its people, language, or culture 2 designating or of a classical (Greek or Roman) order of architecture, distinguished by simplicity of form, esp. by fluted columns with simple capitals —*n.* 1 the Greek dialect of Doris 2 a rustic English dialect as contrasted with Standard English

Dor·is¹ (dôr′is) *n.* ⟦after fol.⟧ a feminine name

Dor·is² (dôr′is) ⟦L < Gr *Dōris*⟧ ancient mountainous region in what is now WC Greece: regarded as the home of the Dorians

dork (dôrk) *n.* ⟦< ?⟧ [Slang] ☆1 the penis: somewhat vulgar 2 a person regarded as stupid, foolish, awkward, clumsy, etc. —**dork′y** *adj.* **dork′i·er, dork′i·est**

Dor·king (dôr′kiŋ) *n.* ⟦after *Dorking,* town in Surrey, England⟧ any of a breed of domestic chicken, having a large body, short legs, and five-toed feet

☆**dorm** (dôrm) *n.* [Informal] DORMITORY

dor·mant (dôr′mənt) *adj.* ⟦ME < OFr prp. of *dormir* < LL *dormire* < IE base **dre-,* to sleep > Sans *ni-dra,* sleep⟧ 1 sleeping 2 as if asleep; quiet; still 3 inoperative; inactive 4 *Biol.* *a)* torpid in winter; in a state of suspended animation *b)* live, but not actively growing 5 *Heraldry* lying down in a sleeping position [a lion *dormant*]: cf. COUCHANT —***SYN.*** LATENT —**dor′man·cy** (-mən sē) *n.*

dor·mer (dôr′mər) *n.* ⟦OFr *dormeour* < L *dormitorium*: see DORMITORY⟧ 1 a window set upright in a sloping roof: also **dormer window** 2 the roofed projection in which this window is set

dormer

dor·mie (dôr′mē) *adj.* ⟦< ?⟧ *Golf* in match play, ahead of an opponent by as many holes as are yet to be played

Dor·mi·tion (dôr mish′ən) *n.* ⟦Fr *dormition* < L *dormitionem,* a falling asleep < *dormire,* to sleep: see DORMANT⟧ *Eastern Orthodox Ch.* 1 the death and bodily assumption of the Virgin Mary 2 a church festival on Aug. 15 commemorating this

dor·mi·to·ry (dôr′mə tôr′ē) *n., pl.* **-ries** ⟦ME *dormitorie* < L *dormitorium,* place for sleeping < *dormitorius,* of or for sleeping < pp. of *dormire*: see DORMANT⟧ 1 a room, building, or part of a building with sleeping accommodations for a number of people ☆2 a building with many rooms that provide sleeping and living accommodations for a number of people, as at college —*adj.* [Chiefly Brit.] designating a suburb or small town whose residents travel daily to their jobs in the city

dor·mouse (dôr′mous′) *n., pl.* **-mice′** (-mīs′) ⟦ME *dormous* ? altered by folk etym. (after *mous,* MOUSE) < OFr *dormeuse,* sleepy, sluggish < *dormir*: see DORMANT⟧ any of a family (Gliridae) of small, furry-tailed, mostly tree-dwelling Old World rodents

dormy (dôr′mē) *adj. alt. sp. of* DORMIE

dor·nick¹ (dôr′nik) *n.* ⟦after *Doornik,* Fl name of Tournai, Belgium, where orig. made⟧ a heavy damask formerly used for hangings, vestments, etc.

☆**dor·nick²** (dôr′nik) *n.* ⟦Ir *dornóg,* Gael *doirneag* < *dorn,* hand⟧ a stone or small rock

Dor·o·the·a (dôr′ə thē′ə, där′-) *n.* ⟦L < Gr *Dōrothea,* lit., gift of God < *dōron,* gift (see DATE¹) + *theos,* God⟧ a feminine name: see DOROTHY

Dor·o·thy (dôr′ə thē, där′-; dôr′thē) *n.* a feminine name: dim. *Dolly, Dora, Dot, Dotty*; var. *Dorothea*

dorp (dôrp) *n.* ⟦Du, akin to Ger *dorf,* THORP⟧ [Chiefly South Afr.] a village

dor·sa (dôr′sə) *n. pl. of* DORSUM

dor·sad (dôr′sad′) *adv.* ⟦< L *dorsum,* the back + -AD²⟧ moving from the front of the body toward the back or posterior part

dor·sal¹ (dôr′səl) *adj.* ⟦ME < ML *dorsalis* < L *dorsualis* < *dorsum,* the back⟧ 1 of, on, or near the back 2 *Bot.* *a)* of or relating to the side of a leaf or other structure away from the axis; abaxial *b)* of or relating to the upper side of a thallus, as in liverworts or lichens —**dor′sal·ly** *adv.*

dor·sal² or **dor·sel** (dôr′səl) *n.* DOSSAL

dorsal lip that part of the rim of the blastopore that lies on the future dorsal side of the embryo: in vertebrates it contains the organizer that determines the position of the future nerve cord

dorsal root the more posterior of two roots that merge to form each spinal nerve: it contains the nerve fibers that transmit sensation

Dor·set¹ (dôr′sət) *n.* any of a breed of medium-sized sheep, originally from Dorset: formerly, both male and female had horns (hence the former name **Dorset Horn**), but today the polled variety prevails

Dor·set² (dôr′sət) county in SW England, on the English Channel: 1,024 sq mi (2,652 sq km): also **Dor′set·shire′** (-shir′, -shər)

dor·si- (dôr′si, -sə) ⟦see DORSO-⟧ *combining form* 1 of, on, or along the back 2 DORSO-

dor·si·ven·tral (dôr′si ven′trəl) *adj.* 1 *Bot.* having both dorsal and ventral surfaces 2 *Zool.* DORSOVENTRAL

dor·so- (dôr′sō, -sə) ⟦< L *dorsum,* the back⟧ *combining form* 1 the back and 2 DORSI-

dor·so·ve·lar (dôr′sō vē′lər) *adj.* *Phonet.* articulated with the back of the tongue touching or near the soft palate, as (k) and (ŋ) —*n.* a dorsovelar consonant

dor·so·ven·tral (dôr′sō ven′trəl) *adj.* 1 *Bot.* DORSIVENTRAL 2 *Zool.* extending from the dorsal to the ventral side

dor·sum (dôr′səm) *n., pl.* **-sa** (-sə) ⟦L⟧ 1 the back (of an animal) 2 any part corresponding to or like the back [the *dorsum* of the hand]

Dort (dôrt) *var. of* DORDRECHT

Dort·mund (dôrt′mənd; *Ger* dôrt′mo͝ont) city in W Germany, in the valley of the Ruhr River in the state of North Rhine-Westphalia

do·ry¹ (dôr′ē) *n., pl.* **-ries** ⟦AmInd (Central America) *dori, duri,* a dugout⟧ a flat-bottomed rowboat with high, flaring sides, used chiefly in commercial fishing

do·ry² (dôr′ē) *n., pl.* **-ries** ⟦ME *dorre* < MFr *dorée,* lit., gilt, fem. of *doré,* pp. of *dorer* < LL *deaurare,* to gild < L *de-,* intens. + *aurare,* to gild < *aurum,* gold: see AUROUS⟧ JOHN DORY

DOS (dôs, däs) *n.* ⟦*d(isk) o(perating) s(ystem)*⟧ *Comput.* an OPERATING SYSTEM that resides on a disk: term used primarily in connection with microcomputers

dos-à-dos (dō′zē dō′) *adv.* ⟦Fr⟧ back to back —*n., pl.* **dos′-a-dos′** (-dōz′) DO-SI-DO

dos·age (dōs′ij) *n.* 1 a dosing or being dosed 2 the system to be followed in taking doses, as of medicine [the prescribed *dosage* is ½ teaspoon every hour] 3 the amount used in a dose

dose (dōs) *n.* ⟦ME < OFr < ML *dosis* < Gr, orig., a giving < IE base **do-,* to give: see DATE¹⟧ 1 exact amount of a medicine or extent of some other treatment to be given or taken at one time or at stated intervals 2 amount of a punishment or other unpleasant experience undergone at one time 3 the amount of radiation delivered to a particular area or to a given part of the body 4 [Slang] a venereal infection, esp. gonorrhea —*vt.* **dosed, dos′ing** ⟦< the *n.*⟧ 1 to give a dose or doses to 2 to give (medicine, etc.) in doses —*vi.* to take a dose or doses of medicine

☆**do-si-do** (dō′sē dō′) *n., pl.* **-dos′** ⟦< DOS-À-DOS⟧ a movement in various folk dances, in which two dancers approach each other, pass back to back, and return to their original positions — *vt., vi.* **-doed′, -do′ing** to execute a do-si-do (with)

do·sim·e·ter (dō sim′ət ər) *n.* ⟦see DOSE & -METER⟧ a device for measuring the total absorbed dose from exposure to ionizing radiation —**do′si·met′ric** (-sə me′trik) *adj.* —**do·sim′e·try** (-sim′ə trē) *n.*

Dos Pas·sos (dəs pas′əs), **John (Roderigo)** 1896-1970; U.S. writer

doss (däs) [Brit. Slang] *n.* ⟦< L *dorsum,* the back⟧ a bed or bunk, esp. in a dosshouse —*vi.* to sleep, esp. in a dosshouse

dos·sal or **dos·sel** (däs′əl) ***n.*** ⟦ML *dossale*, var. of *dorsale* < *dorsalis*: see DORSAL[1]⟧ **1** [Historical] an ornamental upholstery at the back of a chair, throne, etc. **2** an ornamental cloth, as one hung behind an altar

dos·ser[1] (däs′ər) ***n.*** ⟦ME < OFr *dossier* < *dos*, the back: see DOSS⟧ **1** PANNIER (sense 1) **2** DOSSAL

doss·er[2] (däs′ər) ***n.*** [Brit. Slang] a destitute person who sleeps in a doss-house, outdoors, etc.; derelict; vagrant

doss·house (däs′hous′) ***n.*** ⟦see DOSS⟧ [Brit. Slang] a place where a night's lodging can be had very cheaply

dos·si·er (dä′sē ā′, dô′-; däs′yā′, dôs-) ***n.*** ⟦Fr < *dos*, the back < L *dorsum*: so named because labeled on the back⟧ a collection of documents concerning a particular person or matter

dos·sil (däs′il) ***n.*** ⟦ME *dosel*, a barrel spigot < OFr *doisil* < VL **duciculus*, dim. < L *ducere*, to lead: see DUCT⟧ a plug, wad, or fold of cotton or cloth, as for a wound

dost (dust) ***vt., vi.*** *archaic 2d pers. sing., pres. indic., of* DO[1]: used with *thou* (chiefly as an auxiliary)

Dos·to·ev·sky or **Dos·to·yev·sky** (dôs′tô yef′skē), **Fyo·dor (or Feo·dor) Mi·khai·lo·vich** (fyô′dôr mi khī′lô vich) 1821-81; Russ. novelist: also sp. **Dos′to·ev′ski** or **Dos′to·yev′ski**

dot[1] (dät) ***n.*** ⟦OE *dott*, head of boil: prob. reinforced (16th c.) by Du *dot*, akin to Ger *dütte*, nipple, Du *dodde*, a plug, Norw, LowG *dott*, little heap or swelling⟧ **1** a tiny spot, speck, or mark, esp. one made with or as with a pointed object **2** a point used in orthography or punctuation; specif., *a)* the mark placed above an *i* or *j* in writing or printing *b)* a period, as in a Web address **3** any small, round spot [polka *dots*] **4** *Math. a)* a decimal point *b)* a point used as a symbol of multiplication **5** *Music a)* a point after a note or rest, increasing its time value by one half *b)* a point put above or below a note to show that it is staccato **6** *Telegraphy* a short sound or click, as in Morse code: cf. DASH[1] —***vt.*** **dot′ted, dot′ting 1** to mark with or as with a dot **2** to make or form with dots [a *dotted* line] **3** to cover with or as with dots; appear as dotlike parts in [gas stations *dotted* the landscape] —***vi.*** to make a dot or dots —**connect the dots** ⟦in allusion to a children's pastime of connecting printed, prearranged dots with hand-drawn lines, to form a picture⟧ to put discrete or seemingly unrelated pieces of information together to form a theory, explanation, etc. —**dot one's i's and cross one's t's** to be minutely correct or detailed in doing or saying something —**on the dot** [Informal] at the exact time or point —**dot′ter *n.***

dot[2] (dôt) ***n.*** ⟦Fr < L *dos* (gen. *dotis*) < *dare*, to give: see DATE[1]⟧ a woman's marriage dowry —**do·tal** (dôt′'l) ***adj.***

DOT *abbrev.* Department of Transportation

dot·age (dōt′ij) ***n.*** ⟦ME < *doten*, DOTE⟧ **1** feeble and childish state due to old age; senility **2** a doting; foolish or excessive affection

dot·ard (dōt′ərd) ***n.*** ⟦ME < *doten*, DOTE⟧ a person in his or her dotage; foolish and doddering old person

dot-com (dät′käm′) [Informal] *Comput. adj.* ⟦< ".com", a typical ending for commercial Web addresses⟧ designating or of a company doing business primarily on the World Wide Web —***n.*** such a company Also written **dot.com** —**dot′-com′mer** (-käm′ər) ***n.***

dote (dōt) ***vi.*** **dot′ed, dot′ing** ⟦ME *doten*, akin to MDu, to dote & *dotten*, to be insane: for IE base see DODDER[1]⟧ **1** [Archaic] to be foolish or weak-minded, esp. because of old age **2** to be excessively or foolishly fond: with *on* or *upon* —**dot′er *n.***

doth (duth) ***vt., vi.*** [see DOETH] *archaic 3d pers. sing., pres. indic., of* DO[1]: chiefly as an auxiliary

dot·ing (dōt′iŋ) ***adj.*** foolishly or excessively fond —**dot′ing·ly *adv.***

dot-ma·trix (dät′mā′triks) ***adj.*** of or pertaining to a system of printing, as by certain computer printers, in which characters are formed of individual dots printed close together by means of columns of small hammers that are moved across the page

☆**dotted swiss** a type of fine, sheer, crisp fabric, as of cotton, with dots on the surface: it is used for blouses, curtains, etc.

dot·ter·el (dät′ər əl) ***n., pl.*** **-els** or **-el** ⟦ME *doterel* < *doten*, DOTE: so called because regarded as stupid and easy to catch⟧ **1** any of various plovers; esp., a European and Asian species (*Eudromias morinellus*) **2** [Brit. Dial.] an easy dupe

dot·tle or **dot·tel** (dät′'l) ***n.*** ⟦ME *dotelle*, var. of *dosel*, DOSSIL⟧ the tobacco residue left in a pipe after it has been smoked

dot·ty[1] (dät′ē) ***adj.*** **-ti·er, -ti·est** ⟦< DOT[1] + -Y[2]⟧ dotted

dotty[2] (dät′ē) ***adj.*** **-ti·er, -ti·est** ⟦< ME *dotti-*, silly < *doten*, DOTE⟧ [Informal] feebleminded or crazy

Dou (dou), **Ge·rard** (gā′rärt) or **Ger·rit** (gar′it) 1613-75; Du. painter

Dou·ai (do͞o ā′) city in N France: formerly sp. **Douay**

Dou·a·la (do͞o ä′lə) seaport in Cameroon, on the Bight of Biafra

Dou·ay Bible (do͞o′ā, do͞o ā′) an English version of the Bible translated from the Latin Vulgate edition for the use of Roman Catholics: the New Testament was orig. published at Reims (1582) and the Old Testament at Douai (1609-10): also called **Douay Version, Douay-Reims Version**

dou·ble (dub′əl) ***adj.*** ⟦ME < OFr < L *duplus*, lit., twofold (akin to Gr *diploos*) < *duo*, TWO + *-plus* < IE **plo-*, -fold < base **pel-*, to FOLD[1]⟧ **1** two combined; twofold; duplex **2** having two layers; folded in two **3** *a)* having two of one kind; paired; repeated [a *double* consonant] *b)* of or involving two or both [a *double* mastectomy] **4** being of two kinds; dual [a *double* standard] **5** having two meanings; ambiguous **6** twice as much, as many, as large, etc. [pay *double* fare] **7** of extra size, value, strength, or quantity **8** designed or made for two [a *double* bed] **9** characterized by duplicity; two-faced; deceiving [leading a *double* life] **10** having a tone an octave lower [*double* bass] **11** *Bot.* having more than one set of petals —***adv.*** **1** to twice the extent or degree; twofold **2** two together; in or by pairs [to ride *double*] —***n.*** **1** anything twice as much, as many, or as large as normal **2** a person or thing looking very much like another; duplicate; counterpart **3** a substitute actor or singer **4** a stand-in or substitute, as in films **5** a fold; second ply **6** a sharp turn or shift of direction **7** an evasive trick **8** [*pl.*] a game of tennis, handball, etc. with two players on each side ☆**9** *Baseball* a hit on which the batter reaches second base **10** *Bridge* the doubling of an opponent's bid —***vt.*** **-bled, -bling 1** to make double; make twice as much or as many; multiply by two **2** to fold so as to add another ply to [*double* the bandage] **3** to repeat or duplicate **4** to be the double of ☆**5** *Baseball a)* to put out (the second runner) in executing a double play *b)* to advance (a runner) by hitting a double **6** *Bridge* to increase the point value or penalty of (an opponent's bid) by saying "double" when it is one's turn to bid **7** *Music* to supply the upper or lower octave to (another part or voice) [*double* the tenor in brass] **8** *Naut.* to sail around [they *doubled* Cape Horn] —***vi.*** **1** to become double; increase twofold **2** to bend or turn sharply back in the direction from which one came [the animal *doubled* back on its tracks] **3** to serve as a double **4** to serve an additional purpose ☆**5** [Informal] to double-date ☆**6** *Baseball* to hit a double **7** *Music* to play one or more instruments in addition to one's principal instrument: often with *on* —**double down** ⟦< the optional play in BLACKJACK of doubling one's bet and receiving one card only⟧ [Informal] **1** to double one's original bet, investment, etc. so as to recover a past loss in addition to winning an amount equal to that loss **2** to improve one's chances of success, as by intensifying one's efforts —**double one's fist** to clench one's hand to form a fist —☆**double in brass** [Slang] to do or be capable of doing something additional to one's specialty —**double up 1** to bend over, as in laughter or pain: also **double over 2** [Informal] to share a room, etc. with someone —**on (or at) the double** [Informal] **1** in DOUBLE TIME (sense 2) **2** quickly

double agent a spy employed by two rival espionage organizations: cf. MOLE[2] (*n.* 2)

double bar *Music* two adjacent, parallel vertical lines drawn through the staff to indicate the end of a section or composition

dou·ble-bar·reled (-bar′əld) ***adj.*** **1** having two barrels, esp. side by side, as a kind of shotgun **2** having two purposes **3** that can be taken in two ways; ambiguous

double bass (bās) the largest and deepest-toned instrument of the violin family (formerly, of the viol family), with a range of approximately three octaves

double bass

double bassoon CONTRABASSOON

☆**double bind** ⟦see BIND, *n.* 2⟧ **1** a situation in which a person is faced with contradictory demands or expectations, so that any action taken will appear to be wrong **2** DILEMMA (sense 2)

double Blackwall hitch a kind of knot

☆**dou·ble-blind** (-blīnd′) ***adj.*** designating or of a technique used to test objectively the effects of a drug, course of treatment, etc. in which neither the subjects nor the researchers know during the testing who is actually receiving the drug, treatment, etc. and who is not, as in an experiment involving a drug and a placebo: cf. SINGLE-BLIND

double bogey *Golf* a score of two strokes more than par on a hole

☆**double boiler** a pair of saucepans, one of which fits over and partly inside the other: food is cooked in the upper pan while the water boiling in the lower one keeps it from scorching

double bond *Chem.* the sharing of two pairs of electrons between two atoms, usually represented in structural formulas by dots or dashes, as C:C or C=C

dou·ble-breast·ed (-bres′tid) ***adj.*** overlapping so as to provide a double thickness of material across the chest, and having a double row of buttons: said as of a coat

☆**dou·ble-check** (-chek′) ***vt., vi.*** to check again; verify —***n.*** the act of double-checking

double chin a fold of excess flesh beneath the chin

double counterpoint *Music* a type of counterpoint in which either part may be made the higher or the lower part

double cross 1 *Genetics* a new hybrid produced by crossing two existing hybrids (A × B → AB, C × D → CD, AB × CD → ABCD) **2** [Informal] a double-crossing; treachery

dou·ble-cross (-krôs′) ***vt.*** [Informal] to betray (a person) by doing the opposite of, or intentionally failing to do, what one has promised —**dou′ble-cross′er *n.***

double dagger a symbol (‡) used as a reference mark; diesis: cf. DAGGER

☆**double date** [Informal] a DATE[1] (*n.* 6*b*) shared by two couples —**dou′ble-date′** ***vi., vt.*** **-dat′ed, -dat′ing**

Dou·ble·day (dub′əl dā′), **Abner** 1819-93; U.S. army officer: traditionally regarded as the inventor of baseball

dou·ble-deal·ing (dub′əl dēl′iŋ) ***n.*** the act or practice of doing the opposite of what one pretends to do; duplicity; deceit —**dou′ble-deal′er *n.***

dou·ble-deck·er (-dek′ər) ***n.*** **1** any structure or vehicle with an upper deck or floor ☆**2** [Informal] a sandwich with two layers of filling and three slices of bread

double decomposition *Chem.* METATHESIS (sense *b*)

dou·ble-dig·it (-dij′it) ***adj.*** having two digits; specif., *a)* amounting to ten or more, but fewer than 100 [*double-digit* temperatures] *b)* amounting to ten percent or more, but less than 100 percent [*double-digit* inflation]

double dipping the practice of receiving compensation, benefits, etc. from two or more sources in a way regarded as unethical, as from a military pension and a government job —**double dipper**

☆**double dribble** *Basketball* the illegal act either of dribbling the ball with both hands simultaneously or of resuming dribbling after having stopped

double Dutch a children's game of jump-rope in which two turners swing two ropes simultaneously in a crisscross pattern for the person jumping: also **double dutch** or **Double Dutch**

☆**double eagle** ⟦because worth twice as much as an EAGLE (*n.* 3)⟧ a former U.S. gold coin equal to $20

dou·ble-edged (-ejd′) ***adj.*** **1** having two cutting edges **2** that can be understood or interpreted in two ways [a *double-edged* remark] **3** having or able to have both favorable and unfavorable results: often used fig. in the phrase **double-edged sword**, something, as an action, that has or can have such results [giving a child an allowance can be a *double-edged sword*]

dou·ble-en·ten·dre (dub′əl än tän′drə; do͞o′blôn tôn′drə) ***n.*** ⟦Fr (now obs.), double meaning⟧ **1** a term with two meanings, esp. when one of them has a risqué or indecorous connotation **2** the use of such a term or terms; ambiguity

double entry a system of bookkeeping in which every transaction is entered as both a debit and a credit in conformity with the underlying accounting equation which states that assets equal liabilities plus net worth —**dou′ble-en′try** ***adj.***

double exposure *Photog.* **1** the making of two exposures on the same film or plate, either by mistake or for a composite photograph **2** such a photograph

dou·ble-faced (dub′əl fāst′) ***adj.*** **1** having two faces or aspects **2** having a finished nap on both sides: said of cloth **3** hypocritical; insincere; two-faced

double fault *Racket Sports* the act of serving twice improperly, resulting in the loss of the point, the loss of the serve, or both —**dou′ble-fault′** ***vi.***

☆**double feature** two full-length films shown for a single admission price

double flat a sign (♭♭) placed before a note to show that it is to be lowered two semitones

dou·ble-glaz·ing (dub′əl glā′ziŋ) ***n.*** window glazing with two panes of glass having space between them to allow air to act as an insulator

☆**dou·ble-head·er** (-hed′ər) ***n.*** **1** a train pulled by two locomotives **2** a pair of games played in succession on the same day, usually by the same two teams

double helix the characteristic helical structure of the two complementary chains of nucleotides in DNA: the chains are linked by hydrogen bonds and coil around a single axis

dou·ble-hung (dub′əl huŋ′) ***adj.*** designating or of a kind of window having two sashes that slide up and down, each balanced by counterweights and covering a different part of the window space —***n.*** such a window

☆**double indemnity** a clause in life insurance policies providing for the payment of twice the face value of the contract in the case of accidental death

☆**double jeopardy** *Law* exposure of a defendant to a second prosecution for the same offense or crime: prohibited by the U.S. Constitution

dou·ble-joint·ed (-joint′id) ***adj.*** having joints that permit limbs, fingers, etc. to bend at other than the usual angles

dou·ble-knit (-nit′) ***adj.*** knit with a double stitch, which gives extra thickness to the fabric

dou·ble-mind·ed (-mīn′did) ***adj.*** undecided; vacillating

double mordent *see* MORDENT

double negative the use of two negatives in a single statement having a negative force (Ex.: "I didn't hear nothing"): a double negative is now generally regarded as grammatically nonstandard

☆**dou·ble-park** (-pärk′) ***vt., vi.*** to park (a vehicle) beside and parallel to another that is parked alongside a curb

☆**double play** *Baseball* a play in which two players are put out

double pneumonia pneumonia of both lungs

dou·ble-quick (-kwik′) ***adj.*** very quick —***n.*** a very quick marching pace; specif., DOUBLE TIME (sense 2) —☆***vi., vt.*** to march at such a pace —***adv.*** at this pace

dou·ble-reed (-rēd′) ***adj.*** designating or of any of a group of woodwind instruments, as the oboe or bassoon, having two reeds that are separated by a narrow opening and vibrated against each other by the breath —***n.*** a double-reed instrument

double refraction BIREFRINGENCE

double salt *Chem.* **1** a salt, as Rochelle salt, which in solution produces two different cations or anions **2** any compound regarded as a combination of two salts

double sharp a sign (𝄪 or ×) placed before a note to show that it is to be raised two semitones

dou·ble-space (-spās′) ***vt., vi.*** **-spaced′**, **-spac′ing** to type or write so as to leave a full space between lines

dou·ble·speak (-spēk′) ***n.*** ⟦coined with DOUBLE-THINK⟧ obscure or ambiguous language, esp. if meant to deceive

double standard a system, code, criterion, etc. applied unequally; specif., a code of behavior that is stricter for women than for men, esp. in matters of sex

double star **1** BINARY STAR **2** two stars, along the same line of sight, that look like one star, or a binary star, but actually are very distant from each other and physically unrelated; optical double

dou·ble-stop (-stäp′) ***vi.*** to produce two tones simultaneously on a stringed instrument by drawing the bow over two strings at the same time —***n.*** **1** the two tones thus produced **2** the notes showing these

dou·blet (dub′lit) ***n.*** ⟦ME < OFr, dim. of *double*, orig., something folded, a kind of material: see DOUBLE⟧ **1** a man's closefitting jacket with or without sleeves, worn chiefly from the 14th to the 16th cent. **2** either of a pair of similar things **3** a pair; couple **4** [*often pl.*] a pair of thrown dice with identical sides uppermost **5** a simulated gem produced by cementing together two smaller stones, crystals, or pieces of colored glass **6** *Linguis.* either of two words that derive ultimately from the same source but by different processes (Ex.: *regal, royal; skirt, shirt*) **7** *Radio* DIPOLE (*n.* 3)

doublet

double tackle a pulley block with two grooved wheels

☆**double take** a delayed reaction to some remark, situation, etc., in which there is at first unthinking acceptance and then startled surprise or a second glance as the real meaning or actual situation suddenly becomes clear: often used as a comic device in acting

☆**double talk** **1** ambiguous and deceptive talk **2** deliberately confusing or unintelligible talk made up of a mixture of real words and meaningless syllables

☆**dou·ble-team** (-tēm′) ***vt.*** ⟦after TEAM, *n.* 2⟧ *Sports* to use two players to guard or block (a single opposing player)

dou·ble-think or **dou·ble·think** (-thiŋk′) ***n.*** ⟦coined by George ORWELL in his novel *Nineteen Eighty-four* (published 1949)⟧ illogical or deliberately perverse thinking in terms that distort or reverse the truth to make it more acceptable

double time ☆**1** a rate of payment twice as high as usual, as for work on Sundays **2** a marching cadence of 180 three-foot steps a minute: normal cadence is 120 steps a minute **3** *Music a)* duple time *b)* twice as fast as the preceding tempo

dou·ble·ton (-tən) ***n.*** ⟦DOUBLE + *-ton*, as in SINGLETON⟧ two playing cards of the same suit that are the only cards of that suit in a hand dealt to a player

dou·ble-tongue (-tuŋ′) ***vi.*** **-tongued′**, **-tongu′ing** to alternate quickly and regularly the use of the tip and base of the tongue in playing a flute, trumpet, etc. to facilitate rapid articulation

dou·ble-tongued (-tuŋd′) ***adj.*** deceitful

☆**dou·ble·tree** (-trē′) ***n.*** ⟦DOUBLE + (SINGLE)TREE⟧ a crossbar on a wagon, carriage, plow, etc., to each end of which the singletrees are attached when two horses are harnessed abreast

double vision DIPLOPIA

dou·ble-wide (-wīd′) ***n.*** a mobile home consisting of two modular sections connected lengthwise, making the width double that of a typical mobile home: sometimes written **dou′ble·wide′**

dou·bloon (də blo͞on′) ***n.*** ⟦Fr *doublon* < Sp *doblón* < *dobla*, an old Sp gold coin < *doble* < L *duplus*, DOUBLE⟧ an obsolete Spanish gold coin

dou·bly (dub′lē) ***adv.*** **1** twice; to twice the degree or quantity **2** two at a time

doubly serrate BISERRATE

Doubs (do͞o) river in E France, flowing from the Jura Mountains generally southwest into the Saône: *c.* 270 mi (435 km)

doubt (dout) ***vi.*** ⟦ME *douten* < OFr *douter* < L *dubitare*, to waver in opinion < *dubius*, DUBIOUS; *-b-* reintroduced, after L, in 16th c.⟧ **1** to be uncertain in opinion or belief; be undecided **2** to be inclined to disbelief **3** [Archaic] to hesitate —***vt.*** **1** to be uncertain about; question; feel distrust of **2** to be inclined to disbelieve; be skeptical of **3** [Archaic] to be fearful or suspicious of —***n.*** **1** *a)* a wavering of opinion or belief; lack of conviction; uncertainty *b)* lack of trust or confidence **2** a condition of uncertainty [the outcome was in *doubt*] **3** [Obs.] apprehension or fear —***SYN.*** UNCERTAINTY —**beyond** (or **without**) **(a) doubt** certainly —**no doubt** **1** certainly **2** very likely; probably —**doubt′a·ble** ***adj.*** —**doubt′er** ***n.*** —**doubt′ing·ly** ***adv.***

doubt·ful (dout′fəl) ***adj.*** ⟦ME *douteful*⟧ **1** in doubt; not clear or definite; ambiguous **2** not clearly predictable; uncertain; unsure **3** giving rise to doubt or suspicion; questionable, as in reputation **4** feeling doubt; unsettled in opinion or belief —**doubt′ful·ly** ***adv.*** —**doubt′ful·ness** ***n.***

SYN.—**doubtful** implies strong uncertainty as to the probability, value, honesty, validity, etc. of something [a *doubtful* remedy]; **dubious** is less strong, suggesting merely vague suspicion or hesitancy [*dubious* about the future]; **questionable** strictly suggests only that there is some reason for doubt, but it is often used as a euphemism to imply strong suspicion, almost amounting to certainty, of immorality, dishonesty, etc. [a *questionable* reputation]; **problematic** implies only uncertainty with no suggestion of a moral question [a *problematic* success] —***ANT.*** **certain, sure**

doubting Thomas ⟦after the Apostle THOMAS[1]⟧ a person who habitually doubts; chronic skeptic

doubt·less (dout′lis) ***adj.*** ⟦ME *douteles*⟧ [Rare] free from doubt; sure —***adv.*** **1** without doubt; certainly **2** probably —**doubt′less·ly** ***adv.*** —**doubt′less·ness** ***n.***

douce (do͞os) ***adj.*** ⟦ME < OFr, fem. of *douz* < L *dulcis*: see DULCET⟧ **1** [Obs.] pleasant or hospitable **2** [Scot.] sedate; sober

dou·ceur (do͞o sʉr′) ***n.*** ⟦Fr, sweetness: see prec.⟧ a gratuity or bribe

douche (do͞osh) ***n.*** ⟦Fr < It *doccia*, shower bath, orig., conduit, back-form. < *doccione*, water pipe < L *ductio*, a leading away < *ductus*: see DUCT⟧ **1** a jet of liquid applied externally or internally to some part of the body, esp. as a bath or treatment **2** a bath or treatment of this kind; esp., a stream of water, often containing a special preparation, introduced into the vagina to cleanse it **3** a device for douching ☆**4** [Slang] *short for* DOUCHEBAG: mildly vulgar — ***vt., vi.* douched, douch′ing** to apply a douche to (some part of the body, esp. the vagina)

douche·bag (do͞osh′bag′) ***n.*** ☆[Slang] an unpleasant, offensive, or contemptible person: a mildly vulgar term: also written **douche bag**

dough (dō) ***n.*** ⟦ME < OE *dag*, akin to Goth *daigs*, Ger *teig* < IE base **dheiĝh-*, to knead, form > Gr *teichos*, wall, L *fingere*, to form⟧ **1** a mixture of flour, liquid, leavening, and other ingredients, worked into a soft, thick mass for baking into bread, pastry, etc. **2** any pasty mass like this ☆**3** [Slang] money

dough·boy (-boi′) ***n.*** **1** a boiled dumpling ☆**2** [Informal] a U.S. infantryman, esp. of WWI

☆**dough·face** (-fās′) ***n.*** ⟦DOUGH + FACE⟧ in the Civil War, a Northerner who sided with the South on the slavery issue

dough·nut (-nut′) ***n.*** ⟦DOUGH + NUT: so named from original nutlike shape⟧ a small, typically ring-shaped cake of sweetened, leavened dough, fried in deep fat

dough·ty (dout′ē) ***adj.*** **-ti·er, -ti·est** ⟦ME < OE *dohtig*, altered < *dyhtig* (after *dohte*, pt. of *dugan*, to avail), akin to Ger *tüchtig*, fit, good, excellent < IE base **dheugh-*, to press, give abundantly⟧ [Now Rare] valiant; brave **—dough′ti·ly *adv.*** **—dough′ti·ness *n.***

Dough·ty (dout′ē), **C(harles) M(ontagu)** 1843-1926; Eng. travel writer

dough·y (dō′ē) ***adj.*** **dough′i·er, dough′i·est** of or like dough; soft, pasty, flabby, etc. **—dough′i·ness *n.***

Doug·las[1] (dug′ləs) ***n.*** ⟦< Gael, lit., black stream⟧ a masculine name: dim. *Doug*

Doug·las[2] (dug′ləs) **1** Sir **James** 1286?-1330; Scot. military leader: called *Black Douglas* **2** Sir **James** 1358?-88; Scot. military leader **3 Stephen A(rnold)** 1813-61; U.S. politician: noted for his debates with Lincoln in Illinois senatorial campaign (1858) **4 William O(rville)** 1898-1980; associate justice, U.S. Supreme Court (1939-75)

Doug·las[3] (dug′ləs) capital of the Isle of Man

Douglas fir (*or* **spruce, pine,** *or* **hemlock)** ⟦after D. *Douglas* (1798-1834), Scot botanist in U.S.⟧ any of a genus (*Pseudotsuga*) of giant evergreen trees of the pine family, found in W North America and valued for their wood, esp. a popular Christmas tree (*P. menziesii*)

Doug·lass (dug′ləs), **Frederick** (born *Frederick Augustus Washington Bailey*) 1817?-95; U.S. abolitionist, writer, & statesman

Dou·kho·bor (do͞o′kə bôr′) ***n.*** *alt. sp. of* DUKHOBOR

dou·la (do͞o′lə) ***n.*** ⟦< ModGr, female servant⟧ a woman trained to give nonmedical assistance to a woman during labor, providing emotional and physical support throughout the process of childbirth

doum (do͞om) ***n.*** ⟦Fr < Ar *dawm*⟧ an African palm tree (*Hyphaene thebaica*) bearing an edible fruit that has a taste and consistency somewhat like gingerbread; gingerbread palm

doup·pi·o·ni or **dou·pi·o·ni** (do͞o′pē ō′nē) ***n.*** ⟦It *doppioni*, pl. of *doppione*, a double cocoon < *doppio*, double < L *duplus*, DOUBLE: sp. infl. by Fr *doupion* < It⟧ a thick silk yarn of irregular ply, used chiefly for suit fabrics

dour (door, dour) ***adj.*** ⟦ME < L *durus*: see DURABLE⟧ **1** [Scot.] hard; stern; severe **2** [Scot.] obstinate **3** sullen; gloomy; forbidding **—dour′ly *adv.*** **—dour′ness *n.***

dou·rine (doo rēn′) ***n.*** ⟦Fr⟧ a sexually transmitted disease of horses and donkeys, caused by a protozoan (*Trypanosoma equiperdum*) and characterized by inflammation of the genitals and lymph nodes, and paralysis of the hind legs

Dou·ro (dō′roo) river flowing from NC Spain across N Portugal into the Atlantic: *c.* 500 mi (805 km)

douse[1] (dous) ***vt.*** **doused, dous′ing** ⟦16th-c. slang, ? akin to MDu *dossen*, to beat noisily⟧ **1** [Obs.] to hit forcefully **2** *Naut.* to lower (sails) quickly **3** [Informal] to pull off (shoes, clothes, etc.) **4** [Informal] to put out (a light or fire) quickly

douse[2] (dous) ***vt.*** **doused, dous′ing** ⟦< ? prec.⟧ **1** to plunge or thrust suddenly into liquid **2** to drench; pour liquid over **—*vi.*** to get immersed or drenched **—*n.*** a drenching

douse[3] (douz) ***vi.*** **doused, dous′ing** DOWSE[2]

dove[1] (duv) ***n.*** ⟦ME *douve* < OE **dufe* or ON *dūfa*, akin to Goth *dūbo*, Ger *taube* < IE **dheubh-*, obscured, dark (of color) < base **dheu-*: see DULL⟧ **1** PIGEON[1], esp. the smaller species: it is often used as a symbol of peace ☆**2** an advocate of measures in international affairs designed to avoid or reduce open hostilities: cf. HAWK[1] **3** a person regarded as gentle, innocent, or beloved **—dov′ish *adj.***

dove[2] (dōv) ***vi., vt.*** *alt. pt. of* DIVE

dove·cote (duv′kōt′, -kät′) ***n.*** ⟦ME *douvecote*: see DOVE[1] & COT[2]⟧ a small house or box with compartments for nesting pigeons, usually on a pole: also **dove′cot′** (-kät′)

dove·kie or **dove·key** (duv′kē′) ***n.*** ⟦DOVE[1] + *-kie, key*, dim. suffix⟧ a small auk (*Alle alle*) of the Arctic and N Atlantic coasts

do·ven (dä′vən) ***vi.*** *alt. sp. of* DAVEN

Do·ver (dō′vər) **1** seaport in Kent, SE England, on the Strait of Dover **2** ⟦after the seaport⟧ capital of Del., in the central part **3 Strait** (or **Straits) of** strait between France and England, joining the North Sea and the English Channel: narrowest point, 21 mi (34 km)

Dover sole ⟦prob. after prec. (the seaport)⟧ **1** a common European sole (*Solea vulgaris*, family Soleidae), highly valued as a food fish **2** a North American flounder (*Microstomus pacificus*, family Pleuronectidae), widely used as a food fish in the U.S.

Dover's powder ⟦after T. *Dover* (1660-1742), Brit physician⟧ a preparation of opium, ipecac, etc., formerly used to relieve pain and induce perspiration

dove·tail (duv′tāl′) ***n.*** **1** a part or thing shaped like a dove's tail; specif., a projecting, wedge-shaped part (*tenon*) that fits into a corresponding cut-out space (*mortise*) to form an interlocking joint **2** a joint thus formed **—*vt.*** **1** to join or fasten together by means of dovetails **2** to piece together (facts, etc.) so as to make a logically connected whole **—*vi.*** to fit together closely or logically

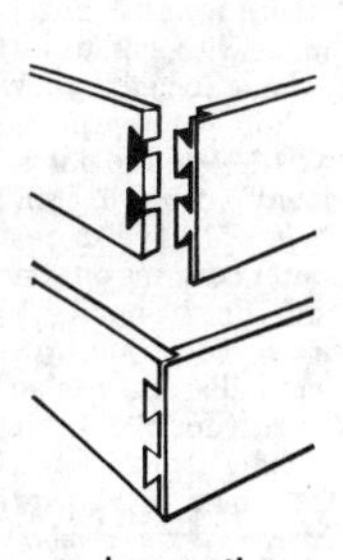

dovetail

Dow (dou), **Gerard** *alt. sp. of* Gerard Dou

dow·a·ger (dou′ə jər) ***n.*** ⟦OFr *douagiere* < *douage*, dowry < *douer*, to give a dowry < L *dotare*, to endow < *dos*: see DOT[2]⟧ **1** a widow with a title or property derived from her dead husband: often used in comb. with the title [queen *dowager*, *dowager* duchess] **2** an elderly woman of wealth and dignity

dowager's hump ⟦so called because often seen in older women⟧ a condition caused by osteoporosis in which the shoulders are rounded and the spine becomes prominently bowed, forming a hump in the upper back

Dow·den (dou′dən), **Edward** 1843-1913; Ir. critic, biographer, & Shakespearean scholar

dow·dy (dou′dē) ***adj.*** **-di·er, -di·est** ⟦< ME *doude*, an unattractive woman + -Y[2]⟧ not neat or stylish in dress or appearance; shabby **—*n., pl.*** **-dies 1** a dowdy woman ☆**2** PANDOWDY **—dow′di·ly *adv.*** **—dow′di·ness *n.***

dow·el (dou′əl) ***n.*** ⟦ME *doule*, prob. akin to MLowG *dövel*, Ger *döbel*, a plug < IE base **dheubh-*, a peg, wooden pin > DUB[1]⟧ a short cylinder of wood, metal, etc., usually fitted into corresponding holes in two pieces to fasten them together **—*vt.*** **-eled** or **-elled, -el·ing** or **-el·ling** to fasten or furnish with dowels

dowel

dow·er (dou′ər) ***n.*** ⟦ME *douere* < OFr *douaire* < ML *dotarium* < L *dos*: see DOT[2]⟧ **1** that part of a man's property which his widow inherits for life **2** a dowry **3** a natural talent, gift, or endowment **—*vt.*** **1** to give a dower to **2** to endow (*with*)

☆**dow·itch·er** (dou′ich ər) ***n., pl.*** **-ers** or **-er** ⟦< name in an Iroquoian language⟧ a medium-sized, long-legged, long-billed snipe (genus *Limnodromus*) of North America and Asia

Dow Jones industrial average ⟦< *The Dow Jones Averages*, trademark of Dow Jones & Company, Inc.⟧ a stock market index based upon the current prices of thirty selected industrial stocks traded on the New York Stock Exchange: also **Dow (Jones) Industrials** or **the Dow**

Dow·land (dou′lənd), **John** 1563?-1626; Eng. lutenist & composer of songs

down[1] (doun) ***adv.*** ⟦ME *doun* < *adune*, adown < OE *adune*, *ofdune*, from the hill < *a-*, *of-*, off, from + *dune*, dat. of *dun*, hill: see DOWN[3]⟧ **1** from a higher to a lower place; toward the ground **2** in, on, or to a lower position or level; specif., to a sitting or reclining position **3** *a)* in or to a place thought of as lower or below; often, specif., southward [to go *down* to Florida] *b)* out of one's hand [put it *down*] **4** below the horizon **5** from an earlier to a later period or person [*down* through the years] **6** into a low or dejected emotional condition **7** into a low or prostrate physical condition [to come *down* with a cold] **8** in or into an inferior position or condition [held *down* by harsh laws] **9** to a lower amount, value, or bulk [to come *down* in price] **10** *a)* to a less excited or active condition; into a tranquil or quiet state [to settle *down*] *b)* to a lower volume of sound [turn *down* the radio] **11** in a serious or earnest manner [to get *down* to work] **12** completely; to the full extent [loaded *down*] **13** in cash or as a down payment [fifty dollars *down* and the remainder in installments] **14** in writing; on record [take *down* his name] **15** in a way that renders something or someone rejected or defeated [vote a measure *down*, shout someone *down* in an argument] **—*adj.*** **1** descending; directed toward a lower position **2** in a lower place; on the ground **3** gone, brought, pulled, etc. down **4** *a)* depressed; dejected *b)* [Slang] depressing or downbeat [a *down* atmosphere] **5** dejected; discouraged **6** prostrate; ill **7** completed; finished [four *down*, six to go] **8** inoperative [the computer is *down*] **9** characterized by low or falling prices **10** [Slang] *a) a generalized term of approval meaning variously* nice, good, excellent, etc. *b)* sophisticated, stylish, etc.; cool; hip **11** *Sports* ☆*a)* no longer in play (said of a football) ☆*b) Football* tackled or otherwise stopped, thus ending the play (said of a player carrying the ball) *c)* trailing an opponent by a specified number of points, strokes, etc. ☆*d) Baseball* put out **—*prep.*** down or downward, along, through, into, or upon [*down* the street, *down* the chimney, *down*

the river, *down* the stairs] —*vt.* 1 *a)* to put, bring, get, throw, or knock down *b)* to defeat, as in a game 2 to gulp or eat rapidly —*vi.* [Rare] to go, come, or get down —*n.* 1 a downward movement or depressed condition; defeat, misfortune, etc.: see UPS AND DOWNS, at UP[1] ☆2 *Football a)* one of four consecutive plays in which a team, in order to keep possession of the ball, must either score or advance the ball at least ten yards *b)* the declaring of the ball as down, or no longer in play 3 [Slang] a barbiturate or other depressant drug; downer —☆**down and out** 1 *Boxing* knocked out 2 lacking enough money, shelter, a job, etc.; destitute or impoverished —**down on** [Informal] hostile to; angry or annoyed with —**down to the ground** thoroughly; completely —**down with** 1 overthrow! do away with! [*down with* the king!] ☆2 [Slang] in approval or acceptance of, in agreement with, enthusiastic about, etc. [I'm *down with* our new councilman] —**have something down** ⟦< HAVE DOWN PAT (see phrase at PAT[1])⟧ [Informal] to know or have memorized thoroughly
NOTE—See also phrases under BREAK, PUT, TRACK, etc.

down[2] (doun) *n.* ⟦ME *doun* < ON *dūnn*, akin to Goth *dauns*, fume < IE base **dheu-*, to fly like dust, be turbid: see DULL⟧ 1 soft, fluffy feathers, as the outer covering on young birds or an inner layer of feathers on adult birds 2 soft, fine hair or hairy growth

down[3] (doun) *n.* ⟦ME *doun* < OE *dun*, a hill, akin to ODu *duna*, LowG *düne*, sandhill: see DUNE⟧ an expanse of open, high, grassy land: *usually used in pl.*

Down (doun) 1 former county of E Northern Ireland: *c.* 952 sq mi (2,466 sq km) 2 district in E Northern Ireland, in the S part of the former county: 249 sq mi (645 sq km)

down- (doun) *combining form* down, downward [*downhill*]

down-and-dirt·y (doun′ən durt′ē) *adj.* [Slang] 1 realistic; unvarnished 2 earthy, coarse, uninhibited, etc. 3 unscrupulous 4 fiercely competitive Sometimes written **down and dirty**

down·beat (doun′bēt′) *n.* 1 a downward trend; downswing 2 *Music a)* the downward stroke of the conductor's hand or baton indicating the first beat of each measure *b)* such a beat —☆*adj.* [Informal] gloomy, discouraging, depressing, grim, etc.

down-bow (-bō′) *n.* 1 a stroke on a violin, cello, etc. in which the bow is drawn across the strings from the frog to the tip 2 a sign (⌐) indicating this

down·cast (-kast′) *adj.* 1 directed downward 2 very unhappy or discouraged; sad; dejected

down·court (-kôrt′) *adv., adj.* ☆*Basketball* into, toward, or in the opposite half of the court [dribbling *downcourt*]

down·draft (-draft′) *n.* a downward air current

☆**Down East** [*also* **d- e-**] [Informal] in or into New England, esp. Maine —**down′-east′er** *n.*

down·er (dou′nər) *n.* [Slang] 1 any depressant drug, as a tranquilizer or barbiturate ☆2 a depressing experience, person, etc.

Dow·ney (dou′nē) ⟦after J. G. *Downey*, governor of Calif., 1860-62⟧ city in SW Calif.: suburb of Los Angeles

down·fall (doun′fôl′) *n.* 1 *a)* a sudden fall, as from prosperity or power *b)* the cause of such a fall 2 a sudden, heavy fall, as of snow

down·fall·en (-fôl′ən) *adj.* fallen; ruined

down·field (-fēld′) *adv., adj. Football, Soccer, etc.* into, toward, or in the opposite end of the field, esp. the defensive end [to pass, kick, or run *downfield*]

☆**down·grade** (-grād′) *n.* 1 a downward slope, esp. in a road 2 a lowering in rank, value, etc. — *adj., adv.* downhill; downward —*vt.* **-grad′ed**, **-grad′ing** 1 to demote to a less skilled job at lower pay 2 to lower in importance, value, esteem, etc. 3 to belittle —**on the downgrade** losing status, influence, health, etc.; declining

down·haul (-hôl′) *n.* a rope, wire, or tackle for hauling something down, as a sail

down·heart·ed (-härt′id) *adj.* in low spirits; discouraged; dejected —**down′heart′ed·ly** *adv.*

down·hill (-hil′) *adv.* 1 toward the bottom of a hill 2 to a poorer condition, status, etc. —*adj.* 1 sloping or going downward 2 without difficulty; easy 3 of or having to do with skiing downhill or, specif., the DOWNHILL (*n.* 2) —*n.* 1 [Obs.] DESCENT (sense 4) 2 *Skiing* a timed downhill race on a very long, steep course with wide gates: see also SLALOM —**go downhill** to decline or deteriorate —**down′hill′er** *n.*

☆**down-home** (-hōm′) *adj.* 1 of, from, or associated with a rural, esp. Southern, area 2 having characteristics associated with rural people; simple, warm, direct, etc.

down·i·ness (dou′nē nis) *n.* the quality of being downy

Down·ing Street (dou′niŋ) ⟦after Sir George *Downing* (1623-84), who owned property there⟧ street in Westminster, London, location of some of the principal government offices of the United Kingdom, including the official residence of the prime minister (Number 10): often used fig. of the British government or the prime minister

down·land (doun′land′, -lənd) *n.* DOWN[3]

down·link (doun′liŋk′) *n.* 1 an electronic link by which signals are received on the earth's surface from an orbiting satellite, spacecraft, etc. 2 the site, facility, etc. which receives such signals —*vi.* to connect to a satellite, spacecraft, etc. using such a link —*vt.* to receive (signals, data, etc.) using such a link Cf. UPLINK

down·load (-lōd′) *vt.* to transfer electronically (a copy of a file or program) from a central computer, a website, etc. to a terminal, personal computer, etc.: distinguished from UPLOAD —*vi.* 1 to transfer a copy of a file or program in this way 2 to be transferred in this way [the program takes two hours to *download*] —*n.* the act or an instance of transferring copies of files or programs in this way —**down′load′a·ble** *adj.*

down-mar·ket (-mär′kit) *adj.* [Chiefly Brit.] DOWNSCALE

☆**down payment** an initial, partial payment on a purchase

down·play (-plā′) *vt.* to play down; minimize

down·pour (-pôr′) *n.* a heavy rain

down quark *Particle Physics* a type of quark with a mass of *c.* 0.005 to 0.015 GeV/c^2, a negative charge that is $^1/_3$ the charge of an electron, zero charm, and zero strangeness: see FLAVOR (sense 5)

☆**down·range** (-rānj′) *adv., adj.* along the course away from the launching site

down·right (doun′rīt′) *adv.* ⟦ME *doun riht*: see DOWN[1] & RIGHT⟧ 1 thoroughly; utterly 2 [Archaic] straight down —*adj.* 1 absolute; thoroughgoing [a *downright* insult] 2 straightforward; plain; frank 3 [Archaic] going straight downward

down·riv·er (-riv′ər) *adv., adj.* toward the mouth of a river; with or in the current of a river

Downs (dounz), **the** 1 ⟦< DOWN[3]⟧ two parallel ranges of low, grassy hills (**North Downs** & **South Downs**) in SE England 2 ⟦because adjacent to the end of the North *Downs* on the coast⟧ naturally protected anchorage in the Strait of Dover, England

☆**down·scale** (doun′skāl′) *adj.* designating, of, or for people who are relatively unstylish, not affluent, etc. — *vt., vi.* **-scaled′**, **-scal′ing** to reduce (something) in size, amount, extent, cost, etc.; downsize

down·shift (-shift′) *vi.* to shift the transmission of a motor vehicle to a lower gear or arrangement —*n.* an instance of shifting gears in this way

down·side (-sīd′) *n.* 1 the lower side or part 2 a downward trend or financial loss, as on an investment 3 any or all of the drawbacks or disadvantages

☆**down·size** (-sīz′) *vt.* **-sized′**, **-siz′ing** 1 to design or manufacture a smaller version of 2 to reduce in size, extent, etc. [to *downsize* a company by eliminating jobs] 3 [Informal] to fire (an employee) in an attempt to reduce expenditures —*vi.* to become smaller in size or extent, as by eliminating employees or reducing expenditures

down·slope (-slōp′) *adv., adj.* toward the bottom of a hill; downhill

☆**down·spout** (-spout′) *n.* a vertical pipe for carrying rainwater from a roof gutter to ground level

down·stage (-stāj′) *adv.* toward the front of the stage —*adj.* having to do with the front of the stage

down·stairs (-sterz′) *adv.* 1 down the stairs 2 on or to a lower floor —*adj.* situated on a lower floor —*n.* a lower floor or floors

☆**down·state** (-stāt′) *n.* that part of a state farther to the south — *adj., adv.* in, to, or from downstate —**down′stat′er** *n.*

down·stream (-strēm′) *adv., adj.* 1 in the direction of the current of a stream 2 at or toward the end of some process, course of activity, etc.

down·swing (-swiŋ′) *n.* 1 the downward part of a swing, as of a golf club 2 a downward trend, as in business

Down syndrome (doun) ⟦after J. L. H. *Down* (1828-96), Brit physician⟧ a congenital condition characterized by abnormal chromosomes, mental deficiency, a broad face, slanting eyes, a short fifth finger, etc.: also called **Down's syndrome**

down·throw (doun′thrō′) *n. Geol.* that side of a fault which has moved downward relative to the other side

☆**down·tick** (-tik′) *n.* ⟦see DOWN- & UPTICK⟧ 1 a stock transaction at a price lower than that of the preceding transaction 2 a decrease or downturn

down·time (-tīm′) *n.* 1 the time during which a machine, factory, etc. is shut down for repairs or the like 2 the time during which a computer or computer system is down, or inoperative, due to hardware or software failure 3 *a)* time spent not working; free or leisure time *b)* a brief period of inactivity occurring between tasks or obligations; rest, pause, break, etc. *c)* an unproductive period caused as by illness, unexpected difficulties, etc.: also written **down time** or **down-time**

down-to-earth (-tə urth′) *adj.* 1 realistic or practical 2 without affectation; natural, sincere, etc.

☆**down·town** (doun′toun′; *for adj., also* doun′toun′) *adj.* 1 of, in, like, or relating to the lower part or main business section of a city or town 2 [Informal] trendy or hip [*downtown* styles, *downtown* music] —*n.* the downtown section of a city or town —*adv.* in, to, or toward downtown

down·town·er (doun′tou′nər) *n.* a person living or working downtown or actively involved in life or culture there

down·trend (doun′trend′) *n.* a downward trend, esp. a financial one

down·trod·den (-träd′'n) *adj.* 1 trampled on or down 2 oppressed; subjugated; tyrannized over

down·turn (-turn′) *n.* a downward trend, as in business activity

down under [Informal] in or into Australia or New Zealand

Down Under ⟦orig. an adv., with ref. to its position relative to England on a globe⟧ [*also* **d- u-**] *informal name for* Australia and New Zealand

down·ward (-wərd) *adv., adj.* ⟦ME *dounward* < OE *aduneweard*: see DOWN[1] & -WARD⟧ 1 toward a lower place, position, state, etc. 2 from an earlier to a later time Also **down′wards** *adv.* —**down′ward·ly** *adv.*

down·wash (-wôsh′) *n.* the downward deflection of air as by an airfoil

down·wind (-wind′) *adv., adj.* in the direction in which the wind is blowing or usually blows

down·y (dou′nē) *adj.* **down′i·er**, **down′i·est** 1 of or covered with soft, fine feathers or hair 2 soft and fluffy, like down

☆**downy mildew** a disease of angiosperms characterized by the appearance of whitish or downy patches of fungus on the surfaces of plant parts, caused by various fungi (family Peronosporaceae)

downy woodpecker a small, black-and-white North American woodpecker (*Picoides pubescens*)

dow·ry (dou′rē) ***n.***, *pl.* **-ries** ⟦ME *douerie* < Anglo-Fr & OFr *douarie*: see DOWER⟧ **1** the property that a woman brings to her husband at marriage: now chiefly historical or metaphorical **2** a natural talent, gift, or endowment **3** [Archaic] a widow's dower **4** [Archaic] a gift by a man to his bride

dowse[1] (dous) ***vt.*** **dowsed, dows′ing** *alt. sp. of* DOUSE[1]

dowse[2] (douz) ***vi.*** **dowsed, dows′ing** ⟦< ?⟧ to search for a source of water or minerals by walking about while holding a divining rod (**dowsing rod**) —**dows′er** ***n.***

dox·ol·o·gy (däks äl′ə jē) ***n.***, *pl.* **-gies** ⟦ML(Ec) *doxologia* < Gr(Ec), a praising < *doxologos*, giving praise < *doxa*, praise, opinion (< *dokein*, to seem: see DECENT) + *logos*, word, thought (see LOGIC)⟧ a hymn of praise to God; specif., *a)* the **greater doxology**, which (in Latin) begins *Gloria in excelsis Deo* (glory to God in the highest) *b)* the **lesser doxology**, which (in Latin) begins *Gloria Patri* (glory to the Father) *c)* a hymn beginning "Praise God from whom all blessings flow"

dox·y (däk′sē) ***n.***, *pl.* **dox′ies** ⟦< ? obs. *docke*, rump, or archaic Du *docke*, doll⟧ [Old Slang] a woman of low morals; specif., a prostitute

dox·y·cy·cline (däk′sē sī′klēn′, -klin) ***n.*** ⟦D(E)OXY- + (TETRA)CYCLINE⟧ a synthetic form of tetracycline, $C_{22}H_{25}ClN_2O_8$, used as a broad-spectrum antibiotic: in full **doxycycline hydrochloride**

doy·en (doi′ən, -en′; dwä yen′) ***n.*** ⟦Fr: see DEAN⟧ the senior member of a group, esp. one regarded as an authority because of superior knowledge and long experience

doy·enne (doi en′, dwä yen′) ***n.*** a doyen who is a woman

Doyle (doil), Sir **Arthur Co·nan** (kō′nən) 1859-1930; Eng. writer of popular fiction: known esp. for his SHERLOCK HOLMES stories

doy·ley (doi′lē) ***n.*** *alt. sp. of* DOILY: also sp. **doy′ly**, *pl.* **-lies**

D'Oyly Carte, Richard *see* CARTE, Richard D'Oyly

doz *abbrev.* dozen(s)

doze[1] (dōz) ***vi.*** **dozed, doz′ing** ⟦prob. < Scand, as in Ice (& Swed dial.) *dusa*: for IE base, see DIZZY⟧ to sleep lightly or fitfully; nap; be half asleep —***vt.*** to spend (time) in dozing: usually with *away* —***n.*** a light sleep; nap —**doze off** to fall into a light sleep —**doz′er** ***n.***

doze[2] (dōz) ***vt.*** **dozed, doz′ing** [Informal] *short for* BULLDOZE (sense 2) —**doz′er** ***n.***

doz·en (duz′ən) ***n.***, *pl.* **-ens** or, esp. after a number, **-en** ⟦ME *dozeine* < OFr *dozaine* < *douze*, twelve < L *duodecim*, twelve < *duo*, TWO + *decem*, TEN⟧ **1** a set of twelve: see also BAKER'S DOZEN **2** [*often pl.*] a large number —☆**the dozens** [Slang] a form of verbal play in which the participants exchange witty, ribald taunts and insults, often specif. about each other's mother: often in the phrase **play the dozens**: used first, and chiefly, by African-Americans —**doz′enth** ***adj.***

doz·y (dō′zē) ***adj.*** **doz′i·er, doz′i·est** ⟦see DOZE[1]⟧ sleepy; drowsy —**doz′i·ly** ***adv.*** —**doz′i·ness** ***n.***

DP *abbrev.* **1** data processing: also **dp** **2** dew point **3** DISPLACED PERSON **4** *Baseball* double play **5** *Film* Director of Photography

DPH or **D.P.H.** *abbrev.* [Brit.] Doctor of Public Health

DPhil, DPh, D.Phil., *or* **D.Ph.** *abbrev.* Doctor of Philosophy

dpi *abbrev. Comput.* dots per inch (a measure of screen or printer resolution)

DPM or **D.P.M.** *abbrev.* Doctor of Podiatric Medicine

dpt *abbrev.* **1** department **2** deponent

DPT *abbrev.* diphtheria, pertussis, and tetanus (vaccine or vaccination)

dr *abbrev.* **1** debit **2** debtor **3** drachma(s) **4** dram(s)

Dr or **Dr.** *abbrev.* **1** Doctor **2** Drive

DR *abbrev.* **1** dead reckoning: also **D/R** **2** Dominican Republic

drab[1] (drab) ***n.*** ⟦< OFr *drap*, cloth < VL *drappus* < IE **drop-* < base **der-*, to skin⟧ **1** a kind of cloth, esp. a yellowish-brown wool **2** a dull yellowish-brown color —***adj.*** **drab′ber, drab′best** **1** of a dull yellowish-brown color **2** not bright or lively; dull, dreary, or monotonous —**drab′ly** ***adv.*** —**drab′ness** ***n.***

drab[2] (drab) ***n.*** ⟦< Celt, as in Ir *drabog*, Gael *drabag*, slattern⟧ [Obs.] **1** a slovenly woman; slattern **2** a prostitute —***vi.*** **drabbed, drab′bing** ⟦< the *n.*⟧ [Obs.] to fornicate with prostitutes

drab·bet (drab′it) ***n.*** ⟦< DRAB[1]⟧ [Brit.] a coarse, unbleached linen

drab·ble (drab′əl) ***vt.*** **-bled, -bling** ⟦ME *drabelen*, akin to (or < ?) LowG *drabbeln*, to walk in mud or water⟧ to make wet and dirty by dragging in mud and water; draggle —***vi.*** to become drabbled

dra·cae·na (drə sē′nə) ***n.*** ⟦ModL < LL, she-dragon < Gr *drakaina*, fem. of *drakōn*, DRAGON⟧ any of a genus (*Dracaena*) of tropical shrubs and trees of the agave family

drachm (dram) ***n.*** ⟦ME *dragme* < OFr < L *drachma* < Gr⟧ **1** DRACHMA **2** DRAM

drach·ma (drak′mə) ***n.***, *pl.* **-mas, -mae** (-mē), or **-mai** (-mī′) ⟦L < Gr *drachmē*, lit., a handful < *drassesthai*, to grasp, take by handfuls < IE base **dergh-*, to grip > TARGE⟧ **1** an ancient Greek silver coin **2** an ancient Greek unit of weight approximately equal to the weight of this coin **3** any of several modern weights or measures: see DRAM **4** the former basic monetary unit of modern Greece

Draco[1] (drā′kō) ***n.*** ⟦L: see DRAGON⟧ a large N constellation containing the north pole of the ecliptic; the Dragon

Dra·co[2] (drā′kō) 7th cent. B.C.; Athenian statesman & lawgiver: also called **Dra′con′** (-kän′)

Dra·co·ni·an (drə kō′nē ən, drā-) ***adj.*** **1** of Draco or the harsh code of laws attributed to him **2** [*often* **d-**] extremely severe or cruel

dra·con·ic (drə kän′ik, drā-) ***adj.*** ⟦< L *draco*: see DRAGON⟧ **1** of or like a dragon **2** [*usually* **D-**] draconian

Drac·u·la (drak′yə lə) ***n.*** the title character in a novel (1897) by Bram Stoker: a Transylvanian count and vampire

draff (draf) ***n.*** ⟦ME *draf* < ON, akin to Ger dial. *treber* (pl.), dregs < IE **dhrābh-* < base **dher-*, dirty, somber > DARK⟧ refuse or dregs, esp. of malt after brewing

draft (draft, dräft) ***n.*** ⟦ME *draught*, a drawing, pulling, stroke < base of OE *dragan*, DRAW⟧ **1** *a)* a drawing or pulling, as of a vehicle or load *b)* the thing, quantity, or load pulled **2** *a)* a drawing in of a fish net *b)* the amount of fish caught in one draw **3** *a)* a taking of liquid into the mouth; drinking *b)* the amount taken at one drink **4** *a)* a portion of liquid for drinking; specif., a dose of medicine *b)* [Informal] a portion of beer, ale, etc. drawn from a keg **5** *a)* a drawing into the lungs, as of air or tobacco smoke *b)* the amount of air, smoke, etc., drawn in **6** a rough or preliminary sketch of a piece of writing **7** a plan or drawing of a work to be done **8** a current of air, as in a room, heating system, etc. **9** a device for regulating the current of air in a heating system **10** a written order issued by one person, bank, firm, etc., directing the payment of money to another; check **11** a demand or drain made on something **12** *a)* the choosing or taking of an individual or individuals from a group for some special purpose, esp. for compulsory military service *b)* the condition of being so taken ☆*c)* a group of these so taken ☆**13** the demand made by a political party for a person to accept, sometimes reluctantly, a candidacy **14** *a)* the area of reduced air resistance behind a moving vehicle *b)* the act or instance of closely following a race car, truck, etc. to avoid wind resistance and conserve fuel **15** *Commerce* a deduction allowed for waste or loss in weight **16** *Hydraulics* the size of an opening for the flow of water **17** *Masonry* a narrow strip along the edge or across the face of a stone, serving as a guide in leveling the surface **18** *Mech.* the taper given to a pattern or die so that the work can be removed easily **19** *Naut.* the depth of water that a vessel draws, or needs in order to float, esp. when loaded ☆**20** *Sports* a system by which a league, as of professional teams, allots to each team the right to contract specified individuals in a group of players, esp. new players, usually by giving each team a turn to select one player until each roster is full —***vt.*** **1** to choose or take for some special purpose, as compulsory military service, by drawing from a group ☆**2** to persuade or compel (a person) to become a candidate for public office **3** to make a preliminary sketch of or working plans for **4** *Sports* to select (a player) during or in a DRAFT (*n.* 20) —***vi.*** ☆to drive very closely behind another vehicle while racing, so as to take advantage of the reduced air resistance behind it —***adj.*** **1** used for pulling loads [*draft* animals] **2** drawn from a keg on order [*draft* beer] **3** in a preliminary or rough form [*a draft* resolution] —**on draft** ready to be drawn directly from the keg —**draft′a·ble** ***adj.*** —**draft′er** ***n.***

☆**draft board** an official board of civilians designated to select qualified persons for compulsory service in the U.S. armed forces

draft dodger ☆a person who avoids or tries to avoid being drafted into the armed forces

☆**draft·ee** (draf tē′) ***n.*** a person drafted, esp. one drafted for service in the armed forces

drafts·man (drafts′mən) ***n.***, *pl.* **-men** (-mən) **1** a person who draws plans of structures or machinery **2** a person who draws up legal documents, speeches, etc. **3** an artist skillful in drawing —**drafts′man·ship′** ***n.***

drafts·per·son (-pur′sən) ***n.*** DRAFTSMAN (sense 1): used to avoid the masculine implication of *draftsman*

draft·y (draf′tē) ***adj.*** **draft′i·er, draft′i·est** letting in, having, or exposed to a draft or drafts of air, esp. an unwanted draft —**draft′i·ly** ***adv.*** —**draft′i·ness** ***n.***

drag (drag) ***vt.*** **dragged, drag′ging** ⟦ME *draggen* < ON *draga* (or OE *dragan*): see DRAW⟧ **1** to pull or draw with force or effort, esp. along the ground; haul **2** *a)* to move (oneself) with effort *b)* to force into some situation, action, etc. **3** to pull a grapnel, net, etc. over the bottom of (a river, lake, etc.) in searching for something; dredge **4** to draw a harrow over (land) **5** to draw (something) out over a period of time; protract tediously or painfully **6** to bring (a subject) into conversation, a piece of writing, etc. unnecessarily or as if by force ☆**7** *Baseball* to hit (a ball) in executing a DRAG BUNT **8** *Comput.* on a GUI screen, *a)* to move (an icon), esp. by means of a mouse, in such a way that its course can be followed *b)* to relocate or process (a file, etc.) by so moving its icon —***vi.*** **1** to be dragged; be pulled along the ground or other surface; trail **2** to lag behind **3** to be prolonged tediously; move or pass too slowly **4** to search a body of water with a grapnel, net, etc. **5** [Slang] to draw deeply (*on* a cigarette, pipe, etc.) **6** [Slang] to participate in or as if in a drag race —***n.*** **1** something dragged or pulled along the ground; specif., *a)* a harrow used for breaking ground *b)* a heavy sledge, or sled *c)* a type of private stagecoach of the 19th cent., with seats inside and on top, drawn by four horses **2** a device used to catch and haul up something under water; grapnel, dragnet, etc. **3** a thing that checks motion, as a brake on the wheel of a carriage **4** anything that hinders or obstructs [*a drag* on his resources] **5** the amount by which anything drags **6** the act of dragging; slow, cumbersome movement ☆**7** [Slang] influence that gains special or undeserved favors; pull ☆**8** [Slang] *a)* a deep puff of a cigarette, pipe, etc. *b)* a swallow of liquid ☆**9** [Slang] a dance **10** [Slang] a street; road [the main *drag*] ☆**11** [Slang] DRAG RACE ☆**12** [Slang] a dull or boring person, situation, etc. **13**

[Slang] *a)* clothing of the opposite sex, esp. as worn by a male homosexual *b)* clothing, esp. clothing typical of a certain country, period, occupation, etc. **14** *Aeron., Engineering* a resisting force exerted on an aircraft, motor vehicle, etc. parallel to its airstream and opposite in direction to its motion **15** *Hunting a)* a trail of scent left by an animal *b)* something dragged over the ground to leave a trail of scent *c)* a hunt over such a trail (in full **drag hunt**) —**SYN.** PULL —**drag on (or out)** to prolong or be prolonged tediously —☆**drag one's feet (or heels)** [Informal] to act with deliberate slowness or obvious reluctance; be uncooperative

drag-and-drop (drag′ən dräp′) *adj. Comput.* of or done with a GUI technique in which a file, portion of text, etc. is relocated or processed by dragging its icon and depositing it into another window, onto another icon, etc.: see DRAG (*vt.* 8)

drag bunt ⟦in ref. to the relatively low position of the bat⟧ *Baseball* a bunt executed by the batter while already moving toward first base, made typically for a base hit rather than a sacrifice

dra·gée (dra zhā′) *n.* ⟦Fr: see DREDGE²⟧ **1** a sugar-coated candy, nut, or pill **2** a small, silver-colored ball used as a decoration, as on a wedding cake

drag·ger (drag′ər) *n.* **1** one that drags ☆**2** a fishing vessel that employs a dragnet

drag·gle (drag′əl) *vt.* **-gled, -gling** ⟦freq. of DRAG⟧ to make wet and dirty by dragging in mud or water —*vi.* **1** to be or become draggled; trail on the ground **2** to lag behind; straggle

drag·gy (drag′ē) *adj.* **-gi·er, -gi·est** that drags; slow-moving, lethargic, dull, boring, etc.

drag·line (drag′līn′) *n.* **1** DRAGROPE **2** a machine for excavating

drag link a link connecting the cranks of two shafts, esp. in steering linkage

drag·net (drag′net′) *n.* **1** a net dragged along the bottom of a river, lake, etc. for catching fish **2** a net for catching small game ☆**3** an organized system or network for gathering in or catching criminals or others wanted by the authorities

drag·o·man (drag′ə mən) *n., pl.* **-mans** or **-men** (-mən) ⟦ME *drogeman* < OFr < It *dragomanno* < MGr *dragomanos* < Ar *tarjumān*, interpreter⟧ in the Near East, an interpreter or professional guide

drag·on (drag′ən) *n.* ⟦ME *dragoun* < OFr *dragon* < L *draco* < Gr *drakōn*, dragon, serpent, lit., the seeing one < *derkesthai*, to see < IE base **derk-*, to see > OIr *derc*, eye⟧ **1** a mythical monster, usually represented as a large reptile with wings and claws, breathing out fire and smoke **2** a fierce person; esp., a fiercely watchful female guardian or chaperone **3** [Historical] *a)* a short musket carried hooked to a soldier's belt *b)* a soldier armed with such a musket; dragoon **4** [Obs.] a large serpent or snake **5** [Obs.] *Bible* a word used to translate several Hebrew words now understood to mean *serpent, jackal, Old Serpent* (Satan), etc. **6** *Zool.* any of a genus (*Draco*) of small tree lizards of Southeast Asia, with winglike membranes used in gliding from tree to tree —**the Dragon** the constellation Draco

drag·on·et (drag′ə nit, drag′ə net′) *n.* ⟦ME < OFr, dim. of prec.⟧ **1** a small dragon **2** any of a percoid family (Callionymidae) of small, brightly colored, scaleless, tropical reef fishes

drag·on·fly (drag′ən flī′) *n., pl.* **-flies′** any of an order (Odonata) or suborder (Anisoptera) of large insects, harmless to people, having narrow, transparent, net-veined wings and feeding mostly on flies, mosquitoes, etc. while in flight: see also DAMSELFLY

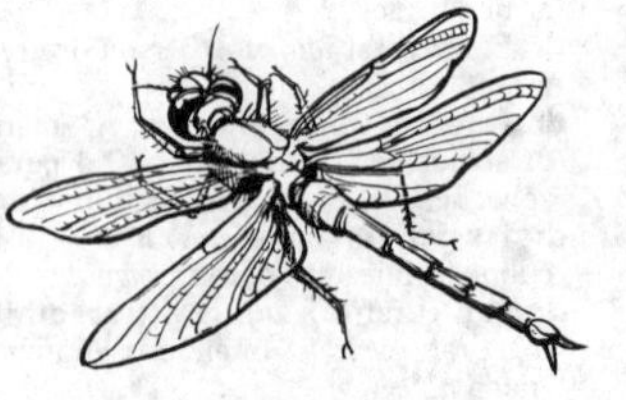

dragonfly

drag·on·head (-hed′) *n.* any of a genus (*Dracocephalum*) of plants of the mint family, with dense spikes of white or bluish flowers: also **drag′on's-head′**

dragon's blood any of several red, resinous substances obtained from various tropical plants and trees, esp. a Malaysian palm tree (*Daemonorops draco*), and used for coloring varnishes and in photoengraving

dragon tree DRACAENA

dra·goon (drə go͞on′) *n.* ⟦Fr *dragon* (see DRAGON): ? so called from their fire-breathing weapons⟧ **1** [Historical] *a)* a mounted soldier armed with a short musket (called a *dragon*), capable of fighting on horseback or on foot *b)* a heavily armed cavalryman **2** a member of a Canadian armored cavalry regiment —*vt.* **1** [Historical] to use dragoons to harass or persecute (someone) **2** to force (someone) *into* doing something; coerce

drag queen [Informal] a man, frequently a homosexual, who dresses, often flamboyantly, in women's clothing

☆**drag race** a race between vehicles to test their acceleration from a complete stop, esp. between specially designed cars on a short, straight course (**drag strip**) —**drag′-race′** *vi.* **-raced′, -rac′ing**

drag·rope (drag′rōp′) *n.* **1** a rope for dragging something, as a cannon **2** a rope hung from a balloon or airship for use as a variable ballast or mooring line

☆**drag·ster** (drag′stər) *n.* **1** a vehicle used in a drag race **2** a person who drives such a vehicle

drain (drān) *vt.* ⟦ME *dreinen* < OE *dreahnian*, to strain off, lit., to dry out < base of *dryge*, DRY⟧ **1** to draw off (liquid) gradually **2** to draw water or any liquid from gradually so as to dry or empty [*to drain swamps*] **3** to receive the waters of [*the St. Lawrence drains the Great Lakes*] **4** to drink all the liquid from (a cup, glass, etc.) **5** to exhaust (strength, emotions, or resources) gradually **6** [Obs.] to filter —*vi.* **1** to flow off gradually **2** to become dry by the drawing or flowing off of liquid **3** to disappear gradually [*his courage drained away*] **4** to discharge its waters [*central Europe drains into the Danube*] —*n.* **1** a channel or pipe for carrying off water, sewage, etc. **2** a draining or exhausting **3** that which gradually exhausts strength, resources, etc. **4** *Surgery* a tube or other device for drawing off discharge, fluid, etc. from a cavity, wound, etc. —**down the drain** lost in a wasteful, heedless way —**drain′er** *n.*

drain·age (drān′ij) *n.* **1** the act, process, or method of draining **2** a system of drains; arrangement of pipes, etc. for carrying off waste matter **3** that which is drained off **4** a region or area drained, as by a river

☆**drainage basin** the region or area drained by a river system

drain·board (drān′bôrd′) *n.* a wide board or surface, usually grooved and set at a slight angle, situated beside a sink, as in a kitchen, and used to allow wet dishes, vegetables, etc. to drain

drain·pipe (drān′pīp′) *n.* a pipe for carrying off water, sewage, etc.

drake¹ (drāk) *n.* ⟦ME < WGmc **drako*, male, as in OHG *anutrehho*, lit., duck-male⟧ a male duck

drake² (drāk) *n.* ⟦ME, dragon < OE *draca* < L *draco*, DRAGON⟧ **1** a small cannon of the 17th and 18th cent. **2** [Obs.] a dragon

Drake (drāk), Sir **Francis** 1540?-96; Eng. admiral & buccaneer: 1st Englishman to sail around the world

Dra·kens·berg (drä′kənz burg′) mountain range in E South Africa: highest peak, 11,425 ft (3,482 m): also **Drakensberg Mountains (or Range)**

Drake Passage ⟦after Sir Francis DRAKE⟧ strait between Cape Horn & the South Shetland Islands: *c.* 400 mi (644 km) wide

dram (dram) *n.* ⟦ME < OFr *dragme* < ML *dragma* < L *drachma*: see DRACHMA⟧ **1** *a)* a unit of weight, equal to 1⁄16 ounce avoirdupois or 27.3437 grains (1.772 grams) *b)* a unit of weight, equal to 1⁄8 ounce apothecaries' or 3 scruples (3.888 grams) *c)* FLUID DRAM: abbrev. *dr.* **2** a small drink of alcoholic liquor **3** a small amount of anything **4** the basic monetary unit of Armenia: see the table of monetary units in the Reference Supplement

DRAM (dē′ram′, dram) *n., pl.* **DRAMs** ⟦D(YNAMIC) + RAM¹⟧ a random-access memory chip that must be recharged continually in order for stored data to be retained

dra·ma (drä′mə, dram′ə) *n.* ⟦LL < Gr, an action, drama < *dran*, to do < IE base **drā-*, to work > Latvian *darīt*, to do⟧ **1** a literary composition that tells a story, usually of human conflict, by means of dialogue and action to be performed by actors; play; now often specif., any play that is not a comedy **2** the art or profession of writing, acting in, or producing plays **3** plays collectively [*Elizabethan drama*] **4** a series of events so interesting, vivid, melodramatic, etc. as to resemble those of a play **5** the quality of being dramatic

☆**Dram·a·mine** (dram′ə mēn′) *trademark for* DIMENHYDRINATE

drama queen [Slang] a woman or girl characterized by excessively temperamental responses

dra·mat·ic (drə mat′ik) *adj.* ⟦LL *dramaticus* < Gr *dramatikos*⟧ **1** of or connected with drama **2** *a)* having such characteristics of a drama as conflict or suspense *b)* filled with action, emotion, or exciting qualities; vivid, striking, etc. *c)* great, marked, strong, etc. [*a dramatic increase in prices*] Also [Archaic] **dra·mat′i·cal** —**dra·mat′i·cal·ly** *adv.*

dramatic monologue a poetic monologue which presents a character and a situation solely by means of that character's own words

dra·mat·ics (drə mat′iks) *pl.n.* ⟦< DRAMATIC: with ref. orig. to dramatic works, later to the art itself⟧ **1** [*usually with sing. v.*] the art of performing or producing plays **2** plays performed and produced by amateurs **3** dramatic effect; esp., exaggerated emotionalism

dram·a·tis per·so·nae (dram′ə tis pər sō′nē, drä′mə-; -nī) ⟦ModL < LL *dramatis*, gen. of *drama*, DRAMA + L *personae*, pl. of *persona*, character, PERSON⟧ the characters in a play, or a list of these

dram·a·tist (dram′ə tist, drä′mə-) *n.* ⟦see DRAMA⟧ a playwright

dram·a·ti·za·tion (dram′ə ti zā′shən, drä′mə-) *n.* **1** the act of dramatizing **2** a dramatized version, as of a novel

dram·a·tize (dram′ə tīz′, drä′mə-) *vt.* **-tized′, -tiz′ing** ⟦< LL *drama* (gen. *dramatis*), DRAMA + -IZE⟧ **1** to make into a drama; adapt (a story, events, etc.) for performance on the stage, in a film, etc. **2** to regard or present (actions, oneself, etc.) as though in a play; give dramatic quality to —*vi.* **1** to be capable of being dramatized **2** to dramatize oneself

dram·a·turge (dram′ə turj′, drä′mə-) *n.* ⟦Fr < Gr *dramatourgos*, writer of dramas, contriver < *drama*, DRAMA + *ergon*, WORK⟧ **1** a playwright, esp. one associated with a particular theater: also **dram′a·tur′gist** (-tur′jist) **2** a literary advisor for a theater, who works with playwrights, selects and edits scripts, etc.: also sp. **dram′a·turg′** (-turj′)

dram·a·tur·gy (dram′ə tur′jē, drä′mə-) *n.* ⟦Ger *dramaturgie* < Gr *dramatourgia* < *dramatourgos*, dramatist, orig., contriver < *drama* (see DRAMA) + *ergon*, WORK⟧ the art of writing plays or producing them —**dram′a·tur′gic** *adj.*, **dram′a·tur′gi·cal** —**dram′a·tur′gi·cal·ly** *adv.*

dra·me·dy (drä′mə dē, dram′ə dē) *n., pl.* **-dies** ⟦a blend of DRAMA & COMEDY⟧ a TV program combining elements of comedy and serious drama, esp. one in situation-comedy format

dram·shop (dram′shäp′) *n.* [Archaic] a bar; saloon —*adj.* designating or of a law holding businesses that serve alcoholic beverages to minors, or to persons already intoxicated, liable for damages

drank (draŋk) *vt., vi. pt. & often informal pp. of* DRINK

drape (drāp) *vt.* **draped, drap′ing** ⟦ME *drapen*, to weave into cloth, drape <

OFr *draper* < *drap*: see DRAB[1]⟧ 1 to cover, hang, or decorate with or as with cloth or clothes in loose folds 2 to arrange (a garment, cloth, etc.) artistically in folds or hangings —*vi.* to hang or fall in folds, as a garment, cloth, etc. —*n.* ⟦Fr *drap*, cloth⟧ 1 *a)* cloth hanging in loose folds, or hanging loosely from the thing that it covers [a surgical *drape*] *b)* a heavy curtain that hangs in loose folds; esp., either of a pair of such curtains 2 the manner in which cloth hangs or is cut to hang, as in a garment

drap·er (drā′pər) *n.* ⟦ME < OFr *drapier*: see prec.⟧ 1 [Obs.] a maker of cloth 2 [Brit.] a dealer in cloth and dry goods

Dra·per (drā′pər) 1 **Henry** 1837-82; U.S. astronomer 2 **John William** 1811-82; U.S. historian & scientist, born in England: father of Henry

drap·er·y (drā′pər ē) *n., pl.* **-er·ies** ⟦ME & OFr *draperie*: see DRAPE & -ERY⟧ 1 [Brit.] DRY GOODS 2 [Brit.] the business of a draper 3 *a)* hangings, covering, or clothing arranged in loose folds *b)* an artistic arrangement of such hangings, etc., esp. as represented in sculpture, painting, etc. ☆4 [*pl.*] curtains of heavy material

dras·tic (dras′tik) *adj.* ⟦Gr *drastikos*, active < *dran*, to do: see DRAMA⟧ acting with force; having a strong or violent effect; severe; harsh; extreme —**dras′ti·cal·ly** *adv.*

drat (drat) *interj.* ⟦aphetic < *'od rot* < *God rot*⟧ darn: a mild oath

drat·ted (drat′id) *adj.* ⟦see prec.⟧ [Informal] confounded; darned

draught (draft, dräft) *n., vt., adj. now chiefly Brit. sp. of* DRAFT

draughts (drafts, dräfts) *n.* [Brit.] the game of checkers

draughts·man (-mən) *n., pl.* **-men** (-mən) 1 *Brit. sp. of* DRAFTSMAN 2 [Brit.] any of the pieces used in playing draughts —**draughts′man·ship′** *n.*

draught·y (draf′tē, dräf′-) *adj.* **draught′i·er, draught′i·est** *Brit. sp. of* DRAFTY —**draught′i·ly** *adv.* —**draught′i·ness** *n.*

Dra·va (drä′vä) river in SC Europe, flowing from the Alps of Austria southeastward through Slovenia & Croatia into the Danube: *c.* 450 mi (724 km)

drave (drāv) *vt., vi. archaic pt. of* DRIVE

Dra·vid·i·an (drə vid′ē ən) *n.* ⟦after Sans *Drāviḍa*, Tamil language⟧ 1 *a)* any of a group of intermixed peoples chiefly in S India and N Sri Lanka *b)* a member of any of these peoples 2 the family of about 25 non-Indo-European languages spoken by these peoples, including Tamil, Malayalam, and Telugu —*adj.* of the Dravidians or their languages or cultures: also **Dra·vid′ic**

draw (drô) *vt.* **drew, drawn, draw′ing** ⟦ME *drawen* < OE *dragan*, akin to ON *draga*, to drag, Ger *tragen*, to bear, carry < IE base **dheragh-*, to pull, draw along > L *trahere*, to pull, draw⟧ **I.** *indicating traction* 1 to make move toward one or along with one by or as by exerting force; pull; haul; drag [a horse *draws* the cart] 2 *a)* to pull up (a sail, drawbridge, etc.) *b)* to pull down (a window shade, etc.) *c)* to pull in (a dragnet, etc.) *d)* to pull aside or together (a curtain, etc.) *e)* to pull across, as a violin bow over strings 3 to pull back the bowstring of (an archer's bow) 4 to need (a specified depth of water) to float in: said of a ship 5 *Billiards* to cause (the cue ball) to reverse direction after it hits an object ball, by imparting backspin to it 6 *Cricket* to deflect (the ball) to the side of the field on which the batsman stands, by a slight turn of the bat 7 *Golf* to deliberately cause (a ball) to hook slightly **II.** *indicating attraction* 1 *a)* to attract; charm; entice *b)* to attract (audiences of a specified size or kind) 2 to take (air, smoke, etc.) into the mouth or lungs; breathe in, inhale, etc. 3 to provoke (a person) into speaking, responding, taking action, etc.: usually in the passive 4 to bring forth; elicit [his challenge *drew* no reply] 5 to bring about as a result; bring on; provoke [to *draw* the enemy's fire] 6 *Med.* to cause a flow of (blood, pus, etc.) to some part **III.** *indicating extraction* 1 to pull out; take out; remove; extract, as a tooth, cork, weapon, etc. 2 *a)* to remove (a liquid, etc.) by sucking, draining, distilling, seeping, etc. *b)* to bring up, as water from a well *c)* to cause (liquid) to flow from an opening, tap, etc. [to *draw* a bath, to *draw* blood] 3 to take out the viscera of; disembowel 4 to get or receive from some source [to *draw* a good salary] 5 to withdraw (money) held in an account 6 to have accruing to it [savings that *draw* interest] 7 to write (a check or draft) 8 to reach (a conclusion or inference); deduce 9 to get or pick (a number, straw, prize, etc.) at random, as in a lottery 10 to bring (a contest or game) to a tie 11 *Card Games a)* to take or get (a card or cards) *b)* to cause (a card or cards) to be played out [*draw* your opponent's trump] **IV.** *indicating tension* 1 to pull out to its fullest extent; make tense; stretch; extend [to *draw* a rope tight] 2 to pull out of shape; distort 3 to stretch, flatten, or shape (metal) by die stamping, hammering, etc. 4 to make metal into (wire) by pulling it through holes **V.** *indicating delineation* (to "pull" across paper, etc.) 1 to make (lines, figures, pictures, etc.), as with a pencil, pen, brush, or stylus; diagram 2 to describe in words 3 to make (comparisons, etc.); formulate —*vi.* 1 to draw something (in various senses of the *vt.*) 2 to be drawn or have a drawing effect 3 to come; move; approach [to *draw* nearer] 4 to shrink or contract 5 to allow a draft of air, smoke, etc. to move through [the chimney *draws* well] 6 to suck (*on* a tobacco pipe, etc.) 7 to attract audiences 8 to become filled with wind: said of sails 9 to steep: said of tea 10 to make a demand or demands (*on* or *upon*) 11 *Hunting a)* to track game by following its scent *b)* to move slowly toward the game after pointing (said of hounds) —*n.* 1 a drawing or being drawn (in various senses) 2 the result of drawing 3 a thing drawn 4 the cards dealt as replacements in draw poker 5 ⟦from, formerly, the withdrawal of stakes in such a case⟧ a tie; stalemate [the game ended in a *draw*] 6 a thing that attracts interest, audiences, etc. ☆7 the movable part of a drawbridge 8 a shallow gully or ravine, as one that water drains into or through ☆9 *Football* a play in which the quarterback moves back to pass and then quickly gives the ball to a running back or quickly reverses direction and runs with the ball —*SYN.* PULL —☆**beat to the draw** to be quicker than (another) in doing something, as in drawing one's weapon —**draw and quarter** [Historical] 1 to execute by tying each arm and leg to a different horse, and then driving the horses in four different directions 2 to eviscerate and cut into pieces after hanging —**draw away** to move away or ahead —**draw back** to withdraw; retreat —**draw down** 1 to reduce in number [to *draw down* troops] 2 to deplete [he *drew down* the available funds] —**draw on** (or **nigh**) to approach —**draw oneself up** 1 to assume a straighter posture; stand or sit straight 2 to bridle —**draw out** 1 to extend; lengthen; prolong 2 to take out; extract 3 to get (a person) to answer or talk —**draw up** 1 to arrange in order; marshal 2 to compose (a document) in proper form; draft 3 to bring or come to a stop 4 to raise one's shoulders and pull one's limbs close to the body; huddle

draw·back (drô′bak′) *n.* ☆1 money paid back from a charge previously made; refund, esp. of import duties when the taxed commodities are later exported 2 anything that prevents or lessens full satisfaction; shortcoming

☆**draw·bar** (-bär′) *n.* 1 COUPLER (sense *a*) 2 a bar at the rear of a tractor for attaching a plow, harrow, etc.

draw·bore (-bôr′) *n.* a hole bored through a mortise-and-tenon joint so that a pin driven into it will force the tenon more securely into the mortise

draw·bridge (-brij′) *n.* a bridge that can be raised or drawn aside to permit passage of watercraft or prevent access, as to a fort

draw·down (-doun′) *n.* 1 a lowering of the water level of a well, reservoir, etc., as in supplying industry with water 2 a reduction or depletion

draw·ee (drô′ē′) *n.* the party that the drawer directs, by means of a bill of exchange, order, draft, etc., to pay money over to a third party (called *payee*)

draw·er (drô′ər; *for 5*, drôr) *n.* 1 a person or thing that draws 2 [Archaic] TAPSTER 3 a person who draws an order for the payment of money 4 a draftsman 5 a sliding storage box in a table, bureau, chest, etc., that can be drawn out and then pushed back into place

drawers (drôrz) *pl.n.* ⟦< DRAW: because one draws them on⟧ an undergarment, long or short, for the lower part of the body, with a separate opening for each leg; underpants

draw·ing (drô′iŋ) *n.* 1 the act of one that draws; specif., the art of representing something by lines made on a surface with a pencil, pen, etc. 2 a picture, design, sketch, etc. thus made 3 a lottery

drawing account an account of or for money paid for expenses, advances on salary, etc., as to a salesman

drawing board a flat, smooth board on which paper, canvas, etc. is fastened for making drawings —**back to the drawing board** [Informal] back to the beginning or to the planning stage for a fresh approach or to find out what went wrong —**on the drawing board** in the planning stage

☆**drawing card** an entertainer, speaker, show, etc. that normally can be expected to draw a large audience

drawing room ⟦< *withdrawing room*: orig., name for room to which guests withdrew after dinner⟧ 1 a room where guests are received or entertained; living room or parlor 2 a formal reception ☆3 a private compartment on a railroad sleeping car, with accommodations for a few people

draw·knife (drô′nīf′) *n., pl.* **-knives′** (-nīvz′) a knife with a handle at each end of the blade, which is drawn toward the user in shaving a surface: also **drawing knife**

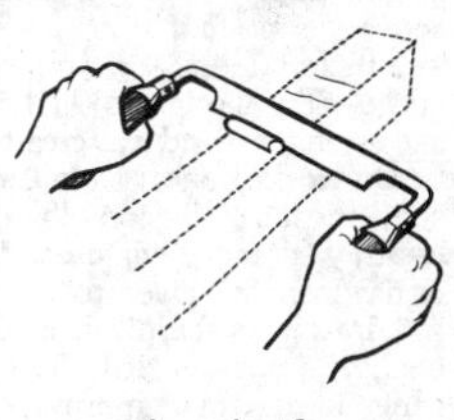
drawknife

drawl (drôl) *vt., vi.* ⟦prob. freq. of DRAW⟧ to speak slowly, prolonging the vowels —*n.* a slow manner of speech characterized by prolongation of vowels —**drawl′er** *n.* —**drawl′ing·ly** *adv.*

drawn (drôn) *vt., vi. pp. of* DRAW —*adj.* 1 pulled out of the sheath 2 with neither side winning or losing; even; tied 3 disemboweled; eviscerated 4 tense; haggard

☆**drawn butter** melted clarified butter, often seasoned, used as a sauce

drawn·work (drôn′wurk′) *n.* ornamental work done on textiles by pulling out threads to produce a lacelike design

draw·plate (drô′plāt′) *n.* a metal plate with holes through which wire is drawn to get the desired thickness

☆**draw poker** a form of poker in which each player is dealt five cards face down, and may be dealt replacements for any unwanted cards (usually not more than three): cf. STUD POKER

draw·shave (-shāv′) *n.* DRAWKNIFE

draw·string (-striŋ′) *n.* a string drawn through a hem, as in the waist of a garment or mouth of a bag, to tighten or close it by taking up the fullness

draw·tube (-to͞ob′, -tyo͞ob′) *n.* a tube sliding within another tube, as in the eyepiece of a microscope

dray (drā) *n.* ⟦ME *dreye*, orig., a drag, sled < OE *dræge*, lit., something drawn, dragnet < *dragan*, to DRAW⟧ a low, sturdily built cart with detachable sides, for carrying heavy loads —*vt.* to carry or haul on a dray —*vi.* to drive a dray

dray·age (drā′ij) *n.* 1 the hauling of a load by dray ☆2 the charge made for this

dray·man (-mən) *n., pl.* **-men** (-mən) a person whose work is hauling loads by dray

Dray·ton (drāt′'n), **Michael** 1563-1631; Eng. poet
dread (dred) *vt.* ⟦ME *dreden* < Late OE (WS) *drædan*, aphetic for *ondrædan* (akin to OS *andradan*, OHG *intraten*) < *ond-*, in, on, against + base < ?⟧ **1** to anticipate with anxiety, alarm, or apprehension; fear intensely **2** to face (something disagreeable) with reluctance **3** [Archaic] to regard with awe —*vi.* [Archaic] to be very fearful —*n.* **1** intense fear, esp. of something which may happen **2** fear mixed with awe or reverence **3** reluctance and uneasiness **4** something dreaded —*adj.* **1** dreaded or dreadful **2** inspiring awe or reverence; awesome —*SYN.* AWE, FEAR
dread·ful (dred′fəl) *adj.* ⟦ME *dredeful*⟧ **1** inspiring dread; terrible or awesome **2** very bad, offensive, disagreeable, etc. —**dread′ful·ness** *n.*
dread·ful·ly (-fəl ē) *adv.* **1** in a dreadful manner **2** very; extremely [*dreadfully* tired]
dread·locks (dred′läks′) *pl.n.* long, thin braids or uncombed, twisted locks of a style worn originally by Rastafarians
dread·nought or **dread·naught** (-nôt′) *n.* **1** *a)* a coat made of a thick woolen cloth *b)* the cloth **2** ⟦after *Dreadnought*, the first of such a class of British battleships, built in 1906⟧ any large, heavily armored battleship with many powerful guns
dreads (dredz) *pl.n.* [Informal] *short for* DREADLOCKS
dream (drēm) *n.* ⟦ME *dream, dreme*: form < OE *dream*, joy, music < IE base **dher-*, to buzz, hum (> DORBEETLE); meaning < ON *draumr*, akin to Ger *traum*, Du *droom* < IE base **dhreugh-*, to deceive⟧ **1** a sequence of sensations, images, thoughts, etc. passing through a sleeping person's mind **2** a fanciful vision of the conscious mind; daydream; fantasy; reverie **3** the state, as of abstraction or reverie, in which such a daydream occurs **4** a fond hope or aspiration **5** anything so lovely, charming, transitory, etc. as to seem dreamlike —*vi.* **dreamed** or **dreamt** (dremt), **dream′ing** **1** to have a dream or dreams **2** to have daydreams **3** to think (*of*) as at all possible, desirable, etc. [I wouldn't *dream* of going] —*vt.* **1** *a)* to have (a dream or dreams) *b)* to have a dream of **2** to spend in dreaming: with *away* or *out* **3** to imagine as possible; fancy; suppose —*adj.* that realizes one's fondest hopes; ideal [her *dream* house] —**dream up** [Informal] to conceive of or devise, as by giving free rein to the imagination —**dream′ful** *adj.* —**dream′like′** *adj.*
☆**dream·boat** (drēm′bōt′) *n.* [Slang] a person regarded as being very attractive
dream·book (-bʊk′) *n.* a reference book or booklet designed to interpret the symbols in one's dreams and, often, specif., to assign lucky numbers to such symbols
dream catcher ⟦so called from the belief that when hung over a bed, it *catches* bad *dreams*, but allows good dreams to pass through to the sleeper⟧ a traditional North American Indian artifact consisting of a hoop strung with a loose net or web and decorated with beads, feathers, etc.
dream·er (drēm′ər) *n.* **1** a person who dreams **2** a person given to daydreaming **3** a person who has ideas or schemes considered impractical; visionary
dream·land (-land′) *n.* **1** any lovely but imaginary place, as one seen in a dream **2** the state of being asleep: a humorous or whimsical usage
dream·less (-lis) *adj.* followed by no memory of having dreamed [a *dreamless* sleep]
dream·scape (-skāp′) *n.* an imaginary, surrealistic, or dreamlike scene or setting, as in a film
dream·time (-tīm′) *n.* ⟦transl. of *alcheringa*, name for this age in a language of the Aborigines⟧ in the mythology of the Australian Aborigines, the age when the world was created: often **the Dreamtime**
dream world **1** DREAMLAND **2** the realm of fantasy; the world as seen by someone full of illusions about life
dream·y (drēm′ē) *adj.* **dream′i·er**, **dream′i·est** **1** filled with dreams **2** fond of daydreaming; given to reverie; visionary; impractical **3** like something in a dream; not sharply defined; misty, vague, etc. **4** having a soft, soothing quality [*dreamy* music] ☆**5** [Slang] excellent, wonderful, delightful, etc.: a generalized term of approval —**dream′i·ly** *adv.* —**dream′i·ness** *n.*
drear (drir) *adj.* [Old Poet.] dreary; melancholy
drear·y (drir′ē) *adj.* **drear′i·er**, **drear′i·est** ⟦ME *dreri* < OE *dreorig*, sad, orig., bloody, gory < *dreor*, blood < base of *dreosan*, to drip < IE base **dhreu-*, break off > DRIP, DROWSE⟧ gloomy; cheerless; depressing; dismal; dull —**drear′i·ly** *adv.* —**drear′i·ness** *n.*
dreck (drek) *n.* ⟦Yiddish *drek* < Ger *dreck*, dirt < IE **(s)treg-* < base **(s)ter-*, unclean matter > L *stercus*, excrement⟧ [Slang] trash; rubbish
dredge[1] (drej) *n.* ⟦prob. < MDu *dregge*, akin to DRAG⟧ **1** a device consisting of a net attached to a frame, dragged along the bottom of a river, bay, etc. to gather shellfish, marine plant specimens, etc. **2** an apparatus for scooping or sucking up mud, sand, rocks, etc., as in deepening or clearing channels, harbors, etc. **3** a barge or other boat equipped with a dredge —*vt.* **dredged**, **dredg′ing** **1** to search for or gather (*up*) with or as with a dredge **2** to enlarge or clean out (a river channel, harbor, etc.) with a dredge —*vi.* **1** to use a dredge **2** to search as with a dredge —**dredg′er** *n.*
dredge[2] (drej) *vt.* **dredged**, **dredg′ing** ⟦< ME *dragge*, sweetmeat < OFr *dragie* < ML *dragium*, earlier *dragetum* < L *tragemata* < Gr *tragēmata*, pl. of *tragēma*, dried fruit, dessert < *trōgein*, to gnaw < IE **trog-* < base **ter-*, to rub: see THROW⟧ **1** to coat (food) with flour or the like, as by sprinkling **2** to sprinkle (flour, etc.) —**dredg′er** *n.*
dree (drē) [Now Chiefly Scot.] *vt.* **dreed**, **dree′ing** ⟦ME *drien* < OE *dreogan* < IE **dhereugh* < base **dher-*, to hold firm: see FIRM[1]⟧ to endure; suffer —*adj.* dreary; tedious
dreg·gy (dreg′ē) *adj.* **-gi·er**, **-gi·est** full of, or having the nature of, dregs; foul —**dreg′gi·ness** *n.*
D region the lowest atmospheric zone within the ionosphere, at an altitude of *c.* 55 to 90 km (*c.* 34 to 56 mi), containing the D layer
dregs (dregz) *pl.n., sing.* **dreg** ⟦ME *dregges*, pl. of *dregge* < ON *dregg*, barm, lees < IE **dherĕgh*, residue: for base see DARK⟧ **1** the particles of solid matter that settle at the bottom in a liquid; lees **2** the most worthless part [the *dregs* of society] **3** [*sing.*] a small amount remaining; residue
drei·del (drā′dəl) *n.* ⟦Yiddish *dreydl* < MHG *dræjen*, to turn, akin to Ger *drehen*: see THROW⟧ **1** a small top with Hebrew letters on each of four sides, spun in a game played by children, esp. during the Jewish festival of Hanukkah **2** the game using this top
Drei·ser (drī′sər, -zər), **Theodore (Herman Albert)** 1871-1945; U.S. novelist
drek (drek) *n.* [Slang] *alt. sp. of* DRECK
drench (drench) *vt.* ⟦ME *drenchen* < OE *drencan*, to make drink, drown, caus. of *drincan*, to drink < Gmc **drank-*, pret. stem of **drinkan*, DRINK + *-jan*, caus. suffix⟧ **1** to make (a horse, cow, etc.) swallow a medicinal liquid **2** to make wet all over; soak or saturate in liquid —*n.* **1** a large liquid dose, esp. for a sick animal **2** a drenching or soaking **3** a solution for soaking —*SYN.* SOAK
Dres·den[1] (drez′dən) *n.* a fine porcelain made near Dresden, Germany —*adj.* designating or of such porcelain
Dres·den[2] (drez′dən) city in E Germany, on the Elbe: capital of the state of Saxony
dress (dres) *vt.* ⟦ME *dressen*, to make straight, direct < OFr *drecier*, to set up, arrange < VL **directiare* < L *directus*: see DIRECT⟧ **1** to put clothes on; clothe **2** to provide with clothing **3** to decorate; trim; adorn **4** to arrange a display in [to *dress* a store window] **5** to arrange or do up (the hair) **6** to arrange (troops) in a straight line or lines **7** to apply medicines and bandages to (a wound, sore, etc.) **8** to treat as required in preparing for use, grooming, etc.; esp., *a)* to clean and eviscerate (a fowl, deer, etc.) *b)* to till, cultivate, or fertilize (fields or plants) *c)* to curry (a horse, leather, etc.) *d)* to smooth, finish, shape, etc. (stone, wood, etc.) —*vi.* **1** to put on clothes; wear clothes **2** to dress in formal clothes **3** to get into a straight line or proper alignment: said of troops —*n.* **1** clothes, clothing, or apparel, esp. as suitable for certain occasions [casual *dress*] or for a certain place or time [modern *dress*] **2** an outer garment for women, having a skirt and usually made in one piece: formerly and traditionally the usual garment for women **3** formal clothes **4** external covering or appearance —*adj.* **1** of or for dresses [*dress* material] **2** worn on formal occasions [a *dress* suit] **3** requiring formal clothes [a *dress* occasion] —**dress down** **1** to scold severely; reprimand **2** to wear casual clothes to an activity, job, etc. that ordinarily requires more formal dress —**dress ship** to raise the ensign at each masthead and the flagstaff and, often, string signal flags over the mastheads from bow to stern —**dress up** **1** to dress in formal clothes, or in clothes more elegant, showy, etc. than one usually wears **2** to improve the appearance of, as by decorating
dres·sage (dre säzh′) *n.* ⟦Fr, training < *dresser*, to arrange, train < OFr *drecier*: see prec.⟧ exhibition riding or horsemanship in which the horse is controlled in certain difficult steps and gaits by very slight movements of the rider
dress circle a section of seats in a theater or concert hall, usually a tier partly encircling and above the orchestra: formal dress was formerly customary there
dress code a standard of dress established for a given environment, as in the military, in a school or business, or in a cultural group
dress-down (dres′doun′) *adj.* of or relating to a policy allowing casual attire in an activity, job, etc. that ordinarily requires more formal dress
dress·er[1] (dres′ər) *n.* **1** a person who dresses another; esp., one who helps actors and actresses put on their costumes **2** a person who dresses something, as store windows, leather, wounds, etc. **3** a person who dresses elegantly or in a certain way [a fancy *dresser*]
dress·er[2] (dres′ər) *n.* ⟦ME *dressour* < OFr *dreceur* < *drecier*, arrange: see DRESS⟧ **1** [Archaic] SIDEBOARD **2** a cupboard for dishes and kitchen utensils ☆**3** a chest of drawers, typically with a mirror
dress·i·ly (dres′ə lē) *adv.* in a dressy manner
dress·i·ness (dres′ē nis) *n.* the quality of being dressy
dress·ing (dres′iŋ) *n.* **1** the act of one that dresses **2** that which is used to dress something, as manure applied to soil, or medicines and bandages applied to wounds **3** a substance used to stiffen fabric during manufacture **4** a sauce as for salads **5** a mixture as of bread and seasoning, used for stuffing roast fowl, etc.
dress·ing-down (dres′iŋ doun′) *n.* a sound scolding
dressing gown a loose robe for wear when one is not fully clothed, as before dressing or when lounging
dressing room a room for getting dressed in; specif., *a)* a room backstage where actors dress and put on makeup *b)* a room, as in a store or tailor shop, for trying on clothes
dressing table a low table with a mirror, for use while putting on cosmetics, grooming the hair, etc.
dress·mak·er (dres′māk′ər) *n.* a person who makes women's dresses and other clothes to order —☆*adj.* designating or of a woman's suit, coat, etc. not cut on severe, mannish lines: cf. TAILORED —**dress′mak′ing** *n.*
☆**dress parade** a military parade in dress uniform
dress rehearsal a final rehearsal, as of a play or ceremony, performed exactly as it is to take place

dress shield a pad worn at the armpit to protect a garment from perspiration

dress suit a man's formal suit for evening wear

dress uniform a military uniform worn on formal occasions

dress·y (dres′ē) ***adj.*** **dress′i·er, dress′i·est** [Informal] **1** showy or elaborate in dress or appearance **2** stylish, elegant, smart, etc.

drew (dro͞o) ***vt., vi.*** *pt. of* DRAW

Drey·fus (drā′fəs, drī′-), **Alfred** 1859-1935; Fr. army officer convicted of treason and imprisoned but later exonerated when proved to be the victim of anti-Semitism and conspiracy

DRG (dē′är′jē′) ***n.*** ⟦*d(iagnostic) r(elated) g(roup)*⟧ any of the diagnostic categories in a system of Medicare reimbursement to hospitals: rates are determined by the average cost of treatment, hospital stay, etc. for a specific problem or category

drib (drib) ***vi., vt.*** **dribbed, drib′bing** ⟦< DRIP⟧ [Obs.] to fall or let fall, in or as if in driblets —**dribs and drabs** ⟦< N Eng *drib*, driblet, droplet + *drab* for *drap*, dial. form of DROP⟧ small amounts

drib·ble (drib′əl) ***vi., vt.*** **-bled, -bling** ⟦freq. of prec.⟧ **1** to flow, or let flow, in drops or driblets; trickle **2** to come forth or let out a little at a time **3** to let (saliva, liquid, etc.) drip from the mouth; drool **4** to keep (a ball or puck) in motion or move (it) forward by a rapid succession of bounces (in basketball), short kicks (in soccer), or light taps with a stick (in hockey) —***n.*** **1** a small drop, or a flowing in small drops **2** a very small amount **3** the act of dribbling a ball or puck **4** a drizzling rain —**drib′bler** ***n.***

drib·let (drib′lit) ***n.*** ⟦dim. of DRIB⟧ a small amount; bit *[*to pay one's debts in *driblets]*

dried (drīd) ***vt., vi.*** *pt. & pp. of* DRY

driegh (drēkh) ***adj.*** [Scot.] *var. of* DREE

dri·er (drī′ər) ***n.*** **1** a substance added to paint, varnish, etc. to make it dry fast **2** *alt. sp. of* DRYER —***adj.*** *compar. of* DRY

dri·est (-ist) ***adj.*** *superl. of* DRY

drift (drift) ***n.*** ⟦ME (akin to ON & MDu *drift*, OHG *trift*) < OE *drifan*, DRIVE⟧ **1** a being driven or carried along, as by a current of air or water or by circumstances **2** the course on which something is directed or driven **3** the deviation of a ship, airplane, rocket, etc. from its path, caused by side currents or winds **4** *a)* the velocity of a current of water *b)* a slow ocean current **5** *a)* a gradual shifting in position *b)* a random course, variation, or deviation **6** a gradual movement or change in some direction or toward some end or purpose; trend; tendency **7** general meaning of what is said or done; intent; tenor **8** something driven, as *a)* rain, snow, or smoke driven before the wind *b)* floating matter driven by water currents *c)* a heap of snow, sand, etc. piled up by the wind *d)* floating matter washed ashore ☆**9** *Electronics* a deviation or variation of a quantity, as voltage, from its assigned value **10** *Geol.* sand, gravel, boulders, etc. moved and deposited by a glacier or by water arising from its melting ice **11** *Linguis.* a gradual change along a certain line of development in the various elements of a language **12** *Mech.* *a)* a tool used for ramming or driving down a heavy object *b)* a tool for enlarging or shaping holes **13** *Mining* *a)* a horizontal passageway driven into or along the path of a vein or rock layer *b)* a small tunnel connecting two larger shafts —***vi.*** **1** to be carried along by or as by a current **2** to be carried along by circumstances; go along aimlessly **3** to wander about from place to place, from job to job, etc. **4** to accumulate in heaps by force of wind or water **5** to become heaped with drifting snow, sand, etc. **6** to move easily or gradually away from a set position ☆**7** [West] to range far afield in a drove, as in seeking pasture or escaping a storm: said of cattle —***vt.*** **1** to cause to drift **2** to cover with drifts —***SYN.*** TENDENCY, WASH —**drift apart** to gradually lose interest in or affection for each other —**drift off** to fall asleep

drift·age (drif′tij) ***n.*** **1** the action of something that drifts **2** the deviation caused by drifting **3** that which has drifted or has washed ashore

drift anchor SEA ANCHOR

drift·er (drif′tər) ***n.*** a person, often one without close friends or family ties, who moves about aimlessly from place to place

drift net a very large net used by commercial fishermen, suspended from floats and designed to drift freely: also written **drift′net′** ***n.***

drift·wood (drift′wood′) ***n.*** wood that is drifting in the water or that has been washed ashore

drift·y (drif′tē) ***adj.*** **drift′i·er, drift′i·est** having drifts or a tendency to form drifts

drill[1] (dril) ***n.*** ⟦Du *dril* < *drillen*, to bore, ult. < IE base **ter-*, to rub (esp. with turning motion) > THROW⟧ **1** a tool or apparatus for boring holes in wood, metal, stone, teeth, etc. **2** the sound of drilling or boring ☆**3** any of various genera of snails, esp. a saltwater species (*Urosalpinx cinerea*), that bores through the shells of oysters and other shellfish and consumes their flesh **4** *a)* military or physical training, esp. of a group, as in marching, the manual of arms, or gymnastic exercises *b)* a single exercise in such training **5** *a)* the process of training or teaching by the continued repetition of an exercise *b)* a single exercise in such training or teaching **6** the method or style of drilling **7** [Informal] the accepted or usual way of doing something —***vt.*** ⟦Du *drillen*⟧ **1** to bore (a hole) in (something) with or as with a drill **2** to train in military or physical exercise; specif., to exercise (troops) in close-order drill **3** to teach or train by putting through repeated exercises **4** to instill (ideas, facts, etc.) *into* someone by repeated exercises ☆**5** [Informal] to hit sharply *[*she *drilled* the ball past the pitcher; I *drilled* him with the ball*]* ☆**6** [Slang] to penetrate with bullets —***vi.*** **1** to bore a hole or holes **2** to engage in, or be put through, military, physical, or mental exercises —***SYN.*** PRACTICE —**drill′er** ***n.***

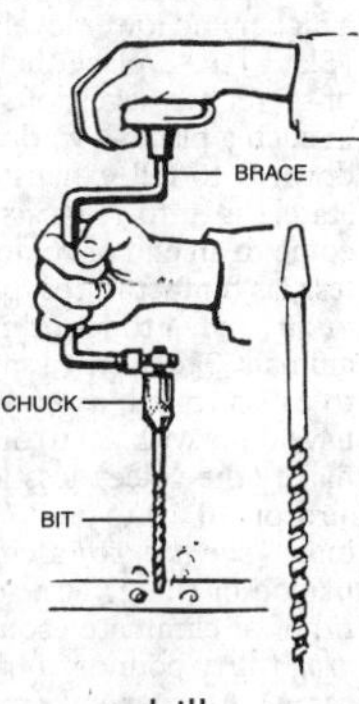

drill

drill[2] (dril) ***n.*** ⟦< ?⟧ **1** a furrow in which seeds are planted **2** a row of planted seeds **3** a machine for making holes or furrows, dropping seeds into them, and covering them —***vt.*** **1** to sow (seeds) in rows to improve growth and efficiency **2** to plant (a field) in drills: cf. BROADCAST (***vt.*** 1)

drill[3] (dril) ***n.*** ⟦< earlier *drilling* < Ger *drillich* < OHG *drilich*, made of three threads < L *trilix* (gen. *trilicis*) < *tri-*, TRI- + *licium*, thread⟧ a coarse linen or cotton cloth with a diagonal weave, used for work clothes, uniforms, etc.

drill[4] (dril) ***n.*** ⟦< ? native term⟧ a short-tailed, bright-cheeked monkey (*Mandrillus leucophaeus*) native to W Africa, resembling the mandrill but smaller

☆**drilling mud** a suspension of fine-grained mineral matter, usually in water, circulated in oil-well drilling to cool and lubricate the drill bit, plug up porous surfaces, etc.

drill·mas·ter (dril′mas′tər) ***n.*** **1** an instructor in military drill, esp. in close-order drill **2** any person who teaches by drilling and using strict discipline

drill press a machine tool for drilling holes in metal, etc.

drill·stock (dril′stäk′) ***n.*** that part of a drilling machine or tool which holds the shank of a drill or bit; chuck

dri·ly (drī′lē) ***adv.*** *alt. sp. of* DRYLY

D-ring (dē′riŋ′) ***n.*** any of various D-shaped fasteners, usually of metal and used as for attaching something to a garment, as a guide for laces or straps, or in pairs to form a closure as on a belt

drink (driŋk) ***vt.*** **drank, drunk** or now informal **drank, drink′ing** ⟦ME *drinken* < OE *drincan*, akin to OHG *trinkan*, Goth *drigkan* < ? IE base **dhreĝ-*, to draw > Sans *dhrájas-*, draft⟧ **1** to take (liquid) into the mouth and swallow it **2** to absorb (liquid or moisture) **3** to swallow the contents of **4** to propose or take part in (a toast) *[*to *drink* someone's health*]* **5** to bring into a specified condition by drinking *[*to *drink* oneself into a stupor*]* **6** to use (*up*) or spend by drinking alcoholic liquor —***vi.*** **1** to take liquid into the mouth and swallow it **2** to absorb anything as if in drinking **3** to drink alcoholic liquor, sometimes specif. as a matter of habit or to excess —***n.*** **1** any liquid for drinking; beverage: cf. FOOD (sense 2) **2** alcoholic liquor **3** habitual or excessive use of alcoholic liquor **4** a portion of liquid drunk or for drinking, specif. one containing alcohol *[*to stop somewhere for a *drink* after work*]* —**drink deep (of)** to take in a large amount (of) by or as by drinking —**drink in** to take in with the senses or the mind, esp. in an eager manner —**drink to** to drink in honor of; drink a toast to —☆**the drink** [Informal] any body of water, esp. the ocean

drink·a·ble (driŋk′ə bəl) ***adj.*** fit for drinking —***n.*** a liquid fit for drinking; beverage: *usually used in pl.*

drink·er (driŋk′ər) ***n.*** **1** a person who drinks **2** a person who drinks alcoholic liquor habitually or excessively

drinking fountain a device for providing a small jet or flow of drinking water, as in a public place

drinking song a song celebrating the pleasures of drinking alcoholic liquors; song for a drinking party

drip (drip) ***vi.*** **dripped, drip′ping** ⟦ME *dryppen* < OE *dryppan*, intens. form (< Gmc **drupjan*), akin to *dreopan* (Ger *triefen*), to drop, drip < IE **dhreub-* < base **dhreu-*, to break away > DREARY⟧ **1** to fall in or as in drops **2** to let drops of liquid fall **3** to be so soaked or filled with liquid as to have some trickle down or over —***vt.*** to let fall in drops —***n.*** **1** a falling in drops; trickling **2** moisture or liquid falling in drops **3** the sound made by liquid falling in drops **4** *a)* a channel cut on the underside of a sill, cornice, etc. for carrying off rainwater *b)* such a sill, cornice, etc. **5** [Slang] a person regarded as unpleasant or insipid **6** *Med.* a continuous giving of a solution of salt, sugar, etc., esp. intravenously —**drip′per** ***n.***

DRIP (drip) ***n.*** ⟦*d(ividend) r(e)i(nvestment) p(lan)*⟧ a company-sponsored investment program through which the shareholders may reinvest their dividends and buy additional shares, either occasionally or at regular intervals

drip-dry (drip′drī′) ***adj.*** designating or of fabrics or garments that dry quickly when hung soaking wet and require little or no ironing —***vi.*** **-dried′, -dry′ing** to launder as a drip-dry fabric does

☆**drip grind** a fine grind of coffee, for use in filter coffee makers, in which the brew drips through a filter into the serving pot

drip·less (drip′ləs) ***adj.*** made or designed so as not to drip when in use *[dripless* candles*]*

drip·ping (drip′iŋ) ***adv.*** so as to drip; thoroughly *[dripping* wet*]* —***n.*** **1** a falling of liquid drop by drop **2** [*usually pl.*] anything that drips, esp. the fat and juices that drip from roasting meat

dripping pan a pan to catch drippings: also **drip pan**

☆**drip·py** (drip′ē) ***adj.*** **-pi·er, -pi·est** **1** characterized by dripping water, rain, etc. **2** [Slang] overly sentimental, stupid, etc.

drip·stone (drip′stōn′) ***n.*** **1** a DRIP (sense 4) made of stone **2** calcite or a similar mineral, as that forming a stalactite or stalagmite, deposited by dripping or flowing water: cf. FLOWSTONE, TRAVERTINE

drive (drīv) ***vt.*** **drove, driv′en, driv′ing** ⟦ME *driven* < OE *drifan*, akin to

Goth *dreiban*, Ger *treiben*, ON *drīfa* < IE base **dhreibh-*, to push⟧ **1** to force to go; urge onward; push forward **2** to force into or from a state or act [*driven* mad] **3** to force to work, usually to excess **4** *a)* to force by or as by a blow, thrust, or stroke *b)* to throw, hit, or cast hard and swiftly *c)* *Golf* to hit from the tee, usually with a driver **5** to cause to go through; make penetrate **6** to make or produce by penetrating [to *drive* a hole through metal] **7** to control the movement or direct the course of (an automobile, horse and wagon, locomotive, etc.) **8** to transport in an automobile or other vehicle **9** *a)* to impel or propel as motive power; set or keep going; cause to function [a gasoline engine *drives* the motorboat] *b)* to compel, motivate, influence, direct, etc. [the investigation is *driven* by political rivalry] **10** to carry on with vigor; push (a bargain, etc.) through ☆**11** *Basketball* to DRIVE (*vi.* 7) through (the lane) **12** *Hunting* *a)* to chase (game) from thickets into the clear or into nets, traps, etc. *b)* to cover (an area) in this way —*vi.* **1** to advance violently; dash **2** to work or try hard, as to reach a goal **3** to drive a blow, ball, missile, etc. **4** to be driven; operate: said of a motor vehicle **5** to go or be conveyed in a vehicle **6** to operate a motor vehicle ☆**7** *Basketball* to move quickly and aggressively, while dribbling, past defenders and to the basket —*n.* **1** the act or an instance of driving **2** a trip in a vehicle **3** *a)* a road for automobiles, etc. *b)* a driveway ☆**4** *a)* a rounding up or moving of animals on foot for branding, slaughter, etc. *b)* the animals rounded up or moved **5** *a)* a hard, swift blow, thrust, etc., as of a ball in a game *b)* *Golf* a shot from the tee, usually with a driver ☆**6** *a)* an organized movement to achieve some purpose; campaign *b)* a large-scale military offensive to gain an objective *c)* *Football* a series of plays that advances the ball, often, specif., one resulting in a field goal or touchdown ☆**7** the power or energy to get things done; enthusiastic or aggressive vigor **8** that which is urgent or pressing; pressure ☆**9** a collection of logs being floated down a river to a sawmill **10** *a)* any apparatus that transmits power in a motor vehicle [a gear *drive*] *b)* that arrangement in an automatic transmission of a motor vehicle which allows movement forward at varying speeds **11** a device that communicates motion to a machine or machine part **12** *Comput.* a unit that reads and writes data on magnetic tape, a disk, etc. **13** *Psychol.* any of the basic biological impulses or urges, such as self-preservation, hunger, sex, etc. —**drive at** **1** to aim at **2** to mean; intend —**drive in** **1** to force in, as by a blow ☆**2** *Baseball* to cause (a runner) to score or (a run) to be scored, as by getting a hit —**driv′a·ble** *adj.*, **drive′a·ble** —**driv′a·bil′i·ty** *n.*, **drive′a·bil′i·ty**

drive-by (drīv′bī′) *adj.* designating or of a shooting in which the gun is fired from a passing vehicle —*n., pl.* **-bys′** a drive-by shooting

☆**drive-in** (drīv′in′) *adj.* designating or of a restaurant, outdoor film theater, etc. designed to render its services to persons who drive up and remain seated in their cars —*n.* such a restaurant, outdoor theater, etc.

driv·el (driv′əl) *vi.* **-eled** or **-elled**, **-el·ing** or **-el·ling** ⟦ME *drivelen* < OE *dreflian*, to slobber, prob. akin to DRAFF⟧ **1** to let saliva flow from one's mouth; drool; slobber **2** to speak in a silly or stupid manner —*vt.* to say in a silly or stupid manner —*n.* **1** [Now Rare] saliva running from the mouth **2** silly, stupid talk; childish nonsense; twaddle —**driv′el·er** *n.*, **driv′el·ler**

drive·line (drīv′līn′) *n.* DRIVETRAIN

driv·en (driv′ən) *vt., vi. pp. of* DRIVE —*adj.* **1** moved along and piled up by the wind [*driven* snow] **2** having, or caused to act or function by, a sense of urgency or compulsion [a *driven* person]

-driv·en (driv′ən) *combining form* **1** powered by [steam-*driven*] **2** controlled by [mouse-*driven*, management-*driven*] **3** motivated, impelled, or kept in force by [market-*driven*, guilt-*driven*]

driv·er (drī′vər) *n.* **1** a person who drives; specif., *a)* one who drives an automobile, team of horses, etc. *b)* one who herds cattle **2** a thing that drives; specif., *a)* a mallet, hammer, etc. *b)* *Golf* a WOOD[1] with little loft, used in hitting a ball from the tee (also called *number one wood*) *c)* any machine part that communicates motion to another part **3** *Comput.* a program designed to enable a computer to control the operation of a peripheral [a printer *driver*] —**the driver's seat** the position of control or dominance

driver ant ARMY ANT

drive shaft a shaft that transmits rotary motion or power, as from the transmission to the rear axle in an automobile: also written **drive′shaft′** *n.*

drive-through (drīv′thro͞o′) *adj.* **1** designating or of a window from which service is provided to those who drive up in their motor vehicles **2** of a restaurant, bank, etc. or its employee that provides such a service [a *drive-through* teller] —*n.* such a window, restaurant, bank, etc. or the service provided: also sp. [Informal] **drive-thru**

☆**drive time** either of the two weekday time periods during which many people commute by car: term used chiefly in connection with radio programming —**drive′-time′** *adj.*

drive·train (drīv′trān′) *n.* the system that transmits an engine's turning power to the wheels, propeller, etc.

☆**drive·way** (drīv′wā′) *n.* a private way or road for cars, leading from a street or road to a garage, house, etc.

driv·ing (drī′viŋ) *adj.* **1** transmitting force or motion **2** moving with force and violence [a *driving* rain] **3** vigorous; energetic [a *driving* jazz solo] —*n.* the way one drives an automobile, etc.

driving wheel a wheel that transmits motion, as one of the large wheels of a locomotive which receive power from the engine by means of the connecting rod

driz·zle (driz′əl) *vi.* **-zled**, **-zling** ⟦prob. freq. of ME **drisnen* (found only as ger. *drisning*), to fall as dew, akin to Norw dial. *drysja*, to drizzle & OE *dreosan*: see DREARY⟧ to rain in fine, mistlike drops —*vt.* **1** to let fall in fine, mistlike drops **2** *Cooking* to drip or pour (a liquid) in a fine stream onto (a food) —*n.* a fine, mistlike rain —**driz′zly** *adj.*

Dro·ghe·da (drô′ə də) seaport in E Ireland, at the mouth of the Boyne: captured (1649) by Cromwell, who massacred its Royalist garrison

drogue (drōg) *n.* ⟦prob. altered < Scot *drug*, dial. var. of DRAG⟧ **1** SEA ANCHOR **2** a funnel-shaped device towed behind an aircraft or spacecraft for its drag effect (also **drogue parachute**), for use as a target, for use in certain refueling operations, etc.: see also BALLUTE

droid (droid) *n.* [Slang] **1** *short for* ANDROID **2** a person who acts in a mechanical, unimaginative way; automaton; robot

droit (droit; *Fr* drwȧ) *n.* ⟦ME < OFr < ML *directum*, right, justice < L *directus*: see DIRECT⟧ **1** a legal right **2** that to which one has legal claim

droit du sei·gneur (drwȧ dü se nyër′) ⟦Fr, right of the lord⟧ **1** an alleged right, reputedly claimed by some feudal lords, to deflower the bride or daughter of a vassal **2** any alleged right arrogantly presumed

droll (drōl) *adj.* ⟦Fr *drôle*, orig. *n.*, buffoon, jester < MDu *drol*, short, stout fellow, lit., bowling pin⟧ amusing in an odd or wry way —*n.* [Now Rare] a droll person; jester —*vi.* [Now Rare] to joke; play the jester —**SYN.** FUNNY —**droll′ness** *n.* —**drol′ly** *adv.*

droll·er·y (drōl′ər ē) *n., pl.* **-er·ies** ⟦Fr *drôlerie*⟧ **1** a droll act, remark, story, etc. **2** the act of joking **3** quaint or wry humor

-drome (drōm) ⟦< Gr *dromos*, running race, racecourse: see fol.⟧ *combining form* **1** a track or racecourse [*motordrome*] **2** a large field or arena [*airdrome, hippodrome*]

drom·e·dar·y (dräm′ə der′ē) *n., pl.* **-dar′ies** ⟦ME *dromedarie* < OFr *dromedaire* < LL(Ec) *dromedarius (camelus)*, dromedary (camel) < L *dromas*, dromedary (+ *-arius*, -ARY) < Gr *dromas, dromos*, a runner, running < *dramein*, to run < IE **drem-* < base **drā-*, to run > Sans *drámati*, (he) runs⟧ an Arabian camel, esp. one trained for fast riding

-dro·mous (drə məs) ⟦< Gr *-dromos* < *dramein*, to run: see prec.⟧ *combining form* running, moving [*catadromous*]

drone[1] (drōn) *n.* ⟦ME < OE *dran*, akin to OS *dran*, MLowG *drone* < IE **dhren-* < base **dher-*, to buzz, hum > OE *dora* (see DORBEETLE)⟧ **1** a male bee or ant which serves only in a reproductive capacity and does no work **2** an idle person who lives by the work of others; parasite; loafer **3** a person whose work is routine, monotonous, etc.; drudge **4** a pilotless airplane that is directed in flight by remote control —*vi.* **droned**, **dron′ing** to live in idleness; loaf

drone[2] (drōn) *vi.* **droned**, **dron′ing** ⟦LME *dronen* < prec.⟧ **1** to make a continuous and monotonous humming or buzzing sound **2** to talk on and on in a dull, monotonous way —*vt.* to utter in a dull, monotonous tone —*n.* **1** a continuous and monotonous humming or buzzing sound **2** *a)* a bagpipe *b)* any of the pipes of fixed tone in a bagpipe **3** *a)* a bass voice or part, sustaining a single low tone *b)* such a tone

drool (dro͞ol) *vi.* ⟦< DRIVEL⟧ **1** to let saliva flow from one's mouth; drivel **2** to flow from the mouth, as saliva **3** [Slang] to speak in a silly or stupid way **4** [Slang] to be overly enthusiastic, eager, etc. —*vt.* **1** to let drivel from the mouth **2** [Slang] to say in a silly or stupid way —*n.* **1** saliva running from the mouth ☆**2** [Slang] silly, stupid talk; nonsense

droop (dro͞op) *vi.* ⟦ME *droupen* < ON *drūpa*: for IE base see DRIP⟧ **1** to sink down; hang or bend down **2** to lose vitality or strength; become weakened; languish **3** to become dejected or dispirited —*vt.* to let sink or hang down —*n.* an act or instance of drooping

droop·y (dro͞o′pē) *adj.* **droop′i·er**, **droop′i·est** **1** drooping or tending to droop **2** [Informal] tired or dejected —**droop′i·ly** *adv.* —**droop′i·ness** *n.*

drop (dräp) *n.* ⟦ME *drope* < OE *dropa*, akin to ON *drūpa*, DROOP, Ger *triefen*: for IE base see DRIP⟧ **1** a small quantity of liquid that is somewhat spherical, as when falling **2** a very small quantity of liquid **3** [*pl.*] liquid medicine taken or applied in drops **4** a very small quantity of anything **5** a thing like a drop in shape or size, as a pendent earring or a small piece of candy **6** the act or fact of dropping; a fall, descent, slump, or decrease [a *drop* in prices] **7** the dropping of troops or supplies by parachute; airdrop **8** anything that drops or is used for dropping or covering something, as a drop curtain or piece of theater scenery, a drop hammer, or a trapdoor **9** a receptacle or slot into which something is dropped **10** the distance between a higher and lower level; distance through which anything falls or sinks ☆**11** [Slang] *a)* a place that is used for the clandestine depositing or holding of secret messages, of something stolen or illegal, etc. *b)* a deposit made in such a place —*vi.* **dropped**, **drop′ping** **1** to fall in drops **2** to fall; come down **3** to fall exhausted, wounded, or dead **4** to pass into a specified state, esp. into a less active or less desirable one [to *drop* off to sleep] **5** to come to an end or to nothing [to let a matter *drop*] **6** to become lower or less, as temperatures, prices, etc. **7** to move down with a current of water or air —*vt.* **1** to let or make fall; release hold of **2** to give birth to: said of animals **3** to utter (a suggestion, hint, etc.) casually **4** to send (a letter) **5** to cause to fall, as by wounding, killing, or hitting **6** *a)* to stop, end, or have done with *b)* to dismiss **7** to make lower or less; lower or lessen **8** to make (the voice) less loud **9** to drop (troops or supplies) by parachute; airdrop **10** *a)* to omit (a letter or sound) in a word *b)* to cut out; remove; omit [she *dropped* a chapter when she rewrote the book] **11** to leave (a person or thing) at a specified place: often with *off* **12** [Informal] to get rid of or eliminate (something unneeded, unwanted, or problematic) [to *drop* thirty pounds, a bad habit, etc.] **13** [Slang] *a)* to lose (money or a game) *b)* to spend (money) **14** [Slang] to take (a hallucinogenic drug, barbiturate, etc.) orally —**a drop in the bucket** [Informal] an insufficient or trifling amount —☆**at the drop of a hat** immediately; at the slightest provocation —**drop back** 1 to move back; retreat 2 DROP BEHIND —**drop behind** to be outdistanced; fall behind —**drop in** (or **over** or **by**) to pay a casual or unexpected visit —**drop off** 1 to become fewer or less; decline; decrease 2 [Informal] to fall asleep —**drop out** to stop being a member or participant; specif., to withdraw from school, esp. high school, before graduating —☆**get** (or **have**) **the drop on** [Informal] 1 to draw and aim one's gun at (another) more quickly than the person can draw and aim at one 2 to get (or have) any advantage over

☆**drop·cloth** (dräp′klôth′) ***n.*** a large piece of cloth or plastic, used to cover floors, furniture, etc. as a protection against dripping paint, etc.

☆**drop cookie** any of various cookies made from dough that is dropped from a spoon onto a baking sheet

drop curtain a theater curtain that is lowered and raised rather than drawn

drop-dead (dräp′ded′) [Slang] ***adj.*** ⟦prob. suggesting the shocked viewer's reaction: see DROP (*vi.* 3)⟧ spectacular; striking; very impressive [a *drop-dead* wardrobe] —***adv.*** extremely; spectacularly [*drop-dead* handsome]

drop-down (-doun′) ***adj.*** ⟦because the list of menu options seems to drop downward into position⟧ *Comput.* PULL-DOWN

drop-forge (-fôrj′) ***vt.*** **-forged′**, **-forg′ing** to pound or shape (heated metal) between dies with a drop hammer or a press —**drop′-forg′er** ***n.***

drop forging a product made by drop-forging

drop-front (dräp′frunt′) ***adj.*** designating a desk with a front panel fitted with hinges on its bottom edge so that it can be pivoted forward and down to form a surface for writing

☆**drop hammer** 1 a machine for pounding metal into shape, with a heavy weight that is raised and then dropped on the metal 2 this weight

drop-in (dräp′in′) ***adj.*** 1 providing treatment, information, or other services to those who drop in without appointment or referral [a *drop-in* center for the homeless] 2 designed for easy insertion and immediate use [a *drop-in* ink cartridge] —***n.*** [Informal] a person who drops in [a restaurant welcoming *drop-ins*]

drop kick *Football, Rugby* a kick in which the ball is dropped and kicked just as it hits the ground —**drop′-kick′** ***vt., vi.*** —**drop′-kick′er** ***n.***

☆**drop leaf** a hinged board attached to the side or end of a table as an extension of the surface: it hangs down when not in use —**drop′-leaf′** ***adj.***

drop·let (dräp′lit) ***n.*** a very small drop, esp. of liquid

droplet infection disease spread by dispersion into the air of droplets, as from an infected respiratory tract

☆**drop·light** (dräp′līt′) ***n.*** a light so suspended from a fixture that it can be raised or lowered as desired

drop-off (dräp′ôf′) ***n.*** 1 a very steep drop 2 a decline or decrease, as in sales, prices, etc. 3 ⟦see DROP (*vt.* 11)⟧ a location where a person or thing can be dropped off [a *drop-off* for rental cars]

☆**drop·out** (dräp′out′) ***n.*** one who drops out; specif., a person who withdraws from school, esp. high school, before graduating

drop·per (dräp′ər) ***n.*** 1 a person or thing that drops ☆2 a small glass or plastic tube usually capped by a hollow rubber bulb at one end, used to measure out a liquid in drops

dropper

drop·ping (dräp′iŋ) ***n.*** 1 the act of a person or thing that drops 2 that which drops or falls in drops 3 [*pl.*] dung of animals

☆**drop press** DROP HAMMER

drop shot 1 shot made by letting molten metal fall in drops to solidify in a container of water below 2 *Tennis, Volleyball, etc.* a shot hit lightly in which the ball drops just over the net with very little bounce

drop·sonde (dräp′sänd′) ***n.*** ⟦DROP + (RADIO)SONDE⟧ a radiosonde dropped by parachute from an aircraft

drop·sy (dräp′sē) ***n.*** ⟦ME *dropesie* < *ydropesie* < OFr *idropisie* < L *hydropisis* < Gr *hydrōps*, dropsy < *hydōr*, WATER⟧ *former term for* EDEMA —**drop′si·cal** (-si kəl) ***adj.***, **drop′sied** (-sēd) —**drop′si·cal·ly** ***adv.***

drop·wort (dräp′wʉrt′) ***n.*** a tall plant (*Filipendula vulgaris*) of the rose family, with fernlike leaves and white or reddish flowers: it resembles the meadowsweet

dros·er·a (dräs′ər ə) ***n.*** ⟦ModL < Gr *droserē*, fem. of *droseros*, dewy < *drosos*, dew⟧ 1 SUNDEW 2 a preparation extracted from this plant, used as in folk medicine

drosh·ky (dräsh′kē) ***n.***, *pl.* **-kies** ⟦Russ *drožki*, dim. of *drogi*, wagon < *doroga*, road, way < IE base **dheragh-*, DRAW, pull⟧ any of various, usually open, carriages; specif., a low, four-wheeled carriage with a narrow bench which the passengers straddle, used formerly in Russia Also **dros′ky** (dräs′-), *pl.* **-kies**

dro·soph·i·la (drə säf′i lə, drō-) ***n.***, *pl.* **-lae′** (-lē′) ⟦ModL < Gr *drosos*, dew + *phila*, fem. of *philos*, loving⟧ any of a genus (*Drosophila*, family Drosophilidae) of tiny fruit flies used in laboratory experiments in heredity because of their short life cycle, giant chromosomes, and great reproductive capacity

dross (drôs, dräs) ***n.*** ⟦ME & OE *dros*, dregs, akin to ON *dregg*, DREGS⟧ 1 a scum formed on the surface of molten metal 2 waste matter; worthless stuff; rubbish —**dross′i·ness** ***n.*** —**dross′y** ***adj.*** **dross′i·er**, **dross′i·est**

drought (drout) ***n.*** ⟦ME < OE *drugoth*, dryness < *drugian*, to dry up; akin to *dryge*, DRY⟧ 1 a prolonged period of dry weather; lack of rain 2 a prolonged or serious shortage or deficiency 3 [Archaic] thirst —**drought′y** ***adj.*** **drought′i·er**, **drought′i·est**

drouth (drouth, drout) ***n.*** *archaic var. of* DROUGHT

drove[1] (drōv) ***n.*** ⟦ME < OE *draf* < *drifan*, DRIVE⟧ 1 a number of cattle, hogs, sheep, etc. driven or moving along as a group; flock; herd 2 a crowd or body of people, esp. when moving or acting together: *usually used in pl.* 3 *a)* a broad-faced chisel for grooving or dressing stone (also **drove chisel**) *b)* a grooved surface made with this chisel (also **drove work**) —***vt., vi.*** **droved**, **drov′ing** to finish (stone) with a drove chisel —**SYN.** GROUP

drove[2] (drōv) ***vt., vi.*** *pt. of* DRIVE

dro·ver (drō′vər) ***n.*** a person who herds droves of animals, esp. to market

drown (droun) ***vi.*** ⟦ME *drounen*, prob. < var. of ON *drukna*, drown, akin to OE *druncnian*, to become drunk, be drowned < *druncen*, pp. of *drincan*, DRINK⟧ to die by suffocation in water or other liquid —***vt.*** 1 to kill by suffocation in water or other liquid 2 *a)* to cover with water; flood; inundate *b)* to overwhelm 3 to be so loud as to overwhelm (another sound): usually with *out* 4 to cause to disappear; get rid of [to *drown* one's worries in drink]

drowse (drouz) ***vi.*** **drowsed**, **drows′ing** ⟦< OE *drusian*, to become sluggish < base of *dreosan*, to drip: see DREARY⟧ to sleep lightly; be half asleep; doze —***vt.*** 1 [Rare] to make sleepy or sluggish 2 to spend (time) in drowsing —***n.*** the act or an instance of drowsing

drows·y (drou′zē) ***adj.*** **-i·er**, **-i·est** 1 *a)* sleepy or half asleep; lethargic *b)* making drowsy; soporific 2 brought on by sleepiness 3 peacefully quiet or inactive [a *drowsy* village] —**SYN.** SLEEPY —**drows′i·ly** ***adv.*** —**drows′i·ness** ***n.***

drub (drub) ***vt.*** **drubbed**, **drub′bing** ⟦? via Turk *durb* < Ar *darb*, a beating < *daraba*, to cudgel, bastinado⟧ 1 to beat as with a stick or club; cudgel; thrash 2 to defeat soundly in a fight, contest, etc. —***vi.*** to drum or tap —***n.*** a blow as with a club; thump —**drub′ber** ***n.***

drub·bing (drub′iŋ) ***n.*** a thorough beating or defeat

drudge (druj) ***n.*** ⟦ME *druggen*, prob. < OE *dreogan*: see DREE⟧ a person who does hard, menial, or tedious work —***vi.*** **drudged**, **drudg′ing** to do such work

drudg·er·y (druj′ər ē) ***n.***, *pl.* **-er·ies** ⟦see prec. & -ERY⟧ work that is hard, menial, or tiresome

drug (drug) ***n.*** ⟦ME *drogge* < OFr *drogue* < ? LowG *drooge (fat)*, dry (cask), the adj. mistaken as the name of the contents: see DRY⟧ 1 any substance used as a medicine or as an ingredient in a medicine, which kills or inactivates germs or affects any bodily function or organ 2 [Obs.] any substance used in chemistry, dyeing, etc. 3 a narcotic, hallucinogen, etc., esp. one that is habit-forming —***vt.*** **drugged**, **drug′ging** 1 to put a harmful drug in (a food, drink, etc.) 2 to administer a drug to 3 to stupefy with or as with a drug —**drug on the market** a commodity for which there is little or no demand because the supply is so plentiful

drug addict a habitual user of narcotics

☆**drug·a·lys·er** (drug′ə lī′zər) ***n.*** ⟦< trademark *Drugalyzer* < DRUG + (AN)ALYZER (prob. modeled after the trademark BREATHALYZER)⟧ any of various devices designed to measure the presence of certain drugs as in a driver's or employee's body or blood

drugged-out (drugd′out′) ***adj.*** [Slang] under the influence of a drug, esp. a narcotic or hallucinogenic drug

drug·get (drug′it) ***n.*** ⟦Fr *droguet*, dim. of *drogue*, stuff, trash < OFr: see DRUG⟧ 1 a woolen or part-woolen material formerly used for clothing 2 a coarse fabric used as a floor covering, carpet lining, etc. 3 a coarse rug from India made of jute or cotton and hair

☆**drug·gie** (drug′ē) ***n.*** [Slang] a habitual user of drugs

drug·gist (drug′ist) ***n.*** ⟦Fr *droguiste* < OFr *drogue*, DRUG⟧ 1 a dealer in drugs, medical equipment, etc. 2 a person authorized to fill prescriptions; pharmacist ☆3 an owner or manager of a drugstore

☆**drug·gy** (drug′ē) [Slang] ***adj.*** **-gi·er**, **-gi·est** 1 addicted to or under the influence of drugs 2 of or like one in a drugged state —***n.***, *pl.* **-gies** DRUGGIE

drug·mak·er (drug′māk′ər) ***n.*** a manufacturing company that produces pharmaceuticals

☆**drug·store** (drug′stôr′) ***n.*** a store where medical prescriptions are filled and drugs, medical supplies, toiletries, etc. are sold

☆**drugstore cowboy** [Slang] 1 a man who dresses like a cowboy but has never worked as one 2 a man who loiters in public places, as on street corners, esp. in order to flirt with women

dru·id (droo͞′id) ***n.*** ⟦Fr *druide* < L *druides*, pl. < Celt, as in OIr *drūi* < IE **dru-wid-*, lit., oak-wise (< base **deru-*, oak, TREE + **wid-*, know, WISE[1])⟧ [*often* **D-**] a member of a literate and influential class in Celtic society that included priests, soothsayers, judges, poets, etc. in ancient Britain, Ireland, and France —**dru·id·ic** (droo͞ id′ik) ***adj.***, **dru·id′i·cal**

dru·id·ism (-iz′əm) ***n.*** [*often* **D-**] the religious and philosophic beliefs of the druids

drum[1] (drum) ***n.*** ⟦< Du *trom*, akin to MLowG *trumme*, drum, OHG *trumba*, of echoic orig.⟧ 1 *a)* a percussion instrument consisting of a hollow cylinder or hemisphere with a membrane stretched tightly over the end or ends, played by beating with the hands, sticks, etc. *b)* [*pl.*] a set of drums and cymbals played by one person in a jazz, rock, or dance band 2 the sound produced by beating a drum, or any sound like this 3 any of various drumlike cylindrical objects; specif., *a)* a metal spool or cylinder around which cable, etc. is wound in a machine *b)* a barrel-like metal container for oil, etc. *c)* any of the cylindrical blocks making up the shaft of a stone column *d)* the circular or polygonal wall supporting a dome ☆**4** any of a family (Sciaenidae) of marine and freshwater percoid fishes that make a drumming sound **5** *Anat. a)* MIDDLE EAR *b)* TYMPANIC MEMBRANE —*vi.* **drummed, drum′ming 1** to beat a drum **2** to beat or tap continually or rhythmically, as with the fingers ☆**3** to make a loud, reverberating sound by quivering the wings: said of the ruffed grouse, etc. —*vt.* **1** to play (a tune, rhythm, etc.) on or as on a drum **2** to beat or tap continually **3** to assemble by beating a drum **4** to instill (ideas, facts, etc.) *into* by continued repetition —☆**beat the drum for** [Informal] to seek to arouse interest in or enthusiasm for —**drum out of 1** [Historical] to expel from (the army) with drums beating **2** to expel from in disgrace —**drum up 1** to summon by or as by beating a drum **2** [Informal] to get (business, etc.) by soliciting —**on drums** playing drums: see DRUM[1] (*n.* 1*b*)

drum[2] (drum) *n.* ⟦see DRUMLIN⟧ [Scot. or Irish] **1** a narrow hill or ridge **2** DRUMLIN

drum-and-bass (drum′ən bās′) *n.* a form of electronic dance music that evolved from JUNGLE (*n.* 3) in the mid-1990s in England, characterized by complex, driving drum beats and deep, pulsing bass lines: also written **drum 'n' bass**

drum·beat (drum′bēt′) *n.* a sound made by beating a drum

drum·beat·er (-bēt′ər) *n.* ☆[Informal] one who actively publicizes or advocates something, as a press agent —**drum′beat′ing** *n.*

drum·fire (-fīr′) *n.* heavy and continuous gunfire, thought of as resembling a drumroll

drum·head (-hed′) *n.* the membrane stretched over the open end or ends of a drum

drumhead court-martial ⟦from the former use of a drum as the judges' table⟧ a summary court-martial held in the field for trial of offenses committed during military operations or troop movements

drum·lin (drum′lin) *n.* ⟦< Ir *druim*, narrow ridge + *-lin*, dim. suffix < -LING[1]⟧ any one of a series of low, flattened, oval mounds or hills formed by an advancing glacier

drum machine an electronic device designed to simulate the sound of a drum or to play back prerecorded drum and percussion sounds, especially in a programmable sequence

drum major a person who leads a marching band, keeping time with a baton

☆**drum majorette 1** a female drum major **2** a girl or woman who twirls a baton and accompanies a marching band

drum·mer (drum′ər) *n.* **1** a drum player **2** any of various fish or insects that make a drumming sound **3** ⟦see DRUM[1], phr. *drum up*⟧ [Old Informal] a traveling salesman

drum·roll (-rōl′) *n.* a rapid succession of light blows on a drum

drum·stick (-stik′) *n.* **1** a stick for beating a drum **2** the lower half of the leg of a cooked fowl

drunk (druŋk) *vt., vi.* ⟦ME *dronke* < *dronken*, DRUNKEN⟧ *pp. & archaic pt. of* DRINK —*adj.* **1** overcome by alcoholic liquor to the point of losing control over one's faculties; intoxicated **2** overcome by any powerful emotion [*drunk* with joy] **3** [Informal] DRUNKEN (sense 2) Usually used in the predicate —*n.* **1** [Informal] *a)* a drunken person *b)* a person who regularly drinks alcoholic liquor to excess; drunkard **2** [Slang] a drinking spree

SYN.—**drunk** is the simple, direct word, usually used in the predicate, for one who is overcome by alcoholic liquor [he is *drunk*]; **drunken**, usually used attributively, is equivalent to **drunk** but sometimes implies habitual, intemperate drinking of liquor [a *drunken* bum]; **intoxicated** and **inebriated** are more formal or neutral terms; there are many euphemistic and slang terms in English expressing varying degrees of drunkenness: e.g., **tipsy** (slight), **tight** (moderate, but without great loss of muscular coordination), **blind drunk** (great), **blotto** (to the point of unconsciousness), etc. —*ANT.* **sober**

drunk·ard (druŋk′ərd) *n.* ⟦DRUNK + -ARD: ? after Du *dronkaard*⟧ a person who often gets drunk; inebriate

drunk·en (druŋk′ən) *vt., vi.* ⟦ME *dronken* < OE *druncen*, pp. of *drincan*, to DRINK⟧ *archaic pp. of* DRINK —*adj.* **1** intoxicated or habitually intoxicated; drunk **2** caused by, characterized by, or occurring during intoxication [*drunken* driving] Used before a noun —*SYN.* DRUNK —**drunk′en·ly** *adv.* —**drunk′en·ness** *n.*

☆**drunk·om·e·ter** (druŋk äm′ət ər) *n.* ⟦DRUNK + -O- + -METER⟧ a device for testing a sample of exhaled breath to indicate the amount of alcohol in the blood

drupe (dro͞op) *n.* ⟦ModL *drupa* < L *drupa (oliva)*, overripe (olive) < Gr *druppa (elaa)* olive, orig., (olive) ripened on tree, contr. < *drupepēs*⟧ any fruit with a soft, fleshy part (*mesocarp*) covered by a skinlike outer layer (*exocarp*, or *epicarp*) and surrounding an inner stone (*endocarp*) that contains the seed, as an apricot, cherry, plum, etc. —**dru·pa·ceous** (dro͞o pā′shəs) *adj.*

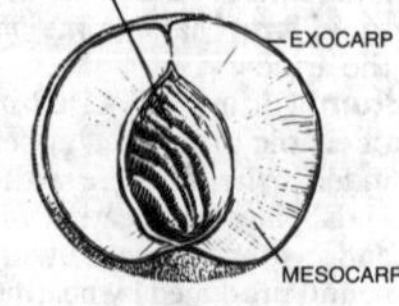

drupe (peach)

drupe·let (-lit) *n.* a small drupe: a single blackberry consists of many drupelets

druse (dro͞oz) *n.* ⟦Ger < MHG *druos*, a boil, swelling, gland < OHG, akin to Du *droes*, goiter⟧ a crystalline crust, usually quartz, lining the sides of a small rock cavity

Druse or **Druze** (dro͞oz) *n.* ⟦Ar *Durūz*, pl., after Ismail al-*Darazī* (lit., tailor), the founder (11th c.)⟧ a member of a religious sect primarily in Syria and Lebanon: their beliefs, though drawn from several sources, are primarily Muslim —**Dru·si·an** *adj.*, **Dru·zi·an, Dru·se·an,** or **Dru·ze·an** (dro͞o′zē ən)

druth·ers (druth′ərz) *n.* ⟦contr. < *I'd rather*, with sound infl. by OTHER⟧ ☆[Informal or Dial.] a choice or preference [if I had my *druthers*]

dry (drī) *adj.* **dri′er, dri′est** ⟦ME *drie* < OE *dryge*, akin to Ger *trocken*, Du *droog* < IE **dhereugh-*, fast, firm, solid (< base **dher-*, to hold out, hold fast > FIRM[1])⟧ **1** not watery; not under water [*dry* land] **2** having no moisture; not wet or damp **3** not shedding tears **4** lacking rain or water [a *dry* summer] **5** having lost liquid or moisture; specif., *a)* arid; withered *b)* empty of water or other liquid *c)* dehydrated **6** needing water or drink; thirsty **7** not yielding milk [a *dry* cow] **8** without butter, jam, etc. on it [*dry* toast] **9** solid; not liquid **10** not sweet; unsweetened; *sec* [*dry* wine] **11** having no mucous or watery discharge [a *dry* cough] ☆**12** prohibiting or opposed to the manufacture or sale of alcoholic beverages [a *dry* town] **13** not colored by emotion, prejudice, etc.; plain; matter-of-fact [*dry* facts] **14** clever and shrewd but ironic or subtle [*dry* wit] **15** not producing results; unfruitful [a *dry* interview] **16** boring, dull, or tedious [a *dry* lecture] **17** harsh; grating: said of a sound **18** [Obs.] without bleeding [a *dry* death] —*n.* **1** [Rare] dryness or drought **2** [Rare] dry land ☆**3** *pl.* **drys** [Informal] a prohibitionist —*vt., vi.* **dried, dry′ing** to make or become dry —**dry out 1** to make or become thoroughly dry **2** [Slang] to withdraw from addiction to alcohol or a narcotic —**dry up 1** to make or become thoroughly dry; parch or wither **2** to make or become unproductive, uncreative, etc. ☆**3** [Slang] to stop talking —**not dry behind the ears** [Informal] immature; inexperienced; naive

SYN.—**dry** suggests a lack or insufficiency of moisture, in either a favorable or unfavorable sense [a *dry* climate, a *dry* riverbed]; **arid** implies an abnormal, intense dryness, esp. with reference to a region or climate, and connotes barrenness or lifelessness [an *arid* waste] —*ANT.* **wet, moist**

dry·a·ble (drī′ə bəl) *adj.* that may be dried in a clothes dryer

dry·ad (drī′ad′, -əd) *n., pl.* **-ads′** or **-a·des′** (-ə dēz′) ⟦L *dryas* (gen. *dryadis*) < Gr < *drys*, an oak, TREE⟧ [*also* **D-**] *Class. Myth.* any of the nymphs living in trees; wood nymph —**dry·ad·ic** (drī ad′ik) *adj.*

dry·as·dust (drī′əz dust′) *n.* ⟦after Dr. Jonas *Dryasdust*, fictional person to whom Sir Walter SCOTT[2] dedicates some of his novels < phr. *dry as dust*⟧ a dull, pedantic person —*adj.* dull and boring

dry battery 1 an electric battery made up of several connected dry cells **2** a dry cell

dry-bulb thermometer (drī′bulb′) a thermometer that is not covered with a wet cloth: see WET-BULB THERMOMETER

dry cell a voltaic cell in which the electrolyte is in the form of a moist paste or gel that cannot spill

dry-clean (drī′klēn′) *vt.* to clean (garments, fabrics, etc.) with some solvent other than water, as naphtha or carbon tetrachloride —**dry cleaner**

dry cleaning 1 the process of cleaning fabrics with a chemical solvent other than water **2** garments, fabrics, etc. that need to be, or have been, subjected to such a process for cleaning

Dry·den (drīd′'n), **John** 1631-1700; Eng. poet, critic, & playwright: poet laureate (1670-88)

dry dock a dock from which the water can be emptied, used for building and repairing ships

dry-dock (drī′däk′) *vt., vi.* to place or go into a dry dock

dry·er (drī′ər) *n.* **1** a person or thing that dries; specif., *a)* a frame or rack for drying clothes, etc. *b)* an apparatus for drying by heating or blowing air, esp. an appliance for drying clothes **2** DRIER

dry-eyed (drī′īd′) *adj.* not weeping; shedding no tears

☆**dry farming** farming in an almost rainless region without the help of irrigation: it is done by conserving the natural moisture of the soil and by planting crops that can resist drought —**dry′-farm′** *vt., vi.* —**dry farmer**

dry fly *see* FLY[2] (sense 2)

dry gangrene gangrene in which the involved body part does not become infected, but mummifies

dry goods cloth, cloth products, thread, etc.

☆**dry-gulch** (drī′gulch′) *vt.* [West] to attack and kill from ambush in a deserted place, as a dry gulch

dry hole 1 an oil, water, or gas well that is not commercially profitable **2** an unsuccessful attempt to accomplish some objective in business, politics, etc.

☆**dry ice** ⟦< *Dry Ice*, former trademark⟧ carbon dioxide solidified and compressed into snowlike cakes that vaporize at −78.5°C without passing through a liquid state: used as a refrigerant

drying oil an organic oil that, when applied in a thin film, dries to form a hard but elastic solid: widely used in paints and varnishes

dry kiln an enclosed place in which lumber is dried and seasoned by artificial heat

dry·land farming (drī′land′) DRY FARMING

dry·ly (drī′lē) *adv.* in a dry manner; matter-of-factly

dry measure a system for measuring the volume of dry things such as grain or vegetables, in which 2 pints = 1 quart, 8 quarts = 1 peck, and 4 pecks = 1 bushel: see the table of weights and measures in the Reference Supplement

dry·ness (drī′nis) *n.* the quality or state of being dry

dry nurse a nurse who takes care of a baby but does not breast-feed it: cf. WET NURSE —**dry′-nurse′** *vt.* **-nursed′, -nurs′ing**

dry·o·pith·e·cine (drī′ō pith′ə sēn′, -sīn′, -sin) ***adj.*** ⟦< ModL *Dryopithecinae*, name of the subfamily < *Dryopithecus*, type genus < Gr *drys*, TREE + ModL *-pithecus*, ape (see PITHECANTHROPUS ERECTUS) + *-inae*, suffix for members of a subfamily < L, fem. pl. of *-inus*, -INE[1]⟧ of or belonging to a genus (*Dryopithecus*) of fossil apelike animals —***n.*** a dryopithecine ape

dry·point (drī′point′) ***n.*** **1** a fine, hard needle for engraving lines on a copper plate without using acid **2** a picture printed from such a plate **3** this way of engraving

dry rot **1** a fungous decay causing seasoned timber to become brittle and crumble to powder **2** a similar fungous disease of plants, fruits, and vegetables **3** any of various fungi causing such decay **4** any internal moral or social decay, thought of as resulting generally from lack of new or progressive influences —**dry′-rot′** ***vi., vt.*** **-rot′ted, -rot′ting**

☆**dry run** **1** [Mil. Slang] practice in firing without using live ammunition **2** [Informal] a simulated or practice performance; rehearsal

dry-salt (drī′sôlt′) ***vt.*** to salt and dry (meat, etc.) in order to preserve it

dry·salt·er (-sôl′tər) ***n.*** [Brit.] a dealer in chemical products, dyes, etc. or, formerly, in dried or salted foods

dry·salt·er·y (-sôl′tə rē) ***n.,*** *pl.* **-er·ies** [Brit.] the stock, shop, or trade of a drysalter

dry-shod (-shäd′) ***adj.*** having dry shoes or feet

dry sink a kitchen cabinet with a shallow basin on top for holding a dishpan, used esp. in the U.S. in the 19th cent.

dry socket a tooth socket in which the blood clot either has broken down after extraction of a tooth or has never formed, resulting in delayed and very painful healing

dry suit a waterproof, usually one-piece suit of rubber or nylon, worn for diving and watersports, under which clothes can be worn for warmth: also written **dry′suit′** ***n.***

Dry Tor·tu·gas (tôr to͞o′gəz) ⟦orig., *Tortugas* < Sp, pl. of *tortuga*, tortoise: so named by PONCE DE LEÓN, discoverer, for the abundant turtles; sailors later called them *dry* because they lack fresh water⟧ group of small islands of Fla. in the Gulf of Mexico, west of Key West

☆**dry·wall** (drī′wôl′) ***n.*** PLASTERBOARD —***vt., vi.*** to cover (a wall, partition, etc.) with plasterboard

☆**dry wash** a dry stream bed

dry well *Building* a covered pit filled with gravel or loose stone, into which drainage from roofs, areaways, etc. is piped to seep into the surrounding soil

ds *abbrev. Commerce* days after sight

Ds *Chem. symbol for* darmstadtium

DS[1] *abbrev.* Doctor of Science: also **DSc** or **D.S.** or **D.Sc.**

DS[2] *abbrev.* ⟦It *dal segno*⟧ *Musical Direction* (repeat) from the sign

DSC *abbrev.* Distinguished Service Cross

DSL (dē′es′el′) ***n.*** ⟦*d(igital) s(ubscriber) l(ine)*⟧ a kind of connection to the internet that permits the transfer of digital data over ordinary telephone lines at a higher rate of speed

DSM *abbrev.* Distinguished Service Medal

DSO *abbrev.* Distinguished Service Order

DSP *abbrev.* digital signal processing

DSS *abbrev.* digital satellite system

DST *abbrev.* daylight saving time

dt *abbrev.* **1** delirium tremens **2** double time

Dt *abbrev. Bible* Deuteronomy

DT *abbrev. Football* defensive tackle: sometimes written **dt**

DTh, DTheol, D.Th., *or* **D.Theol.** *abbrev.* Doctor of Theology

DTP *abbrev.* **1** desktop publishing **2** diphtheria, tetanus, and pertussis (vaccine or vaccination)

d.t.'s (dē′tēz′) ***pl.n.*** [Slang] delirium tremens: usually preceded by *the*: often written **D.T.'s**

DTV *abbrev.* digital television

DU *abbrev.* Dobson unit(s)

Du *abbrev.* **1** Duke **2** Dutch

du·ad (do͞o′ad′, dyo͞o′-) ***n.*** two together; pair; couple

du·al (do͞o′əl, dyo͞o′-) ***adj.*** ⟦L *dualis* < *duo*, TWO⟧ **1** of two **2** having or composed of two parts or kinds, like or unlike; double; twofold [*a dual nature*] —***n.*** *Linguis.* **1** DUAL NUMBER **2** a word having dual number —**du·al·i·ty** (do͞o al′ə tē, dyo͞o-) ***n.*** —**du′al·ly** ***adv.***

du·al·ism (-iz′əm) ***n.*** **1** the state of being dual; duality **2** *Philos.* the theory that the world is ultimately composed of, or explicable in terms of, two basic entities, as mind and matter **3** *Theol.* *a)* the doctrine that there are two mutually antagonistic principles in the universe, good and evil *b)* the doctrine that man has two natures, physical and spiritual —**du′al·ist** (-ist) ***n.***

du·al·is·tic (do͞o′əl is′tik, dyo͞o′-) ***adj.*** **1** of or based on dualism **2** dual —**du′al·is′ti·cal·ly** ***adv.***

du·al·ize (do͞o′əl īz′, dyo͞o′-) ***vt.*** **-ized′, -iz′ing** to make, or consider as, dual

dual number a grammatical number category referring to exactly two persons or things: distinguished by inflection, in such languages as classical Greek and Old English, from *singular* and *plural*

du·al-pur·pose (do͞o′əl pur′pəs, dyo͞o′-) ***adj.*** having, or meant to have, two uses

du·al-use (-yo͞os′) ***adj.*** DUAL-PURPOSE; specif., designating or of machinery, technology, etc. having both civilian and military applications

dub[1] (dub) ***vt.*** **dubbed, dub′bing** ⟦ME *dubben* < OE *dubbian*, to strike (akin to ON *dubba*, to dub, EFris *dubben*, push) < IE base **dheubh-*, a club, wooden pin > DOWEL⟧ **1** [Obs.] to hit; strike **2** to confer knighthood on by tapping on the shoulder with a sword **3** *a)* to confer a title or rank upon *b)* to call, name, or nickname **4** to make (wood, etc.) smooth, as by hammering or scraping **5** to dress (leather) by rubbing **6** [Slang] to bungle (a golf stroke, etc.) —***n.*** ☆[Slang] a clumsy, unskillful person —**dub′ber** ***n.***

☆**dub**[2] (dub) ***vt.*** **dubbed, dub′bing** ⟦contr. < DOUBLE⟧ **1** to rerecord the sound from (an old recording): distinguished from RE-PRESS **2** to provide with a soundtrack **3** to insert in (a film) a soundtrack with synchronized dialogue in another language —***n.*** **1** dialogue, music, etc. inserted in a film's soundtrack **2** a copy of a recording made for testing the sound or content —**dub in** *Film, Radio, TV* to insert (dialogue, music, etc.) in the soundtrack —**dub′ber** ***n.***

dub[3] (dub, do͝ob) ***n.*** ⟦prob. < Scand, akin to Norw *dobbe*, swampy land, MDu *doppe*, shell, MLowG *dobbe*, pool: for IE base see DIMPLE⟧ [Scot. or North Eng.] a small pool or puddle

dub[4] (dub) ***n.*** a form of reggae produced by remixing original recordings with overdubbed sound effects, spoken words, fragments of other music, etc.

Du·bai (do͞o bī′) **1** one of the emirates that constitute the United Arab Emirates: 1,510 sq mi (3,911 sq km) **2** its chief city, a seaport on the Persian Gulf

du Bar·ry (do͞o bar′ē; *Fr* dü bȧ rē′), Comtesse (born *Marie Jeanne Bécu*) 1743?-93; mistress of Louis XV of France

dub·bin (dub′in) ***n.*** ⟦< *dubbing*: see DUB[1], ***vt.*** 5⟧ a greasy preparation for softening and waterproofing leather: also **dub′bing** (-iŋ, -in)

du·bi·e·ty (do͞o bī′ə tē, dyo͞o-) ***n.*** ⟦LL *dubietas*⟧ **1** the quality of being dubious; doubtfulness **2** *pl.* **-ties** a doubtful thing —***SYN.*** UNCERTAINTY

du·bi·os·i·ty (do͞o′bē äs′ə tē, dyo͞o′-) ***n.,*** *pl.* **-ties** vague doubt or uncertainty —***SYN.*** UNCERTAINTY

du·bi·ous (do͞o′bē əs, dyo͞o′-) ***adj.*** ⟦L *dubiosus*, doubtful < *dubius*, doubting, uncertain < *du-* < or akin to *duo*, TWO + IE base **bhu-*, **bheu-*, to BE⟧ **1** causing doubt; ambiguous; vague [*a dubious remark*] **2** feeling doubt; hesitating; skeptical **3** with the outcome undecided or hanging in the balance [*dubious battle*] **4** rousing suspicion; questionable; shady [*a dubious character*] —***SYN.*** DOUBTFUL —**du′bi·ous·ly** ***adv.*** —**du′bi·ous·ness** ***n.***

du·bi·ta·ble (do͞o′bi tə bəl, dyo͞o′-) ***adj.*** ⟦L *dubitabilis*⟧ that is to be doubted; uncertain —**du′bi·ta·bly** ***adv.***

Dub·lin (dub′lən) **1** capital of Ireland: seaport on the Irish Sea **2** county in Leinster province, E Ireland, on the Irish Sea: 356 sq mi (922 sq km); county seat, Dublin

dub·ni·um (do͝ob′nē əm, dub′-) ***n.*** ⟦ModL, after *Dubna*, Russia, where important work in nuclear physics took place + -IUM⟧ a radioactive chemical element with a very short half-life: a transactinide produced by bombarding californium or berkelium with high-energy nuclear particles: symbol, Db; at. no. 105: see the periodic table of elements in the Reference Supplement

du Bois (do͞o bwä′), **Guy Pène** (gē pen) 1884-1958; U.S. painter & art critic

Du Bois (do͞o bois′), **W(illiam) E(dward) B(urghardt)** 1868-1963; U.S. historian, educator, & civil rights leader

Du·brov·nik (do͞o brôv′nik, do͞o′brôv nik) seaport in S Croatia, on the Adriatic

Du·buf·fet (dü bü fā′), **Jean(-Philippe-Arthur)** (zhän) 1901-85; Fr. painter

du·cal (do͞o′kəl, dyo͞o′-) ***adj.*** ⟦OFr < LL *ducalis*, of a leader < L *dux*: see DUCT⟧ of a duke or dukedom —**du′cal·ly** ***adv.***

duc·at (duk′ət) ***n.*** ⟦ME & OFr < It *ducato*, ducat, coin bearing image of a duke < LL *ducatus*: see DUCHY⟧ **1** any of several gold or silver coins formerly used in some European countries **2** [Slang] a piece of money **3** [Slang] a ticket, esp. an admission ticket

du·ce (do͞o′che) ***n.*** ⟦It < L *dux* (gen. *ducis*): see DUCT⟧ leader: title (*Il Duce*) assumed by Benito Mussolini as head of Fascist Italy

Du·champ (dü shän′), **Mar·cel** (mȧr sel′) 1887-1968; U.S. artist, born in France

Du·chenne muscular dystrophy (do͞o shen′) ⟦after G. *Duchenne* (1806-75), Fr neurologist who first described it⟧ a common hereditary form of muscular dystrophy, usually affecting young males, characterized by the severe weakening of the skeletal muscles, esp. the respiratory muscles: also called **Duchenne's muscular dystrophy**

duch·ess (duch′is) ***n.*** ⟦ME & OFr *duchesse*, fem. of *duc*, DUKE[1]⟧ **1** the wife or widow of a duke **2** a woman who has the rank of a duke

duch·y (duch′ē) ***n.,*** *pl.* **duch′ies** ⟦ME & OFr *duchee* < LL *ducatus*, military command, territory of a duke < L *dux*: see DUCT⟧ the territory ruled by a duke or duchess; dukedom

duck[1] (duk) ***n.*** ⟦ME *doke* < OE *duce*, lit., diver, ducker < base of **ducan*, to plunge, dive (see fol.); replaces OE *ened* (akin to Ger *ente*), common Gmc word for the bird⟧ **1** *pl.* **ducks** or **duck** any of a large number of relatively small waterfowl with a flat bill, short neck and legs, and webbed feet **2** a female duck: opposed to DRAKE[1] **3** the flesh of a duck as food **4** [Informal, Chiefly Brit.] a darling; dear ☆**5** [Slang] a person, esp. one qualified as being "odd," "harmless," "funny," etc. —☆**have (or get) one's ducks in a row** ⟦prob. in allusion to a mother duck leading a line of her ducklings⟧ to be (or become) thoroughly organized or prepared —**like water off a duck's back** with no effect or reaction

duck[2] (duk) ***vt., vi.*** ⟦ME *douken* < OE **ducan*, to plunge, dive, akin to OHG *tūhan* (Ger *tauchen*), MLowG *dūken*, Du *duiken*, to dive⟧ **1** to plunge or dip under water for a moment **2** to lower, turn, or bend (the head, body, etc.) suddenly, as in avoiding a blow or in hiding ☆3 [Informal] to avoid or evade [the candidate *ducked* the issue] 4 [Slang] to move (*in* or *out*) quickly —*n.* the act of ducking —**duck′er** *n.*

duck[3] (duk) *n.* ⟦Du *doek*, akin to Ger *tuch*, cloth⟧ 1 a cotton or linen cloth somewhat like canvas but finer and lighter in weight 2 [*pl.*] clothes, esp. white trousers, made of this cloth

duck[4] (duk) *n.* ⟦altered (infl. by DUCK[1]) < *DUKW*, military code name⟧ ☆[Mil. Slang] an amphibious motor vehicle used during WWII

duck·bill (duk′bil′) *n.* PLATYPUS

duck-billed dinosaur (duk′bild′) any of various ornithopod dinosaurs having a flat head, a ducklike bill, and numerous, small, flat teeth for grinding plants

duck·board (-bôrd′) *n.* a board or boards forming a slightly raised surface or flooring, as on a muddy road or along the bottom of a military trench: *often used in pl.*

duck·foot·ed (-fo͝ot′id) *adj.* 1 having the hind toe pointing forward, as on a duck's foot: said of fowl 2 having the feet turned outward; FLAT-FOOTED (*adj.* 2) —*adv.* with the feet turned outward

duck hawk ☆PEREGRINE FALCON

ducking stool ⟦altered (infl. by DUCK[2]) < CUCKING STOOL⟧ [Historical] a chair at the end of a plank, in which a culprit was tied and then ducked into water as a punishment

duck·ling (-liŋ) *n.* ⟦DUCK[1] + -LING[1]⟧ a young duck

duck·pins (-pinz′) *n.* ⟦because the pins have a short, squat shape, suggestive of that of a DUCK[1]⟧ a game like tenpins, played with smaller pins and balls —*pl.n.* the pins used in this game

duck plague an acute, highly fatal disease of ducks caused by a herpesvirus

ducks and drakes the game of throwing a small, flat stone so that it will skim or skip along the surface of water —**make ducks and drakes of** to deal with recklessly or squander: also **play ducks and drakes with**

☆**duck soup** [Old Slang] something that is easy to do; cinch

duck·tail (-tāl′) *n.* a style of man's haircut in which the hair is cut long on the sides and swept back, somewhat resembling a duck's tail: also [Vulgar] **duck's ass** —**duck′tailed′** *adj.*, **duck′-tailed′**

duck·walk (-wôk′) *vi.* to walk in a crouching or squatting position

duck·weed (-wēd′) *n.* any of a family (Lemnaceae, order Arales) of monocotyledonous, minute flowering plants that float on ponds and sluggish streams and reproduce by a kind of budding: so called because eaten by ducks

duck·y (duk′ē) *adj.* **duck′i·er**, **duck′i·est** ⟦early 19th-c. term of endearment < DUCK[1] + -Y[2]⟧ [Old Slang] pleasing, delightful, darling, etc.: often used ironically

duct (dukt) *n.* ⟦ML *ducta*, conduit < L *ductus*, a leading, conducting, pp. of *ducere*, to lead < IE base **deuk-*, to pull > TOW[1], TUG, L *dux*, leader⟧ 1 a tube, channel, or canal through which a gas or liquid moves 2 a tube in the body for the passage of excretions or secretions [a tear *duct*, bile *duct*] 3 a conducting tubule in plant tissues, esp. one containing resin, latex, etc. 4 a pipe or conduit through which wires or cables are run, air is circulated or exhausted, etc. —**duct′less** *adj.*

duc·tile (duk′təl, -tīl′) *adj.* ⟦ME *ductil* < L *ductilis* < *ductus*: see prec.⟧ 1 that can be stretched, drawn, or hammered thin without breaking; not brittle: said of metals 2 easily molded; plastic; pliant 3 easily led; tractable —*SYN.* PLIABLE —**duc·til·i·ty** (duk til′ə tē) *n.*

ductless gland an endocrine gland

duct tape a very strong adhesive tape with a waterproof backing, used to seal ducts, hoses, etc.

duct·ule (duk′tyo͞ol′) *n.* a small duct

duct·work (dukt′wʉrk′) *n.* a system of ducts, as in a building, used to circulate air for heating, cooling, or ventilation

dud (dud) [Informal] *n.* ⟦prob. < Du *dood*, dead⟧ 1 a bomb or shell that fails to explode 2 a person or thing that fails or is ineffectual —*adj.* worthless

☆**dude** (do͞od, dyo͞od) *n.* ⟦< ? Ger dial. *dude*, a fool⟧ 1 a man too much concerned with his clothes and appearance; dandy; fop 2 [West Slang] a city fellow or tourist, esp. an Easterner who is vacationing on a ranch 3 [Slang] any man or boy: often used as a casual term of address, as from one young man to another —*vt.* **dud′ed**, **dud′ing** [Slang] 1 to dress up, esp. in showy or flashy clothes 2 to add showy ornamentation to Usually used with *up* —*vi.* [Slang] to dress up, esp. in showy or flashy clothes: usually used with *up* —**dud′ish** *adj.* —**dud′ish·ly** *adv.*

du·deen (do͞o dēn′, tho͞o-) *n.* ⟦< Ir *dúidín*, a little pipe < *dúd*, a pipe⟧ [Irish] a short-stemmed clay tobacco pipe

☆**dude ranch** a ranch or farm operated as a vacation resort, with horseback riding and similar sports

Dude·vant (düd vän′), Baronne *see* SAND, George

dudg·eon[1] (duj′ən) *n.* ⟦16th-c. (*take*) *in dudgeon*, also *endugine*, prob. Anglo-Fr *en digeon*, with ref. to the hand on the dagger hilt: see fol.⟧ anger or resentment: now chiefly in the phrase **in high dudgeon**, very angry, offended, or resentful

dudg·eon[2] (duj′ən) *n.* ⟦ME *dogeon* < Anglo-Fr *digeon*⟧ [Obs.] 1 a wood, perhaps boxwood, used for dagger hilts 2 a hilt of this wood or a dagger with such a hilt

Dud·ley[1] (dud′lē) *n.* ⟦< the surname (earlier place name) *Dudley*, orig. *Dudda's lea*⟧ a masculine name

Dud·ley[2] (dud′lē), **Robert** *see* LEICESTER[2], Earl of

Dud·ley[3] (dud′lē) city in West Midlands, WC England, near Birmingham

duds (dudz) *pl.n.* ⟦ME *dudde*, cloth, cloak < ?⟧ [Informal] 1 clothes 2 trappings; belongings

due (do͞o, dyo͞o) *adj.* ⟦ME < OFr *deu*, pp. of *devoir*, to owe < L *debere*, to owe: see DEBT⟧ 1 owed or owing as a debt, right, etc.; payable [the first payment is *due*] 2 suitable; fitting; proper; usual [with all *due* respect, in *due* time] 3 as much as is required; enough; adequate [*due* care] 4 expected or scheduled to arrive or be ready; timed for a certain hour or date [the plane is *due* at 6:30 P.M.] —*adv.* exactly; directly [*due* west] —*n.* anything due or owed; specif., *a)* deserved recognition [to give a man his *due*] *b)* [*pl.*] fees, taxes, or other charges [membership *dues*] —**become** (or **fall**) **due** to become payable as previously arranged —☆**due to** 1 caused by; resulting from [an omission *due to* oversight] 2 because of [the name was omitted *due to* oversight] —☆**pay one's dues** [Informal] to earn certain rights, privileges, etc. as because of one's accomplishments or struggles

☆**due bill** a written acknowledgment of a debt to a person named, but neither payable to that person's order nor transferable by endorsement; often, such an acknowledgment exchangeable for merchandise or services only

due diligence 1 the degree of care that is reasonably to be expected or that is legally required, esp. of persons giving professional advice 2 an assessing, evaluating, etc. conducted with prudent or requisite care

du·el (do͞o′əl, dyo͞o′-) *n.* ⟦ME *duelle* < ML *duellum* < OL *dvellum* (L *bellum*), war < IE base **dāu-*, **deu-*, to injure, destroy, burn > Sans *dū*, pain, OE *teona*, harm⟧ 1 a formal fight between two persons armed with deadly weapons: it is prearranged and witnessed by two others (called *seconds*), each representing a combatant 2 any contest or encounter suggesting such a fight, usually between two persons [a verbal *duel*] — *vi.*, *vt.* **-eled** or **-elled**, **-el·ing** or **-el·ling** to fight a duel with (a person or persons) —**du′el·ist** or **du′el·list**, **du′el·er** or **du′el·ler** *n.*

du·el·lo (do͞o el′ō, dyo͞o-) *n.*, *pl.* **-los** ⟦It < ML *duellum*, prec.⟧ 1 the art, rules, or code of dueling 2 [Obs.] a duel

duen·de (dwen′de) *n.* ⟦Sp, lit., goblin, spirit⟧ a special quality or charm that makes a person irresistibly attractive

du·en·na (do͞o en′ə, dyo͞o-) *n.* ⟦Sp *dueña* < L *domina*, mistress: see DAME⟧ 1 an elderly woman who has charge of the girls and young unmarried women of a Spanish or Portuguese family 2 a chaperone or governess

due process (of law) the course of legal proceedings established by the legal system of a nation or state to protect individual rights and liberties

Due·ro (dwe′rô) *Sp. name for* DOURO

du·et (do͞o et′, dyo͞o-) *n.* ⟦It *duetto*, dim. of *duo*, duet < L, TWO⟧ *Music* 1 a composition for two voices or two instruments 2 a performance involving two voices or instruments —*vi.* **du·et′ted**, **du·et′ting** to perform a duet

Du·fay or **Du Fay** (do͞o fā′), **Guil·laume** (gē yōm′) 1397?-74; Fr. composer

duff[1] (duf) *n.* ⟦dial. var. of DOUGH, with *-ff* for ME *-gh* (see LAUGH), orig. pronounced (kh); senses 2 & 3 < ?⟧ 1 a thick flour pudding boiled in a cloth bag or steamed, often containing dried fruit 2 decaying vegetable matter on the ground in a forest 3 coal dust or slack

☆**duff**[2] (duf) *n.* ⟦< ?⟧ [Slang] the buttocks

duff[3] (duf) *adj.* [Brit. Informal] 1 of poor quality; inferior; worthless 2 incorrect; wrong

duf·fel or **duf·fle** (duf′əl) *n.* ⟦Du, after *Duffel*, town in N Belgium⟧ 1 a coarse woolen cloth with a thick nap ☆2 clothing and equipment carried by a sportsman, soldier, camper, etc. ☆3 DUFFEL BAG 4 DUFFLE COAT

☆**duffel (*or* duffle) bag** a large, cylindrical cloth bag, esp. of waterproof canvas or duck, for carrying clothing and personal belongings

duff·er (duf′ər) *n.* ⟦< thieves' slang *duff*, to counterfeit, fake⟧ 1 [Old Slang] a peddler, as of cheap trinkets 2 [Old Slang] anything counterfeit or worthless 3 [Informal] a person, now often elderly, who is incompetent, ineffectual, or dawdling 4 [Informal] a relatively unskilled golfer

duffle coat a knee-length, hooded coat made of duffel or other wool cloth: also **duffel coat**

du·fus (do͞o′fəs) *n.* [Slang] *alt. sp. of* DOOFUS

Du·fy (dü fē′), **Ra·oul (Ernest Joseph)** (rä o͞ol′) 1877-1953; Fr. painter

dug[1] (dug) *vt.*, *vi. pt. & pp. of* DIG[1]

dug[2] (dug) *n.* ⟦< same base as Dan *daegge*, to suckle, caus. of *die*, to suck < IE base **dhē-*: see FEMALE⟧ a female animal's nipple, teat, or udder: sometimes used contemptuously of a woman's breast

du·gong (do͞o′gôŋ′) *n.* ⟦ModL < Malay *duyong*⟧ any of a genus (*Dugong*) of large tropical sirenian mammals that live along the shores of the Indian Ocean and feed mostly on seaweed

☆**dug·out** (dug′out′) *n.* 1 a boat or canoe hollowed out of a log 2 a shelter, as in warfare, dug in the ground or in a hillside 3 *Baseball* either of two covered shelters near the diamond for the players of opposing teams to sit in when not at bat or in the field

duh (du) *interj.* [Slang] 1 used, jocularly, to signify a lack of knowledge or comprehension 2 used in response to something said that is too obvious to need to be mentioned ["Physics is really hard." "Well, *duh*."]

DUI (dē′yo͞o′ī′) *n.* ⟦*d*(*riving*) *u*(*nder the*) *i*(*nfluence*)⟧ a traffic citation issued to a person accused of driving under the influence of alcohol, drugs, etc.

dui·ker (dī′kər) *n.*, *pl.* **-kers** or **-ker** ⟦Du *duiker*, lit., a diver < *duiken*, to DUCK[2]⟧ any of several small African antelopes (as genera *Cephalophus* and *Sylvicapra*) common south of the Sahara

Duis·burg (dyo͞os′bʉrg; *Ger* düs′bo͝ork) city in W Germany, at the junction of the Rhine & Ruhr rivers, in the state of North Rhine-Westphalia

du jour (do͞o zho͝or′, dyo͞o; *Fr* dü zho͝or′) ⟦Fr, lit., of the day⟧ available or offered on this day [a restaurant's soup *du jour*]: often used dismissively for something regarded as one in a series of passing fads [the literary theory *du jour*]

duke[1] (do͞ok, dyo͞ok) ***n.*** ⟦ME *duk* < OFr *duc* < L *dux*, leader < *ducere*, to lead: see DUCT⟧ **1** a prince who rules an independent duchy **2** a nobleman of the highest hereditary rank below that of prince **3** any of several varieties of cherry created by crossing a sweet cherry with a sour cherry —**duke′dom** (-dəm) ***n.***

duke[2] (do͞ok, dyo͞ok) [Slang] ***n.*** ⟦< prec., short for *Duke of York*, used in 19th-c. E rhyming slang for *fork*, hence fingers, hence fist⟧ [*pl.*] the fists or hands — ***vt., vi.*** **duked**, **duking** to hit or fight with the fists —**duke it out** to fight, esp. with the fists

Du·kho·bor (do͞o′kə bôr′) ***n.***, *pl.* **Du′kho·bors′** or **Du′kho·bor′tsy** (-bôrt′ sē) a member of a pacifistic, nonritualistic, mystical religious sect that separated (1785) from the Eastern Orthodox Church: in the 1890s, many members emigrated to W Canada

dul·cet (dul′sit) ***adj.*** ⟦ME *doucet* < OFr, dim. of *douz*, sweet < L *dulcis*, sweet < ? IE base **dl̥ku-*, sweet > Gr *glykys*⟧ **1** soothing or pleasant to hear; sweet-sounding; melodious **2** [Archaic] sweet to taste or smell —**dul′cet·ly** ***adv.***

dul·ci·fy (dul′sə fī′) ***vt.*** **-fied′**, **-fy′ing** ⟦< L *dulcis* (see prec.) + -FY⟧ [Rare] **1** to sweeten **2** to make pleasant or agreeable; mollify

dul·ci·mer (dul′sə mər) ***n.*** ⟦ME *doucemer* < OFr *doulcemer* < Sp *dulcemele* < L *dulce-melos* < *dulce*, neut. of *dulcis*, sweet (see DULCET) + *melos* < Gr, a song, strain⟧ **1** a zither having a usually trapezoidal shape and a number of metal strings, which are struck with two small hammers by the player **2** a zither of the S Appalachians, often long and hourglass-shaped, played on the lap or a table by plucking with a wooden plectrum or goose quill: also **dul′ci·more′** (-môr′) **3** *Bible* a musical instrument, variously interpreted to be a harp, bagpipe, etc.: see Dan. 3:5

dulcimer
(sense 2)

Dul·ci·ne·a (dul′sə nē′ə, -nā′-) ***n.*** ⟦Sp < *dulce*, sweet < L *dulcis*: see DULCET⟧ the name given by Don Quixote to a coarse peasant girl whom he imagines to be a beautiful lady and falls in love with

du·li·a (do͞o lī′ə, dyo͞o-) ***n.*** ⟦ME < ML < Gr *douleia*, service < *doulos*, a slave⟧ *R.C.Ch.* veneration given to angels and saints: distinguished from LATRIA

dull (dul) ***adj.*** ⟦ME *dul* < OE *dol*, stupid, akin to Ger *toll* < IE **dh(e)wel-* < base **dheu-*, blow, be turbid > DUMB, DWELL, OIr *dall*, blind, Gr *thanatos*, death⟧ **1** mentally slow; stupid **2** lacking sensitivity; blunted in feeling or perception [*dull* to grief] **3** physically slow; slow-moving; sluggish **4** lacking spirit, zest, etc.; not lively; listless, insipid, etc. **5** not active or busy; slack [a *dull* period for sales] **6** causing boredom; tedious [a *dull* party] **7** not pointed or sharp; blunt; not keen [a *dull* blade] **8** not felt keenly; not acute [a *dull* headache] **9** *a)* not vivid; not brilliant; dim [a *dull* color] *b)* not shiny or glossy; lusterless [a *dull* finish] **10** not distinct, resonant, etc.; muffled [a *dull* thud] **11** gloomy; cloudy [*dull* weather] — ***vt., vi.*** to make or become dull —**dull′ish** ***adj.*** —**dull′ness** ***n.***, **dul′ness** —**dul′ly** ***adv.***

SYN.—**dull** is specifically applied to a point or edge that has lost its previous sharpness [a *dull* knife] and generally connotes a lack of keenness, zest, spirit, intensity, etc. [a *dull* book, pain, etc.]; **blunt** is often equivalent to **dull**, but specifically refers to a point or edge that is intentionally not sharp [a *blunt* fencing saber]; **obtuse** literally applies to a pointed end whose sides form an angle greater than 90°, and figuratively connotes great dullness of understanding or lack of sensitivity [too *obtuse* to comprehend] See also **stupid** —*ANT.* **sharp, keen**

dull·ard (dul′ərd) ***n.*** ⟦ME: see prec. & -ARD⟧ a stupid person

Dul·les (dul′əs), **John Foster** 1888-1959; U.S. diplomat: secretary of state (1953-59)

☆**dulls·ville** (dulz′vil′) [*also* **D-**] [Slang] ***n.*** a person, condition, etc. that is very dull or boring —***adj.*** very dull, boring, tedious, etc.

dull-wit·ted (dul′wit′əd) ***adj.*** slow-witted —**dull′-wit′ted·ness** ***n.***

dulse (duls) ***n.*** ⟦Ir & Gael *duileasg*⟧ any of several edible red algae (esp. *Rhodymenia palmata*) with large, wedge-shaped fronds

Du·luth (də lo͞oth′) ⟦after Daniel G. *Du Lhut* (or *Du Luth*), 1636-1710, Fr explorer⟧ city and port in NE Minn., on Lake Superior

du·ly (do͞o′lē, dyo͞o′-) ***adv.*** in a due manner; specif., *a)* as due; rightfully *b)* when due; at the right time *c)* as required; sufficiently

Du·ma (do͞o′mä) ***n.*** ⟦Russ < Gmc, as in Goth *doms*, ON *domr*, OE *dom*, judgment: see DOOM[1]⟧ **1** the legislative assembly of czarist Russia (1905-17) **2** the lower chamber of the parliament in Russia (since 1993)

Du·mas (do͞o mä′, do͞o′mä; *Fr* dü mȧ′) **1 Al·ex·an·dre** (al′ig zan′dər) 1802-70; Fr. novelist & playwright: called *Dumas père* **2 Alexandre** 1824-95; Fr. playwright & novelist: called *Dumas fils*: son of *Dumas père*

du Mau·ri·er (do͞o môr′ē ā′, dyo͞o-) **1** Dame **Daphne** 1907-89; Eng. novelist **2 George (Louis Palmella Busson)** 1834-96; Eng. illustrator & novelist, born in France: grandfather of Daphne

dumb (dum) ***adj.*** ⟦ME & OE, akin to Ger *dumm* (Goth *dumbs*), mute, stupid < nasalized var. of IE **dheubh* < base **dheu-*: see DULL⟧ **1** lacking the power of speech; mute: now regarded as offensive **2** unwilling to talk; silent **3** not accompanied by speech **4** temporarily speechless, as from fear **5** producing no sound **6** lacking some normal part, characteristic, or quality ☆**7** ⟦Ger *dumm*⟧ [Informal] stupid; moronic **8** completely undirected by intelligence or foresight [*dumb* luck] **9** *Comput.* incapable of some independent functioning because not equipped with a microprocessor or computer [a *dumb* computer terminal]: contrasted with INTELLIGENT (sense 3) and SMART (*adj.* 9) —☆**dumb down** [Informal] to make or become less intelligent or intellectually demanding —**dumb′ly** ***adv.*** —**dumb′ness** ***n.***

☆**dumb·ass** or **dumb-ass** (dum′as′) [Slang] ***n.*** a stupid or foolish person —***adj.*** stupid or foolish Regarded as mildly vulgar by some

dumb·bell (dum′bel′) ***n.*** ⟦DUMB + BELL[1]: from orig. shape⟧ **1** a device usually used in pairs, consisting of round weights joined by a short bar, by which it is lifted or swung about in the hand for muscular exercise ☆**2** ⟦cf. DUMB, sense 7⟧ [Slang] a stupid person

dumb·found or **dum·found** (dum′found′, dum found′) ***vt.*** ⟦DUMB + (CON)FOUND⟧ to make speechless by shocking; amaze; astonish —*SYN.* PUZZLE

dumb show **1** [Historical] a part of a play done in pantomime **2** gestures without speech

dumb·struck (dum′struk′) ***adj.*** so shocked as to be speechless: also **dumb′strick′en** (-strik′ən)

dumb·wait·er (-wāt′ər) ***n.*** **1** a small, portable stand for serving food, often with shelves ☆**2** a small elevator for sending food, trash, etc. from one floor to another

☆**dum-dum** (dum′dum′) ***n.*** [Slang] a stupid person; dumbbell

dum·dum (bullet) (dum′dum′) ⟦after *Dumdum*, arsenal near Calcutta (now called Kolkata), India < Hindi *damdama*, hill, fortification⟧ a soft-nosed bullet that expands when it hits, inflicting a large, jagged wound

Dum·fries (dum frēs′) former county of S Scotland, on Solway Firth: now part of DUMFRIES AND GALLOWAY

Dumfries and Galloway administrative division of S Scotland

☆**dumm·kopf** (do͝om′kôpf′, -kôf′; dum′-) ***n.*** ⟦Ger⟧ [*also in italics*] [Informal] a stupid person; blockhead

dum·my (dum′ē) ***n.***, *pl.* **-mies** ⟦< DUMB + -Y[2]⟧ **1** [Old Slang] a person unable to talk; mute: an offensive term **2** a figure made in human form, as for displaying clothing, for practicing tackling in football, etc. **3** an imitation or sham; substitute for the real thing, as an empty container or false drawer **4** a person secretly acting for another while apparently representing his or her own interests **5** [Slang] a stupid person **6** *Bridge* *a)* the declarer's partner, whose hand is arranged face up on the table and played by the declarer *b)* such a hand **7** *Printing* *a)* a set of pages with the layout, as for a magazine *b)* a bound volume with blank pages, used as a model for a planned book —***adj.*** **1** imitation; sham; fictitious **2** secretly acting as a front for another [a *dummy* corporation] —***vi.*** **-mied**, **-my·ing** [Slang] *used only in the phrase* **dummy up**, to refuse to talk or tell what one knows

dump[1] (dump) ***vt.*** ⟦ME *dompen*, to plunge, throw down; prob. < ON base akin to Dan *dumpe*, Swed *dompa*: for IE base see DEEP⟧ **1** to throw down or out roughly; empty out or unload as in a heap or mass **2** *a)* to throw away (garbage, rubbish, etc.), esp. in a place set apart for the purpose *b)* to get rid of in an abrupt, rough, or careless manner *c)* [Informal] to end a romantic relationship with (someone) abruptly **3** to sell (a commodity) in a large quantity at a low price, esp. in a foreign market at a price below that of the domestic market ☆**4** *a)* to transfer (data in a computer memory) to another section of storage or to another storage medium *b)* to print out (data in a computer memory) ☆**5** *Football* to throw (a short pass) into the flat —***vi.*** **1** to fall in a heap or mass **2** to unload rubbish **3** to dump commodities ☆**4** [Slang] to defecate: somewhat vulgar —***n.*** **1** a rubbish pile ☆**2** a place for dumping rubbish, etc. ☆**3** a copy, esp. a printout, of data stored in a computer **4** *Mil.* a temporary storage center in the field, as for ammunition, food, or clothing ☆**5** [Slang] a bowel movement: somewhat vulgar: mainly in the phrase **take a dump** ☆**6** [Informal] a place that is unpleasant, ugly, run-down, etc. —☆**dump on** [Slang] to treat with contempt; demean

dump[2] (dump) ***n.*** ⟦prob. < Du *domp*, haze, dullness, akin to DAMP⟧ [Obs.] a sad tune or song —**(down) in the dumps** [Informal] in low spirits; depressed

dump·er (dum′pər) ***n.*** [Slang] a container into which refuse is dumped

dump·ling (dump′liŋ) ***n.*** ⟦< ?⟧ **1** a small piece of dough, steamed or boiled and served with meat or soup **2** a crust of dough filled with fruit and steamed or baked **3** [Informal] a short, fat person or animal

dump·site (dump′sīt′) ***n.*** a DUMP[1] (***n.*** 2), landfill, etc.

☆**dump·ster** (dump′stər) ***n.*** ⟦< *Dumpster*, a former trademark⟧ a large metal trash bin, often of a kind that is emptied, or transported to a dump, by a specially equipped truck

☆**dump truck** a truck with a back end that can be tilted backward to dump a load through the opened tailgate

dump·y (dum′pē) ***adj.*** **dump′i·er**, **dump′i·est** ⟦prob. < DUMP[1]⟧ **1** short and thick; squat; stumpy **2** [Informal] ugly, run-down, etc. —**dump′i·ly** ***adv.*** —**dump′i·ness** ***n.***

dumpy level a surveyor's level with a telescope fixed to a spirit level that rotates in a lateral plane

Dum·yat (do͝om′yät′) *Ar. name for* DAMIETTA

dun[1] (dun) ***adj.*** ⟦ME & OE, akin to OS, chestnut-brown, ult. (? via Celt) < IE **dhus-no* < base **dhus-*, dust-colored: see FURY⟧ dull grayish-brown —***n.*** **1** a dull grayish-brown color **2** a dun horse **3** an artificial fishing fly of this color **4** the mayfly in its stage just before final molting —**dun′ness** ***n.***

dun[2] (dun) ***vt., vi.*** **dunned**, **dun′ning** ⟦? dial. var. of DIN⟧ **1** to ask (a debtor) insistently or repeatedly for payment **2** to annoy constantly —***n.*** **1** a person who duns **2** an insistent demand, esp. for payment of a debt

Du·na (do͞o′nä) *Hung. name for the* DANUBE
Du·nai (do͞o′nī′) *Russ. name for the* DANUBE
Du·naj (do͞o′nī) *Czech name for the* DANUBE
du·nam (do͞on′əm) *n.* in Israel, a unit of land measure equal to 1,000 square meters (about ¼ acre)
☆**Dun & Brad·street** (dun′ən brad′strēt′) ⟦after R. G. *Dun* (1826-1900) & J. M. *Bradstreet* (1815-63), U.S. businessmen whose companies merged in 1933⟧ *service mark for* an agency furnishing subscribers with information as to the financial standing and credit rating of businesses
Du·nant (dü nän′), **Jean Hen·ri** (zhän än rē′) 1828-1910; Swiss philanthropist: founder of the Red Cross society
Du·nă·rea (do͞o′nər yä) *Romanian name for the* DANUBE
Du·nav (do͞o′näv′) *Bulg. name for the* DANUBE
Dun·bar (dun′bär) **1 Paul Laurence** 1872-1906; U.S. poet **2 William** 1460-1520; Scot. poet
Dun·bar·ton (dun bärt′′n) former county of W Scotland
Dun·can[1] (duŋk′ən) *n.* ⟦Gael *Donnchadh*, lit., brown warrior⟧ a masculine name
Dun·can[2] (duŋk′ən), **Isadora** 1878-1927; U.S. dancer
Duncan Phyfe designating or of furniture in a modified Empire and Directoire style designed by Duncan PHYFE
dunce (duns) *n.* ⟦after John DUNS SCOTUS: his followers, called *Dunsmen, Dunses, Dunces,* were regarded as foes of Renaissance humanism⟧ a slow-witted person
dunce cap [Historical] a cone-shaped hat that children slow at learning were forced to wear in school
Dun·dee (dun dē′) seaport in E Scotland, on the Firth of Tay
dun·der·head (dun′dər hed′) *n.* ⟦< Du *donder*, thunder, assoc. by rhyme with BLUNDER (see BLUNDERBUSS) + HEAD⟧ a stupid person; dunce —**dun′der·head′ed** *adj.*
dune (do͞on, dyo͞on) *n.* ⟦Fr < MDu: for IE base see DOWN[3]⟧ a rounded hill, ridge, or mound of windblown material, usually sand
☆**dune buggy** ⟦so called because orig. made for driving on sand dunes⟧ a small off-road vehicle made from a compact-automobile chassis, with an open fiberglass body and oversize tires
Dun·e·din (də nēd′′n) city on the SE coast of South Island, New Zealand
Dun·ferm·line (dən fʉrm′lin) city in E Scotland, on the Firth of Forth
dung (duŋ) *n.* ⟦ME & OE, prob. identical with *dung*, a prison, orig., cellar covered with dung for warmth, as in OS *dung*, OHG *tung*, cellar where women weave < IE base **dheng-*, to cover⟧ **1** animal excrement **2** filth —*vt.* to spread or cover with dung, as in fertilizing
dun·ga·ree (duŋ′gə rē′, duŋ′gə rē′) *n.* ⟦Hindi *dungrī*⟧ **1** a coarse cotton fabric; specif., blue denim **2** [*pl.*] work trousers or overalls made of this cloth
dung beetle any of various scarab beetles that breed in dung and feed on it
Dun·ge·ness crab (dun′jə nes′) ⟦after *Dungeness*, fishing village in NW Washington⟧ a large, edible crab (*Cancer magister*) of the NW coast of North America
dun·geon (dun′jən) *n.* ⟦ME *dongoun* < OFr *donjon*, prob. < Frank **dungjo*, earth-covered cellar for storing fruits: see DUNG⟧ **1** DONJON **2** a dark underground cell, vault, or prison —*vt.* [Rare] to confine in a dungeon
dung·hill (duŋ′hil′) *n.* **1** a heap of dung **2** anything vile or filthy
dung·y (duŋ′ē) *adj.* **dung′i·er, dung′i·est** of, like, or soiled with dung; filthy; vile
dun·ite (dun′īt′, do͞on′-) *n.* ⟦after Mt. *Dun*, in New Zealand + -ITE[1]⟧ a dense, intrusive igneous rock consisting largely of olivine
☆**dunk** (duŋk) *vt.* ⟦Ger *tunken*, to steep, dip, soak < OHG *dunchôn*: for IE base see TINGE⟧ **1** to dip (bread, cake, etc.) into coffee or other liquid before eating it **2** to immerse in a liquid for a short time **3** *Basketball* to put (the ball) into the basket by means of a dunk shot —*n.* **1** a dunking; immersion **2** DUNK SHOT
Dun·kerque (dën kerk′) *Fr. name for* DUNKIRK
☆**Dunk·ers** (duŋ′kərz) *pl.n. old or informal name for* CHURCH OF THE BRETHREN: also **Dunk′ards** (-kərdz)
Dun·kirk (dun′kʉrk′) seaport in N France, on the North Sea: scene of the evacuation of over 300,000 Allied troops under fire (1940) as France fell to Germany
☆**dunk shot** *Basketball* a shot in which the shooter leaps up and throws the ball down through the basket
dun·lin (dun′lin) *n., pl.* **-lins** or **-lin** ⟦< *dunling* < DUN[1] + -LING[1]⟧ a small sandpiper (*Calidris alpina*) with breeding plumage marked by a reddish back, a black patch on the belly, and a striped breast
dun·nage (dun′ij) *n.* ⟦ML *dennagium* < ?⟧ **1** a loose packing of any bulky material put around cargo for protection **2** personal baggage or belongings
☆**dun·nite** (dun′īt) *n.* ⟦after B. W. *Dunn* (1860-1936), U.S. army officer + -ITE[1]⟧ ammonium picrate, a high explosive, $C_6H_2(NO_2)_3ONH_4$, used esp. in armor-piercing shells because of its relative insensitivity to shock
dunno (də nō′) *v. phonetic sp. of* don't know (in informal pronunciation): usually used in the first person
Dun·si·nane (dun′sə nān′) hill in central Scotland: ruined fortress at its summit is the reputed site of Macbeth's defeat as related in Shakespeare's play
Duns Sco·tus (dunz skōt′əs), **John** or **Jo·han·nes** (yō hän′əs) 1265?-1308; Scot. scholastic philosopher and theologian
Duns·tan (dun′stən), Saint (A.D. 924?-988); Eng. prelate: archbishop of Canterbury (959-988): his day is May 19

du·o (do͞o′ō, dyo͞o′ō) *n., pl.* **du′os** ⟦It⟧ **1** the two performers of a DUET, or any two musicians playing together **2** a pair; couple
du·o- (do͞o′ō, -ə; dyo͞o′-) ⟦< L *duo*, TWO⟧ *combining form* two, double [*duologue*]
du·o·dec·i·mal (do͞o′ō des′ə məl, dyo͞o′-) *adj.* ⟦< L *duodecim*, twelve (< *duo*, TWO + *decem*, TEN) + -AL⟧ **1** relating to twelve or twelfths **2** consisting of or counting by twelves or powers of twelve —*n.* **1** one twelfth **2** [*pl.*] *Math.* a system of numeration with twelve as its base, rather than ten as in the decimal system
du·o·dec·i·mo (-mō′) *n., pl.* **-mos′** ⟦short for L *in duodecimo*, in twelve: see prec.⟧ **1** a page size (about 5 by 7½ in), ¹⁄₁₂ of a printer's sheet **2** a book with pages of this size Also called *twelvemo*, and written *12mo* or *12°* —*adj.* with pages of this size
du·o·de·nal (do͞o′ō dē′nəl, dyo͞o′-; do͞o äd′′n əl, dyo͞o-) *adj.* in or of the duodenum
du·o·de·num (do͞o′ō dē′nəm, dyo͞o′-; do͞o äd′′n əm, dyo͞o-) *n., pl.* **-de′na** (-nə) or **-de′nums** ⟦ME < ML < L *duodeni*, twelve each: its length is about twelve fingers' breadth⟧ the first section of the small intestine, between the stomach and the jejunum
du·o·logue (do͞o′ə lôg′, dyo͞o′-) *n.* ⟦DUO- + (MONO)LOGUE⟧ a conversation between two people, esp. in a dramatic performance
duo·mo (dwô′mô) *n., pl.* **-mi** (-mē) ⟦It: see DOME⟧ a cathedral
du·op·o·ly (do͞o äp′ə lē, dyo͞o-) *n.* ⟦DUO- + (MONO)POLY⟧ control of a commodity or service in a given market by only two producers or suppliers
du·o·tone (do͞o′ō tōn′, dyo͞o′-) *n. Printing* a halftone illustration made by using two negatives shot at slightly different angles so as to print in two tones of the same color or in two colors
dup *abbrev.* duplicate
dupe[1] (do͞op, dyo͞op) *n.* ⟦Fr < OFr *duppe*, cant alteration of L *upupa*, hoopoe, stupid bird⟧ a person easily tricked or fooled —*vt.* **duped, dup′ing** ⟦Fr *duper* < the n.⟧ to deceive by trickery; fool or cheat —*SYN.* CHEAT —**dup′a·ble** *adj.* —**dup′er** *n.*
dupe[2] (do͞op, dyo͞op) *n., vt.* **duped, dup′ing** *short for* DUPLICATE
dup·er·y (do͞op′ər ē, dyo͞op′-) *n., pl.* **-ies** a duping or being duped
du·ple (do͞o′pəl, dyo͞o′-) *adj.* ⟦L *duplus*: see DOUBLE⟧ **1** double; twofold **2** *Music* containing two (or a multiple of two) beats to the measure [*duple time*]
Du·ples·sis-Mor·nay (dü ple sē′môr nā′) *see* MORNAY, Philippe de
du·plex (do͞o′pleks′, dyo͞o′-) *adj.* ⟦L, consisting of two leaves, double < *duo*, TWO + *-plex*, -fold < *plicare*, to fold < IE base **plak-*, **plag-* > FLAG[2], Gr *plax*, surface, infl. by early assoc. with *duplus*, DOUBLE⟧ **1** double; twofold **2** designating or of a system of telegraphy in which two messages may be sent simultaneously in opposite directions over a single circuit **3** *Machinery* having two units operating in the same way or simultaneously —☆*n.* **1** DUPLEX HOUSE **2** DUPLEX APARTMENT —**du·plex′i·ty** *n.*
☆**duplex apartment** an apartment with rooms on two floors and a private inner staircase
☆**duplex house** a house consisting of two separate family units
du·pli·cate (do͞o′pli kit, dyo͞o′-; *for v.*, -kāt′) *adj.* ⟦ME *duplicaten* < L *duplicatus*, pp. of *duplicare*, to double: see DUPLEX⟧ **1** double **2** having two similar parts **3** corresponding exactly **4** designating a way of playing bridge in which, for comparative scoring, the same hands are played off again by players who did not hold them originally —*n.* **1** an exact copy or reproduction; replica; facsimile **2** a counterpart or double **3** the game of duplicate bridge ☆**4** TAX DUPLICATE —*vt.* **-cat′ed, -cat′ing** **1** to make double or twofold **2** to make an exact copy or copies of **3** to make, do, or cause to happen again —*SYN.* COPY —**in duplicate** in two identical copies —**du′pli·ca·ble** (-kə bəl) *adj.*, **du′pli·cat′a·ble**
duplicating machine a machine for making exact copies of a letter, photograph, drawing, etc.
du·pli·ca·tion (do͞o′pli kā′shən, dyo͞o′-) *n.* ⟦ME *duplicacioun* < L *duplicatio*⟧ **1** a duplicating or being duplicated **2** a copy; replica —**du′pli·ca′tive** *adj.*
du·pli·ca·tor (do͞o′pli kāt′ər, dyo͞o′-) *n.* ⟦LL, one that doubles < *duplicare*, DUPLICATE⟧ one that duplicates; specif., DUPLICATING MACHINE
du·plic·i·tous (do͞o plis′ə təs, dyo͞o-) *adj.* having duplicity; deceitful
du·plic·i·ty (do͞o plis′ə tē, dyo͞o-) *n., pl.* **-ties** ⟦ME *duplicite* < OFr *duplicité* < LL *duplicitas* < L *duplicare*: see DUPLEX⟧ hypocritical cunning or deception; double-dealing
du Pont (do͞o pänt′, dyo͞o-), **É(leuthère) I(rénée)** 1771-1834; Am. industrialist, born in France
du·ra (door′ə, dyoor′-) *n.* DURA MATER
du·ra·ble (door′ə bəl, dyoor′-) *adj.* ⟦ME & OFr < L *durabilis* < *durare*, to last, harden < IE **duros*, long < base **deu-*, to move forward (> TIRE[1]): meaning infl. in L by *durus*, hard: see DURESS⟧ **1** lasting in spite of hard wear or frequent use **2** continuing to exist; stable **3** designating a power of attorney that remains in effect after the person who authorized it becomes incompetent —*n.* [*pl.*] DURABLE GOODS —**du′ra·bil′i·ty** *n.* —**du′ra·bly** *adv.*
durable goods goods usable for a relatively long time, as machinery, automobiles, or household appliances
☆**du·ra·ble-press** (-pres′) *adj.* PERMANENT-PRESS
du·ral (door′əl, dyoor′-) *adj.* of the dura mater
du·ral·u·min (do͞o ral′yo͞o min, dyo͞o-) *n.* ⟦DUR(ABLE) + ALUMIN(UM)⟧ a strong, lightweight alloy of aluminum with copper, manganese, magnesium, and silicon
du·ra ma·ter (door′ə māt′ər, dyoor′-) ⟦ME < ML, lit., hard mother, transl.

of Ar term⟧ the outermost, toughest, and most fibrous of the three membranes covering the brain and spinal cord

du·ra·men (do͞o rā′mən, dyo͞o-) *n.* ⟦L, hardness < *durare*: see DURABLE⟧ HEARTWOOD

dur·ance (door′əns, dyoor′-) *n.* ⟦ME *duraunce* < OFr < L *durans*, prp. of *durare*, to last: see DURABLE⟧ [Archaic] imprisonment, esp. when long continued: mainly in **durance vile**

Du·ran·go (doo raŋ′gō, də-; *Sp* do͞o räŋ′gô) 1 state of NW Mexico: 46,196 sq mi (119,647 sq km) 2 its capital: in full **Vic·to·ri·a de Du·ran·go** (vēk tô′rē ä de do͞o räŋ′gô)

du·ra·tion (doo rā′shən, dyoo-) *n.* ⟦ME *duracioun* < ML *duratio* < pp. of L *durare*: see DURABLE⟧ 1 continuance in time 2 the time that a thing continues or lasts

Dur·ban (dur′bən) seaport in KwaZulu-Natal province, on the E coast of South Africa

dur·bar (dur′bär′) *n.* ⟦Hindi < *darbār* < Pers, a ruler's court < *dar*, portal (for IE base see DOOR) + *bār*, court⟧ [Historical] in India or Africa, an official reception or audience held by a native prince, or by a British ruler or governor

Dü·rer (dü′rər; *E* dyo͞or′ər), **Al·brecht** (äl′brеHt) 1471-1528; Ger. painter & wood engraver

du·ress (doo res′, dyoo-) *n.* ⟦ME *dures* < OFr *durece* < L *duritia*, hardness, harshness < *durus*, hard < IE base **deru-*, tree, oak (orig. ? hard) > TREE⟧ 1 imprisonment 2 the use of force or threats; compulsion [a confession signed under *duress*]

Dur·ga·pur (door′gə poor′) city in West Bengal, E India

Dur·ham[1] (dur′əm) *n.* ⟦see fol.: after the county, where orig. bred⟧ *former name for* SHORTHORN

Dur·ham[2] (dur′əm) 1 county in N England, on the North Sea: 938 sq mi (2,429 sq km) 2 its county seat, on the Wear 3 city in north central N.C.

du·ri·an or **du·ri·on** (do͞o′rē ən) *n.* ⟦Malay < *dūri*, thorn, prickle⟧ 1 the oval, spiny, edible fruit of an East Indian tree (*Durio zibethinus*) of the bombax family 2 the tree

dur·ing (door′iŋ, dyoor′-, dur′-) *prep.* ⟦ME *duringe*, prep., orig. prp. of *duren*, ENDURE⟧ 1 throughout the entire time of; all through [food was scarce *during* the war] 2 at some point in the entire time of; in the course of [he left *during* the lecture]

Durk·heim (dur′kem, durk′hīm), **Émile** 1858-1917; Fr. sociologist

dur·mast (dur′mast′) *n.* ⟦? for *dun mast oak*, dark-acorned oak: see DUN[1] & MAST[2]⟧ any of several European oaks valued for their heavy, tough wood

durn (durn) *vt., vi., n., adj., adv., interj. chiefly dial. var. of* DARN[2]

du·ro (do͞o′rō) *n., pl.* **-ros** ⟦Sp, for *peso duro*, lit., hard peso⟧ the silver peso, or dollar, of Spain and Spanish America

☆**Du·roc** (door′äk, dyoor′-) *n.* ⟦after *Duroc*, name of a famous 19th-c. stallion owned by a farmer who also had a herd of progenitor pigs⟧ any of a breed of large red or reddish-brown hog

dur·ra (door′ə) *n.* ⟦Ar *dhura*⟧ a variety of grain-producing sorghum (*Sorghum bicolor*) widely grown in Asia and Africa

Dur·rell (dur′əl, də rel′), **Lawrence (George)** 1912-90; Brit. writer

Dür·ren·matt (dür′ən mät′), **Frie·drich** (frē′driH) 1921-90; Swiss playwright & novelist

Dur·rës (door′əs) seaport in W Albania, on the Adriatic: as *Epidamnus*, an ancient Corinthian colony

dur·rie (dur′ē, dur′-) *n. alt. sp. of* DHURRIE

durst (durst) *vi., vt. now chiefly dial. pt. of* DARE

du·rum (door′əm, dyoor′-, dur′-) *n.* ⟦ModL < L, neut. of *durus*, hard: see DURESS⟧ a hard emmer wheat (*Triticum durum*) that yields flour and semolina used in macaroni, spaghetti, etc.

Du·se (do͞o′ze), **E·le·o·no·ra** (e′le ô nô′rä) 1859-1924; It. actress

Du·shan·be (do͞o shäm′bā, -shän′-) capital of Tajikistan, in the W part

dusk (dusk) *adj.* ⟦ME, by metathesis < OE *dox*, dark-colored: for IE base see DUN[1]⟧ [Old Poet.] dark in color; dusky; shadowy —*n.* 1 the time of evening when it is beginning to get dark; dim part of twilight 2 gloom; dusky quality — *vt., vi.* to make or become dusky or shadowy

dusk·y (dus′kē) *adj.* **dusk′i·er, dusk′i·est** 1 somewhat dark in color; esp., swarthy 2 lacking light; dim; shadowy 3 gloomy; melancholy —**dusk′i·ly** *adv.* —**dusk′i·ness** *n.*

SYN.—**dusky** suggests a darkness of color or an absence of light, verging on blackness [*dusky* twilight]; **swarthy** and **tawny** both refer only to color, **swarthy** suggesting a dark brown verging on black [a *swarthy* complexion] and **tawny**, a yellowish brown or tan [*tawny* hair] See also **dark**

Düs·sel·dorf (do͞os′əl dôrf′) city in W Germany, on the Rhine: capital of North Rhine-Westphalia

dust (dust) *n.* ⟦ME < OE, akin to MLowG: for IE base see DUN[1]⟧ 1 powdery earth or other matter in bits fine enough to be easily suspended in air 2 a cloud of such matter 3 confusion; turmoil 4 *a)* earth, esp. as the place of burial *b)* mortal remains disintegrated or thought of as disintegrating to earth or dust 5 a humble or abject condition 6 anything worthless 7 [Brit.] ashes, rubbish, etc. 8 pollen ☆9 GOLD DUST 10 [Archaic] a particle —*vt.* 1 to sprinkle with dust or a fine powdery substance [to *dust* crops with an insecticide] 2 to sprinkle (powder, etc.) on something 3 to rid of dust, as by brushing, shaking, or wiping: often with *off* 4 [Archaic] to make dusty —*vi.* 1 to remove dust, esp. from furniture, floors, etc. 2 to bathe in dust: said of a bird —**bite the dust** [Informal] 1 to die, esp. in battle 2 to stop existing or functioning; fail, break, etc. —**dust off** [Informal] to prepare to use —**leave in the dust** ⟦in ref. to the cloud of *dust* raised as by runners in a race⟧ [Informal] to surpass or outstrip readily —**lick the dust** to be servile; grovel: cf. Mic. 7:17 —**make the dust fly** 1 to act energetically 2 to move swiftly —**shake the dust off one's feet** to leave with disdain or contempt: cf. Matt. 10:14 —**throw dust in someone's eyes** to mislead or deceive someone

dust·bin (dust′bin′) *n.* [Brit.] a container for household rubbish

☆**dust bowl** any arid region characterized by the occurrence of frequent dust storms

☆**Dust Bowl** region in SC U.S., including parts of Okla. & Tex., where eroded topsoil was blown away by winds during a drought in the 1930s

☆**dust bunny** [Informal] any of the small, light balls of dust, hair, etc. that collect on unswept floors, as underneath furniture

dust devil a small whirlwind that raises dust in a narrow column

dust·er (dus′tər) *n.* 1 a person or thing that dusts 2 a brush or cloth for removing dust from furniture, etc. 3 a device for sprinkling on a powder, as for applying an insecticide ☆4 a lightweight coat worn to protect the clothes from dust, as formerly in open automobiles ☆5 a short, loose, lightweight housecoat

dust·heap (dust′hēp′) *n.* 1 a heap of refuse 2 the condition of being forgotten, unwanted, disregarded, etc.; oblivion or obscurity [his former fame consigned to the *dustheap*]

dusting powder any fine, light powder used as an insecticide, medicine, toiletry, etc., or used to prevent sticking

dust jacket 1 a detachable paper cover for a book to protect its binding and now usually designed to promote its contents 2 SLEEVE (*n.* 3)

dust·less (dust′lis) *adj.* having or causing no dust

dust·man (dust′mən) *n., pl.* **-men** (-mən) [Brit.] a man whose work is removing rubbish, ashes, garbage, etc.

dust·pan (dust′pan′) *n.* a pan like a small shovel, usually with a short handle, into which dirt or debris from the floor is swept

dust·proof (-pro͞of′) *adj.* keeping out dust

☆**dust ruffle** a ruffled skirt hung from under the mattress and extending to the floor around the sides of a bed as a decoration

☆**dust storm** a windstorm that sweeps up clouds of dust when passing over an arid region

dust-up (dust′up′) *n.* [Slang] a commotion, quarrel, or fight: also written **dustup**

dust wrapper DUST JACKET (sense 1)

dust·y (dus′tē) *adj.* **dust′i·er, dust′i·est** ⟦ME *dusti* < OE *dustig*⟧ 1 covered with dust; full of dust 2 like dust; powdery 3 muted with gray: said of a color [*dusty* pink] —**dust′i·ly** *adv.* —**dust′i·ness** *n.*

dusty miller any of various garden plants having foliage covered with white, woolly hairs

Dutch (duch) *adj.* ⟦ME *Duch* < MDu *Duutsch*, Dutch, German, akin to Ger *Deutsch*: see DEUTSCHLAND⟧ 1 of the Netherlands or its people, language, or culture ☆2 of the Pennsylvania Dutch or their language or culture —*n.* the West Germanic language spoken in the Netherlands —☆**go Dutch** [Informal] to have every participant pay his or her own expenses —☆**in Dutch** [Informal] in trouble or disfavor —**the Dutch** 1 the people of the Netherlands ☆2 the Pennsylvania Dutch

Dutch Antilles NETHERLANDS ANTILLES

Dutch auction an auction in which an initially high offering price is lowered by increments until a buyer or, as in U.S. Treasury sales of securities, sufficient buyers are found

Dutch Belted any of a breed of dairy cattle that are black with a white stripe around the body

☆**Dutch bob (*or* boy)** a style of haircut with bangs and a straight, even bob that covers the ears

Dutch Borneo the part of Borneo that belonged to the Netherlands: now Kalimantan, Indonesia

Dutch colonial [*also* **D- C-**] a colonial-style house having a gambrel roof, often with flared eaves that overhang porches along the structure's front and back: this style originated among early 17th-cent. Dutch settlers in the U.S.

Dutch courage [Slang] 1 courage resulting from the drinking of an alcoholic beverage 2 an alcoholic beverage

Dutch door a door with upper and lower halves that can be opened separately

Dutch East Indies NETHERLANDS (EAST) INDIES

☆**Dutch elm disease** ⟦from its first appearance in the Netherlands⟧ a virulent and widespread disease of elms caused by a fungus (*Ceratocystis ulmi*) that produces wilting and drying of the leaves and, ultimately, death of the tree

Dutch Guiana *former name for* SURINAME, when it was a dependent territory of the Netherlands (1667-1954)

Dutch·man (duch′mən) *n., pl.* **-men** (-mən) 1 a person born or living in the Netherlands; Hollander 2 a Dutch ship 3 [Obs.] a German

Dutch·man's-breech·es (duch′mənz brich′iz) *n., pl.* **-breech′es** ⟦so named from resemblance of the flower to a tiny pair of knickerbockers⟧ ☆a spring dicentra (*Dicentra cucullaria*) with pinkish, double-spurred flowers, found in E U.S.

Dutch·man's-pipe (-pīp′) *n.* ⟦so named from resemblance of the blossom to the curved bowl of an old-fashioned clay *pipe*⟧ any of several hardy, woody twining vines (genus *Aristolochia*) of the birthwort family having large, brownish or purple, U-shaped flowers with a pouchlike base

Dutch metal tombac, an alloy of copper and zinc
Dutch New Guinea NETHERLANDS NEW GUINEA
Dutch oven **1** a heavy metal or enamelware pot with a high, arched lid, for cooking pot roasts, etc. **2** a metal container for roasting meats, etc., with an open side placed so that it is toward the fire **3** a brick oven whose walls are preheated for cooking
Dutch Republic UNITED PROVINCES
☆**Dutch treat** [Informal] with each participant paying his or her own expenses: said of a date, social outing, etc.
Dutch uncle [Informal] a person who bluntly and sternly lectures or scolds someone, often with benevolent intent
du·te·ous (do͞ot′ē əs, dyo͞ot′-) ***adj.*** dutiful —**du′te·ous·ly** ***adv.***
du·ti·a·ble (do͞ot′ē ə bəl, dyo͞ot′-) ***adj.*** necessitating payment of a duty or tax: said as of imported goods
du·ti·ful (do͞ot′i fəl, dyo͞ot′-) ***adj.*** **1** showing, or resulting from, a sense of duty **2** having a proper sense of duty; obedient —**du′ti·ful·ly** ***adv.*** —**du′ti·ful·ness** ***n.***
du·ty (do͞ot′ē, dyo͞ot′ē) ***n.***, *pl.* **-ties** ⟦ME *duete* < Anglo-Fr *dueté*, what is due (owing): see DUE & -TY[1]⟧ **1** the obedience or respect that one should show toward one's parents, older people, etc. **2** conduct based on moral or legal obligation, or a sense of propriety [one's *duty* to vote] **3** any action, task, etc. required by or relating to one's occupation or position [the *duties* of a secretary] **4** a sense or feeling of obligation [*duty* calls] **5** service, esp. military service [overseas *duty*] **6** a payment due to the government, esp. a tax imposed on imports, exports, or manufactured goods **7** [Brit.] the performance of a machine as measured by the output of work per unit of fuel **8** the amount of work that a machine is meant to do; rated efficiency under specified conditions ☆**9** *Agric.* the amount of water needed for irrigation per acre per crop: also **duty of water** **10** *Mil., etc.* an assigned period of responsibility, as a watch or sentry duty: often used attributively [a *duty* sergeant] —***SYN.*** FUNCTION —**do duty for** to substitute for; serve as —**on (or off) duty** officially engaged (or not officially engaged) in one's duties
du·ty-free (-frē′) ***adj.*** designating or of goods on which no duty or tax must be paid, or a shop selling such goods —***adv.*** with no payment of a duty or tax required
du·um·vir (do͞o um′vir, dyo͞o-) ***n.***, *pl.* **-virs** or **-vi·ri′** (-vi rī′) ⟦L, back-form. < *duum virum*, gen. pl. of *duo viri*, two men < *duo*, TWO + *vir*, a man⟧ **1** either of two magistrates in ancient Rome who held office jointly **2** either member of any duumvirate
du·um·vi·rate (do͞o um′vi rit, dyo͞o-) ***n.*** ⟦L *duumviratus*: see prec. & -ATE[2]⟧ **1** governmental position or authority held jointly by two persons **2** two such persons
du·vet (do͞o vā′, dyo͞o-) ***n.*** a style of comforter, often filled with down, having a slipcover and used in place of a top sheet and blankets
du·ve·tyn or **du·ve·tyne** (do͞o′və tēn′, dyo͞o′-) ***n.*** ⟦Fr *duvetine* < *duvet*, eiderdown < MFr, altered < *dumet* < OFr *dum, dun*, altered (? after *plume*) < ON *dunn*, DOWN[2]⟧ a soft textile with a short, velvety nap, originally made of cotton with a spun-silk filling
dux·elles (do͝ok sel′) ***n.*** ⟦after the Marquis *d'Uxelles* (1652-1730), Fr nobleman⟧ a seasoned mixture of finely chopped mushrooms and shallots, sautéed and used as a garnish or in stuffing, sauce, etc.: also **dux·elle** (do͝ok sel′)
DV *abbrev.* **1** Daily Value: an updated and modified version of the Recommended Daily Allowance, developed by the FDA and placed on the labels of foods, vitamins, etc.: see RDA **2** Douay Version (of the Bible) **3** ⟦L *Deo volente*⟧ God willing **4** digital video
DVD (dē′vē′dē′) ***n.***, *pl.* **DVDs** ⟦< *d(igital) v(ideo) d(isc)* or *d(igital) v(ersatile) d(isc)*⟧ a digital disk on which images, sounds, or data may be recorded for reproduction by a player connected as to a TV, stereo, or computer; specif., such a disk on which a film is commercially recorded
Dvi·na (dvē nä′) **1** river in NW Russia, flowing northwest into Dvina Bay near Arkhangelsk: 460 mi (740 km): often called **Northern Dvina** **2** river in W Russia, flowing from the Valdai Hills northwest through Belarus & Latvia into the Gulf of Riga: 635 mi (1,022 km): Latvian name *Daugava*: often called **Western Dvina**
Dvina Bay arm of the White Sea, in NW Russia: *c.* 65 mi (105 km) long
Dvinsk (dvēnsk) *Russ. name for* DAUGAVPILS
DVM or **D.V.M.** *abbrev.* Doctor of Veterinary Medicine
Dvo·řák (dvôr′zhäk, -zhak; vôr′-), **An·to·nín** (än′tô nin) 1841-1904; Czech composer
DVR (dē′vē′är′) ***n.*** DIGITAL VIDEO RECORDER
dwarf (dwôrf) ***n.***, *pl.* **dwarfs** or **dwarves** (dwôrvz) ⟦ME *dwerf, dwergh* < OE *dweorg*, akin to Ger *zwerg* < IE **dhwergh-*, prob. < base **dhwer-*, to trick, injure > Sans *dhvarati*, (he) injures⟧ **1** any human being, animal, or plant that is much smaller than the usual one of its species **2** *Folklore* a little being in human form, usually ugly or malformed, to whom magic powers are attributed **3** a star of relatively small size or mass and low luminosity: see also WHITE DWARF, BLACK DWARF —***vt.*** **1** to keep from growing to full natural size **2** to make small or insignificant **3** to make seem small by comparison —***vi.*** to become stunted or dwarfed —***adj.*** **1** much smaller than the usual one of its kind **2** undersized; stunted —**dwarf′ish** ***adj.*** —**dwarf′ish·ness** ***n.*** —**dwarf′ism′** ***n.***

SYN.—**dwarf** refers to any individual that is considerably smaller than the average for the species and sometimes implies malformation or disproportion of parts; **midget**, now regarded as somewhat offensive or insulting, refers to a proportionate but diminutive human being; **Pygmy** strictly refers to a member of any of several small-sized African or Asian peoples, but it is sometimes used (written **pygmy**) as a synonym for **dwarf** or **midget**. The term **little person** (pl., **little people**) has been gaining in currency

☆**dwarf chestnut** **1** a chinquapin (*Castanea pumila*) native to SE U.S. **2** its edible nut
dwarf planet a solid body, approximately spherical but typically smaller than a conventional planet, that orbits a star: its general orbital area may be shared by other bodies of significant size
Dwayne (dwān) ***n.*** a masculine name
dweeb (dwēb) ***n.*** ⟦< ?⟧ [Slang] a person regarded as socially dull, unsophisticated, foolish, awkward, etc. —**dweeb′ish** ***adj.*** —**dweeb′y** ***adj.***
dwell (dwel) ***vi.*** **dwelt** or **dwelled**, **dwell′ing** ⟦ME *dwellen* < OE *dwellan*, to lead astray, hinder, akin to ON *dvelja*, to delay < IE **dh(e)wel-*, to obscure, make DULL⟧ to make one's home; reside; live —**dwell on (or upon)** to linger over in thought or speech; think about or discuss at length —**dwell′er** ***n.***
dwell·ing (dwel′iŋ) ***n.*** ⟦ME: see prec.⟧ a place to live in; residence; house; abode: also **dwelling place**
DWI (dē′dub′əl yo͞o′ī′) ***n.*** ⟦*d(riving) w(hile) i(ntoxicated)*⟧ a traffic citation issued to a person accused of driving while intoxicated
Dwight (dwīt) ***n.*** ⟦orig. a surname < ?⟧ a masculine name
dwin·dle (dwin′dəl) ***vi., vt.*** **-dled**, **-dling** ⟦freq. of obs. *dwine*, to languish, fade < ME *dwinen* < OE *dwīnan*, akin to ON *dvína* < IE base **dheu-*: see DIE[1]⟧ to keep on becoming or making smaller or less; diminish; shrink —***SYN.*** DECREASE
dwt *abbrev.* ⟦*d(enarius) w(eigh)t*⟧ pennyweight, pennyweights
Dx *symbol* **1** diagnosis **2** diagnostic
DX *abbrev. Radio* **1** distance **2** distant
Dy *Chem. symbol for* dysprosium
dy·ad (dī′ad′) ***n.*** ⟦LL *dyas* (gen. *dyadis*) < Gr *dyo*, TWO⟧ **1** two units regarded as one; pair **2** *Biol.* a double chromosome resulting from the division of a tetrad in meiosis; half of a tetrad **3** *Chem.* an atom, element, or radical with a valence of two ☆**4** *Sociology* two persons in a continuing relationship involving interaction —***adj.*** consisting of two —**dy·ad′ic** ***adj.***
Dy·ak (dī′ak′) ***n.*** ⟦Malay *dayak*, savage⟧ **1** a member of any of a number of aboriginal peoples living in the interior of Borneo **2** the Austronesian language of these peoples
dy·ar·chy (dī′är′kē) ***n.***, *pl.* **-chies** ⟦< Gr *dyo*, two + -ARCHY⟧ government shared by two rulers, powers, etc.
dyb·buk (dib′ək) ***n.*** ⟦Heb *dibbūq* < *dābhaq*, to cleave, hold to⟧ *Jewish Folklore* the spirit of a dead person that enters the body of a living person and possesses it
dye (dī) ***n.*** ⟦ME *deie* < OE *deag*, akin to OHG *tougal*, dark, secret < IE **dhwek-*, dark color, secret < base **dheu-*: see DULL⟧ **1** color produced in a substance by saturating it with a coloring agent; tint; hue **2** any substance used to give color to fabric, hair, etc.; coloring matter or a solution containing it —***vt.*** **dyed**, **dye′ing** ⟦ME *deien* < OE *deagian*⟧ to color with or as with a dye —***vi.*** to take on color in dyeing —**of (the) deepest dye** of the most marked, esp. the worst, sort —**dy′er** ***n.***
dyed-in-the-wool (dīd′in *th*ə wo͝ol′) ***adj.*** **1** dyed before being woven ☆**2** thoroughgoing or unchanging
dye·ing (dī′iŋ) ***vt., vi.*** *prp. of* DYE —***n.*** the process or work of coloring fabrics with dyes
dy·er's-weed (-wēd′) ***n.*** any of a number of plants that yield a dyestuff, as woadwaxen
dye·stuff (dī′stuf′) ***n.*** any substance constituting or yielding a dye
dye·wood (-wo͝od′) ***n.*** any wood yielding a dye
Dy·fed (div′əd) county of SW Wales, on the Bristol & St. George's channels: 2,226 sq mi (5,765 sq km)
dy·ing (dī′iŋ) ***vi.*** *prp. of* DIE[1] —***adj.*** **1** coming near to an end [a *dying* culture] **2** of or at the time of death [his *dying* words] —***n.*** a ceasing to live or exist; death
dyke[1] (dīk) ***n., vt.*** *alt. sp. of* DIKE[1]
dyke[2] (dīk) ***n.*** ⟦contr. < *morphodyke, morphodite*, altered < HERMAPHRODITE⟧ [Slang] a lesbian, esp. one with physical characteristics traditionally thought of as belonging to men: usually a term of contempt and hostility —**dyk′ey** ***adj.***
Dy·lan (dil′ən), **Bob** (born *Robert Allen Zimmerman*) 1941- ; U.S. folk-rock singer & composer
dyn *abbrev.* dyne(s)
dy·na- (dī′nə) ⟦< Gr *dynamis*, power: see DYNAMIC⟧ *combining form* power [*dynameter*]: also, before a vowel, **dyn-**
dy·nam- (dī nam′) *combining form* DYNAMO-: used before a vowel
dy·nam·e·ter (dī nam′ət ər) ***n.*** ⟦DYNA- + -METER⟧ an instrument for finding the magnifying power of a telescope
dy·nam·ic (dī nam′ik) ***adj.*** ⟦Fr *dynamique* < Gr *dynamikos* < *dynamis*, power, strength < *dynasthai*, to be able or strong⟧ **1** relating to an object, or objects, in motion: opposed to STATIC **2** energetic; vigorous; forceful **3** relating to or tending toward change or productive activity **4** *Comput.* *a)* designating or of an event that occurs during the execution of a program [*dynamic* dump] *b)* designating or of memory that requires periodic renewal of its stored data **5** *Electronics* designating or of a speaker, microphone, etc. in which a diaphragm or cone is attached to a coil that vibrates within a fixed magnetic field Also **dy·nam′i·cal** —***n.*** DYNAMICS (sense 2*a*) —**dy·nam′i·cal·ly** ***adv.***

dy·nam·ics (dī nam′iks) ***n.*** ⟦formed < prec., as in names of other sciences and areas of study: see -ICS⟧ [*with pl. v. for 2a & b*] **1** the branch of mechanics dealing with the motions of material bodies under the action of given forces; kinetics **2** *a)* the various forces, physical, oral, economic, etc., operating in any field *b)* the way such forces shift or change in relation to one another *c)* the study of such forces **3** the effect of varying degrees of loudness or softness in the performance of music

dy·na·mism (dī′nə miz′əm) ***n.*** ⟦DYNAM(O)- + -ISM⟧ **1** the theory that force or energy, rather than mass or motion, is the basic principle of all phenomena **2** the quality of being energetic, vigorous, etc. —**dy′na·mis′tic** (-mis′tik) ***adj.***

dy·na·mite (dī′nə mīt′) ***n.*** ⟦coined (1866 or 1867) by Alfred Bernhard NOBEL < Gr *dynamis*: see DYNAMIC⟧ **1** a powerful explosive made by soaking nitroglycerin into some absorbent, such as ammonium nitrate and wood pulp **2** [Informal] anything potentially dangerous —***vt.*** **-mit′ed, -mit′ing** to blow up or destroy with dynamite —☆***adj.*** [Slang] outstanding; very exciting, effective, etc. —**dy′na·mit′er *n.***

dy·na·mo (dī′nə mō′) ***n.**, pl.* **-mos′** ⟦< *dynamoelectric machine*⟧ **1** *former term for* GENERATOR (sense 1*b*) **2** a forceful, dynamic person

dy·na·mo- (dī′nə mō′) ⟦< Gr *dynamis*: see DYNAMIC⟧ *combining form* power [*dynamometer*]

dy·na·mo·e·lec·tric (dī′nə mō′i lek′trik) ***adj.*** having to do with the production of electrical energy from mechanical energy, or vice versa: also **dy′na·mo′e·lec′tri·cal**

dy·na·mom·e·ter (dī′nə mäm′ət ər) ***n.*** ⟦Fr *dynamomètre*: see DYNAMO- & -METER⟧ an apparatus for measuring force or power, esp. one for measuring mechanical power, as of an engine

dy·na·mom·e·try (dī′nə mäm′ə trē) ***n.*** ⟦DYNAMO- + -METRY⟧ the process of measuring forces at work —**dy′na·mo′met′ric** (-mō′me′trik) ***adj.***

dy·na·mo·tor (dī′nə mōt′ər) ***n.*** an electrical machine combining generator and motor within one housing, usually used to convert direct current to alternating current

dy·nast (dī′nast′, -nəst) ***n.*** ⟦L *dynastes* < Gr *dynastēs* < *dynasthai*: see DYNAMIC⟧ a ruler, esp. a hereditary ruler

dy·nas·ty (dī′nəs tē) ***n.**, pl.* **-ties** ⟦ME *dinastie* < ML *dynastia* < Gr *dynasteia*, lordship, rule < *dynastēs*: see prec.⟧ **1** a succession of rulers who are members of the same family **2** the period during which a certain family reigns —**dy·nas·tic** (dī nas′tik) ***adj.***, **dy·nas′ti·cal** —**dy·nas′ti·cal·ly *adv.***

dy·na·tron (dī′nə trän′) ***n.*** ⟦DYNA- + (ELEC)TRON⟧ an electron tube, usually a tetrode, that produces an oscillating current at certain frequencies

dyne (dīn) ***n.*** ⟦Fr < Gr *dynamis*, power⟧ the basic unit of force in the CGS system, equal to the amount of force that imparts to a mass of one gram an acceleration of one centimeter per second per second (0.00001 newton): abbrev. *dyn*

☆**dy·nel** (dī nel′) ***n.*** **1** a synthetic fiber made from vinyl chloride and acrylonitrile **2** a hairlike yarn or fabric made from this fiber

dy·node (dī′nōd′) ***n.*** ⟦< Gr *dyn(amis)*, power (see DYNAMIC) + -ODE[1]⟧ an electrode in a photomultiplier electron tube designed so that each impinging electron causes the emission of two or more secondary electrons

dy·nor·phin (dī nôr′fin) ***n.*** ⟦DYN(A)- + (M)ORPHIN(E)⟧ any of a group of brain peptides that are powerful pain relievers: though similar to endorphins, they differ in derivation, effectiveness, etc.

dys- (dis) ⟦Gr, bad, hard, unlucky < IE base *dus-, bad, ill > Goth *tuz-*, OHG *zur-* (Ger *zer-*), Sans *duṣ-*⟧ *prefix* bad, ill, abnormal, impaired, difficult, etc. [*dysfunction*]

dys·cal·cu·li·a (dis′kal kyo͞o′lē ə) ***n.*** ⟦ModL < prec. + *calculare*, to reckon + -IA⟧ impairment of the ability to do arithmetic calculations, often as the result of genetic defect or brain injury

dys·cra·si·a (dis krā′zhə, -zhē ə, -zē ə) ***n.*** ⟦ModL < ML, distemper, disease < Gr *dyskrasia*, bad temperament < *dys-*, DYS- + *krasis*, a mixing < *kerannynai*, to mix: see IDIOSYNCRASY⟧ an abnormal imbalance in some part of the body, esp. in the blood

dys·en·ter·y (dis′ən ter′ē) ***n.*** ⟦ME *dissenterie* < OFr < L *dysenteria* < Gr < *dys-*, DYS- + *enteron*, pl. *entera*, bowels: see INTER-⟧ any of various intestinal inflammations characterized by abdominal pain and frequent and intense diarrhea with bloody, mucous feces —**dys′en·ter′ic *adj.***

dys·func·tion (dis fuŋk′shən) ***n.*** abnormal, impaired, or incomplete functioning, as of a bodily organ or part

dys·func·tion·al (-shə nəl) ***adj.*** **1** unable to function normally, properly, etc. **2** of or characterized by abnormal or impaired psychosocial functioning [*a dysfunctional* family, *dysfunctional* behavior]

dys·gen·ic (dis jen′ik) ***adj.*** causing deterioration of hereditary qualities of a stock: cf. EUGENIC

dys·gen·ics (dis jen′iks) ***n.*** the study of dysgenic trends in a population

dys·graph·i·a (dis graf′ē ə) ***n.*** ⟦< DYS- + Gr *graphia*, writing < *graphein*: see GRAPHIC⟧ impairment of the ability to write, as a result of brain dysfunction

dys·ki·ne·sia (dis′kə nē′zhə) ***n.*** ⟦< DYS- + Gr *kinēsis*, motion + -IA⟧ impairment of bodily movements: cf. TARDIVE DYSKINESIA

dys·lex·i·a (dis lek′sē ə) ***n.*** ⟦ModL < DYS- + Gr *lexis*, speech < *legein*, to speak: see LOGIC⟧ impairment of the ability to read, often as the result of genetic defect or brain injury —**dys·lex′ic** (-lek′sik) ***adj.**, **n.***, **dys·lec′tic** (-lek′tik)

dys·lo·gis·tic (dis′lō jis′tik) ***adj.*** ⟦DYS- + (EU)LOGISTIC⟧ [Rare] disapproving; opprobrious: opposed to EULOGISTIC

dys·men·or·rhe·a (dis′men ə rē′ə) ***n.*** ⟦ModL < DYS- + Gr *mēn*, MONTH + -RRHEA⟧ painful or difficult menstruation

dys·pa·reu·ni·a (dis′pə ro͞o′nē ə) ***n.*** ⟦ModL < DYS- + Gr *pareunos*, lying beside < *para*, beside (see PARA-[1]) + *eunē*, bed⟧ sexual intercourse that is physically painful or difficult

dys·pep·si·a (dis pep′sē ə; *also*, -shə) ***n.*** ⟦L < Gr *dyspepsia* < *dys-*, DYS- + *pepsis*, cooking, digestion < *peptein*, to soften, COOK⟧ impaired digestion; indigestion: cf. EUPEPSIA: also [Dial.] **dys·pep′sy** (-sē)

dys·pep·tic (dis pep′tik) ***adj.*** ⟦< Gr *dyspeptos* (see prec.) + -IC⟧ **1** of, causing, or having dyspepsia **2** morose; grouchy —***n.*** a person who suffers from dyspepsia —**dys·pep′ti·cal·ly *adv.***

dys·pha·gi·a (dis fā′jə, -jē ə) ***n.*** ⟦ModL < DYS- + Gr *phag(ein)*, to eat + -IA⟧ *Med.* difficulty in swallowing —**dys·phag′ic** (-faj′ik) ***adj.***

dys·pha·si·a (dis fā′zhə, -zhē ə, -zē ə) ***n.*** ⟦ModL < DYS- + -PHASIA⟧ impairment of the ability to speak or, sometimes, to understand language, as the result of brain injury, a brain tumor, etc. —**dys·pha′sic** (-fā′zik) ***adj.**, **n.***

dys·phe·mism (dis′fə miz′əm) ***n.*** ⟦DYS- + (EU)PHEMISM⟧ **1** the use of a word or phrase that is considered more distasteful, more offensive, etc. than another **2** a word or phrase so substituted (Ex.: *stiff* for *corpse*) —**dys′phe·mis′tic *adj.***

dys·pho·ni·a (dis fō′nē ə) ***n.*** ⟦ModL < Gr *dysphōnia* < *dys-*, DYS- + *phōnē*, voice: see PHONO-⟧ impairment of the ability to produce speech sounds, as because of hoarseness —**dys·phon′ic** (-fän′ik) ***adj.***

dys·pho·ri·a (dis fôr′ē ə) ***n.*** ⟦ModL < Gr *dysphoria* < *dys-*, DYS- + *pherein*, to BEAR[1]⟧ *Psychol.* a generalized feeling of ill-being; esp., an abnormal feeling of anxiety, discontent, physical discomfort, etc. —**dys·phor′ic** (-fôr′ik) ***adj.***

dys·pla·si·a (dis plā′zhə, -zhē ə, -zē ə) ***n.*** ⟦ModL: see DYS- & -PLASIA⟧ a disordered growth or faulty development of various tissues or body parts —**dys·plas′tic** (-plas′tik) ***adj.***

dysp·ne·a (disp nē′ə) ***n.*** ⟦L *dispnoea* < Gr *dyspnoia* < *dys-*, DYS- + *pnoē*, breathing < *pnein*, to breathe: see PNEUMA⟧ shortness of breath: see APNEA —**dysp·ne′al *adj.***, **dysp·ne′ic**

dys·prax·i·a (dis prak′sē ə) ***n.*** ⟦ModL < Gr, lack of success: see DIS- & PRAXIS⟧ *Med.* partial inability to perform certain coordinated actions, often, specif., as associated with speech —**dys·prax′ic** (-prak′sik) ***adj.***

dys·pro·si·um (dis prō′zē əm, -sē-) ***n.*** ⟦ModL < Gr *dysprositos*, difficult of access < *dys-*, DYS- + *prositos*, approachable < *prosienai*, come to < *pros*, toward + *ienai*, to go (see ION): so named (1886) by its discoverer, Fr chemist P.-E. Lecoq de Boisbaudran (1838-1912)⟧ a silver-white chemical element, one of the rare-earth elements, with a great capacity to absorb neutrons and with strong magnetic properties, esp. at very low temperatures: symbol, Dy; at. no. 66: see the periodic table of elements in the Reference Supplement

dys·rhyth·mi·a (dis rith′mē ə) ***n.*** a lack of rhythm, as of the brain waves or in speech patterns

dys·thy·mi·a (dis thī′mē ə) ***n.*** ⟦ModL < Gr, despondency, ult. < *dys-*, DYS- + *thymos*, spirit, mind: see THYMINE⟧ a mild, chronic form of mental depression: also **dysthymic disorder** —**dys·thy′mic *adj.**, **n.***

dys·to·ni·a (dis tō′ne ə) ***n.*** a lack of normal muscle tone due to disease or infection of the nervous system —**dys·ton·ic** (-tän′ik) ***adj.***

dys·to·pi·a (dis tō′pē ə) ***n.*** ⟦DYS- + (U)TOPIA⟧ ☆**1** a hypothetical place, society, or situation in which conditions and the quality of life are dreadful **2** a novel or other work depicting a dystopian society or place Cf. UTOPIA —**dys·to′pi·an *adj.***, **dys·to′pic**

dys·troph·ic (dis träf′ik, -trō′fik) ***adj.*** **1** of or caused by dystrophy **2** of a lake or pond derived from a bog and characterized by brown, humic matter, high acidity, and poorly developed fauna and flora

dys·tro·phin (dis trō′fin) ***n.*** ⟦< fol. + -IN[1]⟧ a protein normally found in muscle tissue: its absence or deficiency has been linked to muscular dystrophy

dys·tro·phy (dis′trə fē) ***n.*** ⟦ModL *dystrophia* < Gr: see DYS- & -TROPHY⟧ **1** faulty nutrition **2** faulty development, or degeneration: cf. MUSCULAR DYSTROPHY

dys·u·ri·a (dis yoor′ē ə) ***n.*** ⟦LL < Gr *dysouria*: see DYS- & -URIA⟧ difficult or painful urination

dz *abbrev.* dozen(s)

Dzer·zhinsk (dzir zhinsk′) city in central European Russia, near Gorki

Dzham·bul (jäm bo͞ol′) city in SE Kazakhstan

Dzun·ga·ri·a (zoon ger′ē ə) *former name for* JUNGGAR PENDI

e[1] or E (ē) *n., pl.* **e's, E's 1** the fifth letter of the English alphabet: from the Greek *epsilon*, a borrowing from the Phoenician **2** any of the speech sounds that this letter represents, as, in English, the vowel (e) of *bed* or (ē) of *equal*, or, when unstressed, (ə) as in *father* **3** a type or impression for *e* or E **4** the fifth in a sequence or group **5** an object shaped like E —*adj.* **1** of *e* or E **2** fifth in a sequence or group **3** shaped like E

e[2] (ē) *n. Math.* the number used as the base of the system of natural logarithms, approximately 2.71828

e[3] *abbrev. Physics* electron

E[1] (ē) *n.* **1** *Educ. a)* a grade indicating below-average work, often equivalent to *condition b)* sometimes, a grade indicating excellence **2** *Music a)* the third tone or note in the ascending scale of C major *b)* a key, string, etc. producing this tone *c)* the scale having this tone as the keynote

E[2] *abbrev.* **1** Earl **2** earth **3** east **4** eastern **5** [Slang] Ecstasy (the drug) **6** empty **7** *Football* end **8** England **9** English **10** *Baseball* error(s) **11** exa- **12** excellent **13** *Physics a)* energy (see MATTER, *n.* 2) *b)* the modulus of elasticity *c)* electromotive force or voltage Also, for 2-4, 6-7, 10, 12, & 13*a*, **e**

e-[1] (ē) *prefix* EX-[1]: used before *b, d, g, j, l, m, n, r,* or *v [eject, emit]*

e-[2] (ē) ⟦E(LECTRONIC)⟧ *prefix* done, made, purchased, etc. electronically, specif. over the internet *[e-banking, airline e-tickets]*

ea *abbrev.* each

each (ēch) *adj., pron.* ⟦ME *ech, elc*, each, every < OE *ælc* < **agilic*, akin to OHG *iogilith* (Ger *jeglich*) < PGmc **aiw-galic*: see AYE[1] & ALIKE⟧ every one of two or more considered separately *[each (one) of you will be notified]* —*adv.* apiece *[give them two apples each]* —**each other 1** each one the other *[my partner and I assist each other]* **2** each one the others; one another *[members of the platoon look out for each other]* ➥Some speakers use *each other* only of two individuals and *one another* only of more than two, but in common usage no distinction is made

Eads (ēdz), **James Buchanan** 1820-87; U.S. engineer: noted for bridge construction & river control

ea·ger[1] (ē′gər) *adj.* ⟦ME *egre* < OFr *aigre* < L *acer*, sharp, acute, ardent, eager: see ACID⟧ **1** feeling or showing keen desire; impatient or anxious to do or get; ardent **2** [Archaic] sharp; keen —**ea′ger·ly** *adv.* —**ea′ger·ness** *n.*

SYN.—**eager** implies great enthusiasm, zeal, or sometimes impatience, in the desire for a pursuit of something *[eager to begin work]*; **avid** suggests an intense, sometimes greedy, desire to enjoy or possess something *[avid for power]*; **keen** implies deep interest and a spirited readiness to achieve something *[the team was keen on winning]*; **anxious**, in this connection, suggests eagerness, but with some uneasiness over the outcome *[anxious to excel]*

ea·ger[2] (ē′gər, ā′-) *n.* [Brit.] *alt. sp. of* EAGRE

☆**eager beaver** [Slang] a person characterized by much, or too much, industry, initiative, or enthusiasm

ea·gle (ē′gəl) *n.* ⟦ME *egle* < OFr *aigle* < L *aquila*, eagle⟧ **1** any of a number of large, strong, flesh-eating accipitrine birds of prey noted for their sharp vision and powerful wings, as the bald eagle **2** a representation of the eagle, used as a symbol or emblem of a nation, etc.; esp., *a)* the military standard of the Roman Empire ☆*b)* the national emblem of the U.S. ☆*c)* the military insigne of a colonel in the U.S. armed forces (captain in the U.S. Navy) ☆**3** ⟦so named from the image of an *eagle* inscribed on the obverse⟧ a former U.S. gold coin worth $10 ☆**4** *Golf* a score of two under par on any hole —*vt.* **eagled, eagling** *Golf* to score an eagle on (a given hole)

ea·gle-eyed (-īd′) *adj.* having keen vision

eagle ray any of a family (Myliobatidae, order Myliobatiformes) of sharp-headed rays with flat teeth and a notched spine on the tail

☆**Eagle Scout 1** the highest rank attainable in the Boy Scouts **2** a Scout having this rank

ea·glet (ē′glit) *n.* ⟦Fr *aiglette*, dim. of *aigle*⟧ a young eagle

ea·gle·wood (e′gəl wood′) *n.* LIGNALOES

ea·gre (ē′gər, ā′-) *n.* ⟦Brit dial. form, prob. ult. < OE *eagor*, flood, high tide, akin to ON *ægir*, ocean < IE **ēkw-*, var. of base **akwa-*, water > L *aqua*⟧ [Brit.] a high tidal wave in an estuary; bore

Ea·kins (ā′kinz), **Thomas** 1844-1916; U.S. painter & sculptor

eal·dor·man (ôl′dər mən, äl′-) *n. Anglo-Saxon History* the chief officer in a shire; alderman

Ea·ling (ē′liŋ) borough of Greater London, England

☆**Eames chair** (ēmz) ⟦< *Eames*, a trademark for such a chair; after C. *Eames* (1907-78) & R. *Eames* (1912-88), its U.S. designers⟧ any of a variety of plywood, plastic, metal, or upholstered chairs contoured to fit the body

-e·an (ē′ən) ⟦< L *-ae-, -e-, -i-* & Gr *-ai-, -ei-* (stem endings of nouns and adjectives) + -AN⟧ *suffix* of, belonging to, like *[European, Aegean]*

E & OE *abbrev.* errors and omissions excepted

ear[1] (ir) *n.* ⟦ME *ere* < OE *ēare* akin to Goth *ausō*, Ger *ohr* < IE base **ous-*, ear > L *auris*, Gr *ous*, OIr *au*⟧ **1** the part of the body specialized for the perception of sound; organ of hearing: the human ear consists of the external ear, the middle ear (tympanum), and the inner ear (labyrinth), which also senses one's state of equilibrium **2** the visible, external part of the ear **3** anything shaped or placed like an ear, as the handle of a pitcher or a small box in the upper corner of a newspaper page **4** the sense of hearing **5** the ability to recognize slight differences in sound, esp. in the pitch, rhythm, etc. of musical tones **6** the ability to perceive or make distinctions; discrimination or taste *[a good ear for a well-written poem]* —**be all ears** [Informal] to be listening attentively or eagerly —☆**bend someone's ear** [Slang] to talk excessively to someone —**fall on deaf ears** to be ignored or unheeded —**give (or lend) ear** to give attention, esp. favorable attention; listen; heed —☆**have (or keep) an ear to the ground** to give careful attention to the trends of public opinion —**have the ear of** to be in a favorable position to talk to and influence; be heeded by —**in one ear and out the other** heard but without effect —**play by ear** to play (a musical instrument or piece) without the use of notation, improvising an arrangement —**play it by ear** [Informal] to act as the situation demands, without a preconceived plan; improvise —**set on its ear** [Informal] to cause excitement, upheaval, etc. in —**turn a deaf ear** to be unwilling to listen or heed

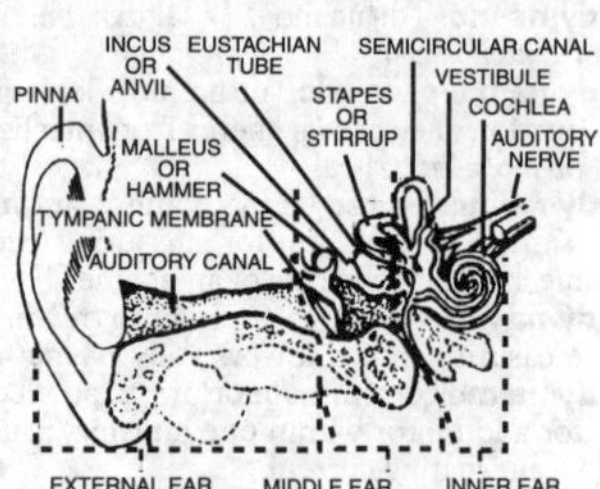

human ear

ear[2] (ir) *n.* ⟦ME *er* < OE *ēar*, akin to Ger *ähre*, Goth *ahs* < IE **aces* (< base **ak-*, sharp) > L *acus*, chaff⟧ the grain-bearing spike of a cereal plant, esp. of corn —*vi.* to sprout ears; form ears

ear·ache (ir′āk′) *n.* an ache or pain in the ear; otalgia

ear·bud (-bud′) *n.* an earphone designed to be inserted into or to rest just outside of the outer ear canal: *usually used in pl.*

ear·drop (-dräp′) *n.* **1** an earring or hanging ornament for the ear **2** [*pl.*] any of various liquid medicines put into the ear in drops

ear·drum (-drum′) *n.* TYMPANUM (sense 1)

eared (ird) *adj.* **1** having ears **2** having (a specified kind of) ears: used in hyphenated compounds *[long-eared]*

eared seal any of various seals (family Otariidae) with distinct external ears and hind limbs used in locomotion, including fur seals and sea lions

ear·flap (ir′flap′) *n.* either of a pair of cloth or fur flaps on a cap, turned down to protect the ears from cold

☆**ear·ful** (-fool′) *n.* [Informal] **1** enough or too much of what is heard **2** important or startling news or gossip **3** a scolding

Ear·hart (er′härt′), **Amelia** 1897-1937; U.S. pioneer aviator

ear·ing (ir′iŋ) *n.* ⟦< EAR[1], sense 3⟧ a small rope passed through a cringle and used to attach the corner of a sail to a yard, gaff, or boom or to reef a sail

earl (url) *n.* ⟦ME *erl*, nobleman, count < OE *eorl*, warrior, akin to ON *jarl*, leader, noble⟧ a British nobleman ranking above a viscount and below a marquess: the wife or widow of an earl is called a *countess* —**earl′dom** *n.*

Earl (url) *n.* ⟦see prec.⟧ a masculine name

ear·lap (ir′lap′) *n.* **1** EARFLAP **2** the ear lobe **3** the external ear

ear·less seal (ir′lis) any of a family (Phocidae) of seals with inconspicuous ears and rudimentary hind limbs

Earl Marshal a high officer of state in England, marshal of state ceremonies and head of the Heralds' College

ear·lobe (ir′lōb′) *n.* the fleshy, lower part of the external ear: often written **ear lobe**

ear·lock (ir′läk′) *n.* a length of hair hanging just in front of the ear, as worn by some Orthodox Jewish males

ear·ly (ur′lē) *adv., adj.* **-li·er, -li·est** ⟦ME *erli* < OE *ærlic*, adv. (> *ærlic*, adj.) < *ær*, before (see ERE) + *-lice*, adv. suffix (see -LY[2], LIKE[1])⟧ **1** near the beginning of a given period of time or of a series, as of events; soon after the start **2** before the expected or customary time **3** in the far distant past; in ancient or remote times **4** in the near future; before much time has passed —**early on** at an early stage; near the beginning —**ear′li·ness** *n.*

Ear·ly (ʉr′lē), **Jubal Anderson** 1816-94; Confederate general in the Civil War

early adopter one who is among the first to use or purchase a new product incorporating the latest technological innovations

Early American [*also* **e- A-**] of or characteristic of the early, especially the Colonial, period of U.S. history; specif., of a plain or sturdy style in furniture, arts, and crafts of this period

early bird [Informal] a person who arrives early, or one who gets up early in the morning

early days [Informal, Chiefly Brit.] *used in the phrase* **it is** (or **these are**) **early days,** it is too soon to know what will happen

early modern designating or of the period of European history from the end of the Middle Ages (*c.* 1450) to *c.* 1750

Early Modern English the English language as spoken and written from about 1500 to about 1700

early music music of the medieval and Renaissance periods, now sometimes including baroque and early classical music

ear·ly-mu·sic (ʉr′lē myo͞o′zik) *adj.* of EARLY MUSIC, esp. as revived and played on period instruments

ear·mark (ir′märk′) *n.* **1** an identification mark put on, or cut into, the ear of a domestic animal to show ownership **2** any identifying mark or feature; characteristic; sign **3** something specially set aside or reserved; often, specif., a government spending appropriation inserted into a bill, committee report, etc. and directed toward or benefiting a particular recipient: term often used to suggest political patronage —*vt.* **1** to mark the ears of (livestock) for identification, usually by cropping or notching the ears in a distinctive way **2** to set a distinctive or informative mark upon; identify **3** to set aside or reserve for a special purpose or recipient

☆**ear·muffs** (-mufs′) *pl.n.* cloth or fur coverings worn over the ears to keep them warm in cold weather

earn (ʉrn) *vt.* ⟦ME *ernen* < OE *earnian,* to gain, labor for, lit., to harvest, akin to Ger *ernte,* harvest, OHG *arnōn,* to bring to harvest < IE base **es-en,* summer, harvest time⟧ **1** to receive (salary, wages, etc.) for one's labor or service **2** to get or deserve as a result of something one has done **3** to receive (interest, dividends, etc.) as a return —**earn′er** *n.*

☆**earned run** *Baseball* a run scored against a pitcher that is not the result of a fielding error: cf. UNEARNED RUN

☆**earned run average** *Baseball* the average number of earned runs allowed by a pitcher for each nine innings pitched

ear·nest[1] (ʉr′nist) *adj.* ⟦ME *ernest* < OE *eornoste* < *eornost,* earnestness, zeal, akin to Ger *ernst,* seriousness (OHG *ernust*) < IE base **er-,* to set oneself in motion, arouse > RUN⟧ serious and intense; not joking or playful; sincere, ardent, etc. —*SYN.* SERIOUS —**in earnest 1** serious; not joking **2** in a serious or determined manner —**ear′nest·ly** *adv.* —**ear′nest·ness** *n.*

ear·nest[2] (ʉr′nist) *n.* ⟦altered (after prec.) < ME *ernes* < OFr *erres* < L *arrae,* pl. of *arra, arrabo,* earnest money < Gr *arrabōn* < Heb *eravon* < *arav,* to guarantee, pledge⟧ **1** money given as a part payment and pledge in binding a bargain: in full **earnest money 2** something given or done as an indication or assurance of what is to come; token —*SYN.* PLEDGE

earn·ings (ʉrn′iŋz) *pl.n.* **1** wages, salary, or other recompense earned by working **2** money made by an investment or an enterprise; profits

Earp (ʉrp), **Wy·att (Berry Stapp)** (wī′ət) 1848-1929; U.S. lawman

ear·phone (ir′fōn′) *n.* a receiver for radio, telephone, a hearing aid, etc., either held to the ear or put into the ear

ear·piece (ir′pēs′) *n.* **1** either of the two parts of a frame for eyeglasses, that extend over the ears **2** EARPHONE

ear·plug (-plug′) *n.* a plug inserted in the outer ear, as to deaden excessive noise or keep out water when swimming

ear·ring (ir′riŋ′, ir′iŋ) *n.* a ring or other small ornament for the lobe of the ear, either passed through a hole pierced in the lobe or fastened with a screw or clip

ear shell 1 ABALONE **2** the shell of the abalone, shaped somewhat like the human ear

ear·shot (ir′shät′) *n.* ⟦by analogy with BOWSHOT⟧ the distance within which a sound, esp. that of the unaided human voice, can be heard; range of hearing

ear·split·ting (-split′iŋ) *adj.* so loud as to hurt the ears; deafening

earth (ʉrth) *n.* ⟦ME *erthe* < OE *eorthe,* akin to Ger *erde* < IE base **er-* > Gr *era,* earth, Welsh *erw,* field⟧ **1** [*often* **E-**] the planet that we live on; terrestrial globe: it is the fifth largest planet of the solar system and the third in distance from the sun: diameter, *c.* 12,760 km (*c.* 7,930 mi); period of revolution, one earth year; period of rotation, 24 hours; one satellite; symbol, ⊕: often with *the* **2** this world, as distinguished from heaven and hell **3** all the people on earth **4** land, as distinguished from sea or sky; the ground **5** the soft, granular or crumbly part of land; soil; ground **6** [Old Poet.] *a)* the substance of the human body *b)* the human body *c)* the concerns, interests, etc. of human life; worldly matters **7** the hole of a burrowing animal; lair **8** [Obs.] a land or country **9** *Chem.* any of the metallic oxides, formerly classed as elements, which are reduced with difficulty to an alkaline-earth metal, rare-earth element, or certain other metals **10** *Elec.* [Brit.] GROUND[1] —*vt.* **1** to cover (*up*) with soil for protection, as seeds or plants **2** to chase (an animal) into a hole or burrow —*vi.* to hide in a burrow: said of a fox, etc. —**come back** (or **down**) **to earth** to stop being impractical; return to reality —**down to earth 1** practical; realistic **2** sincere; without affectation —**go to earth** [Chiefly Brit.] to go into hiding —**on earth** of all things: an intensive used mainly after interrogative pronouns [what *on earth* do you mean?] —**run to earth** ⟦< use in fox hunting⟧ **1** to hunt down **2** to find by search

SYN.—**earth** is applied to the globe or planet we live on, but in religious use is opposed to heaven or hell; **universe** refers to the whole system of planets, stars, space, etc. and to everything that exists in it; **world** is equivalent to **earth,** esp. as relates to human activities, but is sometimes a generalized synonym for **universe**

earth·born (ʉrth′bôrn′) *adj.* **1** born on or springing from the earth **2** human; mortal

earth·bound (-bound′) *adj.* **1** confined to or by the earth or earthly things **2** headed for the earth

☆**Earth Day** April 22, a day on which environmentalist concerns are variously acknowledged

earth·en (ʉrth′ən) *adj.* **1** made of earth or of baked clay **2** earthly

earth·en·ware (-wer′) *n.* the coarser sort of containers, tableware, etc. made of baked clay

earth·i·ness (ʉrth′ē nis) *n.* an earthy quality or state

earth·light (ʉrth′līt′) *n.* EARTHSHINE

earth·ling (ʉrth′liŋ) *n.* **1** a person who lives on earth; human being: now used mainly in science fiction **2** a worldly person

earth·ly (ʉrth′lē) *adj.* **1** of the earth; specif., *a)* terrestrial *b)* worldly *c)* temporal or secular **2** conceivable; possible [a thing of no *earthly* good] —**earth′li·ness** *n.*

SYN.—**earthly** is applied to that which belongs to the earth or to the present life and is chiefly contrasted with *heavenly* [*earthly* pleasures]; **terrestrial,** having as its opposite *celestial* (both Latin-derived parallels of the preceding terms), has special application in formal and scientific usage [*terrestrial* magnetism]; **worldly** implies reference to the material concerns or pursuits of humankind and is chiefly contrasted with *spiritual* [*worldly* wisdom]; **mundane,** although often used as a close synonym of **worldly,** now esp. stresses the commonplace or practical aspects of life [to return to *mundane* matters after a flight of fancy]

earth·man (ʉrth′man′) *n., pl.* **-men′** (-men′) a human being on or from the planet earth, as in science fiction

earth mother [*also* **E- M-**] **1** the planet earth regarded, as in mythology, as the source of all life **2** figuratively, any buxom, sensuous woman who is inclined to mother others

☆**earth·mov·er** (ʉrth′mo͞o′vər) *n.* a bulldozer or other large machine for excavating or moving large quantities of earth

earth·nut (-nut′) *n.* **1** the root, tuber, or underground pod of various plants, as the peanut **2** TRUFFLE

earth·quake (-kwāk′) *n.* a shaking or trembling of the crust of the earth, caused by underground volcanic forces or by breaking and shifting of rock beneath the surface

earth·rise (ʉrth′rīz′) *n.* the rising of the upper limb of the earth above the horizon of the moon, as seen from the moon

earth science any of various sciences, as geology or meteorology, dealing with the earth or its components —**earth scientist**

earth·shak·ing (-shāk′iŋ) *adj.* profound or basic in significance, effect, or influence; momentous

earth·shine (-shīn′) *n.* the faint illumination of the dark part of the moon by sunlight reflected from the earth

earth·star (-stär′) *n.* any of a family (Geastraceae) of puffball fungi, in which the outer wall of the spore fruit splits into a starlike form surrounding the spore sac

earth station a dish antenna, amplifier, and transmitter or receiver used for sending or receiving signals directly to or from communications satellites

earth tone any of various soft colors like those found in nature in soil, vegetation, etc.; esp., brown, tan, or beige

earth·ward (-wərd) *adv., adj.* toward the earth

earth·wards (-wərdz) *adv.* EARTHWARD

earth·work (-wʉrk′) *n.* **1** an embankment made by piling up earth, esp. as a fortification **2** *Engineering* the work of excavating or building embankments **3** a work of art, usually massive in scale, incorporating a natural feature of an area, as a groove sculpted into a desert mesa or a wheat field planted in geometric patterns

earth·worm (-wʉrm′) *n.* any of a number of oligochaetous worms that burrow in the soil, esp. any of a genus (*Lumbricus*) very important in aerating and fertilizing the soil

earth·y (ʉrth′ē) *adj.* **earth′i·er, earth′i·est 1** of or like earth or soil **2** [Archaic] worldly **3** *a)* coarse; unrefined *b)* simple and natural; hearty

ear trumpet a hand-held funnel-shaped or horn-shaped device, used formerly by the partially deaf to improve hearing

ear·wax (ir′waks′) *n.* the yellowish, waxlike secretion found in the canal of the external ear; cerumen

ear·wig (ir′wig′) *n.* ⟦ME *erwig* < OE *earwicga* < *eare,* EAR[1] + *wicga,* beetle, worm < IE base **weik-,* to wind, bend > L *vicia,* VETCH: so named from the incorrect belief that it crawls into the human *ear* and enters the brain⟧ any of an order (Dermaptera) of widely distributed insects with short, horny forewings, a pair of forceps at the terminal end of the abdomen, and biting mouthparts

ease (ēz) ***n.*** ⟦ME *ese* < OFr *aise* < VL **adjaces* < L *adjacens*, lying nearby, hence easy to reach: see ADJACENT⟧ **1** freedom from pain, worry, or trouble; comfort **2** freedom from stiffness, formality, or awkwardness; natural, easy manner; poise **3** freedom from difficulty; facility; adroitness [to write with *ease*] **4** freedom from poverty; state of being financially secure; affluence **5** rest; leisure; relaxation —***vt.*** **eased, eas′ing 1** to free from pain, worry, or trouble; comfort **2** to lessen or alleviate (pain, anxiety, etc.) **3** to make easier; facilitate **4** *a)* to reduce the strain, tension, or pressure of or on; loosen; slacken *b)* to reduce (the strain, tension, pressure, etc.) on (a rope, sail, etc.) **5** to fit or move by careful shifting, slow pressure, etc. [to *ease* a piano into place] —***vi.*** **1** to move or be moved by careful shifting, slow pressure, etc. **2** to lessen in tension, speed, pain, etc. **3** to reduce strain, tension, or pressure: often with *up, off,* etc. —**at ease 1** having no anxiety, pain, or discomfort **2** *Mil. a)* in a relaxed position but maintaining silence and staying in place *b)* the command to assume this position —**ease out** to tactfully persuade (an employee, tenant, etc.) to leave —**ease the rudder** (or **helm**) *Naut.* to reduce the angle the rudder makes with the fore-and-aft line so that the vessel will turn more gradually —**take one's ease** to relax and be comfortable

ease·ful (-fəl) ***adj.*** characterized by, promoting, or full of ease —**ease′ful·ly** ***adv.***

ea·sel (ē′zəl) ***n.*** ⟦17th c. < Du *ezel* (Ger *esel*), ass, ult. < L *asellus*, dim. of *asinus*, ASS[1]: for sense, cf. Fr *chevalet*, easel, lit., little horse & SAWHORSE⟧ an upright frame or tripod to hold an artist's canvas, a picture on display, etc.

ease·ment (ēz′mənt) ***n.*** ⟦ME *esement* < OFr *aisement*⟧ **1** an easing or being eased **2** something that gives ease; a comfort, relief, or convenience **3** *Law* a legal interest in real property that grants the right to use in some specified manner the property of another; often, specif., *a)* the right to enter upon or pass over another's land *b)* a portion of land subject to such a right

eas·i·ly (ē′zə lē) ***adv.*** ⟦ME *esili*⟧ **1** in an easy manner; with little or no difficulty, discomfort, awkwardness, etc. **2** without a doubt; by far [*easily* the best of the lot] **3** very likely [it may *easily* snow again before spring]

eas·i·ness (ē′zē nis) ***n.*** the quality or state of being easy to do or get, or of being at ease

east (ēst) ***n.*** ⟦ME *est* < OE *east*, akin to Ger *osten*, ON *austr* < Gmc base **aust-*, dawn < IE base **awes-*, to shine, dawn > L *aurora*, dawn, *aurum*, gold⟧ **1** the direction to the right of a person facing north; direction in which sunrise occurs: it is properly the point on the horizon at which the center of the sun rises at the equinox **2** the point on a compass at 90°, directly opposite west **3** a region or district in or toward this direction —***adj.*** **1** in, of, to, toward, or facing the east **2** from the east [an *east* wind] **3** [**E-**] designating the eastern part of a continent, country, etc. [*East* Africa] **4** in, of, or toward the altar of a church —***adv.*** in or toward the east; in an easterly direction —**the East** ☆**1** the eastern part of the U.S.; specif., *a)* the part east of the Allegheny Mountains, from Me. through Md. *b)* the part east of the Mississippi and north of the Ohio **2** the Eastern Hemisphere; specif., Asia and the nearby islands

East Anglia 1 former Anglo-Saxon kingdom in E England **2** corresponding section in modern England, chiefly comprising the counties of Norfolk and Suffolk

East Asia countries of E Asia, including China, Japan, North & South Korea, and Mongolia —**East Asian**

East Berlin *see* BERLIN[2]

☆**east·bound** (ēst′bound′) ***adj.*** bound east; going eastward

east by north the direction, or the point on a mariner's compass, halfway between due east and east-northeast; 11°15′ north of due east

east by south the direction, or the point on a mariner's compass, halfway between due east and east-southeast; 11°15′ south of due east

East China Sea part of the Pacific Ocean east of China and west of Kyushu, Japan, and the Ryukyu Islands: 256,600 sq mi (664,591 sq km)

East Coast coastal region of E U.S., esp. the region between Boston and Washington, D.C.

Eas·ter (ēs′tər) ***n.*** ⟦ME *ester* < OE *eastre*, pl. *eastron*, spring, Easter; orig., name of pagan vernal festival almost coincident in date with paschal festival of the church < *Eastre*, dawn goddess < PGmc **Austro* (> Ger *Ostern*) < IE base **awes-*: see EAST⟧ **1** an annual Christian festival celebrating the resurrection of Jesus, held on the first Sunday after the date of the first full moon that occurs during or after the vernal equinox **2** the Sunday of this festival: also **Easter Sunday**

☆**Easter Bunny** [*also* **E- b-**] *Folklore* the rabbit that brings Easter eggs, candy, etc. to children at Easter: with *the*

Easter egg 1 a colored egg or an egg-shaped piece of candy, etc., used as an Easter gift or ornament **2** ⟦by analogy with the candy eggs hidden for children to find at Easter⟧ an often playful feature, image, message, etc. hidden within a video game, computer program, website, etc. and activated or revealed variously, as by a particular sequence of keystrokes

Easter Island ⟦from the fact that it was discovered on *Easter* Sunday, 1722⟧ island in the South Pacific, *c.* 1,864 mi (3,000 km) west of Valparaiso, Chile, & governed as an integral part of Chile: 46 sq mi (119 sq km)

Easter lily any of several species of white-flowered lilies (esp. *Lilium longiflorum*), commonly grown for Easter display

east·er·ly (ēs′tər lē) ***adj., adv.*** **1** in or toward the east **2** from the east, as a wind —***n., pl.*** **-lies** a wind from the east

east·ern (ēs′tərn) ***adj.*** ⟦ME *esterne* < OE *easterne*⟧ **1** in, of, to, toward, or facing the east **2** from the east [an *eastern* wind] **3** [*also* **E-**] *a)* of or characteristic of the East *b)* of the Eastern Church

Eastern Church 1 [Historical] the Christian Church in much of the eastern part of the Roman Empire, consisting of the four patriarchates in E Europe, W Asia, and Egypt, headed by the bishops of Constantinople, Alexandria, Antioch, and Jerusalem: distinguished from the WESTERN CHURCH (sense 2) **2** EASTERN ORTHODOX CHURCH **3** collectively, the Eastern Christian churches in communion with the Western churches

east·ern·er (ēs′tər nər) ***n.*** **1** a person born or living in the east ☆**2** [*also* **E-**] a person born or living in the E part of the U.S.

Eastern Hemisphere that half of the earth which includes Europe, Africa, Asia, and Australia

east·ern·ize (ēs′tərn īz′) ***vt.*** **-ized′, -iz′ing** to make eastern in character, habits, ideas, etc. —**east′ern·i·za′tion** ***n.***

east·ern·most (-mōst′) ***adj.*** farthest east

Eastern Orthodox Church the Christian church dominant in E Europe, W Asia, and N Africa, originally made up of four patriarchates (Constantinople, Alexandria, Antioch, Jerusalem) rejecting the authority of the Roman see in 1054 and now also including certain autonomous churches of Russia, Greece, Romania, Bulgaria, etc.

Eastern Roman Empire Byzantine Empire, esp. so called from A.D. 395, when the Roman Empire was divided, until A.D. 476, when the Western Roman emperor was deposed

Eastern Shore 1 E shore of Chesapeake Bay, including all of Md. and Va. east of the Bay **2** sometimes, the entire Delmarva Peninsula

☆**Eastern Standard Time** a standard time used in the zone which includes the Eastern states of the U.S., corresponding to the mean solar time of the 75th meridian west of Greenwich, England: it is five hours behind Greenwich time

☆**Eastern Time** [*also* **e- t-**] standard time or daylight saving time in the time zone which includes the Eastern states of the U.S.

Eastern Transvaal *former name* (1994-95) *for* MPUMALANGA

Eastern Turkestan CHINESE TURKESTAN

Easter Rising an insurrection against the British government in Dublin on Easter Monday, 1916

Eas·ter·tide (ēs′tər tīd′) ***n.*** ⟦EASTER + TIDE[1]⟧ the period after Easter, extending in various churches to Ascension Day, Pentecost Sunday, or Trinity Sunday

East Flanders province of NW Belgium: 1,151 sq mi (2,981 sq km); cap. Ghent

East Germany *see* GERMANY

East India Company any of several European companies for carrying on trade with the East Indies; esp., such an English company chartered in 1600 and dissolved in 1874

East Indies 1 Malay Archipelago; esp., the islands of Indonesia **2** [Historical] India, Indochina, and the Malay Archipelago: also **East India** —**East Indian**

east·ing (ēs′tiŋ) ***n.*** **1** *Naut.* the distance due east covered by a vessel traveling on any easterly course **2** an easterly direction

East Lothian administrative division of SE Scotland: formerly a county & district

East·man (ēst′mən), **George** 1854-1932; U.S. industrialist & inventor of photographic equipment

east-north·east (ēst′nôrth′ēst′; *naut.,* -nôr-) ***n.*** the direction, or the point on a mariner's compass, halfway between due east and northeast; 22°30′ north of due east — ***adj., adv.*** **1** in or toward this direction **2** from this direction, as a wind

East Pakistan former province of Pakistan: since 1971, the country of Bangladesh

East Prussia former province of Prussia, in NE Germany, on the Baltic Sea, separated from the rest of Germany (1919-39) by the Polish Corridor: in 1945, it was divided between Poland and the U.S.S.R.

East Riding former division of Yorkshire county, England

East River strait in SE N.Y., connecting Long Island Sound and Upper New York Bay and separating Manhattan Island from Long Island: 16 mi (25.7 km) long

East Sea *alt. name for* Sea of JAPAN

East Siberian Sea part of the Arctic Ocean, off the NE coast of Russia, east of the New Siberian Islands

east-south·east (ēst′south′ēst′; *naut.,* -sou-) ***n.*** the direction, or the point on a mariner's compass, halfway between due east and southeast; 22°30′ south of due east — ***adj., adv.*** **1** in or toward this direction **2** from this direction, as a wind

East Sussex county in SE England, on the English Channel: 693 sq mi (1,795 sq km)

East Timor country occupying the E half of the island of Timor, & nearby islands, including an enclave in West Timor: independent since 2002: 5,794 sq mi (15,006 sq km); cap. Dili

east·ward (ēst′wərd) ***adv., adj.*** toward the east —***n.*** an eastward direction, point, or region

east·ward·ly (-lē) ***adv., adj.*** **1** toward the east **2** from the east

east·wards (ēst′wərdz) ***adv.*** *var. of* EASTWARD

East York ⟦orig. the E portion of the county of *York*, after the House of YORK[1]⟧ former city in SE Ontario, Canada, now part of Toronto

eas·y (ē′zē) ***adj.*** **eas′i·er, eas′i·est** ⟦ME *esi* < OFr *aisé*, pp. of *aisier* (& *aa-*

sié, pp. of *aaisier* < *a-* + *aisier*) < *aise:* see EASE] 1 *a)* that can be done, gotten, mastered, endured, etc. with ease; not difficult; not exacting *b)* characterized by insufficient effort or thought [a politician's *easy* answers to complex questions] 2 free from trouble, anxiety, pain, etc. [an *easy* life] 3 conducive to comfort or rest; comfortable [an *easy* carriage] 4 fond of comfort, ease, or idleness 5 free from constraint; not stiff, awkward, or embarrassed [an *easy* manner] 6 not strict, harsh, or severe; lenient [*easy* terms] 7 readily influenced; compliant or credulous [an *easy* mark] 8 *a)* unhurried; not fast [an *easy* pace] *b)* not steep; gradual [an *easy* descent] 9 *a)* in little demand (said of a commodity) *b)* lacking firmness in prices (said of a market) *c)* with funds plentiful and interest rates low (said of a money market) 10 [Informal] consenting to sexual activity readily and, usually, indiscriminately —*adv.* **eas′i·er, eas′i·est** [Informal] 1 easily 2 slowly and carefully —**easy come, easy go** gotten and spent or lost with equal ease: implying a carefree attitude toward money —**easy does it!** [Informal] be careful! go slowly! etc. —☆**easy on the eyes** [Informal] pleasant to look at; attractive —☆**go easy on** [Informal] 1 to use or consume with restraint [*go easy on* the table salt] 2 to deal with leniently [to *go easy on* traffic violators] —**have (got) it easy** [Informal] to be in comfortable, relatively carefree circumstances —**take it easy** [Informal] 1 to refrain from anger, haste, etc. 2 to refrain from hard work; relax; rest Sometimes used as a farewell

SYN.—**easy** is the broadest term here in its application to that which demands little effort or presents little difficulty [*easy* work]; **facile** means occurring, moving, working, etc. easily and quickly, sometimes unfavorably suggesting a lack of thoroughness or depth [a *facile* style]; **effortless**, in contrast, favorably suggests expert skill or knowledge as responsible for performance that seems to require no effort [the *effortless* grace of the skater]; **smooth** suggests freedom from or riddance of irregularities, obstacles, or difficulties as bringing ease of movement [a *smooth* path to success]; **simple**, in this connection, suggests freedom from complication or elaboration as making something easy to understand [a *simple* recipe] —*ANT.* **difficult, hard**

easy chair a stuffed or padded armchair

eas·y·go·ing (ē′zē gō′iŋ) *adj.* 1 dealing with things in a relaxed manner; not hurried or agitated 2 not strict; lenient

☆**easy street** [*sometimes* **E- S-**] [Informal] a condition of ease, usually one marked by financial security or, specif., affluence: chiefly in the phrase **on easy street**, living a life of ease; financially secure or, specif., affluent

easy virtue sexually promiscuous habits [a woman of *easy virtue*]

eat (ēt) *vt.* **ate** (āt; *Brit usually* et), **eat·en** (ēt′'n), **eat′ing** [ME *eten* < OE *etan*, akin to Ger *essen* < IE base **ed-*, to eat > L *edere*, Gr *edmenai*] 1 to put (food) in the mouth, chew if necessary, and swallow 2 to use up, devour, destroy, or waste as by eating; consume or ravage: usually with *away* or *up* 3 to penetrate and destroy, as acid does; corrode 4 to make by or as by eating [the acid *ate* holes in the cloth] 5 to bring into a specified condition by eating [to *eat* oneself sick] 6 [Informal] to absorb (a financial loss); accept responsibility for losses resulting from (unsold goods, bad debts, etc.) ☆7 [Slang] to worry or bother [what's *eating* him?] 8 [Vulgar Slang] to perform fellatio or cunnilingus on —*vi.* 1 to eat food; have a meal or meals 2 to destroy or use up something gradually: often with *into* —**eat one's words** to retract something said earlier —☆**eat out** to have a meal in a restaurant —☆**eat someone out** 1 [Slang] to rebuke; reprimand 2 [Vulgar Slang] to perform cunnilingus on —**eat up** 1 to consume all of 2 [Informal] to respond to with avid, uncritical interest or delight —**eat′er** *n.*

eat·a·ble (ēt′ə bəl) *adj.* fit to be eaten; edible —*n.* a thing fit to be eaten; food: *usually used in pl.*

☆**eat·er·y** (ēt′ər ē) *n., pl.* **-er·ies** [EAT + -ERY] [Informal] a restaurant

eat·ing (ēt′iŋ) *n.* 1 the action of a person or thing that eats 2 something edible, with reference to its quality as food —*adj.* 1 that eats or consumes 2 good for eating uncooked [*eating* apples] 3 used for eating or dining [*eating* utensils, an *eating* place]

eating disorder any of various psychological disorders, as anorexia, bulimia, or compulsive overeating, characterized by extreme, often obsessive, eating behaviors

Ea·ton (ēt′'n), **Cyrus S(tephen)** 1883-1979; U.S. industrialist & financier, born in Canada

☆**eats** (ēts) *pl.n.* [Informal] things to eat; food; meals

eau (ō) *n., pl.* **eaux** (ō) [Fr < L *aqua*, water] water

eau de Co·logne (ō′ də kə lōn′) [Fr, lit., water of Cologne: orig. made at COLOGNE] COLOGNE

eau de vie (ōd vē′) *pl.* **eaux de vie** (ōd vē′) [Fr, lit., water of life] brandy, esp. a clear spirit distilled from fruit other than grapes

eaves (ēvz) *pl.n., sing.* **eave** [orig. sing., ME *eves* (pl. *evesen*) < OE *efes*, edge, border, eaves, akin to ON *ups*, church porch, OHG *obiza*, porch < IE **upes-* < base **upo-*, up from behind > UP[1], L *summus*] the lower edge or edges of a roof, usually projecting beyond the sides of a building

eaves·drop (ēvz′dräp′) *n.* [ME *evesdrop*, altered (after *drop*, DROP) < OE *yfesdrype*: see prec. & DRIP] [Rare] water that drips from the eaves, or the ground on which it drips —*vi.* **-dropped′**, **-drop′ping** [prob. back-form. < *eavesdropper*, lit., one who stands on the eavesdrop to listen] to listen secretly to the private conversation of others —**eaves′drop′per** *n.*

ebb (eb) *n.* [ME *ebbe* < OE *ebba* (common LowG, as in MLowG *ebbe* > Ger *ebbe*, OFris *ebba*) < Gmc **abjan*, a going back < IE base **apo-*, from, away from > OFF[1]] 1 the flow of water back toward the sea, as the tide falls 2 a weakening or lessening; decline [the *ebb* of faith] —*vi.* [ME *ebben* < OE *ebbian*] 1 to flow back; recede, as the tide 2 to weaken or lessen; decline —*SYN.* WANE

ebb tide the outgoing or falling tide: cf. FLOOD TIDE

☆**EBCDIC** (eb′sə dik′) *n.* a standard computer code for the alphanumeric representation of data

Eb·en·e·zer (eb′ə nē′zər) *n.* [Heb *even-haezer*, lit., stone of the help: see 1 Sam. 7:12] a masculine name

Ebitda or **EBITDA** *abbrev.* earnings before interest, taxes, depreciation, and amortization

Eb·lis (eb′lis) *n.* [Ar *Iblīs*] *Islam* Satan

EbN *abbrev.* east by north

E·bo·la (virus) (ē bō′lə) [after *Ebola* River, Democratic Republic of the Congo, near which there was an outbreak of the virus in 1976] an RNA virus (family Filoviridae) that causes fever, internal bleeding, and, often, death

eb·on (eb′ən) *adj., n.* [ME *eban* < L *ebenus, hebenus* < Gr *ebenos* < Egypt *hbny* (> Heb *hovne*)] [Old Poet.] EBONY

☆**E·bon·ics** (ē bän′iks) *n.* [blend of EBONY & PHONICS] BLACK ENGLISH, esp. as differentiated from Standard American English: term used chiefly by educators

eb·on·ite (eb′ə nīt′) *n.* [EBON(Y) + -ITE[1]] HARD RUBBER

eb·on·ize (eb′ə nīz′) *vt.* **-ized′**, **-iz′ing** to blacken with paint or stain so as to make look like ebony

eb·on·y (eb′ə nē) *n., pl.* **-on·ies** [ME *ebenif* < LL(Ec) *ebenius* < *ebenus*: see EBON] 1 the hard, heavy, dark, durable wood of any of various trees, esp. of a group of persimmons native to tropical Africa, Asia, and Sri Lanka: it is used for furniture and decorative woodwork 2 any tree that yields this wood 3 black or very dark brown —*adj.* 1 made of ebony 2 like ebony, esp. in color; dark or black 3 designating a family (Ebenaceae, order Ebenales) of dicotyledonous tropical trees and shrubs, including the persimmon

e-book (ē′book′) *n.* [< E(LECTRONIC) + BOOK] 1 a written work whose text, etc. is published in digital form 2 a portable electronic device with a video screen, for reading such a work

E·bo·ra·cum (i bôr′ə kəm) *ancient name for* YORK[2], England: chief city of the Roman province of Britain

E·bro (ā′brô; *E* ē′brō) river in N Spain, flowing southeast into the Mediterranean: *c.* 575 mi (925 km)

EbS *abbrev.* east by south

e·bul·lient (i bool′yənt, -bul′-) *adj.* [L *ebulliens*, prp. of *ebullire*, to boil up < *e-*, out + *bullire*, BOIL[1]] 1 bubbling; boiling 2 overflowing with enthusiasm, high spirits, etc.; exuberant —**e·bul′lience** *n.*, **e·bul′lien·cy** —**e·bul′lient·ly** *adv.*

eb·ul·li·tion (eb′ə lish′ən, eb′yoo-) *n.* [ME *ebullitioun* < LL *ebullitio* < pp. of *ebullire*: see prec.] 1 a boiling or bubbling up; effervescence 2 a sudden outburst, as of some emotion

e·bur·na·tion (ē′bər nā′shən, eb′ər-) *n.* [< L *eburnus*, of ivory (< *ebur*, IVORY) + -ATION] an abnormal condition of bone or cartilage in which it becomes very dense and smooth like ivory

Ec *abbrev.* 1 *Bible* Ecclesiastes 2 Ecuador

EC *abbrev.* European Community

ec- (ek, ik) *prefix* EX-[1] (sense 1): used before *c* or *s* [*eccentric*]

ECB *abbrev.* European Central Bank

Ec·bat·a·na (ek bat′'n ə) capital of ancient Media, on the site of modern HAMADAN (Iran)

ec·bol·ic (ek bäl′ik) *adj.* [Gr *ekbolē*, a throwing out < *ek-*, out + *ballein*, to throw (see BALL[2]) + -IC] helping to bring forth the fetus in birth, or causing abortion, by contracting the uterus: said of certain drugs —*n.* an ecbolic drug

ec·ce (ek′ā; *Eccles.* et′chā) *v. imper.* [L] behold; lo; see: used to form exclamations

ec·ce ho·mo (et′chā hō′mō, ek′ā-) [L, behold the man: the Vulgate version of Pilate's words when he presented Jesus to the populace before the Crucifixion: John 19:5] a picture or statue of Jesus wearing the crown of thorns

ec·cen·tric (ek sen′trik, ik-) *adj.* [ME *eccentrik* < ML *eccentricus* < LL *eccentros*, out of the center, eccentric < Gr *ekkentros* < *ek-*, out of (see EX-[1]) + *kentron*, CENTER] 1 not having the same center, as two circles one inside the other: opposed to CONCENTRIC 2 not having the axis exactly in the center; off-center [an *eccentric* wheel] 3 not exactly circular in shape or motion 4 deviating from the norm, as in conduct; odd; unconventional —*n.* 1 a disk set off center on a shaft and revolving inside a strap that is attached to one end of a rod, thereby converting the circular motion of the shaft into back-and-forth motion of the rod 2 an odd or unconventional person —**ec·cen′tri·cal·ly** *adv.*

ec·cen·tric·i·ty (ek′sen tris′ə tē, -sən-) *n., pl.* **-ties** [see prec.] 1 the state, quality, or amount of being eccentric 2 *a)* deviation from what is ordinary or customary, as in conduct or manner; oddity; unconventionality *b)* an eccentric trait or habit; peculiarity 3 *Math.* the ratio of the distances from any point of a conic section to the focus and to the directrix: the value of this ratio determines the type of conic section (zero = circle, between zero and one = ellipse, one = parabola, more than one = hyperbola) 4 *Mech.* the distance between the center of a shaft and the center of its eccentric wheel: sometimes, erroneously, called a *throw* —*SYN.* IDIOSYNCRASY

ec·chy·mo·sis (ek′i mō′sis) *n., pl.* **-ses′** (-sēz′) [ModL < Gr *ekchymōsis* < *ekchymousthai*, to pour out, extravasate < *ek-*, out of (see EX-[1]) + *cheein*, to pour: see FOUND[2]⟧ *Med.* 1 an oozing of blood from a ruptured blood vessel into the tissues 2 a black-and-blue or yellowish mark caused by this —**ec′chy·mot′ic** (-mät′ik) ***adj.***

eccl or **eccles** *abbrev.* 1 ecclesiastic 2 ecclesiastical

Eccl or **Eccles** *abbrev. Bible* Ecclesiastes

Ec·cles (ek′əlz), Sir **John Ca·rew** (kə ro͞o′) 1903-97; Brit. neurobiologist, born in Australia

ec·cle·si·a (e klē′zē ə, -klā′-; i-) ***n.***, *pl.* **-si·ae′** (-ē′) ⟦L, assembly, in LL(Ec), assembly of Christians < Gr *ekklēsia*, assembly (in N.T., the church as a body of Christians) < *ekklētos*, summoned < *ekkalein*, to summon < *ek-*, out (see EX-[2]) + *kalein*, to call (see CLAMOR)⟧ 1 in ancient Greek states, a political assembly of citizens 2 *Eccles. a)* the members of a church *b)* a church building

ec·cle·si·al (e klē′zē əl, i-) ***adj.*** of or pertaining to a church

Ec·cle·si·as·tes (e klē′zē as′tēz′, i-) ***n.*** ⟦LL(Ec) < Gr *ekklēsiastēs*, member of an ecclesia (see ECCLESIA): used in LXX for Heb *kohelet*, he who calls together an assembly < *kahal*, assembly⟧ *Bible* a book of teachings, written as if by Solomon: abbrev. *Eccles, Eccl*, or *Ec*

ec·cle·si·as·tic (e klē′zē as′tik, i-) ***adj.*** ⟦LL(Ec) *ecclesiasticus* < Gr *ekklēsiastikos*: see ECCLESIA⟧ ECCLESIASTICAL —***n.*** a member of the clergy

ec·cle·si·as·ti·cal (-ti kəl) ***adj.*** ⟦ME: see prec. & -AL⟧ 1 of a church, its organization, or its clergy 2 used chiefly in early writings relating to Christianity [*ecclesiastical* Latin (or Greek)] —**ec·cle′si·as′ti·cal·ly *adv.***

ec·cle·si·as·ti·cism (-tə siz′əm) ***n.*** 1 ecclesiastical principles, rituals, customs, etc. 2 strong attachment to these things

Ec·cle·si·as·ti·cus (e klē′zē as′ti kəs, i-) ***n.*** ⟦LL(Ec), short for *ecclesiasticus liber*, lit., the church book (see ECCLESIASTIC): from its frequent use for catechetical teaching⟧ a book of proverbs in the Old Testament Apocrypha and the Douay Bible: abbrev. *Ecclus*

ec·cle·si·ol·o·gy (e klē′zē äl′ə jē, i-) ***n.*** ⟦< ECCLESIA + -LOGY⟧ 1 the study of church architecture, art, and decoration 2 the study of the nature and organization of the Christian Church

Ecclus *abbrev. Bible* Ecclesiasticus

ec·crine (ek′rin, -rīn′, -rēn′) ***adj.*** ⟦< Gr *ekkrinein*, to separate, secrete: see EX-[1] & ENDOCRINE⟧ designating or of the common sweat glands of the human body that secrete the clear, watery sweat important in heat regulation: see APOCRINE

☆**ec·dys·i·ast** (ek diz′ē ast′) ***n.*** ⟦coined (1940) by H. L. MENCKEN < fol. + *-ast*, one occupied with (< ME *-aste* < L *-astes* < Gr *-astēs*)⟧ a stripteaser

ec·dy·sis (ek′də sis) ***n.*** ⟦ModL < Gr *ekdysis*, a stripping < *ekdyein*, to strip off < *ek-*, out of + *dyein*, to enter⟧ *Zool.* the shedding of an outer layer of skin or integument, as by snakes or insects

ec·dy·sone (ek′də sōn′) ***n.*** ⟦prec. + -ONE⟧ a hormone produced in the prothoracic glands of insects or in similar glands in crustaceans, for stimulating growth and the molting of the exoskeleton

☆**e·ce·sis** (ē sē′sis) ***n.*** ⟦< Gr *oikēsis*, act of dwelling, residence < *oikein*, to inhabit < *oikos*, house (see ECO-) + *-sis*, fem. suffix of action⟧ the successful establishment of a plant or animal in a new locality

ECG *abbrev.* electrocardiogram

ech·e·lon (esh′ə län′) ***n.*** ⟦Fr *échelon*, ladder rung < *échelle* < OFr *eschelle* < L *scala*, ladder: see SCALE[1]⟧ 1 *a)* a steplike formation of ships or troops, in which each unit or row is slightly to the left or right of the one preceding it *b)* a similar formation of aircraft with each unit at a higher or lower level 2 any of the units in such a formation 3 a subdivision of a military force, according to position [*rear echelon*] or to function [*command echelon*] 4 *a)* any of the levels of responsibility or importance in an organization *b)* the persons at one of these levels — ***vt., vi.*** to assemble, or assume position, in echelon

ech·e·ve·ri·a (ech′ə vir′ē ə, ek′-) ***n.*** ⟦ModL, after *Echeveri*, Mex illustrator of 19th-c. botanical works⟧ any of a large genus (*Echeveria*) of tropical American plants of the orpine family, with dense rosettes of thick, fleshy leaves

e·chid·na (ē kid′nə) ***n.*** ⟦ModL < L, adder, viper < Gr, ult. < IE base **eĝhi-*, snake > Ger *egel*, leech⟧ any of a family (Tachyglossidae) of small, toothless Australasian monotremes with a long, tapering snout and a sticky, extensible tongue; spiny anteater

ech·i·na·cea (ek′ə nā′shə) ***n.*** 1 any of a genus (*Echinacea*) of North American plants of the composite family, esp. a coneflower (*E. purpurea*) with purple flowers 2 a medicinal herb made from the roots, leaves, etc. of certain of these plants

ech·i·nate (ek′i nāt′, e kī′nit) ***adj.*** ⟦L *echinatus* < *echinus*, ECHINUS⟧ covered with prickles; bristling, as a porcupine: also **ech′i·nat′ed**

e·chi·no- (ē kī′nō, -nə; ek′i nō, -nə) ⟦< Gr *echinos*, sea urchin, hedgehog: see ECHINUS⟧ *combining form* prickly, spiny [*echinoderm*]: also, before a vowel, **e·chin-**

e·chi·no·coc·cus (ē kī′nō käk′əs, ek′i nō-) ***n.*** ⟦ModL < prec. + -COCCUS⟧ any of a genus (*Echinococcus*) of tapeworms that cause disease in mammals: see HYDATID

e·chi·no·derm (ē kī′nō durm′, ek′i nō-) ***n.*** ⟦< ModL *Echinodermata*: see ECHINO- & -DERM⟧ any of a phylum (Echinodermata) of marine animals with a water-vascular system, and usually with a hard, spiny skeleton and radial body, including the starfishes and sea urchins —**e·chi′no·der′ma·tous** (-dur′mə təs) ***adj.***

e·chi·noid (ē kī′noid′, ek′ə-) ***adj.*** ⟦ECHIN(O)- + -OID⟧ of or like a sea urchin —***n.*** any of a class (Echinoidea) of echinoderms, including the sea urchins and sand dollars

e·chi·nus (ē kī′nəs) ***n.***, *pl.* **e·chi′ni′** (-nī′) ⟦L < Gr *echinos* < IE **eĝhinos*, of snakes < base **eĝhi-*, snake⟧ 1 SEA URCHIN 2 *Archit. a)* molding under the abacus of the capital of a Doric column *b)* any of several similar moldings

ech·o (ek′ō) ***n.***, *pl.* **-oes** ⟦ME *ecco* < L *echo* < Gr *ēchō* < IE base **(s)waĝh-*, var. of **wag-*, to cry out > L *vagire*, OE *swogan*, to sound, roar⟧ 1 *a)* the repetition of a sound by reflection of sound waves from a surface *b)* a sound so produced 2 *a)* any repetition or imitation of the words, style, ideas, etc. of another *b)* a person who thus repeats or imitates 3 sympathetic response 4 *Electronics* a radar wave reflected from an object, appearing as a spot of light on a radarscope 5 [**E-**] *Gr. Myth.* a nymph who, because of her unreturned love for Narcissus, pines away until only her voice remains 6 *Music a)* a soft repetition of a phrase *b)* an organ stop for producing the effect of echo 7 *Radio, TV* the reception of two similar and almost simultaneous signals because one of them has been delayed slightly by reflection from the E layer in transmission —***vi.*** **-oed, -o·ing** 1 to resound with an echo; reverberate 2 to be repeated as or like an echo —***vt.*** 1 *a)* to repeat (another's words, ideas, etc.) *b)* to repeat the words, etc. of (another person) 2 to repeat or reflect (sound) from a surface —**ech·o·ey** (ek′ō ē′) ***adj.***

ech·o·car·di·og·ra·phy (ek′ō kär′dē äg′rə fē) ***n.***, *pl.* **-phies** a technique for examining the internal structure of the heart, using reflections from high-frequency sound waves to form a picture or display (**ech′o·car′di·o·gram′**) —**ech′o·car′di·o·graph′ic** (-dē ə graf′ik) ***adj.*** —**ech′o·car′di·ol′o·gy** (-dē äl′ə jē) ***n.***

echo chamber a room used in recording and broadcasting to increase resonance, produce echo effects, etc.

☆**ech·o·gram** (ek′ō gram′) ***n.*** ⟦ECHO + -GRAM⟧ a display or record produced on an oscilloscope by the reflection of ultrasonic waves from tissue: with this procedure, abnormal and healthy tissue can be distinguished

e·cho·ic (e kō′ik) ***adj.*** ⟦ECHO + -IC⟧ 1 having the nature of an echo 2 imitative in sound; onomatopoeic: a term used, as in the etymologies of this dictionary, to indicate that a word, as TINKLE, is formed in approximate imitation of some sound —**ech·o·ism** (ek′ō iz′əm) ***n.***

ech·o·la·li·a (ek′ō lā′lē ə) ***n.*** ⟦ModL < *echo* (see ECHO) + *-lalia*, speech defect < Gr *lalia*, speech < *lalein*, to talk, prattle < redupl. of IE echoic **la-* (as in L *lallare*, Ger *lallen*, to lull)⟧ the automatic repetition by someone of words spoken in his or her presence, esp. as a symptom of mental disorder

ech·o·lo·ca·tion (ek′ō lō kā′shən) ***n.*** the determination, as by a bat, of the position of an object by the emission of sound waves which are reflected back to the sender as echoes —**ech′o·lo′cate′** ***vt., vi.*** **-cat′ed, -cat′ing**

echo sounding the determining of depth of water by means of a device (**echo sounder**) that measures the time required for a sound wave to be reflected from the bottom: a similar process (**echo ranging**) is used to measure the distance to an underwater object

ech·o·vi·rus (ek′ō vī′rəs) ***n.*** ⟦< earlier *ECHO virus* < E(NTERIC) + *c(ytopathogenic)* (< CYTO- + PATHOGENIC) + H(UMAN) + O(RPHAN) (in extended use)⟧ any of a group of enteroviruses that includes viruses which cause mild forms of meningitis, gastroenteritis, etc.

echo word *Linguis.* a word that is ECHOIC (sense 2), or onomatopoeic

echt (eHt) ***adj.*** ⟦Ger⟧ genuine; real; authentic

e·cig·a·rette (ē′sig′ə ret′) ***n.*** ⟦E-[2] + CIGARETTE⟧ a small, battery-powered cartridge shaped like a cigarette and designed to deliver vaporized liquid nicotine in lieu of tobacco smoke: also [Informal] **e-cig** (ē′sig′)

Eck (ek), **Jo·hann (Maier)** (yō′hän′) 1486-1543; Ger. Catholic theologian

Eck·hart (ek′härt′), **Jo·han·nes** (yô hän′əs) 1260?-1327?; Ger. theologian & mystic: called *Meister Eckhart*

é·clair (ā kler′; *also* i-, ē-) ***n.*** ⟦Fr, lit., flash of lightning: connection uncert.⟧ a small, oblong pastry shell filled with flavored custard or whipped cream and covered with frosting

é·clair·cisse·ment (ā kler sēs män′) ***n.*** ⟦Fr < *éclaircir*, to clear up < OFr *esclarcir* < VL **exclaricire* < L *ex-*, intens. + *claricare*, to gleam < *clarus*, CLEAR⟧ a clearing up, as of a disputed or difficult point; clarification

ec·lamp·si·a (ek lamp′sē ə) ***n.*** ⟦ModL < Gr *eklampsis*, a shining forth < *ek-*, out + *lampein*, to shine: see LAMP⟧ an attack of convulsions; specif., a disorder that may occur late in pregnancy, characterized by convulsions, edema, and elevated blood pressure

é·clat (ā klä′; *also* i-, ē-) ***n.*** ⟦Fr, noise, clap, splendor < *éclater*, to burst (out), shine, prob. < Gmc base seen in Langobardic *slaitan*, to tear, split, akin to SLIT⟧ 1 brilliant or conspicuous success 2 dazzling display; striking effect 3 approval; acclaim 4 fame; renown

ec·lec·tic (ek lek′tik) ***adj.*** ⟦Gr *eklektikos* < *eklegein*, to select < *ek-*, out + *legein*, to choose, pick: see LOGIC⟧ 1 selecting from various systems, doctrines, or sources 2 composed of material gathered from various sources, systems, etc. —***n.*** a person who uses eclectic methods in philosophy, science, or art —**ec·lec′ti·cal·ly *adv.***

ec·lec·ti·cism (ek lek′tə siz′əm) ***n.*** 1 an eclectic method or system of thought 2 the using or upholding of such a method or system

e·clipse (i klips′, ē-) ***n.*** ⟦ME < OFr < L *eclipsis* < Gr *ekleipsis*, an abandoning, eclipse < *ekleipein*,

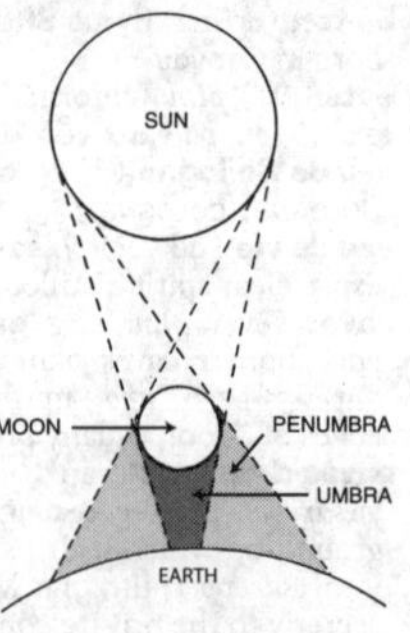

solar eclipse

to leave out, fail < *ek-*, out + *leipein*, to leave < IE base **leikw-*, to leave > LOAN, L *linquere*⟧ 1 the partial or total obscuring of one celestial body by another, esp. of the sun when the moon comes between it and the earth (called **solar eclipse**), or of the moon when the earth's shadow is cast upon it (called **lunar eclipse**) 2 any overshadowing or cutting off of light 3 a dimming or extinction, as of fame or glory —*vt.* **e·clipsed′**, **e·clips′ing** ⟦ME *eclipsen*⟧ 1 to cause an eclipse of; darken or obscure 2 to make seem less brilliant, famous, etc. by being even more so; overshadow; outshine; surpass

e·clip·tic (i klip′tik, ē-) *n.* ⟦ME *ecliptik* < ML *ecliptica* < LL (*linea*) *ecliptica* < Gr *ekleiptikos*, of an eclipse⟧ 1 the great circle on the celestial sphere intersecting the celestial equator at about 23½° and representing the changing position of the sun with respect to the background stars, as seen from the orbiting earth during one year 2 the plane of the earth's orbit extended infinitely —*adj.* of eclipses or the ecliptic

ec·logue (ek′lôg′) *n.* ⟦ME *eclog* < L *ecloga*, a short poem (esp. one of the *Eclogae*, bucolic poems of Virgil) < Gr *eklogē*, selection, esp. of poems < *eklegein*: see ECLECTIC⟧ a short, usually pastoral, poem, often in the form of a dialogue between two shepherds

e·clo·sion (ē klō′zhən) *n.* ⟦Fr *éclosion* < *éclore*, to hatch, be hatched < OFr *esclore* < VL **exclaudere*, to hatch out, altered (as if < L *ex-* + *claudere*, to CLOSE[2]) < L *excludere* to hatch, drive out, EXCLUDE⟧ the emergence of an insect from its egg or from the pupal case

ec·o- (ē′kō, ek′ō) ⟦LL *oeco-* < Gr *oiko-* < *oikos*, house: < IE base **weiko*, house, settlement > OE *wic*, house, village, L *vicus*, group of houses, *villa*, country house, farm⟧ *combining form* 1 environment or habitat [*ecotype*] 2 ecology; ecological: often used in nonce compounds [*eco*-tourism, *ecohero*]

e·co·ca·tas·tro·phe (ē′kō kə tas′trə fē, ek′ō-) *n.* a widespread disturbance or destruction of an ecological system, caused as by an invasive organism or, esp., by human activity: also written **e′co-ca·tas′tro·phe**

☆**e·co·cide** (ē′kō sīd′, ek′ō-) *n.* ⟦ECO- + -CIDE⟧ the destruction of the environment or of ecosystems, as by the use of defoliants or the emission of pollutants —**e′co·ci′dal** *adj.*

e·co·fem·i·nism (ē′kō fem′ə niz′əm, ek′ō-) *n.* ⟦Fr *éco-féminisme* < *éco*(*logie*), ECOLOGY + *féminisme*, FEMINISM: coined by F. d'Eaubonne (1920-2005), Fr writer⟧ the principle or movement that relates feminist concerns to those of environmentalism, viewing the devaluation and exploitation of both women and the environment as rooted in patriarchal values and institutions —**e′co·fem′i·nist** *n., adj.*

ecol *abbrev.* 1 ecological 2 ecology

é·cole (ā kôl′) *n.* ⟦Fr < L *schola*⟧ school

E. co·li (ē kō′lī′) ⟦ModL *E*(*scherichia*) *coli* after T. Escherich (1857-1911), Ger physician + L *coli*, of the colon⟧ a species of Gram-negative bacteria normally present in the intestines of all vertebrates and widely used in biological research: its presence in water in certain quantities indicates fecal pollution that can cause diarrhea

e·co·log·i·cal (ē′kə läj′i kəl, ek′ə-) *adj.* of or having to do with ecology or an ecology; often, specif., of or promoting environmentalist concerns: also **e′co·log′ic** —**e′co·log′i·cal·ly** *adv.*

e·col·o·gy (ē käl′ə jē) *n.* ⟦Ger *ökologie* < Gr *oikos* (see ECO-) + *-logia*, -LOGY⟧ 1 *a*) the branch of biology that deals with the relations between living organisms and their environment *b*) the complex of relations between a specific organism and its environment 2 *Sociology* the study of the relationship and adjustment of human groups to their geographical and social environments —**e·col′o·gist** *n.*

e-com·merce (ē′käm′ərs) *n.* [*often* **E-**] the buying and selling of goods and services over the internet

econ *abbrev.* 1 economic 2 economics 3 economy

e·con·o·met·rics (ē kän′ə me′triks′, i-) *n.* ⟦ECONO(MY) + METRICS⟧ the use of mathematical and statistical methods in the field of economics to verify and develop economic theories —**e·con′o·met′ric** *adj.* —**e·con′o·me·tri′cian** (-mə trish′ən) *n.*

ec·o·nom·ic (ek′ə näm′ik, ē′kə-) *adj.* ⟦L *oeconomicus* < Gr *oikonomikos* < *oikonomia*: see ECONOMY⟧ 1 of or having to do with the management of the income, expenditures, etc. of a household, business, community, or government 2 of or having to do with the production, distribution, and consumption of wealth 3 of or having to do with economics 4 of or having to do with the satisfaction of people's material needs [*economic* biology] 5 ECONOMICAL (sense 2)

ec·o·nom·i·cal (-i kəl) *adj.* 1 not wasting money, time, fuel, etc.; thrifty [an *economical* person, an *economical* stove] 2 expressed or done with economy, as by using few words [an *economical* style] 3 of economics; economic —*SYN.* THRIFTY —**ec′o·nom′i·cal·ly** *adv.*

economic geography the branch of geography that deals with the relation of economic conditions to physical geography and natural resources

ec·o·nom·ics (ek′ə näm′iks, ē′kə-) *n.* ⟦< obs. sing.n. *economic* + -s (sense 1); patterned on Gr *ta oikonomika*, household management, title of treatise by ARISTOTLE < neut. pl. of *oikonomikos*, skilled in household management < *oikonomia*: see ECONOMY⟧ the science that deals with the production, distribution, and consumption of wealth, and with the various related problems of labor, finance, taxation, etc. —*pl.n.* economic factors

economies of scale circumstances, conditions, etc. which encourage mass production of a commodity by lowering its unit cost as greater quantities are produced

e·con·o·mist (i kän′ə mist, ē-) *n.* 1 a specialist in economics 2 [Archaic] an economical or thrifty person

e·con·o·mize (i kän′ə mīz′, ē-) *vi.* **-mized′**, **-miz′ing** to avoid waste or needless expenditure; reduce expenses —*vt.* to manage or use with thrift —**e·con′o·miz′er** *n.*

e·con·o·my (i kän′ə mē, ē-) *n., pl.* **-mies** ⟦L *oeconomia* < Gr *oikonomia*, management of a household or state, public revenue < *oikonomos*, manager < *oikos*, house (see ECO-) + *-nomia*, -NOMY⟧ 1 the management of the income, expenditures, etc. of a household, business, community, or government 2 *a*) careful management of wealth, resources, etc.; avoidance of waste by careful planning and use; thrift or thrifty use *b*) restrained or efficient use of one's materials, technique, etc., esp. by an artist *c*) an instance of such management or use, or a way of economizing 3 an orderly management or arrangement of parts; organization or system [the *economy* of the human body] 4 *a*) a system of producing, distributing, and consuming wealth *b*) the condition of such a system [a healthy *economy*] —*adj.* 1 costing less than the standard or traditional kind [an *economy* car, an *economy* flight] 2 providing more of a product at a lower unit price [an *economy* package]

ECOSOC *abbrev.* Economic and Social Council (of the United Nations)

e·co·spe·cies (ē′kō spē′shēz, -sēz; ek′ō-) *n.* ⟦ECO- + SPECIES⟧ a biological species distinguished from its close relatives, with which it can interbreed, by its adaptations to its particular environment —**e′co·spe·cif′ic** *adj.*

☆**e·co·sphere** (-sfir′) *n.* ⟦ECO- + SPHERE⟧ the zone of the earth, a planet, a star, etc. which contains or is theoretically capable of containing living organisms; specif., the BIOSPHERE

e·co·sys·tem (-sis′təm) *n.* ⟦ECO- + SYSTEM⟧ a system made up of a community of animals, plants, and bacteria interrelated together with its physical and chemical environment

e·co·ter·ror·ism (ē′kō ter′ər iz′əm, ek′ō-) *n.* the threat or use of violence, vandalism, etc. to bring awareness to environmental causes; often, specif., sabotage directed against a company or agency perceived as engaging in practices harmful to the environment —**e′co·ter′ror·ist** *n., adj.*

☆**e·co·tone** (ē′kō tōn′, ek′ō-) *n.* ⟦< ECO- + Gr *tonos*, a stretching: see TONE⟧ a transitional zone between two adjacent communities, containing species characteristic of either as well as other species occurring only within the zone

e·co-tour·ism or **e·co·tour·ism** (ē′kō toor′iz′əm, ek′ō-) *n.* tourism intended to promote ecological awareness and done in a manner that limits damage to the environment —**e′co-tour′ist** *n.*, **e′co·tour′ist**

e·co·tox·i·col·o·gy (ē′kō täk′si käl′ə jē, ek′ō-) *n.* the branch of ecology that deals with toxic chemicals and their impact on the environment —**e′co·tox′i·co·log′i·cal** (-kə läj′i kəl) *adj.* —**e′co·tox′i·col′o·gist** *n.*

e·co·type (ē′kō tīp′, ek′ō-) *n.* ⟦ECO- + TYPE⟧ a group, or race, within a species, having unique physical characteristics genetically adapted to particular environmental conditions —**e′co·typ′ic** (-tip′ik) *adj.* —**e′co·typ′i·cal·ly** *adv.*

e·co-war·ri·or (ē′kō wôr′yər, ek′ō-; -wôr′ē ər) *n.* an environmentalist, often, specif., a radical one

ec·ru (ek′roo′, ā′kroo′) *adj., n.* ⟦Fr *écru*, unbleached, raw < OFr *escru* < *es-* (L *ex-*), intens. + *cru*, raw < L *crudus* (see CRUDE): in reference to the color of unbleached linen⟧ light tan; beige

ec·sta·sy (ek′stə sē) *n., pl.* **-sies** ⟦ME & OFr *extasie* < LL(Ec) *ecstasis* < Gr *ekstasis*, a being put out of its place, distraction, trance < *ek-*, out + *histanai*, to set: see STAND⟧ 1 a state of being overpowered by emotion, as by joy, grief, or passion [an *ecstasy* of delight] 2 a feeling of overpowering joy; great delight; rapture 3 a trance, esp. one resulting from religious fervor 4 [*usually* **E-**] [Slang] an illegal, mildly psychedelic derivative of amphetamine, $C_{11}H_{15}NO_2$, that slows down reactions and thought; MDMA

SYN.—**ecstasy** implies extreme emotional exaltation, now usually intense delight, that overpowers the senses and lifts one into a trancelike state; **bliss** implies a state of great happiness and contentment, often suggesting heavenly joy; **rapture** now generally suggests the mental exaltation experienced when one's entire attention is captured by something that evokes great joy or pleasure; **transport** implies a being carried away by any powerful emotion

ec·stat·ic (ek stat′ik, ik-) *adj.* ⟦ML *ecstaticus* < Gr *ekstatikos*⟧ 1 of, having the nature of, or characterized by ecstasy 2 causing, or caused by, ecstasy 3 subject to ecstasy —**ec·stat′i·cal·ly** *adv.*

ECT *abbrev.* electroconvulsive therapy

ec·to- (ek′tō, -tə) ⟦ModL < Gr *ektos*, outside < IE **eĝhs-*, out > L *ex*⟧ *combining form* outside, external [*ectoderm*]: also, before a vowel, **ect-**

ec·to·blast (ek′tō blast′, -tə-) *n.* EPIBLAST

ec·to·com·men·sal (ek′tə kə men′səl) *n.* a commensal living on the outer surface of the host organism

ec·to·derm (ek′tō durm′, -tə-) *n.* ⟦ECTO- + -DERM⟧ 1 the outer layer of cells of an animal embryo, from which the nervous system, skin, hair, teeth, etc. are developed 2 the layer or layers of cells composing the skin, nervous system, etc. in all animals except protozoans and sponges —**ec′to·der′mal** *adj.*, **ec′to·der′mic**

ec·to·gen·e·sis (ek′tō jen′ə sis, -tə-) *n., pl.* **-ses′** (-sēz′) the growth process of embryonic tissue placed in an artificial environment, as a test tube —**ec′to·ge·net′ic** (-jə net′ik) *adj.*

ec·tog·e·nous (ek täj′ə nəs) *adj.* that can develop outside the host: said of certain parasitic bacteria: also **ec·to·gen·ic** (ek′tō jen′ik, -tə-)

ec·to·mere (ek′tō mir′, -tə-) *n.* ⟦ECTO- + -MERE⟧ any of the blastomeres that contribute to the formation of the ectoderm of an embryo —**ec′to·mer′ic** (-mer′ik) *adj.*

ec·to·morph (-môrf′) *n.* an ectomorphic individual —**ec′to·mor′phy** *n.*

ec·to·mor·phic (ek′tō môr′fik, -tə-) *adj.* ⟦ECTO- + -MORPHIC⟧ designating or of the slender physical type, characterized by predominance of the structures developed from the ectodermal layer of the embryo, as skin, nerves, brain, and sense organs: cf. ENDOMORPHIC, MESOMORPHIC —**ec′to·mor′phi·cal·ly** *adv.*

-ec·to·my (ek′tə mē) ⟦< Gr *ektomē*, a cutting out < *ek-*, out + *temnein*, to cut: see -TOMY⟧ *combining form* a surgical excision of

ec·to·par·a·site (ek′tō par′ə sīt′, -tə-) *n.* any parasite that lives on the outer surface of an animal: opposed to ENDOPARASITE —**ec′to·par′a·sit′ic** (-sit′ik) *adj.*

ec·to·pi·a (ek tō′pē ə) *n.* ⟦ModL < Gr *ektopos*, away from a place < *ek-*, out of (see EX-[1]) + *topos*, a place (see TOPIC) + ModL *-ia*, -IA⟧ an abnormal position of a body part or organ, esp. at birth —**ec·top·ic** (ek täp′ik) *adj.*

☆**ectopic pregnancy** a pregnancy with the fertilized ovum developing outside the uterus, as in a fallopian tube

ec·to·plasm (ek′tō plaz′əm, -tə-) *n.* ⟦ECTO- + -PLASM⟧ **1** the outer layer of the cytoplasm of a cell: distinguished from ENDOPLASM **2** the luminous, vaporous substance believed by spiritualists to emanate from a medium in a trance —**ec′to·plas′mic** *adj.*

ec·to·proct (-präkt′) *n.* ⟦< ModL *Ectoprocta* < *ecto-* (see ECTO-) + Gr *prōktos*, anus⟧ BRYOZOAN —**ec′to·proc′tan** *adj.*

ec·to·sarc (-särk′) *n.* ⟦< ECTO- + Gr *sarx* (gen. *sarkos*), flesh⟧ the ectoplasm of one-celled animals

ec·to·ther·mal (ek′tō thur′məl, -tə-) *adj.* COLDBLOODED (sense 1) —**ec′to·therm′** (-thurm′) *n.* —**ec′to·ther′my** (-thur′mē) *n.*

ec·type (ek′tīp′) *n.* ⟦L *ectypus* < Gr *ektypos*, engraved in relief < *ek-*, out (see EX-[1]) + *typos*, a figure (see TYPE)⟧ a reproduction of an original; copy

ECU or **ecu** (ā′kyoo͞′, ē′sē′yoo͞′) *n.* ⟦< *E(uropean) C(urrency) U(nit)*⟧ a money of account of the European Community through 1998: see EURO

é·cu (ā kü′) *n., pl.* **-cus′** (-kü′) ⟦Fr < OFr *escu* < L *scutum*, a shield⟧ any of various French silver or gold coins, esp. a silver crown of the 17th-18th cent.

Ecua *abbrev.* Ecuador

Ec·ua·dor (ek′wə dôr′) country on the NW coast of South America: independent since 1830: 109,483 sq mi (283,560 sq km); cap. Quito —**Ec′ua·do′re·an** *adj., n.*, **Ec′ua·do′ri·an**, or **Ec′ua·dor′an**

ec·u·men·i·cal (ek′yə men′i kəl, -yoo͞-) *adj.* ⟦LL *oecumenicus* < Gr *oikoumenikos*, of or from the whole world < *oikoumenē* (*gē*), the inhabited (world) < *oikein*, to dwell, inhabit < *oikos*: see ECO-⟧ **1** of or concerning the Christian Church or Christendom as a whole **2** *a)* furthering or intended to further the unity or unification of Christian churches *b)* of or having to do with ecumenism —**ec′u·men′i·cal·ism′** *n.* —**ec′u·men′i·cal·ly** *adv.*

Ecumenical Patriarch *Eastern Orthodox Ch.* the Patriarch of Constantinople, the highest-ranking dignitary of the Church

ec·u·men·i·cism (ek′yə men′ə siz′əm, -yoo͞-) *n.* ECUMENISM

ec·u·men·ism (e kyoo͞′mə niz′əm, ek′yə mə niz′əm) *n.* **1** the ecumenical movement among Christian churches **2** the principles or practice of promoting cooperation or better understanding among differing religious faiths Also **ec·u·me·nic·i·ty** (ek′yə mə nis′ə tē, -yoo͞-) —**ec·u′men·ist** *n.*

ec·ze·ma (ek′sə mə, eg′zə-) *n.* ⟦ModL < Gr *ekzema* < *ek-*, out + *zein*, to boil: see YEAST⟧ any of various noncontagious skin disorders characterized by inflammation, itching, and the formation of scales —**ec·zem·a·tous** (ek sem′ə təs, eg zem′-) *adj.*

ed[1] (ed) *n.* [Informal] education: used chiefly in compounds [drivers *ed*, sex-*ed* classes]

ed[2] *abbrev.* **1** edited (by) **2** *a)* edition *b)* editor **3** education

ED *abbrev.* **1** Department of Education **2** erectile dysfunction

-ed (ed, id, əd, *as a separate syllable, esp. after t or d*; d *after a voiced sound in the same syllable*; t *after a voiceless sound in the same syllable*) *suffix* **1** ⟦as ending of past tense < ME < OE *-ede, -ode, -ade, -de*; as ending of past participles and analogous forms < ME < OE *-ed, -od, -ad*⟧ forming the past tense of weak verbs [*walked, wanted*] **2** ⟦< OE *-ede*⟧ *a)* forming the past participle of weak verbs *b)* forming analogous adjectives from nouns and verbs and from adjectives ending in *-ate* [*cultured* people, *measured* cadences; *echinated*] **3** *forming adjectives from nouns* that is provided with or characterized by [*bearded, diseased*]

EDA *abbrev.* Economic Development Administration

e·da·cious (ē dā′shəs, i-) *adj.* ⟦< L *edax* (gen. *edacis*) < *edere*, EAT + -IOUS⟧ voracious; consuming; devouring

e·dac·i·ty (ē das′ə tē, i-) *n.* ⟦L *edacitas*⟧ the state of being edacious; huge capacity for eating: now a humorous usage

ed·a·ma·me (ed′ə mä′mā′, -mē) *n.* ⟦Jpn, lit., beans on a branch: the pods are sometimes served still attached to the branch⟧ **1** *pl.* **-me′** a type of green soybean that is boiled and salted in the pod and eaten as a snack or appetizer **2** this snack or appetizer

E·dam (cheese) (ē′dəm, -dam′; ä däm′) ⟦after *Edam*, town in NW Netherlands, where orig. made⟧ a mild, yellow cheese, made in a round mold and usually having a coating of red paraffin

e·daph·ic (ē daf′ik, i-) *adj.* ⟦< Gr *edaphos*, soil, earth, bottom (prob. < or akin to *hedos*, seat, chair < IE **sedos-* < base **sed-*, SIT) + -IC⟧ *Ecol.* pertaining to the chemical and physical characteristics of the soil, without reference to climate

EDB (ē′dē′bē′) *n.* ⟦*e(thylene) d(i)b(romide)*⟧ a carcinogenic, colorless liquid, $BrCH_2CH_2Br$, used as an additive to remove the lead during the burning of leaded gasoline and, formerly, as a fumigant to protect stored food, esp. grain and fruit, from insects, rodents, etc.

EdB or **Ed.B.** *abbrev.* Bachelor of Education

EdD or **Ed.D.** *abbrev.* Doctor of Education

Ed·da (ed′ə) *n.* ⟦ON⟧ either of two early Icelandic literary works: *a)* the **Prose (or Younger) Edda** (*c.* 1230), a summary of Norse mythology with two treatises on skaldic poetry, attributed to Snorri Sturluson *b)* the **Poetic (or Elder) Edda**, a collection (made *c.* 1200) of Old Norse poetry —**Eddic** (ed′ik) *adj.*, **Ed·da·ic** (e dā′ik, i-)

Ed·ding·ton (ed′iŋ tən), Sir **Arthur Stanley** 1882-1944; Eng. astronomer & astrophysicist

ed·do (ed′ō) *n., pl.* **-does** ⟦prob. < name in a language of W Africa⟧ the edible corm of the taro

ed·dy (ed′ē) *n., pl.* **-dies** ⟦ME *ydy*, prob. < ON *itha*, an eddy, whirlpool < IE base **eti*, and, furthermore > L *et*⟧ **1** a current of air, water, etc. moving against the main current and with a circular motion; little whirlpool or whirlwind **2** a contrary movement or trend, limited in importance or effect —*vi.* **-died, -dy·ing** to move with a circular motion against the main current; move in an eddy

Ed·dy (ed′ē), **Mary Baker** (born *Mary Morse Baker*) 1821-1910; U.S. founder of Christian Science

Ed·dy·stone Light (ed′i stən) lighthouse on dangerous rocks (**Eddystone Rocks**) just off the SE coast of Cornwall, in the English Channel

E·de (ā′də) city in central Netherlands

e·del·weiss (ā′dəl vīs′, ād′′l-) *n.* ⟦Ger < *edel*, noble, precious + *weiss*, WHITE⟧ a small, flowering plant (*Leontopodium alpinum*) of the composite family, native to the high mountains of Europe and central Asia, esp. the Alps, with leaves and petal-like bracts that are white and woolly

e·de·ma (ē dē′mə, i-) *n., pl.* **-mas** or **-ma·ta** (-mə tə) ⟦ModL < Gr *oidēma*, a swelling, tumor < IE base **oid-*, to swell > OE *ator*, poison⟧ **1** an abnormal accumulation of fluid in cells, tissues, or cavities of the body, resulting in swelling **2** a similar swelling in plant cells or tissues —**e·dem·a·tous** (ē dem′ə təs, i-) *adj.*

E·den[1] (ēd′′n) *n.* ⟦LL < Heb, lit., delight⟧ **1** *Bible* the garden where Adam and Eve first lived; Paradise: Gen. 2:8 **2** any delightful place or state; a paradise —**E·den·ic** *adj.*, **e·den·ic** (ē den′ik)

E·den[2] (ēd′′n), **(Robert) Anthony** Earl of Avon 1897-1977; Brit. statesman: prime minister (1955-57)

e·den·tate (ē den′tāt′, i-) *adj.* ⟦ModL *edentatus* < L, pp. of *edentare*, to render toothless < *e-*, out + *dens* (gen. *dentis*), TOOTH + -ATE[1]⟧ **1** without teeth **2** of the edentates —*n.* any of an order (Edentata) of mammals having only molars or no teeth at all, as the sloths, armadillos, and anteaters

e·den·tu·lous (ē den′tyoo͞ ləs, i-; -den′chə-) *adj.* ⟦L *edentulus* < *e-*, out + *dens*, TOOTH⟧ without teeth

E·des·sa (ē des′ə; i-) ancient city in NW Mesopotamia, on the site of modern SANLIURFA (Turkey)

Ed·gar[1] (ed′gər) *n.* ⟦OE *Eadgar* < *ead*, riches, prosperity, happiness (< Gmc **autha-* > Goth *audags*, fortunate, OHG *ot*, wealth) + *gar*, a spear: see GORE[3]⟧ a masculine name: dim. *Ed, Ned*

Ed·gar[2] (ed′gər) *n.* ⟦after *Edgar* Allan POE⟧ any of the statuettes awarded annually in the U.S. for the best mystery novel, short story, etc.

edge (ej) *n.* ⟦ME *egge* < OE *ecg*, akin to ON *egg*, Ger *ecke*, corner < IE base **ak-*, sharp: see ACID⟧ **1** the thin, sharp, cutting part of a blade **2** the quality of being sharp or keen **3** the projecting ledge or brink, as of a cliff **4** the part farthest from the middle; line where something begins or ends; border, or part nearest the border; margin **5** the verge or brink, as of a condition **6** an intense, harsh, or irritable quality [his voice had a distinct *edge*] **7** *Geom.* a line or line segment at which two plane surfaces meet ☆**8** [Informal] advantage [you have an *edge* on me] **9** [Informal] the quality of being EDGY (sense 4) —*vt.* **edged, edg′ing 1** *a)* to form or put an edge on; provide an edge for *b)* to trim the edge of **2** to make (one's way) sideways, as through a crowd **3** to move gradually or cautiously **4** [Informal] to defeat in a contest by a narrow margin: often with *out* ☆**5** *Skiing* to tilt (a ski) so that one edge bites into the snow, as in traversing a slope —*vi.* **1** to move sideways **2** to move gradually or cautiously [to *edge* away from danger] —*SYN.* BORDER —**on edge 1** so tense or nervous as to be easily upset; irritable **2** eager; impatient —**set someone's teeth on edge 1** to give a sensation of tingling discomfort, as the sound of a fingernail scraped on a slate does **2** to irritate; provoke —**take the edge off** to dull the intensity, force, or pleasure of —**edge′less** *adj.*

☆**edge city** ⟦< *Edge City: Life on the New Frontier* (1991), book by J. Garreau, U.S. journalist⟧ a concentration of comparatively recent commercial and retail development on the outskirts of an urban area, that provides the employment, shopping, etc. customarily sought in a central city

edg·er (ej′ər) *n.* one that edges; specif., a tool for trimming the edge of a lawn, as along a sidewalk

edge species *Ecol.* a species of animal or plant living primarily in an ecotone

edge tool a tool with a cutting edge, as a chisel

edge·wise (ej′wīz′) *adv.* with the edge foremost; on, by, with, or toward the edge: also [Chiefly Brit.] **edge′ways′** (-wāz′) —**get a word in edgewise** to manage to say something in a conversation being monopolized by another or others

Edge·worth (ej′wərth), **Maria** 1767-1849; Ir. novelist, born in England

edg·ing (ej′iŋ) *n.* something forming an edge or placed along the edge; fringe, trimming, etc. for a border

edg·y (ej′ē) *adj.* **edg′i·er, edg′i·est 1** having an edge or edges; sharp **2** irritable; on edge **3** having outlines that are too sharp: said of drawings, paintings, etc. 4 ⟦< CUTTING EDGE⟧ [Informal] innovative, daring, unconventional, etc. —**edg′i·ly** *adv.* —**edg′i·ness** *n.*

edh (*eth*) *n.* 1 a letter of the Old English alphabet (ð, Ð), from Roman *d, D*, used to represent the voiced or voiceless apicodental fricative: in Middle English it was replaced by *th* 2 the lowercase form of this letter as used in some phonetic alphabets, as the IPA, to represent the voiced apicodental fricative (*th*)

ed·i·ble (ed′ə bəl) *adj.* ⟦LL *edibilis* < L *edere*, EAT⟧ fit to be eaten —*n.* anything fit to be eaten; food: *usually used in pl.* —**ed′i·bil′i·ty** (-bil′ə tē) *n.*, **ed′i·ble·ness**

e·dict (ē′dikt′) *n.* ⟦L *edictum*, neut. pp. of *edicere*, to proclaim < *e-*, out + *dicere*, to speak: see DICTION⟧ 1 an official public proclamation or order issued by authority; decree 2 any command or order —**e·dic·tal** (ē dik′təl) *adj.*

ed·i·fi·ca·tion (ed′i fi kā′shən) *n.* ⟦ME *edificacioun* < LL(Ec) *aedificatio* < L, act of building⟧ an edifying or being edified; instruction; esp., moral or spiritual instruction

ed·i·fice (ed′i fis) *n.* ⟦ME < OFr < L *aedificium*, a building < *aedificare*: see fol.⟧ 1 a building, esp. a large, imposing one 2 any elaborately constructed institution, organization, etc. —**SYN.** BUILDING

ed·i·fy (ed′i fī′) *vt.* **-fied′**, **-fy′ing** ⟦ME *edifien* < OFr *edifier* < L *aedificare*, to build, construct (in LL(Ec) to edify) < *aedes*, a dwelling, house, temple, orig., hearth, fireplace < IE base **ai-dh-*, to burn (> Gr *aithein*, to burn, OE *ad*, pyre) + *-ficare* < *facere*, to make, DO[1]⟧ 1 to instruct in such a way as to improve, enlighten, or uplift morally, spiritually, or intellectually 2 [Archaic] to build; establish —**ed′i·fi′er** *n.*

Ed·in·burgh (ed′'n bur′ə, -ō) capital of Scotland, in the E part, on the Firth of Forth

E·dir·ne (e dir′nə) city in NW European Turkey, near the Greek border, on the site of an ancient Roman city (*Adrianopolis*) founded by the emperor Hadrian (A.D. 125?)

Ed·i·son[1] (ed′i sən), **Thomas Al·va** (al′və) 1847-1931; U.S. inventor, esp. of electrical & communication devices, including the incandescent lamp, phonograph, & microphone

Ed·i·son[2] (ed′i sən) ⟦after prec., who had his first laboratory here⟧ urban township in NC N.J.

ed·it[1] (ed′it) *vt.* ⟦back-form. < EDITOR⟧ 1 to prepare (an author's works, journals, letters, etc.) for publication, by selection, arrangement, and annotation 2 to revise and make ready (a manuscript) for publication 3 to supervise the publication of and set the policy for (a newspaper, periodical, reference book, etc.) ☆4 to prepare (a film, tape, or recording) for presentation by cutting and splicing, dubbing, rearranging, etc. 5 to make additions, deletions, or other changes in (a computer file) —*n.* [Informal] an act of editing [*a cut made in the edit*] —☆**edit out** to delete in editing

edit[2] *abbrev.* 1 edited (by) 2 edition 3 editor

E·dith (ē′dith) *n.* ⟦OE *Eadgyth* < *ead* (see EDGAR[1]) + *guth*, combat, battle, war⟧ a feminine name: dim. *Edie*

e·di·tion (i dish′ən) *n.* ⟦ME *edicion* < L *editio*, a bringing forth, publishing < *edere*: see fol.⟧ 1 the size, style, or form in which a book is published [*a pocket edition*] 2 *a)* the total number of copies of a book or the like printed from the same plates, type, etc. and published at about the same time *b)* a single copy of such a printing 3 any of the versions of a textbook, reference book, etc. that is maintained by periodic revision [*the fourth edition of a handbook*] 4 the issue of a standard work or of the writings of a well-known author, distinguished by its editor, publisher, etc. [*the Skeat edition of Chaucer*] 5 any of the various regular issues of a newspaper [*the Sunday edition*] ☆6 any set of like items made and offered for sale at one time [*a limited edition of commemorative plates*]

ed·i·tor (ed′it ər) *n.* ⟦L < *editus*, pp. of *edere*, to give out, publish < *e-*, out + *dare*, to give: see DATE[1]⟧ 1 a person who edits; often, specif., one whose work is procuring and editing manuscripts ☆2 the head of a department of a newspaper, magazine, etc. ☆3 a device for editing film, videotape, etc. as by viewing, cutting, and splicing —**ed′i·tor·ship′** *n.*

ed·i·to·ri·al (ed′i tôr′ē əl) *adj.* 1 *a)* of or by an editor *b)* of or for editing 2 characteristic of an editor or editorial; expressing opinion in the manner of an editor [*an editorial comment*] 3 denoting or of the stories, articles, etc. of a publication, as distinct from advertisements, pictures, etc. —☆*n.* a statement of opinion in a newspaper or magazine, or on radio or television, as by an editor, publisher, or owner —**ed′i·to′ri·al·ly** *adv.*

☆**ed·i·to·ri·al·ist** (-ist) *n.* a writer of editorials

☆**ed·i·to·ri·al·ize** (-īz′) *vi.* **-ized′**, **-iz′ing** 1 to express editorial opinions about something 2 to insert editorial opinions into what is supposed to be a factual account —**ed′i·to′ri·al·i·za′tion** *n.* —**ed′i·to′ri·al·iz′er** *n.*

editor in chief *pl.* **editors in chief** the editor who heads or supervises the editorial staff of a publication: also written **ed′i·tor-in-chief′** *n.*

EdM or **Ed.M.** *abbrev.* Master of Education

Ed·mon·ton (ed′mən tən) ⟦prob. after *Edmonton*, former borough of London, England⟧ capital of Alberta, Canada, in the central part

Ed·mund or **Ed·mond** (ed′mənd) *n.* ⟦OE *Eadmund* < *ead* (see EDGAR[1]) + *mund*, hand, protection: see MANUAL⟧ a masculine name: dim. *Ed, Ned*

Ed·na (ed′nə) *n.* ⟦Gr < Heb, delight: see EDEN[1]⟧ a feminine name

E·do[1] (ē′dō) *n.* 1 a member of a people living in the Benin region of S Nigeria 2 the Kwa language of this people

Ed·o[2] (ed′ō) *former name for* TOKYO

E·dom[1] (ē′dəm) *n. Bible* Esau, Jacob's brother: Gen. 25:30

E·dom[2] (ē′dəm) ancient kingdom in SW Asia, south of the Dead Sea

E·dom·ite (-īt′) *n. Bible* a descendant of Edom, or Esau; inhabitant of Edom: Gen. 36 —**E′dom·it′ish** *adj.*

EDP *abbrev.* electronic data processing

☆**Ed·sel** (ed′səl) *n.* ⟦< *Edsel*, automobile produced (1957-59) by the Ford Motor Company & named after *Edsel* Ford (1893-1943), son of Henry Ford⟧ a product, project, etc. that fails to gain public acceptance despite high expectations, costly promotional efforts, etc.

EDT *abbrev.* Eastern Daylight Time

EDTA (ē′dē′tē′ā′) *n.* ⟦*e(thylene)d(iamine)t(etraacetic) a(cid)*⟧ a colorless, crystalline solid, $C_{10}H_{16}N_2O_8$, used as an industrial chelating agent, food preservative, etc. and in medicine to chelate lead, copper, etc. in metal poisoning, to prevent coagulation of blood, etc.

.edu *abbrev. Comput.* education: a U.S. domain name

educ *abbrev.* 1 education 2 educational

ed·u·ca·ble (ej′o͞o kə bəl, ej′ə-) *adj.* that can be educated or trained —**ed′u·ca·bil′i·ty** *n.*

ed·u·cate (ej′o͞o kāt′, ej′ə-) *vt.* **-cat′ed**, **-cat′ing** ⟦ME *educaten* < L *educatus*, pp. of *educare*, to bring up, rear, or train < *educere* < *e-*, out + *ducere*, to lead: see DUCT⟧ 1 to train or develop the knowledge, skill, mind, or character of, esp. by formal schooling or study; teach; instruct 2 to form and develop (one's taste, etc.) 3 to pay for the schooling of (a person) —**SYN.** TEACH

ed·u·cat·ed (-kāt′id) *adj.* 1 having obtained an education: often in compounds [*self-educated, a Harvard-educated attorney*] 2 having, or showing the results of, a good education ☆3 based on knowledge or experience [*an educated guess*]

ed·u·ca·tion (ej′o͞o kā′shən, ej′ə-) *n.* ⟦L *educatio*: see EDUCATE⟧ 1 the process of training and developing the knowledge, skill, mind, character, etc., esp. by formal schooling; teaching; training 2 knowledge, ability, etc. thus developed 3 *a)* formal schooling at an institution of learning *b)* a stage of this [*a high-school education*] 4 systematic study of the methods and theories of teaching and learning

ed·u·ca·tion·al (-shə nəl) *adj.* 1 relating to education 2 giving instruction or information; educating [*an educational film*] —**ed′u·ca′tion·al·ly** *adv.*

☆**educational park** a centralized, integrated educational facility in a metropolitan area, designed for students from widespread areas throughout the community and consisting variously of schools from kindergarten through college on one campus

ed·u·ca·tion·ist (-shən ist) *n.* an educator; esp., an authority on educational theory: also **ed′u·ca′tion·al·ist** (-shə nə list)

ed·u·ca·tive (ej′o͞o kāt′iv, ej′ə-) *adj.* 1 educating or tending to educate; instructive 2 of education; educational

ed·u·ca·tor (-kāt′ər) *n.* ⟦L⟧ 1 a person whose work is to educate others; teacher 2 a specialist in the theories and methods of education

e·duce (ē do͞os′, -dyo͞os′) *vt.* **-duced′**, **-duc′ing** ⟦L *educere*: see EDUCATE⟧ 1 to draw out; elicit 2 to infer from data; deduce —**SYN.** EXTRACT —**e·duc·i·ble** *adj.* —**e·duc·tion** (ē duk′shən) *n.*

e·duct (ē′dukt′) *n.* ⟦L *eductum*, neut. pp. of *educere*⟧ 1 something educed 2 a substance separated unchanged from another substance: distinguished from PRODUCT

Ed·ward[1] (ed′wərd) *n.* ⟦OE *Eadweard* < *ead* (see EDGAR[1]) + *weard*, guardian, protector (see WARD): hence, wealthy (or fortunate) guardian⟧ a masculine name: dim. *Ed, Eddie, Ned, Ted, Teddy*; equiv. Fr. *Édouard*, Ger. *Eduard*, It. & Sp. *Eduardo*, Scand. *Edvard*

Ed·ward[2] (ed′wərd) 1 1330-76; Prince of Wales: son of Edward III: called the *Black Prince* 2 **Edward I** 1239-1307; king of England (1272-1307): son of Henry III 3 **Edward II** 1284-1327; king of England (1307-27): son of Edward I 4 **Edward III** 1312-77; king of England (1327-77): son of Edward II 5 **Edward IV** 1442-83; king of England (1461-70; 1471-83): son of Richard, duke of York 6 **Edward V** 1470-83; king of England (1483): son of Edward IV: reputed to have been murdered by order of Richard III 7 **Edward VI** 1537-53; king of England & Ireland (1547-53): son of Henry VIII & Jane Seymour 8 **Edward VII** 1841-1910; king of Great Britain & Ireland (1901-10): son of Queen Victoria 9 **Edward VIII** *see* WINDSOR[2], Duke of

Ed·ward[3] (ed′wərd), **Lake** lake in EC Africa, between the Democratic Republic of the Congo & Uganda: 830 sq mi (2,150 sq km)

Ed·ward·i·an (ed wär′dē ən, -wôr′-) *adj.* designating or of the reigns of any of the English kings named Edward; specif., *a)* designating, or in the style of, the architecture of the period of the first three Edwards *b)* ⟦after EDWARD VII⟧ of or characteristic of the period in Great Britain from about 1901 to the beginning of WWI, esp. with reference to literature, art, and fashion

Ed·wards (ed′wərdz), **Jonathan** 1703-58; Am. theologian

Edward the Confessor 1004?-66; king of England (1042-66): canonized: his day is Oct. 13

Ed·win (ed′win) *n.* ⟦OE *Eadwine* < *ead* (see EDGAR[1]) + *wine*, friend < Gmc **weniz* < IE base **wen-*, to strive, desire, love (> WIN(SOME), WISH, L *Venus*): lit., rich friend⟧ a masculine name: dim. *Ed, Eddie*; fem. *Edwina*

Ed·wi·na (ed wē′nə, -win′ə) *n.* ⟦fem. of prec.⟧ a feminine name: dim. *Winnie*: see EDWIN

EE *abbrev.* Electrical Engineer

-ee[1] (ē) ⟦< Anglo-Fr & OFr *-é*, orig. masc. ending of pp. of verbs in *-er* < L *-atus*: see -ATE[2]⟧ *suffix forming nouns* 1 the recipient of a (specified) action, grant, or benefit [*appointee, selectee, mortgagee*] 2 a person in a (specified) condition [*absentee, employee*] 3 a person or thing associated in some way with another [*bargee, goatee*] 4 a person that performs the (specified) action [*standee*]

-ee[2] (ē) *suffix* forming an old-fashioned nonstandard, and now often insulting, form of nouns of nationality ending in -ESE [*Chinee, Portugee*]
EEC *abbrev.* European Economic Community
EEG *abbrev.* 1 electroencephalogram 2 electroencephalograph
E85 (ē′āt′ē fīv′) *n.* ⟦E(THANOL) + 85 (*percent*)⟧ a blended automotive fuel containing up to 85 percent ethanol produced from corn or other crops
eek (ēk) *interj.* ⟦echoic of a scream or squeal⟧ used to signify surprise or sudden fright
eel (ēl) *n., pl.* **eels** or **eel** ⟦ME *ele* < OE *æl*, akin to Ger *aal*⟧ 1 any of an order (Anguilliformes) of bony fishes with long, slippery, snakelike bodies and no pelvic fins 2 any of various other snakelike fishes, including the electric eel and lamprey —**eel·y** (ēl′ē) *adj.*
☆**eel·grass** (ēl′gras′) *n.* 1 a flowering plant (*Zostera marina*) of the pondweed family, that grows underwater and has long, grasslike leaves 2 TAPE GRASS
eel·pout (-pout′) *n., pl.* **-pout′** or **-pouts′** ⟦OE *ælepute*: see EEL & POUT[2]⟧ 1 any of a family (Zoarcidae, order Gadiformes) of marine bony fishes that resemble eels 2 BURBOT
eel·worm (-wurm′) *n.* any of a large number of nematode worms that are either free-living or parasitic on plants
e'en (ēn) *adv.* [Old Poet.] EVEN[1] —*n.* [Old Poet. or Dial.] even(ing)
een·sy (ēn′sē) *adj.* **-si·er, -si·est** ⟦alteration < *teensy*: see TEENY & TEENY-WEENY⟧ [Informal] very small; tiny: a facetious imitation of child's talk: also **een′sy-ween′sy** (-wēn′sē)
EEO *abbrev.* equal employment opportunity
EEOC *abbrev.* Equal Employment Opportunity Commission
EER *abbrev.* energy efficiency ratio
e'er (er, ar, ār) *adv.* [Old Poet.] EVER
-eer (ir) ⟦Fr *-ier* < L *-arius*⟧ *suffix* 1 *forming nouns* *a)* a person or thing that has to do with [*auctioneer, mountaineer*] *b)* a person who writes, makes, etc. (sometimes used derogatorily) [*pamphleteer, profiteer*] 2 *forming verbs* to have to do with [*electioneer*]
ee·rie or **ee·ry** (ir′ē, ē′rē) *adj.* **-ri·er, -ri·est** ⟦N Eng dial & Scot < ME *eri*, filled with dread, prob. var. of *erg*, cowardly, timid < OE *earg*, akin to Ger *arg*, bad, wicked: for IE base see ORCHESTRA⟧ 1 [Now Rare] timid or frightened; uneasy because of superstitious fear 2 mysterious, uncanny, or weird, esp. in such a way as to frighten or disturb —*SYN.* WEIRD —**ee′ri·ly** *adv.* —**ee′ri·ness** *n.*
ef- (ef, if, əf) *prefix* EX-[1]: used before *f* [*efface*]
ef·face (ə fās′, i-) *vt.* **-faced′, -fac′ing** ⟦Fr *effacer* < *e-* (see prec.) + *face*: see FACE⟧ 1 to rub out, as from a surface; erase; wipe out; obliterate [time *effaced* the memory] 2 to make (oneself) inconspicuous; withdraw (oneself) from notice —*SYN.* ERASE —**ef·face′a·ble** *adj.* —**ef·face′ment** *n.* —**ef·fac′er** *n.*
ef·fect (e fekt′, i-) *n.* ⟦ME < OFr (& L) < L *effectus*, orig., pp. of *efficere*, to bring to pass, accomplish < *ex-*, out + *facere*, DO[1]⟧ 1 anything brought about by a cause or agent; result 2 the power or ability to bring about results; efficacy [a law of little *effect*] 3 influence or action on something [the drug had a cathartic *effect*] 4 general meaning; purport [he spoke to this *effect*] 5 *a)* the impression produced on the mind of the observer or hearer, as by artistic design or manner of speaking, acting, etc. [to do something just for *effect*] *b)* something, as a design, aspect of nature, etc., that produces a particular impression [striking cloud *effects*] *c)* a scientific phenomenon [the Doppler *effect*] 6 the condition or fact of being operative or in force [the law goes into *effect* today] 7 [*pl.*] belongings; property [household *effects*] —*vt.* to bring about; produce as a result; cause; accomplish [to *effect* a compromise] —**give effect to** to put into practice; make operative —**in effect** 1 in result; actually; in fact 2 in essence; virtually 3 in operation; in force —**take effect** to begin to produce results; become operative —**to the effect** with the purport or meaning —**ef·fect′er** *n.*

SYN.—**effect** is applied to that which is directly produced by an action, process, or agent and is the exact correlative of *cause*; **consequence** suggests that which follows something else on which it is dependent in some way, but does not connote as direct a connection with *cause*; **result** stresses that which is finally brought about by the effects or consequences of an action, process, etc.; **issue**, in this connection, suggests a result in which there is emergence from difficulties or conflict; **outcome** refers to the result of something that was in doubt See also **perform** —*ANT.* **cause**

ef·fec·tive (e fek′tiv, i-) *adj.* ⟦ME & OFr *effectif* < L *effectivus*⟧ 1 having an effect; producing a result 2 producing a definite or desired result; efficient 3 in effect; operative; active 4 actual, not merely potential or theoretical 5 making a striking impression; impressive 6 equipped and ready for combat —*n.* a soldier, unit, etc. equipped and ready for combat: *usually used in pl.* —**ef·fec′tive·ness** *n.*

SYN.—**effective** is applied to that which produces a definite effect or result [an *effective* speaker]; **efficacious** refers to that which is capable of producing the desired effect or result [an *efficacious* remedy]; **effectual** specifically implies the production of the desired effect or result in a decisive manner [an *effectual* reply to his charge]; **efficient** implies skill and economy of energy in producing the desired result and is often applied to persons [an *efficient* worker] —*ANT.* **futile**

ef·fec·tive·ly (e fek′tiv lē, i-) *adv.* 1 in an effective way 2 in effect; for all practical purposes
ef·fec·tor (e fek′tər, i-) *n.* ⟦L, a producer < *effectus*: see EFFECT⟧ 1 a muscle, gland, cell, etc. capable of responding to a stimulus, esp. to a nerve impulse 2 that part of a nerve which transmits an impulse to an organ of response
ef·fec·tu·al (e fek′cho͞o əl, i-) *adj.* ⟦ME < OFr *effectuel* < ML *effectualis*⟧ 1 producing, or able to produce, the desired effect 2 having legal force; valid —*SYN.* EFFECTIVE —**ef·fec′tu·al′i·ty** (-al′ə tē) *n.*
ef·fec·tu·al·ly (-ə lē) *adv.* with the desired effect; completely; effectively
ef·fec·tu·ate (-āt′) *vt.* **-at′ed, -at′ing** ⟦< Fr *effectuer* (< L *effectus*: see EFFECT), with ending after verbs in *-ate* (e.g., ACTUATE)⟧ to bring about; cause to happen; effect —**ef·fec′tu·a′tion** *n.*
ef·fem·i·na·cy (e fem′ə nə sē, i-) *n.* the quality or state of being effeminate
ef·fem·i·nate (e fem′ə nit, i-) *adj.* ⟦ME *effeminat* < L *effeminatus* pp. of *effeminare*, to make womanish < *ex-*, out + *femina*, a woman: see FEMALE⟧ 1 having the qualities generally attributed to women, as weakness, timidity, delicacy, etc.; unmanly; not virile 2 characterized by such qualities; weak; soft, decadent, etc. [*effeminate* art] —*SYN.* FEMALE —**ef·fem′i·nate·ly** *adv.*
ef·fen·di (e fen′dē) *n., pl.* **-dis** ⟦Turk *efendi* < ModGr *aphentēs* < Gr *authentēs*, a master: see AUTHENTIC⟧ 1 Sir; Mr.: a former Turkish title of respect 2 in countries of the E Mediterranean, a man of high social status as a result of wealth, education, or position in the government
ef·fer·ent (ef′ər ənt) *adj.* ⟦< L *efferens*, prp. of *efferre*, to carry out < *ex-*, out + *ferre*, BEAR[1]⟧ *Physiol.* carrying away from a central part; specif., designating nerves that carry impulses away from a nerve center: opposed to AFFERENT —*n.* an efferent nerve, duct, etc.
ef·fer·vesce (ef′ər ves′) *vi.* **-vesced′, -vesc′ing** ⟦L *effervescere*, to boil up, foam up < *ex-*, out + *fervescere*, to begin to boil < *fervere*, to boil: see FERVENT⟧ 1 to give off gas bubbles, as carbonated beverages; bubble; foam 2 to rise and come out in bubbles, as gas in a liquid 3 to be lively and high-spirited
ef·fer·ves·cent (-ves′ənt) *adj.* ⟦L *effervescens*, prp.: see prec.⟧ 1 giving off gas bubbles; bubbling up; foaming 2 lively and high-spirited; vivacious —**ef′fer·ves′cence** *n.* —**ef′fer·ves′cent·ly** *adv.*
ef·fete (e fēt′, i-) *adj.* ⟦L *effetus*, that has brought forth offspring, exhausted < *ex-*, out + *fetus*, productive: for IE base see FEMALE⟧ 1 no longer capable of producing; spent and sterile 2 lacking vigor, force of character, moral stamina, etc.; decadent, soft, overrefined, etc. 3 effeminate; unmanly —**ef·fete′ly** *adv.* —**ef·fete′ness** *n.*
ef·fi·ca·cious (ef′i kā′shəs) *adj.* ⟦L *efficax* (gen. *efficacis*) < *efficere*, to bring to pass, accomplish (see EFFECT) + -OUS⟧ producing or capable of producing the desired effect; having the intended result; effective [an *efficacious* drug] —*SYN.* EFFECTIVE —**ef′fi·ca′cious·ly** *adv.* —**ef′fi·ca′cious·ness** *n.*
ef·fi·ca·cy (ef′i kə sē) *n.* ⟦ME & OFr *efficace* < L *efficacia* < *efficax*: see prec.⟧ power to produce effects or intended results; effectiveness
ef·fi·cien·cy (e fish′ən sē, i-) *n., pl.* **-cies** ⟦L *efficientia*: see EFFICIENT⟧ 1 ability to produce a desired effect, product, etc. with a minimum of effort, expense, or waste; quality or fact of being efficient 2 the ratio of effective work to the energy expended in producing it, as of a machine; output divided by input ☆3 *short for* EFFICIENCY APARTMENT
☆**efficiency apartment** a small apartment consisting basically, apart from a bathroom, of a single room with a kitchenette
☆**efficiency engineer (***or* **expert)** a person whose work is to increase the productive efficiency of a business or industry by finding better methods of performing various operations, reducing waste and costs, etc.
ef·fi·cient (e fish′ənt, i-) *adj.* ⟦ME & OFr < L *efficiens*, prp. of *efficere*: see EFFECT⟧ producing a desired effect, product, etc. with a minimum of effort, expense, or waste; working well —*SYN.* EFFECTIVE —**ef·fi′cient·ly** *adv.*
-ef·fi·cient (e fish′ənt, i-; *often*, ē-, ə-) *combining form* working or operating efficiently with regard to; making efficient use of [*cost-efficient, energy-efficient*]
efficient cause in Aristotelian philosophy, the person or agent by which a thing is made or done
ef·fi·gy (ef′i jē) *n., pl.* **-gies** ⟦Fr *effigie* < L *effigies*, a copy, image < *effingere* < *ex-*, out + *fingere*, to form: see FIGURE⟧ a portrait, statue, or the like, esp. of a person; likeness; often, a crude representation of a despised person —**burn (or hang) in effigy** to burn (or hang) an image of (a person) in public, as a way of protesting, as against that person's policies
ef·flo·resce (ef′lə res′) *vi.* **-resced′, -resc′ing** ⟦L *efflorescere*, to blossom, flourish < *ex-*, out + *florescere*, to begin to blossom < *florere*, to blossom < *flos* (gen. *floris*), a flower: see BLOOM[1]⟧ 1 to blossom out; flower; bloom 2 *Chem.* *a)* to change from a crystalline to a powdery state through loss of the water of crystallization when exposed to air *b)* to develop a powdery crust as a result of evaporation or chemical change
ef·flo·res·cence (-res′əns) *n.* ⟦Fr < L *efflorescens*, prp. of *efflorescere*: see prec.⟧ 1 a flowering; blooming 2 the time of flowering 3 the peak or fulfillment, as of a career 4 *Chem.* *a)* the changing of certain crystalline compounds to a whitish powder or powdery crust through loss of their water of crystallization *b)* the powder or crust thus formed 5 *Med.* an eruption on the skin; rash or other skin lesion —**ef′flo·res′cent** *adj.*
ef·flu·ence (ef′lo͞o əns) *n.* ⟦ME < ML *effluentia* < L *effluens*, prp. of *effluere*, to flow out < *ex-*, out + *fluere*, to flow: see FLUENT⟧ 1 a flowing out or forth 2 a thing that flows out or forth; emanation
ef·flu·ent (-ənt) *adj.* ⟦ME < L *effluens*: see prec.⟧ a flowing out or forth —*n.* a thing that flows out or forth; specif., *a)* a stream flowing out of a body of water (opposed to AFFLUENT, *n.* 1) *b)* the outflow of a sewer, septic tank, etc.
ef·flu·vi·um (e flo͞o′vē əm, i-) *n., pl.* **-vi·a** (-ə) or **-vi·ums** ⟦L, a flowing out,

outlet < *effluere:* see EFFLUENCE] 1 a real or supposed outflow in the form of a vapor or stream of invisible particles; aura 2 a disagreeable or noxious vapor or odor —**ef·flu′vi·al** *adj.*
ef·flux (ef′luks′) [< L *effluxus,* pp. of *effluere:* see EFFLUENCE] *n.* 1 a flowing out, or emanating 2 a thing that flows out; outflow; emanation 3 an ending; expiration Also **ef·flux·ion** (e fluk′shən)
ef·fort (ef′ərt) *n.* [Fr < OFr *esforz* < *esforcier,* to make an effort < VL **exfortiare* < *ex-,* intens. + **fortiare:* see FORCE] 1 the using of energy to get something done; exertion of strength or mental power 2 a try, esp. a hard try; attempt; endeavor 3 a product or result of working or trying; achievement —**ef′fort·ful** *adj.*

SYN.—**effort** implies a conscious attempt to achieve a particular end [make some *effort* to be friendly]; **exertion** implies an energetic, even violent, use of power, strength, etc., often without reference to any particular end [she feels faint after any *exertion*]; **endeavor** suggests an earnest, sustained attempt to accomplish a particular, usually meritorious, end [a life spent in the *endeavor* to do good]; **pains** (see PAIN, *n.* 5) suggests a laborious, diligent attempt [to take *pains* with one's work] —*ANT.* **ease**

ef·fort·less (-lis) *adj.* making, requiring, or showing virtually no effort —*SYN.* EASY —**ef′fort·less·ly** *adv.* —**ef′fort·less·ness** *n.*
ef·fron·ter·y (e frunt′ər ē, i-) *n.* [Fr *effronterie* < *effronté,* shameless, bold < L *effrons,* barefaced, shameless < *ex-,* from + *frons,* forehead: see FRONT[1]] 1 unashamed boldness; impudence; audacity; presumption 2 *pl.* **-ter·ies** an act or instance of this —*SYN.* TEMERITY
ef·ful·gence (e ful′jəns, i-) *n.* [< L *effulgere,* prp. of *effulgere* < *ex-,* forth + *fulgere,* to shine: see FLAGRANT] great brightness; radiance; brilliance —**ef·ful′gent** *adj.*
ef·fuse (e fyo͞oz′, i-; *for adj.,* -fyo͞os′) *vt., vi.* **-fused′, -fus′ing** [< L *effusus,* pp. of *effundere,* to pour forth < *ex-,* out + *fundere,* to pour: see FOUND[2]] 1 to pour out or forth 2 to spread out; diffuse; radiate —*adj.* 1 [Obs.] poured or spread out freely 2 *Bot.* spread out loosely and flat, without form: said esp. of inflorescences
ef·fu·sion (e fyo͞o′zhən, i-) *n.* [ME & OFr < L *effusio:* see prec.] 1 a pouring forth 2 unrestrained or emotional expression in speaking or writing 3 *a)* an escape of fluid that is bloody, serous, etc. into body cavities or tissues *b)* this fluid 4 the passage of a gas under pressure through an orifice whose size is smaller than the mean free path of the gas molecules, as in measuring low vapor pressures
ef·fu·sive (e fyo͞o′siv, i-) *adj.* 1 [Archaic] pouring out or forth; overflowing 2 expressing excessive emotion in an unrestrained manner; too demonstrative 3 *Geol.* EXTRUSIVE (sense 2) —**ef·fu′sive·ly** *adv.* —**ef·fu′sive·ness** *n.*
Ef·ik (ef′ik) *n., pl.* **Ef′iks** or **Ef′ik** 1 a member of a people of SE Nigeria 2 the Niger-Congo language of this people
eft[1] (eft) *n.* [ME *euete* < OE *efeta,* older, dial., literary form of NEWT] NEWT
eft[2] (eft) *adv.* [ME < OE, orig. compar. (Gmc **aftis*) of AFT[1]] [Obs.] 1 again 2 afterward
EFT *abbrev.* electronic fund transfer
EFTA *abbrev.* European Free Trade Association
EFTS *abbrev.* electronic fund transfer system
eft·soons (eft so͞onz′) *adv.* [ME *eftsones, eftsone* < OE *eftsona* < EFT[2] + *sona:* see SOON] 1 [Archaic] *a)* soon afterward *b)* immediately 2 [Obs.] repeatedly 3 [Obs.] again Also **eft·soon** (eft so͞on′)
Eg *abbrev.* 1 Egypt 2 Egyptian
e.g. *abbrev.* [L *exempli gratia*] for the sake of example; for example
egad (ē gad′) *interj.* [prob. < *oh God*] [Archaic] used as a softened or euphemistic oath
e·gal·i·tar·i·an (ē gal′ə ter′ē ən) *adj.* [< Fr *égalitaire* < *égalité* < OFr *equalité* (see EQUALITY) + -IAN] of, advocating, or characterized by the belief that all people should have equal political, social, and economic rights —*n.* an advocate or supporter of this belief —**e·gal′i·tar′i·an·ism′** *n.*
é·ga·li·té (ā gȧ lē tā′) *n.* [Fr] equality
Eg·bert[1] (eg′bərt) *n.* [OE *Ecgbeorht* < *ecg* (see EDGE) + *beorht* (see BRIGHT): hence, bright sword] a masculine name: dim. *Bert*
Eg·bert[2] (eg′bərt) died A.D. 839; king of the West Saxons (802-839) & first king of the English (829-839)
E·ge·ri·a (ē jir′ē ə) *n.* [L < Gr *Ēgeria*] 1 *Rom. Myth.* a nymph who advised Numa, second king of Rome 2 any woman who acts as an advisor
e·gest (ē jest′) *vt.* [< L *egestus,* pp. of *egerere,* to bear out, discharge < *e-,* out + *gerere,* to bear] to pass off (perspiration, excrement, etc.); excrete —**e·ges′tion** *n.*
e·ges·ta (ē jes′tə) *pl.n.* [ModL < L, neut. pl. of *egestus:* see prec.] egested matter; feces, perspiration, etc.
egg[1] (eg, āg) *n.* [ME < ON, replacing native *ey* < OE *æg,* akin to Ger *ei* (pl. *eier*), prob. < IE base **owjom-, *ojom-,* of a bird (> L *ovum,* Gr *ōion*) < **awei-,* bird (> L *avis*)] 1 the oval or round body laid by a female bird, fish, reptile, insect, etc., containing a supply of nutrients, a protective membrane, and, when fertilized, the embryo of a new individual: many kinds of eggs have a thin, brittle shell as an outer covering 2 a reproductive cell produced by a female animal or plant; ovum: also called **egg cell** 3 the egg of a domestic fowl; specif., the liquid contents of a hen's egg, as used in cooking 4 a thing resembling a hen's egg 5 [Slang] a person [he's a good egg] —*vt.* 1 to mix or cover with the yolk or white of eggs, as in cooking ☆2 [Informal] to throw eggs at —**egg on one's face** [Informal] embarrassment due to an obvious blunder —☆**lay an egg** [Informal] to fail completely: said of a joke, theatrical performance, entertainer, etc. —**put** (or **have**) **all one's eggs in one basket** to risk all that one has on a single venture, method, etc.

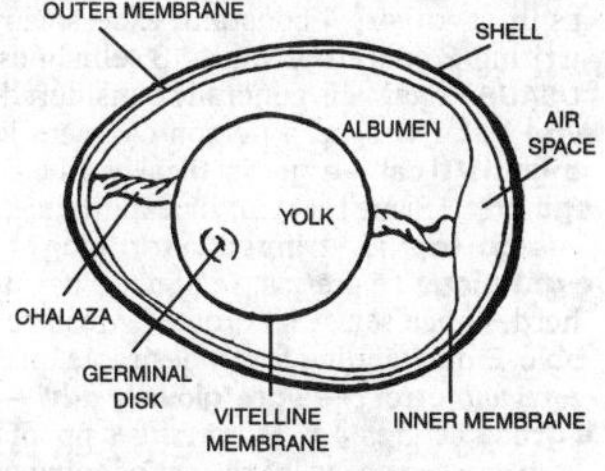

hen's egg

egg[2] (eg, āg) *vt.* [ME *eggen* < ON *eggja,* lit., to give edge to < *egg,* EDGE] to urge or incite: with *on*
egg and dart a decorative molding used in architecture and cabinetwork, consisting of an egg-shaped form alternating with a form shaped like an arrow, anchor, or tongue: also **egg and anchor** or **egg and tongue**
☆**egg·beat·er** (eg′bēt′ər, āg′-) *n.* 1 a kitchen utensil, esp. one with rotary blades, for beating eggs, whipping cream, etc. 2 [Slang] a helicopter
☆**egg coal** coal that is about 2 to 4 inches (5.08 to 10.16 cm) in diameter
☆**egg cream** [so called prob. because the foam on top resembles beaten *egg* white] [Chiefly New York City] a drink made from chocolate syrup, soda water, and milk, mixed to produce a white, foamy head
egg·cup (eg′kup′, āg′-) *n.* a small cup, usually on a base or foot, for holding a soft-boiled egg so that it can be eaten from the shell with a spoon: also written **egg cup**
☆**egg foo yong** (*or* **young** *or* **yung**) (eg′fo͞o yuŋ′, āg′-) a Chinese-American dish consisting of beaten eggs cooked with bean sprouts, onions, minced pork or shrimp, etc.
☆**egg·head** (eg′hed′, āg′-) *n.* [Slang] an intellectual: usually a term of mild derision as used by anti-intellectuals
☆**egg·nog** (eg′näg′, āg′-) *n.* [EGG[1] + NOG[2]] a thick drink made of beaten eggs, milk, sugar, and nutmeg, often containing whiskey, rum, etc.
egg·plant (-plant′) *n.* [so named from its shape; orig. applied to a white-skinned variety] 1 a perennial plant (*Solanum melongena*) of the nightshade family, with large, ovoid, usually purple-skinned fruits that are eaten as a vegetable 2 the fruit
☆**egg roll** a Chinese-American dish consisting of a thin egg pancake wrapped around minced vegetables, meat, shrimp, etc. to form a small roll that is fried in deep fat
☆**eggs Benedict** [< ?] poached eggs served over ham on a split, toasted English muffin, topped with hollandaise sauce
egg·shell (eg′shel′, āg′-) *n.* 1 the hard, brittle outer covering of an egg of a reptile, bird, or monotreme 2 yellowish white —*adj.* 1 fragile and thin, like eggshell 2 yellowish-white —**walk on eggshells** to behave in an esp. wary manner, as from fear of reprisal or of a harsh reaction
egg tooth a tooth-like structure on the nose or beak of young reptiles and birds used to break the egg membrane or shell at the time of hatching
egg·y (eg′ē, āg′-) *adj.* 1 containing eggs, often, specif., beaten eggs [*eggy* bread] 2 having the taste or smell of eggs 3 smeared or covered with egg [*eggy* spoons]
eg·lan·tine (eg′lən tīn′, -tēn′) *n.* [Fr *églantine* < OFr *aiglent* < LL **aculentus* < L *aculeus,* a sting, prickle, dim. of *acus,* a point, sting: see ACUITY] a European rose (*Rosa eglanteria*) with hooked spines, sweet-scented leaves, and usually pink flowers; sweetbrier: naturalized in W U.S.
Eg·mont (eg′mänt′; *Du* ekh′mônt), Count of (born *Lamoral Egmont*) 1522-68; Fl. statesman & general
e·go (ē′gō, eg′ō) *n., pl.* **e′gos** [L: see I[2]] 1 the self; the individual as self-aware 2 *a)* egotism; conceit *b)* self-esteem; self-respect 3 *Philos.* the self, variously conceived as a spiritual substance on which experience is superimposed, the series of acts and mental states introspectively recognized, etc. 4 *Psychoanalysis* that part of the psyche which experiences the external world, or reality, through the senses, organizes the thought processes rationally, and governs action: it mediates between the impulses of the id, the demands of the environment, and the standards of the superego
e·go·cen·tric (ē′gō sen′trik, eg′ō-) *adj.* 1 viewing everything in relation to oneself; self-centered 2 *Philos.* based on the belief that the world exists or can be known only in relation to the individual's mind —*n.* an egocentric person —**e′go·cen′tri·cal·ly** *adv.* —**e′go·cen·tric′i·ty** (-tris′ə tē) *n.* —**e′go·cen′trism′** (-triz′əm) *n.*
ego ideal *Psychoanalysis* the ego's conception of a better or more successful future self, based on identification with parents or parental substitutes
e·go·ism (ē′gō iz′əm, eg′ō-) *n.* [Fr *égoïsme* < L *ego:* see I[2]] 1 the tendency to be self-centered, or to consider only oneself and one's own interests; selfishness 2 egotism; conceit 3 *Ethics* the doctrine that self-interest is the proper goal of all human actions: opposed to ALTRUISM
e·go·ist (-ist) *n.* [Fr *égoïste* < L *ego:* see I[2]] 1 a person who is self-centered or selfish 2 a conceited person; egotist 3 a person who accepts the doctrine of egoism
e·go·is·tic (ē′gō is′tik, eg′ō-) *adj.* 1 self-centered or selfish 2 egotistic; conceited 3 of an egoist or egoism Also **e′go·is′ti·cal** —**e′go·is′ti·cal·ly** *adv.*
e·go·ma·ni·a (ē′gō mā′nē ə, eg′ō-; -mān′yə) *n.* [EGO + -MANIA] abnormally excessive egotism —**e′go·ma′ni·ac′** (-nē ak′) *adj.,* **e′go·ma·ni′a·cal** (-mə nī′ə kəl)
ego psychology the study of the adaptive and mediating functions of the ego and their role in personality development and emotional disorders

e·go·tism (ē′gō tiz′əm, eg′ō-; ē′gə-, eg′ə-) ***n.*** ⟦L *ego*, I[2] + *-tism* (for -ISM), as in NEPOTISM⟧ **1** constant, excessive reference to oneself in speaking or writing **2** conceit or vanity **3** selfishness
USAGE—egotism is generally considered more opprobrious than *egoism*

e·go·tist (-tist) ***n.*** a person characterized by egotism —**e′go·tis′tic** ***adj.***, **e′go·tis′ti·cal** —**e′go·tis′ti·cal·ly** ***adv.***

☆**ego trip** [Slang] a trip, or experience, that gratifies or indulges the ego —**e′go-trip′** ***vi.*** **-tripped′**, **-trip′ping**

e·gre·gious (ē grē′jəs, i-; *also*, -jē əs) ***adj.*** ⟦L *egregius*, separated from the herd, hence select < *e-*, out + *grex*: see GREGARIOUS⟧ **1** [Archaic] remarkable **2** outstanding for undesirable qualities; remarkably bad; flagrant [an *egregious* error] —**e·gre′gious·ly** ***adv.*** —**e·gre′gious·ness** ***n.***

e·gress (ē′gres′) ***n.*** ⟦L *egressus* < pp. of *egredi*, to go out < *e-*, out + *gradi*, to step, go: see GRADE⟧ **1** the act of going out or forth; emergence: also **e·gres·sion** (ē gresh′ən) **2** the right to go out **3** a way out; exit

e·gret (ē′grit, -gret′) ***n.***, ***pl.*** **-grets** or **-gret** ⟦ME < OFr *aigrette*, kind of heron, tuft of feathers < Prov *aigreta* < *aigron* < Frank **heigro*: see HERON⟧ **1** any of several herons (esp. genus *Egretta*), usually with long, white plumes **2** AIGRETTE (sense 1)

E·gypt[1] (ē′jipt) country in NE Africa, on the Mediterranean and Red seas: ancient Egyptian dynasties may date back as far as 4500 B.C.; in modern times, occupied by the British in 1882 & achieved independence in 1922: 386,662 sq mi (1,001,450 sq km); cap. Cairo

Egypt[2] *abbrev.* Egyptian

E·gyp·tian (ē jip′shən, i-) ***adj.*** **1** of Egypt, its people, or their culture **2** of the language of the ancient Egyptians —***n.*** **1** a person born or living in Egypt **2** the Afroasiatic language spoken by ancient Egyptians

Egyptian mau (mou) any of a breed of domestic cat, prob. originating in ancient Egypt, with almond-shaped, usually green eyes and a light-colored coat with a pattern of dark spots and stripes

E·gyp·tol·o·gy (ē′jip täl′ə jē) ***n.*** the science or study of ancient Egyptian architecture, inscriptions, language, customs, etc. —**E′gyp·tol′o·gist** ***n.***

eh (ā, e, en) ***interj.*** **1** used to express doubt or surprise **2** used to make an inquiry and equivalent to "What did you say?" or "Don't you agree?"

EHF or **ehf** *abbrev.* extremely high frequency

Ehr·en·burg (er′ən burg′), **Il·ya (Grigoryevich)** (ēl′yä′) 1891-1967; Soviet writer

Ehr·lich (er′lik) **1 Paul** 1854-1915; Ger. bacteriologist: pioneer in immunology & chemotherapy **2 Paul R(alph)** 1932- ; U.S. biologist

EHV *abbrev.* extra high voltage

Eich·mann (īk′mən, īkh′-), **(Karl) Ad·olf** (ad′ôlf′, ä′dôlf′) 1906-62; Ger. SS officer: administered the deportation of Jews to the Nazi concentration camps

ei·der (ī′dər) ***n.***, ***pl.*** **-ders** or **-der** ⟦ult. < ON *æthar*, gen of *æthr*, eider duck⟧ **1** any of several large sea ducks (esp. genus *Somateria*) that live in northern regions of Europe, Asia, and North America: often **eider duck** **2** EIDERDOWN (sense 1)

ei·der·down (-doun′) ***n.*** ⟦< ON *æthar-dūn*: see prec. & DOWN[2]⟧ **1** the soft, fine breast feathers, or down, of the eider, used as a stuffing for quilts, pillows, etc. **2** a quilt stuffed with such feathers

ei·det·ic (ī det′ik) ***adj.*** ⟦Gr *eidētikos*, constituting a figure < *eidos*, what is seen, shape: see -OID⟧ designating or of mental images that are unusually vivid and almost photographically exact —**ei·det′i·cal·ly** ***adv.***

ei·do·lon (ī dō′lən) ***n.***, ***pl.*** **-lons** or **-la** (-lə) ⟦Gr *eidōlon*, an image: see IDOL⟧ **1** an image without real existence; phantom; apparition ☆**2** an ideal person or thing —**ei·dol′ic** (-däl′ik) ***adj.***

Eif·fel Tower (ī′fəl) ⟦after A. G. *Eiffel* (1832-1923), Fr engineer who designed it⟧ tower of iron framework in Paris, built for the International Exposition of 1889: 984 ft (300 m) high

ei·gen·val·ue (ī′gən val′yōō) ***n.*** ⟦partial transl. of Ger *eigenwert* < *eigen*, own, particular + *wert*, value⟧ *Math., Physics* any of the possible values of a quantity derived from a differential or integral equation having solutions that satisfy certain special conditions

eight (āt) ***adj.*** ⟦ME *eighte* < OE *eahta*, akin to Ger *acht* < IE base **oktō(u)*- L *octo*, Gr *oktō*, OIr *ocht*⟧ totaling one more than seven —***n.*** **1** the cardinal number between seven and nine; 8; VIII **2** any group of eight people or things, as a crew of eight oarsmen **3** *a)* something numbered eight or having eight units, as a playing card, throw of dice, etc. *b)* an engine with eight cylinders or an automobile with such an engine **4** anything shaped like an **8**, as a figure in skating

☆**eight ball** *Pool* **1** a black ball with the number eight on it **2** a form of pool in which a player who inadvertently pockets the eight ball before pocketing all of his or her balls immediately loses the game: also written **8-ball** or **eight-ball** —**behind the eight ball** [Slang] in a very unfavorable position

eight·een (ā′tēn′) ***adj.*** ⟦ME *eightetene* < OE *eahtatiene*: see EIGHT & TEEN[1]⟧ totaling eight more than ten —***n.*** the cardinal number between seventeen and nineteen; 18; XVIII

eight·een·mo (ā′tēn′mō′) ***n.***, ***pl.*** **-mos′** ⟦prec. + *-mo*, as in OCTODECIMO⟧ **1** the page size of a book made up of printer's sheets folded into eighteen leaves, each leaf being approximately 4 by 6½ inches **2** a book consisting of pages of this size Usually written *18mo* or *18°* —***adj.*** OCTODECIMO

eight·eenth (ā′tēnth′) ***adj.*** ⟦ME *eihtetenthe*: see EIGHTEEN & -TH[2]⟧ **1** preceded by seventeen others in a series; 18th **2** designating any of the eighteen equal parts of something —***n.*** **1** the one following the seventeenth **2** any one of the eighteen equal parts of something; 1⁄18 —***adv.*** in the eighteenth place, rank, group, etc.

eight·een-wheel·er (ā′tēn′hwēl′ər, -wēl′-) ***n.*** [Informal] a tractor-trailer having eighteen wheels: often **18-wheeler**

eight·fold (āt′fōld′) ***adj.*** ⟦EIGHT + -FOLD⟧ **1** having eight parts **2** having eight times as much or as many —***adv.*** eight times as much or as many

eighth (ātth, āth) ***adj.*** ⟦ME *eightethe* < OE *eahtotha* < *eahta*: see EIGHT & -TH[2]⟧ **1** preceded by seven others in a series; 8th **2** designating any of the eight equal parts of something —***n.*** **1** the one following the seventh **2** any of the eight equal parts of something; ⅛ **3** *Music* OCTAVE —***adv.*** in the eighth place, rank, group, etc. —**eighth′ly** ***adv.***

eighth note *Music* a note having one eighth the duration of a whole note

800 number a toll-free telephone number, specif. one with an 800, 866, 877, etc. prefix

eight·i·eth (āt′ē ith) ***adj.*** ⟦ME *eightetithe*: see EIGHTY & -TH[2]⟧ **1** preceded by seventy-nine others in a series; 80th **2** designating any of the eighty equal parts of something —***n.*** **1** the one following the seventy-ninth **2** any one of the eighty equal parts of something; 1⁄80 —***adv.*** in the eightieth place, rank, group, etc.

eight·vo (āt′vō′) ***adj.***, ***n.***, ***pl.*** **-vos′** OCTAVO

eight·y (āt′ē) ***adj.*** ⟦ME *eighteti* < OE *(hund)eahtatig*: see EIGHT & -TY[2]⟧ eight times ten —***n.***, ***pl.*** **eight′ies** the cardinal number between seventy-nine and eighty-one; 80; LXXX —**the eighties** the numbers or years, as of a century, from eighty through eighty-nine

☆**eight·y-six** (āt′ē siks′) ***vt.*** [Slang] **1** to eject from, or refuse to serve at, a place where alcoholic drinks are sold, as because of drunkenness **2** to cut off, eject, cancel, eliminate, kill, etc. Also written **86**

Ei·leen (ī lēn′, ā-) ***n.*** ⟦Ir *Eibhlīn*⟧ a feminine name; var. *Aileen*

-ein (ēn, ē in) ⟦altered < -IN[1] & -INE[3]⟧ *Chem. suffix* **1** used to differentiate a compound from another having a similar spelling but ending in *-in* or *-ine* **2** used to indicate a compound containing an internal anhydride Also **-eine**

Eind·ho·ven (īnt′hō′vən) city in S Netherlands

ein·korn (īn′kôrn′) ***n.*** ⟦Ger < *ein*, ONE + *korn*, seed, grain, akin to CORN[1]⟧ any of certain primitive forms of wheat (esp., *Triticum monococcum*) cultivated by some prehistoric peoples

Ein·stein[1] (īn′stīn′) ***n.*** ⟦after fol.⟧ [*sometimes* **e-**] a highly intelligent person

Ein·stein[2] (īn′stīn′), **Albert** 1879-1955; Ger. physicist, in the U.S. after 1933: formulated theory of relativity —**Ein·stein′i·an** (-stīn′ē ən) ***adj.***

☆**ein·stein·i·um** (īn stīn′ē əm) ***n.*** ⟦ModL, after prec. (in honor of his theoretical studies of mass and energy) + -IUM: so named (1955) by A. Ghiorso and co-workers, who identified it⟧ a radioactive, metallic chemical element, one of the actinides, discovered in the debris of the first thermonuclear explosion in 1952, but now produced by bombarding plutonium with neutrons: symbol, Es; at. no. 99: see the periodic table of elements in the Reference Supplement

Eir·e (er′ə) *Ir. name for* IRELAND: also, the former official name (1937-49) of the country of Ireland

ei·ren·ic (ī ren′ik, ī rē′nik) ***adj.*** *var. sp. of* IRENIC: also **ei·ren′ic·al**

Ei·sen·how·er (ī′zen hou′ər), **Dwight D(avid)** 1890-1969; U.S. general & 34th president of the U.S. (1953-61): commander of Allied forces in Europe (1943-45; 1951-52)

☆**Eisenhower jacket** ⟦after General EISENHOWER, with whom the style originated⟧ **1** a waist-length, form-fitting jacket, worn by American servicemen in WWII **2** a casual jacket resembling this

Ei·sen·staedt (ī′zən stat′), **Alfred** 1898-1995; U.S. photographer, born in Germany

Ei·sen·stein (ī′zən stīn′), **Ser·gei (Mikhailovich)** (ser′gā) 1898-1948; Russ. film director & producer

eis·tedd·fod (īs teth′vôd′) ***n.***, ***pl.*** **-fods′** or Welsh **eis·tedd·fod·au** (īs′teth vôd′ī′) ⟦Welsh, a sitting, session < **eistedd*, to sit < **eitsedd* < IE **aty-en-sed-* < base **sed-* > L *sedere*, SIT⟧ a yearly meeting in Wales of poets, musicians, etc., at which prizes are given for compositions and performances: 19th-cent. revival of an old Welsh custom

ei·ther (ē′thər, ī′-) ***adj.*** ⟦ME < OE *æghwæther* < a (æ), always (see AY) + *gehwæther*, each of two (see WHETHER): akin to, and of same formation as, OHG *eogihwedar*⟧ **1** one or the other (of two) [use *either* hand] **2** each (of two); the one and the other [he had a tool in *either* hand] —***pron.*** one or the other (of two) —***conj.*** the first element of the pair of disjunctive correlatives *either ... or*, implying a choice of alternatives [*either* go or stay]: *either ... or* is sometimes used to refer to more than two, although this use is objected to by some [bring *either* cookies, doughnuts, or some other kind of pastry] —***adv.*** **1** any more than the other; also: used after negative expressions [if you don't go, I won't *either*] **2** [Informal] certainly; indeed: used as an intensifier in a negative statement ["It's mine." "It isn't *either*!"]

ei·ther-or (-ôr′) ***adj.*** designating a proposition, situation, etc. limited to only two alternatives: also written **either/or**

e·jac·u·late (ē jak′yōō lāt′, i-; -yə-; *for n.*, -lit) ***vt.***, ***vi.*** **-lat′ed**, **-lat′ing** ⟦< L *ejaculatus*, pp. of *ejaculari*, to throw out < *e-*, out + *jaculari*, to throw < *jaculum*, a dart, missile < *jacere*, to throw: see JET[1]⟧ **1** to eject or discharge (esp. semen) **2** to utter suddenly and vehemently; exclaim —***n.*** discharged semen; specif., the semen discharged during a single ejaculation —**e·jac′u·la′tive** ***adj.*** —**e·jac′u·la′tor** ***n.***

e·jac·u·la·tion (ē jak′yōō lā′shən, i-; -yə-) ***n.*** ⟦see prec.⟧ **1** a sudden ejection of fluid, esp. of semen, from the body **2** a sudden vehement utterance; exclamation **3** *R.C.Ch.* any very brief private prayer

e·jac·u·la·to·ry (ē jak′yōō lə tôr′ē, i-; -yə-) ***adj.*** **1** ejaculating; of or for ejaculation [an *ejaculatory* duct] 2 of the nature of an ejaculation; exclamatory [*ejaculatory* words]

e·ject (ē jekt′, i-) ***vt.*** ⟦< L *ejectus*, pp. of *ejicere*, to throw out < *e-*, out (see EX-[1]) + *jacere*, to throw (see JET[1])⟧ 1 to throw out; cast out; expel; emit; discharge [the chimney *ejects* smoke] 2 to drive out; evict [to *eject* a heckler] —***vi.*** to be ejected from an aircraft as by means of an ejection seat —**e·ject′a·ble** ***adj.*** —**e·jec′tion** ***n.*** —**e·jec′tive** ***adj.*** —**e·jec′tor** ***n.***

SYN.—**eject**, the term of broadest application here, implies generally a throwing or casting out from within [to *eject* saliva from the mouth]; **expel** suggests a driving out, as by force, specif. a forcing out of a country, organization, etc., often in disgrace [*expelled* from school]; **evict** refers to the forcing out, as of a tenant, by legal procedure; **dismiss**, in this connection, refers to the removal of an employee, etc. but does not in itself suggest the reason for the separation [*dismissed* for incompetence]; **oust** implies the getting rid of something undesirable, as by force or the action of law [to *oust* corrupt officials]

e·jec·ta (ē jek′tə) ***pl.n.*** ⟦ModL < neut. pl. of *ejectus*⟧ ejected matter, as from the body, a volcano, etc.

ejection seat a seat designed to be ejected with its occupant from an aircraft in an emergency and parachuted to the ground

e·ject·ment (ē jekt′mənt, i-) ***n.*** 1 an ejecting or ousting; eviction 2 *Law* an action to secure or recover possession of real property by the true owner

e·ji·do (e hē′dô) ***n.***, *pl.* **-dos** (-dôs) ⟦Sp⟧ in Mexico, the communal farmland of a village, usually assigned in small parcels to the villagers to be farmed under a federally supported system of communal land tenure

eke[1] (ēk) ***vt.*** **eked, ek′ing** ⟦ME *eken*, to increase < OE *eacan* & *eacian*: see WAX[2]⟧ [Now Dial.] to make larger or longer; increase —**eke out** 1 to add to so as to make sufficient; supplement [to *eke out* an income with a second job] 2 to manage to make (a living) with difficulty 3 to use (a supply) frugally

eke[2] (ēk) ***adv.*** ⟦ME < OE *eac*, akin to Ger *auch* < IE base **au-*, again, on the other hand > L *aut*, Gr *au*, on the other hand⟧ [Archaic] also

EKG *abbrev.* ⟦Ger *elektrokardiogramm*⟧ electrocardiogram

☆**e·kis·tics** (ē kis′tiks, i-) ***n.*** ⟦< Gr *oikos*, house (see ECO-) + -ICS⟧ the science of city and area planning, dealing with the integration of the basic needs of both the individual and the entire community, as transportation, communication, entertainment, etc. —**e·kis′ti·cal** ***adj.***

el (el) ***n.*** 1 ELL[1] (sense 1) ☆2 ⟦< EL(EVATED)⟧ [Informal] an elevated railway

e·lab·o·rate (ē lab′ə rit, i-; *for v.*, -ə rāt′) ***adj.*** ⟦L *elaboratus*, pp. of *elaborare*, to work out, labor greatly < *e-*, out + *laborare* < *labor*, LABOR⟧ 1 worked out carefully; developed in great detail 2 highly wrought or ornamented; complicated 3 painstaking —***vt.*** **-rat′ed, -rat′ing** 1 to produce by effort 2 to work out carefully; develop in great detail 3 to change (food or substances in the body) into compounds that can be assimilated, excreted, etc. —***vi.*** to state something in detail or add more details: usually with *on* or *upon* —**e·lab′o·rate·ly** ***adv.*** —**e·lab′o·rate·ness** ***n.*** —**e·lab′o·ra′tion** ***n.*** —**e·lab·o·ra·tive** (ē lab′ə rāt′iv, -ə rə tiv) ***adj.*** —**e·lab′o·ra′tor** ***n.***

el·ae·op·tene (el′ē äp′tēn′) ***n.*** ELEOPTENE

El·a·gab·a·lus (el′ə gab′ə ləs) (born *Varius Avitus Bassianus*) A.D. 205?-222; Rom. emperor (218-222)

E·laine (ē lān′, i-) ***n.*** ⟦OFr⟧ 1 a feminine name: see HELEN 2 *Arthurian Legend* *a)* a woman of Astolat, who loves Lancelot *b)* the mother of Galahad

E·lam (ē′ləm) ancient kingdom of SW Asia, at the head of the Persian Gulf (fl. 13th & 12th cent. B.C.)

E·lam·ite (ē′ləm īt′) ***n.*** 1 a person born or living in Elam 2 the extinct language of the Elamites: it is not known to be related to any other language: also **E·lam·it·ic** (ē′ləm it′ik) —***adj.*** of Elam or its people, language, or culture

Elam (8th cent. B.C.)

é·lan (ā län′, -län′) ***n.*** ⟦Fr, a start, outburst, impetuosity < *élancer*, to dart, throw < *é-*, out + *lancer*, to throw a lance, hence throw < LL (Ec) *lanceare* < *lancea*, LANCE⟧ spirited self-assurance; verve; dash; enthusiasm

e·land (ē′lənd) ***n.***, *pl.* **e′land** or **e′lands** ⟦Afrik < Du, elk < obs. Ger *elen(d)* < Lith *élnis*: see ELK⟧ either of two large, oxlike African antelopes (genus *Taurotragus*) with spirally twisted horns

é·lan vi·tal (ā län vē tȧl′) ⟦Fr, lit., vital force⟧ in Bergsonian philosophy, the original vital impulse which is the substance of consciousness and nature

el·a·pine (el′ə pīn′, -pin, -pēn′) ***adj.*** ⟦< ModL *Elapinae*, name of the subfamily < *Elaps*, a genus of venomous snakes (< MGr *elaps* serpent, fish, altered < Gr *ellops* + *-inae*, -INAE⟧ of or pertaining to a family (Elapidae) of poisonous snakes with small, erect fangs, including the cobras and coral snakes —**el′a·pid′** (-pid′) ***n.***

e·lapse (ē laps′, i-) ***vi.*** **e·lapsed′, e·laps′ing** ⟦< L *elapsus*, pp. of *elabi*, to glide away < *e-*, out + *labi*, to glide, fall: see LABOR⟧ to slip by; pass: said of time

e·las·mo·branch (ē las′mō braŋk′, -laz′-) ***adj.*** ⟦< ModL *Elasmobranchii* < Gr *elasmos*, beaten metal (akin to ELASTIC) + L *branchia*, gills⟧ designating or of a class (Chondrichthyes) of fishes characterized by cartilaginous skeletons, placoid scales, and lack of air bladders —***n.*** any fish of this class, as the shark, skate, or ray

e·las·tase (i las′tās′, -tāz′) ***n.*** ⟦ELAST(IN) + -ASE⟧ an enzyme, produced esp. in the pancreas, that digests elastin

e·las·tic (ē las′tik, i-) ***adj.*** ⟦ModL *elasticus* < LGr *elastikos* < Gr *elaunein*, to set in motion, beat out < IE base **el-*, to drive, move, go >? LANE[1]⟧ 1 able to spring back to its original size, shape, or position after being stretched, squeezed, flexed, expanded, etc.; flexible; springy 2 able to recover easily from dejection, fatigue, etc.; buoyant [an *elastic* temperament] 3 readily changed or changing to suit circumstances; adaptable [*elastic* regulations] 4 *Econ.* responding to changes in price: said of the demand for, or supply of, particular goods or services —***n.*** 1 an elastic fabric made flexible by strands of rubber or a rubberlike synthetic running through it 2 a band, garter, etc. of this material 3 a rubber band —**e·las′ti·cal·ly** ***adv.***

SYN.—**elastic** implies ability to return without permanent injury to the original size or shape after being stretched, expanded, etc. [an *elastic* garter]; **resilient** implies ability to spring back quickly into shape after being deformed, esp. by compression [a healthy, *resilient* skin]; **flexible** refers to anything that can be bent without breaking, whether or not it returns to its original form [a *flexible* wire]; **supple** is applied to that which is easily bent, twisted, or folded without breaking, cracking, etc. [kidskin is *supple*] —ANT. **rigid, stiff**

e·las·tic·i·ty (ē′las tis′ə tē, i las′-) ***n.***, *pl.* **-ties** 1 the quality or condition of being elastic; specif., *a)* springiness; flexibility; resilience *b)* buoyancy of spirit *c)* adaptability 2 *Econ.* the degree to which the demand for, or supply of, particular goods or services responds to a change in price

e·las·ti·cize (ē las′tə sīz′, i-) ***vt.*** **-cized′, -ciz′ing** to make (fabric) elastic, as by interweaving with rubber strands

elastic tissue a connective tissue consisting largely of yellow, elastic fibers, occurring especially in the walls of arteries and veins

e·las·tin (ē las′tin) ***n.*** ⟦see ELASTIC & -IN[1]⟧ a yellow, fibrous protein that is the basic constituent of elastic connective tissue, as in a lung or artery

☆**e·las·to·mer** (ē las′tə mər) ***n.*** ⟦< ELAST(IC) + -O- + (POLY)MER⟧ a rubberlike synthetic polymer, as silicone rubber —**e·las′to·mer′ic** (-mer′ik) ***adj.***

E·lat or **E·lath** (ā lät′) *alt. sp. of* EILAT

e·late (ē lāt′, i-) ***vt.*** **-lat′ed, -lat′ing** ⟦< L *elatus*, pp. of *efferre*, to bring out, lift up < *ex-*, out + *ferre*, BEAR[1]⟧ to raise the spirits of; make very proud, happy, or joyful —***adj.*** [Old Poet.] filled with elation —**e·lat′ed·ly** ***adv.*** —**e·lat′ed·ness** ***n.***

el·a·ter (el′ə tər) ***n.*** ⟦ModL < Gr *elatēr*, driver < *elaunein*: see ELASTIC⟧ 1 an elastic filament that scatters the ripe spores, found in certain plants, as in the capsule of a liverwort 2 CLICK BEETLE

e·lat·er·id (ē lat′ər id) ***n.*** CLICK BEETLE —***adj.*** of the family of click beetles

e·lat·er·ite (ē lat′ər īt′) ***n.*** ⟦ELATER, sense 1 + -ITE[1]⟧ a dark-brown hydrocarbon that is soft and elastic until it hardens when exposed to air

el·a·te·ri·um (el′ə tir′ē əm) ***n.*** ⟦L < Gr *elatērion*, neut. of *elatērios*, driving < *elaunein*: see ELASTIC⟧ a cathartic obtained from the dried juice of the squirting cucumber of the gourd family

e·la·tion (ē lā′shən, i-) ***n.*** ⟦L *elatio*: see ELATE⟧ a feeling of exultant joy or pride; high spirits

E layer a dense layer of ions in the E region of the ionosphere at an altitude of *c.* 100 km (*c.* 62 mi), capable of reflecting shortwave radio waves

E·la·zig (el′ə zig′) city in EC Turkey

El·ba (el′bə) Italian island in the Tyrrhenian Sea, between Corsica & Italy: site of Napoleon's first exile (1814-15): 86 sq mi (223 sq km)

El·be (el′bə, elb) river in central Europe, flowing from the NW Czech Republic through Germany into the North Sea at Hamburg: *c.* 725 mi (1,167 km)

El·bert (el′bərt), **Mount** ⟦after S. H. *Elbert*, territorial gov. of Colo. (1873-74)⟧ peak of the Sawatch range, central Colo.: highest peak of the Rocky Mountains of the conterminous U.S.: 14,443 ft (4,402 m)

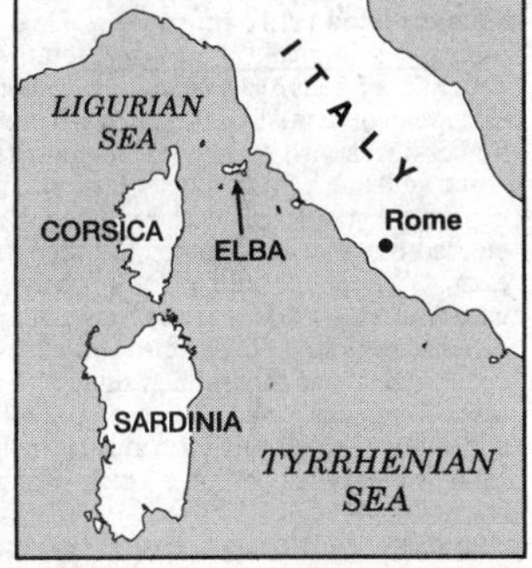

Elba

el·bow (el′bō′) ***n.*** ⟦ME *elbowe* < OE *elboga* < PGmc **alino-boga* (> Ger *ellenbogen*): see ELL[2] & BOW[2]⟧ 1 *a)* the joint between the upper and lower arm; esp., the outer part of the angle made by a bent arm *b)* the joint corresponding to this in the forelimb of quadrupeds 2 the part of a sleeve covering the elbow 3 anything bent like an elbow, as a fitting for joining plumbing pipes at a 45° or 90° angle —***vt.*** 1 to shove or jostle with or as with elbows 2 to push (one's way) with the elbows or rudely —***vi.*** 1 to make one's way by shoving or jostling 2 to form an angle —**at someone's elbow** very close to someone; easy to reach —**out at (the) elbows** shabby; poverty-stricken —**up to the elbows** [Informal] deeply engaged (*in* work, etc.)

elbow grease [Informal] vigorous physical effort, as that used in scrubbing or polishing something

el·bow·room (el′bō ro͞om′) *n.* room enough to move or work in; ample space or scope

El·brus (el′bro͝os, -bro͞oz′), **Mount** mountain of the Caucasus range, in SW Russia: highest peak in Europe, 18,513 ft (5,643 m): also sp. **El′brus**

El·burz Mountains (el bo͝orz′) mountain range in N Iran, along the Caspian Sea: highest peak, Mt. Damavand

El·che (el′chā′) city in SE Spain, near Alicante

eld (eld) *n.* ⟦ME *elde* < OE *eldo* < base of *ald, eald,* OLD⟧ [Archaic] **1** old age **2** ancient times; antiquity; days of yore

eld·er[1] (el′dər) *adj.* ⟦ME < OE (Mercian) *eldra, ældra,* compar. < base of *ald, eald,* OLD⟧ **1** born or brought forth earlier than another or others; exceeding another in age; senior; older **2** [Obs.] of longer standing or superior rank, position, validity, etc. **3** [Now Rare] earlier; former; ancient —*n.* **1** an older person **2** an aged person **3** a forefather; ancestor; predecessor **4** an older person with some authority or dignity in a tribe or community **5** *a)* an officer in an early Christian church *b)* in some Protestant churches, a minister; also, a member appointed to the ruling body who may also assist at Communion ☆*c) Mormon Ch.* a member of the Melchizedek priesthood

el·der[2] (el′dər) *n.* ⟦ME *ellerne* & (with intrusive *-d-* as in ALDER) *eldore* < OE *ellern, ellen,* akin to MLowG *ellern, eldern* < IE base **el-* > ELM, ALDER, L *alnus,* elder⟧ **1** any of a genus (*Sambucus*) of shrubs and small trees of the honeysuckle family, with compound leaves and flat-topped clusters of small white flowers followed by red or purple berries **2** any of various unrelated plants, as the box elder or the marsh elder

el·der·ber·ry (-ber′ē) *n., pl.* **-ries** **1** ELDER[2] (sense 1) **2** its berry, or drupe, used for making wine, jelly, etc.

☆**el·der·care** (el′dər ker′) *n.* provision of care for the elderly

eld·er·ly (el′dər lē) *adj.* **1** somewhat old; past middle age; approaching old age **2** quite old; already in old age; aged **3** not current; outmoded —**the elderly** elderly people as a group —**eld′er·li·ness** *n.*

eld·er·ship (el′dər ship′) *n.* ⟦ELDER[1] + -SHIP⟧ **1** the position or duties of an elder in a church **2** a group of elders; presbytery

elder statesman **1** [Historical] in Japan, any of a number of retired statesmen who served informally as a group of advisors to the emperor **2** any elderly retired statesman who continues to be consulted unofficially on governmental matters

eld·est (el′dist) *adj.* ⟦ME < OE *eldest(a), ieldest(a),* superl. of *ald, eald:* see OLD⟧ oldest; esp., firstborn or oldest surviving

El Do·ra·do or **El·do·ra·do** (el′də rä′dō, -rā′dō, -rad′ō) ⟦Sp, the gilded; *dorado,* pp. of *dorar,* to gild < LL *deaurare,* to gild + L *de-,* intens. + *aurum,* gold⟧ **1** a legendary country in South America, supposed to be rich in gold and precious stones and sought by early Spanish explorers ☆**2** *pl.* **-dos** any place that is, or is supposed to be, rich in gold, opportunity, etc.

el·dritch (el′drich′) *adj.* ⟦Early ModE *elrich,* prob. < ME *elf, elve,* elf + *rice,* realm: see -RIC⟧ weird; eerie

El·ea·nor (el′ə nər, -nôr′) *n.* ⟦OFr *Elienor:* see HELEN⟧ a feminine name: dim. *Ella, Nell, Nora;* var. *Leonora*

Eleanor of Aquitaine 1122?-1204; queen of France (1137-52) as the wife of Louis VII & queen of England (1154-89) as the wife of Henry II

El·e·at·ic (el′ē at′ik) *adj.* ⟦L *Eleaticus,* after *Elea* (Velia), ancient Gr colony in Italy⟧ designating or of an ancient Greek school of philosophy which held that true being is singular and unchanging and that plurality, change, and motion are illusory: Parmenides and Zeno were its best-known adherents —*n.* an Eleatic philosopher —**El′e·at′i·cism′** (-at′i siz′əm) *n.*

El·e·a·zar (el′ē ā′zər) *n.* ⟦LL(Ec) *Eleazar* < Gr(Ec) < Heb *elazar,* lit., God has helped⟧ *Bible* Aaron's son and successor as high priest: Num. 20:28

elec *abbrev.* **1** electric **2** electrical **3** electricity

el·e·cam·pane (el′i kam pān′) *n.* ⟦ME *elena campana,* altered < ML *enula campana* < L *inula* (altered by metathesis < Gr *helenion,* prob. < *Helenē,* daughter of Zeus) + *campana* (< *campus,* field: see CAMPUS)⟧ a tall, hairy European perennial plant (*Inula helenium*) of the composite family, having flower heads with many slender, yellow rays: naturalized in the NE U.S.

e·lect (ē lekt′, i-) *adj.* ⟦ME < L *electus,* pp. of *eligere,* to pick out, choose < *e-,* out + *legere,* to pick, choose: see LOGIC⟧ **1** chosen; given preference **2** elected but not yet installed in office: usually used in comb. [the mayor-*elect*] **3** *Theol.* chosen by God for salvation and eternal life —*n.* a person who is elect —*vt.* **1** to select for some office by voting **2** to choose; select [we *elected* to stay] **3** *Theol.* to choose for eternal salvation: only in the passive, with *God* as the implied subject —*vi.* to make a choice; choose —**the elect** **1** persons belonging to a specially privileged group **2** *Theol.* those chosen by God for salvation and eternal life

e·lect·a·ble (ē lek′tə bəl, i-) *adj.* capable of being elected —**e·lect′a·bil′i·ty** *n.*

e·lec·tion (ē lek′shən, i-) *n.* ⟦ME *eleccioun* < OFr *election* < L *electio,* a choice, in LL(Ec), the election of believers: see ELECT⟧ **1** a choosing or choice **2** *a)* a choosing or being chosen for office by vote *b)* a voting, as in a municipality, on some proposition, issue, etc. **3** *Theol.* the selection by God of certain people for salvation and eternal life

Election Day a day on which elections for public officials are held, specif., in the U.S., the first Tuesday after the first Monday in November

e·lec·tion·eer (ē lek′shə nir′, i-) *vi.* to canvass votes for, or otherwise work for the success of, a candidate, political party, etc. in an election —**e·lec′tion·eer′er** *n.*

e·lec·tive (ē lek′tiv, i-) *adj.* ⟦ME < LL *electivus*⟧ **1** *a)* filled by election [an *elective* office] *b)* chosen by election; elected **2** of or based on election **3** having the power to choose **4** that may be chosen but is not required; optional **5** [Now Rare] having or referring to a tendency to attract or combine with certain substances in preference to others —☆*n.* an optional course or subject in a school or college curriculum —**e·lec′tive·ly** *adv.*

e·lec·tor (ē lek′tər, i-) *n.* ⟦ME *electour* < L *elector*⟧ **1** a person who elects; specif., a qualified voter **2** a member of the electoral college **3** ⟦transl. of Ger *Kurfürst,* lit., choosing prince⟧ [*usually* **E-**] any of the German princes of the Holy Roman Empire who took part in the election of the emperor

e·lec·tor·al (ē lek′tər əl, i-; *often* ē′lek tôr′əl, i lek′-) *adj.* **1** of an election or electors **2** made up of electors

electoral college [*often* **E- C-**] ☆an assembly elected by the voters to perform the formal duty of electing the president and the vice president of the United States: the electors of each state, equal in number to its members in Congress, are expected to cast their votes for the candidates selected by the popular vote in their state

e·lec·tor·ate (ē lek′tər it, i-) *n.* ⟦ML *electoratus*⟧ **1** all those qualified to vote in an election **2** the rank or territory of an elector in the Holy Roman Empire

E·lec·tra (ē lek′trə, i-) *n.* ⟦L < Gr *Elektra,* lit., shining one: see ELECTRIC⟧ *Gr. Myth.* a daughter of Agamemnon and Clytemnestra: she encourages her brother, Orestes, to kill their mother and their mother's lover, who together murdered Agamemnon

Electra complex [Obs.] *Psychoanalysis* the unconscious tendency of a daughter to be attached to her father and hostile toward her mother: cf. OEDIPUS COMPLEX

e·lec·tret (ē lek′trit, -tret′; i-) *n.* ⟦ELECTR(ICITY) + (MAGN)ET⟧ any of certain solid, dielectric materials that have a permanent electric charge after being melted and resolidified in a strong electric field: used in telephones, microphones, etc.

e·lec·tric (ē lek′trik, i-) *adj.* ⟦ModL *electricus* (coined, 1600, by William GILBERT[2]), lit., produced from amber by rubbing < ML, of amber < L *electrum,* amber, electrum < Gr *ēlektron,* akin to *ēlektōr,* shining, the sun < ?⟧ **1** of, charged with, or conducting electricity [*an electric* wire] **2** producing, or produced by, electricity [an *electric* generator] **3** operated by electricity [an *electric* iron] **4** made or designed to generate sound primarily through electronic amplification: said of certain musical instruments [*electric* guitar, bass, etc.] **5** very tense or exciting; electrifying **6** designating a color that is very bright or metallic [*electric* blue] —*n.* ☆a train, car, etc. operated by electricity

e·lec·tri·cal (-tri kəl) *adj.* **1** ELECTRIC **2** connected with the science or use of electricity

electrical engineering the branch of engineering having to do with the generation and use of electrical energy —**electrical engineer**

e·lec·tri·cal·ly (-tri kəl ē) *adv.* by or with electricity

electrical storm [Informal] a thunderstorm, esp. one with a great deal of lightning: sometimes called **electric storm**

electrical tape a plastic adhesive tape for insulating or securing electrical wires: also **electrician's tape**

electric arc ARC (sense 3)

☆**electric chair** **1** an apparatus in the form of a chair, used in electrocuting persons sentenced to death **2** the death sentence by electrocution Often preceded by *the*

electric eel any of a family (Electrophoridae) of large, eel-shaped cyprinoid fishes of N South America, having special organs that can give severe electric shocks

☆**electric eye** PHOTOELECTRIC CELL

electric field the electrically charged region of space surrounding an electrically charged body

electric furnace a furnace heated to high temperatures by an electric current, used in smelting, melting metals, steel making, manufacturing carbides, etc.

☆**e·lec·tri·cian** (ē′lek trish′ən; ē lek′-, i-) *n.* a person whose work is the construction, repair, or installation of electric apparatus

e·lec·tric·i·ty (ē′lek tris′i tē; ē lek′-, i-) *n.* ⟦see ELECTRIC⟧ **1** a property of certain fundamental particles of all matter, as electrons (negative charges) and protons or positrons (positive charges) that have a force field associated with them and that can be separated by the expenditure of energy: electrical charge can be generated by friction, induction, or chemical change and is manifested by an accumulation of electrons on an atom or body, constituting a negative charge, and a loss of electrons, constituting a corresponding positive charge **2** *a)* an electric current (see CURRENT, *n.* 3) *b)* an electric charge (see CHARGE, *n.* I, 3) **3** the branch of physics dealing with electricity **4** electric current supplied as a public utility for lighting, heating, etc. **5** strong emotional tension, excitement, etc.

electric needle a high-frequency electrode in the form of a needle, used in surgery to cauterize tissue

electric ray any of an order (Torpediniformes) of cartilaginous fishes with special organs that can produce strong electrical discharges used to paralyze or stun its enemies or prey

e·lec·tri·fy (ē lek′trə fī′, i-) *vt.* **-fied′, -fy′ing** **1** to charge with electricity **2** to give an electric shock to **3** to give a shock of excitement to; thrill **4** to equip for the use of electricity; provide with electric power —**e·lec′tri·fi′a·ble** *adj.* —**e·lec′tri·fi·ca′tion** *n.* —**e·lec′tri·fi′er** *n.*

e·lec·tro (ē lek′trō′, i-) *n., pl.* **-tros′** ⟦< Gr *ēlektron* (with sense of ModL *electricus*): see ELECTRIC⟧ *short for* ELECTROTYPE

e·lec·tro- (ē lek′trō, -trə; i-) *combining form* **1** electric *[electromagnet]* **2** electrically *[electrocute]* **3** electricity *[electrostatics]* **4** electrolysis *[electrodeposit]*

e·lec·tro·a·cous·tics (ē lek′trō ə ko͞os′tiks, i-) *n.* a branch of acoustics that deals with the conversion of sound into electricity and vice versa, as in a microphone or a speaker —**e·lec′tro·a·cous′tic** *adj.*, **e·lec′tro·a·cous′ti·cal**

e·lec·tro·a·nal·y·sis (-ə nal′ə sis) *n., pl.* **-ses′** (-sēz′) a chemical analysis of an electrolyte by means of electrolysis —**e·lec′tro·an′a·lyt′ic** (-an′ə lit′ ik) *adj.*, **e·lec′tro·an′a·lyt′i·cal**

e·lec·tro·car·di·o·gram (-kär′dē ə gram′) *n.* a graphic tracing showing the variations in electric force which trigger the contractions of the heart: it is used in the diagnosis of heart disease

e·lec·tro·car·di·o·graph (-kär′dē ə graf′) *n.* an instrument for making an electrocardiogram —**e·lec′tro·car′di·o·graph′ic** *adj.* —**e·lec′tro·car′di·o·graph′i·cal·ly** *adv.* —**e·lec′tro·car′di·og′ra·phy** *n.*

e·lec·tro·chem·is·try (-kem′is trē) *n.* the science that deals with the use of electrical energy to bring about a chemical reaction or with the generation of electrical energy by means of chemical action —**e·lec′tro·chem′i·cal** *adj.* —**e·lec′tro·chem′i·cal·ly** *adv.*

e·lec·tro·con·vul·sive therapy (-kən vul′siv) a procedure used to treat serious mental illness, as severe depression or mania, in which an electric current is passed through the brain to cause a brief, controlled surge in electrical activity

☆**e·lec·tro·cute** (ē lek′trə kyo͞ot′, i-) *vt.* **-cut′ed, -cut′ing** ⟦ELECTRO- + (EXE)CUTE⟧ to kill with a charge of electricity; specif., to execute in the electric chair —**e·lec′tro·cu′tion** *n.*

e·lec·trode (ē lek′trōd′, i-) *n.* ⟦coined by Michael FARADAY < ELECTR(O)- + -ODE[1]⟧ any terminal that conducts an electric current into or away from various conducting substances in a circuit, as the anode or cathode in a battery or the carbons in an arc lamp, or that emits, collects, or controls the flow of electrons in an electron tube, as the cathode, plate, or grid

e·lec·tro·de·pos·it (ē lek′trō dē päz′it, i-; -trə-) *vt.* to deposit (a metal, etc.) electrolytically —*n.* a deposit made by an electric current, as in electroplating —**e·lec′tro·dep′o·si′tion** (-dep′ə zish′ən) *n.*

e·lec·tro·di·al·y·sis (-dī al′ə sis) *n., pl.* **-ses′** (-sēz′) a type of dialysis in which undesired ions are removed from solution by means of a direct current passing between two electrodes, one on each side of the membrane

e·lec·tro·dy·nam·ics (-dī nam′iks) *n.* the branch of physics dealing with the phenomena of electric currents and associated magnetic forces —**e·lec′tro·dy·nam′ic** *adj.* —**e·lec′tro·dy·nam′i·cal·ly** *adv.*

e·lec·tro·dy·na·mom·e·ter (-dī′nə mäm′ət ər) *n.* an instrument in which the magnetic forces between two parts of the same circuit are used for detecting or measuring an electric current

e·lec·tro·en·ceph·a·lo·gram (-en sef′ə lō gram′) *n.* ⟦ELECTRO- + ENCEPHALO- + -GRAM⟧ a graphic tracing of minute voltage changes resulting from bioelectric activity in the brain: abbrev. *EEG*

e·lec·tro·en·ceph·a·lo·graph (-en sef′ə lə graf′) *n.* an instrument for making electroencephalograms: abbrev. *EEG* —**e·lec′tro·en·ceph′a·lo·graph′ic** *adj.* —**e·lec′tro·en·ceph′a·log′ra·phy** (-ə läg′rə fē) *n.*

☆**e·lec·tro·form·ing** (ē lek′trō fôr′miŋ, i-) *n.* the production or reproduction of articles by the electrolytic deposition of a metal on a conducting mold

e·lec·tro·hy·drau·lic (ē lek′trō hī drô′lik, i-; -trə-) *adj.* designating or of a process for converting electrical energy to high-pressure, mechanical shock waves by the discharge of a high-voltage arc under the surface of a liquid medium: used in metal shaping, breaking up rock, etc.

e·lec·tro·jet (ē lek′trō jet′, i-; -trə-) *n.* a narrow, high-velocity stream of electric energy that girdles the earth in the ionosphere above the magnetic equator and near the auroral displays

e·lec·tro·ki·net·ics (ē lek′trō ki net′iks, i-; -trə-) *n.* the branch of electrodynamics dealing with electricity in motion, or electric currents: cf. ELECTROSTATICS

e·lec·trol·o·gist (ē′lek träl′ə jist; ē lek′-, i-) *n.* a practitioner of ELECTROLYSIS (sense 2)

e·lec·tro·lu·mi·nes·cence (ē lek′trō lo͞o′mə nes′əns, i-; -trə-) *n.* the emission of cold light by certain substances when acted upon by an alternating electric field —**e·lec′tro·lu′mi·nes′cent** *adj.*

e·lec·trol·y·sis (ē′lek träl′ə sis; ē lek′-, i-) *n.* ⟦ELECTRO- + -LYSIS⟧ **1** the decomposition of an electrolyte by the action of an electric current passing through it **2** a cosmetic procedure in which unwanted hair is removed from the body by destroying the hair roots with an electrified needle

e·lec·tro·lyte (ē lek′trō līt′, i-; -trə-) *n.* ⟦ELECTRO- + -LYTE[1]⟧ **1** any chemical compound that ionizes when molten or in solution, allowing it to conduct electricity **2** *Physiol.* any ionized compound, as of sodium, potassium, or calcium, essential in maintaining certain metabolic processes

e·lec·tro·lyt·ic (ē lek′trō lit′ik, i-; -trə-) *adj.* **1** of or produced by electrolysis **2** of or containing an electrolyte —**e·lec′tro·lyt′i·cal·ly** *adv.*

e·lec·tro·lyze (ē lek′trō līz′, i-; -trə-) *vt.* **-lyzed′, -lyz′ing** to subject to, or decompose by, electrolysis

e·lec·tro·mag·net (ē lek′trō mag′nit, i-; -trə-) *n.* a soft iron or steel core surrounded by a coil of wire, that temporarily becomes a magnet when an electric current flows through the wire

e·lec·tro·mag·net·ic (ē lek′trō mag net′ik, i-; -trə-) *adj.* of, produced by, or having to do with electromagnetism or an electromagnet —**e·lec′tro·mag·net′i·cal·ly** *adv.*

electromagnetic interaction (*or* force) *Particle Physics* the relatively long-range interaction between elementary particles resulting from their electric and magnetic fields, responsible for molecular structure, chemical reactions, and other electromagnetic phenomena: see STRONG INTERACTION, WEAK INTERACTION

electromagnetic spectrum the complete range of frequencies of electromagnetic waves from the lowest to the highest, including, in order, radio, infrared, visible light, ultraviolet, X-ray, and gamma ray waves

electromagnetic wave a wave propagated through space or matter by oscillating electric and magnetic fields: in a vacuum it travels at the speed of light

e·lec·tro·mag·net·ism (-mag′nə tiz′əm) *n.* **1** magnetism produced by an electric current **2** *a)* the interaction between a magnetic field and an electric field *b)* the phenomena produced by such an interaction **3** the branch of physics that deals with electricity and magnetism

e·lec·tro·me·chan·i·cal (-mə kan′i kəl) *adj.* designating or of a mechanical device or operation that is activated or regulated by electricity

e·lec·tro·met·al·lur·gy (-met′ə lur′jē) *n.* the branch of metallurgy having to do with the use of electricity, as for producing heat in smelting, refining, etc., or for refining, plating, or depositing metals by electrolysis

e·lec·trom·e·ter (ē′lek träm′ət ər; ē lek′-, i-) *n.* **1** a device for detecting or measuring differences of potential by means of electrostatic forces **2** an active circuit arrangement for measuring differences of potential without drawing appreciable current

e·lec·tro·mo·tive (ē lek′trō mōt′iv, i-; -trə-) *adj.* **1** producing an electric current through differences in potential **2** relating to electromotive force

electromotive force the force or electric pressure that causes or tends to cause a current to flow in a circuit, equivalent to the potential difference between the terminals and commonly measured in volts: abbrev. *E, EMF*, or *emf*

☆**e·lec·tro·my·o·graph** (-mī′ō graf′, -mī′ə-) *n.* an instrument that displays and records a graphic tracing (**e·lec′tro·my′o·gram′**) of the minute voltage changes in muscle tissue, used in the diagnosis of muscle and nerve disorders: the tracing is made audible by connecting the voltage to a speaker —**e·lec′tro·my′o·graph′ic** *adj.* —**e·lec′tro·my·og′ra·phy** (-äg′rə fē) *n.*

e·lec·tron (ē lek′trän′, i-; *also*, -trən) *n.* ⟦coined (1891) by G. J. Stoney (1826-1911), Ir physicist < ELECTR(IC) + -ON⟧ *Particle Physics* the lightest elementary particle with an electric charge: it is a lepton with a negative charge of *c.* 1.602×10^{-19} coulomb and a rest mass of *c.* 9.109×10^{-31} kg (*c.* 0.511 MeV/c^2), which is *c.* $\frac{1}{1836}$ of the mass of a proton: ordinarily an atom has the same number of negative electrons around the nucleus as the number of positive protons in the nucleus: see also POSITRON, NEGATRON

e·lec·tro·neg·a·tive (ē lek′trō neg′ə tiv, i-; -trə-) *adj.* **1** having a negative electrical charge; tending to move to the positive electrode, or anode, in electrolysis **2** having the ability to attract electrons, esp. in forming a chemical bond —*n.* an electronegative substance

electron gun the part of an electron tube, esp. a cathode-ray tube, that emits, accelerates, and controls a beam of electrons

e·lec·tron·ic (ē′lek trän′ik, ē lek′-, i-; *also* el′ek-) *adj.* **1** of or having to do with electrons **2** operating, produced, or done by the action of electrons or other carriers in semiconductors, vacuum tubes, etc. **3** carried on by or making use of electronic equipment *[electronic* banking, *electronic* journalism*]* —**e·lec′tron′i·cal·ly** *adv.*

e·lec·tron·i·ca (-i kə) *n.* any of various kinds of popular electronic dance music that rely heavily on synthesizers, sequencers, drum machines, sampling techniques, etc.

electronic mail EMAIL (*n.* 1)

electronic music music in which the sounds are created, organized, or altered by electronic devices

☆**electronic organ** a musical instrument with a console like that of a pipe organ, but producing tones by means of electronic devices instead of pipes

electronic publishing the publishing of information, books, etc. in a format accessible by computer

e·lec·tron·ics (-iks) *n.* the science that deals with the behavior and control of electrons in vacuums and gases, and with the use of electron tubes, photoelectric cells, transistors, etc. —*pl.n.* electronic equipment, systems, etc.

electron lens a configuration of electric or magnetic fields, or a combination of both, that serves to focus or deflect an electron beam, as in an electron microscpe

electron microscope an instrument that focuses a beam of electrons on an object, using electric or magnetic fields, to form an enlarged image of the object on a fluorescent screen, photographic plate, or cathode-ray tube; specif., such an instrument in which the beam of electrons passes directly through an extremely thin object and forms a two-dimensional image: it is much more powerful than any optical microscope: cf. SCANNING ELECTRON MICROSCOPE

electron multiplier a device that amplifies a stream of electrons by causing it to strike electrodes at successively higher potentials: secondary electrons produced at each electrode increase the quantity of electrons in the stream

electron optics the branch of electronics having to do with the focusing and deflection of beams of electrons by means of electric and magnetic fields, which act upon the beams in the same way that lenses act on light rays

electron telescope an instrument using a cathode-ray tube to form a visible image of infrared rays brought into focus from a distant object by optical lenses

electron tube a sealed tube, usually of glass, containing a vacuum or a gas and electrodes that are connected to pinlike terminals that protrude from the base, used as a plug-in component in an electronic device to control the flow of electrons

electron volt a unit of energy equal to that attained by an electron falling unimpeded through a potential difference of one volt; 1.602×10^{-19} joule: abbrev. *eV*: often written **e·lec′tron·volt′** *n.* or **e·lec′tron-volt′**

e·lec·tro·op·tics (ē lek′trō äp′tiks, i-) *n.* the technology that deals with the production, control, and detection of light by electrical devices —**e·lec′tro·op′tic** *adj.*, **e·lec′tro·op′ti·cal** —**e·lec′tro·op′ti·cal·ly** *adv.*

e·lec·tro·os·mo·sis (-äs mō′sis, -äz-) *n.* osmosis through a membrane that is caused by the action of an electric field, usually such a field generated by two electrodes, one on each side of the membrane —**e·lec′tro·os·mot′ic** (-mät′ik) *adj.*

e·lec·tro·phil·ic (-fil′ik) *adj.* designating or of a chemical, ion, etc. that accepts additional electrons

e·lec·tro·pho·re·sis (-fə rē′sis) *n.* ⟦ModL < ELECTRO- + (CATA)PHORESIS⟧ the migration of charged colloidal particles or of molecules through a fluid or gel subjected to an electric field —**e·lec′tro·pho·ret′ic** (-fə ret′ik) *adj.*

e·lec·troph·o·rus (ē′lek träf′ə rəs; ē lek′-, i-) *n.*, *pl.* **-ri′** (-rī′) ⟦ModL < ELECTRO- + Gr *-phoros*, bearing < *pherein*, BEAR[1]⟧ an apparatus consisting of an insulated resin disk and a metal plate, used in generating static electricity by induction

e·lec·tro·phys·i·ol·o·gy (ē lek′trō fiz′ē äl′ə jē, i-; -trə-) *n.* 1 the study of the electrical properties of living cells 2 the study of the production of electric currents by living organisms —**e·lec′tro·phys′i·o·log′i·cal** (-fiz′ē ə läj′i kəl) *adj.* —**e·lec′tro·phys′i·ol′o·gist** *n.*

e·lec·tro·plate (ē lek′trō plāt′, i-; -trə-) *vt.* **-plat′ed**, **-plat′ing** to deposit a coating of metal on by electrolysis

e·lec·tro·pos·i·tive (ē lek′trō päz′ə tiv, i-) *adj.* 1 having a positive electrical charge; tending to move toward the negative electrode, or cathode, in electrolysis 2 having the ability to give up electrons, esp. in forming a chemical bond —*n.* an electropositive substance

e·lec·tro·scope (ē lek′trō skōp′, i-; -trə-) *n.* an instrument for detecting very small charges of electricity, electric fields, or radiation: it can indicate whether they are positive or negative, as by the divergence of electrically charged strips of gold leaf: when fitted with optical means for quantitative observation of the divergence, an electroscope serves as an electrometer —**e·lec′tro·scop′ic** (-skäp′ik) *adj.*

GOLD LEAF

electroscope

e·lec·tro·shock therapy (-shäk′) ELECTROCONVULSIVE THERAPY

e·lec·tro·stat·ic (ē lek′trō stat′ik, i-; -trə-) *adj.* 1 of or having to do with electrostatics 2 designating or of a speaker in which electric force is applied to metal plates, causing a diaphragm suspended between them to vibrate —**e·lec′tro·stat′i·cal·ly** *adv.*

electrostatic generator a generator which produces high-voltage electricity by electrostatic induction: sometimes used to accelerate charged particles for nuclear reactions

e·lec·tro·stat·ics (-stat′iks) *n.* the branch of electromagnetic theory dealing with electric charges at rest, or static electricity: cf. ELECTROKINETICS

electrostatic units the system of CGS electric and magnetic units that assigns the value of one to the dielectric constant of a vacuum

e·lec·tro·sur·ger·y (-sur′jər ē) *n.* the use of electricity in surgery, as in cauterizing

e·lec·tro·syn·the·sis (-sin′thə sis) *n.* *Chem.* synthesis produced by means of an electric current

e·lec·tro·ther·a·py (-ther′ə pē) *n.* the treatment of disease by means of the application of electric currents to specific parts of the body —**e·lec′tro·ther′a·pist** *n.*

e·lec·tro·ther·mal (-thur′məl) *adj.* using, relating to, or generating heat from electric energy

e·lec·tro·ther·mics (-thur′miks) *n.* the branch of science which deals with the direct transformations of electric energy and heat, as in the heating chamber of certain rockets —**e·lec′tro·ther′mic** *adj.*

e·lec·trot·o·nus (ē′lek trät′ə nəs, -trät′n əs; ē lek′-, i-) *n.* ⟦ModL: see ELECTRO- & TONE⟧ the changed electrical state of a nerve or muscle when an electric current is passed through it —**e·lec′tro·ton′ic** (-trō tän′ik, -trə-) *adj.*

e·lec·tro·type (ē lek′trō tīp′, i-; -trə-) *n.* *Printing* 1 a plate made by electroplating a wax or plastic impression of the original page of type, etc. 2 a print made from such a plate — *vt., vi.* **-typed′**, **-typ′ing** to make an electrotype of —**e·lec′tro·typ′er** *n.* —**e·lec′tro·typ′ic** (-tip′ik) *adj.*

e·lec·tro·va·lence (ē lek′trō vā′ləns, i-; -trə-) *n.* 1 the number of electrons an atom gains or loses in forming a compound during a chemical reaction 2 IONIC BOND: also **e·lec′tro·va′lent bond** (-lənt)

e·lec·tro·weak (ē lek′trō wēk′, i-) *adj.* designating or of the theory that combines the electromagnetic interaction with the weak interaction and predicts the behavior of the W and Z particles

e·lec·trum (ē lek′trəm, i-) *n.* ⟦L < Gr *ēlektron*: see ELECTRIC⟧ a light-yellow alloy of gold and silver

e·lec·tu·ar·y (ē lek′choo͞ er′ē, i-) *n.*, *pl.* **-ar′ies** ⟦ME *electuarie* < LL *electuarium* < Gr *ekleikton* < *ekleichein*, to lick out < *ek-*, out + *leichein*, to LICK⟧ a medicine made by mixing drugs with honey or syrup to form a paste

el·ee·mos·y·nar·y (el′i mäs′ə ner′ē, el′ē ə mäs′-) *adj.* ⟦ML *eleemosynarius* < LL(Ec) *eleemosyna*, ALMS⟧ [Old-fashioned] 1 of or for charity or alms; charitable 2 supported by or dependent on charity 3 given as charity; free

el·e·gance (el′ə gəns) *n.* ⟦Fr *élégance* < L *elegantia*⟧ 1 the quality of being elegant; specif., *a)* dignified richness and grace, as of design *b)* polished fastidiousness or refined grace, as in manners *c)* clever aptness and simplicity 2 anything elegant Also, esp. for sense 2, **el′e·gan·cy** *pl.* **-cies**

el·e·gant (el′ə gənt) *adj.* ⟦Fr *élégant* < L *elegans* prp. of **elegare* < *e-*, out + **legare*, var. of *legere*, to choose: see LOGIC⟧ 1 characterized by dignified richness and grace, as of design, dress, style, etc.; luxurious or opulent in a restrained, tasteful manner 2 characterized by a sense of propriety or refinement; impressively fastidious in manners and tastes 3 marked by concision, incisiveness, and ingenuity; cleverly apt and simple [an *elegant* solution to a complex problem] 4 [Informal] excellent; fine; first-rate —**el′e·gant·ly** *adv.*

el·e·gi·ac (el ē′jē ak′, i lē′-; el′ə jī′ak′, -ək) *adj.* ⟦LL *elegiacus* < Gr *elegeiakos* < *elegeia*: see ELEGY⟧ 1 *Gr. & Latin Prosody* of or composed in dactylic-hexameter couplets, the second line (sometimes called a *pentameter*) having only an accented syllable in the third and sixth feet: the form was used for elegies and various other lyric poems 2 of, like, or fit for an elegy 3 sad; mournful; plaintive Also **el·e·gi·a·cal** (el′ə jī′ə kəl) —*n.* 1 an elegiac couplet 2 [*pl.*] a series of such couplets; poem or poems written in such couplets

el·e·gist (el′ə jist) *n.* a writer of an elegy or elegies

e·le·git (ē lē′jit) *n.* ⟦L, 3d pers. sing., perf. indic., of *eligere*, to choose: see ELECT⟧ *Law* a writ of execution by which a plaintiff is given possession of the defendant's goods until the plaintiff's claim is satisfied

el·e·gize (el′ə jīz′) *vi.* **-gized′**, **-giz′ing** to write an elegy —*vt.* to commemorate or lament as in an elegy

el·e·gy (el′ə jē) *n.*, *pl.* **-gies** ⟦Fr *élégie* < L *elegia* < Gr *elegeia* < *elegos*, a lament < ? IE base **el-* > ALMS⟧ 1 any poem in elegiac verse 2 a poem or song of lament and praise for the dead, as Shelley's "Adonais" 3 any poem, song, etc. in a mournfully contemplative tone [Gray's "*Elegy* Written in a Country Churchyard"]

elem *abbrev.* 1 element(s) 2 elementary

el·e·ment (el′ə mənt) *n.* ⟦ME < OFr < L *elementum*, first principle, element⟧ 1 any of the four substances (earth, air, fire, and water) formerly believed to constitute all physical matter 2 any of these four substances thought of as the natural environment of a class of living beings 3 the natural or suitable environment, situation, etc. for a person or thing: often in the phrase **in (or out of) one's element** 4 *a)* a component part or quality, often one that is basic or essential [a good story has an *element* of suspense] *b)* a constituent group of a specified kind [the criminal *element* in a city] *c)* a determining factor *d)* any of the data needed or used to make certain calculations, solve a particular problem, etc. 5 on certain electric typewriters, a hollow, metal ball with raised letters, symbols, etc. that print as the corresponding keys are depressed 6 *Chem.* any substance that cannot be separated into different substances by ordinary chemical methods: all matter is composed of such substances: elements can be transformed into other elements by radioactive decay or by nuclear reactions 7 *Comput.* one item of data, as in an ARRAY (sense 5) 8 [*pl.*] *Eccles.* the bread and wine of Communion 9 *Elec.* *a)* any device with terminals at which it can be connected with other electrical devices *b)* the wire coil that becomes glowing hot, as in an electric oven 10 *Math.* *a)* an infinitesimal part of any magnitude; differential *b)* the point, line, etc. that generates a line, surface, etc. *c)* a part of a set or configuration, as a side of a triangle or a number in a matrix 11 *Mil.* a subdivision of a unit or formation —**the elements** 1 the first or basic principles; rudiments 2 wind, rain, and the other forces of nature that make the weather

SYN.—**element**, in its general use, is the broadest term for any of the basic, irreducible parts or principles of anything, concrete or abstract [the *elements* of a science]; **component** and **constituent** both refer to any of the simple or compound parts of some complex thing or concept, but **constituent** also implies that the part is essential to the complex [hemoglobin is a *constituent* of blood]; **ingredient** refers to any of the substances (sometimes nonessential) that are mixed together in preparing a food, medicine, etc. [the *ingredients* of a cocktail]; **factor** applies to any of the component parts that are instrumental in determining the nature of the complex [luck was a *factor* in his success]

el·e·men·tal (el′ə ment′'l) *adj.* ⟦ME < ML *elementalis*⟧ 1 of any or all of the four elements: see ELEMENT (sense 1) 2 of or like natural forces; characteristic of the physical universe 3 basic and powerful; not subtle or refined; primal [hunger and sex are *elemental* drives] 4 ELEMENTARY (sense 2*a*) 5 being an essential or basic part or parts 6 being a chemical element in uncombined form —*n.* a basic principle; rudiment: *usually used in pl.* —**el′e·men′tal·ly** *adv.*

el·e·men·ta·ry (el′ə ment′ə rē, -men′trē) *adj.* ⟦ME *elementare* < L *elementarius*⟧ 1 ELEMENTAL 2 *a)* of first principles, rudiments, or fundamentals; introductory; basic; simple *b)* of or having to do with the formal instruction of children in basic subjects [*elementary* education] —**el·e·men·ta·ri·ly** (el′ə ment′ə rə lē, -men′ter′ə lē) *adv.* —**el′e·men′ta·ri·ness** *n.*

elementary particle *Particle Physics* a subatomic particle that cannot be divided, as a lepton, quark, weakon, or classon: in the past any subatomic particle was thought to be an elementary particle: see also HADRON

elementary school a school of the first six grades (sometimes, the first five or eight grades), where basic subjects are taught

el·e·mi (el′ə mē) ***n.*** ⟦Fr *élémi* < Sp *elemi* < Ar *al-lāmī*⟧ any of various resins from tropical trees of the bursera family, used esp. in varnishes, ointments, and inks

e·len·chus (ē leŋ′kəs) ***n.***, *pl.* **-chi′** (-kī′) ⟦L < Gr *elenchos*, cross-examination, refutation < *elenchein*, to shame, refute⟧ a logical refutation, esp. one that disproves a proposition by proving the direct contrary of its conclusion —**e·lenc′tic** ***adj.***, **e·lench′tic** (-leŋk′tik)

el·e·op·tene (el′ē äp′tēn′) ***n.*** ⟦< Gr *elaion*, olive oil, OIL + *ptēnos*, winged; akin to *pteron*, wing, FEATHER⟧ that part of an essential oil which does not become solid: cf. STEAROPTENE

el·e·phant (el′ə fənt) ***n.***, *pl.* **-phants** or **-phant** ⟦ME *elefaunt* < L *elephantus* < Gr *elephas* (gen. *elephantos*), elephant, ivory < ? Berber *elu*, elephant + Egypt *ȝbw*, elephant, ivory⟧ any of an order (Proboscidea) of huge, thick-skinned, almost hairless mammals, the largest of extant four-footed animals, with a long, flexible snout (called a *trunk*) and, usually, two ivory tusks growing out of the upper jaw: the existing species are the endangered **Asian** (or **Indian**) **elephant** (*Elephas maximus*), which is commonly domesticated, and two species of **African elephant** (*Loxodonta africana* and *Loxodonta cyclotis*), which have a flatter head and larger ears —**elephant in the room** an obvious, crucial factor or fact that is being ignored deliberately, as because it is unpleasant or disconcerting

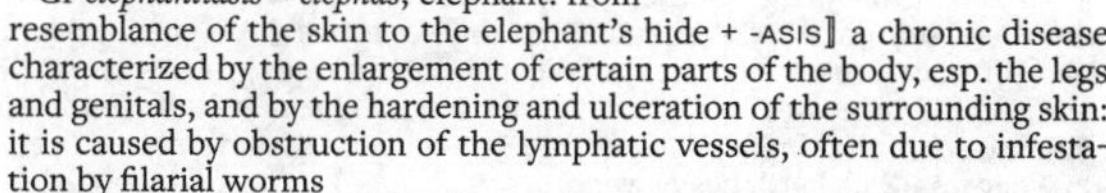

elephants

elephant grass any of various tall grasses or grasslike plants; esp., a perennial, tropical grass (*Pennisetum purpureum*) native to Africa that is cultivated for fodder

el·e·phan·ti·a·sis (el′ə fən tī′ə sis) ***n.*** ⟦L < Gr *elephantiasis* < *elephas*, elephant: from resemblance of the skin to the elephant's hide + -ASIS⟧ a chronic disease characterized by the enlargement of certain parts of the body, esp. the legs and genitals, and by the hardening and ulceration of the surrounding skin: it is caused by obstruction of the lymphatic vessels, often due to infestation by filarial worms

el·e·phan·tine (el′ə fan′tēn′, el′ə fən tēn′; -tīn′) ***adj.*** ⟦L *elephantinus* < Gr *elephantinos*⟧ **1** of an elephant or elephants **2** like an elephant in size or gait; huge, heavy, slow, clumsy, ungainly, etc.

El·e·phan·ti·ne (el′ə fan tī′nē, -tē′-) small island in the Nile, opposite Aswan: site of ancient ruins

elephant seal SEA ELEPHANT

el·e·phant's-ear (el′ə fənts ir′) ***n.*** **1** any of several plants (genus *Colocasia*) of the arum family, esp. an ornamental (*C. antiquorum*) having enormous heart-shaped leaves **2** any of various cultivated begonias with large, showy leaves

El·eu·sin·i·an (el′yoo͞ sin′ē ən) ***adj.*** **1** of Eleusis **2** designating or of the secret religious rites (**Eleusinian mysteries**) celebrated at the ancient Greek city of Eleusis in honor of Demeter and Persephone

E·leu·sis (e lo͞o′sis) town in Greece, northwest of Athens: site of an ancient Greek city (also called **Eleusis**), seat of the Eleusinian mysteries

elev *abbrev.* elevation

el·e·vate (el′ə vāt′) ***vt.*** **-vat′ed**, **-vat′ing** ⟦ME *elevaten* < L *elevatus*, pp. of *elevare*, to raise < *e-*, out + *levare*, to make light, lift < *levis*, LIGHT[2]⟧ **1** to lift up; raise **2** to raise the pitch or volume of (esp. the voice) **3** to raise (a person) in rank or position; promote **4** to raise to a higher intellectual or moral level **5** to raise the spirits of; elate; exhilarate —***adj.*** [Archaic] elevated —***SYN.*** LIFT

el·e·vat·ed (-vāt′id) ***adj.*** **1** lifted up; raised; high **2** exalted; dignified; lofty **3** high-spirited; exhilarated **4** higher than normal [an *elevated* temperature] —☆***n.*** ELEVATED RAILWAY

☆**elevated railway** (*or* **railroad**) a railway elevated on a framework, leaving the street below free for other traffic

el·e·va·tion (el′ə vā′shən) ***n.*** ⟦ME *elevacioun* < OFr *elevacion* < L *elevatio*⟧ **1** an elevating or being elevated **2** a high place or position **3** a raised portion of the earth's surface; hill, mountain, etc. **4** height above a surface, as of the earth **5** *a)* the ability of a dancer to attain height in the air while executing a leap *b)* the height thus attained **6** dignity; eminence; loftiness **7** a flat scale drawing of the front, rear, or side of a building, etc. **8** *Aeron.* the angular altitude of any object above the horizon **9** *Geog.* height above sea level; altitude **10** *Mil.* angular distance of the muzzle of a gun above the horizontal —***SYN.*** HEIGHT

el·e·va·tor (el′ə vāt′ər) ***n.*** ⟦LL(Ec), one who raises up, a deliverer: see ELEVATE⟧ **1** a person or thing that raises or lifts up ☆**2** a platform, cage, or boxlike structure suspended by motor-operated cables, for hoisting or lowering people or things, as in a building or mine ☆**3** a machine, usually consisting of buckets or scoops fastened to an endless belt or chain, for hoisting grain, etc., as in a warehouse ☆**4** GRAIN ELEVATOR **5** a pilot-controlled airfoil attached to the trailing edge of the tail section's horizontal stabilizers, used to make an aircraft go up or down and to control pitching

elevator music recorded popular music played in the background in public places such as elevators, variously regarded as bland, monotonous, etc.

elevator shoe a shoe designed to increase the wearer's height

e·lev·en (ē lev′ən, i-) ***adj.*** ⟦ME *elleven* < OE *endleofan*, akin to OFris *andlofa*, OHG *einlif* (Ger *elf*) < Gmc **ainlif*, lit., one left over (after ten) < **ain-* (OE *an*: see A[2], AN[1] + *-*lif*, left over, prob. < IE base **leikw-*, to leave behind > LOAN⟧ totaling one more than ten —***n.*** **1** the cardinal number between ten and twelve; 11; XI **2** any group of eleven people or things; esp., a football or cricket team **3** something numbered eleven or having eleven units, as a throw of dice

e·lev·en-plus (-plus′) ***n.*** [Brit.] an examination given in school, esp. formerly, at about the age of eleven to determine whether a pupil will go to a vocational or academic secondary school

e·lev·ens·es (i lev′ən ziz) ***pl.n.*** ⟦pl. of *elevens*, luncheon, pl. of ELEVEN: orig. an eleven-o'clock meal⟧ [Brit. Informal] tea, a light snack, etc. served in the late morning

e·lev·enth (ē lev′ənth, i-) ***adj.*** ⟦ME *elleventhe* < OE *endlyfta*: see ELEVEN & -TH[2]⟧ **1** preceded by ten others in a series; 11th **2** designating any of the eleven equal parts of something —***n.*** **1** the one following the tenth **2** any of the eleven equal parts of something; 1/11 —***adv.*** in the eleventh place, rank, etc. —**at the eleventh hour** ⟦see Matt. 20:1-16⟧ at the last moment; just before it is too late

e·lev·en·ty (ē lev′ən tē, i-) ***n.*** ⟦ELEVEN + -TY[2]: coined by J. R. R. TOLKIEN in his book *The Fellowship of the Ring* (1954)⟧ the cardinal number 110: a humorous usage suggesting any unusually large size or quantity

el·e·von (el′ə vän′) ***n.*** ⟦ELEV(ATOR) + (AILER)ON⟧ an aileron on a tailless airplane, that also serves as an elevator

elf (elf) ***n.***, *pl.* **elves** (elvz) ⟦ME < OE *ælf*, akin to OHG *alb* (Ger, nightmare), prob. < IE base **albho-*, white > L *albus*, white: prob. basic sense "whitish figure" (in the mist)⟧ **1** *Folklore* a tiny, often prankish being in human form, exercising magic powers and haunting woods and hills; sprite **2** a small child or being, esp. a mischievous one —**elf′like′** ***adj.***

ELF *abbrev.* extremely low frequency

El Faiyûm *see* FAIYÛM

elf·in (elf′in) ***adj.*** ⟦prob. < ME *elvene*, gen. pl.: see ELF⟧ of or like an elf; tiny, delicate, etc. —***n.*** an elf

elf·ish (elf′ish) ***adj.*** like or characteristic of an elf; elfin or prankish —**elf′ish·ly** ***adv.*** —**elf′ish·ness** ***n.***

elf·lock (elf′läk′) ***n.*** a lock of hair tangled as if by elves: a poetic or fanciful usage

El·gar (el′gər, -gär′), Sir **Edward (William)** 1857-1934; Eng. composer

El·gin (el′jin) ⟦after the title of a Scots hymn written in honor of the town of *Elgin, Scotland*⟧ city in NE Ill., near Chicago

El·gin marbles (el′gin) ⟦after 7th Earl of *Elgin* (1766-1841), who brought them to England⟧ a collection of ancient Athenian marble sculptures taken chiefly from the Parthenon, in the British Museum since 1816

El·gon (el′gän′), **Mount** extinct volcano on the Kenyan-Ugandan border: 14,178 ft (4,321 m): crater, 5 mi (8 km) wide

El Gre·co (el grek′ō) (born *Domenikos Theotokopoulos*) 1541?-1614?; painter in Italy (*c.* 1560-75) & Spain, born in Crete

E·li (ē′lī′) ***n.*** ⟦Heb, lit., high⟧ **1** a masculine name **2** *Bible* a high priest of Israel and teacher of Samuel: 1 Sam. 3

El·i·a·de (el′i ä′de, il′ē ä′dä), **Mir·cea** (mir′chä, mir sē′ə) 1907-86; Romanian scholar & writer, esp. on mythology & comparative religion, in the U.S. after 1956

E·li·as (ē lī′əs, i-) ***n.*** ⟦L < Gr *Elias* < Heb: see ELIJAH⟧ *Bible var. of* ELIJAH

e·lic·it (ē lis′it, i-) ***vt.*** ⟦< L *elicitus*, pp. of *elicere*, to draw out < *e-*, out + *lacere*, to entice, akin to *laqueus*: see LACE⟧ **1** to draw forth; evoke [to *elicit* an angry reply] **2** to cause to be revealed [to *elicit* facts] —***SYN.*** EXTRACT —**e·lic′it·a·ble** ***adj.*** —**e·lic′i·ta′tion** ***n.*** —**e·lic′i·tor** ***n.***

e·lide (ē līd′, i-) ***vt.*** **e·lid′ed**, **e·lid′ing** ⟦L *elidere*, to strike out < *e-*, out + *laedere*, to strike⟧ **1** to leave out; suppress, omit, or ignore **2** to leave out or slur over (a vowel, syllable, etc.) in pronunciation

el·i·gi·ble (el′i jə bəl) ***adj.*** ⟦ME < ML *eligibilis* < L *eligere*: see ELECT⟧ **1** fit to be chosen; legally or morally qualified **2** suitable or desirable, esp. for marriage ☆**3** *Football* allowed by the rules to catch a forward pass —***n.*** an eligible person —**el′i·gi·bil′i·ty** ***n.*** —**el′i·gi·bly** ***adv.***

E·li·hu (ē lī′hyo͞o′, i-; el′i hyo͞o′) ***n.*** ⟦Heb, lit., my God is he⟧ *Bible* one of Job's visitors in his affliction: Job 32-37

E·li·jah (ē lī′jə, i-) ***n.*** ⟦Heb *eliyahu*, lit., Jehovah is God⟧ **1** a masculine name: dim. *Lige*; var. *Elias, Ellis, Eliot* **2** *Bible* a prophet of Israel in the 9th century B.C.: 1 Kings 17-19; 2 Kings 2:1-11

e·lim·i·nate (ē lim′ə nāt′, i-) ***vt.*** **-nat′ed**, **-nat′ing** ⟦< L *eliminatus*, pp. of *eliminare*, to turn out of doors, banish < *e-*, out + *limen*, threshold (akin to *limes*, boundary) < IE base *(*e*)*lei-*, to bend > LIMB[1]⟧ **1** to take out; remove; get rid of **2** to leave out of consideration; reject; omit **3** to drop (a person, team, etc. losing a round or match in a contest) from further competition **4** *Algebra* to get rid of (an unknown quantity) by combining equations **5** *Physiol.* to expel (waste products) from the body; excrete —***SYN.*** EXCLUDE —**e·lim′i·na′tion** ***n.*** —**e·lim′i·na′tive** ***adj.*** —**e·lim′i·na′tor** ***n.*** —**e·lim′i·na·to′ry** (-nə tôr′ē) ***adj.***

El·i·nor (el′ə nər, -nôr′) ***n.*** a feminine name: see ELEANOR

el·int (el′int) ***n.*** ⟦< *el(ectronic) int(elligence)*⟧ the gathering of intelligence by monitoring with electronic equipment from airplanes, ships, satellites, etc.

El·i·ot[1] (el′ē ət, el′yət) ***n.*** ⟦dim. of ELLIS[1]⟧ a masculine name: see ELLIS[1]

El·i·ot[2] (el′ē ət, el′yət) **1 Charles William** 1834-1926; U.S. educator: president of Harvard University (1869-1909) **2 George** (pseud. of *Mary Ann*

Evans) 1819-80; Eng. novelist **3 John** 1604-90; Am. clergyman, born in England: known for missionary work among the Am. Indians **4 T(homas) S(tearns)** 1888-1965; Brit. poet & critic, born in the U.S.

El·i·ot·ic (el′ē ät′ik) ***adj.*** of, like, or characteristic of T. S. Eliot or his style

E·lis (ē′lis) ancient country in the W Peloponnesus, in which Olympia was located

E·lis·a·beth (ē liz′ə bəth, i-) ***n.*** a feminine name: see ELIZABETH[1]

E·li·sha (ē lī′shə, i-) ***n.*** ⟦Heb, lit., God is salvation⟧ **1** a masculine name: var. *Ellis* **2** *Bible* a prophet of Israel, ordained by Elijah as his successor: 1 Kings 19:16, 19; 2 Kings 2

e·li·sion (ē lizh′ən, i-) ***n.*** ⟦L *elisio*, a striking out (in LL, elision) < pp. of *elidere*: see ELIDE⟧ **1** the omission, assimilation, or slurring over of a vowel, syllable, etc. in pronunciation: often used in poetry to preserve meter, as when a word ends with a vowel before another word beginning with a vowel (Ex.: "th' inevitable hour") **2** any act or instance of leaving out or omitting a part or parts

e·lite (i lēt′, ā-) ***n.*** ⟦Fr *élite* < OFr *eslite*, fem. pp. of *eslire*, to choose < VL **exligere*, for L *eligere*: see ELECT⟧ **1** [*also with pl. v.*] the group or part of a group selected or regarded as the finest, best, most distinguished, most powerful, etc. **2** a size of type for typewriters, measuring twelve characters to the linear inch —***adj.*** of, forming, or suitable for an elite

e·lit·ism (-iz′əm) ***n.*** **1** government or control by an elite **2** advocacy of control by, or privileges for, an elite **3** the fact of sensing or believing that one is a member of an elite

e·lit·ist (-ist) ***adj.*** of, having, or advocating elitism —***n.*** **1** one who advocates elitism **2** a person who is or who believes himself or herself to be a member of an elite group

e·lix·ir (i lik′sər) ***n.*** ⟦ME < ML < Ar *al-iksīr* < *al*, the + *iksīr*, philosopher's stone, prob. < Gr *xērion*, powder for drying wounds < *xēros*, dry: see XERO-⟧ **1** a substance sought by medieval alchemists because it was thought to have the power to change base metals into gold or (in full **elixir of life**) to prolong life indefinitely **2** [Rare] the quintessence; underlying principle **3** a supposed remedy for all ailments; panacea **4** *Pharmacy a)* a sweetened, aromatic solution used as a vehicle for a medicine or alcohol, or as a nonmedicated flavoring *b)* a medication containing such a solution [a cough *elixir*]

Eliz *abbrev.* Elizabethan

E·li·za (ē lī′zə, i-) ***n.*** a feminine name: dim. *Liza*: see ELIZABETH[1]

E·liz·a·beth[1] (ē liz′ə bəth, i-) ***n.*** ⟦LL(Ec) *Elizabetha* < Gr(Ec) *Elisabet* < Heb *elisheva*, lit., God is (my) oath⟧ **1** a feminine name: dim. *Bess, Bessie, Beth, Betsy, Betty, Elsie, Libby, Lisa, Liz*; var. *Elisabeth, Eliza* **2** *Bible* the mother of John the Baptist and a kinswoman of Mary: Luke 1

E·liz·a·beth[2] (ē liz′ə bəth′, i-) **2 Elizabeth I** 1533-1603; queen of England (1558-1603): daughter of Henry VIII & Anne Boleyn **3 Elizabeth II** (born *Elizabeth Alexandra Mary*) 1926- ; queen of Great Britain & Northern Ireland (1952-); head of the Commonwealth; daughter of George VI

E·liz·a·beth[3] (ē liz′ə bəth, i-) ⟦after the wife of Sir George Carteret (1610?-80), proprietor of a colony in the region⟧ city in NE N.J., adjacent to Newark

E·liz·a·be·than (ē liz′ə bē′thən, i-) ***adj.*** of or characteristic of the time when Elizabeth I was queen of England —***n.*** an English person, esp. a writer, of the time of Queen Elizabeth I

Elizabethan sonnet SHAKESPEAREAN SONNET

Elizabeth Pe·trov·na (pə trōv′nə) 1709-62; empress of Russia (1741-62): daughter of Peter I

elk (elk) ***n.***, *pl.* **elk** or **elks** ⟦ME, irreg. development (with *-k* for *-ch*) < OE *eolh*, akin to Ger *elch*, ON *elgr* < Gmc base **alchis* < IE base **el-*, stag, hart > Welsh *elain*, doe, Lith *élnis*, Gr *elaphos*, deer⟧ **1** MOOSE: the common term in Europe ☆**2** WAPITI **3** a light, flexible leather of cowhide or calfskin

Elk Grove city in central Calif.: suburb of Sacramento

elk·hound (elk′hound′) ***n.*** NORWEGIAN ELKHOUND

ell[1] (el) ***n.*** ☆**1** an extension or wing at right angles to the main structure **2** an L-shaped pipe or conduit fitting

ell[2] (el) ***n.*** ⟦ME *elle, elne* < OE *eln*, akin to Ger *elle* < Gmc **alinō*, lit., arm, hence arm's length < IE base **elei-*, to bend, **olina*, elbow > L *ulna*, arm, elbow, Gr *ōlenē*, elbow⟧ a former English unit of measure, mainly for cloth, equal to 45 inches, or any of various other European measures of different lengths

El·la (el′ə) ***n.*** a feminine name: see ELEANOR

El·len (el′ən) ***n.*** a feminine name: dim. *Ellie*: see HELEN

Elles·mere (elz′mir′) ⟦after F. Egerton (1800-57), 1st Earl of *Ellesmere*, Eng statesman⟧ northernmost island of the Arctic Archipelago, in the Baffin region of Nunavut, Canada: 75,767 sq mi (196,236 sq km)

El·lice Islands (el′is) group of islands in the WC Pacific, north of Fiji: under British control, 1892-1978; name changed to TUVALU in 1976 and as such became independent in 1978

El·ling·ton (el′iŋ tən), **Duke** (born *Edward Kennedy Ellington*) 1899-1974; U.S. jazz pianist, bandleader, & composer

El·li·ot or **El·li·ott** (el′ē ət) ***n.*** a masculine name: see ELIOT[1]

el·lipse (e lips′, i-) ***n.***, *pl.* **-lip′ses′** (-lip′sēz′) ⟦ModL *ellipsis* < Gr *elleipsis*, a defect, ellipse < *elleipein*, to fall short < *en-*, in + *leipein*, to leave (see LOAN): so named from falling short of a perfect circle⟧ *Geom.* the path of a point that moves so that the sum of its distances from two fixed points, the foci, is constant; closed curve formed by the section of a cone cut by a plane less steeply inclined than the side of the cone

el·lip·sis (e lip′sis, i-) ***n.***, *pl.* **-ses′** (-sēz′) ⟦L < Gr *elleipsis*: see prec.⟧ **1** *Gram.* the omission of a word or words necessary for complete grammatical construction but understood in the context (Ex.: "if possible" for "if it is possible") **2** ELLIPSIS POINTS

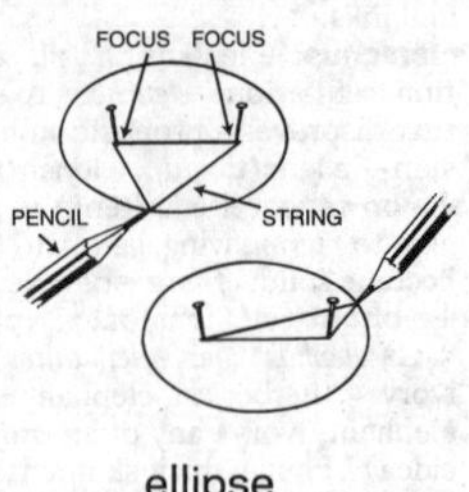

ellipse

ellipsis points (*or* **dots**) ⟦see POINT (*n.* 2)⟧ the characters (... or formerly ***) forming a punctuation mark indicating an intentional omission of words or letters or an abrupt change of thought, lapse of time, incomplete statement, etc.

el·lip·soid (e lip′soid′, i-) ***n.*** ⟦Fr *ellipsoïde*: see ELLIPSE & -OID⟧ *Geom.* **1** a solid formed by rotating an ellipse around either axis: its plane sections are all ellipses or circles **2** the surface of such a solid —***adj.*** of or shaped like an ellipsoid: also **el·lip·soi·dal** (e′lip soid′'l)

el·lip·ti·cal (e lip′ti kəl, i-) ***adj.*** ⟦< Gr *elleiptikos* (see ELLIPSE) + -AL⟧ **1** of, or having the form of, an ellipse, as some leaves **2** of or characterized by ellipsis; with a word or words omitted, with obscure, incomplete constructions, etc. Also **el·lip′tic** —**el·lip′ti·cal·ly** ***adv.***

el·lip·tic·i·ty (el′ip tis′ə tē) ***n.*** **1** the condition of being elliptical; elliptical form **2** the degree of deviation of an ellipse, elliptical orbit, etc. from circular form, or of a spheroid from spherical form

El·lis[1] (el′is) ***n.*** a masculine name: dim. *Eliot*: see ELIJAH, ELISHA

El·lis[2] (el′is), **(Henry) Have·lock** (hav′läk, -lək) 1859-1939; Eng. psychologist & writer, esp. on human sexual behavior

El·lis Island ⟦after S. *Ellis* (1712-94), New York merchant who owned it in the late 1700s⟧ small, government-owned island in Upper New York Bay: former (1892-1943) examination center for immigrants seeking to enter the U.S.: 27 acres (11 hectares)

El·li·son (el′i sən), **Ralph (Waldo)** 1914-94; U.S. writer

Ells·worth (elz′wurth′) **1 Lincoln** 1880-1951; U.S. polar explorer **2 Oliver** 1745-1807; chief justice of the U.S. (1796-1800)

elm (elm) ***adj.*** ⟦ME & OE, akin to OHG *elm*: see ELDER[2]⟧ designating a family (Ulmaceae, order Urticales) of dicotyledonous trees growing largely in the North Temperate Zone —***n.*** **1** any of a genus (*Ulmus*) of tall, deciduous shade trees of the elm family, once widely planted as a lawn tree: see DUTCH ELM DISEASE **2** its hard, heavy wood

El·man (el′mən), **Mi·scha** (mish′ə) 1891-1967; U.S. violinist, born in Russia

☆**elm bark beetle** the bark-boring beetle (*Scolytus multistriatus*) that feeds on the bark of elm trees and carries Dutch elm disease

El·mer (el′mər) ***n.*** ⟦ult. < ? OE *Æthelmær* (< *æthel*, noble + *mære* famous), or < ? *Egilmær* (< *egil-* < *ege*, awe, dread + *mære*)⟧ a masculine name

El Mis·ti (el mē′stē) dormant volcano in S Peru: *c.* 19,100 ft (5,822 m)

☆**elm leaf beetle** a beetle (*Pyrrhalta luteola*) that feeds on the leaves of elm trees while in both its larval and adult stages

El Mon·te (el män′tē) ⟦Sp, the thicket: from a dense clump of willows there⟧ city in SW Calif.: suburb of Los Angeles

El Ni·ño (el nēn′yō) ⟦Sp, the (Christ) Child: because it occurs near Christmas⟧ a warm inshore current annually flowing south along the coast of Ecuador and, about every seven to ten years, extending down the coast of Peru, where it has a devastating effect (**El Niño Effect**) on weather, crops, fish, etc.: cf. LA NIÑA

El O·beid (el ō bād′) city in central Sudan

el·o·cu·tion (el′ə kyōō′shən) ***n.*** ⟦ME *ellocucioun* < L *elocutio* < pp. of *eloqui*: see ELOQUENT⟧ **1** style or manner of speaking or reading in public **2** the art of public speaking or declaiming: now often associated with a studied or artificial style of speaking —**el′o·cu′tion·ar′y** ***adj.*** —**el′o·cu′tion·ist** ***n.***

e·lo·de·a (ē lō′dē ə, i-; el′ə dē′ə) ***n.*** ⟦ModL < Gr *helōdēs*, swampy < *helos*, a swamp < IE base **selos-* > Sans *sáras-*, a lake, pool⟧ any of a genus (*Elodea*) of submerged water plants of the frog's-bit family, with whorls of short, grasslike leaves: often used in aquariums because it releases large amounts of oxygen

E·lo·him (e′lō him′, -hēm′; e lō′him′, -hēm′) ***n.*** ⟦Heb *elohim*, pl. of *eloah*, God⟧ God: name used in parts of the Jewish scriptures: see JEHOVAH

E·lo·hist (e′lō hist′, e lō′-) the otherwise unidentified author of those parts of the Hebrew scriptures in which the name *Elohim*, instead of *Yahweh* (Jehovah), is used for God: see YAHWIST —**El·o·his·tic** (el′ō his′tik) ***adj.***

e·loign or **e·loin** (ē loin′, i-; *also, esp. for n.*, ē′loin′) ***vt.*** ⟦ME *eloinen* < OFr *esloignier* < *es-* (L *ex-*) + L *longe*, far (adv.): see LONG[1]⟧ **1** [Archaic] to seclude (oneself) **2** *a)* to carry away (property) *b) Law* to remove (property) beyond the jurisdiction of a sheriff —**e·loign′ment *n.***, **e·loin′ment**

El·o·ise (el′ō ēz′, el′ō ēz′) ***n.*** a feminine name: equiv. Fr. *Héloïse*: see LOUISE[1]

e·lon·gate (ē lôŋ′gāt′, i-) ***vt., vi.*** **-gat′ed**, **-gat′ing** ⟦< LL *elongatus*, pp. of *elongare*, to prolong < L *e-*, out + *longus*, LONG[1]⟧ to make or become longer; stretch —***adj.*** **1** lengthened; stretched **2** *Bot.* long and narrow: said as of certain leaves —**SYN.** EXTEND

e·lon·ga·tion (ē′lôŋ gā′shən, i′lôŋ-) ***n.*** ⟦ME *elongacioun* < ML *elongatio*⟧ **1** an elongating or being elongated; lengthening; extension **2** something elongated; lengthened part; continuation **3** the angular distance in degrees of a planet or the moon from the sun, as viewed from the earth

e·lope (ē lōp′, i-) ***vi.*** **e·loped′**, **e·lop′ing** ⟦Anglo-Fr *aloper*, prob. < ME **aleapen*, to leap up, run away < OE *ahleapan* (infl. ? by ON *hlaupa*, to run > LOPE)

< *a-*, away + *hleapan*, to run, LEAP⟧ **1** to run away secretly, esp. in order to get married **2** to run away; escape; abscond —**e·lope′ment** ***n.*** —**e·lop′er** ***n.***

el·o·quence (el′ə kwəns) ***n.*** ⟦ME & OFr < L *eloquentia*: see fol.⟧ **1** speech or writing that is vivid, forceful, fluent, graceful, and persuasive **2** the art or manner of such speech or writing **3** persuasive power

el·o·quent (el′ə kwənt) ***adj.*** ⟦ME & OFr < L *eloquens*, prp. of *eloqui*, to speak out, utter < *e-*, out + *loqui*, to speak⟧ **1** having, or characterized by, eloquence; fluent, forceful, and persuasive **2** vividly expressive [*an eloquent* sigh] —**el′o·quent·ly** ***adv.***

El Pas·o (el pas′ō) ⟦Sp, after *El Paso del Norte*, ford (of the river) of the north; i.e., the Rio Grande⟧ city in westernmost Tex., on the Rio Grande

El·sa (el′sə) ***n.*** ⟦Ger < ?⟧ a feminine name

El Sal or **El Salv** *abbrev.* El Salvador

El Sal·va·dor (el sal′və dôr′; el′ säl′və dôr′) country in Central America, southwest of Honduras, on the Pacific: declared itself independent from Spain in 1821; became a fully independent republic in 1841: 8,124 sq mi (21,040 sq km); cap. San Salvador

else (els) ***adj.*** ⟦ME & OE *elles*, adv. gen. of n. base *el-*, other (as in OE *el-land*, foreign land), akin to Goth *aljis*, OHG *elles*, of same formation < IE base **al-*, that, yonder one > L *alius*, another, *alienus*, belonging to another, Gr *allos*, other⟧ **1** different; other [somebody *else*] **2** in addition; more [is there anything *else?*] *Else* follows the word modified and after a pronoun takes the possessive inflection [anybody *else's*] —***adv.*** **1** in a different or additional time, place, or manner; differently [where *else* can I go?] **2** otherwise; if not: now somewhat formal or archaic without *or* (see the phrase OR ELSE below) [study, *else* you will fail] —**or else 1** otherwise; if not [study, *or else* you will fail] **2** or face undesirable consequences: often used as a threat [obey the law, *or else!*] *Or else* is also used somewhat informally as a coordinating conjunction introducing an alternative [take either the red one *or else* the blue one]

else·where (els′hwer′, -wer′) ***adv.*** ⟦ME *elleswher* < OE *elleshwær*⟧ in or to some other place; somewhere else

El·sie (el′sē) ***n.*** a feminine name: see ALICE, ELIZABETH[1]

El·si·nore (el′sə nôr′) HELSINGØR: name used in Shakespeare's *Hamlet*

É·lu·ard (ā lü ȧr′), **Paul** (pôl) (pseud. of *Eugène Grindel*) 1895-1952; Fr. poet

el·u·ate (el′yoo it, -āt′) ***n.*** the solution that results from eluting

e·lu·ci·date (ə lo͞o′sə dāt′, i-) ***vt., vi.*** **-dat′ed, -dat′ing** ⟦< LL *elucidatus*, pp. of *elucidare*, to make light or clear < L *e-*, out + *lucidus*: see LUCID⟧ to make clear (esp. something abstruse); explain —***SYN.*** EXPLAIN —**e·lu′ci·da′tion** ***n.*** —**e·lu′ci·da′tive** ***adj.*** —**e·lu′ci·da′tor** ***n.***

e·lu·cu·bra·tion (ē lo͞o′kə brā′shən, -kyo͞o-; i-) ***n.*** LUCUBRATION

e·lude (ē lo͞od′, i-) ***vt.*** **e·lud′ed, e·lud′ing** ⟦L *eludere*, to finish play, parry a blow, frustrate < *e-*, out + *ludere*, to play: see LUDICROUS⟧ **1** to avoid or escape from by quickness, cunning, etc.; evade **2** *a)* to escape detection, notice, or understanding by *b)* to escape recollection by [his name *eludes* me] **3** to be unobtained or unachieved by [critical acclaim would always *elude* her] —***SYN.*** ESCAPE

El·ul (e lo͞ol′, el′ool′) ***n.*** ⟦Heb *elul*, akin to Akkadian *elul*, *elūlu*, month name and festival of that month; ? also akin to Aram *'alal*, he brought in⟧ the twelfth month of the Jewish year: see the Jewish calendar in the Reference Supplement

e·lu·sion (ē lo͞o′zhən, i-) ***n.*** ⟦LL *elusio* < L *elusus*, pp. of *eludere*⟧ an eluding; escape or avoidance by quickness or cunning; evasion

e·lu·sive (ē lo͞o′siv, i-) ***adj.*** ⟦< L *elusus* (see prec.) + -IVE⟧ **1** tending to elude **2** hard to grasp or retain mentally; baffling Also [Rare] **e·lu′so·ry** (-sə rē) —**e·lu′sive·ly** ***adv.*** —**e·lu′sive·ness** ***n.***

e·lute (ē lo͞ot′, i-) ***vt.*** **e·lut′ed, e·lut′ing** ⟦< L *elutus*, pp. of *eluere*, to wash out: see fol.⟧ to remove (adsorbed material) by use of a solvent —**e·lu′tion** ***n.***

e·lu·tri·ate (ē lo͞o′trē āt′, i-) ***vt.*** **-at′ed, -at′ing** ⟦< L *elutriatus*, pp. of *elutriare*, to wash out, rack off < *eluere* < *e-*, out + *luere*, var. of *lavare*, to LAVE⟧ to purify (an insoluble powder) by washing and straining or by decanting —**e·lu′tri·a′tion** ***n.***

e·lu·vi·al (ē lo͞o′vē əl, i-) ***adj.*** of or relating to eluvium or to eluviation

e·lu·vi·ate (ē lo͞o′vē āt′, i-) ***vi.*** **-at′ed, -at′ing** to be subjected to eluviation

☆**e·lu·vi·a·tion** (ē lo͞o′vē ā′shən, i-) ***n.*** ⟦see fol. & -ATION⟧ the movement of various dissolved or suspended chemicals, minerals, etc. downward through the soil due to the movement of ground water

e·lu·vi·um (ē lo͞o′vē əm, i-) ***n.*** ⟦ModL < L *eluere* (see ELUTRIATE), after L *alluvium*: see ALLUVIUM⟧ an accumulation of dust and soil particles caused by the weathering and disintegration of rocks in place, or deposited by the wind: distinguished from ALLUVIUM

el·ver (el′vər) ***n.*** ⟦for *eelfare*, the passage of young eels up a stream⟧ a young eel, esp. a young freshwater eel that has migrated from salt water, where it first develops by metamorphosis from a larva

elves (elvz) ***n.*** *pl. of* ELF

El·vis (el′vis) *informal form of the name* Elvis PRESLEY

elv·ish (el′vish) ***adj.*** *var. of* ELFISH —**elv′ish·ly** ***adv.***

E·ly (ē′lē), **Isle of** former county of EC England, now part of Cambridgeshire

E·ly·si·an (ē lizh′ən, -liz′ē ən; i-) ***adj.*** [*also* **e–**] **1** in or like Elysium **2** happy; blissful; delightful

E·ly·si·um (ē lizh′əm, -liz′ē əm; i-) ***n.*** ⟦L < Gr *Ēlysion (pedion)*, Elysian (plain), plain of the departed, of non-IE orig.⟧ **1** *Gr. Myth.* the dwelling place of virtuous people after death **2** any place or condition of ideal bliss or complete happiness; paradise Also **Elysian (or elysian) fields**

el·y·tron (el′i trän′) ***n.***, *pl.* **-tra** (-trə) ⟦ModL < Gr a covering, sheath < IE **welutrom* < base **wel-*, to roll > WALK⟧ either of the front pair of modified, usually thickened, wings in certain insects, esp. beetles, which act as protective covering for the rear wings: also **el′y·trum** (-trəm), *pl.* **-tra** (-trə)

El·ze·vir (el′zə vir′) ***n.*** name of a family of Du. printers & publishers of the 16th & 17th cent.

em (em) ***n.*** **1** the letter M **2** *Printing* a unit of measure the width of a capital M in a type font

EM *abbrev.* **1** electromagnetic **2** engineer of mines **3** enlisted man (or men)

'em (əm) ***pron.*** ⟦taken as corruption of THEM, but also < ME *hem*, dat. pl. of 3d pers. pron. used as acc. & later replaced by THEM⟧ [Informal] them

em- (em, im) *prefix* EN-[1]: used before *b*, *m*, or *p* [*emboss, empower*]

e·ma·ci·ate (ē mā′shē āt′, -sē-; i-) ***vt.*** **-at′ed, -at′ing** ⟦< L *emaciatus*, pp. of *emaciare*, to make lean < *e-*, out + *macies*, leanness < *macer*, lean < IE base **mak-* > OE *mæger*, lean⟧ to cause to become abnormally lean; cause to lose much flesh or weight, as by starvation or disease —**e·ma′ci·a′tion** (-sē ā′shən, -shē ā′shən) ***n.***

e·mail (ē′māl′) ***n.*** ⟦< E(LECTRONIC) + MAIL[1]⟧ **1** a system for sending messages, as via a network, from one computer or terminal to a receiving computer or terminal and for storing such messages **2** a message or messages sent or stored in such a system — ***vt., vi.*** to send (a message) to (someone) by e-mail Also written **e′-mail′**

em·a·lan·gen·i (em′ə läŋ gen′ē) ***n.*** *pl. of* LILANGENI

em·a·nate (em′ə nāt′) ***vi.*** **-nat′ed, -nat′ing** ⟦< L *emanatus*, pp. of *emanare*, to flow out, arise < *e-*, out + *manare*, to flow < IE base **mano-*, damp, wet > Welsh *mawn*, peat⟧ to come forth; issue, as from a source —***vt.*** to send forth; emit —***SYN.*** RISE

em·a·na·tion (em′ə nā′shən) ***n.*** ⟦LL *emanatio*⟧ **1** the act of emanating **2** something that comes forth from a source; thing emitted **3** *Chem.* *a) former name for* RADON *b)* a heavy, gaseous isotope that results from the decay of a radioactive element —**em′a·na′tive** ***adj.***

e·man·ci·pate (ē man′sə pāt′, i-) ***vt.*** **-pat′ed, -pat′ing** ⟦< L *emancipatus*, pp. of *emancipare* < *e-*, out + *mancipare*, to deliver up or make over as property < *manceps*, purchaser < *manus*, the hand (see MANUAL) + *capere*, to take (see HAVE)⟧ **1** to set free (a slave, etc.); release from bondage, servitude, or serfdom **2** to free from restraint or control, as of social convention **3** *Law* to release (a child) from parental control and supervision —***SYN.*** FREE —**e·man′ci·pa′tion** ***n.*** —**e·man′ci·pa′tive** ***adj.***, **e·man′ci·pa·to′ry** (-pe tôr′ē) —**e·man′ci·pa′tor** ***n.***

☆**Emancipation Proclamation** a proclamation issued by President Lincoln in September, 1862, effective January 1, 1863, freeing the slaves in all territory still at war with the Union

E·man·u·el (i man′yo͞o el′, -əl) ***n.*** *var. of* EMMANUEL

e·mar·gi·nate (ē mär′jə nit, -nāt′, i-) ***adj.*** ⟦L *emarginatus*, pp. of *emarginare*, to deprive of its edge: see E-[1] & MARGINATE⟧ having a notched margin or tip, as some leaves or wings: also **e·mar′gi·nat·ed**

e·mas·cu·late (ē mas′kyo͞o lāt′, -kyə-; i-; *for adj.*, -lit) ***vt.*** **-lat′ed, -lat′ing** ⟦< L *emasculatus*, pp. of *emasculare* < *e-*, out + *masculus*, MASCULINE⟧ **1** to deprive (a male) of the power to reproduce, as by removing the testicles; castrate; geld **2** to destroy the strength or force of; weaken [a novel *emasculated* by censorship] —***adj.*** deprived of virility, strength, or vigor; effeminate —**e·mas′cu·la′tion** ***n.*** —**e·mas′cu·la′tive** ***adj.***, **e·mas′cu·la·to′ry** (-lə tôr′ē) —**e·mas′cu·la′tor** ***n.***

em·balm (em bäm′, im-; -bälm′) ***vt.*** ⟦ME *embaumen* < OFr *embaumer*: see EN-[1] & BALM⟧ **1** to treat (a dead body) with various chemicals, usually after removing the viscera, etc., to keep it from decaying rapidly **2** to preserve in memory **3** to make fragrant; perfume —**em·balm′er** ***n.*** —**em·balm′ment** ***n.***

em·bank (em baŋk′, im-) ***vt.*** to protect, support, or enclose with a bank or banks of earth, rubble, etc.

em·bank·ment (em baŋk′mənt, im-) ***n.*** **1** the act or process of embanking **2** a bank of earth, rubble, etc. used to keep back water, to hold up a roadway, or as part of a fortification

☆**em·bar·ca·der·o** (em bär′kə der′ō) ***n.***, *pl.* **-der′os** ⟦Sp < pp. of *embarcar*, EMBARK⟧ a wharf or other landing place

em·bar·go (em bär′gō, im-) ***n.***, *pl.* **-goes** ⟦Sp < *embargar* < VL **imbarricare* < L *in-*, in, on + ML *barra*, BAR[1]⟧ **1** a government order prohibiting the entry or departure of commercial ships at its ports, esp. as a war measure **2** any restriction or restraint, esp. one imposed on commerce by law; specif., *a)* a prohibition of trade in a particular commodity *b)* a prohibition or restriction of freight transport —***vt.*** **-goed, -go·ing** to put an embargo upon

em·bark (em bärk′, im-) ***vt.*** ⟦Fr *embarquer* < Sp or OProv *embarcar* < *em-* (L *in-*) + L *barca*, BARK[3]⟧ **1** to put or take (passengers or goods) aboard a ship, aircraft, etc. **2** to engage (a person) or invest (money, etc.) in an enterprise —***vi.*** **1** to go aboard a ship, aircraft, etc. **2** to begin a journey **3** to make a beginning; start [to *embark* on a new career] —**em·bar·ka·tion** ***n.***, **em·bar·ca·tion** (em′bär kā′shən), or **em·bark′ment**

em·bar·ras de ri·chesses (än bȧ räd rē shes′) ⟦Fr⟧ literally, an embarrassment of wealth (of good things); hence, too much to choose from: also **embarrassment of riches**

em·bar·rass (em bar′əs, im-) ***vt.*** ⟦Fr *embarrasser*, lit., to encumber, obstruct < Sp *embarazar* < It *imbarrazzare* < *imbarrare*, to bar, impede < *in-* (L *in-*) + ML *barra*, BAR[1]⟧ **1** to cause to feel self-conscious, confused, and ill at ease; disconcert; fluster **2** to cause difficulties to; hinder; impede **3** to cause to be in debt; cause financial difficulties to **4** to make more difficult; complicate —*vi.* to become flustered, self-conscious, etc. [the child *embarrasses* easily] —**em·bar′rass·ing** *adj.* —**em·bar′rass·ing·ly** *adv.* —**em·bar′rass·ment** *n.*

SYN.—to **embarrass** is to cause to feel ill at ease so as to result in a loss of composure [*embarrassed* by their compliments]; **abash** implies a sudden loss of self-confidence and a growing feeling of shame or inadequacy [I stood *abashed* at his rebukes]; **discomfit** implies a frustration of plans or expectations and often connotes a resultant feeling of discomposure or humiliation; to **disconcert** is to cause someone to lose self-possession quickly, resulting in confusion or mental disorganization [his interruptions were *disconcerting*]; **rattle** and **faze** are equivalents for **disconcert**, but the former emphasizes emotional agitation, and the latter is most commonly used in negative constructions [danger does not *faze* him] —*ANT.* **compose, assure**

em·bar·rassed (em bar′əst, im-) *adj.* caused by or displaying an awkward or uneasy self-consciousness [her *embarrassed* silence] —**em·bar′rassed·ly** *adv.*

em·bas·sage (em′bə sij) *n. archaic var. of* EMBASSY

em·bas·sy (em′bə sē) *n., pl.* **-sies** ⟦earlier *ambassy* < MFr *ambassée* < OIt *ambasciata* < Prov *ambaissada* < **ambaissa*: see AMBASSADOR⟧ **1** the position, functions, or business of an ambassador **2** the official residence or offices of an ambassador in a foreign country **3** an ambassador and his or her staff **4** a person or group sent on an official mission to a foreign government **5** any important or official mission, errand, or message

em·bat·tle (em bat′'l) *vt.* **-tled, -tling** ⟦ME *embataillen*: see EN-[1] & BATTLEMENT⟧ **1** to prepare, array, or set in line for battle **2** to fortify **3** to provide with battlements —**em·bat′tle·ment** *n.*

em·bat·tled (em bat′'ld) *adj.* **1** prepared or arrayed for battle **2** engaged in a battle, conflict, or controversy **3** being subjected to attack, criticism, etc.

em·bay (em bā′) *vt.* **1** to shelter or confine (a vessel) in a bay **2** to shut in; enclose or surround, as in a bay

em·bay·ment (-mənt) *n.* a bay or baylike formation

em·bed (em bed′, im-; *for n.* em′bed′) *vt.* **-bed′ded, -bed′ding** **1** to set (flowers, etc.) in earth **2** to set or fix firmly in a surrounding mass [to *embed* tiles in cement] **3** to fix in the mind, memory, etc. **4** *Comput.* to insert (an identification code, a virus, a routine for monitoring access, etc.) into a software program **5** to assign (an observer) to a group engaged in some activity [to *embed* journalists with a combat unit] —*n.* a person who has been embedded —**em·bed′ment** *n.*

em·bel·lish (em bel′ish, im-) *vt.* ⟦ME *embelishen* < extended stem of OFr *embellir* < *em-* (L *in*) + *bel* < L *bellus*, beautiful⟧ **1** to decorate or improve by adding detail; ornament; adorn **2** to add grace notes, syncopated accents, trills, etc. to (a melody) **3** to improve (an account or report) by adding details, often of a fictitious or imaginary kind; touch up —SYN. ADORN

em·bel·lish·ment (-mənt) *n.* **1** an embellishing or being embellished; ornamentation **2** something that embellishes, as an ornament, a fictitious touch added to a factual account, a musical phrase, etc.

em·ber[1] (em′bər) *n.* ⟦ME *eymere* & (with intrusive *-b*) *eymbre* < OE *æmerge* (& ON *eimyrja*) < *æm-* (akin to ON *eimr*, steam) + *-yrge* (akin to ON *ysja*, fire) < IE base **eus-*, to burn > L *urere*, to burn⟧ **1** a glowing piece of coal, wood, etc. from a fire; esp., such a piece smoldering among ashes **2** [*pl.*] the smoldering remains of a fire

em·ber[2] (em′bər) *adj.* ⟦ME (SE dial.) *embyr-*, as in *embyr-dayes* < OE *ymbren*, lit., a coming around < *ymbryne*, circuit, revolution < *ymb*, round (akin to AMBI-) + *ryne*, a running (< base of RUN)⟧ [*often* **E-**] designating or of three days (Wednesday, Friday, and Saturday) set aside for prayer and fasting in a specified week of each of the four seasons of the year in various Christian churches

em·bez·zle (em bez′əl, im-) *vt.* **-zled, -zling** ⟦ME *embesilen* < Anglo-Fr *enbesiler* < OFr *embesillier* < *en-* (see EN-[1]) + *besillier*, to destroy⟧ to steal (money, etc. entrusted to one's care); take by fraud for one's own use —**em·bez′zle·ment** *n.* —**em·bez′zler** *n.*

em·bit·ter (em bit′ər, im-) *vt.* **1** to make bitter; make resentful or morose **2** to make more bitter; exacerbate; aggravate —**em·bit′ter·ment** *n.*

em·blaze[1] (em blāz′) *vt.* **-blazed′, -blaz′ing** ⟦EM- (see EN-[1]) + BLAZE[1]⟧ [Archaic] **1** to light up; illuminate **2** to set on fire; kindle

em·blaze[2] (em blāz′) *vt.* **-blazed′, -blaz′ing** ⟦EM- (see EN-[1]) + BLAZE[3]⟧ *archaic var. of* EMBLAZON

em·bla·zon (em blā′zən, im-) *vt.* ⟦EM- (see EN-[1]) + BLAZON⟧ **1** to decorate or adorn (*with* coats of arms, etc.) **2** to display brilliantly; decorate with bright colors **3** to spread the fame of; praise; celebrate —**em·bla′zon·ment** *n.*

em·bla·zon·ry (-rē) *n., pl.* **-ries** **1** heraldic decoration **2** any brilliant decoration or display

em·blem (em′bləm) *n.* ⟦orig., inlaid work < L *emblema* < Gr *emblēma*, insertion < *emballein* < *en-*, in + *ballein*, to throw, put: see BALL[2]⟧ **1** [Historical] a picture with a motto or verses, allegorically suggesting some moral truth, etc. **2** a visible symbol of a thing, idea, class of people, etc.; object or representation that stands for or suggests something else [the cross is an *emblem* of Christianity] **3** a sign, badge, or device —*vt.* [Rare] to emblematize

em·blem·at·ic (em′blə mat′ik) *adj.* of or serving as an emblem; symbolic: also **em′blem·at′i·cal** —**em′blem·at′i·cal·ly** *adv.*

em·blem·a·tize (em blem′ə tīz′) *vt.* **-tized′, -tiz′ing** **1** to be an emblem of; symbolize **2** to represent by or as by an emblem Also **em·blem·ize** (em′blə mīz′) **-ized′, -iz′ing**

em·ble·ments (em′blə mənts) *pl.n.* ⟦ME *enblaymentez* < OFr *emblaement* (sing.) < *emblaer* < *en-* (L *in*) + *blee*, grain < WGmc base akin to Ger *blatt*, leaf, MDu *blat*, BLADE⟧ **1** *Law* cultivated growing crops which are produced annually **2** the profits from such crops

em·bod·i·ment (em bäd′i mənt, -bäd′ē-; im-) *n.* **1** an embodying or being embodied **2** that in which something is embodied; concrete expression of some idea, quality, etc. [she is the *embodiment* of virtue]

em·bod·y (em bäd′ē, im-) *vt.* **-bod′ied, -bod′y·ing** **1** to give bodily form to; make corporeal; incarnate **2** to give definite, tangible, or visible form to; make concrete [a speech *embodying* democratic ideals] **3** to bring together into an organized whole [the laws *embodied* in a legal code] **4** to make part of an organized whole; incorporate [the latest findings *embodied* in the new book]

em·bold·en (em bōl′dən, im-) *vt.* ⟦EM- (see EN-[1]) + BOLD + -EN⟧ to give courage to; cause to be bold or bolder

em·bo·lec·to·my (em′bō lek′tə mē) *n.* the surgical removal of an embolus

em·bol·ic (em bäl′ik) *adj.* **1** of or caused by embolism or an embolus **2** of or during emboly

em·bo·lism (em′bə liz′əm) *n.* ⟦ME *embolisme* < LL *embolismus* < Gr *embolismos*, intercalary < *embolos*: see fol.⟧ **1** the intercalation of a day, month, etc. into a calendar, as in leap year **2** the time intercalated **3** *Med.* *a)* the obstruction of a blood vessel by an embolus too large to pass through it *b)* loosely, an embolus

em·bo·lus (em′bə ləs) *n., pl.* **-li′** (-lī′) ⟦ModL < Gr *embolos*, anything put in, wedge < *emballein* < *en-*, in + *ballein*, to throw: see BALL[2]⟧ any foreign matter, as a blood clot or air bubble, carried in the bloodstream and capable of causing an embolism

em·bo·ly (em′bə lē) *n.* ⟦< Gr *embolē*, insertion, lit., a putting in < *emballein*: see prec.⟧ *Embryology* the process by which cells move inward during gastrulation to form the archenteron

em·bon·point (än bōn pwan′) *n.* ⟦Fr < OFr *en bon point*, in good condition⟧ plumpness; corpulence

em·bos·om (em bo͝oz′əm) *vt.* **1** [Archaic] to take to one's bosom; embrace; cherish **2** to enclose protectively; surround; shelter

em·boss (em bôs′, -bäs′; im-) *vt.* ⟦ME *embocen* < OFr *embocer*: see EN-[1] & BOSS[2]⟧ **1** to decorate or cover with designs, patterns, etc. raised above the surface **2** to carve, raise, or print (a design, etc.) so that it is raised above the surface; raise in relief **3** to embellish; ornament —**em·boss′er** *n.* —**em·boss′ment** *n.*

em·bou·chure (äm′bo͞o sho͝or′) *n.* ⟦Fr < *emboucher*, to put into the mouth < VL **imbuccare* < L *in*, in + *bucca*, the cheek: see BUCCAL⟧ **1** the mouth of a river **2** *Music* *a)* the mouthpiece of a wind instrument *b)* the method of applying the lips and tongue to the mouthpiece of a wind instrument

em·bour·geoise·ment (em bo͝or′zhwäz mənt; *Fr* än bo͝or zhwȧz män′) *n.* ⟦Fr < *embourgeoiser*, to make or become BOURGEOIS⟧ the process of becoming middle-class in economic status, social attitudes, etc.

em·bow (em bō′) *vt.* ⟦ME *embouen*: see EN-[1] & BOW[2]⟧ to bend into the form of an arch or bow: now only in pp. [a dolphin *embowed* on the shield]

em·bow·el (em bou′əl) *vt.* **-eled** or **-elled, -el·ing** or **-el·ling** ⟦OFr *enboweler*, altered < *esboueler* < *es-* (L *ex*), out of + *bouel*, BOWEL⟧ **1** *rare var. of* DISEMBOWEL **2** [Obs.] to embed deeply

em·bow·er (em bou′ər) *vt.* to enclose or shelter in or as in a bower

em·brace[1] (em brās′, im-) *vt.* **-braced′, -brac′ing** ⟦ME *embracen* < OFr *embracier* < VL **imbrachiare* < L *im-*, in + *brachium*, an arm: see BRACE[1]⟧ **1** to clasp in the arms, usually as an expression of affection or desire; hug **2** to accept readily; avail oneself of [to *embrace* an opportunity] **3** to take up or adopt, esp. eagerly or seriously [to *embrace* a new profession] **4** to encircle; surround; enclose [an isle *embraced* by the sea] **5** to include; contain [biology *embraces* botany and zoology] **6** to take in mentally; perceive [his glance *embraced* the scene] —*vi.* to clasp or hug each other in the arms —*n.* an embracing; hug —SYN. INCLUDE —**em·brace′a·ble** *adj.* —**em·brace′ment** *n.* —**em·brac′er** *n.*

em·brace[2] (em brās′) *vt.* **-braced′, -brac′ing** ⟦ME *embrasen* < OFr *embraser*, to set on fire, incite < *en-*, in + *braise*, live coals: see BRAISE⟧ *Law* to try illegally to influence or instruct (a jury)

em·brace·or or **em·bra·cer** (em brā′sər) *n.* ⟦ME *embracer* < OFr *embraseor*: see prec.⟧ *Law* a person guilty of embracery

em·brac·er·y (em brā′sər ē) *n.* ⟦ME *embracerie*: see EMBRACE[2]⟧ *Law* an illegal attempt to influence or instruct a jury

em·branch·ment (em branch′mənt) *n.* a branching out or off, as of a river, etc.; ramification

em·bran·gle (em braŋ′gəl, im-) *vt.* **-gled, -gling** ⟦EM- (see EN-[1]) + dial. *brangle*, to wrangle, prob. var. of WRANGLE[1], infl. ? by Fr *branler*, to confuse⟧ to entangle; mix up; confuse; perplex —**em·bran′gle·ment** *n.*

em·bra·sure (em brā′zhər, im-) *n.* ⟦Fr < obs. *embraser*, to widen an opening, earlier *ébraser* < ?⟧ **1** an opening (for a door, window, etc.), esp. one with the sides slanted so that it is wider on the inside than on the outside **2** an opening (in a wall or parapet) with the sides slanting outward to increase the angle of fire of a gun

em·bro·cate (em′brō kāt′, -brə-) *vt.* **-cat′ed, -cat′ing** ⟦< LL *embrocatus*, pp. of *embrocare*, to foment < L *embrocha*, wet poultice < Gr *embrochē* < *embrechein* < *en-*, in + *brechein*, to wet < IE base **meregh-* > Czech *mrholiti*, to drizzle⟧ to moisten and rub (a part of the body) with an oil, liniment, etc.

em·bro·ca·tion (em′brō kā′shən, -brə-) ***n.*** **1** the process of rubbing an oil, etc. on the body **2** a liquid used in this way; liniment, etc.

em·broi·der (em broi′dər, im-) ***vt.*** ⟦ME *embrouderen* < OFr *embroder:* see EN-[1] & BROIDER⟧ **1** to ornament (fabric) with a design using special decorative stitches **2** to make (a design, etc.) on fabric with such stitches **3** to embellish (an account or report); add fanciful details to; exaggerate —***vi.*** **1** to do embroidery **2** to exaggerate —**em·broi′der·er** ***n.***

em·broi·der·y (em broi′dər ē, im-) ***n., pl.*** **-der·ies** ⟦ME *embrouderie:* see prec. & -ERY⟧ **1** the art or work of ornamenting fabric with designs in special decorative stitches; embroidering **2** embroidered work or fabric; ornamental needlework **3** embellishment, as of an account **4** something superficial or unnecessary but attractive or desirable

em·broil (em broil′, im-) ***vt.*** ⟦Fr *embrouiller:* see EN-[1] & BROIL[2]⟧ **1** to confuse (affairs, etc.); mix up; muddle **2** to draw into a conflict or fight; involve in trouble —**em·broil′ment** ***n.***

em·brown (em broun′) ***vt.*** to make darker in color; esp., to make brown or tan

em·brue (em broo′) ***vt.*** **-brued′, -bru′ing** IMBRUE

em·bry·ec·to·my (em′brē ek′tə mē) ***n., pl.*** **-ec′to·mies** ⟦EMBRY(O)- + -ECTOMY⟧ the surgical removal of an embryo, esp. in cases of pregnancy outside of the uterus

em·bry·o (em′brē ō′) ***n., pl.*** **-os′** ⟦ME *embrio* < ML *embryo* < Gr *embryon,* embryo, fetus, thing newly born, neut. of *embryos,* growing in < *en-,* in + *bryein,* to swell, be full⟧ **1** an animal in the earliest stages of its development in the uterus or the egg, specif., in humans, from conception to about the eighth week: see FETUS **2** *a)* an early or undeveloped stage of something *b)* anything in such a stage **3** the rudimentary plant contained in a seed, usually made up of hypocotyl, radicle, plumule, and cotyledons —***adj.*** EMBRYONIC

em·bry·o- (em′brē ō′) *combining form* embryo, embryonic [*embryology*]: also, before a vowel, **em′bry-**

em·bry·og·e·ny (em′brē äj′ə nē) ***n.*** ⟦prec. + -GENY⟧ the formation and development of the embryo: also **em′bry·o′gen′e·sis** (-ō′jen′ə sis) —**em′bry·o′gen′ic** (-jen′ik) ***adj.,*** **em′bry·o·ge·net′ic** (-jə net′ik)

em·bry·ol·o·gy (em′brē äl′ə jē) ***n.*** ⟦EMBRYO- + -LOGY⟧ the branch of biology dealing with the formation and development of embryos —**em′bry·o·log′ic** (-ə läj′ik) ***adj.,*** **em′bry·o·log′i·cal** —**em′bry·o·log′i·cal·ly** ***adv.*** —**em′bry·ol′o·gist** ***n.***

em·bry·on·ic (em′brē än′ik) ***adj.*** **1** of or like an embryo: also **em·bry·o·nal** (em′brē ə nəl) **2** in an early stage; undeveloped; rudimentary

embryonic membrane any of several living membranes enclosing or closely associated with the developing vertebrate embryo, as the allantois, amnion, yolk sac, etc.

em·bry·o·phyte (em′brē ō fīt′) ***n.*** any of a subkingdom (Embryobionta) of plants, having an enclosed embryo, as within a seed or archegonium, including bryophytes, ferns, gymnosperms, and angiosperms: cf. THALLOPHYTE

embryo sac *Bot.* the female gametophyte of a flowering plant, consisting typically of a microscopic elongated sac that is situated within the ovule and contains eight nuclei in seven cells: it gives rise to the embryo and endosperm of the seed after fertilization

☆**em·cee** (em′sē′) ***vt., vi.*** **-ceed′, -cee′ing** ⟦< MC, sense 1⟧ to act as master of ceremonies (for) —***n.*** a master of ceremonies

em dash (em) *Printing* a dash (—) the width of a capital M in a given type font

-eme (ēm) ⟦Fr *-ème,* unit, sound < *phonème,* PHONEME⟧ *combining form Linguis.* a distinctive unit of language structure at a (specified) level of analysis, generally characterized as a class consisting of all the variant forms of the given unit [the *grapheme* <w> consists of all the possible written forms of the letter *w*]

e·meer (e mir′, ə-) ***n.*** *alt. sp. of* EMIR —**e·meer′ate′** (-āt′, -it) ***n.***

e·mend (ē mend′, i-) ***vt.*** ⟦ME *emenden* < L *emendare,* AMEND < *e-,* out (see EX-[1]) + *menda,* a defect, error < IE **mend-,* a flaw⟧ **1** [Rare] to correct or improve **2** to make scholarly corrections or improvements in (a text)

e·men·date (ē′men dāt′, -mən-; ē men′dāt, i-) ***vt.*** **-dat′ed, -dat′ing** ⟦< L *emendatus,* pp. of *emendare*⟧ EMEND (sense 2) —**e′men·da′tor** ***n.*** —**e·men′da·to′ry** (-də tôr′ē) ***adj.***

e·men·da·tion (ē′men dā′shən, -mən-; *also* em′en-, -ən-) ***n.*** ⟦ME *emendacioun* < L *emendatio*⟧ **1** the act of emending **2** correction or change made in a text, as in an attempt to restore the original reading

em·er·ald (em′ər əld, em′rəld) ***n.*** ⟦ME & OFr *emeralde* < VL *smaraldus,* for L *smaragdus* < Gr *smaragdos,* of non-European orig.⟧ **1** a transparent, bright-green precious stone; green variety of beryl **2** a similar variety of corundum **3** bright green —***adj.*** **1** bright-green **2** made of or with an emerald or emeralds **3** designating or of a rectangular cut for gems used esp. with emeralds

Emerald Isle ⟦from its green landscape⟧ *name for* IRELAND

e·merge (ē murj′, i-) ***vi.*** **e·merged′, e·merg′ing** ⟦L *emergere* < *e-,* out + *mergere,* to dip, immerse: see MERGE⟧ **1** to rise from or as from a surrounding fluid **2** *a)* to come forth into view; become visible *b)* to become apparent or known **3** to develop or evolve as something new, improved, etc. [a strong breed *emerged*]

e·mer·gence (ē mur′jəns, i-) ***n.*** ⟦< L *emergens,* prp. of *emergere*⟧ **1** an emerging **2** an outgrowth from beneath the outer layer of a plant, as a rose prickle

e·mer·gen·cy (ē mur′jən sē, i-) ***n., pl.*** **-cies** ⟦orig. sense, "emergence": see prec.⟧ a sudden, generally unexpected occurrence or set of circumstances demanding immediate action —***adj.*** for use in case of sudden necessity [an *emergency* brake]

SYN.—emergency refers to any sudden or unforeseen situation that requires immediate action [the flood had created an *emergency*]; **exigency** may refer either to such a situation or to the need or urgency arising from it [the *exigencies* of the moment require drastic action]; **contingency** is used of an emergency regarded as remotely possible in the future [prepare for any *contingency*]; **crisis** refers to an event regarded as a turning point which will decisively determine an outcome [an economic *crisis*]; **strait** (or **straits**) refers to a trying situation from which it is difficult to extricate oneself [the loss left them in dire *straits*]

emergency room the part of a hospital designed and used for the treatment of people requiring immediate medical attention, as victims of accidents or heart attacks

e·mer·gent (ē mur′jənt, i-) ***adj.*** ⟦< L *emergens,* prp. of *emergere*⟧ **1** emerging **2** arising unexpectedly or as a new or improved development **3** recently founded or newly independent [an *emergent* nation]

e·mer·i·ta (ē mer′ə tə, i-) ***adj., n., pl.*** **-tae′** (-tē′) ⟦L, fem. of fol.⟧ EMERITUS: used only of a woman

e·mer·i·tus (ē mer′ə təs, i-) ***adj.*** ⟦L, pp. of *emereri,* to serve out one's time < *e-,* out + *mereri,* to serve, earn, MERIT⟧ retired from active service, usually for age, but retaining one's rank or title [professor *emeritus*] —***n., pl.*** **-ti′** (-tī′) a person thus retired

e·mersed (ē murst′) ***adj.*** ⟦< L *emersus* (pp. of *emergere,* EMERGE) + -ED⟧ having emerged above the surface; specif., standing out above the water, as the leaves of certain aquatic plants

e·mer·sion (ē mur′zhən, -shən) ***n.*** ⟦< L *emersus:* see prec.⟧ an emerging; emergence

Em·er·son (em′ər sən), **Ralph Waldo** 1803-82; U.S. essayist, philosopher, & poet —**Em′er·so′ni·an** (-sō′nē ən) ***adj.***

em·er·y (em′ər ē) ***n.*** ⟦Fr *émeri* < OFr *emeril* < It *smeriglio* < MGr *smeri,* for Gr *smyris,* emery < IE base **smer-,* SMEAR⟧ a dark, impure, coarse variety of corundum used for grinding, polishing, etc.

emery board a small, flat stick coated with powdered emery, used as a manicuring instrument

emery cloth cloth coated with a mixture of powdered emery and glue, used for polishing and cleaning metal

emery wheel a wheel composed of emery or surfaced with emery, used in grinding, polishing, cutting, etc.

em·e·sis (em′ə sis) ***n., pl.*** **-ses′** (-sēz′) ⟦ModL < Gr *emesis:* see fol.⟧ vomiting

e·met·ic (ē met′ik, i-) ***adj.*** ⟦L *emeticus* < Gr *emetikos* < *emein,* to vomit < IE base **wemē-,* VOMIT⟧ causing vomiting —***n.*** an emetic medicine or other substance

em·e·tine (em′ə tēn′, -tin) ***n.*** ⟦prec. + -INE[3]⟧ an emetic alkaloid, $C_{29}H_{40}N_2O_4$, obtained from ipecac root, used chiefly in the treatment of amebiasis

e·meu (ē′myoo′) ***n.*** *alt. sp. of* EMU

é·meute (ā möt′) ***n.*** ⟦Fr < pp. of *émouvoir,* to agitate: see EMOTION⟧ an uprising or riot

EMF *abbrev.* **1** electromagnetic field **2** electromotive force: also **emf**

EMG *abbrev.* **1** electromyogram **2** electromyograph **3** electromyography

-e·mi·a (ē′mē ə) ⟦ModL < Gr *-aimia* < *haima,* blood: see HEMO-⟧ *combining form* a (specified) condition or disease of the blood [*leukemia*]

em·i·grant (em′i grənt) ***adj.*** ⟦L *emigrans,* prp. of *emigrare*⟧ **1** emigrating **2** of emigrants or emigration —***n.*** a person who emigrates

em·i·grate (em′i grāt′) ***vi.*** **-grat′ed, -grat′ing** ⟦< L *emigratus,* pp. of *emigrare,* to move away < *e-,* out + *migrare,* to move, MIGRATE⟧ to leave one country or region to settle in another: opposed to IMMIGRATE —**SYN.** MIGRATE

em·i·gra·tion (em′i grā′shən) ***n.*** ⟦LL *emigratio*⟧ **1** the act of emigrating **2** emigrants collectively

é·mi·gré or **e·mi·gré** (em′i grā′, em′i grā′) ***n.*** ⟦Fr < pp. of *émigrer* < L *emigrare:* see EMIGRATE⟧ **1** an emigrant **2** a person forced to flee his or her country for political reasons, as a Royalist during the French Revolution —**SYN.** ALIEN

E·mil (ē′məl, ā′-; em′əl; ā mēl′) ***n.*** ⟦Ger < Fr *Émile* < L *Aemilius,* name of a Roman gens < L *aemulus:* see EMULATE⟧ a masculine name: fem. *Emily:* also **É·mile** (ā mēl′)

E·mil·ia-Ro·ma·gna (ā mēl′yä′rō män′yä′) region in NC Italy, near the head of the Adriatic: 8,541 sq mi (22,121 sq km); cap. Bologna

Em·i·ly (em′ə lē) ***n.*** ⟦Fr *Émilie* < L *Aemilia,* fem. of *Aemilius:* see EMIL⟧ a feminine name: var. *Emilia, Emeline, Emmeline*

em·i·nence (em′i nəns) ***n.*** ⟦ME < OFr < L *eminentia* < *eminens,* excellent, prominent, prp. of *eminere,* to stand out < *e-,* out + **minere,* to project, add, for *minari:* see MENACE⟧ **1** a high or lofty place, thing, etc., as a hill **2** *a)* superiority in rank, position, character, achievement, etc.; greatness; celebrity *b)* a person of eminence **3** [**E-**] *R.C.Ch.* a title of honor used in speaking to or of a cardinal: preceded by *Your* or *His* **4** *Anat.* a raised area, usually on the surface of a bone

é·mi·nence grise (ā mē näns grēz′) ⟦Fr, lit., gray eminence, nickname of François Leclerc du Tremblay (1577-1638), Fr monk and confidential agent of, and an assumed influence over, RICHELIEU: so called from the color of his habit⟧ a person who wields great power and influence, but secretly or unofficially

em·i·nen·cy (em′i nən sē) *n., pl.* **-cies** [Obs.] eminence

em·i·nent (em′ə nənt) *adj.* ⟦ME < L *eminens*: see EMINENCE⟧ **1** rising above other things or places; high; lofty **2** projecting; prominent; protruding **3** standing high by comparison with others, as in rank or achievement; renowned; exalted; distinguished **4** outstanding; remarkable; noteworthy [a man of *eminent* courage] **—SYN.** FAMOUS **—em′i·nent·ly** *adv.*

eminent domain ☆*Law* the right of a government to take, or to authorize the taking of, private property for public use, just compensation being given to the owner

e·mir (e mir′, ə-) *n.* ⟦Ar *amīr* < *amara*, to command⟧ **1** any of certain Muslim rulers, princes, or commanders; also, a title for such a person **2** a title given Muhammad's descendants through his daughter Fatima: see FATIMID

em·ir·ate (em′ər ət, -āt′; e mir′-) *n.* ⟦prec. + -ATE²⟧ a state or territory under the rule of an emir

em·is·sar·y (em′i ser′ē) *n., pl.* **-sar′ies** ⟦L *emissarius* < pp. of *emittere*: see EMIT⟧ a person or agent sent on a specific mission **—*adj.*** of, or serving as, an emissary or emissaries

e·mis·sion (ē mish′ən, i-) *n.* ⟦L *emissio* < pp. of *emittere*⟧ **1** the act of emitting; issuance; specif., *a)* the transmission of radio waves *b)* the ejection of electrons from a surface by heat, radiation, etc. *c)* a discharge of fluid from the body; esp., an involuntary discharge of semen **2** something emitted; discharge; often, specif., exhaust from a gasoline or diesel engine

e·mis·sive (ē mis′iv, i-) *adj.* ⟦ML *emissivus* < L *emissus*, pp. of *emittere*⟧ emitting or able to emit

e·mis·siv·i·ty (ē′mi siv′ə tē, em′i-) *n.* the relative ability of a surface to radiate energy as compared with that of an ideally black surface under the same conditions

e·mit (ē mit′, i-) *vt.* **e·mit′ted, e·mit′ting** ⟦L *emittere* < *e-*, out (see EX-¹) + *mittere*, to send: see MISSION⟧ **1** to send out; give forth; discharge [geysers *emit* water] **2** to utter (words or sounds) **3** to transmit (a signal) as by radio waves **4** to give off (electrons) under the influence of heat, radiation, etc. **5** to issue (paper money or the like); put into circulation

e·mit·ter (-ər) *n.* **1** one that emits; specif., a substance that emits particles [a beta *emitter*] **2** in some transistors, the region or layer of semiconductor material, acting as an electrode, that sends electric current to the base

Em·ma (em′ə) *n.* ⟦Ger < *Erma* < names beginning with *Erm-* (e.g., *Ermenhilde*): see IRMA⟧ a feminine name

Em·man·u·el (i man′yoo el′, -əl) *n.* ⟦Gr *Emmanouēl* < Heb *imanuel*, lit., God with us⟧ **1** a masculine name: dim. *Manny*; var. *Emanuel, Immanuel, Manuel* **2** the Messiah: see IMMANUEL

Em·men (em′ən) city in NE Netherlands

em·men·a·gogue (e men′ə gäg′, -mē′nə-; ə-) *n.* ⟦< Gr *emmēna*, pl.n., menses (< *en-*, in + *mēn*, MONTH) + -AGOGUE⟧ anything used to stimulate the menstrual flow

Em·men·thal *or* **Em·men·tal (cheese)** (em′ən täl) ⟦transl. of Ger *Emmentaler käse* (formerly sp. *Emmenthaler*) < *Emmental*, region of Switzerland⟧ a hard, pale-yellow Swiss cheese with a mild flavor and large holes: also **Em′men·thal′er** or **Em′men·tal′er (cheese)** (-täl′ər)

em·mer (em′ər) *n.* ⟦Ger < OHG *amari*⟧ any of a group of wheat species having 14 pairs of chromosomes, esp. a wild species (*Triticum dicoccum*) having a spike broken up into segments and grains that do not thresh free of the chaff: see DURUM

em·met (em′it) *n.* ⟦see ANT¹⟧ [Archaic] an ant

em·me·tro·pi·a (em′ə trō′pē ə) *n.* ⟦ModL < Gr *emmetros*, in measure, fit < *en-*, in + *metron*, MEASURE + -OPIA⟧ the condition of normal refraction of light in the eye, in which vision is perfect **—em′me·trop′ic** (-träp′ik) *adj.*

Em·my (em′ē) ☆⟦altered < *Immy*, slang for the image-orthicon camera: name proposed (1948) in contrast to OSCAR² by H. R. Lubcke, U.S. TV engineer⟧ *trademark for:* **1** any of the annual awards given by the Academy of Television Arts and Sciences for special achievement in programming, acting, etc. **2** any of the statuettes given to those receiving such awards

☆**e·mo** (ē′mō) *n.* ⟦< *emo*(*tional hardcore*)⟧ **1** a form of music derived from punk rock and characterized by often sentimental lyrics conveying angst, desperation, etc. **2** *pl.* **-mos** a person who is a fan of emo music

e·mo·ji (ē mō′jē) *n.* ⟦Jpn⟧ **1** a standardized set of Japanese emoticons (see EMOTICON, sense 2) and other stylized images **2** *pl.* **-ji** or **-jis** an emoticon or other image in such a set

e·mol·li·ent (ē mäl′yənt, -ē ənt; i-; *also*, -mōl′-) *adj.* ⟦L *emolliens*, prp. of *emollire*, to soften < *e-* out + *mollire*, to soften < *mollis*, soft: see MILL¹⟧ softening; soothing **—*n.*** something that has a softening or soothing effect; esp., an emollient preparation or medicine applied to surface tissues of the body

e·mol·u·ment (ē mäl′yoo mənt, i-; -yə-) *n.* ⟦ME < L *emolumentum*, the result of exertion, gain, profit < *emolere*, to grind out < *e-*, out + *molere*, to grind: see MILL¹⟧ gain from employment or position; payment received for work; salary, wages, fees, etc. **—SYN.** WAGE

Em·or·y (em′ər ē) *n.* ⟦prob. via OFr *Aimeri* < OHG *Amalrich*, lit., work ruler < **amal-*, work (in battle) + **rich*, ruler (akin to L *rex*, king: see RIGHT)⟧ a masculine name: var. *Emery*; equiv. Ger. *Emmerich*, It. *Amerigo*

☆**e·mote** (ē mōt′, i-) *vi.* **e·mot′ed, e·mot′ing** ⟦back-form. < EMOTION⟧ [Informal] to act in an emotional or theatrical manner while, or as though, playing a role in a drama: often used humorously

e·mo·ti·con (ē mōt′i kän′, i-) ⟦fol. + ICON⟧ **1** a combination of typed keyboard characters used, as in email, to represent a stylized face meant to convey the writer's tone: for example, :) suggests happiness | ;) suggests irony | :(suggests sadness **2** any of a set of icons, representing stylized faces, that are incorporated within a character set or font

e·mo·tion (ē mō′shən, i-) *n.* ⟦Fr (prob. after *motion*) < *émouvoir*, to agitate, stir up < VL **exmovere*, for L *emovere* < *e-*, out + *movere*, MOVE⟧ **1** *a)* strong feeling; excitement *b)* a state of consciousness having to do with the arousal of feelings, distinguished from other mental states, as cognition, volition, and awareness of physical sensation **2** any specific feeling; any of various complex reactions with both mental and physical manifestations, as love, hate, fear, anger, etc. **—SYN.** FEELING **—e·mo′tion·less** *adj.*

e·mo·tion·al (ē mō′shə nəl, i-) *adj.* **1** of or having to do with emotion or the emotions **2** showing emotion, esp. strong emotion **3** easily aroused to emotion; quick to weep, be angry, etc. **4** appealing to the emotions; moving people to tears, anger, etc. **—e·mo′tion·al·ly** *adv.*

e·mo·tion·al·ism (-nəl iz′əm) *n.* **1** the tendency to be emotional or to show emotion quickly and easily **2** display of emotion **3** an appeal to emotion, esp. to sway an audience to some belief

e·mo·tion·al·ist (-nəl ist) *n.* **1** a very emotional person **2** a person who uses or relies on emotion or emotional effects, as in art

e·mo·tion·al·i·ty (ē mō′shə nal′ə tē, i-) *n.* the quality or state of being emotional

e·mo·tion·al·ize (ē mō′shə nəl īz′, i-) *vt.* **-ized′, -iz′ing** to treat, present, or interpret in an emotional way **—e·mo′tion·al·i·za′tion** *n.*

e·mo·tive (ē mōt′iv, i-) *adj.* **1** characterized by, expressing, or producing emotion **2** relating to the emotions **—e·mo′tive·ly** *adv.*

Emp *abbrev.* **1** Emperor **2** Empress

EMP *abbrev.* electromagnetic pulse: an immense surge of electromagnetic radiation caused by a nuclear explosion

em·pale (em pāl′) *vt.* **-paled′, -pal′ing** IMPALE

em·pa·na·da (em pə nä′də) *n.* ⟦Sp < adj., wrapped in pastry, breaded, fem. of *empanado* < pp. of *empanar* < *pan*, bread < L *panis*: see FOOD⟧ any of various pastry turnovers of Spain and Latin America, filled as with chopped meat and vegetables or with chopped fruit, then sealed and deep-fried

em·pan·el (em pan′əl) *vt.* **-eled** or **-elled, -el·ing** or **-el·ling** IMPANEL

em·pa·thet·ic (em′pə thet′ik) *adj.* of or characterized by empathy **—em′pa·thet′i·cal·ly** *adv.*

em·path·ic (em path′ik) *adj.* EMPATHETIC **—em·path′i·cal·ly** *adv.*

em·pa·thize (em′pə thīz′) *vt.* **-thized′, -thiz′ing** ⟦< fol., after SYMPATHIZE⟧ to undergo or feel empathy (*with* another or others)

em·pa·thy (em′pə thē) *n.* ⟦< Gr *empatheia*, affection, passion < *en-*, in + *pathos*, feeling: used to transl. Ger *einfühlung* (< *ein-*, in + *fühlung*, feeling)⟧ **1** the projection of one's own personality into the personality of another in order to understand the person better; ability to share in another's emotions, thoughts, or feelings **2** the projection of one's own personality into an object, with the attribution to the object of one's own emotions, responses, etc.

Em·ped·o·cles (em ped′ə klēz′) 495?-435? B.C.; Gr. philosopher & poet

em·pen·nage (em′pə nij′, em pen′ij′; em′pə näzh′, äm′-) *n.* ⟦Fr < OFr *empenner*, to feather an arrow < *em-*, in + *penne*, a feather: see PEN⟧ the tail assembly of an airplane, consisting of vertical and horizontal stabilizers, and including the fin, rudder, and elevators

em·per·or (em′pər ər) *n.* ⟦ME *emperour* < OFr *empereor*, ruler (of the Holy Roman Empire) < L *imperator*, commander in chief < pp. of *imperare*, to command < *in-*, in + *parare*, to set in order, PREPARE⟧ **1** the supreme ruler of an empire **2** any of various butterflies (family Nymphalidae) and moths (family Saturniidae) **—em′per·or·ship′** *n.*

emperor penguin the largest penguin (*Aptenodytes forsteri*), found only in Antarctica and growing to four feet in height

em·per·y (em′pər ē) *n., pl.* **-per·ies** ⟦ME & OFr *emperie* < L *imperium* < *imperare*: see EMPEROR⟧ [Old Poet.] broad dominion or authority

em·pha·sis (em′fə sis) *n., pl.* **-ses′** (-sēz′) ⟦L < Gr *emphasis*, an appearing in, outward appearance < *emphainein*, to indicate < *en-*, in + *phainein*, to show < IE base **bha-*, to shine > OE *bonian*, to polish⟧ **1** force of expression, thought, feeling, action, etc. **2** special stress given as to a syllable, word, or phrase in speaking **3** special attention given to something so as to make it stand out; importance; stress; weight

em·pha·size (em′fə sīz′) *vt.* **-sized′, -siz′ing** to give emphasis to; give special force or prominence to; stress

em·phat·ic (em fat′ik, im-) *adj.* ⟦Gr *emphatikos*⟧ **1** expressed, felt, or done with emphasis **2** using emphasis in speaking, expressing, etc. **3** very striking; forcible; definite [an *emphatic* defeat] **4** *Gram.* designating or of a present tense or past tense in which a form of *do* is used as an auxiliary for emphasis (Ex.: I *do* care, we *did* go) **—em·phat′i·cal·ly** *adv.*

em·phy·se·ma (em′fə sē′mə; -zē′-) *n.* ⟦ModL < Gr *emphysēma*, inflation < *emphysaein*, to inflate, blow in < *en-*, in + *physaein*, to blow < IE **phus-* < base **pu-*, **phu-*, echoic of blowing with puffed cheeks⟧ **1** an abnormal swelling of bodily tissues caused by the accumulation of air; esp., such a swelling of the lung tissue, due to the destruction or permanent loss of elasticity of the alveoli, which seriously impairs respiration **2** HEAVES **—em′phy·se′ma·tous** (-sē′mə təs, -sem′-) *adj.* **—em′phy·se′mic** *adj., n.*

em·pire (em′pīr′; *for adj., also* ôm pē′ər, -pir′; äm-) *n.* ⟦ME & OFr < L *imperium* < *imperare*: see EMPEROR⟧ **1** supreme rule; absolute power or authority; dominion **2** *a)* government by an emperor or empress *b)* the period during which such government prevails **3** *a)* a group of states or territories under the sovereign power of an emperor or empress *b)* a state uniting many territories and peoples under a single sovereign power **4** an extensive social or economic organization under the control of a single person, family, or corporation **—*adj.*** [E-] of or characteristic of the first

French Empire (1804-15) under Napoleon; specif., *a)* designating a style of furniture of this period, characterized by massiveness, bronze ornamentation, and motifs of ancient Greece, Rome, and Egypt *b)* designating a gown in the style of the period, with a short waist, décolleté bodice, flowing skirt, and short, puffed sleeves

Empire Day a former holiday celebrated in the British Empire on May 24, Queen Victoria's birthday

☆**Empire State** *name for* NEW YORK State

em·pir·ic (em pir′ik) *n.* ⟦L *empiricus* < Gr *empeirikos*, experienced < *empeiria*, experience < *en-*, in + *peira*, a trial, experiment: see FARE⟧ **1** a person who relies solely on practical experience rather than on scientific principles **2** [Archaic] a charlatan; quack —*adj.* empirical

em·pir·i·cal (em pir′i kəl) *adj.* ⟦prec. + -AL⟧ **1** relying or based solely on experiment and observation rather than theory [the *empirical* method] **2** relying or based on practical experience without reference to scientific principles [an *empirical* remedy] —**em·pir′i·cal·ly** *adv.*

empirical formula a chemical formula which gives the composition of elements in a molecule in their lowest relative proportions but does not specify the structural arrangement or true molecular weight (Ex.: CH for benzene or acetylene)

em·pir·i·cism (em pir′i siz′əm) *n.* **1** experimental method; search for knowledge by observation and experiment **2** *a)* a disregarding of scientific methods and relying solely on experience *b)* [Archaic] quackery **3** *Philos.* the theory that sense experience is the only source of knowledge —**em·pir′i·cist** *n.*

em·place (em plās′, im-) *vt.* **-placed′**, **-plac′ing** ⟦back-form. < fol.⟧ to place in position

em·place·ment (-mənt) *n.* ⟦Fr < *emplacer*, to put in position: see EN-[1] & PLACE⟧ **1** the act of emplacing; placement **2** the position in which something is placed; specif., the prepared position from which a heavy gun or guns are fired

em·plane (em plān′, im-) *vi.* **-planed′**, **-plan′ing** ENPLANE

em·ploy (em ploi′, im-) *vt.* ⟦ME *emploien* < OFr *emploier* < L *implicare*, to enfold, engage: see IMPLY⟧ **1** to make use of; use **2** to keep busy or occupied; take up the attention, time, etc. of; devote [to *employ* oneself in study] **3** to provide work and pay for [mining *employs* fewer men now] **4** to engage the services or labor of for pay; hire —*n.* **1** the state of being employed, esp. for pay; paid service; employment **2** [Archaic] work or occupation —*SYN.* USE

em·ploy·a·ble (-ə bəl) *adj.* that can be employed; specif., *a)* physically or mentally fit to be hired for work *b)* meeting the minimum requirements for a specified kind of work or position of employment —**em·ploy′a·bil′i·ty** (-ə bil′ə tē) *n.*

em·ploy·ee or **em·ploy·e** (em ploi′ē, im-; em ploi′ē′, im-; em′ploi ē′) *n.* ⟦altered (after -EE[1]) < earlier *employé, employée* < Fr, pp. of *employer*, to employ⟧ a person hired by another, or by a business firm, etc., to work for wages or salary

em·ploy·er (em ploi′ər, im-) *n.* one who employs; esp., a person, business firm, etc. that hires one or more persons to work for wages or salary

em·ploy·ment (em ploi′mənt, im-) *n.* **1** an employing or being employed **2** the thing at which one is employed; work; occupation; profession; job **3** the number or percentage of persons gainfully employed **4** [Archaic] purpose to which something is put

em·poi·son (em poi′zən) *vt.* ⟦ME *empoisounen* < OFr *empoisoner*: see EN-[1] & POISON⟧ **1** [Archaic] to make poisonous; taint or corrupt **2** to embitter; envenom

em·po·ri·um (em pôr′ē əm) *n., pl.* **-ri·ums** or **-ri·a** (-ə) ⟦L < Gr *emporion*, trading place, mart < *emporios*, pertaining to trade, commerce < *emporos*, traveler, merchant < *en-*, in + *poros*, way: see FARE⟧ **1** a place of commerce; trading center; marketplace **2** a large store with a wide variety of things for sale

em·pow·er (em pou′ər, im-) *vt.* **1** to give power or authority to; authorize [Congress is *empowered* to levy taxes] **2** to give ability to; enable; permit **3** to provide (someone regarded as weak or oppressed) with the means or opportunities to improve his or her situation —**em·pow′er·ment** *n.*

em·press (em′pris) *n.* ⟦ME *emperesse* < OFr, fem. of *empereor*, EMPEROR⟧ **1** the wife of an emperor **2** a woman ruler of an empire **3** a woman with great power or influence [the *empress* of his heart]

em·presse·ment (än pres män′) *n.* ⟦Fr, eagerness < *s'empresser*, to be eager, hasten: see IMPRESS[2]⟧ great or extreme attentiveness, care, or cordiality

em·prise or **em·prize** (em prīz′) *n.* ⟦ME *emprise* < OFr < pp. of *emprendre*, to undertake < VL **imprehendere* < L *im-*, in + *prehendere*, to take: see PREHENSILE⟧ [Archaic] **1** an enterprise or adventure **2** prowess or daring [knights of great *emprise*]

emp·ty (emp′tē) *adj.* **-ti·er**, **-ti·est** ⟦ME *emti* & (with intrusive *-p-*) *empti* < OE *æmettig*, unoccupied, lit., at leisure < *æmetta*, leisure (< *æ-*, without + base of *motan*, to have to: see MUST[1]) + *-ig*, -Y[2]⟧ **1** containing nothing; having nothing in it **2** having no one in it; unoccupied; vacant [an *empty* house] **3** carrying or bearing nothing; bare **4** having no worth or purpose; useless or unsatisfying [*empty* pleasure] **5** without meaning or force; insincere; vain [*empty* promises] **6** [Informal] hungry —*vt.* **-tied**, **-ty·ing** **1** to make empty **2** *a)* to pour out or remove (the contents) from something *b)* to transfer (the contents) *into, onto,* or *on* something else **3** to unburden or discharge (oneself or itself) —*vi.* **1** to become empty **2** to pour out; discharge [the river *empties* into the sea] —*n., pl.* **-ties** an empty freight car, truck, bottle, etc. —**empty of** lacking; without; devoid of —**run on empty** ⟦by analogy with a car operating with very little fuel left in the tank and the gauge reading "*empty*"⟧ to be at a level of energy, creativity, etc. that is inadequate to sustain worthwhile activity or achievement —**emp′ti·ly** *adv.* —**emp′ti·ness** *n.*

SYN.—**empty** means having nothing in it [an *empty* box, street, stomach, etc.]; **vacant** means lacking that which appropriately or customarily occupies or fills it [a *vacant* apartment, position, etc.]; **void**, as discriminated here, specifically stresses complete or vast emptiness [*void* of judgment]; **vacuous**, now rare in its physical sense, suggests the emptiness of a vacuum See also **vain** —*ANT.* **full**

emp·ty-hand·ed (-han′did) *adj.* bringing, gaining, or carrying away nothing

emp·ty-head·ed (-hed′id) *adj.* frivolous and stupid; silly and ignorant

☆**empty nester** a person whose children have grown up and left home

☆**emp·ty-nest syndrome** (emp′tē nest′) a form of mental depression said to be caused in parents by the loss felt when their children grow up and leave home

em·pur·ple (em pur′pəl) *vt., vi.* **-pled**, **-pling** to make or become purple

em·py·e·ma (em′pī ē′mə, -pē ē′-) *n., pl.* **-ma·ta** (-mə tə) or **-mas** ⟦altered (infl. by Gr) < ME *empima* < ML *empyema* < Gr *empyēma* < *empyein*, to suppurate < *en-*, in + *pyon*, PUS⟧ the accumulation of pus in a body cavity, esp. in the pleural cavity —**em′py·e′ma·tous** (-ē′mə təs, -em′ə-) *adj.*, **em′py·e′mic** (-ē′mik, -em′ik)

em·pyr·e·al (em pir′ē əl; em′pī rē′əl, -pə-) *adj.* ⟦LL *empyrius, empyreus* < Gr *empyrios*, in fire < *en*, in + *pyr*, FIRE⟧ of the empyrean; heavenly; sublime

em·py·re·an (em pir′ē ən; em′pī rē′ən, -pə-) *n.* ⟦see prec. & -AN⟧ **1** the highest heaven; specif., *a)* among the ancients, the sphere of pure light or fire *b)* among Christian poets, the abode of God **2** the sky; the celestial vault; firmament —*adj.* EMPYREAL

Ems (emz) river in NW Germany, flowing northward into the North Sea: *c.* 200 mi (322 km)

EMS *abbrev.* **1** Emergency Medical Service **2** European Monetary System: a system linking the currencies within the European Community

EMT (ē′em′tē′) *n., pl.* **EMTs** an emergency medical technician

e·mu (ē′myōō′) *n.* ⟦< Port *ema (di gei)*, crane (of the ground) < ?⟧ any of a family (Dromaiidae) of large, flightless Australian birds: see CASSOWARY

EMU or **emu** *abbrev.* electromagnetic units

em·u·late (em′yōō lāt′, -yə-; *for adj.*, -lit) *vt.* **-lat′ed**, **-lat′ing** ⟦< L *aemulatus*, pp. of *aemulari* < *aemulus*, trying to equal or excel < IE base **ai-* to give, accept, take > Gr *ainymai*, take⟧ **1** to try, often by imitating or copying, to equal or surpass **2** to imitate (a person or thing admired) **3** to rival successfully **4** *Comput.* to use an emulator to perform the functions of —*adj.* [Obs.] ambitious

em·u·la·tion (em′yōō lā′shən, -yə-) *n.* ⟦L *aemulatio*⟧ **1** the act of emulating **2** desire or ambition to equal or surpass **3** [Obs.] *a)* ambitious rivalry *b)* envious dislike **4** *Comput.* the act or an instance of using an emulator —*SYN.* COMPETITION —**em′u·la′tive** *adj.* —**em′u·la′tive·ly** *adv.*

em·u·la·tor (em′yōō lāt′ər, -yə-) *n.* **1** one that emulates **2** software or hardware that allows one computer to perform the functions of, or execute programs designed for, another type of computer

em·u·lous (em′yōō ləs, -yə-) *adj.* ⟦L *aemulus*: see EMULATE⟧ **1** desirous of equaling or surpassing **2** characterized or caused by emulation **3** [Obs.] jealous; envious —*SYN.* AMBITIOUS —**em′u·lous·ly** *adv.* —**em′u·lous·ness** *n.*

e·mul·si·fi·a·ble (ē mul′sə fī′ə bəl, i-) *adj.* that can be emulsified: also **e·mul′si·ble** (-sə bəl)

e·mul·si·fy (ē mul′sə fī′, i-) *vt., vi.* **-fied′**, **-fy′ing** to form into an emulsion —**e·mul′si·fi·ca′tion** *n.* —**e·mul′si·fi′er** *n.*

e·mul·sion (ē mul′shən, i-) *n.* ⟦ModL *emulsio* < L *emulsus*, pp. of *emulgere*, to milk or drain out < *e-*, out + *mulgere*, to MILK⟧ a stable colloidal suspension, as milk, consisting of an immiscible liquid dispersed and held in another liquid by substances called emulsifiers; specif., *a)* *Pharmacy* such a suspension used as a vehicle for medication *b)* *Photog.* a suspension of a salt of silver, platinum, etc. in gelatin or collodion, used to coat plates, film, and paper —**e·mul′sive** (-siv) *adj.*

e·mul·soid (-soid′) *n.* a lyophilic emulsion

e·munc·to·ry (ē muŋk′tə rē) *n., pl.* **-ries** ⟦ModL *emunctorium* < pp. of L *emungere*, to blow the nose, cleanse < *e-*, out + *mungere*, to blow the nose: for IE base see MUCUS⟧ any organ or part of the body that gives off waste products, as the kidneys, lungs, or skin —*adj.* giving off waste products; excretory

en (en) *n.* **1** the letter N **2** *Printing* a space half the width of an em

-en (ən, ′n) *suffix* **1** ⟦ME < *-en, -ien* < OE *-nian*⟧ *forming verbs* *a)* to become or cause to be (added to adjectives) [*darken, weaken*] *b)* to come to have, cause to have (added to nouns) [*heighten, hearten, strengthen*] **2** ⟦ME & OE, akin to L *-inus*, Gr *-inos*⟧ *forming adjectives* made of: added to concrete nouns [*wooden, waxen*] **3** ⟦ME & OE⟧ forming the past participle of strong verbs [*risen, written*] **4** ⟦OE *-an*⟧ forming the plural of certain nouns [*children, oxen*] **5** ⟦OE⟧ forming the feminine of certain nouns [*vixen*] **6** ⟦OE⟧ forming certain old diminutives [*chicken*]

en-[1] (en, in) ⟦ME < OFr < L *in-* < *in*, IN[1]⟧ *prefix forming verbs* **1** *a)* to put or get into or on [*enthrone, enplane*] *b)* to cover or wrap with [*enrobe*]: added to nouns **2** to make, make into or like, cause to be: added to nouns and adjectives [*endanger, enthrall*] **3** in or into: added to verbs [*encase*] **4** used as an intensifier [*encourage*] Often becomes *em-* before *b, m,* or *p* Many words beginning with *en-* are also spelled with *in-* [*enquire, inquire*]

en-[2] (en, in) ⟦Gr *en-* < *en*, IN[1]⟧ *prefix* in: used chiefly in Greek derivatives *[endemic]*

en·a·ble (en āʹbəl, in-) *vt.* **-bled, -bling 1** *a)* to make able; provide with means, opportunity, power, or authority *[financial aid enabled Lou to attend college]* *b)* to authorize, allow, or permit *[legislation enabling free trade, software enabling computer network access]* **2** to make possible or effective; specif., to make possible or support the dysfunctional behavior of (someone), as by denying it exists or compensating for it in some way **3** *Comput.* to activate (a device, a software function or feature, etc.): opposed to DISABLE (sense 3) —**en·aʹbler** *n.*

en·act (en aktʹ, in-) *vt.* **1** to make (a bill, etc.) into a law; pass (a law); decree; ordain **2** to represent or perform in or as in a play; act out —**en·acʹtor** *n.*

en·ac·tive (-akʹtiv) *adj.* enacting or having the power to enact

en·act·ment (en aktʹmənt, in-) *n.* **1** an enacting or being enacted **2** something enacted, as a law or decree

en·am·el (e namʹəl, i-) *n.* ⟦ME < the v.⟧ **1** a glassy, colored, opaque substance fused to surfaces of metals, glass, and pottery as an ornamental or protective coating **2** any smooth, hard, glossy coating or surface like enamel **3** the hard, white, glossy coating of the crown of a tooth **4** anything enameled; enameled ware or a piece of jewelry, etc. produced in enamel **5** paint that produces a smooth, hard, glossy surface when it dries —*vt.* **-eled** or **-elled, -el·ing** or **-el·ling** ⟦ME *enamelen* < Anglo-Fr *enamayller* < *en-* (see EN-[1]) + *amayl* < OFr *esmail*, enamel < Gmc **smalts*, a glaze, melted substance: for IE base see SMELT[1]⟧ **1** to inlay or cover with enamel **2** to decorate in various colors, as if with enamel **3** to form an enamel-like surface on

en·am·el·er or **en·am·el·ler** (-ər) *n.* **1** a person whose work is applying enamel, as to metal surfaces **2** an artist who designs and produces jewelry and other fine objects in enamel: now usually **en·amʹel·ist** or **en·amʹel·list**

en·am·el·ware (-werʹ) *n.* kitchen utensils, etc. made of enameled metal

en·am·or (en amʹər, in-) *vt.* ⟦ME *enamouren* < OFr *enamourer* < *en-*, in + *amour* < L *amor*, love⟧ to fill with love and desire; charm; captivate: now mainly in the passive voice, with *of [much enamored of her]*

en·an·ti·o·mer (en anʹtē ō mər) *n.* ⟦altered < ENANTIOMORPH < Ger < Gr *enantios*, opposite (< *en*, IN[1] + *anti*, against, ANTI-) + Ger *-morph*, -MORPH⟧ either of two isomers that are, partly or completely, mirror images of each other: they usually have nearly identical properties, although one form is dextrorotatory and the other levorotatory: also called **en·anʹti·o·morphʹ** (-môrfʹ) —**en·anʹti·o·merʹic** (-merʹik) *adj.* —**en·anʹti·o·merʹismʹ** *n.*

en ar·rière (än nȧ ryerʹ) ⟦Fr⟧ **1** behind **2** in arrears

en·ar·thro·sis (enʹär thrōʹsis) *n., pl.* **-ses**ʹ (-sēzʹ) ⟦ModL < Gr *enarthrōsis* < *enarthros*, jointed < *en-*, in + *arthron*, a joint: see ARTHRO-⟧ BALL-AND-SOCKET JOINT

en a·vant (än nȧ vänʹ) ⟦Fr, lit., in front; before⟧ forward; onward; ahead

en banc (en baŋkʹ, än bäŋkʹ) ⟦Fr, on the bench⟧ in full court; by all the judges *[an appeal decided en banc, an en banc hearing]*

en bloc (en bläkʹ; *Fr* än blôkʹ) ⟦Fr, lit., in a block⟧ in a mass; as a whole; all together

en bro·chette (än brô shetʹ) ⟦Fr, lit., on (a) skewer⟧ broiled on small spits or skewers

en brosse (än brôsʹ) ⟦Fr, lit., like a brush⟧ cut short so as to stand up like brush bristles: said of hair

enc *abbrev.* enclosure

en·cae·ni·a (en sēʹnē ə, -sēnʹyə) *pl.n.* ⟦altered (after L) < ME *encennia* < L *encaenia* < Gr *enkainia* < *en-*, EN-[2] + *kainos*, new: see -CENE⟧ *[often with sing. v.]* **1** a festival commemorating the founding of a city, church, university, etc. **2** [E-] the annual ceremony commemorating the founding of Oxford University

en·cage (en kājʹ) *vt.* **-caged**ʹ, **-cagʹing** to shut up in a cage; confine

en·camp (en kampʹ, in-) *vi.* to set up a camp —*vt.* **1** to put in a camp **2** to form into a camp

en·camp·ment (-mənt) *n.* **1** an encamping or being encamped **2** a camp or campsite

en·cap·su·late (en kapʹsə lātʹ, -syo͞o-) *vt.* **-latʹed, -latʹing 1** to enclose in or as if in a capsule **2** to put in concise form; condense Also **en·capʹsule** (-səl, -syo͞olʹ) **-suled, -sul·ing** —**en·capʹsu·laʹtion** *n.*

en·car·nal·ize (en kärʹnəl īzʹ) *vt.* **-ized**ʹ, **-izʹing 1** to incarnate **2** to make carnal; make sensual

en·case (en kāsʹ, in-) *vt.* **-cased**ʹ, **-casʹing 1** to cover completely; enclose **2** to put into a case or cases —**en·caseʹment** *n.*

en cas·se·role (en kasʹə rōlʹ; *Fr* än kȧs rôlʹ) ⟦Fr⟧ (baked and served) in a casserole

en·caus·tic (en kôsʹtik) *adj.* ⟦L *encausticus* < Gr *enkaustikos* < *enkaustos*, burnt in < *enkaiein*, to burn in < *en-*, in + *kaiein*, to burn⟧ done by a process of burning in or applying heat *[encaustic tile]* —*n.* a method of painting in which colors in wax are fused to a surface with hot irons —**en·causʹti·cal·ly** *adv.*

-ence (əns, ʼns) ⟦ME < OFr *-ence* & L *-entia* < *-ent-* (see -ENT) + *-ia*, n. ending⟧ *suffix* act, fact, quality, state, result, or degree *[conference, excellence]*

en·ceinte[1] (en santʹ; *Fr* än santʹ) *n.* ⟦Fr < pp. of *enceindre* < L *incingere*, to gird about < *in*, in + *cingere*, to surround⟧ **1** the line of works enclosing a fortified place **2** the space so enclosed

en·ceinte[2] (än santʹ; *E* en santʹ) *adj.* ⟦Fr < ML *incincta*, orig. fem. of *incinctus*, ungirt < L *in-*, not + *cinctus*, pp. of *cingere*, to gird, surround: see CINCH⟧ pregnant; with child

En·cel·a·dus (en selʹə dəs) *n.* ⟦L < Gr *Enkelados*⟧ a smooth satellite of Saturn having more reflective brightness than any other celestial body in the solar system

en·ce·phal·ic (enʹsə falʹik) *adj.* ⟦ENCEPHAL(O)- + -IC⟧ of or near the brain

en·ceph·a·li·tis (en sefʹə lītʹis, enʹsef-) *n.* ⟦ENCEPHAL(O)- + -ITIS⟧ inflammation of the brain —**en·cephʹa·litʹic** (-litʹik) *adj.*

encephalitis le·thar·gi·ca (li thärʹji kə) a form of encephalitis, or sleeping sickness, epidemic in the period from 1915 to 1926

en·ceph·a·lo- (en sefʹə lōʹ, -lə) ⟦< Gr *enkephalos*: see ENCEPHALON⟧ *combining form* of the brain: also, before a vowel, **en·cephʹal-**

en·ceph·a·lo·gram (en sefʹə lō gramʹ, -lə-) *n. short for* PNEUMOENCEPHALOGRAM

en·ceph·a·lo·my·e·li·tis (en sefʹə lōʹmīʹə lītʹis) *n.* ⟦ENCEPHALO- + MYELITIS⟧ inflammation of the brain and spinal cord; specif., a viral disease of horses and other animals sometimes communicable to people

en·ceph·a·lon (en sefʹə länʹ, -lən) *n., pl.* **-la** (-lə) ⟦ModL < Gr *enkephalos*, (what is) in the head < *en-*, in + *kephalē*, the head: see CEPHALIC⟧ *Anat.* the brain

en·ceph·a·lop·a·thy (en sefʹə läpʹə thē) *n., pl.* **-thies** any disease of the brain —**en·cephʹa·lo·pathʹic** (-lōʹpathʹik) *adj.*

en·chain (en chānʹ) *vt.* ⟦ME *encheinen* < OFr *enchainer*: see EN-[1] & CHAIN⟧ **1** to bind or hold with chains; fetter **2** to hold fast; captivate —**en·chainʹment** *n.*

en·chant (en chantʹ, -chäntʹ; in-) *vt.* ⟦ME *enchanten* < OFr *enchanter* < L *incantare*, to bewitch < *in-* (intens.) + *cantare*, sing: see CHANT⟧ **1** to cast a spell over, as by magic; bewitch **2** to charm greatly; delight —**SYN.** ATTRACT —**en·chantʹer** *n.*

en·chant·ing (en chanʹtiŋ, in-) *adj.* **1** charming; delightful **2** bewitching; fascinating —**en·chantʹing·ly** *adv.*

en·chant·ment (en chantʹmənt, in-) *n.* ⟦ME & OFr *enchantement*: see ENCHANT & -MENT⟧ **1** an enchanting or being enchanted **2** a magic spell or charm **3** something that charms or delights greatly **4** great delight or pleasure

en·chant·ress (en chanʹtris, in-) *n.* ⟦ME & OFr *enchanteresse*: see ENCHANT⟧ **1** a sorceress; witch **2** a fascinating or charming woman

en·chase (en chāsʹ) *vt.* **-chased**ʹ, **-chasʹing** ⟦MFr *enchasser* < OFr < *en-*, EN-[1] + *châsse*: see CHASE[2]⟧ **1** to put in a setting or serve as a setting for **2** to ornament by engraving, embossing, or inlaying with gems, etc. **3** to engrave or carve (designs, etc.)

☆**en·chi·la·da** (enʹchi läʹdə) *n.* ⟦AmSp < *en-* (see EN-[1]) + *chile* (see CHILI) + *-ada* (see -ADE)⟧ a tortilla usually rolled with meat inside and served with a chili-flavored sauce —**the whole enchilada** [Slang] all of it; everything; the entirety of something

en·chi·rid·i·on (enʹki ridʹē ən, -kī-) *n.* ⟦LL < Gr *encheiridion* < *en-*, in + *cheir*, hand (see CHIRO-) + *-idion*, dim. suffix⟧ [Rare] a handbook; manual

en·chon·dro·ma (enʹkän drōʹmə) *n., pl.* **-ma·ta** (-mə tə) or **-mas** ⟦ModL < Gr *en*, in + *chondros*, cartilage (see CHONDRO-) + -OMA⟧ a benign cartilaginous tumor —**enʹchon·dromʹa·tous** (-drämʹə təs, -drōʹmə təs) *adj.*

en·cho·ri·al (en kôrʹē əl) *adj.* ⟦< Gr *enchōrios*, native (< *en-*, in + *chōra*, country, place, akin to *chōros*: see CHOROGRAPHY) + -AL⟧ of or used in a particular country; native; popular; esp., DEMOTIC (sense 1)

☆**en·ci·na** (en sēʹnə) *n.* ⟦Sp < VL *ilicina*, holm oak < L *ilex*, ILEX⟧ a live oak of the SW U.S.

en·ci·pher (en sīʹfər) *vt.* to convert (a message, information, etc.) into cipher

en·cir·cle (en surʹkəl, in-) *vt.* **-cled, -cling 1** to make a circle around; enclose within a circle; surround **2** to move in a circle around —**en·cirʹcle·ment** *n.*

encl *abbrev.* enclosure

en clair (än klerʹ) ⟦Fr, lit., in clear⟧ not in code or cipher; in plain language *[a message sent en clair]*

en·clasp (en klaspʹ) *vt.* to hold in a clasp; embrace

en·clave (enʹklāvʹ, änʹ-) *n.* ⟦Fr < OFr < *enclaver*, to enclose, lock in < VL **inclavare* < L *in*, in + *clavis*, a key: see LOT⟧ **1** a territory surrounded or nearly surrounded by the territory of another country *[San Marino is an enclave within Italy]*: cf. EXCLAVE **2** a minority culture group living as an entity within a larger group

en·clit·ic (en klitʹik) *adj.* ⟦LL *encliticus* < Gr *enklitikos* < *enklinein*, to lean toward, incline < *en-*, in + *klinein*, to LEAN[1]⟧ *Gram.* dependent on the preceding word for its stress: said as of a word that has lost its stress in comb. (Ex.: *man* in *layman*), or of certain particles, as in classical Greek —*n.* any such word or particle Cf. PROCLITIC

en·close (en klōzʹ, in-) *vt.* **-closed**ʹ, **-closʹing** ⟦ME *enclosen*, prob. < *enclos*, an enclosure < OFr, orig. pp. of *enclore*, to enclose < VL **inclaudere*, for L *includere*, INCLUDE⟧ **1** to shut in all around; hem in; fence in; surround **2** to insert in an envelope, wrapper, etc., often along with something else *[to enclose a check with one's order]* **3** to contain

en·clo·sure (en klōʹzhər, in-) *n.* ⟦ME & OE: see prec. & -URE⟧ **1** an enclosing or being enclosed **2** something, as a fence or wall, that encloses **3** something enclosed; specif., *a)* an enclosed place or area *b)* a document, money, etc. enclosed as with a letter **4** a boxlike container for a SPEAKER (sense 2a) **5** [Historical] in England, the gradual process by which communal land was divided into privately owned parcels enclosed by hedges and fences

en·code (en kōdʹ, in-) *vt.* **-codʹed, -codʹing 1** to convert (a message, information, etc.) into code **2** to convert (data) by applying an electronic code —**en·codʹer** *n.*

en·co·mi·ast (en kō′mē ast′, -əst) ***n.*** ⟦Gr *enkōmiastēs* < *enkōmiazein*, to praise < *enkōmion*⟧ a person who speaks or writes encomiums; eulogist

en·co·mi·as·tic (en kō′mē as′tik) ***adj.*** **1** of an encomiast **2** of or like an encomium; eulogistic

en·co·mi·um (en kō′mē əm) ***n., pl.*** **-mi·ums** or **-mi·a** (-ə) ⟦L < Gr *enkōmion*, hymn to a victor, neut. of *enkōmios* < *en-*, in + *kōmos*, a revel⟧ a formal, often enthusiastic, expression of high praise

en·com·pass (en kum′pəs, in-) ***vt.*** **1** to shut in all around; surround; encircle **2** to contain; include **3** to bring about; achieve; contrive [to *encompass* its destruction] —**en·com′pass·ment** ***n.***

en·core (än′kôr′) ***interj.*** ⟦Fr, again, still < OFr *ancor*, prob. < L (*hinc*) *hac hora* (from that time) to the present hour⟧ again; once more: in English, used by an audience to demand a repetition or an additional performance —***n.*** **1** a demand by the audience, shown by continued applause, for the repetition of a piece of music, etc., or for another appearance of the performer or performers **2** the repetition, further performance, etc. in answer to such a demand **3** the piece of music, etc. performed in answer to such a demand —***vt.*** **-cored′**, **-cor′ing** [Now Rare] to demand further performance of or by —***vi.*** [Informal] to give an encore

en·coun·ter (en koun′tər, in-) ***vt.*** ⟦ME *encontren* < OFr *encontrer* < *encontre*, against < VL **incontra* < L *in*, in + *contra*, against⟧ **1** to meet unexpectedly; come upon **2** to meet in conflict or battle **3** to meet with; face (difficulties, trouble, etc.) —***vi.*** to meet accidentally or in opposition —***n.*** **1** a direct meeting, as in conflict or battle **2** a meeting with another, esp. when unexpected or by chance —***adj.*** designating or of a small group that meets for a kind of therapy in personal interrelationship, involving a release of inhibitions, an open exchange of intimate feelings, etc. —***SYN.*** BATTLE[1]

en·cour·age (en kur′ij, in-) ***vt.*** **-aged**, **-ag·ing** ⟦ME *encouragen* < OFr *encoragier*: see EN-[1] & COURAGE⟧ **1** to give courage, hope, or confidence to; embolden; hearten **2** to give support to; be favorable to; foster; help

en·cour·age·ment (-mənt) ***n.*** **1** an encouraging or being encouraged **2** something that encourages

en·cour·ag·ing (en kur′ij iŋ, in-) ***adj.*** giving courage, hope, or confidence —**en·cour′ag·ing·ly** ***adv.***

en·crim·son (en krim′zən) ***vt.*** to make crimson

en·cri·nite (en′kri nīt′) ***n.*** ⟦ModL *encrinites* < Gr *en*, in + *krinon*, lily⟧ a crinoid, esp. a fossil crinoid (genus *Encrinus*)

en·croach (en krōch′, in-) ***vi.*** ⟦ME *encrochen* < OFr *encrochier*, to seize upon, take < *en-*, in + *croc*, *croche*, a hook: see CROSIER⟧ **1** to trespass or intrude (*on* or *upon* the rights, property, etc. of another), esp. in a gradual or sneaking way **2** to advance beyond the proper, original, or customary limits; make inroads (*on* or *upon*) —***SYN.*** TRESPASS —**en·croach′ment** ***n.***

en croûte (än krōōt′; *Fr* än krōōt′) ⟦Fr, lit., in crust⟧ wrapped in pastry and baked: said esp. of meats [pâté *en croûte*]

en·crust (en krust′) ***vt.*** ⟦OFr *encrouster* < L *incrustare*: see IN-[1] & CRUST⟧ **1** to cover with or as with a crust, or hard coating **2** to decorate elaborately, esp. with gems —***vi.*** to form a crust

en·crus·ta·tion (en′krus tā′shən) ***n.*** ⟦LL *incrustatio*⟧ **1** an encrusting or being encrusted **2** a crust; hard layer or coating **3** an elaborate decorative coating, inlay, etc. **4** *Med.* a crust, scale, scab, etc.

en·crypt (en kript′) ***vt.*** ⟦< EN-[1] + CRYPT(OGRAM)⟧ **1** to encode or encipher **2** *Comput.* to add an electronic digital code to (data) being sent over a public network to prevent its unauthorized detection, use, copying, etc. —**en·cryp′tion** ***n.***

en·cul·tu·rate (en kul′chə rāt′, in-) ***vt.*** **-rat′ed**, **-rat′ing** to cause to adapt to the prevailing cultural patterns of one's society; socialize —**en·cul′tu·ra′tion** ***n.***

en·cum·ber (en kum′bər, in-) ***vt.*** ⟦ME *encombren* < OFr *encombrer*: see EN-[1] & CUMBER⟧ **1** to hold back the motion or action of, as with a burden; hinder; hamper **2** to fill in such a way as to obstruct; block up; obstruct **3** to load or weigh down, as with claims, debts, etc.; burden

en·cum·brance (en kum′brəns, in-) ***n.*** ⟦ME & OFr *encombraunce*⟧ **1** something that encumbers; hindrance; obstruction; burden **2** [Rare] a dependent, esp. a child **3** *Law* a lien, charge, or claim attached to real property, as a mortgage

ency or **encyc** *abbrev.* encyclopedia

-en·cy (ən sē, 'n sē) ⟦L *-entia*⟧ *suffix* -ENCE [*dependency, emergency, efficiency*]

en·cyc·li·cal (en sik′li kəl, in-; *occas.*, -sī′kli-) ***adj.*** ⟦LL *encyclicus* < Gr *enkyklios*, in a circle, general, common < *en-*, in + *kyklos*, a circle: see CYCLE⟧ for general circulation: also **en·cyc′lic** —***n.*** *R.C.Ch.* a papal document addressed to the bishops, generally dealing with doctrinal matters

en·cy·clo·pe·di·a or **en·cy·clo·pae·di·a** (en sī′klə pē′dē ə, in-) ***n.*** ⟦ModL (1508) *encyclopaedia* < Gr *enkyklopaideia*, false reading for *enkyklios paideia*, instruction in the circle of the arts and sciences < *enkyklios* (*en-*, in + *kyklos*, a circle: see CYCLE) in a circle, general + *paideia*, education < *paideuein*, to educate, bring up a child < *pais* (gen. *paidos*), child: see PEDO-[1]⟧ **1** a book or set of books giving information on all or many branches of knowledge, generally in articles alphabetically arranged **2** a similar work giving information in a particular field of knowledge [an *encyclopedia* of philosophy]

en·cy·clo·pe·dic or **en·cy·clo·pae·dic** (-pē′dik) ***adj.*** of or like an encyclopedia; esp., giving information about many subjects; comprehensive in scope —**en·cy′clo·pe′di·cal·ly** ***adv.***, **en·cy′clo·pae′di·cal·ly**

en·cy·clo·pe·dism or **en·cy·clo·pae·dism** (-pē′diz′əm) ***n.*** encyclopedic knowledge or learning

en·cy·clo·pe·dist or **en·cy·clo·pae·dist** (-pē′dist) ***n.*** a person who compiles or helps compile an encyclopedia —**the Encyclopedists** the writers of the French Encyclopedia (1751-72) edited by Diderot and d'Alembert, which contained the advanced ideas of the period

en·cyst (en sist′) ***vt., vi.*** to enclose or become enclosed in a cyst, capsule, or sac —**en·cyst′ment** ***n.***, **en′cys·ta′tion** (-sis tā′shən)

end[1] (end) ***n.*** ⟦ME & OE *ende*, akin to Ger *ende*, Goth *andeis* < IE **antyos*, opposite, lying ahead < **anti-*, opposite, facing (< base **ants*, front, forehead) > OHG *endi*, forehead, Gr *anti*, L *ante*⟧ **1** a limit or limiting part; point of beginning or stopping; boundary **2** the last part of anything; final point; finish; completion; conclusion [the *end* of the day] **3** *a)* a ceasing to exist; death or destruction *b)* the cause or manner of this **4** the part at, toward, or near either of the extremities of anything; tip **5** *a)* an outer district or region [the west *end* of town] *b)* a division, sector, area of responsibility, etc., as in an organization **6** what is desired or hoped for; object; purpose; intention **7** an outcome; result; upshot; consequence **8** a piece left over; fragment; remnant [odds and *ends*] **9** the reason for being; final cause ☆**10** *Football* *a)* a player at either end of the line *b)* this position —***vt.*** ⟦ME *enden* < OE *endian*⟧ **1** to bring to an end; finish; stop; conclude **2** to be or form the end of —***vi.*** **1** to come to an end; terminate [will this storm ever *end?*] **2** to die —***adj.*** at the end; final [*end* man, *end* product] —***SYN.*** CLOSE[2], INTENTION —**end for end** with the ends, or the position, reversed —**ends of the earth** remote regions —**end to end** in a line so that the ends touch or meet —**end up** to come to a particular end or condition [they *ended up* in jail] —**in the end** finally; ultimately —**keep one's end up** [Informal] to do one's share —**make an end of 1** to finish; stop **2** to do away with —**make (both) ends meet** ⟦as in Fr *joindre les deux bouts*⟧ to manage to keep one's expenses within one's income —**no end** [Informal] extremely; very much or many —**on end 1** in an upright position **2** without interruption [for days *on end*] —**put an end to 1** to stop **2** to do away with —**to end** that surpasses or exceeds [a trip *to end* all trips]

end[2] *abbrev.* **1** endorse **2** endorsement

end-all (end′ôl′) ***n.*** *see* BE-ALL AND END-ALL

en·dam·age (en dam′ij) ***vt.*** **-aged**, **-ag·ing** [Archaic] to cause damage or injury to

en·da·me·ba (en′də mē′bə) ***n.*** ⟦ModL: see ENDO- & AMOEBA⟧ any of a genus (*Endamoeba*) of amoebas parasitic in invertebrates, as in the digestive tract of cockroaches and termites: see ENTAMEBA

en·dan·ger (en dān′jər, in-) ***vt.*** **1** to expose to danger, harm, or loss; imperil **2** to threaten with extinction —**en·dan′ger·ment** ***n.***

endangered species a species of animal or plant in danger of becoming extinct

end·arch (en′därk′) ***adj.*** ⟦< END(O)- + Gr *archē*, beginning⟧ *Bot.* having the primary xylem maturing from the center of the stem toward the outside: cf. EXARCH[2]

end around *Football* a play in which an offensive end or wide receiver, after running across the field behind the line of scrimmage and taking a handoff from the quarterback, attempts to advance downfield

end·ar·ter·ec·to·my (end är′tər ek′tə mē) ***n., pl.*** **-mies** ⟦END(O)- + ARTER(Y) + -ECTOMY⟧ the removal of plaque deposits and the inner lining of a blood vessel by surgery or pressurized carbon dioxide to improve blood circulation

en dash ⟦see EN⟧ *Printing* a short dash (–), half the length of an em dash

end·brain (end′brān′) ***n.*** TELENCEPHALON

en·dear (en dir′, in-) ***vt.*** to make dear, beloved, or well liked [to *endear* oneself by acts of generosity]

en·dear·ing (-iŋ) ***adj.*** **1** that makes dear or well liked **2** expressing affection [*endearing* tones]

en·dear·ment (en dir′mənt, in-) ***n.*** **1** an endearing or being endeared; affection **2** a word or act expressing affection

en·deav·or (en dev′ər, in-) ***vi.*** ⟦ME *endever* < *en-* (see EN-[1]) + *dever* < OFr *deveir*, duty, as in *se mettre en deveir*, to try to do: see DEVOIR⟧ to make an earnest attempt; strive: now usually with an infinitive [to *endeavor* to finish first] —***vt.*** [Archaic] to try to achieve —***n.*** an earnest attempt or effort Brit. sp. **en·deav′our** —***SYN.*** EFFORT, TRY

en·dem·ic (en dem′ik) ***adj.*** ⟦Fr *endémique* < *endémie*, endemic disease < Gr *endēmia*, a dwelling in < *endēmos*, native < *en-*, in + *dēmos*, the people: see DEMOCRACY⟧ **1** native to a particular country, nation, or region: said of plants, animals, and, sometimes, customs, etc. **2** constantly present in a particular region: said of a disease that is generally under control: cf. EPIDEMIC Also **en·dem′i·cal** —***n.*** **1** an endemic plant or animal **2** an endemic disease —***SYN.*** NATIVE —**en·dem′i·cal·ly** ***adv.*** —**en·de·mic·i·ty** (en′də mis′i tē) ***n.***, **en·dem′ism′**

En·der·by Land (en′dər bē) region of Antarctica, opposite the tip of Africa: claimed by Australia

en·der·gon·ic (en′dər gän′ik) ***adj.*** ⟦END(O)- + Gr *ergon*, WORK + -IC⟧ of or having to do with a biochemical reaction requiring the absorption of energy, as photosynthesis or anabolism: opposed to EXERGONIC

en·der·mic (en dur′mik) ***adj.*** ⟦< Gr *en*, in + *derma*, the skin (see DERMA[1]) + -IC⟧ designating or of a medicine, chemical, etc. that is absorbed through the skin —**en·der′mi·cal·ly** ***adv.***

En·ders (en′dərz), **John F(ranklin)** 1897-1985; U.S. bacteriologist

end·game (end′gām′) ***n.*** **1** the final stage of a game of chess, in which each player has only a few pieces left **2** the final stage of anything

end·ing (en′diŋ) ***n.*** ⟦OE *endung*: see END[2]⟧ **1** an end; specif., *a)* the last part; finish; conclusion *b)* death **2** *Gram.* the letter(s) or syllable(s) added to the end of a word or base to make a derived or inflected form ["-ed" is the *ending* in "wanted"]

en·dive (en′dīv′, än′dēv′) *n.* ⟦ME & OFr < ML *endivia* < MGr *endivi* < L *intibus* < Gr *entybon*, prob. < Egypt *t'-"bt*, January (when it is said to grow in Egypt)⟧ 1 *a)* a cultivated, lettucelike plant (*Cichorium endivia*) of the composite family: its curled, narrow leaves are cooked or blanched and used for salads *b)* another form of this vegetable with wide, smooth leaves, used as a potherb or in salads 2 the young leaves of CHICORY (sense 1) blanched for salads

end·less (end′lis) *adj.* ⟦ME *endeles* < OE *endeleas*: see END[2] & -LESS⟧ 1 having no end; going on forever; infinite 2 lasting too long [an *endless* speech] 3 continual [*endless* interruptions] 4 with the ends joined to form a closed unit that can move continuously over wheels, etc. [an *endless* chain] —**end′less·ly** *adv.* —**end′less·ness** *n.*

end line *Basketball, Football* a line at either end of a court or playing field, marking the limits of the playing area: see also BASE LINE

end·long (-lôŋ′) *adv.* [Archaic] 1 lengthwise 2 on end

end man 1 a man at the end of a row ☆2 in a minstrel show, the comic performer at each end of the first row, for whom the interlocutor serves as a foil

end·most (end′mōst′) *adj.* at the end; farthest; last

end·note (-nōt′) *n.* a note of comment or reference placed at the end of a chapter or, usually, a book: cf. FOOTNOTE

en·do- (en′dō, -də) ⟦< Gr *endon*, within < *en*, in + (?) **dom*, locative of base seen in L *domus*, house: hence, orig., in the house⟧ *combining form* within, inner [*endoderm*]: also, before a vowel, **end-**

en·do·bi·ot·ic (en′dō bī ät′ik, -bē-) *adj.* ⟦prec. + BIOTIC⟧ living within the body or tissues of a host organism

en·do·blast (en′dō blast′) *n.* ⟦ENDO- + -BLAST⟧ ENDODERM

en·do·car·di·al (en′dō kär′dē əl) *adj.* 1 within the heart 2 of the endocardium

en·do·car·di·tis (en′dō kär dīt′is) *n.* ⟦ModL: see -ITIS⟧ inflammation of the endocardium

en·do·car·di·um (en′dō kär′dē əm) *n.* ⟦ModL < ENDO- + Gr *kardia*, HEART⟧ the thin endothelial membrane lining the cavities of the heart

en·do·carp (en′dō kärp′) *n.* ⟦ENDO- + -CARP⟧ the inner layer of the pericarp of a ripened ovary or fruit, as the pit surrounding the seed of a drupe

en·do·com·men·sal (en′dō kə men′səl) *n.* a commensal living within the body of the host organism

en·do·cra·ni·um (en′dō krā′nē əm) *n., pl.* **-ni·a** (-ə) or **-ni·ums** 1 DURA MATER 2 the processes supporting the brain in the head capsule of an insect

en·do·crine (en′dō krin′, -krīn′, -krēn′; -də-) *adj.* ⟦ENDO- + Gr *krinein*, to separate: see CRISIS⟧ 1 designating or of any gland producing one or more hormones 2 designating or of such a hormone —*n.* any such gland or hormone, as the thyroid or its thyroxine

en·do·cri·nol·o·gy (en′dō kri näl′ə jē, -krī-) *n.* the branch of medicine dealing with the endocrine glands and their hormones —**en′do·crin′o·log′i·cal** (-krin′ə läj′i kəl, -krī′nə-) *adj.* —**en′do·cri·nol′o·gist** *n.*

en·do·cy·to·sis (-sī tō′sis) *n.* ⟦ENDO- + CYT(O)- + -OSIS⟧ a process in which a cell engulfs a large molecule, bacterium, etc. and forms a vesicle around it: opposed to EXOCYTOSIS —**en′do·cyt′ic** (-sit′ik) *adj.* —**en′do·cy′tose′** (-sī′tōs′, -tōz′) *vt., vi.* **-tosed′**, **-tos′ing** —**en′do·cy·tot′ic** (-sī tät′ik) *adj.*

en·do·derm (en′dō durm′) *n.* ⟦ENDO- + -DERM⟧ the inner layer of cells of the embryo, from which is formed the lining of the digestive tract, of other internal organs, and of certain glands —**en′do·der′mal** *adj.*, **en′do·der′mic**

en·do·der·mis (en′dō dur′mis) *n.* the specialized innermost layer of cells of the cortex in roots and many stems

☆**en·do·don·tics** (en′dō dän′tiks) *n.* ⟦END(O)- + -ODONT + -ICS⟧ the branch of dentistry that treats disorders of the pulp; root-canal therapy: also **en′do·don′tia** (-shə) —**en′do·don′tic** *adj.* —**en′do·don′tist** *n.*

en·do·en·zyme (en′dō en′zīm′) *n.* an enzyme that functions within the cell

en·dog·a·my (en däg′ə mē) *n.* ⟦ENDO- + -GAMY⟧ 1 the custom of marrying only within one's own group, as a clan, tribe, etc.: opposed to EXOGAMY 2 self-pollination among flowers of the same plant —**en·dog′a·mous** *adj.*, **en·do·gam·ic** (en′dō gam′ik)

en·do·gen (en′dō jən) *n.* ⟦Fr *endogène* (see ENDO- & -GEN): the stems were formerly believed to grow from within⟧ *former term for* MONOCOTYLEDON

en·dog·e·nous (en däj′ə nəs) *adj.* ⟦prec. + -OUS⟧ 1 developing from within; originating internally 2 *Biol.* growing or developing from or on the inside 3 *Biochem., Physiol.* of the anabolism of cells

en·dog·e·ny (en däj′ə nē) *n.* ⟦ENDO- + -GENY⟧ *Biol.* growth from within; endogenous formation of cells

en·do·lymph (en′dō limf′) *n.* ⟦ENDO- + LYMPH⟧ *Anat.* the fluid in the membranous labyrinth of the inner ear: cf. PERILYMPH

en·do·me·tri·o·sis (en′dō mē′trē ō′sis) *n., pl.* **-ses′** (-sēz′) ⟦see fol. & -OSIS⟧ the growth of endometrial tissue in abnormal locations, as on the ovaries or within the peritoneal cavity

en·do·me·tri·um (-mē′trē əm) *n., pl.* **-tri·a** (-trē ə) ⟦ENDO- + Gr *mētra*, uterus; akin to *mētēr*, MOTHER[1]⟧ the inner lining of the uterus —**en′do·me′tri·al** *adj.*

en·do·mix·is (en′dō miks′is) *n.* ⟦ENDO- + ModL *-mixis*, a mixing < Gr *mixis* < base of *meignynai*, to MIX⟧ a periodic reorganization of the nucleus in the cells of certain ciliates, not caused by conjugation

en·do·morph (en′dō môrf′) *n.* ⟦ENDO- + -MORPH⟧ 1 a mineral, esp. a crystal, enclosed within another 2 a person of the endomorphic physical type —**en′do·mor′phy** (-fē) *n.*

en·do·mor·phic (en′dō môr′fik) *adj.* 1 of an endomorph 2 of or caused by endomorphism 3 designating or of the round, fat physical type characterized by predominance of the structures developed from the endodermal layer of the embryo, as the internal organs: cf. ECTOMORPHIC, MESOMORPHIC

en·do·mor·phism (-môr′fiz′əm) *n.* a type of metamorphism in which intrusive igneous rock is changed by the action of the surrounding rock

en·do·nu·cle·ase (en′dō no͞o′klē ās′, -nyo͞o′-) *n.* a RESTRICTION ENZYME used to analyze gene structure, mutations, etc.

en·do·par·a·site (en′dō par′ə sīt′) *n.* a parasite that inhabits the internal organs or tissues of an animal or plant

en·do·pep·ti·dase (-pep′tə dās′) *n.* any enzyme, as pepsin, that starts to hydrolyze peptide bonds in the interior of a peptide chain

en·do·phyte (en′dō fīt′) *n.* ⟦ENDO- + -PHYTE⟧ an organism, as any of certain fungi or algae, living within a plant —**en′do·phyt′ic** (-fit′ik) *adj.*

en·do·plasm (en′dō plaz′əm) *n.* ⟦ENDO- + -PLASM⟧ the inner part of the cytoplasm of a cell: distinguished from ECTOPLASM —**en′do·plas′mic** *adj.*

endoplasmic reticulum a system of folded membranes, channels, and flattened sacs in the cytoplasm of eukaryotic cells, involved in the synthesis, storage, and transport of various substances necessary to cell function: as the point of attachment for ribosomes, it is especially associated with protein synthesis

en·do·proct (en′dō präkt′) *n.* ENTOPROCT

end organ any specialized structure at the peripheral end of nerve fibers having either sensory or motor functions

en·dor·phin (en dôr′fin) *n.* ⟦< *end(ogenous m)orphin(elike substance)* or *end(ogenous m)orphin(e)*⟧ any of several peptides secreted in the brain that have a pain-relieving effect like that of morphine

en·dorse (en dôrs′, in-) *vt.* **-dorsed′**, **-dors′ing** ⟦altered (after L) < ME *endosen* < OFr *endosser* < ML *indorsare* < L *in*, on, upon + *dorsum*, the back⟧ 1 to write on the back of (a document); specif., *a)* to sign (one's name) as payee on the back of (a check, money order, etc.) *b)* to make (a check, etc.) payable to another person by thus signing one's name and specifying the payee 2 to write a note, title, etc. on (a document) 3 *a)* to give approval to; support; sanction [to *endorse* a candidate] *b)* to state, as in an advertisement, that one approves of (a product, service, etc.), often in return for a fee —***SYN.*** APPROVE —**en·dors′a·ble** *adj.* —**en·dors′er** *n.*

en·dors·ee (en′dôr sē′) *n.* the person to whom a check, note, etc. is made over by endorsement

en·dorse·ment (en dôrs′mənt, in-) *n.* ⟦ME *endosement*⟧ 1 the act of endorsing something 2 something written in endorsing; specif., *a)* the signature of a payee on the back of a check, note, etc. *b)* a change, as of coverage or beneficiary, written on or added to an insurance policy *c)* a statement endorsing a person, product, etc., as in an advertisement

en·do·scope (en′dō skōp′, -də-) *n.* ⟦ENDO- + -SCOPE⟧ an instrument for examining visually the inside of a hollow organ or cavity of the body, as the bladder or rectum —**en′do·scop′ic** (-skäp′ik) *adj.* —**en·dos·co·py** (en däs′kə pē) *n.*

en·do·skel·e·ton (en′dō skel′ə tən) *n.* the internal bony, cartilaginous, or chitinous supporting structure in vertebrates, echinoderms, etc.: distinguished from EXOSKELETON —**en′do·skel′e·tal** *adj.*

en·dos·mo·sis (en′däs mō′sis) *n.* ⟦altered (after OSMOSIS) < Fr *endosmose* < *endo-*, ENDO- + Gr *ōsmos*: see OSMOSIS⟧ in osmosis, the more rapid, inward diffusion of the less dense fluid through the semipermeable membrane to mingle with the more dense: opposed to EXOSMOSIS —**en′dos·mot′ic** (-mät′ik) *adj.*

en·do·sperm (en′dō spurm′) *n.* ⟦ENDO- + SPERM[1]⟧ a tissue which surrounds the developing embryo of a seed and provides food for its growth —**en′do·sper′mic** *adj.*, **en′do·sper′mous**

en·do·spore (en′dō spôr′) *n.* 1 an asexual spore formed within the cell wall of the parent cell, as in certain bacteria, fungi, and algae 2 the inner wall of a spore or pollen grain; intine: also **en′do·spo′ri·um** (-spôr′ē əm), *pl.* **-ri·a** (-ə) —**en′do·spor′ous** *adj.*

en·dos·te·um (en däs′tē əm) *n., pl.* **-te·a** (-ə) ⟦ModL < END(O)- + Gr *osteon*, a bone: see OSSIFY⟧ the vascular connective tissue lining the marrow cavities of bones —**en·dos′te·al** *adj.*

en·dos·to·sis (en′däs tō′sis) *n., pl.* **-ses′** (-sēz′) ⟦ModL < END(O)- + OSTOSIS⟧ the formation of bone within cartilage

en·do·sym·bi·o·sis (en′dō sim′bī ō′sis, -bē-) *n.* ⟦see ENDO-⟧ a type of mutually beneficial symbiosis in which one symbiont lives within the body of the other —**en′do·sym′bi·ot′ic** (-ät′ik) *adj.*

en·do·the·ci·um (en′dō thē′shē əm, -sē-) *n., pl.* **-ci·a** (-ə) ⟦ENDO- + ModL *-thecium*, a fine enclosing structure < Gr *thēkion*, a small case, dim. of *thēkē*: see THECA⟧ an inner layer, as the inner wall of a pollen grain or the inner layer of a moss capsule

en·do·the·li·um (en′dō thē′lē əm) *n., pl.* **-li·a** (-ə) ⟦ModL < ENDO- + (EPI)THELIUM⟧ the layer of cells lining the inside of blood and lymph vessels, of the heart, and of some other closed cavities —**en′do·the′li·al** *adj.* —**en′do·the′li·oid′** *adj.*, **en·doth·e·loid** (en däth′ə loid′)

en·do·ther·mal (-thur′məl) *adj.* 1 WARMBLOODED (sense 1) 2 endothermic —**en′do·therm′** (-thurm′) *n.*, **en′do·ther′my** (-thur′mē)

en·do·ther·mic (en′dō thur′mik) *adj.* ⟦ENDO- + THERMIC⟧ designating, of, or produced by a chemical change in which there is an absorption of heat

en·do·tox·in (en′dō täks′in) *n.* ⟦ENDO- + TOXIN⟧ the polysaccharide that is combined with a lipid and released from the cell walls of Gram-negative bacteria, producing toxic effects causing fever, shock, etc. in many animals

en·do·tra·che·al (en′dō trā′kē əl, -trə kē′-) *adj.* within the trachea: said of devices thus placed for administering anesthetic gases, for examination, etc.

en·dow (en dou′, in-) ***vt.*** ⟦ME *endouen* < Anglo-Fr *endouer* < OFr *en-*, in + *dotare*, to endow < *dos*: see DOT²⟧ **1** to provide with some talent, quality, etc. [*endowed* with courage] **2** to think of as having some quality or characteristic [to *endow* gods with human traits] **3** to give money or property so as to provide an income for the support of (a college, hospital, etc.) **4** [Obs.] to provide with a dower

en·dow·ment (en dou′mənt, in-) ***n.*** ⟦ME *endouement*⟧ **1** the act of endowing **2** that with which something is endowed; specif., any bequest or gift that provides an income for an institution or person **3** a gift of nature; inherent talent, ability, quality, etc.

☆**endowment policy** an insurance policy by which a stated amount is paid to the insured after the period of time specified in the contract, or to the beneficiaries in case the insured dies within the time specified

end·pa·per (end′pā′pər) ***n.*** a folded sheet of paper one half of which is pasted to the inside of the front (or back) cover of a book, the other half to the inside edge of the first (or last) page of the book

end plate the area of specialized tissue that forms the junction between an individual muscle fiber and its motor nerve

end·point (end′point′) ***n.*** **1** a point of termination or completion **2** the point of furthest progress, advancement, etc.

end product the final result of any series of changes, processes, or chemical reactions

end rhyme a rhyming of the ends of two or more lines of verse

☆**en·drin** (en′drin) ***n.*** ⟦< ? EN-¹ + (AL)DRIN⟧ a highly toxic isomer of dieldrin, used as an insecticide

end run **1** *Football* SWEEP (*n.* 16) **2** an attempt to bypass red tape, opposition, etc.

end-stopped (end′stäpt′) ***adj.*** *Prosody* designating or of a line of verse that ends with a natural syntactic pause, usually indicated by a mark of punctuation: cf. ENJAMBMENT, RUN-ON (*adj.* 2)

☆**end table** a small table to be placed at either end of a sofa, beside a chair, etc.

end-time (end′tīm′) ***adj.*** of, having to do with, or taking place in the END TIMES

End Times [*also* **e- t-**] *Christian Theol.* the times immediately preceding the end of life on earth and the SECOND COMING, during which it is believed, esp. by many millennialist Christians, that certain events foretold in the Book of Revelation will take place

en·due (en do͞o′, -dyo͞o′; in-) ***vt.*** **-dued′**, **-du′ing** ⟦ME *endeuen* < OFr *enduire* < L *inducere*, to lead in (see INDUCE): form and sense infl. by L *induere* (see INDUE) & ENDOW⟧ **1** [Now Rare] to put on (a garment) **2** to provide (*with* something); specif., to endow (*with* qualities, talents, etc.)

en·dur·a·ble (en door′ə bəl, -dyoor′-; in-) ***adj.*** that can be endured; bearable —**en·dur′a·bly** ***adv.***

en·dur·ance (en door′əns, -dyoor′-; in-) ***n.*** **1** the act of enduring **2** the power of enduring; specif., *a)* ability to last, continue, or remain *b)* ability to stand pain, distress, fatigue, etc.; fortitude **3** duration **4** [Rare] that which is endured; hardship —***SYN.*** PATIENCE

en·dure (en door′, -dyoor′; in-) ***vt.*** **-dured′**, **-dur′ing** ⟦ME *duren* < OFr *endurer* < LL (Ec) *indurare*, to harden the heart < LL, to harden, hold out, last < *durus*, hard: see DURABLE⟧ **1** to hold up under (pain, fatigue, etc.); stand; bear; undergo **2** to put up with; tolerate —***vi.*** **1** to continue in existence; last; remain **2** to bear pain, etc. without flinching; hold out —***SYN.*** BEAR¹, CONTINUE

en·dur·ing (-iŋ) ***adj.*** lasting; permanent; durable —**en·dur′ing·ly** ***adv.***

end-us·er (end′yo͞o′zər) ***n.*** the user of a product; specif., the user of a computer system or network

end·ways (end′wāz′) ***adv.*** **1** on end; upright **2** with the end foremost **3** lengthwise **4** end to end Also **end′wise′** (-wīz′)

En·dym·i·on (en dim′ē ən) ***n.*** ⟦L < Gr *Endymiōn*⟧ *Gr. Myth.* a beautiful young shepherd loved by Selene

☆**end zone** *Football* the rectangular area between the goal line and the end line at each end of the playing field

ENE or **ene** *abbrev.* east-northeast

-ene (ēn) ⟦after L *-enus*, Gr *-enos*, adj. suffix⟧ *Chem. suffix forming nouns* **1** any open-chain hydrocarbon containing one double bond [*propylene*] **2** any of certain other unsaturated compounds containing one or more double bonds [*benzene, pinene*] **3** any of certain commercial products

en·e·ma (en′ə mə) ***n.***, *pl.* **-mas** or **-ma·ta** (-mə tə) ⟦LL < Gr, injection < *enienai*, to send in < *en-*, in + *hienai*, to send: see JET¹⟧ **1** a liquid forced into the colon through the anus, as a purgative, medicine, etc.; clyster **2** the forcing of a liquid into the colon in such a way

en·e·my (en′ə mē) ***n.***, *pl.* **-mies** ⟦ME & OFr *enemi* < L *inimicus*, unfriendly, enemy < *in-*, not + *amicus*, friend: see AMIABLE⟧ **1** a person who hates another, and wishes or tries to injure him; foe **2** *a)* a nation or force hostile to another; military or wartime adversary *b)* troops, fleet, ship, member, etc. of a hostile nation **3** a person hostile to an idea, cause, etc. **4** anything injurious or harmful —***adj.*** **1** [Obs.] hostile **2** of an enemy; of a hostile nation —***SYN.*** OPPONENT

enemy alien an alien residing or interned in a country with which his or her own country is at war

en·er·get·ic (en′ər jet′ik) ***adj.*** ⟦Gr *energētikos*⟧ of, having, or showing energy; vigorous; forceful —***SYN.*** ACTIVE —**en′er·get′i·cal·ly** ***adv.***

en·er·get·ics (-iks) ***n.*** the science that deals with the laws of energy and its transformations

en·er·gid (en′ər jid′, en ʉr′-) ***n.*** ⟦Ger < Gr *energos*, active (see ENERGY) + Ger *-id*, -ID⟧ the nucleus of a cell together with the mass of protoplasm around it

en·er·gize (en′ər jīz′) ***vt.*** **-gized′**, **-giz′ing** **1** to give energy to; activate; invigorate **2** *Elec.* to supply voltage or current to (a circuit, component, etc.) —***vi.*** to show energy; be active —**en′er·giz′er** ***n.***

en·er·gu·men (en′ər gyo͞o′mən) ***n.*** ⟦LL(Ec) *energumenos* < Gr *energoumenos*, prp. pass. of *energein*, to work on: see fol.⟧ **1** a person supposedly possessed by an evil spirit; demoniac **2** a fanatic; enthusiast

en·er·gy (en′ər jē) ***n.***, *pl.* **-gies** ⟦LL *energia* < Gr *energeia* < *energēs*, active, at work < *en-*, in + *ergon*, WORK⟧ **1** force of expression or utterance **2** *a)* potential forces; inherent power; capacity for vigorous action *b)* [*often pl.*] such forces or power, esp. in action [to apply all one's *energies*] **3** strength or power efficiently exerted **4** *a)* those resources, as petroleum, coal, gas, wind, nuclear fuel, and sunlight, from which energy in the form of electricity, heat, etc. can be produced *b)* the available supply of such usable resources [an *energy* shortage] **5** *Physics* the capacity for doing work: abbrev. *E*: see MATTER (sense 2) —***SYN.*** STRENGTH

energy level *Physics* a state in which the energy of a physical system is well defined by quantum mechanics

en·er·vate (en′ər vāt′; *for adj.* ē nʉr′vit, -vāt′) ***vt.*** **-vat′ed**, **-vat′ing** ⟦< L *enervatus*, pp. of *enervare* < *enervis*, nerveless, weak < *e-*, out + *nervus*, NERVE⟧ to deprive of strength, force, vigor, etc.; weaken physically, mentally, or morally; devitalize; debilitate —***adj.*** enervated; weakened —***SYN.*** UNNERVE, WEAKEN —**en′er·va′tion** ***n.*** —**en′er·va′tor** ***n.***

E·ne·sco (i nes′kō), **Georges** (zhôrzh) 1881-1955; Romanian violinist, composer, & conductor

En·e·we·tak (en′ə wē′täk) atoll in the Marshall Islands: site of U.S. atomic & hydrogen bomb tests (1948-54)

en·face (en fās′, in-) ***vt.*** **-faced′**, **-fac′ing** [Brit.] to write or print on the face of (a document, check, etc.)

en fa·mille (än fà mē′y′) ⟦Fr⟧ **1** with one's family; at home **2** in an informal way

en·fant ter·ri·ble (än fän te rē′bl′) *pl.* ***en·fants ter·ri·bles*** (än fän te rē′bl′) ⟦Fr⟧ **1** an unmanageable, mischievous child **2** anyone constantly vexing, startling, or embarrassing others, as, in the arts, by outraging conventional opinion or expectations

en·fee·ble (en fē′bəl, in-) ***vt.*** **-fee′bled**, **-fee′bling** ⟦ME *enfeblen* < OFr *enfeblir*⟧ to make feeble —**en·fee′ble·ment** ***n.***

en·feoff (en fef′, -fēf′) ***vt.*** ⟦ME *enfeffen* (Anglo-Fr *enfeoffer*) < OFr *enfeffer*: see EN-¹ & FIEF⟧ *Law* to invest with an estate held in fee —**en·feoff′ment** ***n.***

en·fet·ter (en fet′ər) ***vt.*** to bind in or as in fetters

En·field (en′fēld) borough of Greater London, England

en·fi·lade (en′fə lād′, en′fə läd′) ***n.*** ⟦Fr < *enfiler*, to thread, string, rake with fire < OFr < *en-* (L *in*) + *fil* (L *filum*), a thread⟧ **1** gunfire, from either flank, directed along the length of a column or line of troops **2** a disposition or placement of troops that makes them vulnerable to such fire —***vt.*** **-lad′ed**, **-lad′ing** to direct such gunfire at

en·fleu·rage (än′flə räzh′, *Fr* än flë ràzh′) ***n.*** ⟦Fr < *en-*, in + *fleur*, FLOWER⟧ a process of extracting perfumes by having fats absorb the exhalations of certain flowers

en·fold (en fōld′, in-) ***vt.*** **1** to wrap in folds; wrap up; envelop **2** to embrace —**en·fold′ment** ***n.***

en·force (en fôrs′, in-) ***vt.*** **-forced′**, **-forc′ing** ⟦ME *enforcen* < OFr *enforcier* < *en-*, in + *force*, FORCE⟧ **1** to give force to; urge [to *enforce* an argument by analogies] **2** to bring about or impose by force [to *enforce* one's will on a child] **3** to compel observance of (a law, etc.) —**en·force′a·ble** ***adj.*** —**en·force′ment** ***n.*** —**en·forc′er** ***n.***

en·fran·chise (en fran′chīz′, in-) ***vt.*** **-chised′**, **-chis′ing** ⟦ME *enfraunchisen* < OFr *enfranchiss-*, stem of *enfranchir*, to set free, enfranchise < *en-*, in + *franchir*, to set free < *franc*: see FRANK¹⟧ **1** to free from slavery, bondage, legal obligation, etc. **2** to give a franchise to; specif., to admit to citizenship, esp. to the right to vote —**en·fran′chise′ment** (-chīz′mənt, -chiz-) ***n.***

eng *abbrev.* **1** engine **2** engineer **3** engineering **4** engraved

Eng *abbrev.* **1** England **2** English

ENG (ē′en′jē′) ***n.*** ⟦< *e*(*lectronic*) *n*(*ews*) *g*(*athering*)⟧ the use of small TV cameras, videotape recorders, and transmission equipment in covering news events

En·ga·dine (en′gə dēn′) valley of the upper Inn River, E Switzerland: site of many resorts: *c.* 60 mi (97 km) long

en·gage (en gāj′, in-) ***vt.*** **-gaged′**, **-gag′ing** ⟦ME *engagen* < OFr *engagier*: see EN-¹ & GAGE¹⟧ **1** [Obs.] to give or assign as security for a debt, etc. **2** to bind (oneself) by a promise; pledge; specif. (now only in the passive), to bind by a promise of marriage; betroth [he is *engaged* to Ann] **3** to arrange for the services of; hire; employ [to *engage* a lawyer] **4** to arrange for the use of; reserve [to *engage* a hotel room] **5** to draw into; involve [to *engage* him in conversation] **6** to attract and hold (the attention, etc.) **7** to employ or keep busy; occupy [reading *engages* his spare time] **8** to enter into conflict with (the enemy) **9** *a)* to interlock with or cause to come into frictional driving contact with *b)* to mesh together [*engage* the gears] **10** [Obs.] to entangle; ensnare —***vi.*** **1** to pledge oneself; promise; undertake; agree [to *engage* to do something] **2** to occupy or involve oneself; take part; be active [to *engage* in dramatics] **3** to enter into conflict **4** to interlock; mesh

en·ga·gé (än gà zhā′) ***adj.*** ⟦Fr, committed < pp. of *engager*⟧ committed to supporting some aim, cause, etc.

en·gaged (en gājd′, in-) ***adj.*** **1** pledged; esp., pledged in marriage; betrothed [an *engaged* couple] 2 not at leisure; occupied; employed; busy 3 *a)* involved in combat, as troops *b)* voluntarily committed or personally involved (cf. ENGAGÉ) 4 attached to or partly set into a wall, etc. [*engaged* columns] 5 in gear; interlocked; meshed

en·gage·ment (en gāj′mənt, in-) ***n.*** 1 an engaging or being engaged; specif., *a)* a promise; pledge *b)* a promise of marriage; betrothal *c)* an arrangement to go somewhere, do something, meet someone, etc.; appointment *d)* employment or period of employment, esp. in the performing arts *e)* a conflict; battle *f)* [*usually pl.*] financial obligations; commitments *g)* state of being in gear 2 something that engages —**SYN.** BATTLE[1]

en·gag·ing (-iŋ) ***adj.*** attractive; pleasant; winning; charming —**en·gag′ing·ly** ***adv.***

en garde (än gärd′) ⟦Fr⟧ *Fencing* 1 on guard: a direction to fencers 2 the opening position from which one may either attack or defend

en·gar·land (en gär′lənd) ***vt.*** [Old Poet.] to deck or adorn with or as with a garland

En·gels[1] (eŋ′gəlz; *Ger* eŋ′əls), **Frie·drich** (frē′driH) 1820-95; Ger. socialist leader & writer, in England after 1850: close associate of Karl Marx

En·gels[2] (eŋ′gəlz) city in SC European Russia, on the Volga, opposite Saratov

en·gen·der (en jen′dər, in-) ***vt.*** ⟦ME *engendren* < OFr *engendrer* < L *ingenerare,* to beget < *in-,* in + *generare*: see GENERATE⟧ 1 [Archaic] to beget 2 to bring into being; bring about; cause; produce [pity *engendered* love] —***vi.*** [Obs.] to be produced; originate

engin *abbrev.* 1 engineer 2 engineering

en·gine (en′jən) ***n.*** ⟦ME *engin,* native talent, hence something produced by this < OFr < L *ingenium,* natural ability, genius < *in-,* in + base of *gignere,* to beget: see GENUS⟧ 1 any machine that uses energy to develop mechanical power; esp., a machine for transmitting motion to some other machine 2 a railroad locomotive 3 any instrument or machine; apparatus [*engines* of warfare, *engines* of torture] 4 FIRE ENGINE 5 [Archaic] any means or device 6 *Comput.* any software designed to perform a basic function: see also SEARCH ENGINE

engine block BLOCK (*n.* 13)

engine brake (*or* braking) a technique for slowing a vehicle by allowing compressed air to escape from the cylinders: in large vehicles powered by diesel engines, this technique can produce a loud, explosive sound

en·gi·neer (en′jə nir′) ***n.*** ⟦earlier *enginer* < ME *enginour* < OFr *engigneur*⟧ 1 [Now Rare] a person who makes engines 2 a person skilled or occupied in some branch of engineering [a mechanical *engineer*] 3 *a)* a person who operates or supervises the operation of engines or technical equipment [a locomotive *engineer,* radio *engineer*] *b)* a specialist in planning and directing operations in some technical field 4 a skillful or clever manager 5 *Mil.* a member of a military engineering unit trained in the construction and demolition of bridges, roads, airfields, etc. —***vt.*** ☆1 to plan, construct, or manage as an engineer ☆2 to plan and direct skillfully; superintend; guide (a measure, action, etc. *through*)

en·gi·neer·ing (en′jə nir′iŋ) ***n.*** 1 *a)* the science concerned with putting scientific knowledge to practical uses, divided into different branches, as civil, electrical, mechanical, and chemical engineering *b)* the planning, designing, construction, or management of machinery, roads, bridges, buildings, etc. 2 the act of maneuvering or managing

☆**engine house** a building in which engines, as fire engines, railroad locomotives, etc., are housed

en·gine·ry (en′jin rē) ***n.*** [Now Rare] engines or machinery collectively; esp., instruments of war

en·gird (en gurd′) ***vt.*** **-girt′** or **-gird′ed, -gird′ing** [Archaic] to encircle; encompass; gird: also **en·gir′dle** (-′l), **-gir′dled, -gir′dling**

en·gla·cial (en glā′shəl) ***adj.*** within a glacier

Eng·land (iŋ′glənd; *also* iŋ′lənd) ⟦ME *Englonde, Yngelonde* (with vowel change as in WING < ME *weng*) < OE *Engla land,* lit., land of the Angles (as opposed to the Saxons), hence England: see ANGLE⟧ 1 division of the United Kingdom of Great Britain & Northern Ireland, occupying most of the S half of the island of Great Britain: 50,637 sq mi (131,149 sq km); cap. London 2 England & Wales, considered an administrative unit 3 UNITED KINGDOM

Eng·lish (iŋ′glish; *also* iŋ′lish) ***adj.*** ⟦ME < OE *Englisc,* lit., of the Angles: see ANGLE & -ISH⟧ 1 of England or its people or culture 2 of the language of England and the U.S. ☆3 of or pertaining to those residents of the U.S. and Canada who are not Amish: term used by the Amish —***n.*** 1 the West Germanic language spoken by the people of England and the U.S., and in the Commonwealth, Liberia, etc. 2 the English language of a specific period or place: see AMERICAN ENGLISH, BRITISH ENGLISH, CANADIAN ENGLISH, OLD ENGLISH, MIDDLE ENGLISH, MODERN ENGLISH 3 a characteristic way of using this language [broken *English*] 4 the equivalent in the English language; English translation 5 a school course or class in the English language or its literature ☆6 [*sometimes* **e-**] *Billiards, Bowling, etc.* a spinning motion given to a ball, as by striking it on one side 7 [Archaic] a size of printing type, 14 point —***vt.*** 1 to translate into English 2 to apply the principles of English pronunciation, spelling, etc. to; Anglicize (a foreign word) ☆3 [*sometimes* **e-**] *Billiards, Bowling, etc.* to give English to (a ball) —**the English** 1 the people of England ☆2 those residents of the U.S. and Canada who are not Amish: term used by the Amish

English bulldog BULLDOG (sense 1)

English Channel arm of the Atlantic, between S England & NW France: 21-150 mi (34-241 km) wide; *c.* 350 mi (563 km) long

English cocker spaniel any of a breed of small spaniel, similar to and the progenitor of the cocker spaniel

☆**English daisy** a small perennial plant (*Bellis perennis*) of the composite family, having single stalked heads with white or pinkish ray flowers

English horn a double-reed woodwind instrument similar to the oboe but larger and a fifth lower in pitch

Eng·lish·ism (-iz′əm) ***n.*** 1 BRITICISM 2 an attachment to the British ways and things

☆**English ivy** IVY (sense 1)

Eng·lish·man (-mən) ***n.,*** *pl.* **-men** (-mən) 1 a person born or living in England, esp. a man 2 an English ship

☆**English muffin** a large, somewhat flat yeast roll, often baked on a griddle, and served split and toasted

English saddle a lightweight saddle with a low cantle and pommel and no horn, designed to place the rider's weight forward onto the withers

English setter any of a breed of setter with flat, white, silky hair spotted or speckled with black, tan, or orange and forming fringes on the neck, tail, legs, and buttocks

English sonnet SHAKESPEAREAN SONNET

☆**English sparrow** the common, small Old World sparrow (*Passer domesticus*) with brownish-gray feathers, now found extensively in North America; house sparrow

English springer spaniel any of a breed of medium-sized spaniel with a long, glossy, black-and-white or liver-and-white coat, used as a hunting dog: traditionally the tail is docked

English system ⟦because developed in England from about the 13th c.⟧ the foot-pound-second system of measurement

English toy spaniel any of a breed of small spaniel, usually with a thick mane

☆**English walnut** 1 an Asian walnut tree (*Juglans regia*) now grown in Europe and North America 2 its nut

Eng·lish·wom·an (-woom′ən) ***n.,*** *pl.* **-wom′en** (-wim′in) a woman born or living in England

en·glut (en glut′) ***vt.*** **-glut′ted, -glut′ting** ⟦OFr *englotir* < LL *ingluttire*: see EN-[1] & GLUT⟧ [Archaic] 1 to gulp down; swallow 2 to glut

en·gorge (en gôrj′, in-) ***vt.*** **-gorged′, -gorg′ing** ⟦Fr *engorger* < OFr < *en-,* in + *gorge,* GORGE⟧ 1 to gorge; glut 2 to devour greedily 3 *Med.* to congest (a blood vessel, tissue, etc.) with fluid, as blood, milk, etc. —***vi.*** to eat greedily; feed ravenously —**en·gorge′ment** ***n.***

engr *abbrev.* 1 engineer 2 engineering 3 engraved 4 engraver 5 engraving

en·graft (en graft′, -gräft′; in-) ***vt.*** 1 to graft (a shoot, etc.) from one plant onto another 2 to establish firmly; implant

en·grail (en grāl′) ***vt.*** ⟦ME *engrelen* (only in pp.) < OFr *engresler* < *en-,* in + *gresle,* slender < L *gracilis*: see GRACILE⟧ 1 to indent (an edge or rim) with concave, curved notches 2 to ornament the edge of with such a pattern —**en·grailed′** ***adj.*** —**en·grail′ment** ***n.***

en·grain (en grān′) ***vt.*** ⟦ME *engreinen* < OFr *engrainer,* to dye scarlet < *en-* (see EN-[1]) + *graine,* seed, cochineal dye; assoc. in both Fr & E with *grain* (texture): see GRAIN⟧ INGRAIN

en·gram (en′gram′) ***n.*** ⟦EN-[1] + -GRAM⟧ 1 *Biol.* a hypothetical permanent change produced by a stimulus in the protoplasm of a tissue 2 *Psychol.* a permanent effect produced in the psyche by stimulation, assumed in explaining persistence of memory —**en·gram′mic** ***adj.***

en·grave (en grāv′, in-) ***vt.*** **-graved′, -grav′ing** ⟦Fr *engraver* < *en-,* in + *graver,* to incise < OFr *grafe,* stylus < L *graphium* < Gr *graphion,* graving tool < *graphein*: see GRAPHIC⟧ 1 to cut or incise letters, designs, etc. in or on (a surface) 2 to impress deeply or permanently on the mind or memory, as though by engraving 3 to cut or incise (a picture, letters, etc.) into a metal plate, wooden block, etc. for printing 4 to print with such a plate, block, etc. 5 PHOTOENGRAVE —**en·grav′er** ***n.***

en·grav·ing (en grāv′iŋ, in-) ***n.*** 1 the act, process, or art of one who engraves 2 an engraved plate, drawing, or design 3 a print made from an engraved surface

en·gross (en grōs′, in-) ***vt.*** ⟦ME *engrossen* < OFr *engrosser,* to acquire in large quantity (< *en-,* in + *gros,* large < L *grossus*) & *engroissier,* to become thick < *en-* + *groisse,* thickness < VL **grossia* < L *grossus*: see GROSS⟧ 1 *a)* to write out in large letters of a kind once used for legal documents *b)* to make a final fair copy of (esp. a legislative bill) 2 to express formally or in legal form 3 to take the entire attention of; occupy wholly; absorb [*engrossed* in a book] 4 [Archaic] *a)* to buy all of so as to monopolize *b)* to take or require all of —**en·gross′er** ***n.*** —**en·gross′ment** ***n.***

en·gross·ing (-iŋ) ***adj.*** taking one's entire attention; very interesting; absorbing

en·gulf (en gulf′, in-) ***vt.*** ⟦EN-[1] + GULF⟧ 1 to swallow up; overwhelm 2 to plunge, as into a gulf

en·hance (en hans′, -häns′; in-) ***vt.*** **-hanced′, -hanc′ing** ⟦ME *enhauncen* < Anglo-Fr *enhauncer* < OFr *enhaucier* < VL **inaltiare* < *in-,* EN-[1] + **altiare,* to raise < L *altus,* high⟧ 1 to make greater, as in cost, value, attractiveness, etc.; heighten; augment 2 to improve the quality or condition of 3 to improve electronically the quality or clarity of (a photograph or other image) as by means of a computer —**SYN.** INTENSIFY —**en·hance′ment** ***n.*** —**en·hanc′er** ***n.***

en·har·mon·ic (en′här män′ik) ***adj.*** ⟦L *enharmonicus* < Gr *enarmonikos*: see EN-[1] & HARMONY⟧ in equal temperament, designating or of tones, as C♯ and D♭, that are identical in pitch but are written differently according to the key in which each occurs: enharmonic tones are especially important in instruments of fixed pitch, as the piano —**en′har·mon′i·cal·ly** ***adv.***

E·nid (ē′nid) ***n.*** ⟦prob. < OWelsh *enaid*, soul, used as term of endearment⟧ **1** a feminine name **2** *Arthurian Legend* the wife of Geraint: she is a model of constancy

e·nig·ma (i nig′mə, e-) ***n.*** ⟦L *aenigma* < Gr *ainigma* < *ainissesthai*, to speak in riddles < *ainos*, tale, story < ? IE base **ai-*, **oi-*, meaningful speech > ? MIr *ōeth*, OATH⟧ **1** a perplexing, usually ambiguous, statement; riddle **2** a perplexing, baffling, or seemingly inexplicable matter, person, etc. —***SYN.*** MYSTERY[1]

en·ig·mat·ic (en′ig mat′ik; *also* ē′nig-) ***adj.*** ⟦Fr *énigmatique* < LL *aenigmaticus*⟧ of or like an enigma; perplexing; baffling: also **e′nig·mat′i·cal** —***SYN.*** OBSCURE —**e′nig·mat′i·cal·ly** ***adv.***

en·isle (en īl′) ***vt.*** **-isled′**, **-isl′ing** [Old Poet.] **1** to make into or like an island **2** to place on or as on an island; isolate

En·i·we·tok (en′ə wē′täk′) *former sp. of* ENEWETAK

en·jamb·ment or **en·jambe·ment** (en jam′mənt) ***n.*** ⟦Fr *enjambement* < *enjamber*, to encroach < *en-* (see EN-[1]) + *jambe*, leg: see JAMB⟧ *Prosody* the use of a RUN-ON line of verse: cf. END-STOPPED

en·join (en join′, in-) ***vt.*** ⟦ME *enjoinen* < OFr *enjoindre* < L *injungere*, to join into, put upon < *in-*, in + *jungere*, JOIN⟧ **1** to urge or impose with authority; order; enforce [to *enjoin* silence on a class] **2** to prohibit, esp. by legal injunction; forbid [the company was *enjoined* from using false advertising] **3** to order (someone) authoritatively to do something, esp. by legal injunction —***SYN.*** COMMAND, FORBID

en·join·der (-dər) ***n.*** anything imposed, enforced, or prohibited by an injunction

en·joy (en joi′, in-) ***vt.*** ⟦ME *enjoien* < OFr *enjoir* < *en-*, in + *joir*, to rejoice < L *gaudere*, to be glad: see JOY⟧ **1** to have or experience with joy; get pleasure from; relish **2** to have the use or benefit of; have as one's lot or advantage [the book *enjoyed* large sales] —***vi.*** to have or experience something with pleasure: often used imperatively —**enjoy oneself** to have a good time; have pleasure

en·joy·a·ble (-ə bəl) ***adj.*** giving or capable of giving enjoyment; pleasurable —***SYN.*** PLEASANT —**en·joy′a·ble·ness** ***n.*** —**en·joy′a·bly** ***adv.***

en·joy·ment (en joi′mənt, in-) ***n.*** **1** the act or state of enjoying; specif., *a)* the possession, use, or benefit of something *b)* a pleasurable experiencing of something **2** something enjoyed **3** pleasure; gratification; joy —***SYN.*** PLEASURE

en·keph·a·lin (en kef′ə lin) ***n.*** an endorphin that occurs at nerve endings and may serve as a neurotransmitter

en·kin·dle (en kin′dəl, in-) ***vt.*** **-dled**, **-dling** **1** to set on fire; make blaze up **2** to stir up; arouse; excite

enl *abbrev.* **1** enlarged **2** enlisted

en·lace (en lās′, in-) ***vt.*** **-laced′**, **-lac′ing** ⟦ME *enlacen* < OFr *enlacer* < *en-*, in + *lacer*, to tie, tangle < L *laqueare* < *laqueus*, a noose: see LACE⟧ **1** to wind about as with a lace or laces; encircle; enfold **2** to entangle; interlace **3** to cover as with lace or netting —**en·lace′ment** ***n.***

en·large (en lärj′, in-) ***vt.*** **-larged′**, **-larg′ing** ⟦ME *enlargen* < OFr *enlargier*: see EN-[1] & LARGE⟧ **1** to make larger; increase in size, volume, extent, etc.; broaden; expand **2** *Photog.* to reproduce on a larger scale —***vi.*** **1** to become larger; increase in size, extent, etc.; expand **2** to speak or write at greater length or in greater detail; expatiate (*on* or *upon*) —***SYN.*** INCREASE —**en·larg′er** ***n.***

en·large·ment (-mənt) ***n.*** **1** an enlarging or being enlarged **2** something that enlarges by being added **3** a reproduction, as of a photograph, on a larger scale

en·light·en (en līt′'n, in-) ***vt.*** **1** *a)* to give the light of fact and knowledge to; free from ignorance, prejudice, or superstition *b)* *Religion* to give spiritual insight and understanding to **2** to make clear to (a person) the facts or nature of something; inform **3** [Archaic] to light up; illuminate —**en·light′en·er** ***n.***

en·light·en·ment (-mənt) ***n.*** an enlightening or being enlightened —**the Enlightenment** **1** a mainly 18th-cent. European philosophical movement characterized by a reliance on reason and experience rather than dogma and tradition and by an emphasis on humanitarian political goals and social progress **2** the period of this movement: also **Age of Enlightenment**

en·list (en list′, in-) ***vt.*** **1** to enroll for service in some branch of the armed forces **2** to win the support of; get the help or services of [to *enlist* men in a cause] **3** to get (another's help, support, aid, etc.) —***vi.*** **1** to join some branch of the armed forces **2** to join or support a cause or movement: with *in* —**en·list·ee** (en lis′tē, in-; en′lis tē′, in′-) ***n.***

en·list·ed (-lis′tid) ***adj.*** of or having to do with a person in the armed forces who is not a commissioned officer or warrant officer

en·list·ment (en list′mənt, in-) ***n.*** **1** an enlisting or being enlisted ☆**2** the period of time for which one enlists

en·liv·en (en lī′vən, in-) ***vt.*** to make active, vivacious, interesting, or cheerful; liven up or brighten —**en·liv′en·er** ***n.*** —**en·liv′en·ment** ***n.***

en masse (än mäs′, en mas′) ⟦Fr, lit., in mass⟧ in a group; as a whole; all together

en·mesh (en mesh′, in-) ***vt.*** to catch in or as in the meshes of a net; entangle

en·mi·ty (en′mə tē) ***n.***, *pl.* **-ties** ⟦ME *enemite* < OFr *enemistie* < VL **inimicitas* < L *inimicus*: see ENEMY⟧ the bitter attitude or feelings of an enemy or of mutual enemies; hostility; antagonism

SYN.—**enmity** denotes a strong, settled feeling of hatred, whether concealed, displayed, or latent; **hostility** usually suggests enmity expressed in active opposition, attacks, etc.; **animosity** suggests bitterness of feeling that tends to break out in open hostility; **antagonism** stresses the mutual hostility or enmity of persons, forces, etc.

en·ne·ad (en′ē ad′) ***n.*** ⟦Gr *enneas* (gen. *enneados*) < *ennea*, NINE⟧ a group or set of nine (books, gods, etc.)

en·no·ble (e nō′bəl, i-) ***vt.*** **-bled**, **-bling** ⟦ME *ennoblen* (only in pp.) < OFr *ennoblir*: see EN-[1] & NOBLE⟧ **1** to raise to the rank of nobleman **2** to give a noble quality to; dignify —**en·no′ble·ment** ***n.*** —**en·no′bler** ***n.***

en·nui (än′wē′, än wē′) ***n.*** ⟦Fr: see ANNOY⟧ weariness and dissatisfaction resulting from inactivity or lack of interest; boredom

E·noch (ē′näk′, -nək) ***n.*** ⟦Gr *Enōch* < Heb *chanoch*, lit., dedicated⟧ **1** a masculine name **2** *Bible* *a)* the eldest son of Cain: Gen. 4:17 *b)* the father of Methuselah: Gen. 5:21

e·no·ki (e nō′kē) ***n.*** ⟦Jpn *enoki(take)* < *enoki*, hackberry + *take*, mushroom⟧ an edible mushroom (*Flammulina velutipes*) with a long, slender stem, a small, yellowish cap, and yellowish gills: also **e·no·ki·ta·ke** (e nō′kē tä′kē)

e·nol (ē′nôl′, -nōl′) ***n.*** ⟦< -ENE + -OL[1]⟧ the form of a tautomeric compound containing the group C:C(OH) —**e·nol′ic** (-näl′ik, -nō′lik) ***adj.***

e·nol·o·gy (ē näl′ə jē) ***n.*** ⟦< Gr *oinos*, wine (akin to *oinē*, VINE) + -LOGY⟧ OENOLOGY —**e·nol′o·gist** ***n.*** —**e·no·log·i·cal** (ē′nə läj′i kəl) ***adj.***

e·no·phile (ē′nə fīl′) ***n.*** *alt. sp. of* OENOPHILE

e·nor·mi·ty (ē nôr′mə tē, i-) ***n.*** ⟦Fr *enormité* < L *enormitas* < *enormis*, irregular, immoderate, immense < *e-*, out + *norma*, rule: see NORM⟧ **1** great wickedness [the *enormity* of a crime] **2** *pl.* **-ties** a monstrous or outrageous act; very wicked crime **3** enormous size or extent; vastness: in modern use, considered a loose usage by some

e·nor·mous (ē nôr′məs, i-) ***adj.*** ⟦ME *enormyouse* < L *enormis* (see prec.) + -OUS⟧ **1** very much exceeding the usual size, number, or degree; of great size; huge; vast; immense **2** [Archaic] very wicked; outrageous —**e·nor′mous·ly** ***adv.*** —**e·nor′mous·ness** ***n.***

SYN.—**enormous** implies an exceeding by far what is normal in size, amount, or degree [an *enormous* nose, *enormous* expenses]; **immense**, basically implying immeasurability, suggests size beyond the regular run of measurements but does not connote abnormality in that which is very large [redwoods are *immense* trees]; **huge** usually suggests an immense mass or bulk [a *huge* building, *huge* profits]; **gigantic**, **colossal**, and **mammoth** basically imply a likeness to specific objects of great size (respectively, a giant, the Colossus of Rhodes, and the huge, extinct elephant) and therefore emphasize the idea of great magnitude, force, importance, etc., now often hyperbolically; **tremendous**, literally suggesting that which inspires awe or amazement because of its great size, is also used loosely as an intensive term

E·nos (ē′nəs) ***n.*** ⟦Gr *Enōs* < Heb *enosh*, lit., man, mankind⟧ **1** a masculine name **2** *Bible* a son of Seth: Gen. 4:26

e·no·sis (e nō′sis) ***n.*** ⟦ModGr⟧ union; specif., the proposed political union of Cyprus and Greece

e·nough (ē nuf′, i-) ***adj.*** ⟦ME *inough* < OE *genoh* < Gmc comp. (seen also in Ger *genug-*, ON *gnogr*, Goth *ganohs*) < *ge-*, intens. + **noh*, enough < IE base **enek-*, **nek-*, to attain, achieve > L *nactus*, attained, Sans *nákṣati*, (he) attains⟧ as much or as many as necessary, desirable, or tolerable; sufficient —***n.*** the amount or number needed, desired, or allowed; sufficiency —***adv.*** **1** as much or as often as necessary; to the required degree or amount; sufficiently **2** fully; quite [oddly *enough*] **3** just adequately; tolerably; fairly [he played well *enough*] —***SYN.*** SUFFICIENT —**enough said** [Informal] no further explanation or discussion is needed

e·nounce (ē nouns′, i-) ***vt.*** **e·nounced′**, **e·nounc′ing** ⟦Fr *énoncer* < L *enuntiare*⟧ ENUNCIATE

☆**E·no·vid** (ē′nō vid, -nə-) ***n.*** ⟦former trademark: arbitrary coinage, based on EN-[1] & OVI- & -ID⟧ a hormonal compound formerly used to regulate the menstrual cycle and as an oral contraceptive

e·now (ē nou′, i-; -nō′) ***adj.***, ***n.***, ***adv.*** ⟦ME *ynoghe*, *inou* < OE *genog*, early form of *genoh* (see ENOUGH): considered in Scot dial. as pl.⟧ [Archaic] enough

en pas·sant (än pä sän′; *E* än′pə sänt′, en′-) ⟦Fr⟧ in passing; by the way: used, in chess, of the capture of a pawn which has just taken a first move of two squares, passing an opponent's pawn that dominates the first of those squares and that makes the capture by moving to that square

en·phy·tot·ic (en′fī tät′ik) ***adj.*** ⟦< EN-[2] + Gr *phyton*, a plant (see -PHYTE) + -IC⟧ affecting certain plants of an area at regular intervals: said of various diseases: see EPIPHYTOTIC

en·plane (en plān′, in-) ***vi.*** **-planed′**, **-plan′ing** ⟦EN-[1] + PLANE[4], after ENTRAIN[1]⟧ to board an airplane

en prise (än prēz′; *E* än prēz′, en-) ⟦Fr, lit., within grasp < *en*, in + *prise*, a taking hold⟧ *Chess* in a position to be taken

en·quire (en kwīr′, in-) ***vt.***, ***vi.*** **-quired′**, **-quir′ing** INQUIRE —**en·quir·y** (en kwīr′ē, in-; en′kwī rē, in′-) ***n.***, *pl.* **-quir′ies**

en·rage (en rāj′, in-) ***vt.*** **-raged′**, **-rag′ing** ⟦OFr *enrager*⟧ to put into a rage; make very angry; infuriate —**en·rag′ed·ly** (-rā′jid lē) ***adv.*** —**en·rage′ment** ***n.***

en rap·port (än rà pôr′; *E* än′rə pôr′) ⟦Fr, in harmony < *en*, in + *rapport*, agreement: see RAPPORT⟧ in a mutually understanding and harmonious relationship; in accord

en·rapt (en rapt′, in-) ***adj.*** enraptured; rapt

en·rap·ture (en rap′chər, in-) ***vt.*** **-tured**, **-tur·ing** to fill with great pleasure or delight; entrance; enchant: also **en·rav′ish** (-rav′ish)

en·reg·is·ter (en rej′is tər) *vt.* ⟦Fr *enregistrer*⟧ to enter in a register; enroll; record

en rè·gle (än re′gl') ⟦Fr⟧ in proper form or order

en·rich (en rich′, in-) *vt.* ⟦ME *enrichen* < OFr *enrichier*⟧ to make rich or richer; specif., *a)* to give more wealth to *b)* to give greater value, importance, effectiveness, etc. to [to *enrich* a curriculum] *c)* to decorate; adorn *d)* to fertilize (soil) *e)* to add vitamins, minerals, etc. to (bread, flour, etc.) so as to increase the nutritional value *f)* to concentrate (a radioactive isotope) in the making of nuclear fuel —**en·rich′ment** *n.*

en·robe (en rōb′, in-) *vt.* **-robed′**, **-rob′ing** to dress in or as in a robe

en·roll (en rōl′, in-) *vt.* **-rolled′**, **-roll′ing** ⟦ME *enrollen* < OFr *enroller*: see EN-[1] & ROLL⟧ **1** to record in a list **2** to enlist **3** to accept as or cause to be a member **4** [Archaic] to roll up; wrap up ☆**5** to make a final fair copy of (a bill passed by a legislature) —*vi.* to enroll oneself or become enrolled; register; enlist; become a member Also [Chiefly Brit.] **en·rol′ -rolled′**, **-roll′ing**

en·roll·ee (en′rōl ē′, en rōl′ē) *n.* a person who is enrolled

en·roll·ment or **en·rol·ment** (en rōl′mənt, in-) *n.* **1** an enrolling or being enrolled **2** a list of those enrolled **3** the number of those enrolled

en·root (en ro͞ot′, in-) *vt.* ⟦EN-[1] + ROOT[1]⟧ to implant firmly or deeply: used chiefly in the passive

en route (än ro͞ot′, en-) ⟦Fr⟧ on the way; along the way

ens (enz) *n.* ⟦LL *ens* (gen. *entis*), a being < prp. of *esse*, to be⟧ *Philos.* abstract being; existence, in the most general sense

Ens *abbrev.* Ensign

en·sam·ple (en sam′pəl) *n.* ⟦ME *ensaumple* < OFr *ensample*: see EXAMPLE⟧ [Archaic] EXAMPLE

en·san·guine (en saŋ′gwin) *vt.* **-guined**, **-guin·ing** ⟦EN-[1] + SANGUINE⟧ to stain with blood; make bloody

En·sche·de (en′skə dā′) city in E Netherlands, near the German border

en·sconce (en skäns′, in-) *vt.* **-sconced′**, **-sconc′ing** ⟦EN-[1] + SCONCE[2]⟧ **1** [Now Rare] to hide; conceal; shelter **2** to place or settle comfortably, snugly, or securely [to *ensconce* oneself in an armchair]

en·sem·ble (än säm′bəl) *n.* ⟦Fr < OFr, together < L *insimul*, at the same time < *in-*, in + *simul*, at the same time: see SAME⟧ **1** all the parts considered as a whole; total effect **2** a whole costume, esp. one of matching or complementary articles of dress **3** *a)* a company of actors, dancers, etc., or all but the featured stars *b)* their performance together **4** *Music a)* a small group of musicians playing or singing together *b)* the instruments or voices constituting such a group *c)* the performance together of such a group, or of all the members of an orchestra, chorus, etc.

En·se·na·da (en′sə näd′ə) seaport in N Baja California, Mexico, on the Pacific

en·sheathe (en shēth′) *vt.* **-sheathed′**, **-sheath′ing** to put in or cover with or as with a sheath

en·shrine (en shrīn′, in-) *vt.* **-shrined′**, **-shrin′ing** **1** to enclose in or as in a shrine **2** to hold as sacred; cherish [*enshrined* in memory] —**en·shrine′ment** *n.*

en·shroud (en shroud′, in-) *vt.* to cover as if with a shroud; hide; veil; obscure

en·si·form (en′si fôrm′) *adj.* ⟦< L *ensis*, sword (< IE **nsi-s* > Sans *así-*) + -FORM⟧ sword-shaped, as an iris leaf; xiphoid

en·sign (en′sən; *chiefly Brit*, -sīn′) *n.* ⟦ME & OFr *enseigne* < L *insignia*: see INSIGNIA⟧ **1** a badge, symbol, or token of office or authority **2** a flag or banner; specif., a national flag, as one displayed on a ship **3** [Historical] *Brit. Army* a commissioned officer who served as standard-bearer ☆**4** ⟦after Fr *enseigne de vaisseau*, ship's ensign, midshipman⟧ *U.S. Navy* a commissioned officer of the lowest rank, ranking just below a lieutenant junior grade —**en′sign·ship** *n.*, **en′sign·cy**

en·si·lage (en′sə lij) *n.* ⟦Fr < *ensiler*, to preserve in an underground granary < *en-* + *silo*: see SILO⟧ **1** the preserving of green fodder by storage in a silo **2** SILAGE —*vt.* **-laged**, **-lag·ing** ENSILE

en·sile (en sīl′, en′sīl′) *vt.* **-siled′**, **-sil′ing** ⟦Fr *ensiler*: see prec.⟧ to store (green fodder) in a silo, or orig. a pit, for preservation

en·slave (en slāv′, in-) *vt.* **-slaved′**, **-slav′ing** **1** to put into slavery; make a slave of **2** to dominate; subjugate —**en·slave′ment** *n.* —**en·slav′er** *n.*

en·snare (en sner′, in-) *vt.* **-snared′**, **-snar′ing** to catch in or as in a snare; trap —**en·snare′ment** *n.*

en·snarl (en snärl′, in-) *vt.* to draw into a snarl or tangle

En·sor (en′sôr′), **James Sydney** 1860-1949; Belgian painter

en·sor·cell or **en·sor·cel** (en sôr′səl) *vt.* **-celled** or **-celed**, **-cell·ing** or **-cel·ing** ⟦OFr *ensorceler*, for **ensorcerer*: see EN-[1] & SORCERY⟧ [Literary] to bewitch

en·soul (en sōl′) *vt.* **1** to take or put into the soul **2** to endow with a soul —**en·soul′ment** *n.*

en·sphere (en sfir′) *vt.* **-sphered′**, **-spher′ing** to enclose in or as in a sphere

en·sta·tite (en′stə tīt′) *n.* ⟦Ger *enstatit* < Gr *enstatēs*, opponent + Ger *-it*, -ITE[1]: from its refractory nature⟧ a hard, brittle, orthorhombic pyroxene, $MgSiO_3$, found in igneous rocks and in meteorites; magnesium silicate

en·sue (en so͞o′, -syo͞o′; in-) *vi.* **-sued′**, **-su′ing** ⟦ME *ensuen* < stem of OFr *ensuivre* < VL **insequere* < L *insequi* < *in-* + *sequi*, to follow: see SEQUENT⟧ **1** to come afterward; follow immediately **2** to happen as a consequence; result —*vt.* [Archaic] to strive for; follow; pursue —**SYN.** FOLLOW

en suite (än swēt′, en-) ⟦Fr⟧ **1** in, or as part of, a series, set, or unit **2** [Brit.] being part of a suite of rooms [hotel accommodations with a bathroom *en suite*]

en·sure (en shoor′, in-) *vt.* **-sured′**, **-sur′ing** ⟦ME *ensuren* < Anglo-Fr *enseurer* (for OFr *asseurer*: see ASSURE) < *en-* (see EN-[1]) + OFr *seur*, SURE⟧ **1** to make sure or certain; guarantee; secure [measures to *ensure* accuracy] **2** to make safe; protect [safety devices to *ensure* workers against accidents] **3** *obs. var. of* INSURE (sense 1)

en·swathe (en swäth′, -swāth′) *vt.* **-swathed′**, **-swath′ing** to wrap or bind in or as in a bandage; swathe

ENT *abbrev. Med.* ear, nose, and throat

ent- (ent) *combining form* ENTO-: used before a vowel

-ent (ənt, ′nt) ⟦< OFr *-ent*, L *-ens* (gen. *-entis*), stem ending of certain present participles⟧ *suffix* **1** *forming adjectives* that has, shows, or does [*insistent*] **2** *forming nouns* a person or thing that [*superintendent, solvent*] See also -ANT

en·tab·la·ture (en tab′lə chər) *n.* ⟦MFr < It *intavolatura* < *intavolare* < *in-*, in + *tavola*, table, base < L *tabula*: see TABLE⟧ *Archit.* **1** a horizontal superstructure supported by columns and composed of architrave, frieze, and cornice **2** any structure like this

CORNICE
FRIEZE
ARCHI-TRAVE

entablature

en·ta·ble·ment (en tā′bəl mənt) *n.* ⟦Fr < OFr < *entabler*: see EN-[1], TABLE, & -MENT⟧ **1** *obs. var. of* ENTABLATURE **2** the platform or series of platforms directly beneath a statue and on top of the dado and the base

en·tail (en tāl′, in-) *vt.* ⟦ME *entailen* < *en-*, in + *taile, talie*, an agreement < OFr *taillié*, pp. of *taillier*, to cut: see TAILOR⟧ **1** *Law* to limit the inheritance of (real property) to a specific line or class of heirs **2** to cause or require as a necessary consequence; involve; necessitate [the plan *entails* work] —*n.* **1** an entailing or being entailed **2** that which is entailed, as an estate **3** necessary sequence, as the order of descent for an entailed inheritance —**en·tail′ment** *n.*

en·ta·me·ba (en′tə mē′bə) *n.* ⟦ModL: see ENTO- & AMOEBA⟧ any of a genus (*Entamoeba*) of amoebas parasitic in vertebrates, esp. a species (*E. histolytica*) causing amoebic dysentery: see ENDAMEBA

en·tan·gle (en taŋ′gəl, in-) *vt.* **-gled**, **-gling** **1** to involve in or as in a tangle; catch, as in a net, vine, etc., so that escape is difficult; ensnare **2** to involve in difficulty **3** to confuse mentally; perplex **4** to cause to be tangled or confused; complicate —**en·tan′gle·ment** *n.*

en·ta·sis (en′tə sis) *n.*, *pl.* **-ses′** (-sēz′) ⟦ModL < Gr *entasis*, lit., a stretching < *enteinein*, to stretch tight < *en-*, in + *teinein*: see THIN⟧ *Archit.* a slight, convex swelling in the shaft of a column: it prevents the illusion of concavity produced by a perfectly straight shaft

En·teb·be (en teb′ə, -ē) city in S Uganda, on Lake Victoria: capital of Uganda when it was a British protectorate (1894-1962)

en·tel·e·chy (en tel′i kē) *n.*, *pl.* **-chies** ⟦< L *entelechia* < Gr *entelecheia*, actuality < *en telei echein*, to be complete < *en*, in + *telei*, dat. of *telos*, end, completion + *echein*, to hold: see SCHEME⟧ **1** in Aristotelian philosophy, the actualization of potentiality or of essence **2** in vitalism, the inherent force which controls and directs the activities and development of a living being

en·tel·lus (en tel′əs) *n.*, *pl.* **-lus·es** ⟦ModL, after *Entellus*, ancient Sicilian athletic hero⟧ HANUMAN

en·tente (än tänt′; *Fr* än tänt′) *n.* ⟦Fr < OFr < *entendre*, to understand: see INTENT⟧ **1** an understanding or agreement, as between nations **2** the parties to this

en·ter (ent′ər) *vt.* ⟦ME *entren* < OFr *entrer* < L *intrare* < *intra*, within, inside: see INTRA-⟧ **1** to come or go in or into **2** to force a way into; penetrate; pierce [the bullet *entered* his body] **3** to put into; insert **4** to write down in a record, list, diary, etc.; make an entry of **5** *a)* to list as a participant in a competition, race, etc. *b)* to become a participant in (a contest) **6** to join; become a part or member of (a political party, school, club, etc.) **7** to get (a person, etc.) admitted **8** to start upon; begin [to *enter* a career] **9** to present for consideration; submit, esp. formally or officially [to *enter* a protest] **10** to register (a ship or cargo) at a customhouse **11** to input (data, a password, etc.) into a computer or other electronic device **12** *Law a)* to place on record before a court *b)* to go upon or into (land or property) and take possession ☆*c)* to file a claim for (a parcel of public land) —*vi.* **1** to come or go into some place; make an entrance: also used as a stage direction meaning "he (or she) comes, or they come, on stage" **2** to pierce; penetrate —**enter into** **1** to engage in; take part in [to *enter into* a conversation] **2** to form a part or component of; be or become a factor in **3** to deal with; discuss **4** to sympathize with; appreciate and share [to *enter into* the spirit of an occasion] —**enter on** (or **upon**) **1** to begin; set out on; start **2** to begin to possess or enjoy; take possession of

en·ter·ic (en ter′ik) *adj.* **1** intestinal; of the enteron: also **en·ter·al** (en′tər əl) **2** *Pharmacy* designating or of a tablet or capsule with a protective coating that delays the release of the medicine until it enters the small intestines

enteric fever *former term for* TYPHOID

en·ter·i·tis (ent′ər īt′is) *n.* ⟦fol. + -ITIS⟧ inflammation of the intestine, esp. the small intestine

en·ter·o- (en′tər ō′, -tər ə) ⟦< Gr *enteron*, intestine: see INTER-⟧ *combining form* intestine [*enterocolitis*]: also, often before a vowel, **enter-**

en·ter·o·bac·te·ri·um (en′tər ō bak tir′ē əm) *n.*, *pl.* **-ri·a** (-ē ə) any of a family (Enterobacteriaceae) of Gram-negative, rod-shaped bacteria that includes normally occurring and pathogenic intestinal bacteria, as E. coli and salmonella

en·ter·o·bi·a·sis (en′tər ō′bī′ə sis) ***n.*** ⟦ModL < *Enterobius*, name of the genus (< ENTERO- + Gr *bios*, life: see BIO-) + -IASIS⟧ infestation with pinworms

en·ter·o·coc·cus (-käk′əs) ***n., pl.*** **-coc′ci′** (-käk′sī′) ⟦ModL < ENTERO- + -COCCUS⟧ a streptococcus normally present in the intestinal tract, that may be a cause of disease when found in other parts of the body —**en′ter·o·coc′cal** (-käk′əl) ***adj.***

en·ter·o·coele or **en·ter·o·coel** (en′tər ō sēl′) ***n.*** ⟦ENTERO- + -COELE⟧ a coelomic cavity, as in starfishes and sea urchins, formed from a pouchlike outward fold of the wall of the archenteron

en·ter·o·co·li·tis (en′tər ō′kō līt′is) ***n.*** ⟦ModL < ENTERO- + COLITIS⟧ inflammation of the colon and the small intestine

en·ter·o·gas·trone (-gas′trōn′) ***n.*** ⟦ENTERO- + GASTR- + -ONE⟧ a hormone secreted by the upper intestinal mucosa, that inhibits the secretion of gastric juice and stomach movements, thereby slowing digestion, esp. of fats

en·ter·o·ki·nase (-kī′nās′, -kin′ās′) ***n.*** ⟦Ger < *entero-*, ENTERO- + *kinase* < *kin(etisch)*, KINETIC + *-ase*, -ASE⟧ an enzyme produced by the small intestine that transforms trypsinogen into trypsin

en·ter·on (en′tər än′, -ən) ***n.*** ⟦Gr *enteron*: see INTER-⟧ the alimentary canal

en·ter·os·to·my (en′tər äs′tə mē) ***n., pl.*** **-mies** ⟦ENTERO- + -STOMY⟧ the surgical operation of making an artificial opening into the intestine through the abdominal wall, as for drainage

en·ter·o·vi·rus (en′tər ō′vī′rəs) ***n.*** ⟦ENTERO- + VIRUS⟧ any of a genus (*Enterovirus*) of picornaviruses, including the polioviruses, echoviruses, and coxsackieviruses

en·ter·prise (ent′ər prīz′) ***n.*** ⟦ME < OFr *entreprise* < fem. pp. of *entreprendre*, to undertake < *entre-* (L *inter*), in, between + *prendre* < L *prehendere*: see PREHENSILE⟧ **1** an undertaking; project; specif., *a)* a bold, difficult, dangerous, or important undertaking *b)* a business venture or company **2** willingness to undertake new or risky projects; energy and initiative **3** active participation in projects

En·ter·prise (ent′ər prīz′) town in SE Nev., near Las Vegas

en·ter·pris·er (-prī′zər) ***n.*** ENTREPRENEUR

enterprise zone a depressed urban area in which employers receive tax reductions or other incentives for establishing businesses and employing the disadvantaged

en·ter·pris·ing (ent′ər prī′ziŋ) ***adj.*** ⟦< archaic v. *enterprise*, to undertake < the n.⟧ showing enterprise; full of energy and initiative; willing to undertake new projects —***SYN.*** AMBITIOUS —**en′ter·pris′ing·ly** ***adv.***

en·ter·tain (ent′ər tān′) ***vt.*** ⟦ME *entretinen* < OFr *entretenir*, to maintain, hold together < *entre* (L *inter*), between + *tenir* < L *tenere*, to hold: see THIN⟧ **1** [Archaic] to keep up; maintain **2** to hold the interest of and give pleasure to; divert; amuse **3** to give hospitality to; have as a guest **4** to allow oneself to think about; have in mind; consider [to *entertain* an idea] —***vi.*** to give hospitality to guests —***SYN.*** AMUSE

en·ter·tain·er (-ər) ***n.*** a person who entertains others, esp. professionally; a popular singer, dancer, comedian, etc.

en·ter·tain·ing (-iŋ) ***adj.*** interesting and pleasurable; diverting; amusing —**en′ter·tain′ing·ly** ***adv.***

en·ter·tain·ment (ent′ər tān′mənt) ***n.*** ⟦ME & OFr *entretenement*⟧ **1** an entertaining or being entertained **2** something that entertains; interesting, diverting, or amusing thing; esp., a show or performance

entertainment center any of various free-standing cabinets with adjustable shelves and compartments for holding video and audio devices and materials, as a TV, a DVD player, CDs, etc.

en·thal·py (en thal′pē, en′thəl pē) ***n.*** ⟦Gr *enthalpein*, to warm in (< *en-*, EN-[2] < *en*, IN[1] + *thalpein*, to heat) + -Y[4]⟧ a measure of the energy content of a system per unit mass

en·thrall or **en·thral** (en thrôl′, in-) ***vt.*** **-thralled′, -thrall′ing** ⟦ME *enthrallen*: see EN-[1] & THRALL⟧ **1** [Now Rare] to make a slave of; enslave **2** to hold as if in a spell; captivate; fascinate —**en·thrall′ment** ***n.***, **en·thral′ment**

en·throne (en thrōn′, in-) ***vt.*** **-throned′, -thron′ing 1** to place on a throne; make a king or bishop of **2** to accord the highest place to; exalt —**en·throne′ment** ***n.***

☆**en·thuse** (en tho͞oz′, -thyo͞oz′; in-) [Informal] ***vi.*** **-thused′, -thus′ing** ⟦back-form. < fol.⟧ to express enthusiasm —***vt.*** to make enthusiastic

en·thu·si·asm (en tho͞o′zē az′əm, -thyo͞o′-; in-) ***n.*** ⟦Gr *enthousiasmos* < *enthousiazein*, to be inspired, be possessed by a god, inspire < *enthous*, *entheos*, possessed by a god < *en-*, in + *theos*, god: see THEO-⟧ **1** [Historical] supernatural inspiration or possession; inspired prophetic or poetic ecstasy **2** [Obs.] religious fanaticism **3** intense or eager interest; zeal; fervor **4** something arousing such interest or zeal —***SYN.*** PASSION

en·thu·si·ast (-ast′, -əst) ***n.*** ⟦Gr *enthousiastēs*⟧ a person full of enthusiasm; specif., *a)* [Archaic] a religious fanatic or zealot *b)* an ardent supporter —***SYN.*** ZEALOT

en·thu·si·as·tic (en tho͞o′zē as′tik, -thyo͞o′-; in-) ***adj.*** ⟦Gr *enthousiastikos*⟧ **1** having or showing enthusiasm; ardent **2** of, or having the nature of, enthusiasm —**en·thu′si·as′ti·cal·ly** ***adv.***

en·thy·meme (en′thi mēm′) ***n.*** ⟦L *enthymema* < Gr *enthymēma* < *enthymeisthai*, to consider, reflect upon < *en-*, in + *thymos*, mind < IE **dhūmos* < base **dheu-* > DULL⟧ *Logic* a syllogism in which one of the premises or the conclusion is not expressed but implied —**en′thy·me·mat′ic** (-thə mē mat′ik) ***adj.***

en·tice (en tīs′, in-) ***vt.*** **-ticed′, -tic′ing** ⟦ME *enticen* < OFr *enticier*, to set afire, hence excite, entice, prob. < VL **intitiare* < L *in* + *titio*, a burning brand⟧ to attract by offering hope of reward or pleasure; tempt; allure —***SYN.*** LURE —**en·tice′ment** ***n.*** —**en·tic′er** ***n.*** —**en·tic′ing·ly** ***adv.***

en·tire (en tīr′, in-) ***adj.*** ⟦ME *enter* < OFr *entier* < L *integer*, whole, untouched, undiminished: see INTEGER⟧ **1** *a)* not lacking any of the parts; whole *b)* complete; thorough; absolute [*entire* confidence] **2** unbroken; intact **3** being wholly of one piece; undivided; continuous **4** not castrated **5** [Obs.] not mixed or alloyed; pure **6** *Bot.* having an unbroken margin, without notches or indentations, as some leaves —***n.*** **1** [Now Rare] the whole; entirety **2** a stallion —***SYN.*** COMPLETE —**en·tire′ness** ***n.***

en·tire·ly (en tīr′lē, in-) ***adv.*** **1** wholly; completely; totally; fully **2** solely; only

en·tire·ty (en tīr′tē, in-) ***n., pl.*** **-ties** ⟦ME *enterete* < OFr *entiereté*⟧ **1** the state or fact of being entire; wholeness; completeness **2** an entire thing; whole; total **3** *Law* undivided or sole possession —**in its entirety** as a whole; completely

en·ti·tle (en tīt′'l, in-) ***vt.*** **-tled, -tling** ⟦ME *entitlen* < OFr *entituler* < LL *intitulare* < L *in*, in + *titulus*, TITLE⟧ **1** to give a title or name to **2** to honor or dignify by a title **3** to give a right or legal title to; qualify (a person) *to* something

en·ti·tle·ment (-mənt) ***n.*** **1** the condition or state of being entitled **2** something to which a person is entitled; specif., any of various benefits provided to qualifying persons under certain government programs, as Medicare

en·ti·ty (en′tə tē) ***n.*** ⟦< Fr *entité* or ML *entitas* < L *ens* (gen. *entis*), prp. of *esse*, to be: see IS[1]⟧ **1** being; existence **2** ***pl.*** **-ties** a thing that has definite, individual existence outside or within the mind; anything real in itself

en·to- (en′tō, -tə) ⟦ModL < Gr *entos*, within < IE **entos* < base **en-*, IN[1]⟧ *combining form* within or inner [*entozoon*]

en·to·blast (en′tō blast′) ***n.*** ⟦prec. + -BLAST⟧ ENDODERM: also **en′to·derm′** (-durm′)

en·toil (en toil′) ***vt.*** [Archaic] to trap in toils or snares; ensnare

en·tomb (en to͞om′, in-) ***vt.*** ⟦ME *entoumben* < OFr *entoumber*: see EN-[1] & TOMB⟧ **1** to place in a tomb or grave; bury **2** to be a tomb for —**en·tomb′ment** ***n.***

en·to·mo- (en′tō mō′, -tə mə) ⟦Fr < Gr *entoma* (*zōa*), notched (animals), insects < *entomos*, cut, notched (< *en*, IN[1]) + *temnein*, to cut (see -TOMY); so named from their structure: see INSECT⟧ *combining form* insect or insects [*entomology*]: also, before a vowel, **entom-**

entomol *abbrev.* entomological

en·to·mol·o·gy (en′tə mäl′ə jē) ***n.*** ⟦Fr *entomologie*: see ENTOMO- & -LOGY⟧ the branch of zoology that deals with insects —**en′to·mo·log′i·cal** (-mə läj′i kəl) ***adj.***, **en′to·mo·log′ic** —**en′to·mo·log′i·cal·ly** ***adv.*** —**en′to·mol′o·gist** ***n.***

en·to·moph·a·gous (-mäf′ə gəs) ***adj.*** ⟦ENTOMO- + -PHAGOUS⟧ feeding chiefly on insects

en·to·moph·i·lous (-mäf′ə ləs) ***adj.*** ⟦ENTOMO- + -PHILOUS⟧ pollinated by insects

en·to·mos·tra·can (-mäs′trə kən) ***n.*** ⟦< ModL < *entomo-* (see ENTOMO-) + Gr *ostrakon*, a shell (see OSTRACIZE) + -AN⟧ any of a large variety of small crustaceans, as the copepods, barnacles, etc., formerly constituting a subclass (Entomostraca)

en·to·phyte (en′tə fīt′) ***n.*** ⟦ENTO- + -PHYTE⟧ ENDOPHYTE —**en′to·phyt′ic** (-fit′ik) ***adj.***

en·to·proct (-präkt′) ***n.*** ⟦ENTO- + Gr *prōktos*, anus⟧ any of a phylum (Entoprocta) of small, mosslike aquatic invertebrates with a complete digestive tract and an anus opening near the mouth and within the circlet of oral tentacles

en·tou·rage (än′to͝o räzh′, än′to͝o räzh′) ***n.*** ⟦Fr < *entourer*, to surround < *en tour*, around < *en*, in + *tour*, turn, round + -AGE⟧ **1** [Now Rare] surroundings; environment **2** a group of accompanying attendants, assistants, or associates; retinue

en·to·zo·on (en′tə zō′än′, -ən) ***n., pl.*** **-zo′a** (-ə) ⟦ENTO- + Gr *zōion*, animal: see BIO-⟧ an internal animal parasite, esp. a parasitic worm infesting the intestines, muscles, etc. —**en′to·zo′al** (-əl) ***adj.***, **en′to·zo′ic** (-ik)

en·tr'acte (än trakt′, än′trakt′; *Fr* än trakt′) ***n.*** ⟦Fr < *entre-*, between + *acte*, an act⟧ **1** the interval between two acts of a play, opera, etc.; intermission **2** a musical selection, dance, etc. performed during this interval

en·trails (en′trālz′, -trəlz) ***pl.n.*** ⟦ME & OFr *entrailles* < ML *intralia* < L *interanea*, pl. of *interaneum*, intestine < *interaneus*, internal < *inter*, between: see INTER-⟧ **1** the inner organs of humans or animals; specif., the intestines; viscera; guts **2** the inner parts of a thing

en·train[1] (en trān′, in-) ***vt.*** ⟦coined after EMBARK⟧ to put (troops, etc.) aboard a train —***vi.*** to go aboard a train

en·train[2] (en trān′) ***vt.*** ⟦< Fr *entraîner* < *en-* (< L *inde*), away + *trainer*, to drag < OFr *trahiner*: see TRAIN⟧ **1** [Rare] to drag along after oneself **2** *Chem.* to suspend (a liquid in the form of fine droplets) in a vapor, so that the vapor will carry the liquid away, as during distillation or evaporation —**en·train′ment** ***n.***

en·trance[1] (en′trəns) ***n.*** ⟦ME *entraunce* < OFr *entrant*, prp. of *entrer*: see ENTER⟧ **1** the act or point of entering [to make an *entrance*] **2** a place for entering; door, gate, etc. **3** permission, right, or power to enter; admission

en·trance[2] (en trans′, -träns′; in-) ***vt.*** **-tranced′, -tranc′ing** ⟦EN-[1] + TRANCE⟧ **1** to put into a trance **2** to fill with rapture or delight; enchant; charm; enrapture —**en·trance′ment** ***n.*** —**en·tranc′ing·ly** ***adv.***

en·trance·way (en′trəns wā′) ***n.*** ENTRYWAY

en·trant (en′trənt) ***n.*** ⟦Fr < OFr: see ENTRANCE[1]⟧ a person who enters, esp. one who enters a contest

en·trap (en trap′, in-) ***vt.*** **-trapped′, -trap′ping** ⟦OFr *entraper*⟧ **1** to catch in or as in a trap 2 to deceive or trick into difficulty, as into incriminating oneself —**en·trap′ment** *n.*

en tra·ves·ti (än trȧ ves tē′) *adv., adj.* ⟦Fr, lit., in disguise⟧ as or by someone of the opposite sex: said of an actor, a role, etc. [Peter Pan played *en travesti* by a woman]

en·treat (en trēt′, in-) *vt.* ⟦ME *entreten,* to treat, deal with, beseech < Anglo-Fr *entretier* < OFr *entraiter* < *en-,* in + *traiter:* see TREAT⟧ 1 [Archaic] to behave toward; treat 2 to ask earnestly; beg; beseech; implore —*vi.* 1 to make an earnest appeal; plead 2 [Obs.] to speak or write (*of*) —*SYN.* BEG —**en·treat′ing·ly** *adv.* —**en·treat′ment** *n.*

en·treat·y (en trēt′ē, in-) *n., pl.* **-treat′ies** ⟦ME *entrete:* see prec.⟧ an earnest request; supplication; prayer

en·tre·chat (än′trə shä′, än′trə shä′; *Fr* än trə shȧ′) *n.* ⟦Fr earlier *entrechasse,* altered (as if < *entre,* between, among + *chasser* < OFr *chacier,* CHASE[1]) < It (*capriola*) *intrecciata,* lit., intertwined (leap) < *intrecciare* < *in-,* in + *treccia,* a plait: see TRESS⟧ *Ballet* a leap straight upward during which the dancer crosses the legs and beats the calves together a number of times

en·tre·côte (än′trə kōt′, än′trə kōt′; *Fr* än trə kōt′) *n.* ⟦Fr, between-rib < *entre-,* INTER- + *côte,* a rib < L *costa*⟧ a boned rib steak

en·tree or **en·trée** (än′trā′, än trā′; *Fr* än trā′) *n.* ⟦Fr *entrée* < OFr < fem. pp. of *entrer,* ENTER⟧ 1 *a)* the act of entering *b)* right, permission, or freedom to enter, use, or take part in; access 2 *a)* the main course of a meal *b)* in some countries, a dish served before the main course or between the fish and meat courses

en·tre·mets (än′trə mā′, än′trə mā′; *Fr* än trə me′) *n., pl.* **en·tre·mets** (än′trə māz′, än′trə māz′; *Fr* än trə me′) ⟦ME *entermes* < OFr *entre,* between (< L *inter*) + *mes,* a dish: see MESS⟧ a dish served between the main courses or as a side dish

en·trench (en trench′, in-) *vt.* ⟦EN-[1] + TRENCH⟧ 1 to surround or fortify with a trench or trenches 2 to establish securely: used in the passive voice or with a reflexive pronoun [an official *entrenched* in office] 3 to cut down into, as by erosion, so as to form a trough or trench —*vi.* to encroach or infringe (*on* or *upon*) —**en·trench′ment** *n.*

en·tre nous (än′trə no͞o′; *Fr* än trə no͞o′) ⟦Fr, lit., between us⟧ between ourselves; confidentially

en·tre·pôt (än′trə pō′, än′trə pō′) *n.* ⟦Fr < OFr *entreposer,* to place in (temporary) storage, orig., to interpose, infl. by *dépot* (see DEPOT) < *entre-,* between (< L *inter-,* INTER-) + *poser,* to put in place: see POSE[1]⟧ 1 a place for the storage of goods; warehouse 2 a distributing center for goods

en·tre·pre·neur (än′trə prə nʉr′, -no͝or′, -nyo͝or′) *n.* ⟦Fr < OFr *entreprendre:* see ENTERPRISE⟧ a person who organizes and manages a business undertaking, assuming the risk for the sake of the profit —**en′tre·pre·neur′i·al** *adj.* —**en′tre·pre·neur′i·al·ism′** *n.* —**en′tre·pre·neur′ship** *n.*

en·tre·sol (än′trə säl′, än′trə säl′) *n.* ⟦Fr < *entre-,* between + *sol,* ground < L *solum* > SOIL[1]⟧ a low story or floor just above the street floor; mezzanine

en·tro·py (en′trə pē) *n.* ⟦Ger *entropie,* arbitrary use (by R. J. E. Clausius, 1822-88, Ger physicist) of Gr *entropē,* a turning toward, as if < Ger *en(ergie),* ENERGY + Gr *tropē,* a turning: see TROPE⟧ 1 a thermodynamic measure of the amount of energy unavailable for useful work in a system undergoing change 2 a measure of the degree of disorder in a substance or a system: entropy always increases and available energy diminishes in a closed system, as the universe 3 in information theory, a measure of the information content of a message evaluated as to its uncertainty 4 a process of degeneration marked variously by increasing degrees of uncertainty, disorder, fragmentation, chaos, etc.; specif., such a process regarded as the inevitable, terminal stage in the life of a social system or structure —**en·trop′ic** (-träp′ik) *adj.*

en·trust (en trust′, in-) *vt.* 1 to charge or invest with a trust or duty [*entrust* a lawyer with records] 2 to assign the care of; turn over for safekeeping [*entrust* the key to me] —*SYN.* COMMIT —**en·trust′ment** *n.*

en·try (en′trē) *n., pl.* **-tries** ⟦ME < OFr *entree* < fem. pp. of *entrer:* see ENTER⟧ 1 *a)* the act of entering; entrance *b)* the right or freedom to enter; entree 2 a way or passage by which to enter; door, hall, etc.; entryway 3 *a)* the recording of an item, note, etc. in a list, journal, etc. or of data in a computer file *b)* an item thus recorded 4 the registration of a ship or cargo at a customhouse 5 *a)* one entered in a race, competition, etc.; entrant *b)* two or more horses belonging to the same owner, entered in the same race, and constituting a unit for betting purposes 6 *a)* a term defined, or a person, place, abbreviation, etc. identified, in a dictionary *b)* the heading under which an encyclopedia article is entered 7 *Card Games* a card that can win a trick and thus gain the lead 8 *Law a)* the taking possession of buildings, land, etc. by entering or setting foot upon them *b)* the entering upon premises with the intention of committing burglary or some other crime

en·try-lev·el (en′trē lev′əl) *adj.* 1 designating or of a job or position offered to an inexperienced person, that usually pays low wages but provides training and experience and the prospect of future advancement 2 basic; introductory [an *entry-level* course in psychology]

☆**en·try·way** (-wā′) *n.* a way or passage by which to enter

en·twine (en twīn′, in-) *vt., vi.* **-twined′, -twin′ing** to twine, weave, or twist together or around

en·twist (en twist′, in-) *vt.* 1 to twist together or in (*with*) 2 to make into a twist

e·nu·cle·ate (ē no͞o′klē āt′, -nyo͞o′-; i-; *for adj.,* -it, -āt′) *vt.* **-at′ed, -at′ing** ⟦< L *enucleatus,* pp. of *enucleare,* to remove kernels < *e-,* out + *nucleus:* see NUCLEUS⟧ 1 [Archaic] to make clear; explain 2 *Biol.* to remove the nucleus from (a cell) 3 *Surgery* to remove (a tumor, organ, etc.) as a whole from its enclosing sac —*adj.* enucleated —**e·nu′cle·a′tion** *n.*

e·nu·mer·ate (ē no͞o′mər āt′, -nyo͞o′-; i-) *vt.* **-at′ed, -at′ing** ⟦< L *enumeratus,* pp. of *enumerare* < *e-,* out + *numerare,* to count < *numerus,* NUMBER⟧ 1 to determine the number of; count 2 to name one by one; specify, as in a list —**e·nu′mer·a·ble** (-mər ə bəl) *adj.* —**e·nu′mer·a′tion** *n.* —**e·nu′mer·a′tive** *adj.* —**e·nu′mer·a′tor** *n.*

e·nun·ci·a·ble (ē nun′sē ə bəl, i-; *also,* -shē-) *adj.* ⟦ML *enuntiabilis*⟧ that can be enunciated

e·nun·ci·ate (ē nun′sē āt′, i-; *also,* -shē-) *vt.* **-at′ed, -at′ing** ⟦< L *enuntiatus,* pp. of *enuntiare* < *e-,* out + *nuntiare,* to announce < *nuntius,* a messenger⟧ 1 to state definitely; express in a systematic way [to *enunciate* a theory] 2 to announce; proclaim 3 to pronounce (words), esp. clearly and distinctly —*vi.* to pronounce words, esp. clearly and distinctly; articulate —*SYN.* UTTER[2] —**e·nun′ci·a′tion** (-sē ā′-) *n.* —**e·nun′ci·a′tive** (-āt′iv, -ə tiv) *adj.* —**e·nun′ci·a′tor** *n.*

en·ure (ən yo͝or′) *vt., vi.* **-ured′, -ur′ing** INURE

en·u·re·sis (en′yo͞o rē′sis) *n., pl.* **-ses′** (-sēz′) ⟦ModL < Gr *enourein,* to urinate in: see EN-[1] & URINE⟧ inability to control urination; esp., involuntary bed-wetting —**en′u·ret′ic** (-ret′ik) *adj.*

env *abbrev.* envelope

en·vel·op (en vel′əp, in-) *vt.* ⟦ME *envolupen* < OFr *envoluper:* see EN-[1] & DEVELOP⟧ 1 to wrap up; cover completely 2 to surround 3 to conceal; hide —**en·vel′op·ment** *n.*

en·ve·lope (än′və lōp′, en′-) *n.* ⟦Fr & OFr *enveloppe* < OFr *envoluper:* see prec.⟧ 1 a thing that envelops; wrapper; covering 2 a folded paper container as for a letter, usually with a gummed flap for sealing 3 *a)* the outer covering of a rigid airship *b)* the bag that contains the gas in a balloon or nonrigid airship 4 the set of limitations, as for a particular aircraft, system, etc., within the boundaries of which it can operate safely and efficiently 5 a set of limits or boundaries: usually in the informal phrase **push the envelope,** to go beyond or attempt to go beyond established rules, limits, expectations, etc. 6 *Astron.* a cloudy mass surrounding the nucleus of a comet; coma 7 *Biol.* any enclosing membrane, skin, shell, etc. 8 *Math.* a curve that is tangent to every one of a family of curves, or a surface that is tangent to every one of a family of surfaces

en·ven·om (en ven′əm, in-) *vt.* ⟦ME *envenimen* < OFr *envenimer*⟧ 1 to put venom or poison on or into; make poisonous 2 to fill with hate; embitter

en·vi·a·ble (en′vē ə bəl) *adj.* good enough to be envied or desired —**en′vi·a·bly** *adv.*

en·vi·er (en′vē ər) *n.* a person who envies

en·vi·ous (en′vē əs) *adj.* ⟦ME < OFr *envieus* < L *invidiosus* < *invidia,* ENVY⟧ 1 characterized by envy; feeling, showing, or resulting from envy 2 [Obs.] *a)* emulous *b)* enviable —**en′vi·ous·ly** *adv.* —**en′vi·ous·ness** *n.*

en·vi·ro (en vī′rō, in-) [Slang] *n., pl.* **-ros** *short for* ENVIRONMENTALIST (sense 2) —*adj. short for* ENVIRONMENTAL (sense 2)

en·vi·ro- (en vī′rō, in-) *combining form* of, relating to, or serving to protect the earth's environment

en·vi·ron (en vī′rən, in-) *vt.* ⟦ME *envirounen* < OFr *environner* < *environ,* about: see ENVIRONS⟧ to surround; encircle

en·vi·ron·ment (en vī′rən mənt, in-; *often,* -vī′ərn-) *n.* ⟦prec. + -MENT⟧ 1 [Rare] a surrounding or being surrounded 2 something that surrounds; surroundings 3 *a)* all the conditions, circumstances, and influences surrounding, and affecting the development of, an organism or group of organisms *b)* all of the conditions, circumstances, etc. that surround and influence life on earth, including atmospheric conditions, food chains, and the water cycle (usually with *the*)

en·vi·ron·men·tal (-ment′'l) *adj.* 1 of or having to do with an environment 2 of or having to do with the environment or with the concerns of an ENVIRONMENTALIST (sense 2) —**en·vi′ron·men′tal·ly** *adv.*

☆**en·vi·ron·men·tal·ist** (en vī′rən ment′'l ist, in-) *n.* 1 a person who accepts the theory that environment is of overriding importance in determining individual characteristics 2 a person working to solve environmental problems, as air and water pollution, the exhaustion of natural resources, and uncontrolled population growth —*adj.* of or being an ENVIRONMENTALIST (sense 2) —**en·vi′ron·men′tal·ism′** *n.*

en·vi·rons (en vī′rənz, in-) *pl.n.* ⟦ME *environ* (sing.) < OFr *environ,* orig. adv., around < *en-,* EN-[1] + *viron,* a circuit < *virer,* to turn: see VEER[1]⟧ 1 the districts surrounding a town or city; suburbs or outskirts 2 surrounding area; vicinity

en·vis·age (en viz′ij, in-) *vt.* **-aged, -ag·ing** ⟦Fr *envisager:* see EN-[1] & VISAGE⟧ 1 [Rare] to face; confront 2 to form an image of in the mind; visualize; imagine

en·vi·sion (en vizh′ən, in-) *vt.* ⟦EN-[1] + VISION⟧ to imagine (something not yet in existence); picture in the mind

en·voi (än′voi′, en′-) *n.* ⟦Fr⟧ 1 ENVOY[2] 2 something said or done in farewell or conclusion

en·voy[1] (än′voi′, en′-) *n.* ⟦Fr *envoyé* < pp. of *envoyer,* to send < OFr *envoier* < *en-* (L *in*), in + *voie* (L *via:* see VIA), way⟧ 1 a messenger; agent 2 an agent sent by a government or ruler to transact diplomatic business; specif., a diplomat (**envoy extraordinary**) ranking just below an ambassador

en·voy[2] (än′voi′, en′-) *n.* ⟦ME *envoye* < OFr *envoy,* lit., a sending < *envoier:* see prec.⟧ a postscript to a poem, essay, or book, containing a dedication, climactic summary, explanation, etc.; specif., a short, concluding stanza of this kind added to a ballade and some other verse forms

en·vy (en′vē) *n.* ⟦ME & OFr *envie* < L *invidia* < *invidus,* having hatred or ill will < *invidere*, to look askance at < *in-*, in, upon + *videre*, to look: see WISE[2]] 1 a feeling of discontent and ill will because of another's advantages, possessions, etc.; resentful dislike of another who has something that one desires 2 desire for some advantage, quality, etc. that another has 3 an object of envious feeling [*her new role makes her the envy of every actress in town*] 4 [Obs.] ill will; spite —*vt.* **-vied**, **-vy·ing** to feel envy toward, at, or because of; regard with envy —*vi.* [Obs.] to feel or show envy —**en′vy·ing·ly** *adv.*

SYN.—to **envy** another is to feel ill will, jealousy, or discontent at the person's possession of something that one keenly desires to have or achieve oneself; **begrudge** implies an unwillingness that someone should possess or enjoy something that is needed or deserved; to **covet** is to long ardently and wrongfully for something that belongs to another

en·wind (en wīnd′) *vt.* **-wound′**, **-wind′ing** to wind around

en·womb (en wo͞om′) *vt.* to enclose in or as in a womb

en·wrap (en rap′) *vt.* **-wrapped′**, **-wrap′ping** to wrap; envelop

en·wreathe (en rēth′) *vt.* **-wreathed′**, **-wreath′ing** to encircle or surround with or as with a wreath

en·zo·ot·ic (en′zō ät′ik) *adj.* ⟦< Gr *en-*, in + *zōion*, animal (see BIO-) + *-otic*, as in EPIZOOTIC⟧ affecting animals in a certain area, climate, or season: said of diseases —*n.* an enzootic disease Cf. EPIZOOTIC

en·zyme (en′zīm′) *n.* ⟦Ger *enzym* < LGr *enzymos*, leavened < Gr *en-*, in + *zymē*, leaven (see ZYME)⟧ any of various proteins, formed in plant and animal cells or made synthetically, that act as organic catalysts in initiating or speeding up specific chemical reactions and that usually become inactive or unstable above *c.* 50°C (122°F) —**en′zy·mat′ic** (-zī mat′ik, -zi-) *adj.*, **en·zy′mic** (-zī′mik)

en·zy·mol·o·gy (en′zī mäl′ə jē, -zi-) *n.* the science dealing with the structure and properties of enzymes and the chemical reactions they catalyze —**en′zy·mol′o·gist** *n.*

e·o- (ē′ō, ē′ə) ⟦< Gr *ēōs*, dawn < IE base **awes-*, to shine > EASTER, L *aurora*⟧ *prefix* early, early part of a period [*Eocene, Eolithic*]

e·o·bi·ont (ē′ō bī′änt′, -ənt) *n.* ⟦coined by J. D. Bernal (1901-71), Brit physicist < prec. + Gr *biount-*, stem of *biōn*, living, prp. of *bioun*, to live < *bios*, life: see BIO-⟧ a hypothetical precursor of living organisms in the chemical evolution preceding the occurrence of life

E·o·cene (ē′ō sēn′, ē′ə-) *adj.* ⟦EO- + -CENE⟧ [*sometimes* **e-**] designating or of the second geologic epoch of the Paleogene, characterized by a warm climate and the development of mammals —**the Eocene** the Eocene Epoch or its rocks: see the geologic time chart in the Reference Supplement

EOE *abbrev.* equal opportunity employer (or employment)

e·o·hip·pus (ē′ō hip′əs) *n.* ⟦ModL < EO- + -HIPPUS⟧ an extinct progenitor (genus *Hyracotherium*) of the modern horse, found in the Lower Eocene of W U.S.: it was about the size of a fox and had four toes on the front feet and three on the hind

E·o·li·an (ē ō′lē ən, -ōl′yən) *adj.* 1 *alt. sp. of* AEOLIAN 2 [*usually* **e-**] carried, formed, eroded, or deposited by the wind, as sand dunes, sediment, etc. —*n. alt. sp. of* AEOLIAN

E·ol·ic (ē äl′ik) *n., adj. alt. sp. of* AEOLIC

e·o·lith (ē′ō lith′, ē′ə-) *n.* ⟦EO- + -LITH⟧ any of the crude stone tools used during the Eolithic period

E·o·lith·ic (ē′ō lith′ik, ē′ə-) *adj.* ⟦see prec. & -IC⟧ designating or of the earliest period of the Stone Age, during which crude stone tools were first used

EOM or **eom** *abbrev.* end of (the) month

e·on (ē′ən, ē′än′) *n.* ⟦LL < Gr *aiōn*, an age, lifetime, eternity < IE base **aiw-*, vitality: see AYE[1]⟧ 1 an extremely long, indefinite period of time; thousands and thousands of years 2 *Geol.* *a)* the major unit of geologic time, usually subdivided into eras (see the geologic time chart in the Reference Supplement) *b)* a billion years —**SYN.** PERIOD

e·o·ni·an (ē ō′nē ən) *adj. alt. sp. of* AEONIAN

E·os (ē′äs′) *n.* ⟦L < Gr *Ēōs*: see EO-⟧ *Gr. Myth.* the goddess of dawn: identified with the Roman goddess Aurora

e·o·sin (ē′ō sin, ē′ə-) *n.* ⟦< Gr *ēōs*, dawn (see EO-) + -IN[1]⟧ 1 *a)* a rose-colored dye, $C_{20}H_8O_5Br_4$, prepared by brominating fluorescein and used to color inks, fabrics, etc. and to stain tissues *b)* its sodium or potassium salt, used as a reddish dye and as a stain in microscopy 2 any of various similar red dyes Also **e′o·sine** (-sin, -sēn′) —**e′o·sin′ic** *adj.*

e·o·sin·o·phil (ē′ō sin′ə fil′) *n.* ⟦prec. + -O- + -PHIL⟧ *Biol.* any structure, cell, etc. readily stainable with eosin; esp., the granular white blood cells that increase greatly in number in certain allergic and parasitic diseases: also **e′o·sin′o·phile′** (-fīl′) —**e′o·sin′o·phil′ic** (-fil′ik) *adj.*

e·o·sin·o·phile (-fīl′) *adj.* ⟦see prec.⟧ *Chem.* easily stained by eosin: also **e′o·sin′o·phil′** (-fil′)

-e·ous (ē əs) ⟦< L *-eus* + -OUS⟧ *suffix var. of* -OUS [*gaseous*]

Ep *abbrev. Bible* Ephesians

EP *abbrev.* extended play (record, tape, etc.)

ep- (ep) *prefix* EPI-: used before a vowel [*epoxy*]

EPA *abbrev.* Environmental Protection Agency

e·pact (ē′pakt′) *n.* ⟦Fr *épacte* < LL *epactae* < Gr *epaktai (hemerai)*, intercalary (days) < *epagein*, to bring in, intercalate < *epi-*, on, in + *agein*, to bring, lead: see ACT[1]⟧ 1 the period of about eleven days by which the solar year exceeds the lunar year of twelve months 2 the age, in days, of the calendar moon on the first of the year

E·pam·i·non·das (i pam′ə nän′dəs) 418?-362 B.C.; Theban (Gr.) general & statesman

ep·arch (ep′ärk′) *n.* ⟦Gr *eparchos* < *epi-*, over + *archos*, ruler: see -ARCH⟧ 1 in the Byzantine Empire, the governor of an eparchy 2 *Eastern Orthodox Ch.* a metropolitan or bishop

ep·arch·y (ep′är kē, -är′-) *n., pl.* **-arch·ies** ⟦Gr *eparchia* < *eparchos*: see prec.⟧ 1 *a)* in the Byzantine Empire, an administrative district *b)* in modern Greece, a political subdivision of a province 2 *Eastern Orthodox Ch.* a diocese —**ep·ar′chi·al** (-kē əl) *adj.*

é·pa·ter (ā pȧ tā′) *vt.* ⟦Fr⟧ to outrage or shock the complacent or conventional sensibilities of

ep·au·let (ep′ə let′, ep′ə let′) *n.* ⟦Fr *épaulette*, dim. of *épaule*, shoulder < OFr *espale* < L *spatula*: see SPATULA⟧ 1 a shoulder ornament for certain uniforms, esp. military uniforms 2 an ornamental strip or tab on the shoulder of a coat, dress, etc. Also [Chiefly Brit.] **ep′au·lette′**

epaulets

ep·a·zote (ep′ə zōt′) *n.* ⟦MexSp < Nahuatl *epazōtl*⟧ American wormseed (see WORMSEED, *n.* 1); esp., the aromatic leaves of this plant used as an herb in Mexican cooking

e·pee or **é·pée** (ā pā′) *n.* ⟦Fr *épée* < OFr *espee* < L *spatha*, broad, two-edged sword without a point < Gr *spathē*, any broad blade: see SPADE[1]⟧ a sword, esp. a thin, pointed sword without a cutting edge, like a foil but heavier and more rigid, used in fencing —**e·pee′ist** *n.*, **é·pée′ist**

ep·ei·rog·e·ny (ep′ī räj′ə nē) *n.* ⟦< Gr *ēpeiros*, mainland + -GENY⟧ movements of uplift or depression affecting large areas of the earth's crust and producing continents, ocean basins, etc. —**e·pei·ro·gen·ic** (e pī′rō jen′ik) *adj.*, **e·pei′ro·ge·net′ic** (-jə net′ik)

ep·en·ceph·a·lon (ep′ən sef′ə län′, -lən) *n.* ⟦ModL < EP- + ENCEPHALON⟧ 1 METENCEPHALON 2 [Rare] the cerebellum

ep·en·dy·ma (ep en′di mə) *n.* ⟦ModL, arbitrary use by Rudolf Virchow (1821-1902, Ger pathologist) of Gr *ependyma*, an upper garment < *ependyein*, to put on over < *epi-*, over + *endyein* < *en-*, on + *dyein*, dip into, put on < IE base **deu-*, to sink into, penetrate⟧ the membrane lining the central cavities of the brain and spinal cord

ep·en·the·sis (e pen′thə sis) *n., pl.* **-ses′** (-sēz′) ⟦LL < Gr < *epi-*, upon + *en-*, in + *thesis*, a placing: see THESIS⟧ 1 *Phonet.* a change which involves the insertion of an unhistoric sound or letter in a word, as the *b* in *mumble* or the extra syllable in the pronunciation (ath′ə lēt′) for *athlete* 2 the inserted sound or letter —**ep·en·thet·ic** (ep′ən thet′ik) *adj.*

e·pergne (ē purn′, ā pern′) *n.* ⟦prob. < Fr *épargne*, a saving < *épargner*, to save < Frank **sparanjan*, akin to Ger *sparen*, to save⟧ an ornamental stand with several separate dishes, trays, etc., used as a table centerpiece for holding fruit, flowers, etc.

ep·ex·e·ge·sis (ep′ek′sə jē′sis) *n.* ⟦Gr *epexēgēsis*, detailed account < *epexēgeisthai*, to recount in detail < *epi-*, on, in + *exēgeisthai*, to point out: see EXEGESIS⟧ additional explanation; further clarification, as by the addition of a word or words —**ep′ex′e·get′i·cal** (-jet′i kəl) *adj.*, **ep′ex′e·get′ic**

Eph *abbrev. Bible* Ephesians

eph- (ef) *prefix* EPI- [*ephemeral*]

e·phah or **e·pha** (ē′fə) *n.* ⟦ME *ephi* < LL(Ec) < Heb *efa*⟧ an ancient Hebrew unit of dry measure, estimated at from ⅓ bushel to a little over one bushel

e·phebe (e fēb′, ef′ēb′) *n.* ⟦< L *ephebus*, fol.⟧ a young man; specif., an ephebus

e·phe·bus (e fē′bəs) *n., pl.* **-bi′** (-bī′) ⟦L < Gr *ephēbos* < *epi-*, at, upon + *hēbē*, early manhood⟧ in ancient Athens, a young citizen (18 to 20 years) undergoing physical and military training —**e·phe′bic** *adj.*

e·phe·dra (e fe′drə) *n.* ⟦ModL < L *ephedra*, the horsetail plant < Gr *ephedros*, sitting by < *epi-*, on, near + *hedra*, a seat⟧ 1 any of a large genus (*Ephedra*) of low, leafless, green gymnospermous shrubs (family Ephedraceae): the dried rhizomes and roots are used as a natural source of ephedrine 2 any stimulant herb derived from this shrub and used in medicine

e·phed·rine (e fe′drin; *chiefly Brit*, ef′ə drēn′, -drin) *n.* ⟦< prec. + -INE[3]⟧ an alkaloid, $C_{10}H_{15}NO$, derived from certain ephedras or synthesized, and used to relieve nasal congestion and asthma and to constrict certain blood vessels

e·phem·er·a (e fem′ər ə, i-) *n., pl.* **-er·as** or **-er·ae′** (-ē′) ⟦ModL < Gr *ephēmeron*: see EPHEMERON⟧ 1 MAYFLY 2 *a)* an ephemeral thing *b)* [*with pl. v.*] ephemeral things collectively 3 printed matter (as theater programs, posters, guidebooks) meant to be of use for only a short time but preserved by collectors

e·phem·er·al (e fem′ər əl; i-, ē-) *adj.* ⟦< Gr *ephēmeros* (see EPHEMERON) + -AL⟧ 1 lasting only one day 2 short-lived; transitory [*ephemeral glory*] —*n.* an ephemeral thing; specif., an organism with a brief life cycle —**SYN.** TRANSIENT —**e·phem′er·al′i·ty** (-al′ə tē) *n.*, **e·phem′er·al·ness** —**e·phem′er·al·ly** *adv.*

e·phem·er·id (e fem′ər id′, i-) *n.* ⟦EPHEMER(A) + -ID⟧ MAYFLY

e·phem·er·is (e fem′ər is, i-) *n., pl.* **eph·e·mer·i·des** (ef′ə mer′ə dēz′) ⟦L < Gr *ephēmeris*, diary, calendar < *ephēmeros*: see fol.⟧ 1 a table giving the computed positions of a celestial body for every day of a given period 2 an astronomical almanac containing such tables 3 [Obs.] a calendar or diary

e·phem·er·on (e fem′ər än′, -ən; i-) *n., pl.* **-er·a** (-ə) or **-er·ons′** ⟦Gr *ephēmeron*, short-lived insect < *ephēmeros*, for the day, short-lived < *epi-*, upon + *hēmera*, day⟧ MAYFLY

E·phe·sian (e fē′zhən, i-) *adj.* of Ephesus or its people —*n.* a person born or living in Ephesus

E·phe·sians (e fē′zhənz, i-) ***n.*** a book of the New Testament: a letter from the Apostle Paul to the Christians of Ephesus: abbrev. *Ep* or *Eph*

Eph·e·sus (ef′i səs) ancient Greek city in W Asia Minor, near what is now Izmir, Turkey: site of a large temple of Artemis (*c.* 550 B.C.–A.D. 260)

eph·od (ef′äd′, ēf′-) ***n.*** ⟦ME < LL(Ec) < Heb *efod* < *afad*, to put on⟧ a richly embroidered outer vestment worn by Jewish priests in ancient times: Ex. 28:28

eph·or (ef′ôr′) ***n., pl.*** **-ors′** or **-o·ri′** (-ō rī′) ⟦L *ephorus* < Gr *ephoros*, overseer < *ephoran* < *epi-*, over + *horan*, to see < IE **woros*, attentive < base **wer-*, to heed > WARN⟧ in ancient Sparta, any of a body of five magistrates annually elected by the people of Sparta

E·phra·im (ē′frā im, -frē əm; -frəm; *also, for sense 1,* ef′rəm) ***n.*** ⟦LL(Ec) < Gr(Ec) < Heb *efrayim*, lit., very fruitful⟧ **1** a masculine name **2** *Bible a)* the younger son of Joseph: Gen. 41:51 *b)* the tribe of Israel descended from this son: Num. 1:32 *c)* the kingdom of Israel

E·phra·im·ite (ē′frā im īt′, -frē əm-) ***n.*** a descendant of Ephraim; member of the tribe of Ephraim

ep·i- (ep′i, -ə) ⟦< Gr *epi*, at, on, to, upon, over, besides < IE base **epi* > Sans *ápi*, L *ob*⟧ *prefix* on, upon, over, on the outside, anterior, beside, besides, among: it becomes *ep-* before a vowel and, as *eph-*, it reflects an original combining with a word containing an initial aspirate (represented by English *h*) *[epiglottis, epidemic, epidermis]*

ep·i·ben·thos (ep′i ben′thäs′, -thəs) ***n.*** ⟦prec. + BENTHOS⟧ the animals and plants living on the sea bottom between the low tide level and a depth of 100 fathoms

ep·i·blast (ep′i blast′) ***n.*** ⟦EPI- + -BLAST⟧ the outer layer of cells of an embryo

e·pib·o·ly (ē pib′ə lē) ***n.*** ⟦Gr *epibolē*, a throwing upon < *epiballein*, to throw upon < *epi-*, on, upon + *ballein*, to throw: see BALL[2]⟧ *Embryology* the growth of a group of cells around another group, resulting from the more rapid division of the former, as in forming a gastrula —**ep·i·bol·ic** (ep′i bäl′ik) ***adj.***

ep·ic (ep′ik) ***n.*** ⟦L *epicus* < Gr *epikos*, (adj.) epic < *epos*, a word, speech, song, epic < IE **wekwos-*, word < base **wekw-*, to speak > L *vox*, OE *woma*, noise⟧ **1** a long narrative poem in a dignified style about the deeds of a traditional or historical hero or heroes; typically, *a)* a poem like the *Iliad* or the *Odyssey*, with certain formal characteristics (beginning *in medias res*, catalog passages, invocations of the muse, etc.) (called **classical epic**) *b)* a poem like Milton's *Paradise Lost*, in which such characteristics are applied to later or different materials (called **art epic** or **literary epic**) *c)* a poem like *Beowulf*, considered as expressing the early ideals and traditions of a people or nation (called **folk epic** or **national epic**) **2** any long narrative poem regarded as having the style, structure, and importance of an epic, as Dante's *Divine Comedy* **3** a prose narrative, play, film, etc. regarded as having certain qualities of an epic, as great length, a wide variety of characters and incidents, serious themes, etc. **4** a series of events regarded as a proper subject for an epic —***adj.*** **1** of an epic **2** having the nature of an epic; specif., *a)* heroic; grand; majestic; imposing *b)* dealing with or characterized by events of historical or legendary importance: also **ep′i·cal** —**ep′i·cal·ly** ***adv.***

ep·i·ca·lyx (ep′i kā′liks′) ***n., pl.*** **-lyx′es** or **-ly·ces′** (-li sēz′) ⟦EPI- + CALYX⟧ a ring of small bracts at the base of certain flowers, resembling an extra outer calyx, as in the mallows

ep·i·can·thus (ep′i kan′thəs) ***n.*** ⟦EPI- + CANTHUS⟧ a small normal fold of skin from the upper eyelid sometimes covering the inner corner of the eye, as in many Asian peoples: also occurs with certain abnormal conditions, as Down syndrome —**ep′i·can′thic** ***adj.***

ep·i·car·di·um (ep′i kär′dē əm) ***n., pl.*** **-di·a** (-ə) ⟦ModL < EPI- + Gr *kardia*, HEART⟧ the innermost layer of the pericardium —**ep′i·car′di·al** ***adj.***

ep·i·carp (ep′i kärp′) ***n.*** ⟦EPI- + -CARP⟧ *var. of* EXOCARP

ep·i·ce·di·um (ep′i sē′dē əm, -si dī′əm) ***n., pl.*** **-di·a** (-ə) ⟦L < Gr *epikēdeion* < *epikēdeios*, funereal < *epi-*, in, on + *kēdos*, grief, funeral rites: see HATE⟧ a funeral ode or hymn; dirge

ep·i·cene (ep′i sēn′) ***adj.*** ⟦ME < L *epicoenus* < Gr *epikoinos*, common < *epi-*, upon, to + *koinos*, common: see COM-⟧ **1** designating a noun, as in Latin or Greek, having only one grammatical form to denote an individual of either sex **2** belonging to one sex but having characteristics of the other, or of neither; specif., effeminate; unmanly —***n.*** an epicene person

ep·i·cen·ter (ep′i sent′ər) ***n.*** ⟦< ModL *epicentrum* < EPI- + L *centrum*, CENTER⟧ **1** the area of the earth's surface directly above the place of origin, or focus, of an earthquake **2** a focal or central point Also **ep′i·cen′trum** (-sen′trəm), *pl.* **-tra** (-trə) —**ep′i·cen′tral** (-sen′trəl) ***adj.***

ep·i·cot·yl (ep′i kät′'l) ***n.*** ⟦< EPI- + COTYL(EDON)⟧ *Bot.* that part of the stem of a seedling or embryo just above the cotyledons —**ep′i·cot′yl·e′don·ar′y** (-ēd′'n er′ē) ***adj.***

ep·i·cra·ni·um (ep′i krā′nē əm) ***n., pl.*** **-ni·a** (-ə) **1** *Anat.* the structures covering the cranium **2** *Entomology* the upper portion of the head of an insect between the frons and the neck —**ep′i·cra′ni·al** ***adj.***

ep·i·crit·ic (ep′i krit′ik) ***adj.*** ⟦Gr *epikritikos*, determinative < *epikrisis*, judgment < *epikrinein*, to judge < *epi-*, upon + *krinein*, to judge: see CRISIS⟧ designating or of the nerve fibers in the skin that transmit the finer sensations of touch and temperature

Ep·ic·te·tus (ep′ik tēt′əs) A.D. 50?-135?; Gr. Stoic philosopher in Rome & Epirus

ep·i·cure (ep′i kyoor′) ***n.*** ⟦< L *Epicurus* < Gr *Epikouros*: see EPICURUS⟧ **1** a person who enjoys and has a discriminating taste for fine foods and beverages **2** [Archaic] a person who is especially fond of luxury and sensuous pleasure

SYN.—an **epicure** is a person who has a highly refined taste for fine foods and beverages and takes great pleasure in indulging it; a **gourmet** is a connoisseur in eating and drinking who appreciates subtle differences in flavor or quality; **gourmand**, occasionally equivalent to **gourmet**, is more often applied to a person who has a hearty liking for good food or one who is inclined to eat to excess; a **gastronome** is an expert in all phases of the art or science of good eating; a **glutton** is a greedy, voracious eater and drinker

Ep·i·cu·re·an (ep′i kyoo rē′ən, -kyoor′ē ən) ***adj.*** ⟦ME *Epicurien* < L *Epicureus* < Gr *Epikoureios* < *Epikouros*⟧ **1** of Epicurus or his philosophy **2** [**e-**] *a)* fond of luxury and sensuous pleasure, esp. that of eating and drinking *b)* suited to or characteristic of an epicure —***n.*** **1** a follower of Epicurus or his philosophy **2** [**e-**] an epicure —***SYN.*** SENSUOUS

Ep·i·cu·re·an·ism (-iz′əm) ***n.*** **1** the philosophy of Epicurus or his school **2** adherence to or practice of this philosophy **3** [**e-**] EPICURISM

ep·i·cur·ism (ep′i kyoor iz′əm) ***n.*** the tastes, habits, or pursuits of an epicure

Ep·i·cu·rus (ep′ə kyoor′əs) 341-270 B.C.; Gr. philosopher: founder of the Epicurean school, which held that the goal of man should be a life characterized by serenity of mind and the enjoyment of moderate pleasure

ep·i·cy·cle (ep′ə sī′kəl) ***n.*** ⟦ME *epicicle* < LL *epicyclus* < Gr *epikyklos* < *epi-*, upon + *kyklos*, a circle: see CYCLE⟧ **1** a circle whose center moves along the circumference of another, larger circle: term used to describe planetary motions in the Ptolemaic system **2** *Geom.* a circle which generates a hypocycloid or epicycloid by rolling around the circumference of a fixed circle —**ep′i·cy′clic** (-sīk′lik) ***adj.***, **ep′i·cy′cli·cal**

epicyclic train a system of gears, belt pulleys, etc., in which at least one gear or pulley axis moves around the circumference of another fixed or moving axis, permitting an unusually high or low velocity ratio with relative simplicity of parts

ep·i·cy·cloid (ep′ə sī′kloid′) ***n.*** ⟦EPICYCL(E) + -OID⟧ *Geom.* the curve traced by a point on the circumference of an epicycle that rolls around the outside of a fixed circle: cf. HYPOCYCLOID —**ep′i·cy·cloi′dal** (-kloid′'l) ***adj.***

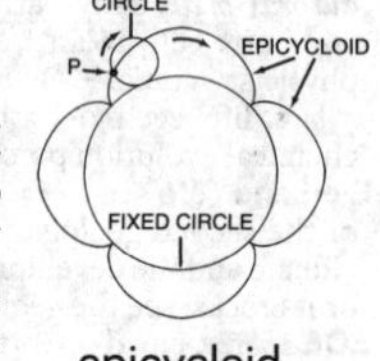

epicycloid

epicycloidal gear a gear of an epicyclic train

Ep·i·dam·nus (ep′ə dam′nəs) *see* DURRËS

ep·i·deic·tic (ep′ə dīk′tik) ***adj.*** ⟦Gr *epideiktikos*, declamatory < *epideikt(os)*, verbal adj. (< *epideiknynai*, to display < *epi-*: see EPI- + *deiknynai*, to show: see DICTION) + *-ikos*, -IC⟧ intended for display, esp. rhetorical display; designed to impress

ep·i·dem·ic (ep′ə dem′ik) ***adj.*** ⟦Fr *épidémique* < MFr < ML *epidemicus* < *epidemia* < Gr *epidēmia* < *epidēmios*, among the people, general < *epi-*, EPI- + *dēmos*, people: see DEMOCRACY⟧ prevalent and spreading rapidly among many individuals in a community at the same time: said esp. of a serious human contagious disease: cf. ENDEMIC: also **ep′i·dem′i·cal** —***n.*** **1** an epidemic disease **2** the rapid spreading of such a disease **3** a rapid, widespread occurrence or growth —**ep′i·dem′i·cal·ly** ***adv.***

epidemic encephalitis any type of widespread encephalitis caused by various viruses

ep·i·de·mi·ol·o·gy (ep′ə dē′mē äl′ə jē, -dem′ē-) ***n.*** ⟦Gr *epidēmios* (see EPIDEMIC) + -LOGY⟧ **1** the branch of medicine that investigates the causes and control of epidemics **2** all the elements contributing to the occurrence or nonoccurrence of a disease in a population; ecology of a disease —**ep′i·de′mi·o·log′ic** (-ə läj′ik) ***adj.***, **ep′i·de′mi·o·log′i·cal** —**ep′i·de′mi·ol′o·gist** ***n.***

ep·i·den·drum (ep′i den′drəm) ***n.*** ⟦ModL < *epi-*, EPI- + Gr *dendron*, tree: see DENDRO-⟧ any of a genus (*Epidendrum*) of small-flowered, chiefly tropical American, epiphytic orchids

ep·i·der·mis (ep′ə dur′mis) ***n.*** ⟦LL < Gr < *epi-*, upon (see EPI-) + *derma*, the skin: see DERMA[1]⟧ **1** the outermost layer of the skin in vertebrates, having no blood vessels and consisting of several layers of cells, covering the dermis **2** the outermost layer of cells covering seed plants and ferns **3** any of various other integuments —**ep′i·der′mal** ***adj.***, **ep′i·der′mic**

ep·i·der·moid (ep′ə dur′moid′) ***adj.*** like, or having the nature of, epidermis: also **ep′i·der·moid′al**

ep·i·di·a·scope (ep′ə dī′ə skōp′) ***n.*** ⟦EPI- + DIA- + -SCOPE⟧ an optical device for projecting on a screen a magnified image of an opaque or transparent object

ep·i·did·y·mis (ep′ə did′i mis) ***n., pl.*** **ep′i·di·dym′i·des′** (-di dim′i dēz′) ⟦ModL < Gr < *epi-*, upon + *didymoi*, testicles, orig. pl. of *didymos*, double, redupl. of *duo*, TWO⟧ a long, oval-shaped structure attached to the rear upper surface of each testicle, consisting mainly of the sperm ducts of the testicles —**ep′i·did′y·mal** ***adj.***

ep·i·dote (ep′ə dōt′) ***n.*** ⟦Fr *épidote* < Gr *epididonai*, to give besides, increase < *epi-*, over + *didonai*, to give (see DATE[1]): so named by R.-J. Haüy (1743-1822), Fr mineralogist; from the enlarged base of some of the crystal forms⟧ hydrous calcium aluminum iron silicate, a yellowish-green to black mineral, $Ca_2(AlFe)_3Si_3O_{12}(OH)$, found as monoclinic crystals, grains, or masses and sometimes used as a gem —**ep′i·dot′ic** (-dät′ik) ***adj.***

ep·i·du·ral (ep′ə door′əl, -dyoor′-) ***adj.*** ⟦EPI- + DUR(A MATER) + -AL⟧ on or outside the dura mater —***n.*** anesthesia, usually of the lower part of the body, by the epidural injection of a local anesthetic: in full **epidural anesthesia**

ep·i·fau·na (ep′i fô′nə) ***n., pl.*** **-nas** or **-nae** (-nē) ⟦EPI- + FAUNA⟧ the animals living on the surface of marine or freshwater sediments: cf. INFAUNA

ep·i·fo·cal (ep′ə fō′kəl) *adj.* over the focus, or center of disturbance, of an earthquake; epicentral

ep·i·gas·tric (ep′i gas′trik) *adj.* **1** of or located within the epigastrium **2** of or pertaining to the front walls of the abdomen

ep·i·gas·tri·um (-gas′trē əm) *n., pl.* **-tri·a** (-ə) ⟦ModL < Gr *epigastrion*, neut. of *epigastrios*, over the stomach < *epi-*, upon + *gastēr*, the stomach: see GASTRO-⟧ *Anat.* the upper middle portion of the abdomen, including the area over and in front of the stomach

ep·i·ge·al (ep′i jē′əl) *adj.* ⟦Gr *epigeios*, on the earth (< *epi-*, upon + *gē*, the earth) + -AL⟧ **1** *Bot. a)* growing on or close to the ground *b)* emerging from the ground after germination (said of cotyledons) **2** *Zool.* living or developing on the exposed surface of the earth or in shallow water See HYPOGEAL Also **ep′i·ge′an**

ep·i·gene (ep′i jēn′) *adj.* ⟦Fr *épigène* < Gr *epigenēs*, born late: see EPI- & -GEN⟧ *Geol.* produced or formed on or near the earth's surface [*epigene* rocks]

ep·i·gen·e·sis (ep′i jen′ə sis) *n.* ⟦ModL: see EPI- & -GENESIS⟧ **1** *Biol.* the theory that the embryo, influenced by its internal and external environment, develops progressively by stages, forming structures that were not originally present in the egg: cf. PREFORMATION **2** *Geol.* a type of metamorphism in which the mineral content of a rock changes as a result of external influences **3** *Med. a)* the appearing of secondary symptoms *b)* a secondary symptom

ep·i·ge·net·ic (-jə net′ik) *adj.* **1** of, or having the nature of, epigenesis **2** *Geol. a)* produced on or near the surface of the earth *b)* formed or deposited later than the enclosing rocks: said of ore deposits, structures, etc.

e·pig·e·nous (e pij′ə nəs, ē-) *adj.* ⟦EPI- + -GENOUS⟧ *Bot.* growing on the surface of a leaf or other plant part, esp. on the upper surface, as some fungi: see HYPOGENOUS

ep·i·ge·ous (ep′i jē′əs) *adj.* EPIGEAL

ep·i·glot·tis (ep′ə glät′is) *n.* ⟦ModL < Gr *epiglōttis*: see EPI- & GLOTTIS⟧ the thin, triangular, lidlike piece of cartilage that folds back over the opening of the windpipe during swallowing, thus preventing food, etc. from entering the lungs —**ep′i·glot′tal** *adj.*, **ep′i·glot′tic**

ep·i·gone (ep′ə gōn′) *n., pl.* **-gones′** or *Gr. Myth.* **e·pig·o·ni** (e pig′ə nī′, ē-) ⟦Ger, sing. of *epigonen* < Gr (*hoi*) *Epigonoi*, lit., (the) Afterborn, epithet of the sons of the seven chiefs who led the first war against Thebes: pl. of *epigonos*, orig. adj., born after: see EPI- & GONO-⟧ an inferior descendant, follower, or imitator —**the Epigoni** *Gr. Myth.* the sons of the SEVEN AGAINST THEBES: they resumed the conflict a decade later and razed Thebes —**ep′i·gon′ic** *adj.*

ep·i·gram (ep′ə gram′) *n.* ⟦ME < OFr *epigramme* < L *epigramma* < Gr, inscription, epigram < *epigraphein* < *epi-*, upon + *graphein*, to write: see GRAPHIC⟧ **1** a short poem with a witty or satirical point **2** any terse, witty, pointed statement, often with a clever twist in thought (Ex.: "Experience is the name everyone gives to his mistakes") **3** use of the epigram —*SYN.* SAYING

ep·i·gram·mat·ic (ep′ə grə mat′ik) *adj.* ⟦L *epigrammaticus* < Gr *epigrammatikos*⟧ **1** of the epigram or full of epigrams **2** having the nature of an epigram; terse, witty, etc. Also **ep′i·gram·mat′i·cal** —**ep′i·gram·mat′i·cal·ly** *adv.*

ep·i·gram·ma·tism (ep′ə gram′ə tiz′əm) *n.* the use of epigrams, or a style characterized by epigram —**ep′i·gram′ma·tist** *n.*

ep·i·gram·ma·tize (-tīz′) *vt., vi.* **-tized′**, **-tiz′ing** to express (something) epigrammatically; make epigrams (about)

ep·i·graph (ep′ə graf′) *n.* ⟦Gr *epigraphē*, inscription < *epigraphein*: see EPIGRAM⟧ **1** an inscription on a building, monument, etc. **2** a brief quotation placed at the beginning of a book, chapter, etc.

ep·i·graph·ic (ep′ə graf′ik) *adj.* of or having to do with an epigraph or epigraphy: also **ep′i·graph′i·cal** —**ep′i·graph′i·cal·ly** *adv.*

e·pig·ra·phist (ē pig′rə fist, i-) *n.* a specialist in epigraphy: also **e·pig′ra·pher**

e·pig·ra·phy (ē pig′rə fē, i-) *n.* ⟦EPIGRAPH + -Y³: form infl. by -GRAPHY⟧ **1** inscriptions collectively **2** the study that deals with deciphering, interpreting, and classifying inscriptions, esp. ancient inscriptions

e·pig·y·nous (ē pij′ə nəs) *adj.* ⟦EPI- + -GYNOUS⟧ designating petals, sepals, and stamens that are attached to the top of the ovary, as in a sunflower: see PERIGYNOUS, HYPOGYNOUS —**e·pig′y·ny** *n.*

ep·i·lep·sy (ep′ə lep′sē) *n.* ⟦OFr *epilepsie* < LL *epilepsia* < Gr *epilēpsia*, *epilēpsis*, lit., a seizure, hence epilepsy < *epilambanein*, to seize upon < *epi-*, upon + *lambanein*, to seize: see LATCH⟧ a recurrent disorder of the nervous system, characterized by seizures of excessive brain activity which cause mental and physical dysfunction, as convulsions, unconsciousness, etc.: see GRAND MAL, PETIT MAL, PSYCHOMOTOR (sense 2)

ep·i·lep·tic (ep′ə lep′tik) *adj.* ⟦Fr *épileptique* < L *epilepticus* < Gr *epilēptikos*⟧ **1** of, like, or having the nature of epilepsy **2** having epilepsy —*n.* a person who has epilepsy —**ep′i·lep′ti·cal·ly** *adv.*

ep·i·lep·toid (ep′ə lep′toid′) *adj.* resembling epilepsy: also **ep′i·lep′ti·form′** (-tə fôrm′)

☆**ep·i·lim·ni·on** (ep′ə lim′nē än′, -ən) *n.* ⟦ModL < EPI- + Gr *limnion*, dim. of *limnē*, marshy lake, prob. < IE base *(*e*)*lei-*, to bend > LIMB¹⟧ an unfrozen lake's warm, upper layer of oxygen-rich water that is above the thermocline: see HYPOLIMNION

ep·i·logue or **ep·i·log** (ep′ə lôg′) *n.* ⟦ME *epiloge* < OFr *epilogue* < L *epilogus* < Gr *epilogos*, conclusion, epilogue < *epilegein*, to say in addition, add < *epi-*, upon + *legein*, to say, speak: see LOGIC⟧ **1** a closing section added to a novel, play, etc., providing further comment, interpretation, or information **2** a short speech or poem spoken to the audience by one of the actors at the end of a play **3** the actor or actors who speak this

ep·i·mere (ep′ə mir′) *n.* ⟦EPI- + -MERE⟧ the dorsal portion of the mesodermal mass in the early development of chordate embryos that gives rise to the skeletal muscles

ep·i·mys·i·um (ep′ə mis′ē əm) *n., pl.* **-i·a** (-ē ə) ⟦ModL < EPI- + Gr *mys*, muscle (see MYO-) + ModL *-ium* (see -IUM)⟧ the sheath of connective tissue surrounding a muscle

ep·i·nas·ty (ep′ə nas′tē) *n.* ⟦EPI- + -NASTY⟧ *Bot.* the condition in which an organ, as a leaf, turns downward because of the more rapid growth of the upper layers of cells: opposed to HYPONASTY —**ep′i·nas′tic** *adj.*

☆**ep·i·neph·rine** (ep′ə nef′rin, -rēn′) *n.* ⟦EPI- + NEPHR(O)- + -INE³⟧ a hormone, $C_9H_{13}NO_3$, secreted by the medulla of the adrenal gland, that stimulates the heart, increases blood sugar, muscular strength, and endurance, etc.; adrenaline: it is extracted from animal adrenals or prepared synthetically

ep·i·neu·ri·um (ep′ə noor′ē əm, -nyoor′-) *n.* ⟦ModL < EPI- + Gr *neuron*, a NERVE⟧ the layer of connective tissue surrounding a peripheral nerve

E·piph·a·ny (ē pif′ə nē, i-) *n., pl.* **-nies** ⟦ME & OFr *epiphanie* < LL(Ec) *epiphania* < Gr(Ec) *epiphaneia*, appearance < *epiphainein*, to show forth, manifest < *epi-*, upon + *phainein*, to show: see FANTASY⟧ **1** [**e-**] an appearance or manifestation of a god or other supernatural being **2** in many Christian churches, a yearly festival, held January 6, commemorating both the revealing of Jesus as the Christ to the Gentiles in the persons of the Magi and the baptism of Jesus: also called TWELFTH DAY **3** ⟦popularized by James JOYCE²⟧ [**e-**] *a)* a moment of sudden intuitive understanding; flash of insight *b)* a scene, experience, etc. that occasions such a moment —**ep·i·phan·ic** (ep′ə fan′ik) *adj.*

ep·i·phe·nom·e·nal·ism (ep′ə fə näm′ə nəl iz′əm) *n.* the theory that mental or conscious processes simply accompany certain neural processes as epiphenomena

☆**ep·i·phe·nom·e·non** (-fə näm′ə nən, -nän′) *n., pl.* **-na** (-nə) ⟦EPI- + PHENOMENON⟧ **1** a phenomenon that occurs with and seems to result from another but has no reciprocal effect or subsequent influence **2** *Med.* a secondary or additional occurrence in the course of a disease, usually unrelated to the disease —**ep′i·phe·nom′e·nal** *adj.* —**ep′i·phe·nom′e·nal·ly** *adv.*

e·piph·y·sis (ē pif′ə sis) *n., pl.* **-ses′** (-sēz′) ⟦ModL < Gr *epiphysis*, a growth upon, excrescence < *epiphyein*, to grow upon < *epi-*, upon + *phyein*, to grow: see BONDAGE⟧ **1** the end part of a long bone which is at first separated from the main part by cartilage, but later fuses with it by ossification **2** the pineal body: in full **epiphysis cer·e·bri** (ser′ə brī′) —**ep·i·phys·e·al** *adj.*, **ep·i·phys·i·al** (ep′ə fiz′ē əl)

ep·i·phyte (ep′ə fīt′) *n.* ⟦EPI- + -PHYTE⟧ **1** a plant that grows on another plant but is not a parasite and produces its own food by photosynthesis, as certain orchids, mosses, and lichens; air plant **2** a plant parasitic on the external surface of an animal body —**ep′i·phyt′ic** (-fit′ik) *adj.*

ep·i·phy·tol·o·gy (ep′i fī täl′ə jē) *n.* ⟦< prec. + -LOGY⟧ the study of epidemic plant diseases

ep·i·phy·tot·ic (-fī tät′ik) *adj.* ⟦< EPI- + Gr *phyton*, a plant (see -PHYTE) + -OTIC⟧ epidemic among plants —*n.* an epiphytotic disease

ep·i·rog·e·ny (ep′ī räj′ə nē) *n.* EPEIROGENY —**e·pi·ro·gen·ic** (e pī′rō jen′ik) *adj.*

E·pi·rus (i pī′rəs) **1** ancient kingdom on the E coast of the Ionian Sea, in what is now S Albania & NW Greece (fl. 3d cent. B.C.) **2** region of modern Greece, in the same general area

Epis or **Episc** *abbrev.* **1** Episcopal **2** Episcopalian

e·pis·ci·a (e pish′ə, -ē ə; ē-, i-) *n.* ⟦ModL < Gr *episkia*, fem. of *episkios*, shaded < *epi-*, EPI- + *skia*, shadow < IE **skiya-*, var. of base **skāi*, to gleam softly > SHINE⟧ any of a genus (*Episcia*) of tropical American plants of the gesneria family with elliptical, hairy leaves and white to red flowers

e·pis·co·pa·cy (ē pis′kə pə sē, i-) *n., pl.* **-cies** ⟦< LL(Ec) *episcopatus*, office of a bishop < *episcopus*, BISHOP⟧ **1** the system of church government by bishops **2** EPISCOPATE

e·pis·co·pal (ē pis′kə pəl, i-) *adj.* ⟦ME < LL(Ec) *episcopalis*⟧ **1** of or governed by bishops **2** [**E-**] designating or of any of various churches governed by bishops, including the Protestant Episcopal and the Anglican Church —**e·pis′co·pal·ly** *adv.*

E·pis·co·pa·lian (ē pis′kə pāl′yən, i-) *adj.* ⟦prec. + -IAN⟧ **1** [**e-**] of church government by bishops **2** Episcopal: see EPISCOPAL (sense 2) —*n.* **1** [**e-**] any member of an episcopal church or a person believing in episcopal government ☆**2** any member of the Protestant Episcopal Church —**E·pis′co·pa′lian·ism′** *n.*

e·pis·co·pal·ism (ē pis′kə pəl iz′əm, i-) *n.* the theory or doctrine that the authority to govern a church rests in a body of bishops and not in any individual

e·pis·co·pate (ē pis′kə pit, -pāt′; i-) *n.* ⟦see EPISCOPACY⟧ **1** the position, rank, or term of office of a bishop **2** a bishop's see **3** bishops collectively

e·pi·si·ot·o·my (i pē′zē ät′ə mē, -piz′ē-) *n., pl.* **-mies** ⟦< Gr *epision*, pubic region + -TOMY⟧ an incision of the perineum, often performed during childbirth to prevent injury to the vagina

ep·i·sode (ep′ə sōd′) *n.* ⟦Gr *epeisodion*, addition, episode, orig. neut. of *epeisodios*, following upon the entrance < *epi-*, upon + *eisodos*, an entrance < *eis-*, into + *hodos*, way, road < IE base **sed-*, to go⟧ **1** the part of an ancient Greek tragedy between two choric songs: it corresponds to an act **2** in a novel, narrative poem, etc., a portion of the story considered as a unit **3** any event or series of events complete in itself but forming part of a larger one [an *episode* in the war] **4** any installment of a serialized story or drama **5** *Music* a passage or section digressing from a main theme, as in a fugue or rondo —**SYN.** OCCURRENCE

ep·i·sod·ic (ep′ə säd′ik) *adj.* **1** having the nature of an episode; incidental **2** divided into episodes, often not closely related or well integrated Also **ep′i·sod′i·cal** —**ep′i·sod′i·cal·ly** *adv.*

ep·i·some (ep′ə sōm′) *n.* ⟦EPI- + -SOME[3]⟧ a small genetic element or unit of DNA that is not essential to the life of the cell: it can be lost or transferred, and it can replicate independently

e·pis·ta·sis (ē pis′tə sis) *n.* ⟦ModL < Gr, a stopping < *ephistanai*, to stop, orig. to place upon < *epi-*, EPI- + *histanai*, to STAND⟧ *Genetics* the suppression of gene expression by one or more other genes —**ep·i·stat·ic** (ep′ə stat′ik) *adj.*

ep·i·stax·is (ep′i stak′sis) *n.* ⟦ModL < Gr *epistazein*, to bleed at the nose < *epi-*, upon + *stazein*, to fall in drops: see STAGNATE⟧ *Med.* nosebleed

ep·i·ste·mic (ep′i stē′mik) *adj.* ⟦< Gr *epistēmē* (see fol.) + -IC⟧ of or having to do with knowledge or the act or ways of knowing —**ep′i·ste′mi·cal·ly** *adv.*

e·pis·te·mol·o·gy (ē pis′tə mäl′ə jē, i-) *n., pl.* **-gies** ⟦< Gr *epistēmē*, knowledge < *epistanai*, to understand, believe (< *epi-* + *histanai*, orig., to stand before, confront: see STAND) + -LOGY⟧ the study or theory of the nature, sources, and limits of knowledge —**e·pis′te·mo·log′i·cal** (-mə läj′i kəl) *adj.* —**e·pis′te·mo·log′i·cal·ly** *adv.* —**e·pis′te·mol′o·gist** *n.*

ep·i·ster·num (ep′i stur′nəm) *n., pl.* **-na** (-nə) ⟦ModL: see EPI- & STERNUM⟧ **1** the most anterior part of the sternum in amphibians and mammals **2** in some lizards, a dermal bone lying ventral to the sternum

e·pis·tle (ē pis′əl) *n.* ⟦ME *epistel* < OFr *epistle* (& OE *epistol*) < L *epistola*, *epistula* < Gr *epistolē*, a letter, message < *epistellein*, to send to < *epi-*, to + *stellein*, to send, summon: see STALK[1]⟧ **1** a letter, esp. a long, formal, instructive letter: now generally a facetious use **2** [**E-**] *a)* any of the letters in the New Testament *b)* a selection, usually from these Epistles, read in various churches

e·pis·tler (ē pis′lər, -əl ər; -pist′lər) *n.* **1** a letter writer **2** [*usually* **E-**] the person who reads the Epistle during Mass, etc.: also **e·pis·to·ler** (ē pis′tə lər)

e·pis·to·lar·y (ē pis′tə ler′ē) *adj.* ⟦Fr *épistolaire* < L *epistolaris* < *epistola*, EPISTLE⟧ **1** of or suitable to letters or letter writing **2** contained in or conducted by letters **3** written in the form of a series of letters exchanged by the characters, as certain novels of the 18th cent.

ep·i·style (ep′i stīl′) *n.* ⟦L *epistylium* < Gr *epistylion* < *epi-*, upon + *stylos*, column: see STYLITE⟧ ARCHITRAVE (sense 1)

ep·i·taph (ep′ə taf′, -täf′) *n.* ⟦ME & OFr *epitaphe* < L *epitaphium*, eulogy < Gr *epitaphion* < *epi*, upon, at + *taphos*, tomb < *thaptein*, to bury⟧ **1** an inscription on a tomb or gravestone in memory of the person buried there **2** a short composition in prose or verse, written as a tribute to a dead person, past event, etc. —**ep′i·taph′ic** *adj.*, **ep′i·taph′i·al**

e·pit·a·sis (ē pit′ə sis) *n.* ⟦ModL < Gr, a stretching, intensity < *epiteinein*, to stretch, intensify < *epi-*, EPI- + *teinein*, to stretch: see THIN⟧ that part of a play, esp. in classical drama, between the protasis, or exposition, and the catastrophe or denouement

ep·i·tax·y (ep′i tak′sē) *n.* ⟦EPI- + *-taxy*, an arranging < Gr *-taxia* < *taxis*: see TAXIS⟧ the growth of crystals of one mineral on top of the crystals of another, both crystal patterns having a similar structure —**ep′i·tax′i·al** *adj.*, **ep′i·tax′ic**

ep·i·tha·la·mi·um (ep′i thə lā′mē əm) *n., pl.* **-mi·ums** or **-mi·a** (-ə) ⟦L < Gr *epithalamion* < *epithalamios*, nuptial < *epi-*, at + *thalamos*, bridal chamber < IE base **dhel-*, an arch, hollow > DALE, DELL⟧ a song or poem in honor of a bride or bridegroom, or of both; nuptial song: also **ep′i·tha·la′mi·on′** (-än′, -ən), *pl.* **-mi·a** (-ə)

ep·i·the·li·al (ep′i thē′lē əl) *adj.* of, or like, epithelium

ep·i·the·li·oid (-oid′) *adj.* resembling epithelium

ep·i·the·li·o·ma (ep′i thē′lē ō′mə) *n., pl.* **-ma·ta** (-mə tə) or **-mas** ⟦ModL < fol. + -OMA⟧ any tumor composed mostly of epithelial cells: a former term for a malignant tumor of the skin

ep·i·the·li·um (ep′i thē′lē əm) *n., pl.* **-li·ums** or **-li·a** (-ə) ⟦ModL < Gr *epi-*, upon + *thēlē*, nipple: see FEMALE⟧ cellular tissue covering external body surfaces, as the epidermis, or lining internal surfaces, as hollow organs, vessels, etc.: it consists of one or more layers of cells with little intercellular material

ep·i·the·lize (ep′i thē′līz′) *vt.* **-lized′**, **-liz′ing** to cover with epithelium: also **ep′i·the′li·al·ize′**, **-ized′**, **-iz′ing**

ep·i·thet (ep′ə thet′, -thət) *n.* ⟦L *epitheton* < Gr, lit., that which is added < *epitithenai*, to put on, add < *epi-*, on + *tithenai*, to put, DO[1]⟧ **1** an adjective, noun, or phrase, often specif. a disparaging one, used to characterize some person or thing (Ex.: "egghead" for an intellectual) **2** a descriptive name or title (Ex.: Philip the Fair, America the Beautiful) —**ep′i·thet′ic** *adj.*, **ep′i·thet′i·cal**

e·pit·o·me (ē pit′ə mē′, i-) *n.* ⟦L < Gr *epitomē*, abridgment < *epitemnein*, to cut short < *epi-*, upon + *temnein*, to cut: see -TOMY⟧ **1** a short statement of the main points of a book, report, incident, etc.; abstract; summary **2** a person or thing that shows all the typical qualities of something —**SYN.** ABRIDGMENT

e·pit·o·mize (-mīz′) *vt.* **-mized′**, **-miz′ing** to make or be an epitome of —**e·pit′o·miz′er** *n.*

ep·i·tope (ep′i tōp′) *n.* ⟦< EPI- + Gr *topos*, place: see TOPIC⟧ *Immunology* the site on an antigen to which an antibody attaches: its structure determines the antibody for which it is a receptor

ep·i·zo·ic (ep′i zō′ik) *adj.* living on or attached to the external surface of an animal, but not parasitic —**ep′i·zo′ite′** (-īt′) *n.*

ep·i·zo·on (-zō′än′, -ən) *n., pl.* **-zo′a** (-ə) ⟦ModL < EPI- + Gr *zōion*, animal: see QUICK⟧ a parasite or commensal living on the outside of an animal's body

ep·i·zo·ot·ic (-zō ät′ik) *adj.* ⟦Fr *épizootique* < *épizootie* (formed by analogy with *épidémie*: see EPIDEMIC) < prec.⟧ epidemic among animals —*n.* an epizootic disease Cf. ENZOOTIC

ep·i·zo·ot·i·ol·o·gy (ep′i zō ät′ē äl′ə jē) *n.* ⟦< prec. + -O- + -LOGY⟧ the study of epidemic animal diseases

e plu·ri·bus u·num (ē′ ploor′ə boos′ ōō′nəm) ⟦L⟧ out of many, one: a motto of the U.S.

EPO *abbrev.* erythropoietin

ep·och (ep′ək; *also* ep′äk′; *Cdn & Brit usually* ē′päk′) *n.* ⟦ML *epocha* < Gr *epochē*, a check, cessation < *epechein*, to hold in, check < *epi-*, upon + *echein*, to hold: see SCHEME⟧ **1** the beginning of a new and important period in the history of anything [the first earth satellite marked a new *epoch* in the study of the universe] **2** a period of time considered in terms of noteworthy and characteristic events, developments, persons, etc. [an *epoch* of social revolution] **3** a point in time or a precise date **4** *Astron.* the time at which observations are made, as of the positions of planets or stars **5** *Geol.* a subdivision of a period in geologic time corresponding to the rock strata of a SERIES (*n.* 6) —**SYN.** PERIOD —**ep′och·al** *adj.* —**ep′och·al·ly** *adv.*

ep·ode (ep′ōd′) *n.* ⟦MFr *épode* < L *epodos* < Gr *epōidos*, incantation, lit., song sung after < *epi-*, upon, after + *aeidein*, to sing: see ODE⟧ **1** a form of lyric poem, as of Horace, in which a short line follows a longer one **2** the stanza that follows the strophe and antistrophe in a Pindaric or ancient Greek ode

ep·o·nym (ep′ə nim′) *n.* ⟦< Gr *epōnymos*, eponymous < *epi-*, upon + *onyma*, NAME⟧ **1** a real or mythical person from whose name the name of a nation, institution, etc. is derived [Sir William Penn, father of William Penn, is the *eponym* of Pennsylvania] **2** a person whose name has become identified with some period, movement, theory, etc. **3** a noun or name derived from a person's name (Ex.: *Jacksonville* after Andrew Jackson; *seaborgium* after Glenn T. Seaborg; *Lou Gehrig's disease*) —**ep·o·nym·ic** (ep′ə nim′ik) *adj.*

e·pon·y·mous (ē pän′ə məs, i-) *adj.* of, having to do with, or being an eponym [Hamlet is the *eponymous* character of Shakespeare's tragic play] —**e·pon′y·mous·ly** *adv.*

e·pon·y·my (ē pän′ə mē, i-) *n.* ⟦EPONYM + -Y[3]⟧ derivation from an eponym

ep·o·pee (ep′ə pē′, ep′ə pē′) *n.* ⟦Fr *épopée* < Gr *epopoiia*, the making of epics < *epopoios*, epic poet < *epos* (see EPIC) song + *poiein*, to make (see POET[2])⟧ **1** an epic poem **2** epic poetry

ep·os (ep′äs′) *n.* ⟦L < Gr: see EPIC⟧ **1** an epic poem **2** epic poetry **3** a collection of poems of a primitive epic nature, handed down orally **4** a series of epic events

ep·ox·ide (ep äk′sīd′) *n.* a compound containing the epoxy group

ep·ox·i·dize (-sə dīz′) *vt.* **-dized′**, **-diz′ing** to convert (an unsaturated compound) into an epoxide —**ep·ox′i·da′tion** *n.*

ep·ox·y (ē päk′sē, i-, e-) *adj.* ⟦EP(I)- + OXY(GEN)⟧ designating or of a compound in which an oxygen atom is joined to each of two attached atoms, usually carbon; specif., designating any of various thermosetting resins, containing epoxy groups, that are blended with other chemicals to form strong, hard, chemically resistant adhesives, enamel coatings, etc. —*n.*, *pl.* **-ox′ies** an epoxy resin —*vt.* **-ox′ied**, **-ox′y·ing** to glue with epoxy resin

EPROM (ē′präm′) *n.* ⟦E(RASABLE) + PROM⟧ a type of PROM chip whose bit patterns can be erased and reprogrammed by the user

E-prop·o·si·tion (ē′ präp′ə zish′ən) *n. Logic* a universal, negative proposition

EPS *abbrev.* earnings per share

ep·si·lon (ep′sə län′, -lən) *n.* ⟦LGr *e psilon*, lit., plain *e*: so named to distinguish it from *ai*, which had come to have the same pronun.⟧ the fifth letter of the Greek alphabet (Ε, ε)

Ep·som (ep′səm) town in Surrey, England, southwest of London: site of **Epsom Downs**, where the Derby is run: now part of the district of **Epsom and Ewell**

Epsom salts (*or* **salt**) ⟦after prec.⟧ a white, crystalline salt, magnesium sulfate, $MgSO_4 \cdot 7H_2O$, used as an anticonvulsant or cathartic, as an ingredient in bath salts, etc.

Ep·stein (ep′stīn), Sir **Jacob** 1880-1959; Brit. sculptor, born in the U.S.

Ep·stein-Barr virus (-bär′) ⟦after M. A. *Epstein* & Y. M. *Barr*, Brit scientists who isolated it in 1964⟧ a herpesvirus that causes infectious mononucleosis and may cause various forms of cancer

eq *abbrev.* **1** equal **2** equalization **3** equalize **4** equalizer **5** equation **6** equivalent Also, for 2-4, **EQ**

eqpt *abbrev.* equipment

eq·ua·ble (ek′wə bəl, ē′kwə-) *adj.* ⟦L *aequabilis* < *aequare*, to make equal < *aequus*, fol.⟧ **1** not varying or fluctuating much; steady; uniform [an *equable* temperature] **2** not readily upset; even; tranquil; serene [an *equable* temperament] —**SYN.** STEADY —**eq′ua·bil′i·ty** (-bil′ə tē) *n.* —**eq′ua·bly** *adv.*

e·qual (ē′kwəl) *adj.* ⟦ME < L *aequalis*, equal < *aequus*, level, even, flat⟧ **1** of the same quantity, size, number, value, degree, intensity, quality, etc. **2** having the same rights, privileges, ability, rank, etc. **3** evenly proportioned; balanced or uniform in effect or operation **4** having the necessary ability, strength, power, capacity, or courage: with *to* [*equal* to the challenge] **5** [Archaic] fair; just; impartial **6** [Archaic] smooth and flat; level **7** [Archaic] equable —*n.* any thing or person that is equal [to be the *equal* of another] —*vt.* **e′qualed** or **e′qualled**, **e′qual·ing** or **e′qual·ling** **1** to be equal to; match in value, degree, etc. **2** to do or make something equal to [to *equal* a record] **3** [Archaic] to make equal; equalize —**SYN.** SAME

e·qual-ar·e·a (ē′kwəl er′ē ə) *adj.* designating any of several map projections in which areas enclosed between corresponding meridians and parallels are proportionally equal to areas on the earth's surface, but distances and directions are distorted

e·qual·i·tar·i·an (ē kwäl′ə ter′ē ən, -kwôl′-; i-) *adj., n.* EGALITARIAN —**e·qual′i·tar′i·an·ism′** *n.*

e·qual·i·ty (ē kwôl′ə tē, -kwäl′-; i-) *n., pl.* **-ties** ⟦ME *equalite* < OFr *equalité* < L *aequalitas*⟧ the condition of being equal, esp. of having the same political, social, and economic rights

e·qual·ize (ē′kwəl īz′) *vt.* **-ized′**, **-iz′ing** **1** to make equal **2** to make uniform **3** to compensate for or correct (varying frequency response characteristics) in recording, playback, etc. —**e′qual·i·za′tion** *n.*

e·qual·iz·er (-ər) *n.* **1** a person who equalizes **2** a thing that equalizes, as a group of components inserted in a circuit so as to change the frequency response; specif., an electronic device that amplifies or reduces particular ranges of audio frequencies ☆**3** [Slang] a gun

e·qual·ly (ē′kwəl ē) *adv.* in an equal manner; in or to an equal extent or degree; uniformly, impartially, etc.

e·qual-op·por·tu·ni·ty (ē′kwəl äp′ər to͞o′nə tē, -tyo͞o′-) *adj.* **1** treating all employees and applicants for employment equally, without discriminating in terms of race, sex, religion, etc. **2** random or impartial in action or effect; not selective: often used humorously or ironically [an *equal-opportunity* disease]

Equal Rights Amendment a proposed amendment to the U.S. Constitution stating that civil rights may not be denied to a resident of the U.S. on account of sex

equal sign the sign (=) used to indicate that the terms on either side of it are equal or equivalent

e·qua·nim·i·ty (ek′wə nim′ə tē, ē′kwə-) *n.* ⟦L *aequanimitas* < *aequanimis* < *aequus*, even, plain + *animus*, the mind: see ANIMAL⟧ the quality of remaining calm and undisturbed; evenness of mind or temper; composure

SYN.—**equanimity** implies an inherent evenness of temper or disposition that is not easily disturbed; **composure** implies the disciplining of one's emotions in a trying situation or habitual self-possession in the face of excitement; **serenity** implies a lofty, clear peace of mind that is not easily clouded by ordinary stresses or excitements; **nonchalance** implies a casual indifference to or a cool detachment from situations that might be expected to disturb one emotionally; **sang-froid** implies great coolness and presence of mind in dangerous or trying circumstances

e·quate (ē kwāt′, i-) *vt.* **e·quat′ed**, **e·quat′ing** ⟦ME *equaten* < L *aequatus*, pp. of *aequare*, to make equal < *aequus*, plain, even⟧ **1** *a)* to make equal or equivalent; equalize *b)* to treat, regard, or express as equal, equivalent, identical, or closely related [to *equate* wealth with happiness] **2** *Math.* to state or express the equality of; put in the form of an equation —*vi.* to be equal —**e·quat′a·ble** *adj.*

Equat Gui or **Equat Guin** *abbrev.* Equatorial Guinea

e·qua·tion (ē kwā′zhən, i-) *n.* ⟦ME *equacioun* < L *aequatio*⟧ **1** the act of equating; equalization **2** the state of being equated; equality, equivalence, or balance; also, identification or association **3** *a)* a complex whole [the human *equation*] *b)* an element in a complex whole (see also PERSONAL EQUATION) **4** a statement of equality between two quantities, as shown by the equal sign (=) [a quadratic *equation*] **5** an expression in which symbols and formulas are used to represent a balanced chemical reaction (Ex.: $H_2SO_4 + 2NaCl = 2HCl + Na_2SO_4$) —**e·qua′tion·al** *adj.*

equation of time *Astron.* the constantly changing difference between the true sundial (**apparent solar time**) and mean solar time: the apparent solar time may be as much as 16 minutes ahead or behind: see ANALEMMA

e·qua·tor (ē kwāt′ər, i-) *n.* ⟦ME < ML < LL *aequator*, lit., one who makes equal: see EQUATE⟧ **1** an imaginary circle around the earth, equally distant at all points from both the North and South Poles: it divides the earth's surface into the Northern and Southern Hemispheres **2** a circle like this around any celestial body **3** any circle that divides a sphere or other body into two equal and symmetrical parts **4** CELESTIAL EQUATOR

e·qua·to·ri·al (ē′kwə tôr′ē əl, ek′wə-) *adj.* **1** of or near the earth's equator **2** of any equator **3** like or characteristic of conditions near the earth's equator [*equatorial* heat] **4** designating or of a telescope mounted in such a way as to have two axes of motion, one (called *polar axis*) parallel to the earth's axis, the other (called *declination axis*) perpendicular to it: by rotation about the polar axis it can follow the apparent motion of a celestial body —*n.* an equatorial telescope

Equatorial Guinea country in WC Africa, consisting of a mainland section (unofficially *Río Muni*) between Gabon & Cameroon, & five islands (including *Bioko*) in the Gulf of Guinea: formerly (until 1968) a Spanish possession: 10,831 sq mi (28,051 sq km); cap. Malabo

eq·uer·ry (ek′wər ē, ē kwer′ē) *n., pl.* **-ries** ⟦altered (after L *equus*, horse) < Fr *écurie* < OFr *escuerie*, status of a squire: see ESQUIRE⟧ **1** [Historical] an officer in charge of the horses of a royal or noble household **2** an officer who is a personal attendant on some member of a royal family

e·ques·tri·an (ē kwes′trē ən, i-) *adj.* ⟦< L *equestris* (< *eques*, horseman < *equus*, horse: see HIPPO-) + -AN⟧ **1** of horses, horsemen, horseback riding, or horsemanship **2** depicting a person on horseback [an *equestrian* statue] **3** *a)* of the ancient Roman equites *b)* of or made up of knights —*n.* a rider on horseback, esp. one performing acrobatics on horseback, as in a circus —**e·ques′tri·an·ism′** *n.*

e·ques·tri·enne (ē kwes′trē en′, i-) *n.* a female equestrian

e·qui- (ē′kwi, -kwə; *also* ek′wi, -wə) ⟦L *aequi-*, comb. form of *aequus*, level, even⟧ *combining form* equal, equally [*equidistant*]

e·qui·an·gu·lar (ē′kwi aŋ′gyo͞o lər) *adj.* having all angles equal

e·qui·dis·tant (ē′kwi dis′tənt) *adj.* equally distant —**e′qui·dis′tance** *n.* —**e′qui·dis′tant·ly** *adv.*

e·qui·lat·er·al (ē′kwi lat′ər əl) *adj.* ⟦LL *aequilateralis* < L *aequus* (see EQUAL) + *latus*, side: see LATERAL⟧ having all sides equal [an *equilateral* triangle] —*n.* **1** a figure having equal sides **2** a side exactly equal to another or others

e·quil·i·brant (ē kwil′ə brənt, i-) *n.* ⟦Fr *équilibrant*, prp. of *équilibrer*, to equilibrate < *équilibre*, equilibrium < L *aequilibrium*, EQUILIBRIUM⟧ *Physics* a force or combination of forces that can balance another force or other forces

e·quil·i·brate (ē kwil′ə brāt′, i-; *also* ē′kwi lī′brāt′) *vt., vi.* **-brat′ed**, **-brat′ing** ⟦< LL *aequilibratus*, in equilibrium, level, pp. of **aequilibrare*⟧ to bring into or be in equilibrium; balance or counterbalance —**e·quil′i·bra′tion** *n.* —**e·quil′i·bra′tor** *n.*

e·quil·i·brist (ē kwil′ə brist, i-) *n.* ⟦Fr *équilibriste* < *équilibre*: see EQUILIBRANT⟧ a performer who does tricks of balancing, as a tightrope walker

e·qui·lib·ri·um (ē′kwi lib′rē əm; *also* ek′wi-) *n., pl.* **-ri·ums** or **-ri·a** (-ə) ⟦L *aequilibrium* < *aequilibris*, evenly balanced < *aequus* (see EQUAL) + *libra*, a balance⟧ **1** a state of balance or equality between opposing forces **2** a state of balance or adjustment of conflicting desires, interests, etc. **3** *a)* the ability of the animal body to keep itself properly oriented or positioned; bodily stability or balance *b)* mental or emotional stability or balance; poise **4** the condition in a reversible chemical reaction in which the products of the reaction are consumed by the reverse reaction at the same rate as they are formed, and there is no net change in the concentrations of the products or the reactants **5** the stage of a radioactive material at which the rate of disintegration and the rate of formation are equal for each intermediate product in the radioactive decay series

e·qui·mo·lal (ē′kwi mō′ləl) *adj.* having the same molal concentration of solute in a solvent

e·qui·mo·lar (-mō′lər) *adj.* **1** having the same molar concentration of solute in a solvent **2** having the same number of moles of a given substance

e·qui·mo·lec·u·lar (ē′kwi mō lek′yo͞o lər) *adj.* having an equal number of molecules

e·quine (ē′kwīn′; *also* e′kwīn′) *adj.* ⟦L *equinus* < *equus*: see EQUESTRIAN⟧ of, like, or characteristic of a horse —*n.* a horse

equine infectious anemia a viral disease of horses, similar to malaria, characterized by sudden fever, swelling, and anemia; swamp fever

e·qui·noc·tial (ē′kwi näk′shəl) *adj.* ⟦ME & OFr *equinoxial* < L *aequinoctialis*⟧ **1** relating to either of the equinoxes or to equal periods of day and night **2** occurring at or about the time of an equinox **3** equatorial —*n.* **1** CELESTIAL EQUATOR **2** a storm occurring at or about the time of an equinox

equinoctial circle (*or* **line**) CELESTIAL EQUATOR

equinoctial year *see* YEAR (sense 2)

e·qui·nox (ē′kwi näks′, ek′wə näks′) *n.* ⟦ME < OFr *equinoxe* < ML *aequinoxium* < L *aequinoctium* < *aequus* (see EQUAL) + *nox*, NIGHT⟧ **1** the time when the sun in its apparent annual movement along the ecliptic crosses the celestial equator, making night and day of equal length in all parts of the earth: in the Northern Hemisphere the **vernal equinox** occurs about March 21 and marks the beginning of spring, and the **autumnal equinox** occurs about September 22 and marks the beginning of autumn **2** either of the two points on the celestial sphere where the sun's path crosses the celestial equator: also called **equinoctial point**

e·quip[1] (ē kwip′, i-) *vt.* **e·quipped′**, **e·quip′ping** ⟦Fr *équiper* < OFr *esquiper*, to embark, put out to sea, prob. < ON *skipa*, to arrange, make ready < *skip*, SHIP⟧ **1** to provide with what is needed; outfit [troops *equipped* for battle] **2** to prepare by training, instruction, etc. **3** to dress (oneself) for a certain purpose —**SYN.** FURNISH

equip[2] *abbrev.* equipment

eq·ui·page (ek′wə pij) *n.* ⟦MFr < *esquiper*: see prec.⟧ **1** the furnishings, accessories, or outfit of a ship, army, expedition, etc.; equipment **2** a carriage, esp. one with horses and liveried servants **3** [Archaic] *a)* toilet articles *b)* a case for these **4** [Archaic] retinue; body of attendants

e·quip·ment (ē kwip′mənt, i-) *n.* **1** an equipping or being equipped **2** whatever a person, group, or thing is equipped with; the special things needed for some purpose; supplies, furnishings, apparatus, etc. **3** goods used in providing service, esp. in transportation, as the rolling stock of a railroad **4** one's abilities, knowledge, etc.

eq·ui·poise (ek′wi poiz′, ē′kwi-) *n.* ⟦EQUI- + POISE[1]⟧ **1** equal distribution of weight; state of balance, or equilibrium **2** a weight or force that balances another; counterbalance

e·qui·pol·lent (ē′kwi päl′ənt) *adj.* ⟦ME & OFr *equipolent* < L *aequipollens* < *aequus* (see EQUAL) + *pollens*, prp. of *pollere*, to be strong⟧ **1** equal in force, weight, or validity **2** equivalent in meaning or result —*n.* something equipollent —**e′qui·pol′lence** *n.*, **e′qui·pol′len·cy**

e·qui·pon·der·ant (ē′kwi pän′dər ənt) *adj.* ⟦ML *aequiponderans*, prp. of *aequiponderare* < L *aequus* (see EQUAL) + *ponderare*, to weigh: see PONDER⟧ of the same weight; evenly balanced —**e′qui·pon′der·ance** *n.*

e·qui·pon·der·ate (-pän′dər āt′) *vt.* **-at′ed**, **-at′ing** ⟦< pp. of ML *aequiponderare*: see prec.⟧ **1** to counterbalance **2** to make evenly balanced

e·qui·po·ten·tial (-pō ten′shəl) *adj.* 1 having equal potentiality or power 2 *Physics* of the same potential at all points

eq·ui·se·tum (ek′wi sēt′əm) *n., pl.* **-tums** or **-ta** (-ə) ⟦ModL < L *equisaetum*, the plant horsetail < *equus*, horse (see HIPPO-) + *saeta*, bristle: see SINEW⟧ HORSETAIL

eq·ui·ta·ble (ek′wit ə bəl) *adj.* ⟦Fr *équitable* < *équité*⟧ 1 characterized by equity; fair; just: said of actions, results of actions, etc. 2 *Law a)* having to do with equity, as distinguished from common or statute law *b)* valid in equity —**eq′ui·ta·ble·ness** *n.* —**eq′ui·ta·bly** *adv.*

eq·ui·tant (ek′wi tənt) *adj.* ⟦L *equitans*, prp. of *equitare*: see fol.⟧ *Bot.* overlapping: said of a leaf whose base overlaps and covers partly the leaf above it, as in the iris

eq·ui·ta·tion (ek′wi tā′shən) *n.* ⟦L *equitatio* < *equitatus*, pp. of *equitare*, to ride < *eques*: see EQUESTRIAN⟧ the art of riding on horseback; horsemanship

eq·ui·tes (ek′wi tēz′) *pl.n.* ⟦L, pl. of *eques*: see EQUESTRIAN⟧ members of a specially privileged class of citizens in ancient Rome, from which the cavalry was formed; equestrian order of knights

eq·ui·ty (ek′wit ē) *n., pl.* **-ties** ⟦ME *equite* < OFr *équité* < L *aequitas*, equality < *aequus*: see EQUAL⟧ 1 fairness; impartiality; justice 2 anything that is fair or equitable ☆3 the value of property beyond the total amount owed on it in mortgages, liens, etc. 4 *Accounting, Finance a)* assets minus liabilities; net worth; capital *b)* that portion of a company's net worth belonging to its owners or shareholders *[shareholders' equity] c)* [*pl.*] shares of stock *[bonds and equities]* 5 *Law a)* resort to general principles of fairness and justice whenever existing law is inadequate *b)* a system of rules and doctrines, as in the U.S., supplementing common and statute law and superseding such law when it proves inadequate for just settlement *c)* a right or claim recognized in a court of equity *d)* EQUITY OF REDEMPTION —*adj.* of or relating to stocks, stock markets, etc. *[equity financing]*

☆**equity capital** funds contributed by the owners of a business

equity of redemption the right of a mortgagor in default to redeem the mortgaged property by paying the principal, interest, and costs within a specified reasonable time

equiv *abbrev.* equivalent

e·quiv·a·lence (ē kwiv′ə ləns, i-) *n.* ⟦Fr *équivalence* < ML *aequivalentia*⟧ 1 the condition of being equivalent; equality of quantity, value, force, meaning, etc. 2 *Chem.* equality of combining capacity; the principle that different weights of different substances are equivalent in chemical reactions Also **e·quiv′a·len·cy**

e·quiv·a·lent (ē kwiv′ə lənt, i-) *adj.* ⟦ME < OFr < LL *aequivalens*, prp. of *aequivalere*, to have equal power: see EQUI- & VALUE⟧ 1 equal in quantity, value, force, meaning, etc. 2 *Chem.* having the same valence 3 *Geom.* equal in area, volume, etc., but not of the same shape —*n.* 1 an equivalent thing 2 *Chem. a)* the quantity by weight (of a substance) that combines with 8 grams of oxygen or 1.008 grams of hydrogen *b)* the weight obtained by dividing the atomic weight by the valence —**SYN.** SAME —**e·quiv′a·lent·ly** *adv.*

e·quiv·o·cal (ē kwiv′ə kəl, i-) *adj.* ⟦< LL *aequivocus* (see fol.) & -AL⟧ 1 that can have more than one interpretation; having two or more meanings; purposely vague, misleading, or ambiguous *[an equivocal reply]* 2 uncertain; undecided; doubtful *[an equivocal outcome]* 3 suspicious; questionable *[equivocal conduct]* —**SYN.** OBSCURE —**e·quiv′o·cal′i·ty** (-kal′ə tē) *n.*, **e·quiv′o·cal·ness** —**e·quiv′o·cal·ly** *adv.*

e·quiv·o·cate (ē kwiv′ə kāt′, i-) *vi.* **-cat′ed**, **-cat′ing** ⟦ME *equivocaten* < ML *aequivocatus*, pp. of *aequivocari*, to have the same sound < LL *aequivocus*, of like sound < L *aequus* (see EQUAL) + *vox*, VOICE⟧ to use equivocal terms in order to deceive, mislead, hedge, etc.; be deliberately ambiguous —**SYN.** LIE[2] —**e·quiv′o·ca′tion** *n.* —**e·quiv′o·ca′tor** *n.*

eq·ui·voque or **eq·ui·voke** (ek′wi vōk′, ē′kwi-) *n.* ⟦Fr *équivoque*, orig. adj., equivocal < LL *aequivocus*: see prec.⟧ [Now Rare] 1 an ambiguous expression or term 2 a pun or punning 3 verbal ambiguity; double meaning

E·quu·le·us (ē kwoo͝l′ē əs) *n.* ⟦L, dim. of *equus*, horse: see HIPPO-⟧ a very small N constellation near the celestial equator and Pegasus

er (*variously* u, ə, ä, *etc.*; ʉr, ər *are spelling pronunciations*) *interj.* used when hesitating in speaking, as while searching for a word or collecting one's thoughts: a conventionalized representation of the sound

Er *Chem. symbol for* erbium

ER *abbrev.* 1 *Baseball* earned run 2 emergency room

'er (ʉr, ər) *pron. dial. or slang var. of* HER[1]

-er (ər) *suffix* 1 ⟦ME *-er(e)* < OE *-ere* < WGmc **-arj*, **-ārj* < or akin to, and reinforced by, L *-arius*, *-arium*, agentive suffixes (Anglo-Fr *-er*, *-ier*), L *-ar* (OFr *-er*), L *-atur* (OFr *-ëure*), L *-atorium* (OFr *-ëor*, Fr *-oir*), L *-ator* (OFr *-ëor*)⟧ *forming nouns a)* a person having to do with, esp. as an occupation or profession (added to nouns) *[hatter, geographer]* (see also -IER, -YER) *b)* a person native to or living in (added to place names and nouns) *[New Yorker, cottager] c)* a thing or action connected with (added to nouns, noun compounds, and noun phrases) *d)* a person or thing that ____s (added to verbs) *[roller]* (see also -AR, -OR) 2 ⟦ME *-re*, *-er* < OE *-ra*⟧ forming the comparative degree of many adjectives and adverbs *[later, greater]* 3 ⟦ME < Anglo-Fr inf. suffix⟧ the action of ____ing: added to verb bases in legal language *[demurrer, repleader]* 4 ⟦ME *-ren*, *-rien* < OE *-rian*, freq. suffix⟧ repeatedly: added to verbs and verb bases *[flicker, patter]*

e·ra (ir′ə, er′ə; *also* ē′rə) *n.* ⟦LL *aera*, era, earlier senses, "counters," "items of account" < pl. of L *aes* (gen. *aeris*), copper: see ORE⟧ 1 a system of reckoning time by numbering the years from some important occurrence or given point of time *[the Christian Era]* 2 an event or date that marks the beginning of a new or important period in the history of something 3 a period of time measured from some important occurrence or date 4 a period of time considered in terms of noteworthy and characteristic events, developments, individuals, etc. *[an era of progress]* 5 *Geol.* a subdivision of an eon: see the geologic time chart in the Reference Supplement —**SYN.** PERIOD

ERA *abbrev.* 1 *Baseball* earned run average: also **era** 2 Equal Rights Amendment

e·ra·di·ate (ē rā′dē āt′, i-) *vi., vt.* **-at′ed**, **-at′ing** to shoot out, as light rays; radiate —**e·ra′di·a′tion** *n.*

e·rad·i·cate (ē rad′i kāt′, i-) *vt.* **-cat′ed**, **-cat′ing** ⟦ME *eradicaten* < L *eradicatus*, pp. of *eradicare*, to root out < *e-*, out + *radix* (gen. *radicis*), ROOT[1]⟧ 1 to tear out by the roots; uproot 2 to get rid of; wipe out; destroy —**SYN.** EXTERMINATE —**e·rad′i·ca·ble** (-kə bəl) *adj.* —**e·rad′i·ca′tion** *n.* —**e·rad′i·ca′tive** *adj.* —**e·rad′i·ca′tor** *n.*

e·rase (ē rās′, i-) *vt.* **e·rased′**, **e·ras′ing** ⟦< L *erasus*, pp. of *eradere*, to scratch out < *e-*, out + *radere*, to scrape, scratch: see RAT⟧ 1 to rub, scrape, or wipe out (esp. written or engraved letters); efface; expunge 2 to remove (something recorded) from (magnetic tape) 3 to remove any sign of; obliterate, as from the mind 4 to remove (data) from a computer storage device 5 [Slang] to kill —**e·ras′a·ble** *adj.*

SYN.—erase implies a scraping or rubbing out of something written or drawn, or figuratively, the removal of an impression; to **expunge** is to remove or wipe out completely; **efface** implies a rubbing out from a surface, and, in extended use, suggests a destroying of the distinguishing marks, or even of the very existence, of something; **obliterate** implies a thorough blotting out of something so that all visible traces of it are removed; **delete** implies the marking of written or printed matter for removal, or the removal of the matter itself

---

e·ras·er (ē rā′sər, i-) *n.* a thing that erases; specif., a device made of rubber for erasing ink or pencil marks, or a pad of felt or cloth for removing chalk marks from a blackboard

e·ra·sion (ē rā′zhən, i-) *n.* ⟦ML *erasio*⟧ 1 the act of erasing 2 *Surgery* the removal of diseased tissue by scraping, as with a curet

E·ras·mus (i raz′məs), **Des·i·der·i·us** (des′ə dir′ē əs) (born *Gerhard Gerhards*) 1466?-1536; Du. humanist, scholar, & theologian —**E·ras′mi·an** (-mē ən) *adj., n.*

E·ras·ti·an (ē ras′tē ən) *adj.* 1 of or supporting Thomas Erastus or his doctrines 2 advocating the supreme authority of the state in church matters —*n.* a follower of Erastus or his doctrines —**E·ras′tian·ism′** *n.*

E·ras·tus (i ras′təs), **Thomas** (born *Thomas Liebler* or *Lieber*) 1524-83; Ger. theologian & physician

e·ra·sure (ē rā′shər, i-) *n.* 1 the act of erasing 2 an erased word, mark, etc. 3 the place on a surface where something has been erased

Er·a·to (er′ə tō′) *n.* ⟦L < Gr *Eratō* < *eratos*, beloved < *eran*, to love⟧ *Gr. Myth.* the Muse of erotic lyric poetry

Er·a·tos·the·nes (er′ə täs′thə nēz′) 275?-195? B.C.; Gr. geographer, astronomer, & mathematician

Er·bil (er′bil) *var. of* IRBIL

er·bi·um (ʉr′bē əm) *n.* ⟦ModL: so named (1843) by C. G. Mosander (1797-1858), Swed chemist, after *Ytterby*, village in Sweden where the rare-earth minerals were first found + -IUM⟧ a trivalent chemical element, one of the rare-earth elements: symbol, Er; at. no. 68: see the periodic table of elements in the Reference Supplement

ere (er) [Old Poet.] *prep.* ⟦ME *er* < OE *ær*, adv., prep., conj., akin to Ger *eher*, *ehe*, orig. compar. as seen in Goth *airis*, earlier < *air*, early < IE **aier-*, dawn < base **ai-*, to burn, shine⟧ before (in time) —*conj.* 1 before 2 sooner than; rather than

Er·e·bus[1] (er′ə bəs) *n.* ⟦L < Gr *Erebos* < IE base **regwos-*, darkness > Arm *erekoy*, evening, Goth *rigis*, darkness⟧ *Gr. Myth.* the dark place under the earth through which the dead pass before entering Hades

Er·e·bus[2] (er′ə bəs), **Mount** volcanic mountain on Ross Island, near Victoria Land, Antarctica: *c.* 12,500 ft (3,810 m)

Er·ech·the·um (er′ek thē′əm) *n.* ⟦Gr *Erechtheion* < *Erechtheus*, lit., the render, a mythical king of Athens supposedly entombed there < *erechthein*, to rend, break < IE base **rekth-*, to harm > Sans *ráksas-*, torment⟧ temple on the Acropolis in Athens, built 5th cent. B.C.: it contains famous examples of Ionic architecture

e·rect (ē rekt′, i-) *adj.* ⟦ME < L *erectus*, pp. of *erigere*, to set up < *e-*, out, up + *regere*, to make straight: see RIGHT⟧ 1 not bending or leaning; straight up; upright; vertical 2 sticking out or up; bristling; stiff 3 [Archaic] *a)* not depressed; uplifted *b)* alert —*vt.* 1 to raise or construct (a building, etc.) 2 to set up; cause to arise *[to erect arbitrary social barriers]* 3 to set in an upright position; raise 4 to set up; assemble 5 [Archaic] to establish; found 6 *Geom.* to construct or draw (a perpendicular, figure, etc.) upon a base line 7 *Physiol.* to cause to become swollen and rigid by being filled with blood —**e·rect′ly** *adv.* —**e·rect′ness** *n.*

e·rec·tile (ē rek′təl, i-; -tīl′) *adj.* ⟦Fr < L *erectus*⟧ 1 that can become erect *[erectile feathers]* 2 of or designating tissue, as in the penis or clitoris, that becomes swollen and rigid when filled with blood 3 having to do with an erection of the penis *[erectile dysfunction]* —**e·rec·til·i·ty** (ē′rek til′ə tē, i rek′-) *n.*

e·rec·tion (ē rek′shən, i-) *n.* 1 an erecting or being erected 2 something erected; structure, building, etc. 3 *Physiol.* a being or becoming rigid and erect by filling with blood; specif., such a condition of the penis or clitoris

e·rec·tor (ē rek′tər, i-) ***n.*** a person or thing that erects; specif., a muscle that causes erection

E region the atmospheric zone within the ionosphere at an altitude of *c.* 90 to 140 km (*c.* 56 to 90 mi), containing the E layer

ere·long (er′lôŋ′) ***adv.*** [Archaic] before long; soon

er·e·mite (er′ə mīt′) ***n.*** ⟦ME < OFr or LL; OFr *ermite, hermite*: see HERMIT⟧ a religious recluse; hermit —**er′e·mit′ic** (-mit′ik) ***adj.***, **er′e·mit′i·cal**

er·e·mu·rus (er′ə myoor′əs) ***n., pl.*** **-mu′ri′** (-ī′) ⟦ModL < Gr *erēmos*, desolate (see HERMIT) + ModL *-urus* < Gr *oura*, tail: see URO-²⟧ any of a genus (*Eremurus*) of perennial plants of the lily family, cultivated for their tall spikes of small, white or colored flowers

ere·now (er′nou′) ***adv.*** [Archaic] before now; heretofore

e·rep·sin (ē rep′sin) ***n.*** ⟦Ger < L *ereptus*, pp. of *eripere*, to snatch away (< *e-*, out + *rapere*, to snatch: see RAPE¹) + Ger *pepsin*, PEPSIN⟧ an enzyme mixture once thought to be one enzyme, secreted by the small intestine and involved in the breaking down of proteins into their component amino acids

er·e·thism (er′ə thiz′əm) ***n.*** ⟦Fr *éréthisme* < Gr *erethismos*, irritation < *erethizein*, to irritate < IE base **er-* > RISE, RUN⟧ [Rare] *Physiol.* an abnormal extreme irritability or sensitivity of an organ, tissue, etc.

ere·while (er′hwīl′) ***adv.*** ⟦ME *er whil*⟧ [Archaic] a short while before; a short time ago: also **ere′whiles′** (-hwīlz′)

Er·furt (er′foort) city in central Germany, in the state of Thuringia

erg¹ (urg) ***n.*** ⟦< Gr *ergon*, WORK⟧ the basic unit of energy or work in the CGS system, equal to the amount of work done by a force of one dyne acting through a distance of one centimeter (10^{-7} joule)

erg² (urg) ***n.*** a vast desert area of deep, rolling sand dunes

er·ga·tive (ur′gə tiv) *Gram.* ***adj.*** ⟦< Gr *ergatēs*, worker (< *ergon*, WORK) + -IVE⟧ **1** designating, of, or in the case that is taken by the subject of a transitive verb in some languages, as Basque or Georgian, in which the direct object of a transitive verb and the subject of the related intransitive share the same case **2** designating or of a verb or language whose transitive and intransitive uses are related in this way

er·go (er′gō, ur′-) ***adv.*** ⟦L⟧ therefore; hence: often used as a conjunctive adverb

er·go·cal·cif·er·ol (ur′gō kal sif′ər ôl′, -ōl′) ***n.*** ⟦ERGO(STEROL) + CALCIFEROL⟧ a crystalline sterol, $C_{28}H_{43}OH$, formed by the ultraviolet irradiation of ergosterol; vitamin D_2

er·god·ic (ur gäd′ik) ***adj.*** ⟦< Gr *ergon*, work + *hodos*, path⟧ **1** designating or of the theory that any large enough statistical sample can be representative of the whole **2** of or having to do with a system or process that demonstrates such a theory

er·go·graph (ur′gō graf′) ***n.*** ⟦< Gr *ergon*, WORK + -GRAPH⟧ an instrument for measuring and recording the amount of work that a muscle is capable of doing

er·gom·e·ter (ur gäm′ət ər) ***n.*** ⟦< Gr *ergon*, WORK + -METER⟧ an instrument for measuring the amount of work done by a muscle or muscles over a period of time —**er·gom′e·try** (-trē) ***n.***

er·go·nom·ics (ur′gə näm′iks) ***n.*** ⟦< Gr *ergon*, WORK + (EC)ONOMICS⟧ the study of the problems of people in adjusting to their environment; esp., the science that seeks to adapt work or working conditions to suit the worker —***pl.n.*** [*with sing. or pl. v.*] ergonomic factors or arrangement —**er′go·nom′ic** ***adj.***, **er′go·nom′i·cal** —**er′go·nom′i·cal·ly** ***adv.*** —**er·gon′o·mist** (-gän′ə məst) ***n.***

☆**er·go·no·vine** (ur′gō nō′vēn′, -vin) ***n.*** ⟦*ergo-* (< Fr < *ergot*, ERGOT) + *nov-* (< L *novus*, NEW) + -INE³⟧ a water-soluble alkaloid of ergot, $C_{19}H_{23}N_3O_2$, used to increase contraction of the uterus during childbirth and prevent uterine hemorrhage

er·gos·ter·ol (ur gäs′tər ôl′, -ōl′) ***n.*** ⟦< fol. + STEROL⟧ a crystalline plant sterol, $C_{28}H_{43}OH$, formerly prepared from ergot but now chiefly from yeast: when exposed to ultraviolet rays it produces a vitamin (D_2) used to prevent or cure rickets

er·got (ur′gət, -gät′) ***n.*** ⟦Fr < OFr *argot*, a rooster's spur, hence (from the shape) the disease growth in the plant⟧ **1** the hard, reddish-brown or black, grainlike masses (*sclerotia*) of certain parasitic fungi (esp. genus *Claviceps*) that replace the kernels of rye or other cereal plants **2** the disease in which this occurs; specif., the disease of rye caused by a species (*Claviceps purpurea*) of this fungus **3** the dried sclerotia of the rye fungus from which several alkaloids are extracted that have the ability to contract blood vessels and smooth muscle tissue **4** any of these alkaloids —**er·got·ic** (ur gät′ik) ***adj.***

er·got·a·mine (ur gät′ə mēn′, -min) ***n.*** ⟦prec. + AMINE⟧ an alkaloid, $C_{33}H_{35}O_5N_5$, isolated from ergot and used esp. in the treatment of migraine headaches

er·got·ism (ur′gət iz′əm) ***n.*** an acute or chronic poisoning resulting from the excessive or improper use of ergot or the eating of grain or grain products infested with ergot fungus

Er·ic (er′ik) ***n.*** ⟦Scand < ON *Eirìkr* < Gmc **aizo*, honor (akin to Ger *ehre*, honor) + base akin to L *rex* (see RIGHT): hence, lit., honorable ruler⟧ a masculine name: var. *Erik*; fem. *Erica, Erika*

Er·i·ca (er′i kə) ***n.*** ⟦fem. of prec.⟧ a feminine name: var. *Erika*: see ERIC

er·i·ca·ceous (er′i kā′shəs) ***adj.*** ⟦< ModL *Erica*, genus name (< L *erica*, heath < Gr *ereikē*) + -ACEOUS⟧ of the heath family of plants

Er·ic·son (er′ik sən), **Leif** *alt. sp. of* Leif ERIKSON

Er·ics·son (er′ik sən) **1 John** 1803-89; U.S. naval engineer & inventor, born in Sweden: builder of the *Monitor* **2 Leif** *alt. sp. of* Leif ERIKSON

Eric the Red fl. 10th cent.; Norw. explorer & adventurer: discovered & colonized Greenland

E·rid·a·nus (ē rid′ə nəs) ***n.*** ⟦L < Gr *Ēridanos*, poetic name of the Po River⟧ a long S constellation extending from the celestial equator to Hydrus and including the bright star Achernar

Er·ie¹ (ir′ē) ***n., pl.*** **Eries** or **Erie** ⟦see fol.⟧ a member of an Iroquoian North American Indian people that lived in an area east and southeast of Lake Erie

Er·ie² (ir′ē) ⟦NAmFr *Erie, Erié* < Huron name of the village called *Rigué* by the Iroquois⟧ **1** port on Lake Erie, in NW Pa. **2 Lake** one of the Great Lakes, between Lake Huron & Lake Ontario: 9,940 sq mi (25,745 sq km)

Erie Canal canal connecting the Hudson River with the Niagara River as part of the NEW YORK STATE CANAL SYSTEM: *c.* 340 mi (547 km) long: the original canal, parts of which coincide with the present-day canal, was completed in 1825

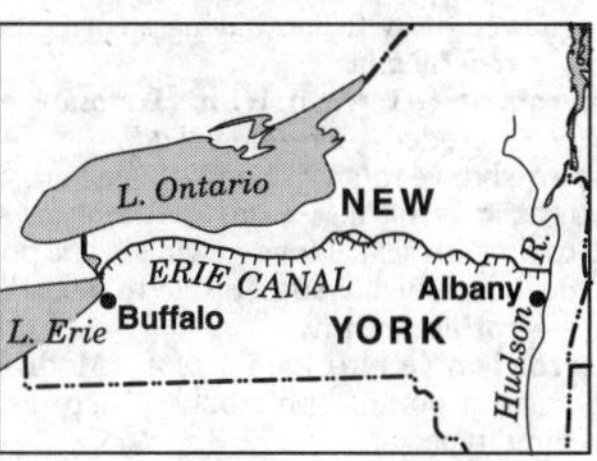

Erie Canal

E·rig·e·na (i rij′ə nə), **Jo·han·nes Sco·tus** (jō hän′əs skōt′əs) A.D. 810-877; Ir. theologian & philosopher at the court of Charlemagne: also **Er·iu·ge·na** (er yoo′jə nə)

e·rig·er·on (ē rij′ər än′) ***n.*** ⟦ModL < L, groundsel < Gr *ērigerōn* < *ēri*, early + *gerōn*, old man (see CORN¹): from the hoary down on some varieties⟧ any of a genus (*Erigeron*) of plants of the composite family having daisylike, yellow flower heads with white, rose, or violet rays

Er·ik·son (er′ik sən), **Leif** fl. 1000; Norw. explorer & adventurer: discovered Vinland, believed to be part of North America: son of Eric the Red: also **Leif Er′iks·son**

Er·in¹ (er′in) ***n.*** ⟦see fol.⟧ a feminine name

Er·in² (er′in) ⟦OIr *Ērinn*, dat. of *Ēriu*, Eire⟧ *old poet. name for* IRELAND

Erin go bragh (er′in gō brä′) ⟦Ir⟧ Ireland forever: a slogan

E·rin·y·es (ē rin′i ēz′, er in′-) ***pl.n., sing.*** **E·rin·ys** (ē rin′is, er in′-) ⟦L < Gr *Erinys*⟧ *Gr. Myth.* FURIES

E·ris (ē′ris, er′is) ***n.*** ⟦L < Gr *Eris*, lit., strife < IE **erei-* < base **er-*, to set in motion > RUN⟧ **1** *Gr. Myth.* the goddess of strife and discord **2** a large dwarf planet of the solar system, orbiting beyond, & roughly the size of, Pluto: diameter, *c.* 2,330 km (*c.* 1,450 mi); one satellite

ERISA (ə ris′ə, ē-) ***abbrev.*** Employee Retirement Income Security Act: also **Erisa**

er·is·tic (er is′tik) ***adj.*** ⟦Gr *eristikos* < *erizein*, to strive, dispute < *eris*, strife: see ERIS⟧ of or provoking controversy or given to sophistical argument and specious reasoning —***n.*** **1** eristic discourse or argument **2** a person who engages in such discourse or argument

Er·i·tre·a (er′ə trē′ə) country in E Africa, on the Red Sea: formerly part of Ethiopia, it became independent in 1993: 46,842 sq mi (121,320 sq km); cap. Asmara —**Er′i·tre′an** ***adj., n.***

Er·i·van (er′ə vän′) *var. of* YEREVAN

Er·lang·en (er′läŋ ən) city in SE Germany, near Nuremberg, in the state of Bavaria

Er·len·mey·er flask (ur′lən mī′ər, er′-) ⟦after Emil *Erlenmeyer* (1825-1909), Ger chemist⟧ [*also* **e- f-**] a conical laboratory flask with a flat bottom and a short, straight neck

erl·king (url′kiŋ′, erl′-) ***n.*** ⟦partial transl. of Ger *erlkönig*, lit., alder king, from Herder's poem; a misunderstanding by Herder (1778) of Dan *ellerkonge*, var. of *elverkonge*, king of the elves⟧ *Gmc. Folklore* a spirit who does mischief and evil, esp. to children: originally a literary character

er·mine (ur′min) ***n., pl.*** **-mines** or **-mine** ⟦ME & OFr *ermin*; OFr *ermine, hermine*, prob. < MHG *hermin*, erminelike < *harme*, ermine < OHG *harmo*, weasel (OE *hearma*): infl. by folk-etym. assoc. with L (*mus*) *Armenius*, Armenian (mouse)⟧ **1** any of several northern weasels having brown fur in summer and white fur with a black-tipped tail in winter, as the stoat **2** the soft, white fur of this animal, used for women's coats, trimming, etc. **3** the position, rank, or functions of some European judges or peers, whose state robe is trimmed with ermine **4** *Heraldry* a representation of a fur indicated by black spots on a white field

er·mined (-mind) ***adj.*** wearing or trimmed with ermine

erne or **ern** (urn) ***n.*** ⟦ME *ern* < OE *earn*, akin to MLowG *arn* < IE base **er-*, **or-*, great bird, eagle > Ger *aar*, eagle & Gr *ornis*, bird⟧ a sea eagle; esp., the European white-tailed eagle (*Haliaeetus albicilla*) which lives near the sea, lakes, or rivers

Er·nest (ur′nist) ***n.*** ⟦Ger *Ernst* < OHG *Ernust, Ernost*, lit., resolute < *ernust*: see EARNEST¹⟧ a masculine name: dim. *Ernie*; var. *Earnest*; equiv. It. & Sp. *Ernesto*, Ger. *Ernst*; fem. *Ernestine*

Er·nes·tine (ur′nis tēn′) ***n.*** ⟦Ger, fem. < *Ernst*: see prec.⟧ a feminine name: dim. *Tina*

Ernst (ernst), **Max** (mäks) 1891-1976; Ger. surrealist painter, in France & the U.S.

e·rode (ē rōd′, ī-) ***vt.*** **e·rod′ed**, **e·rod′ing** ⟦Fr *éroder* < L *erodere* < *e-*, out, off + *rodere*, to gnaw: see RAT⟧ **1** to eat into; wear away; disintegrate [*acid erodes metal*] **2** to form by wearing away gradually [*the running water eroded a gully*] **3** to cause to deteriorate, decay, or vanish —***vi.*** to become eroded —**e·rod′i·ble** ***adj.***

E·rode (i rōd′) city in Tamil Nadu state, S India, on the Cauvery River

e·rog·e·nous (ē räj′ə nəs, i-) ***adj.*** ⟦< Gr *erōs*, love + -GENOUS⟧ designating or of those areas of the body that are particularly sensitive to sexual stimulation: also **er·o·gen·ic** (er′ō jen′ik)

☆**-er·oo** (ə ro͞o′) ⟦prob. < BUCKAROO⟧ *suffix* forming humorous slangy nouns from other nouns [*switcheroo*]

E·ros (er′äs′, ir′-) ***n.*** ⟦L < Gr *Erōs* < *erōs*, love⟧ **1** *Gr. Myth.* the god of love, son of Aphrodite: identified with the Roman god Cupid **2** [**e-**] sexual love or desire **3** *Psychoanalysis* the life instinct, based on the libido, sublimated impulses, and self-preservation

e·rose (ē rōs′) ***adj.*** ⟦L *erosus*, pp. of *erodere*: see ERODE⟧ **1** irregular, as if gnawed away **2** *Bot.* having an irregularly notched edge, as some leaves —**e·rose′ly** ***adv.***

e·ro·sion (ē rō′zhən, i-) ***n.*** ⟦L *erosio* < *erosus*, pp. of *erodere*⟧ an eroding or being eroded —**e·ro′sion·al** ***adj.***

e·ro·sive (ē rō′siv, i-) ***adj.*** causing erosion; eroding

e·rot·ic (ē rät′ik, i-) ***adj.*** ⟦Gr *erōtikos* < *erōs* (gen. *erōtos*), love⟧ **1** having to do with sexual love [*Ovid's erotic poems*] **2** arousing sexual feelings or desires **3** highly susceptible to sexual stimulation —***n.*** an erotic person —**e·rot′i·cal·ly** ***adv.***

e·rot·i·ca (ē rät′i kə, i-) ***pl.n.*** ⟦ModL < Gr *erōtika*, neut. pl.⟧ [*often with sing. v.*] pornographic books, pictures, etc., esp. of a stylish or sophisticated type

e·rot·i·cism (ē rät′ə siz′əm, i-) ***n.*** **1** erotic quality or character **2** *a)* sexual instincts or desire *b)* sexual excitement or behavior **3** preoccupation with sex Also, and for 2 now usually, **er·o·tism** (er′ə tiz′əm)

e·rot·i·cize (-ə sīz′) ***vt.*** **-cized′**, **-ciz′ing** to make erotic or arouse sexual feelings in —**e·rot′i·ci·za′tion** ***n.***

er·o·tize (er′ə tīz′) ***vt.*** **-tized′**, **-tiz′ing** to give sexual significance to or create sexual feeling in; eroticize —**e·ro·ti·za·tion** (er′ə ti zā′shən) ***n.***

e·ro·to·gen·ic (er′ə tō′jen′ik; ē rät′ō-, i-) ***adj.*** ⟦*eroto-*, sexual desire (< Gr *erōto-* < stem of *erōs*, love) + -GENIC⟧ EROGENOUS

e·ro·to·ma·ni·a (er′ə tō′mā′nē ə, -mān′yə; ē rät′ō-, i-) ***n.*** ⟦ModL: see prec. & -MANIA⟧ abnormally strong sexual desire

err (ʉr, er) ***vi.*** ⟦ME *erren* < OFr *errer* < L *errare*, to wander, go astray, err < IE **eras-* > RACE[1], Ger *irren*, to err⟧ **1** to be wrong or mistaken; fall into error **2** to deviate from the established moral code; do wrong **3** [Obs.] to go astray; wander

er·ran·cy (er′ən sē) ***n.***, *pl.* **-cies** ⟦LL *errantia* < L *errans*, prp. of *errare*, ERR⟧ **1** the state or an instance of erring **2** a tendency to err

er·rand (er′ənd) ***n.*** ⟦ME *erende* < OE *ærende*, message, mission, news, lit., that delivered by messenger < base of *ar*, messenger; akin to OS *ārundi*, OHG *ārunti*⟧ **1** a trip to carry a message or do a definite thing, often esp. for someone else **2** the thing to be done on such a trip; purpose or object for which one goes or is sent

er·rant (er′ənt) ***adj.*** ⟦ME *erraunt* < OFr *errant*, prp. of *errer* < ML *iterare*, to travel < L *iter*, a journey: see ITINERANT⟧ **1** roving or wandering, esp. in search of adventure; itinerant [*a knight-errant*] **2** *a)* ⟦OFr, prp. of *errer* (see ERR), confused with *errer*, to rove, travel⟧ erring or straying from what is right or the right course *b)* shifting about [*an errant wind*] **3** *obs. sp. of* ARRANT —**er′rant·ly** ***adv.***

er·rant·ry (er′ən trē) ***n.*** the condition or behavior of a knight-errant; spirit or deeds of chivalry

er·ra·ta (e rät′ə, -rāt′-, -rat′-) ***n.*** **1** *pl. of* ERRATUM **2** a list of errors with their corrections, inserted on a separate page (**errata page**) of a published work

er·rat·ic (i rat′ik) ***adj.*** ⟦ME *erratik* < OFr *erratique* < L *erraticus*, wandering < pp. of *errare*: see ERR⟧ **1** having no fixed course or purpose; irregular; random; wandering **2** deviating from the normal, conventional, or customary course; eccentric; queer **3** *Geol.* designating a boulder or rock formation transported some distance from its original source, as by a glacier —***n.*** an erratic person —**er·rat′i·cal·ly** ***adv.***

er·ra·tum (e rät′əm, -rāt′-, -rat′-) ***n.***, *pl.* **-ta** (-ə) ⟦L, neut. of *erratus* < pp. of *errare*: see ERR⟧ an error discovered in a work already printed: see ERRATA

Er Rif *another name for* RIF

Er·rol (er′əl) ***n.*** a masculine name

er·ro·ne·ous (e rō′nē əs, ə-) ***adj.*** ⟦ME < L *erroneus*, wandering about < *errare*: see ERR⟧ containing or based on error; mistaken; wrong —**er·ro′ne·ous·ly** ***adv.***

er·ror (er′ər) ***n.*** ⟦ME & OFr *errour* < L *error* < *errare*: see ERR⟧ **1** the state of believing what is untrue, incorrect, or wrong **2** a wrong belief; incorrect opinion **3** something incorrectly done through ignorance or carelessness; mistake **4** a departure from the accepted moral code; transgression; wrongdoing; sin **5** *a)* the difference between a computed or estimated result and the actual value, as in mathematics *b)* the amount by which something deviates from what is required ☆**6** *Baseball* a misplay in fielding or throwing a ball which allows a runner to reach base or to advance to the next base: neither a WILD PITCH nor a PASSED BALL is an error **7** *Law* a mistake in judgment or procedure of a court of record, usually prejudicial to one of the parties **8** *Philately* a flaw in a stamp or stamps from a defect in a printing plate, a difference in color, etc. —**er′ror·less** ***adj.***

SYN.—**error** implies deviation from truth, accuracy, correctness, right, etc. and is the broadest term in this comparison [*an error in judgment, in computation, etc.*]; **mistake** suggests an error resulting from carelessness, inattention, misunderstanding, etc. and does not in itself carry a strong implication of criticism [*a mistake in reading a blueprint*]; **blunder** implies stupidity, clumsiness, inefficiency, etc. and carries a suggestion of more severe criticism [*a tactical blunder cost them the war*]; a **slip** is a mistake, usually slight, made inadvertently in speaking or writing; a **faux pas** is a social blunder or error in etiquette that causes embarrassment; **boner** and **boo-boo**, slang terms, are applied to a silly or ridiculous blunder

er·satz (er′zäts′, er zäts′; ʉr′zäts′, ʉr zäts′) ***n.***, ***adj.*** ⟦Ger, lit., replacement < *ersetzen*, to replace < *er-* (< OHG *ir-*, re-) + *setzen*, to place, SET⟧ substitute or synthetic: the word usually suggests inferior quality —SYN. ARTIFICIAL

Erse (ʉrs) ***adj.***, ***n.*** ⟦ME *Erish*, var. of *Irisc*, IRISH⟧ (of) GAELIC (***n.*** 1 and, sometimes, ***n.*** 3)

erst (ʉrst) ***adv.*** ⟦ME *erest* < OE *ærest*, superl. of *ær*: see ERE⟧ **1** [Obs.] at first; originally **2** [Archaic] formerly —***adj.*** [Obs.] first

erst·while (ʉrst′hwīl′) ***adv.*** [Archaic] some time ago; formerly —***adj.*** of an earlier time; former [*my erstwhile friend*]

ERT *abbrev.* estrogen replacement therapy

Er·té (er′tā) (pseud. of *Romain de Tirtoff*) 1892-1990; Fr. illustrator & fashion designer, born in Russia

e·ruct (ē rukt′) ***vt.***, ***vi.*** ⟦L *eructare* < *e-*, out + *ructare*, to belch < IE base **reug-* > OE *rocettan*⟧ to belch: also **e·ruc·tate** (ē ruk′tāt′), **-tat′ed**, **-tat′ing** —**e·ruc·ta·tion** (ē′ruk tā′shən, ē ruk′-) ***n.***

er·u·dite (er′yo͞o dīt′, er′o͞o-; er′yə-, er′ə-) ***adj.*** ⟦ME *erudit* < L *eruditus*, pp. of *erudire*, to instruct, lit., free from roughness < *e-*, out + *rudis*, RUDE⟧ having or showing a wide knowledge gained from reading; learned; scholarly —**er′u·dite′ly** ***adv.***

er·u·di·tion (er′yo͞o dish′ən, er′o͞o-; er′yə-, er′ə-) ***n.*** ⟦ME *erudicioun* < L *eruditio*: see prec.⟧ learning acquired by reading and study; scholarship —SYN. INFORMATION

e·rum·pent (ē rum′pənt) ***adj.*** ⟦< L *erumpens*, prp. of *erumpere*, to burst forth: see fol.⟧ *Bot.* bursting out, as certain spores, seeds, etc.

e·rupt (ē rupt′, i-) ***vi.*** ⟦< L *eruptus*, pp. of *erumpere*, to break out, burst forth < *e-*, out + *rumpere*, to break: see RUPTURE⟧ **1** to burst forth or out, as from some restraint [*erupting lava; a riot erupted*] **2** to throw forth lava, water, steam, etc., as a volcano or geyser **3** to break out in a rash **4** to break through the gums and become visible: said of new teeth —***vt.*** to cause to burst forth; throw forth; eject —**e·rupt′i·ble** ***adj.***

e·rup·tion (ē rup′shən, i-) ***n.*** ⟦ME *erupcioun* < L *eruptio*: see prec.⟧ **1** a bursting forth or out, as of lava from a volcano **2** a throwing forth of lava, water, steam, etc. **3** a sudden outburst, as of emotion or social discontent **4** *Med.* *a)* a breaking out in a rash *b)* a rash

e·rup·tive (ē rup′tiv, i-) ***adj.*** **1** erupting or tending to erupt **2** of, produced by, or formed by eruption [*eruptive rock*] **3** *Med.* causing or characterized by a skin eruption —***n.*** *Geol.* a rock thrown out by volcanic eruption —**e·rup′tive·ly** ***adv.***

Er·win (ʉr′win) ***n.*** ⟦Ger *Erwin*, earlier *Herwin* < OHG *hari*, host, crowd (akin to OE *here*: see HARRY) + *wini*, *wine* (see EDWIN)⟧ a masculine name: var. *Irwin*

-er·y (ər ē, er′ē) ⟦ME *-erie* < OFr *-erie* < LL *-aria*, or by addition of *-ie* (L *-ia*) to OFr nouns of agency in *-ier*⟧ *suffix* **1** a place to [*tannery, brewery*] **2** a place for [*nunnery, vinery*] **3** the practice, act, or occupation of [*robbery, midwifery*] **4** the product or goods of [*pottery, millinery*] **5** a collection of [*greenery, crockery*] **6** the state or condition of [*drudgery, slavery*] **7** the behavior or qualities of [*tomfoolery*]

Er·y·man·thus (er′ə man′thəs), **Mount** mountain in the NW Peloponnesus, Greece: 7,297 ft (2,224 m): in Greek mythology, haunt of a savage boar captured by Hercules —**Er′y·man′thi·an** (-thē ən) ***adj.***

e·ryn·go (ē riŋ′gō, i-) ***n.***, *pl.* **-goes** ⟦via Sp or It *eringio* < L *eryngium* < Gr *eryngion*, dim. of *ēryngos*, prob. < *ear*, *eros*, spring, hence spring flower⟧ **1** any of a genus (*Eryngium*) of plants of the umbel family, with flowers in dense heads and usually stiff, spiny leaves **2** [Obs.] the candied root of the sea holly, formerly used as an aphrodisiac

er·y·sip·e·las (er′i sip′ə ləs, ir′-) ***n.*** ⟦ME *erisipela* < L *erysipelas* < Gr < base of *erythros*, RED + *-pelas*, akin to L *pellis*: see FELL[4]⟧ an acute infectious disease of the skin or mucous membranes caused by a streptococcus and characterized by local inflammation and fever —**er′y·si·pel′a·tous** (-si pel′ə təs) ***adj.***

er·y·sip·e·loid (er′i sip′ə loid′, ir′-) ***n.*** ⟦see prec. & -OID⟧ an infectious skin disease caused by bacteria (*Erysipelothrix rhusiopathiae*) and characterized by red-colored lesions

er·y·the·ma (er′i thē′mə) ***n.*** ⟦ModL < Gr *erythēma* < *erythainein*, to redden, blush < *erythros*, RED⟧ an abnormal redness of the skin caused by various agents, as sunlight, drugs, etc., that irritate and congest the capillaries —**er′y·the′mic** (-mik) ***adj.***, **er·y·them·a·tous** (er′i them′ə təs, -thē′mə-)

er·y·thrism (er′i thriz′əm) ***n.*** ⟦ERYTHR(O)- + -ISM⟧ unusual redness, esp. of the hair of mammals or the feathers of birds —**er·y·thris·mal** (er′i thriz′məl) ***adj.*** —**er′y·thris′tic** (-thris′tik) ***adj.***

er·y·thrite (er′i thrīt′) ***n.*** ⟦ERYTHR(O)- + -ITE[1]⟧ **1** ERYTHRITOL **2** a reddish or pinkish, very soft, monoclinic mineral, $Co_3(AsO_4)_2 \cdot 8H_2O$, that usually forms as a crust near cobalt deposits; hydrous cobalt arsenate: cf. ANNABERGITE

e·ryth·ri·tol (e rith′ri tôl′, -tōl′) ***n.*** ⟦< prec. + -OL[1]⟧ a sweet, colorless crystalline alcohol, $CH_2OH(CHOH)_2CH_2OH$, obtained from some lichens and algae and by synthesis

e·ryth·ro- (e rith′rō, -rə; ē-, i-) ⟦< Gr *erythros*, RED⟧ *combining form* **1** red [*erythrocyte*] **2** erythrocyte [*erythroblast*] Also, before a vowel, **erythr-**

e·ryth·ro·blast (e rith′rō blast′) ***n.*** ⟦prec. + -BLAST⟧ a small nucleated cell, found normally in the marrow of bones, from which an erythrocyte develops —**e·ryth′ro·blas′tic** ***adj.***

e·ryth·ro·blas·to·sis (e rith′rō blas tō′sis) ***n.*** **1** the appearance of immature, nucleated, red-colored blood cells in the circulating blood **2** a disease of the developing fetus and newborn infant, characterized by a hemolytic anemia and jaundice and caused by an incompatibility of blood types between mother and fetus, usually involving the Rh factor: also called **erythroblastosis fe·tal·is** (fi tal′is)

e·ryth·ro·cyte (e rith′rō sīt′) ***n.*** ⟦ERYTHRO- + -CYTE⟧ a mature, red-colored blood cell containing hemoglobin and normally lacking a nucleus; red blood cell: it is a very small, circular disk with both faces concave —**e·ryth′ro·cyt′ic** (-sit′ik) ***adj.***

er·y·throid (er′i throid′) ***adj.*** ⟦ERYTHR(O)- + -OID⟧ **1** reddish in color **2** pertaining to erythrocytes or the primitive cells from which they develop

☆**e·ryth·ro·my·cin** (e rith′rō mī′sin) ***n.*** ⟦ERYTHRO- + -MYCIN⟧ an antibiotic, $C_{37}H_{67}NO_{13}$, isolated from a soil bacterium (*Streptomyces erythreus*), used in treating various bacterial diseases

er·y·thron (er′i thrän′, -thrən) ***n.*** ⟦ModL < Gr *erythron*, neut. of *erythros*, RED⟧ the red blood cell system as an organic unit, comprising the erythrocytes, their sources of production and destruction, etc.

e·ryth·ro·poi·e·sis (e rith′rō poi ē′sis) ***n.*** ⟦ModL < ERYTHRO- + Gr *poiēsis*, a making: see POESY⟧ the body process of developing red blood cells —**e·ryth′ro·poi·et′ic** (-poi et′ik) ***adj.***

e·ryth·ro·poi·e·tin (-poi′ə tin) ***n.*** a hormone that stimulates erythropoiesis, produced mainly in the kidneys of higher organisms

e·ryth·ro·sine (e rith′rō sin, -sēn′) ***n.*** ⟦ERYTHRO- + (EO)SIN⟧ a sodium or potassium salt, $C_{20}H_6I_4O_5Na_2$, formed from an iodine derivative of fluorescein and used in making food colors, biological stains, etc.

Erz·ge·bir·ge (erts′gə bir′gə) mountain range along the border of Germany & the Czech Republic: highest peak, 4,080 ft (1,244 m)

Er·zu·rum (er′zə ro͞om′) city in NE Turkey

Es[1] *abbrev. Bible* Esther

Es[2] *Chem. symbol for* einsteinium

es- (es, is, əs) *prefix* EX-[1] (sense 1): occurs in many words of French origin [*escape*]

-es (iz, əz, z) ⟦ME < OE *-as*, pl. inflection of masc. nouns⟧ *suffix* **1** forming the plural of nouns ending in the sounds (s), (z), (sh), and (ch): an apostrophe can then be added to form the possessive plural [*glasses, buzzes, fishes; witches′*] **2** ⟦ME < Northumbrian OE *-s*, 3d pers. sing., pres. tense inflection of verbs⟧ forming the 3d person sing., pres. indic., of certain verbs [he *kisses*]

ESA *abbrev.* European Space Agency

E·sau (ē′sô′) ***n.*** ⟦L < Gr *Ēsau* < Heb *esav*, lit., hairy⟧ *Bible* the son of Isaac and Rebecca, who sold his birthright to his younger twin brother, Jacob: Gen. 25:21-34, 27

Esc *abbrev.* escape: a key on a standard computer keyboard

es·ca·beche (es′kə bāsh′, -bā′che) ***n.*** ⟦Sp, lit., brine for pickling⟧ **1** any of various dishes, esp. of fish, prepared with a sauce or marinade of onions, peppers, spices, oil, and vinegar **2** a Mexican condiment of pickled vegetables

es·ca·drille (es′kə dril′) ***n.*** ⟦Fr < Sp *escudrilla*, dim. of *escuadra*, squad, orig., square < VL **exquadra*: see SQUARE⟧ a squadron of airplanes, usually six, with their men and equipment, as in the French armed forces of WWI

es·ca·lade (es′kə lād′) ***n.*** ⟦Fr < It *scalata* < *scalare*, to climb < L *scala*, ladder: see SCALE[1]⟧ the act of scaling or climbing the walls of a fortified place by ladders —***vt.*** **-lad′ed, -lad′ing** to climb (a wall, etc.) or enter (a fortified place) by ladders

☆**es·ca·late** (es′kə lāt′) ***vi.*** **-lat′ed, -lat′ing** ⟦back-form. < fol.⟧ **1** to rise on or as on an escalator **2** to expand step by step, as from a limited or local conflict into a general, esp. nuclear, war **3** to grow or increase rapidly, often to the point of becoming unmanageable, as prices or wages —***vt.*** to cause to escalate —**es′ca·la′tion** ***n.*** —**es′ca·la·to′ry** (-lə tôr′ē) ***adj.***

☆**es·ca·la·tor** (es′kə lāt′ər) ***n.*** ⟦coined as a trademark (1895) < ESCALA(DE) + *-tor*, as in (ELEVA)TOR⟧ **1** a moving stairway consisting of treads linked in an endless belt, used in department stores, subway stations, etc. **2** ESCALATOR CLAUSE

☆**escalator clause** a clause in a contract providing for increases or decreases in wages, prices, etc. based on fluctuations in the cost of living, production costs, etc.

es·cal·lo·ni·a (es′kə lō′nē ə) ***n.*** ⟦ModL, after *Escallón*, name of a Sp traveler who discovered the shrub in Colombia⟧ any of a genus (*Escallonia*) of shrubs of the saxifrage family, with white, pink, or red flowers

es·cal·lop or **es·cal·op** (e skäl′əp, -skal′-) ***n., vt.*** ⟦OFr *escalope*, a shell: see SCALLOP⟧ SCALLOP

es·ca·pade (es′kə pād′) ***n.*** ⟦Fr < Sp *escapada* < *escapar*, to escape, flee < VL **excappare*: see fol.⟧ **1** [Archaic] an escape from restraint or confinement **2** a reckless adventure or prank

es·cape (e skāp′, i-) ***vi.*** **-caped′, -cap′ing** ⟦ME *escapen* < NormFr *escaper*, var. of *eschaper* < VL **excappare* < L *ex-*, out of (see EX-[1]) + LL *cappa*, cloak (i.e., leave one's cloak behind)⟧ **1** to get free; get away; get out; break loose, as from a prison **2** to avoid an illness, accident, pain, etc. [two were injured, but he *escaped*] **3** to flow, drain, or leak away [gas *escaping* from a pipe] **4** to slip away; disappear [the image *escaped* from her memory] **5** to come forth involuntarily or unintentionally [a scream *escaped* from her lips] **6** *Bot.* to grow wild, as a plant from a condition of cultivation —***vt.*** **1** to get away from; flee from [to *escape* pursuers] **2** to manage to keep away from; avoid [to *escape* punishment] **3** to come from involuntarily or unintentionally [a scream *escaped* her lips] **4** to slip away from; be missed, unperceived, or forgotten by [his name *escapes* me] —***n.*** ⟦ME *escap*⟧ **1** an act or instance or escaping **2** the state of having escaped **3** a means or way of escape **4** an outward flow or leakage **5** a temporary mental release from reality [movies are her *escape*] **6** *Bot.* a garden plant growing wild —***adj.*** **1** giving temporary mental release from reality **2** *a)* making escape possible [an *escape* hatch] *b)* giving a basis for evading or circumventing a claim, responsibility, etc. [an *escape* clause] —**es·cap′a·ble** ***adj.*** —**es·cap′er** ***n.***

SYN.—**escape**, as compared here, implies a getting out of, a keeping away from, or simply a remaining unaffected by an impending or present danger, evil, confinement, etc. [to *escape* death, criticism, etc.]; to **avoid** is to make a conscious effort to keep clear of something undesirable or harmful [to *avoid* crowds during a flu epidemic]; to **evade** is to escape or avoid by artifice, cunning, adroitness, etc. [to *evade* pursuit, one's duty, etc.]; to **elude** is to escape the grasp of someone or something by artful or slippery dodges or because of a baffling quality [the criminal *eluded* the police; the meaning *eluded* him]

escape artist an entertainer, as in vaudeville, who is skilled at escaping from shackles or other confinement

es·cap·ee (e skā′pē′, -skā′pē′, i-; es′kā pē′) ***n.*** a person who has escaped, esp. from confinement

escape mechanism a kind of defense mechanism by which a person avoids unpleasant thoughts, responsibilities, etc., as through daydreaming

es·cape·ment (e skāp′mənt, i-) ***n.*** ⟦ESCAPE + -MENT, after Fr *échappement*⟧ **1** [Rare] the action of escaping or a means of escape **2** the part in a mechanical clock or watch that controls the speed and regularity of the balance wheel or pendulum, and thereby of the entire mechanism, by the movement of a notched wheel (**escape wheel**), one tooth of which is permitted to escape from the detaining catch at a time **3** a ratchet mechanism, esp. one in typewriters that regulates the horizontal movement of the carriage

escapement

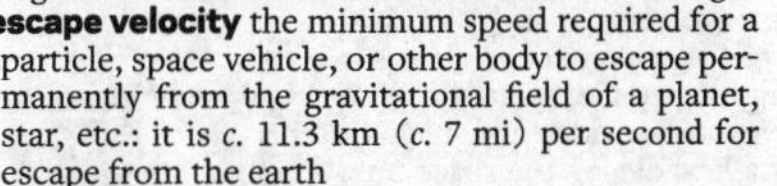

escape velocity the minimum speed required for a particle, space vehicle, or other body to escape permanently from the gravitational field of a planet, star, etc.: it is *c.* 11.3 km (*c.* 7 mi) per second for escape from the earth

es·cap·ism (e skāp′iz′əm, i-) ***n.*** **1** a tendency to escape from reality, the responsibilities and routine of real life, etc., esp. by unrealistic imaginative activity **2** behavior characterized by this tendency

es·cap·ist (-ist) ***adj.*** characterized by, expressing, or catering to escapism —***n.*** a person whose behavior, writing, etc. is escapist

es·cap·ol·o·gist (es′kā päl′ə jist) ***n.*** one who is adept at escaping; escape artist —**es′cap·ol′o·gy** ***n.***

es·car·got (es′kär gō′) ***n.*** ⟦Fr⟧ a snail, esp. an edible variety

es·ca·role (es′kə rōl′) ***n.*** ⟦Fr < ML *escariola* < L *escarius*, pertaining to food < *esca*, food: see ESCULENT⟧ ENDIVE (sense 1)

es·carp (e skärp′) ***n., vt.*** ⟦Fr n. *escarpe* < It *scarpa*: see SCARP⟧ SCARP

es·carp·ment (-mənt) ***n.*** ⟦Fr *escarpement* < *escarpe*: see prec.⟧ **1** a steep slope or cliff formed by erosion or, less often, by faulting **2** ground formed into a steep slope on the exterior of a fortification See also SCARP

Es·caut (e skō′) *Fr. name for* SCHELDT

-es·cence (es′əns) ⟦L *-escentia* < *-escens*: see fol.⟧ *suffix forming nouns* the process of becoming or beginning [*obsolescence*]

-es·cent (es′ənt) ⟦L *-escens* (gen. *-escentis*), prp. ending of inceptive or inchoative verbs in *-escere*⟧ *suffix forming adjectives* **1** in the process of ___ing; starting to be, being, or becoming (as specified) [*obsolescent*] **2** giving off or reflecting light, or showing a play of color (as specified) [*phosphorescent*]

esch·a·lot (esh′ə lät′, esh′ə lät′) ***n.*** ⟦Fr *eschallotte*: see SHALLOT⟧ SHALLOT

es·char (es′kär′, -kər) ***n.*** ⟦altered (after L) < ME *escare* < OFr < LL *eschara*: see SCAR[1]⟧ a dry scab that forms as a result of a burn or of corrosive action

es·cha·rot·ic (es′kə rät′ik) ***adj.*** ⟦LL *escharoticus* < Gr *escharōtikos*⟧ producing or tending to produce an eschar; corrosive; caustic —***n.*** a corrosive or caustic substance

es·cha·tol·o·gy (es′kə täl′ə jē) ***n.*** ⟦< Gr *eschatos*, furthest (< *ex-*, out < IE base **eǵhs* > L *ex*) + -LOGY⟧ **1** the branch of theology dealing with last things, such as death, immortality, resurrection, judgment, and the end of the world **2** the doctrines concerning these —**es·cha·to·log·i·cal** (es′kə tə läj′i kəl, -kat′ə-) ***adj.***

es·cheat (es chēt′) ***n.*** ⟦ME *eschete* < OFr, lit., that which falls to one < pp. of *escheoir*, to fall to one's share < VL **excadere*, to fall upon < L *ex-*, out + *cadere*, to fall: see CASE[1]⟧ *Law* **1** the reverting of property to the lord of the manor (in feudal law), to the crown (in England), or to the government (in the U.S.) when there are no legal heirs **2** property so reverting —***vt.*** to cause to escheat; confiscate —***vi.*** to revert or go by escheat —**es·cheat′a·ble** ***adj.***

Es·cher (esh′ər), **M(aurits) C(ornelis)** 1898-1972; Du. graphic artist

es·chew (es cho͞o′) ***vt.*** ⟦ME *eschewen* < Anglo-Fr *eschuer* < OFr *eschiver* < OHG *sciuhan*, to fear: akin to SHY[1]⟧ to keep away from (something harmful or disliked); shun; avoid; abstain from —**es·chew′al** ***n.***

Es·cof·fier (es kô fyā′), **Au·guste** (ô güst′) 1847-1935; Fr. chef & writer on cooking

☆**es·co·lar** (es′kə lär′) ***n.*** ⟦Sp, lit., scholar (< LL *scholaris:* see SCHOLAR): so named because the rings around the eyes resemble spectacles⟧ any of a family (Gempylidae) of large, deep-water, marine percoid fishes

Es·con·di·do (es′kən dē′dō) ⟦Sp, hidden: after nearby *Escondido* Creek, whose source was difficult to find⟧ city in S Calif., near San Diego

Es·co·ri·al (es kôr′ē əl; *Sp* es′kô ryäl′) ***n.*** ⟦Sp *escorial,* lit., place where a mine has been exhausted < *escoria* < L *scoria,* dross < Gr *skōria,* SCORIA⟧ huge quadrangle of granite buildings near Madrid, built (16th cent.) by Philip II of Spain: it encloses a palace, church, monastery, etc.

es·cort (es′kôrt′; *for v.* i skôrt′) ***n.*** ⟦Fr *escorte* < It *scorta* < *scorgere,* to perceive, lead < LL **excorrigere* < L *ex-,* out + *corrigere,* to set right, CORRECT⟧ **1** one or more persons (or cars, ships, airplanes, etc.) accompanying another or others to give protection or show honor **2** *a)* a man or boy accompanying a woman or girl, as to a party *b)* a person, esp. a woman, employed through a business (**escort service**) to act as a date for a social activity, often, specif., covert illicit sexual activity **3** accompaniment by an escort —***vt.*** ⟦Fr *escorter* < It *scortare*⟧ to go with as an escort; accompany to protect or show honor or courtesy to —***SYN.*** ACCOMPANY

es·cri·toire (es′kri twär′) ***n.*** ⟦OFr *escriptoire* < LL *scriptorium,* metallic style for writing on wax tablets < pp. of L *scribere,* to write: see SCRIBE⟧ a writing desk or table; secretary

es·crow (es′krō′) ***n.*** ⟦OFr *escroue,* roll of writings, bond < ML *scroda* < MDu *schrot,* piece cut off: see SHRED⟧ *Law* a written agreement or something of value put in the care of a third party and not delivered until certain conditions are fulfilled —☆**in escrow** *Law* put in the care of a third party until certain conditions are fulfilled: said of a deed, money, etc.

es·cu·do (es kōō′dō; *Sp* es kōō′thô; *Port* ish kōō′dōō) ***n., pl.*** **-dos** ⟦Sp & Port, a shield, gold coin < L *scutum,* shield: so named from the inscription on the obverse⟧ **1** any of several obsolete coins of Spain, Portugal, and their former colonies **2** the former basic monetary unit of Portugal and Cape Verde

es·cu·lent (es′kyōō lənt, -kyə-) ***adj.*** ⟦L *esculentus* < *esca,* food < IE **ēdes-* < base **ed-,* to eat > L *edere,* EAT⟧ fit for food; edible —***n.*** something fit for food, esp. a vegetable

Es·cu·ri·al (es kyoor′ē əl) ***n.*** *var. of* ESCORIAL

es·cutch·eon (e skuch′ən, i-) ***n.*** ⟦NormFr *escuchon* < VL **scutio* < L *scutum,* shield < ? IE base **skeu-,* to cover > SKY⟧ **1** a shield or shield-shaped surface on which a coat of arms is displayed **2** something shaped like an escutcheon; specif., *a)* a protective, often ornamental shield or plate, as that around a keyhole *b)* the space on a ship's stern bearing the name —**a blot on one's escutcheon** a stain on one's honor; disgrace to one's reputation

escutcheon

Es·dra·e·lon (ez′drə ē′lən, es′-) plain in N Israel, extending from the Jordan River valley to a coastal plain near Mt. Carmel: also, & in the Bible always, called JEZREEL

Es·dras (ez′drəs) ***n.*** ⟦Gr *Esdras,* Ezra⟧ *Bible* either of two books in the Apocrypha about EZRA: abbrev. *Esd*

ESE or **ese** *abbrev.* east-southeast

-ese (ēz, ēs) ⟦OFr *-eis,* It *-ese* < L *-ensis*⟧ *suffix* **1** *forming adjectives a)* of a country or place *[Javanese] b)* in the language or dialect of *[Cantonese] c)* in the style of *[Carlylese]* **2** *forming nouns a)* a person born or living in *[Portuguese] b)* the language or dialect of *[Brooklynese] c)* the style of or the jargon associated with (often used jocularly or derogatorily to form nonce words) *[journalese]*

es·em·plas·tic (es′əm plas′tik) ***adj.*** ⟦coined by COLERIDGE < Gr *es,* into + *hen,* one (see HENDECA-) + *plastikos,* adj. < *plassein,* to mold⟧ bringing together or able to bring together different concepts and thoughts into a unified whole *[the esemplastic ability of the imagination]*

es·er·ine (es′ər ēn′, -in) ***n.*** ⟦Fr *ésérine* < *ésér-* (prob. < name in a language of W Africa) + *-ine,* -INE[3]⟧ PHYSOSTIGMINE

Es·fa·hán (es′fä han′) city in WC Iran: capital of Persia in the 17th cent.

Esk *abbrev.* Eskimo

es·ker (es′kər) ***n.*** ⟦Ir *eiscir,* a ridge⟧ a winding, narrow ridge of sand or gravel, probably deposited by a stream flowing in or under glacial ice: sometimes called **es·kar** (es′kär′, -kər)

Es·ki·mo (es′kə mō′) ***n.*** ⟦earlier *Esquimaw(es),* prob. via Fr < Sp *esquimao(s)* (used by 16th-c. Basque fishermen in Labrador) < Montagnais *ayashkimew,* lit., ? snowshoe net makers⟧ **1** *pl.* **-mos′** or **-mo′** a member of a group of indigenous North American peoples thinly scattered in areas extending from Greenland across N Canada and Alaska through the NE tip of Asia: cf. INUIT (***n.*** 1 & 3) **2** any of the languages of the Eskimos, belonging to the Eskimo-Aleut language family —***adj.*** of the Eskimos or their languages or cultures See also INUIT —**Es′ki·mo′an** ***adj.***

Es·ki·mo-Al·e·ut (-al′ē ōōt′, -al′yōōt′, -ə lōōt′) ***n., adj.*** (designating or of) a family of languages including Aleut and the Eskimo languages

Eskimo dog any of several large, strong dogs of the Arctic regions of E Asia and North America, characterized by erect ears, a heavy coat, and a wolf-like appearance, used especially for pulling sleds

Es·ki·şe·hir (es kē′she hir′) city in WC Turkey

ESL *abbrev.* English as a second language

ESOP (ē′säp) ***n.*** Employee Stock Ownership Plan: a compensation plan set up by a company and funded with its tax-deductible contributions by which qualified employees accumulate shares of the company's stock

e·soph·a·gus (i säf′ə gəs, ē-) ***n., pl.*** **-a·gi′** (-jī′) ⟦altered (after ML) < ME *ysophagus,* OFr *ysofague* < ML *oesophagus* < Gr *oisophagos,* lit., passage for food < *oisein,* fut. inf. of *pherein,* to carry (see BEAR[1]) + *phagein,* to eat: see -PHAGOUS⟧ the tube through which food passes from the pharynx to the stomach; gullet —**e·soph·a·ge·al** (i säf′ə jē′əl, ē′sə faj′ē əl) ***adj.***

es·o·ter·ic (es′ə ter′ik) ***adj.*** ⟦Gr *esōterikos* < *esōteros,* inner, compar. of *esō,* within < *es, eis,* into⟧ **1** *a)* intended for or understood by only a chosen few, as an inner group of disciples or initiates (said of ideas, literature, etc.) *b)* beyond the understanding or knowledge of most people; abstruse **2** confidential; private; withheld *[an esoteric plan]* Opposed to EXOTERIC —**es′o·ter′i·cal·ly** ***adv.***

☆**es·o·ter·i·ca** (-i kə) ***pl.n.*** esoteric facts or things

es·o·tro·pi·a (es′ō trō′pē ə) ***n.*** ⟦ModL < Gr *esō,* within + ModL *-tropia,* -TROPY⟧ a condition in which only one eye fixes on an object while the other turns inward, producing the appearance of cross-eye: cf. EXOTROPIA

ESP (ē′es′pē′) ***n.*** extrasensory perception

esp. *abbrev.* especially

es·pa·drille (es′pə dril′) ***n.*** ⟦Fr, altered by metathesis < *espardille* < dial. (Gascon) *espartilho,* dim. < Sp *esparto,* ESPARTO⟧ a kind of shoe for casual wear, with a canvas upper and a sole of twisted rope

es·pal·ier (es pal′yər, -yā′; is-) ***n.*** ⟦Fr < It *spalliera,* support for the shoulders < *spalla,* the shoulder < L *spatula:* see SPATULA⟧ **1** a lattice or trellis on which trees and shrubs are trained to grow flat **2** a plant, tree, etc. so trained —***vt.*** **1** to train as or on an espalier **2** to provide with an espalier

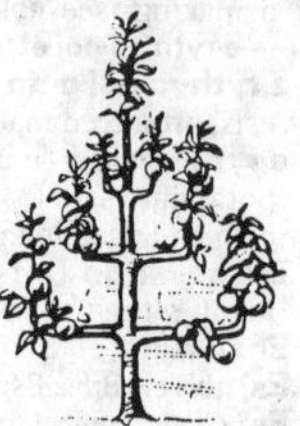
espalier (sense 2)

Es·pa·ña (es pä′nyä) *Sp. name for* SPAIN

es·par·to (es pär′tō) ***n.*** ⟦Sp < L *spartum* < Gr *sparton, spartos* < IE base **sper-,* to turn > SPIRAL⟧ either of two kinds of long, coarse grass (*Stipa tenacissima* or *Lygeum spartum*) growing in Spain and N Africa, used to make cordage, baskets, shoes, and paper: also **esparto grass**

es·pe·cial (e spesh′əl, i-) ***adj.*** ⟦ME & OFr < L *specialis*⟧ special; particular; outstanding; exceptional —***SYN.*** SPECIAL

es·pe·cial·ly (-əl ē) ***adv.*** particularly; mainly; to a marked degree; unusually

Es·pe·ran·to (es′pə rän′tō, -ran′-) ***n.*** ⟦after pseud. of the inventor, lit. (in Esperanto), one who hopes < prp. of *esperi,* to hope < Romance forms (Fr *espérer,* Sp *esperar,* etc.) < L *sperare,* to hope⟧ an invented language, devised (1887) by Pol. physician L. L. Zamenhof (1859-1917), and proposed for use as an international (chiefly European) auxiliary language: it uses word bases common to the main European languages, and it has self-evident parts of speech (all nouns end in *-o,* all adjectives in *-a,* etc.), a single and regular conjugation of verbs, a few simplified inflections, etc.

es·pi·al (e spī′əl, i-) ***n.*** ⟦ME *espiaille* < OFr < *espier:* see SPY⟧ **1** an espying or being espied; observation **2** discovery **3** [Obs.] a spy

es·pi·o·nage (es′pē ə näzh′, -näj′) ***n.*** ⟦Fr *espionnage* < *espionner,* to spy < *espion* < It *spione* < *spia,* spy < Gmc **speha,* akin to OHG *spehon:* see SPY⟧ **1** the act of spying **2** the use of spies by a government to learn the military secrets of other nations ☆**3** the use of spies in industry or commerce to learn the secrets of other companies

Es·pí·ri·to San·to (i spē′rē too sän′too) state of E Brazil, on the Atlantic: 17,832 sq mi (46,185 sq km); cap. Vitória

es·pla·nade (es′plə näd′, -näd′) ***n.*** ⟦Fr < It *spianata* < *spianare,* to level < L *explanare,* to level: see EXPLAIN⟧ a level, open space of ground, esp. one serving as a public walk or roadway, often along a shore

ESPN *service mark* Entertainment and Sports Programming Network

Es·poo (es′pō) city in S Finland, just west of Helsinki

es·pous·al (e spou′zəl, i-) ***n.*** ⟦ME *espousaile* < OFr *espousailles (pl.)* < L *sponsalia* < *sponsus* (fem. *sponsa*): see SPOUSE⟧ **1** [*often pl.*] *a)* a betrothal or betrothal ceremony *b)* a marriage or wedding **2** an espousing (of some cause, idea, etc.); advocacy

es·pouse (e spouz′, i-) ***vt.*** **-poused′, -pous′ing** ⟦ME *espousen* < OFr *espouser* < LL *sponsare* < L *sponsus:* see SPOUSE⟧ **1** to take as a spouse, esp. as a wife; marry **2** to give in marriage **3** to take up, support, or advocate (some cause, idea, etc.) —**es·pous′er** ***n.***

es·pres·so (e spres′ō) ***n., pl.*** **-sos** ⟦It *(caffè) espresso,* pressed-out (coffee), pp. of *esprimere,* to press out, express < L *exprimere:* see EXPRESS⟧ coffee prepared in a special machine from finely ground coffee beans, through which steam under high pressure is forced

es·prit (e sprē′) ***n.*** ⟦Fr⟧ **1** spirit **2** lively intelligence or wit

esprit de corps (-də kôr′) ⟦Fr, lit., spirit of a body (of persons)⟧ group spirit; sense of pride, honor, etc. shared by those in the same group or undertaking

es·prit d'es·ca·lier (es prē des kȧ lyā′) ⟦Fr, wit of the staircase (i.e., as one is leaving)⟧ clever repartee one thinks of too late

es·py (e spī′, i-) ***vt.*** **-pied′, -py′ing** ⟦ME *espien* < OFr *espier:* see SPY⟧ to catch sight of; make out; spy; descry —***SYN.*** SEE[1]

Esq or **Esqr** *abbrev.* Esquire

-esque (esk) ⟦Fr < It *-esco* < Gmc suffix akin to OHG *-isc,* -ISH⟧ *suffix forming adjectives* **1** in the manner or style of *[Romanesque]* **2** having the quality of; like *[statuesque]*

Es·qui·line (es′kwə līn′) ⟦L *(Mons) esquilinus,* after *Esquiliae,* name of the hill < base akin to *colere,* to till: see CULT⟧ *see* SEVEN HILLS OF ROME

Es·qui·mau (es′kə mō′) *n., pl.* **-maux′** (-mō′, -mōz′) or **-mau′** *archaic sp. of* ESKIMO

es·quire (es′kwīr′; e skwīr′, i-) *n.* ⟦ME *esquier* < OFr *escuier* < LL *scutarius*, a squire, shield-bearer < L *scutum*, a shield: see ESCUTCHEON⟧ **1** [Historical] a candidate for knighthood, acting as attendant and shield-bearer for a knight; squire **2** in England, a member of the gentry ranking just below a knight **3** [E-] a title of courtesy, usually abbreviated *Esq., Esqr.*, placed after a man's surname and corresponding more ceremoniously to *Mr.*: in the U.S., now specif. used for lawyers, male and female **4** [Archaic] a landed country gentleman; squire

ess (es) *n., pl.* **ess′es 1** the letter S **2** something shaped like S

-ess (es, is, əs) ⟦ME *-esse, -isse* < OFr *-esse* < LL *-issa* < Gr⟧ *suffix forming nouns* female [*lioness*]: in nouns of agent ending in *-tor* or *-ter*, the vowel is usually dropped before *-ess* is added [*actress*]

USAGE—as applied to persons, now often avoided as patronizing or discriminatory [*poetess, Negress*]

es·say (e sā′; *for n. 1 usually, & for n. 2 always,* es′ā) *vt.* ⟦OFr *essayer* < VL **exagiare* < LL *exagium*, a weight, weighing < *ex-*, out of + *agere*, to do: see ACT[1]⟧ **1** to test the nature or quality of; try out **2** to try; attempt —*n.* ⟦OFr *essai* < LL *exagium*⟧ **1** *a)* a trying or testing *b)* an attempt; trial **2** a short literary composition of an analytical, interpretive, or reflective kind, dealing with its subject in a nontechnical, limited, often unsystematic way and, usually, expressive of the author's outlook and personality **3** a proposed design for a new postage stamp or piece of paper money —**SYN.** TRY —**es·say′er** *n.*

es·say·ist (es′ā ist) *n.* one who writes essays

es·say·is·tic (es′ā is′tik) *adj.* having the style or tone of an essay

es·se (es′ē, -ā) *n.* ⟦L, to be⟧ being; existence; essence

Es·sen (es′ən) city in W Germany, in the Ruhr valley, in the state of North Rhine-Westphalia

es·sence (es′əns) *n.* ⟦ME < OFr & L *essentia* < *esse*, to be: for IE base see IS[1]⟧ **1** something that is, or exists; entity **2** that which makes something what it is; intrinsic, fundamental nature or most important quality (of something); essential being **3** *a)* a substance that keeps, in concentrated form, the flavor, fragrance, or other properties of the plant, drug, food, etc. from which it is extracted; essential oil *b)* a solution of such a substance or oil in alcohol *c)* a perfume **4** *Philos. a)* the inward nature of anything, underlying its manifestations; true substance *b)* the indispensable conceptual characteristics and relations of anything —**in essence** essentially —**of the essence** of the greatest importance

Es·sene (es′ēn′, e sēn′) *n.* ⟦L *Esseni* < Gr *Essēnoi*, said (by Philo) to be < *hosios*, holy, pious, but < Syr *ḥsēn*, pl. < *ḥsī*, pious, holy⟧ a member of an ancient Jewish sect of ascetics and mystics, which existed to the middle of the 1st century A.D. —**Es·se·ni·an** (e sē′nē ən) *adj.*, **Es·sen·ic** (e sen′ik, -sē′nik)

es·sen·tial (ə sen′shəl, i-) *adj.* ⟦ME *essencial* < LL *essentialis*: see ESSENCE⟧ **1** of or constituting the intrinsic, fundamental nature of something; basic; inherent [an *essential* difference] **2** absolute; complete; perfect **3** absolutely necessary; indispensable; requisite **4** containing, or having the properties of, a concentrated extract of a plant, drug, food, etc. [an *essential* oil] **5** *Biochem.* needed for life or health but not synthesized within the body, as an amino acid or vitamin that must be consumed —*n.* something necessary or fundamental; indispensable, inherent, or basic feature or principle —**es·sen′tial·ly** *adv.*

SYN.—**essential**, in strict usage, is applicable to that which constitutes the absolute essence or the fundamental nature of a thing and therefore must be present for the thing to exist, function, etc. [food is *essential* to life]; an **indispensable** person or thing cannot be done without if the specified or implied purpose is to be achieved; **requisite** is applied to that which is required by the circumstances or for the purpose and generally suggests a requirement that is imposed externally rather than an inherent need [the *requisite* experience for a position]; **necessary** implies a pressing need but does not always connote absolute indispensability

es·sen·tial·ism (-iz′əm) *n.* **1** *Philos.* a theory in which things are conceived of in terms of their essence, or indispensable conceptual characteristics, rather than their concrete, experienced existence **2** *a)* any theory that views certain ideas, behaviors, or traits as being natural to or inherent in either sex, in an ethnic group, etc. *b)* an instance of applying such a theory —**es·sen′tial·ist** *n., adj.*

es·sen·ti·al·i·ty (i sen′shē al′ə tē) *n., pl.* **-ties** essential quality, fact, or thing

es·sen·tial·ize (i sen′shəl īz′) *vt.* **-ized′**, **-iz′ing** to concentrate on the essential meanings or aspects of

essential oil any volatile oil that gives distinctive odor, flavor, etc. to a plant, flower, or fruit

Es·se·qui·bo (es′ə kē′bō) river in Guyana, flowing from the Guiana highlands northward to the Atlantic: *c.* 600 mi (966 km)

Es·sex[1] (es′iks), 2d Earl of (*Robert Devereux*) 1566-1601; Eng. soldier & courtier: executed for treason

Es·sex[2] (es′iks) **1** former Anglo-Saxon kingdom in E England **2** county in SE England, on the North Sea: 1,419 sq mi (3,675 sq km)

es·so·nite (es′ə nīt′) *n.* ⟦< Gr *hēssōn*, inferior (i.e., to real hyacinth) + -ITE[1]⟧ a dark-brown kind of garnet

est *abbrev.* **1** established: also **estab 2** estate **3** estimate **4** estimated

Est *abbrev.* **1** *Bible* Esther **2** Estonia **3** Estonian

EST *abbrev.* Eastern Standard Time

-est (est, ist, əst) *suffix* **1** ⟦ME < OE *-est, -ost, -ast*, superl. suffix of adj. & adv., akin to OHG *-isto* < IE **-istho-* (> Gr *-isto-*, Sans *-iṣṭha-*)⟧ forming the superlative degree of most adjectives and adverbs of one or two syllables [*greatest, soonest*] **2** ⟦ME < OE *-est, -ast*, 2d pers. sing., pres. tense inflection < IE **-si, *-s* + initial dental of enclitic pron.: see THOU[1]⟧ forming the archaic 2d pers. sing. of verbs [*goest*]: in certain cases, it becomes *-st* [*hadst*]

es·tab·lish (ə stab′lish, i-) *vt.* ⟦ME *establissen* < extended stem of OFr *establir* < L *stabilire* < *stabilis*, STABLE[1]⟧ **1** to make stable; make firm; settle [to *establish* a habit] **2** to order, ordain, or enact (a law, statute, etc.) permanently **3** to set up (a government, nation, business, etc.); found; institute **4** to cause to be or happen; bring about [efforts to *establish* a friendship] **5** to settle in an office or position, or set up as in business or a profession **6** to make a state institution of (a church) **7** to set up (a precedent, theory, reputation, etc.) permanently; cause to be accepted or recognized **8** to prove; demonstrate [to *establish* one's cause at law] **9** *Card Games* to win control of (a suit) so that one is sure of taking all the remaining tricks in it —**es·tab′lish·er** *n.*

established church 1 a church officially recognized by the government and supported as a national institution **2** [E- C-] the Church of England

establishing shot *Film, TV* a shot, typically a wide shot at the beginning of a SCENE (*n.* 5*b*), intended to establish the location and the main characters in that scene

es·tab·lish·ment (-mənt) *n.* **1** an establishing or being established **2** a thing established, or set up; specif., a place of business [a coalition of downtown dining *establishments*] —**the Establishment 1** the dominant group or forces of a society or nation, characterized esp. by opposition to change **2** the ruling inner circle or dominant group of any field of endeavor, organization, institution, etc. **3** ESTABLISHED CHURCH

es·tab·lish·men·tar·i·an (ə stab′lish mən ter′ē ən, i-) [*also* E-] *n.* a member or supporter of the Establishment —*adj.* belonging to, supporting, or characteristic of the Establishment

es·ta·mi·net (es tȧ mē ne′) *n.* ⟦Fr⟧ a small café

es·tan·cia (es tän′syä) *n., pl.* **-cias** ⟦Sp, orig., a stopping place⟧ a large estate, esp. a cattle ranch, in Spanish America

es·tate (ə stāt′, i-) *n.* ⟦ME & OFr *estat*, STATE⟧ **1** *a)* state or condition [to restore the theater to its former *estate*] *b)* a condition or stage of life [to come to man's *estate*] *c)* status or rank **2** [Historical] esp. in feudal times, any of the three social classes having specific political powers: the first estate was the Lords Spiritual (clergy), the second estate the Lords Temporal (nobility), and the third estate the Commons (bourgeoisie): see also FOURTH ESTATE **3** property; possessions; capital; fortune **4** the assets and liabilities of a dead or bankrupt person **5** landed property; individually owned piece of land containing a residence, esp. one that is large and maintained by great wealth **6** [Brit.] a real-estate development **7** [Archaic] display of wealth; pomp **8** *Law a)* the degree, nature, extent, and quality of interest or ownership that a person has in land or other property *b)* all the property, real or personal, owned by a person

estate agent [Brit.] **1** a real-estate agent or broker **2** a person who manages a landed estate for its owner

estate car [Brit.] STATION WAGON

Es·tates-Gen·er·al (ə stāts′ jen′ər əl, i-) *n.* STATES-GENERAL (sense 1)

estate tax a tax levied on a deceased person's estate

es·teem (ə stēm′, i-) *vt.* ⟦ME *estemen* < OFr *estimer* < L *aestimare*, to value, appraise, estimate; prob. < **ais-temos*, one who cuts copper, mints money < IE **ayos-* (L *aes*), brass, copper (see ORE) + **tem-*, to cut: see -TOMY⟧ **1** to have great regard for; value highly; respect **2** to hold to be; consider; regard [we *esteem* it an honor to be invited] —*n.* **1** favorable opinion; high regard; respect [to be held in high *esteem*] **2** [Archaic] an opinion; estimation —**SYN.** APPRECIATE, REGARD

Es·telle (e stel′, i-) *n.* ⟦Fr, ult. < L *stella*, STAR⟧ a feminine name; var. *Estella, Stella*

es·ter (es′tər) *n.* ⟦Ger, contr. < *essigäther* < *essig*, vinegar (< L *acetum*: see ACETO-) + *äther* (< L *aether*), ETHER⟧ an organic compound, comparable to an inorganic salt: generally, HR (inorganic acid) + R^1OH (alcohol) = RR^1 (ester) + H_2O (water) or RCOOH (organic acid) + R^1OH = $RCOOR^1$ (ester) + H_2O

es·ter·ase (es′tər ās′) *n.* ⟦prec. + -ASE⟧ any hydrolase enzyme that acts as a catalyst in chemical reactions involving the hydrolysis of an ester

es·ter·i·fy (es ter′ə fī′) *vt., vi.* **-fied′**, **-fy′ing** to change into an ester —**es·ter′i·fi·ca′tion** *n.*

Esth *abbrev. Bible* Esther

Es·ther (es′tər) *n.* ⟦LL(Ec) *Esthera* < Gr(Ec) *Esthēr* < Heb *ester*, prob. < Pers *sitareh*, star < IE base **ster-*, STAR⟧ **1** a feminine name: var. *Hester* **2** *Bible a)* the Jewish wife of the Persian king Ahasuerus: she saved her people from slaughter by Haman *b)* the Old Testament book telling her story (abbrev. *Esth, Es, Est*)

es·the·si·a (es thē′zhə, -zhē ə, -zē ə) *n.* ⟦ModL < Gr *aisthēsis*, perception, sense-impression < *aisthanesthai*: see AESTHETIC⟧ the ability to feel sensations

es·the·si·om·e·ter (es thē′zē äm′ə tər, -sē-) *n.* ⟦< ModL *aesthesia*, AESTHESIA + -METER⟧ an instrument for measuring the sensitivity of the sense of touch, esp. one for testing how far apart two points pressed against the skin have to be for the points to be felt as separate

es·thete (es′thēt′) *n.* AESTHETE

es·thet·ic (es thet′ik) ***adj.*** ⟦see AESTHETIC⟧ **1** AESTHETIC **2** of esthesia; having to do with sensation **—*n.*** AESTHETIC **—es·thet′i·cal·ly *adv.***
es·the·ti·cian (es′thə tish′ən) ***n.*** AESTHETICIAN
es·thet·i·cism (es thet′ə siz′əm) ***n.*** AESTHETICISM
es·thet·ics (es thet′iks) ***pl.n.*** AESTHETICS
Es·tho·ni·a (es tō′nē ə, -thō′-) *former var. of* ESTONIA
es·ti·ma·ble (es′tə mə bəl) ***adj.*** ⟦ME & OFr < L *aestimabilis* < *aestimare*: see ESTEEM⟧ **1** [Obs.] that can be estimated or evaluated; calculable **2** worthy of esteem; deserving to be respected or valued **—es′ti·ma·bly *adv.***
es·ti·mate (es′tə māt′; *for n.*, -mit) ***vt.* -mat′ed, -mat′ing** ⟦< L *aestimatus*, pp. of *aestimare*: see ESTEEM⟧ **1** to form an opinion or judgment about **2** to judge or determine generally but carefully (size, value, cost, requirements, etc.); calculate approximately **—*vi.*** to make an estimate or estimates **—*n.* 1** a general calculation of size, value, etc.; esp., an approximate computation of the probable cost of a piece of work made by a person undertaking to do the work **2** an opinion or judgment **—es′ti·ma′tive *adj.* —es′ti·ma′tor *n.***

***SYN.*—estimate**, in this comparison, refers broadly to the forming of a personal opinion or judgment; **appraise** implies the aim of giving an accurate or expert judgment, as of value or worth [to *appraise* a new house]; **evaluate** also connotes an attempt at an exact judgment, but rarely with reference to value in terms of money [let us *evaluate* the evidence]; **rate** implies assignment of comparative value, quality, etc. [he is *rated* the best in his field] See also **calculate**

es·ti·ma·tion (es′tə mā′shən) ***n.*** ⟦ME *estimacioun* < OFr *estimacion* < L *aestimatio*⟧ **1** the act of estimating **2** an estimate, opinion, or judgment **3** esteem; regard
es·ti·val (es′tə vəl, es tī′vəl) ***adj.*** ⟦L *aestivalis* < *aestivus* < *aestas*, summer < IE base **ai-dh-*, to burn: see EDIFY⟧ of or pertaining to summer
es·ti·vate (es′tə vāt′) ***vi.* -vat′ed, -vat′ing** ⟦< L *aestivatus*, pp. of *aestivare* < *aestas*: see prec.⟧ **1** to spend the summer **2** to pass the summer in a dormant state, as snails: cf. HIBERNATE
es·ti·va·tion (es′tə vā′shən) ***n.* 1** *Zool.* the state of an estivating creature **2** *Bot.* the arrangement of petals in a flower bud before it opens
Es·to·ni·a (e stō′nē ə, -stōn′yə) country in N Europe, on the Baltic Sea: from 1940 to 1991 it was a republic of the U.S.S.R.: 17,462 sq mi (45,226 sq km); cap. Tallinn: formerly, **Estonian Soviet Socialist Republic**
Es·to·ni·an (e stō′nē ən, -stōn′yən) ***adj.*** of Estonia or its people, language, or culture **—*n.* 1** a person born or living in Estonia **2** the Finnic language spoken in Estonia
es·top (e stäp′) ***vt.* -topped′, -top′ping** ⟦ME *estoppen* < Anglo-Fr & OFr *estoper* < VL **stuppare*, to stop with tow: see STOP⟧ **1** [Archaic] *a)* to stop up *b)* [Rare] to stop; prevent; bar **2** *Law* to bar or prevent by estoppel
es·top·pel (e stäp′əl) ***n.*** ⟦OFr *estoupail*, stopper, bung < *estoper*: see prec.⟧ the barring of a person, in a legal proceeding, from making allegations or denials which are contrary either to a previous statement or act by that person or to a previous adjudication
es·to·vers (es tō′vərz) ***pl.n.*** ⟦ME < OFr *estovoir*, to be necessary (inf. used as n.) < L *est opus*, it is needed⟧ certain reasonable necessities allowed by law, as wood taken by a tenant for fuel or repairs
es·tra·di·ol (es′trə dī′ôl′, -ōl′) ***n.*** ⟦ESTR(ONE) + *-a-* + DI-[1] + -OL[1]⟧ a female sex hormone, $C_{18}H_{24}O_2$, used in correcting female hormone deficiency
es·trange (e strānj′, i-) ***vt.* -tranged′, -trang′ing** ⟦OFr *estranger*, to remove < ML *extraneare*, to treat as a stranger < L *extraneus*, STRANGE⟧ **1** to remove, as from usual surroundings or associates; keep apart or away **2** to turn (a person) from an affectionate or friendly attitude to an indifferent, unfriendly, or hostile one; alienate the affections of **—es·trange′ment *n.***
es·tranged (e strānjd′, i-) ***adj.*** living apart because no longer in a loving or amicable relationship: said of a spouse or family member [an interview with the celebrity's *estranged* wife]
es·tray (ə strā′) ***n.*** ⟦Anglo-Fr < *estraier*: see STRAY⟧ **1** any person or thing out of its usual place **2** *Law* a stray and unclaimed domestic animal **—*vi.*** [Archaic] to stray
es·treat (es trēt′) ***n.*** ⟦ME & Anglo-Fr *estrete* < OFr *estraite* < ML *extracta* < pp. of L *extrahere*: see EXTRACT⟧ a true copy or extract of an original record entered in a law court, as of fines **—*vt.* 1** to take from the records of a law court for purposes of prosecution **2** to take as a levy, fine, etc.
Es·tre·ma·dur·a (es′trə mə door′ə) **1** region of WC Spain, on the Portuguese border: 16,063 sq mi (41,603 sq km) **2** region of W Portugal, on the Atlantic: chief city, Lisbon
es·tri·ol (es′trī ôl′, -ōl′; -trē-) ***n.*** ⟦ES(TRUS) + TRI- + -OL[1]⟧ a female sex hormone, $C_{18}H_{24}O_3$, present in the urine during pregnancy, thus indicating normal fetal and placental activity
es·tro·gen (es′trə jən, -jen′) ***n.*** ⟦< ESTRUS + -GEN⟧ any of several female sex hormones or synthetic compounds that cause estrus
es·tro·gen·ic (es′trə jen′ik) ***adj.* 1** of estrogen **2** of or producing estrus
es·trone (es′trōn′) ***n.*** ⟦ESTR(US) + -ONE⟧ a female sex hormone, $C_{18}H_{22}O_2$
es·trous (es′trəs; *Brit usually* ē′strəs) ***adj.*** of, or having the characteristics of, estrus
estrous cycle the regular female reproductive cycle of most placental mammals that is under hormonal control and includes a period of heat, followed by ovulation and complex changes of the uterine lining
es·trus (es′trəs; *Brit usually* ē′strəs) ***n.*** ⟦ModL < L *oestrus*, gadfly, horsefly, frenzy < Gr *oistros*, gadfly, sting, frenzy < IE base **eis-*, to move violently > ON *eisa*, to rush on, L *ira*, ire, Lith *aistra*, violent passion⟧ **1** the periodic sexual excitement of most female placental mammals, corresponding to *rut* in males; heat **2** the period of this, when the female will accept mating with the male, characterized by changes in the sex organs Also **es′trum**
es·tu·a·rine (es′tyoo͞ ə rin, -choo͞-; -rīn′) ***adj.* 1** of an estuary **2** formed or deposited in an estuary
es·tu·ar·y (es′tyoo͞ er′ē, -choo͞-) ***n.*, *pl.* -ar′ies** ⟦L *aestuarium* < *aestus*, the tide, orig., a boiling, akin to *aestas*, summer heat: see ESTIVAL⟧ an inlet or arm of the sea; esp., the lower portion or wide mouth of a river, where the salty tide meets the freshwater current **—es′tu·ar′i·al *adj.***
esu *abbrev.* electrostatic unit(s)
e·su·ri·ent (ē soor′ē ənt, -syoor′-) ***adj.*** ⟦< L *esuriens*, prp. of *esurire*, to be hungry < pp. of *edere*, EAT⟧ hungry; voracious; greedy **—e·su′ri·ence *n.*, e·su′ri·en·cy —e·su′ri·ent·ly *adv.***
Et *Chem. symbol for* ETHYL
ET[1] (ē′tē′) ***n.*, *pl.* ETs** ⟦E(XTRA)T(ERRESTRIAL)⟧ an extraterrestrial being, as in science fiction
ET[2] *abbrev.* Eastern Time
-et (et, it, ət) ⟦ME *-et* < OFr *-et*, masc., *-ete* (Fr *-ette*), fem. < LL *-itus*, *-ita*⟧ *suffix* little: used to form nouns from other nouns [*islet, eaglet*]
e·ta (āt′ə, ēt′ə) ***n.*** ⟦LL < Gr *ēta* < Sem, as in Heb *chet*, HET⟧ the seventh letter of the Greek alphabet (Η, η): in English transliteration, as in the etymologies of this dictionary, it is shown as *ē*
ETA *abbrev.* estimated time of arrival
é·ta·gère or **e·ta·gere** (ā′tä zher′) ***n.*** ⟦Fr⟧ a free-standing set of open shelves for displaying small art objects, ornaments, etc.
e-tail·er (ē′tā′lər) ***n.*** ⟦E-[2] + *(re)tailer*: see RETAIL⟧ a retail business that sells goods online over the internet from a website
et al. *abbrev.* **1** ⟦L *et alibi*⟧ and elsewhere **2** ⟦L *et alii*⟧ and others
e·ta·lon (āt′ə län′) ***n.*** ⟦Fr *étalon*, a standard of weights and measures < OFr *estalon*: see STALLION⟧ an optical instrument with two plane parallel reflecting surfaces, used for the precise measurement of distance or the wavelength of light
et·a·mine (et′ə mēn′) ***n.*** ⟦Fr *étamine* < VL **staminea* < L *stamineus*, full of threads < *stamen*, thread⟧ a loosely woven cotton or worsted cloth, used for dresses, curtains, etc.
etc. *abbrev.* et cetera
et cet·er·a (et set′ər ə, -se′trə) ⟦L⟧ **1** and others; and the like; and the rest; and so forth **2** or the like; or others of the same kind; or something similar ➥Usually written *etc.*
et·cet·er·as (et set′ər əz, -se′trəz) ***pl.n.*** [Informal] additional things or persons
etch (ech) ***vt.*** ⟦Du *etsen* < Ger *ätzen*, to corrode < MHG *etzen*, to cause to eat, caus. of *ezzen* (Ger *essen*), EAT⟧ **1** to make (a drawing, design, etc.) on metal, glass, etc. by the action of an acid, esp. by coating the surface with wax and letting acid eat into the lines or areas laid bare with a special needle **2** to prepare (a metal plate, glass, etc.) in this way, for use in printing such drawings or designs **3** to engrave using a laser **4** to depict or impress sharply and distinctly **—*vi.*** to make etchings **—etch′er *n.***
etch·ant (ech′ənt) ***n.*** a substance, as an acid, used in etching
etch·ing (ech′iŋ) ***n.* 1** the art or act of one who etches **2** an etched plate, drawing, or design **3** a print made from an etched surface
ETD *abbrev.* estimated time of departure
E·te·o·cles (ē tē′ə klēz′) ***n.*** ⟦L < Gr *Eteoklēs*⟧ *Gr. Myth.* a son of Oedipus and Jocasta: see SEVEN AGAINST THEBES
e·ter·nal (ē tur′nəl, i-) ***adj.*** ⟦ME < OFr < LL *aeternalis* < L *aeturnus* < *aevum*, an age < IE base **aiw-*, **āju-*, a life, vital force > AYE[1]⟧ **1** without beginning or end; existing through all time; everlasting **2** of eternity **3** forever the same; always true or valid; unchanging [the *eternal* verities] **4** always going on; never stopping; perpetual [*eternal* rest] **5** seeming never to stop; happening very often [her *eternal* complaints] **6** *Philos.*, *Theol.* outside or beyond time or time relationships; timeless **—*SYN.*** CONTINUAL **—the Eternal** name for God **—e·ter′nal·ly *adv.* —e·ter′nal·ness *n.***
Eternal City *name for* ROME[2]
e·terne (ē turn′, i-) ***adj.*** [Archaic] eternal
e·ter·ni·ty (ē tur′nə tē, i-) ***n.*, *pl.* -ties** ⟦ME *eternite* < OFr *eternité* < L *aeternitas*⟧ **1** the quality, state, or fact of being eternal; eternal existence or duration; continuance without end **2** infinite time; time without beginning or end **3** a long period of time that seems endless [an *eternity* of waiting] **4** the endless time after death
e·ter·nize (ē tur′nīz′, i-; ē′tər-) ***vt.* -nized′, -niz′ing** ⟦Fr *éterniser* < ML *aeternizare* < L *aeternus*⟧ **1** to make eternal; cause to last forever **2** to make famous forever; immortalize Also **e·ter′nal·ize′, -ized′, -iz′ing —e·ter′ni·za′tion *n.***
e·te·si·an (ē tē′zhən, -zē ən) ***adj.*** ⟦L *etesius* < Gr *etēsios* < *etos*, year < IE base **wet-* > L *vetus*, old, Goth *withrus*, yearling lamb⟧ annual: said of certain Mediterranean winds that blow from the north for several weeks every summer
ETF (ē′tē′ef′) ***n.*** ⟦*e(xchange-)t(raded) f(und)*⟧ a fund made up of a number of stocks or other securities for which fractional shares are issued to investors, similar to a mutual fund, but with the shares tradeable on an exchange, similar to ordinary shares of common stock
eth (*eth*) ***n.*** *alt. sp. of* EDH
Eth *abbrev.* **1** Ethiopia **2** Ethiopic
-eth[1] (ith, əth) ⟦see -TH[2]⟧ *suffix* -TH[2]: used with bases ending in a vowel [*fortieth*]

-eth² (ith, əth) ⟦ME -(e)th < OE -(a)th (ult. < IE *ti- > L -(i)t, Sans -ti)⟧ *suffix* forming the archaic 3d pers. sing., pres. indic., of verbs [*asketh, bringeth*]: see also -TH³

E·than (ē′thən) ***n.*** ⟦LL(Ec) < Heb *etan*, lit., strength, firmness⟧ a masculine name

eth·ane (eth′ān′; *Brit usually* ē′thān′) ***n.*** ⟦ETH(YL) + -ANE⟧ an odorless, colorless, gaseous alkane, CH_3CH_3, found in natural gas and used as a refrigerant and in fuel mixtures

eth·a·nol (eth′ə nôl′, -nōl′; *Brit also* ē′thə-) ***n.*** ⟦prec. + -OL¹⟧ ALCOHOL (sense 1)

Eth·el (eth′əl) ***n.*** ⟦short for *Ethelinda, Etheldred*, and other names compounded < OE *Æthelu* < *æthele*, noble⟧ a feminine name

Eth·el·bert (eth′əl bərt) A.D. 552?-616; king of Kent (560-616)

Eth·el·red II (eth′əl red′) A.D. 968-1016; king of England (978-1016): called *the Unready*

eth·ene (eth′ēn′) ***n.*** ETHYLENE

e·ther (ē′thər) ***n.*** ⟦ME < L *aether* < Gr *aithēr* < *aithein*, to kindle, burn < IE base **aidh-* > L *aestas*, summer, OE *ætan*, to burn⟧ **1** a substance hypothesized by the ancients as filling all space beyond the SPHERE (***n.*** 5) of the moon, and making up the stars and planets **2** the upper regions of space; clear sky **3** [Rare] the air **4** *Chem.* any of a series of organic compounds having an oxygen atom linking two carbon atoms from two hydrocarbon radicals, generally ROR¹; esp., ethyl ether, a volatile, colorless, highly flammable liquid, $H_5C_2OC_2H_5$, prepared by the reaction of sulfuric acid and ethyl alcohol and used as an anesthetic and a solvent for resins and fats **5** *Physics* a hypothetical diffuse, invisible medium formerly thought to pervade space and transmit light, heat, etc. —**e·ther·ic** (i ther′ik, -thir′-) ***adj.***

e·the·re·al (ē thir′ē əl, i-) ***adj.*** ⟦< L *aetherius* < Gr *aitherios* + -AL⟧ **1** of or like the ether, or upper regions of space **2** very light; airy; delicate [*ethereal* music] **3** not earthly; heavenly; celestial **4** *Chem.* of, like, or containing ether, esp. if mixed with an essential oil —**e·the′re·al′i·ty** (-al′ə tē) ***n.***, **e·the′re·al·ness** —**e·the′re·al·ly** ***adv.***

e·the·re·al·ize (-īz′) ***vt.*** **-ized′**, **-iz′ing** to make, or treat as being, ethereal —**e·the′re·al·i·za′tion** ***n.***

Eth·er·ege (eth′ər ij), Sir **George** 1635?-91; Eng. playwright of the Restoration

e·ther·i·fy (ē ther′ə fī′, i-; ē′thər-) ***vt.*** **-fied′**, **-fy′ing** to change (an alcohol) into ether —**e·ther′i·fi·ca′tion** ***n.***

e·ther·ize (ē′thər īz′) ***vt.*** **-ized′**, **-iz′ing** ☆to anesthetize (a patient) with ether fumes —**e′ther·i·za′tion** ***n.***

E·ther·net (ē′thər net′) ***n.*** ⟦ETHER (prob. sense 5) + NET(WORK)⟧ a system for connecting and coordinating the components of a LOCAL AREA NETWORK

eth·ic (eth′ik) ***n.*** ⟦ME *ethik* < OFr *ethique* < LL *ethica* < Gr *ēthikē* (*technē*), ethical (art): see fol.⟧ **1** a system of moral standards or values [the humanist *ethic*] **2** a particular moral standard or value [the success *ethic*]

eth·i·cal (eth′i kəl) ***adj.*** ⟦ME *ethik* (< L *ethicus* < Gr *ēthikos* < *ēthos*, character, custom < IE base **swedh-*, essential quality, own character > Goth *swes*, L *suus*, one's own & *suescere*, to become accustomed) + -AL⟧ **1** having to do with ethics or morality; of or conforming to moral standards **2** conforming to the standards of conduct of a given profession or group **3** designating or of a drug obtainable only on a doctor's prescription —***SYN.*** MORAL —**eth′i·cal′i·ty** (-kal′ə tē) ***n.***, **eth′i·cal·ness** —**eth′i·cal·ly** ***adv.***

eth·i·cist (eth′ə sist) ***n.*** **1** a person specializing in the study of ethics: also **eth·i·cian** (eth ish′ən) **2** a person trained to advise on ethical issues of healthcare, as in a hospital

eth·ics (eth′iks) ***n.*** **1** the study of standards of conduct and moral judgment; moral philosophy **2** a treatise on this study **3** [*with sing. or pl. v.*] the system or code of morals of a particular person, religion, group, profession, etc.

E·thi·op (ē′thē äp′) ***adj.***, ***n.*** [Archaic] ETHIOPIAN: also **E′thi·ope′** (-ōp′)

E·thi·o·pi·a (ē′thē ō′pē ə) **1** ancient kingdom (possibly dating to the 10th cent. B.C.) in NE Africa, on the Red Sea, corresponding to modern Sudan & N Ethiopia (the country) **2** country in E Africa: established, 1855: 435,186 sq mi (1,127,127 sq km); cap. Addis Ababa

E·thi·o·pi·an (-ō′pē ən) ***adj.*** **1** of Ethiopia or its people or culture **2** [Archaic] BLACK (***adj.*** *2a*) **3** designating or of the biogeographic realm that includes Madagascar and all of Africa, except some parts of N Africa in the Palearctic realm —***n.*** **1** a person born or living in Ethiopia **2** [Archaic] a black person

E·thi·op·ic (-äp′ik, -ō′pik) ***adj.*** ⟦< L *aethiopicus* < Gr *aithiopikos* < *Aithiops*, Ethiopian, lit., with burnt face < *aithein*, to burn (see ETHER) + *ōps*, face, EYE⟧ **1** ETHIOPIAN **2** designating or of the group of Semitic languages spoken in Ethiopia —***n.*** **1** the classical Semitic language of Ethiopia, still used as the liturgical language of the Christian church in Ethiopia; Ge'ez **2** the group of Semitic languages spoken in Ethiopia, including classical Ethiopic

eth·moid (eth′moid′) ***adj.*** ⟦Gr *ēthmoeidēs* < *ēthmos*, strainer, sieve (< *ēthein*, to strain < IE base **se(i)-*) + *eidos*, -OID⟧ designating or of the perforated bone or bones that form part of the septum and walls of the nasal cavity: the olfactory nerves pass through the perforations —***n.*** an ethmoid bone

eth·nic (eth′nik) ***adj.*** ⟦ME *ethnik* < LL(Ec) *ethnicus*, pagan < Gr *ethnikos*, national (in LGr(Ec), gentile, heathen) < *ethnos*, nation, people, *ta ethnē*, nations (in LXX, non-Jews, in N.T., gentile Christians): akin to *ēthos*: see ETHICAL⟧ **1** [Now Rare] heathen **2** designating or of a population subgroup having a common cultural heritage or nationality, as distinguished by customs, characteristics, language, common history, etc. **3** being or designating a member of a specific ethnic group in relation to the dominant group in a nation, region, etc. [an *ethnic* Ukrainian in Poland] **4** of or for ethnics, often, specif., nonwhite ethnics as a consumer or marketing group [a radio station playing *ethnic* music, *ethnic* haircare products, a candidate's appeal to the *ethnic* vote] —***n.*** a member of an ethnic group, esp. a member of a minority or nationality group that is part of a larger community —**eth′ni·cal·ly** ***adv.***

ethnic cleansing the systematic attempt to eliminate an ethnic group from a country or region as by forced expulsion or mass execution

eth·nic·i·ty (eth nis′ə tē) ***n.*** ⟦ETHNIC + -ITY⟧ ethnic classification or affiliation

eth·no- (eth′nō, -nə) ⟦Fr < Gr *ethnos*: see ETHNIC⟧ *combining form* ethnic group or division; people or peoples [*ethnology*]: also, before a vowel, **ethn-**

eth·no·bot·a·ny (eth′nō bät′n ē) ***n.*** ⟦prec. + BOTANY⟧ the study of how plants are used in a particular culture —**eth′no·bo·tan′i·cal** ***adj.*** —**eth′no·bot′a·nist** ***n.***

eth·no·cen·trism (eth′nō sen′triz′əm, -nə-) ***n.*** ⟦ETHNO- + CENTR(O)- + -ISM⟧ the belief that one's own ethnic group, nation, or culture is superior —**eth′no·cen′tric** ***adj.*** —**eth′no·cen′tri·cal·ly** ***adv.*** —**eth′no·cen·tric′i·ty** (-tris′ə tē) ***n.***

eth·nog·ra·phy (eth näg′rə fē) ***n.*** ⟦Fr *ethnographie*: see ETHNO- & -GRAPHY⟧ **1** the branch of anthropology that deals descriptively with specific cultures, esp. those of nonliterate peoples or groups **2** *a)* ethnographic research *b)* *pl.* **-phies** an ethnographic report, monograph, etc. —**eth·nog′ra·pher** ***n.*** —**eth′no·graph′ic** (-nə graf′ik) ***adj.***, **eth′no·graph′i·cal** —**eth′no·graph′i·cal·ly** ***adv.***

eth·nol·o·gy (eth näl′ə jē) ***n.*** ⟦ETHNO- + -LOGY⟧ the branch of anthropology that studies comparatively the cultures of contemporary, or recent, societies or language groups —**eth′no·log′i·cal** (-nə läj′i kəl) ***adj.***, **eth′no·log′ic** —**eth′no·log′i·cal·ly** ***adv.*** —**eth·nol′o·gist** ***n.***

eth·no·mu·si·col·o·gy (eth′nō myo͞o′zi käl′ə jē) ***n.*** **1** the study of the music of a particular region and its sociocultural implications, esp. of music outside the European art tradition **2** the comparative study of the music of different cultural groups —**eth′no·mu′si·col′o·gist** ***n.***

e·tho·gram (ē′thə gram′) ***n.*** ⟦< Gr *ēthos* (see ETHOS) + -GRAM⟧ *Zool.* a detailed list of the known behaviors and activities of a given species

e·thol·o·gy (ē thäl′ə jē) ***n.*** ⟦L *ethologia*, character portrayal < Gr *ēthologia*: see fol. & -LOGY⟧ the scientific study of the characteristic behavior patterns of animals —**e·tho·log·i·cal** (ē′thə läj′i kəl) ***adj.*** —**e·thol′o·gist** ***n.***

e·thos (ē′thäs′) ***n.*** ⟦Gr *ēthos*, disposition, character: see ETHICAL⟧ the characteristic and distinguishing attitudes, habits, beliefs, etc. of an individual or of a group

eth·yl (eth′əl) ***n.*** ⟦ETH(ER) + -YL⟧ the monovalent radical C_2H_5, which forms the base of many compounds, as ethyl alcohol and ether —**eth·yl·ic** (i thil′ik) ***adj.***

ethyl acetate a colorless, fruity-smelling liquid ester, $CH_3COOC_2H_5$, formed from acetic acid and ethyl alcohol and used as a solvent, in flavoring, in manufacturing synthetic resins, etc.

ethyl alcohol ALCOHOL (sense 1)

eth·yl·ate (eth′əl āt′; *for n.*, -it) ***vt.*** **-at′ed**, **-at′ing** to compound with one or more ethyl groups —***n.*** a compound formed by the replacement of the hydrogen atom in the hydroxyl group of ethyl alcohol by an active metal —**eth′yl·a′tion** ***n.***

ethyl cellulose an ethyl ether of cellulose obtained as a white granular solid by treating wood pulp soaked in sodium hydroxide (**alkali cellulose**) with ethyl chloride: used in adhesives, plastics, insulation, etc.

ethyl chloride a colorless liquid, C_2H_5Cl, prepared by heating ethyl alcohol with hydrogen chloride in the presence of zinc chloride: used in preparing tetraethyl lead and ethyl cellulose, and as a local anesthetic

☆**eth·yl·ene** (eth′əl ēn′) ***n.*** ⟦ETHYL + -ENE⟧ a colorless, flammable, gaseous alkene, $H_2C{:}CH_2$, obtained by the cracking of natural or coal gas, by the dehydration of alcohol, etc.: it is the simplest alkene and is used to synthesize organic chemicals, esp. polyethylene, to hasten the ripening of fruits, and as an anesthetic

☆**ethylene glycol** a colorless, viscous liquid, $HOCH_2CH_2OH$, used as an antifreeze, as a solvent, in resins, etc.

ethylene series a group of similar hydrocarbons: see ALKENE

ethyl ether *see* ETHER (sense 4)

eth·yl-par·a-a·mi·no·ben·zo·ate (eth′əl par′ə am′ə nō ben′zō āt′, -it) ***n.*** BENZOCAINE

e·ti·o·late (ē′tē ə lāt′) ***vt.*** **-lat′ed**, **-lat′ing** ⟦Fr *étioler* < dial. var. of *éteule*, stubble, straw < OFr *estouble*: see STUBBLE⟧ **1** to cause to be pale and unhealthy **2** to deprive of strength; weaken **3** *Bot.* to blanch or bleach by depriving of sunlight —**e′ti·o·la′tion** ***n.***

e·ti·ol·o·gy (ēt′ē äl′ə jē) ***n.***, *pl.* **-gies** ⟦LL *aetiologia* < Gr *aitiologia* < *aitia*, cause (< base of *aisa*, fate: see DIET¹) + *logia*, description: see -LOGY⟧ **1** the assignment of a cause, or the cause assigned [the *etiology* of a folkway] **2** *a)* the science of the causes or origins of disease *b)* the causes of a specific disease —**e′ti·o·log′ic** (-ə läj′ik) ***adj.***, **e′ti·o·log′i·cal** —**e′ti·o·log′i·cal·ly** ***adv.***

et·i·quette (et′i kit, -ket) ***n.*** ⟦Fr *étiquette*, lit., TICKET⟧ **1** the forms, manners, and ceremonies established by convention as acceptable or required in social relations, in a profession, or in official life **2** the rules for such forms, manners, and ceremonies —***SYN.*** DECORUM

Et·na (et′nə), **Mount** volcanic mountain in E Sicily: 10,900 ft (3,322 m)

E·to·bi·coke (i tō′bi kō′) ⟦ult. < Ojibwa (? *Wahdobekaug* or *Wadopikang*), place where the black alders grow]] former city in SE Ontario, Canada, now part of Toronto

E·ton (ēt′'n) town in Berkshire, England, on the Thames, near London: site of a private preparatory school for boys (**Eton College**)

Eton collar a broad, white linen collar worn with an Eton jacket, or a collar resembling this

E·to·ni·an (ē tō′nē ən) *adj.* of Eton College —*n.* a student or former student at Eton College

Eton jacket (*or* **coat**) a black, waist-length jacket with broad lapels, left open in front, as that worn by students at Eton College

é·touf·fée (ā′to͞o fā′) *n.* [[Fr, a stew < *étouffer,* to smother: see STIFLE[1]]] a Cajun stew, typically of crayfish or shrimp in a sauce of vegetables, spices, and a well-browned roux, served over rice

E·tru·ri·a (i tro͝or′ē ə) [[L]] ancient country (fl. 6th cent. B.C.) occupying what is now Tuscany & part of Umbria in WC Italy

E·trus·can (i trus′kən) *adj.* [[< L *Etruscus* < ? Etr **etrsco-*]] of Etruria or its people, language, or culture —*n.* **1** a person born or living in Etruria **2** the language of the ancient Etruscans: it is not known to be related to any other language Also **E·tru·ri·an** (i tro͝or′ē ən)

ETS *trademark* Educational Testing Service

et seq. *abbrev.* **1** [[L *et sequens*]] and the following **2** [[L *et sequentes* or *et sequentia*]] and those that follow

-ette (et) [[Fr: see -ET]] *suffix forming nouns* **1** little *[statuette]* ☆**2** female *[majorette]*: as applied to persons, now often avoided as patronizing *[suffragette]* **3** a substitute for *[leatherette]*

é·tude (ā′to͞od′, -tyo͞od′) *n.* [[Fr, STUDY]] a musical composition for a solo instrument, designed to give practice in some special point of technique, but often performed for its artistic worth

e·tui (ā twē′, e-; e′twē′) *n.* [[Fr *étui* < OFr *estui* < *estuier,* to place in a cover, enclose < VL **studiare,* to treat with care < L *studium*: see STUDY]] an ornamental case for small articles, as needles

ETV *abbrev.* educational television

ety or **etym** *abbrev.* etymology

et·y·mo·log·i·cal (et′ə mə läj′i kəl) *adj.* [[< L *etymologicus* < Gr *etymologikos* + -AL]] of or according to the etymology, or to the principles of etymology —**et′y·mo·log′i·cal·ly** *adv.*

et·y·mol·o·gist (et′ə mäl′ə jist) *n.* an expert in etymology

et·y·mol·o·gize (-jīz′) *vt., vi.* **-gized′**, **-giz′ing** to trace the etymology of, or give or suggest an etymology for (a word or words)

et·y·mol·o·gy (-jē) *n., pl.* **-gies** [[ME & OFr *ethimologie* < L *etymologia* < Gr: see fol. & -LOGY]] **1** the origin and development of a word, affix, phrase, etc.; the tracing of a word or other form back as far as possible in its own language and to its source in contemporary or earlier languages: in this dictionary etymologies are given in doubled brackets preceding the senses to which they apply **2** the branch of linguistics dealing with word origin and development

et·y·mon (et′ə män′) *n., pl.* **-mons′** or **-ma** (-mə) [[L < Gr *etymon,* literal sense of a word, etymology, neut. of *etymos,* true < IE **seto-* < base **es-,* to be > IS[1], L *sum, est*]] **1** an earlier form of a word, as at an earlier period in the development of a language: in this dictionary etymons are shown in italic type within the etymologies (Ex.: Old English "*eage*" is the etymon of Modern English "eye") **2** a word or morpheme from which derivatives or compounds have developed

Eu *Chem. symbol for* europium

EU *abbrev.* European Union

eu- (yo͞o, yoo) [[Fr & ModL < Gr *eu-,* good, well < IE base **esu-,* good]] *prefix* good, well *[eulogy, euphony]*

Eu·boe·a (yo͞o bē′ə) large island in the Aegean Sea, off the E coast of Greece: 1,411 sq mi (3,654 sq km)

eu·caine (yo͞o′kān′, yo͞o kān′) *n.* [[EU- + (CO)CAINE]] either of two cocaine-like synthetic alkaloids, **alpha-eucaine**, $C_{19}H_{27}NO_4$, or **beta-eucaine**, $C_{15}H_{21}NO_2$, made from piperidine: the hydrochloride of beta-eucaine is used as a local anesthetic for animals and was formerly used for humans

eu·ca·lyp·tol or **eu·ca·lyp·tole** (yo͞o′kə lip′tôl, -tōl) *n.* [[fol. + -OL[1], -OLE]] an essential oil, $C_{10}H_{18}O$, with a camphorlike odor and spicy taste, used in medicines and perfumes: the chief component of eucalyptus oil

eu·ca·lyp·tus (yo͞o′kə lip′təs) *n., pl.* **-tus·es** or **-ti′** (-tī′) [[ModL < EU- + Gr *kalyptos,* covered (from the covering of the buds) < *kalyptein,* to cover, CONCEAL]] any of a genus (*Eucalyptus*) of tall, aromatic, chiefly Australian evergreen trees of the myrtle family, bearing pendent leaves and umbels of white, red, or pink flowers and valued for their timber, gum, and oil: also **eu′ca·lypt′**

eucalyptus oil an essential oil derived from eucalyptus leaves, used as an antiseptic and expectorant

eu·car·y·ote (yo͞o kar′ē ōt′) *n. alt. sp. of* EUKARYOTE

eu·cha·ris (yo͞o′kə ris) *n.* [[ModL < Gr, charming, gracious < *eu-* (see EU-) + *charis,* favor (see fol.)]] any of a genus (*Eucharis*) of South American plants of the lily family, with white flowers

Eu·cha·rist (yo͞o′kə rist) *n.* [[ME *eukarist* < OFr *eucariste* < LL(Ec) *eucharistia* < Gr, gratitude (in N.T., the Eucharist) < *eucharistos,* grateful < *eu-,* well (see EU-) + *charizesthai,* to show favor to]] **1** the central Christian rite, in which bread and wine are consecrated and distributed as the body and blood of Jesus or as symbols of them **2** the consecrated bread and wine, or either of these —**Eu′cha·ris′tic** *adj.*

☆**eu·chre** (yo͞o′kər) *n.* [[earlier also *yuker, uker* < ?]] **1** a card game basically for two, three, or four players, played with thirty-two cards (sevens up through aces), five cards being dealt to each player **2** a euchring or being euchred —*vt.* **-chred**, **-chring 1** to prevent (the trump-naming opponent at euchre) from taking the required three tricks **2** [Informal] to outwit or cheat *[they were euchred out of their savings]*

eu·chro·ma·tin (yo͞o krō′mə tin) *n.* [[Ger: see EU- & CHROMATIN]] *Biol.* the portion of the chromatin that accepts a light stain and contains most of the active genetic material: cf. HETEROCHROMATIN

eu·clase (yo͞o′klās′) *n.* [[Fr < *eu-* (see EU-) + Gr *klasis,* a breaking < *klan,* to break (see CLASTIC): so named from breaking easily]] a very hard, brittle, monoclinic mineral, hydrous beryllium aluminum silicate, $BeAlSiO_4(OH)$, sometimes used as a gem

Eu·clid (yo͞o′klid) [[L *Euclides* < Gr *Eukleidēs*]] fl. 300 B.C.; Gr. mathematician: author of a basic work in geometry —**Eu·clid′e·an** (-ē ən) *adj.*, **Eu·clid′i·an**

eu·crite (yo͞o′krīt′) *n.* [[Ger *eukrit* < Gr *eukritos,* easy to discern < *eu-,* EU- + *kritos,* pp. of *krinein,* to separate: see CRISIS]] a class of rare achondritic meteorite composed of basalt and believed to have been formed in lava flows on either the moon, Mars, or an asteroid —**eu·crit·ic** (yo͞o krit′ik) *adj.*

eu·dae·mo·ni·a or **eu·de·mo·ni·a** (yo͞o′di mō′nē ə) *n.* [[Gr *eudaimonia,* happiness < *eudaimōn,* blessed with a good genius, fortunate < *eu-* (see EU-) + *daimōn* (see DAEMON)]] happiness or well-being; specif., in Aristotle's philosophy, happiness or well-being, the main universal goal, distinct from pleasure and derived from a life of activity governed by reason

eu·dae·mon·ism (yo͞o dē′mən iz′əm) *n.* [[Gr *eudaimonismos,* a calling happy < *eudaimonizein,* to call happy < *eudaimōn*: see prec.]] the ethical doctrine that personal happiness is the chief good and the proper aim of action, esp. such happiness conceived of in terms of well-being based on virtuous and rational self-realization: also **eu·de′mon·ism′** —**eu·dae′mon·ist** *n., adj.* —**eu·dae′mon·is′tic** *adj.*

eu·di·om·e·ter (yo͞o′dē äm′ət ər) *n.* [[< Gr *eudios,* clear, fair (< *eudia,* fair weather < *eu-* (see EU-) + *dia,* day < IE **diw-,* glowing day < base *dei-,* to shine > DEITY) + -METER]] an instrument for measuring and analyzing gases volumetrically, originally for measuring the amount of oxygen in the air to determine its purity —**eu′di·o·met′ric** (-ə met′rik) *adj.*, **eu′di·o·met′ri·cal** —**eu′di·om′e·try** *n.*

Eu·gene[1] (yoo jēn′, yo͞o′jēn) *n.* [[Fr *Eugène* < L *Eugenius* < Gr *Eugenios* < *eugenēs,* well-born: see EU- & GENUS]] a masculine name: dim. *Gene*; fem. *Eugenia*

Eu·gene[2] (yo͞o jēn′, yo͞o′jēn), Prince (*François Eugène de Savoie-Carignan*) 1663-1736; Austrian general, born in France

Eu·gene[3] (yo͞o jēn′, yoo′jēn) [[after *Eugene* F. Skinner (1809-64), farmer who built the first cabin there (1846)]] city in W Oreg.

eu·ge·ni·a (yoo jē′nē ə, -jēn′yə) *n.* any of various tropical evergreen trees and shrubs of the myrtle family with colorful, cherrylike fruit which is often edible

Eu·ge·ni·a (yo͞o jē′nē ə, -jēn′yə) *n.* [[L < Gr *Eugenia*: see EUGENE[1]]] a feminine name: dim. *Genie*

eu·gen·ic (yo͞o jen′ik) *adj.* [[< Gr *eugenēs,* well-born (see EUGENE[1]): used in causative sense (1883) by F. GALTON]] **1** causing improvement of hereditary qualities of a stock: cf. DYSGENIC **2** of, relating to, or improved by eugenics Also **eu·gen′i·cal** —**eu·gen′i·cal·ly** *adv.*

eu·gen·i·cist (yo͞o jen′ə sist) *n.* a specialist in or advocate of eugenics: also **eu·gen·ist** (yo͞o′jə nist)

eu·gen·ics (yo͞o jen′iks) *n.* [[< Gr *eugenēs* (see EUGENE[1]) + -ICS: coined (1883) by F. GALTON]] the movement devoted to improving the human species through the control of hereditary factors in mating

Eu·gé·nie (yoo jē′nē; *Fr* ö zhā nē′), Empress (born *Eugenia María de Montijo de Guzmán*) 1826-1920; wife of Louis Napoleon & empress of France (1853-71), born in Spain

eu·ge·nol (yo͞o′jə nôl′, -nōl′) *n.* [[< ModL *Eugenia,* a genus of tropical trees + -OL[1]]] a colorless, aromatic liquid phenol, $C_{10}H_{12}O_2$, found in oil of cloves and used in perfumes, as an antiseptic in dentistry, etc.

eu·gle·na (yo͞o glē′nə) *n.* [[ModL < EU- + Gr *glēnē,* pupil of the eye < IE base **ĝel-,* **ĝlē-,* to gleam > CLEAN]] any of a genus (*Euglena*) of green protists with a single flagellum, a reddish eyespot, and a flexible body shape

eu·gle·noid movement (yo͞o glē′noid′) the expansion and contraction of the cell body of various flagellates

eu·he·mer·ism (yo͞o hē′mər iz′əm, -hem′ər-) *n.* [[< L *Euhemerus* (< Gr *Euhēmeros*) + -ISM]] the theory of the Greek writer Euhemerus (4th cent. B.C.) that the gods of mythology were deified human beings; theory that myths are based on traditional accounts of real people and events —**eu·he′mer·ist** *n., adj.* —**eu·he′mer·is′tic** *adj.*

eu·he·mer·ize (-īz′) *vt.* **-ized′**, **-iz′ing** to interpret (myths, etc.) by euhemerism

eu·kar·y·ote (yo͞o kar′ē ōt′) *n.* [[< Gr *eu-,* good + *karyōtis,* a date < *karyon,* a nut, fruit stone, kernel]] a living organism made up of cells with true nuclei that divide by mitosis: in some systems of biological classification, any of a superkingdom (Eukaryotae) of living organisms, including the plants and animals: cf. PROKARYOTE —**eu·kar′y·ot′ic** (-ät′ik) *adj.*

☆**eu·la·chon** (yo͞o′lə kän′) *n.* [[Chinook jargon *ulâkân*]] CANDLEFISH

Eu·ler (oi′lər), **Le·on·hard** (lā′ôn härt′) 1707-83; Swiss mathematician

eu·lo·gi·a (yo͞o lō′jē ə, -jə) *n.* [[ML, food, blessing (in ML(Ec), the Eucharist): see EULOGY]] bread blessed but not consecrated, and given in small pieces to the noncommunicants at the Eucharistic service, esp. in the Eastern Orthodox Church

eu·lo·gis·tic (yo͞o′lə jis′tik) *adj.* of or expressing eulogy; praising highly; laudatory —**eu′lo·gis′ti·cal·ly** *adv.*

eu·lo·gi·um (yoo lō′jē əm) ***n.***, *pl.* **-gi·ums** or **-gi·a** (-jē ə, -jə) ⟦ML⟧ EULOGY

eu·lo·gize (yoo͞′lə jīz′) ***vt.*** **-gized′**, **-giz′ing** to praise highly; compose a eulogy about; extol —***SYN.*** PRAISE —**eu′lo·gist** ***n.***, **eu′lo·giz′er**

eu·lo·gy (yoo͞′lə jē) ***n.***, *pl.* **-gies** ⟦ME *euloge* < ML *eulogia* < Gr, praise, lit., fine language (in LXX & N.T., blessing) < *eulegein*, to speak well of, bless: see EU- & -LOGY⟧ speech or writing in praise of a person, event, or thing; esp., a formal speech praising a person who has recently died

Eu·men·i·des (yoo͞ men′i dēz′) ***pl.n.*** ⟦L < Gr, lit., the gracious ones < *eumenēs*, well-disposed, gracious < *eu-* (see EU-) + *menos*, the mind, temper: a propitiatory euphemism⟧ *Gr. Myth.* FURIES

Eu·nice (yoo͞′nis) ***n.*** ⟦LL(Ec) < Gr *Eunikē*, lit., good victory < *eu-* (see EU-) + *nikē*, victory⟧ a feminine name

eu·nuch (yoo͞′nək) ***n.*** ⟦ME *eunuk* < L *eunuchus* < Gr *eunouchos*, guardian of the bed, chamberlain, eunuch < *eunē*, bed + *echein*, to have, hold: see SCHEME⟧ **1** a castrated man in charge of a harem or employed as a chamberlain or high officer in the court of an emperor or potentate **2** any man or boy lacking normal function of the testes, as through castration or disease

eu·on·y·mus (yoo͞ än′ə məs) ***n.*** ⟦ModL, used by LINNAEUS < L, the spindle tree < Gr *euōnymos*, lit., of good name, lucky < *eu-* (see EU-) + *onyma*, dial. form of *onoma*, NAME⟧ any of a genus (*Euonymus*) of deciduous or evergreen shrubs and woody vines of the staff-tree family, with colorful seeds and pods

eu·pa·to·ri·um (yoo͞′pə tôr′ē əm) ***n.*** ⟦ModL < Gr *eupatorion*, hemp agrimony, named in honor of Mithridates *Eupatōr*, king of Pontus⟧ any of a genus (*Eupatorium*) of plants of the composite family, including the mistflower, joe-pye weed, and boneset

eu·pat·rid (yoo͞ pa′trid, yoo͞′pə trid) ***n.***, *pl.* **eu·pat′ri·dae′** (-tri dē′) or **eu′pat·rids** ⟦Gr *eupatridēs* < *eu-* (see EU-) + *patēr*, FATHER⟧ [*also* **E-**] any of the hereditary aristocrats of ancient Athens or other Greek states

eu·pep·si·a (yoo͞ pep′sē ə; *also*, -shə) ***n.*** ⟦ModL < Gr, digestibility: see EU- & DYSPEPSIA⟧ normal digestion: cf. DYSPEPSIA

eu·pep·tic (yoo͞ pep′tik) ***adj.*** ⟦< Gr *eupeptos* (< *eu-* (see EU-) + *peptein*, to digest: see COOK) + -IC⟧ **1** of or having normal digestion **2** healthy and happy; cheerful

eu·pha·u·si·id (yoo͞′fə yoo͞′sē id′) ***n.*** ⟦< ModL *Euphausia*, name of the genus < Gr *eu-* (see EU-) + ? *pha(inein)*, to show (see -PHANE) + *ousia*, substance (see HOMOIOUSIAN) + -ID⟧ KRILL: also **eu·pha·u′sid′** (-sid′)

eu·phe·mism (yoo͞′fə miz′əm) ***n.*** ⟦Gr *euphēmismos* < *euphēmizein*, to use words of good omen < *euphēmos*, of good sound or omen < *eu-* (see EU-) + *phēmē*, speech < *phanai*, say: see BAN[1]⟧ **1** the use of a word or phrase that is less expressive or direct but considered less distasteful, less offensive, etc. than another **2** a word or phrase so substituted (Ex.: *remains* for *corpse*) —**eu′phe·mist** ***n.*** —**eu′phe·mis′tic** ***adj.***, **eu′phe·mis′ti·cal** —**eu′phe·mis′ti·cal·ly** ***adv.***

eu·phe·mize (-mīz′) ***vt.***, ***vi.*** **-mized′**, **-miz′ing** to speak or write (of) euphemistically

☆**eu·phen·ics** (yoo͞ fen′iks) ***n.*** ⟦coined (1963) by Joshua Lederberg, U.S. geneticist < EU- + *phen-* (as in PHENOTYPE) + -ICS, after EUGENICS⟧ a movement seeking to improve the human species by modifying the biological development of the individual, as through prenatal gene manipulation with chemicals

eu·phon·ic (yoo͞ fän′ik) ***adj.*** ⟦ML *euphonicus*⟧ **1** of or having to do with euphony **2** euphonious Also **eu·phon′i·cal** —**eu·phon′i·cal·ly** ***adv.***

eu·pho·ni·ous (yoo͞ fō′nē əs) ***adj.*** characterized by euphony; having a pleasant sound; harmonious —**eu·pho′ni·ous·ly** ***adv.***

eu·pho·ni·um (yoo͞ fō′nē əm) ***n.*** ⟦< Gr *euphōnos*, musical (see fol.) + (HARMON)IUM⟧ a valved brass instrument like the baritone but more mellow in tone, due to a larger bore

eu·pho·ny (yoo͞′fə nē) ***n.***, *pl.* **-nies** ⟦Fr *euphonie* < LL *euphonia* < Gr *euphōnia* < *euphōnos*, sweet-voiced, musical < *eu-* (see EU-) + *phōnē*, voice: see PHONE[1]⟧ **1** the quality of having a pleasing sound **2** pleasant combination of agreeable sounds in spoken words **3** such a combination of words

eu·phor·bi·a (yoo͞ fôr′bē ə) ***n.*** ⟦ME *euforbia* < L *euphorbea*, said to be named after *Euphorbus*, physician of 1st c. A.D., who used it medically⟧ SPURGE

eu·pho·ri·a (yoo͞ fôr′ē ə) ***n.*** ⟦ModL < Gr, power of bearing easily < *euphoros*, bearing well < *eu-* (see EU-) + *pherein*, BEAR[1]⟧ a feeling of vigor, well-being, or high spirits —**eu·phor′ic** (-fôr′ik) ***adj.***

eu·pho·ri·ant (-ənt) ***n.*** *Med.* a drug or other agent that produces euphoria

eu·pho·tic (yoo͞ fōt′ik) ***adj.*** ⟦EU- + PHOTIC⟧ *Ecol.* of or pertaining to the uppermost portion of a body of water that receives sufficient sunlight for photosynthesis: see APHOTIC

eu·phra·sy (yoo͞′frə sē) ***n.***, *pl.* **-sies** ⟦ME *eufrasie* < ML *euphrasia* < Gr < *euphrainein*, to cheer < *eu-* (see EU-) + *phrēn*, mind (see PHRENO-⟧ EYEBRIGHT

Eu·phra·tes (yoo͞ frāt′ēz) river flowing from EC Turkey generally southward through Syria & Iraq, joining the Tigris to form the Shatt-al-Arab: *c.* 1,700 mi (2,736 km)

Eu·phros·y·ne (yoo͞ fräs′i nē′) ***n.*** ⟦L < Gr *Euphrosynē* < *euphrōn*, cheerful < *eu-* (see EU-) + *phrēn*, mind⟧ *Gr. Myth.* Joy, one of the three Graces

eu·phu·ism (yoo͞′fyoo͞ iz′əm) ***n.*** ⟦after *Euphues* (main character in two prose romances by John LYLY) < Gr *euphyēs*, shapely, graceful < *eu-* (see EU-) + *phyē*, growth < *phyein*, to grow: see BONDAGE⟧ **1** the artificial, affected, high-flown style of speaking or writing used by John Lyly and his imitators, characterized by alliteration, balanced sentences, far-fetched figures of speech, etc. **2** any artificial, high-flown style of speech or writing **3** an instance of this —**eu′phu·ist** ***n.***

eu·phu·is·tic (yoo͞′fyoo͞ is′tik) ***adj.*** of, having the nature of, or characterized by euphuism —***SYN.*** BOMBASTIC —**eu′phu·is′ti·cal** ***adj.*** —**eu′phu·is′ti·cal·ly** ***adv.***

eu·plas·tic (yoo͞ plas′tik) ***adj.*** ⟦EU- + -PLASTIC⟧ *Physiol.* easily formed into or adapted to the formation of tissue —***n.*** a euplastic material

eu·ploid (yoo͞′ploid′) ***adj.*** ⟦EU- + -PLOID⟧ with the complement of chromosomes being an exact multiple of the haploid number, as diploid, triploid, etc.: see HETEROPLOID —**eu′ploid′y** (-ploi′dē) ***n.***

eup·ne·a or **eup·noe·a** (yoo͞p nē′ə) ***n.*** ⟦ModL < Gr *eupnoia* < *eu-* (see EU-) + *pnoē*, breathing < *pnein*, to breathe: see PNEUMA⟧ [Obs.] normal breathing: see APNEA, DYSPNEA

Eur *abbrev.* **1** Europe **2** European

EUR *abbrev.* euro

Eur·a·sia (yoor ā′zhə) land mass made up of the continents of Europe & Asia

Eur·a·sian (-zhən) ***adj.*** **1** of Eurasia **2** of mixed European and Asian descent —***n.*** **1** a person who has one European parent and one Asian parent, or a person who is generally of mixed European and Asian descent **2** a member of a people of both Europe and Asia

Eur·a·tom (yoor at′əm) ***n.*** European Atomic Energy Community, a unit of the European Community

eu·re·ka (yoo rē′kə) ***interj.*** ⟦Gr *heurēka*, I have found, perf. of *heuriskein*, to find, discover < IE base **wer-*, to find, take > Arm *gerem*, (I) capture, OIr *fūar*, I have found⟧ **1** I have found (it): believed to have been uttered by Archimedes when he discovered a way to determine the purity of gold by applying the principle of specific gravity **2** I've got it; yes; that's it: used to express triumphant achievement, success, or discovery

eu·rhyth·mics (yoo rith′miks) ***n.*** *alt. sp. of* EURYTHMICS —**eu·rhyth′mic** ***adj.*** —**eu·rhyth′my** ***n.***

Eu·rip·i·des (yoo rip′ə dēz′) 480-406 B.C.; Gr. writer of tragedies —**Eu·rip′i·de′an** (-dē′ən) ***adj.***

eu·ri·pus (yoo rī′pəs) ***n.***, *pl.* **-pi′** (-pī′) ⟦L < Gr *euripos* < *eu-* (see EU-) + *rhipē*, rush, impetus, orig., turning motion < IE **wrei-* < base **wer-*, to turn > L *vertere*, Ger *reiben*, to grate⟧ a strait or channel with a violent current or tide

eu·ro (yoor′ō) ***n.*** ⟦shortened < EUROPE or EUROPEAN⟧ **1** the basic monetary unit of the European Monetary Union and of various other countries: symbol, €: see the table of monetary units in the Reference Supplement **2** [**E-**] [Informal] EUROPEAN (***n.*** 1) —***adj.*** [**E-**] [Informal] EUROPEAN

Eu·ro- (yoor′ō, -ə) *combining form* **1** European, European and [*Euromart, Euro*-American]: also, before a vowel, **Eur-** **2** [*also* **e-**] European Union, European Monetary Union [*Euromart, eurozone*]

Eu·ro-A·mer·i·can (yoor′ō ə mer′i kən) ***n.***, ***adj.*** EUROPEAN AMERICAN

Eu·ro·bond (yoor′ō bänd′) ***n.*** a bond issued in an international, usually European, market and repayable in the currency of issue

Eu·ro·cen·tric (yoor′ō sen′trik) ***adj.*** centering on Europe or emphasizing the values, history, perspective, etc. of the European tradition, sometimes so as to exclude other cultural groups within a society —**Eu′ro·cen′trism′** ***n.***

Eu·roc·ly·don (yoo räk′li dän′, -dən) ***n.*** ⟦Gr(Ec) *euroklydōn*, prob. in error (as if < *euros*, east wind + *klydōn*, wave, billow), for *eurakylōn*, a northeast wind < *euros* (see EURUS) + L *aquilo*, the north (or north-by-east) wind < *aquilus*, dark, stormy, orig., watery < *aqua*, water⟧ **1** *Bible* a stormy northeast wind of the Mediterranean: Acts 27:14 **2** any stormy wind

Eu·ro·com·mu·nism (yoor′ō käm′yə niz′əm) ***n.*** a former policy of some W European Communist parties stressing their independence from the Soviet Union, support of democratic political procedures, etc. —**Eu′ro·com′mu·nist** ***adj.***, ***n.***

Eu·ro·crat (yoor′ə krat′) ***n.*** ⟦EURO- + -CRAT, with implied pun on BUREAUCRAT⟧ any of the officials or employees of the European Economic Community

Eu·ro·cur·ren·cy (yoor′ō kur′ən sē) ***n.***, *pl.* **-cies** deposits denominated in the currency of, but held in banks outside of, their country of origin, esp. in Europe

Eu·ro·dol·lars (yoor′ō däl′ərz) ***pl.n.*** deposits of U.S. dollars in banks outside the U.S., especially in Europe —**Eu′ro·dol′lar** ***adj.***

Eu·ro·mart (yoor′ō märt′) ***n.*** EUROPEAN ECONOMIC COMMUNITY: also **Eu′ro·mar′ket** (-mär′kit)

Eu·ro·pa (yoo rō′pə) ***n.*** ⟦L < Gr *Eurōpē*⟧ **1** *Gr. Myth.* a Phoenician princess loved by Zeus: he, disguised as a white bull, carries her off across the sea to Crete **2** the fourth largest satellite of Jupiter: discovered in 1610 by Galileo

Eu·rope (yoor′əp) ⟦L *Europa* < Gr *Eurōpē*⟧ **1** continent between Asia & the Atlantic Ocean: the Ural Mountains & the Ural River are generally considered the E boundary: *c.* 3,837,000 sq mi (9,938,000 sq km) **2** EUROPEAN COMMUNITY

Eu·ro·pe·an (yoor′ə pē′ən) ***adj.*** of Europe or its peoples, languages, or cultures —***n.*** **1** a person born or living in Europe **2** in Africa and Asia, any Caucasian, or white person

European American **1** an American of European ancestry; often, specif., a white American **2** of or relating to both Europe and the U.S. Also written **Eu′ro·pe′an-A·mer′i·can** ***n.***, ***adj.***

European Community an organization of European nations, originally, Belgium, the Federal Republic of Germany, France, Italy, Luxembourg, and the Netherlands, for advancing economic integration and political cooperation: it was established by the merger in 1967 of the *European Coal and Steel Community* (created in 1951), the EUROPEAN ECONOMIC COMMUNITY, and the *European Atomic Energy Community* (created in 1957); in 1993 it became the EUROPEAN UNION: also **European Communities**

European Economic Community an organization of European nations, created in 1957, for advancing economic integration as by eliminating trade barriers: abbrev. *EEC*

Eu·ro·pe·an·ism (-iz′əm) *n.* belief in or advocacy of political unification and economic integration among European nations —**Eu′ro·pe′an·ist** *adj., n.*

Eu·ro·pe·an·ize (-īz′) *vt.* **-ized′**, **-iz′ing** **1** to make European, as in culture **2** to integrate (the economy of a European nation) with that of other European nations —**Eu′ro·pe′an·i·za′tion** *n.*

European Monetary Union the union of those members of the European Union that have adopted the euro as their legal currency

☆**European plan** a system of hotel operation in which the rate charged to guests covers rooms and service but not meals: distinguished from AMERICAN PLAN

European Union a union of European nations created by treaty and put into effect in 1993 for the purpose of working gradually toward an economic and political unification of Europe by means of a unified monetary policy, a common currency, standardized laws of commerce and trade, etc.: see EUROPEAN COMMUNITY

eu·ro·pi·um (yoo͞ rō′pē əm) *n.* ⟦ModL: so named (1901) by E. A. Demarçay (1852-1904), Fr chemist < EUROPE + -IUM⟧ a chemical element, one of the rare-earth elements, used as the red phosphor in color TVs: symbol, Eu; at. no. 63: see the periodic table of elements in the Reference Supplement

Eu·ro·trash (yoor′ō trash′) [Slang] *pl.n.* fashionable Europeans, traveling or living abroad, of a type regarded variously as pretentious, shallow, sexually promiscuous, irresponsible, etc. —*adj.* of or belonging to this type

eu·ro·zone (yoor′ō zōn′) [*also* **E-**] loosely, those nations of the European Union that have adopted the euro as their legal currency: often **euro zone**

Eu·rus (yoo͞′rəs) *n.* ⟦ME < L < Gr *euros*, prob. ult. < IE base **eus-*, to burn > L *urere*, to burn⟧ *Gr. Myth.* the god of the east wind or southeast wind

eu·ry- (yoo͞′ri, -rə; yoor′i, -ə) ⟦ModL < Gr < *eurys*, wide, broad < IE base **wer-*, broad > Sans *uru*⟧ *combining form* wide, broad [*euryhaline*]

eu·ry·bath (yoo͞′ri bath′, yoor′ə-) *n.* ⟦prec. + Gr *bathos*, depth⟧ *Biol.* an organism that can live in a wide range of water depths: opposed to STENOBATH —**eu′ry·bath′ic** *adj.*

Eu·ryd·i·ce (yoo͞ rid′i sē′) *n.* ⟦L < Gr *Eurydikē*⟧ *Gr. Myth.* the wife of ORPHEUS

eu·ry·ha·line (yoo͞′ri hā′līn′, -hal′in′, yoor′ə-) *adj.* ⟦Ger *euryhalin* < *eury-*, EURY- + Gr *halinos*, saline < *hals*, SALT⟧ *Biol.* able to exist in waters widely varying in salt content: opposed to STENOHALINE

eu·ry·hy·gric (-hī′grik) *adj.* ⟦EURY- + HYGR- + -IC⟧ *Biol.* able to withstand a wide range of humidity: opposed to STENOHYGRIC

eu·ryph·a·gous (yoo͞ rif′ə gəs) *adj.* ⟦EURY- + -PHAGOUS⟧ *Biol.* eating a wide variety of foods: opposed to STENOPHAGOUS

eu·ryp·ter·id (yoo͞ rip′tər id′) *n.* ⟦< ModL *Eurypterida* < Gr *eurys*, broad + *pteron*, FEATHER, wing: so named from a pair of broad swimming appendages⟧ any of an extinct order (Eurypterida) of large, aquatic arthropods of the Paleozoic Era, similar to the horseshoe crab and sometimes reaching a length of *c.* 1.8 m (*c.* 6 ft)

eu·ry·therm (yoo͞′ri thurm′, yoor′ə-) *n.* ⟦Ger, independent of temperature variations: see EURY- & THERM⟧ *Biol.* an organism that can live in a wide range of temperatures: opposed to STENOTHERM —**eu′ry·ther′mal** (-thur′məl) *adj.*, **eu′ry·ther′mous** (-məs), or **eu′ry·ther′mic** (-mik)

eu·ryth·mic (yoo͞ rith′mik) *adj.* **1** characterized by perfect proportion and harmony, or by movement in rhythm **2** of eurhythmics or eurythmy Also **eu·ryth′mi·cal**

eu·ryth·mics (-miks) *n.* ⟦< EURHYTHMY + -ICS⟧ the art of performing various bodily movements in rhythm, usually to musical accompaniment

eu·ryth·my (yoo͞ rith′mē) *n.* ⟦L *eurythmia* < Gr < *eurythmos*, rhythmic < *eu-* (see EU-) + *rhythmos*, RHYTHM⟧ **1** rhythmic movement **2** harmonious proportion **3** a method of teaching dancing or rhythmic movement, esp. to the recitation of verse or prose

eu·ry·top·ic (yoo͞′ri täp′ik, yoor′ə-) *adj.* ⟦< Ger *eurytop*, widely distributed (< EURY- + *-top* < Gr *topos*, place: see TOPIC) + -IC⟧ *Biol.* able to withstand a wide range of environmental conditions: opposed to STENOTOPIC —**eu′ry·to·pic′i·ty** (-tō pis′ə tē) *n.*

Eu·se·bi·us (Pam·phi·li) (yoo͞ sē′bē əs pam′fə lī′) A.D. 264?-340; Gr. ecclesiastical historian

eu·so·cial (yoo͞ sō′shəl) *adj.* ⟦see EU-⟧ of or having to do with a type of animal, as the ant or termite, that forms a colony in which one female produces all the offspring —**eu·so′ci·al′i·ty** (-shē al′ə tē) *n.*

eu·sta·chian tube (yoo͞ stā′shən, -stā′shē ən, -stā′kē ən) ⟦after Bartolomeo *Eustachio* (1520-74), It anatomist⟧ [*also* **E- t-**] a slender tube between the middle ear and the pharynx, which serves to equalize air pressure on both sides of the eardrum

eu·sta·sy or **eu·sta·cy** (yoo͞′stə sē) *n., pl.* **-sies**, **-cies** a uniform, worldwide change in the water level of the oceans —**eu·stat·ic** (yoo͞ stat′ik) *adj.*

eu·stele (yoo͞′stēl, yoo͞ stē′lē) *n.* ⟦EU- + STELE⟧ the typical vascular cylinder of a dicotyledonous plant or a gymnosperm, consisting of a ring of collateral bundles of xylem, cambium, and phloem

eu·tec·tic (yoo͞ tek′tik) *adj.* ⟦< Gr *eutēktos*, easily fused < *eu-* (see EU-) + *tēkein*, to melt (< IE **tāk-* < base **tā-*, to melt > THAW) + -IC⟧ fusing at the lowest possible temperature; specif., designating or of a mixture or alloy with a melting point lower than that of any other combination of the same components —*n.* a eutectic mixture or alloy —**eu·tec′toid′** (-toid′) *adj., n.*

Eu·ter·pe (yoo͞ tur′pē) *n.* ⟦L < Gr *Euterpē* < *euterpēs*, charming < *eu-* (see EU-) + *terpein*, to delight, charm < IE base **terp-*, enjoy⟧ *Gr. Myth.* the Muse of music and lyric poetry

eu·tha·na·si·a (yoo͞′thə nā′zhə, -zhē ə, -zē ə) *n.* ⟦Gr, painless, happy death < *eu-* (see EU-) + *thanatos*, death: see DULL⟧ **1** [Now Rare] an easy and painless death **2** act or practice of causing death painlessly, so as to end suffering: advocated by some as a way to deal with persons dying of incurable, painful diseases

☆**eu·tha·nize** (yoo͞′thə nīz′) *vt.* **-nized′**, **-niz′ing** ⟦< prec. + -IZE⟧ to put to death by euthanasia

☆**eu·then·ics** (yoo͞ then′iks) *n.* ⟦< Gr *euthēnein*, to flourish (< *eu-* (see EU-) + IE base **gwhen-*, to swell > Pers *āganiš*, full) + -ICS⟧ the science of improving the human species through control of environmental factors

eu·thy·roid (yoo͞ thī′roid′) *n.* of, characterized by, or having a normal thyroid: see HYPERTHYROID, HYPOTHYROID

eu·troph·ic (yoo͞ träf′ik, -trō′fik) *adj.* ⟦EU- + TROPHIC⟧ designating or of a body of water, esp. a lake or pond, rich in nutrients which cause excessive growth of aquatic plants, esp. algae: the resulting bacteria consume nearly all the oxygen, esp. during warm weather, choking the fish, etc.: see also MESOTROPHIC —**eu·troph′i·ca′tion** *n.*

eux·e·nite (yoo͞k′sə nīt′) *n.* ⟦Ger *euxenit* < Gr *euxenos*, hospitable (< *eu-* (see EU-) + *xenos*, stranger, guest) + -ITE[1]: so named from containing several rare elements⟧ a dark-colored, hard, orthorhombic mineral, $(Y,Ca,Ce,U,Th)(Nb,Ta,Ti)_2O_6$, containing oxides of several chemical elements, esp. of calcium, uranium, titanium, and certain rare-earth elements

Eux·ine Sea (yoo͞k′sən, -sīn′) ⟦L *Pontus Euxinus*⟧ *ancient name for* the BLACK SEA

eV or **ev** *abbrev.* electron volt

EV (ē′vē′) *n., pl.* **EVs** ⟦*e*(*lectric*) *v*(*ehicle*)⟧ an automotive vehicle with an engine driven by a rechargeable electric battery or batteries

E·va (ē′və) *n.* a feminine name: see EVE

EVA *abbrev.* extravehicular activity

e·vac·u·ant (ē vak′yoo͞ ənt, i-) *adj.* ⟦L *evacuans*, prp. of *evacuare*: see fol.⟧ causing evacuation, esp. of the bowels; cathartic or emetic —*n.* an evacuant medicine

e·vac·u·ate (ē vak′yoo͞ āt′, i-) *vt.* **-at′ed**, **-at′ing** ⟦< L *evacuatus*, pp. of *evacuare* < *e-*, out + *vacuare*, to make empty < *vacuus*, empty⟧ **1** to make empty; remove the contents of; specif., to remove air from so as to make a vacuum **2** to discharge (bodily waste, esp. feces) **3** *a)* to remove (inhabitants, etc.) from (a place or area), as for protective purposes *b)* to give up military occupation of; withdraw from —*vi.* **1** to withdraw, as from a besieged town or area of danger **2** to discharge bodily waste, esp. feces —**e·vac′u·a′tive** *adj.* —**e·vac′u·a′tor** *n.*

e·vac·u·a·tion (ē vak′yoo͞ ā′shən, i-) *n.* ⟦ME *evacuacioun* < L *evacuatio*⟧ **1** an evacuating or being evacuated **2** something evacuated; specif., feces

e·vac·u·ee (ē vak′yoo͞ ē′, -vak′yoo͞ ē′; i-) *n.* a person evacuated from an area of danger

e·vade (ē vād′, i-) *vi.* **e·vad′ed**, **e·vad′ing** ⟦Fr *évader* < L *evadere* < *e-*, out, from + *vadere*, to go: see WADE⟧ **1** [Rare] to escape; get away **2** to be deceitful or clever in avoiding or escaping something; use evasion —*vt.* **1** to avoid or escape from by deceit or cleverness; elude [*to evade* a pursuer] **2** to avoid doing or answering directly; get around; get out of [*to evade* a question, to *evade* payment of a tax] —**SYN.** ESCAPE —**e·vad′a·ble** *adj.* —**e·vad′er** *n.*

e·vag·i·nate (ē vaj′ə nāt′, i-) *vt.* **-nat′ed**, **-nat′ing** ⟦< L *evaginatus*, pp. of *evaginare*, to unsheathe < *e-*, from + *vagina*, a sheath⟧ **1** to turn inside out **2** to cause to protrude by turning inside out —**e·vag′i·na′tion** *n.*

e·val·u·ate (ē val′yoo͞ āt′, i-) *vt.* **-at′ed**, **-at′ing** ⟦back-form. < fol.⟧ **1** to find the value or amount of **2** to judge or determine the worth or quality of; appraise **3** *Math.* to find the numerical value of; express in numbers —**SYN.** ESTIMATE —**e·val′u·a′tive** *adj.* —**e·val′u·a′tor** *n.*

e·val·u·a·tion (ē val′yoo͞ ā′shən, i-) *n.* ⟦Fr *évaluation* < OFr *évaluer* < *value* < *valu*: see VALUE⟧ the process of evaluating something or an instance of this

Ev·an (ev′ən) *n.* ⟦Welsh, var. of JOHN[1]⟧ a masculine name

ev·a·nesce (ev′ə nes′) *vi.* **-nesced′**, **-nesc′ing** ⟦L *evanescere* < *e-*, out + *vanescere*, to vanish < *vanus*, VAIN⟧ to pass away or fade from sight like mist or smoke; disappear slowly

ev·a·nes·cence (-nes′əns) *n.* ⟦ML *evanescentia*: see fol.⟧ **1** a gradual disappearance **2** a tendency to evanesce; evanescent quality; transitoriness

ev·a·nes·cent (-nes′ənt) *adj.* ⟦< L *evanescens*, prp.: see EVANESCE⟧ tending to pass away or fade from sight like mist or smoke; ephemeral —**SYN.** TRANSIENT —**ev′a·nes′cent·ly** *adv.*

e·van·gel (ē van′jəl, i-) *n.* ⟦ME & OFr *evangile* < L *evangelium*, good news (in LL(Ec), gospel) < Gr *euangelion*, good news (in N.T., gospel) < *euangelos*, bringing good news < *eu-*, well + *angelos*, messenger: see ANGEL⟧ **1** the gospel **2** [**E-**] any of the four Gospels **3** ⟦Gr *euangelos*⟧ an evangelist

e·van·gel·i·cal (ē′van jel′i kəl, ev′ən-) *adj.* ⟦< LL(Ec) *evangelicus* < Gr *euangelikos* < *euangelion* (see prec.) + -AL⟧ **1** in, of, or according to the Gospels or the teaching of the New Testament **2** *a)* of a Protestant tradition that emphasizes salvation by faith and rejects the efficacy of the sacraments and good works alone *b)* [**E-**] designating or of any of various Protestant sects with this belief **3** of the Low Church party in the Church of England **4** of or promoting evangelism; evangelistic Also **e′van·gel′**

ic —*n.* [E-] a member of an evangelical church —**e′van·gel′i·cal·ism′** *n.* —**e′van·gel′i·cal·ly** *adv.*

E·van·ge·line (ē van′jə lēn′, -līn′, -lin) *n.* ⟦Fr *Évangeline* < LL(Ec) *evangelium*: see EVANGEL⟧ a feminine name

e·van·ge·lism (ē van′jə liz′əm, i-) *n.* ⟦LGr(Ec) *euangelismos*⟧ **1** a preaching of, or zealous effort to spread, the gospel, as in revival meetings or by televised services **2** any zealous effort in propagandizing for a cause —**e·van′ge·lis′tic** (-lis′tik) *adj.* —**e·van′ge·lis′ti·cal·ly** *adv.*

e·van·ge·list (-list) *n.* ⟦ME & OFr *evangeliste* < LL(Ec) *evangelista* < Gr *euangelistēs*, bringer of good news (in N.T., evangelist): see EVANGEL⟧ **1** [E-] any of the four writers of the Gospels: Matthew, Mark, Luke, or John **2** a revivalist or a preacher who holds large public services in various cities, now often televised

e·van·ge·lize (ē van′jə līz′, i-) *vt.* **-lized′**, **-liz′ing** ⟦ME *evangelisen* < OFr *evangeliser* < LL(Ec) *evangelizare* < LGr(Ec) *euangelizein* < *euangelion*: see EVANGEL⟧ **1** to preach the gospel to **2** to convert or try to convert to Christianity —*vi.* to preach the gospel —**e·van′ge·li·za′tion** *n.*

e·van·ish (ē van′ish) *vi.* ⟦ME *evanishen* < OFr *evaniss-*, extended stem of *esvanir* < VL **exvanire*, for L *evanescere*, EVANESCE⟧ [Old Poet.] VANISH

Ev·ans (ev′ənz) **1** Sir **Arthur John** 1851-1941; Eng. archaeologist **2 Herbert McLean** (mə klān′) 1882-1971; U.S. anatomist & biologist **3 Mary Ann** *see* ELIOT², George **4 Maurice** 1901-89; U.S. actor, born in England **5 Walker** 1903-75; U.S. photographer

Ev·ans·ville (ev′ənz vil′) ⟦after Gen. R. M. *Evans*, a founder, who served in the War of 1812⟧ city in SW Ind., on the Ohio River

e·vap·o·ra·ble (ē vap′ə rə bəl, i-) *adj.* ⟦ML *evaporabilis*⟧ that can be evaporated —**e·vap′o·ra·bil′i·ty** *n.*

e·vap·o·rate (ē vap′ə rāt′, i-) *vt.* **-rat′ed**, **-rat′ing** ⟦ME *evaporaten* < L *evaporatus*, pp. of *evaporare* < *e-*, out, from + *vaporare*, to emit vapor < *vapor*, VAPOR⟧ **1** to change (a liquid or solid) into vapor; drive out or draw off in the form of vapor **2** to remove moisture from (milk, vegetables, fruits, etc.) by heating or drying so as to get a concentrated product **3** *a)* to deposit (a metal, metallic salts, etc.) by sublimation *b)* to drive out (neutrons, electrons, etc.) —*vi.* **1** to become vapor; pass off in the form of vapor **2** to give off vapor **3** to disappear like vapor; vanish —**e·vap′o·ra′tion** *n.* —**e·vap′o·ra′tive** *adj.* —**e·vap′o·ra′tor** *n.*

☆**evaporated milk** unsweetened milk thickened by evaporation to about half its weight, and then canned and sterilized: cf. CONDENSED MILK

e·vap·o·rite (ē vap′ə rīt′, i-) *n.* a type of sedimentary rock, as halite or gypsum, formed by the evaporation of salt water

☆**e·vap·o·tran·spi·ra·tion** (ē vap′ō tran′spə rā′shən) *n.* ⟦EVAPO(RATION) + TRANSPIRATION⟧ the total water loss from the soil, including that by direct evaporation and that by transpiration from the surfaces of plants

e·va·sion (ē vā′zhən, i-) *n.* ⟦ME & OFr < L *evasio* < *evasus*, pp. of *evadere*: see EVADE⟧ **1** an evading; specif., an avoiding of a duty, question, etc. by deceit or cleverness **2** a way of doing this; subterfuge

e·va·sive (ē vā′siv, i-) *adj.* ⟦< L *evasus* (see prec.) + -IVE⟧ **1** tending or seeking to evade; not straightforward; tricky; equivocal **2** hard to catch, grasp, etc.; elusive —**e·va′sive·ly** *adv.* —**e·va′sive·ness** *n.*

eve (ēv) *n.* ⟦ME, var. of *even* < OE *æfen*, EVENING⟧ **1** [Old Poet.] evening **2** [*often* E-] the evening or day before a holiday [Christmas *Eve*] **3** the period immediately before some event [on the *eve* of victory]

Eve (ēv) *n.* ⟦ME < LL(Ec) *Eva*, *Heva* < Heb *Ḥawwāh*, lit., life, living being⟧ **1** a feminine name: var. *Eva* **2** *Bible* the first woman, Adam's wife: Gen. 3:20

e·vec·tion (ē vek′shən, i-) *n.* ⟦L *evectio*, a going up, carrying out < *evectus*, pp. of *evehere* < *e-*, out, from + *vehere*, to carry: see WAY⟧ a periodical variation in the motion of the moon in its orbit, caused by the attraction of the sun —**e·vec′tion·al** *adj.*

Ev·e·lyn¹ (ev′ə lin; *Brit usually*, ēv′lin) *n.* a feminine and masculine name: fem. var. *Evelina*, *Eveline*

Ev·e·lyn² (ēv′lin), **John** 1620-1706; Eng. diarist

e·ven¹ (ē′vən) *adj.* ⟦ME < OE *efne*, *efen*, akin to Ger *eben*, Goth *ibns* < ? IE base **yem-*, hold together > MIr *emon*, twins⟧ **1** flat; level; smooth [*even* country] **2** not irregular; not varying; uniform; constant [an *even* tempo] **3** calm; tranquil; serene; placid [an *even* disposition] **4** in the same plane or line; in line [water *even* with the rim] **5** equally balanced **6** *a)* owing and being owed nothing *b)* with neither a profit nor a loss **7** revenged for a wrong, insult, etc. **8** just; equitable; fair [an *even* exchange] **9** equal or identical in number, quantity, degree, score, etc. **10** exactly divisible by two: said of numbers: opposed to ODD **11** exact [an *even* mile] —*adv.* **1** [Obs.] in an even manner **2** *used as an intensive or emphatic particle meaning*: *a)* though it may seem improbable; moreover; indeed; fully [*even* unto death; *even* a fool could understand] *b)* exactly; precisely; just; in no other way but [it happened *even* as I expected] *c)* just as; while; already [*even* as he spoke, she entered] *d)* still; yet (used in emphasizing a comparison) [an *even* worse mistake] *e)* [Archaic] namely; particularly [one there was, *even* John] — *vt.*, *vi.* to make, become, or be even; level off; equalize or be equalized: often with *off*, *out*, or *up* —*SYN.* LEVEL, STEADY —**even if** supposing that; though —**even so** in spite of that; nonetheless —**e′ven·ly** *adv.* —**e′ven·ness** *n.*

e·ven² (ē′vən) *n.* ⟦see EVE⟧ [Archaic] evening

e·ven·fall (-fôl′) *n.* [Old Poet.] twilight; dusk

e·ven·hand·ed (-han′did) *adj.* impartial; fair; just

eve·ning (ēv′niŋ) *n.* ⟦ME < OE *æfnung*, verbal n. < *æfnian*, to grow toward evening < *æfen*, evening, akin to Ger *abend*, prob. < IE base **epi-*, **opi-*, after, later (> Gr *epi*, L *ob*): basic sense "later part of the day"⟧ **1** the last part of the day; close of the day and early part of night; period between sunset or the last meal of the day and bedtime **2** in some parts of the South, in rural areas, and in parts of England, the period from noon through sunset and twilight **3** the last period, as of life, a career, etc. **4** a part of the night spent in a specified way [a musical *evening*] —*adj.* of, in, or for the evening [an *evening* gown]

evening dress (*or* clothes) formal clothes worn on formal occasions in the evening

evening prayer [*often* E- P-] **1** *R.C.Ch.* the sixth of the seven canonical hours; vespers **2** *Anglican Ch.* EVENSONG

evening primrose any of a genus (*Oenothera*) of plants of the evening-primrose family, with yellow, pink, or white flowers, many of which open in the evening

eve·ning-prim·rose (-prim′rōz′) *adj.* designating a family (Onagraceae, order Myrtales) of dicotyledonous plants found chiefly in temperate America, including the fuchsia, sundrops, and willow herbs

eve·nings (ēv′niŋz) *adv.* during every evening or most evenings

evening star a bright planet, esp. Venus, that can be seen in the W sky soon after sunset

even money equal stakes in betting, with no odds

even-pin·nate (ē′vən pin′āt′, -it) *adj.* with pinnate leaflets that are symmetrically paired

e·ven·song (ē′vən sôŋ′) *n.* ⟦ME < OE *æfensang*: see EVENING & SONG⟧ **1** [*often* E-] *a)* *R.C.Ch.* vespers (see VESPER, sense 2*a*) *b)* *Anglican Ch.* the worship service assigned to the evening **2** a song sung at evening **3** [Archaic] evening

e·ven-ste·ven or **e·ven-ste·phen** (ē′vən stē′vən) *adj.* ⟦rhyming slang < EVEN¹ + STEVEN⟧ [*often* **even-S-**] [Informal] EVEN¹ (*adj.* 4-9): also written **even steven** or **even stephen**

e·vent (ē vent′, i-) *n.* ⟦OFr < L *eventus*, event, pp. of *evenire*, to happen < *e-*, out + *venire*, COME⟧ **1** a happening or occurrence, esp. when important **2** a particular contest or item in a program [the pole vault, high jump, and other *events*] **3** any organized activity, celebration, etc. for members of the general public or a particular group [the social *event* of the year] **4** [Archaic] a result; outcome —*SYN.* OCCURRENCE —**in any event** no matter what happens; anyhow: also **at all events** —**in the event** [Chiefly Brit.] as it turns out or turned out —**in the event of** if there should happen to be; in case of —**in the event that** if it should happen that

e·ven-tem·pered (ē′vən tem′pərd) *adj.* not quickly angered or excited; placid; calm

e·vent·ful (ē vent′fəl, i-) *adj.* **1** full of outstanding events [an *eventful* year] **2** having an important outcome; momentous [an *eventful* conversation] —**e·vent′ful·ly** *adv.* —**e·vent′ful·ness** *n.*

event horizon *Astron.* the spherical boundary surrounding a black hole, within which there is such strong gravity that nothing, not even light, can escape

e·ven·tide (ē′vən tīd′) *n.* ⟦ME < OE *æfentid*: see EVENING & TIDE¹⟧ [Archaic] evening

e·ven·tu·al (ē ven′cho͞o əl, -sho͞o-; i-) *adj.* ⟦< L *eventus* (see EVENT) + -AL⟧ **1** [Archaic] contingent or possible **2** happening at the end of, or as a result of, a series of events; ultimate; final [*eventual* success]

e·ven·tu·al·i·ty (ē ven′cho͞o al′ə tē, -sho͞o-; i-) *n.*, *pl.* **-ties** a possible event, outcome, or condition; contingency

e·ven·tu·al·ly (ē ven′cho͞o əl ē, -sho͞o-; -chə lē) *adv.* finally; ultimately; in the end

☆**e·ven·tu·ate** (ē ven′cho͞o āt′, -sho͞o-; i-) *vi.* **-at′ed**, **-at′ing** ⟦< L *eventus* (see EVENT) + -ATE¹⟧ to happen in the end; result: often with *in*

ev·er (ev′ər) *adv.* ⟦ME < OE *æfre*, prob. < WGmc bases of OE *a*, always, ever (see AYE¹) + ? *feorr*, FAR⟧ **1** at all times; always [lived happily *ever* after] **2** continually or continuously: usually in comb., often hyphenated [an *ever* worsening conflict] **3** at any time [have you *ever* seen an eclipse?] **4** at all; by any chance; in any way [how can I *ever* repay you?] *Ever* is also used informally as an intensifier [was she *ever* tired!] —**ever and anon** (or **again**) [Archaic] now and then; occasionally —**ever so** [Informal] very; extremely —**for ever and ever** always: also **for ever and a day**

Ev·er·est (ev′ər ist, ev′rist), **Mount** peak of the Himalayas, on the border of Nepal & Tibet: highest mountain in the world: 29,035 ft (8,850 m)

Ev·er·ett¹ (ev′ər it, ev′rit) *n.* ⟦Du *Evert*, *Everhart* < OFr *Everart* < OHG *Eburhart* < *ebur*, wild boar + *harto*, strong (see HARD): hence, lit., strong (as a) wild boar⟧ a masculine name

Ev·er·ett² (ev′ər it, ev′rit), **Edward** 1794-1865; U.S. statesman, orator, & clergyman

Ev·er·ett³ (ev′ər it, ev′rit) ⟦named (1891) after *Everett* Colby (1874-1943), Am lawyer, the son of a founder⟧ port in NW Wash., on Puget Sound

☆**ev·er·glade** (ev′ər glād′) *n.* ⟦EVER (in sense "unending") + GLADE⟧ a tract of marshy land covered in places with tall grass; swampland —**the Everglades** large tract of subtropical marshland in S Fla.

ev·er·green (ev′ər grēn′) *adj.* **1** having leaves that are green all year: opposed to DECIDUOUS **2** that remains fresh, vital, interesting, applicable, etc.; timeless —*n.* **1** an evergreen plant or tree, including most conifers and many broad-leaved plants, as some rhododendrons, hollies, etc. **2** [*pl.*] the branches and twigs of evergreens, used for decoration **3** an evergreen, or timeless, person or thing

ev·er·last·ing (ev′ər las′tiŋ) *adj.* **1** never coming to an end; lasting forever; eternal **2** going on for a long time; lasting indefinitely; durable **3** going on too long or happening too often; seeming never to stop —*n.* **1** eternity 2 *a)* any of various plants, mostly of the composite family, whose blossoms keep their color and shape when dried; esp., the strawflower *b)* the blossom of such a plant —**the Everlasting** God —**ev′er·last′ing·ly** *adv.* —**ev′er·last′ing·ness** *n.*

ev·er·more (ev′ər môr′, ev′ər môr′) *adv.* ⟦ME *evermor,* earlier *efre ma* < OE *æfre ma:* see EVER & MORE⟧ 1 [Archaic] forever; constantly 2 [Obs.] for all future time —**for evermore** forever; always

e·ver·si·ble (ē vur′sə bəl) *adj.* ⟦< L *eversus* (see fol.) + -IBLE⟧ that can be everted

e·ver·sion (ē vur′zhən, -shən) *n.* ⟦ME & OFr < L *eversio* < *eversus,* pp. of *evertere*⟧ an everting or being everted

e·vert (ē vurt′) *vt.* ⟦L *evertere* < *e-,* out + *vertere,* to turn: see VERSE⟧ to turn outward or inside out, as an eyelid

e·ver·tor (ē vurt′ər) *n.* a muscle that everts or rotates a part, esp. the foot, outward

ev·er·y (ev′rē) *adj.* ⟦ME *everiche* < OE *æfre ælc,* lit., ever each⟧ 1 each, individually and separately; each, and including all *[every* man among you*]* 2 the fullest possible; all that there could be *[*given *every* chance to do the job*]* 3 each group or interval (a specified number or time) *[*take a pill *every* three hours*]* —**every now and then** from time to time; occasionally: also [Informal] **every so often** —**every other** each alternate, as the first, third, fifth, etc. —☆**every which way** [Informal] 1 in every direction 2 in complete disorder

ev·er·y·bod·y (ev′rē bäd′ē, -bud′ē) *pron.* every person; everyone

ev·er·y·day (ev′rē dā′) *adj.* 1 daily *[*one's *everyday* routine*]* 2 suitable for ordinary days *[everyday* shoes*]* 3 usual; common *[*an *everyday* occurrence*]*

Ev·er·y·man (ev′rē man′) *n.* ⟦after the title character in a 15th-c. Eng morality play⟧ [*often* **e-**] a person or fictional character regarded as representing the human race or the common person

ev·er·y·one (ev′rē wun′) *pron.* every person; everybody

every one every person or thing of those named *[*to remind *every one* of the students*]*

☆**ev·er·y·place** (ev′rē plās′) *adv.* [Informal] in or to every place; everywhere

ev·er·y·thing (ev′rē thiŋ′) *pron.* 1 every thing; all things; all 2 all things pertinent to a specified matter 3 the most important thing *[*money is *everything* to him*]* —**with everything** having all the available options, toppings, etc. *[*to order a hamburger *with everything]*

ev·er·y·where (ev′rē hwer′, -wer′) *adv.* in or to every place

Ev·er·y·wom·an (ev′rē woom′ən) *n.* ⟦after EVERYMAN⟧ [*often* **e-**] a woman or female fictional character regarded as representing all women or the average woman

e·vict (ē vikt′, i-) *vt.* ⟦ME *evicten* < L *evictus,* pp. of *evincere,* EVINCE⟧ to remove (a tenant) from leased premises by legal procedure, as for failure to pay rent —*SYN.* EJECT —**e·vic′tion** *n.*

ev·i·dence (ev′ə dəns, -dens′) *n.* ⟦ME < OFr < L *evidentia* < *evidens,* clear, evident < *e-,* from + *videns,* prp. of *videre,* to see: see WISE[2]⟧ 1 [Archaic] the condition of being evident 2 something that makes another thing evident; indication; sign 3 something that tends to prove; ground for belief 4 *Law* something presented in a legal proceeding, as a statement of a witness, an object, etc., which bears on or establishes a point in question: distinguished from TESTIMONY and PROOF: see also STATE'S EVIDENCE —*vt.* **-denced, -denc·ing** 1 to make evident; indicate; show 2 to bear witness to; attest —*SYN.* PROOF —**in evidence** plainly visible or perceptible

ev·i·dent (ev′ə dənt, -dent′) *adj.* ⟦ME < OFr < L *evidens* (gen. *evidentis*): see prec.⟧ easy to see or perceive; clear; obvious; plain

SYN.—**evident** and **apparent** apply to that which can be readily perceived or easily inferred, but **evident** implies the existence of external signs *[*his *evident* disappointment*]* and **apparent** suggests the use of deductive reasoning *[*it's *apparent* he'll win*]*; **manifest** applies to that which is immediately, often intuitively, clear to the understanding; **obvious** refers to that which is so noticeable or obtrusive that no one can fail to perceive it; **palpable** applies esp. to that which can be perceived through some sense other than that of sight *[palpable* signs of fever*]*; **clear** implies that there is no confusion or obscurity to hinder understanding *[clear* proof*]*; **plain** implies such simplicity or lack of complexity as to be easily perceptible *[*the *plain* facts are these*]*

ev·i·den·tial (ev′ə den′shəl) *adj.* ⟦ML *evidentialis* < L *evidentia,* EVIDENCE + *-alis,* -AL⟧ EVIDENTIARY —**ev′i·den′tial·ly** *adv.*

ev·i·den·ti·ar·y (-shə rē, -shē er′ē) *adj.* ⟦< L *evidentia,* EVIDENCE + -ARY⟧ 1 of, serving as, or based on evidence 2 providing, or having the nature of, evidence

ev·i·dent·ly (ev′ə dent′lē, ev′ə dənt lē) *adv.* 1 [Now Rare] obviously; clearly 2 apparently (but not necessarily); seemingly

e·vil (ē′vəl) *adj.* ⟦ME *ivel* < OE *yfel,* akin to Ger *übel* < IE **upelo-* < base **upo-,* up from under > UP[1], Sans *upa,* toward⟧ 1 *a)* morally bad or wrong; wicked; depraved *b)* resulting from or based on conduct regarded as immoral *[*an *evil* reputation*]* 2 causing pain or trouble; harmful; injurious 3 offensive or disgusting *[*an *evil* odor*]* 4 threatening or bringing misfortune; unlucky; disastrous; unfortunate *[*an *evil* hour*]* 5 angry, irritable, disagreeable, etc. *[*in an *evil* mood*]* —*adv.* in an evil, wicked, or offensive way: now only in hyphenated compounds *[evil*-hearted*]* —*n.* 1 moral wickedness; depravity; sin 2 anything that causes harm, pain, misery, disaster, etc. —*SYN.* BAD[1] —**the Evil One** the Devil; Satan —**e′vil·ly** *adv.* —**e′vil·ness** *n.*

e·vil·do·er (-doo′ər) *n.* a person who does evil, esp. habitually —**e′vil·do′ing** *n.*

evil eye 1 a look believed by some to be able to harm or bewitch the one stared at 2 the power to cast such a look With *the*

e·vil-mind·ed (-mīn′did) *adj.* having an evil mind or disposition; specif., *a)* malicious or wicked *b)* habitually putting an evil interpretation, esp. a salacious or prurient one, on even innocent things —**e′vil-mind′ed·ly** *adv.* —**e′vil-mind′ed·ness** *n.*

e·vince (ē vins′, i-) *vt.* **e·vinced′, e·vinc′ing** ⟦L *evincere,* to conquer, win one's point < *e-,* intens. + *vincere,* to conquer: see VICTOR⟧ 1 [Obs.] to overcome 2 to show plainly; indicate; make manifest; esp., to show that one has (a specified quality, feeling, etc.) —**e·vin′ci·ble** *adj.* —**e·vin′cive** *adj.*

e·vis·cer·ate (ē vis′ər āt′, i-) *vt.* **-at′ed, -at′ing** ⟦< L *evisceratus,* pp. of *eviscerare* < *e-,* out + *viscera,* VISCERA⟧ 1 to remove the viscera from; disembowel 2 to deprive of an essential part; take away the force, significance, etc. of 3 *Surgery* to remove the contents of (an organ) —*vi.* 1 to protrude through a surgical incision or deep wound: said as of the viscera 2 to experience such a protrusion —**e·vis′cer·a′tion** *n.*

ev·i·ta·ble (ev′i tə bəl) *adj.* ⟦L *evitabilis* < *evitare,* to shun < *e-,* from + *vitare,* to avoid: see WIDE⟧ avoidable

ev·o·ca·ble (ev′ə kə bəl) *adj.* ⟦Fr *évocable:* see EVOKE⟧ that can be evoked

ev·o·ca·tion (ev′ə kā′shən, ē′vō-) *n.* ⟦ME *evocacion* < L *evocatio* < pp. of *evocare*⟧ 1 an evoking, or calling forth 2 INDUCTION (sense 5)

e·voc·a·tive (ē väk′ə tiv, i-) *adj.* ⟦L *evocativus*⟧ 1 tending to evoke a reaction or response, esp. an emotional one 2 vivid and seemingly realistic as in the artistic representation of a particular time, place, etc. —**e·voc′a·tive·ly** *adv.* —**e·voc′a·tive·ness** *n.*

ev·o·ca·tor (ev′ə kāt′ər, ē′vō-) *n.* a person who evokes

e·voke (ē vōk′, i-) *vt.* **e·voked′, e·vok′ing** ⟦Fr *évoquer* < L *evocare* < *e-,* out, from + *vocare,* to call < *vox,* VOICE⟧ 1 to call forth or summon (a spirit, demon, etc.), as by chanting magical words; conjure up 2 to draw forth or elicit (a particular mental image, reaction, etc.) —*SYN.* EXTRACT

ev·o·lute (ev′ə loot′) *n.* ⟦< L *evolutus:* see fol.⟧ *Geom.* a curve that is the locus of the center of curvature of another curve (called the *involute*); the envelope of the perpendiculars, or normals, of the involute: see INVOLUTE

ev·o·lu·tion (ev′ə loo′shən; *occas.* ē′və-) *n.* ⟦L *evolutio,* an unrolling or opening < *evolutus,* pp. of *evolvere:* see EVOLVE⟧ 1 an unfolding, opening out, or working out; process of development, as from a simple to a complex form, or of gradual, progressive change, as in a social and economic structure 2 a result or product of this; thing evolved 3 *a)* a movement that is part of a series or pattern *b)* a pattern produced, or seemingly produced, by such a series of movements *[*the *evolutions* of a fancy skater*]* 4 a setting free or giving off, as of gas in a chemical reaction 5 *Biol. a)* the development of a species, organism, or organ from its original or primitive state to its present or specialized state; phylogeny or ontogeny *b)* DARWINIAN THEORY (see also LAMARCKISM, MUTATION) 6 *Math.* the extracting of a root of a given number: opposed to INVOLUTION 7 ⟦Fr *évolution*⟧ *Mil.* any of various movements or maneuvers by which troops, ships, etc. change formation —**ev′o·lu′tion·al** *adj.* —**ev′o·lu′tion·al·ly** *adv.* —**ev′o·lu′tion·ar′y** *adj.*

evolutionary psychology the study of human behavior in relation to the theory that mental functions, as perception, memory, and the capacity for language, are the result of natural selection —**evolutionary psychologist**

ev·o·lu·tion·ist (-ist) *n.* 1 a person who accepts the principles of biological evolution 2 a person who believes in the possibility of political and social progress by gradual, peaceful steps —*adj.* 1 of the theory of evolution 2 of evolutionists —**ev′o·lu′tion·ism′** *n.* —**ev′o·lu′tion·is′tic** *adj.* —**ev′o·lu′tion·is′ti·cal·ly** *adv.*

e·volve (ē välv′, -vôlv′; i-) *vt.* **e·volved′, e·volv′ing** ⟦L *evolvere,* to roll out or forth < *e-,* out + *volvere,* to roll: see WALK⟧ 1 to develop gradually *[*to *evolve* a comprehensive plan*]* 2 to set free or give off (gas, heat, etc.) 3 to produce by evolution —*vi.* to develop gradually by a process of growth and change —**e·volve′ment** *n.*

e·vul·sion (ē vul′shən) *n.* ⟦ME *evulsioun* < *evulsio* < pp. of *evellere,* to pull out < *e-,* out + *vellere,* to pluck < IE base **wel-,* to tear, injure > OE *wæl,* slaughter⟧ a pulling out by force, or uprooting

Ev·voi·a (ev′ē ə) *var. of* EUBOEA

ev·zone (ev′zōn′) *n.* ⟦< ModGr *euzōnos* < Gr, well-equipped, lit., well-girdled < *eu-,* well (see EU-) + *zōnē,* a girdle: see ZONE⟧ a member of a special unit of riflemen in the Greek army whose uniform includes a wide skirt

ewe (yoo) *n.* ⟦ME *ewe* < OE *eowu,* fem. of *eow,* sheep, akin to Ger dial. *aue,* a ewe < IE base **owi-s,* sheep, L *ovis*⟧ a female sheep

E·we (ā′wā′, ā′vā′) *n., pl.* **E′wes′** or **E′we′** 1 a member of a people of Togo and parts of Ghana and Benin 2 the Kwa language of this people

Ew·ell (yoo′əl), **Richard Stod·dert** (städ′ərt) 1817-72; Confederate general in the Civil War

ewe-neck (yoo′nek′) *n.* a thin, badly arched neck sometimes occurring in horses and dogs —**ewe′-necked′** *adj.*

ew·er (yoo′ər) *n.* ⟦ME < Anglo-Fr < OFr *evier* < ML *aquarium,* water pitcher < L: see AQUARIUM⟧ a large water pitcher with a wide mouth

ex[1] (eks) *prep.* ⟦L⟧ 1 without; exclusive of *[ex* dividend, *ex* interest*]* 2 out of; free of *[ex warehouse* means "free of charges until removed from the warehouse"*]* ☆3 of the (specified) college class, but not having graduated with it *[*Wm. Jones, Yale *ex* '61*]* —*n., pl.* **ex′es** [Informal] one's divorced husband or wife

ex[2] (eks) *n., pl.* **ex′es** the letter X

ex[3] *abbrev.* 1 examined 2 example 3 exchange 4 executive 5 express 6 extra

Ex *abbrev. Bible* Exodus

ex-[1] (*for 1* eks, iks, egz, igz; *for 2* eks) ⟦ME < OFr or L, akin to Gr *ex-*, *exō-*, *ek-* < IE base **eĝhs*, out⟧ *prefix* **1** *a)* forth, from, out [*extubate*] *b)* beyond [*exurb*] *c)* away from, out of [*explant*] *d)* thoroughly *e)* upward *f)* without, not having [*exsanguine*]: it becomes *ef-* before *f*; *e-* before *b, d, g, j, l, m, n, r,* or *v*; often *ec-* before *c* or *s*; and, in many words of French origin, *es-* **2** former, previous, previously: used in hyphenated compounds [*ex*-president, *ex*-convict, *ex*-wife]

ex-[2] (eks) *prefix* EXO-: used before a vowel

ex·a- (ek′sə, eg′zə) *combining form* ⟦< HEXA-: because the number is 1,000 to the sixth power⟧ one quintillion; the factor 10^{18} [*exajoule*]

ex·ac·er·bate (eg zas′ər bāt′, ig-) *vt.* **-bat′ed, -bat′ing** ⟦< L *exacerbatus*, pp. of *exacerbare*, to exasperate, make angry < *ex-*, intens. + *acerbus*, bitter: see ACERBITY⟧ **1** to make more intense or sharp; aggravate (disease, pain, annoyance, etc.) **2** to exasperate; annoy; irritate; embitter —**ex·ac′er·ba′tion** *n.*

ex·act (eg zakt′, ig-) *adj.* ⟦L *exactus* < pp. of *exigere*, to drive out, measure, determine < *ex-*, out + *agere*, to do: see ACT[1]⟧ **1** characterized by, requiring, or capable of accuracy of detail; very accurate; methodical; correct [*an exact* science] **2** not deviating in form or content; without variation; precise [an *exact* replica] **3** being the very (one specified or understood) [the *exact* spot where I put it] **4** strict; severe; rigorous [an *exact* disciplinarian] —*vt.* ⟦ME *exacten*⟧ **1** to force payment of; extort: with *from* or *of* **2** to demand and get by authority or force; insist on: with *from* or *of* **3** to call for; make necessary; require —*SYN.* CORRECT, DEMAND, EXPLICIT —**ex·act′a·ble** *adj.* —**ex·act′ness** *n.* —**ex·ac′tor** *n.*, **ex·act′er**

☆**ex·ac·ta** (eg zak′tə, ig-) *n.* PERFECTA

ex·act·ing (eg zak′tiŋ, ig-) *adj.* **1** making severe or excessive demands; not easily satisfied; strict [an *exacting* teacher] **2** demanding great care, patience, effort, etc.; arduous [an *exacting* job] —*SYN.* ONEROUS —**ex·act′ing·ly** *adv.*

ex·ac·tion (eg zak′shən, ig-) *n.* ⟦ME < OFr < L *exactio*⟧ **1** an exacting, as of money, time, etc. **2** an excessive demand; extortion **3** an exacted fee, tax, etc.

ex·ac·ti·tude (eg zak′tə to͞od′, -tyo͞od′; ig-) *n.* ⟦Fr⟧ the quality of being exact; precision; accuracy

ex·act·ly (eg zakt′lē, ig-) *adv.* in an exact manner; accurately; correctly; precisely —*interj.* used in affirmation, equivalent to "I agree" or "quite true"

ex·ag·ger·ate (eg zaj′ər āt′, ig-) *vt.* **-at′ed, -at′ing** ⟦< L *exaggeratus*, pp. of *exaggerare*, to increase, exaggerate < *ex-*, out, up + *aggerare*, to heap up < *agger*, a heap < *aggerere*, to bring toward < *ad-*, to + *gerere*, to carry: see GESTURE⟧ **1** to think, speak, or write of as greater than is really so; magnify beyond the fact; overstate **2** to increase or enlarge to an extreme or abnormal degree; overemphasize; intensify —*vi.* to give an exaggerated description or account —**ex·ag′ger·at′ed·ly** *adv.* —**ex·ag′ger·a′tion** *n.* —**ex·ag′ger·a′tive** *adj.* —**ex·ag′ger·a′tor** *n.*

ex·alt (eg zôlt′, ig-) *vt.* ⟦ME *exalten* < OFr *exalter* < LL (chiefly Ec) *exaltare* < *ex-*, out, up + *altus*, high: see OLD⟧ to raise on high; elevate; lift up; specif., *a)* to raise in status, dignity, power, honor, wealth, etc. *b)* to praise; glorify; extol *c)* to fill with joy, pride, etc.; elate (used in the passive or in participial form) *d)* to heighten or intensify the action or effect of —**ex·alt′ed·ly** *adv.* —**ex·alt′er** *n.*

ex·al·ta·tion (eg′zôl tā′shən) *n.* ⟦ME *exaltacioun* < LL(Ec) *exaltatio*⟧ **1** an exalting or being exalted **2** a feeling of great joy, pride, power, etc.; elation; rapture

ex·am (eg zam′, ig-) *n. short for* EXAMINATION

ex·a·men (eg zā′mən, ig-) *n.* ⟦L: see EXAMINE⟧ **1** an examination or detailed study **2** *Eccles.* a methodical scrutiny of one's conscience

ex·am·i·na·tion (eg zam′ə nā′shən, ig-) *n.* ⟦ME *examinacioun* < OFr *examination* < L *examinatio*: see EXAMINE⟧ **1** an examining or being examined; investigation; inspection; checkup; scrutiny; inquiry; testing **2** a set of questions asked in testing or interrogating; test

ex·am·i·na·to·ri·al (-nə tôr′ē əl) *adj.* of or having to do with an examiner or examination

ex·am·ine (eg zam′ən, ig-) *vt.* **-ined, -in·ing** ⟦ME *examinen* < OFr *examiner* < L *examinare*, to weigh, ponder, examine < *examen*, tongue of a balance, examination < *ex-*, out + base of *agere*, to lead, move: see ACT[1]⟧ **1** to look at or into critically or methodically in order to find out the facts, condition, etc. of; investigate; inspect; scrutinize; inquire into **2** to test by carefully questioning in order to find out the knowledge, skill, qualifications, etc. of (a student, witness, job applicant, etc.) —*SYN.* SCRUTINIZE —**ex·am′i·na·ble** *adj.*

ex·am·i·nee (eg zam′ə nē′, ig-) *n.* a person being or to be examined

ex·am·in·er (eg zam′ə nər, ig-) *n.* a person who examines, specif. one whose work is examining records, people, etc.: also **ex·am′i·nant** (-nənt)

ex·am·ple (eg zam′pəl, ig-) *n.* ⟦ME < OFr *example*, *essample* < L *exemplum*, sample, example < *eximere*, to take out < *ex-*, out + *emere*, to buy < IE base **em-*, to take > Lith *imù*⟧ **1** something selected to show the nature or character of the rest; single part or unit used as a sample; typical instance **2** a case, punishment, etc. that serves as a warning or caution [to fine a speeder as an *example* to others] **3** a person or thing to be imitated; model; pattern; precedent **4** a problem, as in mathematics, designed to illustrate a principle or method —*vt.* **-pled, -pling** to exemplify: obs., except in the passive —*SYN.* INSTANCE, MODEL —**for example** as an example; by way of illustration —**set an example** to be, or behave so as to be, a pattern or model for others to imitate

ex·an·i·mate (eks an′ə mit) *adj.* ⟦L *exanimatus*, pp. of *exanimare*, to deprive of air, kill < *ex-*, out of + *anima*, air, spirit (see ANIMAL) + -ATE[1]⟧ **1** dead; inanimate **2** without animation; spiritless; inert

ex·an·them (eks an′thəm) *n.* ⟦< LL *exanthema* < Gr *exanthēma*, efflorescence, eruption < *exanthein*, to bloom < *ex-*, out + *anthein*, to flower < *anthos*: see ANTHO-⟧ **1** a skin eruption or rash occurring in certain infectious diseases, as measles **2** an infectious disease characterized by such eruptions Also **ex·an·the·ma** (eks′an thē′mə) *n., pl.* **-mas** or **-ma·ta** (-mə tə)

ex·arch[1] (eks′ärk′) *n.* ⟦LL *exarchus*, overseer of monasteries < Gr *exarchos*, leader, chief (in LGr, prefect, bishop): see EX-[1] & -ARCH⟧ **1** a governor of an outlying province in the ancient Byzantine Empire **2** the supreme head of the independent Orthodox Church of Bulgaria **3** *Eastern Orthodox Ch. a)* [Historical] an archbishop or patriarch *b)* now, a bishop or other member of the clergy serving as a patriarch's deputy or legate —**ex′arch′al** *adj.*

ex·arch[2] (eks′ärk′) *adj.* ⟦< EX-[1] + Gr *archē*, beginning⟧ *Bot.* having the primary xylem maturing from the outer part of a stem toward the center: cf. ENDARCH

ex·arch·ate (eks är′kit, -kāt′; eks′är′-) *n.* ⟦ML *exarchatus*⟧ the position, rank, or province of an exarch

ex·as·per·ate[1] (eg zas′pər āt′, ig-) *vt.* **-at′ed, -at′ing** ⟦< L *exasperatus*, pp. of *exasperare* < *ex-*, out, from + *asperare*, to roughen < *asper*, rough: see ASPERITY⟧ **1** to irritate or annoy very much; make angry; vex **2** [Archaic] to intensify (a feeling, disease, etc.); aggravate —*SYN.* IRRITATE

ex·as·per·ate[2] (eg zas′pər it, -āt′) *adj.* ⟦< L *exasperatus*: see prec.⟧ **1** [Archaic] exasperated **2** *Bot.* having rough and prickly skin

ex·as·per·a·tion (eg zas′pər ā′shən, ig-) *n.* an exasperating or being exasperated; great irritation or annoyance

exc *abbrev.* except

Ex·cal·i·bur (eks kal′i bər) *n.* ⟦ME < OFr *Escalibor* < ML *Caliburnus* < Celt⟧ *Arthurian Legend* King Arthur's sword: in one version of the legend, he draws it out of a stone; in another, it is given to him by the Lady of the Lake

ex ca·the·dra (eks ka′thi drə; *often*, -kə thē′-) ⟦ModL, lit., from the chair < L *ex*, from + *cathedra*, CHAIR, esp. of a teacher (in LL(Ec), of a bishop)⟧ with the authority that comes from one's rank or office: often specif. with reference to papal pronouncements, on matters of faith or morals, that have authoritative finality

ex·ca·vate (eks′kə vāt′) *vt.* **-vat′ed, -vat′ing** ⟦< L *excavatus*, pp. of *excavare* < *ex-*, out + *cavare*, to make hollow < *cavus*, hollow: see CAVE⟧ **1** to make a hole or cavity in, as by digging; hollow out **2** to form by hollowing out; dig [to *excavate* a tunnel] **3** to uncover or expose by digging; unearth [to *excavate* ancient ruins] **4** to dig out (earth, soil, etc.) —*vi.* to make an excavation

ex·ca·va·tion (eks′kə vā′shən) *n.* ⟦L *excavatio*⟧ **1** an excavating or being excavated **2** a hole or hollow made by excavating **3** something unearthed by excavating —*SYN.* HOLE

ex·ca·va·tor (eks′kə vāt′ər) *n.* a person or thing that excavates; specif., a power shovel, dredge, etc.

ex·ceed (ek sēd′, ik-) *vt.* ⟦ME *exceden* < OFr *exceder* < L *excedere* < *ex-*, out, beyond + *cedere*, to go: see CEDE⟧ **1** to go or be beyond (a limit, limiting regulation, measure, etc.) [to *exceed* a speed limit] **2** to be more than or greater than; surpass; outdo [to *exceed* one's expectations] —*vi.* [Now Rare] to surpass others, as in a quality or quantity; be outstanding

ex·ceed·ing (-iŋ) *adj.* surpassing; extraordinary; extreme —*adv.* [Archaic] EXCEEDINGLY

ex·ceed·ing·ly (-iŋ lē) *adv.* extremely; to a great degree; extraordinarily; very

ex·cel (ek sel′, ik-) *vi., vt.* **-celled′, -cel′ling** ⟦ME *excellen* < OFr *exceller* < L *excellere*, to raise, surpass, excel < *ex-*, out of, from + *-cellere*, to rise, project < IE base **kel-*, to project > HILL, Gr *kolophōn*⟧ to be better or greater than, or superior to (another or others)

SYN.—**excel** implies superiority in some quality, skill, achievement, etc. over all or over the one (or ones) specified [to *excel* at chess]; **surpass** implies a going beyond (someone or something specified) in degree, amount, or quality [no one *surpasses* him in generosity]; **transcend** suggests a surpassing to an extreme degree [it *transcends* all understanding]; **outdo** implies a going beyond someone else or a previous record in performance [he will not be *outdone* in bravery]

ex·cel·lence (ek′sə ləns) *n.* ⟦ME < OFr < L *excellentia* < prp. of *excellere*⟧ **1** the fact or condition of excelling; superiority; surpassing goodness, merit, etc. **2** [Now Rare] something in which a person or thing excels; particular virtue **3** [**E-**] EXCELLENCY (sense 1)

ex·cel·len·cy (ek′sə lən sē) *n., pl.* **-cies** ⟦ME *excellencie* < L *excellentia*⟧ **1** [**E-**] a title of honor applied to various persons of high position, as an ambassador, bishop, or governor: preceded by *Your* or by *His* or *Her* **2** [Now Rare] EXCELLENCE (sense 2)

ex·cel·lent (ek′sə lənt) *adj.* ⟦ME < OFr < L *excellens*, prp. of *excellere*, EXCEL⟧ **1** [Obs.] excelling; surpassing **2** outstandingly good of its kind; of exceptional merit, virtue, etc. —**ex′cel·lent·ly** *adv.*

☆**ex·cel·si·or** (ek sel′sē ôr′, ik-; *for n.*, -ər) *interj.* ⟦L, compar. of *excelsus*, lofty, high < pp. of *excellere*, EXCEL⟧ higher; always upward: used as a motto (as on the New York State seal) —*n.* ⟦orig. a trademark⟧ long, thin wood shavings used for packing breakable things or as stuffing in some furniture

ex·cept (ek sept′, ik-) *vt.* ⟦ME *excepten* < OFr *excepter* < L *exceptare*, to take out, except < *exceptus*, pp. of *excipere* < *ex-*, out + *capere*, to take: see HAVE⟧ to leave out or take out; make an exception of; exclude; omit —*vi.*

[Now Rare] to object; take exception: with *to* or *against* [to *except* to a remark] —***prep.*** ⟦ME < L *exceptus*⟧ leaving out; omitting; other than; but [to everyone *except* me] —***conj.*** **1** [Archaic] unless **2** [Informal] were it not true; only: often followed by *that* [I'd quit *except* that I need the money] **3** otherwise than [she doesn't leave home *except* to attend church] —**except for** if it were not for

ex·cept·ing (-sep′tiŋ) ***prep., conj.*** EXCEPT

ex·cep·tion (ek sep′shən, ik-) ***n.*** ⟦ME *excepcioun* < OFr *exception* < L *exceptio*⟧ **1** an excepting or being excepted; omission; exclusion **2** anything that is excepted; specif., *a)* a case to which a rule, general principle, etc. does not apply *b)* a person or thing different from or treated differently from others of the same class **3** objection or opposition **4** *Law* a formal objection or reservation to court action or opinion in the course of a trial —**take exception 1** to object; demur **2** to resent something; feel offended —**the exception (that) proves the rule** the exception (that) tests the rule (see PROVE, ***vt.*** 1): now usually understood to mean "the exception (that) validates the rule"

ex·cep·tion·a·ble (-ə bəl) ***adj.*** liable to exception; open to objection —**ex·cep′tion·a·bly** ***adv.***

ex·cep·tion·al (ek sep′shə nəl, ik-) ***adj.*** **1** constituting, or occurring as, an exception; not ordinary or average; esp., much above average in quality, ability, etc. [*exceptional* talents] ☆**2** needing special attention or presenting a special problem, as in education, because mentally gifted or, esp., because mentally, physically, or emotionally handicapped —**ex·cep′tion·al′i·ty** (-nal′ə tē) ***n.,*** *pl.* **-ties** —**ex·cep′tion·al·ly** ***adv.***

ex·cep·tion·al·ism (ek sep′shə nəl iz′əm, ik-) ***n.*** **1** the condition of being exceptional **2** *a)* an exceptional or unique nature ascribed to a nation, culture, etc. and regarded as giving it a special role in history, world affairs, etc. *b)* the belief in this

ex·cep·tive (ek sep′tiv, ik-) ***adj.*** ⟦ML *exceptivus*⟧ **1** of, containing, or forming an exception **2** [Rare] inclined to take exception; captious

ex·cerpt (ek surpt′, ik-; *also, and for n. always,* ek′surpt′) ***vt.*** ⟦< L *excerptus*, pp. of *excerpere*, to pick out, choose < *ex-*, out + *carpere*, to pick, pluck < IE **kerp-* < base **(s)ker-*, to cut, scrape > HARVEST⟧ to select, take out, or quote (passages from a book, sequences from a film, etc.); extract —***n.*** a passage or sequence selected or quoted from a book, article, film, etc.; extract —**ex·cerp′tion** ***n.***

ex·cess (ek ses′, ik-; *also, esp. for adj.,* ek′ses′) ***n.*** ⟦ME & OFr *exces* < L *excessus* < pp. of *excedere*: see EXCEED⟧ **1** action or conduct that goes beyond the usual, reasonable, or lawful limit **2** lack of moderation; intemperance; overindulgence **3** an amount or quantity greater than is necessary, desirable, usable, etc.; too much; superfluity **4** the amount or degree by which one thing exceeds another; remainder; surplus —***adj.*** more than usual; extra; surplus [*excess* profits] —***vt.*** to do away with the position or job of [the science center *excessed* many researchers] —**in excess of** more than —**to excess** to too great an extent or degree; too much

ex·ces·sive (ek ses′iv, ik-) ***adj.*** ⟦ME & OFr *excessif* < ML *excessivus*⟧ characterized by excess; being too much or too great; immoderate; inordinate —**ex·ces′sive·ly** ***adv.*** —**ex·ces′sive·ness** ***n.***

SYN.—**excessive** applies to that which goes beyond what is proper, right, or usual [*excessive* demands]; **exorbitant** is applied to that which is unreasonably excessive and often connotes a greedy desire for more than is just or due [*exorbitant* prices]; **extravagant** and **immoderate** both imply excessiveness resulting from lack of restraint or of prudence [*extravagant* praise, *immoderate* laughter]; **inordinate** implies a going beyond the orderly limits of convention or the bounds of good taste [his *inordinate* pride]

exch *abbrev.* exchange

ex·change (eks chānj′, iks-) ***vt.*** **-changed′**, **-chang′ing** ⟦ME *eschaungen* < OFr *eschangier* < VL **excambiare*: see EX-[1] & CHANGE⟧ **1** *a)* to give, hand over, or transfer (*for* another thing in return) *b)* to receive or give another thing for (something returned) **2** to give and receive (equivalent or similar things); interchange [to *exchange* gifts] **3** to give up for a substitute or alternative [to *exchange* honor for wealth] —***vi.*** **1** to make an exchange; barter; trade **2** *Finance* to pass in exchange [currency that *exchanges* at par] —***n.*** **1** a giving or taking of one thing for another; trade; barter **2** a giving to one another of similar things [an *exchange* of greetings] **3** the substituting of one thing for another [an *exchange* of tears for smiles] **4** a thing given or received in exchange **5** a place for exchanging; esp., a place where trade is carried on in securities or commodities by brokers, merchants, etc. [a stock *exchange*] ☆**6** a central office, or a system operated by it, providing telephone communication in a community or in part of a city **7** *Commerce, Finance a)* the payment of debts by negotiable drafts or bills of exchange, without actual transfer of money *b)* a bill of exchange *c)* a fee paid for settling accounts or collecting a draft, bill of exchange, etc. *d)* an exchanging of a sum of money of one country or of a depreciated issue for the equivalent in the money of another country or of a current issue *e)* EXCHANGE RATE *f)* difference in value between currencies *g)* [*pl.*] the checks, drafts, etc. presented to a clearinghouse for exchange and settlement —***adj.*** **1** exchanged; interchanged **2** having to do with an exchange [an *exchange* broker] —**ex·change′a·bil′i·ty** ***n.*** —**ex·change′a·ble** ***adj.*** —**ex·chang′er** ***n.***

exchange rate the rate, based on relative values, at which the currency of one country or region may be exchanged for that of another country or region

exchange student a student studying for a time in a foreign country as part of a program in which schools send and, in turn, host students who wish to study abroad

ex·cheq·uer (eks chek′ər, iks-; eks′chek′ər) ***n.*** ⟦ME *escheker*, lit., chessboard, court of revenue, treasury < OFr *eschekier*: see CHECKER[1]⟧ **1** [**E-**] *a)* under the Norman kings of England, an administrative and judicial state department in charge of revenue (so called from a table marked into squares, on which accounts of revenue were kept with counters) *b)* later, the British Court of Exchequer, which had jurisdiction over all cases relating to government revenue, now merged in the Queen's Bench Division of the High Court of Justice *c)* [*often* **E-**] the British state department in charge of the national revenue **2** the funds in the British treasury **3** a treasury, as of a country or organization **4** money in one's possession; funds; finances

ex·cide (ek sīd′, ik-) ***vt.*** **-cid′ed**, **-cid′ing** ⟦L *excidere* < *ex-*, out + *caedere*, to cut: see -CIDE⟧ [Rare] to cut out

ex·ci·mer (ek′sə mər) ***n.*** ⟦EXCI(TED) (***adj.*** 2) + (DI)MER⟧ a dimer formed through the bonding of an electrically excited molecule with an unexcited one: such a bond decays rapidly into a dissociative ground state, resulting in radiation emission

excimer laser a kind of laser in which a mixture of noble and halogen gas molecules are electrically stimulated to produce brief, intense pulses of ultraviolet light: used in semiconductor manufacturing, eye surgery, etc.

ex·cip·i·ent (ek sip′ē ənt) ***n.*** ⟦< L *excipiens*, prp. of *excipere*: see EXCEPT⟧ *Pharmacy* any of various inert substances added to a prescription to give the desired consistency or form

ex·cis·a·ble (ek sī′zə bəl, ik-; *also, esp. for 1,* ek′sī′-) ***adj.*** **1** subject to an excise tax **2** that can be excised, or cut out

ex·cise[1] (ek′sīz′; *occas.,* -sīs′) ***n.*** ⟦altered (after fol.) < earlier *accise* < MDu *accijs*, earlier *assijs* < OFr *assise*: see ASSIZE⟧ **1** a tax or duty on the manufacture, sale, or consumption of various commodities, as liquor or tobacco, within a country: also **excise tax** **2** a fee paid for a license to carry on certain occupations, sports, etc. —***vt.*** **-cised′**, **-cis′ing** to put an excise on

ex·cise[2] (ek sīz′, ik-) ***vt.*** **-cised′**, **-cis′ing** ⟦< L *excisus*, pp. of *excidere*: see EXCIDE⟧ to cut out or away; specif., to remove (a tumor, organ, etc.) surgically —**ex·ci′sion** (-sizh′ən) ***n.***

ex·cise·man (ek′sīz′man′) ***n.,*** *pl.* **-men′** (-men′) in Great Britain, a government official who collects excises and enforces the laws concerning them

ex·cit·a·ble (ek sīt′ə bəl, ik-) ***adj.*** **1** that is easily excited **2** *Physiol.* capable of responding to the proper stimulus; irritable —**ex·cit′a·bil′i·ty** ***n.*** —**ex·cit′a·bly** ***adv.***

ex·cit·ant (ek sīt′′nt, ik-; ek′sə tənt) ***adj.*** ⟦L *excitans*, prp. of *excitare*: see EXCITE⟧ stimulating —***n.*** a stimulant

ex·ci·ta·tion (ek′sī tā′shən) ***n.*** ⟦ME *excitacioun* < LL *excitatio*⟧ an exciting or being excited: see EXCITE (esp. senses 4, 5, 6)

ex·cit·a·to·ry (-ə tôr′ē) ***adj.*** exciting or tending to excite: also **ex·cit·a·tive** (ik sīt′ə tiv)

ex·cite (ek sīt′, ik-) ***vt.*** **-cit′ed**, **-cit′ing** ⟦ME *exciten* < OFr *exciter* < L *excitare*, to call forth, excite, freq. of *exciere*, to call forth < *ex-*, out + pp. of *ciere*, to call, summon: see CITE⟧ **1** to put into motion or activity; stir up [tapping on the hive *excited* the bees] **2** to call forth; arouse; provoke [the rumors *excited* her curiosity] **3** to arouse the feelings or passions of [the news *excited* us] **4** *Elec. a)* to supply electric current to (the field winding of a motor, generator, or other device) *b)* to thus produce a magnetic field in *c)* to supply a signal to (any stage of a vacuum-tube or transistor circuit) **5** *Physics* to raise (a nucleus, atom, etc.) to a higher energy state **6** *Physiol.* to produce or increase the response of (an organism, organ, tissue, etc.) to a proper stimulus —*SYN.* PROVOKE

ex·cit·ed (-id) ***adj.*** **1** emotionally aroused; agitated **2** *Physics* in a state of excitation —**ex·cit′ed·ly** ***adv.***

ex·cite·ment (ek sīt′mənt, ik-) ***n.*** ⟦ME < OFr⟧ **1** an exciting or being excited; agitation **2** something that excites

ex·cit·er (ek sīt′ər, ik-) ***n.*** **1** a person or thing that excites **2** *Elec. a)* a small generator that provides direct current for the field winding of a larger AC generator *b)* an oscillator that provides the carrier frequency voltage driving the various stages, as in a radio transmitter

ex·cit·ing (ek sīt′iŋ, ik-) ***adj.*** causing excitement or agitation; stirring, thrilling, etc. —**ex·cit′ing·ly** ***adv.***

ex·ci·ton (ek sī′tän, ek′sə tän′) ***n.*** ⟦EXCIT(ATION) + -ON: see EXCITE (***vt.*** 5)⟧ a localized, electrically neutral, excited state that allows the transfer of energy but not electric charge through a semiconductor, insulator, etc., as an electron bound to a positive hole —**ex′ci·ton′ic** ***adj.***

ex·ci·tor (ek sīt′ər, ik-; *also, esp. for 2,* -sī′tôr′) ***n.*** ⟦ME *exciter*⟧ **1** EXCITER **2** *Physiol.* a nerve which, when stimulated, causes increased activity of the part that it supplies

excl *abbrev.* **1** exclude **2** excluded **3** excluding **4** exclusive

ex·claim (ek sklām′, ik-) ***vi., vt.*** ⟦Fr *exclamer* < L *exclamare* < *ex-*, out + *clamare*, to cry, shout: see CLAMOR⟧ to cry out; speak or say suddenly and vehemently, as in surprise, anger, etc. —**ex·claim′er** ***n.***

ex·cla·ma·tion (ek′sklə mā′shən) ***n.*** ⟦ME *exclamacioun* < L *exclamatio*⟧ **1** the act of exclaiming; sudden, vehement utterance; outcry **2** something exclaimed; exclamatory word or phrase; interjection

☆**exclamation point (*or* mark)** a mark (!) used after a word or sentence in writing or printing to express surprise, strong emotion, determination, etc.

ex·clam·a·to·ry (eks klam′ə tôr′ē, iks-) ***adj.*** ⟦< L *exclamatus*, pp. of *exclamare* (see EXCLAIM) + -ORY⟧ of, containing, expressing, or using exclamation

ex·clave (eks′klāv′) ***n.*** ⟦EX-[1] + (EN)CLAVE⟧ a territory (of a nearby specified country) surrounded by foreign territory [East Prussia was an *exclave* of Germany]: cf. ENCLAVE

ex·clo·sure (eks klō′zhər) ***n.*** ⟦EX-[1] + (EN)CLOSURE⟧ an area protected against the entrance of intruders, as animals

ex·clude (eks klo͞od′, iks-) ***vt.*** **-clud′ed, -clud′ing** ⟦ME *excluden* < L *excludere* < *ex-*, out + *claudere*, CLOSE[3]⟧ **1** to refuse to admit, consider, include, etc.; shut out; keep from entering, happening, or being; reject; bar **2** to put out; force out; expel —**ex·clud′a·ble** ***adj.*** —**ex·clud′er** ***n.***

SYN.—**exclude** implies a keeping out or prohibiting of that which is not yet in [to *exclude* someone from membership]; **debar** connotes the existence of some barrier, as legal authority or force, which excludes someone from a privilege, right, etc. [to *debar* certain groups from voting]; **disbar** refers only to the expulsion of a lawyer from the group of those who are permitted to practice law; **eliminate** implies the removal of that which is already in, usually connoting its undesirability or irrelevance [to *eliminate* waste products]; **suspend** refers to the removal, usually temporary, of someone from some organization, institution, etc., as for the infraction of some rule [to *suspend* a student from school] —***ANT.*** **admit, include**

ex·clud·ing (eks klo͞o′diŋ, iks-) ***prep.*** not including; not taking into account; excepting; rejecting

ex·clu·sion (eks klo͞o′zhən, iks-) ***n.*** ⟦ME *exclusioun* < L *exclusio* < pp. of *excludere*⟧ **1** an excluding or being excluded **2** a thing excluded —**to the exclusion of** so as to keep out, bar, etc. —**ex·clu′sion·ar′y** ***adj.***

exclusionary rule a legal rule that evidence obtained illegally, as from a search without a warrant, may not be introduced at trial

ex·clu·sion·ist (-ist) ***n.*** a person in favor of excluding another or others, as from some privilege —***adj.*** of, favoring, or causing exclusion —**ex·clu′sion·ism′** ***n.***

exclusion principle PAULI EXCLUSION PRINCIPLE

ex·clu·sive (eks klo͞o′siv, iks-) ***adj.*** ⟦ML *exclusivus* < L *exclusus*, pp. of *excludere*: see EXCLUDE⟧ **1** excluding or tending to exclude all others; shutting out other considerations, happenings, existences, etc. [an *exclusive* interest in sports] **2** excluding all but what is specified ["only" is an *exclusive* particle] **3** given or belonging to no other; not shared or divided; sole [an *exclusive* right to sell something] **4** *a)* excluding certain people or groups, as for social or economic reasons [an *exclusive* club] *b)* snobbish; undemocratic **5** dealing only in costly items [an *exclusive* shop] **6** being the only one of its kind [an *exclusive* dress] —***n.*** something exclusive; specif., *a)* a news item, feature, etc. printed or broadcast by only one newspaper, station, etc. *b)* an exclusive right, as to the sale of something —**exclusive of** not including or allowing for; ignoring [the cost *exclusive of* taxes] —**ex·clu′sive·ly** ***adv.*** —**ex·clu′sive·ness** ***n.***

ex·clu·siv·i·ty (eks′klo͞o siv′i tē) ***n.*** **1** the condition or practice of being exclusive; esp., clannishness or isolationism **2** exclusive rights to something; monopoly Also **ex·clu′siv·ism′** —**ex·clu′siv·ist** ***n., adj.*** —**ex·clu′siv·is′tic** ***adj.***

ex·cog·i·tate (eks käj′ə tāt′) ***vt.*** **-tat′ed, -tat′ing** ⟦< L *excogitatus*, pp. of *excogitare*: see EX-[1] & COGITATE⟧ **1** to think out carefully and fully **2** to contrive, devise, or invent by such thought —**ex·cog′i·ta′tion** ***n.*** —**ex·cog′i·ta′tive** ***adj.***

ex·com·mu·ni·cate (eks′kə myo͞o′ni kāt′; *for adj. & n., usually*, -nə kit) ***vt.*** **-cat′ed, -cat′ing** ⟦ME *excommunicaten* < LL(Ec) *excommunicatus*, pp. of *excommunicare*: see EX-[1] & COMMUNICATE⟧ to exclude, by an act of ecclesiastical authority, from the sacraments, rights, and privileges of a church; censure by cutting off from communion with a church —***adj.*** excommunicated —***n.*** an excommunicated person —**ex′com·mu′ni·ca′tion** ***n.*** —**ex′com·mu′ni·ca′tive** (-kāt′iv, -kə tiv) ***adj.*** —**ex′com·mu′ni·ca′tor** ***n.*** —**ex′com·mu′ni·ca·to′ry** (-kə tôr′ē) ***adj.***

ex·co·ri·ate (ek skôr′ē āt′, ik-) ***vt.*** **-at′ed, -at′ing** ⟦ME *excoriaten* < L *excoriatus*, pp. of *excoriare* < *ex-*, out, off + *corium*, the skin: see CORIUM⟧ **1** to strip, scratch, or rub off the skin of; flay, abrade, chafe, etc. **2** to denounce harshly —**ex·co′ri·a′tion** ***n.***

ex·cre·ment (eks′krə mənt) ***n.*** ⟦Fr *excrément* < L *excrementum*, that which is sifted out, refuse < *excretus*: see EXCRETE⟧ waste matter from the bowels; feces —**ex′cre·men′tal** (-ment′'l) ***adj.***, **ex′cre·men·ti′tious** (-men tish′əs, -mən-)

ex·cres·cence (eks kres′əns, iks-) ***n.*** ⟦ME < OFr < L *excrescentia*, excrescences < *excrescere*, to grow out < *ex-*, out + *crescere*, to grow: see CRESCENT⟧ **1** [Now Rare] a normal outgrowth; natural appendage, as a fingernail **2** an abnormal or disfiguring outgrowth or addition, as a bunion

ex·cres·cen·cy (-kres′ən sē) ***n.*** **1** the condition of being excrescent **2** *pl.* **-cies** EXCRESCENCE

ex·cres·cent (eks kres′ənt, iks-) ***adj.*** ⟦ME < L *excrescens*, prp. of *excrescere*⟧ **1** forming an excrescence; growing abnormally; superfluous **2** *Phonet.* designating or of an epenthetic sound or letter in a word

ex·cre·ta (eks krēt′ə) ***pl.n.*** ⟦L, neut. pl. of *excretus*⟧ waste matter excreted from the body, as sweat or urine —**ex·cre′tal** ***adj.***

ex·crete (eks krēt′, iks-) ***vt., vi.*** **-cret′ed, -cret′ing** ⟦< L *excretus*, pp. of *excernere*, to sift out < *ex-*, out of + *cernere*, to sift: see HARVEST⟧ **1** to separate (waste matter) from the blood or tissue and eliminate from the body, as through the kidneys or sweat glands **2** *Bot.* to eliminate (waste matter) from the cells

ex·cre·tion (eks krē′shən, iks-) ***n.*** ⟦VL *excretio*⟧ **1** the act or process of excreting **2** waste matter excreted; sweat, urine, etc.

ex·cre·to·ry (eks′krə tôr′ē) ***adj.*** ⟦VL *excretorius*⟧ of or for excretion —***n.***, *pl.* **-ries** an excretory organ

ex·cru·ci·ate (eks kro͞o′shē āt′, iks-) ***vt.*** **-at′ed, -at′ing** ⟦< L *excruciatus*, pp. of *excruciare* < *ex-*, intens. + *cruciare*, to torture, crucify < *crux*, CROSS⟧ **1** to cause intense bodily pain to; torture **2** to subject to mental anguish; torment —**ex·cru′ci·a′tion** ***n.***

ex·cru·ci·at·ing (-āt′iŋ) ***adj.*** **1** causing intense physical or mental pain; agonizing **2** intense or extreme [with *excruciating* attention to detail] —**ex·cru′ci·at′ing·ly** ***adv.***

ex·cul·pate (eks′kəl pāt′, ik skul′pāt′) ***vt.*** **-pat′ed, -pat′ing** ⟦< L *ex*, out + *culpatus*, pp. of *culpare*, to blame < *culpa*, fault⟧ to free from blame; declare or prove guiltless —**ex·cul·pa·ble** (ik skul′pə bəl) ***adj.*** —**ex′cul·pa′tion** ***n.*** —**ex·cul′pa·to′ry** ***adj.***

ex·cur·rent (eks kur′ənt) ***adj.*** ⟦L *excurrens*, prp. of *excurrere*, to run out, project < *ex-*, out + *currere*, to run: see CURRENT⟧ **1** running out or forth **2** *Bot. a)* projecting beyond the tip, as the midrib of certain leaves *b)* having an undivided projecting main stem, as fir trees **3** *Zool.* of ducts, tubes, or passages whose contents flow outward

ex·cur·sion (eks kur′zhən, -shən; iks-) ***n.*** ⟦L *excursio*, a running out or forth < *excursus*, pp. of *excurrere*: see prec.⟧ **1** [Obs.] a military sortie; raid **2** a short trip taken with the intention of returning to the point of departure; short journey, as for pleasure; jaunt **3** a round trip (on a train, bus, ship, etc.) at reduced rates, usually with limits set on the dates of departure and return **4** a group taking such a trip **5** a deviation or digression **6** *Physics a)* a single movement outward from the mean position in an oscillating or alternating motion *b)* the distance involved in such a movement *c)* a sudden, very rapid rise in the neutron flux and power of a nuclear reactor **7** *Med.* the extent of movement from a central position, as of the eyes from a midmost location or of the chest during respiration —***adj.*** of or for an excursion [*excursion* rates] —**ex·cur′sion·ist** (-ist) ***n.***

ex·cur·sive (eks kur′siv) ***adj.*** rambling; desultory; digressive —**ex·cur′sive·ly** ***adv.*** —**ex·cur′sive·ness** ***n.***

ex·cur·sus (eks kur′səs) ***n.***, *pl.* **-sus·es** or **-sus** ⟦L, a running forth, digression, pp. of *excurrere*: see EXCURRENT⟧ **1** a detailed discussion of some point in a work, added as an appendix **2** a lengthy digression, as in a literary work

ex·cus·a·ble (ek skyo͞o′zə bəl, ik-) ***adj.*** ⟦ME < OFr < *excusabilis*⟧ that can be excused; pardonable; justifiable —**ex·cus′a·bly** ***adv.***

ex·cus·a·to·ry (-zə tôr′ē) ***adj.*** ⟦ML *excusatorius*⟧ of or containing an excuse or excuses; apologetic

ex·cuse (ek skyo͞oz′, ik-; *for n.*, -skyo͞os′) ***vt.*** **-cused′, -cus′ing** ⟦ME *excusen* < OFr *escuser* & L *excusare*, to free from a charge < L *ex-*, from + *causa*, a charge: see CAUSE⟧ **1** to try to free (a person) of blame; seek to exonerate **2** to try to minimize or pardon (a fault); apologize or give reasons for **3** to consider (an offense or fault) as not important; overlook; pardon [*excuse* my rudeness] **4** to release from an obligation, duty, promise, etc. **5** to permit to leave **6** to serve as an explanation or justification for; justify; exculpate; absolve [a selfish act that nothing will *excuse*] —***n.*** **1** a plea in defense of or explanation for some action or behavior; apology **2** a release from obligation, duty, etc. **3** something that excuses; extenuating or justifying factor **4** a pretended reason for conduct; pretext —**a poor** (or **bad**, etc.) **excuse for** a very inferior example of —**excuse me** **1** I am sorry; pardon me: a mild apology or a courteous request, as to allow one to pass **2** please repeat or clarify what you just said: often spoken with the rising intonation of a question —**excuse oneself** **1** to ask that one's fault be overlooked; apologize **2** to ask for permission to leave —**make one's excuses** to express one's regret over not being able to attend a social gathering, etc.

ex-di·rec·to·ry (eks′də rek′tə rē) ***adj.*** [Brit.] **1** designating a telephone number not listed in the telephone directory **2** designating a person with such a number

ex-div·i·dend (eks div′ə dend′, -dənd) ***adj.*** designating a period during which the buyers of a company's stock are not entitled to receive a forthcoming dividend —***adv.*** without the buyers being entitled to the forthcoming dividend [stock selling *ex-dividend*]

ex·ec[1] (eg zek′) ***n.*** [Informal] **1** an executive officer **2** an executive

exec[2] *abbrev.* **1** executive **2** executor

ex·e·cra·ble (ek′si krə bəl) ***adj.*** ⟦L *execrabilis*⟧ **1** deserving to be execrated; abominable; detestable **2** very inferior; of poorest quality —**ex′e·cra·bly** ***adv.***

ex·e·crate (ek′si krāt′) ***vt.*** **-crat′ed, -crat′ing** ⟦< L *execratus*, pp. of *execrare*, to curse < *ex-*, out + *sacrare*, to consecrate < *sacer*, SACRED⟧ **1** to call down evil upon; curse **2** to speak abusively or contemptuously of; denounce scathingly **3** to loathe; detest; abhor —***vi.*** to curse —***SYN.*** CURSE —**ex′e·cra′tive** ***adj.***, **ex′e·cra·to′ry** (-krə tôr′ē) —**ex′e·cra′tor** ***n.***

ex·e·cra·tion (ek′si krā′shən) ***n.*** ⟦L *execratio* < *execrare*: see prec.⟧ **1** the act of execrating; a cursing, denouncing, etc. **2** a curse **3** a person or thing cursed or detested

ex·ec·u·tant (eg zek′yo͞o tənt, ig-; -yə-) ***n.*** ⟦Fr *exécutant*, prp. of *exécuter*: see fol.⟧ a person who gets something done; esp., a performer, as on a musical instrument

ex·e·cute (ek′si kyo͞ot′) ***vt.*** **-cut′ed, -cut′ing** ⟦ME *executen* < OFr *executer*, back-form. < *executeur*: see EXECUTOR⟧ **1** to follow out or carry out; do; perform; fulfill [to *execute* another's orders] **2** to carry into effect; administer (laws, etc.) **3** to put to death as in accordance with a legally imposed sentence **4** to create or produce in accordance with an idea, plan, blueprint, etc. [to *execute* a statue in marble] **5** to perform (a piece of music, a part in a play, etc.) **6** *Comput.* to perform the operations indicated in (an instruction or program) **7** *Law* to complete or make valid (a deed, contract, etc.) as by signing, sealing, and delivering —***vi.*** *Comput.* to run an instruction or program —SYN. KILL[1], PERFORM —**ex′e·cut′a·ble** ***adj.***

ex·e·cut·er (ek′si kyo͞ot′ər) ***n.*** *alt. sp. of* EXECUTOR (sense 1)

ex·e·cu·tion (ek′si kyo͞o′shən) ***n.*** ⟦ME *execucion* < Anglo-Fr < OFr *execution* < L *executio, exsecutio*: see EXECUTOR⟧ **1** the act of executing; specif., *a)* a carrying out, doing, producing, etc. *b)* a putting to death as in accordance with a legally imposed sentence **2** the manner of doing or producing something, as of performing a piece of music or a role in a play **3** [Archaic] effective action, esp. of a destructive nature **4** *Law* *a)* a writ or order, issued by a court, giving authority to put a judgment into effect *b)* the legal method afforded for the enforcement of a judgment of a court *c)* the act of carrying out the provisions of such a writ or order *d)* the making valid of a legal instrument, as by signing, sealing, and delivering

ex·e·cu·tion·er (-ər) ***n.*** a person who carries out the death penalty as imposed by a court

ex·ec·u·tive (eg zek′yo͞o tiv, ig-; -yə-) ***adj.*** ⟦ME < ML *executivus* < L *executus*: see EXECUTOR⟧ **1** of, capable of, or concerned with carrying out duties, functions, etc. or managing affairs, as in a business organization **2** empowered and required to administer (laws, government affairs, etc.); administrative: distinguished from LEGISLATIVE, JUDICIAL **3** of upper-level administrative or managerial personnel or functions —***n.*** **1** the person, group of people, or branch of government empowered and required to administer the laws and affairs of a nation **2** any person whose function is to administer or manage affairs, as of a corporation, school, etc.; specif., a person overseeing middle managers

☆**Executive Mansion** **1** the White House (in Washington, D.C.), official home of the President of the U.S. **2** the official home of the governor of a state

executive officer *Mil.* an officer who is chief assistant to the commanding officer

executive order an order or regulation issued by the President or an agency of the executive branch, having the force of law

executive privilege the right of a President to withhold from the legislature or judiciary certain important information relating to the activities of the executive

executive secretary a secretary, as in a corporation, having administrative duties

executive session a session, as of a legislative body, commission, etc., that is not open to the public

ex·ec·u·tor (ek′si kyo͞ot′ər; *for 2* eg zek′yo͞o tər, ig-; -yə-) ***n.*** ⟦ME *executour* < OFr & ML *executor*, both < L *executus, exsecutus*, pp. of *exequi, exsequi*, to follow up, pursue < *ex-*, intens. + *sequi*, to follow: see SEQUENT⟧ **1** a person who gets something done or produced **2** a person appointed to carry out the provisions and directions in a testator's will: cf. ADMINISTRATOR —**ex·ec′u·to′ri·al** (-tôr′ē əl) ***adj.***

ex·ec·u·to·ry (eg zek′yo͞o tôr′ē, ig-; -yə-) ***adj.*** ⟦LL *exsecutorius* < L *exsecutus*: see prec.⟧ **1** executive; administrative **2** *Law* designed to be, or capable of being, put into effect at the appropriate time

ex·ec·u·trix (eg zek′yo͞o triks′, ig-; -yə-) ***n.***, *pl.* **-trix′es** or **ex·ec′u·tri′ces′** (-trī′sēz′) a woman who is an EXECUTOR (sense 2)

ex·e·dra (ek′si drə, ek sē′-) ***n.***, *pl.* **-drae′** (-drē′) ⟦L < Gr *exedra* < *ex-*, out + *hedra*, a seat⟧ in ancient Greece, a room, building, or outdoor area with seats, where conversations were held

ex·e·ge·sis (ek′sə jē′sis) ***n.*** ⟦Gr *exēgēsis*, explanation < *exēgeisthai*, to lead, explain < *ex-*, out + *hēgeisthai*, to lead, guide < IE base **seg-*, **sag-*, to trace, suspect > SEEK, L *sagire*, to perceive quickly⟧ **1** explanation or critical analysis of a written text, usually, specif., a Biblical or literary text **2** *pl.* **-ses′** (-sēz′) an instance of this —**ex′e·get′ic** (-jet′ik) ***adj.***, **ex′e·get′i·cal** —**ex′e·get′i·cal·ly** ***adv.***

ex·e·gete (ek′sə jēt′) ***n.*** ⟦< Gr *exēgētēs*, interpreter < *exēgeisthai*: see prec.⟧ an expert in exegesis

ex·e·get·ics (ek′sə jet′iks) ***n.*** the science, study, or practice of exegesis

ex·em·plar (eg zem′plər, -plär′; ig-) ***n.*** ⟦ME < OFr *exemplaire* < LL *exemplarium* < L *exemplum*, a pattern, EXAMPLE⟧ **1** a person or thing regarded as worthy of imitation; model; pattern; archetype **2** a typical specimen or example **3** a copy of a book, pamphlet, etc.

ex·em·pla·ry (eg zem′plə rē, ig-) ***adj.*** ⟦LL *exemplaris*: see prec.⟧ **1** serving as a model or example; worth imitating [*exemplary* behavior] **2** serving as a warning or deterrent [*exemplary* punishment] **3** serving as a sample, instance, type, etc.; illustrative [*exemplary* extracts] —**ex·em·pla·ri·ly** (eg zem′plər ə lē, eg′zem pler′ə lē) ***adv.*** —**ex·em′pla·ri·ness** ***n.***

exemplary damages *Law* damages awarded to the plaintiff beyond the actual loss, imposed as a punishment for the defendant's wrong

ex·em·pli·fi·ca·tion (eg zem′plə fi kā′shən, ig-) ***n.*** ⟦ME < ML *exemplificatio*: see fol.⟧ **1** a showing by example **2** something that exemplifies; example **3** *Law* a legally attested or certified copy or transcript

ex·em·pli·fy (eg zem′plə fī′, ig-) ***vt.*** **-fied′**, **-fy′ing** ⟦ME *exemplifien* < OFr *exemplifier* < ML *exemplificare* < L *exemplum*, an example + *facere*, to make, DO[1]⟧ **1** to show by example; serve as an example of **2** to make a legally attested or certified copy or transcript of (a document) under seal

ex·em·plum (eg zem′pləm, ig-) ***n.***, *pl.* **-pla** (-plə) ⟦L, EXAMPLE⟧ **1** an example; illustration **2** a moralized tale or anecdote, esp. one included in a medieval sermon

ex·empt (eg zempt′, ig-) ***vt.*** ⟦ME *exempten* < Anglo-Fr *exempter* < L *exemptus*, pp. of *eximere*, to take out: see EXAMPLE⟧ to free from a rule or obligation which applies to others; excuse; release —***adj.*** ⟦L *exemptus*⟧ not subject to or bound by a rule, obligation, etc. applying to others —***n.*** an exempted person —**ex·empt′i·ble** ***adj.***

ex·emp·tion (eg zemp′shən, ig-) ***n.*** ⟦ME *exempcioun* < OFr *exemption* < L *exemptio*⟧ **1** an exempting or being exempted; freedom or release from a liability, obligation, etc.; immunity **2** *a)* the exempting from an individual's taxable income of a specified sum for the taxpayer and each dependent *b)* the sum specified *c)* any such dependent

SYN.—**exemption** implies release from some obligation or legal requirement, esp. where others are not so released [*exemption* from the military draft]; **immunity** implies freedom from or protection against something disagreeable or menacing to which all or many are liable [*immunity* from a penalty, disease, taxes]; **impunity** specifically implies escape or freedom from punishment [to commit a crime with *impunity*] —ANT. **liability**

ex·en·ter·ate (eks en′tər āt′) ***vt.*** **-at′ed**, **-at′ing** ⟦< L *exenteratus*, pp. of *exenterare* < Gr *exenterizein* < *ex-*, out + *enteron*, bowel: see INTER-⟧ **1** [Obs.] to disembowel **2** *Surgery* to take out (an organ) —**ex·en′ter·a′tion** ***n.***

ex·e·qua·tur (eks′i kwāt′ər) ***n.*** ⟦L, 3d pers. sing., pres. subj., of *exequi, exsequi*, to follow out, perform: see EXECUTOR⟧ an official document given to a consul or commercial agent by the government of the country to which the person is assigned, authorizing the performance of duties there

ex·e·quies (eks′i kwēz′) ***pl.n.*** ⟦ME *exequies*, pl. < OFr < L *exequiae* < *exequi*: see EXECUTOR⟧ *former var. of* OBSEQUIES

ex·er·cise (ek′sər sīz′) ***n.*** ⟦ME & OFr *exercice* < L *exercitium* < pp. of *exercere*, to drive out (farm animals to work), hence drill, exercise < *ex-*, out + *arcere*, to enclose < IE base **areq-*, to protect, enclose > Gr *arkein*⟧ **1** active use or operation; employment [the *exercise* of an option] **2** performance (of duties, functions, etc.) **3** activity for the purpose of training or developing the body or mind; systematic practice; esp., bodily exertion for the sake of health **4** a regular series of specific movements designed to strengthen or develop some part of the body or some faculty [finger *exercises* for the piano] **5** a problem or group of written examples, passages, etc. to be studied and worked out for developing technical skill, as in mathematics, grammar, etc. ☆**6** [*pl.*] a set program of formal ceremonies, speeches, etc. [graduation *exercises*] —***vt.*** **-cised′**, **-cis′ing** **1** to put into action; use; employ [to *exercise* self-control] **2** to carry out (duties, etc.); perform; fulfill **3** [Now Rare] to use habitually; practice; train: used reflexively or in the passive [she was *exercised* in virtue] **4** to put (the body, a muscle, the mind, a skill, etc.) into use so as to develop or train **5** to drill (troops) **6** to engage the attention and energy of, esp. so as to worry, perplex, or harass: used esp. in the passive [greatly *exercised* about the decision] **7** to exert or have (influence, control, authority, etc.) **8** to use the right to buy or sell something, renew a contract, etc. under the terms of (an option contract) —***vi.*** to take exercise; do exercises —SYN. PRACTICE —**ex′er·cis′a·ble** ***adj.***

exercise bike a stationary exercise machine having a pair of handles, a padded seat, and rotating pedals: it simulates the activity of pedaling a bicycle

exercise price *Finance* STRIKE PRICE

ex·er·cis·er (-ər) ***n.*** **1** one who exercises **2** any of various types of apparatus used for exercising, as an exercycle

ex·er·ci·ta·tion (eg zʉr′sə tā′shən, ig-) ***n.*** ⟦ME *exercitacioun* < OFr *exercitation* < L *exercitatio* < pp. of *exercitare*, intens. of *exercere*: see EXERCISE⟧ [Now Rare] exercise; esp., the exercising or display of special abilities, skills, etc.

ex·er·cy·cle (ek′sər sī′kəl) ***n.*** ⟦< *Exercycle*, former trademark, prob. blend of EXERCISE & BICYCLE⟧ EXERCISE BIKE

ex·er·gon·ic (ek′sər gän′ik) ***adj.*** ⟦< EX-[1] + Gr *ergon*, WORK + -IC⟧ of or having to do with a biochemical, energy-releasing reaction, such as respiration or catabolism: opposed to ENDERGONIC

ex·ergue (eks′ʉrg′, eg′zʉrg′) ***n.*** ⟦Fr, lit., that which is out of the work < ModL *exergum* < Gr *ex*, out, outside of + *ergon*, WORK⟧ **1** the space on a coin or medal below or around the pictures or designs, often used for the date, place, etc. **2** the inscription in this space

ex·ert (eg zʉrt′, ig-) ***vt.*** ⟦L *exsertare*, freq. of *exserere*, to stretch out, put forth < *ex-*, out + *serere*, to join, fasten together: see SERIES⟧ **1** to put forth or use energetically; put into action or use [to *exert* strength, influence, etc.] **2** to apply (oneself) with great energy or straining effort —**ex·er′tive** ***adj.***

ex·er·tion (eg zʉr′shən, ig-) ***n.*** **1** the act, fact, or process of exerting; active use of strength, power, etc.; exercise **2** energetic activity; effort —SYN. EFFORT

Ex·e·ter (eks′ə tər) city in Devonshire, SW England

ex·e·unt (ek′sē oont′, -unt′) ⟦L, 3d pers. pl., pres. indic., of *exire*: see EXIT, *vi.* 1⟧ they (two or more specified characters) leave the stage: a stage direction

exeunt om·nes (äm′nēz′) ⟦L⟧ all (of the characters who are on stage) leave: a stage direction

ex·fil·tra·tion (eks′fil trā′shən) ***n.*** the act of removing something or someone by means of stealth

ex·fo·li·ant (eks fō′lē ənt) ***n.*** ⟦< fol. + -ANT⟧ a soap, moisturizer, cosmetic treatment, etc. designed to remove dead cells from the surface of the skin

ex·fo·li·ate (eks fō′lē āt′) ***vt., vi.*** **-at′ed**, **-at′ing** ⟦< LL *exfoliatus*, pp. of *exfoliare*, to strip of leaves < L *ex-*, out + *folium*, a leaf: see FOIL[2]⟧ to cast or come off in flakes, scales, or layers: said of skin, bark, rock, etc. —**ex·fo′li·a′tion** *n.* —**ex·fo′li·a′tive** *adj.*

ex gra·ti·a (eks grä′shē ə) ⟦L, from favor⟧ as a favor, with no legal obligation [an *ex gratia* payment]

ex·hal·ant (eks hāl′ənt) *adj.* ⟦L *exhalans*, prp. of *exhalare*⟧ of or for exhalation —*n.* an organ or duct used for exhalation

ex·ha·la·tion (eks′hə lā′shən, ek′sə-) *n.* ⟦L *exhalatio*⟧ **1** an exhaling or being exhaled; expiration or evaporation **2** something exhaled, as air, steam, or an odor; emanation; effluvium

ex·hale (eks hāl′, eks′hāl′) *vi.* **-haled′**, **-hal′ing** ⟦Fr *exhaler* < L *exhalare* < *ex-*, out + *halare*, to breathe < IE base **an-* > Gr *anemos*, L *animus*⟧ **1** to breathe out **2** to be given off or rise into the air as vapor; evaporate —*vt.* **1** to breathe out (air, cigarette smoke, etc.) **2** to give off (vapor, fumes, etc.)

ex·haust (eg zôst′, ig-) *vt.* ⟦< L *exhaustus*, pp. of *exhaurire*, to draw out, exhaust < *ex-*, out + *haurire*, to draw, drain < IE base **aus-* > ON *ausa*⟧ **1** to draw off or let out completely (air, gas, etc.), as from a container **2** to use up; expend completely [to *exhaust* one's resources] **3** *a)* to empty completely; draw off the contents of; drain [to *exhaust* a well] *b)* to create a vacuum in **4** to drain of power, resources, etc. [war *exhausted* the nation] **5** to tire out; make very weary; weaken **6** to deal with, study, or develop completely and thoroughly [to *exhaust* a subject] —*vi.* to be discharged or let out, as gas or steam from an engine —*n.* **1** *a)* the withdrawing of air, gas, etc. from a container or enclosure, as by means of a fan or pump *b)* an apparatus for doing this, as in getting rid of fumes, dust, stale air, etc. **2** *a)* the discharge or release of used steam, gas, etc. from a steam or gas turbine or from the cylinders of an engine at the end of every working stroke of the pistons *b)* the system of pipes, including mufflers, catalytic converters, etc. through which such steam, gas, etc. is released **3** something given off or let out, as fumes from a gasoline engine —**ex·haust′i·bil′i·ty** *n.* —**ex·haust′i·ble** *adj.* —**ex·haust′less** *adj.*

ex·haus·tion (eg zôs′chən, ig-) *n.* ⟦LL *exhaustio*⟧ **1** the act of exhausting **2** the state of being exhausted; esp., *a)* great fatigue or weariness *b)* the condition of being used up; complete consumption

ex·haus·tive (eg zôs′tiv, ig-) *adj.* ⟦ML *exhaustivus*⟧ leaving nothing out; covering every possible detail; thorough —**ex·haus′tive·ly** *adv.*

ex·hib·it (eg zib′it, ig-) *vt.* ⟦ME *exhibiten* < L *exhibitus*, pp. of *exhibere*, to hold forth, present < *ex-*, out + *habere*, to hold: see HABIT⟧ **1** to present or expose to view; show; display **2** to present to public view for entertainment, instruction, advertising, judgment in a competition, etc. **3** to give evidence of; reveal [to *exhibit* impatience] **4** *Law* to present (a document or an object) formally to a court **5** *Med.* to administer (a drug, etc.) as a remedy —*vi.* to put pictures, wares, etc. on public display —*n.* **1** a show; display; presentation **2** a thing exhibited; esp., an object or objects displayed publicly **3** *Law* a document or object produced as evidence in a court —**SYN.** PROOF, SHOW

Exhibit A ⟦in allusion to the alphabetical labeling of *exhibits* presented as evidence in court⟧ something or someone regarded or presented as primary evidence in support of an argument or proposition

exhibiter (-ər) *n. alt. sp. of* EXHIBITOR

ex·hi·bi·tion (ek′sə bish′ən) *n.* ⟦ME & OFr *exhibicion* < LL *exhibitio* < pp. of L *exhibere*: see EXHIBIT⟧ **1** the act or fact of exhibiting **2** the thing or things exhibited **3** a public show or display, as of art, industrial products, athletic feats, etc. **4** [Brit.] a sum of money awarded by a school or university to help support a student

ex·hi·bi·tion·er (-ər) *n.* [Brit.] a student who is awarded an EXHIBITION (sense 4)

exhibition game *Sports* a game between two teams, specif. professional teams, played under regular game conditions, in which the outcome has no effect on official records or standings

ex·hi·bi·tion·ism (-iz′əm) *n.* **1** a tendency to call attention to oneself or show off one's talents, skill, etc. **2** *Psychol.* *a)* a tendency to expose parts of the body that are conventionally concealed, esp. in seeking sexual stimulation or gratification *b)* an instance of such exposure —**ex′hi·bi′tion·ist** *n.* —**ex′hi·bi′tion·is′tic** *adj.*

ex·hib·i·tive (eg zib′i tiv, ig-) *adj.* serving or tending to exhibit: usually with *of*

ex·hib·i·tor (eg zib′it ər, ig-) *n.* one that exhibits; esp., *a)* a person, company, etc. that enters an exhibit as in a fair, show, or competition ☆*b)* the owner or manager of a theater showing films

ex·hib·i·to·ry (-i tôr′ē) *adj.* ⟦LL *exhibitorius*⟧ **1** exhibiting **2** of or for exhibition

ex·hil·a·rant (eg zil′ə rənt, ig-) *adj.* ⟦Fr < L *exhilarans*, prp. of *exhilarare*: see fol.⟧ that exhilarates; exhilarating —*n.* a thing that exhilarates

ex·hil·a·rate (eg zil′ə rāt′, ig-) *vt.* **-rat′ed**, **-rat′ing** ⟦< L *exhilaratus*, pp. of *exhilarare*, to gladden < *ex-*, intens. + *hilarare*, to gladden < *hilaris*, glad: see HILARIOUS⟧ **1** to make cheerful, merry, or lively **2** to invigorate or stimulate —**SYN.** ANIMATE —**ex·hil′a·ra′tive** *adj.*

ex·hil·a·ra·tion (eg zil′ə rā′shən, ig-) *n.* ⟦LL *exhilaratio*⟧ **1** the act of exhilarating **2** an exhilarated condition or feeling; liveliness; high spirits; stimulation

ex·hort (eg zôrt′, ig-) *vt., vi.* ⟦ME *exhorten* < L *exhortari*, to exhort < *ex-*, out + *hortari*, to urge: see HORTATORY⟧ to urge earnestly by advice, warning, etc. (*to* do what is proper or required); admonish strongly —**SYN.** URGE

ex·hor·ta·tion (eg′zôr tā′shən, -zər-; ek′sôr-, -sər-) *n.* ⟦ME *exhortacion* < OFr < L *exhortatio*⟧ **1** the act of exhorting **2** a plea, sermon, etc. that exhorts

ex·hor·ta·to·ry (eg zôr′tə tôr′ē, ig-) *adj.* ⟦ME < LL *exhortatorius*⟧ of, or having the nature of, exhortation; meant to exhort; admonitory: also **ex·hor′ta·tive** (-tiv)

ex·hume (eks hyo͞om′, ik syo͞om′; eg zyo͞om′, ig-) *vt.* **-humed′**, **-hum′ing** ⟦ME *exhumen* < ML *exhumare* < L *ex*, out + *humus*, the ground: see HUMUS[2]⟧ **1** to dig out of the earth; disinter **2** to bring to light; disclose; reveal —**ex·hu·ma·tion** (eks′hyo͞o mā′shən, eks′yo͞o-; eg′zyo͞o-) *n.*

ex·i·gen·cy (ek′sə jən sē; *also* eg zij′ən-, ig-) *n., pl.* **-cies** ⟦ML *exigentia*⟧ **1** the condition or quality of being exigent; urgency **2** a situation calling for immediate action or attention **3** [*pl.*] pressing needs; demands; requirements Also **ex′i·gence** (-jəns) —**SYN.** EMERGENCY, NEED

ex·i·gent (ek′sə jənt) *adj.* ⟦L *exigens*, prp. of *exigere*, to drive out: see EXACT⟧ **1** calling for immediate action or attention; urgent; critical **2** requiring more than is reasonable; demanding; exacting —**ex′i·gent·ly** *adv.*

ex·i·gi·ble (ek′sə jə bəl) *adj.* ⟦Fr < L *exigere*: see EXACT⟧ that can be demanded or exacted

ex·ig·u·ous (eg zig′yo͞o əs, ig-) *adj.* ⟦L *exiguus*, small < *exigere*: see EXACT⟧ scanty; little; small; meager —**ex·i·gu·i·ty** (ek′sə gyo͞o′ə tē) *n.*

ex·ile (ek′sīl′, eg′zīl′) *n.* ⟦ME & OFr *exil* < L *exilium* < *exul*, an exile, one banished < *ex-*, out + IE base **al-*, to wander aimlessly > Gr *alaomai*, I wander, am banished⟧ **1** a prolonged living away from one's country, community, etc., usually enforced; banishment, sometimes self-imposed **2** a person in exile **3** the span of time in exile —*vt.* **-iled′**, **-il′ing** to force (someone) to leave his or her own country, community, etc.; banish —**SYN.** BANISH —**in exile** **1** banished **2** taking refuge [a government *in exile*] —**the Exile** the period in the 6th cent. B.C. during which the Jews were held captive in Babylonia

ex·il·ic (ek sil′ik, eg zil′ik) *adj.* of exile, esp. the exile of the Jews in Babylonia

ex·ist (eg zist′, ig-) *vi.* ⟦Fr *exister* < L *existere*, *exsistere*, to come forth, stand forth < *ex-*, out + *sistere*, to cause to stand, set, place, caus. of *stare*, STAND⟧ **1** to have reality or actual being; be **2** to occur or be present [the qualities that *exist* in a person] **3** to continue being; live [the refugees barely *exist*]

ex·ist·ence (eg zis′təns, ig-) *n.* ⟦ME < OFr < ML *existentia* < prp. of L *existere*⟧ **1** the act of existing; state or fact of being **2** continuance of being; life; living **3** occurrence; specific manifestation **4** a manner of existing, being, or living [derelicts have a poor *existence*] **5** a being; entity; thing that exists

ex·ist·ent (eg zis′tənt, ig-) *adj.* ⟦L *existens*, prp. of *existere*, EXIST⟧ **1** having existence or being; existing **2** existing now; present; immediate

ex·is·ten·tial (eg′zis ten′shəl, ek′sis-; -chəl) *adj.* ⟦ModL *existentialis*⟧ **1** of, based on, or expressing existence **2** of, relating to, or as conceived of in, existentialism: now often used to refer in general to the human condition as characterized by feelings of uncertainty, anxiety, depression, etc. **3** *Logic* implicitly or explicitly asserting actuality as opposed to conceptual possibility

ex·is·ten·tial·ism (-iz′əm) *n.* ⟦Fr *existentialisme* < *existenciel*⟧ a philosophical and literary movement, variously religious or atheistic, stemming from Kierkegaard and represented by Sartre, Heidegger, etc.: it is based on the doctrine that concrete, individual existence takes precedence over abstract, conceptual essence and holds that human beings are totally free and responsible for their acts and that this responsibility is the source of their feelings of dread and anguish —**ex′is·ten′tial·ist** *adj., n.*

ex·it (ek′sit, eg′zit) *n.* ⟦L *exitus*, orig. pp. of *exire*, to go out < *ex-*, out + *ire*, to go < IE base **ei-* > YEAR, Sans *ēmi*, Goth *iddja* (I went)⟧ **1** an actor's departure from the stage **2** a going out; departure **3** a way out; doorway or passage leading out ☆**4** a ramp or road leading from an expressway —*vi.* **1** ⟦L, 3d pers. sing., pres. indic., of *exire*⟧ he (or she) leaves the stage: a direction in a play script **2** to leave; depart —*vt.* **1** to leave (a building, road, vehicle, etc.) [she will *exit* the plane at Atlanta] **2** *Comput.* to finish using and close (a program)

exit poll a poll taken of a small percentage of voters as they leave their voting places, with the pollster asking if they voted for or against certain candidates or issues

ex li·bris (eks lē′bris) *pl.* **ex libris** ⟦L, lit., from the books (of)⟧ a bookplate

Ex·moor (eks′moor) hilly region of moors in SW England, mostly in Somerset

ex ni·hil·o (eks′ nī′ə lō′, -ni′hil ō′; -nē′-) ⟦L⟧ out of nothing [the poet does not write *ex nihilo*]

ex·o- (eks′ō, -ə) ⟦< Gr *exō*, without < *ex-*, EX-[1]⟧ *prefix* outside, outer, outer part [*exogamy*]

ex·o·bi·ol·o·gy (eks′ō bī äl′ə jē) *n.* the branch of biology investigating the possibility of extraterrestrial life and the effects of extraterrestrial environments on living organisms from the earth —**ex′o·bi′o·log′i·cal** *adj.* —**ex′o·bi·ol′o·gist** *n.*

ex·o·carp (eks′ō kärp′) *n.* ⟦EXO- + -CARP⟧ the outer layer of a ripened ovary or fruit, as the skin of a plum; epicarp

ex·o·crine (eks′ō krin′, -krīn′, -krēn′) *adj.* ⟦EXO- + *-crine*, as in ENDOCRINE⟧ designating or of any gland secreting externally, either directly or through a duct —*n.* any such gland, as a sweat gland, or its secretion

ex·o·cy·to·sis (ek′sō sī tō′sis) *n.* ⟦EXO- + CYT(O)- + -OSIS⟧ a process in which a cell releases a large molecule, particle, etc.: opposed to ENDOCYTOSIS —**ex′o·cy·tose′** (-tōs′, -tōz′) *vt., vi.* **-tosed′**, **-tos′ing** —**ex′o·cy·tot′ic** (-tät′ik) *adj.*

Exod *abbrev. Bible* Exodus

☆**ex·o·don·tics** (eks′ō dän′tiks) *n.* ⟦ModL < L *ex*, out + Gr *odōn* (gen. *odon-*

tos), TOOTH + -ICS] the branch of dentistry having to do with the extraction of teeth: also **ex′o·don′ti·a** (-shə, -shē ə) —**ex′o·don′tist** ***n.***

ex·o·dus (eks′ə dəs; *also* eg′zə-) ***n.*** [< LL *Exodus* (O.T. book) < Gr *Exodus*, lit., a going out < *ex*-, out + *hodos*, way: see -ODE[1]] **1** [**E-**] the departure of the Israelites from Egypt: with *the* **2** [**E-**] the second book of the Pentateuch in the Bible, which describes this and gives the law of Moses: abbrev. *Ex* or *Exod* **3** a going out or forth, esp. in a large group

ex of·fi·ci·o (eks′ ə fish′ē ō′, -fis′-) [L, lit., from office] by virtue of one's office, or position

ex·og·a·my (eks äg′ə mē) ***n.*** [EXO- + -GAMY] **1** the custom, often inviolable, of marrying only outside one's own clan, tribe, etc.: opposed to ENDOGAMY **2** *Bot.* cross-pollination —**ex·og′a·mous** ***adj.***, **ex·o·gam·ic** (eks′ə gam′ik)

ex·o·gen (ek′sə jən, -jen′) ***n.*** [< Fr *exogène*: see EXO- & -GEN] *former term for* DICOTYLEDON

ex·og·e·nous (eks äj′ə nəs) ***adj.*** [prec. + -OUS] **1** developing from without; originating externally **2** *Biol.* of or relating to external factors, as food or light, that have an effect upon an organism —**ex·og′e·nous·ly** ***adv.***

ex·on (ek′sän) ***n.*** a sequence in the genetic code that supplies the information for protein formation

ex·on·er·ate (eg zän′ər āt′, ig-) ***vt.*** **-at′ed**, **-at′ing** [< L *exoneratus*, pp. of *exonerare*, to disburden < *ex*-, out + *onerare*, to load < *onus* (gen. *oneris*), a burden: see ONUS] **1** to relieve of (a duty, obligation, etc.) **2** to free from a charge or the imputation of guilt; declare or prove blameless; exculpate —***SYN.*** ABSOLVE —**ex·on′er·a′tion** ***n.*** —**ex·on′er·a′tive** ***adj.*** —**ex·on′er·a′tor** ***n.***

☆**ex·o·num·i·a** (ek′sə no͞o′mē ə) ***n.*** *Numismatics* collectible items other than coins or paper money, as medals or tokens —**ex′o·num′ist** ***n.***

ex·o·pep·ti·dase (eks′ō pep′tə dās′) ***n.*** any of a number of enzymes that split off the terminal amino acids of a protein

exophthalmic goiter a disease of unknown cause characterized by enlargement of the thyroid gland, overproduction of the thyroid hormone, and abnormal protrusion of the eyeballs

ex·oph·thal·mos (eks′äf thal′məs) ***n.*** [ModL < Gr, with prominent eyes < *ex*-, out + *ophthalmos*, an eye: see OPHTHALMIA] abnormal protrusion of the eyeball, caused by various disorders: also **ex′oph·thal′mus** (-məs) or **ex′oph·thal′mi·a** (-mē ə) —**ex′oph·thal′mic** ***adj.***

ex·o·plan·et (ek′sō plan′it) ***n.*** [EXO- + PLANET] any planet that orbits a star outside our solar system

ex·o·ra·ble (eks′ə rə bəl) ***adj.*** [L *exorabilis* < *exorare*, to move by entreaty < *ex*-, out + *orare*: see ORATION] that can be persuaded or moved by pleas

ex·or·bi·tance (eg zôr′bi təns, ig-) ***n.*** [ME *exorbitaunce*: see fol.] **1** a going beyond what is right or reasonable, as in demands, prices, etc.; extravagance **2** [Archaic] lawlessness Also **ex·or′bi·tan·cy**, *pl.* **-cies**

ex·or·bi·tant (-tənt) ***adj.*** [ME < L *exorbitans*, prp. of *exorbitare*, to go out of the track < *ex*-, out + *orbita*, a track, ORBIT] going beyond what is reasonable, just, proper, usual, etc.; excessive; extravagant: said esp. of charges, prices, etc. —***SYN.*** EXCESSIVE —**ex·or′bi·tant·ly** ***adv.***

ex·or·cise or **ex·or·cize** (eks′ôr sīz′) ***vt.*** **-cised′** or **-cized′**, **-cis′ing** or **-ciz′ing** [ME *exorcisen* < LL(Ec) *exorcizare* < Gr *exorkizein*, to swear a person (in N.T., to banish an evil spirit) < *ex*-, out + *horkizein*, to make one swear < *horkos*, an oath, akin to *horkanē*, enclosure, *herkos*, fence, prob. < IE base **ser*-, wickerwork > L *sarcire*, to patch] **1** to drive (an evil spirit or spirits) out or away by ritual prayers, incantations, etc. **2** [Rare] to adjure (such a spirit or spirits) **3** to free from such a spirit or spirits

ex·or·cism (eks′ôr siz′əm, -ər-) ***n.*** [ME *exorcisme* < LL(Ec) *exorcismus* < Gr *exorkismos*] **1** the act of exorcising **2** a verbal formula or ritual used in exorcising

ex·or·cist (-sist) ***n.*** [ME < LL *exorcista* < Gr *exorkistēs*] **1** a person who exorcises **2** *R.C.Ch.* a member of the second highest of the four former minor orders

ex·or·di·um (eg zôr′dē əm, ig-; eks-, iks-) ***n.***, *pl.* **-di·ums** or **-di·a** (-ə) [L < *exordiri*, to begin a web, begin < *ex*-, from + *ordiri*, to lay the warp, begin: for IE base see ORDER] the opening part of an oration, treatise, etc. —**ex·or′di·al** ***adj.***

ex·o·skel·e·ton (eks′ō skel′ə tən) ***n.*** any hard, external, secreted supporting structure, as the shell of an oyster or the cuticle of a lobster: cf. ENDOSKELETON —**ex′o·skel′e·tal** (-təl) ***adj.***

ex·os·mo·sis (eks′äs mō′sis, -äz-) ***n.*** [altered (after OSMOSIS) < *exosmose* < Fr < Gr *exo*, out + *ōsmos*, impulse: see OSMOSIS] in osmosis, the slower, outward diffusion of the more dense fluid through the semipermeable membrane to mingle with the less dense: opposed to ENDOSMOSIS —**ex′os·mot′ic** (-äz mät′ik) ***adj.***

☆**ex·o·sphere** (eks′ō sfir′, eks′ə-) ***n.*** [EXO- + SPHERE] the outermost portion of a planet's, esp. the earth's, atmosphere, consisting of a hot layer of light atoms often moving at escape velocity

ex·o·spore (eks′ō spôr′) ***n.*** [EXO- + SPORE] *Bot.* **1** the outer layer of the covering of a spore **2** CONIDIUM

ex·os·to·sis (eks′äs tō′sis) ***n.***, *pl.* **-ses′** (-sēz′) [ModL < Gr *exostōsis* < *ex*-, outside + *osteon*, a bone: see OSTEO-] an abnormal bony growth on the surface of a bone or tooth

ex·o·ter·ic (eks′ə ter′ik) ***adj.*** [LL *exotericus* < Gr *exōterikos*, external < compar. of *exō*, outside: see EX-[1]] **1** of the outside world; external **2** not limited to a select few or an inner group of disciples; suitable for the uninitiated **3** that can be understood by the public; popular Opposed to ESOTERIC —**ex′o·ter′i·cal·ly** ***adv.***

ex·o·ther·mic (ek′sō thʉr′mik, -sə-) ***adj.*** [EXO- + THERMIC] designating or of a chemical change in which there is a liberation of heat, as in combustion: also **ex′o·ther′mal**

ex·ot·ic (eg zät′ik, ig-) ***adj.*** [L *exoticus* < Gr *exōtikos* < *exō*, outside: see EX-[1]] **1** foreign; not native **2** strange or different in a way that is striking or fascinating; strangely beautiful, enticing, etc. —***n.*** **1** a foreign or imported thing **2** a plant that is not native **3** EXOTIC DANCER —**ex·ot′i·cal·ly** ***adv.*** —**ex·ot′i·cism′** (-ə siz′əm) ***n.***

ex·ot·i·ca (-i kə) ***pl.n.*** [ModL < L, neut. pl. of *exoticus*, prec.] foreign or unfamiliar things, as curious or rare art objects, strange customs, etc.

☆**exotic dancer** a dancer whose state of undress and suggestive movements are intended to arouse erotic feelings in an audience; often, specif., a stripteaser

exotic shorthair any of a breed of domestic cat, bred by crossing a Persian cat and an American shorthair, with a dense, soft coat, longer than that of other shorthairs, and round eyes

ex·o·tox·in (eks′ō täk′sin) ***n.*** [EXO- + TOXIN] *Bacteriology* a protein toxin, as tetanus or diphtheria, secreted by bacteria

ex·o·tro·pi·a (ek′sō trō′pē ə, -sə-) ***n.*** [ModL < EXO- + *-tropia*, -TROPY] a condition in which only one eye fixes on an object while the other turns outward; walleye: cf. ESOTROPIA

exp *abbrev.* **1** expenses **2** experience **3** experiment **4** expiration **5** expires **6** export **7** express

ex·pand (ek spand′, ik-) ***vt.*** [ME *expanden* < L *expandere* < *ex*-, out + *pandere*, to spread, extend; akin to *patere*: see FATHOM] **1** to spread out; open out; stretch out; unfold [the eagle *expanded* its wings] **2** to make greater in size, bulk, scope, etc.; enlarge; dilate; extend **3** to enlarge upon (a topic, idea, etc.); develop in detail **4** to work out or show the full form of (a contraction, mathematical equation, etc.) —***vi.*** **1** to become expanded; spread out, unfold, enlarge, etc. **2** to become affable, warmly communicative, etc. —**ex·pand′a·ble** ***adj.*** —**ex·pand′a·bil′i·ty** ***n.*** —**ex·pand′er** ***n.***

SYN.—**expand** implies an increasing in size, bulk, or volume and is the broadest term here, being applicable when the enlarging force operates from either the inside or the outside or when the increase comes about by unfolding, puffing out, spreading, or opening; **swell** implies expansion beyond the normal limits or size; **distend** implies a swelling as a result of pressure from within that forces a bulging outward; **inflate** suggests the use of air or gas, or of something insubstantial, to distend or swell a thing; **dilate** suggests a widening or stretching of something circular —***ANT.*** **contract**

ex·pand·ed (-span′did) ***adj.*** **1** increased in size, area, scope, etc. **2** *Printing* EXTENDED (sense 4)

expanded metal sheet metal that has been cut into parallel, attached strips and stretched into a latticelike form; used to reinforce concrete, as for plastering, lath, etc.

ex·panse (ek spans′, ik-) ***n.*** [ME *expans* < L *expansum*, neut. pp. of *expandere*: see EXPAND] **1** a large, open area or unbroken surface; wide extent; great breadth **2** expansion

ex·pan·si·ble (ek span′sə bəl, ik-) ***adj.*** that can be expanded —**ex·pan′si·bil′i·ty** ***n.***

ex·pan·sile (-sil) ***adj.*** **1** tending to expand **2** of or characteristic of expansion

ex·pan·sion (-shen) ***n.*** [LL *expansio* < L *expansus*: see EXPANSE] **1** an expanding or being expanded; enlargement; dilation **2** an expanded thing or part **3** the amount, degree, or extent of expansion **4** a development or full treatment, as of a topic **5** the process or result of working out or giving the full form of a contraction, equation, etc. **6** *Mech.* the expanding in volume of steam in the cylinder of a steam engine after cutoff, or of gas in the cylinder of an internal-combustion engine after explosion **7** *Sports* the act or an instance of increasing the number of teams in a league —***adj.*** *Sports* designating or of a team added during the expansion of a league

ex·pan·sion·ar·y (-shə ner′ē) ***adj.*** directed toward expansion

expansion bolt a bolt with an attachment that expands as the bolt is screwed in so as to anchor it in place, used in holes drilled in stone, concrete, etc.

ex·pan·sion·ism (-shən iz′əm) ***n.*** the policy of expanding a nation's territory or its sphere of influence, often at the expense of other nations —**ex·pan′sion·ist** ***adj., n.*** —**ex·pan′sion·is′tic** ***adj.***

ex·pan·sive (-siv) ***adj.*** [< L *expansus* (see EXPANSE) + -IVE] **1** tending or being able to expand **2** of, or working by means of, expansion **3** widely extended; broad; extensive; comprehensive **4** characterized by a free and generous nature; sympathetic; demonstrative; open [an *expansive* person] **5** *Psychiatry* in or of a state characterized by overestimation of oneself, overgenerosity, euphoria, and, at times, delusions of grandeur —**ex·pan′sive·ly** ***adv.*** —**ex·pan′sive·ness** ***n.***, **ex·pan·siv·i·ty** (ek′span siv′ə tē)

ex par·te (eks pär′tē) [L, lit., from the side or party: see EX-[1] & PART[2]] on, or in the interest of, one side only; one-sided

ex·pat (eks′pat′) ***n.*** [Informal, Chiefly Brit.] *short for* EXPATRIATE

ex·pa·ti·ate (ek spā′shē āt′, ik-) ***vi.*** **-at′ed**, **-at′ing** [< L *expatiatus*, pp. of *expatiari, exspatiari*, to go out of one's course, wander < *ex*-, out + *spatiari*, to walk, roam < *spatium*, SPACE] **1** [Archaic] to roam or wander freely **2** to speak or write in great detail; elaborate or enlarge (*on* or *upon*) —**ex·pa′ti·a′tion** ***n.***

ex·pa·tri·ate (eks pā′trē āt′; *for adj. & n., usually*, -it) ***vt., vi.*** **-at′ed**, **-at′ing** [< pp. of ML *expatriare*, to leave the homeland < L *ex*, out of + *patria*, fatherland < *pater*, FATHER⟧ 1 to drive (a person) from his or her native land; exile 2 to withdraw (oneself) from one's native land or from allegiance to it —*adj.* that has become an expatriate; expatriated —*n.* 1 an expatriated person 2 a person who lives outside his or her native country or country of citizenship —SYN. BANISH —**ex·pa'tri·a'tion** *n.*

ex·pect (ek spekt', ik-) *vt.* ⟦L *expectare, exspectare* < *ex-*, out + *spectare*, to look, freq. of *specere*, to see: see SPECTACLE⟧ 1 to look for as likely to occur or appear; look forward to; anticipate [I *expected* you sooner] 2 to look for as due, proper, or necessary [to *expect* a reward] 3 [Informal] to suppose; presume; guess 4 [Obs.] to wait for —**be expecting** [Informal] to be pregnant —**ex·pect'a·ble** *adj.*

SYN.—**expect** implies a considerable degree of confidence that a particular event will happen [to *expect* guests for dinner]; **anticipate** implies a looking forward to something with a foretaste of the pleasure or distress it promises, or a realizing of something in advance, and a taking of steps to meet it [to *anticipate* trouble]; **hope** implies a desire for something, accompanied by some confidence in the belief that it can be realized [to *hope* for the best]; **await** implies a waiting for, or a being ready for, a person or thing [a hearty welcome *awaits* you]

ex·pect·an·cy (ek spek'tən sē, ik-) *n., pl.* **-cies** ⟦ML *expectantia* < L *expectans*: see fol.⟧ 1 an expecting or being expected; expectation 2 that which is expected, esp. on a statistical basis [life *expectancy*] Also **ex·pect'ance** (-təns)

ex·pect·ant (ek spek'tənt, ik-) *adj.* ⟦ME < OFr < L *expectans*, prp. of *expectare*⟧ expecting; specif., *a)* having or showing expectation *b)* waiting, as for the birth of a child or for an inheritance —*n.* a person who expects something —**ex·pect'ant·ly** *adv.*

ex·pec·ta·tion (ek'spek tā'shən) *n.* ⟦L *expectatio* < pp. of *expectare*: see EXPECT⟧ 1 a looking forward to; anticipation 2 a looking for as due, proper, or necessary 3 a thing looked forward to 4 [*also pl.*] a reason or warrant for looking forward to something; prospect for the future, as of advancement or prosperity 5 the probability of the occurrence, duration, etc. of something, esp. as indicated by statistics —**ex·pect·a·tive** (ek spek'tə tiv, ik-) *adj.*

ex·pec·to·rant (ek spek'tə rənt, ik-) *adj.* ⟦L *expectorans*, prp. of *expectorare*: see fol.⟧ causing or easing the bringing up of phlegm, mucus, etc. from the respiratory tract —*n.* an expectorant medicine

ex·pec·to·rate (ek spek'tə rāt', ik-) *vt., vi.* **-rat'ed, -rat'ing** ⟦< L *expectoratus*, pp. of *expectorare*, to expel from the breast < *ex-*, out + *pectus* (gen. *pectoris*), breast⟧ 1 to cough up and spit out (phlegm, mucus, etc.) 2 to spit —**ex·pec'to·ra'tion** *n.*

ex·pe·di·en·cy (ek spē'dē ən sē, ik-) *n.* 1 the quality or state of being expedient; suitability for a given purpose; appropriateness to the conditions 2 the doing or consideration of what is of selfish use or advantage rather than of what is right or just; self-interest 3 *pl.* **-cies** an expedient Also **ex·pe'di·ence**

ex·pe·di·ent (ek spē'dē ənt, ik-) *adj.* ⟦ME < OFr < L *expediens*, prp. of *expedire*: see EXPEDITE⟧ 1 useful for effecting a desired result; suited to the circumstances or the occasion; advantageous; convenient 2 based on or offering what is of use or advantage rather than what is right or just; guided by self-interest; politic —*n.* 1 an expedient thing; means to an end 2 a device used in an emergency; makeshift; resource —SYN. RESOURCE —**ex·pe'di·ent·ly** *adv.*

ex·pe·di·en·tial (ek spē'dē en'shəl, ik-) *adj.* based on or guided by expediency

ex·pe·dite (eks'pə dīt') *vt.* **-dit'ed, -dit'ing** ⟦< L *expeditus*, pp. of *expedire*, lit., to free one caught by the feet, hence hasten, dispatch < *ex-*, out + *pes* (gen. *pedis*), FOOT⟧ 1 to speed up or make easy the progress or action of; hasten; facilitate 2 to do quickly 3 [Rare] to send off; issue officially; dispatch —*adj.* [Obs.] 1 not impeded 2 prompt, ready, or alert

ex·pe·dit·er (-ər) *n.* a person who expedites; esp., one employed to ensure the steady progress to completion of a project or the efficient movement of materials, freight, etc. within a system: also sp. **ex'pe·di'tor**

ex·pe·di·tion (eks'pə dish'ən) *n.* ⟦ME *expedicioun* < OFr *expedition* < L *expeditio* < pp. of *expedire*: see EXPEDITE⟧ 1 *a)* a sending forth or starting out on a journey, voyage, march, etc. for some definite purpose, as exploration or battle *b)* the journey, etc. itself *c)* the people, ships, equipment, etc. on such a journey 2 efficient speed; dispatch —SYN. HASTE, TRIP —**ex'pe·di'tion·ar'y** *adj.*

ex·pe·di·tious (eks'pə dish'əs) *adj.* done with or characterized by expedition; efficient and speedy; prompt —**ex'pe·di'tious·ly** *adv.*

ex·pel (ek spel', ik-) *vt.* **-pelled', -pel'ling** ⟦ME *expellen* < L *expellere* < *ex-*, out + *pellere*, to thrust: see PULSE[1]⟧ 1 to drive out by force; force out; eject 2 to dismiss or send away by authority; deprive of rights, membership, etc. —SYN. EJECT —**ex·pel'la·ble** *adj.* —**ex·pel·lee** (eks'pel ē') *n.* —**ex·pel'ler** *n.*

ex·pel·lant or **ex·pel·lent** (-ənt) *adj.* ⟦< L *expellans*, prp. of *expellere*⟧ expelling or tending to expel —*n.* an expellant medicine

ex·pend (ek spend', ik-) *vt.* ⟦ME *expenden* < L *expendere*, to weigh out, pay out < *ex-*, out + *pendere*, to weigh: see PENDANT⟧ 1 to spend 2 to consume by using; use up

ex·pend·a·ble (ek spen'də bəl, ik-) *adj.* 1 that can be expended 2 *Mil.* designating or of equipment or personnel considered worth sacrificing to achieve an objective 3 regarded as having too little value or usefulness to be worth keeping 4 designating or of a person or thing regarded as worth sacrificing under particular circumstances —*n.* a person or thing considered expendable —**ex·pend'a·bil'i·ty** *n.*

ex·pend·i·ture (ek spen'di chər, ik-) *n.* ⟦< ML *expenditus*, irreg. pp. for L *expendere* + -URE⟧ 1 the act of expending; a spending or using up of money, time, etc. 2 the amount of money, time, etc. expended; expense

ex·pense (ek spens', ik-) *n.* ⟦ME < Anglo-Fr < LL *expensa (pecunia)*, paid out (money) < L *expensum*, neut. pp. of *expendere*: see EXPEND⟧ 1 [Obs.] the act of expending; a spending or using up 2 financial cost; fee; charge 3 any cost or sacrifice 4 [*pl.*] *a)* charges or costs met with in running a business, doing one's work, maintaining property, etc. *b)* money to pay for these charges 5 a cause of spending; drain on one's finances [a car can be a considerable *expense*] —*vt.* **-pensed', -pens'ing** 1 to charge or record as an expense 2 to charge to an expense account —**at the expense of** with the payment, onus, loss, etc. borne by

☆**expense account** 1 an arrangement whereby business-related expenses of an employee are paid for by the employer 2 a record of such expenses

ex·pen·sive (ek spen'siv, ik-) *adj.* requiring or involving much expense; high-priced; dear —SYN. COSTLY —**ex·pen'sive·ly** *adv.* —**ex·pen'sive·ness** *n.*

ex·pe·ri·ence (ek spir'ē əns, ik-) *n.* ⟦ME < OFr < L *experientia*, trial, proof, experiment < *experiens*, prp. of *experiri*, to try, test: see PERIL⟧ 1 the act of living through an event or events; personal involvement in or observation of events as they occur 2 anything observed or lived through [an *experience* he'll never forget] 3 *a)* all that has happened in one's life to date [not within his *experience*] *b)* everything done or undergone by a group, people in general, etc. 4 the effect on a person of anything or everything that has happened to that person; individual reaction to events, feelings, etc. 5 *a)* activity that includes training, observation of practice, and personal participation *b)* the period of such activity *c)* knowledge, skill, or practice resulting from this —*vt.* **-enced, -enc·ing** to have experience of; personally encounter or feel; meet with; undergo

ex·pe·ri·enced (-ənst) *adj.* 1 having had much experience, as in a particular occupation or activity 2 having learned from experience; made wise, competent, etc. by experience

ex·pe·ri·en·tial (ek spir'ē en'shəl, ik-; -chəl) *adj.* ⟦< L *experientia* + -AL⟧ of or based on experience; empirical —**ex·pe'ri·en'tial·ly** *adv.*

ex·per·i·ment (ek sper'ə mənt, ik-; *also, & for v. usually*, -ment; *often*, -spir'-) *n.* ⟦ME < OFr < L *experimentum*, a trial, test < *experiri*: see PERIL⟧ 1 a test or trial of something; specif., *a)* any action or process undertaken to discover something not yet known or to demonstrate something known *b)* any action or process designed to find out whether something is effective, workable, valid, etc. 2 the conducting of such tests or trials; experimentation —*vi.* to make an experiment or experiments —SYN. TRIAL —**ex·per'i·ment'er** *n.*

ex·per·i·men·tal (ek sper'ə ment''l, ik-; *often*, -spir'-) *adj.* ⟦ME < ML *experimentalis*: see prec.⟧ 1 of or based on experience rather than on theory or authority 2 based on, tested by, or having the nature of, experiment 3 for the sake of experiment; designed to test 4 tentative 5 of or used for experiments —**ex·per'i·men'tal·ly** *adv.*

ex·per·i·men·tal·ism (-iz'əm) *n.* 1 the theory or practice of depending on experimentation; empiricism 2 fondness for experimenting or for new experiences, procedures, etc. —**ex·per'i·men'tal·ist** *n., adj.*

ex·per·i·men·ta·tion (ek sper'ə mən tā'shən, -men-; ik-; *often*, -spir'-) *n.* ⟦ML *experimentatio*⟧ the conducting of experiments

ex·pert (eks'pərt; *for adj., also* eks purt', ik spurt') *adj.* ⟦ME < OFr < L *expertus*, pp. of *experiri*: see PERIL⟧ 1 very skillful; having much training and knowledge in some special field 2 of or from an expert [an *expert* opinion] —*n.* [Fr] a person who is very skillful or highly trained and informed in some special field —**ex'pert·ly** *adv.* —**ex'pert·ness** *n.*

ex·per·tise (eks'pər tēz', -tēs') *n.* ⟦Fr⟧ the skill, knowledge, judgment, etc. of an expert

ex·pert·ize (eks'pər tīz') *vi., vt.* **-ized', -iz'ing** ⟦EXPERT + -IZE⟧ to give an expert opinion of the genuineness, value, etc. of (a painting, collectible postage stamp, etc.) —**ex'pert·i·za'tion** *n.*

expert system computer software based on the expertise and problem-solving strategies of specialists in a particular field and designed to provide advice or solutions in that field

ex·pi·a·ble (eks'pē ə bəl) *adj.* ⟦Fr⟧ that can be expiated

ex·pi·ate (eks'pē āt') *vt.* **-at'ed, -at'ing** ⟦< L *expiatus*, pp. of *expiare*, to make satisfaction or atonement < *ex-*, out + *piare*, to appease, akin to *pius*, PIOUS⟧ 1 to make amends or reparation for (wrongdoing or guilt); atone for 2 to pay the penalty of; suffer for —**ex'pi·a'tion** *n.* —**ex'pi·a'tor** *n.*

ex·pi·a·to·ry (eks'pē ə tôr'ē) *adj.* ⟦LL *expiatorius*⟧ that expiates or is meant to expiate

ex·pi·ra·tion (eks'pə rā'shən) *n.* ⟦ME *expiracioun* < L *expiratio, exspiratio* < pp. of *exspirare*, EXPIRE⟧ 1 a breathing out, as of air from the lungs 2 *a)* something breathed out *b)* a sound, etc. made by breathing out 3 a breathing one's last; dying 4 a coming to an end; close 5 a formal termination on a closing date, as of a contract or subscription

ex·pir·a·to·ry (ek spī'rə tôr'ē, -spī'ər ə-; ik-) *adj.* of expiration; relating to breathing out air from the lungs

ex·pire (ek spīr', ik-) *vt.* **-pired', -pir'ing** ⟦ME *expiren* < L *exspirare* < *ex-*, out + *spirare*, to breathe: see SPIRIT⟧ 1 to breathe out (air from the lungs) 2 [Obs.] to give off (an odor, etc.) —*vi.* 1 to breathe out air 2 to breathe one's last breath; die 3 to come to an end; terminate; cease [the lease *expired*] —SYN. DIE[1]

ex·pi·ry (ek spī'rē, eks'pə rē) *n., pl.* **-ries** ⟦prec. + -Y[1]⟧ 1 [Brit.] a coming to an end; termination 2 [Archaic] death

ex·plain (ek splān′, ik-) ***vt.*** ⟦ME *explanen* < L *explanare,* to flatten < *ex-,* out + *planare,* to make level < *planus,* level (see PLANE[2]): sp. infl. by PLAIN[1]⟧ **1** to make clear, plain, or understandable **2** to give the meaning or interpretation of; expound **3** to account for; state reasons for —***vi.*** to give an explanation —**explain away** to state reasons for so as to justify, often by minimizing, or make understandable —**explain oneself 1** to make clear what one means **2** to give reasons justifying one's conduct —**ex·plain′a·ble** ***adj.***

SYN.—**explain** implies a making clear or intelligible of something that is not known or understood [to *explain* how a machine operates]; **expound** implies a systematic and thorough explanation, often one made by a person having expert knowledge [to *expound* a theory]; **explicate** implies a scholarly analysis or exposition that is developed in detail [the *explication* of a Biblical passage]; **elucidate** implies a shedding light upon by clear and specific explanation, illustration, etc. [to *elucidate* the country's foreign policy]; to **interpret** is to bring out meanings not immediately apparent, as by translation, searching insight, or special knowledge [how do you *interpret* his silence?]; **construe** suggests a particular interpretation of something whose meaning is ambiguous [his statement is not to be lightly *construed*]

ex·pla·na·tion (eks′plə nā′shən) ***n.*** ⟦ME *explanacioun* < L *explanatio* < pp. of *explanare*⟧ **1** the act of explaining **2** something that explains **3** the interpretation, meaning, or sense given in explaining **4** a mutual defining of terms, declaration of motives, etc. to clear up a misunderstanding or settle a dispute

ex·plan·a·to·ry (ek splan′ə tôr′ē, ik-) ***adj.*** ⟦LL *explanatorius*⟧ explaining or intended to explain: also **ex·plan′a·tive** (-ə tiv) —**ex·plan′a·to′ri·ly** ***adv.***

ex·plant (eks plant′) ***vt.*** ⟦EX-[1] + PLANT, ***vt.***⟧ to transfer (living tissue) for culture in an artificial medium —***n.*** this tissue or culture —**ex′plan·ta′tion** (-plan tā′shən) ***n.***

ex·ple·tive (eks′plə tiv) ***n.*** ⟦LL *expletivus,* serving to fill < L *expletus,* pp. of *explere,* to fill < *ex-,* out, up + *plere,* to fill: see FULL[1]⟧ **1** an oath or exclamation, esp. an obscenity **2** a word, phrase, etc. not needed for the sense but used merely to fill out a sentence or metrical line, for grammar, rhythm, balance, etc. [*there* in "there is nothing left" is an *expletive*] **3** [Rare] anything serving as a filler —***adj.*** used to fill out a sentence, line, etc.: also **ex′ple·to′ry** (-tôr′ē)

ex·pli·ca·ble (eks′pli kə bəl, ik splik′ə bəl) ***adj.*** ⟦L *explicabilis* < *explicare:* see fol.⟧ that can be explained; explainable

ex·pli·cate (eks′pli kāt′) ***vt.*** **-cat′ed, -cat′ing** ⟦< L *explicatus,* pp. of *explicare,* to unfold < *ex-,* out + *plicare,* to fold: see FLAX⟧ to make clear or explicit (something obscure or implied); explain fully —*SYN.* EXPLAIN —**ex′pli·ca′tion** ***n.*** —**ex·pli·ca·tive** (eks′pli kāt′iv, ik splik′ə tiv) ***adj.***, **ex·pli·ca·to·ry** (eks′pli kə tôr′ē, ik splik′ə-) —**ex′pli·ca′tor** ***n.***

ex·pli·ca·ti·on de texte (ek splē kä syōnt tekst′) *pl.* **ex·pli·ca·tions de texte** (ek splē kä syōnt tekst′) ⟦Fr⟧ an intensive scrutiny and interpretation of the interrelated details of a written work, esp. a literary one

ex·plic·it (eks plis′it, ik splis′-) ***adj.*** ⟦OFr *explicite* < ML *explicitus* < L, pp. of *explicare:* see EXPLICATE⟧ **1** clearly stated and leaving nothing implied; distinctly expressed; definite: distinguished from IMPLICIT **2** saying what is meant, without reservation or disguise; outspoken **3** plain to see; readily observable **4** graphic in the portrayal of nudity or sexual activity —***v.*** (here) ends: a word sometimes placed at the end of a medieval manuscript —**ex·plic′it·ly** ***adv.*** —**ex·plic′it·ness** ***n.***

SYN.—**explicit** is applied to that which is so clearly stated or distinctly set forth that there should be no doubt as to the meaning; **express** adds to **explicit** the ideas of directness and positiveness; **exact** and **precise**, in this connection, both suggest that which is strictly defined, accurately stated, or made unmistakably clear; **definite** implies precise limitations as to the nature, character, meaning, etc. of something; **specific** implies the pointing up of details or the particularizing of references —*ANT.* **vague, ambiguous**

explicit function *Math.* a function whose values may be computed directly, as $y = x^2 + 1$: compare IMPLICIT FUNCTION

ex·plode (ek splōd′, ik-) ***vt.*** **-plod′ed, -plod′ing** ⟦orig., to drive off the stage by clapping and hooting < L *explodere* < *ex-,* off + *plaudere,* to applaud⟧ **1** to cause to be rejected; expose as false; discredit [to *explode* a theory] **2** to make burst with a loud noise; blow up; detonate **3** to cause to change suddenly and violently from a solid or liquid to a quickly expanding gas **4** to cause rapid nuclear fusion or fission in, with accompanying destructive force **5** *Golf* to hit (a ball) from a sand trap with an explosion shot —***vi.*** **1** to be exploded; burst noisily and violently **2** to break forth noisily [to *explode* with anger] **3** to increase very rapidly [the area's population is *exploding*] —**ex·plod′a·ble** ***adj.*** —**ex·plod′er** ***n.***

exploded view a photograph or drawing showing separately but in proper sequence and relationship the various parts of an assembly, as of a machine

ex·ploit (eks′ploit′; *also, and for v. usually,* ek sploit′, ik-) ***n.*** ⟦ME & OFr *esploit,* an exploit, action < L *explicitum,* neut. pp. of *explicare:* see EXPLICATE⟧ an act remarkable for brilliance or daring; bold deed —***vt.*** **1** to make use of; turn to account; utilize productively **2** to make unethical use of for one's own advantage or profit; specif., to make profit from the labor of (others) without giving a just return **3** to stir up interest in or promote, as in advertising [to *exploit* a new product] —**ex·ploit′a·ble** ***adj.*** —**ex·ploit′er** ***n.***

ex·ploi·ta·tion (eks′ploi tā′shən) ***n.*** an exploiting or being exploited (in various senses)

ex·ploit·a·tive (ek sploit′ə tiv, ik-) ***adj.*** **1** exploiting **2** of exploitation Also **ex·ploi′tive** (-sploit′iv)

ex·plo·ra·tion (eks′plə rā′shən, -plôr ā′-) ***n.*** ⟦L *exploratio* < pp. of *explorare:* see EXPLORE⟧ an exploring or being explored

ex·plor·a·to·ry (ek splôr′ə tôr′ē, ik-) ***adj.*** ⟦ME < L *exploratorius*⟧ of, in, or for exploration: also **ex·plor′a·tive** (-tiv)

ex·plore (ek splôr′, ik-) ***vt.*** **-plored′, -plor′ing** ⟦L *explorare,* to search out < *ex-,* out + *plorare,* to cry out, wail⟧ **1** to look into closely; examine carefully; investigate **2** to travel in (a region previously unknown or little known) in order to learn about its natural features, inhabitants, etc. **3** *Med.* to examine (an organ, wound, etc.) by operation, probing, etc., as in order to make a diagnosis —***vi.*** **1** to explore new regions, etc. **2** to search carefully, systematically, or scientifically *for* oil, minerals, treasure, etc.

ex·plor·er (-ər) ***n.*** a person who explores; esp., one who explores an unknown or little-known region

ex·plo·sion (ek splō′zhən, ik-) ***n.*** ⟦L *explosio* < pp. of *explodere:* see EXPLODE⟧ **1** an exploding; esp., a blowing up, or bursting with a loud noise; detonation **2** the noise made by exploding **3** a noisy outburst; loud breaking forth [an *explosion* of wrath] **4** a sudden, rapid, and widespread increase [a population *explosion*] **5** *Phonet.* PLOSION

explosion shot *Golf* a shot used in hitting a ball from a sand trap, in which the sand just behind the ball rather than the ball itself is struck with full force

ex·plo·sive (ek splō′siv, ik-) ***adj.*** **1** of, causing, or having the nature of, an explosion **2** tending to explode; esp., tending to burst forth noisily **3** likely to explode, as in violence [an *explosive* situation] **4** *Phonet.* PLOSIVE —***n.*** **1** a substance that can explode, as gunpowder **2** *Phonet.* PLOSIVE —**ex·plo′sive·ly** ***adv.*** —**ex·plo′sive·ness** ***n.***

ex·po (eks′pō) ***n.*** [Informal] *short for* EXPOSITION (sense 3)

ex·po·nent (ek spōn′ənt, ik-; *also, esp. for n. 3,* eks′pōn′-) ***adj.*** ⟦L *exponens,* prp. of *exponere:* see EXPOUND⟧ explaining, interpreting, or expounding —***n.*** **1** a person who sets forth, expounds, or promotes principles, methods, etc. **2** a person or thing that is an example or symbol (*of* something); representative **3** *Algebra* a small figure or symbol placed above and at the right of another figure or symbol to show how many times the latter is to be used as a factor (Ex.: $b^3 = b \times b \times b$): zero, negative, and fractional exponents have special rules (Ex.: $a^0 = 1$, $a^{-2} = 1/a^2$, $a^{1/2} = \sqrt{a}$)

ex·po·nen·tial (eks′pō nen′shəl, -chəl) ***adj.*** **1** *a)* of or relating to an algebraic exponent *b)* involving a variable or unknown quantity as an algebraic exponent **2** of or increasing by extraordinary proportions —**ex′po·nen′tial·ly** ***adv.***

ex·po·nen·ti·a·tion (eks′pō nen′shē ā′shən) ***n.*** the mathematical operation of raising a number, quantity, etc. to a power

ex·port (ek spôrt′, ik-; *also, and for n. & adj. always,* eks′pôrt′) ***vt.*** ⟦L *exportare* < *ex-,* out + *portare,* to carry: see PORT[2]⟧ **1** to carry or send (goods) to another country or other countries, esp. for purposes of sale **2** to carry or send (ideas, culture, etc.) from one place to another **3** [Obs.] to carry off; transport —***n.*** **1** something exported **2** the act or process of exporting —***adj.*** of or for exporting or exports —**ex·port′a·ble** ***adj.*** —**ex·port′er** ***n.***

ex·por·ta·tion (eks′pôr tā′shən) ***n.*** ⟦L *exportatio*⟧ **1** the act or process of exporting **2** anything exported

ex·pose (ek spōz′, ik-) ***vt.*** **-posed′, -pos′ing** ⟦ME *exposen* < OFr *exposer* < L *expositus,* pp. of *exponere* (see EXPOUND) but infl. by OFr *poser:* see POSE[1]⟧ **1** *a)* to lay open (*to* danger, attack, ridicule, etc.); leave unprotected *b)* to make accessible or subject (*to* an influence or action) **2** to put or leave out in an unprotected place; abandon [some ancient peoples *exposed* unwanted infants] **3** to allow to be seen; disclose; reveal; exhibit; display **4** *a)* to make (a crime, fraud, etc.) known; unmask *b)* to make known the crimes, etc. of **5** *Photog.* to subject (a sensitized film or plate) to radiation having a photochemical effect —*SYN.* SHOW —**expose oneself** to display one's genitalia, as in exhibitionism —**ex·pos′er** ***n.***

ex·po·sé (eks′pō zā′, eks′pō zā′) ***n.*** ⟦Fr < pp. of *exposer:* see prec.⟧ a public disclosure of a scandal, crime, etc.

ex·po·si·tion (eks′pə zish′ən) ***n.*** ⟦ME *exposicioun* < OFr *exposition* < L *expositio* < *expositus,* pp. of *exponere:* see EXPOUND⟧ **1** a setting forth of facts, ideas, etc.; detailed explanation **2** writing or speaking that sets forth or explains **3** [< Fr] an exhibition; esp., a large public exhibition or show, often international in scope **4** that part of a play, etc. which reveals what has happened before, who the characters are, etc. **5** the first section of certain musical forms, which introduces the main theme or themes, as in a sonata, or all the voices, as in a fugue —**ex′po·si′tion·al** ***adj.***

ex·pos·i·tor (ek späz′ət ər, ik-) ***n.*** ⟦ME *expositour* < OFr *expositeur* < L *expositor* < *expositus:* see prec.⟧ a person who expounds or explains

ex·pos·i·to·ry (ek späz′ə tôr′ē, ik-) ***adj.*** ⟦ML *expositorius*⟧ of, like, or containing exposition; explanatory: also **ex·pos′i·tive** (-ə tiv)

ex post fac·to (eks′ pōst fak′tō) ⟦L, from (the thing) done afterward⟧ done or made afterward, esp. when having retroactive effect [an *ex post facto* law]

ex·pos·tu·late (ek späs′chə lāt′, ik-) ***vi.*** **-lat′ed, -lat′ing** ⟦< L *expostulatus,* pp. of *expostulare,* to demand vehemently, require < *ex-,* intens. + *postulare:* see POSTULATE⟧ to reason with a person earnestly, objecting to that person's actions or intentions; remonstrate (*with*) —*SYN.* OBJECT —**ex·pos′tu·la′tion** ***n.*** —**ex·pos′tu·la′tor** ***n.*** —**ex·pos′tu·la·to′ry** (-lə tôr′ē) ***adj.***

ex·po·sure (ek spō′zhər, ik-) ***n.*** ⟦EXPOS(E) + -URE⟧ **1** an exposing or being exposed; specif., *a)* a being exposed to harsh weather conditions without protection *b)* the act or an instance of exposing a part of the body conventionally concealed, as in exhibitionism [indecent *exposure*] **2** a location, as of a house, in relation to the sun, winds, etc. [an eastern *exposure*] **3** appearance, esp. frequent appearance, before the public, as in the theater, on radio and TV, etc. **4** *Photog.* *a)* the subjection of a sensitized film or plate to the action of light rays, X-rays, etc. *b)* a sensitized surface or section of film for making one picture *c)* the time during which such a surface or section of film is exposed

exposure meter *Photog.* an instrument that measures the intensity of light striking, or reflecting from, the subject, used to find the correct exposure settings; light meter

ex·pound (ek spound′, ik-) ***vt.*** ⟦ME *expounden* < OFr *expondre* < L *exponere,* to put forth, expound < *ex-*, out + *ponere,* to put: see POSITION⟧ **1** to set forth point by point; state in detail **2** to explain or interpret; clarify —***vi.*** to comment (*on*); make a statement —***SYN.*** EXPLAIN —**ex·pound′er** ***n.***

ex·press (ek spres′, ik-) ***vt.*** ⟦ME *expressen* < ML *expressare* < L *expressus,* pp. of *exprimere,* to express, lit., force out < *ex-*, out + *premere*: see PRESS[1]⟧ **1** to press out or squeeze out (juice, etc.) **2** to get by pressure; elicit by force; extort **3** to put into words; represent by language; state **4** to make known; reveal; show [his face *expressed* sorrow] **5** to picture, represent, or symbolize in music, art, etc. **6** to show by sign; symbolize; signify [the sign + *expresses* addition] ☆**7** to send by express **8** *Genetics* *a)* to manifest (a genetic trait) *b)* to manifest a trait caused by (a particular gene) —***adj.*** ⟦ME & OFr *expres* < L *expressus*⟧ **1** *a)* expressed and not implied; explicit [to give *express* orders] *b)* specific [his *express* reason for going] **2** exact [she is the *express* image of her aunt] **3** made for or suited to a special purpose [*express* regulations] **4** ⟦orig., for the *express* purpose of running to one station⟧ fast, direct, and making few stops [an *express* train] **5** characterized by speed or velocity; specif., *a)* for fast driving [an *express* highway] *b)* high-speed [an *express* bullet] *c)* for high-speed projectiles [an *express* rifle] *d)* having to do with railway express, pony express, etc. *e)* for expedited service [*express* checkout] —***adv.*** by express —***n.*** **1** [Chiefly Brit.] *a)* a special messenger; courier *b)* a message delivered by such a messenger; dispatch sent swiftly **2** *a)* an express train, bus, elevator, etc. *b)* an express rifle **3** the pony express ☆**4** *a)* a method or service for transporting goods or sending money or mail rapidly, but at extra cost *b)* the goods transported or money sent by express *c)* a business concern operating such a service **5** any method or means of swift transmission —***SYN.*** EXPLICIT, UTTER[2] —**express oneself 1** to state one's thoughts **2** to give expression to one's feelings, imagination, etc., in creative or artistic activity —**ex·press′er** ***n.*** —**ex·press′i·ble** ***adj.***

☆**ex·press·age** (-ij) ***n.*** **1** the carrying of packages, etc. by express **2** the charge for this

ex·pres·sion (ek spresh′ən, ik-) ***n.*** ⟦ME *expressioun* < L *expressio* < *expressus*: see EXPRESS⟧ **1** a pressing out or squeezing out, as of juice **2** a putting into words or representing in language **3** a picturing, representing, or symbolizing in art, music, etc. **4** a manner of expressing; esp., a meaningful and eloquent manner of speaking, singing, etc. [to read with *expression*] **5** a particular word, phrase, or sentence ["catch cold" is an idiomatic *expression*] **6** a showing of feeling, character, etc. [laughter as an *expression* of joy] **7** a look, intonation, sign, etc. that conveys meaning or feeling [a quizzical *expression* on the face] **8** a symbol or set of symbols expressing some mathematical fact, as a quantity or operation **9** a showing by a symbol, sign, figures, etc. **10** *Genetics* the manifestation of a trait caused by a particular gene

ex·pres·sion·ism (-iz′əm) ***n.*** [*often* **E-**] an early 20th-cent. movement in art, literature, and drama, characterized by distortion of reality and the use of symbols, stylization, etc. to give objective expression to inner experience —**ex·pres′sion·ist** ***adj., n.*** —**ex·pres′sion·is′tic** ***adj.*** —**ex·pres′sion·is′ti·cal·ly** ***adv.***

ex·pres·sion·less (-lis) ***adj.*** lacking expression; blank and impassive —**ex·pres′sion·less·ly** ***adv.***

ex·pres·sive (ek spres′iv, ik-) ***adj.*** ⟦ME < ML *expressivus*⟧ **1** of or characterized by expression **2** that expresses or shows; indicative (*of*) [a song *expressive* of joy] **3** full of meaning or feeling [an *expressive* nod] —**ex·pres′sive·ly** ***adv.*** —**ex·pres′sive·ness** ***n.***

ex·pres·siv·i·ty (eks′pres siv′ə tē) ***n.*** **1** the quality of being expressive **2** *Genetics* the relative degree to which a trait caused by a gene is manifested in an individual

ex·press·ly (ek spres′lē, ik-) ***adv.*** **1** in a plain and definite way; explicitly **2** for the specific purpose; particularly

☆**ex·press·man** (ek spres′mən, ik-) ***n., pl.*** **-men** (-mən) a person employed by an express company; esp., a driver of an express truck, who collects and delivers packages

ex·pres·so (ek spres′ō) ***n.*** ESPRESSO

express rifle a hunting rifle using a large charge and a light bullet of large caliber, discharged with a high initial velocity; used to kill large game at short range

☆**ex·press·way** (ek spres′wā′, ik-) ***n.*** ⟦EXPRESS + (HIGH)WAY⟧ a divided highway for through traffic, with full or partial control of access and generally with overpasses or underpasses at intersections

ex·pro·pri·ate (eks prō′prē āt′) ***vt.*** **-at′ed, -at′ing** ⟦< ML *expropriatus,* pp. of *expropriare,* to deprive of one's own < L *ex-*, out + *proprius,* one's own⟧ **1** to take (land, property, etc.) from its owner; esp., to take for public use or in the public interest, as by right of eminent domain **2** to transfer (property) from another to oneself **3** to deprive of ownership; dispossess —**ex·pro′pri·a′tion** ***n.*** —**ex·pro′pri·a′tor** ***n.***

ex·pul·sion (ek spul′shən, ik-) ***n.*** ⟦ME *expulsioun* < OFr *expulsion* < L *expulsio* < *expulsus,* pp. of *expellere*⟧ an expelling, or forcing out, or the condition of being expelled —**ex·pul′sive** (-siv) ***adj.***

ex·punc·tion (ek spunk′shən, ik-) ***n.*** ⟦LL *expunctio* < L *expunctus*⟧ an expunging or being expunged

ex·punge (ek spunj′, ik-) ***vt.*** **-punged′, -pung′ing** ⟦L *expungere* (pp. *expunctus*), to mark (with points) for omission, erase < *ex-*, out + *pungere,* to prick: see POINT⟧ to erase or remove completely; blot out or strike out; delete; cancel —***SYN.*** ERASE

ex·pur·gate (eks′pər gāt′) ***vt.*** **-gat′ed, -gat′ing** ⟦< L *expurgatus,* pp. of *expurgare,* to purge, cleanse < *ex-*, out + *purgare,* PURGE⟧ **1** to remove passages considered obscene or otherwise objectionable from (a book, etc.) **2** to expunge (objectionable material) *from*; delete —**ex′pur·ga′tion** ***n.*** —**ex′pur·ga′tor** ***n.*** —**ex·pur′ga·to′ry** (-gə tôr′ē) ***adj.***

ex·qui·site (eks′kwiz it, ek skwiz′it) ***adj.*** ⟦ME, carefully sought out < L *exquisitus,* pp. of *exquirere,* to search out < *ex-*, out + *quaerere,* to ask⟧ **1** carefully done or elaborately made [an *exquisite* design] **2** very beautiful or lovely, esp. in a delicate or carefully wrought way [*exquisite* lace] **3** of highest quality; consummate [*exquisite* technique] **4** highly sensitive; keenly discriminating; fastidious [an *exquisite* ear for music] **5** sharply intense; keen [*exquisite* pain] —***n.*** a person who makes a great show of being refined and fastidious in matters of taste, etc. —***SYN.*** DELICATE —**ex′qui·site·ly** ***adv.*** —**ex′qui·site·ness** ***n.***

exr *abbrev.* executor

ex·san·guine (eks saŋ′gwin) ***adj.*** ⟦EX-[1] + L *sanguis* (gen. *sanguinis*), blood⟧ bloodless; anemic

ex·scind (ek sind′) ***vt.*** ⟦L *exscindere* < *ex-*, out + *scindere,* to cut: see SCISSION⟧ to cut out; excise; extirpate

ex·sect (ek sekt′) ***vt.*** ⟦< L *exsectus,* pp. of *exsecare* < *ex-*, out + *secare,* to cut: see SAW[2]⟧ to cut out —**ex·sec′tion** ***n.***

ex·sert (ek surt′) ***vt.*** ⟦< L *exsertus,* pp. of *exserere,* to stretch out: see EXERT⟧ to thrust out; protrude; project —***adj.*** EXSERTED —**ex·ser′tile** (-surt′'l) ***adj.*** —**ex·ser′tion** ***n.***

ex·sert·ed (-id) ***adj.*** projecting, as from a sheath or pod

ex·sic·cate (ek′si kāt′) ***vt., vi.*** **-cat′ed, -cat′ing** ⟦ME *exsiccaten* < L *exsiccatus,* pp. of *exsiccare,* to make dry < *ex-*, out + *siccare,* to dry < *siccus,* dry: see DESICCATE⟧ to dry up —**ex′sic·ca′tion** ***n.***

ex·stip·u·late (ek stip′yoo lit, -lāt′) ***adj.*** *Bot.* having no stipules

ex·stro·phy (ek′strə fē) ***n.*** ⟦< EX-[1] + Gr *strophē,* a turning: see STROPHE⟧ *Med.* the turning inside out of an organ; esp., such a congenital condition of the urinary bladder

ext *abbrev.* **1** extension **2** exterior **3** external **4** extra **5** extract

ex·tant (eks′tənt; ek stant′, ik-) ***adj.*** ⟦L *extans, exstans,* prp. of *exstare,* to stand out or forth < *ex-*, out + *stare,* STAND⟧ **1** still existing; not extinct; not lost or destroyed **2** [Archaic] standing out; conspicuous

ex·tem·po·ral (ek stem′pə rəl) ***adj.*** ⟦L *extemporalis*: see EXTEMPORE⟧ *archaic var. of* EXTEMPORANEOUS

ex·tem·po·ra·ne·ous (eks′tem′pə rā′nē əs, ik stem′-) ***adj.*** ⟦LL *extemporaneus*: see EXTEMPORE⟧ **1** made, done, or spoken without any preparation; unpremeditated; offhand [an *extemporaneous* speech] **2** spoken with some preparation but not written out or memorized: distinguished from IMPROMPTU **3** speaking or adept at speaking without preparation **4** made for the occasion; improvised —***SYN.*** IMPROMPTU —**ex′tem′po·ra′ne·ous·ly** ***adv.***

ex·tem·po·rar·y (ek stem′pə rer′ē, ik-) ***adj.*** EXTEMPORANEOUS —***SYN.*** IMPROMPTU —**ex·tem′po·rar′i·ly** ***adv.*** —**ex·tem′po·rar′i·ness** ***n.***

ex·tem·po·re (ek stem′pə rē, ik-) ***adv., adj.*** ⟦L, lit., out of the time < *ex-*, from, out of + *tempore,* abl. of *tempus,* time: see TEMPER⟧ without preparation; offhand [a speech given *extempore*] —***SYN.*** IMPROMPTU

ex·tem·po·rize (-rīz′) ***vi., vt.*** **-rized′, -riz′ing** **1** to speak, perform, or compose extempore; improvise **2** to furnish or contrive (things) in a makeshift way to meet a pressing need —**ex·tem′po·ri·za′tion** ***n.*** —**ex·tem′po·riz′er** ***n.***

ex·tend (ek stend′, ik-) ***vt.*** ⟦ME *extended* < L *extendere* < *ex-*, out + *tendere,* to stretch: see THIN⟧ **1** to stretch out or draw out to a certain point, or for a certain distance or time **2** to enlarge in area, scope, influence, meaning, effect, etc.; widen; broaden; expand; spread **3** to stretch or thrust forth; hold out; proffer **4** to present for acceptance; offer; accord; grant **5** to stretch or straighten out (a flexed limb of the body) **6** *a)* to make longer in time or space; prolong *b)* to allow a period of time for the payment of (a loan, mortgage, etc.) beyond that originally set **7** to make (oneself) work or try very hard **8** to give added bulk or body to (a substance) by adding another, usually cheaper or inferior, substance **9** [Obs.] to gain control of by force **10** *Commerce* to calculate (an amount on an invoice) by multiplying quantity by price —***vi.*** **1** to be extended **2** to lie or stretch [the fence *extends* to the meadow]

SYN.—**extend** and **lengthen** both imply a making longer in space or time, but **extend**, in addition, may signify an enlarging in area, scope, influence, meaning, etc.; **elongate** is a synonym for **lengthen** in the spatial sense and is more commonly used in technical applications; **prolong** and **protract** both primarily imply an extending in time, **prolong** suggesting continuation beyond the usual or expected time, and **protract** a being drawn out needlessly or wearingly

ex·tend·ed (-sten′did) ***adj.*** **1** stretched out; spread out **2** prolonged; continued **3** enlarged in influence, meaning, scope, effect, etc.; extensive **4** *Printing* designating type with a wider face than is standard for the height

extended care nursing care provided for a limited time after a hospital stay, as in a special facility

☆**extended family** a nuclear family together with other relatives living with them or nearby

ex·tend·er (-dər) ***n.*** **1** a substance or ingredient added to another to give more bulk or body or to adulterate or dilute it **2** a part added or attached, for lengthening

ex·tend·i·ble (-də bəl) ***adj.*** EXTENSIBLE: also **ex·tend′a·ble** —**ex·tend′i·bil′i·ty** (-bil′ə tē) ***n.***, **ex·tend′a·bil′i·ty**

ex·ten·si·ble (ek sten′sə bəl, ik-) ***adj.*** ⟦Fr < ML *extensibilis* < L *extensus*, pp. of *extendere*⟧ that can be extended: also **ex·ten′sile** (-səl) —**ex·ten′si·bil′i·ty** ***n.***

ex·ten·sion (-shən) ***n.*** ⟦ME *extensioun* < L *extensio* < pp. of *extendere*: see EXTEND⟧ **1** an extending or being extended **2** the amount or degree to which something is or can be extended; range; extent **3** a part that forms a continuation or addition [an *extension* to a factory] **4** an extra period of time allowed a debtor for making payment **5** a branch of a university for students who cannot attend the university proper **6** *a)* an extra telephone connected to the same line as the main telephone *b)* any of the telephones connected to a PBX or other telephone system, each having a number assigned for direct calling; also, the number so assigned **7** *a)* the straightening of a flexed limb *b)* traction applied to a fractured or dislocated limb so as to bring it into its normal position **8** a length of natural or synthetic hair added to a person's hair, as by weaving, gluing, or attaching with a comb at the scalp, to create a longer or fuller style: *usually used in the pl.* **9** *Ballet a)* the act or an instance of extending either leg at any angle from the body *b)* the capability of a dancer to so extend a leg, specif. at a difficult angle for a period of time **10** *Commerce a)* an amount on an invoice calculated by multiplying quantity by price *b)* the calculation of such an amount **11** *Logic* the class of all particular objects to which a term refers; denotation: cf. INTENSION (sense 3) **12** *Physics* that property of a body by which it occupies space —☆***adj.*** designating a device that can be extended or that extends something else [*extension* ladder, *extension* cord] —**ex·ten′sion·al** ***adj.***

ex·ten·si·ty (ek sten′sə tē, ik-) ***n.*** **1** the quality of having extension **2** *Psychol.* that quality of sensation which permits the perception of space or size

ex·ten·sive (ek sten′siv, ik-) ***adj.*** ⟦ME < L *extensivus* < *extensus*: see EXTENSIBLE⟧ **1** having great extent; covering a large area; vast **2** having a wide scope, effect, influence, etc.; far-reaching; comprehensive **3** of or characterized by extension **4** designating or of farming in which large areas of land are used with minimum expense, resulting in a low yield per acre: see INTENSIVE (sense 4) —**ex·ten′sive·ly** ***adv.*** —**ex·ten′sive·ness** ***n.***

ex·ten·som·e·ter (eks′ten säm′ət ər) ***n.*** ⟦< L *extensus* (see EXTENSIBLE) + -METER⟧ an instrument for measuring extremely small degrees of expansion, contraction, or deformation, as in a test piece of metal subjected to tension

ex·ten·sor (ek sten′sər, -sôr′; ik-) ***n.*** ⟦LL *extensor*, stretcher < L *extensus*: see EXTENSIBLE⟧ a muscle that extends or straightens some part of the body, esp. a flexed arm or leg

ex·tent (ek stent′, ik-) ***n.*** ⟦ME *extente* < Anglo-Fr < OFr *estente* < *estendre* < L *extendere*⟧ **1** the space, amount, or degree to which a thing extends; size; length; breadth **2** range or limits of anything; scope; coverage **3** an extended space; vast area [an *extent* of woodland] **4** [Historical] *Eng. Law a)* a writ directing the seizure of a debtor's property to compel payment of the debt *b)* a valuation of property, as one made in connection with such a writ —**to some extent** somewhat

ex·ten·u·ate (ek sten′yo͞o āt′, ik-) ***vt.*** **-at′ed, -at′ing** ⟦< L *extenuatus*, pp. of *extenuare* < *ex-*, out + *tenuare*, to make thin < *tenuis*, THIN⟧ **1** [Archaic] to make thin or lean **2** [Now Rare] to diminish or weaken **3** to lessen or seem to lessen the seriousness of (an offense, guilt, etc.) by giving excuses or serving as an excuse [*extenuating* circumstances] **4** [Archaic] to underrate; underestimate **5** [Obs.] to belittle or disparage —**ex·ten′u·a′tor** ***n.***

ex·ten·u·a·tion (ek sten′yo͞o ā′shən, ik-) ***n.*** ⟦ME *extenuacioun* < L *extenuatio*⟧ **1** an extenuating or being extenuated; esp., mitigation, as of the seriousness of a crime, offense, etc. **2** a thing that extenuates; partial excuse

ex·ten·u·a·to·ry (ek sten′yo͞o ə tôr′ē, ik-) ***adj.*** extenuating or tending to extenuate: also **ex·ten′u·a′tive** (-āt′iv)

ex·te·ri·or (ek stir′ē ər, ik-) ***adj.*** ⟦L, compar. of *exter, exterus*, on the outside: see EXTERNAL⟧ **1** *a)* on the outside; outer; outermost [an *exterior* wall] *b)* to be used on the outside [*exterior* paint] **2** originating outside; acting or coming from without [*exterior* forces] —***n.*** **1** an outside or outside surface **2** an outward appearance [a misleading *exterior*] ☆**3** a picture, view, stage setting, etc. of a scene outdoors —**ex·te′ri·or·ly** ***adv.***

exterior angle **1** any of the four angles formed on the outside of two straight lines when crossed by a transversal **2** an angle formed by any side of a polygon and the extension of the adjacent side

ex·te·ri·or·i·ty (ek stir′ē ôr′ə tē, ik-) ***n.*** **1** the state or quality of being exterior or exteriorized **2** external aspect

ex·te·ri·or·ize (ek stir′ē ər īz′, ik-) ***vt.*** **-ized′, -iz′ing** **1** to give or attribute an external form or objective character outside the self to (states of mind, attitudes, etc.) **2** EXTERNALIZE —**ex·te′ri·or·i·za′tion** ***n.***

ex·ter·mi·nate (ek stʉr′mə nāt′, ik-) ***vt.*** **-nat′ed, -nat′ing** ⟦< L *exterminatus*, pp. of *exterminare*, lit., to drive beyond the boundaries, hence drive out, destroy < *ex-*, out + *terminus*, boundary: see TERM[1]⟧ to destroy or get rid of entirely, as by killing; wipe out; annihilate —**ex·ter′mi·na′tion** ***n.***

SYN.—**exterminate** implies the complete, wholesale destruction of things or living beings whose existence is considered undesirable; **extirpate** and **eradicate** both suggest the extinction or abolition of something, **extirpate** implying a deliberate and violent destruction at the very source so that the thing cannot be regenerated, and **eradicate** connoting less violence and, often, the working of natural processes or a methodical plan

ex·ter·mi·na·tor (ek stʉr′mə nāt′ər, ik-) ***n.*** ⟦LL(Ec)⟧ a person or thing that exterminates; specif., ☆*a)* a person whose work or business is exterminating rats, cockroaches, and other vermin ☆*b)* a powder, liquid, etc. for exterminating vermin

ex·ter·mi·na·to·ry (-mə nə tôr′ē) ***adj.*** exterminating or tending to exterminate: also **ex·ter′mi·na′tive** (-mə nāt′iv, -mə nə tiv)

ex·tern (eks′tʉrn′) ***n.*** ⟦Fr *externe* < L *externus*: see fol.⟧ a person connected with, but not living in, an institution, as a nonresident doctor in a hospital: opposed to INTERN

ex·ter·nal (ek stʉr′nəl, ik-) ***adj.*** ⟦ME < L *externus*, outward, external < *exter, exterus*, on the outside, compar. form < *ex*, out of (see EX-[1]) + -AL⟧ **1** on or having to do with the outside; outer; exterior **2** on, or for use on, the outside of the body [a medicine for *external* use only] **3** *a)* outwardly visible *b)* existing apart from the mind; material [*external* reality] **4** originating outside; acting or coming from without [an *external* force] **5** *a)* for outward appearance or show; superficial [*external* politeness] *b)* not basic or essential [*external* factors] **6** having to do with foreign countries and international affairs —***n.*** **1** an outside or outward surface or part **2** [*pl.*] outward appearance or behavior; superficialities —**ex·ter′nal·ly** ***adv.***

ex·ter·nal-com·bus·tion engine (-kəm bus′chən) an engine, as a steam engine, that obtains its power from heat produced by burning fuel outside the cylinder, turbine, etc.

external degree a college or university degree granted to a non-resident student who has earned credits for work experience, non-academic training, independent study, and the passing of proficiency examinations, but has spent little or no time in formal classroom sessions

external ear the part of the ear outside the tympanic membrane

external galaxy any galaxy beyond our own galaxy

ex·ter·nal·ism (ek stʉr′nəl iz′əm, ik-) ***n.*** **1** EXTERNALITY (sense 1) **2** too great a regard for externals

ex·ter·nal·i·ty (eks′tər nal′ə tē) ***n., pl.*** **-ties** **1** the quality or state of being external **2** an external thing **3** *Econ.* a cost to society, as of pollution or diminished public health, that is not accounted for in the price of a product sold to the public

ex·ter·nal·ize (ek stʉr′nəl īz′, ik-) ***vt.*** **-ized′, -iz′ing** **1** to make external; embody **2** EXTERIORIZE —**ex·ter′nal·i·za′tion** ***n.***

external respiration exchange of oxygen and carbon dioxide across external or respiratory surfaces, as gills or lungs, in multicellular organisms: cf. INTERNAL RESPIRATION

ex·ter·o·cep·tor (eks′tər ō sep′tər) ***n.*** ⟦L *exter* (see EXTERNAL) + -O- + (RE)CEPTOR⟧ a sense organ receiving stimuli from the external environment, as the eye or the heat receptors in the skin —**ex′ter·o·cep′tive** (-tiv) ***adj.***

ex·ter·ri·to·ri·al (eks′ter ə tôr′ē əl) ***adj.*** EXTRATERRITORIAL

ex·tinct (ek stiŋkt′, ik-) ***adj.*** ⟦ME < L *extinctus, exstinctus*, pp. of *exstinguere*: see EXTINGUISH⟧ **1** *a)* having died down or burned out; extinguished [an *extinct* fire] *b)* no longer active [an *extinct* volcano] **2** no longer in existence or use; specif., having no living examples [an *extinct* species] **3** that no living person holds or can claim: said of offices, titles, etc. **4** no longer spoken as a native language —*SYN.* DEAD

ex·tinc·tion (ek stiŋk′shən, ik-) ***n.*** ⟦ME *extinccioun* < L *exstinctio* < *exstinctus*: see prec.⟧ **1** a putting out or being put out, as of a fire **2** a destroying or being destroyed; annihilation; abolition **3** the fact or state of being or becoming extinct **4** a dying out: said as of a biological species **5** *Physiol., Psychol.* the weakening and disappearance of a conditioned response that is no longer being reinforced

ex·tinc·tive (-tiv) ***adj.*** ⟦ME *extinctif*: see EXTINCT⟧ serving or tending to extinguish

ex·tin·guish (ek stiŋ′gwish, ik-) ***vt.*** ⟦L *extinguere, exstinguere*, to quench, destroy < *ex-*, out + *stinguere*, to extinguish (for IE base see STICK) + -ISH⟧ **1** to put out (a fire, etc.); quench; smother **2** to put an end to; destroy or cause to die out **3** to put in the shade; eclipse; obscure **4** *Law a)* to make void; nullify *b)* to settle (a debt) —**ex·tin′guish·a·ble** ***adj.*** —**ex·tin′guish·ment** ***n.***

ex·tin·guish·er (-ər) ***n.*** a person or thing that extinguishes; esp., FIRE EXTINGUISHER

ex·tir·pate (eks′tər pāt′; *also* ek stʉr′-) ***vt.*** **-pat′ed, -pat′ing** ⟦< L *extirpatus*, pp. of *extirpare, exstirpare*, to root out < *ex-*, out + *stirps*, lower part of a tree, root < IE base **ster-*, stiff > STARE, STARVE, STARK⟧ **1** to pull up by the roots; root out **2** to destroy or remove completely; exterminate; abolish —*SYN.* EXTERMINATE —**ex′tir·pa′tion** ***n.*** —**ex′tir·pa′tive** ***adj.*** —**ex′tir·pa′tor** ***n.***

ex·tol or **ex·toll** (ek stōl′, -stäl′; ik-) ***vt.*** **-tolled′, -tol′ling** ⟦ME *extollen* < L *extollere*, to raise up < *ex-*, out, up + *tollere*, to raise: see TOLERATE⟧ to praise highly; laud —*SYN.* PRAISE —**ex·tol′ler** ***n.*** —**ex·tol′ment** ***n.***, **ex·toll′ment**

ex·tort (ek stôrt′, ik-) ***vt.*** ⟦< L *extortus*, pp. of *extorquere*, to twist or turn out < *ex-*, out + *torquere*, to twist: see TORT⟧ to get (money, etc.) from someone by violence, threats, misuse of authority, etc.; exact or wrest (*from*) —*SYN.* EXTRACT —**ex·tort′er** ***n.*** —**ex·tor′tive** ***adj.***

ex·tor·tion (ek stôr′shən, ik-) ***n.*** ⟦ME *extorcioun* < OFr *extorcion* < LL(Ec) *extorsio* < L *extortus*⟧ **1** *a)* the act of extorting, or getting money, etc. by threats, misuse of authority, etc. (sometimes applied to the exaction of too high a price) *b)* the legal offense committed by an official who extorts **2** something extorted —**ex·tor′tion·ist** *n.*, **ex·tor′tion·er**

ex·tor·tion·ate (-shə nit) *adj.* **1** characterized by, or having the nature of, extortion: also **ex·tor′tion·ar′y** (-ner′ē) **2** excessive; exorbitant [an *extortionate* price]

ex·tra (eks′trə) *adj.* ⟦contr. < EXTRAORDINARY; also < L *extra*, additional, extra < *extra*, adv., more than, outside: see fol.⟧ **1** more, larger, or better than is expected, usual, or necessary; additional or superior **2** requiring payment of an added charge —*n.* an extra person or thing; specif., *a)* an additional charge (*often used in pl.*) ☆*b)* a special edition of a newspaper as formerly put out between regular editions to cover news of unusual importance *c)* an additional benefit or feature *d)* a spare or leftover copy of something *e)* an extra worker *f) Cricket* a run not made from a hit, as a bye *g) Film* an actor hired by the day to play a minor part, as a member of a crowd scene, etc. —*adv.* more than usually; esp., exceptionally [*extra* good quality]

ex·tra- (eks′trə) ⟦L < *exter, exterus*: see EXTERNAL⟧ *prefix* outside, outside the scope or region of, beyond, besides: added to adjectives The list below contains some common compounds formed with this prefix that do not have special meanings:

extracellular
extrachromosomal
extracontinental
extracorporeal
extracranial
extrafamilial
extragovernmental
extrahepatic
extralinguistic
extramusical
extraofficial
extraplanetary

☆**ex·tra-base hit** (eks′trə bās′) *Baseball* any hit greater than a single; double, triple, or home run

ex·tra·bold (-bōld′) *n. Printing* a style of type heavier than boldface

ex·tra·ca·non·i·cal (eks′trə kə nän′i kəl) *adj.* not included in the canon; not among the authorized books

ex·tract (ek strakt′, ik-; *for n.* eks′trakt′) *vt.* ⟦ME *extracten* < L *extractus*, pp. of *extrahere*, to draw out < *ex-*, out + *trahere*, to DRAW⟧ **1** to draw out by effort; pull out [to *extract* a tooth, to *extract* a promise from someone] **2** to remove or separate (metal) from ore **3** to obtain (a substance, esp. an essence or concentrate) by pressing, distilling, using a solvent, etc. [to *extract* juice from fruit] **4** to obtain as if by drawing out; deduce (a principle), derive or elicit (information, pleasure, etc.), or the like **5** to copy out or quote (a passage from a book, etc.); excerpt **6** *Math.* to compute (the root of a quantity) —*n.* something extracted; specif., *a)* a concentrated form, whether solid, viscid, or liquid, of a food, flavoring, etc. [beef *extract*] *b)* a passage selected from a book, etc.; excerpt; quotation *c) Pharmacy* the concentrated substance obtained by dissolving a drug in some solvent, as ether or alcohol, and then evaporating the preparation —**ex·tract′a·ble** *adj.*, **ex·tract′i·ble**

SYN.—**extract** implies a drawing out of something, as if by pulling, sucking, etc. [to *extract* a promise]; **educe** suggests a drawing out or evolving of something that is latent or undeveloped [laws were *educed* from tribal customs]; **elicit** connotes difficulty or skill in drawing out something hidden or buried [his jokes *elicited* no smiles]; **evoke** implies a calling forth or summoning, as of a mental image, by stimulating the emotions [the odor *evoked* a memory of childhood]; **extort** suggests a forcing or wresting of something, as by violence or threats [to *extort* a ransom]

ex·trac·tion (ek strak′shən, ik-) *n.* ⟦ME *extraccioun* < ML *extractio*⟧ **1** the act or process of extracting; specif., the extracting of a tooth by a dentist **2** origin; lineage; descent [of Navajo *extraction*] **3** a thing extracted; extract

ex·trac·tive (ek strak′tiv, ik-) *adj.* ⟦ME *extractif* < ML *extractivus*⟧ **1** extracting or having to do with extraction **2** capable of being extracted **3** having the nature of an extract —*n.* **1** an extractive substance **2** an extract

ex·trac·tor (ek strak′tər, ik-) *n.* a person or thing that extracts; specif., the part of a breech-loading gun that withdraws the cartridge or shell case from the chamber

☆**ex·tra·cur·ric·u·lar** (eks′trə kə rik′yoo lər, -yə-) *adj.* **1** not part of the required curriculum; outside the regular course of study but under the supervision of the school [dramatics, athletics, and other *extracurricular* activities] **2** not part of the normal, or one's regular, work, routine, etc.: often humorous or ironic [a husband's *extracurricular* liaisons]

ex·tra·dit·a·ble (eks′trə dīt′ə bəl) *adj.* **1** that can be extradited **2** making liable to extradition

ex·tra·dite (eks′trə dīt′) *vt.* **-dit′ed**, **-dit′ing** ⟦back-form. < fol.⟧ **1** to turn over as according to procedures established in an existing treaty (a person accused or convicted of a crime) to the country having jurisdiction over that crime **2** to obtain the extradition of

ex·tra·di·tion (eks′trə dish′ən) *n.* ⟦Fr < L *ex*, out + *traditio*, a surrender: see TRADITION⟧ the act of extraditing, as according to procedures established in an existing treaty, a person accused or convicted of a crime

ex·tra·dos (ek strä′däs′) *n.* ⟦Fr < L *extra*, beyond + Fr *dos* < L *dorsum*, back⟧ *Archit.* the outside curve of an arch

ex·tra·ga·lac·tic (eks′trə gə lak′tik) *adj.* outside or beyond our own galaxy

ex·tra·ju·di·cial (-joo dish′əl) *adj.* **1** outside or beyond the jurisdiction of a court **2** outside the usual course of justice —**ex′tra·ju·di′cial·ly** *adv.*

ex·tra·le·gal (-lē′gəl) *adj.* outside of legal control or authority; not regulated by law —**ex′tra·le′gal·ly** *adv.*

ex·tra·mar·i·tal (-mar′ət′l) *adj.* of or relating to sexual intercourse with someone other than one's spouse [*extramarital* affairs]

ex·tra·mun·dane (-mun′dān′) *adj.* ⟦LL *extramundanus*: see EXTRA- & MUNDANE⟧ outside the physical world; not of this world

ex·tra·mu·ral (-myoor′əl) *adj.* ⟦see EXTRA- & MURAL⟧ outside the walls or limits of a city, school, etc. [*extramural* activities]

ex·tra·ne·ous (ek strā′nē əs, ik-) *adj.* ⟦L *extraneus*, external, foreign < *extra*: see EXTRA-⟧ **1** coming from outside; foreign [an *extraneous* substance] **2** not truly or properly belonging; not essential **3** not pertinent; irrelevant —*SYN.* EXTRINSIC —**ex·tra′ne·ous·ly** *adv.* —**ex·tra′ne·ous·ness** *n.*

ex·tra·net (ek′strə net′) *n.* an intranet in which access is granted to certain outside users, as to customers or business partners

ex·tra·nu·cle·ar (eks′trə noo′klē ər, -nyoo′-) *adj.* located or occurring outside of the nucleus of a cell

ex·tra·or·di·naire (ik strôr′də ner′) *adj.* ⟦Fr⟧ extraordinary: used after the noun

ex·tra·or·di·nar·y (ek strôrd′'n er′ē, ik-; -strôr′də ner′ē; *also* eks′trə ôrd′'n er′ē, -ôr′də ner′ē) *adj.* ⟦ME *extraordinari* < L *extraordinarius* < *extra ordinem*, out of the usual order < *extra* + acc. of *ordo*, ORDER⟧ **1** not according to the usual custom or regular plan [an *extraordinary* session of Congress] **2** going far beyond the ordinary degree, measure, limit, etc.; very unusual; exceptional; remarkable **3** outside the regular staff; sent on a special errand; having special authority or responsibility [a minister *extraordinary*] —**ex·tra·or′di·nar′i·ly** *adv.* —**ex·tra·or′di·nar′i·ness** *n.*

☆**extraordinary rendition** the process by which a country seizes a person suspected as of terrorist activity and transports him or her for detention or interrogation to a country affording fewer legal protections against torture, etc.

extra point CONVERSION (sense 3)

ex·trap·o·late (ek strap′ə lāt′, ik-) *vt., vi.* **-lat′ed**, **-lat′ing** ⟦L *extra* (see EXTRA-) + (INTER)POLATE⟧ **1** *Statistics* to estimate or infer (a value, quantity, etc. beyond the known range) on the basis of certain variables within the known range, from which the estimated value is assumed to follow **2** to arrive at (conclusions or results) by hypothesizing from known facts or observations **3** to speculate as to consequences on the basis of (known facts or observations) —**ex·trap′o·la′tion** *n.* —**ex·trap′o·la′tive** *adj.* —**ex·trap′o·la′tor** *n.*

ex·tra·sen·so·ry (eks′trə sen′sə rē) *adj.* occurring or seeming to occur apart from, or in addition to, the normal function of the usual senses [*extrasensory* perception]

ex·tra·so·lar (-sō′lər) *adj.* outside or beyond the solar system [*extrasolar* planets]

ex·tra·sys·to·le (-sis′tə lē′) *n.* ⟦EXTRA- + SYSTOLE⟧ a disturbance of heart rhythm resulting in an extra contraction of the heart between regular beats —**ex′tra·sys·tol′ic** (-sis täl′ik) *adj.*

ex·tra·ter·res·tri·al (-tə res′trē əl) *adj.* existing, taking place, or coming from outside the limits of the earth —*n.* an extraterrestrial being, as in science fiction

ex·tra·ter·ri·to·ri·al (-ter′ə tôr′ē əl) *adj.* **1** outside the territorial limits or jurisdiction of the country, state, etc. **2** of extraterritoriality [*extraterritorial* rights] —**ex′tra·ter′ri·to′ri·al·ly** *adv.*

ex·tra·ter·ri·to·ri·al·i·ty (-ter′ə tôr′ē al′ə tē) *n.* **1** freedom from the jurisdiction of the country in which one is living, as in the case of foreign diplomats **2** jurisdiction of a country over its citizens in foreign lands

ex·tra·u·ter·ine (-yoot′ər in) *adj.* outside the uterus

ex·trav·a·gance (ek strav′ə gəns, ik-) *n.* ⟦Fr: see fol.⟧ **1** a going beyond reasonable or proper limits in conduct or speech; unreasonable excess **2** a spending of more than is reasonable or necessary; excessive expenditure; wastefulness **3** an instance of excess in spending, behavior, or speech Also **ex·trav′a·gan·cy**, *pl.* **-cies**

ex·trav·a·gant (-gənt) *adj.* ⟦ME & Anglo-Fr *extravagaunt* < ML *extravagans*, prp. of *extravagari*, to stray < L *extra*, beyond + *vagari*, to wander < *vagus*: see VAGUE⟧ **1** [Obs.] straying beyond bounds; wandering **2** going beyond reasonable limits; excessive or unrestrained [*extravagant* demands] **3** too ornate or showy [*extravagant* designs] **4** costing or spending too much; wasteful —*SYN.* EXCESSIVE, PROFUSE —**ex·trav′a·gant·ly** *adv.*

ex·trav·a·gan·za (ek strav′ə gan′zə, ik-) *n.* ⟦respelled by analogy with L *ex-* < It *estravaganza*, extravagance < *estravagante* < ML *extravagans*: see prec.⟧ **1** a literary, musical, or dramatic fantasy characterized by a loose structure and farce **2** a spectacular, elaborate theatrical production, as some musicals

ex·trav·a·gate (ek strav′ə gāt′) *vi.* **-gat′ed**, **-gat′ing** ⟦< ML *extravagatus*, pp.: see EXTRAVAGANT⟧ [Rare] **1** to stray; wander **2** to go beyond reasonable limits; be extravagant —**ex·trav′a·ga′tion** *n.*

ex·trav·a·sate (ek strav′ə sāt′) *vt.* **-sat′ed**, **-sat′ing** ⟦L *extra* (see EXTRA-) + *vas*, a vessel + -ATE[1]⟧ to allow or force (blood, etc.) to flow from its normal vessels into the surrounding tissues —*vi.* **1** to flow out or escape into surrounding tissues: said of blood, lymph, etc. **2** to flow out, as lava from a vent —**ex·trav′a·sa′tion** *n.*

ex·tra·vas·cu·lar (eks′trə vas′kyoo lər) *adj.* outside the vascular system, or the blood and lymph vessels

☆**ex·tra·ve·hic·u·lar** (-vē hik′yoo lər) *adj.* designating or of activity by an astronaut outside a vehicle in space

ex·tra·ver·sion (-vur′zhən) *n.* EXTROVERSION (sense 2) —**ex′tra·vert′** (-vurt′) *n., adj.*

ex·tra-vir·gin (-vur′jən) *adj.* ⟦< It (*olio*) *extra vergine* (*di oliva*), (oil) extra virgin (adj.) (of the olive)⟧ designating VIRGIN (*adj.* 8*a*) olive oil with the least acid and the best flavor, aroma, color, etc.

Ex·tre·ma·du·ra (ek′strə mə do͝or′ə) *Sp. name for* ESTREMADURA

ex·treme (ek strēm′, ik-) *adj.* ⟦ME & OFr < L *extremus*, last, outermost, superl. of *exterus*, outer: see EXTERNAL⟧ **1** at the end or outermost point; farthest away; most remote; utmost **2** *a)* in or to the greatest degree; very great or greatest [*extreme* pain] *b)* to an excessive degree; immoderate **3** far from what is usual or conventional **4** deviating to the greatest degree from the center of opinion, as in politics **5** very severe; drastic [*extreme* measures] **6** designating or of sports that involve high speeds, unusually risky actions, and considerable exposure to physical injury **7** [Archaic] last; final —*n.* **1** either of two things that are as different or far as possible from each other **2** an extreme degree **3** an extreme act, expedient, etc. **4** an extreme state or condition [an *extreme* of distress] **5** [Obs.] an extreme point; extremity **6** *Math. a)* the first or last term of a proportion *b)* EXTREMUM —**go to extremes** to be excessive or immoderate in speech or action —**in the extreme** to the utmost degree —**ex·treme′ly** *adv.* —**ex·treme′ness** *n.*

extremely high frequency *Radio* any frequency between 30,000 and 300,000 megahertz

Ex·treme Unction (ek′strēm) ANOINTING OF THE SICK

ex·trem·ism (ek strēm′iz′əm, ik-) *n.* the quality or state of going to extremes, esp. the extreme right or extreme left in politics —**ex·trem′ist** *adj., n.*

ex·trem·i·ty (ek strem′ə tē, ik-) *n., pl.* **-ties** ⟦ME & OFr *extremite* < L *extremitas* < *extremus*: see EXTREME⟧ **1** the outermost or utmost point or part; end **2** the greatest degree **3** a state of extreme necessity, danger, etc. **4** [Archaic] the end of life; dying **5** an extreme measure; severe or strong action: *usually used in pl.* **6** *a)* a body limb *b)* [*pl.*] the hands and feet

ex·tre·mum (ek strē′məm) *n., pl.* **-tre′ma** (-mə) ⟦ModL < L, an end, neut. of *extremus*: see EXTREME⟧ *Math.* the maximum or minimum value of a function

ex·tri·cate (eks′tri kāt′) *vt.* **-cat′ed, -cat′ing** ⟦< L *extricatus*, pp. of *extricare*, to disentangle < *ex-*, out + *tricae*, vexations: see TRICK⟧ to set free; release or disentangle (*from* a net, difficulty, etc.) —**ex′tri·ca·bil′i·ty** *n.* —**ex′tri·ca·ble** (-kə bəl) *adj.* —**ex′tri·ca′tion** *n.*

ex·trin·sic (ek strin′sik, -zik; ik-) *adj.* ⟦Fr *extrinseque* < L *extrinsecus*, from without, outer < *exter*, without + *secus*, following, otherwise < base of *sequi*, to follow: see SEQUENT⟧ **1** not really belonging to the thing with which it is connected; not inherent **2** being, coming, or acting from the outside; extraneous Opposed to INTRINSIC —**ex·trin′si·cal·ly** *adv.*

SYN.—**extrinsic** refers to that which may be connected to something else but is not an essential part of it [much of the discussion was *extrinsic* to the main issue]; **extraneous** also implies that something is not essential and often that it can be easily done without [in his second portrait, the artist left out *extraneous* details]; **foreign** refers to something regarded as not belonging in or with something else because it is very different [bragging is *foreign* to his nature; *foreign* matter in a solution]; **alien** suggests something so different that it cannot or should not be associated with something else [a practice *alien* to our tradition] —***ANT.*** **intrinsic**

extrinsic factor vitamin B_{12}

ex·tro- (eks′trō, -trə) *prefix* EXTRA- (when opposed to INTRO-)

ex·trorse (ek strôrs′) *adj.* ⟦Fr < LL *extrorsus* < L *extra*, outside + *versus*, pp. of *vertere*, to turn: see VERSE⟧ *Bot.* turned outward or away from the axis of growth: opposed to INTRORSE —**ex·trorse′ly** *adv.*

ex·tro·ver·sion (eks′trə vʉr′zhən, -shən) *n.* ⟦altered < Ger *extraversion* < L *extra-* (see EXTRA-) + ML *versio*, a turning < L *versus*: see VERSE⟧ **1** *Med.* EXSTROPHY **2** ⟦Ger⟧ *Psychol.* an attitude in which one's interest is directed to things outside oneself and to other persons rather than to oneself or one's experiences **3** a tendency to be outgoing and socially active Opposed to INTROVERSION

ex·tro·vert (eks′trə vʉrt′) *n.* ⟦see prec.⟧ **1** *Psychol.* someone characterized by EXTROVERSION (sense 2) **2** someone characterized by a tendency to be outgoing and socially active Opposed to INTROVERT —*adj.* EXTROVERTED

ex·tro·vert·ed (-id) *adj.* **1** *Psychol.* characterized by EXTROVERSION (sense 2) **2** outgoing and socially active Opposed to INTROVERTED

ex·trude (ek stro͞od′, ik-) *vt.* **-trud′ed, -trud′ing** ⟦L *extrudere*, to thrust out or forth < *ex-*, out + *trudere*, THRUST⟧ **1** to push or force out; expel **2** to force (metal, plastic, etc.) through a die or very small holes to give it a certain shape —*vi.* **1** to be extruded **2** to protrude —**ex·trud′er** *n.* —**ex·tru′sion** *n.*

ex·tru·sive (ek stro͞o′siv) *adj.* **1** extruding or tending to extrude **2** *Geol.* designating or of igneous rock formed from lava that hardened on the surface of the earth, moon, etc.: cf. INTRUSIVE (sense 2)

ex·tu·bate (ek sto͞o′bāt′, -styo͞o′-) *vt.* **-bat′ed, -bat′ing** ⟦EX-[1] + TUB(E) + -ATE[1]⟧ to remove a previously inserted tube from (a part of the body, as an air passage) —**ex′tu·ba′tion** *n.*

ex·u·ber·ance (eg zo͞o′bər əns, -zyo͞o′-; ig-) *n.* ⟦Fr *exubérance* < L *exuberantia* < *exuberans*, prp. of *exuberare*, to come forth in abundance < *ex-*, intens. + *uberare*, to bear abundantly < *uber*, UDDER⟧ **1** the state or quality of being exuberant; great abundance; luxuriance **2** an instance of this; esp., action or speech showing high spirits Also **ex·u′ber·an·cy** (-ən sē), *pl.* **-cies**

ex·u·ber·ant (-ənt) *adj.* ⟦ME < L *exuberans*: see prec.⟧ **1** growing profusely; luxuriant or prolific [*exuberant* vegetation] **2** characterized by good health and high spirits; full of life; uninhibited **3** overly elaborate; flowery **4** very great; extreme —**ex·u′ber·ant·ly** *adv.*

ex·u·ber·ate (-āt′) *vi.* **-at′ed, -at′ing** ⟦ME *exuberaten* < L *exuberatus*, pp. of *exuberare*⟧ [Rare] to be exuberant; abound

ex·u·date (eks′yo͞o dāt′, -dit; egz′yo͞o-) *n.* ⟦L *exudatus*, pp. of *exudare*: see EXUDE⟧ matter exuded

ex·u·da·tion (eks′yo͞o dā′shən, egz′yo͞o-) *n.* ⟦< prec. + -ION⟧ **1** the act of exuding **2** something exuded, as sweat

ex·ude (eg zyo͞od′, -zo͞od′; ig-) *vt., vi.* **-ud′ed, -ud′ing** ⟦L *exudare*, *exsudare* < *ex-*, out + *sudare*, to sweat < *sudor*, SWEAT⟧ **1** to pass out in drops through pores, an incision, etc.; ooze; discharge **2** to diffuse or seem to radiate [to *exude* joy]

ex·ult (eg zult′, ig-) *vi.* ⟦Fr *exulter* < L *exultare*, *exsultare*, to leap up, leap for joy < *ex-*, intens. + *saltare*, freq. of *salire*: see SALIENT⟧ **1** to rejoice greatly; be jubilant; glory **2** [Obs.] to leap up; leap with joy —**ex·ult′ing·ly** *adv.*

ex·ult·ant (eg zult′'nt, ig-) *adj.* ⟦L *exsultans*, prp. of *exsultare*⟧ exulting; triumphant; jubilant —**ex·ult′ant·ly** *adv.*

ex·ul·ta·tion (egz′əl tā′shən, eks′əl-) *n.* ⟦ME *exultacion* < L *exultatio*, *exsultatio* < pp. of *exsultare*⟧ the act of exulting; rejoicing; jubilation; triumph: also **ex·ult·ance** (eg zult′'ns, ig-) or **ex·ult′an·cy** (-zult′'n sē)

☆**ex·urb** (eks′ʉrb′) *n.* ⟦EX-[1] + (SUB)URB: coined (1955) by A. C. Spectorsky (1910-72), U.S. author and editor⟧ a region, generally semirural, beyond the suburbs of a city, inhabited largely by persons in the upper-income group —**ex·ur′ban** *adj.*

☆**ex·ur·ban·ite** (eks ʉr′bən īt′) *n.* ⟦coined (1955) by A. C. Spectorsky (see prec.) < EX-[1] + (SUB)URBANITE⟧ a person living in an exurb; esp., one commuting to the city as a business or professional person —*adj.* a characteristic of exurbia or exurbanites

☆**ex·ur·bi·a** (eks ʉr′bē ə) *n.* the exurbs collectively: usually used to connote an affluent lifestyle regarded as characteristic of exurbanites

ex·u·vi·ae (ik so͞o′vē ē, -syo͞o′-; ig zo͞o′-) *pl.n., sing.* **-vi·a** (-ə) ⟦L, that which is stripped off, spoils < *exuere*, to strip off < *ex-*, away + IE base **eu-*, to put on > Lith *aviù*, to wear footwear⟧ *Zool.* castoff coverings of animals, as crab shells or the skins of snakes —**ex·u′vi·al** *adj.*

ex·u·vi·ate (-vē āt′) *vt., vi.* **-vi·at′ed, -vi·at′ing** ⟦prec. + -ATE[1]⟧ to cast off (a skin, shell, etc.); molt —**ex·u′vi·a′tion** *n.*

ex·vo·to (eks′vō′tō) *n., pl.* **-tos** ⟦L⟧ **1** a votive offering **2** a painting or other artwork, usually nonprofessional, placed in a church as a token of thanks for blessings

-ey (ē, i) *suffix* -Y[3]: used esp. after a word ending in *y* [*clayey*, *gooey*]

ey·as (ī′əs) *n.* ⟦ME, by faulty division (infl. by *ey*, egg) of *a nyas*, *a niais* < OFr *niais*, nestling < VL **nidax* < L *nidus*, NEST⟧ an unfledged bird; nestling; esp., a young hawk taken from its nest for training in falconry

eye (ī) *n.* ⟦ME *ey*, *eie* < OE *ēage*, akin to Ger *auge* < IE base **okw-*, to see > Gr *osse*, eyes, *ōps*, face, eye, L *oculus*⟧ **1** the organ of sight in humans and animals **2** *a)* the eyeball *b)* the iris [brown *eyes*] *c)* the eyeball as it appears within the face [big *eyes*, narrow *eyes*, slanted *eyes*] **3** the area around the eye, including the eyelids [to get a black *eye*] **4** [*often pl.*] the power of seeing; sight; vision [weak *eyes*] **5** a look; glance; gaze [to cast an *eye* on something] **6** attention; regard; observation **7** the power of judging, estimating, discriminating, etc. by eyesight [a good *eye* for distances] **8** [*often pl.*] judgment; opinion; estimation [in the *eyes* of the law] **9** a thing like an eye in appearance or function; specif., *a)* a bud of a tuber, as a potato *b)* the spot on a peacock's tail feather *c)* the center of a flower; disk *d)* a hole in a tool, as for a handle *e)* the threading hole in a needle *f)* a loop of metal, rope, or thread [hook and *eye*] *g)* an organ sensitive to light, as in certain lower forms of life *h)* PHOTOELECTRIC CELL *i)* a section of any of certain cuts of meat [*eye* of round] *j)* a hole, as in certain cheeses **10** [Old Slang] a private detective; private eye **11** *Meteorol.* the calm, low-pressure area at the center of a strong tropical cyclone, hurricane, or typhoon, around which winds of high velocity move **12** [*pl.*] *Naut.* the part of the main deck of a vessel that is farthest forward —*vt.* **eyed, eye′ing** or **ey′ing** **1** to look at; watch carefully; observe **2** to provide with eyes, or holes —*vi.* [Obs.] to appear (to the eyes) —**all eyes** extremely attentive —**an eye for an eye** punishment or retaliation similar or equivalent to the injury suffered —**catch someone's eye** to attract someone's attention —**eyes right (or left)** *Mil.* a command to snap the head to the right (or left) while marching, as a salute when passing in review —☆**give someone the eye** [Slang] to look at someone, esp. in an admiring or inviting way —**have an eye for** to have a keen appreciation of —**have an eye to** to watch out for; attend to —**have eyes for** [Informal] to be very interested in and want —☆**in a pig's eye!** [Slang] never; under no circumstances: an exclamation indicating skepticism, strong disapproval, etc. —**in the eye of the wind** *Naut.* directly against the wind —**in the public eye** **1** much seen in public **2** often brought to public attention; well-known —**keep an eye on** to look after; watch carefully —☆**keep an eye out for** to be watchful for — **keep one's eyes (or an eye) open (or peeled or skinned)** to be on the lookout; be watchful —**lay (or set or clap) eyes on** to see; look at —**look someone in the eye** to look directly and assertively into the eyes of another [out of shame he couldn't *look me in the eye*] —**make eyes at** to look

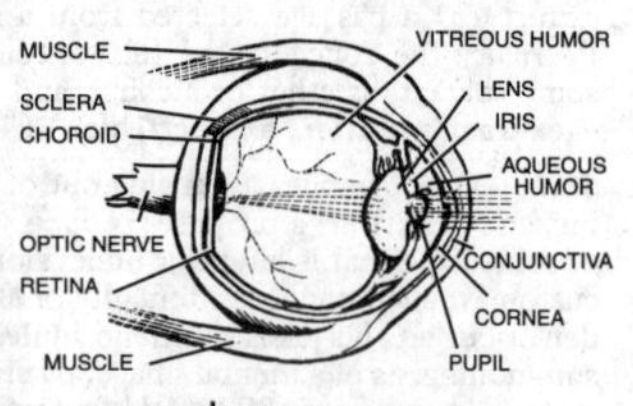

human eye

at amorously or flirtatiously —**my eye!** [Slang] an exclamation of contradiction, astonishment, etc. —**open someone's eyes** to make someone aware of the facts, real reasons, etc. —**run one's eye over** to glance at hurriedly —**see eye to eye** to agree completely —**see with half an eye** to see or understand (something) easily because it is so evident —**shut (or close) one's eyes to** to refuse to see or think about —**turn a blind eye (to)** to ignore or pretend not to notice (something) —**with an eye to** paying attention to; considering

eye·ball (ī′bôl′) *n.* **1** the ball-shaped part of the eye, enclosed by the socket and eyelids **2** a viewer of a TV program, website, etc. —☆*vt., vi.* [Informal] to observe, examine, measure, etc. (something) visually —**eyeball to eyeball** [Slang] in direct personal contact; person to person

eye bank a place at which corneas obtained from human bodies immediately after death are stored and preserved for later transplantation to patients with corneal defects

eye bath EYECUP

eye·beam (-bēm′) *n.* [Archaic] a beam, or glance, of the eye; quick look

eye black a kind of black grease applied under the eyes as by athletes to reduce glare

eye bolt a bolt with a loop for a head

eye·bright (-brīt′) *n.* any of a genus (*Euphrasia*) of plants of the figwort family, esp. a small plant (*E. americana*) of NE U.S. having pale lavender flowers in leafy clusters: formerly used in treating eye disorders

eye·brow (-brou′) *n.* ⟦ME *eiebrou*: see EYE + BROW⟧ **1** the bony arch over each eye **2** the arch of hair growing on this —**raise (or lift) an eyebrow** to appear or feel skeptical, surprised, mildly scandalized, etc.

☆**eye candy** [Slang] a person or thing regarded as superficially pleasing or attractive to look at

☆**eye-catch·er** (-kach′ər) *n.* something that especially attracts one's attention —**eye′-catch′ing** *adj.*

eye chart a chart used to test vision from a specified distance: it consists typically of rows of letters of decreasing size

eye contact direct visual contact with the eyes of another person

☆**eye·cup** (-kup′) *n.* a small cup whose rim is shaped to fit over the eye, used in applying medicine to the eyes or in washing them

eyed (īd) *adj.* **1** having eyes (of a specified kind) [*blue-eyed*] **2** having markings that look like eyes; spotted

eye dialect nonstandard respelling of words to suggest dialectal or informal pronunciation

☆**eye·drop·per** (ī′dräp′ər) *n.* a DROPPER (sense 2), specif. one for applying eyedrops

eye·drops (-dräps′) *pl.n.* liquid medicine for the eyes, applied as with an eyedropper

eye·ful (-fo͝ol′) *n.* **1** a quantity of something squirted or blown into the eye **2** a full look at something; good look **3** [Slang] a person or thing that looks striking or unusual

eye·glass (-glas′) *n.* **1** a lens designed to be worn to help or correct faulty vision; specif., a monocle **2** [*pl.*] a pair of such lenses, usually in a frame; glasses **3** EYEPIECE **4** [Chiefly Brit.] EYECUP

eye·hole (-hōl′) *n.* **1** the socket for the eyeball **2** a peephole **3** EYELET (sense 1)

eye·lash (-lash′) *n.* **1** any of the hairs on the edge of the eyelid **2** a fringe of these hairs

eye·less (-lis) *adj.* **1** without eyes **2** [Literary] blind

eye·let (-lit) *n.* ⟦ME *oylet* < OFr *oeillet*, dim. of *oeil*, eye < L *oculus*, EYE⟧ **1** a small hole for receiving a shoestring, rope, cord, hook, etc. **2** a metal ring or short tube for reinforcing such a hole **3** *a)* a small hole edged by stitching in embroidered work *b)* a lightweight fabric of machine-embroidered eyelets in rows or patterns **4** a peephole or loophole **5** a small eye; ocellus —*vt.* to provide with eyelets

eye level a height that is level with the eyes, as for ease of viewing [*museum paintings hung at eye level*]

eye·lid (-lid′) *n.* ⟦ME *eielid, eien lidd*: see EYE & LID⟧ either of the two movable folds of flesh that cover and uncover the front of the eyeball

eye·lift (-lift′) *n.* a plastic surgery operation for removing wrinkles, sagging flesh, etc. from around the eyes: cf. BLEPHAROPLASTY

eye·lin·er (-līn′ər) *n.* a cosmetic preparation applied in a thin line on the eyelid at the base of the eyelashes

ey·en (ī′ən) *n. archaic pl. of* EYE

☆**eye-o·pen·er** (ī′ō′pə nər) *n.* **1** a surprising piece of news, a sudden realization, etc. **2** [Informal] an alcoholic drink, esp. one taken early in the day —**eye′-o′pen·ing** *adj.*

eye·piece (-pēs′) *n.* in a telescope, microscope, or other optical instrument, the lens or lenses nearest the viewer's eye

eye·pop·per or **eye-pop·per** (-päp′ər) *n.* ⟦see POP[1] (*vi.* 3)⟧ [Informal] something that causes wonder or amazement or that draws particular notice —**eye′-pop′ping** *adj.*

eye rhyme similarity in the spelling, rather than the pronunciation, of the ends of words or lines of verse (Ex.: lone, none; though, cough)

eye·shade (-shād′) *n.* SUN VISOR

☆**eye shadow** a cosmetic preparation of any of various colors applied to the upper eyelids

eye·shot (-shät′) *n.* the distance that a person can see; range of vision

eye·sight (-sīt′) *n.* **1** the power of seeing; sight; vision **2** the range of vision

eyes-on·ly (īz′ōn′lē) *adj.* [Informal] confidential: said of a business or government report, memorandum, etc. not to be made public

eye·sore (ī′sôr′) *n.* ⟦ME *eie sor*⟧ a thing that is unpleasant to look at

eye splice a splice made by turning back the end of a rope and interlacing its strands into the body of the rope so as to form an end loop, or eye

eye·spot (-spät′) *n.* **1** a spot of color that looks like an eye **2** a small spot of pigment associated with sensitivity to light, found in many invertebrates

eye·stalk (-stôk′) *n.* a movable stalk with a compound eye at the tip, as in lobsters, shrimps, snails, and certain other crustaceans and mollusks

eye·strain (-strān′) *n.* a tired or strained condition of the eye muscles, caused as by too much use of the eyes, uncorrected visual defects, or reading in dim light

eye·tooth (-to͞oth′) *n., pl.* **-teeth′** ⟦so called from being located directly below the *eye*⟧ either of the two pointed teeth in the upper jaw between the bicuspids and the incisors; upper canine tooth —**cut one's eyeteeth** to become experienced or sophisticated

eye·wall (ī′wôl′) *n.* the inner wall-like boundary of rotating cumulonimbus clouds that rapidly swirl around the eye of a strong tropical cyclone, hurricane, or typhoon

eye·wash (-wôsh′) *n.* **1** a medicated solution for the eyes **2** [Slang] *a)* nonsense *b)* flattery *c)* something done only to impress an observer

eye·wear (-wer′) *n.* devices worn to protect the eyes or improve the vision; eyeglasses, sunglasses, safety goggles, etc.

eye·wink (-wiŋk′) *n.* **1** a wink of the eye **2** an instant

eye·wit·ness (-wit′nis) *n.* **1** a person who sees or has seen something happen, as an accident, crime, etc. **2** a person who testifies to what he or she has seen

eyre (er) *n.* ⟦ME & Anglo-Fr *eire* < OFr *erre* < *errer*, to travel: see ERRANT⟧ *Eng. History* **1** a tour or circuit: chiefly in the phrase **justices in eyre** **2** a circuit court held by justices in eyre

Eyre (er), **Lake** shallow salt lake in NE South Australia, varying from frequently dry to *c.* 3,700 sq mi (9,583 sq km)

Eyre Peninsula peninsula in S South Australia, east of the Great Australian Bight: base, 200 mi (322 km) across

ey·rie or **ey·ry** (er′ē, ir′ē) *n., pl.* **-ries** AERIE

ey·rir (ā′rir′) *n., pl.* **au·rar** (ou′rär′) ⟦Ice < ON, a coin, unit of weight < L *aureus*, a gold coin, orig. adj., golden: see AUREATE⟧ a monetary unit of Iceland, equal to $\frac{1}{100}$ of a krona

Ez *abbrev. Bible* **1** Ezekiel: also **Eze** or **Ezek** **2** Ezra: also **Ezr**

E·ze·ki·el[1] (i zē′kē əl) *n.* ⟦LL(Ec) *Ezechiel* < Gr *Iezekiēl* < Heb *yechezkel*, lit., God strengthens⟧ **1** a masculine name: dim. *Zeke* **2** *Bible a)* a Hebrew prophet of the 6th cent. B.C. *b)* the book of his prophecies (abbrev. *Ezek, Ezk, Ez,* or *Eze*)

E·ze·ki·el[2] (i zē′kē əl), **Moses Jacob** 1844-1917; U.S. sculptor

Ezk *abbrev. Bible* Ezekiel

Ez·ra (ez′rə) *n.* ⟦LL(Ec) < Heb *ezra*, lit., help⟧ **1** a masculine name **2** *Bible a)* a Hebrew scribe, prophet, and religious reformer of the 5th cent. B.C. *b)* the book telling of his life and teachings (abbrev. *Ez* or *Ezr*)

f[1] or **F** (ef) ***n.**, pl.* **f's, F's** **1** the sixth letter of the English alphabet: a modification of the Old Greek digamma (F), ultimately from the Phoenician **2** any of the speech sounds that this letter represents, as, in English, the (f) of *fire* **3** a type or impression for *f* or F **4** the sixth in a sequence or group **5** an object shaped like F —***adj.*** **1** of *f* or F **2** sixth in a sequence or group **3** shaped like F

f[2] *abbrev.* **1** femto- **2** *Physics* frequency **3** *Math.* function of **4** furlong(s)

f[3] *abbrev.* ⟦It *forte*⟧ *Musical Direction* loud(ly)

F[1] (ef) ***n.*** **1** *Educ.* *a)* a grade indicating failing work *b)* sometimes, a grade indicating fair or average work **2** *Music* *a)* the fourth tone or note in the ascending scale of C major *b)* the scale having this tone as a keynote *c)* a note representing this tone *d)* a key, string, etc. producing this tone

F[2] *abbrev.* **1** Fahrenheit **2** farad(s) **3** faraday(s) **4** Father **5** February **6** Fellow (of a learned society) **7** female or feminine **8** *Genetics* filial generation **9** fine **10** *Insurance* fire **11** *Photog.* f-number **12** folio(s) **13** following **14** *Physics* force **15** *Sports* forward **16** franc(s) **17** French **18** Friar **19** Friday **20** full **21** *Comput., Math.* function **22** *Pharmacy* *a)* ⟦L *fiat*⟧ let there be made *b)* ⟦L *fac*⟧ make Also, for 7, 9, 11-13, 15-16, & 22, **f**

F[3] *Chem. symbol for* fluorine

F/, f/, *or* **F:** *abbrev. Photog.* f-number

F- (ef) *prefix* fighter: used in designations for aircraft *[F-16]*

fa (fä) ***n.*** ⟦ME < ML < *fa(muli)*: see GAMUT⟧ *Music* a syllable representing the fourth tone of the diatonic scale: see SOLFEGGIO

FAA *abbrev.* Federal Aviation Administration

fab[1] (fab) ***adj.*** [Informal] *short for* FABULOUS (sense 3)

fab[2] (fab) ***n.*** ⟦prob. < *fabrication plant*⟧ a manufacturing facility for the production of microchips

fa·ba·ceous (fə bā′shəs) ***adj.*** ⟦L *fabaceus* < *faba*, BEAN⟧ of the legume order of plants; leguminous

Fa·bi·an (fā′bē ən) ***adj.*** ⟦L *Fabianus*, of Fabius: see FABIUS⟧ ☆**1** using a cautious strategy of delay and avoidance of battle **2** of the Fabian Society —***n.*** a member of the Fabian Society —**Fa′bi·an·ism′** ***n.***

Fabian Society ⟦after fol.⟧ an organization of English socialists, established in 1884, aiming to bring about socialism by gradual reforms rather than revolutionary action

Fa·bi·us (fā′bē əs) (full name *Quintus Fabius Maximus Verrucosus*) died 203 B.C.; Rom. general & statesman: defeated Hannibal in the second Punic War by a cautious strategy of delay and avoidance of direct encounter: called *Cunctator* (the Delayer)

fa·ble (fā′bəl) ***n.*** ⟦ME < OFr < L *fabula*, a story < *fari*, to speak: see FAME⟧ **1** a fictitious story meant to teach a moral lesson: the characters are usually talking animals **2** a myth or legend **3** a story that is not true; falsehood **4** [Archaic] the plot of a literary work — ***vi., vt.*** **-bled, -bling** to write or tell (fables, legends, or falsehoods) —**fa′bler** ***n.***

fa·bled (-bəld) ***adj.*** **1** told of in fables or legends; mythical; legendary **2** unreal; fictitious

fab·li·au (fa′blē ō′; *Fr* fȧ blē ō′) ***n.**, pl.* **-aux′** (-ōz′; *Fr*, -ō′) ⟦Fr < OFr, dial. form of *fablel*, dim. of *fable*, FABLE⟧ in medieval literature, esp. French and English literature, a short story in verse telling comic incidents of ordinary life, usually with earthy realism

fab·ric (fab′rik) ***n.*** ⟦MFr *fabrique* < L *fabrica*, a workshop, trade, product, fabric < *faber*, a workman < IE base **dhabh-*, to fit together > OE *(ge)dæfte*, fit⟧ **1** *a)* anything constructed or made of parts put together; structure; building *b)* the framework or basic structure of anything **2** the style or plan of construction **3** *a)* a material made from fibers or threads by weaving, knitting, felting, etc., as any cloth, felt, lace, or the like *b)* the texture of such material **4** [Brit.] the construction and upkeep of a church building

fab·ri·cate (fab′ri kāt′) ***vt.*** **-cat′ed, -cat′ing** ⟦ME *fabricaten* < L *fabricatus*, pp. of *fabricari*, to construct, build < *fabrica*: see prec.⟧ **1** to make, build, construct, etc., esp. by assembling parts; manufacture **2** to make up (a story, reason, lie, etc.); invent —***SYN.*** LIE[2], MAKE[1] —**fab′ri·ca′tor** ***n.***

fab·ri·ca·tion (fab′ri kā′shən) ***n.*** ⟦ME *fabricacioun* < L *fabricatio*⟧ **1** a fabricating or being fabricated; construction; manufacture **2** a fabricated thing; esp., a falsehood, false excuse, etc.

fab·u·late (fab′yə lāt′) ***vi.*** ⟦< L *fabulari*, to speak (in fables) < *fabula*, FABLE⟧ to write or tell fictitious stories, esp. highly allegorical or fantastic ones —**fab′u·la′tion** ***n.*** —**fab′u·la′tor** ***n.***

fab·u·list (fab′yə list) ***n.*** ⟦Fr *fabuliste* < L *fabula*: see FABLE⟧ **1** a person who writes or tells fables **2** a liar

fab·u·lous (fab′yə ləs) ***adj.*** ⟦ME < L *fabulosus*, fabled < *fabula*⟧ **1** of or like a fable; imaginary, fictitious, or legendary **2** hard to believe; incredible; astounding **3** [Informal] very good; wonderful —***SYN.*** FICTITIOUS —**fab′u·lous·ly** ***adv.*** —**fab′u·lous·ness** ***n.***

fa·cade or **fa·çade** (fə säd′) ***n.*** ⟦Fr < It *facciata* < *faccia* < VL *facia*: see fol.⟧ **1** the front of a building; part of a building facing a street, courtyard, etc. **2** the front part of anything: often used fig., with implications of an imposing appearance concealing something inferior

face (fās) ***n.*** ⟦ME < OFr < VL *facia* < L *facies*, the face, appearance < base of *facere*, DO[1]⟧ **1** the front of the head from the top of the forehead to the bottom of the chin, and from ear to ear; visage; countenance **2** the expression of the countenance **3** a surface of a thing; esp., *a)* the front, upper, or outer surface or part *b)* any one of the surfaces of a geometric figure or crystal **4** the side or surface that is marked, as of a clock, playing card, domino, etc., or that is finished, as of fabric, leather, etc. **5** the appearance; outward aspect; semblance **6** facial makeup; cosmetics: used chiefly in the phrases **do one's face** and **put one's face on** **7** dignity; self-respect; prestige: used chiefly in the phrase **lose (**or **save) face** **8** the topography (of an area) **9** the functional or striking surface (of a tool, golf club, etc.) **10** what is shown by the language of a document, without explanation or addition **11** [Informal] effrontery; audacity **12** *Mining* the end of a tunnel, drift, etc., where work is being done **13** *Printing* *a)* the type surface on which a letter is cut; printing part of a letter or plate *b)* the full selection of type of a certain design —***vt.*** **faced, fac′ing** ⟦ME *facen* < the *n.*⟧ **1** to turn, or have the face or front turned, toward *[the building faces the square]* **2** to meet or confront squarely or face to face **3** to confront with boldness, courage, etc. **4** to acknowledge and accept (facts, the truth, etc.) **5** to put another material on the surface of **6** to level and smooth the surface of (esp. a block of stone) **7** to turn (a card, etc.) with the face up **8** *Mil.* to cause (a formation of soldiers) to pivot by giving the appropriate command **9** *Sewing* to apply a facing to (a collar, edge, etc.) —***vi.*** **1** to turn, or have the face turned, toward a specified thing or person, or in a specified direction **2** *Mil.* to pivot in a specified direction: usually in the form of a command *[right face!]* —☆**be (**or **get) in someone's face** [Slang] to behave in a confrontational or annoyingly direct or persistent manner toward someone —**face down** **1** with the face or front turned downward *[to slip and land face down in a pile of leaves]* **2** to disconcert or overcome by a confident, bold manner —**face off** **1** *Hockey* to start or resume play with a face-off **2** [Informal] to confront one another as opponents or adversaries *[candidates face off in an election]* **3** [Informal] to take a position opposing: with *against* or *with* *[Congress faced off against the President]* —**face to face** **1** confronting each other **2** very near to; in the presence of: followed by *with* —**face up** with the face or front turned upward; on its or one's back *[to deal playing cards face up]* —**face up to** **1** to face with courage; confront and resist **2** to realize and be ready to meet (a condition, fact, etc.) —**fly in the face of** to be rashly defiant of —**in someone's face** (in a manner that is) direct and confrontational *[the door was slammed in my face]* —**in the face of** **1** in the presence of **2** in spite of —**make a face** to distort the face, esp. in a way expressing contempt, distaste, humor, etc.: also [Chiefly Brit.] **pull a face** —**on the face of it** to all appearances; apparently —**pull (**or **wear) a long face** to look sad, glum, disapproving, etc. —**put a bold face on** to seem bold or confident about —**set one's face against** to be determinedly against; disapprove of; resist —**show one's face** to come and be seen; appear —**to someone's face** in someone's presence; openly and without fear

SYN.—**face** is the basic, direct word for the front of the head; **countenance** refers to the face as it reflects the emotions or feelings and is, hence, often applied to the facial expression *[his happy countenance]*; **visage** refers to the form, proportions, and expression of the face, especially as indicative of general temperament *[a man of stern visage]*; **physiognomy** refers to the general cast of features, esp. as characteristic of an ethnic group or as supposedly indicative of character *[the physiognomy of an honest man]*

face card any king, queen, or jack in a deck of cards

☆**face cord** a measure of wood cut for fuel, as arranged in a pile 8 feet wide, 4 feet high, and with pieces 12 to 18 inches in length

-faced (fāst) *combining form* having a (specified kind of) face *[round-faced]*

face·down (fās′doun′; *for n.*, -doun′) ***adv.*** with the face or front turned downward —***n.*** ⟦< FACE DOWN (see phr. under FACE)⟧ a confrontation between rivals or opponents

face-hard·en (fās′härd′′n) ***vt.*** CASEHARDEN (sense 1)

face·less (fās′lis) *adj.* 1 lacking a face 2 lacking a distinct character; without individuality; anonymous

☆**face-lift** (fās′lift′) *n.* 1 a cosmetic surgery operation for removing wrinkles, sagging flesh, etc. from the face 2 a renovation or redesign of the exterior of something, as a building Also written **face lift** —*vt.* to renovate or redesign the exterior of

face mask a protective covering of plastic or metal for the face, worn in football, hockey, etc.: sometimes written **face′mask′** *n.*

face-off (fās′ôf′) *n.* 1 *Ice Hockey* the act of starting or resuming play when the referee drops the puck between two opposing players 2 [Informal] a confrontation of persons or groups in opposition

face·plate (fās′plāt′) *n.* 1 a disk fastened to the spindle of a lathe that holds in place work to be turned 2 a protective cover, as over a light switch, journal box, etc.

face powder a cosmetic powder, as of talcum, applied to the face

fac·er (fās′ər) *n.* 1 a person or thing that faces 2 [Brit. Informal] any sudden, unexpected difficulty or defeat

face-sav·ing (fās′sā′viŋ) *adj.* preserving or intended to preserve one's dignity, self-respect, or good reputation

fac·et (fas′it) *n.* ⟦Fr *facette*, dim. of *face*, FACE⟧ 1 any of the small, polished plane surfaces of a cut gem 2 any of a number of sides or aspects, as of a personality 3 *Anat.* any small, smooth surface on a bone or other hard part 4 *Archit.* the raised plane between the flutes of a column 5 *Zool.* the outer surface of an ommatidium of a compound eye, as in many insects and crustaceans —*vt.* **-et·ed** or **-et·ted**, **-et·ing** or **-et·ting** to cut or make facets on —**SYN.** PHASE[1]

fa·ce·ti·ae (fə sē′shē ē′) *pl.n.* ⟦L, pl. of *facetia*, a jest < *facetus*, elegant, witty, akin to *fax*, torch < IE base **ĝhwok-*, to gleam > Gr *phaos*, light⟧ [Rare] witty sayings

☆**face time** [Informal] 1 a period of meeting or speaking with someone in person 2 the length of time someone gets to appear on TV

fa·ce·tious (fə sē′shəs) *adj.* ⟦Fr *facétieux* < L *facetia*: see FACETIAE & -OUS⟧ joking or trying to be jocular, esp. at an inappropriate time —**SYN.** WITTY —**fa·ce′tious·ly** *adv.* —**fa·ce′tious·ness** *n.*

face-to-face (fās′tə fās′) *adj., adv.* 1 in the close presence of or facing each other [*face-to-face* customer service, standing *face-to-face*] 2 in direct confrontation [come *face-to-face* with the issues, fight the enemy *face-to-face*] —*n.* an occasion of two people meeting or confronting each other in person

face·up (fās′up′) *adv.* with the face or front turned upward

face value 1 the value printed or stamped on a bill, bond, coin, etc. 2 the amount of the death benefits of a life insurance policy 3 the seeming value [to take a promise at *face value*]

fa·ci·a (fā′shē ə, -shə) *n. chiefly Brit. var. of* FASCIA

fa·cial (fā′shəl) *adj.* ⟦Fr < ML *facialis* < VL *facia*, FACE⟧ of or for the face —☆*n.* a treatment intended to improve the appearance of the skin of the face, as by massage, the application of creams and astringents, etc. —**fa′cial·ly** *adv.*

facial angle the angle made by the intersection of two lines drawn from the base of the nostrils, one to the ear opening and the other to the most prominent part of the forehead

facial index the ratio of the height to the width of the face; (height × 100) ÷ width: cf. CEPHALIC INDEX

☆**facial tissue** a sheet of soft tissue paper used for cleansing, as a handkerchief, etc.

-fa·cient (fā′shənt) ⟦< L *faciens* (gen. *facientis*), prp. of *facere*, to make, DO[1]⟧ *combining form forming adjectives* making or causing to become [*liquefacient*]

fa·ci·es (fā′shē ēz′, -shēz′; *also, esp. for 2*, -sēz′) *n., pl.* **fa′ci·es′** ⟦L, FACE⟧ 1 the general appearance, aspect, or nature of anything 2 *Ecol.* a particular modification of the appearance or composition of a community 3 *Geol.* the characteristics of a rock body or part of a rock body that differentiate it from others, as in appearance, composition, etc. 4 *Med. a)* the appearance of the face as indicative of a specific disease or condition *b)* a surface

fac·ile (fas′əl) *adj.* ⟦Fr < L *facilis* < *facere*, DO[1]⟧ 1 not hard to do or achieve; easy 2 acting, working, or done easily, or in a quick, smooth way; fluent; ready [a *facile* wit] 3 using or showing little effort and not sincere or profound; superficial [a *facile* solution, *facile* emotions] 4 [Now Rare] easy to influence or persuade; affable —**SYN.** EASY —**fac′ile·ly** *adv.* —**fac′ile·ness** *n.*

fa·cil·i·tate (fə sil′ə tāt′) *vt.* **-tat′ed**, **-tat′ing** ⟦< Fr *faciliter* < It *facilitare* < L *facilis* (see prec.) + -ATE[1]⟧ to make easy or easier —**fa·cil′i·ta′tor** *n.*

fa·cil·i·ta·tion (fə sil′ə tā′shən) *n.* 1 the act of facilitating 2 *Psychol.* increased ease of performance of any action, resulting from the lessening of nerve resistance by the continued successive application of the necessary stimulus —**fa·cil′i·ta′tive** *adj.*

fa·cil·i·ty (fə sil′ə tē) *n., pl.* **-ties** ⟦ME & OFr *facilite* < L *facilitas*, easiness < *facilis*, FACILE⟧ 1 ease of doing or making; absence of difficulty 2 a ready ability; skill; dexterity; fluency 3 [*usually pl.*] the means by which something can be done [poor transportation *facilities*] 4 a building, special room, etc. that is built or designed for some activity [a new *facility* for outpatient treatment] 5 [*usually pl.*] LAVATORY (sense 2*a*) 6 an arrangement in which a bank agrees to extend a service to a company, government, etc., esp. one in which a certain amount of credit can be drawn on as funds are needed [credit *facility*]

fac·ing (fās′iŋ) *n.* 1 a lining, often decorative, sewn on the inside edge of a garment or on a part that is turned back, as a collar 2 any material used for this 3 a covering of contrasting material to decorate or protect a building, brick wall, etc. 4 [*pl.*] the trimmings, collar, and cuffs of certain military coats

fac·sim·i·le (fak sim′ə lē) *n.* ⟦L *fac*, imper. of *facere*, DO[1] + *simile*, neut. of *similis*, SIMILAR⟧ 1 an exact reproduction or copy 2 the transmission and reproduction of graphic matter by electrical means, as by radio or wire —*adj.* of or having the nature of a facsimile —*vt.* **-led**, **-le·ing** to make a facsimile of —**SYN.** COPY

fact (fakt) *n.* ⟦L *factum*, that which is done, deed, fact, neut. pp. of *facere*, DO[1]⟧ 1 a deed; act: now esp. in the sense of "a criminal deed" in the phrases **after the fact** and **before the fact** [an accessory *after the fact*] 2 a thing that has actually happened or that is really true; thing that has been or is 3 the state of things as they are; reality; actuality; truth [*fact* as distinct from fancy] 4 something said to have occurred or supposed to be true [to check the accuracy of one's *facts*] 5 *Law* an actual or alleged incident or condition, as distinguished from its legal consequence —**as a matter of fact** in reality; really; actually: also **in fact** or **in point of fact** —☆**the facts of life** 1 basic information about sexual reproduction 2 the harsh, unpleasant facts about a situation in life

fact-check (fakt′chek′) *vt., vi.* to confirm, prior to publication, the accuracy of facts, quotations, etc. in (a newspaper story, magazine article, etc.) —**fact′-check′er** *n.*

fact-find·ing (fakt′fīn′diŋ) *n.* the gathering of information; specif., preliminary research to gather facts for a later, full investigation, hearing, etc. —*adj.* of, resulting from, or for the purpose of such research [a *fact-finding* trip prior to a Congressional hearing] —**fact′-find′er** *n.*

fac·tic·i·ty (fak tis′ə tē) *n.* ⟦Fr *facticité* < Ger *faktizität* < L *factum*, FACT⟧ the quality or state of being a fact or factual; factuality

fac·tion[1] (fak′shən) *n.* ⟦< Fr *faction* & L *factio*, a making, doing, group of this kind < pp. of L *facere*, DO[1]⟧ 1 a group of people inside a political party, club, government, etc. working in a common cause against other such groups or against the main body 2 partisan conflict within an organization or a country; dissension —**fac′tion·al** *adj.* —**fac′tion·al·ly** *adv.*

☆**fac·tion[2]** (fak′shən) *n.* ⟦a blend of FACT & FICTION⟧ a kind of fiction based on or incorporating recognizable historical events, real people, etc.

fac·tion·al·ism (-əl iz′əm) *n.* 1 factional dissension 2 affiliation with a faction —**fac′tion·al·ist** *n., adj.*

fac·tion·al·ize (-əl īz′) *vt., vi.* **-ized′**, **-iz′ing** to divide into factions —**fac′tion·al·i·za′tion** *n.*

fac·tious (fak′shəs) *adj.* ⟦L *factiosus* < *factio*⟧ 1 producing or tending to produce faction; causing dissension 2 produced or characterized by faction —**fac′tious·ly** *adv.* —**fac′tious·ness** *n.*

fac·ti·tious (fak tish′əs) *adj.* ⟦L *facticius* < pp. of *facere*, DO[1]⟧ not natural, genuine, or spontaneous; forced or artificial [*factitious* needs created by advertising] —**fac·ti′tious·ly** *adv.* —**fac·ti′tious·ness** *n.*

fac·ti·tive (fak′tə tiv) *adj.* ⟦ModL, *factitivus*, irreg. < L *factus*, pp. of *facere*, DO[1]⟧ *Gram.* designating or of a verb that expresses the idea of making, calling, or thinking something to be of a certain character, using a noun, pronoun, or adjective as a complement to its direct object (Ex.: *make* the dress *short*, *elect* him *mayor*)

☆**fac·toid** (fak′toid′) *n.* ⟦coined (1973) by N. MAILER < FACT + -OID⟧ a single fact or statistic variously regarded as being trivial, useless, unsubstantiated, etc.

fac·tor (fak′tər) *n.* ⟦ME *factour* < OFr *facteur* < L *factor*, doer, maker < pp. of *facere*, DO[1]⟧ 1 *a)* a person who carries on business transactions for another; commission merchant; agent for the sale of goods entrusted to his possession *b)* an agent, as a banking or finance company, engaged in financing the operations of certain companies, or in financing wholesale and retail sales, through the purchase of accounts receivable 2 ⟦fig. use of *n.* 4⟧ any of the circumstances, conditions, etc. that bring about a result; element or constituent that makes a thing what it is 3 *Biol. a)* GENE *b)* a substance that has a particular effect on the body physiologically, as the Rh factor in clotting blood 4 *Math.* any of two or more quantities which form a product when multiplied together —*vt.* ☆*Math.* to resolve into factors —*vi.* to act in the capacity of a factor —**SYN.** AGENT, ELEMENT —**factor in** (or **into**) to include as a factor —**factor out** to exclude as a factor —**fac′tor·a·ble** *adj.* —**fac′tor·ship′** *n.*

fac·tor·age (-ij) *n.* 1 the business of a factor; buying and selling on commission 2 a factor's commission

fac·to·ri·al (fak tôr′ē əl) *adj.* 1 of a factor 2 *Math.* of factors or factorials —*n. Math.* the product of a given series of consecutive whole numbers beginning with 1 and ending with the specified number [the *factorial* of 5 (5!) is 1 × 2 × 3 × 4 × 5, or 120]

fac·tor·ize (fak′tər īz′) *vt.* **-ized′**, **-iz′ing** *Math.* FACTOR —**fac′tor·i·za′tion** *n.*

factor of safety the ratio of the maximum strength of a piece of material or a part to the probable maximum load to be applied to it

factor VIII an inherited plasma protein that is usually defective or missing in hemophiliacs, needed to stop excessive internal bleeding

fac·to·ry (fak′tə rē; *often* fak′trē) *n., pl.* **-ries** ⟦Fr *factorie* < *facteur*: see FACTOR⟧ 1 a building or buildings in which things are manufactured; manufacturing plant 2 ⟦< Port *feitoria*⟧ a trading settlement maintained by factors

factory farm a large livestock farm, often owned by a corporation, aimed at expeditious processing of a high volume of animals: term used chiefly by those who regard such farms as objectionable due to their harmful effects on the environment and their abusive treatment of animals, particularly by confinement —**factory farming**

fac·to·tum (fak tōt′əm) ***n.*** ⟦ModL < L *fac*, imper. of *facere*, DO[1] + *totum*, neut. of *totus*, all, the whole⟧ a person hired to do all sorts of work; handyman

fac·tu·al (fak′cho͞o əl) ***adj.*** ⟦FACT + (ACT)UAL⟧ **1** of or containing facts **2** having the nature of fact; real; actual —**fac′tu·al′i·ty** ***n.*** —**fac′tu·al·ly** ***adv.***

fac·tu·al·ism (-iz′əm) ***n.*** adherence or devotion to facts

fac·ture (fak′chər) ***n.*** ⟦ME < OFr < L *factura* < *facere*, to make, DO[1]⟧ the manner in which something, esp. a painting, is made or executed

fac·u·lae (fak′yo͞o lē′) ***pl.n.***, *sing.* **-la** (-lə) ⟦L, dim. of *fax* (gen. *facis*), torch: see FACETIAE⟧ bright areas visible on the surface of the sun, esp. near its edge

fac·ul·ta·tive (fak′əl tāt′iv) ***adj.*** ⟦Fr *facultatif* < L *facultas*: see fol.⟧ **1** *a)* granting a faculty, or permission; permissive *b)* optional **2** that may or may not happen or be; contingent **3** having to do with a faculty or faculties **4** *Biol.* capable of living under varying conditions; e.g., able to live independently and as a parasite: opposed to OBLIGATE (***adj.*** 2)

fac·ul·ty (fak′əl tē) ***n.***, *pl.* **-ties** ⟦ME & OFr *faculte* < L *facultas* < *facilis*: see FACILE⟧ **1** [Obs.] the power to do; ability to perform an action **2** any natural or specialized power of a living organism; sense *[the faculty of hearing, speech, etc.]* **3** power or ability to do some particular thing; special aptitude or skill *[a faculty for making friends]* **4** ⟦ME < ML *facultas*, transl. of Aristotle's *dynamis*, branch of learning⟧ in Canada, a college or school of a university ☆**5** all the teachers of a school, college, or university or of one of its departments or divisions **6** all the members of any of the learned professions **7** *a)* a power or privilege conferred by authority *b)* [*usually pl.*] *R.C.Ch.* authorization granted to a bishop, priest, etc. permitting the performance of certain acts or functions otherwise prohibited to him **8** [Archaic] what a person is trained to do **9** any of the powers of the mind, as will or reason —***SYN.*** TALENT

fad (fad) ***n.*** ⟦19th c. < Brit Midland dial.⟧ a custom, style, etc. that many people are interested in for a short time; passing fashion; craze —***SYN.*** FASHION —**fad′dy** ***adj.***

fad·dish (-ish) ***adj.*** **1** having the nature of a fad **2** fond of fads; following fads —**fad′dish·ly** ***adv.*** —**fad′dish·ness** ***n.***

fad·dism (-iz′əm) ***n.*** the practice of following fads, or a tendency to do so —**fad′dist** ***n.***

fade (fād) ***vi.*** **fad′ed, fad′ing** ⟦ME *faden* < OFr *fader* < *fade*, pale < VL **fatidus*, prob. < L *fatuus* (see FATUOUS); infl. by *vapidus*, VAPID⟧ **1** to become less distinct; lose color, brilliance, etc. **2** to lose freshness or strength; wither; wane **3** to disappear slowly; die out **4** to lose braking power: said of brakes that heat and glaze the lining in repeated hard use **5** to curve from its direct course **6** *Radio, TV* to vary in intensity: said of a signal —***vt.*** **1** to cause to fade ☆**2** [Slang] to meet the bet of; cover: a dice player's term **3** *Golf* to deliberately cause (a ball) to slice slightly —***n.*** **1** the act of fading **2** any of several styles of haircut in which the hair is cut so as to be very close on the sides of the head and progressively longer toward the top of the head **3** *Film, Radio, TV* a FADE-IN or FADE-OUT **4** *Golf* the path of a ball that is faded or that slices slightly —***SYN.*** VANISH —☆**fade back** *Football* to move back from the line of scrimmage, as in order to throw a forward pass —☆**fade in (or out)** *Film, Radio, TV* to appear or cause to appear (or disappear) gradually; make or become more (or less) distinct

☆**fade·a·way** (fād′ə wā′) ***n.*** **1** *Baseball former term for* SCREWBALL (***n.*** 1) **2** *Basketball* a type of shot in which the shooter leans or jumps away from the basket while shooting

☆**fade-in** (-in′) ***n.*** *Film, Radio, TV* a fading in; gradual appearance or becoming distinct of a scene or sound

fade·less (-lis) ***adj.*** that will not fade; unfading

☆**fade-out** (-out′) ***n.*** *Film, Radio, TV* a fading out; gradual disappearance or becoming indistinct of a scene or sound

fa·do (fä′do͞o) ***n.*** ⟦Port, lit., fate < L *fatum*: see FATE⟧ a kind of Portuguese folk song, usually melancholy and nostalgic

fae·ces (fē′sēz′) ***pl.n.*** *alt. sp. of* FECES —**fae·cal** (fē′kəl) ***adj.***

fa·e·na (fä ā′nä) ***n.*** ⟦Sp, lit., work⟧ in bullfighting, the series of passes at the bull immediately before the kill, for displaying the matador's skill

fa·er·ie or **fa·er·y** (fā′ər ē, fer′ē) ***n.*** ⟦OFr *faerie* (see FAIRY): E use due to Spenser⟧ [Archaic] **1** fairyland **2** *pl.* **-ies** a fairy —***adj.*** [Archaic] fairy Also written **faërie** or **faëry**

Faer·oe Islands (fer′ō) *alt. sp. of* FAROE ISLANDS: also **Faer′oes**

Faer·o·ese (fer′ō ēz′, -ēs′) ***n.*** **1** *pl.* **-ese′** a person born or living in the Faroe Islands **2** the North Germanic language spoken in the Faroe Islands, related to Icelandic —***adj.*** of the Faroe Islands or their people, language, or culture

Faf·nir (fäv′nir′) ***n.*** ⟦ON *Fāfnir*⟧ *Norse Myth.* a giant who, in the form of a dragon, guards the Nibelung treasure: he is killed by Sigurd

fag[1] (fag) ***vi.*** **fagged, fag′ging** ⟦< ? FAG END⟧ **1** to work hard and become very tired **2** [Brit. Informal] to serve as a fag or servant —***vt.*** **1** to make tired by hard work **2** [Brit. Informal] to employ (a boy) as a fag or servant —***n.*** **1** [Brit. Informal] *a)* hard, tiring work; drudgery *b)* fatigue; weariness *c)* a boy in an English public school who acts as a servant for another boy in a higher form, or class *d)* a menial worker; drudge ☆**2** [Slang] a male homosexual: a term of contempt and hostility —**fag′gy** ***adj.***

fag[2] (fag) ***n.*** ⟦< fol.⟧ [Informal, Now Chiefly Brit.] a cigarette

fag end ⟦< ME *fagge*, broken thread⟧ **1** *a)* the last part or coarse end of a piece of cloth *b)* the frayed, untwisted end of a rope **2** the last and worst part of anything; remnant

fag·got[1] (fag′ət) ***n., vt.*** *alt. sp. of* FAGOT

☆**fag·got**[2] (fag′ət) ***n.*** ⟦prob. extended < *fag* (homosexual), on the pattern of prec.⟧ [Slang] a male homosexual: a term of contempt and hostility —**fag′got·y** ***adj.***

☆**fag hag** [Slang] a heterosexual woman who prefers the company of homosexual men: a jocular or disparaging term

fag·ot (fag′ət) ***n.*** ⟦ME < OFr, with change of suffix < VL **facellum* < Gr *phakelos*, a bundle⟧ **1** a bundle of sticks, twigs, or branches, esp. for use as fuel **2** *Metallurgy* a bundle or heap of iron or steel pieces to be worked into bars by hammering or rolling at welding temperature —***vt.*** **1** to make into a fagot; form fagots of **2** *Sewing* to decorate with fagoting

fag·ot·ing or **fag·got·ing** (fag′ət iŋ) ***n.*** **1** a kind of drawnwork or hemstitch with wide spaces **2** openwork decoration in which the thread is drawn in crisscross or barlike stitches across the open seam

Fahr·en·heit (fer′ən hīt′) ***adj.*** ⟦after G. D. *Fahrenheit* (1686-1736), Ger physicist who devised the scale⟧ designating or of a thermometer on which 32° is the freezing point and 212° is the boiling point of water: abbrev. *F*: the formula for converting a Fahrenheit temperature to Celsius is °C = 5/9(°F−32) —***n.*** this thermometer or its scale

fa·ience (fā äns′, fī-; *Fr* fā yäns′) ***n.*** ⟦Fr, after *Faenza*, Italy, original place of its manufacture⟧ opaquely glazed earthenware

fail (fāl) ***vi.*** ⟦ME *failen* < OFr *faillir*, to fail, miss < L *fallere*, to deceive, disappoint < IE base **ĝhwel-*, to bend, deviate > Sans *hválati*, (he) loses the way, errs, Gr *phēloein*, to deceive⟧ **1** to be lacking or insufficient; fall short *[the water supply is failing]* **2** to lose power or strength; weaken; die away **3** to stop operating or working *[the brakes failed]* **4** to be deficient or negligent in an obligation, duty, or expectation; default **5** to be unsuccessful in obtaining a desired end; be unable to do or become; miss **6** to become bankrupt **7** *Educ.* to get a grade of failure; not pass —***vt.*** **1** to be useless or not helpful to; be inadequate for; disappoint **2** to leave; abandon *[his courage failed him]* **3** to miss, neglect, or omit: used with an infinitive *[he failed to go]* **4** *Educ.* *a)* to give a grade of failure to (a pupil) *b)* to get a grade of failure in (a subject) —***n.*** ⟦ME *faile* < OFr *faile* < the v.⟧ failure: now only in the phrase **without fail**, without failing (to occur, do something, etc.) —**fail of** to fail to achieve; be without

fail·ing (-iŋ) ***n.*** **1** a failure **2** a slight fault or defect; weakness —***prep.*** without; lacking *[failing a good voter turnout, our candidate will lose]* —***SYN.*** FAULT

faille (fīl, fāl; *Fr* fä′y′) ***n.*** ⟦Fr⟧ a soft, ribbed, plainly woven fabric of silk or rayon, for dresses, coats, etc.

fail-safe (fāl′sāf′) ***adj.*** ⟦FAIL, v. + SAFE, ***adj.***⟧ designating, of, or involving a procedure or mechanism designed to prevent malfunctioning or unintentional operation, often specif. of nuclear-armed aircraft —***n.*** such a procedure or mechanism

fail·ure (fāl′yər) ***n.*** ⟦< earlier *failer* < Anglo-Fr < OFr *faillir*: see FAIL⟧ **1** the act of failing or the state or condition resulting from having failed; specif., *a)* a falling short *b)* a losing of power or strength *c)* a breakdown in operation or function *d)* neglect or omission *e)* a not succeeding in doing or becoming *f)* a becoming bankrupt **2** a person or thing that fails **3** *Educ.* *a)* a failing to pass ☆*b)* a grade or mark (usually F) indicating a failing to pass

fain (fān) ***adj.*** ⟦ME joyful, joyfully < OE *fægen*, glad, akin to ON *feginn* < IE base **pek-*, to be satisfied > FAIR[1]⟧ [Archaic] **1** glad; ready **2** reluctantly willing **3** eager —***adv.*** [Archaic] with eagerness; gladly: used with *would* *[he would fain stay]*

fai·né·ant (fā′nē ənt; *Fr* fe nā än′) ***adj.*** ⟦Fr < OFr *faignant*, an idler, orig. prp. of *feindre* (see FEIGN); altered by folk etym. as if < Fr *fait*, (he) does + *néant*, nothing⟧ lazy; idle —***n.*** a lazy, idle person

faint (fānt) ***adj.*** ⟦ME *feint* < OFr, sluggish, orig. pp. of *feindre*: see FEIGN⟧ **1** without strength; weak; feeble **2** without courage or hope; timid **3** done without strength, vigor, or enthusiasm; halfhearted **4** feeling weak and dizzy, as if about to swoon **5** dim; indistinct; unclear **6** far from certain *[a faint chance]* —***n.*** **1** a condition of temporary loss of consciousness as a result of an inadequate flow of blood to the brain; swoon **2** [*pl.*] the crude, impure spirits given off in the first and last stages of the distillation of liquor —***vi.*** **1** to fall into a faint; swoon: often with *away* **2** [Archaic] *a)* to weaken; languish *b)* to lose courage or hope —**faint′ish** ***adj.*** —**faint′ly** ***adv.*** —**faint′ness** ***n.***

faint·heart·ed (-härt′id) ***adj.*** cowardly; timid; shy —**faint′heart′ed·ly** ***adv.*** —**faint′heart′ed·ness** ***n.***

fair[1] (fer) ***adj.*** ⟦ME < OE *fæger*, akin to FAIN, Goth *fagrs*, apt, fit < IE base **pek-*, to be content, make (something) pretty > Lith *púošiu*, to ornament⟧ **1** attractive; beautiful; lovely **2** unblemished; clean *[a fair name]* **3** ⟦< notion that light coloring was desirable⟧ light in color; blond *[fair hair]* **4** clear and sunny; free from storm or the threat of storm **5** easy to read; clear *[a fair hand]* **6** just and honest; impartial; unprejudiced; specif., free from discrimination based on race, religion, sex, etc. *[fair employment practices, fair housing]* **7** according to the rules *[a fair blow]* **8** likely; promising; advantageous *[he is in a fair way to make money]* **9** pleasant and courteous **10** favorable; helpful *[a fair wind]* **11** of moderately good size *[a fair fortune]* **12** neither very bad nor very good; average *[in fair condition]* **13** apparently favorable but really false; specious *[fair words]* **14** [Archaic] without obstacles; clear and open *[a fair road]* **15** *Baseball* of or having to do with the part of the field on or between the foul lines, including home plate —*n.* 1 [Obs.] beauty 2 [Archaic] a woman 3 [Archaic] something fair, or good —*adv.* 1 in a fair manner 2 straight; squarely [struck *fair* in the face] 3 *Baseball* in or into the part of the field that is on or between the foul lines, including home plate —*vi.* [Dial.] to become clear: said of the weather —*vt.* to give a smooth or streamlined surface to —**fair and square** [Informal] with justice and honesty —**fair to middling** [Informal] moderately good; passable —**no fair** not according to the rules: often used as an interjection —**fair′ness** *n.*

SYN.—fair, the general word, implies the treating of both or all sides alike, without reference to one's own feelings or interests [a *fair* exchange]; **just** implies adherence to a standard of rightness or lawfulness without reference to one's own inclinations [a *just* decision]; **impartial** and **unbiased** both imply freedom from prejudice for or against any side [an *impartial* chairman, an *unbiased* account]; **dispassionate** implies the absence of passion or strong emotion, hence, connotes cool, disinterested judgment [a *dispassionate* critic]; **objective** implies a viewing of persons or things without reference to oneself, one's interests, etc. [an *objective* newspaper] See also **beautiful** —*ANT.* **prejudiced, biased**

fair² (fer) *n.* ⟦ME *feire* < OFr < ML *feria* < LL, holiday (in LL(Ec), weekday) < L *feriae*, pl., festivals < OL *fesiae*, akin to L *festus* (see FEAST) < IE base **dhēs-*, used in religious terms > Oscan *fíísnu*, temple, Arm *dik'*, gods⟧ 1 [Historical] a gathering of people held at regular intervals for barter and sale of goods 2 a festival or carnival where there is entertainment and things are sold, often for charity; bazaar ☆3 *a)* an event consisting of a usually competitive exhibition of livestock, handicrafts, garden produce, etc. plus amusement facilities and educational displays *b) short for* WORLD'S FAIR *c)* any of various shows or conventions on a particular theme, typically consisting of booths, educational exhibits, vendors, etc.: usually in combination [science *fair*, book *fair*]

☆**fair ball** *Baseball* a batted ball that is touched in fair territory, that lands in the outfield, that comes to rest in the infield, or that is ruled a home run

Fair·banks¹ (fer′baŋks′), **Douglas (Elton)** 1883-1939; U.S. film actor

Fair·banks² (fer′baŋks′) ⟦after C. W. *Fairbanks* (1852-1918), prominent political figure⟧ city in EC Alas.

☆**fair catch** *Football* a catch of a kicked ball made after signaling that no attempt will be made to run with the ball: opposing players are penalized if they interfere with the catcher

fair copy ⟦< FAIR¹ (see *adj.* 2 & 5): opposed to *foul copy* (see FOUL, *adj.* 14)⟧ an exact copy of a document, manuscript, etc. after final corrections have been made on it

Fair·field (fer′fēld′) 1 ⟦after an Eng village of the same name⟧ city in SW Conn., near Bridgeport 2 ⟦after *Fairfield*, Conn.⟧ city in W Calif., near Vallejo

fair game 1 game that may lawfully be hunted 2 any legitimate object of attack or pursuit

fair·ground (fer′ground′) *n.* [*often pl.*] an open space where fairs are held

fair-haired (fer′herd′) *adj.* 1 having blond hair ☆2 [Informal] favorite [the *fair-haired* boy of the family]

fair·ing¹ (fer′iŋ) *n.* ⟦see FAIR¹, *vt.*⟧ *Engineering* an additional part or structure added to an aircraft, tractor-trailer, etc. to smooth the outline and thus reduce drag

fair·ing² (fer′iŋ) *n.* [Brit.] a gift, esp. one gotten at a fair

fair·ish (fer′ish) *adj.* moderately good, well, large, etc.

Fair Isle ⟦after *Fair Isle*, Scot island where pattern originated⟧ knitted in a pattern of colorful bands; esp., designating a wool sweater with a patterned yoke

fair-lead (fer′lēd′) *n.* ⟦< earlier *fair-leader*⟧ *Naut.* a pulley block, metal ring, etc. used to guide a line and cause it to run easily without chafing

fair·ly (fer′lē) *adv.* ⟦ME: see FAIR¹ & -LY²⟧ 1 justly; equitably 2 moderately; somewhat [*fairly* hot] 3 clearly; distinctly 4 virtually; in effect [he *fairly* flew across the room] 5 [Obs.] *a)* softly *b)* courteously

fair-mind·ed (fer′mīn′did) *adj.* just; impartial; unbiased —**fair′-mind′ed·ly** *adv.* —**fair′-mind′ed·ness** *n.*

Fairness Doctrine [*often* **f- d-**] a rule (1949-87) of the Federal Communications Commission under which TV and radio stations must provide broadcast time for the airing of opposing views on controversial issues

fair play the act or fact of abiding by the rules as in sports or games; fairness and honor in dealing with competitors, customers, etc.

fair sex women collectively: used with *the*: now sometimes considered a patronizing term

☆**fair shake** [Informal] fair, just, or equitable treatment

fair-spo·ken (fer′spōk′ən) *adj.* speaking or spoken courteously

fair trade trade done within the stipulations of a FAIR-TRADE agreement

fair-trade (fer′trād′) *adj.* ☆1 designating or of an agreement whereby a seller undertakes to charge no less than the minimum price set by a manufacturer on a specified trademarked or brand-name commodity: most U.S. states no longer permit such agreements 2 *a)* designating or of goods, as food or clothing, that are produced in developing countries and traded under an agreement in which a buyer in a developed country pays a price to the producer that is higher than the free-market price *b)* of such an agreement, or of a social movement advocating it —*vt.* **-trad′ed, -trad′ing** to sell (a commodity or goods) under such an agreement

fair use *Law* the use of copyrighted material according to defined limits so as not to require permission from the copyright holder

fair·way (fer′wā′) *n.* 1 a navigable channel in a river, harbor, etc.; often, specif., the middle of such a channel 2 the mowed part of a golf course between a tee and a green

Fair·weath·er (fer′weth′ər), **Mount** ⟦named by James COOK¹ in allusion to the state of the weather⟧ mountain on the border between SE Alaska and NW British Columbia: 15,300 ft (4,663 m)

fair-weath·er (fer′weth′ər) *adj.* 1 suitable only for fair weather 2 helpful, dependable, etc. only in agreeable, easy circumstances [*fair-weather* friends]

fair·y (fer′ē) *n., pl.* **fair′ies** ⟦ME, fairyland, fairy < OFr *faerie* < *fée*: see FAY¹⟧ 1 *Folklore* a being usually in human form and having magic powers, specif. one that is tiny, graceful, and delicate 2 [Slang] a male homosexual: term of contempt or derision —*adj.* 1 of fairies 2 fairylike; graceful; delicate —**fair′y·like′** *adj.*

fair·y·land (-land′) *n.* 1 the imaginary land where the fairies live 2 a lovely, enchanting place

fairy ring a circle of mushrooms often seen on grassy ground, originating from one initial mycelium and often accompanied by a circle of darker grass: so called because formerly thought to have been made by the dancing of fairies

fairy shrimp any of an order (Anostraca) of crustaceans, often found in temporary freshwater pools in early spring, having delicate colors and a graceful swimming motion

fairy tale 1 a story about fairies, giants, magic deeds, etc. 2 an account regarded as highly romantic or as fantastic or unbelievable —**fair′y-tale′** *adj.*

Fai·sa·la·bad (fī′säl′ə bäd′, -sal′ə bad′) city in NE Pakistan, near Lahore

fait ac·com·pli (fe tȧ kōn plē′; *E* fāt′ə käm′plē′) *pl.* ***faits ac·com·plis*** (fe tȧ kōn plē′; *E* fāt′ə käm′plē′) ⟦Fr, an accomplished fact⟧ something already done or in effect, making opposition or argument useless

faith (fāth) *n.* ⟦ME *feith* < OFr *feid, fei* < L *fides*, confidence, belief (in LL(Ec), the Christian religion) < *fidere*, to trust < IE base **bheidh-*, to urge, be convinced > BIDE, Gr *peithein*, to persuade, L *foedus*, a compact⟧ 1 unquestioning belief that does not require proof or evidence 2 unquestioning belief in God, religious tenets, etc. 3 a religion or a system of religious beliefs 4 anything believed 5 complete trust, confidence, or reliance 6 allegiance to some person or thing; loyalty See also BAD FAITH and GOOD FAITH —*interj.* [Archaic] indeed; in faith —*SYN.* BELIEF —**break** (or **keep**) **faith** 1 to be disloyal (or loyal) to one's beliefs, principles, etc. 2 to break (or keep) a promise —**in faith** indeed; really —**on faith** through trust; without proof or evidence

Faith (fāth) *n.* ⟦see prec.⟧ a feminine name

☆**faith-based** (fāth′bāst′) *adj.* affiliated with or sponsored by a church or other religious organization

☆**faith cure** FAITH HEALING

faith·ful (fāth′fəl) *adj.* ⟦ME⟧ 1 keeping faith; maintaining allegiance; constant; loyal [*faithful* friends] 2 marked by or showing a strong sense of duty or responsibility; conscientious [*faithful* attendance] 3 accurate; reliable; exact [a *faithful* copy] 4 [Obs.] full of faith, esp. religious faith —**the faithful** 1 the true believers (in any specified religion) 2 the loyal adherents or supporters —**faith′ful·ly** *adv.* —**faith′ful·ness** *n.*

SYN.—faithful implies steadfast adherence to a person or thing to which one is bound as by an oath or obligation [a *faithful* wife]; **loyal** implies undeviating allegiance to a person, cause, institution, etc. which one feels morally bound to support or defend [a *loyal* friend]; **constant** suggests freedom from fickleness in affections or loyalties [a *constant* lover]; **staunch** (or **stanch**) implies such strong allegiance to one's principles or purposes as not to be turned aside by any cause [a *staunch* defender of the truth]; **resolute** stresses unwavering determination, often in adhering to one's personal ends or aims [*resolute* in one's decision] —*ANT.* **faithless**

☆**faith healing** *Religion* the act or an instance of healing an illness or injury by means of prayer or religious faith —**faith healer**

faith·less (fāth′lis) *adj.* ⟦ME *feithles*⟧ 1 not keeping faith; dishonest; disloyal 2 unreliable; undependable 3 lacking faith; unbelieving —**faith′less·ly** *adv.* —**faith′less·ness** *n.*

SYN.—faithless implies failure to adhere as to an oath or obligation [a *faithless* wife]; **false**, in this connection more or less synonymous with **faithless**, stresses failure in devotion to someone or something that has a moral claim to one's support [a *false* friend]; **disloyal** implies a breach of allegiance to a person, cause, institution, etc. [*disloyal* to one's family]; **traitorous** strictly implies the commission of treason; **treacherous** suggests an inclination or tendency to betray a trust [his *treacherous* colleagues]; **perfidious** adds to the meaning of **treacherous** a connotation of sordidness or depravity [a *perfidious* informer] —*ANT.* **faithful**

faits di·vers (fe dē ver′) *sing.* ***fait divers*** (fe dē ver′) ⟦Fr⟧ brief news stories, as those typically found in some French newspapers, that are sensational, lurid, etc.

Fai·yûm (fī yo͞om′, fā-) city in N Egypt, just west of the Nile: also **El Faiyûm**

☆**fa·ji·ta** (fā hē′tä, fə hēt′ə) *n.* ⟦AmSp⟧ a Tex-Mex dish consisting of grilled strips of beef or chicken, often served wrapped in a soft tortilla with vegetable slices or a sauce

fake¹ (fāk) *vt., vi.* **faked, fak′ing** ⟦earlier *feague, feake*, ult. < ? Ger *fegen*, polish, sweep, in 17th-c. thieves' slang, to clean out a (victim's) purse⟧ 1 *a)* to make (something) seem real, satisfactory, etc. by any sort of deception or tampering *b)* to practice deception by pretending or simulating (something) ☆2 to improvise —*n.* 1 anything or anyone not genuine; fraud; counterfeit 2 [Informal] a deceptive act, movement, etc. —*adj.* 1 fraudulent; not genuine; sham; false 2 artificial; not real; specif., made of synthetic fibers, to resemble animal fur [*fake* fur] —*SYN.* FALSE, QUACK[2] —**fake out** [Informal] to deceive or outmaneuver as by a feint, bluff, or deceptive act —**fak'er** *n.* —**fak'er·y** *n.*

fake[2] (fāk) *vt.* **faked, fak'ing** ⟦< ?⟧ *Naut.* to lay out (a line) in long, parallel, partly overlapping lengths so that it will run out freely without kinking: usually with *down*

faking

fak·ey (fā'kē) *adj.* [Informal] inauthentic, hypocritical, phony, etc.

fa·kir (fə kir') *n.* ⟦Ar *faqīr*, lit., poor, a poor man⟧ 1 a member of a Muslim holy sect who lives by begging 2 a Hindu ascetic 3 any Muslim or Hindu itinerant beggar, often one reputed to perform marvels Also sp. **fa·keer'**

fa la (fä lä') 1 syllables used as a refrain in some old songs 2 a type of 16th- and 17th-cent. part song with this refrain Also sp. **fal la**

fa·la·fel (fə läf'əl) *n., pl.* **-fel** ⟦Ar *falāfil*⟧ 1 a small croquette or patty of ground chickpeas and other vegetables, seasoned with spices and deep-fried in oil 2 a sandwich made by stuffing this into the pocket of a pita

Fa·lange (fə lanj', -länj') *n.* ⟦Sp, lit., phalanx < L *phalanx*, PHALANX⟧ a fascist organization, founded in 1933, that became the only official political party of Spain under Franco

Fa·lan·gist (fə lan'jist) *n.* a member of the Falange

Fa·la·sha (fə lä'shə) *n.* ⟦Amharic, lit., exile, immigrant⟧ a member of a people formerly living chiefly in Ethiopia and now in Israel and practicing a form of the Jewish faith: also called *Ethiopian Jew*: the group calls itself *Beta Israel*, "the House of Israel"

fal·cate (fal'kāt', -kit) *adj.* ⟦L *falcatus* < *falx* (gen. *falcis*), a sickle < ? IE base **dhelg-*, to pierce, needle > Ger *dolch*, dagger⟧ sickle-shaped; curved; hooked

fal·chion (fôl'chən, -shən) *n.* ⟦ME & OFr *fauchon* < VL **falcio* < L *falx*: see prec.⟧ 1 a medieval sword with a short, broad, slightly curved blade 2 [Old Poet.] any sword

fal·ci·form (fal'si fôrm') *adj.* ⟦< L *falx*, a sickle (see FALCATE) + -FORM⟧ FALCATE

fal·con (fal'kən; fôl'-, fäl'-, fô'-) *n.* ⟦ME < OFr *faucon* < LL *falco* (gen. *falconis*), deriv. by folk etym. < L *falx* (see FALCATE) because of its curved beak and talons, but prob. < Gmc **falco* (OHG *falcho*) < IE base **pel-*, FALLOW[2]⟧ 1 any bird of prey trained to hunt and kill small game: in falconry the female is called a *falcon*, the male a *tiercel* 2 any of various birds of prey (family Falconidae), with long, pointed wings and a short, curved, notched beak 3 ⟦from the former practice of naming kinds of firearms after birds of prey⟧ a small cannon used from the 15th to the 17th cent.

fal·con·er (-ər) *n.* ⟦ME < OFr *fauconnier*⟧ 1 a person who breeds and trains falcons 2 a person who hunts with falcons

fal·con·et (fal'kə net', fôl'-) *n.* 1 ⟦dim. of FALCON⟧ *Zool.* any small falcon, esp. any of various Asian kinds 2 ⟦It *falconetto* < OIt *falcone*, FALCON: see sense 3⟧ an obsolete type of light cannon, smaller than the falcon

fal·con-gen·tle (fal'kən jent''l, fôl'-) *n.* ⟦ME *faucoun gentil* < Fr: see FALCON & GENTLE⟧ a female falcon, esp. a female peregrine falcon

fal·con·ry (-rē) *n.* ⟦OFr *fauconnerie*⟧ 1 the art of training falcons to hunt game 2 the sport of hunting with falcons

fal·de·ral (fäl'də räl') *n. alt. sp. of* FOLDEROL

fald·stool (fôld'sto͞ol') *n.* ⟦ME *foldstol* < ML *faldistolium*, prob. via OFr *faldestoel* < Frank **faldistol* (see FOLD[1] & STOOL), akin to OHG *faltstuol*, OE *fyldestol*⟧ 1 a portable stool or desk used in praying 2 *R.C.Ch.* a backless chair used as by a bishop when officiating in a church not his own 3 *Anglican Ch.* a desk at which the litany is read

Fal·kirk (fôl'kərk, fô'-) city in E Scotland: site of a battle (1298) in which the Scots under Wallace were defeated by the English

Falk Is *abbrev.* Falkland Islands

Falk·land Islands (fôk'lənd) British crown colony consisting of a group of islands in the S Atlantic, east of the tip of South America: also claimed by Argentina: 4,710 sq mi (12,200 sq km): also **Falklands**: Sp. name MALVINAS

fall (fôl) *vi.* **fell, fall'en, fall'ing** ⟦ME *fallen* < OE *feallan*, to fall, akin to Ger *fallen* < IE base **phol-*, to fall > Lith *púolu*, to fall⟧ I. *to come down by the force of gravity; drop; descend* 1 to come down because detached, pushed, dropped, etc.; move down and land forcibly [apples *fall* from the tree] 2 to come down suddenly from a standing or sitting position; tumble; topple; become prostrate 3 to be wounded or killed in battle 4 to come down in ruins; collapse [the building *fell*] 5 to hang down [hair *falling* about her shoulders] II. *to pass to a position, condition, etc. regarded as lower* 1 to take a downward direction [land *falling* away to the sea] 2 to become lower in amount, number, degree, intensity, value, etc.; drop; abate [prices *fell*] 3 to lose power; be overthrown [the government has *fallen*] 4 to lose status, reputation, dignity, etc. 5 to yield to temptation; do wrong; sin; specif. in earlier use (esp. of women), to lose chastity 6 to be captured or conquered 7 to take on a look of disappointment or dejection [his face *fell*] 8 to become lower in pitch or volume [her voice *fell*] III. *to happen as if by dropping* 1 to take place; occur [the meeting *fell* on a Friday] 2 to come by lot, distribution, inheritance, etc. [the estate *falls* to the son] 3 to pass into a specified condition; become [to *fall* ill, to *fall* in love] 4 to occur at a specified place [the accent *falls* on the third syllable] 5 to be directed by chance [his eye *fell* on a misspelled word] 6 to be spoken in an involuntary way [the news *fell* from his lips] 7 to be born: said of animals 8 to be divided (*into*) [to *fall* into two classes] —*vt.* [Dial.] to fell (a tree, etc.) —*n.* ⟦< the v.⟧ 1 a dropping; descending; coming down 2 a coming down suddenly from a standing or sitting position 3 a hanging down, or a part hanging down 4 a downward direction or slope 5 a becoming lower or less; reduction in value, price, etc. 6 a lowering of the voice in pitch or volume 7 a capture; overthrow; ruin 8 a loss of status, reputation, etc. 9 a yielding to temptation; wrongdoing; moral lapse 10 *a)* a birth (said of animals) *b)* the number of animals born at one birth; litter 11 *a)* something that has fallen [a *fall* of leaves] *b)* a felling of trees, or timber felled at one time 12 that season of the year in which many trees lose their leaves; autumn: in the North Temperate Zone, generally regarded as including the months of September, October, and November 13 the amount of what has fallen [a six-inch *fall* of snow] 14 the distance that something falls 15 [*usually pl., often with sing. v.*] water falling over a cliff, etc.; cascade 16 a broad, turned-down ruff or collar worn in the 17th cent. 17 *a)* [Now Rare] a kind of veil hanging from the back of a woman's hat *b)* lace, ruffles, or other trimming on a dress, usually hanging from the collar 18 a long tress of hair, often synthetic, used by a woman to fill out her coiffure 19 *Mech.* the loose end of the rope, cable, etc. used in a block and tackle 20 *Naut. a)* either of the lines used to lower or hoist a boat at the davits *b)* in a TACKLE (*n.* 2), the part of a rope between the free end and a pulley or between pulleys 21 *Wrestling a)* the act of holding an opponent down so that both shoulders touch the mat for a specified time period; pin *b)* a bout or a division of a match —*adj.* of, in, for, or characteristic of the fall season —**fall about (laughing)** [Brit. Informal] to laugh uproariously or uncontrollably —☆**fall (all) over oneself** [Informal] to behave in too eager or zealous a manner —**fall among** to come among by chance —**fall apart** to crumble, disintegrate, disunite, etc. —**fall away** 1 to take away friendship, support, etc.; desert a person, cause, etc. 2 to become less in size, strength, etc.; specif., to grow thin and weak —**fall back** to withdraw; give way; retreat —**fall back on (or upon)** 1 to turn, or return, to for security or help 2 to retreat to —**fall behind** 1 to be outdistanced; drop behind 2 to fail to pay on time; be in arrears —☆**fall down on** [Slang] to fail or be unsuccessful in (a job, etc.) —☆**fall for** [Informal] 1 to fall in love with; become infatuated with 2 to be tricked or deceived by —**fall foul (or afoul) of** 1 to collide with or become entangled with 2 to get into trouble or conflict with —**fall in** 1 to collapse inward; cave in 2 to agree 3 *Mil.* to line up in proper formation —**fall in with** 1 to meet by chance 2 to meet and join 3 to agree with; comply with —**fall off** 1 to become smaller, less, lighter, etc. 2 to become worse; decline 3 *Naut.* to swing away from the heading, often, specif., to leeward —**fall on (or upon)** 1 to attack 2 to be the duty of —**fall out** 1 to have a disagreement or quarrel, as with a friend or relative, that leads to a breach with that person 2 to happen; result 3 *Mil.* to leave one's place in a formation —**fall short** 1 to be lacking 2 to fail to meet a standard or goal: with *of* —**fall through** to come to nothing; fail —**fall to** to begin; start; specif., *a)* to start attacking *b)* to start eating —**fall under** 1 to come under (an influence, etc.) 2 to be listed or classified as —**ride for a fall** to behave in a manner likely to cause one trouble or injury —☆**take the fall** [Informal] to take the blame or suffer the consequences in place of someone else —**the Fall (of Man)** *Christian Theol.* Adam's sin of yielding to temptation in eating the forbidden fruit, and his subsequent loss of grace: see ORIGINAL SIN —**the fall of the cards** the chance distribution of cards in a given deal

Fa·lla (fä'lyä), **Ma·nuel de** (mä nwel' *th*ə) 1876-1946; Sp. composer

fal·la·cious (fə lā'shəs) *adj.* ⟦L *fallaciosus*⟧ 1 containing a fallacy; erroneous [*fallacious* reasoning] 2 *a)* misleading or deceptive *b)* causing disappointment; delusive —**fal·la'cious·ly** *adv.* —**fal·la'cious·ness** *n.*

fal·la·cy (fal'ə sē) *n., pl.* **-cies** ⟦ME *fallace* < OFr < L *fallacia*, deception, artifice < *fallax* (gen. *fallacis*), deceitful < *fallere*, to deceive: see FAIL⟧ 1 [Obs.] deception 2 aptness to mislead; deceptive or delusive quality [the *fallacy* of the senses] 3 a false or mistaken idea, opinion, etc.; error 4 *a)* an error in reasoning; flaw or defect in argument *b)* *Logic* an argument which does not conform to the rules of logic, esp. one that appears to be sound

fal-lal (fäl läl') *n.* ⟦? contr. < rare *falbala* < Fr, FURBELOW⟧ a useless piece of finery or frippery

fall·a·way (fôl'ə wā') *Basketball* ☆*adj.* designating or of a JUMP SHOT in which the player shoots while leaning back, away from the basket, on his or her descent —*n.* ☆a fallaway shot

fall·back (fôl'bak') *n.* 1 something in reserve that one can turn to for help 2 a withdrawing; retreat

fall·en (fôl'ən) *vi. pp. of* FALL —*adj.* ⟦ME, pp. of *fallen*, to FALL⟧ 1 having come down; dropped 2 on the ground; prostrate 3 having lost status or moral reputation; degraded 4 captured; overthrown 5 ruined; destroyed 6 dead

fall·er (fôl'ər) *n.* 1 a device, as in a stamping machine, that works by falling 2 a person who fells trees

☆**fall·fish** (fôl'fish') *n., pl.* **-fish'** ⟦prob. so named because often found near falls or rapids⟧ a freshwater minnow (*Semotilis corporalis*) found in clear waters of the NE U.S.

☆**fall guy** [Slang] a person made to or left to face the consequences, as of a scheme that has miscarried

fal·li·ble (fal′ə bəl) ***adj.*** ⟦ME < ML *fallibilis* < L *fallere*, to deceive: see FAIL⟧ **1** capable of making a mistake or being deceived **2** liable to be erroneous or inaccurate —**fal′li·bil′i·ty** (-bil′ə tē) ***n.***, **fal′li·ble·ness** —**fal′li·bly** ***adv.***

fall·ing-out (fôl′iŋ out′) ***n.***, *pl.* **fall′ing-outs′** or **fall′ings-out′** a disagreement or quarrel that causes a breach between persons formerly close

falling sickness *former name for* EPILEPSY

falling star METEOR[1] (sense 1)

☆**fall line** **1** the geographical line indicating the beginning of a plateau, usually marked by many waterfalls and rapids **2** *Skiing* the line of direct descent down a hill

Fall Line the line east of the Appalachian Mountains, marking the end of the coastal plains and the beginning of the Piedmont Plateau

☆**fall·off** (fôl′ôf′) ***n.*** the act of becoming less or worse; decline

fal·lo·pi·an tube (fə lō′pē ən) ⟦after Gabriel *Fallopius* (L form of Gabriello *Fallopio*), 1523-62, It anatomist⟧ [*also* **F- t-**] either of two slender tubes that carry ova from the ovaries to the uterus

fall·out (fôl′out′) ***n.*** ☆**1** the descent to earth of radioactive particles, as after a nuclear explosion ☆**2** these particles **3** the negative consequences of any action or decision

fal·low[1] (fal′ō) ***n.*** ⟦ME *falow* < OE *fealh*, akin to *fealh*, harrow, felly (of wheel) < IE base **pelk-*, to turn > Gael *olca*, fallow land⟧ **1** land plowed but not seeded for one or more growing seasons, as to kill weeds or make the soil richer **2** the plowing of land to be left idle in this way —***adj.*** **1** left uncultivated or unplanted **2** untrained; inactive: said esp. of the mind —***vt.*** ⟦ME *falwen* < OE *fealgian* < *fealh*, fallow land; infl. by *fealwian*, to fade < *fealo*: see fol.⟧ to leave (land) unplanted after plowing —**lie fallow** to remain uncultivated, unused, unproductive, etc. for a time —**fal′low·ness** ***n.***

fal·low[2] (fal′ō) ***adj.*** ⟦ME *falwe* < OE *fealo*, akin to Ger *fahl*, fallow < Gmc **falwa* < IE base **pel-*, gray, pale > L *pallidus*⟧ pale-yellow; brownish-yellow

fallow deer ⟦see prec.⟧ a small European deer (*Dama dama*) having a yellowish coat spotted with white in summer

Fall River ⟦transl. of Algonquian name of the Taunton River, which flows into the ocean here⟧ seaport in SE Mass.

Fal·mouth (fal′məth) seaport & resort in Cornwall, SW England, on an inlet (**Falmouth Bay**) of the English Channel

false (fôls) ***adj.*** **fals′er**, **fals′est** ⟦ME < OFr < *fals* < L *falsus*, pp. of *fallere*, to deceive: see FAIL⟧ **1** not true; in error; incorrect; mistaken [*a false argument*] **2** untruthful; lying; dishonest [*a false witness*] **3** disloyal; unfaithful [*a false friend*] **4** deceiving or meant to deceive; misleading [*a false scent*] **5** not real; artificial; counterfeit [*false teeth*] **6** not properly so named; deceptively resembling [*false jasmine*] **7** based on wrong or mistaken ideas [*false pride*] **8** *Mech.* temporary, nonessential, or added on for protection, disguise, etc. [*a false drawer*] **9** *Music* pitched inaccurately —***adv.*** **fals′er**, **fals′est** in a false manner —**play someone false** to deceive, cheat, hoodwink, or betray someone —**put in a false position** to cause misunderstanding of the intentions, opinions, etc. of —**false′ly** ***adv.*** —**false′ness** ***n.***

SYN.—false, in this comparison, refers to anything that is not in essence that which it purports to be and may or may not connote deliberate deception [*false hair*]; **sham** refers to an imitation or simulation of something and usually connotes intent to deceive [*sham piety*]; **counterfeit** and the informal **bogus** apply to a very careful imitation and always imply intent to deceive or defraud [*counterfeit*, or *bogus*, money]; **fake** is a less formal term for any person or thing that is not genuine [*a fake doctor, fireplace, etc.*] See also **faithless** —***ANT.*** **genuine, real**

false arrest *Law* any unlawful detention or restraint of a person by one claiming legal power or authority

false bottom **1** a horizontal partition inside a box, trunk, etc. that fits above the actual bottom, forming a secret compartment **2** the bottom of a glass, as one in which whiskey is served, designed to give the illusion that the glass holds more than it does

false·face (fôls′fās′) ***n.*** a mask, esp. a comical or grotesque one

false fruit *Bot.* a fruit derived from the separate carpels of one flower, the uniting of a cluster of flowers, or tissue other than the ovary; pseudocarp: see TRUE FRUIT, ACCESSORY FRUIT

false·heart·ed (-härt′id) ***adj.*** disloyal; deceitful

false·hood (-hood′) ***n.*** ⟦ME *falshod*: see FALSE & -HOOD⟧ **1** lack of accuracy or truth; falsity; deception **2** the telling of lies; lying **3** a false statement; lie **4** a false belief, theory, idea, etc.

false imprisonment *Law* any unlawful detention or restraint of another person

false keel a narrow keel below the main keel, for protection and increased stability

false pregnancy PSEUDOCYESIS

false pretenses **1** *Law* deliberate misrepresentation of fact in speech or action in order to obtain another's property **2** any deceptive claims or methods used in order to attain a desired result [*votes obtained under false pretenses*]

false relation CROSS RELATION

false ribs the five lower ribs on each side of the human body: so called because not directly attached to the sternum

false start in a race, the act of starting to run, swim, etc. before the official signal has been given —**false′-start′** ***adj., vi.***

false step **1** a misstep; stumble **2** a social blunder

false teeth an artificial denture, esp. a complete one

fal·set·to (fôl set′ō) ***n.***, *pl.* **-tos** ⟦It, dim. of *falso*, false < L *falsus*, FALSE⟧ **1** an artificial way of singing or speaking, in which the voice is placed in a register much higher than that of the natural voice **2** the voice used in such singing, esp. by tenors, usually having a soft, colorless quality **3** a person singing or speaking in falsetto: also **fal·set′tist** —***adj.*** of or singing in falsetto —***adv.*** in falsetto

☆**fals·ies** (fôl′sēz′) ***pl.n.*** [Informal] devices, as pads or breast-shaped forms, worn inside a bra to make the breasts look fuller

fal·si·fi·a·ble (fôl′sə fī′ə bəl) ***adj.*** *Philos.* designating or of a statement, theory, etc. that is so formulated as to permit empirical testing and, therefore, is open to being proven false —**fal′si·fi′a·bil′i·ty** ***n.***

fal·si·fy (fôl′sə fī′) ***n.*** **-fied′**, **-fy′ing** ⟦ME *falsifien* < OFr *falsifier* < ML *falsificare* < L *falsificus*, that acts falsely < *falsus*, FALSE + *facere*, to make, DO[1]⟧ **1** to make false; specif., *a)* to give an untrue or misleading account of; misrepresent *b)* to alter (a record, etc.) fraudulently **2** to prove or show to be untrue or unfounded [*to falsify their hopes*] —***vi.*** to tell falsehoods; lie —**fal′si·fi·ca′tion** ***n.*** —**fal′si·fi′er** ***n.***

fal·si·ty (fôl′sə tē) ***n.*** ⟦ME *falsete* < OFr < L *falsitas*⟧ **1** the condition or quality of being false; specif., *a)* incorrectness *b)* dishonesty *c)* deceitfulness *d)* disloyalty **2** *pl.* **-ties** something false; esp., a lie

Fal·staff (fôl′staf′), **Sir John** in Shakespeare's *Henry IV* and *The Merry Wives of Windsor*, a fat, witty, boastful knight, convivial but dissolute —**Fal·staff′i·an** ***adj.***

Fal·ster (fäl′stər) one of the islands of Denmark, in the Baltic Sea: 198 sq mi (513 sq km)

falt·boat (fält′bōt′) ***n.*** ⟦Ger *faltboot* < *falten*, FOLD[1] + *boot*, BOAT⟧ FOLDBOAT

fal·ter (fôl′tər) ***vi.*** ⟦ME *faltren*, prob. < ON, as in *faltra(sk)*, be uncertain⟧ **1** to move uncertainly or unsteadily; totter; stumble **2** to stumble in speech; speak haltingly; stammer **3** to act hesitantly; show uncertainty; waver; flinch [*to falter under enemy fire*] **4** to lose strength, certainty, etc.; weaken [*the economy faltered*] —***vt.*** to say hesitantly or timidly —***n.*** **1** a faltering **2** a faltering sound —**fal′ter·er** ***n.*** —**fal′ter·ing·ly** ***adv.***

F.A.M. *abbrev.* Free and Accepted Masons

fame (fām) ***n.*** ⟦ME < OFr < L *fama*, fame, reputation, akin to *fari*, to speak < IE base **bhā-*, to speak > BAN[1], BOON[1], Gr *phēmē*, utterance, report⟧ **1** [Rare or Archaic] public report; rumor **2** reputation, esp. good reputation **3** the state of being widely known or much talked about; renown; celebrity —***vt.*** **famed**, **fam′ing** [Archaic] to make famous

famed (fāmd) ***adj.*** ⟦pp. of prec.⟧ much talked about or widely known; famous; renowned (*for* something)

fa·mil·ial (fə mil′yəl, -mil′ē əl) ***adj.*** ⟦Fr: see FAMILY & -AL⟧ of, involving, or common to a family

fa·mil·iar (fə mil′yər) ***adj.*** ⟦ME *familier* < OFr < L *familiaris*, of a household, domestic < *familia*, FAMILY⟧ **1** [Archaic] having to do with a family **2** friendly, informal, or intimate [*to be on familiar terms*] **3** too friendly; unduly intimate or bold; presumptuous **4** having an intimate knowledge of; closely acquainted (*with*) [*familiar with the Bible*] **5** well-known; common; ordinary [*a familiar sight*] **6** domesticated: said of animals —***n.*** **1** *a)* a close friend or associate *b)* [Rare] HABITUÉ *c)* [Archaic] an ecclesiastical servant or agent **2** *Folklore* a spirit or demon constantly attending someone and typically dwelling within, or taking the form of, an animal; also, the animal within which such a spirit or demon dwells —**fa·mil′iar·ly** ***adv.***

SYN.—familiar is applied to that which is known through constant association, and, with reference to persons, suggests informality or even presumption, such as might prevail among members of a family; **close** is applied to persons or things very near to one in affection, attraction, interests, etc.; **intimate** implies very close association, acquaintance, relationship, etc. or suggests something of a very personal or private nature; **confidential** implies a relationship in which there is mutual trust and a sharing of private thoughts, problems, etc. See also **common**

fa·mil·i·ar·i·ty (fə mil′ē er′ə tē, -ar′-) ***n.*** ⟦ME *familiarite* < OFr < L *familiaritas* < *familiaris*: see prec.⟧ **1** close association; intimacy **2** free and intimate behavior; absence of formality and ceremony **3** intimacy that is too bold or unwelcome **4** *pl.* **-ties** a highly intimate act, remark, etc.; often, specif., a caress or other act of sexual intimacy **5** close acquaintance (*with* something)

fa·mil·i·ar·ize (fə mil′yər īz′, -mil′ē ər-) ***vt.*** **-ized′**, **-iz′ing** **1** to make commonly known **2** to make (another or oneself) accustomed or fully acquainted *with* something —**fa·mil′i·ar·i·za′tion** ***n.***

familiar spirit FAMILIAR (*n.* 2)

fam·i·lism (fam′ə liz′əm) ***n.*** a form of social structure in which the needs of the family as a group are more important than the needs of any individual family member —**fam′i·lis′tic** ***adj.***

fam·i·ly (fam′ə lē, fam′lē) ***n.***, *pl.* **-lies** ⟦ME *familie* < L *familia*, household establishment, akin to *famulus*, servant < ? IE **dhe-mo-*, house (< base **dhē-*: see DO[1]) > Sans *dhāman*, household⟧ **1** [Obs.] all the people living in the same house; household: see also EXTENDED FAMILY **2** *a)* a social unit consisting of parents and the children they rear (see also NUCLEAR FAMILY) *b)* the children of the same parents *c)* one's spouse and children **3** a group of people related by ancestry or marriage; relatives **4** all those claiming descent from a common ancestor; tribe or clan; lineage **5** a criminal syndicate under a single leader [*a Mafia family*] **6** a COMMUNE[2] (sense 5) living in one household, esp. under one head **7** a group of things having a common source or similar features; specif., *a) Biol.* a major category in the classification of animals, plants, etc., ranking above a genus and below an order: it can include one genus or many similar genera: the Latinized family names are capitalized but not italicized (Ex.: Felidae, cats) *b) Chem.* a group of chemical elements having similar properties, forming one of the vertical columns of the periodic table *c) Ecol.* a community composed of organisms of the same species *d) Linguis.* a parent language and all the languages and dialects descended from it *e) Math.* a set of curves, functions, or other entities with some shared property —*adj.* **1** of or for a family [a *family* picnic, the *family* car] **2** characteristic of or suitable for a family, esp. one regarded as traditional or typical; wholesome, middle-class, etc. [*family* entertainment] —**in a (or the) family way** [Informal] pregnant; with child

family Bible a large Bible containing pages for recording family births, deaths, and marriages

family circle **1** the close members of a family and intimate friends ☆**2** a section of less expensive seats in the upper balcony of a theater or concert hall

family doctor a doctor, typically a GENERAL PRACTITIONER or FAMILY PRACTITIONER, who looks after the health of the members of a family

family jewels ☆[Slang] the testicles: a jocular usage

family leave temporary leave from work, granted to an employee as to care for a newborn or a sick family member

family man **1** a man who has a wife and children **2** a man devoted to his family and home

family name **1** the name of one's family, used after one's given name; surname **2** a first or middle name that is or was a surname within the family, as the mother's maiden name

family planning the regulation, as by birth control methods, of the number, etc. of children that a family will have

family practitioner a practicing physician who specializes in treating the general medical needs of the whole family

family romance ⟦loose transl. of Ger *Der Familienroman der Neurotiker*, lit., of the family-novel of neurotics, title of a paper by FREUD⟧ **1** *Psychoanalysis* a type of fantasy in which a person maintains that he or she is not the child of his or her real parents but of parents of a higher social class **2** loosely, the system of relationships within a family group

☆**family room** a room in a home, with informal furnishings, used for relaxation and recreation

☆**family style** **1** a way of serving food, as in boardinghouses and some restaurants, in which the people at the table help themselves from large dishes passed around from hand to hand **2** (served) in this way

family tree **1** a genealogical chart showing the relationship of ancestors and descendants in a given family **2** all the ancestors and descendants in a given family

☆**family values** principles or standards regarded as fundamental to the traditional nuclear family

fam·ine (fam′in) *n.* ⟦ME < OFr < VL **famina* < L *fames*, hunger < IE base **dhē-*, to wither away > DAZE⟧ **1** an acute and general shortage of food, or a period of this **2** any acute shortage **3** [Archaic] starvation

fam·ish (fam′ish) *vt., vi.* ⟦ME *famishen*, altered (after verbs ending in *-ish*: see -ISH) < *famen*, aphetic < OFr *afamer* < VL **affamare* < L *ad*, to + *fames*, hunger: see prec.⟧ **1** to make or be very hungry; make or become weak from hunger **2** [Obs.] to starve to death —**fam′ish·ment** *n.*

fa·mous (fā′məs) *adj.* ⟦ME < L *famosus* < *fama*: see FAME⟧ **1** much talked about; having fame, or celebrity; renowned **2** [Informal] excellent; very good; first-rate **3** [Archaic] notorious

SYN.—**famous** is applied to persons or things that have received wide public attention and are generally known and talked about; **renowned** suggests a being named publicly again and again as for some outstanding quality, achievement, etc.; **celebrated** is applied to persons or things that have received much public honor or praise; **noted** implies a being brought to the wide notice of the public for some particular quality; **notorious**, in current usage, suggests a being widely but unfavorably known or talked about; **distinguished** implies a being noted as superior in its class or of its kind; **eminent** more strongly stresses the conspicuous superiority of persons or things; **illustrious** suggests a reputation based on brilliance of achievement or splendidness of character —*ANT.* **obscure, unknown**

fa·mous·ly (fā′məs lē) *adv.* **1** in a manner that is or that has become famous or notorious **2** in words that have become famous [as Patrick Henry *famously* said, "Give me liberty, or give me death!"] **3** excellently; very well [they got along *famously*]

fam·u·lus (fam′yoo ləs) *n., pl.* **-li′** (-lī′) ⟦< L, a servant: see FAMILY⟧ an assistant, esp. of a medieval scholar or sorcerer

fan[1] (fan) *n.* ⟦ME *fanne* < OE *fann* < L *vannus*, basket for winnowing grain < IE base **wē-*, to blow, flutter > WIND[2], WINNOW⟧ **1** [Historical] a device for winnowing grain **2** any device or machine used to set up a current of air for ventilating or cooling; specif., *a)* any flat surface moved by hand *b)* a folding device made of paper, cloth, etc. which when opened has the shape of a sector of a circle *c)* a device consisting of one or more revolving blades or vanes attached to a rotary hub and operated by a motor **3** anything in the shape of a FAN[1] (*n.* 2*b*), as the tail of a bird **4** in a windmill, a small vane that keeps the large vanes, or sails, at right angles to the wind —*vt.* **fanned**, **fan′ning** ⟦ME *fannen* < OE *fannian*⟧ **1** to move or agitate (air) with or as with a fan **2** to direct, with or as with a fan, a current of air toward or on **3** to stir up; excite **4** to blow or drive away with a fan **5** to spread out into the shape of a FAN[1] (*n.* 2*b*) **6** to separate (grain) from chaff ☆**7** [Slang] to spank ☆**8** [Informal] to fire (a pistol) several times quickly in succession by slapping the hammer back as with the alternate hand between shots ☆**9** [Slang] *Baseball* to strike (a batter) out —*vi.* ☆[Slang] *Baseball* to strike out —**fan out** to scatter or spread out like an open FAN[1] (*n.* 2*b*) —**fan the air** to strike at but fail to hit something

☆**fan**[2] (fan) *n.* ⟦contr. < fol.⟧ a person enthusiastic about a specified sport, pastime, or performer; devotee [a baseball *fan*, movie *fan*]

fa·nat·ic (fə nat′ik) *adj.* ⟦< L *fanaticus*, of a temple, hence enthusiastic, inspired < *fanum*, a temple: see FANE⟧ FANATICAL —*n.* a person whose extreme zeal, piety, etc. goes beyond what is reasonable; zealot —*SYN.* ZEALOT

fa·nat·i·cal (-i kəl) *adj.* unreasonably enthusiastic; overly zealous —**fa·nat′i·cal·ly** *adv.*

fa·nat·i·cism (-ə siz′əm) *n.* excessive and unreasonable zeal

fa·nat·i·cize (-ə sīz′) *vt., vi.* **-cized′**, **-ciz′ing** to make or become fanatical

fan belt a tough, thin belt on most automotive engines connecting the crankshaft to the cooling fan, alternator, etc.

☆**fan·boy** (fan′boi′) *n.* [Slang] a man or boy who is a devoted fan, as of comic books, science fiction, or certain types of computer technology: often a humorous or dismissive term

fan·cied (fan′sēd) *adj.* imaginary; imagined

fan·ci·er (fan′sē ər) *n.* a person with a special interest in and knowledge of something, particularly of the breeding of plants or animals [a dog *fancier*]

fan·ci·ful (fan′sə fəl) *adj.* **1** full of fancy; indulging in fancies; imaginative in a playful way; whimsical **2** created in the fancy; imaginary; not real [a *fanciful* tale] **3** showing fancy in construction or design; quaint; odd [*fanciful* costumes] —**fan′ci·ful·ly** *adv.* —**fan′ci·ful·ness** *n.*

fan·cy (fan′sē) *n., pl.* **-cies** ⟦ME *fantsy*, contr. < *fantasie*: see FANTASY⟧ **1** imagination, now esp. light, playful, or whimsical imagination **2** illusion or delusion **3** a mental image **4** an arbitrary idea; notion; caprice; whim **5** an inclination, liking, or fondness, often transient [to take a *fancy* to someone] **6** [Rare] critical taste or judgment in art, dress, etc. —*adj.* **-ci·er**, **-ci·est** **1** based on fancy; capricious; whimsical; fanciful **2** higher than real value; extravagant [a *fancy* price] **3** made or added to please the fancy; ornamental; decorated; not plain; elaborate [a *fancy* necktie] **4** of superior skill; intricate and difficult [*fancy* diving] **5** of superior quality, and therefore more expensive [canned goods graded *fancy*] **6** bred for some special feature or excellence of type: said of animals —*vt.* **-cied**, **-cy·ing** **1** to form an idea of; imagine **2** to have a liking for; be fond of [to *fancy* rich desserts] **3** to believe something without being sure; suppose [they are, I *fancy*, still friends] —**fancy (that)!** can you imagine (that)! —**the fancy** [Obs.] the enthusiasts of some sport or hobby, esp. boxing —**fan′ci·less** *adj.* —**fan′ci·ly** *adv.* —**fan′ci·ness** *n.*

☆**fan·cy dan** ⟦prec. + (prob.) *Dan*, nickname for DANIEL[1]⟧ [Slang] a flashy, ostentatious person, often one who lacks real skill

fancy dress a masquerade costume

fan·cy-free (fan′sē frē′) *adj.* **1** free to fall in love; not married, engaged, etc. **2** free from worry; carefree

fancy man [Old Informal] a man supported by a woman; esp., a pimp

fancy woman [Old Informal] **1** a mistress **2** a prostitute

fan·cy·work (fan′sē wurk′) *n.* embroidery, crocheting, and other ornamental needlework

F & AM or **F & M** *abbrev.* Free and Accepted Masons

fan·dan·go (fan daŋ′gō′) *n., pl.* **-gos′** ⟦Sp⟧ **1** a lively Spanish dance in rhythm varying from slow to quick 3/4 time **2** music for this **3** a foolish act

☆**fan·dom** (fan′dəm) *n.* fans collectively, as of a sport or entertainer

F & WS *abbrev.* Fish and Wildlife Service

fane (fān) *n.* ⟦L *fanum*, sanctuary, temple < **fasnom* < IE base **dhēs-*: see FAIR[2]⟧ [Archaic] a temple or church

fan·fare (fan′fer′) *n.* ⟦Fr < *fanfarer*, to blow trumpets, prob. < *fanfaron*, braggart: see fol.⟧ **1** *a)* a loud flourish of trumpets *b)* a very brief musical piece serving as to introduce a dignitary or announcement **2** noisy or showy display

fan·fa·ron·ade (fan′fə rə nād′) *n.* ⟦Fr *fanfaronnade* < Sp *fanfarronada* < *fanfarrón*, boaster, prob. < Ar *farfār*, loquacious⟧ boasting talk or showy action; bluster

fan·fold paper (fan′fōld′) ⟦in allusion to the way in which a paper FAN[1] is folded⟧ paper that is perforated at regular intervals and folded on the perforations in alternating directions, designed to lie in flat stacks for continuous feeding, as into a computer printer

fang (faŋ) *n.* ⟦ME, that which is seized < OE < base of *fon*, to take, catch, akin to Ger *fangen* < IE base **pak*, **paĝ*, to fasten, tie > L *pangere* (see PEACE), Sans *pāś-*, noose⟧ **1** *a)* one of the long, pointed teeth with which meat-eating animals seize and tear their prey; canine tooth *b)* one of the long, hollow or grooved teeth through which poisonous snakes inject their venom *c)* the root of a tooth **2** the pointed part of something —*SYN.* TOOTH —**fanged** (faŋd) *adj.*

FANGS

Fang (faŋ, fäŋ) *n.* ⟦< Fr *Fan*, apparently < *Fang Pangwe*, self-designation⟧ **1** *pl.* **Fang** or **Fangs** a member of an African people living in N Gabon, S Cameroon, and Equatorial Guinea **2** the Bantu language of this people

fan·jet (fan′jet′) *n.* **1** TURBOFAN (sense 1) **2** an aircraft propelled by such an engine

fan·light (fan′līt′) ***n.*** a semicircular window, often with sash bars in a fanlike arrangement, over a door or larger window

☆**fan mail** letters, esp. of praise or adulation from strangers, received by a prominent or well-known person

fan·ner (fan′ər) ***n.*** a person or thing that fans

Fan·nie or **Fan·ny** (fan′ē) ***n.*** a feminine name: see FRANCES

☆**Fannie Mae** (mā′) ⟦altered (as if a given name) < pronun. of its abbrev., *FNMA*⟧ *informal name for* Federal National Mortgage Association: a government-sponsored corporation, formerly a federal agency, which purchases mortgages from lending institutions and sells mortgage-backed securities to investors

☆**fan·ny** (fan′ē) ***n.,*** *pl.* **-nies** ⟦< ? FAN[1], *vt.* 7⟧ [Informal] the buttocks

fanny pack ⟦< prec.: so called because often worn at the back of the waist⟧ a small, usually zippered purse or pouch worn at the waist, for carrying keys, a wallet, etc.

fan·on (fan′ən) ***n.*** ⟦ME *fanoun* < OFr *fanon* < Frank *fano,* piece of cloth, akin to Ger *fahne,* banner < IE base **pan-,* fabric > Gr *pēnos,* L *pannus*⟧ a capelike vestment worn by the pope when celebrating a High Mass

fan palm any palm tree with broad, fan-shaped leaves: see FEATHER PALM

☆**fan·tab·u·lous** (fan tab′yoo ləs, -yə-) ***adj.*** ⟦FANT(ASTIC) + (F)ABULOUS⟧ [Slang] remarkably good

fan·tail (fan′tāl′) ***n.*** **1** a part, tail, or end spread out like an opened fan **2** *Naut. a)* the overhanging portion of the stern on some ships *b)* the part of the main deck at the stern **3** any of various birds with a very broad tail, as a variety of pigeon

fan-tan (fan′tan′) ***n.*** ⟦Chin *fan t'an,* lit., repeated divisions⟧ **1** a Chinese gambling game in which the players bet on the number of beans, etc. that will be left from a pile after it has been counted off in fours **2** a card game in which the players seek to discard all their cards in proper sequence Also written **fan tan**

fan·ta·sia (fan tā′zhə, -zē ə; fant′ə zē′ə) ***n.*** ⟦It < L *phantasia:* see FANTASY⟧ **1** *a)* any of a number of predominantly improvisational musical compositions, with a structure determined by the composer's fancy *b)* a literary work similarly constructed **2** a medley of familiar tunes

fan·ta·sist (fan′tə sist, -zist; fan tā′zhist) ***n.*** a person who creates a fantasy or fantasies

fan·ta·size (fant′ə sīz′) ***vt.*** **-sized′, -siz′ing** ⟦FANTAS(Y) + -IZE⟧ to create or imagine in a fantasy; have daydreams about —***vi.*** to indulge in fantasies

fan·tasm (fan′taz′əm) ***n.*** *archaic sp. of* PHANTASM

fan·tast (-tast′) ***n.*** an impractical dreamer; visionary

fan·tas·tic (fan tas′tik) ***adj.*** ⟦ME *fantastik* < OFr *fantastique* < ML *fantasticus* < LL *phantasticus* < Gr *phantastikos,* able to present or represent to the mind < *phantazein,* to make visible < *phainein,* to show: see FANTASY⟧ **1** existing in the imagination; imaginary; unreal *[fantastic* terrors*]* **2** having a strange or weird appearance; grotesque; odd *[fantastic* designs*]* **3** strange and unusual; extravagant; capricious; eccentric *[*a *fantastic* plan*]* **4** seemingly impossible; incredible *[fantastic* progress in science*]* Also **fan·tas′ti·cal** —***n.*** [Archaic] a person who is fantastic in behavior, dress, etc.; eccentric —**fan·tas′ti·cal·ly** ***adv.*** —**fan·tas′ti·cal·ness** ***n.***

SYN.—**fantastic** implies a lack of restraint in imagination, suggesting that which is extravagantly fanciful or unreal in design, conception, construction, etc. *[fantastic* notions*]*; **bizarre** suggests that which is extraordinarily eccentric or strange because of startling incongruities, extreme contrasts, etc. *[*music with a *bizarre* atonality*]*; **grotesque** suggests a ludicrously unnatural distortion of the normal or real, or a fantastic combination of elements *[*the *grotesque* grimaces of the comedian*]*

fan·tas·ti·cate (-ti kāt′) ***vt.*** **-cat′ed, -cat′ing** to make fantastic —**fan·tas′ti·ca′tion** ***n.***

fan·ta·sy (fant′ə sē, -zē) ***n.,*** *pl.* **-sies** ⟦ME *fantasie* < OFr < L *phantasia,* idea, notion < Gr, appearance of a thing < *phainein,* to show, appear < IE base **bhā-,* to gleam, shine > OE *bonian,* to ornament⟧ **1** imagination or fancy; esp., wild, visionary fancy **2** an unnatural or bizarre mental image; illusion; phantasm **3** an odd notion; whim; caprice **4** *a)* a work of fiction portraying highly IMAGINATIVE (sense 3) characters or settings that have no counterparts in the real world *b)* such works, collectively, as a literary form; specif., those works dealing with dragons, elves, ghosts, etc. **5** *Music* FANTASIA (sense 1*a*) **6** *Psychol. a)* a more-or-less connected series of mental images, as in a daydream, usually involving some unfulfilled desire *b)* the activity of forming such images —***vt.*** **-sied, -sy·ing** to form fantasies about —***vi.*** to indulge in fantasies, as by daydreaming —***adj.*** **1** of or like a fantasy **2** of or pertaining to any of various games in which scoring is keyed statistically to the performances of actual players in a particular sport

fan·ta·sy·land (-land′) ***n.*** any fantastic or unreal place, as one imagined in a fantasy

fan·tod (fan′täd′) ***n.*** ⟦prob. < FANT(ASTIC) + *-od* < ?⟧ [Informal] a nervous condition: usually in the humorous phrase **the fantods,** a state of restless anxiety

fan tracery the decoration on fan vaulting

fan vaulting *Archit.* vaulting in which the ribs are spread out like those of a fan

fan·wise (fan′wīz′) ***adv.*** opened out like a folding fan

☆**fan·zine** (fan′zēn′) ***n.*** ⟦FAN[2] + (MAGA)ZINE⟧ a magazine, usually produced by amateurs, devoted to a special-interest group, such as fans of science fiction or comic books

FAO *abbrev.* Food and Agriculture Organization (of the United Nations)

FAQ (fak) ***n.,*** *pl.* **FAQs** ⟦*f(requently) a(sked) q(uestions)*⟧ **1** a series of questions paired with answers, as in an online document, that provides basic information about something **2** any such question

far (fär) ***adj.*** **far′ther, far′thest**: see also FURTHER, FURTHEST ⟦ME *farr, fer* (> dial. form *fur*) < OE *feorr,* akin to OHG *ferro* < IE base **per-,* forward, beyond > L *per,* Gr *per*⟧ **1** distant in space or time; not near; remote **2** extending a long way *[*a *far* journey*]* **3** more distant *[*the *far* side of the room*]* **4** very different in quality or nature *[far* from poor*]* —***adv.*** **far′ther far′thest**: see also FURTHER, FURTHEST **1** very distant in space, time, or degree **2** to or from a great distance in time or position **3** very much; considerably *[far* better*]* **4** to a certain distance or degree *[*how *far* did you go?*]* —***n.*** a distant place *[*to come from *far]* —**as far as 1** to the distance, extent, or degree that or of *[*the bus goes *as far as* the county line; *as far as* I'm concerned, let's skip lunch*]* **2** [Informal] with reference to; concerning; as for *[as far as* the weather, bring a jacket*]* —**by far** considerably; to a great degree; very much: also **far and away** —**far and near** everywhere —**far and wide** widely; everywhere —**far be it from me** I would not presume or wish —**far gone** *see phrase under* GONE —**far out** FAR-OUT —**go far 1** to cover much extent; last long **2** to accomplish much; achieve much success —**go too far** to improperly exceed normal or expected bounds —**in so far as** to the extent or degree that —**so far** up to this place, time, or degree: also **thus far** —**so far as** to the extent or point that —**so far, so good** up to this point everything is or has been all right

SYN.—**far** generally suggests that which is an indefinitely long way off in space, time, relation, etc. *[far* lands*]*; **distant,** although also suggesting a considerable interval of separation *[*a *distant* sound*]*, is the term used when the measure of any interval is specified *[*desks four feet *distant* from one another*]*; **remote** is applied to that which is far off in space, time, connection, etc. from a place, thing, or person understood as a point of reference *[*a *remote* village*]*; **removed,** used in the predicate, stresses separateness, distinctness, or lack of connection more strongly than **remote** —*ANT.* **near, close**

far·ad (far′ad′, -əd) ***n.*** ⟦after Michael FARADAY⟧ the basic unit of electric capacitance in the SI and MKS systems, equal to the capacitance of a capacitor that stores a charge of one coulomb when one volt is applied: abbrev. F

far·a·day (far′ə dā′) ***n.*** ⟦after fol.⟧ a unit of quantity of electricity, used especially in electrolysis, equal to the amount of charge needed to free one mole of a univalent element (*c.* 96,485 coulombs): abbrev. *F:* often called **Faraday constant**

Far·a·day (far′ə dā′), **Michael** 1791-1867; Eng. scientist: noted esp. for his work in electricity & magnetism

fa·rad·ic (fə rad′ik) ***adj.*** ⟦see FARAD⟧ *Elec.* of or pertaining to an intermittent, asymmetrical alternating current produced by the secondary winding of an induction coil

far·a·dize (far′ə dīz′) ***vt.*** **-dized′, -diz′ing** ⟦after Michael FARADAY: see -IZE⟧ to treat or stimulate (a muscle or nerve) with faradic current —**far′a·di·za′tion** ***n.***

far·an·dole (far′ən dōl′) ***n.*** ⟦Fr < Prov *farandoulo*⟧ **1** a lively dance of S France, in 6/8 time, by a winding chain of dancers **2** the music for this dance

far·a·way (fär′ə wā′) ***adj.*** **1** distant in time, place, degree, etc. **2** dreamy; abstracted *[*a *faraway* look*]*

farce (färs) ***n.*** ⟦Fr, stuffing, hence farce < VL **farsa* < pp. of L *farcire,* to stuff: early farces were comic interludes between acts of plays⟧ **1** [Now Rare] stuffing, as for a fowl **2** an exaggerated comedy based on broadly humorous, highly unlikely situations **3** broad humor of the kind found in such plays **4** something absurd or ridiculous, as an obvious pretense *[*his show of grief was a *farce]* —***vt.*** **farced, farc′ing** to fill out with or as with stuffing or seasoning *[*to *farce* a play with old jokes*]*

far·ceur (fär sʉr′; -sōōr′, -soor′) ***n.*** ⟦Fr⟧ **1** an actor in farces **2** a writer of farces **3** a joker; humorist; wag

far·ci·cal (fär′si kəl) ***adj.*** of, or having the nature of, a farce; absurd, ridiculous, etc. —*SYN.* FUNNY —**far′ci·cal′i·ty** (-kal′ə tē) ***n.,*** *pl.* **-ties** —**far′ci·cal·ly** ***adv.***

far·cy (fär′sē) ***n.*** ⟦ME *farsine* < OFr *farcin* < ML *farcina* (for LL *farciminum*) < L *farcimen,* a sausage < *farcire,* to stuff⟧ a chronic form of glanders characterized by skin ulcers and swollen lymph vessels

far·del (färd′'l) ***n.*** ⟦ME < OFr < OIt *fardello,* dim. < *fardo,* a bundle, pack < Ar *farda,* a bundle, camel's load⟧ [Archaic] **1** a pack; bundle **2** a burden; misfortune

fare (fer) ***vi.*** **fared, far′ing** ⟦ME *faren* < OE *faran,* to go, wander, akin to Ger *fahren* & Du *raren* < IE base **per-,* to come over, transport > L *portare,* to carry, Gr *peran,* to pass over, *peira,* a trial, *poros,* a way⟧ **1** [Old Poet.] to travel; go **2** to happen; result *[*how did it *fare* with him?*]* **3** to be in a specified condition or position; get on; go through an experience *[*he *fared* well on his trip*]* **4** to eat or be given food —***n.*** **1** money paid or to be paid for transportation in a train, taxi, plane, etc. **2** a passenger who pays a fare **3** *a)* food available to be eaten *b)* the usual kind of diet **4** [Archaic] the condition of things —*SYN.* FOOD

Far East EAST ASIA: the term sometimes includes the countries of Southeast Asia & the Malay Archipelago

fare·box (fer′bäks′) ***n.*** a boxlike device used to collect fares on a bus, in a subway system, etc.

fare-thee-well (fer′thē wel′) ***n.*** ☆the highest or ultimate degree: used chiefly in the phrase **to a fare-thee-well**: also **fare-you-well**

fare·well (fer wel′; *for adj.* fer′wel′) *interj.* ⟦FARE (imper.) + WELL[2]⟧ used in parting with another or others, usually to express good wishes —*n.* **1** words spoken at parting, usually of good wishes **2** a leaving or going away —*adj.* parting; last; final [*a farewell gesture*]

Farewell, Cape southernmost tip of Greenland

☆**fare·well-to-spring** (-tə spriŋ′) *n.* a W American plant (*Clarkia amoena*) of the evening-primrose family, with showy purple, pink, or white flowers

far·fal·le (fär fä′lā′, -lē) *n.* ⟦It, pl. of *farfalla*, lit., butterfly⟧ pasta in a shape suggestive of butterflies or bow ties

far·fel (fär′fəl) *n.* ⟦Yiddish *farfal, ferfel* < MHG *varvelen*, soup with fragments of dough or beaten egg⟧ noodle dough formed into small grains or pellets

far-fetched (fär′fecht′) *adj.* **1** [Archaic] brought from a distance **2** that is barely believable based on logical or normal thinking

far-flung (-fluŋ′) *adj.* extending over a wide area

Far·go (fär′gō) ⟦after W. G. *Fargo*, of Wells, Fargo & Co., express shippers⟧ city in E N.Dak., on the Red River of the North

fa·ri·na (fə rē′nə) *n.* ⟦ME < L, ground grain, meal < *far*, sort of grain, spelt < IE base **bhares-* > OE *bere*, BARLEY⟧ **1** flour or meal made from cereal grains (esp. whole wheat), potatoes, nuts, etc. and eaten as a cooked cereal **2** potato starch or other starch

far·i·na·ceous (far′ə nā′shəs) *adj.* ⟦LL *farinaceus* < L *farina*: see prec.⟧ **1** containing, consisting of, or made from flour or meal **2** like meal **3** containing starch

far·i·nose (far′ə nōs′) *adj.* ⟦LL *farinosus*⟧ **1** producing farina **2** full of meal; mealy **3** *Biol.* producing or covered with a powderlike substance

☆**far·kle·ber·ry** (fär′kəl ber′ē) *n., pl.* **-ries** ⟦< ?⟧ an evergreen shrub or small tree (*Vaccinium arboreum*) of the heath family, with bell-shaped, white flowers and round, black berries, found in the S U.S.

farm (färm) *n.* ⟦ME < OFr *ferme* < ML *firma*, fixed payment, farm < *firmare*, to farm, lease, orig., to make a contract < L, to make firm, secure < *firmus*, FIRM[1]⟧ **1** *a)* [Obs.] a fixed sum payable at regular intervals, as rent or taxes *b)* the letting out, for a fixed amount, of the collection of taxes, with the privilege of keeping all that is collected *c)* the condition of being let out at a fixed rent **2** a district of a country leased out by a government for the collection of taxes **3** a piece of land (with house, barns, etc.) on which crops or animals are raised: orig., such land let out to tenants **4** any place where certain things are raised [*a tract of water for raising fish is a fish farm*] **5** *a)* an area containing a group of units for storage, production, etc. [*a tank farm, the turbines on a wind farm*] *b)* [Slang] a place or institution characterized by a specified type of customer, patient, service, etc. (often jocular or deprecating) [*funny farm, fat farm*] **6** *Sports* a minor-league team, esp. a baseball team, having an agreement with a major-league team to train its young or inexperienced players: in full **farm club (***or* **team)** —*vt.* **1** to cultivate (land) **2** to cultivate or rear (plants or animals) on a farm **3** to collect the taxes and other fees of (a business) on a commission basis or for a fixed amount **4** to turn over to another for a fee —*vi.* to work on or operate a farm; raise crops or animals on a farm —**farm out 1** to rent (land, a business, etc.) in return for a fixed payment **2** to send (work) from a shop, office, etc. to workers on the outside **3** to let out the labor of (a convict, etc.) for a fixed amount **4** to destroy the fertility of (land), as by failing to rotate crops ☆**5** *Baseball* to assign to a FARM (*n.* 6) —**farm′a·ble** *adj.*

farm·er (fär′mər) *n.* ⟦ME *fermour*, farmer, bailiff < Anglo-Fr *fermer* < OFr *fermier* < *ferme*: see prec.⟧ **1** a person who earns a living by farming; esp., one who manages or owns a farm **2** [Historical] a person who pays for a right, as to collect and keep taxes

Far·mer (fär′mər), **Fannie (Merritt)** 1857-1915; U.S. teacher & writer on cooking

farmer (*or* **farmer's) cheese** a mild, firm cheese, somewhat like cottage cheese with most of the liquid pressed out: also called **farm cheese**

farm·hand (färm′hand′) *n.* **1** a hired laborer on a farm **2** a player on a farm club: see FARM (*n.* 6)

farm·house (-hous′) *n.* a house on a farm; esp., the main dwelling house on a farm

farm·ing (fär′miŋ) *adj.* of or for agriculture —*n.* **1** the business of operating a FARM (*n.* 3 & 4) **2** the letting out to farm of land, revenue, etc.

farm·land (färm′land′) *n.* land used or suitable for use in farming

farm·stead (-sted′) *n.* the land and buildings of a farm

farm·work·er (-wurk′ər) *n.* FARMHAND (sense 1)

farm·yard (-yärd′) *n.* the yard surrounding or enclosed by the farm buildings

far·o (fer′ō) *n.* ⟦Fr *pharaon*, PHARAOH (< LL(Ec) *Pharao*); so named from the picture of a Pharaoh (as the king) on French playing cards orig. used for the game⟧ a gambling game in which the players bet on the cards to be uncovered by the removal of cards from the top of the dealer's pack

Far·oe Islands (fer′ō) group of Danish islands in the N Atlantic, between Iceland & the Shetland Islands: 540 sq mi (1,399 sq km)

Far·o·ese (fer′ō ēz′, -ēs′) *n., pl.* **-ese′**, *adj. alt. sp. of* FAEROESE

far-off (fär′ôf′) *adj.* distant; remote

fa·rouche (fə ro͞osh′) *adj.* ⟦Fr < OFr *forasche*, ill-tamed < VL *forasticus*, out-of-doors < L *foras*, outside, out-of-doors, akin to *foris*, DOOR⟧ **1** wild; savage; fierce **2** unsociable in a fierce or surly way; lacking social grace

far-out (fär′out′) *adj.* ☆[Informal] very advanced, experimental, or nonconformist; esp., avant-garde

far point the farthest point at which vision is distinct when the lens, muscles, etc. of the eye are relaxed

Far·quhar (fär′kwər, -kər), **George** 1678-1707; Brit. playwright, born in Ireland

far·ra·go (fə rä′gō, -rā′-) *n., pl.* **-goes** ⟦L, mixed fodder for cattle, mixture, medley < *far*: see FARINA⟧ a confused mixture; jumble; hodgepodge —**far·rag′i·nous** (-raj′ə nəs) *adj.*

Far·ra·gut (far′ə gət), **David Glasgow** (born *James Glasgow Farragut*) 1801-70; U.S. admiral: Union naval commander in the Civil War

far-reach·ing (fär′rēch′iŋ) *adj.* having a wide range, extent, influence, or effect

Far·rell (far′əl), **James T(homas)** 1904-79; U.S. novelist

far·ri·er (far′ē ər) *n.* ⟦ME *ferrour* < OFr *ferreor* < ML *ferrator* < VL **ferrare*, to shoe horses < L *ferrum*, iron⟧ [Chiefly Brit.] a person who shoes horses; blacksmith; also, sometimes, one who treats the diseases of horses

far·ri·er·y (-ē) *n., pl.* **-er·ies** [Chiefly Brit.] the work or shop of a farrier

far·row[1] (far′ō) *n.* ⟦altered (after *v.*) < OE *fearh*, young pig < IE **porkos*, pig (< base **perk-*, to root up, dig) > L *porcus*, PORK, MIr *orc*⟧ **1** [Obs.] a young pig **2** a litter of pigs —*vt., vi.* ⟦ME *farwen*⟧ to give birth to (a litter of pigs)

far·row[2] (far′ō) *adj.* ⟦earlier *ferow*, prob. akin to obs. Du *verrekoe*, barren cow, Ger *färse*, heifer, OE *fearr*, bull⟧ [Chiefly Scot. or North Eng.] not bearing a calf in a given season

far·see·ing (fär′sē′iŋ) *adj.* FARSIGHTED (senses 1 & 2)

Far·si (fär′sē) *n.* the modern Iranian language spoken in Iran and Afghanistan, developed after Old Persian and Pehlevi; Persian

far·sight·ed (-sīt′id; *also, esp. for 2*, -sīt′əd) *adj.* **1** capable of seeing far **2** having or showing prudent judgment and foresight **3** having better vision for distant objects than for near ones; hyperopic —**far′sight′ed·ly** *adv.* —**far′sight′ed·ness** *n.*

fart (färt) *vi.* ⟦ME *ferten* < OE **feortan*, akin to OHG *ferzan* < IE base **perd-* > Sans *párdatē*, Gr *perdomai*⟧ to pass, or emit, gas from the intestines through the anus —*n.* ⟦ME⟧ **1** such a passing of gas **2** [Slang] a person, esp. an old one, regarded as a fool, nuisance, etc. ➥Now somewhat vulgar in all uses —**fart around** [Slang] to spend time idly, foolishly, etc.

far·ther (fär′thər) *adj.* ⟦ME *ferther*, var. of *further*, substituted for regular *ferrer* (compar. of *fer*) < OE *fyrre*, compar. of *feorr*, FAR⟧ **1** *compar. of* FAR **2** more distant or remote **3** additional; further —*adv.* **1** *compar. of* FAR **2** at or to a greater distance or more remote point in space or time **3** to a greater degree or extent; further **4** [Archaic] in addition; further

USAGE—in sense 3 of the *adj.* and senses 3 and 4 of the *adv.*, FURTHER is more commonly used

far·ther·most (-mōst′) *adj.* most distant; farthest

far·thest (fär′thist) *adj.* ⟦ME *ferthest*: see FARTHER⟧ **1** *superl. of* FAR **2** most distant; most remote **3** [Rare] most extended; longest —*adv.* **1** *superl. of* FAR **2** at or to the greatest distance or most remote point in space or time **3** to the greatest degree or extent; most

far·thing (fär′thiŋ) *n.* ⟦ME *ferthing* < OE *feorthing*, lit., a fourthling, fourth part, dim. of *feortha*, FOURTH⟧ **1** a former small British coin, equal to one fourth of a penny **2** a thing of little value; the least amount

far·thin·gale (fär′thiŋ gāl′) *n.* ⟦OFr *verdugalle*, farthingale < Sp *verdugado*, provided with hoops, farthingale < *verdugo*, young shoot of a tree, rod, hoop < *verde* < L *viridis*, green⟧ **1** a hoop, openwork frame, or circular pad worn under the skirt, about the hips, by women in the 16th and 17th cent. **2** the skirt or petticoat worn over this

FAS *abbrev.* **1** fetal alcohol syndrome **2** Foreign Agricultural Service **3** free alongside ship: also **fas**

FASB *service mark* Financial Accounting Standards Board

fasc *abbrev.* fascicle

fas·ces (fas′ēz′) *pl.n.* ⟦L, pl. of *fascis*, a bundle, fagot, packet < IE base **bhasko-*, bundle > MIr *basc*, neckband⟧ a bundle of rods bound about an ax with projecting blade, carried before ancient Roman magistrates as a symbol of authority: later, the symbol of Italian fascism

fasces

Fa·sching (fä′shiŋ) *n.* ⟦Ger < MHG *vastschang* < *vast*, fast + *schanc*, a pouring out, hence, draft (of beer, liquor)⟧ the pre-Lenten period of revelry celebrated in Austria and parts of Germany

fas·ci·a (fash′ē ə, fash′ə; *for 2, 4*, fā′shē ə, -shə) *n., pl.* **-ci·ae′** (-ē) or **-ci·as** ⟦L, a band, sash⟧ **1** a flat strip; band; fillet **2** [Brit.] *a)* an instrument panel or dashboard, as of an automobile *b)* a board over a shop front, bearing the proprietor's name, etc. **3** *Anat.* a thin layer of connective tissue covering, supporting, or connecting the muscles or inner organs of the body **4** *Archit.* a flat, horizontal band or board, specif. *a)* one of two or three making up an architrave *b)* one covering the outer edge of the eaves (also **fascia board**) **5** *Biol.* a distinct band of color —**fas′ci·al** *adj.*

fas·ci·ate (fash′ē āt′) *adj.* ⟦L *fasciatus*, pp. of *fasciare*, to swathe, wrap with bands < *fascia*: see prec.⟧ **1** bound with a band or fillet **2** *Bot.* *a)* abnormally enlarged and flattened, as some plant stems *b)* growing in a fascicle **3** *Zool.* marked by broad, colored bands Also **fas′ci·at′ed**

fas·ci·a·tion (fash′ē ā′shən) *n.* ⟦Fr⟧ **1** the condition of being fasciate **2** a binding up **3** *Bot.* an abnormal broadening, flattening, and clumping of plant stems, as in broccoli

fas·ci·cle (fas′i kəl) *n.* ⟦ME < OFr < L *fasciculus*, dim. of *fascis*: see

FASCES⟧ 1 any of the sections of a book being brought out in installments prior to its publication in completed form 2 a small bundle 3 *Bot.* a small tuft or cluster of fibers, leaves, stems, roots, etc.

fas·cic·u·late (fə sik′yo͞o lit, -lāt′) ***adj.*** ⟦< L *fasciculus*, dim. of *fascis* (see FASCES) + -ATE[1]⟧ formed of, or growing in, bundles or clusters: also **fas·cic′u·lat′ed** (-lāt′id) or **fas·cic′u·lar** (-lər)

fas·cic·u·lus (fə sik′yo͞o ləs) ***n., pl.*** **-u·li′** (-lī′) ⟦L, dim. of *fascis*, a bundle: see FASCES⟧ 1 a small bundle of fibers; specif., a bundle of nerve fibers in the central nervous system 2 FASCICLE (sense 1)

fas·ci·i·tis (fash′ē īt′is) ***n.*** ⟦ModL: see FASCIA & -ITIS⟧ *Med.* inflammation of a fascia [plantar *fasciitis*]

fas·ci·nate (fas′ə nāt′) ***vt.*** **-nat′ed, -nat′ing** ⟦< L *fascinatus*, pp. of *fascinare*, to bewitch, charm < *fascinum*, a charm < ? or akin to Gr *baskanos*, sorcerer⟧ 1 [Obs.] to put under a spell; bewitch 2 to attract or hold motionless, as by a fixed look or by inspiring terror 3 to hold the attention of by being very interesting or delightful; charm; captivate —**SYN.** ATTRACT —**fas′ci·nat′ing·ly** ***adv.***

fas·ci·na·tion (fas′ə nā′shən) ***n.*** 1 a fascinating or being fascinated 2 strong attraction; charm; allure

fas·ci·na·tor (fas′ə nāt′ər) ***n.*** ⟦L, an enchanter⟧ 1 a person who fascinates ☆2 [Old-fashioned] a woman's light scarf, usually knitted or crocheted, worn around the head or neck

fas·cine (fa sēn′) ***n.*** ⟦Fr < OFr < L *fascina*, a bundle of sticks, a fagot < *fascis*: see FASCES⟧ a bundle of sticks bound together, formerly used to fill ditches, strengthen the sides of trenches, etc.

fas·cism (fash′iz′əm) ***n.*** ⟦It *fascismo* < *fascio*, political group < L *fascis*: see FASCES⟧ 1 [**F-**] the doctrines, methods, or movement of the Fascisti 2 [*sometimes* **F-**] a system of government characterized by rigid one-party dictatorship, forcible suppression of opposition, private economic enterprise under centralized governmental control, belligerent nationalism, racism, and militarism, etc. 3 *a)* a political movement based on such policies *b)* fascist behavior See also NAZI

fas·cist (-ist) ***n.*** ⟦It *fascista*: see fol.⟧ 1 [**F-**] *a)* a member of the Fascisti *b)* a member of some similar party; Nazi, Falangist, etc. 2 a person who believes in or practices fascism —***adj.*** 1 [**F-**] of Fascists or Fascism 2 of, believing in, or practicing fascism —**fa·scis·tic** (fə shis′tik, fa-) ***adj.*** —**fa·scis′ti·cal·ly** ***adv.***

Fa·scis·ti (fa shis′tē, fä shē′stē) ***pl.n.*** ⟦It, pl. of *fascista*, a Fascist < L *fascis*: see FASCES⟧ an Italian political organization which seized power and set up a fascist dictatorship (1922-43) under Mussolini

fash (fash) ***vt., vi.*** ⟦< MFr *fascher*, to vex < VL **fasticare* < L *fastidire*, to feel loathing < L *fastidium*: see FASTIDIOUS⟧ [Scot.] to trouble; annoy; vex —***n.*** vexation

fash·ion (fash′ən) ***n.*** ⟦ME *fasoun* < OFr *faceon* < L *factio*, a making: see FACTION[1]⟧ 1 the make, form, or shape of a thing 2 [Now Rare] kind; sort 3 the way in which something is made or done; manner 4 the current style or mode of dress, speech, conduct, etc. 5 something, esp. a garment, in the current style 6 fashionable people as a group [gentlemen of *fashion*] —***vt.*** 1 to make in a certain way; give a certain form to; shape; mold 2 to fit; accommodate (*to*) [music *fashioned* to popular taste] 3 [Obs.] to think up; contrive —**after** (or **in**) **a fashion** in some way or to some extent, but not thoroughly or very well —**fash′ion·er** ***n.***

SYN.—**fashion** is the prevailing custom in dress, manners, speech, etc. of a particular place or time, esp. as established by the dominant section of society or the leaders in the fields of art, literature, etc.; **style**, often a close synonym for **fashion**, in discriminating use suggests a distinctive fashion, esp. the way of dressing, living, etc. that distinguishes persons with money and taste; **mode**, the French word expressing this idea, suggests the height of fashion in dress, behavior, etc. at any particular time; **vogue** stresses the general acceptance or great popularity of a certain fashion; **fad** stresses the impulsive enthusiasm with which a fashion is taken up for a short time; **rage** and **craze** both stress an intense, sometimes irrational enthusiasm for a passing fashion See also **make**

fash·ion·a·ble (-ə bəl) ***adj.*** 1 following the current style; in fashion; stylish 2 of, characteristic of, or used by people who follow the current fashion —**fash′ion·a·ble·ness** ***n.*** —**fash′ion·a·bly** ***adv.***

☆**fash·ion-for·ward** (-fôr′wərd) ***adj.*** 1 stylish; fashionable 2 knowledgeable about the latest styles in clothing, cosmetics, etc.

☆**fash·ion·is·ta** (fash′ən ēs′tə) ***n.*** ⟦FASHION + Sp *-ista*, -IST[1]⟧ [Informal] a person who sets or eagerly follows the latest trends as in clothing and accessories: often a humorous or derisive term

☆**fashion plate** 1 a picture showing a current style in dress 2 a person who dresses fashionably

Fass·bin·der (fas′bin′dər, fäs′-), **Rai·ner Wer·ner** (rī′nər ver′nər) 1945-82; Ger. film director & actor

fast[1] (fast, fäst) ***adj.*** ⟦ME < OE *fæst*, akin to Ger *fest*, firm, stable < IE base **pasto-*, fixed, secure > Arm *hast*⟧ 1 not easily moved, freed, or separated; firm, fixed, or stuck [the ship was *fast* on the rocks] 2 firmly fastened or shut [make the shutters *fast*] 3 loyal; devoted [*fast* friends] 4 that will not fade [*fast* colors] 5 rapid in movement or action; swift; quick; speedy 6 permitting or facilitating swift movement [a *fast* racetrack] 7 taking or lasting a short time [a *fast* lunch] 8 showing or keeping to a time in advance of a standard or scheduled time [his watch is *fast*] 9 *a)* living in a reckless, wild, dissipated way [a *fast* crowd] *b)* promiscuous sexually ☆10 [Informal] glib and deceptive [a *fast* talker] 11 [Slang] acting, gotten, done, etc. quickly and often dishonestly [out for a *fast* buck] 12 *Bacteriology* resistant to dissolution or decolorization, as certain bacteria 13 *Photog.* adapted to or allowing very short exposure time [a *fast* lens, *fast* film] 14 [Now Dial.] complete; sound [a *fast* sleep] —***adv.*** ⟦ME *faste* < OE *fæste* < adj.⟧ 1 firmly; fixedly 2 thoroughly; soundly [*fast* asleep] 3 rapidly; swiftly; quickly; speedily 4 ahead of time 5 in a reckless, dissipated way; wildly 6 [Obs. or Old Poet.] close; near [*fast* by the river] —***n.*** *Naut.* a rope for mooring [a stern *fast*] —☆**a fast one** [Slang] an act intended to deceive; trick; ploy [to pull *a fast one* on someone] —**play fast and loose** to behave with reckless duplicity or insincerity

SYN.—**fast** and **rapid** are generally interchangeable in expressing the idea of a relatively high rate of movement or action, but **fast** more often refers to the person or thing that moves or acts, and **rapid** to the action [a *fast* typist, *rapid* transcription]; **swift** implies great rapidity, but in addition often connotes smooth, easy movement; **fleet** suggests a nimbleness or lightness in that which moves swiftly; **quick** implies promptness of action, or occurrence in a brief space of time, rather than velocity [a *quick* reply]; **speedy** intensifies the idea of quickness, but may also connote high velocity [a *speedy* recovery, a *speedy* flight]; **hasty** suggests hurried action and may connote carelessness, rashness, or impatience —**ANT. slow**

fast[2] (fast, fäst) ***vi.*** ⟦ME *fasten* < OE *fæstan*, akin to Ger *fasten*, Goth *fastan*, lit., hold fast < base of prec.⟧ 1 to abstain from all or certain foods, as in observing a holy day 2 to eat very little or nothing —***n.*** 1 the act of fasting 2 a day or period of fasting —**break one's fast** to eat food for the first time after fasting, or for the first time in the day

☆**fast·back** (fast′bak′) ***n.*** an automobile body which slopes from the roof to the rear bumper

☆**fast·ball** (-bäl′) ***n.*** *Baseball* a pitch thrown with great velocity and that travels in a relatively straight line

☆**fast break** a play, as in basketball, in which a team quickly moves down the playing area in an attempt to score before an adequate defense can be set up

fast day a religious holy day, etc. observed by fasting

fas·ten (fas′ən, fäs′-) ***vt.*** ⟦ME *fastnen* < OE *fæstnian* < base of *fæst*: see FAST[1]⟧ 1 to join (one thing *to* another); attach; connect 2 to make fast or secure, as by locking, shutting, buttoning, etc.; fix firmly in place 3 to hold, fix, or direct (the attention, gaze, etc.) steadily *on* something 4 to cause to be connected or attributed; impute [to *fasten* a crime on someone] 5 to force (oneself) *on* or *upon* another in an annoying way —***vi.*** 1 to become attached or joined 2 to take a firm hold (*on* or *upon*); seize; cling 3 to concentrate (*on* or *upon*) —**SYN.** TIE

fas·ten·er (-ər) ***n.*** 1 a person who fastens 2 any of various devices for fastening things together; fastening

fas·ten·ing (-iŋ) ***n.*** 1 the act or way of making something fast, or secure 2 anything used to fasten; bolt, clasp, hook, lock, button, etc.

☆**fast-food** (fast′fo͞od′) ***adj.*** designating or of a type of restaurant specializing in low-cost carryout food (**fast food**) that is prepared and served quickly

fast forward 1 the setting on an electronic playback device, allowing the user to skip portions and advance at an accelerated speed to a later section of a disc, tape, etc. 2 the act or condition of speeding up and advancing

fast-for·ward (-fôr′wərd) ***vi., vt.*** to advance to a later time at an accelerated speed —***n.*** FAST FORWARD

fas·tid·i·ous (fa stid′ē əs, fə-) ***adj.*** ⟦ME < L *fastidiosus* < *fastidium*, a loathing, disgust < *fastus*, disdain, contempt, pride (< ? IE base **bhars-*, projection, point, BRISTLE) + *taedium*: see TEDIUM⟧ 1 not easy to please; overly exacting or discriminating 2 refined in a dainty or oversensitive way —**SYN.** DAINTY —**fas·tid′i·ous·ly** ***adv.*** —**fas·tid′i·ous·ness** ***n.***

fas·tig·i·ate (fa stij′ē it, -āt′) ***adj.*** ⟦LL *fastigiatus*, for L *fastigatus* < *fastigium*, a slope, roof < IE **bharsti-* < base **bhars-*: see prec.⟧ having a narrow, spirelike shape, as certain kinds of trees

fast lane 1 a lane on an expressway for moving at higher speeds or passing other vehicles 2 a way of living variously regarded as fast-paced, success-oriented, sophisticated, risk-taking, etc.

fast·ness (fast′nis, fäst′-) ***n.*** ⟦ME *fastnesse* < OE *fæstnes*: see FAST[1] & -NESS⟧ 1 the quality or condition of being fast 2 a secure place; stronghold

fast pitch a variety of softball in which the ball is pitched at a high speed with an underhand motion: cf. SLOW PITCH

fast reactor a type of nuclear reactor which makes little or no use of a moderator to slow down the high-energy neutrons

☆**fast-talk** (-tôk′) ***vt.*** [Informal] to persuade with fast, smooth, but often deceitful talk —**fast′-talk′ing** ***adj.***

☆**fast time** [Informal] DAYLIGHT SAVING TIME

fast track 1 FAST LANE (sense 2) 2 a career path offering rapid advancement 3 a building method in which construction begins even before plans and designs are completed

fast-track (-trak′) ***adj.*** 1 speedy or accelerated; expeditious [*fast-track* approval of a new drug] 2 designating or having to do with the power to enter into agreements that are not subject to Congressional modification [the President's *fast-track* authority in trade negotiations] —***vt.*** to speed up the progress of

fas·tu·ous (fas′tyo͞o əs) ***adj.*** ⟦L *fastuosus* < *fastus*: see FASTIDIOUS⟧ 1 haughty; lofty 2 ostentatious; pretentious

fat (fat) ***adj.*** **fat′ter, fat′test** ⟦ME < OE *fætt*, pp. of *fætan*, to fatten, akin to Ger *feist*, plump < OHG *feizzen*, to make fat < IE **poid-* < base **pi-*, to be fat, distended > Gr *pimelē*, lard, Sans *pīná-*, fat⟧ 1 *a)* containing or full of fat; oily, greasy, etc. *b)* having much fat in relation to lean (said of meat) *c)* containing volatile oil *[fat* coal*]* *d)* containing much resin *[fat* wood*]* 2 *a)* fleshy; plump *b)* too plump; corpulent; obese 3 thick; broad *[*the *fat* part of a baseball bat, a *fat* cigar*]* 4 containing something valuable in great quantity; fertile; productive *[fat* land*]* 5 *a)* profitable; lucrative *[*a *fat* job*]* *b)* prosperous *c)* supplied plentifully; ample 6 [Slang] desirable because large or important *[*a *fat* role for an actor*]* —*n.* 1 any of various mixtures of solid or semisolid triglycerides found in adipose animal tissue or in the seeds of plants: they are insoluble in water but soluble in organic solvents 2 any such substance used in cooking 3 fleshiness; plumpness; corpulence 4 the richest or finest part of anything 5 anything unnecessary or superfluous that can be trimmed away 6 *Chem.* a class of neutral lipids consisting of the various triglycerides: they are called *oils* if in the liquid state — *vt., vi.* **fat′ted, fat′ting** ⟦ME *fatten* < OE *fættian*⟧ to make or become fat: now usually FATTEN —**a fat lot** ⟦see *adj.* 5c: used ironically⟧ [Slang] very little or nothing —**chew the fat** [Slang] to talk together; chat —☆**(a) fat chance** ⟦see *adj.* 5c: used ironically⟧ [Slang] very little or no chance —**live off** (or **on**) **the fat of the land** ⟦after LL(Ec) *medulla terrae*, Gen. 45:18⟧ to have, use, or enjoy the finest things, in abundance; live in luxury —**the fat is in the fire** the unfortunate thing has happened and cannot be undone —**fat′ly** *adv.* —**fat′ness** *n.*

Fa·tah (fə tä′, fät′ə) *n.* ⟦Ar, lit., victory, conquest: used as a reverse acronym of *ḥarakat taḥrīr Filasṭīn*, Movement for the Liberation of Palestine⟧ a militant, nationalist Palestinian political faction opposed to the state of Israel

fa·tal (fāt′'l) *adj.* ⟦ME < OFr & < L *fatalis* < *fatum*, FATE⟧ 1 [Obs.] fated; destined; inevitable 2 important in its outcome; fateful; decisive *[*the *fatal* day arrived*]* 3 resulting in death 4 very destructive; most unfortunate; disastrous 5 concerned with or determining fate —**fa′tal·ness** *n.*

SYN.—**fatal** implies the inevitability or actual occurrence of death or disaster *[*a *fatal* disease, a *fatal* mistake*]*; **deadly** is applied to a thing that can and probably (but not inevitably) will cause death *[*a *deadly* poison*]*; **mortal** implies that death has occurred and is applied to the immediate cause of death *[*he has received a *mortal* blow*]*; **lethal** is applied to that which by its very nature or purpose may be a cause of death *[*a *lethal* weapon*]*

fa·tal·ism (-iz′əm) *n.* 1 the belief that all events are determined by fate and, therefore, inevitable 2 acceptance of, or submission to, events as being inevitable —**fa′tal·ist** *n.* —**fa′tal·is′tic** *adj.* —**fa′tal·is′ti·cal·ly** *adv.*

fa·tal·i·ty (fā tal′ə tē, fə-) *n., pl.* **-ties** ⟦Fr *fatalité* < LL *fatalitas* < L *fatalis*, FATAL⟧ 1 fate or necessity; subjection to fate 2 something caused by fate 3 a strong likelihood of ending in disaster 4 a fatal quality; deadly effect; deadliness *[*the *fatality* of any specified disease*]* 5 a death caused by a disaster, as in an accident, war, etc.

fa·tal·ly (fāt′'l ē) *adv.* 1 as determined by fate; inevitably 2 so as to cause death or disaster; mortally

fa·ta mor·ga·na (fät′ə môr gän′ə) ⟦It, lit., MORGAN LE FAY: such mirages were formerly believed to be caused by her⟧ a mirage, esp. one sometimes seen off the coast of Sicily near the Strait of Messina

☆**fat·back** (fat′bak′) *n.* 1 fat from the back of a hog, usually dried and salted in strips 2 MENHADEN

☆**fat cat** [Slang] a wealthy, influential person, specif. one who is a heavy contributor to a political party or campaign

fat cell a cell in connective tissue specialized for the synthesis of glucose, fatty acids, etc. and storage of the derived globules of fat

☆**fat city** ⟦< FAT, *adj.* 5⟧ [*also* **F- C-**] [Slang] a place or condition of prosperity, comfort, success, etc.

fate (fāt) *n.* ⟦ME < L *fatum*, prophetic declaration, oracle < neut. pp. of *fari*, to speak: see FAME⟧ 1 the power or agency supposed to determine the outcome of events before they occur; destiny 2 *a)* something inevitable, supposedly determined by this power *b)* what happens or has happened to a person or entity; lot; fortune 3 final outcome 4 death; destruction; doom 5 [**F-**] any of the three FATES —*vt.* **fat′ed, fat′ing** to destine: now usually in the passive

SYN.—**fate** refers to the inevitability of a course of events as supposedly predetermined by a god or other agency beyond human control; **destiny** also refers to an inevitable succession of events as determined supernaturally or by necessity, but often implies a favorable outcome *[*it was her *destiny* to become famous*]*; **portion** and **lot** refer to what is supposedly distributed in the determining of fate, but **portion** implies an equitable apportionment and **lot** implies a random assignment; **doom** always connotes an unfavorable or disastrous fate

fat·ed (fāt′id) *adj.* 1 ordained or determined by fate; destined 2 destined to destruction; doomed

fate·ful (-fəl) *adj.* 1 [Archaic] revealing what is to come; prophetic 2 having important consequences; often, specif., bringing death or destruction —SYN. OMINOUS —**fate′ful·ly** *adv.* —**fate′ful·ness** *n.*

Fates (fāts) *pl.n. Class. Myth.* the three goddesses who control human destiny and life: see CLOTHO, LACHESIS, ATROPOS

☆**fat farm** [Informal] a resort or spa where people go to lose weight through a regimen of diet and exercise

fath *abbrev.* fathom(s)

fat·head (fat′hed′) *n.* [Slang] a stupid person; blockhead —**fat′head′ed** *adj.*

fa·ther (fä′thər) *n.* ⟦ME *fader* < OE *fæder*, akin to ON *fathir*, OHG *fater*, Goth *fadar* < IE **pətēr* > L *pater*, Gr *patēr*, Sans *pitár*: ult. origin prob. echoic of baby talk, as in PAPA, Hindi *bābū*⟧ 1 a man who has begotten a child; esp., a man as he is related to his child or children 2 *a)* a stepfather *b)* an adoptive father *c)* a father-in-law 3 the male parent of a plant or animal 4 a person regarded as a male parent; protector 5 [**F-**] God, or God as the first person in the Trinity 6 a forefather; ancestor: *usually used in pl.* 7 an originator, founder, or inventor 8 any man deserving of respect or reverence because of age, position, etc. 9 a senator of ancient Rome 10 any of the leaders of a city, assembly, etc.: *usually used in pl.* 11 [*often* **F-**] any of the early Christian religious writers considered reliable authorities on the doctrines and teachings of the Church 12 [*often* **F-**] a Christian priest: used esp. as a title —*vt.* 1 to be the father of; beget 2 to look after or care for as a father does 3 to bring into being; found, originate, or invent 4 to take the responsibility for

Father Christmas *Brit. name for* SANTA CLAUS

father confessor 1 a priest who hears confessions, as in the Roman Catholic Church 2 a person whom one consults, esp. regularly, as about personal difficulties

father figure (*or* **image**) a person who serves as an emotional substitute for one's father

fa·ther·hood (-hood′) *n.* ⟦ME *faderhod*: see -HOOD⟧ 1 the state of being a father; paternity 2 the qualities or character of a father 3 fathers collectively

fa·ther-in-law (-in lô′) *n., pl.* **fa′thers-in-law′** the father of one's wife or husband

fa·ther·land (-land′) *n.* ⟦prob. < Du *vaderland*, Ger *vaterland*⟧ 1 a person's native land or country 2 the land or country of one's ancestors

fa·ther·less (-lis) *adj.* ⟦ME *faderles* < OE *fæderleas*⟧ 1 not having a father living, or lacking a father's protection 2 not knowing the identity of one's father

fa·ther·ly (-lē) *adj.* ⟦ME *faderly* < OE *fæderlic*⟧ 1 of a father 2 having traits considered typical of fathers; kind, protective, wise, etc.; paternal —*adv.* [Archaic] as a father —**fa′ther·li·ness** *n.*

☆**Father's Day** the third Sunday in June, a day set aside (in the U.S.) in honor of fathers

Father Time time personified as a very old man carrying a scythe and an hourglass

fath·om (fath′əm) *n.* ⟦ME *fadme* < OE *fæthm* (akin to OFris *fethm*, OS pl. *fathmōs*), the two arms outstretched (to embrace, measure), akin to Ger *faden*, thread < IE base **pet-*, to stretch out > L *patere*, to stretch out⟧ a unit of length used to measure the depth of water or the length of a nautical rope or cable, equal to 6 ft (1.8288 m) —*vt.* 1 to measure the depth of; sound 2 to get to the bottom of; understand thoroughly —**fath′om·a·ble** *adj.*

☆**fa·thom·e·ter** (fa thäm′ət ər) *n.* ⟦< *Fathometer*, former trademark < prec. + -METER⟧ [*occas.* **F-**] a type of echo sounder

fath·om·less (fath′əm lis) *adj.* 1 too deep to be measured 2 incomprehensible —**fath′om·less·ness** *n.*

fa·tid·ic (fā tid′ik, fə-) *adj.* ⟦L *fatidicus*, prophesying < *fatum*, FATE + *dicere*, to say: see DICTION⟧ of divination or prophecy; prophetic: also **fa·tid′i·cal**

fat·i·ga·ble (fat′i gə bəl) *adj.* that can be fatigued or easily tired —**fat′i·ga·bil′i·ty** *n.*

fa·tigue (fə tēg′) *n.* ⟦Fr < *fatiguer* < L *fatigare*, to weary < **fatis*, exhaustion < base of *fames*, hunger (see FAMINE) + *agere*, to drive, make (see ACT[1])⟧ 1 physical or mental exhaustion; weariness 2 the cause of this; hard work; toil 3 any manual labor or menial duty, other than drill or instruction, assigned to soldiers: in full **fatigue duty** 4 [*pl.*] sturdy work clothing worn by soldiers doing fatigue duty: also **fatigue clothes** (or **clothing**) 5 the tendency of a metal or other material to crack and fail under repeated applications of stress 6 *Physiol.* the decreased ability to function or the inability to respond, due to prolonged exertion or repeated stimulation: said of an organism or one of its parts — *vt., vi.* **-tigued′, -tigu′ing** 1 to make or become tired or exhausted; weary 2 to subject to or undergo fatigue

Fat·i·ma (fat′i mə, fät′-; fə tē′mə) A.D. 606?-632; daughter of Muhammad

Fat·i·mid (fat′i mid′) *adj.* 1 descended from Muhammad's daughter Fatima 2 designating or of a dynasty of Muslim rulers, descended from Fatima and Ali, that ruled over Egyptian Islam and parts of N Africa (A.D. 909-1171) —*n.* any Fatimid ruler or descendant Also **Fat′i·mite′** (-mīt′)

fat·ling (fat′liŋ) *n.* ⟦FAT + -LING[1]⟧ a calf, lamb, kid, or young pig fattened for slaughter

☆**fat·so** (fat′sō) *n., pl.* **-sos, -soes** [Slang] a fat person: somewhat derisive or contemptuous, often used as a term of address

fat-sol·u·ble (fat′säl′yoo bəl) *adj.* soluble in fats or in solvents for fats

fat·ten (fat′'n) *vt.* 1 to make fat, or plump, as by feeding; specif., to make (cattle, etc.) fat for slaughter 2 to make (land) fertile 3 to make richer, fuller, etc. —*vi.* to become fat —**fat′ten·er** *n.*

fat·tish (-ish) *adj.* somewhat fat

Fat Tuesday ⟦lit. transl. of Fr *Mardi gras*⟧ MARDI GRAS (sense 1)

fat·ty (fat′ē) *adj.* **-ti·er, -ti·est** 1 containing, consisting of, or made of fat 2 very plump; obese 3 resembling fat; greasy; oily —*n., pl.* **-ties** [Informal] a fat person: somewhat derisive or contemptuous, often used as a term of address —**fat′ti·ness** *n.*

fatty acid any of a class of lipids consisting of various saturated or unsaturated, monobasic organic acids, generally R·COOH, usually in a straight chain: they occur naturally in the form of glycerol esters in animal or vegetable fats and oils

fatty degeneration the abnormal occurrence of fat particles in tissue

fa·tu·i·ty (fə to͞o′ə tē, -tyo͞o′-; fa-) *n., pl.* **-ties** ⟦Fr *fatuité* < L *fatuitas* < *fatuus*: see fol.⟧ **1** stupidity, esp. complacent stupidity; smug foolishness **2** a fatuous remark, act, etc. **3** [Archaic] idiocy or imbecility —**fa·tu′i·tous** *adj.*

fat·u·ous (fach′o͞o əs) *adj.* ⟦L *fatuus*, foolish < IE base **bhāt-*, to strike > BATTER[1]⟧ complacently stupid or inane; silly; foolish —*SYN.* SILLY —**fat′u·ous·ly** *adv.* —**fat′u·ous·ness** *n.*

fat·wa (fät′wä, fat′wə) *n.* ⟦Ar⟧ [*also in roman type*] **1** *Islam* a religious and legal decree or edict issued by a council of religious leaders **2** loosely, a death sentence imposed through, or as through, such a decree

fat-wit·ted (fat′wit′id) *adj.* thick-headed; dull; stupid

fat·wood (fat′wood′) *n.* ⟦FAT (*adj.* 1d) + WOOD[1]⟧ [Chiefly South] LIGHTWOOD

fau·bourg (fō bo͞or′; *E* fō′boor′, -boorg′) *n.* ⟦Fr for earlier *faux bourg*, lit., false town, folk-etym. form of OFr *forsbourc*, lit., outside town, hence suburb < *fors* (Fr *hors*), outside + *bourg*, town⟧ in France, *a)* a suburb *b)* a city district that was at one time a suburb

fau·cal (fô′kəl) *adj.* ⟦< fol. + -AL⟧ *Phonet.* of or articulated in the fauces: said of certain speech sounds, as guttural sounds in the Semitic languages

fau·ces (fô′sēz′) *n.* ⟦L, throat, gullet⟧ the passage leading from the back of the mouth into the pharynx —**fau′cial** (-shəl) *adj.*

fau·cet (fô′sit, fä′-) *n.* ⟦ME < OFr *fausset*, prob. < *faulser*, to make a breach in, falsify < LL *falsare* < L *falsus*, FALSE⟧ a device with a hand-operated valve for regulating the flow of a liquid from a pipe, barrel, etc.; cock; tap

faugh (fô: *conventionalized pronun.; actually, an expulsion of air, often with vibration of the lips*) *interj.* used to express disgust, scorn, etc.

Faulk·ner (fôk′nər), **William** (born *William Cuthbert Falkner*) 1897-1962; U.S. novelist —**Faulk·ner·i·an** (fôk nir′ē ən, -ner′-) *adj.*

fault (fôlt) *n.* ⟦ME *faute* < OFr *faulte*, a lack < VL **fallita* < **fallitus*, for L *falsus*: see FALSE⟧ **1** [Obs.] failure to have or do what is required; lack **2** something that mars the appearance, character, structure, etc.; defect or failing **3** something done wrongly; specif., *a)* a misdeed; offense *b)* an error; mistake **4** responsibility for something wrong; blame [*it's her fault that they are late*] **5** *Elec.* a defect or point of defect in the wiring or connections of a circuit, which prevents the current from following the intended path **6** *Geol.* a fracture or zone of fractures in rock strata, characterized by tectonic movement that displaces the sides relative to one another **7** *Hunting* a break in the line of the scent **8** *Volleyball, Tennis, etc.* an improper serve; specif., a serve that hits the net or lands outside the court —*vt.* **1** to find fault with; blame or criticize **2** *Geol.* to cause a fault in —*vi.* **1** to commit a fault: archaic except in racket sports **2** *Geol.* to develop a fault —**at fault 1** unable to find the scent: said of hunting dogs **2** [Archaic] not knowing what to do; perplexed **3** guilty of error; deserving blame: also **in fault** —**find fault (with)** to seek and point out faults (of); complain (about); criticize —**to a fault** too much; excessively

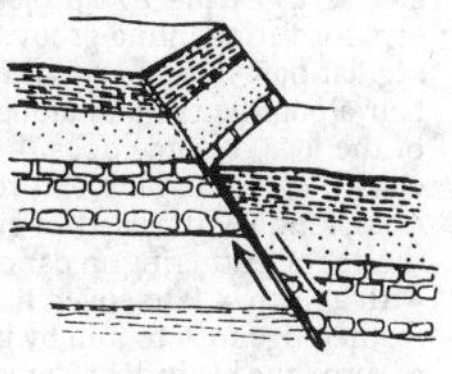
fault (sense 6)

SYN.—**fault**, in this comparison, refers to a definite, although not strongly condemnatory, imperfection in character [*her only fault is stubbornness*]; **failing** implies an even less serious shortcoming, usually one of those common to mankind [*tardiness was one of his failings*]; **weakness** applies to a minor shortcoming that results from a lack of perfect self-control [*talking too much is my weakness*]; **foible** refers to a slight weakness that is regarded more as an amusing idiosyncrasy than an actual defect in character [*eating desserts first is one of his foibles*]; **vice**, although stronger in its implication of moral failure than any of the preceding terms, does not in this connection suggest actual depravity or wickedness [*gambling is his only vice*] —*ANT.* **virtue**

fault·find·er (fôlt′fīn′dər) *n.* a person given to finding fault; chronic, captious complainer

fault·find·ing (-fīn′diŋ) *n., adj.* (a) finding fault; calling attention to defects —*SYN.* CRITICAL

fault·less (-lis) *adj.* without any fault or defect; perfect —**fault′less·ly** *adv.* —**fault′less·ness** *n.*

fault line 1 *Geol.* the line formed along the surface of the ground by a fault **2** any division or rift, as based on philosophical, religious, or ethnic differences, that is perceived as leading inevitably to violent confrontation

fault·y (fôl′tē) *adj.* **fault′i·er, fault′i·est** ⟦ME *fauti*⟧ having a fault or faults; defective, blemished, imperfect, or erroneous —**fault′i·ly** *adv.* —**fault′i·ness** *n.*

faun (fôn) *n.* ⟦ME < L *faunus*: see FAUNUS⟧ any of a class of minor Roman deities, usually represented as having the trunk of a man and the horns, pointed ears, tail, and hind legs of a goat: cf. SATYR

fau·na (fô′nə) *n., pl.* **-nas** or **-nae** (-nē) ⟦ModL < LL *Fauna*, sister of fol.: adopted by LINNAEUS (1746) as term parallel to FLORA⟧ **1** the animals of a specified region or time [*the fauna of North America*] **2** a descriptive list of such animals —**fau′nal** *adj.*

Fau·nus (fô′nəs) *n.* ⟦L < ? IE **dhaunos*, wolf, strangler < base **dhau-*, to strangle > Gr *Daunos*; infl. by Roman folk-etym. assoc. with L *favere*, to favor⟧ *Rom. Myth.* a god of nature, the patron of farming and animals: identified with the Greek Pan

Fau·ré (fô rā′), **Gabriel (Urbain)** 1845-1924; Fr. composer

Faust (foust) *n.* ⟦Ger < L *faustus*, fortunate < base of *favere*: see FAVOR⟧ the hero of several medieval legends and later literary and operatic works, a philosopher who sells his soul to the devil in exchange for knowledge and power: also **Faus·tus** (fous′təs, fôs′-) —**Faust·i·an** (fous′tē ən, fôs′-) *adj.*

faute de mieux (fōt də myö′) ⟦Fr⟧ for want of (something) better

fau·teuil (fō të′y′) *n.* ⟦Fr < OFr *faldestoel*, FALDSTOOL⟧ an upholstered chair, esp. one with open arms

fauve (fōv) [*often* **F-**] *n.* a fauvist painter —*adj.* of or having to do with fauvism

fau·vism (fō′viz′əm) *n.* ⟦Fr *fauvisme* < *fauve*, wild beast, orig. adj., fawn-colored, dun < OFr < Frank **falw* < Gmc **falwa*, FALLOW[2]⟧ [*often* **F-**] a French expressionist movement in painting at the beginning of the 20th cent., involving Matisse, Derain, Vlaminck, etc.: it was characterized by bold distortion of form and the use of strong, pure color —**fau′vist** *n., adj.*

faux (fō) *adj.* ⟦Fr⟧ false or artificial [*carvings of faux ivory*]

faux-na·ïf (fō nä ēf′) *adj.* ⟦Fr⟧ **1** artificially or affectedly naive **2** of a literary or artistic style that pretends to be simple, childlike, or unsophisticated —*n.* a faux-naïf person, style, etc.

faux pas (fō pä′) *pl.* **faux pas** (fō päz′) ⟦Fr, lit., false step⟧ a social blunder; error in etiquette; tactless act or remark —*SYN.* ERROR

fa·va bean (fä′və) ⟦It *fava*, bean (< L *faba*, BEAN)⟧ BROAD BEAN

☆**fave** (fāv) *n., adj.* [Slang] *short for* FAVORITE

fa·ve·la (fə ve′lə) *n.* ⟦Port⟧ in Brazil, a slum at the edge of a city

fa·ve·o·late (fə vē′ə lit′, -lāt′) *adj.* ⟦< ModL *faveolus*, dim. of L *favus*, honeycomb⟧ honeycombed; containing cells; alveolate

fa·vism (fä′viz′əm, fā′-) *n.* ⟦< It *favismo* < *fava*, FAVA BEAN⟧ an acute anemia in certain people, caused by their reaction to the fava bean or its pollen

fa·vo·ni·an (fə vō′nē ən) *adj.* ⟦L *Favonianus* < *Favonius*, west wind < *favere*: see fol.⟧ of or like the west wind; specif., gentle, mild, etc.

fa·vor (fā′vər) *n.* ⟦ME *favour* < OFr < L *favor* < *favere*, to favor < IE base **ghow-*, to perceive > OE (*ofer*) *gumian*, to neglect, Czech *hověti*, to take precautions (with), spare⟧ **1** friendly or kind regard; good will; approval; liking **2** unfair partiality; favoritism **3** a kind, obliging, friendly, or generous act [*to do someone a favor*] **4** [*pl.*] sexual privileges granted by a woman **5** *a)* a small gift, souvenir, or token *b)* [Archaic] a token of love, as to a knight from a female admirer **6** [Archaic] a business letter or note [*your favor of the 15th June*] **7** [Archaic] *a)* appearance or look *b)* face or countenance **8** [Obs.] attractiveness; charm —*vt.* **1** to regard with favor; approve or like **2** to be indulgent or too indulgent toward; be partial to; prefer unfairly **3** to be for; support; advocate; endorse **4** to make easier; help; assist [*rain favored his escape*] **5** to do a kindness for **6** to look like; resemble in facial features [*to favor one's mother*] **7** to use gently; spare [*to favor an injured leg*] —**find favor with** to be regarded with favor by; be pleasing to —**in favor** favored; liked —**in favor of 1** approving; supporting; endorsing **2** to the advantage of **3** payable to, as a check, etc. —**in someone's favor** to someone's advantage or credit —**out of favor** no longer popular or a favorite; no longer in good standing —**fa′vor·er** *n.*

fa·vor·a·ble (fā′vər ə bəl) *adj.* ⟦ME < OFr < L *favorabilis*⟧ **1** approving or commending **2** advantageous **3** pleasing or desirable [*a favorable impression*] —**fa′vor·a·ble·ness** *n.* —**fa′vor·a·bly** *adv.*

SYN.—**favorable** applies to that which is distinctly helpful or advantageous in gaining an end [*a favorable climate for citrus fruits*]; **auspicious** refers to something regarded as a good omen of some undertaking [*he made an auspicious debut*]; **propitious** is now usually applied to a circumstance or a time that appears favorable for doing or beginning something [*a propitious moment*] —*ANT.* **adverse, unfavorable**

fa·vored (fā′vərd) *adj.* **1** regarded or treated with favor; specif., *a)* provided with advantages; talented *b)* specially privileged **2** having (specified) features: often in hyphenated compounds [*ill-favored*]

fa·vor·ite (fā′vər it; *also* fāv′rit) *n.* ⟦MFr < It *favorito*, pp. of *favorire*, to favor < *favore* < L *favor*, FAVOR⟧ **1** a person or thing regarded with special liking, or more highly than others; specif., a person liked very much and granted special privileges as by a monarch, high official, etc. **2** a contestant regarded as most likely to win —*adj.* held in special regard; best liked; preferred

☆**favorite son 1** a famous man honored and praised in his native city, district, etc. because of his achievements **2** *a)* a candidate favored by the political leaders of his own state, city, etc., as for presidential nomination *b)* a candidate at a political convention who controls a state's votes for brokering, or who is available as a compromise nominee

fa·vor·it·ism (fā′vər ə tiz′əm) *n.* **1** the showing of more kindness and indulgence to some person or persons than to others; act of being unfairly partial **2** the condition of being a favorite

fa·vour (fā′vər) *n., vt. Brit. sp. of* FAVOR

fa·vus (fā′vəs) *n.* ⟦ModL < L, honeycomb⟧ an infectious skin disease of humans and many animals, esp. fowl, caused by an imperfect fungus (esp. *Trichophyton schoenleinii*) and characterized by itching and the formation of yellow crusts usually about the hair follicles, esp. on the head

Fawkes (fôks), **Guy** 1570-1606; Eng. conspirator: executed for participating in the GUNPOWDER PLOT

fawn[1] (fôn) *vi.* ⟦ME *faunen* < OE *fagnian* < *fagen*, var. of *fægen*: see FAIN⟧ **1** to show friendliness by licking hands, wagging its tail, etc.: said of a dog **2** to try to gain favor by acting servilely; cringe and flatter [*courtiers fawning on a king*] **3** to show affection in a solicitous or exaggerated way: usually with *over* —**fawn′er** *n.* —**fawn′ing·ly** *adv.*

fawn[2] (fôn) ***n.*** ⟦ME < OFr *faon, feon* < LL **feto* (gen. **fetonis*), young animal, child < L FETUS: see FETUS⟧ **1** a young deer less than one year old **2** a pale yellowish-brown color —***adj.*** of this color — ***vi., vt.*** to bring forth (young): said of a deer

☆**fawn lily** DOGTOOTH VIOLET

fax (faks) ***n.*** ⟦< FACSIMILE⟧ **1** the transmission of graphic matter by electrical or electronic means, as over a telephone line, for reception and reproduction; facsimile **2** graphic matter in the form of electronic data transmitted in this way, that has been reproduced by printing out or stored as a computer file **3** a device for producing such copies: also **fax machine** —***adj.*** **1** of or for a fax **2** by fax [*a fax* sales order] —***vt.*** **1** to transmit by fax **2** to send to by fax

fay[1] (fā) ***n.*** ⟦ME *faie* < OFr *fée* < VL *fata*, one of the Fates < L *fatum*: see FATE⟧ [Literary] a fairy

fay[2] (fā) ***n.*** ⟦ME *fei* < OFr: see FAITH⟧ [Archaic] faith: used in oaths

fay[3] (fā) ***vt., vi.*** ⟦ME *feien* < OE *fegan*, to join, fit, akin to *fæger*, FAIR[1]⟧ *Shipbuilding* to fit closely or exactly; join

Fay or **Faye** (fā) ***n.*** ⟦< ? ME *faie* (see FAY[1]) or ? ME *fei*, FAY[2]⟧ a feminine name

Fay·ette·ville (fā′ət vil′) ⟦after the Marquis de (LA)FAYETTE⟧ city in SC N.C.

Fay·um or **Fay·yum** (fī yo͞om′, fā-) *alt. sp. of* FAIYÛM

faze (fāz) ***vt.*** **fazed, faz′ing** ⟦var. of FEEZE, obs. vt., to drive off⟧ to disturb; disconcert —***SYN.*** EMBARRASS

FB *abbrev. Football* fullback: sometimes written **fb**

FBI *abbrev.* FEDERAL BUREAU OF INVESTIGATION

fbm *abbrev.* feet board measure

fc *abbrev.* **1** *Printing* follow copy **2** foot-candle

FC *abbrev.* **1** *Baseball* fielder's choice **2** fluorocarbon(s)

FCA *abbrev.* Farm Credit Administration

fcap or **fcp** *abbrev.* foolscap

FCC *abbrev.* FEDERAL COMMUNICATIONS COMMISSION

FCIC *abbrev.* Federal Crop Insurance Corporation

F clef BASS CLEF

FCSC *abbrev.* Foreign Claims Settlement Commission

FD *abbrev.* Fire Department

FDA *abbrev.* Food and Drug Administration

FDIC *abbrev.* Federal Deposit Insurance Corporation

FDN or **fdn** *abbrev.* foundation

FDR *abbrev.* Franklin Delano Roosevelt

fe (fā) ***n.*** [Heb] *see* PE

Fe ⟦L *ferrum*⟧ *Chem. symbol for* iron

fe·al·ty (fē′əl tē) ***n., pl.*** **-ties** ⟦ME *feute, fealtye* < OFr *feauté, fealté* < L *fidelitas*, FIDELITY⟧ **1** *a)* the duty and loyalty owed by a vassal or tenant to his feudal lord *b)* an oath of such loyalty **2** [Archaic] loyalty; fidelity —***SYN.*** ALLEGIANCE

fear (fir) ***n.*** ⟦ME *fer* < OE *fær*, lit., sudden attack, akin to OHG *fāra*, ambush, snare: for IE base see PERIL⟧ **1** a feeling of anxiety and agitation caused by the presence or nearness of danger, evil, pain, etc.; timidity; dread; terror; fright; apprehension **2** respectful dread; awe; reverence **3** a feeling of uneasiness or apprehension; concern [*a fear* that it will rain] **4** a cause for fear; possibility; chance [there was no *fear* of difficulty] —***vt.*** **1** [Obs.] to fill with fear; frighten **2** to be afraid of; dread **3** to feel reverence or awe for **4** to expect with misgiving; suspect [*I fear* I am late] —***vi.*** **1** to feel fear; be afraid **2** to be uneasy, anxious, or doubtful —**for fear of** in order to avoid or prevent; lest

SYN.—**fear** is the general term for the anxiety and agitation felt at the presence of danger; **dread** refers to the fear or depression felt in anticipating something dangerous or disagreeable [to live in *dread* of poverty]; **fright** applies to a sudden, shocking, usually momentary fear [the mouse gave her a *fright*]; **horror** refers to a more profound fear, as of something nightmarish or supernatural [to feel *horror* at the prospect of a ghost at one's back]; **alarm** implies the fright felt at the sudden realization of danger [he felt *alarm* at the sight of the pistol]; **terror** applies to an overwhelming, often paralyzing fear [the *terror* of soldiers in combat]; **panic** refers to a frantic, unreasoning fear, often one that spreads quickly and leads to irrational, aimless action [the cry of "Fire!" created a *panic*]

Fear (fir), **Cape** cape on an island off the SE coast of N.C.

fear·ful (fir′fəl) ***adj.*** **1** causing fear; terrifying; dreadful **2** feeling fear; afraid **3** showing or resulting from fear [*a fearful* look] **4** [Informal] very bad, offensive, great, etc. [*a fearful* liar] —***SYN.*** AFRAID —**fear′ful·ness** ***n.***

fear·ful·ly (-fəl ē) ***adv.*** **1** in a fearful manner **2** to a fearful extent **3** [Informal] very much; very [*fearfully* busy]

fear·less (-lis) ***adj.*** without fear; not afraid; brave; intrepid —**fear′less·ly** ***adv.*** —**fear′less·ness** ***n.***

fear·some (fir′səm) ***adj.*** **1** causing fear; dreadful; horrible **2** [Now Rare] frightened; timid —**fear′some·ly** ***adv.*** —**fear′some·ness** ***n.***

fea·sance (fē′zəns) ***n.*** ⟦Anglo-Fr *fesance* (Fr *faisance*) < stem of *faire*, to do: see fol.⟧ *Law* the performance of an act, condition, obligation, etc.

fea·si·ble (fē′zə bəl) ***adj.*** ⟦ME *faisible* < OFr < stem of *faire*, to do < L *facere*: see DO[1]⟧ **1** capable of being done or carried out; practicable; possible [*a feasible* scheme] **2** within reason; likely or probable: a usage objected to by some [*a feasible* story] **3** capable of being used or dealt with successfully; suitable [land *feasible* for cultivation] —***SYN.*** POSSIBLE —**fea′si·bil′i·ty** ***n., pl.*** **-ties** —**fea′si·ble·ness** ***n.*** —**fea′si·bly** ***adv.***

feast (fēst) ***n.*** ⟦ME *feste* < OFr < VL *festa* < pl. of L *festum*, festival < *festus*, festal, joyful, orig., of days for religious observance: see FAIR[2]⟧ **1** a celebration or festival; esp., a periodic religious celebration, as in honor of God or a saint **2** a rich and elaborate meal; banquet **3** anything that gives pleasure because of its abundance or richness —***vi.*** ⟦ME *festen* < OFr *fester* < the *n.*⟧ **1** to eat a rich, elaborate meal **2** to have a special treat —***vt.*** **1** to entertain at a feast or banquet **2** to gratify or delight as with a feast [*feast* your eyes on this!] —**feast′er** ***n.***

feast day **1** FEAST (sense 1) **2** NAME DAY

Feast of Lots PURIM

Feast of Tabernacles SUKKOT

feat[1] (fēt) ***n.*** ⟦ME *fet* < Anglo-Fr < OFr *fait* < L *factum*, a deed < neut. pp. of *facere*: see DO[1]⟧ an act or accomplishment showing unusual daring, skill, endurance, etc.; remarkable deed; exploit

feat[2] (fēt) ***adj.*** ⟦ME *fet* < OFr *fait*, pp. of *faire*, to do < L *facere*: see DO[1]⟧ [Archaic] **1** fitting **2** neat or neatly dressed **3** skillful

feath·er (feth′ər) ***n.*** ⟦ME *fether* < OE; akin to Ger *feder* < IE base **pet-*, to fall, fly > Gr *pteron*, wing, *piptein*, L *petere*, to fall, Sans *pátati*, (he) flies⟧ **1** any of the growths covering the body of a bird or making up a large part of the wing surface, as down or contour feathers: a typical contour feather consists of a horny central shaft, partly hollow, from which light, soft, narrow barbs, with interlocking barbules and barbicels, extend to form a thin, flat surface **2** a feather or featherlike part fastened to the shaft of an arrow to help control its flight **3** anything like or suggesting a feather or feathers in appearance, lightness, etc., as *a)* a trifle *b)* a projecting part, esp. for fitting into a groove *c)* an irregular flaw in a gem *d)* the fringe of hair along the tail and along the back of the legs of some dogs **4** [*pl.*] [Archaic] *a)* plumage *b)* attire; dress **5** class; kind [enthusiasts of every *feather*] **6** frame of mind; temper; vein **7** the act of feathering an oar or propeller —***vt.*** **1** to provide (an arrow, etc.) with a feather **2** to cover, fit, or fringe with or as with feathers **3** to give a featheredge to **4** to join by inserting a wedge-shaped part into a groove **5** to turn (the blade of an oar) parallel to the line of movement in recovering after a stroke, so as to offer the least resistance to air or water **6** to cut or style (hair) so as to give it a feathery look or texture, as with wispy curls **7** *Aeron.* *a)* to turn (the blade of a propeller) on its shaft so that its leading and trailing edges are nearly parallel with the airplane's line of flight, thus preventing engine damage caused by airflow turning the propeller during an engine failure *b)* to change the angle of the blades of a helicopter rotor —***vi.*** **1** to grow, or become covered with, feathers **2** to move, grow, or extend like feathers **3** to look like feathers **4** to feather an oar or propeller —**feather in one's cap** a distinctive accomplishment; achievement worthy of pride —**feather one's nest** to grow rich by taking advantage of circumstances —**in feather** feathered —**in fine** (or **high** or **good**) **feather** in very good humor, health, or form —**feath′er·less** ***adj.***

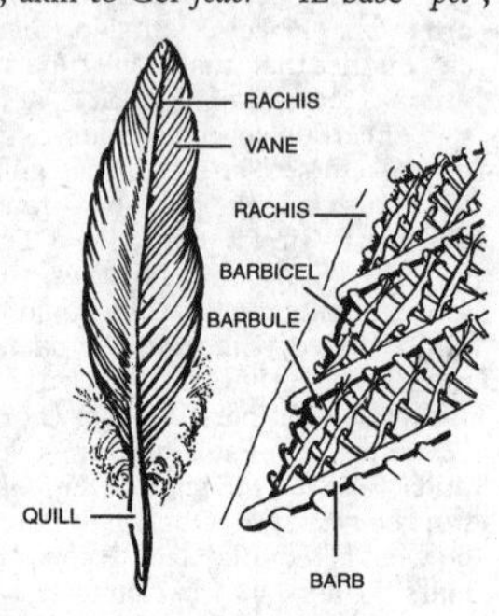

parts of a feather

feath·er·bed (-bed′) ***adj.*** ☆of, facilitating, or having to do with featherbedding —☆***vi., vt.*** **-bed′ded, -bed′ding** to engage in or subject to featherbedding

feather bed a type of cloth bedding thickly filled with feathers or down, used as, or on top of, a mattress

☆**feath·er·bed·ding** (-bed′iŋ) ***n.*** the practice of limiting output or of requiring extra workers, as by union contract, in order to provide more jobs and prevent unemployment

feath·er·brain (-brān′) ***n.*** a silly, foolish, or frivolous person —**feath′er·brained′** ***adj.***

☆**feath·er·cut** (-kut′) ***n.*** a style of woman's haircut characterized by curls with feathery tips

feath·er·edge (-ej′) ***n.*** a very thin edge, as on a board or tool —***vt.*** **-edged′, -edg′ing** to give such an edge to

feath·er·head (-hed′) ***n.*** FEATHERBRAIN

feath·er·ing (-iŋ) ***n.*** **1** the act of one who feathers **2** feathers collectively **3** long hair on the ears, legs, tail, or body of a dog

feather palm any palm with featherlike, or pinnate, leaves: see FAN PALM

feather star ⟦descriptive: from the *feathery* arms of its somewhat *star*-shaped body⟧ any of an order (Comatulida) of unattached, free-swimming crinoids; comatulid

feath·er·stitch (-stich′) ***n.*** ⟦so called from resemblance to the arrangement of barbs on a *feather*⟧ an embroidery stitch forming a zigzag line —***vt., vi.*** to embroider with such a stitch

feath·er·weight (-wāt′) ***n.*** **1** any person or thing of comparatively light weight or small size **2** an unimportant person or thing **3** a boxer between a junior featherweight and a junior lightweight, with a maximum weight of 126 pounds (57.15 kg) **4** the minimum weight that a racehorse may carry in a handicap —***adj.*** **1** of featherweights **2** light or trivial

feath·er·y (-ē) ***adj.*** **1** covered with or as with feathers **2** resembling feathers; soft, light, etc. —**feath′er·i·ness** ***n.***

feat·ly (fēt′lē) [Now Rare] ***adv.*** ⟦ME *fetli* < *fet*: see FEAT[2]⟧ **1** suitably; aptly **2** neatly **3** skillfully; adroitly —***adj.*** neat; graceful

fea·ture (fē′chər) ***n.*** ⟦ME *feture* < OFr *faiture* < L *factura*, a making, formation < pp. of *facere*, to make, DO[1]⟧ **1** *a)* [Archaic] the make, shape, form, or appearance of a person or thing *b)* [Obs.] attractive appearance; physical beauty **2** *a)* [*pl.*] the form or look of the face; facial appearance *b)* any of the parts of the face, as the eyes, nose, mouth, etc. **3** a distinct or outstanding part, quality, or characteristic of something ☆**4** a prominently displayed or publicized attraction, as at an entertainment or sale ☆**5** a special story, article, etc. in a newspaper or magazine, often prominently displayed ☆**6** a film, usually fictional, running 40 minutes or longer, esp. as the main presentation in a theater: in full **feature film** —***vt.* -tured, -tur·ing** ☆**1** to give prominence to; make a feature of **2** to sketch or show the features of **3** to be a feature of ☆**4** [Slang] to conceive of; imagine **5** [Dial.] to look like; favor —☆***vi.*** to have a prominent part —**fea′ture·less** ***adj.***

fea·tured (-chərd) ***adj.*** **1** having (a specified kind of) facial features [broad-*featured*] ☆**2** given special prominence as a main attraction

☆**fea·ture-length** (fē′chər leŋth′) ***adj.*** of the usual length of a feature: said of a film, magazine article, etc.

fea·tur·ette (fē′chər et′) ***n.*** a short film, often a documentary about the making of a feature film

feaze (fēz, fāz) ***vt.* feazed, feaz′ing** *var. of* FAZE

Feb *abbrev.* February

feb·ri- (feb′ri, -rə) ⟦< L *febris*, FEVER⟧ *combining form* fever [*febrifuge*]

fe·brif·ic (fē brif′ik) ***adj.*** ⟦< Fr *febrifique*: see prec. + -FIC⟧ [Archaic] having or producing a fever

feb·ri·fuge (feb′ri fyo͞oj′) ***n.*** ⟦Fr *fébrifuge* (see FEBRI- & -FUGE), after LL *febrifugia* (see FEVERFEW), the centaury, regarded as an antipyretic⟧ any substance for reducing fever; antipyretic —***adj.*** reducing fever

fe·brile (fē′brəl, feb′rəl; fē′brīl′, feb′rīl′) ***adj.*** ⟦Fr *fébrile* < L *febris*, FEVER⟧ **1** of or characterized by fever; feverish **2** caused by fever

Feb·ru·ar·y (feb′ro͞o er′ē, feb′yo͞o er′ē) ***n.***, *pl.* **-ar′ies** or **-ar′ys** ⟦ME *Feb-ruarie* < L *Februarius (mensis)*, orig., month of expiation < *februa*, Roman festival of purification held Feb. 15, pl. of *februum*, means of purification, prob. < IE **dhwes-*, to stir up, blow, eddy > DEER, DIZZY⟧ the second month of the year, having 28 days in regular years and 29 days in leap years: abbrev. *Feb* or *F*

FEC *abbrev.* Federal Election Commission

fe·cal (fē′kəl) ***adj.*** of or consisting of feces

fe·ces (fē′sēz′) ***pl.n.*** ⟦L *faeces*, pl. of *faex*, dregs, lees⟧ waste matter expelled from the bowels; excrement

feck·less (fek′lis) ***adj.*** ⟦Scot < *feck* (aphetic for EFFECT) + -LESS⟧ **1** weak; ineffective **2** careless; irresponsible —**feck′less·ly** ***adv.*** —**feck′less·ness** ***n.***

fec·u·lence (fek′yo͞o ləns) ***n.*** ⟦Fr *féculence* < L *faeculentia*: see fol.⟧ **1** the state or quality of being feculent **2** *a)* dregs; sediment *b)* filth

fec·u·lent (-lənt) ***adj.*** ⟦ME < L *faeculentus* < *faecula*, dim. < *faex*: see FECES⟧ **1** containing, or having the nature of, feces **2** filthy; foul

fe·cund (fē′kənd, fek′ənd) ***adj.*** ⟦ME *fecound* < OFr *fecond* < L *fecundus*, fertile: for IE base see FETUS⟧ fruitful or fertile; productive; prolific —***SYN.*** FERTILE —**fe·cun·di·ty** (fi kun′də tē, fē-) ***n.***

fe·cun·date (fē′kən dāt′, fek′ən-) ***vt.* -dat′ed, -dat′ing** ⟦< L *fecundatus*, pp. of *fecundare*, to make fruitful < *fecundus*: see prec.⟧ **1** to make fecund **2** to fertilize; impregnate; pollinate —**fe′cun·da′tion** ***n.***

fed[1] (fed) ***vt., vi. pt. & pp. of*** FEED —**fed up** [Informal] having had enough to become disgusted, bored, or annoyed

fed[2] (fed) ***n.*** ⟦< FEDERAL⟧ ☆[*often* **F-**] [Slang] a U.S. federal agent or officer: *usually used in pl.* —☆**the Fed** [Informal] the Federal Reserve System

Fed *abbrev.* **1** Federal **2** Federation

fed·a·yeen (fed′ä yēn′) ***pl.n.*** ⟦Ar *fidā′īyīn*, pl. of *fidā′ī*, lit., one who sacrifices himself (esp. for his country)⟧ Arab irregulars or guerrillas in the Middle East

fed·er·al (fed′ər əl; *also* fed′rəl) ***adj.*** ⟦< L *foedus* (gen. *foederis*), a league, compact, treaty: see FAITH & -AL⟧ **1** of or formed by a compact; specif., designating or of a union of states, groups, etc. in which each member agrees to subordinate its governmental power to that of the central authority in certain specified common affairs **2** *a)* designating, of, or having to do with a central authority or government in such a union ☆*b)* [*often* **F-**] designating, of, or having to do with the central government of the U.S. ☆**3** [**F-**] of or supporting the Federalist Party or its principle of strong centralized government ☆**4** [**F-**] of or pertaining to the style in architecture and furniture based on classical Roman models that flourished in the U.S. from 1780 into the 1830s ☆**5** [**F-**] of or supporting the government of the U.S. in the Civil War; Union; pro-Union —***n.*** ☆**1** [**F-**] a Federalist ☆**2** [**F-**] a supporter or soldier of the U.S. government in the Civil War ☆**3** [*often* **F-**] a U.S. federal agent or officer —**fed′er·al·ly** ***adv.***

☆**Federal Bureau of Investigation** a branch of the U.S. Department of Justice whose duty is to investigate violations of certain federal laws

federal case ⟦in ref. to a *federal* court *case*⟧ *used in the informal phrase* ☆**make a federal case (out) of**, to overreact to or exaggerate (a problem or concern)

☆**Federal Communications Commission** a U.S. federal agency whose duty is to regulate communication by telephone, telegraph, radio, TV, cable TV, and satellite

federal funds rate a rate of interest for short-term interbank loans, adjusted periodically by a committee of the Federal Reserve System: also [Informal] **fed funds rate**

fed·er·al·ism (fed′ər əl iz′əm) ***n.*** **1** *a)* the federal principle of government or organization *b)* support of this principle ☆**2** [**F-**] the principles of the Federalist Party

fed·er·al·ist (-ist) ***n.*** **1** a person who believes in or supports federalism ☆**2** [**F-**] a member or supporter of the Federalist Party —***adj.*** **1** of or supporting federalism ☆**2** [**F-**] of or supporting the Federalist Party or its principles Also **fed′er·al·is′tic** —☆**The Federalist (Papers)** a set of 85 articles by Alexander Hamilton, James Madison, and John Jay, published in 1787 and 1788, analyzing the proposed U.S. Constitution and urging its adoption

☆**Federalist (*or* Federal) Party** a political party in the U.S. (1789-1816), led by Alexander Hamilton and John Adams, which advocated the adoption of the Constitution and the establishment of a strong, centralized government

fed·er·al·ize (fed′ər əl īz′) ***vt.* -ized′, -iz′ing** **1** to unite (states, etc.) into or within a federal union **2** to put under the authority of a federal government —**fed′er·al·i·za′tion** ***n.***

Federal Republic of Germany *see* GERMANY

☆**Federal Reserve Bank** any of the twelve district banks of the Federal Reserve System

☆**Federal Reserve note** any of the notes issued by the individual Federal Reserve Banks in various denominations: Federal Reserve notes are the prevailing U.S. paper currency

☆**Federal Reserve System** a centralized banking system in the U.S. under a Board of Governors (formerly called the **Federal Reserve Board**) with supervisory powers over twelve Federal Reserve Banks, each a central bank for its district: established in 1913, it is intended to regulate banking and the economy by controlling the supply of money and credit

☆**Federal Trade Commission** a U.S. federal agency whose duty is to investigate unfair methods of competition in business, fraudulent advertising, etc., and to restrain or prosecute those charged with such practices

fed·er·ate (fed′ər it; *for v.*, -ər āt′) ***adj.*** ⟦L *foederatus*, pp. of *foederare*, to league together < *foedus*: see FAITH⟧ united by common agreement under a central government or authority — ***vt., vi.* -at′ed, -at′ing** to unite in a federation

fed·er·a·tion (fed′ər ā′shən) ***n.*** ⟦Fr *fédération* < ML *federatio* < L *foederatus*: see prec.⟧ **1** the act of uniting or of forming a union of states, groups, etc. by agreement of each member to subordinate its power to that of the central authority in common affairs **2** an organization formed by such an act; league; specif., a federal union of states, nations, etc.

fed·er·a·tive (fed′ər āt′iv, -ər ə tiv) ***adj.*** of, forming, or having the nature of a federation —**fed′er·a′tive·ly** ***adv.***

☆**fe·do·ra** (fə dôr′ə) ***n.*** ⟦Fr, after *Fédora* (1882), play by V. SARDOU: the hat style was worn by one of the characters⟧ a man's soft felt hat with the crown creased lengthwise and a somewhat curved brim

fee (fē) ***n.*** ⟦ME, estate, fief, payment < Anglo-Fr (< OFr *feu*, *fief* < Gmc, as in OHG *feho*, *fihu*, akin to OE *feoh*) < IE base **pek-* > OE *feoh*, cattle, property⟧ **1** *a)* [Historical] heritable land held from a feudal lord in return for service; fief; feudal benefice *b)* [Historical] the right to hold such land *c)* [Obs.] payment, service, or homage due a superior **2** payment asked or given for professional services, admissions, licenses, tuition, etc.; charge **3** [Now Rare] a present of money; tip; gratuity **4** an inheritable estate in real property: see FEE SIMPLE, FEE TAIL —***vt.* feed, fee′ing** [Now Rare] to give a fee, or tip, to —***SYN.*** WAGE —**hold in fee** to own; possess

☆**feeb** (fēb) ***n.*** ⟦< fol.⟧ [Slang] a weak, ineffectual person; wimp

fee·ble (fē′bəl) ***adj.* -bler, -blest** ⟦ME *feble* < OFr *faible*, *feble* < L *flebilis*, to be wept over < *flere*, to weep < IE base **bhlē-*, to howl > BLEAT, BLARE⟧ weak; not strong; specif., *a)* infirm [a *feeble* old man] *b)* without force or effectiveness [a *feeble* light, a *feeble* attempt] *c)* easily broken; frail [a *feeble* barrier] —***SYN.*** WEAK —**fee′ble·ness** ***n.*** —**fee′bly** ***adv.***

fee·ble·mind·ed (-mīn′did) ***adj.*** **1** mentally retarded; subnormal in intelligence: term no longer used in psychology **2** slow-witted, as from old age —**fee′ble·mind′ed·ly** ***adv.*** —**fee′ble·mind′ed·ness** ***n.***

feed (fēd) ***vt.* fed, feed′ing** ⟦ME *feden* < OE *fedan* < base of *foda*, FOOD⟧ **1** to give food to; provide food for **2** *a)* to provide as food [to *feed* oats to horses] *b)* to serve as food for [a can of soup *feeds* two people] **3** to provide something necessary for the growth, development, or existence of; nourish; sustain [to *feed* one's anger] **4** to provide (material to be used up, processed, etc.) [to *feed* coal into a stove] **5** to provide with material [*feed* the stove] **6** to provide satisfaction for; gratify [to *feed* one's vanity] **7** *Sports* to pass (the ball, puck, etc.) to (a teammate intending to make a shot, try for a goal, etc.) **8** *Theater* to supply (an actor) with (cue lines) —***vi.*** **1** to eat: said chiefly of animals **2** to flow steadily, as into a machine for use, processing, etc. —***n.*** **1** *a)* food given to animals; fodder *b)* the amount of fodder given at one time **2** *a)* the material fed into a machine *b)* the part of the machine supplying this material *c)* the supplying of this material **3** [Informal] a meal **4** *Radio, TV* a transmission by satellite, landlines, etc., as that sent by a network to individual stations for broadcast **5** *Comput.* a notification sent out by a website to alert subscribers about updated information: such notifications are received typically through a web browser: in full **web feed** or **news feed** —**feed on (**or **upon) 1** to take as food; eat: said chiefly of animals **2** to get satisfaction, support, etc. from —**off one's feed** [Slang] without appetite for food; somewhat sick

feed·back (fēd′bak′) ***n.*** **1** *Elec.* the transfer of part of the output of an active circuit or device back to the input, either as an unwanted effect or in an intentional use, as to reduce distortion **2** *a)* a process in which the factors that produce a result are themselves modified, corrected, strengthened, etc. by that result *b)* a response, as one that sets such a process in motion

☆**feed bag** a bag filled with grain, fastened over a horse's muzzle for feeding —**put on the feed bag** [Slang] to eat a meal

feed·er (fēd′ər) ***n.*** **1** a person or thing that feeds; specif., *a)* a device that feeds material into a machine *b)* a device that supplies food to animals or birds **2** an animal, esp. a steer, being fattened **3** anything that supplies or leads into something else; tributary; specif., a branch transportation line (in full **feeder line**) **4** *Elec.* a conductor supplying current or signals to a substation, antenna, etc.

feeding frenzy ⟦in allusion to the behavior of sharks⟧ [Informal] an energetic attack on, or pursuit of, someone or something by a group

feed·lot (-lät′) ***n.*** an enclosed area where livestock, esp. cattle or hogs, are fed and fattened before being slaughtered for food

☆**feed·stock** (-stäk′) ***n.*** raw material for industrial processing; often, specif., any of various petroleum products used in making petrochemicals and gasoline

feel (fēl) ***vt.*** **felt**, **feel′ing** ⟦ME *felen* < OE *felan*, akin to Ger *fühlen* & L *palpare*, to stroke < ? IE base **pel-*, to fly, flutter, cause to tremble > OE *fifealde*, Ger *falter*, butterfly⟧ **1** to touch or handle in order to become aware of; examine or test by touching or handling **2** to perceive or be aware of through physical sensation *[to feel rain on one's face]* **3** *a)* to experience (an emotion or condition) *[to feel joy, pain, etc.]* *b)* to be moved by or be very sensitive to *[to feel death keenly]* **4** to be aware of through intellectual perception *[to feel the weight of an argument]* **5** to think or believe, often for unanalyzed or emotional reasons *[he feels that we should go]* —***vi.*** **1** to have physical sensation; be sentient **2** to appear to be to the senses, esp. to the sense of touch *[the water feels warm]* **3** to have the indicated emotional effect *[it feels good to be needed]* **4** to try to find something by touching; grope (*for*) **5** to be, or be aware of being *[to feel sad, sick, certain, etc.]* **6** to be moved to sympathy, pity, etc. (*for*) —***n.*** **1** the act of feeling; perception by the senses **2** the sense of touch **3** the nature of a thing as perceived through touch *[the feel of wet sawdust]* **4** an emotional sensation or effect *[the feel of happiness]* **5** an instinctive ability or appreciation *[a feel for floral arrangement]* **6** [Slang] the act or an instance of touching, handling, groping, etc. *[have a feel of this fabric]* —☆**feel like 1** [Informal] to have an inclination or desire for *[I feel like some ice cream]* **2** [Dial.] to think or believe that *[I feel like he's a fool]* —**feel (like) oneself** to feel normally healthy, fit, etc. —☆**feel out** [Informal] to find out the opinions or attitude of by a cautious and indirect approach —**feel strongly about** to have decided opinions concerning —**feel up** [Slang] to fondle sexually: a mildly vulgar usage —**feel one's way** to move or advance cautiously, by or as if by groping

feel·er (fēl′ər) ***n.*** **1** a person or thing that feels **2** a specialized sensory organ that projects typically from the head of an animal, esp. an insect **3** [Informal] a remark, question, offer, etc. made to feel out another: *usually used in pl.*

feel-good (fēl′go͝od′) ***adj.*** [Informal] that evokes a feeling of well-being or satisfaction: often implying superficiality or smugness

feel·ing (fēl′iŋ) ***adj.*** ⟦ME *feling*: see FEEL & -ING⟧ full of or expressing emotion or sensitivity; sympathetic —***n.*** **1** that one of the senses by which sensations of contact, pressure, temperature, and pain are transmitted through the skin; sense of touch **2** the power or faculty of experiencing physical sensation **3** an awareness; consciousness; sensation *[a feeling of pain]* **4** *a)* emotion or sensitivity *[to sing with feeling]* *b)* an emotion **5** [*pl.*] the power or faculty of experiencing emotions and subjective responses *[to hurt someone's feelings]* **6** a kindly, generous attitude; sympathy, pity, etc. **7** *a)* an opinion or sentiment *[a feeling that he is honest]* *b)* a premonition *[a feeling that we will win]* **8** an impression or emotional quality; air; atmosphere *[the lonely feeling of the city at night]* **9** a natural ability or sensitive appreciation *[a feeling for music]* **10** the emotional quality in a work of art —**have feelings for** [Informal] to feel romantically about (someone); be in love with or be infatuated with —**feel′ing·ly** ***adv.***

SYN.—**feeling**, when unqualified in the context, refers to any of the subjective reactions, pleasant or unpleasant, that one may have to a situation and usually connotes an absence of reasoning [I can't trust my own *feelings*]; **emotion** implies an intense feeling with physical as well as mental manifestations [her breast heaved with *emotion*]; **passion** refers to a strong or overpowering emotion, connoting especially sexual love or intense anger; **sentiment** applies to a feeling, often a tender one, accompanied by some thought or reasoning [what are your *sentiments* in this matter?]

fee simple ⟦Anglo-Fr: see FEE & SIMPLE⟧ absolute ownership of real property with unrestricted rights of disposition

☆**fee-split·ting** (fē′split′iŋ) ***n.*** the practice of giving part of the fee charged a referred client or patient to a colleague who makes the referral: it is considered an unethical practice in the medical profession

feet (fēt) ***n.*** *pl. of* FOOT —**feet of clay** ⟦in allusion to the feet of the idol in Nebuchadnezzar's dream: see Dan. 2:33⟧ a weakness or defect of character (in an otherwise strong person) —**get one's feet wet** to have or get one's first experience in some activity or pursuit —**have one's feet on the ground** to be practical, realistic, etc. —**on one's feet 1** in a standing position **2** firmly established **3** in a sound or recovered condition **4** alert(ly) **5** without preparation; readily or extemporaneously *[an able attorney can think on her feet]* —**put one's feet up** to relax; specif., to assume a relaxing position as with a footrest or on a recliner —**sit at the feet of** to be an admiring disciple of —**stand on one's own (two) feet** to be independent —**sweep (or carry) someone off his (or her) feet** to inspire strong and immediate enthusiasm, love, etc. in someone —**to one's feet** to a standing position

fee tail ⟦Anglo-Fr *fee tailé* < *fee* (see FEE) + *tailé*, pp. of *taillir*, to cut, limit (OFr *taillier*): see TAILOR⟧ an estate in real property which may be inherited only by a specified class of heirs, usually the natural children of the owner

feeze (fēz, fāz) ***n.*** ⟦< obs. vt., to drive off < ME *fesen*, to drive, put to flight < OE *fesian*, to drive < *fus*, eager < IE base **pent-*, to go toward > FIND⟧ **1** [Brit. Dial.] a rush, hard impact, or rub **2** [Informal] perturbation

feh (fe) ***interj.*** ⟦Yiddish⟧ used to express disgust, contempt, or scorn

Feh·ling's solution (fā′liŋz) ⟦after H. von *Fehling* (1811-85), Ger chemist⟧ a blue solution of copper sulfate, Rochelle salt, and sodium hydroxide, used to test for the presence of a sugar, aldehyde, etc.: also called **Fehling's reagent**

feign (fān) ***vt.*** ⟦ME *feinen* < OFr *feindre* (prp. *feignant*) < L *fingere*, to touch, handle, shape: see FIGURE⟧ **1** [Obs.] to form; shape **2** to make up (a story, excuse, etc.); invent; fabricate **3** to make a false show of; pretend; imitate; simulate **4** [Archaic] to imagine —***vi.*** to pretend; dissemble —***SYN.*** ASSUME —**feign′er** ***n.***

feigned (fānd) ***adj.*** **1** [Now Rare] fictitious; imagined **2** pretended; simulated; sham

fei·joa·da (fā zhwä′dä) ***n.*** ⟦Port⟧ a Brazilian stew of black beans, pork, sausage, onions, spices, and cassava: served over rice

Fei·ning·er (fī′niŋ ər), **Ly·o·nel (Charles Adrian)** (lī′ə nəl) 1871-1956; U.S. painter

feint (fānt) ***n.*** ⟦Fr *feint* < pp. of *feindre*: see FEIGN⟧ **1** a false show; sham **2** a pretended blow or attack intended to put the opponent off guard, as in boxing or warfare — ***vi., vt.*** to deliver (such a blow or attack)

☆**feist** (fīst) ***n.*** ⟦orig., lit., a fart < ME *fist* < OE *fisten*, akin to Du *veest*, ON *fisa* < IE base **(s)peis-*, to blow: see SPIRIT⟧ [Dial.] a small, snappish dog

☆**feist·y** (fīs′tē) ***adj.*** **feist′i·er**, **feist′i·est** ⟦prec. + -Y[2]⟧ full of spirit; specif., *a)* quarrelsome, aggressive, belligerent, etc. *b)* lively, energetic, assertive, etc. —**feist′i·ly** ***adv.*** —**feist′i·ness** ***n.***

fe·la·fel (fə läf′əl) ***n.*** *alt. sp. of* FALAFEL

feld·sher (feld′shər) ***n.*** ⟦Russ *fel′dšer* < Ger *feldscher*, *feldscherer*, field surgeon < *feld*, FIELD + *scherer*, barber, surgeon, akin to *scheren, to clip*, SHEAR⟧ a medical worker, esp. in Russia, who acts as an assistant to a physician and is qualified by practical training to perform certain tasks: also sp. **feld′scher**

feld·spar (feld′spär′) ***n.*** ⟦altered < Ger *feldspath* (now *feldspat*) < *feld*, FIELD + *spath*, spar < IE base **spe-*, long, flat board > SPOON, SPADE[1]⟧ any of several light-colored, hard, glassy, monoclinic or triclinic minerals made up of aluminum silicates with sodium, potassium, or calcium, found in all types of rock —**feld·spath′ic** (-spath′ik) ***adj.***

Fe·li·ci·a (fə lish′ə, -ē ə; -lē′shə, -shē ə; -lis′ē ə) ***n.*** a feminine name: see FELIX

fe·li·cif·ic (fē′li sif′ik) ***adj.*** ⟦< L *felix* (see FELICITY) + -FIC⟧ [Rare] producing or tending to produce happiness

fe·lic·i·tate (fə lis′i tāt′) ***vt.*** **-tat′ed**, **-tat′ing** ⟦< L *felicitatus*, pp. of *felicitare*, to make happy < *felix*: see prec.⟧ **1** [Archaic] to make happy **2** to wish happiness to; congratulate —***adj.*** [Obs.] made happy —**fe·lic′i·ta′tion** ***n.*** —**fe·lic′i·ta′tor** ***n.***

fe·lic·i·tous (fə lis′i təs) ***adj.*** ⟦< fol. + -OUS⟧ **1** used or expressed in a way suitable to the occasion; aptly chosen; appropriate; apt **2** having the knack of appropriate and pleasing expression —**fe·lic′i·tous·ly** ***adv.*** —**fe·lic′i·tous·ness** ***n.***

fe·lic·i·ty (fə lis′i tē) ***n.***, *pl.* **-ties** ⟦ME *felicite* < OFr *felicité* < L *felicitas*, happiness < *felix* (gen. *felicis*), happy, orig., fertile, fruitful, nourishing: for IE base see FEMALE⟧ **1** happiness; bliss **2** anything producing happiness; good fortune **3** a quality or knack of appropriate and pleasing expression in writing, speaking, painting, etc. **4** an apt expression or thought

fe·lid (fē′lid) ***n.*** ⟦< ModL *Felidae*, the cat family < L *felis*: see fol.⟧ any animal of the cat family

fe·line (fē′līn) ***adj.*** ⟦L *felinus* < *feles*, cat⟧ **1** of a cat or the cat family **2** catlike; esp., *a)* crafty, sly, stealthy, etc. *b)* graceful in a sleek way —***n.*** any animal of the cat family —**fe′line′ly** ***adv.*** —**fe·lin·i·ty** (fē lin′ə tē) ***n.***

Fe·lix (fē′liks) ***n.*** ⟦L, lit., happy: see FELICITY⟧ a masculine name: fem. *Felicia*

fell[1] (fel) ***vi., vt.*** *pt. of* FALL

fell[2] (fel) ***vt.*** ⟦ME *fellen* < OE *fællan*, *fellan* (< Gmc **falljan*), caus. of *feallan* (< Gmc **fallan*), FALL⟧ **1** to cause to fall; knock down *[to fell an opponent with a blow]* **2** to cut down (a tree or trees) **3** *Sewing* to turn over (the rough edge of a seam) and sew down flat on the underside —***n.*** **1** the trees cut down in one season **2** *Sewing* a felled seam —**fell′a·ble** ***adj.*** —**fell′er** ***n.***

fell[3] (fel) ***adj.*** ⟦ME *fel* < OFr < ML *fello*: see FELON[1]⟧ **1** fierce; terrible; cruel **2** deadly: archaic except in the phrase **at (or in) one fell swoop**, with a single effort or action that is completely effective, devastating, etc. —**fell′ness** ***n.***

fell[4] (fel) ***n.*** ⟦ME *fel* < OE, akin to Ger *fell* < IE base **pel-*, skin, hide > FILM, L *pellis*, skin⟧ **1** an animal's hide or skin **2** a thin membrane of connective tissue under the hide

fell[5] (fel) ***n.*** ⟦ME *fel* < Scand, as in ON *fjall*, mountain, akin to Ger *fels*, rock, cliff < IE base **pels-* > MIr *all*, crag, Gr *pella*, stone⟧ [Brit.] **1** a rocky or barren hill **2** a moor; down

fel·la (fel′ə) ***n.*** [Slang] *phonetic sp. of* FELLOW

fel·lah (fel′ə) ***n.***, *pl.* **fel′lahs**, **fel·la·heen** or **fel·la·hin** (fel′ə hēn′) ⟦Ar *fallāh* (pl. *fallāḥīn*), peasant, farmer < *falaḥa*, to plow⟧ a peasant or farm laborer in an Arab country

fel·late (fel′āt′, fel āt′) *vt.* **-lat′ed, -lat′ing** ⟦back-form. < fol.⟧ to perform fellatio on

fel·la·ti·o (fə lā′shō, -shē ō′) *n.* ⟦ModL < L *fellatus*, pp. of *fellare*, to suck < IE base **dhē-*: see FEMALE⟧ a sexual activity involving oral contact with the penis

fel·la·tor (fə lāt′ər) *n.* the sexual partner performing fellatio

fel·la·trice (fə lā′tris) *n.* a female fellator: also **fel·la′trix** (-triks)

Fel·li·ni (fə lē′nē; *It* fel lē′nē), **Fe·de·ri·co** (fe′də rē′kō; *It* fe′de rē′kô) 1920-93; It. film director

fell·mon·ger (fel′muŋ′gər) *n.* ⟦FELL[4] + MONGER⟧ [Chiefly Brit.] a person who deals in or prepares animal skins

fel·loe (fel′ō) *n.* FELLY[1]

fel·low (fel′ō; *also, for n.,* fel′ə) *n.* ⟦ME *felaghe* < Late OE *feolaga*, partner < *feoh* (see FEE) + *laga*, a laying down (see LAW), after ON *félagi*: basic sense, "one laying down wealth for a joint undertaking"; senses 5, 6, 7 < transl. of L *socius*: see ASSOCIATE⟧ **1** [Obs.] a person who shares; partner or accomplice **2** a companion; associate **3** a person of the same class or rank; equal; peer **4** either of a pair of corresponding things; mate **5** a graduate student who holds a fellowship in a university or college **6** a member of a learned society **7** at some British and U.S. universities, *a)* a faculty member who is a member of the governing body *b)* a scholar, journalist, etc. who is appointed on a fellowship for a given period of research, teaching, or both **8** [Obs.] *a)* a person of a lower social class *b)* a coarse, rough man **9** [Informal] *a)* a man or boy (often in familiar address) *b)* a person; one *[a fellow must eat]* **10** [Informal] a suitor; beau —*adj.* **1** having the same ideas, position, work, etc. **2** in the same condition or of the same nature; associated or kindred *[fellow workers, one's fellow man]*

fellow feeling a feeling of fellowship, kinship, comradeship, etc.

fel·low·ship (fel′ō ship′) *n.* ⟦ME *felauship*⟧ **1** companionship; friendly association **2** a mutual sharing, as of experience, activity, interest, etc. **3** a group of people with the same interests; company; brotherhood **4** an endowment, or a sum of money paid from such an endowment, for the support of a graduate student, scholar, etc. doing advanced study in some field **5** the rank or position of a fellow in a university or college

fellow traveler ⟦transl. of Russ *poputčik*⟧ a person who espouses the cause of a party, esp. a Communist Party, without being a member; sympathizer

fel·ly[1] (fel′ē) *n., pl.* **-lies** ⟦ME *felwe* < OE *felg*, akin to Ger *felge* < IE **pelk̑-*, to turn > FALLOW[1]⟧ the rim of a spoked wheel, or a segment of the rim

fel·ly[2] (fel′lē) *adv.* in a fell manner; with cruelty

fel·on[1] (fel′ən) *n.* ⟦ME < OFr < ML *felo*, earlier *fello* < ?⟧ **1** [Obs.] a villain **2** *Law* a person guilty of a major crime; criminal —*adj.* [Old Poet.] wicked; base; criminal

fel·on[2] (fel′ən) *n.* ⟦ME < ? same base as prec.⟧ a painful abscess or infection at the end of a finger or toe, near the nail; whitlow

fe·lo·ni·ous (fə lō′nē əs) *adj.* ⟦altered (after FELONY) < ME *felonous* < OFr *feloneus*⟧ **1** [Old Poet.] wicked; base **2** *Law* of, like, or constituting a felony

fel·on·ry (fel′ən rē) *n.* felons collectively

fel·o·ny (fel′ə nē) *n., pl.* **-nies** ⟦ME *felonie* < OFr < ML *felonia*, treason, treachery < *felo*, FELON[1]⟧ a major crime, as murder, arson, or rape, for which statute usually provides a greater punishment than for a misdemeanor: the usual minimum penalty is imprisonment for one year

fel·sen·meer (fel′zən mir′) *n.* ⟦Ger, lit., sea of rock < *fels, felsen*, rock (see FELL[5]) + *meer*, sea⟧ an area that is usually found on gentle slopes above the timberline, covered with a layer of weathered rocks and boulders

fel·site (fel′sīt′) *n.* ⟦< fol. + -ITE[1]⟧ a light-colored, dense, fine-grained igneous rock consisting mainly of feldspar and quartz

fel·spar (fel′spär′) *n.* ⟦altered < FELDSPAR, after Ger *fels*, rock⟧ FELDSPAR

felt[1] (felt) *n.* ⟦ME < OE, akin to Ger *filz*, Du *filt* (basic sense, "cloth made by pounding or beating") < IE base **pel-*, to beat, strike > L *pellere*, to beat, drive⟧ **1** a fabric of wool, often mixed with fur or hair or with cotton, rayon, etc., the fibers being worked together by pressure, heat, chemical action, etc. instead of by weaving or knitting **2** any fabric or material with a fuzzy, springy surface like that of felt; esp., a heavy insulating material made of asbestos fibers matted together **3** anything made of felt —*adj.* made of felt —*vt.* **1** *a)* to make into felt *b)* to cover with felt **2** to cause (fibers) to mat together —*vi.* to become matted together

felt[2] (felt) *vt., vi. pt. and pp. of* FEEL

felt·ing (fel′tiŋ) *n.* **1** the making of felt **2** the material of which felt is made **3** felted cloth

felt-tip (pen) (felt′tip′, fel′-) a kind of pen having a writing tip of compressed felt that picks up ink from an interior reservoir —**felt′-tipped′** *adj.*

fe·luc·ca (fə luk′ə) *n.* ⟦< Sp < Ar *falūka* < ? Gr *epholkion*, small boat towed behind a ship⟧ a small, narrow ship propelled by oars or lateen sails and used esp. in the Mediterranean

fem *abbrev.* **1** female **2** feminine

FEMA (fē′mə) *abbrev.* Federal Emergency Management Agency

fe·male (fē′māl′) *adj.* ⟦ME, altered after MALE < *femelle* < OFr < L *femella*, dim. of *femina*, a woman < IE base **dhē-*, to suck, suckle > L *fellare*, to suck, *filius*, son, *fetus*, progeny, Gr *thēlazein*, to suckle, *thele*, nipple⟧ **1** designating or of the sex that produces ova and bears offspring: biological symbol, ♀: cf. MALE **2** of, characteristic of, or suitable to members of this sex; feminine **3** consisting of women or girls **4** designating or having a hollow part shaped to receive a corresponding inserted part (called *male*): said of pipe fittings, electric sockets, etc. **5** *Bot.* *a)* having pistils, archegonia, or oogonia, but no stamens or antheridia *b)* designating or of a reproductive structure or part containing large gametes (eggs) that can be fertilized by smaller, motile gametes (sperms) *c)* designating or of any structure or part that produces fruit after it is fertilized —*n.* **1** a female person; woman or girl **2** a female animal or plant —**fe′male·ness** *n.*

SYN.—**female** is the basic term applied to members of the sex that is biologically distinguished from the male sex and is used of animals or plants as well as of human beings; **feminine** is now the preferred term for references, other than those basically biological, to qualities thought to be characteristic of or suitable to women, as delicacy, gentleness, etc.; **womanly** suggests the noble qualities one associates with a woman, esp. one who has maturity of character; **womanish**, in contrast, suggests the weaknesses and faults that are regarded as characteristic of women; **effeminate**, used chiefly in reference to a man, implies delicacy, softness, or lack of virility; **ladylike** refers to manners, conduct, etc. such as are expected from a refined or well-bred woman See also **woman** —*ANT.* **male, masculine, manly, mannish**

feme cov·ert (fem′ kuv′ərt) ⟦OFr, lit., woman covered⟧ *Law* a married woman

feme sole (fem′ sōl′) ⟦OFr, lit., woman alone⟧ *Law* an unmarried woman; spinster, divorcée, or widow

fem·i·nine (fem′ə nin) *adj.* ⟦ME < OFr < L *femininus* < *femina*, woman⟧ **1** female; of women or girls **2** having qualities regarded as characteristic of women and girls, as gentleness, weakness, delicacy, or modesty **3** suitable to or characteristic of a woman; womanly **4** effeminate; womanish: said of a man **5** *Gram.* designating, of, or belonging to the gender of words denoting, or referring to, females as well as many other words to which no distinction of sex is attributed **6** *Music* designating or of a cadence ending on an unaccented note or chord **7** *Prosody* *a)* ending with an unstressed syllable, as a line of verse *b)* designating or of a rhyme in which the rhyming elements have two, or sometimes three, syllables of which only the first is stressed (Ex.: danger, stranger) —*n. Gram.* **1** the feminine gender **2** a word or form in this gender —*SYN.* FEMALE —**fem′i·nine·ly** *adv.* —**fem′i·nin′i·ty** *n.*

fem·i·nism (fem′ə niz′əm) *n.* ⟦< L *femina*, woman + -ISM⟧ **1** [Rare] feminine qualities **2** *a)* the principle that women should have political, economic, and social rights equal to those of men *b)* the movement to win such rights for women —**fem′i·nist** *n., adj.*

fem·i·nize (fem′ə nīz′) *vt., vi.* **-nized′, -niz′ing** ⟦< L *femina*, woman + -IZE⟧ to make or become feminine or effeminate —**fem′i·ni·za′tion** *n.*

femme (fem) *n.* [Fr] [Slang] **1** a woman or wife **2** a person, esp. a lesbian, who dresses and behaves in a way regarded as traditionally feminine or effeminate

femme de cham·bre (fȧm də shän′br′) [Fr] **1** a chambermaid **2** a lady's maid

femme fa·tale (fȧm fȧ tȧl′) [Fr, lit., deadly woman] *pl.* **femmes fa·tales** (fȧm fȧ tȧl′) an alluring woman, esp. one who leads men to their downfall or ruin

fem·to- (fem′tō) ⟦< Dan *femten*, fifteen < ODan *femtan* < *fem*, five + *-tjan*, akin to OE *-tyne*, -TEEN⟧ *combining form* one quadrillionth part of; the factor 10^{-15} *[femtosecond]*

fe·mur (fē′mər) *n., pl.* **fe′murs** or **fem·o·ra** (fem′ə rə) ⟦ModL < L, thigh⟧ **1** the largest, longest, and heaviest bone in the body, extending from the hip to the knee; thighbone **2** a long leg segment in various animals, connecting the leg to the body —**fem·o·ral** (fem′ə rəl) *adj.*

fen[1] (fen) *n.* ⟦ME < OE, akin to Ger *fenne*, marsh, Goth *fani*, mud < IE base **pen-*, wet, slime, mire > Ger *feucht*, damp⟧ an area of low, flat, marshy land; swamp; bog

fen[2] (fun) *n.* ⟦Chin⟧ a monetary unit of China, equal to 1⁄100 of a yuan

fe·na·gle (fə nā′gəl) *vi., vt.* **-gled, -gling** *alt. sp. of* FINAGLE

fence (fens) *n.* ⟦ME *fens*, aphetic for *defens*, DEFENSE⟧ **1** [Obs.] a protection; defense **2** a barrier, as of wooden or metal posts, rails, wire mesh, etc., used as a boundary or means of protection or confinement **3** the art of self-defense with foil, saber, or epee; fencing **4** *a)* a person who deals in stolen goods *b)* a place where stolen goods are bought and sold ☆**5** *Baseball* the fence, wall, etc. at the back of the outfield: a hit over this is a home run —*vt.* **fenced, fenc′ing** **1** to enclose, restrict, or hamper with or as with a fence: with *in, off*, etc. **2** to keep (*out*) by or as by a fence **3** [Archaic] to ward off; protect; defend **4** to sell (stolen property) to a fence —*vi.* **1** to practice the art of fencing **2** to avoid giving a direct reply; be evasive (*with*); parry **3** to deal in stolen goods —☆**mend one's fences** to engage in politicking; look after one's political interests —☆**on the fence** uncommitted or undecided in a controversy —**fence′less** *adj.*

fence-mend·ing (fens′men′diŋ) *n.* the act or process of repairing or reestablishing relations, as between political factions

fenc·er (fen′sər) *n.* **1** a person who fences with a foil, saber, or epee **2** one who makes or repairs fences

☆**fence-sit·ter** (fens′sit′ər) *n.* ⟦from the idea of being ON THE FENCE (see phr. under FENCE)⟧ a person who is uncommitted or undecided about an issue, esp. one who is stubbornly or habitually so —**fence′-sit′ting** *n.*

fenc·ing (fen′siŋ) *n.* ⟦< FENCE, v.⟧ **1** the art or sport of fighting with a foil, saber, or epee **2** *a)* material for making fences *b)* a system of fences

fend (fend) *vt.* ⟦ME *fenden*, aphetic for *defenden*, DEFEND⟧ [Archaic] to defend —*vi.* to resist; parry —**fend for oneself** to manage by oneself; get along without help —**fend off** to ward off

fend·er (fen′dər) *n.* anything that fends off or protects something else;

specif., ☆*a)* a metal or plastic enclosure over the wheels of an automobile or other vehicle to protect against splashing mud, etc. ☆*b)* a device on the front of a streetcar or locomotive to catch or push aside anything on the track *c)* a low screen or frame in front of a fireplace to keep the hot coals in *d)* a pad or cushion of canvas, rope, wood, etc. hung over a ship's side to protect it when going alongside a pier or another ship

☆**fender bender** [Informal] an automobile accident in which the automobile sustains little damage

Fé·ne·lon (fān lōn′; *E* fen′ə län′), **Fran·çois (de Salignac de La Mothe)** (frän swȧ′) 1651-1715; Fr. clergyman & writer

fe·nes·tra (fi nes′trə) ***n.***, *pl.* **-trae′** (-trē′) ⟦ModL < L, window, prob. < Etr **fnestra*⟧ **1** a small opening, as any of the covered oval openings in the inner wall of the middle ear **2** a small, transparent spot, as in the wings of some insects **3** any small opening in a membrane —**fe·nes′tral** ***adj.***

fe·nes·trat·ed (fi nes′trāt′id, fen′es trāt′id) ***adj.*** ⟦pp. of rare v. < L *fenestratus*, pp. of *fenestrare*, to furnish with openings < *fenestra*, window: see prec.⟧ **1** having windows, openings, or perforations **2** *Biol.* having fenestrae Also **fe·nes′trate** (-trit; -trāt′)

fen·es·tra·tion (fen′es trā′shən) ***n.*** ⟦see prec. & -ION⟧ **1** the arrangement of windows and doors in a building **2** *Surgery* the act of perforating or making an opening, esp. into the inner ear in certain cases of otosclerosis

feng shui (fuŋ′shwā′, -shwē′) ⟦Chin *feng*, wind + *shui*, water⟧ the Chinese practice of choosing, designing, and furnishing work and living spaces to achieve balance, promote comfort, etc.

Fe·ni·an (fē′nē ən, fēn′yən) ***n.*** ⟦< pl. of Ir Gael *Fiann*, the old militia of Ireland, after *Finn, Fionn*, hero of Irish tradition: assoc. with OIr *fēne*, inhabitant of Ireland⟧ **1** any of a group of legendary military heroes of ancient Ireland ☆**2** a member of a secret revolutionary movement formed in New York and Ireland to free Ireland from English rule: the movement was most active in the 1860s and continued until WWI —***adj.*** of the Fenians —**Fe′ni·an·ism′** ***n.***

fen·ing (fen′iŋ) ***n.*** ⟦Serb, akin to Ger *pfennig*: see PENNY⟧ a monetary unit of Bosnia and Herzegovina, equal to $^1/_{100}$ of a marka

fen·nec (fen′ek′) ***n.*** ⟦Ar *fanak*⟧ a small, fawn-colored desert fox (*Fennecus zerda*) of N Africa and Arabia, with large eyes and ears

fen·nel (fen′əl) ***n.*** ⟦ME *fenel* < OE *finul* < L *faeniculum*, dim. of *faenum*, earlier *fenum*, hay⟧ a tall herb (*Foeniculum vulgare*) of the umbel family, with feathery leaves and yellow flowers: its foliage and aromatic seeds are used to flavor foods and medicines

fen·nel·flow·er (-flou′ər) ***n.*** ⟦so named from being confused with prec.⟧ any of a genus (*Nigella*) of plants of the buttercup family, with finely divided foliage and blue, yellow, or white flowers

Fen·no·scan·di·a (fen′ō skan′dē ə) ⟦ult. < L *Fenni*, Finns + *Scandia*, all or a part of Scandinavia⟧ region in N Europe, including Scandinavia, Finland, and the part of NW Russia west of the White Sea: sometimes **Fen′no-Scan′di·a** —**Fen′no·scan′di·an** ***adj.***

fen·ny (fen′ē) ***adj.*** ⟦ME *fenni* < OE *fennig*⟧ **1** full of fens; marshy; boggy **2** of or found in fens

Fen·ris (fen′ris) ***n.*** ⟦ON⟧ *Norse Myth.* a great wolf, bound by the gods with a magic rope: also **Fen·rir** (fen′rir′)

fen·ta·nyl (fen′tə nil′) ***n.*** a powerful, synthetic, short-acting narcotic drug, $C_{22}H_{28}N_2O{\cdot}C_6H_8O_7$, used for severe pain and as a general anesthetic: in full **fentanyl citrate**

fen·u·greek (fen′yoo grēk′) ***n.*** ⟦ME *fenugrek* < OFr *fenugrec* < L *faenumgraecum*, lit., Greek hay⟧ a leguminous herb (*Trigonella foenumgraecum*) native to SE Europe and W Asia, used for forage and formerly in medicine and having seeds used in cooking

feoff (fef, fēf) ***vt.*** ⟦Early ME *feoffen* < Anglo-Fr *feoffer* < OFr *fieuffer, fieffer* < *fieu*, fief: see FEE⟧ [Historical] ENFEOFF —***n. var. of*** FIEF —**feoff′ment** ***n.*** —**feof′for** ***n.***, **feoff′er**

feoff·ee (fef ē′, fēf ē′) ***n.*** ⟦ME *feoffe* < Anglo-Fr *feoffé*, pp. of *feoffer*⟧ a person granted a fief

-fer (fər) ⟦< Fr *-fère* or L *-fer* < *ferre*, BEAR[1]⟧ *suffix forming nouns* bearer, producer [*conifer*]

fe·rae na·tu·rae (fē′rē nə tyoo′rē, fer′ā nə too′rä) ⟦L, of a wild nature⟧ *Law* nondomesticated animals and fowls that are no one's private property

fe·ral (fir′əl, fer′-) ***adj.*** ⟦ML *feralis* < L *fera*, wild animal < *ferus*, FIERCE + -AL⟧ **1** *a)* untamed; wild *b)* having returned to a wild condition **2** savage; fierce

fer·bam (fur′bam′) ***n.*** ⟦*fer(ric dimethyldithiocar)bam(ate)*⟧ a fungicide, $FeC_9H_{18}N_3S_6$, used to control certain diseases, esp. of fruit trees

fer-de-lance (fer′də lans′) ***n.*** ⟦Fr, iron tip of a lance (from the shape of the head)⟧ a large, poisonous pit viper (*Bothrops atrox*) found in tropical America

Fer·di·nand[1] (furd′'n and) ***n.*** ⟦Fr; prob. < Gmc **farthi-*, journey < *faran*, to travel (see FARE) + **nanths*, courage > Goth *(ana)nanthjan*, to be bold, OE *nethan*, to dare; hence, lit., ? bold traveler⟧ a masculine name

Fer·di·nand[2] (furd′'n and) **1 Ferdinand I** 1000?-65; king of Castile (1035-65) & of León (1037-65): called *the Great* **2 Ferdinand I** 1503-64; emperor of the Holy Roman Empire (1558-64), born in Spain **3 Ferdinand I** (born *Maximilian Karl Leopold Maria*) 1861-1948; king of Bulgaria (1908-18); abdicated **4 Ferdinand II** 1578-1637; emperor of the Holy Roman Empire (1619-37) **5 Ferdinand V** 1452-1516; king of Castile (1474-1504); (as **Ferdinand II**) king of Aragon & Sicily (1479-1516); (as **Ferdinand III**) king of Naples (1504-16): husband of Isabella I of Castile: called *the Catholic*

fere (fēr) ***n.*** ⟦ME *fere* < OE (Anglian) *fera*, aphetic for *gefera* < *ge-*, together + *-fera* < base of *faran*, to go: see FARE⟧ [Archaic] **1** a companion; mate **2** a husband or wife; spouse

fer·e·to·ry (fer′ə tôr′ē) ***n.***, *pl.* **-ries** ⟦altered < ME *fertre* < OFr *fiertre* < L *feretrum*, a litter, bier < Gr *pheretron* < *pherein*, BEAR[1]⟧ **1** a portable reliquary **2** a place for keeping this

fe·ri·a (fir′ē ə, fer′-) ***n.***, *pl.* **-ri·as** or **-ri·ae′** (-ē′) ⟦LL: see FAIR[2]⟧ **1** [*pl.*] in ancient Rome, holidays or festivals **2** *Eccles.* any weekday, except Saturday, that is not a feast day or vigil —**fe′ri·al** ***adj.***

fe·rine (fir′īn, -in) ***adj.*** ⟦L *ferinus* < *ferus*, FIERCE⟧ FERAL

fer·i·ty (fer′i tē) ***n.*** ⟦L *feritas* < *ferus*, FIERCE⟧ the state or quality of being wild, savage, or untamed

Fer·man·agh (fər man′ə) **1** former county of SW Northern Ireland: 724 sq mi (1,875 sq km) **2** district in SW Northern Ireland, occupying the same area: 724 sq mi (1,875 sq km)

Fer·mat (fer mä′), **Pierre de** (pyer də) 1601-65; Fr. mathematician

fer·ma·ta (fer mät′ə) ***n.*** ⟦It < *fermare*, to stop, confirm < L *firmare*, to make firm < *firmus*, FIRM[1]⟧ *Music* PAUSE (sense 4)

fer·ment (fur′ment′; *for v.* fər ment′) ***n.*** ⟦ME < OFr < L *fermentum*, leaven, yeast < *fervere*, to boil, be agitated: see BARM⟧ **1** a substance or organism causing fermentation, as yeast, bacteria, enzymes, etc. **2** FERMENTATION **3** a state of excitement or agitation —***vt.*** **1** to cause fermentation in **2** to excite; agitate —***vi.*** **1** to be in the process of fermentation **2** to be excited or agitated; seethe —**fer·ment′a·ble** ***adj.***

fer·men·ta·tion (fur′mən tā′shən) ***n.*** ⟦ME *fermentacioun* < LL *fermentatio*: see prec.⟧ **1** the breakdown of complex molecules in organic compounds, caused by the influence of a ferment [*bacteria cause milk to curdle by fermentation*] **2** excitement; agitation

fer·ment·a·tive (fər ment′ə tiv) ***adj.*** of, causing, or resulting from fermentation

fer·mi (fer′mē, fur′-) ***n.*** ⟦after fol.⟧ *Physics* a unit of length equal to 10^{-15} meter: see FEMTO-

Fer·mi (fer′mē), **En·ri·co** (en rē′kō) 1901-54; U.S. nuclear physicist, born in Italy

fer·mi·on (fer′mē än′, fur′-) ***n.*** ⟦after prec. + -ON⟧ *Particle Physics* any of a class of subatomic particles that obey the Pauli exclusion principle and have fractional spin, including the leptons, quarks, and baryons: see BOSON

☆**fer·mi·um** (fer′mē əm, fur′-) ***n.*** ⟦ModL: so named (1955) by A. Ghiorso and co-workers, after E. FERMI (in honor of his studies in nuclear physics) + -IUM⟧ a radioactive, metallic chemical element, one of the actinides, produced by intense neutron bombardment of plutonium, as in a cyclotron: symbol, Fm; at. no. 100: see the periodic table of elements in the Reference Supplement

fern (furn) ***n.*** ⟦ME < OE *fearn* < IE **porno-*, leaf, feather (> Sans *parna*, feather, leaf) < base **per-*, to transport, fly > FARE⟧ any of a widespread division (Filicophyta) of nonflowering embryophytes having roots, stems, and fronds, and reproducing by spores instead of by seeds —**fern′y** ***adj.***

fern

Fer·nan·do de No·ro·nha (fer nän′doo də nô rô′nyə) island in the S Atlantic, northeast of Natal, Brazil: with neighboring islets, part of Pernambuco state, Brazil: 10 sq mi (25.9 sq km)

Fer·nan·do Pó·o (fer nän′dô pô′ô) *former name for* BIOKO

fern bar a fashionable bar or restaurant decorated mainly with plants, including ferns

fern·er·y (furn′ər ē) ***n.***, *pl.* **-er·ies** **1** a place where ferns are grown **2** a collection of growing ferns

fern seed the dustlike spores of ferns: formerly believed to make the person who carried them invisible

fe·ro·cious (fə rō′shəs) ***adj.*** ⟦< L *ferox* (gen. *ferocis*), wild, untamed < *ferus*, FIERCE + base akin to *oculus*, EYE + -OUS⟧ **1** fierce; savage; violently cruel **2** [Informal] very great [*a ferocious appetite*] —**fe·ro′cious·ly** ***adv.*** —**fe·ro′cious·ness** ***n.***

fe·roc·i·ty (fə räs′ə tē) ***n.*** ⟦Fr *férocité* < L *ferocitas*⟧ the state or quality of being ferocious

-fer·ous (fər əs) ⟦L *-fer* < *ferre*, BEAR[1] + -OUS⟧ *suffix forming adjectives* bearing, producing [*coniferous*]

Fer·ra·ra (fə rär′ə) commune in NC Italy, in the Emilia-Romagna region

fer·rate (fer′āt′) ***n.*** ⟦< L *ferrum*, iron (see FERRO-) + -ATE[2]⟧ a salt of the hypothetical ferric acid, containing the divalent negative radical FeO_4

fer·re·dox·in (fer′ə däk′sin) ***n.*** ⟦FER(RO)- + REDOX + -IN[1]⟧ a protein, containing iron, that is found in chloroplasts and transports electrons in photosynthesis, nitrogen fixation, and other biological processes

fer·re·ous (fer′ē əs) ***adj.*** ⟦L *ferreus* < *ferrum*, iron + -OUS⟧ of, like, or containing iron

fer·ret[1] (fer′ət) ***n.*** ⟦< It *fioretti*, floss silk, orig. pl. of *fioretto*, dim. of *fiore*, a flower < L *flos*, FLOWER⟧ a narrow ribbon of cotton, wool, silk, etc.: also **fer′ret·ing**

fer·ret[2] (fer′ət) ***n.*** ⟦ME *feret* < OFr *furet* < LL *furetus*, dim. of *furo*, a ferret < L *fur*, thief: see FURTIVE⟧ **1** a small, domesticated European polecat with pink eyes and yellowish fur, easily tamed for hunting rabbits, rats, etc. **2** a rare, black-footed weasel (*Mustela nigripes*) of the W U.S. —*vt.* **1** to force out of hiding with or as if with a ferret **2** to search for persistently and discover (facts, the truth, etc.); search: with *out* **3** [Archaic] to keep after; harass —*vi.* **1** to hunt with ferrets **2** to search around —**fer′ret·er** *n.* —**fer′ret·y** (-ē) *adj.*

fer·ri- (fer′ī, -i, -ə) ⟦< L *ferrum:* see FERRO-⟧ *combining form* containing ferric iron [*ferricyanide*]: see FERRO-

fer·ri·age (fer′ē ij) *n.* ⟦< FERRY + -AGE⟧ **1** transportation by ferry **2** the charge for this

fer·ric (fer′ik) *adj.* ⟦< L *ferrum*, iron (see FERRO-) + -IC⟧ **1** of, containing, or derived from iron **2** *Chem.* designating or of trivalent iron, or compounds containing such iron: distinguished from FERROUS

ferric oxide a brown or reddish oxide of iron, Fe_2O_3, occurring naturally as hematite or prepared by the oxidation of iron: used as a pigment, in polishing compounds, in magnetic tapes, etc.

fer·ri·cy·an·ic acid (fer′ī sī an′ik, fer′i-) ⟦FERRI- + CYANIC⟧ a brown, crystalline, unstable acid, $H_3Fe(CN)_6$

fer·ri·cy·a·nide (-sī′ə nīd′) *n.* a salt of ferricyanic acid containing the trivalent negative radical $Fe(CN)_6$, in which the iron is trivalent

fer·rif·er·ous (fə rif′ər əs) *adj.* ⟦FERRI- + -FEROUS⟧ bearing or containing iron

fer·ri·mag·net·ic (fer′ī mag net′ik, fer′ē-) *adj.* designating a material, as magnetite, having a weak, permanent magnetism: used in recording tape —**fer′ri·mag′net·ism′** (-mag′nə tiz′əm) *n.*

☆**Fer·ris wheel** (fer′is) ⟦after George W. G. *Ferris* (1859-96), U.S. engineer who constructed the first one for the World's Fair in Chicago in 1893⟧ an amusement-park ride consisting of a large, upright, revolving wheel with seats for the riders attached at equidistant points along its rim

fer·rite (fer′īt′) *n.* ⟦< L *ferrum*, iron + -ITE[1]⟧ **1** one of the forms of pure metallic iron, having high magnetic permeability and occurring as a constituent of ordinary iron and steel **2** any of various ceramic, magnetic materials with poor electrical conductivity, containing ferric oxide and another metallic oxide: used in recording tape and computer memories **3** *Geol.* a grain, scale, or bit of red, brown, or yellow iron oxide in a rock

fer·ri·tin (fer′i tin) *n.* an iron-storing protein found in certain bodily tissue

fer·ro- (fer′ō, -ə) ⟦< L *ferrum*, iron, prob. via Etr < Sem base seen in Heb-Phoen *barzel*, Assyr *parz-illu*⟧ *combining form* **1** iron [*ferromagnetic*] **2** iron and [*ferromanganese*] **3** containing ferrous iron [*ferrocyanide*]: see FERRI-

fer·ro·al·loy (fer′ō al′oi′, -ə loi′) *n.* any of various alloys of iron used in the manufacture of steel: named from the added metal, as ferrochromium, ferromanganese, etc.

fer·ro·chro·mi·um (-krō′mē əm) *n.* an alloy of iron and chromium: also **fer′ro·chrome′** (-krōm′)

fer·ro·con·crete (-kän′krēt′) *n.* REINFORCED CONCRETE

fer·ro·cy·a·nide (-sī′ə nīd′, -nid) *n.* a salt of $H_4Fe(CN)_6$, containing the tetravalent negative radical $Fe(CN)_6$, in which the iron is divalent

☆**fer·ro·e·lec·tric** (-ē lek′trik) *adj.* of or relating to a crystalline dielectric substance, as Rochelle salt, that is capable of retaining the electric polarization of an applied electric field: used in making transducers, capacitors, etc. —*n.* a ferroelectric substance —**fer′ro·e′lec·tric′i·ty** *n.*

Ferrol *see* EL FERROL

fer·ro·mag·ne·sian (fer′ō mag nē′shən, -nē′zhən) *adj.* ⟦< FERRO- + MAGNESI(UM) + -AN⟧ *Mineralogy* containing iron and magnesium

fer·ro·mag·net·ic (-mag net′ik) *adj.* designating a material, as iron, nickel, or cobalt, having a high magnetic permeability which varies with the magnetizing force —**fer′ro·mag′net·ism′** (-mag′nə tiz′əm) *n.*

fer·ro·man·ga·nese (-maŋ′gə nēs′, -nēz′) *n.* an alloy of iron and manganese, used for making hard steel

fer·ro·sil·i·con (-sil′i kän′) *n.* a compound of iron and silicon, used in making steel, as a deoxidizing agent, etc.

fer·ro·type (fer′ō tīp′, fer′ə-) *n.* ⟦FERRO- + -TYPE⟧ **1** a positive photograph taken directly on a thin plate of black-enameled iron coated with a sensitized emulsion; tintype **2** the process of making such photographs —*vt.* **-typed′**, **-typ′ing** to give a glossy finish to (a photographic print) by squeezing into contact with a highly polished surface, usually chromium-plated steel, stainless steel, or plastic

fer·rous (fer′əs) *adj.* ⟦< L *ferrum*, iron (see FERRO-) + -OUS⟧ **1** of, containing, or derived from iron **2** *Chem.* designating or of divalent iron, or compounds containing it: distinguished from FERRIC

ferrous oxide the black, powdery monoxide of iron, FeO

ferrous sulfate a green, crystalline compound, $FeSO_4{\cdot}7H_2O$, used in dyeing, the making of ink, etc.; copperas

fer·ru·gi·nous (fə ro͞o′ji nəs) *adj.* ⟦L *ferruginus* < *ferrugo*, iron rust, color of iron rust < *ferrum*, iron: see FERRO-⟧ **1** of, containing, or having the nature of, iron **2** having the color of iron rust; reddish-brown

fer·rule (fer′əl, -o͞ol′) *n.* ⟦formerly *verrel* < ME & OFr *virole*, iron ring on a staff < L *viriola*, dim. of *viriae*, bracelets, via Celt < IE **weir-*, wire, twisted work (> WIRE) < base **wei-*, to bend, twist > L *viere*, to twist, bind around; sp. altered after L *ferrum*, iron⟧ **1** a metal ring or cap put around the end of a cane, tool handle, etc. to prevent splitting or to give added strength **2** *Mech.* a short tube or bushing for tightening a joint —*vt.* **-ruled**, **-rul·ing** to furnish with a ferrule

fer·ry (fer′ē) *vt.* **-ried**, **-ry·ing** ⟦ME *ferien* < OE *ferian*, to carry, convey, esp. by water, caus. of *faran*, to go: see FARE⟧ **1** to take (people, cars, etc.) across a river or narrow body of water in a boat, raft, etc. **2** to cross (a river, etc.) on a ferry **3** to deliver (airplanes) by flying to the destination **4** to transport by airplane —*vi.* to cross a river, etc. by ferry —*n., pl.* **-ries** **1** a system for carrying people, cars, or goods across a river, etc. by boat **2** a boat used for this **3** the place where a ferry docks on either shore **4** the legal right to transport by ferry for a fee **5** the delivery of airplanes to their destination by flying them

fer·ry·boat (-bōt′) *n.* FERRY (*n.* 2)

fer·ry·man (-mən) *n., pl.* **-men** (-mən) a person who owns, manages, or works on a ferry

fer·tile (furt′'l; *chiefly Brit & Cdn* fur′tīl′) *adj.* ⟦ME < OFr < L *fertilis* < stem of *ferre*, BEAR[1]⟧ **1** producing abundantly; rich in resources or invention; fruitful; prolific **2** causing or helping fertility [the sun's *fertile* warmth] **3** able to produce young, seeds, fruit, pollen, spores, etc. **4** capable of development into a new individual; fertilized [*fertile* eggs] **5** designating or of material, as uranium-238 or thorium-232, that can be made fissile by a neutron-induced nuclear reaction —**fer′tile·ly** *adv.* —**fer′tile·ness** *n.*

SYN.—**fertile** implies a producing, or power of producing, fruit or offspring, and may be used figuratively of the mind; **fecund** implies the abundant production of offspring or fruit, or, figuratively, of creations of the mind; **fruitful** specifically suggests the bearing of much fruit, but it is also used to imply fertility (of soil), favorable or profitable results, etc.; **prolific**, a close synonym for **fecund**, more often carries derogatory connotations of overly rapid production or reproduction —*ANT.* **sterile, barren**

Fertile Crescent historical crescent-shaped region in the Middle East, extending from the E end of the Mediterranean Sea along the Tigris & Euphrates rivers to the Persian Gulf: significant as the birthplace of several ancient civilizations

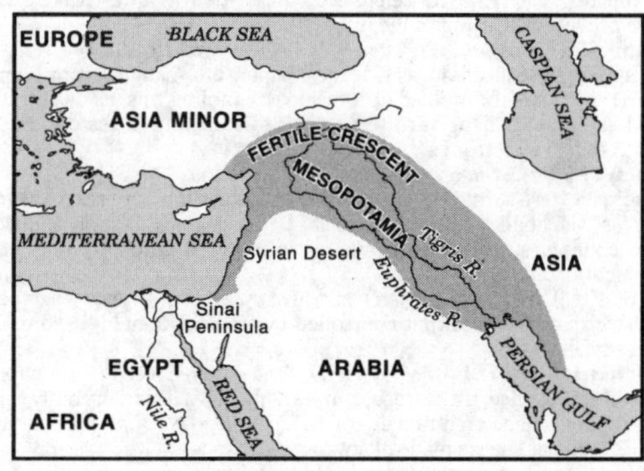

Fertile Crescent

fer·til·i·ty (fər til′ə tē) *n.* **1** the quality, state, or degree of being fertile; fecundity **2** the birthrate of a given population

fer·til·ize (furt′'l īz′) *vt.* **-ized′**, **-iz′ing** **1** to make fertile; make fruitful or productive; enrich [nitrates *fertilize* soil] **2** to spread fertilizer on **3** *Biol.* to make (the female reproductive cell or female individual) fruitful by pollinating, or impregnating, with the male gamete —**fer′til·iz′a·ble** *adj.* —**fer′til·i·za′tion** *n.*

fer·til·iz·er (-ī′zər) *n.* a person or thing that fertilizes; specif., any material, as manure, chemicals, etc., put on or in the soil to improve the quality or quantity of plant growth

fer·u·la (fer′yo͞o lə, fer′o͞o-) *n., pl.* **-lae′** (-lē′) ⟦ModL < L, giant fennel, hence, stick, whip, rod, prob. akin to *festuca*, blade of grass⟧ **1** any of a genus (*Ferula*) of plants of the umbel family, valuable as a source of various gums, as asafetida **2** FERULE

fer·ule (fer′əl, -o͞ol′, -yo͞ol′) *n.* ⟦ME *ferul* < L *ferula*: see prec.⟧ a flat stick or ruler used for punishing children —*vt.* **-uled**, **-ul·ing** to strike or punish with a ferule

fer·ven·cy (fur′vən sē) *n.* ⟦ME < OFr *fervence* < L *fervens*: see fol.⟧ great warmth of feeling; ardor

fer·vent (fur′vənt) *adj.* ⟦ME + OFr & < L *fervens* (gen. *ferventis*), prp. of *fervere*, to glow, boil, rage < IE **bhreu-*, to boil up < base **bher-*, to boil > BREW, BURN[1]⟧ **1** hot; burning; glowing **2** having or showing great warmth of feeling; intensely devoted or earnest; ardent —*SYN.* PASSIONATE —**fer′vent·ly** *adv.*

fer·vid (fur′vid) *adj.* ⟦L *fervidus* < *fervere*: see prec.⟧ **1** hot; glowing **2** impassioned; fervent —*SYN.* PASSIONATE —**fer′vid·ly** *adv.* —**fer′vid·ness** *n.*

fer·vor (fur′vər) *n.* ⟦ME < OFr < L < *fervere*: see FERVENT⟧ **1** intense heat **2** great warmth of emotion; ardor; zeal Brit. sp. **fer′vour** —*SYN.* PASSION

Fès (fes) *var. of* FEZ

fes·cue (fes′kyo͞o′) *n.* ⟦ME *festu* < OFr < L *festuca*, a straw, blade of grass⟧ **1** [Rare] a long stick, straw, etc., used as a teacher's pointer **2** any of a genus (*Festuca*) of grasses, many of which are used in the temperate zone as lawn and pasture grasses

fess or **fesse** (fes) *n.* ⟦ME *fesse* < OFr < L *fascia*, a band, FASCIA⟧ *Heraldry* a horizontal band forming the middle third of a shield

☆**fess up** or **'fess up** (fes) ⟦aphetic for CONFESS⟧ [Informal] to admit or acknowledge something; confess

☆**fest** (fest) ***n.*** [Informal] *short for* FESTIVAL (*n.* 2): sometimes used in an ironic or humorous way [a love *fest* between political rivals]

☆**-fest** (fest) *combining form* **1** ⟦< Ger *fest*, a celebration < L *festum*: see FEAST⟧ a festival, event, or gathering with a (specified) purpose or focus [*songfest*] **2** an occasion of much or many (of the thing specified): often used to form informal or slang words [*slugfest*]

fes·ta (fes′tə) ***n.***, *pl.* **-te** (-tā) ⟦It⟧ a holiday celebration; festival

fes·tal (fes′təl) ***adj.*** ⟦< L *festum* (see FEAST) + -AL⟧ of or like a joyous celebration; festive —**fes′tal·ly** ***adv.***

fes·ter (fes′tər) ***n.*** ⟦ME *festre* < OFr < L *fistula*: see FISTULA⟧ a small sore filled with pus; pustule —***vi.*** ⟦ME *festren* < the n.⟧ **1** to form pus; ulcerate **2** *a)* to grow embittered; rankle *b)* to grow or increase in virulence **3** to decay —***vt.*** **1** to cause the formation of pus in **2** to cause to rankle; embitter

fes·ti·nate (fes′tə nāt′; *for adj.*, -nit) [Rare] ***vt., vi.*** **-nat′ed, -nat′ing** ⟦< L *festinatus*, pp. of *festinare*, to hurry < IE base **bheres*, quick > MIr *bras*, swift⟧ to hurry; speed —***adj.*** hurried

fes·ti·na·tion (fes′tə nā′shən) ***n.*** ⟦L *festinatio*, haste: see prec.⟧ an involuntary inclination to hurry in walking, esp. seen in certain nervous diseases, as Parkinson's disease

fes·ti·val (fes′tə vəl) ***n.*** ⟦ME, n. & adj. < OFr < ML *festivalis* < L *festivus*: see fol.⟧ **1** a time or day of feasting or celebration; esp., a periodic religious celebration **2** a celebration, entertainment, or series of performances of a certain kind, often held periodically [a Bach *festival*] **3** merrymaking; festivity —***adj.*** of, for, or fit for a festival

fes·tive (fes′tiv) ***adj.*** ⟦L *festivus* < *festum*: see FEAST⟧ **1** of, for, or suited to a feast or festival **2** merry; joyous —**fes′tive·ly** ***adv.*** —**fes′tive·ness** ***n.***

fes·tiv·i·ty (fes tiv′ə tē) ***n.*** ⟦ME *festivite* < OFr < L *festivus*: see prec.⟧ **1** merrymaking; gaiety; joyful celebration **2** *pl.* **-ties** *a)* a festival *b)* [*pl.*] festive proceedings; things done in celebration

fes·toon (fes to͞on′) ***n.*** ⟦Fr *feston* < It *festone* < *festa* < VL: see FEAST⟧ **1** a wreath or garland of flowers, leaves, paper, etc. hanging in a loop or curve **2** any carved or molded decoration resembling this, as on furniture —***vt.*** **1** to adorn or hang with festoons **2** to form into a festoon or festoons **3** to join by festoons

fes·toon·er·y (-ər ē) ***n.*** an arrangement of festoons

Fest·schrift (fest′shrift′) ***n.***, *pl.* **-schrift′en** (-shrif′tən) or **-schrifts′** ⟦Ger < *fest*, festival, holiday + *schrift*, a writing⟧ [*also* **f-**] a collection of articles by the colleagues, former students, etc. of a noted scholar, published in his or her honor

FET (ef′ē′tē′) ***n.*** ⟦*f*(*ield-*)*e*(*ffect*) *t*(*ransistor*) < FIELD-EFFECT⟧ a type of transistor that has its output controlled by an electric field, used to amplify a signal

fet·a (cheese) (fet′ə) ⟦< ModGr (*tyri*) *pheta* < *tyri*, cheese (< Gr *tyros*) + *pheta* < It *fetta*, a slice, ult. < L *offa*, a morsel, piece⟧ **1** a soft, crumbly, white Greek cheese, made traditionally of sheep's or goat's milk and cured in brine **2** a similar cheese made of cow's milk

fe·tal (fēt′'l) ***adj.*** of, pertaining to, or like a fetus

fetal alcohol syndrome a condition affecting infants, characterized variously by INTELLECTUAL DISABILITY, heart defects, physical malformations, etc. and caused by excessive consumption of alcohol by the mother during pregnancy: also called, in less severe cases, **fetal alcohol effect**

fetal position a position resembling that of the human fetus in the uterus, in which the arms and legs of a person lying on one side are drawn in to the chest and the head is bent down

fe·ta·tion (fē tā′shən) ***n.*** **1** fetal development **2** pregnancy

fetch[1] (fech) ***vt.*** ⟦ME *fecchen* < OE *feccan*, earlier *fetian* < IE **pedyo-* (extension of base **ped-*, FOOT) > Ger *fassen*, to grasp⟧ **1** to go after and come back with; bring; get **2** to cause to come; produce; elicit **3** to draw (a breath) or heave (a sigh, groan, etc.) **4** [Rare] to derive or infer **5** to arrive at; reach, esp. when sailing against the wind or tide **6** to bring as a price; sell for **7** [Informal] to attract; charm; captivate **8** [Informal] to deliver or deal (a blow, stroke, etc.) —***vi.*** **1** to go after things and bring them back; specif., to retrieve game: said of hounds **2** *Naut.* *a)* to take or hold a course *b)* to veer —***n.*** **1** the act of fetching **2** a trick; dodge **3** the distance a wind blows unobstructed over water, esp. as a factor affecting the buildup of waves —*SYN.* BRING —**fetch and carry** to do minor tasks or chores —**fetch up** **1** [Informal] to come to a stop; arrive at a destination or stopping place; end up **2** [Dial.] to bring up or raise (a child, pet, etc.) —**fetch′er** ***n.***

fetch[2] (fech) ***n.*** ⟦< ?⟧ the apparition of a living person; wraith

fetch·ing (fech′iŋ) ***adj.*** attractive; charming —**fetch′ing·ly** ***adv.***

fete or **fête** (fāt, fet) ***n.*** ⟦Fr *fête* < OFr *feste*: see FEAST⟧ a festival; entertainment; esp., a gala entertainment held outdoors —***vt.*** **fet′ed** or **fêt′ed, fet′ing** or **fêt′ing** to celebrate or honor with a fete; entertain

fête cham·pê·tre (fet shän pe′tr′) ⟦Fr, rural festival⟧ an outdoor feast or entertainment

☆**fet·e·ri·ta** (fet′ə rēt′ə) ***n.*** ⟦prob. < Ar dial. name⟧ a cultivated sorghum (*Sorghum bicolor* var. *caudatum*) with large white, yellow, or red seeds, grown for grain and forage in the SW U.S.

fe·ti- (fēt′i, -ə) *combining form* fetus [*fetiparous*]

fe·tial (fē′shəl) ***n.*** ⟦L *fetialis* < *fetiales*, pl., college of priests < OL **fetis* < IE **dhē-ti-s*, statute < base **dhē-*: see DO[1]⟧ in ancient Rome, any of a group of priests who gave advice in the conduct of war, diplomatic negotiations, etc. —***adj.*** of these priests

fet·ich (fet′ish; *also* fēt′-) ***n.*** *archaic sp. of* FETISH —**fet′ich·ism′** ***n.***

fe·ti·cide (fēt′ə sīd′) ***n.*** ⟦< FETUS + -CIDE⟧ the killing of a fetus; illegal abortion —**fe′ti·ci′dal** (-sīd′'l) ***adj.***

fet·id (fet′id; *also* fēt′-) ***adj.*** ⟦ME < L *fetidus, foetidus* < L *foetere*, to stink < IE **dhwoitos* < base **dheu-*, to blow about > DULL⟧ having a bad smell, as of decay; putrid —**fet′id·ly** ***adv.*** —**fet′id·ness** ***n.***

fe·tip·a·rous (fē tip′ə rəs) ***adj.*** ⟦FETI- + -PAROUS⟧ designating or of animals whose young are born incompletely developed: said as of marsupials

fet·ish (fet′ish; *also* fēt′-) ***n.*** ⟦Fr *fétiche* < Port *feitiço*, a charm, sorcery; orig. adj. < L *facticius*, made by art, FACTITIOUS⟧ **1** any object believed by some person or group to have magic power **2** any thing or activity to which one is excessively or irrationally devoted [to make a *fetish* of sports] **3** *a)* an habitual sexual response by a person to any object (as a glove) or body part (as the foot) not conventionally regarded as erotic *b)* the object, body part, etc. eliciting such a response

fet·ish·ism (-iz′əm) ***n.*** ⟦Fr *fétichisme*⟧ **1** worship of or belief in fetishes **2** *Psychiatry* FETISH (sense 3*a*) —**fet′ish·ist** ***n.*** —**fet′ish·is′tic** ***adj.***

fet·ish·ize (-īz′) ***vt.*** **-ized′, -iz′ing** **1** to make a fetish of **2** to treat with unwarranted respect; overvalue —**fet′ish·i·za′tion** ***n.***

fet·lock (fet′läk′) ***n.*** ⟦ME *fitlok* (understood in ME as comp. of *fet*, FEET + *lok*, LOCK[2]) < MDu or MLowG cognate of MHG *vizzeloch* < *vissel*, dim. (< base of OHG *fuoz*, FOOT) + *-och*, -OCK⟧ **1** a tuft of hair on the back of the leg of a horse, donkey, etc., just above the hoof **2** the joint or projection bearing this tuft

fe·to- (fēt′ō, -ə) *combining form* FETI-

fe·tol·o·gy (fē täl′ə jē) ***n.*** ⟦*feto-* (var. of FETI-) + -LOGY⟧ the branch of embryology that deals with the fetus —**fe·tol′o·gist** ***n.***

fe·tor (fēt′ər, fē′tôr′) ***n.*** ⟦L *fetor, foetor* < *foetere*: see FETID⟧ a strong, disagreeable smell; stench

fe·to·scope (fē′tə skōp′) ***n.*** **1** an endoscope used to examine a fetus in the womb **2** a special stethoscope used to listen to the fetal heartbeat —**fe·to·scop·ic** (fē′tə skäp′ik) ***adj.*** —**fe·tos·co·py** (fē täs′kə pē) ***n.***

fet·ter (fet′ər) ***n.*** ⟦ME *feter* < OE < base of *fot*, FOOT, akin to Ger *fessel*⟧ [*often pl.*] **1** a shackle or chain for the feet **2** anything that holds in check; restraint —***vt.*** ⟦ME *feterien* < OE (*ge*)*feterian*⟧ **1** to bind with fetters; shackle; chain **2** to hold in check; restrain; confine

☆**fet·ter·bush** (fet′ər boosh′) ***n.*** **1** any of a genus (*Leucothoe*) of plants of the heath family, found in E U.S., with white, bell-shaped flowers **2** any of various other plants of the heath family

fet·tle (fet′'l) ***vt.*** **-tled, -tling** ⟦ME *fetlen*, to make ready, prob. < OE *fetel*, belt (akin to *feter*, FETTER), confused with *fætel*, container < *fæt*, VAT⟧ **1** [Dial.] to put in order or readiness; arrange **2** to line or cover (the hearth of a puddling furnace) with fettling —***n.*** **1** condition of body and mind [in fine *fettle*] **2** FETTLING

fet·tling (fet′liŋ) ***n.*** ⟦see prec.⟧ a loose material, as silica, used to fettle a puddling furnace

fet·tuc·ci·ne (fet′ə chē′nē) ***n.*** ⟦It, lit., little ribbons < *fetta*: see FETA⟧ pasta in thin, flat strips, wider than linguine, often served with butter, cheese, etc.: also sp. **fet′tu·ci′ne** or **fet′tu·ci′ni**

fe·tus (fēt′əs) ***n.***, *pl.* **-tus·es** ⟦ME < L *fetus, foetus*, a bringing forth, progeny; as adj., pregnant, fruitful: see FEMALE⟧ an unborn offspring of a vertebrate animal that is still in the uterus or egg, esp. in its later stages and specif., in humans, from about the eighth week after conception until birth: see EMBRYO

feu (fyo͞o) ***n.*** ⟦Scot for FEE⟧ *Scot. Law* **1** [Historical] a right to hold land for which the holder must pay in grain or money rather than in military service **2** a right to use land in perpetuity for a fixed annual payment **3** the land so held or used —***vt.*** to grant (land) on feu

feud[1] (fyo͞od) ***n.*** ⟦ME *fede* < OFr *faide* < Frank **faida*, akin to OHG *fehida*, enmity, revenge < IE base **peik-*, hostile > FOE, Lith *pìktas*, angry⟧ **1** a bitter, protracted, and violent quarrel, esp. between clans or families, often characterized by killings and counterkillings **2** any dispute or rivalry, esp. when bitter or protracted —***vi.*** to carry on a feud; quarrel

feud[2] (fyo͞od) ***n.*** ⟦ME < ML *feodum* < Frank **fehu-* (akin to OHG *feho*, cattle, property: see FEE) + **od*, **ot*, wealth, akin to OE *ead*⟧ land held from a feudal lord in return for service; fief

feu·dal[1] (fyo͞od′'l) ***adj.*** ⟦ML *feudalis*⟧ **1** of a feud (land) **2** of or like feudalism —**feu′dal·ly** ***adv.***

feu·dal[2] (fyo͞od′'l) ***adj.*** of or like a feud (quarrel)

feu·dal·ism (fyo͞od′'l iz′əm) ***n.*** **1** the economic, political, and social system in medieval Europe, in which land, worked by serfs who were bound to it, was held by vassals in exchange for military and other services given to overlords **2** a society organized like that in medieval Europe —**feu′dal·ist** ***n.*** —**feu′dal·is′tic** ***adj.***

feu·dal·i·ty (fyo͞o dal′ə tē) ***n.***, *pl.* **-ties** ⟦Fr *feodalité*⟧ **1** the quality or state of being feudal **2** a feudal holding or estate; fief

feu·dal·ize (fyo͞od′'l īz′) ***vt.*** **-ized′, -iz′ing** to make feudal; establish feudalism in —**feu′dal·i·za′tion** ***n.***

feudal system FEUDALISM

feu·da·to·ry (fyo͞o′də tôr′ē) ***n.***, *pl.* **-ries** ⟦ML *feodatorius* < *feodare*, to enfeoff < *feodum*, *feudum*: see FEUD[2]⟧ **1** a person holding land by feudal tenure **2** the land held; fief —***adj.*** **1** of the feudal relationship between vassal and lord **2** owing feudal allegiance (*to*)

☆**feud·ist**[1] (fyo͞od′ist) ***n.*** a participant in a feud (quarrel)

feud·ist[2] (fyo͞od′ist) ***n.*** a specialist in feudal law

feuil·le·ton (fëy′ tôn′) ***n.*** ⟦Fr < *feuillet*, a leaf, sheet < dim. of OFr *fuil*: see FOIL[2]⟧ **1** that part of a French newspaper which contains serialized fiction, light reviews, etc. **2** a piece printed in this section **3** any light, popular piece of writing

feuil·le·ton·ist (fu'yə tən ist) ***n.*** a writer of *feuilletons*

Feul·gen reaction (foil'gən) ⟦after R. *Feulgen* (1884-1955), Ger biochemist⟧ *Cytology* a reaction in which an aldehyde combines with a modified Schiff's reagent to produce a purplish compound: used especially to test for the presence of DNA

fe·ver (fē'vər) ***n.*** ⟦ME < OE *fefer* & OFr *fievre*, both < L *febris* < IE base **dhegwh-*, to burn > L *fovere*, to warm, MIr *daig*, fire⟧ **1** a body temperature that is higher than normal, caused by an infection, ovulation, vigorous exercise, etc.; pyrexia **2** any of various diseases characterized by a high fever [yellow *fever*] **3** a condition of nervousness or restless excitement —***vt.*** to cause fever in —**fe'vered** ***adj.***

fever blister (*or* **sore**) COLD SORE

fe·ver·few (fē'vər fyo͞o') ***n.*** ⟦ME *fevyrfue* < OE *feverfuge* & Anglo-Fr **fewerfue*, both < LL *febrifugia* < L *febris*, FEVER + *fugia* < *fugare*, to drive away; akin to *fugere*, to flee: see FUGITIVE⟧ a bushy plant (*Chrysanthemum parthenium*) of the composite family, with finely divided foliage and flowers with white florets around a yellow disk

fe·ver·ish (fē'vər ish') ***adj.*** **1** having fever, esp. slight fever **2** of, like, or caused by fever **3** causing fever **4** greatly excited or agitated Also **fe'ver·ous** —**fe'ver·ish·ly** ***adv.*** —**fe'ver·ish·ness** ***n.***

fe·ver·wort (fē'vər wurt') ***n.*** ☆HORSE GENTIAN: also **fe'ver·root'** (-ro͞ot')

few (fyo͞o) ***adj.*** ⟦ME *fewe* < OE *feawe, feawa*, pl., akin to OFris *fē*, Goth *fawai*, pl. < IE base **pōu-*, small, little > L *paucus*, Gr *pauros*, little⟧ not many; a small number of [*few* seats were left, a *few* people came] —***pron.*** not many; a small number [many left, *few* stayed; a *few* of the men are wearing hats] —**few and far between** scarce; rare —**the few** the minority; esp., a small, select group —**few'ness** ***n.***

few·er (-ər) ***adj. compar. of*** FEW —***pron.*** a smaller number [some left, *fewer* stayed] —**fewer and fewer** an ever-decreasing number (of) [*fewer and fewer* men are wearing hats]

USAGE—see the note at LESS

fey (fā) ***adj.*** ⟦ME *feie* < OE *fæge*, fated, akin to Ger *feige*, cowardly (OHG *feigi*, doomed) < IE base **peik-*, hostile > FOE, FEUD[1], L *piger*, averse⟧ **1** [Now Chiefly Scot.] *a)* fated; doomed to death (archaic except in Scottish usage) *b)* in an unusually excited state, formerly believed to portend sudden death **2** strange or unusual in any of certain ways, as, variously, eccentric, whimsical, visionary, elfin, shy, otherworldly —**fey'ly** ***adv.*** —**fey'ness** ***n.***

Fey·deau (fā dō'), **Georges** (zhôrzh) 1862-1921; Fr. writer of farces

Feyn·man (fīn'mən), **Richard Phillips** 1918-88; U.S. physicist

fez (fez) ***n., pl.*** **fez'zes** ⟦Fr < Turk *fes*, after fol.⟧ a brimless felt hat shaped like a truncated cone, usually red, with a flat crown from which a long, black tassel hangs: the Turkish national headdress of men in the 19th and early 20th cent.

Fez (fez) city in NC Morocco

Fez·zan (fe zan') region of SW Libya, in the Sahara

ff[1] *abbrev.* **1** folios **2** following (pages, lines, etc.)

ff[2] *abbrev.* ⟦It *fortissimo*⟧ *Musical Direction* very loud(ly)

FFA *abbrev.* Future Farmers of America

FFV *abbrev.* flex(ible) fuel vehicle

FG *abbrev. Basketball, Football* field goal: sometimes written **fg**

FHA *abbrev.* Federal Housing Administration

FHLBB *abbrev.* Federal Home Loan Bank Board

F.I. *abbrev.* Falkland Islands

fi·a·cre (fē ä'kər; *Fr* fyȧ'kr') ***n.*** ⟦Fr, after the *Hôtel St-Fiacre* in Paris, location of the first office for renting such vehicles⟧ in France, a small carriage for hire: used in the 17th-19th cent.

fi·an·cé (fē'än sā'; *also* fē än'sā', fē'än sā') ***n.*** ⟦Fr, pp. of *fiancer* < OFr *fiance*, a promise < *fier*, to trust < VL **fidare*, for L *fidere*: see FAITH⟧ the man to whom one is engaged to be married

fi·an·cée (fē'än sā'; *also* fē än'sā, fē'än sā') ***n.*** ⟦Fr, fem. pp. of *fiancer*: see prec.⟧ the woman to whom one is engaged to be married

fi·an·chet·to (fē'ən ket'ō, -chet'ō) ***vt., vi.*** **-toed, -to·ing** ⟦It, dim. of *fianco*, flank, side⟧ *Chess* to move (a bishop) from its initial position diagonally into the adjacent knight's file

fi·as·co[1] (fē as'kō) ***n., pl.*** **-coes** or **-cos** ⟦Fr < It (*far*) *fiasco*, to fail (lit., to make a bottle: ref. uncert.) < *fiasco*, bottle: see fol.)⟧ a complete failure; esp., an ambitious project that ends as a ridiculous failure

fi·as·co[2] (fē äs'kō) ***n., pl.*** **-coes** or **-chi** (-kē) ⟦It < Gmc **flasko*, FLASK⟧ a bottle; esp., a long-necked wine bottle with a rounded lower portion covered in woven straw

fi·at (fē'ät, -at, -ət; fī'at', -ət) ***n.*** ⟦L, 3d pers. sing., pres. subj., of *fieri*, to become, come into existence < IE base **bheu-* > BE⟧ **1** an order issued by legal authority, traditionally beginning with the word *fiat* ("let it be done"); decree **2** a sanction; authorization **3** any arbitrary order

☆**fiat money** currency made legal tender by fiat and neither backed by, nor necessarily convertible into, gold or silver

fib (fib) ***n.*** ⟦16th- & 17th-c. slang: said to be clipped form of obs. *fible-fable*, redupl. form of FABLE⟧ a small or trivial lie —***vi.*** **fibbed, fib'bing** to tell such a lie or lies —***SYN.*** LIE[2] —**fib'ber** ***n.***

fi·ber (fī'bər) ***n.*** ⟦Fr *fibre* < L *fibra*, akin to *filum*, thread: see FILE[1]⟧ **1** *a)* a slender, threadlike structure that combines with others to form animal or vegetable tissue *b)* the tissue so formed [muscle *fiber*] **2** a slender, threadlike structure made from a mineral or synthetically [rayon *fibers*] **3** *a)* any substance that can be separated into threads or threadlike structures for spinning, weaving, etc. [cotton *fiber*] *b)* any such thread or structure [wool *fibers*] **4** a threadlike root **5** the texture of something [a fabric of coarse *fiber*] **6** character or nature; quality [a man of strong moral *fiber*] **7** ROUGHAGE —**fi'ber·like'** ***adj.***

fiber art **1** *a)* the creative art of making wall hangings, sculpture, etc. out of thread, yarn, rope, etc., often by using multiple techniques for weaving or knotting the materials *b)* objects so made collectively **2** handcrafted work, as sweaters or comforters, made by knitting, weaving, etc. —**fiber artist**

☆**fi·ber·board** (-bôrd') ***n.*** **1** a building material consisting of wood or other vegetable fibers compressed into stiff sheets **2** a sheet of this material

☆**fi·ber·fill** (-fil') ***n.*** a resilient, lightweight, fluffy filling for quilts, etc., made of synthetic fibers

☆**Fi·ber·glas** (-glas') *trademark for* finespun filaments of glass made into yarn that is woven into textiles, used in woolly masses as insulation, and pressed and molded as plastic material —***n.*** this substance

fi·ber·glass (-glas') ***n.*** ⟦< prec.⟧ finespun filaments of glass like Fiberglas: sometimes **fiber glass**; Brit. sp. **fi'bre·glass'**

fiber optics **1** *a)* the branch of optics dealing with the transmission of light and images, as around bends and curves, through transparent optical fibers *b)* the technology using this fiber as for the transmission of data at high speeds and in large amounts **2** such fibers bound together and used to send data, images, etc. —**fi'ber-op'tic** ***adj.***, **fiber optic**

fi·ber·scope (-skōp') ***n.*** a fiber-optic device for use in places difficult to see or reach, as an endoscope for a biopsy

Fi·bo·nac·ci series (fē'bə nä'chē) ⟦after L. *Fibonacci*, 13th-c. It. mathematician, who developed it⟧ a sequence of integers in which each integer (**Fibonacci number**) after the second is the sum of the two preceding integers; specif., the series 1, 1, 2, 3, 5, 8, 13, . . .

fi·br- *combining form* FIBRO-: used before a vowel

fi·branne (fī'brăn', -bran') ***n.*** ⟦Fr < *fibre*, FIBER⟧ a fabric of spun rayon, often woven to resemble linen

fi·bre (fī'bər) ***n.*** *Brit. sp. of* FIBER

fi·bril (fī'brəl) ***n.*** ⟦< ModL *fibrilla*, dim. of L *fibra*, FIBER⟧ **1** a small fiber, esp. a component of a larger fiber **2** a root hair —**fi'bril·lar** (-brə lər) ***adj.***, **fi'bril·lar'y** (-brə ler'ē)

fi·bril·late (fib'ri lāt') ***vi., vt.*** **-lat'ed, -lat'ing** to experience or cause to experience fibrillation

fi·bril·la·tion (fib'ri lā'shən, fī'bri-) ***n.*** ⟦< FIBRIL + -ATION: with ref. to fibers of the heart muscle⟧ a rapid, uncoordinated series of contractions of a muscle; esp., such contractions of some portion of the heart muscle, causing irregular heartbeats and sometimes ineffectual pumping of blood

fi·bril·lose (fī'brə lōs') ***adj.*** of or like fibrils

fi·brin (fī'brin) ***n.*** ⟦FIBR(E) + -IN[1]⟧ a fibrous, insoluble blood protein: in the clotting process, thrombin converts fibrinogen to fibrin monomers which polymerize to form clots

fi·bri·no- (fī'bri nō', -nə; -brə-) *combining form* fibrin [*fibrinogen*]

fi·brin·o·gen (fī brin'ə jən, -jen') ***n.*** ⟦prec. + -GEN⟧ a soluble protein of the blood plasma that is converted to fibrin by the action of the enzyme thrombin in the clotting of blood

fi·brin·o·gen·ic (fī brin'ə jen'ik, fī'brə nō'-) ***adj.*** **1** of or like fibrinogen **2** able to form fibrin Also **fi'bri·nog'e·nous** (-näj'ə nəs)

fi·bri·nol·y·sin (fī'brə näl'ə sin) ***n.*** ⟦FIBRINO- + LYSIN⟧ any of various enzymes, esp. plasmin, capable of digesting fibrin in the bloodstream

fi·bri·nol·y·sis (-sis) ***n.*** ⟦FIBRINO- + -LYSIS⟧ the digestion or dissolution of fibrin by an enzyme —**fi'bri·no·lyt'ic** (-nō lit'ik) ***adj.***

fi·brin·ous (fī'brə nəs) ***adj.*** of, like, or containing fibrin

fi·bro- (fī'brō, -brə) ⟦< L *fibra*, FIBER⟧ *combining form* fibrous matter or structure [*fibroblast*]

fi·bro·blast (fī'brō blast') ***n.*** ⟦prec. + -BLAST⟧ a large, flat, oval cell found in connective tissue and responsible for the formation of fibers —**fi'bro·blas'tic** ***adj.***

fi·bro·cyst·ic (fī'brō sis'tik) ***adj.*** designating or of a condition characterized by fibrosis and the development of benign cysts, esp. in the breasts

fi·broid (fī'broid') ***adj.*** ⟦FIBR(O)- + -OID⟧ like, composed of, or forming fibrous tissue —***n.*** a fibrous tumor, esp. a benign tumor of the uterus

fi·bro·in (fī'brō in) ***n.*** ⟦FIBRO- + -IN[1]⟧ a pale-yellow, albuminoid protein forming almost the entire thread of a spider and the core of raw silk

fi·bro·ma (fī brō'mə) ***n., pl.*** **-mas** or **-ma·ta** (-mə tə) ⟦ModL < FIBR(O)- + -OMA⟧ a benign tumor derived from, or composed mostly of, fibrous tissue —**fi·brom'a·tous** (-bräm'ə təs, -brō'mə-) ***adj.***

fi·bro·my·al·gia (fī'brō mī al'jə) ***n.*** a chronic condition characterized by pain, tenderness, and stiffness of the muscles and joints along with fatigue and anxiety

fi·bro·nec·tin (fī'brō nek'tin) ***n.*** ⟦< FIBRO- + L *nectere*, to fasten⟧ an adhesive glycoprotein that helps destroy bacteria, etc. in the blood or that helps structure connective tissue

fi·bro·pla·si·a (-plā'zhə, -plā'zhē ə, -plā'zē ə) ***n.*** ⟦ModL: see FIBRO- & -PLASIA⟧ the growth of fibrous tissue, as in wound healing or in certain diseases

fi·bro·sis (fī brō'sis) ***n.*** ⟦ModL < FIBR(O)- + -OSIS⟧ an excessive growth of fibrous connective tissue in an organ, part, or tissue, esp. in response to an injury —**fi·brot'ic** (-brät'ik) ***adj.***

fi·bro·si·tis (fī'brō sīt'is) ***n.*** ⟦ModL < *fibrosus*, fol. + -ITIS⟧ an excessive growth of white fibrous tissue, as of the muscle sheaths, resulting from inflammation; muscular rheumatism

fi·brous (fī'brəs) ***adj.*** ⟦< ModL *fibrosus*⟧ **1** containing or composed of fibers **2** like fiber

fi·bro·vas·cu·lar (fī′brō vas′kyo͞o lər) *adj. Bot.* having or composed of fibers and ducts for transporting a fluid, as sap

fib·u·la (fib′yo͞o lə) *n., pl.* **-lae′** (-lē′) or **-las** ⟦L, a clasp, pin (< base of *figere*, to fasten, FIX): the bone, as it appears in man, is like a clasp⟧ **1** the long, thin outer bone of the human leg between the knee and the ankle **2** a similar bone in the hind leg of other animals **3** in ancient Greece or Rome, a buckle or clasp for fastening garments —**fib′u·lar** (-lər) *adj.*

-fic (fik) ⟦< Fr & L; Fr *-fique* < L *-ficus* < unstressed form of *facere*, to make, DO[1]⟧ *suffix forming adjectives* making, creating *[terrific, scientific]*

FICA (fī′kə) *abbrev.* Federal Insurance Contributions Act

-fi·ca·tion (fi kā′shən) ⟦< Fr & L; Fr *-fication* < L *-ficatio* < *-ficare*, unstressed combining form of *facere*, to make, DO[1]⟧ *suffix forming nouns* a making, creating, causing *[calcification, glorification]*

fiche (fēsh) *n., pl.* **fich′es** or **fiche** *short for* MICROFICHE

Fich·te (fiH′tə), **Jo·hann Gott·lieb** (yō′hän′ gôt′lēp) 1762-1814; Ger. philosopher

fich·u (fish′o͞o; *Fr* fē shü′) *n.* ⟦Fr < pp. of *ficher*, to thrust in, attach < VL **figicare*, for L *figere*, FIX⟧ a three-cornered lace or muslin cape for women, worn with the ends fastened or crossed in front

fick·le (fik′əl) *adj.* ⟦ME *fikel* < OE *ficol*, tricky < base of *befician*, to deceive, akin to *gefic*, betrayal, deceit: for IE base see FEY⟧ changeable or unstable in affection, interest, loyalty, etc.; capricious —*SYN.* INCONSTANT —**fick′le·ness** *n.*

fict *abbrev.* **1** fiction **2** fictitious

fic·tile (fik′til, -təl) *adj.* ⟦L *fictilis* < pp. of *fingere*: see fol.⟧ **1** that can be molded; plastic **2** formed of molded clay, earth, etc. **3** of pottery or ceramics

fic·tion (fik′shən) *n.* ⟦ME *ficcioun* < OFr *fiction* < L *fictio*, a making, counterfeiting < pp. of *fingere*, to form, mold: see DOUGH⟧ **1** a making up of imaginary happenings; feigning **2** anything made up or imagined, as a statement, story, etc. **3** *a)* literary narratives, collectively, which portray imaginary characters or events, specif. novels and short stories *b)* a narrative of this kind **4** something accepted as fact for the sake of convenience, although not necessarily true —**fic′tion·al** *adj.* —**fic′tion·al·ly** *adv.* —**fic′tion·eer′** *n.* —**fic′tion·ist** *n.*

fic·tion·al·ize (fik′shə nəl īz′) *vt.* **-ized′**, **-iz′ing** to deal with (historical events, a person's life, etc.) in fictional form, as in a narrative that includes imaginary events, characters, dialogue, etc.: also **fic′tion·ize′** —**fic′tion·al·i·za′tion** *n.*

fic·ti·tious (fik tish′əs) *adj.* ⟦L *ficticius* < pp. of *fingere*, to form, devise: see DOUGH⟧ **1** of or like fiction; imaginary **2** not real; pretended; false *[fictitious joy]* **3** assumed for disguise or deception *[a fictitious name]* —**fic·ti′tious·ly** *adv.*

SYN.—**fictitious** refers to that which is invented by the imagination and is therefore not real, true, or actually existent *[Gulliver is a fictitious character]*; **fabulous** suggests that which is incredible or astounding, but does not necessarily connote nonexistence *[the man's wealth is fabulous]*; **legendary** refers to something that may have a historical basis in fact but, in popular tradition, has undergone great elaboration and exaggeration *[the legendary amours of Don Juan]*; **mythical** basically applies to the highly imaginary explanation of natural or historical phenomena by a people and, therefore, connotes that what it qualifies is a product of the imagination; **apocryphal** suggests that which is of doubtful authenticity or authorship —*ANT.* **real, true, factual**

fic·tive (fik′tiv) *adj.* ⟦Fr *fictif* < ML *fictivus*⟧ **1** of fiction or the production of fiction **2** not real; imaginary; feigned —**fic′tive·ly** *adv.*

fi·cus (fī′kəs) *n., pl.* **fi′cus** ⟦ModL < L, fig tree⟧ any of a genus (*Ficus*) of tropical shrubs, trees, and climbing plants of the mulberry family, with glossy, leathery leaves, including the rubber plant: often grown indoors as an ornamental

fid (fid) *n.* ⟦Early ModE naut. term < ?⟧ **1** a round, pointed wooden tool for separating the strands of a rope in splicing **2** a square wooden or metal bar for supporting a topmast

-fid (fid) ⟦L *-fidus*, split < base of *findere*: see FISSION⟧ *combining form* split or separated into (a specified number or kind of) parts *[palmatifid]*

fid·dle (fid′'l) *n.* ⟦ME *fithele* < OE < VL *vitula* < L *vitulari*, to rejoice: *vi-* (< IE **woi-*, **wi-*, outcry > OE *wi*, Gr *ia*) + ? base of *tollere*, to raise, exalt⟧ **1** [Informal] any stringed instrument played with a bow, esp. the violin ☆**2** [Slang] a petty swindle **3** *Naut.* a frame or railing on a ship's table to keep dishes, etc. from sliding off in rough weather —*vt.* **-dled**, **-dling 1** [Informal] to play (a tune) on a fiddle **2** [Slang] to swindle in a petty way —*vi.* **1** [Informal] to play a fiddle **2** to play or tinker (*with*), esp. in a nervous way —**fiddle around** [Informal] to pass time aimlessly —**fiddle away** to waste (time) —**fit as a fiddle** in excellent health; physically fit

fid·dle·dee·dee (fid′'l dē dē′) *n., interj.* ⟦prob. < prec., with addition of nonsense syllables⟧ nonsense

fid·dle-fad·dle (fid′'l fad′'l) *n., interj.* ⟦redupl. of FIDDLE or obs. *faddle*, to trifle⟧ nonsense —*vi.* **-dled**, **-dling** [Informal] to be concerned with trifles; fuss

fid·dle·head (-hed′) *n.* **1** a carved decoration on a ship's bow, curved like the scroll of a violin head **2** ⟦so named from its shape⟧ the coiled tip of a young fern of any of certain species, often cooked and eaten as a vegetable; crosier: also called **fiddlehead fern**

fid·dler (fid′lər) *n.* **1** a person who fiddles **2** FIDDLER CRAB

☆**fiddler crab** a small, burrowing crab (genus *Uca*), the male of which has one claw much larger than the other

fid·dle·sticks (fid′'l stiks′) *interj.* ⟦< *fiddlestick*, a bow for a FIDDLE⟧ nonsense!

fid·dle·wood (-wood′) *n.* **1** any of several tropical American timber trees of the verbena family, valuable for their hard wood **2** the wood

fid·dling (fid′liŋ) *adj.* trifling; useless; petty

fid·dly (fid′lē) *adj.* ⟦see FIDDLE (*vi.* 2)⟧ [Chiefly Brit.] of or characterized by small, typically fussy or annoying, details

fi·de·ism (fē′dā iz′əm, fī′dē-) *n.* ⟦ModL *fideismus* < L *fides*, FAITH + *-ismus*, -ISM⟧ the view that everything that can be known with certainty about God or divine things is known only or primarily by faith and never by reason alone —**fi′de·ist** *n.* —**fi′de·is′tic** *adj.*

☆**Fi·del·is·mo** (fē′del iz′mō′) *n.* ⟦AmSp, after *Fidel* CASTRO + *-ismo*, -ISM⟧ *[also* **f-***]* the social revolution in Cuba led by Fidel Castro, or its principles

Fi·del·is·ta (-is′tə) *n.* *[also* **f-***]* an adherent of Fidelismo

fi·del·i·ty (fə del′ə tē, fī-) *n., pl.* **-ties** ⟦ME *fidelite* < OFr < L *fidelitas* < *fidelis*, faithful, trusty < *fides*, FAITH⟧ **1** faithful devotion to duty or to one's obligations or vows; loyalty; faithfulness **2** accuracy of a description, translation, etc. or of the reproduction of sound, an image, etc. —*SYN.* ALLEGIANCE

fidg·et (fij′it) *n.* ⟦< obs. *fidge*, to fidget < ME *fichen* < ? or akin to ON *fikja*, to fidget⟧ **1** the state of being restless, nervous, or uneasy **2** a fidgety person —*vi.* to move about in a restless, nervous, or impatient way —**the fidgets** behavior characterized by restlessness, nervous movements, etc.

fidg·et·y (-it ē) *adj.* nervous; uneasy —**fidg′et·i·ness** *n.*

Fi·do (fī′dō) *n.* ⟦< L *fidus*, faithful < *fides*, FAITH⟧ a traditional name for a pet dog: often used informally to refer to the typical pet dog

fi·du·cial (fi do͞o′shəl, -dyo͞o′-; fī-) *adj.* ⟦L *fiducialis* < *fiducia*, trust: see fol.⟧ **1** based on firm faith **2** used as a standard of reference for measurement or calculation *[a fiducial point]* **3** FIDUCIARY

fi·du·ci·ar·y (fi do͞o′shē er′ē, -dyo͞o′-; -shə rē) *adj.* ⟦L *fiduciarius* < *fiducia*, trust, thing held in trust < *fidere*, to trust: see FAITH⟧ **1** designating or of a person who holds something in trust for another; of a trustee or trusteeship *[a fiduciary guardian for a minor child]* **2** held in trust *[fiduciary property]* **3** valuable only because of public confidence and support: said of certain money —*n., pl.* **-ar′ies** TRUSTEE (sense 1)

fie (fī) *interj.* ⟦ME *fi* < OFr, of echoic orig., as in L *fu*, Gr *phy*⟧ [Archaic] for shame: now used mainly in mock reproach

Fied·ler (fēd′lər), **Arthur** 1894-1979; U.S. orchestra conductor

fief (fēf) *n.* ⟦Fr: see FEE⟧ under feudalism, heritable land held from a lord in return for service

fief·dom (fēf′dəm) *n.* **1** FIEF **2** anything under a person's complete control or authority

field (fēld) *n.* ⟦ME *feld* < OE, akin to Ger *feld*, Du *veld* < IE **pelt-* < base **pele-*, **pla-*, flat and broad > L *planus*, plane, Gr *palamē*, flat hand⟧ **1** a wide stretch of open land; plain **2** a piece of cleared land, set off or enclosed, for raising crops or pasturing livestock **3** a piece of land used for some particular purpose *[a landing field]* **4** an area of land producing some natural resource *[a gold field]* **5** any wide, unbroken expanse *[a field of ice]* **6** *a)* a battlefield *b)* a battle **7** *a)* an area of military operations *b)* a military area away from the post or headquarters **8** *a)* an area where practical work is done, as by a social worker, geologist, etc., away from the central office, laboratory, or the like (usually with *the*) *[camping equipment tested in the field]* *b)* a realm of knowledge or of special work or opportunity *[the field of electronics]* **9** an area of observation *[the field of vision of the human eyes, the field of view of a microscope]* **10** the background, as on a flag or coin **11** *a)* an area where games or athletic events are held *b)* the part of such an area, usually inside a closed racing track, where contests in the high jump, long jump, shot put, pole vault, etc. are held ☆*c)* in baseball, any part of the outfield *[a batter who hits to all fields]* *d)* all the entrants in a contest *e)* all the entrants in a contest except the one(s) specified **12** *Comput.* any of the units of storage that are grouped to form a RECORD (*n.* 7) **13** *Heraldry* the surface or part of the surface of a shield **14** *Horse Racing* those horses, in a race with more than twelve entrants, that are grouped together to function as a unit for betting purposes **15** *Math.* a set of numbers or other algebraic elements for which arithmetic operations (except for division by zero) are defined in a consistent manner to yield another element of the set **16** *Physics* a region, volume, or space where a specific, measurable force, as gravity or magnetism, exists **17** *TV* *a)* the area viewed by the camera *b)* the area that the scanning element covers in one vertical sweep —*adj.* **1** of, operating in, or held on the field or fields **2** growing in fields; having a field as its habitat —*vt.* **1** *a)* *Baseball, etc.* to catch, grab, or handle (a ball that has been batted, thrown, etc.) *b)* to put (a team or player) in the field for a game or competition **2** to position in a given location *[to field an army]* **3** [Informal] *a)* to answer (a question) extemporaneously *b)* to deal with; handle *[to field phone calls]* —*vi. Baseball, etc.* to play as a fielder — **keep (or hold) the field** to continue activity, as in games or military operations —☆**play the field 1** to take a broad area of operations; not confine one's activities to one object **2** [Informal] to date several people casually over a period of time —**take (or leave) the field** to begin (or withdraw from) activity in a game, military operation, etc.

Field (fēld) **1 Cyrus West** 1819-92; U.S. industrialist: promoted the first transatlantic cable **2 Eugene** 1850-95; U.S. writer

field artillery movable artillery capable of accompanying an army into battle

☆**field corn** any variety of corn grown for feeding livestock

field day **1** a day devoted to military exercises and display **2** a day of athletic events and contests ☆**3** a day spent in outdoor scientific study **4** an occasion of enjoyably exciting events, extraordinary opportunity, or highly successful activity [the press had a *field day* with the senator's confession]

field-dress (fēld′dres′) ***vt.*** to DRESS (***vt.*** 8*a*) (a fowl, deer, etc.) while still at the hunting site

field-effect (fēld′e fekt′) ***adj.*** designating or of an electronic component or device, esp. a transistor, controlled by an external electric field

field·er (fēl′dər) ***n.*** *Baseball, Cricket* a player in the field whose chief purpose is to stop or catch batted balls

☆**fielder's choice** *Baseball* an attempt by a fielder to retire a runner already on base rather than the batter: the batter is not credited with a base hit if he reaches first base safely

field event any of the contests held on the field in a track meet, as the high jump or shot put

field·fare (fēld′fer′) ***n.*** ⟦ME *feldefare,* altered (after *faren,* FARE) < OE *feldeware,* lit., "field-dweller" < *feld,* FIELD + ? *wærian,* to guard, inhabit: ? folk etym.⟧ a European thrush (*Turdus pilaris*) with a grayish head and brown wings

field glasses binoculars for outdoor use: often **field glass**

☆**field goal** **1** *Basketball* a shot made while the ball is in play, scoring two points or, if made from a certain distance (in professional basketball, at least 23 feet), three points **2** *Football* a kick that passes through or above the space between the uprights, scoring three points

field guide a handbook, usually illustrated, for use in identifying birds, plants, etc., as while hiking or camping

field gun a mobile cannon

☆**field hand** **1** [Historical] a plantation slave who worked in the fields **2** a hired farm laborer

field hockey HOCKEY (sense 2)

field hospital a temporary military hospital near the combat zone, for emergency treatment

☆**field house** **1** a building near an athletic field, with lockers, showers, etc. for the athletes' use **2** a large building for basketball games, indoor track meets, etc.

Field·ing (fēl′diŋ), **Henry** 1707-54; Eng. novelist

fielding average *Baseball* a figure expressing the average fielding efficiency of a player or team, figured by dividing the number of putouts and assists by the number of putouts, assists, and errors

field judge *Football* an official who makes rulings regarding pass receptions, fair catches, field goals, etc.

field magnet the magnet used to create and maintain the magnetic field in a motor or generator

field marshal in some armies, an officer of the highest rank

field mouse any of several kinds of mice that live in fields

field officer *Mil.* a colonel, lieutenant colonel, or major

field of force FIELD (*n.* 16)

field of honor **1** a dueling place **2** a battlefield

field pea a strain of the common pea (*Pisum sativum* var. *arvense*) with mottled leaves and purplish flowers, grown for forage

field·piece (fēld′pēs′) ***n.*** FIELD GUN

Fields (fēldz), **W. C.** (born *William Claude Dukenfield*) 1880-1946; U.S. actor & comedian

fields·man (fēldz′mən) ***n.,*** *pl.* **-men** (-mən) a fielder in cricket

field spaniel any of a breed of medium-sized spaniel, usually black, with a silky coat fringed on the legs and ears, often used as a hunting dog

field sparrow ☆a rust-colored North American sparrow (*Spizella pusilla*) with a whitish belly and pink bill

field·stone (fēld′stōn′) ***n.*** stone that has been left in its natural state, used typically to build walls, walks, etc.

☆**field-strip** (-strip′) ***vt.*** **-stripped′**, **-strip′ping** to disassemble (a firearm) for cleaning and inspection

☆**field-test** (-test′) ***vt.*** to test (a device, method, etc.) under actual operating conditions

field theory *Physics* a theory in which the basic quantities are physical fields

field trial a competition in which the performance of hunting dogs is tested in the field

field trip an educational trip away from the classroom, as to give students firsthand experience

field winding the winding of a field magnet

field·work (fēld′wurk′) ***n.*** **1** any temporary fortification, as an earthen barrier, made by troops in the field **2** the work of collecting scientific data in the field, as by a geologist or botanist —**field′work′er** ***n.***

fiend (fēnd) ***n.*** ⟦ME *fend, feend* < OE *feond,* lit., the one hating, orig. prp. < base of *feogan,* to hate, akin to Goth *fijands* < *fijan,* to hate < IE base **pē(i)-,* to harm⟧ **1** an evil spirit; devil **2** an inhumanly wicked or cruel person ☆**3** [Informal] *a)* a person addicted to some activity, habit, etc. [a fresh-air *fiend*] *b)* a person who is excellent at some activity [a *fiend* at tennis] —**the Fiend** Satan

fiend·ish (fēn′dish) ***adj.*** **1** of or like a fiend; devilish; inhumanly wicked or cruel **2** extremely vexatious or difficult —**fiend′ish·ly** ***adv.*** —**fiend′ish·ness** ***n.***

fierce (firs) ***adj.*** **fierc′er, fierc′est** ⟦ME *fers* < OFr *fers, fier* < L *ferus,* wild, savage < IE base **ĝhwer-,* wild animal > Gr *thēr,* animal⟧ **1** of a violently cruel nature; savage; wild [a *fierce* dog] **2** violent; uncontrolled [a *fierce* storm] **3** intensely eager; intense; ardent [a *fierce* embrace] ☆**4** [Informal] very distasteful, disagreeable, bad, etc. —**fierce′ly** ***adv.*** —**fierce′ness** ***n.***

fi·er·y (fī′ər ē, fī′rē) ***adj.*** **-er·i·er, -er·i·est** ⟦ME *firi*⟧ **1** containing or consisting of fire **2** like fire; glaring, hot, etc. **3** characterized by strong emotion; ardent; spirited [*fiery* words] **4** easily stirred up; excitable [a *fiery* nature] **5** easily set on fire; flammable [*fiery* fumes] **6** inflamed [a *fiery* sore] —**fi′er·i·ly** ***adv.*** —**fi′er·i·ness** ***n.***

fiery cross **1** a wooden cross with charred or bloody ends, used by ancient Scottish clans as a signal calling men to battle ☆**2** a burning cross, used by the Ku Klux Klan as an emblem or to inspire terror

Fie·so·le (fye′zô le), **Gio·van·ni da** (jô vän′nē dä) *see* ANGELICO, Fra

☆**fi·es·ta** (fē es′tə) ***n.*** ⟦Sp < VL *festa:* see FEAST⟧ **1** a religious festival; esp., a saint's day **2** any gala celebration; holiday

FIFA (fē′fə) ⟦< Fr⟧ *service mark Fédération Internationale de Football Association:* governing body for international soccer competition

fife (fīf) ***n.*** ⟦Ger *pfeife,* a pipe, fife < MHG *pfife* < OHG *pfifa* < VL **pipa,* PIPE⟧ a small flute having from six to eight finger holes, and usually no keys, used mainly with drums in playing marches — ***vt., vi.*** **fifed, fif′ing** to play on a fife —**fif′er** ***n.***

Fife (fīf) administrative unit of E Scotland: formerly a county

fife rail *Naut.* an inboard rail with holes for belaying pins

☆**FIFO** (fī′fō′) ***n.*** ⟦*f(irst) i(n,) f(irst) o(ut)*⟧ a method of valuing inventories in which items sold or used are priced at the cost of earliest acquisitions and those remaining are valued at the cost of most recent acquisitions: cf. LIFO

fif·teen (fif′tēn′) ***adj.*** ⟦ME *fiftene* < OE: see FIVE & -TEEN⟧ totaling five more than ten —***n.*** the cardinal number between fourteen and sixteen; 15; XV

15 minutes (of fame) ⟦from a statement made by Andy WARHOL (*c.* 1968)⟧ the very brief period of fame facetiously deemed to be allotted to each person in the modern age of telecommunications, broadcast news, etc.

fif·teenth (fif′tēnth′) ***adj.*** ⟦ME *fiftenthe* < *fifteotha* < *fiftene:* see FIFTEEN & -TH²⟧ **1** preceded by fourteen others in a series; 15th **2** designating any of the fifteen equal parts of something —***n.*** **1** the one following the fourteenth **2** any of the fifteen equal parts of something; $\frac{1}{15}$ —***adv.*** in the fifteenth place, rank, group, etc.

fifth (fifth) ***adj.*** ⟦ME *fifte* < OE *fifta* < *fif,* FIVE⟧ **1** preceded by four others in a series; 5th **2** designating any of the five equal parts of something —***n.*** **1** the one following the fourth **2** any of the five equal parts of something; $\frac{1}{5}$ ☆**3** *a)* a unit of liquid measure for alcoholic beverages, equal to a fifth of a gallon (0.757 liter) *b)* a bottle of alcohol with a capacity of one fifth of a gallon **4** *Music* *a)* the fifth tone of an ascending diatonic scale, or a tone four degrees above or below any given tone in such a scale; dominant *b)* the interval between two such tones, or a combination of them ☆**5** [F-] [Informal] FIFTH AMENDMENT —***adv.*** in the fifth place, rank, group, etc. —☆**plead (or take) the Fifth** [Informal] to invoke the Fifth Amendment in refusing to testify against oneself —**fifth′ly** ***adv.***

☆**Fifth Amendment** an amendment to the U.S. Constitution mainly guaranteeing certain protections in criminal cases, specif. the clause protecting persons from being compelled to testify against themselves

fifth column ⟦transl. of Sp *quinta columna:* first used (1936) by the Sp Nationalist General Mola, who, besieging Madrid with four columns from the outside, boasted of having a "fifth column" of civilian supporters within⟧ a group of people who aid the enemy from within their own country —**fifth columnist**

Fifth Republic the republic established in France in 1958: its constitution strengthened the presidential role

fifth wheel **1** *a)* a horizontal wheel-like structure placed over the front axle of a carriage or wagon to support it on turns ☆*b)* a similar structure on the rear of the cab of a tractor-trailer, serving as a coupling for attaching the trailer **2** an unnecessary or superfluous person or thing

fif·ti·eth (fif′tē ith) ***adj.*** ⟦ME *fiftithe* < OE *fiftigotha* < *fiftig:* see fol. & -TH²⟧ **1** preceded by forty-nine others in a series; 50th **2** designating any of the fifty equal parts of something —***n.*** **1** the one following the forty-ninth **2** any of fifty equal parts of something; $\frac{1}{50}$ —***adv.*** in the fiftieth place, rank, group, etc.

fif·ty (fif′tē) ***adj.*** ⟦ME *fifti* < OE *fiftig:* see FIVE & -TY²⟧ five times ten —***n.,*** *pl.* **-ties** the cardinal number between forty-nine and fifty-one; 50; L —**the fifties** the numbers or years, as of a century, from fifty through fifty-nine

☆**fif·ty-fif·ty** (fif′tē fif′tē) [Informal] ***adj.*** shared equally between two persons or things; equal; even —***adv.*** equally; half-and-half

fig¹ (fig) ***n.*** ⟦ME *fige* < OFr < VL **fica,* for L *ficus,* fig tree, fig⟧ **1** the hollow, pear-shaped false fruit (syconium) of the fig tree, with sweet, pulpy flesh containing numerous tiny, seedlike true fruits (achenes) **2** any of a genus (*Ficus*) of fig-bearing trees of the mulberry family, esp. any of the many cultivated varieties of a tree (*F. carica*) bearing edible figs **3** a trifling amount; little bit [not worth a *fig*] **4** a gesture of contempt or disdain made as by placing the thumb between the first two fingers or under the upper teeth

fig² (fig) ***vt.*** **figged, fig′ging** ⟦altered < obs. *feague,* to whip, polish; confused with the contr. for FIGURE, prob. from the use of this contracted form in reference to plates in books of fashions⟧ to dress showily: with *out* or *up* —***n.*** [Informal] **1** dress; appearance **2** shape; condition —**in full fig** [Informal] completely dressed or outfitted, esp. in a showy manner

fig³ *abbrev.* **1** figurative **2** figuratively **3** figure(s)

fig·eat·er (fig′ēt′ər) ***n.*** ☆a large, green, velvety scarab beetle (*Cotinis nitida*) of the S U.S., the adults of which feed on ripe fruit; June bug

fight (fīt) *vi.* **fought, fight′ing** ⟦ME *fighten* < OE *feohtan*, akin to Ger *fechten* < IE base **pek-*, to pluck hair or wool > OE *feoh* (see FEE) & L *pecten*, a comb, *pecu*, cattle⟧ **1** *a)* to take part in a physical struggle or battle; struggle *b)* to box, esp. professionally **2** to struggle or work hard in trying to beat or overcome someone or something; contend **3** to argue or quarrel; dispute: often with *about* or *over* —*vt.* **1** *a)* to oppose physically or in battle, as with fists, weapons, etc. *b)* to box with in a contest **2** to try to overcome; struggle against or contend with [to *fight* a head cold, legislation to *fight* poverty] **3** to engage in or carry on (a war, conflict, case, etc.) **4** to gain by struggle [to *fight* one's way to the top] **5** to cause to fight; manage (a boxer, gamecock, etc.) —*n.* ⟦ME < OE *feoht*⟧ **1** a physical struggle; battle; combat **2** any struggle, contest, or quarrel **3** power or readiness to fight; pugnacious spirit [full of *fight*] —***SYN.*** CONFLICT —**fight it out** to fight until one side is defeated —**fight off 1** to repel an attack by **2** to struggle to avoid [to *fight off* starvation]

fight·back (fīt′bak′) *n.* [Chiefly Brit.] the act or an instance of fighting back from a weaker position

fight·er (fīt′ər) *n.* **1** one that fights or is inclined to fight **2** a prizefighter; pugilist **3** a small, fast, highly maneuverable airplane for aerial combat that may be equipped with bombs, rockets, etc.

☆**fighting chance** a chance to win or succeed, but only after a hard struggle

☆**fighting words** [Informal] a remark that stirs up antagonism

fight-or-flight (fīt′ôr flīt′) *adj.* designating or of an animal's overall instinctive response to danger, that prepares it either to confront or to flee the threat: among the common physical reactions are a release of epinephrine into the bloodstream and increased blood flow to the muscles

fig leaf 1 a leaf of a fig tree **2** a representation of such a leaf used, as in sculpture, to conceal the genitals of a nude **3** any blatant or inadequate attempt to cover up or disguise something

fig marigold any of a genus (*Mesembryanthemum*) of fleshy plants of the carpetweed family, with showy flowers, grown in warm, dry climates

fig·ment (fig′mənt) *n.* ⟦ME < L *figmentum* < *fingere*, to form: see DOUGH⟧ something merely imagined or made up in the mind

fig·ur·al (fig′yoor əl, -yər-) *adj.* **1** FIGURATIVE (sense 3) **2** of or made up of human or animal figures, as a painting; representational

fig·u·rant (fig′yo͞o rənt, -ränt′; fig′yo͞o ränt′) *n.* ⟦Fr, masc. prp. of *figurer*, to FIGURE⟧ **1** a member of a corps de ballet **2** a supernumerary on the stage

fig·u·ra·tion (fig′yo͞o rā′shən, -yə-) *n.* ⟦ME *figuracioun* < L *figuratio* < *figuratus*: see fol.⟧ **1** a forming; shaping **2** form; appearance **3** representation or symbolization **4** *Music* the repetition of a figure or motif, esp. in variations on a theme —**fig′u·ra′tion·al** *adj.*

fig·ur·a·tive (fig′yoor ə tiv′, -yər-) *adj.* ⟦ME < OFr *figuratif* < LL *figurativus* < L *figuratus*, pp. of *figurare*, to form, fashion < *figura*, fol.⟧ **1** representing by means of a figure, symbol, or likeness **2** having to do with figure drawing, painting, etc. **3** not in its original, usual, literal, or exact sense; representing one concept in terms of another that may be thought of as analogous with it; metaphoric [in "screaming headlines," the word "screaming" is a *figurative* use] **4** containing figures of speech —**fig′ur·a·tive′ly** *adv.*

fig·ure (fig′yər, -yoor; *often, esp. for v., & Brit always,* fig′ər) *n.* ⟦ME < OFr < L *figura* < *fingere*, to form, shape: see DOUGH⟧ **1** the outline or shape of something; form **2** *a)* the shape of the human body; human form *b)* an indistinct human form [two *figures* seen from a distance] *c)* a particular person's shape with respect to its physical attractiveness [a woman with a good *figure*] **3** a person, esp. one seen or thought of in a specified way [a great social *figure*] **4** a likeness or representation of a person or thing **5** an illustration; diagram; picture; drawing **6** an artistic design in fabrics, etc.; pattern **7** *a)* the symbol for a number [the *figure* 5] *b)* [*pl.*] calculation with such symbols; arithmetic [very good at *figures*] *c)* [Informal] a general quantity of money as expressed by a specified number of digits (often used in comb.) [a six-*figure* salary is at least $100,000] **8** a sum of money **9** *Dancing, Skating* a series or pattern of steps or movements **10** *Geom.* a surface or space bounded on all sides by lines or planes **11** *Logic* the form of a syllogism with reference to the use of the middle term as variously the subject or the predicate of the premises **12** *Music* a series of consecutive tones or chords forming a distinct group which with other similar groups completes a phrase or theme; motif **13** *Rhetoric* FIGURE OF SPEECH —*vt.* **-ured, -ur·ing** ⟦ME *figuren* < the n.⟧ **1** to represent in definite form; give a shape to **2** to represent mentally; imagine **3** to ornament with a design **4** to compute with figures **5** [Informal] to believe; consider; decide **6** *Music* to indicate chords for (the bass) by writing the appropriate figures next to the notes —*vi.* **1** *a)* to appear, often prominently (with *in*) [you *figure* in all my dreams] *b)* to be a causal factor (with *in*) [poor food *figured* in his ill health] **2** to do arithmetic ☆**3** [Informal] to consider; calculate ☆**4** [Informal] to be just as expected or as anticipated: often used in a sarcastic or pessimistic way [it *figures* that I miss my flight but my baggage gets loaded!] —***SYN.*** FORM —**figure in** ☆to add in; include —☆**figure on** [Informal] **1** to count on; rely on **2** to consider as part of a scheme or project; plan on —☆**figure out 1** to solve; compute **2** to understand; reason out —☆**figure up** to add; total —☆**go figure!** [Slang] try to understand; try to figure it out —**fig′ur·er** *n.*

fig·ured (-yərd) *adj.* **1** shaped; formed **2** represented or shown by a picture, diagram, etc. **3** having a design or pattern **4** *Music* marked with figures (Arabic numerals) representing the appropriate accompanying chords: said of the bass

figure eight a pattern, form, or course that resembles the shape of the numeral eight (8) —**fig′ure-eight′** *adj.*

fig·ure-eight knot (fig′yər āt′) a kind of knot: also **fig′ure-of-eight′ knot**

fig·ure·head (fig′yər hed′) *n.* **1** a carved figure on the bow of a ship **2** a person put in a position of leadership because of name, rank, etc., but having no real power, authority, or responsibility

figure of speech an expression, as a metaphor or simile, using words in a nonliteral sense or unusual manner to add vividness, beauty, etc. to what is said or written

figure skating ice skating with emphasis, esp. formerly, on the tracing of elaborate figures on the ice by the performer and, now, on athletic leaps and spins, displays of agility, etc. —**figure skater**

fig·u·rine (fig′yo͞o rēn′, -yə-) *n.* ⟦Fr < It *figurina*, dim. of *figura* < L: see FIGURE⟧ a small sculptured or molded figure; statuette

fig wasp any of a family (Agaonidae) of small wasps living in certain figs, esp. a wasp (*Blastophaga psenes*) active in the pollination of certain cultivated strains

fig·wort (fig′wurt′) *adj.* designating a large family (Scrophulariaceae, order Scrophulariales) of dicotyledonous plants, including the foxglove and snapdragon —*n.* any of a genus (*Scrophularia*) of plants of the figwort family, with square stems and small flowers

Fi·ji (fē′jē) country occupying a group of islands (**Fiji Islands**) in the SW Pacific, north of New Zealand: 7,054 sq mi (18,270 sq km); cap. Suva

Fi·ji·an (fē′jē ən, fē jē′ən) *adj.* ⟦< Fijian *Viti*, the Fijians' name for their country + -AN⟧ of the Fiji Islands or their people, language, or culture —*n.* **1** a person born or living in the Fiji Islands **2** the Austronesian language spoken in the Fiji Islands

fi·la (fī′lə) *n. pl. of* FILUM

fil·a·ment (fil′ə mənt) *n.* ⟦Fr < ML *filamentum* < LL *filare*, to spin < L *filum*: see FILE[1]⟧ **1** a very slender thread or fiber **2** a threadlike part; specif., *a)* the fine metal wire in a lightbulb, which becomes incandescent when heated by an electric current *b)* the cathode of a thermionic tube, usually in the form of a wire, which may be electrically heated **3** *Bot.* the stalk of a stamen bearing the anther —**fil′a·men′ta·ry** (-men′tə rē) *adj.* —**fil′a·men′tous** (-men′təs) *adj.*

fi·lar (fī′lər) *adj.* ⟦< L *filum*, a thread (see FILE[1]) + -AR⟧ **1** of a thread **2** having fine threads or hairs stretched across the field of view, as a micrometer

☆**fil·a·ree** (fil′ə rē′) *n.* ALFILARIA

fi·lar·i·a (fi ler′ē ə) *n., pl.* **-i·ae′** (-ē ē′) ⟦ModL < L *filum*: see FILE[1]⟧ any of a superfamily (Filarioidea) of threadlike, parasitic nematode worms that live in the blood and tissues of vertebrate animals: they are carried and transmitted by mosquitoes and other invertebrates —**fi·lar′i·al** *adj.*, **fi·lar′i·an**

fil·a·ri·a·sis (fil′ə rī′ə sis) *n.* ⟦ModL: see prec.⟧ a disease, the most common form of elephantiasis, caused by filarial worms transmitted by mosquitoes: the worms invade lymphatic vessels and lymphoid tissue, causing chronic swelling of the lower extremities and other parts of the body

fil·a·ture (fil′ə chər) *n.* ⟦Fr < pp. of LL *filare*, to spin: see FILE[1]⟧ **1** a spinning into threads **2** *a)* a reeling of raw silk from cocoons *b)* a reel for this *c)* a place where this is done

fil·bert (fil′bərt) *n.* ⟦ME *filberde*, *philliberd*, prob. via NormFr (*noix de*) *filbert*, (nut of) Philibert, after St. *Philibert*, whose feast came in the nutting season⟧ **1** the edible nut of a hazel, esp. of a cultivated European tree (*Corylus avellana* or *C. maxima*); hazelnut **2** a tree bearing this nut

filch (filch) *vt.* ⟦ME *filchen*⟧ to steal (usually something small or petty); pilfer

file[1] (fīl) *vt.* **filed, fil′ing** ⟦ME *filen* < OFr *filer*, to string documents on thread, orig., to spin thread < LL *filare*, to spin < L *filum*, thread < IE base **gwhislo-* > Lith *gýsla*, sinew⟧ **1** *a)* to arrange (papers, etc.) in order for future reference *b)* to put (a paper, etc.) in its proper place or order ☆**2** to dispatch (a news story) to a newspaper, news agency, etc. **3** to register (an application, etc.) **4** to put (a document) on public record, esp. as required by law **5** to initiate (a divorce suit or other legal action) —*vi.* **1** to move in a line [to *file* out of a building] ☆**2** to register oneself as a candidate (*for* a political office) **3** to make application (*for* divorce proceedings, etc.) —*n.* ⟦senses 1, 2, & 5 < the v.; 3 & 4 < Fr *file* < L *filum*⟧ **1** a container, as a folder, cabinet, etc., for keeping papers in order **2** an orderly arrangement of papers, cards, etc., as for reference **3** a line of persons or things situated one behind another: cf. RANK[1] **4** any of the rows of squares on a chessboard extending from one player's end to the other **5** *Comput.* a collection of data (or, often, of logically related records) stored and dealt with as a single, named unit: cf. RECORD (*n.* 7), FIELD (*n.* 12) —**in file** in line, one behind another —**on file** (kept) in or as in a file for reference —**file′a·ble** *adj.* —**fil′er** *n.*

file[2] (fīl) *n.* ⟦ME < OE *feol* (Mercian *fil*), akin to Ger *feile* < Du *vijl*, prob. < IE base **peik-*, var. of **peig-*, to scratch, prick > PAINT⟧ **1** a steel tool with a rough, ridged surface for smoothing, grinding down, or cutting through something **2** [Brit. Slang] a crafty rascal —*vt.* **filed, fil′ing** to smooth, grind down, or cut through as with a file

file[3] (fīl) *vt.* **filed, fil′ing** ⟦ME *filen* < OE *-fylan* < *ful*, dirty, FOUL⟧ [Archaic] to make foul; defile

☆**fi·lé** (fē lā′) *n.* ⟦AmFr < Fr, pp. of *filer*, to twist, spin < L *filare* < *filum*, a thread: see FILE[1]⟧ powdered sassafras leaves, used in Creole cooking

file clerk a person hired to keep office files in order

file·fish (fīl′fish′) *n., pl.* **-fish′** or **-fish′es** (see FISH) any of various fishes (family Balistidae) of the same order (Tetraodontiformes) as the puffer fish, with a compressed body and very small, rough scales

fi·let (fi lā′, fil′ā′) *n.* ⟦ME < OFr: see FILLET⟧ **1** a net or lace with a simple pattern on a square mesh background **2** FILLET (*n.* 6) —*vt.* **-let′ed**, **-let′ing** FILLET (*vt.* 2)

fi·let mi·gnon (fi lā′min yōn′, -yän′) ⟦Fr, lit., tiny fillet⟧ a thick, round cut of lean beef tenderloin broiled, often with a bacon strip wrapped around it

fil·i·al (fil′ē əl, fil′yəl) *adj.* ⟦ME < LL(Ec) *filialis*, of a son or daughter < L *filius*, son, *filia*, daughter < base of *femina*, *fetus*: see FEMALE⟧ **1** of, suitable to, or due from a son or daughter [*filial* devotion] **2** *Genetics* designating or of any generation following the parental: the first filial generation is designated F_1, the second (produced from the first) F_2, etc.

fil·i·a·tion (fil′ē ā′shən) *n.* ⟦ME *filiacion* < OFr *filiation* < LL *filiatio* < L *filius*: see prec.⟧ **1** the state or fact of being a son or daughter; relation of a child to its parent **2** descent from or as from a parent; derivation **3** *a)* the forming of a new branch of a society, etc. *b)* such a branch **4** *Law* the determination by a court of the paternity of a child

fil·i·beg (fil′i beg′) *n.* ⟦Gael *feileadh beag* < *feileadh*, a fold + *beag*, little⟧ a kilt

fil·i·bus·ter (fil′i bus′tər) *n.* ⟦Sp *filibustero* < Fr *flibustier*, earlier *fribustier* < MDu *vrijbuiter*, FREEBOOTER⟧ **1** an adventurer who engages in unauthorized warfare against a country with which his own country is at peace; specif., any of the 19th-cent. U.S. adventurers who led armed expeditions into Latin American countries; freebooter ☆**2** *a)* the making of long speeches, introduction of irrelevant issues, etc. in order to obstruct the passage of a bill in the Senate *b)* a member of the Senate who uses such methods (also **fil′i·bus′ter·er**) —*vi.* **1** to engage in unauthorized warfare as a freebooter ☆**2** to engage in a filibuster —*vt.* ☆to obstruct the passage of (a bill) by a filibuster

fil·i·form (fil′i fôrm′, fī′li-) *adj.* ⟦< L *filum*, a thread (see FILE[1]) + -FORM⟧ having the form of a thread or filament

fil·i·gree (fil′i grē′) *n.* ⟦altered from earlier *filigrain* < Fr *filigrane* < It *filigrana* < L *filum*, a thread (see FILE[1]) + *granum*, GRAIN⟧ **1** delicate, lacelike ornamental work of intertwined wire of gold, silver, etc. **2** any delicate work or design like this —*adj.* like, made of, or made into filigree —*vt.* **-greed′**, **-gree′ing** to ornament with filigree

fil·ing (fil′iŋ) *n.* **1** a small piece, as of metal, scraped off with a file: *usually used in pl.* **2** a document filed as with a court, government agency, etc.

fil·i·o·pi·e·tis·tic (fil′ē ō pī′ə tis′tik) *adj.* ⟦< L *filius*, son (see FILIAL) + -O- + PIETISTIC⟧ of, having to do with, or characterized by great, often excessive, reverence for ancestors or tradition

Fil·i·pi·na (fil′i pē′nə) *n.*, *pl.* **-nas** ⟦Sp⟧ a woman or girl born or living in the Philippines —*adj.* of Filipinas

Fil·i·pi·no (fil′i pē′nō) *n.* ⟦Sp⟧ **1** *pl.* **-nos** a person born or living in the Philippines **2** *var. of* PILIPINO —*adj.* of the Philippine Islands or their people or culture

fill (fil) *vt.* ⟦ME *fillen*, *fullen* < OE *fyllan* < Gmc **fulljan*, to make full < **fulla-* (> Goth *fulls*, FULL[1]) + *-jan*, caus. suffix⟧ **1** *a)* to put as much as possible into; make full *b)* to put a considerable quantity of something into [to *fill* the tub for a bath, to *fill* one's life with joy] **2** *a)* to take up or occupy all or nearly all the capacity, area, or extent of [the crowd *filled* the room] *b)* to spread or be diffused throughout **3** *a)* to occupy (an office, position, etc.) *b)* to put a person into (an office, position, etc.) ☆**4** to fulfill (an engagement to perform, speak, etc.) ☆**5** *a)* to supply the things needed or called for in (an order, prescription, etc.) *b)* to satisfy (a need, requirement, etc.) **6** *a)* to close or plug (holes, cracks, etc.) *b)* to insert a filling in (a tooth) **7** to satisfy the hunger or desire of; feed or satiate ☆**8** to raise the level of (low land) by adding earth, gravel, etc. **9** *Naut.* *a)* to cause (a sail) to swell out *b)* to adjust (a sail) so that the wind strikes its after side ☆**10** *Poker* to draw the card or cards needed to complete (a straight, flush, or full house) —*vi.* to become full —*n.* **1** all that is needed to make full **2** all that is needed to satisfy [to eat or drink one's *fill*] ☆**3** anything that fills or is used to fill; esp., earth, gravel, etc. used for filling a hole or depression ☆**4** a piece of land artificially raised to a required level, as a railroad embankment —**fill in 1** to fill with some substance **2** to make complete by inserting or supplying something **3** to insert or supply for completion ☆**4** to be a substitute —**fill out 1** to make or become larger, rounder, shapelier, etc. ☆**2** to make (a document, etc.) complete by inserting or supplying information —☆**fill someone in (on)** [Informal] to provide someone with additional facts, details, etc. (about) —**fill up** to make or become completely full

fille de joie (fē′y′ də zhwȧ′) ⟦Fr, lit., girl of joy⟧ a prostitute

filled gold brass or other base metal covered with a layer of gold

☆**filled milk** skimmed milk with vegetable oils added to increase the fat content

fill·er (fil′ər) *n.* a person or thing that fills; specif., *a)* matter added to some other to increase bulk, improve consistency, etc. *b)* a preparation used to fill in the cracks, grain, etc. of wood before painting or varnishing *c)* the bunch of blended tobacco held together by a binder leaf to form a cigar *d)* a short, space-filling item as in a newspaper; squib *e)* the paper to be inserted into a loose-leaf notebook, etc. *f)* *Archit.* a plate put in to fill a space, as between two structural parts

fil·lér (fēl′lär′) *n.*, *pl.* **-lér** or **-lérs** ⟦Hung⟧ a monetary unit of Hungary, equal to 1/100 of a forint

fil·let (fil′it; *for n. 6 & vt. 2, usually* fi lā′, fil′ā′) *n.* ⟦ME *filet* < OFr, dim. of *fil*: see FILE[1]⟧ **1** a narrow band worn around the head as to hold the hair in place **2** a thin strip or band **3** FAIRING[1] **4** *Archit.* *a)* a flat, square molding separating other moldings *b)* a narrow band between two flutings in a column **5** *Bookbinding* an ornamental line impressed on a book cover **6** *Cooking* *a)* a lean, boneless piece of meat *b)* a flat, boneless slice cut lengthwise from the side of a fish —*vt.* **1** to bind or decorate with a band, molding, etc. **2** to bone and slice (meat or fish)

fill-in (fil′in′) *n.* a person or thing that fills a vacancy or gap, often temporarily

fill·ing (fil′iŋ) *n.* **1** the act of one that fills **2** a thing used to fill something else or to supply what is lacking; specif., *a)* the metal, plastic, etc. inserted by a dentist into a prepared cavity in a tooth *b)* the foodstuff used between the slices of a sandwich, in a pastry shell, etc. ☆**3** the crosswise threads, or weft, in a woven fabric

☆**filling station** SERVICE STATION (sense 2)

fil·lip (fil′ip) *n.* ⟦echoic extension of FLIP[1]: see CHIRRUP, CHIRP⟧ **1** the snap made by a finger which is held down toward the palm by the thumb and then suddenly released **2** a light blow or tap given in this way **3** anything that stimulates or livens up; piquant element —*vt.* **1** to strike, impel, or snap with a fillip **2** to stimulate or liven up —*vi.* to make a fillip

fillip

fil·lis·ter (fil′is tər) *n.* ⟦< ?⟧ **1** a plane for cutting grooves in wood **2** a groove, as one in a window frame for holding the glass

Fill·more (fil′môr), **Mill·ard** (mil′ərd) 1800-74; 13th president of the U.S. (1850-53)

fil·lo (fē′lō, fī′-) *n. alt. sp. of* PHYLLO

fil·ly (fil′ē) *n.*, *pl.* **-lies** ⟦ME *filli* < ON *fylja*, fem. of *foli*, FOAL⟧ **1** a young female horse, specif. one under five years of age **2** [Informal] a vivacious young woman or girl

film (film) *n.* ⟦ME < OE *filmen*, membrane, foreskin: for IE base see FELL[4]⟧ **1** a fine, thin skin, surface, layer, or coating **2** a sheet or roll of a flexible cellulose material coated with an emulsion sensitive to light and used to capture an image for a photograph or FILM (*n.* 5a) **3** a thin veil, haze, or blur **4** an opacity of the cornea **5** *a)* a sequence of photographs or drawings projected on a screen in such rapid succession that they create the optical illusion (because of the persistence of vision) of moving persons and objects *b)* a play, story, etc. photographed as such a sequence *c)* [*pl.*] the business of making films **6** [Rare] *a)* a fine filament *b)* a gauzy web of filaments —*vt.* **1** to cover with or as with a film **2** *a)* to take a photograph or FILM (*n.* 5a) of *b)* to make an electronic recording of (an image or images), as with a digital camera **3** to make a FILM (*n.* 5b) of (a novel, play, etc.) —*vi.* **1** to become covered with a film **2** *a)* to make a FILM (*n.* 5a & b) *b)* to be filmed or suitable for filming [this novel won't *film* well] —**film′er** *n.*

film badge a badgelike safety device worn by people who work with ionizing radiation: it contains a strip of photographic film that indicates the amount of radiation received

film·dom (film′dəm) *n.* the film industry, esp. the U.S. film industry, regarded as a sphere or domain

film·go·er (-gō′ər) *n.* MOVIEGOER

film·ic (film′ik) *adj.* **1** of or having to do with films or the art of making them **2** of the visual qualities of a film as distinct from the theme, dialogue, story, etc. **3** visually exciting or expressive —**film′i·cal·ly** *adv.*

film·mak·er (film′māk′ər) *n.* a person who makes films, esp. a producer, director, etc. —**film′mak′ing** *n.*

film noir (film′ nwär′) ⟦Fr, lit., black film⟧ **1** a type of film, esp. of the 1940s and 1950s, fatalistic, pessimistic, or cynical in mood and often dealing melodramatically with urban crime and corruption **2** *pl.* **films noirs**, **film noirs**, or **films noir** a film of this type

film·og·ra·phy (fil mäg′rə fē) *n.* ⟦FILM + (BIBLI)OGRAPHY⟧ a list of the films of a particular actor, director, genre, etc.

film pack several sheets of photographic film in a frame that fits in the back of a camera

film·strip (film′strip′) *n.* a length of film containing still photographs, often of illustrations, diagrams, charts, etc., arranged in sequence for projection separately and used as a teaching aid

film·y (fil′mē) *adj.* **film′i·er**, **film′i·est 1** gauzy; sheer; very thin **2** blurred or hazy —**film′i·ly** *adv.* —**film′i·ness** *n.*

fi·lo (fē′lō, fī′-) *n. alt. sp. of* PHYLLO

fil·o·po·di·um (fil′ō pō′dē əm, fī′lō-) *n.*, *pl.* **-di·a** (-ə) ⟦ModL < L *filum*, thread (see FILE[1]) + -PODIUM⟧ a thin, narrow pseudopodium consisting primarily of ectoplasm

fi·lose (fī′lōs′) *adj.* ⟦< L *filum* (see FILE[1]) + -OSE[2]⟧ **1** threadlike **2** having a threadlike projection

fils[1] (fēls, fils) *n.*, *pl.* **fils** ⟦Ar, earlier *fals* < LGr *phollis*, a small coin, 1/288 of a solidus⟧ any of the monetary units of: *a)* Bahrain, Iraq, Jordan, and Kuwait, equal to 1/1000 of a dinar *b)* the United Arab Emirates, equal to 1/100 of a dirham *c)* Yemen, equal to 1/100 of a rial

fils[2] (fēs) *n.* ⟦Fr < L *filius*: see FILIAL⟧ a son or a youth: often used like English "Jr." [Alexandre Dumas *fils*]

fil·ter (fil′tər) *n.* ⟦ME *filtre* < OFr < ML *filtrum*, *feltrum*, felt, fulled wool (used for straining liquors) < Gmc: see FELT[1]⟧ **1** a device for separating solid particles, impurities, etc. from a liquid or gas by passing it through a porous substance **2** any porous substance used or suitable for this, as sand, charcoal, felt, etc. **3** *Comput.* software variously designed to examine data, email messages, etc. and to process, delete, block, etc. those satisfying certain criteria [a spam *filter* that deletes spam sent to one's PC] **4** *Physics a)* a device or substance that passes electric currents of certain frequencies or frequency ranges while preventing the passage of others *b)* a device or substance that partially or completely absorbs certain light rays [a color *filter* for a camera lens] —*vt.* ⟦Fr *filtrer* < the *n.*⟧ **1** to pass through or as if through a filter **2** to remove or separate by means of a filter: often with *out* **3** to act as a filter for —*vi.* **1** to pass through or as if through a filter **2** to move or pass slowly [the news *filtered* through town] —**fil′ter·less** *adj.*

fil·ter·a·ble (fil′tər ə bəl) *adj.* that can be filtered —**fil′ter·a·bil′i·ty** *n.*

filterable virus any virus: so called because most viruses are capable of passing through fine filters that bacteria cannot pass through

filter bed a tank, covered trench, etc. with a sand or gravel bottom, used to filter water, sewage, etc.

filter feeder an animal that feeds by filtering small organisms or food particles from the water or air, as a clam, baleen whale, or sponge

filter paper porous paper for filtering liquids

☆**filter tip** **1** a cigarette tip containing cellulose, cotton, charcoal, etc. and serving as a mouthpiece through which the smoke is filtered **2** a cigarette having such a tip —**fil′ter-tip′** *adj.*, **fil′ter-tipped′**

filth (filth) *n.* ⟦ME < OE *fylthe* < base of *ful* (see FOUL) + -TH[1]⟧ **1** disgustingly offensive dirt, garbage, etc. **2** anything considered as foul as this; esp., anything viewed as grossly indecent or obscene **3** gross moral corruption

filth·y (fil′thē) *adj.* **filth′i·er**, **filth′i·est** ⟦ME *filthi*⟧ **1** full of filth; disgustingly foul **2** grossly obscene **3** morally vicious or corrupt —*adv.* [Informal] to an inordinate extent; extremely [*filthy* rich] —*SYN.* DIRTY —**filth′i·ly** *adv.* —**filth′i·ness** *n.*

fil·tra·ble (fil′trə bəl) *adj.* FILTERABLE —**fil′tra·bil′i·ty** *n.*

fil·trate (fil′trāt′) *vt.* **-trat′ed**, **-trat′ing** ⟦< ML *filtratus*, pp. of *filtrare* < *filtrum*, FILTER⟧ to filter —*n.* a filtered liquid —**fil·tra′tion** *n.*

fi·lum (fī′ləm) *n.*, *pl.* **fi′la** (-lə) ⟦L, a thread: see FILE[1]⟧ *Anat.* any threadlike part; filament

fim·bri·a (fim′brē ə) *n.*, *pl.* **-bri·ae′** (-brē ē′) ⟦ModL < L, fiber, fringe⟧ *Biol.* a fringe or border of hairs, fibers, etc. or a fringelike process, esp. at the opening of an oviduct in mammals

fim·bri·ate (fim′brē āt′) *adj.* ⟦L *fimbriatus*, fringed: see prec.⟧ having a fringe of hairs, fibers, etc. —**fim′bri·a′tion** *n.*

fin[1] (fin) *n.* ⟦ME < OE *finn*, akin to Du *vin*, Ger *finne* < IE **(s)pina-*, point < base **(s)p(h)ei-*, pointed stick > SPIT[1], SPIKE[1]⟧ **1** any of several winglike, membranous organs on the body of a fish, dolphin, etc., used in swimming, turning, and balancing **2** anything like a fin in shape or use; specif., *a)* any narrow edge or ridge formed in manufacturing, as on a casting by metal forced through the halves of the mold *b)* any vertical airfoil, fixed or movable, whose chief function is to give stability in flight *c)* a stabilizing or steering projection on boats or submarines *d)* [Slang] a hand or arm —*vi.* **finned**, **fin′ning** to move the fins, esp. in a violent way

☆**fin[2]** (fin) *n.* ⟦shortened < W Yiddish *finef*, five (cf. E Yiddish *finf*) < MHG *vinf* < OHG *fimf*, FIVE⟧ [Slang] a five-dollar bill

fin[3] (fan) *n.* ⟦Fr⟧ the end; finish; conclusion

fin[4] *abbrev.* **1** finance **2** financial **3** finished

Fin *abbrev.* **1** Finland **2** Finnish

fin·a·ble (fīn′ə bəl) *adj.* liable to a fine

fi·na·gle (fə nā′gəl) *vt.* **-gled**, **-gling** ⟦< ?⟧ [Informal] to get, arrange, or maneuver by cleverness, persuasion, etc., or esp. by craftiness, trickery, etc. —*vi.* to use craftiness, trickery, etc. —**fi·na′gler** *n.*

fi·nal (fī′nəl) *adj.* ⟦ME < OFr < L *finalis* < *finis*, end: see FINISH⟧ **1** of or coming at the end; last; concluding [the *final* chapter] **2** leaving no further chance for action, discussion, or change; deciding; conclusive [a *final* decree] **3** having to do with the basic or ultimate purpose, aim, or end [the *final* destination] —*n.* **1** anything final **2** [*pl.*] the last of a series of contests, trials, etc. **3** a final or concluding examination

final cause in Aristotelian philosophy, the purpose for which a thing is made or done

fi·na·le (fə nal′ē; -nä′lā, -lē) *n.* ⟦It, orig. adj. < L *finalis*, FINAL⟧ **1** the concluding part of a musical composition **2** the last scene or feature of an entertainment **3** the conclusion or last part; end

fi·nal·ist (fī′nəl ist) *n.* a contestant who participates in the final and deciding contest or contests of a series

fi·nal·i·ty (fī nal′ə tē, fə-) *n.* ⟦LL *finalitas*⟧ **1** the quality or condition of being final, settled, or complete; conclusiveness **2** *pl.* **-ties** anything final

fi·nal·ize (fī′nəl īz′) *vt.* **-ized′**, **-iz′ing** ⟦FINAL + -IZE⟧ to make final; bring to completion —**fi′nal·i·za′tion** *n.*

fi·nal·ly (fī′nəl ē; *often* fīn′lē) *adv.* **1** at the end; in conclusion **2** decisively; conclusively; irrevocably **3** at last; eventually [after many seasons, our team *finally* won a championship]

Final Solution, the ⟦transl. of Ger *endlösung* < *end-* (< *ende*, END[1]) + *lösung*, solution⟧ the Nazi program for killing all Jews in German-controlled lands

final straw *var. of* LAST STRAW

fi·nance (fī′nans′, fə nans′) *n.* ⟦ME *finaunce*, a fine, forfeit < OFr *finance*, wealth, revenue < *finer*, to end, settle accounts, pay ransom < *fin*: see FINE[2]⟧ **1** [*pl.*] the money resources, income, etc. of a nation, organization, or person **2** the managing or science of managing money matters, credit, etc. —*vt.* **-nanced′**, **-nanc′ing** **1** to supply money, credit, or capital to or for **2** to obtain money, credit, or capital for

☆**finance company** a company specializing in the lending of money to consumers, the purchasing of accounts receivable, and the extension of credit to businesses

fi·nan·cial (fī nan′shəl, fə-) *adj.* of finance, finances, or financiers —**fi·nan′cial·ly** *adv.*

SYN.—**financial** implies reference to money matters, esp. where large sums are involved [a *financial* success]; **fiscal** is used with reference to government revenues and expenditures or the administering of the financial affairs of an organization or corporation [a *fiscal* year]; **monetary** refers directly to money itself and is used in connection with coinage, circulation, standards, relative values, etc. [the *monetary* unit of a country]; **pecuniary** is applied to money matters of a practical or personal nature [*pecuniary* motives]

financial planner a person whose business is advising individuals in the management of their financial affairs

fi·nan·cials (fī nan′shəlz) *pl.n.* **1** financial data **2** shares of stock in financial companies, including banks, insurers, etc.

fin·an·cier (fin′ən sir′, fī′nən-; fī nan′sir, fī-) *n.* ⟦Fr⟧ **1** a person trained or skilled in finance **2** a person who engages in financial operations on a large scale —*vi.* to engage in financial operations, often specif. in a dishonest way

fi·nas·ter·ide (fə nas′tər īd′) *n.* a white, crystalline drug, $C_{23}H_{36}N_2O_2$, that reduces the amount of testosterone produced by the body, used to treat BPH and male-pattern baldness

☆**fin·back whale** (fin′bak′) RORQUAL

fin·ca (fēŋ′kä′) *n.*, *pl.* **-cas** ⟦Sp < *fincar*, to buy real estate < VL **figicare*, to attach: see FISHPLATE⟧ an estate or plantation in Spain or Spanish America

finch (finch) *n.* ⟦ME < OE *finc*, akin to Ger *fink* < IE echoic base **(s)pingo-*, chirping bird > Welsh *pink*, Gr *spingos*, finch⟧ any of various small, short-beaked, seed-eating passerine birds (esp. family Fringillidae), including redpolls, canaries, crossbills, goldfinches, and chaffinches

find (fīnd) *vt.* **found**, **find′ing** ⟦ME *finden* < OE *findan*, akin to Ger *finden*, Goth *finthan* < IE base **pent-*, to walk, happen upon, find > L *pons*, a plank causeway, bridge⟧ **1** to happen on; come upon; meet with; discover by chance **2** to get by searching or by making an effort [*find* the answer] **3** to get sight or knowledge of; perceive; learn [I *find* that I was wrong] **4** to experience or feel [to *find* pleasure in music] **5** *a)* to get or recover (something lost) [to *find* a missing book] *b)* to get or recover the use of [we *found* our sea legs] **6** to realize as being; consider; think [to *find* a book boring] **7** to get to; reach; attain [the blow *found* his chin] **8** to declare after careful thought [the jury *found* him innocent] **9** to supply; furnish: cf. FOUND[1] —*vi.* to reach and announce a decision [the jury *found* for the accused] —*n.* **1** the act of finding **2** something found, esp. something interesting or valuable —**find oneself** **1** to learn what one's real talents and inclinations are, and begin to apply them **2** to become aware of being [to *find oneself* in trouble] —**find out** **1** to discover; learn **2** to learn the true character or identity of (someone or something)

find·er (fīn′dər) *n.* **1** a person or thing that finds **2** VIEWFINDER **3** a small, low-powered telescope attached to a larger one, used to locate objects for closer view with the more powerful telescope ☆**4** a person who, for a fee (**finder's fee**), initiates a business deal between others

fin de siè·cle (fant sye′kl′) ⟦Fr, end of the century⟧ of or characteristic of the last years of the 19th cent.: formerly used to refer to progressive ideas and customs, but now generally used to indicate decadence: also written **fin-de-siècle** *adj.*

find·ing (fīn′diŋ) *n.* ⟦ME: see FIND⟧ **1** the act of one who finds; discovery **2** something found or discovered **3** [*pl.*] miscellaneous small articles or materials used in making garments, shoes, jewelry, etc., as buttons, buckles, or clasps **4** [*often pl.*] the conclusion reached after an examination or consideration of facts or data by a judge, coroner, scholar, etc.

fine[1] (fīn) *adj.* **fin′er**, **fin′est** ⟦ME *fin* < OFr < ML *finus*, for L *finis*, an end, limit: see FINISH⟧ **1** [Obs.] finished; perfected **2** superior in quality; better than average; excellent; very good [a *fine* sample] **3** of exceptional character or ability [a *fine* teacher] **4** with no impurities; refined **5** containing a specified proportion of pure metal: said usually of gold or silver **6** in good health; very well **7** clear and bright: said of the weather **8** *a)* not heavy or gross *b)* not coarse; in very small particles [*fine* sand] **9** *a)* very thin or slender [*fine* thread] *b)* very small [*fine* print] **10** sharp; keen [a knife with a *fine* edge] **11** *a)* discriminating; subtle [*fine* distinctions] *b)* involving precise accuracy [a *fine* adjustment] **12** of delicate or subtle composition or character [*fine* lace] **13** [Now Rare] attractive; handsome [a *fine* child] **14** trained and developed physically to the maximum extent: said of athletes, horses, etc. **15** *a)* elegant [*fine* writing] *b)* too elegant; showy [her *fine* ways] **16** acceptable; satisfactory —*adv.* **fin′er**, **fin′est** **1** FINELY **2** [Informal] very well; all right — *vt.*, *vi.* **fined**, **fin′ing** to make or become fine or finer

fine[2] (fīn) *n.* ⟦ME < OFr *fin* < L *finis*: see FINISH⟧ **1** a finish; end; conclusion: obs. except in IN FINE (see phrase below) **2** a sum of money paid to settle a matter; esp., a sum required to be paid as punishment or penalty for an offense —*vt.* **fined**, **fin′ing** to require the payment of a fine from —**in fine** **1** in conclusion **2** in brief

fi·ne[3] (fē′nā) *n.* ⟦It < L *finis*: see FINISH⟧ *Musical Direction* the end: a note marking the close of a repetition

fine·a·ble (fīn′ə bəl) *adj. alt. sp. of* FINABLE

fine art ⟦orig. considered purely aesthetic, as distinguished from the "useful" arts⟧ **1** any of the art forms that include drawing, painting, sculpture, and ceramics, and, occas., architecture, literature, music, dramatic art, or dancing: *usually used in pl.* **2** artistic objects, as paintings, sculpture, etc. collectively [an exhibition of *fine art*] **3** any highly creative or intricate skill

fine-drawn (-drôn′) ***adj.*** **1** drawn out until very fine, as wire **2** extended to a high degree of subtleness: said of reasoning, arguments, etc.

fine-grained (-grānd′) ***adj.*** having a fine, smooth grain, as some kinds of woods, leather, etc.

fine·ly (fīn′lē) ***adv.*** ⟦ME *finliche*⟧ in a fine manner

fine·ness (fīn′nis) ***n.*** **1** the quality or state of being fine **2** the proportion of pure gold or silver in an alloy

fine print **1** a section of a document, as a contract, warranty, or advertisement, in smaller print than the main body: although it includes additional conditions, limits, etc., this section may not be read carefully because it is typically terse or in legalese **2** any additional details, conditions, etc. regarded as obscure or, often, deliberately obscure

fin·er·y[1] (fīn′ər ē) ***n.***, *pl.* **-er·ies** showy, elaborate decoration, esp. clothes, jewelry, etc.

fin·er·y[2] (fīn′ər ē) ***n.***, *pl.* **-er·ies** ⟦Fr *finerie* < *finer*, to refine < ML *finire*, to refine < L, FINISH⟧ a refinery where malleable iron or steel is made

fines (fīnz) ***pl.n.*** fine fragments or tiny particles, as of crushed rock, esp. when separated by screening

fines herbes (fēn zerb′) ⟦Fr, lit., fine herbs⟧ mixed chopped herbs, traditionally parsley, chives, tarragon, and chervil, used as a seasoning, as in an omelet

fine·spun (fīn′spun′) ***adj.*** **1** spun or drawn out to extreme fineness; delicate; fragile **2** extremely or overly subtle

fi·nesse (fə nes′) ***n.*** ⟦Fr < OFr *fin*, FINE[1]⟧ **1** adroitness and delicacy of performance **2** the ability to handle delicate and difficult situations skillfully and diplomatically **3** cunning; skill; artfulness; craft **4** *Bridge* an attempt to take a trick with a lower card while holding a higher card not in sequence with it, made in the hope that the intervening card is in the hand of the opponent who has already played —***vt.*** **-nessed′**, **-ness′ing** **1** to manage, bring about, or deal with by finesse: sometimes with *into* **2** to evade or bypass (a problem, issue, etc.) **3** *Bridge a)* to make a finesse with (a specified card) *b)* to play a card lower than (the specified intervening card) in making a finesse —***vi.*** to use finesse or make a finesse

fin·est (fīn′ist) ***adj., adv. superl. of*** FINE[1] —***pl.n.*** [Informal] the members of the police force (of a specified city) [one of New York's *finest*]

☆**fine-toothed comb** (fīn′to͞otht′) a comb with fine, closely set teeth: also **fine-tooth comb** (-to͞oth′) —**go over with a fine-toothed comb** to examine very carefully and thoroughly

fine-tune (-to͞on′, -tyo͞on′) ***vt.*** **-tuned′**, **-tun′ing** **1** to adjust a control on (a TV or radio set) for better reception **2** to adjust (a device, system, policy, etc.) for greater effectiveness

fin·fish (fin′fish′) ***n.***, *pl.* **-fish′** or **-fish′es** (see FISH) any fish with fins, as distinguished from other kinds of fish, esp. shellfish

Fin·gal's Cave (fiŋ′gəlz) large cavern on an islet (called *Staffa*) west of Mull in the Hebrides, W Scotland

fin·ger (fiŋ′gər) ***n.*** ⟦ME < OE, akin to Ger *finger*, Goth *figgrs*, prob. < IE base **penkwe*, FIVE⟧ **1** any of the five jointed parts projecting from the palm of the hand; esp., any of these other than the thumb **2** the part of a glove that covers one of these parts **3** anything resembling a finger in shape or use; specif., a short strip of chicken, fish, etc., breaded and deep-fried ☆**4** a rough unit of measure based on *a)* the breadth of a finger (¾ inch to 1 inch), as in measuring whiskey in a glass *b)* [Now Rare] the length of a man's middle finger (about 4½ inches) **5** *Mech.* a projecting part coming into contact with another part and controlling its motion —***vt.*** **1** to touch or handle with the fingers; use the fingers on **2** [Now Rare] to take; steal ☆**3** [Slang] to point out; indicate or designate, specif. in senses of PUT THE FINGER ON (see phrase below) **4** *Music a)* to play (an instrument, chord, etc.) by using the fingers in a certain way or sequence on strings, keys, etc. *b)* to mark (a score) with directions for the way to use the fingers —***vi.*** **1** to use the fingers in a certain way or sequence on a musical instrument **2** to be fingered: said of musical instruments **3** to extend (*out, across*, etc.) like a finger —**burn one's fingers** to cause oneself trouble by being too inquisitive, meddlesome, etc. —**give someone the finger** [Slang] to express anger, contempt, etc. for someone by gesturing vulgarly with the middle finger held upright from a clenched fist —**have a finger in the pie** **1** to help do something; participate **2** to be meddlesome —**have** (or **keep**) **one's fingers crossed** ⟦see CROSS ONE'S FINGERS at CROSS⟧ to be hoping that something happens in a certain way —**lift a finger** to make even the slightest effort —**point a** (or **the**) **finger at** [Informal] to accuse or blame —**put one's finger on** to indicate or ascertain exactly —☆**put the finger on** [Slang] **1** to identify as for the police; inform on **2** to indicate as the place to be robbed, victim to be killed, etc.

fin·ger·board (-bôrd′) ***n.*** a strip of ebony or other hardwood fixed to the neck of a stringed instrument, against which the strings are pressed, as with the fingers, to produce the desired notes

finger bowl a small bowl to hold water for rinsing the fingers at table after a meal

fin·ger·breadth (-bredth′) ***n.*** the breadth of a finger, roughly ¾ inch to 1 inch in measure

fin·gered (fiŋ′gərd) ***adj.*** **1** having fingers (of a specified kind or number): used in hyphenated compounds [light-*fingered*] **2** soiled or marred by touching **3** *Bot. a)* digitate *b)* fingerlike in form **4** *Music* marked to show the fingering: said of a score

finger food a food or foods intended to be eaten while held in the fingers, as hors d'oeuvres served at a cocktail party

fin·ger·ing (fiŋ′gər iŋ) ***n.*** **1** a touching or handling with the fingers **2** *Music a)* act or technique of applying the fingers to the strings, keys, etc. of an instrument to produce the tones *b)* directions on a musical score for using the fingers in a certain way or sequence

Finger Lakes ⟦so named because long and narrow, like the *fingers* of a hand⟧ group of long, narrow glacial lakes in WC N.Y.

fin·ger·ling (fiŋ′gər liŋ) ***n.*** ⟦ME: see FINGER & -LING[1]⟧ **1** anything very small or trifling **2** a small fish about the length of a finger, or a young fish up to the end of the first year

fin·ger·nail (-nāl′) ***n.*** the horny substance growing on the upper part of the end joint of a finger

☆**finger painting** **1** the art or process of painting by using the fingers, hand, or arm to spread, on moistened paper, paints (**finger paints**) made of starch, glycerin, and pigments **2** a painting made in this manner —**fin′ger-paint′** ***vi., vt.***

fin·ger·pick (fiŋ′gər pik′) ***n.*** a special pick of plastic or metal, designed to be worn on a finger and used in fingerpicking — ***vt., vi.*** to play using a fingerpick

fin·ger·pick·ing (-pik′iŋ) ***n.*** a style of guitar playing, esp. in folk music, in which the thumb plays bass notes while the index and middle fingers play a syncopated treble melody, often with the use of several fingerpicks

fin·ger-point·ing (-point′iŋ) ***n.*** the act of assigning blame as for a harmful policy or unwise decision to another or others, often in an effort to deflect blame from oneself

finger post a post with a sign, often shaped like a pointing finger or hand, indicating a direction

fin·ger·print (-print′) ***n.*** **1** an impression of the lines and whorls on the inner surface of the end joint of the finger, used as by the police in the identification of a person **2** any characteristic or set of characteristics that distinguishes or unambiguously identifies a person or thing; signature —***vt.*** to take the fingerprints of

fin·ger·stall (-stôl′) ***n.*** ⟦ME *fingir stall*: see STALL[1]⟧ a protective covering of rubber, leather, etc. for an injured finger

fin·ger·tip (-tip′) ***n.*** **1** the tip of a finger **2** something used to protect the end of a finger —**have at one's fingertips** **1** to have available for instant use **2** to be completely familiar with —**to one's** (or **the**) **fingertips** entirely; altogether

☆**finger wave** a loose wave made by dampening and shaping the hair without heat, using only fingers and comb

fi·ni (fē nē′) ***adj.*** ⟦Fr⟧ finished; through; at an end

fin·i·al (fin′ē əl; *Brit* fī′nē-) ***n.*** ⟦ME, orig. adj., FINAL⟧ a decorative part at the tip of a spire, gable, lampshade support, etc., or projecting upward from the top of a cabinet, breakfront, etc.

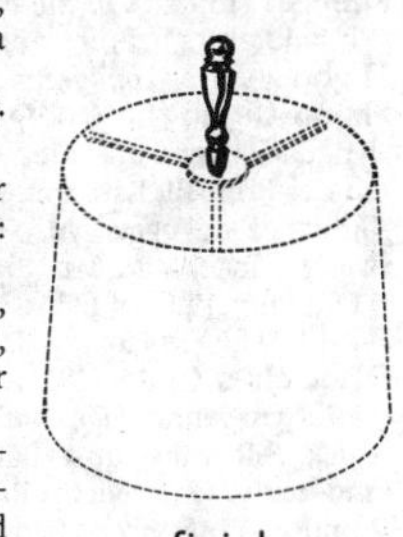
finial

fin·i·cal (fin′i kəl) ***adj.*** ⟦< FINE[1]⟧ FINICKY —**fin′i·cal′i·ty** (-i kal′ə tē) ***n.*** —**fin′i·cal·ly** ***adv.***

fin·ick·y (fin′i kē) ***adj.*** ⟦< prec.⟧ too particular or exacting; overly dainty or fastidious; fussy: also **fin′ick·ing** (-kiŋ) —**fin′ick·i·ness** ***n.***

fin·ing (fīn′iŋ) ***n.*** ⟦ME < *finen*, to refine < *fin*, FINE[1]⟧ **1** the refining or clarifying of liquids, metals, etc. **2** [*pl.*] any substance used for clarifying liquors

fi·nis (fin′is, fī′nis; *often, because taken erroneously as Fr*, fē nē′) ***n.*** ⟦L: see fol.⟧ the end; finish; conclusion: used, esp. formerly, at the end of some movies and books

fin·ish (fin′ish) ***vt.*** ⟦ME *finishen* < extended stem of OFr *finir* < L *finire*, to end < *finis*, an end, limit, orig., boundary (post), something fixed in the ground < IE base **dhigw-*, to stick in > DIKE[1], L *figere*, FIX⟧ **1** *a)* to bring to an end; complete [to *finish* the work] *b)* to come to the end of [to *finish* a book] **2** to use up; consume entirely [*finish* your milk] **3** to give final touches to; embellish or perfect **4** to treat (a cut edge, esp. of a garment), as by pinking, serging, or binding, in order to prevent raveling **5** to give (cloth, leather, wood, etc.) a desired surface effect **6** *a)* to cause the defeat, collapse, death, etc. of *b)* to render worthless, useless, helpless, etc. —***vi.*** **1** to come to an end; terminate **2** to complete something being done **3** to complete a contest in a specified position [to *finish* last] —***n.*** **1** the last part; end **2** anything used to give a desired surface effect, as paint, varnish, polish, wax, etc. **3** completeness; perfection **4** the manner or method of completion **5** *a)* the surface given to wood, metal, etc. as by painting, varnishing, etc. [a walnut *finish*, matte *finish*] *b)* any surface texture and appearance [cloth with a satiny *finish*] **6** refinement as in manners, speech, etc.; polish in social or cultural matters **7** defeat, collapse, etc. or that which brings it about; downfall **8** the taste a wine leaves in the mouth after it has been swallowed **9** *Carpentry* joiner work, as the installation of doors, stairs, panels, etc., which completes the interior of a building —***SYN.*** CLOSE[2] —**finish off** **1** to end or complete **2** [Informal] to kill or destroy —**finish up** **1** to end or complete **2** to consume all of —**finish with** **1** to end or complete **2** to end relations with; become indifferent to —**in at the finish** being present or taking part at the conclusion, as of a contest —**fin′ish·er** ***n.***

fin·ished (fin′isht) ***adj.*** **1** ended; concluded **2** completed **3** highly skilled or polished; perfected; accomplished **4** given a certain kind of finish or surface, as of paint, wax, etc. **5** defeated, ruined, dying, etc. ☆**6** done with a task, activity, or concern [they were *finished* by noon]

finishing nail a slender nail with a very small head, used in finish carpentry, or joinery

finishing school a private school for young women that emphasizes training in cultured behavior, social graces, etc.

finish line a line that marks the end of a race

Fin·is·terre (fin′is ter′), **Cape** promontory at the westernmost point of Spain

fi·nite (fī′nīt′) ***adj.*** ⟦ME *finit* < L *finitus*, pp. of *finire*, FINISH⟧ **1** having measurable or definable limits; not infinite **2** *Gram.* having limits of person, number, and tense: said of a verb that can be used in a predicate **3** *Math. a)* capable of being reached, completed, or surpassed by counting (said of numbers or sets) *b)* neither infinite nor infinitesimal (said of a magnitude) —***n.*** anything that has measurable limits; finite thing —**fi′nite′ly** ***adv.*** —**fi′nite′ness** ***n.***

fi·ni·to (fē nē′tō) ***adj.*** ⟦It⟧ [*often not in italics*] finished; over; at an end

fin·i·tude (fin′i to͞od′, -tyo͞od′; *Brit* fī′ni-) ***n.*** the state or quality of being finite

☆**fink** (fiŋk) [Slang] ***n.*** ⟦Ger, lit., FINCH, used since the 17th c. as generalized pejorative; adopted (*c.* 1740) by students at Jena for nonmembers of fraternities (prob. in allusion to the wild bird in contrast to the caged canary); later extended to those not in organizations, esp. unions⟧ **1** an informer **2** a strikebreaker; esp., a professional strikebreaker **3** a person regarded as contemptible, obnoxious, etc. —***vi.*** to inform (*on*) —**fink out** **1** to withdraw; back out **2** to fail

Fin·land (fin′lənd) **1** country in N Europe, northeast of the Baltic Sea: 130,559 sq mi (338,145 sq km); cap. Helsinki: Finn. name SUOMI **2 Gulf of** arm of the Baltic Sea, south of Finland: *c.* 250 mi (402 km) long

Fin·land·ize (fin′lən dīz′) ***vt.*** **-ized′**, **-iz′ing** ⟦in allusion to an allegedly similar relationship between Finland and the U.S.S.R. after WWII⟧ to cause (a country) to accommodate its foreign policy to that of the U.S.S.R. as in order to maintain its autonomy —**Fin′land·i·za′tion** ***n.***

Finn[1] (fin) ***n.*** **1** a person born or living in Finland **2** a person who speaks a Finnic language

Finn[2] *abbrev.* Finnish

fin·nan had·die (fin′ən had′ē) ⟦prob. < *Findhorn haddock*, after fishing port and river of *Findhorn*, Scotland; often assoc. with *Findon*, Scotland⟧ smoked haddock: also **finnan haddock**

finned (find) ***adj.*** having a fin or fins

Finn·ic (fin′ik) ***n.*** **1** a group of languages of the Finno-Ugric language subfamily, including Finnish, Estonian, and Lapp **2** [Rare] Finnish —***adj.*** designating or of this group of languages

fin·nick·y (fin′ik ē) ***adj.*** *alt. sp. of* FINICKY

Finn·ish (fin′ish) ***n.*** the Finno-Ugric language spoken in Finland —***adj.*** of Finland or its people, language, or culture

Fin·no- (fin′ō) *combining form* Finnish, Finnish and [*Finno*-Ugric]

Fin·no-U·gric (fin′ō o͞o′grik, -yo͞o′-) ***n.*** a subfamily of the Uralic family of languages, spoken chiefly in NE Europe, W Siberia, and Hungary: it includes Finnish, Estonian, and Hungarian —***adj.*** designating or of this subfamily of languages Also **Fin′no-U′gri·an** (-grē ən)

fin·ny (fin′ē) ***adj.*** **1** *a)* having fins *b)* like a fin **2** *a)* of or being fish *b)* [Old Poet.] full of fish

fi·no (fē′nō) ***n.*** ⟦Sp < adj., fine⟧ a very pale and dry sherry

fi·noc·chi·o (fi nō′kē ō′) ***n.*** ⟦It < VL **fenuculum* < L *feniculum*, FENNEL⟧ a variety of fennel (*Foeniculum vulgare* var. *dulce*), cooked as a vegetable: its thick, celerylike, anise-flavored stalks are also eaten raw

Fins·bur·y (finz′ber′ē; *Brit*, -bə ri) former metropolitan borough of EC London, now part of Islington

Fin·ster·aar·horn (fin′stər är′hôrn) mountain in SC Switzerland: highest peak in the Bernese Alps: 14,026 ft (4,275 m)

Fi·o·na (fē ō′nə) ***n.*** ⟦after a character in OSSIAN by James MACPHERSON; prob. infl. by Gael *fionn*, white, fair⟧ a feminine name

fiord (fyôrd) ***n.*** ⟦Norw *fjord* < ON *fjörthr*, akin to OE *ford*, FORD⟧ a narrow inlet or arm of the sea bordered by steep cliffs, esp. in Norway

fio·ri·tu·ra (fyô′rē to͞o′rä) ***n.***, *pl.* ***-tu′re*** (-re) ⟦It, lit., blossoming⟧ *Music* a written or improvised embellishment of a melody, as in a coloratura aria, a cadenza, or a roulade

fip·ple flute (fip′əl) ⟦< ?⟧ any of a class of vertical flutes, as the recorder, in which a wedgelike plug (**fipple**) near the mouthpiece diverts part of the breath in producing the tones

fir[1] (fur) ***n.*** ⟦ME *firre* < OE *fyrh*, akin to Ger *föhre* < IE base **perkwus*, name of the tree, oak > L *quercus*, oak⟧ **1** any of a genus (*Abies*) of cone-bearing evergreen trees of the pine family, having flattened needles and upright cones whose scales fall off at maturity **2** any of various other coniferous trees, as the Douglas fir **3** the wood of any of these trees —**fir′ry** ***adj.***

fiord

fir[2] *abbrev.* firkin

Fir·bank (fur′baŋk), **(Arthur Annesley) Ronald** 1886-1926; Eng. novelist

Fir·dau·si (fir dou′sē) (born *Abul Kasim Mansur*) A.D. 940?-1020; Pers. epic poet: also **Fir·du′si** (-do͞o′sē)

fire (fīr) ***n.*** ⟦ME *fyr* < OE, akin to Ger *feuer* < IE base **pewōr-* > Gr *pyra*, PYRE, Czech *pýř*, glowing embers⟧ **1** the active principle of burning, characterized by the heat and light of combustion **2** fuel burning in a furnace, fireplace, etc. **3** an instance of burning that is undesired, uncontrolled, and destructive [a forest *fire*] **4** any preparation that will burn and make a brilliant display [Greek *fire*] **5** *a)* anything like fire, as in heat or brilliance *b)* firelike brilliance **6** death, torture, or trial by burning **7** extreme suffering or distress that tries one's endurance; tribulation or ordeal **8** a feverish or inflamed condition of the body **9** strong feeling; excitement; ardor [a speech full of *fire*] **10** vivid imagination **11** *a)* discharge of firearms or artillery; shooting *b)* anything like this in speed and continuity of action [a *fire* of criticism] —***vt.*** **fired**, **fir′ing** ⟦ME *firen* < OE *fyrian*⟧ **1** to apply fire to; make burn; ignite **2** to supply with fuel; tend the fire of [to *fire* a furnace] **3** to bake (bricks, pottery, etc.) in a kiln **4** to dry by heat **5** to make bright or illuminate, as if by fire **6** *a)* to animate or inspire *b)* to excite, stimulate, or inflame (often with *up*) **7** *a)* to shoot or discharge (a gun, bullet, etc.) *b)* to make explode by igniting **8** to hurl or direct with force and suddenness [*fire* a rock, *fire* questions] ☆**9** ⟦pun on *discharge*⟧ to dismiss from an office, position, or employment; discharge —***vi.*** **1** to start burning; flame **2** to become excited or aroused **3** to react in a specified way to firing in a kiln [a glaze that *fires* bright blue] **4** to shoot a firearm **5** to discharge a projectile [the gun *fired* accidentally] **6** to become yellow prematurely, as corn or grain —**between two fires** between two attacks; shot at, criticized, etc. from both sides —**catch (on) fire** to begin burning; ignite —**fire away** [Informal] to begin; start: used esp. to invite questions or criticism —**fire up** **1** to start a fire in a furnace, stove, etc. **2** to start or warm up (an engine, etc.) **3** [Archaic] to become suddenly angry or impassioned —**go through fire and water** to undergo great difficulties or dangers —**on fire** **1** burning **2** greatly excited; full of ardor **3** having an extraordinary run of success —**open fire** to begin to shoot firearms, artillery, etc. —**play with fire** to do something risky —**set fire to** to make burn; ignite —**set the world on fire** to become famous through brilliant achievements —**strike fire** to make a spark, as with tinder —**take fire** **1** to begin to burn **2** to become excited —**under fire** **1** under attack, as by gunfire **2** subjected to criticism or hostility; embattled —**fir′er** ***n.***

fire alarm **1** a signal to announce the outbreak of a fire, the activation of a smoke detector, etc. **2** a bell, siren, whistle, flashing light, etc. to give this signal

fire-and-brim·stone (fīr′ən brim′stōn′) ***adj.*** characterized by an impassioned emphasis on damnation and eternal punishment [a *fire-and-brimstone* sermon]

fire ant any of a genus (*Solenopsis*) of ants whose sting causes a burning sensation, esp. a South American species (*S. invicta*) that has become a severe pest in the S U.S.

fire·arm (fīr′ärm′) ***n.*** any weapon from which a shot is fired by the force of an explosion; esp., such a weapon small enough to be carried, as a rifle or pistol

fire·ball (-bôl′) ***n.*** **1** something resembling a ball of fire; specif., *a)* a large, bright meteor (see BOLIDE) *b)* BALL LIGHTNING *c)* a high-temperature, luminous ball of gas which forms shortly after a nuclear explosion **2** [Historical] a ball of explosive or combustible material thrown as a weapon in battle ☆**3** [Informal] a vigorous, energetic person

☆**fire·ball·er** (-bôl′ər) ***n.*** [Slang] *Baseball* a pitcher who throws an exceptionally rapid fastball —**fire′ball′ing** ***adj.***

☆**fire·base** (-bās′) ***n.*** a military base in a combat zone, from which artillery, rockets, etc. are fired

fire·bird (-burd′) ***n.*** ☆any of various birds with brilliant coloring, as the scarlet tanager or the Baltimore oriole

fire blight ☆a disease of fruit trees, as the pear or apple, caused by a bacterium (*Erwinia amylovora*): it kills the branches and blackens the leaves

☆**fire·boat** (-bōt′) ***n.*** a boat equipped with firefighting equipment, used in harbors, etc.

fire·bomb (-bäm′) ***n.*** a bomb or missile intended to start a fire; incendiary bomb —***vt.*** to attack, damage, or destroy with a firebomb

fire·box (-bäks′) ***n.*** **1** the place for the fire in a locomotive engine, stove, etc. **2** [Obs.] a tinderbox

fire·brand (-brand′) ***n.*** **1** a piece of burning wood **2** a person who stirs up others to rebellion or strife

fire·brat (-brat′) ***n.*** any of various small thysanuran insects (*Thermobia domestica*) resembling silverfish, found in hot areas, as around steam pipes or fireplaces

fire·break (-brāk′) ***n.*** a strip of land cleared or plowed to stop the spread of fire, as in a forest or prairie

fire-breath·ing (-brē′thiŋ) ***adj.*** impassioned, outspoken, etc., esp. in political matters; fiery [a *fire-breathing* radical]

fire·brick (-brik′) ***n.*** a brick made to withstand great heat, used to line fireplaces, furnaces, etc.

fire brigade *chiefly Brit. var. of* FIRE COMPANY (sense 1)

☆**fire·bug** (-bug′) ***n.*** [Informal] a person who deliberately sets fire to buildings, etc.; pyromaniac; incendiary

☆**fire chief** the officer in charge of a fire department

fire·clay (-klā′) ***n.*** a kind of clay capable of resisting intense heat, used for making firebricks, furnace linings, etc.

fire company 1 a body of men organized to fight fires, esp. one of a number of such groups constituting a fire department 2 [Brit.] a business firm selling fire insurance

fire control supervision of the aiming and firing of weapons at military targets

☆**fire·crack·er** (-krak′ər) *n.* a usually small paper cylinder that contains an explosive and an attached fuse and makes a sharp noise when exploded: used at celebrations, etc.

☆**fire-cure** (-kyoor′) *vt.* **-cured′**, **-cur′ing** to cure (tobacco, etc.) by direct exposure to the smoke of wood fires

fire·damp (-damp′) *n.* a gas, largely methane, formed in coal mines, which is explosive when mixed with air

☆**fire department** a municipal department, usually consisting of one or more fire companies, whose work is fighting fires and preventing their occurrence

fire·dog (-dôg′) *n.* ⟦sense development as in Fr *chenet*, andiron, dim. of *chien*, dog⟧ ANDIRON

fire door ☆a door of metal or other fire-resistant material designed to keep a fire from spreading

fire·drake (-drāk′) *n.* ⟦see FIRE & DRAKE[2]⟧ *Gmc. Myth.* a fire-breathing dragon

fire drill ☆a drill in which buildings are vacated, fire stations manned, etc. in a quick, orderly way to teach proper procedures in case of fire

fire-eat·er (-ēt′ər) *n.* 1 a performer at circuses, etc. who pretends to eat fire 2 a hot-tempered person always ready to quarrel or fight

fire engine 1 a motor truck with a special pumping apparatus for spraying water, chemicals, etc. on fires to put them out 2 loosely, any motor truck for carrying firemen and equipment to a fire

fire escape 1 a stairway, typically an open, metal one down an outside wall, designed to provide a means of escape from a burning building 2 a ladder, chute, rope, etc. used for the same purpose

fire extinguisher a portable device containing chemicals that can be sprayed on a fire to put it out

fire·fight (-fīt′) *n.* an intense, usually brief, exchange of gunfire between soldiers of small military units

fire·fight·er (-fīt′ər) *n.* a person whose work is fighting fires; esp., a member of a fire department —**fire′fight′ing** *n.*

fire·fly (-flī′) *n.*, *pl.* **-flies′** any of a family (Lampyridae) of winged beetles, active at night, whose abdomens glow with a luminescent light: see GLOWWORM

fire·guard (-gärd′) *n.* FIRE SCREEN

fire·hall (-hôl′) *n.* [Chiefly Cdn.] FIRE STATION

☆**fire·house** (-hous′) *n.* FIRE STATION

☆**fire hydrant** FIREPLUG

fire insurance insurance against loss or damage resulting from fire

fire irons the poker, shovel, and tongs used for tending a fireplace

fire·less (-lis) *adj.* without a fire

fire·light (-līt′) *n.* light from a fire, esp. an open fire

fire·lit (-lit′) *adj.* illuminated by firelight

fire·lock (-läk′) *n.* 1 an early type of gunlock in which the priming was ignited by sparks; wheel lock or flintlock 2 an early type of musket with such a lock

fire·man (-mən) *n.*, *pl.* **-men** (-mən) 1 FIREFIGHTER 2 a person who tends a fire in a furnace or boiler ☆3 *U.S. Navy* an enlisted person ranking below a petty officer third class, whose general duties are concerned with ships' engines, boilers, etc. ☆4 [Slang] *Baseball* a relief pitcher

☆**fire marshal** the officer in charge of a fire prevention bureau, as within a fire department

Fi·ren·ze (fē ren′dze) *It. name for* FLORENCE[2]

fire opal a reddish opal usually exhibiting a brilliant play of colors in bright light

fire·place (fīr′plās′) *n.* 1 a place for a fire, esp. an open place built in a wall, at the base of a chimney 2 a masonry structure or metal frame with a grill for outdoor cooking over an open fire

fire·plug (-plug′) *n.* a street hydrant to which a hose can be attached for fighting fires

fire·pow·er (-pou′ər) *n.* *Mil.* the capacity of a given weapon, unit, etc. to deliver fire

fire·proof (-pro͞of′) *adj.* that does not burn or is not easily destroyed by fire —*vt.* to make fireproof

☆**fire sale** 1 a sale at reduced prices of goods damaged in a fire 2 a sale of something, as property or stocks, at very low prices

fire screen a screen to be set in front of a fire to protect against heat or sparks

fire ship [Historical] a ship filled with explosive materials, set afire and floated among an enemy's ships to destroy them

fire·side (-sīd′) *n.* 1 the part of a room near a fireplace or hearth 2 the home or domestic life

fire station a place where fire engines are kept and where firefighters stay when on duty

fire·stone (-stōn′) *n.* 1 [Historical] flint or iron pyrites used for striking fire 2 a stone that can withstand intense heat

fire·storm (-stôrm′) *n.* 1 an intense fire over a large area, as one initiated by an atomic explosion, that is sustained and spread by inrushing winds created by a strong draft of rising hot air 2 a strong, often violent, outburst, disturbance, or upheaval

☆**fire·thorn** (-thôrn′) *n.* any of a genus (*Pyracantha*) of thorny Eurasian plants of the rose family, grown widely in the U.S. for the masses of brilliant red or orange fruits

fire tower a tower, usually in a forest, where a lookout is posted to watch for fires and give the alarm

fire·trap (-trap′) *n.* a building particularly unsafe in case of fire because it will burn easily or lacks adequate exits or fire escapes

☆**fire·truck** (-truk′) *n.* FIRE ENGINE

☆**fire wall** 1 a fireproof wall to prevent the spread of fire, as from one room or compartment to the next 2 anything serving as a protective barrier; specif., a program or system designed to protect a computer network from unauthorized access, as over the internet Also, and for sense 2 usually, **fire′wall′** *n.*

☆**fire warden** an official assigned to prevent or fight fires, as in a forest, logging operation, camp, or town

☆**fire·wa·ter** (-wôt′ər) *n.* ⟦calque of Ojibwa *ishkodewaaboo*, ardent spirits (rum, brandy, whiskey) < *ishkodew-*, fire + *-aaboo*, water, liquid⟧ alcoholic liquor: now humorous

☆**fire·weed** (-wēd′) *n.* any of a number of plants that grow readily on cleared or burned-over land; esp., a species (*Epilobium angustifolium*) of willow herb, with purplish-red flowers

fire·wood (-wood′) *n.* wood used as fuel

fire·works (-wurks′) *pl.n.* 1 *sing.* **-work′** firecrackers, rockets, etc., exploded or burned, as in celebrations, to produce noises or brilliant lighting effects: *sometimes used in sing.* 2 a display of fireworks 3 a noisy quarrel or display of anger

fir·ing (fīr′iŋ) *n.* 1 the application of heat to harden or glaze pottery 2 the stoking of a fire, furnace, etc. 3 the shooting of firearms, etc. 4 fuel for a fire ☆5 the scorching of plants, as from heat, drought, or disease

firing line 1 the line from which gunfire is directed against the enemy 2 the troops stationed along this line 3 the forefront in any kind of activity

firing order the order in which explosions occur in the cylinders of an internal-combustion engine

firing pin that part in the bolt or breech of a firearm which strikes the primer and explodes the charge

firing squad (*or* party) 1 a group of soldiers detailed to shoot someone to death as a form of execution 2 *Mil.* a group detailed to fire a volley of shots over the grave at a military funeral

fir·kin (fur′kin) *n.* ⟦ME, contr. < *firdekyn* < MDu, dim. of *vierdel*, fourth⟧ 1 a small, wooden tub for butter, lard, etc. 2 a unit of capacity equal to ¼ barrel

firm[1] (furm) *adj.* ⟦ME *ferm* < OFr < L *firmus* < IE base **dher-*, to hold, support > Sans *dhárma*, precept, law, Gr *thronos*, armchair⟧ 1 not yielding easily under pressure; solid; hard 2 not moved or shaken easily; fixed; stable 3 continued steadily; remaining the same *[a firm friendship]* 4 unchanging; resolute; constant *[firm faith]* 5 showing determination, strength, etc. *[a firm command]* 6 legally or formally concluded; definite; final *[a firm contract, a firm order]* 7 *Commerce* not rising or falling very much; steady: said of prices, etc. —*vt., vi.* to make or become firm, or solid, steady, stable, definite, etc.: often with *up* —**stand (or hold) firm** to be or remain steadfast in conviction despite attack, efforts to persuade, etc. —**firm′ly** *adv.* —**firm′ness** *n.*

SYN.—**firm**, in referring to material consistency, suggests a compactness that does not yield easily to, or is very resilient under, pressure *[firm flesh]*; **hard** is applied to that which is so firm that it is not easily penetrated, cut, or crushed *[hard as rock]*; **solid** suggests a dense consistency throughout a mass or substance that is firm or hard and often connotes heaviness or substantiality *[a solid brick front]*; **stiff** implies resistance to bending or stretching *[a stiff collar]*

firm[2] (furm) *n.* ⟦It *firma*, signature, hence title of a business < L *firmare*, to strengthen < *firmus*: see prec.⟧ 1 a business company or partnership of two or more persons: distinguished from a CORPORATION in that a firm is not legally recognized as a person apart from the members forming it 2 popularly, any business company, whether or not unincorporated

fir·ma·ment (fur′mə mənt) *n.* ⟦ME < OFr < LL(Ec) *firmamentum* < L, a strengthening, support < *firmare*: see prec.⟧ the sky, viewed poetically as a solid arch or vault —**fir′ma·men′tal** (-ment′'l) *adj.*

firm·er (fur′mər) *adj.* ⟦Fr *fermoir*, altered < *formoir* < *former*, to FORM⟧ designating a carpenter's chisel or gouge with a thin blade fixed in a handle —*n.* a firmer chisel or gouge

firm·ware (furm′wer′) *n.* ⟦FIRM[1] + -WARE⟧ a computer program stored on a ROM chip

firn (firn) *n.* ⟦Ger < *firn*, of last year, old, akin to OE *fyrn*, former < IE base **per-*, beyond > FAR, fol.⟧ the granular snow, not in a completely compacted mass, that accumulates at the top of a glacier

first (furst) *adj.* ⟦ME < OE *fyrst*, lit., foremost, superl. of *fore*, before (see FORE), akin to OHG *furist*, Ger *fürst*, prince, lit., foremost < IE base **per-*, beyond > L *prae*, before, Gr *para*, beside, beyond⟧ 1 preceding all others in a series; before any other; 1st: used as the ordinal of ONE 2 happening or acting before all others; earliest 3 ranking before all others; foremost in rank, quality, importance, etc.; principal 4 designating the slowest forward gear ratio of a motor vehicle transmission; LOW[1] (*adj.* 20) 5 *Music* playing or singing the leading part or the part highest in pitch —*adv.* 1 *a)* before any other person or thing; at the beginning *b)* before doing anything else 2 as the first point; to begin with 3 for the first time 4 sooner; preferably 5 with (a specified part) in the front or lead [to plunge into a pool feet *first*] —*n.* **1** that one before the second **2** any person, thing, class, place, etc. that is first **3** the first day of a month **4** the beginning; start **5** a first happening or thing of its kind **6** [*pl.*] the best quality of merchandise **7** the winning place in a race or competition **8** the FIRST (*adj.* 4) gear of a motor vehicle transmission; LOW[1] (*n. a*) ☆**9** *Baseball short for* FIRST BASE **10** *Music* the highest or leading voice or instrument in an ensemble —**first thing** as the first thing; before anything else —**in the first place** firstly; to begin with

first aid emergency treatment for injury or sudden illness, before regular medical care is available —**first′-aid′** *adj.*

☆**first base** *Baseball* **1** the base to the left of the pitcher, the first of the four bases that a base runner attempts to reach safely **2** the defensive position played by the first baseman —**get to first base** [Slang] to accomplish the first step of an undertaking, often, specif., a romantic or sexual one

☆**first baseman** *Baseball* the infielder who plays near first base and usually covers first base, esp. on ground balls

first·born (furst′bôrn′, -bôrn′) *adj.* born first in a family; eldest (of the offspring) —*n.* the firstborn child

first cause **1** a primary cause of anything; source **2** [**F- C-**] *Theol.* God as the uncaused cause of all being

first-class (furst′klas′) *adj.* **1** of the highest class, rank, excellence, etc.; of the best quality **2** designating or of the most expensive accommodations [a *first-class* cabin on a ship] ☆**3** designating or of a class of mail that includes letters, postcards, large envelopes, and small packages —*adv.* **1** with the most expensive accommodations [to travel *first-class*] **2** as or by first-class mail

first cousin the son or daughter of one's uncle or aunt

First day [*sometimes* **F- D-**] Sunday: term used by the Society of Friends

first-day cover (furst′dā′) *Philately* an envelope, postal card, etc., bearing a newly issued stamp and a postmark for the first day the stamp was issued: also **first day cover**

first-degree burn (furst′di grē′) *see* BURN[1] (*n.* 1)

first down *Football* **1** the first play of the set of four downs allowed to the offensive team: see DOWN[1] (*n.* 2*a*) **2** a gain which earns the offensive team a new set of four downs

first estate *see* ESTATE (sense 2)

☆**first family** [*often* **F- F-**] **1** a family considered to have prestige because of descent, social status, etc. [one of the *first families* of Boston] **2** the family of the U.S. president

first finger the finger next to the thumb; index finger

first floor **1** the ground floor of a building **2** in Great Britain and certain other countries, the floor above this

first fruits ⟦orig. transl. of Vulg. *primitiae*: see Ex. 23:16⟧ **1** the earliest produce of the season, esp. when offered to a deity **2** the first products, results, or profits of any activity

first-gen·er·a·tion (furst′jen′ər ā′shən) *adj.* **1** of or being an immigrant taking up permanent residence in a country; often, specif., of or being a naturalized, foreign-born citizen of a country **2** of or being a native-born citizen of a country whose parents had immigrated into that country

first·hand (furst′hand′) *adj., adv.* from the original producer or source; direct

☆**first lady** [*often* **F- L-**] **1** the wife or official hostess of a chief official, esp. of the U.S. president, a state governor, or a mayor **2** a woman considered to be foremost in her profession or art

first lieutenant **1** *U.S. Mil.* an officer ranking above a second lieutenant and below a captain **2** *U.S. Navy* the officer in charge of maintenance of a ship or shore station

first light early morning, when light starts to appear; dawn; daybreak

first·ling (furst′liŋ) *n.* **1** the first of a kind **2** the first fruit, produce, etc. **3** the first offspring of an animal

first·ly (furst′lē) *adv.* in the first place; first: used chiefly in enumerating topics

first mate a merchant ship's officer next in rank below the captain: also **first officer**

first milk COLOSTRUM

first mortgage a mortgage having priority over all other liens or encumbrances on the same property, except those, as real estate taxes, given priority by statute

☆**first name** the first of one's given names

first night the opening night of a play, opera, etc.

first-night·er (furst′nīt′ər) *n.* a person who attends the opening performance of a play, opera, etc., esp. one who regularly attends first nights

first offender a person convicted for the first time of an offense against the law

first person **1** *Gram.* *a)* the form of a pronoun (as *I*) or verb (as *am*) that refers to the speaker or writer or, in the plural, also to those for whom the speaker or writer serves as spokesperson *b)* a category consisting of such forms **2** narration characterized by the general use of such forms

first quarter **1** the time of month between new moon and first half-moon **2** the phase of the moon after the waxing crescent when only the right half of its face, when viewed from the Northern Hemisphere, reflects sunlight to the earth

first-rate (furst′rāt′) *adj.* ⟦orig. applied to the highest of the rates, or classes, of warships⟧ of the highest class, rank, or quality; very good; excellent —*adv.* [Informal] very well

First Republic the republic established in France in 1792 after the Revolution, and lasting until the establishment of the Empire by Napoleon in 1804

first responder ☆any of those charged with responding first to the scene of an emergency, as police officers, firefighters, and ambulance medics

first-run (furst′run′) *adj.* designating or of: *a)* a film in its first schedule of performances *b)* a theater that shows first-run films *c)* a TV program or series being telecast for the first time

☆**first sergeant** *U.S. Army, U.S. Marine Corps* the noncommissioned officer, usually a master sergeant, serving as chief administrative assistant to the commander of a company, battery, etc.

first strike a surprise attack with nuclear weapons, made with the intention of destroying an enemy nation's means of effective retaliation —**first′-strike′** *adj.*

☆**first-string** (furst′striŋ′) *adj.* ⟦see STRING, *n.* 5⟧ [Informal] **1** *Sports* that is the first choice for regular play at a specified position **2** first-class; excellent

first water ⟦see WATER, *n.* 8*a*⟧ the best quality and purest luster: said of diamonds, pearls, etc., but also used fig.

First World [*occas.* **f- w-**] the countries of the world that are well developed economically and industrially and that have a relatively high standard of living

First World War WORLD WAR I

firth (furth) *n.* ⟦ME < ON *fjörthr*, akin to OE *ford*, FORD⟧ a narrow inlet or arm of the sea; estuary

FISA (fī′zə) *abbrev.* Foreign Intelligence Surveillance Act

fisc (fisk) *n.* ⟦Fr < L *fiscus*: see fol.⟧ [Rare] a royal or state treasury; exchequer

fis·cal (fis′kəl) *adj.* ⟦Fr < LL *fiscalis* < L *fiscus*, basket of rushes, public chest < IE **bhidh-*, pot (> ON *bitha*, milk jug) < base **bheidh-*, to weave, tie⟧ **1** having to do with the public treasury or revenues **2** financial **3** designating or of government policies of spending and taxation designed to maintain economic stability, promote full employment, etc.: see also KEYNESIAN —*n.* in some countries, a public prosecutor or other official —**SYN.** FINANCIAL —**fis′cal·ly** *adv.*

fis·cal·ist (-ist) *n.* an adherent of FISCAL (sense 3) policies; Keynesian: opposed to MONETARIST

☆**fiscal year** a twelve-month period between settlements of financial accounts: the U.S. government fiscal year legally ends September 30

Fisch·er (fish′ər) **1 Emil** 1852-1919; Ger. organic chemist **2 Hans** 1881-1945; Ger. organic chemist

fish (fish) *n., pl.* **fish**; in referring to different species, **fish′es** ⟦ME < OE *fisc*, akin to Ger *fisch*, Du *visch* < IE base **pisk-* > L *piscis*⟧ **1** any of three classes (jawless, cartilaginous, and bony fishes) of coldblooded vertebrate animals living in water and having fins, permanent gills for breathing, and, usually, scales **2** loosely, any animal living in water only, as a dolphin, crab, or oyster: often used in comb. [*shellfish, jellyfish*] **3** the flesh of a fish used as food **4** [Informal] a person thought of as like a fish, as in being easily lured by bait, lacking intelligence or emotion, etc. —*vi.* ⟦OE *fiscian*⟧ **1** to catch or try to catch fish, or shrimps, lobsters, etc. **2** to try to get something indirectly or by cunning: often with *for* **3** to grope: often with *for* —*vt.* **1** to catch or try to catch fish, shrimps, etc. in [to *fish* a stream] **2** to get by or as by fishing **3** to grope for, find, and bring to view: often with *out* or *up* [to *fish* a coin from one's pocket] **4** *Naut.* to pull (an old-fashioned anchor) to the gunwale, as from the cathead, preparatory to securing it —*adj.* **1** of fish or fishing **2** selling fish —**bigger (or other) fish to fry** other, more important things to attend to —**drink like a fish** to drink heavily, esp. alcoholic liquor —**fish in troubled waters** to try to gain something by taking advantage of a confused or troubled situation —**fish or cut bait** to proceed energetically with a task or give it up altogether —**fish out** to deplete the stock of fish in (a lake, etc.) —**like a fish out of water** out of one's element; in a situation or surroundings not suited to one —**neither fish nor fowl** not belonging to a distinct or recognizable category or class —**the Fishes** Pisces, the constellation and twelfth sign of the zodiac —**fish′a·ble** *adj.* —**fish′like′** *adj.*

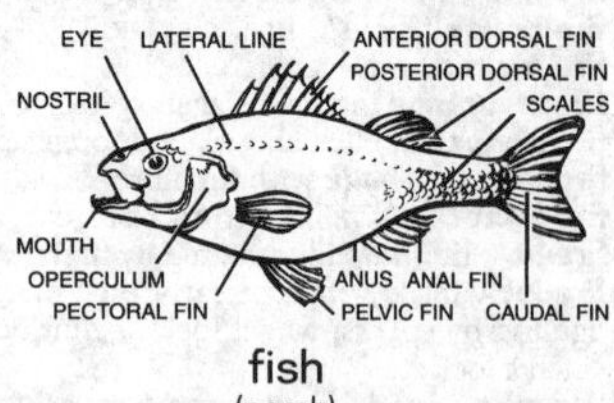

fish
(perch)

Fish (fish), **Hamilton** 1808-93; U.S. statesman

fish and chips [*with sing. or pl. v.*] fried, batter-coated fillets of fish served with French-fried potatoes

☆**fish ball (*or* cake)** a fried ball (or patty) of minced fish, often mixed with mashed potatoes

fish·bowl (fish′bōl′) *n.* **1** a glass bowl in which goldfish, snails, etc. are kept; small aquarium **2** any place where one's activities are open to public view

☆**fish crow** a fish-eating crow (*Corvus ossifragus*) of the Atlantic and Gulf coasts of the U.S.

fish·er (fish′ər) *n.* **1** a person who fishes; fisherman **2** *pl.* **fish′ers** or **fish′er** *a)* the largest marten (*Martes pennanti*), noted for its thick, dark fur *b)* this fur

fish·er·folk (fish′ər fōk′) *pl.n.* people, as of a coastal community, engaged in fishing as a living

fish·er·man (fish′ər mən) ***n.***, *pl.* **-men** (-mən) **1** a person who fishes for sport or for a living **2** a commercial fishing vessel —***adj.*** designating or of a style of bulky sweater knit in a combination of stitches and having a wide collar or turtleneck: also **fisherman (**or **fisherman's) knit**

fisherman's bend a kind of knot

fish·er·y (fish′ər ē) ***n.***, *pl.* **-er·ies** **1** the business of catching, packing, or selling fish, or lobsters, shrimp, etc. **2** a place where fish, etc. are caught; fishing ground **3** the legal right to catch fish in certain waters or at certain times **4** a place where fish are bred

fish·eye lens (fish′ī′) a camera lens designed to record up to a 180-degree field of vision

fish farm a facility where fish and shellfish are bred commercially, as in ponds or tanks, for use as food —**fish farming, fish′-farm′ing *n.***

fish finger [Brit.] FISH STICK

fish flake [Cdn.] a platform for drying fish

☆**fish flour** fish-protein concentrate in pulverized form

☆**fish fry** a picnic or cookout where fried fish is prepared and eaten; also, a meal served indoors at which fried fish is the featured dish

fish hawk OSPREY

fish·hook (fish′hook′) ***n.*** a hook, usually barbed, for catching fish

fish·ing (fish′iŋ) ***n.*** **1** the catching of fish for sport or for a living **2** a place to fish

fishing banks (*or* **grounds)** a place where fish are abundant, as off Newfoundland

fishing expedition ☆a wide-ranging, often unwarranted investigation, interrogation, etc. carried out in the hope of uncovering any unspecified incriminating or compromising information

☆**fishing pole** a simple device for fishing, often one that is improvised, consisting of a pole, line, and hook

fishing rod a slender pole with an attached line, hook, and usually a reel, used in fishing

fishing tackle the equipment, as hooks, lines, rods, reels, etc., used in fishing

fish joint a joint between two timbers, railroad rails, etc. that meet end to end and are fastened together by a fishplate or fishplates: also **fished joint**

☆**fish ladder** an ascending series of pools so arranged as to permit fish to leap or swim upward from level to level and thus pass over dams and waterfalls

fish line a line, usually with a hook at one end, used in fishing

fish meal ground, dried fish, used as fertilizer or fodder

fish·mon·ger (fish′muŋ′gər, -mäŋ′-) ***n.*** [Chiefly Brit.] a dealer in food fish

fish·net (fish′net′) ***n.*** **1** a net for fishing **2** an open-weave, usually coarse, fabric —***adj.*** made of fishnet fabric [*fishnet* stockings]

fish oil oil from certain fishes, as sardines and herring, which contains high concentrations of omega-3 fatty acids and is often used as a nutritional supplement

fish·plate (fish′plāt′) ***n.*** ⟦prob. < Fr *fiche*, means of fixing < *ficher*, to fix < OFr *fichier* < VL **figicare*, intens. for L *figere*: see FIX⟧ a wood or metal piece used to fasten together two timbers, railroad rails, etc. that meet end to end

fishplate

fish·pond (fish′pänd′) ***n.*** a pond where fish are kept or bred

fish·skin disease (fish′skin′) ICHTHYOSIS

☆**fish stick** a small, oblong fillet or cake of fish breaded and fried

☆**fish story** ⟦from the conventional exaggeration by fishermen of the size of fish that escaped being caught⟧ [Informal] an unbelievable story; exaggeration

fish·tail (fish′tāl′) ***vi.*** **1** to swing the tail of an airplane from side to side in order to reduce speed after landing **2** to move forward with a side-to-side, swinging motion of the rear end [the car *fishtailed* on the icy hill]

fish·wife (fish′wīf′) ***n.***, *pl.* **-wives′** (-wīvz′) **1** a woman who sells fish **2** a coarse, scolding woman

☆**fish·worm** (-wurm′) ***n.*** ANGLEWORM

fish·y (fish′ē) ***adj.*** **fish′i·er, fish′i·est** **1** full of fish **2** like a fish in odor, taste, etc., specif., strongly or undesirably so **3** dull or expressionless [*fishy* eyes] **4** ⟦< FISH STORY⟧ [Informal] *a)* causing doubt or suspicion; questionable [*fishy* behavior] *b)* expressing doubt or suspicion [a *fishy* glance] —**fish′i·ly *adv.*** —**fish′i·ness *n.***

Fiske (fisk), **John** (born *Edmund Fisk Green*) 1842-1901; U.S. historian & philosopher

fis·sile (fis′il; *chiefly Brit*, -īl′) ***adj.*** ⟦L *fissilis* < *fissus*, pp. of *findere*, to cleave: see fol.⟧ that can be split; fissionable: said of atoms, cells, etc. —**fis·sil·i·ty** (fi sil′i tē) ***n.***

fis·sion (fish′ən, fizh′-) ***n.*** ⟦L *fissio* < *fissus*, pp. of *findere*, to cleave, split < IE base **bheid-*, to split > BITE⟧ **1** a splitting apart; division into parts **2** NUCLEAR FISSION **3** *Biol.* a form of asexual reproduction, found in various simple plants and animals, in which the parent organism divides into two or more approximately equal parts, each becoming an independent individual — ***vi., vt.*** to undergo or cause to undergo nuclear fission —**fis′sion·a·ble *adj.***

fis·sip·a·rous (fi sip′ə rəs) ***adj.*** ⟦< L *fissus* (see prec.) + -PAROUS⟧ *Biol.* reproducing by fission

fis·si·ped (fis′i ped′) ***adj.*** ⟦< L *fissipes* (gen. *fissipedis*), cloven-footed < *fissus* (see FISSION) + *pes*, FOOT⟧ *Zool.* having the toes separated from each other: also **fis·sip·e·dal** (fi sip′ə dəl, fis′i pēd′'l)

fis·si·ros·tral (fis′i räs′trəl) ***adj.*** ⟦< L *fissi-*, cloven (< *fissus*: see FISSION) + *rostrum*, beak (see ROSTRUM) + -AL⟧ having a broad and deeply cleft beak, as a swift or nighthawk

fis·sure (fish′ər) ***n.*** ⟦ME < OFr < L *fissura* < *fissus*: see FISSION⟧ **1** a long, narrow, deep cleft or crack **2** a dividing or breaking into parts **3** *Anat.* a groove between lobes or parts of an organ, as in the brain **4** *Med.* a break or ulceration where skin and mucous membrane join [anal *fissure*] — ***vt., vi.*** **-sured, -sur·ing** to break into parts; crack or split apart

fist (fist) ***n.*** ⟦ME < OE *fyst*, akin to Ger *faust* (OHG *fūst*), prob. < IE **pn̥ksti* < ? base **penkwe*, FIVE, in sense "clenched five (fingers)"⟧ **1** a hand with the fingers closed tightly into the palm, as for hitting; clenched hand **2** [Informal] *a)* a hand *b)* the grasp **3** *Printing* a sign (☞) used to direct special attention to something —***vt.*** **1** to hit with the fist **2** to grasp or handle —**make a good (**or **poor,** etc.**) fist of** [Brit. Informal] to make or be a good (or poor, etc.) attempt or effort at [a biography that *makes a good fist of* a complicated life]

fist·fight (fist′fīt′) ***n.*** a fight with the fists

fist·ful (-fool′) ***n.***, *pl.* **-fuls′** HANDFUL

fist·ic (fis′tik) ***adj.*** having to do with boxing; fought with the fists; pugilistic

fist·i·cuffs (fis′ti kufs′) ***pl.n.*** ⟦< FIST + CUFF[2]⟧ the act or skill of fighting with the fists

fis·tu·la (fis′tyoo lə, -chə lə) ***n.***, *pl.* **-las** or **-lae′** (-lē′) ⟦ME < OFr < L, a pipe, ulcer⟧ **1** [Rare] a pipe or tube **2** an abnormal passage from an abscess, cavity, or hollow organ to the skin or to another abscess, cavity, or organ

fis·tu·lous (-ləs) ***adj.*** ⟦ME < L *fistulosus* < *fistula*⟧ **1** shaped like a pipe or tube; tubular **2** of or like a fistula Also **fis′tu·lar** (-lər)

fit[1] (fit) ***vt.*** **fit′ted** or **fit, fit′ting** ⟦ME *fitten* < ? or akin ? to ON *fitja*, to knit, tie ends of thread, akin to OHG *fizza*, skein of thread, ult. < IE **pedyo-*, fetter, lit., of the foot < base **ped-*, FOOT⟧ **1** to be suitable or adapted to; be in accord with [let the punishment *fit* the crime] **2** to be the proper size, shape, etc. for **3** *a)* to make or alter so as to be suitable or proper *b)* to measure (a person) for something that must be FITTED [*fit* him for a new suit] **4** to make suitable or qualified [his training *fits* him for the job] **5** *a)* to insert, as into a receptacle [to *fit* a key into a lock] *b)* to make a place for (with *in* or *into*) [to *fit* one more passenger into the crowded car] **6** to equip; outfit: often with *out* —***vi.*** **1** [Archaic] to be suitable or proper **2** to be suitably adapted; be in accord or harmony: often with *in* or *into* **3** to have the proper size or shape for a particular figure, space, etc. [his coat *fits* well; this won't *fit* into the box] —***adj.*** **fit′ter, fit′test** ⟦ME *fyt*⟧ **1** adapted, adjusted, qualified, or suited to some purpose, function, situation, etc. [food *fit* to eat] **2** proper; right; appropriate **3** in good physical condition; healthy **4** [Informal] disturbed enough; inclined [she was *fit* to scream] —***n.*** ⟦prob. < the v.⟧ **1** the condition of fitting or being fitted **2** the manner or degree of fitting or of fitting together [a good *fit*, a tight *fit*] **3** anything that fits —☆**fit to be tied** [Informal] extremely frustrated and angry —☆**fit to kill** [Informal] **1** excessively; immoderately **2** strikingly or showily [dressed *fit to kill*]

SYN.—**fit**, the broadest term here, means having the qualities or qualifications to meet some condition, circumstance, purpose, or demand [*fit* for a king]; **suitable** is applied to that which accords with the requirements or needs of the occasion or circumstances [shoes *suitable* for hiking]; **proper** implies reference to that which naturally or rightfully belongs to something or suggests a fitness or suitability dictated by good judgment [*proper* respect for one's elders]; that is **appropriate** which is especially or distinctively fit or suitable; **fitting** is applied to that which accords harmoniously with the character, spirit, or tone of something; **apt**, in this connection, is used of that which is exactly suited to the purpose [an *apt* phrase]

fit[2] (fit) ***n.*** ⟦ME < OE (rare) *fitt*, conflict⟧ **1** any sudden, uncontrollable attack; paroxysm [a *fit* of coughing] **2** *a)* a sharp, brief display of feeling [a *fit* of anger] *b)* a transient mood [a *fit* of the blues] **3** a temporary burst of activity **4** a seizure in which the victim loses consciousness, has convulsions, etc.: a somewhat dated term —**by fits (and starts)** in an irregular way; in bursts of activity followed by periods of inactivity —**have a fit** [Informal] to become very angry or upset: also ☆**throw a fit**

fit[3] (fit) ***n.*** ⟦ME *fitte* < OE *fitt*, akin to OS (Latinized) pl. *vitteas*, sections of a poem (the *Heliand*), OHG *fizza*: see FIT[1]⟧ [Obs.] a section of a poem, ballad, or song

fitch (fich) ***n.*** ⟦ME *ficheu* < OFr *fichau* < MDu *vitsche*, *visse* < Gmc **wisjo* < IE base **weis-* > VIRUS, WEASEL⟧ **1** POLECAT (sense 1) **2** the pelt or fur of this animal Also [Archaic or Dial.] **fitch′et** (-it) or **fitch′ew** (-oo)

Fitch (fich) **1 (William) Clyde** 1865-1909; U.S. playwright **2 John** 1743-98; U.S. inventor of a steamboat

fit·ful (fit′fəl) ***adj.*** ⟦FIT[2] + -FUL⟧ characterized by irregular or intermittent activity, impulses, etc.; spasmodic; restless —**fit′ful·ly *adv.*** —**fit′ful·ness *n.***

fit·ly (fit′lē) ***adv.*** **1** in a fit manner; suitably **2** at the right time

fit·ment (fit′mənt) ***n.*** [Chiefly Brit.] any of various furnishings, fixtures, or detachable parts

fit·ness (fit′nis) ***n.*** the condition of being fit; suitability, appropriateness, healthiness, etc.

fit·ted (fit′id) *adj.* designed to conform to the contours of that which it covers [*fitted* bed sheets, a *fitted* shirt]

fit·ter (fit′ər) *n.* a person who fits; specif., *a)* a person who alters or adjusts garments to fit *b)* a person who installs or adjusts machinery, pipes, etc.

fit·ting (fit′iŋ) *adj.* suitable; proper; appropriate —*n.* **1** an adjustment or trying on of clothes, etc. for fit **2** a small part used to join, adjust, or adapt other parts, as in a system of pipes **3** [*pl.*] the fixtures, furnishings, or decorations of a house, office, automobile, etc. —**SYN.** FIT[1] —**fit′ting·ly** *adv.*

Fitz·ger·ald (fits jer′əld) **1 Ella** 1917-96; U.S. jazz singer **2 F(rancis) Scott (Key)** 1896-1940; U.S. writer

Fitz·Ger·ald (fits jer′əld), **Edward** (born *Edward Purcell*) 1809-83; Eng. poet & translator of *The Rubáiyát*: also written **Fitzgerald**

Fiu·me (fyo͞o′me) *It. name for* RIJEKA

five (fiv) *adj.* ⟦ME < OE *fif*, with assimilated nasal, akin to Ger *fünf* (OHG, Goth *fimf*) < IE base **penkwe* > Sans *páñca*, Gr *pente*, L *quinque*⟧ totaling one more than four —*n.* **1** the cardinal number between four and six; 5; V **2** *a)* any group of five people or things ☆*b)* a basketball team **3** something numbered five or having five units, as a playing card, domino, face of a die, etc. ☆**4** [Informal] a five-dollar bill

☆**five-and-ten-cent store** (fīv′ən ten′sent′) ⟦such stores orig. carried many articles priced at five or ten cents⟧ a store that sells a wide variety of inexpensive merchandise: also **five′-and-ten′** or **five′-and-dime′** (-ən dīm′) *n.*

five-card stud (fīv′kärd′) a variety of stud poker in which five cards are dealt to each player, the first face down, the others face up, the betting being done after each round of cards dealt face up

☆**Five Civilized Tribes** the Cherokees, Chickasaws, Choctaws, Creeks, and Seminoles of the Indian Territory

five-fin·ger (fīv′fiŋ′gər) *n.* ⟦OE *fiffingre*⟧ any of various plants having leaves with five parts or flowers with five petals; esp., the cinquefoils and WOODBINE (sense 2)

five·fold (fīv′fōld′) *adj.* ⟦FIVE + -FOLD⟧ **1** having five parts **2** having five times as much or as many —*adv.* five times as much or as many

five hundred ☆a variety of euchre or rummy in which the object is to score five hundred points

☆**Five Nations** the Mohawks, Oneidas, Onondagas, Cayugas, and Senecas as a group, constituting an early confederation of Iroquoian peoples: see also SIX NATIONS

five o'clock shadow [Informal] a slight growth of beard, as that which would be visible in the late afternoon on the face of a man who had shaved in the morning

fiv·er (fīv′ər) *n.* [Informal] ☆**1** a five-dollar bill **2** [Brit.] a five-pound note

fives (fīvz) *n.* ⟦prob. because orig. played by teams of five⟧ a kind of handball played in England

five-star (fīv′stär′) *adj.* ⟦see STAR (*n.* 3)⟧ **1** indicating the highest classification, based on a given set of criteria for determining excellence [a *five-star* rating] **2** having or deserving to have a five-star rating [a *five-star* hotel]

fix (fiks) *vt.* **fixed**, **fix′ing** ⟦ME *fixen* < *fix*, fixed < L *fixus*, pp. of *figere*, to fasten, attach: see FINISH⟧ **1** *a)* to make firm, stable, or secure *b)* to fasten or attach firmly **2** to set firmly in the mind **3** *a)* to direct steadily [to *fix* the eyes on a target] *b)* to direct one's eyes steadily at [to *fix* the target] **4** to make rigid or stiff [to *fix* one's jaw] **5** to make permanent or lasting [color is *fixed* in dyeing] **6** *a)* to arrange or establish definitely; set [to *fix* the date of a wedding] *b)* to determine with certainty [to *fix* the period of the dinosaurs' existence] *c)* to assign or ascribe [the jury must *fix* guilt] **7** to arrange properly or in a certain way; set in order; adjust **8** to restore to proper condition; repair, mend, remedy, heal, etc. **9** to bank, refuel, and tend (a fire) **10** to prepare and cook (food or meals) **11** to preserve (a specimen) so that its tissue, etc. can be used for microscopic study ☆**12** [Informal] to influence the result or action of (a horse race, jury, election, etc.) to one's advantage by bribery, trickery, etc. ☆**13** [Informal] to revenge oneself on; get even with; punish or chastise **14** [Informal] to spay or castrate **15** *Chem. a)* to make solid, permanent, or nonvolatile *b)* to cause (atmospheric nitrogen) to combine with other elements or compounds to form nitrates, ammonia, etc. **16** *Photog.* to make (a film, print, etc.) permanent and prevent from fading by washing in a chemical solution —*vi.* **1** to become fixed, firm, or stable **2** [Informal or Dial.] to prepare or intend [I'm *fixing* to go hunting] —*n.* **1** the position of a ship or aircraft determined from the bearings of two or more known points, from astronomical observations, or from radio signals, etc. ☆**2** [Informal] a difficult or awkward situation; predicament **3** [Informal] an adjustment, repair, improvement, etc. [a short-term *fix*] **4** [Informal] a clear understanding or evaluation [to get a *fix* on the problem] ☆**5** [Slang] *a)* the act of fixing the outcome of a contest, situation, etc. *b)* a contest, situation, etc. that has been fixed ☆**6** [Slang] an injection of a narcotic, as heroin, by an addict: often used fig. for anything that temporarily satisfies a craving —**SYN.** PREDICAMENT —**fix on (or upon) 1** to choose; settle on **2** to focus on —**fix someone up** [Informal] to arrange a meeting or date for someone [she *fixed him up* with her sister] —**fix up** [Informal] **1** to repair, mend, remedy, etc. **2** to arrange properly; set in order **3** to make arrangements for —**fix′a·ble** *adj.*

fix·ate (fik′sāt′) *vt., vi.* **-at′ed**, **-at′ing** ⟦< ML *fixatus*, pp. of *fixare* < *fixus*: see prec.⟧ to make or become fixed; specif., *a)* to direct and focus (the eyes) on (a point or object) *b) Psychoanalysis* to attach or arrest (the expression of the libidinal or aggressive drive) at an early stage of psychosexual development *c)* to focus *on*, or become preoccupied with, something, often obsessively so

fix·a·tion (fik sā′shən) *n.* ⟦ME *fixacioun* < ML *fixatio* < *fixatus*: see prec.⟧ **1** a fixating or a being fixated; specif., *a)* the directing and focusing of the eyes *b)* an exaggerated preoccupation; obsession **2** *Chem. a)* reduction into a solid, permanent, or nonvolatile form *b)* NITROGEN FIXATION **3** *Photog.* the treatment of a film, print, etc. to make it permanent **4** *Psychoanalysis* an arrest of the expression of the libidinal or aggressive drive at an early stage of psychosexual development, or a persistent attachment to some object or person that derives from this

fix·a·tive (fik′sə tiv) *adj.* ⟦FIX + -ATIVE⟧ that is able or tends to make permanent, prevent fading, etc. —*n.* a substance that makes something permanent, prevents fading, etc., as a mordant or a preservative used in microscopy

fixed (fikst) *adj.* **1** firmly placed or attached; not movable **2** established; settled; set [a *fixed* price] **3** steady; unmoving; resolute [a *fixed* purpose] **4** remaining in the same position relative to the earth [a *fixed* satellite] **5** persisting obstinately in the mind and tending to control the thoughts and actions; obsessive [a *fixed* idea] **6** *Chem. a)* nonvolatile, as a vegetable oil *b)* incorporated into a stable compound from its free state, as atmospheric nitrogen *c)* permanently held, as a fabric dye ☆**7** [Informal] supplied with something needed, specif. money [comfortably *fixed* for life] ☆**8** [Slang] with the outcome dishonestly arranged beforehand [a *fixed* race] —**fix·ed·ly** (fik′sid lē) *adv.* —**fix′ed·ness** *n.*

☆**fixed charge** any of certain charges, as taxes, rent, interest, etc., which must be paid, usually at regular intervals, without being changed and without reference to the amount of business done

fixed oil a nonvolatile oil, esp. one found in fatty animal tissue and the seeds of various plants, including cotton, corn, flax, sunflowers, peanuts, coconuts, and olives

fixed-point (fikst′point′) *adj.* designating, of, or having to do with a system of arithmetic, used esp. in computer science, having its numbers expressed with a given, fixed decimal or binary point

fixed star *former term for* STAR (*n.* 1): so called by early astronomers to distinguish it from a PLANET (sense 1), which was thought to be a moving star

☆**fixed-wing** (fikst′wiŋ′) *adj.* designating an aircraft having its wings fastened to the fuselage, as distinguished from a helicopter

fix·er (fik′sər) *n.* **1** a person or thing that fixes ☆**2** [Informal] a person who pays bribes or uses personal influence to manipulate results, as in keeping others from being punished for illegal acts ☆**3** ⟦see FIX, *n.* 6⟧ [Slang] a person who sells narcotics illegally to addicts

fix·er-up·per (fik′sər up′ər) *n.* [Informal] a house in poor repair but suitable for restoration, that is for sale at a bargain price

fix·ings (fik′siŋz′, -sinz′) *pl.n.* ☆[Informal] accessories or trimmings [a Thanksgiving dinner of roast turkey and all the *fixings*]

☆**fix-it** (fiks′it) *adj.* [Informal] of or having to do with fixing or repairing things: also **fix′it**

fix·i·ty (fik′si tē) *n.* **1** the quality or state of being fixed; steadiness or permanence **2** *pl.* **-ties** anything fixed, or unmoving

fix·ture (fiks′chər) *n.* ⟦< ME *fixure* (< LL *fixura* < L *fixus*: see FIX), altered by analogy with MIXTURE⟧ **1** anything firmly in place **2** any of the fittings or furniture of a house, store, etc. attached to the building and, ordinarily, considered legally a part of it [bathroom *fixtures*] **3** any person or thing that has remained in a situation or place so long as to seem fixed there **4** [Chiefly Brit.] a well-established, regularly occurring sports or social event

fizz (fiz) *n.* ⟦? akin to fol.⟧ **1** a hissing, sputtering sound, as of an effervescent drink **2** an effervescent drink —*vi.* **1** to make a hissing or bubbling sound **2** to give off gas bubbles; effervesce

fiz·zle (fiz′əl) *vi.* **-zled**, **-zling** ⟦ME *fesilen*, to break wind silently, akin to *fisten*: see FEIST⟧ **1** to make a hissing or sputtering sound **2** [Informal] to fail, esp. after a successful beginning: often with *out* —*n.* ☆[Informal] an attempt that ends in failure

fizz·y (fiz′ē) *adj.* **fizz′i·er**, **fizz′i·est** fizzing; effervescent

fjeld (fyeld, fyel) *n.* ⟦Norw < ON *fiall*, *fjall*, FELL[5]⟧ a barren plateau in Scandinavian countries

fjord (fyôrd) *n. alt. sp. of* FIORD

fl *abbrev.* **1** floor **2** florin(s) **3** ⟦L *floruit*⟧ (he or she) flourished **4** fluid

Fl[1] *abbrev.* Flemish

Fl[2] *Chem. symbol for* flerovium

FL *abbrev.* **1** *Football* flanker: sometimes written **fl** **2** Florida

Fla *abbrev.* Florida

flab (flab) *n.* ⟦back-form. < FLABBY⟧ [Informal] sagging, flaccid flesh

flab·ber·gast (flab′ər gast′) *vt.* ⟦18th-c. slang < ? fol. + AGHAST⟧ to make speechless with amazement; astonish —**SYN.** SURPRISE

flab·by (flab′ē) *adj.* **-bi·er**, **-bi·est** ⟦var. of *flappy* < FLAP⟧ **1** lacking firmness; limp and soft; flaccid [*flabby* muscles] **2** lacking force; weak —**flab′bi·ly** *adv.* —**flab′bi·ness** *n.*

fla·bel·late (flə bel′āt′, -it) *adj.* ⟦< fol. + -ATE[1]⟧ fan-shaped: also **fla·bel′li·form′** (-i fôrm′)

fla·bel·lum (flə bel′əm) *n., pl.* **-bel′la** (-ə) ⟦L, a fan, dim. of *flabrum*, a breeze < *flare*, to blow < IE **bhlē-*: see BLAST⟧ **1** a large fan carried by the pope's attendants on ceremonial occasions **2** *Zool.* a fan-shaped organ or structure of the body

flac·cid (flas′id; *often* flak′sid) *adj.* ⟦L *flaccidus* < *flaccus*, flabby⟧ **1** hanging in loose folds or wrinkles; soft and limp; flabby [*flaccid* muscles] **2** lacking force; weak; feeble —**flac·cid′i·ty** *n.* —**flac′cid·ly** *adv.*

☆**flack**[1] (flak) [Slang] ***n.*** ⟦< ?⟧ PRESS AGENT —***vi.*** to serve as a press agent —**flack′er·y** ***n.***

flack[2] (flak) ***n.*** *alt. sp. of* FLAK

fla·con (flak′ən; *Fr* flȧ kōn′) ***n.***, *pl.* **-ons** (-ənz; *Fr*, -kōn′) ⟦Fr: see FLAGON⟧ a small flask with a stopper, as for holding perfume

fla·court·i·a (flə kurt′ē ə, -kôr-) ***adj.*** ⟦NL, after É. de *Flacourt* (1607-60), Fr botanist & governor of Fr colony in Madagascar⟧ designating a family (Flacourtiaceae, order Violales) of dicotyledonous tropical trees and shrubs

flag[1] (flag) ***n.*** ⟦LME *flagge* < FLAG[4], in obs. sense "to flutter"⟧ **1** a piece of cloth or bunting, often attached to a staff, with distinctive colors, patterns, or symbolic devices, used as a national or state symbol, as a signal, etc.; banner; standard; ensign **2** [*pl.*] [Now Rare] long feathers or quills, as on a hawk **3** the tail of a deer **4** the bushy tail of certain dogs, as setters and some hounds **5** something, as a tab of metal or cardboard, that is attached to a card, folder, etc. so that it may be found easily, as in a file **6** *Comput.* a character, symbol, etc. used to mark data or a record for special attention ☆**7** *Football a)* a piece of colored cloth tosssed by an official to signal a rule infraction (in full **penalty flag**) *b)* a strip of cloth worn by players in FLAG FOOTBALL: a person carrying the ball is considered down when an opponent snatches his or her flag **8** *Music* any of the lines extending from a stem, indicating whether the note is an eighth, sixteenth, etc. —***vt.*** **flagged, flag′ging 1** to decorate or mark with flags **2** to signal with or as with a flag; esp., to signal (the driver of a vehicle) to stop: often with *down* **3** to send (a message) by signaling **4** to mark with or as with a FLAG[1] (***n.*** 5 & 6) ☆**5** ⟦see ***n.*** 7⟧ *Football* to penalize (a player, coach, etc.) during a game for a rule infraction —**dip the flag** to salute by lowering a flag briefly

flag[2] (flag) ***n.*** ⟦ME *flagge* < ON *flaga*, slab of stone < IE **plāk-*, to spread out, flat < base **plā* > PLAIN[1]⟧ FLAGSTONE

flag[3] (flag) ***n.*** ⟦ME *flagge* < ?⟧ **1** *a)* any of various wild irises with flat fans of sword-shaped leaves and white, blue, or yellow flowers *b)* any of various cultivated irises **2** SWEET FLAG **3** CATTAIL **4** the flower or leaf of any of these plants

flag[4] (flag) ***vi.*** **flagged, flag′ging** ⟦16th c., prob. < ON *flǫgra*, to flutter < IE base **plāk-*, to strike > FLAW[2]⟧ **1** to become limp; droop **2** to lose strength; grow weak or tired [*his energy flagged*]

☆**Flag Day 1** June 14, anniversary of the day in 1777 when the U.S. flag was adopted **2** [**f- d-**] in England, any day when people give to some special fund for charity and get small flags in token of their contribution

flag·el·lant (flaj′ə lənt, flə jel′ənt) ***n.*** ⟦< L *flagellans*, prp. of *flagellare*: see fol.⟧ a person who engages in or submits to flagellation

flag·el·late (flaj′ə lāt′; *for adj., also* flaj′ə lit *or* flə jel′it) ***vt.*** **-lat′ed, -lat′ing** ⟦< L *flagellatus*, pp. of *flagellare*, to whip, scourge < *flagellum*, a whip, dim. of *flagrum* < IE base **bhlag̑-*, to beat > ON *bluk*, a slap⟧ to subject to flagellation —***adj.*** **1** having a flagellum or flagella: also **flag′el·lat′ed 2** shaped like a flagellum —***n.*** a flagellate organism —**flag′el·la′tor** ***n.***

flag·el·la·tion (flaj′ə lā′shən) ***n.*** ⟦ME *flagellacioun* < LL(Ec) *flagellatio*: see prec.⟧ a whipping or flogging, esp. as a religious discipline or for sexual stimulation —**flag′el·la·to′ry** (-lə tôr′ē) ***adj.***

fla·gel·li·form (flə jel′i fôrm′) ***adj.*** ⟦< FLAGELLUM + -FORM⟧ shaped like a flagellum

fla·gel·lin (flə jel′in, -ən) ***n.*** the protein that forms the flagella of bacteria

fla·gel·lum (flə jel′əm) ***n.***, *pl.* **-la** (-ə) or **-lums** ⟦L, a whip: see FLAGELLATE⟧ **1** *Biol.* a whiplike part or process of some cells, esp. of certain bacteria, protozoans, etc., that is an organ of locomotion or that produces a current in the surrounding fluid **2** *Bot.* a threadlike shoot or runner **3** *Zool.* the terminal, lashlike portion of the antenna in many insects

flag·eo·let[1] (flaj′ə let′) ***n.*** ⟦Fr, dim. of OFr *flageol, flajeol*, a pipe, flute < VL **flabeolum*, a flute < L *flare*, to blow: see BLAST⟧ a small fipple flute, similar to a recorder

flag·eo·let[2] (flaj′ə let′; *Fr* flȧ zhô le′) ***n.*** ⟦Fr, ult. < L *faseolus*: see FRIJOL⟧ **1** a variety of kidney bean, cultivated for its seed **2** the pale-green, immature seed, used esp. in French cooking

☆**flag football** a variety of football in which a defensive player stops a play by snatching a strip of cloth (*flag*) worn by the ballcarrier, rather than by tackling

flag·ger (flag′ər) ***n.*** a person or thing that signals with a flag; specif., a person who directs traffic around or past a construction site

flag·ging[1] (flag′iŋ) ***adj.*** ⟦prp. of FLAG[4]⟧ weakening or drooping —**flag′ging·ly** ***adv.***

flag·ging[2] (flag′iŋ) ***n.*** flagstones or a pavement made of flagstones

fla·gi·tious (flə jish′əs) ***adj.*** ⟦ME *flagicious* < L *flagitiosus* < *flagitium*, shameful act < *flagitare*, to demand, akin to *flagrum*: see FLAGELLATE⟧ shamefully wicked; vile and scandalous —**fla·gi′tious·ly** ***adv.*** —**fla·gi′tious·ness** ***n.***

flag·man (flag′mən) ***n.***, *pl.* **-men** (-mən) a person whose work is signaling with a flag or lantern, as with a railroad

flag of convenience the flag of the foreign country in which a fishing vessel, tanker, etc. is registered, usually so as to avoid taxes, regulations, etc. in the home country of the vessel's owner

flag officer ☆*U.S. Navy* any officer above the rank of captain, entitled to display a flag indicating rank

flag of truce a white flag shown to an enemy to indicate a desire to confer or parley

flag·on (flag′ən) ***n.*** ⟦ME < OFr *flacon* < LL *flasco*: see FLASK⟧ **1** a container for liquids, with a handle, a narrow neck, a spout, and, sometimes, a lid **2** the contents of a flagon

flag·pole (flag′pōl′) ***n.*** a pole on which a flag is raised and flown

fla·gran·cy (flā′grən sē) ***n.*** the quality or state of being flagrant: also **fla′grance**

fla·grant (flā′grənt) ***adj.*** ⟦L *flagrans*, prp. of *flagrare*, to flame, blaze < IE base **bhleg-*, to shine, burn > BLACK⟧ **1** glaringly bad; notorious; outrageous **2** [Archaic] flaming; blazing —**SYN.** OUTRAGEOUS —**fla′grant·ly** ***adv.***

flagrante delicto *see* IN FLAGRANTE DELICTO

flag·ship (flag′ship′) ***n.*** **1** the ship that carries the commander of a fleet or other large naval unit and displays his flag **2** the finest, largest, or newest ship of a steamship line **3** the finest, largest, or most important member or part as of a group or a broadcast network

Flag·stad (flag′stad′; *Norw* fläg′stä′), **Kir·sten** (kir′sten; *Norw* kish′tən) 1895-1962; Norw. soprano

flag·staff (flag′staf′) ***n.*** a flagpole

☆**flag·stick** (flag′stik′) ***n.*** *Golf* PIN (sense 10)

flag·stone (flag′stōn′) ***n.*** ⟦FLAG[2] + STONE⟧ **1** any hard stone that splits into flat pieces **2** a piece of such stone for use in paving walks, terraces, etc.

☆**flag stop** ⟦< *flag down*: see FLAG[1] (***vt.*** 2)⟧ a place at which a bus, train, etc. stops only when signaled

flag-wav·ing (flag′wāv′iŋ) ***n.*** **1** an effort to arouse intense patriotic or nationalist feelings by a deliberate appeal to the emotions **2** a conspicuous show of patriotism —**flag′-wav′er** ***n.***

Fla·her·ty (fla′ər tē), **Robert (Joseph)** 1884-1951; U.S. film director, esp. of documentaries

flail (flāl) ***n.*** ⟦ME *fleil* < OFr *flaiel* & OE **flegel*, both < L *flagellum*, a whip, scourge: see FLAGELLATE⟧ a farm tool consisting of a free-swinging stick tied to the end of a long handle, used to thresh grain — ***vt., vi.*** **1** to thresh with a flail **2** to strike or beat as with a flail **3** to move (one's arms) about like flails: often used fig. of futile or awkward struggling of any kind [*flailing about in vain attempts to establish a career*]

flair (fler) ***n.*** ⟦ME, odor, fragrance < OFr < *flairer*, to emit an odor < LL *flagrare*, for L *fragrare*, to smell, reek < IE **bhrag-*, prob. < base **bher-*, to boil up > BARM, BREATH⟧ **1** [Obs.] sense of smell; hence, keen, natural discernment **2** a natural talent or ability; aptitude; knack **3** a sense of what is stylish and striking

flak (flak) ***n.*** ⟦Ger < *Fl(ieger)a(bwehr)k(anone)*, lit., flyer defense gun⟧ **1** the fire of antiaircraft guns **2** [Informal] strong, clamorous criticism, opposition, etc.

flake[1] (flāk) ***n.*** ⟦ME < Scand, as in Norw *flak*, ice floe, ON *flakna*, to flake off < IE **plāg*, flat < base **plā-* > PLAIN[1]⟧ **1** a small, thin mass [*a flake of snow*] **2** a thin piece or layer split off or peeled off from anything; chip ☆**3** [Slang] an eccentric, unbalanced, or irrational person — ***vt., vi.*** **flaked, flak′ing 1** to form into flakes **2** to chip or peel off in flakes **3** to make or become spotted with flakes —**flak′er** ***n.***

flake[2] (flāk) ***n.*** ⟦ME *flake, fleke* < ON *flaki, fleki*, hurdle < IE base **pel-*, to cover > FELL[4]⟧ a platform or rack for storing or drying food

flake[3] (flāk) ***vt.*** **flaked, flak′ing** ⟦prob. specialized use of FLAKE[1]⟧ *rare var. of* FAKE[2] —**flake out** [Slang] **1** to fall asleep **2** to faint

flak jacket a vestlike, bulletproof jacket worn as by soldiers

flak·y (flāk′ē) ***adj.*** **flak′i·er, flak′i·est 1** containing or made up of flakes **2** breaking easily into flakes ☆**3** [Slang] very eccentric, erratic, irrational, etc. —**flak′i·ly** ***adv.*** —**flak′i·ness** ***n.***

flam (flam) ***n.*** ⟦prob. echoic⟧ a drumbeat made by striking the head of a drum with both drumsticks almost simultaneously

flam·bé (fläm bā′, *Fr* flän bā′) ***adj.*** ⟦Fr, lit., flamed < pp. of *flamber*, to flame⟧ served with a sauce of flaming brandy, rum, etc. —***n.*** a dessert or other dish so served —***vt.*** **-béed′, -bé′ing** to add brandy, etc. to and serve flaming —**flam·béed′** ***adj.***

flam·beau (flam′bō′) ***n.***, *pl.* **-beaux′** (-bōz′) or **-beaus′** ⟦Fr, dim. of OFr *flambe*: see FLAME⟧ **1** a lighted torch **2** a large, ornamental candlestick

flam·boy·ant (flam boi′ənt) ***adj.*** ⟦Fr, prp. of OFr *flamboyer* < *flambe*: see fol.⟧ **1** designating or of a kind of architecture, as late French Gothic, characterized by flamelike tracery of windows and florid decoration **2** flamelike or brilliant in form or color **3** too showy or ornate; florid, extravagant, etc. [*a flamboyant costume, an actor's flamboyant gestures*] —***n.*** ROYAL POINCIANA —**flam·boy′ance** ***n.***, **flam·boy′an·cy** —**flam·boy′ant·ly** ***adv.***

flame (flām) ***n.*** ⟦ME < OFr *flamme* (< L *flamma*) & *flambe* < L *flammula*, dim. of *flamma* < base of *flagrare*, to burn: see FLAGRANT⟧ **1** the burning gas or vapor of a fire, seen as a flickering light of various colors; blaze **2** a tongue of light rising from a fire **3** [*often pl.*] the state of burning with a blaze of light [*to burst into flame*] **4** *a)* a thing like a flame in heat, brilliance, etc. *b)* brilliance or bright coloring **5** an intense emotion; strong passion **6** [Informal] an angry, insulting, or harshly critical electronic message **7** [Informal] a sweetheart —***vi.*** **flamed, flam′ing** ⟦ME *flammen* < OFr *flamer* < L *flammare*⟧ **1** to burn with a blaze of light; burst into flame **2** to light up with color as if blazing; grow red or hot [*a face flaming with anger*] **3** to show intense emotion; become very excited **4** [Informal] to send an angry, insulting, or harshly critical electronic message —***vt.*** **1** [Now Rare] to burn or heat with flame **2** to treat with flame **3** [Informal] to attack, insult, or harshly criticize by means of an electronic message **4** *Cooking* to douse with alcoholic liquor and set afire [*flame the roast with brandy*] —**SYN.** BLAZE[1] —**flame out** to experience a flameout —**go down in flames** ⟦in allusion to aerial combat⟧ to fail in a spectacular or dramatic fashion —**in flames** burning; on fire —**flame′less** ***adj.***

flame cell a hollow cell in the excretory tubules of many lower animals, as flatworms, with an internal tuft of cilia that produces movement of the excretory products

fla·men (flā′men) *n., pl.* **fla′mens** or **flam·i·nes** (flam′i nēz′) ⟦ME *flamin* < L *flamen* < IE base *bhlagmen-, priest, magician > Sans *brahmán-*⟧ in ancient Rome, a priest serving one particular god

fla·men·co (flə meŋ′kō, -men′-) *n.* ⟦Sp, lit., Flemish < MDu *Flaming*, a FLEMING[1]⟧ **1** *a)* the Spanish gypsy style of dance, characterized by stamping and typically performed while clapping or playing castanets *b)* music in this style, often performed on a guitar **2** *pl.* **-cos** a song or dance in this style

flame·out (flām′out′) ☆*n.* **1** the stopping of combustion in a jet engine as a result of some abnormal flight condition **2** a sudden and complete, usually conspicuous, failure

flame·proof (-pro͞of′) *adj.* **1** not readily damaged by fire **2** not catching fire

flame stitch ⟦see BARGELLO, sense 2⟧ BARGELLO (senses 1 & 2)

flame·throw·er (-thrō′ər) *n.* ⟦transl. of Ger *flammenwerfer*⟧ a weapon for shooting a stream of flaming gasoline, oil, napalm, etc.

flame tree **1** a bottletree (*Brachychiton acerifolium*) with large, lobed leaves and brilliant scarlet flowers **2** any of various trees with brilliant red flowers

flam·ing (flām′iŋ) *adj.* **1** burning with flames; blazing **2** like a flame in brilliance or heat [*flaming* colors] **3** intensely emotional; ardent; passionate **4** *a)* startling or flagrant *b)* flamboyantly effeminate (said as of a male homosexual) —**flam′ing·ly** *adv.*

fla·min·go (flə miŋ′gō′) *n., pl.* **-gos′** or **-goes′** ⟦Port *flamingo* < Sp *flamenco*, lit., Flemish (see FLAMENCO): assoc. with *flama*, FLAME, because of its color⟧ any of an order (Phoenicopteriformes) of large, tropical birds with long legs, webbed feet, long necks, downward-curving beaks, and bright pink or red feathers

flamingo

Fla·min·i·an Way (flə min′ē ən) ⟦after the Roman censor Gaius *Flaminius*⟧ ancient Roman paved highway from Rome to Ariminum (Rimini): *c.* 210 mi (338 km)

flam·ma·ble (flam′ə bəl) *adj.* ⟦L *flammare*, to FLAME + -ABLE⟧ easily set on fire; that will burn readily or quickly: term now preferred to INFLAMMABLE in commerce, industry, etc. —**flam′ma·bil′i·ty** *n.*

Flam·ma·rion (flȧ mȧ ryōn′), **Camille** 1842-1925; Fr. astronomer

flan (flan, flän) *n.* ⟦Fr < OFr *flaon* (> ME *flawn*, flan) < ML *flado* (gen. *fladonis*) < OHG, *flado*, flat cake, akin to ME *flathen*: for IE base see FLAT[1]⟧ **1** a piece of shaped metal ready to be made into a coin by the stamp of a die; blank **2** *a)* a tart filled with custard, fruit, etc., or with a savory mixture *b)* a Spanish dessert of custard covered with a burnt-sugar syrup

Flan·a·gan (flan′ə gən), **E(dward) J(oseph)** 1886-1948; U.S. Rom. Catholic clergyman; founder of Boys Town: called *Father Flanagan*

Flan·ders (flan′dərz) region (in medieval times a county) in NW Europe, on the North Sea, including a part of NW France & the provinces of East Flanders & West Flanders in Belgium

flâ·ne·rie (flän rē′, flä nə-) *n.* ⟦Fr: see fol.⟧ idle strolling

flâ·neur (flä nër′) *n.* ⟦Fr < *flâner*, to stroll < ON *flana*: see FLAUNT⟧ a person who strolls about idly, as along the fashionable boulevards of Paris

flange (flanj) *n.* ⟦< ? ME *flaunch*, a lenticular space on a coat of arms < OFr *flanche*, side, var. of *flanc*: see fol.⟧ a projecting rim or collar on a wheel, pipe, rail, etc., that serves to hold it in place, give it strength, guide it, or attach it to something else —*vt.* **flanged**, **flang′ing** to put a flange on

flank (flaŋk) *n.* ⟦ME *flanke* < OFr *flanc* < Frank **hlanka*, akin to OHG *hlanka*, a hip, flank: for IE base see LANK⟧ **1** the fleshy side of a person or animal between the ribs and the hip **2** a cut of beef from this part **3** loosely, the outer side of the upper part of the human thigh **4** the side of anything **5** *Mil.* the right or left side of a formation or force, or of the projection of a bastion —*adj.* of or having to do with the flank —*vt.* **1** to be at the side of **2** to place at the side, or on either side, of **3** *Mil.* *a)* to protect the side of (a friendly unit) *b)* to attack the side of (an enemy unit) *c)* to pass around the side of (an enemy unit) —*vi.* to be located at the side: with *on* or *upon*

flan·ken (flaŋ′kən, fläŋ′-) *n.* ⟦Yiddish, pl. of *flank*, flank < Ger *flanke*, flank < OFr *flanc*: see prec.⟧ a cut of beef from the PLATE (*n.* 15)

flank·er (flaŋk′ər) *n.* **1** *Mil.* *a)* a fortified position at either flank for protection or attack *b)* any of several soldiers detailed to protect the flanks of a marching column ☆**2** *Football* an offensive back who takes a position closer to the sideline than the rest of the team

flan·nel (flan′əl) *n.* ⟦ME, akin to or < *flanen* < Welsh *gwlanen* < *gwlan*, wool < IE base **wel-*, hair, WOOL⟧ **1** a soft, lightweight, loosely woven woolen cloth with a slightly napped surface **2** COTTON FLANNEL **3** [*pl.*] *a)* trousers, etc. made of light flannel *b)* heavy woolen underwear **4** [Brit. Informal] vague, indirect speech or writing, used as to avoid answering a question —*vt.* **-neled** or **-nelled**, **-nel·ing** or **-nel·ling** to wrap or clothe in flannel —**flan′nel·ly** *adj.*

flan·nel·ette or **flan·nel·et** (flan′əl et′) *n.* a soft cotton cloth like cotton flannel but lighter in weight

flan·nel-mouthed (flan′əl mouthd′, -moutht′) *adj.* **1** speaking thickly, as if one's mouth were full of flannel **2** garrulous, esp. in an insincere or deceptive way

flap (flap) *n.* ⟦ME *flappe* < the v.⟧ **1** anything flat and broad that is attached at one end and hangs loose or covers an opening [the *flap* of a pocket] **2** the motion or slapping sound of a swinging flap [the *flap* of an awning in the breeze] **3** [Archaic] a blow with something broad and flat; slap **4** either of the two parts of a book's dust jacket that fold inside the book's covers, typically containing a summary of the book's contents and a brief biographical sketch of its author **5** [Informal] a state of excitement, controversy, or agitation **6** *Aeron.* a pilot-controlled airfoil; esp., a section hinged to the trailing edge of a wing between the aileron and the fuselage, usually used to increase lift or drag **7** *Phonet.* a sound articulated with a single rapid touch of the tongue against the roof of the mouth **8** *Surgery* a piece of tissue partly detached from the surrounding tissue, as for grafting —*vt.* **flapped**, **flap′ping** ⟦ME *flappen*: prob. echoic⟧ **1** to strike with something flat and broad; slap **2** to move back and forth or up and down as in beating the air, usually with some noise [a bird *flapping* its wings] **3** to throw, fling, slam, etc. abruptly or noisily —*vi.* **1** to move back and forth or up and down, as in the wind; flutter **2** to fly or try to fly by flapping the wings **3** to hang down as a flap **4** [Slang, Chiefly Brit.] to become excited or confused —**flap′less** *adj.* —**flap′py** *adj.*

flap·doo·dle (flap′do͞od′'l) *n.* ⟦arbitrary formation⟧ [Informal] foolish talk; nonsense

flap·jack (flap′jak′) *n.* a pancake or griddlecake

flap·per (flap′ər) *n.* **1** a person or thing that flaps; esp., *a)* a flap *b)* a flipper *c)* something broad and flat for striking **2** *a)* a young wild duck, partridge, etc. just learning to fly *b)* [Informal] in the 1920s, a young woman considered bold and unconventional

flare (fler) *vi.* **flared**, **flar′ing** ⟦ME *fleare* < ?⟧ **1** *a)* to blaze up with a sudden, bright light *b)* to burn unsteadily, as a flame whipped about by the wind **2** to burst out suddenly in anger, violence, etc.: often with *up* or *out* **3** to curve or spread outward, as the bell of a trumpet —*vt.* **1** to make flare **2** to signal with a flare —*n.* **1** a bright, unsteady blaze of light lasting only a little while; outburst of flame **2** a device for producing a very bright light, used as a distress signal, to light up a landing field, etc. **3** a sudden, brief outburst, as of emotion or sound **4** *a)* a curving or spreading outward, as of a skirt *b)* a part that curves or spreads outward **5** [*pl.*] pants with legs that widen near or at the ankles **6** *Astron.* *a)* a short-lived, spotlike outburst of increased brightness on the sun, seen esp. near sunspots and often accompanied by X-rays, gamma rays, etc. *b)* a sudden, temporary increase in the brightness of any star **7** *Photog.* a foggy spot on film, caused by a reflection of light from the lens —*SYN.* BLAZE[1]

flare·back (fler′bak′) *n.* a flame shooting out backward or in some other abnormal way from a furnace, cannon, etc.

flare-up (-up′) *n.* **1** a sudden outburst of flame **2** a sudden, brief outburst of anger, trouble, etc.

flar·ing (fler′iŋ) *adj.* **1** blazing unsteadily for a little while **2** gaudy; lurid **3** curving or spreading outward

flash (flash) *vi.* ⟦ME *flashen*, to splash, sprinkle; of echoic orig.⟧ **1** to send out or reflect a sudden, brief blaze or light, esp. at intervals **2** to sparkle or gleam [eyes *flashing* with anger] **3** to speak abruptly, esp. in anger: usually with *out* **4** to come, move, or pass swiftly and suddenly; be seen or realized for an instant like a flash of light [an idea *flashed* through his mind] **5** [Informal] to expose one's genitals, breasts, etc. briefly and deliberately in public **6** [Informal] to have a sudden idea, thought, insight, or recollection: usually with *on* —*vt.* **1** to send out (light, etc.) in sudden, brief spurts **2** to cause to flash **3** to signal with light or reflected light **4** to send (news, messages, etc.) swiftly or suddenly, as by radio **5** to put flashing on so as to make weatherproof **6** in glassmaking, *a)* to put (a colored film of glass) on other glass *b)* to coat with a colored film of glass **7** [Informal] to show briefly or ostentatiously [to *flash* a roll of money] **8** [Informal] to expose (one's genitals, breasts, etc.) briefly and deliberately to (someone) **9** [Archaic] to splash or dash (water) —*n.* **1** *a)* a sudden, brief light *b)* a sudden burst of flame or heat **2** a brief time; moment **3** a sudden, brief display of thought, understanding, feeling, etc. [a *flash* of wit] ☆**4** a brief news report of something that has just happened **5** a gaudy display; showiness **6** a preparation containing burnt sugar, used for coloring liquors **7** a device that produces a brief, illuminating light, used when taking photographs in dim lighting conditions **8** [Informal] *a)* a flashlight *b)* a person very quick or adept at something —*adj.* **1** *a)* [Informal, Now Chiefly Brit.] flashy; showy; sporty *b)* [Old Informal] of thieves or other social outcasts **2** that flashes; happening swiftly or suddenly [a *flash* warning] **3** working with a coordinated flash of light [a *flash* camera] **4** *Comput.* designating or of an erasable memory device that retains stored data when power is turned off —*adv.* quickly, esp. by means of an intense application of some process, as heating or cooling [*flash*-frozen vegetables] —**flash in the pan** ⟦orig. of an ineffectual flash of powder in the pan of a flintlock⟧ a person, effort, etc. that is successful or famous for only a short time

SYN.—**flash** implies a sudden, brief, brilliant light; **glance** refers to a darting light, esp. one that is reflected from a surface at an angle; **gleam** suggests a steady, narrow ray of light shining through a background of relative darkness; **sparkle** implies a number of brief, bright, intermittent flashes; **glitter** implies the reflection of such bright, intermittent flashes; **glisten** suggests the reflection of a lustrous light, as from a wet surface; **shimmer** refers to a soft, tremulous reflection, as from a slightly disturbed body of water

☆**flash·back** (flash′bak′) ***n.*** **1** *a)* an interruption in the continuity of a story, play, film, etc. by an episode portraying a chronologically earlier occurrence *b)* such an episode **2** a vivid, spontaneous recollection of a past experience, often, specif., of a traumatic experience

flash-bang (flash′baŋ′) ***n.*** a kind of grenade designed to emit a loud sound and a flash of light, to disorient people temporarily rather than cause serious injury

flash·board (-bôrd′) ***n.*** a board or boards placed at the top of a dam to increase the depth or force of the stream

flash·bulb (-bulb′) ***n.*** an electric lightbulb giving a brief, illuminating light, for taking photographs

flash burn damage to bodily tissue caused by exposure to a flash of intense radiant heat, esp. the heat of a nuclear explosion

☆**flash·card** (-kärd′) ***n.*** ⟦see FLASH, ***vt.*** 7⟧ any of a set of cards with facts, simple arithmetic problems, etc. on them, which are displayed one by one for quick response, as in a classroom drill

☆**flash·cube** (-kyo͞ob′) ***n.*** a rotating cube with a flashbulb in each of its four sides, used with certain flash cameras

flash drive *Comput.* a solid-state data storage device; specif., a very small, portable memory device that plugs into a USB port: see also FLASH (***adj.*** 4)

flash·er (flash′ər) ***n.*** a person or thing that flashes; specif., *a)* a device for causing lights to go on and off intermittently, or a light that flashes in this way *b)* [Informal] an exhibitionist who flashes (see FLASH, ***vi.*** 5)

flash fiction a genre of fiction consisting of very short stories, typically of fewer than 1,000 words

☆**flash flood** a sudden, violent flood, as after a heavy rain

flash-for·ward (flash′fôr′wərd) ***n.*** **1** an interruption in the continuity of a story, play, film, etc. by an episode portraying a chronologically later occurrence **2** such an episode

☆**flash gun** a device that sets off a flashbulb simultaneously with the opening of the camera shutter

flash·ing (flash′iŋ) ***n.*** **1** the action of a person or thing that flashes **2** sheets of metal or other material used to weatherproof joints formed where exterior surfaces, as of a roof and a wall, meet at an angle

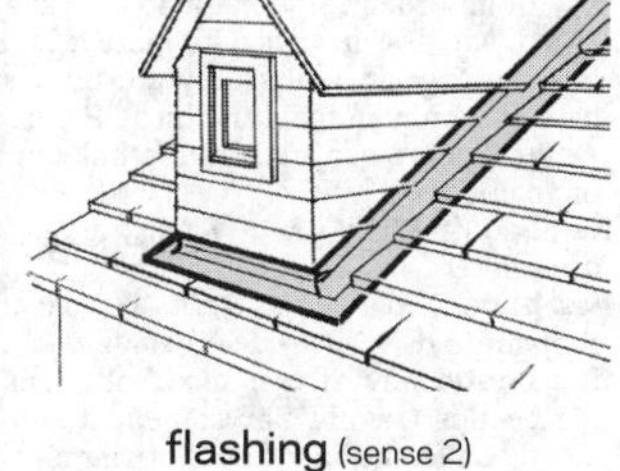

flashing (sense 2)

flash·light (flash′līt′) ***n.*** ☆**1** a portable electric light, usually operated by batteries **2** a light that shines in flashes, used for signaling, as in lighthouses, airplane beacons, etc.: in nautical usage, usually **flashing light** **3** a brief, dazzling light for taking photographs at night or indoors

flash mob an often impromptu and unannounced gathering of people in a public place, organized by means of social media

flash·o·ver (-ō′vər) ***n.*** an undesired electrical discharge across an insulator, between a high potential and the ground, etc.

flash·point (-point′) ***n.*** **1** the lowest temperature at which a volatile solid or the vapor of a liquid will flash when exposed to a brief flame under certain conditions **2** a critical moment, place, or event at which someone or something bursts forth into activity or existence Also, esp. for sense 1, **flash point**

flash tube a gaseous discharge tube designed to emit extremely short bursts of very intense light

flash·y (flash′ē) ***adj.*** **flash′i·er**, **flash′i·est** **1** dazzling or bright for a little while **2** ostentatious and vulgar; gaudy —**flash′i·ly** ***adv.*** —**flash′i·ness** ***n.***

flask (flask, fläsk) ***n.*** ⟦ME < ML *flasco* & OE *flasce*, both < LL *flasco* (gen. *flasconis*) < *flasca* < Gmc **flasko*, bottle, wicker-enclosed jug, prob. < base of OHG *flechtan*, to weave: for IE base see FLAX⟧ **1** any small, bottle-shaped container with a narrow neck, used in laboratories, etc. **2** a small, flattened container for liquor, etc., to be carried in the pocket **3** the frame for a mold of sand in a foundry

flask·et (flas′kit) ***n.*** ⟦ME < OFr *flasquet*, dim. of *flasque* < Gmc **flasko*: see prec.⟧ a small flask

flat[1] (flat) ***adj.*** **flat′ter**, **flat′test** ⟦ME < ON *flatr*, akin to OHG *flaz* < IE **plāt*, **plēt-*, wide, flat (> Gr *platys*, broad, OE *flet*, floor) < base **plā-*, broad⟧ **1** having a smooth, level surface; having little or no depression or elevation **2** *a)* lying extended at full length *b)* spread out smooth and level **3** touching at as many points as possible [with his back *flat* against the wall] **4** *a)* having little depth or thickness; broad, even, and thin *b)* having a flat heel or no heel [*flat* shoes] **5** designating or having an almost straight or level trajectory or flight **6** absolute; positive [a *flat* denial] **7** not variable; fixed [a *flat* rate, a *flat* fee] **8** without much business activity [a *flat* market] **9** *a)* having little or no taste; insipid *b)* having lost effervescence **10** having little or no interest; monotonous; dull **11** not clear or full; blurred [a *flat* sound] ☆**12** emptied of air [a *flat* tire] **13** without gloss [*flat* paint] ☆**14** [Slang] completely without money; penniless **15** *Art* *a)* lacking relief, depth, or perspective *b)* uniform in tint or shade **16** *Gram.* *a)* not having the marker *to* (said of an infinitive: Ex.: *go* in "make it go") *b)* not having an inflectional ending (said esp. of certain adverbs: Ex.: he drove *fast*) **17** *Music* *a)* lower in pitch by a half step [D-*flat* (D♭)] *b)* out of tune by being below the true or proper pitch **18** *Phonet.* designating the vowel *a* when it represents the sound (a) as in *had* or *hat*, articulated with the tongue in a relatively level position **19** *Photog.* lacking in contrast —***adv.*** **flat′ter**, **flat′test** **1** in a flat manner; flatly (in various senses) **2** in or to a flat condition **3** in a prone or supine position **4** *a)* exactly; precisely [to run a race in ten seconds *flat*] *b)* bluntly; abruptly [she left him *flat*] **5** [Informal] absolutely; completely [a business that is *flat* broke] ☆**6** *Finance* with no interest **7** *Music* below the true or proper pitch —***n.*** **1** a flat surface or part [the *flat* of the hand, of a sword, etc.] **2** [*often pl.*] an expanse of level land **3** a low-lying marsh **4** a shallow; shoal **5** any of various flat things; specif., *a)* a shallow box or container, as for growing seedlings ☆*b)* *short for* FLATCAR *c)* a piece of theatrical scenery on a flat frame ☆*d)* a deflated tire *e)* [*pl.*] women's flat-heeled shoes or slippers **6** *Football* the area flanking either end of the offensive line **7** *Music* *a)* a note or tone one half step below another *b)* the sign (♭) indicating such a note —***vt.*** **flat′ted**, **flat′ting** *Music* to make flat; lower a half step —***vi.*** to sing or play below the true or proper pitch —***SYN.*** INSIPID, LEVEL —**fall flat** to fail in the desired effect; be completely unsuccessful —**flat out** [Informal] **1** at full speed, with maximum effort, etc. **2** clear(ly); definite(ly) —**flat′ly** ***adv.*** —**flat′ness** ***n.***

flat[2] (flat) ***n.*** ⟦altered < Scot dial. *flet* (ME & OE *flet*), a floor (of a dwelling): see prec.⟧ [Chiefly Brit.] an apartment or suite of rooms on one floor of a building

flat·bed (flat′bed′) ***adj.*** ☆**1** designating or of a truck, trailer, etc. having a bed or platform without sides or stakes **2** *Printing* designating or of a press having a plane or horizontal printing surface: cf. ROTARY PRESS —***n.*** ☆**1** a flatbed truck, trailer, etc. **2** a flatbed press

flat·boat (-bōt′) ***n.*** a boat with a flat bottom, for carrying freight in shallow waters or on rivers

flat·bread (flat′bred′) ***n.*** bread made in thin, circular pieces or sheets, often unleavened, as pita or matzo

☆**flat·car** (-kär′) ***n.*** a railroad car without sides or a roof, for carrying certain kinds of freight

flat-coat·ed retriever (-kōt′id) any of a breed of medium-sized retriever with a dense, flat coat of black or liver, developed principally from the Labrador retriever and the Newfoundland

flat-earth·er (-ʉrth′ər) ***n.*** ⟦orig. referring to someone holding on to the belief that the earth is flat⟧ a person whose beliefs are regarded as outmoded, irrational, reactionary, etc.

flat·fish (-fish′) ***n.***, *pl.* **-fish′** or **-fish′es** (see FISH) any of an order (Pleuronectiformes) of marine bony fishes, including flounders and soles, having a laterally flattened, asymmetrical body with, as an adult, both the eyes and the mouth on the upper side

flat·foot (-fo͝ot′) ***n.*** **1** a condition in which a foot has a flat or dropped instep arch, with the entire sole meeting the ground **2** *pl.* **-foots′** or **-feet′** [Slang] a policeman: so called from the notion that flat feet result from walking a beat

flat foot a foot having a flattened instep arch, with the entire sole meeting the ground

flat-foot·ed (-fo͝ot′id) ***adj.*** **1** having flatfoot **2** designating a manner of walking, with the toes pointed outward, as by people with flatfoot ☆**3** [Informal] downright and firm; plain and uncompromising **4** [Informal] *a)* awkward or clumsy *b)* tedious, plodding, etc. —☆***adv.*** [Informal] firmly, directly, or abruptly —☆**catch someone flat-footed** [Informal] to catch someone who is unprepared; take by surprise —**flat′-foot′ed·ly** ***adv.*** —**flat′-foot′ed·ness** ***n.***

☆**Flat·head** (-hed′) ***n.***, *pl.* **-heads′** or **-head′** **1** a member of any of various North American Indian peoples who bound the skulls of their infants so as to produce a flattened forehead **2** a Salish people of NW Montana that is not known to have practiced head flattening

-fla·tion (flā′shən) *combining form* inflation: used in many nonce compounds [*oilflation, medflation*]

flat·i·ron (flat′ī′ərn) ***n.*** an old-fashioned IRON (***n.*** 2a), heated externally and typically triangular in shape

flat·land (-land′) ***n.*** [*also pl.*] land or a region of land that is extremely level —**flat′land′er** ***n.***

flat·line (-līn′) ***vi.*** **-lined′**, **-lin′ing** ⟦< FLAT[1] + LINE[1]: from earlier use as n., for the unfluctuating readout line on a medical monitor, indicating a cessation of heartbeat⟧ [Informal] to cease to live, flourish, or succeed; die literally or figuratively

flat·ling (-liŋ) ***adv.*** ⟦ME: see FLAT[1] & -LING[2]⟧ [Now Brit. Dial.] **1** at full length **2** with the flat side, as of a sword Also **flat′lings** or **flat′long′** (-lôŋ′)

flat·mate (-māt′) ***n.*** [Chiefly Brit.] a person who shares a FLAT[2] with another or others

flat-out (-out′) ***adj.*** [Informal] **1** at full speed, with maximum effort, etc. **2** absolute; thorough; definite

flat-pan·el (-pan′əl) ***adj.*** being or of a thin, flat, electronic display device, as an LCD screen, serving as a computer monitor, TV screen, etc.

flat race a race, usually for horses, run over a level track without artificial obstructions: cf. STEEPLECHASE

flat-screen (-skrēn′) ***adj.*** FLAT-PANEL

☆**flat silver** silver knives, forks, spoons, etc., as distinguished from silver trays, teapots, bowls, etc.

flat tax an income tax with a single rate for all taxpayers, regardless of income
flat taxer a proponent of a FLAT TAX: also written **flat′-tax′er** *n.*
flat·ten (flat′'n) *vt.* **1** to make flat or flatter **2** [Informal] to knock down; make prostrate **3** to level to the ground —*vi.* **1** to become flat or flatter **2** to become prostrate —**flatten out 1** to make or become flat or flatter by spreading out **2** *Aeron.* LEVEL OFF (sense 2) (at LEVEL) —**flat′ten·er** *n.*
flat·ter[1] (flat′ər) *vt.* ⟦ME *flateren* < OFr *flater*, to smooth, caress with flat hand < Frank **flat*, akin to OHG *flaz*, FLAT[1]⟧ **1** to praise too much, untruly, or insincerely, as in order to win favor **2** to try to please, or ingratiate oneself with, by praise and attention **3** to make seem better or more attractive than is so [*his portrait flatters him*] **4** to make feel pleased or honored; gratify the vanity of [*it's flattering to be remembered*] **5** to please or gratify (the eye, ear, senses, etc.) **6** to encourage, esp. falsely —*vi.* to use flattery —**flatter oneself** to hold the self-satisfying or self-deluding belief (*that*) —**flat′ter·er** *n.* —**flat′ter·ing·ly** *adv.*
flat·ter[2] (flat′ər) *n.* **1** a person who flattens something **2** a drawplate for forming flat strips **3** a smith's forging tool with a broad, flat face
flat·ter[3] (flat′ər) *adj., adv. compar. of* FLAT[1]
flat·ter·y (flat′ər ē) *n., pl.* **-ter·ies** ⟦ME & OFr *flaterie* (Fr *flatterie*) < *flater*: see FLATTER[1]⟧ **1** the act of flattering **2** excessive, untrue, or insincere praise; exaggerated compliment or attention
flat·tish (flat′ish) *adj.* somewhat flat
☆**flat·top** (flat′täp′) *n.* something having a flat or level surface, platform, etc.; specif., *a)* [Slang] an aircraft carrier *b)* a style of man's haircut in which the hair on top of the head is cropped so that it bristles up to form a flat surface
flat·u·lent (flach′ə lənt) *adj.* ⟦Fr < ModL *flatulentus* < L *flatus*: see fol.⟧ **1** of or having gas in the stomach or intestines **2** producing gas in the stomach or intestines, as certain foods **3** windy or empty in speech; pompous; pretentious —**flat′u·lence** *n.*, **flat′u·len·cy** —**flat′u·lent·ly** *adv.*
fla·tus (flāt′əs) *n.* ⟦L < *flare*, to blow: see BLAST⟧ gas in, or expelled from, the stomach or intestines
flat·ware (flat′wer′) *n.* relatively flat tableware; specif., ☆*a)* knives, forks, spoons, etc. ☆*b)* flat plates, platters, etc.: cf. HOLLOWARE
flat·wise (-wīz′) *adv.* with the flat side foremost, uppermost, or in contact: also **flat′ways′** (-wāz′)
☆**flat·work** (-wurk′) *n.* laundered articles, as sheets, napkins, and other flat pieces, that can be pressed quickly in a mangle
flat·worm (-wurm′) *n.* PLATYHELMINTH
Flau·bert (flō ber′), **Gus·tave** (güs tȧv′) 1821-80; Fr. novelist —**Flau·ber·tian** (flō ber′shən, -bert′ē ən) *adj.*
flaunt (flônt) *vi.* ⟦15th & 16th c., prob. < dial. *flant*, to strut coquettishly, akin to Norw *flanta* < ON *flana*, run back and forth < IE **plano-* < base **pla-*, broad, flat, spread out > Gr *planos*, wandering⟧ **1** to make a gaudy, ostentatious, conspicuous, impudent, or defiant display **2** to flutter or wave freely —*vt.* **1** to show off proudly, defiantly, or impudently [*to flaunt one's guilt*] **2** ⟦through confusion in form and meaning⟧ FLOUT: usage objected to by many —*n.* [Archaic] the act of flaunting —*SYN.* SHOW —**flaunt′ing·ly** *adv.* — [Rare] **flaunt′y** *adj.*
flau·ta (flou′tä) *n.* ⟦MexSp < Sp, lit., flute⟧ a Mexican dish consisting of a tortilla rolled tightly around a filling as of shredded chicken or beef and deep-fried
flau·tist (flôt′ist, flout′-) *n.* ⟦It *flautista* < *flauto*, FLUTE⟧ *var. of* FLUTIST
fla·va·none (flā′və nōn′) *n.* ⟦fol. + -AN(E) + -ONE⟧ **1** a complex, colorless, crystalline ketone, $C_{15}H_{12}O_2$, derived from flavone **2** any of the derivatives of flavanone, many of which are found in various plants
fla·vin (flā′vin) *n.* ⟦< L *flavus*, yellow (see FLAVONE) + -IN[1]⟧ **1** a complex heterocyclic ketone, $C_{10}H_6N_4O_2$ **2** any of a group of yellow pigments, derived from this ketone and occurring in certain plant and animal products or prepared by synthesis; specif., riboflavin **3** QUERCETIN
fla·vine (flā′vēn′) *n.* **1** FLAVIN **2** ACRIFLAVINE
fla·vone (flā′vōn′) *n.* ⟦Ger *flavon* < L *flavus*, yellow (< IE base **bhlē-wos*, used of light colors > BLUE) + Ger *-on*, -ONE⟧ **1** a colorless, crystalline ketone, $C_{15}H_{10}O_2$, obtained from certain plants or prepared synthetically: it forms a base for some yellow dyes **2** any derivative of this compound
fla·vo·noid (flā′və noid′) *n.* any of a large group of aromatic compounds occurring naturally, chiefly as pigments in higher plants, as anthocyanin
fla·vo·nol (flā′və nôl′, -nōl′) *n.* ⟦< FLAVON(E) + -OL[1]⟧ **1** a yellow, crystalline hydroxy derivative of flavone, $C_{15}H_{10}O_3$: also **fla′va·nol 2** any of various derivatives of flavonol, used as yellow pigments and dyes and frequently found in plants
fla·vo·pro·tein (flā′vō prō′tēn′) *n.* any of a group of enzymes involved in tissue respiration and consisting of a protein and a flavin group
fla·vo·pur·pu·rin (-pur′pə rin) *n.* ⟦< L *flavus*, yellow (see FLAVONE) + PURPURIN⟧ a yellowish, crystalline chemical compound, $C_{14}H_8O_5$, used in making dyes
fla·vor (flā′vər) *n.* ⟦ME *flavour*, an odor, altered (by analogy with *savour*, SAVOR) < OFr *flaur* < VL **flator*, odor < L *flatare*, to blow, freq. of *flare*, blow (see BLAST), prob. infl. by *foetor*, foul odor⟧ **1** [Archaic] an odor; smell; aroma **2** *a)* that quality of a substance that is a mixing of its characteristic taste and smell *b)* taste in general [*a soup lacking flavor*] **3** any substance added to a food, medicine, etc. to give it a particular taste; flavoring **4** the characteristic quality of something; distinctive nature [*the flavor of a small town*] **5** *Particle Physics* any of the six basic types of quarks or leptons: *down quark, up quark, charmed quark, strange quark, top quark,* or *bottom quark* —*vt.* to give flavor to —**fla′vor·less** *adj.*
fla·vor·ful (-fəl) *adj.* having a rich, pleasing flavor; savory: also **fla′vor·some** (-səm), **fla′vor·ous**, or **fla′vor·y** —**fla′vor·ful·ly** *adv.*
fla·vor·ing (-iŋ) *n.* an essence, extract, etc. added to a food or drink to give it a certain taste
fla·vor·ist (-ist) *n.* a chemist who specializes in producing flavorings for foods, beverages, medicines, etc.
fla·vour (flā′vər) *n., vt. Brit. sp. of* FLAVOR
flaw[1] (flô) *n.* ⟦ME, a flake, scale, splinter, prob. < or akin to ON *flaga*, thin layer: for IE base see FLAKE[1]⟧ **1** a break, scratch, crack, etc. that spoils something; blemish [*a flaw in a diamond*] **2** a defect; fault; error [*a flaw in a legal document, in one's reasoning, etc.*] —*vt., vi.* to make or become faulty —*SYN.* DEFECT —**flaw′less** *adj.* —**flaw′less·ly** *adv.* —**flaw′less·ness** *n.*
flaw[2] (flô) *n.* ⟦< or akin to ON *flaga*, sudden onset < IE base **plāk-*, **plāg-*, to strike, beat > FLICKER[1], L *plangere*, to beat (the breast)⟧ a sudden, brief gust of wind, often with rain or snow; squall
flax (flaks) *adj.* ⟦ME < OE *fleax*, akin to Ger *flachs* < IE base **plek-*, to plait, interweave > L *plectere*, *plicare*, Ger *flechten*⟧ designating a family (Linaceae, order Linales) of dicotyledonous plants and shrubs usually having narrow leaves and five-part flowers —*n.* **1** any of a genus (*Linum*) of the flax family; esp. a slender, erect annual plant (*L. usitatissimum*) with delicate, blue flowers: the seeds are used to make linseed oil, and the fibers of the stem are spun into linen thread **2** the threadlike fibers of these plants, ready for spinning **3** any of a number of flaxlike plants
flax·en (flak′sən) *adj.* ⟦ME < OE *fleaxen*⟧ **1** of or made of flax **2** like flax in color; pale-yellow; straw-colored
Flax·man (flaks′mən), **John** 1755-1826; Eng. sculptor & illustrator
flax·seed (flak′sēd′) *n.* the seed of the flax; linseed
flax·y (flak′sē) *adj.* like flax; flaxen
flay (flā) *vt.* ⟦ME *flan* < OE *flean*, akin to MDu *vlaen*, ON *fla* < IE base **plēk̂-*, to tear off > FLITCH⟧ **1** to strip off the skin or hide of, as by whipping **2** to criticize or scold mercilessly **3** to rob; pillage
F layer the two dense layers of ions in the F region of the ionosphere that are used to reflect long-range radio signals: the **F_1 layer**, at an altitude of *c.* 200 to 300 km (*c.* 125 to 185 miles), exists during the day, and the permanent **F_2 layer**, or Appleton layer, is at *c.* 225 to 400 km (*c.* 140 to 250 miles)
fl dr *abbrev.* fluid dram(s)
flea (flē) *n.* ⟦ME *fle* < OE *fleah*, akin to Ger *floh* < same Gmc base as FLEE⟧ **1** any of an order (Siphonaptera) of small, flattened, wingless insects with large legs adapted for jumping: as adults they are bloodsucking parasites on mammals and birds **2** FLEA BEETLE —**flea in one's ear** a stinging rebuke or rebuff, or an annoying hint

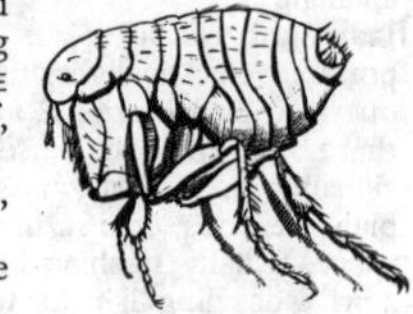
flea (sense 1)

flea·bag (flē′bag′) *n.* ☆[Slang] a very cheap, dirty hotel
flea·bane (-bān′) *n.* ⟦FLEA + BANE: once thought to drive away fleas⟧ ERIGERON
flea beetle any of a number of small jumping beetles (family Chrysomelidae) that feed chiefly on leaves and shoots of plants
flea·bite (-bīt′) *n.* **1** the bite of a flea **2** the red spot on the skin caused by the bite of a flea **3** a minor pain or trifling inconvenience
flea-bit·ten (-bit′'n) *adj.* **1** bitten by a flea or fleas **2** infested with fleas **3** wretched; decrepit; shabby **4** light-colored with reddish-brown spots: said of horses
☆**flea circus** an act, as for a carnival sideshow, featuring tricks performed, or purportedly performed, by trained fleas
flea-flick·er (-flik′ər) *n. Football* any of various deceptive plays involving both a lateral pass and a forward pass, esp. one in which the quarterback, after handing the ball off, receives a lateral pass and then throws a forward pass
☆**flea·hop·per** (-häp′ər) *n.* any of several small, jumping hemipterous bugs (family Miridae), many of which damage cotton and other cultivated plants
fleam (flēm) *n.* ⟦ME *fleme* < OFr *flieme* < VL **fleutomum* for LL *phlebotomus*: see PHLEBOTOMY⟧ a sharp lancet formerly used for bloodletting
flea market a bazaar, usually outdoors, dealing mainly in cheap, second-hand goods
flea·pit (flē′pit′) *n.* [Informal] a public place, esp. a hotel or theater, that is cheap, run-down, inferior, etc.
flea·wort (flē′wurt′) *n.* **1** any of several plants that supposedly ward off fleas, as a European aromatic plant (*Inula conyza*) of the composite family with rough leaves and yellow flowers **2** a European plantain (*Plantago psyllium*) whose seeds, which more or less resemble fleas, are used as a laxative
flèche (flesh, flāsh) *n.* ⟦Fr, lit., an arrow < OFr *fleche* < MDu *vleke*, an arrow, akin to OE *flacor*, flying (of arrows): for IE base see FLAW[2]⟧ a slender spire, esp. one over the intersection of the nave and the transept in some Gothic churches
flé·chette (flā shet′) *n.* ⟦Fr, a dart, dim. of *flèche*, arrow: see prec.⟧ a small, dartlike projectile, now usually shot from a gun or discharged in clusters by means of a bomb
fleck (flek) *n.* ⟦ON *flekkr*, akin to MDu *vlecke*, Ger *fleck* < IE **plīk-*, var. of base **plēk̂-*: see FLAY⟧ **1** a spot or small patch of color, etc.; speck [*flecks of*

sunlight] 2 a small piece; particle; flake —*vt.* ⟦ME **flekken* (found only in pp. *flekked*), prob. < ON *flekka* < *flekkr*⟧ to cover or sprinkle with flecks; speckle

flec·tion (flek′shən) *n.* ⟦L *flexio* < pp. of *flectere*, to bend⟧ 1 a bending; flexing 2 a bend or bent part 3 *Anat.* FLEXION 4 *Gram.* inflection

fled (fled) *vi., vt. pt. & pp. of* FLEE

fledge (flej) *vi.* **fledged, fledg′ing** ⟦< ME *flegge*, ready to fly < OE *(un)-flycge*, (un)fledged, akin to MHG *vlücke*, MDu *vlugghe*: for IE base see FLY[1]⟧ to grow the feathers necessary for flying —*vt.* 1 to rear (a young bird) until it is able to fly 2 to supply or adorn with or as if with feathers or down; specif., to fit (an arrow, etc.) with feathers

fledg·ling (flej′liŋ) *n.* 1 a young bird just fledged 2 a young, inexperienced person —*adj.* recent and, hence, characterized by immaturity, inexperience, etc. [*a fledgling* company] Also [Chiefly Brit.] **fledge′ling**

flee (flē) *vi.* **fled, flee′ing** ⟦ME *fleen* < OE *fleon*: see FLOW⟧ 1 to run away or escape from danger, pursuit, unpleasantness, etc. 2 to pass away swiftly; vanish [night had *fled*] 3 to move rapidly; go swiftly —*vt.* to run away or try to escape from —**fle·er** (flē′ər) *n.*

fleece (flēs) *n.* ⟦ME *flees* < OE *fleos*, akin to Ger *vlies* < IE base **pleus-*, to pluck out > L *pluma*, a feather, down⟧ 1 the wool covering a sheep or similar animal 2 the amount of wool cut from a sheep in one shearing 3 a covering like a sheep's, as of woolly hair 4 a soft, warm, napped fabric, used for garments, linings, etc. —*vt.* **fleeced, fleec′ing** 1 to shear the fleece from (sheep, etc.) 2 [Informal] to steal from by fraud; swindle 3 to cover or fleck with fleecy masses —**fleec′er** *n.*

fleec·y (flēs′ē) *adj.* **fleec′i·er, fleec′i·est** 1 made of or covered with fleece 2 like fleece; soft and light [*fleecy* snow] —**fleec′i·ly** *adv.* —**fleec′i·ness** *n.*

fleer (flir) *vi., vt.* ⟦ME *flerien*, prob. < Scand, as in Dan dial., Norw *flire*, to snicker, laugh, prob. < IE base **plēi-*, bald, bare⟧ to laugh derisively (at); sneer or jeer (at) —*n.* a derisive grimace, laugh, etc.; gibe —**fleer′ing·ly** *adv.*

fleet[1] (flēt) *n.* ⟦ME *flete* < OE *fleot* < *fleotan*, to float: see fol.⟧ 1 *a)* a number of warships under one command, usually in a definite area of operation *b)* the entire naval force of a country; navy 2 any group of ships, trucks, buses, airplanes, etc. acting together or under one control

fleet[2] (flēt) *vi.* ⟦ME *fleten* < OE *fleotan*, akin to Ger *fliessen* < IE **pleud-* < base **pleu-*, FLOW⟧ 1 [Obs.] to float; swim 2 to move swiftly; flit; fly 3 [Archaic] to pass away swiftly; disappear —*vt.* 1 [Rare] to pass away (time) 2 *Naut.* to change the position of (a rope, pulley block, etc.) —*adj.* 1 swift; rapid 2 [Old Poet.] evanescent —*SYN.* FAST[1] —**fleet′ly** *adv.* —**fleet′ness** *n.*

fleet[3] (flēt) *n.* ⟦ME *flete* < OE *fleot*, akin to Du *vliet*: base as in prec.⟧ [Now Brit. Dial.] a small inlet; creek —**the Fleet** 1 a former small creek in London, now a covered sewer 2 a debtor's prison which stood near this creek: also **Fleet Prison**

☆**fleet admiral** *U.S. Navy* an officer of the highest rank, a specially conferred one above that of admiral: the rank, created during WWII, has not been conferred since

fleet·ing (flēt′iŋ) *adj.* ⟦OE *fleotende*, floating: see FLEET[2]⟧ passing swiftly; not lasting —*SYN.* TRANSIENT —**fleet′ing·ly** *adv.* —**fleet′ing·ness** *n.*

Fleet Street ⟦after THE FLEET (see FLEET[3]), which crosses beneath it⟧ 1 old street in central London, where several newspaper & printing offices are located 2 the London press

fleh·men (flā′mən) *n.* ⟦Ger, to curl the upper lip⟧ a response of certain mammals, including horses and cats, involving a curling back of the lips to direct scents and, specif., pheromones toward the vomeronasal organ: also **flehmen response**

Flem·ing[1] (flem′iŋ) *n.* ⟦ME < OFris or MDu *Vlaming*⟧ 1 a person born or living in Flanders 2 a Belgian who speaks Flemish

Flem·ing[2] (flem′iŋ) 1 Sir **Alexander** 1881-1955; Brit. bacteriologist: discovered penicillin together with Sir Howard Walter Florey 2 **Ian (Lancaster)** 1908-64; Brit. writer, esp. of the JAMES BOND stories

Flem·ish (flem′ish) *n.* the West Germanic language spoken in Flanders, very closely related to Dutch —*adj.* of Flanders or its people, language, or culture —**the Flemish** the people of Flanders

flense (flens) *vt.* **flensed, flens′ing** ⟦< Du *vlensen* or Dan *flense*⟧ to cut blubber skin from (a whale, seal, etc.): also **flench** (flench)

fler·o·vi·um (fle rō′vē əm) *n.* ⟦< the *Flerov* Laboratory of Nuclear Reactions in Russia, after G. *Flerov* (1913-90), Russ physicist⟧ a radioactive, metallic chemical element, one of the noble gases: a transactinide produced by bombarding plutonium with calcium ions: symbol, Fl; at. no. 114: see the periodic table of elements in the Reference Supplement

flesh (flesh) *n.* ⟦ME < OE *flæsc*, akin to Ger *fleisch* < ? IE base **plēk-*, to tear off > FLAY⟧ 1 *a)* the soft substance of the body (of a person or animal) between the skin and the bones; esp., the muscular tissue *b)* the surface or skin of the body [to feel one's *flesh* crawl] 2 the flesh of any animal as food; meat; esp., meat other than fish or fowl 3 the pulpy or edible part of fruits and vegetables 4 the human body, as distinguished from the soul [more than *flesh* can bear] 5 human nature, esp. in its sensual aspect 6 all living beings, esp. all humankind 7 kindred or relatives: now mainly in *one's (own) flesh and blood*: see phrase at FLESH AND BLOOD 8 the typical color of a white person's skin; ranging from beige or tan to yellowish pink 9 [Informal] plumpness; fat [you've been putting on *flesh*] —*vt.* 1 to feed (animals) with flesh so as to incite them to hunt or kill 2 to prepare for or incite to bloodshed, etc. by a foretaste 3 to harden; inure 4 to plunge (a weapon) into flesh 5 to put flesh on; fatten 6 to fill out as if with flesh; realize or make full, as by the addition of details: usually with *out* 7 to remove flesh from (a hide) —*vi.* to grow fleshy or fat: usually with *out* or *up* —**in the flesh** 1 alive 2 actually present; in person —☆**press the flesh** [Informal] to shake hands or embrace, mingle, etc. effusively in crowds, esp. in politicking

flesh and blood the human body, esp. as subject to its natural limitations —**one's (own) flesh and blood** one's close relatives

flesh-and-blood (flesh′ən blud′) *adj.* 1 alive; living 2 real; actual; true 3 actually present; in person

flesh-col·ored (flesh′kul′ərd) *adj.* 1 having any of the shades of color of human skin 2 having the typical color of a white person's skin, ranging from beige or tan to yellowish pink

flesh-eat·ing (-ēt′iŋ) *adj.* habitually eating flesh; carnivorous

flesh fly any of a family (Sarcophagidae) of dipterous flies that deposit their maggots on flesh, carrion, dung, etc.

flesh·ings (flesh′iŋz) *pl.n.* 1 flesh-colored tights, worn by acrobats, etc. 2 pieces of flesh scraped from hides

flesh·ly (flesh′lē) *adj.* **-li·er, -li·est** ⟦ME *fleschlich* < OE *flæsclic*: see FLESH & -LY[1]⟧ 1 of the body and its nature; corporeal 2 fond of bodily pleasures; sensual 3 [Obs.] FLESHY —*SYN.* CARNAL —**flesh′li·ness** *n.*

flesh meat the meat of birds or of animals other than fish, clams, etc., used as food

flesh·pot (flesh′pät′) *n.* ⟦after Ex. 16:3⟧ 1 [*pl.*] bodily comfort and pleasure; luxury 2 a place where carnal pleasures are provided: *usually used in pl.*

flesh wound a wound that does not reach the bones or vital organs

flesh·y (flesh′ē) *adj.* **flesh′i·er, flesh′i·est** 1 having much flesh; fat; plump 2 of or like flesh 3 having a firm pulp, as some fruits —**flesh′i·ness** *n.*

fletch (flech) *vt.* ⟦altered (after fol.) < FLEDGE⟧ to fit a feather on (an arrow)

fletch·er (flech′ər) *n.* ⟦ME < OFr *flechier* < *fleche*, an arrow < Frank **fliugika*, akin to MDu *vlieke* < base of *vlegen*, FLY[1]⟧ [Archaic] a person who makes arrows

Fletch·er (flech′ər), **John** 1579-1625; Eng. playwright: collaborated with Francis Beaumont

fleur-de-lis (flʉr′də lē′, -lēs′) *n., pl.* **fleurs-de-lis** (flʉr′də lē′, -lēz′, -lēs′) ⟦altered, after Fr *fleur* < ME *flour de lyce* < OFr *flor de lis*, lit., flower of the lily⟧ 1 IRIS (senses 4 & 5) 2 the coat of arms of the former French royal family 3 *Heraldry* an emblem resembling a lily or iris Also sp. **fleur-de-lys**

fleur-de-lis

Fleu·ry (flë rē′) 1 **An·dré Her·cule de** (än drā er kül′ də) 1653-1743; Fr. cardinal & statesman: prime minister (1726-43) under Louis XV 2 **Claude** (klōd) 1640-1723; Fr. ecclesiastical historian

Fle·vo·land (flē′vō land′) province of the WC Netherlands, on the IJsselmeer: 931 sq mi (2,411 sq km)

flew (flo͞o) *vi., vt. pt. of* FLY[1]

flews (flo͞oz) *pl.n.* ⟦< ?⟧ the loose, hanging parts of the upper lip of a hound or other dog

flex[1] (fleks) *vt., vi.* ⟦< L *flexus*, pp. of *flectere*, to bend, curve⟧ 1 to bend (an arm, knee, etc.) 2 to tense (a muscle) by contraction

flex[2] (fleks) *n.* ⟦< FLEXIBLE⟧ [Brit.] flexible, insulated electric cord

flex fuel any automotive fuel that contains ethanol produced from corn or other crops: often **flexible fuel**

flex·i·ble (flek′sə bəl) *adj.* ⟦ME < OFr < L *flexibilis* < *flexus*: see FLEX[1]⟧ 1 able to bend without breaking; not stiff or rigid; easily bent; pliant 2 able to bend the body easily; limber; supple 3 easily persuaded or influenced; tractable 4 adjustable to change; capable of modification [a *flexible* voice] —*SYN.* ELASTIC —**flex′i·bil′i·ty** *n.* —**flex′i·bly** *adv.*

flex·ile (fleks′il) *adj.* ⟦L *flexilis*⟧ flexible; pliant; mobile

flex·ion (flek′shən) *n.* 1 FLECTION 2 *Anat.* the bending of a joint or limb by contraction of flexor muscles

flex·or (fleks′ər, -ôr′) *n.* ⟦ModL < L *flexus*: see FLEX[1]⟧ a muscle that bends a limb or other part of the body

flex·time (fleks′tīm′) *n.* ⟦FLEX(IBLE) + TIME⟧ a system allowing individual employees some flexibility in choosing the time, but not the number, of their working hours: also **flex′i·time′** (-i tīm′)

flex·u·ous (fleks′yo͞o əs, flek′sho͞o-) *adj.* ⟦L *flexuosus* < *flexus*: see FLEX[1]⟧ winding or wavering —**flex′u·ous·ly** *adv.*

flex·ure (flek′shər) *n.* ⟦L *flexura*⟧ 1 a bending, curving, or flexing, as of a heavy object under its own weight 2 a bend, curve, or fold —**flex′ur·al** *adj.*

flib·ber·ti·gib·bet (flib′ər tē jib′it) *n.* ⟦extended < ME *flypergebet* < ?⟧ an irresponsible, flighty person

flic (flēk) *n.* ⟦Fr⟧ [Informal] a policeman

flick[1] (flik) *n.* ⟦echoic, but infl. by FLICKER[1]⟧ 1 a light, quick stroke, as with a whip; sudden, jerky movement; snap 2 a light, snapping sound, as of the flick of a whip 3 a fleck; splotch; streak —*vt.* 1 to strike, propel, remove, etc. with a light, quick, snapping stroke, as with the fingernail 2 to make a light, quick, snapping stroke with (a whip, etc.) —*vi.* to move quickly and jerkily; flutter

flick[2] (flik) [Slang] *n.* ⟦< fol.⟧ a FILM (*n.* 5) —**the flicks** 1 films collectively 2 a showing of a film

flick·er[1] (flik′ər) ***vi.*** ⟦ME *flikeren* < OE *flicorian*, akin to *flacor*, flying, ON *flǫkta*, to flutter: for IE base see FLAW[2]⟧ **1** to flap the wings rapidly, as in hovering; flutter: said of a bird **2** to move with a quick, light, wavering motion **3** to burn or shine unsteadily, as a candle in the wind —***vt.*** to cause to flicker or waver —***n.*** **1** an act or instance of flickering **2** a dart of flame or light, as in a flickering fire **3** a look or feeling that comes and goes quickly [a *flicker* of fear crossed his face] **4** any of various visual effects, as a fluctuation in brightness on a video screen or in the clarity of the image being projected on a film screen —**SYN.** BLAZE[1] —**flick′er·y** ***adj.***

☆**flick·er**[2] (flik′ər) ***n.*** ⟦echoic of its cry⟧ any of several North American woodpeckers (genus *Colaptes*); esp., the yellow-shafted flicker

flick-knife (-nīf′) ***n.*** [Brit.] SWITCHBLADE (KNIFE)

flied (flīd) ***vi. pt. & pp. of*** FLY[1] (***vi.*** 10)

fli·er (flī′ər) ***n.*** **1** *alt. sp. of* FLYER (senses 1-4) ☆**2** ⟦< archaic *flyer, flier*, a flying leap⟧ [Informal] a risky, sometimes reckless, gamble or speculation: often in the phrase **take a flier**

flies[1] (flīz) ***n.*** **1** *pl. of* FLY[1] **2** [Brit.] *see* FLY[1] (***n.*** *2b*)

flies[2] (flīz) ***n. pl. of*** FLY[2]

flight[1] (flīt) ***n.*** ⟦ME *fliht* < OE *flyht* (akin to OS *fluht*, Du *vlucht*) < base of *fleogan*, FLY[1]⟧ **1** the act, manner, or power of flying or moving through space **2** the distance covered or that can be covered at one time by an airplane, bird, projectile, etc. **3** a group of things flying through the air together [a *flight* of birds, arrows, etc.] **4** *a)* a military flight formation *b)* the smallest tactical unit in an air force; specif., in the U.S. Air Force, a subdivision of a squadron **5** an airplane scheduled to fly a certain route at a certain time **6** a trip by airplane or spacecraft **7** an outburst or soaring above the ordinary [a *flight* of fancy] **8** a set of stairs, as between landings or floors **9** a flight arrow: see FLIGHT SHOOTING **10** *Sports* a division of contestants grouped according to ability —***vi.*** to fly in numbers: said of birds —**SYN.** GROUP —**take flight** to take wing, take off, etc.; become airborne and fly

flight[2] (flīt) ***n.*** ⟦ME *fliht, fluht* < OE *flyht* < base of *fleon*, FLEE⟧ a fleeing from or as from danger —**put to flight** to force to flee —**take (to) flight** to run away; flee

flight attendant an attendant on an airplane, employed to look after the passengers' comfort and safety

☆**flight bag** **1** a lightweight, compact, flexible piece of luggage with outside pockets, designed to fit beneath or above a passenger seat on an airliner **2** a small bag with a zipper top for carrying incidentals

flight control **1** the control from the ground, as by radio, of aircraft in flight **2** a station exercising such control

flight crew AIRCREW

☆**flight deck** **1** the upper deck of an aircraft carrier, that serves as a runway **2** the front compartment of some airplanes, for the crew

flight engineer *Aeron.* a crew member who is in charge of mechanical operation during flight

flight feather any of the large feathers of the wings or tail that support a bird in flight

flight·less (flīt′lis) ***adj.*** not able to fly

flight line the portion of an airfield where planes are parked and serviced

flight plan a pilot's oral or written report to an air-traffic controller, stating the proposed speed, altitude, destination, etc. of an upcoming flight

flight recorder an electronic module, designed to survive a crash, fire, etc., that records flight data, as altitude, airspeed, and aircrew conversations

flight shooting *Archery* the sport of distance shooting, using a bow (**flight bow**) and arrow (**flight arrow**) designed for maximum distance rather than maximum accuracy

☆**flight strip** an emergency runway; airstrip

☆**flight surgeon** a military medical officer specializing in aviation medicine

flight-test (flīt′test′) ***vt.*** to put (an aircraft, rocket, etc.) through an actual test (**flight test**) of flight performance

flight·y (flīt′ē) ***adj.*** **flight′i·er, flight′i·est** ⟦FLIGHT[1] + -Y[2]⟧ **1** given to sudden whims; not taking things seriously; frivolous or irresponsible **2** easily excited, upset, etc. —**flight′i·ly** ***adv.*** —**flight′i·ness** ***n.***

flim·flam (flim′flam′) ***n.*** ⟦? redupl. < *flam*, deceptive trick⟧ **1** nonsense; rubbish; humbug **2** a sly trick or deception —***vt.*** **-flammed′, -flam′ming** [Informal] to trick, swindle, or cheat —**flim′flam′mer·y** ***n.***

flim·sy (flim′zē) ***adj.*** **-si·er, -si·est** ⟦? altered < FILM + -SY⟧ **1** thin and easily broken or damaged; poorly made and fragile; frail **2** ill-conceived and inadequate; ineffectual [a *flimsy* excuse] —***n.***, *pl.* **-sies** [Chiefly Brit.] **1** a sheet of thin paper, as used for carbon copies **2** written or typed copy on such paper —**flim′si·ly** ***adv.*** —**flim′si·ness** ***n.***

flinch (flinch) ***vi.*** ⟦earlier also *flench* < OFr *flenchir*, to bend aside < Frank **hlankjan*, akin to Ger *lenken*, OE *hlencan*, to twist, bend: see LANK⟧ **1** to draw back, as from a blow, difficulty, etc. **2** to wince, as from pain —***n.*** an act of flinching

flin·ders (flin′dərz) ***pl.n.*** ⟦ME (northern) *flender* < Scand, as in Norw *flindra*, splinter < IE base *(s)plei-*, to split > SPLIT, SPLINT, FLINT⟧ splinters or fragments: chiefly in **break (or fly) into flinders**

fling (fliŋ) ***vt.*** **flung, fling′ing** ⟦ME *flingen*, to rush < ON *flengja*, to whip (Norw dial., to throw) < IE base **plāk-*: see FLAW[2]⟧ **1** to throw, esp. with force or violence; hurl; cast **2** to put abruptly or violently [to be *flung* into confusion] **3** to move (one's arms, legs, head, etc.) suddenly or impulsively **4** to throw (oneself) energetically (*into* a task) **5** to throw aside; disregard [to *fling* caution to the winds] **6** [Old Poet.] to emit or diffuse —***vi.*** **1** to move suddenly and violently; rush; dash **2** to kick and plunge, as a horse does: often with *out* —***n.*** **1** an act of flinging **2** a brief time of unrestrained pleasures or dissipation **3** a spirited dance [the Highland *fling*] **4** [Informal] a trial effort; try [to have a *fling* at acting] **5** [Informal] a brief love affair —**SYN.** THROW —**fling′er** ***n.***

flint (flint) ***n.*** ⟦ME < OE, akin to Norw, stone splinter: see FLINDERS⟧ **1** a dark-colored variety of chert that produces sparks when struck with steel and that breaks into pieces with sharp cutting edges **2** a piece of this stone, used to start a fire, for primitive tools, etc. **3** a small piece of metal consisting of iron and misch metal, used to strike the spark in a cigarette lighter **4** anything extremely hard or firm like flint

Flint (flint) ⟦after the nearby *Flint* River, so called from the *flint* rocks in it⟧ city in SE Mich.

☆**flint corn** a variety of corn (*Zea mays* var. *indurata*) with very hard kernels not dented at the tip

flint glass a hard, bright glass having a high index of refraction, used as for lenses

flint·lock (flint′läk′) ***n.*** **1** a gunlock in which a flint in the hammer strikes a metal plate to produce a spark that ignites the powder **2** an old-fashioned gun with such a lock

Flint·shire (flint′shir) former county of NE Wales, now part of Clwyd county

flint·y (flin′tē) ***adj.*** **flint′i·er, flint′i·est** **1** made of or containing flint **2** like flint; extremely hard and firm; inflexible [a *flinty* heart] —**flint′i·ly** ***adv.*** —**flint′i·ness** ***n.***

flip[1] (flip) ***vt.*** **flipped, flip′ping** ⟦echoic⟧ **1** to toss or move with a quick jerk; flick [*flip* the drawer shut] **2** to snap (a coin) into the air with the thumb, as in betting on which side will land uppermost **3** to turn or turn over [to *flip* pages in a book] **4** [Informal] to look at a series of (TV channels) by switching from one to another quickly and randomly **5** [Informal] to buy and sell (a house, stock, etc.) for a quick profit —***vi.*** **1** to make a quick, light stroke, as with the finger or a whip; snap **2** to move jerkily **3** to flip a coin, as in letting chance decide something **4** to turn over quickly; specif., to execute a flip **5** to look (*through*) in a quick, random manner ☆**6** [Slang] to lose self-control as a result of excitement, anger, madness, etc.: also **flip out** —***n.*** **1** the act or motion of flipping; snap, tap, jerk, or toss **2** a somersault in the air **3** a woman's hairstyle in which the hair is worn straight, with the ends rolled outward at the neck or shoulders —**flip on (or off)** [Informal] to turn something on (or off) with or as with a push button —☆**flip one's lid (or wig)** [Slang] to lose self-control; go berserk

flip[2] (flip) ***n.*** ⟦prob. < prec.⟧ a sweetened mixed drink of beer, wine, or liquor with eggs, spices, etc.

flip[3] (flip) ***adj.*** **flip′per, flip′pest** ⟦contr. < FLIPPANT⟧ [Informal] flippant; saucy; impertinent

flip·book (flip′book′) ***n.*** a booklet, tablet, etc. with one of a series of drawings on each page, the drawings forming an animated-cartoonlike sequence when the pages are flipped rapidly with the thumb: also written **flip book**

flip chart a series of large paper sheets containing charts, information, etc., fastened loosely to allow them to be turned over, and held by a frame for display, as to illustrate a lecture

flip-flop (flip′fläp′) ***n.*** ☆**1** an acrobatic spring backward from the feet to the hands and back to the feet **2** an abrupt change, as to an opposite opinion **3** a flapping noise **4** ⟦redupl. of FLIP[1]: descriptive of flapping motion or echoic of flapping sound produced as the wearer walks in it⟧ a kind of sandal consisting usually of a flat rubber sole held on the foot by a strap slipped between the big toe and the toe next to it **5** *Electronics* a circuit having two stable states and remaining in one until a signal causes it to switch to the other —***vi.*** **-flopped′, -flop′ping** to do a flip-flop

flip·pan·cy (flip′ən sē) ***n.*** **1** the quality or state of being flippant **2** *pl.* **-cies** a flippant act or remark

flip·pant (flip′ənt) ***adj.*** ⟦Early ModE, nimble, prob. < FLIP[1]⟧ **1** [Obs.] glib; talkative **2** frivolous and disrespectful; saucy; impertinent —**flip′pant·ly** ***adv.***

flip·per (flip′ər) ***n.*** ⟦< FLIP[1]⟧ **1** a broad, flat part or limb adapted for swimming, as in seals or whales ☆**2** a large, flat, paddlelike rubber device worn on each foot by a swimmer or skin diver to increase the force of the kick

☆**flip side** [Informal] **1** the reverse side (of a phonograph record), esp. the less important or less popular side **2** the reverse or opposite, often sharply contrasting, side, aspect, effect, etc. of something or someone

FLIR or **flir** (flir) ***n.*** ⟦*f(orward) l(ooking) i(nfra)r(ed)*⟧ an electronic heat sensor able to detect and display on a TV-like screen a distant scene despite darkness, smoke, etc.: used esp. in military aircraft

flirt (flurt) ***vt.*** ⟦earlier *flert, flurt* < ? OFr *fleureter*, to touch lightly, lit., move from flower to flower < *fleur*, FLOWER⟧ **1** [Now Rare] to toss or flick quickly **2** to move jerkily back and forth [the bird *flirted* its tail] —***vi.*** **1** to move jerkily or unevenly **2** to behave as though romantically or sexually attracted to someone, often, specif., without serious intentions or emotional commitment —***n.*** **1** a quick, jerky movement; flutter **2** a person who flirts with others —**SYN.** TRIFLE —**flirt with** **1** to engage in flirtatious behavior toward (someone) **2** to engage in or become interested in (something) briefly or superficially [an actor *flirting with* politics] **3** to expose oneself to in a careless manner [a sky diver *flirting with* danger]

flir·ta·tion (flər tā′shən) ***n.*** **1** the act or an instance of flirting **2** a brief and frivolous love affair

flir·ta·tious (flər tā′shəs) ***adj.*** **1** inclined to flirt **2** of or characteristic of flirtation Also **flirt·y** (flurt′ē) —**flir·ta′tious·ly** ***adv.***

flit (flit) ***vi.*** **flit′ted, flit′ting** ⟦ME *flitten* < ON *flytja*, akin to OE *fleotan*,

FLEET[2]⟧ 1 to pass lightly and rapidly [memories *flitted* through his mind] 2 to fly lightly and rapidly; flutter 3 [Scot. or North Eng.] to move to other quarters, esp. by stealth 4 [Brit. Informal] to leave quickly, as to escape creditors —*vt.* [Scot. or North Eng.] to move to other quarters —*n.* 1 the act or an instance of flitting ☆2 [Slang] a male homosexual: a dismissive or mildly contemptuous term

flitch (fliçh) *n.* ⟦ME *flicche* < OE *flicce*, akin to ON *flikki* < IE base **plēk-*, **plēik-*, to tear (off) > FLAY⟧ 1 the cured and salted side of a hog; side of bacon 2 a lengthwise strip or beam cut from a tree trunk 3 either of two thick boards bolted together with a steel plate between them to form a beam (**flitch beam**) —*vt.* ⟦< the *n.*⟧ to cut so as to form flitches

flit·ter[1] (flit′ər) *vi., vt.* ⟦ME *flitteren*, freq. of *flitten*, FLIT⟧ FLUTTER

flit·ter[2] (flit′ər) *n.* a person or thing that flits

☆**fliv·ver** (fliv′ər) *n.* ⟦< ?⟧ [Old Slang] a small, cheap automobile, esp. an old one

float (flōt) *n.* ⟦ME *flote* < OE *flota*, that which floats, ship, fleet < base of *fleotan*: see FLEET[2]⟧ 1 anything that stays, or causes something else to stay, on the surface of a liquid or suspended near the surface; specif., *a)* an air-filled bladder, as in a fish *b)* a cork on a fishing line *c)* a floating ball or device that regulates the valve controlling water level, as in a tank, or fuel supply, as in a carburetor *d)* a raftlike platform anchored near a shore, as for use by swimmers ☆*e)* a life preserver *f)* a buoyant device on an aircraft to enable it to land or remain on water 2 *a)* a low, flat, decorated vehicle for carrying exhibits, tableaux, etc. in a parade *b)* this vehicle together with its exhibit, tableau, etc. 3 a flat tool for smoothing or spreading cement, plaster, etc. 4 a thread that is brought to the surface of a cloth in weaving, esp. to form a pattern ☆5 a cold beverage, typically a soft drink, served with a scoop of ice cream in it [a root beer *float*] 6 the act or an instance of floating 7 any of the various styles of floating executed by swimmers 8 the act of allowing a currency to float on the market ☆9 *Banking* the total value of checks or drafts in transit and not yet collected —*vi.* ⟦ME *flotien* < OE *flotian*⟧ 1 to stay on the surface of a liquid or suspended near the surface 2 to drift or move slowly or easily on water, in air, etc. [leaves *floating* down from the trees] ☆3 to move or drift about vaguely and without purpose [idle thoughts *floating* through the mind] 4 to fluctuate freely in relationship to other currencies, as determined by supply and demand: said of a currency —*vt.* 1 *a)* to cause to stay on the surface of a liquid or suspended near the surface *b)* to bring to the surface and cause to stay there 2 [Now Rare] to cover (land) with water; flood 3 *a)* to put into circulation; place on the market [to *float* a bond issue] *b)* to establish or start (a business, etc.) 4 to arrange for (a loan) 5 to smooth or spread (cement, plaster, etc.) 6 to allow the exchange value of (a currency) to fluctuate freely in relationship to other currencies —**float′a·ble** *adj.*

float·age (flōt′ij) *n. alt. sp. of* FLOTAGE

float·a·tion (flō tā′shən) *n. alt. sp. of* FLOTATION

float·er (flōt′ər) *n.* 1 a person or thing that floats ☆2 a person who illegally casts a vote at each of several polling places ☆3 a person who changes his or her place of residence or work at frequent intervals; drifter; esp., a transient laborer 4 an employee who works at various tasks, times, or locations, as required by an employer 5 an insurance policy covering movable property irrespective of its location at the time of loss 6 a speck that appears to float before the eye, caused by a defect or impurity in the vitreous humor: *usually used in pl.*

float·ing (flōt′iŋ) *adj.* 1 that floats 2 not fixed; not remaining in one place; moving about 3 *Finance a)* designating an unfunded, short-term debt resulting from current operations and having no specified date for repayment *b)* not permanently invested; available for current expenses [*floating* capital] 4 *Mech.* designating or of parts, as in a suspension, that reduce force or vibration 5 *Med.* displaced from the normal position and moving more freely [a *floating* kidney]

floating (dry) dock a dock that floats and can be lowered in the water for the entrance of a ship, and then raised for use as a dry dock

floating island ☆1 a floating mass of vegetation resembling an island 2 a dessert of boiled custard topped with a dab or dabs of meringue or whipped cream

float·ing-point (flōt′iŋ point′) *adj.* ⟦in ref. to the decimal *point*⟧ designating or of a system of arithmetic, used esp. in computer science, having its numbers expressed in scientific notation (Ex.: 0.0003 becomes 3×10^{-4})

floating dry dock

floating ribs the eleventh and twelfth pairs of ribs, not attached to the breastbone or to other ribs but only to the vertebrae

float·plane (flōt′plān′) *n.* a seaplane equipped with pontoons or floats

float valve a valve regulated by a float

float·y (flōt′ē) *adj.* [Informal] 1 able to float; buoyant 2 lightweight and delicate: said as of fabric

floc (fläk) *n.* ⟦contr. < FLOCCULE⟧ 1 a very fine, fluffy mass formed by the aggregation of fine suspended particles, as in a precipitate 2 FLOCK[2] (senses 1, 2, & 3)

floc·cose (fläk′ōs′) *adj.* ⟦LL *floccosus* < L *floccus*: see FLOCCUS⟧ covered with soft wool or wool-like tufts

floc·cu·lant (fläk′yə lənt) *n.* a substance causing flocculation, as a chemical used in treating waste water: also called **flocculating agent**

floc·cu·late (fläk′yə lāt′; *for n.*, -lət) *vt., vi.* **-lat′ed**, **-lat′ing** to form small, individual masses, as in a suspension —*n.* a flocculated mass —**floc′cu·la′tion** *n.*

floc·cule (fläk′yo͞ol′) *n.* ⟦see FLOCCULUS⟧ a small mass of matter resembling a soft tuft of wool, as in a suspension

floc·cu·lent (fläk′yə lənt) *adj.* ⟦< L *floccus* (see FLOCCUS) + -ULENT⟧ 1 like wool or tufts of wool; fluffy 2 containing or consisting of small woolly masses 3 covered with a wool-like substance, as some insects —**floc′cu·lence** *n.*

floc·cu·lus (fläk′yə ləs) *n., pl.* **-li′** (-lī′) ⟦ModL, dim. < L *floccus*, flock of wool: see fol.⟧ 1 a small, woolly or hairy tuft or mass 2 *Anat.* a small lobe on the underside of each half of the cerebellum ☆3 *Astron. a former term for* PLAGE[2]

floc·cus (fläk′əs) *n., pl.* **floc·ci** (fläk′sī′) ⟦L, flock of wool < IE **bhlok-* > OHG *blaha*, coarse linen cloth⟧ a woolly or hairy tuft or mass

flock[1] (fläk) *n.* ⟦ME *floc* < OE *flocc*, a troop, band, akin to ON *flokkr*, prob. < var. of IE base **pel-*, to pour, fill > L *plere*, to fill⟧ 1 a group of certain animals, as goats or sheep, or of birds, living, feeding, or moving together 2 any group, esp. a large one, as the members of a church or the children in a family —*vi.* to assemble or travel in a flock or crowd —*SYN.* GROUP

flock[2] (fläk) *n.* ⟦ME *flocke* < OFr *floc* < L *floccus*: see FLOCCUS⟧ 1 a small tuft of wool, cotton, etc. 2 wool or cotton waste used to stuff upholstered furniture, mattresses, etc. 3 tiny, fine fibers of wool, rayon, etc. applied to a fabric, wallpaper, or the like to form a velvetlike pattern 4 FLOC (sense 1) —*vt.* to stuff or decorate with flock

flock·ing (fläk′iŋ) *n.* 1 FLOCK[2] (*n.* 3) 2 a material or surface with flock applied to it

flock·y (fläk′ē) *adj.* **flock′i·er**, **flock′i·est** flocculent; floccose

Flod·den (fläd′'n) hilly field in N Northumberland, England: site of a battle (1513) in which the English defeated James IV of Scotland

floe (flō) *n.* ⟦prob. < Norw *flo*, layer, expanse < ON < IE base **plā-*, > FLAG[2]⟧ ICE FLOE

flog (fläg, flôg) *vt.* **flogged**, **flog′ging** ⟦? cant abbrev. of L *flagellare*, to whip: see FLAGELLATE⟧ 1 to beat with a strap, stick, whip, etc., esp. as punishment 2 [Informal] to actively promote or deal in —*SYN.* BEAT —**flog′ger** *n.*

flo·ka·ti (flō kä′tē) *n.* ⟦< ModGr *phlokatē*, peasant's blanket⟧ [*also* **F-**] a rug with a thick, rough nap, that originated as a hand-woven, white wool rug in Greece, but is now also made in a variety of colors with synthetic fibers

flood (flud) *n.* ⟦ME *flode* < OE *flod*, akin to Ger *flut*: for IE base see FLOW⟧ 1 an overflowing of water on an area normally dry; inundation; deluge 2 the flowing in of water from the sea as the tide rises 3 a great flow or outpouring [a *flood* of words] 4 [Informal] *short for* FLOODLIGHT 5 [Archaic] *a)* water, as opposed to land *b)* a large body of water, as a sea or broad river —*vt.* 1 to cover or fill with or as with a flood; overflow; inundate [rain *flooded* the valley; music *flooded* the room] 2 to put much or too much water, fuel, etc. on or in [to *flood* a carburetor] —*vi.* 1 to rise, flow, or gush out in or as in a flood 2 to become flooded —**the Flood** *Bible* the great flood in Noah's time: Gen. 7

☆**flood control** the protection of land from floods, as by soil conservation, reforestation, the construction of dams, reservoirs, river embankments, etc.

flood·gate (flud′gāt′) *n.* 1 a gate in a stream or canal, to control the height and flow of the water; sluice 2 anything like this in controlling a flow or an outburst: *often used in pl.*

flood·light (flud′līt′) *n.* 1 an artificial light of high intensity, usually with a reflector that causes it to shine in a broad beam 2 such a beam of light —*vt.* **-light′ed** or **-lit′**, **-light′ing** to illuminate by a floodlight or floodlights

flood plain a plain that borders a river, formed from sediment deposited by floods: also written **flood′plain′** *n.*

flood tide the incoming or rising tide: cf. EBB TIDE

flood·wa·ter (flud′wôt′ər) *n.* [*often pl.*] the water that overflows during a flood

☆**floo·ey** or **floo·ie** (flo͞o′ē) *adj.* [Slang] BLOOEY

floor (flôr) *n.* ⟦ME *flor* < OE, akin to Ger *flur*, a plain < IE base **plā-*, broad, flat > PLAIN[1]⟧ 1 the inside bottom surface of a room, hall, etc., on which one stands or walks 2 the bottom surface of anything [the ocean *floor*] 3 the platform of a bridge, pier, etc. 4 a level or story in a building [an office on the sixth *floor*] 5 *a)* the part of a legislative chamber, stock exchange, etc. occupied by the members and not including the gallery or platform *b)* such members as a group: with *the* 6 the part of a factory, store, etc. where the main activity of the business takes place 7 *a)* that portion of a ballroom, nightclub, etc. on which the patrons dance (in full **dance floor**) *b)* that portion of a casino where patrons gamble ☆8 permission or the right to speak in an assembly: with *the* [to ask a chairman for the *floor*] 9 a lower limit set on anything, as by official regulation —*vt.* 1 to cover or furnish with a floor 2 to knock down 3 [Informal] *a)* to be the victor over; defeat *b)* to flabbergast; astound 4 [Informal] to press down to the floor: often in the phrase **floor it**, to depress the accelerator of a vehicle to the floorboard in order to go as fast as possible —☆**from the floor** *Basketball* during the time of a game when active defense is permitted [the team shot 56% *from the floor*]

floor·age (flôr′ij) ***n.*** the area of a floor: also **floor space**
floor·board (flôr′bôrd′) ***n.*** **1** a board in a floor **2** the floor of an automobile, etc.
floor exercise *Gym.* an event in which a gymnast performs, without apparatus, a routine involving a series of tumbling movements, acrobatic leaps, and balletic displays
floor·ing (flôr′iŋ) ***n.*** **1** a floor **2** floors collectively **3** material for making a floor
floor lamp a tall lamp that stands on the floor
☆**floor leader** a member of a legislature chosen by a political party to direct its actions on the floor
floor-length (flôr′leŋkth′, -leŋth′) ***adj.*** extending to the floor [a *floor-length* mirror, *floor-length* gown]
floor·man (-man′, -mən) ***n., pl.*** **-men′** (-men′, -mən) a person whose work is supervising a gaming table in a casino
floor model (or **sample**) a sample sale item, as a piece of furniture or an appliance, on display in a store; often, specif., such an item offered for sale at a reduced price
floor plan a scale drawing of the layout of rooms, halls, etc. on one floor of a building
floor show a show presenting singers, dancers, etc. in a restaurant, nightclub, etc.
☆**floor-through** (flôr′thro͞o′) ***n.*** an apartment that takes up the entire floor of a building
☆**floor·walk·er** (flôr′wôk′ər) ***n.*** a person employed by a department store to direct customers, supervise sales, etc.: now usually **floor** (or **sales**) **manager**
☆**floo·zy** or **floo·zie** (flo͞o′zē) ***n., pl.*** **-zies** ⟦< FLOSSY⟧ [Slang] a disreputable woman or girl, esp. one who is promiscuous or a prostitute: also sp. **floo′sy** or **floo′sie**, *pl.* **-sies**
flop (fläp) ***vt.*** **flopped**, **flop′ping** ⟦echoic var. of FLAP⟧ **1** to flap, strike, throw, or cause to drop noisily and clumsily **2** *Photoengraving* to turn (a film negative) face down before exposure to a metal plate, in order to create a desired mirror image —***vi.*** **1** to move or flap around loosely or clumsily, usually with a thud or thuds **2** to fall or drop in this way [to *flop* into a chair] ☆**3** to make a sudden change **4** [Informal] to be a failure ☆**5** [Slang] to sleep [the guest *flopped* on the sofa all night] —***n.*** **1** the act or sound of flopping ☆**2** [Informal] a failure ☆**3** [Slang] a place to sleep **4** [Slang] dung or a piece of dung [cow *flop*] —***adv.*** with a flop —**flop′per** ***n.***
☆**flop·house** (fläp′hous′) ***n.*** [Informal] a very cheap hotel frequented chiefly by indigents
flop·py (fläp′ē) ***adj.*** **-pi·er**, **-pi·est** [Informal] flopping or inclined to flop; soft and flexible —***n.*** *short for* FLOPPY DISK —**flop′pi·ly** ***adv.*** —**flop′pi·ness** ***n.***
floppy disk ⟦in contrast to a HARD DISK, which is rigid⟧ a thin, portable, plastic disk for storing data files, designed esp. for use with smaller computers
flops (fläps) ***n., pl.*** **flops** ⟦*fl(oating-point) o(perations) p(er) s(econd)*⟧ a unit for measuring the number of floating-point operations that a computer can perform in a second: chiefly in comb. [*megaflops, gigaflops*]
☆**flop sweat** ⟦see FLOP (***vi.*** 4, ***n.*** 2)⟧ [Slang] profuse nervous sweating by a comedian, actor, etc. while on stage in response to an apparently failing performance
flo·ra (flôr′ə, flō′rə) ***n.*** ⟦L < *flos*, FLOWER: adopted by LINNAEUS (1745) as term for the plants of a region⟧ **1** [**F-**] a feminine name **2** [**F-**] *Rom. Myth.* the goddess of flowers **3** *a) pl.* **-ras** or **-rae** (-ē) the plants of a specified region or time [the *flora* of Africa] *b)* a descriptive, systematic list of such plants
flo·ral (flôr′əl, flō′rəl) ***adj.*** ⟦L *floralis*, of the goddess Flora: see prec.⟧ of, made of, or like flowers —***n.*** **1** *a)* a pattern or design incorporating representations of flowers *b)* a fabric, rug, etc. with such a pattern or design **2** a perfume with a floral aroma —**flo′ral·ly** ***adv.***
floral envelope PERIANTH
Flor·ence[1] (flôr′əns, flär′-) ***n.*** ⟦Fr < L *Florentia*, lit., a blooming < *florens*, prp. of *florere*, to bloom < *flos*: see BLOOM[1]⟧ a feminine name: dim. *Flo, Flossie*; equiv. Ger. *Florenz*, It. *Fiorenza*, Sp. *Florencia*
Flor·ence[2] (flôr′əns, flär′-) ⟦ult. < L *Florentia*: see prec.⟧ commune in Tuscany, central Italy, on the Arno River: It. name FIRENZE
Florence flask ⟦after prec.: so named because similar in shape to certain bottles used in Italy to hold wine or olive oil⟧ a spherical glass flask with a long neck, used in laboratories to heat or mix chemicals
Flor·en·tine (-ən tēn′, -tīn′) ***adj.*** **1** of Florence, Italy, or its people or culture **2** [*often* **f-**] designating a metal finish, as for jewelry, with finely incised lines that impart a dull luster **3** [*also* **f-**] prepared or served with cooked spinach, and, often, covered with a light cheese sauce [chicken *Florentine*] —***n.*** a person born or living in Florence, Italy
Flo·res (flō′rēz, flôr′is) **1** island of Indonesia, west of Timor & south of Sulawesi: 5,500 sq mi (14,245 sq km) **2** westernmost island of the Azores: 55 sq mi (142 sq km)
flo·res·cence (flō res′əns, flô-, flə-) ***n.*** ⟦< L *florescens*, prp. of *florescere*, to begin to bloom, inceptive of *florere*, to bloom < *flos*: see BLOOM[1]⟧ **1** the act, condition, or period of blooming **2** a period of success or achievement —**flo·res′cent** (-ənt) ***adj.***
Flores Sea part of the Pacific, between the islands of Sulawesi & Flores in Indonesia
flo·ret (flôr′it, flō′rit) ***n.*** ⟦ME *flourette* < OFr *florete*, dim. of *flor*, FLOWER⟧ **1** a small flower **2** any of the individual flowers making up the head of a plant of the composite family **3** the flowering unit of a grass spikelet, consisting of the flower and its two enveloping bracts
Flo·rey (flôr′ē), Sir **Howard Walter** 1898-1968; Brit. pathologist, born in Australia: developed penicillin together with Sir Alexander Fleming
Flo·ri·a·nó·po·lis (flôr′ē ə näp′ə lis) city on an island just off the SE coast of Brazil: capital of Santa Catarina state
flo·ri·at·ed (flôr′ē āt′id, flō′rē-) ***adj.*** having floral decorations —**flo′ri·a′tion** ***n.***
flo·ri·bun·da (flôr′i bun′də, flō′ri-) ***n.*** ⟦ModL, fem. of **floribundus*, abounding in blossoms < L *flos*, FLOWER + *-bundus* (as in *moribundus*, MORIBUND), taken to mean "producing": sense infl. by ABUNDANT⟧ any of a group of rose varieties created by crossing polyantha and hybrid tea roses and characterized by clusters of small to medium-sized flowers produced in profusion
flo·ri·cul·ture (flôr′i kul′chər, flō′ri-) ***n.*** ⟦< L *flos* (gen. *floris*): see BLOOM[1] & CULTURE⟧ the cultivation of flowers, esp. ones to be cut and sold —**flo′ri·cul′tur·al** ***adj.*** —**flo′ri·cul′tur·ist** ***n.***
flor·id (flôr′id, flär′-) ***adj.*** ⟦L *floridus*, flowery < *flos*, a FLOWER⟧ **1** flushed with red or pink; rosy; ruddy: said of the complexion **2** highly decorated; gaudy; showy; ornate [a *florid* musical passage] **3** [Obs.] decorated with flowers; flowery —**flo·rid·i·ty** (flō rid′ə tē, flô-, flə-) ***n.***, **flor′id·ness** —**flor′id·ly** ***adv.***
Flor·i·da (flôr′ə də, flär′-) ⟦Sp < L, lit., abounding in flowers < *flos* (gen. *floris*): see BLOOM[1]: so named by PONCE DE LEÓN⟧ **1** Southern state of the SE U.S., mostly on a peninsula between the Atlantic & the Gulf of Mexico: admitted 1845; 53,927 sq mi (139,670 sq km); cap. Tallahassee: abbrev. *FL* or *Fla* **2 Straits of** strait between the S tip of Fla. & Cuba on the south & the Bahamas on the southeast: it connects the Atlantic & the Gulf of Mexico: also called **Florida Strait**
Florida Keys chain of small islands extending southwest from the S tip of Fla.
Flo·rid·i·an (flô rid′ē ən) ***adj.*** of Florida: usually used in the predicate —***n.*** a person born or living in Florida Also **Flor·i·dan** (flôr′ə dən)
flo·rif·er·ous (flō rif′ər əs, flô-, flə-) ***adj.*** ⟦L *florifer* (< *flos*, a FLOWER + *ferre*, BEAR[1]) + -OUS⟧ bearing flowers; blooming abundantly
☆**flor·i·gen** (flôr′ə jən, -jen′) ***n.*** ⟦< L *flos* (gen. *floris*), FLOWER + -GEN: so named at California Institute of Technology⟧ a plant hormone thought to stimulate the flowering of plants
flor·i·le·gi·um (flôr′ə lē′jē əm, flō′rə-) ***n.*** ⟦ModL < L *florilegus*, picking flowers < *flos, flori-*, FLOWER + *legere*, to gather, collect (see LEGAL): parallel to formation, in Gr, of ANTHOLOGY⟧ a compilation of choice or representative selections, as from an author's writings; anthology
flor·in (flôr′in) ***n.*** ⟦ME < OFr < It *fiorino* < *fiore*, a flower < L *flos* (gen. *floris*), FLOWER: from the figure of a lily stamped on the original coins⟧ **1** a gold coin of medieval Florence, issued in 1252 **2** a British coin originally equal to two shillings: coinage discontinued in 1971 **3** any of various European or South African silver or gold coins
Flo·ri·o (flôr′ē ō′), **John** 1553?-1625; Eng. writer & lexicographer: translator of Montaigne
flo·rist (flôr′ist, flär′-; flō′rist) ***n.*** ⟦< L *flos* (gen. *floris*): see BLOOM[1] & -IST[1]⟧ a person who cultivates or sells flowers —**flo′ris·try** (-is trē) ***n.***
flo·ris·tic (flō ris′tik, flô-, flə-) ***adj.*** ⟦FLOR(A) + -ISTIC⟧ of or having to do with flowers or floristics —**flo·ris′ti·cal·ly** ***adv.***
flo·ris·tics (-tiks) ***n.*** ⟦< prec. + -ICS⟧ the branch of botany dealing with the kinds and number of plant species in particular areas and their distribution
-flo·rous (flə rəs) ⟦< LL *-florus* < L *flos* (gen. *floris*): see BLOOM[1]⟧ *combining form* having a (specified) number or kind of flowers [*triflorous, tubuliflorous*]
floss (flôs, fläs) ***n.*** ⟦earlier also *flosh* < Fr *floche*, downy, woolly (in *soie floche*, floss silk), ult. < L *floccus*: see FLOCCUS⟧ **1** the rough silk covering a silkworm's cocoon **2** the short, downy waste fibers of silk **3** a soft, loosely twisted thread or yarn, as of silk (**floss silk**) or cotton, used in embroidery: in full **embroidery floss** **4** a soft, silky substance resembling floss, as in milkweed pods **5** DENTAL FLOSS — ***vt., vi.*** to clean (the teeth) with dental floss
floss·y (flôs′ē, fläs′ē) ***adj.*** **floss′i·er**, **floss′i·est** **1** of or like floss; downy; light; fluffy ☆**2** [Slang] stylish in a showy way
flo·tage (flōt′ij) ***n.*** ⟦< FLOAT, *v.* + -AGE, after OFr⟧ **1** the act, condition, or power of floating **2** anything that floats; esp., floating debris; flotsam
flo·ta·tion (flō tā′shən) ***n.*** ⟦earlier *floatation*, respelled as if < Fr *flottaison*⟧ **1** the act or condition of floating; specif., the act of beginning or financing a business, etc., as by selling an entire issue of bonds, securities, etc. **2** the capacity to stay on the surface of soft material, as sand or snow: said of a tire on a motor vehicle **3** *Mining* a method of ore separation in which finely powdered ore is introduced into a bubbling solution to which oils are added: certain minerals float on the surface, and others sink
flo·til·la (flō til′ə) ***n.*** ⟦Sp, dim. of *flota*, a fleet < OFr *flote* < ON *floti* < Gmc **flutan*: for IE base see FLOW⟧ **1** a small fleet **2** a fleet of boats or small ships ☆**3** *U.S. Navy* a unit consisting of two or more squadrons of destroyers or smaller vessels
Flo·tow (flō′tō), Baron **Frie·drich von** (frē′driH fôn) 1812-83; Ger. operatic composer
flot·sam (flät′səm) ***n.*** ⟦Anglo-Fr *floteson* < OFr *flotaison*, a floating < *floter*, to float < MDu *vloten* (or OE *flotian*), to FLOAT⟧ **1** the wreckage of a ship or its cargo floating at sea **2** odds and ends **3** unemployed people who drift from place to place The term **flotsam and jetsam**, which combines the marine senses of the two words, is also used for senses 2 & 3 of FLOTSAM

flounce[1] (flouns) *vi.* **flounced, flounc′ing** ⟦Early ModE, orig., to dive: < ? Scand, as in Swed dial. *flunsa*, to dive, dip; ? infl. by BOUNCE⟧ **1** to move with quick, flinging motions of the body, as in anger **2** to twist or turn abruptly; jerk —*n.* the act of flouncing

flounce[2] (flouns) *n.* ⟦earlier *frounce* < ME < OFr *fronce* < *froncir*, to wrinkle < Frank **hrunkja*, wrinkle, akin to Ger *runzel*⟧ a piece of cloth, often gathered or pleated, sewn on by its upper edge to a skirt, sleeve, etc.; wide, ornamental ruffle —*vt.* **flounced, flounc′ing** to trim with a flounce or flounces —**flounc′y** *adj.*

flounc·ing (floun′siŋ) *n.* **1** material for making flounces **2** a flounce, or flounces collectively

floun·der[1] (floun′dər) *vi.* ⟦earlier *flunder*, ? blend of BLUNDER + FOUNDER[1]⟧ **1** to struggle awkwardly to move, as in deep mud or snow; plunge about in a stumbling manner **2** to speak or act in an awkward, confused manner, with hesitation and frequent mistakes —*n.* the act of floundering

floun·der[2] (floun′dər) *n., pl.* **-der** or **-ders** ⟦ME < Scand as in Swed *flundra*, akin to Ger *flunder* < IE base **plāt-*, FLAT[1]⟧ any of two families (Bothidae and Pleuronectidae) of flatfishes, including halibut, plaice, and turbot

flour (flour) *n.* ⟦ME (see FLOWER): a fig. use as "best, prime" in "flour of wheat," after Fr *fleur de farine*, lit., flower of meal⟧ **1** a fine, powdery substance, or meal, produced by grinding and sifting grain, esp. wheat, or any of various edible roots, nuts, etc. **2** any finely powdered substance —*vt.* **1** to put flour in or on **2** to make into flour

flour·ish (flur′ish) *vi.* ⟦ME *florishen* < extended stem of OFr *florir*, to blossom < LL **florire* < L *florere* < *flos*, FLOWER⟧ **1** [Obs.] to blossom **2** to grow vigorously; succeed; thrive; prosper **3** to be at the peak of development, activity, influence, production, etc.; be in one's prime **4** to make showy, wavy motions, as of the arms **5** [Now Rare] *a)* to write in an ornamental style *b)* to perform a fanfare, as of trumpets —*vt.* **1** to ornament with something flowery or fanciful **2** ⟦first so used by John WYCLIFFE⟧ to wave (a sword, arm, hat, etc.) in the air; brandish —*n.* **1** [Rare] a thriving state; success; prosperity **2** anything done in a showy way, as a sweeping movement of the limbs or body **3** a waving in the air; brandishing **4** a decorative or curved line or lines in handwriting **5** an ornate musical passage; fanfare **6** [Obs.] a blooming or a bloom —**flour′ish·er** *n.* —**flour′ish·ing** *adj.*

flour·y (flour′ē) *adj.* **1** of flour **2** like flour in color or texture; powdery or white **3** covered with flour

flout (flout) *vt.* ⟦prob. special use of ME *flouten*, to play the flute, hence, whistle (at)⟧ **1** to mock or scoff at; show scorn or contempt for **2** to openly disregard, as by rejecting, defying, or ignoring —*vi.* to be scornful; show contempt; jeer; scoff —*n.* a scornful or contemptuous action or speech; mockery; scoffing; insult —**flout′er** *n.* —**flout′ing·ly** *adv.*

flow (flō) *vi.* ⟦ME *flouen* < OE *flowan*, akin to ON *floa*, to flood, OHG *flouwen*, to wash < IE base **pleu-*, to run, flow, fly > FLOOD, FLY[1], FLEE, FLEET[2], FLOAT, L *pluere*, to rain⟧ **1** to move as a liquid does; move in a stream, like water **2** to move in a way suggestive of a liquid; stream *[crowds flowed past]* **3** *a)* to move gently, smoothly, and easily; glide *b)* to have smooth and pleasing continuity *[the lines in the painting flowed]* **4** to stream forth; pour out **5** to be derived; spring; proceed **6** to fall in waves; hang loose *[her long hair flowed down her back]* **7** to come in; rise, as the tide **8** to be overflowing or plentiful **9** *Geol.* to change in shape under pressure without breaking or splitting, as ice in a glacier or rocks deep in the earth —*vt.* **1** to overflow; flood **2** [Archaic] to cause to flow —*n.* **1** the act or manner of flowing **2** the rate of flowing **3** anything that flows; stream or current **4** a continuous production *[a flow of ideas]* **5** the rising of the tide —*SYN.* RISE —**go with the flow** [Informal] to conform to or accept, rather than resist, a trend, condition, development, etc. —**flow′ing·ly** *adv.*

flow·age (flō′ij) ☆*n.* **1** a flowing, overflowing, or flooding **2** a flooded condition **3** what flows or overflows **4** *Geol.* a gradual change in shape of rocks that occurs without breakage

☆**flow·chart** (-chärt′) *n.* a diagram, often using geometric symbols, showing steps in a sequence of operations, as in manufacturing or in a computer program

flow·er (flou′ər) *n.* ⟦ME *flowre, flour*, OFr *flor, flour* (Fr *fleur*) < L *flos* (gen. *floris*), a flower: see BLOOM[1]⟧ **1** *a)* the seed-producing structure of an angiosperm, consisting of a shortened stem usually bearing four layers of organs, with the leaflike sepals, colorful petals, and pollen-bearing stamens unfolding around the pistils *b)* a blossom; bloom *c)* the reproductive structure of any plant **2** a plant cultivated for its blossoms; flowering plant **3** the best or finest part or example *[the flower of a country's youth]* **4** the best period of a person or thing; time of flourishing **5** something decorative; esp., a figure of speech **6** [*pl.*] *Chem.* a substance in powder form, made from condensed vapors *[flowers of sulfur]* —*vi.* **1** to produce blossoms; bloom **2** to reach the best or most vigorous stage *[his genius flowered early]* —*vt.* to decorate with flowers or floral patterns —**in flower** in a state of flowering —**flow′er·less** *adj.* —**flow′er·like′** *adj.*

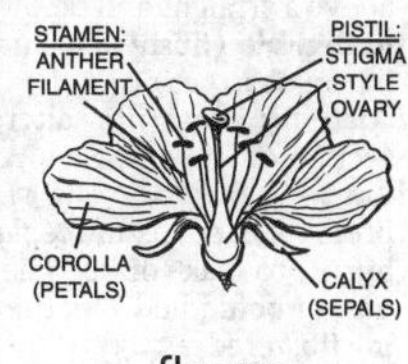

flower

flow·er·age (-ij) *n.* **1** flowers collectively **2** the act or condition of flowering

flower bud a bud from which only flowers develop: cf. LEAF BUD, MIXED BUD

☆**flower child** [Slang] HIPPIE

flow·ered (flou′ərd) *adj.* **1** bearing or containing flowers **2** decorated with a design like flowers

flow·er·et (flou′ər it) *n.* ⟦ME *flourette*, dim. of *flour*, FLOWER⟧ FLORET

flower girl **1** a girl or woman who sells flowers in the streets **2** a young girl who carries flowers and attends the bride at a wedding

flower head *Bot.* HEAD (*n.* 17*a*)

flow·er·ing (flou′ər iŋ) *adj.* **1** having flowers; in bloom **2** bearing showy or profuse flowers

flowering crab any of several species and varieties of crab apple trees with small fruits and abundant spring flowers ranging from white to reddish purple

flowering dogwood a small dogwood tree (*Cornus florida*) of the E U.S., with groups of small flowers surrounded by four large white or pink, petal-like bracts

flowering quince JAPANESE QUINCE

☆**flower-of-an-hour** (-əv ən our′) *n.* a weedlike annual plant (*Hibiscus trionum*) of the mallow family, having yellow or white flowers with dark centers

flow·er·pot (flou′ər pät′) *n.* a container made of porous clay or of plastic, in which to grow plants

flow·er·y (flou′ər ē) *adj.* **-er·i·er, -er·i·est** **1** covered or decorated with flowers **2** of or like flowers **3** full of figurative and ornate expressions and fine words: said of language, style, etc. —*SYN.* BOMBASTIC —**flow′er·i·ly** *adv.* —**flow′er·i·ness** *n.*

flown[1] (flōn) *vi., vt. pp. of* FLY[1]: sometimes used to form hyphenated adjectives *[far-flown, high-flown]*

flown[2] (flōn) *adj.* ⟦obs. pp. of FLOW⟧ filled too full

flow sheet FLOWCHART

flow·stone (flō′stōn′) *n.* any mineral deposit, esp. of calcium carbonate, formed in a cave by flowing water: cf. DRIPSTONE, TRAVERTINE

Floyd (floid) *n.* ⟦var. of LLOYD: *Fl-* for the fricative represented by Welsh *Ll-*⟧ a masculine name

fl oz *abbrev.* fluid ounce(s)

FLSA *abbrev.* Fair Labor Standards Act

flt *abbrev.* flight

flu (flo͞o) *n.* **1** *short for* INFLUENZA **2** popularly, any of various respiratory or intestinal infections caused by a virus Often with *the* —**flu′-like′** *adj.*

☆**flub** (flub) [Informal] *vt., vi.* **flubbed, flub′bing** ⟦< ? FL(OP) + (D)UB⟧ to make a botch of (a job, chance, stroke, etc.); bungle —*n.* a mistake or blunder

fluc·tu·ate (fluk′cho͞o āt′) *vi.* **-at′ed, -at′ing** ⟦< L *fluctuatus*, pp. of *fluctuare* < *fluctus*, a flowing, wave < pp. stem of *fluere*, to flow < IE **bhleu-*, to swell up, flow (> BLUSTER) < base **bhel-*, to swell up > BALL[1]⟧ **1** to move back and forth or up and down; rise and fall; undulate, as waves **2** to be continually changing or varying in an irregular way *[prices fluctuated wildly]* —*vt.* to cause to fluctuate —*SYN.* SWING —**fluc′tu·ant** *adj.* —**fluc′tu·a′tion** *n.*

flue[1] (flo͞o) *n.* ⟦< ? OFr *fluie*, a flowing, stream⟧ **1** a tube, pipe, or shaft for the passage of smoke, hot air, exhaust fumes, etc., esp. in a chimney **2** ⟦ME, mouthpiece of a hunting horn⟧ *a)* a flue pipe in an organ *b)* the opening or passage for air in such a flue pipe

flue[2] (flo͞o) *n.* ⟦altered < ? FLUKE[2]⟧ a barbed point; fluke

flue[3] (flo͞o) *n.* ⟦< Fl *vluwe* < Fr *velu*, woolly < VL *villutus*, shaggy < L *villus*, shaggy hair⟧ a loose, downy mass; fluff

flue[4] (flo͞o) *n.* ⟦ME *flew* < MDu *vluwe*⟧ a kind of fishing net

☆**flue-cured** (flo͞o′kyoord′) *adj.* cured or dried by hot air passed through flues: said of tobacco

flue·gel·horn or **flü·gel·horn** (flo͞o′gəl hôrn′) *n.* ⟦Ger < *flügel*, wing < *horn*, horn: because of shape⟧ a brass instrument like the cornet in design and pitch but with a wider bore, larger bell, and mellower tone

flu·en·cy (flo͞o′ən sē) *n.* ⟦LL *fluentia* < L *fluens*: see fol.⟧ the quality or condition of being fluent, esp. in speech or writing

flu·ent (flo͞o′ənt) *adj.* ⟦L *fluens* (gen. *fluentis*), prp. of *fluere*, to flow: see FLUCTUATE⟧ **1** flowing or moving smoothly and easily *[fluent verse]* **2** able to write or speak easily, smoothly, and expressively *[fluent in French]* —**flu′ent·ly** *adv.*

flue pipe an organ pipe in which the tone is produced by a current of air striking the lip of the mouth, or opening, in the pipe

fluff (fluf) *n.* ⟦? blend of FLUE[3] + PUFF⟧ **1** soft, light down **2** a loose, soft, downy mass of hair, feathers, cotton, dust, etc. **3** any light or trivial matter or talk **4** *Radio, Theater, TV* an error in speaking or reading a line —*vt.* **1** to shake or pat until loose, feathery, and fluffy **2** *Radio, Theater, TV* to make an error in speaking or reading (a word, one's lines, etc.) **3** to make a botch of; flub —*vi.* **1** to become fluffy **2** to make a mistake —**bit** (or **piece**) **of fluff** [Slang] a girl or young woman: now often regarded as patronizing

fluff·y (fluf′ē) *adj.* **fluff′i·er, fluff′i·est** **1** soft and light like fluff; feathery **2** covered with fluff **3** frothy; foamy —**fluff′i·ness** *n.*

flu·id (flo͞o′id) *adj.* ⟦ME < L *fluidus* < *fluere*, to flow: see FLUCTUATE⟧ **1** that can flow; not solid; able to move and change shape without separating when under pressure **2** of a fluid or fluids **3** like a fluid; that can change rapidly or easily; not settled or fixed *[fluid plans]* **4** marked by or using graceful movements **5** available for investment *[fluid capital]* **6** available as cash *[fluid assets]* —*n.* **1** any substance that can flow; a gas or, esp., a liquid **2** a liquid in the body —**flu·id·ic** (flo͞o id′ik) *adj.* —**flu·id′i·ty** *n.*, **flu′id·ness** —**flu′id·ly** *adv.*

fluid dram a unit of liquid measure, equal to ⅛ fluid ounce or 60 minims (3.6967 milliliters): abbrev. *fl dr*

☆**flu·id·ex·tract** (-ek′strakt′) ***n.*** *Pharmacy* a solution containing dissolved vegetable drugs, alcohol, and water, of such strength that one cm^3 is equal to one gram of the dried drug: also written **fluid extract**

flu·id·ics (flo͞o id′iks) ***n.*** ⟦FLUID + -ICS⟧ the science or technology dealing with the control of a flow of air or some other fluid, used like an electronic circuit to perform functions of sensing, control, computing, etc.

flu·id·ize (flo͞o′ə dīz′) ***vt.*** **-ized′**, **-iz′ing** **1** to make fluid **2** to give fluid properties to (a solid), as by pulverizing

flu·id·ized-bed (flo͞o′ə dīzd′bed′) ***adj.*** designating, of, or having to do with a process for burning coal, garbage, etc. to produce electricity, using a rising stream of hot air to support, churn, and burn a fluidlike bed of fuel particles mixed with sand, ash, etc.

fluid mechanics the study of the pressures, velocities, etc. of liquids and gases when they are in motion or at rest

fluid ounce a unit of liquid measure, equal to ¼ gill or 1/16 pint or 8 fluid drams (29.5734 milliliters): the British and Canadian imperial fluid ounce equals 1/20 of an imperial pint or 28.4122 milliliters: abbrev. *fl oz*

flu·ish (flo͞o′ish) ***adj.*** having flulike symptoms

fluke[1] (flo͞ok) ***n.*** ⟦ME *floke* < OE *floc*, akin to ON *floki* < IE base **plāg-*, broad, flat > FLAG[2], Ger *flach*, flat, level⟧ **1** any of various flatfishes, esp. a genus (*Paralichthys*) of flounders **2** TREMATODE

fluke[2] (flo͞ok) ***n.*** ⟦prob. < prec., with reference to shape⟧ **1** a pointed part of an anchor, designed to catch in the ground ☆**2** a barb or barbed head of an arrow, harpoon, etc. **3** either of the two lobes of a whale's tail

fluke[3] (flo͞ok) ***n.*** ⟦< ?⟧ **1** [Old Slang] an accidentally good or lucky stroke in billiards, pool, etc. **2** [Informal] a result, esp. a successful one, brought about by accident; stroke of luck —***vt.*** **fluked**, **fluk′ing** [Informal] to hit or get by a fluke

fluk·y (flo͞o′kē) ***adj.*** **fluk′i·er**, **fluk′i·est** ⟦< prec.⟧ [Informal] **1** resulting from chance rather than skill or design; lucky **2** constantly changing; uncertain; fitful *[a fluky breeze]* —**fluk′i·ness** ***n.***

flume (flo͞om) ***n.*** ⟦ME *flum*, river, stream < OFr < L *flumen* < *fluere*, to flow: see FLUCTUATE⟧ ☆**1** an artificial channel, usually an inclined chute or trough, for carrying water to furnish power, transport logs down a mountainside, etc. ☆**2** a narrow gorge or ravine with a stream running through it —☆***vt.*** **flumed**, **flum′ing** to send (logs, water, etc.) down or through a flume

flum·mer·y (flum′ər ē) ***n.***, *pl.* **-mer·ies** ⟦Welsh *llymru*, soured oatmeal < *llymus*, of a sharp quality⟧ **1** any soft, easily eaten food; esp., *a)* [Historical] thick, boiled oatmeal or flour *b)* a soft custard or blancmange **2** meaningless flattery or silly talk

flum·mox (flum′əks) ***vt.*** ⟦< ?⟧ [Old Slang] to confuse; perplex

flump (flump) ***vt.***, ***vi.*** ⟦prob. echoic⟧ to drop or move heavily and noisily —***n.*** the act or sound of flumping

flung (fluŋ) ***vt.***, ***vi.*** *pt. & pp. of* FLING

☆**flunk** (fluŋk) ***vt.*** ⟦19th-c. college slang < ? FUNK[1] or echoic⟧ [Informal] **1** to fail in (schoolwork) *[to flunk a science examination]* **2** to give a mark of *failure* to (a student) —***vi.*** [Informal] **1** to fail, esp. in schoolwork **2** to give up; retreat —***n.*** [Old Informal] **1** a failure **2** a mark or grade of *failure* —**flunk out** [Informal] to send or be sent away from school or college because of unsatisfactory work

flunk·y (fluŋ′kē) ***n.***, *pl.* **flunk′ies** ⟦orig. Scot < ? Fr *flanquer*, to flank, be at the side of, as to render aid < OFr *flanc*, FLANK⟧ **1** a liveried manservant: term of contempt **2** *a)* a person who obeys superiors in a servile, cringing way ☆*b)* a person with very minor or menial tasks Also sp. **flunk′ey**, *pl.* **-eys** —**flunk′y·ism′** ***n.***

fluo- (flō, flo͝o) *combining form* FLUORO-

flu·or (flo͞o′ôr) ***n.*** ⟦ModL < L, flux < *fluere*, to flow (see FLUCTUATE): transl. of Ger *fluss*, orig. applied to minerals used as smelting fluxes, but later limited to those containing fluorine⟧ [Chiefly Brit.] FLUORITE

fluor- (flôr, flo͝or) *combining form* FLUORO-: used before a vowel

fluo·resce (flō res′, flo͝o-) ***vi.*** **-resced′**, **-resc′ing** ⟦back-form. < FLUORESCENCE⟧ to produce, show, or undergo fluorescence; be or become fluorescent

fluo·res·ce·in (flo͝o res′ē in) ***n.*** ⟦< prec. + -IN[1]: from its bright fluorescence in solution⟧ a yellowish-red, crystalline compound, $C_{20}H_{12}O_5$, made synthetically from resorcinol and phthalic anhydride: a dilute alkaline solution appears green by reflected light and red by transmitted light: used as a textile dye, a liquid coloring, and, in medicine, an intravenous diagnostic aid

fluo·res·cence (flo͝o res′əns) ***n.*** ⟦< FLUOR(SPAR) + -ESCENCE⟧ **1** the property of a substance, such as fluorite, of producing light while it is being acted upon by ultraviolet rays, X-rays, or other forms of radiant energy **2** the production of such light **3** light so produced

fluo·res·cent (flo͝o res′ənt) ***adj.*** **1** producing light when acted upon by radiant energy **2** of or having to do with fluorescent light or lighting **3** glowing and vivid *[fluorescent colors]*

☆**fluorescent lamp** (*or* **tube**) a glass tube coated on the inside with a fluorescent substance that gives off a bright light (**fluorescent light**) when a vapor, usually mercury vapor, in the tube is acted upon by a stream of electrons from the cathode

☆**fluo·ri·date** (flôr′ə dāt′, flo͝or′-) ***vt.*** **-dat′ed**, **-dat′ing** to add fluorides to (a supply of drinking water) in order to reduce the incidence of caries in the teeth —**fluo′ri·da′tion** (-dā′shən) ***n.***

fluo·ride (flôr′īd′, flo͝or′-) ***n.*** **1** a compound of fluorine and another element, radical, etc. **2** such a compound put in drinking water or toothpaste to prevent tooth decay

☆**fluo·ri·nate** (flôr′ə nāt′, flo͝or′-) ***vt.*** **-nat′ed**, **-nat′ing** **1** to introduce fluorine into or cause to combine with fluorine **2** FLUORIDATE —**fluo′ri·na′tion** (-nā′shən) ***n.***

fluo·rine (flôr′ēn′, flo͝or′-) ***n.*** ⟦FLUOR + -INE[3]⟧ a corrosive, toxic, greenish-yellow, gaseous chemical element, one of the halogens and the most reactive nonmetallic element, forming fluorides with almost all known elements: symbol, F; at. no. 9: see the periodic table of elements in the Reference Supplement

fluo·rite (flôr′īt′, flo͝or′-) ***n.*** ⟦fol. + -ITE[1]⟧ a crystalline mineral, CaF_2, with perfect cleavage, used as a flux, in glassmaking, etc. and as the principal source of fluorine; calcium fluoride: see MOHS SCALE

fluo·ro- (flôr′ō-, flo͝or′ō; -ə) *combining form* **1** fluorine *[fluorosis]* **2** fluorescence *[fluoroscope]*

☆**fluo·ro·car·bon** (flôr′ə kär′bən, flo͝or′-) ***n.*** any of various nonreactive halocarbons containing carbon, fluorine, and, in some cases, hydrogen: used as aerosols, lubricants, electrical insulators, etc.

fluo·ro·chrome (flôr′ə krōm′, flo͝or′-) ***n.*** any of a number of fluorescent substances used to stain biological specimens for study

fluo·rog·ra·phy (flō räg′rə fē, flo͝o-) ***n.*** PHOTOFLUOROGRAPHY

☆**fluo·rom·e·ter** (flō räm′ət ər, flo͝o-) ***n.*** an instrument for measuring the wavelength and intensity of fluorescence —**fluo·ro·met·ric** (flôr′ə me′trik, flo͝or-) ***adj.*** —**fluo·rom′e·try** (-ə trē) ***n.***

☆**fluo·ro·scope** (flôr′ə skōp′, flo͝or′-) ***n.*** ⟦FLUORO- + -SCOPE⟧ a machine that uses X-rays to cast shadows of the internal structure of people, animals, raw material, welds, etc. on a fluorescent screen: the shadows vary in intensity according to the density of the object or part —***vt.*** **-scoped′**, **-scop′ing** to examine with a fluoroscope —**fluo′ro·scop′ic** (-skäp′ik) ***adj.*** —**fluo′ro·scop′i·cal·ly** ***adv.***

☆**fluo·ros·co·py** (flō räs′kə pē, flo͝o-) ***n.*** examination by means of a fluoroscope —**fluo·ros′co·pist** ***n.***

fluo·ro·sis (flō rō′sis, flo͝o-) ***n.***, *pl.* **-ses′** (-sēz′) ⟦ModL: see FLUOR(O)- & -OSIS⟧ a disorder resulting from the absorption of too much fluorine, usually characterized by mottled or stained teeth

fluor·spar (flo͝or′spär′, flôr′-, flo͞o′ər-) ***n.*** FLUORITE

flu·ox·e·tine (flo͞o äk′sə tēn′, -tin) ***n.*** a white, crystalline drug, $C_{17}H_{18}F_3NO \cdot HCl$, used to treat depression, eating disorders, obsessive-complusive neurosis, etc.: in full **fluoxetine hydrochloride**

flur·ry (flur′ē) ***n.***, *pl.* **-ries** ⟦< obs. *flurr*, to scatter (? echoic), prob. after HURRY⟧ ☆**1** a sudden, brief rush of wind; gust ☆**2** a gust of rain or snow **3** a sudden confusion or commotion ☆**4** a brief fluctuation in stock market prices or increase in trading —***vt.*** **-ried**, **-ry·ing** to confuse; agitate —***vi.*** to move in a quick, flustered way

flush[1] (flush) ***vi.*** ⟦complex of several words, with senses FLASH & ME *flusshen*, to fly up suddenly, blended with echoic elements; "flow" senses < ? or akin to OFr *fluir* (stem *fluiss-*), to flow⟧ **1** to flow and spread suddenly and rapidly **2** to become red in the face, as with embarrassment or anger; blush **3** to glow **4** to become cleaned, washed, or emptied out with a sudden flow of water, etc. **5** to use the flushing device in a toilet **6** to start up from cover: said of birds —***vt.*** **1** to make flow **2** to clean, wash, or empty out with a sudden flow of water, etc.; specif., *a)* to empty the contents of (a toilet) with a flow of water, etc. *b)* to empty (a toilet's contents) with a flow of water, etc. **3** to make blush or glow **4** to excite; animate; exhilarate: usually in the passive voice *[flushed with victory]* **5** to drive from cover or hiding **6** to make level or even —***n.*** **1** a sudden and rapid flow, as of water in washing out something; specif., the emptying and rinsing of a toilet bowl with a flow of water, etc. **2** a sudden, vigorous growth *[the first flush of youth]* **3** a sudden feeling of excitement or exhilaration **4** a blush; glow **5** a sudden feeling of great heat, as in a fever —***adj.*** **1** well supplied, esp. with money **2** abundant; plentiful **3** [Dial.] lavish; profuse **4** [Rare] full of vigor **5** [Rare] having a ruddy color; glowing **6** *a)* making an even or unbroken line or surface; being even or on the same line or plane *[a door flush with the walls]* *b)* even with a margin or edge **7** direct; full —***adv.*** **1** in an even manner; so as to be level or in alignment **2** directly; squarely *[it hit him flush in the face]*

flush[2] (flush) ***n.*** ⟦Fr *flux*: see FLUX⟧ **1** a hand of cards all of the same suit **2** *Poker* such a hand in which the cards are not in sequence: it ranks just above a straight and below a full house: cf. STRAIGHT FLUSH

flush·a·ble (flush′ə bəl) ***adj.*** able to be flushed down a toilet without causing an obstruction

Flush·ing (flush′iŋ) ⟦altered < Du *Vlissingen*, town in the Netherlands⟧ N section of Queens, New York City, on the East River

flus·ter (flus′tər) ***vt.***, ***vi.*** ⟦ME *flosteren*, prob. < Scand, as in Ice *flaustra*, to bustle, hurry⟧ to make or become confused, nervous, or befuddled —***n.*** the condition of being flustered

flute (flo͞ot) ***n.*** ⟦ME *floute* < OFr *fleüte*, *flaute* < Prov *fläut*, prob. < *flaujol* (OFr *flajeol*: see FLAGEOLET[1]) + *laüt*, LUTE[1]⟧ **1** *a)* a high-pitched wind instrument consisting of a long, slender tube, played by blowing across a hole near one end: by fingering the holes and keys along its length, the player can produce various tones *b)* any of various similar instruments, as the fipple flute **2** *a)* an ornamental groove or pleat in cloth, etc. *b)* *Archit.* a long, verti-

flute

cal, rounded groove in the shaft of a column **3** *a)* a flue pipe *b)* a flue organ stop with a flutelike tone **4** a tall, slender wineglass, used esp. for champagne —*vt.* **flut′ed, flut′ing 1** to sing, speak, whistle, etc. in a flutelike tone **2** to play on the flute **3** to make long, rounded grooves in (a column, etc.) —*vi.* **1** to play on the flute **2** to sing, speak, whistle, etc. in a flutelike tone —**flute′like′** *adj.*

flut·ed (flo͞ot′id) *adj.* **1** having a flutelike tone; fluty **2** having long, rounded grooves

flut·er (flo͞ot′ər) *n.* ⟦ME *floutour* < OFr *flauteur*⟧ **1** [Rare] a flutist **2** a person or tool that makes flutings

flut·ing (flo͞ot′iŋ) *n.* **1** a decoration consisting of long, rounded grooves, as in a column **2** such grooves or the act of making them **3** the act of playing the flute or singing, etc. in a flutelike tone

flut·ist (flo͞ot′ist) *n.* a person who plays the flute; flautist

flut·ter (flut′ər) *vi.* ⟦ME *floteren* < OE *flotorian*, freq. of *flotian* < base of *fleotan*: see FLEET[2]⟧ **1** to flap the wings rapidly, as in short flight or without flying at all **2** to wave or vibrate rapidly and irregularly *[*a flag *fluttering* in the wind*]* **3** to move with quick vibrations, flaps, etc. **4** to be in a state of tremulous excitement; tremble; quiver **5** to move restlessly; bustle —*vt.* **1** to cause to move in quick, irregular motions **2** to throw into a state of excitement, alarm, or confusion —*n.* **1** a fluttering movement; vibration **2** a state of excitement or confusion **3** a condition of the heart in which the contractions are very rapid but generally regular **4** a potentially destructive vibration of a part of an aircraft, as the wing, caused by aerodynamic forces **5** [Brit.] a small gamble or speculation **6** *a)* a rapid fluctuation in the amplitude of a reproduced sound (cf. WOW[2]) *b)* a flicker in the image on a television screen —**flut′ter·er** *n.* —**flut′ter·y** *adj.*

flutter kick *Swimming* a kick in which the legs are moved up and down in short, rapid, steady strokes

flut·y (flo͞ot′ē) *adj.* **flut′i·er, flut′i·est** flutelike in tone; soft, clear, and high-pitched

flu·vi·al (flo͞o′vē əl) *adj.* ⟦ME < L *fluvialis* < *fluvius*, a river < *fluere*, to flow: see FLUCTUATE⟧ of, found in, or produced by a river: also **flu′vi·a·tile** (-ə til)

flu·vi·o- (flo͞o′vē ō, -ə) ⟦< L *fluvius*: see prec.⟧ *combining form* **1** by the combined action of a river and *[fluvioglacial]* **2** of a river, stream, etc. *[fluviology]*

flux (fluks) *n.* ⟦ME < OFr < L *fluxus*, a flowing, flow < pp. of *fluere*, to flow: see FLUCTUATE⟧ **1** a flowing or flow **2** the rate of flow of water, as the tide or current, through a defined area **3** a continuous movement or continual change *[*fashion is always in a state of *flux]* **4** any excessive or unnatural discharge of fluid body matter, esp. from the bowels **5** *a)* a substance, as borax or rosin, used to help metals fuse together by preventing oxidation, as in soldering *b)* in metallurgy, a substance added to metals while they are in a furnace, to remove impurities, promote fusing, etc., as a nonmetallic material added to a furnace charge that has the ability to fuse with undesired matter and form a liquid slag that can run off more easily **6** *Physics* the rate of flow of energy, fluids, etc. across a surface —*vt.* **1** to make (a solid) melt **2** to fuse (metals) by melting —*vi.* [Archaic] to flow or stream out

flux density the FLUX (*n.* 6) through a unit of surface area

flux gate an instrument used to measure the force and direction of the earth's magnetic field

flux·ion (fluk′shən) *n.* ⟦Fr < VL *fluxio*, for L *fluctio*, a flowing < pp. of *fluere*, to flow: see FLUCTUATE⟧ **1** something that flows; esp., an abnormal flow of bodily fluids; discharge **2** [Archaic] *Math. a)* the rate of continuous change in variable quantities *b)* DERIVATIVE (sense 5) —**flux′ion·al** *adj.*, **flux′ion·ar′y**

fly[1] (flī) *vi.* **flew** or, for *vi.* 10, **flied, flown** or, for *vi.* 10, **flied, fly′ing** ⟦ME *flien, flegen* < OE *fleogan*, akin to MDu *vlegen*, Ger *fliegen* < IE **pleuk-* < base **pleu-*: see FLOW⟧ **1** to move through the air; specif., *a)* to move through the air by using wings, as a bird does *b)* to travel through the air in an aircraft or through space in a spacecraft *c)* to be propelled through the air **2** to operate an aircraft or spacecraft **3** to wave or float in the air, as a flag or kite does **4** to move swiftly *[*the door *flew* open*]* **5** to appear to pass swiftly *[*time *flies]* **6** to be used up swiftly: said of money, etc. **7** to run away; flee **8** [Informal] to be successful, acceptable, etc. *[*that explanation just won't *fly]* **9** to hunt with a hawk **10** *Baseball* to hit a fly —*vt.* **1** *a)* to cause to float in the air *[fly* a kite*]* *b)* to display (a flag) as from a pole **2** to operate (an aircraft or spacecraft) **3** *a)* to travel over in an aircraft *b)* to travel via (a particular airline, aircraft, etc.) **4** to carry or transport in an aircraft **5** to run away from; flee from; avoid **6** to use (a hawk) to hunt game **7** *Theater* to suspend (flats, lights, etc.) in the space above the stage —*n., pl.* **flies 1** [Rare] the act of flying; flight **2** ⟦from the idea of a thing, as a flag, attached at one edge⟧ *a)* a garment closure consisting of a zipper, buttons, etc. and typically concealed by a fold or flap of cloth *b)* such a closure in the front of a pair of men's or boys' trousers (in full **fly front**: also [Brit.] **flies**) *c)* such a fold or flap **3** *a)* a flap serving as the door of a tent *b)* a piece of fabric serving as an outer or second top on a tent **4** *a)* the length of an extended flag measured from the staff outward *b)* the outside edge of a flag **5** a regulating device, as for a clockwork mechanism, consisting of vanes radiating from a rotating shaft **6** *a)* FLYWHEEL *b)* FLYLEAF **7** [Brit.] a hackney carriage **8** *Baseball* a ball batted high in the air, esp. within the foul lines **9** *Football* a pass pattern in which the receiver runs straight up the field at full speed **10** [*pl.*] *Theater* the space behind and above the proscenium arch, containing overhead lights, raised flats, etc. —**fly at** to attack suddenly by or as by flying or springing toward —**fly into** to have a violent outburst of *[fly into* a rage*]* —**fly off** to go away quickly or suddenly; hurry off —☆**fly out** *pt. & pp.* **flied** *Baseball* to be put out by hitting a fly that is caught by a fielder —**let fly (at) 1** to shoot or throw (at) **2** to direct a verbal attack (at) —**on the fly 1** while in flight **2** [Informal] while in a hurry or while doing something else

fly[2] (flī) *n., pl.* **flies** ⟦ME *flie* < OE *fleoge* (akin to Ger *fliege*) < base *fleogan*: see prec.⟧ **1** *a)* any dipterous insect; esp., the housefly *b)* any of several four-winged insects from various orders, as the mayfly or caddis fly **2** a hook covered with feathers, colored silk, etc. to resemble an insect, used as a lure in fishing: a *wet fly* drifts below the surface of the water, and a *dry fly* floats on it **3** *Printing* a device on a flatbed press for removing and stacking the printed sheets —**fly in the ointment** anything, esp. a little thing, that reduces or destroys the value or usefulness of something else

fly[3] (flī) *adj.* **fli′er, fli′est** ⟦orig., thieves' slang < ? FLY[1]⟧ **1** [Slang, Chiefly Brit.] alert and knowing; sharp; quick **2** [Slang] fashionable, stylish, attractive, etc.

Fly (flī) river in S New Guinea, flowing through Papua New Guinea into the Coral Sea: *c.* 650 mi (1,046 km)

fly·a·ble (flī′ə bəl) *adj.* suitable or ready for flying *[flyable* weather, a *flyable* airplane*]*

fly agaric ⟦orig. used as a fly poison⟧ a poisonous mushroom (*Amanita muscaria*) usually having an orange or russet cap with white flakes and white gills: also **fly amanita**

fly ash airborne bits of unburnable ash, esp. as a factor in air pollution

fly·a·way (flī′ə wā′) *adj.* **1** *a)* loose and streaming, as if blown by the wind *b)* fine and unmanageable (said of human hair) **2** flighty **3** ready for flight

fly ball FLY[1] (*n.* 8)

fly·blow (flī′blō′) *n.* a blowfly's egg or larva — *vt., vi.* **-blew′, -blown′, -blow′ing 1** to deposit flyblows in (meat, etc.) **2** to contaminate; spoil; taint

fly·blown (flī′blōn′) *adj.* **1** full of flies' eggs or larvae; maggoty **2** contaminated; spoiled; tainted **3** [Informal] shabby, dingy, disreputable, etc.

fly book a booklike case to hold artificial fishing flies

☆**fly·boy** (flī′boi′) *n.* [Slang] an aviator, esp. in the Air Force

☆**fly·by** or **fly-by** (flī′bī′) *n., pl.* **-bys′** a flight past a designated point or place by an aircraft or spacecraft

fly-by-night (flī′bī nīt′) *adj.* not trustworthy; esp., financially irresponsible —*n.* a fly-by-night person; esp., a debtor who runs away to escape debts

☆**fly-by-wire** (flī′bī wīr′) *adj.* designating or of a control system for an airplane or spacecraft, in which the controls are actuated by electrical impulses, as from a computer

fly-cast (flī′kast′) *vt.* **-cast′, -cast′ing** to fish by casting artificial flies, using a lightweight, resilient rod

fly·catch·er (flī′kach′ər) *n.* **1** any of an Old World family (Muscicapidae) of small passerine birds that catch insects in flight **2** TYRANT FLYCATCHER

fly·er (flī′ər) *n.* **1** a person or thing that flies; specif., an aviator ☆**2** a bus, train, etc. that has a fast schedule **3** any step in a straight stairway ☆**4** a small circular or handbill widely distributed ☆**5** [Informal] *alt. sp. of* FLIER (sense 2)

fly fisherman one who fishes by fly-casting

fly-fish·ing (flī′fish′iŋ) *n.* the act, technique, or an instance of fly-casting

fly·ing (flī′iŋ) *adj.* **1** that flies or can fly **2** moving as if flying; moving swiftly; fast **3** like flight through the air **4** hasty and brief *[*a *flying* trip*]* **5** of or for aircraft or aviators **6** organized to act quickly, as in an emergency *[*a *flying* squad*]* —*n.* the action of a person or thing that flies

flying boat an airplane with a hull that permits it to land on and take off from water

flying bridge *Naut.* a small, often open structure over the main bridge, from which a vessel may be conned

flying buttress a buttress connected with a wall at some distance from it by an arch or part of an arch: it serves to resist outward pressure

flying colors flags flying in the air —**with flying colors** with notable victory or success

Flying Dutchman 1 a fabled Dutch sailor condemned to sail the seas off the Cape of Good Hope until Judgment Day **2** his ghostly ship, considered a bad omen by sailors who think they see it

flying field a field prepared for the landing, taking off, and minor servicing of smaller aircraft

fly·ing·fish (flī′iŋ fish′) *n., pl.* **-fish′** or **fish′es** (see FISH) any of a family (Exocoetidae, order Atheriniformes) of chiefly warm-water, marine bony fishes with winglike pectoral fins that enable them to glide through the air: also written **flying fish**

flying fox any of a genus (*Pteropus*, family Pteropodidae) of fruit bats with a foxlike head, living in Africa, Australia, and S Asia

flying frog any of several tree frogs (esp., genus *Rhacophorus*) of the East Indies that have large webbed feet which enable them to make long, gliding leaps

flying buttress

flying gurnard any of an order (Dactylopteriformes) of marine bony fishes with winglike pectoral fins, capable of gliding in the air for short distances

flying jib a small, triangular sail in front of the jib, usually on an extension of the jib boom or bowsprit

flying lemur any of an order (Dermoptera) of tree-dwelling mammals of Southeast Asia, having a broad fold of skin on each side of the body between the forelimbs and the tail, that enables it to make long, gliding leaps
flying machine *former term for* an airplane or other aircraft
flying mare a throw made in exhibition wrestling by seizing the opponent's wrist, turning, and throwing the opponent over one's back
flying phalanger any of several phalangers (family Petauridae) with a thin membrane along the sides of the body that enables them to make long, gliding leaps
☆**flying saucer** a UFO, orig. and typically saucer-shaped, that is thought to be an alien spacecraft
flying squad [Informal] a small, select team trained and equipped to take action quickly as in an emergency
☆**flying squirrel 1** any of a number of squirrels (esp. genus *Glaucomys*) with winglike folds of skin attached to the legs and body, which enable them to make long, gliding leaps **2** FLYING PHALANGER
flying start 1 the start of a race in which the contestants are already moving as they pass the starting line **2** any rapid beginning
fly·leaf (flī′lēf′) *n., pl.* **-leaves′** (-lēvz′) a blank leaf at the beginning or end of a book, usually the free half of an endpaper
Flynn (flin), **Errol (Leslie Thomson)** 1909-1959; U.S. film actor, born in Tasmania —☆**in like Flynn** ⟦prob. in allusion to his off-screen sexual exploits⟧ [Slang] IN[1] (*adj.* 8)
fly·off (flī′ôf′) *n.* a competitive program for testing various engineering models, as, esp., of military aircraft or missiles, to determine which design will be awarded a production contract
fly-on-the-wall (flī′än *th*ə wôl′) *adj.* ⟦from FLY[2], *n.* 1⟧ making use of a perspective which provides an unusually intimate view of a subject *[a fly-on-the-wall* documentary covering 24 hours of prison life*]*
fly·o·ver (flī′ō′vər) *n.* **1** [Brit.] an overpass or cloverleaf **2** a flight by one or more aircraft over a particular area or point
fly·pa·per (flī′pā′pər) *n.* a sticky or poisonous paper set out to catch or kill flies
fly sheet ⟦< earlier *flying sheet*⟧ a pamphlet
fly·speck (flī′spek′) *n.* **1** a speck of excrement left by a fly **2** any tiny spot **3** a petty or insignificant error or flaw —*vt.* to make flyspecks on
flyt·ing (flīt′iŋ) *n.* ⟦< *flyte, flite,* to contend, strive < OE *flītan;* akin to MHG *vlīzen,* to quarrel, Ger *fleiss,* diligence⟧ a formalized exchange of taunts, insults, etc., as between warriors or rivals in medieval poetry
fly·trap (flī′trap′) *n.* **1** any device for catching flies **2** a plant that catches insects, as the Venus' flytrap
☆**fly·way** (flī′wā′) *n.* a flying route taken regularly by migratory birds going to and from their breeding grounds
fly·weight (flī′wāt′) *n.* a boxer between a junior flyweight and a bantamweight, with a maximum weight of 112 pounds (50.81 kg) —*adj.* of flyweights
fly·wheel (flī′hwēl′) *n.* a heavy wheel for regulating the speed and uniformity of motion of the machine to which it is attached
fm *abbrev.* fathom(s)
Fm *Chem. symbol for* fermium
FM[1] (ef′em′) *n.* frequency-modulation broadcasting or sound transmission characterized by high fidelity and a low level of noise and static: cf. AM[2]
FM[2] *abbrev.* frequency modulation
FMB *abbrev.* Federal Maritime Board
FMC *abbrev.* Federal Maritime Commission
FMCS *abbrev.* Federal Mediation and Conciliation Service
FmHA *abbrev.* Farmers Home Administration: also **FMHA**
fMRI (ef′em′är′ī′) *n.* ⟦*f(unctional) m(agnetic) r(esonance) i(maging)*⟧ a specialized type of MRI that measures brain activity by detecting changes in blood oxygenation and flow that occur during certain neural processes
fn *abbrev.* footnote
Fn *abbrev. Comput.* function
FN *abbrev. U.S. Navy* fireman
FNMA *abbrev. see* FANNIE MAE
f-num·ber (ef′num′bər) *n. Photog.* a number that represents the relative aperture of a lens, equal to the focal length divided by the effective diameter of the lens aperture: a higher number indicates a smaller opening
fo *abbrev.* folio(s)
FO *abbrev.* Foreign Office
foal (fōl) *n.* ⟦ME *fole* < OE *fola,* akin to ON *foli,* OHG *folo* (Ger *fohlen*) < IE base **pōu-,* little, small > FEW, FILLY, L *paucus,* little⟧ a young horse, mule, donkey, etc.; colt or filly — *vt., vi.* to give birth to (a foal)
foal·ing (fōl′iŋ) *n.* the period when foals are born on a farm, ranch, etc.
foam (fōm) *n.* ⟦ME *fom* < OE *fam,* akin to Ger *feim,* scum < IE base **(s)poimno-,* foam > Sans *phēna-,* L *spuma*⟧ **1** the whitish mass of bubbles formed on or in liquids by agitation, fermentation, etc. **2** something like foam, as the heavy sweat of horses, or frothy saliva **3** [Old Poet.] the sea **4** a kind of colloid in which a gas is suspended in a liquid or solid matter, having a texture ranging from soft and liquid, as whipped cream, to firm and elastic, as foam rubber: cf. GEL (sense 1) —*vi.* to form, produce, or gather foam; froth —*vt.* to cause to foam —**foam at the mouth** to be very angry; rage —**foam′less** *adj.*
☆**foam·flow·er** (fōm′flou′ər) *n.* a small plant (*Tiarella cordifolia*) of the saxifrage family, with white flowers that bloom in the spring, found in E North America
foam rubber rubber that has been treated to form a firm, spongy foam, used in upholstered seats, mattresses, etc.
foam·y (fōm′ē) *adj.* **foam′i·er, foam′i·est** ⟦ME *fomi* < OE *famig*⟧ **1** foaming or covered with foam **2** consisting of or like foam —**foam′i·ly** *adv.* —**foam′i·ness** *n.*
fob[1] (fäb) *n.* ⟦prob. < dial. Ger *fuppe,* a pocket⟧ **1** a small pocket in the front of a pair of trousers, for carrying a watch, etc.; watch pocket ☆**2** *a)* a short ribbon or chain attached to a watch and hanging out of such a pocket *b)* any ornament worn at the end of such a ribbon or chain **3** any small trinket or device attached or made to attach to a key ring or keychain, specif., a small remote-control device that operates the doors, alarm, etc. of an automobile: in full **key fob**
fob[2] (fäb) *vt.* **fobbed, fob′bing** ⟦< ME *fobben,* to cheat, trick, prob. akin to Ger *foppen,* orig. a cant term⟧ [Obs.] to cheat; trick; deceive —**fob off 1** to trick or put off (a person) with second-rate articles, lies, excuses, etc. **2** to get rid of (something worthless) by deceit or trickery; palm off
FOB or **fob** *abbrev.* free on board
fo·cac·cia (fō kä′chə, -chē ə) *n.* ⟦It⟧ a round, flat Italian yeast bread with a crisp crust, containing olive oil, herbs, etc.
fo·cal (fō′kəl) *adj.* of or at a focus —**fo′cal·ly** *adv.*
focal infection a localized infection, as in the gallbladder, teeth, or tonsils, which may spread to other parts of the body through the blood
fo·cal·ize (fō′kəl īz′) *vt., vi.* **-ized′, -iz′ing 1** to adjust or become adjusted to a focus **2** *Med.* to limit or be limited to a small area; localize: said of an infection —**fo′cal·i·za′tion** *n.*
focal length the distance from the optical center of a lens or curved mirror to the point where light rays from a very distant object converge: also **focal distance**
focal point 1 the point at which light, sound, etc. is focused **2** any center of activity, attention, etc.
Foch (fôsh), **Fer·di·nand** (fer dē nän′) 1851-1929; Fr. marshal: commander in chief of Allied forces (1918)
fo′c′sle or **fo′c's′le** (fōk′səl) *n. phonetic sp. of* FORECASTLE
fo·cus (fō′kəs) *n., pl.* **fo′cus·es** or **fo′ci′** (-sī′) ⟦ModL, adopted in math. senses by Johannes KEPLER (1604) < L, fireplace, hearth < ? IE base **bhok-,* to flame, burn > ? Arm *boç,* flame⟧ **1** the point where rays of light, heat, etc. or waves of sound come together, or from which they spread or seem to spread; specif., the point where rays of light reflected by a mirror or refracted by a lens meet (called *real focus*) or the point where they would meet if prolonged backward through the lens or mirror (called *virtual focus*) **2** FOCAL LENGTH **3** an adjustment of the focal length to make a clear image *[to* bring a camera into *focus]* **4** any center of activity, attention, etc. **5** a part of the body where a disease process, as an infection, tumor, etc., is localized or most active **6** the starting point of an earthquake **7** *Math. a)* either of the two fixed points used in determining an ellipse *b)* any analogous point for a parabola or hyperbola (see ECCENTRICITY, sense 3) —*vt.* **-cused** or **-cussed, -cus·ing** or **-cus·sing 1** to bring into focus **2** to adjust the focal length of (the eye, a lens, etc.) in order to produce a clear image **3** to fix or settle on one thing; concentrate *[to focus* one's attention on a question*]* —*vi.* **1** to meet at a focus **2** to adjust one's eye or a lens so as to make a clear image **3** to direct one's thoughts or efforts; concentrate —**in focus** clear; distinct; sharply defined —**out of focus** indistinct; blurred —**fo′cus·er** *n.*

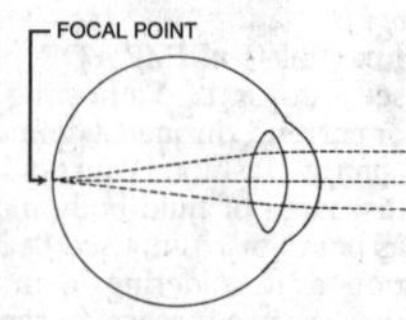

focus
(of light through the lens of an eye)

focus group a form of market research in which a small group of people is gathered to engage in controlled discussions and interviews in order to elicit opinions about particular products or services, candidates or issues, etc.
fod·der (fäd′ər) *n.* ⟦ME < OE *fodor* (akin to Ger *futter*) < base of *foda,* FOOD⟧ **1** coarse food for cattle, horses, sheep, etc., as cornstalks, hay, and straw **2** *a)* something, esp. information, that is thought of as being in large supply and, often, inferior, raw or coarse, etc. *[*promotional *fodder* in mass media*]* *b)* the basis or basic material for something *[fodder* for celebrity gossip*]* —*vt.* to feed with fodder
foe (fō) *n.* ⟦ME *fo, ifo* < OE *fah,* hostile, *(ge)fah,* enemy, akin to OHG *gefēh,* at feud, hostile: for IE base see FEUD[1]⟧ ENEMY (in all senses)
FOE *abbrev.* Fraternal Order of Eagles
foehn (fān; *Ger* fön) *n.* ⟦Ger dial. *föhn* < MHG *phönne* < OHG *fonno* < LL **faunjo* < L *Favonius,* west wind: see FAVONIAN⟧ a warm, dry wind blowing down into the valleys of a mountain, esp. in the Alps
foe·man (fō′mən) *n., pl.* **-men** (-mən) ⟦ME *foman* < OE *fahmann,* lit., hostile person⟧ [Archaic] an enemy in war; foe
foe·ti- (fēt′i, -ə) *combining form alt. sp. of* FETI-: also **foe·to-** (fēt′ō, -ə)
foe·tid (fet′id; *also* fēt′-) *adj. alt. sp. of* FETID
foe·tus (fēt′əs) *n. alt. sp. of* FETUS —**foe′tal** *adj.*
fog[1] (fôg, fäg) *n.* ⟦prob. < Scand, as in ON *fok,* Dan *(sne)fog,* driving snow, Norw dial. *fuka,* sea mist < IE base **pū-,* to puff up, blow, of echoic orig.⟧ **1** a large mass of water vapor condensed to fine particles, at or just above the earth's surface; thick, obscuring mist **2** a similar mass of smoke, dust, etc. obscuring the atmosphere **3** a vaporized liquid, as insecticide, dispersed over a large area **4** a state of mental dimness and confusion; blurred, be-

wildered state **5** a grayish area on a photograph or film —*vi.* **fogged, fog′ging 1** to become surrounded or covered by fog **2** to be or become blurred, dimmed, or obscured —*vt.* **1** to surround or cover with fog **2** to blur; dim; obscure **3** to confuse; bewilder **4** [Slang] to hurl (a baseball, etc.) **5** to make (a photograph, etc.) grayish in certain areas —**SYN.** MIST

fog[2] (fôg, fäg) *n.* ⟦ME *fogge*, prob. < Scand as in Norw dial. *fogg*, long grass in moist place, akin to Ger *feucht*, damp: see FEN[1]⟧ **1** a new growth of grass after cutting or grazing **2** long, rank grass left uncut or left standing **3** [Scot.] moss

fog bank a dense mass of fog as seen from a distance, usually at sea

fog·bound (fôg′bound′) *adj.* **1** surrounded or covered by fog **2** prevented from sailing, flying, etc. because of fog

fog·bow (-bō′) *n.* a phenomenon like a white or slightly tinted rainbow, sometimes seen in a fog

fog·dog (-dôg′) *n.* a bright spot sometimes seen at the horizon as a fog starts to dissipate

fo·gey (fō′gē) *n., pl.* **-geys** *alt. sp. of* FOGY

fog·ger (fôg′ər, fäg′-) *n.* a device for dispersing a vaporized liquid, as certain insecticides, over a large area

Fog·gia (fôd′jä) commune in Apulia, SE Italy

fog·gy (fôg′ē, fäg′-) *adj.* **-gi·er, -gi·est 1** full of fog; misty; murky **2** dim; blurred; clouded **3** confused; perplexed —**fog′gi·ly** *adv.* —**fog′gi·ness** *n.*

☆**Foggy Bottom** ⟦< name orig. given to the swampland on which U.S. State Department offices were built⟧ [Informal] the U.S. State Department

fog·horn (-hôrn′) *n.* **1** a horn on a ship, lighthouse, buoy, etc. sounded as a warning during a fog **2** a loud, strident voice

fo·gy (fō′gē) *n., pl.* **-gies** ⟦< ?⟧ a person who is old-fashioned or highly conservative in ideas and actions: usually used with *old* —**fo′gy·ish** *adj.* —**fo′gy·ism′** *n.*

foh (fô) *interj.* FAUGH

FOIA *abbrev.* Freedom of Information Act

foi·ble (foi′bəl) *n.* ⟦obs. var. of Fr *faible*: see FEEBLE⟧ **1** a small weakness; slight frailty in character **2** the weakest part of a sword blade, from the middle to the point: cf. FORTE[1] (sense 1) —**SYN.** FAULT

foie gras (fwä grä′) ⟦Fr⟧ the enlarged liver of a force-fed goose, or, sometimes, duck, often made into pâté de foie gras

foil[1] (foil) *vt.* ⟦ME *foilen* < OFr *fuler*, to trample on, subdue: see FULL[2]⟧ **1** to keep from being successful; thwart; frustrate **2** *Hunting* to make (a scent, trail, etc.) confused, as by recrossing, in order to balk the pursuers —*n.* **1** [Archaic] the scent or trail of an animal **2** [Archaic] a thwarting —**SYN.** FRUSTRATE

foil[2] (foil) *n.* ⟦ME < OFr *fuil* (Fr *feuille*), a leaf < L *folia* < *folium*, leaf: see FOLIATE⟧ **1** a leaflike, rounded space or design between cusps or in windows, etc., as in Gothic architecture **2** a very thin sheet or leaf of metal; specif., such a sheet, as of aluminum, used for wrapping food, etc. **3** the metal coating on the back of a mirror **4** a thin leaf of polished metal placed under an inferior or artificial gem to give it brilliance **5** a person or thing that sets off or enhances another by contrast —*vt.* **1** to cover or back with foil **2** [Rare] to serve as a contrast to **3** to decorate (windows, etc.) with foils

foil[3] (foil) *n.* ⟦< ?⟧ **1** a long, thin fencing sword with a button on the point to prevent injury **2** [*pl.*] the art or sport of fencing with foils

foils·man (foilz′mən) *n., pl.* **-men** (-mən) a fencer who uses a FOIL[3] (sense 1)

foin (foin) *vi., n.* ⟦ME *foinen* < *foin*, a thrust, stab < OFr *foisne*, fish spear < L *fuscina*, a trident⟧ [Archaic] lunge or thrust, as in fencing

foi·son (foi′zən) *n.* ⟦ME *foisoun* < OFr *foison, fuison* < L *fusio*, a pouring: see FUSION⟧ **1** [Archaic] a plentiful crop; good harvest; plenty **2** [Now Dial.] *a)* vitality; strength; ability *b)* [*pl.*] resources

foist (foist) *vt.* ⟦prob. < dial. Du *vuisten*, to hold in the hand; hence, in dicing, to hide or palm in the hand < *vuist*, a fist, akin to FIST⟧ **1** to put in slyly or surreptitiously, as a clause into a contract **2** to get (a thing) accepted, sold, etc. by fraud, deception, etc.; palm off: with *on* or *upon*

Fo·kine (fô kēn′), **Mi·chel** (mē shel′) (born *Mikhail Mikhailovich Fokin*) 1880-1942; U.S. choreographer, born in Russia

Fok·ker (fäk′ər), **Anthony Herman Gerard** 1890-1939; U.S. aircraft designer, born in Dutch East Indies: built airplanes for Germany & the Netherlands, 1911-21

fol *abbrev.* **1** folio(s) **2** following

fo·la·cin (fō′lə sin) *n.* ⟦FOL(IC) AC(ID) + -IN[1]⟧ FOLIC ACID

fo·late (fō′lāt′) *n.* ⟦FOL(IC ACID) + -ATE[2]⟧ a B vitamin, the natural form of folic acid, that is needed to produce and maintain new cells, found in spinach, beans, citrus fruits, etc.

fold[1] (fōld) *vt.* ⟦ME *folden* < OE *faldan* (WS *fealdan*), akin to Ger *falten* < IE **pel-to* < base **pel-*, to fold > (SIM)PLE, (TRI)PLE⟧ **1** *a)* to bend or press (something) so that one part is over another; double up on itself [*to fold a sheet*] *b)* to make more compact by so doubling a number of times *c)* UNFOLD (*vt.* 1) [*fold open a map, fold out a centerfold*] **2** to draw together and intertwine [*to fold the arms*] **3** to draw (wings) close to the body **4** to clasp in the arms; embrace **5** to wrap up; envelop —*vi.* **1** to be or become folded ☆**2** [Informal] to fail; specif., *a)* to be forced to close, as a business, play, etc. *b)* to succumb, as to exhaustion; collapse ☆**3** *Poker* to withdraw from the betting on a hand, specif. by turning over one's exposed cards —*n.* **1** a folded part or layer **2** a mark made by folding **3** a hollow or crease produced by folded parts or layers **4** [Brit.] a hollow; small valley **5** *Geol.* a rock layer folded by pressure —**fold in** *Cooking* to blend (an ingredient) into a mixture, using gentle, cutting strokes

fold[2] (fōld) *n.* ⟦ME < OE *fald*, akin to Du *vaalt*, enclosed place, Dan *fold*, sheep pen⟧ **1** a pen in which to keep sheep **2** sheep kept together; flock of sheep **3** a group or organization with common interests, aims, faith, etc., as a church —*vt.* to keep or confine in a pen

-fold (fōld) ⟦ME *-fold, -fald* < OE *-feald*: see FOLD[1]⟧ *suffix* **1** *forming adjectives* having (a specified number of) parts [*a tenfold division*] **2** *forming adjectives and adverbs* (a specified number of) times as many, as much, as large [*to profit tenfold*]

☆**fold·a·way** (fōld′ə wā′) *adj.* that can be folded together for easy storage [*a foldaway cot*]

fold·boat (fōld′bōt′) *n.* a lightweight, collapsible, folding kayak

fold·er (fōl′dər) *n.* **1** a person or thing that folds **2** a sheet of cardboard or heavy paper folded for holding loose papers, as in a file **3** *Comput.* any of the places, within a DIRECTORY, in which files are stored and grouped as by topic ☆**4** a circular with one or more folds, each section of which is a separate printed page

fol·de·rol (fäl′də räl′) *n.* ⟦orig., *fal-de-ral, fol-de-rol*, nonsense syllables forming the refrain in songs⟧ **1** a showy but worthless trinket **2** mere nonsense

folding door a door with hinged leaves or accordion pleats that can be folded back

folding knife a knife with a blade that folds into the handle

☆**folding money** [Informal] PAPER MONEY

☆**fold·out** (fōld′out′) *n.* **1** GATEFOLD **2** designed to open out for use by folding [*a sofa with a foldout cot inside*]

fo·ley (fō′lē) *adj.* ⟦after J. *Foley* (1891-1967), Hollywood sound-effects specialist⟧ [*also* **F-**] of or having to do with the creation or editing of sound effects for the soundtracks of films [*a foley walker dubs footsteps*]

fo·li·a (fō′lē ə) *n. alt. pl. of* FOLIUM

fo·li·a·ceous (fō′lē ā′shəs) *adj.* ⟦L *foliaceus* < *folium*, a leaf: see FOLIATE⟧ **1** of or like the leaf of a plant **2** having leaves **3** consisting of thin layers, as certain rocks

fo·li·age (fō′lē ij) *n.* ⟦ME *foilage* < OFr *feuillage* < *feuille*, a leaf < L *folia* < *folium*: see FOLIATE⟧ **1** leaves, as of a plant or tree; mass of leaves; leafage **2** a decoration consisting of a representation of leaves, branches, flowers, etc.

fo·li·aged (-ijd) *adj.* having foliage: often in hyphenated compounds [*dark-foliaged*]

fo·li·ar (fō′lē ər) *adj.* ⟦ModL *foliaris* < L *folium*: see fol.⟧ of or like a leaf or leaves

fo·li·ate (fō′lē āt′; *for adj., usually,* -it) *vt.* **-at′ed, -at′ing** ⟦< L *foliatus*, leafy < *folium*, a leaf < IE base **bhel-*, **bhlō-*, to swell, blossom > BLADE, BLOOM[1]⟧ **1** *a)* to divide into thin layers *b)* to beat into foil **2** to decorate with leaflike layers or ornamentation **3** to number the leaves of (a book or manuscript) —*vi.* **1** to separate into layers **2** to send out leaves —*adj.* **1** having or covered with leaves **2** like a leaf or leaves

fo·li·a·tion (fō′lē ā′shən) *n.* ⟦ML *foliatio*: see prec.⟧ **1** a growing of or developing into a leaf or leaves; leaf formation **2** the state of being in leaf **3** the way leaves are arranged in the bud; vernation **4** the act or process of beating metal into layers **5** *a)* a splitting into leaflike layers (said of certain minerals) *b)* the property of splitting into such layers *c)* such layers **6** the process of backing glass as with metal foil to make a mirror **7** the consecutive numbering of leaves, rather than pages, of a book **8** *a)* a decorating with leaflike ornamentation *b)* a leaflike decoration consisting of small arcs or foils

fo·lic acid (fō′lik) ⟦< L *folium*, a leaf (see FOLIATE) + -IC⟧ a crystalline substance, $C_{19}H_{19}N_7O_6$, found in green leaves and in certain other plant and animal tissues, exhibiting vitamin B activity: used in medicine, esp. for treating certain anemias

fo·lie à deux (fô lē à dö′) ⟦Fr, lit., double insanity⟧ *Psychiatry* a condition in which two closely associated people who are mentally ill share the same delusional beliefs

fo·lie de gran·deur (fô lē də grän dër′) ⟦Fr⟧ delusions of grandeur; megalomania

fo·li·ic·o·lous (fō′lē ik′ə ləs) *adj.* ⟦*folii-* (< L *folium*, leaf: see FOLIATE) + -COLOUS⟧ growing on leaves, as certain lichens, fungi, and algae

fo·lin·ic acid (fō lin′ik) ⟦FOL(IC ACID) + -IN[1] + -IC⟧ the active substance, $C_{20}H_{23}N_7O_7$, into which folic acid is converted in bodily tissue

fo·li·o (fō′lē ō′; *also* fōl′yō′) *n., pl.* **-os′** ⟦ME < L (*in*) *folio*, (in) a sheet, abl. of *folium*, a leaf (in LL, leaf of paper): see FOLIATE⟧ **1** *Bookkeeping* a page of a ledger, or facing pages with the same number **2** *Law* a set number of words (100 in the U.S., 72 or 90 in England) considered as a unit of measuring the length of a legal or official document **3** *Printing* *a)* a large sheet of paper folded once, so that it forms two leaves, or four pages, of a book, manuscript, etc. *b)* a large size of book, about 12 by 15 inches, made of sheets folded in this way *c)* a leaf of a manuscript, book, etc. numbered on only one side *d)* the number of a page in a book, etc. —*adj.* having sheets folded once; of the size of a folio —*vt.* **-li·oed′, -li·o′ing** to number the pages of (a book, etc.) consecutively; page —**in folio** in the form or size of a folio

fo·li·o·late (fō′lē ə lit, -lāt′) *adj.* ⟦< *foliole*, a leaflet (< Fr < L *foliolum*, dim. of L *folium*, leaf: see FOLIATE) + -ATE[1]⟧ *Bot.* having or relating to leaflets

fo·li·ose (fō′lē ōs′) *adj.* ⟦L *foliosus*, leafy < *folium*, a leaf: see FOLIATE⟧ covered with leaves; leafy

-fo·li·ous (fō′lē əs) ⟦< L *folium*, a leaf + -OUS⟧ *combining form* having (a specified number or kind of) leaves

fo·li·um (fō′lē əm) *n., pl.* **-li·ums** or **-li·a** (-ə) ⟦L: see FOLIATE⟧ **1** *Geol.* a thin layer of stratum, as in metamorphic rock **2** *Geom.* the looping, closed part of a curve extending from a node

folk (fōk) ***pl.n.*** ⟦ME < OE *folc*, akin to Ger *volk* < Gmc **fulca-*, army, group of warriors < ?⟧ **1** *a)* a people or nation; ethnic group [a peaceful *folk*] *b)* the large body of the common people of such a group (with *the*) **2** people in general; persons [city *folk* sometimes vacation in the country; *folks* differ in their tastes]: also **folks** (fōks) **—*n.*** *short for* FOLK MUSIC **—*adj.*** of, originating among, or having to do with the common people, who transmit the general culture of the group through succeeding generations [*folk* art] **—just (plain) folks** [Informal] people who are regarded as simple, unassuming, not snobbish, etc. **—one's (or the) folks** [Informal] one's family or relatives; esp., one's parents

folk dance **1** a traditional dance of the common people of a country or region **2** music for this

Fol·ke·ting or **Fol·ke·thing** (fōl′kə tiŋ′) ***n.*** ⟦Dan < *folke*, people (see FOLK) + *ting, thing*, assembly (see THING²)⟧ **1** [Historical] the lower branch of the Danish legislature **2** now, the unicameral legislature of Denmark

folk etymology unscientific etymology; popular but incorrect notion of the origin and derivation of a word: folk etymology may bring about change, as in the case of "cole slaw" becoming "cold slaw"

folk·ie (fōk′ē) ***n.*** [Informal] a performer or devotee of folk music or folk songs

folk·lore (fōk′lôr′) ***n.*** ⟦FOLK + LORE¹: suggested (1846) by W. J. Thoms (1803-85), Eng antiquary, to replace earlier *popular antiquities*⟧ **1** all of the unwritten traditional beliefs, legends, sayings, customs, etc. of a culture **2** the study and scientific investigation of these **—folk′lor′ic *adj.* —folk′lor′ist *n.* —folk′lor·is′tic *adj.***

folk medicine the treatment of illness with traditional, rather than modern medical, methods and remedies: folk medicine is typically characterized by the use of herbs and other natural substances

folk·moot (fōk′mo͞ot′) ***n.*** ⟦OE *folcmot, fologemot*: see FOLK & MOOT⟧ [Historical] a general meeting of the people of a town, shire, etc. of medieval England: also **folk′mote′** (-mōt′)

folk music **1** traditional music made and handed down among the common people **2** music composed in the style of this

☆**folk-rock** (-räk′) ***n.*** music with a rhythmic rock-and-roll beat combined with words in folk-song style

folks (fōks) ***pl.n.*** *see* FOLK

folk song ⟦calque of Ger *volkslied*, loan transl. (by Johann Gottfried von Herder, 1771) of E *popular song*⟧ **1** a song made and handed down among the common people: folk songs are usually of anonymous authorship and often have many versions **2** a song composed in the style of such a traditional song Also written **folk′song′ *n.* —folk singer, folk′sing′er *n.***

☆**folk·sy** (fōk′sē) ***adj.*** **-si·er, -si·est** [Informal] friendly or sociable in a simple, direct manner: sometimes used in a derogatory way of affected or exaggerated familiarity **—folk′si·ly *adv.* —folk′si·ness *n.***

folk tale (*or* story) a story, usually of anonymous authorship and containing legendary elements, made and handed down orally among the common people

☆**folk·way** (-wā′) ***n.*** ⟦first used (1906) by W. G. SUMNER⟧ any way of thinking, feeling, behaving, etc. common to members of the same social group: see MORES

folk·y (fō′kē) ***adj.*** **1** FOLK **2** of or having to do with FOLK MUSIC, esp. as it is variously regarded as being soft or quiet, sensitively written or performed, etc.

fol·li·cle (fäl′i kəl) ***n.*** ⟦ModL *folliculus* < L, a small bag, husk, pod, dim. of *follis*, bellows < IE base **bhel-*, to blow up, swell > BALL¹, BULL¹⟧ **1** *Anat. a)* any small sac, cavity, or gland for excretion or secretion [a hair *follicle*] *b)* [Obs.] a lymph nodule **2** *Bot.* a dry seed pod with a single cavity, that splits open along only one seam to release its seeds, as a milkweed pod **—fol·lic·u·lar** (fə lik′yo͞o lər, -yə-) ***adj.*** **—fol·lic′u·late** (-lit, -lāt′) ***adj.***, **fol·lic′u·lat′ed**

follicle mite any of a genus (*Demodex*) of small, wormlike mites living as parasites in the hair follicles of mammals; esp., a species (*D. folliculorum*) that infests humans

fol·li·cle-stim·u·lat·ing hormone (-stim′yo͞o lāt′iŋ) a hormone, secreted by the anterior pituitary gland, which stimulates the development of ova in the female and testicular function in the male: abbrev. *FSH*

fol·lic·u·lin (fə lik′yo͞o lin, -yə-) ***n.*** ESTRONE

fol·lies (fäl′ēz′) ***n.*** ⟦pl. of FOLLY⟧ ☆a revue: usually used as part of the title

fol·low (fäl′ō) ***vt.*** ⟦ME *folwen* < OE *folgian*, akin to Ger *folgen* & (?) Welsh *olafiad*, follower⟧ **1** to come or go after **2** to go after in order to catch; chase; pursue **3** to go along [*follow* the right road] **4** to come or occur after in time, in a series, etc. **5** to provide *with* something that comes after [to *follow* praise with blame] **6** to take the place of in rank, position, etc. [Monroe *followed* Madison as president] **7** to take up; engage in [to *follow* a trade] **8** to come or happen as a result of [disease often *follows* malnutrition] **9** to take as a model; act in accordance with; imitate **10** to accept the authority of; obey [to *follow* rules] **11** to support or advocate the ideas, opinions, etc. of **12** to watch or listen to closely; observe [to *follow* a conversation intently] **13** to be interested in or attentive to current developments in [to *follow* local politics] **14** to understand the continuity or logic of [do you *follow* me?] **—*vi.*** **1** to come, go, or happen after or next after some thing or person in place, sequence, or time **2** to occur as a natural or logical consequence; result **—*n.*** **1** the act of following **2** *Billiards* a shot that imparts a forward spin to the cue ball so that it continues rolling in the same direction after striking the object ball: also **follow shot** **—as follows** as will next be told or explained **—follow out** to carry out fully or completely **—follow through** **1** to continue and complete a stroke or swing after hitting or releasing the ball or puck **2** to continue and complete an action **—follow up** **1** to follow closely and persistently **2** to carry out fully **3** to add to the effectiveness of by doing something more

SYN.—follow is the general word meaning to come or occur after, but it does not necessarily imply a causal relationship with what goes before [sunshine *followed* by rain]; **ensue** implies that what follows comes as a logical consequence of what preceded [clouds appeared and rain *ensued*]; **succeed** implies that what follows takes the place of what preceded [who *succeeded* Polk to the presidency?]; **result** stresses a definite relationship of cause and effect between what follows and what preceded [superstition *results* from ignorance] **—ANT. precede**

fol·low·er (fäl′ō ər) ***n.*** ⟦ME *folwere* < OE *folgere*⟧ **1** a person or thing that follows; specif., *a)* a person who follows another's beliefs or teachings; disciple *b)* a servant or attendant **2** a gear or part of a machine that is given motion by another part, esp. the last driven part

SYN.—follower is the general term for one who follows or believes in the teachings or theories of someone [a *follower* of Freud]; **supporter** applies to one who upholds or defends opinions or theories that are disputed or under attack [a *supporter* of technocracy]; **adherent** refers to a close, active follower of some theory, cause, etc. [the *adherents* of a political party]; **disciple** implies a personal, devoted relationship to the teacher of some doctrine or leader of some movement [Plato was a *disciple* of Socrates]; **partisan**, in this connection, refers to an unswerving, often blindly devoted, adherent of some person or cause

fol·low·er·ship (-ship′) ***n.*** the ability to follow a leader

fol·low·ing (fäl′ō iŋ) ***adj.*** **1** that follows; next after [the *following* year] **2** to be mentioned immediately; to be dealt with next [the *following* people were chosen] **3** moving in the same direction that a ship is moving: said of the tide or wind **—*n.*** a group of followers or adherents **—*prep.*** after [*following* lunch he left] **—the following** **1** the one or ones to be mentioned immediately **2** what follows

fol·low-on (-än′) ***adj.*** designating or of anything that follows something else as a consequence or natural development; follow-up [*follow-on* negotiations]

fol·low-through (-thro͞o′) ***n.*** **1** *a)* the act or manner of continuing the swing or stroke of a club, a racket, the arm, etc. to its natural end after striking or releasing the ball, puck, etc. *b)* this final part of the stroke **2** the continuing of a process, activity, etc. to completion

fol·low-up (-up′) ***adj.*** designating or of anything that follows something else as a review, addition, etc. [*follow-up* examinations, a *follow-up* letter] **—*n.*** **1** a follow-up thing or event **2** the use of follow-up letters, visits, etc. **3** a following up

fol·ly (fäl′ē) ***n.***, *pl.* **-lies** ⟦ME *folie* < OFr < *fol*: see FOOL¹⟧ **1** a lack of understanding, sense, or rational conduct; foolishness **2** any foolish action or belief **3** any foolish and useless but expensive undertaking **4** *a)* [Obs.] wickedness or evil; also, lewdness *b)* action that ends or can end in disaster **5** an unconventional or extravagant, and often largely purposeless, building or structure See also FOLLIES

☆**Fol·som** (fōl′səm) ***adj.*** ⟦after *Folsom*, village in N.Mex., where such spearheads have been found⟧ of or having to do with a North American culture of the late Pleistocene Epoch characterized by the use of stone spearheads with fluted sides

Fo·mal·haut (fō′məl hôt′, -məl ōt′) ***n.*** ⟦Fr < Ar *fum al-ḥūt*, lit., mouth of the fish⟧ the brightest star in the constellation Piscis Austrinus: magnitude, 1.17

FOMC *abbrev.* Federal Open Market Committee

fo·ment (fō ment′) ***vt.*** ⟦ME *fomenten* < OFr *fomenter* < LL *fomentare* < L *fomentum*, poultice < *fovere*, to keep warm < IE **dhogwh-* < base **dhegwh-*, to burn > Sans *dáhati*, (it) burns, MIr *daig*, fire⟧ **1** to treat with warm water, medicated lotions, etc. **2** to stir up (trouble); instigate; incite [to *foment* a riot] **—*SYN.*** INCITE **—fo·ment′er *n.***

fo·men·ta·tion (fō′men tā′shən, -mən-) ***n.*** ⟦ME *fomentacioun* < LL *fomentatio* < L *fomentum*: see prec.⟧ **1** treatment of bodily pain or injury by the application of warm, moist substances, as in a lotion or compress **2** a lotion, compress, etc. so applied **3** a stirring up of trouble; incitement

fond¹ (fänd) ***adj.*** ⟦ME, contr. of *fonned*, foolish, pp. of *fonnen*, to be foolish⟧ **1** [Now Rare] foolish, esp. foolishly naive or hopeful **2** *a)* tender and affectionate; loving; dear [*fond* memories] *b)* affectionate in a foolish or overly indulgent way **3** cherished with great or unreasoning affection; doted on [a *fond* hope] **—fond of** having a liking for

fond² (fänd; *Fr* fōn) ***n.*** ⟦Fr: see FUND⟧ **1** foundation; basis; background **2** [Obs.] supply; fund

Fon·da (fän′də), **Henry (Jaynes)** 1905-82; U.S. film actor

fon·dant (fän′dənt; *Fr* fōn dän′) ***n.*** ⟦Fr < prp. of *fondre*, to melt: see FOUND³⟧ a soft, creamy confection made of sugar, water, and cream of tartar, used as an icing and a candy, and esp. as a filling for other candies

fon·dle (fän′dəl) ***vt., vi.*** **-dled, -dling** ⟦freq. of obs. v. *fond* < FOND¹⟧ **1** to stroke or handle (someone or something) in a tender and loving way; caress **2** to touch or stroke (someone), often inappropriately, in making sexual advances **3** [Obs.] to pamper **—*SYN.*** CARESS **—fon′dler *n.***

fond·ly (fänd′lē) ***adv.*** ⟦ME: see FOND¹ & -LY²⟧ **1** with simple trust; naively **2** lovingly **3** [Archaic] foolishly

fond·ness (fänd′nis) ***n.*** **1** tender or doting affection **2** an inclination; taste **3** [Archaic] foolishness

fon·due or **fon·du** (fän do͞o′, fän′do͞o′) ***n.*** ⟦Fr < pp. of *fondre*, to melt: see FOUND[3]⟧ **1** a dish made by melting cheese in wine, with a little brandy and seasoning added, used as a dip for cubes of bread **2** any of various other dishes, as one in which cubes of meat are dipped in simmering oil until cooked **3** cheese soufflé with bread crumbs

Fon·se·ca (fän sā′kä), **Gulf of** inlet of the Pacific in W Central America

fons et o·ri·go (fänz′ et ō rī′gō, -rē′gō) ⟦L⟧ source and origin

font[1] (fänt) ***n.*** ⟦ME < OE < L *fons* (gen. *fontis*), spring, FOUNTAIN⟧ **1** *a)* a large basin, now typically supported by a pedestal, for holding water to be used in baptizing *b)* an open container, as at a church entrance, for holding holy water **2** [Archaic] a fountain or spring **3** a source or origin —**font′al** ***adj.***

font[2] (fänt) ***n.*** ⟦Fr *fonte* < *fondre*, to cast, FOUND[3]⟧ *Printing* a complete assortment of type in one size and style

Fon·taine·bleau (fōn ten blō′; *E* fänt′'n blō′, -blo͞o′) town in N France, near Paris: site of a palace of former kings of France

Fon·tan·a (fän tan′ə) ⟦< ?⟧ city in SW Calif.

fon·ta·nel or **fon·ta·nelle** (fänt′'n el′) ***n.*** ⟦ME *fontinel*, a hollow, pit (of the body) < OFr *fontanele*, dim. of *fontaine*, FOUNTAIN⟧ **1** [Obs.] an opening in the body for the discharge of secretions **2** any of the soft, boneless areas in the skull of a baby or young animal, which are later closed up by the formation of bone

FONTANELS

Fon·tanne (fän tan′), **Lynn** 1887?-1983; U.S. actress: wife of Alfred Lunt

Fon·teyn (fän tān′), Dame **Margot** (born *Margaret Hookham*) 1919-91; Eng. ballerina

fon·ti·na (fän tē′nə) ***n.*** ⟦It⟧ [*also* **F-**] a pale, semisoft to hard Italian cheese, made, esp. originally, of ewe's milk

Foo·chow (fo͞o′chou′, fo͞o′jō′) *a former transliteration of* FUZHOU

food (fo͞od) ***n.*** ⟦ME *fode* < OE *foda* < IE *pāt-*, to feed, eat < base **pā-*, to pasture cattle > L *pastor, pabulum, pascere*, to feed, *panis*, bread⟧ **1** any substance taken into and assimilated by a plant or animal to keep it alive and enable it to grow and repair tissue; nourishment; nutriment **2** solid substances of this sort: distinguished from DRINK **3** a specified kind of food **4** anything that nourishes or stimulates; whatever helps something to keep active, grow, etc. [*food* for thought] —***adj.*** **1** of or relating to food **2** used as food

---

SYN.—**food** is the general term for all matter that is taken into the body for nourishment; **fare** refers to the range of foods eaten by a particular organism or available at a particular time and place [the *fare* of horses, a bill of *fare*]; **victuals** (see VICTUAL, ***n.*** 2) is a dialectal or informal word for human fare or diet; **provisions** (see PROVISION, ***n.*** 2*b*), in this connection, refers to a stock of food assembled in advance [*provisions* for the hike]; **ration** refers to a fixed allowance or allotment of food [the weekly *ration*] and in the plural (**rations**) to food in general [how are the *rations* in this outfit?]

---

food bank a place where food is stored for regular distribution to the needy

food chain *Ecol.* a sequence (as grass, rabbit, fox) of organisms in a community in which each member feeds on the one below it

food court an area, as in an enclosed shopping center, with fast-food stalls surrounding tables and chairs for common use

food cycle *Ecol.* FOOD WEB

food fish any fish used primarily as a commercial source of food

food·ie (fo͞o′dē) ***n.*** [Slang] a person having an enthusiastic interest in the preparation and consumption of fine foods

foo dog (fo͞o) **1** a fierce-looking dog with a lion's mane, used as a motif in East Asian art **2** a figurine or statue in the form of this dog

food poisoning **1** the sickness resulting from eating food contaminated either by bacterial toxins or by certain bacteria, esp. salmonella, often causing vomiting, diarrhea, and prostration **2** poisoning resulting from naturally poisonous foods, as certain mushrooms, or from chemical contaminants in food

food processor an electrical appliance that can mix, blend, purée, slice, grate, chop, etc. foods rapidly

food pyramid **1** a pyramid-shaped representation of the FOOD CHAIN with many food-producing organisms, esp. green plants, at the base and decreasing numbers of food-consuming organisms, esp. animals, at each higher level ☆**2** a pyramid-shaped diagram showing basic food groups and recommended servings constituting a balanced diet, typically including grains, fruits and vegetables, dairy, meat and fish, etc.

☆**food stamp** any of the federal coupons given to qualifying low-income persons for use in buying food

food·stuff (fo͞od′stuf′) ***n.*** any substance used as food

food web *Ecol.* all the individual food chains in a community

☆**foo·fa·raw** (fo͞o′fə rô′) ***n.*** ⟦altered < Fr *fanfaron*, a swaggering < Sp *fanfarrón*: see FANFARONADE⟧ [Slang] **1** unnecessary things added for show; frills **2** stir or fuss over something trivial

fool[1] (fo͞ol) ***n.*** ⟦ME *fol* < OFr (Fr *fou*) < LL *follis* < L, windbag, bellows: see FOLLICLE⟧ **1** *a)* a person with little or no judgment, common sense, wisdom, etc.; silly or stupid person; simpleton *b)* [Obs.] a mentally retarded person **2** a man formerly kept in the household of a nobleman or king to entertain by joking and clowning; professional jester **3** a victim of a joke or trick; dupe **4** a person especially devoted to or skilled in some activity [a dancing *fool*] —***adj.*** [Informal] foolish —***vi.*** **1** to act like a fool; be silly **2** to speak, act, etc. in jest; joke **3** [Informal] to trifle or meddle (*with*) —***vt.*** to make a fool of; trick; deceive; dupe —**be no** (or **nobody's**) **fool** to be shrewd and capable —☆**fool around** [Informal] **1** to spend time in trifling or pointless activity **2** to trifle or meddle **3** to engage in casual sexual activity —**fool away** [Informal] to fritter away foolishly —**play** (or **act**) **the fool** to act like a fool; do silly things; clown

fool[2] (fo͞ol) ***n.*** ⟦Early ModE < ? prec.⟧ [Brit.] crushed stewed fruit mixed with cream, esp. whipped cream

fool·er·y (fo͞ol′ər ē) ***n., pl.*** **-er·ies** foolish behavior or a foolish action

fool·har·dy (fo͞ol′här′dē) ***adj.*** **-di·er**, **-di·est** ⟦ME *folhardi* < OFr *fol hardi* < *fol*, FOOL[1] + *hardi*: see HARDY[1]⟧ bold or daring in a foolish way; rash; reckless —**fool′har′di·ly** ***adv.*** —**fool′har′di·ness** ***n.***

☆**fool hen** ⟦so called because regarded as an easy target for hunters⟧ SPRUCE GROUSE

fool·ish (fo͞ol′ish) ***adj.*** ⟦ME *folish*⟧ **1** without good sense; silly; unwise **2** *a)* ridiculous; absurd *b)* abashed; embarrassed **3** [Archaic] humble —***SYN.*** ABSURD —**fool′ish·ly** ***adv.*** —**fool′ish·ness** ***n.***

☆**fool·proof** (fo͞ol′pro͞of′) ***adj.*** so simple, well-designed, or sturdily made as not to be mishandled, damaged, misunderstood, etc. even by a fool

fools·cap (fo͞olz′kap′) ***n.*** ⟦so called from the former watermark, a *fool's* head and *cap*⟧ **1** any of various sizes of writing paper; esp., in the U.S., a size measuring 13 by 16 inches **2** FOOL'S CAP

fool's cap a cap, usually with bells, formerly worn by a court fool or jester

fool's errand a foolish, fruitless task or undertaking

☆**fool's gold** pyrite or chalcopyrite, both of which resemble gold in color

fool's paradise a state of deceptive happiness, based on illusions or delusions

fool's-pars·ley (-pärs′lē) ***n.*** a poisonous, foul-smelling European weed (*Aethusa cynapium*) of the umbel family: also written **fool's parsley**

foos·ball (fo͞os′bôl′) ***n.*** ⟦altered < Ger *tischfussball*, table soccer < *tisch*, table + *fussball*, soccer (lit., football) < *fuss*, fol. + *ball*, BALL[1]⟧ a soccerlike game played on a special rectangular table containing a series of parallel rods to which are attached paddles typically in the shape of miniature soccer players: the rods are turned in an attempt to strike the ball into a goal

foot (fo͝ot) ***n., pl.*** **feet** ⟦ME *fot* < OE, akin to Ger *fuss* < IE **pōd-*, var. of base **pĕd-*, foot, to go > Sans *pad-*, Gr *pous*, L *pes*⟧ **1** the end part of the leg, on which a person or animal stands or moves **2** a thing like a foot in some way; specif., *a)* the part that a thing stands on; base *b)* the lowest part; bottom [the *foot* of a page] *c)* the last of a series [go to the *foot* of the line] *d)* the part of a sewing machine that presses down on the cloth as it is moved forward and stitched *e)* the part of the body of a mollusk that is normally muscular and ventrally located, used for attachment, burrowing, and locomotion, or, as in cephalopods, serving as the basis for the arms, tentacles, eyes, and mouth **3** the end of a bed, grave, etc. toward which the feet are directed **4** the end opposite to the end designated the head [at the *foot* of the table] **5** the part of a stocking, boot, etc. that covers the foot **6** a unit of length in the FPS system, equal to 12 inches or ⅓ yard (0.3048 meter): symbol, ′: abbrev. *ft*: pl. sometimes **foot** following a number [50 *foot* of lumber] and always in attributive use [a six-*foot* athlete] **7** [*with pl. v.*] [Brit.] foot soldiers; infantry **8** ***pl.*** **foots** the sediment in a liquid: *usually used in pl.* **9** a group of syllables serving as a unit of meter in verse; esp., such a unit having a specified placement of the stressed syllable or syllables —***vi.*** **1** *a)* to dance *b)* to go on foot (now rare exc. in phr. **foot it**: see below) **2** to move ahead, esp. with speed: said of a sailboat —***vt.*** **1** to walk, dance, or run on, over, or through; tread **2** to make or repair the foot of (a stocking, etc.) **3** to add (a column of figures) and set down a total: often with *up* ☆**4** [Informal] to pay (costs, expenses, etc.) [to *foot* the bill] —**a** (or **one's**) **foot in the door** an opportunity, as to gain access to something or begin an undertaking —**foot it** [Informal] to dance, walk, or run —**of foot** in walking or running [swift *of foot*] —**on foot** **1** walking or running **2** going on; in process —**on the wrong foot** in an inept or unfavorable way at the very beginning —**put one's best foot forward** [Informal] **1** to do the best that one can **2** to try to appear at one's best —**put one's foot down** [Informal] to be firm; act decisively —**put one's foot in it** [Informal] to make an embarrassing or troublesome blunder —**put one's foot in one's mouth** [Informal] to make an embarrassing or tactless statement —**under foot** **1** on the surface of the ground; on the floor, etc. **2** in the way

NOTE—For phrases using *feet*, see FEET

foot·age (fo͝ot′ij) ***n.*** ⟦prec. + -AGE⟧ ☆**1** the length expressed in feet: said esp. of portions of film **2** the length of film that has been exposed during shooting

foot-and-mouth disease (fo͝ot′'n mouth′) an acute, highly contagious viral disease of cloven-footed animals, characterized by fever and by blisters in the mouth and around the hoofs; hoof-and-mouth disease: it is sometimes transmitted to humans

foot·ball (fo͝ot′bôl′) ***n.*** ⟦ME *foteballe*⟧ **1** *a)* [Brit.] SOCCER *b)* [Brit.] RUGBY[1] (sense 2) *c)* in the U.S., a game played on a field that is 100 yards long, with 2 teams of 11 players and a goal at each end: the players may attempt to score a touchdown by running or passing the ball, kick a field goal, etc. *d)* CANADIAN FOOTBALL **2** the oval, inflated, leather or rubber ball used in playing football in the U.S. or Canada **3** any issue, problem, etc. that is passed about or shunted from one group to another [a political *football*]

foot·ball·er (-ər) ***n.*** [Chiefly Brit.] a football player, esp. a soccer player

foot·board (-bôrd′) ***n.*** **1** a board or small platform for supporting the feet or for standing on **2** a vertical piece across the foot of a bed

foot·boy (-boi′) ***n.*** ⟦see FOOTMAN⟧ a young manservant or page

foot brake a brake, as on a bicycle, worked by pressure of the foot

foot·bridge (-brij′) ***n.*** a bridge for pedestrians

foot-can·dle (foot′kan′dəl) ***n.*** a unit of illumination, equal to one lumen per square foot (10.764 lux), or the amount of light from a source of one candela directly thrown on a square foot of surface at a distance of one foot: abbrev. *fc*

foot·cloth (foot′klôth′) ***n.***, *pl.* **-cloths′** (-klôthz′) **1** [Historical] a low-hanging, ornamental cloth over a horse's back **2** [Now Rare] a carpet or rug

foot-drag·ging (foot′drag′iŋ) ***n.*** deliberate slowness or delay; stalling

foot·ed (foot′id) ***adj.*** **1** having a foot or feet [a *footed* goblet] **2** having (a specified number or kind of) feet: used in hyphenated compounds [four-*footed*, sure-*footed*]

foot·er (foot′ər) ***n.*** **1** FOOTING (*n.* 6) **2** in word processing, a line or lines of text, typically consisting of the topic, date, page number, etc., printed at the bottom of each page of a document

-foot·er (foot′ər) *combining form* a person or thing (a specified number of) feet tall, high, long, etc.: used in hyphenated compounds [six-*footer*]

foot·fall (foot′fôl′) ***n.*** the sound of a footstep

foot fault *Tennis* a rule violation consisting of failure to keep both feet behind the base line, or to keep at least one foot on the ground, when serving

foot·gear (foot′gir′) ***n.*** covering for the feet; shoes, boots, etc.

☆**foot·hill** (-hil′) ***n.*** a low hill at or near the foot of a mountain or mountain range

foot·hold (-hōld′) ***n.*** **1** a place to put a foot down securely, as in climbing **2** a secure position from which it is difficult to be dislodged

☆**foot·ie** (foot′ē) ***n.*** **1** FOOTSIE **2** a very short sock, extending to or below the ankle

foot·ing (foot′iŋ) ***n.*** ⟦ME *fotinge*: see FOOT & -ING⟧ **1** [Now Rare] a moving on the feet; walking, dancing, etc. **2** a secure placing of the feet [to lose one's *footing*] **3** *a)* the condition of a surface with regard to its suitability, for walking, running, etc. [poor *footing* following the rain] *b)* a secure place to put the feet; foothold **4** *a)* a position or basis [the business is on a sound *footing*] *b)* a basis for relationship [a friendly *footing*, an equal *footing*] **5** *a)* the adding of a column of figures *b)* the sum obtained **6** *Archit.* the projecting base or enlarged foundation put under a column, wall, etc. to spread its weight and prevent settling

foo·tle (fo͞ot′'l, foot′'l) ***vi.*** **-tled, -tling** ⟦altered (prob. after FUTILE) < dial. *footer*, to trifle < Fr *foutre*, orig., to copulate with < L *futuere* < IE **bhaut-* < base **bhau-* > BEAT⟧ [Informal, Chiefly Brit.] to act or talk foolishly —***n.*** [Informal, Chiefly Brit.] foolishness; nonsense; twaddle

foot·less (foot′lis) ***adj.*** ⟦ME *fotles*⟧ **1** without a foot or feet **2** not supported; without basis or substance **3** [Informal] not skillful or efficient; clumsy; inept —**foot′less·ly** ***adv.*** —**foot′less·ness** ***n.***

foot·lights (foot′līts′) ***pl.n.*** a row of lights along the front of a stage at the actors' foot level, formerly common in stage lighting —**the footlights** the theater, or acting as a profession

foo·tling (fo͞ot′liŋ, foot′-) ***adj.*** ⟦prp. of FOOTLE⟧ [Informal] silly and unimportant; trivial; trifling

☆**foot·lock·er** (foot′läk′ər) ***n.*** a small trunk for personal belongings, usually kept at the foot of the bed of a soldier or camper

foot·loose (foot′lo͞os′) ***adj.*** free to go wherever one likes or to do as one likes

foot·man (foot′mən) ***n.***, *pl.* **-men** (-mən) ⟦orig., a man who ran on foot beside his master's horse or carriage⟧ **1** a male servant who assists the butler in a large household **2** [Archaic] a foot soldier; infantryman

foot·mark (foot′märk′) ***n.*** *var. of* FOOTPRINT

foot·note (foot′nōt′) ***n.*** **1** a note of comment or reference at the bottom of a page or, now often, at the end of a chapter or book: cf. ENDNOTE **2** an additional comment, remark, etc. —***vt.*** **-not′ed, -not′ing** to add a footnote or footnotes to

foot·pace (foot′pās′) ***n.*** **1** a normal walking pace **2** ⟦< PACE[1] in an old sense, "a step, platform"⟧ a raised platform

foot·pad (-pad′) ***n.*** ⟦see PAD[4]⟧ a highwayman who traveled on foot

foot·path (-path′) ***n.*** a narrow path for use by pedestrians only

foot-pound (foot′pound′) ***n.*** a basic unit of energy or work in the FPS system, equal to the amount of work needed to raise a weight of one pound a distance of one foot (1.3558 joule): symbol, ft-lb

foot-pound·al (foot′poun′dəl) ***n.*** a basic unit of energy or work in the FPS system, equal to the amount of work done by a force of one poundal acting through a distance of one foot (0.0421 joule): abbrev. *ft-pdl*

foot-pound-sec·ond (foot′pound′sek′ənd) ***adj.*** designating or of the British, Canadian, and U.S. system of measurement in which the foot, pound, and second are used as the units of length, mass, and time, respectively: abbrev. *FPS*: see the table of weights and measures in the Reference Supplement

foot·print (foot′print′) ***n.*** **1** an impression or mark made by a foot or shoe, as in sand **2** an area, or its shape, which something affects, occupies, etc., as the space taken up by a computer, the coverage pattern of a communications satellite, etc. See also CARBON FOOTPRINT

foot·race (-rās′) ***n.*** a race between runners on foot —**foot′rac′ing** ***n.***

foot·rest (-rest′) ***n.*** a support to rest the feet on

foot·rope (-rōp′) ***n.*** **1** the part of a boltrope sewn into the lower edge of the sail **2** a piece of wire rope supported beneath a yard, upon which sailors stand when furling or reefing sail

foot rot ☆**1** an infection which causes rotting of the stem base and crown of a plant, caused by various microorganisms **2** a disease of cattle and sheep caused by a bacterium (*Sphaerophorus necrophorus*) and characterized by necrosis of the tissue in and around the hoofs

☆**foot·sie** (foot′sē) ***n.*** the foot: a child's term —**play footsie (with)** [Informal] **1** to touch feet or rub knees (with) in a caressing way, as under the table **2** to flirt (with) or have surreptitious, usually underhanded dealings (with)

foot·slog (foot′släg′) ***vi.*** **-slogged′, -slog′ging** to march or plod through or as through mud —**foot′slog′ger** ***n.***

foot soldier **1** a soldier who moves and fights largely on foot; infantryman **2** a person who does the hard or routine work at the lowest levels of an organization, group, etc.

foot·sore (foot′sôr′) ***adj.*** having sore or tender feet, as from much walking

foot·stalk (-stôk′) ***n.*** the stalk of a flower or leaf; pedicel

foot·stall (-stôl′) ***n.*** the pedestal or base of a column

foot·step (foot′step′) ***n.*** **1** a person's step **2** the distance covered in a step **3** the sound of a step; footfall **4** a footprint **5** a step in a stairway —**follow in someone's footsteps** to follow someone's example, vocation, etc.; be or try to be like some predecessor

foot·stock (foot′stäk′) ***n.*** TAILSTOCK

foot·stone (foot′stōn′) ***n.*** a stone put at the foot of a grave

foot·stool (foot′sto͞ol′) ***n.*** a low stool for supporting the feet of a seated person

☆**foot·sy** (foot′sē) ***n.***, *pl.* **foot′sies** *alt. sp. of* FOOTSIE

foot-ton (foot′tun′) ***n.*** a unit of energy, equal to the amount of energy required to raise a weight of one long ton a distance of one foot; 2,240 foot-pounds

foot·wall (foot′wôl′) ***n.*** the side beneath an inclined fault, vein, lode, or other type of ore body

foot·way (foot′wā′) ***n.*** FOOTPATH

☆**foot·wear** (foot′wer′) ***n.*** foot coverings, as shoes or slippers

foot·work (foot′wurk′) ***n.*** the act or manner of moving or using the feet, as in walking, boxing, dancing, etc.

foot·worn (-wôrn′) ***adj.*** **1** having tired feet, as from much walking **2** worn down by feet [*footworn* stairs]

foo·ty[1] (fo͞ot′ē, foot′ē) ***adj.*** ⟦altered (as if < FOOT + -Y[3]) < Fr *foutu*, wretched, orig. pp. of *foutre*, to copulate: see FOOTLE⟧ [Dial.] of little or no importance; paltry; mean

☆**foot·y**[2] (foot′ē) ***n.***, *pl.* **foot′ies** *var. of* FOOTSIE

foo·zle (fo͞o′zəl) ***vt., vi.*** **-zled, -zling** ⟦< Ger *fuseln*, to bungle⟧ to make or do (something) awkwardly; esp., to bungle (a stroke in golf) —***n.*** an act of foozling; esp., a bad stroke in golf —**foo′zler** ***n.***

fop (fäp) ***n.*** ⟦ME *foppe*, a fool, prob. akin to FOB[2]⟧ **1** [Obs.] a foolish person **2** a vain, affected man who pays too much attention to his clothes, appearance, etc.; dandy —**fop′pish** ***adj.*** —**fop′pish·ly** ***adv.*** —**fop′pish·ness** ***n.***

FOP *abbrev.* Fraternal Order of Police

fop·per·y (fäp′ər ē) ***n.*** **1** the actions, dress, etc. of a fop **2** *pl.* **-per·ies** something foppish

for[1] (fôr, fur) ***prep.*** ⟦ME < OE, akin to Ger *für* & Du *ver-* < IE base **per-* > L *per-*, *pro-*, *prae-*, Gr *pro*, Sans *pári*⟧ **1** in place of; instead of [to use blankets *for* coats] **2** as the representative of; in the interest of [acting *for* another] **3** in defense of; in favor of [fight *for* our cause; vote *for* the levy] **4** in honor of [to give a banquet *for* someone] **5** with the aim or for the purpose of [to carry a gun *for* protection] **6** for the purpose of going to [he left *for* home] **7** in order to be, become, get, have, keep, etc. [to walk *for* exercise, to fight *for* one's life] **8** in search of [to look *for* a lost article] **9** meant to be received by (a specified person or thing), or to be used in (a specified way) [flowers *for* Mother, money *for* paying bills] **10** suitable to; appropriate to [a room *for* sleeping] **11** *a)* pertaining to; concerning [a need *for* improvement, an ear *for* music, a desire *for* power] *b)* as regards [*for* one thing, it costs too much; *for* another, we don't really need it] **12** as being [I know it *for* a fact] **13** considering the general nature of [cool *for* July, clever *for* a child] **14** because of; as a result of [to cry *for* pain] **15** in proportion to; corresponding to [two dollars spent *for* every dollar earned] **16** to the amount of; equal to [a bill *for* $50]: when preceded and followed by the same noun, *for* indicates equality between things being compared or contrasted (dollar *for* dollar) **17** *a)* at the price or by the payment of [sold *for* $20,000] *b)* in exchange with respect to [our thanks *for* your help] **18** to the length, duration, or extent of; throughout; through [to walk *for* an hour] **19** at (a specified time) [an appointment *for* two o'clock] **20** [Obs.] before —***conj.*** because; seeing that; since: more formal than *because* and used to introduce evidence or explanation for an immediately preceding statement [comfort him, *for* he is sad] —**for all** in spite of; notwithstanding [stupid *for all* their learning] —**for one** as one individual or example [I, *for one*, like the idea] —**O! for** I wish that I had

for[2] *abbrev.* **1** foreign **2** forestry

for- (fôr, fər) ⟦ME < OE, replacing *fer-*, *fær-* (akin to Ger *ver-* < IE base **per-*, as in FOR[1]) & < OFr *for-* (as in FORFEIT) < L *foris*, beyond, from without⟧ *prefix* **1** away, apart, off [*forbid, forget, forgo*] **2** very much, intensely [*forlorn*] A prefix of Old and Middle English, much of whose original force is now obscured

fo·ra (fôr′ə) ***n.*** *alt. pl. of* FORUM

for·age (fôr′ij, fär′-) ***n.*** ⟦ME < OFr *fourage* < *forre*, *fuerre*, fodder < Frank **fodr*, food, akin to OE *fodor*, FODDER⟧ **1** food for domestic animals; fodder **2** a search for food or provisions ***—vi.*** **-aged**, **-ag·ing** ⟦Fr *fourrager* < the *n.*⟧ **1** to search for food or provisions **2** to search for what one needs or wants ***—vt.*** **1** *a)* to get or take food or provisions from *b)* [Now Rare] to ravage; plunder **2** to provide with forage; feed **3** to get by foraging **—for′ag·er** ***n.***

forage acre a measure of the vegetation available for grazing on a range or pasture, equal to the total area multiplied by the percentage of surface covered by usable vegetation (Ex.: 10 acres × 30% coverage = 3 forage acres)

For·a·ker (fôr′ə kər), **Mount** ⟦after J. B. *Foraker* (1846-1917), prominent politician⟧ mountain in the Alaska Range, SC Alas.: 17,395 ft (5,302 m)

for·am (fôr′əm) ***n.*** *short for* FORAMINIFER

fo·ra·men (fō rā′mən, fə-) ***n.***, *pl.* **-ram′i·na** (-ram′ə nə) or **-ra′mens** ⟦L, a hole < *forare*, BORE⟧ a small opening or perforation, esp. in a bone or in a plant ovule **—fo·ram′i·nal** (-ram′i nəl) ***adj.***, **fo·ram′i·nate** (-nit)

foramen mag·num (mag′nəm) ⟦ModL, large opening⟧ the opening at the base of the skull where the spinal cord merges with the medulla oblongata

foramen o·va·le (ō vā′lē) ⟦ModL, oval opening⟧ the small, oval opening in the wall that separates the atria of the heart in a normal fetus: it allows blood to bypass the nonfunctioning fetal lungs until the time of birth when it gradually closes up

for·a·min·i·fer (fôr′ə min′i fər) ***n.***, *pl.* **fo·ram·i·nif·er·a** (fə ram′ə nif′ər ə) ⟦< L *foramen* (gen. *foraminis*): see FORAMEN & -FER⟧ any of an order (Foraminiferida) of marine protozoans with calcareous shells full of tiny holes through which slender filaments project: they form the main component of chalk and many deep-sea oozes: also called **fo·ram·i·nif·er·an** (fō ram′ə nif′ər ən) **—fo·ram′i·nif′er·al** ***adj.***, **fo·ram′i·nif′er·ous**

for·as·much (fôr′az much′) ***conj.*** inasmuch (*as*)

for·ay (fôr′ā) ***vi.*** ⟦ME *forraien*, prob. back-form. < *forreier*, *forager* < OFr *forrier* < *forrer*, to forage < *forre*: see FORAGE⟧ to make a foray (*into* enemy territory, an unfamiliar situation, etc.) ***—n.*** **1** ⟦ME *forrai*⟧ a sudden attack or raid into enemy territory, as to seize something or to plunder **2** a venturing into any new or unfamiliar situation or undertaking

☆**forb** (fôrb) ***n.*** ⟦Gr *phorbē*, fodder < *pherbein*, to feed, graze⟧ a broad-leaved herbaceous plant, as distinguished from the grasses, sedges, shrubs, and trees

for·bade or **for·bad** (fər bad′, fôr-) ***vt.*** *pt. of* FORBID

for·bear[1] (fôr ber′) ***vt.*** **-bore′** or [Archaic] **-bare′**, **-borne′**, **-bear′ing** ⟦ME *forberen* < OE *forberan*: see FOR- & BEAR[1]⟧ **1** to refrain from; avoid or cease (doing, saying, etc.) **2** [Now Chiefly Dial.] to endure; tolerate ***—vi.*** **1** to refrain or abstain **2** to keep oneself in check; control oneself under provocation —*SYN.* REFRAIN[1] **—for·bear′er** ***n.*** **—for·bear′ing·ly** ***adv.***

for·bear[2] (fôr′ber′) ***n.*** *alt. sp. of* FOREBEAR

for·bear·ance (fôr ber′əns) ***n.*** **1** the act of forbearing **2** the quality of being forbearing; self-control; patient restraint **3** *Law* the act by which a creditor extends time for payment of a debt or forgoes for a time the right to enforce legal action on the debt —*SYN.* PATIENCE

for·bid (fər bid′, fôr-) ***vt.*** **-bade′** or **-bad′**, **-bid′den** or [Archaic] **-bid′**, **-bid′ding** ⟦ME *forbeden* < OE *forbeodan*: see FOR- & BID[1]⟧ **1** to rule against; not permit; prohibit **2** to command to stay away from; exclude or bar from **3** to make impossible; prevent

SYN.—**forbid** is the basic, direct word meaning to command a person to refrain from some action; **prohibit** implies a forbidding by law or official decree; **interdict** implies legal or ecclesiastical prohibition, usually for a limited time, as an exemplary punishment or to forestall unfavorable developments; **enjoin** implies a legal order from a court prohibiting (or ordering) a given action, under penalty; **ban** implies legal or ecclesiastical prohibition with an added connotation of strong condemnation or censure —*ANT.* **permit**, **allow**

for·bid·dance (-bid′ns) ***n.*** the act of forbidding; prohibition

for·bid·den (-bid′n) ***adj.*** not permitted; prohibited

forbidden fruit **1** *Bible* the fruit of the tree of knowledge of good and evil, forbidden to Adam and Eve: Gen. 2:17; 3:3 **2** any sinful or forbidden pleasure

for·bid·ding (fər bid′iŋ, fôr-) ***adj.*** looking dangerous, threatening, or disagreeable; repellent **—for·bid′ding·ly** ***adv.***

for·bore (fôr bôr′) ***vt.***, ***vi.*** *pt. of* FORBEAR[1]

for·borne (-bôrn′) ***vt.***, ***vi.*** *pp. of* FORBEAR[1]

for·by or **for·bye** (fôr bī′) ***prep.***, ***adv.*** ⟦ME *forbi* (see FOR- & BY), akin to Ger *vorbei*⟧ [Chiefly Scot.] besides

force (fôrs, fōrs) ***n.*** ⟦ME < OFr < VL **fortia*, **forcia* < L *fortis*, strong: see FORT[1]⟧ **1** strength; energy; vigor; power **2** the intensity of power; impetus [the *force* of a blow] **3** *a)* physical power or strength exerted against a person or thing [to use *force* in opening a door] *b)* the use of physical power to overcome or restrain a person; physical coercion; violence [to resort to *force* in dispersing a mob] **4** the power of a person to act effectively and vigorously; moral or intellectual strength [*force* of character] **5** *a)* the power to control, persuade, influence, etc.; effectiveness [the *force* of circumstances, an argument lacking *force*] *b)* a person, thing, or group having a certain influence, power, etc. [a *force* for good] **6** the real or precise meaning; basic point [to miss the *force* of something said] **7** *a)* military, naval, or air power *b)* the collective armed strength, as of a nation *c)* any organized group of soldiers, sailors, etc. **8** any group of people organized for some activity [a sales *force*, a police *force*] **9** *Law* binding power; validity **10** *Physics* the cause, or agent, that puts an object at rest into motion or alters the motion of a moving object: abbrev. *F* ***—vt.*** **forced**, **forc′ing** ⟦ME *forcen* < OFr *forcer* < VL **fortiare* < **fortia*, **forcia*: see the *n.*⟧ **1** to cause to do something by or as if by force; compel **2** to rape (a woman) **3** *a)* to break open, into, or through by force [to *force* a lock] *b)* to make (a way, etc.) by force *c)* to overpower or capture by breaking into, through, etc. [to *force* the enemy's stronghold] **4** to get or take by force; wrest; extort [*forcing* the gun from his hand] **5** to drive by or as by force; cause to move against resistance; impel [to *force* an article into a filled box] **6** to impose by or as by force: with *on* or *upon* [to *force* one's attentions on another] **7** to effect or produce by or as by force; produce by unusual or unnatural effort [to *force* a smile] **8** to exert beyond the natural limits or capacity; strain [to *force* one's voice] **9** to cause (plants, fruit, etc.) to develop or grow faster by artificial means **10** [Obs.] *a)* to give or add force to *b)* to put in force ☆**11** *Baseball* *a)* to cause (a base runner) to be put out by a force-out (said of a batter) *b)* to cause (a runner) to score or (a run) to be scored by walking the batter with the bases full (often with *in*) **12** *a)* *Card Games* to cause (an opponent) to play (a particular card) *b)* *Bridge* to make a bid that requires (one's partner) to bid in response **—in force** **1** in full strength; in full number **2** in effect; operative; valid **—force′a·ble** ***adj.*** **—force′less** ***adj.*** **—forc′er** ***n.***

SYN.—**force** implies the exertion of power in causing a person or thing to act, move, or comply against his or its resistance and may refer to physical strength or to any impelling motive [circumstances *forced* him to lie]; **compel** implies a driving irresistibly to some action, condition, etc.; to **coerce** is to compel submission or obedience by the use of superior power, intimidation, threats, etc.; **constrain** implies the operation of a restricting force and therefore suggests a strained, repressed, or unnatural quality in that which results [a *constrained* laugh] See also **strength**

forced (fôrst) ***adj.*** **1** done or brought about by force; not voluntary; compulsory [*forced* labor] **2** produced or kept up by unusual effort; not natural or spontaneous; strained or constrained [a *forced* smile] **3** due to necessity or emergency [a *forced* landing] **4** at a pace faster than usual [a *forced* march] **—forc·ed·ly** (fôr′sid lē) ***adv.***

☆**force-feed** (fôrs′fēd′) ***vt.*** **-fed′**, **-feed′ing** to feed by force, esp. by means of a tube passing down the throat to the stomach

force·ful (fôrs′fəl) ***adj.*** full of force; powerful, vigorous, effective, cogent, etc. **—force′ful·ly** ***adv.*** **—force′ful·ness** ***n.***

force ma·jeure (fôrs mȧ zhër′) ⟦Fr⟧ **1** superior or overwhelming power **2** an unanticipated or uncontrollable event or effect which releases one from fulfillment of a contractual obligation

force·meat (fôrs′mēt′) ***n.*** ⟦altered < *farce meat* < FARCE, *vt.*⟧ meat or fish chopped up and seasoned, usually for stuffing

☆**force-out** (fôrs′out′) ***n.*** *Baseball* an out that results when a base runner who has been forced from a base when a teammate hits the ball fails to reach the next base before the ball does

for·ceps (fôr′seps′, -səps) ***n.***, *pl.* **-ceps′** ⟦L, orig., smith's tongs < *formus*, WARM + *capere*, to take: see HAVE⟧ tongs or pincers for grasping, compressing, and pulling, used esp. by surgeons and dentists

force pump a pump with a valveless plunger for forcing a liquid through a pipe, esp. for sending water under pressure to a considerable height

for·ci·ble (fôr′sə bəl) ***adj.*** ⟦ME < OFr⟧ **1** done or effected by force; involving the use of force **2** having force; forceful **—for′ci·ble·ness** ***n.*** **—for′ci·bly** ***adv.***

ford (fôrd) ***n.*** ⟦ME < OE, akin to Ger *furt* < IE *pr̥tu*, passage < base **per-*, to transport > FARE, L *portus*, Goth **faran*⟧ a shallow place in a stream, river, etc., where one can cross by wading or by riding on horseback, in an automobile, etc. ***—vt.*** to cross at a ford **—ford′a·ble** ***adj.***

Ford (fôrd) **1 Ford Ma·dox** (mad′əks) (born *Ford Madox Hueffer*) 1873-1939; Eng. writer & editor **2 Gerald R(udolph), Jr.** (born *Leslie Lynch King, Jr.*) 1913-2006; 38th president of the U.S. (1974-77) **3 Henry** 1863-1947; U.S. automobile manufacturer **4 John** 1586-1639?; Eng. dramatist **5 John** (born *John Martin Feeney*) 1894-1973; U.S. film director

for·do (fôr do͞o′) ***vt.*** **-did′**, **-done′**, **-do′ing** ⟦ME *fordon* < OE: see FOR- & DO[1]⟧ [Archaic] **1** to destroy, kill, ruin, etc. **2** to cause to become exhausted: only in the pp.

fore (fôr, fōr) ***adv.*** ⟦ME < OE *fore*, *foran*, akin to Ger *vor* < IE base **per-*, through, throughout, before > FOR[1], FOR-, L *per*⟧ **1** at, in, or toward the bow of a ship: only in FORE AND AFT **2** [Obs.] previously ***—adj.*** **1** situated in front or in front of some other thing or part **2** [Obs.] previous; former ***—n.*** the thing or part in front ***—prep.*** [Obs.] in the sight of; before: used chiefly in oaths, as in a court of law ***—interj.*** *Golf* used as a shout warning players who are farther ahead that one is about to hit the ball **—to the fore** to the front; into view or into prominence

'fore (fôr, fōr) ***prep.*** [Old Poet.] *short for* BEFORE

fore- (fôr, fōr) ⟦ME < OE: see FORE⟧ *prefix* **1** before in time, place, order, or rank [*forenoon*, *foreman*] **2** the front part of [*forehead*]

fore and aft *Naut.* **1** from the bow to the stern; lengthwise [sails rigged *fore and aft*] **2** at, in, or toward both the bow and the stern [lifeboats located *fore and aft*]

fore-and-aft (fôr′ən aft′) ***adj.*** *Naut.* from the bow to the stern; lengthwise or set lengthwise, as sails

fore-and-aft·er (-af′tər) ***n.*** a schooner, ketch, or other ship with fore-and-aft rig

fore·arm[1] (fôr′ärm′) ***n.*** the part of the arm between the elbow and the wrist

fore·arm[2] (fôr ärm′) ***vt.*** to arm in advance; prepare beforehand for a fight or any difficulty

fore·bear (fôr′ber′) ***n.*** ⟦< FORE + BE + -ER⟧ an ancestor

fore·bear·er (-ər) ***n.*** *disputed var. of* FOREBEAR

fore·bode (fôr bōd′) ***vt., vi.*** **-bod′ed, -bod′ing** ⟦OE *forebodian*: see FORE- & BIDED⟧ **1** to indicate beforehand; portend; foretell; predict (esp. something bad or harmful) **2** to have a presentiment of (something bad or harmful) —**fore·bod′er** ***n.***

fore·bod·ing (fôr bōd′iŋ, fôr′bōd′-) ***n.*** ⟦OE *forebodung*⟧ a prediction, portent, or presentiment, esp. of something bad or harmful —***adj.*** characterized by foreboding —***SYN.*** OMINOUS —**fore·bod′ing·ly** ***adv.***

fore·brain (fôr′brān′) ***n.*** **1** the front part of the three primary divisions of the brain of a vertebrate embryo **2** the part of the fully developed brain evolved from this, consisting of the diencephalon and the telencephalon

fore·cast (fôr′kast′; *for v., also* fôr kast′) ***vt.*** **-cast′** or **-cast′ed, -cast′ing** ⟦ME *forecasten* < *fore* (see FORE) + *casten*, to contrive: see CAST⟧ **1** [Archaic] to foresee **2** to estimate or calculate in advance; predict or seek to predict (weather, business conditions, etc.) **3** to serve as a prediction or prophecy of —***vi.*** to make a forecast —***n.*** **1** [Archaic] foresight; forethought **2** a prediction, as of weather conditions —**fore′cast′er** ***n.***

fore·cas·tle (fōk′səl, fôr′kas′əl) ***n.*** ⟦FORE + CASTLE: from the foremost of the two castlelike structures on the hull of a medieval vessel⟧ **1** the upper deck of a ship in front of the foremast **2** the front part of a merchant ship, where the crew's quarters are located

fore·check (fôr′chek′) ***vt.*** *Hockey* to check (an opponent) in the area around the opponent's goal, usually in an effort to prevent an offensive play from developing: cf. BACKCHECK

fore·close (fôr klōz′) ***vt.*** **-closed′, -clos′ing** ⟦ME *forclosen* < OFr *forclos*, pp. of *forclore*, to exclude < *fors* (< L *foris*: see DOOR), outside + *clore* (< L *claudere*), CLOSE[3]⟧ **1** to shut out; exclude; bar **2** to extinguish the right to redeem (a mortgage) by foreclosure **3** to deprive (a mortgagor) of this right by foreclosure **4** to hinder or prevent **5** to claim exclusively —***vi.*** to foreclose a mortgage —**fore·clos′a·ble** ***adj.***

fore·clo·sure (fôr klō′zhər) ***n.*** the legal procedure for satisfying claims against a mortgagor in default who has not redeemed the mortgage: satisfaction may be obtained from the proceeds of a forced sale of the property

fore·court (fôr′kôrt′) ***n.*** **1** a court at the front of a building ☆**2** *Basketball* the half of the court which contains the basket toward which the ball is shot in attempting to score **3** *Tennis, etc.* the part of the court nearest the net

fore·deck (-dek′) ***n.*** the forepart of a ship's main deck

fore·do (fôr do͞o′) ***vt.*** *alt. sp. of* FORDO

fore·doom (fôr do͞om′; *for n.* fôr′do͞om′) ***vt.*** to doom in advance; condemn beforehand —***n.*** [Archaic] a sentence or judgment in advance; destiny

fore·fa·ther (fôr′fä′thər) ***n.*** ⟦ME *forefader*: see FORE- & FATHER⟧ an ancestor

fore·feel (fôr fēl′) ***vt.*** **-felt′, -feel′ing** to feel beforehand; have a premonition of

fore·fend (fôr fend′) ***vt.*** *alt. sp. of* FORFEND

fore·fin·ger (fôr′fiŋ′gər) ***n.*** ⟦ME⟧ the finger nearest the thumb; index finger; first finger

fore·foot (-fo͝ot′) ***n., pl.*** **-feet′** ⟦ME *forefot*⟧ **1** either of the front feet of an animal with four or more feet **2** the meeting point of the keel and the stem of a ship

fore·front (-frunt′) ***n.*** **1** the extreme front **2** the position of most activity, importance, etc.

fore·gath·er (fôr gath′ər) ***vi.*** *alt. sp. of* FORGATHER

fore·go[1] (-gō′) ***vt., vi.*** **-went′, -gone′, -go′ing** ⟦ME *forgon* < OE *foregan*⟧ to go before in place, time, or degree; precede

fore·go[2] (-gō′) ***vt.*** *alt. sp. of* FORGO

fore·go·ing (fôr′gō′iŋ, fôr gō′-) ***adj.*** previously said, written, etc.; preceding —**the foregoing 1** the one or ones previously mentioned **2** what has already been said or written

fore·gone (fôr gôn′, fôr′gôn′) ***adj.*** **1** that has gone before; previous; former **2** previously determined or confidently anticipated; also, inevitable or unavoidable: said of a conclusion

fore·ground (fôr′ground′) ***n.*** **1** the part of a scene, landscape, etc. nearest, or represented in perspective as nearest, to the viewer **2** the most noticeable or conspicuous position —☆***vt.*** to bring to or place in the foreground; emphasize; highlight

fore·gut (-gut′) ***n.*** the front part of the alimentary canal in vertebrate embryos: the duodenum, stomach, esophagus, pharynx, etc. develop from it

fore·hand (fôr′hand′) ***n.*** **1** [Archaic] the position in front or above; advantage **2** the part of a horse in front of the rider **3** a kind of stroke, as in tennis, made with the arm extended and the palm of the hand turned forward —***adj.*** **1** [Obs.] done or given earlier **2** foremost; front **3** done or performed as or with a forehand —***adv.*** with a forehand

fore·hand·ed (fôr′han′did′, -han′-) ***adj.*** **1** looking ahead to, or making provision for, the future; thrifty; prudent **2** well-to-do; well-off; prosperous **3** FOREHAND (*adj.* 3) —**fore′hand′ed·ly** ***adv.*** —**fore′hand′ed·ness** ***n.***

fore·head (fôr′ed′, -hed′; fär′-; -id) ***n.*** ⟦ME *forhed* < OE *forheafod*: see FORE- & HEAD⟧ **1** the part of the face between the eyebrows and the line where the hair normally begins **2** [Old Poet.] the front part of anything

for·eign (fôr′in, fär′-) ***adj.*** ⟦ME *forein* < OFr *forein, forain* < LL *foranus*, foreign, orig., external < L *foras*, out-of-doors, orig. acc. pl. of OL *fora*, DOOR⟧ **1** situated outside one's own country, province, locality, etc. [*foreign* lands] **2** of, from, or characteristic of another country or countries [*foreign* languages] **3** having to do with the relations of one country to another country or countries [*foreign* affairs, *foreign* trade]: often opposed to DOMESTIC **4** not subject to the laws or jurisdiction of the specified country **5** *a)* not natural to the person or thing specified; not belonging; not characteristic [a trait *foreign* to one's nature] *b)* not pertinent; irrelevant **6** not organically belonging; introduced from outside: said of substances found in parts of the body or in organisms where they do not naturally occur —***SYN.*** EXTRINSIC —**for′eign·ness** ***n.***

foreign bill (of exchange) a bill of exchange drawn in one state or country and payable in another, as one arising from foreign trade operations

for·eign-born (-bôrn′) ***adj.*** born in some other country; not native —**the foreign-born** immigrants of a country

foreign correspondent a journalist who reports news from a foreign country

for·eign·er (fôr′in ər, fär′-) ***n.*** **1** a person from another country, thought of as an outsider; alien **2** any person regarded as an outsider or stranger —***SYN.*** ALIEN

foreign exchange 1 the transfer of credits to a foreign country to settle debts or accounts between residents of the home country and those of the foreign country **2** foreign bills, currencies, etc. used to settle such accounts

☆**for·eign·ism** (fôr′in iz′əm, fär′-) ***n.*** a foreign idiom, mannerism, custom, etc.

foreign legion 1 a military force composed mainly of volunteers from foreign countries **2** [**F- L-**] such a French force, originally based in N Africa

foreign minister a member of a governmental cabinet in charge of foreign affairs for the country

foreign mission 1 a religious, esp. Christian, mission sent by a church to do missionary work esp. in a non-Christian country **2** a group sent on diplomatic or other business to a foreign nation

foreign office in some countries, the office of government in charge of foreign affairs

fore·judge[1] (fôr juj′) ***vt.*** **-judged′, -judg′ing** to consider or decide before knowing the facts; judge beforehand

fore·judge[2] (fôr juj′) ***vt.*** **-judged′, -judg′ing** ⟦ME *forjugen* < OFr *forjugier* < *fors*, outside (< L *foris*: see FORFEIT) + *jugier*: see JUDGE⟧ *Law* to expel or dispossess by court judgment

fore·know (fôr nō′) ***vt.*** **-knew′, -known′, -know′ing** to know beforehand —**fore·know′a·ble** ***adj.***

fore·knowl·edge (fôr′näl′ij, fôr näl′ij) ***n.*** knowledge of something before it happens or exists

☆**fore·la·dy** (fôr′lā′dē) ***n., pl.*** **-dies** a forewoman in charge of a department or group of workers

fore·land (fôr′lənd) ***n.*** ⟦ME⟧ **1** a headland; promontory **2** land in relation to the territory behind it

fore·leg (fôr′leg′, -lāg′) ***n.*** either of the front legs of an animal with four or more legs

fore·limb (-lim′) ***n.*** a front limb, as an arm, foreleg, wing, or flipper

fore·lock (-läk′) ***n.*** a lock of hair growing just above, or hanging over, the forehead

fore·man (fôr′mən) ***n., pl.*** **-men** (-mən) ⟦orig., foremost man, leader⟧ **1** the chairman and spokesman of a jury **2** a person in charge of a department or group of workers in a factory, mill, etc. —**fore′man·ship′** ***n.***

fore·mast (fôr′mast′, -məst) ***n.*** the mast nearest the bow of a ship

fore·most (fôr′mōst′; *also*, -məst) ***adj.*** ⟦ME *foremeste* < OE *formest* (akin to OFris *formest*, Goth *frumists*), superl. of OE *forma*, itself a superl. of *fore* (see FORE); later understood and spelled as FORE + MOST⟧ **1** first in place or time **2** first in rank or importance; leading —***adv.*** before all else; first —***SYN.*** CHIEF

fore·moth·er (fôr′muth′ər) ***n.*** ⟦< FORE- + MOTHER[1], by analogy with FOREFATHER⟧ a female ancestor

fore·name (fôr′nām′) ***n.*** a given name; personal name; name before the surname

fore·named (-nāmd′) ***adj.*** named or mentioned before

fore·noon (fôr′no͞on′, fôr′no͞on′) ***n.*** the time of day from sunrise to noon; morning, esp. the late morning —***adj.*** of, in, or for the forenoon

fo·ren·sic (fə ren′sik, -zik) ***adj.*** ⟦< L *forensis*, public < *forum* (see FORUM) + adj. suffix *-ensis* + -IC⟧ **1** of, characteristic of, or suitable for a law court, public debate, or formal argumentation **2** specializing in or having to do with the application of scientific, esp. medical, knowledge to legal matters, as in the investigation of crime —***n.*** [*pl., with sing. v.*] **1** debate or formal argumentation **2** the use of knowledge and techniques derived from various sciences, as ballistics and medicine, in the investigation of crime —**fo·ren′si·cal·ly** ***adv.***

fore·or·dain (fôr′ôr dān′) ***vt.*** to ordain beforehand; predestine —**fore′or′di·na′tion** (-ôrd′′n ā′shən) ***n.***

fore·part (fôr′pärt′) ***n.*** **1** the first or early part **2** the part in front

fore·passed or **fore·past** (fôr past′) ***adj.*** [Rare] past; bygone

fore·paw (fôr′pô′) ***n.*** an animal's front paw

fore·peak (-pēk′) ***n.*** the part of a ship's interior in the angle of the bow

fore·per·son (fôr′pur′sən) ***n.*** FOREMAN: used to avoid the masculine implication of *foreman*

fore·play (fôr′plā′) ***n.*** mutual sexual stimulation preceding sexual intercourse

fore·quar·ter (-kwôrt′ər) ***n.*** **1** the front half of a side of beef or the like **2** [*pl.*] the front quarters of a horse or other animal, including the forelegs

fore·reach (fôr rēch′) ***vt.*** to overtake and pass, esp. in a sailboat —***vi.*** to keep moving forward while heading into the wind: said esp. of a sailing vessel that is coming about

fore·run (-run′) ***vt.*** **-ran′**, **-run′**, **-run′ning** [Now Rare] **1** to run before; go before; precede **2** to be the precursor of; be a prediction or sign of (a thing to follow); foreshadow **3** to forestall

fore·run·ner (fôr′run′ər, fôr run′ər) ***n.*** ⟦ME *forerenner*, after L *praecursor*⟧ **1** a person sent before or going before to announce or prepare the way for another or for something to follow; herald **2** a sign that tells or warns of something to follow; prognostic **3** *a)* a predecessor *b)* an ancestor

fore·said (fôr′sed′) ***adj.*** *archaic var. of* AFORESAID

fore·sail (fôr′sāl′; *naut.*, -səl) ***n.*** **1** the lowest sail on the foremast of a square-rigged ship **2** the main triangular sail on the foremast of a schooner **3** a JIB[2]

fore·see (fôr sē′) ***vt.*** **-saw′**, **-seen′**, **-see′ing** ⟦ME *forseyn* < OE *foreseon*⟧ to see beforehand; know beforehand; foreknow —**fore·see′a·ble** ***adj.*** —**fore·se′er** ***n.***

fore·shad·ow (-shad′ō) ***vt.*** ⟦FORE- + SHADOW (*vt.* 4): that is, to be the shadow thrown ahead of (something)⟧ to be a sign of (something to come); indicate or suggest beforehand; prefigure; presage

fore·shank (fôr′shaŋk′) ***n.*** **1** the upper part of the front legs of cattle **2** meat from this part

fore·sheet (fôr′shēt′) ***n.*** **1** one of the ropes used to trim a foresail **2** [*pl.*] the space forward in an open boat

fore·shock (-shäk′) ***n.*** a minor earthquake preceding a greater one and originating at or near the same place

fore·shore (-shôr′) ***n.*** **1** the part of a shore closest to the water **2** the part of a shore between the high-water and low-water marks

fore·short·en (fôr shôrt′′n) ***vt.*** **1** in painting, drawing, etc., to represent some lines of (an object) as shorter than they actually are in order to give the illusion of proper relative size, in accordance with the principles of perspective **2** to present in condensed form; abridge

foreshortened arm

fore·show (-shō′) ***vt.*** **-showed′**, **-shown′** or **-showed′**, **-show′ing** ⟦ME *foreshewen* < OE *foresceawian*⟧ to show or indicate beforehand; foretell; prefigure

fore·side (fôr′sīd′) ***n.*** ⟦ME⟧ [Now Rare] the front or upper side

fore·sight (fôr′sīt′) ***n.*** ⟦ME, prob. transl. of L *providentia*⟧ **1** *a)* the act of foreseeing *b)* the power to foresee **2** a looking forward **3** thoughtful regard or provision for the future; prudent forethought —**fore′sight′ed** ***adj.*** —**fore′sight′ed·ly** ***adv.*** —**fore′sight′ed·ness** ***n.***

fore·skin (fôr′skin′) ***n.*** the fold of skin that covers the glans of the penis; prepuce: in circumcision it is completely or partly removed

fore·speak (fôr spēk′) ***vt.*** **-spoke′** or [Archaic] **-spake′**, **-spok′en** or [Archaic] **-spoke′**, **-speak′ing** ⟦ME *forspeken*: see FORE- & SPEAK⟧ [Rare] **1** to foretell; prophesy; predict **2** to apply for or demand in advance; bespeak

for·est (fôr′ist, fär′-) ***n.*** ⟦ME < OFr (Fr *forêt*) < ML (*silva*) *forestis*, as if (wood) unenclosed (< L *foris*, out-of-doors), but prob. (wood) under court control (< L *forum*, court, FORUM)⟧ **1** a thick growth of trees and underbrush covering an extensive tract of land; large woods: often used fig. **2** [Brit. Historical] any of certain tracts of woodland or wasteland, usually the property of the sovereign, preserved for game —***adj.*** of or in a forest; sylvan —***vt.*** to plant with trees; change into a forest; afforest

fore·stage (fôr′stāj′) ***n.*** the part of a stage in front of the curtain; apron

fore·stall (fôr stôl′) ***vt.*** ⟦ME *forestallen* < *forestal*, ambush < OE *foresteall*: see FORE & STALL[2]⟧ **1** to prevent or hinder by doing something ahead of time **2** to act in advance of; get ahead of; anticipate **3** to interfere with the trading in (a market) by buying up goods in advance, getting sellers to raise prices, etc. **4** [Obs.] *a)* to intercept *b)* to obstruct by force —***SYN.*** PREVENT —**fore·stall′er** ***n.*** —**fore·stall′ment** ***n.***

☆**for·est·a·tion** (fôr′is tā′shən, fär′-) ***n.*** the planting or care of forests; afforestation

fore·stay (fôr′stā′) ***n.*** ⟦ME *forstay*: see FORE- & STAY[1]⟧ a rope or cable reaching from the head of a ship's foremast to the bowsprit, for supporting the foremast

fore·stay·sail (fôr′stā′sāl′, *naut.*, -səl) ***n.*** a triangular sail set from the forestay

for·est·ed (fôr′is təd, fär′-) ***adj.*** covered with a thick growth of trees and underbrush [*a forested* mountainside]

for·est·er (fôr′is tər, fär′-) ***n.*** ⟦ME < OFr *forestier* < ML *forestarius*⟧ **1** a person trained in forestry **2** a person in charge of a forest or trees **3** a person or animal that lives in a forest **4** any of a family (Agaristidae) of metallic-green or velvety-black moths

For·es·ter (fôr′is tər, fär′-), **C(ecil) S(cott)** 1899-1966; Eng. novelist

forest green ⟦first used by Sir Walter SCOTT[2] in ref. to the color of clothing worn by ROBIN HOOD and his men⟧ a deep green color

for·est·land (fôr′ist land′, fär′-) ***n.*** an area or region covered with forests or reserved for forests

for·est·ry (fôr′is trē, fär′-) ***n.*** **1** [Rare] wooded land; forest land **2** the science of planting and taking care of forests **3** systematic forest management for the production of timber, conservation, etc.

fore·taste (fôr′tāst′; *for v.* fôr tāst′) ***n.*** ⟦ME *fortaste*⟧ a preliminary or first taste; slight experience of something to be enjoyed, endured, etc. in the future; anticipation —***vt.*** **-tast′ed**, **-tast′ing** [Rare] to taste beforehand; have a foretaste of

fore·tell (fôr tel′) ***vt.*** **-told′**, **-tell′ing** ⟦ME *foretellen*, prob. transl. of L *praedicere*⟧ to tell, announce, or indicate beforehand; prophesy; predict —**fore·tell′er** ***n.***

fore·thought (fôr′thôt′) ***n.*** ⟦ME: see FORE- & THOUGHT⟧ **1** a thinking or planning beforehand; premeditation **2** prudent thought for the future; foresight —***adj.*** planned beforehand

fore·time (fôr′tīm′) ***n.*** the past; former time

fore·to·ken (fôr′tō′kən; *for v.* fôr tō′kən) ***n.*** ⟦ME *foretokne* < OE *foretacn*: see FORE- & TOKEN⟧ a prophetic sign; omen; prognostic —***vt.*** to be a prophetic sign or omen of; foreshadow

fore·told (fôr tōld′) ***vt.*** *pt. & pp. of* FORETELL

fore·tooth (fôr′to͞oth′) ***n.***, *pl.* **-teeth′** ⟦ME *foretoth* < OE⟧ a front tooth; incisor

fore·top (-täp′; *also, for 1 naut.*, -təp) ***n.*** ⟦ME: see FORE- & TOP[1]⟧ **1** a platform at the top of a ship's foremast **2** a horse's (or, formerly, a person's) forelock

fore-top·gal·lant (fôr′täp′gal′ənt′; *naut.*, -tə gal′-) ***adj.*** designating or of the mast, sail, yard, etc. just above the fore-topmast

fore-top·mast (fôr′täp′mast′; *naut.*, -məst) ***n.*** the section of the foremast just above the bottommost section

fore-top·sail (-sāl; *naut.*, -səl) ***n.*** the sail set on the fore-topmast, above the foresail

for·ev·er (fôr ev′ər, fər-) ***adv.*** **1** for eternity; for always; endlessly **2** at all times; always —***n.*** [Informal] a period of time that seems to have no end: a hyperbolic use [we stood in line *forever*]

for·ev·er·more (fôr ev′ər môr′, fər-) ***adv.*** for eternity; for always; forever

fore·warn (fôr wôrn′) ***vt.*** to warn beforehand

fore·went (-went′) ***vt.***, ***vi.*** *pt. of* FOREGO[1]

fore·wing (fôr′wiŋ′) ***n.*** either of the front pair of wings present in most insects and sometimes forming a cover for the hind pair

fore·wom·an (-wo͝om′ən) ***n.***, *pl.* **-wom′en** (-wim′in) a woman serving as a foreman

fore·word (-wərd) ***n.*** ⟦transl. of Ger *vorwort* < *vor*, FORE + *wort*, WORD⟧ an introductory statement to a book, esp. one written by someone other than the book's author —***SYN.*** INTRODUCTION

fore·worn (fôr wôrn′) ***adj.*** *alt. sp. of* FORWORN

fore·yard (for′yärd′) ***n.*** the lowest yard on the foremast, from which the foresail is set

For·far (fôr′fər) *former name for* ANGUS[2]: also **For′far·shire′** (-shir′)

for·feit (fôr′fit) ***n.*** ⟦ME *forfet* < OFr *forfait*, pp. of *forfaire*, to transgress < ML *forisfacere*, to do wrong, lit., to do beyond < L *foris*, *foras*, out-of-doors, beyond (see FOREIGN) + *facere* (see FACT)⟧ **1** something that one loses or has to give up because of some crime, fault, or neglect of duty; specif., a fine or penalty **2** *a)* a thing taken away as a penalty for making some mistake in a game, and redeemable by a specified action *b)* [*pl.*] any game in which such forfeits are taken **3** the act of forfeiting; forfeiture —***adj.*** lost, given up, or taken away as a forfeit —***vt.*** to lose, give up, or be deprived of as a forfeit for some crime, fault, etc. —**for′feit·a·ble** ***adj.*** —**for′feit·er** ***n.***

for·fei·ture (fôr′fə chər) ***n.*** **1** the act of forfeiting **2** anything forfeited; penalty or fine

for·fend (fôr fend′) ***vt.*** ⟦ME *forfenden*: see FOR- & FEND⟧ [Archaic] **1** to forbid **2** to ward off; prevent

for·fi·cate (fôr′fi kit, -kāt′) ***adj.*** ⟦< L *forfex* (gen. *forficis*), pair of shears + -ATE[1]⟧ deeply notched or forked, as some birds' tails

for·gat (fər gat′) ***vt.***, ***vi.*** *archaic pt. of* FORGET

for·gath·er (fôr gath′ər) ***vi.*** ⟦FOR[1] + GATHER, after Du *vergaderen*⟧ **1** to come together; meet; assemble **2** to meet by chance; encounter **3** to associate or have friendly social relations (*with*)

for·gave (fər gāv′, fôr-) ***vt.***, ***vi.*** *pt. of* FORGIVE

forge[1] (fôrj) ***n.*** ⟦ME < OFr < L *fabrica*, workshop, fabric < *faber*, workman < IE base **dhabh-*, to join, fit > DAFT⟧ **1** a furnace for heating metal to be wrought **2** a place where metal is heated and hammered or wrought into shape; smithy **3** a place where wrought iron is made from pig iron or iron ore —***vt.*** **forged**, **forg′ing** ⟦ME *forgen* < OFr *forgier* < L *fabricare*, to make < *fabrica*⟧ **1** to form or shape (metal) with blows or pressure from a hammer, press, or other machine, usually after heating **2** to make (something) by or as by this method; form; shape; produce **3** to make (something false) or imitate (something genuine) for purposes of deception or fraud; esp., to counterfeit (a check, signature, etc.) —***vi.*** **1** to work at a forge **2** to commit forgery

forge[2] (fôrj) ***vi.*** **forged**, **forg′ing** ⟦prob. altered < FORCE⟧ **1** to move forward steadily, as if against difficulties **2** to move in a sudden spurt of speed and energy Often with *ahead*

forg·er (fôr′jər) ***n.*** a person who forges; specif., *a)* one who tells false stories *b)* one who forges metal *c)* one who commits forgery

for·ger·y (fôr′jər ē) *n., pl.* **-ger·ies** **1** the act or legal offense of imitating or counterfeiting documents, signatures, works of art, etc. to deceive **2** anything forged **3** [Archaic] invention

for·get (fər get′, fôr-) *vt.* **-got′, -got′ten** or **-got′, -get′ting** ⟦ME *forgeten* < OE *forgietan* (see FOR- & GET): orig. sense, "to fail to hold"⟧ **1** to lose (facts, knowledge, etc.) from the mind; fail to recall; be unable to remember **2** to fail to do, bring, etc. as because of carelessness; overlook, omit, or neglect unintentionally [don't *forget* to write] **3** to overlook, omit, or neglect intentionally [let's *forget* our differences] —*vi.* to forget things; be forgetful —*SYN.* NEGLECT —☆**forget it!** never mind! it doesn't matter! —**forget oneself** **1** to think only of others; be altruistic or unselfish **2** to behave in an improper or unseemly manner —**for·get′ta·ble** *adj.* —**for·get′ter** *n.*

for·get·ful (fər get′fəl) *adj.* ⟦ME⟧ **1** apt to forget; having a poor memory **2** heedless or negligent **3** [Old Poet.] causing to forget [*forgetful* sleep] —**for·get′ful·ly** *adv.* —**for·get′ful·ness** *n.*

for·get-me-not (fər get′mē nät′) *n.* **1** any of a genus (*Myosotis*) of marsh plants of the borage family, with clusters of small blue, white, or pink flowers: an emblem of faithfulness and friendship **2** any of a number of other plants related or similar to this

forg·ing (fôr′jiŋ) *n.* **1** something forged; esp., a forged piece of metal **2** the act of one that forges

for·give (fər giv′, fôr-) *vt.* **-gave′, -giv′en, -giv′ing** ⟦ME *forgeven* < OE *forgiefan, forgifan* (akin to Ger *vergeben*): see FOR- & GIVE⟧ **1** to give up resentment against or the desire to punish; stop being angry with; pardon **2** to give up all claim to punish or exact penalty for (an offense); overlook **3** to cancel or remit (a debt) —*vi.* to show forgiveness; be inclined to forgive —*SYN.* ABSOLVE —**for·giv′a·ble** *adj.* —**for·giv′a·bly** *adv.* —**for·giv′er** *n.*

for·give·ness (fər giv′nis) *n.* **1** a forgiving or being forgiven; pardon **2** inclination to forgive or pardon

for·giv·ing (fər giv′iŋ) *adj.* **1** that forgives; inclined to forgive **2** allowing for or accommodating adjustments, errors, imperfections, weakness, etc.; not exacting or harsh [*forgiving* recipes for the novice chef] —**for·giv′ing·ly** *adv.* —**for·giv′ing·ness** *n.*

for·go (fôr gō′) *vt.* **-went′, -gone′, -go′ing** ⟦ME *forgon* < OE *forgan*: see FOR- & GO[2]⟧ **1** [Obs.] *a)* to go past *b)* to overlook; neglect **2** to do without; abstain from; give up —*SYN.* RELINQUISH —**for·go′er** *n.*

for·got (fər gät′, fôr-) *vt., vi. pt. & alt. pp. of* FORGET

for·got·ten (fər gät′'n) *vt., vi. alt. pp. of* FORGET

for·int (fôr′int) *n.* ⟦Hung < It *fiorino,* FLORIN⟧ the basic monetary unit of Hungary: see the table of monetary units in the Reference Supplement

for·judge (fôr juj′) *vt.* **-judged′, -judg′ing** FOREJUDGE[2]

fork (fôrk) *n.* ⟦ME *forke* < OE *forca* & Anglo-Fr *forque* (Fr *fourche*), both < L *furca,* two-pronged fork⟧ **1** an instrument of greatly varying size with a handle at one end and two or more pointed prongs at the other: forks are variously used as eating utensils and for pitching hay, breaking up soil, etc. **2** something resembling a fork in shape [tuning *fork*] **3** a division into branches; bifurcation ☆**4** the point where a river, road, etc. is divided into two or more branches, or where branches join to form a river, road, etc. **5** any of these branches —*vi.* to divide into branches; be bifurcated [where the road *forks*] —*vt.* **1** to make into the shape of a fork **2** to pick up, spear, or pitch with a fork **3** *Chess* to attack (two chessmen) simultaneously with a single chessman —☆**fork over** (or **out** or **up**) [Informal] to pay out or hand over —**fork′ful′** *n., pl.* **-fuls′**

☆**fork·ball** (fôrk′bôl′) *n. Baseball* a breaking pitch made by holding the ball with the middle and index fingers spread apart

forked (fôrkt) *adj.* **1** having a fork or forks; divided into branches; cleft [*forked* lightning] **2** having prongs: often in hyphenated compounds [*five-forked*] Also **fork′y, fork′i·er, fork′i·est**

☆**forked tongue** ⟦prob. transl. of AmInd expression⟧ lying or deceitful talk [to speak with a *forked tongue*]

☆**fork·lift** (fôrk′lift′) *n.* **1** a device, usually mounted on a small vehicle, for lifting, stacking, etc. heavy objects: it consists typically of projecting prongs that are slid under the load and then raised or lowered **2** a vehicle equipped with such a device —*vt.* to lift or raise (pallets, etc.) in this way

For·lì (fôr lē′) commune in Emilia-Romagna region, NC Italy

for·lorn (fôr lôrn′, fər-) *adj.* ⟦ME *forloren* < OE, pp. of *forleosan,* to lose utterly: see FOR- & LOSE⟧ **1** abandoned or deserted **2** *a)* lonely and sad; unhappy and neglected *b)* without hope; desperate **3** bereft or deprived (*of*) —**for·lorn′ly** *adv.* —**for·lorn′ness** *n.*

forlorn hope ⟦altered < Du *verloren hoop,* lit., lost group < *verloren,* pp. of *verliezen,* to lose (akin to prec.) + *hoop,* a band, group; akin to HEAP⟧ **1** a group of soldiers detached from the main group for a very dangerous mission **2** a desperate undertaking; enterprise with very little chance of success **3** ⟦through confusion with HOPE⟧ a faint hope

form (fôrm) *n.* ⟦ME *forme* < OFr < L *forma,* a shape, figure, image < ? (via Etr) Gr *morphē*⟧ **1** the shape, outline, or configuration of anything; structure as apart from color, material, etc. **2** *a)* the body or figure of a person or animal *b)* a model of the human figure, esp. one used to display or fit clothes **3** anything used to give shape to something else; mold; specif., a temporary structure of boards or metal into which concrete is poured to set **4** the particular mode of existence a thing has or takes [water in the *form* of vapor] **5** *a)* arrangement; esp., orderly arrangement; way in which parts of a whole are organized; pattern; style (distinguished from CONTENT[2]) *b)* a specific arrangement, esp. a conventional one **6** a way of doing something requiring skill; specif., the style or technique of an athlete, esp. when it is the standard or approved one **7** a customary or conventional way of acting or behaving; ceremony; ritual; formality **8** a fixed order of words; formula [the *form* of a wedding announcement] **9** a printed document with blank spaces to be filled in [an application *form*] **10** a particular kind, type, species, or variety [man is a *form* of animal life] **11** physical or mental condition with respect to one's performance or effectiveness [in good *form* for the game] **12** *a)* RACING FORM *b)* what is or was to be expected, based on past performances [to react according to *form*] **13** the lair or hiding place of a hare, etc. **14** a long, wooden bench without a back, as formerly in a schoolroom **15** a grade or class in some private schools and in British secondary schools **16** [Archaic] beauty **17** *Gram.* any of the different variations in which a word may appear due to changes of inflection, spelling, or pronunciation ["am" is a *form* of the verb "be"] **18** *Linguis.* LINGUISTIC FORM **19** *Philos.* the ideal nature or essential character of a thing as distinguished from its material manifestation; specif., in Plato, an IDEA (sense 7) **20** *Printing* the type, engravings, etc. locked in a frame, or chase, for printing or plating —*vt.* ⟦ME *formen* < OFr *fourmer* < L *formare* < the *n.*⟧ **1** to give shape or form to; fashion; make, as in some particular way **2** to mold or shape by training and discipline; train; instruct **3** to develop (habits) **4** to think of; frame in the mind; conceive **5** to come together into; organize into [to *form* a club] **6** to make up; act as; create out of separate elements; constitute [thirteen states *formed* the original Union] **7** *Gram.* *a)* to build (words) from bases, affixes, etc. *b)* to construct or make up (a phrase, sentence, etc.) —*vi.* **1** to be formed; assume shape **2** to come into being; take form **3** to take a definite or specific form or shape —**good** (or **bad**) **form** conduct in (or not in) accord with social custom —**form′a·ble** *adj.*

SYN.—**form** denotes the arrangement of the parts of a thing that gives it its distinctive appearance and is the broadest term here, applying also to abstract concepts; **figure** is applied to physical form as determined by the bounding lines or surfaces; **outline** is used of the lines bounding the limits of an object and, in an extended sense, suggests a general plan without detail; **shape**, although also stressing outline, is usually applied to something that has mass or bulk and may refer to nonphysical concepts; **configuration** stresses the relative disposition of the inequalities of a surface See also **make**

-form (fôrm) ⟦OFr *-forme* < L *forma,* prec.⟧ *combining form* **1** having the form of; shaped like [*dentiform*] **2** having (a specified number of) forms [*triform*]

for·mal (fôr′məl) *adj.* ⟦ME < L *formalis* < *forma,* FORM⟧ **1** of external form or structure, rather than nature or content **2** of the internal form; relating to the intrinsic or essential character or nature **3** of or according to prescribed or fixed customs, rules, ceremonies, etc. [a *formal* wedding] **4** *a)* having the appearance of being suitable, correct, etc., but not really so *b)* stiff in manner; not warm or relaxed **5** *a)* designed for use or wear at ceremonies, elaborate parties, etc. [*formal* dress] *b)* requiring clothes of this kind [a *formal* dance] **6** done or made in orderly, regular fashion; methodical **7** very regular or orderly in arrangement, pattern, etc.; rigidly symmetrical [a *formal* garden] **8** done or made according to the forms that make explicit, definite, valid, etc. [a *formal* contract] **9** designating education in schools, colleges, etc. **10** designating or of the level of language usage characterized by expanded vocabulary, complete syntactic constructions, complex sentences, etc.: distinguished from COLLOQUIAL or INFORMAL —*n.* **1** a formal dance or ball **2** a woman's evening dress —**go formal** [Informal] to go dressed in evening clothes

formal cause in Aristotelian philosophy, the form into which a thing is made

form·al·de·hyde (fôr mal′də hīd′, fər-) *n.* ⟦FORM(IC) + ALDEHYDE⟧ a pungent gas, HCHO, used in solution as a strong disinfectant and preservative, and in the manufacture of synthetic resins, dyes, etc.

for·ma·lin (fôr′mə lin) *n.* ⟦< ? former trademark < prec. + -IN[1]⟧ a solution of formaldehyde in water, varying from 37% to 50% by volume and usually containing some methanol

for·mal·ism (fôr′məl iz′əm) *n.* **1** strict or excessive attention to or insistence on outward forms, as in art, or established traditions, as in religion **2** an instance of this —**for′mal·ist** *n., adj.* —**for′mal·is′tic** *adj.*

for·mal·i·ty (fôr mal′ə tē) *n.* ⟦Fr *formalité*⟧ **1** the quality or state of being formal; specif., *a)* a following or observing of prescribed customs, rules, ceremonies, etc.; propriety *b)* careful or too careful attention to order, regularity, precision, or conventionality; stiffness **2** *pl.* **-ties** a formal or conventional act or requirement; ceremony or form, often without practical meaning —*SYN.* CEREMONY

for·mal·ize (fôr′mə līz′) *vt.* **-ized′, -iz′ing** **1** to give definite form to **2** to make formal **3** to make official, valid, etc. by use of an appropriate form [to *formalize* an agreement] —**for′mal·i·za′tion** *n.*

formal logic the branch of logic that examines patterns of reasoning to determine which ones necessarily result in valid, or formally correct, conclusions

for·mal·ly (fôr′məl ē) *adv.* ⟦ME *formali, formeliche*⟧ **1** in a formal manner **2** with regard to form

for·mal·wear (fôr′məl wer′) *n.* formal clothes, as evening gowns and tuxedos, worn on formal occasions

for·mant (fôr′mənt) *n.* ⟦Ger < L *formans* (gen. *formantis*), prp. of *formare,* FORM⟧ *Phonet.* any one of the group of frequencies characterizing a given vowel sound

for·mat (fôr′mat′) *n.* ⟦Ger < L *formatus,* pp. of *formare*: see FORM⟧ **1** the shape, size, binding, typeface, paper, and general makeup or arrangement of a book, magazine, etc. **2** a basic form, style, or medium **3** a specific arrangement in accordance with which computer data is processed, stored, printed, etc. **4** a particular audio or video recording and playback system, as VHS —*vt.* **-mat′ted, -mat′ting** to arrange according to a format

for·mate (fôr′māt′) *n.* **1** a salt of formic acid containing the monovalent negative radical HCOO **2** an uncharged ester of this acid

for·ma·tion (fôr mā′shən) *n.* ⟦ME *formacioun* < OFr *formation* < L *formatio* < pp. of *formare*: see FORM⟧ **1** a forming or being formed **2** a thing formed **3** the way in which something is formed or arranged; structure **4** an arrangement or positioning, as of troops, ships, airplanes in flight, football players, etc. **5** *Ecol.* the major unit of vegetation usually extending over a large area, as the prairie, deciduous forest, tundra, etc.: see BIOME **6** *Geol.* a rock unit distinguished from adjacent deposits by some common character, as composition, origin, type of fossil, etc.

form·a·tive (fôr′mə tiv) *adj.* ⟦OFr *formatif* < ML *formativus* < L *formatus*, pp. of *formare*: see FORM⟧ **1** giving or able to give form; helping to shape, develop, or mold [the *formative* influence of a teacher] **2** of formation or development [a child's *formative* years] **3** *Linguis.* serving to form words, as a prefix or suffix —*n.* *Linguis.* a bound form, as a prefix or suffix —**form′a·tive·ly** *adv.*

☆**form class** *Linguis.* a class made up of words that occur in a distinctive position in constructions and have certain formal features in common, as the form class *noun* in English, made up of all words to which both the plural and possessive suffixes may be added

form criticism critical analysis of the literary forms of Biblical texts, designed to reconstruct the original oral or written material from which the texts emerged so as to evaluate the authenticity and accuracy of the existing texts

for·mer[1] (fôr′mər) *adj.* ⟦ME *formere*, compar. of *forme*, first < OE *forma*: see FOREMOST⟧ **1** preceding in time; earlier; past [in *former* times] **2** first mentioned of two: often used absolutely (with *the*) [Jack and Bill are twins, but the *former* is taller than the latter]: opposed to LATTER (sense 3) —*SYN.* PREVIOUS

form·er[2] (fôrm′ər) *n.* a person or thing that forms

for·mer·ly (fôr′mər lē) *adv.* at or in a former or earlier time; in the past

form-fit·ting (fôrm′fit′iŋ) *adj.* fitting closely the contours of the body: said esp. of clothing: also written **form′fit′ting**

form genus a genus consisting of species superficially resembling each other but probably not closely related in their evolutionary origin

for·mic (fôr′mik) *adj.* ⟦< L *formica*, an ant < IE **morm-*, var. of *morwi-* > OIr *moirb*, ON *maurr*, ant: see PISMIRE⟧ **1** of ants **2** designating or of a colorless acid, HCOOH, that is extremely irritating to the skin: it is found in living organisms, as ants, spiders, and nettles, and is prepared commercially for use in dyeing textiles, treating leather, preserving food, etc.

☆**For·mi·ca** (fôr mī′kə) ⟦orig. uncert.⟧ *trademark for* a laminated, heat-resistant thermosetting plastic used for table and sink tops, etc. —*n.* **[f-]** a surface of such plastic

for·mi·car·y (fôr′mi ker′ē) *n., pl.* **-car′ies** ⟦ML *formicarium* < **formicarius*, of ants < L *formica*, ant: see FORMIC⟧ an anthill or ants' nest: also **for′mi·car′i·um** (-ē əm) *n., pl.* **-car′i·a** (-ē ə)

for·mi·da·ble (fôr′mə də bəl, fôr mid′ə bəl) *adj.* ⟦ME < OFr < L *formidabilis* < *formidare*, to fear, dread < *formido*, fear < IE **mormo-*, to feel horror > Gr *mormoros*, fear⟧ **1** causing fear or dread **2** hard to handle or overcome **3** awe-inspiring in size, excellence, etc.; strikingly impressive —**for′mi·da·bil′i·ty** *n.*, **for′mi·da·ble·ness** —**for′mi·da·bly** *adv.*

form·less (fôrm′lis) *adj.* having no definite or regular form or plan; shapeless —**form′less·ly** *adv.* —**form′less·ness** *n.*

☆**form letter** any of a number of standardized, printed or duplicated letters, often with the date, name, and address filled in separately

For·mo·sa (fôr mō′sə, -zə) *former (Port.) name for* TAIWAN —**For·mo′san** *adj., n.*

Formosa Strait *former name for* TAIWAN STRAIT

for·mu·la (fôr′myo͞o lə, -myə-) *n., pl.* **-las** or **-lae′** (-lē′, -lī′) ⟦L, dim. of *forma*, FORM⟧ **1** a fixed form of words, esp. one that has lost its original meaning or force and is now used only as a conventional or ceremonial expression ["Very truly yours" is a *formula* used in letters] **2** a rule or method for doing something, esp. when conventional and used or repeated without thought [a *formula* for musical comedies] **3** an exact statement of religious faith or doctrine **4** *a)* directions for preparing a medicine, a paint, a baby's food, etc. *b)* something prepared from such directions; often specif., a milk preparation for feeding a baby **5** a set of algebraic symbols expressing a mathematical fact, principle, rule, etc. [$A = \pi r^2$ is the *formula* for determining the area of a circle] **6** *Chem.* an expression of the composition of a compound (or a radical, etc.) by a combination of symbols and figures to show the constituents: see EMPIRICAL FORMULA, MOLECULAR FORMULA, STRUCTURAL FORMULA —*adj.* designating or of any of various classes of racing car or motorcycle specially designed to conform to a particular set of specifications governing size, weight, engine displacement, etc.

☆**for·mu·la·ic** (fôr′myo͞o lā′ik, -myə-) *adj.* consisting of, or made or expressed according to, a formula or formulas

for·mu·lar·ize (fôr′myo͞o lər īz′, -myə-) *vt.* **-ized′, -iz′ing** FORMULATE (sense 1) —**for′mu·lar·i·za′tion** (-lər i zā′shən, -ī zā′-) *n.*

for·mu·lar·y (fôr′myo͞o ler′ē, -myə-) *n., pl.* **-lar′ies** ⟦Fr *formulaire* < L *formula*, FORMULA⟧ **1** a collection of fixed or prescribed forms or formulas, as in a book **2** a fixed or prescribed form or formula **3** *Pharmacy* a list of medicines with their formulas and directions for compounding them —*adj.* of or like a formula or formulary

for·mu·late (fôr′myo͞o lāt′, -myə-) *vt.* **-lat′ed, -lat′ing** **1** to express in or reduce to a formula **2** to express (a theory, plan, etc.) in a systematic way **3** to work out or form in one's mind; devise, develop, contrive, etc. —**for′mu·la′tion** *n.* —**for′mu·la′tor** *n.*

for·mu·lism (fôr′myo͞o liz′əm, -myə-) *n.* reliance on or belief in formulas —**for′mu·list** *n.* —**for′mu·lis′tic** *adj.*

for·mu·lize (-līz′) *vt.* **-lized′, -liz′ing** *var. of* FORMULATE (sense 1) —**for′mu·li·za′tion** *n.*

for·myl (fôr′mil) *n.* ⟦FORM(IC) + -YL⟧ the monovalent radical HCO of formic acid

For·nax (fôr′naks′) *n.* ⟦L, lit., FURNACE⟧ a S constellation between Eridanus and Cetus

for·ni·cate[1] (fôr′ni kāt′) *vi.* **-cat′ed, -cat′ing** ⟦< LL(Ec) *fornicatus*, pp. of *fornicari*, to fornicate < L *fornix* (gen. *fornicis*), a brothel, orig., vault < *fornus*, an oven, akin to *fornax*, FURNACE⟧ to commit fornication —**for′ni·ca′tor** *n.*

for·ni·cate[2] (fôr′ni kit, -kāt′) *adj.* ⟦L *fornicatus* < *fornix*: see prec.⟧ arched or vaulted

for·ni·ca·tion (fôr′ni kā′shən) *n.* ⟦ME *fornicacioun* < OFr *fornication* < LL(Ec) *fornicatio* < *fornicatus*: see FORNICATE[1]⟧ **1** voluntary sexual intercourse between persons not married to each other **2** *Bible* *a)* any unlawful sexual intercourse, including adultery *b)* worship of idols

for·nix (fôr′niks) *n., pl.* **for′ni·ces′** (-nə sēz′) ⟦ModL < L, an arch⟧ any of several anatomical arches or folds, such as the vault of the pharynx or the upper part of the vagina

for-prof·it (fôr′präf′it) *adj.* established for earning a profit: used esp. of a business enterprise of a kind that is typically nonprofit [a *for-profit* school, hospital, etc.] —*n.* a for-profit enterprise

for·sake (fôr sāk′, fər-) *vt.* **-sook′, -sak′en, -sak′ing** ⟦ME *forsaken* < OE *forsacan*, to oppose, forsake < *for-*, FOR- + *sacan*, to contend, strive < *sacu*: see SAKE[1]⟧ **1** to give up; renounce (a habit, idea, etc.) **2** to leave; abandon —*SYN.* ABANDON

for·sak·en (fər sā′kən, fôr-) *adj.* abandoned; desolate; forlorn

for·sook (fôr so͝ok′) *vt. pt. of* FORSAKE

for·sooth (fôr so͞oth′, fər-) *adv.* ⟦ME *forsoth* < OE prep. *for* + *soth*, truth: see SOOTH⟧ [Archaic] in truth; no doubt; indeed: in later use, mainly ironic

for·spent (fôr spent′) *adj.* ⟦pp. of obs. *forspend* < OE *forspendan*, to use up: see FOR- & SPEND⟧ [Archaic] exhausted with toil; fatigued

For·ster (fô′stər; *in the US, usually* fôr′stər), **E(dward) M(organ)** 1879-1970; Eng. novelist

for·swear (fôr swer′) *vt.* **-swore′** (-swôr′), **-sworn′, -swear′ing** ⟦ME *forswerien* < OE *forswerian*: see FOR- & SWEAR⟧ **1** to renounce on oath; promise earnestly to give up **2** to deny earnestly or on oath —*vi.* to swear falsely; commit perjury —**forswear oneself** to swear falsely; perjure oneself

for·sworn (-swôrn′) *vt., vi. pp. of* FORSWEAR —*adj.* perjured

for·syth·i·a (fôr sith′ē ə, fər-; -sī′thē ə) *n.* ⟦ModL, after W. *Forsyth* (1737-1804), Eng botanist⟧ any of a genus (*Forsythia*) of shrubs of the olive family, having yellow, bell-shaped flowers that bloom in early spring

fort[1] (fôrt) *n.* ⟦ME *forte*, orig. adj., strong < L *fortis* < OL *forctus* < IE base **bhereĝh-*, high, elevated > Sans *bṛṁhati*, (it) strengthens, elevates, OHG *berg*, hill⟧ **1** an enclosed place or fortified building for military defense, equipped as with earthworks, guns, etc. ☆**2** a permanent army post, as distinguished from a temporary camp —☆**hold the fort** **1** to make a defensive stand **2** [Informal] to keep things in operation; remain on duty, etc.

fort[2] *abbrev.* **1** fortification **2** fortified

For·ta·le·za (fôr′tə lā′zə) seaport in NE Brazil, on the Atlantic: capital of Ceará state

for·ta·lice (fôr′tə lis) *n.* ⟦ME < ML *fortalitia* < L *fortis*, strong: see FORT[1]⟧ [Archaic] **1** a small fort **2** a fortress

Fort Collins ⟦after Lt. Col. W. O. *Collins* (1809-80), military commander at Fort Laramie, Wyo. (early 1860s)⟧ city in N Colo., north of Denver

Fort-de-France (fôr də fräns′) seaport & capital of Martinique, in the Windward Islands

forte[1] (fôrt, fōrt; *for 2 often* fôr′tā′) *n.* ⟦Fr, fem. of *fort*, replacing ME, strength < OFr: see FORT[1]⟧ **1** the strongest part of the blade of a sword, between the middle and the hilt: cf. FOIBLE (sense 2) **2** a thing that a person does particularly well; special accomplishment or strong point

for·te[2] (fôr′tā′) [*also in italics*] *Music adj., adv.* ⟦It < L *fortis*, strong: see FORT[1]⟧ loud(ly): opposed to PIANO[1]: often used as a musical direction —*n.* a forte passage

for·te·pi·an·o[1] (fôr′tā pē an′ō, -än′-) *n.* ⟦see fol.⟧ the piano of the 18th and early 19th cent.

for·te·pia·no[2] (fôr′tā pyä′nō) *adj., adv.* ⟦It: see FORTE[2] & PIANO[2]⟧ *Musical Direction* loud(ly) and then soft(ly)

forth (fôrth, fōrth) *adv.* ⟦ME < OE, akin to FORE⟧ **1** forward in place, time, or degree; onward [from that day *forth*] **2** out; esp., out into view, as from hiding **3** [Obs.] abroad —*prep.* [Archaic] out from; out of See also idiomatic phrases under BACK[1], GIVE, HOLD[1], etc. —**and so forth** and so on; and other such things; et cetera

Forth (fôrth) **1** river in SE Scotland, flowing east into the Firth of Forth: 65 mi (105 km) **2 Firth of** long estuary of the Forth, flowing into the North Sea: 51 mi (82 km)

forth·com·ing (fôrth′kum′iŋ) *adj.* **1** about to appear; approaching [the author's *forthcoming* book] 2 available or ready when needed [the promised help was not *forthcoming*] 3 *a)* friendly, communicative, outgoing, etc. *b)* open; frank; direct —*n.* a coming forth; approach

forth·right (fôrth′rīt′) *adj.* ⟦ME < OE *forth riht*: see FORTH & RIGHT⟧ 1 [Archaic] going straight forward 2 straightforward; direct; frank —*adv.* 1 straight forward; directly onward 2 [Archaic] immediately; at once —*n.* [Archaic] a straight path or course —**forth′right′ly** *adv.* —**forth′right′ness** *n.*

forth·with (fôrth with′, -with′) *adv.* ⟦ME *forth with* (for OE *forth mid*): see FORTH & WITH⟧ immediately; at once

for·ti·eth (fôrt′ē ith) *adj.* ⟦ME *fourtithe* < OE *feowertigotha*: see FORTY & -TH[2]⟧ 1 preceded by thirty-nine others in a series; 40th 2 designating any of the forty equal parts of something —*n.* 1 the one following the thirty-ninth 2 any of the forty equal parts of something; 1/40 —*adv.* in the fortieth place, rank, group, etc.

for·ti·fi·ca·tion (fôrt′ə fi kā′shən) *n.* ⟦ME *fortificacioun* < OFr *fortification* < LL *fortificatio* < pp. of *fortificare*: see FORTIFY⟧ 1 the act or science of fortifying 2 something used in fortifying; esp., a fort or defensive earthwork, wall, etc. 3 a fortified place or position

fortified wine any wine, as sherry, port, or Madeira, to which brandy or other alcohol has been added to raise its alcoholic content

for·ti·fy (fôrt′ə fī′) *vt.* **-fied′**, **-fy′ing** ⟦ME *fortifien* < OFr *fortifier* < LL *fortificare* < L *fortis*, strong (see FORT[1]) + *facere*, to make, DO[1]⟧ 1 to make strong or stronger; strengthen physically, emotionally, etc. 2 to strengthen against attack, as by building or furnishing with forts, walls, etc. 3 to support; corroborate [to *fortify* an argument with statistics] 4 to strengthen (wine, etc.) by adding alcohol 5 to add vitamins, minerals, etc. to (milk, etc.) so as to increase the nutritional value; enrich —*vi.* to build military defenses —**for′ti·fi′a·ble** *adj.* —**for′ti·fi′er** *n.*

for·tis (fôr′tis) *adj.* ⟦L, strong: see FORT[1]⟧ *Phonet.* articulated with much muscle tension and, usually, with strong aspiration, as initial (p) and (t) in English —*n.* a fortis sound Opposed to LENIS

for·tis·si·mo (fôr tis′ə mō′; *It* fôr tēs′sē mô′) [*also in italics*] *Music adj., adv.* ⟦It, superl. of *forte*, FORTE[2]⟧ very loud(ly): opposed to PIANISSIMO: often used as a musical direction —*n., pl.* **-mos′** or It. **-mi′** (-mē′) a fortissimo passage

for·ti·tude (fôrt′ə to͞od′, -tyo͞od′) *n.* ⟦ME < L *fortitudo* < *fortis*, strong: see FORT[1]⟧ the strength to bear misfortune, pain, etc. calmly and patiently; firm courage —**for′ti·tu′di·nous** (-to͞od′'n əs, -tyo͞od′-) *adj.*

SYN.—**fortitude** refers to the courage that permits one to endure patiently misfortune, pain, etc. [to face a calamity with *fortitude*]; **grit** applies to an obstinate sort of courage that refuses to succumb under any circumstances; **backbone** refers to the strength of character and resoluteness that permits one to face opposition unflinchingly; **pluck** and **guts** (see GUT, *n.* 7*a*) both refer originally to visceral organs, hence **pluck** implies a strong heart in the face of danger or difficulty and **guts**, an informal word, suggests the sort of stamina that permits one to "stomach" a disagreeable or frightening experience See also **patience** —*ANT.* **cowardice**

Fort Knox ⟦see KNOXVILLE⟧ military reservation in N Ky., near Louisville: site of U.S. gold bullion depository

Fort Lau·der·dale (lô′dər dāl′) ⟦after original *fort* built (1838) during a campaign led by Maj. W. *Lauderdale* (1782?-1838)⟧ city on the SE coast of Fla., near Miami

Fort Mc·Hen·ry (mək hen′rē) ⟦after J. *McHenry*, U.S. Secretary of War, 1796-1800⟧ fort in Baltimore harbor, Md., where the British were repulsed in 1814

fort·night (fôrt′nīt′) *n.* ⟦ME *fourte(n) niht* < OE *feowertyn niht*, lit., fourteen nights⟧ [Chiefly Brit.] a period of two weeks

fort·night·ly (fôrt′nīt′lē; *also, esp. for adv.* fôrt nīt′lē) [Chiefly Brit.] *adj., adv.* once in every fortnight, or at two-week intervals —*n., pl.* **-lies** a periodical issued at two-week intervals

☆**FORTRAN** (fôr′tran′) *n.* ⟦*for(mula) tran(slation)*⟧ a high-level computer language employing algebraic formulas

for·tress (fôr′tris) *n.* ⟦ME *forteresse* < OFr < VL **fortaricia* < L *fortis*, strong: see FORT[1]⟧ a fortified place; fort: often used fig. [a mighty *fortress* is our God] —*vt.* to protect by or furnish with a fortress

Fort Smith region of S Northwest Territories, Canada

Fort Sum·ter (sum′tər) ⟦after General T. *Sumter* (1734-1832)⟧ fort in Charleston harbor, S.C., where Confederate troops fired the first shots of the Civil War (April 12, 1861)

for·tu·i·tous (fôr to͞o′ə təs, -tyo͞o′-) *adj.* ⟦L *fortuitus* < *forte*, by chance < *fors* (gen. *fortis*), chance, luck < IE **bhr̥tis* < base **bher-*, to bring > BEAR[1]⟧ 1 happening by chance; accidental 2 bringing, or happening by, good luck; fortunate —*SYN.* ACCIDENTAL —**for·tu′i·tous·ly** *adv.* —**for·tu′i·tous·ness** *n.*

for·tu·i·ty (fôr to͞o′ə tē, -tyo͞o′-) *n., pl.* **-ties** ⟦< L *fortuitus* (see prec.) + -ITY⟧ 1 the quality or condition of being fortuitous 2 chance or chance occurrence

For·tu·na (fôr to͞o′nə, -tyo͞o′-) *n.* ⟦L < *fortuna*⟧ *Rom. Myth.* the goddess of fortune

for·tu·nate (fôr′chə nət) *adj.* ⟦ME *fortunat* < L *fortunatus*, pp. of *fortunare*, to make fortunate < *fortuna*, fol.⟧ 1 having good luck; lucky 2 bringing, or coming by, good luck; favorable; auspicious —**for′tu·nate·ly** *adv.* —**for′tu·nate·ness** *n.*

for·tune (fôr′chən) *n.* ⟦ME < OFr < L *fortuna*, chance, fate, fortune < *fors*, chance: see FORTUITOUS⟧ 1 the entity or power believed by some to bring good or bad luck to people; luck; chance; fate: often personified 2 [*also pl.*] what happens or is going to happen to one; one's lot, good or bad, esp. one's future lot 3 good luck; success; prosperity 4 a large quantity of money or possessions; wealth; riches —*vt.* **-tuned**, **-tun·ing** [Archaic] to provide with wealth —*vi.* [Archaic] to happen; chance —**a small fortune** a very high price or cost —**tell someone's fortune** to profess to tell what is going to happen in someone's life, as by palmistry, cards, etc. —**for′tune·less** *adj.*

☆**fortune cookie** a crisp, hollow E Asian cookie containing a slip of paper giving advice, a prediction, etc. and typically served in Chinese restaurants

☆**Fortune 500 (or 1000 or 100, etc.)** ⟦from annual listings in *Fortune*, a U.S. business magazine⟧ the 500 (or 1000, 100, etc.) largest U.S. corporations as ranked according to sales volume

fortune hunter a person who tries to become rich, esp. by marrying someone rich

for·tune·tell·er or **for·tune-tell·er** (fôr′chən tel′ər) *n.* a person who professes to foretell events, esp. events in other people's lives —**for′tune·tell′ing** *n., adj.*, **for′tune-tell′ing**

Fort Wayne ⟦after Anthony WAYNE[2]⟧ city in NE Ind.

Fort William ⟦after *William* McGillivray, a director of the North West Co.⟧ *see* THUNDER BAY

Fort Worth ⟦after W. J. *Worth* (1794-1849)⟧ city in N Tex.

for·ty (fôrt′ē) *adj.* ⟦ME *fourti* < OE *feowertig*, akin to Ger *vierzig*, Goth *fidwor tigjus*: see FOUR & -TY[2]⟧ four times ten —*n., pl.* **-ties** the cardinal number between thirty-nine and forty-one; 40; XL —**the forties** the numbers or years, as of a century, from forty through forty-nine

for·ty-five (fôrt′ē fīv′) *n.* ☆1 a .45-caliber handgun: usually written **.45** 2 a phonograph record for playing at 45 revolutions per minute: usually written **45**

☆**for·ty-nin·er** or **For·ty-Nin·er** (fôrt′ē nīn′ər) *n.* a person who went to California in the gold rush of 1849

forty winks [Informal] a short sleep; nap

fo·rum (fôr′əm, fō′rəm) *n.* ⟦L, area out-of-doors, marketplace, orig. ? area with board fence < *forus*, board < IE **bhoros*: see BAR[1]⟧ 1 *pl.* **-rums** or **-ra** (-ə) the public square or marketplace of an ancient Roman city or town, where legal and political business was conducted 2 a law court; tribunal 3 *a)* an assembly, place, radio program, internet site, etc. for the discussion of public matters or current questions *b)* an opportunity for open discussion —**the Forum** the forum of ancient Rome

for·ward (fôr′wərd) *adj.* ⟦ME *foreward* < OE adj. & adv. *foreweard*: see FORE & -WARD⟧ 1 at, toward, or of the front, or forepart 2 advanced; specif., *a)* mentally advanced; precocious *b)* advanced socially, politically, etc.; progressive or radical *c)* [Now Rare] ahead of time; early 3 moving toward a point in front; onward; advancing 4 ready or eager; prompt 5 too bold or free in manners; pushing; presumptuous 6 of or for the future [*forward* buying] —*adv.* 1 toward the front or a point in front or before; ahead 2 to an earlier time or date [to move a meeting *forward*] 3 to or toward a later time [set your clock *forward* one hour] 4 toward the future [a commencement speaker looking *forward*] 5 into view or prominence [to bring *forward* an opinion] —*n.* *Basketball, Hockey, Soccer, etc.* any of the players positioned ahead of the rest of the team when they are at the offensive end of the court, field, etc.: see also POWER FORWARD, SMALL FORWARD —*vt.* 1 to help advance; promote 2 to send on, as to another address [to *forward* mail] —*SYN.* ADVANCE —**going forward** from now on; henceforth: chiefly a business usage —**for′ward′a·ble** *adj.* —**for′ward·ness** *n.*

for·ward·er (fôr′wər dər) *n.* a person or thing that forwards; specif., a person or agency that receives goods and expedites their delivery, as by arranging for warehousing, shipping in carload lots, transshipping, etc.

for·ward-look·ing (fôr′wərd lo͝ok′iŋ) *adj.* anticipating or making provision for the future; progressive

for·ward·ly (fôr′wərd lē) *adv.* 1 boldly; presumptuously ☆2 [Now Rare] at or toward the front 3 [Archaic] readily; eagerly

for·ward·most (-mōst′) *adj.* farthest in front; first

☆**forward pass** *Football* a pass made from behind the line of scrimmage to a teammate in a position forward of the thrower

for·wards (fôr′wərdz) *adv.* ⟦ME *forewardes* < *foreward* + adv. gen. *-es*, akin to Ger *vorwärts*⟧ FORWARD

for·went (fôr went′) *vt. pt. of* FORGO

for·why (fôr hwī′) *adv.* ⟦ME *forwhi* < OE *for hwy*, wherefore: see FOR[1] & WHY⟧ [Now Dial.] why; wherefore —*conj.* [Obs.] because

for·worn (fôr wôrn′) *adj.* ⟦Early ModE *forworen*, pp. of obs. *forwear*: see FOR- & WEAR[1]⟧ [Archaic] worn out

for·zan·do (fôr tsän′dō) *adj., adv.* ⟦It < *forzare*, to force < LL **fortiare*: see FORCE⟧ [*also in italics*] *Musical Direction* SFORZANDO

fos·sa (fäs′ə, fôs′ə) *n., pl.* **-sae** (-ē, -ī) ⟦ModL < L, a ditch, trench < *fossus*: see FOSSIL⟧ *Anat.* a cavity, pit, or small hollow —**fos′sate′** (-āt′, -it) *adj.*

fosse or **foss** (fäs, fôs) *n.* ⟦ME < OFr < L *fossa* < *fossa (terra)*, dug (earth) < *fossus*: see FOSSIL⟧ a ditch or moat, esp. one used in fortifications

fos·sette (fä set′, fô-) *n.* ⟦Fr, dim. of *fosse*: see prec.⟧ 1 a small hollow 2 a dimple

fos·sick (fäs′ik) *vi.* ⟦Eng dial., prob. ult. < FUSS⟧ [Austral.] 1 to prospect or search, as for gold 2 to search about; rummage —*vt.* to search for; seek out

fos·sil (fäs′əl) *n.* ⟦Fr *fossile* < L *fossilis*, dug out, dug up < *fossus*, pp. of *fodere*, to dig up < IE **bhedh-*, to dig in the earth > Welsh *bedd*, grave, OE *bedd*, BED⟧ 1 [Obs.] any rock or mineral dug out of the earth 2 any hardened remains or imprints of plant or animal life of some previous geologic period, preserved in the earth's crust, including petrified wood and various resins **3** anything fossilized or like a fossil **4** a person who is old-fashioned or has outmoded, fixed ideas —***adj.*** **1** of, having the nature of, or forming a fossil or fossils **2** belonging to the past; unchanged by progress; antiquated

fossil fuel an organic substance, as coal, petroleum, etc., found underground in deposits formed in a previous geologic period and used as a source of energy

fos·sil·if·er·ous (fäs′əl if′ər əs) ***adj.*** ⟦FOSSIL + -I- + -FEROUS⟧ containing fossils

fos·sil·ize (fäs′əl īz′) ***vt.*** **-ized′, -iz′ing** **1** to change into a fossil or fossils; petrify **2** to make out of date, rigid, or incapable of change —***vi.*** to become fossilized —**fos′sil·i·za′tion** ***n.***

fos·so·ri·al (fä sôr′ē əl) ***adj.*** ⟦< LL *fossorius* < L *fossor*, digger < *fossus* (see FOSSIL) + -AL⟧ digging or adapted for digging; burrowing [*fossorial* claws]

fos·ter (fôs′tər, fäs′-) ***vt.*** ⟦ME *fostren* < OE *fostrian*, to nourish, bring up < *fostor*, food, nourishment < base of *foda*, FOOD⟧ **1** to bring up with care; rear **2** to help to grow or develop; stimulate; promote [to *foster* discontent] **3** to cling to in one's mind; cherish [*foster* a hope] —***adj.*** **1** having the standing of a specified member of the family, though not by birth or adoption, and giving, receiving, or sharing the care appropriate to that standing [*foster* parent, *foster* brother] **2** designating or relating to such care —**fos′ter·er** ***n.***

Fos·ter (fôs′tər, fäs′-) **1 Stephen (Collins)** 1826-64; U.S. composer of popular songs **2 William Z(ebulon)** 1881-1964; U.S. Communist Party leader

fos·ter·age (fôs′tər ij′) ***n.*** **1** the rearing of a foster child **2** the state of being a foster child **3** a promoting, stimulating, or encouraging

foster home a home in which a child or children are raised by people other than their natural or adoptive parents

fos·ter·ling (fôs′tər liŋ) ***n.*** ⟦ME < OE *fostorling*: see -LING[1]⟧ [Now Rare] a foster child

Fou·cault (fo͞o kō′) **1 Jean Ber·nard Lé·on** (zhän ber nȧr′ lā ōn′) 1819-68; Fr. physicist **2 Mi·chel** (mē shel′) 1926-84; Fr. philosopher

Foucault (*or* Foucault's) pendulum a pendulum consisting of a heavy weight on the end of a long wire hanging from a fixed point, of the kind invented by Jean Foucault to demonstrate that the earth is rotating: although the weight continues to swing within a single plane, its path appears to an observer to shift progressively over time

fou·droy·ant (fo͞o droi′ənt; *Fr* fo͞o drwȧ yän′) ***adj.*** ⟦Fr, prp. of *foudroyer*, to strike by lightning < *foudre*, lightning, ult. < L *fulgur*, akin to *flagrare*, to burn: see FLAME⟧ **1** [Rare] dazzling or stunning **2** *Med. obs. var. of* FULMINANT

fouet·té (fwe tā′) ***n.*** ⟦Fr, pp. of *fouetter*, to whip < *fouet*, a whip < MFr, dim. of OFr *fou*, beech < L *fagus*, BEECH⟧ *Ballet* a whipping movement of one leg made while turning on the other leg

fought (fôt) ***vi., vt.*** ⟦ME *fauht* < OE *feaht*, 3d pers. sing., past indic., of *feohtan*⟧ *pt. & pp. of* FIGHT

foul (foul) ***adj.*** ⟦ME < OE *ful*, akin to Ger *faul*, rotten, lazy < IE base **pū-*, **pu-*, to stink (< ? exclamation of disgust) > L *putere*, to rot, Gr *pyon*, PUS⟧ **1** so offensive to the senses as to cause disgust; stinking; loathsome [a *foul* odor] **2** extremely dirty or impure; disgustingly filthy **3** full of or blocked up with dirt or foreign objects [a *foul* pipe] **4** putrid; rotten: said of food **5** not decent; obscene; profane [*foul* language] **6** very wicked; abominable [a *foul* murder] **7** not clear; stormy; unfavorable [*foul* weather, winds, etc.] **8** tangled or snarled; caught [a *foul* rope] **9** not according to the rules of a game; unfair, by either accident or intention **10** treacherous; dishonest **11** [Now Dial., Chiefly Brit.] ugly **12** [Informal] unpleasant, disagreeable, etc. ☆**13** *Baseball* of or having to do with the part of the field that lies outside the foul lines: see FAIR[1] (*adj.* 15), FAIR BALL **14** *Printing* containing errors or marked with changes [*foul* copy or proof] —***adv.*** **1** in a foul way **2** *Baseball* in or into the part of the field that lies outside the foul lines —***n.*** anything foul; specif., *a)* a collision of boats, contestants, etc. *b)* an infraction of the rules, as of a game or sport *c)* *Baseball* FOUL BALL —***vt.*** **1** to make foul; dirty; soil; defile **2** to dishonor or disgrace **3** to impede or obstruct; specif., *a)* to fill up; encrust; choke [to *foul* a drain with grease] *b)* to cover (the bottom of a ship) with barnacles, seaweed, etc. *c)* to entangle; catch [a rope *fouled* in the shrouds] **4** to make a foul against in a contest or game ☆**5** *Baseball* to bat (the ball) so that it falls outside the foul lines —***vi.*** **1** to become dirty, filthy, or rotten **2** to be clogged or choked **3** to become tangled **4** to break the rules of a game **5** *Baseball* to bat the ball so that it falls outside the foul lines or is caught there [to *foul* to the third baseman] —***SYN.*** DIRTY —☆**foul out** **1** *Baseball* to be retired as batter by the catch of a foul ball **2** *Basketball* to be disqualified from further play for having committed a specified number of personal fouls —☆**foul up** [Informal] to make a mess of; make disordered or confused; bungle —**run (or fall) foul of** **1** to collide with or become entangled in **2** to get into trouble with —**foul′ly** ***adv.*** —**foul′ness** ***n.***

fou·lard (fo͞o lärd′) ***n.*** ⟦Fr < ? dial. *foulat*, lit., fulled (cloth) < *fouler*, to full < ML *fullare*, to FULL[2]⟧ **1** a lightweight material of silk, rayon, or sometimes cotton in a plain or twill weave, usually printed with a small design **2** a necktie, scarf, etc. made of this material

☆**foul ball** *Baseball* a batted ball that is not a fair ball: see FAIR BALL

foul·brood (foul′bro͞od′) ***n.*** a deadly bacterial disease of the larvae of honeybees

☆**foul line** **1** *Baseball* either of the lines extending from home plate through the outside corners of first base or third base and onward to the end of the outfield **2** *Basketball* a free-throw line: see FREE THROW **3** *Bowling, Tennis, etc.* any of various lines bounding the playing area, outside of which the ball must not be hit, the player must not go, etc.

foul·mouthed (foul′mouthd′, -moutht′) ***adj.*** using obscene, profane, or scurrilous language

foul play **1** unfair play; action that breaks the rules of the game **2** criminal action or violence; esp., murder

☆**foul pole** *Baseball* either of the tall poles that mark the ends of the foul lines in the outfield: see also FAIR BALL

☆**foul shot** FREE THROW

☆**foul tip** *Baseball* a foul ball barely tipped by the bat: it is counted as a strike, but to be counted as a third strike, it must be caught by the catcher

☆**foul-up** (foul′up′) ***n.*** [Informal] a mix-up; botch; mess

found[1] (found) ⟦ME *funden* < OE *funden*, pp. of *findan*⟧ ***vt., vi. pp. & pt. of*** FIND —***adj.*** designating or of an object displayed as or as part of a work of art, that is a natural object or an ordinary man-made article —☆**and found** [Informal] with room and board in addition to wages: also [Chiefly Brit.] **all found**

found[2] (found) ***vt.*** ⟦ME *founden* < OFr *fonder* < L *fundare* < *fundus*, bottom < IE **bhundhos* < base **bhudh-* > Sans *budhnáḥ*, BOTTOM⟧ **1** to lay the base of; set for support; base [a statement *founded* on facts] **2** to begin to build or organize; bring into being; establish [to *found* a college] —***vi.*** [Rare] to be based (*on* or *upon*)

found[3] (found) ***vt.*** ⟦ME *founden* < OFr *fondre* < L *fundere*, to pour, melt (metal) < IE base **ĝheu-* > OE *geotan*, Gr *cheein*, pour⟧ **1** to melt and pour (metal or materials for glass) into a mold **2** to make by pouring molten metal into a mold; cast

foun·da·tion (foun dā′shən) ***n.*** ⟦ME *foundacioun* < OFr *fondation* < L *fundatio* < pp. of *fundare*: see FOUND[2]⟧ **1** a founding or being founded; establishment **2** *a)* an organization established to maintain, assist, or finance institutions or projects of a social, educational, charitable, religious, etc. nature, as by the making of grants *b)* the fund or endowment used by such an organization to carry out its programs *c)* an institution maintained by such a fund **3** the base on which something rests; specif., the supporting part of a wall, house, etc., usually of masonry, concrete, etc., and at least partially underground **4** the fundamental principle on which something is founded; basis **5** a supporting material or part beneath an outer part **6** FOUNDATION GARMENT **7** a cosmetic cream, liquid, etc. over which other makeup is applied —***SYN.*** BASE[1] —**foun·da′tion·al** ***adj.***

foundation garment a woman's corset or girdle, esp. one with an attached bra

foun·der[1] (foun′dər) ***vi.*** ⟦ME *foundren* < OFr *fondrer*, to fall in, sink < *fond*, bottom < L *fundus*, bottom: see FOUND[2]⟧ **1** to stumble, fall, or go lame **2** to become stuck as in soft ground; bog down **3** to fill with water, as during a storm, and sink: said of a ship or boat **4** to become sick from overeating: used esp. of livestock **5** to break down; fail —***vt.*** to cause to founder —***n.*** ⟦< the *vi.*, 1⟧ LAMINITIS

found·er[2] (foun′dər) ***n.*** **1** a person who founds, or establishes **2** [*usually* **F-**] FOUNDING FATHER (sense 2)

found·er[3] (foun′dər) ***n.*** a person who founds, or casts, metals, glass, etc.

☆**founding father** **1** someone who founds or is instrumental in founding an institution, nation, etc. **2** [*usually* **F- F-**] a participant in the U.S. Constitutional Convention of 1787, esp. one who signed the document

found·ling (found′liŋ′) ***n.*** ⟦ME *foundeling* < *founde(n)*, pp. of *finden*, FIND + *-ling*⟧ an infant of unknown parents that has been found abandoned

found object OBJET TROUVÉ

found·ry (foun′drē) ***n., pl.*** **-ries** ⟦see FOUND[3] & -ERY⟧ **1** the act, process, or work of melting and molding metals; casting **2** metal castings **3** a place where metal is cast

foundry proof *Printing* proof from a locked form, submitted for a final reading before plates are cast

fount[1] (fount) ***n.*** ⟦ME *font* < OFr < L *fons*, FOUNTAIN⟧ **1** [Old Poet.] a fountain or spring **2** a source

fount[2] (fount) ***n.*** [Brit.] FONT[2]

foun·tain (fount′'n) ***n.*** ⟦ME < OFr *fontaine* < LL *fontana* < fem. of L *fontanus* < *fons* (gen. *fontis*), spring, prob. < IE base **dhen-*, to run, flow > Sans *dhanáyati*, (he) runs⟧ **1** a natural spring of water **2** the source or beginning of a stream **3** a source or origin of anything [a *fountain* of knowledge] **4** *a)* an artificial spring, jet, or flow of water *b)* the basin, pipes, etc. where this flows *c)* DRINKING FOUNTAIN **5** a container or reservoir, as for ink or oil

foun·tain·head (-hed′) ***n.*** **1** a spring that is the source of a stream **2** the original or main source of anything

Fountain of Youth a legendary spring supposed to restore the health and youth of anyone who drinks from it: it was sought in America by Ponce de León and other explorers

fountain pen a pen in which a nib at the end is fed ink from a supply in a reservoir or cartridge

four (fôr, fōr) ***adj.*** ⟦ME < OE *feower*, akin to Ger *vier*, Goth *fidwōr* < IE base **kwetwor-* > L *quattuor*, Welsh *pedwar*⟧ totaling one more than three —***n.*** **1** the cardinal number between three and five; 4; IV **2** any group of four people or things **3** something numbered four or having four units, as a playing card, face of a die, etc. —**on all fours** **1** on all four feet **2** on hands and knees (or feet) **3** exactly equatable (*with*)

☆**four-bag·ger** (fôr′bag′ər) ***n.*** ⟦see BAG (*n.* 12)⟧ [Slang] HOME RUN

4x4 (fôr′bī fôr′) ***n., pl.*** **4x4s, 4x4's** ⟦see X[5] (sense 1)⟧ a four-wheel-drive vehicle

four·chette (foor shet′) *n.* ⟦Fr, dim. of *fourche*: see FORK⟧ 1 the side strip of a finger in a glove 2 *Anat.* a small fold of skin at the posterior end of the vulva

four-col·or (fôr′kul′ər) *adj.* designating or of a printing process using separate plates in yellow, red, blue, and black, so as to produce any color or colors

four-cy·cle (fôr′sī′kəl) *adj.* FOUR-STROKE

four-di·men·sion·al (fôr′də men′shə nəl) *adj.* of or in four dimensions, esp. in relativity theory where four coordinates are used to record the space location and time of occurrence of each event

Four·drin·i·er (foor drin′ē ər) *adj.* ⟦after Sealy and Henry *Fourdrinier*, 19th-c. Eng papermakers, for whom the machine was developed⟧ designating or of a papermaking machine that produces paper in a continuous strip or roll —*n.* such a machine

Four Eyes [*also* **f- e-**] [Slang] a person wearing eyeglasses: a term of derision, used esp. in direct address —**four′-eyed′** *adj.*

☆**four-flush** (fôr′flush′) *vi.* 1 *Stud Poker* to bluff when one holds four cards of the same suit (**four flush**) instead of the five in a true flush 2 [Informal] to pretend to be, have, or intend something so as to deceive; bluff —**four′-flush′er** *n.*

four·fold (fôr′fōld′) *adj.* ⟦FOUR + -FOLD⟧ 1 having four parts 2 having four times as much or as many —*adv.* four times as much or as many

four-foot·ed (-foot′id) *adj.* having four feet; quadruped

four·gon (fōōr gōn′) *n.* ⟦Fr⟧ a wagon or car for baggage

☆**4-H** (fôr′āch′) *n.* ⟦so named from its goal of improving members' *h*(*ead*), *h*(*eart*), *h*(*ands*), and *h*(*ealth*)⟧ a program for young people sponsored by the U.S. Department of Agriculture, offering training in agriculture, home economics, conservation, citizenship, etc. through local organizations (**4-H clubs**) and related activities

four-hand·ed (fôr′han′did) *adj.* 1 having four hands 2 for four players, as some card games 3 *Music* for two performers, as a piano duet Also **four′-hand′**

Four Horsemen of the Apocalypse *Bible* four figures representing pestilence, war, famine, and death, whose appearance signals that the end of the world is near: Rev. 6:2-8

☆**four hundred** ⟦popularized by C. J. Allen, New York *Sun* society reporter, from a remark by Ward McAllister: "There are only 400 people in New York that one really knows"; prob. from limited capacity of Mrs. J. J. Astor's ballroom⟧ [*also* **F- H-**] the exclusive social set of a particular place: preceded by *the*

Fou·rier (fōō ryā′; *E* foor′ē ər) 1 **Fran·çois Ma·rie Charles** (frän swȧ′ mȧ rē′ shȧrl) 1772-1837; Fr. socialist & reformer 2 Baron **Jean Bap·tiste Jo·seph** (zhän bȧ tēst′ zhō zef′) 1768-1830; Fr. mathematician & physicist

☆**Fou·ri·er·ism** (foor′ē ər iz′əm) *n.* the doctrines of F. M. C. FOURIER, esp. his proposed system for reorganizing society into small, self-sufficient, cooperative agricultural communities

Fou·ri·er series (foor′ē ər) ⟦formulated by Baron FOURIER⟧ *Math.* the expansion of a periodic function into a series of sines and cosines

four-in-hand (fôr′in hand′) *n.* 1 *a*) a team of four horses driven by one person *b*) a coach drawn by such a team ☆2 a necktie tied in a slipknot with the ends left hanging —*adj.* designating or of a four-in-hand

four-leaf clover (fôr′lēf′) a leaf of clover with four leaflets on one leafstalk, popularly believed to bring good luck to the finder

☆**four-let·ter word** (fôr′let′ər) any of several short words having to do with sex or excrement and generally regarded as offensive or objectionable

four-o'clock (fôr′ə kläk′) *adj.* designating a family (Nyctaginaceae, order Caryophyllales) of dicotyledonous plants, including the bougainvilleas —*n.* any of a genus (*Mirabilis*) of chiefly tropical American plants of the four-o'clock family, bearing petal-less flowers and, often, brightly colored leaves; esp., a garden plant (*M. jalapa*) with long-tubed blossoms that generally open in the late afternoon

401(k) (fôr′ō′wun′kā′) *n., pl.* **401(k)s** or **401(k)'s** ⟦< designation of section of U.S. Internal Revenue Code on which it is based⟧ 1 a type of retirement plan in which each eligible employee is allowed to put a percentage of wages or salary into a tax-deferred account that typically offers a variety of savings and investment options 2 such an account Also written **401(K)**, **401K**

four·pence (fôr′pəns) *n.* 1 the sum of four British pennies 2 a former silver coin of this value

four·pen·ny (fôr′pə nē; *for adj.* 2 fôr′pen′ē) *adj.* 1 costing or valued at fourpence 2 *Carpentry* designating a size of nail: see PENNY —*n.* fourpence

four-post·er (fôr′pōs′tər) *n.* a bedstead with tall corner posts that sometimes support a canopy or curtains

four·ra·gère (fōō rȧ zher′) *n.* ⟦Fr < *fourrager*: see FORAGE, *vi.*⟧ a colored, braided cord worn about the shoulder of a uniform; esp., such a cord awarded as a decoration to an entire unit of troops

four·score (fôr′skôr′) *adj., n.* ⟦ME⟧ [Archaic] four times twenty; eighty

four·some (fôr′səm) *adj.* ⟦FOUR + -SOME[2]⟧ of or engaged in by four —*n.* 1 a group of four persons 2 *Golf* a game involving four players, often two to a team

four·square (fôr′skwer′) *adj.* 1 perfectly square 2 unyielding; unhesitating; firm 3 frank; honest; forthright —*adv.* 1 in a square form or manner; squarely 2 forthrightly —*n.* [Archaic] a square

☆**four-star** (fôr′stär′) *adj.* 1 designating a general or admiral whose insignia bears four stars 2 especially important or good, highly recommended, etc.

four-stroke (fôr′strōk′) *adj.* designating or having to do with an internal-combustion engine in which a complete fuel cycle in a cylinder requires four separate piston strokes

four·teen (fôr′tēn′) *adj.* ⟦ME *fourtene* < OE *feowertyne*: see FOUR & -TEEN⟧ totaling four more than ten —*n.* the cardinal number between thirteen and fifteen; 14; XIV

four·teenth (fôr′tēnth′) *adj.* ⟦ME *fourtenthe*, altered (after prec.) < OE *feowerteotha*⟧ 1 preceded by thirteen others in a series; 14th 2 designating any of the fourteen equal parts of something —*n.* 1 the one following the thirteenth 2 any of the fourteen equal parts of something; $1/_{14}$ —*adv.* in the fourteenth place, rank, group, etc.

fourth (fôrth, fōrth) *adj.* ⟦ME *feorthe, ferthe* < OE *feortha*: see FOUR & -TH[2]⟧ 1 preceded by three others in a series; 4th 2 designating any of the four equal parts of something 3 designating the forward gear ratio of a motor vehicle next after third gear —*n.* 1 the one following the third 2 any of the four equal parts of something; ¼ 3 *Music a*) the fourth tone of an ascending diatonic scale, or a tone three degrees above or below any given tone in such a scale; subdominant *b*) the interval between two such tones, or a combination of them —*adv.* in the fourth place, rank, group, etc. —**fourth′ly** *adv.*

fourth-class (fôrth′klas′) *adj.* 1 of the class, rank, excellence, etc. next below the third ☆2 designating or of a former class of mail consisting of merchandise, printed matter, etc.; parcel post —☆*adv.* as or by fourth-class mail

fourth dimension a dimension in addition to the ordinary three space coordinates of length, width, and depth: in the theory of relativity, time is regarded as the fourth dimension: see SPACE-TIME (sense 1) —**fourth′-di·men′sion·al** *adj.*

fourth estate ⟦see ESTATE (sense 2)⟧ [*often* **F- E-**] journalism or journalists

☆**Fourth of July** *see* INDEPENDENCE DAY

Fourth Republic the republic established in France in 1946 and lasting until 1958

fourth wall ⟦in ref. to the typical stage enclosed on three sides⟧ the traditional imaginary barrier between a performing actor, as on a stage or set, and the audience: often in the phrase **break the fourth wall**, to address or otherwise acknowledge the audience during a performance

fourth world [*often* **F- W-**] the poorest, most underdeveloped countries of the Third World

four-wall·ing (fôr′wôl′iŋ) *n.* ⟦< the *four walls* of a theater⟧ a form of distribution and exhibition, esp. of films, in which a distributor or producer rents a theater for a fixed amount, pays all advertising and operating costs, and collects all box-office receipts

four-way (fôr′wā′) *adj.* 1 giving passage in four directions [*a four-way valve*] 2 involving four participants or elements [*a four-way debate*]

4WD *abbrev.* 1 four-wheel drive 2 four-wheel-drive vehicle

four-wheel (-hwēl′, -wēl′) *adj.* having or running on four wheels: also **four′-wheeled′** —**four′-wheel′er** *n.*

four-wheel drive an automotive power-delivery system capable of providing driving power to all four wheels simultaneously

FOV *abbrev.* field of view

fo·ve·a (fō′vē ə) *n., pl.* **-ve·ae′** (-ē′, -ī′) or **-ve·as** ⟦ModL < L⟧ 1 *Biol.* a small pit, hollow, or depression 2 FOVEA CENTRALIS —**fo′ve·al** (-əl) *adj.*, **fo′ve·ate** (-it, -āt′) —**fo·ve·i·form** (fō vē′i fôrm′) *adj.*

fovea cen·tra·lis (sen trā′lis) a depression toward the center of the retina in some vertebrates, the point where the vision is most acute

fo·ve·o·la (fō vē′ə lə) *n., pl.* **-lae′** (-lē′, -lī′) or **-las** ⟦ModL, dim. of *fovea*⟧ a small fovea, or pit: also **fo·ve·ole** (fō′vē ōl′) —**fo·ve′o·late** (-lit, -lāt′) *adj.*, **fo′ve·o·lat′ed** (-lāt′id)

fowl (foul) *n., pl.* **fowls** or **fowl** ⟦ME *foule, foghel* < OE *fugol*, akin to Ger *vogel*, bird < Gmc **fuglaz*, altered by dissimulation < **fluglaz* < **flug-*, **fleug-* < IE **pleuk-* > FLY[1]⟧ 1 any bird: now only in comb. [*wildfowl*] 2 any of various domestic birds used as food; specif., *a*) the chicken *b*) the duck, goose, turkey, etc. *c*) a full-grown chicken, as distinguished from a springer, etc. 3 the flesh of any of these birds used for food —*vi.* to catch, trap, hunt, or shoot wild birds for food or sport —**fowl′er** *n.* —**fowl′ing** *n.*

Fow·ler (fou′lər), **H(enry) W(atson)** 1858-1933; Eng. lexicographer & arbiter of linguistic usage

fowling piece a type of shotgun for hunting wild fowl

fox (fäks) *n., pl.* **fox′es** or **fox** ⟦ME < OE, akin to Ger *fuchs* < Gmc base **fuh-* < IE base **puk-*, thick-haired, bushy > Sans *púccha*, tail⟧ 1 any of various small, wild canines (esp. genera *Vulpes* or *Urocyon*) with bushy tails and, commonly, reddish-brown or gray fur: the fox is conventionally thought of as sly and crafty 2 the fur of a fox 3 a sly, crafty, deceitful person 4 ⟦concept from "The Fox and the Hedgehog," essay by Sir Isaiah Berlin (1907–97), Brit philosopher & historian, born in Russia: in ref. to phr. "the fox knows many things, but the hedgehog knows one big thing," transl. of fragment attributed to Gr poet Archilochus (fl. 7th c. B.C.)⟧ a person regarded as being of a type characterized by wide-ranging knowledge and by adherence to no particular viewpoint or philosophy: opposed to HEDGEHOG (*n.* 3) ☆5 [Slang] a person, esp. a woman, who is attractive, esp. sexually attractive —*vt.* 1 to make (beer, etc.) sour by fermenting 2 ⟦from the color of a fox⟧ to cause (book leaves, prints, etc.) to become stained with reddish-brown or yellowish discolorations 3 to trick or deceive by slyness or craftiness 4 to bewilder or baffle 5 *a*) to repair (boots, shoes, etc.) with new upper leather *b*) to trim (the upper of a shoe) with leather 6 [Obs.] to intoxicate —*vi.* 1 to become sour: said of beer, etc. 2 to become stained: said of book leaves, etc. —**foxed** *adj.*

Fox[1] (fäks) ***n.*** ⟦transl. of Fr *Renard*, which is transl. of Huron *Skenchiohronon*, lit., red-fox people (prob. with ref. to a clan or moiety; cf. the modern clan name *waakosheehaki*, lit., foxes)⟧ ☆**1** a member of a North American Indian people formerly living in Wisconsin and Illinois, now living in Iowa ☆**2** the Algonquian language spoken by the Fox, Sauk, and Kickapoo peoples; esp., the dialect spoken by the Fox

Fox[2] (fäks) **1 Charles James** 1749-1806; Eng. statesman & orator **2 George** 1624-91; Eng. religious leader: founder of the Society of Friends

Foxe Basin (fäks) arm of the Atlantic Ocean, in NE Canada, west of Baffin Island: *c.* 340 mi (547 km) long

fox fire the luminescence of decaying wood and plant remains, caused by various fungi

fox·glove (fäks′gluv′) ***n.*** ⟦ME *foxes glove* < OE *foxes glofa*, fox's glove⟧ DIGITALIS

☆**fox grape** a common wild grape (*Vitis labrusca*) native to E North America with leaves whose undersides are covered with whitish or reddish woolly hairs: it is the parent of many American vineyard grapes, as the Concord and Catawba

☆**fox·hole** (fäks′hōl′) ***n.*** a hole dug in the ground as a temporary protection for one or two soldiers against enemy gunfire or tanks

fox·hound (-hound′) ***n.*** a hound of either of two breeds (*American foxhound* and *English foxhound*) with a close, dense coat of black, tan, and white and ears set close to the head: the English breed has a heavier build, but both are noted for their endurance and have been trained to hunt foxes and other game

fox hunt a sport in which hunters on horses ride after dogs in pursuit of a fox —**fox′-hunt′** ***vi.***

☆**fox snake** a common, harmless rat snake (*Elaphe vulpina*), with a yellowish background color and a series of dark blotches on the back

☆**fox squirrel** a variously colored tree squirrel (*Sciurus niger*) of E North America

fox·tail (fäks′tāl′) ***n.*** **1** the bushy tail of a fox **2** any of various grasses (esp. genus *Setaria*) having cylindrical spikes bearing spikelets interspersed with stiff bristles

foxtail lily EREMURUS

☆**foxtail millet** a cultivated annual grass (*Setaria italica*) with dense, lobed, bristly spikes containing small grains, grown in Eurasia for grain and forage and in America mainly for birdseed

fox terrier any of a breed of terrier having a long, lean head, a white coat with dark markings, and an erect tail, formerly trained to drive foxes out of hiding: there are two varieties, the *smooth*, with a flat, dense coat, and the *wire* (or *wire-haired*)

☆**fox trot** **1** a slow gait in which a horse moves its forelegs in a trot and its hind legs in a long-striding pace **2** *a)* a dance for couples in 4/4 time with a variety of steps, both fast and slow *b)* the music for such a dance —**fox′-trot′** ***vi.*** **-trot′ted, -trot′ting**

fox·y (fäk′sē) ***adj.*** **fox′i·er, fox′i·est** **1** foxlike; crafty; wily; sly **2** having the reddish-brown color of a fox **3** discolored by brownish or yellowish stains, as the leaves of an old book ☆**4** having the characteristic flavor of fox grapes: said of certain wines ☆**5** [Slang] attractive, stylish, etc.; specif., sexually attractive: used esp. of women —***SYN.*** SLY —**fox′i·ly** ***adv.*** —**fox′i·ness** ***n.***

foy (foi) ***n.*** ⟦MDu *foy, fooi, voye*, prob. < OFr *voie* < L *via*, way, journey: see VIA⟧ [Now Chiefly Scot.] **1** a feast, present, etc. given by or to a person departing on a journey **2** a feast at the end of a harvest or fishing season

foy·er (foi′ər; *also* foi′ā′, -yā′; foi ā′, -yā′) ***n.*** ⟦Fr, lobby, greenroom, lit., hearth < ML *focarium* < *focarius*, of the hearth < L *focus*, hearth: see FOCUS⟧ an entrance hall or lobby, esp. in a theater, hotel, or apartment house

fp[1] *abbrev.* **1** foot-pound(s): also **FP** **2** freezing point

fp[2] *abbrev.* ⟦It⟧ *Musical Direction* FORTEPIANO[2]

FPC *abbrev.* **1** Federal Power Commission (1920-77) **2** fish protein concentrate: see FISH FLOUR

fpm *abbrev.* feet per minute

FPO *abbrev. U.S. Navy* Fleet Post Office

fps *abbrev.* **1** feet per second **2** foot-pound-second (system): usually **FPS**: see the table of weights and measures in the Reference Supplement **3** *Photog.* frames per second

fr *abbrev.* **1** fragment **2** franc(s) **3** frequent **4** from

Fr[1] *abbrev.* **1** ⟦L *frater*⟧ Brother **2** Father **3** France **4** ⟦Ger⟧ *Frau* **5** French **6** Friar **7** Friday

Fr[2] *Chem. symbol for* francium

Fra (frä) ***n.*** ⟦It, abbrev. of *frate* < L *frater*, BROTHER⟧ brother: title given to an Italian monk or friar

frab·jous (frab′jəs) ***adj.*** ⟦coined by Lewis CARROLL in *Through the Looking-Glass*⟧ [Informal] splendid; magnificent

frac (frak) *adj.* related to FRACKING —***vi.*** **fracked, frack′ing** *alt. sp. of* FRACK

fra·cas (frā′kəs, fra′-; *Brit* fra′kä′) ***n.*** ⟦Fr < It *fracasso* < *fracassare*, to smash, prob. blend < *frangere* (< L: see BREAK) + *cassare*, to quash, break < L *quassare*: see QUASH[2]⟧ a noisy fight or loud quarrel; brawl

frack (frak) ***adj.*** *alt. sp. of* FRAC —***vi.*** to produce gas and oil by means of FRACKING

frack·ing (frak′iŋ) ***n.*** ⟦< *hydraulic fracturing*⟧ the injection of water at high pressure into a borehole, in order to open underground fissures for the extraction of natural gas or oil

☆**frac·tal** (frak′təl) ***n.*** ⟦via Fr < L *fractus* (see FRACTUS) + -AL: coined (1975) by B. Mandelbrot: see MANDELBROT⟧ *Geom.* an extremely irregular line or surface formed by the infinite repetition of a geometric pattern that becomes smaller and smaller with each repetition

frac·tion (frak′shən) ***n.*** ⟦ME < L *fractio*, a breaking < pp. of *frangere*, BREAK⟧ **1** a breaking or dividing, specif., of the Host in the Mass **2** *a)* a small part broken off; fragment; scrap *b)* a small part, amount, degree, etc.; portion **3** *Chem.* a part separated by fractional crystallization, distillation, etc. **4** *Math.* *a)* a number expressed as a quotient of two whole numbers, as $^{13}/_{4}$ or $^{2}/_{5}$: all fractions are rational numbers (see also DECIMAL, ***n.*** 1) *b)* any quantity expressed in terms of a numerator and denominator, as x/y —***vt.*** to separate into fractions

frac·tion·al (frak′shə nəl) ***adj.*** **1** of or forming a fraction or fractions **2** very small; unimportant; insignificant **3** *Chem.* designating or of any of various processes for separating the constituents of a mixture by taking advantage of differences in their solubility, boiling points, etc. [*fractional* distillation] —**frac′tion·al·ly** ***adv.***

☆**fractional currency** small coins or paper money of a denomination less than the standard monetary unit [dimes and pennies are *fractional currency*]

frac·tion·al·ize (-nəl īz′) ***vt.*** **-ized′, -iz′ing** to divide into fractions, or parts: also **frac′tion·ize′, -ized′, -iz′ing** —**frac′tion·al·i·za′tion** ***n.***, **frac′tion·i·za′tion**

frac·tion·ate (frak′shən āt′) ***vt.*** **-at′ed, -at′ing** **1** to separate into fractions, or parts **2** *Chem.* to separate into fractions by crystallization, distillation, etc. —**frac′tion·a′tion** ***n.***

frac·tious (frak′shəs) ***adj.*** ⟦prob. < FRACTION (in obs. sense "discord") + -OUS⟧ **1** hard to manage; unruly; rebellious; refractory **2** peevish; irritable; cross —**frac′tious·ly** ***adv.*** —**frac′tious·ness** ***n.***

frac·tur (fräk toor′) ***n.*** [*sometimes* **F-**] FRAKTUR (sense 2)

frac·ture (frak′chər) ***n.*** ⟦ME < OFr < L *fractura*, a breaking, breach, cleft < pp. of *frangere*, BREAK⟧ **1** a breaking or being broken **2** a break, crack, or split **3** a break in a body part, esp. in a bone, or a tear in a cartilage: see COMPOUND FRACTURE **4** the texture, shape, etc. of the broken surface of a mineral as distinct from when it breaks along its cleavage plane [conchoidal *fracture*] —***vt.*** **-tured, -tur·ing** **1** to break, crack, or split **2** to break up; disrupt **3** to violate (rules or conventions) flagrantly or thoroughly [a nonnative speaker who *fractures* the language] —***vi.*** **1** to break, crack, or split **2** to break up; disintegrate —***SYN.*** BREAK —**frac′tur·al** ***adj.***

frac·tus (frak′təs) ***n.*** ⟦L, pp. of *frangere*, BREAK⟧ a species of cumulus clouds (**cumulus fractus**) or stratus clouds (**stratus fractus**) with a ragged, shredded appearance

frae (frā) ***prep.*** [Scot.] from

frae·num (frē′nəm) ***n.***, *pl.* **-nums** or **-na** (-nə) FRENUM

☆**frag** (frag) ***vt.*** **fragged, frag′ging** ⟦< *frag(mentation grenade)*⟧ [Mil. Slang] to intentionally kill or wound (one's superior officer, etc.), esp. with a hand grenade

frag·ile (fraj′əl; *chiefly Brit & Cdn*, -īl) ***adj.*** ⟦< OFr < L *fragilis* < *frangere*, BREAK⟧ **1** easily broken, damaged, or destroyed **2** physically weak; frail; delicate **3** tenuous; flimsy [a *fragile* hope] —**fra·gil·i·ty** (frə jil′ə tē) ***n.***

SYN.—**fragile** implies such delicacy of structure as to be easily broken [a *fragile* china teacup]; **frangible** adds to this the connotation of liability to being broken because of the use to which the thing is put [the handle on this ax seems *frangible*]; **brittle** implies such inelasticity as to be easily broken or shattered by pressure or a blow [the bones of the body become *brittle* with age]; **crisp** suggests a desirable sort of brittleness, as of fresh celery or soda crackers; **friable** is applied to something that is easily crumbled or crushed into powder [*friable* rock] —***ANT.*** **tough, sturdy**

fragile X syndrome a congenital disorder caused by a mutation in a gene on the X chromosome and characterized by any of various levels of INTELLECTUAL DISABILITY, autism, etc.

frag·ment (frag′mənt; *for v. also* frag′ment′, frag ment′) ***n.*** ⟦ME < L *fragmentum* < *frangere*, BREAK⟧ **1** a part broken away from a whole; broken piece **2** a detached, isolated, or incomplete part [a *fragment* of a song] **3** the part that exists of a literary or other work left unfinished —***vt., vi.*** to break into fragments; break up —***SYN.*** PART[1] —**frag′ment′ed** ***adj.***

frag·men·tal (frag ment′'l) ***adj.*** **1** FRAGMENTARY **2** *Geol.* CLASTIC —**frag·men′tal·ly** ***adv.***

frag·men·tar·y (frag′mən ter′ē, frag ment′ə rē) ***adj.*** consisting of fragments; not complete; disconnected —**frag′men·tar′i·ly** ***adv.*** —**frag′men·tar′i·ness** ***n.***

frag·men·tate (frag′mən tāt′) ***vt., vi.*** **-tat′ed, -tat′ing** to break into fragments —**frag′men·ta′tion** ***n.***

fragmentation bomb a bomb that scatters in broken, jagged pieces over a wide area when it explodes

frag·ment·ize (frag′mən tīz′) ***vt., vi.*** **-ized′, -iz′ing** to break into fragments —**frag′ment·i·za′tion** ***n.***

Fra·go·nard (frȧ gô nȧr′), **Jean Ho·no·ré** (zhän ô nô rā′) 1732-1806; Fr. painter

fra·grance (frā′grəns) ***n.*** ⟦L *fragrantia*⟧ **1** the quality of being fragrant **2** a sweet smell; pleasant odor Also [Now Rare] **fra′gran·cy**, *pl.* **-cies** —***SYN.*** SCENT

fra·grant (frā′grənt) ***adj.*** ⟦ME < L *fragrans* (gen. *fragrantis*), prp. of *fragrare*, to emit a (sweet) smell < IE base **bhrag-*, to smell > OHG *braccho*, bloodhound⟧ having a pleasant odor; sweet-smelling —**fra′grant·ly** ***adv.***

fraid·y-cat (frā′dē kat′) ***n.*** ⟦< AFRAID + CAT[1]⟧ [Informal] a person easily frightened: a child's term

frail[1] (frāl) ***adj.*** ⟦ME *frele* < OFr < L *fragilis*, FRAGILE⟧ **1** easily broken, shattered, damaged, or destroyed; fragile; delicate **2** slender and delicate; not robust; weak **3** easily tempted to do wrong; morally weak —***SYN.*** WEAK —**frail′ly** ***adv.*** —**frail′ness** ***n.***

frail[2] (frāl) ***n.*** ⟦ME *fraiel* < OFr *frael*, rush basket < ML *fraellum* < L *flagellum*, young branch, whip: see FLAGELLUM⟧ a basket made of rushes, for packing figs, raisins, etc.

frail·ty (frāl′tē) ***n.*** ⟦ME *frelete* < OFr *fraileté* < L *fragilitas*, fragility⟧ **1** the quality or condition of being frail; weakness, specif. moral weakness **2** *pl.* **-ties** any fault or failing arising from such weakness

fraise (frāz) ***n.*** ⟦Fr, orig., a ruff < *fraiser*, to ruffle⟧ **1** a ruff or high collar of a kind worn esp. in the 16th cent. **2** *Mil.* a barrier consisting of an inclined or horizontal fence as of wooden stakes

fraises des bois (frez dā bwȧ′) ⟦Fr⟧ wild strawberries

Frak·tur (fräk to͝or′) ***n.*** ⟦Ger < L *fractura* (see FRACTURE): so named from its angular, broken lines⟧ **1** [*sometimes* **f-**] a style of German black-letter type **2** [*usually* **f-**] *a)* a type of Pennsylvania Dutch folk art consisting of documents, as marriage or baptismal certificates, framed mottoes, etc. written in Fraktur lettering and illuminated with colorful flowers, birds, and other motifs *b)* an example of this

fram·be·sia or **fram·boe·sia** (fram bē′zhə, -zhē ə) ***n.*** ⟦ModL < Fr *framboise*, raspberry, altered (after *fraise*, strawberry) < Frank **brambasi*, akin to Ger *brombeere*: see BRAMBLE & BERRY⟧ YAWS

fram·boise (frän bwȧz′) ***n.*** ⟦Fr: see prec.⟧ raspberry liqueur

frame (frām) ***vt.*** **framed**, **fram′ing** ⟦ME *framen* < *frame*, a structure, frame, prob. < ON *frami*, profit, benefit, akin to *frama*, to further < *fram*, forward (akin to OE *fram*, FROM); some senses < OE *framian*, to be helpful: see FURNISH⟧ **1** to shape, fashion, or form, usually according to a pattern; design [to *frame* a constitution] **2** to put together the parts of; construct **3** to put into words; compose; devise; contrive; conceive [to *frame* an excuse] **4** to utter [his lips *framed* the words] **5** to adapt for a particular use; adjust; fit [a law *framed* to equalize the tax burden] **6** to enclose in a border; provide a border for (a mirror, picture, etc.) **7** to photograph or film (objects or activity) within the limits of the FRAME (*n.* 13*b*) ☆**8** [Informal] to falsify evidence, testimony, etc. beforehand in order to make (an innocent person) appear guilty **9** [Obs.] to bring about; cause —***vi.*** [Obs.] to proceed or succeed; go —***n.*** ⟦ME: see the ***vt.***⟧ **1** *a)* [Archaic] anything made of parts fitted together according to a design *b)* body structure in general; build **2** basic or skeletal structure around which a thing is built and that gives the thing its shape; framework, as of a house **3** *a)* the skeletal framework of an automotive chassis, on which the body and various mechanical components are mounted *b)* COLD FRAME *c)* the case or border into which a window, door, etc. is set and which serves as a structural support *d)* a border, often ornamental, surrounding a picture, etc.; also, the picture or other matter inside such a border *e)* [*pl.*] the framing of a pair of eyeglasses; rims **4** any of various machines built on or in a framework **5** the way that anything is constructed or put together; organization; form **6** a set of circumstances that serve as background to an event **7** condition; state [a bad *frame* of mind] **8** an established order or system ☆**9** [Informal] *Baseball* an inning ☆**10** [Informal] the act of framing an innocent person; frame-up: see FRAME (***vt.*** 8) **11** *Bowling, etc.* any of the ten divisions of a game, in each of which the pins are set up anew **12** *Linguis.* a syntactic construction with a blank left in it for testing which words will occur there ☆**13** *Film a)* each of the small exposures composing a strip of film *b)* the rectangular image on a film screen, or the particular objects or activity focused on by the camera **14** *Pool a)* RACK[1] *b)* the period of play required to pocket all the balls **15** *Shipbuilding* any of the transverse strengthening members of a ship's hull that extend from the gunwale to the keel **16** *TV* a single scanning of the field of vision by the electron beam —***adj.*** ☆having a wooden framework, usually covered with boards [a *frame* house]

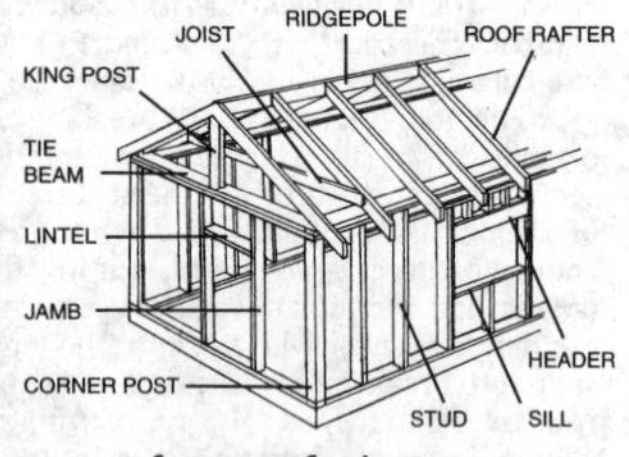

frame of a house

frame of reference **1** *Math.* the fixed points, lines, or planes from which coordinates are measured **2** the set of ideas, experiences, and circumstances forming the basis of someone's judgments, values, etc.

fram·er (frām′ər) ***n.*** **1** a person or thing that frames **2** [*usually* **F-**] any of the delegates who participated in the framing of the U.S. Constitution; Founding Father

frame·shift mutation (frām′shift′) a mutation of a gene caused by the addition or deletion of any number of nucleotides other than three or multiples of three in a DNA sequence: messenger RNA derived from such DNA will carry faulty instructions for the synthesis of proteins

☆**frame-up** (frām′up′) ***n.*** [Informal] **1** a falsifying of evidence, testimony, etc. to make an innocent person seem guilty **2** a surreptitious, underhanded, prearranged scheme

frame·work (frām′wurk′) ***n.*** **1** a structure, usually rigid, serving to hold the parts of something together or to support something constructed or stretched over or around it **2** the basic structure, arrangement, or system **3** FRAME OF REFERENCE (sense 2)

fram·ing (frām′iŋ) ***n.*** **1** the act of a person or thing that frames **2** the way in which something is framed **3** *a)* a frame or framework *b)* a system of frames

franc (fraŋk; *Fr* frän) ***n.*** ⟦Fr < L *Francorum rex*, king of the French, device on the coin in 1360⟧ **1** the former basic monetary unit of Belgium, France, and Luxembourg, superseded in 2002 by the EURO **2** the basic monetary unit of: *a)* Democratic Republic of the Congo *b)* Liechtenstein *c)* Switzerland **3** any of the basic monetary units of various countries formerly ruled by France or Belgium, as Benin, Burundi, Chad, Gabon, Niger, and the Republic of the Congo See the table of monetary units in the Reference Supplement

France[1] (frans, fräns), **A·na·tole** (an′ə tōl′) (pseud. of *Jacques Anatole François Thibault*) 1844-1924; Fr. novelist & literary critic

France[2] (frans, fräns) country in W Europe, on the Atlantic & the Mediterranean Sea: 211,209 sq mi (547,030 sq km); cap. Paris: Fr. name **Ré·pub·lique Fran·çaise** (rā pü blēk′ frän sez′)

Fran·ces (fran′sis, frän′-) ***n.*** ⟦OFr fem. form of *Franceis*: see FRANCIS[1]⟧ a feminine name: dim. *Fran, Fannie, Fanny*

Fran·ces·ca (frän ches′kä), **Pie·ro del·la** (pye′rô del′lä) 1412?-92; It. painter

Francesca da Ri·mi·ni (dä rē′mē nē′) 13th-cent. It. woman famous for her adulterous love affair with her brother-in-law, Paolo

Franche-Com·té (fränsh kōn tā′) **1** historical region of E France, on the border of Switzerland **2** metropolitan region of modern France, in the same general area: 6,256 sq mi (16,203 sq km); chief city, Besançon

fran·chise (fran′chīz′) ***n.*** ⟦ME < OFr < *franc*, free: see FRANK[1]⟧ **1** [Archaic] freedom from some restriction, servitude, etc. **2** any special right, privilege, or exemption granted by the government, as to be a corporation, operate a public utility, etc. **3** the right to vote; suffrage: usually preceded by *the* **4** *a)* the right to market a product or provide a service, often exclusive for a specified area, as granted by a manufacturer or company *b)* a business granted such a right ☆**5** *a)* the right to own a member team as granted by a league in certain professional sports *b)* such a member team —***vt.*** **-chised′**, **-chis′ing** to grant a franchise to —***adj.*** designating a player on a professional team who is regarded as being essential to that team's success

fran·chi·see (fran′chī zē′) ***n.*** a person, business, etc. that has been granted a franchise

fran·chis·er (fran′chī′zər) ***n.*** **1** a company or manufacturer that grants franchises: also sp. **fran′chi·sor** **2** [Rare] FRANCHISEE

Fran·cis[1] (fran′sis) ***n.*** ⟦OFr *Franceis* < ML *Franciscus* < Gmc **Franco*: see FRANK[2]⟧ a masculine name: dim. *Frank*; equiv. Fr. *François*, Ger. *Franz*, It. *Francesco, Franco*, Sp. *Francisco*; fem. *Frances, Francine*

Fran·cis[2] (fran′sis) **1 Francis** (born *Jorge Mario Bergoglio*) 1936- ; pope (2013-) **2 Francis I** 1494-1547; king of France (1515-47) **3 Francis II** 1768-1835; last emperor of the Holy Roman Empire (1792-1806) and, as **Francis I**, first emperor of Austria (1804-35)

Fran·cis·can (fran sis′kən) ***adj.*** ⟦< ML *Franciscus*: see FRANCIS[1]⟧ **1** of Saint Francis of Assisi **2** designating or of the religious order founded by him in 1209: it is now divided into three branches —***n.*** any member of this order

Francis Ferdinand 1863-1914; archduke of Austria: his assassination led to the outbreak of WWI

Francis Joseph I 1830-1916; emperor of Austria (1848-1916) and king of Hungary (1867-1916): uncle of Francis Ferdinand

Francis of Assisi, Saint (born *Giovanni di Bernardone*) (1181?-1226); It. friar: founder of the Franciscan Order: his day is Oct. 4

Francis of Sales (sālz), Saint (1567-1622); Fr. bishop & writer: his day is Jan. 29

Francis Xavier, Saint *see* XAVIER, Saint Francis

fran·ci·um (fran′sē əm) ***n.*** ⟦ModL < FRANCE[2] + -IUM⟧ a radioactive chemical element, an alkali metal, existing in minute amounts in nature as a decay product of actinium: symbol, Fr; at. no. 87: see the periodic table of elements in the Reference Supplement

Franck (fränk), **Cé·sar (Auguste)** (sā zȧr′) 1822-90; Fr. composer & organist, born in Belgium

Fran·co (fraŋ′kō), **Fran·cis·co** (fran sis′kō) (born *Francisco Paulino Hermenegildo Teódulo Franco Bahamonde*) 1892-1975; Sp. general: dictator of Spain (1939-75)

Fran·co- (fraŋ′kō) ⟦ML < LL *Francus*, a Frank⟧ *combining form* **1** Frankish **2** French, French and [*Francophobe, Franco*-Prussian War]

fran·co·lin (fraŋ′kō lin) ***n.*** ⟦Fr < It *francolino*⟧ any of a genus (*Francolinus*, family Phasianidae) of African and Asian partridges

Fran·co·ni·a (fraŋ kō′nē ə) region of central Germany, a duchy in the Middle Ages —**Fran·co′ni·an** ***adj., n.***

Fran·co·phile (fraŋ′kə fīl′) ***n.*** ⟦FRANCO- + -PHILE⟧ a person who strongly admires France or its people, culture, customs, influence, etc.: also **Fran′co·phil** (-fil)

Fran·co·phobe (-fōb′) ***n.*** ⟦FRANCO- + -PHOBE⟧ a person who hates or fears France or its people, culture, customs, influence, etc. —**Fran′co·pho′bi·a** ***n.*** —**Fran′co·pho′bic** ***adj.***

Fran·co·phone (fraŋ′kə fōn′) [*also* **f-**] ***adj.*** ⟦FRANCO- + Gr *phōnē*, a voice⟧ of or having to do with speakers of French —***n.*** a person who speaks French —**Fran′co·phon′ic** (-fän′ik) ***adj.***

Fran·co-Prus·sian War (fraŋ′kō prush′ən) a war (1870-71) in which Prussia defeated France

franc·ti·reur (frän tē rër′) *n., pl.* **francs-ti·reurs** (frän tē rër′) ⟦Fr < *franc,* free + *tireur,* a gunner < *tirer,* to shoot⟧ a French irregular soldier, specif. one who is a guerrilla or sniper

fran·gi·ble (fran′jə bəl) *adj.* ⟦ME < OFr < ML *frangibilis* < L *frangere,* BREAK⟧ breakable; fragile —*SYN.* FRAGILE —**fran′gi·bil′i·ty** *n.*

fran·gi·pan·i (fran′ji pan′ē, -pän′-) *n., pl.* **-pan′i** or **-pan′is** ⟦It, after Marquis *Frangipani* (16th-c. It nobleman), said to have invented the perfume⟧ **1** any of a genus (*Plumeria*) of tropical American shrubs and trees of the dogbane family, with large, funnel-shaped flowers and milky sap; specif., a small tree (*P. rubra*) with fragrant, reddish flowers that are used, in Hawaii, to make leis **2** a perfume obtained from, or scented like, such flowers **3** a custard dessert or a custard filling for cakes and tarts, usually flavored with ground almonds Also **fran′gi·pane′** (-pān′)

Fran·glais (frän glā′; *Fr* frän gle′) *n.* ⟦Fr, coined (1964) by René Étiemble, Fr writer < *Fran(çais),* French + *(An)glais,* English⟧ [*often* **f-**] French that contains a significant quantity of English words and phrases: a mildly contemptuous term

frank[1] (fraŋk) *adj.* ⟦ME < OFr *franc,* free, frank < ML *francus* < LL *Francus,* a Frank, hence free man (i.e., member of the ruling race in Gaul) < Gmc **Frank* (> OHG *Franco*) < ? or akin to **franco,* a spear, javelin > OE *franca,* ON *frakka*⟧ **1** [Archaic] free in giving; generous **2** open and honest in expressing what one thinks or feels; straightforward; candid **3** free from reserve, disguise, or guile; clearly evident; plain [*showing frank distaste*] —*vt.* **1** *a)* to send (mail) free of postage, as by virtue of an official position *b)* to mark (mail) as with one's signature so that it can be sent free *c)* to put a stamp on or meter (mail) to prepay postage **2** to make easy the passage of (a person); allow to pass freely —*n.* **1** the privilege of sending mail free **2** a mark, signature, or stamp on mail for, or in place of, postage **3** an envelope, etc. that has been franked —**frank′ness** *n.*

SYN.—**frank** applies to a person, remark, etc. that is free or blunt in expressing the truth or an opinion, unhampered by conventional reticence [*a frank criticism*]; **candid** implies a basic honesty that makes deceit or evasion impossible, sometimes to the embarrassment of the listener [*a candid opinion*]; **open** implies a lack of concealment and often connotes an ingenuous quality [*her open admiration for him*]; **outspoken** suggests a lack of restraint or reserve in speech, esp. when reticence might be preferable

☆**frank**[2] (fraŋk) *n.* [Informal] *short for* FRANKFURTER

Frank[1] (fraŋk) *n.* ⟦shortened & altered < FRANCIS[1]⟧ a masculine name: dim. *Frankie:* see FRANCIS[1]

Frank[2] (fraŋk) *n.* ⟦ME < OE *Franca* & < OFr *Franc* < LL *Francus:* see FRANK[1]⟧ a member of the group of related Germanic peoples that established the Frankish Empire, which, at its height (beginning of the 9th cent. A.D.), extended over what is now France, Germany, and Italy

Frank[3] (fraŋk), **Anne** 1929-45; Jewish victim of the Holocaust, born in Germany: known for diary (published 1947) kept while in hiding in Amsterdam (1942-44): died in Bergen-Belsen

Frank[4] *abbrev.* Frankish

Frank·en·food (fraŋ′kən fo͞od′) *n.* ⟦< fol. + FOOD⟧ a food that has been altered by genetic engineering: a term used derisively

Frank·en·stein (fraŋ′kən stīn′) *n.* **1** the title character in a novel (1818) by Mary Wollstonecraft SHELLEY[2]: he is a young medical student who creates a monster that destroys him **2** popularly, Frankenstein's monster **3** any person destroyed by his or her own creation **4** anything that becomes dangerous to its creator

Frank·fort (fraŋk′fərt) **1** ⟦orig. *Frank's Ford,* prob. after Stephen *Frank,* a pioneer killed there (1780)⟧ capital of Ky., in the NC part **2** FRANKFURT

Frank·furt (fraŋk′fərt; *Ger* fräŋk′foort) **1** city in W Germany, on the Main River, in the state of Hesse: also **Frankfurt am Main** (äm mīn′) **2** city in E Germany, on the Oder River, in the state of Brandenburg: also **Frankfurt an der Oder** (än dur ō′dər)

☆**frank·furt·er** (fraŋk′fər tər) *n.* ⟦Ger, after prec.⟧ a smoked sausage of beef, pork, chicken, etc., enclosed in a membranous casing and made in cylindrical links a few inches long: the casing is now usually removed before packaging

Frank·furt·er (fraŋk′fər tər), **Felix** 1882-1965; associate justice, U.S. Supreme Court (1939-62), born in Austria

frank·in·cense (fraŋ′kin sens′) *n.* ⟦ME < OFr *franc encens* (in sense "pure, high-grade" incense): see FRANK[1] & INCENSE[1]⟧ a gum resin obtained from various Arabian and African trees (genus *Boswellia*) of the bursera family and used in perfumes and as incense; olibanum

Frank·ish (fraŋ′kish) *n.* the West Germanic language of the Franks —*adj.* of the Franks or their language or culture

frank·lin (fraŋk′lin) *n.* ⟦ME *frankelein* < Anglo-Fr *fraunkelain* < ML *francelengus* < *francus* (see FRANK[1]) + Gmc *-*ling* (see -LING[1])⟧ a freeholder; specif., in England in the 14th-15th cent., a landowner of free but not noble birth, ranking just below the gentry

Frank·lin[1] (fraŋk′lin) *n.* ⟦see prec.⟧ a masculine name

Frank·lin[2] (fraŋk′lin) **1 Benjamin** 1706-90; Am. statesman, scientist, inventor, & writer **2 Sir John** 1786-1847; Eng. arctic explorer

Frank·lin[3] (fraŋk′lin) ⟦see FRANKLIN⟧ former district of the Northwest Territories, Canada

☆**frank·lin·ite** (fraŋk′lin īt′) *n.* ⟦after *Franklin,* N.J., where found⟧ a dark-colored, hard, very heavy, magnetic mineral, zinc manganese iron oxide, $(Zn,Fe,Mn)(Fe,Mn)_2O_4$, an ore of zinc and manganese

☆**Franklin stove** ⟦after Benjamin FRANKLIN[2], who invented it⟧ a cast-iron heating stove resembling an open fireplace

Franklin stove

frank·ly (fraŋk′lē) *adv.* **1** in a frank manner **2** in truth; to be frank [*frankly, he's a bore*]

frank·pledge (fraŋk′plej′) *n.* ⟦ME *frank-plege* < Anglo-Fr *fraunc plege* (see FRANK[1] & PLEDGE): prob. orig. a mistransl. of OE *frith-borh,* lit., peace pledge⟧ **1** the system in old English law which made each man in a tithing responsible for the actions of other members **2** a member under this system **3** the tithing

fran·se·ri·a (fran sir′ē ə) *n.* ⟦ModL, after A. *Franseri,* 18th-c. Sp botanist⟧ ☆any of a genus (*Franseria*) of W American plants of the composite family

fran·tic (fran′tik) *adj.* ⟦ME *frantik, frenetik:* see PHRENETIC⟧ **1** wild with anger, pain, worry, etc.; frenzied **2** marked by frenzy; resulting from wild emotion **3** [Archaic] insane —**fran′ti·cal·ly** *adv.,* [Rare] **fran′tic·ly**

Franz Jo·sef I (fränts yō′zef; *E* fränts jō′zəf) *Ger. name for* FRANCIS JOSEPH I

Franz Josef Land (fränts jō′zəf) group of islands of Russia, in the Arctic Ocean, north of Novaya Zemlya: *c.* 6,229 sq mi (16,133 sq km)

frap (frap) *vt.* **frapped, frap′ping** ⟦ME *frapen* < OFr *fraper,* to strike⟧ *Naut.* to pass ropes, cables, etc. around in order to strengthen, support, steady, etc.

☆**frap·pé** (fra pā′) *adj.* ⟦Fr, pp. of *frapper,* to strike⟧ partly frozen; iced; cooled —*n.* **1** a dessert made of partly frozen beverages, fruit juices, etc. **2** a drink made of some beverage poured over shaved ice **3** [New England] a milkshake Also, esp. for 3, **frappe** (frap)

Fra·sca·ti (frə skät′ē) *n.* a white Italian wine, usually dry, produced in and around the town of Frascati southeast of Rome

Fra·ser (frā′zər) river in British Columbia, Canada, flowing southward into the Strait of Georgia: 850 mi (1,368 km)

frass (fras) *n.* ⟦Ger < *fressen,* to devour: see FRET[1]⟧ the mixture of fecal material and plant matter left by an animal, esp. an insect, after it has eaten its way into a tree, plant, etc.

☆**frat** (frat) *n.* [Informal] a fraternity, as at a college

fra·ter[1] (frāt′ər) *n.* ⟦ME *freitour* < Anglo-Fr *fraitur,* aphetic for OFr *refreitor, refeitor* < ML *refectorium*⟧ [Obs.] the eating room, or refectory, in a monastery

fra·ter[2] (frāt′ər; *also* frāt′-) *n.* ⟦L, lit., BROTHER⟧ **1** a brother or comrade, esp. as in a fraternity **2** [Obs.] a friar

fra·ter·nal (frə tur′nəl) *adj.* ⟦ME < ML *fraternalis* < L *fraternus,* brotherly < *frater,* BROTHER⟧ **1** of or characteristic of a brother or brothers; brotherly **2** of or like a fraternal order or a fraternity **3** designating twins, of either the same or different sexes, developed from separately fertilized ova and thus having hereditary characteristics not necessarily the same: cf. IDENTICAL (sense 3) —**fra·ter′nal·ism′** *n.* —**fra·ter′nal·ly** *adv.*

☆**fraternal order** (*or* **organization, association,** *etc.*) a society of members banded together for mutual benefit or for work toward a common goal

fra·ter·ni·ty (frə tur′nə tē) *n., pl.* **-ties** ⟦ME *fraternite* < OFr *fraternité* < L *fraternitas* < *fraternus:* see FRATERNAL⟧ **1** the state or quality of being brothers; fraternal relationship or spirit; brotherliness **2** a group of men (or, sometimes, men and women) joined together by common interests, for fellowship, etc.; specif., a Greek-letter college organization **3** a group of people with the same beliefs, interests, work, etc. [*the medical fraternity*]

frat·er·nize (frat′ər nīz′) *vi.* **-nized′, -niz′ing** ⟦Fr *fraterniser* < L *fraternus:* see FRATERNAL⟧ **1** to associate in a brotherly manner; be on friendly terms **2** to have intimate or friendly relations with any of the enemy: said of soldiers occupying enemy territory —**frat′er·ni·za′tion** *n.* —**frat′er·niz′er** *n.*

frat·ri·cide (fra′trə sīd′) *n.* ⟦Fr < LL(Ec) *fratricidium* < L *fratricida,* one who kills a brother < *frater,* BROTHER + *caedere,* to kill (see -CIDE)⟧ **1** *a)* the act of killing one's own brother or sister *b)* the act of killing relatives or fellow-countrymen, as in a civil war **2** ⟦ME < OFr < L *fratricida*⟧ a person who kills his or her own brother or sister —**frat′ri·ci′dal** (-sīd′'l) *adj.*

Frau (frou) *n., pl.* **Frau′en** (-ən) ⟦Ger < OHG *frouwa,* mistress < IE **prōwo-* < base **per-,* beyond > FAR, FIRST, FORE⟧ **1** Mrs.; Madam: German title of respect used to address a married woman: now also used to address a single woman, esp. in business **2** a married woman **3** a wife

fraud (frôd) *n.* ⟦ME *fraude* < OFr < L *fraus* (gen. *fraudis*) < IE base **dhwer-,* to trick > Sans *dhvárati,* (he) injures⟧ **1** *a)* deceit; trickery; cheating *b)* *Law* intentional deception to cause a person to give up property or some lawful right **2** something said or done to deceive; trick; artifice **3** a person who deceives or who is not what he or she pretends to be; impostor; cheat —*SYN.* DECEPTION

fraud·ster (frôd′stər) *n.* [Chiefly Brit.] a person who commits fraud; cheat; swindler

fraud·u·lent (frô′jə lənt) *adj.* ⟦ME < OFr < L *fraudulentus* < *fraus,* FRAUD⟧ **1** acting with fraud; deceitful **2** based on or characterized by fraud [*a fraudulent scheme*] **3** done or obtained by fraud [*their fraudulent wealth*] —**fraud′u·lence** *n.,* **fraud′u·len·cy** —**fraud′u·lent·ly** *adv.*

fraught (frôt) *adj.* ⟦ME *fraught,* pp. of *fraughten,* to freight < MDu *vrachten* < *vracht,* a load < Gmc **fraaichtiz* < **fra-* (akin to FOR[1]) + **aig-,* to have > Goth *aigan,* OWE⟧ **1** filled, charged, or loaded (*with*) [*a life fraught with hardship*] **2** emotional, tense, anxious, distressing, etc.

Fräu·lein (froi′līn′; *E* froi′-, frou′-) ***n.***, *pl.* **-lein′** or Eng. **-leins′** ⟦Ger < *frau* (see FRAU) + dim. suffix *-lein*⟧ **1** Miss: a German title of respect **2** an unmarried woman or a girl: cf. the note at FRAU (sense 1)

Fraun·ho·fer lines (froun′hō′fər) ⟦after Joseph von *Fraunhofer* (1787-1826), Bavarian optician, who first mapped them accurately⟧ the dark lines visible in the spectrum of the sun or a star

frax·i·nel·la (frak′si nel′ə) ***n.*** ⟦ModL, dim. of L *fraxinus*, ash tree (the leaves resemble those of the ash): for IE base see BIRCH⟧ GAS PLANT

fray[1] (frā) ***n.*** ⟦ME *frai*, aphetic < *affrai*, AFFRAY⟧ a noisy quarrel or fight; brawl —***vt.*** ⟦ME *fraien*⟧ [Archaic] to frighten

fray[2] (frā) ***vt., vi.*** ⟦ME *fraien* < OFr *freier* < L *fricare*, to rub: see FRICTION⟧ **1** to make or become worn, ragged, or raveled by rubbing **2** to make or become weakened or strained —***n.*** a frayed place, as in cloth

Fra·zer (frā′zər), Sir **James (George)** 1854-1941; Scot. anthropologist: wrote *The Golden Bough*

☆**fra·zil (ice)** (frāz′il, frə zil′) ⟦CdnFr *frasil* < Fr *fraisil*, charcoal cinders, altered (prob. after *fraiser*, to ruffle) < OFr *faisil* < VL **facilis* < L *fax* (gen. *facis*), a torch < IE base **ĝhwok-*, to gleam, glow⟧ tiny, round or pointed ice crystals formed in supercooled waters and prevented from coagulating by turbulence

fraz·zle (fraz′əl) [Informal] ***vt., vi.*** **-zled**, **-zling** ⟦Brit (E Anglian) dial. & U.S., prob. altered (after FRAY[2]) < dial. *fazle* < ME *faselen*, to fray < *fasel*, frayed edge < *fas* < OE *fæs*, a fringe⟧ **1** to wear or become worn to rags or tatters; fray **2** to make or become physically or emotionally exhausted —☆***n.*** the state of being frazzled

freak[1] (frēk) ***n.*** ⟦Early ModE < ? OE *frician*, to dance (> ME *freking*, whim, capricious conduct)⟧ **1** *a)* a sudden fancy; odd notion; whim *b)* an odd or unusual happening **2** any abnormal animal, person, or plant; monstrosity ☆**3** [Slang] *a)* a user of a specified narcotic, hallucinogen, etc. [*an acid freak*] *b)* a devotee or buff [*a reggae freak*] *c)* HIPPIE **4** [Archaic] capriciousness **5** *Philately* a postage stamp with an error that occurred in the printing or perforation process and is unique to the one stamp —***adj.*** oddly different from what is usual or normal; odd; abnormal [*freak weather*] —***vt., vi.*** [Slang] FREAK OUT (see phrase) —**freak out** [Slang] **1** to experience, esp. in an extreme way, the mental reactions, hallucinations, etc. induced by a psychedelic drug **2** to make or become very excited, distressed, disorganized, etc.

freak[2] (frēk) ***vt.*** ⟦ult. < IE **(s)p(h)ereg-* > FRECKLE⟧ [Rare] to streak or fleck

freak·ing (frēk′iŋ) ***adj., adv.*** [Slang] *euphemism for* FUCKING

freak·ish (frēk′ish) ***adj.*** **1** full of or characterized by freaks; whimsical; capricious **2** having the nature of a freak; odd; peculiar —**freak′ish·ly** ***adv.*** —**freak′ish·ness** ***n.***

freak·out (frēk′out′) ***n.*** [Slang] the act or an instance of freaking out

☆**freak show** an exhibit of freaks, as in a carnival sideshow

freak·y (frēk′ē) ***adj.*** **freak′i·er**, **freak′i·est** [Informal] FREAKISH

freck·le (frek′əl) ***n.*** ⟦ME *frekel*, altered < *frakene* < Scand, as in Norw dial. *frokle*, freckle & Norw *frekna*, Dan *fregne*, Swed *fräkne*, ON *freknōttr*, freckled < IE base **(s)p(h)ereg-*, to strew: see SPARK[1]⟧ a small, brownish spot on the skin, esp. as a result of exposure to the sun —***vt.*** **-led**, **-ling** to cause freckles to appear on —***vi.*** to become spotted with freckles —**freck′led** ***adj.***, **freck′ly**

Fre·da (frē′də) ***n.*** a feminine name: see FRIEDA

☆**Fred·die Mac** (fred′ē mak′) ⟦altered (as if a given name, after FANNIE MAE) < pronun. of parts of its abbrev., *FHLMC*, ? infl. by pronun. of *federal*⟧ **1** *informal name for* Federal Home Loan Mortgage Corporation: a corporation sponsored by the federal government which issues securities backed by pools of residential mortgages purchased from lending institutions **2** any of the securities issued by this corporation: *usually used in pl.*

Fred·er·i·ca (fred′ər ē′kə) ***n.*** ⟦see fol.⟧ a feminine name

Fred·er·ick[1] (fred′rik, -ər ik) ***n.*** ⟦Fr *Frédéric* < Ger *Friedrich* < OHG *Fridurih* < Gmc **frithu-*, peace (< *fri-*, to love, protect + *-thu-*, substantive particle) + **rik-*, king, ruler (akin to L *rex*, Ger *reich*): see RIGHT⟧ a masculine name: dim. *Fred, Freddie, Freddy*; equiv. Fr. *Frédéric*, Ger. *Friedrich, Fritz*, It. & Sp. *Federico*; fem. *Frederica*: also **Frederic**, **Fredric**, or **Fredrick**

Fred·er·ick[2] (fred′rik, -ər ik) **1 Frederick I** 1123?-90; king of Germany (1152-90) & emperor of the Holy Roman Empire (1155-90): called *Frederick Barbarossa* **2 Frederick I** 1657-1713; 1st king of Prussia (1701-13) &, as **Frederick III**, elector of Brandenburg (1688-1701): son of Frederick William, the Great Elector **3 Frederick II** 1194-1250; emperor of the Holy Roman Empire (1215-50): king of Sicily (1197-1250) **4 Frederick II** FREDERICK THE GREAT **5 Frederick III** 1463-1525; elector of Saxony (1486-1525): protector of Luther after the diet at Worms **6 Frederick IX** 1899-1972; king of Denmark (1947-72)

Fred·ericks·burg (fred′riks burg′) ⟦after *Frederick* Louis (1707-51), father of GEORGE III⟧ city in NE Va., on the Rappahannock: scene of a Civil War battle (Dec., 1862) in which Confederate forces were victorious

Frederick the Great 1712-86; king of Prussia (1740-86): son of Frederick William I

Frederick William **1** 1620-88; elector of Brandenburg (1640-88): called *the Great Elector* **2 Frederick William I** 1688-1740; king of Prussia (1713-40) **3 Frederick William II** 1744-97; king of Prussia (1786-97) **4 Frederick William III** 1770-1840; king of Prussia (1797-1840)

Fred·er·ic·ton (fred′ə rik tən) capital of New Brunswick, Canada, on the Saint John River

free (frē) ***adj.*** **fre′er**, **fre′est** ⟦ME *fre* < OE *freo*, not in bondage, noble, glad, illustrious, akin to Ger *frei*, Du *vrij* < IE base **prei-*, to be fond of, hold dear > FRIEND, Sans *priyá-*, dear, desired⟧ **1** *a)* not under the control of some other person or some arbitrary power; able to act or think without compulsion or arbitrary restriction; having liberty; independent *b)* characterized by or resulting from liberty **2** *a)* having, or existing under, a government that does not impose arbitrary restrictions on the right to speak, assemble, petition, vote, etc.; having civil and political liberty [*a free people*] *b)* not under control of a foreign government **3** able to move in any direction; not held, as in chains, etc.; not kept from motion; loose **4** not held or confined by a court, the police, etc.; acquitted **5** not held or burdened by obligations, debts, discomforts, etc.; unhindered; unhampered [*free from pain*] **6** at liberty; allowed [*free to leave at any time*] **7** not confined to the usual rules or patterns; not limited by convention or tradition [*free verse*] **8** not literal; not exact [*a free translation*] **9** not held or confined by prejudice or bias **10** not restricted by anything except its own limitations or nature [*free will*] **11** not busy or not in use; available for other work, use, etc. **12** readily done or made; spontaneous [*a free offer*] **13** not constrained or stilted; easy and graceful [*a free gait*] **14** *a)* generous; liberal; lavish [*a free spender*] *b)* profuse; copious **15** frank; straightforward **16** too frank or familiar in speech, action, etc.; forward **17** with no charge or cost; gratis [*a free ticket*] **18** not liable to (trade restrictions, etc.); exempt from certain impositions, as taxes or duties **19** clear of obstructions; open and unimpeded [*a free road ahead*] **20** open to all; esp., without restrictions as to trade [*a free market, free port*] **21** not in contact or connection; not fastened [*the free end of a rope*] **22** not united; not combined [*free oxygen*] **23** *Games* additional; extra [*a free turn*] **24** *Jazz* designating or of improvisation unrestricted by set harmonic structure, rhythmic patterns, tempo, etc. **25** *Linguis.* designating a minimum form, or morpheme, that may occur alone as an independent word [*in "boys," boy is a free form, but -s is not*]: opposed to BOUND[2] (***adj.*** 8) **26** *Navigation* not opposed; favorable: said of a wind blowing from a direction more than six points from straight ahead —***adv.*** **fre′er**, **fre′est** **1** without cost or payment **2** in a free manner; without obstruction, burden, obligation, etc. **3** *Naut.* with a favorable wind —***vt.*** **freed**, **free′ing** to make free; specif., *a)* to release from bondage or arbitrary power, authority, obligation, etc. *b)* to clear of obstruction, entanglement, etc.; disengage —☆**for free** [Informal] without cost or payments; gratis —**free and easy** not constrained by formality or conventionality; informal; unceremonious —**free from** (or **of**) **1** lacking; without **2** released or removed from **3** beyond; outside of —**free up** to release, or make available, for use [*to free up funds*] —**give** (or **have**) **a free hand** to give (or have) liberty to act according to one's judgment —**make free with** **1** to use or treat as if one owned; use freely **2** to take liberties with —**set free** to cause to be free; release; liberate —**with a free hand** with generosity; lavishly —**free′ly** ***adv.*** —**free′ness** ***n.***

SYN.—**free** is the general term meaning to set loose from any sort of restraint, entanglement, burden, etc. [*to free a convict, one's conscience, etc.*]; **release**, more or less interchangeable with **free**, stresses a setting loose from confinement, literally or figuratively [*release me from my promise*]; **liberate** emphasizes the state of liberty into which the freed person or thing is brought [*to liberate prisoners of war*]; **emancipate** refers to a freeing from the bondage of slavery or of social institutions or conventions regarded as equivalent to slavery [*emancipated from medieval superstition*]; **discharge**, in this connection, implies a being permitted to leave that which confines or restrains [*discharged at last from the army*] —ANT. **restrain, bind, confine**

-free (frē) *combining form* free of or from, exempt from, without: used in hyphenated compounds [*tax-free income*]

free agent ☆an athlete eligible to play a professional sport who is free to sign a contract with any team —**free agency**

free alongside ship (*or* vessel) delivered to the dock with freight charges paid by the shipper

free-as·so·ci·ate (frē′ə sō′shē āt′, -sē-) ***vi.*** **-at′ed**, **-at′ing** to engage in free association

free association **1** *Psychoanalysis* the technique of having the patient talk spontaneously, expressing without inhibition whatever ideas, memories, etc. come to mind: used to discover repressed material in the unconscious **2** any process of mental association in which spontaneous or nonlogical linking takes place

☆**free·base** (frē′bās′) ***n.*** a concentrated form of cocaine for smoking, prepared by extracting, or freeing, the alkaloid, or base, from a salt of the drug — ***vt., vi.*** **-based′**, **-bas′ing** to prepare or use such a form of (cocaine) Also written **free-base**

☆**free·bie** or **free·bee** (frē′bē) ***n.*** ⟦arbitrary extension of FREE⟧ [Slang] something given or gotten free of charge, as a complimentary theater ticket

free·board (frē′bôrd′) ***n.*** the distance from the main deck or gunwale to the waterline of a ship

free·boot (frē′bo͞ot′) ***vi.*** ⟦back-form. < fol.⟧ to act as a freebooter

free·boot·er (-bo͞ot′ər) ***n.*** ⟦Du *vrijbuiter* < *vrijbuiten*, to plunder < *vrij*, free + *buit*, plunder⟧ a plunderer; specif., a pirate

free·born (frē′bôrn′) ***adj.*** **1** born free, not in slavery or serfdom **2** of or fit for a person so born

free central placentation *Bot.* a type of placenta structure in an ovary, in which the ovules cluster freely around a columnlike central placenta which is attached at the base of the ovary: cf. AXILE PLACENTATION, PARIETAL (sense 3)

free city a semi-autonomous city under international control, as Danzig between WWI and WWII

☆**free coinage** the system by which a government is legally required to coin for a person, either free or at cost, any gold, silver, etc. that the person brings to the mint

freed·man (frēd′mən) *n., pl.* **-men** (-mən) a man legally freed from slavery or bondage

free·dom (frē′dəm) *n.* ⟦ME *fredom* < OE *freodom*: see FREE & -DOM⟧ **1** the state or quality of being free; esp., *a)* exemption or liberation from the control of some other person or some arbitrary power; liberty; independence *b)* exemption from arbitrary restrictions on a specified civil right; civil or political liberty [*freedom* of speech] *c)* exemption or immunity from a specified obligation, discomfort, etc. [*freedom* from want] *d)* exemption or release from imprisonment *e)* a being able to act, move, use, etc. without hindrance or restraint [to have the *freedom* of the house] *f)* a being able of itself to choose or determine action freely [*freedom* of the will] *g)* ease of movement or performance; facility *h)* a being free from the usual rules, patterns, etc. *i)* frankness or easiness of manner; sometimes, an excessive frankness or familiarity **2** a right or privilege

SYN.—freedom, the broadest in scope of these words, implies the absence of hindrance, restraint, confinement, or repression [*freedom* of speech]; **liberty**, often interchangeable with **freedom**, strictly connotes past or potential restriction, repression, etc. [civil *liberties*]; **license** implies freedom that consists in violating the usual rules, laws, or practices, either by consent [poetic *license*] or as an abuse of liberty [slander is *license* of the tongue] —***ANT.*** **repression, constraint**

freedom fighter a person who, typically as part of an organized movement, revolts against or forcibly resists an oppressive political or social system

☆**freedom of the press** the right to publish newspapers, magazines, books, etc. without government interference or prior censorship

freedom of the seas the principle that all merchant ships may freely travel the open seas at any time

freed·wom·an (frēd′woom′ən) *n., pl.* **-wom′en** (-wim′in) a woman legally freed from slavery or bondage

free enterprise the economic doctrine or practice of permitting private industry to operate under freely competitive conditions with a minimum of governmental control

free fall 1 the unchecked fall of anything through space, the atmosphere, a vacuum, etc., specif., the part of a parachutist's jump before the parachute is opened **2** any unchecked, usually rapid, decline, as in value, status, or stability

free-fall (frē′fôl′) *n.* FREE FALL (sense 2) —*vi.* **-fell′** (-fel′), **-fall′en** (-fôl′ən), **-fall′ing** to undergo, experience, or move in a free fall

free-fire zone (frē′fīr′) **1** a military area in which no restrictions are imposed on rifle or artillery fire, bombing, etc. **2** [Informal] a situation, activity, debate, etc. with no set rules or limits

free flight any flight or part of a flight, as of a rocket, occurring without propulsion —**free′-flight′** *adj.*

free-float·ing (frē′flōt′iŋ) *adj.* [Informal] **1** undecided, uncommitted, or without a definite focus **2** likely to be experienced although without an evident cause [*free-floating* fear]

☆**free-for-all** (frē′fər ôl′) *n.* **1** a contest, race, etc. that anyone may enter **2** a disorganized fight in which many take part; brawl —*adj.* open to anyone

free-form (frē′fôrm′) *adj.* **1** having an irregular, usually curvilinear form or outline **2** not conforming to or restricted by conventional rules, structure, etc.; spontaneous, unrestrained, etc.

free·hand (frē′hand′) *adj.* drawn or done by hand without the use of instruments, measurements, etc.

free·hand·ed (-han′did) *adj.* generous; openhanded

free·heart·ed (-härt′id) *adj.* ⟦ME *frehertet*⟧ frank, open, generous, impulsive, etc.

free·hold (frē′hōld′) *n.* ⟦ME *fre holde*, after Anglo-Fr *franc tenement*⟧ **1** an estate in land held for life or with the right to pass it on through inheritance: distinguished from LEASEHOLD **2** the holding of an estate, office, etc. in this way —*adj.* of or held by freehold —**free′hold′er** *n.*

free indirect style a method of narration, used in works of fiction, in which the story is told in the THIRD PERSON (sense 2), but which also incorporates subtle indications of the point of view, feelings, unspoken thoughts, etc. of a character, thereby making possible a more intimate understanding of the character's inner nature: also **free indirect discourse**

free jazz jazz involving FREE (*adj.* 24) improvisation

free kick 1 *Football* a kick, usually a kickoff, after which the ball may be recovered by either team **2** *Soccer* any kick awarded to a team due to a penalty by an opponent

free·lance or **free-lance** (frē′lans′) *n.* ⟦< fol.⟧ FREELANCER —*adj.* of or working as a freelancer —*vi.* **-lanced′**, **-lanc′ing** to work as a freelancer —*vt.* to produce or work on as a freelancer

free lance 1 a medieval soldier who sold his services to any state or military leader **2** an independent, as in political adherence

free·lanc·er or **free-lanc·er** (frē′lan′sər) *n.* ⟦< prec.⟧ a writer, musician, artist, etc. who is not under contract for regular work but whose writings or services are sold to individual buyers

free list ☆a list of goods not subject to tariff duties

free-liv·ing (frē′liv′iŋ) *adj.* **1** indulging freely in eating, drinking, and other sensual pleasures **2** *Biol.* living independently of any other organism: not parasitic or symbiotic

☆**free·load·er** (frē′lōd′ər) *n.* [Informal] a person who habitually imposes on others for free food, lodging, etc.; sponger —**free′load′** *vi.* —**free′load′ing** *adj.*

☆**free love** the practice or advocacy of sexual relations that are unrestricted by marriage or other legal obligations

☆**free lunch** ⟦from the former practice in some saloons of offering free lunches to purchasers of drinks⟧ [Informal] something beneficial that comes at no cost or that carries no obligations ["there's no such thing as a *free lunch*"]

free·man (frē′mən) *n., pl.* **-men** (-mən) ⟦ME *fre man* < OE *freomon*⟧ **1** a person not in slavery or bondage **2** a person who has full civil and political rights; citizen

free market any market where buying and selling can be carried on without restrictions as to price, etc.: often used fig. [the *free market* of ideas]

free·mar·tin (frē′märt′′n) *n.* ⟦< ? FREE + Gael *mart*, cow⟧ an imperfectly developed female calf, usually sterile, born as the twin of a male

Free·ma·son (frē′mā′sən) *n.* ⟦< obs. *freemason*, a skilled itinerant mason, free to move from town to town without restraint by local guilds⟧ a member of an international fraternal order dating from the 18th cent. and retaining architectural symbolism and various secret rituals: also **Free and Accepted Mason**

Free·ma·son·ry (-rē) *n.* **1** the principles, rituals, etc. of Freemasons **2** the Freemasons **3** [**f-**] a natural sympathy and understanding among persons with like experiences

free on board delivered (by the seller) aboard the train, ship, etc. at the point of shipment, without charge to the buyer

free port 1 a port open equally to ships of all countries **2** a port or zone where goods may be unloaded, stored, and reshipped without payment of customs or duties, if they are not imported

fre·er (frē′ər) *adj. compar. of* FREE —*n.* a person or thing that frees

free radical an atom or molecule having at least one unpaired electron: free radicals are typically very reactive and unstable, and can damage healthy tissue cells

free-range (frē′rānj′) *adj.* **1** allowed to range for food, as in a field, rather than being confined: said of livestock **2** of or produced by such livestock [*free-range* eggs, beef, etc.]

☆**free ride** [Informal] the use, enjoyment, etc. of something without the usual expenditure of money or effort

☆**free safety** *Football* the safety who is without an assignment of covering a particular player on the other team and is, typically, responsible for defending against long pass plays

free·sia (frē′zhə, -zhē ə; frē′sē ə, -zē ə) *n.* ⟦ModL, after F. H. T. *Freese*, 19th-c. Ger physician⟧ any of a genus (*Freesia*) of South African bulbous plants of the iris family, with fragrant, usually white or yellow, funnel-shaped flowers

☆**free silver** the free coinage of silver, esp. at a fixed ratio to the gold coined in the same period

☆**free soil** [Historical] territory in which there is no slavery; esp., any territory in the U.S. where slavery was prohibited before the Civil War

☆**Free-Soil** (frē′soil′) *adj.* [*also* **f- s-**] opposed to the extension of slavery; specif., designating or of a former (1848-54) political party (**Free-Soil Party**) that opposed the spread of slavery into the Territories —**Free′-Soil′er** *n.*

free spirit a person who lives according to his or her own wishes and beliefs, unconstrained by society's conventions; nonconformist —**free-spir·ited** *adj.*

free-spo·ken (frē′spō′kən) *adj.* free in expressing opinions; frank; outspoken

fre·est (frē′ist) *adj. superl. of* FREE

free-stand·ing (frē′stand′iŋ) *adj.* **1** resting on its own support, without attachment or added support **2** independent; unaffiliated [a *free-standing* store, company, etc.]

free state ☆[*often* **F- S-**] any state of the U.S. in which slavery was forbidden before the Civil War

free·stone (frē′stōn′) *n.* **1** ⟦ME *fre ston*, after OFr *fraunche piere*⟧ a stone, esp. sandstone or limestone, that can be cut easily without splitting **2** ⟦FREE + STONE⟧ *a)* a peach, plum, etc. in which the pit does not cling to the pulp of the ripened fruit *b)* such a pit —*adj.* having such a pit

free·style (frē′stīl′) *adj. Sports* not limited to a specified style, pattern of movement, etc. —*n.* **1** *a)* a freestyle competition *b) Swimming* a race in which contestants may use any stroke: the crawl is typically used in such races **2** a style of wrestling in which any hold or throw is allowed

free-swim·ming (-swim′iŋ) *adj.* capable of swimming about freely: said as of certain protozoans

free·think·er (-thiŋk′ər) *n.* a person who forms opinions about religion, politics, morals, etc., independently of or counter to tradition, authority, or established belief —***SYN.*** ATHEIST —**free′think′ing** *n., adj.* —**free thought**

☆**free throw** *Basketball* a free, or unhindered, shot at the basket from a designated line (**free throw line**), allowed to a player as a penalty imposed on the opponents for some rule infraction: each successful shot counts for one point

☆**free throw lane** *Basketball* a rectangular area under each basket between the free throw line and the end line, used to line up the players during a free throw

Free·town (frē′toun′) seaport & capital of Sierra Leone, on the Atlantic

free trade trade between countries carried on without quotas on imports or exports, without protective tariffs, etc.

free verse poetry without regular meter, rhyme, or stanzaic forms

free·ware (frē′wer′) *n.* ⟦FREE + -WARE⟧ copyrighted computer software that is available free of charge but whose distribution, resale, etc. typically are restricted

☆**free·way** (frē′wā′) *n.* **1** a multiple-lane divided highway with fully controlled access, as by cloverleafs **2** a highway without toll charges

free weight a weight used in WEIGHT LIFTING, as a barbell or dumbbell, not attached to a machine or other device

free·wheel (frē′hwēl′, -wēl′) *n.* **1** a mechanism attached to the rear hub of a bicycle, that permits the wheel to go on turning when the cyclist stops pedaling **2** in some automobiles, helicopters, etc., a device that permits the speed of the drive shaft or rotor to exceed that of the engine shaft, thus producing greater speeds with no increase in power

free·wheel·ing (-iŋ) *adj.* **1** of or having a freewheel **2** unrestrained in manner, actions, etc.; uninhibited

free·will (frē′wil′) *adj.* freely given or done; voluntary [a *freewill* donation instead of an admission fee]

free will **1** freedom of decision or of choice between alternatives **2** *a)* the freedom of the will to choose a course of action without external coercion but in accordance with the ideals or moral outlook of the individual *b)* the doctrine that people have such freedom (opposed to DETERMINISM)

freeze (frēz) *vi.* **froze, fro′zen, freez′ing** ⟦ME *fresen* < OE *freosan*, akin to OHG *friosan* (Ger *frieren*) < IE base **preus-*, to freeze, burn like cold > L *pruina*, hoarfrost, *pruna*, glowing coals⟧ **1** to be formed into ice; be hardened or solidified by cold **2** to become covered or clogged with ice **3** to be or become very cold **4** to become attached by freezing [wheels *frozen* to the ground] **5** to die or be damaged by exposure to cold ☆**6** to become motionless or fixed **7** to be made momentarily speechless or unable to move or act by a strong, sudden emotion [to *freeze* with terror] **8** to become formal, haughty, or unfriendly **9** *Mech.* to stick or become tight as a result of expansion from overheating, of increased friction due to corrosion, etc. —*vt.* **1** to cause to form into ice; harden or solidify by cold **2** to cover or clog with ice **3** to make very cold; chill **4** to remove sensation from, as with a local anesthetic **5** to preserve (food) by solidifying it through rapid refrigeration; quick-freeze **6** to make fixed or attached by freezing **7** to kill or damage by exposure to cold **8** to make or keep motionless or stiff ☆**9** to frighten or discourage by cool behavior, unfriendliness, etc. **10** to make formal, haughty, or unfriendly ☆**11** *a)* to fix (prices, employment, an employee, etc.) at a given level or place by authoritative regulation *b)* to stop consumer production or use of (a critical material), as in wartime *c)* to make (funds, assets, etc.) unavailable to the owners *d)* to suspend the production of (weapons, esp. nuclear weapons) —*n.* **1** a freezing or being frozen **2** a period of cold, freezing weather; a frost —**freeze out** ☆**1** to die out through freezing, as plants do ☆**2** [Informal] to keep out or force out by a cold manner, by competition, etc. —**freez′a·ble** *adj.*

freeze-dry (frēz′drī′) *vt.* **-dried′, -dry′ing** to subject (food, vaccines, etc.) to quick-freezing followed by drying under high vacuum at a low temperature: a freeze-dried product, as food, will keep for long periods at room temperature

freeze frame a single frame of a film repeated a number of times so as to stop motion and create the effect of a still photograph for dramatic emphasis: also **freeze′-frame′** (-frām′) *n.* —**freeze′-frame′** *vt.* **-framed′, -fram′ing**

freez·er (frē′zər) *n.* ☆**1** a refrigerator, compartment, or room that can maintain freezing or subfreezing temperatures, for freezing and storing perishable foods **2** a hand-cranked or electrically operated device for making ice cream and sherbet

freezer burn discoloration appearing on improperly or inadequately packaged frozen food, caused by evaporation of moisture

freezing point the temperature at which a liquid freezes or becomes solid: the freezing point of water is 32°F or 0°C: cf. MELTING POINT

free zone FREE PORT (sense 2)

Fre·ge (frā′gə), **Gott·lob** (gôt′lôp) 1848-1925; Ger. philosopher & mathematician

F region the highest atmospheric zone within the ionosphere, at an altitude of *c.* 140 to 400 km (*c.* 90 to 250 mi), containing the F layers

Frei·burg (frī′boork) **1** city in SW Germany, in the state of Baden-Württemberg: also **Freiburg im Breis·gau** (im brīs′gou) **2** *Ger. name for* FRIBOURG

freight (frāt) *n.* ⟦ME *freit, fraught* < MDu *vracht*: see FRAUGHT⟧ **1** a method or service for transporting goods, esp. bulky goods, by water, land, or air: freight is usually cheaper but slower than express **2** the cost for such transportation **3** the goods transported; lading; cargo ☆**4** FREIGHT TRAIN **5** any load or burden —*vt.* **1** to load with freight **2** to load; burden **3** to transport as or send by freight

freight·age (-ij) *n.* **1** the charge for transporting goods **2** freight; cargo **3** the transportation of goods

☆**freight car** a railroad car for transporting freight

freight·er (-ər) *n.* **1** a person who sends goods by freight **2** a ship or aircraft for carrying freight

☆**freight house** a depot where freight is received and stored

freight ton TON[1] (sense 5)

☆**freight train** a railroad train made up of freight cars

frem·i·tus (frem′i təs) *n.* ⟦ModL < L, a roaring < *fremere*, to roar < IE base **bherem-*, to murmur > Welsh *brefu*, to bray, Ger *brummen*, to grumble⟧ *Med.* a vibration, esp. one felt in palpation of the chest

Fre·mont (frē′mänt) ⟦after fol.⟧ city in W Calif., on San Francisco Bay: suburb of Oakland

Fré·mont (frē′mänt), **John Charles** 1813-90; U.S. politician, general, & explorer, esp. in the West

fre·na (frē′nə) *n. alt. pl. of* FRENUM

French[1] (french) *n.* ⟦ME *Frensh* < OE *Frencisc* < *Franca*, a FRANK[2]⟧ **1** the Romance language spoken chiefly in France, French Canada, and certain parts of Belgium, Switzerland, and Africa **2** [*often* **f-**] [Brit.] dry vermouth —*adj.* of France or its people, language, or culture —*vt.* [*often* **f-**] ☆**1** to trim the meat from the end of the bone of (a lamb or veal chop) ☆**2** to cut (string beans) into long, thin slices before cooking —**the French** the people of France

French[2] (french), **Daniel Chester** 1850-1931; U.S. sculptor

☆**French and Indian War** the American phase (1754-63) of the SEVEN YEARS' WAR

☆**French braid** a hairstyle in which the hair is gathered in increasingly greater amounts into a single braid that begins at the crown and extends down the back of the head

French bread ⟦because typical of the loaf commonly accompanying meals in French cuisine⟧ a bread made with white flour in a long, slender loaf with a hard, crisp crust

French bulldog any of a breed of small, short-haired dog, developed in France, with a square head, mouselike ears, and short legs

French Canadian **1** a Canadian of French ancestry **2** CANADIAN FRENCH

French chalk a very soft soapstone chalk used for marking lines on cloth or removing grease spots

French Community former political union (formed in 1958) comprising France & several of its former territories, & related African republics: defunct by the 1970s

French cuff a double cuff, as on the sleeve of a shirt, that is turned back on itself and fastened with a cuff link

French curve a template for drawing curved lines

French doors two adjoining doors that have glass panes from top to bottom and are hinged at opposite sides of a doorway so that they open in the middle

☆**French dressing** **1** [Now Chiefly Brit.] VINAIGRETTE **2** a creamy, orange-colored salad dressing made commercially, or a homemade version consisting mainly of mayonnaise and chili or tomato sauce

☆**French endive** CHICORY (sense 1)

French Equatorial Africa former federation of French colonies in central Africa

☆**French fries** *sing.* **French fry** [*often* **f- f-**] strips of potato that have been French fried

☆**French fry** [*often* **f- f-**] to fry in very hot deep fat until crisp —**French′-fried′** *adj.*

French Guiana French overseas department in NE South America, on the Atlantic: 33,025 sq mi (85,534 sq km); cap. Cayenne

French Guinea Guinea when it was under French control

French heel a curved high heel on a woman's shoe

French horn a brass instrument with a mellow tone, consisting of a long, spiral tube ending in a flaring bell, three valves, and a funnel-shaped mouthpiece: *horn* is the term preferred in classical music

French·i·fy (fren′chi fī′) *vt., vi.* **-fied′, -fy′ing** to make or become French or like the French in customs, ideas, manners, etc. —**French′i·fi·ca′tion** *n.*

French India former French territory in India

French Indochina Indochina when it was under French control

French kiss a passionate kiss with the lips parted and the tongues touching —**French′-kiss′** *vt., vi.*

French knot an embroidery stitch forming a raised dot, made by winding the thread around the needle and reinserting it very close to the point where it came up through the fabric

French leave ⟦< 18th-c. custom, prevalent in France, of leaving receptions without taking leave of the host or hostess⟧ an unauthorized, unnoticed, or unceremonious departure; act of leaving secretly or in haste

French letter [Brit. Slang] CONDOM

French·man (french′mən) *n., pl.* **-men** (-mən) **1** a person born or living in France, esp. a man **2** a French ship

French marigold a small, bushy marigold (*Tagetes patula*) with solitary ray flowers whose yellow petals are blotched with red

French Morocco the former (1912-56) French zone of Morocco, making up most of the country: with Spanish Morocco & Tangier, it became the country of Morocco

French pastry rich pastry, usually filled with preserved fruit, whipped cream, etc.

French polish a preparation, usually shellac dissolved in alcohol, applied to furniture for a glossy finish

French Polynesia French overseas territory in the South Pacific, consisting principally of five archipelagoes: 1,609 sq mi (4,167 sq km); cap. Papeete: formerly called **French (Settlements in) Oceania**

☆**French Provincial** [*also* **f- p-**] a style of furniture, architecture, etc. of or based on that of the French provinces, esp. in the mid-18th century, based in turn on Parisian style

French Revolution the revolution of the people against the monarchy in

France: it began in 1789, resulted in the establishment of a republic, and ended in 1799 with the Consulate under Napoleon

French Revolutionary calendar the official calendar (1793-1805) of the first French republic

French roll FRENCH TWIST

French seam a seam in which the raw edge of the cloth is turned under and sewn in place on the inner side of the material

French Somaliland former French overseas territory in E Africa: called *French Territory of the Afars and the Issas* from 1967 until 1977, when it became the country of Djibouti

French Sudan former French overseas territory in W Africa: since 1960, the republic of Mali

☆**French telephone** any telephone having a HANDSET; specif., one consisting of an often ornate, boxlike base having a pronged cradle for holding the handset

☆**French toast** sliced bread dipped in a batter of egg and milk and then fried

French twist a woman's hairstyle in which the hair is pulled back and twisted into a vertical coil running down the back of the head

French Union former political union (1946-58) of France, its overseas departments & territories, & its protectorates & associated states: succeeded by the FRENCH COMMUNITY

French West Africa former French overseas territory in W Africa, including the present countries of Senegal, Mali, Mauritania, Guinea, Ivory Coast, Burkina Faso, Benin, & Niger

French West Indies islands in the West Indies, possessions of France, including two overseas departments (Martinique & Guadeloupe) & several former dependencies of Guadeloupe

French windows a pair of casement windows designed like French doors and usually extending to the floor

French·wom·an (french′woom′ən) ***n.**, pl.* **-wom′en** (-wim′in) a woman born or living in France

French·y (fren′chē) ***adj.*** **French′i·er, French′i·est** [Informal] of, characteristic of, or like the French —***n.**, pl.* **French′ies** [Slang] a Frenchman

Fre·neau (fri nō′), **Philip (Morin)** 1752-1832; U.S. poet & journalist

☆**fren·e·my** (fren′ə mē) ***n.**, pl.* **-mies** ⟦blend of FRIEND & ENEMY⟧ [Informal] a person who is seemingly friendly or collegial with someone but who is actually hostile or competitive

fre·net·ic (frə net′ik) ***adj.*** ⟦ME *frenetik* < OFr *frenetique* < L *phreneticus* < Gr *phrenētikos,* mad, suffering with inflammation of the brain < *phrenitis,* delirium, madness < *phrēn,* mind (see PHRENO-) + *-itis,* -ITIS⟧ frantic; frenzied: also **fre·net′i·cal** —**fre·net′i·cal·ly** ***adv.***

fren·u·lum (fren′yoo ləm, -yə-) ***n.**, pl.* **-lums** or **-la** (-lə) ⟦ModL, dim. of *frenum:* see fol.⟧ **1** a small frenum **2** *Zool.* a stiff bristle or group of bristles extending from the hind wing of some moths and interlocking with a structure on the front wing, linking the wings together in flight

fre·num (frē′nəm) ***n.**, pl.* **-nums** or **-na** (-nə) ⟦L, lit., a bridle < IE base **dher-,* to hold > FIRM[1]⟧ a fold of skin or mucous membrane that checks or controls the movement of an organ or part, as the fold under the tongue

fren·zy (fren′zē) ***n.**, pl.* **-zies** ⟦ME *frenesie* < OFr < ML *phrenesia* < L *phrenesis* < LGr *phrenēsis* < Gr *phrenitis,* madness: see FRENETIC⟧ wild or frantic outburst of feeling or action —***vt.*** **-zied, -zy·ing** to make frantic; drive mad —**SYN.** MANIA —**fren′zied** ***adj.*** —**fren′zied·ly** ***adv.***

☆**Fre·on** (frē′än′) ⟦F(LUORINE) + RE(FRIGERANT) + *-on,* as in NEON⟧ *trademark for* any of a series of gaseous or low-boiling, inert, nonflammable compounds of fluorine, carbon, and often chlorine: used as refrigerants, solvents, and aerosol propellants

freq *abbrev.* **1** frequency **2** frequent **3** frequentative

fre·quen·cy (frē′kwən sē) ***n.**, pl.* **-cies** ⟦ME < Fr < L *frequentia* < *frequens:* see FREQUENT⟧ **1** [Obs.] *a)* the condition of being crowded *b)* a crowd **2** the fact of occurring often or repeatedly **3** the number of times any action or occurrence is repeated in a given period **4** *Math., Statistics a)* the number of times an event, value, or characteristic occurs in a given period *b)* the ratio of the number of times a characteristic occurs to the number of trials in which it can potentially occur (in full **relative frequency**) **5** *Physics* the number of periodic oscillations, vibrations, or waves per unit of time: usually expressed in hertz: abbrev. *f* Also **fre′quence** (-kwəns)

frequency distribution a numerical tabulation in which the different observed values of a variable, or the different outcomes of an event, are grouped into classes, and the frequencies for each of these classes are given

frequency modulation **1** the variation of the frequency of a carrier wave in accordance with the signal being broadcast **2** a broadcasting system that uses this Abbrev. *FM* Cf. AMPLITUDE MODULATION

frequency response a measurement of the capability of a device, as an amplifier or speaker, to reproduce sound, expressed in hertz

fre·quent (frē′kwənt; *for v., also* frē kwent′) ***adj.*** ⟦ME < OFr < L *frequens* (gen. *frequentis*), ? akin to *farcire,* to stuff: see FARCE⟧ **1** [Obs.] crowded; filled **2** occurring often; happening repeatedly at brief intervals **3** constant; habitual —***vt.*** to go to constantly; be at often [to *frequent* the theater] —**fre′quen·ta′tion** ***n.*** —**fre·quent·er** (frē′kwən tər, frē kwen′tər) ***n.***

fre·quen·ta·tive (frē kwen′tə tiv) ***adj.*** ⟦L *frequentativus* < *frequentare,* to frequent⟧ *Gram.* expressing frequent and repeated action —***n.*** *Gram.* a frequentative verb ["sparkle" is a *frequentative* of "spark"]

fre·quent-fli·er or **fre·quent-fly·er** (frē′kwənt flī′ər) ***adj.*** designating or related to a program in which an airline awards points to customers for miles flown or for other approved expenditures and then redeems them for free air travel when sufficient points have been accumulated

fre·quent·ly (frē′kwənt lē) ***adv.*** at frequent or brief intervals; often

frère (frer) ***n.*** ⟦Fr⟧ **1** a brother **2** a friar

fres·co (fres′kō) ***n.**, pl.* **-coes** or **-cos** ⟦It, fresh < OHG *frisc:* see fol.⟧ **1** the art or technique of painting with watercolors on wet plaster **2** a painting or design so made —***vt.*** to paint in fresco

fresh[1] (fresh) ***adj.*** ⟦ME < OE *fersc,* but altered under infl. of OFr *fres, fresche* < Gmc **friska* (> Ger *frisch* & OE *fersc*)⟧ **1** *a)* recently produced, obtained, or arrived *b)* newly made [a *fresh* pot of coffee] **2** having original strength, vigor, quality, taste, etc.; esp., *a)* not preserved by being salted, pickled, canned, or frozen [*fresh* meat, *fresh* vegetables] *b)* not spoiled, rotten, or stale *c)* not tired; vigorous; lively [to feel *fresh* after a nap] *d)* not worn, soiled, faded, etc.; vivid; bright; clean *e)* youthful or healthy in appearance [a *fresh* complexion] **3** not known before; new; recent [*fresh* information] **4** additional; further [a *fresh* start] **5** *a)* inexperienced; unaccustomed *b)* having just arrived **6** original, spontaneous, and stimulating [*fresh* ideas] **7** cool and refreshing; invigorating [a *fresh* spring day] **8** brisk; strong: said of the wind **9** not salt: said of water **10** designating or of a cow that has just begun to give milk, as after having borne a calf —***n.*** **1** the fresh part **2** a freshet **3** a pool or stream of fresh water —***adv.*** in a fresh manner — ***vi., vt.*** to make or become fresh —**SYN.** NEW —**fresh out (of)** [Informal] having just sold or used up the last one or part (of) —**fresh′ness** ***n.***

☆**fresh**[2] (fresh) ***adj.*** ⟦< Ger *frech,* bold, impudent (akin to OE *fræc* < IE base **preg-,* bold, greedy): confused with prec.⟧ [Informal] bold; impertinent; impudent —**fresh′ly** ***adv.*** —**fresh′ness** ***n.***

fresh breeze a wind whose speed is 19 to 24 miles per hour: see the Beaufort scale in the Reference Supplement

fresh·en (fresh′ən) ***vt.*** to make fresh, or vigorous, clean, etc. —***vi.*** **1** to become fresh **2** to increase in strength: said of the wind ☆**3** to begin to give milk, as a cow after having a calf —**freshen up** to bathe oneself, change into fresh clothes, etc.

fresh·en·er (fresh′ən ər, fresh′nər) ***n.*** anything that freshens or refreshes

fresh·et (fresh′it) ***n.*** ⟦see FRESH[1] & -ET⟧ **1** a stream or rush of fresh water flowing into the sea ☆**2** a sudden overflowing of a stream because of melting snow or heavy rain

fresh gale a wind whose speed is 39 to 46 miles per hour: see the Beaufort scale in the Reference Supplement

fresh·ly (fresh′lē) ***adv.*** ⟦ME *freschli*⟧ **1** in a fresh manner **2** just now; recently: followed by a past participle [bread *freshly* baked]

fresh·man (fresh′mən) ***n.**, pl.* **-men** (-mən) ⟦FRESH[1] + MAN⟧ **1** a beginner; novice **2** a student in the first year of college or the ninth grade in high school ☆**3** a person in the first year, term, etc. of some enterprise [a *freshman* in Congress] —***adj.*** of, for, or having to do with a freshman or freshmen

fresh·wa·ter (fresh′wôt′ər) ***adj.*** **1** of or living in water that is not salty **2** accustomed to sailing only on inland waters, not on the sea

freshwater eel any of a family (Anguillidae) of eels that live in streams, lakes, etc. and migrate to the sea to spawn

Fres·nel (frā nel′), **Au·gus·tin Jean** (ō güs tan′ zhän) 1788-1827; Fr. physicist

Fresnel lens ⟦after prec.⟧ a thin optical lens of many concentric rings, having the properties of a much thicker and heavier lens: used in cameras, lighthouse beacons, etc.

Fresnel mirrors ⟦after A. J. FRESNEL⟧ *Optics* two plane mirrors so linked that a beam of light falling on them is reflected in slightly different directions, thus producing interference fringes in the area where this reflected light overlaps

Fres·no (frez′nō) ⟦< Sp *fresno,* ash tree < L *fraxinus:* see FRAXINELLA⟧ city in central Calif.

fret[1] (fret) ***vt.*** **fret′ted, fret′ting** ⟦ME *freten* < OE *fretan,* to devour, akin to Ger *fressen,* Goth *fra-itan* < Gmc prefix **fra-* (OE *for-:* see FOR-) + **itan,* to eat (OE *etan:* see EAT)⟧ **1** to eat away; gnaw **2** to wear away by gnawing, rubbing, corroding, etc. **3** to make or form by wearing away **4** to make rough; disturb [wind *fretting* the water] **5** to irritate; vex; annoy; worry —***vi.*** **1** to gnaw (*into, on,* or *upon*) **2** to become eaten, corroded, worn, frayed, etc. **3** to become rough or disturbed **4** to be irritated, annoyed, or querulous; worry —***n.*** **1** a wearing away **2** a worn place **3** irritation; worry —**fret′ter** ***n.***

fret[2] (fret) ***n.*** ⟦ME *frette,* prob. merging of OFr *frete* (Fr *frette*), interlaced work, with OE *frætwa,* ornament (> ? OFr *frete*)⟧ **1** an ornamental net or network, esp. one formerly worn by women as a headdress **2** an ornamental pattern of small, straight bars intersecting or joining one another, usually at right angles, to form a regular design, as for a border or in an architectural relief —***vt.*** **fret′ted, fret′ting** to ornament with a fret

fret[3] (fret) ***n.*** ⟦OFr *frette,* a band, ferrule⟧ any of several narrow, lateral ridges fixed across the fingerboard of a banjo, guitar, mandolin, etc. to regulate the fingering —***vt.*** **fret′ted, fret′ting** **1** to furnish with frets **2** to press the strings (of a banjo, etc.) against the frets —**fret′less** ***adj.***

fret·ful (fret′fəl) ***adj.*** having or showing a tendency to fret; irritable and discontented; peevish —**fret′ful·ly** ***adv.*** —**fret′ful·ness** ***n.***

fret saw a handsaw with a narrow, fine-toothed blade in a U-shaped frame, for cutting curved patterns in thin boards or metal plates

fret·work (-wurk′) ***n.*** work ornamented with frets; decorative carving or openwork, as of interlacing lines

Freud (froid) **1 Lucian (Michael)** 1922-2011; Brit. painter: grandson of Sigmund **2 Sigmund** 1856-1939; Austrian physician & neurologist: founder of psychoanalysis

Freud·i·an (froi′dē ən) ***adj.*** of or according to Freud or his theories and practice —***n.*** a person who believes in Freud's theories or uses Freud's methods in psychoanalysis, literary criticism, etc. —**Freud′i·an·ism′** ***n.***

Freudian slip a mistake made in speaking or writing by which, it is thought, a person inadvertently reveals unconscious motives, desires, etc.

Frey (frā) ***n.*** *Norse Myth.* the god of crops, fruitfulness, love, peace, and prosperity: also **Freyr** (frār)

Frey·a (frā′ə, -ä′) ***n.*** *Norse Myth.* the goddess of love and beauty, sister of Frey: also **Frey′ja′** (-yä′)

FRG *abbrev.* Federal Republic of Germany (West Germany)

Fri *abbrev.* Friday

fri·a·ble (frī′ə bəl) ***adj.*** ⟦Fr < L *friabilis* < *friare,* to rub, crumble < IE base **bhrēi-,* to cut, scrape > Russ *brit',* to shave, L *fricare,* to rub⟧ easily crumbled or crushed into powder —**SYN.** FRAGILE —**fri′a·bil′i·ty** ***n.,*** **fri′a·ble·ness**

fri·ar (frī′ər) ***n.*** ⟦ME *frer, frier* < OFr *frere* < L *frater,* BROTHER⟧ a member of any of various mendicant orders, as a Franciscan or Dominican —**fri′ar·ly** ***adj.***

fri·ar·bird (-burd′) ***n.*** any of a genus (*Philemon*) of honeyeaters of the SW Pacific and Australia that have a naked, featherless head

Friar Minor *pl.* **Friars Minor** a member of the branch of the Franciscan order that follows the original rule: see CAPUCHIN, CONVENTUAL

fri·ar·y (frī′ər ē) ***n., pl.*** **-ar·ies 1** a house of friars **2** a brotherhood of friars

frib·ble (frib′əl) ***adj.*** ⟦< ?⟧ of little importance; trifling —***n.*** **1** a person who wastes time **2** any trifling act or thought —***vi.*** **frib′bled, frib′bling** to waste time; trifle —**fribble away** to use wastefully

Fri·bourg (frē boor′) canton of WC Switzerland: 645 sq mi (1,671 sq km)

fric·an·deau (frik′ən dō′, frik′ən dō′) ***n., pl.*** **-deaux′** (-dōz′) ⟦Fr, irreg. < ? fol.⟧ meat, esp. veal, larded and roasted or braised

fric·as·see (frik′ə sē′, frik′ə sē′) ***n.*** ⟦Fr *fricassée,* fem. pp. of *fricasser,* to cut up and fry < *frire,* FRY[1] + *casser,* to break: see CASHIER[2]⟧ a dish consisting of meat cut into pieces, stewed or fried, and served in a sauce of its own gravy —***vt.*** **-seed′, -see′ing** to prepare (meat) by this method

fric·a·tive (frik′ə tiv) ***adj.*** ⟦< L *fricatus,* pp. of *fricare* (see FRIABLE) + -IVE⟧ *Phonet.* articulated by means of breath forced through a narrow slit formed at some point in the mouth, producing friction, as in (f, v, th, z, h) —***n.*** a fricative consonant

Frick (frik), **Henry Clay** 1849-1919; U.S. industrialist & philanthropist

fric·tion (frik′shən) ***n.*** ⟦Fr < L *frictio* < pp. of *fricare,* to rub: see FRIABLE⟧ **1** a rubbing, esp. of one object against another **2** ill will or conflict because of differences of opinion, temperament, etc. **3** *Mech.* the resistance to motion of two moving objects or surfaces that touch —**fric′tion·less** ***adj.***

fric·tion·al (frik′shə nəl) ***adj.*** of or caused by friction

fric·tion·al·ly (-nəl ē) ***adv.*** by or with friction

friction clutch a mechanical clutch in which the rotating coaxial shafts are engaged through frictional contact of their surfaces

☆**friction match** a match that lights by friction: includes all modern matches

friction tape a thick, cloth-based, moisture-resistant adhesive tape, used as on a handle to improve one's grip and, esp. formerly, for insulating or securing electrical wires

Fri·day (frī′dā; *occas.,* -dē) ***n.*** ⟦ME *fridai* < OE *frigedæg,* lit., day of the goddess FRIGG, akin to Ger *Freitag,* Du *Vrijdag,* Swed *Fredag*: transl. of LL *Veneris dies* (Fr *vendredi*), Venus' day⟧ **1** the sixth day of the week: abbrev. *Fri* or *F* **2** [after the devoted servant of ROBINSON CRUSOE] a faithful follower or efficient helper: usually **man (or girl) Friday**

Fri·days (-dāz; *occas.,* -dēz) ***adv.*** during every Friday or most Fridays

fridge (frij) ***n.*** [Informal] a refrigerator

fried (frīd) ***vt., vi.*** *pt. & pp. of* FRY[1] —***adj.*** ⟦ME *ifrid,* pp. of *frien,* FRY[1]⟧ ☆[Slang] quite intoxicated by drugs or alcohol

Frie·da (frē′də) ***n.*** ⟦Ger < OHG *fridu,* peace: see FREDERICK[1]⟧ a feminine name: var. *Freda*

☆**fried·cake** (frīd′kāk′) ***n.*** a small cake fried in deep fat; doughnut

Fried·man (frēd′mən), **Milton** 1912-2006; U.S. economist

Frie·drich (frē′driH), **Cas·par Da·vid** (käs′pär′ dä′vēt′) 1774-1840; Ger. painter

friend (frend) ***n.*** ⟦ME *frend* < OE *freond,* friend, lover, akin to Ger *freund,* prp. of Gmc **frijon,* to love (> OE *freon*): for IE base see FREE⟧ **1** a person whom one knows well and is fond of; intimate associate; close acquaintance **2** a person on the same side in a struggle; one who is not an enemy or foe; ally **3** a supporter or sympathizer [a *friend* of labor unions] **4** something thought of as like a friend in being helpful, reliable, etc. **5** [**F-**] any member of the Society of Friends; Quaker —***vt.*** to act as a friend to; befriend: now archaic except in social networking —**make (or be) friends with** to become (or be) a friend of —**man's best friend** DOG (*n.* 1*a*): an affectionate or proverbial use —**friend′less** ***adj.*** —**friend′less·ness** ***n.***

friend at court a person in an influential position who is friendly toward and able to help one

friend·ly (frend′lē) ***adj.*** **-li·er, -li·est** ⟦ME *frendli* < OE *freondlice*⟧ **1** like, characteristic of, or suitable for a friend, friends, or friendship; kindly **2** not hostile; amicable **3** supporting; helping; favorable [a *friendly* wind] **4** showing friendly feelings; ready to be a friend **5** [Informal] easy to use, operate, or understand [a *friendly* set of computer icons] —***adv.*** **-li·er, -li·est** in a friendly manner; as a friend —***n., pl.*** **-lies** a person or thing that is friendly —**friend′li·ly** ***adv.*** —**friend′li·ness** ***n.***

-friend·ly (frend′lē) *combining form* **1** easily used or understood by [learner-*friendly*] **2** *a)* helpful to or safe for [child-*friendly*] *b)* not harmful to [environment-*friendly*] Sometimes with an adverb or a combining form [environmentally-*friendly,* eco-*friendly*]

friendly fire a discharge of weapons which, although aimed at an enemy, results in casualties to the side firing the weapons

Friendly Islands TONGA

friend of the court AMICUS CURIAE

Friends (frendz) ***adj.*** of or having to do with Friends, or Quakers

friend·ship (frend′ship′) ***n.*** ⟦ME *frendship* < OE *freondscipe*⟧ **1** the state of being friends **2** attachment between friends **3** friendly feeling or attitude; friendliness

fri·er (frī′ər) ***n.*** *alt. sp. of* FRYER

☆**fries** (frīz) ***pl.n.*** [Informal] *short for* FRENCH FRIES

Frie·sian (frē′zhən) ***n., adj.*** *var. of* FRISIAN

Fries·land (frēz′lənd, -land′; *Du* frēs′länt′) province of the N Netherlands, on the North Sea: 2,217 sq mi (5,742 sq km); cap. Leeuwarden

frieze[1] (frēz) ***n.*** ⟦Fr *frise* < ML *frisium* < ? Frank **frisi,* a curl, akin to OE *fris,* crisped, curled; ? confused in folk-etym. by assoc. with ML *frigium* < L *Phrygium,* Phrygian: Phrygia was noted for embroidery in gold⟧ **1** a decoration or series of decorations forming an ornamental band around a room, mantel, etc. **2** *Archit.* a horizontal band, often decorated with sculpture, between the architrave and cornice of a building

frieze[2] (frēz) ***n.*** ⟦ME *frise* < OFr < MDu, prob. akin to prec.⟧ a heavy wool cloth with a shaggy, uncut nap on one side

frig[1] (frig) ***vt.*** **frigged, frig′ging** [Slang] **1** to engage in sexual intercourse with: somewhat vulgar **2** to cheat, trick, etc. —***vi.*** to spend time idly, foolishly, etc.: usually with *around*

frig[2] (frij) ***n.*** [Informal, Chiefly Brit.] *alt. sp. of* FRIDGE

frig·ate (frig′it) ***n.*** ⟦Fr *frégate* < It *fregata*⟧ **1** a fast, medium-sized sailing warship of the 18th and early 19th cent., which carried from 24 to 60 guns **2** a Brit. warship between a corvette and a destroyer **3** *a)* until 1975, a U.S. warship larger than a destroyer and smaller than a light cruiser *b)* since 1975, a U.S. warship smaller than a destroyer, used chiefly for escort duty

frigate bird any of a family (Fregatidae) of large, tropical pelecaniform birds with extremely long wings and tail and a hooked beak: it commonly robs other birds of their prey

Frigg (frig) ***n.*** ⟦ON, akin to OHG *Fria* & Sans *priyā,* beloved: for IE base see FREE⟧ the wife of Odin and goddess of the skies, presiding over marriage and the home: also **Frig·ga** (frig′ə)

frig·ging (frig′iŋ) ***adj., adv.*** ⟦prp. of vulgar *frig,* to copulate, orig. to rub, prob. ult. < L *fricare,* to rub: see FRIABLE⟧ [Slang] *euphemism for* FUCKING

fright (frīt) ***n.*** ⟦ME < OE *fyrhto, fryhto,* fear, akin to Ger *furcht,* fear, Goth *faúrhts* < IE base **perg-,* fear, to be afraid⟧ **1** sudden fear or terror; alarm **2** an ugly, ridiculous, startling, or unusual person or thing —***vt.*** ⟦ME *frighten* < OE *fyrhtan*⟧ [Archaic] to frighten; terrify —**SYN.** FEAR

fright·en (frīt′'n) ***vt.*** **1** to cause to feel fright; make suddenly afraid; scare; terrify **2** to force (*away, out,* or *off*) or bring (*into* a specified condition) by making afraid [to *frighten* someone into confessing] —***vi.*** to become suddenly afraid —**fright′en·ing·ly** ***adv.***

SYN.—frighten is the broadest of these terms and implies, usually, a sudden, temporary feeling of fear [*frightened* by a mouse] but sometimes, a state of continued dread [she's *frightened* when she's alone]; **scare,** often equivalent to **frighten,** in stricter use implies a fear that causes one to flee or to stop doing something [I *scared* him from the room]; **alarm** suggests a sudden fear or apprehension at the realization of an approaching danger [*alarmed* by his warning]; to **terrify** is to cause to feel an overwhelming, often paralyzing fear [*terrified* at the thought of war]; **terrorize** implies deliberate intention to terrify by threat or intimidation [gangsters *terrorized* the city]

fright·ened (-'nd) ***adj.*** filled with fright; terrified —**SYN.** AFRAID

fright·ful (frīt′fəl) ***adj.*** **1** causing fright; terrifying; alarming **2** shocking; terrible **3** [Informal] *a)* unpleasant; annoying *b)* great [in a *frightful* hurry] —**fright′ful·ly** ***adv.*** —**fright′ful·ness** ***n.***

fright wig ⟦so called because it gives the wearer an appearance of sudden fear: see HAIR-RAISING⟧ [Slang] a wig made of synthetic, often brightly colored fibers that stick out from the head

frig·id (frij′id) ***adj.*** ⟦ME < L *frigidus* < *frigere,* to be cold < *frigus,* coldness, frost < IE base **srīg-,* coldness > Gr *rhigos,* frost⟧ **1** extremely cold; without heat or warmth **2** without warmth of feeling or manner; stiff and formal **3** habitually failing to become sexually aroused, or abnormally repelled by sexual activity: said of a woman —**fri·gid·i·ty** (fri jid′ə tē) ***n.,*** **frig′id·ness** —**frig′id·ly** ***adv.***

☆**Frig·id·aire** (frij′i der′) ⟦arbitrary coinage < prec. + AIR⟧ *trademark for* an electric refrigerator —***n.*** [**f-**] [Old-fashioned] an electric refrigerator

Frigid Zone either of two zones of the earth (**North Frigid Zone** & **South Frigid Zone**) between the polar circles and the poles

frig·o·rif·ic (frig′ə rif′ik) ***adj.*** ⟦Fr *frigorifique* < L *frigorificus* < *frigus* (see FRIGID) + *facere,* to make (see DO[1])⟧ making cold; freezing or cooling

☆**fri·jol** (frē′hōl′; *also* frē hōl′) ***n., pl.*** **fri·jo·les** (frē hō′lēz′, -lāz′, -lās′; *also* frē′hō′lēz′, -hōlz′) ⟦Sp *frijol, fréjol* < L *faseolus,* earlier *phaselus* < Gr *phasēlos,* kind of bean⟧ **1** any of various beans used for food, esp. any of certain kidney beans so used in Mexico and the SW U.S.: also **fri·jo·le** (frē hō′lē; frē′hōl′, frē hōl′) **2** [*pl.*] REFRIED BEANS

frill (fril) ***n.*** ⟦< ?⟧ **1** a fold of skin around the neck of a reptile, a fringe of feathers around the neck of a bird, etc. **2** any unnecessary ornament; superfluous thing added for show **3** an edging or trimming of lace, etc., gathered or pleated and attached along one edge but free at the other; ruffle **4** *Photog.* a wrinkling of the edge of a film, plate, etc. —*vt.* **1** to make a ruffle of; crimp **2** to decorate with a frill —*vi. Photog.* to become wrinkled, as a film, due to a separation of the emulsion from the base —**frill′y** *adj.* **frill′i·er, frill′i·est**

Friml (frim′əl), **(Charles) Rudolf** 1879-1972; U.S. composer, born in Bohemia

fringe (frinj) *n.* ⟦ME *frenge* < OFr *frenge, fringe* < VL **frimbia*, metathesis of LL *fimbria*, a fringe, border < L *fimbriae*, shreds, fibers⟧ **1** a border or trimming of cords or threads, hanging loose or tied in bunches **2** *a)* anything like this [a *fringe* of hair] *b)* an outer edge; border; margin [at the *fringes* of the slums] **3** a part considered to be peripheral, extreme, or minor in relation to the main part [the radical *fringe* of a political party] ☆**4** FRINGE BENEFIT **5** *Optics* any of the light or dark bands resulting from the interference or diffraction of light —*vt.* **fringed, fring′ing 1** to decorate with or as with fringe **2** to be a fringe for; line [trees *fringed* the lawn] —*adj.* **1** at the outer edge or border [a *fringe* area of television reception] ☆**2** additional [*fringe* costs] ☆**3** less important; minor [*fringe* industries]

☆**fringe benefit** any form of employee compensation provided in addition to wages or base salary, as a pension, insurance coverage, vacation time, etc.

☆**fringed gentian** any of several gentians having blue flowers with fringed petals, native to the N U.S. and Canada

☆**fringed polygala** a trailing perennial milkwort (*Polygala paucifolia*) with rosy-lavender flowers having a fringed lower lip, growing in the woods of E North America

☆**fringe tree** any of a genus (*Chionanthus*) of the olive family; esp., a small tree (*C. virginicus*) native to the SE U.S., having large clusters of drooping white flowers

fringing reef a coral reef growing outward from the shore with little or no water between it and the shore: cf. BARRIER REEF

fring·y (frin′jē) *adj.* **fring′i·er, fring′i·est 1** like a fringe **2** having a fringe or fringes

frip·per·y (frip′ər ē) *n., pl.* **-per·ies** ⟦orig., castoff clothes < Fr *friperie* < OFr *freperie* < *frepe*, a rag < ? ML *faluppa*, a shaving, straw⟧ **1** cheap, gaudy clothes; tawdry finery **2** showy display in dress, manners, speech, etc.; affectation of elegance

Fris *abbrev.* Frisian

☆**Fris·bee** (friz′bē) ⟦altered < *Frisbie*, name of a bakery in Bridgeport, Conn.: tins from "Mother Frisbie's" pies were orig. used for the game by students at Yale University⟧ *trademark for* a plastic, saucer-shaped disk sailed back and forth between players in a simple game —*n.* [*also* **f-**] **1** such a disk **2** the game played with it

Fris·co (fris′kō) **1** city in NE Tex.: suburb of Dallas **2** *informal name for* SAN FRANCISCO: not a local usage

fri·sé (frē zā′, fri-) *n.* ⟦Fr < *friser*, to curl, prob. < Frank **frisi*: see FRIEZE[1]⟧ a type of upholstery fabric having a thick pile consisting of uncut loops, or, sometimes, of some loops cut to form a design

fri·sée (frē zā′, fri-) *n.* ⟦Fr, shortened < *chicorée frisée*, curly chicory⟧ a light-green, feathery form of endive with a somewhat bitter taste, often used in mesclun

fri·seur (frē zër′) *n.* ⟦Fr < *friser*: see FRISÉ⟧ a hairdresser

Fri·sian (frizh′ən, frē′zhən) *n.* ⟦< L *Frisii*, the Frisians < OFris *Frisa* < Gmc **frisi*, curl: so named from their hair style⟧ **1** a person born or living in Friesland or the Frisian Islands **2** a member of an ancient Germanic people of N Holland **3** the West Germanic language spoken by the Frisians, closely related to Dutch and Old English —*adj.* designating or of Friesland or the Frisian Islands, or their people, language, or culture

Frisian Islands island chain in the North Sea, extending along the coast of NW Europe: it is divided into three groups, one belonging to the Netherlands (**West Frisian Islands**), one belonging to Germany (**East Frisian Islands**), & one divided between Germany & Denmark (**North Frisian Islands**)

frisk (frisk) *adj.* ⟦ME < OFr *frisque* < OHG *frisc*, new, cheerful, lively: see FRESH[1]⟧ [Obs.] lively; frisky —*n.* **1** a lively, playful movement; frolic; gambol **2** [Informal] the act or an instance of frisking a person —*vt.* **1** to move in a playful, lively manner [the colt *frisked* its tail] **2** to search (a person) as for concealed weapons or stolen articles by passing the hands quickly over the person's clothing —*vi.* to dance or move about in a playful, lively manner; frolic

frisk·y (fris′kē) *adj.* **frisk′i·er, frisk′i·est 1** inclined to frisk about **2** lively; playful; frolicsome —**frisk′i·ly** *adv.* —**frisk′i·ness** *n.*

fris·son (frē sōn′; *Fr* frē sōn′) *n.* ⟦Fr, lit., a shiver⟧ a brief sensation or feeling, as of excitement, fear, or pleasure, often accompanied by a shudder or shiver

frit (frit) *n.* ⟦Fr *fritte* < It *fritta*, fried, pp. of *friggere* < L *frigere*, FRY[1]⟧ **1** the partly fused mixture of sand and fluxes, of which glass is made **2** a partly fused vitreous substance, ground and used as a basis for glazes and enamels — *vt., vi.* **frit′ted, frit′ting** to prepare (materials for glass) by heating; make into frit

frites (frēts; *Fr* frĕt) *pl.n.* ⟦Fr⟧ [*often in italics*] FRENCH FRIES

frit fly ⟦< ? FRIT, in ref. to the glazed, shining appearance of the fly's body⟧ any of a family (Chloropidae) of tiny dipterous flies, esp. a black species (*Oscinella frit*), whose larvae destroy grain

frith (frith) *n.* ⟦var. of FIRTH⟧ a narrow inlet or arm of the sea

frit·il·lar·y (frit′'l er′ē; *Brit* fri til′ə ri) *n., pl.* **-lar′ies** ⟦< ModL *Fritillaria* < L *fritillus*, dice box: from markings on the petals or wings⟧ **1** any of a genus (*Fritillaria*) of perennial, bulbous plants of the lily family, with nodding, bell-shaped flowers: also **frit·il·lar·i·a** (frit′'l er′ē ə) **2** any of certain medium-sized nymphalid butterflies, typically having brownish or orange wings with silver spots on the undersides

frit·ta·ta (frē tä′tə) *n.* ⟦It, omelet < *fritto*, fried < pp. of *friggere*, to fry < L *frigere*: see FRY[1]⟧ an omelet with pieces of vegetables, meat, etc. in the egg mixture, cooked slowly until fluffy and served without folding

frit·ter[1] (frit′ər) *n.* ⟦< ? OFr *fraiture* < L *fractura*: see FRACTURE⟧ [Rare] a small piece; shred —*vt.* ⟦< the *n.*⟧ **1** [Rare] to break or tear into small pieces **2** to waste (money, time, etc.) bit by bit on petty things: usually with *away* —**frit′ter·er** *n.*

frit·ter[2] (frit′ər) *n.* ⟦ME *friture* < OFr < VL **frictura* < pp. of L *frigere*, FRY[1]⟧ a small cake of fried batter, usually containing corn, fruit, fish or meat, etc.

frit·to mi·sto (frēt′tô mē′stô; *E* frē′tō mē′stō) ⟦It < *fritto*, fried (see FRITTATA) + *misto*, mixed⟧ [*sometimes not in italics*] an Italian dish consisting of meat or seafood and sliced vegetables dipped in a batter and deep-fried

☆**fritz** (frits) *n.* ⟦< Ger, nickname for *Friedrich*: orig. meant a German; current sense in allusion to cheap German goods exported to U.S. before WWI⟧ ☆[Slang] a broken or nonfunctioning state: only in the phrase **on the fritz**, not in working order

Fri·u·li-Ve·ne·zia Giu·lia (frē ōō′lē ve ne′tsyä jōō′lyä) region of NE Italy, on the Adriatic: 3,029 sq mi (7,845 sq km); cap. Trieste

friv·ol (friv′əl) *vi.* **-oled** or **-olled, -ol·ing** or **-ol·ling** ⟦back-form. < FRIVOLOUS⟧ [Informal] to waste time on frivolous things

fri·vol·i·ty (fri väl′ə tē) *n.* ⟦Fr *frivolité*⟧ **1** the quality or condition of being frivolous **2** *pl.* **-ties** a frivolous act or thing

friv·o·lous (friv′ə ləs) *adj.* ⟦ME < *frivol* (< OFr *frivole* < L *frivolus*, fragile, silly, akin to *friare*: see FRIABLE) + -OUS⟧ **1** of little value or importance; trifling; trivial **2** not properly serious or sensible; silly and light-minded; giddy [a *frivolous* remark, a *frivolous* youth] **3** having no basis in law because of the lack of sound legal arguments, facts, etc. or not brought to court in good faith —**friv′o·lous·ly** *adv.* —**friv′o·lous·ness** *n.*

frizz[1] or **friz** (friz) *vt., vi.* **frizzed, friz′zing** ⟦Fr *friser*, to curl: see FRIEZE[1]⟧ to form into small, tight curls —*n.* hair, etc. that is frizzed

frizz[2] (friz) *vt., vi.* ⟦echoic alteration of FRY[1]⟧ to fry with a sputtering, hissing noise; sizzle

friz·zle[1] (friz′əl) *vi., vt.* **-zled, -zling** ⟦echoic alteration of FRY[1], after SIZZLE⟧ **1** to make or cause to make a sputtering, hissing noise, as in frying; sizzle **2** to become or make crisp by broiling or frying thoroughly

friz·zle[2] (friz′əl) *vt., vi.* **-zled, -zling** ⟦prob. akin to Fris *frislen*, to plait (the hair)⟧ to form into small, tight curls; frizz; crimp —*n.* a small, tight curl

friz·zly (friz′lē) *adj.* **-zli·er, -zli·est** ⟦< prec. + -Y[3]⟧ FRIZZY

friz·zy (friz′ē) *adj.* **-zi·er, -zi·est** full of or covered with small, tight curls —**friz′zi·ly** *adv.* —**friz′zi·ness** *n.*

fro (frō) *adv.* ⟦ME *fra, fro* < ON *frā*, akin to OE *fram*, FROM⟧ away; backward; back: now only in TO AND FRO (see phrase under TO[1])

Fro·bish·er (frō′bi shər), Sir **Martin** 1535?-94; Eng. navigator & explorer

Frobisher Bay ⟦after prec.⟧ **1** inlet of the N Atlantic, on the SE coast of Baffin Island, Canada **2** *former name for* IQALUIT

frock (fräk) *n.* ⟦ME *frok* < OFr *froc*, monk's habit (or ML *froccus*) < Frank **hrokk*, cloak⟧ **1** a robe worn by friars, monks, etc. **2** any of various other garments; specif., *a)* a tunic, mantle, or long coat formerly worn by men *b)* a smock or smock frock *c)* a girl's or woman's dress *d)* FROCK COAT —*vt.* to clothe in a frock

frock coat a man's double-breasted dress coat with a full skirt reaching to the knees, worn chiefly in the 19th cent.

froe (frō) *n.* ⟦also *frow* (*frower*): ? contr. of FROWARD, in sense "handle turned away"⟧ a cleaving tool with the handle set into the blade at right angles to the cutting edge

Froe·bel or **Frö·bel** (frö′bəl; *E* frā′bəl), **Frie·drich (Wilhelm August)** (frē′driH) 1782-1852; Ger. educator: originated the kindergarten system

frog (frôg, fräg) *n.* ⟦ME *frogge* < OE *frogga*, akin to Ger *frosch*, ON *froskr* < IE base **preu-*, to jump > Sans *právatē*, (he) hops⟧ **1** *a)* any of various families of tailless, leaping anuran amphibians with long, powerful hind legs, short forelegs, a smooth skin, and webbed feet: it develops from a tadpole, and most species, when grown, are able to live either in water or on land that is near water *b)* a toad **2** the triangular, horny pad in the posterior half of the sole of a horse's foot **3** a fastening on a belt for carrying a sword, bayonet, etc. **4** a corded or braided loop used as a fastener or decoration on clothing ☆**5** a device on railroad tracks for keeping cars on the proper rails at intersections or switches **6** a device placed in a bowl or vase to hold the stems of flowers **7** that part of the bow of a stringed instrument, including the nut, by which the bow is held **8** ⟦from the stereotypical notion that the French are fond of eating *frogs*⟧ [*sometimes* **F-**] [Slang] a French person: term of contempt or derision —**have a frog in one's throat** [Informal] to experience temporary hoarseness

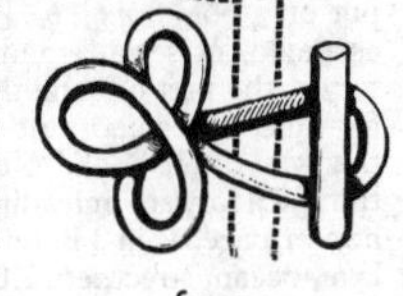
frog
(sense 4)

frog·fish (frôg′fish′) *n., pl.* **-fish′** or **-fish′es** (see FISH) any of a family (Antennariidae) of tropical angler fishes with a globular, scaleless body bearing many fleshy appendages

frog·gy (frôg′ē) *adj.* **-gi·er, -gi·est** of or characteristic of a frog
frog·hop·per (frôg′häp′ər) *n.* SPITTLEBUG
frog kick *Swimming* a kick in which the legs are drawn up and spread outward at the knees and then extended and brought together with a snap
frog·man (frôg′man′) *n., pl.* **-men′** (-men′) a person trained and equipped, as with a rubber suit and scuba apparatus, for underwater demolition, exploration, etc.
frog-march (-märch) *vt.* ⟦from the ungainly positions of the victim's limbs⟧ [Informal, Chiefly Brit.] to grasp by the arm from behind and force to walk along
frog's-bit (frôgz′bit′) *adj.* designating a family (Hydrocharitaceae, order Hydrocharitales) of submerged, monocotyledonous aquatic plants, including elodea and tape grass
frog spit (*or* **spittle)** 1 CUCKOO SPIT 2 mats of filamentous algae floating on the surface of ponds and containing bubbles of oxygen
Froh·man (frō′mən), **Charles** 1860-1915; U.S. theatrical manager & producer
froi·deur (frwȧ dër′) *n.* ⟦Fr⟧ coldness or coolness of manner; reserve; aloofness
Frois·sart (frwȧ sȧr′; *E* froi′särt), **Jean** (zhän) 1337-1410?; Fr. chronicler & poet
frol·ic (fräl′ik) *adj.* ⟦Du *vroolijk* < MDu *vrō*, merry, akin to Ger *froh*, prob. < IE base **preu-*, to leap > FROG⟧ [Archaic] full of fun and pranks; merry —*n.* 1 a playful trick; prank 2 a lively party or game 3 merriment; gaiety; fun —*vi.* **-icked, -ick·ing** 1 to make merry; have fun 2 to play or romp about in a happy, carefree way —**frol′ick·er** *n.*
frol·ic·some (-səm) *adj.* ⟦prec. + -SOME[1]⟧ full of gaiety or high spirits; playful; merry: also **frol′ick·y**
from (frum) *prep.* ⟦ME < OE *from, fram*, akin to Goth *fram*, forward, away, ON *frā* < IE base **pro-*, var. of **per-*, beyond, ahead > FOR[1], FORE, FIRST⟧ *a particle used with verbs or other words to indicate:* 1 *a)* beginning at (a point of departure as for motion, duration, or action) [leaving *from* the station] *b)* at a certain distance away with respect to [a mile *from* town] 2 starting with (the first of two named limits) [*from* noon to midnight] 3 out of; derived or coming out of [he took a comb *from* his pocket; lava spewed *from* the volcano] 4 with (a person or thing) as the source, maker, sender, speaker, teacher, etc. [a crate made *from* wood, a letter *from* Mary, facts learned *from* reading] 5 at a place not near to; out of contact with: used to express absence, removal, separation, etc. [away *from* danger, far *from* home] 6 out of the whole of; out of unity or alliance with [take two *from* four; he withdrew *from* the class] 7 out of the possibility of; prevented or excluded with respect to [kept *from* going on the hike] 8 out of the possession or control of; free with respect to [released *from* jail] 9 as not being like: used to express difference, distinction, etc. [to tell one sister *from* the other] 10 because of; caused by; having the reason or motive of [to tremble *from* fear] ☆11 ⟦adaptation of Yiddish locution⟧ [Slang] about: used with *know* [they don't know *from* good taste]
Fromm (främ), **Er·ich** (er′ik) 1900-80; U.S. psychoanalyst, born in Germany
frond (fränd) *n.* ⟦L *frons* (gen. *frondis*), leafy branch, foliage⟧ 1 a leaf; specif., *a)* the leaf of a fern *b)* the leaf of a palm 2 the leaflike part, or shoot, of a lichen, seaweed, duckweed, etc. —**frond′ed** *adj.*
Fronde (frōnd) *n.* ⟦Fr, lit., a sling⟧ a French political movement organized during the minority of Louis XIV to oppose the court and Cardinal Mazarin; also, the rebellions (1648-53) fomented by it
fron·des·cence (frän des′əns) *n.* ⟦< ModL *frondescentia* < L *frondescens*, prp. of *frondescere*, to become leafy < *frondere*, to put forth leaves < *frons*: see FROND⟧ 1 the process, state, or period of putting forth leaves 2 leaves; foliage —**fron·des′cent** *adj.*
frons (fränz) *n., pl.* **fron·tes** (frän′tēz) ⟦L: see fol.⟧ the upper front portion of the head of an insect, human being, etc.; forehead
front[1] (frunt) *n.* ⟦ME < OFr < L *frons* (gen. *frontis*), forehead, front < IE **bhren-*, to project > OE *brant*, steep, high⟧ 1 [Now Rare] *a)* the forehead *b)* the face; countenance 2 *a)* attitude or appearance, as of the face, indicating state of mind; external behavior when facing a problem, etc. [to put on a bold *front*] *b)* [Informal] an appearance, usually pretended or assumed, of social standing, wealth, etc. 3 [Rare] impudence; effrontery 4 the part of something that faces forward or is regarded as facing forward; most important side; forepart 5 the first part; beginning [toward the *front* of the book] 6 the place or position directly before a person or thing 7 a forward or leading position or situation ☆8 the first available bellhop or page, as in a hotel: generally used as a call 9 the land bordering a lake, ocean, street, etc. 10 [Brit.] a promenade along a body of water 11 the advanced line, or the whole area, of contact between opposing sides in warfare; combat zone 12 a specified area of activity [the home *front*, the political *front*] 13 a broad movement in which different groups are united for the achievement of certain common political or social aims ☆14 a person who serves as a public representative of a business, group, etc., usually because of his or her prestige ☆15 a person or group used to cover or obscure the activity or objectives of another, controlling person or group 16 a stiff shirt bosom, worn with formal clothes 17 *Archit.* a face of a building; esp., the face with the principal entrance 18 *Meteorol.* the boundary between two air masses of different density and temperature —*adj.* 1 at, to, in, on, or of the front 2 *Phonet.* articulated with the tongue in a position toward the front of the mouth: said of certain vowels, as (i) in *bid* —*vt.* 1 to face; be opposite to 2 to be before in place 3 to meet; confront 4 to defy; oppose 5 to supply or serve as a front, or facing, of 6 *a)* to be the leader or most prominent member of (a musical band, an organization, etc.) *b)* to conduct or host (a radio or TV show) —*vi.* 1 to face in a certain direction [a castle *fronting* on the sea] ☆2 to act as a FRONT[1] (senses 14 & 15): with *for* —**front and center** 1 (in or to) a central place at the front of a group or row: often used in the imperative 2 (in or into) any prominent or conspicuous position —**in front of** before; in a position ahead of
front[2] *abbrev.* frontispiece
front·age (frunt′ij) *n.* 1 the front part of a building 2 the direction toward which this faces; exposure 3 the land between the front edge of a building and the street 4 *a)* the front boundary line of a lot facing a street *b)* the length of this line 5 land bordering a street, river, lake, etc.
fron·tal[1] (frunt′'l) *adj.* ⟦ModL *frontalis*⟧ 1 of the front; in, on, at, or against the front 2 of, or situated at or near, the forehead [the *frontal* cortex of the brain] 3 involving the front of the human body [a movie scene with *frontal* nudity] —*n.* FRONTAL BONE —**fron′tal·ly** *adv.*
fron·tal[2] (frunt′'l) *n.* ⟦ME *frountel* < OFr *frontel* < ML *frontellum*, dim. for *frontale* < L *frontalia*, frontlet < *frons*: see FRONT[1] & -AL⟧ 1 an ornamental band worn on the forehead 2 an ornamental cloth hung over the front of an altar 3 *a)* a facade *b)* a small pediment over a door, window, etc.
frontal bone the bone comprising the front part of the skull and forming the forehead in humans
fron·tal·i·ty (frun tal′ə tē) *n.* ⟦transl. of Dan *frontalitet*: see FRONTAL[1] & -ITY⟧ the condition or quality of facing forward or outward, directly toward the viewer: said of a figure or object as depicted in a painting, sculpture, film, etc.
frontal lobe the part of the cerebrum covered by the frontal bone
front·bench·er (frunt′ben′chər) *n.* a member of the British House of Commons who is a leader in a party and occupies a seat near the speaker
front burner ⟦in ref. to a pot placed on a near, or front, burner of a kitchen stove⟧ a state of high priority or importance: usually in the phrase **on the front burner**, in or into such a state
☆**front·court** (frunt′kôrt′) *n. Basketball* 1 the half of the court with the basket that a team shoots at to score 2 the players on a team who play center and forward
Fron·te·nac (frōnt nȧk′; *E* frän′tə nak′), Comte **de (Frontenac et de Palluau)** (born *Louis de Buade*) 1620-98; Fr. colonial governor in North America (1672-82; 1689-98)
front-end (frunt′end′) *adj.* designating, of, or having to do with a contract, financial arrangement, etc. in which specified payments, costs, etc. are payable in advance
☆**front-end loader** a tractor with a large, hinged bucket mounted on the front at the end of a pair of jointed arms, for scooping and loading earth, gravel, debris, etc.
fron·tes (frän′tēz) *n. pl. of* FRONS
fron·tier (frun tir′; *also* frän-) *n.* ⟦ME *frontere* < OFr *frontier* < *front*: see FRONT[1]⟧ 1 the border between two countries ☆2 *a)* that part of a settled, civilized country which lies next to an unexplored or undeveloped region *b)* the developing, often still uncivilized or lawless, region of a country 3 any new field of learning, thought, etc. or any part of a field that is still incompletely investigated: *often used in pl.* [the *frontiers* of medicine] —*adj.* of, on, or near a frontier
☆**fron·tiers·man** (-tirz′mən) *n., pl.* **-men** (-mən) a person, esp. a man, who lives in a frontier region
fron·tis·piece (frunt′is pēs′) *n.* ⟦OFr < LL *frontispicium*, front of a church, front view < L *frons*, FRONT[1] + *specere*, to look: see SPY⟧ 1 [Obs.] the first page, esp. the title page, of a book 2 an illustration facing the title page of a book 3 *Archit.* *a)* the main facade *b)* a pediment over a door, window, etc.
front·let (frunt′lit) *n.* ⟦OFr *frontelet*, dim. of *frontel*, FRONTAL[2]⟧ 1 a frontal or a phylactery worn on the forehead 2 the forehead of an animal 3 the forehead of a bird, when distinguishable by the color or texture of the plumage 4 an ornamental border for an altar frontal
front·line or **front-line** (frunt′līn′) *adj.* of, at, on, or forming a front line [*frontline* soldiers, *frontline* research]
front line 1 a line or position of direct and immediate contact or confrontation as with an enemy 2 a line or position of furthest progress or advancement
front·list (frunt′list′) *n.* a list of a publisher's new titles, often, specif., those thought to appeal to a large number of people: distinguished from BACKLIST
front-load (frunt′lōd′) *vt.* to put or concentrate (efforts, costs, expenditures, etc.) at the beginning of (a contract, project, etc.) —*adj.* designating or of a washing machine with the lid in the front
front·man (frunt′man′) *n., pl.* **-men′** (-men′) 1 the most prominent or visible member of a group of musicians, as a lead singer ☆2 a person who lends his or her prestige to a group by acting as its public representative or nominal leader; often, such a person used as a cover for illegal or subversive activity
front money money paid in advance, as in a front-end contract
front nine in an 18-hole golf course, those holes numbered 1 through 9, regarded as a unit: cf. BACK NINE
fron·to- (frän′tō, frun′-) ⟦< L *frons*: see FRONT[1]⟧ *combining form* 1 of the frontal bone or region and [*frontoparietal*] 2 of or connected with a meteorological front [*frontogenesis*]
☆**front office** the management or administration, as of a company

fron·to·gen·e·sis (frän′tō jen′ə sis; *also* frun′-) ***n.*** ⟦ModL < FRONTO- + GENESIS⟧ the formation of a weather front as a result of contact between two different air masses, usually with resultant clouds and precipitation

fron·tol·y·sis (frun täl′ə sis; *also* frän-) ***n.*** ⟦ModL < FRONTO- + -LYSIS⟧ the process that tends to destroy a weather front, as by mixture of the frontal air

fron·ton (frän′tän′; *Sp* frôn tôn′) ***n.*** ⟦Sp *frontón*, orig., wall of a handball court, orig., a pediment < It *frontone*, aug. deriv. < *fronte*, forehead < L *frons*: see FRONT[1]⟧ a building containing a jai alai court or courts

fron·to·pal·a·tal (frun′tō pal′ə təl, -ət′l) ***adj.*** *Phonet.* articulated with the portion of the tongue that is just behind the tip touching or near the alveolar ridge and hard palate, as (sh) and (zh) —***n.*** a frontopalatal consonant

fron·to·pa·ri·e·tal (frun′tō pə rī′ə təl) ***adj.*** of the frontal and parietal bones of the skull

☆**front-page** (frunt′pāj′) ***adj.*** **1** on the front page of a newspaper **2** suitable for the front page of a newspaper, as in being important or sensational —***vt.*** **-paged′**, **-pag′ing** to print on the front page of a newspaper

Front Range range on the E edge of the Rockies, in SE Wyo. & NC Colo.: highest peak, 14,274 ft (4,351 m)

front room a room in the front of a house, esp. a living room

front-run·ner (frunt′run′ər) ***n.*** **1** one who is leading in a race or competition **2** a contestant or entry that runs best when in the lead ☆**3** a person who supports a political candidate, sports team, etc. because they are leading their race or competition

front-run·ning (-run′iŋ) ***n.*** the illegal brokering practice of trading on one's own behalf, based on advance knowledge of impending trades or recommendations, before informing or acting on behalf of one's clients —***adj.*** **1** leading in a race or competition ☆**2** supporting a political candidate, sports team, etc. because they are leading their race or competition [*front-running* fans]

front·ward (frunt′wərd) ***adv.*** ⟦FRONT[1] + -WARD⟧ **1** toward the front; ahead **2** with the front or face foremost —***adj.*** turned or directed toward the front

front·wards (-wərdz) ***adv.*** FRONTWARD

front-wheel drive (frunt′hwēl′, -wēl′) an automotive power-delivery system that provides driving power only to the front wheels

frore (frōr) ***adj.*** ⟦ME *frore(n)*, frozen, pp. of *fresen*, FREEZE⟧ [Archaic] very cold; frosty; frozen

☆**frosh** (fräsh) ***n., pl.*** **frosh** ⟦altered < FRESHMAN⟧ [Informal] a high-school or college freshman

frost (frôst, fräst) ***n.*** ⟦ME < OE *forst, frost* (akin to Ger *frost*) < pp. base of *freosan* (see FREEZE) + *-t* (Gmc *-*ta*), nominal suffix⟧ **1** a freezing or state of being frozen **2** a temperature low enough to cause freezing **3** the icy crystals that form directly on a freezing surface as moist air contacts it; rime; hoarfrost **4** coolness of action, feeling, manner, etc. **5** [Informal] a book, play, etc. that is poorly received by the public; failure —***vt.*** **1** to cover with frost **2** to damage, wither, or kill by freezing **3** to cover with frosting, or icing **4** to give a frostlike, opaque surface to (glass or metal) **5** to apply lighter coloring to selected strands of (hair) using a chemical dye **6** [Slang] to make angry, annoy, irritate, etc.

Frost (frôst, fräst), **Robert (Lee)** 1874-1963; U.S. poet

☆**Frost·belt** (frôst′belt′) SNOWBELT: also **Frost Belt**

frost·bite (frôst′bīt′) ***n.*** tissue damage caused by exposure to intense cold

frost·bit·ten (-bit′′n) ***adj.*** suffering from frostbite: also **frost′bit′**

☆**frost·fish** (-fish′) ***n., pl.*** **-fish′** or **-fish′es** (see FISH) **1** TOMCOD **2** any of various fishes that appear in the early fall

☆**frost·flow·er** (-flou′ər) ***n.*** any of various asters

frost·ing (frôs′tiŋ) ***n.*** **1** a mixture variously of sugar, butter, flavoring, water or other liquid, egg whites, etc. for covering a cake or pastries; icing **2** a dull, frostlike finish on glass, metal, etc. **3** a mixture of ground glass, varnish, etc. used in ornamental work

☆**frost line** the limit of penetration of soil by frost

frost·work (frôst′wurk′) ***n.*** **1** the tracery formed by frost on glass, etc. **2** ornamentation like this, as on silver

frost·y (frôs′tē) ***adj.*** **frost′i·er**, **frost′i·est** **1** producing frost or cold enough to produce frost; freezing **2** covered with or as with frost; hoary, glistening, etc. **3** cold in manner or feeling; austere; unfriendly —**frost′i·ly** ***adv.*** —**frost′i·ness** ***n.***

froth (frôth, fräth; *for v., also* frôth, fräth) ***n.*** ⟦ME *frothe* < ON *frotha*, akin to OE *(a)-freothan*, to froth up < IE **preu-th*, a snorting, slavering < base **per-*, to sprinkle, scatter > Gr *prēmainein*, to blow hard⟧ **1** a whitish mass of bubbles; foam **2** foaming saliva caused by disease or great excitement **3** light, trifling, or worthless talk, ideas, etc. —***vt.*** ⟦< the *n.*⟧ **1** to cause to foam **2** to cover with foam **3** to spill forth like foam —***vi.*** ⟦ME *frothen*⟧ to produce froth; foam

froth·y (frôth′ē, frôth′ē) ***adj.*** **froth′i·er**, **froth′i·est** **1** of, like, or covered with froth; foamy **2** light; trifling; worthless —**froth′i·ly** ***adv.*** —**froth′i·ness** ***n.***

frot·tage (frə täzh′) ***n.*** ⟦Fr, a rubbing, chafing < *frotter*, to rub⟧ **1** sexual gratification from rubbing against the body of another person, often, specif., from rubbing against a stranger in a public place **2** an artistic rubbing or tracing from a surface that is textured, raised, etc.

Froude (frōōd), **J(ames) A(nthony)** 1818-94; Eng. historian & biographer

frou·frou (frōō′frōō′) ***n.*** ⟦Fr; echoic⟧ **1** a rustling or swishing, as of a silk skirt ☆**2** [Informal] excessive ornateness or affected elegance

frounce (frouns) ***vt., vi.*** **frounced**, **frounc′ing** ⟦ME *frouncen* < OFr *froncir*, to wrinkle < Frank **hrunkja*, a wrinkle, akin to ON *hrukka*⟧ [Obs.] to curl, crease, or wrinkle

frow (frō) ***n.*** *alt. sp. of* FROE

fro·ward (frō′wərd; *also* frō′ərd) ***adj.*** ⟦ME, turned away, unruly: see FRO & -WARD⟧ **1** not easily controlled; stubbornly willful; contrary **2** [Obs.] adverse —**fro′ward·ly** ***adv.*** —**fro′ward·ness** ***n.***

frown (froun) ***vi.*** ⟦ME *frounen* < OFr *frognier* < *froigne*, sullen face < Gaul **frogna*, nostrils, akin to OIr *srón*, nose⟧ **1** to contract the brows and lower the corners of the mouth, as in displeasure, sternness, or concentration **2** to look with displeasure or disapproval (*on* or *upon*) —***vt.*** **1** [Now Rare] to silence, subdue, etc. with a disapproving look **2** to express (disapproval, disgust, etc.) by frowning —***n.*** **1** a facial expression conveying displeasure, sternness, or concentration, and consisting typically of a contracting of the brows and a lowering of the corners of the mouth **2** any expression of displeasure or disapproval —**frown′er** ***n.*** —**frown′ing·ly** ***adv.***

frowst (froust) [Brit. Informal] ***n.*** ⟦back-form. < fol.⟧ stale, musty air —***vi.*** to lounge about in a hot, stuffy room

frowst·y (frous′tē) ***adj.*** **frowst′i·er**, **frowst′i·est** ⟦prob. altered < fol.⟧ [Brit.] musty or stuffy —**frowst′i·ness** ***n.***

frow·zy (frou′zē) ***adj.*** **-zi·er**, **-zi·est** ⟦< ?⟧ dirty and untidy; slovenly; unkempt: also sp. **frow′sy** —**frow′zi·ly** ***adv.*** —**frow′zi·ness** ***n.***

froze (frōz) ***vi., vt.*** *pt. of* FREEZE

fro·zen (frō′zən) ***vi., vt.*** *pp. of* FREEZE —***adj.*** ⟦ME⟧ **1** turned into or covered with ice; congealed by cold **2** injured, damaged, or killed by freezing **3** having heavy frosts and extreme cold [the *frozen* polar wastes] **4** preserved or prepared by freezing, as food **5** affected as if turned into ice; made motionless [*frozen* with terror] **6** without warmth or affection in behavior, manners, etc. **7** arbitrarily kept at a fixed level or in a fixed position **8** not capable of being spent, transferred, sold, etc., as a result of legal action [*frozen* assets]

☆**frozen custard** a frozen dessert resembling ice cream, but having a lower butterfat content and a flowing consistency

☆**frozen yogurt** a frozen dessert made from yogurt, milk, and sweeteners

Frs *abbrev.* Frisian

FRS *abbrev.* **1** Federal Reserve System **2** Fellow of the Royal Society

frt *abbrev.* freight

fruc·tif·er·ous (fruk tif′ər əs) ***adj.*** ⟦< L *fructifer* (< *fructus*, FRUIT + *ferre*, to BEAR[1]) + -OUS⟧ producing fruit; fruit-bearing

fruc·ti·fy (fruk′tə fī′) ***vi.*** **-fied′**, **-fy′ing** ⟦ME *fructifien* < OFr *fructifier* < L *fructificare*: see FRUIT & -FY⟧ to bear fruit; become fruitful —***vt.*** to cause to bear fruit; fertilize —**fruc′ti·fi·ca′tion** ***n.***

fruc·tose (fruk′tōs′, frook′-) ***n.*** ⟦< L *fructus*, FRUIT + -OSE[1]⟧ a crystalline monosaccharide found in sweet fruits and in honey; fruit sugar; levulose

fruc·tu·ous (fruk′chōō əs) ***adj.*** ⟦ME < OFr < L *fructuosus* < *fructus*, FRUIT⟧ fruitful; productive

fru·gal (frōō′gəl) ***adj.*** ⟦L *frugalis* < *frugi*, fit for food, hence proper, worthy, frugal, orig. dat. of *frux* (gen. *frugis*), fruits, produce: for IE base see FRUIT⟧ **1** not wasteful; not spending freely or unnecessarily; thrifty; economical **2** not costly or luxurious; inexpensive or meager [a *frugal* meal] —*SYN.* THRIFTY —**fru·gal′i·ty** (-gal′ə tē) ***n., pl.*** **-ties** —**fru′gal·ly** ***adv.***

fru·giv·o·rous (frōō jiv′ə rəs) ***adj.*** ⟦< L *frux* (see prec.) + -VOROUS⟧ fruit-eating

fruit (frōōt) ***n., pl.*** **fruit** or **fruits** ⟦ME < OFr < L *fructus*, enjoyment, means of enjoyment, fruit, produce, profit < pp. of *frui*, to partake of, enjoy < IE base **bhrūg-*, fruit, to enjoy > BROOK[2]⟧ **1** any plant product, as grain, flax, vegetables, etc.: *usually used in pl.* **2** the edible plant structure of a mature ovary of a flowering plant, usually eaten raw: many fruits which are not sweet, as tomatoes, beans, green peppers, etc., are popularly called *vegetables* **3** the quality of being FRUITY (sense 1*b*); fruitiness: said of wine **4** the result, product, or consequence of any action [*fruit* of hard work] ☆**5** [Slang] a male homosexual: term of contempt or derision **6** [Archaic] offspring; young **7** *Bot.* the mature ovary of a flowering plant, together with its contents, and any closely connected parts, as the whole peach, pea pod, cucumber, etc.: see TRUE FRUIT, FALSE FRUIT — ***vi., vt.*** to bear or cause to bear fruit

fruit·age (frōōt′ij) ***n.*** ⟦OFr: see -AGE⟧ **1** bearing of fruit; fruiting **2** a crop of fruit; fruits collectively **3** a result; product; consequence

fruit·ar·i·an (frōō ter′ē ən) ***n.*** a person whose diet consists chiefly or exclusively of fruit

fruit bat any fruit-eating bat (esp. family Pteropodidae), as the flying fox

fruit·cake (frōōt′kāk′) ***n.*** **1** a rich, dense cake containing nuts, preserved fruit, citron, spices, etc. **2** [Slang] a foolish, eccentric, or crazy person ☆**3** [Slang] a male homosexual: term of contempt or derision

fruit cup ☆mixed diced fruits served in a sherbet glass, etc. as an appetizer or dessert: also **fruit cocktail**

fruit·er (frōōt′ər) ***n.*** ⟦ME *fruter* < OFr *fruitier*⟧ a tree that bears fruit

fruit·er·er (-ər ər) ***n.*** ⟦ME *fruterer* (with redundant *-er*) < prec.⟧ [Chiefly Brit.] a person who deals in fruit

fruit fly **1** any of a family (Tephritidae) of small dipterous flies whose larvae feed on fruits and vegetables **2** DROSOPHILA

fruit·ful (frōōt′fəl) ***adj.*** ⟦ME⟧ **1** bearing much fruit **2** producing much; productive; prolific **3** producing results; profitable [a *fruitful* plan] —*SYN.* FERTILE —**fruit′ful·ly** ***adv.*** —**fruit′ful·ness** ***n.***

fruit·ing body (frōōt′iŋ) the spore-bearing structure of a fungus

fru·i·tion (frōō ish′ən) ***n.*** ⟦ME *fruicioun* < OFr *fruition* < LL *fruitio*, enjoyment < *frui*: see FRUIT⟧ **1** a pleasure obtained from using or possessing something; enjoyment 2 ⟦by assoc. with FRUIT⟧ the bearing of fruit 3 a coming to fulfillment; realization [a book that is the *fruition* of years of research]

☆**fruit jar** a glass jar for canning fruit, vegetables, etc., sealed airtight with a cap

fruit·less (fro͞ot′lis) *adj.* ⟦ME *fruitles*⟧ 1 without results; unprofitable; unsuccessful; vain 2 bearing no fruit; sterile; barren —*SYN.* FUTILE —**fruit′less·ly** *adv.* —**fruit′less·ness** *n.*

fruit machine ⟦so called from the use of pictures of various *fruits* as symbols in many such machines⟧ [Brit.] SLOT MACHINE (sense *b*)

fruit sugar FRUCTOSE

fruit tree a tree that bears edible fruit

fruit·wood (fro͞ot′wood′) *n.* the wood of any of various fruit trees, used in furniture, paneling, etc.

fruit·y (fro͞ot′ē) *adj.* **fruit′i·er, fruit′i·est** 1 *a)* like fruit in taste or smell *b)* suggesting the flavor or aroma of ripe fruit (said of wine) 2 rich or mellow in tone, esp. excessively so [a *fruity* voice] 3 rich in interest; spicy; juicy 4 [Slang] *a)* eccentric or crazy ☆*b)* of or like a male homosexual (term of contempt or derision) —**fruit′i·ly** *adv.* —**fruit′i·ness** *n.*

fru·men·ta·ceous (fro͞o′men tā′shəs, -mən-) *adj.* ⟦LL *frumentaceus* < L *frumentum*, grain < base of *frui*: see FRUIT⟧ of, having the nature of, or like wheat or other grain

fru·men·ty (fro͞o′mən tē) *n.* ⟦ME *frumente* < OFr *frumentée* < L *frumentum*: see prec.⟧ an English dish consisting of hulled wheat boiled in milk, sweetened, and flavored with spice

frump (frump) *n.* ⟦prob. shortened n. form < ME *fromplen*, to wrinkle < earlier Du *frompelen, verrompelen* < *ver-*, FOR- + *rompelen*: see RUMPLE⟧ a dowdy, unattractive woman —**frump′ish** *adj.* —**frump′y** *adj.* **frump′i·er, frump′i·est**

Frun·ze (fro͞on′ze) *name* (1926-91) *for* BISHKEK

frus·trate (frus′trāt′) *vt.* **-trat′ed, -trat′ing** ⟦ME *frustraten* < L *frustratus*, pp. of *frustrare, frustrari*, to disappoint, deceive < *frustra*, in vain: for IE base see FRAUD⟧ 1 to cause to have no effect; bring to nothing; counteract; nullify [to *frustrate* plans] 2 to prevent from achieving an objective; foil; baffle; defeat [to *frustrate* an opponent] 3 *Psychol.* to prevent from gratifying certain impulses or desires, either conscious or unconscious 4 to cause (someone) to feel the impatience, impotence, annoyance, anger, etc. commonly felt when desires or needs are not satisfied —*vi.* to become frustrated —*adj.* [Now Rare] frustrated; baffled; defeated —**frus′trat′ing** *adj.* —**frus′trat′ing·ly** *adv.*

SYN.—to **frustrate** means to deprive of effect or render worthless an effort directed to some end; **thwart** and **balk** both mean to frustrate by blocking someone or something moving toward some objective; **foil** means to throw off course so as to discourage further effort or render it of no avail; to **baffle** is to defeat the efforts of by bewildering or confusing [the crime *baffled* the police]

frus·tra·tion (frə strā′shən) *n.* ⟦ME *frustracioun* < L *frustratio*⟧ 1 a frustrating or being frustrated 2 something that frustrates

frus·tule (frus′tyo͞ol′, -cho͞ol′) *n.* ⟦Fr < L *frustulum*, dim. of *frustum*, a piece: see fol.⟧ either of the two interlocking halves of the hard, siliceous shell of a diatom cell

frus·tum (frus′təm) *n., pl.* **-tums** or **-ta** (-tə) ⟦L, a piece, bit < IE **bhreus-*, to break, crush < base **bher-*, to split, cut > BORE⟧ 1 a solid figure consisting of the bottom part of a cone or pyramid, the top of which has been cut off by a plane parallel to the base 2 the part of a solid figure contained between two parallel planes See TRUNCATED

fru·tes·cent (fro͞o tes′ənt) *adj.* ⟦< L *frutex*, a shrub < IE base **bhreu-*, to sprout (> MHG *briezen*, to bud) + -ESCENT⟧ shrubby or becoming shrubby —**fru·tes′cence** *n.*

fru·ti·cose (fro͞ot′i kōs′) *adj.* ⟦L *fruticosus* < *frutex*: see prec.⟧ of or like a shrub; shrubby

fry[1] (frī) *vt., vi.* **fried, fry′ing** ⟦ME *frien* < OFr *frire* < L *frigere*, to fry < IE base **bher-*, to bake, roast > Pers *birištan*, to fry⟧ 1 to cook or be cooked in a pan or on a griddle over direct heat, usually in hot fat or oil 2 to subject or be subjected to the painful or destructive effects of intense heat 3 [Slang] to electrocute or be electrocuted —*n., pl.* **fries** 1 *a)* a fried food *b)* [*pl.*] fried potatoes ☆2 a social gathering at which food is fried and eaten [a fish *fry*]

fry[2] (frī) *pl.n., sing.* **fry** ⟦ME *frie*, prob. a merging of ON *frjo*, seed, offspring (akin to Goth *fraiw*) with Anglo-Fr *frei* (Fr *frai*) < OFr *freier*, to rub, spawn < VL **frictiare* < L *fricare*, to rub: see FRIABLE⟧ 1 young fish 2 small adult fish, esp. when in large groups *Sometimes used in sing.*

Fry (frī) 1 **Christopher** (born *Christopher Hammond*) 1907-2005; Eng. playwright 2 **Elizabeth** 1780-1845; Eng. philanthropist & prison reformer

fry bread a flat wheat bread that is cooked by frying in deep fat until light brown and puffed on both sides: originally made by North American Indians of the SW U.S.: also written **fry′bread′** *n.*

fry·er (frī′ər) *n.* 1 a person or thing that fries; specif., a utensil for deep-frying foods 2 food to be cooked by frying; esp., a chicken young and tender enough to fry

frying pan a shallow pan with a handle, for frying food: also **fry′pan′** *n.* —**out of the frying pan into the fire** from a bad situation into a worse one

fry-up (frī′up′) *n.* [Brit. Informal] a dish consisting of several fried foods served together, as eggs, sausage, and kidneys

FS *abbrev.* 1 Forest Service 2 *Football* free safety: sometimes written **fs**

FSC *abbrev.* ⟦L *Fratres Scholarum Christianarum*⟧ Brothers of the Christian Schools; Christian Brothers

FSH *abbrev.* follicle-stimulating hormone

FSLIC *abbrev.* Federal Savings and Loan Insurance Corporation

f-stop (ef′stäp′) *n. Photog.* any of the calibrated settings for an f-number

ft *abbrev.* foot; feet

Ft *abbrev.* Fort

FT *abbrev. Basketball* free throw(s)

FTC *abbrev.* FEDERAL TRADE COMMISSION

ft-c *abbrev.* foot-candle

fth or **fthm** *abbrev.* fathom(s)

ft-lb *abbrev.* foot-pound

FTP *abbrev.* file transfer protocol

ft-pdl *abbrev.* foot-poundal(s)

FTSE (foot′sē) *service mark* ⟦*F(inancial) T(imes) S(tock) E(xchange)*⟧ an index based upon the current prices of selected companies traded on the London Stock Exchange: also **FTSE index**

fub·sy (fub′zē) *adj.* **-si·er, -si·est** ⟦< obs. *fub*, plump child⟧ [Brit.] fat and squat; plump

fuch·sia (fyo͞o′shə) *n.* ⟦ModL, so named by LINNAEUS after L. *Fuchs* (1501-66), Ger botanist⟧ 1 any of a genus (*Fuchsia*) of shrubby plants of the evening-primrose family, usually with pink, red, or purple flowers hanging from the ends of the branches 2 purplish red —*adj.* purplish-red

fuch·sin (fook′sin) *n.* ⟦Fr *fuchsine* < prec. + *-ine*, -IN[1]: from the color⟧ a purplish-red aniline dye, $C_{20}H_{19}N_3HCl$, used as a coloring agent in inks, stains, and dyes: also **fuch′sine** (-sin, -sēn′)

fuck (fuk) [Vulgar] *vi.* ⟦Early ModE *fuck, fuk*, < ME **fuken* < Gmc: akin to MDu *fokken*, to strike, copulate, Swed dial. *fock*, penis⟧ 1 to engage in sexual intercourse 2 [Slang] to meddle (*with*) —*vt.* 1 to engage in sexual intercourse with 2 [Slang] to treat (someone) with great, usually malicious, unfairness; esp., to cheat: sometimes with *over* —*n.* 1 an act or instance of sexual intercourse 2 [Slang] a person with whom one engages in sexual intercourse, often, specif., one of specified competence 3 [Slang] an undesirable or contemptible person —*interj.* [Slang] used to express anger, disappointment, frustration, etc. ➥*Fuck* is also widely used interjectionally in various combinations to express irritation, anger, etc. [*fuck*, no!], and in various ways, esp. after *the*, to express surprise, disbelief, disgust, etc. [who the *fuck* is he? what the *fuck!*] —**fuck around** [Slang] 1 to spend time idly, foolishly, etc. 2 to meddle (*with*) —**fuck off** [Slang] 1 to idle; loaf 2 go away! —**fuck up** [Slang] 1 to make a mess (of); bungle or blunder 2 to confuse or disturb, esp. mentally or emotionally

USAGE—although hundreds of years old, *fuck* has only rarely been recorded in print until recent years; even in print its use is still confined largely to reported speech, and the term is considered to be at least somewhat vulgar in all uses

fuck·er (-ər) *n.* [Slang] 1 a person who fucks: a vulgar use 2 an unpleasant or contemptible person: considered vulgar by many 3 any person or thing: considered vulgar by many

fuck·ing (-iŋ) *adj., adv.* [Slang] 1 damned 2 extreme(ly) Often used simply as a strong intensive [a *fucking* shame] Considered vulgar by many

fuck·up (-up′) *n.* [Slang] a person who habitually bungles or blunders: somewhat vulgar

fu·coid (fyo͞o′koid′) *adj.* ⟦< fol. + -OID⟧ of or like seaweed, esp. rockweed —*n.* a seaweed; esp., rockweed

fu·cus (fyo͞o′kəs) *n., pl.* **fu′ci′** (-sī′) or **fu′cus·es** ⟦ModL < L, rock lichen; also, red or purple paint obtained from it < Gr *phykos*, rock lichen, rouge < Sem, as in Heb *puch*, cosmetic for the eyes⟧ 1 [Obs.] *a)* a kind of paint for the face *b)* any paint or dye 2 any of a genus (*Fucus*, order Fucales) of brown algae with a flattened and forking plant body that bears swollen bladders

fud (fud) *n.* [Informal] FUDDY-DUDDY

fud·dle (fud′'l) *vt.* **-dled, -dling** ⟦akin? to Ger dial. *fuddeln*, to swindle⟧ to confuse or stupefy as with alcoholic liquor; befuddle —*vi.* [Rare] to drink heavily; tipple —*n.* a fuddled condition

fud·dy-dud·dy (fud′ē dud′ē) *n., pl.* **-dies** ⟦redupl., prob. based on dial. *fud*, buttocks⟧ [Informal] 1 a fussy, critical person 2 a person regarded as being limited by old-fashioned customs, tastes, beliefs, etc.

fudge (fuj) *n.* ⟦? echoic, as in Ger *futsch*, gone, ruined⟧ 1 empty, foolish talk; nonsense ☆2 ⟦< ?⟧ *a)* a soft candy made of butter, milk, sugar, and chocolate or other flavoring, etc. *b)* a rich, sweet chocolate sauce used as a topping for ice cream or as an ingredient in cakes and cookies (usually used attributively) [a *fudge* sundae] 3 *Printing* a short piece of last-minute news or other matter inserted in a newspaper page 4 the act or an instance of fudging —*vt.* **fudged, fudg′ing** to make or put together dishonestly or carelessly; fake —*vi.* ☆1 to refuse to commit oneself or give a direct answer; hedge [to *fudge* on an issue] ☆2 to be dishonest; cheat —*interj.* [Old-fashioned] nonsense

fudge factor ⟦see prec.⟧ [Informal] a term or quantity introduced into a calculation to represent or compensate for something unpredictable, or to ensure a desired result

fudg·y (fuj′ē) *adj.* **-i·er, -i·est** having the rich chocolate flavor and moist, dense texture typical of fudge [a recipe for *fudgy* brownies]

Fu·e·gi·an (fyo͞o ē′jē ən, fwā′-) *adj.* of Tierra del Fuego or its people or culture —*n.* a member of a South American Indian people living in Tierra del Fuego

Fueh·rer (fü′rər; E fyo͞or′ər) *n.* [*also in roman type*] *alt. sp. of* FÜHRER

fu·el (fyōō′əl, fyōōl) ***n.*** ⟦ME *fewell* < OFr *fouaille* < ML *fuale, focale* < *foca,* hearth, for L *focus,* fireplace: see FOCUS⟧ **1** any material, as coal, oil, gas, wood, etc., burned to supply heat or power **2** fissile material from which nuclear energy can be obtained, as in a nuclear reactor **3** anything that maintains or intensifies strong feeling, etc. —***vt.*** **fu′eled** or **fu′elled, fu′el·ing** or **fu′el·ling** to supply with fuel —***vi.*** to get fuel —**fu′el·er** ***n.,*** **fu′el·ler**

fuel cell an electrochemical generator that produces direct current from a chemical reaction, as from combining oxygen and hydrogen

fuel-ef·fi·cient (-ə fish′ənt) ***adj.*** designating a type of vehicle, engine, etc. that delivers superior mileage per gallon of fuel —**fuel′-ef·fi′cien·cy** ***n.***

fuel injection **1** a system in which a fine spray of fuel is injected directly into each combustion chamber of an engine **2** such injection of fuel —**fu′el-in·ject′ed** ***adj.***

☆**fuel oil** any oil used for fuel; esp., a petroleum distillate used in diesel engines

fuel rod a rod-shaped metal assembly containing fissile fuel, used in nuclear reactors

Fuen·tes (fwen′tās, -tes), **Carlos** 1928-2012; Mex. novelist

fug (fug) ***n.*** ⟦altered < ? FOG[1]⟧ [Chiefly Brit.] the heavy air in a closed room, regarded as either oppressive and murky or warm and cozy —**fug′gy** ***adj.*** —**fug′gi·ly** ***adv.***

fu·ga·cious (fyōō gā′shəs) ***adj.*** ⟦< L *fugax* (gen. *fugacis*) < *fugere* (see FUGITIVE) + -IOUS⟧ **1** passing quickly away; fleeting; ephemeral **2** *Bot.* falling soon after blooming, as some flowers —**fu·gac′i·ty** (-gas′ə tē) ***n.***

fu·gal (fyōō′gəl) ***adj.*** of, or having the nature of, a fugue

-fuge (fyōōj) ⟦Fr < L *fugere,* to flee: see fol.⟧ *combining form* something that drives away or out *[febrifuge, vermifuge]*

fu·gi·tive (fyōō′ji tiv) ***adj.*** ⟦ME *fugitif* < OFr < L *fugitivus* < pp. of *fugere,* to flee < IE base **bheug-,* to flee > Gr *phygē,* flight⟧ **1** fleeing, apt to flee, or having fled, as from danger, justice, etc. **2** passing quickly away; fleeting; evanescent **3** having to do with matters of temporary interest *[fugitive* essays*]* **4** roaming; shifting —***n.*** **1** a person who flees or has fled from danger, justice, etc. **2** a fleeting or elusive thing —**fu′gi·tive·ly** ***adv.***

fu·gle·man (fyōō′gəl mən) ***n., pl.*** **-men** (-mən) ⟦altered by dissimilation < Ger *flügelmann,* file-leader, lit., wing-man < *flügel,* wing + *mann,* man⟧ **1** [Historical] a soldier expert in drilling, detailed to stand at the head of a unit and serve as a model and guide for others **2** a leader or exemplar

fu·gu (fōō′gōō) ***n.*** ⟦Jpn⟧ a Japanese puffer containing a deadly toxin, tetrodotoxin, in its skin and organs: the white flesh of this fish is served raw as a delicacy, esp. in Japan

fugue (fyōōg) ***n.*** ⟦Fr < It *fuga* < L, a flight < *fugere:* see FUGITIVE⟧ **1** a musical composition for a definite number of parts or voices, in which a subject is announced in one voice, imitated in succession by each of the other voices, and developed contrapuntally **2** *Psychiatry* a state of psychological amnesia during which the subject seems to behave in a conscious and rational way, but, upon return to normal consciousness, cannot remember the period of time nor what he or she did during it —**fu′guist** ***n.***

Füh·rer (fü′rər; *E* fyoor′ər) ***n.*** ⟦Ger < *führen,* to lead < Gmc **forjan,* caus. of *faran,* to go, travel > FARE⟧ *[also in roman type]* leader: title assumed by Adolf Hitler as head of Nazi Germany (1934-45)

Fuji (fōō′jē), **Mount** dormant volcano on Honshu island, Japan, southwest of Tokyo: highest peak in Japan: 12,388 ft (3,776 m): also **Fu·ji·ya·ma** (fōō′jē yä′mə) or **Fu′ji·san′** (-sän′)

Fu·jian (fōō′jyän′) province of SE China, on Taiwan Strait: 47,529 sq mi (123,100 sq km); cap. Fuzhou: former transliteration **Fu·kien** (fōō′kyen′)

Fu·ji·ta scale (fōō jēt′ə) ⟦after T. T. *Fujita* (1920-98), U.S. meteorologist who devised it⟧ a numerical scale for measuring the wind speed and corresponding destructive power of a tornado, ranging from F0 (40-72 mph) to F6 (319-380 mph): see the Tornado Damage Potential Scale in the Reference Supplement

Fu·ku·o·ka (fōō′kōō ō′kə) seaport on the N coast of Kyushu island, Japan

-ful (fəl; *for 2, usually* fool) ⟦ME < OE < *full,* FULL[1]⟧ *suffix* **1** *forming adjectives a)* full of, characterized by, having *[joyful, painful] b)* having the qualities of *[masterful] c)* having the ability or tendency to, apt to *[helpful, forgetful]* **2** *forming nouns* the quantity that fills or would fill: the plural is formed by adding *-s* to the resulting word *[teaspoonfuls, handfuls]* or, sometimes, by adding *-s-* between the noun stem and the suffix *[cupsful]*

Fu·la (fōō′lä′, -lə) ***n.*** ⟦< native name⟧ the Niger-Congo language spoken by the Fulanis: also **Fu′lah′**

Fu·la·ni (fōō′lä nē, -lə-; fōō lä′-) ***n.*** **1** *pl.* **-nis** or **-ni** a member of a people living chiefly in Nigeria, Mali, Guinea, Cameroon, and Niger **2** FULA —***adj.*** of the Fulanis or their language or culture

Ful·bright (fool′brīt′) ***adj.*** ⟦after U.S. Senator J. W. *Fulbright* (1905-95), originator of legislation creating the program⟧ designating, of, or holding a scholarship or grant in a U.S. government program for the exchange of U.S. and foreign scholars, teachers, etc. —***n.*** a Fulbright scholarship, grant, or scholar

ful·crum (fool′krəm, ful′-) ***n., pl.*** **-crums** or **-cra** (-krə) ⟦L, bedpost, support, akin to *fulcire:* see BALK⟧ **1** *a)* the support or point of support on which a lever turns in raising or moving something *b) Zool.* any structure that supports or acts like a fulcrum **2** a means of exerting influence, pressure, etc.

ful·fill (fool fil′) ***vt.*** **-filled′, -fill′ing** ⟦ME *fulfillen* < OE *fullfyllan:* a pleonasm: see FULL[1] & FILL⟧ **1** to carry out (something promised, desired, predicted, etc.); cause to be or happen **2** to do (something required); obey **3** to satisfy (a condition) or answer (a purpose) Brit. sp. **ful·fil′, -filled′, -fill′ing** —**SYN.** PERFORM —**fulfill oneself** to realize completely one's ambitions, potentialities, etc. —**ful·fill′er** ***n.*** —**ful·fill′ment** ***n.,*** [Brit.] **ful·fil′ment**

ful·gent (ful′jənt) ***adj.*** ⟦ME < L *fulgens* (gen. *fulgentis*), prp. of *fulgere,* to flash, shine < IE **bhleg-,* to shine, gleam > FLAME, BLACK⟧ [Literary] very bright; radiant —**ful′gent·ly** ***adv.***

ful·gu·rate (ful′gyoo rāt′) ***vi.*** **-rat′ed, -rat′ing** ⟦< L *fulguratus,* pp. of *fulgurare,* to flash < *fulgur,* lightning, akin to prec.⟧ [Rare] to give off flashes of or like lightning —***vt.*** **1** to give off in flashes **2** *Med.* to destroy (tissue) by electrical means —**ful′gu·ra′tion** ***n.***

ful·gu·rat·ing (-rāt′iŋ) ***adj.*** flashing or sudden, like lightning *[a fulgurating* pain*]*: also **ful′gu·rant** (-rənt)

ful·gu·rite (ful′gyoo rīt′) ***n.*** ⟦L *fulgur* (see FULGURATE) + -ITE[1]⟧ a glassy substance, usually tube-shaped, formed by fusion when sand, rock, etc. are struck by lightning

ful·gu·rous (ful′gyoo rəs) ***adj.*** ⟦L *fulgur* (see FULGURATE) + -OUS⟧ like or full of lightning; flashing

Ful·ham (fool′əm) former metropolitan borough of SW London, now part of Hammersmith

fu·lig·i·nous (fyōō lij′ə nəs) ***adj.*** ⟦LL *fuliginosus* < L *fuligo,* soot < IE **dhuli-* < base **dheu-,* to blow, smoke > DULL⟧ **1** full of smoke or soot **2** dark; dusky

full[1] (fool) ***adj.*** ⟦ME < OE, akin to Ger *voll,* Goth *fulls* < IE base **pel-,* to fill > L *plenus,* full & *plere,* to fill, Gr *plēthein,* to be full, Welsh *llawn,* full⟧ **1** having in it all there is space for; holding or containing as much as possible; filled *[a full* jar*]* **2** *a)* having eaten all that one wants *b)* having had more than one can stand *(of)* **3** using or occupying all of a given space *[a full* load*]* **4** having a great deal or number *(of)*; crowded *[a* room *full* of people*]* **5** *a)* well supplied, stocked, or provided; rich or abounding (with *of*) *[woods full* of game*] b)* rich in detail *[full* information*]* **6** *a)* filling the required number, capacity, measure, etc.; complete *[a full* dozen*] b)* thorough; absolute *[to come to a full* stop*]* **7** *a)* having reached the greatest development, size, extent, intensity, etc. *[a full* moon, *full* speed*]* ☆*b)* having attained the highest regular rank *[a full* professor*]* **8** having the same parents *[full* brothers*]* **9** having clearness, volume, and depth *[a full* tone*]* **10** plump; round; filled out *[a full* face*]* **11** with loose, wide folds; ample; flowing *[a full* skirt*]* **12** *a)* greatly affected by emotion, etc. *b)* occupied or engrossed with ideas, thoughts, etc. ☆**13** *Baseball a)* designating a count of three balls and two strikes on the batter *b)* with a runner at each of the three bases —***n.*** the greatest amount, extent, number, size, etc. *[to enjoy life to the full]* —***adv.*** **1** to the greatest degree; completely; fully *[a full-*grown boy*]* **2** directly; exactly *[to be hit full* in the face*]* **3** very *[full* well*]* —***vt.*** to sew loose folds into (a skirt); gather —***vi.*** to become full: said of the moon —**SYN.** COMPLETE —**at the full** at the state or time of fullness —**in full** **1** to, for, or with the full amount, value, etc. **2** with all the words or letters; not abbreviated or condensed

full[2] (fool) ***vt., vi.*** ⟦ME *fullen* < OFr *fuler* < ML *fullare,* to full < L *fullo,* cloth fuller⟧ to shrink and thicken (cloth, esp. wool) with moisture, heat, and pressure

full·back (fool′bak′) ***n.*** **1** *Football* one of the running backs, used typically for blocking **2** *Soccer, Rugby, etc.* a defensive player who generally plays back in the defensive end of the field near the goal so as to prevent the opponent's forwards from scoring

☆**full blood** ⟦from obs. notion that blood is the medium of heredity⟧ **1** the relationship between offspring of the same parents **2** unmixed breed or race

☆**full-blood·ed** (fool′blud′id) ***adj.*** **1** of unmixed breed or race; purebred: also **full′-blood′** **2** vigorous; lusty **3** genuine; authentic **4** rich and full

full-blown (fool′blōn′) ***adj.*** **1** in full bloom; open: said of flowers **2** fully grown or developed; matured *[a full-blown* case of AIDS*]* **3** having all the necessary features; thorough

full-bod·ied (fool′bäd′ēd) ***adj.*** **1** having a rich flavor and much strength *[a full-bodied* wine*]* **2** large or broad in body or substance

full-bore (fool′bôr′) ***adv.*** to the greatest degree or extent; at full speed, with the greatest power or effort, etc. *[a factory running full-bore]* —***adj.*** complete or thorough; all-out *[a full-bore* effort*]*

full-court press (fool′kôrt′) *Basketball* a PRESS[1] (***n.*** 8) over the entire length of the court

full dress formal clothes worn on important or ceremonial occasions; esp., formal evening clothes

full-dress (fool′dres′) ***adj.*** **1** of or requiring full dress; formal *[a full-dress* dinner*]* **2** complete and thorough *[a full-dress* inquiry*]*

full·er[1] (fool′ər) ***n.*** ⟦ME < OE *fullere* < L *fullo,* prob. < IE **bheld-,* to strike > BOLT[1]⟧ a person whose work is to full cloth: see FULL[2]

full·er[2] (fool′ər) ***n.*** ⟦< ? obs. *full,* to make full, complete < FULL[1]⟧ **1** a tool used by blacksmiths to hammer grooves into iron **2** a groove so made

Ful·ler (fool′ər) **1 R(ichard) Buck·min·ster** (buk′min stər) 1895-1983; U.S. engineer, inventor, & philosopher **2 (Sarah) Margaret** (*Marchioness Ossoli*) 1810-50; U.S. writer, critic, & social reformer **3 Melville Wes·ton** (wes′tən) 1833-1910; chief justice of the U.S. (1888-1910)

ful·ler·ene (fool′ə rēn′, fool′ə rēn′) ***n.*** ⟦after Buckminster FULLER + -ENE⟧ any of a class of hollow, tube-shaped or ball-shaped molecules, consisting of 32 or more carbon atoms and having extraordinary strength and stability

fuller's earth a highly absorbent, opaque clay used to remove grease from woolen cloth in fulling, to clarify fats and oils, etc.

Ful·ler·ton (fool′ər tən) ⟦after G. H. *Fullerton* (1853-1929), railroad agent, land developer, & a founder of the town (1887)⟧ city in SW Calif.: suburb of Los Angeles

full-fash·ioned (fo͝ol′fash′ənd) ***adj.*** knitted to conform to the contours of the body: said as of hosiery or sweaters
full-fig·ured (fo͝ol′fig′yərd) ***adj.*** having a plump figure [lingerie for the *full-figured* woman]
full-fledged (fo͝ol′flejd′) ***adj.*** **1** having a complete set of feathers: said of birds **2** completely developed or trained; of full rank or status **3** having all the necessary features; thoroughgoing
full-fron·tal (fo͝ol′frunt′'l) ***adj.*** **1** fully facing or exposing the front; specif., designating or characterized by nudity, as in a film, in which the pubes is exposed **2** completely frank or candid
full-grown (fo͝ol′grōn′) ***adj.*** having reached full size or maturity; fully grown
☆**full house** *Poker* a hand containing three of a kind and a pair, as three jacks and two fives: it ranks just above a flush and below four of a kind
full-length (fo͝ol′leŋkth′, -leŋth′) ***adj.*** **1** made or designed to show the entire length of an object or of a person's figure: said of a portrait or mirror **2** extending to or nearly to the floor [a *full-length* gown] **3** of the original, unabridged, or standard length; not shortened [a *full-length* novel]
full marks [Brit.] **1** the highest grade or rating possible, as for schoolwork **2** figuratively, very high praise
full moon **1** the phase of the moon when it is on the side of the earth away from the sun, with its entire face reflecting sunlight to the earth **2** the time of month when such a moon is seen
full-mouthed (-mouthd′, -moutht′) ***adj.*** **1** having a full set of teeth: said of cattle, etc. **2** uttered loudly
full nelson ⟦< surname *Nelson*⟧ *Wrestling* a hold in which both arms are placed under the opponent's armpits from behind with the hands pressed against the back of the opponent's neck
full·ness (fo͝ol′nis) ***n.*** ⟦ME *fulnesse*⟧ the quality or state of being full —**in the fullness of time** [Literary] **1** at the appointed or allotted time **2** eventually
full professor PROFESSOR (sense 2*a*)
full-rigged (fo͝ol′rigd′) ***adj.*** **1** having three or more masts, all carrying square sails **2** fully equipped
full sail **1** the complete number of sails **2** with every sail set **3** with maximum speed and energy
full-scale (fo͝ol′skāl′) ***adj.*** **1** of or according to the original or standard scale or measure [a *full-scale* drawing] **2** to the utmost limit, degree, etc.; complete and thorough; all-out [*full-scale* war]
full-serve (fo͝ol′sʉrv′) ***adj.*** [Informal] *short for* FULL-SERVICE
full-serv·ice (fo͝ol′sʉr′vis) ***adj.*** **1** offering the complete range of services for a business of its type [a *full-service* bank] **2** offering service; not self-service [a *full-service* gas station]
full-size (fo͝ol′sīz′) ***adj.*** **1** of or being the usual or standard size, length, etc. **2** of or being a large size [a *full-size* sedan] **3** designating or for a bed that is 54 by 75 inches Also **full′-sized′** (-sīzd′)
full stop a period (punctuation mark)
full-throat·ed (fo͝ol′thrōt′id) ***adj.*** **1** having or producing a full, deep, or rich sound; sonorous **2** complete and unmitigated; thoroughgoing [a *full-throated* opponent of the plan]
full throttle *used in the phrase* **at full throttle**, at full speed or with great intensity
full-throt·tle (fo͝ol′thrät′'l) ***adj., adv.*** (going, acting, happening, etc.) at full speed or with great intensity
full-tilt (fo͝ol′tilt′) ***adj., adv.*** ⟦< (AT) FULL TILT (see phr. under TILT[1])⟧ at full speed or with the greatest energy, dedication, etc.: also, for ***adv.***, **full tilt**
full time as a full-time employee, student, etc. [to work *full time*]
full-time (fo͝ol′tīm′) ***adj.*** designating, of, or engaged in work, study, etc. for certain time periods regarded as constituting one's full regular working hours
full·y (fo͝ol′ē) ***adv.*** ⟦ME *fulli* < OE *fullice* < *full*, FULL[1]⟧ **1** to the full; completely; entirely; thoroughly **2** abundantly; amply **3** at least [*fully* two hours later]
ful·mar (fo͝ol′mər) ***n.*** ⟦ON < *fūll*, foul, unpleasant + *mār*, sea gull⟧ any of various tubenose birds (family Procellariidae); esp., a gray sea bird (*Fulmarus glacialis*) common in arctic regions
ful·mi·nant (ful′mə nənt) ***adj.*** ⟦L *fulminans*, prp.: see fol.⟧ **1** fulminating **2** *Med.* developing suddenly and severely, as a disease
ful·mi·nate (ful′mə nāt′, fo͝ol′-) ***vi.*** **-nat′ed**, **-nat′ing** ⟦ME *fulminaten* < L *fulminatus*, pp. of *fulminare*, to flash or strike with lightning < *fulmen*, lightning, thunderbolt, akin to *fulgere*: see FULGENT⟧ **1** [Archaic] to thunder and lighten **2** to explode with sudden violence; detonate **3** to express strong disapproval; inveigh: usually with *against* [to *fulminate* against political corruption] —***vt.*** **1** to cause to explode **2** to shout forth (denunciations, decrees, etc.) —***n.*** an explosive salt of fulminic acid, containing the monovalent negative radical CNO and used in detonators and percussion caps —**ful′mi·na′tion** ***n.*** —**ful′mi·na′tor** ***n.***
fulminating powder an explosive material used as a detonator, esp. one containing mercuric fulminate
ful·mine (ful′min) ***vi., vt.*** **-mined**, **-min·ing** ⟦Fr *fulminer*⟧ *archaic var. of* FULMINATE
ful·min·ic acid (ful min′ik) ⟦< L *fulmen*, lightning (see FULMINATE) + -IC⟧ an unstable isomer of cyanic acid, known chiefly in the form of highly explosive, shock-sensitive salts used as detonators
ful·ness (fo͝ol′nis) ***n.*** *alt. sp. of* FULLNESS
ful·some (fo͝ol′səm) ***adj.*** ⟦ME *fulsom*, abundant, disgustingly excessive < *ful*, FULL[1] + *-som*, -SOME[1], but infl. by *ful*, FOUL⟧ **1** disgusting or offensive, esp. because excessive or insincere [*fulsome* praise] **2** ⟦apparent revival of the orig. sense, obs. since 16th c.⟧ full; ample; abundant: usage objected to by some —**ful′some·ly** ***adv.*** —**ful′some·ness** ***n.***
Ful·ton (fo͝ol′tən), **Robert** 1765-1815; U.S. inventor & engineer: designer of the first commercially successful U.S. steamboat, the *Clermont* (launched 1807)
ful·vous (ful′vəs) ***adj.*** ⟦L *fulvus* < IE base **bhlē-wos* > BLUE, L *flavus*, yellow⟧ dull reddish-yellow or brownish-yellow; tawny
☆**Fu Man·chu (mustache)** (fo͞o′man cho͞o′) ⟦after *Fu-Manchu*, a character usually depicted with such a mustache, in a series of novels by Eng author Sax Rohmer (pseud. of A. S. Ward) (1883-1959)⟧ a mustache that droops down along the sides of the mouth, usually to the chin or below
fu·mar·ic acid (fyo͞o mar′ik) ⟦< ModL *Fumaria*, fumitory (< L *fumarium*: see fol.) + -IC⟧ a colorless, crystalline, unsaturated organic acid, HOOCCH:CHCOOH, occurring in various plants or produced synthetically from maleic acid: used in making resins, as a stabilizer for foods, etc.
fu·ma·role (fyo͞o′mə rōl′) ***n.*** ⟦It *fumaruolo* < LL *fumariolum*, smoke hole, dim. of LL *fumarium*, chimney < *fumus*, smoke: see FUME⟧ a vent in a volcanic area, from which smoke and gases arise —**fu′ma·rol′ic** (-räl′ik) ***adj.***
fum·ble (fum′bəl) ***vi., vt.*** **-bled**, **-bling** ⟦var. of ME *famelen*, prob. < ON *famla*, akin to Du *fommeln*, Ger *fummeln*⟧ **1** to search (*for* a thing) by feeling about awkwardly with the hands; grope clumsily **2** to handle (a thing) clumsily or unskillfully; bungle **3** to lose one's grasp on (a football, etc.) while trying to catch or hold it **4** to make (one's way) clumsily or by groping —***n.*** **1** the act or fact of fumbling **2** a football, etc. that has been fumbled —**fum′bler** ***n.*** —**fum′bling·ly** ***adv.***
fume (fyo͞om) ***n.*** ⟦ME < OFr *fum* < L *fumus* < IE base **dheu-*, to blow, smoke, be turbid > DULL⟧ **1** [*often pl.*] a gas, smoke, or vapor, esp. if offensive or suffocating **2** [Rare] an outburst of anger, annoyance, etc. **3** *Chem.* a number of solid or liquid particles within a gas —***vi.*** **fumed**, **fum′ing** ⟦ME *fumen* < OFr *fumer* < L *fumare* < *fumus*⟧ **1** to give off gas, smoke, or vapor **2** to rise up or pass off in fumes **3** to feel, show, or give way to anger, annoyance, etc. —***vt.*** **1** to expose to fumes **2** to give off as fumes —**fum′ing·ly** ***adv.***
fu·mé blanc (fo͞o′mā bläŋk′, fyo͞o′-; *Fr* fü mā blän′) SAUVIGNON BLANC (sense 2): name used by some California wineries
fumed oak oak wood given a darker color and more distinct marking by exposure to ammonia fumes
fu·met (fyo͞o mā′) ***n.*** ⟦Fr, lit., aroma as of meat being cooked < *fumer*, FUME (***vi.***)⟧ a rich, concentrated broth made by boiling the bones of fish, chicken, game birds, etc. with wine and herbs: used in sauces and in braising
fu·mi·gant (fyo͞o′mə gənt) ***n.*** ⟦< L *fumigans*, prp. of *fumigare*⟧ any substance used in fumigating
fu·mi·gate (fyo͞o′mə gāt′) ***vt.*** **-gat′ed**, **-gat′ing** ⟦< L *fumigatus*, pp. of *fumigare*, to smoke < *fumus*, smoke (see FUME) + *agere*, to do: see ACT[1]⟧ **1** to expose to the action of fumes, esp. in order to disinfect or kill the vermin in **2** [Archaic] to perfume —**fu′mi·ga′tion** ***n.*** —☆**fu′mi·ga′tor** ***n.***
fu·mi·to·ry (fyo͞o′mə tôr′ē) ***n.***, *pl.* **-ries** ⟦ME *fumeter* < OFr *fumeterre* < ML *fumus terrae*, lit., smoke of the earth (see FUME & TERRAIN): so called from its smell⟧ any of a genus (*Fumaria*) of plants of the fumitory family, with watery juice and spurred flowers, formerly used in medicine —***adj.*** designating a family (Fumariaceae, order Papaverales) of dicotyledonous plants, including the dicentras and corydalises
fum·y (fyo͞o′mē) ***adj.*** **fum′i·er**, **fum′i·est** full of fumes; producing fumes; vaporous
fun (fun) ***n.*** ⟦< ME *fonne*, a fool, foolish, or *fonnen*, to be foolish < ?⟧ **1** *a)* lively, joyous play or playfulness; amusement, sport, recreation, etc. *b)* enjoyment or pleasure **2** a source or cause of amusement or merriment, as an amusing person or thing —☆***adj.*** [Informal] intended for, or giving, pleasure or amusement [a *fun* gift] —***vi.*** **funned**, **fun′ning** ⟦< the ***n.***⟧ [Informal] to have or make fun; play or joke —**for** (or **in**) **fun** just for amusement; not seriously —**like fun!** [Slang] by no means! not at all!: used to express emphatic negation or doubt —**make fun of** to mock or tease laughingly; ridicule: also **poke fun at**
Fun·a·fu·ti (fo͞on′ə fo͞o′tē) capital of Tuvalu
fu·nam·bu·list (fyo͞o nam′byo͞o list) ***n.*** ⟦< L *funambulus* < *funis*, a rope + *ambulare* + -IST[1]⟧ a tightrope walker
Fun·chal (fo͞on shäl′) capital of Madeira, Portugal
func·tion (fuŋk′shən) ***n.*** ⟦OFr < L *functio* < pp. of *fungi*, to perform < IE base **bheug-*, to enjoy > Sans *bhuṅktē*, (he) enjoys⟧ **1** the normal or characteristic action of anything; esp., any of the natural, specialized actions of a system, organ, or part of an animal or plant [the procreative *function*] **2** a special duty or performance required in the course of work or activity [the *function* of an auditor, the *function* of the brakes] **3** occupation or employment **4** a formal ceremony or elaborate social occasion **5** a thing that depends on and varies with something else **6** *a)* an action which is part of a series leading to a resulting action *b)* an operational instruction for programming an electronic device, as a digital watch, computer, etc.; also, an operation performed by such a device as a result of such an instruction **7** any of the roles that a linguistic form can fulfill in an utterance **8** *Math.* an association between two sets in which each element of one set has one assigned element in the other set: any selected element becomes the independent variable and its as-

sociated element is the dependent variable [y = f(x) means y is a *function* of x] **—*vi.*** **1** to act in a required or expected manner; work **2** to have a function; serve or be used (*as*) **—func′tion·less *adj.***

SYN.—function is the broad, general term for the natural, required, or expected activity of a person or thing [the *function* of the liver, of the public schools, etc.]; **office**, in this connection, refers to the function of a person, as determined by his position, profession, or employment [the *office* of a priest]; **duty** is applied to a task necessary in or appropriate to one's occupation, rank, status, etc. and carries a strong connotation of obligation [the *duties* of a vicar]; **capacity** refers to a specific function or status, not necessarily the usual or customary one [the judge spoke to him in the *capacity* of a friend]

func·tion·al (fuŋk′shə nəl) ***adj.*** **1** of or relating to a function or functions **2** *a)* performing or able to perform a function *b)* useful or intended to be useful **3** *Med.* affecting a function of some organ without apparent structural or organic changes [a *functional* disease] **—func′tion·al·ly *adv.***

functional food a food or beverage product to which vitamins, phytochemicals, etc. have been added so as to increase its health-promoting properties

☆**functional illiterate** a person who does not meet minimum standards of literacy and thus finds it difficult or impossible to carry out everyday activities that require reading or writing

func·tion·al·ism (fuŋk′shə nəl iz′əm) ***n.*** **1** the theory or practice in art, architecture, and design that the structure or design of anything should be manifestly related to its function **2** the social theory which holds that a society's beliefs, behavior, social structure, etc. are interrelated and function as a means to achieve its common goals and protect its social values **—func′tion·al·ist *n., adj.*** **—func′tion·al·is′tic *adj.***

func·tion·al·i·ty (fuŋk′shə nal′ə tē) ***n.***, *pl.* **-ties** **1** the quality or state of being functional; usefulness **2** an operation or set of operations performed as by software or by an electronic device

functional shift the conversion of a linguistic form from one part of speech to another, as the use of a noun as a verb

func·tion·ar·y (fuŋk′shə ner′ē) ***n.***, *pl.* **-ar′ies** ⟦FUNCTION + -ARY, after Fr *fonctionnaire*⟧ a person who performs a certain function; esp., an official

function word a word, as an article or conjunction, having little or no lexical meaning but used to show syntactic relation

fund (fund) ***n.*** ⟦L *fundus*, bottom, land, estate (< IE **bhundhos* < base **bhudh-* > BOTTOM): meaning infl. by Fr *fond*, stock, provision < same source⟧ **1** a supply that can be drawn upon; stock; store [a *fund* of good humor] **2** *a)* a sum of money set aside for some particular purpose *b)* an organization that administers such a fund *c)* [*pl.*] money available for use, as in a checking account **3** [*pl.*] the British national debt, regarded as stock held by investors: with *the* **—*vt.*** **1** to provide money for the payment of principal or interest on (a debt) **2** to put or convert into a long-term debt that bears interest **3** to put in a fund; accumulate **4** to provide funds or funding for

fun·da·ment (fun′də mənt) ***n.*** ⟦ME *foundement* < OFr < L *fundamentum* < *fundare*, to lay the bottom < *fundus*: see prec.⟧ **1** a base or foundation **2** the buttocks **3** the anus

fun·da·men·tal (fun′də ment′'l) ***adj.*** ⟦LME < ML *fundamentalis* < L *fundamentum*: see prec.⟧ **1** of or forming a foundation or basis; basic; essential [the *fundamental* rules of art] **2** relating to what is basic; radical [a *fundamental* alteration] **3** on which others are based; primary; original [a *fundamental* type] **4** most important; chief [his *fundamental* needs] **5** *Music a)* designating or of the lowest, or root, tone of a chord *b)* designating the prime or main tone of a harmonic series **6** *Physics* designating or of a fundamental **—*n.*** **1** a principle, theory, law, etc. serving as a basis; essential part **2** *Music a)* the lowest, or root, tone of a chord *b)* the prime or main tone of a harmonic series **3** *Physics* the lowest frequency at which a system, as an air column or stretched string, will freely vibrate **—fun′da·men′tal·ly *adv.***

fundamental bass *Music* a theoretical bass line of the roots of a succession of chords

☆**fun·da·men·tal·ism** (-iz′əm) ***n.*** [*sometimes* **F-**] **1** *a)* religious beliefs based on a literal interpretation of the Bible *b)* the 20th-cent. movement among some American Protestants, based on these beliefs **2** any strict adherence to or interpretation of a doctrine, set of principles, etc. **—fun′da·men′tal·ist *n., adj.***

fundamental law a law or laws, as a constitution, regarded as basic and, often, irrevocable by ordinary judicial or legislative action; organic law

fundamental particle *Particle Physics* ELEMENTARY PARTICLE

fun·der (fun′dər) ***n.*** a provider of funds, as for the support of a charitable or nonprofit organization

fund·ing (fun′diŋ) ***n.*** **1** money set aside to pay for or finance something **2** the arranging for or providing of such money

fund·rais·er (fund′rā′zər) ***n.*** **1** a person or organization engaged in fundraising **2** an event organized for the purpose of fundraising Also **fund′-rais′er *n.***

fund·rais·ing (fund′rā′ziŋ) ***n.*** the act or occupation of soliciting money for charitable organizations, political parties, etc.: also written **fund-raising**

fun·dus (fun′dəs) ***n.***, *pl.* **fun′di′** (-dī′) ⟦ModL < L, bottom: see FUND⟧ *Anat.* the base of a hollow organ, or the part farthest from the opening, as that part of the uterus farthest from the cervix **—fun′dic *adj.***

Fun·dy (fun′dē), **Bay of** arm of the Atlantic, between New Brunswick & Nova Scotia, Canada: *c.* 140 mi (225 km) long: noted for its high tides of 60-70 ft (18-21 m)

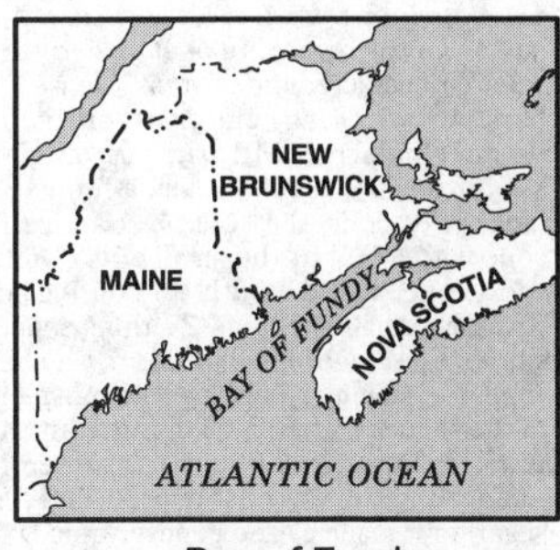

Bay of Fundy

Fü·nen (fü′nən) *Ger. name for* FYN

fu·ner·al (fyoo͞′nər əl) ***adj.*** ⟦ME < LL *funeralis* < L *funus* (gen. *funeris*), a funeral < ? IE **dheu-*, to pass away, DIE[1]⟧ of or having to do with a funeral **—*n.*** ⟦ME *funerelles* (pl.) < OFr *funerailles* < ML *funeralia* < neut. pl. of *funeralis*⟧ **1** the sequence of rituals and ceremonies connected with the burial or cremation of a dead person **2** the procession accompanying the body to the place of burial or cremation —☆**be someone's funeral** [Informal] to be someone's problem, worry, etc. and not another's

☆**funeral director** a person, usually a licensed embalmer, who manages a funeral home

☆**funeral home** a business establishment where the bodies of the dead are prepared for burial or cremation and where viewings and funeral services can be held: also, esp. formerly, **funeral parlor**

fu·ner·ar·y (fyoo͞′nər er′ē) ***adj.*** ⟦LL *funerarius*⟧ of or having to do with a funeral or burial

fu·ne·re·al (fyoo͞ nir′ē əl) ***adj.*** ⟦< L *funereus* < *funus* (see FUNERAL) + -AL⟧ of or suitable for a funeral; esp., sad and solemn; gloomy; dismal **—fu·ne′re·al·ly *adv.***

fun·fair (fun′fer′) ***n.*** [Brit.] an amusement park or carnival with rides, games, sideshows, etc.

fun·gal (fuŋ′gəl) ***adj.*** of, like, or caused by a fungus or fungi

fun·ghi (foon′gē) ***pl.n.*** ⟦It⟧ mushrooms

fun·gi (fun′jī′, fuŋ′gī′) ***n.*** *alt. pl. of* FUNGUS

fun·gi- (fun′ji, -jə; fun′gi, -gə) *combining form* fungus or fungi [*fungicide*]: also, before a vowel, **fung-**

fun·gi·ble (fun′jə bəl) ***adj.*** ⟦ML *fungibilis* < L *fungi*, to perform: see FUNCTION⟧ *Law* designating movable goods, as grain or lumber, units or portions of which are interchangeable, as in discharging a debt **—*n.*** ⟦ME (*res*) *fungibilis*⟧ a fungible thing **—fun′gi·bil′i·ty *n.***

fun·gi·cide (fun′jə sīd′, fuŋ′gə-) ***n.*** ⟦FUNGI- + -CIDE⟧ any substance that kills fungi or their spores **—fun′gi·ci′dal *adj.***

fun·gi·form (-fôrm′) ***adj.*** ⟦FUNGI- + -FORM⟧ having the form of a fungus

fun·gi·stat (fun′ji stat′, fuŋ′gə-) ***n.*** any substance that inhibits the growth of fungi **—fun′gi·stat′ic *adj.***

☆**fun·go** (fuŋ′gō) ***n.***, *pl.* **-goes** ⟦< ? Scot *fung*, to toss⟧ *Baseball* a batted ball, esp. a fly ball, hit for fielding practice: the ball is not pitched, but rather is tossed into the air by the batter and then struck as it descends

☆**fungo bat** a relatively long, thin bat specially designed for hitting fungoes

fun·goid (fuŋ′goid) ***adj.*** like or characteristic of a fungus **—*n.*** a fungus

fun·gous (fuŋ′gəs) ***adj.*** ⟦ME < L *fungosus*, spongy < *fungus*): see fol.⟧ FUNGAL

fun·gus (fuŋ′gəs) ***n.***, *pl.* **fun·gi** (fun′jī′, fuŋ′gī′) or **fun′gus·es** ⟦L, a mushroom, fungus < Gr dial. (Attic) *sphongos*, var. of Gr *spongos*, SPONGE⟧ **1** any of a large division (Eumycota) of thallophytes, including molds, mildews, mushrooms, rusts, and smuts, that are parasites on living organisms or that feed upon dead organic material: fungi lack chlorophyll, true roots, stems, and leaves, and reproduce by means of spores: in some systems of biological classification, these organisms are placed in a separate kingdom (Fungi) and are not considered to be plants **2** something that grows suddenly and rapidly like a fungus **—*adj.*** of, like, or caused by a fungus; fungous

☆**fun house** an attraction at an amusement park consisting of a series of rooms and passageways with sloping or moving floors, distorting mirrors, and other devices designed to surprise or amuse

fu·ni·cle (fyoo͞′ni kəl) ***n.*** ⟦L *funiculus*, dim. of *funis*, a cord, rope⟧ a little cord or fiber; specif., a funiculus

fu·nic·u·lar (fyoo͞ nik′yoo͞ lər) ***adj.*** ⟦< L *funiculus* (see prec.) + -AR⟧ **1** of or like a funiculus or funiculi **2** of, worked by, or hanging from a rope or cable **—*n.*** a mountain railway on which counterbalanced cars on parallel sets of rails are pulled up and lowered by cables: also **funicular railway**

fu·nic·u·lus (fyoo͞ nik′yoo͞ ləs) ***n.***, *pl.* **-li′** (-lī′) ⟦L, small cord, dim. of *funis*, a cord, rope⟧ **1** *Anat.* any cordlike structure; esp., *a)* any of various bundles of white matter in the spinal cord *b)* [Obs.] the umbilical or spermatic cord **2** *Bot.* the slender stalk of an ovule or seed **—fu·nic′u·late** (-lit, -lāt′) ***adj.***

funk[1] (fuŋk) [Informal] ***n.*** ⟦< ? Fl *fonck*, dismay⟧ **1** the condition of being greatly afraid or in a panic **2** a low, depressed mood: also **blue funk** **—*vi.*** [Old-fashioned] to be afraid **—*vt.*** [Chiefly Brit.] to avoid as because of fear; shrink from

funk[2] (fuŋk) ***n.*** ⟦back-form. < fol.⟧ **1** [Obs.] a musty odor, as of moldy tobacco ☆**2** funky jazz ☆**3** a form of rhythm and blues originating in the 1970s in which highly syncopated polyrhythms are combined with a prominent, jerky bass line, minimal harmonic structure, and declamatory vocalizing

funk·y (fuŋ′kē) ***adj.*** **-i·er, -i·est** ⟦orig. black slang, lit., smelly, hence musty, earthy < obs. *funk*, smell, smoke, prob. < Fr dial. *funkier*, to smoke < VL **fumicare*, for L *fumigare*: see FUMIGATE⟧ **1** [Dial.] smelly; musty ☆**2** *Jazz* having an earthy quality or style derived from early blues or gospel music ☆**3** of or characteristic of FUNK[2] (sense 3) ☆**4** [Slang] unconventional, offbeat, etc. ☆**5** [Slang] emotional or soulful —**funk′i·ness *n.***

fun·nel (fun′əl) ***n.*** ⟦ME *fonel* < (prob. via an OFr form) Prov *fonilh, enfonilh* < L *fundibulum, infundibulum*, a funnel < *infundere*, to pour in < *in-*, IN-[1] + *fundere*, to pour: see FOUND[3]⟧ **1** an instrument consisting of an inverted cone with a hole at the small end, or a tapering or cylindrical tube with a wide, cone-shaped mouth, for pouring liquids and powders into containers that have small openings **2** a thing shaped like a funnel **3** *a)* a cylindrical smokestack, as of a steamship *b)* a chimney or flue — ***vi., vt.*** **-neled** or **-nelled, -nel·ing** or **-nel·ling 1** to move or pour through a funnel **2** to form in the shape of a funnel **3** to move into a channel or to a central point

☆**funnel cake** a round, flat cake made from batter that is poured through a funnel or spout into hot fat, fried, and then often sprinkled with powdered sugar: first made by the Pennsylvania Dutch

funnel cloud a slender, rotating, funnel-shaped cloud extending downward from a cumulus or cumulonimbus cloud: such a cloud becomes a tornado if it contacts the ground while rotating at very high speed

fun·nel·form (-fôrm′) ***adj.*** shaped like a funnel

fun·nies (fun′ēz) ***pl.n.*** [Informal] **1** comic strips **2** the section or supplement of a newspaper containing comic strips: with *the*

fun·ny (fun′ē) ***adj.*** **-ni·er, -ni·est** ⟦see FUN & -Y[2]⟧ **1** causing laughter; laughable; amusing; humorous **2** out of the ordinary, esp. in a puzzling or suspicious way **3** [Informal] peculiar, eccentric, crazy, etc. —***adv.*** [Informal] in a funny manner —☆***n.*** *pl.* **-nies** [Informal] a joke or witticism —☆**get funny with** [Slang] to be impudent to —**fun′ni·ly *adv.*** —**fun′ni·ness *n.***

SYN.—**funny** is the simple, general term for anything that excites laughter or mirth; **laughable** applies to that which is fit to be laughed at and may connote contempt or scorn; that is **amusing** which provokes smiles, laughter, or pleasure by its pleasant, entertaining quality; that is **droll** which amuses one because of its quaintness or strangeness, or its wry or waggish humor; **comic** is applied to that which contains the elements of comedy (in a dramatic or literary sense) and amuses one in a thoughtful way; **comical** suggests that which evokes laughter of a more spontaneous, unrestrained kind; **farcical** suggests a broad comical quality based on nonsense, extravagantly boisterous humor, etc.

funny bone ⟦from its reaction to impact, but prob. also suggested by the pun on *humerus/humorous*⟧ **1** a place on the inner elbow where the ulnar nerve passes close to the surface: a sharp impact at this place causes a strange, tingling sensation in the arm **2** inclination to laughter; (one's) risibilities

funny book [Informal] COMIC BOOK

☆**funny car** a dragster that resembles a standard automobile except in having large rear tires and a one-piece fiberglass body that must be raised for access

funny farm [Slang] an institution for hospitalizing the mentally ill

fun·ny·man (fun′ē man′) ***n.***, *pl.* **-men′** (-men′) a comedian, often, specif., one who does stand-up comedy

☆**funny money** [Informal] **1** bills, vouchers, etc. resembling or used as a substitute for legal currency **2** money that is illegal or that is tainted by illegal activity; specif., counterfeit money **3** currency, securities, etc. regarded as being of uncertain or decreasing value, as because of inflationary fiscal policy, highly leveraged financing, etc.

☆**funny paper** [*also pl.*] [Informal] FUNNIES (sense 2)

fur[1] (fʉr) ***n.*** ⟦ME *furre*, prob. contr. < *furrure*, fur lining or blanket OFr *fourrure* < *fuerre*, sheath, lining < Frank **fodr*, akin to Ger *futter* < IE base **po-*, to tend flocks, cover, protect > Gr *poimēn*, Sans *pālá-*, shepherd⟧ **1** the soft, thick hair covering the body of many mammals **2** a skin bearing such hair, when stripped and processed for making, lining, or trimming garments; dressed pelt **3** any garment, neckpiece, trimming, etc. made of such skins **4** any furlike or fuzzy coating, as diseased matter on the tongue in illness —***adj.*** of or having to do with fur —***vt.*** **furred, fur′ring 1** to line, cover, make, or trim with fur **2** to coat with any smooth, furlike deposit **3** to use furring in constructing (a floor, wall, etc.) —***vi.*** to become coated with a deposit —☆**make the fur fly** [Informal] **1** to cause dissension or fighting **2** to accomplish much quickly

fur[2] *abbrev.* furlong(s)

fu·ran (fyoo̅′ran′, fyoo̅ ran′; fyoor′an′) ***n.*** ⟦contr. < FURFURAN⟧ a colorless, liquid heterocyclic compound, C_4H_4O, prepared from wood tar or furfural, and used in organic synthesis

fur·be·low (fʉr′bə lō′) ***n.*** ⟦altered (by assoc. with FUR[2]) < Prov *farbello*, a fringe, flounce, var. of Fr *falbala*, furbelow⟧ **1** a flounce or ruffle **2** a showy, useless decoration or elaboration: *usually used in pl.* —***vt.*** to decorate with or as with furbelows

fur·bish (fʉr′bish) ***vt.*** ⟦ME *furbishen* < extended stem of OFr *forbir* < WGmc **furbjan*, to clean > MHG *vürben*⟧ **1** [Now Rare] to brighten by rubbing or scouring; polish; burnish **2** to make usable or attractive again; refurbish: usually with *up* —**fur′bish·er *n.***

☆**Fur·bish lousewort** (fʉr′bish) ⟦after Kate *Furbish* (1834-1931), U.S. naturalist & artist who discovered it (1880)⟧ a rare lousewort (*Pedicularis furbishiae*) with greenish-yellow flowers, found in Maine and Canada

fur·cate (fʉr′kāt′; *for adj., also,* -kit) ***adj.*** ⟦ML *furcatus*, cloven < L *furca*, a fork⟧ forked —***vi.*** **-cat′ed, -cat′ing** to branch; fork —**fur′cate′ly *adv.*** —**fur·ca′tion *n.***

fur·cu·la (fʉr′kyoo̅ lə) ***n.***, *pl.* **-lae** (-lē, -lī′) ⟦ModL, forked support, dim. of L *furca*, a fork⟧ *Anat., Zool.* any forked part or organ, as the wishbone of birds or the forked tail of certain springing insects —**fur′cu·lar** (-lər) ***adj.***

fur·cu·lum (fʉr′kyoo̅ ləm) ***n.***, *pl.* **-la** (-lə) ⟦ModL, dim. of L *furca*, a fork⟧ FURCULA

fur·fur (fʉr′fər) ***n.***, *pl.* **-fu·res′** (-fyoo̅ rēz′, -fə-) ⟦L, bran, redupl. < IE base **gher-*, to rub > Gr *cheras*, gravel⟧ **1** dandruff; scurf **2** [*pl.*] scaly bits; esp., dandruff scales

fur·fu·ra·ceous (fʉr′fyoo̅ rā′shəs, -fə-) ***adj.*** ⟦LL *furfuraceus*: see prec.⟧ **1** of or like bran **2** covered with dandruff

fur·fu·ral (fʉr′fyoo̅ ral′, fʉr′fyoo̅ ral′; -fə-) ***n.*** ⟦FURFUR + -AL⟧ a colorless, sweet-smelling, oily liquid, C_4H_3OCHO, produced from corncobs, oat hulls, and other cereal wastes, used as a solvent and to make dyes, lacquers, synthetic resins, etc.

fur·fu·ran (fʉr′fyoo̅ ran′, fʉr′fyoo̅ ran′; -fə-) ***n.*** ⟦prec. + -AN⟧ FURAN

Fu·ries (fyoor′ēz) ***pl.n.*** ⟦ME < L *Furiae*, pl. of *furia*, FURY⟧ *Class. Myth.* the three terrible female spirits with snaky hair (Alecto, Tisiphone, and Megaera) who punish the doers of unavenged crimes

fu·ri·ous (fyoor′ē əs) ***adj.*** ⟦ME < OFr *furieus* < L *furiosus*⟧ **1** full of fury or wild rage; violently angry **2** moving violently; violently overpowering [*a furious* attack] **3** very great; intense [with *furious* speed] —**fu′ri·ous·ly *adv.*** —**fu′ri·ous·ness *n.***

furl (fʉrl) ***vt.*** ⟦< OFr *ferlier* < *fermlier*, to tie up < *ferm* (< L *firmus*, FIRM[1]) + *lier* (< L *ligare*, to tie: see LIGATURE)⟧ to roll up tightly and make secure, as a flag to a staff or a sail to a spar —***vi.*** to become curled or rolled up —***n.*** **1** a roll or coil of something furled **2** a furling or being furled

fur·long (fʉr′lôŋ′) ***n.*** ⟦ME < OE *furlang*, a measure, lit., length of a furrow < *furh*, FURROW + *lang*, LONG[1]⟧ a unit of length in the FPS system, equal to 220 yards or ⅛ statute mile (201.168 meters): one square furlong equals ten acres: abbrev. *fur*

fur·lough (fʉr′lō) ***n.*** ⟦earlier *furloff* < Du *verlof*, modeled on Ger *verlaub* < MHG *verlouben*, to permit < *ver-*, FOR- + *loube*, permission, akin to LEAVE[2]⟧ **1** a leave of absence; esp., a leave granted to military enlisted personnel for a specified period **2** a period of time, specif. a day (**furlough day**), in which business is suspended and employees are not paid, as a means to cut labor costs —☆***vt.*** **1** to grant a furlough to **2** to impose a furlough on (employees); esp., to lay off temporarily

fur·men·ty (fʉr′mən tē) ***n.*** FRUMENTY: also **fur′me·ty** (-mə tē) or **fur′mi·ty** (-mə tē)

fur·nace (fʉr′nəs) ***n.*** ⟦ME *furnaise* < OFr *fornais* < L *fornax* (gen. *fornacis*), furnace: see WARM⟧ **1** an enclosed chamber or structure in which heat is produced, as by burning fuel, for warming a building, reducing ores and metals, etc. **2** any extremely hot place **3** a grueling test or trial

Fur·ness (fʉr′nis), **Horace Howard** 1833-1912; U.S. Shakespearean scholar

fur·nish (fʉr′nish) ***vt.*** ⟦ME *furnishen* < extended stem of OFr *furnir* (Fr *fournir*) < Frank **frumjan* (akin to OE *framian*, Ger *frommen*, to benefit), caus. < **fruma* (akin to ON *frami*, profit): for IE base see FROM⟧ **1** to supply, provide, or equip *with* whatever is necessary or useful; esp., to put furniture into (a room, apartment, etc.) **2** to supply; provide; give [to *furnish* information] —**fur′nish·er *n.***

SYN.—**furnish**, as compared here, implies the provision of all the things requisite for a particular service, action, etc. [to *furnish* a house]; to **equip** is to furnish with what is requisite for efficient action [a car *equipped* with overdrive]; to **outfit** is to equip completely with the articles needed for a specific undertaking, occupation, etc. [to *outfit* a hunting expedition]; **appoint**, a formal word now generally used in the past participle, implies the provision of all the requisites and accessories for proper service [a well-*appointed* studio]; **arm** literally implies equipment with weapons, etc. for war but, in extended use, connotes provision with what is necessary to meet any circumstance

fur·nish·ings (fʉr′nish iŋz) ***pl.n.*** **1** the furniture, carpets, and the like for a room, apartment, etc. **2** articles or accessories of dress; things to wear [men's *furnishings*]

fur·ni·ture (fʉr′ni chər) ***n.*** ⟦Fr *fourniture* < *fournir*, FURNISH⟧ **1** [Obs.] the act of furnishing **2** the things, usually movable, in a room, apartment, etc. which equip it for living, as chairs, sofas, tables, beds, etc. **3** the necessary equipment of a machine, ship, trade, etc. **4** [Archaic] full equipment for a man and horse, as armor, harness, etc. **5** *Printing* pieces of wood, metal, or plastic used to fill in blank areas in type forms

Fur·ni·vall (fʉr′ni vəl), **Frederick James** 1825-1910; Eng. philologist & editor

fu·ror (fyoor′ôr′, -ər) ***n.*** ⟦ME *furour* < OFr *fureur* < L *furor*, rage, madness < *furere*: see FURY⟧ **1** fury; rage; frenzy **2** *a)* a great, widespread outburst of admiration or enthusiasm; craze; rage *b)* a state of excitement or confusion; commotion or uproar Also [Chiefly Brit.] **fu·rore** (fyoor′ôr′, -ər; *Brit* fyoo rô′rē)

fu·ro·se·mide (fyoo̅ rō′sə mīd′) ***n.*** a diuretic, $C_{12}H_{11}ClN_2O_5S$, used to treat edema and hypertension

furred (fʉrd) ***adj.*** **1** made, trimmed, or lined with fur **2** having fur: said of an animal **3** wearing fur **4** coated with diseased or waste matter: said as of the tongue in illness **5** provided with furring strips

fur·ri·er (fʉr′ē ər) ***n.*** ⟦ME *furrere*⟧ **1** a dealer in furs **2** a person who processes furs or makes, repairs, alters, etc. fur garments

fur·ri·er·y (fur′ē ər ē) *n., pl.* **-er·ies** 1 [Obs.] furs collectively 2 the business or work of a furrier
fur·ring (fur′iŋ) *n.* 1 fur used for trimming or lining 2 the act of trimming, lining, etc. with fur 3 a coating of diseased or waste matter, as on the tongue 4 *a)* the fastening of thin strips of wood or metal as to joists, studs, or masonry walls in order to form a level backing for flooring, plaster, etc. or to provide air spaces *b)* the strips so used (in full **furring strips**)
fur·row (fur′ō) *n.* ⟦ME *forwe* < OE *furh*, akin to Ger *furche* (OHG *furuh*) < IE base **perk-*, to dig up, furrow > **porkos*, L *porca*, furrow, *porcus*, pig (lit., digger)⟧ 1 a narrow groove made in the ground by a plow 2 anything resembling this, as a deep, narrow rut made by a wheel, a deep wrinkle on the face, etc. 3 [Obs.] plowed land —*vt.* ⟦< the *n.*⟧ to make a furrow or furrows in —*vi.* 1 to make furrows 2 to become wrinkled
fur·ry (fur′ē) *adj.* **-ri·er, -ri·est** 1 of or made of fur 2 covered with or wearing fur 3 *a)* like fur, as in texture *b)* having a furlike coating —**fur′ri·ness** *n.*
fur seal any of several eared seals (esp. genus *Callorhinus*) with soft, thick underfur
fur·ther (fur′thər) *adj.* ⟦ME < OE *furthor* (akin to Ger *vorder*) < base of *fore*, FORE + compar. suffix < IE *-*tero-* (as in AFTER, OTHER)⟧ 1 *alt. compar. of* FAR 2 additional; more 3 more distant or remote; farther —*adv.* ⟦ME < OE *further*, orig. a neut. acc. of the adj.⟧ 1 *alt. compar. of* FAR 2 to a greater degree or extent 3 in addition; moreover 4 at or to a greater distance or more remote point in space or time; farther ➡In sense 3 of the *adj.* and sense 4 of the *adv.*, FARTHER is more commonly used —*vt.* ⟦ME *furthren* < OE *fyrthrian* < *furthra, furthor*⟧ to give aid to; promote —*SYN.* ADVANCE —**fur′ther·er** *n.*
fur·ther·ance (fur′*th*ər əns) *n.* ⟦ME⟧ a furthering, or helping forward; advancement; promotion
fur·ther·more (fur′*th*ər môr′) *adv.* ⟦ME *further more*⟧ in addition; besides; moreover: used with conjunctive force
fur·ther·most (fur′*th*ər mōst′; *also*, -məst) *adj.* most distant; furthest
fur·thest (fur′*th*ist) *adj.* ⟦ME, formed as superl. on analogy of *further*⟧ 1 *alt. superl. of* FAR 2 most distant; farthest —*adv.* 1 *alt. superl. of* FAR 2 at or to the greatest distance or most remote point in space or time 3 to the greatest degree or extent; most
fur·tive (fur′tiv) *adj.* ⟦Fr *furtif* < L *furtivus*, stolen, hidden < *furtum*, theft < *fur*, a thief < IE **bhōr-* (> Gr *phōr*) < base **bher-*, to BEAR[1]: hence, orig., one who carries off⟧ done or acting in a stealthy manner, as if to hinder observation; surreptitious; stealthy; sneaky —*SYN.* SECRET —**fur′tive·ly** *adv.* —**fur′tive·ness** *n.*
Furt·wäng·ler (foort′veŋ′lər), **Wilhelm** 1886-1954; Ger. orchestra conductor
fu·run·cle (fyoo′ruŋ kəl, fyoor′uŋ′-) *n.* ⟦L *furunculus*, petty thief, boil, dim. of *fur*, thief: see FURTIVE⟧ BOIL[2] —**fu·run′cu·lar** (-kyoo lər) *adj.*, **fu·run′cu·lous** (-ləs)
fu·run·cu·lo·sis (fyoo ruŋ′kyoo lō′sis) *n.* ⟦< prec. + -OSIS⟧ the disorder characterized by the recurrent appearance of furuncles
fu·ry (fyoor′ē) *n., pl.* **-ries** ⟦ME *furie* < OFr < L *furia* < *furere*, to rage, prob. < IE **dhus-*, to rage, storm, dust-colored < base **dheu-*, to blow: see DULL⟧ 1 *a)* violent anger; wild rage *b)* a fit of this 2 violence; vehemence; fierceness [the *fury* of a storm] 3 a violent or vengeful person; esp., such a woman 4 [F-] any of the FURIES 5 [Archaic] inspired frenzy —*SYN.* ANGER —**like fury** [Informal] with great violence, speed, etc.
furze (furz) *n.* ⟦ME *firs* < OE *fyrs* < IE base **pūro-*, cereal > Czech *pýr*, couch grass⟧ a prickly evergreen shrub (*Ulex europaeus*) of the pea family, with dark-green spines and yellow flowers, native to European wastelands; gorse; whin —**fur′zy** *adj.*
fu·sain (fyoo′zān′, fyoo zān′) *n.* ⟦Fr, orig., spindle tree < VL **fusago* (gen. **fusaginis*) < L *fusus*, a spindle⟧ 1 a type of fine charcoal pencil prepared from the wood of the spindle tree 2 a drawing made with this 3 a type of brittle, porous, black bituminous coal having a silky luster and a fibrous structure
Fu·san (foo′sän′) *a former transliteration of* BUSAN
fu·sar·i·um wilt (fyoo sär′ē əm, -zär′-) ⟦< ModL *Fusarium* < L *fusus*, spindle⟧ a fungus disease (genus *Fusarium*) that destroys various plants, esp. tomatoes, bananas, and lawn grasses
fus·cous (fus′kəs) *adj.* ⟦L *fuscus*: see OBFUSCATE⟧ dark-gray or grayish-brown in color; dusky
fuse[1] (fyooz) *vt., vi.* **fused, fus′ing** ⟦< L *fusus*, pp. of *fundere*, to pour out, shed: see FOUND[3]⟧ 1 to melt, or to join by melting 2 to unite as if by melting together; blend 3 to unite (atomic nuclei) in the process of NUCLEAR FUSION —*SYN.* MIX
fuse[2] (fyooz) *n.* ⟦It *fuso*, a cord, tube, casing < L *fusus*, hollow spindle⟧ 1 a narrow tube filled with combustible material, or a wick saturated with such material, for setting off an explosive charge 2 FUZE[2] (*n.* 2) 3 *Elec.* a safety device placed in a circuit, consisting of a replaceable plug or tube containing wire or metal that will melt and break the circuit if the current exceeds a specified amperage —*vt.* **fused, fus′ing** to connect a fuse to —**blow a fuse** 1 to have an electrical fuse melt 2 [Informal] to become very angry
fused quartz a clear, strong vitreous material obtained when silica is fused at high temperature: used in devices, as crucibles or molds, that are to be subjected to high or rapidly changing temperatures
fused silica SILICA GLASS
fu·see (fyoo zē′, fyoo′zē′) *n.* ⟦Fr *fusée*, spindle, rocket, hence fusee < ML *fusata* < L *fusus*: see FUSE[2]⟧ 1 [Archaic] a friction match with a large head, able to burn in a wind ☆2 a colored flare used as a signal by trainmen, truck drivers, etc. 3 in an old-fashioned clock or watch, a grooved cone upon which the cord from the spring container was unwound to equalize the force of the spring 4 FUSE[2] (*n.* 1)
fu·se·lage (fyoo′sə läzh′; -zə-; -läj′, -lij′) *n.* ⟦Fr < *fuselé*, tapering (< OFr *fus*, spindle < L *fusus*) + *-age*, -AGE⟧ the body of an airplane, exclusive of the wings, tail assembly, and engines
Fu·se·li (fyoo′zə lē, fyoo zel′ē), **Henry** (born *Johann Heinrich Füssli*) 1741-1825; Eng. painter, born in Switzerland
fu·sel oil (fyoo′zəl, -səl) ⟦Ger *fusel*, inferior liquor < L *fusilis*, FUSIL[1]⟧ an oily, acrid, poisonous liquid occurring in imperfectly distilled alcoholic products and consisting chiefly of amyl alcohols: small amounts contribute to the characteristic flavor of a whiskey
Fu·shun (foo′shoon′) city in Liaoning province, NE China
fu·si·ble (fyoo′zə bəl) *adj.* ⟦ME < OFr⟧ that can be fused or easily melted —**fu′si·bil′i·ty** *n.* —**fu′si·bly** *adv.*
fu·si·form (fyoo′zi fôrm′, -si-) *adj.* ⟦< L *fusus*, a spindle + -FORM⟧ rounded, broadest in the middle, and tapering toward each end; spindle-shaped
fu·sil[1] (fyoo′zil, -sil) *adj.* ⟦L *fusilis* < *fusus*: see FUSE[1]⟧ [Archaic] 1 fusible or fusing 2 *a)* fused; melted *b)* made by melting and molding, or casting; founded Also **fu′sile** (-zil, -sil; -zīl′, -sīl′)
fu·sil[2] (fyoo′zil) *n.* ⟦Fr, orig., steel for striking sparks < ML *focile* < L *focus*, hearth (in LL, fire): see FOCUS⟧ a light flintlock musket
fu·si·lier or **fu·sil·eer** (fyoo′zə lir′) *n.* ⟦Fr *fusilier* < *fusil*: see prec.⟧ [Historical] a soldier armed with a fusil: the term *Fusiliers* is still applied to certain British regiments formerly so armed
fu·sil·lade (fyoo′sə läd′, -lād′;) *n.* ⟦Fr < *fusiller*, to shoot < *fusil*: see FUSIL[2]⟧ 1 a simultaneous or rapid and continuous discharge of many firearms 2 something like this; barrage [a *fusillade* of questions] —*vt.* **-lad′ed, -lad′ing** to shoot down or attack with a fusillade
fu·sil·li (fyoo sē′lē, foo-) *n.* ⟦It, pl. of *fusillo*, dim. of *fuso*, spindle < L *fusus*⟧ pasta in the shape of spirals
fu·sion (fyoo′zhən) *n.* ⟦L *fusio*⟧ 1 a fusing or melting together 2 *a)* the union of different things by or as if by melting; blending; coalition [a *fusion* of political parties] *b)* the state or fact of being so united 3 anything made by fusing 4 NUCLEAR FUSION 5 *Linguis.* *a)* in some languages, the use of morphemes that combine different semantic categories (Ex.: in Latin *amō*, "I love," *-ō* indicates simultaneously first person subject, singular subject, and present tense) (distinguished from AGGLUTINATION, sense 3) *b)* a joining of morphemes with a marked adjustment of sounds at the point of juncture ☆6 a style of popular music originating in the 1970s that blends improvisational elements of jazz with the rhythms, harmonic structure, and bass lines of rock or funk, sometimes adding elements from other musical styles, and usually emphasizing the use of electronic keyboard instruments, electronic modifications in recordings, etc. 7 a style of cooking that combines techniques, ingredients, etc. of more than one regional or national cuisine: also **fusion cuisine**
fusion bomb a nuclear bomb in which the principal energy source is the fusion reaction that follows the initial fission reaction: see HYDROGEN BOMB
fu·sion·ism (-iz′əm) *n.* the theory or practice of bringing about a fusion, or coalition, of political parties, factions, etc. —**fu′sion·ist** *n., adj.*
fuss (fus) *n.* ⟦17th-c. slang, prob. echoic⟧ 1 a flurry of nervous, excited, often needless activity; bustle 2 a state of excessive nervousness, agitation, etc. ☆3 a quarrel or argument 4 a showy display of delight, approval, interest, etc. 5 trouble, difficulty, or bother —*vi.* 1 to cause or make a fuss 2 to bustle about or worry, esp. over trifles 3 to whine, fret, etc.: said esp. of a baby —*vt.* to bother or worry unnecessarily —**fuss around** to engage in idle, aimless, or annoying activity —**fuss′er** *n.*
☆**fuss·budg·et** (-buj′it) *n.* ⟦prec. + BUDGET, prob. in sense "bag, sack"⟧ [Informal] a fussy person: also [Informal, Chiefly Brit.] **fuss′pot′**
fuss·y (fus′ē) *adj.* **fuss′i·er, fuss′i·est** 1 *a)* habitually fussing; bustling about or worrying over trifles *b)* overly exacting and hard to please *c)* whining, fretting, etc., as a baby 2 showing or needing careful attention 3 full of unnecessary details —**fuss′i·ly** *adv.* —**fuss′i·ness** *n.*
fus·tian (fus′chən, fust′yən) *n.* ⟦ME < OFr *fustaigne* < ML *fustaneum* (< L *fustis*, wooden stick) used as transl. of Gr *xylinon* < *xylinos*, wooden (in LXX, cotton)⟧ 1 [Historical] a coarse cloth of cotton and linen 2 a thick cotton cloth with a short nap, as corduroy, velveteen, etc. 3 pompous, pretentious talk or writing; bombast; rant —*adj.* 1 made of fustian 2 pompous and pretentious
fus·tic (fus′tik) *n.* ⟦ME *fustik* < OFr *fustoc* < Ar *fustuq* < Pers *fistik* > Gr *pistakē*, pistachio⟧ ☆1 a tropical American tree (*Chlorophora tinctoria*) of the mulberry family: dyes are extracted from its yellow wood 2 any of these dyes 3 any of several other woods which yield dyes
fus·ti·gate (fus′ti gāt′) *vt.* **-gat′ed, -gat′ing** ⟦< L *fustigatus*, pp. of *fustigare* < *fustis*, a stick + *agere*: see ACT[1]⟧ to beat with a stick; cudgel —**fus′ti·ga′tion** *n.*
fus·ty (fus′tē) *adj.* **fus′ti·er, fus′ti·est** ⟦< *fust*, a musty smell < Early ModE, a cask (ME *foist*) < OFr cask, orig. tree trunk < L *fustis*, wooden stick⟧ 1 smelling stale or stuffy; musty; moldy 2 not up-to-date; old-fashioned; conservative —**fus′ti·ly** *adv.* —**fus′ti·ness** *n.*
fut *abbrev.* future
fu·thark (foo′thärk′) *n.* ⟦< the first six letters: *f, u, þ (th), a* (or *o*), *r, k* (or *c*)⟧ the runic alphabet: also **fu′thorc′** (-thôrk′) or **fu′thork′** (-thôrk′)
fu·tile (fyoot′'l; *chiefly Brit & Cdn*, fyoo′tīl′) *adj.* ⟦< Fr or L: Fr *futile* < L *futi-*

lis, lit., that easily pours out, hence untrustworthy, worthless, futile < base of *fundere*: see FOUND[3]⟧ 1 *a)* that could not succeed; useless; vain *b)* lacking vigor or purpose; inept or ineffective 2 trifling or unimportant —**fu′tile·ly** *adv.* —**fu′tile·ness** *n.*

SYN.—**futile** is applied to that which fails completely of the desired end or is incapable of producing any result; **vain** also implies failure but does not have as strong a connotation of intrinsic inefficacy as **futile**; **fruitless** stresses the idea of great and prolonged effort that is profitless or fails to yield results; that is **abortive** which fails to succeed or miscarries at an early stage of its development; that is **useless** which has proved to be ineffectual in practice or is theoretically considered to be of no avail —*ANT.* **effective, fruitful, effectual**

fu·til·i·ty (fyo͞o til′ə tē) *n., pl.* **-ties** 1 the quality of being futile 2 a futile act, thing, etc.

fu·ton (fo͞o′tän′) *n.* ⟦SinoJpn, orig. round cushions filled with cattail flower spikes < Chin *fu*, cattail + *ton*, round⟧ 1 a thin mattress like a quilt, placed on the floor or on a very low platform frame, for use as a bed or chair 2 any of various kinds of low couch or chair that can be unfolded to serve as a simple platform bed

fut·tock (fut′ək) *n.* ⟦ME *futtek, fottek* < ? **fot-hok*, foot hook⟧ any of the curved timbers that make up a rib of a wooden ship

futtock plate an iron plate put horizontally around the top of a ship's lower mast to hold the futtock shrouds

futtock shroud one of the short iron rods extending from a futtock plate to a band around the lower mast to brace the topmast where it joins the lower mast

Fu·tu·na (fə to͞o′nə) *see* WALLIS AND FUTUNA

fu·ture (fyo͞o′chər) *adj.* ⟦ME *futur* < OFr < L *futurus*, about to be, used as fut. part. of *esse*, to be⟧ 1 that is to be or come; of days, months, or years ahead 2 *Gram.* indicating time to come [the *future* tense of a verb] —*n.* 1 the time that is to come; days, months, or years ahead 2 what will happen; what is going to be [to claim to foretell the *future*] 3 the prospective or potential condition of a person or thing; esp., the chance to achieve, succeed, etc. [to have a great *future* in politics] 4 [*usually pl.*] a contract for a specific commodity or derivative bought or sold for delivery at a later date 5 *Gram. a)* the future tense *b)* a verb form or phrase in this tense

fu·ture·less (-lis) *adj.* having no hopes or prospects for the future

future life *Religion* the life following death

future perfect 1 a tense indicating an action as completed or a state as having ended, in relation to a specified time in the future 2 a verb form in this tense (Ex.: *will have gone*, expressed analytically in English)

☆**future shock** ⟦from the title of a book (1970) by A. Toffler, U.S. writer & futurist⟧ the inability to cope with the rapid and myriad changes of modern society, or the distress resulting from this

fu·tur·ism (fyo͞o′chər iz′əm) *n.* ⟦It *futurismo* < *futuro*, FUTURE⟧ [*often* **F-**] a movement in the arts, originated by Italian painters shortly before WWI: they opposed traditionalism and sought to depict dynamic movement by eliminating conventional form and by stressing the speed, flux, and violence of the machine age

fu·tur·ist (fyo͞o′chər ist) *n.* 1 an adherent of futurism 2 a person engaged in futurological speculation —*adj.* of futurists or futurism

fu·tur·is·tic (fyo͞o′chər is′tik) *adj.* 1 of or having to do with the future, futurism, or futurology 2 so advanced in design, form, concept, etc. as to seem suited for some future time; ultramodern —**fu′tur·is′ti·cal·ly** *adv.*

fu·tu·ri·ty (fyo͞o to͝or′ə tē, -tyo͝or′-, -cho͝or′-) *n., pl.* **-ties** 1 *a)* the future *b)* a future condition or event 2 the quality of being future 3 FUTURITY RACE

☆**futurity race** a race for two-year-old horses in which the entries are selected before birth

☆**fu·tur·ol·o·gy** (fyo͞o′chər äl′ə jē) *n.* ⟦FUTUR(E) + -OLOGY⟧ the speculative study of probable or presumed future conditions, as extrapolated from known facts and trends —**fu′tur·o·log′i·cal** *adj.* —**fu′tur·ol′o·gist** *n.*

☆**futz** (futs) *vi.* ⟦? shortening of E Yiddish *arumfartsn zikh*, fart around⟧ [Slang] to trifle or meddle; fool (*around*)

fuze[1] (fyo͞oz) *vt., vi.* **fuzed, fuz′ing** *alt. sp. of* FUSE[1]

fuze[2] (fyo͞oz) *n.* 1 *alt. sp. of* FUSE[2] (*n.* 1) 2 any of various devices for detonating bombs, projectiles, or explosive charges —*vt.* **fuzed, fuz′ing** to connect a fuze to

fu·zee (fyo͞o zē′, fyo͞o′zē′) *n. alt. sp. of* FUSEE

Fu·zhou (fo͞o′jō′) city in SE China; capital of Fujian province

fuzz (fuz) *n.* ⟦< ? Du *voos*, spongy, or back-form. < fol.⟧ 1 very loose, light particles of down, wool, etc.; fine hairs or fibers [the *fuzz* on a peach] 2 a blurred, distorted audio effect deliberately produced when amplifying the sounds of an electronic musical instrument, as by overloading an amplification circuit: also **fuzz′tone′** (-tōn′) — *vi., vt.* 1 to cover or become covered with fuzz 2 to make or become fuzzy —☆**the fuzz** ⟦< ? FUSS, in sense "a fussy (i.e., hard to please) person"⟧ [Slang] a policeman or the police

fuzz·y (fuz′ē) *adj.* **fuzz′i·er, fuzz′i·est** ⟦prob. < LowG *fussig*, fibrous, spongy, akin to Du *voos*, spongy < IE **pus-* < base **pu-*, to rot > FOUL⟧ 1 of, like, or covered with fuzz 2 not clear, distinct, or precise; blurred [*fuzzy* thinking, a *fuzzy* sound] 3 using or having to do with FUZZY LOGIC 4 [Informal] characterized by tenderness; compassionate, sentimental, cuddly, etc.: usually in the phrase **warm and fuzzy** —**fuzz′i·ly** *adv.* —**fuzz′i·ness** *n.*

☆**fuzzy logic** ⟦< *fuzzy (set)*, coined (1965) by L. A. Zadeh, U.S. computer scientist: see prec.⟧ a type of logic used in computers and other electronic devices for processing imprecise or variable data: in place of the traditional binary values, fuzzy logic employs a range of values for greater flexibility

f.v. *abbrev.* ⟦L *folio verso*⟧ on the back of the page

fwd *abbrev.* forward

F-word (ef′wurd′), **the** [Informal] the word FUCK: a euphemism

FX *abbrev.* 1 foreign exchange 2 *Film* special effects: also **F/X**

FY *abbrev.* fiscal year

-fy (fī) ⟦ME *fyen, -fien* < OFr *-fier* < L *-ficare* < *facere*, to make, DO[1]: see FACT⟧ *suffix forming verbs* 1 to make; cause to be or become [*liquefy*] 2 to cause to have or feel; imbue with [*glorify*] 3 to become [*putrefy*]

☆**fyce** (fīs) *n.* [Dial.] *var. of* FEIST

☆**FYI** *abbrev.* for your information

☆**fyke** (fīk) *n.* ⟦Du *fuik*, a bow net⟧ a fishnet in the form of a long bag reinforced with hoops

fyl·fot (fil′fät′) *n.* ⟦< FILL + FOOT: so called because used to fill the foot of a colored window⟧ SWASTIKA (sense 1)

Fyn (fün) island of Denmark, between Jutland & Zealand: 1,149 sq mi (2,976 sq km)

g[1] or G (jē) ***n.***, *pl.* **g's, G's 1** the seventh letter of the English alphabet: from the Greek *gamma,* a borrowing from the Phoenician **2** any of the speech sounds that this letter represents, as, in English, the (g) of *get* or (j) of *gem* **3** a type or impression for *g* or *G* **4** the seventh in a sequence or group **5** an object shaped like G —***adj.*** **1** of *g* or *G* **2** seventh in a sequence or group **3** shaped like G

g[2] (jē) ***n.*** **1** acceleration of gravity **2** G-FORCE

g[3] *abbrev.* gram(s)

G[1] (jē) ***n.*** **1** ⟦< G(RAND), ***n.*** 2⟧ [Slang] one thousand dollars **2** *Educ.* a grade meaning *good* **3** *Music a)* the fifth tone or note in the ascending scale of C major *b)* a key, string, etc. producing this tone *c)* the scale having this tone as the keynote **4** *Physics a)* the gravitational constant in Newton's law of gravitation *b)* G-FORCE

G[2] a film rating meaning "general audience": it indicates that the film is considered suitable for persons of all ages

G[3] *abbrev.* **1** game(s) **2** gauge **3** gauss(es) **4** German **5** giga- **6** goal(s) **7** goalkeeper **8** guanine **9** *Basketball, Football* guard **10** guilder(s) **11** guinea(s) **12** gulf **13** specific gravity Also, except for 3, 4, & 12, **g**

G[4] *symbol Elec.* conductance

Ga[1] *abbrev.* **1** *Bible* Galatians **2** Georgia

Ga[2] *Chem. symbol for* gallium

GA *abbrev.* **1** General Agent **2** General Assembly **3** general average: also **ga** or **G/A 4** Georgia

GAAP (gap) *abbrev.* Generally Accepted Accounting Principles (or Procedures)

gab (gab) [Informal] ***vt.* gabbed, gab′bing** ⟦ME *gabben,* to lie, scoff, talk nonsense < ON *gabba,* to mock (& < OFr *gaber* < ON), akin to OE *gaffetung,* a scoffing & *gaf-spræc,* foolish speech < IE **ĝhebh-* < base **ghē-* > GAP, GAPE, GASP⟧ to talk much or idly; chatter; gabble —***n.*** idle talk; chatter —**gift of (the) gab** the ability to speak fluently or glibly —**gab′ber *n.***

GABA (gab′ə; gä′bə, -bä′) ***n.*** ⟦*g(amma-)a(mino)b(utyric) a(cid)*⟧ an amino acid, $H_2N(CH_2)_3COOH$, found in plants and in nervous tissue, esp. in the brain, where it acts as a neurotransmitter that suppresses nerve activity

gab·ar·dine (gab′ər dēn′, gab′ər dēn′) ***n.*** ⟦var. of GABERDINE⟧ **1** a cloth of wool, cotton, rayon, etc. twilled on one side and having a fine, diagonal weave, used for suits, coats, dresses, etc. **2** a garment made of this cloth **3** *alt. sp. of* GABERDINE (sense 1)

gab·ble (gab′əl) ***vi.* -bled, -bling** ⟦freq. of GAB⟧ **1** to talk rapidly and incoherently; jabber; chatter **2** to utter rapid, meaningless sounds, as a goose does —***vt.*** to utter rapidly and incoherently —***n.*** rapid, incoherent talk or meaningless utterance —**gab′bler *n.***

gab·bro (gab′rō) ***n.*** ⟦It < L *glaber,* bare: see GLABROUS⟧ any of a group of usually dark, coarsegrained, igneous rocks, composed chiefly of pyroxene and plagioclase

gab·by (gab′ē) ***adj.* -bi·er, -bi·est** [Informal] inclined to chatter; talkative —**gab′bi·ness *n.***

ga·belle (gə bel′) ***n.*** ⟦ME < OFr < OIt *gabella* < Ar *ḳabāla,* tax < *qabala,* to receive; akin to Heb *kibel*: see CABALA⟧ a tax levied on salt in France before the Revolution

gab·er·dine (gab′ər dēn′, gab′ər dēn′) ***n.*** ⟦earlier *gawbardyne* < OFr *gaverdine,* kind of cloak < ? MHG *walvart,* pilgrimage < *wallen,* to wander about (< IE **wē-,* var. of base *awē,* to blow, flutter) + *vart,* a trip < *varen,* FARE⟧ **1** a loose coat of coarse cloth, worn in the Middle Ages and later associated with Jews **2** *chiefly Brit. sp. of* GABARDINE (senses 1 & 2)

gab·er·lun·zie (gab′ər lun′zē, -lo͞on′yē) ***n.*** ⟦Scot; printing form of *gaberlunyie* (with printed *z* for *y* as in name *Menzies*) < ?⟧ a wandering beggar

☆**gab·fest** (gab′fest′) ***n.*** ⟦GAB + -FEST⟧ [Informal] **1** an informal gathering of people to talk with one another **2** their talk

ga·bi·on (gā′bē ən) ***n.*** ⟦Fr < It *gabbione,* large cage < *gabbia,* cage, coop < L *cavea:* see CAGE⟧ **1** a cylinder of wicker filled with earth or stones, formerly used in building fortifications **2** a similar cylinder of metal, used as in building dams and dikes

ga·ble (gā′bəl) ***n.*** ⟦ME < OFr < Gmc, as in ON *gafl,* gable, akin to Ger *giebel* < IE base **ghebhel-,* gable, head > Gr *kephalē*⟧ **1** *a)* the triangular wall enclosed by the sloping ends of a ridged roof *b)* popularly, the whole section, including wall, roof, and space enclosed **2** the end wall of a building, the upper part of which is a gable **3** *Archit.* a triangular decorative feature, such as that over a door or window —***vt.* -bled, -bling** to put a gable or gables on

gable

Ga·ble (gā′bəl), **(William) Clark** 1901-60; U.S. film actor

gable roof a ridged roof forming a gable at each end

gable window 1 a window in a GABLE (sense 2) **2** a window with a GABLE (sense 3) over it

Ga·bo (gä′bō), **Na·um** (nä′o͞om) (born *Naum Pevsner*) 1890-1977; U.S. sculptor, born in Russia

Ga·bon (ga bōn′) country in WC Africa, on the Gulf of Guinea: formerly a French territory, it became independent in 1960: 103,347 sq mi (267,667 sq km); cap. Libreville —**Gab·o·nese** (gab′ə nēz′) ***adj., n., pl.* -nese′**

Ga·bor (gä′bôr, gə bôr′), **Dennis** 1900-79; Brit. physicist, born in Hungary

Ga·bo·ro·ne (gä′bə rō′nā) capital of Botswana, in the SE part

Ga·bri·el (gā′brē əl) ***n.*** ⟦Heb *gavriel,* lit. ? man of God < *gever,* man + *el,* God⟧ **1** a masculine name; dim. *Gabe*; fem. *Gabriella, Gabrielle* **2** *Bible* one of the archangels, the herald of good news: Dan. 8:16; Luke 1:26

Ga·bri·el·i (gä′brē el′ē), **Gio·van·ni** (jô vä′nē, jē′ō-) 1557?-1612; It. composer & organist

Ga·bri·elle (gāb′rē el′, ga′brē-) ***n.*** ⟦Fr, fem. of *Gabriel,* GABRIEL⟧ a feminine name: equiv. It. & Sp. *Gabriella*: see GABRIEL

ga·by (gā′bē) ***n.*, *pl.* -bies** ⟦< Brit Midland dial. < ? ON *gapi,* a gaper < *gapa,* GAPE⟧ a simpleton

gad[1] (gad) ***vi.* gad′ded, gad′ding** ⟦LME *gadden,* to hurry, ? back-form. < *gadeling,* companion in arms < OE *gædeling*: for IE base see GATHER⟧ to wander about in an idle or restless way, as in seeking amusement —***n.*** an act of gadding: chiefly in the phrase **on (or upon) the gad**, gadding about —**gad′der *n.***

gad[2] (gad) ***n.*** ⟦ME *gadd* < ON *gaddr,* infl. in sense by OE *gad* (see GOAD); akin to Goth *gazds,* thorn < IE base **ĝhasto-,* rod, pole > YARD[1], L *hasta,* rod, shaft⟧ *Bible* **1** GOAD **2** any of several chisel-like or pointed bars used in mining —***vt.* gad′ded, gad′ding** to break up or loosen (ore) with a gad

Gad[1] (gad) ***interj.*** ⟦euphemism for God⟧ used to express surprise, disgust, etc.: a mild oath

Gad[2] (gad) ***n.*** ⟦Heb *gad,* lit., good fortune⟧ *Bible* **1** Jacob's seventh son, whose mother was Zilpah: Gen. 30:11 **2** the tribe of Israel descended from him: Num. 1:24

gad·a·bout (gad′ə bout′) ***n.*** a person who gads about; restless seeker after fun —***adj.*** fond of gadding

Gad·a·rene (gad′ə rēn′) ***adj.*** ⟦after the *Gadarene* swine (Luke 8:26-39) that ran into the sea after demons possessed them⟧ moving rapidly and without control; headlong

Gad·da·fi (gə dä′fē) *see* QADDAFI

gad·fly (gad′flī′) ***n.*, *pl.* -flies′** ⟦GAD[2] + FLY[2]⟧ **1** any of several large flies, as the horsefly, that bite livestock **2** a person who annoys others, esp. by rousing them from complacency

gadg·et (gaj′it) ***n.*** ⟦< ? Fr *gâchette,* catch (of a lock), tumbler, dim. of *gâche,* a bolt, catch⟧ **1** any small, esp. mechanical contrivance or device **2** any interesting but relatively useless or unnecessary object —**gadg′et·y *adj.***

☆**gadg·et·eer** (gaj′i tir′) ***n.*** ⟦prec. + -EER⟧ a person who contrives, or takes a special delight in, gadgets

gadg·et·ry (gaj′i trē) ***n.*** **1** gadgets collectively **2** preoccupation with mere gadgets

Ga·dhel·ic (gə del′ik) ***n., adj.*** *var. of* GOIDELIC

ga·doid (gā′doid′) ***adj.*** ⟦< ModL *gadus,* cod (< Gr *gados,* kind of fish) + -OID⟧ of or like the family (Gadidae, order Gadiformes) of bony fishes including cod, hake, and burbot —***n.*** any fish of this family

gad·o·lin·ite (gad′ō lin īt′) ***n.*** ⟦Ger *gadolinit,* after J. *Gadolin* (1760-1852), Finn chemist who isolated it⟧ a dark green to black, hard, radioactive mineral, beryllium iron yttrium silicate, $Be_2FeY_2Si_2O_{10}$, that is an ore of various rare-earth elements

gad·o·lin·i·um (gad′ō lin′ē əm) ***n.*** ⟦ModL, earlier *gadolinia*: so named (1886) by P. E. L. de Boisbaudran (1838-1912), Fr chemist, and J.-C. G. de Marignac (1817-94), Swiss chemist, who had each isolated it, in honor of J. *Gadolin* (see prec.) + -IUM⟧ a chemical element, one of the rare-earth elements, that is highly magnetic at low temperatures, superconductive, and has the highest rate of neutron absorption of any element: symbol, Gd; at. no. 64: see the periodic table of elements in the Reference Supplement

ga·droon (gə dro͞on′) ***n.*** ⟦Fr *godron,* prob. < *godet,* small cup without handle, bowl < MDu *kodde,* wooden cylinder, rounded object: for IE base see

CUD⟧ any of various oval-shaped beadings, flutings, or reedings used to decorate molding, silverware, etc. —**ga·droon′ing** *n.*

Gads·den (gadz′dən), **James** 1788-1858; U.S. diplomat: negotiated (1853) a purchase of land (**Gadsden Purchase**) from Mexico, which became part of N.Mex. & Ariz.

gad·wall (gad′wôl′) *n., pl.* **-walls′** or **-wall′** ⟦< ?⟧ a grayish-brown wild duck (*Anas strepera*) of the freshwater regions of North America

Gad·zooks (gad zo͞oks′, -zo͝oks′) *interj.* ⟦< *God's hooks*, nails of the Cross⟧ [Archaic] used as a mild oath

gae[1] (gā) *vi.* **gaed** (gād), **gaen** (gān), **gae′ing** [Scot.] GO[1]

gae[2] (gā) *vt., vi.* [Scot.] *alt. pt. of* GIE (give)

Gae·a (jē′ə) *n.* ⟦Gr *Gaia* < *gē*, earth⟧ *Gr. Myth.* a goddess who is the personification of the earth, the mother of the Titans: identified with the Roman Tellus

Gael (gāl) *n.* ⟦contr. < Gael *Gaidheal*, akin to Ir *Gaedheal*, OIr *Góidel*, Welsh *gwyddel*⟧ a Celt of Scotland, Ireland, or the Isle of Man; esp., a Celt of the Scottish Highlands

Gael·ic (gā′lik) *n.* ⟦< Gael *Gaidhealach*⟧ **1** the Celtic language of Scotland **2** the Goidelic languages as a group **3** IRISH (*n.* 1) —*adj.* **1** of the Gaels **2** designating or of the Goidelic languages

gaff[1] (gaf) *n.* ⟦ME *gaffe* < OFr < OProv *gaf* or Sp *gafa* < Goth *gafah*, a catch < *ga-*, intens. + *fahan*, to catch, akin to FANG⟧ **1** a large, strong hook on a pole, or a barbed spear, used in landing large fish **2** *a)* a sharp metal spur fastened to the leg of a gamecock *b)* any of the steel points on a lineman's climbing iron **3** *a)* a spar or pole extending from the after side of a mast and supporting a fore-and-aft sail *b) U.S. Navy* a similarly located spar on the mainmast, from which the ensign is flown when a ship is underway **4** [Slang] any secret device for cheating **5** ⟦earlier in sense of "a fair": ? because visitors were *gaffed* there⟧ [Brit. Slang] a cheap theater, dance hall, etc. —*vt.* **1** to strike or land (a fish) with a gaff **2** [Slang, Chiefly Brit.] to cheat; hoax; trick **3** [Slang] *Naut.* to rig with a gaff —☆**stand the gaff** [Slang] to bear up well under difficulties, punishment, ridicule, etc.; be game

gaff[2] (gaf) [Brit. Slang] *n.* ⟦prob. altered < earlier *gab*, mockery < ME, deceit: see GAB⟧ foolish talk; nonsense —**blow the gaff** to reveal a secret

gaffe (gaf) *n.* ⟦Fr < OProv *gaf*: see GAFF[1]⟧ a blunder; faux pas

gaf·fer (gaf′ər) *n.* ⟦altered < GODFATHER⟧ **1** an old man, esp. one from the country: now usually humorous: cf. GAMMER **2** a master glass blower ☆**3** chief electrician in charge of lighting on a TV or film set **4** [Brit.] a foreman of a group of workers

gaff-top·sail (gaf′täp′sāl′; *naut.*, -səl) *n.* a topsail the lower edge of which is attached to a gaff

gag (gag) *vt.* **gagged**, **gag′ging** ⟦ME *gaggen*, of echoic orig.⟧ **1** to cause to retch or choke **2** to put something over or into the mouth of, so as to keep from talking, crying out, etc. **3** to keep from speaking or expressing oneself freely, as by intimidation **4** to prevent or limit speech in (a legislative body) **5** *Mech.* to choke or stop up (a valve, etc.) —*vi.* **1** to retch or choke **2** [Informal] to make a gag or gags; joke —*n.* **1** something put into or over the mouth to prevent talking, crying out, etc. ☆**2** any restraint of free speech **3** a device for holding the jaws open for dental work or for any surgery inside the mouth **4** *a)* a comical remark or act; joke, as one interpolated by an actor on the stage *b)* a practical joke or hoax

ga·ga (gä′gä′) *adj.* ⟦Fr, orig., a fool: echoic of ? stammering, muttering, etc.⟧ [Slang] **1** mentally confused; crazy **2** carried away as by love or enthusiasm

ga·ga·ku (gä gä′ko͞o) *n.* ⟦Jpn < *ga*, refined, noble + *gaku*, music⟧ an ancient music of East Asia associated chiefly with Japan's imperial court

Ga·ga·rin (gä gär′in), **Yu·ri A·lek·se·ye·vich** (yo͞o′rē ä′lyek sā′yə vich) 1934-68; Soviet cosmonaut: 1st man to orbit the earth in a space flight (1961)

gage[1] (gāj) *n.* ⟦ME < OFr, a pledge, pawn < (? via ML *wagium*) Frank **waddi* or Goth *wadi*, pledge < IE base **wadh-*: see WED⟧ **1** [Archaic] something deposited or pledged to ensure that an obligation will be fulfilled; security **2** [Historical] a pledge to appear and fight, as a glove thrown down by a knight challenging another **3** [Archaic] a challenge —*vt.* **gaged**, **gag′ing** [Archaic] **1** to offer as a pledge; wager **2** to bind by a pledge

gage[2] (gāj) *n., vt.* **gaged**, **gag′ing** *alt. sp. of* GAUGE

gage[3] (gāj) *n. short for* GREENGAGE

Gage (gāj), **Thomas** 1721-87; Brit. general in the American Revolution

gag·ger (gag′ər) *n.* a person or thing that gags; specif., a piece of iron to keep a core in place in a mold

gag·gle (gag′əl) *n.* ⟦ME *gagel* < *gagelen*, to cackle: orig. echoic⟧ **1** a flock of geese **2** any group or cluster

gag·man (gag′man′) *n., pl.* **-men′** (-men′) a person who devises jokes, bits of comic business, etc., as for entertainers

☆**gag order** a judge's order prohibiting public discussion of a case by the parties, witnesses, etc. involved in it

☆**gag rule (***or* **law)** a rule or law limiting or preventing discussion, as in a legislative body

gag·ster (gag′stər) *n.* **1** GAGMAN **2** a person fond of making jokes (gags)

gahn·ite (gän′īt′) *n.* ⟦Ger *gahnit*, after J. G. *Gahn* (1745-1818), Swed chemist⟧ a dark green to black, very hard, brittle, crystalline mineral, $ZnAl_2O_4$, found in schists, pegmatites, etc.; zinc spinel

Gai·a (gā′ə, gī′ə) *n. var. of* GAEA

Gaia hypothesis (gī′ə, gā′ə) the theory that the earth is a group of interdependent organisms and environmental systems that function as a single, self-regulating organism

gai·e·ty (gā′ə tē) *n.* ⟦Fr *gaieté*⟧ **1** the state or quality of being GAY (*adj.* 1); cheerfulness **2** *pl.* **-ties** merrymaking; festivity **3** finery; showy brightness

gai·jin (gī jēn′) *n., pl.* **-jin′** ⟦Jpn⟧ in Japan, a foreigner: often a term of derision or contempt

Gail (gāl) *n.* a feminine name: var. *Gayle*: see ABIGAIL

Gail·lard Cut (gāl′yərd, gā′lärd) ⟦after D. D. *Gaillard* (1859-1913), U.S. army engineer in charge of its excavation⟧ S section of the Panama Canal cut through the Continental Divide: *c.* 8 mi (12.9 km) long

☆**gail·lar·di·a** (gā lär′dē ə) *n.* ⟦ModL, after *Gaillard* de Marentonneau, 18th-c. Fr botanist⟧ any of a genus (*Gaillardia*) of American plants of the composite family, having large, showy flower heads with yellow or reddish rays and disks

gai·ly (gā′lē) *adv.* ⟦ME⟧ in a gay manner; specif., *a)* happily; merrily; joyously *b)* brightly; in bright colors

gain[1] (gān) *n.* ⟦ME < OFr *gaaigne* < *gaaignier*: see the *vt.*⟧ **1** an increase; addition; specif., *a)* [*often pl.*] an increase in wealth, earnings, etc.; profit; winnings *b)* an increase in advantage; advantage; improvement **2** the act of getting something; acquisition; accumulation **3** *Electronics a)* an increase in signal strength when transmitted from one point to another: often expressed in decibels *b)* the ratio of the output current, voltage, or power of an amplifier, receiver, etc. to the respective input —*vt.* ⟦ME *gainen*, to profit, be of use < OFr *gaaignier* < Frank **waidanjan*, to work, earn, akin to OHG *weidenen*, to pasture < *weide*, pasture < IE **witi-*, a hunting after < base **wei-*, to go, hunt > L *via*, way, *vis*, strength⟧ **1** to get by labor; earn [to *gain* a livelihood] **2** *a)* to get by effort or merit, as in competition; win *b)* to cause to be directed toward oneself or itself; attract [to *gain* one's interest] **3** to get as an increase, addition, profit, or advantage [to *gain* ten pounds] **4** to make an increase in [to *gain* speed] **5** to go faster by [my watch *gained* two minutes] **6** to get to; arrive at; reach —*vi.* **1** to make progress; improve or advance, as in health, business, etc. **2** to acquire wealth or profit **3** to increase in weight; become heavier **4** to be fast; said of a clock, etc. —**SYN.** GET, REACH —**gain on 1** to draw nearer to (an opponent in a race, etc.) **2** to make more progress than (a competitor) —**gain over** to win over to one's side

☆**gain**[2] (gān) *n.* ⟦< ?⟧ *Carpentry* a groove or mortise, as in a piece of wood, into which another piece can be fitted

gain·er (gān′ər) *n.* **1** a person or thing that gains **2** a dive in which the diver faces forward and does a backward somersault in the air

Gaines·ville (gānz′vil) ⟦after Gen. E. P. *Gaines* (1777-1849)⟧ city in NC Fla.

gain·ful (gān′fəl) *adj.* producing gain; profitable —**gain′ful·ly** *adv.* —**gain′ful·ness** *n.*

gain·ly (gān′lē) *adj.* **-li·er**, **-li·est** ⟦ME *geinli* < *gein*, convenient, ready < ON *gegn*, straight, fit⟧ shapely and graceful; comely —**gain′li·ness** *n.*

gain·say (gān′sā′, gān′sā′) *vt.* **-said′** (-sed′), **-say′ing** ⟦ME *geinseggen* < *gein-* < OE *gegn*, against (see AGAIN) + *secgan* (see SAY)⟧ **1** to deny **2** to contradict **3** to speak or act against; oppose —*n.* a gainsaying —**SYN.** DENY —**gain′say′er** *n.*

Gains·bor·ough (gānz′bur′ō, -bər ə), **Thomas** 1727-88; Eng. painter

'gainst or **gainst** (genst, gānst) *prep.* [Old Poet.] *short for* AGAINST

Gai·ser·ic (gī′zə rik) *var. of* GENSERIC

gait (gāt) *n.* ⟦ME *gate*, a going, gait, orig., path < ON *gata*, path between hedges, street, akin to Ger *gasse*, lane⟧ **1** manner of moving on foot; way of walking or running **2** any of the various foot movements of a horse, as a trot, pace, canter, or gallop —*vt.* **1** to train (a horse) to a particular gait or gaits **2** to lead (a dog) before the judges at a dog show so as to exhibit its gait, bearing, etc.

gait·ed (gāt′id) *adj.* **1** having a (specified) gait or gaits: used in hyphenated compounds [heavy-*gaited*] **2** designating a horse trained to use a specific gait

gai·ter (gāt′ər) *n.* ⟦altered (after GAIT) < Fr *guêtre*, earlier *guietre*, prob. < Frank **wrist*, instep, akin to WRIST⟧ **1** a cloth or leather covering for the instep and ankle, and, sometimes, the calf of the leg; spat or legging ☆**2** a shoe with elastic in the sides and no lacing ☆**3** a high overshoe with cloth upper

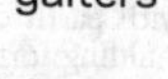

gaiters

Ga·ius[1] (gī′əs, gā′-) *n.* ⟦L⟧ *Rom. History* a masculine praenomen

Ga·ius[2] (gī′əs, gā′-) A.D. 110?-180?; Rom. jurist

gal[1] (gal) *n.* ⟦altered < dial. pronun. of GIRL⟧ [Slang] a girl or woman

gal[2] (gal) *n.* ⟦< GAL(ILEO)⟧ a unit of acceleration equal to one centimeter per second per second: used in gravimetry

gal[3] *abbrev.* gallon(s)

Gal *abbrev. Bible* Galatians

ga·la (gā′lə, gal′ə, gä′lə) *n.* ⟦< Fr or It *gala* < Sp < ? Ar *khilá*, a royal presentation robe⟧ **1** a festive occasion; festival; celebration **2** a public entertainment **3** [**G-**] a red to red-and-gold variety of apple with sweet, crisp flesh —*adj.* festive, or suitable for a festive occasion —**in gala** in festive dress

ga·la·bi·a or **ga·la·bi·ya** (gə lä′bē ə) *n.* ⟦< informal Egypt Ar var. of Ar *jallābīya*⟧ *var. of* DJELLABA

ga·lac·ta·gogue (gə lak′tə gäg′) *n.* ⟦GALACT(O)- + -AGOGUE⟧ an agent that stimulates or increases the secretion of milk

ga·lac·tic (gə lak′tik) *adj.* ⟦Gr *galaktikos*, milky < *gala* (gen. *galaktos*), milk < IE base **glak-* > L *lac*, milk⟧ 1 of or obtained from milk; lactic 2 *Astron.* of or pertaining to the Milky Way or some other galaxy

galactic noise radio waves emanating from sources outside the solar system but within the Milky Way galaxy

ga·lac·to- (gə lak′tō, -tə) ⟦Gr *gala*: see GALACTIC⟧ *combining form* milk, milky [*galactometer*]: also, before a vowel, **ga·lact-** (gə lakt′)

gal·ac·tom·e·ter (gal′ak täm′ə tər) *n.* LACTOMETER

ga·lac·tor·rhe·a (gə lak′tə rē′ə) *n.* ⟦GALACTO- + -RRHEA⟧ persistent flow of milk from the breasts

ga·lac·tose (gə lak′tōs′) *n.* ⟦GALACT(O)- + -OSE²⟧ a white, crystalline monosaccharide, prepared by the hydrolysis of lactose

ga·lac·to·se·mi·a (gə lak′tō sē′mē ə) *n.* ⟦prec. + -EMIA⟧ a congenital disease caused by the genetic lack of an enzyme needed to metabolize galactose into glucose and producing INTELLECTUAL DISABILITY, cataracts, and liver damage

ga·lac·to·side (gə lak′tə sīd′) *n.* ⟦GALACTOS(E) + -IDE⟧ any glycoside which contains galactose

ga·lah (gə lä′) *n.* ⟦< native name⟧ a pink and gray cockatoo (*Cacatua roseicapilla*) that is widely distributed in inland Australia and is popular as a cage bird

Gal·a·had (gal′ə had′) *n.* 1 *Arthurian Legend* a knight who is successful in the quest for the Holy Grail because of his purity and nobility of spirit: he is the son of Lancelot and Elaine 2 any man regarded as very pure and noble

ga·lan·gal (gal′ən gal′) *n.* ⟦ME *galingale* < OFr *galingal* < ML *galingala* < Ar *khulungān*, ult. < ? Chin⟧ 1 either of two plants (genus *Alpinia*) of the ginger family, whose dried rhizomes yield aromatic substances used in medicines and flavorings 2 any of various plants (genus *Cyperus*) of the sedge family, some of which have aromatic rootstocks

gal·an·tine (gal′ən tēn′) *n.* ⟦ME *galentine* < OFr < ML *galatina*, jelly < L *gelata*, fem. pp. of *gelare*: see GELATIN⟧ a mold of boned, seasoned, boiled white meat, as chicken or veal, chilled and served in its own jelly or with aspic

ga·lan·ty show (gə lan′tē) ⟦earlier also *galanté*, prob. < It *galante*, gallant: from the stories portrayed⟧ a pantomime made by throwing the shadows of puppet figures on a screen or wall

Ga·lá·pa·gos Islands (gə lä′pə gōs′) group of islands belonging to Ecuador, in the Pacific on the equator: 3,093 sq mi (8,011 sq km)

Ga·la·ta (gal′ə tə) commercial section of Istanbul, Turkey, on the Golden Horn

gal·a·te·a (gal′ə tē′ə) *n.* ⟦after the 19th-c. Eng warship H.M.S. *Galatea*: the fabric was used to make sailor suits for little boys⟧ a strong, twilled cotton cloth, often striped, used for play clothes, uniforms, etc.

Gal·a·te·a (gal′ə tē′ə) *n. Gr. Myth.* a statue of a maiden which is given life by Aphrodite after its sculptor, Pygmalion, falls in love with it: name applied in post-classical times

Ga·la·ți (gä läts′) city in E Romania, on the Danube

Ga·la·tia (gə lā′shə) ancient kingdom in central Asia Minor, made a Roman province *c.* 25 B.C. —**Ga·la′tian** *adj., n.*

Ga·la·tians (gə lā′shənz) *n.* a book of the New Testament, a letter from the Apostle Paul to the Christians of Galatia: abbrev. *Gal* or *Ga*

gal·a·vant (gal′ə vant′) *vi. alt. sp. of* GALLIVANT

☆**ga·lax** (gā′laks′) *n.* ⟦ModL, prob. < Gr *gala*, milk (see GALACTIC): from its white flower⟧ a dicotyledonous evergreen plant (*Galax aphylla*) of the SE U.S., with shiny leaves (often used in wreaths) and small, white flowers

gal·ax·y (gal′ək sē) *n., pl.* for 2 & 3 **gal′ax·ies** ⟦ME *galaxie* < LL *galaxias* < Gr, Milky Way < *gala*, milk: see GALACTIC⟧ 1 [*usually* **G-**] the MILKY WAY: often with *the* 2 a large, independent system of stars, typically containing millions to hundreds of billions of stars: the four classes of galaxies are spiral, barred spiral, elliptical, or irregular, depending on their shape 3 *a)* an assembly of brilliant or famous people *b)* a brilliant array of things

Gal·ba (gal′bə, gôl′-), **(Servius Sulpicius)** 3? B.C.-A.D. 69; Rom. emperor (68-69)

gal·ba·num (gal′bə nəm) *n.* ⟦ME < L < Gr *chalbanē* < Heb *chelbenah*⟧ a bitter, bad-smelling Asian gum resin, obtained from various plants (genus *Ferula*) of the umbel family, formerly used in medicine

Gal·braith (gal′brāth′), **John Kenneth** 1908-2006; U.S. economist

gale¹ (gāl) *n.* ⟦prob. < Scand, as in Shetland Is. dial. *galder*, howling wind, OIce *gal*, a howling: for IE base see YELL⟧ 1 *a)* a strong wind *b)* *Meteorol.* a wind ranging in speed from 32 to 63 miles per hour (see the Beaufort scale in the Reference Supplement) 2 [Archaic] a breeze ☆3 a loud outburst [*a gale of laughter*] —*SYN.* WIND²

gale² (gāl) *n.* ⟦ME *gawel* < OE *gagel*, akin to Ger *gagel*⟧ SWEET GALE

ga·le·a (gā′lē ə) *n., pl.* **ga′le·ae′** (-ē′) ⟦ModL < L, a helmet: prob. < Gr *galeē*, a weasel, marten (hence, leather, hide, then article made of leather)⟧ *Biol.* a helmet-shaped part, esp. of a corolla or calyx

ga·le·ate (-āt′) *adj.* ⟦L *galeatus*, pp. of *galeare*, to cover with a helmet < *galea*, a helmet⟧ 1 wearing a helmet 2 helmet-shaped 3 having a galea Also **ga′le·at′ed**

Ga·len (gā′lən) (L. name *Claudius Galenus*) A.D. 130?-200?; Gr. physician & writer on medicine & philosophy —**Ga·len·ic** (gə len′ik) *adj.*, **Ga·len′i·cal**

ga·le·na (gə lē′nə) *n.* ⟦L, lead ore, dross of melted lead < ?⟧ a soft, lead-gray, very heavy, crystalline mineral, lead sulfide, PbS, with a bright metallic luster, that is the chief ore of lead: see GLANCE²

ga·len·i·cal (gə len′i kəl) *n.* ⟦after GALEN⟧ a medicine prepared from plants, according to a fixed recipe, as opposed to drugs of known chemical composition

Ga·len·ism (gā′lən iz′əm) *n.* the system of medical practice originated by Galen —**Ga′len·ist** *n.*

ga·le·nite (gə lē′nīt′) *n. var. of* GALENA

ga·lère (gà ler′) *n.* ⟦Fr, lit., GALLEY (*n.* 1)⟧ a group of people of the same sort or class

ga·lette (gä let′) *n.* ⟦Fr⟧ 1 a round, flat cake, esp. an elaborate one made for a holiday 2 a pancake, esp. one of those typically made with buckwheat flour in Brittany

Ga·li·bi (gä lē′bē) *n.* 1 *pl.* **-bis** or **-bi** a member of an Amerindian people living in Guiana 2 the Cariban language of this people

Ga·li·cia (gə lish′ə) 1 region of SE Poland & NW Ukraine: formerly an Austrian crown land 2 region of NW Spain: 11,365 sq mi (29,435 sq km): a former medieval kingdom

Ga·li·ci·an (gə lish′ən, -ē ən) *adj.* 1 of Galicia in NW Spain, or its people, language, or culture 2 of Galicia in E Europe, or its people or culture —*n.* 1 a person born or living in Galicia in Spain 2 the Romance language of this region, closely related to Portuguese 3 a person born or living in Galicia in E Europe

Gal·i·le·an¹ (gal′ə lē′ən) *adj.* of Galilee or its people or culture —*n.* 1 a person born or living in Galilee 2 [Archaic] a Christian —**the Galilean** Jesus

Gal·i·le·an² (gal′ə lā′ən, -lē′-) *adj.* of Galileo

gal·i·lee (gal′ə lē′) *n.* ⟦ME *galilie* < ML *galilaea* < L *Galilaea*, Galilee: ? because, being at the less sacred western end, it was compared with the scriptural "Galilee of the Gentiles"⟧ a porch or chapel at the western entrance of certain medieval churches

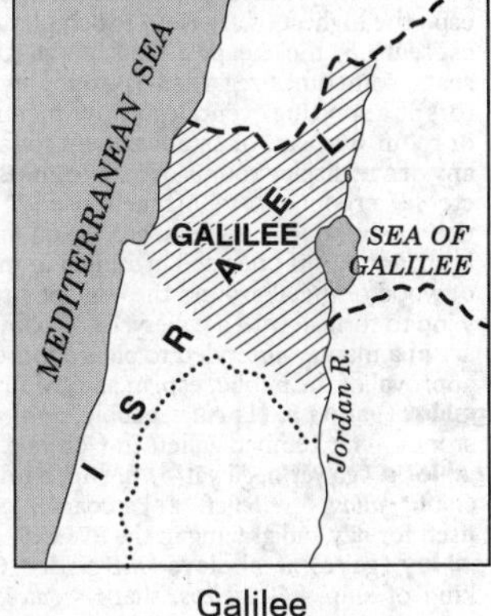

Galilee

Gal·i·lee (gal′ə lē′) ⟦L *Galilaea* < Gr *Galilaia* < Heb *hagalil* < *gelil* (*hagoyim*), lit., district (of the Gentiles)⟧ 1 region of N Israel 2 **Sea of** lake in NE Israel, on the Syrian border: *c.* 13 mi (21 km) long

Gal·i·le·o (gal′ə lā′ō, -lē′-) (born *Galileo Galilei*) 1564-1642; It. astronomer, mathematician, & physicist: with the telescope, which he improved, he demonstrated the truth of the Copernican theory: condemned for heresy by the Inquisition

gal·i·ma·ti·as (gal′i mā′shē əs, -mat′ē əs) *n.* ⟦< ModL *gallimathia* < Fr, prob. < L *gallus*, lit., a cock, 16th-c. student slang for a candidate engaged in doctoral disputations + Gr *-mathia*, learning < *mathēma*: see MATHEMATICAL⟧ meaningless talk; gibberish

gal·in·gale (gal′in gāl′) *n. var. of* GALANGAL

gal·i·ot (gal′ē ət) *n. alt. sp. of* GALLIOT

gal·i·pot (gal′i pät′) *n.* ⟦Fr, earlier *garipot*, prob. altered < MDu *harpois*, boiled resin⟧ crude turpentine from a pine tree (*Pinus pinaster*) of S Europe

gall¹ (gôl) *n.* ⟦ME *galle* < OE (Anglian) *galla* (WS *gealla*), akin to Ger *galle* < IE base **ĝhel-*, to shine, YELLOW > L *fel*, gall, Gr *cholē*, bile⟧ 1 BILE (sense 1) 2 [Archaic] the gallbladder 3 something that is bitter or distasteful 4 bitter feeling; rancor ☆5 rude boldness; impudence; audacity —*SYN.* TEMERITY

gall² (gôl) *n.* ⟦ME *galle* < OE *gealla* < L *galla*: see fol.⟧ 1 a sore on the skin, esp. of a horse's back, caused by rubbing or chafing 2 irritation or annoyance, or a cause of this —*vt.* ⟦ME *gallen* < the *n.* (or < OFr *galer*, to scratch < *galle* < L *galla*)⟧ 1 to injure or make sore by rubbing; chafe 2 to irritate; annoy; vex —*vi.* [Rare] to become sore from rubbing or chafing

gall³ (gôl) *n.* ⟦ME *galle* < OFr < L *galla*, gallnut, orig., spherical growth < IE base **gel-*, to form into a ball > CLAY, CLOT⟧ a tumor on plant tissue caused by stimulation by fungi, insects, or bacteria: galls formed on oak trees have a high tannic acid content and are used commercially

Gal·la (gal′ə) *n., pl.* **-las** or **-la** ⟦earlier *Gaallaa* < ?⟧ *former name for* OROMO: now often considered offensive

gal·lant (gal′ənt; *for adj.* 4 & *n. usually, and for v. always,* gə lant′, -länt′) *adj.* ⟦ME *galaunt* < OFr *galant*, merry, brave, prp. of *galer*, to rejoice, make merry < *gala*: see GALA⟧ 1 showy and lively in dress or manner 2 stately; imposing [*a gallant ship*] 3 brave and noble; high-spirited and daring 4 *a)* polite and attentive to women in a courtly way *b)* having to do with love; amorous —*n.* 1 [Now Rare] a high-spirited, stylish man 2 a man attentive and polite to women 3 a lover or paramour —*vt.* 1 [Now Rare] to court (a woman) 2 to escort or accompany (a woman) —*vi.* [Now Rare] to court a woman —*SYN.* CIVIL —**gal′lant·ly** *adv.*

gal·lant·ry (gal′ən trē) *n., pl.* **-ries** ⟦Fr *galanterie* < OFr *galant*: see prec.⟧ 1 nobility of behavior or spirit; heroic courage 2 the courtly manner of a gallant 3 an act or speech characteristic of a gallant 4 amorous intrigue 5 [Archaic] showy appearance

Gal·la·tin (gal′ə tin), **(Abraham Alfonse) Albert** 1761-1849; U.S. statesman & financier, born in Switzerland: secretary of the treasury (1801-13)

Gal·lau·det (gal′ə det′), **Thomas Hopkins** 1787-1851; U.S. educator: noted for his work with those having hearing and speech impairments

gall·blad·der (gôl′blad′ər) *n.* a membranous sac closely connected by various ducts to the liver, in which excess gall, or bile, is stored and concentrated

gal·le·ass (gal′ē as′) *n.* ⟦Fr *galéasse* < OFr *galeace* < It *galeazza* < ML: see GALLEY⟧ a large, three-masted vessel having sails and oars and carrying heavy guns: used in the Mediterranean in the 16th and 17th cent.

gal·le·in (gal′ē in, gal′ēn) *n.* ⟦GALL(IC ACID) + (PHTHAL)EIN⟧ a violet dye, $C_{20}H_{12}O_7$, formed by heating pyrogallol with phthalic anhydride, used as an indicator and as a mordant dye

gal·le·on (gal′ē ən, gal′yən) *n.* ⟦Sp *galeón* < ML *galea*: see GALLEY⟧ a large sailing ship with three or four masts and a high forecastle and stern, developed in the 15th and 16th cent., and used as both a warship and a trader

gal·le·ri·a (gal′ə rē′ə) *n.* ⟦< It, gallery < ML *galeria*: see GALLERY⟧ a large arcade or court, sometimes with a glass roof, used for displaying artworks, as a passageway to shops or offices, as a location for restaurants, boutiques, etc.

gal·ler·ied (gal′ər ēd) *adj.* having a gallery or galleries

gal·ler·y (gal′ər ē; *often* gal′rē) *n., pl.* **-ler·ies** ⟦ME < OFr *galerie, gallerie*, long portico, gallery < ML *galeria*, prob. < *galilaea*: see GALILEE (porch)⟧ **1** *a)* a covered walk open at one side or having the roof supported by pillars; colonnade *b)* [Chiefly South] a veranda or porch **2** a long, narrow balcony on the outside of a building **3** a platform projecting at either quarter or around the stern of an early sailing ship **4** *a)* a platform or projecting upper floor attached to the back wall or sides of a church, theater, etc.; esp., the highest of a series of such platforms in a theater, with the cheapest seats *b)* the cheapest seats in a theater *c)* the people occupying these seats, sometimes regarded as exemplifying popular tastes *d)* the spectators at a sporting event, legislative meeting, etc. **5** a long, narrow corridor or room **6** a place or establishment for exhibiting or dealing in artworks **7** any of the display rooms of a museum **8** a collection of paintings, statues, etc. ☆**9** a room or establishment used as a photographer's studio, for practice in shooting at targets, etc. **10** an underground passage, as one made by an animal, or one used in mining or military engineering **11** a low railing of wood or metal around the edge of a table, shelf, etc. —*vt.* **-ler·ied**, **-ler·y·ing** to furnish with a gallery, or balcony —**play to the gallery 1** *Theater* to act in a manner intended to please those in the gallery **2** to try to win the approval of the public, esp. in an obvious or showy way

gal·let (gal′it) *n.* ⟦Fr *galet*, pebble, dim. < dial. *gal*, stone: see fol.⟧ a chip of stone —*vt.* to embed gallets in (joints of fresh masonry)

☆**gal·let·a** (gə yet′ə, gä yāt′ə) *n.* ⟦Sp, hardtack < OFr *galette* < *gal*, a stone (< Gaul **gallos*) + *-ette*: cf. -ET⟧ a coarse, tough forage grass (*Hilaria jamesii*) used for hay and grazing in the SW U.S.

gal·ley (gal′ē) *n., pl.* **-leys** ⟦ME *galeie* < OFr *galie* < ML *galea* < MGr *galaia*, kind of ship < Gr *galeos*, shark < *galeē*, weasel (in reference to its speed)⟧ **1** a long, low, usually single-decked ship propelled by oars and sails, used esp. in ancient and medieval times: the oars were usually manned by chained slaves or convicts **2** *a)* the kitchen of a ship, boat, or airplane *b)* a small, compact, or cramped kitchen **3** [Brit.] a large rowboat **4** *Printing a)* a shallow, oblong tray for holding composed type before it is put into a form *b)* GALLEY PROOF

galley

galley proof printer's proof, originally that taken from type in a galley, now usually a single column of copy printed out to permit correction of errors before being made up in pages

☆**gal·ley-west** (gal′ē west′) *adv.* ⟦< dial. *colly-west* < ?⟧ [Informal] into confusion or inaction: chiefly in the phrase **knock galley-west**

gall·fly (gôl′flī′) *n., pl.* **-flies′** an insect whose eggs or larvae cause galls when deposited in plant stems, or one which lays its eggs in galls produced by other insects

Gal·li·a (gal′ē ə, gä′lē ä′) *Latin name for* GAUL[2]

gal·liard (gal′yərd) *adj.* ⟦ME *gaillard* < OFr, brave < ML **galia*, strength < IE base **gal-*, to be able⟧ [Obs.] **1** valiant; sturdy **2** lively —*n.* **1** a lively French dance in triple time, for two dancers, popular in the 16th and 17th cent. **2** music for this

gal·lic (gal′ik) *adj. Chem.* of or containing trivalent gallium

Gal·lic (gal′ik) *adj.* ⟦L *Gallicus* < *Galli*, the Gauls⟧ **1** of ancient Gaul or its people or culture **2** French

gallic acid ⟦Fr *gallique* < *galle*, GALL[3]⟧ a nearly colorless, crystalline acid, $(OH)_3C_6H_2COOH$, prepared from tannins, etc. and used in photography and the manufacture of inks, dyes, etc.

Gal·li·can (gal′i kən) *adj.* ⟦ME < OFr < L *Gallicanus*, of the Roman province of *Gallia* < *Gallicus*⟧ **1** GALLIC **2** of the Roman Catholic Church in France, esp. before 1870 **3** of Gallicanism —*n.* a supporter of Gallicanism

Gal·li·can·ism (-iz′əm) *n.* the principles enunciated by the French Roman Catholic Church in 1682, claiming limited autonomy: opposed to ULTRAMONTANISM

Gal·li·cism (gal′i siz′əm) *n.* ⟦Fr *Gallicisme* < L *Gallicus*, GALLIC⟧ [*also* **g-**] **1** a word, phrase, grammatical construction, or other feature originating in or peculiar to the French language **2** a French custom, way of thought, etc.

Gal·li·cize (gal′i sīz′) *vt., vi.* **-cized′**, **-ciz′ing** ⟦see GALLIC⟧ [*also* **g-**] to make or become French or like the French in thought, language, etc.

gal·li·gas·kins (gal′i gas′kinz) *pl.n.* ⟦altered < Fr *garguesque* < OFr *greguesque* < It *grechesca* < *Grechesca*, Grecian (hence, orig., "Grecian breeches")⟧ **1** loosely fitting breeches worn in the 16th and 17th cent.: later applied humorously to any loose breeches **2** [Brit. Dial.] leggings or gaiters

gal·li·mau·fry (gal′i mô′frē) *n., pl.* **-fries** ⟦Fr *galimafrée*, prob. < OFr *galer* (see GALLANT) + dial. (Picardy) *mafrer*, to eat much < MDu *maffelen*⟧ **1** [Archaic] a hash made of meat scraps **2** a hodgepodge; jumble

gal·li·na·cean (gal′i nā′shən) *adj.* GALLINACEOUS —*n.* any gallinaceous bird

gal·li·na·ceous (gal′i nā′shəs) *adj.* ⟦L *gallinaceus* < *gallina*, hen < *gallus*, a cock⟧ of an order (Galliformes) of birds that nest on the ground, including turkeys, chickens, pheasants, and grouse

gall·ing (gôl′iŋ) *adj.* ⟦prp. of GALL[2]⟧ chafing; very annoying; irritating; vexing —**gall′ing·ly** *adv.*

☆**gal·li·nip·per** (gal′i nip′ər) *n.* ⟦prob. altered (infl. by GALLEY) < *gurnipper* < ?⟧ [Dial.] any of various insects, esp. a large one that bites

gal·li·nule (gal′i no͞ol′, -nyo͞ol′) *n.* ⟦ModL < L *gallinula*, pullet, dim. of *gallina*: see GALLINACEOUS⟧ any of various gruiform marsh birds (family Rallidae) that both swim and wade; esp., the moorhen

gal·li·ot (gal′ē ət) *n.* ⟦ME < OFr *galiot*, dim. of *galie* < ML *galea*, GALLEY⟧ **1** a small, swift galley with sails and oars, formerly used on the Mediterranean **2** a light Dutch merchant vessel of shallow draft, with a mainmast and jigger

Gal·lip·o·li (gə lip′ə lē) *var. of* GELIBOLU

Gallipoli Peninsula peninsula in S European Turkey, forming the NW shore of the Dardanelles: *c.* 55 mi (89 km) long

gal·li·pot[1] (gal′i pät′) *n.* ⟦ME *galy pott*, prob. < *galeie*, GALLEY + *pott*, POT[1]: ? because shipped in galleys from Italy⟧ a small pot or jar of glazed earthenware, esp. one used by druggists as a container for medicine

gal·li·pot[2] (gal′i pät′) *n. alt. sp. of* GALIPOT

gal·li·um (gal′ē əm) *n.* ⟦ModL: so named (1875) by P. E. Lecoq de Boisbaudran (1838-1912), Fr chemist, after L *Gallia*, France, and as a pun on his name *Lecoq* (in L, *gallus*, a cock) + -IUM⟧ a bluish-white, metallic chemical element, often a supercooled liquid at room temperature, used in semiconductors, LED's, lasers, etc., and as a substitute for mercury in high-temperature thermometers: symbol, Ga; at. no. 31: see the periodic table of elements in the Reference Supplement

gallium arsenide a dark gray, crystalline compound, GaAs, used in making semiconductors, lasers, etc.

gal·li·vant (gal′ə vant′) *vi.* ⟦arbitrary elaboration of GALLANT⟧ **1** [Archaic] to gad about with members of the opposite sex **2** to go about in search of amusement or excitement —**gal′li·vant′er** *n.*

gal·li·wasp (gal′ə wäsp′) *n.* ⟦< ?⟧ **1** any of a genus (*Diploglossus*, family Anguidae) of large, harmless lizards found in marshes in the West Indies and Central America **2** a Caribbean lizardfish (*Synodus foetens*)

gall midge (*or* **gnat**) any of a family (Cecidomyiidae) of tiny midges that often produce galls on plants

gall mite any of various mites (family Eriophyidae) that have only two pairs of legs and produce galls on plants

☆**gall·nut** (gôl′nut′) *n.* NUTGALL

Gal·lo- (gal′ō, -ə) ⟦L < *Gallus*, a Gaul⟧ *combining form* French, French and [*Gallophile*]

gal·lo·glass (gal′ō glas′) *n.* ⟦Ir *gallōglach*, servant, soldier < *gall*, foreigner + *ōglach*, a youth, servant, soldier < OIr *ōac*, YOUNG⟧ an armed follower of any of the old Irish chieftains

gal·lon (gal′ən) *n.* ⟦ME *galoun* < NormFr *galon* < OFr *jalon* < VL **gallone* < stem of LL *galleta*, a jug⟧ **1** *a)* a unit of liquid measure, equal to 4 liquid quarts (3.7854 liquid liters): the British and Canadian imperial gallon equals 4.54596 liquid liters *b)* a unit of dry measure, equal to ½ peck or 4 dry quarts (4.4048 dry liters or 0.1556 cubic foot): abbrev. *gal* **2** any container with a capacity of one gallon

gal·lon·age (-ij) *n.* amount or capacity in gallons

gal·loon (gə lo͞on′) *n.* ⟦Fr *galon* < *galonner*, to braid, adorn with lace, altered (? infl. by *gala*: see GALA) < OFr **garlonner* < *garlander*, to ornament < *garlande*, GARLAND⟧ a braid or ribbon, as of cotton or silk or of gold or silver thread, used for trimming or binding

gal·lop (gal′əp) *vi.* ⟦ME *galopen* < OFr *galoper* < Frank **walahlaupan*, to run well < **wala*, akin to WELL[2] + **hlaupan*, to run, akin to LEAP⟧ **1** to go at a gallop **2** to move, progress, or act very fast; hurry —*vt.* to cause to gallop —*n.* ⟦OFr *galop*⟧ **1** the fastest gait of a horse or other animal, consisting of a succession of leaping strides with all the feet off the ground at one time **2** a ride on a galloping animal **3** any fast pace, speedy action, or rapid progression —**gal′lop·er** *n.* —**gal′lop·ing** *adj.*

gal·lo·pade (gal′ə pād′) *n.* ⟦Fr *galopade* < *galoper*: see prec. & -ADE⟧ GALOP

gal·lous (gal′əs) *adj.* ⟦GALL(IUM) + -OUS⟧ *Chem.* of or containing divalent gallium

Gal·lo·way[1] (gal′ə wā′) *n.* any of a breed of polled beef cattle, usually black with a curly coat, resembling the Aberdeen Angus and originating in the district of Galloway

Gal·lo·way[2] (gal′ə wā′) former district of SW Scotland: now part of DUMFRIES AND GALLOWAY

gal·low·glass (gal′ō glas′) *n. alt. sp. of* GALLOGLASS

gal·lows (gal′ōz) *n., pl.* **-lows** or **-lows·es** ⟦ME *galwes*, pl. of *galwe* < OE *galga*, akin to Ger *galgen* < IE base **ĝhalgh-*, pliant tree branch > Lith *žalgà*, long, thin pole: the earliest gallows was a pulled-down branch that carried the victim with it when allowed to spring up⟧ 1 an upright frame with a crossbeam and a rope, for hanging condemned persons 2 any structure like this, used for suspending or supporting 3 the death sentence by hanging

gallows bird [Informal] a person who deserves hanging

☆**gallows humor** amused cynicism by one facing disaster; morbid or cynical humor

gallows tree ⟦ME *galwetre* < OE *galgtreow*⟧ a gallows

gall·stone (gôl′stōn′) ***n.*** a small, solid mass formed in some gallbladders or bile ducts; biliary calculus: it is formed of cholesterol, or, occasionally, of calcium salts, and can obstruct the flow of bile, causing pain, jaundice, and other symptoms

Gal·lup (gal′əp), **George Horace** 1901-84; U.S. statistician

gal·lus·es (gal′əs iz) ***pl.n.*** ⟦< *gallus*, dial. var. of GALLOWS⟧ [Informal] suspenders; braces

gall wasp any of a family (Cynipidae) of tiny hymenopteran insects whose larvae produce galls in plants, esp. oaks and roses

Ga·lois theory (gal wä′) ⟦after E. *Galois* (1811-32), Fr mathematician⟧ a branch of algebra that determines if an algebraic equation can be solved in terms of radicals

ga·loot (gə lo͞ot′) ***n.*** ⟦orig., naval slang < ?⟧ [Slang] a person, esp. an awkward, ungainly person

gal·op (gal′əp; *Fr* gȧ lō′) ***n.*** ⟦Fr: see GALLOP⟧ 1 a lively round dance in 2/4 time 2 music for this —***vi.*** to dance a galop

ga·lore (gə lôr′) ***adj.*** ⟦Ir *go leōr*, enough < *go*, to + *leōr*, enough⟧ in abundance: used postpositively [*a menu with salads galore*]

ga·losh or **ga·loshe** (gə läsh′) ***n.*** ⟦ME *galoche* < OFr < ML *galochium*, shoe with a wooden sole < VL **calopus* < Gr *kalopous*, lit., wooden foot < *kalon*, wood + *pous*, FOOT⟧ 1 either of a pair of overshoes, esp. a high, warmly lined overshoe of rubber and fabric: *usually used in pl.* 2 [Obs.] any heavy shoe or boot

Gals·wor·thy (gôlz′wur′thē, galz′-), **John** 1867-1933; Eng. novelist & playwright

Gal·ton (gôlt′'n), Sir **Francis** 1822-1911; Eng. scientist & writer: pioneer in eugenics

ga·lumph (gə lumf′) ***vi.*** ⟦coined by Lewis CARROLL < GAL(LOP) + (TRI)UMPH⟧ 1 [Now Rare] to march or bound along in a self-satisfied, triumphant manner 2 to move or walk heavily and clumsily

Gal·va·ni (gal vä′nē), **Lu·i·gi** (lo͞o wē′jē) 1737-98; It. physiologist & physicist

gal·van·ic (gal van′ik) ***adj.*** ⟦GALVAN(ISM) + -IC⟧ 1 of or having to do with direct current that is produced by a chemical reaction, as in a storage battery or dry cell 2 stimulating or stimulated as if by electric shock; startling or convulsive Also **gal·van′i·cal** —**gal·van′i·cal·ly** ***adv.***

gal·va·nism (gal′və niz′əm) ***n.*** ⟦Fr *galvanisme* < It *galvanismo*: so called after L. GALVANI⟧ 1 electricity produced by a chemical reaction 2 *Med.* direct electrical current used to stimulate nerves and muscles

gal·va·nize (gal′və nīz′) ***vt.*** **-nized′**, **-niz′ing** ⟦Fr *galvaniser* < *galvanisme*: see prec.⟧ 1 to apply an electric current to 2 to stimulate as if by electric shock; rouse; stir; spur 3 to plate (metal) with zinc, originally by galvanic action —**gal′va·ni·za′tion** ***n.***

gal·va·no- (gal′və nō′, gal van′ō) *combining form* galvanic, galvanism [*galvanometer*]

gal·va·no·mag·net·ic (gal′və nō mag net′ik) ***adj.*** designating or of any electrical or thermal effect resulting from a current that is passing through a conductor or semiconductor in a magnetic field

gal·va·nom·e·ter (gal′və näm′ət ər) ***n.*** an instrument for detecting and measuring a small electric current —**gal′va·no·met′ric** (-və nō me′trik) ***adj.*** —**gal′va·nom′e·try** (-trē) ***n.***

Gal·ves·ton (gal′və stən) ⟦< fol.⟧ seaport in SE Tex., on an island (**Galveston Island**) at the mouth of Galveston Bay

Galveston Bay ⟦after Bernardo de *Gálvez* (1746-86), gov. of Louisiana⟧ inlet of the Gulf of Mexico, in SE Tex.

Gal·way (gôl′wā) 1 county in Connacht province, W Ireland: 2,293 sq mi (5,939 sq km) 2 its county seat, on an inlet of the Atlantic (**Galway Bay**)

Gal·we·gian (gal wē′jən) ***adj.*** 1 of Galloway or its people 2 of Galway or its people —***n.*** a person born or living in Galloway or Galway

gal·yak or **gal·yac** (gal′yak′) ***n.*** ⟦< word used in a region of Uzbekistan for a premature lamb < Russ *golyak*, bare, naked < IE base **gal-* > CALLOW⟧ a flat, glossy fur made from the pelts of lambs or kids

☆**gam**[1] (gam) ***n.*** ⟦prob. < Scand, as in Norw, Swed dial. *gams*, loose conversation < ON *gems*, akin to GAME[1]⟧ 1 a social visit 2 a social visit or conversation between the crews of ships, esp. whaling ships, at sea 3 a school of whales —***vi.*** **gammed**, **gam′ming** 1 to take part in a gam 2 to come together; congregate: said of whales

gam[2] (gam) ***n.*** ⟦var. of GAMB⟧ a leg; often, specif., a woman's shapely leg

Gama, **Vasco da** *see* DA GAMA, Vasco

☆**ga·ma grass** (gä′mə) ⟦altered < *grama grass*: see GRAMA⟧ any of several tall, perennial, American grasses (genus *Tripsacum*), used for forage

Ga·ma·li·el (gə mā′lē əl, -māl′yəl) ***n.*** ⟦LL < Gr *Gamaliēl* < Heb *gamliel*, lit., reward of God⟧ *Bible* a teacher of Saul of Tarsus: Acts 22:3

ga·may (ga mā′) ***n.*** ⟦after *Gamay*, village in Burgundy⟧ [*sometimes* **G-**] 1 a red grape used esp. in making Beaujolais 2 any of several wines made from this grape

gamb or **gambe** (gamb) ***n.*** ⟦dial. Fr *gambe* (Fr *jambe*) < ML *gamba*, a leg (in LL, a hoof) < Gr *kampē*, a turn, bend: see CAMPUS⟧ an animal's leg or shank, esp. on a coat of arms

gam·ba·do (gam bā′dō) ***n.***, *pl.* **-dos** or **-does** 1 ⟦altered < Fr *gambade* < Prov *gambado* < It *gambata*, a kick < *gamba*, leg: see prec.⟧ *a)* a curvetting leap, as by a horse *b)* a prank or antic 2 ⟦< It *gamba*, a leg⟧ a long legging, esp. one attached to a saddle to serve as a stirrup

gam·be·son (gam′bi sən) ***n.*** ⟦ME < OFr < ML *wambasium* < LGr *bambax*, cotton: see BOMBAST⟧ a medieval coat, made of leather or quilted cloth, worn as armor

Gam·bi·a (gam′bē ə) 1 country on the W coast of Africa, surrounded on three sides by Senegal: formerly a British colony & protectorate, it became independent (1965) & a member of the Commonwealth: 4,363 sq mi (11,300 sq km); cap. Banjul: official name **The Gambia** 2 river in W Africa, flowing from N Guinea, through Senegal & Gambia, into the Atlantic: *c.* 700 mi (1,127 km)

gam·bier or **gam·bir** (gam′bir) ***n.*** ⟦Malay *gambir*⟧ an astringent substance extracted from various S Asian plants (genus *Uncaria*) of the madder family, chewed with the betel nut: used in tanning and dyeing and, formerly, in medicine

gam·bit (gam′bit) ***n.*** ⟦Fr < OFr *gambet* < Sp *gambito*, a tripping < It *gamba*, a leg < ML *gamba*: see GAMB⟧ 1 *Chess* an opening in which a pawn or other piece is sacrificed to get an advantage in position 2 an opening maneuver, action, or remark intended to gain an advantage or to offer an opinion

gam·ble (gam′bəl) ***vi.*** **-bled**, **-bling** ⟦prob. back-form. < obs. *gamler*, a gambler < *gamel*, to play (altered < ME *gamen*, to play < *game*, GAME[1]) + -ER: akin to Ger dial. *gammeln*, to sport, make merry⟧ 1 to play games of chance for money or some other stake 2 to take a risk in order to gain some advantage —***vt.*** to risk in gambling; bet; wager —***n.*** an act or undertaking involving risk of a loss —**gamble away** to squander or lose in gambling —**gam′bler** (-blər) ***n.***

gam·boge (gam′bōj′, -bo͞oj′, -bo͞ozh′) ***n.*** ⟦ModL *gambogium*, after CAMBODIA, where first obtained⟧ a gum resin obtained from a tropical Asian tree (*Garcinia hanburyi*) of the St. Johnswort family, used as a yellow pigment and as a cathartic

gam·bol (gam′bəl) ***n.*** ⟦earlier *gambolde* < Fr *gambade*, a gambol: see GAMBADO⟧ a jumping and skipping about in play; frolic —***vi.*** **-boled** or **-bolled**, **-bol·ing** or **-bol·ling** to jump and skip about in play; frolic

gam·brel (gam′brəl) ***n.*** ⟦NormFr < OFr *gambe*: see GAMB⟧ 1 the hock of a horse or similar animal 2 a frame shaped like a horse's hind leg, used by butchers for hanging carcasses ☆3 GAMBREL ROOF

☆**gambrel roof** a roof with two slopes on each of its two sides, the lower steeper than the upper

gam·bu·si·a (gam byo͞o′zē ə, -sē ə) ***n.*** ⟦ModL, altered from Cuban Sp *gambusino*⟧ ☆any of a genus (*Gambusia*) of livebearers, including the mosquitofish, useful in mosquito control

gambrel roof

game[1] (gām) ***n.*** ⟦ME < OE *gamen*, akin to OFris *game*, OHG *gaman* < ? IE base **gwhemb-*, to leap merrily⟧ 1 any form of play or way of playing; amusement; recreation; sport; frolic; play 2 *a)* any specific contest, engagement, amusement, computer simulation, or sport involving physical or mental competition under specific rules, as football, chess, or war games *b)* a single contest in such a competition [to win two out of three *games*] *c)* *Tennis* a subdivision of a SET (***n.*** 6*h*), consisting of a series of at least four consecutive serves by a single player *d)* a subdivision of any of certain other contests 3 *a)* the number of points required for winning [the *game* is 25] *b)* the score at any given point in a competition [at the half the *game* was 7 to 6] 4 that which is gained by winning; victory; win 5 a set of equipment for a competitive amusement [to sell toys and *games*] 6 a way or quality of playing in competition [to play a good *game*] 7 any test of skill, courage, or endurance [the *game* of life] 8 a project; scheme; plan [to see through another's *game*] 9 *a)* wild birds or animals hunted for sport or for use as food (see also BIG GAME) *b)* the flesh of such creatures used as food 10 FAIR GAME (sense 2) 11 [Informal] a business or vocation, esp. one with an element of risk [the stock-market *game*] —***vi.*** **gamed**, **gam′ing** 1 to play cards, etc. for stakes; gamble 2 to play computer or video games —***vt.*** [Informal] to take advantage of or manipulate to one's own advantage [to *game* the system, *game* an election] —***adj.*** 1 designating or of wild birds or animals hunted for sport or for use as food: see also GAME FISH, GAME FOWL 2 **gam′er**, **gam′est** *a)* plucky; courageous *b)* having enough spirit or enthusiasm; ready (*for* something) —☆**ahead of the game** [Informal] in the position of winning, esp. in gambling —**die game** to die bravely and still fighting —**game away** to squander or lose in gambling —**make game of** to make fun of; make the butt of jokes, teasing, etc.; ridicule —**off one's game** not performing up to one's usual level —**play the game** [Informal] 1 to act according to the rules of a game 2 to behave as fairness or custom requires —**The Game** charades —**the game is up** all chances for success are gone

game[2] (gām) ***adj.*** ⟦< ?⟧ [Informal] lame or injured: said esp. of a leg

game·cock (gām′käk′) ***n.*** a specially bred rooster trained for cockfighting

☆**game face** [Informal] an athlete's facial expression during or just before competition, when it indicates resolution and concentration: often used fig. [put on your *game face* and get to work]

game fish any fish regularly caught for sport

game fowl any of a breed of fowl trained for cockfighting

game·keep·er (gām′kēp′ər) ***n.*** a person employed to breed and take care of game birds and animals on private estates, game preserves, etc.
gam·e·lan (gam′ə lan′) ***n.*** ⟦Javanese, a bamboo xylophone⟧ a musical ensemble of Indonesia, consisting of wind, string, and percussion instruments, as flute, lute, gongs, drums, and bamboo xylophones
game laws laws regulating hunting and fishing in order to preserve game
game·ly (gām′lē) ***adv.*** in a game, or plucky, manner
game·ness (-nis) ***n.*** a game, or plucky, quality
game of chance any game entirely or chiefly dependent upon the element of chance, as through the use of dice, a roulette wheel, playing cards, a lottery, etc.: games of chance often involve gambling
game plan **1** the strategy planned before a game, esp. a football game **2** any long-range strategy to reach an objective
game·play (gām′plā′) ***n.*** the way a particular video game is designed and played
☆**game point** *Tennis* **1** a situation in which the next point scored can decide the winner of the GAME[1] (*n.* 2c) **2** the point that wins the game
gam·er (gām′ər) ***n.*** [Slang] **1** an athlete who is GAME[1] (*adj.* 2); specif., one who is highly competitive, steadfast and reliable, etc., esp. in difficult situations **2** a person who plays computer and video games, board games, etc.
game show *Radio, TV* a program in which audience participants compete for prizes
games·man·ship (gāmz′mən ship′) ***n.*** ⟦< GAME[1] + (SPORT)SMANSHIP⟧ skill in using ploys to gain a victory or advantage over another person
game·some (gām′səm) ***adj.*** ⟦ME *gamsum:* see GAME[1] & -SOME[1]⟧ playful; sportive; frolicsome —**game′some·ly** ***adv.***
game·ster (gām′stər) ***n.*** ⟦GAME[1] + -STER⟧ a gambler
gam·e·tan·gi·um (gam′ə tan′jē əm) ***n.***, *pl.* **-gi·a** (-ə) ⟦ModL: see fol. & ANGIO-⟧ a plant structure in which gametes are produced
gam·ete (gam′ēt, gə mēt′) ***n.*** ⟦ModL *gameta* < Gr *gametē*, a wife < *gamein*, to marry < *gamos:* see GAMO-⟧ a reproductive cell that is haploid and can unite with another gamete to form the cell (*zygote*) that develops into a new individual —**ga·met·ic** (gə met′ik) ***adj.***
game theory a method of using mathematical analysis to select the best available strategy in order to minimize one's maximum losses or maximize one's minimum winnings in a game, war, business competition, etc.
ga·me·to- (gə mēt′ō, -ə) *combining form* gamete *[gametophore]*
ga·me·to·cyte (gə mēt′ə sīt′) ***n.*** a parent cell, which undergoes meiosis and produces gametes
ga·me·to·gen·e·sis (gə mēt′ō jen′ə sis) ***n.*** the entire process of consecutive cell divisions and differentiation by which mature eggs or sperm are developed —**ga·me′to·gen′ic** (-jen′ik) ***adj.***, **gam·e·tog·e·nous** (gam′ə täj′ə nəs) —**gam′e·tog′e·ny** (-nē) ***n.***
ga·me·to·phore (gə mēt′ə fôr′) ***n.*** that part of a plant bearing the organs that produce gametes —**ga·me′to·phor′ic** ***adj.***
ga·me·to·phyte (-fīt′) ***n.*** in plants, the gamete-bearing generation that is haploid and reproduces by eggs and sperms: distinguished from SPOROPHYTE —**ga·me′to·phyt′ic** (-fit′ik) ***adj.***
gam·ey (gām′ē) ***adj.*** *alt. sp. of* GAMY
gam·ic (gam′ik) ***adj.*** ⟦< Gr *gamos*, marriage (see GAMO-) + -IC⟧ *Biol.* that can develop only after fertilization: said of such an ovum
gam·i·ly (gām′ə lē) ***adv.*** in a gamy manner; esp., pluckily
gam·in (gam′in; *Fr* gȧ man′) ***n.*** ⟦Fr⟧ **1** a neglected child left to roam the streets; street urchin **2** a girl with a roguish, saucy charm: also **ga·mine** (ga mēn′)
gam·i·ness (gām′ē nis) ***n.*** the quality of being gamy
gam·ing (gām′iŋ) ***n.*** **1** the act or practice of gambling **2** playing games that imitate possible business situations or war maneuvers, as preparation or training **3** the act or practice of playing computer or video games
gam·ma (gam′ə) ***n.*** ⟦ME < Gr < Sem, as in Heb *gimel*, akin to *gamal*, camel⟧ **1** the third letter of the Greek alphabet (Γ, γ) **2** the third of a group or series **3** a microgram **4** a number indicating the degree of contrast between the darkest and lightest parts of a photographic image **5** a unit of magnetic field intensity equal to 10^{-5} — ***adj.*** *Chem. see* ALPHA
gam·ma·di·on (gə mā′dē ən) ***n.***, *pl.* **-di·a** (-ə) ⟦MGr, dim. < Gr *gamma*⟧ a figure made by four capital gammas radiating from a center; esp., a swastika
gamma globulin that fraction of blood serum which contains most antibodies, used in the temporary prevention of several infectious diseases, as measles and hepatitis
gamma ray **1** electromagnetic radiation having a wavelength of 10^{-9} centimeters or less: may be produced by the reactions of nuclei or elementary particles or by the interaction of high energy electrons with matter **2** a stream of gamma rays
gam·mer (gam′ər) ***n.*** ⟦altered < GODMOTHER⟧ an old woman, esp. one from the country: now usually humorous: cf. GAFFER
gam·mon[1] (gam′ən) ***n.*** ⟦ME *gambon* < NormFr < dial. Fr *gambe:* see GAMB⟧ **1** the bottom end of a side of bacon **2** a smoked or cured ham or side of bacon
gam·mon[2] (gam′ən) ***n.*** ⟦ME *gammen*, var. of *game, gamen:* see GAME[1]⟧ *Backgammon* a victory in which the winner gets rid of all pieces before his or her opponent gets rid of any —***vt.*** to defeat by scoring a gammon
gam·mon[3] (gam′ən) ***vt.*** ⟦< *gammon*, a lashing up < ?⟧ to secure (the bowsprit) to the stem of a vessel
gam·mon[4] (gam′ən) ***n.*** ⟦prob. orig. thieves' cant < ?⟧ [Brit. Informal] nonsense intended to deceive; humbug — ***vt., vi.*** **1** to talk humbug (to) **2** to deceive or mislead
gam·my (gam′ē) ***adj.*** ⟦altered < ? GAME[2]⟧ [Brit. Informal] GAME[2]
gam·o- (gam′ō, -ə) ⟦< Gr *gamos*, marriage < IE base *ĝem-, to marry, be related > Sans *jārá-h*, suitor, *jāmā*, daughter-in-law, L *gener*, son-in-law⟧ *combining form* **1** sexually united *[gamogenesis]* **2** joined or united *[gamosepalous]* Also, before a vowel, **gam-** (gam)
gam·o·gen·e·sis (gam′ō jen′ə sis) ***n.*** reproduction by the uniting of gametes; sexual reproduction —**gam′o·ge·net′ic** (-jə net′ik) ***adj.*** —**gam′o·ge·net′i·cal·ly** ***adv.***
gam·o·pet·al·ous (-pet′′l əs) ***adj.*** having the petals united so as to form a tubelike corolla as a morning glory
gam·o·phyl·lous (-fil′əs) ***adj.*** having leaves or leaflike organs joined by their edges
gam·o·sep·al·ous (-sep′əl əs) ***adj.*** having the sepals united; monosepalous
-ga·mous (gə məs) ⟦< Gr *gamos* (see GAMO-) + -OUS⟧ *combining form forming adjectives* marrying, uniting sexually *[heterogamous, polygamous]*
Ga·mow (gam′ôf, -äf), **George Antony** 1904-68; U.S. astrophysicist, born in Russia
gamp (gamp) ***n.*** ⟦in allusion to the umbrella of Mrs. *Gamp* in Dickens' *Martin Chuzzlewit*⟧ [Brit.] a large umbrella, esp. one that is bulky or awkwardly wrapped
gam·ut (gam′ət) ***n.*** ⟦ML *gamma ut* < *gamma*, the gamut, name used by GUIDO D'AREZZO for the lowest note of his scale (< Gr *gamma*, GAMMA) + *ut* < L *ut*, that, used as a musical note, taken from a medieval song whose phrases began on successive ascending major tones: *Ut* queant laxis *Re*sonare fibris, *Mi*ra gestorum *Fa*muli tuorum, *Sol*ve polluti *La*bii reatum, Sancte Iohannes⟧ **1** *Music* *a)* the lowest note of the medieval scale, corresponding to modern G below middle C *b)* the complete medieval scale *c)* the entire series of recognized notes in modern music *d)* any complete musical scale, esp. the major scale **2** the entire range or extent, as of emotions —***SYN.*** RANGE
gam·y (gām′ē) ***adj.*** **gam′i·er**, **gam′i·est** **1** having a strong, tangy flavor like that of cooked game **2** strong in smell or taste; slightly tainted **3** plucky; game **4** *a)* risqué or racy *b)* salacious, coarse, or crude
-ga·my (gə mē) ⟦Gr *-gamia* < *gamos:* see GAMO-⟧ *combining form forming nouns* marriage, sexual union *[polygamy]*
gan (gan) ***vt., vi.*** *pt. of* GIN[3]
ga·nache (gə näsh′) ***n.*** ⟦Fr⟧ a rich, thick filling or frosting of heavy cream and usually chocolate
Gand (gän) *Fr. name for* GHENT
Gan·da (gän′də, gan′-) ***n.*** **1** *pl.* **-das** or **-da** a member of an agricultural people of S Uganda **2** the Bantu language of this people
gan·der (gan′dər) ***n.*** ⟦ME < OE *gan(d)ra*, akin to Ger dial., Du, LowG *gander*, akin to Ger *gans*, GOOSE⟧ **1** a male goose **2** a stupid or silly fellow **3** [Slang] a look: chiefly in the phrase **take a gander**
Gan·dhi (gän′dē, gan′-) **1** Mrs. **In·di·ra (Nehru)** (in dir′ə) 1917-84; Indian statesman: prime minister of India (1966-77; 1980-84): assassinated: daughter of Jawaharlal Nehru **2** **Mo·han·das K(aramchand)** (mō hän′dəs) 1869-1948; Hindu nationalist leader & social reformer: assassinated: called *Mahatma Gandhi* —**Gan′dhi·an** ***adj.***
Gan·dhi·ism (-iz′əm) ***n.*** the political theories of Mohandas Gandhi, esp. his theories of passive resistance and civil disobedience to achieve reform
Gan·dhi·na·gar (gun′də nug′ər) city in W India: capital of Gujarat state
☆**gan·dy dancer** (gan′dē) ⟦prob. so named because of movements while using tools from the *Gandy* Manufacturing Co. (Chicago)⟧ [Old Slang] a worker in a railroad section gang
ga·nef (gä′nəf) ***n.*** ⟦Yiddish *ganef* < Heb *ganav* < *ganav*, to steal⟧ [Slang] a thief
Ga·nesh (gə näsh′, -nesh′) ***n.*** ⟦< Sans *Gaṇeśa*, lord of the ganas, or attendants of Siva⟧ a Hindu god, typically depicted with the head of an elephant: also **Ga·ne′sha** (-nā′shə)
gang[1] (gaŋ) ***n.*** ⟦ME, a band or company, orig., a going, journey < OE < base of *gangan:* see fol.⟧ **1** a group of people associated together in some way; specif., *a)* a group of workers directed by a foreman *b)* an organized group of criminals *c)* a squad of convicts at work *d)* a group of youths from one neighborhood banded together for social reasons; often specif., a band of juvenile delinquents **2** a set of like tools, machines, components, etc., designed or arranged to work together: often used attributively *[gang drills]* **3** a very large number of persons or things —***vi.*** ☆to form, or be associated in, a gang (with *up*) —***vt.*** ☆**1** [Informal] to attack as a gang ☆**2** to arrange in a gang, or coordinated set —☆**gang up on** [Informal] to attack or oppose as a group
gang[2] (gaŋ) ***vi.*** ⟦ME *gangen* < OE *gangan*, akin to ON *ganga*, Goth *gaggan*, to go < IE base *ĝhengh- > Sans *jáṁhas-*, a step⟧ [Scot.] to go or work
gang·bang (gaŋ′baŋ′) ***n.*** [Slang] **1** sexual intercourse with, or, esp., rape of, one woman by several men in rapid succession: term considered vulgar by some **2** a sexual orgy in which men and women change partners: term considered vulgar by some ☆**3** a gang fight
☆**gang·bang·er** (gaŋ′baŋ′ər) ***n.*** [Slang] a member of a youth gang
☆**gang·bust·er** (-bus′tər) [Slang] ***n.*** a police officer or official engaged in combating criminal gangs —***adj.*** strikingly forceful, effective, or successful —**like gangbusters** very forcefully, energetically, or effectively
gang·er (gaŋ′ər) ***n.*** a foreman of a gang of workers
Gan·ges (gan′jēz) river in N India & Bangladesh, flowing from the Himalayas into the Bay of Bengal: *c.* 1,560 mi (2,511 km) —**Gan·get·ic** (gan jet′ik) ***adj.***
☆**gang hook** a multiple fishhook consisting of several, usually three, hooks with their shanks joined

☆**gang·land** (gaŋ′land′) ***n.*** the sphere of criminal gangs: now usually used attributively [*a gangland slaying*]

gan·gli·at·ed (gaŋ′glē āt′id) ***adj.*** having ganglia: also **gan′gli·ate** (-it, -āt′)

gan·gling (gaŋ′gliŋ) ***adj.*** ⟦? altered (? infl. by DANGLE) < GANGREL, in obs. sense, "lanky person"⟧ thin, tall, and awkward; of loose, lanky build: also **gan′gly** (-glē)

gan·gli·o- (gaŋ′glē ō, -ə) *combining form* ganglion: also, before a vowel, **gangli-**

gan·gli·on (gaŋ′glē ən, -än′) ***n.***, *pl.* **-gli·a** (-ə) or **-gli·ons** ⟦special use of LL *ganglion*, a swelling < Gr, tumor, prob. redupl. < IE base **gel-*, to form into a ball > CLING, CLOD⟧ **1** a mass of nerve cells serving as a center from which nerve impulses are transmitted **2** a center of force, energy, activity, etc. **3** a cystic tumor on a tendon sheath —**gan′gli·on′ic** (-än′ik) ***adj.***

gan·gli·o·side (-ə sīd′) ***n.*** ⟦GANGLI(O)- + -OSE[1] + -IDE⟧ any of a group of complex lipids found mainly on the membranes of nervous tissue and in the liver, spleen, and kidney

☆**gang·plank** (gaŋ′plaŋk′) ***n.*** ⟦< *gang*, a going (see GANG[1]) + PLANK⟧ a narrow, movable platform or ramp forming a bridge by which to board or leave a ship

☆**gang plow** a plow with a number of shares fastened side by side for making several furrows at a time

gan·grel (gaŋ′grəl, gaŋ′rəl) ***n.*** ⟦ME, a vagabond, tramp, prob. < *gangen* (see GANG[2]) + ending seen also in *wastrel*⟧ [Now Chiefly Dial.] a roving beggar; vagrant

gan·grene (gaŋ′grēn′, gaŋ grēn′) ***n.*** ⟦Fr *gangrène* < L *gangraena* < Gr *gangraina*, redupl. < *gran*, to gnaw < IE base **gras-* > L *gramen*, grass, fodder⟧ decay of tissue in a part of the body when the blood supply is obstructed by injury, disease, etc. — ***vt., vi.*** **-grened′**, **-gren′ing** [Now Rare] to develop gangrene (in) —**gan′gre·nous** (-grə nəs) ***adj.***

gang·sta (gaŋ′stə) ***n.*** ⟦< fol.⟧ **1** a variety of rap music that is distinguished by an emphasis on themes of violence, criminality, and machismo: also **gangsta rap** **2** a person who writes and performs this music: also **gangsta rapper**

☆**gang·ster** (gaŋ′stər) ***n.*** ⟦see -STER⟧ a member of a gang of criminals —**gang′ster·ism′** ***n.***

Gang·tok (guŋ′täk′) city in E India: capital of Sikkim state

gangue (gaŋ) ***n.*** ⟦Fr < Ger *gang*, metallic vein, passage, lit., a going, akin to GANG[1]⟧ the commercially worthless mineral matter associated with economically valuable metallic minerals in a deposit

gang·way (gaŋ′wā′; *for interj.* gaŋ′wā′) ***n.*** ⟦OE *gangweg*, thoroughfare (< GANG[1], in obs. sense "a going" & WAY)⟧ **1** a passageway for entering, leaving, or going past **2** *a)* an opening in a vessel's bulwarks or railing that allows passage on or off *b)* GANGPLANK **3** a main level in a mine ☆**4** an incline for logs, leading up to a sawmill **5** [Brit.] a passageway between rows of seats; aisle; specif., in the House of Commons, the aisle separating frontbenchers from backbenchers —***interj.*** make room; clear the way

gan·is·ter (gan′is tər) ***n.*** ⟦Ger dial. *ganster* < MHG, a spark, akin to OE *gnast*, spark: see GNEISS⟧ a hard, siliceous sedimentary rock sometimes found underlying coal beds, used in making brick for refractory linings of metallurgical furnaces

gan·ja or **gan·jah** (gän′jə) ***n.*** ⟦Hindi *gā̃ja* < Sans *gañjā*⟧ MARIJUANA

gan·net (gan′it) ***n.***, *pl.* **-nets** or **-net** ⟦ME *ganat* < OE *ganot*, solan goose, lit., a gander, akin to Du *gent*, OHG *ganazzo*, gander: for IE base see GOOSE⟧ any of a genus (*Morus*, family Sulidae) of pelecaniform birds; esp., a white, gooselike, web-footed bird (*M. bassanus*) that breeds on cliffs along the N Atlantic coasts

gan·nis·ter (gan′is tər) ***n.*** *alt. sp. of* GANISTER

gan·oid (gan′oid′) ***adj.*** ⟦Fr *ganoïde* < Gr *ganos*, brightness (prob. < IE base **gāu-*, to rejoice > L *gaudium*, JOY) + *-eidēs*, -OID⟧ of or having growing scales with a hard glossy surface of many layers of enamel, as in many extinct and some living fishes —***n.*** a fish having such scales, as the sturgeons, gars, and paddlefishes

Gan·su (gän′sü′) province of NW China: 141,506 sq mi (366,499 sq km): cap. Lanzhou

gant·let[1] (gônt′lit, gänt′-, gant′-) ***n.*** ⟦earlier *gantlope* < Swed *gatlopp*, a running down a lane < *gata*, lane (akin to Ger *gasse*: see GAIT) + *lopp*, a run, akin to LEAP⟧ **1** *a)* a former military punishment in which the offender had to run between two rows of men who struck him with clubs, etc. as he passed *b)* a series of troubles or difficulties (in these senses, now spelled equally *gauntlet*) **2** a section of railroad track through a narrow passage where two lines of track overlap, one rail of each line being within the rails of the other —***vt.*** to overlap (railroad tracks) so as to make a gantlet —**run the gantlet** **1** to be punished by means of the gantlet **2** to proceed while under attack from both sides, as by criticism

gant·let[2] (gônt′lit, gänt′-, gant′-) ***n.*** *var. of* GAUNTLET[1]

gant·line (gant′līn′) ***n.*** ⟦altered < ? *girtline* (< GIRT[2] + LINE[2])⟧ *Naut.* a rope passing through an overhead pulley, used as for hoisting gear aloft

gan·try (gan′trē) ***n.***, *pl.* **-tries** ⟦ME *gauntre*, altered (prob. infl. by *tre*, TREE) < OFr *gantier, chantier* < L *canterius*, beast of burden, trellis < Gr *kanthēlios*, a pack ass⟧ **1** a frame on which barrels can be set horizontally **2** a framework that spans a distance, often moving on wheels at each end, used for carrying a traveling crane **3** a bridgelike framework over railroad tracks, for supporting signals or for loading ☆**4** a wheeled framework with a crane, platforms at different levels, etc., used for assembling, positioning, and servicing a large rocket at its launching site

Gan·y·mede (gan′i mēd′) ***n.*** ⟦Gr *Ganymēdēs*⟧ **1** *Gr. Myth.* a beautiful youth carried off by Zeus to be the cupbearer to the gods **2** the largest satellite of Jupiter: discovered in 1610 by Galileo

GAO *abbrev.* Government Accountability Office (since July, 2004); formerly, General Accounting Office

gaol (jāl) ***n.*** *Brit. sp. of* JAIL —**gaol′er** ***n.***

gap (gap) ***n.*** ⟦ME < ON < *gapa*, to yawn, fol.⟧ **1** a hole or opening, as in a wall or fence, made by breaking or parting; breach **2** a mountain pass, cleft, or ravine **3** an interruption of continuity in space or time; hiatus; lacuna **4** a lag or disparity between conditions, ideas, natures, etc. **5** SPARK GAP —***vt.*** **gapped**, **gap′ping** to make an opening in; breach —***vi.*** to come apart; open

gape (gāp; *occas.* gap) ***vi.*** **gaped**, **gap′ing** ⟦ME *gapen* < ON *gapa* < IE **ghēp-* < IE **ghēp-* < base **ghe-*, to yawn, gape > GAB, Gr *chasma*, abyss, L *hiatus*⟧ **1** to open the mouth wide, as in yawning or from hunger **2** to stare with the mouth open, as in wonder or surprise **3** to open or be opened wide, as a chasm —***n.*** **1** the act of gaping; specif., *a)* an open-mouthed stare *b)* a yawn **2** a wide gap or opening **3** *Zool.* the measure of the widest possible opening of a mouth or beak —**the gapes** **1** a disease of young poultry and birds, characterized by gasping and choking and caused by gapeworms **2** a fit of yawning —**gap′er** ***n.*** —**gap′ing·ly** ***adv.***

gape·worm (gāp′wurm′) ***n.*** a roundworm (*Syngamus trachea*) parasitic in the respiratory passage of young poultry and other birds and causing the gapes

gap·toothed (gap′to͞otht′) ***adj.*** having a gap between two teeth, as because of a missing tooth

☆**gar** (gär) ***n.***, *pl.* **gar** or **gars** ⟦contr. < GARFISH⟧ **1** any of an order (Semionotiformes) of North American freshwater bony fishes having an elongated body covered with ganoid scales, a long beaklike snout, and many sharp teeth **2** NEEDLEFISH

GAR *abbrev.* Grand Army of the Republic: a fraternal order of Union veterans of the Civil War

ga·rage (gə räzh′, -räj′; *Brit* gar′äzh′, -ij) ***n.*** ⟦Fr < *garer*, to protect, preserve < Gmc, as in OHG *waron*, to watch over: for IE base see WARN⟧ **1** a closed shelter for a motor vehicle or vehicles **2** a business establishment where motor vehicles are stored, repaired, serviced, etc. —***adj.*** **1** designating or of a kind of loud, fast rock music originating in the U.S. in the 1960s, characterized by crude instrumental and vocal techniques associated with young, amateur musicians **2** designating or of a band that plays such music —***vt.*** **-raged′**, **-rag′ing** to put or keep in a garage

☆**garage sale** a sale of used or unwanted possessions, as household articles, often held in the garage of a house

ga·ram masala (gə räm′, gär′əm) ⟦Hindi & Urdu, lit., hot spices: see MASALA⟧ a hot spice mixture, usually of ground coriander, cumin, cinnamon, cloves, cardamom, and pepper, used in Indian cooking

Gar·a·mond (gar′ə mänd′) ***n.*** a style of type orig. designed by Claude Garamond, 16th-cent. Fr. type founder

☆**Gar·and rifle** (gar′ənd, gə rand′) ⟦after J. C. *Garand*, U.S. engineer who invented it⟧ a semiautomatic, rapid-firing, .30-caliber rifle: the former standard infantry weapon of the U.S. Army: see also SPRINGFIELD RIFLE

garb (gärb) ***n.*** ⟦OFr *garbe*, gracefulness < It *garbo*, elegance < ? Gmc **garwī* > OHG *gar(a)wen*, to prepare, dress, ornament⟧ **1** manner or style of clothing, esp. as characteristic of an occupation, profession, or rank [*clerical garb*] **2** external form or appearance **3** [Obs.] style; manner —***vt.*** to clothe; dress; attire

gar·bage (gär′bij) ***n.*** ⟦ME, entrails of fowls < ?⟧ **1** things or something thrown away, specif. spoiled or waste food **2** any worthless, unnecessary, or offensive matter [*literary garbage*] —**gar′bag·ey** ***adj.***, **gar′bag·y**

gar·bage·man (gär′bij man′) ***n.***, *pl.* **-men′** (-men′) a person whose job is to pick up and dispose of garbage

gar·ban·zo (gär bän′zō) ***n.***, *pl.* **-zos** ⟦Sp < Gr *erebinthos* < *orobos*, chickpea (+ *-inthos*, suffix of Pelasgian orig.) < IE **eregw(h)o-*, pea > Ger *erbse*⟧ CHICKPEA

gar·ble (gär′bəl) ***vt.*** **-bled**, **-bling** ⟦ME *garbelen* < It *garbellare*, to sift < *garbello*, a sieve < Ar *gharbāl*, earlier *ghirbāl* < LL *cribellum*, small sieve, dim. of L *cribrum*, a sieve, akin to *cernere*: see CRITIC⟧ **1** *a)* [Obs.] to sort by sifting *b)* [Rare] to select the best parts of **2** to suppress or distort parts of (a story, etc.) in telling, so as to mislead or misrepresent **3** to confuse or mix up (a quotation, story, message, etc.) unintentionally, as through inaccurate copying or poor radio transmission —***n.*** the act or result of garbling —**gar′bler** ***n.***

Gar·bo (gär′bō), **Greta** (born *Greta Lovisa Gustafsson*) 1905-90; U.S. film actress, born in Sweden

gar·board (strake) (gär′bôrd′) ⟦Du *gaarbord* < *garen* (contr. of *gaderen*, to GATHER) + *boord*, BOARD⟧ the strake adjoining the keel

Gar·cí·a Lor·ca (gär thē′ä lôr′kä; *E* gär sē′ə lôr′kə), **Fe·de·ri·co** (fe′de rē′kô) 1899-1936; Sp. poet & playwright

Gar·cí·a Már·quez (gär sē′ä mär′kes; *E* gär sē′ə mär′kez), **Ga·bri·el** (gä′vrē el′; *E* gā′brē əl, gä′brē el′) 1928-2014; Colombian writer

gar·çon (gȧr sōn′) ***n.***, *pl.* **-çons′** (-sōn′) ⟦Fr, old acc. of *gars*, boy: see GASKET⟧ **1** a boy, youth, or young man **2** a waiter or servant

gar·çon·nière (gȧr sô nyer′) ***n.*** ⟦Fr⟧ a bachelor's apartment or quarters

Gar·da (gär′də), **Lake** lake in N Italy, on the Lombardy-Veneto border: 143 sq mi (370 sq km)

gar·dant (gär′dənt, gärd′′nt) ***adj.*** *alt. sp. of* GUARDANT

garde-man·ger (gȧrd män zhā′; *E* gärd′män′zhā′) ***n.***, *pl.* **garde-man·ger′** or Eng. **garde′-man′gers′** ⟦Fr⟧ a cook (as on the staff of a restaurant or cruise ship) who prepares the cold foods such as salads, hors d'oeuvres, and fish

gar·den (gärd′'n) ***n.*** ⟦ME < NormFr *gardin* < Frank **gardo*, akin to Ger *garten*, OE *geard*: see YARD[2], GARTH⟧ **1** a piece of ground, usually close to a house, for growing vegetables, fruits, flowers, ornamental shrubs or trees, etc. **2** a well-cultivated region; area of fertile, developed land: also **garden spot 3** [*often pl.*] a place outdoors for public enjoyment, planted with trees, flowers, etc., and sometimes having special displays of plants, a zoo, a duck pond, etc. **—*vi.*** to make, work in, or take care of a garden, lawn, etc. **—*vt.*** to make a garden of **—*adj.*** **1** of, for, used in, or grown in a garden **2** *a)* ordinary; commonplace *b)* hardy **—lead down the garden path** to mislead or deceive

☆**garden apartment 1** a low-rise apartment building, often one in a complex, having extensive areas of lawn or landscaping **2** a unit within such a building or complex

garden balsam a fleshy annual garden impatiens (*Impatiens balsamina*) with roselike white, lavender, yellow, pink, or red blossoms borne along the main stem in leaf axils

garden cress an annual plant (*Lepidium sativum*) of the crucifer family, sometimes grown as a salad plant

gar·den·er (gärd′'n ər, gärd′nər) ***n.*** **1** a person who likes or is skilled at working in a garden **2** a person whose occupation is making and tending gardens

Garden Grove ⟦name, orig. that of the first school, on *Garden Grove* Blvd., was proposed by city founder A. G. Cook (1839-1932), who donated the land⟧ city in SW Calif.

garden heliotrope a tall valerian (*Valeriana officinalis*) with small, very fragrant, white, pink, or lavender flowers and a strong-smelling root formerly used in medicine

☆**gar·de·ni·a** (gär dēn′yə, -dē′nē ə) ***n.*** ⟦ModL, after A. *Garden* (1730-91), Am botanist⟧ any of a genus (*Gardenia*) of chiefly subtropical Old World plants of the madder family, with glossy leaves and highly fragrant, white or yellow, waxy flowers

Garden of Eden EDEN[1]

garden sage *see* SAGE[2] (sense 1)

gar·den-va·ri·e·ty (gärd′'n və rī′ə tē) ***adj.*** ⟦see GARDEN, ***adj.*** **2*a***⟧ ordinary; commonplace [*a garden-variety* novelist]

Gard·ner (gärd′nər), **Erle Stanley** (ʉrl) 1889-1970; U.S. writer

gar·dy·loo (gär′dē lo͞o′) ***interj.*** ⟦< Fr *garde à l'eau*, beware (of) the water⟧ [Historical] in Edinburgh, used as a warning to people below that slops were about to be thrown from a window into the street

Gar·eth (gar′ith) ***n.*** *Arthurian Legend* a knight of the Round Table, nephew of King Arthur

Gar·field (gär′fēld′), **James A(bram)** 1831-81; 20th president of the U.S. (1881): assassinated

gar·fish (gär′fish′) ***n.***, *pl.* **-fish′** or **-fish′es** (see FISH) ⟦ME < *gare*, spear (< OE *gar*: see GORE[3]) + *fish*, FISH⟧ GAR

gar·ga·ney (gär′gə nē) ***n.*** ⟦prob. < It dial. *garganello* < echoic base **garg-*: see GARGLE⟧ a small freshwater European duck (*Anas querquedula*) resembling the American blue-winged teal

Gar·gan·tu·a (gär gan′cho͞o ə, -tyo͞o ə) ***n.*** ⟦Fr < Sp *garganta*, throat, gullet < echoic base **garg-*: see GARGLE⟧ a giant king, noted for his size and prodigious feats and appetite, in *Gargantua and Pantagruel*, a satire by Rabelais (1552)

gar·gan·tu·an (gär gan′cho͞o ən) ***adj.*** ⟦after prec.⟧ enormous; gigantic

gar·get (gär′git) ***n.*** ⟦ME < OFr *gargate*, throat < echoic base **garg-*: see fol.⟧ an inflammation of the udders of cows, ewes, etc., usually caused by bacteria

gar·gle (gär′gəl) ***vt., vi.*** **-gled, -gling** ⟦Fr *gargouiller* < *gargouille*, throat, waterspout, gargoyle < echoic base **garg-* > Gr *gargarizein*, to gargle, Sans *gharghara-h*, gurgling⟧ **1** to rinse or wash (the throat) with a liquid kept in motion by the slow expulsion of air from the lungs **2** to utter or speak with the sound of gargling **—*n.*** **1** a liquid used for gargling **2** a gargling sound

gar·goyle (gär′goil′) ***n.*** ⟦ME *gargule*, throat < OFr *gargouille*: see prec.⟧ **1** a waterspout, usually in the form of a grotesquely carved animal or fantastic creature, projecting from the gutter of a building **2** a projecting ornament (on a building) that looks like this **3** a person with grotesque features **—gar′goyled′** ***adj.***

gargoyles

gar·i·bal·di (gar′ə bôl′dē, -bal′-) ***n.*** a woman's loose, high-necked blouse with full sleeves, patterned after the red shirts worn by the followers of Garibaldi

Gar·i·bal·di (gar′ə bôl′dē; *It* gä′rē bäl′dē), **Giu·sep·pe** (jo͞o zep′pe) 1807-82; It. patriot & general: leader in the movement to unify Italy

gar·ish (gar′ish, ger′-) ***adj.*** ⟦earlier *gaurish*, prob. < ME *gauren*, to stare⟧ **1** too bright or gaudy; showy; glaring [*garish* colors] **2** gaudily or showily dressed, decorated, written, etc. **—gar′ish·ly** ***adv.*** **—gar′ish·ness** ***n.***

gar·land (gär′lənd) ***n.*** ⟦ME < OFr *garlande*⟧ **1** a wreath or woven chain of flowers, leaves, etc. worn on the head or used as decoration, esp. as a symbol of victory, honor, etc. **2** anthology of poems, songs, etc. **3** *Naut.* a band or ring of rope used as to hoist spars or prevent chafing **—*vt.*** to form into or decorate with a garland or garlands

Gar·land[1] (gär′lənd) **1 (Hannibal) Ham·lin** (ham′lin) 1860-1940; U.S. novelist & short-story writer **2 Judy** (born *Frances Gumm*) 1922-69; U.S. film actress & singer

Gar·land[2] (gär′lənd) ⟦after A. H. *Garland*, U.S. attorney general (1885-89)⟧ city in NE Tex.: suburb of Dallas

gar·lic (gär′lik) ***n.*** ⟦ME *garlek* < OE *garleac* < *gar*, a spear (see GORE[3]) + *leac*, LEEK: from the spearlike leaves⟧ **1** a bulbous herb (*Allium sativum*) of the lily family **2** the strong-smelling bulb of this plant, made up of small sections called cloves, used as seasoning in meats, salads, etc. **—gar′lick·y** (-lik ē) ***adj.***

gar·licked (gär′likt) ***adj.*** seasoned with garlic

gar·ment (gär′mənt) ***n.*** ⟦ME, contr. < OFr *garnement* < *garnir*: see GARNISH⟧ **1** *a)* any article of clothing *b)* [*pl.*] clothes; costume **2** a covering **—*vt.*** to cover with, or as with, a garment; clothe

gar·ner (gär′nər) ***n.*** ⟦ME *gerner* < OFr *grenier* < L *granarium*, granary < *granum*, GRAIN⟧ a place for storing grain; granary **—*vt.*** **1** to gather up and store in or as in a granary **2** to get or earn **3** to collect or gather

gar·net[1] (gär′nit) ***n.*** ⟦ME *gernet* < OFr *grenat* < ML *granatus* < *granatum*, garnet, lit., pomegranate < L (see POMEGRANATE): from the resemblance in color⟧ **1** any of a group of very hard silicate minerals having the general formula $A_3B_2(SiO_4)_3$, occurring chiefly as well-formed crystals in metamorphic rocks: red varieties are often used as gems, ordinary varieties as abrasives: see MOHS SCALE (sense 2) **2** a single-crystal synthetic form used in lasers, electronics, etc. **3** a deep red

gar·net[2] (gär′nit) ***n.*** ⟦LME *garnett*, prob. < or akin to Du *garnaat*⟧ *Naut.* a hoisting tackle for loading cargo

Gar·nett (gär′nit, gär net′), **Constance** (born *Constance Clara Black*) (1861-1946) Eng. translator of Russ. literature

gar·ni (gär nē′) ***adj.*** ⟦Fr, pp. of *garnir*, to garnish⟧ garnished: said of food

gar·ni·er·ite (gär′nē ər īt′) ***n.*** ⟦after J. *Garnier*, 19th-c. Fr geologist⟧ a green, soft, amorphous nickel magnesium silicate, $(Ni, Mg)_3Si_2O_5(OH)_4$, that is an ore of nickel and is used as a gem

gar·nish (gär′nish) ***vt.*** ⟦ME *garnischen* < extended stem of OFr *garnir*, to furnish, protect < Gmc **warnjan* > WARN⟧ **1** to decorate; adorn; embellish; trim **2** to decorate (food) with something that adds color or flavor [a steak *garnished* with parsley] **3** *Law* to attach as a result of a garnishment **—*n.*** **1** a decoration; ornament **2** something put on or around food to add color or flavor, as parsley or watercress **3** [Obs.] a fee, esp. one formerly extorted from new prisoners by inmates of English jails or by the jailer **—gar′nish·er** ***n.***

gar·nish·ee (gär′ni shē′) ***n.*** ⟦prec. + -EE[1]⟧ *Law* the third party in a GARNISHMENT (sense 2) **—*vt.*** **-eed′, -ee′ing** GARNISH (***vt.*** 3): now rare in U.S. legal usage

gar·nish·ment (gär′nish mənt) ***n.*** **1** a decoration; embellishment **2** *Law* a proceeding by which a creditor plaintiff seeks to attach money or property in the possession of a third party in order to satisfy a debt owed by the defendant

gar·ni·ture (gär′ni chər) ***n.*** ⟦Fr < OFr *garnir*: see GARNISH⟧ an ornament; decoration; embellishment; trimming

Ga·ronne (gȧ rôn′) river in SW France, flowing from the Pyrenees into the Gironde: *c.* 400 mi (644 km)

☆**gar·pike** (gär′pīk′) ***n.*** GAR

gar·ret (gar′it) ***n.*** ⟦ME *garite*, a watchtower, loft < OFr < *garir*, to watch < Frank **warjan*, to protect, akin to OE *warian*: for IE base see WARN⟧ the space, room, or rooms just below the roof of a house, esp. a sloping roof; attic

Gar·rick (gar′ik), **David** 1717-79; Eng. actor & theater manager

gar·ri·son (gar′ə sən) ***n.*** ⟦ME *garison* < OFr < *garir* (see GARRET); meaning infl. by assoc. with ME & OFr *garnison*, a garrison, provisions < *garnir*, to furnish: see GARNISH⟧ **1** troops stationed in a fort or fortified place **2** a fortified place with troops, guns, etc.; military post or station **—*vt.*** **1** *a)* to station troops in (a fortified place) for its defense *b)* to occupy and control by sending troops into **2** to place (troops) on duty in a garrison

Gar·ri·son (gar′ə sən), **William Lloyd** 1805-79; U.S. editor, lecturer, & abolitionist leader

garrison cap 1 OVERSEAS CAP **2** SERVICE CAP

☆**Garrison finish** ⟦after Snapper *Garrison*, 19th-c. U.S. jockey⟧ a close finish, as in a horse race, in which the winner comes from behind at the last moment

gar·rote (gə rät′, -rōt′) ***n.*** ⟦Sp, orig., a stick used to wind a cord, prob. < OFr *garrot*, crossbow bolt, for earlier *guaroc* < *garokier*, to garrote < Frank **wrokkan*, to twist < IE **werĝh-*, to twist, choke < base **wer-*, to turn > WORM, WRENCH⟧ **1** *a)* a method of execution, as formerly in Spain, with an iron collar tightened about the neck by a screw *b)* the iron collar so used **2** *a)* a cord, thong, or length of wire for strangling a robbery victim, enemy sentry, etc. in a surprise attack *b)* a disabling by strangling in this way; strangulation **—*vt.*** **-rot′ed** or **-rot′ted, -rot′ing** or **-rot′ting 1** to execute or attack with a garrote or by strangling **2** to disable by strangling, as in an attack for robbery Also sp. **ga·rotte′** or **gar·rotte′** **—gar·rot′er** ***n.***

gar·ru·lous (gar′ə ləs, -yo͞o-, -yə-) ***adj.*** ⟦L *garrulus* < *garrire*, to chatter: for IE base see CARE⟧ talking much or too much, esp. about unimportant things; loquacious **—SYN.** TALKATIVE **—gar·ru·li·ty** (gə ro͞o′lə tē) ***n.***, **gar′ru·lous·ness** **—gar′ru·lous·ly** ***adv.***

gar·ter (gärt′ər) ***n.*** ⟦ME < NormFr *gartier* < OFr *garet, jaret*, small of the leg behind the knee < Celt, as in Bret *gar*, shank of the leg⟧ 1 an elastic band, or a fastener suspended from a band, girdle, etc., for holding a stocking or sock in position 2 an elastic band formerly worn to keep a shirt sleeve pushed up 3 [**G-**] *a)* the badge of the Order of the Garter *b)* the order itself *c)* membership in it —*vt.* to bind, support, or fasten with or as with a garter

☆**garter belt** a wide belt, usually of elastic fabric, with garters suspended from it, worn by women

☆**garter snake** ⟦so named from the stripes, suggestive of *garters*, running the length of its body⟧ any of various small, harmless, striped colubrid snakes (genus *Thamnophis*) common in North America

garth (gärth) *n.* ⟦ME < ON *garthr*, akin to OE *geard*, YARD[2]⟧ [Archaic] an enclosed yard or garden

Gar·vey (gär′vē), **Marcus** 1887-1940; Jamaican black nationalist leader in the U.S.

Gar·y[1] (ger′ē, gar′ē) *n.* ⟦< OE **Garwig*, lit., spear (of) battle < *gar*, a spear + *wig* < Gmc **wiga-*, battle < IE base **wīk-*, to be bold > L *vincere*, to conquer⟧ a masculine name: var. *Garry*

Gar·y[2] (ger′ē, gar′ē) ⟦after E. H. *Gary* (1846-1927), U.S. industrialist⟧ city in NW Ind., on Lake Michigan

gas (gas) *n., pl.* **gas·es** or **gas·ses** (gas′iz) ⟦ModL, altered by Van Helmont (1577-1644), Belgian chemist (with *g-* pronounced, as in Du, as a voiced fricative) < Gr *chaos*, air (see CHAOS), term used by Paracelsus⟧ 1 the fluid form of a substance in which it can expand indefinitely and completely fill its container; form that is neither liquid nor solid; vapor 2 any mixture of flammable gases used for lighting, heating, or cooking 3 any gas, as nitrous oxide, used as an anesthetic 4 any substance, as phosgene, intentionally dispersed through the atmosphere, as in war, to act as a poison, irritant, or asphyxiant 5 any gaseous substance formed by decaying or decomposing matter 6 *a)* a gaseous substance formed in the bowels, stomach, etc. during digestion *b)* a condition resulting from indigestion in which such gas causes abdominal bloating, flatulence, etc. 7 [Informal] *short for* GASOLINE 8 [Informal] energy, power, force, drive, etc. [*by game's end, the players had run out of gas*] ☆9 [Slang] *a)* idle or boastful talk *b)* something or someone that is very pleasing, exciting, amusing, etc. [*the movie was a gas*] 10 *Mining* a mixture of firedamp with air, that explodes if ignited —*vt.* **gassed**, **gas′sing** 1 to supply with gas 2 to subject to the action of gas 3 to injure or kill by gas, as in war ☆4 [Slang] to thrill, delight, amuse greatly, etc. —*vi.* 1 to give off gas ☆2 [Slang] to talk in an idle or boastful way —*adj.* of, using, or operated by gas —☆**gas up** [Informal] to put gasoline into the tank of (a vehicle) —☆**step on the gas** 1 [Informal] to press on the accelerator of an automobile 2 [Slang] to hurry; move or act faster

gas bacillus a rod-shaped microorganism (genus *Clostridium*) that infects wounds and causes gas to form in them

gas·bag (gas′bag′) *n.* 1 a bag to hold gas, as in a balloon ☆2 [Slang] a person who talks too much

gas black CARBON BLACK

gas burner GAS JET (sense 2)

gas chamber a room in which people are put to be killed with poison gas

gas chromatography chromatography in which a gas, often nitrogen, combines with a vaporized mixture that is then passed through a long column of adsorbent material to identify its constituents

gas coal bituminous coal used to make any flammable gas

Gas·cogne (gȧs kôn′y′) *Fr. name for* GASCONY

Gas·con (gas′kən) *adj.* ⟦Fr < L *Vasco* (gen. *Vasconis*), a BASQUE⟧ 1 of Gascony or its people or culture 2 [**g-**] like or characteristic of this people, reputed to be boastful —*n.* 1 a person born or living in Gascony 2 [**g-**] a boaster; swaggerer

gas·con·ade (gas′kə nād′) *n.* ⟦Fr *gasconnade*: see prec. & -ADE⟧ boastful or blustering talk —*vi.* **-ad′ed**, **-ad′ing** to boast or bluster

Gas·co·ny (gas′kə nē) ⟦ME *Gascoyne* < OFr *Gascogne* < LL *Vasconia* < L *Vascones*, pl., the Basques⟧ historical region in SW France, on the Bay of Biscay

gas·e·lier (gas′ə lir′) *n.* ⟦GAS + (CHAND)ELIER⟧ an early type of ornamental chandelier with branches ending in gas jets

gas·e·ous (gas′ē əs, gash′əs) *adj.* 1 of, having the nature of, or in the form of, gas 2 [Informal] GASSY (sense 1) —**gas′e·ous·ness** *n.*

gas fitter a person whose work is installing and repairing gas pipes and fixtures

gas fixture a heating or lighting fixture that uses gas

gas furnace 1 a furnace or reactor that distills gas from coal, etc. 2 a furnace that burns gas as fuel

gas gangrene a gangrene in which gas bacilli multiply in extensive, dirty wounds, producing severe pain, swollen, gas-filled tissue, and toxemia

gas guzzler [Slang] an automotive vehicle that has low fuel mileage —**gas-guz·zling** (gas′guz′′liŋ) *adj.*

gash (gash) *vt.* ⟦earlier *garse* < ME *garsen* < OFr *garser* < VL **charassare* < Gr *charassein*, to cut, engrave⟧ to make a long, deep cut in; slash —*n.* ⟦ME *garse* < OFr⟧ a long, deep cut

☆**gas·house** (gas′hous′) *n.* GASWORKS: formerly used fig. to suggest slum areas, rowdiness, etc.

gas·i·form (gas′i fôrm′) *adj.* in the form of gas; gaseous

gas·i·fy (gas′i fī′) *vt., vi.* **gas′i·fied′**, **-fy′ing** to change into gas —**gas′i·fi·ca′tion** *n.*

gas jet 1 a flame of illuminating gas 2 a nozzle or burner at the end of a gas fixture

Gas·kell (gas′kəl), Mrs. **Elizabeth (Cleghorn)** (born *Elizabeth Cleghorn Stevenson*) 1810-65; Eng. novelist

gas·ket (gas′kit) *n.* ⟦prob. altered < Fr *garcette* < OFr *garcete*, small cord, orig., little girl, dim. of *garce*, fem. of *gars*, boy < ML **warkjone* < Frank **wrakjo*, mercenary soldier; akin to OE *wrecca*, WRETCH⟧ 1 a piece or ring of rubber, metal, paper, etc. placed at a joint to make it leakproof 2 *Naut.* a length of rope or canvas for securing a furled sail to a yard or boom —**blow a gasket** [Slang] to become enraged

gas·kin (gas′kin) *n.* ⟦contr. < GALLIGASKINS⟧ 1 [*pl.*] [Obs.] galligaskins 2 the upper part of the hind leg of a horse or other hoofed animal

gas·light (gas′līt′) *n.* 1 the light produced by burning illuminating gas 2 a gas jet or burner —*adj.* of or suggesting the period when gaslight was used for lighting [*gaslight melodrama*]

gas·lit (gas′lit′) *adj.* lighted or as if lighted by gaslight

☆**gas log** an imitation log in the form of a hollow, perforated cylinder, used as a gas burner in a fireplace

gas main a large underground pipe that conducts gas into smaller pipes leading into houses, factories, etc.

gas·man (gas′man′) *n., pl.* **-men′** (-men′) 1 an employee of a gas company who reads consumers' gas meters for billing purposes 2 GAS FITTER 3 *Mining* an inspector who checks the ventilation and guards against firedamp

gas mantle a MANTLE (*n.* 3) to be used over a gas burner

gas mask a device, worn over the face, designed to prevent inhalation of poisonous gases by chemically filtering them out of the air

gas meter an instrument for measuring the quantity of a gas, esp. of illuminating gas consumed as fuel

☆**gas·o·hol** (gas′ə hôl′, -häl′) *n.* ⟦GAS(OLINE) + (ALC)OHOL⟧ a motor fuel mixture with about 90 percent unleaded gasoline and 10 percent ethyl alcohol

☆**gas oil** an oily liquid obtained in the fractional distillation of petroleum, boiling between the kerosene and lubricating oil fractions: used esp. as a diesel fuel and heating oil

gas·o·lier (gas′ə lir′) *n. alt. sp. of* GASELIER

☆**gas·o·line** (gas′ə lēn′, gas′ə lēn′) *n.* ⟦GAS + -OL[2] + -INE[3]⟧ a volatile, highly flammable, colorless liquid mixture of hydrocarbons produced by the fractional distillation of petroleum and used chiefly as a fuel in internal-combustion engines: sometimes sp. **gas′o·lene′**

gas·om·e·ter (ga säm′ət ər) *n.* ⟦Fr *gazomètre*: see GAS & -METER⟧ 1 a container for holding and measuring gas 2 a tank or reservoir for storing gas

gasp (gasp) *vi.* ⟦ME *gaspen* < ON *geispa*, to yawn, prob. by metathesis of **geipsa* < *geipa*, to gossip: for IE base see GAPE⟧ to inhale suddenly, as in surprise, or breathe with effort, as in choking —*vt.* to say or tell with gasps —*n.* a gasping; catching of the breath with difficulty —**at the last gasp** 1 just before death 2 just before the end; at the last moment

Gas·pé Peninsula (gas pā′) ⟦Fr < Algonquian (Micmac) *gachepe*, the end⟧ peninsula in S Quebec, Canada, extending into the Gulf of St. Lawrence: *c.* 150 mi (241 km) long

gasp·er (gäs′pər) *n.* [Brit. Slang] a cheap cigarette

gas plant a perennial plant (*Dictamnus albus*) of the rue family, with fragrant white, pink, or purple flowers that on hot nights give off a flammable gas

gassed (gast) *adj.* ☆[Slang] drunk; intoxicated

gas·ser (gas′ər) *n.* ☆1 an oil well that produces gas 2 [Slang] *a)* a person who talks a great deal ☆*b)* someone or something that is remarkable, very funny, etc.

Gasset, José Ortega y *see* ORTEGA Y GASSET, José

☆**gas station** a SERVICE STATION (sense 2); specif., one that primarily or only sells gasoline for motor vehicles

gas·sy (gas′ē) *adj.* **-si·er**, **-si·est** 1 full of, containing, or producing gas; esp., flatulent 2 like gas 3 [Informal] full of talk, esp. boastful talk

gas·ter·o- (gas′tər ō′, -ə) *combining form* GASTRO-

Gast·haus (gäst′hous′) *n., pl.* **-häus′er** (-hoi′zər) ⟦Ger, lit., guest house⟧ an inn

gastr- (gastr) *combining form* GASTRO-: used before a vowel

gas·trae·a or **gas·tre·a** (gas trē′ə) ⟦ModL < Gr *gastēr*, stomach⟧ *n.* the hypothetical ancestral form of flatworms, structured like the gastrula stage in embryology

gas·trec·to·my (gas trek′tə mē) *n., pl.* **-mies** ⟦GASTR(O)- + -ECTOMY: see GASTRO-⟧ the surgical removal of all, or esp. part, of the stomach

gas·tric (gas′trik) *adj.* ⟦GASTR(O)- + -IC⟧ of, in, or near the stomach

gastric juice the clear digestive fluid produced by glands in the mucous membrane lining the stomach: it contains enzymes and hydrochloric acid and has a pH of *c.* 2.0

gastric ulcer an ulcer in the lining of the stomach

gas·trin (gas′trin) *n.* ⟦GASTR(O)- + -IN[1]⟧ a polypeptide hormone secreted in the stomach, that stimulates production of gastric juice

gas·tri·tis (gas trīt′is) *n.* ⟦ModL < fol. + -ITIS⟧ inflammation of the stomach, esp. of the stomach lining

gas·tro- (gas′trō, -trə) ⟦< Gr *gastēr*, the stomach < **grastēr*, lit., eater, gnawer < *gran*, to gnaw, devour < IE base **gras-*, to devour > L *gramen*, grass⟧ *combining form* 1 stomach [*gastroscope*] 2 stomach and [*gastrocolic*]

gas·troc·ne·mi·us (gas′träk nē′mē əs) *n., pl.* **-mi·i′** (-mē ī′) ⟦ModL < Gr *gastroknēmia*, calf < *gastēr*, the belly + *knēmē*, lower part of the leg: so named from the protruding, or *bellying*, shape of the calf⟧ the large muscle on the back of the lower leg, that connects with the Achilles tendon and extends the foot

gas·tro·col·ic (gas′trō käl′ik) *adj.* of or attached to the stomach and the transverse colon

gas·tro·derm (gas′trō durm′) *n.* ENDODERM

gas·tro·en·ter·i·tis (gas′trō en′tər īt′is) *n.* ⟦ModL < GASTRO- + ENTER(O)- + -ITIS⟧ inflammation of the stomach and the intestines

gas·tro·en·ter·ol·o·gy (-en′tər äl′ə jē) *n.* ⟦GASTRO- + ENTER(O)- + -OLOGY⟧ the medical specialty that is concerned with disorders of the digestive system —**gas′tro·en′ter·ol′o·gist** *n.*

gas·tro·in·tes·ti·nal (-in tes′tə nəl) *adj.* of the stomach and the intestines

gas·tro·lith (gas′trō lith) *n.* ⟦GASTRO- + -LITH⟧ a stony concretion formed in the stomach

gas·tro·nome (gas′trə nōm′) *n.* ⟦Fr < *gastronomie*: see fol.⟧ a person who enjoys and has a discriminating taste for foods: also **gas·tron·o·mer** (gas trän′ə mər) or **gas·tron′o·mist** (-mist) —*SYN.* EPICURE

gas·tron·o·my (gas trän′ə mē) *n.* ⟦Fr *gastronomie*, after Gr *Gastronomia*, poem by Archestratus (4th c. B.C.): see GASTRO- & -NOMY⟧ the art or science of good eating; epicurism —**gas′tro·nom′ic** (-trə näm′ik) *adj.*, **gas′tro·nom′i·cal** —**gas′tro·nom′i·cal·ly** *adv.*

gas·tro·pod (gas′trə päd′) *n.* ⟦< ModL *Gastropoda* < GASTRO- + -POD⟧ any of a large class (Gastropoda) of mollusks having one-piece, straight or spiral shells, as snails, limpets, etc., or having no shells or greatly reduced shells, as certain slugs: most gastropods move by means of a broad, muscular, ventral foot —**gas·trop·o·dan** (gas träp′ə dən) *adj.*, **gas·trop′o·dous** (-dəs)

gas·tro·scope (gas′trə skōp′) *n.* ⟦GASTRO- + -SCOPE⟧ a fiber-optic endoscope inserted through the mouth for visually inspecting the inside of the stomach —**gas′tro·scop′ic** (-skäp′ik) *adj.* —**gas·tros·co·pist** (gas träs′kə pist) *n.* —**gas·tros·co·py** (gas träs′kə pē) *n.*

gas·trot·o·my (gas trät′ə mē) *n.*, *pl.* **-mies** ⟦GASTRO- + -TOMY⟧ surgical incision into the stomach

gas·tro·trich (gas′trō trik) *n.* ⟦< ModL *Gastrotricha* < GASTRO- + *-tricha*, ciliate creatures < Gr neut. pl. of *-trichos*, haired < *thrix* (gen. *trichos*), hair⟧ any of a phylum (Gastrotricha) of minute, aquatic, wormlike animals that swim by means of cilia

gas·tro·vas·cu·lar (gas′trō vas′kyoo lər) *adj. Zool.* having both a digestive and a circulatory function

gas·tru·la (gas′troo lə) *n.*, *pl.* **-lae′** (-lē′, -lī) or **-las** ⟦ModL, dim. < Gr *gastēr*, the stomach⟧ an embryo in an early stage of development, consisting of a sac with two layers, the ectoderm and endoderm, enclosing a central cavity, the archenteron, that opens to the outside through the blastopore

gas·tru·la·tion (gas′troo lā′shən) *n.* the process of forming a gastrula from a blastula, as by epiboly

gas turbine a turbine driven by the pressure of a burning mixture of compressed air and fuel

gas·works (gas′wurks′) *n.* a plant where gas for heating and lighting is prepared

gat[1] (gat) *vt., vi. archaic pt. of* GET

gat[2] (gat) *n.* ⟦< Scand, as in Dan, Swed, ON *gat*, an opening, passage, akin to OE *geat*: see GATE[1]⟧ a narrow channel of water as between cliffs or sandbanks

☆**gat**[3] (gat) *n.* ⟦< GAT(LING GUN)⟧ [Old Slang] a pistol

gate[1] (gāt) *n.* ⟦ME < OE *gatu*, pl. of *geat*, a gate, akin to OFris *jet*, Du & ON *gat*, opening⟧ **1** a movable framework or solid structure, esp. one that swings on hinges, controlling entrance or exit through an opening in a fence or wall **2** an opening providing passageway through a fence or wall, with or without such a structure; gateway **3** any means of entrance, exit, or access; specif., any of the numbered areas at an airport terminal, typically including a waiting area, from which passengers board and exit an airplane **4** a mountain pass **5** a movable barrier, as at a railroad crossing or for controlling the start of a horse race **6** a structure controlling the flow of water, as in a pipe, canal, etc. ☆**7** a frame in which a saw or saws are set **8** in Alpine racing, an opening between two upright poles through which the skier must pass **9** *a)* the total amount of money received in admission prices to a performance or exhibition *b)* the total number of spectators who pay to see such an event **10** *Elec. a)* a circuit with one output and two or more inputs, whose output is energized only when certain input conditions are satisfied *b)* an electrode in some semiconductors, esp. an FET, that controls the flow of current —*vt.* **gat′ed**, **gat′ing** [Brit.] to confine (a student) to the college grounds —☆**give (or get) the gate** [Slang] to subject (or be subjected) to dismissal

gate[2] (gāt) *n.* ⟦altered (infl. by prec.) < OE *gyte*, a pouring forth, akin to *geotan*, to pour: for IE base see FOUND[3]⟧ **1** a channel through which molten metal is poured into a mold **2** the waste part of a casting formed at this channel

gate[3] (gāt) *n.* ⟦ME < ON *gata*: see GAIT⟧ [Now Dial.] **1** a road or path **2** a way of doing something

☆**-gate** (gāt) ⟦< (WATER)GATE⟧ *combining form* a scandal characterized by charges of corruption or illegal acts carried out, usually in a covert manner, by people with power or influence [*Koreagate*]

gâ·teau or **ga·teau** (ga tō′) *n.*, *pl.* **-teaux′** (-tō′, -tōz′) ⟦Fr, cake < OFr *gastel* < Frank **wastil*⟧ **1** a rich layer cake or a pastry shell filled as with custard or mousse **2** a meat, fish, or vegetable preparation shaped like a cake

☆**gate-crash·er** (gāt′krash′ər) *n.* [Informal] a person who attends a social affair without an invitation or attends a performance, etc. without paying admission —**gate′-crash′** *vt., vi.*

gat·ed (gāt′id) *adj.* designating or of a private, residential community, access to which is restricted and controlled by a gate, fences or walls, security guards, etc.

☆**gate·fold** (gāt′fōld′) *n.* a page larger than the others in a magazine or book, bound so it can be unfolded and opened out like a gate

gate·house (gāt′hous′) *n.* a house beside or over a gateway, used as a porter's lodge, etc.

gate·keep·er (gāt′kēp′ər) *n.* **1** a person in charge of a gate to control passage through it: also **gate′man** (-mən) *pl.* **-men** (-mən) **2** any person or thing that controls access or otherwise regulates

gate·leg table (gāt′leg′, -lāg′) a table with drop leaves supported by gatelike legs swung back against the frame to permit the leaves to drop: also **gate′legged′ table**

gateleg table

gate·post (gāt′pōst′) *n.* the post on which a gate is hung or the one to which it is fastened when closed

Gates (gāts), **Horatio** 1728?-1806; Am. general in the Revolutionary War

Gates·head (gāts′hed′) city in Tyne and Wear, NE England

gate·way (gāt′wā′) *n.* **1** an entrance as in a wall, fitted with a gate **2** a means of access

Gath (gath) *n.* ⟦Heb, lit., wine press⟧ *Bible* one of the cities of the Philistines: 2 Sam. 1:20

gath·er (gath′ər) *vt.* ⟦ME *gaderen* < OE *gad(e)rian*, akin to OFris *gaduria*, Du *gaderen* < IE base **ghedh-*, to unite, join > (TO)GETHER, GOOD, Ger *gatte*, spouse⟧ **1** to cause to come together in one place or group **2** to get or collect gradually from various places, sources, etc.; amass; accumulate [to *gather* information] **3** to bring close [to *gather* a blanket about one's legs] **4** to pick, pluck, or collect by picking; harvest [to *gather* crops] **5** to prepare to collect (oneself, one's energies) to meet a situation **6** to gain or acquire gradually [to *gather* speed] **7** to draw (cloth) on a thread loosely stitched across it into fixed folds or puckers **8** to wrinkle (one's brow) **9** to put (the pages or signatures of a book) in proper order for binding **10** [Informal] to get as an idea or impression; infer; conclude [I *gather* that you disagree] —*vi.* **1** to come together; assemble [to *gather* for lunch] **2** to form pus; come to a head, as a boil; fester **3** to increase [clouds *gathered*] **4** to become wrinkled: said of the brow —*n.* a pucker or fold made in cloth —**be gathered to one's fathers** to die: cf. Judg. 2:10 —**gather up 1** to pick up and assemble **2** to draw together; make more compact —**gath′er·er** *n.*

SYN.—**gather** is the general term for a bringing or coming together [to *gather* scattered objects, people *gathered* at the corners]; **collect** usually implies careful choice in gathering from various sources, a bringing into an orderly arrangement, etc. [he *collects* coins]; **assemble** applies especially to the gathering together of persons for some special purpose [*assemble* the students in the auditorium]; **muster** applies to a formal assembling, especially of troops for inspection, roll call, etc. See also **infer**

gath·er·ing (-iŋ) *n.* **1** the act of one that gathers **2** what is gathered; specif., *a)* a meeting; assemblage; crowd *b)* a gather in cloth **3** a boil or abscess

Gat·i·neau (gat′′n ō; *Fr* gȧ tē nō′) city in S Quebec, Canada, near Ottawa

☆**Gat·ling gun** (gat′liŋ) ⟦after R. J. *Gatling* (1818-1903), U.S. inventor⟧ an early kind of machine gun having a cluster of barrels designed to be successively discharged automatically when rotated about an axis

ga·tor or **'ga·tor** (gāt′ər) *n.* [Informal] *short for* ALLIGATOR

GATT (gat) *n.* ⟦*G(eneral) A(greement on) T(ariffs and) T(rade)*, adopted in 1947⟧ an international organization which promotes free trade, chiefly by facilitating negotiations among nations for the reduction or elimination of trade barriers

Ga·tun (gä toon′) town in central Panama: site of a dam (**Gatun Dam**) which forms a lake (**Gatun Lake**), 163 sq mi (422 sq km), that is part of the route of the Panama Canal

gauche (gōsh) *adj.* ⟦Fr, fig. meaning (lit., on the left) < MFr *gauchir*, to become crooked, warped, ult. < Frank **wankjan*, to totter (akin to Ger *wanken*), confused with **walken*, to beat, full (cloth)⟧ lacking grace, esp. social grace; awkward; tactless —**gauche′ly** *adv.* —**gauche′ness** *n.*

gau·che·rie (gō′shə rē, gō′shə rē′) *n.* ⟦Fr: see prec.⟧ **1** awkwardness; tactlessness **2** a gauche act or expression

gau·cho (gou′chō) *n.*, *pl.* **-chos** ⟦AmSp, prob. of Araucanian orig.⟧ a cowboy, usually of mixed Indian and Spanish ancestry, living on the South American pampas

gaud (gôd) *n.* ⟦ME *gaude*, a large bead in a rosary, trinket, prob. ult. < L *gaudium*, JOY⟧ a cheap, showy trinket

gaud·er·y (gôd′ər ē) *n.*, *pl.* **-er·ies** gaudy, or ostentatious, appearance, clothes, etc.; finery

Gau·dí (i Cor·net) (gou dē′ē kôr′net), **An·to·nio** (än tô′nyô) 1852-1926; Sp. architect

gaud·y[1] (gôd′ē) *adj.* **gaud′i·er**, **gaud′i·est** ⟦GAUD + -Y[3]⟧ bright and showy, but lacking in good taste; cheaply brilliant and ornate —**gaud′i·ly** *adv.* —**gaud′i·ness** *n.*

gaud·y[2] (gôd′ē) *n.*, *pl.* **gaud′ies** ⟦< L *gaudium*, JOY⟧ a feast; esp., an annual dinner or reunion at a British university

gauf·fer (gôf′ər, gäf′-) *vt., n. alt. sp. of* GOFFER

gauge (gāj) *n.* ⟦ME < NormFr: see the *vt.*⟧ **1** a standard measure or scale of measurement **2** dimensions, capacity, thickness, etc. **3** any device for measuring something, as the thickness of wire, the dimensions of a machined part, the amount of liquid in a container, steam pressure, etc. **4** any means of estimating or judging **5** the distance between the rails of a rail track: cf. STANDARD GAUGE, BROAD GAUGE, NARROW GAUGE **6** the distance between parallel wheels at opposite ends of an axle **7** the size of a bore, esp. of a shotgun, expressed in terms of the number per pound of round lead balls of a diameter equal to that of the bore **8** the thickness of sheet metal, diameter of wire, etc. **9** *a)* a measure of the fineness of a knitted or crocheted fabric *b)* the fineness of a machine-knitted fabric expressed in terms of the number of loops per 1½ inches **10** *Naut.* the position of a ship in relation to another ship and the wind [a sailboat that has the weather *gauge* of another boat is to windward of it] **11** *Plastering* the amount of plaster of Paris used with common plaster to hasten its setting Usually GAGE[1] in technical senses —*vt.* **gauged**, **gaug′ing** ⟦ME *gaugen* < NormFr *gaugier*, prob. < VL **gallicare* < ?⟧ **1** to measure accurately by means of a gauge **2** to measure the size, amount, extent, or capacity of **3** to estimate; judge; appraise **4** to bring to correct gauge; make conform with a standard **5** *Masonry* to cut or rub (bricks or stone) to a desired shape **6** *Plastering* to mix (plaster) in the proportions required for a specified setting time —*SYN.* STANDARD —**gauge′a·ble** *adj.*

gaug·er (gā′jər) *n.* ⟦ME < Anglo-Fr *gaugeour* < prec.⟧ **1** a person or thing that gauges **2** [Chiefly Brit.] an official who measures the contents of casks of liquor, etc. to be taxed **3** a collector of excise taxes

Gau·guin (gō gan′), **(Eugène Henri) Paul** (pôl) 1848-1903; Fr. painter, in Tahiti after 1891

Gaul[1] (gôl) *n.* **1** a member of the Celtic-speaking people of ancient Gaul **2** a Frenchman

Gaul[2] (gôl) ⟦Fr < Frank **walha*, Romans, foreigners, orig., Celts < WGmc **walhos* < Celt name > WALES, WELSH, L *Volcae*⟧ **1** ancient region in W Europe, consisting of what is now mainly France & Belgium: after 5th cent. B.C., also called **Transalpine Gaul** **2** ancient region in N Italy, occupied by the Gauls (4th cent. B.C.): in full **Cisalpine Gaul** **3** ancient division of the Roman Empire, including Cisalpine Gaul & Transalpine Gaul (1st-5th cent. A.D.)

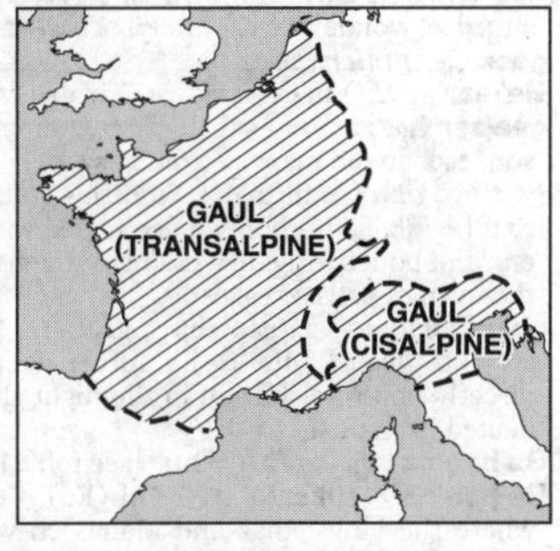

Gaul

Gaul·ish (gôl′ish) *n.* the Celtic language of ancient Gaul —*adj.* of Gaul or its people, language, or culture

Gaull·ism (gôl′iz′əm) *n.* the political policies of Charles de Gaulle, characterized by extreme nationalism —**Gaull′ist** *n., adj.*

gaul·the·ri·a (gôl thir′ē ə) *n.* ⟦ModL, after M. *Gaulthier*, 18th-c. Cdn physician⟧ any of a large genus (*Gaultheria*) of evergreen shrubs of the heath family, including various wintergreens and the salal

gaunt (gônt, gänt) *adj.* ⟦ME *gawnte*, earlier *gant*, slender, thin, gaunt < ?⟧ **1** thin and bony; hollow-eyed and haggard, as from great hunger or age; emaciated **2** looking grim, forbidding, or desolate —**gaunt′ly** *adv.* —**gaunt′ness** *n.*

gaunt·let[1] (gônt′lit, gänt′-) *n.* ⟦ME < OFr *gantelet*, dim. of *gant*, a glove < Frank **want*, a mitten, akin to EFris *wante*⟧ **1** a medieval glove, usually of leather covered with metal plates, worn by knights in armor to protect the hand in combat **2** *a)* a long glove with a flaring cuff covering the lower part of the arm *b)* the flaring cuff —**take up the gauntlet** **1** to accept a challenge **2** to undertake the defense of a person, etc. —**throw down the gauntlet** to challenge, as to combat

gaunt·let[2] (gônt′lit, gänt′-) *n. see* GANTLET[1] (*n.* 1)

gaunt·let·ed (-id) *adj.* wearing a gauntlet, or glove

gaun·try (gôn′trē) *n., pl.* **-tries** *var. of* GANTRY

gaur (gour) *n., pl.* **gaur** or **gaurs** ⟦Hindi < Sans *gaura*, akin to *gáuh*, cow[1]⟧ a wild ox of India (*Bos gaurus*), the world's largest type of cattle

gauss (gous) *n., pl.* **gauss** or **gauss′es** ⟦after C. F. *Gauss* (1777-1855), Ger mathematician & astronomer⟧ the basic unit of magnetic flux density in the CGS system, equal to one line of magnetic flux per square centimeter or one maxwell per square centimeter (0.0001 tesla): abbrev. *G*

Gauss·i·an curve (gou′sē ən) ⟦see prec.⟧ BELL CURVE

Gau·ta·ma (gou′tə mə, gô′-) *see* BUDDHA[2]

Gau·teng (gou′teŋ′) province of South Africa, in the N part: 7,263 sq mi (18,810 sq km); cap. Johannesburg

Gau·tier (gō tyā′), **Thé·o·phile** (tā ô fēl′) 1811-72; Fr. poet, novelist, & critic

gauze (gôz) *n.* ⟦Fr *gaze* < Sp *gasa* < Ar *ḳazz*, raw silk < Pers *kāž*⟧ **1** any very thin, light, transparent, loosely woven material, as of cotton or silk **2** any similar but stiff material, as of thin wire **3** a thin mist

gauz·y (gô′zē) *adj.* **gauz′i·er**, **gauz′i·est** thin, light, and transparent, like gauze; diaphanous —**gauz′i·ly** *adv.* —**gauz′i·ness** *n.*

ga·vage (gə väzh′) *n.* ⟦Fr < *gaver*, to stuff: see GAVOTTE⟧ the administration of liquids through a stomach tube, as in forced feeding

gave (gāv) *vt., vi. pt. of* GIVE

☆**gav·el** (gav′əl) *n.* ⟦? dial. var. of Scot *gable*, a fork, tool with forked handle < ME < OE *gafol*, akin to Ger *gabel*⟧ a small mallet rapped on the table by a presiding officer in calling for attention or silence, or by an auctioneer —*vt.* **-eled** or **-elled**, **-el·ing** or **-el·ling** **1** to strike with or as with a gavel **2** to cause (a meeting) to end, be in order, etc. by striking a gavel —*vi.* to strike a gavel

gav·el·kind (gav′əl kīnd′) *n.* ⟦ME *gavelkynde* (orig. Kentish) < *gavel*, tribute, tax, rent (< OE *gafol* < base of *giefan*: see GIVE) + *kynde*, KIND⟧ [Historical] in Great Britain, a system of land tenure by which: *a)* the property of a man dying intestate was divided equally among his sons *b)* the tenant could dispose of his land by feoffment at the age of fifteen *c)* the land did not escheat upon the conviction of the tenant as a felon

gav·el-to-gav·el (gav′əl tə gav′əl) *adj.* ⟦with ref. to the striking of a GAVEL to open and close a session⟧ *Radio, TV* designating or of live news coverage of court trials, legislative hearings, political conventions, etc. that lasts from beginning to end

ga·vi·al (gā′vē əl) *n.* ⟦< Fr, altered < Hindi *ghaṛiyāl*⟧ *var. of* GHARIAL

ga·votte (gə vät′) *n.* ⟦Fr < Prov *gavoto*, dance of the *Gavots*, name used for a people of Hautes-Alpes, France, lit., boors, gluttons < *gaver*, to stuff, force-feed (poultry) < OProv *gava*, crop⟧ **1** a 17th-cent. dance like the minuet, but faster and livelier **2** the music for this, in 4/4 time Also sp. **ga·vot′**

GAW *abbrev.* guaranteed annual wage

Ga·wain (gə wān′; gä′wān′, -win) *n.* ⟦OFr *Gauvain* < ? Gmc **Gawin*⟧ *Arthurian Legend* a knight of the Round Table, nephew of King Arthur

gawk (gôk) *n.* ⟦prob. var. of GOWK⟧ a clumsy, stupid fellow; simpleton —*vi.* to stare stupidly, like a gawk —**gawk′ish** *adj.*

gawk·y (gô′kē) *adj.* **gawk′i·er**, **gawk′i·est** ⟦prob. < ME *gouki*, foolish < *gouk*: see GOWK⟧ awkward or ungainly, often, specif., from being disproportionately tall —**gawk′i·ly** *adv.* —**gawk′i·ness** *n.*

gawp (gôp) *vi.* ⟦dial., altered < ME *galpen*, to yawn, gape⟧ [Slang] to stare open-mouthed; gawk or gape

gay (gā) *adj.* ⟦ME *gai* < OFr < ? Frank **gahi*, swift, impetuous, akin to Ger *jäh*⟧ **1** joyous and lively; merry; happy; lighthearted **2** bright; brilliant [*gay* colors] **3** given to social life and pleasures [a *gay* life] **4** [Old-fashioned] wanton; licentious ☆**5** *a)* homosexual (now often used specif. of male homosexuals) *b)* of, for, or relating to homosexuals, often, specif., male homosexuals [*gay* liberation] ☆**6** [Slang] odd, inept, pathetic, etc.: often regarded as offensive because of its derivation from sense 5 —☆*n.* a homosexual; esp., a homosexual man —**gay′ness** *n.*

Gay (gā), **John** 1685-1732; Eng. poet & playwright

Ga·ya (gä′yə) city in central Bihar, NE India

gay·dar (gā′där′) *n.* ⟦GAY (*adj.* 5*b*) + (RA)DAR⟧ [Informal] the ability to detect homosexuality in others: a humorous term

gay·e·ty (gā′ə tē) *n., pl.* **-ties** *alt. sp. of* GAIETY

Gayle (gāl) *n.* a feminine name: see GAIL

Gay-Lus·sac (gā lü sák′), **Jo·seph Louis** (zhô zef′ lwē) 1778-1850; Fr. chemist & physicist

Gay-Lus·sac's law (gā′lə saks′) ⟦after prec.⟧ **1** the statement that the volumes of two or more gases that combine to give a gaseous product are in the proportion of small whole numbers to each other and to the volume of the product **2** CHARLES'S LAW

gay·ly (gā′lē) *adv. alt. sp. of* GAILY

☆**gay·wings** (gā′wiŋz′) *n.* a trailing pink or white milkwort (*Polygala paucifolia*) found in the E U.S. and Canada

gaz *abbrev.* gazetteer

Ga·za (gäz′ə, gaz′ə) city in SW Asia, at the SE end of the Mediterranean: in ancient times, one of the chief cities of the Philistines; Biblical site of Samson's death (Judg. 16:21-30): the city and a surrounding strip of land (**Gaza Strip**) were alternately occupied by Egypt & Israel (1949-67); under Israeli administration (1967-94); an agreement in 1994 provided for a transfer of authority in stages that would result in self-rule —**Ga′zan** *n., adj.*

☆**ga·za·bo** (gə zā′bō) *n., pl.* **-bos** or **-boes** ⟦< Sp *gazapo*, an artful knave, back-form. < *gazapatón*, foolish talk, ult. < Gr *kakemphaton*, neut. of *kakemphatos*, ill-sounding, equivocal⟧ [Old Slang] a fellow; guy: often derogatory

ga·za·ni·a (gə zā′nē ə, -nyə) *n.* ⟦ModL, after Theodorus *Gaza* (1398-1478), Greek scholar & translator⟧ any of a genus (*Gazania*) of plants of the composite family, having large, colorful, daisylike flower heads

ga·zar (gə zär′) *n.* a sheer, lightweight cloth of silk or, sometimes, a synthetic fiber, having a glazelike sheen and moderate stiffness

gaze (gāz) *vi.* **gazed**, **gaz′ing** ⟦ME *gazen* < Scand, as in Norw & Swed dial. *gasa*, to stare < ON *gas*, GOOSE⟧ to look intently and steadily; stare, as in wonder or expectancy —*n.* a steady look —**gaz′er** *n.*

ga·ze·bo (gə zē′bō, -zā′-) *n., pl.* **-bos** or **-boes** ⟦jocular formation < prec., after L *videbo*, I shall see⟧ a turret, windowed balcony, or summerhouse from which one can gaze at the surrounding scenery; specif., a small, open building with a roof, typically located in a garden park

gaze·hound (gāz′hound′) *n.* [Archaic] a dog that hunts by sight instead of scent, as a greyhound

ga·zelle (gə zel′) *n., pl.* **-zelles′** or **-zelle′** ⟦Fr < Ar *ghazāl*⟧ any of various small, swift, graceful antelopes (esp. genera *Gazella* and *Procapra*) of Africa, the Near East, and Asia with spirally twisted, backward-pointing horns and large, lustrous eyes

ga·zette (gə zet′) *n.* ⟦Fr < It *gazzetta* < dial. (Venetian) *gazeta*, a small coin, price of the newspaper, orig., prob. dim. of L *gaza*, treasure < Gr < Pers, the royal treasure⟧ **1** a newspaper: now used mainly in some newspaper titles **2** [Brit.] any of various official publications containing announcements and bulletins —*vt.* **-zet′ted**, **-zet′ting** [Brit.] to publish, announce, or list in a gazette

gaz·et·teer (gaz′ə tir′) ***n.*** ⟦Fr *gazettier*⟧ **1** [Archaic] a person who writes for a gazette **2** ⟦prob. after L. Echard's use for his geographical dictionary (*c.* 1700)⟧ a dictionary or index of geographical names

Ga·zi·an·tep (gä′zē än tep′) city in S Turkey, near the Syrian border

☆**ga·zil·lion** (gə zil′yən) ***n.*** ⟦arbitrary coinage < ZILLION⟧ [Slang] a very large, indefinite number

gaz·pa·cho (gə spä′chō, gəz pä′chō) ***n.*** ⟦Sp⟧ a Spanish soup made with tomatoes, cucumbers, peppers, and onions, chopped up raw with oil, vinegar, etc. and served cold

Gb *abbrev.* **1** gigabit(s) **2** gilbert

GB[1] (jē′bē′) ***n.*** ⟦U.S. Army code name⟧ SARIN

GB[2] *abbrev.* **1** gigabyte(s) **2** Great Britain

GBP *abbrev.* ⟦< *G*(*reat*) *B*(*ritain*) *p*(*ound*)⟧ pound sterling: see POUND[1] (***n.*** 2)

Gbps *abbrev.* gigabits per second

GCA *abbrev. Aeron.* ground-controlled approach

g-cal *abbrev.* gram calorie(s)

GCD or **gcd** *abbrev.* greatest common divisor

GCF or **gcf** *abbrev.* greatest common factor

G clef TREBLE CLEF

gcs *abbrev.* gigacycles per second

gd *abbrev.* guard

Gd *Chem. symbol for* gadolinium

Gdańsk (gə dänsk′, -dansk′) seaport in N Poland, on the Baltic Sea: Ger. name DANZIG

gdn *abbrev.* garden

GDP *abbrev.* gross domestic product

GDR *abbrev.* German Democratic Republic (East Germany)

gds *abbrev.* goods

Gdy·nia (gə dēn′yä) seaport in N Poland, on the Baltic Sea

Ge[1] (zhā) ***n.*** a family of South American Indian languages of Brazil, many now extinct

Ge[2] (jē; gā) ⟦Gr *gē*, earth⟧ *var. of* GAEA

Ge[3] *abbrev. Bible* Genesis

Ge[4] *Chem. symbol for* germanium

ge·an·ti·cline (jē an′ti klīn′) ***n.*** ⟦Gr *gē*, earth + ANTICLINE⟧ *Geol.* a great upward folding of the earth's crust, larger and more complex than an anticline, commonly measured in tens or hundreds of miles —**ge′an′ti·cli′nal** (-klī′nəl) ***adj.***

gear (gir) ***n.*** ⟦ME *gere*, prob. < ON *gervi*, preparation, ornament, akin to OE *gearo*, YARE⟧ **1** *a)* [Obs.] the clothing and equipment of a soldier, knight, etc. *b)* clothing; apparel **2** movable property; esp., apparatus or equipment for some particular task, as a workman's tools, the rigging of a ship, a harness, etc. **3** *a)* a toothed wheel, disk, etc. designed to mesh with another or with the thread of a worm *b)* [*often pl.*] a system of two or more gears meshed together so that the motion of one controls the speed and torque of another *c)* a specific adjustment of such a system *d)* any part of a mechanism performing a specific function [*the steering gear*] —***adj.*** [Slang, Chiefly Brit.] highly acceptable, attractive, etc. —***vt.*** **1** to furnish with gear; harness **2** to adapt (one thing) so as to conform with another [*to gear production to demand*] **3** *Mech.* *a)* to connect by gears *b)* to furnish with gears *c)* to put into gear —***vi.*** *Mech.* to be in, or come into, proper adjustment or working order —**gear down** to adjust gears so that the driven element goes slower than the driving element, with a consequent increase in torque —**gear up 1** to adjust gears so that the driven element goes faster than the driving element, with a consequent decrease in torque **2** to accelerate; increase efficiency (of) [*the factory geared up production*] —☆**high gear 1** the arrangement of gears providing the greatest speed but little torque **2** [Informal] high speed or efficiency —**in** (or **out of**) **gear 1** (not) connected to the motor **2** (not) in proper adjustment or working order —☆**low gear 1** the arrangement of gears providing little speed but great torque **2** [Informal] low speed or efficiency —**reverse gear** the arrangement of gears providing reverse, or backward, motion —☆**shift gears 1** to change from one gear arrangement to another **2** to change one's approach or focus

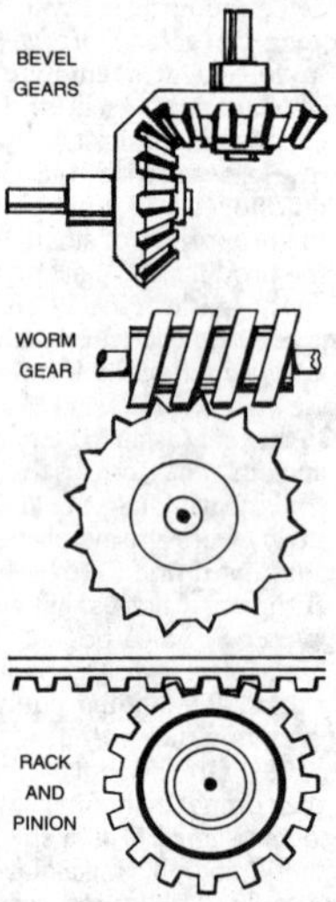

BEVEL GEARS
WORM GEAR
RACK AND PINION
gears

gear·box (gir′bäks′) ***n.*** **1** TRANSMISSION (sense 2) **2** a case enclosing gears to protect them from dirt

gear·ing (gir′iŋ) ***n.*** **1** the act or manner of fitting a machine with gears **2** a system of gears or other parts for transmitting motion

gear ratio the fixed relationship between the rotating speeds of two gears indicating available torque

☆**gear·shift** (gir′shift′) ***n.*** the lever used to engage or disengage any of a number of sets of transmission gears to a motor, etc.

gear·wheel (-hwēl′, -wēl′) ***n.*** a toothed wheel in a system of gears

geck·o (gek′ō) ***n.***, *pl.* **-os** or **-oes** ⟦prob. < Malay *ge'kok*, ? echoic of its cry⟧ any of a family (Gekkonidae) of soft-skinned, insect-eating, tropical and subtropical lizards with a short, stout body, a large head, and suction pads on the feet

GED[1] *trademark* General Educational Development

GED[2] *abbrev.* general equivalency diploma

Ged·des (ged′ēz), **Norman Bel** (bel) 1893-1958; U.S. theatrical & industrial designer

gee[1] (jē) ***interj., n.*** ⟦Early ModE < ?⟧ (used as) a command to a horse, ox, etc., meaning *a)* "turn right" *b)* "go ahead" (in this sense, usually **gee up**) — ***vt., vi.*** **geed, gee′ing** to turn to the right Opposed to HAW[2]

☆**gee**[2] (jē) ***interj.*** ⟦euphemistic contr. < JE(SUS)⟧ [Slang] used to signify surprise, wonder, etc.

gee[3] (jē) ***n.*** **1** the letter G ☆**2** ⟦G(RAND), ***n.*** 2⟧ [Slang] one thousand dollars

gee·gaw (gē′gô) ***n.*** *var. of* GEWGAW

☆**geek** (gēk) ***n.*** ⟦< dial. *geck*, fool < Du *gek*, madman, fool < MLowG *geck*: orig. echoic of unintelligible cries⟧ **1** a performer of grotesque or depraved acts in a carnival, etc., such as biting off the head of a live chicken **2** [Slang] any person considered to be different from others in a negative or bizarre way, as a teenager seen as being socially or physically awkward **3** [Slang] a person regarded as being especially enthusiastic, knowledgeable, and skillful, esp. in technical matters —**geek·y** (gē′kē) ***adj.*** **geek′i·er, geek′i·est**

Gee·long (jē lôŋ′) seaport in S Victoria, Australia

Geel·vink Bay (khāl′viŋk) *former name for* SARERA BAY

geese (gēs) ***n.*** *pl. of* GOOSE

☆**gee whiz** ⟦euphemistic alt. of JESUS[2]⟧ exclamation used variously to express surprise, wonder, enthusiasm, protest, etc.

☆**gee-whiz** (jē′hwiz′, -wiz′) ***adj.*** ⟦< prec.⟧ **1** naively enthusiastic **2** causing surprise, wonder, etc. —***interj.*** GEE WHIZ

geez (jēz) ***interj.*** JEEZ

Ge′·ez (gē ez′) ***n.*** ETHIOPIC (***n.*** 1): also written **Geez** or **Ge'ez**

gee·zer (gē′zər) ***n.*** ⟦< dial. *guiser*, a mummer < GUISE⟧ [Slang] an old person, esp. an old man: also **old geezer**

☆**ge·fil·te fish** (gə fil′tə) ⟦E Yiddish < *gefilte*, inflected adj. form of pp. of *filn*, to fill + *fish*, fish⟧ chopped fish mixed with chopped onion, egg, seasoning, etc. and boiled, orig. in a casing of the fish skin: it is usually served cold in the form of balls or cakes

ge·gen·schein (gā′gən shīn′, geg′ən-) ***n.*** ⟦Ger < *gegen*, against + *schein*, a SHINE, gleam⟧ [*also* **G-**] a diffuse, faint light, sometimes visible almost directly opposite the sun in the night sky, and thought to be sunlight reflected from dust

Ge·hen·na[1] (gi hen′ə, gə-) ***n.*** ⟦see fol.⟧ **1** a place of torment **2** hell

Ge·hen·na[2] (gi hen′ə, gə-) ⟦LL(Ec) < Gr *Geenna*, hell < Heb *gey hinom*, where the kings Ahaz and Manasseh were said to have sacrificed their sons to Moloch⟧ the valley of Hinnom, near Jerusalem, where refuse was burned in biblical times

Geh·rig (ger′ig), **(Henry) Lou(is)** (lo͞o) (born *Heinrich Ludwig Gehrig II*) 1903-41; U.S. baseball player

Geh·ry (ger′ē), **Frank** (born *Ephraim Owen Goldberg*) 1929- ; U.S. architect, born in Canada

Gei·ger counter (gī′gər) ⟦after H. *Geiger* (1882-1945), Ger physicist⟧ an instrument for detecting and counting ionizing particles that pass through it: it consists of a needlelike electrode inside a hollow metallic cylinder filled with gas which, when ionized by the radiation, sets up a current in an electric field: a refined version (**Geiger-Müller counter**) with an amplifying system is used for detecting and measuring radioactivity

G-8 (jē′āt′) ***n.*** ⟦< *G*(*roup of*) *Eight*⟧ the successor to the G-7, consisting of the G-7 countries and Russia

Gei·sel (gī′zəl), **Theodor Seuss** (so͞os) (pseud. *Dr. Seuss*) 1904-91; U.S. writer & illustrator, esp. of children's books

gei·sha (gā′shə; *also* gē′-) ***n.***, *pl.* **-sha** or **-shas** ⟦Jpn < SinoJpn *gei*, art (of dancing, singing) + *sha*, person⟧ a Japanese woman trained in singing, dancing, the art of conversation, etc., to serve as a hired companion to men: sometimes [Informal] **geisha girl**

Geiss·ler tube (gīs′lər) ⟦after H. *Geissler* (1814-79), Ger inventor⟧ a glass tube having two electrodes and containing a gas which, when electrified, takes on a luminous glow of a color characteristic of the gas: used in spectroscopy, etc.

gel (jel) ***n.*** ⟦< GELATIN⟧ **1** a colloidal form of matter having a jellylike texture, usually formed by cooling a colloidal solution into a solid or semisolid phase: cf. SOL[3], FOAM (sense 4) **2** any of various jellylike preparations used to style hair, clean teeth, etc. **3** GELATIN (***n.*** 3) —***vi.*** **gelled, gel′ling 1** to form a gel **2** [Brit.] JELL (***vi.*** 2)

gel·a·da (jel′ə də, jə lä′-) ***n.*** ⟦ModL, the species name; of Sem orig.⟧ an Ethiopian baboon (*Theropithecus gelada*) characterized by a bare red patch on the chest: also **gelada baboon**

Ge·län·de·sprung (gə len′də shpro͝oŋ′) ***n.*** ⟦Ger < *gelände*, open terrain + *sprung*, a leap⟧ *Skiing* a jump, as over an obstacle, made from a crouching position by propelling oneself with the ski poles

gel·a·tin (jel′ə tin) ***n.*** ⟦Fr *gélatine* < It *gelatina* < *gelata*, a jelly < pp. of L *gelare*, to freeze < IE base **gel-*, to freeze > COOL, L *gelu*, frost⟧ **1** the tasteless, odorless, brittle mixture of proteins extracted by boiling skin, bones, horns, etc.; also, a similar vegetable substance: gelatin dissolves in hot water, forming a jellylike substance when cool, and is used in the preparation of various foods, medicine capsules, photographic film, etc. **2** something, as a jelly, made with gelatin **3** a sheet of translucent, colored material, placed over stage lights for special effects Also **gel′a·tine** (-tin, *Brit* -tēn′)

ge·lat·i·nize (jə lat′'n īz′, jel′ə tin īz′) ***vt.*** **-nized′**, **-niz′ing** **1** to change into gelatin or gelatinous matter **2** *Photog.* to coat with gelatin —***vi.*** to be changed into gelatin or gelatinous matter —**ge·lat′i·ni·za′tion** ***n.***

ge·lat·i·noid (jə lat′'n oid′) ***adj.*** like gelatin —***n.*** a gelatinoid substance

ge·lat·i·nous (jə lat′'n əs) ***adj.*** **1** of or containing gelatin **2** like gelatin or jelly; having the consistency of gelatin or jelly; viscous —**ge·lat′i·nous·ness** ***n.***

ge·la·tion[1] (jē lā′shən) ***n.*** ⟦L *gelatio* < pp. of *gelare*, to freeze: see GELATIN⟧ solidification by cooling or freezing

gel·a·tion[2] (jel ā′shən) ***n.*** ⟦GEL + -ATION⟧ the coagulation of a sol to form a gel

ge·la·to (jə lät′ō) ***n.***, *pl.* **-ti** (-ē) or **-tos** ⟦It < adj., frozen < pp. of *gelare*, to freeze < L: see GELATIN⟧ [*often in italics*] an Italian sherbet made of whole milk, sugar, gelatin, and flavoring

gel·cap (jel′kap′) ***n.*** ⟦GEL(ATIN) + CAP(SULE)⟧ **1** CAPSULE (sense 2) **2** SOFTGEL

geld[1] (geld) ***vt.*** **geld′ed** or **gelt, geld′ing** ⟦ME *gelden* < ON *gelda*, to castrate < *geldr*, barren < IE base **ĝhel-*, to cut > OWelsh *gylym*, knife, ON *gylta*, sow, Goth *giltha*, scythe⟧ **1** to castrate (esp. a horse) **2** to deprive of anything essential; weaken

geld[2] (geld) ***n.*** ⟦ML (Domesday Book) *geldum* < OE *gield*, payment (akin to Ger *geld*, money): for IE base see YIELD⟧ a tax paid to the crown by English landholders in Anglo-Saxon and Norman times

Gel·der·land (gel′dər land′; *Du* khel′dər länt′) province of E Netherlands: 1,986 sq mi (5,144 sq km); cap. Arnhem

geld·ing (gel′diŋ) ***n.*** ⟦ME < ON *geldingr*: see GELD[1] & -ING⟧ **1** a gelded animal; esp., a castrated male horse **2** [Archaic] a eunuch

Ge·li·bo·lu (gel′ē bô lo͞o′) seaport in S European Turkey, on the Gallipoli Peninsula: strategic point in the defense of the Dardanelles and Bosporus straits

gel·id (jel′id) ***adj.*** ⟦L *gelidus* < *gelu*, frost: see GELATIN⟧ extremely cold; frozen —**ge·lid·i·ty** (jē lid′ə tē) ***n.***

gel·ig·nite (jel′ig nīt′, jə lig′-) ***n.*** ⟦GEL(ATIN) + L *ign(is)*, fire + -ITE[1]⟧ a sensitive blasting explosive that is a mixture of nitroglycerin, nitrocellulose, etc.: also called **gelatin dynamite**

Gell-Mann (gel män′, -man′), **Murray** 1929- ; U.S. physicist

gel·se·mi·um (jel sē′mē əm) ***n.*** ⟦ModL < It *gelsomino*, jessamine < Ar *yāsamīn*: see JASMINE⟧ **1** any of a genus (*Gelsemium*) of twining shrubs of the logania family, bearing fragrant yellow flowers **2** the poisonous root of one variety, once used medicinally

Gel·sen·kir·chen (gel′zən kir′Hən) city in WC Germany, in the state of North Rhine-Westphalia

gelt[1] (gelt) ***vt.*** *alt. pt. & pp. of* GELD[1]

gelt[2] (gelt) ***n.*** ⟦Yiddish *geld* < Ger (a late-19th-c. borrowing): orig. (16th c.) > Ger or Du *geld*, but fell out of use except dialectally: cf. GELD[2]⟧ [Slang] money

gem (jem) ***n.*** ⟦ME *gemme* < OFr < L *gemma*, a swelling, bud, precious stone < IE **ĝembhna* < base **ĝembh-*, to bite, tooth > COMB[1]⟧ **1** *a)* a cut and polished gemstone or a pearl, used for ornamentation *b)* GEMSTONE [*a fortune in uncut gems*] **2** anything prized for its beauty and value, esp. if small and perfect of its kind **3** a highly valued person ☆**4** a kind of muffin —***vt.*** **gemmed, gem′ming** to adorn or set with or as with gems

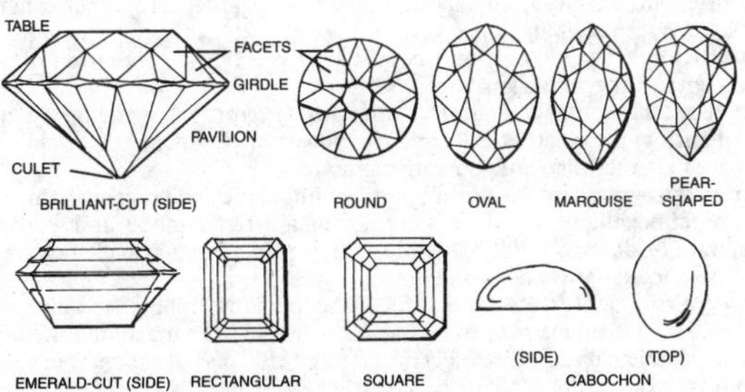

Ge·ma·ra (gə mä rä′; gə mä′rä, -môr′ə) ***n.*** ⟦< Heb-Aram *gemara* < Aram *gemara*, lit., study, learning < verb root *gmr*, to finish⟧ **1** the second and supplementary part of the Talmud, providing a commentary on the first part (the MISHNA) **2** loosely, the Talmud

Ge·mein·schaft (gə mīn′shäft′) ***n.***, *pl.* **-schaf′ten** (-shäf′tən) ⟦Ger, community < *gemein*, common + *-schaft*, -SHIP⟧ [*sometimes* **g-**] a social relationship between individuals which is based on common feeling, kinship, or membership in a community: opposed to GESELLSCHAFT

gem·i·nate (jem′ə nāt′) ***adj.*** ⟦< L *geminatus*, pp. of *geminare*, to double < *geminus*, twin⟧ growing or combined in pairs; coupled —***vt.*** **-nat′ed, -nat′ing** to arrange in pairs; double —***vi.*** to become doubled or paired —**gem′i·na′tion** ***n.***

Gem·i·ni (jem′ə nī′, -nē′) ***n.*** ⟦L, twins, pl. of *geminus*⟧ **1** a N constellation between Cancer and Taurus, containing the bright stars Castor and Pollux; the Twins **2** the third sign of the zodiac, entered by the sun about May 21: also called *the Twins* **3** a person born under this sign

gem·ma (jem′ə) ***n.***, *pl.* **-mae** (-ē) ⟦L: see GEM⟧ *Biol.* a budlike outgrowth which becomes detached and develops into a new organism, as in certain liverworts —**gem·ma·ceous** (jem ā′shəs) ***adj.***

gem·mate (jem′āt′) ***adj.*** ⟦L *gemmatus*, pp. of *gemmare*, to put forth buds < *gemma*, a bud: see GEM⟧ having, or reproducing by, gemmae —***vi.*** **-mat′ed, -mat′ing** to have, or reproduce by, gemmae; bud —**gem·ma′tion** ***n.***

gem·mif·er·ous (je mif′ər əs) ***adj.*** producing or reproducing by buds or gemmae; gemmiparous

gem·mip·a·rous (je mip′ə rəs) ***adj.*** ⟦< L *gemma*, a bud (see GEM) + -I- + -PAROUS⟧ *Biol.* of or reproducing by gemmation; budding

gem·mu·la·tion (jem′yo͞o lā′shən) ***n.*** *Biol.* formation of or reproduction by gemmules

gem·mule (jem′yo͞ol′) ***n.*** ⟦Fr < L *gemmula*, dim. of *gemma*, a bud: see GEM⟧ *Biol.* a bud of a moss or a reproductive body of an alga or of certain sponges; small gemma

gem·my (jem′ē) ***adj.*** ⟦ME⟧ **1** set with gems **2** like a gem; glittering

gem·ol·o·gy or **gem·mol·o·gy** (je mäl′ə jē) ***n.*** ⟦< L *gemma* (see GEM) + -O- + -LOGY: sp. infl. by GEM⟧ the science or study of gems and gemstones —**gem′o·log′i·cal** ***adj.***, **gem′mo·log′i·cal** —**gem·ol′o·gist** ***n.***, **gem·mol′o·gist**

ge·mot or **ge·mote** (gə mōt′) ***n.*** ⟦OE < *ge-*, collective prefix (akin to L *cum*: see COM-) + *mōt*, assembly: see MOOT⟧ an early English public assembly or court, before the Norman Conquest; moot

gems·bok (gemz′bäk′) ***n.***, *pl.* **-bok′** or **-boks′** ⟦Afrik < Ger *gemsbock* < *gemse*, chamois < OHG **gamuz* < LL *camox* (see CHAMOIS) + *bock*, BUCK[1]⟧ a large antelope (*Oryx gazella*) of S Africa, with long, straight horns and a tufted tail

gem·stone (jem′stōn′) ***n.*** any mineral or petrified substance that can be cut and polished for setting into a piece of jewelry

ge·müt·lich (gə müt′liH) ***adj.*** ⟦Ger⟧ agreeable, cheerful, cozy, etc.

Ge·müt·lich·keit (gə müt′likh kīt′) ***n.*** ⟦Ger < prec. + *-keit*, var. of *-heit*, noun suffix akin to E -HOOD⟧ the quality of being agreeable, friendly, or congenial; warm cordiality

gen[1] (jen) ***n.*** ⟦prob. < *gen(eral information)*⟧ [Informal, Chiefly Brit.] the basic or general information about someone or something

gen[2] *abbrev.* **1** gender **2** genera **3** general **4** generic **5** genitive **6** genus

Gen *abbrev.* **1** General **2** *Bible* Genesis

-gen (jən, jen) ⟦Fr *-gène* < Gr *-genēs*, born < base of *gignesthai*, to be born, become: see GENUS⟧ *suffix forming nouns* **1** something that produces [*hydrogen*] **2** something produced (in a specified way) [*pathogen*] Also **-gene**

gen·darme (zhän därm′, zhän′därm′; *Fr* zhän dȧrm′) ***n.***, *pl.* **-darmes′** (-därmz′; *Fr*, -dȧrm′) ⟦Fr < *gens d'armes*, men-at-arms < L *gens*, GENS + *de*, of + *arma*, arms⟧ **1** [Historical] a French cavalryman commanding a squad **2** in France, Belgium, etc., *a)* a soldier serving as an armed policeman *b)* a police officer; esp., a French police officer

gen·dar·me·rie (zhän′där′mə rē′, zhän där′mə rē; *Fr* zhän dȧr mə rē′) ***n.*** ⟦Fr⟧ gendarmes collectively: also **gen·dar′mer·y**

gen·der[1] (jen′dər) ***n.*** ⟦ME < OFr *gendre*, with unhistoric *-d-* < L *genus* (gen. *generis*), descent, origin, transl. Gr *genos*, race, class, sex: see GENUS⟧ **1** *Gram.* *a)* the formal classification by which nouns are grouped and inflected, or changed in form, so as to reflect certain syntactic relationships: pronouns, modifiers, and verbs may also be so inflected: although gender is not a formal feature of English, some nouns and the third person singular pronouns are distinguished according to sex or the lack of sex (Ex.: *man* or *he*, masculine gender; *woman* or *she*, feminine gender; *door* or *it*, neuter gender): in most Indo-European languages, as well as in many others, gender is not necessarily correlated with sex *b)* any one of such groupings, or an inflectional form showing membership in such a group **2** *a)* either of the two sexual divisions, male or female, into which human beings are divided *b)* the fact or condition of being a male or a female human being, esp. with regard to how this affects or determines a person's self-image, social status, goals, etc.

gen·der[2] (jen′dər) ***vt., vi.*** *archaic var. of* ENGENDER

gen·der-ben·der (jen′dər ben′dər) ***n.*** [Slang] a person who looks or behaves in a way regarded as androgynous or as typical of the opposite sex —**gen·der-bend·ing** (jen′dər ben′diŋ) ***n.***

gender dysphoria dysphoria associated with one's gender identity

gen·dered (jen′dərd) ***adj.*** characterized or determined by issues or factors of GENDER[1] (sense 2*b*) [*a gendered analysis of the last election*]

☆**gender gap** the apparent disparity between men and women in values, attitudes, voting patterns, etc.

gen·der-spe·cif·ic (jen′dər spə sif′ik) ***adj.*** of or limited to either males or females [*eye and hair color are not gender-specific*]

☆**gene** (jēn) ***n.*** ⟦< Ger *gen*, short for *pangen* (< *pan-*, PAN- + *-gen*, -GEN, after PANGENESIS)⟧ *Genetics* any of the units occurring at specific points on the chromosomes, by which hereditary characters are transmitted and determined: each is regarded as a particular state of organization of the chromatin in the chromosome, consisting primarily of DNA and protein: see DOMINANT, RECESSIVE

Gene (jēn) ***n.*** a masculine name: see EUGENE[1]

geneal *abbrev.* genealogy

ge·ne·a·log·i·cal (jē′nē ə läj′i kəl, jen′ē-) ***adj.*** **1** of genealogy **2** tracing a line of descent —**ge′ne·a·log′i·cal·ly** ***adv.***

ge·ne·al·o·gy (jē′nē äl′ə jē, -al′-; jen′ē-) ***n.***, *pl.* **-gies** ⟦ME *genelogi* < OFr *genealogie* < LL *genealogia* < Gr < *genea*, race, descent (akin to *genos*: see GENUS) + *-logia*, -LOGY⟧ **1** a chart or recorded history of the descent of a person or family from an ancestor or ancestors **2** the science or study of family descent 3 descent from an ancestor; pedigree; lineage —**ge′ne·al′o·gist** *n.*

gene flow the passage of particular genes through a population of animals or plants as a result of cross-fertilizations within the population

gene map a graphic representation of the linear sequence of genes, and of the relative distances between them, on a chromosome or chromosome segment

gene pool the stock of genes of a species or of the members of a species population

gen·er·a (jen′ər ə) *n. pl. of* GENUS

gen·er·a·ble (jen′ər ə bəl) *adj.* ⟦L *generabilis*⟧ that can be generated

gen·er·al (jen′ər əl, jen′rəl) *adj.* ⟦ME < OFr < L *generalis* < *genus* (gen. *generis*), kind, class: see GENUS⟧ 1 of, for, or from the whole or all; not particular or local *[a general anesthetic, the general welfare]* 2 of, for, or applying to a whole genus, kind, class, order, or race *[the general classifications of matter]* 3 existing or occurring extensively; common; widespread *[a general unrest]* 4 most common; usual *[the general spelling of a word]* 5 concerned with the main or overall features; lacking in details; not specific *[the general features of a plan]* 6 not precise; vague *[to speak in general terms]* 7 senior or highest in rank *[a general manager, an attorney general]* 8 not connected with or limited to one branch or department of learning, business, etc.; not specialized *[a general store]* —*n.* 1 the main or overall fact, condition, idea, etc.: opposed to PARTICULAR 2 the head of some religious orders 3 [Archaic] the public; populace 4 any of various military officers ranking above a colonel; specif., *a) U.S. Air Force, U.S. Army* such an officer, with an insignia of four stars, ranking above a lieutenant general (see also BRIGADIER GENERAL, MAJOR GENERAL) *b) U.S. Marine Corps* an officer of the highest rank 5 an anesthetic that makes a patient unconscious: cf. LOCAL (*n.* 6): in full **general anesthetic** —*SYN.* COMMON, UNIVERSAL —**in general** 1 in the main; usually 2 without specific details 3 with reference to all spoken of

general admission 1 admission for usually unreserved seats, as in a theater, stadium, etc. 2 the section of a theater, stadium, etc. where these seats are located

☆**General American** American English as conversationally spoken by most people in the greater part of the U.S., exclusive of much of New England and most of the South: a nontechnical term

general anesthesia *see* ANESTHESIA (sense 2)

general anesthetic *see* GENERAL (*n.* 5)

general assembly ☆1 [*often* **G- A-**] in some states of the U.S., the legislative assembly 2 [**G- A-**] the deliberative assembly of the United Nations 3 the highest governing body of the Presbyterian Church or the national association of certain other Protestant denominations

general aviation aviation that includes the operation of all nonmilitary aircraft except for commercial passenger and cargo airliners

general contractor a person who contracts to construct a building or buildings, for a stipulated sum, in accordance with certain plans and specifications, or to remodel or build an addition to a building

☆**General Court** 1 [Historical] a Colonial legislative assembly with limited judicial powers 2 now, the legislature of New Hampshire or Massachusetts: the official title

general court-martial the highest military court, for judging the gravest offenses: it consists of five or more officers or enlisted persons, and can impose the death sentence

gen·er·al·cy (jen′ər əl sē) *n., pl.* **-cies** the rank, commission, tenure of office, or authority of a general

☆**general delivery** 1 delivery of mail at the post office to addressees who come there to collect it 2 the department of the post office that handles this mail 3 mail sent to general delivery

☆**general election** 1 an election to choose from among candidates previously nominated in a primary election, by party convention, etc. 2 a nationwide or statewide election

general headquarters *Mil.* the headquarters of a commanding general in the field

gen·er·al·is·si·mo (jen′ər ə lis′i mō′) *n., pl.* **-mos′** ⟦It, superl. of *generale*, GENERAL⟧ in certain countries, the commander in chief of all the armed forces

gen·er·al·ist (jen′ər ə list) *n.* an administrator, teacher, etc. with broad general knowledge and experience in several disciplines or areas, as opposed to a specialist —**gen′er·al·ism′** *n.*

gen·er·al·i·ty (jen′ər al′ə tē) *n., pl.* **-ties** ⟦ME *generalte* < OFr *généralité* < LL *generalitas* < L *generalis*⟧ 1 the condition or quality of being general, or applicable to all 2 a general statement, idea, etc., specif. *a)* one that is vague or inadequate *b)* GENERALIZATION 3 the bulk; main body

gen·er·al·i·za·tion (jen′ər ə li zā′shən, jen′rəl i-) *n.* 1 the act or process of generalizing 2 a general idea, statement, etc. resulting from this; inference applied generally

gen·er·al·ize (jen′ər əl īz′, jen′rəl īz′) *vt.* **-ized′, -iz′ing** ⟦ME *generalisen*⟧ to make general; esp., *a)* to state in terms of a general law or precept *b)* to infer or derive (a general law or precept) from (particular instances) *c)* to emphasize the general character rather than specific details of *d)* to cause to be widely known or used; popularize —*vi.* 1 to formulate general principles or inferences from particulars 2 to talk in generalities 3 to become general or spread throughout a body or area —**gen′er·al·iz′a·ble** *adj.*

gen·er·al·ly (jen′ər əl ē, jen′rə lē, jen′ər lē) *adv.* 1 to or by most people; widely; popularly; extensively *[a generally accepted usage]* 2 in most instances; usually; as a rule 3 in a general way or sense; without reference to details or individual cases; not specifically

general officer *Mil.* any officer above a colonel in rank

☆**general of the air force** *U.S. Air Force* an officer of the highest rank, with an insignia of five stars: a WWII rank

☆**general of the army** *U.S. Army* an officer of the highest rank, with an insignia of five stars: a WWII rank

general order *Mil.* 1 any of a numbered series of orders under competent authority, including general directives, announcements, etc. 2 any of the permanent orders giving in general the duties of sentries

general paresis (*or* **paralysis**) PARESIS (sense 2)

general practitioner a practicing physician who does not specialize in any particular field of medicine

gen·er·al-pur·pose (jen′ər əl pur′pəs) *adj.* having a variety of uses; suitable for general use

general quarters *Navy* the positioning of a ship's personnel in their BATTLE STATIONS

General Secretary the head of the Communist Party of the Soviet Union

gen·er·al·ship (jen′ər əl ship′) *n.* ⟦see -SHIP⟧ 1 *a)* the rank, tenure, or authority of a general *b)* the military skill of a general 2 highly skillful leadership

general staff *Mil.* a group of officers who assist the commander of a high unit in planning, coordinating, and supervising operations

☆**general store** a store where many sorts of merchandise are sold, but not in separate departments

general strike a strike by the workers in an entire industry or, esp., throughout an entire community or country

general theory of relativity *see* RELATIVITY (sense 4): also called **general relativity**

gen·er·ate (jen′ər āt′) *vt.* **-at′ed, -at′ing** ⟦< L *generatus*, pp. of *generare*, to beget, produce < *genus* (gen. *generis*): see GENUS⟧ 1 to produce (offspring); beget; procreate 2 to bring into being; cause to be *[to generate hope]* 3 *a)* to originate or produce by a physical, chemical, mechanical, electronic, or mathematical process *[to generate electricity, software that generates graphs]* *b)* to produce in great quantities *[an office that generates a lot of paperwork]* 4 *Geom.* to trace out or form (a curve, plane, or figure) by the motion of a point, line, or plane

gen·er·a·tion (jen′ər ā′shən) *n.* ⟦ME *generacioun* < OFr *generacion* < L *generatio* < *generatus*: see prec.⟧ 1 the act or process of producing offspring; procreation 2 a bringing into being; production 3 a single stage or degree in the succession of natural descent *[father and son are two generations]* 4 the average period (about thirty years) between the birth of one generation and that of the next 5 *a)* all the people born and living at about the same time *b)* a group of such people with the same experience, attitude, etc. in common *[the computer generation]* 6 any of the stages of successive improvement in the development of a product, system, etc. 7 *Geom.* the formation of a curve, plane, or figure by the motion of a point, line, or plane: see GENERATRIX —**gen′er·a′tion·al** *adj.*

generation gap the set of differences in ideals, attitudes, experiences, etc. that exist between an older and a younger generation of people living at the same time

Generation X (eks) ⟦popularized as title of novel (1991) by D. Coupland, Cdn writer⟧ the generation of persons born in the 1960s and 1970s, the children of the baby boomers, often variously regarded as apathetic, materialistic, irresponsible, etc.

Generation Y (wī) ⟦because it comes after prec.⟧ the generation of persons born in the 1980s and early 1990s

gen·er·a·tive (jen′ər ə tiv, -āt′iv) *adj.* ⟦ME *generatif*⟧ 1 of the production of offspring; procreative 2 having the power of producing or originating ☆3 of or characteristic of generative grammar

☆**generative grammar** *Linguis.* a system of linguistic analysis consisting of a limited, unchanging set of rules employing a list of symbols and words to generate or describe every possible sentence in a language: cf. TRANSFORMATIONAL (GENERATIVE) GRAMMAR

gen·er·a·tor (jen′ər āt′ər) *n.* ⟦L⟧ 1 a person or thing that generates; specif., *a)* a machine for producing gas or steam *b)* a machine for changing mechanical energy into electrical energy; dynamo 2 GENERATRIX

gen·er·a·trix (jen′ər ā′triks) *n., pl.* **-tri·ces′** (-tri sēz′) ⟦L, fem. of prec.⟧ *Math.* a point, line, or plane whose motion generates a curve, plane, or figure

ge·ner·ic (jə ner′ik) *adj.* ⟦ML *genericus*: see GENUS & -IC⟧ 1 of, applied to, or referring to a whole kind, class, or group; inclusive or general 2 without a brand name 3 without individual character or distinctive characteristics 4 *Biol.* of or characteristic of a genus —*n.* a product, as a drug or grocery item, without a brand name —*SYN.* UNIVERSAL —**ge·ner′i·cal·ly** *adv.*

gen·er·os·i·ty (jen′ər äs′ə tē) *n.* ⟦ME *generosite* < L *generositas* < *generosus*⟧ 1 the quality of being generous; specif., *a)* nobility of mind; magnanimity *b)* willingness to give or share; unselfishness 2 *pl.* **-ties** a generous act

gen·er·ous (jen′ər əs) *adj.* ⟦L *generosus*, of noble birth, excellent, generous < *genus*: see GENUS⟧ 1 [Obs.] of noble birth 2 having qualities attributed to people of noble birth; noble-minded; gracious; magnanimous 3 giving or sharing liberally and willingly; openhanded 4 large; ample *[generous portions of food]* 5 rich in yield; fertile 6 full-flavored and strong: said of wine —**gen′er·ous·ly** *adv.* —**gen′er·ous·ness** *n.*

Gen·e·see (jen′ə sē′) ⟦< Seneca, ? beautiful valley⟧ river flowing from N Pa. across W N.Y. into Lake Ontario: *c.* 150 mi (241 km)

gen·e·sis (jen′ə sis) ***n.*** ⟦ME < OE & LL(Ec) < L, birth, generation < Gr (used in LXX for Gen.) < base of *gignesthai*, to be born: see GENUS⟧ **1** [**G-**] the first book of the Bible, giving an account of the Creation: abbrev. *Gen, Gn,* or *Ge* **2** *pl.* **-ses′** (-sēz′) the way in which something comes to be; beginning; origin

-gen·e·sis (jen′ə sis) ⟦see prec.⟧ *combining form forming nouns* origination, creation, formation, evolution (of something specified) [*psychogenesis*]

gene splicing any technique or procedure used in genetic engineering to create recombinant DNA

gen·et (jen′it, jə net′) ***n.*** ⟦ME < OFr *genette* < Sp *gineta* < Ar *jarnayṭ*⟧ **1** any of a genus (*Genetta*) of small, spotted African carnivores in the same family (Viverridae) as the civet **2** its fur

Ge·net (zhə nā′), **Jean** 1910-86; Fr. playwright & novelist

Ge·nêt (zhə nā′), **Ed·mond Charles É·douard** (ed mōn′ shȧrl ā dwȧr′) 1763-1834; Fr. diplomat, in the U.S. after 1793: called *Citizen Genêt*

gene therapy the experimental treatment of a disease by the use of techniques associated with genetic engineering, as to modify or replace the disease-causing genes of certain cells

ge·net·ic (jə net′ik) ***adj.*** ⟦< GENESIS⟧ **1** of the genesis, or origin, of something **2** of or having to do with genetics **3** GENIC Also **ge·net′i·cal** —**ge·net′i·cal·ly** ***adv.***

genetic code the biochemical code in DNA or RNA that determines the characteristics of an organism, made up of a long chain or sequence of nucleotides, codons, and genes

genetic counseling the medical counseling of prospective parents regarding the existence of genetic abnormalities in a fetus or the possible transmission of genetic defects

genetic drift in evolution, *a)* a random change in gene frequency within a small population, resulting in mutations which, regardless of their adaptive value, become fixed within the group *b)* any such process

genetic engineering the branch of biology dealing with the splicing and recombining of specific genetic units from the DNA of living organisms as in order to produce new species or biochemicals

genetic fingerprinting DNA FINGERPRINTING

ge·net·i·cist (jə net′ə sist) ***n.*** a specialist in genetics

genetic marker any allele or gene associated with a specific chromosome and used in genetic research, as in the identification and location of the other genes in a linkage group

ge·net·ics (jə net′iks) ***n.*** ⟦GENET(IC) + -ICS: coined by W. Bateson (1861-1926), Eng biologist⟧ **1** the branch of biology that deals with heredity and variation in similar or related animals and plants **2** the genetic features or constitution of an individual, group, or kind

ge·ne·va (jə nē′və) ***n.*** ⟦Du *genever* < OFr *genevre*, juniper berry < L *juniperus*, JUNIPER⟧ HOLLANDS

Ge·ne·va (jə nē′və) **1** city in SW Switzerland, on Lake Geneva **2** canton of SW Switzerland, largely the city of Geneva & its suburbs: 109 sq mi (282 sq km) **3 Lake (of)** lake in SW Switzerland, on the French border: 224 sq mi (580 sq km): see LEMAN, Lake

Geneva bands ⟦after the clerical garb of *Geneva* Calvinists⟧ two white cloth strips hanging from the front of the collar, worn by some Protestant clergy

Geneva Convention an international agreement signed at Geneva in 1864, establishing a code, later revised, for the care and treatment in wartime of the sick, wounded, and dead, and of prisoners of war, including protection of civilians and of hospitals, etc. having the emblem of the Red Cross

Geneva cross RED CROSS (sense 1)

Geneva gown ⟦see GENEVA BANDS⟧ a long, loose, wide-sleeved black gown, worn by many Protestant clergy

Ge·ne·van (jə nē′vən) ***adj.*** **1** of Geneva, Switzerland, esp. at the time of the Reformation **2** of or having to do with Calvinism —***n.*** **1** a person born or living in Geneva **2** a follower of John Calvin

Ge·nève (zhə nev′) *Fr. name for* GENEVA (the city & the canton)

Gen·e·vieve[1] (jen′ə vēv′) ***n.*** ⟦Fr *Geneviève* < LL *Genovefa* < ? Celt⟧ a feminine name

Gen·e·vieve[2] (jen′ə vēv′), Saint (A.D. 422?-512?); Fr. nun; patron saint of Paris: her day is Jan. 3

Genf (genf) *Ger. name for* GENEVA (the city & the canton)

Gen·ghis Khan (geŋ′gis, jeŋ′-) (born *Temuchin*) 1162?-1227; Mongol conqueror of central Asia

gen·i·al[1] (jēn′yəl, jē′nē əl) ***adj.*** ⟦L *genialis*, of generation or birth < *genius*, guardian deity: see GENIUS⟧ **1** [Obs.] of marriage or procreation **2** promoting life and growth; pleasantly warm, mild, and healthful [*a genial climate*] **3** cheerful, friendly, and sympathetic; amiable **4** [Rare] of or characterized by genius —**SYN.** AMIABLE —**ge·ni·al·i·ty** (jē′nē al′ə tē) ***n.*** —**gen′i·al·ly** ***adv.***

ge·ni·al[2] (jē nī′əl) ***adj.*** ⟦< Gr *geneion*, a chin (< *genys*, a jaw: see CHIN) + -AL⟧ having to do with the chin

gen·ic (jen′ik) ***adj.*** of, having the nature of, or caused by a gene or genes; genetic

-gen·ic (jen′ik) *combining form forming adjectives* **1** pertaining to production or generation [*phylogenic*] **2** suitable to [*photogenic*]

ge·nic·u·late (jə nik′yoo lit, -lāt′) ***adj.*** ⟦L *geniculatus* < *geniculum*, dim. of *genu*, KNEE⟧ **1** having a kneelike joint **2** bent sharply Also **ge·nic′u·lat′ed** (-lāt′id)

ge·nie (jē′nē) ***n.*** ⟦Fr *génie* (< L *genius*: see GENIUS), used to translate Ar *jinnī*, JINNI < *jinn*, JINN⟧ a JINN, now, esp., one in fables and stories who is confined to a lamp or bottle and who grants the wishes of whoever releases him

ge·ni·i (jē′nē ī′) ***n.*** *pl. of* GENIUS (senses 1 & 2)

gen·i·pap (jen′i pap′) ***n.*** ⟦Port *genipapo* < the WInd (Tupí) name⟧ **1** the brown, edible fruit of a tropical American tree (*Genipa americana*) of the madder family **2** the tree itself

gen·i·tal (jen′i təl) ***adj.*** ⟦ME < OFr < L *genitalis* < *genitus*, pp. of *genere, gignere*, to beget: see GENUS⟧ **1** of reproduction or the sexual organs **2** *Psychoanalysis a)* designating or of the third stage of infantile psychosexual development in which interest centers around the genital organs *b)* designating or of the adult or final stage of psychosexual development in which conflicts have been resolved, libidinal drives regulated, and character structure integrated: cf. ANAL[1], ORAL

gen·i·ta·li·a (jen′i tā′lē ə, -tāl′yə) ***pl.n.*** ⟦L, short for *genitalia (membra)*, genital (members)⟧ GENITALS

gen·i·tals (jen′i təlz) ***pl.n.*** ⟦< GENITAL⟧ the reproductive organs; esp., the external sex organs

gen·i·ti·val (jen′i tī′vəl) ***adj.*** of or in the genitive case

gen·i·tive (jen′i tiv) *Gram.* ***adj.*** ⟦ME *genitif* < OFr < L *(casus) genitivus*, lit., (case) of origin < *genitus* (see GENITAL): mistransl. < Gr *genikē*, generic (case), (case) of genus < Gr *genos*, GENUS⟧ designating, of, or in a relational case typically expressing possession, source, or a partitive concept: cf. POSSESSIVE —***n.*** **1** the genitive case: expressed by inflection in languages such as Latin and either by an analytical construction or by inflection in English (Ex.: the sons *of the queen*, the *queen's* sons) **2** a word or phrase in this case

gen·i·to- (jen′i tō) *combining form* genital and [*genitourinary*]

gen·i·to·u·ri·nar·y (jen′i tō yoor′ə ner′ē) ***adj.*** designating or of the genital and urinary organs together

gen·ius (jēn′yəs; *also, esp. for 1-2*, jē′nē əs) ***n.***, *pl.* for 3–6, **gen′ius·es**; for 1 & 2, **ge·ni·i** (jē′nē ī′) ⟦L, guardian spirit, natural ability, genius < base of *genere, gignere*, to produce: see GENUS⟧ **1** *a)* [*often* **G-**] according to ancient Roman belief, a guardian spirit assigned to a person at birth; tutelary deity *b)* [*often* **G-**] the guardian spirit of any person, place, etc. *c)* either of two spirits, one good and one evil, supposed to influence one's destiny *d)* a person considered as having strong influence over another **2** JINN **3** the personification of a quality **4** particular character or essential spirit or nature of a nation, place, age, etc. **5** a great natural ability (*for* a particular activity); strong disposition or inclination **6** *a)* great mental capacity and inventive ability; esp., great and original creative ability in some art, science, etc. *b)* a person having such capacity or ability *c)* popularly, any person with a very high IQ —**SYN.** TALENT

ge·ni·us lo·ci (jē′nē əs lō′sī′, -lō′kē) ⟦L, the (guardian) spirit of a place⟧ the general atmosphere of a place

genl *abbrev.* general

☆**gen·o·a** (jen′ə wə) ***n.*** ⟦after fol.⟧ [*often* **G-**] *Naut.* a large jib used as on a racing yacht: also **genoa jib**

Gen·o·a (jen′ə wə) **1** seaport in NW Italy, at the head of the Gulf of Genoa: It. name GENOVA **2 Gulf of** N part of the Ligurian Sea, off NW Italy

gen·o·cide (jen′ə sīd′) ***n.*** ⟦< Gr *genos*, race, kind (see GENUS) + -CIDE: coined by R. Lemkin (1900-59), lawyer & human-rights advocate, born in Poland, to characterize the attempted extermination of the Jews by Nazi Germany⟧ the systematic destruction of a national or ethnic group, specif. by means of execution or murder —**gen′o·ci′dal** (-sīd′'l) ***adj.***

Gen·o·ese (jen′ə wēz′, -wēs′) ***adj.*** of Genoa or its people or culture —***n.***, *pl.* **-ese′** a person born or living in Genoa

gé·noise (zhā nwäz′) ***n.*** ⟦Fr < adj., fem. of *génois*, prec.⟧ a rich, moist spongecake, often with a creamy filling, jam, etc. between its layers

ge·nome (jē′nōm′) ***n.*** ⟦Ger *genom* < *gen*, GENE + *(chromos)om*, CHROMOSOME⟧ **1** one complete haploid set of chromosomes of an organism **2** the total genetic information present in a somatic cell and unique to any specific organism —**ge·nom′ic** (-nō′mik, -näm′ik) ***adj.***

ge·no·mics (jē nō′miks) ***n.*** ⟦< prec. + -ICS⟧ the science that deals with genomes and their functions

gen·o·type (jen′ə tīp′, jē′nə-) ***n.*** ⟦< Gr *genos*, race, kind (see GENUS) + -TYPE⟧ **1** the fundamental constitution of an organism in terms of its hereditary factors **2** a group of organisms each having the same hereditary characteristics **3** the type species of a genus —**gen′o·typ′ic** (-tip′ik) ***adj.***, **gen′o·typ′i·cal** —**gen′o·typ′i·cal·ly** ***adv.***

-gen·ous (jə nəs) ⟦-GEN + -OUS⟧ *combining form forming adjectives* **1** producing, generating [*nitrogenous*] **2** produced by, generated in [*autogenous*]

Ge·no·va (je′nô vä′) *It. name for* GENOA

gen·re (zhän′rə) ***n.*** ⟦Fr < L *genus* (gen. *generis*): see GENUS⟧ a kind, or type, as of works of literature, art, etc. —***adj.*** **1** designating or of a type of book, film, etc. which is distinguished by subject, theme, or style, as science fiction, mystery, western, etc. **2** designating or of a kind of painting in which subjects or scenes from everyday life are treated realistically

gen·ro (gen′rō′) ***pl.n.*** ⟦Jpn *genrō*, lit., first elder < SinoJpn *gen*, original + *rō*, old⟧ the former elder statesmen of Japan: see ELDER STATESMAN

gens (jenz) ***n.***, *pl.* **gen·tes** (jen′tēz′) ⟦L, orig., that belonging together by birth < base of *gignere*, to beget: see GENUS⟧ **1** in ancient Rome, a clan united by descent through the male line from a common ancestor and having both name and religious observances in common **2** any tribe or clan; esp., an exogamous group claiming descent through the male line

Gen·ser·ic (jen′sər ik, gen′-) A.D. 400?-477; king of the Vandals (427-477): conqueror in N Africa & of Rome

gent[1] (jent) ***n.*** [Informal] a gentleman; man —**the Gents** [*also* **the g-**] [Informal, Chiefly Brit.] MEN'S ROOM

gent[2] (jent) *adj.* ⟦ME < OFr < L *genitus*, born, pp. of *gignere*, to beget, produce: see GENUS⟧ [Obs.] pretty; graceful

Gent (khent) *Fl. name for* GHENT

gen·ta·mi·cin (jent′ə mī′sin) *n.* ⟦< GENTIAN VIOLET (with ref. to the color of the organism) + *-micin*, altered < -MYCIN⟧ a broad-spectrum antibiotic obtained from soil actinomycetes (genus *Micromonospora*), used in treating a wide variety of serious infections

gen·teel (jen tēl′) *adj.* ⟦< OFr *gentil* (of same orig. as GENTLE & JAUNTY, but borrowed again in 16th c.)⟧ 1 having or showing the good taste and refinement associated with polite society; elegant, fashionable, etc. 2 excessively or affectedly refined, polite, etc. —**gen·teel′ly** *adv.* —**gen·teel′ness** *n.*

gen·tian (jen′shən) *adj.* ⟦ME *genciane* < OFr *gentiane* < L *gentiana*, of Illyrian orig.⟧ designating a family (Gentianaceae, order Gentianales) of dicotyledonous plants, including the fringed gentians and the closed gentians —*n.* 1 any of a large genus (*Gentiana*) of plants of the gentian family, with blue, white, red, or yellow flowers 2 the bitter root of the **yellow gentian** (*G. lutea*), used as a gastrointestinal tonic

gentian violet a violet dye used as an antiseptic and as a stain in microscopy

gen·tile (jen′tīl′) *n.* ⟦< Fr & L; Fr *gentil* < L *gentilis*, of the same gens, clan, or race; also, foreigner (in opposition to Roman); in LL(Ec), pagan, heathen (in opposition to Jew and Christian): see GENTLE⟧ [*also* **G-**] 1 any person not a Jew; often, specif., a Christian 2 [Historical] among Christians, a heathen or pagan ☆3 among Mormons, any person not a Mormon —*adj.* [*also* **G-** *for senses* 1, 2, & 3] 1 not Jewish 2 heathen; pagan ☆3 not Mormon: term used by the Mormons 4 of a clan, tribe, or nation 5 *Gram.* designating a nationality or country [“French” is a *gentile* adjective] —***SYN.*** PAGAN

gen·ti·lesse (jen′ti les′) *n.* ⟦ME < OFr *gentillise* < *gentil*: see GENTLE⟧ [Archaic] good breeding and courteous behavior

gen·til·i·ty (jen til′ə tē) *n.*, *pl.* **-ties** ⟦ME *gentilete* < OFr < L *gentilitas* < *gentilis*: see GENTLE⟧ 1 *a)* the condition of belonging by birth to the upper classes *b)* members of the upper class, collectively 2 the quality of being genteel; now, specif., excessive or affected refinement and elegance

gen·tis·ic acid (jen tis′ik) ⟦< *gentisin*, pigment derived from gentian root < ModL *Gentiana*, GENTIAN + (TRYP)SIN⟧ a crystalline, water-soluble acid, $C_6H_3(OH)_2COOH$, whose sodium salt has been used in medicine as an analgesic

gen·tle (jent′'l) *adj.* **-tler**, **-tlest** ⟦ME *gentil* < OFr, of noble birth < L *gentilis*, of the same gens (in LL, of a good family) < *gens*: see GENS⟧ 1 belonging to the upper classes or polite society 2 like or suitable to polite society; refined, courteous, etc. 3 [Archaic] noble; chivalrous [*a gentle* knight] 4 generous; kind [*gentle* reader] 5 easily handled; tame [*a gentle* dog] 6 kindly; serene; patient [*a gentle* disposition] 7 not violent, harsh, or rough [*a gentle* tap, *a gentle* rebuke] 8 gradual [*a gentle* slope] —*n.* [Archaic] a person of the upper classes —*vt.* **-tled**, **-tling** 1 to make gentle, mild, or pleasant 2 to tame or train (a horse or other animal) 3 to calm or soothe as by stroking 4 [Obs.] to raise to the social status of a gentleman —***SYN.*** SOFT —**the gentle craft** (or **art**) 1 fishing 2 [Obs.] shoemaking —**gen′tle·ness** *n.*

gentle breeze *Meteorol.* a wind whose speed is 8 to 12 miles per hour: see the Beaufort scale in the Reference Supplement

gen·tle·folk (jent′'l fōk′) *pl.n.* people of high social standing: also **gen′tle·folks′**

☆**gen·tle·la·dy** (jent′'l lā′dē) *n.*, *pl.* **-dies** GENTLEWOMAN (*n.* 4): often in the phrase **the gentlelady from** (a specified state)

gen·tle·man (jent′'l mən) *n.*, *pl.* **-men** (-mən) ⟦ME *gentilman* (after OFr *gentilz hom*): see GENTLE & MAN⟧ 1 *a)* [Obs.] a man born into a family of high social standing *b)* any man of independent means who does not work for a living 2 a courteous, gracious man with a strong sense of honor 3 a man's personal servant; valet: chiefly in the phrase **gentleman's gentleman** 4 any man: a polite term, esp. as (in pl.) a form of address ☆5 a member of the U.S. House of Representatives: usually a form of address: often in the phrase **the gentleman from** (a specified state)

gen·tle·man-at-arms (-at ärmz′) *n.*, *pl.* **gen′tle·men-at-arms′** any of a corps of men of rank, traditionally forty, who accompany the British sovereign as a military guard on important occasions

gen·tle·man-farm·er (-fär′mər) *n.*, *pl.* **gen′tle·men-farm′ers** a wealthy man who farms as an avocation

gen·tle·man·ly (-lē) *adj.* ⟦ME⟧ of, characteristic of, or fit for a gentleman; well-mannered: also **gen′tle·man·like′** —**gen′tle·man·li·ness** *n.*

gentleman of fortune ADVENTURER

☆**gentlemen's** (*or* **gentleman's**) **agreement** 1 an unwritten agreement secured only by the parties' pledge of honor and not legally binding 2 such an agreement to discriminate against members of certain minority groups

gentlemen's (*or* **gentleman's**) **club** a typically upscale nightclub or bar featuring female strippers, lap dancers, etc. for a male clientele

gen·tle·wom·an (jent′'l woom′ən) *n.*, *pl.* **-wom′en** (-wim′in) ⟦ME *gentil womman*⟧ 1 [Obs.] a woman born into a family of high social standing; lady 2 a courteous, gracious woman 3 [Historical] a woman in attendance on a lady of rank ☆4 a female member of the U.S. House of Representatives: usually a form of address: often in the phrase **the gentlewoman from** (a specified state)

gen·tly (jent′lē) *adv.* ⟦ME *gentilly*⟧ in a gentle manner or to a gentle degree

Gen·too (jen to͞o′) *adj.*, *n.*, *pl.* **-toos′** ⟦Port *gentio*, heathen, gentile < L *gentilis*: see GENTILE⟧ [Archaic] HINDU

gen·tri·fy (jen′tri fī′) *vt.* **-fied′**, **-fy′ing** ⟦< fol. + -FY⟧ 1 to convert (a deteriorated or aging area in a city) into a more affluent middle-class neighborhood, as by remodeling dwellings, resulting in increased property values and in displacement of the poor 2 to raise to a higher status or condition; improve, uplift, etc. —**gen′tri·fi·ca′tion** *n.* —**gen′tri·fi′er** *n.*

gen·try (jen′trē) *n.* ⟦ME *genterie*, noble or high birth; prob. taken as sing. of *genterise*, gentility of birth < OFr, var. of *gentilise* < *gentil*: see GENTLE⟧ 1 [Obs.] rank resulting from birth; esp., high rank 2 people of high social standing; esp., in Great Britain, the class of landowning people ranking just below the nobility 3 people of a particular class or group [the newspaper *gentry*]

ge·nu (jē′no͞o′) *n.*, *pl.* **gen·u·a** (jen′yo͞o ə) ⟦L, KNEE⟧ *Anat.* 1 the knee 2 a kneelike or sharply bent part, as in the facial nerve

gen·u·flect (jen′yə flekt′) *vi.* ⟦ML(Ec) *genuflectere* < L *genu*, KNEE + *flectere*, to bend: see FLEX[1]⟧ 1 to touch one bent knee to the ground and lower one's body as an act of reverence, as when one enters a church 2 to act in a submissive or servile way —**gen′u·flec′tion** *n.*

gen·u·ine (jen′yo͞o in; *dial.* -wīn′) *adj.* ⟦L *genuinus*, orig., inborn, native, hence authentic < base of *gignere*, to be born: see fol.⟧ 1 of the original stock; purebred 2 really being what it is said to be or coming from the alleged source or origin; not counterfeit or artificial; real; true; authentic 3 sincere and frank; honest and forthright —***SYN.*** AUTHENTIC —**gen′u·ine·ly** *adv.* —**gen′u·ine·ness** *n.*

ge·nus (jē′nəs) *n.*, *pl.* **gen·er·a** (jen′ər ə) or **ge′nus·es** ⟦L, birth, origin, race, species, kind < IE base **ĝen-*, to beget, produce > L *gignere*, to beget, *gens*, clan, Gr *genos*, race, *gignesthai*, to be born, Ger *kind*, child, OE *(ge)cynd*, KIND, *cennan*, to beget; also, with loss of initial *g-*, L *nasci*, to be born, *natura*, nature⟧ 1 a class; kind; sort 2 *Biol.* a major category in the classification of animals, plants, etc., ranking above a species and below a family: it can include one species or many similar species: the Latinized genus name is capitalized and italicized, and precedes the species name, which is italicized but not capitalized (Ex.: *Homo sapiens*, modern man) 3 *Logic* a class of things made up of subordinate classes or SPECIES

-gen·y (jə nē) ⟦Gr *-geneia* < *-genēs*: see -GEN⟧ *combining form forming nouns* origin, production, development [*phylogeny*]

ge·o- (jē′ō, -ə) ⟦Gr *geō-* < *gaia*, *gē*, the earth⟧ *combining form* 1 earth, of the earth [*geocentric*, *geophyte*] 2 geographical [*geopolitics*]

☆**ge·o·bot·a·ny** (jē′ō bät′'n ē) *n.* 1 the science dealing with the relationship between specific plant species and the substrata from which they receive their nourishment 2 PHYTOGEOGRAPHY —**ge′o·bo·tan′i·cal** *adj.*

ge·o·cen·tric (jē′ō sen′trik) *adj.* ⟦GEO- + -CENTRIC⟧ 1 measured or viewed as from the center of the earth 2 having or regarding the earth as a center Also **ge′o·cen′tri·cal** —**ge′o·cen′tri·cal·ly** *adv.*

ge·o·chem·is·try (-kem′is trē) *n.* the branch of chemistry dealing with the chemical composition of the earth's crust and the chemical changes that occur there —**ge′o·chem′i·cal** *adj.* —**ge′o·chem′ist** *n.*

ge·o·chro·nol·o·gy (-krə näl′ə jē) *n.* ⟦GEO- + CHRONOLOGY⟧ the branch of geology dealing with the age of the earth and its materials, the dating of evolutionary stages in plant and animal development, etc. —**ge′o·chron′o·log′i·cal** (-krän′ə läj′i kəl) *adj.*

ge·o·chro·nom·e·try (-krə näm′ə trē) *n.* ⟦GEO- + CHRONOMETRY⟧ the measurement of geologic time, as from the decay of radioactive elements

ge·o·co·ro·na (-kə rō′nə) *n.* the envelope of ionized gases, esp. hydrogen, surrounding the earth at the outer limit of the atmosphere

ge·ode (jē′ōd′) *n.* ⟦Fr *géode* < L *geodes*, a precious stone < Gr *geoidēs*, earthlike < *gē*, earth + *-eidos*, -OID⟧ 1 a globular stone having a cavity lined with inward-growing crystals or layers of silica 2 *a)* such a cavity *b)* any formation like this —**ge·od′ic** (-äd′ik) *adj.*

ge·o·des·ic (jē′ə des′ik, -dē′sik) *adj.* 1 GEODETIC (sense 1) 2 *a)* designating the shortest surface line between two points on a surface, esp. a curved surface *b)* of or pertaining to the geometry of such lines ☆3 *Archit.* having a structurally strong surface made up of short, straight, lightweight bars that form a grid of polygons [*geodesic* dome] —*n.* a geodesic line

ge·od·e·sy (jē äd′ə sē) *n.* ⟦Gr *geōdaisia* < *gē*, the earth + *daiein*, to divide < IE base **dā-*, *dā(i)-*, to divide > TIDE[1]⟧ the branch of applied mathematics concerned with measuring, or determining the shape of, the earth or a large part of its surface, or with locating points on its surface with precision —**ge·od′e·sist** *n.*

ge·o·det·ic (jē′ə det′ik) *adj.* 1 of or determined by geodesy 2 GEODESIC (sense 2) Also **ge′o·det′i·cal** —**ge′o·det′i·cal·ly** *adv.*

☆**ge·o·duck** (go͞o′ē duk′) *n.* ⟦< AmInd (Chinook) name⟧ a very large, burrowing, edible clam (*Panope generosa*) of intertidal beaches of W North America

ge·o·dy·nam·ics (jē′ō dī nam′iks) *n.* a branch of geophysics dealing with the activity and forces inside the earth —**ge′o·dy·nam′ic** *adj.*

ge·o·ec·o·nom·ics (jē′ō ek′ə näm′iks, -ē′kə-) *n.* 1 economics in its relationship to such geographical conditions as location and natural resources 2 a condition of economic rivalry among nations —**ge′o·ec′o·nom′ic** *adj.*

Geof·frey (jef′rē) *n.* ⟦ME *Geffrey* < OFr *Geoffroi* < Gmc *Walafrid* < **wala-*, traveler + **frithu*, peace (> Ger *friede*)⟧ a masculine name: dim. *Geoff*, *Jeff*; var. *Jeffrey*

Geoffrey of Monmouth 1100?-54; Brit. bishop & chronicler: preserver of the Arthurian legend

geog *abbrev.* 1 geographer 2 geographical 3 geography

ge·og·no·sy (jē äg′nə sē) *n.* ⟦Fr *géognosie* < Gr *gē*, earth + *gnōsis*, knowledge: see GNOSIS⟧ *former term for* GEOLOGY (senses 1 & 2)

ge·og·ra·pher (jē äg′rə fər) *n.* a specialist in geography

ge·o·graph·i·cal (jē′ə graf′i kəl) *adj.* **1** of or according to geography **2** with reference to the geography of a particular region Also **ge′o·graph′ic** —**ge′o·graph′i·cal·ly** *adv.*

ge·og·ra·phy (jē äg′rə fē) *n., pl.* **-phies** ⟦L *geographia* < Gr *geōgraphia*, geography < *geō-* (see GEO-) + *graphein*, to write: see GRAPHIC⟧ **1** the descriptive science dealing with the surface of the earth, its division into continents and countries, and the climate, plants, animals, natural resources, inhabitants, and industries of the various divisions **2** the physical features, esp. the surface features, of a region, area, or place **3** a book about geography

ge·oid (jē′oid′) *n.* ⟦Ger *geoide* < Gr *geoeidēs*, earthlike: see GEODE⟧ in geodesy, the earth viewed as a hypothetical ellipsoid with the surface represented as a mean sea level

geol *abbrev.* **1** geologic(al) **2** geologist **3** geology

ge·o·log·ic (jē′ə läj′ik) *adj.* of or according to geology: also **ge′o·log′i·cal** —**ge′o·log′i·cal·ly** *adv.*

geologic time the time period (*c.* 4.55 billion years) representing the earth's geologic history: see the geologic time chart in the Reference Supplement

ge·ol·o·gist (jē äl′ə jist) *n.* a specialist in geology

ge·ol·o·gize (-jīz′) *vi., vt.* **-gized′**, **-giz′ing** [Rare] to study geology or make a geologic survey of (an area)

ge·ol·o·gy (jē äl′ə jē) *n., pl.* **-gies** ⟦ML *geologia*: see GEO- & -LOGY⟧ **1** the science dealing with the physical nature and history of the earth, including the structure and development of its crust, the composition of its interior, individual rock types, the forms of life found as fossils, etc. **2** the structure of the earth's crust in a given region, area, or place **3** a book about geology

geom *abbrev.* **1** geometric **2** geometry

ge·o·mag·net·ic (jē′ō mag net′ik) *adj.* of or pertaining to the magnetic properties of the earth —**ge′o·mag′ne·tism′** *n.*

ge·o·man·cy (jē′ō man′sē) *n.* ⟦ME *geomancie* < OFr < ML *geomantia* < LGr *geōmanteia*: see GEO- & -MANCY⟧ divination by random figures formed when a handful of earth is thrown to the ground, or as by lines drawn at random —**ge′o·man′cer** *n.* —**ge′o·man′tic** *adj.*

ge·o·met·ric (jē′ə me′trik) *adj.* ⟦L *geometricus* < Gr *geōmetrikos*⟧ **1** of or according to geometry **2** characterized by or using straight lines, triangles, circles, or similar regular shapes or forms [*a geometric* pattern] Also **ge′o·met′ri·cal** —*n.* a geometric design, pattern, etc.: *usually used in pl.* —**ge′o·met′ri·cal·ly** *adv.*

ge·om·e·tri·cian (jē äm′ə trish′ən, jē′ə mə-) *n.* a specialist in geometry: also **ge·om·e·ter** (jē äm′ə tər)

geometric mean *Math.* the *n*th root of the product of *n* factors [the *geometric mean* of 2 and 8 (or the mean proportional between 2 and 8) is 2×8, or $\sqrt{4}$]

geometric progression a sequence of terms in which the ratio of each term to the preceding one is the same throughout the sequence (Ex.: 1, 2, 4, 8, 16, 32)

ge·om·e·trid (jē äm′ə trid) *n.* ⟦< ModL *Geometridae* < L *geometres*: see GEOMETRY⟧ any of a large family (Geometridae) of moths, typically having broad wings: the slender larvae are called *measuring worms, inchworms*, etc.: see MEASURING WORM

ge·om·e·trize (-trīz′) *vi.* **-trized′**, **-triz′ing** [Rare] to use geometric principles —*vt.* [Rare] to work out geometrically

ge·om·e·try (jē äm′ə trē) *n., pl.* **-tries** ⟦ME *geometrie* < OFr < L *geometria* < Gr *geōmetria* < *geōmetrein*, to measure the earth < *gē*, earth + *metria*, measurement < *metrein*, to measure: for IE base, see METER[1]⟧ **1** the branch of mathematics that deals with points, lines, planes, and figures, and examines their properties, measurement, and mutual relations in space: see PLANE GEOMETRY, SOLID GEOMETRY **2** a book about geometry **3** a specific system of geometry

ge·o·mor·phic (jē′ō môr′fik) *adj.* ⟦GEO- + -MORPHIC⟧ of or pertaining to the shape of the earth or its topography

ge·o·mor·phol·o·gy (-môr fäl′ə jē) *n.* ⟦GEO- + MORPHOLOGY⟧ the science dealing with the nature and origin of the earth's topographic features —**ge′o·mor′pho·log′ic** (-môr′fə läj′ik) *adj.*, **ge′o·mor′pho·log′i·cal**

ge·oph·a·gy (jē äf′ə jē) *n.* ⟦GEO- + -PHAGY⟧ the eating of earth to make up for lack of food, as in famine areas

☆**ge·o·phone** (jē′ə fōn′) *n.* ⟦GEO- + -PHONE⟧ an electronic receiver designed to pick up seismic vibrations transmitted through rock, ice, etc.

ge·o·phys·ics (jē′ō fiz′iks) *n.* the science that deals with the physics of the earth, including weather, winds, tides, earthquakes, volcanoes, etc. and their effect on the planet earth —**ge′o·phys′i·cal** *adj.* —**ge′o·phys′i·cist** *n.*

ge·o·phyte (jē′ə fīt′) *n.* ⟦GEO- + -PHYTE⟧ a plant that grows in earth; esp., a perennial whose buds live underground throughout the winter

ge·o·pol·i·tics (jē′ō päl′i tiks′) *n.* ⟦< Ger *geopolitik*: see GEO- & POLITICS⟧ **1** political relations among nations, esp. as they involve claims and disputes pertaining to borders, territories, etc. **2** the Nazi policy of aggressive territorial expansion: see LEBENSRAUM —**ge′o·po·lit′i·cal** (-pə lit′i kəl) *adj.* —**ge′o·pol′i·ti′cian** *n.*

ge·o·pon·ic (jē′ō pän′ik) *adj.* ⟦Gr *geōponikos* < *geōponein*, to till the ground < *geō-* (see GEO-) + *ponein*, to toil < *ponos*, work, toil < IE base **(s)pen(d)-*, to pull, draw > SPIN⟧ [Rare] related to agriculture

ge·o·pres·sured (-presh′ərd) *adj.* of or having to do with substances, as methane or water, within the earth's crust that are forced upward by geologic pressures: also **ge′o·pres′sur·ized′** (-presh′ər īzd′)

Geor·die (jôr′dē) *n.* ⟦< dim. of fol.⟧ **1** [Brit.] a person born or living in or near Newcastle-upon-Tyne **2** the variety of Brit. English spoken there

George[1] (jôrj) *n.* ⟦< Fr & L; Fr *Georges* < LL *Georgius* < Gr *Geōrgios* < *geōrgos*, husbandman, lit., earthworker < *gaia, gē*, earth + base of *ergon*, WORK⟧ a masculine name: dim. *Georgie*; equiv. Fr. *Georges*, Ger. & Scand. *Georg*, It. *Giorgio*, Sp. *Jorge*; fem. *Georgette, Georgia, Georgina*

George[2] (jôrj) **1** Saint (died A.D. 303?); Christian martyr, possibly from Cappadocia: patron saint of England: his day is April 23 **2 George I** 1660-1727; king of Great Britain & Ireland (1714-27), born in Germany: great-grandson of James I **3 George II** 1683-1760; king of Great Britain & Ireland (1727-60), born in Germany: son of George I **4 George III** 1738-1820; king of Great Britain & Ireland (1760-1820): grandson of George II **5 George IV** 1762-1830; king of Great Britain & Ireland (1820-30); regent (1811-20): son of George III **6 George V** 1865-1936; king of Great Britain & Ireland (1910-36): son of Edward VII **7 George VI** 1895-1952; king of Great Britain & Northern Ireland (1936-52): son of George V **8 David Lloyd** *see* LLOYD GEORGE, David **9 Henry** 1839-97; U.S. political economist: advocate of the single tax

George[3] (jôrj), **Lake** lake in NE N.Y.: 33 mi (53 km) long

George·town (jôrj′toun′) **1** seaport & capital of Guyana, on the Atlantic **2** section of Washington, D.C. **3** *former name for* PENANG (the seaport): also **George Town**

geor·gette (jôr jet′) *n.* ⟦after *Georgette* de la Plante, Parisian modiste⟧ a thin, durable, slightly crinkled fabric, used for women's dresses, blouses, etc.: also **georgette crepe**

Geor·gia[1] (jôr′jə) *n.* ⟦fem. of GEORGE[1]⟧ a feminine name; dim. *Georgie*: see GEORGE[1]

Geor·gia[2] (jôr′jə) **1** ⟦after GEORGE II⟧ Southern state of the SE U.S.: one of the 13 original states: 57,906 sq mi (149,976 sq km); cap. Atlanta: abbrev. *GA* or *Ga* **2** ⟦orig. uncert.⟧ region in SE Europe on the Black Sea **3** GEORGIAN SOVIET SOCIALIST REPUBLIC **4** ⟦see sense 2⟧ country in Transcaucasia, on the Black Sea: became independent upon the breakup of the U.S.S.R. (1991): 26,911 sq mi (69,700 sq km); cap. Tbilisi: formerly, *Georgian Soviet Socialist Republic* **5 Strait of** ⟦after GEORGE III⟧ arm of the Pacific, between Vancouver Island & British Columbia, Canada: *c.* 150 mi (241 km) long: also **Georgia Strait**

Geor·gian[1] (jôr′jən) *adj.* **1** *a)* of the reigns of George I, II, III, and IV of England (1714-1830) *b)* designating or of the artistic style of this period **2** of or characteristic of the period of the reign of George V of England, specif. with reference to literature **3** of the state of Georgia: usually used in the predicate —*n.* ☆a person born or living in the state of Georgia

Geor·gian[2] (jôr′jən) *adj.* of the country of Georgia or its people, language, or culture —*n.* **1** a person born or living in the country of Georgia **2** the South Caucasian language spoken in the country of Georgia

Georgian Bay NE arm of Lake Huron, in Ontario, Canada

Georgian Soviet Socialist Republic a republic of the U.S.S.R.: now GEORGIA[2]

geor·gic (jôr′jik) *adj.* ⟦L *georgicus* < Gr *geōrgikos*, agricultural < *geōrgos*, husbandman, farmer: see GEORGE[1]⟧ having to do with agriculture or husbandry —*n.* ⟦L (Virgil) *georgicum (carmen)*, georgic (song)⟧ a poem dealing with farming or rural life

ge·o·sci·ence (jē′ō sī′əns) *n.* **1** the geological sciences as a whole; geology **2** any earth science —**ge′o·sci′en·tist** *n.*

☆**ge·o·sta·tion·ar·y** (jē′ō stā′shə ner′ē) *adj.* designating or of a satellite or spacecraft in an orbit above the equator, revolving at a rate of speed synchronous with that of the earth's rotation so that it always stays above the same place on the earth's surface: also **ge′o·syn′chro·nous** (-siŋ′krə nəs)

ge·o·stroph·ic (jē′ō sträf′ik) *adj.* ⟦< GEO- + Gr *strophē* (see STROPHE) + -IC⟧ designating or of a force producing deflection as a result of the earth's rotation

ge·o·syn·cline (-sin′klīn′) *n.* ⟦GEO- + SYNCLINE⟧ a very large, troughlike depression in the earth's surface containing masses of sedimentary and volcanic rocks

ge·o·tax·is (-tak′sis) *n.* ⟦ModL: see GEO- & -TAXIS⟧ the positive (or negative) response of a freely moving organism to (or against) gravity —**ge′o·tac′tic** (-tak′tik) *adj.* —**ge′o·tac′ti·cal·ly** *adv.*

ge·o·tec·ton·ic (-tek tän′ik) *adj.* ⟦GEO- + TECTONIC⟧ TECTONIC (sense 3)

ge·o·ther·mal (-thur′məl) *adj.* ⟦GEO- + THERMAL⟧ having to do with the heat of the earth's interior: sometimes **ge′o·ther′mic** (-thur′mik)

ge·ot·ro·pism (jē ä′trə piz′əm) *n.* ⟦GEO- + -TROPISM⟧ any positive (or negative) movement or growth of a plant or sessile animal in response to (or against) the force of gravity —**ge·o·trop·ic** (jē′ō träp′ik) *adj.*

ger *abbrev.* gerund

Ger *abbrev.* **1** German **2** Germany

Ge·ra (gā′rä) city in E Germany, in the state of Thuringia

ge·rah (gē′rə) *n.* ⟦Heb *gera*, lit., a bean⟧ an ancient Hebrew coin and weight equal to 1⁄20 of a shekel

Ge·raint (jə rānt′) *n.* ⟦< Celt⟧ *Arthurian Legend* a knight of the Round Table, husband of Enid

Ger·ald (jer′əld) *n.* ⟦< OFr or OHG; OFr *Giraut, Giralt* < OHG *Gerald, Gerwald* < *ger*, spear (akin to OE *gar*: see GORE[3]) + base of *waldan*, to rule: for IE base see WIELD⟧ a masculine name: dim. *Gerry, Jerry*; fem. *Geraldine*

ge·ra·ni·ol (jə rā′nē ôl′, -ōl′) *n.* ⟦< ModL *Geranium* (see fol.) + -OL[1]: so named because derived from geranium leaves⟧ a terpene alcohol, $C_{10}H_{18}O$, found in many essential oils and having an odor resembling that of roses: used in perfumery

ge·ra·ni·um (jə rā′nē əm) *adj.* ⟦L < Gr *geranion*, cranesbill, dim. < *geranos*, a crane < IE base **ger-*, echoic of hoarse cry > CRANE⟧ designating a family

(Geraniaceae, order Geraniales) of dicotyledonous plants, including the pelargonium —*n.* 1 any of a large genus (*Geranium*) of plants of the geranium family, having pink or purple flowers, long bill-shaped seeds, and leaves with many lobes; cranesbill 2 PELARGONIUM: the florist's geranium 3 an intense red

Ge·rard (jə rärd′) *n.* ⟦OFr *Girart* < OHG *Gerhart* < *ger* (see GERALD) + *hart*, HARD⟧ a masculine name: dim. *Gerry, Jerry*

☆**ge·rar·di·a** (jə rär′dē ə) *n.* ⟦ModL, after J. *Gerard* (1545-1612), Eng botanist⟧ any of a genus (*Gerardia*) of American plants of the figwort family, with showy yellow, white, or pinkish flowers: it is sometimes parasitic on roots

ger·be·ra (jər bir′ə, gər-; jur′bə rə, gur′-) *n.* ⟦ModL: so named after T. *Gerber*, 18th-c. Ger physician and naturalist⟧ an African plant (*Gerbera jamesonii*) of the composite family, with basal rosettes of leaves and single flower heads with numerous long, narrow ray flowers in white, pink, orange, salmon, or violet

ger·bil or **ger·bille** (jur′bəl) *n.* ⟦Fr *gerbille* < ModL *gerbillus* < *gerbo*, JERBOA⟧ any of a subfamily (Gerbillinae, family Cricetidae) of burrowing rodents, with long hind legs and hairy tail, native to Africa and Asia: often kept as a pet

ge·rent (jir′ənt) *n.* ⟦< L *gerens* (gen. *gerentis*), prp. of *gerere*, to bear, conduct⟧ [Rare] a person who manages, directs, or rules

ger·e·nuk (ger′ə no͝ok′) *n.* ⟦< Somali *garanug*⟧ a small antelope (*Litocranius walleri*) of E Africa, with a long neck and long legs

ger·fal·con (jur′fôl′kən, -fô′kən; -fal′-) *n. alt. sp. of* GYRFALCON

☆**ger·i·a·tri·cian** (jer′ē ə trish′ən) *n.* a doctor who specializes in geriatrics: also **ger·i·at·rist** (jer′ē a′trist)

☆**ger·i·at·rics** (jer′ē a′triks) *n.* ⟦< Gr *gēras*, old age, *gerōn*, old man (< IE base **ĝer-*, to grow ripe, age > CORN[1], CHURL, Sans *járant-*, feeble, old) + -IATRICS⟧ the branch of medicine that deals with the diseases and problems of old age: see GERONTOLOGY —**ger′i·at′ric** *adj.*

Gé·ri·cault (zhä rē kō′), **(Jean-Louis-André-)Thé·o·dore** (tā ō dôr′) 1791-1824; Fr. painter

germ (jurm) *n.* ⟦ME *germe*, a bud, sprout < OFr < L *germen*, sprig, bud, germ, embryo < IE **gen-men* (> Sans *janiman-*, birth, origin) < base **ĝen-*: see GENUS⟧ 1 the rudimentary form from which a new organism is developed; seed; bud 2 any microscopic organism, esp. one of the bacteria, that can cause disease 3 that from which something can develop or grow; basis [the *germ* of an idea]

ger·man (jur′mən) *adj.* ⟦ME *germain*, *german* < OFr *germain* < L *germanus*, akin to *germen*, a sprout, prec.⟧ closely related: now chiefly in compounds, meaning *a)* having the same parents [a brother-*german*] *b)* having the same grandparents on either the father's side or the mother's [a cousin-*german* is a first cousin]

Ger·man (jur′mən) *n.* ⟦ME (only in pl.) < ML *Germanus* < L, prob. < Celt⟧ 1 a person born or living in Germany 2 the West Germanic language spoken chiefly in Germany, Austria, and certain parts of Switzerland, technically called *New High German*: see also OLD HIGH GERMAN, MIDDLE HIGH GERMAN, HIGH GERMAN, LOW GERMAN 3 [g-] *a)* a complicated dance for many couples in which partners are changed often *b)* a party at which the german is danced —*adj.* of Germany or its people, language, or culture

German cockroach CROTON BUG

German Democratic Republic *see* GERMANY

ger·man·der (jər man′dər) *n.* ⟦ME *germandre* < OFr *germandree* < ML *germandra* < Gr *chamaidrys* < *chamai*, on the ground (< IE base **ĝhm-, ĝhthem-* > L *humus* & OE *guma*, man) + *drys*, TREE⟧ any of a genus (*Teucrium*) of plants of the mint family, with spikes of flowers that lack an upper lip

ger·mane (jər mān′) *adj.* ⟦var. of GERMAN⟧ 1 truly relevant; pertinent; to the point 2 [Obs.] akin; german —***SYN.*** RELEVANT

German East Africa former colony of the German Empire, in E Africa: it was the territory now consisting chiefly of Tanzania, Rwanda, & Burundi

Ger·man·ic (jər man′ik) *adj.* ⟦L *Germanicus*, of the Germans: orig. applied to a particular tribe, prob. Celtic⟧ 1 [Now Rare] German 2 designating or of a group of N European peoples including the Germans, Scandinavians, Dutch, English, etc., or the peoples from whom they are descended 3 designating or of the language group Germanic —*n.* 1 [Obs.] PROTO-GERMANIC 2 a principal branch of the Indo-European family of languages, comprising the languages descended from Proto-Germanic: it is divided into three groups: **East Germanic** (including Gothic), **North Germanic** (Norwegian, Danish, Swedish, Icelandic, Old Norse, etc.), and **West Germanic** (English, Dutch, German, Yiddish, Frisian, etc.)

Ger·man·i·cus Caesar (jər man′i kəs) 15 B.C.-A.D. 19; Rom. general: father of Caligula

Ger·man·ism (jur′mən iz′əm) *n.* 1 a word, phrase, grammatical construction, or other feature originating in or peculiar to the German language 2 a German custom, belief, etc. 3 fondness for or imitation of German ways

Ger·man·ist (-ist) *n.* a specialist in the study of German life and culture or Germanic linguistics and literature

ger·ma·ni·um (jər mā′nē əm) *n.* ⟦ModL < L *Germania*, Germany⟧ a grayish-white, nonmetallic chemical element of the carbon family used in semiconductors, transistors, infrared equipment, etc.: symbol, Ge; at. no. 32: see the periodic table of elements in the Reference Supplement

Ger·man·ize (jur′mən īz′) *vt.* **-ized′**, **-iz′ing** 1 to make German or like the Germans in thought, language, etc. 2 [Archaic] to translate into German —*vi.* to adopt German methods, attitudes, etc. —**Ger′man·i·za′tion** *n.*

German measles RUBELLA

Ger·man·o- (jər man′ō) *combining form* German, German and [*Germanophobe*]

Ger·man·o·phile (jər man′ə fil′) *n.* ⟦prec. + -PHILE⟧ a person who strongly admires Germany or its people, culture, customs, influence, etc.

Ger·man·o·phobe (-fōb′) *n.* ⟦GERMANO- + -PHOBE⟧ a person who hates or fears Germany or its people, culture, influence, etc. —**Ger·man′o·pho′bi·a** *n.*

German shepherd any of a breed of large dog somewhat resembling a wolf, with a bushy tail and erect ears, developed in Germany to herd sheep, now often used as a guard dog, a police dog, and a guide for the blind

German short·haired pointer (shôrt′herd′) any of a breed of large, lean hunting dog similar to, and probably descended from the same stock as, the pointer, with a short, thick coat, liver or liver-and-white in color

German silver NICKEL SILVER

German Southwest Africa *former name for* NAMIBIA

Ger·man·town (jur′mən toun′) NW section of Philadelphia, Pa.: formerly a separate town, scene of an American defeat in a Revolutionary War battle (1777)

German wirehaired pointer any of a breed of large, lean hunting dog developed from the pointer and other breeds, having a wiry coat of liver-and-white, bushy eyebrows, and a beard

Ger·ma·ny (jur′mə nē), *pl.* **-nys** or **-nies**: used to refer to the divided countries (1945-90) ⟦L *Germania*⟧ country in NC Europe, on the North and Baltic Seas, comprising 16 states: Germany was divided into four zones of occupation after WWII (1945), administered respectively by France, Britain, the U.S., & the U.S.S.R., and in 1949 was partitioned into two countries, the **Federal Republic of Germany** (also called **West Germany**), made up of the former French, British, & U.S. zones, and the **German Democratic Republic** (also called **East Germany**), comprising the former Soviet zone: the two countries reunited in 1990: 137,847 sq mi (357,021 sq km); cap. Berlin

germ cell any of various cells, esp. an egg or sperm cell, from which a new organism can develop: opposed to SOMATIC CELL

ger·men (jur′mən) *n., pl.* **-mens** or **-mi·na** (-mi nə) ⟦L: see GERM⟧ [Archaic] a rudimentary form; embryo

ger·mi·cide (jur′mə sīd′) *n.* ⟦< GERM + -CIDE⟧ any antiseptic, etc. used to destroy germs —**ger′mi·ci′dal** (jur′mə sīd′'l) *adj.*

ger·mi·nal (jur′mə nəl) *adj.* ⟦Fr < ML *germinalis* < L *germen* (gen. *germinis*): see GERM⟧ 1 of, like, or characteristic of germs or germ cells 2 in an embryonic stage; in the first stage of growth or development 3 being, or serving as, a productive source or influence —**ger′mi·nal·ly** *adv.*

germinal disk 1 a disklike spot in a fertilized ovum in which the first traces of the embryo are visible 2 the disklike spot on the yolk of a heavily yolked egg where segmentation begins after fertilization

germinal vesicle the greatly enlarged nucleus of an egg in the prophase of the first meiotic division

ger·mi·nant (jur′mə nənt) *adj.* that germinates; sprouting

ger·mi·nate (-nāt′) *vi., vt.* **-nat′ed**, **-nat′ing** ⟦< L *germinatus*, pp. of *germinare*, to sprout < *germen*, a sprout, GERM⟧ 1 to sprout or cause to sprout, as from a spore, seed, or bud 2 to start developing or growing —**ger′mi·na′tion** *n.* —**ger′mi·na′tive** *adj.*

Ger·mis·ton (jur′mis tən) city in central Gauteng province, South Africa

germ layer *Embryology* any of the three primary layers of cells (ectoderm, endoderm, and mesoderm) from which the various organs and parts of the organism develop by further differentiation

germ plasm the reproductive cells of an organism, particularly that portion of the reproductive cells involved in heredity: cf. SOMATOPLASM

germ theory [Old-fashioned] the theory that certain diseases are transmitted by specific germs, or microorganisms

germ warfare the deliberate contamination of enemy territory with disease germs during a war

germ·y (jur′mē) *adj.* **germ′i·er**, **germ′i·est** full of germs

Ge·ron·i·mo (jə rän′ə mō′) ⟦Sp, Jerome, used as a nickname by the Mexicans⟧ 1829?-1909; Apache Indian leader

ger·on·toc·ra·cy (jer′ən tä′krə sē) *n.* ⟦altered (modeled on -CRACY) < Fr *gérontocratie* < Gr *geronto-* (see fol.) + *-kratia*, -CRACY⟧ 1 government by old men 2 *pl.* **-cies** a governing group composed of old men —**ger·on·to·crat·ic** (jə rän′tə krat′ik) *adj.*

ger·on·tol·o·gy (jer′ən täl′ə jē) *n.* ⟦Gr *geronto-* < *gerōn* (see GERIATRICS) + -LOGY⟧ the scientific study of the process of aging and of the problems of aged people: see GERIATRICS —**ger′on·to·log′i·cal** (-tə läj′i kəl) *adj.* —**ger′on·tol′o·gist** *n.*

ge·ron·to·mor·pho·sis (jə rän′tō môr′fə sis) *n.* ⟦*geronto-* (see prec.) + MORPHOSIS⟧ evolutionary development that produces extreme specialization and, ultimately, extinction of a species or race, as of the large dinosaurs

ger·o·psy·chol·o·gy (jer′ō sī käl′ə jē) *n.* the branch of psychology that specializes in the mental and emotional processes of the elderly —**ger′o·psy·chol′o·gist** *n.*

-ger·ous (jər əs) ⟦L *-ger* < *gerere*, to bear + -OUS⟧ *suffix* producing or bearing [*dentigerous*]

Ger·ry (ger′ē), **El·bridge** (el′brij) 1744-1814; Am. statesman: signer of the Declaration of Independence: vice president of the U.S. (1813-14)

☆**ger·ry·man·der** (jer′ē man′dər; *orig.* ger′-) *vt.* ⟦satirical coinage after E. GERRY, governor of Mass. when the method was employed (1812) + (SALA)MANDER (the shape of the redistricted Essex County)⟧ 1 to divide (a voting area) so as to give one political party a majority in as many districts as possible or weaken the voting strength of an ethnic or racial group, urban population, etc. **2** to manipulate unfairly so as to gain advantage —*vi.* to engage in gerrymandering —*n.* a redistricting of voting districts to the advantage of one party or disadvantage of a group, region, etc.

Gersh·win (gursh′win), **George** (born *Jacob Gershvin*) 1898-1937; U.S. composer

Ger·trude (gur′tro͞od′) *n.* ⟦< Fr & Ger: Fr *Gertrude* < Ger *Gertrud* < OHG *Geretrudis* < *ger*, spear + *trut*, dear⟧ a feminine name: dim. *Gert, Gertie, Trudy*

ger·und (jer′ənd) *n.* ⟦LL *gerundium* < L *gerundus*, ger. of *gerere*, to do, carry out⟧ *Gram.* **1** in Latin, a verbal noun in the singular of all cases but the nominative, used to indicate continuing or generalized action (Ex.: *probandi* in *onus probandi*, "the burden of proving") **2** in other languages, any of various forms analogous to this; specif., an English verbal noun ending in *-ing* that has all the uses of the noun but retains certain syntactic characteristics of the verb, such as the ability to take an object or an adverbial modifier (Ex.: *playing* in "Playing golf is his only exercise") —**ge·run·di·al** (jə run′dē əl) *adj.*

ge·run·dive (jə run′div) *n.* ⟦ME *gerundif* < LL *gerundivus* < *gerundium*: see prec.⟧ *Gram.* **1** in Latin, a verbal adjective with a typical gerund stem form, used as a future passive participle expressing duty, necessity, fitness, etc. (Ex.: *delenda* in *delenda est Carthago*, "Carthage must be destroyed") **2** in other languages, any of various forms analogous to this —**ger·un·di·val** (jer′ən dī′vəl) *adj.*

Ge·ry·on (jē′rē än′; ger′ē ən) *n.* ⟦L < Gr *Gēryōn* or *Gēryonēs*⟧ *Gr. Myth.* a winged, three-bodied monster killed by Hercules as one of his twelve labors

Ge·samt·kunst·werk (gə zämt′ko͝onst′verk) *n.* ⟦Ger, synthesis of the arts < *gesamt*, total + *kunstwerk*, work of art⟧ in the aesthetic theory of Richard Wagner, an ideal synthesis of performing arts, including music, drama, decor, etc., into a kind of total theater, as in opera

Ge·sell (gə zel′), **Arnold L(ucius)** 1880-1961; U.S. psychologist: authority on child behavior

Ge·sell·schaft (gə zel′shäft′) *n., pl.* **-schaf′ten** (-shäf′tən) ⟦Ger, society < *gesell(e)*, fellow, companion, member of a group + *-schaft*, -SHIP⟧ [*sometimes* **g-**] the societal form of association in which rational order, neutral involvement, and obligations to institutions are dominant: opposed to GEMEINSCHAFT

ges·ne·ri·a (jes nir′ē ə, ges-) *adj.* ⟦ModL, after K. V. *Gesner* (1516-65), Swiss naturalist⟧ designating a tropical family (Gesneriaceae, order Scrophulariales) of woody or fleshy dicotyledonous plants with showy tubular flowers, including the African violets, the gloxinias, and the episcias —**ges·ne′ri·ad** *adj., n.*

ges·so (jes′ō) *n.* ⟦It, gypsum, chalk < L *gypsum*, GYPSUM⟧ plaster of Paris (or, now, chalk) mixed with glue and applied to flat or carved surfaces or as bas-reliefs, etc. and then painted, gilded, etc.

gest[1] or **geste** (jest) *n.* ⟦ME *geste* < OFr < L *gesta*, deeds, pl. of *gestus* < pp. of *gerere*, to do, act⟧ **1** [Archaic] an adventure; deed; exploit **2** a romantic story of daring adventures, esp. a medieval tale in verse

gest[2] (jest) *n.* ⟦Fr *geste* < L *gestus*, posture, gesture < pp. of *gerere*, to bear, behave⟧ [Archaic] **1** bearing; deportment **2** a gesture

gest[3] *abbrev.* ⟦Ger *gestorben*, lit., dead, deceased, pp. of *sterben*, to die⟧ died: used with the year of a person's death

ge·stalt (gə shtält′, -stält′; -shtôlt′, -stôlt′) *n., pl.* **-stalt′en** (-ən) or **-stalts′** ⟦Ger, lit., shape, form < MHG pp. of *stellen*, to arrange, fix⟧ [*also* **G-**] in Gestalt psychology, any of the integrated structures or patterns that make up all experience and have specific properties which can neither be derived from the elements of the whole nor be considered simply as the sum of these elements

Gestalt psychology a school of psychology, developed in Germany, which affirms that all experience consists of gestalten, and that the response of an organism to a situation is a complete and unanalyzable whole rather than a sum of the responses to specific elements in the situation

Ge·sta·po (gə stä′pō, -stap′ō) *n.* ⟦< Ger *Ge(heime) Sta(ats)po(lizei)*, secret state police⟧ **1** [*sometimes* **g-**] the secret police force of the German Nazi state, notorious for its terrorism, brutality, etc. **2** [*also* **g-**] any secret police **3** [*also* **g-**] [Slang] any police force or other authority regarded variously as sinister, ruthless, brutal, etc.

Ges·ta Ro·ma·no·rum (jes′tə rō′mə nôr′əm) ⟦ML, doings of the Romans⟧ a 14th-cent. European collection of tales in Latin, used as a source of plots by Chaucer, Shakespeare, etc.

ges·tate (jes′tāt′) *vt.* **-tat′ed, -tat′ing** ⟦back-form. < fol.⟧ to carry in the uterus during pregnancy

ges·ta·tion (jes tā′shən) *n.* ⟦L *gestatio* < pp. of *gestare*, freq. of *gerere*, to bear, carry⟧ **1** the act or period of carrying young in the uterus from conception to birth; pregnancy **2** a development, as of a plan in the mind

ges·tic (jes′tik) *adj.* ⟦GEST[2] + -IC⟧ having to do with bodily movement and gestures, esp. dancing: also **ges′ti·cal**

ges·tic·u·late (jes tik′yo͞o lāt′, -yə-) *vi.* **-lat′ed, -lat′ing** ⟦< L *gesticulatus*, pp. of *gesticulari*, to make mimic gestures < *gesticulus*, dim. of *gestus*, a gesture < pp. of *gerere*, to bear, carry, do⟧ to make or use gestures, esp. with the hands and arms, as in adding nuances or force to one's speech, or as a substitute for speech —*vt.* to express by gesticulating —**ges·tic′u·la′tive** *adj.* —**ges·tic′u·la′tor** *n.*

ges·tic·u·la·tion (jes tik′yo͞o lā′shən, -yə-) *n.* ⟦L *gesticulatio*⟧ **1** a gesticulating **2** a gesture, esp. an energetic one —**ges·tic′u·la·to′ry** (-lə tôr′ē) *adj.*

ges·ture (jes′chər) *n.* ⟦ME < ML *gestura*, mode of action < L *gestus*, pp. of *gerere*, to bear, carry⟧ **1** a movement, or movements collectively, of the body, or of part of the body, to express or emphasize ideas, emotions, etc. **2** anything said or done to convey a state of mind, intention, etc.; often, something said or done merely for effect or as a formality [*a gesture* of sympathy] —*vi.* **-tured, -tur·ing** to make or use a gesture or gestures —*vt.* to express with a gesture or gestures —**ges′tur·al** *adj.* —**ges′tur·er** *n.*

ge·sund·heit (gə zo͝ont′hīt′) *interj.* ⟦Ger⟧ used to wish good health to someone who has just sneezed

get (get; *also, although it is considered nonstandard by some,* git) *vt.* **got, got′ten, get′ting**: see usage note at **got′ten** ⟦ME *geten* < ON *geta*, to get, beget, akin to OE *-gietan* (see BEGET, FORGET), Ger *-gessen* in *vergessen*, forget < IE base **ghend-*, to seize, get hold of > L *(pre)hendere*, to grasp, understand⟧ **1** to come into the state of having; become the owner or receiver of; receive, win, gain, obtain, acquire, etc. **2** to reach; arrive at (a place or condition) [to *get* home early] **3** to set up communication with, as by radio or telephone [to *get* Paris] **4** *a)* to go and bring *b)* to bring [go *get* your books] **5** *a)* to catch; capture; gain hold of *b)* to become afflicted with (a disease) **6** to learn; commit to memory **7** to obtain as a result, by means of experiment or calculation [add 2 and 2 to *get* 4] **8** to influence or persuade (a person) to do something [*get* him to leave] **9** to cause to act in a certain way [*get* the door to shut properly] **10** *a)* to cause to be [to *get* one's hands dirty] *b)* to cause to arrive at [*get* the copy to the printer] **11** to take (oneself) away: often used absolutely **12** to be sentenced to [to *get* ten years for robbery] **13** to prepare [to *get* lunch] **14** BEGET: said of animals **15** to manage or contrive: with an infinitive object [to *get* to do something] **16** [Informal] to be obliged; feel a necessity: preceded by *have* or *has* and followed by an infinitive object [he's *got* to pass the test] **17** [Informal] to own; possess: with *have* or *has* [he's *got* red hair] **18** [Informal] to be or become the master of; esp., *a)* to overpower; have complete control of [his illness finally *got* him] *b)* to puzzle; baffle [this problem *gets* me] *c)* to take into custody, wound, or kill *d)* to inflict (unspecified) harm or damage against [I'll *get* you yet!] ☆*e) Baseball* to put (an opponent) out, as by catching a batted ball **19** [Informal] to strike; hit [the blow *got* him in the eye] **20** [Informal] to catch the meaning or import of; understand **21** [Slang] to cause an emotional response in; irritate, please, thrill, etc. [her singing really *gets* me] ☆**22** [Slang] to notice or observe [*get* the look on his face] —*vi.* **1** to come, go, or arrive [to *get* to work on time] **2** to be or become; come to be (doing something); come to be (in a situation, condition, etc.) [to *get* caught in the rain; *get* in touch with me] **3** [Informal] to leave at once: commonly pronounced (git) when used in the imperative or infinitive ➡*Get* is used as a linking verb in idiomatic phrases, and as an informal auxiliary for emphasis in passive constructions [he *got* fired from his job] —*n.* **1** the young of an animal; offspring; breed **2** a begetting **3** *Tennis, etc.* a retrieving of a shot seemingly out of reach —**get about** **1** to move from place to place **2** to go to many social events, places, etc. **3** to circulate widely, as news or a rumor does —**get across** [Informal] **1** to clarify or explain convincingly **2** to be clear; be understood **3** to succeed, as in making oneself understood or conveying one's personality to an audience —**get after** [Informal] **1** to pursue or attack **2** to urge or goad persistently —**get along** *see phrase under* ALONG —**get anywhere (**or **anyplace)** to have any success or make any progress —**get around** **1** to get about (in all senses) ☆**2** to circumvent or overcome **3** to influence, outwit, or gain favor with by cajoling, flattering, etc. —**get around to** **1** to find time or occasion for **2** to get started on, esp. after a delay —**get at** **1** to approach or reach ☆**2** to apply oneself to (work, etc.) **3** to find out **4** to imply or suggest **5** [Informal] to influence by bribery or intimidation —**get away** **1** to go away; leave **2** to escape **3** to start, as in a race —**get away from it all** [Informal] to go away, as on a vacation, and leave behind one's problems, worries, etc. —☆**get away with** [Informal] to succeed in doing or taking without being discovered or punished —**get back** **1** to return **2** to recover ☆**3** [Slang] to retaliate; get revenge: usually with *at* —**get someone back** ☆[Slang] to get revenge against someone —**get behind** **1** to move to the rear of **2** to endorse or support **3** to fall into arrears, as in making a payment —**get by** **1** to be fairly adequate or acceptable ☆**2** [Informal] to succeed without being discovered or punished **3** [Informal] to survive; manage —**get down** **1** to descend **2** to dismount ☆**3** [Slang] *a)* to relax and take part in social activity, play music, dance, etc. *b)* to act or behave naturally, casually, without pretense, etc. —**get down to** to begin to consider or act on —**get in** **1** to enter **2** to join or cause to join (an activity, group, etc.): also **get in on** **3** to arrive **4** to put in **5** to become familiar or closely associated (*with*) —**get into it** [Informal] to engage in an argument or fight —**get it** [Informal] ☆**1** to understand **2** to be punished —**get it on** [Slang] to have sexual intercourse: often with *with* —**get nowhere** to make no progress; accomplish nothing —**get off** **1** to come off, down, or out of **2** to leave; go away **3** to take off **4** to escape **5** *a)* to help escape sentence or punishment *b)* to lessen the sentence or punishment of **6** to start, as in a race ☆**7** to utter (a joke, retort, etc.) **8** to have a holiday; have time off **9** [Slang] to experience euphoria, an orgasm, etc. —**get (someone) off** [Slang] to cause to experience euphoria, intoxication, an orgasm, etc. —**get off on** [Slang] to experience or receive pleasure and satisfaction from; enjoy —**get on** **1** to go on or into **2** to put on **3** to proceed; make progress **4** to grow older **5** to succeed, as in making a living **6** to agree; be compatible —**get on for** [Brit.] to approach (a time, amount, age, etc.) —**get (right) on it** [Informal] to begin doing a task (immediately) —**get out** **1** to go out **2** to go away **3** to take out ☆**4** to become no longer a secret **5** to publish —**get out of 1** to go out from **2** *a)* to escape from or avoid *b)* to help escape from or avoid **3** to go beyond (sight, etc.) **4** to find out from, as by force —**get over 1** to recover from **2** to forget or overlook **3** [Informal] to get across (in all senses) —**get one's own back** *see phrase under* OWN —**get somewhere** to accomplish something; succeed —☆**get so (that)** [Informal] to reach the point or state where —**get there** ☆[Informal] to succeed —**get through 1** to finish **2** to manage to survive **3** to secure favorable action upon (a bill, etc.) **4** to establish communication, or make oneself clear (*to*) —**get to 1** to succeed in reaching or communicating with ☆**2** to influence, as by bribery or intimidation **3** *a)* to stir the emotions of *b)* to annoy or irritate —**get together 1** to bring together; accumulate **2** to come together; gather ☆**3** [Informal] to reach an agreement —**get up 1** to rise from a chair, from sleep, etc. **2** to contrive; organize **3** to dress elaborately **4** to advance; make progress **5** to climb or mount ☆**6** go forward: used as a command to a horse —**get with** to go along with: often in the phrase **get with the program**, to go along with the assigned or predetermined plan of action —**get′ta·ble** *adj.*, **get′a·ble**

SYN.—**get** is the word of broadest application meaning to come into possession of, with or without effort or volition [to *get* a job, an idea, a headache, etc.]; **obtain** implies that there is effort or desire in the getting [he has *obtained* aid]; **procure** suggests active effort or contrivance in getting or bringing to pass [to *procure* a settlement of the dispute]; **secure**, in strict discrimination, implies difficulty in obtaining something and in retaining it [to *secure* a lasting peace]; **acquire** implies a lengthy process in the getting and connotes collection or accretion [he *acquired* a fine education]; **gain** always implies effort in the getting of something advantageous or profitable [to *gain* fame] —*ANT.* **lose, forgo**

ge·ta (get′ə, -ä) *n., pl.* **ge′ta** or **ge′tas** ⟦Jpn < ?⟧ in Japan, a high wooden clog fastened to the foot by a thong between the first and second toes

get·at·a·ble (get at′ə bəl) *adj.* ⟦< GET AT (see phr. under GET) + -ABLE⟧ [Informal] easy to reach or ascertain; accessible —**get·at′a·bil′i·ty** *n.*

get·a·way (get′ə wā′) *n.* **1** the act of starting, as in a race **2** the act of escaping, as from the police **3** *a)* a period of rest and relaxation, esp. a short one [a weekend *getaway*] *b)* the place to which one goes for this [a favorite *getaway* in the mountains]

get-go (get′gō′) *n.* ⟦< phr. *get going*, to begin⟧ [Informal] earliest stage; beginning; start: used mainly in the phrase **from the get-go**

Geth·sem·a·ne (geth sem′ə nē) *n.* ⟦Gr *Gethsēmanē* < Aram *gat shemanin*, lit., oil press: ? because such a press was located there⟧ **1** *Bible* a garden on the Mount of Olives, east of Jerusalem, scene of the agony, betrayal, and arrest of Jesus: Matt. 26:36 **2** [*often* **g-**] any scene or occasion of agony

get-out (get′out′) *n.* escape from an unpleasant situation —☆**all get-out** [Informal] the extreme degree, quality, etc. [big as *all get-out*]

get·ter (get′ər) *n.* **1** one that gets **2** a substance, esp. a metal, added in small amounts to a semiconductor, vacuum tube, etc. to attract and remove unwanted or residual impurities **3** [Cdn.] poisoned bait for farm pests

☆**get-to·geth·er** (get′tə geth′ər) *n.* an informal social gathering or meeting

Get·tys·burg (get′iz burg′) ⟦after J. *Gettys*, its 18th-c. founder⟧ town in S Pa.: site of a crucial battle (July, 1863) of the Civil War and of a famous address (Nov., 1863) by Abraham Lincoln dedicating a National Cemetery

get-up (get′up′) *n.* [Informal] **1** general arrangement or composition **2** costume; outfit; dress ☆**3** driving ambition; vigor; energy: also **get′-up′-and-go′** (-ən gō′)

ge·um (jē′əm) *n.* ⟦ModL < L⟧ AVENS

GeV or **Gev** *abbrev.* one billion (10^9) electron volts

ge·valt or **ge·vald** (gə vält′) *interj.* ⟦< E Yiddish *g'vald* < MHG *gewalt*, force, violence⟧ help: an exclamation of alarm

gew·gaw (gyoo̅′gô′) *n.* ⟦ME *giuegoue, gugaw*, redupl. < ?⟧ something showy but useless and of little value; trinket —*adj.* showy but useless

Ge·würz·tra·mi·ner (gə vurts′trə mēn′ər; *Ger* gə vürts′trä mē′nər) *n.* ⟦Ger < *gewürz*, spice + *traminer*, variety of white grape, after *Tramin* (It *Termeno*), town in N Italy where it prob. originated⟧ [*also* **g-**] **1** a dry, fruity white wine with a spicy flavor and bouquet, produced orig. in Alsace and N Italy and now also elsewhere **2** the pinkish grape from which it is made

gey (gā) [Scot.] *adj.* ⟦var. of GAY⟧ considerable —*adv.* very

gey·ser (gī′zər; *Brit* gē′-) *n.* ⟦Ice *Geysir*, name of a certain hot spring in Iceland, lit., gusher < ON *gjosa*, to GUSH⟧ **1** a spring from which columns of boiling water and steam gush into the air at intervals **2** [Brit.] a small hot-water heater of the coil type

gey·ser·ite (gī′zər īt′) *n.* siliceous material, usually opaline silica, deposited on the edges of geysers and hot springs

Ge·zi·ra (jə zir′ə) former administrative region of EC Sudan, between the Blue Nile & the White Nile

GFCI (jē′ef′sē′ī′) *n.* ground-fault circuit-interrupter: see GROUND-FAULT INTERRUPTER

GFI (jē′ef′ī′) *n.* GROUND-FAULT INTERRUPTER

G-force (jē′ fôrs′) *n.* ⟦< *g(ravity)*⟧ a unit measuring the inertial stress on a body undergoing rapid acceleration, expressed in multiples of the acceleration of gravity: also written **g-force**

Gha·na (gä′nə) country in W Africa, on the Gulf of Guinea: formed (1957) by a merger of the Gold Coast & part of Togoland: member of the Commonwealth: 92,456 sq mi (239,460 sq km); cap. Accra —**Gha·na·ian** (gä nē′ən, -nā′-) *adj., n.*

ghar·i·al (ger′ē əl) *n.* ⟦< Hindi *ghaṛiyāl*⟧ any of the only species (*Gavialis gangeticus*) of a subfamily (Gavialinae) of large crocodilian reptiles: it has a very long, slender snout and lives in N India

ghar·ry or **ghar·ri** (gar′ē) *n., pl.* **-ries** ⟦Hindi *gāṛī*⟧ in India, a vehicle, esp. a cab for hire: often used in comb. [a horse-*gharry*]

ghast·ly (gast′lē, gäst′-) *adj.* **-li·er**, **-li·est** ⟦ME *gastli* < *gast*, frightened, pp. of *gasten*, to frighten < OE *gæstan* < *gæst*, var. of *gast* (see GHOST): meaning infl. in ME by *gostlich*, GHOSTLY⟧ **1** horrible; frightful **2** ghostlike; pale; haggard **3** [Informal] very bad or unpleasant —**ghast′li·ness** *n.*

ghat or **ghaut** (gôt, gät) *n.* ⟦Hindi *ghāṭ*⟧ in India, *a)* a mountain pass *b)* a flight of steps leading down to a river landing for ritual bathers

Ghats (gôts, gäts) two mountain ranges (**Eastern Ghats** and **Western Ghats**) forming the east & west edges of the Deccan Plateau, India: highest peak, 8,841 ft (2,695 m)

gha·zi (gä′zē) *n.* ⟦Ar *ghāzī*, prp. of *ghazā*, to fight⟧ a Muslim hero, esp. one who wars against infidels

GHB (jē′āch′bē′) *n.* ⟦*g(amma-)h(ydroxy)b(utyrate)*⟧ a depressant of the central nervous system, $C_4H_8O_3$, used illegally as a date-rape drug, in bodybuilding, etc.

ghee (gē) *n.* ⟦Hindi *ghī*⟧ in India, the liquid butter remaining when butter from cow's milk or buffalo milk is melted, boiled, and strained

Ghent (gent) city in NW Belgium: capital of East Flanders

gher·kin (gur′kin) *n.* ⟦< Du or LowG *gurken*, cucumber < Pol *ogórek* < ModGr *angouri* < LGr *angourion*, watermelon < Pers *angārah*⟧ **1** a plant (*Cucumis anguria*) of the gourd family bearing small, prickly, cucumber-like fruit **2** the fruit of this plant, used for pickles **3** the immature fruit of the cucumber when pickled

ghet·to (get′ō) *n., pl.* **-tos** or **-toes** ⟦It, lit., foundry (< *gettare*, to pour < VL **jectare*, for L *jactare*, to throw, cast), name of a quarter in Venice occupied by Jews, orig. location of a cannon foundry⟧ **1** in certain European cities, a section to which Jews were formerly restricted **2** any section of a city in which many members of some minority group live, or to which they are restricted as by economic pressure or social discrimination **3** any place or condition regarded as isolating or restricting a particular group of people —*adj.* ☆of, or regarded as characteristic of, impoverished, esp. black, inner-city life, culture, or attitudes

☆**ghetto blaster** ⟦so called from perceived wide use in U.S. urban areas⟧ [Slang] a large, powerful, portable radio and tape or CD player: a mildly offensive term

☆**ghet·to·ize** (-īz′) *vt.* **-ized′**, **-iz′ing 1** to restrict to a ghetto **2** to make into a ghetto —**ghet′to·i·za′tion** *n.*

Ghib·el·line (gib′ə lēn′, -lin, -līn′) *n.* ⟦It *Ghibellino*, for Ger *Waiblingen*, Hohenstaufen estate in Franconia⟧ any member of a political party in medieval Italy that supported the authority of the German emperors in Italy in opposition to the papal party of the Guelphs —*adj.* of this party

Ghi·ber·ti (gē ber′tē), **Lo·ren·zo** (lô ren′tsô) (born *Lorenzo di Cione di Ser Buonaccorso*) 1378-1455; Florentine sculptor, painter, & worker in metals

ghil·lie (gil′ē) *n.* ⟦var. of GILLIE[1]⟧ **1** a tongueless shoe with loops instead of eyelets, and a lace that may be tied around the ankle: also **ghillie tie 2** *alt. sp. of* GILLIE[1]

Ghir·lan·da·io (gir′län dä′yô), **Do·men·i·co** (dô mā′nē kô) (born *Domenico di Tommaso Bigordi*) 1449-94; Florentine painter: also sp. **Ghir′lan·da′jo**

ghost (gōst) *n.* ⟦altered (prob. after Fl *gheest*) < ME *goste* < OE *gast*, soul, spirit, demon, akin to Ger *geist* < IE base **gheizd-*, to be excited, frightened > Sans *hēd-*, to be angry⟧ **1** the spirit or soul: now only in HOLY GHOST and [Literary] **give up the ghost**, to die **2** *Folklore* a dead person's disembodied spirit, esp. when thought of as appearing to the living as a pale, shadowy apparition **3** a haunting memory **4** *a)* a faint, shadowy semblance; inkling *b)* a slight trace [not a *ghost* of a chance] ☆**5** [Informal] GHOSTWRITER **6** *Optics, TV* an unwanted secondary image —*vi.* ☆to work as a ghostwriter —*vt.* **1** to haunt ☆**2** to be the ghostwriter of —**ghost′like′** *adj.*

☆**ghost dance** a North American Indian dance of the 19th cent., performed in connection with a messianic belief

ghost·ly (gōst′lē) *adj.* **-li·er**, **-li·est** ⟦ME *gostlich* < OE *gastlic*, spiritual, spectral⟧ **1** of, like, or characteristic of a ghost; spectral **2** [Now Rare] having to do with the soul or religion; spiritual —**ghost′li·ness** *n.*

☆**ghost town** the remains of a deserted town, permanently abandoned esp. for economic reasons

ghost word ⟦term invented by W. W. SKEAT⟧ a word created through misreading of manuscripts, misunderstanding of grammatical elements, etc. and never really established in a language

☆**ghost·writ·er** (gōst′rīt′ər) *n.* a person who writes books, articles, etc. for another who professes to be the author —**ghost′write′** *vt., vi.* **-wrote′**, **-writ′ten**, **-writ′ing**

ghoul (goo̅l) *n.* ⟦Ar *ghūl*, demon of the desert < *ghāla*, to seize⟧ **1** *Muslim Folklore* an evil spirit that robs graves and feeds on the flesh of the dead **2** a person who robs graves **3** a person who derives pleasure from loathsome acts or things —**ghoul′ish** *adj.* —**ghoul′ish·ly** *adv.* —**ghoul′ish·ness** *n.*

GHQ *abbrev.* General Headquarters

GHz *abbrev.* gigahertz

gi *abbrev.* **1** gastrointestinal **2** general issue **3** gill(s): see GILL[2]

☆**GI**[1] (jē′ī′) *adj.* **1** *Mil.* *a)* galvanized iron [a *GI* can] (originally an abbreviation used in military paperwork) *b)* now, government issue (designating clothing, equipment, etc. issued to military personnel) **2** [Informal] *a)* of or characteristic of the U.S. armed forces or their personnel [a *GI* haircut] *b)* inclined to a strict observance of military regulations and customs [a captain who is very *GI*] *c)* of or for veterans of the U.S. armed forces —*n., pl.* **GI's** or **GIs** [Informal] any member of the U.S. armed forces; esp., an enlisted soldier

GI[2] *abbrev.* **1** gastrointestinal **2** general issue

Gia·co·met·ti (jä′kô met′tē), **Al·ber·to** (äl ber′tô) 1901-66; Swiss sculptor & painter, mainly in France

gi·ant (jī′ənt) *n.* ⟦ME *geant* < NormFr *gaiant* (OFr *jaiant*) < VL **gagante* < L *gigas* (pl. *gigantes*), huge fabled beings (in Vulg., giant) < Gr *gigas* (gen. *gigantos*), in LXX, a man of great size and strength⟧ **1** *Gr. Myth.* any of a race of huge beings of human form who war with the gods **2** any imaginary being of human form but of superhuman size and strength **3** a person or thing of great size, intellect, etc. —*adj.* like a giant; of great size, strength, etc.

giant anteater ANT BEAR (sense 1)

gi·ant·ess (jī′ən tis) *n.* a female giant: see -ESS

gi·ant·ism (jī′ən tiz′əm) *n.* GIGANTISM

giant panda a large, black-and-white carnivore (*Ailuropoda melanoleuca*) of a bearlike family (Ailuropodidae) from China, that normally feeds on bamboo

☆**giant powder** a blasting explosive that is like dynamite

Giant's Causeway headland in N Northern Ireland, consisting of thousands of small, vertical basaltic columns: *c.* 3 mi (4.8 km) long

giant sequoia BIG TREE

giant slalom *Skiing* an Alpine race similar to a SLALOM but with the course set steeper and wider and having fewer gates

giant squid any of a genus (*Architeuthis*) of very large squids that reach a length of 18.3 m (60 ft): it is the largest invertebrate

giaour (jour) *n.* ⟦prob. via It < Turk *giaur* (modern sp. *gâvur*) < Ar *kāfir*, infidel: see KAFFIR⟧ in Muslim usage, a non-Muslim; esp., a Christian

gi·ar·di·a·sis (jē′är dī′ə sis, jär′-) *n., pl.* **-ses** ⟦ModL < *Giardia* (after A. M. *Giard* (1846-1908), Fr biologist) + -IASIS⟧ an intestinal infection by a parasitic protozoan (*Giardia lamblia*) that may cause prolonged pain, diarrhea, etc.

gib[1] (gib) *n.* ⟦ME *gibbe*, a swelling < L *gibba*, a hump < *gibbus*, bent, prob. < IE base **geibh-* > Norw dial. *keiv*, askew⟧ an adjustable piece of metal, etc. for keeping moving parts of a machine in place or for reducing friction —*vt.* **gibbed, gib′bing** to fasten or fit with a gib

gib[2] (gib) *n.* ⟦ME *gibbe*, short for GILBERT[1], used as a proper name for a cat⟧ a male cat; esp., a castrated male cat

gib·ber (jib′ər) *vi., vt.* ⟦echoic⟧ to speak or utter rapidly and incoherently; chatter unintelligibly —*n.* unintelligible chatter; gibberish

gib·ber·el·lic acid (jib′ər el′ik) ⟦< fol. + -IC⟧ an acid, $C_{19}H_{22}O_6$, isolated from various fungi and other plants, and used to increase the growth of plants and seedlings and to improve the yield of certain fruit-bearing plants

gib·ber·el·lin (jib′ər el′in) *n.* ⟦< ModL *Gibberella* (dim. of L *gibber*, hump on the back < *gibbus*: see GIB[1]) + -IN[1]⟧ one of a group of organic compounds, secreted by an ascomycetous fungus (*Gibberella fujikuroi*), which behave like plant hormones in stimulating seed germination, growth of roots, leaves, and stems, etc.

gib·ber·ish (jib′ər ish) *n.* ⟦< GIBBER⟧ rapid and incoherent talk; unintelligible chatter; jargon

gib·bet (jib′it) *n.* ⟦ME *gibet*, gallows, forked stick < OFr, dim. < Frank **gibb*, forked stick⟧ **1** a gallows **2** a structure like a gallows, from which bodies of criminals already executed were hung and exposed to public scorn —*vt.* **1** to execute by hanging **2** to hang on a gibbet **3** to expose to public scorn

gib·bon (gib′ən) *n.* ⟦Fr < native name⟧ any of a family (Hylobatidae) of small, slender, long-armed, tree-dwelling anthropoid apes of India, S China, and the East Indies

Gib·bon (gib′ən), **Edward** 1737-94; Eng. historian

Gib·bons (gib′ənz), **Orlando** 1583-1625; Eng. organist & composer

gib·bos·i·ty (gi bäs′i tē) *n.* ⟦OFr *gibbosite* < ML *gibbositas* < L *gibbosus*⟧ **1** the state or quality of being gibbous **2** *pl.* **-ties** a swelling or protuberance

gib·bous (gib′əs) *adj.* ⟦ME < L *gibbosus* < *gibba*: see GIB[1]⟧ **1** protuberant; rounded and bulging **2** designating the moon, a planet, etc. in that phase in which more than half, but not all, of the face reflects sunlight to the earth **3** humpbacked; kyphotic

Gibbs (gibz), **J(osiah) Willard** 1839-1903; U.S. mathematician & physicist

gibe (jīb) *vi., vt.* **gibed, gib′ing** ⟦< ? OFr *giber*, to handle roughly⟧ to jeer or taunt; scoff (at) —*n.* a jeer; taunt; scoff —**gib′er** *n.*

gib·let (jib′lit) *n.* ⟦ME *gibelet* < OFr, stew made of game, roast game < *gibier*, wild game < *gibois*, game < Frank **gibaiti*, falconry; akin to ON *beita*: see BAIT⟧ any of various edible parts of a fowl, as the heart, gizzard, or neck, that are usually cooked separately or are used in making gravy: *usually used in pl.*

Gi·bral·tar[1] (ji brôl′tər) *n.* ⟦after the fol.⟧ any strong fortification; unassailable fortress

Gi·bral·tar[2] (ji brôl′tər) **1** small peninsula at the southern tip of Spain, extending into the Mediterranean: 2.5 sq mi (6.5 sq km); it consists mostly of a rocky hill (**Rock of Gibraltar**), 1,396 ft (426 m) high **2** British crown colony, including a port & naval base, on this peninsula **3 Strait of** strait between Spain & Morocco, joining the Mediterranean & the Atlantic: *c.* 35 mi (56 km) long

Gib·ran (ji brän′), **Kha·lil** (kä lēl′) (Ar. name *Jubrān Khalil Jubrān*) 1883-1931; Lebanese novelist, poet, & artist, in the U.S. (after 1910)

☆**Gib·son** (gib′sən) *n.* ⟦after H. *Gibson* (1883-1954), U.S. diplomat⟧ [*also* **g-**] a dry martini cocktail served with a tiny pickled onion

Gibson Desert central section of the vast desert region of Western Australia

☆**Gibson girl** the fashionable, young American woman of the 1890s as depicted by Charles Dana Gibson (1867-1944), U.S. illustrator

gid (gid) *n.* ⟦< fol.⟧ a disease, esp. of sheep, caused by the larvae of a tapeworm (*Multiceps multiceps*) in the brain or spinal cord

gid·dy (gid′ē) *adj.* **-di·er, -di·est** ⟦ME *gidie* < OE *gydig*, insane, prob. < base (**gud*) of *god*, GOD + *-ig* (see -Y[2]): hence basic meaning, possessed by a god⟧ **1** feeling dizzy or unsteady **2** causing or likely to cause dizziness [a *giddy* height] **3** turning or circling around very rapidly; whirling **4** *a)* inconstant; fickle *b)* frivolous; flighty; heedless — *vt., vi.* **-died, -dy·ing** to make or become giddy —**gid′di·ly** *adv.* —**gid′di·ness** *n.*

☆**gid·dy·ap** (gid′ē ap′) *interj.* ⟦altered < *get up*⟧ **1** start moving **2** go faster A command to a horse Also **gid′dy·up′** (-up′) or **gid·dap** (gi dap′)

Gide (zhēd), **An·dré (Paul Guillaume)** (än drā′) 1869-1951; Fr. writer

Gid·e·on (gid′ē ən) *n.* ⟦Heb *gidon*, lit., hewer < *gada*, to hew⟧ **1** a masculine name **2** *Bible* a judge of Israel and a leader in the defeat of the Midianites: Judg. 6-8

☆**Gideons International** a Protestant organization for placing Bibles in hotels, motels, hospitals, etc.

gie (gē) *vt., vi.* **gied** or **gae** (gā), **gi·en** (gē′ən), **gie′ing** [Scot. or North Eng.] to give

Giel·gud (gēl′good′), Sir **(Arthur) John** 1904-2000; Eng. actor

gift (gift) *n.* ⟦ME < OE, portion, wedding gift (< *giefan*: see GIVE) & < ON *gipt*, gift (< *gefa*, akin to GIVE), akin to Ger *gift*, poison⟧ **1** something given to show friendship, affection, support, etc.; present **2** the act, power, or right of giving **3** a natural ability; talent [a *gift* for languages] —*vt.* **1** to present a gift to **2** to present as a gift —*SYN.* PRESENT, TALENT —**look a gift horse in the mouth** to be critical of a gift or favor: from the practice of judging a horse's age by its teeth

☆**gift certificate (***or* **card)** a certificate (or machine-readable card) that can be purchased, as from a store, for presentation as a gift: it entitles the recipient to select merchandise in the amount indicated

gift·ed (gif′tid) *adj.* **1** having a natural ability or aptitude; talented **2** notably superior in intelligence —**gift′ed·ness** *n.*

gift of tongues **1** *Bible* a divine gift whereby utterances of the Apostles were heard as though spoken in each of the various native languages of their hearers: Acts 2:1-13 **2** GLOSSOLALIA

gift·ware (gift′wer′) *n.* goods made of crystal, porcelain, silver, etc., as candlesticks, vases, and figurines, often given as gifts

gift-wrap (gift′rap′) *vt.* **-wrapped′, -wrap′ping** to wrap as a gift, with decorative paper, ribbon, etc.

Gi·fu (gē′fo͞o′) city in central Honshu, Japan

gig[1] (gig) *n.* ⟦ME *gigge*, whirligig, prob. < Scand, as in Dan *gig*, whirling object, top, Norw dial. *giga*, to shake, totter < IE **gheigh-* < base **ghei-*, to gape > GAPE, GIGGLE⟧ **1** a light, two-wheeled, open carriage drawn by one horse **2** a long, light ship's boat, esp. one reserved for the commanding officer **3** ⟦for *gig mill*, because the machine has a rotating cylinder⟧ a machine for raising nap on cloth —*vi.* **gigged, gig′ging** to travel in a gig

gig[2] (gig) *n.* ⟦contr. < earlier *fishgig*, *fizgig* < Sp *fisga*, kind of harpoon < *fisgar* < LL **fixicare*, to attach < L *fixare*, fasten < *fixus*: see FIX⟧ **1** a fish spear **2** a fish line with hooks designed to catch fish by jabbing into their bodies —*vt., vi.* **gigged, gig′ging** to spear or jab with or as with a gig

gig[3] (gig) [Slang] *n.* ⟦< ?⟧ **1** an official record or report of a minor delinquency, as in a military school; demerit **2** punishment for such a delinquency —*vt.* **gigged, gig′ging** to give a gig to

☆**gig**[4] (gig) [Slang] *n.* ⟦< ?⟧ **1** a job performing music, esp. jazz or rock **2** any job —*vi.* **gigged, gig′ging** to have a job performing music, esp. jazz or rock

gig[5] (gig) *n.* [Informal] *short for* GIGABYTE

gi·ga- (gig′ə; *also* gī′gə, jig′ə) ⟦< Gr *gigas*, GIANT⟧ *combining form* one billion; the factor 10^9 [*gigaton*]

gi·ga·bit (gig′ə bit′) *n.* ⟦prec. + BIT[4]⟧ *Comput.* one billion bits

gi·ga·byte (-bīt′) *n.* ⟦GIGA- + BYTE⟧ **1** a unit of storage capacity in a computer system, equal to 1,073,741,824 (2^{30}) bytes **2** loosely, one billion bytes Abbrev. *GB*

gi·ga·flops (-fläps′) *n., pl.* **-flops′** ⟦GIGA- + FLOPS⟧ a unit of processing speed in a computer, equal to one billion flops

gi·ga·hertz (-hurts′) *n., pl.* **-hertz′** ⟦GIGA- + HERTZ⟧ one billion hertz: abbrev. *GHz*: formerly **gi′ga·cy′cle** (-sī′kəl)

gi·gan·te·an (jī′gan tē′ən, jī gan′tē ən) *adj.* ⟦< L *giganteus* < *gigas* (see GIANT) + -AN⟧ GIGANTIC

gi·gan·tesque (jī′gan tesk′) *adj.* ⟦Fr < It *gigantesco* < *gigante*: see GIANT⟧ like or fit for a giant; gigantic

gi·gan·tic (jī gan′tik) *adj.* ⟦< L *gigas* (gen. *gigantis*): see GIANT + -IC⟧ **1** of, like, or fit for a giant **2** very big; huge; colossal; enormous; immense —*SYN.* ENORMOUS —**gi·gan′ti·cal·ly** *adv.*

gi·gan·tism (jī gan′tiz′əm, jī′gan-) *n.* ⟦see prec. & -ISM⟧ **1** the quality or state of being gigantic **2** abnormally great growth of the body, due to an excessive production of growth hormone by the anterior lobe of the pituitary gland

gi·gan·tom·a·chy (jī′gan täm′ə kē) *n.* ⟦LL *gigantomachia* < Gr < *gigas* (see GIANT) + *machē*, battle⟧ **1** [**G-**] *Gr. Myth.* the war between the giants and the gods **2** a war between giant powers

gi·ga·ton (gig′ə tun′, jig′-) *n.* ⟦GIGA- + TON[2]⟧ the explosive force of one billion tons of TNT: a unit for measuring the power of thermonuclear weapons: abbrev. *GT*

gi·ga·watt (-wät′) *n.* one billion watts: abbrev. *GW*

gig·gle (gig′əl) *vi.* **-gled, -gling** ⟦16th c., prob. < Du *giggelen*: for IE base see GIG[1]⟧ to laugh with a series of uncontrollable, rapid, high-pitched sounds in a silly or nervous way, as if trying to hold back; titter —*n.* the act or sound of giggling —*SYN.* LAUGH —**gig′gler** *n.* —**gig′gly** *adj.* **-gli·er, -gli·est**

☆**GIGO** (gig′ō; gī′gō, gē′-) *n.* ⟦*g(arbage) i(n,) g(arbage) o(ut)*⟧ an acronym noting the fact that garbled input to a computer results in garbled output

gig·o·lo (jig′ə lō′, zhig′-) *n., pl.* **-los′** ⟦Fr, masc. back-form. < *gigole*, prostitute, orig., tall, thin woman < OFr < *gigue*, long-legged, thin girl, thigh, leg, fiddle: see fol.⟧ **1** a man who is paid to be a dancing partner or escort for women **2** a man who is the lover of a woman and is supported by her

gig·ot (jig′ət, zhē gō′) *n.* ⟦Fr < OFr, leg of mutton, dim. of *gigue*, a fiddle < MHG *giga*, a fiddle: for IE base see JIG[1]⟧ **1** a leg of mutton, lamb, veal, etc. **2** a leg-of-mutton sleeve

gigue (zhēg) *n.* ⟦Fr⟧ a jig, esp., the stylized form used as a movement of a classical suite

☆**GI Joe** ⟦*G.I.*, orig. abbrev. < *g(alvanized) i(ron)*, interpreted as *g(overnment) i(ssue)* + JOE⟧ [Slang] any man in the U.S. armed forces; esp., an enlisted soldier in WWII

Gi·jón (hē hôn′) seaport in NW Spain

Gi·la (hē′lə) ⟦Sp < Yuman name, lit., salty water⟧ river in S Ariz., flowing southwest into the Colorado: 630 mi (1,014 km) long

☆**Gi·la monster** ⟦< prec.⟧ a stout, sluggish, poisonous lizard (*Heloderma suspectum*, family Helodermatidae) having a short, stumpy tail and a body covered with beadlike scales arranged in alternating rings of black and orange, pink, or yellow: found in desert regions of the SW U.S. and in Mexico

☆**gil·bert** (gil′bərt) *n.* ⟦after William GILBERT[2]⟧ the basic unit of magnetomotive force in the CGS system, equal to 0.7958 ampere-turns: abbrev. *Gb*

Gil·bert[1] (gil′bərt) *n.* ⟦OFr *Guillebert* < OHG *Williberht* < *willo*, WILL[1] + *beraht*, BRIGHT⟧ a masculine name: dim. *Gil*

Gil·bert[2] (gil′bərt) **1 Cass** (kas) 1859-1934; U.S. architect **2** Sir **Humphrey** 1539?-83; Eng. navigator and colonizer in North America **3 William** 1544?-1603; Eng. physician & scientist **4** Sir **William Schwenck** (shweŋk) 1836-1911; Eng. humorous poet & librettist: collaborated with Sir Arthur Sullivan in writing comic operas

Gil·bert[3] (gil′bərt) ⟦after W. *Gilbert*, who donated right of way for a railroad siding at this location *c.* 1902⟧ town in SC Ariz., near Phoenix

Gilbert Islands group of islands in the WC Pacific which in 1979 became the independent nation of KIRIBATI

gild[1] (gild) *vt.* **gild′ed** or **gilt**, **gild′ing** ⟦ME *gilden* < OE *gyldan* < Gmc **gulthjan* < **gultha* (> Goth *gulth*, GOLD) + **-jan*, caus. suffix⟧ **1** *a)* to overlay with a thin layer of gold *b)* to coat with a gold color **2** to make appear bright and attractive **3** to make (something) seem more attractive or more valuable than it is —**gild the lily** to attempt to improve something regarded as already excellent or perfect —**gild′er** *n.*

gild[2] (gild) *n. alt. sp. of* GUILD

Gil·da (gil′də) *n.* a feminine name

☆**Gilded Age** ⟦< *The Gilded Age* (1873), satirical novel by Mark TWAIN & C. D. Warner⟧ a period of U.S. history in the 1870s noted for political corruption, financial speculation, and the opulent lives of wealthy industrialists and financiers

gild·ing (gil′diŋ) *n.* **1** *a)* the art or process of applying gold leaf or a substance like gold to a surface *b)* the substance so applied **2** an outward appearance covering unpleasant facts, reality, etc.

Gil·e·ad (gil′ē əd) mountainous region of ancient Palestine, east of the Jordan (Gen. 37:25)

Giles[1] (jīlz) *n.* ⟦OFr *Gilles* < L *Aegidius* < *aegis*: see AEGIS⟧ a masculine name

Giles[2] (jīlz), Saint (*c.* 7th cent. A.D.); semilegendary Athenian hermit in S Gaul: his day is Sept. 1

Gil·ga·mesh (gil′gə mesh′) *n.* ⟦< Bab⟧ *Bab. Legend* an ancient king and hero of an epic (*Gilgamesh Epic*) completed about 2000 B.C.: sometimes **Gil′ga·mish′** (-mish′)

gill[1] (gil) *n.* ⟦ME *gile*, prob. < Anglo-N < or akin to ON *gjǫlnar*, jaws, gills, older Dan (*fiske*) *gaeln*, Swed *gäl* < IE base **ghelunā-*, jaw > Gr *chelynē*, lip, jaw⟧ **1** the organ for breathing of most animals that live in water, as fish, lobsters, or clams, consisting of a simple saclike or complex feathery evagination of the body surface, usually richly supplied with blood **2** [*pl.*] *a)* the red flesh hanging below the beak of a fowl; wattle *b)* the flesh under and about the chin and lower jaw of a person **3** any of the thin, leaflike, radiating plates on the undersurface of a mushroom, on which the basidiospores are produced —**to the gills** [Slang] to the point of being completely or completely full; thoroughly [*soaked to the gills*, *packed to the gills*] —**gilled** (gild) *adj.*

gill[2] (jil) *n.* ⟦ME *gille* < OFr, measure for wine < LL *gillo*, cooling vessel⟧ a unit of liquid measure, equal to ¼ pint or 4 fluid ounces (0.11829375 liquid liter or 118.29375 milliliters): the British and Canadian imperial gill equals 0.1421 liquid liter: abbrev. *gi*

gill[3] (jil) *n.* ⟦contr. of *Gillian*, proper name < L *Juliana*, fem. of *Julianus*: see JULIAN[1]⟧ [*also* **G-**] [Archaic] a girl or woman; esp., a sweetheart

gill[4] (gil) *n.* ⟦ME *gille* < ON *gil* < IE base **ĝheri-*, to gape > YAWN, L *hiatus*⟧ [Brit.] **1** a wooded ravine or glen **2** a narrow stream; brook

gill cleft (gil) **1** VISCERAL CLEFT **2** GILL SLIT

Gil·les·pie (gi les′pē), **Dizzy** (born *John Birks Gillespie*) 1917-93; U.S. jazz trumpeter & composer

Gil·lette (ji let′), **King C(amp)** 1855-1932; U.S. inventor of the safety razor

gill fungus (gil) any basidiomycete having spores that are produced from gills

Gil·li·an (jil′ē ən) *n.* ⟦< Fr *Juliane*, akin to JULIANA[1]⟧ a feminine name

gil·lie[1] or **gil·ly** (gil′ē) *n., pl.* **-lies** ⟦Scot < Gael *gille*, lad, page⟧ in the Scottish Highlands *a)* [Archaic] a male servant *b)* a sportsman's attendant or guide

gil·lie[2] (gil′ē) *n.* ⟦var. of prec.⟧ *alt. sp. of* GHILLIE (sense 1)

gil·li·flow·er (jil′i flou′ər) *n.* ⟦altered (after FLOWER) < ME *gilofre* < OFr *gilofre, girofle*, gilliflower < LL *caryophyllon* < Gr *karyophyllon*, clove tree < *karyon*, nut (see HARD) + *phyllon*, leaf (see BLOOM[1])⟧ **1** any of several plants of various families with clove-scented flowers, as the carnation **2** STOCK (sense 6) **3** WALLFLOWER (sense 1) Also sp. **gil′ly·flow′er**

☆**gill net** (gil) a net set upright in the water to catch fish by entangling their gills in its meshes

gill slit (gil) any of a series of paired, slitlike openings between the pharynx and the area behind the mouth of fishes, some amphibians, etc.

Gil·son·ite (gil′sən īt′) ☆⟦after S. H. *Gilson* (1836-1913), U.S. rancher and one of its discoverers⟧ *trademark for* UINTAHITE

gilt[1] (gilt) *vt. alt. pt. & pp. of* GILD[1] —*adj.* overlaid with gilding —*n.* GILDING

gilt[2] (gilt) *n.* ⟦ME *gilte* < ON *gyltr*: for IE base see GELD[1]⟧ a young female pig; immature sow

gilt-edged (gilt′ejd′) *adj.* **1** having gilded edges, as the pages of a book **2** of the highest quality, grade, or value [*gilt-edged securities*] Also **gilt′-edge′**

gilt·head (gilt′hed′) *n.* any of various marine fishes with gold markings on the head; esp., an edible European porgy (*Sparus aurata*)

gim·bal (gim′bəl, jim′-) *n.* ⟦sing. of *gimbals*, altered < ME *gemelles*, twins < L *gemellus*, dim. of *geminus*, twin⟧ [*usually pl.*] a device consisting of a pivoted ring or rings capable of swinging freely while mounted on a fixed frame, used as to hold a ship's compass, pelorus, etc. level despite any pitch, roll, or yaw: often **gimbal ring** —*vt.* **-baled** or **-balled**, **-bal·ing** or **-bal·ling** to attach to or mount on a gimbal

gim·crack (jim′krak′) *adj.* ⟦altered < ME *gibbecrak*, an ornament, prob. < *gibben*, to be erratic (< OFr *giber*) + *crak*, a bursting sound⟧ showy but cheap and useless —*n.* a cheap, showy, useless thing

gim·crack·er·y (-ər ē) *n.* **1** gimcracks collectively **2** showy but cheap and useless decoration, effects, etc.

gim·el (gim′əl) *n.* ⟦Heb *gīmel*, lit., camel: see GAMMA⟧ the third letter of the Hebrew alphabet (ג)

gim·let (gim′lit) *n.* ⟦ME < OFr *guimbelet*, altered (with dim. suffix *-et*) < *wimbelquin* < MDu *wimmelkijn* < *wimmel*, WIMBLE + dim. suffix *-kijn*, -KIN⟧ **1** a small boring tool with a handle at right angles to a shaft having at the other end a spiral, pointed cutting edge **2** a cocktail made of sweetened lime juice, gin or vodka, and sometimes soda —*vt.* to make a hole in with or as with a gimlet

gim·let-eyed (-īd′) *adj.* having a piercing glance

gim·mal (gim′əl, jim′-) *n.* ⟦see GIMBAL⟧ a ring formed of two or more interlocked circlets

gim·me (gim′ē) *vt. phonetic sp. of* give me (in informal pronunciation) [*gimme a break!*] —*vi.* [Slang] give it to me: used in the imperative —*adj.* [Slang] acquisitive; greedy [*the gimme generation*] —*n., pl.* **-mies** [Slang] **1** *Golf* a putt so short that one's opponent gives one credit for sinking it in a single stroke without one's actually having to shoot it **2** something expected to be so easily achieved as to seem certain or inevitable

☆**gimme cap** a cap displaying a logo, typically given away for promotional purposes

☆**gim·mick** (gim′ik) *n.* ⟦< ? GIMCRACK⟧ **1** *a)* a secret means of controlling a gambling device *b)* anything that tricks or mystifies; deceptive or secret device **2** *a)* an attention-getting device or feature, typically superficial, designed to promote the success of a product, campaign, etc. *b)* any clever little gadget or ruse —*vt.* to use gimmicks in or add gimmicks to — [Informal] **gim′mick·y** *adj.*

☆**gim·mick·ry** (-rē) *n.* **1** gimmicks collectively **2** the use of gimmicks Also **gim′mick·er·y** (-ər ē)

gim·mie (gim′ē) *adj., n.* [Slang] *alt. sp. of* GIMME

gimp[1] (gimp) *n.* ⟦? via Du < Fr *guimpe*, wimple < OFr *guimple* < Frank **wimpil*: for IE base see WIMPLE⟧ a ribbonlike, braided fabric, sometimes stiffened with wire, used to trim garments, furniture, etc.

☆**gimp[2]** (gimp) *n.* ⟦< ?⟧ [Old Slang] fighting spirit; vigor

☆**gimp[3]** (gimp) *n.* ⟦prob. < Norw dial. *gimpa*, to rock, tip over < IE base **gwhemb-*, to jump, hop⟧ **1** [Slang] a lame person: an offensive term of derision **2** [Informal] a halting, lame walk —*vi.* [Informal] to limp —**gimp′y** *adj.*

gin[1] (jin) *n.* ⟦< GENEVA⟧ **1** a strong, aromatic alcoholic liquor distilled from rye and other grains and flavored with juniper berries **2** a similar liquor differently flavored [*sloe gin*] **3** [Archaic] alcoholic liquor generally

gin[2] (jin) *n.* ⟦ME, ingenuity, machine, aphetic < OFr *engin*, ENGINE⟧ **1** a snare, net, or trap, as for game or fish **2** a machine for hoisting heavy objects ☆**3** COTTON GIN —*vt.* **ginned, gin′ning** **1** to catch in a trap **2** to remove seeds from (cotton) with a gin

gin[3] (gin) *vt., vi.* **gan, gin′ning** ⟦ME *ginnen*, aphetic form of *beginnen* (see BEGIN) & *onginnen* (OE *onginnan*, to attempt)⟧ [Archaic] to begin

gin[4] (gin) *conj.* ⟦? contr. < GIVEN, infl. ? by Scot prep. *gin*, by (a certain time)⟧ [Scot.] if; whether

gin[5] (jin) *n.* ☆GIN RUMMY —*vi.* **ginned, gin′ning** ☆to win in gin rummy with no unmatched cards left in one's hand, thus gaining additional points

gin[6] (jin) *vi.* ⟦phr. < ? old slang *gin up*, to become intoxicated < GINGER (*vt.* 2)⟧ [Slang] *used only in the phrase* **gin up**, *a)* to generate, devise, etc. *b)* to stir up, stimulate, enliven, etc.

Gi·na (jē′nə) ***n.*** a feminine name: see REGINA[1]

gin·gel·li or **gin·gel·ly** (jin′jə lē) ***n.*** *var.* *of* GINGILI

gin·ger (jin′jər) ***adj.*** ⟦ME *gingere, gingivere* < OE *gingifer* & OFr *gingivre,* both < ML *gingiber* < L *zingiber* < Gr *zingiberi* < Pali *siṅgivera*⟧ **1** designating a family (Zingiberaceae, order Zingiberales) of aromatic, monocotyledonous tropical plants, including galangal **2** flavored with ginger **3** having sandy, reddish-brown fur or hair —***n.*** **1** an Asian herb (*Zingiber officinale*) of the ginger family, widely cultivated in the tropics for its aromatic rhizome, used as a spice or perfume and in medicine **2** the rhizome, or the spice made from it **3** *a)* a sandy or reddish-brown color *b)* [Informal] an animal, esp. a cat, with ginger fur *c)* [Informal] a person with red hair; redhead ☆**4** [Informal] vigor; spirit —***vt.*** **1** to flavor with ginger **2** [Informal] to invigorate; enliven: usually with *up*

Gin·ger (jin′jər) ***n.*** ⟦altered < VIRGINIA[1]; popularized by U.S. actress *Ginger* Rogers (1911-95), born *Virginia* McMath⟧ a feminine name: see VIRGINIA[1]

ginger ale a sweet, carbonated soft drink flavored with ginger

ginger beer a carbonated drink like ginger ale but with a stronger flavor obtained from fermented ginger

gin·ger·bread (jin′jər bred′) ***n.*** ⟦ME *ginge bred,* altered (after *bred,* BREAD) < *gingebras,* preserved ginger, ginger pudding < OFr *gingembraz* < *gingibre* < ML *gingiber,* GINGER⟧ **1** *a)* a cake flavored with ginger and molasses *b)* a kind of cookie cut from a rolled-out dough flavored with ginger and molasses **2** showy ornamentation, as gaudy or fancy carvings on furniture, gables, etc. —***adj.*** cheap and showy; gaudy: also **gin′ger·bread′y**

gingerbread palm (*or* tree) DOUM

ginger group [Brit.] a group or faction which enlivens or energizes a party, movement, etc., as by the zealousness of its efforts

ginger jar ⟦believed to have been filled with a gift of candy, *ginger,* etc., for Chinese New Year celebrations⟧ a round jar with a domed lid, bulging out from the top and in toward the base, often adapted as a lamp base

gin·ger·ly (jin′jər′lē) ***adv.*** ⟦altered (after GINGER) < ? OFr *genzor,* compar. of *gent,* delicate (see GENT[2]) + -LY[2]⟧ in a very careful or cautious way —***adj.*** very careful; cautious —**gin′ger·li·ness *n.***

gin·ger·snap (jin′jər snap′) ***n.*** a crisp, spicy cookie flavored with ginger and molasses

gin·ger·y (jin′jər ē) ***adj.*** **1** *a)* like or flavored with ginger *b)* spicy; pungent **2** sandy or reddish in color **3** lively, vigorous, sharp, etc.

ging·ham (giŋ′əm) ***n.*** ⟦< Du *gingang* or Fr *guingan,* ult. < Malay *ginggang,* striped (cloth)⟧ a yarn-dyed cotton cloth, usually woven in stripes, checks, or plaids

gin·gi·li (jin′ji lē) ***n.*** ⟦Hindi *jinjalī* < Ar *juljulān*⟧ **1** SESAME **2** the oil of the sesame seed Also sp. **gin′gil·li**

gin·gi·va (jin jī′və) ***n.,*** *pl.* **-vae** (-vē) ⟦L < IE base **geng-,* lump, ball > KINK⟧ GUM[2] —**gin·gi·val** (jin jī′vəl, jin′jə vəl) ***adj.***

gin·gi·vi·tis (jin′jə vīt′is) ***n.*** ⟦ModL < prec. + -ITIS⟧ inflammation of the gums

ging·ko (giŋ′kō) ***n.,*** *pl.* **-koes** *var. of* GINKGO

☆**gink** (giŋk) ***n.*** ⟦< ? dial. *gink,* a trick (> Scot *ginkie,* term of reproach applied to a woman)⟧ [Slang] a man or boy, esp. one seen as odd

gink·go (giŋ′kō; *also* giŋk′gō′) ***n.,*** *pl.* **-goes** ⟦Jpn *ginkyo* < SinoJpn *gin,* silver + *kyō,* apricot⟧ an Asian tree (*Ginkgo biloba*) with fan-shaped leaves and fleshy, yellow, foul-smelling seeds enclosing a silvery, edible inner kernel: the only living member of a class (Ginkgoatae) of gymnosperms

☆**gin mill** (jin) [Slang] a bar or saloon

☆**gin·ner** (jin′ər) ***n.*** a person who operates a cotton gin

Gin·nie or **Gin·ny** (jin′ē) ***n.*** a feminine name: see VIRGINIA[1]

☆**Gin·nie Mae** (jin′ē mā′) ⟦altered (as if a given name, after FANNIE MAE) < pronun. of its abbrev., *GNMA*⟧ **1** *informal name for* Government National Mortgage Association: a federal agency which purchases mortgages from lending institutions with funds raised by the sale of government-backed securities **2** *pl.* **Ginnie Maes** any of the securities issued by this agency

gi·nor·mous (jī nôr′məs) ***adj.*** ⟦blend of GIANT (or GIGANTIC) + ENORMOUS⟧ [Slang] enormous, gigantic, colossal, etc.

☆**gin rummy** (jin) ⟦orig., a play on GIN[1], suggested by *rhum,* early form of RUMMY[1], ***n.***⟧ a variety of rummy in which a hand with unmatched cards totaling no more than 10 points may be exposed: the hand exposed wins or loses points, depending on whether the opponent's unmatched cards add up to a higher or lower total: see also GIN[5]

Gins·berg (ginz′burg′), **(Irwin) Allen** 1926-97; U.S. poet

Gins·burg (ginz′burg′), **Ruth Ba·der** (bā′dər) 1933- ; associate justice, U.S. Supreme Court (1993-)

gin·seng (jin′seŋ′) ***adj.*** ⟦Chin *jēn shēn* < *jēn,* man (from the shape of the root) + *shēn,* the constellation Orion⟧ designating a family (Araliaceae, order Apiales) of dicotyledonous plants, shrubs, and trees, usually having flat clusters of small, white or greenish flowers and, often, fragrant leaves, including Hercules'-club and English ivy —***n.*** **1** any of several perennial herbs (genus *Panax*) of the ginseng family, with thick, forked, aromatic roots, esp. a Chinese species (*P. pseudoginseng*) and a North American species (*P. quinquefolium*) **2** such a root, or a preparation made from it, used as a tonic

Gio·con·da (jō kän′də; *It* jô kôn′dä), **La** (lä) ⟦It, lit., the cheerful one⟧ a portrait by Leonardo da Vinci, more commonly called MONA LISA

gio·co·so (jô kô′sô) ***adj., adv.*** ⟦It, lit., playful, joking < L *jocosus:* see JOCOSE⟧ *Musical Direction* with a lively, playful quality

Gior·gio·ne (jôr jô′ne), **Il** (ēl) (born *Giorgio Barbarelli*) 1478?-1510; Venetian painter

Giot·to (di Bon·do·ne) (jôt′tô dē bôn dô′ne; *E* jät′ō) 1266?-1337; Florentine painter & architect

gip (jip) ***n., vt., vi.*** *alt. sp. of* GYP[1]

gi·pon (ji pän′, jip′än′) ***n.*** ⟦ME < OFr *gipon, jupon:* see JUPON⟧ JUPON

Gip·sy (jip′sē) ***n., adj., vi.*** *alt. sp. of* GYPSY

gi·raffe (jə raf′, -räf′) ***n.,*** *pl.* **-raffes′** or **-raffe′** ⟦Fr < It *giraffa* < Ar *zarāfa*⟧ either of two species (genus *Giraffa,* family Giraffidae) of African ruminants, with a very long neck and long legs: the tallest of existing animals, they often reach a height of 5.5 m (*c.* 18 ft) —**the Giraffe** the constellation Camelopardalis

gir·an·dole (jir′ən dōl′) ***n.*** ⟦Fr < It *girandola* < *girare,* to turn < LL *gyrare* < *gyrus,* a circle < Gr *gyros:* see GYRO-⟧ **1** a revolving cluster of fireworks **2** a revolving water jet **3** a branched candleholder, often attached to a wall mirror **4** a pendant or earring with small stones grouped around a larger one Also **gi·ran·do·la** (ji ran′də lə)

Gi·rard (jə rärd′), **Stephen** 1750-1831; Am. financier & philanthropist, born in France

gir·a·sol (jir′ə sôl′, -säl′, -sōl′) ***n.*** ⟦Fr < It *girasole* < *girare* (see GIRANDOLE) + *sole* (< L *sol,* SUN[1])⟧ **1** JERUSALEM ARTICHOKE **2** FIRE OPAL Also **gir′a·sole′** (-sōl′)

Gi·rau·doux (zhē rō do͞o′), **(Hippolyte) Jean** (zhän) 1882-1944; Fr. playwright & novelist

gird[1] (gurd) ***vt.*** **gird′ed** or **girt, gird′ing** ⟦ME *girden* < OE *gyrdan,* akin to Ger *gürten* < IE base **gherdh-,* to enclose > YARD[2]⟧ **1** to encircle or fasten with a belt or band **2** to surround, encircle, or enclose **3** *a)* to equip, furnish, clothe, etc. *b)* to endow with some attribute **4** to prepare (oneself) for action

gird[2] (gurd) ***n., vi., vt*** ⟦ME *girden,* to strike, assail with words < ? OE **gyrdan* for **gierdan,* lit., to strike with a rod < *gierd, gerd,* a rod (see YARD[1]): infl. by prec.⟧ gibe; scoff; jeer

gird·er (gur′dər) ***n.*** ⟦GIRD[1] + -ER⟧ a large beam, usually horizontal, of timber or steel, for supporting the joists of a floor, the framework of a building, the superstructure of a bridge, etc.

gir·dle (gurd′'l) ***n.*** ⟦ME *girdil* < OE *gyrdel* < base of *gyrdan* (see GIRD[1]): akin to Ger *gürtel*⟧ **1** [Archaic] a belt or sash for the waist **2** anything that surrounds or encircles ☆**3** a woman's elasticized undergarment for supporting or molding the waist and hips **4** the rim of a cut gem ☆**5** a ring made by removing bark around the trunk of a tree, so as to kill it **6** *Anat.* a bony arch or encircling structure supporting the limbs [the pelvic *girdle*] —***vt.*** **-dled, -dling 1** to surround or bind, as with a girdle **2** to encircle ☆**3** to remove a ring of bark from (a tree) as by cutting or chewing

gir·dler (gurd′lər) ***n.*** **1** a person who makes girdles **2** a person or thing that girdles, or encircles ☆**3** any insect that cuts girdles in trees, esp. an American beetle (*Oncideres cingulata*) that lays its eggs in holes bored into twigs

girl (gurl) ***n.*** ⟦ME *girle, gurle,* youngster of either sex < ? OE **gyrele,* prob. akin to LowG *göre,* Ger dial. *gör,* girl < IE base **ĝher-,* small > OIr *gair,* short⟧ **1** a female child **2** a young, unmarried woman **3** a female servant or other employee: sometimes considered a patronizing term **4** [Informal] a woman of any age, married or single: sometimes considered a patronizing term **5** [Informal] GIRLFRIEND (sense 1) **6** [Informal] a daughter

girl Friday *see* FRIDAY (sense 2)

☆**girl·friend** (gurl′frend′) ***n.*** [Informal] **1** a sweetheart who is a girl or woman **2** a girl who is someone's friend **3** a woman friend of a woman

Girl Guide a member of an organization (**Girl Guides**) in Great Britain, Canada, and other countries that is similar to the Girl Scouts

girl·hood (-ho͝od′) ***n.*** **1** the state or time of being a girl **2** girls collectively

girl·ie or **girl·y** (gur′lē) [Slang] ***n.,*** *pl.* **girl′ies** a girl or woman: a playful or patronizing term —☆***adj.*** designating or of magazines, shows, etc. characterized by the erotic display of nude or nearly nude young women

girl·ish (gur′lish) ***adj.*** of, like, or suitable to a girl or girlhood —**girl′ish·ly *adv.*** —**girl′ish·ness *n.***

☆**Girl Scout** a member of the **Girl Scouts of the United States of America,** an organization founded by Juliette Low (as *Girl Guides*) in 1912, which provides healthful, character-building activities for girls five to seventeen years of age

Gi·ronde[1] (jə ränd′; *Fr* zhē rōnd′) ***n.*** the Girondist Party

Gi·ronde[2] (jə ränd′; *Fr* zhē rōnd′) **1** estuary in SW France, formed by the juncture of the Garonne & Dordogne rivers and flowing into the Bay of Biscay: *c.* 45 mi (72 km) long **2** historical region of France, on the Bay of Biscay

Gi·ron·dist (jə rän′dist) ***n.*** ⟦so named because first led by deputies from Gironde⟧ a member of a French political party (1791-93) that advocated moderate republican principles: it was suppressed by the Jacobins —***adj.*** designating or of this party

girt[1] (gurt) ***vt.*** *alt. pt. & pp. of* GIRD[1]

girt[2] (gurt) ***vt.*** ⟦ME *girten,* var. of *girden:* see GIRD[1]⟧ **1** to gird **2** to fasten with a girth **3** to measure the girth of —***vi.*** to measure in girth

girth (gurth) ***n.*** ⟦ME *gerth* < ON *gjörth* < base of *gyrtha,* to encircle, akin to OE *gyrdan:* see GIRD[1]⟧ **1** a band put around the belly of a horse or other animal for holding a saddle, pack, etc. **2** the circumference, as of a tree trunk or person's waist —***vt.*** **1** to girdle; encircle **2** to fasten or bind with a girth —***vi.*** to measure in girth

gi·sarme (gi zärm′) ***n.*** ⟦ME < OFr, prob. < **getsarna* < OHG *getisarn,* lit., weeding iron (< *geten,* to weed + *isarn,* IRON): form infl. by *arme,* ARM[2]⟧ a battle-ax or halberd with a long shaft, formerly carried by foot soldiers

☆**gis·mo** (giz′mō) ***n.,*** *pl.* **-mos** [Slang] *alt. sp. of* GIZMO

Gis·sing (gis′iŋ), **George (Robert)** 1857-1903; Eng. novelist

gist (jist) ***n.*** ⟦ME *giste* < OFr, abode, point at issue < 3d pers. sing., pres. indic., of *gesir*, to lie < L *jacere*, to lie; sense infl. by Anglo-Fr legal phrase *l'action gist*, lit., the action lies⟧ **1** *Law* the grounds for action in a lawsuit **2** the essence or main point, as of an article or argument

git[1] (git) ***vi.*** *dial. or phonetic sp. of* GET (***vi.*** 3): used in the imperative and infinitive

git[2] (git) ***n.*** ⟦ult. < GET (***n.*** 1)⟧ [Brit. Slang] a person regarded as contemptible, coarse, foolish, etc.

Gi·ta (gē′tä) ***n.*** BHAGAVAD-GITA

git·tern (git′ərn) ***n.*** ⟦ME *giterne* < OFr *guiterne*, altered < OSp *guitarra*: see GUITAR⟧ an early instrument of the guitar family, having an oval body and wire strings

give (giv) ***vt.*** **gave, giv′en, giv′ing** ⟦ME *given* (with *g-* < ON *gefa*, to give), *yeven* < OE *giefan*, akin to Ger *geben* < IE base **ghabh-*, to grasp, take > L *habere*, to have: the special Gmc sense of this base results from its use as a substitute for IE **dō-* (as in L *dare*, to give)⟧ **1** to turn over the possession or control of to someone without cost or exchange; make a gift of **2** to hand or pass over into the trust or keeping of someone *[to give the porter a bag to carry, to give a daughter in marriage]* **3** to hand or pass over in exchange for something else; sell (goods, services, etc.) for a price or pay (a price) for goods, services, etc. **4** to relay; pass along *[to give regards to someone]* **5** to produce in a person or thing; cause to have; impart *[to give pleasure, to give someone a cold]* **6** to confer or assign (a title, position, name, etc.) **7** to act as host or sponsor of (a party, dance, etc.) ☆**8** to put in communication with, as by telephone **9** to be the source, origin, or cause of; produce; supply *[cows give milk]* **10** *a)* to part with for some cause; sacrifice *[to give one's life for a cause]* *b)* to devote to some occupation, pursuit, etc. *[to give one's life to art]* **11** to concede; yield *[to give a point in an argument]* **12** to offer or yield (oneself) to a man for sexual intercourse **13** to show; exhibit *[to give every indication of being a fool]* **14** to put forward for acceptance or rejection; offer; proffer *[to give a suggestion]* **15** *a)* to perform *[to give a concert]* *b)* to introduce or present (a speaker, the subject of a toast, etc.) **16** to make (a gesture, movement, etc.) *[to give a leap]* **17** to perform (a physical act) *[to give someone a hug, kiss, etc.]* **18** to administer or dispense (medicine, etc.) **19** *a)* to utter, emit, or produce (words, sounds, etc.) *[to give a grunt]* *b)* to put into words; state *[to give a thoughtful reply]* **20** to inflict or impose (punishment, a sentence, etc.) **21** [Informal] to predict that (something or someone) will last or remain for (a specified period of time) *[I give their marriage one year]* —***vi.*** **1** to make gifts or donations; contribute **2** to bend, sink, move, break down, yield, etc. from force or pressure **3** to be springy; be resilient **4** to provide a view of, or a way of getting to, some place; open: usually with *on*, *upon*, or *onto* *[the window gives on the park]* **5** [Slang] to abandon a claim, fight, etc.; give in or give up —***n.*** **1** a bending, moving, sinking, etc. under pressure **2** a tendency to be springy; resilience —**give and take** to exchange on an even basis —**give away 1** to make a gift of; donate; bestow **2** in a marriage ceremony, to present (the bride) ritually to the bridegroom ☆**3** [Informal] to reveal, expose, or betray —**give back** to return or restore —**give forth** to send forth; emit; issue —**give in 1** to hand in **2** to abandon a claim, fight, or argument; surrender; yield —**give it to** [Informal] to punish; beat or scold —**give off** to send forth or out; emit —**give or take** plus or minus *[a price of $1.00, give or take a few cents]* —**give out 1** to send forth or out; emit **2** to cause to be known; make public **3** to distribute **4** to become worn out or used up; fail to last —**give over 1** to hand over **2** to stop; cease **3** to set apart for some purpose —**give to understand (**or **believe,** etc.**)** to cause to understand (or believe, etc.) —**give up 1** to hand over; turn over; surrender **2** to stop; cease **3** to admit failure and stop trying **4** to lose hope for; despair of **5** to sacrifice; devote wholly —**what gives?** [Slang] what is going on?: a phrase used in requesting an explanation

SYN.—**give** is the general word meaning to transfer from one's own possession to that of another; **grant** implies that there has been a request or an expressed desire for the thing given *[to grant a favor]*; **present** implies a certain formality in the giving and often connotes considerable value in the gift *[he presented the school with a library]*; **donate** is used especially of a giving to some philanthropic or religious cause; **bestow** stresses that the thing is given gratuitously and often implies condescension in the giver *[to bestow charity upon the poor]*; **confer** implies that the giver is a superior and that the thing given is an honor, privilege, etc. *[to confer a title, a college degree, etc.]*

give-and-take (giv′ən tāk′) ***n.*** **1** a yielding and conceding on both sides; compromise **2** an exchange of remarks or retorts on equal terms; repartee; banter

☆**give·a·way** (giv′ə wā′) ***n.*** **1** an unintentional revelation or betrayal **2** something given free or sold cheap so as to attract customers, etc. **3** an instance of giving something away free or for inadequate compensation **4** a radio or television program in which prizes are given to contestants

☆**give·back** (-bak′) ***n.*** a workers' benefit or right, previously gained as through labor negotiations, that is relinquished to management, usually in exchange for a wage increase or some other concession

giv·en (giv′ən) ***vt., vi. pp. of*** GIVE —***adj.*** **1** bestowed; presented **2** accustomed, as from habit or inclination; prone *[given to lying]* **3** stated; specified *[a given date]* **4** taken as a premise; assumed; granted *[given that ABC is a right triangle]* **5** issued or executed (on the specified date by the specified person): used in official documents —***n.*** that which is assumed to be true or is accepted as a fact

given name the name of a person given at birth or baptism, as distinguished from the surname; first name or middle name

giv·er (giv′ər) ***n.*** **1** a person who gives: often in compounds *[lawgiver, almsgiver]* **2** a person who is characterized by unselfishness

Gî·za (gē′zə) city in N Egypt, near Cairo: site of the Sphinx & three pyramids: also sp. **Gîzeh**

☆**giz·mo** (giz′mō) ***n., pl.*** **-mos** ⟦< ? Sp *gisma*, obs. or dial. var. of *chisme*, trifle, jigger, ult. < L *cimex*, a bug⟧ [Slang] any gadget or contrivance

giz·zard (giz′ərd) ***n.*** ⟦ME *giser* (+ unhistoric *-d*) < OFr *gisier* < L *gigeria*, pl., cooked entrails of poultry < ? an Iran base > Pers *džigar*, liver⟧ **1** the second stomach of a bird: it has thick muscular walls and a tough lining for grinding food that has been partially digested in the first stomach **2** [Informal] the stomach: a humorous usage

Gk *abbrev.* Greek

g/l *abbrev.* grams per liter

gla·bel·la (glə bel′ə) ***n., pl.*** **-lae** (-ē, -ī′) ⟦ModL < L, fem. of *glabellus*, without hair < *glaber*: see GLABROUS⟧ smooth prominence on the forehead between the eyebrows and just above the nose —**gla·bel′lar** ***adj.***

gla·brate (glā′brāt′, -brit) ***adj.*** ⟦< L *glabratus*, pp. of *glabrare*, lit., to make smooth, deprive of hair < *glaber*: see fol.⟧ **1** glabrous or nearly glabrous **2** becoming glabrous when old or mature

gla·brous (glā′brəs) ***adj.*** ⟦< L *glaber*, smooth, bald (< IE **ghladh-ros* < **ghlādh-*: see GLAD[1]) + -OUS⟧ *Biol.* without hair, down, or fuzz; bald —**gla′brous·ness** ***n.***

gla·cé (gla sā′) ***adj.*** ⟦Fr, pp. of *glacer*, to freeze < L *glaciare* < *glacies*, ice: see fol.⟧ **1** having a smooth, glossy surface, as certain leathers or silks **2** candied or glazed, as fruits —***vt.*** **-céed′, -cé′ing** to glaze (fruits, etc.)

gla·cial (glā′shəl; *chiefly Brit*, -sē əl) ***adj.*** ⟦L *glacialis*, icy, frozen < *glacies*, ice < IE **glag-*, partial redupl. of base **gel-*, to freeze > COLD⟧ **1** of or like ice or glaciers **2** of or produced by a glacier or a glacial epoch or period **3** freezing; frigid *[glacial weather]* **4** cold and unfriendly *[a glacial stare]* **5** as slow as the movement of a glacier *[glacial progress]* **6** *Chem.* having an icelike, crystalline appearance —**gla′cial·ly** ***adv.***

glacial epoch ICE AGE —**the Glacial Epoch** the Pleistocene Epoch

gla·cial·ist (-ist) ***n.*** a student of glaciers and their action

gla·ci·ate (glā′shē āt′, -sē-) ***vt.*** **-at′ed, -at′ing** ⟦< L *glaciatus*, pp. of *glaciare*, to turn into ice, freeze: see GLACIAL & -ATE[1]⟧ **1** *a)* to cover over with ice or a glacier *b)* to form into ice; freeze **2** to expose to or change by glacial action —**gla′ci·a′tion** ***n.***

gla·cier (glā′shər; *chiefly Brit*, glas′ē ər) ***n.*** ⟦Fr (orig., Savoy dial. > also Ger *gletscher*) < VL **glaciarium* < *glacia*, for L *glacies*, ice: see GLACIAL⟧ a large mass of ice and snow that forms in areas where the rate of snowfall constantly exceeds the rate at which the snow melts: it moves slowly outward from the center of accumulation or down a mountain until it melts or breaks away

☆**gla·ci·ol·o·gy** (glā′shē äl′ə jē, -sē-) ***n.*** ⟦*glacio-* (< prec.) + -LOGY⟧ **1** the scientific study of the formation, movements, etc. of glaciers **2** the glacial formations of a particular region —**gla′ci·o·log′i·cal** (-shē ə läj′i kəl, -sē-) ***adj.*** —**gla′ci·ol′o·gist** ***n.***

gla·cis (glā′sis, glas′is) ***n., pl.*** **-cis′** (-sēz′) or **-cis·es** (-sis iz) ⟦Fr < OFr *glacier*, to slip < *glace*, ice < VL *glacia*: see GLACIER⟧ **1** a gradual slope **2** an embankment sloping gradually up to a fortification, so as to expose attackers to defending gunfire

glad[1] (glad) ***adj.*** **glad′der, glad′dest** ⟦ME < OE *glæd*, akin to Ger *glatt*, smooth (the orig. Gmc sense) < IE **ghlādh-*, shining, smooth < base **ĝhel-*, to shine > GLEAM, GOLD⟧ **1** feeling or characterized by pleasure or joy; happy; pleased **2** causing pleasure or joy; making happy **3** very willing *[I'm glad to help]* **4** bright or beautiful — ***vt., vi.*** **glad′ded, glad′ding** ⟦ME *gladen* < OE *gladian*⟧ [Archaic] to gladden —**SYN.** HAPPY —**glad′ly** ***adv.*** —**glad′ness** ***n.***

glad[2] (glad) ***n.*** *informal var. of* GLADIOLUS (sense 1)

glad·den (glad′'n) ***vt.*** ⟦< GLAD[1] + -EN⟧ to make glad —***vi.*** [Archaic] to be or become glad

glade (glād) ***n.*** ⟦ME < *glad*, GLAD[1]: orig. sense prob. "bright, smooth place," use similar to Ger *lichtung*, glade < *licht*, light, Fr *clairière* < *clair*, clear⟧ **1** an open space in a wood or forest ☆**2** an everglade

☆**glad hand** [Informal] a cordial welcome, esp. one that is effusive or overly demonstrative —**glad′-hand′** ***vt., vi.*** —**glad′-hand′er** ***n.***

gla·di·ate (glā′dē āt′, -it; glad′ē-) ***adj.*** ⟦< L *gladius*, sword (see fol.) + -ATE[1]⟧ *Bot.* sword-shaped

glad·i·a·tor (glad′ē āt′ər) ***n.*** ⟦L < *gladius*, sword, via Celt (as in Welsh *cleddyf*, sword) < IE base **kel-*, to strike > L *calamitas*⟧ **1** in ancient Rome, a man trained to fight animals or other men with weapons in an arena, for the entertainment of spectators **2** any person taking part in a public controversy or fight —**glad·i·a·to·ri·al** (glad′ē ə tôr′ē əl) ***adj.***

glad·i·o·la (glad′ē ō′lə) ***n.*** ⟦mistaken as sing. of fol.⟧ GLADIOLUS (sense 1)

glad·i·o·lus (glad′ē ō′ləs) ***n., pl.*** **-lus·es** or **-li′** (-lī′) ⟦ModL < L, sword lily, small sword, dim. of *gladius*: see GLADIATOR⟧ **1** any of a genus (*Gladiolus*) of plants of the iris family, with swordlike leaves, corms, and tall spikes of funnel-shaped flowers in various colors **2** *Anat.* the central part of the sternum

☆**glad rags** [Slang] fine or dressy clothes

glad·some (glad′səm) ***adj.*** ⟦see GLAD[1], ***adj.*** & -SOME[1]⟧ joyful or cheerful —**glad′some·ly** ***adv.***

Glad·stone[1] (glad′stōn′, -stən) ***n.*** ⟦after fol.⟧ a traveling bag hinged so that it can open flat into two compartments of equal size: in full **Gladstone bag**

Glad·stone[2] (glad′stōn; *Brit,* -stən), **William Ew·art** (yo͞o′ərt) 1809-98; Brit. statesman: prime minister (1868-74; 1880-85; 1886; 1892-94)

Glad·ys (glad′is) ***n.*** ⟦Welsh *Gwladys*, prob. < L *Claudia*: see CLAUDIA⟧ a feminine name

Glag·o·lit·ic (glag′ə lit′ik) ***adj.*** ⟦ModL *glagoliticus* < Serbo-Croatian *glagolitsa*, Glagolitic alphabet < Old Church Slavonic *glagolŭ*, word⟧ designating or of a Slavic alphabet probably predating the Cyrillic alphabet

glai·kit or **glai·ket** (glāk′it) ***adj.*** ⟦ME⟧ [Chiefly Scot.] foolish; flighty; giddy

glair (gler) ***n.*** ⟦ME *glaire* < OFr < VL **claria* < L *clarus*, CLEAR⟧ **1** raw white of egg, used in sizing or glazing **2** a size or glaze made from this **3** any sticky matter resembling raw egg white —***vt.*** to cover with glair —**glair′y** ***adj.***

glaive (glāv) ***n.*** ⟦ME < OFr, a lance < L *gladius*, sword: see GLADIATOR⟧ [Obs.] a sword; esp., a broadsword

glam (glam) [Slang] ***adj. short for*** GLAMOROUS —***n. short for*** GLAMOUR Usually connoting showiness rather than elegance

Gla·mor·gan (glə môr′gən) former county of SE Wales, on the Bristol Channel: now divided into three counties: MID GLAMORGAN, SOUTH GLAMORGAN, and WEST GLAMORGAN: also **Gla·mor′gan·shire′** (-shir′)

☆**glam·or·ize** (glam′ər īz′) ***vt.*** **-ized′**, **-iz′ing** to make glamorous: also sp. **glam′our·ize′** —**glam′or·i·za′tion** ***n.***

glam·or·ous (glam′ər əs) ***adj.*** full of glamour; fascinating; alluring: also sp. **glam′our·ous** —**glam′or·ous·ly** ***adv.***

glam·our (glam′ər) ***n.*** ⟦Scot var. of *grammar* (with sense of GRAMARYE), popularized by Sir Walter SCOTT[2]; orig. esp. in *cast the glamour*, to cast an enchantment⟧ **1** [Archaic] a magic spell or charm ☆**2** seemingly mysterious and elusive fascination or allure; bewitching charm ☆**3** elegance, luxury, high fashion, etc. or their aura around a person, situation, etc. Also sp. **glam′or**

glamour stock a stock which attracts a large number of investors, as because of its continuous or dramatic price appreciation

glance[1] (glans, gläns) ***vi.*** **glanced**, **glanc′ing** ⟦ME *glansen*, *glenchen*, prob. blend of OFr *glacier*, to slip (see GLACIS) & *guenchir*, to elude < Frank **wenkjan*, to totter; akin to OE *wancol*, unstable⟧ **1** to strike a surface obliquely and go off at an angle: usually with *off* **2** to make an indirect or passing reference: with *over*, *at*, etc. **3** to flash or gleam **4** to look suddenly and briefly; take a quick look —***vt.*** to cause (an object) to strike a surface at an angle and be deflected —***n.*** **1** a glancing off; deflected impact **2** a flash or gleam **3** a quick look —**SYN.** FLASH

glance[2] (glans) ***n.*** ⟦Ger *glanz*, lit., luster: for IE base see GLASS⟧ any of various ores with a metallic luster: now applied to only a few metallic ores, such as silver glance (ARGENTITE) and lead glance (GALENA)

glanc·ing (glan′siŋ) ***adj.*** **1** striking obliquely and going off at an angle [*a glancing* blow] **2** indirect or passing —**glanc′ing·ly** ***adv.***

gland[1] (gland) ***n.*** ⟦Fr *glande* < OFr *glandre* < L *glandula*, tonsil, dim. of *glans* (gen. *glandis*), acorn (< IE base **gwel-*, oak, acorn > Gr *balanos*)⟧ **1** any organ or specialized group of cells that produces secretions, as insulin or bile, or excretions, as urine: some glands, as the liver and kidneys, have ducts that empty into an organ: the ductless (or endocrine) glands, as the thyroid and adrenals, secrete hormones **2** loosely, any similar structure that is not a true gland [lymph *glands*] **3** *Bot.* an organ or layer of cells that produces and secretes some substance

gland[2] (gland) ***n.*** ⟦< ?⟧ *Mech.* a movable part that compresses the packing in a stuffing box

glan·dered (glan′dərd) ***adj.*** having glanders

glan·ders (glan′dərz) ***n.*** ⟦OFr *glandres* < L *glandulae*, swollen glands in the neck, pl. of *glandula*: see GLAND[1]⟧ a contagious, chronic or acute disease of horses, mules, etc. characterized by fever, swollen lymph nodes, ulcerous nodules on the skin, inflammation of the nasal mucous membranes, etc.: it is caused by bacteria (*Pseudomonas mallei*) and is transmitted to certain other animals and humans: see FARCY —**glan′der·ous** (-dər əs) ***adj.***

glan·du·lar (glan′jə lər) ***adj.*** ⟦Fr *glandulaire*: see GLANDULE⟧ **1** of, like, or functioning as a gland **2** having or consisting of glands **3** derived from or affected by glands —**glan′du·lar·ly** ***adv.***

glandular fever INFECTIOUS MONONUCLEOSIS

glan·dule (glan′jo͞ol) ***n.*** ⟦Fr < L *glandula*: see GLAND[1]⟧ a small gland

glans (glanz) ***n.***, *pl.* **glan·des** (glan′dēz′) ⟦L, lit., acorn: see GLAND[1]⟧ **1** the head, or end, of the penis: in full **glans penis** **2** the corresponding part of the clitoris

glare[1] (gler) ***vi.*** **glared**, **glar′ing** ⟦ME *glaren* < or akin to MDu, to gleam, glare & OE *glær*, amber: for IE base see GLASS⟧ **1** to shine with a strong, steady, dazzling light **2** to be too bright or showy **3** to stare fiercely or angrily —***vt.*** to send forth or express with a glare —***n.*** **1** a strong, steady, dazzling light or brilliant reflection, as from sunlight **2** a too bright or dazzling display **3** a fierce or angry stare —**SYN.** BLAZE[1]

glare[2] (gler) ***n.*** ⟦prob. < prec.⟧ a smooth, bright, glassy surface, as of ice —***adj.*** smooth, bright, and glassy

glar·ing (gler′iŋ) ***adj.*** **1** shining with a too bright, dazzling light **2** too bright and showy **3** staring in a fierce, angry manner **4** too obvious to be overlooked [*a glaring* mistake] —**glar′ing·ly** ***adv.***

Glar·us (glär′əs) canton in EC Switzerland: 264 sq mi (684 sq km): Fr. name **Gla·ris** (glȧ rēs′)

glar·y (gler′ē) ***adj.*** **glar′i·er**, **glar′i·est** shining with, or reflecting, a too bright light —**glar′i·ness** ***n.***

Gla·ser (glā′zər), **Donald A(rthur)** 1926-2013; U.S. physicist

Glas·gow[1] (glas′kō, glaz′gō), **Ellen (Anderson Gholson)** 1873-1945; U.S. novelist

Glas·gow[2] (glas′kō, glaz′gō; *Brit* gläz′gō) seaport in SC Scotland, on the Clyde

glas·nost (gläs′nôst, -nōst) ***n.*** ⟦Russ *glasnost′*, opportunity to be heard⟧ the Soviet policy of the 1980s of publicly acknowledging the nation's social and economic problems and of allowing open discussion of them

☆**glas·phalt** or **glass·phalt** (glas′fôlt′) ***n.*** ⟦blend of fol. & ASPHALT⟧ an asphalt mixture containing crushed recycled glass, used for paving

glass (glas, gläs) ***n.*** ⟦ME *glas* < OE *glæs*, akin to Ger *glas* < IE base **ĝhel-*, to shine > GOLD, GLINT, GLOW⟧ **1** a hard, brittle substance made by fusing silicates with soda or potash, lime, and, sometimes, various metallic oxides into a molten mass that is cooled rapidly to prevent crystallization or annealed to eliminate stresses: various types of glass can be transparent, translucent, heat-resistant, flexible, shatterproof, photochromic, etc. **2** any substance like glass in composition, transparency, brittleness, etc. **3** GLASSWARE **4** *a)* an article made partly or wholly of glass, as a drinking container, mirror, windowpane, telescope, barometer, etc. *b)* [*pl.*] eyeglasses *c)* [*pl.*] binoculars **5** the quantity contained in a drinking glass ☆**6** [Slang] *Basketball* a backboard, esp. when made of a transparent substance: with *the* —***vt.*** **1** to put into glass jars for preserving **2** to mirror; reflect **3** to equip with glass panes; glaze **4** to look at through a telescope, etc. **5** to make glassy —***vi.*** to become glassy —***adj.*** of, made of or with, or like glass —**glass in** to enclose with glass panes

Glass (glas), **Philip** 1937- ; U.S. composer

glass blowing the art or process of shaping molten glass into various forms by blowing air into a mass of it at the end of a tube —**glass blower**

glass ceiling ⟦so called because often invisible⟧ institutional and social obstacles regarded as a barrier preventing women and certain minorities from advancing to the highest positions in business, government, etc.

glass cutter **1** a person whose work is cutting sheets of glass to desired sizes or shapes **2** a person whose work is etching designs on glass surfaces **3** a tool for cutting glass —**glass cutting**

glass·ful (glas′fo͝ol′) ***n.***, *pl.* **-fuls′** the amount that will fill a drinking glass

glass harmonica a musical instrument consisting of an arranged series of graduated glasses from which tones are produced by rubbing the edges with a wet finger

glass·house (glas′hous′) ***n.*** [Brit.] GREENHOUSE

☆**glass·ine** (gla sēn′, glas′ēn) ***n.*** ⟦GLASS + -INE[1]⟧ a thin but tough, glazed, nearly transparent paper, used as for envelopes

glass·mak·er (glas′māk′ər) ***n.*** a person who makes glass or glassware —**glass′mak′ing** ***n.***

☆**glass snake** any of a genus (*Ophisaurus*, family Anguidae) of snakelike, legless lizards found in the S U.S. and other warm regions: so called because its long tail breaks off easily

glass·ware (glas′wer′) ***n.*** articles made of glass, esp. glass containers, as drinking glasses, serving dishes, or vases

glass wool fine fibers of glass intertwined in a woolly mass, used in filters and as insulation

glass·work (-wurk′) ***n.*** **1** [*pl., with sing. or pl. v.*] a factory for making glass **2** the making or ornamentation of glass and glassware **3** GLASSWARE —**glass′work′er** ***n.***

glass·worm (glas′wurm′) ***n.*** ARROWWORM

glass·wort (glas′wurt′) ***n.*** ⟦GLASS + WORT[2]⟧ any of several fleshy plants (genera *Salicornia* and *Salsola*) of the goosefoot family, often found in saline coastal or desert areas: the ash is called *barilla* and formerly was used in making soap and glass

glass·y (glas′ē, gläs′ē) ***adj.*** **glass′i·er**, **glass′i·est** ⟦ME *glasi*⟧ **1** like glass, as in smoothness or transparency **2** expressionless or lifeless [*a glassy* stare] —**glass′i·ly** ***adv.*** —**glass′i·ness** ***n.***

Glas·we·gi·an (glas wē′jən, -jē ən) ***adj.*** of Glasgow —***n.*** a person born or living in Glasgow

glatt (glät) ⟦< Yiddish < Ger *glatt*, simply⟧ designating or of meat products prepared according to the highest degree of kosher dietary requirements: in full **glatt kosher**

Glau·ber's salt (*or* salts) (glou′bərz) ⟦after J. R. *Glauber* (1604-68), Ger chemist⟧ hydrated sodium sulfate, $Na_2SO_4 \cdot 10H_2O$, a crystalline salt used in medicine as a cathartic or diuretic, and in heating systems, etc.: also **Glauber salt (or salts)**

glau·co- (glô′kō, -kə) ⟦< Gr *glaukos*, bright blue, bluish gray, gleaming < ?⟧ *combining form* bluish-green, silvery, or gray [*glauconite*]: also, before a vowel, **glauc-**

glau·co·ma (glô kō′mə, glou-) ***n.*** ⟦L < Gr *glaukōma* < *glaukos* (see prec.) + -OMA⟧ any of a group of related eye disorders characterized by increased pressure within the eye which impairs the vision and may slowly cause eye damage and total loss of vision —**glau·co′ma·tous** (-kō′mə təs) ***adj.***

glau·co·nite (glô′kə nīt′) ***n.*** ⟦Ger *glaukonit* < Gr *glaukon*, neut. of *glaukos*: see GLAUCO-⟧ a greenish silicate of iron and potassium, a kind of mica found in greensand

glau·cous (glô′kəs) ***adj.*** ⟦L *glaucus* < Gr *glaukos*: see GLAUCO-⟧ **1** bluish-green or yellowish-green **2** *Bot.* covered with a greenish bloom that can be rubbed off, as grapes, plums, cabbage leaves, etc.

glaucous gull a large, white and bluish-gray, arctic gull (*Larus hyperboreus*) that often preys on smaller birds

glaze (glāz) ***vt.*** **glazed**, **glaz′ing** ⟦ME *glasen* < *glas*, GLASS⟧ **1** to fit (windows, etc.) with glass **2** to give a hard, glossy finish or coating to; specif., *a)* to overlay (pottery, etc.) with a substance that gives a glassy finish when fused *b)* to make the surface of (leather, etc.) glossy by polishing, etc. *c)* to cover (foods) with a glassy coating of sugar syrup, gelatin, etc. *d)* to coat (a painted surface) with a semitransparent color **3** to give (the eyes) a glassy look **4** to cover with a thin layer of ice —*vi.* **1** to become glassy or glossy **2** to form a glaze —*n.* **1** *a)* a glassy finish, as on pottery *b)* any substance used to produce this **2** a coat of semitransparent color applied to a painted surface to modify the effect **3** a substance, as hardened sugar syrup or gelatin, forming a glassy coating on foods **4** a film or coating, as on the eyes **5** a thin coating of ice —**glaz′er** *n.*

gla·zi·er (glā′zhər; *chiefly Brit,* -zē ər) *n.* ⟦ME *glasier*: see GLASS & -IER⟧ a person whose work is cutting glass and setting it in windows, etc. —**gla′zi·er·y** (-zhər ē, -zē ər ē) *n.*

glaz·ing (glā′ziŋ) *n.* ⟦ME *glasinge*: see GLASS & -ING⟧ **1** the work of a glazier in fitting windows, etc. with glass **2** glass set or to be set in frames **3** the putty, etc. used to secure glass panes **4** a glaze or application of a glaze

Gla·zu·nov (glä zo͞o nôf′), **A·lek·san·dr Kon·stan·ti·no·vich** (ä lyek sän′dr′ kôn′stän tē′nô vich) 1865-1936; Russ. composer

GLBT *abbrev.* gay, lesbian, bisexual, and transgender

gleam (glēm) *n.* ⟦ME *glem* < OE *glæm* < IE **ghlei-* < **ĝhel-*, to shine, gleam > GOLD, GLASS, GLOW⟧ **1** a flash or beam of light **2** a faint light **3** a reflected brightness, as from a polished surface **4** a brief, faint manifestation or trace, as of hope, understanding, etc. —*vi.* **1** to shine or reflect with a gleam or gleams **2** to appear or be revealed briefly or suddenly —**SYN.** FLASH —**gleam′ing** *adj.* —**gleam′y** *adj.*

glean (glēn) *vt., vi.* ⟦ME *glenen* < OFr *glener* < VL *glennare* < Celt, as in OIr *dīgleinn*, he gleans < IE **ĝhlend-* < base **ĝhel-*: see prec.⟧ **1** to collect (grain, etc. left by reapers) **2** to collect the remaining grain, etc. from (a reaped field) **3** *a)* to collect or find out (facts, etc.) gradually or bit by bit *b)* to examine or go through (books, etc.) so as to collect certain information —**glean′er** *n.*

glean·ings (glēn′iŋz) *pl.n.* that which is gleaned

glebe (glēb) *n.* ⟦ME < L *gleba*, clod, lump of earth (in ML(Ec), glebe), akin to *globus*: see GLOBE⟧ **1** a piece of church land forming part or all of a benefice **2** [Archaic] soil; earth; esp., a piece of cultivated land

glede (glēd) *n.* ⟦ME < OE *glida*, akin to GLIDE, ON *gletha*⟧ the common European red kite (*Milvus milvus*)

glee (glē) *n.* ⟦ME *gle* < OE *gleo*, entertainment, merriment, akin to (rare) ON *glȳ* < IE **ghleu-*, to be merry, jest < base **ghel-*, to cry out > Gr *chleuē*, jest⟧ **1** lively joy; gaiety; merriment **2** an English part song for three or more unaccompanied, usually men's, voices

glee club a group formed to sing glees, part songs, and short choral compositions

gleed (glēd) *n.* ⟦ME *glede* < OE *gled* < base of *glowan*: see GLOW⟧ [Now Chiefly Dial.] a glowing coal

glee·ful (glē′fəl) *adj.* full of glee; merry: also [Now Rare] **glee′some** (-səm) —**glee′ful·ly** *adv.* —**glee′ful·ness** *n.*

glee·man (glē′mən) *n., pl.* **-men** (-mən) ⟦ME *gleman* < OE *gleoman*: see GLEE & MAN⟧ [Obs.] a medieval minstrel

gleet (glēt) *n.* ⟦ME *glete* < OFr < L *glittus*, sticky, akin to LL *glus*, GLUE: see CLAY⟧ **1** [Now Rare] any abnormal discharge from the body of an animal or human **2** chronic inflammation of the urethra, as in gonorrhea, characterized by a mucous discharge

glen (glen) *n.* ⟦ME < Late MScot < Gael **glenn* (now *gleann*), mountain valley, akin to Welsh *glyn*⟧ a narrow, secluded valley

Glen·da (glen′də) *n.* a feminine name

Glen·dale (glen′dāl) ⟦GLEN + DALE⟧ **1** city in SW Calif.: suburb of Los Angeles **2** city in SC Ariz.: suburb of Phoenix

Glen·dow·er (glen′dou ər, glen dou′ər), **Owen** 1359?-1416?; Welsh chieftain: rebelled against Henry IV

glen·gar·ry (glen gar′ē, glen′gar′ē) *n., pl.* **-ries** ⟦after *Glengary* valley in Scotland⟧ [*occas.* **G-**] a Scottish cap for men, creased lengthwise across the top and often having short ribbons at the back: also **glengarry bonnet**

Glen More (glen môr′) valley across N Scotland, traversed by the Caledonian Canal: 60 mi (97 km) long

Glenn[1] or **Glen** (glen) *n.* ⟦Celt: see GLEN⟧ a masculine name

Glenn[2] (glen), **John (Herschel, Jr.)** 1921- ; U.S. astronaut & senator: 1st American to orbit the earth (1962)

gle·noid (glē′noid′, glen′oid′) *adj.* ⟦Gr *glēnoeidēs* < *glēnē*, socket of a joint, eyeball + *-eidēs*, -OID⟧ forming a smooth, shallow cavity or socket for a bone; esp., designating the cavity on the head of the scapula which, together with the head of the humerus, forms the shoulder joint

glen plaid (*or* check) (glen) ⟦after *Glenurquhart*, clan of *Glen Urquhart*, valley in NW Scotland⟧ [*also* **G- p-**] a plaid pattern or cloth with thin cross-barred stripes in black and white and one or more muted colors: also **Glen·ur·quhart** (glen ur′kərt) *n.*

gley (glā) *n.* ⟦earlier *glei* < Ukrainian (cf. Russ *glina*, clay) < IE base **glei-*, to stick together > CLAY⟧ a sticky, compact, clayey soil that sometimes develops in highly humid regions

gli·a (glī′ə; *also* glē′ə) *n. short for* NEUROGLIA —**gli′al** *adj.*

gli·a·din (glī′ə din) *n.* ⟦Fr *gliadine* < MGr *glia*, glue (akin to Gr *gloios*: for base see CLAY) + *-d-* + Fr *-ine*, -IN[1]⟧ any of a group of simple vegetable proteins found in gluten

glib (glib) *adj.* **glib′ber, glib′best** ⟦orig., slippery < or akin to Du *glibberig*, slippery, *glibber*, jelly⟧ **1** done in a smooth, offhand fashion **2** speaking or spoken in a smooth, fluent, easy manner, often in a way that is too smooth and easy to be convincing —**glib′ly** *adv.* —**glib′ness** *n.*

glide (glīd) *vi.* **glid′ed, glid′ing** ⟦ME *gliden* < OE *glidan*, akin to Ger *gleiten*, prob. < IE **ghlei-dh* (< base **ĝhel-*, to shine > GLASS, GLOW)⟧ **1** to flow or move smoothly and easily, as in skating **2** to move by or pass gradually and almost unnoticed, as time **3** *Aeron.* *a)* to fly in a glider *b)* to descend with little or no engine power, using airflow to control lift **4** *Music, Phonet.* to make a glide —*vt.* to cause to glide —*n.* **1** the act of gliding; smooth, easy flow or movement ☆**2** a small disk or ball, as of nylon, attached to the underside of furniture legs, etc. to allow easy sliding **3** *Music* loosely, a slur, portamento, or the like **4** *Phonet.* *a)* an intermediate sound produced in the transition of the speech organs from the position for one sound to that for another *b)* the nonsyllabic vowel in a diphthong: see OFF-GLIDE, ON-GLIDE

glid·er (glīd′ər) *n.* **1** a person or thing that glides **2** a heavier-than-air aircraft without an engine, using airflow to produce free flight ☆**3** a porch seat suspended in a frame so that it can glide or swing back and forth

glim (glim) *n.* ⟦ME *glimme*, radiance, prob. < Scand, as in OSwed *glimma*, akin to GLEAM, MHG *glim*, a spark⟧ [Slang] **1** a light, as a lamp, candle, etc. **2** an eye

glim·mer (glim′ər) *vi.* ⟦ME *glimeren*, to shine, freq. < base of OE *glæm* (see GLEAM), akin to Du *glimmeren*, Ger *glimmern*⟧ **1** to give a faint, flickering light **2** to appear or be seen faintly or dimly —*n.* **1** a faint, flickering light **2** a faint manifestation or dim perception

glim·mer·ing (glim′ər iŋ) *n.* GLIMMER

glimpse (glimps) *vt.* **glimpsed, glimps′ing** ⟦ME *glimsen* (with unhistoric *-p-*) < base of OE *glæm* (see GLEAM), akin to MHG *glimsen*, MDu *glinsen*⟧ to catch a brief, quick view of, as in passing; perceive momentarily and incompletely —*vi.* to look quickly; glance (*at*) —*n.* **1** [Archaic] a brief, sudden shining; flash **2** a faint, fleeting appearance; slight trace **3** a brief, quick view

Glin·ka (glin′kä; *E* gliŋ′kə), **Mi·kha·il I·va·no·vich** (mē khä ēl′ i vä′nô vich) 1804-57; Russ. composer

glint (glint) *vi.* ⟦ME *glenten*, prob. < Scand, as in Swed dial *gläntа*, akin to MHG *glinzen*, to glint, Ger *glänzen*, to shine < IE **ghlendh-* < base **ĝhel-*, to shine > GLOW, GLASS⟧ **1** to shine or reflect with intermittent flashes of light; gleam, flash, or glitter **2** [Archaic] to move quickly, esp. glancingly —*n.* a gleam, flash, or glitter

gli·o·ma (glī ō′mə; *also* glē-) *n., pl.* **-ma·ta** (-mə tə) or **-mas** ⟦ModL < MGr *glia* (see GLIADIN) + *-ōma* (see -OMA)⟧ a tumor of the brain, spinal cord, etc., composed of tissue that normally forms the supporting structure of nerves

glis·sade (gli säd′, -sād′) *n.* ⟦Fr < *glisser*, to slide, glide, prob. blend of Frank **glitan* (for IE base see GLIDE) & OFr *glacier*, to slip (see GLACIS)⟧ **1** an intentional slide by a mountain climber down a steep snow-covered slope **2** *Ballet* a gliding step —*vi.* **-sad′ed, -sad′ing** to make a glissade; slide or glide

glis·san·do (gli sän′dō; *also,* -san′-) *n., pl.* **-di** (-dē) or **-dos** ⟦formed as if It prp. equiv. to Fr *glissant*, prp. of *glisser*, to slide: see prec.⟧ *Music* **1** a sliding effect achieved by sounding a series of adjacent tones in rapid succession, as by running a finger over the white keys of a piano **2** a passage having this effect — *adj., adv. Music* (performed) with such an effect

glis·ten (glis′ən) *vi.* ⟦ME *glistnen* (with unhistoric *-t-*) < OE *glisnian* < base of *glisian*, to shine < IE **ghleis-* < base **ĝhel-* > GLEAM, GLASS⟧ to shine or sparkle with reflected light, as a wet or polished surface does —*n.* a glistening —**SYN.** FLASH

glis·ter (glis′tər) *vi., n.* ⟦ME *glisteren*, prob. < LowG, as in MDu *glinsteren*, MLowG *glistern*, akin to prec.⟧ *archaic var. of* GLISTEN

glitch (glich) *n.* ⟦< Ger colloq. *glitsche*, a slip < *glitschen*, to slip, slide, intens. of Ger *gleiten*: see GLIDE⟧ **1** [Slang] a mishap, error, malfunctioning, etc. **2** a sudden, brief change in the period of a pulsar, believed to be caused by sudden changes in the structure of the rotating star

glit·ter (glit′ər) *vi.* ⟦ME *gliteren*, prob. < ON *glitra*, akin to Ger *glitzern*: for IE base see GLISTEN⟧ **1** to shine with a sparkling light; be bright; glisten; sparkle **2** to be strikingly brilliant, showy, or attractive —*n.* **1** a bright, sparkling light **2** striking or showy brilliance or attractiveness **3** bits of glittering material used for decoration **4** [Cdn.] a glaze of ice formed by quickly freezing rain: also **glitter ice** —**SYN.** FLASH

glit·ter·a·ti (glit′ə rät′ē) *pl.n.* ⟦prec. + (LITER)ATI⟧ [Informal] people who are wealthy, chic, famous, etc.

glit·ter·y (glit′ər ē) *adj.* having glitter; glittering

☆**glitz** (glits) *n.* ⟦< ?⟧ [Informal] gaudy or glittery showiness or attractiveness; ostentation

☆**glitz·y** (glit′sē) *adj.* **glitz′i·er, glitz′i·est** ⟦< ?⟧ [Informal] **1** having glitter; sparkling; glittery **2** attracting attention in an ornate or gaudy way; showy; pretentious

Gli·wi·ce (gli vē′tse) city in S Poland

gloam·ing (glōm′iŋ) *n.* ⟦ME (Scot) *glomyng* < OE *glomung* < *glom*, twilight, akin to *glowan*, to GLOW: adopted in literature < Scot dial.⟧ evening dusk; twilight

gloat (glōt) *vi.* ⟦prob. via dial. < OE **glotian* or ON *glotta*, to grin scornfully, akin to Ger *glotzen*, E dial. *glout*, to stare < IE **ĝhlud-* < base **ĝhel-*, to shine > GLOW⟧ to gaze or think with exultation or malicious pleasure: often with *over* —*n.* the act of gloating

glob (gläb) *n.* ⟦prob. contr. < GLOBULE, modeled on BLOB⟧ a somewhat rounded mass or lump, as of jelly or grease

glob·al (glō′bəl) *adj.* **1** round like a ball; globe-shaped **2** of, relating to, or including the whole earth; worldwide **3** complete or comprehensive **4** being or having to do with a business, operation, system, etc. carried on or extending throughout all or much of the world [*a global* company, *global* communications] **5** *Comput.* pertaining to or including an entire file, database, etc. —**glob′al·ly** *adv.*

☆**glob·al·ism** (-iz′əm) *n.* a policy, outlook, etc. that is worldwide in scope —**glob′al·ist** *n., adj.*

glob·al·i·za·tion (glō′bəl i zā′shən, -ī-) *n.* the process of globalizing something; specif., the expansion of many businesses into markets throughout the world, marked by an increase in international investment, the proliferation of large multinational corporations, worldwide economic integration, etc.

glob·al·ize (glō′bəl īz′) *vt.* **-ized′**, **-iz′ing** to make global; esp., to organize or establish worldwide

global village ⟦term popularized by M. MCLUHAN⟧ the world regarded as having become a single community by the effects of mass media, rapid travel, etc.

global warming a slight but continuing increase in the temperature of the lower atmosphere, usually attributed to an intensifying of the GREENHOUSE EFFECT due to human activity and regarded as ultimately resulting in harmful or devastating climatic conditions

glo·bate (glō′bāt′) *adj.* ⟦L *globatus*, pp. of *globare*, to make into a ball < *globus*, fol.⟧ round like a ball

globe (glōb) *n.* ⟦ME < L *globus*, a ball: for IE base see CLIMB⟧ **1** any round, ball-shaped thing; sphere; specif., *a)* the earth *b)* a spherical model of the earth showing the continents, seas, etc. *c)* a similar model of the heavens, showing the constellations, etc. **2** anything shaped somewhat like a globe; specif., *a)* a round glass container, as for goldfish *b)* a rounded glass cover for a lamp *c)* a small, golden ball used as a symbol of authority — *vt., vi.* **globed**, **glob′ing** to form or gather into a globe —**the Globe** former London theater on the S bank of the Thames: site of the original performances of many of Shakespeare's plays

globe artichoke ARTICHOKE (sense 1)

globe·fish (glōb′fish′) *n., pl.* **-fish′** or **-fish′es** (see FISH) ⟦so named from its shape when inflated with air or water⟧ any puffer fish or porcupinefish

globe·flow·er (-flou′ər) *n.* **1** any of a genus (*Trollius*) of plants of the buttercup family, with white, orange, or yellow globe-shaped flowers **2** KERRIA

globe-trot·ter (glōb′trät′ər) *n.* a person who travels widely about the world, esp. for pleasure —**globe′-trot′ting** *n., adj.*

glo·big·er·i·na ooze (glō bij′ər ī′nə) ⟦ModL *Globigerina*, a genus of foraminifera (< L *globus*, a ball, GLOBE + *ger(ere)*, to bear + ModL *-ina*, taxonomic suffix < L, pl. of *-inus*, -INE[1]) + OOZE[2]⟧ a fine, deep-sea sediment covering approximately one-third of the ocean floors at depths usually between 2,000 and 4,000 m (*c.* 6,560 and 13,120 ft), consisting predominantly of the empty, calcareous shells of a genus (*Globigerina*) of planktonic foraminifera

glo·bin (glō′bin) *n.* ⟦(HEMO)GLOBIN⟧ the protein component of hemoglobin: cf. HEME

glo·boid (glō′boid′) *adj.* shaped somewhat like a globe or ball —*n.* anything globoid

glo·bose (glō′bōs′) *adj.* ⟦ME < L *globosus*⟧ globoid or globular: also **glo′bous** (-bəs) —**glo′bose′ly** *adv.* —**glo·bos′i·ty** (-bäs′i tē) *n.*

glob·u·lar (gläb′yə lər) *adj.* **1** shaped like a globe or ball; spherical; round **2** made up of globules —*SYN.* ROUND[1]

glob·ule (gläb′yo͞ol) *n.* ⟦Fr < L *globulus*, dim. of *globus*, GLOBE⟧ a tiny ball or globe; esp., a drop of liquid

glob·u·lin (gläb′yə lin) *n.* ⟦prec. + -IN[1]⟧ any of a group of proteins, fully soluble only in salt solutions, found in both animal and vegetable tissues: see ALBUMIN

glo·chid·i·um (glō kid′ē əm) *n., pl.* **-i·a** (-ə) ⟦ModL < Gr *glōchis*, point (see GLOSS[2]) + ModL *-idium*, dim. suffix < Gr *-idion*⟧ **1** *Bot.* a barbed hair or bristle, as on certain cactuses or on the spore masses of ferns **2** *Zool.* the parasitic larval stage of freshwater mussels (family Unionidae) which infests the gills, etc. of many fishes —**glo·chid′i·ate** (-it, -āt′) *adj.*

glock·en·spiel (gläk′ən spēl′, -shpēl′) *n.* ⟦Ger < *glocke*, a bell (see CLOCK[1]) + *spiel*, play⟧ a percussion instrument with chromatically tuned, flat metal bars set in a frame, that produce bell-like tones when struck with small hammers

glögg or **glogg** (glög) *n.* ⟦Swed *glögg* < *glödga*, to mull, lit., to burn < OSwed < *glöth*, glowing coal, akin to OE *glæd*: see GLEED⟧ a Swedish drink made by heating wines, brandy, etc. with sugar and spices and adding raisins and almonds as a garnish

glom (gläm) [Slang] *vt.* **glommed**, **glom′ming** ⟦earlier *glaum* < Scot dial., prob. < Gael *glaim*, to snatch⟧ **1** to seize; grab **2** to steal **3** to look over; view; see —**glom onto** to take and hold; obtain

glom·er·ate (gläm′ər it, -āt′) *adj.* ⟦L *glomeratus*, pp. of *glomerare*, to wind or make into a ball < *glomus*, a ball, sphere, akin to *globus*, GLOBE⟧ formed into a rounded mass or ball; clustered

glom·er·a·tion (gläm′ər ā′shən) *n.* ⟦L *glomeratio* < *glomeratus*: see prec.⟧ **1** the act of forming into a rounded mass; agglomeration or conglomeration **2** something formed into a rounded mass; cluster

glo·mer·u·late (glō mer′yo͞o lit, -lāt′) *adj.* ⟦< fol. + -ATE[1]⟧ grouped in small, dense clusters

glom·er·ule (gläm′ər o͞ol′) *n.* ⟦Fr *glomérule* < ModL *glomerulus*, dim. < L *glomus* (gen. *glomeris*), a ball, round knot: see GLOMERATE⟧ **1** a compact cluster, as of a flower head **2** GLOMERULUS

glo·mer·u·lo·ne·phri·tis (glō mer′yo͞o lō′ne frīt′is) *n.* ⟦ModL: see fol. & NEPHRITIS⟧ a type of nephritis characterized by inflamed glomeruli and probably caused by certain antibody-antigen complexes in the blood filtering through the kidney

glo·mer·u·lus (glō mer′yo͞o ləs) *n., pl.* **-li′** (-lī′) ⟦ModL: see GLOMERULE⟧ any cluster or structure of blood vessels or nerves; esp., any of the tiny clusters of capillaries in the kidney which act as filters, initiating the formation of urine —**glo·mer′u·lar** (-lər) *adj.*

Glom·ma (glôm′ə) river in SE Norway, flowing south into the Skagerrak: longest river in Scandinavia: 375 mi (603 km)

glon·o·in (glän′ō in) *n.* ⟦GL(YCERIN) + O(XYGEN) + N(ITR)O(GEN) + -IN[1]⟧ NITROGLYCERIN

gloom (glo͞om) *vi.* ⟦< ME *gloum(b)en*, to look morose, prob. < Scand, as in Norw dial. *glome*, to stare somberly, akin to EFris *glumen*, to peer secretly (< IE **ĝhlu-* < base **ghêl-* > GLEAM, GLOW): meaning infl. by OE *glom*, twilight⟧ **1** to be or look morose, displeased, or dejected **2** to be, become, or appear dark, dim, or dismal —*vt.* to make dark, dismal, dejected, etc. —*n.* **1** darkness; dimness; obscurity **2** a dark or dim place **3** deep sadness or hopelessness

gloom·y (glo͞om′ē) *adj.* **gloom′i·er**, **gloom′i·est** **1** overspread with or enveloped in darkness or dimness **2** *a)* very sad or dejected; hopeless; melancholy *b)* morose or sullen **3** causing gloom; dismal; depressing —*SYN.* DARK —**gloom′i·ly** *adv.* —**gloom′i·ness** *n.*

☆**glop** (gläp) *n.* ⟦< ? GL(UE) + (SL)OP⟧ [Informal] any soft, gluey substance, thick liquid, etc. —**glop′py** *adj.*

Glo·ri·a (glôr′ē ə, glō′rē ə) *n.* ⟦L, glory⟧ **1** a feminine name **2** *short for:* *a)* GLORIA IN EXCELSIS DEO *b)* GLORIA PATRI **3** the music for either of these **4** [**g-**] a halo or its representation in art **5** [**g-**] a glossy, closely woven cloth of cotton, rayon, silk and wool, etc.

Gloria in ex·cel·sis De·o (in ek shel′sis dā′ō, -sel′-) ⟦L⟧ glory (be) to God on high: first words of the greater doxology

Gloria Pa·tri (pä′trē) ⟦L⟧ glory (be) to the Father: first words of the lesser doxology

glo·ri·fy (glôr′ə fī′) *vt.* **-fied′**, **-fy′ing** ⟦ME *glorifien* < OFr *glorifier* < LL(Ec) *glorificare*: see GLORY & -FY⟧ **1** to make glorious; give glory to **2** to exalt and honor (God), as in worship **3** to praise extravagantly; honor; extol **4** to portray or make seem better, larger, finer, etc. than is actually the case: usually in the pp. [their "yacht" was little more than a *glorified* motorboat] —**glo′ri·fi·ca′tion** *n.* —**glo′ri·fi′er** *n.*

glo·ri·ole (glō′rē ōl′, glôr′ē-) *n.* ⟦Fr < L *gloriola*, dim. of *gloria*, glory⟧ GLORY (sense 6)

glo·ri·ous (glôr′ē əs) *adj.* ⟦ME & Anglo-Fr < OFr *glorios* < L *gloriosus*⟧ **1** having, giving, or deserving glory **2** splendid; magnificent **3** [Informal] very delightful or enjoyable —**glo′ri·ous·ly** *adv.* —**glo′ri·ous·ness** *n.*

glo·ry (glôr′ē) *n., pl.* **-ries** ⟦ME *glorie* < OFr < L *gloria*⟧ **1** *a)* great honor and admiration won by doing something important or valuable; fame; renown *b)* anything bringing this **2** worshipful adoration or praise **3** the condition of highest achievement, splendor, prosperity, etc. [Greece in her *glory*] **4** radiant beauty or splendor; magnificence **5** heaven or the bliss of heaven **6** *a)* a halo or its representation in art *b)* any circle of light —*vi.* **-ried**, **-ry·ing** to be very proud; rejoice; exult: with *in* —**gone to glory** dead —**in one's glory** at one's best, happiest, most gratified, etc.

gloss[1] (glôs, gläs) *n.* ⟦prob. < Scand, as in Norw dial. *glosa*, to gleam: for IE base see GLASS⟧ **1** the brightness or luster of a smooth, polished surface; sheen **2** a deceptively smooth or pleasant outward appearance, as in manners or speech **3** *short for* LIP GLOSS —*vt.* **1** to give a polished, shiny surface to; make lustrous **2** ⟦a blend of *vt.* 1 & GLOSS[2]⟧ to smooth over or cover up (an error, inadequacy, fault, etc.); make appear right by specious argument or by minimizing: often with *over* —*vi.* to become shiny —**gloss′er** *n.*

gloss[2] (glôs, gläs) *n.* ⟦ME *glose* < OFr or ML *glosa*, for L *glossa*, foreign or strange word needing explanation < Gr *glōssa*, orig., tongue, language < **glōchia*, pointed object < *glochis*, point < IE base **glogh-*, thorn, point > OSlav *gloge*, thorn⟧ **1** words of explanation or translation inserted between the lines of a text **2** *a)* a note of comment or explanation accompanying a text, as in a footnote or margin *b)* a collection of such notes **3** a false or misleading interpretation —*vt.* **1** to furnish (a text) with glosses **2** to interpret falsely —*vi.* to annotate a text —**gloss′er** *n.*

gloss[3] *abbrev.* glossary

glos·sa (gläs′ə, glôs′-) *n., pl.* **-sae** (-ē, -ī′) or **-sas** ⟦ModL < Gr *glōssa*, tongue: see GLOSS[2]⟧ the tongue of a vertebrate, or any tonguelike structure, as of a butterfly or moth; esp., either of the middle lobes of the labium of an insect

glos·sal (gläs′əl, glôs′-) *adj.* ⟦prec. + -AL⟧ of the tongue

glos·sa·ry (glôs′ə rē, gläs′-) *n., pl.* **-ries** ⟦ME *glosarie* < L *glossarium* < *glossa*: see GLOSS[2]⟧ a list of difficult, technical, or foreign terms with definitions or translations, as for some particular author, field of knowledge, etc., often included in alphabetical listing at the end of a textbook —**glos·sar·i·al** (glô ser′ē əl, glä-) *adj.* —**glos′sar·ist** *n.*

glos·sa·tor (gläs′āt′ər; glôs′-, gläs āt′-, glôs-) *n.* ⟦ME *glosatour* < ML *glossator*⟧ a person who writes textual glosses

glos·si·tis (gläs īt′is, glôs-) *n.* ⟦fol. + -ITIS⟧ *Med.* inflammation of the tongue —**glos·sit′ic** (-it′ik) *adj.*

glos·so- (gläs′ō, glôs′-; -ə) ⟦ModL < Gr *glōssa*: see GLOSS[2]⟧ *combining form* **1** tongue, tongue and [*glossitis*] **2** of words or language [*glossolalia*] Also, before a vowel, **gloss-**

glos·sog·ra·pher (glə säg′rə fər; glô-, glä-) *n.* ⟦Gr *glōssographos* < *glōssa* (see GLOSS[2]) + *graphein*, to write: see GRAPHIC⟧ a writer of glosses or glossaries —**glos·sog′ra·phy** *n.*

glos·so·la·li·a (gläs′ō lā′lē ə, glôs′-) *n.* ⟦ModL < *glosso-* (see GLOSSO-) + Gr *lalia*, a speaking < *lalein*, to speak, prattle, of echoic orig.⟧ **1** ecstatic or apparently ecstatic utterance of usually unintelligible speechlike sounds, as in a religious assembly, viewed by some as a manifestation of deep religious experience **2** GIFT OF TONGUES

gloss·y (glôs′ē, gläs′ē) *adj.* **gloss′i·er, gloss′i·est** ⟦GLOSS[1] + -Y[3]⟧ **1** having a smooth, shiny appearance or finish **2** smooth and plausible; specious —☆*n., pl.* **gloss′ies 1** *Photog.* a print with a glossy finish: opposed to MATTE[2] **2** [Informal] a magazine printed on glossy paper; slick —**gloss′i·ly** *adv.* —**gloss′i·ness** *n.*

glot·tal (glät′'l) *adj.* of or produced in or at the glottis: also **glot′tic** (-ik)

glottal stop *Phonet.* a speech sound (IPA symbol [ʔ]) articulated by a momentary complete closing of the glottis: it is sometimes heard as a variant for medial *t* (as in *bottle* or *water*) in some English dialects, and is the medial sound in the negative expression conventionally spelled *unh-unh* in English

glot·tis (glät′is) *n., pl.* **-tis·es** or **-ti·des′** (-i dēz′) ⟦ModL < Gr *glōttis* < *glōtta*, Attic var. of *glōssa*: see GLOSS[2]⟧ the opening between the vocal cords in the larynx

glot·to- (glät′ō) ⟦< Gr *glōtto-* < *glōtta*, Attic for *glōssa, tongue*: see GLOSS[2]⟧ *combining form* language

☆**glot·to·chro·nol·o·gy** (glät′ō krə näl′ə jē) *n.* ⟦prec. + CHRONOLOGY⟧ a method for estimating the dates when the branches of a family of languages separated from the parent language and from one another

Glouces·ter (gläs′tər, glôs′-) **1** city in SW England, on the Severn **2** GLOUCESTERSHIRE

Glouces·ter·shire (-shir) county in SW England, on Severn estuary: 1,024 sq mi (2,652 sq km)

glove (gluv) *n.* ⟦ME < OE *glof* & ON *glofi* < ? Gmc **ga-lōfa* < **ga-*, together (OE *ge-*) + **lōfa* (Goth *lōfa*), palm of the hand: for IE base see LUFF⟧ **1** a covering for the hand, made of leather, cloth, etc., with a separate sheath for each finger and the thumb ☆**2** *Baseball a)* a similar covering of padded leather worn by players in the field (see also MITT) *b)* the ability to field a batted or thrown ball **3** *Boxing* BOXING GLOVE —*vt.* **gloved, glov′ing 1** to supply with gloves **2** to cover with or as with a glove ☆**3** *Baseball* to catch (a ball) with a glove —**fit like a glove** to fit perfectly —**put on the gloves** [Informal] to engage in BOXING[1]

glove box 1 a sealed enclosure containing a window for viewing and ports with attached gloves for handling toxic, radioactive, sterile, etc. materials inside the enclosure **2** GLOVE COMPARTMENT

glove compartment a compartment built into the dashboard of an automotive vehicle, for storing miscellaneous articles

glov·er (gluv′ər) *n.* one who makes or sells gloves

glow (glō) *vi.* ⟦ME *glowen* < OE *glowan*, akin to Ger *glühen* < IE **ghlō-* < base **ĝhel-*, to shine > GOLD, GLEAM, YELLOW, Gr *chlōros*, light green⟧ **1** to give off a bright light as a result of great heat; be incandescent or red-hot **2** to give out a steady, even light without flame or blaze **3** to be or feel hot; give out heat **4** to radiate health or high spirits **5** to be elated or enlivened by emotion [*to glow with pride*] **6** to show brilliant, conspicuous colors; be bright; specif., *a)* to be flushed, as from emotion, enthusiasm, etc.; be rosy or ruddy *b)* to gleam; flash; light up (said of the eyes) *c)* to be bright or luminescent (said of colors) —*n.* **1** a light given off as the result of great heat; incandescence **2** a steady, even light without flame or blaze **3** brilliance, vividness, or luminescence of color **4** a brightness of skin color, as from good health, emotion, etc.; flush **5** a sensation of warmth and well-being **6** warmth of emotion; ardor, eagerness, etc. —***SYN.*** BLAZE[1] —**glow′ing** *adj.* —**glow′ing·ly** *adv.*

glow·er (glou′ər) *vi.* ⟦ME *glouren*, var. of *gloren*, prob. < ON, as in Norw dial. *glōra*, Swed dial. *glora*, to stare, gape < IE **ĝhlōu-* < base **ĝhel-*: see prec.⟧ to stare with sullen anger; scowl —*n.* a sullen, angry stare; scowl —**glow′er·ing** *adj.* —**glow′er·ing·ly** *adv.*

glow lamp (glō) *Elec.* a discharge lamp, esp. one used to produce a brightly colored light: see DISCHARGE TUBE: sometimes called **glow tube**

glow·worm (glō′wurm′) *n.* any of a number of beetles or beetle larvae that give off a luminescent light; esp., the wingless female or the larva of the firefly

glox·in·i·a (gläk sin′ē ə) *n.* ⟦ModL, after B. P. *Gloxin*, 18th-c. Ger botanist⟧ a cultivated tropical plant (*Sinningia speciosa*) of the gesneria family, with large, downy leaves and bell-shaped flowers of various colors

gloze (glōz) *vt., vi.* **glozed, gloz′ing** ⟦ME *glosen* < OFr *gloser* < *glose*: see GLOSS[2]⟧ **1** [Obs.] to make glosses or comments (on); explain: the original meaning **2** [Now Rare] to explain away or gloss (*over*) **3** [Obs.] to fawn or flatter (someone) —*n.* [Now Rare] **1** a gloss; comment **2** flattery **3** specious talk or insincere action

glu·ca·gon (glo͞o′kə gän′) *n.* ⟦Ger *glukagon* < *glukose* (< Fr *glucose*, GLUCOSE) + Gr *agōn*, a struggle (see AGON): so named from effect on insulin⟧ a hormone formed in the pancreas, or certain cells, that increases the concentration of blood sugar and opposes the action of insulin

Gluck (glo͝ok), **Chris·toph Wil·li·bald** (kris′tôf vil′i bält′) 1714-87; Ger. composer

glu·co·nate (glo͞o′kə nāt′) *n.* **1** a salt of gluconic acid, containing the monovalent negative radical $HOCH_2(CHOH)_5COO$ **2** an uncharged ester of this acid

glu·con·ic acid (glo͞o kän′ik) ⟦fol. + -ON(E) + -IC⟧ a crystalline substance, $CH_2OH(CHOH)_4COOH$, prepared by the oxidation of glucose and used in food products and pharmaceuticals, for cleaning metals, etc.

glu·cose (glo͞o′kōs′) *n.* ⟦Fr < Gr *gleukos*, sweet wine, sweetness, akin to *glykys*, sweet: see GLYCERIN⟧ a crystalline monosaccharide occurring naturally in fruits, honey, and blood: the commercial form, also containing dextrin and maltose, is prepared as a sweet syrup or, upon desiccation, as a white solid, by the hydrolysis of starch in the presence of dilute acids or enzymes

glu·co·side (glo͞o′kə sīd′) *n.* ⟦prec. + -IDE⟧ **1** *former term for* GLYCOSIDE **2** a glycoside whose sugar constituent is glucose —**glu′co·sid′ic** (-sid′ik) *adj.*

glue (glo͞o) *n.* ⟦ME *gleu* < OFr *glu*, birdlime < LL *glus* (gen. *glutis*), glue: see CLAY⟧ **1** a hard, brittle gelatin made by boiling animal skins, bones, hoofs, etc. to a jelly: when heated in water, it forms a sticky, viscous liquid used to stick things together **2** any of various similar adhesive preparations made from casein, resin, etc. —*vt.* **glued, glu′ing 1** to make stick with or as with glue **2** to make fixed or focused: usually in the pp.: with *to* [*glued to the TV all morning*] —**glu′er** *n.*

glue·pot (glo͞o′pät′) *n.* a pot like a double boiler for melting glue

☆**glue-sniff·ing** (-snif′iŋ) *n.* the practice of inhaling the fumes of glue containing toluene or other solvents for the intoxicating and euphoric effects: it may cause damage to the brain, liver, kidneys, etc. —**glue′-sniff′er** *n.*

glu·ey (glo͞o′ē) *adj.* **glu′i·er, glu′i·est 1** like glue; sticky **2** covered with or full of glue —**glu′ey·ness** *n.* —**glu′i·ly** *adv.*

glug (glug) *vi.* **glugged, glug′ging** ⟦echoic⟧ to make the muffled, gurgling sound of liquid flowing in spurts as from a bottle —*vt.* to drink, esp. by taking large gulps of —*n.* **1** a glugging sound **2** a large gulp of liquid

glum (glum) *adj.* **glum′mer, glum′mest** ⟦prob. < ME *glomen*, var. of *gloum(b)en*: see GLOOM⟧ feeling or looking gloomy, sullen, or morose —**glum′ly** *adv.* —**glum′ness** *n.*

glu·ma·ceous (glo͞o mā′shəs) *adj.* **1** having glumes **2** like glumes

glume (glo͞om) *n.* ⟦ModL *gluma* < L, husk < base of *glubere*, to peel, flay: see CLEAVE[1]⟧ either of the two empty sterile bracts at the base of a grass spikelet, or a similar structure on the spikelets of sedges

glu·on (glo͞o′än′) *n.* ⟦GLU(E) + -ON⟧ a quantum of energy or massless particle postulated to carry the force that binds quarks together within subatomic particles

glut (glut) *vi.* **glut′ted, glut′ting** ⟦ME *glutten* < OFr *gloter*, to swallow < L *gluttire*, prob. ult. < IE base **gel-*, to devour > Ger *kehle*, OE *ceole*, throat⟧ to eat like a glutton; overindulge —*vt.* **1** to feed, fill, supply, etc. to excess; surfeit **2** to flood (the market) with certain goods so that the supply is greater than the demand —*n.* ⟦< the v.⟧ **1** a glutting or being glutted **2** a supply of certain goods that is greater than the demand —***SYN.*** SATIATE

glu·ta·mate (glo͞ot′ə māt′) *n.* a salt or ester of glutamic acid

glu·tam·ic acid (glo͞o tam′ik) ⟦GLUT(EN) + AM(INO) + -IC⟧ a nonessential amino acid, $COOH(CH_2)_2CH(NH_2)COOH$: see AMINO ACID

glu·ta·mine (glo͞ot′ə mēn′, -min) *n.* ⟦GLUT(EN) + AMINE⟧ a nonessential amino acid, $H_2NC(O)(CH_2)_2CH(NH_2)COOH$: see AMINO ACID

glu·ta·thi·one (glo͞ot′ə thī′ōn′) *n.* ⟦GLUTAMIC ACID + THIO- + -ONE⟧ a polypeptide, $C_{10}H_{17}O_6N_3S$, containing cysteine, glutamic acid, and glycine and involved, as an antioxidant and coenzyme, in the normal biochemical reactions occurring in plant and animal tissues

glu·te·al (glo͞ot′ē əl; *also* glo͞o tē′-) *adj.* ⟦GLUTE(US) + -AL⟧ of or near the muscles of the buttocks

glu·te·i (glo͞ot′ē ī′; *also* glo͞o tē′ī′) *n. pl. of* GLUTEUS

glu·ten (glo͞ot′'n) *n.* ⟦L *gluten*, glue, akin to LL *glus*, GLUE⟧ a gray, sticky, nutritious mixture of proteins, including gliadin, found in wheat and other grain: it gives dough its tough, elastic quality —**glu′ten·ous** *adj.*

gluten bread bread made from flour rich in gluten and low in starch

glutes (glo͞ots) *pl.n.* [Slang] the muscles of the buttocks; glutei

glu·te·us (glo͞ot′ē əs; *also* glo͞o tē′əs) *n., pl.* **glu·te·i** (glo͞ot′ē ī′; *also* glo͞o tē′ī′) ⟦ModL < Gr *gloutos*, rump, buttock: for IE base see CLIMB⟧ any of the three muscles that form each of the buttocks and act to extend, abduct, and rotate the thigh

gluteus max·i·mus (mak′sə məs) *pl.* **glutei max′i·mi′** (-mī′) ⟦ModL, largest GLUTEUS⟧ the outermost of the glutei, a large, rounded muscle that acts to extend the thigh

glu·ti·nous (glo͞ot′'n əs) *adj.* ⟦ME < L *glutinosus* < *gluten*: see GLUTEN⟧ gluey; sticky —**glu′ti·nous·ly** *adv.*

glut·ton (glut′'n) *n.* ⟦ME *glotoun* < OFr *gloton* < L *gluto, glutto* < *glutire, gluttire*, to devour, akin to *gula*, GULLET⟧ **1** a person who greedily eats too much **2** a person with a great capacity for something [*a glutton for work*] **3** ⟦transl. of Ger *vielfrass*, lit., great devourer⟧ WOLVERINE —***SYN.*** EPICURE —**glut′ton·ize′** *vt., vi.* **-ized′, -iz′ing**

glut·ton·ous (glut′'n əs) *adj.* ⟦ME *glotonous* < OFr *glotonos*: see prec.⟧ of or like a person who is a glutton —**glut′ton·ous·ly** *adv.*

glut·ton·y (glut′'n ē) *n., pl.* **-ton·ies** ⟦ME *glotonie* < OFr < *gloton*, GLUTTON⟧ the habit or act of eating too much

glyc·er·al·de·hyde (glis′ər al′də hīd′) *n.* the simplest aldehyde sugar, $C_3H_6O_3$, used as the standard reference for carbohydrate structure and produced in the body by the oxidation of sugars

gly·cer·ic acid (gli ser′ik, glis′ər ik) a syrupy liquid, $C_3H_6O_4$, occurring in two optically active forms: it is prepared by the oxidation of glycerin

glyc·er·ide (glis′ər īd′, -id) *n.* ⟦fol. + -IDE⟧ an ester of glycerol

glyc·er·in (-in, -ēn′) *n.* ⟦Fr *glycérine* < Gr *glykeros*, sweet < **dlykeros* < ? IE base **dlku-*, sweet > Gr *glykys*, L *dulcis*, sweet⟧ *nontechnical term for* GLYCEROL: also sp. **glyc′er·ine** (-in, -ēn′)

glyc·er·in·ate (glis′ər in āt′) *vt.* **-at′ed, -at′ing** to treat with glycerin —**glyc′er·i·na′tion** *n.*

glyc·er·ol (glis′ər ôl′, -ōl′) *n.* ⟦GLYCER(IN) + -OL[1]⟧ an odorless, colorless, syrupy liquid, $C_3H_5(OH)_3$, prepared by the hydrolysis of fats and oils: it is used as a solvent, skin lotion, food preservative, etc., and in the manufacture of explosives, alkyd resins, etc.: cf. GLYCERIN

glyc·er·yl (glis′ər il′) *n.* ⟦GLYCER(IN) + -YL⟧ the trivalent radical C_3H_5 derived from glycerol

gly·cine (glī′sēn′, -sin; glī sēn′) *n.* ⟦< Gr *glykys*, sweet (see GLYCERIN) + -INE[3]⟧ a sweet nonessential amino acid, $CH_2(NH_2)COOH$: it is the simplest amino acid and does not have mirror image isomeric forms: see AMINO ACID

gly·co- (glī′kō, -kə) ⟦Gr *glyko-* < *glykys*: see GLYCERIN⟧ *combining form* glycerol, sugar, sweet, glycogen, glycine: also, before a vowel, **glyc-** (glīk)

gly·co·gen (glī′kə jən, -jen′) *n.* ⟦prec. + -GEN⟧ a polysaccharide, $(C_6H_{10}O_5)_x$, produced and stored in animal tissues, esp. in the liver and muscles, and changed into glucose as the body needs it

gly·co·gen·e·sis (glī′kō jen′ə sis) *n.* ⟦ModL < prec., after -GENESIS⟧ the formation of glycogen

gly·co·gen·ic (-jen′ik) *adj.* of glycogen or glycogenesis

gly·col (glī′kôl′, -kōl′) *n.* ⟦GLYC(ERIN) + -OL[1]⟧ **1** ETHYLENE GLYCOL **2** any of a group of alcohols with a hydroxyl group attached to each of two carbon atoms, as ethylene glycol

gly·col·ic acid (glī käl′ik) a crystalline acid, $CH_2OHCOOH$, found in sugar cane or prepared by the oxidation of glycol

gly·col·y·sis (glī käl′ə sis) *n.* ⟦GLYCO- + -LYSIS⟧ a complex series of cellular biochemical reactions, not requiring oxygen, that splits glucose, glycogen, or other carbohydrates into pyruvic, or lactic, acid while storing energy in ATP molecules —**gly·co·lyt·ic** (glī′kō lit′ik) *adj.*

gly·co·ne·o·gen·e·sis (glī′kō nē′ō jen′ə sis) *n.* ⟦GLYCO- + NEO- + -GENESIS⟧ the production in the body of carbohydrates, esp. glycogen, from amino acids, fats, and other noncarbohydrates

gly·co·pro·tein (glī′kō prō′tēn′) *n.* any of a class of compounds in which a protein is combined with a carbohydrate group

gly·co·side (glī′kə sīd′) *n.* ⟦Fr < *glycose* (altered after Gr *glykys*), for *glucose*, GLUCOSE + *-ide*, -IDE⟧ any of a group of sugar derivatives, widely distributed in plants, which on hydrolysis yield a sugar and one or more other substances —**gly′co·sid′ic** (-sid′ik) *adj.*

gly·co·su·ri·a (glī′kō soor′ē ə) *n.* ⟦ModL: see GLYCO- & -URIA⟧ the presence of sugar in the urine, often associated with diabetes mellitus —**gly′co·su′ric** *adj.*

glyph (glif) *n.* ⟦Gr *glyphē*, a carving < *glyphein*, to carve, cut < IE base **gleubh-* > CLEAVE[1]⟧ **1** a pictograph or other symbolic character or sign, esp. when cut into a surface or carved in relief **2** *Archit.* a vertical channel or groove —**glyph′ic** *adj.*

glyph·og·ra·phy (glif äg′rə fē) *n.* ⟦< Gr *glyphē* (see prec.) + -GRAPHY⟧ a method of producing a printing plate by engraving on a wax-coated copperplate which is then used to make an electrotype

glyp·tic (glip′tik) *adj.* ⟦Fr *glyptique* < Gr *glyptikos* < Gr *glyptos*, carved < *glyphein*: see GLYPH⟧ having to do with carving or engraving, esp. on gems

glyp·tics (-tiks) *n.* ⟦< prec.⟧ the art of carving or engraving designs on gems, etc.

glyp·to·dont (glip′tə dänt′) *n.* ⟦ModL < Gr *glyptos* (see GLYPTIC) + -ODONT: so called from its fluted teeth⟧ any of a family (Glyptodontidae) of extinct South American edentate mammals, similar to, but much larger than, an armadillo: also **glyp′to·don′**

glyp·to·graph (-graf′) *n.* ⟦< Gr *glyptos* (see GLYPTIC) + -GRAPH⟧ **1** a design cut or engraved on a gem, seal, etc. **2** a gem, seal, etc. so engraved —**glyp·tog·ra·phy** (glip täg′rə fē) *n.*

gm *abbrev.* gram(s)

GM *abbrev.* **1** General Manager **2** general merchandise **3** genetically modified **4** Grand Master

G-man (jē′man′) *n.*, *pl.* **G′-men′** (-men′) ⟦assoc. with *g(overnment) man*, but prob. orig. of officers in the *G* division of the Dublin Police⟧ ☆[Informal] an agent of the Federal Bureau of Investigation

GMAT *abbrev.* Graduate Management Admission Test

Gmc *abbrev.* Germanic

GMT or **Gmt** *abbrev.* Greenwich mean time

gn *abbrev.* guinea(s)

Gn *abbrev. Bible* Genesis

Gnae·us (nī′əs, nā′-) *n.* ⟦L⟧ *Rom. History* a masculine praenomen

gnar or **gnarr** (när) *vi.* **gnarred, gnar′ring** ⟦echoic⟧ [Now Rare] to snarl or growl

gnarl[1] (närl) *n.* ⟦back-form. < GNARLED⟧ a knot on the trunk or branch of a tree —*vt.* to make knotted or twisted; contort —*vi.* to form gnarls

gnarl[2] (närl) *vi.* ⟦freq. of echoic *gnar*⟧ [Obs.] to snarl; growl

gnarled (närld) *adj.* ⟦ult. < ME *knorre*, a knot: see KNUR⟧ **1** knotty and twisted, as the trunk of an old tree **2** roughened, hardened, sinewy, etc., as hands that do rough work Also **gnarl·y** (när′lē) **gnarl′i·er, gnarl′i·est**

gnash (nash) *vt.* ⟦Early ModE for earlier *gnast* < ME *gnasten*, prob. < ON *gnīsta*, to gnash (the teeth), *gnastan*, to gnash, prob. < IE **ghnei-* < base **ghen-* > GNAW⟧ **1** to grind or strike (the teeth) together, as in anger or pain **2** to bite by grinding the teeth —*vi.* to grind the teeth together —*n.* the act of gnashing

gnat (nat) *n.* ⟦ME < OE *gnæt*, akin to Ger dial. *gnatze*, LowG *gnatte* < IE **ghnedh-* < base **ghen-* > GNAW⟧ **1** any of various small insects, esp. certain dipterous flies, which often bite **2** [Brit.] a mosquito —**strain at a gnat** to hesitate or have scruples about trifles: Matt. 23:24 —**gnat′ty** *adj.*

gnath·ic (nath′ik) *adj.* ⟦< Gr *gnathos*, jaw (for IE base see CHIN) + -IC⟧ of the jaw

gnathic index a measurement of the relative amount of protrusion of the jaw, expressed in terms of the ratio of the distance from the nasion to the basion (arbitrarily taken as 100) to the distance from the basion to the middle point of the alveolar process

gna·thite (nā′thīt′, nath′īt′) *n.* ⟦< Gr *gnathos*, jaw + -ITE[1]⟧ a mouth appendage of an arthropod, modified for chewing

gna·thon·ic (nā thän′ik) *adj.* ⟦after *Gnatho*, sycophant in Terence's play *Eunuchus*⟧ [Rare] fawning or flattering

-gna·thous (nə thəs) *combining form* ⟦< Gr *gnathos*: see GNATHIC⟧ having a (specified kind of) jaw *[prognathous]*

gnaw (nô) *vt.* **gnawed, gnawed** or [Rare] **gnawn, gnaw′ing** ⟦ME *gnawen* < OE *gnagen*, akin to Ger *nagen* (OHG *gnagan*) < IE **ghnēgh* < base **ghen-*, to gnaw away, rub away > GNASH, GNAT⟧ **1** to cut, bite, and wear away bit by bit with the teeth **2** to make by gnawing *[to gnaw a hole]* **3** to consume; wear away; corrode **4** to torment, as by constant pain, fear, etc.; harass —*vi.* **1** to bite repeatedly: with *on, away, at*, etc. **2** to produce a biting, consuming, corroding, eroding, tormenting, etc. effect: with *on, at*, etc. *[waves gnawed away at the shore; guilt gnawed at his conscience]*

gnaw·ing (nô′iŋ) *n.* **1** a sensation of dull, constant pain or suffering **2** [*pl.*] pangs, esp. of hunger

gneiss (nīs) *n.* ⟦Ger *gneis* < OHG *gneisto*, a spark, akin to ON *gneisti*, OE *gnast*: from the luster of certain of the components⟧ a coarsegrained metamorphic rock resembling granite, consisting of alternating layers of different minerals, such as feldspar, quartz, mica, and hornblende, and having a banded appearance —**gneiss′ic** *adj.* —**gneiss′oid** *adj.*

GNMA *abbrev.* Government National Mortgage Association: see GINNIE MAE

gnoc·chi (nä′kē, nô′-; *It* nyôk′kē) *n.* ⟦It, pl. of *gnocco*, dumpling, altered < *nocchio*, knot (in wood), prob. < Langobardic; akin to MHG *knoche*, a knot, gnarl: for IE base see KNUCKLE⟧ **1** pasta in the form of small, variously shaped dumplings of flour, and often potato, served with a sauce **2** *pl.* **-chi** or **-chis** one of these dumplings

gnome[1] (nōm) *n.* ⟦Fr < ModL *gnomus* < Gr *gnōmē* (see fol.): so called by PARACELSUS, prob. from the belief that gnomes had occult knowledge of the earth⟧ *Folklore* any of a race of small, misshapen, dwarflike beings that dwell in the earth and guard its treasures —**gnom′ish** *adj.*

gnome[2] (nōm, nō′mē) *n.* ⟦LL, a sentence, maxim < Gr *gnōmē*, thought, judgment, intelligence < *gignōskein*, to KNOW⟧ a wise, pithy saying; maxim

gno·mic (nō′mik, näm′ik) *adj.* ⟦Gr *gnōmikos* < *gnōmē*: see prec.⟧ **1** characterized by aphorisms **2** obscure in meaning; enigmatic

gno·mon (nō′män′) *n.* ⟦L < Gr *gnōmōn*, one who knows or examines, index of a sundial < base of *gignōskein*, to KNOW⟧ **1** a column or pin on a sundial, etc. that casts a shadow indicating the time of day **2** the part of a parallelogram remaining after a similar, smaller parallelogram has been taken from one of its corners

gno·mon·ic (nō män′ik) *adj.* **1** of a gnomon, or sundial **2** of the measurement of time by sundials

-gnomy (-nə mē) ⟦Gr *-gnōmia* < *gnōmē*: see GNOME[2]⟧ *combining form* art or science of judging or determining *[physiognomy]*

gno·sis (nō′sis) *n.* ⟦LL(Ec) < Gr *gnōsis*, knowledge < *gignōskein*, to KNOW⟧ knowledge of spiritual things, esp. a secret and superior knowledge limited to an elite few, such as the Gnostics claimed to have

-gnosis (nō′sis) ⟦< Gr *gnōsis*: see prec.⟧ *combining form* knowledge, recognition *[diagnosis]*

gnos·tic (näs′tik) *adj.* ⟦Gr *gnōstikos* < *gnōsis*: see GNOSIS⟧ **1** of knowledge; specif., of gnosis **2** [*usually* **G-**] of Gnostics or Gnosticism —*n.* ⟦LL(Ec) *gnosticus* < Gr *gnōstikos*⟧ [*usually* **G-**] an adherent of Gnosticism

Gnos·ti·cism (näs′tə siz′əm) *n.* [*often* **g-**] an esoteric system of mystical religious and philosophical doctrines, stressing gnosis as essential to salvation, viewing matter as evil, and variously combining ideas derived from mythology, ancient Greek philosophy, ancient religions, and, eventually, Christianity

gno·to·bi·ot·ics (nō′tō bī ät′iks) *n.* ⟦< Gr *gnōtos*, known (< *gignōskein*, KNOW) + -BIOT(IC) + -ICS⟧ the study of organisms raised in germ-free conditions: often a specific microorganism is also introduced —**gno′to·bi·ot′ic** (-ik) *adj.*

GNP *abbrev.* gross national product

gnu (noo, nyoo) *n.*, *pl.* **gnus** or **gnu** ⟦Fr *gnou* < Xhosa *ngu*⟧ either of two large African antelopes (genus *Connochaetes*) with an oxlike head, horns that curve forward, and a horselike mane and tail; wildebeest

go[1] (gō) *vi.* **went, gone, go′ing** ⟦ME *gon* < OE *gan*, akin to Du *gaan*, Ger *gehen* < IE base **ĝhē-*, orig., to leave behind, go away > Sans *jíhītē*, (he) goes; the pt. WENT is < WEND replacing OE *eode*, ME *yede*⟧ **I.** *indicating motion without reference to destination or point of departure* **1** to move along; travel; proceed *[to go 90 miles an hour]* **2** to be moving *[who goes there?]* **3** *a)* to be in operation, as a mechanism, action, etc. *b)* to work or operate properly; function *[a clock that isn't going]* **4** to behave in a certain way; gesture, act, or make sounds as specified or shown *[the balloon went "pop"]* **5** to take or follow a particular course, line of action, etc.; specif., *a)* to turn out; result *[the war went badly]* *b)* to be guided, regulated, or directed by a procedure, method, etc. *[to go by what someone says]* *c)* to take its course; proceed *[how is the evening going?]*: sometimes used merely to emphasize a following verb *[did you have to go and do that?]* **6** to pass: said of time **7** to pass from person to person [a rumor *went* through the office] **8** to be known or accepted [to *go* by the name of Lindsay] **9** to move about or be in a certain condition or state, usually for some time [to *go* in rags] **10** to pass into a certain condition, state, etc.; become; turn [to *go* mad] **11** to have a certain form, arrangement, etc.; be expressed, phrased, voiced, or sung [as the saying *goes*] **12** to be or act in harmony; fit in [a hat that *goes* well with the dress] **13** to put oneself [to *go* to some trouble] **14** to contribute to a result; tend; help [facts that *go* to prove a case] ☆**15** to have force, validity, acceptance, etc. [that rule still *goes*; anything *goes*] **16** [Informal] to perform in an especially inspired or exciting manner [a jazz band that can really *go*] **II.** *indicating motion from a point of departure* **1** to move off; leave; depart **2** to begin to move off, as in a race: used as a command **3** *a)* to leave a court of justice *b)* to continue (unpunished, unrewarded, unrequited, etc.) **4** to cease to have an effect; come to an end; pass away [the pain has *gone*] **5** to die **6** to be removed or eliminated [the third paragraph had to *go*] **7** to break away; be carried away or broken off [the mast *went* in the storm] **8** to fail; give way [his eyesight is *going*] **9** to be given up or sacrificed [the country house must *go*] **10** to pass into the hands of someone; be allotted, awarded, or given [the prize *goes* to Jean] **11** to be sold (*for* a specified sum) **12** [Informal] to pass bodily waste matter; relieve oneself **III.** *indicating motion toward a place, point, etc.* **1** to move toward a place or person or in a certain direction [to *go* to the back of the room] **2** to move out of sight or out of the presence of the speaker: used as a command **3** to make regularly scheduled trips as specified [a bus that *goes* to Chicago] **4** *a)* to extend, lead, reach, etc. to a place [a road that *goes* to London] *b)* to be able to extend or reach [the belt won't *go* around his waist] **5** to be capable of passing (*through*), fitting (*into*), etc. [it won't *go* through the door] **6** to carry one's case, plan, etc. (*to* an authority) **7** to turn or resort (*to*) [to *go* to war] **8** *a)* to carry one's activity to specified lengths [the pitcher *went* 7 innings] *b)* to extend or reach so far in behavior, action, etc. [to *go* too far in one's protests] **9** to endure; last; hold out **10** to have a particular or regular place or position [the shirts *go* in the top drawer] **11** to approach, enter, or attend, and then engage in or take part in the activities of [you're allowed to *go*, but don't stay out late] ➥Additional meaning is conveyed by the use of a noun governed by *to*, or by a participle [to *go* to college, to *go* swimming]; reason for going is indicated by an infinitive, by *and* with a verb, or by a noun governed by *to* [to *go* to learn, to *go* to breakfast] —*vt.* **1** to travel or proceed along [to *go* Route 90] **2** to bet; wager ☆**3** [Informal] to tolerate; put up with [I can't *go* him] **4** [Informal] to furnish (bail) for an arrested person **5** [Informal] to be willing to pay, bid, etc. (a specified sum) ☆**6** [Informal] to appreciate or enjoy [could you *go* a piece of pie?] **7** [Informal] to say: used to introduce a quotation or paraphrase [He *goes* "When?" and she *goes* "Tonight!"] —*n., pl.* **goes 1** the act of going **2** something that operates successfully; a success [to make a *go* of a marriage] **3** [Informal] the power of going; animation; energy **4** [Informal] a state of affairs ☆**5** [Informal] an agreement, or bargain [is it a *go*?] **6** [Informal] a try; attempt; endeavor **7** [Brit. Informal] a quantity given or taken at one time **8** *Cribbage a)* a call made by a player who cannot play a card because any card in his hand will carry the count above 31 *b)* a point received for playing the last card in any sequence with a count less than 31 —☆***adj.*** ⟦orig. aerospace & astronauts' jargon⟧ [Slang] **1** functioning properly or ready to go **2** all right; OK See also phrases under GOING —**as people** (or **things**) **go** in comparison with how other people (or things) are —☆**from the word "go"** from the outset —**go about 1** to be occupied with; be busy at; do **2** to move from place to place; circulate **3** COME ABOUT (sense 3) (at COME) —**go after** [Informal] to try to catch or get; pursue —**go against** to be or act in opposition to —**go along 1** to proceed; continue **2** to agree; cooperate **3** to accompany: often with *with* —**go around 1** to enclose; surround ☆**2** to be enough to provide a share for each **3** to move from place to place; circulate —**go at 1** to attack **2** to work at —☆**go back on** [Informal] **1** to be faithless or disloyal to; betray **2** to break (a promise, etc.) —**go beyond** to exceed —**go by 1** to pass **2** to be guided or led by **3** to be known or referred to by —**go down 1** to descend; sink; set **2** to suffer defeat; lose **3** to be perpetuated, as in history **4** to fall; decline [prices *went down*] **5** to be swallowed **6** [Informal] to be accepted with approval **7** [Slang] to take place; happen **8** [Brit.] to leave a university, esp. upon graduation —**go down on** [Vulgar Slang] to perform oral sex on —**go for 1** to be regarded or taken as **2** to try to get ☆**3** to advocate; support ☆**4** [Informal] to attack **5** [Informal] to be attracted by; like very much —**go hard with** to cause trouble or pain to —☆**go in for** [Informal] to engage, take part, or indulge in; be given to —**go into 1** to inquire into **2** to take up as a study or occupation **3** to examine or review **4** to be contained in [*5 goes into* 10 twice] —**go in with** to share expenses or obligations with; join —**go it** [Informal] to carry on some activity; proceed; act [to *go it* alone] —**go missing** to become lost or absent, often under suspicious circumstances; disappear: orig. an informal Brit. usage [the ship *went missing* in the dense fog] —**go off 1** to go away; leave, esp. suddenly **2** to explode; detonate **3** to make a noise **4** to happen —**go on 1** to move ahead; proceed; continue **2** to behave **3** to happen; take place **4** [Informal] to chatter or rant **5** *Theater* to make an entrance —☆**go (a person) one better** [Informal] to outdo or surpass (a person) —**go out 1** to come to an end; specif., *a)* to be extinguished *b)* to become outdated **2** *a)* to attend social affairs, the theater, etc. *b)* to have a date or dates [she's agreed to *go out* with him] **3** to go on strike **4** to try out (*for* an athletic team, etc.) **5** *Golf see phrase under* OUT —**go over 1** to examine thoroughly **2** to do again **3** to review ☆**4** [Informal] to be successful —☆**go some** [Informal] to do or achieve quite a lot —**go there** [Informal] to follow a course of action, a line of reasoning, etc.: usually in negative constructions [You're trying to blame me? Don't even *go there!*] —**go through 1** to perform thoroughly **2** to endure; suffer; experience ☆**3** to look through; search ☆**4** to get approval or acceptance **5** to spend —**go through with** to pursue or carry out to the end, despite difficulties, objections, etc. —**go to!** [Archaic] come! indeed!: used to express disapproval, disbelief, etc. —**go together 1** to match; harmonize ☆**2** [Informal] to date only each other —**go under** ☆to fail, as in business —**go up 1** to rise in value, price, etc.; increase **2** [Brit.] to enter a university —**go up in flames** (or **smoke**) to burn —**go with** [Informal] **1** to be a sweetheart of **2** to make use of or proceed with (a particular option) [let's *go with* the blue wallpaper for this room] —**go without** to manage or do without —**have a go at** [Informal] to try; attempt —**let go 1** to set free; let escape **2** to release one's hold or grip **3** to give up; abandon, as one's interest in something **4** to dismiss from a job; fire —**let oneself go 1** to be unrestrained or uninhibited **2** to become negligent in caring for oneself, esp. with respect to one's personal appearance —**no go** [Informal] not possible; without use or value —**on the go** [Informal] in constant motion or action —**to go** [Informal] ☆**1** to be taken out: said of food in a restaurant **2** remaining; still to be completed, etc. [one finished, two *to go*] —☆**what goes?** [Slang] what's happening?

go² (gō) *n.* ⟦SinoJpn⟧ [*also* **G-**] a Japanese game played with black and white stones on a board marked with many intersecting lines

GO *abbrev.* general order(s)

go·a (gō′ə) *n.* ⟦Tibetan *dgoba*⟧ a small, long-haired, brownish-gray antelope (*Procapra picticaudata*) of Tibet

Go·a (gō′ə) state of India, on the SW coast: formerly part of Portuguese India, it later formed (1962-87) with Daman & Diu a territory of India: 1,429 sq mi (3,701 sq km); cap. Panaji —**Go′an** (-ən) ***adj., n.***

goad (gōd) *n.* ⟦ME *gode* < OE *gad*, akin to Langobardic *gaida*, javelin < IE base **ĝhei-*, to throw > Sans *hinvati*, (he) hurls⟧ **1** a sharp-pointed stick used in driving oxen **2** any driving impulse; spur —*vt.* to drive with or as with a goad; prod into action; urge on

☆**go-a·head** (gō′ə hed′) *adj.* **1** advancing; not pausing **2** enterprising; pushing **3** *Sports* that is a score that puts a team into the lead in a game [to score the *go-ahead* run] —*n.* permission or a signal to proceed: usually with *the*

goal (gōl) *n.* ⟦ME *gol*, boundary < ? or akin ? to OE *gælan*, to hinder, impede⟧ **1** the line or place at which a race, trip, etc. is ended **2** an object or end that one strives to attain; aim **3** in certain games, *a)* the line, crossbar, or net over or into which the ball or puck must be passed to score *b)* the act of so scoring *c)* the score made —***SYN.*** INTENTION

goal·keep·er (gōl′kēp′ər) *n.* in certain games, a player stationed at a goal to prevent the ball or puck from crossing or entering it: also **goal·ie** (gōl′ē) or **goal′tend′er** (-ten′dər)

goal kick *Soccer* a free kick by the defensive team from near its goal, awarded after the offensive team plays the ball across the goal line but not into the goal

goal line 1 a line representing the goal in various games **2** *Football* the line separating an end zone from the rest of the playing field

goal post 1 either of the two vertical posts that support a crossbar and form the opening of a goal in soccer, hockey, etc. **2** *Football* the base, crossbar, and uprights that form the goal for a field goal or for an extra point that is kicked

goal·tend·ing (gōl′ten′diŋ) *n.* **1** *Basketball* the illegal touching of a shot after it has begun its downward flight toward the basket or the touching of a free throw at any point in its course **2** *Hockey, Lacrosse* the act of guarding a goal, as a goalkeeper does

go·an·na (gō an′ə) *n.* ⟦altered < IGUANA⟧ an Australian monitor lizard

Goa powder ⟦first used in GOA, *c.* 1852⟧ ARAROBA (sense 1)

go-a·round (gō′ə round′) *n.* GO-ROUND

goat (gōt) *n.* ⟦ME *gote* < OE *gat*, akin to Du *geit*, Ger *geiss* < IE base **ghaido-*, he-goat > L *haedus*, kid goat⟧ **1** *pl.* **goats** or **goat** *a)* any of a genus (*Capra*) of wild or domesticated bovid ruminants with hollow horns ☆*b)* ROCKY MOUNTAIN GOAT **2** a lecherous man ☆**3** [Informal] a person forced to take the blame or punishment for others; scapegoat —☆**get someone's goat** [Informal] to annoy, anger, or irritate someone —**the Goat** Capricornus, the constellation, or Capricorn, the tenth sign of the zodiac

goat antelope any of several bovid ruminants intermediate in their characteristics between goats and antelopes, as the serow, goral, and chamois

☆**goat·ee** (gō tē′) *n.* ⟦< GOAT + -EE¹: from the resemblance to a goat's beard⟧ a small, pointed beard on a man's chin

goat·fish (gōt′fish′) *n., pl.* **-fish′** or **-fish′es** (see FISH) any of a percoid family (Mullidae) of edible, tropical reef fishes with large scales, two barbels on the lower jaw, and bright coloration

goat·herd (gōt′hurd′) *n.* one who herds or tends goats

goat·ish (gōt′ish′) *adj.* **1** like or characteristic of a goat **2** lustful; lecherous —**goat′ish·ly** *adv.* —**goat′ish·ness** *n.*

goats·beard (gōts′bird′) *n.* **1** a hardy plant (*Aruncus dioicus*) of the rose family, with spikes of white flowers in clusters **2** any of a genus (*Tragopogon*) of plants of the composite family, with flower heads and seed heads that resemble large dandelions, as salsify

goat·skin (gōt′skin′) *n.* **1** the skin of a goat **2** leather made from this **3** a container as for wine or water, made of this leather

goat's-rue (gōts′ro͞o′) *n.* ☆**1** a plant (*Tephrosia virginiana*) of the pea family, with yellowish and purple flowers **2** a bushy Old World plant (*Galega* *officinalis*) of the pea family, with thick clusters of white or blue flowers similar to a pea plant's flower

goat·suck·er (gōt′suk′ər) ***n.*** ⟦transl. of L *caprimulgus* < *capri*, goat + *mulgere*, to milk: it was thought to suck milk from goats⟧ any of an order (Caprimulgiformes) of large-mouthed, usually nocturnal birds that feed on insects or fruit; esp., any of the nightjars

gob¹ (gäb) ***n.*** ⟦ME *gobbe* < OFr *gobe*, back-form. < *gobet*: see GOBBET⟧ **1** a lump or mass, as of something soft **2** [*pl.*] [Informal] a large quantity or amount **3** waste material produced in coal mining, consisting of clay, shale, etc.

☆**gob²** (gäb) ***n.*** ⟦< ?⟧ [Slang] a sailor in the U.S. Navy

gob³ (gäb) ***n.*** ⟦< ? Gael *gob*, the mouth, beak⟧ [Brit. Slang] the mouth

gob·bet (gäb′it) ***n.*** ⟦ME *gobet*, small piece < OFr mouthful, prob. < Gaul *gobbo-, mouth⟧ [Now Rare] **1** a fragment or bit, esp. of raw flesh **2** a lump; chunk; mass **3** a mouthful

gob·ble¹ (gäb′əl) ***n.*** ⟦echoic, var. of GABBLE⟧ the characteristic throaty sound made by a male turkey —***vi.*** **-bled**, **-bling** to make this sound

gob·ble² (gäb′əl) ***vt., vi.*** **-bled**, **-bling** ⟦prob. freq. formation on base of OFr *gober*, to swallow < *gobet*, GOBBET⟧ **1** to eat quickly and greedily **2** to seize eagerly; snatch Often with *up*

☆**gob·ble·dy·gook** (gäb′əl dē go͝ok′, -də-; -go͞ok′) ***n.*** ⟦first used in current sense by Maury Maverick (1895-1954), U.S. Congressman: ? echoic of turkey cries⟧ [Informal] talk or writing that is wordy, pompous, etc. and largely incomprehensible or meaningless: also sp. **gob′ble·de·gook′**

gob·bler (gäb′lər) ***n.*** ⟦GOBBL(E) + -ER⟧ a male turkey

gob·by (gäb′ē) ***adj.*** ⟦< GOB³⟧ [Brit. Slang] talkative, outspoken, mouthy, etc.

Gob·e·lin (gäb′ə lin, gō′bə-; *Fr* gô blan′) ***adj.*** designating, of, or like a kind of tapestry made at the Gobelin works in Paris —***n.*** Gobelin tapestry

go-be·tween (gō′bē twēn′) ***n.*** a person who deals with each of two sides in making arrangements between them; intermediary

Go·bi (gō′bē) desert plateau in E Asia, chiefly in Mongolia: *c.* 500,000 sq mi (1,294,995 sq km)

gob·let (gäb′lit) ***n.*** ⟦ME *gobelet* < OFr < *gobel* < ? Bret *gob*, *kop*, cup⟧ **1** [Archaic] a bowl-shaped drinking container without handles **2** a drinking glass with a base and stem

gob·lin (gäb′lin) ***n.*** ⟦ME *gobelin* < OFr < ML *gobelinus* < VL *cobalus < Gr *kobalos*, sprite⟧ *Folklore* an evil or mischievous spirit, often represented in pictures as humanlike and ugly or misshapen in form

☆**go·bo** (gō′bō) ***n., pl.*** **-bos** or **-boes** ⟦< ?⟧ **1** a black screen used to reduce light falling on a camera lens **2** a screen to shield a microphone from unwanted sounds

gob·smacked (gäb′smakt′) ***adj.*** ⟦< Brit slang *gob*, the mouth + SMACK²⟧ [Brit. Informal] astounded, stunned, etc.

go·by (gō′bē) ***n., pl.*** **-bies** or **-by** ⟦L *gobio*, *gobius*, gudgeon < Gr *kōbios*⟧ any of a family (Gobiidae) of small, predatory, spiny-finned percoid fishes of tropical and subtropical seas: the pelvic fins are united as a suction disk that clings to rocky surfaces

go-by (gō′bī′) ***n.*** [Informal] a passing by; esp., an intentional disregard or slight: chiefly in **give (or get) the go-by** to slight (or be slighted)

go-cart (gō′kärt′) ***n.*** **1** *former term for* a child's walker or stroller **2** a former type of light carriage **3** KART (sense 2)

god (gäd, gôd) ***n.*** ⟦ME < OE, akin to Ger *gott*, Goth *guth*, prob. < IE base *ĝhau-, to call out to, invoke > Sans *havaté*, (he) calls upon⟧ **1** any of various beings conceived of as supernatural, immortal, and having special powers over the lives and affairs of people and the course of nature; deity, esp. a male deity: typically considered objects of worship **2** an image that is worshiped; idol **3** a person or thing deified or excessively honored and admired **4** [**G-**] in monotheistic religions, the creator and ruler of the universe, regarded as eternal, infinite, all-powerful, and all-knowing; Supreme Being; the Almighty —***interj.*** [*usually* **G-**] used variously, and in interjectional phrases, as an oath and as an expression of relief, determination, surprise, anger, etc. [*God, I'm glad that's over! I'll see this through, by god! God almighty! my God!*] —**God willing** if God is willing: used to express a wish

Go·da·va·ri (gō dä′və rē) river in central India, flowing from the Western Ghats into the Bay of Bengal: *c.* 900 mi (1,448 km)

god·child (gäd′chīld′) ***n., pl.*** **-chil′dren** (-chil′drən) ⟦ME⟧ the person for whom a godparent is sponsor

god·damned (gäd′damd′, -dam′) ***adj.*** strongly cursed or damned: used as a curse or strong intensive: often shortened to **god′damn′** or **god′dam′** (-dam′)

God·dard (gäd′ərd), **Robert H(utchings)** 1882-1945; U.S. physicist & rocket engineer

god·daugh·ter (gäd′dôt′ər) ***n.*** ⟦ME *goddoughter* < OE *goddohtor*⟧ a female godchild

god·dess (gäd′is) ***n.*** ⟦ME *godesse*⟧ **1** a female god **2** a woman greatly admired, as for her beauty **3** [*also* **G-**] a feminine deity proposed by some as having been worshiped from ancient times and as variously present as a goddess in many of the world's myths and religions: often with *the*

Gö·del (gurd′'l), **Kurt** (kurt) 1906-78; U.S. mathematician, born in Czechoslovakia

Gödel's theorem either of two theorems published by the mathematician Kurt Gödel in 1931 that prove all mathematical systems are incomplete in that their truth or consistency can only be proved using a system of a higher order: also called **Gödel's proof** or **Gödel's incompleteness theorem**

☆**go-dev·il** (gō′dev′əl) ***n.*** **1** a rotary tool for scraping out obstructions from an oil pipeline **2** a metal weight dropped into an oil well to set off an explosive charge **3** a railroad handcar

god·fa·ther (gäd′fä′*th*ər) ***n.*** **1** a male godparent **2** a man who acts as an advisor or mentor to someone ☆**3** [*often* **G-**] *a)* [Informal] the head of a Mafia family or syndicate *b)* [Slang] any person having much influence or authority in some area

God-fear·ing (gäd′fir′iŋ) ***adj.*** [*occas.* **g-**] **1** fearing God **2** devout; pious

God·for·sak·en (-fər sā′kən) ***adj.*** [*also* **g-**] **1** depraved; wicked **2** desolate; forlorn

God·frey (gäd′frē) ***n.*** ⟦OFr *Godefrei* < OHG *Godafrid* < *god*, GOD + *fridu*, peace: hence, lit., peace (of) God⟧ a masculine name: equiv. Ger. *Gottfried*

God-giv·en (gäd′giv′ən) ***adj.*** [*occas.* **g-**] **1** given by God **2** very welcome; suitable or opportune

god·head (gäd′hed′) ***n.*** ⟦ME *godhede*⟧ **1** godhood; divinity **2** [**G-**] God: usually with *the*

god·hood (-ho͝od′) ***n.*** ⟦ME *godhod*: see -HOOD⟧ the state or quality of being a god; divinity

Go·di·va (gə dī′və) ***n.*** *Eng. Legend* an 11th-cent. noblewoman of Coventry who, on the dare of her husband, rode naked through the streets on horseback so that he would abolish a heavy tax

god·less (gäd′lis) ***adj.*** ⟦ME *godles* < OE *godleas*⟧ **1** denying the existence of God or a god; irreligious; atheistic **2** impious; wicked —**god′less·ness** ***n.***

god·like (gäd′līk′) ***adj.*** ⟦ME⟧ like or suitable to God or a god; divine

god·ling (gäd′liŋ) ***n.*** ⟦see -LING¹⟧ a minor god

god·ly (gäd′lē) ***adj.*** **-li·er**, **-li·est** ⟦ME: see GOD & -LY¹⟧ **1** of or from God; divine **2** devoted to God; pious; devout; religious —**god′li·ness** ***n.***

god·moth·er (gäd′mu*th*′ər) ***n.*** **1** a female godparent **2** a woman who acts as an advisor or mentor to someone

go·down (gō′doun′, gō doun′) ***n.*** ⟦Anglo-Ind < Malay *gudang* < Telugu *giḍaṅgi*⟧ in the Far East, a warehouse

god·par·ent (gäd′per′ənt, -par′-) ***n.*** a person who sponsors a child, as at baptism, and, traditionally, assumes responsibility for the child's faith; godmother or godfather

God's acre a burial ground, esp. one in a churchyard

god·send (gäd′send′) ***n.*** ⟦contr. of *God's send*: ME *sande*, mission, message < OE *sand* < *sendan*, to SEND⟧ anything unexpected and needed or desired that comes at the opportune moment, as if sent by God

god·son (gäd′sun′) ***n.*** a male godchild

God·speed (gäd′spēd′) ***n., interj.*** ⟦contr. of *God speed you*: see SPEED, ***vt.*** 5⟧ success; good fortune: a wish for the welfare of a person starting on a journey or venture

Godthåb (gôt′hôp′) capital of Greenland, on the SW coast

Go·du·nov (gô′do͞o nôf′), **Bo·ris Feo·do·ro·vich** (bô rēs′ fyô′dô rô′vich) 1551?-1605; czar of Russia (1598-1605)

God·win¹ (gäd′win) ***n.*** ⟦OE *Godewine*, friend (of) God: see EDWIN⟧ a masculine name

God·win² (gäd′win) **1 Mary Wollstonecraft** *see* WOLLSTONECRAFT, Mary **2 William** 1756-1836; Eng. political philosopher & writer

Godwin Austen ⟦after H. H. *Godwin-Austen* (1834-1923), Brit geologist who first surveyed it⟧ mountain in the Karakoram range, N Jammu and Kashmir, near the border with Xinjiang: second highest mountain in the world: 28,251 ft (8,611 m): commonly called *K2*

god·wit (gäd′wit) ***n.*** ⟦orig. prob. echoic of cry⟧ any of a genus (*Limosa*, family Scolopacidae) of brownish shorebirds with a long bill that curves slightly upward

Goeb·bels (gö′bəls), **Joseph (Paul)** 1897-1945; Ger. Nazi propaganda minister

go·er (gō′ər) ***n.*** one that goes

Goe·ring or **Gö·ring** (gö′riŋ), **Her·mann (Wilhelm)** (her′män′) 1893-1946; Ger. Nazi field marshal

goes (gōz) ***vi., vt.*** *3d pers. sing., pres. indic., of* GO¹

Goe·thals (gō′thəlz), **George Washington** 1858-1928; U.S. army officer & engineer: in charge of building the Panama Canal (1907-14)

Goe·the (gö′tə; *E* gur′tə, gā′tə), **Jo·hann Wolf·gang von** (yō′hän′ vôlf′ gäŋk′ fôn) 1749-1832; Ger. poet & dramatist

goe·thite (gö′thīt′, gur′-; *also*, gō′-) ***n.*** ⟦Ger *göthit*, after prec., in honor of his studies in geology and mineralogy⟧ a hard, brownish, orthorhombic mineral, FeO(OH), an ore of iron; iron hydroxide

☆**go·fer** or **go-fer** (gō′fər) ***n.*** ⟦from being asked to *go for* whatever is needed⟧ [Slang] an employee who performs minor or menial tasks such as running errands

gof·fer (gäf′ər, gôf′-) ***vt.*** ⟦Fr *gaufrer*, to crimp < *gaufre*, waffle < Du *wafel*, WAFFLE¹⟧ to pleat, crimp, or flute (cloth, paper, etc.) —***n.*** **1** an iron used to goffer cloth, etc. **2** the act of pleating or fluting; also, a series of pleats, crimps, or flutes: also **gof′fer·ing**

Gog and Ma·gog (gäg′ ənd mā′gäg′) ⟦Heb *gog*, *magog*: see Ezek. 38:2⟧ *Bible personification of* the nations that, under Satan, are to war against the kingdom of God: Rev. 20:8

☆**go-get·ter** (gō′get′ər) ***n.*** [Informal] an enterprising and aggressive person who usually achieves personal ambitions

gog·gle (gäg′əl) ***vi.*** **-gled**, **-gling** ⟦ME *gogelen*, to look obliquely, freq. formation prob. < Celt base, as in Ir *gog*, a nod, Welsh *gogi*, to shake⟧ **1** *a)* to stare with bulging or wide-open eyes *b)* to roll the eyes **2** *a)* to bulge or open wide in a stare *b)* to roll: said of the eyes —***n.*** **1** a staring with bulging eyes **2** [*pl.*] any of various types of protective eyeglasses, typically fitted with side guards, special lenses, etc. [ski *goggles*] —*adj.* bulging or rolling: said of the eyes

gog·gle-eye (gäg′əl ī′) *n.* ☆any of various fishes with large, bulging eyes, as the rock bass

gog·gle-eyed (-īd′) *adj.* having eyes that bulge or roll

gog·gler (gäg′lər) *n.* **1** one who goggles **2** GOGGLE-EYE

Gogh, Vincent van *see* VAN GOGH, Vincent

gog·let (gäg′lit) *n.* ⟦Port *gorgoleta*, dim., ult. < L *gurgulio*, gullet, akin to *gurges*: see GORGE⟧ a porous earthenware container with a long neck, for keeping water cool by evaporation

go-go (gō′gō′) *adj.* ⟦short for *à gogo* < Fr, in plenty, ad lib., in clover < *à*, to + *gogo*, abundance, jocular redupl. of *gogue*, joy, prob. of echoic orig.⟧ **1** of dancing to rock music, as in discothèques **2** of a dancer, often semi-nude, performing erotic movements to rock music, as in a bar **3** [Informal] *Business, Finance a)* of or characterized by dramatic appreciation or expansion [the *go-go* years for U.S. automakers] *b)* of or characterized by aggressive, often highly speculative, buying and selling [*go-go* mutual funds, a *go-go* stock market]

Go·gol (gô′gôl; *E* gō′gəl), **Ni·ko·lai Va·sil·ie·vich** (nē′kô lī′ vä sēl′yə vich) 1809-52; Russ. novelist & dramatist, born in Ukraine

Goi·â·ni·a (goi ä′nē ə) city in central Brazil; capital of Goiás state

Goi·ás (goi äs′) state of central Brazil: 131,773 sq mi (341,291 sq km); cap. Goiânia

Goi·del·ic (goi del′ik) *n.* ⟦< OIr *Góidel*: see GAEL⟧ the subdivision of the Celtic languages that includes Scottish Gaelic, Irish, and Manx —*adj.* designating or of this group of languages or the peoples that speak them

go·ing (gō′iŋ) *n.* **1** the act of one who goes: usually used in compounds [opera-*going*] **2** a leaving; departure **3** the condition of the ground or land as it affects traveling, walking, etc. **4** circumstances affecting progress **5** [Slang] current situation or course of events in any given area, time, or sphere [tough *going* in the stock market these days] —*adj.* **1** moving; running; working **2** conducting its business successfully [a *going* concern] **3** in existence or available [the best bet *going*] **4** commonly accepted; current [the *going* rate for plumbers] —**be going to** to be intending to; will or shall —☆**get going** [Informal] to start; begin —☆**get someone going** [Slang] to cause a person to be excited, angry, etc. —**going on** [Informal] nearing or nearly (a specified age or time) [a child who is nine, *going on* ten] —☆**have something going for one** [Slang] to have something working to one's advantage

go·ing-ov·er (-ō′vər) *n.* [Informal] ☆**1** an inspection or examination, esp. a thorough one ☆**2** a severe scolding or beating

go·ings-on (gō′iŋz än′) *pl.n.* [Informal] actions or events, esp. when regarded with disapproval

goi·ter (goit′ər) *n.* ⟦Fr *goitre*, back-form. < OFr *goitron*, throat < VL **gutturio* < L *guttur*, throat: see GUTTURAL⟧ an enlargement of the thyroid gland, often visible as a swelling in the lower part of the front of the neck: also [Chiefly Brit.] **goi′tre** —**goi′trous** *adj.*

☆**go-kart** (gō′kärt′) *n.* KART (sense 2)

Go·lan Heights (gō′län′), **the** hilly region northeast of the Sea of Galilee: part of SW Syria until occupation (1967) & annexation (1981) by Israel: also **the Golan**

Gol·con·da[1] (gäl kän′də) *n.* ⟦after the fol.⟧ a source of great wealth, as a mine

Gol·con·da[2] (gäl kän′də) ancient city, now ruins, in SC India, near Hyderabad: noted for diamond cutting in the 16th cent.

gold (gōld) *n.* ⟦ME < OE, akin to Ger *gold*, ON *goll* < IE base **ghel-*, to shine, gleam > GLOW, YELLOW⟧ **1** a heavy, yellow, inert, metallic chemical element that is highly ductile and malleable: it is a precious metal and is used in the manufacture of coins, jewelry, alloys, etc.: symbol, Au; at. no. 79: see the periodic table of elements in the Reference Supplement **2** *a)* gold coin *b)* money; riches; wealth **3** the bright yellow color of gold **4** something regarded as having the value, brilliance, etc. of gold [a voice of pure *gold*] **5** *short for* GOLD MEDAL —*adj.* **1** of, made of, like, or plated with gold **2** having the color of gold **3** secured by or redeemable in gold; based on gold ☆**4** ⟦after the gold-plated copy awarded to the performer(s)⟧ designating a record, tape, disc, etc. which has registered sales of a specified number, as 500,000, or a specified value, as $1,000,000: *gold* reflects a lesser number or value than *platinum*

gold·beat·er (gōld′bēt′ər) *n.* a person who pounds gold into thin leaves for use in gilding —**gold′beat′ing** *n.*

☆**gold beetle** any of various gold-colored beetles

☆**gold·brick** (-brik′) *n.* **1** [Informal] a worthless metal bar gilded and sold as solid gold in a swindle **2** [Informal] anything worthless passed off as genuine or valuable **3** [Mil. Slang] a person who tries to avoid work; shirker; loafer: also **gold′brick′er** —*vi.* [Mil. Slang] to shirk a duty or avoid work; loaf

☆**gold·bug** (-bug′) *n.* GOLD BEETLE

gold bug ⟦see BUG[1] (*n.* 6a)⟧ [Informal] one who buys, or advocates buying, gold as protection against an anticipated collapse in the value of currency, stocks, etc.

☆**gold certificate** [Historical] a type of U.S. paper currency redeemable in gold

☆**Gold Coast**[1] [Informal] a district where rich people live, esp. along a shore, as of a lake

Gold Coast[2] former British territory in W Africa, on the Gulf of Guinea: see GHANA

☆**gold digger** [Informal] a woman who in her personal relations with men tries to get money and gifts from them

gold dust gold in very small bits or as a powder, the normal state in which it is found in placer mining

gold·en (gōl′dən) *adj.* ⟦ME *golden* < *gold* (for earlier *gilden*)⟧ **1** made of, containing, or yielding gold **2** having the color and luster of gold; bright-yellow **3** very valuable or precious; excellent **4** prosperous and joyful; flourishing **5** favorable; auspicious [a *golden* opportunity] **6** marking or celebrating the 50th year [a *golden* anniversary] **7** gifted or favored in a way that promises future success [a new employee has become management's *golden* boy] **8** richly mellow, as a voice —**gold′en·ly** *adv.* —**gold′en·ness** *n.*

Golden Age ⟦after L (Ovid) *aurea aetas*⟧ **1** *Class. Myth.* the early age in which mankind was ideally happy, prosperous, and innocent **2** [**g- a-**] a period of great progress, prosperity, or cultural achievement **3** [**g- a-**] of or for golden agers

golden ag·er (ā′jər) [*also* **G- A-**] [Informal] an elderly person, specif. one who is 65 or older and retired

☆**golden aster** any of a genus (*Chrysopsis*) of North American plants of the composite family, with golden ray flowers

☆**golden bantam corn** a variety of sweet corn with bright-yellow kernels on small ears

golden calf **1** *Bible* a calf of gold worshiped by the Israelites while Moses was at Mount Sinai: 1 Kings 12:28 **2** riches regarded as an object of worship and greedy pursuit

Golden Delicious a variety of yellow apple first grown in W.Va.

gold·en·doo·dle (gōl′dən do͞od′'l) *n.* ⟦< GOLDEN RETRIEVER + POODLE; infl. by LABRADOODLE⟧ a dog crossbred from a golden retriever and a poodle

golden eagle a large, strong eagle (*Aquila chrysaetos*) found in mountainous districts of the Northern Hemisphere, with brown feathers on the back of its head and neck

gold·en·eye (gōl′dən ī′) *n., pl.* **-eyes′** or **-eye′** a swift, diving wild duck (*Bucephala clangula*) of North America and the Old World, with yellow eyes, a dark-green back, and a white breast

Golden Fleece *Gr. Myth.* the fleece of gold that hung in a sacred grove at Colchis, guarded by a dragon until taken away by Jason and the Argonauts

Golden Gate ⟦so named (1846) by J. C. FRÉMONT after the GOLDEN HORN in anticipation of the flow of Asian riches through the strait⟧ strait between San Francisco Bay and the Pacific: 2 mi (3.2 km) wide

☆**golden glow** a tall garden black-eyed Susan (*Rudbeckia laciniata*) with numerous globular, yellow ray flower heads

golden handshake ⟦from the *handshake* as a gesture of farewell⟧ [Informal] payment offered to induce an employee to retire early

Golden Horde ⟦from the splendors of their leader's camp⟧ the Mongol armies that invaded Europe in 1237 and, under the Khans, ruled Russia for two centuries

Golden Horn arm of the Bosporus in European Turkey, forming the harbor of Istanbul

golden mean ⟦transl. of L (Horace) *aurea mediocritas*⟧ **1** the safe, prudent way between extremes; moderation **2** *a)* GOLDEN RATIO (sense 1) *b)* GOLDEN SECTION (sense 1)

golden nematode a small, European nematode worm (*Heterodera rostochiensis*) now found in the E U.S. as a destructive potato parasite

☆**golden oldie** [Informal] something from the past, esp. a popular song, that continues to be popular

golden parachute [Informal] a very large sum of money or other liberal compensation given as severance pay by a corporation to a top executive

golden pheasant a pheasant (*Chrysolophus pictus*) originally of China and Tibet, with brightly colored feathers and an orange crest

gold·en·rain tree (gōl′dən rān′) a small, deciduous Asian tree (*Koelreuteria paniculata*) of the soapberry family having small yellow flowers and papery fruit pods

golden ratio **1** a ratio, equal to 1.61803+: it serves as the basis for the GOLDEN SECTION (sense 1): symbol, φ or τ **2** GOLDEN SECTION (sense 1)

golden retriever any of a breed of medium-sized hunting dog with hanging ears and a dense, golden coat feathered on the legs, neck, and tail

gold·en·rod (gōl′dən räd′) *n.* ⟦descriptive⟧ any of a genus (*Solidago*) of chiefly North American plants of the composite family, typically with long, branching stalks bearing one-sided clusters of small, yellow flower heads through the late summer and fall

golden rule, the [*often* **G- R-**] the precept that one should behave toward others as one would want others to behave toward oneself: see Matt. 7:12; Luke 6:31

☆**gold·en·seal** (-sēl′) *n.* an American plant (*Hydrastis canadensis*) of the buttercup family, with large, round leaves and a thick, yellow rootstock, formerly much used in medicine

golden section **1** a proportion based on the GOLDEN RATIO (sense 1): held to be detectable in nature, classical architecture, Renaissance art, etc. and purported to be aesthetically pleasing to the eye (Ex.: in the line ACB, if AB is to AC as AC is to CB) **2** GOLDEN RATIO (sense 1)

Golden State *name for* CALIFORNIA

Golden Triangle region in Southeast Asia, where the borders of Laos, Myanmar, & Thailand meet: regarded as a major area of cultivation of opium poppies used for heroin production

golden wedding a 50th wedding anniversary

gold-filled (gōld′fild′) *adj.* made of a base metal overlaid with gold

gold·finch (gōld′finch′) ***n.*** ⟦ME < OE *goldfinc*: see GOLD & FINCH⟧ any of various yellow-and-black finches; esp., a Eurasian songbird (*Carduelis carduelis*) or an American species (*C. tristis*)

gold·fish (-fish′) ***n.***, *pl.* **-fish′** a small, golden-yellow or orange, freshwater cyprinoid fish (*Carassius auratus*) often kept in ponds and aquariums and represented by numerous domestic varieties

gold foil ⟦ME *golde foyle*⟧ gold beaten into thin sheets slightly thicker than gold leaf

Gold·i·locks (gōl′dē läks′) ***n.*** **1** ⟦so called because of her blond, or *golden*, hair⟧ a little girl in a folk tale who visits the home of three bears **2** ⟦from the color of its flowers⟧ [**g-**] a European plant (*Linosyris vulgaris*) of the composite family, with clusters of small, yellow flowers

Gol·ding (gōl′ diŋ), Sir **William (Gerald)** 1911-93; Brit. writer

gold leaf gold beaten into very thin sheets, used for gilding

gold medal a medal, typically gold in color or composition, given as an award to the person winning a competition, race, etc.

gold mine **1** a mine from which gold ore is obtained **2** [Informal] a source of something very valuable or profitable

Gol·do·ni (gôl dô′nē), **Car·lo** (kär′lô) 1707-93; It. dramatist

gold plate **1** tableware made of or plated with gold **2** a plating of or with gold *[a pen with accents in gold plate]*

gold-plate (gōld′plāt′) ***vt.*** **-plat′ed**, **-plat′ing** to coat with gold, esp. by electroplating

gold-plat·ed (-plāt′id) ***adj.*** **1** plated with gold **2** [Informal] expensive, splendid, etc., often to an extravagant degree

☆**gold reserve** the gold held by the government of a country, specif., when used, as formerly in the U.S., to secure its currency, support credit expansion, make payments to foreign governments, etc.

☆**gold rush** a rush of people to territory where gold has recently been discovered, as to California in 1849

gold·smith (gōld′smith′) ***n.*** ⟦ME < OE⟧ an artisan who makes and repairs articles of gold

Gold·smith (gōld′smith), **Oliver** 1730?-74; Brit. poet, playwright, & novelist, born in Ireland

goldsmith beetle ☆a large, bright-yellow American scarab beetle (*Cotalpa lanigera*) that feeds on tree foliage

☆**gold standard** **1** a monetary standard solely in terms of gold, in which the basic currency unit is made equal to and redeemable by a specified quantity of gold **2** a thing that serves as a model or standard of excellence against which other things of its type may be measured or judged

☆**gold star** a small, gold-colored star displayed to represent a member of the U.S. armed forces killed in war

gold·stone (gōld′stōn′) ***n.*** AVENTURINE (sense 1)

gold·thread (-thred′) ***n.*** ☆any of a genus (*Coptis*) of North American plants of the buttercup family, esp. a small perennial (*C. groenlandica*) with white flowers and yellow rhizomes, used in folk medicine

gold·tone or **gold-tone** (gōld′tōn′) ***adj.*** made to resemble gold in color, sheen, etc. *[goldtone earrings]*

Gold·wyn (gōld′win′), **Samuel** (born *Schmuel* or *Shmuel Gelbfisz*) 1882-1974; U.S. film producer, born in Poland

go·lem (gō′ləm, -lem′) ***n.*** ⟦Heb, orig., embryo; later, monster (> Yiddish *goylem*, dolt), akin to Ar *ghulām*, lad⟧ *Jewish Folklore* a human being artificially created by cabalistic rites

golf (gôlf, gälf) ***n.*** ⟦LME (Scot) *golf, gouff*, usually deriv. < Du *kolf*, a club, but all early forms have *g-*, and the *-l-* may be unhistoric, hence < ? Scot *gowf*, to strike < *gowf*, a blow (with the open hand)⟧ an outdoor game played on a large course with a small, hard ball and a set of clubs, the object being to hit the ball into each of a series of nine or eighteen holes in turn, using the fewest possible strokes —***vi.*** to play golf —**golf′er** ***n.***

golf ball a small, hard ball with a seamless, dimpled covering, used in the game of golf

golf cart **1** a lightweight cart with two wheels and a long, cylindrical body, used to carry a set of golf clubs **2** a small, electric, carlike vehicle designed to carry two golfers and their clubs around a golf course

golf club **1** an implement consisting of a long, slender shaft and a metal or wooden head, used in golf to hit the ball: see also WOOD[1] (***n.*** 6), IRON (***n.*** 6), PUTTER[2] (sense 1) **2** an organization owning a golf course, clubhouse, etc., for the use of its members

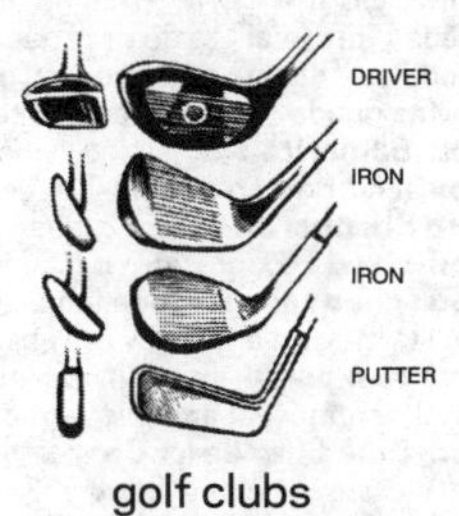

golf clubs

golf course a tract of land for playing golf, with tees, greens, fairways, hazards, etc.: often **golf links**

Gol·gi apparatus (gôl′jē, gōl′jē) ⟦after C. *Golgi* (1844-1926), It neurologist, who first observed it (1909)⟧ a network of stainable cytoplasmic fibers, rods, granules, etc., that can collect proteins and secrete them outside the cell: also **Golgi body**

Gol·go·tha (gäl′gə thə, gôl′-) ***n.*** ⟦LL(Ec) < Gr(Ec) *golgotha* < Aram *gulgulta* < Heb *gulgolet*, skull, place of a skull⟧ *Bible* the place where Jesus was crucified; Calvary: Mark 15:22

gol·iard (gōl′yərd) ***n.*** ⟦contr. < ME *goliardeis* (< OFr *goliardois*) & OFr *goliart*, glutton < *gole* (< L *gula*: see GULLET) + *-art*, -ARD⟧ any of a class of wandering students of the late Middle Ages who wrote satirical Latin verse and often served as minstrels and jesters —**gol·iar·dic** (gōl yär′dik) ***adj.***

Go·li·ath (gə lī′əth) ***n.*** ⟦LL(Ec) < Heb *golyat*⟧ *Bible* the Philistine giant killed by the young David with a stone shot from a sling: 1 Sam. 17:4, 49

goliath grouper a large grouper (*Epinephelus itajara*) found in the Caribbean and the W Atlantic

gol·li·wog (gäl′ē wôg′, -wäg′) ***n.*** ⟦< *Golliwogg* (arbitrary formation, ? related to WOG, ? after POLLIWOG), the name of such a character in a series of children's books by Florence K. Upton (1873-1922)⟧ a type of grotesque rag doll with a black face and woolly hair

gol·ly (gäl′ē) ***interj.*** used to express surprise, wonder, etc.: orig. a euphemism for *God*

go·losh or **go·loshe** (gə läsh′) ***n.*** *Brit. sp. of* GALOSH

gom·been (man) (gäm bēn′) in Ireland, *a)* a shopkeeper who engages in usury on the side *b)* an avaricious and opportunistic businessman, entrepreneur, etc.

gom·broon (gäm bro͞on′) ***n.*** ⟦after *Gombroon* (Bandar Abbas), town on the Persian Gulf⟧ a type of white, semitransparent Persian pottery

Go·mel (gô′mel) city in SE Belarus

gom·er·al (gäm′ər əl) ***n.*** ⟦< ? obs. *gome*, a man (< OE *guma*: see HOMO[1]) + *-(e)rel*, depreciatory suffix < OFr *-erel*⟧ [Scot.] a simpleton; fool

Go·mor·rah (gə môr′ə) ***n.*** ⟦Gr *Gomorrha* < Heb⟧ *see* SODOM

Gom·pers (gäm′pərz), **Samuel** 1850-1924; U.S. labor leader, born in England

gom·pho·sis (gäm fō′sis) ***n.***, *pl.* **-ses′** (-sēz′) ⟦ModL < Gr *gomphōsis*, a nailing together < *gomphos*, a nail, bolt, tooth: see COMB[1]⟧ an immovable joint in which a bone or other hard part, as a tooth, fits into a socket

go·mu·ti (gō mo͞ot′ē) ***n.*** ⟦Malay *gemuti*⟧ **1** a Malayan palm (*Arenga pinnata*) with feathery leaves and a sweet sap from which a crude sugar and an alcoholic beverage, arrack, are made **2** the wiry fibers from the leaf stalks of this palm, used in making ropes, brushes, etc.

-gon (gän, gən) ⟦Gr *-gōnon* < *gōnia*, an angle: see KNEE⟧ *combining form* a figure having (a specified number of) angles *[pentagon]*

go·nad (gō′nad′) ***n.*** ⟦< ModL *gonas* (pl. *gonades*) < Gr *gonē*, a seed, generation < IE **gon-* < base **ĝen-*, to produce > GENUS⟧ an organ or gland in animals that produces reproductive cells; esp., an ovary or testis —**go·nad′al** ***adj.***

go·nad·o·tro·pin (gō nad′ō trō′pin) ***n.*** a hormone that supports and stimulates the function and growth of the gonads: also **go·nad′o·tro′phin** (-fin) —**go·nad′o·trop′ic** (-träp′ik) ***adj.***, **go·nad′o·troph′ic** (-träf′ik, -trō′fik)

Gon·cha·rov (gun′chə rôf′), **I·van A·lek·san·dro·vich** (i vän′ ä′lyek sän′drə vich′) 1812-91; Russ. novelist

Gon·court (gōn ko͞or′) **1 Ed·mond (Louis Antoine Huot de)** (ed mōn′) 1822-96; Fr. novelist & art critic **2 Jules (Alfred Huot de)** (zhül′) 1830-70; Fr. novelist & art critic: brother of Edmond, with whom he collaborated

Gond (gänd, gōnd) ***n.*** ⟦< native (Gondi) name⟧ a member of a group of aboriginal peoples of central India

Gon·di (gän′dē, gōn′-) ***n.*** the Dravidian language spoken by the Gonds, consisting of many dialects

gon·do·la (gän′də lə, gän dō′lə) ***n.*** ⟦It (Venetian) < Rhaeto-Romanic (dial.) *gondolá*, to rock⟧ **1** a long, narrow boat for a few passengers used on the canals of Venice, having a high, pointed prow and stern and propelled by a single long oar at the stern ☆**2** a flat-bottomed river barge ☆**3** a railroad freight car with no top and, often, with low sides: also **gondola car** ☆**4** a cabin suspended under an airship or balloon, for holding the motors, instruments, passengers, etc. ☆**5** a car suspended from and moved along a cable, for holding passengers **6** a car for riders on a Ferris wheel or other amusement-park ride

gondola

gon·do·lier (gän′də lir′) ***n.*** ⟦Fr < It *gondoliere* < *gondola*: see prec.⟧ a person who propels a gondola

Gond·wa·na (gänd wä′nə) ⟦after the *Gondwana Series*, an extensive tillite deposit in *Gondwana*, region in central India < GOND⟧ the Mesozoic landmass in the Southern Hemisphere that included what are now South America, Africa, Australia, and Antarctica: it and Laurasia were the result of the splitting of Pangea: often called **Gond·wa·na·land′** (-land′)

gone (gôn, gän) ***vi.***, ***vt.*** *pp. of* GO[1] —***adj.*** ⟦ME *gon* < OE *gan*⟧ **1** moved away; departed **2** ruined **3** lost **4** dead **5** faint; weak **6** used up; consumed **7** ago; past ☆**8** [Slang] *a)* excellent; first-rate *b)* enraptured or inspired *c)* pregnant —**far gone** **1** in an advanced state of deterioration **2** nearly dead —**gone on** [Informal] infatuated with

gon·ef (gän′əf) ***n.*** [Slang] *alt. sp. of* GANEF

gon·er (gôn′ər) ***n.*** ⟦< GONE + -ER⟧ [Informal] a person or thing that is beyond help or seems certain to die soon, be ruined, etc.

Gon·er·il (gän′ər il) ***n.*** in Shakespeare's *King Lear*, the elder of Lear's two cruel and disloyal daughters

gon·fa·lon (gän′fə län′, -lən) ***n.*** ⟦Fr < OFr *gonfanon*, banner < Frank **gundfano*, battle standard (akin to OE *guthfana*) < *gund*, battle (akin to OE *guth*:

see DEFEND) + *fano* (OE *fana*), banner: see FANON⟧ a flag hanging from a crosspiece instead of an upright staff, usually ending in streamers; esp., such a standard of any of the medieval republics of Italy

gon·fa·lon·ier (gän′fə lən ir′) ***n.*** ⟦< Fr or It: Fr *gonfalonier* < It *gonfaloniere*⟧ **1** the bearer of a gonfalon **2** in some medieval republics of Italy, a high official

gong (gôŋ, gäŋ) ***n.*** ⟦Malay *guṅ*: echoic⟧ **1** a slightly convex metallic disk that gives a loud, resonant tone when struck: used as a signal, percussion instrument, etc. **2** a saucer-shaped bell with such a tone **3** [Brit. Slang] a medal

Gon·go·rism (gäŋ′gə riz′əm) ***n.*** ⟦after the style of Luis de *Góngora* y Argote (1561-1627), Sp poet⟧ a highly mannered Spanish literary style characterized by affected diction and strained figures of speech

go·nid·i·um (gō nid′ē əm) ***n.,*** *pl.* **-i·a** (-ə) ⟦ModL, dim. < Gr *gonos*: for base see GONAD⟧ **1** a reproductive cell produced asexually in certain algae, as tetraspores or zoospores **2** any of the chlorophyll-bearing algal cells in lichens —**go·nid′i·al** ***adj.***

gon·iff or **gon·if** (gän′if) ***n.*** [Slang] *var. of* GANEF

go·ni·o- (gō′nē ō′) ⟦< Gr *gōnia*, an angle: see KNEE⟧ *combining form* angle [*goniometry*]: also **go·ni-** (gō′nē)

go·ni·om·e·ter (gō′nē äm′ə tər) ***n.*** ⟦prec. + -METER⟧ **1** an instrument for measuring angles, esp. of solid bodies **2** *Radio* an electrical device used to determine the direction or angle of signals coming from a transmitting station

go·ni·om·e·try (gō′nē äm′ə trē) ***n.*** ⟦GONIO- + -METRY⟧ the theory or science of measuring angles —**go′ni·o·met′ric** (-nē ə me′trik) ***adj.***

go·ni·on (gō′nē än′) ***n.,*** *pl.* **-ni·a** (-ə) ⟦ModL < Gr *gonia*, an angle: see KNEE⟧ the point where the bottom of the lower jaw curves upward toward the ear

-go·ni·um (gō′nē əm) ⟦ModL < Gr *gonos*: see GONO-⟧ *combining form forming nouns* a cell or structure in which reproductive cells are formed [*archegonium*]

gonna (gôn′ə) ***v.aux.*** *phonetic sp. of* going to (in informal pronunciation) (see BE GOING TO under GOING) [*are you gonna* be quiet?]

gon·o- (gän′ō, -ə) ⟦< Gr *gonos, gonē*, procreation, offspring, semen, seed: see GONAD⟧ *combining form* reproductive, sexual [*gonococcus, gonophore*]: also, before a vowel, **gon-** (gän)

gon·o·coc·cus (gän′ə käk′əs) ***n.,*** *pl.* **-coc′ci′** (-käk′sī′) ⟦ModL < prec. + COCCUS⟧ the bacterium (*Neisseria gonorrhoeae*) that causes gonorrhea —**gon′o·coc′cal** (-käk′əl) ***adj.***

gon·of or **gon·oph** (gän′əf) ***n.*** [Slang] *alt. sp. of* GANEF

gon·o·phore (gän′ə fôr) ***n.*** ⟦GONO- + -PHORE⟧ **1** an extension of the axis of a flower, lifting the pistil and stamens above the floral envelope **2** a hydranth of a hydroid colony, specialized for the asexual production of offspring —**gon′o·phor′ic** (-fôr′ik) ***adj.,*** **go·noph·o·rous** (gō näf′ə rəs)

gon·o·pore (gän′ə pôr′) ***n.*** ⟦GONO- + PORE[2]⟧ an external genital opening through which gametes are released, as in earthworms or insects

gon·or·rhe·a (gän′ə rē′ə) ***n.*** ⟦LL *gonorrhoea* < Gr *gonorrhoia* < *gonos*, a seed, semen (see GONAD) + *rhoia* < *rheein*, to flow: see STREAM⟧ a sexually transmitted disease caused by gonococci, characterized by inflammation of the mucous membrane of the genitourinary tract and a discharge of mucous and pus: it can seriously affect other mucous membranes, esp. those of the eye, as in a baby during childbirth: also [Chiefly Brit.] **gon′or·rhoe′a** —**gon′or·rhe′al** ***adj.,*** [Chiefly Brit.] **gon′or·rhoe′al**

-go·ny (gə nē) ⟦L *-gonia* < Gr < base of *gignesthai*, to be born: see GENUS⟧ *combining form* production, generation, coming into being [*cosmogony, theogony*]

☆**gon·zo** (gän′zō) ***adj.*** ⟦< It, blockhead < ?⟧ [Slang] **1** bizarre, unrestrained, or extravagant: used esp. of a style of personal journalism **2** crazy or foolish

☆**goo** (gōō) ***n.*** ⟦prob. < baby talk⟧ [Informal] **1** anything sticky and viscous, as glue **2** anything sticky and sweet **3** excessive sentimentality

☆**goo·ber** (gōō′bər) ***n.*** ⟦< Kongo *nguba*⟧ [Chiefly South] a peanut

good (good) ***adj.*** **bet′ter, best** ⟦ME *gode* < OE *gōd*, akin to Ger *gut* < IE base **ghedh-*, to unite, be associated, suitable > GATHER⟧ **I.** *a general term of approval or commendation* **1** *a)* suitable to a purpose; effective; efficient [a lamp *good* to read by] *b)* producing favorable results; beneficial; salutary [*good* exercise for the legs] *c)* in accord with prevailing usage [*good* English] *d)* clever or witty [a *good* quip] **2** fertile [*good* soil] **3** fresh; unspoiled; uncontaminated [*good* eggs] **4** valid; genuine; real [*good* money, a *good* excuse] **5** healthy; strong; vigorous [*good* eyesight] **6** financially safe or sound [a *good* investment] **7** honorable; worthy; respectable [one's *good* name] **8** enjoyable, desirable, pleasant, happy, etc. [a *good* life] **9** dependable; reliable; right [*good* advice] **10** thorough; complete [a *good* job of cleaning up] **11** *a)* excellent of its kind [a *good* novel] *b)* best or considered best [her *good* china] **12** adequate; ample; sufficient; satisfying [a *good* meal] **13** morally sound or excellent; specif., *a)* virtuous; honest; just *b)* pious; devout *c)* kind, benevolent, generous, sympathetic, etc. *d)* well-behaved; dutiful **14** *a)* proper; becoming; correct [*good* manners] *b)* socially acceptable [a *good* family] **15** able; skilled; expert [a *good* swimmer] **16** loyal or conforming [a *good* Democrat] **17** [Informal] comfortable, satisfied, etc. ["Would you like some more?" "No, thanks. I'm *good*"] **18** *Law* effectual; valid [*good* title] **II.** *a general intensive* **1** to a considerable amount, extent, or degree [a *good* many, a *good* beating] **2** at least; full [we waited a *good* six hours] —***n.*** something good; specif., *a)* that which is morally right *b)* worth; virtue; merit [the *good* in a man] *c)* something contributing to health, welfare, happiness, etc.; benefit; advantage [the greatest *good* of the greatest number] *d)* something desirable or desired: see also GOODS —***interj.*** used to express satisfaction, pleasure, agreement, etc. and, in some exclamatory phrases, to express surprise, consternation, etc.: orig. a euphemism for *God* —***adv.*** well, completely, fully, etc.: variously regarded as substandard, dialectal, or informal —**as good as** in effect; virtually; nearly —**come to no good** to come to a bad end; end in failure, trouble, etc. —**for good (and all)** for always; finally; permanently —☆**good and** [Informal] very or altogether —**good for 1** able to survive, endure, or be used for (a specified period of time) **2** worth [a coupon *good for* 10¢] **3** able to pay, repay, or give **4** sure to result in [*good for* a laugh] —☆**good for someone!** an exclamation used to express approval for someone who has done or achieved something admirable [*good for you!*] —**no good** useless or worthless —**the good 1** those who are good **2** what is morally good —**to the good** as a profit, benefit, or advantage

good afternoon a phrase used in the afternoon as a greeting or farewell

Good·all (good′ôl′), Dame **Jane** (born *Valerie Jane Morris-Goodall*) 1934- ; Brit. primatologist

Good Book the Bible: usually with *the*

good·bye or **good-bye** (good′bī′) ***interj., n.,*** *pl.* **-byes′** ⟦contr. of *God be with ye*⟧ farewell: the interj. is used at parting: also sp. **good′by′** or **good′-by′**, *pl.* **-bys′**

good cheer 1 merrymaking; revelry **2** good food and drink; feasting **3** cheerful or courageous spirit

☆**Good Conduct Medal** a U.S. military decoration awarded for exemplary behavior, efficiency, and fidelity

good day a phrase used during the day as a greeting or farewell

good evening a phrase used in the evening as a greeting or farewell

good faith absence of malice or any intention to deceive; good intentions; sincerity

good fellow an agreeable, convivial person

good-fel·low·ship (good′fel′ō ship′) ***n.*** ⟦prec. + -SHIP⟧ hearty, convivial companionship

good-for-noth·ing (good′fər nuth′iŋ) ***adj.*** useless or worthless —***n.*** a useless or worthless person

Good Friday the Friday before Easter Sunday, observed in commemoration of the crucifixion of Jesus

good-heart·ed (good′härt′id) ***adj.*** kind and generous —**good′-heart′ed·ly** ***adv.*** —**good′-heart′ed·ness** ***n.***

Good Hope, Cape of cape at the SW tip of Africa, on the Atlantic

good humor a cheerful, agreeable, pleasant mood

good-hu·mored (good′hyōō′mərd) ***adj.*** having or showing good humor; cheerful and agreeable —**good′-hu′mored·ly** ***adv.***

good·ish (good′ish) ***adj.*** **1** fairly good **2** fairly large

good-look·ing (good′look′iŋ) ***adj.*** pleasing in appearance; beautiful or handsome —**SYN.** BEAUTIFUL

good looks attractive personal appearance; esp., pleasing facial features

good·ly (good′lē) ***adj.*** **-li·er, -li·est 1** of attractive appearance; good-looking **2** of good quality; fine **3** rather large; ample [a *goodly* sum] —**good′li·ness** ***n.***

good·man (good′mən) ***n.,*** *pl.* **-men** (-mən) ⟦ME: see GOOD & MAN⟧ [Archaic] **1** a husband or master of a household **2** a title equivalent to *Mr.*, applied to a man ranking below a gentleman

Good·man (good′mən), **Ben·ny** (ben′ē) (born *Benjamin David Goodman*) 1909-86; U.S. clarinetist & bandleader

good morning a phrase used in the morning as a greeting or farewell

good nature a pleasant, agreeable, or kindly disposition; amiability; geniality

good-na·tured (good′nā′chərd) ***adj.*** having or showing good nature; pleasant; agreeable; affable —**SYN.** AMIABLE —**good′-na′tured·ly** ***adv.***

good·ness (good′nis) ***n.*** ⟦ME *goodnesse* < OE *godnes*⟧ **1** the state or quality of being good; specif., *a)* virtue; excellence *b)* kindness; generosity; benevolence **2** the best part, essence, or valuable element of a thing —***interj.*** used to express surprise or wonder: orig. a euphemism for *God*: also used in phrases [for *goodness'* sake!]

good night a phrase used as a farewell at night in parting or going to bed

good old boy [Informal] a man of the S U.S., variously characterized as easygoing, companionable, assertively masculine, and strongly identifying with his regional lifestyle

goods (goodz) ***pl.n.*** **1** movable personal property **2** merchandise; wares **3** fabric; cloth **4** [Brit.] freight: usually used attributively —☆**deliver the goods** [Informal] to do or produce the thing required —☆**get (or have) the goods on** [Slang] to discover (or know) something incriminating about —☆**the goods** [Slang] what is required, genuine, or valid

good Samaritan a person who pities and helps another, typically a stranger, or others unselfishly: see Luke 10:30-37

Good Shepherd *name for* JESUS[2]: John 10:11

good-sized (good′sīzd′) ***adj.*** ample; big or fairly big

good speed success; good luck: a farewell expressing good wishes to a person starting on a journey or venture

good-tem·pered (-tem′pərd) ***adj.*** having a good temper; not easily angered or annoyed; amiable —**good′-tem′pered·ly** ***adv.***

good-time Char·lie (*or* **Char·ley**) (good′tīm′ chär′lē) [Informal] a sociable, pleasure-seeking fellow regarded as carefree or irresponsible

good turn a good deed; friendly, helpful act; favor

good·wife (good′wīf′) ***n.,*** *pl.* **-wives′** (-wīvz′) ⟦ME: see GOOD & WIFE⟧ [Archaic] **1** a wife or a mistress of a household **2** a title equivalent to *Mrs.*, applied to a woman ranking below a lady

good·will (-wil′) ***n.*** **1** a friendly or kindly attitude; benevolence **2** cheerful consent; willingness 3 *Accounting* an intangible asset which takes into account the value added to a business firm as a result of patronage, reputation, etc. Also written **good will**

good·y[1] (good′ē) *n., pl.* **good′ies** [Informal] 1 *a)* something considered very good to eat, as a piece of candy *b)* any gift, perk, etc., esp. a small one: *usually used in pl.* ☆2 GOODY-GOODY *—adj.* [Informal] GOODY-GOODY *—interj.* used to express approval or delight: mainly a child's term

good·y[2] (good′ē) *n., pl.* **good′ies** ⟦< GOODWIFE⟧ [Archaic] a woman, esp. an old woman or housewife, of lowly social status: used as a title with the surname

Good·year (good′yir′), **Charles** 1800-60; U.S. inventor: originated the process for vulcanizing rubber

good·y-good·y (good′ē good′ē) [Informal] *adj.* ⟦redupl. of GOODY[1]⟧ moral or pious in an affected or canting way *—*☆*n.* a goody-goody person

good·y-two-shoes (good′ē to͞o′sho͞oz′) *adj., n.* ⟦after *Goody Two-Shoes,* heroine of a Brit children's story (1766)⟧ [Informal] GOODY-GOODY: also **goody two-shoes** or **Goody Two-shoes**

☆**goo·ey** (go͞o′ē) *adj.* **goo′i·er, goo′i·est** ⟦GOO + -EY⟧ [Informal] 1 *a)* sticky and viscous *b)* sticky and sweet 2 overly sentimental

☆**goof** (go͞of) [Informal] *n.* ⟦prob. < dial. *goff* < Fr *goffe,* stupid < It *goffo*⟧ 1 a stupid, silly, or credulous person 2 a mistake; blunder *—vi.* 1 to make a mistake; blunder, fail, etc.: often with *up* 2 to waste time, shirk one's duties, etc.: usually with *off* or *around* **—goof up** to make a mess of, as by ineptness; bungle

☆**goof·ball** (go͞of′bôl′) *n.* ⟦prec. + BALL[1]⟧ [Slang] 1 a pill containing a barbiturate or, sometimes, a stimulant drug, tranquilizer, etc., esp. when used nonmedicinally: also **goof ball** 2 GOOF (*n.* 1) *—adj.* GOOFY

goof-off (-ôf′) *n.* [Slang] a person who wastes time or avoids work; shirker

goof·y (go͞of′ē) *adj.* **goof′i·er, goof′i·est** [Informal] like or characteristic of a goof; stupid and silly **—goof′i·ly** *adv.* **—goof′i·ness** *n.*

☆**goo·gol** (go͞o′gôl′, -gəl′) *n.* ⟦arbitrary use by E. Kasner (1878-1955), U.S. mathematician, of a word coined, as he reported it, by his young nephew, Milton Sirotta⟧ 1 the number 1 followed by 100 zeros; 10^{100} 2 any very large number

☆**goo·gol·plex** (-pleks′) *n.* ⟦prec. + L *-plex,* -fold⟧ the number 1 followed by 100 zeros; 10 to the power googol

☆**goo-goo** (go͞o′go͞o′) *n.* ⟦< *goo(d) go(vernment)*⟧ [Slang] an idealistic advocate of honest government: usually a somewhat disparaging term

goo-goo eyes (go͞o′go͞o′) [Slang] amorously inviting glances

☆**gook**[1] (gook, go͞ok) *n.* ⟦GOO + (GUN)K⟧ [Slang] any sticky, greasy, or slimy substance

gook[2] (go͞ok) *n.* ⟦< ?⟧ [Slang] an East Asian; specif., a Korean, Vietnamese, Japanese, etc.: a hostile and contemptuous term

goom·bah (go͞om′bä′) *n.* ⟦phonetic sp. of dial. pronun. of It *compare,* godfather, friend⟧ [Slang] a male friend; esp., an older man who is a friend, protector, advisor, etc.

goom·bay (go͞om′bā′) *n.* a dance of the Bahamas done to syncopated rhythms of drums, maracas, sticks, and improvised instruments

☆**goon** (go͞on) *n.* [Informal] 1 ⟦< ?⟧ a ruffian or thug, esp. one hired to help break a strike, etc. 2 ⟦after Alice the *Goon,* grotesque comic-strip figure created by E. C. Segar (1894-1938), U.S. cartoonist⟧ a person who is awkward, grotesque, stupid, etc.

goo·ney bird (go͞o′nē) ⟦< *gooney,* sailors' name for the albatross, orig. simpleton, prob. < or akin to ME *gonen,* to gape < OE *ganian:* see YAWN⟧ ALBATROSS: also sp. **goo′ny bird**

goon·y (go͞o′nē) *adj.* **goon′i·er, goon′i·est** [Slang] awkward, grotesque, stupid, silly, etc.: also sp. **goon′ey**

☆**goop** (go͞op) *n.* ⟦GOO + (SOU)P⟧ [Informal] any sticky, semiliquid substance **—goop′y** *adj.* **goop′i·er, goop′i·est**

goos·an·der (go͞os an′dər) *n.* ⟦prob. < fol., after *bergander,* sheldrake⟧ the common merganser: see MERGANSER

goose (go͞os) *n., pl.* for 1–3, **geese**; for 4 & 5, **goos′es** ⟦ME *gose* < OE *gos,* akin to Du & Ger *gans,* ON *gas* < IE **ĝhans* > L *anser*; *vt.* 1 prob. for the fact that geese sometimes attack children from the rear⟧ 1 any of various long-necked, web-footed, wild or domestic waterfowl that are like ducks but larger; esp., a female as distinguished from a gander 2 the flesh of a goose, used for food 3 a silly person 4 a tailor's pressing iron with a long handle curved somewhat like the neck of a goose 5 [Informal] a sudden, playful prod in the backside *—vt.* **goosed, goos′ing** [Informal] ☆1 to prod suddenly and playfully in the backside so as to startle ☆2 to feed gasoline to (an engine) in irregular spurts ☆3 to prod, or stir, into action **—cook someone's goose** [Informal] to spoil someone's chances, hopes, etc.

goose barnacle ⟦from the old notion that geese grow from them⟧ any of a number of barnacles (genera *Lepas* and *Mitella*) that attach themselves by a long, fleshy stalk to rocks, ship bottoms, etc.

goose·ber·ry (go͞os′ber′ē, -bə rē; go͞oz′-) *n., pl.* **-ries** ⟦as if < GOOSE + BERRY, but prob. folk-etym. form for **grose berie,* akin to dial. *grosel,* gooseberry (< Fr *groseille*), Du *kruisbezie,* Ger *krausbeere*⟧ 1 a small, sour berry used in making preserves, pies, etc.: it resembles a currant but is larger 2 any of various prickly shrubs (genus *Ribes*) of the saxifrage family which produce gooseberries

☆**goose bumps** a roughened condition of the skin in which the papillae are erected, caused by cold, fear, etc.

goose egg ⟦so called from its shape⟧ [Slang] ☆1 zero or a score of zero 2 a large swelling or lump, esp. one caused by a blow

goose·fish (go͞os′fish′) *n., pl.* **-fish′** or **-fish′es** (see FISH) any of a family (Lophiidae) of anglers characterized by large, sharp teeth and a wide, flat body: see MONKFISH

goose flesh *var. of* GOOSE BUMPS

goose·foot (go͞os′foot′) *adj.* ⟦from the resemblance of the shape of the leaf to that of the *foot* of a *goose*⟧ designating a family (Chenopodiaceae, order Caryophyllales) of dicotyledonous plants, including spinach and beets *—n., pl.* **-foots′** any of a genus (*Chenopodium*) of weedy plants of the goosefoot family, with small green flowers and, frequently, scurfy or fleshy foliage

goose·grass (go͞os′gras′) *n.* ⟦name given to various plants once used as food for geese⟧ any of various weeds or weedy grasses, as knotgrass or cleavers

goose·herd (go͞os′hurd′) *n.* ⟦ME *gosherde:* see HERD[2]⟧ a person who tends geese

goose·liv·er (go͞os′liv′ər) *n.* smoked liver sausage

goose·neck (go͞os′nek′) *n.* any of various mechanical devices shaped like a goose's neck, as an iron joint for pipes or a flexible rod for supporting a desk lamp

gooseneck barnacle GOOSE BARNACLE

goose pimples *var. of* GOOSE BUMPS

goose step a marching step, as of troops passing in review, in which the legs are raised high and kept stiff and unbent: often used fig. to connote militarism, fascism, etc. **—goose-step** (go͞os′step′) *vi.* **-stepped′, -step′ping**

goos·ey or **goos·y** (go͞os′ē) *adj.* **goos′i·er, goos′i·est** 1 *a)* like or characteristic of a goose *b)* foolish; stupid 2 [Slang] nervous; jumpy

GOP (jē′ō′pē′) *n.* ⟦*G(rand) O(ld) P(arty)*⟧ *name for* REPUBLICAN PARTY

☆**go·pher**[1] (gō′fər) *n.* ⟦< ? Fr *gaufre,* honeycomb (see GOFFER): so called from its habit of burrowing⟧ 1 any of a family (Geomyidae) of burrowing rodents about the size of a large rat, with wide cheek pouches; pocket gopher 2 any of a number of striped ground squirrels (genus *Citellus*) found on the prairies of North America 3 ⟦earlier *magofer,* prob. < AmInd⟧ a burrowing land tortoise (*Gopherus polyphemus*) found in SE U.S. 4 [**G-**] [Informal] a person born or living in Minnesota, called the **Gopher State**

go·pher[2] (gō′fər) *n.* [Slang] *alt. sp. of* GOFER

gopher ball [Slang] *Baseball* a pitch that is hit for a home run

☆**gopher snake** ⟦so named from its typical prey⟧ 1 [West] *regional var. of* BULLSNAKE 2 INDIGO SNAKE

gopher wood ⟦Heb *gofer*⟧ *Bible* the wood used to make Noah's ark: Gen. 6:14

Go·rakh·pur (gôr′ək poor′) city in E Uttar Pradesh, N India

go·ral (gō′rəl, gôr′əl) *n., pl.* **-rals** or **-ral** ⟦< name in a language of the Himalayas⟧ any of a genus (*Naemorhedus*) of goat antelopes found in Asian mountains from the S Himalayas to Siberia

Gor·ba·chev (gôr′bə chôf′, gôr′bə chôf′), **Mi·kha·il (Sergeyevich)** (mē′khä ēl′) 1931- ; general secretary of the Communist Party of the U.S.S.R. (1985-91)

gor·cock (gôr′käk′) *n.* ⟦prob. < GORE[1] + COCK[1], because of its color⟧ [Brit. Dial.] the male red grouse

Gor·di·an knot (gôr′dē ən) 1 *Gr. Legend* a knot tied by King Gordius of Phrygia, which an oracle reveals will be undone only by the future master of Asia: Alexander the Great, failing to untie it, cuts the knot with his sword 2 any perplexing problem **—cut the Gordian knot** to find a quick, bold solution for a perplexing problem

gor·di·an worm (gôr′dē ən) ⟦in allusion to prec., from the tangled masses the worms sometimes form⟧ any of a phylum (Nematomorpha) of long, thin, worms parasitic in insects when immature and free-swimming as adults; horsehair worm

Gor·don[1] (gôrd′'n) *n.* ⟦Scot < surname *Gordon*⟧ a masculine name

Gor·don[2] (gôrd′'n), **Charles George** 1833-85; Brit. general in China, Egypt, & Sudan: called *Chinese Gordon*

Gordon setter ⟦after a Scot dog fancier, the 4th Duke of *Gordon* (1745?-1827?)⟧ any of a breed of setter having a soft, black coat with tan markings

gore[1] (gôr) *n.* ⟦ME *gore,* filth < OE *gor,* dung, filth, akin to ON *gor,* Welsh *gor,* MDu *gore* < IE base **gwher-,* hot > WARM, L *fornax,* furnace⟧ blood shed from a wound, esp. when clotted

gore[2] (gôr) *vt.* **gored, gor′ing** ⟦ME *goren* < *gore,* a spear < OE *gar:* see fol.⟧ to pierce with or as with a horn or tusk

gore[3] (gôr) *n.* ⟦ME *gore* < OE *gara,* corner < base of *gar,* a spear, akin to MDu *gheere,* Ger *gehre,* gusset < IE base **ghaiso-,* a stake, javelin > Ger *geissel,* a whip⟧ 1 a small, triangular piece of land as where two roads diverge 2 a tapering piece of cloth made or inserted in a skirt, sail, etc. to give it fullness *—vt.* **gored, gor′ing** to make or insert a gore or gores in

Gore-Tex (gôr′teks′) ⟦after W. L. *Gore* & Associates, Inc., its originators + TEX(TILE)⟧ *trademark for* a strong, porous material formed from a polymer, used to make clothing water-repellent, and for electrical insulation, prosthetic devices, etc.

Go·rey (gôr′ē), **Edward (St. John)** 1925-2000; U.S. writer and illustrator

Gor·gas (gôr′gəs), **William Craw·ford** (krô′fərd) 1854-1920; U.S. army medical officer: chief sanitary officer in the Canal Zone during construction of the Panama Canal

gorge (gôrj) *n.* ⟦ME < OFr, throat, gullet < LL **gurga,* throat, narrow pass, for L *gurges,* whirlpool < IE base **gwer-,* to swallow up > L *vorare*⟧ 1 [Archaic] the throat or gullet 2 the crop or stomach of a hawk 3 *a)* the maw or stomach of a voracious being or animal *b)* food or a meal to fill or stuff the stomach *c)* the contents of the stomach (often used fig. in such phrases as **make one's gorge rise**, to sicken, disgust, or anger one) **4** the entrance from the rear into a bastion or projecting section of a fortification **5** a deep, narrow pass between steep heights ☆**6** a mass that blocks up a passage —*vi.* **gorged, gorg′ing** to eat gluttonously —*vt.* **1** to fill the gorge of; glut **2** to swallow greedily

gor·geous (gôr′jəs) *adj.* ⟦ME *gorgeouse*, altered < OFr *gorgias*, beautiful, glorious, ? akin to *gorgiere*, ruff for the neck < *gorge*: see prec.⟧ **1** brilliantly showy; magnificent or sumptuous; splendid **2** [Informal] beautiful, wonderful, delightful, etc.: a generalized term of approval —**gor′geous·ly** *adv.* —**gor′geous·ness** *n.*

gor·ger·in (gôr′jər in) *n.* ⟦Fr < *gorgère* < OFr *gorgiere*: see prec.⟧ *Archit.* the part of a column just below the top molding or between the shaft and the capital

gor·get (gôr′jit) *n.* ⟦ME < OFr *gorgete* < *gorgiere*: see GORGEOUS⟧ **1** a piece of armor to protect the throat **2** a collar **3** an article of clothing covering the neck and breast, formerly worn by women; wimple **4** a patch of color, often iridescent, on the throat of a bird, as on a male hummingbird

Gor·gon (gôr′gən) *n.* ⟦ME < L *Gorgo* (gen. *Gorgonis*) < Gr *Gorgō* < *gorgos*, terrible, fierce⟧ **1** *Gr. Myth.* any of three sisters with snakes for hair, so horrible that the beholder is turned to stone **2** [**g-**] any ugly, terrifying, or repulsive woman —**Gor·go′ni·an** *adj.*

gor·go·ni·an (gôr gō′nē ən) *n.* ⟦ModL *Gorgonia*, name of the genus < L, coral (< *Gorgo*, prec.) + -AN⟧ any of an order (Gorgonacea) of colonial anthozoans with a horny, axial skeleton that branches, as in the sea whips, or forms an open network, as in the sea fans

gor·gon·ize (gôr′gən īz′) *vt.* **-ized′**, **-iz′ing** ⟦GORGON + -IZE⟧ to petrify or stupefy, as with a look

Gor·gon·zo·la (gôr′gən zō′lə) *n.* ⟦It, after *Gorgonzola*, town in Italy near Milan⟧ a white Italian pressed cheese with veins of blue-green mold and a strong flavor

gor·hen (gôr′hen′) *n.* ⟦prob. < GORE[1] + HEN, with reference to the color⟧ the female red grouse; moorhen

☆**go·ril·la** (gə ril′ə) *n.* ⟦ModL, arbitrary use (1847) by T. Savage (1804-80), U.S. physician & clergyman, of assumed nom. sing. of Gr *gorillai*, form used by Gr translators of Hanno, Carthaginian navigator (fl. early 5th c. B.C.), for his name for a tribe of hairy human beings in W Africa (said to be their local name)⟧ **1** the largest and most powerful of the great apes (*Gorilla gorilla*), native to the jungles of equatorial Africa: the adult male weighs up to 225 kg (*c.* 500 lb): it is generally shy, intelligent, and herbivorous **2** [Slang] *a)* a person regarded as like a gorilla in appearance, strength, etc. *b)* a gangster; thug

Gor·ki′ or **Gor·ky** (gôr′kē), **Max·im** (mak′sim) (pseud. of *Aleksei Maximovich Peshkov*) 1868-1936; Russ. novelist & playwright

Gor·ki[2], **Gor·kiy,** *or* **Gor·ky** (gôr′kē) *name* (1932-90) *for* NIZHNY NOVGOROD

Gor·ky (gôr′kē), **Ar·shile** (är′shēl) (born *Vosdanig Manoog Adoian*) 1904-48; U.S. artist, born in Turkish Armenia

Gor·lov·ka (gär lôf′kä) city in SE Ukraine, in the Donets Basin

gor·mand (gôr′mənd) *n. var. of* GOURMAND

gor·mand·ize (gôr′mən dīz′) *n.* ⟦< Fr *gourmandise* < OFr *gourmand*: see GOURMAND⟧ *rare var. of* GOURMANDISE — *vi., vt.* **-ized′**, **-iz′ing** ⟦< the *n.*⟧ to eat or devour like a glutton —**gor′mand·iz′er** *n.*

gorm·less (gôrm′lis) *adj.* ⟦altered < dial. *gaumless* < *gaum, gome*, care < ME *gome* < ON *gaum*, akin to OE *gieme*, care, Goth *gaumjan*, to heed⟧ [Brit. Informal] slow-witted; stupid

go-round (gō′round′) *n.* one of a series of actions, encounters, meetings, etc., often one involving a conflict or fight

☆**gorp** (gôrp) *n.* ⟦< ?⟧ TRAIL MIX

gorse (gôrs) *n.* ⟦ME *gorst* < OE < IE base *ĝhers-, to stiffen, bristle > L *horrere*, to stand on end⟧ FURZE —**gors′y** *adj.*

gor·y (gôr′ē) *adj.* **gor′i·er, gor′i·est** **1** full of, covered with, or like gore; bloody **2** characterized by much bloodshed or slaughter [*a gory* fight] —**the gory details** [Informal] the explicit details about something, esp. when lurid, sensational, intimate, etc. —**gor′i·ly** *adv.* —**gor′i·ness** *n.*

☆**gosh** (gäsh, gôsh) *interj.* [Slang] used to express surprise, wonder, etc.: orig. a euphemism for *God*

gos·hawk (gäs′hôk′) *n.* ⟦ME *goshauk* < OE *goshafoc*: see GOOSE & HAWK[1]⟧ a large, swift, powerful hawk (*Accipiter gentilis*) with short wings and a long, rounded tail

Go·shen (gō′shən) *n.* ⟦Heb⟧ *Bible* the fertile land assigned to the Israelites in Egypt: Gen. 45:10

gos·ling (gäz′liŋ) *n.* ⟦ME *goslynge* (see GOOSE & -LING[1]), for *geslynge* < ON *gæslingr*⟧ **1** a young goose **2** a young and foolish or inexperienced person

gos·pel (gäs′pəl) *n.* ⟦ME *godspell, gospel* (with assimilated *-d-*) < OE *gōdspel*, orig., good story, good news: intended as transl. of LL(Ec) *evangelium* (see EVANGEL), tidings, but later by shortening of *o* it became *gŏdspel* as if < *god*, God + *spel*, story⟧ **1** [*often* **G-**] *a)* the teachings of Jesus and the Apostles; specif., the Christian doctrine of the redemption of man through Jesus as Christ *b)* the history of the life and teachings of Jesus **2** [**G-**] *a)* any of the first four books of the New Testament *b)* an excerpt from any of these books read in a religious service **3** anything proclaimed or accepted as the absolute truth: also **gospel truth** **4** any doctrine or rule widely or ardently maintained **5** an evangelistic Protestant religious music, esp. a kind that evolved from spirituals and the black churches in the U.S.; also, a melismatic singing style characteristic of black gospel, often employing antiphonal patterns —*adj.* [*often* **G-**] **1** of or having to do with the gospel or evangelism **2** of or having to do with gospel music

gos·pel·er (-ər) *n.* ⟦ME *gospellere* < OE *godspellere*⟧ **1** [Now Rare] a reader of the Gospel in a religious service **2** an ardent preacher or supporter of the Gospel or of a gospel: derisive term Also sp. **gos′pel·ler**

gos·po·din (gäs pä dyēn′) *n., pl.* **-da′** (-dä′) ⟦Russ, lit., lord < IE base **ghostis*, stranger, guest: see HOSPICE⟧ [Archaic] a Russian title of respect, more formal than English *Mr.*

gos·sa·mer (gäs′ə mər) *n.* ⟦ME *gosesomer*, lit., goose summer: with allusion to the warm period in fall (*St. Martin's summer*) when geese are in season and gossamer is chiefly noticed⟧ **1** a filmy cobweb floating in the air or spread on bushes or grass **2** a very thin, soft, filmy cloth ☆**3** a lightweight waterproof coat **4** anything like gossamer in lightness, flimsiness, etc. —*adj.* light, thin, and filmy: also **gos′sa·mer·y** (-mər ē)

gos·san (gäs′ən, gäz′-) *n.* ⟦Cornish *gossen* < *gos*, blood < Old Cornish *guit*⟧ *Mining* rusty iron deposits often occurring where the upper part of a vein has been weathered and oxidized

gos·sip (gäs′əp) *n.* ⟦ME *godsip, gossyp* (with assimilated *-d-*) < Late OE *godsibbe*, godparent: see GOD & SIB⟧ **1** [Now Dial.] *a)* a godparent *b)* a close friend **2** a person who chatters or repeats idle talk and rumors, esp. about the private affairs of others **3** *a)* such talk or rumors *b)* chatter —*vi.* to be a gossip or engage in gossip —**gos′sip·y** *adj.*

gos·sip·mon·ger (-muŋ′gər, -mäŋ′-) *n.* GOSSIP (*n.* 2)

gos·soon (gä so͞on′) *n.* ⟦altered < Fr *garçon*, boy, attendant < OFr *gars*: see GASKET⟧ **1** a boy **2** a servant boy

gos·sy·pol (gäs′ə pôl, -pōl′) *n.* ⟦Ger < ModL *Gossypium*, genus name of cotton + *-ol*, -OL[1]⟧ a toxic, phenolic pigment, $C_{30}H_{30}O_8$, in cotton plants: it inhibits sperm production and is used experimentally as a male contraceptive

got (gät) *vt., vi. pt. & alt. pp. of* GET

NOTE—See usage note at GOTTEN

Go·ta·ma (gô′tə mə) *alt. sp. of* GAUTAMA: see BUDDHA[2]

got·cha (gät′chə) *interj.* ⟦phonetic sp. of informal or dial. pronun. of *got you*⟧ used to signify: *a)* that one has caught, captured, or gained power over someone or something *b)* that one understands what someone has just said

Gö·te·borg (yö′tə bôr′y′) seaport in SW Sweden, on the Kattegat

Goth[1] (gäth) *n.* ⟦< LL *Gothi*, pl. (for OE *Gotan*) < Gr *Gothoi*, pl. < base of Goth **Gutans*, pl., or *Gut (thiuda)*, Gothic (people)⟧ **1** a member of a Germanic people that invaded and conquered most of the Roman Empire in the 3d, 4th, and 5th centuries A.D.: see also OSTROGOTH, VISIGOTH **2** an uncouth, uncivilized person; barbarian **3** ⟦< GOTHIC, *adj.* 4⟧ [*usually* **g-**] *a)* a form of music derived from punk rock and characterized by melodramatically morose or morbid lyrics *b)* a style characterized by black clothing, heavy, dark makeup, and a preoccupation with the themes of goth music *c)* a devotee of goth music or fashions —*adj.* [*usually* **g-**] of or having to do with goth music, styles, or attitudes

Goth[2] *abbrev.* Gothic

Goth·am (gōt′əm, gät′-; *for 2* gäth′əm) **1** village near Nottingham, England, whose inhabitants, the "wise men of Gotham," were, according to legend, very foolish **2** ⟦after the Eng village: used satirically by IRVING[2]⟧ *name for* New York City —**Goth′am·ite′** (-īt′) *n.*

Goth·ic (gäth′ik) *adj.* ⟦LL *Gothicus*: see GOTH[1]⟧ **1** of the Goths or their language or culture **2** designating, of, or related to a style of architecture developed in W Europe between the 12th and 16th cent. and characterized by the use of ribbed vaulting, flying buttresses, pointed arches, steep, high roofs, etc. **3** [*sometimes* **g-**] *a)* medieval *b)* not classical *c)* barbarous; uncivilized **4** [*sometimes* **g-**] of or having to do with a type of fiction orig. and esp. of the late 18th and early 19th cent. using remote (and, orig., medieval) settings and a sinister, eerie atmosphere to suggest horror and mystery **5** [*also* **g-**] designating or of a type of ROMANCE (*n.* 3) set typically in the 18th or 19th cent. and relating the melodramatic adventures of the heroine —*n.* **1** the East Germanic language of the Goths: it is known chiefly from the Bible translations of Bishop ULFILAS **2** Gothic style, esp. in architecture **3** *Printing* ☆*a)* [*often* **g-**] a style of sans-serif type *b)* a heavy, ornate style of type, now used especially in calligraphy —**Goth′i·cal·ly** *adv.* —**Goth′ic·ness** *n.*

Gothic arch a pointed arch as in Gothic architecture

Goth·i·cism (-i siz′əm) *n.* **1** barbarism; rudeness **2** conformity to or use of Gothic style —**Goth′i·cist** *n.*

Goth·i·cize (-i sīz′) *vt.* **-cized′**, **-ciz′ing** to make Gothic

Got·land (gät′lənd; *Swed* gôt′-) Swedish island in the Baltic, off the SE coast of Sweden: 1,159 sq mi (3,002 sq km)

☆**go-to** (gō′to͞o′) *adj.* [Informal] trusted to perform dependably or skillfully, esp. in a critical situation [*a quarterback's go-to receiver*]

gotta (gät′ə) *v.aux. phonetic sp. of* (have or has) got to (in informal pronunciation) [*I gotta go; she's gotta be kidding*]

got·ten (gät′'n) *vt., vi. alt. pp. of* GET

USAGE—although both GOTTEN and GOT are accepted past participles for most senses of the verb GET, GOTTEN has become the prevailing form in the U.S. in all speech and writing, especially for the senses of receiving, becoming, or arriving; the gradual acceptance of GOTTEN has probably been facilitated by the desire to distinguish between possession, as in the informal *I've got a car*, and acquisition, as in *I've gotten a car*; these forms are not commonly used in most other English-speaking countries, where the standard form for possession is *have* (*I have a car*) and the standard past participle is GOT (for instance, in Britain, *I have got a car* means *I have acquired a car*)

Göt·ter·däm·mer·ung (göt′ər dem′ər o͝oŋ) ***n.*** ⟦Ger, twilight of the gods⟧ **1** *Ger. name for* RAGNAROK **2** the total, usually violent, collapse of a society, regime, institution, etc.

Göt·ting·en (göt′iŋ ən) city in central Germany, in the state of Lower Saxony

Gott·schalk (gät′shôk′), **Louis Mo·reau** (mô rō′) 1829-69; U.S. composer

gouache (gwäsh) ***n.*** ⟦Fr < It *guazzo*, water color, spray, pool < L *aquatio*, watering, watering place < *aqua*, water: see ISLAND⟧ **1** a way of painting with opaque colors ground in water and mixed with a preparation of gum **2** a pigment of this sort **3** a painting made with such pigments

Gou·da (cheese) (go͞o′də, gou′-) ⟦after *Gouda*, Netherlands, city where orig. produced⟧ a mild, semisoft to hard cheese similar to Edam and sometimes coated with red wax

Gou·dy (gou′dē), **Frederic William** 1865-1947; U.S. printer & designer of printing types

gouge (gouj) ***n.*** ⟦ME < OFr < VL *gubia*, for LL *gulbia* < Celt (as in OIr *gulban*, goad, thorn) < IE base **gelebh-*, to scrape, hollow out > Gr *glaphein*, to carve⟧ **1** a chisel with a curved, hollowed blade, for cutting grooves or holes in wood **2** *a)* an act of gouging *b)* the groove or hole made by gouging **3** any deep groove or hole that is considered a blemish **4** [Informal] an act of overcharging or cheating of money; extortion or swindle —***vt.* gouged, goug′ing 1** to make a groove, hole, etc. in (something) with or as with a gouge **2** to scoop out; dig or force out [*to gouge out dirt*] ☆**3** in fighting, to push one's thumb into the eye of ☆**4** [Informal] to cheat out of money, etc.; also, to overcharge —☆**goug′er *n.***

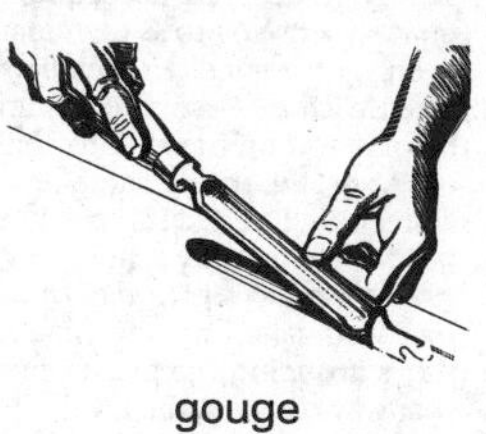
gouge

gou·lash (go͞o′läsh′; *also*, -lash′) ***n.*** ⟦Ger *gulasch* < Hung *gulyás*, lit., cattle herder (< *gulya*, cattle), hence herdsman's food⟧ a stew made of beef or veal and onions, and sometimes other vegetables, and seasoned with paprika: also **Hungarian goulash**

Gould (go͞old) **1 Glenn** (born *Glenn Herbert Gold*) 1932-82; Cdn. pianist **2 Jay** (born *Jason Gould*) 1836-92; U.S. financier **3 Stephen Jay** 1941-2002; U.S. paleontologist & writer

Gou·nod (go͞o nō′, go͞o′nō), **Charles (François)** (shärl) 1818-93; Fr. composer

gou·ra·mi (go͞o rä′mē, go͝or′ə mē) ***n.**, pl.* **-mies** or **-mi** ⟦Malay *gurami*⟧ any of various families of tropical, freshwater percoid fishes; esp., a nest-building food fish (*Osphronemus goramy*) of Southeast Asia

gourd (gôrd, go͝ord) ***adj.*** ⟦ME *gourde* < OFr *gouorde* < L *cucurbita*⟧ designating a family (Cucurbitaceae, order Violales) of dicotyledonous plants, including the squash, melon, cucumber, and pumpkin —***n.* 1** any trailing or climbing plant belonging to the gourd family **2** any of the ornamental, inedible fruits of these or related plants, esp. of a yellow-flowered variety (*Cucurbita pepo ovifera*) of the pumpkin ☆**3** the dried, hollowed-out shell of such a fruit, used as a drinking cup, dipper, etc. **4** [Slang] the head: usually in the phrase **out of one's gourd**, crazy, foolish, etc.

gourde (go͝ord) ***n.*** ⟦Fr < fem. of *gourd*, numb, heavy, dull < L *gurdus*, dull, heavy, stupid⟧ the basic monetary unit of Haiti: see the table of monetary units in the Reference Supplement

gour·mand (go͝or mänd′; go͝or′mänd′, -mənd) ***n.*** ⟦ME *gourmaunt* < OFr *gourmand*, altered < ? *gormet*: see GOURMET⟧ **1** [Obs.] a glutton **2** a person with a hearty liking for good food and drink and a tendency to indulge in them to excess **3** GOURMET —***SYN.*** EPICURE

gour·man·dise (go͝or mən dēz′) ***n.*** ⟦Fr⟧ the tastes or connoisseurship of a gourmand

gour·met (go͝or mā′, gôr-; go͝or′mā, gôr′-) ***n.*** ⟦Fr < OFr *gormet, gromet*, servant, wine taster, vintner's assistant: meaning infl. by GOURMAND⟧ a person who likes and is an excellent judge of fine foods and beverages; epicure —***adj.* 1** that is of a quality fit for a gourmet [*gourmet cheeses*] **2** of or having to do with fine foods and beverages [*gourmet cooking*] —***SYN.*** EPICURE

Gour·mont (go͞or mōn′), **Ré·my de** (rā mē′ də) 1858-1915; Fr. poet, novelist, & literary critic

gout (gout) ***n.*** ⟦ME *goute* < OFr, gout, lit., a drop < L *gutta*, a drop: orig. attributed to a discharge of drops of humors⟧ **1** a hereditary form of recurrent, acute arthritis with swelling and severe pain, characterized by an excess of uric acid in the blood and deposits of uric acid salts, usually in the joints of the feet and hands, esp. in the big toe **2** a large splash, clot, glob, etc.

gout·y (gout′ē) ***adj.* gout′i·er, gout′i·est 1** having, or tending to have, gout **2** resulting from or causing gout **3** swollen with gout —**gout′i·ly *adv.*** —**gout′i·ness *n.***

gov or **Gov** *abbrev.* **1** government **2** governor

.gov (dät′guv′) *abbrev. Comput.* government: a U.S. domain name

gov·ern (guv′ərn) ***vt.*** ⟦ME *governen* < OFr *gouverner* < L *gubernare*, to pilot (a ship), direct, guide < Gr *kybernan*, to steer, govern, prob. of non-IE orig.⟧ **1** to exercise authority over; rule, administer, direct, control, manage, etc. **2** to influence the action or conduct of; guide; sway [*to govern public opinion*] **3** to hold in check; restrain; curb [*to govern one's temper*] **4** to regulate the speed of (an automobile, etc.) by means of a governor **5** to be a rule or law for; determine [*the scientific principles governing a phenomenon*] **6** *Gram. a)* to require (a word) to be in a certain case or mood *b)* to require (a particular case or mood): used as of prepositions with noun cases, esp. in highly inflected languages, and, in English, more loosely, of any interrelationship between forms, as that between a preposition and a following pronoun —***vi.*** to exercise the function of governing; rule —**gov′ern·a·ble *adj.***

SYN.—**govern** implies the exercise of authority in controlling the actions of the members of a body politic and directing the affairs of state, and generally connotes as its purpose the maintenance of public order and the promotion of the common welfare; **rule** now usually signifies the exercise of arbitrary or autocratic power; **administer** implies the orderly management of governmental affairs by executive officials

gov·ern·ance (guv′ər nəns) ***n.*** ⟦ME < OFr *gouvernance* < ML *gubernantia* < prp. of L *gubernare*: see prec.⟧ the action, manner, function, or power of government

gov·ern·ess (guv′ər nis) ***n.*** a woman employed in a private home to train and teach a child or children

gov·ern·ment (guv′ərn mənt, -ər-) ***n.*** ⟦OFr *governement*: see GOVERN & -MENT⟧ **1** *a)* the exercise of authority over a state, district, organization, institution, etc.; direction; control; rule; management *b)* the right, function, or power of governing **2** *a)* a system of ruling, controlling, etc. *b)* an established system of political administration by which a nation, state, district, etc. is governed [*we need honest government*] *c)* the study of such systems; political science **3** all the people or agencies that administer or control the affairs of a nation, state, institution, etc.; administration [*the election resulted in a new government*] **4** [*often* **G-**] the executive or administrative branch of government of a particular nation as constituted by the political party or coalition in power [*a Labor government in Great Britain*] **5** [Now Rare] a governed territory **6** *Gram.* the influence of one word over the case or mood of another —***adj.*** of or relating to government —☆**gov′ern·men′tal *adj.*** —☆**gov′ern·men′tal·ly *adv.***

gov·er·nor (guv′ə nər, -ər-) ***n.*** ⟦ME *governour* < OFr *governeor* < L *gubernator*, a pilot, steersman, governor⟧ **1** a person who governs; esp., *a)* a person appointed to govern a dependency, province, town, fort, etc. ☆*b)* the elected head of any state of the U.S. *c)* any of the group of persons who direct an organization or institution [*the board of governors of a hospital*] *d)* [Chiefly Brit.] the person in charge of an organization or institution, as a prison **2** a mechanical device for automatically controlling the speed of an engine or motor as by regulating the intake of fuel, steam, etc. **3** [Brit. Informal] a person having authority; esp., one's father or employer: as a term of address, somewhat old-fashioned

governor general *pl.* **governors general** or **governor generals 1** a governor who has subordinate or deputy governors, specif., one who is appointed by the British sovereign, as in some countries of the Commonwealth **2** in some countries of the Commonwealth, a person appointed as a symbolic representative of the British sovereign Also [Brit.] **gov′er·nor-gen′er·al *n.**, pl.* gov′er·nors-gen′er·al**

gov·er·nor·ship (-ship′) ***n.*** the position, function, or term of office of a governor

govt or **Govt** *abbrev.* government

gow·an (gou′ən) ***n.*** ⟦< obs. *gollan*, yellow flower < ME < or akin to ON *goll*, GOLD⟧ [Scot.] any yellow or white field flower; esp., the English daisy

Gow·er (gou′ər, gō′ər), **John** 1330-1408; Eng. poet

gowk (gouk, gōk) ***n.*** ⟦ME *goke, gouk* < ON *gaukr*, akin to OE *geac*, Ger *gauch*, of echoic orig.⟧ [Brit. Dial.] **1** a cuckoo **2** a simpleton

gown (goun) ***n.*** ⟦ME *goune* < OFr < LL *gunna*, loose robe, orig., fur cloak⟧ **1** a long, loose outer garment; specif., *a)* DRESSING GOWN *b)* a nightgown, nightshirt, etc. *c)* a cotton smock worn by a surgeon *d)* a flowing robe worn as a symbol of office or status by certain officials, members of the clergy, scholars, etc. **2** a woman's long dress, esp. one that is elegant or formal **3** the members of a college or university as distinct from the other residents of the community [*conflicts between town and gown*] —***vt.*** to dress in a gown, as in an academic or ecclesiastic robe

goy (goi) ***n.**, pl.* **goys** or **goy·im** (goi′im) ⟦Yiddish < Heb, tribe, nation⟧ [Informal] a non-Jew; gentile: often used contemptuously —**goy′ish *adj.***

Go·ya (y Lu·cien·tes) (gô′yä ē lo͞o thyen′tās), **Fran·cis·co Jo·sé de** (frän thēs′kô hô se′ *the*) 1746-1828; Sp. painter

GP or **gp** *abbrev.* general practitioner

GPA *abbrev.* grade-point average

gpm *abbrev.* gallons per minute

GPO *abbrev.* **1** General Post Office **2** General Printing Office

gps *abbrev.* gallons per second

GPS *abbrev.* Global Positioning System: an electronic system using a network of satellites to indicate on a receiver the position of a vehicle, ship, person, etc.

gr *abbrev.* **1** grade **2** grain(s) **3** gram(s) **4** grammar **5** great **6** gross **7** group

Gr *abbrev.* **1** Greece **2** Greek

Graaf·i·an follicle (*or* vesicle) (graf′ē ən, gräf′-) ⟦after R. de *Graaf* (1641-73), Du anatomist⟧ any of the small, round, fluid-filled sacs in the ovary of higher mammals, each of which contains a maturing ovum surrounded by hormone-secreting cells

grab (grab) ***vt.* grabbed, grab′bing** ⟦prob. < MDu *grabben*, akin to ON *grapa*, GRASP < IE base **ghrebh-* > Sans *grabh-*, to seize⟧ **1** to seize or snatch suddenly; take roughly and quickly **2** to get possession of by unscrupulous methods **3** [Informal] to get or take quickly [*to grab a bite to eat*] ☆**4**

[Slang] to attract strongly the attention of; impress greatly *[a performance that grabs an audience]* **—*vi.*** to snatch or try to snatch something: often with *for, at, onto,* etc. **—*n.*** **1** the act of grabbing **2** something grabbed **3** any of various mechanical devices for clutching something to be hoisted **4** [Chiefly Brit.] CLAMSHELL (sense 2) **—*SYN.*** TAKE **—☆up for grabs** [Slang] available to the highest bidder, most aggressive person, etc. **—grab′ber *n.***

☆**grab bag** **1** a container holding various wrapped or bagged articles that are sold unseen: the buyer draws one at random and pays a fixed price **2** something like this in having a variety of things

grab·ble (grab′əl) ***vi.*** **-bled, -bling** ⟦Du *grabbelen,* freq. of MDu *grabben,* GRAB⟧ **1** to feel about with the hands; grope **2** to sprawl

grab·by (grab′ē) ***adj.*** **-bi·er, -bi·est** [Informal] grasping; avaricious

gra·ben (grä′bən) ***n.*** ⟦Ger, a ditch < OHG *grabo* < *graban,* to dig: see GRAVE[2]⟧ a relatively long, narrow area of the earth's crust that has subsided between two bordering faults: cf. HORST

Grac·chus (grak′əs) **1 Gaius Sem·pro·ni·us** (sem prō′nē əs) 153-121 B.C.; Rom. statesman & social reformer **2 Tiberius Sempronius** 163-133 B.C.; Rom. statesman and social reformer: brother of Gaius The two brothers are called **the Grac′chi** (-ī)

grace (grās) ***n.*** ⟦ME < OFr < L *gratia,* pleasing quality, favor, thanks < *gratus,* pleasing < IE base **gwer-,* to lift up the voice, praise > Sans *gṛṇāti,* (he) sings, praises & OIr *bard,* bard⟧ **1** beauty or charm of form, composition, movement, or expression **2** an attractive quality, feature, manner, etc. **3** [**G-**] any of the Graces **4** *a)* a sense of what is right and proper; decency *b)* thoughtfulness toward others **5** goodwill; favor **6** [Archaic] mercy; clemency **7** *a)* a period of time granted beyond the date set for the performance of an act or the payment of an obligation; temporary exemption *b)* favor shown by granting such a delay **8** a short prayer in which blessing is asked, or thanks are given, for a meal **9** [**G-**] a title of respect or reverence used in speaking to or of an archbishop, duke, or duchess: preceded by *Your* or by *His* or *Her* **10** [*pl.*] *Music* ornamental notes or effects collectively, as appoggiaturas, slides, trills, etc. **11** *Theol. a)* the unmerited love and favor of God toward human beings *b)* divine influence acting in a person to make the person pure, morally strong, etc. *c)* the condition of a person brought to God's favor through this influence *d)* a special virtue, gift, or help given to a person by God **—*vt.*** **graced, grac′ing** **1** to give or add grace or graces to; decorate; adorn **2** to bring honor to; dignify **3** *Music* to add a grace note or notes to **—fall from grace** to do wrong; sin **—have the grace** to be so aware of what is proper as (to do something) **—in the good** (or **bad**) **graces of** in favor (or disfavor) with **—with bad grace** sullenly or reluctantly **—with good grace** graciously or willingly

Grace (grās) ***n.*** ⟦see prec.⟧ a feminine name: dim. *Gracie*

grace cup **1** *a)* a cup passed around for drinking a toast after grace at the end of a meal *b)* the toast **2** a parting drink or toast

grace·ful (grās′fəl) ***adj.*** having grace, or beauty of form, composition, movement, or expression; elegant **—grace′ful·ly *adv.*** **—grace′ful·ness *n.***

grace·less (grās′lis) ***adj.*** **1** lacking any sense of what is right or proper **2** without grace; clumsy or inelegant **—grace′less·ly *adv.*** **—grace′less·ness *n.***

grace note *Music* a note not necessary to the melody, added only for ornamentation: it is usually printed as a small note with a slant line through the stem, just before the note that it embellishes

grace period extra time allowed, as for payment of a note, insurance premium, etc. after it is due

Grac·es (grās′iz) ***pl.n.*** ⟦transl. of L *Gratiae* (see GRACE), transl. of Gr *Charites,* pl. of *Charis:* see CHARISMA⟧ *Gr. Myth.* the three sister goddesses who have control over pleasure, charm, and beauty in human life and in nature: Aglaia, Euphrosyne, and Thalia

gra·ci·as (grä′thē äs′, -sē-) ***interj.*** ⟦Sp⟧ thank you

grac·ile (gras′il) ***adj.*** ⟦L *gracilis,* scanty⟧ **1** slender; slim **2** ⟦by assoc. with GRACE⟧ gracefully slender **3** graceful **—gra·cil·i·ty** (gra sil′ə tē, grə-) ***n.***

gra·ci·o·so (grā′shē ō′sō; *Sp* grä thyô′sô) ***n.*** ⟦Sp⟧ a clown or buffoon in Spanish comedies

gra·cious (grā′shəs) ***adj.*** ⟦ME < OFr < L *gratiosus,* in favor, popular, kind < *gratia:* see GRACE⟧ **1** having or showing kindness, courtesy, charm, etc. **2** merciful; compassionate **3** indulgent or polite to those held to be inferiors **4** characterized by the taste, luxury, and social ease associated with prosperity, education, etc. *[gracious living]* **5** [Archaic] having pleasing qualities; attractive **—*interj.*** used to express surprise or dismay **—gra′cious·ly *adv.*** **—gra′cious·ness *n.***

grack·le (grak′əl) ***n.*** ⟦L *graculus,* jackdaw < IE echoic base **ger-* > CRANE, CROW[1]⟧ ☆any of several blackbirds somewhat smaller than a crow; esp., the common grackle (*Quiscalus quiscula*)

☆**grad**[1] (grad) ***n.*** [Informal] a graduate

grad[2] *abbrev.* **1** graduate **2** graduated

gra·date (grā′dāt′) ***vt., vi.*** **-dat′ed, -dat′ing** ⟦back-form. < fol.⟧ to pass or cause to pass by imperceptible degrees from one to another; shade into one another, as colors

gra·da·tion (grā dā′shən, grə-) ***n.*** ⟦Fr < L *gradatio* < *gradatus,* having steps or grades < *gradus:* see fol.⟧ **1** the act or process of forming or arranging in grades, stages, or steps **2** a gradual change by steps or stages from one condition, quality, etc. to another **3** a gradual shading of one tint, tone, or color into another **4** a step, stage, or degree in a graded series; transitional stage *[the many gradations between good and bad]* **5** *Geol.* the process of wearing away high areas of land by erosion and building up low areas by deposition **6** *Linguis.* ABLAUT: in full **vowel gradation** **—gra·da′tion·al *adj.*** **—gra·da′tion·al·ly *adv.***

grade (grād) ***n.*** ⟦Fr < L *gradus,* a step, degree, rank < *gradi,* to step, walk < IE base **ghredh-,* to stride > Goth *griths,* step⟧ **1** any of the stages in an orderly, systematic progression; step; degree **2** *a)* a degree or rating in a scale classifying according to quality, rank, worth, intensity, etc. (often in hyphenated compounds) *[grade A eggs, weapons-grade plutonium]* *b)* any of the official ranks or ratings of officers or enlisted persons *[an army colonel and a navy captain are in grade O-6]* *c)* an accepted standard or level *[up to grade]* *d)* a group of people of the same rank, merit, worth, etc. ☆**3** *a)* the degree of rise or descent of a sloping surface, as of a highway, railroad, etc. *b)* such a sloping surface **4** the ground level around a building ☆**5** *a)* any of the divisions in a school curriculum usually equal to one year; most systems in the U.S. include twelve grades after the kindergarten *b)* a group of pupils forming such a division in a school ☆**6** a mark or rating on an examination, in a school course, etc. ☆**7** *Animal Husbandry* an animal with one parent of pure breed **8** *Linguis.* any of the various forms in which a vowel may appear in grammatically or etymologically related forms as a result of gradation **—*vt.*** **grad′ed, grad′ing** **1** to arrange or classify by grades; rate according to quality, rank, worth, etc.; sort **2** to give a GRADE (sense 6) to **3** to gradate ☆**4** to level or slope (ground, a road, etc.) evenly ☆**5** *Animal Husbandry* to improve by crossing with a pure breed: often with *up* **—*vi.*** **1** to assume an indicated rank or position in a series; be of a certain grade **2** to change gradually; go through a series of stages **—☆at grade** on the same level **—☆make the grade** **1** to get to the top of a steep incline **2** [Informal] to overcome obstacles and succeed **—☆the grades** elementary school

-grade (grād) ⟦< L *gradi,* to walk: see prec.⟧ *combining form forming adjectives* walking or moving (in a specified manner) *[plantigrade]*

☆**grade crossing** the place where a railroad intersects another railroad or a roadway on the same level

grade-point average (grād′point′) the mean of the numerical equivalents of a student's grades for a given period: see POINT SYSTEM (sense 1)

☆**grad·er** (grād′ər) ***n.*** **1** a person or thing that grades **2** a pupil in a (specified) grade at a school *[a fifth grader]*: often hyphenated

☆**grade school** ELEMENTARY SCHOOL **—grade schooler, grade′-school′er *n.***

☆**grade separation** a crossing with an overpass or underpass

gra·di·ent (grā′dē ənt) ***adj.*** ⟦L *gradiens* (gen. *gradientis*), prp. of *gradi,* to step: see GRADE⟧ ascending or descending with a uniform slope **—*n.*** **1** *a)* a slope, as of a road or railroad *b)* the degree of such slope **2** *Biol.* a gradation in rate of growth, metabolism, etc. in an organism, growing part, or developing embryo ☆**3** *Math.* a vector pointing in the direction of the most rapid increase of a function and having coordinates that are the partial derivatives of the function **4** *Physics* the rate of change of a physical quantity, as temperature or pressure, with distance

gra·dine (grä dēn′, grā′dēn′) ***n.*** ⟦Fr < It *gradino,* dim. of *grado* < L *gradus:* see GRADE⟧ **1** one of a series of steps or seats arranged in tiers **2** a shelf at the back of an altar, as for candlesticks Also **gra·din** (grā′din)

grad·u·al (gra′jo͞o əl, -jə wəl) ***adj.*** ⟦ML *gradualis* < L *gradus:* see GRADE⟧ taking place by almost imperceptible steps or degrees; developing little by little, not sharply or suddenly **—*n.*** ⟦ML *graduale,* book of hymns orig. sung on steps of a pulpit < L *gradus*⟧ [*often* **G-**] **1** a set of usually Scriptural verses following the Epistle at Mass **2** an official book containing the words and musical notation for the parts of the Mass sung by participants other than the celebrant: in full **Gra·du·a·le Ro·ma·num** (grä′do͞o ä′lā rō mä′no͝om) **—grad′u·al·ly *adv.*** **—grad′u·al·ness *n.***

☆**grad·u·al·ism** (-iz′əm) ***n.*** the principle of seeking to achieve social or political changes or goals gradually **—grad′u·al·ist *n., adj.*** **—grad′u·al·is′tic *adj.***

grad·u·ate (gra′jo͞o it; *for v.* gra′jo͞o āt′) ***n.*** ⟦< ML *graduatus,* pp. of *graduare,* to graduate < L *gradus:* see GRADE⟧ **1** a person who has completed a course of study at a school or college and has received a degree or diploma **2** a flask, tube, or other container marked with a progressive series of degrees (lines or numbers or both) for measuring liquids or solids **—*vt.*** **-at′ed, -at′ing** **1** to give a degree or diploma to in recognition of the completion of a course of study at a school or college **2** [Informal] to become a graduate of *[to graduate college]* **3** to mark (a flask, tube, gauge, etc.) with degrees for measuring **4** *a)* to arrange or classify into grades according to amount, size, etc. *b)* to arrange in grades or stages *[graduated income tax]* **—*vi.*** **1** to become a graduate of a school or college **2** to change, esp. advance, by degrees **—*adj.*** **1** having been graduated from a school, college, etc. *[a graduate engineer]* ☆**2** designating, of, for, or participating in instruction or research in various fields leading to degrees above the bachelor's *[graduate courses, graduate students]* **—grad′u·a′tor *n.***

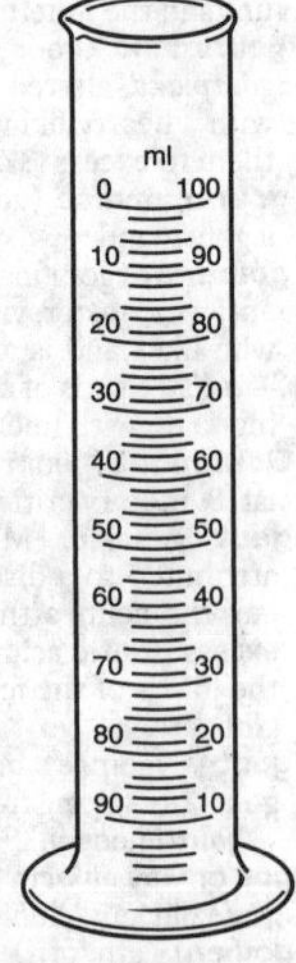

graduated cylinder

graduated cylinder a thin, cylindrical container that is scaled, usually in milliliters: used as in a laboratory to measure and pour exact amounts of a liquid

grad·u·a·tion (gra′jo͞o ā′shən) ***n.*** ⟦ML *graduatio* < pp. of *graduare:* see GRADUATE⟧ **1** *a)* a graduating or being graduated from a school or college *b)* the ceremony connected with this; commencement **2** *a)* a marking of a flask, tube, gauge, etc. with a series of degrees for measuring *b)* one or all of the degrees marked; a degree or scale **3** an arrangement or classification into grades according to amount, size, etc.

gra·dus (grā′dəs) ***n.*** ⟦< L *Gradus (ad Parnassum)*, lit., a step (to Parnassus), title of a book (17th c.) on Latin prosody⟧ **1** a dictionary of prosody for help in writing Greek or Latin poetry **2** a book of piano studies, études, etc. arranged in a progressive order of difficulty

Grae·ae (grē′ē′) ***pl.n.*** ⟦L < Gr *Graiai*, pl. of *graia*, old woman < *grais*, old, akin to *gēras*, old age: see GERIATRICS⟧ *Gr. Myth.* the three old sisters who act as guards for the Gorgons and have only one eye and one tooth to share among them

Grae·cism (grē′siz′əm) ***n.*** *alt. sp. of* GRECISM

Grae·cize (-sīz′) ***vt., vi.*** **-cized′**, **-ciz′ing** *alt. sp. of* GRECIZE

Grae·co- (grē′kō) *combining form* GRECO-

Graf (gräf) ***n.***, *pl.* **Graf·en** (gräf′ən) ⟦Ger⟧ a German, Austrian, or Swedish title of nobility corresponding to *earl* or *count*

graf·fi·ti (grə fēt′ē) ***pl.n.***, *sing.* **-fi′to** (-ō) ⟦It, scribblings < *graffio*, a scratch < L *graphium*: see GRAFT⟧ [*now usually with sing. v.*] inscriptions, slogans, drawings, etc. scratched, scribbled, or drawn, often crudely, on a wall or other public surface

graf·fi·tied (grə fēt′ēd) ***adj.*** having or covered with graffiti

graf·fi·tist (grə fēt′ist) ***n.*** a person who writes or draws graffiti, esp. one whose stylized works are thought of as art

graft (graft, gräft) ***n.*** ⟦with unhistoric *-t*, for earlier *graff* < ME *graffe* < OFr, a pencil < L *graphium* < Gr *grapheion*, stylus (see GRAPHIC): from resemblance of the scion to a pointed pencil⟧ **1** *a)* a shoot or bud of one plant or tree inserted or to be inserted into the stem or trunk of another, where it continues to grow, becoming a permanent part; scion *b)* the act or process of inserting such a bud or shoot *c)* the place on a plant or tree where such a bud or shoot has been inserted *d)* a tree or plant with such an insertion **2** a joining of one thing to another as if by grafting ☆**3** *a)* the act of taking advantage of one's position, esp. a political position, to gain money, property, etc. dishonestly *b)* anything acquired by such illegal methods, as an illicit profit from government business **4** *Surgery a)* a piece of skin, bone, or other living tissue transplanted or to be transplanted from one body, or place on a body, to another, where it grows and becomes a permanent part *b)* such a transplanting —***vt.*** **1** *a)* to insert (a shoot or bud) as a graft *b)* to insert a graft of (one plant) in another *c)* to produce (a fruit, flower, etc.) by means of a graft **2** to join or make as one **3** *Surgery* to transplant (a graft) —***vi.*** **1** to be grafted **2** to make a graft on a plant —**graft′er** ***n.***

graft·age (graf′tij) ***n.*** **1** the act or science of grafting **2** the state of being grafted

☆**gra·ham** (grā′əm, gram) ***adj.*** ⟦after S. *Graham* (1794-1851), U.S. dietary reformer⟧ designating or made of whole-wheat flour

Gra·ham (grā′əm, gram) **1 Billy** (born *William Franklin Graham*) 1918- ; U.S. Christian evangelist **2 Martha** 1893?-1991; U.S. dancer & choreographer

graham cracker ⟦after S. *Graham*, who invented it as an early health food: see GRAHAM⟧ a crisp, somewhat sweet cracker made mainly of graham flour

Gra·hame (grā′əm), **Kenneth** 1859-1932; Brit. writer

Grai·ae (grī′ē′, grā′ē′) ***pl.n.*** *var. of* GRAEAE

Gra·ian Alps (grā′ən) division of the W Alps, along the French-Italian border: highest peak, *c.* 13,320 ft (4,060 m)

Grail (grāl) ***n.*** ⟦ME *graal* < OFr < ML *gradalis*, flat dish, cup < ? VL **cratalis* < L *crater*, mixing bowl: see CRATER⟧ **1** *Medieval Legend* the cup or platter used by Jesus at the Last Supper, and by Joseph of Arimathea to collect drops of Jesus' blood at the Crucifixion: the chivalric quest for the Grail, which later disappeared, is treated in Malory's *Morte Darthur*, Wagner's *Parsifal*, etc. **2** [*usually* **g-**] HOLY GRAIL (sense 2)

grain (grān) ***n.*** ⟦ME *greyne* < OFr *grein*, a seed, grain (< L *granum*, a seed, kernel) & *grainne*, seed or grain collectively (< LL *grana*, fem., orig. pl. of L *granum*) < IE base **ĝer-*, to become ripe > CORN[1], KERNEL⟧ **1** a small, hard seed or seedlike fruit, esp. that of any cereal plant, as wheat, rice, corn, rye, etc. **2** *a)* cereal seeds in general *b)* the seeds of a specific cereal *c)* any plant or plants producing cereal seeds: also called *corn* in Great Britain **3** *a)* a tiny, solid particle, as of salt or sand *b)* a crystal or crystals collectively; also crystallization, esp. of sugar **4** a tiny bit; slightest amount [*a grain of sense*] **5** ⟦orig. from the weight of a grain of wheat⟧ the smallest unit in the system of weights used in the U.S., Great Britain, and Canada, equal to .0648 gram: one pound avoirdupois equals 7,000 grains; one pound troy or apothecaries' weight equals 5,760 grains: abbrev. *gr* **6** *a)* the arrangement or direction of fibers, layers, or particles of wood, leather, stone, paper, etc. *b)* the markings or texture due to a particular arrangement *c)* paint or other surface finish imitating such markings or texture *d)* a granular surface appearance **7** *a)* that side of a piece of leather from which the hair has been removed *b)* the markings on that side **8** *a)* disposition; nature *b)* essential quality **9** [Obs.] *a)* kermes or cochineal *b)* a red dye made from either *c)* any fast dye *d)* [Archaic] color or shade —***vt.*** **1** to form into grains; granulate **2** to paint or otherwise finish (a surface) in imitation of the grain of wood, marble, etc. **3** *a)* to remove the hair from (hides) *b)* to put a finish on the grain surface of (leather) —***vi.*** to form grains —**against the** (or **one's**) **grain** ⟦prob. orig. in allusion to the difficulty of planing or cutting wood in a direction not in line with its GRAIN (*n. 6a*)⟧ contrary to one's feelings or wishes, to prevailing trends or attitudes, etc.

grain alcohol ethyl alcohol, esp. when made from grain

☆**grain elevator** a tall warehouse, often cylindrical, for collecting, storing, and discharging grain

grain·field (grān′fēld′) ***n.*** a field where grain is grown

grain sorghum any of various strains of sorghum grown primarily for grain

grain·y (grān′ē) ***adj.*** **grain′i·er**, **grain′i·est** **1** having a clearly defined grain: said of textures or surfaces, as of wood **2** consisting of grains; coarsely textured; granular —**grain′i·ness** ***n.***

gral·la·to·ri·al (gral′ə tôr′ē əl) ***adj.*** ⟦ModL *grallatorius* < L *grallator*, walker on stilts < *grallae*, stilts (akin to *gradi*: see GRADE) + -IAL⟧ of or pertaining to long-legged water birds of various orders, as herons and cranes

gram[1] (gram) ***n.*** ⟦Fr *gramme* < LL *gramma*, weight of two oboli < Gr, small weight, lit., what is written < *graphein*, to write: see GRAPHIC⟧ the basic unit of mass in the metric system, equal to 0.03527 ounce (0.0022046 pound or 15.4321 grains): now defined in the SI system as 0.001 of the mass of the standard international kilogram (a platinum-iridium cylinder kept in France): one pound equals 453.5924 grams: abbrev. *g*

gram[2] (gram) ***n.*** ⟦Port *grão* < L *granum*: see GRAIN⟧ any of certain leguminous plants, used as fodder; esp., the chickpea

gram[3] (gram) ***n.*** [Informal] *short for* GRANDMOTHER

gram[4] *abbrev.* **1** grammar **2** grammatical

-gram (gram) ⟦< Gr *gramma*: see GRAM[1]⟧ *combining form forming nouns* **1** something written down, drawn, or recorded [*telegram, electrocardiogram*] **2** a telegram or singing telegram, or something resembling this in some way: used esp. in nonce compounds [*Mailgram, Candygram*]

☆**gra·ma** (gram′ə, grä′mə) ***n.*** ⟦Sp < L *gramen*, GRASS⟧ any of a genus (*Bouteloua*) of native range grasses of the W U.S.: also **grama grass**

gram·a·rye or **gram·a·ry** (gram′ə rē) ***n.*** ⟦ME *gramery*, grammar, magic < OFr *gramaire*, GRAMMAR⟧ [Archaic] magic; the occult

gram atom *Chem.* the quantity of an element having a weight in grams numerically equal to the element's atomic weight: a gram atom of copper, the atomic weight of which is 63.54, is a quantity of copper weighing 63.54 grams: also **gram-a·tom·ic weight** (gram′ə täm′ik)

gram calorie CALORIE (sense 1)

gra·mer·cy (grə mʉr′sē, gram′ər sē) ***interj.*** ⟦ME < OFr *grant merci* < *grant*, GRAND + *merci*, thanks: see MERCY⟧ [Archaic] **1** used to express gratitude **2** used to express surprise

☆**gram·i·ci·din** (gram′i sīd′'n) ***n.*** ⟦GRAM(-POSITIVE) + -I- + -CID(E) + -IN[1]⟧ any of a group of chemically related antibiotic polypeptides produced by a soil bacillus (*Bacillus brevis*) and used in medicines to treat various bacterial infections, esp. of the skin and eyes

gra·min·e·ous (grə min′ē əs) ***adj.*** ⟦L *gramineus* < *gramen*, GRASS⟧ **1** of the grass family **2** of or like grass; grassy

gram·i·niv·o·rous (gram′i niv′ə rəs) ***adj.*** ⟦< L *gramen*, GRASS + -I- + -VOROUS⟧ feeding on grasses; grass-eating

gram·mar (gram′ər) ***n.*** ⟦ME *gramer* < OFr *gramaire* < L *grammatica* (*ars*, art) < Gr *grammatikē* (*technē*, art), grammar, learning < *gramma*, something written (see GRAM[1]): in L & Gr a term for the whole apparatus of literary study: in the medieval period, specif., "the study of Latin," hence "all learning as recorded in Latin" (cf. GRAMMAR SCHOOL in Brit usage), and "the occult sciences as assoc. with this learning": see GRAMARYE, GLAMOUR⟧ **1** that part of the study of language which deals with the forms and structure of words (*morphology*), with their customary arrangement in phrases and sentences (*syntax*), and now often with language sounds (*phonology*) and word meanings (*semantics*) **2** the system of a given language at a given time **3** a body of rules imposed on a given language for speaking and writing it, based on the study of its GRAMMAR (sense 2) or on some adaptation of another, esp. Latin, grammar **4** a book or treatise on grammar **5** one's manner of speaking or writing as judged by prescriptive grammatical rules [*his grammar was poor*] **6** *a)* the elementary principles of a field of knowledge *b)* a book or treatise on these

gram·mar·i·an (grə mer′ē ən) ***n.*** ⟦ME *gramarian* < MFr *gramarien*⟧ a specialist or expert in grammar

grammar school ☆**1** [Now Rare] an elementary school: the term was variously applied to different school levels, esp. to that between the fifth and eighth grades **2** in England *a)* [Historical] a school where Latin was taught *b)* a government-supported secondary school preparing pupils for college

gram·mat·i·cal (grə mat′i kəl) ***adj.*** ⟦LL *grammaticalis* < L *grammatica*: see GRAMMAR⟧ **1** of, relating to, or according to grammar **2** conforming to the rules of grammar —**gram·mat′i·cal′i·ty** ***n.*** —**gram·mat′i·cal·ly** ***adv.*** —**gram·mat′i·cal·ness** ***n.***

gramme (gram) ***n.*** *former Brit. var. of* GRAM[1]

gram molecule MOLE[4]: also **gram-mo·lec·u·lar weight** (gram′mə lek′yoo lər)

☆**Gram·my** (gram′ē) ***n.***, *pl.* **-mys** or **-mies** ⟦< *Grammy*, service mark < GRAM(OPHONE) + *-my* (as in EMMY)⟧ **1** any of the annual awards given by the National Academy of Recording Arts & Sciences for special achievement in the recording industry **2** any of the statuettes given to those receiving such awards

Gram-neg·a·tive (gram′neg′ə tiv) ***adj.*** [*also* **g-**] designating bacteria that do not retain the color stain: see GRAM'S METHOD

☆**gram·o·phone** (gram′ə fōn′) ***n.*** ⟦so named (1887) by E. Berliner (1851-1929), U.S. inventor, born in Germany, by arbitrary inversion of PHONOGRAM⟧ *now chiefly Brit. var. of* PHONOGRAPH

Gram·pi·an (gram′pē ən) former administrative region of NE Scotland

Grampian Mountains mountain range across central & N Scotland, dividing the Highlands from the Lowlands: highest peak, Ben Nevis: also **Grampian Hills** or **Grampians**

Gram-pos·i·tive (gram′päz′ə tiv) ***adj.*** [*also* **g-**] designating bacteria that retain the color stain: see GRAM'S METHOD

gramps (gramps) ***n.*** [Informal] *short for* GRANDFATHER

gram·pus (gram′pəs) ***n., pl.*** **-pus·es** ⟦earlier *graundepose*, altered (after GRAND) < ME *grapays* < OFr *graspeis* < L *crassus piscis* < *crassus*, fat (see CRASS) + *piscis*, FISH⟧ **1** a playful, black-and-white dolphin (*Grampus griseus*) **2** KILLER WHALE

Gram·sci (gräm′shē), **An·to·nio** (än tô′nyô) 1891-1937; It. Communist leader & Marxist theoretician

Gram's method (gramz) ⟦after Hans C. J. *Gram* (1853-1938), Dan physician⟧ a method of staining bacteria for the purpose of classification, involving treatment with crystal violet, an iodine solution, and alcohol: the violet stain is retained by Gram-positive bacteria or lost by Gram-negative bacteria when the alcohol is applied

gran (gran) ***n.*** [Informal] *short for* GRANDMOTHER

gra·na (grā′nə) ***n.*** *pl. of* GRANUM

Gra·na·da (grə nä′də; *Sp* grä nä′thä) **1** former Moorish kingdom in S Spain **2** city in this region: site of the Alhambra

gran·a·dil·la (gran′ə dil′ə) ***n.*** ⟦Sp < dim. of *granada*, pomegranate < L *granatus*, containing seeds < *granum*, seed: see GRAIN⟧ the edible fruit of certain passionflowers

Gra·na·dos (grə nä′dōs), **En·ri·que** (en rē′kā) 1867-1916; Sp. composer

gran·a·ry (gran′ə rē, grān′-) ***n., pl.*** **-ries** ⟦L *granarium* < *granum*: see GRANADILLA & -ARY⟧ **1** a building for storing threshed grain **2** a region that produces much grain

Gran Cha·co (grän chä′kô) CHACO

grand (grand) ***adj.*** ⟦ME *graunt* < OFr *grand, grant* < L *grandis*, full-grown, great (replacing *magnus* in LL & Romance languages), prob. < IE base **gwrendh-*, to swell up > Gr *brenthos*, pride⟧ **1** higher in rank, status, or dignity than others having the same title [*a grand duke*] **2** most important; chief; main; principal [*the grand ballroom, grand prize*] **3** imposing because of great size, beauty, and extent; magnificent [*grand scenery*] **4** handsome and luxurious; characterized by splendor and display [*a grand banquet*] **5** eminent; distinguished; illustrious **6** self-important; pretentious; haughty **7** lofty and dignified, as in style **8** complete; overall [*the grand total*] **9** [Informal] very good; excellent, delightful, admirable, etc.: a general term of approval **10** *Music* full; complete [*a grand chorus*] —***n.*** **1** GRAND PIANO ☆**2** *pl.* **grand** [Slang] a thousand dollars —**grand′ly** ***adj.*** —**grand′ness** ***n.***

SYN.—**grand** is applied to that which makes a strong impression because of its greatness (in size or some favorable quality), dignity, and splendor [*the Grand Canyon*]; **magnificent** suggests a surpassing beauty, richness, or splendor, or an exalted or glorious quality [*a magnificent voice*]; **imposing** suggests that which strikingly impresses one by its size, dignity, or excellence of character [*an imposing array of facts*]; **stately** suggests that which is imposing in dignified grace and may imply a greatness of size [*a stately mansion*]; **majestic** adds to stately the idea of lofty grandeur [*the majestic Rockies*]; **august** suggests an exalted dignity or impressiveness such as inspires awe [*an august personage*]; **grandiose** is often used disparagingly of a grandeur that is affected or exaggerated [*a grandiose manner*]

grand- (grand) ⟦OFr (see prec.), replacing OE *ealde-*, ME *olde-*: see OLD⟧ *combining form* of the generation older (or younger) than [*grandmother, grandson*]: see GREAT-

gran·dam (gran′dam′, -dəm) ***n.*** ⟦ME *grandame* < Anglo-Fr *graund dame*: see prec. & DAME⟧ [Now Rare] **1** a grandmother **2** an old woman Also sp. **gran′dame′**

☆**Grand Army of the Republic** an association of Union veterans of the Civil War, formed in 1866: the last member died in 1956

grand·aunt (grand′ant′) ***n.*** GREAT-AUNT

Grand Banks (*or* **Bank**) large shoal in the North Atlantic, southeast of Newfoundland: noted fishing grounds: *c.* 500 mi (805 km) long

Grand Canal **1** canal in NE China, extending from Tianjin to Hangzhou: *c.* 1,000 mi (1,609 km) **2** main canal in Venice

Grand Canyon deep gorge of the Colorado River, in NW Ariz.: over 200 mi (322 km) long; 4-18 mi (6.4-29 km) wide; 1 mi (1.6 km) deep

grand·child (grand′chīld′, gran′-) ***n., pl.*** **-chil′dren** (-chil′dren) a child of one's son or daughter

Grand Cou·lee (ko͞o′lē) dam on the Columbia River, NE Wash.: 550 ft (167 m) high; over 4,000 ft (1,220 m) long

grand·dad, grand-dad, *or* **gran·dad** (gran′dad′) ***n.*** [Informal] *short for* GRANDFATHER

grand·dad·dy (gran′dad′ē) ***n., pl.*** **-dies** [Informal] **1** GRANDDAD **2** *a)* the biggest or best of its kind *b)* the first or oldest of its kind

grand·daugh·ter (-dôt′ər) ***n.*** a daughter of one's son or daughter

grand duchess **1** the wife or widow of a grand duke **2** a woman who has the rank of a grand duke and rules a grand duchy **3** in czarist Russia, a royal princess

grand duchy the territory or a country ruled by a grand duke or a grand duchess

grand duke **1** the sovereign ruler of a grand duchy, ranking just below a king **2** in czarist Russia, a prince of the royal family

grande dame (gränd′däm′) ⟦Fr, great lady⟧ a woman, esp. an older one, of great dignity or prestige

gran·dee (gran dē′) ***n.*** ⟦Sp & Port *grande*: see GRAND⟧ **1** a Spanish or Portuguese nobleman of the highest rank **2** a man of high rank; important personage

Grande-Terre (grän′ter′) E island of the two major islands of Guadeloupe, West Indies: 228 sq mi (591 sq km)

gran·deur (gran′jər, -jo͝or′, -dyo͝or′) ***n.*** ⟦Fr < *grand*: see GRAND⟧ the quality of being grand; specif., *a)* splendor; magnificence *b)* moral or intellectual greatness; nobility

Grand Falls **1** *former name for* CHURCHILL FALLS **2** *see* YELLOWSTONE FALLS

grand·fa·ther (grand′fä′*th*ər, gran′-) ***n.*** **1** the father of one's father or mother: also a term of respectful familiarity to any elderly man **2** a male ancestor; forefather —***vt.*** [Informal] to exempt (an activity, practice, person, etc.) from a new law or regulation by or as by a GRANDFATHER CLAUSE (sense 2): sometimes with *in* or *into*

☆**grandfather clause** **1** a former law in some Southern states waiving electoral literacy requirements for those whose forebears voted before the Civil War, thus keeping the franchise for illiterate whites **2** in some legislation forbidding or regulating a certain activity, a clause which exempts those already engaged in it before the legislation was passed

☆**grandfather (*or* grandfather's) clock** ⟦after such a clock in the song "My *Grandfather's Clock*" (*c.* 1875) by H. C. Work, U.S. songwriter⟧ a large clock with a pendulum, contained in a tall, narrow case

grand·fa·ther·ly (-lē) ***adj.*** **1** of a grandfather **2** having traits considered typical of grandfathers; kindly, indulgent, benign, etc.

Grand Gui·gnol (grän gē nyôl′) ⟦the name of a former theater in Paris noted for such drama⟧ [*often* **g- g-**] [*often not in italics*] any dramatic or literary production designed to shock and horrify its audience with its gruesome or macabre content

gran·di·flo·ra (gran′di flôr′ə) ***adj.*** ⟦ModL < L *grandis*, GRAND + *flos* (gen. *floris*), FLOWER⟧ bearing large flowers —***n.*** any of a group of rose varieties with clusters of large to medium-sized flowers on long stems: created by crossing floribunda and hybrid tea roses

gran·dil·o·quent (gran dil′ə kwənt) ***adj.*** ⟦< L *grandiloquus* < *grandis*, GRAND + *loqui*, to speak, after ELOQUENT⟧ using high-flown, pompous, bombastic words and expressions —*SYN.* BOMBASTIC —**gran·dil′o·quence** ***n.*** —**gran·dil′o·quent·ly** ***adv.***

gran·di·ose (gran′dē ōs′, gran′dē ōs′; *also*, -ōz′) ***adj.*** ⟦Fr < It *grandioso* < L *grandis*, great, GRAND⟧ **1** having grandeur or magnificence; imposing; impressive **2** seeming or trying to seem very important; pompous and showy —*SYN.* GRAND —**gran′di·ose′ly** ***adv.*** —**gran′di·os′i·ty** (-äs′ə tē) ***n.***

gran·di·o·so (grän dyô′sô; *E* gran′dē ō′sō) ***adj., adv.*** ⟦It⟧ *Musical Direction* in a grand, noble style

grand jury a special jury of a statutory number of citizens, usually more than 12, that investigates accusations against persons charged with crime and indicts them for trial before a petit jury if there is sufficient evidence

grand·kid (grand′kid′, gran′-) ***n.*** [Informal] a grandchild

Grand Lama DALAI LAMA

grand larceny *see* LARCENY

grand·ma (gran′mə, -mä′; gra′-, grand′-; -mô′) ***n.*** [Informal] GRANDMOTHER: also **grand′ma·ma′** (-mə mä′, -mä′mə)

grand mal (grän′mäl′, grand′mal′) ⟦Fr, lit., great ailment⟧ a type of epilepsy in which there are convulsions and loss of consciousness: distinguished from PETIT MAL

Grand Ma·nan (mə nan′) island of New Brunswick, Canada, at the entrance to the Bay of Fundy: 55 sq mi (142 sq km)

Grand Mar·nier (grän mär nyā′) *trademark for* a sweet, orange-flavored liqueur, produced in France

grand·mas·ter (grand′mas′tər) ***n.*** **1** a national or, now usually, international title awarded to chess players of the highest ranking **2** a chess player holding this title Also written **grand master**

grand monde (grän mōnd′) ⟦Fr, great world⟧ fashionable society; high society

grand·moth·er (gran′mu*th*′ər, grand′-, gra′-) ***n.*** **1** the mother of one's father or mother: also a term of respectful familiarity to any elderly woman **2** a female ancestor

grand·moth·er·ly (-lē) ***adj.*** **1** of a grandmother **2** having traits considered typical of grandmothers; kindly, indulgent, solicitous, etc. **3** [Informal] fussy

grand·neph·ew (grand′nef′yo͞o, gran′-) ***n.*** the grandson of one's brother or sister; great-nephew

grand·niece (-nēs′) ***n.*** the granddaughter of one's brother or sister; great-niece

grand opera opera, generally on a serious theme, in which the whole text is set to music

grand·pa (gran′pə, -pä′; gram′-, grand′-; -pô′) ***n.*** [Informal] GRANDFATHER: also **grand′pa·pa′** (-pə pä′, -pä′pə)

grand·par·ent (grand′per′ənt, gran′-) ***n.*** a grandfather or grandmother

grand piano a large piano with strings set horizontally in a wing-shaped case supported on three legs

Grand Prairie city in NE Tex.: suburb of Dallas

Grand Pré (gran prā′; *Fr* grän prā′) village in central Nova Scotia, on Minas Basin: site of an early Acadian settlement

grand prix[1] (grän prē′, gran-) *pl.* **grand prix** (-prēz′) or **grands prix** (grän prē′, gran-) ⟦< fol.⟧ **1** [*often* **G- P-**] any of a series of races involving formula cars and leading to an overall championship: often used attributively [*the grand prix circuit*] **2** any competitive event or, often, series of events: usually used as part of the title

grand prix[2] (grän prē′; *E* grän prē′) ⟦Fr, great prize⟧ first prize; highest award in a competition
Grand Rapids ⟦after the *rapids* on the *Grand* River⟧ city in SW Mich.
grand right and left in folk dancing, an interweaving of two concentric circles of dancers, one moving clockwise, the other counterclockwise, giving right and left hands alternately to successive partners
grand·sire (grand′sīr′) ***n.*** [Archaic] **1** a grandfather **2** a male ancestor **3** an old man
grand slam 1 *a)* *Bridge* the winning of all the tricks in a deal by the declarer ☆*b)* the winning of all of a group of select competitions in a particular sport, as golf ☆**2** *Baseball* a home run hit when there is a runner on each base: sometimes called **grand′slam′mer**
grand·son (grand′sun′, gran′-) ***n.*** a son of one's son or daughter
grand·stand (grand′stand′) ***n.*** the main seating structure for spectators at a sporting event, etc. —☆***vi.*** [Informal] to try to gain the applause or admiration of an audience by or as by making an unnecessarily showy play (**grandstand play**), as in baseball —**grand′stand′er *n.***
Grand Terre (grän′ ter′) *alt. sp. of* GRANDE-TERRE
Grand Te·tons (tē′tänz′, -tənz) ⟦< CdnFr *les Trois Tétons,* the three breasts, in ref. to the appearance of the range's three highest peaks: so named by Fr-Cdn trappers⟧ range of the Rocky Mountains, in NW Wyo. and SE Ida.: highest peak (**Grand Teton**), 13,770 ft (4,197 m)
grand theft GRAND LARCENY: see LARCENY
grand tour 1 a tour of continental Europe formerly taken by young men of the British aristocracy to complete their education **2** any tour like this **3** a conducted inspection tour, as of a building
grand·un·cle (grand′uŋ′kəl) ***n.*** GREAT-UNCLE
grand unified (field) theory *Particle Physics* any of various theories postulating that three fundamental forces in the universe (electromagnetism, the strong interaction, and the weak interaction) are actually types of a single high-energy force: also called **grand unification theory**
grange (grānj) ***n.*** ⟦ME < Anglo-Fr *graunge* (OFr *grange*) < ML *granica* < L *granum,* GRAIN⟧ **1** [Archaic] a granary **2** a farm with its dwelling house, barns, etc. ☆**3** [**G-**] any local lodge of the Grange —☆**the Grange** the Patrons of Husbandry, a fraternal organization, orig. of farmers, organized in the U.S. in 1867
grang·er (grān′jər) ***n.*** ☆**1** a farmer ☆**2** [**G-**] a member of the Grange —**grang′er·ism′ *n.***
grang·er·ize (grān′jər īz′) ***vt.* -ized′, -iz′ing** ⟦after J. *Granger,* author of a *Biographical History of England* (1769), which included blank pages for such illustrations⟧ [Rare] **1** to illustrate (a book already printed) with engravings, prints, etc. obtained elsewhere, often by clipping them from other books **2** to damage (a book) by clipping such engravings, etc. —**grang′er·ism′ *n.***
gran·i- (gran′i, -ə) ⟦< L *granum,* GRAIN⟧ *combining form* grain *[granivorous]*
Gra·ni·cus (grə nī′kəs) river in ancient Mysia (W Asia Minor): site of a battle (334 B.C.) in which Alexander the Great defeated the Persians
gra·nif·er·ous (grə nif′ər əs) ***adj.*** ⟦< L *granifer:* see GRAIN & -FEROUS⟧ bearing grain
gra·ni·ta (grə nēt′ə) ***n.*** ⟦It < fem. of *granito:* see fol.⟧ an ice, made as with fruit and juice, that is like a sorbet but coarser in consistency
gran·ite (gran′it) ***n.*** ⟦It *granito,* granite, lit., grained < pp. of *granire,* to reduce to grains < *grano* < L *granum,* a seed, GRAIN⟧ a very hard, coarse-grained, gray to pink, intrusive igneous rock, composed mainly of feldspar, quartz, mica, and hornblende —**gra·nit·ic** (grə nit′ik) ***adj.*** —**gran·it·oid** (gran′i toid′) ***adj.***
gran·ite·ware (-wer′) ***n.*** **1** a variety of ironware for household use, coated with a hard enamel that looks somewhat like granite **2** a variety of fine, hard pottery
gra·niv·o·rous (grə niv′ə rəs) ***adj.*** ⟦GRANI- + -VOROUS⟧ feeding on grain and seeds
gran·ny or **gran·nie** (gran′ē) ***n.,*** *pl.* **-nies** [Informal] **1** a grandmother **2** an old woman **3** any fussy, exacting person ☆**4** [South] a midwife —***adj.*** of a style like that formerly worn by many elderly women *[granny* nightgown*]*; specif., designating eyeglasses (**granny glasses**) with small, often oval, lenses and thin, wirelike metal frames
granny knot a knot like a square knot but with the ends crossed the wrong way: it will slip under strain
Granny Smith ⟦after Maria Ann *Smith* (1799–1870), Austral orchardist, born in England, who discovered the variety on her farm⟧ a popular, bright-green variety of apple with tart flesh
gran·o- (gran′ō, -ə) ⟦Ger *grano-:* see GRANOPHYRE⟧ *combining form* of or like granite *[granolith]*
☆**gran·o·la** (grə nō′lə) ***n.*** ⟦coined (*c.* 1870) < ? L *granum,* grain + *-ola,* It dim. suffix⟧ a breakfast cereal of rolled oats, wheat germ, sesame seeds, brown sugar or honey, raisins, nuts, etc.
gran·o·lith (gran′ə lith′) ***n.*** ⟦GRANO- + -LITH⟧ a concrete used for flooring, pavement, etc., containing crushed or chipped granite or other stone —**gran′o·lith′ic *adj.***
gran·o·phyre (-fīr′) ***n.*** ⟦Ger *granophyr,* arbitrary blend < *granit,* GRANITE + *porphyr,* PORPHYRY⟧ an igneous rock similar to granite in composition and appearance, but containing larger crystals of quartz and feldspar in a matrix of a finer grain —**gran′o·phyr′ic** (-fir′ik) ***adj.***
grant (grant, gränt) ***vt.*** ⟦ME *granten* < OFr *graanter, craanter,* to promise, assure < VL **credentare,* to promise, yield < L *credens,* prp. of *credere,* to believe: see CREED⟧ **1** to give (what is requested, as permission, etc.); assent to; agree to fulfill **2** *a)* to give or confer formally or according to legal procedure *b)* to transfer (property) by a deed **3** to acknowledge for the sake of argument; admit as true without proof; concede —***n.*** **1** the act of granting **2** something granted, as property, a tract of land, an exclusive right or power, money from a fund, etc. ☆**3** a territorial subdivision in Maine, New Hampshire, or Vermont —***SYN.*** GIVE —**take for granted** to consider as true, already settled, requiring no special attention, etc.; accept as a matter of course —**grant′a·ble *adj.*** —**grant′er *n.***
Grant[1] (grant) ***n.*** a masculine name
Grant[2] (grant) **1 Cary** (born *Archibald Leach*) 1904-86; U.S. film actor, born in England **2 Ulysses S(impson)** (born *Hiram Ulysses Grant*) 1822-85; 18th president of the U.S. (1869-77): commander in chief of Union forces in the Civil War
grant·ee (gran tē′) ***n.*** *Law* a person to whom a grant is made
grant-in-aid (grant′in ād′) ***n.,*** *pl.* **grants′-in-aid′** a grant of funds, as by the federal government to a state or by a foundation to a writer, scientist, artist, etc., to support a specific program or project
grant·or (gran′tər, -tôr′) ***n.*** *Law* a person who makes a grant
☆**grants·man·ship** (grants′mən ship′) ***n.*** ⟦< GRANT + -MANSHIP⟧ **1** the art of acquiring grants-in-aid **2** skill in doing this
gran·u·lar (gran′yə lər) ***adj.*** ⟦< LL *granulum* (see GRANULE) + -AR⟧ **1** containing or consisting of grains or granules **2** like grains or granules **3** having a grainy surface —**gran′u·lar′i·ty** (-ler′ə tē) ***n.*** —**gran′u·lar·ly *adv.***
granular snow 1 a rare form of opaque precipitation consisting of very tiny ice crystals **2** CORN SNOW
gran·u·late (gran′yə lāt′) ***vt., vi.* -lat′ed, -lat′ing 1** to form into grains or granules **2** to make or become rough on the surface by the development of granules —**gran′u·la′tor *n.,*** **gran′u·lat′er** —**gran′u·la′tive *adj.***
gran·u·la·tion (gran′yə lā′shən) ***n.*** **1** formation into granules or grains **2** *Med. a)* the formation of a small mass of tiny red granules of newly formed capillaries, as on the surface of a wound that is healing *b)* the mass itself
gran·ule (gran′yo͞ol) ***n.*** ⟦< LL *granulum,* dim. of L *granum,* GRAIN⟧ **1** a small grain **2** a small, grainlike particle or spot; specif., any of the small, bright areas on the sun's photosphere that last only a few minutes
gran·u·lite (gran′yə līt′) ***n.*** ⟦prec. + -ITE[1]⟧ a metamorphic rock consisting of uniformly sized, interlocked mineral grains in which coarse and finer bands may alternate —**gran′u·lit′ic** (-lit′ik) ***adj.***
gran·u·lo·cyte (-lō sīt′) ***n.*** ⟦GRANUL(E) + -O- + -CYTE⟧ any of several types of white blood cells with a granular cytoplasm —**gran′u·lo·cyt′ic *adj.***
gran·u·lo·ma (gran′yə lō′mə) ***n.,*** *pl.* **-mas** or **-ma·ta** (-mə tə) ⟦GRANUL(E) + -OMA⟧ a firm, tumorlike granulation formed as a reaction to chronic inflammation, as from foreign bodies, bacteria, etc. —**gran′u·lo′ma·tous** (-təs) ***adj.***
gran·u·lose (gran′yə lōs′) ***adj.*** GRANULAR
gra·num (grā′nəm) ***n.,*** *pl.* **-na** (-nə) ⟦ModL < L, a seed, GRAIN⟧ any of the stacks of thylakoids in a chloroplast: see THYLAKOID
Gran·ville-Bar·ker (gran′vil bär′kər), **Har·ley** (här′lē) 1877-1946; Eng. playwright, critic, & actor
grape (grāp) ***n.*** ⟦ME *grap,* replacing earlier *winberie* (see WINE & BERRY) < OFr *grape,* bunch of grapes < *graper,* to gather with a hook < Frank **krappo* (OHG *chrapfo*), a hook: for IE base see CRADLE⟧ **1** any of various small, round, smooth-skinned, juicy berries, generally purple, red, or green, growing in clusters on woody vines: grapes are eaten raw, used to make wine, or dried to make raisins **2** any of various vines (genus *Vitis*) of the grape family that bear grapes, including fox grape and muscadine; grapevine **3** a dark purplish-red color **4** GRAPESHOT —***adj.*** designating a family (Vitaceae, order Rhamnales) of dicotyledonous, tendril-bearing, climbing, woody vines, including the Virginia creeper
grape·fruit (grāp′fro͞ot′) ***n.*** ⟦so named because it grows in clusters⟧ **1** a large, round, edible citrus fruit with a pale-yellow rind, juicy pulp, and a somewhat sour taste **2** the semitropical evergreen tree (*Citrus paradisi*) of the rue family, that bears grapefruit
grape hyacinth any of a group of small, hardy, bulbous plants (genus *Muscari*) of the lily family, with spikes of small, bell-shaped flowers of blue or white
grape ivy an evergreen climbing vine (*Cissus incisa*) of the grape family, common as a houseplant
grap·er·y (grāp′ər ē) ***n.,*** *pl.* **-er·ies** a place, esp. an enclosed area or building, where grapes are grown
grape·shot (grāp′shät′) ***n.*** a cluster of small iron balls, formerly fired from a cannon
grape sugar GLUCOSE
grape·vine (grāp′vīn′) ***n.*** **1** any of the woody vines that bear grapes ☆**2** a secret means of spreading or receiving information; also, the spreading of news or gossip from one person to another: with *the*
graph[1] (graf, gräf) ***n.*** ⟦< *graphic formula*⟧ **1** a diagram, as a curve, broken line, or series of bars, representing various kinds of quantitative information and relationships, such as the successive changes in a variable quantity or quantities **2** *Math. a)* a curve or surface showing the values of a function *b)* a diagram consisting of nodes and links and representing logical relationships or sequences of events —***vt.*** to put in the form of, or represent by, a graph

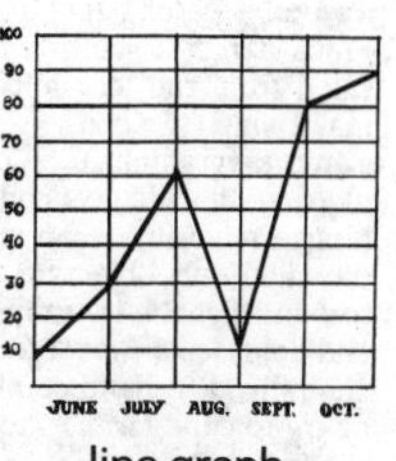

line graph

graph[2] (graf, gräf) ***n.*** ⟦see fol.⟧ a writing-system unit which may be a representation of a phoneme, a syllable, etc.

-graph (graf, gräf) ⟦Gr *-graphos* < *graphein*: see GRAPHIC⟧ *combining form forming nouns* **1** something that writes or records *[telegraph]* **2** something written, drawn, or recorded *[monograph]*

☆**graph·eme** (graf′ēm′) ***n.*** ⟦*graph*, a spelling, occurrence of an allograph (< prec.) + -EME⟧ *Linguis.* a class consisting of all the allographs representing a given unit of a writing system, or all those representing a given phoneme —**gra·phe′mic** ***adj.***

☆**gra·phe·mics** (gra fē′miks) ***n.*** the branch of language study dealing with the relationship between speech sounds and the writing system of a language

graph·ene (graf′ēn′) ***n.*** ⟦GRAPH(ITE) + -ENE⟧ a form of carbon consisting of a film of graphite one atom thick, an unusually strong material and an excellent conductor of electricity and heat

-gra·pher (grə fər) *combining form forming nouns* the agent of a (specified) method or process for recording or describing *[telegrapher, stenographer]*

graph·ic (graf′ik) ***adj.*** ⟦L *graphicus* < Gr *graphikos*, capable of painting or drawing, of writing < *graphē*, a drawing, writing < *graphein*, to write, orig., scratch, incise < IE base **gerebh-* > CARVE, CRAB[1]⟧ **1** *a)* describing or depicting in vivid and realistic detail *[a rather graphic war movie]* *b)* described or depicted in vivid and realistic detail *[graphic details of the battle]* **2** of the GRAPHIC ARTS **3** *a)* of handwriting; used or expressed in handwriting *b)* written, inscribed, or recorded in letters of the alphabet, meaningful symbols, etc. **4** having markings suggestive of written or printed characters *[graphic granite]* **5** *a)* of graphs or diagrams *b)* shown by graphs or diagrams Also **graph′i·cal** —***n.*** an illustration, graph, map, caption, etc. accompanying a newspaper or magazine article, appearing on a computer or TV screen, etc.: *often used in pl.*: see also GRAPHICS —**graph′ic·ness** ***n.***

-graph·ic (graf′ik) *combining form forming adjectives* of or relating to a (specified) method or process for recording or describing *[telegraphic, stenographic]*: also **-graph′i·cal** (-əl)

graph·i·cal·ly (graf′ik lē) ***adv.*** **1** in a graphic way; vivid and realistic **2** of or with graphics

graphic arts **1** any form of visual artistic representation, esp. painting, drawing, photography, etc. **2** those arts in which impressions are printed from various kinds of blocks, plates, screens, etc. as engraving, etching, lithography, serigraphy, dry point, offset, etc. —**graphic artist**

graphic equalizer an electronic equalizer with set ranges of frequencies which may be increased or reduced independently

graphic novel a story of some length in comic-strip format, usually bound as a book

graph·ics (graf′iks) ***n.*** ⟦< GRAPHIC⟧ **1** the art of making drawings, as in architecture or engineering, in accordance with mathematical rules **2** calculation of stresses, etc. from such drawings **3** *a)* design, including the use of typography, as employed in the graphic arts *b)* GRAPHIC ARTS (sense 2) **4** COMPUTER GRAPHICS See also GRAPHIC (*n.*)

graph·ite (graf′īt′) ***n.*** ⟦Ger *graphit* < Gr *graphein*, to write (see GRAPHIC): from its use as writing material⟧ a very soft, black, hexagonal mineral of pure carbon, formed in thin plates and found in metamorphic rocks: used in making electrodes, paints, the lead of pencils, etc. —**gra·phit·ic** (grə fit′ik) ***adj.***

graph·i·tize (graf′i tīz′) ***vt.*** **-tized′**, **-tiz′ing** **1** to change into graphite as by heating **2** to put graphite in or on

graph·o- (graf′ō, -ə) ⟦Fr < Gr *graphē*, a writing: see GRAPHIC⟧ *combining form* writing or drawing *[graphology]*

graph·ol·o·gy (graf äl′ə jē) ***n.*** ⟦Fr *graphologie*: see prec. & -LOGY⟧ the study of handwriting, esp. as a clue to character, aptitudes, etc. —**graph·ol′o·gist** ***n.***

graph paper paper with small ruled squares on which to draw graphs, diagrams, etc.

-gra·phy (grə fē) ⟦L *-graphia* < Gr, writing < *graphein*, to write: see GRAPHIC⟧ *combining form forming nouns* **1** a process or method of writing, recording, or representing (in a specified way) *[calligraphy, photography]* **2** a descriptive science or a treatise dealing with such a science *[geography]*

grap·nel (grap′nəl) ***n.*** ⟦ME *grapnell*, dim. < OFr *grapin, grapil* < Prov < *grapa*, a hook < Frank **krappo*: see GRAPE⟧ a small anchor with usually four or five curved, pointed arms, used for anchoring a small boat, dragging the bottom for objects, or grasping and holding fast to something

grapnel

grap·pa (gräp′pä) ***n.*** ⟦It < Gmc **krappa*, akin to Frank **krappo*: see GRAPE⟧ an Italian brandy distilled from the lees left after pressing grapes to make wine

grap·ple (grap′əl) ***n.*** ⟦OFr *grapil*: see GRAPNEL⟧ **1** GRAPNEL **2** a device consisting of two or more hinged, movable iron prongs for grasping and moving heavy objects **3** a coming to grips; hand-to-hand fight —***vt.*** **grap′pled**, **grap′pling** to grip and hold; seize —***vi.*** **1** to use a GRAPNEL **2** to struggle in hand-to-hand combat; wrestle **3** to struggle or try to cope (*with*) *[to grapple with a problem]* —**grap′pler** ***n.***

grappling iron (*or* hook) GRAPNEL: also **grap′pling** ***n.***

grap·y (grā′pē) ***adj.*** ⟦ME *grapi*⟧ of or like grapes; specif., tasting distinctly of grapes: said of some wines, often with negative intent: see FRUITY (sense 1*b*): also sp. **grap′ey**

☆**GRAS** *abbrev.* generally recognized as safe: designating food additives that cause no known harm when used as intended

grasp (grasp, gräsp) ***vt.*** ⟦ME *graspen*, by metathesis < **grapsen*, prob. < MLowG (as in LowG, Fris *grapsen*), akin to Norw dial. *grapsa*, to scratch, ON *grapa*, to snatch: see GRAB⟧ **1** to take hold of firmly with or as with the hand or arms; grip **2** to take hold of eagerly or greedily; seize **3** to take hold of mentally; understand; comprehend —***vi.*** **1** to reach for and try to seize: with *at* **2** to accept eagerly: with *at* —***n.*** **1** the act of grasping; grip or clasp of the hand or arms **2** a firm hold; control; possession **3** the power to hold or seize; reach **4** power of understanding; comprehension —**SYN.** TAKE —**grasp′a·ble** ***adj.*** —**grasp′er** ***n.***

grasp·ing (gras′piŋ) ***adj.*** **1** that grasps **2** eager for gain; avaricious —**SYN.** GREEDY —**grasp′ing·ly** ***adv.***

grass (gras) ***n.*** ⟦ME *gras* < OE *gærs, græs*, akin to Ger *gras* < IE **ghrō-*, GROW⟧ **1** any of various plants of the grass family that are usually used for food, fodder, or grazing and as lawns **2** any grasslike plant of various families having similar uses **3** ground covered with grass; pasture land or lawn **4** ⟦from the visual resemblance to blades of grass⟧ horizontal lines of clutter on a radarscope caused by electronic noise signals ☆**5** [Slang] marijuana **6** ⟦short for *grasshopper*, rhyming slang for COPPER[2]⟧ [Brit. Slang] an informer; stool pigeon —***adj.*** designating a family (Poaceae, order Cyperales) of monocotyledonous plants with long, narrow leaves, jointed stems, flowers in spikelets, and seedlike fruit, including wheat, rye, barley, oats, corn, sugar cane, bamboo, sorghum, and bluegrass —***vt.*** **1** to put (an animal or animals) out to pasture or graze **2** to grow grass over; cover with grass **3** to lay (textiles, etc.) on the grass for bleaching by the sun **4** [Brit. Slang] to inform against, as to the police —***vi.*** **1** to become covered with grass **2** [Brit. Slang] to act as an informer; inform (*on*) —**go to grass** **1** to graze **2** [Chiefly Brit.] to rest or retire ☆**3** go to the devil! —**let the grass grow under one's feet** to waste one's time or neglect one's opportunities —**put out to grass** [Chiefly Brit.] PUT OUT TO PASTURE (see phrase under PASTURE) —**grass′less** ***adj.*** —**grass′like′** ***adj.***

grass carp ⟦so called from the plants it consumes⟧ a large, weed-eating carp (*Ctenopharyngodon idella*) brought to the U.S. from E Asia to consume the plants in clogged waterways, lakes, etc.; white amur

grass cloth a cloth made of plant fibers, as of jute or hemp

grass·hop·per (gras′häp′ər) ***n.*** ⟦ME *grashoppere*, extended with *-er* suffix (see -ER) < *greshoppe* < OE *gærshoppe* < *gærs* (see GRASS) + base of *hoppian* (see HOP[1])⟧ **1** any of various families (esp. Acrididae) of leaping, plant-eating orthopteran insects with powerful hind legs adapted for jumping **2** a cocktail made of green crème de menthe, cream, and, usually colorless crème de cacao ☆**3** [Mil. Slang] a small, light airplane for scouting, liaison, and observation

grasshopper

grass·land (gras′land′) ***n.*** **1** land with grass growing on it, used for grazing; pasture land **2** land or region where grass predominates; prairie

grass·plot (-plät′) ***n.*** a piece of ground with grass growing on it; esp., a lawn

grass roots ☆**1** the common people, orig. those esp. of rural or nonurban areas, thought of as best representing the basic, direct political interests of the electorate ☆**2** the basic or fundamental source or support, as of a social or political movement —☆***adj.*** of or having to do with the grass roots: also **grass′-roots′** or **grass′root′**

grass snake ☆*a)* GARTER SNAKE ☆*b)* GREEN SNAKE

grass tree any of a genus (*Xanthorrhoea*) of plants of the grass-tree family, native to Australia, with short, thick, woody trunks and grasslike leaves: some produce fragrant resins

grass-tree (gras′trē′) ***adj.*** designating a family (Xanthorrhoeaceae, order Liliales) of monocotyledonous plants

grass widow ⟦Early ModE, discarded mistress (similar to Du *graswedwe*, Ger *strohwittwe*): prob. allusion is to bed of grass or straw as opposed to the conjugal bed⟧ **1** a woman divorced or otherwise separated from her husband **2** a woman whose husband is often away for short periods of time

grass widower **1** a man divorced or otherwise separated from his wife **2** a man whose wife is often away for short periods of time

grass·y (gras′ē) ***adj.*** **grass′i·er**, **grass′i·est** **1** of or consisting of grass **2** covered with or containing grass **3** green like growing grass —**grass′i·ness** ***n.***

grate[1] (grāt) ***vt.*** **grat′ed**, **grat′ing** ⟦ME *graten* < OFr *grater* (Fr *gratter*) < Frank **kratton*, akin to OHG *chrazzōn* (Ger *kratzen*), to scratch < IE base **gred-* > Alb *gërrusë*, scraper⟧ **1** to grind into shreds or particles by rubbing or scraping **2** to rub against (an object) with a harsh, scraping sound **3** to grind (the teeth) together with a rasping sound **4** to irritate; annoy; fret —***vi.*** **1** to grind or rub with a harsh scraping or rasping sound **2** to make a harsh or rasping sound **3** to have an irritating or annoying effect *[a noise that grates on one's nerves]*

grate[2] (grāt) ***n.*** ⟦ME, trellis, lattice < ML *grata, crata* < L *cratis*, a hurdle, CRATE⟧ **1** GRATING[1] (sense 1) **2** a frame of metal bars for holding fuel in a fireplace, stove, or furnace **3** a fireplace **4** *Mining* a screen for grading ores —***vt.*** **grat′ed, grat′ing** to provide with a grate

grate·ful (grāt′fəl) ***adj.*** ⟦obs. *grate,* pleasing (< L *gratus:* see GRACE) + -FUL⟧ **1** feeling or expressing gratitude; thankful; appreciative **2** causing gratitude; welcome; pleasing —**grate′ful·ly** ***adv.*** —**grate′ful·ness** ***n.***

grat·er (grāt′ər) ***n.*** a utensil with a rough surface on which to grate spices, vegetables, cheese, etc.

Gra·tian (grā′shən) (L. name *Flavius Gratianus*) A.D. 359-383; Rom. emperor (375-383)

grat·i·fi·ca·tion (grat′i fi kā′shən) ***n.*** **1** a gratifying or being gratified **2** something that gratifies; cause for satisfaction **3** [Archaic] reward or recompense for services or benefits

grat·i·fy (grat′i fī′) ***vt.*** **-fied′, -fy′ing** ⟦Fr *gratifier* < L *gratificare, gratificari,* to oblige, please < *gratus,* pleasing (see GRACE) + *-ficare,* -FY⟧ **1** to give pleasure or satisfaction **2** to give in to; indulge; humor **3** [Archaic] to reward —***SYN.*** PLEASANT —**grat′i·fi′er** ***n.*** —**grat′i·fy′ing** ***adj.*** —**grat′i·fy′ing·ly** ***adv.***

gra·tin (grät′'n, grat′'n; *Fr* grȧ tan′) ***n.*** ⟦Fr, bread crumbs, scrapings < *gratter,* to scrape, GRATE¹⟧ any dish having a lightly browned, crisp crust on top, esp. one topped with bread crumbs or grated cheese and broiled briefly

gra·ti·né (grät′'n ā′, grat′-) ***adj.*** ⟦Fr < pp. of *gratiner,* to prepare with a crust of breadcrumbs and grated cheese < *gratin:* see prec.⟧ AU GRATIN: also **gra′ti·néed′** (-ād′)

grat·ing¹ (grāt′iŋ) ***n.*** ⟦< GRATE² + -ING⟧ **1** a framework of parallel or latticed bars set in a window, door, etc. **2** parallel bars or crossbars, sometimes curved or patterned, in a framework set in a sidewalk, ship's hatchway, etc. **3** DIFFRACTION GRATING

grat·ing² (grāt′iŋ) ***adj.*** ⟦prp. of GRATE¹⟧ **1** harsh and rasping **2** irritating or annoying —**grat′ing·ly** ***adv.***

gra·tis (grat′is; grät′-, grāt′-) ***adv., adj.*** ⟦L < *gratia,* a favor: see GRACE⟧ without charge or payment; free

grat·i·tude (grat′i to͞od′, -tyo͞od′) ***n.*** ⟦Fr < ML *gratitudo* < L *gratus,* pleasing: see GRACE⟧ a feeling of thankful appreciation for favors or benefits received; thankfulness

Grat·tan (grat′'n), **Henry** 1746-1820; Ir. statesman

gra·tu·i·tous (grə to͞o′i təs, -tyo͞o′-) ***adj.*** ⟦L *gratuitus* < *gratus:* see GRACE⟧ **1** *a)* given or received without charge or payment; free *b)* granted without obligation **2** without cause or justification; uncalled-for —**gra·tu′i·tous·ly** ***adv.*** —**gra·tu′i·tous·ness** ***n.***

gratuitous contract *Law* a contract for the benefit of the person for whom it is made, without a reciprocal promise of benefit to the maker

gra·tu·i·ty (grə to͞o′i tē, -tyo͞o′-) ***n., pl.*** **-ties** ⟦Fr *gratuité* < ML *gratuitas* < L *gratuitus:* see GRATUITOUS⟧ a sum of money, often a percentage of the total billed, given to a server, porter, etc. for a service or favor; tip —***SYN.*** PRESENT

grat·u·late (grach′ə lāt′) ***vt.*** **-lat′ed, -lat′ing** ⟦< L *gratulatus,* pp. of *gratulari,* CONGRATULATE⟧ [Archaic] **1** to express joy or gratification at the sight of **2** to congratulate —**grat′u·la′tion** ***n.*** —**grat′u·la·to′ry** (grach′ə-) ***adj.***

Grau·bün·den (grou′bün′dən) easternmost canton of Switzerland: 2,743 sq mi (7,104 sq km)

grau·pel (grou′pəl) ***n.*** ⟦Ger < *graupeln,* to sleet < *graupelein,* dim. of *graupe,* hulled barley, granule of ice < Slav, as in Pol, Serb *krupa,* kernel of grain, hail < IE **kreup-,* scab, fragment (> ON *hrufa,* scale) < base **kreu-,* to break > RUE¹⟧ *Meteorol.* a kind of precipitation consisting of brittle, white ice particles having a snowlike structure; soft hail

☆**Grau·stark·i·an** (grou stärk′ē ən) ***adj.*** ⟦after *Graustark,* imaginary kingdom in novels by G. B. McCutcheon (1866-1928), U.S. novelist⟧ of, like, or characteristic of colorful, implausible, highly melodramatic and romantic situations or circumstances

gra·va·men (grə vā′mən) ***n., pl.*** **-mens** or **gra·vam′i·na** (-vam′i nə) ⟦LL, lit., a burden, trouble < L *gravare,* to weigh down < *gravis:* see fol.⟧ **1** a grievance **2** *Law* the essential part of a complaint or accusation

grave¹ (grāv) ***adj.*** **grav′er, grav′est** ⟦Fr < L *gravis,* heavy, weighty < IE base **gwer-,* heavy, mill > QUERN, Gr *barys,* heavy, Sans *gurúh,* grave⟧ **1** *a)* requiring serious thought; important; weighty [*grave* doubts] *b)* not light or trifling in nature or in consequence; grievous [a *grave* sin] **2** *a)* seriously threatening health, well-being, or life; critical; dangerous [a *grave* illness] *b)* seriously contrary to what is right or desirable; extremely bad [a *grave* fault] *c) Theol.* so evil as to cause spiritual death; mortal [a *grave* sin] **3** dignified and solemn or sedate in manner or mien **4** somber; dull [*grave* colors] **5** low or deep in pitch —***SYN.*** SERIOUS —**grave′ly** ***adv.*** —**grave′ness** ***n.***

grave² (grāv) ***n.*** ⟦ME < OE *græf* (akin to OFris *gref,* Ger *grab*) < base of *grafan,* to dig: see the ***vt.***⟧ **1** *a)* a hole in the ground in which to bury a dead body *b)* any place of burial; tomb **2** final end or death; extinction —***vt.*** **graved, grav′en** or **graved, grav′ing** ⟦ME *graven* < OE *grafan;* akin to Ger *graben* < IE base **ghrebh-,* to scratch, scrape⟧ **1** [Obs.] *a)* to dig *b)* to bury **2** [Archaic] *a)* to shape by carving; sculpture *b)* to engrave; incise **3** to impress sharply and clearly; fix permanently —**have one foot in the grave** to be very ill, old, or infirm; be near death —**spin (or roll over, turn, turn over, sit up, etc.) in one's grave** to be shocked or distressed: said of someone now deceased: used to convey that the person would be shocked or distressed were he or she alive

grave³ (grāv) ***vt.*** **graved, grav′ing** ⟦ME *graven,* prob. < OFr *grave* (Fr *grève*), beach, coarse sand (see GRAVEL): ships were orig. beached for cleaning the hulls⟧ to clean barnacles, etc. from (the hull of a wooden ship) and coat with pitch or tar

gra·ve⁴ (grä′ve) ***adj., adv.*** ⟦It, lit., grave < L *gravis:* see GRAVE¹⟧ *Musical Direction* slowly and with solemnity

grave accent (gräv, grāv) a mark (`) used to indicate: *a)* the quality or length of a vowel, as in French *chère* *b)* in French, a distinction in meaning, as in *où,* "where" and *ou,* "or" *c)* secondary stress as in *týpewrìter* *d)* full pronunciation of a syllable normally elided in speech, as in *lovèd*

grave·dig·ger (grāv′dig′ər) ***n.*** a person whose work is digging graves

grav·el (grav′əl) ***n.*** ⟦ME < OFr *gravelle,* dim. of *grave,* coarse sand, seashore < or akin to Gaul **grava,* stone < IE base **ghreu-,* to rub hard, pulverize > GRIT⟧ **1** a loose mixture of pebbles and rock fragments coarser than sand, often mixed with clay, etc. **2** *Med.* a deposit of small concretions that form in the kidneys or gallbladder and that may be retained, passed on to the urinary bladder, or passed from the body —***vt.*** **-eled** or **-elled, -el·ing** or **-el·ling** **1** to cover (a walk, driveway, etc.) with gravel **2** to embarrass or perplex ☆**3** [Informal] to irritate or annoy

grav·el·ly (grav′əl ē) ***adj.*** **1** full of, like, or consisting of gravel **2** sounding harsh or rasping [a *gravelly* voice]

grav·en (grāv′ən) ***vt. alt. pp. of*** GRAVE²

Gravenhage *see* 'S GRAVENHAGE

graven image an idol made from stone or wood

Gra·ven·stein (grav′ən stēn′, grä′vən-; -stīn′) ***n.*** ⟦after *Gravenstein,* village in Denmark⟧ a variety of large, yellow apple with red streaks

grav·er (grā′vər) ***n.*** ⟦ME: see GRAVE², ***vt.*** & -ER⟧ **1** a cutting tool used by engravers and sculptors **2** an engraver; esp., a carver in stone

Graves¹ (gräv) ***n.*** a red or white wine from the Graves district of the Bordeaux region

Graves² (grāvz), **Robert (Ranke)** 1895-1985; Eng. poet, novelist, & critic

Graves' disease (grāvz) ⟦after R. J. *Graves* (1797-1853), Ir physician⟧ EXOPHTHALMIC GOITER

☆**grave·side** (grāv′sīd′) ***n.*** the area alongside a grave —***adj.*** being, or taking place, beside a grave

grave·site (-sīt′) ***n.*** a place of burial, or a place reserved for a grave

grave·stone (-stōn′) ***n.*** ⟦ME *graveston*⟧ an engraved stone marking a grave; tombstone

Gra·vet·ti·an (grə vet′ē ən) ***adj.*** ⟦after La *Gravette,* France, site of archaeological discoveries + -IAN⟧ designating or of an Upper Paleolithic culture, characterized by flint points resembling a pointed knife blade with a blunted back

grave·yard (grāv′yärd′) ***n.*** a burial ground; cemetery

☆**graveyard shift** [Informal] a work shift that starts during the night, usually at midnight

grav·id (grav′id) ***adj.*** ⟦L *gravidus* < *gravis,* heavy: see GRAVE¹⟧ pregnant —**gra·vid·i·ty** (grə vid′i tē) ***n.***

gra·vim·e·ter (grə vim′ət ər) ***n.*** ⟦Fr *gravimètre* < L *gravis,* heavy (see GRAVE¹) + Fr *-mètre,* -METER⟧ **1** a device used to determine specific gravity, esp. of liquids **2** an instrument used to measure the earth's gravitational pull at different places on, in, or above the planet

grav·i·met·ric (grav′i me′trik) ***adj.*** ⟦< L *gravis* (see GRAVE¹) + METRIC⟧ **1** of or in terms of measurement by weight **2** of or pertaining to measurements of the pull of gravity Also **grav′i·met′ri·cal** —**grav′i·met′ri·cal·ly** ***adv.***

gra·vim·e·try (grə vim′ə trē) ***n.*** ⟦< L *gravis* (see GRAVE¹) + -METRY⟧ the measurement of weight or density

graving dock [see GRAVE³] DRY DOCK

grav·i·tas (grav′i täs′, gräv′-) ***n.*** ⟦< L, lit., weight < *gravis,* heavy: see GRAVE¹⟧ [*often in italics*] weight, as of a leader or official; dignity, seriousness, credibility, etc.

grav·i·tate (grav′i tāt′) ***vi.*** **-tat′ed, -tat′ing** ⟦< ModL *gravitatus,* pp. of *gravitare* (coined by Sir Isaac NEWTON²) < L *gravitas:* see GRAVITY⟧ **1** to move or tend to move in accordance with the force of gravity **2** [Rare] to sink or settle **3** to be attracted or tend to move (*toward* something or someone) —***vt.*** to cause to gravitate

grav·i·ta·tion (grav′i tā′shən) ***n.*** ⟦ModL *gravitatio:* see prec.⟧ **1** the act, process, or fact of gravitating **2** *Physics* *a)* the force by which every mass or particle of matter, including photons, attracts and is attracted by every other mass or particle of matter *b)* the tendency of these masses or particles to move toward each other —**grav′i·ta′tion·al** ***adj.*** —**grav′i·ta′tion·al·ly** ***adv.***

gravitational lens a massive celestial body, esp. a galaxy or cluster of galaxies, having enough gravity to refract light waves from a more distant object, esp. a quasar, so that an observer sees an amplified or multiple image (**gravitational lensing**)

gravitational wave a hypothetical wave of very weak gravitational energy that travels through space at the speed of light: thought to be caused by the sudden acceleration of a large mass: sometimes called **gravitational radiation**

grav·i·ta·tive (grav′i tāt′iv) ***adj.*** **1** of or caused by gravitation **2** tending or causing to gravitate

grav·i·ton (-tän′) ***n.*** ⟦GRAVIT(ATION) + -ON⟧ *Particle Physics* a theoretical subatomic particle with no charge or mass, postulated as the quantum of gravity: see also CLASSON

grav·i·ty (grav′i tē) ***n., pl.*** **-ties** ⟦L *gravitas,* weight, heaviness < *gravis,* heavy: see GRAVE¹⟧ **1** the state or condition of being grave; esp., *a)* solemnity or sedateness of manner or character; earnestness *b)* danger or threat; ominous quality [the *gravity* of his illness] *c)* seriousness, as of a situation **2** weight; heaviness: see SPECIFIC GRAVITY, CENTER OF GRAVITY **3** lowness of musical pitch **4** gravitation, esp. terrestrial gravitation; force

that tends to draw all bodies in the earth's sphere toward the center of the earth: see ACCELERATION OF GRAVITY —*adj.* operated by the force of gravity
gravity wave GRAVITATIONAL WAVE
grav·lax (gräv′läks′) *n.* ⟦Scand, prob. Swed < *gravad*, cured with spices + *lax*, salmon⟧ sliced salmon rubbed with salt, sugar, pepper, and dill, marinated, and served with a mustard sauce
gra·vure (grə vyoor′, grāv′yər) *n.* ⟦Fr < *graver*, to carve < Frank **graban*, akin to GRAVE[2], *vt.*⟧ **1** *a)* any process using intaglio printing plates *b)* such a plate or a print made by such a process **2** *a)* PHOTOGRAVURE *b)* ROTOGRAVURE
gra·vy (grā′vē) *n., pl.* **-vies** ⟦ME *grave*, ? a misreading of OFr *grané* < ? *grain*, used as a name for cooking ingredients⟧ **1** the juice given off by meat in cooking **2** a sauce made by combining this juice with flour, seasoning, etc. ☆**3** [Slang] *a)* money easily or illegally obtained *b)* any extra benefit or value beyond that expected
gravy boat a long, low sort of pitcher, used to serve gravy, sauce, etc.
☆**gravy train** ⟦< phr. *ride the gravy train*, to achieve financial success easily < GRAVY (*n.* 3*a*)⟧ [Slang] a sinecure, subsidy, etc. that allows one to live luxuriously without much work
gray[1] (grā) *adj.* ⟦ME *grai* < OE *græg*, akin to Ger *grau* < IE base **ĝher-*, to shine, gleam > Czech *zříti*, to see⟧ **1** of a color that is a mixture or blend of black and white **2** *a)* darkish; dull *b)* dreary; dismal **3** *a)* having hair that is gray *b)* old, or old and respected **4** wearing gray garments or uniforms **5** designating a vague, intermediate area, as between morality and immorality —*n.* **1** an achromatic color made by mixing or blending black and white: see COLOR **2** an animal or thing colored gray; esp., a gray horse **3** gray or unbleached fabric or clothing **4** [*often* **G-**] *a)* a person or group wearing a gray uniform *b)* a Confederate soldier **5** *see* GREY WATER — *vt., vi.* to make or become gray —**gray′ly** *adv.* —**gray′ness** *n.*
gray[2] (grā) *n.* ⟦after L. H. *Gray* (1905-65), Eng radiobiologist⟧ the basic unit of an absorbed dose of radiation in the SI system, equal to the absorption of one joule of energy per kilogram of material (100 rads): abbrev. *Gy*
Gray (grā) **1 Asa** 1810-88; U.S. botanist **2 Thomas** 1716-71; Eng. poet
gray·back (grā′bak′) *n.* any of certain birds, fish, whales, etc. with grayish coloring, as the hooded crow, alewife, or gray whale
gray·beard (-bird′) *n.* an old man
gray eminence ÉMINENCE GRISE
☆**gray·fish** (-fish′) *n., pl.* **-fish′** or **-fish′es** (see FISH) a dogfish (shark)
gray fox either of two New World foxes (*Urocyon cinereoargenteus* or *U. littoralis*) having short gray and white hair and able to climb trees
gray-head·ed (-hed′id) *adj.* **1** having gray hair **2** old
gray·ish (grā′ish) *adj.* somewhat gray
gray jay a large North American jay (*Perisoreus canadensis*) with gray and black feathers and no crest
gray·lag (grā′lag′) *n.* ⟦short for *gray lag goose*: from its color and its late migration⟧ the European wild gray goose (*Anser anser*)
gray·ling (grā′liŋ) *n., pl.* **-ling** or **-lings** ⟦GRAY[1] + -LING[1]: from the color⟧ **1** any of a genus (*Thymallus*) of arctic, freshwater game trout with a long dorsal fin **2** any of various large wood nymph butterflies
☆**gray·mail** (grā′māl′) *n.* ⟦GRAY[1] (*adj.* 5) + (BLACK)MAIL⟧ [Informal] social pressure intended to compel someone, esp. a public official, to reveal sensitive information
gray market ⟦GRAY[1] (*adj.* 5) + (BLACK) MARKET⟧ a market, as for imported goods, operating outside the authorized system of distribution —**gray marketeer** (or **marketer**)
gray matter **1** grayish nerve tissue of the brain and spinal cord, consisting chiefly of nerve cells, with few nerve fibers: distinguished from WHITE MATTER **2** [Informal] intellectual capacity; brains
Gray's Inn *see* INNS OF COURT
☆**gray squirrel** any of several large, gray squirrels (genus *Sciurus*), native to the U.S.
gray·wacke (grā′wak′) *n.* ⟦Anglicization of Ger *grauwacke*: see GRAY[1]; E *wacke*, a rock like sandstone < Ger⟧ **1** a nonporous, dark-colored sandstone containing angular particles of other rocks **2** a fine-grained conglomerate resembling sandstone
☆**gray whale** a mostly black, migratory baleen whale (*Eschrichtius robustus*) of the N Pacific: it is the only member of its family (Eschrichtiidae)
☆**gray wolf** a large, gray wolf (*Canis lupus*) that hunts in packs, once common throughout the northern part of the Northern Hemisphere
Graz (gräts) city in SE Austria
graze[1] (grāz) *vt.* **grazed**, **graz′ing** ⟦ME *grasen* < OE *grasian* < base of *græs*, *gærs*, GRASS⟧ **1** to feed on (growing grass, herbage, a pasture, etc.) **2** to put livestock to feed on (growing grass, herbage, etc.) **3** to tend (feeding livestock) **4** to feed on the pasturage of (land) —*vi.* **1** to feed on growing grass, etc. **2** [Informal] *a)* to snack all day instead of eating regular meals *b)* to eat small portions of different foods, as appetizers or samples of entrees —**graz′er** *n.*
graze[2] (grāz) *vt.* **grazed**, **graz′ing** ⟦prob. < prec. in sense "to come close to the grass"⟧ **1** to touch or rub lightly in passing **2** to scrape or scratch in passing [*a bullet* grazed *his thigh*] —*vi.* to scrape, touch, or rub lightly against something in passing —*n.* **1** the act of grazing **2** a slight scratch or scrape caused by grazing
gra·zier (grā′zhər; -zē ər) *n.* [Chiefly Brit.] a person who grazes beef cattle for sale
graz·ing (grā′ziŋ) *n.* **1** land to graze on; pasture **2** [Informal] the eating of snacks all day long or the eating of small portions of different foods
gra·zio·so (grä tsyô′sô) *adj., adv.* ⟦It < L *gratiosus*: see GRACIOUS⟧ *Musical Direction* with grace; (in a) smooth and elegant (manner)
Gr Brit or **Gr Br** *abbrev.* Great Britain
GRE *trademark* Graduate Record Examination
grease (grēs; *for v., also* grēz) *n.* ⟦ME *gresse* < OFr *craisse* < VL **crassia* < L *crassus*, fat, thick: see CRASS⟧ **1** melted animal fat **2** any thick, oily substance or lubricant, esp. the substance that is put on the moving parts of automobiles and other machines to make them run smoothly **3** an inflammation of the skin of a horse's fetlock or pastern characterized by cracked skin and an oily discharge: also **grease heel** **4** *a)* the oily substance in uncleaned wool; suint *b)* an uncleaned fleece (also **grease wool**) —*vt.* **greased**, **greas′ing** **1** to smear or lubricate with grease **2** to influence by giving money to; bribe or tip: chiefly in **grease the palm** (or **hand**) **of** —**in (the) grease** **1** fat and ready to be killed: said of game animals **2** in an uncleaned condition: said of wool or fur
grease·ball (grēs′bôl′) *n.* [Slang] **1** ⟦see GREASER (*n.* 3)⟧ a person of Mediterranean or Latin American origin: a term of contempt or hostility **2** GREASER (sense 2)
grease cup a small cup over a bearing in machinery, for holding a supply of grease to lubricate the bearing
☆**grease monkey** [Slang] a mechanic, esp. one who works on automobiles or airplanes
grease·paint (-pānt′) *n.* a mixture of grease and coloring matter used by performers in making up for the stage, etc.
grease pencil a pencil with a center of compressed grease and coloring matter, used for marking
greas·er (grēs′ər) *n.* **1** a person or thing that greases ☆**2** ⟦< *grease*, oily hair tonic commonly used⟧ [Slang] a poor or working-class youth, esp. in the 1950s, often characterized as being rough in manner, wearing a leather jacket, riding a motorcycle, etc.: usually a somewhat derogatory term **3** ⟦from stereotypical notions that such persons have dark, oily hair⟧ [Slang] a person of Latin American, specif. Mexican, origin: a term of contempt or hostility
☆**grease·wood** (-wood′) *n.* **1** a thorny plant (*Sarcobatus vermiculatus*) of the goosefoot family, found in the desert regions of the W U.S., having fleshy leaves **2** any of several other similar plants
greas·y (grē′sē, grē′zē) *adj.* **greas′i·er**, **greas′i·est** **1** smeared or soiled with grease **2** containing grease, esp. much grease **3** like grease; oily, unctuous, slippery, etc. —**greas′i·ly** *adv.* —**greas′i·ness** *n.*
☆**greasy spoon** [Informal] a small, dingy restaurant that serves cheap food
great (grāt) *adj.* ⟦ME *grete* < OE *great*, akin to Ger *gross*, Du *groot* < IE base **ghrēu-*, rub hard over, crumble > GRIT, Welsh *gro*, sand: basic sense "coarse, coarsegrained"⟧ **1** of much more than ordinary size, extent, volume, etc.; esp., *a)* designating a thing or group of things larger than others of the same kind [*the* great *cats are tigers, lions, etc.; the* Great *Lakes*] *b)* large in number, quantity, etc.; numerous [*a* great *company*] *c)* long in duration [*a* great *while*] **2** much higher in some quality or degree; much above the ordinary or average; esp., *a)* existing in a high degree; intense [*a* great *light,* great *pain*] *b)* very much of a; acting much as (something specified) [*a* great *reader*] *c)* eminent; distinguished; illustrious; superior [*a* great *playwright*] *d)* very impressive or imposing; remarkable [great *ceremony*] *e)* having or showing nobility of mind, purpose, etc.; grand [*a* great *man,* great *ideas*] **3** of most importance; main; chief [*the* great *seal*] **4** [Informal] clever; expert; skillful: usually with *at* [great *at tennis*] ☆**5** [Informal] excellent; splendid; fine **6** [Now Chiefly Dial.] pregnant: chiefly in **great with child** —*adv.* [Informal] very well —*n.* a great or distinguished person: *usually used in pl.* —**SYN.** LARGE —**great on** [Informal] enthusiastic about —**the great** those who are great —**great′ly** *adv.* —**great′ness** *n.*
great- (grāt) *combining form* ⟦< prec., taken as intensifier⟧ older (or younger) by one generation: each additional *great-* shows one further generation removed [great-*aunt,* great-great-*grandson*]
great ape any of a family (Pongidae) of primates consisting of the gorilla, chimpanzee, and orangutan
great auk a large, flightless auk (*Pinguinus impennis*) of the N Atlantic, extinct since 1844
great-aunt (-ant′) *n.* a sister of any of one's grandparents; grandaunt
Great Australian Bight wide bay of the Indian Ocean, indenting S Australia: *c.* 720 mi (1,159 km) wide
Great Barrier Reef coral reef off the NE coast of Queensland, Australia: 1,250 mi (2,012 km) long
Great Basin vast inland region of the W U.S., between the Sierra Nevada & the Wasatch Mountains: the rivers & streams flowing into this region form lakes which have no outlet to the sea: *c.* 200,000 sq mi (517,998 sq km)
Great Bear, the the constellation Ursa Major
Great Bear Lake lake in Fort Smith & Inuvik regions, Northwest Territories, Canada: 12,096 sq mi (31,329 sq km)
Great Britain **1** principal island of the United Kingdom, including England, Scotland, & Wales, & administratively including adjacent islands except the Isle of Man & the Channel Islands **2** popularly, the United Kingdom of Great Britain and Northern Ireland
great calorie CALORIE (sense 2)
great circle any circle described on the surface of a sphere by a plane which passes through the center of the sphere; specif., such a circle on the earth's surface: a course (**great-circle course**) plotted along a great circle of the earth is the shortest route between any two points on the earth's surface

great·coat (grāt′kōt′) ***n.*** a heavy overcoat

Great Dane any of a breed of very large, muscular dog with pointed, erect ears, a square muzzle, and a short, thick, smooth coat

☆**Great Divide 1** a principal mountain watershed: specif., CONTINENTAL DIVIDE **2** any important dividing line —**cross the Great Divide** to die

Great Dividing Range series of mountain ranges along the E coast of Australia: highest peak, Mt. Kosciusko

great egret a large, white heron (*Egretta alba*) found in the marshy areas of most continents

great·en (grāt′'n) ***vt., vi.*** to make or become great or greater

great·er (grāt′ər) ***adj.*** [*often* **G-**] **1** designating a big city and the cities and towns surrounding it, esp. such an area included in the U.S. census [*Greater* Cleveland] **2** designating a country and the nearby states or regions that it claims, has taken by force, etc., as because of their ethnic composition

Greater Antilles group of islands in the West Indies, made up of the N & W Antilles, including the islands of Cuba, Jamaica, Hispaniola, & Puerto Rico

Greater Manchester county in NW England, surrounding Manchester: 496 sq mi (1,285 sq km)

greater omentum *see* OMENTUM

greater yellowlegs *see* YELLOWLEGS

greatest common divisor the number or quantity that is the largest common factor of a given set of numbers or quantities [12 is the *greatest common divisor* of 48, 60, and 96]: also **greatest common factor**

Great Glen of Scotland GLEN MORE

great-grand·child (grāt′grand′chīld′) ***n., pl.*** **-chil′dren** a child of any of one's grandchildren —**great′-grand′daugh′ter** ***n.*** —**great′-grand′son′** ***n.***

great-grand·par·ent (-grand′per′ənt) ***n.*** a parent of any of one's grandparents —**great′-grand′fa′ther** ***n.*** —**great′-grand′moth′er** ***n.***

great-great- (grāt′grāt′) *combining form see* GREAT-

great gross a unit of quantity equal to twelve gross

great·heart·ed (-härt′id) ***adj.*** **1** brave; fearless; courageous **2** generous; magnanimous; unselfish

great horned owl a large, pale gray and brownish American owl (*Bubo virginianus*) with two prominent tufts of black feathers on its head

Great Karroo *see* KARROO

Great Lakes chain of freshwater lakes in EC North America, emptying into the St. Lawrence River; Lakes Superior, Michigan, Huron, Erie, & Ontario

☆**great laurel** a large, E American shrub (*Rhododendron maximum*) of the heath family, with thick, oblong, dark-green leaves and delicate, white or pinkish flowers that grow in cone-shaped clusters

great-neph·ew (grāt′nef′yo͞o) ***n.*** a grandson of one's brother or sister; grandnephew

great-niece (-nēs′) ***n.*** a granddaughter of one's brother or sister; grandniece

Great Plains sloping region of valleys & plains in WC North America, extending from Tex. north to S Alberta, Canada, & stretching east from the base of the Rocky Mountains for *c.* 400 mi (644 km)

great power [*sometimes* **G- P-**] SUPERPOWER (sense 2)

great primer a large size of printing type, 18 point, formerly used esp. for Bibles

Great Pyrenees any of a breed of large dog, somewhat bearlike in appearance, with falling ears and a long, thick white coat, originally used in the Pyrenees to guard sheep and as a guide in snowy regions

Great Rift Valley depression of SW Asia & E Africa, extending from the Jordan River valley across Ethiopia & Somalia to the lakes region of E Africa

great room FAMILY ROOM

Great Russian 1 the Russian language, as distinguished from Ukrainian and Belorussian, the other two East Slavic languages **2** RUSSIAN (***n.*** 2) **3** RUSSIAN (***adj.***)

Great Salt Lake shallow saltwater lake in NW Utah, fluctuating greatly in size from 1,100 sq mi to 2,300 sq mi (2,849 sq km to 5,957 sq km)

Great Sandy Desert N section of the vast desert region of Western Australia

Great Schism 1 the division or conflict in the Roman Catholic Church from 1378 to 1417, when there were rival popes at Avignon and Rome: also called **Schism of the West 2** the separation of the Eastern Church from the Western Church, traditionally dated 1054: also called **Schism of the East**

great seal the chief seal of a nation or state, with which official papers are stamped as proof of having been approved or certified

Great Slave Lake lake in EC Fort Smith region, Northwest Territories, Canada: 10,980 sq mi (28,438 sq km)

Great Smoky Mountains mountain range of the Appalachians, along the Tenn.-N.C. border: highest peak, Clingman's Dome

Great Spirit ⟦transl. of Ojibwa *kitchi manitou* (or *manidoo*): see MANITOU⟧ the supreme deity in the traditional belief system of many North American Indian peoples

Great St. Bernard Pass mountain pass in the Pennine Alps, on the border between SW Switzerland & Italy: 8,110 ft (2,472 m) high

great-un·cle (grāt′uŋ′kəl) ***n.*** a brother of any of one's grandparents; granduncle

Great Victoria Desert S section of the vast desert region of Western Australia

Great Vowel Shift the complex series of sound developments (*c.* 1400 to *c.* 1750) which changed the vowel system of Middle English into that of Modern English: Middle English long high vowels (ē and o͞o) changed to Modern English diphthongs (ī and ou), and long mid and low vowels (ā, ō, and ä) were raised in their tongue positions to the Modern English sounds (ē, o͞o, and ā), but the orthography remained largely the same

Great Wall of China stone & earth wall extending across N China, built as a defense against invaders in the 3d cent. B.C., with later extensions: 15-30 ft (4.5-9 m) high; 12-20 ft (3.5-6 m) wide; *c.* 1,500 mi (2,415 km) long

Great War World War I

☆**Great White Father** name historically given by the American Indians to the president of the U.S.

great white shark WHITE SHARK

☆**Great White Way** the brightly lighted theater district in New York City, on Broadway near Times Square

great world ⟦transl. of Fr *grand monde*⟧ fashionable society and its way of life

great year one full cycle of precession of the equinoxes, equal to *c.* 25,800 years

greave (grēv) ***n.*** ⟦ME *greve* < OFr, shin, shin armor < Ar *jaurab*, stocking⟧ armor for the leg from the ankle to the knee

greaves (grēvz) ***pl.n.*** ⟦whaling term < LowG *greven*, pl., MDu *grēve*, akin to Ger *griebe*: basic sense, "coarse elements that will not melt": for IE base see GREAT⟧ the sediment of skin, etc. formed when animal fat is melted down for tallow; specif., cracklings

grebe (grēb) ***n., pl.*** **grebes** or **grebe** ⟦< Fr *grèbe* < ?⟧ any of a worldwide order (Podicipediformes) of diving and swimming birds with broadly lobed toes and legs set far back on the body

Gre·cian (grē′shən) ***adj.*** ⟦< L *Graecia*, GREECE + -AN⟧ GREEK (***adj.*** 1) —***n.*** **1** a Greek **2** [Archaic] a scholar of Greek

Grecian profile a profile in which the nose and forehead form an almost straight line

Gre·cism (grē′siz′əm) ***n.*** ⟦Fr *grécisme* < ML *Graecismus* < L *Graeci*, the Greeks⟧ **1** *a)* a word, phrase, grammatical construction, etc. originating in or peculiar to Classical Greek *b)* an imitation of this **2** the spirit of Greek culture **3** imitation of Greek style in the arts

Gre·cize (grē′sīz′) ***vt.*** **-cized′**, **-ciz′ing** ⟦Fr *gréciser* < L *Graecizare* < *Graeci*, the Greeks⟧ to make Greek; give a Greek form to; Hellenize —***vi.*** to imitate the Greeks in language, manner, etc. Also **Gre·cian·ize** (grē′shən īz′) **-ized′**, **-iz′ing**

Greco, El *see* EL GRECO

Gre·co- (grek′ō, grē′kō) ⟦< L *Graecus*⟧ *combining form* Greek, Greek and [*Greco*-Roman]

Gre·co-Ro·man (grek′ō rō′mən, grē′kō-) ***adj.*** of or influenced by both Greece and Rome; CLASSICAL (senses 2 & 3) [*Greco-Roman* art, *Greco-Roman* wrestling]

gree[1] (grē) ***n.*** ⟦ME *gre* < OFr *gre, gred* < L *gratum*, neut. of *gratus*: see GRACE⟧ [Obs.] good will —**do** (or **make**) **gree** [Archaic] to give satisfaction for an injury

gree[2] (grē) ***n.*** ⟦ME *gre* < OFr *gré*, a step < L *gradus*, a step: see GRADE⟧ [Scot.] superiority, preeminence, or victory

gree[3] (grē) ***vt., vi.*** **greed**, **gree′ing** ⟦ME *green* < OFr *grëer* < *gré*, pleasure (see AGREE); also aphetic < ME *agreen*⟧ [Dial.] to agree or make agree

Greece (grēs) country in the S Balkan Peninsula, including many islands in the Aegean, Ionian, & Mediterranean seas: in ancient times, the region comprised a number of small monarchies and city-states: 50,942 sq mi (131,940 sq km); cap. Athens

Ancient Greece

greed (grēd) ***n.*** ⟦back-form. < fol.⟧ excessive desire for getting or having, esp. wealth; desire for more than one needs or deserves; avarice; cupidity

greed·y (grēd′ē) ***adj.*** **greed′i·er**, **greed′i·est** ⟦ME *gredie* < OE *grædig* < base of *græd-* (in *grædum*, eagerly) + *-ig* (see -Y[2]), akin to Goth *grēdags*, lit., hungry < IE base **ĝher-*, to crave > Gr *charis*, grace, favor⟧ **1** wanting or taking all that one can get, with no thought of others' needs; desiring more than one needs or deserves; avaricious; covetous **2** having too strong a desire for food and drink; gluttonous; voracious **3** intensely eager —**greed′i·ly** ***adv.*** —**greed′i·ness** ***n.***

SYN.—**greedy** implies an insatiable desire to possess or acquire something to an amount inordinately beyond what one needs or deserves and is the broadest of the terms compared here; **avaricious** stresses greed for money or riches and often connotes miserliness; **grasping** suggests an unscrupulous eagerness for gain that manifests itself in a seizing upon every opportunity to get what one desires; **acquisitive** stresses the exertion of effort in acquiring or accumulating wealth or material possessions to an excessive amount; **covetous** implies greed for something that another person rightfully possesses

Greek (grēk) ***n.*** ⟦ME *Greke* < OE *Grec* < L *Graecus* < Gr *Graikos*, name orig. used by Illyrians for the Dorians in Epirus (< *Grāi, Grāii* < *Grāes*, native name of the people of Epirus); later applied by the people of Italy to all Hellenes⟧ **1** a person born or living in ancient or modern Greece **2** the language of the Greeks, constituting a separate branch of the Indo-European language family: see also LATE GREEK, MEDIEVAL GREEK, MODERN GREEK **3** ancient Greek, esp. that of the classical period (*c.* 8th-4th cent. B.C.) ☆**4** [Informal] a member of a Greek-letter fraternity or sorority —***adj.*** ⟦ME *Grec* < the *n.* & < Fr *grec* < L *Graecus*⟧ **1** of ancient or modern Greece or its people, language, or culture **2** designating or of Greek Catholics or the Greek Orthodox Church ☆**3** [Informal] designating or of a Greek-letter fraternity or sorority —**be (all) Greek to someone** to be incomprehensible or unintelligible to someone

Greek Catholic 1 loosely, a member of certain Eastern Orthodox churches **2** a member of certain Eastern churches in communion with the WESTERN CHURCH (sense 2)

Greek cross a cross with four equal arms at right angles

Greek fire ⟦from its first use by *Greeks* of Byzantium⟧ an incendiary material used in medieval warfare, described as able to burn in water

☆**Greek-let·ter** (grēk′let′ər) ***adj.*** designating or of a student fraternity or sorority whose name is designated by a combination of Greek letters

Greek (Orthodox) Church 1 the established church of Greece, an autonomous part of the Eastern Orthodox Church **2** loosely, the Eastern Orthodox Church

Gree·ley (grē′lē), **Horace** 1811-72; U.S. journalist & political leader

green (grēn) ***adj.*** ⟦ME *grene* < OE, akin to Ger *grün*, Du *groen*: for IE base see GROW⟧ **1** of the color that is characteristic of growing grass **2** *a)* overspread with or characterized by green plants or foliage [*a green field*] *b)* made of green-leaved vegetables [*green salad*] **3** keeping the green grass of summer; without snow; mild [*a green December*] **4** sickly or bilious, as from illness, fear, etc. **5** *a)* flourishing; active [*to keep someone's memory green*] *b)* of the time of one's youth [*the green years*] **6** not mature; unripe [*green bananas*] **7** not trained; inexperienced **8** easily led or deceived; simple; naive **9** not dried, seasoned, or cured; unprocessed [*green lumber*] **10** fresh; new **11** *a)* [*often* **G-**] of, relating to, or advocating ecological awareness, the preservation of natural resources, etc. [*green politics*] *b)* [*usually* **G-**] designating or of a political party or movement having these goals **12** ⟦see GREEN-EYED⟧ [Informal] jealous —***n.* 1** the color of growing grass; any color between blue and yellow in the spectrum: green can be produced by blending blue and yellow pigments **2** any green pigment or dye **3** anything colored green, as clothing **4** [*pl.*] green leaves, branches, etc., used for ornamentation **5** [*pl.*] *a)* lettuce, endive, dandelion leaves, etc. eaten raw, usually with a dressing [*salad greens*] *b)* leaves of the collard, turnip, etc., cooked in various ways **6** an area of smooth turf set aside for special purposes [*a village green*] **7** [*usually* **G-**] an environmentalist; specif., a member of an environmentalist political party ☆**8** [Slang] money, esp. paper money: chiefly in **long green** and **folding green 9** *Golf* the plot of carefully tended turf immediately surrounding each of the holes to facilitate putting — ***vt., vi.*** to make or become green —**green with envy** very envious —**green′ish** ***adj.*** —**green′ish·ness** ***n.*** —**green′ly** ***adv.*** —**green′ness** ***n.***

Green[1] (grēn) **1 Henry** (pseud. of *Henry Vincent Yorke*) 1905-73; Eng. novelist **2 William** 1873-1952; U.S. labor leader

Green[2] (grēn) river flowing from W Wyo. south into the Colorado River in SE Utah: 730 mi (1,175 km)

green algae any of a division (Chlorophycota) of photosynthetic thallophytes in which the chlorophyll is not obscured by other pigments: a type of ALGAE

Green·a·way (grēn′ə wā′), **Kate** 1846-1901; Eng. painter & illustrator, esp. of children's books

☆**green·back** (grēn′bak′) ***n.*** any piece of U.S. paper money printed in green ink on the back

☆**Greenback Party** a political party organized in the U.S. after the Civil War, which advocated that fiat money issued by the federal government be the only currency

Green Bay ⟦transl. of Fr *Baie Verte*⟧ **1** arm of Lake Michigan, extending into NE Wis.: *c.* 100 mi (161 km) long **2** city & port in Wis., on this bay

☆**green bean 1** a variety of kidney bean with long, narrow green pods **2** the edible immature seed pod of this

green·belt (grēn′belt′) ***n.*** a beltlike area around a city, reserved by official authority for park land, farms, etc.

☆**Green Beret** ⟦from the *green beret* worn as part of the uniform⟧ a member of the SPECIAL FORCES of the U.S. Army, popularly known as the **Green Berets**

☆**green·bri·er** (-brī′ər) ***n.*** any of several climbing woody vines (genus *Smilax*) of the lily family, with prickly stems, oval leaves, and, usually, black berries

green card ☆a registration card, originally green, granting an alien permission to reside and be employed in the U.S.

☆**green corn** young ears of sweet corn, in the milky stage

green dragon ☆an American wildflower (*Arisaema dracontium*) of the arum family, with a very long spadix and a slender, greenish spathe

Greene (grēn) **1 (Henry) Graham** 1904-91; Eng. writer, esp. of novels **2 Nathanael** 1742-86; Am. general in the Revolutionary War **3 Robert** 1558?-92; Eng. poet, dramatist, & pamphleteer

green earth 1 any of several earths or clays containing iron silicates used as a pale grayish-green pigment **2** TERRE-VERTE

green·er·y (grēn′ər ē) ***n.,*** *pl.* **-er·ies 1** green vegetation; verdure **2** greens: see GREEN (*n.* 4) **3** a greenhouse

green-eyed (grēn′īd′) ***adj.*** ⟦see Shakespeare's *Merchant of Venice* III, ii and *Othello* III, iii⟧ of or having to do with jealousy: usually in the phrase **green-eyed monster**

green·finch (grēn′finch′) ***n.*** a finch (*Carduelis chloris*) with olive-green and yellow feathers, native to Europe

green flash a sudden, bright flash of greenish light sometimes visible near the horizon at sunset or sunrise on a clear day, caused by the atmospheric refraction of sunlight

green·fly (grēn′flī′) ***n.,*** *pl.* **-flies′** [Brit.] a green aphid

green·gage (grēn′gāj′) ***n.*** ⟦GREEN + *gage*, after Sir William *Gage* (1651-1727), Englishman who imported the trees from France (*c.* 1725)⟧ a large plum with golden-green skin and flesh

green·gro·cer (grēn′grō′sər) ***n.*** [Chiefly Brit.] a retail dealer in fresh vegetables and fruit —**green′gro′cer·y** ***n.,*** *pl.* **-cer·ies**

green·heart (grēn′härt′) ***n.*** ⟦so named from the greenish color of its wood⟧ **1** any of various tropical trees, esp. bebeeru, whose wood is valued for its hardness and resistance to fungi and insects **2** the wood

green·horn (grēn′hôrn′) ***n.*** ⟦orig. with reference to a young animal with immature horns⟧ **1** *a)* an inexperienced person; beginner; novice ☆*b)* [Now Rare] a newly arrived immigrant **2** a person easily deceived; dupe

green·house (grēn′hous′) ***n.*** a building made mainly of glass, in which the temperature and humidity can be regulated for the cultivation of delicate or out-of-season plants —***adj.*** of or contributing to the greenhouse effect [*greenhouse gases*]

greenhouse effect the warming of a planet's surface and lower atmosphere caused by trapped solar radiation: solar shortwave radiation penetrates to the planet's surface and is reradiated into the atmosphere as infrared waves that are then absorbed by carbon dioxide, water vapor, etc.

☆**green·ie** (grēn′ē) ***n.*** ⟦so called from the color of a common type⟧ [Slang] an amphetamine pill, used as a stimulant

green·ing[1] (grēn′iŋ) ***n.*** ⟦MDu *groeninc* < *groen*: see GREEN⟧ any of various apples having greenish-yellow skins when ripe

green·ing[2] (grēn′iŋ) ***n.*** ⟦< *The Greening of America* (1970), book by C. A. Reich, U.S. writer & law professor⟧ ☆a becoming more mature and less naive, esp. in one's understanding of social and political forces

green·keep·er (grēn′kēp′ər) ***n. var. of*** GREENSKEEPER

Green·land (grēn′lənd) ⟦< ON *Grönland*: orig. so called (A.D. 986) by ERIC THE RED⟧ self-governing island northeast of North America; an integral part of Denmark: it is the world's largest island: 836,330 sq mi (2,166,086 sq km): ice-free land 158,475 sq mi (410,449 sq km); cap. Godthåb —**Green′land·er** ***n.***

Greenland Sea part of the Arctic Ocean east of Greenland

☆**green·let** (grēn′lit) ***n.*** any of various tropical vireos

green·light (grēn′līt′) ***vt.*** **-light′ed** or **-lit′**, **-light′ing** ⟦< fol.⟧ [Informal] to approve or give permission to proceed with (a project, funding proposal, etc., esp. a proposed film script)

☆**green light** ⟦in allusion to the green "go" signal of a traffic light⟧ [Informal] permission or authorization to proceed with a proposed undertaking, as the project of making a film from a script that has been submitted: usually in **give (or get) the green light**

green·ling (grēn′liŋ) ***n.*** any of a family (Hexagrammidae) of large, predatory percoid fishes of the N Pacific, with a long dorsal fin

green·mail (-māl′) ***n.*** ⟦< GREEN (*n.* 8) + (BLACK)MAIL⟧ [Informal] the buying of a large amount of a company's stock in anticipation that the management, fearing that the buyer will gain control, will buy it back at a premium over the market price —**green′mail′er** ***n.***

green manure 1 a crop of plants, as clover, plowed under while still green to fertilize the soil **2** fresh manure

green mold any of various species of a fungus (esp. genus *Penicillium*) that produce greenish masses of spores

green monkey a small, ground-dwelling guenon monkey (*Cercopithecus sabaeus*) with greenish fur

☆**Green Mountain Boys** the Vermont soldiers organized and led by Ethan Allen in the American Revolution

Green Mountains ⟦from the abundant evergreen trees covering them⟧ range of the Appalachians, extending the length of Vermont: highest peak, 4,393 ft (1,339 m)

green·ock·ite (grēn′ək īt′) ***n.*** ⟦after C. M. Cathcart, Lord *Greenock* (1783-1859), Brit general who discovered it (1841) + -ITE[1]⟧ a soft, yellowish, hexagonal mineral, CdS, an ore of cadmium; cadmium sulfide

green onion an immature onion with a long stalk and green leaves, often eaten raw as in salads; scallion

Gree·nough (grē′nō), **Horatio** 1805-52; U.S. sculptor

☆**green pepper** the green, immature fruit of any red pepper, esp. any large, bell-shaped variety: see CAPSICUM

☆**green power** ⟦see GREEN, *n.* 8⟧ money as the source of economic power and, hence, social and political power

☆**green revolution** the simultaneous development of new varieties of food plants and improved agricultural techniques, resulting in greatly increased crop yields

☆**Green River Ordinance** ⟦after such an ordinance passed (1931) in *Green River*, Wyo.⟧ a local ordinance prohibiting door-to-door selling

green·room (grēn′ro͞om′) ***n.*** ⟦prob. from such rooms orig. being painted *green*⟧ a waiting room in a theater, concert hall, TV studio, etc., for use by performers when they are offstage

green·sand (-sand′) *n.* a green, sandy deposit containing much glauconite

Greens·bor·o (grēnz′bur′ō) ⟦after Nathanael GREENE⟧ city in NC N.C.

greens fee a fee paid to play golf on a golf course

green·shank (grēn′shaŋk′) *n.* a European sandpiper (*Tringa nebularia*) with greenish legs

green·sick·ness (-sik′nis) *n.* CHLOROSIS (sense 2)

greens·keep·er (grēnz′kēp′ər) *n.* the person in charge of maintaining the turf, bunkers, etc. of a golf course

☆**green snake** any of a genus (*Opheodrys*) of harmless, small and slender, green colubrid snakes of North America

green soap a soft, originally greenish, soap made of potassium hydroxide, certain vegetable oils, and alcohol, used in treating skin diseases

green·stick fracture (grēn′stik′) a type of bone fracture, esp. of the long bones of children, in which the bone is bent and broken only on the convex side

green·stone (grēn′stōn′) *n.* any of various altered basic igneous rocks having a dark-green color

green·sward (-swôrd′) *n.* green, grassy ground or turf

green tea tea that is not fermented before being dried: distinguished from BLACK TEA

☆**green thumb** an apparent skill or talent for growing plants easily

green turtle a large, edible species (*Chelonia mydas*, family Cheloniidae) of marine turtle

green vitriol FERROUS SULFATE

green·way (grēn′wā′) *n.* a protected natural area that connects developed, esp. urban, areas, often providing trails for bicycling, hiking, etc.

Green·wich (gren′ich; *chiefly Brit*, grin′ij) borough of Greater London, England, located on the prime meridian: formerly the site of an astronomical observatory: see HERSTMONCEUX

Greenwich (mean) time mean solar time of the meridian (0° longitude) at Greenwich, England: see also COORDINATED UNIVERSAL TIME, UNIVERSAL TIME

Green·wich Village (gren′ich) ⟦after GREENWICH, England⟧ section of New York City, on the lower west side of Manhattan: noted for once being a bohemian center for artists, writers, etc.: formerly a village

green·wood (grēn′wood′) *n.* a forest in leaf

greet[1] (grēt) *vt.* ⟦ME *greten* < OE *gretan*, *grætan*, akin to Du *groetan*, Ger *grüssen* < IE **ghredh-* < base **gher-*, echoic of outcry > L *hirrire*, to whimper, growl⟧ **1** to speak or write to with expressions of friendliness, respect, pleasure, etc., as in meeting or by letter; hail; welcome **2** to meet, receive, address, or acknowledge (a person, utterance, or event) in a specified way [the speech was *greeted* with cheers; the army was *greeted* by cannon shots] **3** to come or appear to; meet [a roaring sound *greeted* his ears]

greet[2] (grēt) *vi.* ⟦ME *greten* < OE *grætan*, akin to Goth *gretan* and to prec.⟧ [Scot.] to weep; lament

greet·er (grēt′ər) *n.* one who greets; specif., a person employed, as in a retail store, to greet arriving customers

greet·ing (grēt′iŋ) *n.* **1** the act or words of a person who greets; salutation; welcome **2** [*often pl.*] a message of regards from someone absent

greeting card CARD[1] (*n.* 1*h*)

greet·ings (grēt′iŋz) *interj.* hello: used formally, as in the salutation of an official letter, or variously in informal contexts

greg·a·rine (greg′ə rēn′, -rīn′, -rin) *n.* ⟦< ModL *Gregarina* < L *gregarius* (see fol.): name suggested by L. Dufour, 19th-c. Fr zoologist⟧ any of a subclass (Gregarinia) of sporozoan protozoans that are parasites in the digestive tract of insects, crustaceans, earthworms, etc. —*adj.* of or pertaining to these protozoans: also **greg·a·rin·i·an** (greg′ə rin′ē ən)

gre·gar·i·ous (grə ger′ē əs) *adj.* ⟦L *gregarius*, belonging to a flock < *grex* (gen. *gregis*), a flock, herd < IE base **ger-*, to collect > Gr *ageirein*, to assemble⟧ **1** living in herds or flocks **2** fond of the company of others; sociable **3** having to do with a herd, flock, or crowd **4** *Bot.* growing in clusters —**gre·gar′i·ous·ly** *adv.* —**gre·gar′i·ous·ness** *n.*

gre·go (grē′gō, grā′-) *n.* ⟦< It *Greco* or Port *Grego*, both < L *Graecus*, Greek⟧ a short cloak of coarse cloth with an attached hood, worn in the Levant

Gre·go·ri·an (grə gôr′ē ən) *adj.* of or introduced by Pope Gregory I or Pope Gregory XIII

Gregorian calendar a corrected form of the JULIAN CALENDAR, introduced by Pope Gregory XIII in 1582 and now used in most countries of the world: it provides for an ordinary year of 365 days and a leap year of 366 days every fourth, even year, exclusive of the final year of a century, which is a leap year only if exactly divisible by 400

Gregorian chant a ritual plainsong, monophonic and unmeasured, traditionally codified by Pope Gregory I, and formerly widely used in the Roman Catholic Church

Greg·o·ry[1] (greg′ə rē) *n.* ⟦LL *Gregorius* < Gr *Grēgorios*, lit., vigilant, hence, watchman < dial. form of *egeirein*, to awaken < IE base **ger-*, to grow, awaken⟧ a masculine name: dim. *Greg*; var. *Gregg*; equiv. Fr. *Grégoire*, Ger. & Scand. *Gregor*, It. & Sp. *Gregorio*

Greg·o·ry[2] (greg′ə rē) **1 Gregory I** (A.D. 540?-604); pope (590-604): his day is Sept. 3: called *the Great*: also called **Saint Gregory I 2 Gregory VII** (born *Hildebrand*) (1020?-85); pope (1073-85): his day is May 25: also called **Saint Gregory VII 3 Gregory XIII** (born *Ugo Buoncompagni*) 1502-85; pope (1572-85): see GREGORIAN CALENDAR **4** Lady **Augusta** (born *Isabella Augusta Persse*) 1852-1932; Ir. playwright

Gregory of Nys·sa (nis′ə), Saint (A.D. 335?-394?); Gr. theologian & bishop in Cappadocia: his day is March 9: brother of Saint Basil

Gregory of Tours, Saint (A.D. 538?-594?); Frank. historian & bishop: his day is Nov. 17

greige (grāzh) *n.* ⟦Fr *grège*, raw (silk) < It (*seta*) *greggia* < VL **gredius*, raw⟧ **1** unbleached and undyed cloth or yarn **2** a color blending gray and beige —*adj.* grayish-beige

grei·sen (grī′zən) *n.* ⟦Ger, var. of *greiss* < dial. *greissen*, to split⟧ a crystalline, igneous rock consisting mainly of quartz and white mica

gre·mi·al (grē′mē əl) *n.* ⟦LL *gremialis* < L *gremium*, bosom, lap < IE **grem-* < base **ger-*: see GREGARIOUS⟧ a lap cloth placed across the knees of a bishop, as when he sits during the celebration of Mass

grem·lin (grem′lin) *n.* ⟦prob. < Dan **græmling*, imp, dim. of obs. *gram*, a devil < ON *gramr*, angry, akin to OE *gremian*, to enrage: for IE base see GRIM⟧ a small imaginary creature humorously blamed for the faulty operation of airplanes or the disruption of any procedure

Gre·na·da (grə nā′də) **1** southernmost island of the Windward group in the West Indies: 120 sq mi (311 sq km) **2** country consisting of this island & the S Grenadines: formerly a British colony, it became independent (1974) & a member of the Commonwealth: 133 sq mi (344 sq km); cap. St. George's

gre·nade (grə nād′) *n.* ⟦Fr < OFr, pomegranate (said to be so named from its shape) < L (*malum*) *granatum*, (apple) with seeds, pomegranate < *granatus*, seedy < *granum*, seed, GRAIN⟧ **1** a small bomb detonated by a fuze and thrown by hand or fired from a rifle **2** a glass container to be thrown so that it will break and disperse the chemicals inside: used for putting out fires, spreading tear gas, etc.

gren·a·dier (gren′ə dir′) *n.* ⟦Fr < *grenade*: see prec.⟧ **1** [Archaic] an infantry soldier employed to carry and throw grenades **2** a member of a special regiment or corps, as of the Grenadier Guards of the British Army, attached to the royal household **3** any of a family (Macrouridae, order Gadiformes) of deep-sea bony fishes with a long, tapering tail, large head, and soft fins

gren·a·dine[1] (gren′ə dēn′, gren′ə dēn′) *n.* ⟦Fr < *grenade*, pomegranate: see GRENADE⟧ a red syrup made from pomegranate juice, used for flavoring drinks, etc.

gren·a·dine[2] (gren′ə dēn′, gren′ə dēn′) *n.* ⟦Fr < *grenade* (see GRENADE): from being spotted with "grains"⟧ a thin, loosely woven cotton, wool, silk, or rayon cloth

Gren·a·dines (gren′ə dēnz′) chain of small islands of the Windward group in the West Indies: the northern group is part of the nation of St. Vincent and the Grenadines, & the southern group is part of Grenada

Gren·del (gren′dəl) *n.* the male monster slain by BEOWULF

Gren·fell (gren′fel′), Sir **Wilfred Thom·a·son** (täm′ə sən) 1865-1940; Eng. physician, writer, & medical missionary to Labrador

Gre·no·ble (grə nō′bəl; *Fr* grə nô′bl′) city in SE France, in the Alps

Gresh·am (gresh′əm) city in NW Oreg., near Portland

Gresh·am's law (gresh′əmz) ⟦after Sir Thomas *Gresham* (1519-79), Eng financier, formerly thought to have formulated it⟧ the theory that when two or more kinds of money of equal denomination but unequal intrinsic value are in circulation, the one of greater value will tend to be hoarded or exported; popularly, the principle that bad money will drive good money out of circulation

gres·so·ri·al (gre sôr′ē əl) *adj.* ⟦< L *gressus*, pp. of *gradi*, to step, walk: see GRADE⟧ adapted for walking, as the feet of certain birds

Gret·a (gret′ə, grāt′ə) *n.* ⟦Swed or < Ger *Grete*⟧ a feminine name: see MARGARET

Gretch·en (grech′ən) *n.* ⟦Ger, dim. of *Margarete*⟧ a feminine name: see MARGARET

Gret·na Green (gret′nə) border village in Scotland, where, formerly, many eloping English couples went to be married: used fig. of any similar village or town

Greuze (grëz), **Jean Bap·tiste** (zhän bȧ tēst′) 1725-1805; Fr. painter

grew (grōō) *vi., vt.* ⟦ME *greu* < OE *greow*⟧ *pt. of* GROW

grew·some (grōō′səm) *adj. archaic sp. of* GRUESOME

grey (grā) *adj., n., vt., vi. chiefly Brit. sp. of* GRAY[1]

Grey (grā) **1 Charles** 2d Earl Grey 1764-1845; Eng. statesman; prime minister (1830-34) **2** Lady **Jane** Lady Jane Dudley 1537-54; queen of England (July 10-19, 1553): beheaded **3 Zane** (zān) 1875-1939; U.S. writer, esp. of westerns

grey·hen (grā′hen′) *n.* the female of the BLACK GROUSE

grey·hound (grā′hound′) *n.* ⟦ME *grehounde* < OE *grighund*, **grieghund*, akin to ON *greyhundr* < **grieg*, bitch, coward (prob. < IE **gherēu-* < base **ĝher-*, to shine > GRAY[1]) + *hund*, dog, HOUND[1]⟧ any of a breed of tall, slender, swift dog with a long, narrow head and a short, smooth coat, formerly much used in coursing and now very popular as a racing dog

grey·lag (grā′lag′) *n. alt. sp. of* GRAYLAG

grey water household wastewater from sinks, bathtubs, washers, etc.: distinguished from BLACKWATER: also written **grey′wa′ter** *n.*

grib·ble (grib′əl) *n.* ⟦prob. dim. < base of GRUB⟧ a small marine isopod (*Limnoria lignorum*) that bores into wooden objects under water and destroys them

grid (grid) *n.* ⟦short for GRIDIRON⟧ **1** a framework of parallel bars; grating **2** a network of evenly spaced horizontal and vertical bars or lines, esp. one for locating points when placed over a map, chart, etc. **3** a system for distributing electric power throughout a region **4** on a speedway, the order in which racing cars start **5** *Elec.* a conductive framework of metal plates in a storage cell or battery, that contains lead or a lead compound, esp. a lead oxide, and reacts with the electrolyte **6** *Electronics* any gridlike or spiral-shaped electrode positioned between a cathode and anode to control the flow of electrons or ions in an electron tube —☆*adj.* ⟦< GRIDIRON (sense 3)⟧ [Slang] having to do with football

grid bias a steady, direct-current voltage applied to the control grid of an electron tube to make it negative with respect to the cathode

grid current the flow of electrons between a grid and the cathode of an electron tube

☆**grid·der** (grid′ər) *n.* ⟦< GRID, *adj.* & GRIDIRON⟧ [Slang] a football player

grid·dle (grid′'l) *n.* ⟦ME *gredil* < Anglo-Fr *gridil* < OFr **gredil*, var. of *graïl* < L *craticula*, small gridiron < *cratis*, wickerwork: see CRATE⟧ a heavy, flat metal plate with a handle, or a special flat, heated surface on the top of a stove, used for cooking pancakes and other foods —*vt.* **-dled, -dling** to cook on a griddle

grid·dle·cake (-kāk′) *n.* a thin, flat batter cake cooked on a griddle; pancake

gride (grīd) *vt., vi.* **grid′ed, grid′ing** ⟦metathesis of ME *girden*, to pierce (see GIRD[2]): adopted (from John LYDGATE) & popularized by Edmund SPENSER[2]⟧ **1** to scrape or grate with a rasping sound **2** [Obs.] to pierce or wound —*n.* a harsh, rasping sound made by scraping or grating

grid·i·ron (grid′ī′ərn) *n.* ⟦ME *gredirne*, folk etym. on *irne* (see IRON) < *gredire*, var. of *gredil*: see GRIDDLE⟧ **1** a framework of metal bars or wires on which to broil meat or fish; grill **2** any framework or network resembling a gridiron ☆**3** a football field

☆**grid·lock** (grid′läk′) *n.* ⟦GRID + LOCK[1]⟧ **1** a traffic jam, as at an intersection, in which no vehicle can move in any direction **2** any obstructed condition or impasse [airport *gridlock*, *gridlock* in the Senate] —*vt.* to cause gridlock in —**grid′locked′** *adj.*

grief (grēf) *n.* ⟦ME *gref* < OFr, sorrow, grief < *grever*: see GRIEVE⟧ **1** intense emotional suffering caused by loss, disaster, misfortune, etc.; acute sorrow; deep sadness **2** a cause or the subject of such suffering **3** [Informal] *a)* irritation or frustration, esp. from accidents, mishaps, etc. [the *griefs* of a computer operator] *b)* trouble; difficulty [enough *grief* for one day] *c)* a cause of any of these —**come to grief** to fail or be ruined

grief-strick·en (grēf′strik′ən) *adj.* stricken with grief; keenly distressed; sorrowful

Grieg (grēg; *Norw* grig), **Ed·vard (Hagerup)** (ed′värd; *Norw* ed′värt) 1843-1907; Norw. composer

griev·ance (grēv′əns) *n.* ⟦ME *grevaunce* < OFr *grevance* < *grever*: see GRIEVE⟧ **1** a circumstance thought to be unjust or injurious and ground for complaint or resentment **2** complaint or resentment, or a statement expressing this, against a real or imagined wrong **3** a complaint arising from circumstances or conditions relating to one's employment **4** [Obs.] *a)* the inflicting of injury or hardship *b)* a cause of injury or hardship

grievance committee a committee formed to settle grievances according to formal procedures (**grievance procedures**) agreed upon, as by the terms of a collective bargaining agreement

griev·ant (grēv′ənt) *n.* one who presents a grievance, as before a grievance committee

grieve (grēv) *vt.* **grieved, griev′ing** ⟦ME *greven* < OFr *grever* < L *gravare*, to burden, grieve < *gravis*, heavy, grievous: see GRAVE[1]⟧ **1** to cause to feel grief; afflict with deep, acute sorrow or distress **2** to challenge (some action, decision, etc. of management) by filing and pursuing a grievance **3** [Archaic] to harm; injure —*vi.* **1** to feel deep, acute sorrow or distress; mourn **2** to grieve some action, decision, etc. of management

griev·ous (grēv′əs) *adj.* ⟦ME *grevous* < OFr < *grever*: see prec.⟧ **1** causing grief **2** showing or characterized by grief [a *grievous* cry] **3** causing suffering; hard to bear; severe [*grievous* pain] **4** very serious; deplorable [a *grievous* fault] **5** atrocious; heinous [a *grievous* crime] —**griev′ous·ly** *adv.* —**griev′ous·ness** *n.*

griffe (grif) *n.* ⟦Fr, lit., claw < OFr *grif* < Frank **grif*, akin to OHG *grif*: for IE base see GRIPE⟧ *Archit.* a clawlike ornament extending from the base of a column

grif·fin (grif′in) *n.* ⟦ME *griffon* < OFr *grifoun* < OHG or It *grifo*, both < L *gryphus*, earlier *gryps* < Gr *gryps*, griffin < *grypos*, hooked, curved (prob. so called from its hooked beak) < IE base **ger-* > CRANK[1]⟧ a mythical monster with the body and hind legs of a lion and the head, wings, and claws of an eagle

griffin

Grif·fith[1] (grif′ith) *n.* ⟦Welsh *Gruffydd* < ? L *Rufus*: see RUFUS⟧ a masculine name

Grif·fith[2] (grif′ith), **D(avid Lewelyn) W(ark)** 1875-1948; U.S. film producer & director

grif·fon (grif′ən) *n.* ⟦Fr, lit., a griffin⟧ **1** GRIFFIN **2** any of a breed of medium-sized hunting dog, developed by a Dutch breeder in the 19th cent., with a square muzzle and a harsh, bristly coat: in full *wirehaired pointing griffon*

☆**grift** (grift) [Old Slang] *vi.* ⟦altered < now-rare v. *graft*, to gain money by illicit means⟧ to swindle on a small scale —*n.* a petty swindle

☆**grift·er** (grif′tər) *n.* ⟦prec. + -ER⟧ [Slang] a petty swindler, as one who operates a dishonest gambling device at a carnival; confidence man

grig (grig) *n.* ⟦ME *grege*, anything diminutive, dwarf, prob. < Scand, as in Norw *krek*, Swed dial. *krik*, little animal⟧ **1** a lively, animated person **2** [Now Dial.] a small eel **3** [Now Dial.] a grasshopper or cricket

Gri·gnard reagent (grē′nyärd′) ⟦after F. A. V. *Grignard* (1871-1935), Fr chemist⟧ any of a class of reagents with the general formula RMgX, in which R is an organic radical, esp. an alkyl or aryl, and X is a halogen: these reagents react with a great variety of compounds and are used in the synthesis of organic compounds

☆**gri-gri** (grē′grē′) *n. alt. sp. of* GRIS-GRIS

grill[1] (gril) *n.* ⟦Fr *gril* < OFr *graïl*: see GRIDDLE⟧ **1** a cooking unit having parallel metal bars or wires on which to broil meat or fish, as *a)* a portable or stationary outdoor device fueled by gas or charcoal *b)* an indoor unit, sometimes part of a range **2** a large griddle **3** grilled food **4** a restaurant, club, or dining room that makes a specialty of grilled foods —*vt.* ⟦Fr *griller* < the *n.*⟧ **1** to cook on a grill; broil **2** to torture by applying heat ☆**3** to question relentlessly; cross-examine searchingly —*vi.* to be subjected to grilling

grill[2] (gril) *n. alt. sp. of* GRILLE

gril·lage (gril′ij) *n.* ⟦Fr, wirework, grating, frame < *grille*: see fol.⟧ a framework of beams laid crosswise, used as a support or foundation, as for a building on soft ground

grille (gril) *n.* ⟦Fr < OFr *graïlle* < L *craticula*: see GRIDDLE⟧ **1** an open grating of wrought iron, bronze, wood, etc., forming a screen to a door, window, or other opening, or used as a divider **2** a grating or screen at the front of a motor vehicle, that allows air to pass through to the radiator **3** *alt. sp. of* GRILL[1] (*n.* 4) **4** *Court Tennis* a square opening high on the back wall of the court on the hazard side

grilled (grild) *adj.* **1** having a grille **2** cooked on a grill or gridiron; broiled

grill·room (gril′ro͞om′) *n.* GRILL[1] (*n.* 4)

grill·work (gril′wurk′) *n.* a grille, or something worked into the form of a grille

grilse (grils) *n., pl.* **grilse** or **grils′es** ⟦ME *grills*, prob. metathesis of OFr *gisle*, dim. < *gris*, gray: see GRISAILLE⟧ a young salmon on its first return from the sea to fresh water

grim (grim) *adj.* **grim′mer, grim′mest** ⟦ME < OE *grimm*, akin to Ger < IE base **ghrem-*, to make a loud sound, roar angrily > GRUMBLE, Russ *grom*, thunder⟧ **1** fierce; cruel; savage **2** hard and unyielding; relentless; stern; resolute [*grim* courage] **3** appearing stern, forbidding, harsh, etc. [a *grim* face] **4** repellent; uninviting [a *grim* task] **5** dealing with unpleasant subjects; frightful; ghastly [*grim* humor] —**grim′ly** *adv.* —**grim′ness** *n.*

grim·ace (grim′is, gri mās′) *n.* ⟦Fr, altered (with pejorative suffix) < OFr *grimuche*, prob. < Frank **grima*, a mask, akin to OE *grima*: see GRIME⟧ a twisting or distortion of the face, as in expressing pain, contempt, disgust, etc., or a wry look as in seeking to amuse —*vi.* **-aced, -ac·ing** to make grimaces

Gri·mal·di man (gri mäl′dē, -môl′-) ⟦from the remains found near *Grimaldi*, village in Italy⟧ an Aurignacian human, similar to the Cro-Magnon

gri·mal·kin (gri mal′kin, -môl′-) *n.* ⟦earlier *gray malkin*: see MALKIN⟧ **1** a cat; esp., an old female cat **2** a malicious old woman

grime (grīm) *n.* ⟦Early ModE, prob. < Fl *grijm*, akin to OE *grima* < IE **ghrei-* < base **gher-*, to rub hard, smear > Gr *chrisma*, ointment⟧ dirt, esp. sooty dirt, rubbed into or covering a surface, as of the skin —*vt.* **grimed, grim′ing** to make very dirty or grimy

☆**Grimes (Golden)** (grīmz) ⟦short for *Grimes Golden Pippin*, variety grown (*c.* 1790) by T. P. *Grimes*, Va. fruit grower⟧ a yellow autumn eating apple

Grimm (grim) **1 Ja·kob (Ludwig Karl)** (yä′kôp) 1785-1863; Ger. philologist **2 Wil·helm (Karl)** (vil′helm) 1786-1859; Ger. philologist: brother of Jakob, with whom he collaborated in the collection of fairy tales

Grimm's law ⟦after Jakob GRIMM in honor of his formulation (1822) of parallels noted by himself & R. K. RASK⟧ the statement of a series of systematic prehistoric changes of reconstructed Indo-European consonants to Proto-Germanic consonants: these hypothesized prehistoric sound shifts are reflected by consonant correspondences between Germanic words and their cognates in non-Germanic Indo-European languages: (1) IE voiceless stops (p, t, k) = Gmc voiceless fricatives (f, th, h); hence, L *p*ater (cf. PATERNAL) = E *f*ather, L *t*enuis (cf. TENUOUS) = E *th*in, Gr *k*ardia (cf. CARDIAC) = E *h*eart (2) IE voiced stops (b, d, g) = Gmc voiceless stops (p, t, k); hence, L *b*ucca (cf. BUCCAL) = OE *p*ohha, a sack, L *d*ecem (cf. DECIMAL) = E *t*en, L *g*enu (cf. GENUFLECT) = E *k*nee, which has lost the (k) sound (3) IE voiced aspirated stops (b + h, d + h, g + h) = Gmc voiced stops (b, d, g); hence, Sans *bh*rātar = E *b*rother, Sans mā*dh*u, honey = E mea*d*, IE **gh*ostis = E *g*uest These correspondences show the kinship, stressed in the etymologies of this dictionary, between various native English words and the English words borrowed from any of the non-Germanic Indo-European languages

Grim Reaper, the *see* REAPER

grim·y (grīm′ē) *adj.* **grim′i·er, grim′i·est** covered with or full of grime; very dirty —*SYN.* DIRTY —**grim′i·ly** *adv.* —**grim′i·ness** *n.*

grin (grin) *vi.* **grinned, grin′ning** ⟦ME *grennen* < OE *grennian*, to gnash or bare the teeth, akin to OHG *grennan*, to mutter, Ger *greinen*, to weep⟧ **1** to smile broadly as in amusement or pleasure, or, sometimes, in embarrassment **2** to draw back the lips and show the teeth in pain, scorn, etc. —*vt.* to express by grinning —*n.* the act or look of one who grins —**grin and bear it** to accept philosophically something burdensome or painful —**grin′ner** *n.* —**grin′ning·ly** *adv.*

Grinch (grinch) *n.* ⟦after the title character of a children's book, *How the Grinch Stole Christmas!* (1957), by Dr. SEUSS⟧ ☆[*often* **g-**] a person who maliciously spoils the fun of others

grind (grīnd) *vt.* **ground, grind′ing** ⟦ME *grinden* < OE *grindan* < IE **ghrendh* < base **ghren-*, to rub away, pulverize > GROUND[1]⟧ **1** *a)* to crush into bits or fine particles between two hard surfaces; pulverize *b)* to chop into small pieces or fine particles by means of sharp metal blades *[*to *grind* coffee beans*]* **2** to afflict with cruelty, hardship, etc.; crush; oppress: often with *down [*a people *ground* down by tyranny*]* **3** to sharpen, shape, or smooth by friction **4** to press down or together with a crushing, turning motion; rub harshly or gratingly *[*to *grind* one's teeth*]* **5** to operate by turning the crank of *[*to *grind* a coffee mill*]* **6** to make or produce by grinding —*vi.* **1** to perform the act of grinding something **2** to be capable of being ground; undergo grinding **3** to grate **4** [Informal] to work or study hard and steadily ☆**5** [Slang] to move the hips in a circular motion, as in striptease dancing —*n.* **1** the act or operation of grinding **2** the degree of fineness of something ground into particles **3** long, difficult, tedious work or study; drudgery ☆**4** [Informal] a student who studies very hard ☆**5** [Slang] a circular movement of the hips made by or as by a striptease dancer —**grind out** to produce by steady or laborious, often uninspired, effort —**grind to a halt (**or **stop)** to come gradually to a stop or to an end —**grind′ing·ly** *adv.*

☆**grin·de·li·a** (grin dēl′yə, -dē′lē ə) *n.* ⟦ModL, after H. *Grindel* (1776-1836), professor of botany at Riga⟧ any of a genus (*Grindelia*) of coarse plants of the composite family, with large, yellow flower heads: the dried stems and leaves are used medicinally

grind·er (grīn′dər) *n.* ⟦ME & OE *grindere*⟧ **1** a person who grinds; specif., one whose work is sharpening tools, etc. **2** a thing that grinds; specif., *a)* any of various machines for crushing or sharpening *b)* a molar tooth *c)* [*pl.*] [Informal] the teeth ☆**3** *chiefly New England var. of* HERO SANDWICH

grind·stone (grīnd′stōn′) *n.* **1** [Now Rare] a millstone **2** a revolving stone disk for sharpening bladed tools or shaping and polishing things —**keep (**or **have** or **put) one's nose to the grindstone** to work hard and steadily

☆**grin·ga** (griŋ′gə) *n.* ⟦MexSp, fem. of fol.⟧ [*also in italics*] a female gringo: usually a hostile or disparaging term

☆**grin·go** (griŋ′gō) *n., pl.* **-gos** ⟦MexSp < Sp, gibberish, altered < *Griego*, Greek < L *Graecus*, GREEK⟧ in Latin America, a foreigner, esp. an American or Englishman: usually a dismissive or disparaging term

gri·ot (grē′ō) *n.* ⟦Fr < ?⟧ a traditional, W African musician or storyteller who recounts the oral history of a village, family, etc.

grip[1] (grip) *n.* ⟦ME *gripe* < OE *gripa*, a clutch, handful < base of *grīpan*: see GRIPE⟧ **1** the act of taking firmly and holding fast with the hand, teeth, an instrument, etc.; secure grasp; firm hold **2** the manner in which this is done **3** any special manner of clasping hands by which members of a secret or fraternal society identify one another as such ☆**4** the power of grasping firmly *[*to lose one's *grip* on a slippery handle*]* **5** the power of understanding; mental grasp *[*to have a good *grip* on a matter*]* **6** firm control; mastery *[*in the *grip* of disease, to get a *grip* on oneself*]* **7** a mechanical contrivance for clutching or grasping **8** a part by which something is grasped; often, specif., a handle or hilt ☆**9** ⟦short for GRIPSACK⟧ a small bag or satchel for holding clothes, etc. in traveling ☆**10** one who handles properties and scenery on a stage or TV or film set **11** *Sports* the manner of holding a ball, bat, club, racket, etc. —*vt.* **gripped, grip′ping 1** to take firmly and hold fast with the hand, teeth, an instrument, etc. **2** to give a GRIP[1] (*n.* 3) to **3** to fasten or join firmly (*to*) **4** *a)* to get and hold the attention of *b)* to have a strong emotional impact on —*vi.* to get a grip —**come to grips 1** to engage in hand-to-hand fighting **2** to struggle or try to cope (*with*): also [Brit.] **get to grips** —**grip′per** *n.*

grip[2] (grip) *n. alt. sp. of* GRIPPE

gripe (grīp) *vt.* **griped, grip′ing** ⟦ME *gripen* < OE *gripan*, to seize, akin to Ger *greifen* < IE base **ghreib-*, to grasp, akin to base of GRAB⟧ **1** [Archaic] *a)* to grasp; clutch *b)* to distress; oppress; afflict **2** to cause sudden, sharp pain in the bowels of ☆**3** [Informal] to annoy; irritate —*vi.* **1** to feel sharp pains in the bowels ☆**2** [Informal] to complain; grumble —*n.* **1** the pressure or pain of something distressing or afflicting **2** a sudden, sharp pain in the bowels: *usually used in pl.* **3** [Rare] a handle **4** *a)* a device that grips *b)* [*pl.*] *Naut.* hooks, straps, etc. for holding a ship's boat in place ☆**5** [Informal] a complaint **6** [Archaic] *a)* a grasping or clutching *b)* control; mastery —**grip′er** *n.*

grippe (grip) *n.* ⟦Fr, lit., a seizure < *gripper* < Frank **gripan*, akin to prec.⟧ *former term for* INFLUENZA —**grip′py** *adj.* **-pi·er, -pi·est**

grip·ple (grip′əl) *adj.* ⟦ME *gripel* < OE *gripul* < base of *grīpan*: see GRIPE⟧ [Brit. Dial.] miserly; avaricious

☆**grip·sack** (grip′sak′) *n.* ⟦GRIP[1] + SACK[1]⟧ *former term for* GRIP[1] (*n.* 9)

Gris (grēs), **Juan** (born *José Victoriano González*) 1887-1927; Sp. painter, in France after 1906

gri·saille (gri zī′, -zāl′) *n.* ⟦Fr < *gris*, gray < Frank **gris*, akin to Du *grijs*, gray < IE **ĝhrēi-* < base **ĝher-*, to shine, gleam > GRAY[1]⟧ a style of painting, esp. on glass, in monochrome, usually using only gray tints and giving the effect of sculpture in relief

Gri·sel·da (gri zel′də, -sel′-) *n.* ⟦Fr or It < Ger *Griseldis, Grishilda*⟧ **1** a feminine name **2** the heroine of various medieval tales, famous for her meek, long-suffering patience

gris·e·o·ful·vin (gris′ē ō fo͝ol′vin, griz′-) *n.* ⟦< ModL *griseofulvum*, epithet for species of *Penicillium* (see PENICILLIUM) from which it was obtained (< ML *griseus*, gray + L *fulvus*, reddish-yellow) + -IN[1]⟧ an oral antibiotic, $C_{17}H_{17}ClO_6$, taken to treat serious fungal infections of the skin, nails, etc.

gris·e·ous (gris′ē əs, griz′-) *adj.* ⟦ML *griseus*, of Gmc orig.: see GRISAILLE⟧ gray; esp., pearl-gray

gri·sette (grē zet′, gri-) *n.* ⟦Fr, orig., gray woolen cloth used for dresses worn by working-class girls < *gris*, gray: see GRISAILLE⟧ a French working-class girl

☆**gris-gris** (grē′grē′) *n., pl.* **gris′-gris′** ⟦Louisiana Fr, of Afr orig.: ult. < ? Ar *ḥirz al-siḥr*, lit., amulet (of) the witchcraft⟧ an amulet, charm, or spell of African origin

gris·kin (gris′kin) *n.* ⟦dim. of obs. *grice*, pig < ME *gris* < ON *griss*, young pig, hog: ? ult. echoic of a pig's squeal⟧ [Brit.] the lean section of a pork loin

gris·ly (griz′lē) *adj.* **-li·er, -li·est** ⟦ME *grislich* < OE *grislic* (akin to OFris *grislyk*) < base of *a-grisan*, to shudder with fear, prob. < IE **ghrei-*: see GRIME⟧ terrifying; horrible; ghastly —**gris′li·ness** *n.*

Gri·sons (grē zōn′) *Fr. name for* GRAUBÜNDEN

grist (grist) *n.* ⟦ME < OE, akin to OHG *grist-* in *gristgrimmon*, to gnash the teeth: for prob. IE base see GRIME⟧ grain that is to be or has been ground; esp., a batch of such grain —**grist to (**or **for) someone's mill** anything that someone can use profitably

gris·tle (gris′əl) *n.* ⟦ME *gristel* < OE *gristle* (akin to OFris *gristel*) < ? IE **ghrei-*: see GRIME⟧ cartilage, now esp. as found in meat —**gris′tli·ness** *n.* —**gris·tly** (gris′lē) *adj.*

grist·mill (grist′mil′) *n.* a mill for grinding grain, esp. for individual customers

grit (grit) *n.* ⟦with Early ModE vowel shortening < ME *grete* < OE *greot*, akin to Ger *griess* < IE base **ghrēu-*, to rub hard over, crumble > GREAT⟧ **1** rough, hard particles of sand, stone, etc. **2** the texture of stone, with regard to the fineness or coarseness of its grain **3** any of several sandstones with large, sharp grains, often used for grindstones ☆**4** stubborn courage; brave perseverance; pluck **5** [**G-**] [Informal] a member of the Liberal Party of Canada —*vt.* **grit′ted, grit′ting 1** to cover with grit ☆**2** to clench or grind (the teeth) in anger or determination —*vi.* to make a grating sound —*SYN.* FORTITUDE

grith (grith) *n.* ⟦ME < OE < ON, orig., home⟧ [Obs.] **1** security, protection, or peace, esp. as guaranteed by someone or in some place **2** a sanctuary

☆**grits** (grits) *pl.n.* ⟦ME *gryttes* (pl.) < OE *grytte*, akin to Ger *grütze*: for IE base see GRIT⟧ [*often with sing. v.*] corn or other grain, soybeans, etc. ground more coarsely than for flour or meal; esp., in the South, hominy ground coarsely: grits are eaten as porridge, as a side dish, and in casseroles

grit·ty (grit′ē) *adj.* **-ti·er, -ti·est 1** of, like, or containing grit; sandy **2** brave; plucky **3** characterized by detailed, intensely realistic presentation of the subject, characters, etc., esp. in their negative or unpleasant aspects *[*a *gritty* novel*]* —**grit′ti·ly** *adv.* —**grit′ti·ness** *n.*

griv·et (griv′it) *n.* ⟦Fr⟧ a ground-dwelling, olive-green guenon monkey (*Cercopithecus aethiops*)

griz·zle[1] (griz′əl) *n.* ⟦< ME *grisel* < OFr adj. *grisel* < *gris*, gray: see GRISAILLE⟧ **1** [Archaic] *a)* gray hair *b)* a gray wig **2** gray —*vt., vi.* **-zled, -zling** to make or become gray —*adj.* [Archaic] gray

griz·zle[2] (griz′əl) *vt.* **-zled, -zling** [Brit.] **1** to grumble; complain **2** to fret or whimper

griz·zled (griz′əld) *adj.* ⟦< GRIZZLE[1] + -ED⟧ **1** gray or streaked with gray **2** having gray hair

griz·zly (griz′lē) *adj.* **-zli·er, -zli·est** grayish; grizzled —*n., pl.* **-zlies** *short for* GRIZZLY BEAR

grizzly bear ⟦prec. + BEAR[2]: infl. by assoc. with GRISLY⟧ a large, brown bear (*Ursus arctos horribilis*) of W North America, having long front claws

gro *abbrev.* gross

groan (grōn) *vi.* ⟦ME *gronien* < OE *granian*, akin to GRIN, Ger *greinen*, to weep⟧ **1** to utter a deep sound expressing pain, distress, or disapproval **2** to make a creaking or grating sound, as from great strain *[*a heavy gate *groaning* on its hinges*]* **3** to be weighed down, overburdened, or oppressed *[*a table *groaning* beneath a Christmas feast, citizens *groaning* under the weight of tyranny*]* —*vt.* to utter with a groan or groans —*n.* a sound made in groaning —**groan′er** *n.* —**groan′ing·ly** *adv.*

groat (grōt) *n.* ⟦ME *grote* < MDu *groot* or MLowG *grote*, lit., GREAT, mistransl. of MHG *grosse*, short for ML *(denarius) grossus*, lit., gross (i.e., thick) (denarius): see GROSS⟧ **1** an obsolete English silver coin worth fourpence **2** a trifling sum

groats (grōts) *pl.n.* ⟦ME *grotes* < OE *grotan*, pl.: for IE base see GRIT⟧ hulled, or hulled and coarsely cracked, grain, esp. wheat, buckwheat, oats, or barley

gro·cer (grō′sər) *n.* ⟦ME *grosser* < OFr *grossier*, lit., dealer in the gross, wholesaler < ML *grossarius* < LL *grossus*: see GROSS⟧ a storekeeper who sells food and various household supplies

gro·cer·y (grō′sər ē; *often* grōs′rē) *n., pl.* **-cer·ies** ⟦ME *groceryе* < OFr *grosserie*⟧ ☆**1** a grocer's store **2** [*pl.*] the food and supplies sold by a grocer

Grod·no (grôd′nô) city in W Belarus, on the Neman River

grog (gräg) *n.* ⟦after Old *Grog*, nickname of Brit Admiral E. Vernon (1684-1757), who ordered the sailors' rum to be diluted: so called because he wore a *grogram* cloak⟧ **1** an alcoholic liquor, esp. rum, diluted with water **2** any alcoholic liquor

☆**grog·ger·y** (gräg′ər ē) *n., pl.* **-ger·ies** [Archaic] a saloon

grog·gy (gräg′ē) *adj.* **-gi·er, -gi·est** ⟦< GROG + -Y[2]⟧ **1** [Archaic] drunk; intoxicated **2** shaky or dizzy, as from a blow **3** sluggish or dull, as from lack of sleep —**grog′gi·ly** *adv.* —**grog′gi·ness** *n.*

grog·ram (gräg′rəm) *n.* ⟦earlier *grograin* < OFr *gros grain*: see GROSS & GRAIN⟧ **1** a coarse fabric in former use, made of silk, worsted, and mohair, often stiffened with gum **2** an article of clothing made of this

grog·shop (gräg′shäp′) *n.* [Chiefly Brit.] a saloon

groin (groin) *n.* ⟦Early ModE phonetic rendering of *grine*, var. of *grinde*

< ME *grynde*, prob. < OE, abyss, in sense "depression" (akin to *grund*, GROUND[1])] 1 *a)* the hollow or fold where the abdomen joins either thigh *b)* the lower abdomen, where the genitals are located 2 *Archit. a)* the sharp, curved edge formed at the junction of two intersecting vaults *b)* the rib of wood, stone, etc. covering this edge 3 a strong, low sea wall built at a right angle to the coast to reduce shoreline erosion, esp. of a beach —*vt.* to build or provide with groins

grom·met (gräm′it) *n.* [< obs. Fr *gromette* (now *gourmette*), curb chain, bridle < *gourmer*, to curb, prob. < VL **grumus*, throat] 1 a ring of rope or metal used to fasten the edge of a sail to its stay, hold an oar in place, etc. 2 an eyelet, as of metal or plastic, protecting an opening in cloth, leather, etc.

grom·well (gräm′wel′, -wəl) *n.* [altered < ME *gromil* < OFr < ML *gruinum milium*, kind of millet < *gruinus*, of a crane (< L *grus*, crane) + L *milium*, MILLET] any of a genus (*Lithospermum*) of plants of the borage family, with yellow or orange flowers and hard, stonelike nutlets

Gro·my·ko (grə mē′kō), **An·drei (Andreyevich)** (än drā′) 1909-89: Soviet diplomat

Gro·ning·en (grō′niŋ ən; *Du* khrō′niŋ ən) 1 province of N Netherlands: 1,146 sq mi (2,968 sq km) 2 its capital

Grøn·land (grön′län) *Dan. name for* GREENLAND

groom (gro͞om; *also* gro͝om) *n.* [ME *grom*, boy, groom < ?] 1 a person whose work is tending, feeding, and currying horses 2 any of certain officials of the British royal household 3 BRIDEGROOM 4 [Archaic] *a)* a manservant *b)* any man —*vt.* 1 to clean and curry (a horse, dog, etc.) 2 to clean, make neat and tidy, etc. 3 to clean the fur, feathers, etc. of itself or another animal, often as a social activity ☆4 to train for a particular purpose [to *groom* a man for politics]

grooms·man (gro͞omz′mən) *n., pl.* **-men** (-mən) a man who attends the bridegroom at a wedding

groove (gro͞ov) *n.* [ME *grofe* < ON *grof*, a pit & < MDu *groeve*, both akin to Ger *grube*, a pit, hole, ditch: for IE base see GRAVE[2]] 1 a long, narrow furrow or hollow cut in a surface with a tool, as the track cut in a phonograph record for the stylus to follow 2 any channel or rut cut or worn in a surface 3 a habitual way of doing something; settled routine [an athlete getting back into a *groove* after an injury] 4 *Anat.* any narrow furrow, depression, or slit occurring on the surface of an organ, esp. of bone 5 *Printing* the indentation on the bottom of a piece of type —*vt.* **grooved**, **groov′ing** to make a groove or grooves in —*vi.* ☆[Slang] to react with empathy or enjoyment: with *on, to*, etc. [to *groove* to jazz]

☆**groov·y** (gro͞o′vē) *adj.* **groov′i·er**, **groov′i·est** [< slang *in the groove*, working effortlessly] [Slang] very pleasing or attractive

grope (grōp) *vi.* **groped**, **grop′ing** [ME *gropien* < OE *grapian*, to touch, seize, akin to Ger *greifen*, to grasp: for IE base see GRIPE] to feel or search about blindly, hesitantly, or uncertainly; feel one's way —*vt.* 1 to seek or find (one's way) by groping 2 [Slang] to make sexual advances by touching (a person) in a way regarded as rough, awkward, inappropriate, etc. —*n.* an act or instance of groping —**grop′er** *n.* —**grop′ing·ly** *adv.*

Gro·pi·us (grō′pē əs), **Walter** 1883-1969; U.S. architect, born in Germany: founder of the BAUHAUS

gros·beak (grōs′bēk′) *n.* [Fr *grosbec*: see GROSS & BEAK] any of various passerine birds (family Fringillidae or Emberizidae) with a thick, strong, conical bill

gro·schen (grō′shən) *n., pl.* **-schen** [Ger < 14th-c. dial. *grosch(e)* < Czech *groš* < ML *(denarius) grossus*: see GROAT] a former monetary unit of Austria, equal to $\frac{1}{100}$ of a schilling

gros de Lon·dres (or lon·dres) (grō də lôn′drə) [Fr, lit., London gross: see GROGRAM] a shiny fabric of lightweight silk having alternate wide and narrow ribs

gros·grain (grō′grān′) *n.* [Fr: see GROGRAM] a closely woven silk or rayon fabric with prominent, crosswise ribbing, used for ribbons, trimming, etc.

gros point (grō) [Fr, lit., large stitch] 1 a large needlepoint stitch over two vertical and two horizontal threads 2 work done with this stitch

gross (grōs) *adj.* [ME *grose* < OFr *gros*, big, thick, coarse < LL *grossus*, thick] 1 big or fat and coarse-looking; corpulent; obese 2 glaring; flagrant; very bad [a *gross* miscalculation] 3 *a)* lacking fineness, as in texture *b)* lacking fine distinctions or specific details 4 lacking in refinement or perception; insensitive; dull 5 vulgar; obscene; coarse [*gross* language] 6 [Slang] unpleasant, disgusting, offensive, etc. 7 with no deductions; total; entire [*gross* income]: opposed to NET[2] 8 [Archaic] evident; obvious —*n.* [ME *groos* < OFr *grosse*, orig. fem. of *gros*] 1 *pl.* **gross′es** overall total, as of income, before deductions are taken 2 *pl.* **gross** twelve dozen — *vt., vi.* to earn (a specified total amount) before expenses are deducted —***SYN.*** COARSE —☆**gross out** [Slang] to disgust, shock, offend, etc. —**in the gross** 1 in bulk; as a whole 2 wholesale: also **by the gross** —**gross′ly** *adv.* —**gross′ness** *n.*

gross domestic product the total value of the annual output of goods and services produced within a nation's borders: it excludes the foreign output of domestic firms and includes the domestic output of foreign firms

gross·er (grōs′ər) *n.* [Slang] something, esp. a film, with respect to the amount of money it earns: usually with a qualifier [this summer's biggest *grosser*]

gross national product the total value of a nation's annual output of goods and services: it includes the foreign output of domestic firms and excludes the domestic output of foreign firms

☆**gross-out** (grōs′out′) [Slang] *n.* something thought of as being disgusting, repulsive, offensive, etc.: often used attributively [a director specializing in *gross-out* movies]

gross ton [Brit.] TON[1] (sense 2)

gros·su·lar·ite (gräs′yə lər īt′) *n.* [Ger *grossularit* < ModL *grossularia*, orig. gooseberry genus (in reference to the color of some varieties) < Fr *groseille*: see GOOSEBERRY] a kind of garnet, $Ca_3Al_2(SiO_4)_3$, occurring in various colors

gross weight the total weight of a commodity, including the weight of the packaging or container

Gros Ventre (grō′ vänt′) [Fr, lit., big belly] 1 a member of a western group of the Arapaho, now living in Montana: also called **Gros Ventre of the Prairie** 2 HIDATSA: also called **Gros Ventre of the Missouri**

grosz (grôsh) *n., pl.* **grosz′y** (-ē) [Pol, akin to Czech *groš*: see GROSCHEN] a monetary unit of Poland, equal to $\frac{1}{100}$ of a zloty

Grosz (grōs), **George** 1893-1959; U.S. painter & caricaturist, born in Germany

grot (grät) *n.* [Fr *grotte* < It *grotta*] [Old Poet.] a grotto

gro·tesque (grō tesk′) *adj.* [Fr < It *grottesca (pittura)*, orig., (picture) in a cave < *grotta*, GROTTO: from resemblance to designs found in Roman caves] 1 in or of a style of painting, sculpture, etc. in which forms of persons and animals are intermingled as with foliage, flowers, or fruits in a fantastic or bizarre design 2 characterized by distortions or striking incongruities in appearance, shape, or manner; fantastic; bizarre 3 ludicrously eccentric or strange; ridiculous; absurd —*n.* 1 a grotesque painting, sculpture, design, etc. 2 a grotesque person, thing, or quality —***SYN.*** FANTASTIC —**gro·tesque′ly** *adv.* —**gro·tesque′ness** *n.*

gro·tes·que·rie or **gro·tes·que·ry** (grō tes′kə rē) *n., pl.* **-que·ries** [< prec.] 1 a grotesque thing 2 the quality or state of being grotesque

Gro·ti·us (grō′shē əs, grōt′ē əs), **Hugo** (born *Huigh de Groot*) 1583-1645; Du. scholar, jurist, & statesman

grot·to (grät′ō) *n., pl.* **-toes** or **-tos** [It *grotta* < ML *grupta* < VL *crupta*, for L *crypta*, CRYPT] 1 a cave 2 a cavelike summerhouse, shrine, etc.

grot·ty (grät′ē) *adj.* **-ti·er**, **-ti·est** [< GROTESQUE + -Y[2]] [Slang, Chiefly Brit.] dirty, cheap, nasty, disgusting, etc.: a generalized term of disapproval

☆**grouch** (grouch) *vi.* [< earlier *grutch* < ME *grucchen*: see GRUDGE] to grumble or complain in a sulky way —*n.* 1 a person who is habitually grouchy, surly, irritable, etc. 2 a grumbling or sulky mood 3 a complaint

☆**grouch·y** (grou′chē) *adj.* **grouch′i·er**, **grouch′i·est** [< prec.] in a bad-tempered or sulky mood; grumpy —**grouch′i·ly** *adv.* —**grouch′i·ness** *n.*

ground[1] (ground) *n.* [ME *grund* < OE, ground, bottom, akin to Ger *grund*, ON *grunnr*: for IE base see GRIND] 1 *a)* [Obs.] the lowest part, base, or bottom of anything *b)* the bottom of a body of water 2 the surface of the earth, specif. the solid surface 3 the soil of the earth; earth; land 4 *a)* any particular piece of land; esp., one set aside for a specified purpose [a hunting *ground*] *b)* [*pl.*] land surrounding or attached to a house or other building; esp., the lawns, garden, etc. of an estate 5 any particular area of reference, discussion, work, etc.; topic; subject [arguments covering the same *ground*] 6 [*often pl.*] basis; foundation 7 the logical basis of a conclusion, action, etc.; valid reason, motive, or cause: *often used in pl.* 8 the background or surface over which other parts are spread or laid, as the main surface of a painting 9 [*pl.*] the particles that settle to the bottom of a liquid; dregs; sediment [coffee *grounds*] 10 *Elec. a)* a conducting body (as the earth, or an object connected with the earth) whose potential is taken as zero and to which an electric circuit can be connected *b)* the connection of an electrical conductor with a ground *c)* a device, as a stake, iron pipe, etc., that makes such a connection —*adj.* 1 of, on, or near the ground 2 growing or living in or on the ground ☆3 *Football* designating the part of the offensive game plan using running plays —*vt.* 1 to set on, or cause to touch, the ground 2 to cause (a ship, etc.) to run aground 3 to found on a firm basis; establish 4 to base (a claim, argument, etc.) on something specified 5 to instruct (a person) in the elements or first principles of 6 to provide with a background 7 *a)* to keep (an aircraft or pilot) from flying ☆*b)* [Informal] to punish (a young person, esp. a teenager) by not permitting him or her to leave home to engage in social activity 8 *Elec.* to connect (an electrical conductor) to a ground ☆9 *Football* to throw or knock (an opposing player) to the ground —*vi.* 1 to strike the bottom or run ashore: said of a ship ☆2 *Baseball a)* to hit a grounder *b)* to be put out on a grounder (usually with *out*) ☆3 *Football* to throw an incomplete pass intentionally, to avoid being sacked —**break ground** 1 to dig; excavate 2 to plow 3 to start building 4 to start any undertaking —**break new ground** to innovate or pioneer —**cover ground** 1 to move or traverse a certain distance 2 to make a certain amount of progress —**cut the ground from under someone (or someone's feet)** to deprive someone of effective defense or argument —☆**from the ground up** from the first or elementary principles, methods, etc. to the last or most advanced; completely; thoroughly —**gain ground** 1 to move forward 2 to make progress 3 to gain in strength, extent, popularity, etc. —☆**get off the ground** to get (something) started; begin or cause to begin to make progress —**give ground** to withdraw under attack; retreat; yield —**go to ground** [orig. of a fox or other animal entering its burrow] [Chiefly Brit.] to go into hiding or seclusion —**hold (or stand) one's ground** to keep one's position against attack or opposition; not withdraw or retreat —**lose ground** 1 to drop back; fall behind 2 to lose in strength, extent, popularity, etc. —**make up ground** to reduce the distance by which one has fallen behind —**on delicate ground** in a situation requiring tact —**on firm ground** 1 in a safe situation 2 firmly supported by facts or evidence —**on one's own ground** 1 dealing with a situation or subject that one knows well 2 at home —**on the ground** 1 at the site of the action [wartime journalists *on the ground*] 2 under practical conditions; in actual practice —☆**run into the ground** [Informal] **1** to do too long or too often; overdo **2** to mismanage to the point of ruin or near-ruin; destroy —**shift one's ground** to change one's argument or defense —**suit (right) down to the ground** [Informal] to suit completely —**thick on the ground** plentiful; common —**thin on the ground** scarce; uncommon

ground[2] (ground) *vt., vi. pt. & pp. of* GRIND

ground ball GROUNDER

ground bass *Music* a short phrase, usually of four to eight measures, played repeatedly in the bass against the melodies and harmonies of the upper parts

ground beetle any of a large family (Carabidae) of nocturnal beetles that live under rocks, rubbish, etc. and prey on other insects

ground·break·ing (ground′brāk′iŋ) ***adj.*** **1** designating or of the ceremony of breaking ground, as for a new building **2** pioneering —***n.*** a groundbreaking ceremony for a new building —**ground′break′er *n.***

☆**ground-cher·ry** (ground′cher′ē) ***n.*** any of a genus (*Physalis*) of plants of the nightshade family having small cherrylike fruits completely enclosed by a papery calyx

ground control personnel, electronic equipment, etc. on the ground, serving to guide airplanes and spacecraft in takeoff, flight, and landing operations

ground cover any of various low, dense-growing plants, as ivy, pachysandra, etc., used for covering the ground, as in places where it is difficult to grow grass

ground crew a team of people who maintain and repair aircraft

ground·ed (groun′did) ***adj.*** **1** firmly established **2** practical or realistic **3** natural, sincere, etc. **4** stable, secure, etc. **5** kept at home, and forbidden to engage in social activity, as a punishment **6** *Elec.* connected directly to the earth or some other electrical ground: said of electrical wires, circuits, motors, etc.

ground·er (groun′dər) ***n.*** *Baseball, Cricket* a batted ball that strikes the ground almost immediately and rolls or bounces along

ground-fault interrupter (ground′fôlt′) an electronic safety device used in place of a standard electrical outlet in areas where shocks are more likely, as kitchens, bathrooms, and workshops: it immediately breaks the circuit if electricity is being lost: often called **ground′-fault′ cir′cuit-in′ter·rupt′er** (-sur′kit in′tə rup′tər)

ground fir GROUND PINE

ground·fire (ground′fīr′) ***n.*** gunfire directed at aircraft from the ground

ground·fish (-fish′) ***n.,*** *pl.* **-fish′** or **-fish′es** (see FISH) a fish that feeds or lives near the bottom of a body of water, specif. one that is edible and lives in the sea, as a cod or haddock

ground floor that floor of a building which is approximately level with the ground; first floor —☆**in on the ground floor** [Informal] in at the beginning (of a business, etc.) and thus in an especially advantageous position

ground glass **1** glass whose surface has been ground so that it diffuses light and is therefore not transparent **2** glass ground into fine particles

ground hemlock a low, spreading evergreen shrub (*Taxus canadensis*) of the yew family, native to the NE U.S.

☆**ground·hog** (ground′hôg′) ***n.*** ⟦prob. transl. of Afrik *aardvark,* AARDVARK⟧ WOODCHUCK: also written **ground hog**

☆**Groundhog Day** Feb. 2, when, according to tradition, the groundhog comes out of hibernation: if it sees its shadow, it supposedly returns to its hole for six more weeks of winter weather

ground ice ANCHOR ICE

☆**ground ivy** a creeping plant (*Glechoma hederacea*) of the mint family, with round, toothed leaves and blue flowers

ground·less (ground′lis) ***adj.*** without reason or cause; unjustified —**ground′less·ly *adv.*** —**ground′less·ness *n.***

ground·ling (ground′liŋ) ***n.*** **1** *a)* a fish that lives close to the bottom of the water *b)* an animal that lives on or in the ground *c)* a plant that grows close to the ground **2** *a)* in an Elizabethan theater, a person who watched the performance from cheap standing room in the pit *b)* a person lacking critical ability or taste

ground loop a sudden, sharp, unplanned turn made by an airplane on the ground

ground·mass (ground′mas′) ***n.*** *Geol.* the small-grained matrix in which larger crystals are embedded

ground meristem the basic primary tissue of the growing tip of a stem or root, excluding the epidermis and vascular bundles, which gives rise to the cortex, rays, and pith

ground moraine *see* MORAINE

ground·nut (ground′nut′) ***n.*** **1** a plant with edible tubers or tuberlike parts, as the peanut **2** the edible tuber or tuberlike part

ground pine any of several lycopods (genus *Lycopodium*) having forking stems covered with leaves like some evergreen needles

ground plan **1** FLOOR PLAN **2** a first or basic plan

☆**ground plum** a low, perennial, prairie milk vetch (*Astragalus crassicarpus*), with thick-walled, edible pods

ground rent [Chiefly Brit.] rent paid for land on which the occupant can build or make improvements

☆**ground rule** **1** *Baseball* any of a set of rules adapted to playing conditions in a specific ballpark **2** any basic principle or guideline for carrying out a specific activity: *usually used in pl.* [the *ground rules* for running an efficient household]

ground·sel (ground′səl, groun′-) ***n.*** ⟦ME *grundeswylie* < OE *grundeswylige,* altered (after *grund,* GROUND[1]) < earlier *gundeswelge,* ? lit., pus swallower < *gund,* pus + *swelgan,* to SWALLOW[2], from its use in poultices⟧ any of a genus (*Senecio*) of plants of the composite family, with usually yellow, rayed flower heads

ground·sill (ground′səl) ***n.*** the lowest horizontal timber in the framework of a building: also sp. **ground′sel**

☆**grounds·keep·er** (groundz′kēp′ər) ***n.*** a person who tends the grounds of a playing field, estate, cemetery, etc.: also **ground′keep′er**

ground·speed (ground′spēd′) ***n.*** the speed of an aircraft in flight relative to the ground it passes over

☆**ground squirrel** any of various small, burrowing squirrels (esp. genus *Spermophilus*)

ground state the lowest energy state of a particle, atom, etc.

ground stroke a stroke, as in tennis, made in returning the ball after it has struck the ground

ground·swell (ground′swel′) ***n.*** **1** a violent swelling or rolling of the ocean, caused by a distant storm or earthquake **2** a rapidly growing wave of popular sentiment or opinion

ground tack·le (tak′əl; *naut.* tā′kəl) the anchors, anchor cables, and cable fittings used in anchoring a vessel

ground·wa·ter (-wôt′ər) ***n.*** water found underground in porous rock strata and soils, as in a spring: also written **ground water**

ground wave a radio wave that follows the curvature of the earth near the ground

☆**ground wire** a wire acting as a conductor from an electric circuit, antenna, etc. to a ground

ground·work (ground′wurk′) ***n.*** **1** a foundation; basis **2** work done in preparation —*SYN.* BASE[1]

☆**ground zero** **1** the land or water surface area directly below or above the point of detonation, as of a nuclear bomb **2** [Slang] *a)* nothing *b)* the starting point *c)* the most basic condition or level

group (grōōp) ***n.*** ⟦Fr *groupe* < It *gruppo,* a knot, lump, group < Gmc **kruppa,* round mass: see CROP⟧ **1** a number of persons or things gathered closely together and forming a recognizable unit; cluster; aggregation; band [a *group* of houses] **2** a collection of objects or figures forming a design or part of a design, as in a work of art **3** a number of persons or things classified together because of common characteristics, community of interests, etc. **4** *Chem.* *a)* a unit consisting of two or more joined atoms within a molecule; esp., a RADICAL (*n.* 3) *b)* a number of elements with similar properties, forming one of the vertical columns of the periodic table *c)* a number of elements having similar chemical reactions **5** *Geol.* a stratigraphic unit consisting of two or more formations **6** *Math.* a closed set of elements having an associative binary operation (usually multiplication), an identity element (I × a = a × I = a), and an inverse element for each element (a × 1/a = 1/a × a = I) ☆**7** a military aircraft unit; specif., in the U.S. Air Force, a subdivision of a wing, composed of two or more squadrons ☆**8** *U.S. Mil.* a unit made up of two or more battalions or squadrons —***vt., vi.*** to assemble or form into a group or groups —***adj.*** of, characteristic of, or involving a group [*group* attitudes] —**group′age *n.***

SYN.—**group** is the basic, general word expressing the simple idea of an assembly of persons, animals, or things without further connotation; **herd** is applied to a group of cattle, sheep, or similar large animals feeding, living, or moving together; **flock**, to goats, sheep, or birds; **drove**, to cattle, hogs, or sheep; **pack**, to hounds or wolves; **pride**, to lions; **swarm**, to insects; **school**, to fish, porpoises, whales, or the like; **bevy**, to quails; **covey**, to partridges or quails; **flight**, to birds flying together. In extended applications, **flock** connotes guidance and care, **herd** and **pack** are used contemptuously of people, **swarm** suggests a thronging, and **bevy** and **covey** are used of girls or women

group dynamics **1** the personal interrelationships among members of a small group **2** the study of these interrelationships

grou·per (grōō′pər) ***n.,*** *pl.* **-per** or **-pers** ⟦Port *garoupa* < ? a South American Indian language⟧ any of several large sea basses (esp. genera *Epinephelus* and *Mycteroperca*) found in warm seas

group home an establishment, usually resembling a private home and located in a residential neighborhood, for providing a small group of persons with special needs, as handicapped or elderly persons, with lodging and supervised care

group·ie (grōō′pē) ***n.*** [Informal] **1** a young female fan of rock groups or other popular personalities, who follows them about, often in the hope of achieving sexual intimacy **2** an enthusiast; devotee [a tennis *groupie*]

group·i·ng (grōō′piŋ) ***n.*** **1** a group of persons or things, esp. one assembled for some common purpose or function **2** the act of assembling or forming groups

☆**group insurance** insurance, esp. life or health insurance, available to employees or members of an organization as a group at special, low rates

☆**group medicine** **1** the practice of medicine by a number of specialists working together in association **2** medical care provided, esp. by such an association, to the members of a group at a fixed, usually annual, rate

group therapy (*or* psychotherapy) a form of treatment for a group of patients with similar emotional problems or disorders, as by group discussions moderated by a therapist

group·think (grōōp′thiŋk′) ***n.*** the tendency of members of a committee, profession, etc. to conform to those opinions or feelings prevailing in their group

grou·pus·cule (gro͞o′pə skyo͞ol′) *n.* ⟦Fr, small group⟧ a small, activist group or faction

grouse[1] (grous) *n., pl.* **grouse** ⟦Early ModE < ?⟧ any of a family (Tetraonidae) of gallinaceous game birds with a round, plump body, feathered legs, feather-covered nostrils, and mottled feathers, as the ruffed grouse or sage grouse

grouse[2] (grous) [Informal] *vi.* **groused, grous′ing** ⟦orig. Brit army slang < ?⟧ to complain; grumble —*n.* a complaint —**grous′er** *n.*

grout (grout) *n.* ⟦ME < OE *grut,* residue of malt liquor, fine meal, akin to *greot,* GRIT⟧ **1** *a)* coarse meal *b)* [*pl.*] GROATS **2** [*usually pl.*] [Brit.] sediment; dregs **3** a thin mortar used to fill chinks, as between tiles **4** a fine plaster for finishing surfaces —*vt.* to fill or finish with grout —**grout′er** *n.*

grout·y (grout′ē) *adj.* **grout′i·er, grout′i·est** ⟦< dial. *grout,* to grumble + -Y[2]⟧ [Dial.] rough or surly

grove (grōv) *n.* ⟦ME *grof* < OE *graf,* akin to *græfa,* thicket⟧ **1** a small wood or group of trees without undergrowth **2** a group of trees planted and cultivated to bear fruit, nuts, etc.; orchard

grov·el (gräv′əl, gruv′-) *vi.* **-eled** or **-elled, -el·ing** or **-el·ling** ⟦back-form. (first found in Shakespeare) < *grovelling,* down on one's face (assumed to be prp.) < ME *grufelinge* < *gruf,* for *o grufe,* on the face (< ON *á grúfu*) + *-ling,* -LING[2]⟧ **1** to lie prone or crawl in a prostrate position, esp. abjectly **2** to behave humbly or abjectly, as before authority; debase oneself in a servile fashion **3** to wallow in what is low or contemptible —**grov′el·er** *n.,* **grov′el·ler**

grow (grō) *vi.* **grew, grown, grow′ing** ⟦ME *growen* < OE *growan,* akin to ON *grōa,* OHG *gruoen* < IE base **ghrō-,* to grow, turn green > GREEN, GRASS⟧ **1** to come into being or be produced naturally; spring up; sprout **2** to exist as living vegetation; thrive [*cactus grows in sand*] **3** to increase in size and develop toward maturity, as a plant or animal does by assimilating food **4** to increase in size, quantity, or degree, or in some specified manner [*to grow in wisdom*] **5** to come to be, esp. over a period of time [*to grow weary of the daily routine*] **6** to become attached or united by growth —*vt.* **1** *a)* to cause to grow; raise; cultivate *b)* to cause to develop or flourish [*to grow a business*] **2** to cover with a growth: used in the passive [*a yard grown over with weeds*] **3** to allow to grow [*to grow a beard*] **4** to cause to be or to exist; develop —**grow into 1** to develop so as to be [*a boy grows into a man*] **2** to grow or develop so as to fit into or be suited to —**grow on** [Informal] to have a gradually increasing effect on; come gradually to seem more important, dear, or admirable to —**grow out of 1** to develop from **2** to outgrow —**grow up 1** to reach maturity; become adult or attain full growth **2** to come to be; develop; arise —**grow′er** *n.*

growing pains 1 recurrent pains in the joints and muscles, esp. of the legs, of growing children: a loose term with no precise medical meaning **2** *a)* difficulties one experiences in growing up *b)* difficulties encountered in the early stages of a project, venture, etc.

growing point the apex of a stem or root, containing actively dividing and elongating cells

growing season a time of year during which a particular crop grows or crops in general grow

growl (groul) *vi.* ⟦ME *groulen,* to rumble, prob. of echoic orig.⟧ **1** to make a low, rumbling, menacing sound in the throat, as a dog does **2** to complain in an angry or surly manner **3** to rumble, as thunder, cannons, etc. —*vt.* to express by growling —*n.* **1** the act or sound of growling ☆**2** *Jazz* a low, rough, husky, often muted sound produced on a trumpet, trombone, etc. —**growl′ing·ly** *adv.*

growl·er (groul′ər) *n.* **1** a person, animal, or thing that growls ☆**2** [Slang] *a)* a pail or can used to carry out beer bought at a saloon, microbrewery, etc. *b)* a keg of beer, equal to 1/8 barrel **3** a small iceberg ☆**4** an electromagnetic device used to find short circuits in coils and for magnetizing and demagnetizing

grown (grōn) *vi., vt. pp. of* GROW —*adj.* **1** having completed its growth; fully developed; mature **2** covered with a specified growth **3** cultivated as specified [*home-grown*]

grown-up (grōn′up′; *for n.,* -up′) *adj.* **1** that is an adult **2** of, for, or like an adult —*n.* an adult: also written **grown′up′**

growth (grōth) *n.* **1** the process of growing or developing; specif., *a)* gradual development toward maturity *b)* formation and development **2** *a)* degree of increase in size, weight, power, etc. *b)* the full extent of such increase **3** something that grows or has grown [*a thick growth of grass*] **4** an outgrowth or offshoot **5** a tumor or other abnormal mass of tissue developed in or on the body —*adj.* of or designating a stock, mutual fund, etc. or a company, industry, etc. whose value or earnings grow at a rate above average

growth factor any genetic, hormonal, or nutritional factor whose absence prevents normal growth of an organism

growth hormone 1 a polypeptide hormone of the anterior part of the pituitary gland, that promotes normal growth **2** any of various substances that promote growth, as of plants or beef cattle

Groz·ny (grôz′nē) city in Chechnya, Russia, at the foot of the Caucasus Mountains

grrr (gʉr) *interj., n.* ⟦echoic⟧ (used to suggest) a growling sound of or like that of a dog: also sp. **grr**

GRT *abbrev.* gross registered tons

grub (grub) *vi.* **grubbed, grub′bing** ⟦ME *grubben,* to dig, prob. < OE **grybban* (akin to OHG *grubilōn,* to bore into): for IE base see GRAVE[2]⟧ **1** to dig in the ground **2** to work hard, esp. at something menial or tedious; drudge **3** to search about; rummage **4** ⟦< *n.* 3⟧ [Old Slang] to eat —*vt.* **1** to clear (ground) of roots and stumps by digging them up **2** to dig up by or as by the roots; root out; uproot —*n.* ⟦ME *grubbe,* prob. < the v.⟧ **1** the short, fat, wormlike larva of certain insects, esp. of a beetle **2** [Old Informal] a person who does menial or tedious work; drudge **3** ⟦< ? notion "what is grubbed for"⟧ [Slang] food —**grub′ber** *n.*

grub·by (grub′ē) *adj.* **-bi·er, -bi·est 1** infested with grubs, esp. with botfly larvae, as cattle or sheep **2** dirty; messy; untidy **3** inferior, contemptible, mean, etc. —**grub′bi·ly** *adv.* —**grub′bi·ness** *n.*

☆**grub·stake** (grub′stāk′) *n.* ⟦GRUB (*n.* 3) + STAKE⟧ [Informal] **1** money or supplies advanced to a prospector in return for a share in any findings **2** money advanced for any enterprise —*vt.* **-staked′, -stak′ing** [Informal] to provide with a grubstake —**grub′stak′er** *n.*

Grub·street (grub′strēt′) *n.* ⟦after earlier name of a London street where many literary hacks lived⟧ literary hacks collectively —*adj.* [*also* **g-**] of or like literary hacks or their work

grudge (gruj) *vt.* **grudged, grudg′ing** ⟦LME *gruggen,* var. of *grucchen* < OFr *grouchier*⟧ **1** to envy and resent (someone) because of that person's possession or enjoyment of (something); begrudge [*to grudge a person his success*] **2** to give with reluctance [*the miser grudged his dog its food*] —*n.* **1** a strong, continued feeling of hostility or ill will against someone over a real or fancied grievance **2** a reason or cause for this —**grudg′ing·ly** *adv.*

grue (gro͞o) *n.* ⟦see GRUESOME⟧ [Chiefly Scot.] a shudder of fear

gru·el (gro͞o′əl) *n.* ⟦ME < OFr, coarse meal < ML **grutellum,* dim. of *grutum,* meal, mash < Gmc **grut,* hulled dried grain, akin to GROATS⟧ **1** thin, easily digested porridge made by cooking meal in water or milk **2** [Old Brit. Informal] punishment

gru·el·ing or **gru·el·ling** (gro͞o′liŋ, gro͞o′ə liŋ) *adj.* ⟦prp. of obs. v. *gruel,* to punish < prec.⟧ extremely trying; exhausting —*n.* [Brit. Informal] harsh treatment or punishment

grue·some (gro͞o′səm) *adj.* ⟦< dial. *grue,* to shudder (< ME *gruwen,* akin to MHG < IE base **ĝhreu-,* to grind down > GRIT) + -SOME[1]⟧ causing horror or disgust; grisly —**grue′some·ly** *adv.* —**grue′some·ness** *n.*

gruff (gruf) *adj.* ⟦< Du *grof,* akin to Ger *grob,* coarse, surly < OHG *gerob* < *ge-,* intens. + base akin to OE *hreof,* rough, scabby < IE base **kreup-*: see GRAUPEL⟧ **1** rough or surly in manner or speech; brusquely rude **2** harsh and throaty; hoarse —**SYN.** BLUNT —**gruff′ly** *adv.* —**gruff′ness** *n.*

gru·gru (gro͞o′gro͞o′) *n.* ⟦Sp *grugrú,* prob. < Carib name⟧ **1** a West Indian palm tree (*Acrocomia sclerocarpa*) with spiny trunk and leaves and edible nuts **2** the large, wormlike, edible larva of a genus (*Rhynchophorus*) of weevils infesting this palm

gru·i·form (gro͞o′ə fôrm′) *adj.* ⟦< L *grus,* crane + -FORM⟧ designating or of an order (Gruiformes) of marshland or grassland birds, including rails, cranes, and bustards

grum·ble (grum′bəl) *vi.* **-bled, -bling** ⟦prob. < Du *grommelen,* akin to Ger *grummeln,* OE *gremman,* to enrage: for IE base see GRIM⟧ **1** to make low, unintelligible sounds in the throat; growl **2** to mutter or mumble in discontent; complain in a surly or peevish manner **3** to rumble, as thunder —*vt.* to express by grumbling —*n.* **1** the act of grumbling, esp. in complaint **2** a rumble —**grum′bler** *n.* —**grum′bling·ly** *adv.* —**grum′bly** *adj.*

grum·met (grum′it) *n. var. of* GROMMET

grump (grump) *n.* ⟦prob. echoic of ill-tempered cry⟧ **1** [*often pl.*] a fit of bad humor **2** a grumpy person —*vi.* to complain and grumble

grump·y (grum′pē) *adj.* **grump′i·er, grump′i·est** ⟦prec. + -Y[2]⟧ grouchy; peevish; bad-tempered: occas. **grump′ish** —**grump′i·ly** *adv.* —**grump′i·ness** *n.*

Grun·dy (grun′dē), **Mrs.** ⟦a neighbor repeatedly referred to (but never appearing) in Tom Morton's play *Speed the Plough* (1798) with the question "What will Mrs. Grundy say?"⟧ *a personification of* conventional social disapproval, prudishness, narrow-mindedness, etc. —**Grun′dy·ism′** *n.*

Grü·ne·wald (grü′nə vält′), **Mat·thi·as** (mä tē′äs) (born *Mathis Gothardt*) 1470?-1528; Ger. painter

☆**grunge** (grunj) *n.* ⟦prob. back-form. < fol.⟧ **1** [Slang] something grungy; specif., garbage or dirt **2** *a)* a form of rock music that originated in the 1990s, characterized by loud guitar and drum playing and nihilistic lyrics *b)* a fashion style emphasizing used, tattered, and ill-fitting, esp. baggy, clothes and including plaid flannel shirts, heavy boots, etc.

☆**grun·gy** (grun′jē) *adj.* **-gi·er, -gi·est** ⟦? blend of GRIMY, DINGY, & *grunt,* defecate (child's euphemism)⟧ [Slang] dirty, messy, disreputable, etc.; unpleasant in any way

☆**grun·ion** (grun′yən) *n., pl.* **-ion** or **-ions** ⟦prob. < Sp *gruñón,* grumbler < L *grunnire,* to grunt < IE **gru-,* echoic⟧ a silverside fish (*Leuresthes tenuis*) of the California coast: it spawns on sandy beaches during high tides in the spring

grunt (grunt) *vi.* ⟦ME *grunten* < OE *grunnettan* (akin to Ger *grunzen*), freq. of *grunian,* to grunt < IE **gru-,* echoic > L *grunnire*⟧ **1** to make the short, deep, hoarse sound of a hog **2** to make a sound like this, as in annoyance, contempt, effort, etc. —*vt.* to express by grunting [*to grunt one's disapproval*] —*n.* **1** the sound made in grunting **2** any of a family (Haemulidae) of marine percoid fishes that grunt when removed from water ☆**3** [Slang] *a)* a U.S. infantryman, orig. in the war in Vietnam *b)* any person having or performing a low-prestige job involving routine tasks, strenuous labor, etc. —*adj.* by or characteristic of a GRUNT (*n.* 3*b*) [*grunt work*]

grunt·er (grunt′ər) *n.* ⟦ME *gruntare*⟧ **1** a person or animal that makes a grunting sound; esp., a hog **2** GRUNT (*n.* 2)

grun·tled (grunt′'ld) *adj.* ⟦obs. form revived as a facetious back-form. < *disgruntled*: see DISGRUNTLE⟧ not disgruntled; pleased, contented, etc.: a humorous usage

Grus (grōōs) *n.* ⟦L, crane (the bird): see GRUIFORM⟧ a S constellation between Piscis Austrinus and Indus

Gru·yère (cheese) (grōō yer′, grē-; *Fr* grü yer′) ⟦after *Gruyère*, district in W Switzerland, where first produced⟧ [*often* **g- c-**] a light-yellow Swiss cheese, very rich in butterfat

gr wt *abbrev.* gross weight

gryph·on (grif′ən) *n. var. of* GRIFFIN

GS *abbrev.* **1** General Schedule (civil service classification system) **2** general secretary **3** general staff **4** ground speed: also **gs**

GSA *abbrev.* **1** General Services Administration **2** Girl Scouts of America

G-7 (jē′sev′ən) *n.* ⟦< *G(roup of) Seven*⟧ the seven major industrialized nations, including the U.S., Canada, Great Britain, Germany, France, Italy, and Japan, whose leaders and officials convene from time to time to discuss economic and political issues

GSM (jē′es′em′) *n.* ⟦*G(lobal) S(ystem for) M(obile communications)*⟧ **1** a wireless transmission standard for digital cell phones, used worldwide **2** a digital cell-phone system using this standard

G spot ⟦after E. *G(räfenberg)* (1881-1957), Ger gynecologist, who first described it⟧ a supposed area in the vaginal wall that when stimulated produces a distinctive orgasm

☆**G-string** (jē′striŋ′) *n.* ⟦< ?⟧ **1** a narrow loincloth **2** a similar cloth or band, usually with spangles or tassels, as worn by striptease dancers

☆**G-suit** (jē′sōōt′) *n.* ⟦< *g(ravity)*⟧ a garment worn by astronauts and high-speed pilots to avoid blackouts during rapid acceleration: it exerts pressure on the abdomen and legs to prevent the pooling of blood away from the heart and brain

gt *abbrev.* **1** gilt **2** great **3** gross ton(s) **4** *Pharmacy* gutta

GT *abbrev.* gross ton(s)

Gt Brit or **Gt Br** *abbrev.* Great Britain

gtc *abbrev.* good till canceled: added to an order for stocks or securities

Gtd *abbrev.* guaranteed

gtt. *abbrev. Pharmacy* guttae: see GUTTA

GU *abbrev.* **1** genitourinary: also **gu** **2** Guam

☆**gua·ca·mo·le** (gwä′kə mō′lē, -lā) *n.* ⟦AmSp < Nahuatl *a:wakamo:lli* < *a:wakaλ*, AVOCADO + *mo:lli*, a sauce (altered by analogy with Sp *mole*, soft)⟧ a thick sauce or paste of seasoned, mashed or puréed avocados, served as a dip, in salads, etc.

gua·cha·ro (gwä′chə rō′) *n., pl.* **-ros′** ⟦Sp *guácharo*, lit., sickly, whining: prob. so named from its cry⟧ a South American night goatsucker (*Steatornis caripensis*) of a family (Steatornithidae) with only one species; oilbird: the melted fat of the young birds is used for cooking and lighting

gua·co (gwä′kō) *n., pl.* **-cos** ⟦AmSp, prob. < a Mayan language⟧ any of several South American plants (genus *Mikania* of the composite family and genus *Aristolochia* of the birthwort family) used by the natives for asthma, snakebite, etc.

Gua·da·la·ja·ra (gwäd′'l ə här′ə; *Sp* gwä′thä lä hä′rä) city in W Mexico: capital of Jalisco

Gua·dal·ca·nal (gwäd′'l kə nal′) largest island of the Solomon Islands: 2,060 sq mi (5,335 sq km)

Gua·dal·quiv·ir (-kwiv′ər; *Sp* gwä′thäl kē vēr′) river in S Spain, flowing into the Atlantic: *c.* 375 mi (603 km)

Gua·de·loupe (gwä′də lōōp′) overseas department of France in the Leeward Islands, consisting of two large islands (BASSE-TERRE & GRANDE-TERRE) and several smaller islands: 630 sq mi (1,631 sq km); cap. Basse-Terre

Gua·di·a·na (gwä′dē ä′nə) river flowing from SC Spain west & then south into the Atlantic, forming part of the Spanish-Portuguese border: *c.* 510 mi (821 km)

guai·ac (gwī′ak′) *n.* ⟦< GUAIACUM⟧ **1** a greenish-brown resin from the wood of two species of guaiacum (*Guaiacum sanctum* and *G. officinale*) used as a reagent in tests for blood traces, in varnishes, etc. **2** GUAIACUM (sense 2)

guai·a·col (gwī′ə kôl′, -kōl′) *n.* ⟦< fol. + -OL[1]⟧ a whitish, crystalline solid or slightly yellowish, oily liquid, $C_6H_4(OH)OCH_3$, prepared from guaiacum or wood creosote and used in medicine as an expectorant or antiseptic and as a chemical reagent

guai·a·cum (gwī′ə kəm) *n.* ⟦ModL < Sp *guayaco* < Taino *guayacan*⟧ **1** any of a genus (*Guaiacum*) of trees of the caltrop family native to tropical America, with blue or purple flowers and fruit growing in capsules **2** the hard, dense wood of any of these trees: see LIGNUM VITAE **3** GUAIAC (sense 1)

Guam (gwäm) largest of the Mariana Islands, in the W Pacific: an unincorporated territory of the U.S.: 209 sq mi (541 sq km); cap. Agana: abbrev. *GU*

guan (gwän) *n.* ⟦AmSp < the Carib name⟧ any of several gallinaceous game birds (family Cracidae) of Central and South America that feed on fruits

gua·na·co (gwä nä′kō) *n., pl.* **-cos** or **-co** ⟦Sp < Quechua *huanacu*⟧ a woolly, reddish-brown, wild Andean llama (*Lama guanacoe*)

Gua·na·jua·to (gwä′nä hwä′tô) **1** state of central Mexico: rich mining center, esp. for silver: 11,810 sq mi (30,588 sq km) **2** its capital

gua·nay (gwä nī′) *n.* ⟦Sp < the Quechua name⟧ a white-breasted, crested cormorant (*Phalacrocorax bougainvillii*) of Peru and Chile: it is a major source of guano

Guang·dong (gwäŋ′dōōŋ′) province of SE China, on the South China Sea: 76,101 sq mi (197,101 sq km); cap. Guangzhou

Guang·xi (gwäŋ′shē′) autonomous region in S China: 85,097 sq mi (220,400 sq km); cap. Nanning: also **Guang′xi′-Zhuang′** (-jwäŋ′)

Guang·zhou (gwäŋ′jō′) seaport in SE China, in the Zhu River delta; capital of Guangdong province

gua·ni·dine (gwä′nə dēn′, -din) *n.* ⟦< fol.⟧ a strongly poisonous crystalline base, $(NH_2)_2C{:}NH$, normally found in the urine as a result of protein metabolism

gua·nine (gwä′nēn′, -nin) *n.* ⟦< fol. (a commercial source of the base) + -INE[3]⟧ a crystalline purine base, $C_5H_5N_5O$, contained in the nucleic acids of all tissue: it links with cytosine in the DNA structure

gua·no (gwä′nō) *n., pl.* **-nos** ⟦Sp < Quechua *huanu*, dung⟧ **1** dung of seabirds, found especially on islands off the coast of Peru: it is used as a fertilizer **2** any natural or artificial fertilizer resembling this, as bat dung

gua·no·sine (gwä′nə sēn′, -sin) *n.* ⟦blend of GUANINE & RIBOSE⟧ a white, crystalline nucleoside, $C_{10}H_{13}N_5O_5$, condensed from guanine and ribose: it is a major component of RNA

Guan·tá·na·mo (gwän tä′nə mō′) city in SE Cuba

Guantánamo Bay inlet of the Caribbean, on the SE coast of Cuba: site of a U.S. naval station: 12 mi (19.3 km) long

Gua·po·ré (gwä′pô *re*′) river in central South America, flowing from central Brazil northwest along the Brazilian-Bolivian border into the Mamoré: 1,087 mi (1,749 km)

guar[1] (gwär) *n.* ⟦Hindi *guār*⟧ an annual leguminous plant (*Cyamopsis tetragonoloba*) native to India and grown in the SW U.S. for forage

guar[2] *abbrev.* guaranteed

Gua·ra·ní (gwä′rä nē′) *n.* ⟦Guaraní *guariñi*, lit., warrior⟧ **1** *pl.* **-nís′** or **-ní′** a member of a South American Indian people formerly living in an area between the Paraguay River and the Atlantic **2** the language of this people, related to Tupí **3** *pl.* **-nís′** [**g-**] the basic monetary unit of Paraguay: see the table of monetary units in the Reference Supplement

guar·an·tee (gar′ən tē′, gar′ən tē′) *n.* ⟦altered < GUARANTY, after words ending in -EE[1]⟧ **1** GUARANTY (*n.* 1 & 3) **2** a pledge or assurance; specif., *a)* a pledge that something is as represented and will be replaced if it does not meet specifications *b)* a positive assurance that something will be done in the manner specified **3** a guarantor **4** a person who receives a guaranty **5** a sign or portent [the clouds were a *guarantee* of rain] —*vt.* **-teed′**, **-tee′ing** **1** to give a guarantee or guaranty for [to *guarantee* a product] **2** to state with confidence; promise [to *guarantee* that a thing will be done]

guar·an·tor (gar′ən tôr′, gar′ən tôr′) *n.* a person who makes or gives a guaranty or guarantee

guar·an·ty (gar′ən tē) *n., pl.* **-ties** ⟦OFr *garantie* < *garantir*, to guarantee < *garant, warant*, a warrant, supporter < Frank **warand*, prp. of **warjan*, to verify (akin to OHG *werēn* < *wār*, true < IE **weros*, true > L *verus*), infl. also by **warjan*, to defend, akin to OE *werian*: see WEIR⟧ **1** a pledge committing a person to the payment of another's debt or the fulfillment of another's obligation in the event of default **2** an agreement that secures the existence or maintenance of something **3** something given or held as security **4** a guarantor —*vt.* **-tied**, **-ty·ing** GUARANTEE

guard (gärd) *vt.* ⟦LME *garde* < the n.⟧ **1** to keep safe from harm; watch over and protect; defend; shield **2** to watch over; specif., *a)* to keep from escape or trouble *b)* to hold in check; control; restrain *c) Sports* to keep (an opponent) from making a gain or scoring; also, to cover (a goal or area) in defensive play *d)* to supervise entrances and exits through (a door, gate, etc.) **3** to cover (a piece of machinery) with a device to protect the operator **4** [Archaic] to escort —*vi.* **1** to keep watch; take precautions (*against*) **2** to act as a guard —*n.* ⟦ME *garde* < OFr *garder*, to protect < Gmc **wardon* (> Ger *warten*, to wait) < IE base **wer-*, to heed > WARE[2], L *vereri*, to fear⟧ **1** the act or duty of guarding; careful watch; wariness; defense; protection **2** *a)* a posture of alert readiness for defense, as in boxing, fencing, etc. *b)* the arms or weapon in such a posture **3** any device that protects against injury or loss; specif., *a)* the part of the handle of a sword, knife, or fork that protects the hand *b)* a chain or cord attached to a watch, bracelet, etc. to protect against loss *c)* a ring worn to keep a more valuable ring from slipping off the finger *d)* a safety device, as in machinery *e)* an article worn to protect a part of the body, as in a sport [a catcher's shin *guards*] **4** a person or group that guards; specif., *a)* a sentinel or sentry *b)* a railway brakeman or gatekeeper *c)* [Brit.] a railroad conductor *d)* a person who guards prisoners *e)* [*pl.*] a special unit of troops assigned to the British royal household *f)* a military unit with a special ceremonial function [a color *guard*] ☆**5** *Basketball* either of two players who are the main ball handlers and offensive leaders positioned at the rear of the court on offense: see also POINT GUARD ☆**6** *Football* either of two players on offense at the left and the right of the center whose purpose is blocking: see also NOSE GUARD —**mount guard** to go on sentry duty —**off (one's) guard** not alert for protection or defense —**on (one's) guard** alert for protection or defense; vigilant —**stand guard** to do sentry duty —**guard′er** *n.*

guard·ant (gärd′'nt) *adj.* ⟦Fr *gardant*, prp. of *garder*: see prec.⟧ *Heraldry* having the face fully turned toward the observer [a lion *guardant*]

guard cell either of the two bean-shaped cells which surround and control a stoma, or air pore, in the epidermis of a plant

guard·ed (gär′did) *adj.* **1** kept safe; watched over and protected; defended **2** kept from escape or trouble; held in check; supervised **3** cautious; noncommittal [a *guarded* reply] ☆**4** serious and of uncertain prognosis [a patient in *guarded* condition] —**guard′ed·ly** *adv.*

guard hair any of the coarse protective hairs in the outer fur of certain mammals

guard·house (gärd′hous′) *n. Mil.* 1 a building used by the members of a guard when not walking a post 2 a building where personnel are confined for minor offenses or while awaiting court-martial

guard·i·an (gärd′ē ən) *n.* ⟦ME *gardein* < OFr *gardien*, altered (modeled on nouns ending in *-ien* < L *-ianus*) < *gardenc* < Frank **warding* < Gmc **wardon* (see GUARD) + *-ing*, akin to -ING⟧ 1 a person who guards, protects, or takes care of another person, property, etc.; custodian 2 a person legally placed in charge of the affairs of a minor or of a person of unsound mind —*adj.* protecting —**guard′i·an·ship′** *n.*

guard of honor HONOR GUARD

guard·rail (gärd′rāl′) *n.* 1 a railing that serves as a protective barrier, as on a staircase or alongside a highway ☆2 an extra rail alongside the main rail of a railroad at a crossing, etc., as to keep the cars on the track

guard·room (-ro͞om′) *n. Mil.* 1 a room used by the members of a guard when not walking a post 2 a room in which military offenders are confined

guards·man (gärdz′mən) *n., pl.* **-men** (-mən) 1 a member of any military body called a "guard" ☆2 any member of a National Guard

Guar·ne·ri[1] (gwär ne′rē) *n.* (L. name *Guarnerius*) name of a family of violin-makers of Cremona, Italy (fl. 17th-18th cent.)

Guar·ne·ri[2] (gwär ne′rē), **Giu·sep·pe An·to·nio** (jo͞o zep′pe än tô′nyô) 1687?-1745; It. violin-maker

Guar·ner·i·us (gwär ner′ē əs) *n.* a violin made by a member of the Guarneri family

Guat *abbrev.* Guatemala

Gua·te·ma·la (gwät′ə mä′lə) country in Central America, south & east of Mexico: 42,043 sq mi (108,890 sq km); cap. Guatemala City —**Gua′te·ma′lan** *adj., n.*

Guatemala City capital of Guatemala, in the S part

gua·va (gwä′və) *n.* ⟦Sp *guayaba* < Taino *guayavá*, prob. ult. < Tupí⟧ 1 any of several tropical American plants (genus *Psidium*) of the myrtle family, esp. a tree (*P. guajava*) bearing a yellowish, round or pear-shaped, edible fruit 2 the fruit, used for jelly, preserves, etc.

gua·ya·be·ra (gwä′yä ber′ä) *n.* ⟦AmSp⟧ a man's loosefitting, usually white shirt customarily worn hanging free outside the trousers: it is especially popular in Latin America

Guay·a·quil (gwī′ä kēl′) seaport in W Ecuador

☆**gua·yu·le** (gwī o͞o′lē, wī-) *n.* ⟦AmSp < Nahuatl *kʷawolli* < *kʷawiλ*, tree + *olli*, rubber⟧ 1 a small shrub (*Parthenium argentatum*) of the composite family, grown in N Mexico, Texas, etc. for the rubber obtained from it 2 this rubber: also **guayule rubber**

gu·ber·na·to·ri·al (go͞o′bər nə tôr′ē əl, go͞o′bə nə-) *adj.* ⟦L *gubernator*, helmsman, governor < pp. of *gubernare* (see GOVERN) + -IAL⟧ of a governor or the office of governor

☆**guck** (guk) *n.* ⟦< ? G(OO) + (M)UCK⟧ [Slang] any thick, viscous, sticky or slimy substance

gudg·eon[1] (guj′ən) *n.* ⟦ME *gogeon* < OFr *goujon* < L *gobio* < Gr *kōbios*⟧ 1 any of a genus (*Gobio*) of small, European, freshwater cyprinoid fishes that are easily caught and used for bait 2 any of various other fishes, as a goby or killifish

gudg·eon[2] (guj′ən) *n.* ⟦ME *gogoun* < OFr *gojon*, pivot⟧ 1 a metal pin or shaft at the end of an axle, on which a wheel turns 2 the socket of a hinge, into which the pin is fitted 3 the part of a shaft that revolves in a bearing

Gud·run (good′ro͞on′) *n.* ⟦ON *Guthrūn* < *guthr*, war, battle + *runa*, close friend (secret-sharer) < ON *rūn*: see RUNE⟧ *Gmc. Legend* the daughter of the Nibelung king: she lures Sigurd away from the Valkyrie Brynhild and marries him

guel·der·rose (gel′dər rōz′) *n.* ⟦after *Guelderland* (or GELDERLAND)⟧ SNOWBALL (sense 2)

Guelph[1] or **Guelf** (gwelf) *n.* ⟦It *Guelfo*, for MHG *Welf*, a family name < OHG *welf*, a WHELP: the war cry of the anti-imperialists at the battle of Weinsberg (1140)⟧ any member of a political party in medieval Italy that supported the authority of the pope in opposition to the aristocratic party of the Ghibellines

Guelph[2] (gwelf) city in SE Ontario, Canada

gue·non (gə nōn′, -nän′) *n.* ⟦Fr < ?⟧ any of a genus (*Cercopithecus*) of long-tailed African monkeys, including the green monkey and grivet

guer·don (gurd′'n) [Archaic] *n.* ⟦ME *guerdoun* < OFr *gueredon*, altered (after L *donum*, gift) < Frank & OHG *widarlōn* < OHG *widar*, back, counter + *lōn*, reward < IE base **lāu-*, to capture > L *lucrum*, riches⟧ a reward; recompense —*vt.* to reward

Guer·ni·ca (gur′nē kə, ger′-; gwer′ni kə) town in The Basque Country of N Spain: bombed from the air in 1937 by the Nazis in support of the Spanish Nationalists

Guern·sey[1] (gurn′zē) *n., pl.* **-seys** 1 ⟦after fol., where first bred⟧ any of a breed of medium-sized dairy cattle, usually fawn-colored with white markings 2 ⟦orig. made on the island⟧ [**g-**] a closefitting, knitted woolen shirt, worn by seamen

Guern·sey[2] (gurn′zē) second largest of the Channel Islands of the United Kingdom, north and west of Jersey: 25 sq mi (65 sq km)

Guer·re·ro (ge re′rô) state of S Mexico: 24,631 sq mi (63,794 sq km); cap. Chilpancingo

guer·ril·la (gə ril′ə) *n.* ⟦Sp, dim. of *guerra*, war < Fr *guerre* or It *guerra*, both < Frank **werra*: see WAR[1]⟧ 1 [Archaic] warfare carried on by guerrillas 2 any member of a small defensive force of irregular soldiers, usually volunteers, making surprise raids, esp. behind the lines of an invading enemy army —*adj.* 1 of or by guerrillas 2 characteristic of guerrillas; undercover, clandestine, etc. or radical, subversive, etc. Also sp. **gue·ril′la**

guerrilla theater a form of propaganda or political protest in which a group of activists perform satirical skits, sing songs, engage in playful pranks, etc. in the midst of a public event or activity

guess (ges) *vt., vi.* ⟦ME *gessen*, to judge, estimate, prob. < MDu, akin to Dan *gisse*, Swed *gissa*, ON *geta*: for IE base see GET⟧ 1 to form a judgment or estimate of (something) without actual knowledge or enough facts for certainty; conjecture; surmise 2 to judge correctly by doing this 3 to think or suppose [*I guess I can do it*] —*n.* 1 the act of guessing 2 a judgment or estimate formed by guessing; conjecture; surmise —**guess′a·ble** *adj.* —**guess′er** *n.*

SYN.—**guess** implies the forming of a judgment or estimate (often a correct one) haphazardly [*he guessed the number of beans in the jar*]; to **conjecture** is to infer or predict from incomplete or uncertain evidence [*I cannot conjecture what his plans are*]; **surmise** implies a conjecturing through mere intuition or imagination [*she surmised the truth*]

☆**guess·ti·mate** (ges′tə mit; *for v.*, -māt′) [Informal] *n.* ⟦blend of prec. & ESTIMATE⟧ an estimate based on a guess or conjecture —*vt.* **-mat′ed, -mat′ing** to form a guesstimate of Also sp. **gues′ti·mate**

guess·work (ges′wurk′) *n.* 1 the act of guessing 2 a judgment, result, etc. arrived at by guessing

guest (gest) *n.* ⟦ME *gest* < ON *gestr*, akin to OE *gæst*, Ger *gast* < IE base **ghostis*, stranger, guest > L *hostis*⟧ 1 *a)* a person entertained at the home of another; visitor *b)* a person entertained by another acting as host at a restaurant, theater, etc. 2 any paying customer of a hotel, restaurant, etc. 3 a nonmember receiving the hospitality of a club, institution, etc. 4 a person who appears or performs on a program by special invitation 5 INQUILINE —*adj.* 1 for guests 2 performing by special invitation [*a guest artist*] —*vt.* to entertain as a guest —☆*vi.* to be, or perform as, a guest —SYN. VISITOR

guest·house (gest′hous′) *n.* 1 a small house on the same property as a larger main house, used as for guests 2 a free-standing hotel unit, often like a cottage, rented to guests Also written **guest house**

guest of honor 1 the person in whose honor a festivity or ceremony is held 2 a guest attending a festivity or ceremony by special invitation

guest worker a person who works temporarily or seasonally in a foreign country, typically in a menial or unskilled occupation

Gue·va·ra (gā vär′ə, gwə-), **Che** (chā) (born *Ernesto Guevara*) 1928-67; Cuban revolutionary leader, born in Argentina

☆**guff** (guf) *n.* ⟦echoic⟧ [Slang] 1 foolish talk; nonsense 2 brash or insolent talk

guf·faw (gə fô′) *n.* ⟦echoic⟧ a loud, coarse burst of laughter —*vi.* to laugh in this way —SYN. LAUGH

gug·gle (gug′əl) *n., vi., vt.* **-gled, -gling** ⟦echoic⟧ GURGLE

GUI (go͞o′ē) *n.* ⟦*g(raphical) u(ser) i(nterface)*⟧ a type of computer screen display in which commands are entered and functions are selected by means of icons, menus, a mouse, etc.

Gui·a·na (gē an′ə, -ä′nə) 1 region in N South America, including Guyana, Suriname, and French Guiana 2 area including this region, SE Venezuela, & part of N Brazil, bounded by the Orinoco, Negro, & Amazon rivers & the Atlantic Ocean

guid·ance (gīd′'ns) *n.* 1 the act of guiding; direction; leadership 2 something that guides 3 advice or assistance, as that given to students by vocational or educational counselors 4 the process of directing the course of a spacecraft, missile, etc.

guidance counselor a member of the staff of a high school whose job is advising students about course selection, possible careers, preparation for college, etc.

guide (gīd) *vt.* **guid′ed, guid′ing** ⟦ME *giden* < OFr *guider* < *guide* < It *guida* < Goth **wida*, leader, guide < **witan*, to observe, akin to OE *witan*, to see: see WISE[1]⟧ 1 to point out the way for; direct on a course; conduct; lead 2 to direct the course or motion of (a vehicle, implement, etc.) by physical action 3 to give instruction to; train 4 to direct (the policies, actions, etc.) of; manage; regulate —*vi.* to act as a guide —*n.* a person or thing that guides; specif., *a)* a person whose work is conducting strangers or tourists through a region, building, etc. *b)* a person who directs, or serves as the model for, another's conduct, career, etc. *c)* a part that controls the motion of other parts of a machine *d)* a guidebook *e)* a book giving instruction in the elements of some subject; handbook [*a guide to mathematics*] *f) Mil.* a soldier at the right front of a column, who regulates its pace and alignment and indicates its route —**guid′a·ble** *adj.*

guide·book (gīd′book′) *n.* 1 a book containing directions and information for tourists 2 a handbook on some other subject

guided missile a military missile guided during flight to a target by internal preset, or self-reacting, devices or external electronic signals: see BALLISTIC MISSILE

guide dog a dog trained to lead a blind person

guide·line (-līn′) *n.* ☆a standard or principle by which to make a judgment or determine a policy or course of action

guide·post (-pōst′) *n.* 1 a post with a sign and directions for travelers, placed at a roadside or crossroads 2 anything that serves as a guide, standard, example, etc.; guideline

guide·way (-wā′) *n.* ⟦so named because it controls the direction of motion⟧ a track, channel, etc. along which something moves or slides, as a tool or train

guide word a word printed at the top of a page in a dictionary, encyclopedia, etc., usually the first or last entry on the page

Gui·do d'A·rez·zo (gwē′dô dä ret′tsô) A.D. 990?-1050?; It. monk & musical theoretician: also called **Guido A·re·ti·no** (ä′re tē′nô)

gui·don (gī′dən, gī′dän′) ***n.*** ⟦Fr < It *guidone* < *guidare* < *guida*: see GUIDE⟧ **1** [Historical] a small flag or pennant carried by the guide of mounted cavalry **2** the identification flag of a military unit or the soldier carrying it

Gui·enne (gē en′, gwē-) *alt. sp. of* GUYENNE

guild (gild) ***n.*** ⟦ME *gild*, blend of ON *gildi*, guild, guild-feast & OE *gyld*, association (of paying members), akin to OHG *gelt*, OFris *ield*, all < base seen in OE *gieldan*, to pay: see YIELD⟧ **1** in medieval times, a union of men in the same craft or trade to uphold standards and protect the members **2** any association for mutual aid and the promotion of common interests

guil·der (gil′dər) ***n.*** ⟦ME *gilder*, altered < MDu *gulden*: see GULDEN⟧ **1** the former basic monetary unit of the Netherlands, superseded in 2002 by the EURO **2** the former monetary unit of Suriname **3** a former coin of Germany, Austria, etc.

guild·hall (gild′hôl′) ***n.*** ⟦ME *gildhall* < OE *gildheall*⟧ **1** a hall where a guild meets **2** [Brit.] a town hall **3** [**G-**] the hall of the City of London: preceded by *The*

guilds·man (gildz′mən) ***n., pl.* -men** (-mən) a member of a guild

guild socialism a form of socialism proposed in England in the early 20th cent., emphasizing government ownership of all industries, each to be managed by a guild of workers

guile (gīl) ***n.*** ⟦ME *gile* < OFr *guile* < Frank **wigila*, guile, akin to OE *wigle*: see WILE⟧ slyness and cunning in dealing with others

guile·ful (gīl′fəl) ***adj.*** full of guile; deceitful —**guile′ful·ly** ***adv.***

guile·less (gīl′lis) ***adj.*** without guile; candid; frank —**guile′less·ly** ***adv.*** —**guile′less·ness** ***n.***

Gui·lin (gwē′lin′) city in Guangxi province, S China

Guil·lain-Bar·ré syndrome (gē lan′bä rā′, -lan′-) ⟦after G. *Guillain* & J. *Barré*, 20th-c. Fr neurologists⟧ an acute neurological disorder of unknown cause, involving partial paralysis of several muscle groups and occurring rarely after certain viral infections and vaccinations

guil·le·mot (gil′ə mät′) ***n.*** ⟦Fr, dim. of *Guillaume*, William: see ROBIN⟧ any of various narrow-billed, northern alcidine shorebirds (genera *Uria* and *Cepphus*)

guil·loche (gi lōsh′) ***n.*** ⟦Fr *guillochis* < *guillocher*, to ornament with lines < OIt *ghiocciare*, to drop, drip < LL **guttiare* < L *gutta*, a drop⟧ a decorative design in which two or more curved lines or bands are interwoven, forming a series of spaces between them

guil·lo·tine (gil′ə tēn′, gē′ə-; gil′ə tēn′, gē′ə-) ***n.*** ⟦Fr, after J. I. *Guillotin* (1738-1814), Fr physician who advocated its use during the French Revolution in preference to less humane methods⟧ **1** an instrument for beheading by means of a heavy blade dropped between two grooved uprights **2** an instrument, working on a similar principle, as for cutting paper **3** [Brit.] a method of limiting Parliamentary debate on a bill by voting at previously fixed times on specific sections of it —***vt.* -tined′**, **-tin′ing** ⟦Fr *guillotiner* < the n.⟧ to behead with a guillotine

guillotine

guilt (gilt) ***n.*** ⟦ME *gilt* < OE *gylt*, a sin, offense⟧ **1** the state of having done a wrong or committed an offense; culpability, legal or ethical **2** a painful feeling of self-reproach resulting from a belief that one has done something wrong or immoral **3** conduct that involves guilt; crime; sin

guilt·less (gilt′lis) ***adj.*** **1** free from guilt; innocent **2** having no knowledge or experience: with *of* —**guilt′less·ly** ***adv.***

guilt·y (gil′tē) ***adj.*** **guilt′i·er, guilt′i·est** ⟦ME *gilti* < OE *gyltig*⟧ **1** having guilt; deserving blame or punishment; culpable **2** having one's guilt proved; legally judged an offender **3** showing or conscious of guilt [*a guilty look*] **4** of or involving guilt or a sense of guilt [*a guilty conscience; indulging in chocolate is a guilty pleasure of mine*] —**guilt′i·ly** ***adv.*** —**guilt′i·ness** ***n.***

guimpe (gamp, gimp) ***n.*** ⟦Fr: see GIMP[1]⟧ **1** a blouse worn under a pinafore or jumper **2** a wide piece of cloth used in some nuns' habits to cover the neck and shoulders

guin·ea (gin′ē) ***n.*** **1** ⟦after fol. (the region), said to be the source of the gold from which it was first minted for use in trade in that region⟧ a former English gold coin, last minted in 1813, equal to 21 shillings: the word is still used in England in giving prices of luxury items **2** GUINEA FOWL **3** [Slang] an Italian or a person of Italian descent: an offensive term of hostility and contempt

Guin·ea (gin′ē) **1** coastal region of W Africa, between Senegal & Nigeria **2** country in this region: formerly a French colony, it became independent in 1958: 94,926 sq mi (245,857 sq km); cap. Conakry **3 Gulf of** part of the Atlantic, off the W coast of Africa —**Guin′e·an** ***adj., n.***

Guin·ea-Bis·sau (-bi sou′) country in W Africa, on the coast between Guinea & Senegal: formerly a Portuguese territory, it became independent in 1973: 13,946 sq mi (36,120 sq km); cap. Bissau

guinea fowl ⟦so named because orig. imported from GUINEA⟧ any of a family (Numididae) of gallinaceous African birds with a featherless head, rounded body, and dark feathers spotted with white, esp. the widespread domesticated species (*Numida meleagris*)

guinea hen **1** a female guinea fowl **2** any guinea fowl

Guinea pepper **1** any of several African plants (genus *Xylopia*) of the custard-apple family, esp. a tree (*X. aethiopica*) with fruits used in spices and folk medicine **2** the fruit of any of these plants

guinea pig ⟦prob. orig. brought to England by ships plying between England, the region of GUINEA, and South America (where it originated)⟧ **1** any of various small, plump rodents (genus *Cavia*) with short ears and no external tail: often domesticated and used in biological experiments ☆**2** any person or thing used in an experiment or test

Guinea worm ⟦after GUINEA, where orig. found throughout the region⟧ a nematode worm (*Dracunculus medinensis*) of tropical Africa and S Asia, parasitic as an adult in the subcutaneous tissues of humans and other mammals: the female can reach a length of *c.* 90 cm (*c.* 3 ft)

Guin·e·vere (gwin′ə vir′) ***n.*** ⟦< Celt; first element < Welsh *gwen*, white⟧ **1** a feminine name **2** *Arthurian Legend* the wife of King Arthur and lover of Lancelot Also **Guin′e·ver** (-vər)

Guin·ness (gin′əs), Sir **Al·ec** (al′ik) (born *Alec Guinness de Cuffe*) 1914-2000; Eng. actor

gui·pure (gē pyoor′; *Fr* gē pür′) ***n.*** ⟦Fr < *guiper*, to cover with silk < Frank **wipan*, to wind, akin to WHIP⟧ **1** lace without any ground mesh, having the patterns held together by connecting threads **2** a kind of gimp fabric

☆**gui·ro** (gwē′rō, gwir′ō) ***n., pl.* -ros** ⟦AmSp *güiro*, lit., gourd⟧ a Latin American percussion instrument typically consisting of a long-necked gourd that is sounded by scraping a stick along ridges cut into its surface

guise (gīz) ***n.*** ⟦ME *gise* < OFr *guise* < OHG *wisa*, way, manner, akin to WISE[2]⟧ **1** [Archaic] *a)* manner or way *b)* customary behavior, manner, or carriage **2** manner of dress; garb **3** outward aspect; semblance **4** a false or deceiving appearance; pretense [*under the guise of friendship*] —**SYN.** APPEARANCE

Guise[1] (gēz) ***n.*** name of a Fr. ducal family of the 16th & 17th cent.

Guise[2] (gēz) **1 Fran·çois de Lor·raine** (frän swá′ də lô ren′) 2d Duc de Guise 1519-63; Fr. statesman **2 Hen·ri de Lorraine** (än rē′) 3d Duc de Guise 1550-88; Fr. statesman: son of François

gui·tar (gi tär′) ***n.*** ⟦Fr *guitare* < OSp *guitarra* < Ar *qītār* < Gr *kithara*, lyre, lute⟧ a musical instrument related to the lute but having a flat back and usually six strings that are plucked or strummed with the fingers or a plectrum —**gui·tar′ist** ***n.***

☆**gui·tar·fish** (-fish′) ***n., pl.* -fish′** or **-fish′es** (see FISH) ⟦so named from its shape⟧ any of an order (Rhinobatiformes) of cartilaginous fishes with a long, narrow sharklike tail and a broad raylike body

Gui·yang (gwē′yän′) city in S China; capital of Guizhou province

Gui·zhou (gwē′jō′) province of S China: 67,182 sq mi (174,001 sq km); cap. Guiyang

Gu·ja·rat (goo′jə rät′) state of W India: 75,685 sq mi (196,023 sq km); cap. Gandhinagar

Gu·ja·ra·ti (goo′jə rät′ē) ***n.*** **1** a person born or living in Gujarat **2** the Indo-Aryan language spoken in Gujarat —***adj.*** of Gujarat or its people, language, or culture

Guj·ran·wa·la (gooj′rən wäl′ə) city in NE Pakistan

gu·lag (gōō′läg′, -lag′) ***n.*** ⟦Russ *GULAG*, acronym for *Glavnoe upravlenie ispravitel'no-trudovyx lagerej*, Main Administration for Corrective Labor Camps: term popularized by A. SOLZHENITSYN in his multivolume work, *The Gulag Archipelago*⟧ **1** [*also* **G-**] the system of prisons and labor camps, esp. for political prisoners, in the Soviet Union: with *the* **2** such a prison or forced-labor camp, as in the Soviet Union **3** any place or situation regarded as like such a prison

gu·lar (gyōō′lər) ***adj.*** ⟦< L *gula*, throat (see GULLET) + -AR⟧ of or on the throat

☆**gulch** (gulch) ***n.*** ⟦prob. < dial., to swallow greedily < ME *gulchen*, of echoic orig.⟧ a steep-walled valley cut by a swift stream; deep, narrow ravine

gul·den (gool′dən) ***n., pl.* -dens** or **-den** ⟦MDu, short for *gulden florijn*, golden florin⟧ GUILDER

gules (gyōōlz) ***n.*** ⟦ME *goules* < OFr, gules, red-dyed ermine, orig. pl. of *goule*, the mouth < L *gula*, throat: see GULLET⟧ *Heraldry* the color red: indicated in engravings by parallel vertical lines

gulf (gulf) ***n.*** ⟦ME *goulf* < OFr *golfe* < It *golfo* < LGr *kolphos*, for Gr *kolpos*, a fold, bosom, gulf, prob. < IE **kwolpos* < base **kwel-*, to turn > Ger *wölben*, to arch⟧ **1** a large body of sea or ocean water, typically larger than a bay, that is partially enclosed by land **2** a wide, deep chasm or abyss **3** a wide or impassable gap or separation **4** an eddy that draws objects down; whirlpool —***vt.*** to swallow up; engulf —**the Gulf 1** the Persian Gulf or the surrounding region **2** the Gulf of Mexico or the surrounding region

Gulf States **1** states on the Gulf of Mexico; Fla., Ala., Miss., La., & Tex. **2** PERSIAN GULF STATES

Gulf Stream warm ocean current flowing from the Gulf of Mexico along the E coast of the U.S., and turning east at the Grand Banks toward Europe: *c.* 50 mi (80 km) wide

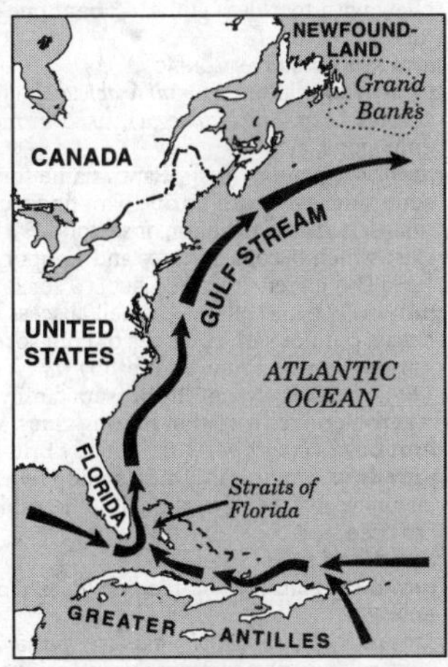

Gulf Stream

Gulf War ⟦after the PERSIAN GULF⟧ the brief war fought in

1991 between Iraq and United Nations allies to free Kuwait from occupying Iraqi forces

Gulf War syndrome a chronic medical condition of unproven origin experienced by some Gulf War (1991) veterans, characterized variously by fatigue, headaches, memory loss, aching joints, etc.

gulf·weed (gulf′wēd′) ***n.*** **1** a brown algae (genus *Sargassum*) with berrylike air sacs, found floating in the Gulf Stream, Pacific Ocean, etc. **2** SARGASSUM

gull[1] (gul) ***n., pl.*** **gulls** or **gull** ⟦ME < Celt, as in Cornish *gullan*, Welsh *gwylan*, Bret *gwelan*⟧ any of various shorebirds of a worldwide family (Laridae), with large wings, slender legs, webbed feet, a strong, hooked bill, and feathers of chiefly white and gray

gull[2] (gul) ***n.*** ⟦ME *gulle*, silly fellow, lit., unfledged bird < *gul*, yellow < ON *gulr*, akin to *goll*, GOLD⟧ a person easily cheated or tricked; dupe —***vt.*** to cheat or trick; dupe

☆**Gul·lah** (gul′ə) ***n.*** ⟦after ? *Gola (Gula)*, tribal group in Liberia, or < ? *Ngola*, tribal group in the Hamba basin in Angola⟧ **1** a member of a group of former slaves and their descendants living on the Sea Islands and in adjacent isolated coastal areas of South Carolina and Georgia **2** the English creole spoken by the Gullahs, containing vocabulary and grammatical features from various West African languages **3** loosely, any variety of black speech of coastal South Carolina or Georgia

gul·let (gul′it) ***n.*** ⟦ME *golet* < OFr *goulet*, throat, narrow passage, dim. of *goule* < L *gula*, throat < IE base **gel-*, to swallow > OE *ceole*, Ger *kehle*, throat⟧ **1** the tube leading from the mouth to the stomach; esophagus **2** the throat or neck **3** any depression or channel like a gullet, as a water gully

gul·li·ble (gul′ə bəl) ***adj.*** ⟦GULL[2], *vt.* + -IBLE⟧ easily cheated or tricked; credulous: also [Rare] **gul′la·ble** —**gul′li·bil′i·ty** ***n.*** —**gul′li·bly** ***adv.***

Gul·li·ver's Travels (gul′ə vərz) a political and social satire (1726) by Jonathan Swift, in the form of a narrative of the voyages of Lemuel Gulliver to four imaginary lands, Lilliput, Brobdingnag, Laputa, and the land of the Houyhnhnms

gul·ly[1] (gul′ē) ***n., pl.*** **-lies** ⟦altered < ME *golet*, water channel, orig., GULLET⟧ a channel or hollow worn by running water; small, narrow ravine —***vt.*** **-lied**, **-ly·ing** to make a gully or gullies in

gul·ly[2] (gul′ē, go͝ol′ē) ***n., pl.*** **-lies** ⟦< ?⟧ [Brit.] a large knife

gu·los·i·ty (gyo͞o läs′ə tē) ***n.*** ⟦LL *gulositas* < *gulosus*, gluttonous < *gula*, GULLET⟧ [Now Rare] greediness

gulp (gulp) ***vt.*** ⟦ME *gulpen*, prob. < MDu *gulpen*, to gulp down, akin to OE *gielpan*: see YELP⟧ **1** to swallow hastily, greedily, or in large amounts **2** to choke back as if swallowing; repress (a sob, etc.) —***vi.*** to catch the breath in or as in swallowing a large amount —***n.*** **1** the act of gulping **2** the amount swallowed at one time —**gulp′er** ***n.*** —**gulp′ing·ly** ***adv.***

gum[1] (gum) ***n.*** ⟦ME *gomme* < OFr < LL *gumma* < L *gummi, cummi* < Gr *kommi* < Egypt *qmyt*⟧ **1** a sticky, colloidal carbohydrate found in certain trees and plants, which dries into an uncrystallized, brittle mass that dissolves or swells in water **2** any similar plant secretion, as resin **3** any plant gum processed for use in industry, art, etc. **4** *a)* an adhesive, as on the back of a postage stamp *b)* any of various sticky or viscous substances or deposits **5** *a)* GUM TREE *b)* the wood of a gum tree **6** [Now Rare] *a)* pure rubber ☆*b)* [*pl.*] rubber overshoes ☆**7** CHEWING GUM ☆**8** [Dial.] a hollowed gum log used as a trough, etc. —***vt.*** **gummed**, **gum′ming** to coat, unite, or stiffen with gum —***vi.*** **1** to secrete or form gum **2** to become sticky or clogged —**by gum!** [Informal] by God!: a euphemism —☆**gum up** [Slang] to put out of working order; cause to go awry

gum[2] (gum; *esp. formerly*, go͞om) ***n.*** ⟦ME *gome* < OE *goma*, akin to Ger *gaumen*, roof of the mouth < IE base **ghēu-, *ghōu-*, to yawn, gape > Gr *chaos*⟧ [*often pl.*] the firm flesh covering the jaws on the inside of the mouth and surrounding the base of the teeth —☆***vt.*** **gummed**, **gum′ming** to bite or chew with toothless gums —☆**beat one's gums** [Slang] to talk much and idly

gum ammoniac AMMONIAC

gum arabic ⟦after L *gummi Arabicum*⟧ a gum obtained from several African acacias (esp. *Acacia senegal*), used in medicine and candy, for stabilizing emulsions, etc.

☆**gum·bo** (gum′bō) ***n.*** ⟦< Bantu name for okra⟧ **1** OKRA (senses 1 & 2) **2** a soup thickened with unripe okra pods, usually made with tomatoes, vegetables, and chicken, ham, or seafood **3** a fine, silty soil of the Western prairies, which becomes sticky and nonporous when wet: also **gumbo soil** **4** [*also* **G-**] a French-based CREOLE (sense 5) spoken in Louisiana

gum·boil (gum′boil′) ***n.*** a small abscess on the gum associated with tooth decay, but not with pyorrhea or cold sores

gum·bo·lim·bo (gum′bō lim′bō) ***n., pl.*** **-lim′bos** a tropical American tree (*Bursera simaruba*) of the bursera family, having reddish, peeling bark and an aromatic resin used in making glues, varnish, incense, etc.

gum·boot (gum′bo͞ot′) ***n.*** [Chiefly Brit.] a high rubber boot

☆**gum·drop** (gum′dräp′) ***n.*** a small piece of candy of a firm, jellylike consistency, made of sweetened gum arabic or gelatin, usually colored and flavored, and covered with sugar

gum elemi ELEMI

gum·line (gum′līn′) ***n.*** the line formed along either gum, where the teeth emerge

gum·ma (gum′ə) ***n., pl.*** **-mas** or **-ma·ta** (-ə tə) ⟦ModL < L *gummi*, GUM[1]⟧ a soft, rubbery tumor occurring in various organs or tissues, esp. in the late stages of syphilis —**gum′ma·tous** ***adj.***

gum·mite (gum′īt′) ***n.*** ⟦so named (1868) by J. D. DANA[1] < L *gummi*, GUM[1] + -ITE[1]⟧ a soft, yellowish or reddish-brown mixture of minerals containing uranium, lead, and thorium

gum·mo·sis (gu mō′sis) ***n.*** ⟦ModL < L *gummi*, GUM[1] + -OSIS⟧ the giving off of gummy substances as a result of cell degeneration: a characteristic of certain plant diseases, esp. of stone fruits

gum·mous (gum′əs) ***adj.*** ⟦L *gummosus*⟧ of or like gum

gum·my (gum′ē) ***adj.*** **-mi·er**, **-mi·est** **1** having the nature of gum; sticky; viscid **2** covered with or containing gum **3** yielding gum —**gum′mi·ness** ***n.***

gump·tion (gump′shən) ***n.*** ⟦< Scot dial. < ? ME *gome*, attention (< ON *gaumr*), with playful Latinate suffix⟧ [Informal] **1** [Obs.] shrewdness in practical matters; common sense **2** courage and initiative; enterprise and boldness

gum resin a mixture of gum and resin, given off by certain trees and plants

☆**gum·shoe** (gum′sho͞o′) ***n.*** ⟦GUM[1] (rubber) + SHOE⟧ **1** *a)* a rubber overshoe *b)* [*pl.*] sneakers **2** [Slang] a detective —***vi.*** **-shoed′**, **-shoe′ing** [Slang] to sneak or go about quietly, as a detective; act with stealth

☆**gum tree** any of various trees that yield gum, as the sweet gum, tupelo, eucalyptus, etc.

gum turpentine TURPENTINE (*n.* 2)

gum·wood (gum′wood′) ***n.*** the wood of a gum tree

gun (gun) ***n.*** ⟦ME *gunne, gonne*, contr. < *gonilde*, a 14th-c. cannon < ON *Gunnhildr*, fem. name (< *gunnr*, older form of *guthr*, war + *hildr*, battle)⟧ **1** a weapon consisting of a metal tube from which a projectile is discharged by the force of an explosive; specif., *a)* technically, a heavy weapon with a relatively long barrel fixed in a mount, as a cannon or machine gun *b)* a rifle ☆*c)* popularly, a pistol or revolver **2** any similar device not discharged by an explosive [*an air gun*] **3** a discharge of a gun in signaling or saluting **4** anything like a gun in shape or use ☆**5** [Slang] GUNMAN (sense 1) **6** [Slang] the throttle of an engine —***vi.*** **gunned**, **gun′ning** to shoot or hunt with a gun; go shooting or hunting —***vt.*** ☆**1** [Informal] to shoot (a person) intentionally: with *down* **2** [Slang] to advance the throttle of (an engine) so as to increase the speed —☆**give it the gun** ⟦from the resemblance of early airplane accelerators to the trigger of a gun⟧ [Slang] to cause something to start or gain speed —**go great guns** [Slang] to act with speed and efficiency —☆**gun for** **1** to hunt for with a gun **2** to look for in order to shoot or harm **3** [Slang] to try to get; seek —**jump the gun** [Informal] **1** to begin a race before the signal has been given **2** to begin anything before the proper time —**spike someone's guns** to frustrate or defeat someone —**stick to one's guns** [Informal] to hold one's position under attack; not withdraw or retreat; be firm —**under the gun** [Informal] in a tense, demanding situation or threatened state, often one involving a deadline

gun·boat (-bōt′) ***n.*** **1** a small armed ship of shallow draft **2** [*pl.*] [Slang] shoes; esp., a pair of large shoes

gunboat diplomacy the use or threatened use of limited military force in place of conventional diplomatic negotiations

gun·cot·ton (-kät′′n) ***n.*** nitrocellulose in a highly nitrated form, used as an explosive substance and propellant

gun dog a dog, as a pointer, setter, or hound, trained to help a hunter by finding or retrieving game

☆**gun·fight** (-fīt′) ***n.*** a fight between persons using pistols or revolvers —☆**gun′fight′er** ***n.***

gun·fire (-fīr′) ***n.*** **1** the firing of a gun or guns **2** the use of firearms or artillery, as distinguished from other military tactics

gun·flint (-flint′) ***n.*** a piece of flint in the hammer of a flintlock, for striking a spark to set off the charge

☆**gung-ho** (guŋ′hō′) ***adj.*** ⟦Chin, *kung-ho*, lit., work together: slogan of Lt. Col. E. F. Carlson's Marine Raiders in WWII⟧ [Informal] enthusiastic, cooperative, enterprising, etc. in an unrestrained, often naive way

☆**gun·ite** (gun′īt′) ***n.*** ⟦< GUN + -ITE[1]⟧ a concrete mixture sprayed under pressure over steel reinforcements, as in making swimming pools

☆**gunk** (guŋk) ***n.*** ⟦< ? G(OO) + (J)UNK⟧ [Slang] any oily, viscous, or thick, messy substance —**gunk′y** ***adj.***

gunk·hole (-hōl′) ***n.*** ⟦< ?⟧ a small, sheltered cove for anchoring small watercraft —***vi.*** **-holed′**, **-hol′ing** to make a series of short pleasure trips by boat, as from island to island

gun lap *Track & Field* the final lap of a race, signaled by the firing of a starter's pistol as the runner in the lead begins the lap

gun·lock (gun′läk′) ***n.*** in some old guns, the mechanism by which the charge is set off

gun·man (-mən) ***n., pl.*** **-men** (-mən) ☆**1** a man armed with a gun, esp. an armed gangster or hired killer **2** a man skilled in the use of a gun

gun·met·al (-met′'l) ***n.*** **1** a kind of bronze formerly used for making cannons **2** any metal or alloy treated to resemble tarnished gunmetal **3** the dark gray color of tarnished gunmetal: also **gunmetal gray** —***adj.*** dark gray

☆**gun moll** ⟦see MOLL⟧ [Old Slang] the mistress or female accomplice of a GUNMAN (sense 1)

Gun·nar (go͞on′när′) ***n.*** ⟦ON *Gunnarr* < *gunnr*: see GUN⟧ *Gmc. Legend* the brother of Gudrun and husband of Brynhild

gun·nel[1] (gun′əl) ***n.*** ⟦< ?⟧ any of a family (Pholidae) of elongated percoid fishes of northern seas

gun·nel[2] (gun′əl) ***n.*** *phonetic sp. of* GUNWALE

gun·ner (gun′ər) ***n.*** ⟦ME *gonner* < *gonne*, GUN⟧ **1** a soldier, sailor, etc. who fires or helps fire an artillery piece **2** a naval warrant officer whose specialty is guns, missiles, torpedoes, etc. and related equipment **3** a hunter who uses a gun

gun·ner·y (gun′ər ē) ***n.*** **1** heavy guns **2** the science of making and using heavy guns and projectiles

☆**gunnery sergeant** *U.S. Marine Corps* a noncommissioned officer ranking above a staff sergeant and below a master sergeant or first sergeant

gun·ny (gun′ē) ***n.***, *pl.* **-nies** ⟦Hindi *gōnī*, gunny bag < Sans, a sack⟧ **1** a coarse, heavy fabric of jute or hemp, used for sacks **2** GUNNYSACK

gun·ny·sack (-sak′) ***n.*** a sack or bag made of gunny: sometimes **gun′ny·bag′** (-bag′)

☆**gun·play** (gun′plā′) ***n.*** an exchange of gunshots, as between gunmen and police

☆**gun·point** (-point′) ***n.*** the muzzle of a gun: chiefly in **at gunpoint**, under threat of being shot with a gun at close range

gun·pow·der (-pou′dər) ***n.*** **1** an explosive powder, esp. a blackish mixture of sulfur, potassium nitrate, and charcoal, used as a charge in cartridges, shells, etc., for blasting, in fireworks, etc. **2** GUNPOWDER TEA

Gunpowder Plot the unsuccessful plot (1605) to blow up King James I of England and both Houses of Parliament

gunpowder tea Chinese green tea whose leaves are rolled into pellets

gun room **1** on British warships, the junior officers' quarters, previously, the quarters of the gunner and his mates **2** a room for displaying a collection of guns

gun·run·ning (-run′iŋ) ***n.*** the smuggling of guns and ammunition into a country —**gun′run′ner** ***n.***

guns and (*or* or) butter *a phrase referring to* the economic policies of a government or society, considered in light of the percentage of resources allocated to military uses as opposed to the percentage allocated to other, nonmilitary spending, as for social welfare

☆**gun·sel** (gun′səl) ***n.*** [Slang] **1** ⟦orig., boy (with implication of perversion), prob. < Yiddish *gendzl*, gosling < MHG *gensel*, dim. of *gans*, GOOSE⟧ a catamite **2** ⟦infl. by GUN⟧ GUNMAN (sense 1)

gun·ship (gun′ship′) ***n.*** ☆a heavily armed helicopter used to support ground troops and assault enemy ground forces

gun·shot (-shät′) ***n.*** ⟦ME *gunnes shott*⟧ **1** a shot fired from a gun **2** the range of a gun —***adj.*** caused by a shot from a gun *[a gunshot wound]*

gun-shy (-shī′) ***adj.*** **1** easily frightened at the firing of a gun *[a gun-shy dog]* **2** frightened, wary, mistrustful, etc., as because of a previous experience —**gun′-shy′ness** ***n.***

☆**gun·sling·er** (-sliŋ′ər) ***n.*** [Slang] a skilled gunfighter in the Old West

gun·smith (-smith′) ***n.*** ⟦GUN + SMITH (in general sense), maker⟧ a person who designs, makes, or repairs small guns

gun·stock (-stäk′) ***n.*** STOCK (*n.* 8*e*)

Gun·ter's chain (gun′tərz) ⟦after E. *Gunter* (1581-1626), Eng mathematician who invented it⟧ a surveyor's chain 66 ft (20.117 m) in length: it consists of 100 links, each 7.92 in (20.117 cm) long

Gun·ther (goon′tər) ***n.*** ⟦Ger < Gmc **gund-*, **gunt-*, war (> ON *gunnr*, *guthr*) + **har-* (> OE *here*), army⟧ in the *Nibelungenlied*, a king of Burgundy and husband of Brunhild

Gun·tur (goon toor′) city in E Andhra Pradesh, SE India, in the Kistna River delta

gun·wale (gun′əl) ***n.*** ⟦LME *gonne walle* (see GUN & WALE[1]): first applied to bulwarks supporting a ship's guns⟧ the upper edge of the side of a ship or boat

gup·py (gup′ē) ***n.***, *pl.* **-pies** ⟦after R. J. L. *Guppy*, of Trinidad, who first provided specimens for the British Museum⟧ a brightly colored livebearer (*Poecilia reticulata*) native to Barbados, Trinidad, and Venezuela

Gurd·jieff (gurd′yef), **G(eorge) I(vanovich)** (born *George S. Georgiades*) 1872?-1949; Armenian writer, occultist, & spiritual leader

gurge (gurj) ***n.*** ⟦L *gurges*: see GORGE⟧ [Now Rare] a whirlpool

gur·gi·ta·tion (gur′jə tā′shən) ***n.*** ⟦< pp. LL *gurgitare*, to flood < L *gurges*, whirlpool: see GORGE⟧ [Now Rare] a whirling or surging, as of liquid

gur·gle (gur′gəl) ***vi.*** **-gled, -gling** ⟦prob. echoic orig., as in Ger *gurgeln*, or? akin to It *gorgogliare* < L *gurgulio*, gullet⟧ **1** to flow with a bubbling or rippling sound, as water from a narrow-necked bottle does **2** to make such a sound in the throat, as a contented baby does —***vt.*** to utter with a gurgling sound —***n.*** the act or sound of gurgling

gur·glet (gurg′lit) ***n.*** ⟦Port *gorgoleta*⟧ *var. of* GOGLET

Gur·kha (goor′kä′) ***n.*** a member of a people living in the mountains of Nepal, famous as soldiers

gur·nard (gur′nərd) ***n.***, *pl.* **-nards** or **-nard** ⟦ME < OFr *gornart* < *grogner*, to grunt (< L *grunnire*): from "grunting" when caught: see GRUNT, *n.* 2⟧ **1** FLYING GURNARD **2** SEA ROBIN

gur·ney (gur′nē) ***n.***, *pl.* **-neys** ⟦< ?⟧ a stretcher or cot on wheels, used in hospitals to move patients

gurn·ing (gur′niŋ) ***n.*** ⟦prp. of ME *girnen*, var. of *grennen*: see GRIN⟧ [Dial., Chiefly Brit.] the act of making a face; snarling, grimacing, etc.

☆**gur·ry** (gur′ē) ***n.*** ⟦< ?⟧ fish offal, as from a fish cannery

gu·ru (goo͞′roo͞′, goor′oo͞′; *also* goo roo͞′, gə-) ***n.*** ⟦Hindi *guru* < Sans *guruḥ*, venerable, orig. heavy < IE **gweru-* < base **gwer-* > GRAVE[1]⟧ **1** in Hinduism, one's personal spiritual advisor or teacher **2** any leader, mentor, etc. who is regarded as being deeply influential or charismatic

gush (gush) ***vi.*** ⟦ME *guschen*, prob. akin to ON *gjosa*, to gush & *gustr*, GUST[1]⟧ **1** to flow out suddenly and plentifully; pour out; spout **2** to have a sudden, plentiful flow of blood, tears, etc. **3** to express oneself with exaggerated enthusiasm or feeling; talk or write effusively —***vt.*** to cause to flow out suddenly and plentifully —***n.*** **1** a sudden, plentiful outflow **2** gushing talk or writing —**gush′ing** ***adj.*** —**gush′ing·ly** ***adv.***

gush·er (gush′ər) ***n.*** **1** a person who gushes ☆**2** an oil well from which oil spouts without being pumped

gush·y (gush′ē) ***adj.*** **gush′i·er, gush′i·est** given to or characterized by gush; effusive —**gush′i·ly** ***adv.*** —**gush′i·ness** ***n.***

gus·set (gus′it) ***n.*** ⟦ME *guschet* < OFr *gousset*⟧ **1** a piece of chain mail or a metal plate protecting the opening of a joint in a suit of armor **2** a triangular or diamond-shaped piece sewn into a garment, glove, etc. to make it stronger or roomier **3** a brace, usually triangular, for reinforcing a corner or angle in the framework of a structure —***vt.*** to furnish with a gusset

gus·sy or **gus·sie** (gus′ē) ***vt.***, ***vi.*** **-sied, -sy·ing** ⟦< ?⟧ [Slang] to dress (*up*) or decorate in a fine or showy way

gust[1] (gust) ***n.*** ⟦ON *gustr*, gust, blast < *gjosa*, to gush, break out < IE **gheus-* < base **ĝheu-*, to pour > GUT, L *fundere*⟧ **1** a sudden, strong rush of air or wind **2** a sudden burst of rain, smoke, fire, sound, etc. **3** an outburst of laughter, rage, etc. —***vi.*** to blow in gusts —***SYN.*** WIND[2]

gust[2] (gust) ***n.*** ⟦ME *guste* < L *gustus*: see GUSTO⟧ [Archaic] **1** taste; relish; flavor; savor **2** enjoyment or appreciation —***vt.*** [Scot.] to taste or relish —**gust′a·ble** ***adj., n.***

Gus·taf (goos′täf) **1 Gustaf V** 1858-1950; king of Sweden (1907-50): also called **Gustav** (or **Gustavus**) **V** **2 Gustaf VI (Adolf)** 1882-1973; king of Sweden (1950-73): also called **Gustav** (or **Gustavus**) **VI**

gus·ta·tion (gəs tā′shən) ***n.*** ⟦L *gustatio* < *gustatus*, pp. of *gustare*, to taste < *gustus*, a taste: see GUSTO⟧ **1** the act of tasting **2** the sense of taste

gus·ta·to·ry (gus′tə tôr′ē) ***adj.*** ⟦< L *gustatus*, pp. (see prec.) + -ORY⟧ of or having to do with tasting or the sense of taste: also **gus′ta·tive** (-tiv)

Gus·ta·vus (gəs tā′vəs, gəs tä′vəs) **1 Gustavus I** (born *Gustavus Eriksson Vasa*) 1496-1560; king of Sweden (1523-60) **2 Gustavus II** (born *Gustavus Adolphus*) 1594-1632; king of Sweden (1611-32): grandson of Gustavus I **3 Gustavus III** 1746-92; king of Sweden (1711-92) **4 Gustavus IV** 1778-1837; king of Sweden (1792-1809); deposed: son of Gustavus III See also GUSTAF

gus·to (gus′tō) ***n.*** ⟦It & Sp < L *gustus*, taste < IE base **ĝeus-*, to enjoy, taste > CHOOSE⟧ **1** taste; liking **2** keen enjoyment; enthusiastic appreciation; zest; relish **3** great vigor or liveliness **4** [Archaic] artistic style

gust·y (gus′tē) ***adj.*** **gust′i·er, gust′i·est** **1** characterized by gusts of air or wind **2** characterized by sudden bursts or outbursts —**gust′i·ly** ***adv.*** —**gust′i·ness** ***n.***

gut (gut) ***n.*** ⟦ME < OE *guttas*, pl. < base of *geotan*, to pour: for IE base see GUST[1]⟧ **1** *a)* [*pl.*] the bowels; entrails *b)* the stomach or belly: now often regarded as an indelicate usage **2** all or part of the alimentary canal, esp. the intestines **3** tough cord made from animal intestines, used for violin strings, surgical sutures, etc.; catgut **4** the little bag of silk removed from a silkworm before it has spun its cocoon: made into strong cord for use in fishing tackle **5** a narrow passage or gully, as of a stream or path **6** [*pl.*] [Informal] the basic, inner or deeper parts **7** [*pl.*] [Informal] *a)* daring, courage, perseverance, vigor, etc. *b)* impudence; effrontery *c)* power or force —***vt.*** **gut′ted, gut′ting** **1** to remove the intestines from; eviscerate **2** to destroy the interior of, as by fire —***adj.*** **1** [Slang] urgent and basic or fundamental *[the gut issues of a campaign]* **2** [Slang] easy; simple *[a gut course in college]* **3** [Informal] based on intuition, instinct, or emotion rather than careful consideration *[a gut feeling, gut reaction]* —***SYN.*** FORTITUDE —**hate someone's guts** [Slang] to hate someone intensely

GUT *abbrev.* GRAND UNIFIED (FIELD) THEORY

☆**gut·buck·et** (gut′buk′it) ***adj.*** ⟦orig., a bucket for food or drink for chain-gang laborers; later used for a pail circulated to collect contributions for beer or food, esp. for itinerant musicians; then, a saloon where such musicians played⟧ designating or of a raucous, unsophisticated style of playing jazz

Gu·ten·berg (goot′'n burg′), **Jo·hann** (yō′hän′) (born *Johannes Gensfleisch*) 1400?-68; Ger. printer: reputedly the first European to print with movable type

Guth·rie (guth′rē), **Wood·y** (wood′ē) (born *Woodrow Wilson Guthrie*) 1912-67; U.S. folk singer, guitarist, & composer

gut·less (gut′lis) ***adj.*** ⟦see GUT, *n.* 7⟧ [Informal] lacking courage, daring, perseverance, etc. —**gut′less·ness** ***n.***

guts·y (gut′sē) ***adj.*** **guts′i·er, guts′i·est** [Informal] full of guts; daring, courageous, forceful, plucky, etc.

gut·ta (gut′ə) ***n.***, *pl.* **-tae** (-ē) ⟦ME, drop of gum < L, a drop⟧ **1** *Pharmacy* a liquid drop **2** any of a series of small, droplike ornaments on a Doric entablature

gut·ta-per·cha (gut′ə pur′chə) ***n.*** ⟦< Malay < *getah*, tree sap, latex + ? *perca*, rag, strip of cloth (so called because sold in strips): form infl. by L *gutta*, a drop⟧ a rubberlike gum produced from the latex of various SE Asian trees (esp. genera *Palaquium* and *Payena*) of the sapodilla family and used in electric insulation, dentistry, golf balls, etc.

gut·tate (gut′āt′) ***adj.*** ⟦L *guttatus* < *gutta*, a drop⟧ **1** in the form of drops **2** spotted, as with drops

gut·ter (gut′ər) ***n.*** ⟦ME *gotere* < OFr *gutiere* < L *gutta*, a drop⟧ **1** a channel along or under the eaves of a roof, to carry off rainwater **2** a narrow channel along the side of a road or street, to carry off water, as to a sewer **3** a place or state of living characterized by filth, poverty, squalor, etc. **4** a channel or groove like a gutter, as the groove on either side of a bowling alley **5** the adjoining inner margins of two facing pages in a book, magazine, etc. —*vt.* to furnish with gutters; make gutters in —*vi.* **1** to flow in a stream **2** to melt rapidly so that the wax runs down the side in channels: said of a candle

gut·ter·snipe (-snīp′) *n.* ⟦orig. (Brit dial.), the common snipe, which picks food out of gutters⟧ a child of the slums who spends most of his or her time in the streets: contemptuous term applied to anyone regarded as having the unsavory manners, morals, etc. sometimes associated with those living in filth, poverty, or squalor

gut·tur·al (gut′ər əl) *adj.* ⟦L *guttur*, throat < IE **gut-*, **gutr*, throat < base **gēu-*, to curve > COD[1]⟧ **1** *a)* harsh; rasping (said of vocal sounds) *b)* characterized by such sounds [*a guttural* language] **2** VELAR (sense 2) —*n.* a guttural sound —**gut′tur·al·ly** *adv.* —**gut′tur·al·ness** *n.*

gut·tur·al·ize (gut′ər əl īz′) *vt.* **-ized′**, **-iz′ing** ⟦prec. + -IZE⟧ to pronounce gutturally —**gut′tur·al·i·za′tion** *n.*

gut·ty (gut′ē) *adj.* **-ti·er**, **-ti·est** [Informal] *var. of* GUTSY

guv (guv) *n. slang var. of* GOVERNOR (esp. senses 1*b* & 3)

guy[1] (gī) *n.* ⟦ME *gie* < OFr *guie*, a guide < *guier*, to guide < *guider*: see GUIDE⟧ a rope, chain, rod, or wire attached to something to steady or guide it —*vt.* to guide or steady with a guy

guy[2] (gī) *n.* ⟦after Guy FAWKES⟧ **1** in England, an effigy of Guy Fawkes displayed and burned on Guy Fawkes Day **2** [Brit.] a person whose appearance or dress is odd ☆**3** [Informal] *a)* a man *b)* [*pl.*] persons, esp. friends or associates; fellows —*vt.* [Informal] to make fun of; ridicule; josh; tease

Guy (gī; *Fr* gē) *n.* ⟦OFr *Gui*, *Guy*, lit., leader: see GUY[1]⟧ a masculine name: equiv. It. & Sp. *Guido*

Guy·a·na (gī an′ə, -än′ə) country in NE South America: formerly a British colony, it became independent in 1966; member of the Commonwealth: 83,000 sq mi (214,970 sq km); cap. Georgetown —**Guy·a·nese** (gī′ə nēz′) *adj.*, *n.*

Guy·enne (gē en′, gwē-) historical region of SW France, roughly corresponding to earlier Aquitaine

Guy Fawkes Day in England, a day (Nov. 5) commemorating the foiling of the Gunpowder Plot: celebrated with fireworks, guys, etc.: see FAWKES, Guy

☆**guy·ot** (gē′ō′, gē ō′) *n.* ⟦after A. H. *Guyot* (1807-84), U.S. geologist⟧ a flat-topped, steeply rising seamount; tablemount

guz·zle (guz′əl) *vi.*, *vt.* **-zled**, **-zling** ⟦< ? OFr *gosillier* < *gosier*, throat < Gaul *geusiae*, throat⟧ to drink (or, rarely, eat) greedily or immoderately —**guz′zler** *n.*

gv *abbrev.* gravimetric volume

GVW *abbrev.* gross vehicle weight

GW or **Gw** *abbrev.* gigawatt(s)

Gwa·li·or (gwä′lē ôr′) city in NC India

Gwang·ju (gwäŋ′jo͞o′) city in SW South Korea

Gwen·do·line (gwen′də lin) *n.* ⟦< Celt: see GUINEVERE⟧ a feminine name: dim. *Gwen*; var. *Gwendolyn*

Gwent (gwent) county in SE Wales, on the Severn estuary: 532 sq mi (1,378 sq km)

Gwin·nett (gwi net′), **But·ton** (but′'n) 1735?-77; Am. patriot, born in England: signer of the Declaration of Independence

Gwyn or **Gwynne** (gwin), **Nell** (born *Eleanor Gwyn*) 1650-87; Eng. actress: mistress of Charles II

Gwyn·edd (gwin′əth) county in NW Wales, on the Irish Sea & St. George's Channel: 1,491 sq mi (3,862 sq km)

Gy *abbrev. Physics* gray(s)

Gyan·dzha (gyän′jə) city in NC Azerbaijan, in Transcaucasia

gybe (jīb) *n.*, *vi.*, *vt.* **gybed**, **gyb′ing** *alt. sp. of* JIBE[1]

gym (jim) *n.* [Informal] **1** *short for* GYMNASIUM ☆**2** PHYSICAL EDUCATION

gym·kha·na (jim kä′nə) *n.* ⟦Anglo-Ind, a place where athletic contests or games are held; altered (by analogy with GYMNASIUM) < Hindustani *gendkhāna*, racket court < *gend*, ball + *khāna*, court, place⟧ **1** a sporting event involving a series of contests on horseback **2** a sporting event involving a series of contests testing auto-racing skills

gym·na·si·arch (jim nā′zē ärk′) *n.* ⟦L *gymnasiarchus* < Gr *gymnasiarchos* < *gymnasion*, GYMNASIUM + *-archos*, -ARCH⟧ in ancient Greece, an official who supervised athletic games, contests, and schools

gym·na·si·ast (gim nä′zē ast′; *for 2* jim nā′zē ast′) *n.* **1** a student in a Gymnasium **2** a gymnast

gym·na·si·um (jim nā′zē əm; *for 2* gim nä′zē o͝om′) *n.*, *pl.* **-si·ums** or **-si·a** (-ə) ⟦L < Gr *gymnasion*, place for exercising < *gymnazein*, to train naked < *gymnos*, naked, stripped < IE base **nogw-* > NAKED, L *nudus*⟧ **1** a room or building equipped for physical training and athletic games and sports **2** [**G-**] in Germany and some other European countries, a secondary school for students preparing to enter a university

gym·nast (jim′nast′, -nəst) *n.* ⟦Gr *gymnastēs*, trainer of athletes⟧ an expert in gymnastics

gym·nas·tic (jim nas′tik) *adj.* ⟦L *gymnasticus* < Gr *gymnastikos* < *gymnazein*: see GYMNASIUM⟧ of or having to do with gymnastics —**gym·nas′ti·cal·ly** *adv.*

gym·nas·tics (-tiks) *n.* ⟦< prec.⟧ a sport combining tumbling and acrobatic feats, usually done with apparatus such as the parallel bars, the balance beam, etc.

gym·no- (jim′nō, jim′nə) ⟦< Gr *gymnos*, naked: see GYMNASIUM⟧ *combining form* naked, stripped, bare [*gymnosperm*]: also, before a vowel, **gymn-**

gym·nos·o·phist (jim näs′ə fist) *n.* ⟦ME *genosophis* < L *gymnosophistae*, pl. < Gr *gymnosophistai*: see prec. & SOPHIST⟧ a member of an ancient Hindu sect of ascetics who wore little or no clothing

gym·no·sperm (jim′nō spurm′, -nə-) *n.* ⟦ModL *gymnospermus* < Gr *gymnospermos*: see GYMNO- & -SPERM⟧ any of a large division (Pinophyta) of seed plants having the ovules borne on open scales, usually in cones, and usually lacking true vessels in the woody tissue, including seed ferns, cycads, conifers, and the ginkgo: see ANGIOSPERM —**gym′no·sper′mous** *adj.* —**gym′no·sper′my** (-ē) *n.*

☆**gym shoe** SNEAKER (sense 2)

GYN *abbrev.* **1** gynecologic(al) **2** gynecologist **3** gynecology Also written Gyn

gyn- (gīn, jin) *combining form* GYNO-: used before a vowel

gyn·ae·ce·um (jin′ə sē′əm, gī′nē-) *n.*, *pl.* **-ce′a** (-ə) ⟦L < Gr *gynaikeion* < *gynaikeios*, of women, feminine < *gynē*, a woman: see GYNO-⟧ **1** in ancient Greek and Roman houses, the section of rooms set apart for women **2** GYNOECIUM

gyn·ae·co- (gī′nə kō′, jin′ə kō′) *combining form* GYNECO-

gy·nan·dro·morph (gī nan′drə môrf′, ji nan′drə môrf′) *n.* ⟦< Gr *gynandros* (see fol.) + -MORPH⟧ an abnormal organism whose physical features are a mixture of male and female characteristics —**gy·nan′dro·mor′phic** *adj.*, **gy·nan′dro·mor′phous** —**gy·nan′dro·mor′phism′** *n.*, **gy·nan′dro·mor′phy**

gy·nan·drous (gī nan′drəs, ji-) *adj.* ⟦Gr *gynandros*, of doubtful sex < *gynē*, a woman (see GYNO-) + *anēr* (gen. *andros*), a man⟧ **1** *Bot.* having the stamen and pistil united in one column, as in the orchids **2** characterized by hermaphroditism

gyn·arch·y (gī′nər kē, jin′ər-) *n.*, *pl.* **-arch·ies** ⟦GYN- + -ARCHY⟧ GYNECOCRACY

gyn·e·co- (gī′nə kō′, jin′ə kō′) ⟦Gr *gynaiko-* < *gynē*, a woman: see GYNO-⟧ *combining form* woman, female [*gynecocracy*]: also, before a vowel, **gynec-**

gyn·e·coc·ra·cy (gī′nə käk′rə sē, jin′ə-) *n.*, *pl.* **-cies** ⟦Gr *gynaikokratia*: see prec. & -CRACY⟧ government by a woman or women

gyn·e·coid (gī′nə koid′, jin′ə-) *adj.* ⟦GYNEC(O)- + -OID⟧ of or characteristic of a woman or women; female

gy·ne·col·o·gy (gī′nə käl′ə jē; *occas.* jin′ə-) *n.* ⟦GYNECO- + -LOGY⟧ the branch of medicine dealing with the study and treatment of the diseases of the female reproductive system, including the breasts —**gy′ne·co·log′i·cal** (-kə läj′i kəl) *adj.*, **gy′ne·co·log′ic** —**gy′ne·col′o·gist** *n.*

gy·ne·co·mas·ti·a (gī′nə kō mas′tē ə) *n.* ⟦< GYNECO- + Gr *mastos*, breast⟧ a condition of overdevelopment of a male's breasts

gyn·e·pho·bi·a (gī′nə fō′bē ə, jin′ə-) *n.* ⟦< Gr *gynē* (see GYNO-) + -PHOBIA⟧ GYNOPHOBIA

gyn·i·at·rics (gī′nē a′triks, jin′ē-) *n.* ⟦< fol. + -IATRICS⟧ the branch of medicine dealing with the treatment of women's diseases

gyn·o- (gī′nō, jin′ō; gī′nə, jin′ə) ⟦< Gr *gynē*, woman < IE **gwenā* > QUEEN⟧ *combining form* **1** woman or female **2** female reproductive organ, ovary, pistil [*gynophore*]

gy·noe·ci·um (ji nē′sē əm, gī-) *n.*, *pl.* **-ci·a** (-ə) ⟦ModL, altered (after Gr *oikos*, house) < L *gynaeceum* < LGr *gynaikeion* < Gr *gynaikeios*, feminine < *gynē*: see prec.⟧ the female organ or organs of a flower; pistil or pistils; the carpels, collectively

gyn·o·pho·bi·a (gī′nō fō′bē ə, jin′ō-; gī′nə-, jin′ə-) *n.* ⟦see GYNEPHOBIA⟧ an abnormal fear of women

gyn·o·phore (gī′nə fôr′, jin′ə-) *n.* ⟦GYNO- + -PHORE⟧ a stalk bearing the gynoecium above the petals and stamens —**gyn′o·phor′ic** *adj.*

-gy·nous (jə nəs) ⟦ModL *-gynus* < Gr *-gynos* < *gynē*, woman: see GYNO-⟧ *combining form forming adjectives* **1** woman or female [*polygynous*] **2** having female organs or pistils as specified [*monogynous, androgynous*]

-gy·ny (jə nē) *combining form forming nouns* **1** the state of having or relating to a (specified) number of women or females at a time [*monogyny*] **2** the state of being located in a (specified) relation to the female organ of a plant

Győr (dyör) city in NW Hungary

☆**gyp**[1] (jip) *n.* ⟦prob. < GYPSY⟧ [Informal] **1** an act of cheating; swindle; fraud **2** a swindler: also **gyp′per** or **gyp′ster** — *vt.*, *vi.* **gypped**, **gyp′ping** [Informal] to swindle; cheat: In all senses often considered offensive

gyp[2] (jip) *n.* ⟦< ? obs. *gippo*, a scullion < Fr *jupeau*, a jacket, jerkin < *jupe* < Ar *jubba*, a long outer garment⟧ [Brit.] a male servant at a college, esp. at Cambridge

gyp·se·ous (jip′sē əs) *adj.* ⟦ME *gipseous* < LL *gypseus* < L *gypsum*⟧ **1** like gypsum **2** containing or consisting of gypsum

gyp·sif·er·ous (jip sif′ər əs) *adj.* ⟦< GYPSUM + -I- + -FEROUS⟧ containing or yielding gypsum

gyp·soph·i·la (jip säf′i lə) *n.* ⟦ModL: see fol. & -PHIL⟧ any of a genus (*Gypsophila*) of plants of the pink family, bearing clusters of small white or pink flowers with a delicate fragrance; baby's breath

gyp·sum (jip′səm) *n.* ⟦ME < L < Gr *gypsos*, chalk, gypsum < Sem⟧ a very soft, monoclinic mineral, $CaSO_4 \cdot 2H_2O$, commonly found with other evaporites in sedimentary rock and used to make plaster of Paris and cement; hydrous calcium sulfate: see MOHS SCALE

gypsum board (*or* wallboard) PLASTERBOARD

Gyp·sy (jip′sē) ***n.***, *pl.* **-sies** ⟦earlier *gypcien*, short for *Egipcien*, Egyptian: orig. thought to have come from Egypt⟧ **1** [*also* **g-**] a member of a nomadic Caucasoid people with dark skin and black hair, found throughout the world and believed to have originated in India: they are conventionally known as metalworkers, musicians, fortunetellers, etc.: now often considered offensive, the word ROM (pl., *Roma*) or ROMANI being preferred **2** ROMANI (*n.* 2) **3** [**g-**] a person whose appearance or habits are like those of a Gypsy **4** ⟦so called by analogy with Gypsies as nomads, because such dancers go from one show to another⟧ [**g-**] a dancer in the chorus of a musical show —***adj.*** **1** [*also* **g-**] of, like, or characteristic of the Gypsies or their language or culture **2** [**g-**] [Informal] unlicensed or nonunion [*a gypsy plumber*] —***vi.*** **-sied, -sy·ing** [**g-**] [Rare] to wander or live like a Gypsy

☆**gypsy cab** [Informal] **1** an unlicensed taxicab operated by an independent driver **2** a licensed taxicab operated by a driver who may respond to telephone calls but may not solicit customers while cruising

gypsy moth a European moth (*Lymantria dispar*), brownish (males) or whitish (females), now common in the E U.S.: its larvae feed on leaves, doing much damage to forest and shade trees

gy·ral (jī′rəl) ***adj.*** ⟦< GYRE + -AL⟧ **1** moving in a circular or spiral path; gyratory **2** of a gyrus

gy·rate (jī′rāt′) ***vi.*** **-rat′ed, -rat′ing** ⟦< L *gyratus*, pp. of *gyrare*, to turn, whirl < *gyrus*, a circle < Gr *gyros* < IE **guros* < base **gēu-*, **gū-*, to bend, arch > COD², COP¹⟧ to move in a circular or spiral path; rotate or revolve on an axis; whirl —***adj.*** spiral, coiled, circular, or convoluted —**gy′ra′tor *n.*** —**gy′ra·to′ry** (-rə tôr′ē) ***adj.***

gy·ra·tion (jī rā′shən) ***n.*** **1** the act of gyrating; circular or spiral motion **2** something gyrate, as a whorl

gyre (jīr) [Old Poet.] ***n.*** ⟦L *gyrus* < Gr *gyros*, a circle: see GYRATE⟧ **1** a circular or spiral motion; whirl; revolution **2** a circular or spiral form; ring or vortex — ***vi., vt.*** **gyred, gyr′ing** to whirl

☆**gy·rene** (jī rēn′) ***n.*** ⟦< ?⟧ [Slang] a member of the U.S. Marine Corps

gyr·fal·con (jur′fôl′kən, -fô′kən; -fal′-) ***n.*** ⟦ME *gerfaucoun* < OFr *girfaucon* < Frank **gerfalko* < **ger* (OHG *gir*, hawk), lit., greedy (one) < IE base **ĝhī*, **ĝhe-* > GAPE + **falko*, FALCON⟧ a large, fierce, strong falcon (*Falco rusticolus*) of the arctic regions

gy·ro¹ (jī′rō′) ***n.*** *short for:* **1** GYROSCOPE **2** GYROCOMPASS

gy·ro² (yir′ō, jir′ō, gir′ō, hyir′ō; jī′rō) ***n.***, *pl.* **-ros** ⟦< ModGr *gyros*, a circle (from rotating meat on a spit), wrongly taken as a pl.⟧ **1** a sort of loaf consisting of layers of lamb or lamb and beef, roasted, as on a vertical spit, and sliced **2** a sandwich consisting of slices of this meat, onions, tomatoes, etc. wrapped in a pita Often **gy·ros** (yir′ôs)

gy·ro- (jī′rō, -rə) ⟦< Gr *gyros*, a circle: see GYRATE⟧ *combining form* **1** gyrating [*gyroscope*] **2** gyroscope [*gyrocompass*] Also, before a vowel, **gyr-**

gy·ro·com·pass (-kum′pəs) ***n.*** a compass consisting of a motor-operated gyroscope whose rotating axis, kept in a horizontal plane, takes a position parallel to the axis of the earth's rotation and thus points to the geographical north pole instead of to the magnetic pole

gyro horizon ARTIFICIAL HORIZON

gy·ro·mag·net·ic (jī′rō mag net′ik) ***adj.*** of or pertaining to the magnetic properties of rotating charged particles

gy·ro·pi·lot (jī′rō pī′lət) ***n.*** AUTOMATIC PILOT

gy·ro·plane (jī′rō plān′) ***n.*** ⟦GYRO- + PLANE²⟧ any aircraft having wings that rotate about a vertical or nearly vertical axis, as the autogiro or helicopter

gy·ro·scope (jī′rō skōp′, -rə-) ***n.*** ⟦GYRO- + -SCOPE⟧ a wheel mounted in a set of rings so that its axis of rotation is free to turn in any direction: when the wheel is spun rapidly, it will keep the original direction of its rotation axis no matter which way the ring is turned: gyroscopes are used in gyrocompasses and to keep moving ships, airplanes, etc. level —**gy′ro·scop′ic** (-skäp′ik) ***adj.*** —**gy′ro·scop′i·cal·ly *adv.***

gy·rose (jī′rōs′) ***adj.*** ⟦< GYRE + -OSE²⟧ *Bot.* marked with wavy lines or convolutions

gy·ro·sta·bi·liz·er (jī′rō stā′bə lī′zər) ***n.*** a device consisting of a gyroscope spinning in a vertical plane, used to stabilize the side-to-side rolling of a ship, spacecraft, etc.

gy·rus (jī′rəs) ***n.***, *pl.* **-ri′** (-rī′) ⟦ModL < L: see GYRE⟧ *Anat.* a convoluted ridge or fold between fissures, or sulci, of the cortex of the brain

Gy Sgt *abbrev.* Gunnery Sergeant

gyve (jīv) ***n., vt.*** **gyved, gyv′ing** ⟦ME *give* < Anglo-Fr *gyves*, pl. < ?⟧ [Archaic] fetter; shackle

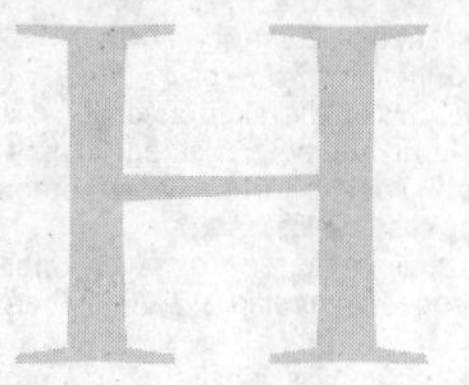

h[1] or H (āch) ***n.***, *pl.* **h's, H's** **1** the eighth letter of the English alphabet: from the Greek *eta*, a borrowing from the Phoenician **2** any of the speech sounds that this letter represents, as, in English, the (h) of *hat* **3** a type or impression for *h* or *H* **4** the eighth in a sequence or group **5** an object shaped like H **—*adj.*** **1** of *h* or *H* **2** eighth in a sequence or group **3** shaped like H

h[2] *abbrev.* hecto-

h[3] *Chem. symbol for* Planck's constant

H[1] *abbrev.* **1** harbor **2** hard **3** hardness **4** height **5** *Physics a)* henry *b)* the horizontal component of terrestrial magnetism **6** [Slang] heroin **7** high **8** *Baseball* hit(s) **9** hot (on water faucets) **10** hour(s) **11** hundred(s) **12** husband **13** husky (width in boys' garments) Also, for 2-4, 5*b*, 7, 8, 10, & 12, **h**

H[2] *abbrev.* ⟦L⟧ *Anthrop.* HOMO[1]

H[3] *Chem. symbol for* hydrogen

H_0 *symbol* Hubble constant

ha[1] (hä) ***interj.*** ⟦echoic⟧ used variously to express surprise, wonder, triumph, anger, etc. **—*n.*** the sound of this exclamation or of a laugh

ha[2] *abbrev.* hectare(s)

Ha *Chem. symbol for* hahnium

h.a. *abbrev.* ⟦L *hoc anno*⟧ in this year

Haa·kon VII (hô′ko͞on) 1872-1957; king of Norway (1905-57)

Haar·lem (här′ləm) city in NW Netherlands: capital of North Holland province

Haar·lem·mer·meer (här′lə mər mer′) city in NW Netherlands, on the site of a former lake

Ha·bak·kuk (hab′ə kuk′, hə bak′ək) ***n.*** ⟦Heb *Ḥabhaqqūq*, prob. < *ḥābaq*, to embrace⟧ *Bible* **1** a Hebrew prophet of *c.* 7th cent. B.C. **2** the book containing his prophecies: abbrev. *Hab* or *Hb*

Ha·ba·na (ä bä′nä), **(La)** *Sp. name for* HAVANA[2]

ha·ba·ne·ra (hä′bə ner′ə; *Sp* ä′bä nā′rä) ***n.*** ⟦< Sp *danza habanera*, dance in the style of Havana < *danza*, a dance + *habanera*, fem. of *habanero*: see fol.⟧ **1** a slow Cuban dance similar to the tango **2** the music for this

ha·ba·ne·ro (ä′bä ner′ō) ***n.***, *pl.* **-ros** ⟦< MexSp *chile habanero* < Sp *chile*, chili (pepper) + *habanero*, of HAVANA[2]⟧ a kind of chili pepper that is small, orange when ripe, and extremely hot: it is used esp. in Latin American cooking: in full **habanero pepper**

ha·be·as cor·pus (hā′bē əs kôr′pəs) ⟦ME < L, (that) you have the body⟧ *Law* any of various writs ordering a person to be brought before a court; specif., a writ requiring that a detained person be brought before a court to decide the legality of the detention or imprisonment

Ha·ber (hä′bər), **Fritz** (frits) 1868-1934; Ger. chemist

hab·er·dash·er (hab′ər dash′ər, hab′ə-) ***n.*** ⟦ME *haberdashere*, prob. < Anglo-Fr *hapertas*, kind of cloth⟧ **1** a person whose work or business is selling men's accessories, such as hats, shirts, neckties, and gloves **2** [Brit.] a dealer in various small articles, such as ribbons, thread, and needles

hab·er·dash·er·y (-ər ē) ***n.***, *pl.* **-er·ies** ⟦ME *haberdasshrie*⟧ **1** things sold by a haberdasher **2** a haberdasher's shop

hab·er·geon (hab′ər jən) ***n.*** ⟦ME *habergoun* < OFr *haubergeon*, dim. of *hauberc*: see HAUBERK⟧ **1** a short, high-necked jacket of mail, usually sleeveless **2** HAUBERK

hab·ile (hab′il) ***adj.*** ⟦ME *habil* < OFr *habile* < L *habilis* < base of *habere*: see HABIT⟧ [Now Rare] able; skillful; handy; clever

ha·bil·i·ment (hə bil′ə mənt) ***n.*** ⟦MFr *habillement* < *habiller*, to clothe, make fit < *habile*: see prec.⟧ **1** [*usually pl.*] clothing; dress; attire **2** [*pl.*] furnishings or equipment; trappings

ha·bil·i·tate (hə bil′ə tāt′) ***vt.*** **-tat′ed, -tat′ing** ⟦< ML *habilitatus*, pp. of *habilitare*, to make suitable < L *habilis*: see HABILE⟧ **1** to clothe; equip; outfit **2** [Archaic] to train; make capable **3** *Mining* to provide (a mine) with the capital and equipment needed to work it **—ha·bil′i·ta′tion *n.*** **—ha·bil′i·ta′tive *adj.***

hab·it (hab′it) ***n.*** ⟦ME < OFr < L *habitus*, condition, appearance, dress < pp. of *habere*, to have, hold < IE base **ghabh-*, to grasp, take > GIVE⟧ **1** [Obs.] costume; dress **2** a particular costume showing rank, status, etc.; specif., *a)* a distinctive religious costume [*a monk's habit*] *b)* a costume worn for certain occasions [*a riding habit*] **3** habitual or characteristic condition of mind or body; disposition **4** *a)* a thing done often and hence, usually, done easily; practice; custom *b)* a pattern of action that is acquired and has become so automatic that it is difficult to break **5** a tendency to perform a certain action or behave in a certain way; usual way of doing something **6** an addiction, esp. to narcotics **7** *Biol.* the tendency of a plant or animal to grow in a certain way; characteristic growth [*a twining habit*] **—*vt.*** **1** [Now Rare] to dress; clothe **2** [Archaic] to inhabit

SYN.—**habit** refers to an act repeated so often by an individual that it has become automatic [*his habit of tugging at his ear*]; **practice** also implies the regular repetition of an act but does not suggest that it is automatic [*the practice of reading in bed*]; **custom** applies to any act or procedure carried on by tradition and often enforced by social disapproval of any violation [*the custom of dressing for dinner*]; **usage** refers to custom or practice that has become sanctioned through being long established [*usage is a chief authority in language*]; **wont** is a literary or somewhat archaic equivalent for **practice** [*it was his wont to rise early*]

hab·it·a·ble (hab′it ə bəl) ***adj.*** ⟦ME < OFr < L *habitabilis* < *habitare*, to have possession of, inhabit: see prec. & -ABLE⟧ that can be inhabited; fit to be lived in **—hab′it·a·bil′i·ty *n.*** **—hab′it·a·bly *adv.***

hab·it·ant (hab′i tənt; *for 2* hab′i tänt′ *or* å bē tän′) ***n.*** ⟦Fr < L *habitans*, prp.: see prec.⟧ **1** an inhabitant; resident **2** a farmer in Louisiana or Canada of French descent: also **ha·bi·tan** (å bē tän′)

hab·i·tat (hab′i tat′) ***n.*** ⟦L, it inhabits: see HABITABLE⟧ **1** the region where a plant or animal naturally grows or lives; native environment **2** the place where a person or thing is ordinarily found

hab·i·ta·tion (hab′i tā′shən) ***n.*** ⟦ME *habitacioun* < OFr *habitacion* < L *habitatio*: see HABITABLE⟧ **1** the act of inhabiting; occupancy **2** a place in which to live; dwelling; home **3** a colony or settlement

hab·it-form·ing (hab′it fôr′miŋ) ***adj.*** resulting in the formation of a habit or in addiction

ha·bit·u·al (hə bich′o͞o əl) ***adj.*** ⟦ML *habitualis*, of habit or dress: see HABIT⟧ **1** formed or acquired by continual use; done by habit or fixed as a habit; customary **2** being or doing a certain thing by habit; steady; inveterate [*a habitual smoker*] **3** much seen, done, or used; usual; frequent **—*SYN.*** USUAL **—ha·bit′u·al·ly *adv.*** **—ha·bit′u·al·ness *n.***

ha·bit·u·ate (hə bich′o͞o āt′) ***vt.*** **-at′ed, -at′ing** ⟦< LL *habituatus*, pp. of *habituare*, to bring into a condition or habit of the body < L *habitus*: see HABIT⟧ **1** to make used (*to*); accustom: often used reflexively [*to habituate oneself to the cold*] ☆**2** [Archaic] to frequent **—*vi.*** to cause addiction **—ha·bit′u·a′tion *n.***

hab·i·tude (hab′i to͞od′, -tyo͞od′) ***n.*** ⟦ME *abitude* < MFr *habitude* < L *habitudo*, condition, habit: see HABIT⟧ **1** habitual or characteristic condition of mind or body; disposition **2** usual way of doing something; custom

ha·bit·u·é (hə bich′o͞o ā′, hə bich′o͞o ā′) ***n.*** ⟦Fr < pp. of *habituer*, to accustom < LL *habituare*: see HABITUATE⟧ a person who frequents a certain place or places [*a habitué of downtown nightclubs*]

hab·i·tus (hab′i təs) ***n.***, *pl.* **-tus** (-təs) ⟦ModL < L, HABIT⟧ **1** HABIT (***n.*** 5 & 7) **2** general physical build and constitution, often, esp. formerly, as related to a predisposition to certain diseases

ha·boob (hə bo͞ob′) ***n.*** ⟦< Ar *habūb*, blowing violently⟧ a violent sandstorm, as in the Sudan or SW U.S.

Habs·burg (haps′burg′; *Ger* häps′bo͝orkh) ***n.*** name of a European dynasty (1278-1918) that ruled the former kingdom of Austria from 1278 and, subsequently, the Holy Roman Empire (1438-1806), Spain (1516-1700), and Austria-Hungary (1867-1918)

ha·ček (hä′chek) ***n.*** ⟦Czech, lit., little hook⟧ a mark (ˇ) used over certain consonant letters in the orthography of some languages to indicate a specific sound, or used in certain systems of symbols for representing speech sounds

ha·cen·da·do (hä′sen dä′dō) ***n.***, *pl.* **-dos** ⟦Sp < *hacienda*, estate: see HACIENDA⟧ the owner or manager of a hacienda: also **ha·ci·en·da·do** (hä′ sē en dä′dō)

Ha·chi·o·ji (häch′ē ō′jē) city in EC Honshu, Japan

ha·chure (ha sho͞or′, hash′yo͝or′, hash′o͝or′; *for v.* ha sho͞or′) ***n.*** ⟦Fr < OFr *hacher*, to chop < *hache*, ax < Frank **hapja*, sickle < IE base **(s)kep-* > SHAFT, L *capo*, capon, Gr *koptein*, to chop⟧ any of a series of short parallel lines used, esp. in map making, to represent a sloping or elevated surface **—*vt.*** **-chured′, -chur′ing** to show by, or shade with, hachures

☆**ha·ci·en·da** (hä′sē en′də, has′ē-) ***n.*** ⟦Sp < OSp *facienda*, employment, estate < L, things to be done < *facere*: see DO[1]⟧ in Spanish America, *a)* a large estate, ranch, or plantation *b)* the main dwelling on any of these

hack[1] (hak) ***vt.*** ⟦ME *hacken* < OE *haccian*, akin to Ger *hacken* < IE base **keg-*, peg, hook > HOOK, HATCHEL⟧ **1** *a)* to chop or cut crudely, roughly, or irregularly, as with a hatchet *b)* to shape, trim, damage, etc. with or as with rough, sweeping strokes **2** to break up (land) as with a hoe or mattock ☆**3** [Slang] to deal with or carry out successfully ☆**4** [Slang] to annoy or irritate: usually with *off* **5** [Slang] *Sports* to foul (an opponent) roughly

—*vi.* 1 to make rough or irregular cuts 2 to give harsh, dry coughs —*n.* 1 a tool for cutting or hacking, as an ax, hoe, mattock, etc. 2 a slash, gash, or notch made by a sharp implement 3 a hacking blow 4 a harsh, dry cough —☆**hack around** [Informal] to engage in aimless activity; spend time idly —☆**hack it** [Slang] to carry out or manage something successfully

hack[2] (hak) *n.* ⟦contr. < HACKNEY⟧ 1 *a)* a horse for hire *b)* a horse for all sorts of work *c)* a saddle horse *d)* an old, worn-out horse 2 a person hired to do routine, often dull, writing ☆3 a worker for a political party, usually holding office through patronage and serving devotedly and unquestioningly 4 a carriage or coach for hire 5 [Informal] *a)* a taxicab *b)* a hackman or cabdriver —*vt.* 1 to employ as a hack 2 to hire out (a horse, etc.) 3 to wear out or make stale by constant use 4 *Comput.* to gain unauthorized access to (a file, network, etc.) [*to hack a company's personnel records*] —*vi.* 1 [Brit.] to jog along on a horse ☆2 [Informal] to drive a taxicab 3 *Comput.* to be a HACKER[2]; specif., to gain unauthorized access (*into* a particular file, network, etc.) [*to hack into a company's personnel files*] —*adj.* 1 employed as a hack [*a hack writer*] 2 done by a hack [*a hack job*] 3 stale; trite; hackneyed [*hack writing*]

hack[3] (hak) *n.* ⟦orig., board on which a falcon's meat was put, var. of HATCH[2]⟧ a grating or rack for drying cheese or fish, holding food for cattle, etc. —*vt.* to place on a hack for drying

☆**hack·a·more** (hak′ə môr′) *n.* ⟦altered < Sp *jáquima*, halter < Ar *shakīma*⟧ [West] a rope or rawhide halter with a headstall, used in breaking horses

hack·ber·ry (hak′ber′ē) *n., pl.* **-ries** ⟦< Scand, as in Dan *hæggebær*, Norw *haggebär*, ON *heggr*: for IE base see HEDGE⟧ ☆1 any of a genus (*Celtis*) of American trees of the elm family, with a small fruit resembling a cherry ☆2 its fruit or its wood

hack·but (hak′but′) *n.* ⟦Fr *haquebut* < obs. Du *hakebus* < *hake, haak*, HOOK + *bus*, a gun, gun barrel: so named from method of support during firing⟧ a kind of harquebus

hack·er[1] (hak′ər) *n.* ⟦HACK[1] + -ER⟧ 1 a person who hacks (see HACK[1]) ☆2 an unskilled golfer, tennis player, etc.

hack·er[2] (hak′ər) *n.* ⟦HACK[2] + -ER⟧ 1 an adept or highly skilled computer enthusiast or programmer 2 a computer user who attempts to gain unauthorized access to files in various systems

☆**hack·ie** (hak′ē) *n.* ⟦see HACK[2]⟧ [Informal] a taxicab driver

hacking jacket ⟦< HACK[2], *vi.* 1⟧ a jacket worn by horseback riders, usually with slanting pockets and side or rear vents

hack·le[1] (hak′əl) *n.* ⟦ME *hechele* (akin to Ger *hechel*) < OE **hæcel* < IE base **keg-*, a peg, hook > HACK[1], HOOK: senses 2, 3, & 4, prob. infl. by dial. *hackle*, bird's plumage, animal's skin < OE *hacele*⟧ 1 a comblike instrument for separating the fibers of flax, hemp, etc. 2 *a)* any of the long, slender feathers at the neck of a rooster, peacock, pigeon, etc. *b)* such feathers, collectively 3 *Fishing a)* a tuft of feathers from a rooster's neck, used in making artificial flies *b)* a fly made with a hackle 4 [*pl.*] the hairs on a dog's neck and back that bristle, as when the dog is ready to fight —*vt.* **-led, -ling** 1 to separate the fibers of (flax, hemp, etc.) with a hackle 2 [Rare] to supply (a fishing fly) with a hackle —**get one's hackles up** to become tense with anger; bristle

hack·le[2] (hak′əl) *vt., vi.* **-led, -ling** ⟦freq. of HACK[1]⟧ to cut roughly; hack; mangle

☆**hack·man** (hak′mən) *n., pl.* **-men** (-mən) the driver of a hack or carriage for hire

☆**hack·ma·tack** (hak′mə tak′) *n.* ⟦< AmInd (Algonquian)⟧ 1 TAMARACK 2 BALSAM POPLAR 3 the wood of these trees

hack·ney (hak′nē) *n., pl.* **-neys** ⟦ME *hakene, hakenei*, after *Hakeney* (now *Hackney*), England⟧ 1 a horse for ordinary driving or riding 2 a carriage for hire 3 [Obs.] a drudge —*adj.* [Obs.] 1 hired out 2 trite; commonplace

Hack·ney (hak′nē) borough of Greater London, England

hack·neyed (-nēd′) *adj.* ⟦pp. of archaic v. *hackney*, hire out, make trite: see HACKNEY⟧ made trite by overuse —*SYN.* TRITE

hack·saw (hak′sô′) *n.* a saw for cutting metal, consisting of a narrow, fine-toothed blade held in a frame: also written **hack saw**

hack·work (hak′wurk′) *n.* routine, often dull, writing done by a HACK[2] (*n.* 2)

had (had) *vt.* ⟦ME *hadde, had* < OE *hæfde*⟧ *pt. & pp. of* HAVE: also used to indicate preference or necessity, with adverbs, adjectives, and phrases of comparison, such as *rather, better, as well* (Ex.: I *had* better leave) —**to be had** ☆[Slang] to be deceived or taken in [*we've been had in that business deal*]

ha·dal (hād′'l) *adj.* ⟦Fr < *Hadès*, Hades + *-al*, -AL⟧ designating or of the ecological zone (**hadal zone**) of the ocean floor trenches below *c.* 19,685 ft (*c.* 6,000 m)

ha·dar·im (khä′dä rēm′) *n. pl. of* HEDER

had·dock (had′ək) *n., pl.* **-dock** or **-docks** ⟦ME *hadok* < ?⟧ an edible gadoid fish (*Melanogrammus aeglefinus*) found off the coasts of Europe and North America

hade (hād) *n.* ⟦< dial. *hade*, to slope, incline < ?⟧ *Geol.* the angle between the plane of a fault or vein and the vertical plane —*vi.* **had′ed, had′ing** *Geol.* to incline from the vertical plane, as a fault, vein, or lode

Ha·de·an (hā′dē ən, hā dē′ən) *adj.* ⟦< fol.: by analogy with the fires and chaos of hell, as described in Christian tradition⟧ [*sometimes* **h-**] designating or of the time on earth when the solar system was forming and the earth was still in a molten state; Precambrian, esp. early Precambrian —**the Hadean** the Hadean time period: see the geologic time chart in the Reference Supplement

Ha·des (hā′dēz′) *n.* ⟦Gr *Haidēs*⟧ 1 *Gr. Myth. a)* the home of the dead, beneath the earth *b)* the god of the underworld 2 *Bible* the state or resting place of the dead: name used in some modern translations of the New Testament 3 [*often* **h-**] hell: a euphemism

Ha·dhra·maut or **Ha·dra·maut** (hä′drä môt′) 1 region on the S coast of Arabia, on the Gulf of Aden: *c.* 58,500 sq mi (151,514 sq km) 2 river valley (**Wadi Hadhramaut**) that crosses this region: *c.* 400 mi (644 km)

ha·dith (hə dēth′) *n., pl.* **-dith′** or **-diths′** ⟦Ar⟧ *Islam* 1 [*often* **H-**] a traditional collection of the sayings of, and biographical anecdotes about, Muhammad 2 any of these sayings or anecdotes

hadj (haj, häj) *n. alt. sp. of* HAJJ

hadj·i (haj′ē, hä′jē) *n. alt. sp. of* HAJJI

Had·ley cell (had′lē) ⟦after George *Hadley* (1685-1768), Eng meteorologist⟧ *Meteorol.* an atmospheric convection pattern in which a current of hot equatorial air rises, divides, cools as it moves toward the poles, descends, and warms as it returns to the equator

had·n't (had′'nt) *contraction* had not

Ha·dri·an (hā′drē ən) (L. name *Publius Aelius Hadrianus*) A.D. 76-138; Rom. emperor (117-138)

Hadrian's Wall stone wall across N England, from Solway Firth to the Tyne: built (A.D. 122-128) by Hadrian to protect Roman Britain from N tribes: 73.5 mi (118.3 km)

had·ron (had′rän′) *n.* ⟦Gr *hadros*, thick, strong + -ON⟧ *Particle Physics* any of a class of subatomic particles, including the proton, neutron, meson, and hyperon, that consist of a combination of quarks and antiquarks: see also STRONG INTERACTION —**had·ron·ic** (ha drän′ik, hə-) *adj.*

had·ro·saur (had′rə sôr′) *n.* ⟦< ModL *Hadrosaurus*, genus name < Gr *hadros*, thick, stout + -SAURUS⟧ any of a family (Hadrosauridae) of large, duck-billed ornithopod dinosaurs of the Cretaceous Period: also **had′ro·sau′rus**

hadst (hadst) *vt. archaic 2d pers. sing., past indic., of* HAVE: used with *thou*

hae (hā, ha) *vt.* [Scot.] to have

haec·ce·i·ty (hek sē′ə tē) *n.* ⟦ML *haecceitas* < L *haec*, fem. of *hic*, this + *-itas*, -ITY⟧ *Philos.* the condition of being a uniquely particular person or thing; individuality

Haeck·el (hek′əl), **Ernst Hein·rich** (ernst hīn′riH) 1834-1919; Ger. biologist & philosopher

haem·a·to- (hem′ə tō, hē′mə-; -tə) *combining form* HEMATO-: also, before a vowel, **haemat-**

hae·ma·tox·y·lon (hē′mə täk′sə län′, hem′ə-) *n.* ⟦ModL < prec. + Gr *xylon*, wood⟧ *var. of* HEMATOXYLIN

-hae·mi·a (hē′mē ə) *combining form* -EMIA

hae·mo- (hē′mō, -mə; hem′ō, -ə) *combining form* HEMO-: also **hae·ma-** or, before a vowel, **haem-**

ha·fiz (hä′fiz′) *n.* ⟦Ar *ḥāfiẓ*, a person who remembers⟧ a Muslim who has memorized the Koran: a title of honor

Ha·fiz (hä fiz′) (born *Shams-ud-Din Mohammed*) 1325?-90?; Pers. lyric poet

haf·ni·um (haf′nē əm) *n.* ⟦ModL: so named (1923) by D. Coster (1889-1950), Du chemist, and G. C. de Hevesy (*c.* 1889-1966), Hung chemist, after *Hafnia*, Latinized name of Dan *København*, COPENHAGEN (where it was discovered) + -IUM⟧ a metallic chemical element found with, and similar to, zirconium: used in the manufacture of light-bulb filaments and in reactor control rods: symbol, Hf; at. no. 72: see the periodic table of elements in the Reference Supplement

haft (haft, häft) *n.* ⟦ME < OE *hæft*, a handle < base of *hebban*: see HEAVE⟧ a handle or hilt of a knife, ax, etc. —*vt.* to fit with, or fix in, a haft

haf·ta·ra or **haf·to·rah** (häf′tə rä′, häf tôr′ə) *n. alt. sp. of* HAPHTARA

hag[1] (hag) *n.* ⟦ME *hagge*, a witch, hag, contr. < OE *hægtes* < *haga*, hedge, akin to Ger *hexe* (OHG *hagazussa*): sense comparable to ON *tūnritha*, lit., hedge rider, hence witch⟧ 1 [Obs.] a female demon or evil spirit 2 [Archaic] a witch; enchantress 3 an ugly, often vicious, old woman 4 HAGFISH

hag[2] (hag, häg) [Scot. or North Eng.] *vt.* ⟦Scot < ME *haggen* < Anglo-N form of ON *höggva*, to cut, hack, akin to OE *heawan*, HEW⟧ to cut; hack —*n.* ⟦< Anglo-N form of ON *högg*, a cutting, chopping < base of the vt.⟧ 1 *a)* a cutting of wood *b)* felled trees 2 *a)* the edge of a cutting in a peat bog *b)* a marsh or marshy spot *c)* a firm spot in a bog or marsh

Hag *abbrev. Bible* Haggai

Ha·gar (hā′gär′, -gər) *n.* ⟦Heb *Hāghār*, lit., prob. fugitive < ? base akin to Ar *hajara*, to forsake: see HEGIRA⟧ 1 a feminine and masculine name 2 *Bible* a concubine of Abraham and slave of Abraham's wife Sarah: see also ISHMAEL

Ha·gat·na (hə gät′nyə) capital of Guam: also sp. **Hagåtña**

Ha·gen[1] (hä′gən) *n.* ⟦Ger⟧ in the *Nibelungenlied*, Gunther's uncle, who murders Siegfried at Brunhild's bidding

Ha·gen[2] (hä′gən) city in W Germany, in the Ruhr valley, in the state of North Rhine-Westphalia

hag·fish (hag′fish′) *n., pl.* **-fish′** or **-fish′es** (see FISH) ⟦HAG[1] + FISH⟧ any of an order (Myxiniformes) of small, marine, eel-like jawless fishes, with a round, sucking mouth and horny teeth

Hag·ga·da (hä′gä dä′, hə gä′də) *n., pl.* **-ga·dot′** (-dōt′) or **Hag·ga′das** ⟦TalmudHeb *hagada* < *higid*, to tell, relate < root *ngd*, to oppose⟧ 1 AGGADA 2 *a)* a narrative of the Exodus read at the Seder during Passover *b)* a book containing this narrative and the Seder ritual Also sp. **Hag′ga·dah′**, *pl.* **-ga·dot′** or **Hag·ga′dahs** —**hag·gad·ic** (hə gad′ik, -gä′dik) *adj.*

hag·ga·dist (hə gä′dist) *n.* a haggadic writer or scholar —**hag·ga·dis·tic** (hag′ə dis′tik) *adj.*

Hag·ga·i (hag′ā ī′, hag′ī′) *n.* ⟦Heb *Ḥaggai*, lit., festal⟧ *Bible* 1 a Hebrew prophet of *c.* 6th cent. B.C. 2 the book of his prophecies: abbrev. *Hag* or Hg

hag·gard (hag′ərd) *adj.* ⟦MFr *hagard,* untamed, untamed hawk⟧ **1** *Falconry* designating a hawk captured after reaching maturity **2** untamed; unruly; wild **3** *a)* wild-eyed *b)* having a wild, wasted, worn look, as from sleeplessness, grief, or illness; gaunt; drawn —*n. Falconry* a haggard hawk —**hag′gard·ly** *adv.* —**hag′gard·ness** *n.*

Hag·gard (hag′ərd), Sir **H(enry) Rider** 1856-1925; Eng. writer, esp. of adventure novels

hag·gis (hag′is) *n.* ⟦ME *hagas,* kind of pudding < ? *haggen,* HAG[2]⟧ a Scottish dish made of the lungs, heart, etc. of a sheep or calf, mixed with suet, seasoning, and oatmeal and boiled in the animal's stomach

hag·gish (hag′ish) *adj.* of, like, or characteristic of a hag —**hag′gish·ly** *adv.* —**hag′gish·ness** *n.*

hag·gle (hag′əl) *vi.* **-gled, -gling** ⟦freq. of HAG[2]⟧ to argue about terms, price, etc.; bargain; wrangle —*n.* the act of haggling —**hag′gler** *n.*

hag·i·arch·y (hag′ē är′kē, hā′jē-) *n., pl.* **-arch′ies** ⟦< fol. + -ARCHY⟧ HAGIOCRACY

hag·i·o- (hag′ē ō′, hā′jē ō′; -ə) ⟦< Gr *hagios,* holy⟧ *combining form* **1** saint [*hagiocracy*] **2** sacred, holy [*hagiographer*] Also, before a vowel, **hag·i-**

hag·i·oc·ra·cy (hag′ē äk′rə sē, hā′jē-) *n., pl.* **-cies** ⟦prec. + -CRACY⟧ rule by priests, saints, or others considered holy; theocracy

Hag·i·og·ra·pha (hag′ē äg′rə fə, hā′jē-) *n.* ⟦LL(Ec) < Gr(Ec) *hagiographa (biblia),* transl. of Heb *ketuvim,* lit., writings: see HAGIO- & -GRAPH⟧ the third and final part of the Jewish Scriptures, those books not in the Law or the Prophets

hag·i·og·ra·pher (hag′ē äg′rə fər, hā′jē-) *n.* **1** any of the authors of the Hagiographa **2** a writer of hagiography

hag·i·o·graph·ic (hag′ē ə graf′ik, hā′jē-) *adj.* **1** of hagiography or the Hagiographa **2** idealizing its subject: said of a biography Also **hag′i·o·graph′i·cal**

hag·i·og·ra·phy (hag′ē äg′rə fē, hā′jē-) *n., pl.* **-phies** ⟦HAGIO- + -GRAPHY⟧ **1** a book or writing, or an assemblage of these, about the lives of saints **2** such books or writings as a field of study **3** a biography or biographical writing that idealizes its subject

hag·i·ol·o·gy (hag′ē äl′ə jē, hā′jē-) *n., pl.* **-gies** ⟦HAGIO- + -LOGY⟧ HAGIOGRAPHY —**hag′i·o·log′ic** (-ə läj′ik) *adj.,* **hag′i·o·log′i·cal**

hag·i·o·scope (hag′ē ə skōp′, hā′jē-) *n.* ⟦HAGIO- + -SCOPE⟧ a narrow opening in an inside wall of a medieval church to let those in a side aisle, or transept, see the main altar

hag·rid·den (hag′rid″n) *adj.* ⟦HAG[1] + RIDDEN⟧ **1** [Obs.] obsessed by a hag, or witch **2** obsessed or harassed, as by fears

Hague (hāg), **The** city in W Netherlands: seat of the government (cf. AMSTERDAM); capital of South Holland province: Du. name 'S GRAVENHAGE

Hague Tribunal the Permanent Court of Arbitration founded in 1899: it selects the nominees for election to the International Court of Justice

hah (hä) *interj., n. alt. sp. of* HA[1]

ha-ha[1] (hä′hä′, hä′hä′) *interj.* used to suggest the sound of laughter, in expressing variously humor, joy, derision, etc. —*n.* this sound

ha-ha[2] (hä′hä′) *n.* ⟦Fr *haha* < ?⟧ a fence, wall, etc. set in a ditch around a garden or park so as not to hide the view from within: also written **haha**

Hahn (hän), **Otto** 1879-1968; Ger. nuclear physicist

Hah·ne·mann (hä′nə mən), **(Christian Friedrich) Samuel** 1755-1843; Ger. physician: founder of homeopathy

☆**hahn·i·um** (hä′nē əm) *n.* ⟦after Otto HAHN⟧ DUBNIUM: symbol, Ha: the name originally proposed by American scientists for this element

hai (hī) *adv., interj.* ⟦Jpn⟧ yes

Hai·da (hī′dä′, -də) *n.* ⟦a self-designation, lit., people⟧ **1** *pl.* **-das′** or **-da′** a member of a North American Indian people living mainly on islands of British Columbia and Alaska **2** the language of this people, of uncertain relationship but thought by some scholars to be distantly related to Tlingit and the Athabaskan languages —*adj.* of the Haidas or their language or culture

Hai·fa (hī′fə) seaport in NW Israel, on the Mediterranean

Haig (hāg), **Douglas** 1st Earl Haig 1861-1928; Brit. commander in chief, WWI

haik (hīk, hāk) *n.* ⟦Ar *ḥāyk* < *ḥāka,* to weave⟧ a sheetlike, woolen or cotton cloth worn by Arabs as an outer garment

Hai·kou (hī′kō′) city in S China, on Hainan island; capital of Hainan province

hai·ku (hī′ko͞o′) *n.* ⟦Jpn⟧ **1** a Japanese verse form, rendered in English as three unrhymed lines of 5, 7, and 5 syllables respectively (total 17 syllables), often on some subject in nature **2** *pl.* **-ku′** a poem in this form

hail[1] (hāl) *vt.* ⟦ME *hailen,* to salute, greet < *hail, heil,* sound, healthy < ON *heill,* whole, sound, akin to OE *hal* (see HALE[1], WHOLE): used as a salutation, approximately, may you be well⟧ **1** to welcome, greet, etc. with or as with cheers; acclaim **2** to name by way of tribute; salute as [they *hailed* him their leader] **3** to call out to or signal to, as in summoning or greeting [to *hail* a taxi] —*n.* **1** the act of hailing or greeting **2** the distance that a shout will carry [within *hail*] —*interj.* used to signify tribute, greeting, etc. —**hail fellow well met** very sociable or friendly to everyone, esp. in a superficial manner: also **hail fellow** or **hail-fellow** —**hail from** to be from; come from (one's birthplace or established residence) —**hail′er** *n.*

hail[2] (hāl) *n.* ⟦ME *haile* < OE *hægel,* var. of *hagol,* akin to Ger *hagel* < IE base **kaghlo-,* small pebble > Gr *kachlēx*⟧ **1** precipitation in the form of pellets of ice larger than 5 mm (.2 in), associated with cumulonimbus clouds: see also SLEET **2** a falling, showering, etc. of hail, or in the manner of hail [a *hail* of bullets] —*vi.* ⟦ME *hailen* < OE *hagalian*⟧ to drop or pour down hail: usually in an impersonal construction [it is *hailing*] —*vt.* to shower, hurl, pour, etc. violently in the manner of hail: often with *on* or *upon* [to *hail* curses on someone]

☆**hail Columbia** ⟦euphemism for HELL, with pun on *hail;* "Hail Columbia" was the former U.S. national anthem⟧ [Old Slang] a severe beating, punishment, scolding, etc.

Hai·le Se·las·sie (hī′lē sə las′ē, -läs′ē) (born *Tafari Makonnen*) 1892-1975; emperor of Ethiopia (1930-36; 1941-74): deposed

Hail Mary (hāl, hal) *pl.* **Hail Mar′ys** ⟦see AVE MARIA⟧ **1** *a)* the first words of the English version of a prayer to the Virgin Mary used in the Roman Catholic Church *b)* this prayer ☆**2** *Football* a long pass thrown into the end zone, as in the final seconds of a game, in the desperate hope that one of the receivers will be able to catch it for a touchdown

hail·stone (hāl′stōn′) *n.* ⟦ME *hawelston*⟧ a pellet of hail

hail·storm (-stôrm′) *n.* a storm in which hail falls

haim·ish (hām′ish, hīm′-) *adj.* ⟦Yiddish < Ger *heimisch,* homelike, domestic: see HOME & -ISH⟧ having qualities associated with the home; simple, warm, relaxed, cozy, unpretentious, etc.

Hai·nan (hī′nän′) island province of China, in the South China Sea: 13,243 sq mi (34,299 sq km); cap. Haikou

Hai·naut (e nō′) province of SW Belgium: 1,462 sq mi (3,787 sq km); cap. Mons

Hai·phong (hī′fäŋ′) seaport in N Vietnam, in the delta of the Red River

hair (her, har) *n.* ⟦ME *here* < OE *hær* (akin to Ger *haar,* Frank **harja*) & < ? OFr *haire,* hair shirt < Frank **harja* < IE base **k̑er(s)-,* to bristle⟧ **1** any of the fine, threadlike outgrowths from the skin of an animal or human being **2** a growth of these; esp., *a)* the growth covering the human head *b)* the growth covering all or part of the skin of most mammals **3** material woven from hair **4** an extremely small space, margin, degree, etc. [to miss by a *hair*] **5** *Bot.* a threadlike growth on a plant; trichome —*adj.* **1** made of or with hair **2** for the care of the hair [*hair* tonic] —☆**get in someone's hair** [Slang] to annoy someone —**hair of the dog (that bit one)** [Informal] a drink of alcoholic liquor taken as a supposed remedy for a hangover —**have (or get) by the short hairs** ⟦< *short hairs,* pubic hair⟧ [Slang] to have (or get) completely at one's mercy: mildly vulgar —**let one's hair down** [Slang] to be very informal, relaxed, and free in behavior —**make someone's hair stand on end** ⟦in ref. to HORRIPILATION⟧ to terrify or horrify someone —**not turn a hair** to show no fear, surprise, embarrassment, etc.; stay calm and unruffled —**split hairs** to make petty distinctions; quibble —**to a hair** exactly; right in every detail —**hair′like′** *adj.*

hair·ball (her′bôl′) *n.* a rounded mass of partially digested hair forming in the stomach or intestines of cats and certain other animals that lick their coat

hair·brained (her′brānd′) *adj.* ⟦by folk etym. after HAREBRAINED⟧ *var. of* HAREBRAINED

hair·breadth (-bredth′) *n.* an extremely small space or amount —*adj.* very narrow; close [a *hairbreadth* escape]

hair·brush (-brush′) *n.* a brush for grooming the hair

hair cell any of the nerve cells of the inner ear having groups of projecting, hairlike receptors that are sensitive to vibrations and sound waves: see also ORGAN OF CORTI

hair·cloth (-klôth′) *n.* cloth woven from horsehair, camel's hair, etc., now used mainly for covering furniture

hair·cut (-kut′) *n.* **1** a cutting or clipping of the hair of the head **2** the style in which the hair is cut **3** [Informal] a financial loss, esp. a substantial one: often in the phrase **take a haircut** —**hair′cut′ter** *n.*

☆**hair·do** (-do͞o′) *n., pl.* **-dos′** the style in which hair is arranged; coiffure

hair·dress·er (-dres′ər) *n.* a person whose work is styling hair —**hair′dress′ing** *n., adj.*

-haired (herd) *combining form* having (a specified kind of) hair [fair-*haired,* short-*haired*]

hair·less (her′lis) *adj.* **1** having little or no hair [a breed of *hairless* dog] **2** having lost the hair; bald

hair·line (her′līn′) *n.* **1** [Historical] a line, cord, etc. made of hair **2** a very thin line **3** *a)* a very thin stripe *b)* cloth patterned with such stripes **4** a very narrow margin or degree of difference **5** the outline of the hair on the head, esp. of the hair above the forehead **6** *Printing* a very thin stroke on a typeface or impression —*adj.* of or characterized by a tiny crack or small difference

hair·net (her′net′) *n.* a net or fine-meshed cap of silk, etc., for covering the hair or keeping the hair in place

hair·piece (-pēs′) *n.* **1** a toupee or wig **2** a switch of hair, often styled, for a woman's hairdo

hair·pin (-pin′) *n.* a small, usually U-shaped, piece of wire, shell, etc., for keeping the hair or a headdress in place —*adj.* characterized by an abrupt, esp. a U-shaped, bend [a road with a *hairpin* turn]

hair-rais·ing (her′rā′ziŋ) *adj.* causing, or thought of as causing, the hair to stand on end; terrifying or shocking —**hair′-rais′er** *n.*

hairs·breadth or **hair's-breadth** (herz′bredth′) *n., adj. var. of* HAIRBREADTH

hair seal EARLESS SEAL

hair shirt [Historical] a shirt of haircloth, worn, as by ascetics, over the skin as a penance

hair space *Printing* the narrowest metal space used between words, equal to about ½ point

hair·split·ting (her′split′iŋ) *adj., n.* (a) making overnice or petty distinctions; quibbling —**hair′split′ter** *n.*

hair spray a liquid sprayed from a spray can onto the hair, to hold it in place: also written **hair′spray′** ***n.***

hair·spring (her′spriŋ′) ***n.*** a very slender, spiral spring that controls the regular movement of the balance wheel in a watch or clock

hair·streak (her′strēk′) ***n.*** any of a number of small, usually dark-colored butterflies (family Lycaenidae) with each hind wing commonly having narrow taillike projections

hair stroke a very fine line in writing or printing

hair·style (her′stīl′) ***n.*** a particular style of hairdressing, often one that is distinctive and fashionable —**hair′styl′ing** ***n.*** —**hair′styl′ist** ***n.***

hair trigger a trigger so delicately adjusted that a very slight pressure on it discharges the firearm

hair-trig·ger (her′trig′ər) ***adj.*** ⟦see prec.⟧ set in motion or operation by a very slight impulse

hair·worm (her′wurm′) ***n.*** GORDIAN WORM

hair·y (her′ē) ***adj.*** **hair′i·er**, **hair′i·est** **1** covered with hair; hirsute **2** of or like hair ☆**3** [Slang] difficult, distressing, harrowing, etc. —**hair′i·ness** ***n.***

hairy vetch a common annual plant (*Vicia villosa*) with hairy foliage and numerous small blue flowers, grown for forage or for use as green manure

Hai·ti (hāt′ē) **1** country occupying the W portion of the island of Hispaniola, West Indies: 10,714 sq mi (27,750 sq km); cap. Port-au-Prince **2** *former name for* HISPANIOLA

Hai·ti·an (hā′shən; *occas.* hāt′ē ən) ***adj.*** of Haiti or its people, language, or culture —***n.*** **1** a person born or living in Haiti **2** the French-based creole language of Haiti: in full **Haitian Creole**

hajj (haj, häj) ***n.*** ⟦Ar *ḥajj* < *ḥajja*, to set out, go on a pilgrimage⟧ the pilgrimage to Mecca that every Muslim is expected to make at least once: also sp. **haj**

haj·ji or **haj·i** (haj′ē, hä′jē) ***n.*** ⟦Ar *ḥajji*, adj. < *ḥajj*, pilgrimage: see prec.⟧ a Muslim who has made a pilgrimage to Mecca: a title of honor

hake (hāk) ***n.***, *pl.* **hake** or **hakes** ⟦ME, prob. < ON *haki*, a hook (from the shape of the jaw) > Norw *hakefisk*, trout, salmon, lit., hook-fish: for IE base see HOOK⟧ any of various gadoid marine food fishes, as the silver hake

ha·kim[1] (hä kēm′; *also* hä′kēm′) ***n.*** ⟦Ar *ḥakīm*, wise, learned, hence physician⟧ a Muslim physician

ha·kim[2] (hä′kēm′; *also* hä kēm′) ***n.*** ⟦Ar *ḥākim*, governor < *ḥakama*, to exercise authority⟧ a Muslim ruler or judge

Hak·luyt (hak′lo͞ot), **Richard** 1552?-1616; Eng. geographer & chronicler of explorations & discoveries

Ha·ko·da·te (hä′kō dä′tā) seaport on the SW coast of Hokkaido, Japan

hal- (hal, hāl) *combining form* HALO-: used before a vowel

Ha·la·kha or **Ha·la·cha** (hä′lä khä′, hə lä′khə) ***n.***, *pl.* **-la·khot′**, **-la·chot′** ⟦Heb *halacha*, rule, law (by which to go, or guide oneself) < verb root *hlk*, to go⟧ **1** any of the laws or ordinances not written down in the Jewish Scriptures but based on an oral interpretation of them **2** the part of the Talmud devoted to such laws and ordinances Also sp. **Ha′la·khah′** See also AGGADA

ha·la·khist or **ha·la·chist** (hä′lä khist′, -lə-; -kist′; hə lä′-) ***n.*** any of the contributors to the Halakha

ha·lal (hä läl′) ***adj.*** [Ar] characterized by adherence to the requirements of Islamic law, as in following proper dietary practices, esp. in slaughtering animals for meat

ha·la·la (hə lä′lə) ***n.***, *pl.* **-la** or **-las** ⟦Ar⟧ a monetary unit of Saudi Arabia, equal to $^1/_{100}$ of a riyal

ha·la·tion (hā lā′shən, ha-) ***n.*** ⟦HAL(O) + -ATION⟧ *Photog.* an undesirable spreading or reflection of light on a negative, appearing like a halo around highlights

hal·a·zone (hal′ə zōn′) ***n.*** ⟦HAL(O)- + AZ(O)- + -ONE⟧ a white, crystalline powder, $C_7H_5Cl_2NO_4S$, with a strong taste and smell of chlorine, usually used in tablet form to disinfect small quantities of drinking water

hal·berd (hal′bərd) ***n.*** ⟦LME *haubert* < OFr *hallebarde* & MDu *hellebaerde*, both < MHG *helmbarte* < *helm*, handle, staff (see HELM[2]) + *barte*, an ax, var. of *bart*, BEARD⟧ a combination spear and battle-ax, used in the 15th and 16th cent.: also **hal′bert** (-bərt) —**hal′berd·ier′** (-bər dir′) ***n.***

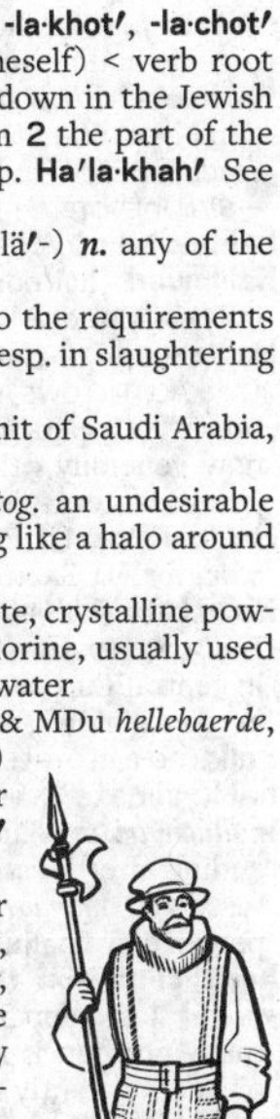

hal·cy·on (hal′sē ən) ***n.*** ⟦ME *alcioun* < L *alcyon* < Gr *alkyōn*, kingfisher, altered by folk etym. after Gr *hals*, sea⟧ **1** a legendary bird, identified with the kingfisher, which is supposed to have a peaceful, calming influence on the sea at the time of the winter solstice **2** *Zool.* any of a genus (*Halcyon*) of kingfishers of S Asia and Australia —***adj.*** **1** of the halcyon **2** tranquil, happy, idyllic, etc.: esp. in phr. **halcyon days**, usually with nostalgic reference to earlier times

Hal·dane (hôl′dān) **1 J(ohn) B(urdon) S(anderson)** 1892-1964; Eng. biologist & writer **2 Richard Bur·don** (bur′dən) 1st Viscount Haldane of Cloan 1856-1928; Scot. statesman & philosopher: uncle of J. B. S. Haldane

hale[1] (hāl) ***adj.*** **hal′er**, **hal′est** ⟦northern ME *hal*, same as Midland *hool* (see WHOLE) < OE *hal*, sound, healthy⟧ sound in body; vigorous and healthy: now said esp. of older persons

halberd

hale[2] (hāl) ***vt.*** **haled**, **hal′ing** ⟦ME *halen*, *halien* < OFr *haler*, prob. < ODu *halen*: see HAUL⟧ **1** [Archaic] to pull forcibly; drag; haul **2** to force (a person) to go [*haled* him into court]

Hale (hāl) **1 Edward Everett** 1822-1909; U.S. clergyman & writer **2 George El·ler·y** (el′ər ē) 1868-1938; U.S. astronomer **3 Nathan** 1755-76; Am. soldier in the Revolutionary War: hanged by the British as a spy

Ha·leb (hä leb′) *Ar. name for* ALEPPO

hal·er (hä′lər, -ler′) ***n.***, *pl.* **-e·ru′** (-lə ro͞o′) or **-ers** ⟦Czech < MHG *haller*: see HELLER[2]⟧ a monetary unit of the Czech Republic, equal to $^1/_{100}$ of a koruna

Ha·lé·vy (å lā vē′), **Jacques** (zhåk) (born *Jacques François Fromental Élie Lévy*) 1799-1862; Fr. composer

half (haf, häf) ***n.***, *pl.* **halves** ⟦ME < OE *healf*, part, half, akin to ON *halfr*, Ger *halb* < IE **(s)kelep-*, lit., divided < base **(s)kel-*, to cut > SCALP, SKILL, HELM[2]⟧ **1** *a)* either of the two equal parts of something [the top *half* of a layer cake] *b)* either of two corresponding or approximately equal parts [the larger *half* of a divided pie] **2** *a)* a half-hour [*half* past one] ☆*b)* a half dollar **3** ☆*a) Baseball* either of the two parts of an inning [the top *half* of the sixth inning] *b) Basketball, Football, etc.* either of the two equal periods of the game, between which the players rest ☆*c) Football* HALFBACK —***adj.*** **1** *a)* being either of the two equal parts of something *b)* being about a half of the amount, length, etc. [a *half* mask covered his eyes] **2** incomplete; fragmentary; partial —***adv.*** **1** to an extent approximately or exactly fifty percent of the whole **2** *a)* to some extent; partly [to be *half* convinced] *b)* to a large extent or degree; nearly (often used hyperbolically) [*half* dead with fatigue] **3** by any means; at all: used with *not* [the concert was not *half* bad] —**by half** considerably; very much —**in half** into halves —**not the half of** only a small part of

half- (haf) *combining form* **1** one half [*half*-life] **2** partly [*half*-baked]

half-and-half (haf′ən haf′) ***n.*** something consisting of fifty percent one substance and fifty percent another substance; esp., ☆*a)* a mixture of equal parts of milk and cream *b)* [Chiefly Brit.] a drink of equal parts of porter and ale or of beer and stout —***adj.*** combining two things equally —***adv.*** in two equal parts

half-assed (haf′ast′) ***adj.*** [Slang] having or showing little thought, care, or foresight: mildly vulgar: also **half′-ass′**

half·back (-bak′) ***n.*** ☆**1** *Football a)* one of the running backs, typically smaller and faster than the fullback *b)* a defensive back, as a cornerback or safety **2** *Soccer, Field Hockey, etc.* a player positioned between the forwards and the fullbacks, who has both offensive and defensive responsibilities

half-baked (-bākt′) ***adj.*** **1** only partly baked **2** not completely planned or thought out [a *half-baked* scheme] **3** having or showing little intelligence and experience

half·beak (-bēk′) ***n.*** any of a family (Hemirhamphidae, order Atheriniformes) of small, long-bodied, tropical marine bony fishes with a greatly extended lower jaw and a short upper jaw

half binding a style of book binding in which leather or other ornamental material covers the spine and corners

half blood **1** kinship through one parent only [sisters of the *half blood*] **2** HALF-BLOOD

half-blood (-blud′) ***n.*** ⟦based on the obs. notion that blood is the medium of heredity⟧ **1** a person related to another through one parent only ☆**2** HALF-BREED: generally regarded as an offensive term ☆**3** *Animal Husbandry* an animal with one parent of poor pedigree in contrast to that of the other —***adj.*** of or having to do with a half-blood: also **half′-blood′ed**

half boot a boot typically extending to just above the ankle

☆**half-breed** (haf′brēd′) ***n.*** a person whose parents are of different races; esp., an offspring of a North American Indian and a person of European ancestry —***adj.*** half-blood ➥Generally regarded as a contemptuous and offensive term

half brother a brother through one parent only

half-caste (haf′kast′) ***adj.***, ***n.*** *former term for* EURASIAN (***adj.*** 2 and ***n.*** 1): generally regarded as an offensive term

half-cell (-sel′) ***n.*** a cell consisting of an electrode immersed in a suitable electrolyte, designed to measure single electrode potentials

half cock the halfway position of the hammer of a firearm, when the trigger is locked and cannot be pulled

half-cocked (haf′käkt′) ***adj.*** having the hammer at half cock: said of a firearm —☆**go off half-cocked** **1** to go off too soon: said of a firearm **2** [Informal] to speak or act thoughtlessly or too hastily: also **go off at half cock**

half crown a former British coin equal to two shillings and sixpence (2½ shillings)

☆**half dollar** a U.S. or Canadian coin, equal to 50 cents: the U.S. half dollar is made largely of copper

☆**half eagle** ⟦because worth *half* as much as an EAGLE (***n.*** 3)⟧ a former gold coin of the U.S., worth $5.00

half-ev·er·green (haf′ev′ər grēn′) ***adj.*** having leaves which may or may not remain green throughout the year

half gainer a dive in which the diver springs from the board facing forward and does a back flip in the air so as to enter the water headfirst, facing the board

half·heart·ed (haf′härt′id) ***adj.*** with little enthusiasm, determination, interest, etc.; spiritless —**half′heart′ed·ly** ***adv.***

half hitch a knot made by passing the end of a rope around the rope and then through the loop thus made

half-hour (haf′our′) ***n.*** **1** 30 minutes **2** the point 30 minutes after any given hour —***adj.*** **1** lasting for 30 minutes **2** occurring every 30 minutes —**half′-hour′ly** ***adj.***, ***adv.***

half-length (-leŋkth′) ***adj.*** **1** of half the full length **2** made or designed to show a person from the waist up: said of a portrait or mirror —***n.*** a half-length portrait

half-life (-līf′) *n.* **1** the constant time period required for the disintegration of half of the atoms in a sample of some specific radioactive substance: also **half life** **2** the time it takes for half of something to decompose, reduce in strength or effectiveness, etc.: often, specif., used of the diminishing concentration of a medication in the body **3** LIFE (*n.* 15)
half-light (-līt′) *n.* dim or subdued light
half-mast (-mast′) *n.* the position of a flag lowered about halfway down a mast, staff, etc., esp. as a sign of mourning —*vt.* to fly (a flag) at half-mast
half-moon (-mo͞on′) *n.* **1** the moon in its first or last quarter phase **2** anything shaped like a half-moon or crescent
half mourning **1** traditionally, the second period of mourning, during which black clothes are lightened or replaced by gray, white, or purple **2** the clothes worn then
half nelson ⟦< surname *Nelson*⟧ a wrestling hold in which an arm is placed under the opponent's arm from behind with one's hand pressed against the back of the opponent's neck: see FULL NELSON
half note *Music* a note having one half the duration of a whole note
half·pen·ny (hāp′nē, hā′pən ē) *n., pl.* **-pence** (hā′pəns) or **-pen·nies** a former British coin equal to half a penny —*adj.* worth a halfpenny, or very little; trifling
half pint **1** a unit of liquid or dry measure equal to 8 ounces or ¼ quart (0.2 liter) ☆**2** [Slang] a small person
half rhyme SLANT RHYME, esp. when the result of consonance
half shell either of the two shells of a bivalve mollusk —**on the half shell** served raw, with seasonings, on a half shell: said of oysters, etc.
half sister a sister through one parent only
half size any of a series of sizes in women's garments for short-waisted, mature, full figures
half slip a woman's slip without a top
half sole a sole (of a shoe or boot) from the arch to the toe
half-sole (haf′sōl′) *vt.* **-soled′**, **-sol′ing** to repair (shoes or boots) by attaching new half soles
half sovereign a former British gold coin equal to ten shillings
☆**half-staff** (haf′staf′) *n.* HALF-MAST
half step **1** *Mil.* a short marching step of fifteen inches (in double time, eighteen inches) **2** *Music* SEMITONE
half tide the condition or period halfway between a high tide and its related low tide
half-tim·bered (-tim′bərd) *adj. Archit.* made of a wooden framework having the spaces filled with plaster, brick, etc.
☆**half·time** (-tīm′) *n.* the rest period between halves of a football game, basketball game, etc.
half title the title of a book, often abbreviated, on the odd page preceding (or sometimes following) the main title page
half·tone (-tōn′) *n.* **1** *Art* a tone or shading between light and dark **2** *Music* SEMITONE **3** *Photoengraving* *a)* a technique of representing shadings by dots produced by photographing the object from behind a fine screen *b)* a photoengraving so made
☆**half-track** (-trak′) *n.* an army truck, armored vehicle, etc. with tractor treads in the rear, but with a pair of wheels in front
half-truth (-tro͞oth′) *n.* a statement or account containing only some of the facts, the rest often being left out so as to deceive
half volley *Racket Sports* a stroke made in returning the ball just as it begins to bounce after striking the ground
half-vol·ley (haf′väl′ē) *vt., vi.* to return (a ball) with a half volley
half·way (haf′wā′, -wā′) *adj.* **1** equally distant between two points, conditions, etc.; midway **2** incomplete; partial [*halfway* measures] —*adv.* **1** half the distance; to the midway point **2** incompletely; partially —**meet halfway** to compromise or be willing to compromise (with)
halfway house **1** a midway inn or stopping place on or as on a journey ☆**2** a place where persons are aided in readjusting to society following a period of imprisonment, hospitalization, etc.
half-wit (haf′wit′) *n.* a stupid or silly person; fool —**half′-wit′ted** *adj.* —**half′-wit′ted·ness** *n.*
hal·i·but (hal′ə bət; *also* häl′-) *n., pl.* **-but** or **-buts** ⟦ME *halybutte* < *hali*, holy + *butt*, a flounder (so called because eaten on holidays): see HOLY + BUTT[1]⟧ any of a genus (*Hippoglossus*, family Pleuronectidae) of large, edible flounders found in northern seas, esp. the Atlantic species (*H. hippoglossus*), which may exceed 45 kg (*c.* 100 lb)
Hal·i·car·nas·sus (hal′ə kär nas′əs) ancient city in SW Asia Minor, on the Aegean: site of the MAUSOLEUM
hal·ide (hal′īd, -id; hā′līd′, -lid) *n.* ⟦HAL(OGEN) + -IDE⟧ a compound in which a halogen is combined with a certain element, radical, etc. —*adj.* HALOID
hal·i·dom (hal′i dəm) *n.* ⟦ME < OE *haligdom*: see HOLY & -DOM⟧ [Archaic] **1** holiness **2** a holy place or thing Also **hal′i·dome′** (-dōm′)
hal·ier (häl′yər) *n.* ⟦Slovak, cent, penny, akin to Czech *haler*: see HALER⟧ the former monetary unit of Slovakia, equal to $\frac{1}{100}$ of a koruna
Hal·i·fax (hal′ə faks′) ⟦after the 2d Earl of *Halifax* (1716-71)⟧ capital of Nova Scotia, Canada: seaport on the Atlantic
hal·ite (hal′īt′, hā′līt′) *n.* ⟦< Gr *hals*, SALT + -ITE[1]⟧ a soft, colorless or white mineral, NaCl; native sodium chloride; rock salt
☆**hal·i·to·sis** (hal′i tō′sis) *n.* ⟦ModL < L *halitus*, breath (< *halare*, to breathe) + -OSIS⟧ bad-smelling breath
hall (hôl) *n.* ⟦ME *halle* < OE *heall* (akin to Ger *halle*), lit., that which is covered < base of *helan*, to cover < IE base **kel-*, to cover > HELL, L *celare*, to conceal⟧ **1** [Historical] *a)* the great central room in the dwelling of a king or chieftain, where banquets, games, etc. were held *b)* the dwelling itself **2** the main dwelling on the estate of a baron, squire, etc. **3** [*sometimes* **H-**] a building containing public offices or the headquarters of an organization, for transacting business, holding meetings, etc. **4** a large public or semipublic room for gatherings, entertainments, etc. **5** [*sometimes* **H-**] a college dormitory, classroom building, eating center, etc. **6** a passageway or room between the entrance and the interior of a building; vestibule, foyer, or lobby **7** a passageway or area onto which rooms open
Hall (hôl) **1 Charles Martin** 1863-1914; U.S. chemist: discovered electrolytic process for reducing aluminum from bauxite **2 G(ranville) Stanley** 1844-1924; U.S. psychologist & educator
hal·lah (khä′lə, hä′-) *n. var. of* CHALLAH
hal·lal (hä läl′) *adj. alt. sp. of* HALAL
Hal·lam (hal′əm), **Henry** 1777-1859; Eng. historian
☆**hall bedroom** a small bedroom off a corridor, esp. a small bedroom formed by partitioning off the end of an upstairs corridor
Hal·le (häl′ə; *E* hal′ē) city in E Germany
hal·lel (häl′el′; *also* hä lel′) *n.* ⟦Heb *halel*, praise⟧ a part of the Jewish religious services consisting of Psalms 113 to 118 inclusive, recited or sung on certain festivals
hal·le·lu·jah or **hal·le·lu·iah** (hal′ə lo͞o′yə) *interj.* ⟦lit., praise (ye) the Lord! < LL(Ec) *alleluja* < Gr(Ec) *hallēlouia* < Heb < *hallelū*, praise (imper.) + *yāh*, JEHOVAH⟧ used to express praise, thanks, or joy, esp. to God as in a hymn or prayer —*n.* an exclamation, hymn, or song of praise to God
Hal·ley (hal′ē; hô′lē, hā′-), **Edmond** 1656-1742; Eng. astronomer
Halley's comet a famous comet, last seen in 1986, whose reappearance about every 76 years was predicted by Edmond HALLEY
hal·liard (hal′yərd) *n. alt. sp. of* HALYARD
hall·mark (hôl′märk′) *n.* **1** an official mark stamped on British gold and silver articles, originally at Goldsmiths' Hall in London, as a guarantee of genuineness **2** any mark or symbol of genuineness or high quality —*vt.* to put a hallmark on
hal·lo or **hal·loa** (hə lō′) *vi., vt., interj., n. var. of* HALLOO
Hall of Fame ⟦orig., a memorial in New York City containing busts and tablets honoring celebrated Americans⟧ **1** a monument or building honoring the renowned achievers in a particular sport or other activity **2** these achievers collectively —**Hall of Fam′er**
hal·loo (hə lo͞o′) *vi., vt.* **-looed′**, **-loo′ing** ⟦ME *halowen* < interj. *halou*: prob. also < OFr *halloer*, to follow after with much noise⟧ **1** to shout or call out in order to attract the attention of (a person) **2** *Hunting* to urge on (hounds) by shouting or calling "halloo" **3** to shout or yell, as in greeting or surprise —*interj., n.* (a shout or call) used esp. to attract a person's attention or to urge on hounds in hunting
hal·low[1] (hal′ō) *vt.* ⟦ME *halowen* < OE *halgian* (used for L *sanctificare*) < Gmc base of *halig* (see HOLY): akin to Ger *heiligen*⟧ **1** to make holy or sacred; sanctify; consecrate **2** to regard as holy; honor as sacred; venerate —*SYN.* DEVOTE
hal·low[2] (hə lō′, hal′ō) *vi., vt., interj., n.* HALLOO
hal·lowed (hal′ōd; *in poetry, also* hal′ō id) *adj.* ⟦pp. of HALLOW[1]⟧ **1** made holy or sacred **2** honored as holy; venerated —*SYN.* HOLY
Hal·low·een or **Hal·low·e'en** (hal′ə wēn′, häl′-) *n.* ⟦contr. < *all hallow even* (see ALLHALLOWS); *hallow* < OE *halga*, definite form of *halig* (see HOLY) in sense "holy person, hence saint"⟧ the day or, esp., the evening of Oct. 31, now generally celebrated by masquerading, trick-or-treating, displaying jack-o'-lanterns, etc.
Hal·low·mas (hal′ō məs, -mas′) *n.* ⟦< *all hallow mass*: see prec.⟧ *former name for* ALL SAINTS' DAY
Hall·statt (häl′stät′, -shtät′; hôl′stät′) *adj.* ⟦from archaeological finds at *Hallstatt*, Austria⟧ designating or of an Iron Age culture (*c.* 700-400 B.C.) in central Europe, characterized by swords of bronze or iron with winged metal terminals, and by the domestication of horses
☆**hall tree** a CLOTHES TREE, esp. one in an entrance hall
hal·lu·ci·nate (hə lo͞o′si nāt′) *vt.* **-nat′ed**, **-nat′ing** ⟦< L *hallucinatus*, pp. of *hallucinari*, to wander mentally, rave < Gr *alyein*, *halyein*, to be confused (+ ending after L *vaticinari*, to prophesy) < IE base **al-*, to wander, be confused > L *ambulare*⟧ **1** [Now Rare] to cause to have hallucinations ☆**2** to perceive in a hallucination —*vi.* to have hallucinations
hal·lu·ci·na·tion (hə lo͞o′si nā′shən) *n.* ⟦L *hallucinatio* < *hallucinari*: see prec.⟧ **1** the apparent perception of sights, sounds, etc. that are not actually present: it may occur in certain mental disorders **2** the imaginary object apparently seen, heard, etc. —*SYN.* DELUSION —**hal·lu′ci·na′tive** *adj.*
hal·lu·ci·na·to·ry (hə lo͞o′si nə tôr′ē) *adj.* **1** of or characterized by hallucination **2** producing hallucination
hal·lu·ci·no·gen (hə lo͞o′si nə jən, -jen′; hal′yo͞o sin′ə-, -yə-) *n.* ⟦< HALLUCIN(ATION) + -O- + -GEN⟧ a drug or other substance that produces hallucinations —**hal·lu′ci·no·gen′ic** *adj.*
hal·lu·ci·no·sis (hə lo͞o′si nō′sis) *n.* ⟦ModL < L *hallucinatio* + -OSIS⟧ a mental disorder characterized by hallucinations
hal·lux (hal′əks) *n., pl.* **-lu·ces′** (-yo͞o sēz′) ⟦ModL < L *hallux*, *hallus*, big toe⟧ the first toe on either of the hind legs of a terrestrial vertebrate; in humans, the large inner toe
☆**hall·way** (hôl′wā′) *n.* **1** a passageway or room between the entrance and the interior of a building; vestibule **2** a passageway; corridor
Hal·ma·he·ra (häl′mə her′ə) largest of the Molucca Islands, Indonesia, east of Sulawesi: 6,865 sq mi (17,780 sq km)
ha·lo (hā′lō) *n., pl.* **-los** or **-loes** ⟦L *halos* (gen. & acc. *halo*) < Gr *halōs*,

circular threshing floor, round disk of the sun or moon, hence halo around the sun or moon < *halein*, to grind < IE base **al-*, to grind > Arm *alam*, grind, Hindi *āṭā*, meal⟧ **1** *a)* a ring of light that seems to encircle the sun, moon, or other luminous body: it results from the refraction of light through ice crystals in our atmosphere *b)* a spherical distribution of stars and star clusters extending beyond the main body of certain galaxies, as the Milky Way **2** a symbolic disk or ring of light shown around or above the head of a saint, etc., as in pictures; nimbus **3** the splendor or glory with which a famed, revered, or idealized person or thing is invested —*vt.* **-loed, -lo·ing** to encircle with a halo

hal·o- (hal′ō, -ə) ⟦< Gr *hals* (gen. *halos*), SALT, hence sea⟧ *combining form* **1** of the sea *[halobiont]* **2** having to do with a salt *[halophyte]* **3** having to do with a halogen *[haloid]*

hal·o·bi·ont (hal′ō bī′änt) *n.* ⟦< prec. + Gr *biount-*, stem of *biōn*, prp. of *bioun*, to live < *bios*, life: see BIO-⟧ an organism living in a saline environment, as in the sea

hal·o·car·bon (hal′ə kär′bən) *n.* any of a class of organic compounds containing carbon, one or more halogens, and sometimes hydrogen: used as an aerosol and refrigerant, and polymerized to make plastics: see CHLOROFLUOROCARBON

hal·o·cline (hal′ə klīn′) *n.* ⟦HALO- + *-cline*, as in ANTICLINE⟧ a level of marked change, esp. increase, in the salinity of seawater at a certain depth

halo effect the tendency for an estimate or judgment to be influenced by an irrelevant or only loosely associated factor, impression, etc.

hal·o·gen (hal′ə jən) *n.* ⟦HALO- + -GEN⟧ any of the five very reactive, nonmetallic chemical elements making up group VIIA of the periodic table: fluorine is the lightest and most reactive of the group, and astatine is the heaviest and least reactive: see the periodic table of elements in the Reference Supplement —**ha·log·e·nous** (ha lä′jə nəs) *adj.*

hal·o·gen·ate (hal′ō jə nāt′, hal′ə-; hə läj′ə nāt′) *vt.* **-at′ed, -at′ing 1** to treat with a halogen or with a hydrogen halogen **2** to introduce a halogen, usually chlorine or bromine, into (a compound) —**hal′o·gen·a′tion** *n.*

hal·o·ge·ton (hal′ə jə tän′, hə läj′ə tän′) *n.* ⟦ModL < HALO- + Gr *geitōn*, neighbor⟧ a poisonous Asian weed (*Halogeton glomeratus*) of the goosefoot family, with fleshy, cylindrical leaves and minute, papery flowers, becoming widespread in the W U.S.

hal·oid (hal′oid′) *adj.* ⟦HAL(O)- + -OID⟧ of, like, or from a halogen

ha·lon (hā′län′) *n.* ⟦HAL(O)- + -ON⟧ any of various halocarbons, esp. those containing bromine, used in fire extinguishers, fertilizers, etc. and thought to harm the ozone layer

hal·o·per·i·dol (hal′ō per′ə dôl, -däl′) *n.* ⟦HALO- + (PI)PERID(INE) + -OL[1]⟧ a powerful tranquilizer, $C_{21}H_{23}ClFNO_2$, used in treating schizophrenia, Tourette's syndrome, nausea, etc.

hal·o·phile (hal′ə fīl′) *n.* ⟦HALO- + -PHILE⟧ an organism living in a salty environment —**hal′o·phil′ic** (-fil′ik) *adj.*, **ha·loph·i·lous** (hə läf′i ləs)

hal·o·phyte (hal′ə fīt′) *n.* ⟦HALO- + -PHYTE⟧ a plant that can grow in salty or alkaline soil

hal·o·thane (hal′ə thān′) *n.* ⟦HALO- + (E)TH(ER) + -ANE⟧ a nonexplosive liquid, $CF_3CHBrCl$, whose vapor is inhaled to produce general anesthesia

Hals (häls), **Frans** (fräns) 1580-1666; Du. painter

Hal·sey (hôl′zē), **William Frederick** 1882-1959; U.S. admiral: called *Bull Halsey*

Häl·sing·borg (hel′siŋ bôr′y′) seaport in SW Sweden, on the Öresund, opposite Helsingør, Denmark

halt[1] (hôlt) *n.* ⟦orig. in phr. *to make halt*, transl. of Ger *halt machen* < imper. of *halten* (see HOLD[1]) + *machen*, MAKE[2]⟧ **1** a stop, esp. a temporary one, as in marching; pause or discontinuance **2** a command to stop — *vi., vt.* to come or bring to a halt; stop, esp. temporarily —☆**call a halt** to order a stop, esp. temporarily

halt[2] (hôlt) *vi.* ⟦ME *halten* < OE *healtian* < *healt* (see the *adj.*), akin to MHG *halzen*⟧ **1** [Archaic] to walk with a crippled gait; limp; hobble **2** to be uncertain; waver; hesitate *[to halt in one's speech]* **3** to have defects; esp., *a)* to have a faulty meter (said of verse) *b)* to be illogical (said of argument) —*adj.* ⟦ME *halte* < OE *healt, halt*, akin to MHG *halz* < IE base **kel-*, to strike, hew (> L *calamitas*): basic sense "lamed by wounding"⟧ [Archaic] limping; crippled; lame —*n.* [Archaic] lameness —**the halt** [Archaic] those crippled by an injured or deformed leg or foot

hal·ter[1] (hôl′tər) *n.* ⟦ME < OE *hælftre* (akin to Ger *halfter*) < base of *helfe* (see HELVE): basic sense "that by which something is held"⟧ **1** *a)* a rope, cord, strap, etc., usually with a headstall, for tying or leading an animal *b)* a bitless headstall, with or without a lead rope **2** *a)* a rope for hanging a person; hangman's noose *b)* execution by hanging **3** a garment held up by a cord or loop around the neck and worn by women and girls to bare the shoulders, arms, and back: also called **halter top** —*vt.* **1** to put a halter on (an animal); tie with a halter **2** to hang (a person)

hal·ter[2] (hôl′tər, hal′-) *n., pl.* **hal·te·res** (-tir′ēz) ⟦ModL < L, lead weights < Gr *haltēr*, weight held (to give impetus) in leaping < *hallesthai*, to leap < IE base **sel-* > L *salire*⟧ either of a pair of knobbed, modified secondary wings serving as balancing organs in dipteran insects: also **hal′tere′** (-tir′)

halt·ing (hôl′tiŋ) *adj.* **1** limping, awkward, or unsteady *[a halting gait]* **2** marked by hesitation or uncertainty; jerky, disconnected, etc. *[halting speech]* —**halt′ing·ly** *adv.*

ha·lutz (khä lo͞ots′, hä-) *n., pl.* **ha′lutz·im′** (-lo͞ot sēm′) ⟦Heb *chaluts*, lit., warrior in the vanguard < root *ḥlc*, to be in the vanguard⟧ a Jewish pioneer in the agricultural settlements of modern Israel

hal·vah or **hal·va** (häl vä′; häl′vä′, -və) *n.* ⟦Turk *helwa* < Ar *halwa*⟧ a Middle Eastern confection, a paste of ground sesame seeds and honey, often mixed as with chopped pistachios, dried fruit, or a flavoring

halve (hav, häv) *vt.* **halved, halv′ing** ⟦ME *halven* < *half*, HALF⟧ **1** to divide into two equal parts **2** to share (something) equally *with* someone *[to halve one's winnings with another]* **3** to reduce by fifty percent; reduce to half **4** *Carpentry* to join (two pieces of wood) by cutting away an end of each to half its thickness and fitting the cut ends together **5** *Golf* in match play, to play (a hole, match, etc.) in the same number of strokes as one's opponent

halves (havz, hävz) *n. pl. of* HALF —**by halves 1** halfway; imperfectly **2** halfheartedly —**go halves** to share expenses, etc. equally

hal·yard (hal′yərd) *n.* ⟦altered (after YARD[1]) < ME *halier* < *halien*: see HALE[2]⟧ a rope or tackle for raising or lowering a flag, sail, etc.

ham (ham) *n.* ⟦ME *hamme* < OE *hamm*, akin to Ger dial. *hamme* < IE base **konemo-*, shin bone (> Gr *knēmē*): *n.* 5 & 6 and *adj.* infl. by AM(ATEUR)⟧ **1** [Archaic] the part of the leg behind the knee **2** *a)* the back of the thigh *b)* the thigh and the buttock together **3** the hock or hind leg of a four-legged animal **4** the upper part of a hog's hind leg, or meat from this, salted, dried, smoked, etc. ☆**5** [Informal] a licensed amateur radio operator ☆**6** ⟦< *hamfatter*, an actor of low grade, said to be so named from former use of ham fat to remove makeup⟧ [Informal] an amateur or incompetent performer, esp. an actor who performs with showy exaggeration — *vi., vt.* **hammed, ham′ming** [Slang] to act with exaggeration: often in **ham it up** —*adj.* ☆[Informal] having to do with licensed amateur radio operation

Ham (ham) *n. Bible* Noah's second son: Gen. 6:10

Ha·ma or **Ha·mah** (hä′mä) city in W Syria

ha·ma·da (hə mä′də) *n. alt. sp. of* HAMMADA

Ha·ma·dan (ham′ə dan′) city in W Iran: noted for carpets and rugs made there

ham·a·dry·ad (ham′ə drī′ad′, -əd) *n.* ⟦L *Hamadryas* < Gr < *hama*, together with + *dryas*, DRYAD⟧ **1** [*also* **H-**] *Gr. Myth.* a dryad; specif., a wood nymph whose life is bound up with that of the tree in which she lives **2** KING COBRA **3** an Arabian and N African baboon (*Papio hamadryas*) with ashy-gray fur: usually called **ham′a·dry′as′** (-as′, -əs)

ha·mal (hə mäl′, -môl′) *n.* ⟦Ar *hammāl* < *ḥamala*, to carry⟧ in the Middle East, a porter: also **ha·maul′** (-môl′)

Ha·ma·ma·tsu (hä′mä mä′tso͞o) city on the SC coast of Honshu, Japan

Ha·man (hā′mən) *n. Bible* a Persian official who sought the destruction of the Jews and was hanged when his plot was exposed to Ahasuerus by Esther: Esth. 7

ha·man·tasch·en (hä′mən täsh′ən) *pl.n., sing.* **-tasch′** ⟦Yiddish < prec. + *tash*, pocket, pouch⟧ triangular pastries filled as with prune purée or poppy seeds, made for Purim

ha·mar·ti·a (hä′mär tē′ə) *n.* ⟦Gr < *hamartanein*, to err⟧ TRAGIC FLAW

Ha·mas (hä mäs′, hä′mäs′) *n.* ⟦Ar, lit., zeal, enthusiasm: used as acronym of *ḥarakat al-muqawamah al-Islamiyya*, Islamic Resistance Movement⟧ a militant Palestinian Islamic organization operating in opposition to Israel

ha·mate bone (hā′māt′) ⟦< L *hamatus*, having or shaped like a hook < *hamus*, a hook⟧ a wedgelike bone on the side of the wrist connecting the wrist with the fourth and fifth metacarpals, which connect to the ring finger and little finger

Ha·math (hā′math) *Bible var. of* HAMA

Ham·ble·to·ni·an (ham′bəl tō′nē ən) *n.* ⟦after the name of a famous American stallion (1849-76)⟧ an annual harness race for three-year-old trotters

ham·bone (ham′bōn′) *n.* **1** the bone of a HAM (*n.* 4) ☆**2** [Slang] HAM (*n.* 6)

Ham·burg[1] (ham′bərg) *n.* ⟦after fol.⟧ any of a variety of small chicken of European origin, having dark plumage with white markings and dark-blue legs

Ham·burg[2] (ham′bərg; *Ger* häm′bo͝orkh) **1** state of N Germany: 292 sq mi (755 sq km) **2** capital of this state: port on the Elbe river

☆**ham·burg·er** (ham′bur′gər) *n.* ⟦earlier *Hamburg steak*, after prec.⟧ **1** ground beef **2** a fried, broiled, or baked patty of such meat **3** a sandwich made with such a patty, usually in a round bun Sometimes **ham′burg**

hame[1] (hām) *n.* ⟦ME < MDu, horse collar, akin to ON *hamr* < IE base **ḱem-*, to cover > HEAVEN⟧ either of the two rigid pieces along the sides of a horse's collar, to which the traces are attached

hame[2] (hām) *n.* [Scot.] home

Ham·e·lin (ham′ə lin) city in NW Germany, in the state of Lower Saxony: see also PIED PIPER (sense 1): Ger. name **Ha·meln** (hä′məln)

ham-hand·ed (ham′han′did) *adj.* clumsy, graceless, or tactless; inept: also [Chiefly Brit.] **ham′-fist′ed** (-fis′tid)

Ham·hung (häm′ho͝oŋ′) city in EC North Korea

Ha·mil·car Bar·ca (hə mil′kär bär′kə, ham′əl kär′-) 270?-228? B.C.; Carthaginian general: father of Hannibal

Ham·il·ton[1] (ham′əl tən) **1 Alexander** 1755?-1804; Am. statesman: 1st secretary of the U.S. treasury (1789-95) **2 Edith** 1867-1963; U.S. educator, writer, & classical scholar

Ham·il·ton[2] (ham′əl tən) **1** ⟦after G. *Hamilton*, local farmer (*c.* 1813)⟧ city & port in SE Ontario, Canada, at the W end of Lake Ontario **2** city in N North Island, New Zealand **3** city in SC Scotland, near Glasgow, on the Clyde **4** capital of Bermuda, on the main island **5** *former name* (1821-1965) *for* the CHURCHILL[2] (river in Labrador, Canada)

Ham·il·to·ni·an (ham′əl tō′nē ən) *adj.* of or characteristic of Alexander Hamilton or his federalist principles —*n.* a follower of Alexander Hamilton

ham·ish (hām′ish) *adj.* ⟦Yiddish⟧ *var. of* HAIMISH

Ham·ite (ham′īt′) *n.* **1** a person regarded as descended from Ham **2** a member of any of several usually dark-skinned Caucasoid peoples indigenous to N and E Africa, including the Egyptians, Berbers, etc.

Ham·it·ic (ham it′ik, hə mit′-) ***n.*** an obsolete grouping within the Afroasiatic language family, including the Berber, Cushitic, and Egyptian languages ***—adj.*** designating or of the Hamites or Hamitic

Ham·i·to-Se·mit·ic (ham′i tō′sə mit′ik) ***adj.*** AFROASIATIC

ham·let (ham′lit) ***n.*** ⟦ME *hamelet* < OFr (Anglo-Fr *hamelete*), dim. of *hamel* (Fr *hameau*), dim. of MLowG *hamm*, enclosed area, akin to OE: for IE base see HEM[1]⟧ a very small village

Ham·let (ham′lit) ***n.*** **1** a tragedy by Shakespeare (*c.* 1602) **2** the hero of this play, a Danish prince who avenges the murder of his father, the king, by killing his uncle Claudius, the murderer

ham·ma·da (hə mä′də) ***n.*** a desert plateau of hard, wind-swept bedrock covered with a thin layer of sand, pebbles, etc.

Ham·mar·skjöld (håm′år shüld′), **Dag (Hjalmar Agne Carl)** (dåg) 1905-61; Swed. statesman: secretary-general of the United Nations (1953-61)

ham·mer (ham′ər) ***n.*** ⟦ME *hamer* < OE *hamor*, akin to Ger *hammer*, ON *hamarr*, crag, cliff < IE **k̂omor-*, stone hammer < base **ak-m-* < **ak̂-*, sharp, sharp stone > Gr *akmē*, point, *akmōn*, anvil⟧ **1** a tool for pounding, usually consisting of a metal head fastened across one end of a handle: one end of the head may be a pronged claw for pulling nails **2** a thing like this tool in shape or use; specif., *a)* the mechanism that strikes the firing pin or percussion cap in a firearm *b)* a device for striking a bell, gong, metal bar, etc. to make a sound *c)* any of the felt-covered mallets that strike against the strings of a piano *d)* a high-speed, hammering power tool fitted with a metal block or chisel, for shaping metal, breaking up paved surfaces, etc. **3** the malleus, one of the three bones of the middle ear **4** an auctioneer's gavel **5** a metal ball weighing usually sixteen pounds, hung from a wire handle and thrown for distance in a track-and-field competition ***—vt.*** **1** *a)* to strike repeatedly with or as with a hammer *b)* to smash, destroy, defeat overwhelmingly, etc. [a tornado *hammered* the region] **2** to make or fasten with a hammer **3** to drive, force, or shape with or as with hammer blows [to *hammer* an idea into someone's head] ***—vi.*** to strike repeated blows with or as with a hammer **—hammer and tongs** ⟦with reference to the work of a blacksmith⟧ with all one's might; very vigorously **—hammer (away) at 1** to work continuously or energetically at **2** to keep emphasizing or talking about **—hammer out 1** to shape, construct, or produce by hammering **2** to make flat by hammering **3** to take out by or as by hammering **4** to develop or work out by careful thought or repeated effort **—under the hammer** ⟦cf. *n.* 4 above⟧ for sale at auction **—ham′mer·er** ***n.***

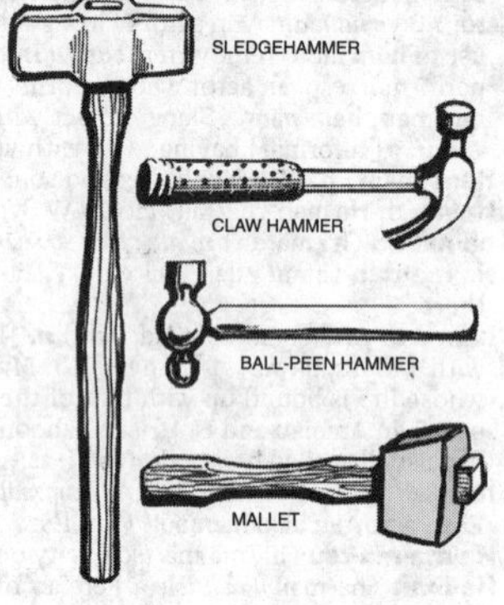

hammers

hammer and sickle the emblem of Communist parties in some countries, consisting of a sickle (symbolizing peasants) placed across a hammer (symbolizing industrial workers)

ham·mered (ham′ərd) ***adj.*** **1** shaped or marked by hammer blows: said of metal work **2** [Slang] drunk; intoxicated

hammered dulcimer DULCIMER (*n.* 1)

Ham·mer·fest (häm′ər fest′) seaport on an island in N Norway: northernmost city in the world

ham·mer·head (ham′ər hed′) ***n.*** **1** the head of a hammer, specif. the part with a flat surface for striking **2** any of a family (Sphyrnidae, order Carcharhiniformes) of large, tropical sharks that have a mallet-shaped head with an eye near the center of each end **3** a very large African fruit bat (*Hypsignathus monstrosus*) with a large horselike head **4** a large, brownish, crested African wading bird (*Scopus umbretta*) of a family (Scopidae) with only one species

ham·mer·less (-lis) ***adj.*** having the hammer or other striking device enclosed: term used esp. of rifles, shotguns, and pistols

ham·mer·lock (-läk′) ***n.*** a wrestling hold in which one arm of the opponent is twisted upward behind the opponent's back

Ham·mer·smith (ham′ər smith′) borough of Greater London, England: in full **Hammersmith and Fulham**

Ham·mer·stein (ham′ər stīn′), **Oscar, II** 1895-1960; U.S. librettist & lyricist of musicals

ham·mer·toe (-tō′) ***n.*** **1** a condition in which the first joint of a toe is permanently bent downward, resulting in a clawlike deformity **2** such a toe

Ham·mett (ham′it), **(Samuel) Da·shiell** (də shēl′, dash′əl) 1894-1961; U.S. detective-story writer

ham·mock[1] (ham′ək) ***n.*** ⟦Sp *hamaca*, of Arawakan orig.⟧ a length of netting, canvas, etc. swung from ropes at both ends and used as a bed or couch

ham·mock[2] (ham′ək) ***n.*** ⟦var. of HUMMOCK⟧ ☆[South] a fertile, raised area with hardwood trees

Ham·mu·ra·bi (hä′moo rä′bē, ham′ə-) fl. 18th cent. B.C.; king of Babylon: a famous code of laws is attributed to him

ham·my (ham′ē) ***adj.*** **-mi·er, -mi·est** ☆[Slang] like or characteristic of a ham (actor); overacting

ham·per[1] (ham′pər) ***vt.*** ⟦northern ME *hampren*, akin to *hamelian*, to maim (with freq. *-er* & intrusive *-p-*) < IE base **kem-*, to press together > HEM[1]⟧ to keep from moving or acting freely; hinder; impede; encumber

ham·per[2] (ham′pər) ***n.*** ⟦var. of HANAPER⟧ a large basket, usually with a cover, as for laundry

Hamp·shire (hamp′shir, ham′-) **1** county on the S coast of England: 1,459 sq mi (3,779 sq km) **2** former county of England including present-day Hampshire & the Isle of Wight

Hamp·stead (-stid, -sted) former metropolitan borough of London, now part of borough of Camden

Hamp·ton[1] (-tən), **Wade** 1818-1902; U.S. politician & Confederate general

Hamp·ton[2] (-tən) ⟦after a town in England⟧ seaport in SE Va., on Hampton Roads

Hampton Roads ⟦see prec. & ROAD (sense 4)⟧ channel & harbor in SE Va., linking the James River estuary with Chesapeake Bay

Hamp·tons (hamp′tənz), **the** ⟦in ref. to villages & towns in the area with names ending in *-hampton*⟧ resort area in SE N.Y., on the E end of Long Island

ham·ster (ham′stər) ***n.*** ⟦Ger < OHG *hamustro*, prob. < OSlav *chomĕstorŭ* < or akin to Iran *hamaēstar*, one who knocks down⟧ any of several burrowing rodents (family Cricetidae) of Europe and Asia, with large cheek pouches: one species (*Mesocricetus auratus*) is used in scientific experiments or is often kept as a pet

ham·string (ham′striŋ′) ***n.*** **1** one of the tendons at the back of the human knee **2** the large tendon at the back of the hock in a four-legged animal **3** any of three large muscles that form the back of the thigh and work together to flex the leg, extend the thigh, etc.: in full **hamstring muscle** ***—vt.*** **-strung′, -string′ing 1** to disable by cutting a hamstring **2** to lessen considerably or destroy the power or effectiveness of

Ham·sun (häm′soon; *E* ham′sən), **Knut** (k′nōōt) (born *Knut Pedersen*) 1859-1952; Norw. novelist

ham·u·lus (ham′yoo ləs) ***n.***, *pl.* **-u·li′** (-lī′) ⟦ModL < L, dim. of *hamus*, a hook⟧ a small hook or hook-shaped part, as at the ends of the barbicels of feathers or at the ends of some bones

ham·za (ham′zə, häm′-) ***n.*** ⟦Ar, lit., a compression⟧ a mark used in Arabic writing to indicate a glottal stop and usually represented in English transliteration by an apostrophe or single quotation mark: in this dictionary, it is represented by (ʾ)

Han[1] (hän) ***n.*** **1** a Chinese dynasty (206 B.C.-A.D. 220) characterized by the introduction of Buddhism, a renewal of the arts, and territorial expansion **2** an ethnic group in China constituting the majority of the Chinese people and distinguished from the Manchus, Mongols, etc.

Han[2] (hän) river in central China, flowing from Shaanxi province southeast into the Chang at Wuhan: *c.* 900 mi (1,448 km)

han·a·per (han′ə pər) ***n.*** ⟦ME *haniper* < OFr *hanapier*, a container for cups < *hanap*, a cup < Frank **hnap*, a beaker (akin to Ger *napf*)⟧ a small wicker container formerly used to hold official papers

Han Cities *see* WUHAN

Han·cock (han′käk) **1 John** 1737-93; Am. statesman: president of the Continental Congress (1775-77) & 1st signer of the Declaration of Independence: see also JOHN HANCOCK **2 Win·field Scott** (win′fēld′) 1824-86; Union general in the Civil War

hand (hand) ***n.*** ⟦ME < OE, akin to Goth *handus* < base of *-hinthan*, to seize (hence, basic sense "grasper") < ? IE base **kent-*, ? to seize⟧ **I. 1** the part of the human body attached to the end of the forearm, including the wrist, palm, fingers, and thumb **2** a corresponding part in some animals; specif., *a)* any of the four feet in apes, monkeys, etc., used like human hands for grasping and gripping *b)* the end part of the forelimb in many of the higher vertebrates *c)* the pincerlike claw of a crustacean **3** a side, direction, or position indicated by one hand or the other [at one's right *hand*] **II.** *denoting some function or activity of the hand* **1** the hand as an instrument for making or producing **2** the hand as a symbol of its grasping or gripping function; specif., *a)* [*pl.*] possession [the documents now in his *hands*] *b)* control; power; authority [to strengthen one's *hand*] *c)* [*pl.*] care; charge; supervision [the matter is in the *hands* of my lawyer] *d)* agency; influence [to see someone's *hand* in this affair] *e)* an active part; share [take a *hand* in the work] **3** the hand as a symbol of promise; specif., *a)* a clasp or handshake as a pledge of agreement, friendship, etc. *b)* a promise to marry [he asked for her *hand*] **III.** *denoting the manner in which the hand is used* **1** skill; ability; dexterity [the work that shows a master's *hand*] **2** manner of doing something [to play the piano with a light *hand*] **IV.** *denoting something produced by the hand* **1** *a)* handwriting *b)* a signature **2** a clapping of hands; applause [to receive a big *hand* for one's performance] **3** assistance; aid; help: with *a* [to lend a *hand*] **V.** *denoting a person as producing or transmitting with the hands* **1** a person whose chief work is done with the hands, esp., one of a staff or crew, as a sailor or a laborer on a farm or ranch **2** a person regarded as having some special skill, expertise, or characteristic [she's quite a *hand* at sewing]: see also OLD HAND **3** a person (or, sometimes, thing) from or through which something comes; source [essays by several *hands*]: often used with an ordinal number: cf. the phrases (AT) FIRST HAND and (AT) SECOND HAND below **VI.** *denoting something like a hand* **1** a conventional drawing of a hand (☞) used on signposts, etc. **2** an indicator; pointer [the *hands* of a clock] **3** the approximate breadth of the adult human palm, used as a unit of measurement, esp. for the height of horses: now usually taken to be 4 inches **4** *Commerce* a banana cluster **VII.** *denoting something held in the hand* **1** *Card Games a)* the cards held by a player at any one time *b)* the conventional number of cards dealt to each player *c)* a player *d)* a round of play ☆**2** a small tied bundle, esp. of tobacco leaves **3** the way cloth held in the hand feels —*adj.* **1** of or for the hand or hands **2** made by hand **3** controlled by hand; manual —*vt.* **1** to pass or give with or as with the hand; transfer; transmit; deliver ☆**2** to give; provide with [it *handed* them a laugh] **3** to help, conduct, steady, etc. by means of the hand [to *hand* a lady into a taxi] **4** *Naut.* to furl (a sail) —**(at) first hand** from the original source; directly —**at hand 1** near; close by **2** immediately available —**(at) second hand 1** not from the original source; indirectly **2** not new; previously used —**at the hand (***or* **hands) of** through the action of —**by hand** not by machines but with the hands —**change hands** to pass from one owner to another —**eat out of someone's hand** to be completely dominated by or devoted to someone —**force someone's hand** ⟦orig. a whist term⟧ to force someone to act, or declare intentions, before he or she is ready —**from hand to hand** from one person's possession to another's —**from hand to mouth** with just enough for immediate needs and nothing left over for the future —**hand and foot 1** so that the hands and feet cannot move [bound *hand and foot*] **2** constantly and diligently [to wait on someone *hand and foot*] —**hand down 1** to give as an inheritance; bequeath ☆**2** to announce or deliver (a verdict, etc.) —**hand in** to give; submit —**hand in (***or* **and) glove** in intimate association; in close agreement or cooperation —**hand in hand 1** holding each other's hand **2** together; in cooperation or correlation —☆**hand it to** [Informal] to give deserved credit to —**hand off** *Sports* to hand (the ball) to a teammate during a play —**hand on** to pass along; transmit —**hand out** to distribute; deal out —**hand over** to give up; deliver —**hand over fist** [Informal] easily and in large amounts —**hands down** without effort; easily —**hands off!** don't touch! don't interfere! —**hands up!** ☆raise your hands over your head!: an order given by a person pointing a gun, etc. —**hand to hand** at close quarters: said of fighting —**hand up** to present (an indictment) to a court: said of a grand jury —**have one's hands full** to be extremely busy; be doing as much as one can —**hold hands** to hold each other's hand, esp. in affection —**in hand 1** in order or control **2** in possession **3** being worked on; in process —**join hands 1** to become associates; enter into partnership **2** to become husband and wife —**keep one's hand in** to keep in practice in order to retain one's skill —**lay hands on 1** to attack, injure, or punish physically **2** to get hold of; seize; take **3** to place the hands on ceremonially, as in blessing or ordaining —**not lift a hand** to do nothing; not even try —**off one's hands** no longer in one's care; out of one's responsibility —**on every hand** on all sides; in all directions —**on hand 1** near ☆**2** available or ready ☆**3** present —**on one's hands** in one's care; being one's responsibility —**on the one hand** from one point of view —**on the other hand** from the opposed point of view —**out of hand 1** out of control **2** immediately; without preliminaries or delay **3** over and done with —**show one's hand** ⟦orig. with reference to card playing⟧ to disclose one's intentions —**take in hand 1** to take control of or responsibility for **2** to take up; handle; treat **3** to try; attempt —**throw in one's hand** [Informal] to admit defeat; give up: from the act, as by a poker player, of tossing one's hand onto the table to signal withdrawal from a round —**throw up one's hands** to give up in despair —**tie someone's hands** [Informal] to hinder or restrict someone from carrying out an action —**to hand 1** near; accessible **2** in one's possession —**turn (***or* **put) one's hand to** to undertake; work at —**wash one's hands of** to refuse to go on with or take responsibility for: see Matt. 27:24 —**with a heavy hand 1** in a heavy manner; without delicacy or grace **2** with severity or sternness —**with a high hand** with arrogance; in an arbitrary or dictatorial manner —**with clean hands** without guilt; as an innocent person

Hand (hand), **(Billings) Lear·ned** (lʉr′nid) 1872-1961; U.S. jurist

hand- (hand) *combining form* of, with, by, or for a hand or hands [*handclasp, handcuff*]

hand ax (*or* **axe) 1** a small ax for use with one hand; hatchet **2** a stone tool of the Paleolithic period rounded at one end for grasping and flaked to a point at the other end

hand·bag (hand′bag′) *n.* **1** a bag, usually of leather or cloth, held in the hand or hung by a strap from the arm or shoulder and used, esp. by women, to carry money, keys, and personal effects **2** a small suitcase or valise

hand·ball (-bôl′) *n.* **1** a game in which a small ball is batted against a wall or walls with the hand, alternately by opposing teams of one or two players **2** the small rubber ball used in this game

hand·bar·row (-bar′ō) *n.* a large tray with handles at either end, for carrying loads

hand·bas·ket (hand′bas′kit) *n.* a small basket with a handle —**to hell in a handbasket** [Slang] to one's doom or to utter ruin

hand·bill (-bil′) *n.* a small printed notice, advertisement, etc. to be passed out by hand

hand·blown (-blōn′) *adj.* shaped individually by a glass blower

hand·book (-book′) *n.* ⟦OE *handboc*, transl. of L *manuale* (see MANUAL): modern senses infl. by Ger *handbuch*⟧ **1** a compact reference book on some subject; manual of facts or instructions **2** GUIDEBOOK (sense 1) ☆**3** a book in which bets are recorded, as on horse races

hand·breadth (-bredth′) *n.* the approximate breadth of the adult human palm: see HAND (*n.* VI, 3)

☆**hand·car** (-kär′) *n.* a small, open car, originally powered manually, used on railroads, as to transport workers

hand·cart (-kärt′) *n.* a small cart, often with only two wheels, pulled or pushed by hand

hand·clasp (-klasp′) *n.* a clasping of each other's hand as in greeting or farewell

hand·craft (-kraft′) *n.* HANDICRAFT —*vt.* to make by hand with craftsmanship —**hand′craft′ed** *adj.*

hand·cuff (hand′kuf′) *n.* either of a pair of connected metal rings that can be locked about the wrists, as in restraining a prisoner: *usually used in pl.* —*vt.* **1** to put handcuffs on; manacle **2** to check or hinder the activities of

-hand·ed (han′did) *combining form* **1** having, or for use by one having, a (specified) handedness [*right-handed*] **2** having or using a (specified) number of hands [*two-handed*] **3** involving (a specified number of) players [*three-handed* pinochle]

hand·ed·ness (-nis) *n.* **1** ability in using one hand more skillfully than, and in preference to, the other **2** *Chem.* the structural property of an asymmetrical molecule or object which has the mirror-image structure of another molecule or object: see also ENANTIOMER

Han·del (han′dəl), **George Fri·der·ic** (frē′dər ik, -drik) (born *Georg Friedrich Händel*) 1685-1759; Eng. composer, born in Germany —**Han·de·li·an** (han del′ē ən, -dē′lē-; -del′yən, -dēl′-) *adj.*

hand·fast (hand′fast′) [Obs.] *n.* ⟦< the *vt.*⟧ **1** a firm hold, as with the hands **2** a contract, esp. of marriage or betrothal, confirmed by a handclasp —*adj.* betrothed or married —*vt.* ⟦ME *handfasten* < OE *handfæstan*, to make fast, ratify & < ON *handfesta*: see HAND & FASTEN⟧ to betroth or marry by joining hands

hand·fast·ing (-fas′tiŋ) *n.* ⟦OE *handfæstunge*: see prec.⟧ [Archaic] **1** a betrothal **2** a form of irregular or trial marriage confirmed by a joining of hands

hand-feed (hand′fēd′) *vt.* **-fed′**, **-feed′ing** to feed (in various senses) by hand

hand·ful (hand′fool′) *n., pl.* **-fuls′** ⟦ME < OE *handfull*⟧ **1** as much or as many as the hand will hold **2** a relatively small number or amount [a mere *handful* of people] **3** [Informal] as much as one is able to manage; someone or something hard to manage

hand glass 1 a magnifying glass **2** a small mirror with a handle

hand grenade a small grenade thrown by hand and exploded by a timed fuze or by impact

hand·grip (hand′grip′) *n.* **1** a handclasp or handshake **2** a handle or a grip, as on a bicycle handlebar —**come to handgrips** to engage in hand-to-hand fighting

hand·gun (hand′gun′) *n.* any firearm, as a pistol, designed to be held and fired with one hand

hand-held (hand′held′) *adj.* small enough to be held in the hand while being used or operated [a *hand-held* computer]: also written **hand′held′**

hand·hold (hand′hōld′) *n.* **1** a secure grip or hold with the hand or hands **2** a part or thing to take hold of

hand-hold·ing (hand′hōl′diŋ) *n.* the providing of attentive support or instruction, as to calm or lessen anxiety or fear —**hand′-hold′er** *n.*

hand·i·cap (han′dē kap′) *n.* ⟦orig. a game in which forfeits were drawn from a cap or hat < *hand in cap*⟧ **1** *a)* a race or other competition in which difficulties are imposed on the superior contestants, or advantages given to the inferior, to make their chances of winning equal *b)* such a difficulty or advantage **2** *a)* something that hampers a person; disadvantage; hindrance *b)* a physical or mental disability —*vt.* **-capped′**, **-cap′ping 1** to give a handicap to (contestants) **2** to cause to be at a disadvantage; hinder; impede

hand·i·capped (-kapt′) *adj.* **1** having handicaps assigned to contestants **2** having a physical or mental disability; disabled —**the handicapped** those who are physically or mentally disabled

hand·i·cap·per (-kap′ər) *n.* **1** an official who assigns handicaps to contestants, as in a tournament ☆**2** a person, as a sports writer, who tries to predict the winners in horse races on the basis of past records, track conditions, etc.

hand·i·craft (han′dē kraft′) *n.* ⟦ME *handiecrafte*, altered (infl. by *handiwerk*, HANDIWORK) < *handcrafte* < OE *handcræft*⟧ **1** expertness with the hands; manual skill **2** an occupation or art calling for skillful use of the hands, as weaving, pottery, etc. **3** work done or articles made by manual skills —**hand′i·crafts′man** (-krafts′mən) *n., pl.* **-men** (-mən)

hand·i·ly (han′də lē) *adv.* **1** in a handy manner; deftly or conveniently **2** with no trouble; easily [to win *handily*]

hand·i·ness (han′dē nis) *n.* the quality of being handy

hand·i·work (han′də wʉrk′, -dē-) *n.* ⟦ME *handiwerk* < OE *handgeweorc* < *hand* (see HAND) + *geweorc* < *ge-*, collective prefix + *weorc*, WORK⟧ **1** HANDWORK **2** anything made or done by a particular person

hand job [Slang] a sexual activity in which one person manually stimulates another's penis: somewhat vulgar

hand·ker·chief (haŋ′kər chif′, -chēf′) *n., pl.* **-chiefs′** (-chifs′, -chivz′, -chēfs′, -chēvz′) or **-chieves′** (-chivz′, -chēvz′) ⟦HAND + KERCHIEF⟧ **1** a small, square piece of linen, cotton, silk, etc., for wiping the nose, eyes, or face, or carried or worn for ornament **2** KERCHIEF

hand-knit (hand′nit′) *adj.* knit by hand instead of by machine: also **hand′-knit′ted**

han·dle (han′dəl) *n.* ⟦ME *handil* < OE *handle* (akin to Du *handel*) < *hand*, HAND⟧ **1** that part of a utensil, tool, etc. which is to be held, turned, lifted, pulled, etc. with the hand **2** a thing like a handle in appearance or use **3** the total amount of money bet over a specified period of time, as at a racetrack ☆**4** [Slang] a person's name, nickname, or title —*vt.* **-dled**, **-dling**

⟦ME *handlien* < OE *handlian*⟧ **1** to touch, lift, etc. with the hand or hands **2** to manage, operate, or use with the hand or hands; manipulate **3** to manage, control, direct, train, etc. **4** *a)* to deal with or treat in a particular way [to *handle* a problem tactfully] *b)* to deal with successfully or appropriately *c)* [Informal] to come to terms with psychologically [he just can't *handle* it] ☆**5** to sell or deal in (a certain commodity) **6** to behave toward; treat —*vi.* to respond or submit to control [the car *handles* well] —☆**fly off the handle** [Informal] to become suddenly or violently angry or excited —**get a handle on** [Informal] to find a means of dealing with, understanding, etc. —**han′dle·less** *adj.*

SYN.—**handle** implies the possession of sufficient (or a specified degree of) skill in managing or operating with or as with the hands [to *handle* a tool or a problem]; **manipulate** suggests skill, dexterity, or craftiness in handling [to *manipulate* a machine or an account]; **wield** implies skill and control in handling effectively [to *wield* an ax, to *wield* influence]; **ply** suggests great diligence in operating [to *ply* an oar, to *ply* one's trade]

han·dle·bar (han′dəl bär′) *n.* **1** [*often pl.*] a bar with handles on the ends, for steering a bicycle, motorcycle, etc. ☆**2** [Informal] a mustache with long, curved ends, resembling a handlebar: in full **handlebar mustache**

han·dler (hand′lər) *n.* a person or thing that handles; specif., ☆*a)* a boxer's trainer and second *b)* a person who trains and manages a horse, dog, etc. in a show or contest ☆*c)* a person employed to advise a politician, celebrity, etc. on what to say or do, as in shaping his or her public image

hand·less (hand′lis) *adj.* **1** not having any hands **2** [Dial.] inexpert, clumsy, or awkward

han·dling (hand′liŋ) *n.* **1** the act or an instance of touching, moving, etc. with the hands **2** the process of packing and sending merchandise to a customer [a fee for shipping and *handling*] **3** the way in which something is done or someone is treated [a temperamental artist requires special *handling*]

hand·list (hand′list′) *n.* a list, as of the contents of a collection, containing few details

hand·made (hand′mād′) *adj.* made by hand, not by machine; made by a process requiring manual skills

hand·maid·en (hand′mād′′n) *n.* **1** a woman or girl servant or attendant: now rare except in poetic or historical use **2** that which accompanies in a useful but subordinate capacity [law is the *handmaiden* of justice] Also **hand′maid′**

hand-me-down (hand′mē doun′) [Informal] *n.* something, esp. an article of clothing, which is used and then passed along to someone else, as to a younger sibling —*adj.* **1** used; secondhand **2** ready-made and cheap

☆**hand·off** (hand′ôf′) *n. Football* an offensive maneuver in which a back, esp. the quarterback, hands the ball directly to another back

☆**hand organ** a barrel organ played by turning a crank by hand

☆**hand·out** (hand′out′) *n.* **1** a gift of food, clothing, etc., as to a beggar **2** a pamphlet, leaflet, etc. handed out as for publicity or information **3** NEWS RELEASE

hand·o·ver (hand′ō′vər) *n.* a transfer or relinquishing of authority, control, possession, etc. [a *handover* of occupied land]

hand·pick (hand′pik′) *vt.* **1** to pick (fruit or vegetables) by hand **2** to choose with care or for a special purpose —**hand′picked′** *adj.*

hand·print (hand′print′) *n.* an impression or mark made by a hand

hand puppet a kind of puppet that fits over the hand and is manipulated from within by moving the fingers

hand·rail (hand′rāl′) *n.* a rail serving as a guard or support to be held by the hand, as along a staircase or ramp

hand-run·ning (hand′run′iŋ) *adv.* [Informal or Dial.] in succession; without break or interruption: also **hand running**

hand·saw (-sô′) *n.* a hand-held saw for manual use

hand's-breadth (handz′bredth′) *n. var. of* HANDBREADTH

hand·sel (hand′səl, han′səl) *n.* ⟦ME *handsel* < OE (rare) *handselen,* a giving into hand & ON *handsal,* sealing of a bargain by a handclasp (transl. of L *mancipatio*: see EMANCIPATION), both < *hand* + IE base of SELL⟧ **1** a present for good luck, as at the new year or on the launching of a new business **2** [Rare] *a)* a first payment or first installment *b)* the first money taken in by a new business or on any day of business **3** the first use or specimen of anything, regarded as a token of what is to follow —*vt.* **-seled** or **-selled**, **-sel·ing** or **-sel·ling** ⟦ME *handsellen* < ON *handselja*⟧ **1** to give a handsel to **2** to begin or launch with ceremony and gifts **3** to use, do, etc. for the first time

☆**hand·set** (hand′set′) *n.* **1** a telephone mouthpiece and receiver in a single hand-held unit; also, such a unit containing a dial or push buttons **2** a hand-held CELL PHONE

hand·shake (-shāk′) *n.* a gripping and shaking of each other's hand in greeting, farewell, agreement, etc.

hands-off (handz′ôf′) *adj.* designating or of a policy, attitude, etc. of not interfering or intervening

hand·some (han′səm, hand′-) *adj.* **-som·er**, **-som·est** ⟦orig., easily handled, convenient < ME *handsom*: see HAND & -SOME[1]⟧ **1** *a)* [Now Rare] moderately large *b)* large; impressive; considerable [a *handsome* sum] **2** generous; magnanimous; gracious [a *handsome* gesture] **3** good-looking; of pleasing appearance: said esp. of attractiveness that is manly, dignified, or impressive rather than delicate and graceful [a *handsome* lad, a *handsome* antique desk] —*SYN.* BEAUTIFUL —**hand′some·ly** *adv.* —**hand′some·ness** *n.*

Handsome Lake 1735-1815; Seneca prophet, social reformer, & founder of a North American Indian religion named after him

hands-on (handz′än′) *adj.* **1** designating or of training, an activity, etc. in which a person actively participates by design **2** designating or of a manager, administrator, etc. who intervenes or otherwise actively participates in the execution of a task or activity

hand·spike (hand′spīk′) *n.* ⟦altered (by assoc. with SPIKE[1]) < Du *handspaeke* (modern Du *handspaak*) < *hand,* hand + *spaeke,* rod, pole⟧ a heavy bar used as a lever, as in turning a capstan

hand·spring (-spriŋ′) *n.* a tumbling feat in which the performer turns over in midair with one or both hands touching the ground, floor, etc.

hand·stamp (-stamp′) *n.* **1** RUBBER STAMP **2** a rubber stamp used to postmark stamps —*vt.* to postmark (a stamp) with a handstamp

hand·stand (-stand′) *n.* a gymnastic feat of supporting oneself upside down on the hands with the body held vertically

hand-to-hand (hand′to͞o hand′) *adj.* in close contact; at close quarters: said of fighting

hand-to-mouth (-mouth′) *adj.* ⟦see FROM HAND TO MOUTH at HAND⟧ characterized by a barely sufficient source of food or income

hand truck a two-wheeled device for moving stacked cartons, crates, etc., consisting of an upright frame with a platform that can be slid under the load: tilting back the frame lifts the load so that it can be wheeled about

hand·work (hand′wurk′) *n.* work done or made by hand, not by machine —**hand′worked′** *adj.*

hand-wo·ven (-wō′vən) *adj.* **1** woven on a loom operated manually, not by machine power **2** woven by hand, as baskets or chair seats

hand-wring·ing or **hand·wring·ing** (hand′riŋ′iŋ) *n.* excessive expressions of distress or anxiety, by or as by clasping and twisting the hands together —**hand′-wring′er** *n.*, **hand′wring′er**

hand·writ·ing (-rīt′iŋ) *n.* **1** writing done by hand, with pen, pencil, etc. **2** a style or way of forming letters and words when writing by hand, often, specif., when writing cursive **3** [Archaic] something written by hand

hand·writ·ten (hand′rit′′n) *adj.* written by hand, with pen, pencil, etc.

hand·y (han′dē) *adj.* **hand′i·er**, **hand′i·est** ⟦HAND + -Y[3]⟧ **1** close at hand; easily reached; conveniently located; accessible **2** easily used; saving time or work; convenient [a *handy* device] **3** easily managed or handled: said of a ship, etc. **4** clever with the hands; deft; adroit **5** capable of making simple repairs to a house, an automobile, electrical appliances, etc. —*SYN.* DEXTEROUS

Han·dy (han′dē), **W(illiam) C(hristopher)** 1873-1958; U.S. composer of popular songs

hand·y·man (han′dē man′) *n., pl.* **-men′** (-men′) a man employed at various small tasks; one who does odd jobs

hang (haŋ) *vt.* **hung**, **hang′ing**; for vt. 3 & vi. 5, **hanged** is the preferred pt. & pp. ⟦ME *hangen,* with form < OE vi. *hangian* & ON vi. *hanga*; senses < these, also < OE vt. *hon* & ON caus. v. *hengja*; akin to Ger vi. *hangen,* vt. *hängen,* to execute (caus.): all ult. < IE base **k̂enk,* to sway, hang (akin to **keg-* > HOOK)⟧ **1** to attach to something above with no support from below; suspend **2** to attach so as to permit free motion at the point of attachment [to *hang* a door on its hinges] **3** to put to death by tying a rope about the neck and suddenly suspending the body so as to snap the neck or cause strangulation **4** to fasten (pictures, etc.) to a wall by hooks, wires, etc. **5** to ornament or cover *with* things suspended [to *hang* a room with pictures and drapes] **6** to paste (wallpaper) to walls **7** to exhibit (pictures) in a museum or gallery **8** to let (one's head) droop downward **9** to fasten (an ax head, scythe blade, etc.) with correct balance **10** to pin and sew the hem of (a dress) evenly at a desired distance from the floor ☆**11** to deadlock (a jury) by one's vote **12** to fix (something) *on* a person or thing ☆**13** *Baseball* to pitch (a breaking ball) that fails to curve sharply and is therefore easy to hit —*vi.* **1** to be attached to something above with no support from below **2** to hover or float in the air, as though suspended **3** to swing, as on a hinge **4** to fall, flow, or drape, as cloth, a coat, etc. **5** to die by hanging **6** *a)* to incline; lean *b)* to droop; bend **7** to be doubtful or undecided; hesitate **8** to have one's pictures exhibited in a museum or gallery **9** [Slang] *a)* to loiter; idle *b)* to engage in social activity: often with *with* [*hanging* with their friends at the mall] — *v. imper.* [Slang] to hell with; damn: used euphemistically in exclamations indicating anger or exasperation —*n.* **1** the way that a thing hangs **2** a pause in, or suspension of, motion —☆**get (or have) the hang of** [Informal] **1** to learn (or have) the knack of **2** to understand the significance or idea of —**hang a left (or right)** [Informal] to turn to the left (or right), as in driving a car —☆**hang around (or about)** **1** to cluster around **2** [Informal] to loiter or linger around **3** [Informal] to associate or socialize with [Don't *hang around* those kids!] —☆**hang around with** [Informal] to associate or socialize with —**hang back (or off)** to be reluctant to advance, as from timidity or shyness —**hang fire** **1** to be slow in firing: said of a gun **2** to be slow in doing something **3** to be unsettled or undecided —**hang five (or ten)** [Slang] to ride a surfboard with the toes of one (or both) feet draped over the front edge of the board —☆**hang in (there)** [Informal] to hold steadfast; persevere —**hang it (all)!** [Slang] to hell with it! damn it!: a euphemistic exclamation of anger or exasperation —**hang it (or them or 'em) up** [Informal] to retire or quit —**hang loose** [Slang] to be relaxed, easygoing, etc. —**hang on** **1** to keep hold **2** [Informal] to hold steadfast; persevere **3** to depend on; be contingent on **4** to listen attentively to [to *hang on* a speaker's every word] —☆**hang one on** [Slang] **1** to hit with a blow **2** to go on a drunken spree —**hang out** **1** to lean out **2** to display, as by suspending **3** [Slang] *a)* to reside *b)* to spend much of one's time; frequent a place **4** [Slang] to loiter; idle —**hang over** **1** to project over; overhang **2** to loom over; threaten **3** to be left from a previous time or state —**hang together** 1 to stick or remain together 2 to make sense in a coherent way —**hang tough** [Informal] to take a firm or defiant stand; be inflexible —**hang up** 1 to put on a hanger, hook, etc., esp. in the proper place ☆2 to put a telephone receiver or handset back in place in ending a call 3 to delay or suspend the progress of [cars that are *hung up* in traffic] —**hang up on someone** [Informal] to end abruptly and rudely a telephone or cell-phone conversation with someone —☆**let it all hang out** [Slang] to go all the way; be uninhibited — **not care (or give) a hang about** [Informal] to not care the least bit about

hang·ar (haŋ′ər) ***n.*** ⟦Fr, a shed, prob. < Frank **haimgard* or MDu **hamgaerd*, enclosed area: see HOME & YARD[2]⟧ a shelter used to house or repair an airplane —***vt.*** to put or keep in a hangar

Hang·chow (haŋ′chou′) *a former transliteration of* HANGZHOU

hang·dog (haŋ′dôg′) ***n.*** 1 [Archaic] a person considered fit only for hanging dogs, or to be hanged like a dog 2 a contemptible, sneaking person —***adj.*** 1 contemptible; sneaking 2 ashamed, dejected, or sheepish [a *hangdog* expression]

hang·er (haŋ′ər) ***n.*** 1 a person who hangs things: often in comb. [a *paperhanger*] 2 [Rare] a hangman; executioner 3 *a)* a thing that hangs down *b)* [Historical] a short sword hung from the belt 4 a thing on which or by means of which objects are, or can be, hung; specif., *a)* a hook, chain, rope, strap, bracket, etc. for this purpose *b)* a small frame on which a garment is hung to keep it in shape

hang·er-on (haŋ′ər än′) ***n., pl.*** **hang′ers-on′** ⟦< HANG ON + -ER⟧ a follower or dependent; specif., *a)* a person who joins another, some group, etc. although not wanted *b)* a sycophant; parasite

☆**hang gliding** the sport of gliding through the air while hanging suspended by a harness from a large kitelike device (**hang glider**)

hang·ing (haŋ′iŋ) ***adj.*** 1 attached to something overhead and not supported from below; suspended; pendulous 2 designed for objects to be hung on 3 leaning over; inclining; overhanging 4 located on a steep slope or slant 5 deserving, causing, or inclined to impose death by hanging [a *hanging* judge] 6 designating or of indentation in which the first line of a paragraph touches the left margin, the other lines being indented beneath it 7 not yet decided; unsettled 8 [Archaic] downcast —***n.*** 1 a suspending or being suspended 2 a putting to death by hanging: see HANG (***vt.*** 3) 3 something hung on a wall, window, etc., as a drapery or tapestry

hang·man (haŋ′mən, -man′) ***n., pl.*** **-men** (-mən) an executioner who hangs criminals condemned to death

hang·nail (haŋ′nāl′) ***n.*** ⟦altered (by popular assoc. with HANG) < AGNAIL⟧ a bit of torn skin hanging at the side or base of a fingernail

☆**hang·out** (haŋ′out′) ***n.*** [Slang] a place frequented by some person or group

☆**hang·o·ver** (haŋ′ō′vər) ***n.*** 1 something remaining from a previous time or state; a survival 2 a condition characterized by headache, nausea, etc. as an aftereffect of drinking much alcoholic liquor

Hang Seng (haŋ′ seŋ′) ⟦after the *Hang Seng* Bank in Hong Kong⟧ *service mark for* an index based upon the current prices of selected companies traded on the Hong Kong Stock Exchange: also **Hang Seng index**

☆**hang·tag** (haŋ′tag′) ***n.*** a tag attached to an article of merchandise, giving instructions for its use and care

☆**hang time** *Sports* 1 the length of time a punted football remains in the air 2 the length of time a leaping athlete, as a basketball player jumping for a dunk shot, remains in midair

☆**hang-up** (haŋ′up′) ***n.*** [Slang] a problem or difficulty, esp. one of a personal or emotional nature that a person seems unable to deal with

Hang·zhou (häŋ′jō′) port in E China; capital of Zhejiang province

hank (haŋk) ***n.*** ⟦LME, prob. < Scand, as in ON *hǫnk*, a coil, skein, *hanki*, hasp, clasp < IE base **keg-*, **kenk-* > HOOK⟧ 1 a loop or coil of something flexible 2 a specific length of coiled thread or yarn: a hank of worsted yarn contains 560 yd; a hank of cotton contains 840 yd 3 *Naut.* a ring or clip for fastening a staysail to its stay

han·ker (haŋ′kər) ***vi.*** ⟦Early ModE, prob. < Du or LowG source, as in Fl *hankeren*, to desire, long for, Du *hunkeren*, freq. formation & metaphoric extension < base of HANG⟧ to crave, long, or yearn: followed by *after, for,* or an infinitive

han·ker·ing (-iŋ) ***n.*** a craving; yearning

han·kie or **han·ky** (haŋ′kē) ***n., pl.*** **-kies** [Informal] a handkerchief

Han·kow (haŋ′kou′) former city in EC China: see WUHAN

han·ky-pan·ky (haŋ′kē paŋ′kē) ***n.*** ⟦altered ? after (SLEIGHT OF) HAND < HOCUS-POCUS⟧ [Informal] questionable behavior, as shady dealings or illicit sexual activity

Han·na (han′ə), **Mark** (born *Marcus Alonzo Hanna*) 1837-1904; U.S. financier & politician

Han·nah or **Han·na** (han′ə) ***n.*** ⟦Heb *Ḥannáh*, lit., graciousness⟧ 1 a feminine name: see ANNA, JOAN 2 *Bible* the mother of Samuel: 1 Sam. 1:20

Han·ni·bal (han′ə bəl) 247-183? B.C.; Carthaginian general: crossed the Alps to invade Italy in 218

Ha·noi (ha noi′, hä-) capital of Vietnam, in the N part

Han·o·ver[1] (han′ō vər) ***n.*** name of the ruling family of England (1714-1901), founded by George I, originally Elector of Hanover

Han·o·ver[2] (han′ō vər) 1 former province (1886-1945) of Prussia, in NW Germany: earlier, an electorate (1692-1815) & a kingdom (1815-86): now part of the German state of Lower Saxony 2 city in NW Germany: capital of Lower Saxony

Han·o·ve·ri·an (han′ō vir′ē ən, han′ə-; -ver′-) ***adj.*** 1 of Hanover, Germany 2 of the English royal house of Hanover —***n.*** a supporter of the house of Hanover

Hans (häns, hänz, hanz) ***n.*** ⟦Ger abbrev. of *Johannes*: equivalent to *Jack*: see JACK (***n.*** 1)⟧ a masculine name

han·sa (han′sə, hän′-) ***n.*** *var. of* HANSE

Han·sard (han′sərd) ***n.*** ⟦after L. *Hansard* (1752-1828) and descendants, by whom the reports were compiled and printed until 1889⟧ the official record of proceedings in the British Parliament

hanse (hans; han′sə, hän′-) ***n.*** ⟦ME < MFr & < ML *hansa*, both < MHG & MLowG *hanse*, association of merchants < OHG *hansa*, band of men, akin to OE *hos*, a troop⟧ 1 a medieval guild of merchants 2 a fee paid to this guild —**the Hanse** a medieval league of free towns in N Europe, formed to promote and protect their economic interests: the leading members were Bremen, Lübeck, and Hamburg: also **the Hansa**; now usually **Hanseatic League**

Han·se·at·ic (han′sē at′ik, -zē-) ***adj.*** ⟦ML *hanseaticus*⟧ of the Hanse or the towns that formed it

han·sel (han′səl) ***n.*** *var. of* HANDSEL

Han·sen's disease (han′sənz) ⟦after A. *Hansen* (1841-1912), Norw physician who discovered its causative bacterium⟧ *technical term for* LEPROSY

han·som (cab) (han′səm) ⟦after J. A. *Hansom* (1803-82), Eng architect & inventor, who designed it⟧ a two-wheeled covered carriage for two passengers, drawn by one horse: the driver's seat is above and behind the passenger compartment

hansom cab

Han·son (han′sən), **Howard** 1896-1981; U.S. composer

hant or **ha'nt** (hant) ***vt., n.*** *dial. var. of* HAUNT

han·ta·vi·rus (han′tə vī′rəs) ***n.*** ⟦after *Hantaan* River in South Korea, where the disease was first identified⟧ any of a group of RNA viruses (family Bunyaviridae); esp., one spread by contact with rodent urine and feces, causing flulike symptoms and sometimes a fatal lung or kidney disease

Hants (hants) *abbrev.* HAMPSHIRE

Ha·nuk·kah (khä′no͞o kä′, -kə; hä′-) ***n.*** ⟦TalmudHeb *chanuka*, lit., dedication < root *ḥnx*, inaugurate, dedicate⟧ a Jewish festival commemorating the rededication of the Temple by Judas Maccabaeus in 165 B.C. and celebrated for 8 days beginning the 25th day of Kislev: also sp. **Ha′nuk·ka′** or **Ha′nu·ka′**

han·u·man (hun′o͞o män′, hän′-; hun′o͞o män′, hän′-) ***n.*** ⟦Hindi *Hanumān* < Sans *hanumant*, having (big) jaws < *hánu-*, jaw < IE base **ĝenu-* > CHIN⟧ 1 [**H-**] *Hindu Myth.* a demigod in the form of a monkey 2 a small, slender-bodied, leaf-eating monkey (*Presbytis entellus*) with a long tail, found in Southeast Asia

Han·yang (hän′yäŋ′) former city in EC China: see WUHAN

ha·o·le (hä′ō lā′) ***n.*** ⟦Haw, foreigner⟧ in Hawaii, a non-Polynesian, esp. a white person, or Caucasian: sometimes a term of contempt

hap[1] (hap) [Archaic] ***n.*** ⟦ME < ON *happ*, akin to OE *(ge)hæp*, convenient, suitable < IE base **kob-*, to be fitted to, suit > OIr *cob*, victory⟧ 1 chance; luck; lot 2 an occurrence or happening, esp. an unfortunate one: *usually used in pl.* —***vi.*** **happed, hap′ping** ⟦ME *happen* < the *n.* or < ? (rare) OE *hæppan*, to go by chance < same base⟧ to occur by chance; happen

hap[2] (häp, hap) [Brit. Dial.] ***vt.*** **happed, hap′ping** ⟦ME *happen* < ?⟧ to cover, as with extra bedclothes —***n.*** any covering

ha·pax le·go·me·non (hā′paks′ li gäm′ə nän′) *pl.* ***-me·na′*** (-nä′, -nə) ⟦Gr, (something) said only once⟧ a word or phrase occurring only once, as in a text or in the written record of a language

hap·haz·ard (hap′haz′ərd) ***n.*** ⟦HAP[1] + HAZARD⟧ mere chance; accident; fortuity —***adj.*** not planned; random —***adv.*** by chance; casually —**SYN.** RANDOM —**hap′haz′ard·ly** ***adv.*** —**hap′haz′ard·ness** ***n.***

haph·ta·ra (häf′tä rä′, häf tôr′ə) ***n., pl.*** **-ta·roth′** (-tə rōt′, -tôr′ōt′) or **-ta′ras** (-tôr′əz) ⟦TalmudHeb *haftara*, dismissal, release < *hiftir*, dismiss < root *ptr*, send away⟧ the part of the Prophets read in synagogue services on the Sabbath and certain major holy days: the selection is related to the part of the Pentateuch read just before it

hap·less (hap′lis) ***adj.*** ⟦HAP[1] + -LESS⟧ unfortunate; unlucky; luckless —**hap′less·ly** ***adv.*** —**hap′less·ness** ***n.***

hap·lo- (hap′lō, -lə) ⟦< Gr *haploos*, single < IE **sm̥plos*, SIMPLE⟧ *combining form* single, simple [*haploid*]: also, before a vowel, **hapl-**

hap·loid (hap′loid′) ***adj.*** ⟦< prec. + -OID⟧ *Biol.* having the full number of chromosomes normally occurring in the mature germ cell, or half the number in the usual somatic cell —***n.*** a haploid cell or gamete —**hap′loi′dy** (-loi′dē) ***n.***

hap·lol·o·gy (hap läl′ə jē) ***n.*** ⟦HAPLO- + -LOGY⟧ the dropping of one of two similar or identical successive syllables or sounds in a word (Ex.: *interpretive* for *interpretative*)

hap·lont (hap′länt′) ***n.*** ⟦HAPL(O)- + *-ont* < Gr *ōn* (gen. *ontos*): see ONTO-⟧ an organism in which the nuclei of the somatic cells are haploid

hap·lo·sis (hap lō′sis) ***n.*** ⟦HAPL(O)- + -OSIS⟧ *Biol.* a halving of the number of chromosomes during meiosis, through the division of a diploid cell into two haploids

hap·lo·type (hap′lō tīp′) ***n.*** a set of alleles inherited by an individual from a single parent

hap·ly (hap′lē) ***adv.*** ⟦ME *hapliche*: see HAP[1] & -LY[2]⟧ [Archaic] by chance or accident; perhaps

hap·pen (hap′ən) ***vi.*** ⟦ME *happenen*: see HAP[1] & -EN⟧ **1** to take place; occur; befall **2** to be or occur by chance or without plan [it *happened* to rain] **3** to have the luck or occasion [I *happened* to catch the exhibit when I was in New York] **4** to come by chance (*along, by, in,* etc.) —**as it (so) happens** as a matter of fact; incidentally —**happen on (**or **upon)** to meet or find by chance —**happen to** to be done to or be the fate of; befall

SYN.—**happen** is the general word meaning to take place or come to pass and may suggest either direct cause or apparent accident; **chance**, more or less equivalent to **happen**, always implies apparent lack of cause in the event; **occur** is somewhat more formal and usually suggests a specific event at a specific time [what *happened?*; the accident *occurred* at four o'clock]; **transpire** is now frequently used as an equivalent for **happen** or **occur** [what *transpired* at the conference], apparently by confusion with its sense of to become known, or leak out [reports on the conference never *transpired*]

hap·pen·ing (hap′ən iŋ; *informally* hap′niŋ) ***n.*** **1** something that happens; occurrence; incident; event ☆**2** *a)* a theatrical performance of unrelated and bizarre or ludicrous actions, often spontaneous and with some participation by the audience *b)* any event regarded as important, entertaining, newsworthy, etc.

☆**hap·pen·stance** (hap′ən stans′) ***n.*** ⟦HAPPEN + (CIRCUM)STANCE⟧ [Informal] **1** chance; fortuity **2** a chance or accidental happening

hap·pi coat (hap′ē) ⟦< Jpn *happi,* coat of this kind + COAT⟧ a short, lightweight Japanese coat worn with a narrow sash over regular clothes, as to protect them from soiling

hap·py (hap′ē) ***adj.*** **-pi·er, -pi·est** ⟦ME *happi* < *hap*: see HAP[1]⟧ **1** favored by circumstances; lucky; fortunate **2** having, showing, or causing a feeling of great pleasure, contentment, joy, etc.; joyous; glad; pleased **3** exactly appropriate to the occasion; suitable and clever; apt; felicitous [a *happy* suggestion] **4** [Slang] *a)* intoxicated, sedated, etc. (often used in comb.) [slap-*happy*] *b)* intoxicating, sedating, etc. [*happy* pills] *c)* irresponsibly quick to act (used in comb.) [trigger-*happy*] —**hap′pi·ly** ***adv.*** —**hap′pi·ness** ***n.***

SYN.—**happy** generally suggests a feeling of great pleasure, contentment, etc. [a *happy* marriage]; **glad** implies more strongly an exultant feeling of joy [your letter made her so *glad*], but both **glad** and **happy** are commonly used in merely polite formulas expressing gratification [I'm *glad*, or *happy*, to have met you]; **cheerful** implies a steady display of bright spirits, optimism, etc. [he's always *cheerful* in the morning]; **joyful** and **joyous** both imply great elation and rejoicing, the former generally because of a particular event, and the latter as a matter of usual temperament [the *joyful* throngs, a *joyous* family] —***ANT.*** **sad**

happy camper [Informal] a person who is content

hap·py-go-luck·y (hap′ē gō luk′ē) ***adj.*** taking things as they come; easygoing; trusting to luck; lighthearted

☆**happy hour** a time, as in the late afternoon, when a bar or tavern features drinks at reduced prices

☆**happy hunting ground** the land of the dead: term used in referring to traditional North American Indian concepts of the afterlife

☆**happy talk** *Radio, TV* a style of news presentation characterized by cheerful commentary and informal conversation among anchors during newscasts

Haps·burg (haps′burg′; *Ger* häps′bo͝orkh) ***n.*** *alt. sp. of* HABSBURG

hap·ten (hap′ten′) ***n.*** ⟦Ger < Gr *haptein,* to fasten, touch + Ger *-en,* -ENE⟧ a compound which, when coupled with a protein or other molecule, can cause the formation of antibodies: also **hap·tene** (hap′tēn′) —**hap·ten·ic** (hap ten′ik) ***adj.***

hap·tic (hap′tik) ***adj.*** ⟦< Gr *haptein,* to touch + -IC⟧ of or having to do with the sense of touch; tactile

hap·to·glo·bin (hap′tə glō′bin) ***n.*** ⟦< Gr *haptein.* to fasten + HEMOGLOBIN⟧ a blood protein that binds with free hemoglobin in the bloodstream or at a wound when red blood cells decompose or are destroyed abnormally in the circulation

har·a-kir·i (här′ə kir′ē, har′ə-; *popularly,* her′ē ker′ē) ***n.*** ⟦Jpn < *hara,* belly + *kiri,* a cutting, cut⟧ ritual suicide by cutting the abdomen: it is called *seppuku* by the Japanese, and was practiced by high-ranking Japanese of the military class in lieu of execution or to avoid disgrace

ha·rangue (hə raŋ′) ***n.*** ⟦ME (Scot) *arang* < OFr *arenge* < OIt *aringa* < *aringo,* site for horse races and public assemblies < Goth **hrings,* circle: see RING[2]⟧ a long, blustering, noisy, or scolding speech; tirade — ***vi., vt.*** **-rangued′, -rangu′ing** to speak or address in a harangue —**ha·rangu′er** ***n.***

Ha·ra·re (hä rä′rē) capital of Zimbabwe, in the NE part

har·ass (har′əs, hə ras′) ***vt.*** ⟦Fr *harasser* < OFr *harer,* to set a dog on < *hare,* cry to incite dogs < OHG *harēn,* to call, cry out⟧ **1** to trouble, worry, or torment, as with cares, debts, repeated questions or demands, etc.: see also SEXUAL HARASSMENT **2** to trouble by repeated raids or attacks, etc.; harry —**har′ass·er** ***n.*** —**har′ass·ment** ***n.***

Har·bin (här′bin) city in NE China, on the Songhua River; capital of Heilongjiang province

har·bin·ger (här′bin jər) ***n.*** ⟦ME *herbergeour* (with intrusive *-n-*) < OFr *herbergeor,* provider of lodging < *herberge,* a shelter < Frank (or OHG) *heriberga,* shelter for soldiers < *heri,* army (see HARRY) + *berga,* a shelter < *bergan,* to protect: see BURY⟧ **1** [Historical] an advance representative of an army or royal party, who arranged for lodging, entertainment, etc. **2** a person or thing that comes before to announce or give an indication of what follows; herald —***vt.*** to serve as harbinger of

har·bor (här′bər) ***n.*** ⟦ME *herberwe* < OE *herebeorg* (& ON *herbergi*), lit., army shelter (< *here,* army + *beorg,* a shelter), akin to OHG *heriberga*: see prec.⟧ **1** a place of refuge, safety, etc.; retreat; shelter **2** a protected inlet, or branch of a sea, lake, etc., where ships can anchor, esp. one with port facilities —***vt.*** **1** to serve as, or provide, a place of protection to; shelter or house; conceal or hide **2** to be the dwelling place or habitat of **3** to hold in the mind; cling to [to *harbor* a grudge] —***vi.*** **1** to take shelter, as in a harbor **2** to live or exist —**har′bor·er** ***n.*** —**har′bor·less** ***adj.***

har·bor·age (-ij) ***n.*** **1** a shelter for ships; port; anchorage **2** shelter or lodgings

harbor master the official in charge of enforcing the regulations governing the use of a harbor

harbor seal an earless seal (*Phoca vitulina*) common in N Atlantic coastal waters

har·bour (här′bər) ***n., vt., vi.*** *Brit. sp. of* HARBOR

hard (härd) ***adj.*** ⟦ME < OE *heard,* akin to Ger *hart* < IE base **kar-,* hard > Gr *karyon,* nut, *kratos,* strength⟧ **1** not easily dented, pierced, cut, or crushed; resistant to pressure; firm and unyielding to the touch; rigid; solid and compact **2** having firm muscles; in good bodily trim; vigorous and robust **3** showing, or done with, great force or strength; powerful; violent; vigorous [a *hard* blow] **4** demanding great physical or mental effort or labor; fatiguing; difficult; specif., *a)* difficult to do [*hard* work] *b)* difficult to understand, explain, or answer [a *hard* question] *c)* difficult to deal with; not easily managed or controlled [a man *hard* to live with] *d)* firmly fastened or tied [a *hard* knot] **5** *a)* not easily moved; unfeeling; callous [a *hard* heart] *b)* unfriendly; hostile [*hard* feelings] **6** practical and shrewd or calculating, esp. in an unyielding way [to drive a *hard* bargain] **7** *a)* firm or definite, esp. in an aggressive way [a *hard* line in foreign policy] *b)* undeniable, reliable, or actual [*hard* facts] *c)* consisting of the basic facts about major events, as opposed to presenting feature stories, opinion, etc. [*hard* news] **8** causing or characterized by pain or discomfort; specif., *a)* difficult to endure; trying [a *hard* life] *b)* harsh; severe; stern [a *hard* master, *hard* words] *c)* characterized by hardship, setbacks, etc. [*hard* luck] **9** very cold, stormy, etc.; inclement [a *hard* winter] **10** *a)* harsh, stiff, and wiry (said of fibers or cotton) *b)* having no nap (said of a finish for fabric) *c)* having a texture that is firm, dense, wiry, etc. [a dog with a *hard* coat] **11** *a)* clearly defined or having sharp contrast; distinct [*hard* outlines] *b)* too clear, bright, or penetrating to be pleasant [a *hard* light] **12** containing mineral salts that interfere with the lathering and cleansing properties of soap, that corrode metals, etc.: said of water **13** energetic and persistent; steady and earnest [a *hard* worker] **14** *a)* fermented; alcoholic [*hard* cider] *b)* containing a relatively high percentage of alcohol; strong [*hard* liquor] ☆*c)* [Informal] of or pertaining to a HARD DRUG **15** *a)* of metal, not paper *b)* of currency or coin, not credit: said of money **16** *a)* that can be exchanged for gold or silver *b)* that is readily accepted as foreign exchange: said of certain currencies **17** *Phonet.* *a)* designating *c* sounded as in *can* or *g* sounded as in *gun* [a *hard* g] *b)* voiceless, as the sound of *s* in *sin* *c)* not palatalized (said as of certain consonants in Slavic languages): not used in these ways as a technical term by phoneticians **18** *Agric.* high in gluten content [*hard* wheat] **19** *Chem.* not easily biodegradable: said of detergents and pesticides **20** *Commerce* high and stable: said of a market, prices, etc. **21** *Mil.* heavily fortified: said as of an underground installation [a *hard* base] **22** *Radiology* of high penetrating power: said of X-rays —***adv.*** **1** energetically and persistently; steadily and earnestly [work *hard*] **2** with strength, violence, or severity [hit *hard*] **3** with difficulty: often used in hyphenated compounds [*hard*-earned, *hard*-sought] **4** so as to withstand much wear, use, etc. [*hard*-wearing clothes] **5** deeply; fully; soundly [sleep *hard*] **6** firmly; tightly [hold on *hard*] **7** close; near [we live *hard* by the woods] **8** so as to be or make firm, solid, or rigid [to freeze *hard*] **9** with vigor and to the fullest extent: used esp. in indicating direction [*hard* alee! turn *hard* right] —**be hard on** **1** to treat severely; be harsh toward **2** to be difficult, unpleasant, or painful for —**be hard put (to it)** to have considerable difficulty or trouble —**hard and fast** invariable; strict; definitive: said of rules, etc. —**hard of hearing** partially deaf —**hard up** [Informal] in great need of something, esp. money —**play hard to get** [Informal] to seem unwilling to accept an offer, romantic advances, etc., as in order to elicit further or stronger appeals

SYN.—**hard**, in this comparison, is the simple and general word for whatever demands great physical or mental effort [*hard* work, a *hard* problem]; **difficult** applies especially to that which requires great skill, intelligence, tact, etc. rather than physical labor [a *difficult* situation]; **arduous** implies the need for diligent, protracted effort [the *arduous* fight ahead of us]; **laborious** suggests long, wearisome toil [the *laborious* task of picking fruit] See also **firm** —***ANT.*** **easy, simple**

hard-ass (härd′as′) [Slang] ***adj.*** tough, inflexible, etc. —***n.*** one who is tough, inflexible, etc. A mildly vulgar term

hard·back (härd′bak′) ***n.*** a hardcover book

☆**hard·ball** (härd′bôl′) ***n.*** **1** *a)* a kind of baseball characterized by hard-thrown overhand pitching *b)* the ball typically used in this game; BASEBALL (sense 2) **2** any ruthless, aggressive, highly competitive form of politics, business, etc.: often in the phrase **play hardball** —***adj.*** of or characterized by ruthlessness, competitiveness, coercion, etc. [*hardball* business practices]

hard-bit·ten (härd′bit′'n) *adj.* 1 [Archaic] that bites hard; tough in fighting: said of dogs 2 tough, cynical, jaded, etc.

☆**hard·board** (härd′bôrd′) *n.* a boardlike building material made by subjecting fibers from wood chips to pressure and heat

hard-boiled (härd′boild′) *adj.* 1 cooked in simmering water until both the white and the yolk solidify: said of eggs ☆2 [Informal] not affected by sentiment, pity, etc.; tough; callous ☆3 of or designating a style of genre fiction dealing in a straightforward, cynical way with criminals, detectives, etc.

☆**hard bop** a style of jazz, esp. in its development from about 1954 to 1967, that further refined bop while introducing more melodies and harmonies based on blues and gospel influences

☆**hard-bound** (-bound′) *adj.* HARDCOVER

hard case [Informal] 1 a rough or tough person 2 one who is firmly established in bad habits 3 a person in an unfortunate condition

hard coal ANTHRACITE

hard copy a computer printout, often supplied along with or instead of a video screen display

hard core the firm, unyielding, or unchanging central part or group

hard·core (härd′kôr′) *adj.* 1 constituting or of a hard core 2 absolute; unqualified [a *hardcore* radical] 3 explicit, rather than suggestive, in the portrayal of sexual acts; graphic [*hardcore* pornography] Often written **hard-core**

☆**hard·cover** (härd′kuv′ər) *adj.* designating any book bound in a relatively stiff cover, as of cloth-covered cardboard —*n.* a hardcover book: distinguished from PAPERBACK

hard disk a computer disk with a rigid metal base

hard drive a computer drive for hard disks, specif., such a drive constituting the primary storage device of a computer

☆**hard drug** [Informal] a potent drug, such as heroin or cocaine, that typically leads to physical or psychological dependency

hard-edge (härd′ej′) *adj.* 1 designating or of any painting or work of art in which there are hard, or clearly defined, edges to the shapes, as of color, on the surface 2 intense or sharp; clearly defined: also **hard′-edged′**

hard·en (härd′'n) *vt.* ⟦ME *hardnen* < ON *harthna* & < ME *hard,* HARD⟧ 1 to make solid, rigid, or firm 2 to make callous [painful experience can *harden* one's heart] 3 to accustom to varying or adverse conditions or climate —*vi.* to become solid, rigid, callous, etc.

hard·ened (härd′'nd) *adj.* 1 made or become hard or harder (in various senses) 2 confirmed or inveterate, esp. in wrong or immoral behavior; habitual —**SYN.** CHRONIC

hard·en·er (härd′'n ər) *n.* a person or thing that hardens something; specif., *a)* a person who tempers metal tools *b)* a substance added to paint, varnish, etc. to give it a harder film

hard·en·ing (härd′'n iŋ) *n.* 1 a making or becoming hard 2 a substance used to harden something

hard-fea·tured (-fē′chərd) *adj.* having coarse, cruel, stern, or harsh features

hard·fist·ed (härd′fist′id) *adj.* stingy; miserly

hard·goods (härd′goodz′) *pl.n.* durable goods, such as automobiles, furniture, etc.: also written **hard goods**

☆**hard·hack** (härd′hak′) *n.* ⟦HARD + HACK[1]⟧ STEEPLEBUSH

hard·hand·ed (härd′han′did) *adj.* 1 having hands made hard by work 2 severe; tyrannical; ruthless: said of a ruler or rule —**hard′hand′ed·ness** *n.*

hard hat ☆1 a protective helmet worn by construction workers, miners, etc. ☆2 [Slang] such a worker —**hard′-hat′** *adj.*

hard·head (härd′hed′) *n.* 1 a shrewd person, not easily moved 2 a stubborn, hardheaded person 3 any of various fishes; esp., a slender river minnow (*Mylopharodon conocephalus*) of central and N California

hard·head·ed (-hed′id) *adj.* 1 shrewd and unsentimental; practical; matter-of-fact 2 stubborn; obstinate; dogged —**hard′head′ed·ly** *adv.* —**hard′head′ed·ness** *n.*

hardhead sponge any of several coarse-fibered sponges from the Caribbean area

hard·heart·ed (härd′härt′id) *adj.* unfeeling; pitiless; cruel —**hard′heart′ed·ly** *adv.* —**hard′heart′ed·ness** *n.*

hard-hit·ting (-hit′iŋ) *adj.* [Informal] forceful, aggressive, boldly frank, etc. [a *hard-hitting* news report]

har·di·hood (här′dē hood′) *n.* ⟦< HARDY[1] + -HOOD⟧ boldness, daring, fortitude, vigor, etc.

har·di·ly (här′də lē) *adv.* in a hardy manner

har·di·ness (här′dē nis) *n.* the quality of being hardy; specif., *a)* physical endurance; strength *b)* hardihood; boldness

Har·ding (här′diŋ), **Warren G(amaliel)** 1865-1923; 29th president of the U.S. (1921-23)

hard labor compulsory physical labor imposed, together with imprisonment, as a punishment for some crimes

☆**hard landing** a landing, as of a rocket on the moon, made at relatively high speed, with an impact that may destroy all or much of the equipment —**hard′-land′** *vi., vt.*

☆**hard-line** (härd′līn′) *adj.* characterized by an aggressive, unyielding position in politics, foreign policy, etc.

☆**hard-lin·er** (-ər) *n.* a person who takes a hard-line position

hard·ly (härd′lē) *adv.* ⟦ME *hardliche* < OE *heardlice*⟧ 1 [Now Rare] *a)* with effort or difficulty *b)* severely; harshly 2 only just; barely; scarcely: often used ironically or politely to mean "not quite," or "not at all" [*hardly* the person to ask]

☆**hard maple** SUGAR MAPLE

hard·ness (härd′nis) *n.* 1 the state or quality of being hard (in various senses) 2 *Mineralogy* the relative capacity of a substance for scratching another or for being scratched by another

☆**hard-nosed** (härd′nōzd′) *adj.* [Informal] 1 indomitable; tough; stubborn 2 shrewd and practical —**hard′nose′** *n.*

hard-on (-än′) *n.* [Slang] an erection of the penis: considered vulgar by some

hard pack (snow) dense, compacted snow

hard palate the bony part of the roof of the mouth, behind the upper teeth-ridge

hard·pan (härd′pan′) *n.* 1 a layer of hard soil cemented by almost insoluble materials that restrict the downward movement of water and roots 2 solid, unplowed ground ☆3 the hard, underlying part of anything; solid foundation

hard-pressed (härd′prest′) *adj.* confronted with a demanding or distressing problem or situation

☆**hard rock** loud, fast rock music with driving, regular rhythms

hard rubber a firm, inelastic substance made by treating crude rubber with a large amount of sulfur and subjecting it to intense heat; ebonite: used for combs, electrical insulation, etc.

hards (härdz) *pl.n.* ⟦ME *hardes* < OE *heordan, pl.,* flax hards, akin to MLowG *herde* < IE base **kes-* to scrape, comb > Gr *keskeon,* tow⟧ TOW[2]

☆**hard sauce** a sweet, creamy mixture of butter, powdered sugar, and a flavoring such as vanilla extract, rum, or brandy, served as with plum pudding or cake

hard science NATURAL SCIENCE: opposed to behavioral science, called SOFT (*adj.* 16)

hard·scrab·ble (härd′skrab′əl) *adj.* producing or earning only a very small amount; barren [a *hardscrabble* farm, life, etc.]

☆**hard sell** [Informal] high-pressure salesmanship —**hard′-sell′** *adj.*

hard-set (härd′set′) *adj.* 1 in trouble or difficulty 2 rigid; fixed; firm 3 stubborn

hard-shell (härd′shel′) *adj.* 1 *a)* having a hard shell *b)* having a shell not recently molted (said of crabs, crayfish, etc.) ☆2 [Informal] strict; strait-laced; uncompromising, esp. in religious matters Also **hard′-shelled′**

hard-shelled (*or* hard-shell) clam QUAHOG

☆**hard-shelled (*or* hard-shell) crab** a crab, esp. an edible sea crab, before it has shed its hard shell

hard·ship (härd′ship′) *n.* ⟦ME *heardschipe:* see HARD & -SHIP⟧ 1 hard circumstances of life 2 a thing hard to bear; specific cause of discomfort or suffering, as poverty, pain, etc. —**SYN.** DIFFICULTY

hard-spun (härd′spun′) *adj.* spun with a firm, close twist: said of yarn

☆**hard·stand** (härd′stand′) *n.* a paved area for parking aircraft or other vehicles

hard·tack (härd′tak′) *n.* ⟦HARD + TACK, *n.* 5⟧ unleavened bread made in very hard, large wafers: it was formerly a part of army and navy rations

☆**hard·top** (härd′täp′) *n.* 1 a motor vehicle with a permanent rigid top or a removable rigid top 2 the rigid top of such a vehicle

hard·ware (härd′wer′) *n.* 1 articles made of metal, as tools, nails, fittings, utensils, etc.; often, specif., hinges, handles, locks, etc. used on doors, windows, etc. ☆2 heavy military equipment, such as weapons, vehicles, missiles, etc. ☆3 *a)* apparatus used for controlling spacecraft, etc. *b) Comput.* the mechanical, magnetic, and electronic design, structure, and devices of a computer or computer system or of other electronic equipment: cf. SOFTWARE

hard wheat wheat with high protein content and hard kernels: see DURUM

hard-wired (härd′wīrd′) *adj.* 1 directly connected to a computer [a *hard-wired* terminal] 2 designating or of a computer device with permanently wired circuitry for performing certain tasks 3 biologically or genetically predetermined, rather than resulting from the effects of experience or environment Also written **hard′wired′**

hard·wood (härd′wood′) *n.* 1 any tough, heavy timber with a compact texture 2 *Forestry* the wood of an angiosperm possessing true vessels, in contrast to the softwood of a gymnosperm, which lacks vessels 3 a tree yielding hardwood

hard·work·ing (härd′wur′kiŋ) *adj.* diligent; industrious: also written **hard-working**

har·dy[1] (här′dē) *adj.* **-di·er, -di·est** ⟦ME & OFr *hardi,* pp. of *hardir,* to make bold < Frank **hardjan,* to make hard < **hard-,* HARD⟧ 1 bold and resolute; daring; courageous 2 too bold; full of temerity; rash 3 able to withstand fatigue, privation, etc.; robust; vigorous 4 able to survive the winter without special care: said of plants

har·dy[2] (här′dē) *n.* ⟦prob. HARD + -Y[3]⟧ a chisel with a square shank, used by blacksmiths: it fits into a square hole (**hardy hole**) in the anvil

Har·dy (här′dē) 1 **Oliver** (born *Norvell Hardy*) 1892-1957; U.S. film comedian: teamed with Stan LAUREL 2 **Thomas** 1840-1928; Eng. novelist & poet

hare (her, har) *n., pl.* **hares** or **hare** ⟦ME < OE *hara,* akin to Ger *hase* < IE **kas-,* gray (hence, lit., the gray animal, euphemism for a taboo name) > L *canus,* hoary⟧ any of a large group of swift mammals (order Lagomorpha) of the same family (Leporidae) as the rabbits, with long ears, soft fur, a cleft upper lip, a short tail, and long, powerful hind legs: it differs from a rabbit in that it is larger, does not burrow, and has furry, active young —*vi.* **hared, har′ing** [Brit. Informal] to run fast or go hurriedly: with *off, away, about,* etc.

hare and hounds a game in which some players, called "hounds," chase others, called "hares," who have left a trail of paper scraps along their route

hare·bell (her′bel′) *n.* ⟦ME *harebelle*: see HARE & BELL[1]⟧ a slender, delicate perennial bellflower (*Campanula rotundifolia*) with clusters of blue, bell-shaped flowers

hare·brained (her′brānd′) *adj.* ⟦< obs. *hare-brain*, heedless person, one having a brain like a hare's + -ED⟧ having or showing little sense; reckless, flighty, giddy, rash, etc.

Ha·re Krishna (hä′rē krish′nə) ⟦< Hindi *Hari*, one of the names of Vishnu + KRISHNA[2]⟧ 1 a cult that holds certain Hindu beliefs and stresses devotion to Krishna: it was founded in the U.S. in 1966 2 a member of this cult

hare·lip (her′lip′) *n.* CLEFT LIP —**hare′lipped′** *adj.*

ha·rem (her′əm, har′-) *n.* ⟦Ar *ḥarīm*, lit., prohibited (place, thing) < *ḥarama*, to forbid⟧ 1 that part of a Muslim household in which the women live; seraglio 2 the wives, concubines, women servants, etc. occupying a harem 3 a number of female animals, as of fur seals, who mate and lodge with one male Also **ha·reem** (hä rēm′)

harem pants ⟦from their resemblance to women's trousers formerly worn in some Muslim countries⟧ a kind of baggy trousers worn by women, made of lightweight fabric and closefitting at the ankles

Har·greaves (här′grēvz, -grävz), **James** died 1778; Eng. inventor of the spinning jenny

Har·ia·na (hər yä′nə) state of NW India: 17,070 sq mi (44,211 sq km); cap. Chandigarh

har·i·cot (har′i kō′) *n.* ⟦Fr < *harigoter*, to cut to pieces < ? MDu **harigod*, sharp tool < *haren*, to sharpen + *god*, a tool⟧ 1 a highly seasoned stew of lamb or mutton and vegetables 2 ⟦altered (infl. by the stew) < ? Nahuatl *ayecotli*, bean⟧ [Chiefly Brit.] *a)* KIDNEY BEAN *b)* the pod or seed of any of various other edible beans

ha·ri·jan (har′i jən, hu′ri-; -jan′) *n.* ⟦Sans *harijana*, person devoted to the god Vishnu < *Hari*, Vishnu + *jana*, person⟧ [*also* **H-**] in India, an untouchable or, later, a member of the Scheduled Castes

har·i-kar·i (här′ē kär′ē, her′ē ker′ē) *n. var. of* HARA-KIRI

Har·in·gey (hä′riŋ gā) borough of Greater London, England

hark (härk) *vi.* ⟦ME *herkien* (akin to Ger *horchen*) < ? OE **heorcian* or < OE *heorcnian*: see HEARKEN⟧ [Now Chiefly Literary] to listen carefully: usually in the imperative, with the effect of an exclamation —*vt.* [Archaic] to listen to; hear —**hark back** 1 to return to an earlier point so as to pick up the scent or trail again 2 to go back in thought or speech; revert

hark·en (här′kən) *vi., vt. alt. sp. of* HEARKEN —**harken back** HEARKEN BACK (see phrase under HEARKEN)

harl (härl) *n.* ⟦ME *herle*, prob. < MLowG *harle*⟧ 1 a filament, esp. of hemp or flax 2 *var. of* HERL

Har·lan[1] (här′lən) *n.* ⟦< the surname *Harlan*⟧ a masculine name

Har·lan[2] (här′lən), **John Marshall** 1899-1971; associate justice, U.S. Supreme Court (1955-71)

Har·lem (här′ləm) ⟦after HAARLEM⟧ section of New York City, in N Manhattan

Harlem Renaissance the period, chiefly the 1920s, of vigorous growth and development of African-American culture, esp. as exemplified by the work of the many writers, musicians, etc. in Harlem

Harlem River tidal river separating Manhattan Island from the Bronx &, with Spuyten Duyvil Creek, connecting the East River with the Hudson: *c.* 8 mi (12.9 km)

Har·le·quin (här′li kwin, -kin) *n.* ⟦Fr *harlequin, arlequin* < OFr *hierlekin, hellequin*, demon: Fr sense & form infl. by It *arlecchino* < same OFr source⟧ 1 a traditional comic character in pantomime, who wears a mask and spangled, diamond-patterned tights of many colors and sometimes carries a wooden wand or sword 2 [**h-**] a clown; buffoon —*adj.* [**h-**] 1 comic; ludicrous 2 of many colors; colorful

Harlequin

har·le·quin·ade (här′li kwi nād′) *n.* ⟦Fr *arlequinade*⟧ 1 that part of a play or pantomime in which the Harlequin and the clown play leading parts 2 comic pranks; lively, mischievous antics; buffoonery

☆**harlequin bug** a black-and-red, hemipterous stink bug (*Murgantia histrionica*) that feeds on cabbages and related plants

☆**harlequin snake** the E American coral snake (*Micrurus fulvius*)

har·lot (här′lət) *n.* ⟦ME (< OFr, rogue, vagabond), orig. a euphemism for *whore*⟧ [Old-fashioned] a promiscuous woman, esp. a prostitute

har·lot·ry (här′lə trē) *n.* [Archaic or Literary] 1 prostitution 2 prostitutes collectively

harm (härm) *n.* ⟦ME < OE *hearm*, akin to Ger *harm* < IE base **k̑ormo-*, pain, torment > MPers *šarm*, shame⟧ 1 hurt; injury; damage 2 moral wrong; evil —*vt.* ⟦ME *harmen* < OE *hearmian* < the *n.*⟧ to do harm to; hurt, damage, etc. —*SYN.* INJURE —**harm′er** *n.*

har·mat·tan (här′mə tan′) *n.* ⟦Sp *harmatán* < the native (Twi) name in W Africa⟧ a dry, dusty wind that blows from the Sahara in N Africa toward the Atlantic, esp. from Nov. to March

harm·ful (härm′fəl) *adj.* causing or able to cause harm; hurtful —**harm′ful·ly** *adv.* —**harm′ful·ness** *n.*

har·mine (här′mēn′) *n.* an alkaloid drug, $C_{13}H_{12}N_2O$, present in ayahuasca and used in medicine as a stimulant

harm·less (härm′lis) *adj.* 1 [Rare] not harmed 2 causing or seeking to cause no harm; not harmful; inoffensive —**harm′less·ly** *adv.* —**harm′less·ness** *n.*

Har·mo·ni·a (här mō′nē ə) *n.* ⟦L < Gr: see HARMONY⟧ *Gr. Myth.* 1 the daughter of Aphrodite and Ares, and wife of Cadmus 2 *personification of* harmony and order

har·mon·ic (här män′ik) *adj.* ⟦L *harmonicus* < Gr *harmonikos* < *harmonia*, HARMONY⟧ 1 harmonious in feeling or effect; agreeing 2 *Math.* designating or of a harmonic progression 3 *Music a)* of or pertaining to harmony rather than to melody or rhythm *b)* of or pertaining to a harmonic —*n.* 1 an alternating-current voltage or current or a component of such voltage or current, whose frequency is some integral multiple of a fundamental frequency 2 *Music* any of the pure tones making up a composite tone, including the upper partials or overtones of the fundamental, and often excluding the fundamental itself —**har·mon′i·cal·ly** *adv.*

☆**har·mon·i·ca** (här män′i kə) *n.* ⟦L, fem. of *harmonicus* (see prec.): name altered < earlier *armonica* (< It, fem. of *armonico*, of same orig.) by Benjamin FRANKLIN[2], who developed this instrument from an earlier form⟧ 1 a small wind instrument played with the mouth; mouth organ: it has a series of graduated metal reeds that vibrate and produce tones when air is blown or sucked across them 2 GLASS HARMONICA

harmonic analysis 1 the study of Fourier series 2 the act of breaking a periodic function into components, each expressed as a sine or cosine function

harmonic mean a number associated with a set of numbers, that is equal to the number of numbers divided by the sum of the reciprocals of the numbers ($h = n \div (\frac{1}{a} + \frac{1}{b} + \frac{1}{c} + ...)$) (Ex.: for $\frac{1}{2}$, $\frac{1}{3}$, and $\frac{1}{4}$, $h = 3 \div (2 + 3 + 4) = \frac{1}{3}$; for $\frac{1}{2}$ and $\frac{1}{3}$, $h = 2 \div (2 + 3) = \frac{2}{5}$)

harmonic motion motion that repeats periodically, as the motion produced by a restoring force proportional to displacement

harmonic progression a series of quantities whose reciprocals form an arithmetic progression (Ex: $\frac{1}{2}$, $\frac{1}{3}$, and $\frac{1}{4}$: the resulting arithmetic progression 2, 3, and 4 is not a harmonic progression)

harmonic series *Music* the series of harmonics, or pure tones, making up a composite tone

har·mo·ni·ous (här mō′nē əs) *adj.* ⟦Fr *harmonieux* < OFr *harmonie*: see HARMONY⟧ 1 having parts combined in a proportionate, orderly, or pleasing arrangement; congruous 2 having similar or conforming feelings, ideas, interests, etc.; in accord 3 having musical tones combined to give a pleasing effect; consonant —**har·mo′ni·ous·ly** *adv.* —**har·mo′ni·ous·ness** *n.*

har·mo·nist (här′mə nist) *n.* 1 a musician expert in harmony 2 a scholar who arranges a HARMONY (sense 4) —**har′mo·nis′tic** *adj.* —**har′mo·nis′ti·cal·ly** *adv.*

har·mo·ni·um (här mō′nē əm) *n.* ⟦Fr: so named by A. F. Debain (1809-77), Fr organ maker < *harmonie*, HARMONY⟧ a small kind of reed organ

har·mo·nize (här′mə nīz′) *vi.* **-nized′**, **-niz′ing** ⟦Fr *harmonizer*: see fol. & -IZE⟧ 1 to be in harmony; accord; agree 2 to sing in harmony —*vt.* 1 to make harmonious; bring into agreement 2 to add chords to (a melody) so as to form a harmony 3 to arrange into a HARMONY (sense 4) —*SYN.* AGREE —**har′mo·ni·za′tion** *n.* —**har′mo·niz′er** *n.*

har·mo·ny (här′mə nē) *n., pl.* **-nies** ⟦ME *armony* < OFr *harmonie* < L *harmonia* < Gr < *harmos*, a fitting < IE base **ar-* > ART[3], ARM[1]⟧ 1 a combination of parts into a pleasing or orderly whole; congruity 2 agreement in feeling, action, ideas, interests, etc.; peaceable or friendly relations 3 a state of agreement or orderly arrangement according to color, size, shape, etc. 4 an arrangement of parallel passages of different authors, esp. of the Scriptures, so as to bring out corresponding ideas, qualities, etc. 5 agreeable sounds; music 6 *Music a)* the simultaneous sounding of two or more tones, esp. when satisfying to the ear *b)* structure in terms of the arrangement, modulation, etc. of chords (distinguished from MELODY, RHYTHM) *c)* the study of this structure —*SYN.* SYMMETRY

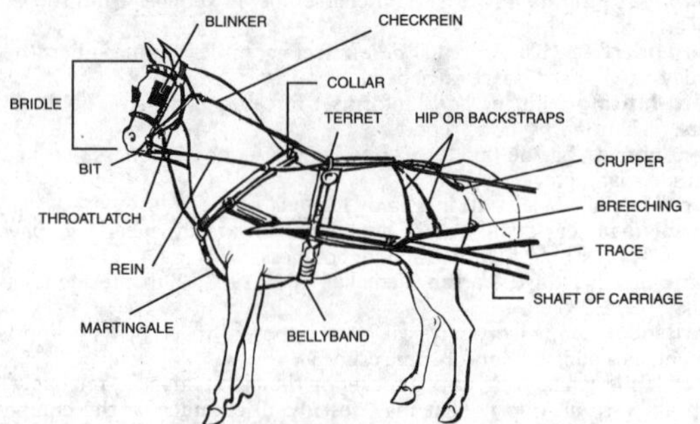

light harness for a carriage

har·ness (här′nis) *n.* ⟦ME *harneis* < OFr, armor < ON **hernest*, military supplies < *herr*, army, akin to HARRY + *nest*, provisions⟧ 1 [Archaic] armor and other military equipment for a man or horse 2 the assemblage of leather straps and metal pieces by which a horse, mule, etc. is fastened to a vehicle, plow, or load 3 any trappings or gear similar to this; specif., *a)* the straps, etc. by which a parachute is fastened to a person or object *b)* a device for raising and lowering the warp threads on a loom **4** a set of electrical wires that can be quickly connected or disconnected as a unit at pluglike junctions **—*vt.* 1** [Obs.] to put armor on **2** *a)* to put harness on (a horse, etc.) *b)* to attach (a horse, etc.) with a harness *to* something, as a wagon **3** to control so as to use the power of [to *harness* one's energy] **—in double harness** in a harness for two animals pulling the same carriage, plow, etc. **—in harness 1** in or at one's routine work **2** in cooperation; in tandem

harness hitch a kind of knot used in hauling

☆**harness race** a horse race between either trotters or pacers, with each horse pulling a sulky and driver

Har·old¹ (har′əld) ***n.*** ⟦OE *Hereweald & Harald* < ON *Haraldr*, both < Gmc **Hariwald*, lit., army chief < **harja-*, army (OE *here*, OHG *heri*) + **waldan*, to rule: see WIELD⟧ a masculine name: dim. *Hal*

Har·old² (har′əld) **1 Harold I** died 1040; king of England (1035-40): son of Canute: called **Harold Hare·foot** (her′foot′) **2 Harold II** 1022?-66; last Saxon king of England (1066): killed in the Battle of Hastings

ha·ro·set (hä rō′set) ***n.*** *var. of* CHAROSET: also **ha·ro′seth** (-seth)

harp (härp) ***n.*** ⟦ME < OE *hearpe*, akin to Ger *harfe* < Gmc **harpa* < IE base **(s)kerb(h)-*, to bend, curve (> SHRIMP): from the shape of the instrument⟧ **1** a musical instrument with strings stretched vertically in an open, triangular frame and played by plucking with the fingers: the modern harp has usually forty-six strings and, to permit the playing of halftones, seven foot-pedals **2** a harp-shaped object or implement **3** *Jazz, etc.* HARMONICA (sense 1) **—*vi.* 1** to play a harp **2** to persist in talking or writing tediously or continuously (*on* or *upon* something) **—the Harp** the constellation Lyra **—harp′er *n.***

harp

Har·per (här′pər), **Stephen (Joseph)** 1959- ; prime minister of Canada (2006-2015)

Har·pers Ferry (här′pərz) ⟦the site of a *ferry* owned (*c.* 1747) by R. *Harper*⟧ town in W.Va., at the juncture of the Potomac & Shenandoah rivers: site of the U.S. arsenal captured by John Brown (1859)

harp·ist (här′pist) ***n.*** a harp player

har·poon (här po͞on′) ***n.*** ⟦MDu *harpoen* < MFr *harpon* < *harper*, to claw, grip < ON *harpa*, to squeeze, cramp: for IE base see HARP⟧ a barbed spear with a line attached to it, used for spearing whales or other large sea animals **—*vt.*** to strike or catch with a harpoon **—har·poon′er *n.***

harp seal ⟦so named from the somewhat *harp*-shaped marking on the back esp. of the male⟧ a migratory, earless arctic seal (*Phoca groenlandica*) having pups with silky, white fur

harp·si·chord (härp′si kôrd′) ***n.*** ⟦obs. Fr *harpechorde* or It *arpicordo* < *arpa* (LL *harpa* < Gmc **harpa*: see HARP) + *corda* (see CORD); *-s-* is intrusive⟧ a stringed musical instrument with a keyboard, often with two manuals: the strings are plucked by points of leather or quill when the keys are pressed, producing short, abrupt tones: cf. CLAVICHORD **—harp′si·chord′ist *n.***

har·py (här′pē) ***n., pl.* -pies** ⟦MFr *harpie* < L *harpyia* < Gr *harpyiai*, pl., lit., snatchers < *harpazein*, to snatch < IE **serp-* < base **ser-*, sickle, curved hook > L *sarpere*, to prune⟧ **1** [**H-**] *Gr. Myth.* any of several hideous, filthy, rapacious winged monsters with the head and trunk of a woman and the tail, legs, and talons of a bird **2** a relentless, greedy, or grasping person **3** a shrewish woman **4** HARPY EAGLE

harpy eagle a large, black-and-white, short-winged tropical American eagle (*Harpia harpyja*) with a double crest and a powerful bill and claws

har·que·bus (här′kwə bəs) ***n.*** ⟦Fr *arquebuse* < It *archibuso* < MFr *harquebusche* < Du *hakebus*: see HACKBUT⟧ an early type of portable gun, supported on a hooked staff or forked rest during firing

har·ri·dan (har′i dən) ***n.*** ⟦prob. altered < Fr *haridelle*, worn-out horse, jade⟧ a nasty, bad-tempered woman, esp. an old one

har·ri·er¹ (har′ē ər) ***n.*** ⟦< HARE + -IER⟧ **1** any of a breed of hound similar to but smaller than the English foxhound, used in packs for hunting hares and rabbits **2** [*pl.*] a pack of such dogs and the hunters in a hunt **3** a cross-country runner

har·ri·er² (har′ē ər) ***n.*** **1** a person who harries **2** any of a genus (*Circus*) of hawks, as the marsh hawk, that prey on small mammals, reptiles, etc.

Har·ri·et (har′ē it) ***n.*** ⟦fem. dim. of HARRY⟧ a feminine name: dim. *Hattie*: see HARRY

Har·ri·man (har′ə mən) **1 Edward Henry** 1849-1909; U.S. financier & railroad magnate **2 W(illiam) Averell** 1891-1986; U.S. diplomat, politician, & businessman: son of Edward Henry

Har·ris¹ (har′is) **1 Joel Chandler** 1848-1908; U.S. writer: author of the *Uncle Remus* stories **2 Roy (Ellsworth)** 1898-1979; U.S. composer

Harris² *see* LEWIS WITH HARRIS

Har·ris·burg (har′is burg′) ⟦after John *Harris*, Jr. (1727-91), a founder⟧ capital of Pa., in the S part, on the Susquehanna

Har·ri·son (har′ə sən) **1 Benjamin** 1726?-91; Am. Revolutionary patriot: signer of the Declaration of Independence: father of William Henry **2 Benjamin** 1833-1901; 23d president of the U.S. (1889-93): grandson of William Henry **3 William Henry** 1773-1841; U.S. general; 9th president of the U.S. (1841): called *Tippecanoe*

Harris tweed ⟦after *Harris* (see LEWIS WITH HARRIS), in the Outer Hebrides, where the cloth is made⟧ *trademark for* a soft, all-wool tweed, hand-woven on the islands of the Outer Hebrides

Har·ro·vi·an (ha rō′vē ən) ***adj.*** of Harrow **—*n.*** a student or former student of Harrow

har·row¹ (har′ō) ***n.*** ⟦ME *harwe* < ? OE **hearwa*: akin to ON *harfr* < IE **(s)kerp-*: see HARVEST⟧ a frame with spikes or sharp-edged disks, drawn by a horse or tractor and used for breaking up and leveling plowed ground, covering seeds, rooting up weeds, etc. **—*vt.* 1** to draw a harrow over (land) **2** to cause mental distress to; torment **—*vi.*** to take harrowing [ground that *harrows* well] **—har′row·er *n.***

disk harrow

har·row² (har′ō) ***vt.*** ⟦ME *harwen, herien* < OE *hergian*: see HARRY⟧ [Archaic] to rob, plunder, or pillage **—the harrowing of hell** *Christianity* Christ's redemption of the righteous souls in hell (or Limbo), just after the Crucifixion

Har·row (har′ō) **1** borough of Greater London, England **2** private preparatory school for boys, in this borough

har·row·ing (har′ō iŋ) ***adj.*** ⟦prp. of HARROW¹⟧ inspiring anguish, terror, etc. **—har′row·ing·ly *adv.***

har·rumph (hə rumpf′: *conventionalized pronun.*) ***vi.*** ⟦echoic⟧ **1** to clear one's throat, esp. in a studied, pompous way **2** to protest or complain in a pompous or self-righteous way **—*n.*** the act or sound of harrumphing **—*interj.*** used to suggest such a sound

har·ry (har′ē) ***vt.* -ried, -ry·ing** ⟦ME *hergien* < OE *hergian* < base of *here*, army < IE **koryos*, army, var. of base **koros*, war > Lith *kãras*, war, MIr *cuire*, host⟧ **1** to raid, esp. repeatedly, and ravage or rob; pillage; plunder **2** to torment or worry; harass **3** to force or push along

Har·ry (har′ē) ***n.*** ⟦ME *Herry* < HENRY¹⟧ a masculine name: fem. *Harriet*

harsh (härsh) ***adj.*** ⟦ME *harsk*, akin to Ger *harsch*, rough, raw < IE base **kars*, to scratch, comb > L *carduus*, thistle, *carrere*, to card (wool)⟧ **1** unpleasantly sharp or rough; specif., *a)* grating to the ear; discordant *b)* too bright or vivid to the eye; glaring *c)* too strong to the taste; bitter *d)* not smooth to the touch; coarse **2** so unpleasantly crude, abrupt, or strained as to be offensive to the mind or feelings [the *harsh* realities of war] **3** rough, crude, or forbidding in appearance [beneath his *harsh* exterior] **4** excessively severe; cruel or unfeeling [a *harsh* punishment] **5** oppressive, inhospitable, inclement, etc. [a *harsh* climate] **—harsh′ly *adv.* —harsh′ness *n.***

hart (härt) ***n., pl.* harts** ⟦ME *hert* < OE *heorot*, akin to Ger *hirsch* < IE base **k̂er-*, head, what is on the head, HORN > REIN(DEER) & L *cervus*, hart⟧ a male of the European red deer, esp. after its fifth year, when the crown antlers are formed; stag

Harte (härt), **Bret** (bret) (born *Francis Brett Hart*) 1836-1902; U.S. writer, esp. of short stories

har·te·beest (här′tə bēst′, härt′bēst′) ***n., pl.* -beests′** or **-beest′** ⟦obs. Afrik < *harte*, hart + *beest*, beast⟧ any of a genus (*Alcelaphus*) of large, swift African antelopes with long horns curved backward at the tips

Hart·ford (härt′fərd) ⟦named after *Hertford*, England, birthplace of Samuel Stone (1602–63), Puritan leader and a founder of the town⟧ capital of Conn., in the central part, on the Connecticut River

harts·horn (härts′hôrn′) ***n.*** **1** a hart's antler **2** ammonium carbonate, used in smelling salts; sal volatile: so called because formerly obtained from deers' antlers

hart's-tongue or **harts-tongue** (-tuŋ′) ***n.*** a fern (*Phyllitis scolopendrium*) with narrow, simple fronds, found in Europe, Asia, and NE North America

ha·rumph (hə rumpf′: *conventionalized pronun.*) ***vi., interj., n.*** *alt. sp. of* HARRUMPH

har·um-scar·um (her′əm sker′əm) ***adj.*** ⟦< ? HARE + SCARE + 'EM⟧ acting or done in a reckless or rash way; irresponsible **—*adv.*** in a harum-scarum manner **—*n.*** a harum-scarum person or action

Ha·run ar-Ra·shid (hä ro͞on′ är rä shēd′) A.D. 764?-809; caliph of Baghdad (786-809): given popular fame as a hero of *The Arabian Nights*: also **Ha·run′ al-Ra·shid′** (-äl-)

ha·rus·pex (hə rus′peks′, har′əs peks′) ***n., pl.* -rus′pi·ces′** (-pə sēz′) ⟦L, lit., inspector of entrails < *haru-* (see YARN) + *-spex* (see AUSPEX)⟧ in ancient Rome, a soothsayer who professed to foretell events by examining the entrails of sacrificial animals

Har·vard (här′vərd), **John** 1607-38; Eng. clergyman, in America: 1st benefactor of Harvard College

har·vest (här′vist) ***n.*** ⟦ME *hervest* < OE *hærfest*, akin to Ger *herbst* (OHG *herbist*) < IE **(s)kerp-* < base **(s)ker-*, to cut > SHEAR, SHORT, L *caro*, flesh, *cernere* & Gr *krinein*, to separate, *karpos*, fruit: basic sense "time of cutting"⟧ **1** the time of the year when matured grain, fruit, vegetables, etc. are reaped and gathered in **2** a season's yield of grain, fruit, etc. when gathered in or ready to be gathered in; crop **3** the gathering in of a crop **4** the outcome or consequence of any effort or series of events **— *vt., vi.* 1** to gather in (a crop, etc.) **2** to gather the crop from (a field) **3** to catch, shoot, trap, etc. (fish or game), usually in an intensive, systematic way, as for commercial purposes 4 to get (something) as the result of an action or effort 5 to remove (body parts) for transplantation —**har′vest·a·ble** *adj.*

har·vest·er (-ər) *n.* 1 a person who gathers in a crop of grain, fruit, etc. ☆2 any of various farm machines for harvesting crops

☆**harvest fly** CICADA

harvest home 1 the bringing home of the last harvest load of the season 2 an English festival celebrating this

har·vest·man (-mən) *n., pl.* **-men** (-mən) 1 a man who harvests 2 any of an order (Opiliones) of spiderlike arachnids with long, thin legs and a short, broad, segmented abdomen; daddy longlegs

☆**harvest mite** CHIGGER

harvest moon the full moon at or about the time of the autumnal equinox

harvest mouse 1 a very small European mouse (*Micromys minutus*) that builds its nest among the stalks of wild plants and growing grain 2 any of a genus (*Reithrodontomys*) of very small New World mice with a very long tail

Har·vey[1] (här′vē) *n.* ⟦Fr *Hervé* < OHG *Herewig,* lit., army battle < Gmc **harja,* army (> OE *here:* see HARRY) + **wig-,* fight, akin to OE *wig* < IE base **weik-* > L *vincere,* conquer⟧ a masculine name

Har·vey[2] (här′vē), **William** 1578-1657; Eng. physician: discovered the circulation of the blood

Har·ya·na (hər yä′nə) *alt. sp. of* HARIANA

Harz Mountains (härts) mountain range in central Germany, extending from Lower Saxony to the Elbe River

has (haz; *also, as before "to",* has) *vt. 3d pers. sing., pres. indic., of* HAVE

Ha·sa (hä′sə) region of NE Saudi Arabia: also **Al Hasa** (äl)

has-been (haz′bin′) *n.* [Informal] a person or thing that was formerly popular or effective but is no longer so: a dismissive term

Has·dru·bal (haz′drōō bəl) 1 died 221 B.C.; Carthaginian general: brother-in-law of Hannibal 2 died 207 B.C.; Carthaginian general: crossed the Alps (207) to aid Hannibal, his brother: son of Hamilcar Barca

Ha·šek (hä′shek), **Ja·ro·slav** (yä′rō släf′) 1883-1923; Czech writer

ha·sen·pfef·fer (häs′ən fef′ər, häz′-; -pfef′-) *n.* ⟦Ger < *hase,* rabbit (see HARE) + *pfeffer,* pepper⟧ a German dish of rabbit meat marinated in vinegar and stewed in the marinade

hash[1] (hash) *vt.* ⟦Fr *hacher,* to chop, mince: see HACHURE⟧ 1 to chop (meat or vegetables) into small pieces for cooking 2 [Informal] to make a mess of; botch; bungle —*n.* 1 a chopped mixture of cooked meat and vegetables, usually baked or browned 2 a mixture, as of things used before in different forms; rehash 3 a hodgepodge; muddle; mess —☆**hash out** [Informal] to settle or resolve by prolonged discussion —☆**hash over** [Informal] to talk over in detail; discuss at length —**make (a) hash of** [Informal] 1 to bungle; botch 2 to destroy or defeat (an opponent, argument, etc.) —**settle someone's hash** [Slang] to deal with decisively, as in getting revenge

hash[2] (hash) *n.* [Slang] *short for* HASHISH

hash[3] (hash) *n.* ⟦prob. < HATCH[3]⟧ [Chiefly Brit.] the symbol (#); pound sign: also **hash sign**

hash browns raw or boiled potatoes that have been hashed and fried in a frying pan: also **hashed browns**

Hash·em·ite or **Hash·im·ite** (hash′əm īt′) *n.* ⟦after *Hāshim,* great-grandfather of Muhammad⟧ a member of an Arabian princely family claiming descent from Muhammad —*adj.* of or pertaining to this family

☆**hash house** [Slang] a cheap restaurant

hash·ish (hash′ēsh′, ha shēsh′) *n.* ⟦Ar *ḥashish,* dried hemp⟧ a drug made from the resin contained in the flowering tops of hemp, chewed or smoked for its intoxicating and euphoric effects: also sp. **hash′eesh′**

☆**hash mark** 1 [Mil. Slang] SERVICE STRIPE 2 *Football* any of the segments of the inbounds line marked on the field at the yard lines: they mark the point at which the ball is put back in play after it has been grounded outside an inbounds line

hash·tag (hash′tag′) *n.* ⟦< HASH[3] + TAG⟧ a word or phrase preceded by the symbol (#), used in social networking to identify the subject of a conversation and to facilitate searches for that subject

Has·i·dim (has′ə dim′, -dēm′, ha sid′im, -sēd′-; *Heb* khä′sē dēm′) *pl.n., sing.* **Has·id** (has′id; *Heb* khä sēd′) the members of a sect of Jewish mystics that originated in Poland in the 18th cent. and that emphasizes joyful worship of an immanent God —**Ha·sid·ic** (ha sid′ik) *adj.* —**Has′i·dism′** *n.*

has·let (has′lit, hāz′-) *n.* ⟦ME *hastelet* < OFr < *haste,* meat cooked on a spit < MDu *harst,* a roast (form and sense infl. by L *hasta,* a spear) < IE base **ker-,* to burn > HEARTH⟧ the heart, liver, lungs, etc. of a pig or other animal, used for food

has·n't (haz′ənt) *contraction* has not

hasp (hasp, häsp) *n.* ⟦ME < OE *hæsp,* by metathesis < *hæpse,* akin to Ger *haspe* < IE base **kap-,* to grasp > HAVE⟧ a hinged metal fastening for a door, window, lid, etc.; esp., a metal piece that fits over a staple and is held in place by a pin or padlock —*vt.* [Rare] to fasten with or as with a hasp

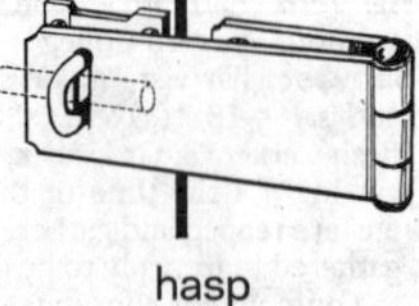
hasp

Has·sam (has′əm), **(Frederick) Childe** (chīld) 1859-1935; U.S. painter & etcher

Has·selt (häs′əlt) commune in NE Belgium: capital of Limburg province

has·si·um (has′ē əm) *n.* ⟦ModL, after the L name for HESSE[2], where new elements were created in a nuclear physics laboratory + -IUM⟧ a radioactive chemical element with a very short half-life: a transactinide produced by bombarding lead with high-energy nuclear particles: symbol, Hs: at. no. 108: see the periodic table of elements in the Reference Supplement

☆**has·sle** (has′əl) [Informal] *n.* ⟦< ?⟧ 1 a heated argument; squabble 2 a troublesome situation —*vi.* **-sled, -sling** to have a hassle —*vt.* to annoy, harass, etc.

has·sock (has′ək) *n.* ⟦ME *hassok* < OE *hassuc,* (clump of) coarse grass < ?⟧ 1 [Now Rare] a thick clump or tuft of grass; tussock 2 a firmly stuffed cushion used as a footstool or seat

hast (hast) *vt. archaic 2d pers. sing., pres. indic., of* HAVE: used with *thou*

has·ta la vis·ta (äs′tä lä vēs′tä) ⟦Sp, lit., until the (next) meeting⟧ goodbye; (I'll) see you again

hasta lue·go (lwe′gô) ⟦Sp, lit., until later, soon⟧ goodbye; (I'll) see you soon

hasta ma·ña·na (mä nyä′nä) ⟦Sp, lit., until tomorrow⟧ goodbye; (I'll) see you tomorrow

has·tate (has′tāt′) *adj.* ⟦L *hastatus* < *hasta,* a spear < IE base **ĝhasto-* a rod, shaft > YARD[1]⟧ having a triangular shape like a spearhead, as some leaves

haste (hāst) *n.* ⟦ME < OFr < Frank **haist,* violence, akin to OE *hæst* < IE base **keibh-,* quick, violent > Sans *śibham,* quick⟧ 1 the act of hurrying; quickness of motion; rapidity 2 the act of hurrying carelessly or recklessly [*haste* makes waste] 3 necessity for hurrying; urgency [an air of *haste* marks the undertaking] — *vt., vi.* **hast′ed, hast′ing** [Rare] HASTEN —**in haste** 1 in a hurry 2 in too great a hurry; without enough care —**make haste** to hasten; hurry

SYN.—**haste** implies quick or precipitate movement or action, as from the pressure of circumstances or intense eagerness; **hurry,** often interchangeable with **haste,** specifically suggests excitement, bustle, or confusion [the *hurry* of city life]; **speed** implies rapidity of movement, operation, etc., suggesting effectiveness and the absence of excitement or confusion [to increase the *speed* of an assembly line]; **expedition** adds to **speed** the implication of efficiency and stresses the facilitation of an action or procedure; **dispatch** comes close to **expedition** in meaning but more strongly stresses promptness in finishing something —*ANT.* **slowness, delay**

has·ten (hās′ən) *vt.* ⟦extended form of prec., v.⟧ to cause to be or come faster; speed up; accelerate —*vi.* to move or act swiftly; hurry

Has·tings[1] (hās′tiŋz), **Warren** 1732-1818; Eng. statesman: 1st governor general of India (1773-84)

Has·tings[2] (hās′tiŋz) city in East Sussex, SE England, on the English Channel: near the site of the decisive battle (**Battle of Hastings,** 1066) in the Norman Conquest of England

hast·y (hās′tē) *adj.* **hast′i·er, hast′i·est** ⟦ME *hasti* < OFr *hasti, hastif:* see HASTE⟧ 1 done or made with haste; quick; hurried [a *hasty* lunch] 2 done or made too quickly and with too little thought; rash; impetuous 3 [Old-fashioned] *a)* short-tempered *b)* showing irritation or impatience —*SYN.* FAST[1] —**hast′i·ly** *adv.* —**hast′i·ness** *n.*

hasty pudding ⟦so called because quickly prepared⟧ ☆1 mush made of cornmeal 2 [Brit.] mush made of flour or oatmeal

hat (hat) *n.* ⟦ME < OE *hætt,* akin to OFris *hat,* Ger *hut* < IE base **kadh-,* to cover, protect > HOOD[1], HEED, L *cassis,* helmet⟧ 1 a covering for the head, usually with a brim and a crown: sometimes distinguished from BONNET, BERET, CAP[1], etc. 2 any of the several titles, positions, jobs, roles, etc. that one person may have —*vt.* **hat′ted, hat′ting** to cover or provide with a hat: used chiefly in the pp. —**hat in hand** in a humble or obsequious manner; abjectly —☆**pass the hat** ⟦in allusion to the use of a hat in which to collect money⟧ [Informal] to take up a collection, as at a meeting —**take one's hat off to** to salute or congratulate —☆**talk through one's hat** [Informal] to make irresponsible or foolish statements; talk nonsense —**throw one's hat into the ring** to enter a contest, esp. one for political office —☆**under one's hat** [Informal] strictly confidential; secret

hat·band (hat′band′) *n.* a band of cloth around the crown of a hat, just above the brim

hat·box (-bäks′) *n.* a box or case for carrying or storing a hat or hats

hatch[1] (hach) *vt.* ⟦ME *hacchen,* akin to Ger *hecken,* to breed & OE *hagan,* the genitals < ? IE base **kak-,* to be able, help > Sans *śaknóti,* (he) can⟧ 1 *a)* to bring forth (young) from an egg or eggs by applying warmth *b)* to bring forth young from (an egg or eggs) 2 to bring (a plan, idea, etc.) into existence; esp., to plan in a secret or underhanded way; plot —*vi.* 1 to bring forth young; develop embryos: said of eggs 2 to come forth from the egg 3 to brood: said of a bird —*n.* 1 the process of hatching 2 the brood hatched 3 a result —**hatch′er** *n.*

hatch[2] (hach) *n.* ⟦ME *hacche* < OE *hæcc,* grating, lattice gate, akin to Du, LowG *hek* < IE base **kagh-,* to enclose, wickerwork > HEDGE⟧ 1 the lower half of a door, gate, etc. that has two separately movable halves 2 HATCHWAY 3 a covering for a ship's hatchway, or a lid or trapdoor for a hatchway in a building 4 a barrier to regulate the flow of water in a stream; floodgate —**down the hatch!** [Informal] drink up!: used as a toast

hatch[3] (hach) *vt.* ⟦OFr *hacher,* to chop: see HACHURE⟧ to mark or engrave with fine, crossed or parallel lines so as to achieve shading —*n.* any of these lines

☆**hatch·back** (hach′bak′) *n.* ⟦HATCH[2] + BACK[1]⟧ 1 an automobile body with a rear door or section that swings up, providing a wide opening into a storage area 2 a car having such a body

☆**hat·check** (hat′chek′) *adj.* of, for, or working in a checkroom for hats, coats, etc.

hatch·el (hach′əl) ***n., vt.*** **-eled** or **-elled, -el·ing** or **-el·ling** HACKLE[1]

hatch·er·y (hach′ər ē) ***n., pl.*** **-er·ies** a place for hatching eggs, esp. those of fish or poultry

hatch·et (hach′it) ***n.*** ⟦ME *hachet* < OFr *hachette*, dim. of *hache*, an ax: see HACHURE⟧ **1** a small ax with a short handle, for use with one hand: often the part of the head opposite the cutting edge is shaped like the striking portion of a hammerhead ☆**2** TOMAHAWK —☆**bury the hatchet** ⟦in allusion to an American Indian peacemaking custom: see sense 2⟧ to stop fighting; make peace

hatchet

☆**hatchet face** a lean, sharp face, suggesting the cutting edge of a hatchet —**hatch′et-faced′** ***adj.***

☆**hatchet job** [Informal] a biased, malicious attack on the character or activities of a person, institution, etc.

☆**hatchet man** [Informal] **1** a person hired to commit murder **2** any person assigned by another to carry out disagreeable or unscrupulous tasks **3** a malicious or harsh writer or critic, as one who attempts to destroy a reputation

hatch·ing (hach′iŋ) ***n.*** ⟦HATCH[3] + -ING⟧ **1** the drawing or engraving of fine, parallel or crossed lines to achieve shading **2** such lines

hatch·ling (-liŋ) ***n.*** a recently hatched bird, fish, turtle, etc.

hatch·ment (hach′mənt) ***n.*** ⟦for earlier *atcheament*, altered < ACHIEVEMENT⟧ *Heraldry* a diamond-shaped panel bearing the coat of arms of a person who has recently died, displayed before the house during mourning

hatch·way (hach′wā′) ***n.*** **1** a covered opening in a ship's deck, through which cargo can be lowered or entrance made to a lower deck **2** a similar opening in the floor or roof of a building

hate (hāt) ***vt.*** **hat′ed, hat′ing** ⟦ME *hatien* < OE *hatian*, akin to Ger *hassen* < IE base **k̂ād-*, bad temper > Gr *kēdein*, to trouble, *kedos*, grief, Welsh *cas*, hate⟧ **1** to have strong dislike or ill will for; loathe; despise **2** to dislike or wish to avoid; have a strong aversion to [to *hate* arguments] —***vi.*** to feel hatred —***n.*** **1** a strong feeling of dislike or ill will; hatred **2** a person or thing hated —***adj.*** based on, expressing, or characterized by hatred, esp. hatred of a particular race, religion, etc. [a *hate* group, a piece of *hate* mail] —**hat′er** ***n.***

SYN.—hate implies a feeling of great dislike or aversion, and, with persons as the object, connotes the bearing of malice; **detest** implies vehement dislike or antipathy; **despise** suggests a looking down with great contempt upon the person or thing one hates; **abhor** implies a feeling of great repugnance or disgust; **loathe** implies utter abhorrence —***ANT.*** **love, like**

hate·a·ble (hāt′ə bəl) ***adj.*** that deserves to be hated

hate crime a crime motivated by hatred of the victim's race, ethnicity, religion, sexual orientation, etc.

hate·ful (hāt′fəl) ***adj.*** **1** [Archaic] feeling or showing hate; malicious; malevolent **2** causing or deserving hate; loathsome; detestable; odious **3** nasty, unpleasant, objectionable, etc. [what a *hateful* thing to say!] —**hate′ful·ly** ***adv.*** —**hate′ful·ness** ***n.***

SYN.—hateful is applied to that which provokes extreme dislike or aversion; **odious** stresses a disagreeable or offensive quality in that which is hateful; **detestable** refers to that which arouses vehement dislike or antipathy; **obnoxious** is applied to that which is very objectionable to one and causes great annoyance or discomfort by its presence; that is **repugnant** which is so distasteful or offensive that one offers strong resistance to it; that is **abhorrent** which is regarded with extreme repugnance or disgust; **abominable** is applied to that which is execrably or degradingly offensive or loathsome

☆**hate·mon·ger** (hāt′muŋ′gər, -mäŋ′-) ***n.*** a propagandist who seeks to provoke hatred and prejudice, as against a minority group or groups

hath (hath) ***vt.*** *archaic 3d pers. sing., pres. indic., of* HAVE

Hath·a·way (hath′ə wā′), **Anne** 1557?-1623; maiden name of the wife of William Shakespeare

hath·a yoga (häth′ə, hath′ə, huth′ə) ⟦Sans < *haṭha*, force + *yoga*, YOGA⟧ YOGA (sense 1)

Hath·or (hath′ôr′) ***n.*** ⟦Gr *Hathōr* < Egypt *Ḥet-Ḥert*, lit., the house above⟧ *Egypt. Myth.* the goddess of love, mirth, and joy, usually represented as having the head or ears of a cow —**Ha·thor·ic** (ha thôr′ik) ***adj.***

hat·pin (hat′pin′) ***n.*** a long, ornamental pin for fastening a woman's hat to her hair

hat·rack (hat′rak′) ***n.*** a rack, set of pegs or hooks, etc. to hold hats

ha·tred (hā′trid) ***n.*** ⟦ME < *hate*, hate + *-red*, *-reden* < OE *-rǣden*, state, condition⟧ strong dislike or ill will; hate

hat·ter (hat′ər) ***n.*** a person who makes, sells, or cleans hats, esp. men's hats

Hat·ter·as (hat′ər əs), **Cape** cape on an island (**Hatteras Island**) of N.C., between Pamlico Sound & the Atlantic

Hat·tie (hat′ē) ***n.*** a feminine name: see HARRIET

☆**hat tree** a stand with arms or hooks to hold hats, coats, etc.

hat trick ⟦orig. term in cricket: from the practice of rewarding with a new hat the feat performed by a bowler taking three wickets on successive balls⟧ **1** *Sports* any of various unusual feats; esp., the act by a single player in ice hockey, soccer, etc. of scoring three goals in one game **2** any remarkable feat, usually one consisting of three separate but related achievements [to pull off a *hat trick* by writing three bestsellers]

hau·ber·geon (hô′bər jən) ***n.*** *obs. var. of* HABERGEON

hau·berk (hô′bərk) ***n.*** ⟦ME *hauberc* < OFr < Frank **halsberg* (akin to OE *healsbeorg*), protection for the neck, gorget < *hals*, the neck (see COLLAR) + *bergan*, to protect⟧ a medieval coat of armor, usually of chain mail

haugh·ty (hôt′ē) ***adj.*** **-ti·er, -ti·est** ⟦ME *haut*, high, haughty < OFr, high < *altus* (with *h-* after Frank **hoh*, high) + -Y[3]: *-gh-* prob. inserted by analogy with NAUGHTY⟧ **1** having or showing great pride in oneself and disdain, contempt, or scorn for others; proud; arrogant; supercilious **2** [Archaic] lofty; noble —***SYN.*** PROUD —**haugh′ti·ly** ***adv.*** —**haugh′ti·ness** ***n.***

haul (hôl) ***vt.*** ⟦17th-c. phonetic sp. of HALE[2] < ME *halen* < OFr *haler*, to draw < ODu *halen*, akin to Ger *holen*, to fetch < IE base **kel-*, to cry out (> L *calare*): basic sense "to call hither"⟧ **1** to pull with force; move by pulling or drawing; tug; drag **2** to transport by wagon, truck, etc. [to *haul* coal for a living] **3** HALE[2] **4** *Naut.* to change the course of (a ship), specif. so as to sail closer to the wind —***vi.*** **1** to pull; tug **2** to shift direction: said of the wind **3** *Naut.* to change the course of a ship, specif. so as to sail closer to the wind —***n.*** **1** the act of hauling; pull; tug **2** *a)* the amount of fish taken in a single pull of a net *b)* [Informal] the amount gained, won, earned, etc. at one time **3** the distance or route over which something is transported or over which one travels **4** a load or quantity transported —***SYN.*** PULL —☆**haul ass** [Slang] to act, go, depart, etc. quickly or hurriedly: mildly vulgar —**haul off** **1** to change a ship's course so as to draw away from something **2** to retreat; withdraw ☆**3** [Informal] to draw the arm back before hitting —**haul up** **1** to sail closer to the wind **2** to come to rest; stop —**haul your** (or **her**, etc.) **wind** to sail closer to the wind: also **haul to the wind** —**in** (or **over**) **the long haul** over a long period of time —**haul′er** ***n.***

haul·age (hôl′ij) ***n.*** **1** the act or process of hauling **2** the charge made for hauling, as by a railroad

haul·ier (hôl′yər) ***n.*** [Brit.] a person or business that transports goods using motor trucks

haulm (hôm) ***n.*** ⟦ME *halm* < OE *healm, halm*, straw, akin to Ger *halm* < IE **k̂olemos*, reed, cane > Gr *kalamos*, L *culmus*⟧ **1** the stalks or stems of cultivated cereal plants, beans, peas, etc., esp. after the crop has been gathered **2** straw or hay used for thatching, bedding, etc. **3** a stem of grass or grain

haunch (hônch, hänch) ***n.*** ⟦ME *haunche* < OFr *hanche* < Gmc, as in MDu *hanke*, haunch⟧ **1** the part of the body including the hip, buttock, and thickest part of the thigh **2** an animal's loin and leg together; joint of venison, mutton, etc. **3** *Archit.* either of the sides of an arch from the point of rising to the vertex

haunch bone the ilium, or hipbone

haunt (hônt, hänt; *for n. 2, usually* hant) ***vt.*** ⟦ME *haunten* < OFr *hanter*, to frequent < Gmc **haimetan* (akin to OE *hamettan*, to domicile) < **haim*, HOME⟧ **1** to visit (a place) often or continually; frequent **2** to seek the company or companionship of; run after **3** to appear or recur repeatedly to, often to the point of obsession [memories *haunted* her] **4** to be associated with; fill the atmosphere of; pervade [memories of former gaiety *haunt* the house] *Haunt* is often used with a ghost, spirit, etc. as its stated or implied subject —***n.*** **1** *a)* a place often visited [to make the library one's *haunt*] *b)* a lair or feeding place of animals **2** [Dial.] a ghost

haunt·ed (hônt′id) ***adj.*** frequented, inhabited, etc. by a ghost or ghosts

haunt·ing (hônt′iŋ) ***adj.*** often recurring to the mind and typically evoking poignant feelings [a *haunting* melody] —**haunt′ing·ly** ***adv.***

Haupt·mann (houpt′män), **Ger·hart** (ger′härt) 1862-1946; Ger. dramatist, novelist, & poet

Hau·sa (hou′sə, -zə) ***n., pl.*** **-sas** or **-sa** **1** a member of a people living chiefly in N Nigeria, Niger, and adjacent areas **2** the Chadic language of this people, used as a trade language in many parts of W Africa

hau·sen (hô′zən, hou′-) ***n.*** ⟦Ger⟧ BELUGA (sense 1)

haus·frau (hous′frou′) ***n.*** ⟦Ger: see HOUSE & FRAU⟧ **1** a German housewife **2** [Informal] a housewife, esp. one regarded as very domestic: a humorous usage

haus·tel·lum (hôs tel′əm) ***n., pl.*** **-tel′la** (-ə) ⟦ModL < L *haustus*, pp. of *haurire*, to drink, draw water⟧ a tubelike sucking organ, or proboscis, as in any of various insects —**haus·tel·late** (hos′tə lāt′, -lit′) ***adj.***

haus·to·ri·um (hôs tôr′ē əm) ***n., pl.*** **-ri·a** (-ə) ⟦ModL < L *haustus*: see prec.⟧ a rootlike outgrowth in certain parasitic plants, through which food is absorbed from the host —**haus·to′ri·al** (-əl) ***adj.***

haut·boy (hō′boi′, ō′-) ***n.*** ⟦Fr *hautbois* < *haut*, high (see HAUGHTY) + *bois*, wood < Frank **busk*, forest: see BUSH[1]⟧ an early type of oboe

haute (ōt) ***adj.*** ⟦Fr, fem. of *haut*, high, grand: see HAUGHTY⟧ of a high level of quality, fashion, etc.: often used to suggest affectation or snobbery

haute cou·ture (ōt′ko͞o to͝or′) ⟦Fr, lit., high sewing⟧ **1** the leading designers and creators of new fashions in clothing for women, collectively **2** the clothing created by them

haute cui·sine (ōt′kwē zēn′) ⟦Fr, lit., high cooking⟧ **1** the preparation of fine food by highly skilled chefs **2** food prepared in this way

Haute-Nor·man·die (ōt nôr män dē′) metropolitan region of NW France: 4,756 sq mi (12,318 sq km); chief city, Rouen

hau·teur (hō tʉr′) ***n.*** ⟦Fr < *haut*: see HAUGHTY⟧ disdainful pride; haughtiness; snobbery

haut monde (ō mōnd′) ⟦Fr⟧ high society

Ha·van·a[1] (hə van′ə) ***n.*** **1** a cigar made in Havana, or in Cuba, or of Cuban tobacco **2** Cuban tobacco

Ha·van·a[2] (hə van′ə) seaport & capital of Cuba, on the Gulf of Mexico: Sp. name HABANA

Havana brown any of a breed of domestic cat with a chestnut-brown coat, a long, tapering muzzle, and forward-tilting ears

Hav·a·nese (hä′vä nēz′) *n., pl.* **-nese′** ⟦after HAVANA[2]: orig. bred in Cuba⟧ any of a breed of toy dog with a long, wavy, silky coat, and a plumed tail that curls over the back

ha·var·ti (hə vär′tē) *n.* ⟦< *Havarti,* place name in Denmark⟧ a semisoft, pale-yellow Danish cheese

have (hav; *also, as before "to",* haf) *vt.* **had** (had; *unstressed,* həd, əd), **hav′ing** ⟦ME *haven* (earlier *habben*) < OE *habban,* akin to OHG *haben,* ON *hafa,* Goth *haban* < IE base **kap-,* to grasp > Gr *kaptein,* to gulp down, L *capere,* to take: primary sense, "to hold, have in hand"⟧ **1** to hold in the hand or in control; own; possess [*to have* wealth] **2** to possess or contain as a part, characteristic, attribute, etc. [she *has* blue eyes; the week *has* seven days] **3** to be affected by or afflicted with [to *have* a cold] **4** to possess by way of experience; experience; undergo [*have* a good time] **5** to possess an understanding of; know [to *have* only a little Spanish] **6** to hold or keep in the mind [to *have* an idea] **7** to declare or state [so gossip *has* it] **8** to gain possession, control, or mastery of **9** *a)* to get, take, receive, or obtain [to *have* news of someone, *have* a look at it] *b)* to consume; eat or drink [*have* some tea] **10** to bear or beget (offspring) **11** to perform; carry on; engage in [to *have* an argument] **12** *a)* to cause to [*have* them walk home] *b)* to cause to be [*have* this done first] **13** to be in (a certain) relation to [to *have* brothers and sisters] **14** to feel and show [*have* pity on her] **15** to permit; tolerate: used in the negative [I won't *have* this nonsense] **16** [Informal] *a)* to hold at a disadvantage or to overcome [I *had* my opponent now] *b)* to engage in sexual intercourse with —*n.* [Informal] a person or nation with relatively much wealth or rich resources [the *haves* and have-nots] —**have at** to attack; strike —**have done** to stop; get through; finish —**have had it** [Informal] **1** to be exhausted, defeated, disgusted, bored, ready to quit, etc. **2** to be no longer popular, useful, accepted, etc. —**have it good** [Informal] to be in comfortable circumstances —**have it off** [Brit. Slang] to have sexual intercourse: somewhat vulgar —**have it out** [Informal] to settle an issue, disagreement, etc. by fighting or discussion —**have on 1** to be wearing; be dressed in **2** [Brit. Informal] to fool (someone) by playing on the person's credulity; trick; kid [you're *having* me *on,* aren't you?] —☆**have to be** [Informal] to be unquestionably or without doubt [this *has to be* the best movie of the year] —**have to do with** *see phrase under* DO[1] —**to have and to hold** to possess for life: phrase used in certain marriage services

USAGE—*have* is used as an auxiliary with past participles to form phrases expressing completed action, as in the perfect tenses (Ex.: I *have* left, I *had* left, I shall *have* left, I would *have* left, etc.), and with infinitives to express obligation or necessity (Ex.: we *have* to go). *Have got* often replaces *have*: see GET. *Have* is conjugated in the present indicative: (I) *have,* (he, she, it) *has,* (we, you, they) *have*; in the past indicative (I, he, she, it, we, you, they) *had.* Archaic forms are: (thou) *hast, hadst,* (he, she, it) *hath*; the present subjunctive is *have,* the past subjunctive *had*

Ha·vel[1] (hä′vəl), **Vá·clav** (vät′släf′) 1936-2011; Czech writer & statesman: president of Czechoslovakia (1989-92) & of the Czech Republic (1993-2003)

Ha·vel[2] (hä′fəl) river in NE Germany, flowing southwest into the Elbe: *c.* 215 mi (346 km)

☆**have·lock** (hav′läk′) *n.* ⟦after Sir Henry *Havelock* (1795-1857), Eng general in India⟧ a light cloth covering for a military cap, falling over the back of the neck for protection against the sun

havelock

ha·ven (hā′vən) *n.* ⟦ME < OE *hæfen,* akin to Ger *hafen,* LowG *haff* < IE **kapnos,* haven < base **kap-*: see HAVE⟧ **1** a port; harbor **2** any sheltered, safe place; refuge —*vt.* to provide a haven for

have-not (hav′nät′, hav′nät′) *n.* [Informal] a person or nation with little wealth or poor resources

have·n't (hav′ənt) *contraction* have not

ha·ver (hā′vər) *vi.* ⟦< ?⟧ [Brit.] **1** to talk foolishly or waste time talking foolishly **2** to waver; vacillate

Ha·ver·ing (hāv′riŋ) borough of Greater London, England

ha·vers (hā′vərz) *interj., n.* [Brit.] nonsense

hav·er·sack (hav′ər sak′) *n.* ⟦Fr *havresac* < Ger *habersack,* lit., sack of oats < *haber* (now *hafer* < LowG), akin to E dial. *haver,* oats (? orig. "goat food" < IE base **kapro-* > L *caper,* goat) + Ger *sack,* SACK[1]⟧ a canvas bag for carrying rations, etc., generally worn over one shoulder, as by soldiers or hikers

Ha·ver·sian (hə vur′zhən, -shən) *adj.* ⟦after C. *Havers* (*c.* 1650-1702), Eng physician⟧ designating or of the canals through which blood vessels and connective tissue pass in bone

hav·oc (hav′ək, -äk′) *n.* ⟦earlier esp. in phrase CRY HAVOC (see below) < ME & Anglo-Fr *havok* < OFr *havot,* prob. < *haver,* to hook, take, *hef,* a hook < Frank **haf-,* to seize: for IE base see HAVE⟧ great destruction and devastation, as that resulting from hurricanes, wars, etc. —*vt.* **-ocked, -ock·ing** [Obs.] to lay waste; devastate —***SYN.*** RUIN —**cry havoc 1** [Archaic] to give (an army) the signal for pillaging **2** to warn of great, impending danger —**play havoc with** to devastate; destroy; ruin

Havre, Le *see* LE HAVRE

haw[1] (hô) *n.* ⟦ME *hawe* < OE *haga,* haw, hedge, akin to *hecg,* HEDGE⟧ **1** the berry of the hawthorn **2** HAWTHORN

haw[2] (hô) *interj., n.* ⟦< ?⟧ (used as) a command to a horse, ox, etc., meaning "turn to the left" — *vt., vi.* to turn to the left Opposed to GEE[1]

haw[3] (hô) *vi.* ⟦echoic⟧ *see* HEM AND HAW *under* HEM[2] — *interj., n.* **1** (used to suggest) the sound a speaker often makes when hesitating briefly **2** *var. of* HA[1]

haw[4] (hô) *n.* ⟦< ?⟧ **1** NICTITATING MEMBRANE **2** [*often pl.*] inflammation of this membrane

Haw *abbrev.* Hawaiian

Ha·wai·i (hə wä′ē, -wī′ē) ⟦Haw *Hawai'i* < Proto-Polynesian **hawaiki*; akin to *Savai'i,* SAVAII⟧ **1** state of the U.S., consisting of a group of islands (**Hawaiian Islands**) in the North Pacific: admitted 1959: 6,423 sq mi (16,635 sq km); cap. Honolulu: abbrev. *HI* **2** largest & southernmost of the islands of Hawaii, southeast of Oahu: 4,028 sq mi (10,432 sq km)

☆**Ha·wai·i-A·leu·tian Standard Time** (-ə lo͞o′shən) a standard time used in the zone which includes Hawaii and the W Aleutian Islands, corresponding to the mean solar time of the 150th meridian west of Greenwich, England: it is ten hours behind Greenwich time

Ha·wai·ian (hə wä′yən, -wī′ən) *adj.* of Hawaii or its people, indigenous language, or culture —*n.* **1** a person born or living in Hawaii **2** a Hawaiian of indigenous Polynesian descent **3** the Austronesian language of the Hawaiians

Hawaiian guitar STEEL GUITAR

Hawaiian shirt a short-sleeved, brightly patterned casual shirt having a collar and buttoned front and usually worn outside the trousers

haw·finch (hô′finch′) *n.* ⟦HAW[1] + FINCH⟧ the common European grosbeak (*Coccothraustes coccothraustes*) of a family (Fringillidae) of finches

hawk[1] (hôk) *n.* ⟦ME *hauk* < OE *hafoc,* akin to Ger *habicht,* Pol *kobuz,* falcon⟧ **1** *a)* any of various accipitrine birds having short, rounded wings and a long tail and legs, as the Cooper's hawk, the goshawk, and the harriers *b)* loosely, any of various other birds of prey, as falcons and ospreys **2** ⟦from the perceived fierceness of this and other birds of prey⟧ a person who advocates an aggressive approach or response to a problem, crisis, etc.; specif., an advocate of military action in an international dispute: cf. DOVE[1] **3** a person regarded as having the preying or grasping nature of a hawk; cheater; swindler —*vi.* **1** to hunt birds or other small game with the help of falcons or other hawks **2** to attack by or as by swooping and striking —*vt.* to attack or prey on as a hawk does —**hawk′ish** *adj.* —**hawk′like′** *adj.*

goshawk

hawk[2] (hôk) *vt.* ⟦back-form. < HAWKER[1]⟧ **1** to advertise or peddle (goods) in the streets by shouting **2** to advertise or sell: a mildly contemptuous term

hawk[3] (hôk) *vi.* ⟦echoic⟧ to clear the throat audibly —*vt.* to bring up (phlegm) by coughing —*n.* an audible clearing of the throat

hawk[4] (hôk) *n.* ⟦prob. fig. use of HAWK[1]⟧ a flat, square piece of wood or metal with a handle underneath, for carrying mortar or plaster

hawk·er[1] (hôk′ər) *n.* ⟦altered by folk etym. < MLowG *hoker,* huckster (Du *heuker,* Ger *höker*) < *hoken,* to peddle, orig., to crouch (as with a burden) < IE base **keu-,* to bend, stoop, arch > HOBBLE, HIGH⟧ a peddler or huckster

hawk·er[2] (hôk′ər) *n.* ⟦OE *hafocere*⟧ a person who uses hawks for hunting; falconer

☆**Hawk·eye** (hôk′ī′) *n.* [Informal] a person born or living in Iowa, called the **Hawkeye State**

hawk-eyed (hôk′īd′) *adj.* keen-sighted like a hawk

hawk·ing (hôk′iŋ) *n.* hunting with hawks; falconry

Hawk·ing (hôk′iŋ), **Stephen W(illiam)** 1942- ; Eng. physicist

Haw·kins (hô′kinz), **Coleman** 1907-69; U.S. jazz saxophonist

hawk moth any of a family (Sphingidae) of moths with a thick, tapering body, slender wings, and a long feeding tube used for sucking the nectar of flowers; sphinx moth

hawk's-beard (hôks′bird′) *n.* any of a genus (*Crepis*) of plants of the composite family, with milky juice and small, red, orange, or yellow flower heads borne in clusters

hawks·bill (turtle) (hôks′bil′) a medium-sized marine turtle (*Eretmochelys imbricata,* family Cheloniidae) having a hawklike beak and a horny shell from which tortoiseshell is obtained

hawk·shaw (hôk′shô′) *n.* ⟦after a character in *The Ticket of Leave Man,* a play by Tom Taylor (1817-80), Eng dramatist⟧ ☆[Old Informal] a detective

Hawks·moor (hôks′moor′), **Nicholas** 1661-1736; Eng. architect

hawk·weed (hôk′wēd′) *n.* any of a genus (*Hieracium*) of plants of the composite family, usually with conspicuous basal leaves and stalked clusters of heads with yellow or scarlet ray flowers, including devil's paintbrush

Ha·worth (härth, hou′ərth), Sir **(Walter) Norman** 1883-1950; Brit. organic chemist

hawse (hôz, hôs) *n.* ⟦LME *halse* < ON *hals,* the neck, part of the bow of a ship: see COLLAR⟧ **1** that part of the bow of a ship containing the hawseholes **2** HAWSEHOLE **3** the space between the bow of an anchored vessel and the point on the surface directly above the anchor **4** the arrangement of the anchor cables when a ship is moored with both a starboard and a port anchor

hawse·hole (-hōl′) *n.* either of the holes in a ship's bow through which a hawser or anchor cable is passed

hawse·pipe (-pīp′) *n.* an iron or steel pipe in a hawsehole, through which a hawser or anchor cable is passed

haw·ser (hô′zər, -sər) *n.* ⟦ME *haucer* < Anglo-Fr *hauceour* < OFr *haucier* < VL **altiare* < L *altus*, high: see ALTITUDE⟧ a large rope used for towing or mooring a ship

haw·ser-laid (-lād′) *adj.* CABLE-LAID

haw·thorn (hô′thôrn′) *n.* ⟦lit., hedge thorn < ME *hagethorn* < OE *hagathorn* < *haga*, hedge, HAW¹ + *thorn*, akin to Ger *hagedorn*⟧ any of a group of thorny shrubs and small trees (genus *Crataegus*) of the rose family, with white, pink, or red flowers and usually red fruits (*haws*) resembling miniature cherries

Haw·thorne (hô′thôrn′), **Nathaniel** 1804-64; U.S. novelist & short-story writer

☆**Hawthorne effect** ⟦after the *Hawthorne* Works of the Western Electric Co. in Cicero, Ill., where studies of worker performance were made in 1927⟧ improvement in performance, as by workers or students, resulting from mere awareness that experimental attempts are being made to bring about improvement

hay¹ (hā) *n.* ⟦ME *hei* < OE *hieg* (akin to Ger *heu*) < base of OE *heawan*, to cut: see HEW⟧ **1** grass, alfalfa, clover, etc. cut and dried for use as fodder ☆**2** [Slang] a negligible amount, esp. of money: in negative constructions [*a hundred dollars ain't hay*] —*vi.* to mow grass, alfalfa, etc., and spread it out to dry —*vt.* [Rare] **1** to furnish with hay **2** to grow grass on (land) for hay —**a roll in the hay** [Slang] the act or an instance of sexual intercourse —☆**hit the hay** [Slang] to go to bed to sleep —**make hay 1** to mow grass, alfalfa, etc., and spread it out to dry **2** to make the most of an opportunity: also **make hay while the sun shines** —**make hay (out) of something** to turn something to one's advantage

hay² (hā) *n.* ⟦OFr *haye*⟧ an old country dance with much winding in and out

Hay (hā), **John (Milton)** 1838-1905; U.S. statesman & writer: secretary of state (1898-1905)

hay·cock (hā′käk′) *n.* a small, conical heap of hay drying in a field

Hay·dn (hīd′'n), **(Franz) Jo·seph** (yō′zef) 1732-1809; Austrian composer

Ha·yek (hī′ək), **F(riedrich) A(ugust von)** 1899-1992; Brit. economist, born in Austria

Hayes (hāz) **1 Helen** (born *Helen Hayes Brown*) 1900-93; U.S. actress **2 Rutherford B(irchard)** 1822-93; 19th president of the U.S. (1877-81)

hay fever an acute inflammation of the eyes and upper respiratory tract, accompanied by sneezing: it is an allergic reaction, caused mainly by the pollen of some grasses and trees; pollinosis

hay·field (hā′fēld′) *n.* a field of grass, alfalfa, etc. to be made into hay

hay·fork (-fôrk′) *n.* **1** PITCHFORK ☆**2** a mechanically operated device for lifting or moving hay

hay·loft (-lôft′) *n.* a loft, or upper story, in a barn or stable, for storing hay

hay·mak·er (-māk′ər) *n.* **1** a person who cuts hay and spreads it out to dry ☆**2** [Slang] a powerful blow with or swing of the fist, intended to cause a knockout

Hay·mar·ket Square (hā′mär′kit) square in Chicago: site of a battle between police & workmen (**Haymarket Riot**) on May 4, 1886, following a demonstration for the eight-hour workday

hay·mow (hā′mou′) *n.* **1** a pile of hay in a barn **2** HAYLOFT

hay·rack (hā′rak′) *n.* **1** a rack or frame from which cattle, horses, etc. eat hay ☆**2** *a)* a framework extending up from a wagon, to permit carrying larger quantities of hay *b)* a wagon having this

hay·rick (-rik′) *n.* a large heap of hay; haystack

☆**hay·ride** (-rīd′) *n.* a pleasure ride in a wagon partly filled with hay, taken by a group on an outing

Hays (hāz), **Arthur Garfield** 1881-1954; U.S. lawyer & civil libertarian

hay·seed (hā′sēd′) *n.* **1** grass seed shaken from mown hay **2** bits of chaff and straw from hay ☆**3** [Slang] an awkward, unsophisticated person regarded as typical of rural areas; yokel: a somewhat contemptuous term

hay·stack (-stak′) *n.* a large heap of hay piled up outdoors

Hay·ward (hā′wərd) ⟦after W. *Hayward* (1815-91), local landowner⟧ city in W Calif.: suburb of Oakland

☆**hay·wire** (hā′wīr′) *n.* wire for tying up bales of hay, straw, etc. —*adj.* ⟦prob. < *haywire outfit*, loggers' term for a camp with poor equipment that had to be held together with haywire⟧ [Informal] **1** out of order; disorganized; confused **2** crazy —**go haywire** [Informal] **1** to behave or perform erratically **2** to become crazy

ha·zan (hä′zən; *Heb* khä zän′) *n., pl.* **ha′zans** or **ha·za·nim** (hä′zə nēm′, -nim′; *Heb* khä zä nēm′) ⟦Yiddish *khazn* < Talmudic Heb *chazan*⟧ a cantor in a synagogue

haz·ard (haz′ərd) *n.* ⟦ME < OFr *hasard*, game of dice, adventure < ? Ar *az-zahr*, for Egypt colloq. Ar *al-zahr*, dice⟧ **1** an early game of chance played with dice, from which craps is derived **2** chance, or a chance occurrence **3** *a)* risk; peril; danger; jeopardy *b)* [Archaic] something risked **4** an obstacle on a golf course, as a sand trap or pond **5** *Court Tennis* any of the three openings on the side (**hazard side**) of the court in which service is received: see WINNING OPENING —*vt.* **1** to expose to danger; chance; risk **2** to attempt or venture [*to hazard a try*] —**SYN.** DANGER

haz·ard·ous (haz′ər dəs) *adj.* **1** of or involving chance **2** risky; dangerous; perilous —**haz′ard·ous·ly** *adv.*

haze¹ (hāz) *n.* ⟦prob. back-form. < HAZY⟧ **1** a dispersion of vapor, smoke, dust, etc. in the air that reduces visibility **2** a slight confusion or vagueness of mind —*vi., vt.* **hazed, haz′ing** to make or become hazy: often with *over* —**SYN.** MIST

haze² (hāz) *vt.* **hazed, haz′ing** ⟦< ? OFr *haser*, to irritate, annoy⟧ **1** [Archaic] *Naut.* to punish or harass by forcing to do hard, unnecessary work ☆**2** to initiate or discipline (a new member of a team, fraternity, etc.) by forcing to do ridiculous, humiliating, or painful things ☆**3** [West] to drive (horses or cattle) while on horseback

ha·zel (hā′zəl) *n.* ⟦ME *hasel* < OE *hæsel*, akin to Ger *hasel* < IE **kos(e)lo-*, hazel > L *corulus*, hazel bush, OIr *coll*, hazel⟧ **1** any of a genus (*Corylus*) of shrubs or trees of the birch family, bearing edible nuts **2** HAZELNUT **3** *a)* the wood of this tree or shrub *b)* a stick of this wood **4** the color of a ripened hazelnut; reddish brown —*adj.* **1** of the hazel tree or its wood **2** light reddish-brown or yellowish-brown **3** greenish-gray or greenish-brown, often with flecks of a third color: said of eyes —**ha′zel·ly** *adj.*

Ha·zel (hā′zəl) *n.* ⟦Heb *Hazā'el*, lit., God sees⟧ a feminine name

ha·zel·hen (-hen′) *n.* a European woodland grouse (*Tetrastes bonasia*) similar to the ruffed grouse: also called **hazel grouse**

ha·zel·nut (-nut′) *n.* FILBERT

Haz·litt (haz′lit), **William** 1778-1830; Eng. essayist

haz·mat (haz′mat′) *n.* ⟦HAZ(ARDOUS) + MAT(ERIAL)⟧ any material being stored or transported, esp. in large quantities, that is toxic, explosive, or otherwise hazardous: often written **HAZMAT**

ha·zy (hā′zē) *adj.* **-zi·er, -zi·est** ⟦prob. < or akin to OE *hasu, haswig*, gray, dusky (akin to MHG *heswe*, pale): cf. HARE⟧ **1** filled with haze; somewhat foggy, misty, or smoky **2** somewhat vague, obscure, confused, or indefinite [*hazy thinking*] —**ha′zi·ly** *adv.* —**ha′zi·ness** *n.*

haz·zan (hä′zən; *Heb* khä zän′) *alt. sp. of* HAZAN

Hb *abbrev.* **1** *Bible* Habakkuk **2** hemoglobin

HB *abbrev.* **1** *Football* halfback: sometimes written **hb 2** hepatitis B (vaccine or vaccination) **3** *Government* House Bill

H-back (āch′bak′) *n. Football* a wingback or slotback

HBCU *abbrev.* historically black college or university

HBM *abbrev.* Her (or His) Britannic Majesty

HBO *service mark* Home Box Office

☆**H-bomb** (āch′bäm′) *n.* HYDROGEN BOMB

HBP *abbrev.* **1** *Pharmacy* high blood pressure **2** *Baseball* hit by pitch (or pitcher)

HC *abbrev.* **1** hardcover: also **hc 2** House of Commons: also **H of C 3** hydrocarbon(s)

h.c. *abbrev.* ⟦L *honoris causa*⟧ for the sake of honor

hcf *abbrev.* highest common factor

HCFC *abbrev.* hydrochlorofluorocarbon

HCG (āch′sē′jē′) *n.* ⟦*h(uman) c(horionic) g(onadotropin)*⟧ a placental hormone that stimulates the ovaries to produce other hormones that prevent menstruation: its presence in the urine indicates pregnancy, and it is used as a fertility drug

hd *abbrev.* head

HD *abbrev.* high-definition

H.D. (pen name of *Hilda Doolittle*) 1886-1961; U.S. poet

hdbk *abbrev.* handbook

HDL (āch′dē′el′) *n.* ⟦*h(igh-)d(ensity) l(ipoprotein)*⟧ a lipoprotein that helps remove cholesterol from the bloodstream and that is believed to reduce the risk of heart disease: cf. LDL

HDPE *abbrev.* high-density polyethylene

hdqrs *abbrev.* headquarters

HDTV *abbrev.* high-definition television

he¹ (hē) *pron., pl.* **they** ⟦OE (where it contrasts with *heo*, she, *hie*, they < same base) < IE **ko-, *kē-*, this one > HERE, HITHER, L *cis*, on this side: orig. a demonstrative⟧ **1** the man, boy, or male animal (or, sometimes, the thing regarded as male) previously mentioned: masculine personal pronoun in the third person singular: *he* is the nominative form, *him* the objective, *his* the possessive, and *himself* the reflexive and intensive; *his* is the possessive pronominal adjective **2** the person; the one; anyone [*he who laughs last laughs best*] **3** the person just mentioned: used following such antecedents as *everyone, somebody*, or *no one* [*everyone ran just as fast as he could*] ➥Senses 2 & 3, although used traditionally without distinction as to gender, are now often objected to by many as carrying a masculine implication —*n., pl.* **hes** a man, boy, or male animal

he² (hā) *n.* ⟦Heb, lit., window⟧ the fifth letter of the Hebrew alphabet (ה)

He¹ *abbrev. Bible* Hebrews

He² *Chem. symbol for* helium

HE *abbrev.* **1** Her (or His) Excellency **2** high explosive **3** His Eminence

he- (hē) *combining form* male: used in hyphenated compounds [*he-dog*]

head (hed) *n.* ⟦ME *hede, heved* < OE *heafod*, akin to Ger *haupt* (OHG *houbit*, Goth *haubith*) < IE base **kaput-* (orig. prob. cup-shaped) > L *caput*: merged in Gmc with word akin to OHG *hūba*, a cap, crest (Ger *haube*) < IE base **keu-*, to bend, curve⟧ **1** *a)* the top part of the body in humans, the apes, etc., or the front part in most other animals: in higher animals it is a bony structure containing the brain, and including the jaws, eyes, ears, nose, and mouth *b)* this part exclusive of the face *c)* the approximate length of the human head, used in height comparisons [*the boy is a head taller than his sister*] **2** *a)* the head as the seat of reason, memory, and imagination;

mind; intelligence [to use one's *head*] *b)* aptitude; ability [to have a *head* for mathematics] *c)* [Informal] a headache, esp. as part of a hangover **3** the head as a symbol for the individual; person [dinner at ten dollars a *head*] **4** *pl.* **head** the head as a unit of counting [fifty *head* of cattle] **5** a representation of a head, as in painting or sculpture **6** the obverse of a coin, usually with such a representation: often **heads 7** the highest or uppermost part or thing; top; specif., *a)* the top of a page, column of figures, etc. *b)* a printed title at the top of a page, section of writing, etc. *c)* a chief point of discussion; topic of a section, chapter, etc. in a speech or written work *d)* a headline for a newspaper story *e)* froth floating on newly poured effervescent beverages, esp. on beer *f)* that end of a cask or barrel which is uppermost at any time *g)* the upper edge or corner of a sail **8** the foremost part of a thing; front; specif., *a)* a part associated with the human head [the *head* of a bed] *b)* the end of a pier farthest from land *c)* the front part of a ship; bow *d)* ⟦because orig. in the ship's *head*, or bow: see sense *c*⟧ *Naut.* a toilet, or latrine *e)* the front position, as of a column of marchers *f)* either end of something; extremity **9** the projecting part of something; specif., *a)* the part designed for holding, pushing, striking, etc. [the *head* of a pin, the *head* of a golf club] *b)* a jutting mass of rock, land, etc. as of a mountain *c)* a point of land; promontory; headland *d)* a projecting place in a boil or other inflammation where pus is about to break through *e)* the part of a tape recorder that records or plays back the magnetic signals on the tape *f)* WARHEAD **10** the membrane stretched across the end of a drum, tambourine, etc.; drumhead **11** the source of a flowing body of water; beginning of a stream, river, etc. **12** *a)* a source of water kept at some height to supply a mill, etc. *b)* the height of such a source of water or the vertical distance through which it falls *c)* a rush of water, as in a riptide **13** the pressure in an enclosed fluid, as steam, from its own weight or applied externally **14** a position of leadership, honor, or first importance [the *head* of the class] **15** the person who is foremost or in charge; leader, ruler, chief, director, etc. **16** a headmaster **17** *Bot. a)* a dense cluster of tiny sessile flowers attached to a common receptacle, as in the composite family *b)* a large, compact bud [a *head* of cabbage] *c)* the uppermost part of a plant's foliage [the *head* of a tree] ☆**18** *Jazz a)* the melody or theme of a composition *b)* an improvised, usually extemporaneous arrangement that is not written down (in full **head arrangement**) **19** *Linguis.* any word or word group in a construction that functions grammatically like the entire construction ["woman" is the *head* of "the woman who wrote that book"] **20** *Mining* HEADING (sense 4) **21** *Music* the rounded part of a note, at the end of the stem ☆**22** [Slang] *a)* a habitual user of a hallucinogen, stimulant, etc., as marijuana or cocaine (often in comb.) [a *head* with an expensive habit, an *acidhead*] *b)* a person devoted to or very enthusiastic about some activity, product, etc. (usually in combination) [*Nethead*] —*adj.* **1** of or having to do with the head **2** most important; principal; commanding; first **3** at the top or front **4** striking against the front [*head* winds] —*vt.* **1** to be chief of or in charge of; command; direct **2** *a)* to be at the top or beginning of; lead; precede (often with *up*) [to *head* a list] *b)* to take a lead over, as in a race or competition **3** to supply (a pin, etc.) with a head **4** [Rare] to behead; decapitate **5** to trim the higher part from (a tree or plant); poll ☆**6** to go around the head of [to *head* a stream] **7** to turn or cause to go in a specified direction [to *head* a car for home] **8** *Soccer* to hit (the ball) with one's head —*vi.* **1** to grow or come to a head **2** to set out; travel in a direction or toward a destination [to *head* eastward, *head* home] ☆**3** to originate, as a river —**bite (**or **snap) someone's head off** [Informal] to speak sharply or harshly to someone —**by a head** by the length of the animal's head, as in horse racing —**by (**or **down by) the head** *Naut.* with the bow deeper in the water than the stern —**come to a head 1** to be about to discharge pus: said of a boil or pimple **2** to culminate, or reach a crisis —**get it through (**or **into) one's head** to understand or realize something —**give head** [Slang] to perform fellatio or cunnilingus (on): considered vulgar by many —**go to someone's head 1** to confuse, excite, or intoxicate someone **2** to make someone vain or overconfident —**hang (**or **hide) one's head** to lower one's head or conceal one's face in or as in shame —**head and shoulders above** clearly superior to —☆**head for 1** to direct one's way toward [she *headed for* home] **2** to be destined for [he's *heading for* trouble] —**head off** to get ahead of and cause to stop or turn away; intercept —**one's head off** [Informal] a great deal; excessively: preceded by a verb [he laughed *his head off*] —**head over heels 1** tumbling as if in a somersault **2** deeply; completely [*head over heels* in love] —**heads up!** [Informal] look out! be careful! —**keep one's head** to keep one's poise, self-control, etc.; not become excited or flustered —**keep one's head above water 1** to remain afloat; not sink **2** to keep oneself alive, out of debt, etc. —**lose one's head** to lose one's poise, self-control, etc.; become excited or flustered —**make head** to make headway; go forward; advance —**make head or tail of** to understand: usually in the negative —**on (**or **upon) someone's head** as someone's burden, responsibility, or misfortune —**out of one's (**or **off one's) head** [Informal] **1** crazy **2** delirious; raving —**over someone's head 1** *a)* too difficult for someone to understand *b)* so that someone cannot understand **2** in spite of someone's prior claim **3** without consulting someone; to a higher authority —**put (**or **lay) heads together** to consult or scheme together —**take it into one's head** to conceive the notion, plan, or intention —**turn someone's head 1** to make someone dizzy **2** to make someone vain or overconfident —**turn heads** to attract much interest or attention

Head (hed), **Edith** (born *Edith Claire Posener*) 1897-1981; U.S. film costume designer

-head[1] (hed) *suffix* -HOOD [*godhead*]

-head[2] (hed) *combining form used to form nouns meaning* a person having a (specified kind of) head or mind, or a head seemingly filled with a (specified) thing [*dumbhead, airhead*]

head·ache (hed′āk′) *n.* ⟦ME *hevedeche* < OE *heafodece*⟧ **1** a continuous pain in the head ☆**2** [Informal] a cause of worry, annoyance, or trouble

head·ach·y or **head·ach·ey** (hed′āk′ē) *adj.* having, feeling, or causing the symptoms of a headache

head·band (hed′band′) *n.* **1** *a)* a band worn around the head *b)* a U-shaped band of flexible plastic, metal, etc. worn on the head to hold the hair in place ☆**2** an ornamental printed band at the top of a page or the beginning of a chapter **3** *Bookbinding* a cloth band fastened under a book's spine at top and bottom

☆**head·bang·er** (hed′baŋ′ər) *n.* ⟦see fol.⟧ [Informal] a fan or performer of HEAVY METAL music

☆**head·bang·ing** or **head-bang·ing** (hed′baŋ′iŋ) *n.* rhythmical moving of the head up and down in dancing to HEAVY METAL —*adj.* [Informal] of or having to do with HEAVY METAL music

head·board (hed′bôrd′) *n.* a board or frame that forms the head of a bed, etc.

☆**head·cheese** (hed′chēz′) *n.* a loaf of jellied, seasoned meat, made from parts of the heads and feet of hogs

head cold a common cold characterized chiefly by congestion of the nasal passages

head count 1 the act of counting the people in a certain category **2** the number of people so counted Also written **head′count′** *n.*

head doctor [Slang] a psychiatrist

head·dress (hed′dres′) *n.* a covering or decoration for the head, esp. one worn ceremonially

head·ed (hed′id) *adj.* **1** formed into a head, as cabbage **2** having a heading

-head·ed (hed′id) *combining form* **1** having a (specified kind of) head [*clearheaded*] **2** having (a specified number of) heads [two-*headed*]

head·er (hed′ər) *n.* **1** a person or device that puts heads on pins, nails, rivets, etc. ☆**2** a machine that takes off the heads of grain and sends them up an inclined plane into a wagon **3** a pipe, tube, etc. that brings together other pipes to direct the flow of a fluid through them, as in an exhaust system **4** in word processing, a line or lines of text, typically consisting of the topic, date, page number, etc., printed at the top of each page of a document **5** [Informal] a headlong fall or dive **6** *Carpentry* a wooden beam, as in flooring, placed between two long beams with the ends of short beams resting against it **7** *Masonry* a brick or building stone laid across the thickness of a wall so that a short end is exposed in the face of the wall **8** *Soccer* a shot or pass made by hitting the ball with the head

head·first (hed′furst′) *adv.* **1** with the head in front; headlong **2** in a reckless way; rashly; impetuously Also **head′fore′most′** (-fôr′mōst′) —*adj.* with or done with the head first or foremost; headlong

☆**head·fish** (hed′fish′) *n., pl.* **-fish′** or **-fish′es** (see FISH) OCEAN SUNFISH

☆**head gate** a gate that controls the flow of water into a canal lock, sluice, etc.

head·gear (hed′gir′) *n.* **1** a covering for the head; hat, cap, headdress, etc. **2** the harness for the head of a horse

head·hunt·er (hed′hunt′ər) *n.* **1** a member of any of certain primitive peoples that remove the heads of slain enemies and preserve them as trophies ☆**2** [Informal] an agent or agency specializing in the recruitment of executive or highly skilled personnel —**head′hunt′ing** *n.*

head·i·ly (hed′′l ē) *adv.* in a heady manner

head·i·ness (hed′ē nis) *n.* the quality or condition of being heady

head·ing (hed′iŋ) *n.* **1** something forming or used to form the head, top, edge, or front; specif., an inscription at the top of a paragraph, chapter, page, section, etc., giving the title or topic **2** a division of a subject; topic or category **3** the horizontal direction in which a moving ship, plane, etc. is pointed, usually expressed as a compass reading in degrees **4** *Mining a)* a drift; gallery *b)* the end of a gallery

☆**head·lamp** (hed′lamp′) *n.* [Chiefly Brit.] HEADLIGHT

head·land (hed′land′; *for 2 usually*, -lənd) *n.* ⟦ME *hedelonde* < OE *heafod lond*⟧ **1** the unbroken soil at the edge of a plowed field, esp. at the ends of the furrows **2** a cape or point of land reaching out into the water; esp., a promontory

head·less (hed′lis) *adj.* ⟦ME *hevedles* < OE *heafodleas*⟧ **1** without a head; specif., *a)* ACEPHALOUS (*adj.* 1) *b)* beheaded **2** without a leader or director

head lettuce lettuce with the leaves formed into a round, compact head

☆**head·light** (hed′līt′) *n.* a light at the front of a vehicle, as for illuminating the way ahead at night

head·line (hed′līn′) *n.* **1** a line at the top of a page in a book, giving the running title, page number, etc. ☆**2** a line or lines, usually in larger type, at the top of a newspaper article, giving a short statement of its contents **3** an important item of news —☆*vt.* **-lined′**, **-lin′ing 1** to provide (a news article) with a headline **2** to give (a performer or performance) featured billing or publicity **3** to be the leading performer or attraction in (a variety show, popular music concert, etc.)

☆**head·lin·er** (hed′līn′ər) *n.* **1** an actor or entertainer advertised as a leading attraction **2** the padded material lining the inside of the roof of an automotive vehicle

head linesman *Football* an official who makes rulings regarding play along the line of scrimmage and who oversees the measurement and marking of yardage gained or lost

head·lock (hed′läk′) ***n.*** *Wrestling* a hold in which one contestant's head is locked between the arm and the body of the other

head·long (hed′lôŋ′) ***adv.*** ⟦LME *hedlong*, altered (by assoc. with ALONG) < ME *hedelinge(s)* < *hede*, head + *-linge*, adv. suffix⟧ **1** with the head first; headfirst **2** with uncontrolled speed and force **3** recklessly; rashly; impetuously —***adj.*** **1** [Old Poet.] steep; dizzy; precipitous [*a headlong* height] **2** with or done with the head first or foremost; headfirst **3** moving with uncontrolled speed and force **4** reckless; impetuous

head louse *see* LOUSE (*n.* 1*a*)

head·man (hed′mən, -man′) ***n.***, *pl.* **-men** (-mən, -men′) ⟦ME *hevidmon* < OE *heafodmann*⟧ **1** a leader, chief, or overseer **2** [Rare] a headsman

head·mas·ter (hed′mas′tər) ***n.*** in certain, esp. private, schools, the man in charge of the school; principal —**head′mas′ter·ship′** ***n.***

head·mis·tress (-mis′tris) ***n.*** in certain, esp. private, schools, the woman in charge of the school; principal

head·most (hed′mōst′) ***adj.*** in the lead; foremost

head·note (hed′nōt′) ***n.*** a brief explanatory note prefacing a chapter, poem, story, legal report, etc.

☆**head-on** (hed′än′) ***adj., adv.*** **1** with the head or front foremost [*a head-on* collision] **2** directly; esp., in direct opposition [to meet a problem *head-on*]

head·phone (hed′fōn′) ***n.*** **1** a listening device consisting of a single small speaker held to the ear by a band over the head **2** [*usually pl.*] a listening device consisting of two such speakers

head·piece (hed′pēs′) ***n.*** **1** a covering for the head, esp. a protective covering; helmet **2** *Printing* an ornamental design at the beginning of a chapter or top of a page

head·pin (-pin′) ***n.*** the pin at the front of a triangular arrangement of bowling pins

head·quar·ters (hed′kwôrt′ərz) ***pl.n.*** [*with sing. or pl. v.*] **1** the main office, or center of operations and control, of anyone in command, as in an army or police force **2** the main office or center of control in any organization —**head′quar′ter** ***vt.***

head·race (hed′rās′) ***n.*** the channel or race furnishing water as to a mill wheel: opposed to TAILRACE

head register the upper register of the voice, in which the higher range of tones is produced

head·rest (hed′rest′) ***n.*** a support for the head, as on a dentist's chair, automobile seat, etc.

head·room (hed′ro͞om′) ***n.*** **1** space or clearance overhead, as in a doorway or tunnel or above the seats of an automobile **2** the temporary increase in volume or power that a high-fidelity audio component can accommodate without distortion

head·sail (hed′sāl′; *naut.*, -səl) ***n.*** any sail forward of the mast or foremast

head-scratch·er (hed′skrach′ər) ***n.*** ⟦< fol.⟧ [Informal] a question, problem, etc. that puzzles

head-scratch·ing (-skrach′iŋ) ***n.*** ⟦see the phrase SCRATCH ONE'S HEAD at SCRATCH⟧ the act of puzzling over a question or problem —***adj.*** [Informal] causing puzzlement

head·set (hed′set′) ***n.*** a headphone, often with a small microphone attached for two-way communication

head·ship (hed′ship′) ***n.*** the position or authority of a chief or leader; leadership; command

☆**head shop** ⟦see HEAD, *n.* 22⟧ [Informal] a shop selling drug paraphernalia

head·shrink·er (hed′shriŋk′ər) ***n.*** **1** a member of a headhunting people who shrink and preserve the heads of slain enemies as trophies ☆**2** [Slang] SHRINK (*n.* 2)

heads·man (hedz′mən) ***n.***, *pl.* **-men** (-mən) ⟦ME *heddysman* < *heddys*, *hefdes* (gen. of *hede, heved*, HEAD) + MAN⟧ an executioner who beheads those condemned to die

head·spring (hed′spriŋ′) ***n.*** ⟦ME *hedspring*: see HEAD & SPRING⟧ a fountain, origin, or source

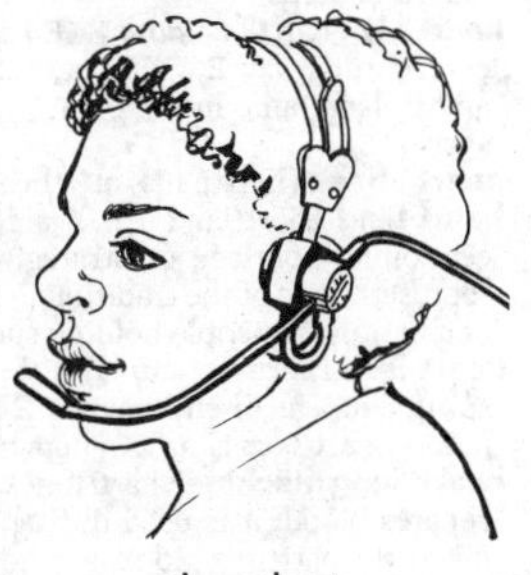
headset

head·stall (-stôl′) ***n.*** ⟦see HEAD & STALL[1]⟧ the part of a bridle or halter that fits over a horse's head

head·stand (-stand′) ***n.*** the act of supporting oneself upright on the head, usually with the help of the hands

head start an early start or other advantage given to or taken by a contestant or competitor

head·stock (hed′stäk′) ***n.*** a bearing or support for a revolving or moving part of a machine; specif., the part of a lathe supporting the spindle

head·stone (-stōn′) ***n.*** **1** [Rare] a cornerstone **2** a stone marker placed at the head of a grave

head·stream (-strēm′) ***n.*** a stream forming the source of another and larger stream or river

head·strong (-strôŋ′) ***adj.*** ⟦ME *heedstronge*: see HEAD & STRONG⟧ **1** determined not to follow orders, advice, etc. but to do as one pleases **2** showing such determination [*headstrong* desire]

heads-up (hedz′up′) [Informal] ***adj.*** ⟦< interjectional phr. HEADS UP!: see HEAD⟧ alert and resourceful [playing *heads-up* baseball] —***n.*** the act or an instance of providing a notice or warning to alert someone, as in advance of difficulty or trouble

head-to-head (hed′to͞o hed′) ***adj., adv.*** ☆in direct confrontation

head tone any of the tones produced in the head register

☆**head trip** [Slang] an exhilarating intellectual experience

head-up display (hed′up′) the display of instrument readings onto the windshield of an aircraft, automobile, etc., so as to afford the pilot or driver with a simultaneous view of the data and of the sky or road: often **heads-up display**

head·wait·er (hed′wāt′ər) ***n.*** a supervisor of waiters and waitresses, often in charge of table reservations

head·wa·ters (hed′wôt′ərz) ***pl.n.*** the headstreams and the beginning of a large stream or river

head·way (hed′wā′) ***n.*** **1** forward motion **2** progress or success in work, etc. **3** HEADROOM ☆**4** the difference in time or distance between two trains, ships, etc. traveling in the same direction over the same course

head wind a wind blowing in the direction directly opposite the course of a ship or aircraft

head·word (hed′wurd′) ***n.*** **1** a word or phrase that is a heading for a paragraph, chapter, etc. **2** *Linguis.* a word functioning as a head in a structure

head·work (hed′wurk′) ***n.*** mental effort; thought

head·y (hed′ē) ***adj.*** **head′i·er, head′i·est** ⟦ME *hevedi*: see HEAD & -Y[3]⟧ **1** [Now Rare] impetuous; rash; willful **2** *a)* tending to affect the senses; intoxicating [*heady* wine] *b)* thrilling; exhilarating [the *heady* days of one's youth] **3** having, showing, or using intelligence or good judgment

heal (hēl) ***vt.*** ⟦ME *helen* < OE *hælan* (akin to Ger *heilen*) < base of *hal*, sound, healthy: see HALE[1], WHOLE⟧ **1** to make sound, well, or healthy again; restore to health [*heal* the sick] **2** *a)* to cure or get rid of (a disease) *b)* to cause (a wound, sore, etc.) to become closed or scarred so as to restore a healthy condition **3** to free from grief, troubles, evil, etc. **4** *a)* to remedy or get rid of (grief, troubles, etc.) *b)* to make up (a breach, differences, etc.); reconcile —***vi.*** **1** to become well or healthy again; be cured **2** to become closed or scarred: said of a wound —***SYN.*** CURE

heal·er (hēl′ər) ***n.*** ⟦ME *helere*⟧ a person or thing that heals; specif., one who tries to heal through prayer or faith

health (helth) ***n.*** ⟦ME *helthe* < OE *hælth* < base of *hal*, sound, healthy (see HALE[1], WHOLE) + -TH[1]⟧ **1** physical and mental well-being; freedom from disease, pain, or defect; normalcy of physical and mental functions; soundness **2** condition of body or mind [good or bad *health*] **3** a wish for a person's health and happiness, as in drinking a toast **4** soundness or vitality, as of a society

health·care (helth′ker′) ***n.*** the prevention and treatment of illness or injury, esp. on a comprehensive, ongoing basis: also written **health care**

health club a private club for physical exercise, with rooms for weight lifting, massage, etc., courts for handball, racquetball, etc., and, often, a swimming pool, sauna, etc.

health farm a place, especially in the country, where people go for a healthful regimen of regular exercise, special diets, etc.

☆**health food** food considered to be especially healthful; often, specif., such food when organically grown and free of chemical additives

health·ful (helth′fəl) ***adj.*** **1** helping to produce, promote, or maintain health; salutary; wholesome **2** [Rare] HEALTHY —**health′ful·ly** ***adv.*** —**health′ful·ness** ***n.***

☆**health maintenance organization** HMO

☆**health physics** a discipline dealing with protection against the potential hazards of harmful radiations in the environment, esp. in the workplace —**health physicist**

health spa a commercial establishment with facilities for physical exercise and, often, a swimming pool, sauna, etc.

health·y (hel′thē) ***adj.*** **health′i·er, health′i·est** **1** having good health; well; sound **2** showing or resulting from good health [a *healthy* complexion] **3** HEALTHFUL **4** vigorous, prosperous, etc. **5** [Informal] *a)* proper; fitting [a *healthy* respect for the law] *b)* abundant, considerable, etc. —**health′i·ly** ***adv.*** —**health′i·ness** ***n.***

Hea·ney (hē′nē), **Sea·mus (Justin)** (shā′məs) 1939-2013; Ir. poet

heap (hēp) ***n.*** ⟦ME *hepe*, a troop, heap < OE *heap*, a troop, band, multitude, akin to Ger *hauf(en)*, Du *hoop* < IE **keub-* < base **keu-*, bend, arch > HOP[1], HIVE⟧ **1** a pile, mass, or mound of things jumbled together **2** [*often pl.*] [Informal] a great number or amount [*a heap* of toys, *heaps* of money] ☆**3** [Slang] an automobile, esp. an old, dilapidated one —***vt.*** **1** to make a heap of; bring together into a pile **2** to give or supply in large amounts; load [to *heap* gifts upon someone] **3** to fill (a plate, dry measure, etc.) full or to overflowing —***vi.*** to accumulate or rise in a heap, or pile

hear (hir) ***vt.*** **heard** (hurd), **hear′ing** ⟦ME *heren* < OE *hieran*, akin to Ger *hören* (Goth *hausjan*) < IE base **keu-*, to notice, observe > L *cavere*, be on one's guard, Gr *koein*, to perceive, hear⟧ **1** to perceive or sense (sounds), esp. through stimulation of auditory nerves in the ear by sound waves **2** to listen to and consider; specif., *a)* to take notice of; pay attention to [*hear* what I tell you] *b)* to listen to officially; give a formal hearing to [to *hear* a child's lessons] *c)* to conduct an examination or hearing of (a law case, etc.); try *d)* to consent to; grant [*hear* my plea] *e)* to understand [I *hear* you] *f)* to be a member of the audience at (an opera, lecture, etc.) **3** to be informed of; be told of; learn of [to *hear* a rumor] —***vi.*** **1** to have a normally functioning ear or ears; be able to hear sounds **2** to listen **3** to be told or informed (*of* or *about*) —**hear from** **1** to get a telephone call, letter, email, etc. from **2** to get a criticism or reprimand from —**hear! hear!**

well said!: an expression of approval or agreement —**hear out** to listen to until the end —**hear tell** [Dial.] to be told; learn —**will (or would) not hear of** to forbid or refuse to consider [my grandfather *would not hear of* such behavior] —**hear′er** *n.*

hear·ing (hir′iŋ) *n.* ⟦ME *heringe*: see prec.⟧ 1 the act or process of perceiving sounds 2 the sense by which sounds are perceived 3 an opportunity to speak, sing, etc.; chance to be heard 4 *a)* a court appearance before a judge or court referee, other than an actual formal trial *b)* a formal meeting, as of an investigative body or legislative committee, before which evidence is presented, testimony is given, etc. 5 the distance that a sound, esp. that of the unaided voice, will carry [to be within *hearing*]

hearing aid a small, battery-powered electronic device that amplifies sound waves, worn in or near the ear of a person who is partially deaf

hear·ing-im·paired (hir′iŋ im perd′) *adj.* physiologically unable to hear, totally or partially; deaf

hark·en (här′kən) *vi.* ⟦ME *herknien* < OE *heorknian, hyrcnian* < base of *hieran*: see HEAR⟧ [Now Literary] to give careful attention; listen carefully: with *to* —*vt.* [Archaic] to heed; hear —**hearken back** to go back in thought or speech; revert; hark back

hear·say (hir′sā′) *n.* ⟦< phrase *to hear say*, parallel to Ger *hörensagen*⟧ 1 something one has heard but does not know to be true; rumor; gossip 2 HEARSAY EVIDENCE —*adj.* based on hearsay

hearsay evidence *Law* testimony, typically inadmissible, given by a witness and consisting of a report of something which someone else has said

hearse (hʉrs) *n.* ⟦ME *herce* < OFr, a harrow, grated portcullis < L *hirpex*, a large rake with iron teeth < dial (Sabine) *irpus*, wolf (hence, lit., wolf-tooth device)⟧ 1 an automobile or carriage, used in a funeral for carrying the corpse 2 *a)* a framelike structure above a coffin or tomb, for candles, hangings, etc. *b)* a triangular framework to hold candles at Tenebrae 3 [Archaic] a bier or coffin

Hearst (hʉrst), **William Randolph** 1863-1951; U.S. newspaper & magazine publisher

heart (härt) *n.* ⟦ME *herte* < OE *heorte*, akin to Ger *herz* < IE base **k̑erd-*, **k̑ṛd-*, heart > L *cor*, (gen. *cordis*), Gr *kardia*, OIr *cride*, Serb *sȓce*⟧ 1 *a)* the hollow, muscular organ in a vertebrate animal that receives blood from the veins and pumps it through the arteries by alternate dilation and contraction *b)* an analogous part in most invertebrate animals 2 the part of the human body thought of as containing the heart; breast; bosom 3 any place or part like a heart, in that it is near the center; specif., *a)* the central core of a plant or vegetable [*hearts* of celery] *b)* the center or innermost part of a place or region [the *heart* of a city] 4 the central, vital, or main part; real meaning; essence; core 5 the human heart considered as the center or source of emotions, personality attributes, etc.; specif., *a)* inmost thought and feeling; consciousness or conscience [to know in one's *heart*] *b)* the source of emotions (contrasted with HEAD, *n.* 2a, the source of intellect) *c)* one's emotional nature; disposition [to have a kind *heart*] *d)* any of various humane feelings; love, devotion, sympathy, etc. *e)* mood; feeling [to have a heavy *heart*] *f)* spirit, resolution, or courage [to lose *heart*] 6 a person, usually one loved or admired in some specified way [he is a valiant *heart*] 7 something like a heart in shape; conventionalized design or representation of a heart, shaped like this: ♡ 8 *a)* any of a suit of playing cards marked with such figures in red *b)* [*pl., with sing. or pl. v.*] this suit of cards ☆*c)* [*pl., with sing. v.*] a card game in which the object is either to avoid winning any hearts or the queen of spades, or to win all the hearts and the queen of spades —*vt.* [Obs.] to hearten, or encourage —**after someone's own heart** in accord with someone's feelings or tastes —**at heart** in one's innermost or hidden nature; secretly or fundamentally —**break someone's heart** to cause someone to be overcome with grief or disappointment, often, specif., by rejecting or spurning his or her love or affection —**by heart** by or from memorization —☆**change of heart** a change of mind, affections, loyalties, etc. —**do someone's heart good** to make someone happy; please or gratify someone —**eat one's heart out** to brood or feel keenly unhappy over some frustration or in regret —**from (the bottom of) one's heart** very sincerely or deeply: also **from the heart** —☆**have a heart** to be sensitive, sympathetic, generous, etc. —**have one's heart in one's mouth (or throat)** to be full of fear or nervous anticipation —**have one's heart in the right place** to be well-intentioned or well-meaning —**heart and soul** with all one's effort, enthusiasm, etc. —**in one's heart of hearts** in one's innermost nature or deepest feelings; fundamentally —**lose one's heart (to)** to fall in love (with) —**near someone's heart** dear or important to someone —**not have the heart** to be insufficiently unfeeling or pitiless to do a particular thing [I do *not have the heart* to turn him away] —**set someone's heart at rest (or ease)** to cause someone to set aside doubts, fears, or worries —**set one's heart on** to have a fixed desire for; long for —**steal someone's heart** to cause someone to feel love or affection —**take heart** to have more courage or confidence; cheer up —**take to heart** 1 to consider seriously 2 to be troubled or grieved by —**to one's heart's content** as much as one desires —**wear one's heart on one's sleeve** to behave so that one's feelings or affections are plainly evident —**with all one's heart** 1 with complete sincerity, devotion, etc. 2 very willingly; with pleasure —**with half a heart** halfheartedly

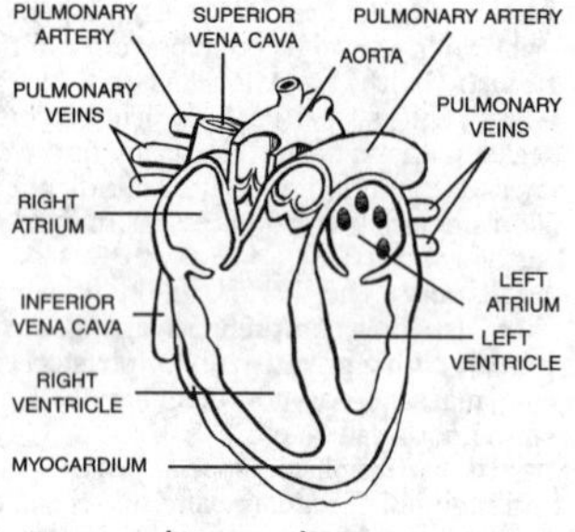

human heart

heart·ache (härt′āk′) *n.* ⟦OE *heortece*: see prec. & ACHE⟧ sorrow or grief; mental anguish

☆**heart attack** any sudden instance of the blood supply to the heart muscle itself becoming inadequate, resulting in heart muscle damage: often a result of a coronary thrombosis

heart·beat (härt′bēt′) *n.* 1 *a)* one pulsation, or full contraction and dilation, of the heart *b)* the continuous series of such pulsations constituting the rhythmic beating of the heart [an irregular *heartbeat*] 2 a very brief period of time; moment; instant [reappeared in a *heartbeat*] 3 the vital core or motivating force

heart block a disorder in which there is defective transmission of impulses regulating the heartbeat, resulting in independent contractions of the atria and ventricles

heart·break (härt′brāk′) *n.* overwhelming sorrow, grief, or disappointment —**heart′break′ing** *adj.*

heart·break·er (-ər) *n.* someone or something that causes heartbreak, specif. a person whose manner and appearance inspire romantic responses, but whose casual, insensitive behavior in a relationship causes heartbreak

heart·bro·ken (härt′brō′kən) *adj.* overwhelmed with sorrow, grief, or disappointment

heart·burn (härt′bʉrn′) *n.* a burning sensation beneath the breastbone resulting from a spastic reflux of stomach acid, food, etc. into the esophagus; pyrosis; brash

heart cherry any of several heart-shaped and soft-fleshed varieties of sweet cherry: cf. BIGARREAU

heart disease disease of the cardiovascular system

-heart·ed (härt′id) ⟦ME⟧ *combining form* having a (specified kind of) heart [*stouthearted*]

heart·en (härt′'n) *vt.* ⟦HEART + -EN⟧ to cheer up; encourage

heart failure 1 the failure of the heart to beat or to pump blood 2 the inability of the heart to pump enough blood to maintain an adequate flow to and from the bodily tissues: see also CONGESTIVE HEART FAILURE

heart·felt (härt′felt′) *adj.* ⟦HEART + pp. of FEEL⟧ with or expressive of deep feeling; sincere

hearth (härth) *n.* ⟦ME *herth* < OE *heorth*, akin to Ger *herd* < IE base **ker-*, to burn, glow > L *carbo*, coal, Lith *kárštas*, hot⟧ 1 the stone or brick floor of a fireplace, often extending out into the room 2 *a)* the fireside as the center of family life *b)* family life; home 3 the part of a brick oven, or of a blacksmith's forge, on which the fire rests 4 *Metallurgy* *a)* the lowest part of a blast furnace, on which the molten metal and slag are deposited *b)* the floor of a furnace on which the ore or metal rests for exposure to the flame

hearth·side (härth′sīd′) *n.* FIRESIDE

hearth·stone (-stōn′) *n.* 1 the stone forming a hearth 2 the home, or home life 3 a soft stone or powdered composition used for scouring a hearth or steps

heart·i·ly (härt′'l ē) *adv.* ⟦ME *hertili*: see HEART & -LY[2]⟧ 1 in a friendly, sincere, cordial way 2 with zest, enthusiasm, or vigor 3 with a good appetite and in large amounts [to eat *heartily*] 4 completely; fully; very [*heartily* sorry]

heart·i·ness (härt′ē nis) *n.* a hearty quality or state

heart·land (härt′land′) *n.* 1 a geographically central area having crucial economic, political, or strategic importance 2 *a)* a region regarded as representative of the traditional, specif. middle-class or small-town, values of a nation *b)* people holding such values, regarded collectively

heart·less (härt′lis) *adj.* ⟦ME *herteles* < OE *heortleas*⟧ 1 [Archaic] lacking spirit, courage, or enthusiasm 2 lacking kindness or feeling; hard and pitiless —**heart′less·ly** *adv.* —**heart′less·ness** *n.*

heart-lung machine (härt′luŋ′) a mechanical device that pumps and oxygenates blood: it is used during open-heart surgery, lung surgery, etc. to divert the patient's blood around the heart and lungs

heart-rend·ing (härt′ren′diŋ) *adj.* causing much grief or mental anguish —**heart′-rend′ing·ly** *adv.*

hearts·ease or **heart's-ease** (härts′ēz′) *n.* ⟦see HEART & EASE⟧ 1 peace of mind; calmness of emotion 2 WILD PANSY: so called because formerly believed to cure the pangs of love

heart·sick (härt′sik′) *adj.* sick at heart; extremely unhappy or despondent: also **heart′sore′** (-sôr′)

heart·some (härt′səm) *adj.* ⟦HEART + -SOME[1]⟧ [Scot.] 1 heartening; cheering 2 cheerful; lively

heart-stop·ping (härt′stäp′iŋ) *adj.* very exciting, deeply moving, etc.; specif., *a)* very beautiful or pleasurable *b)* suspenseful [a *heart-stopping* ninth inning] *c)* terrifying

heart-strick·en (härt′strik′ən) *adj.* deeply grieved or greatly dismayed: also **heart′-struck′** (-struk′)

heart·strings (härt′striŋz′) *pl.n.* ⟦orig., tendons or nerves formerly believed to brace the heart⟧ deepest feelings or affections

heart·throb (-thräb′) *n.* 1 the heartbeat ☆2 [Slang] *a)* tender or mawkish emotion (*usually used in pl.*) *b)* a sweetheart 3 a person, usually a young man, renowned for inspiring feelings of romantic infatuation

heart-to-heart (härt′ to͞o härt′) *adj.* intimate and candid —☆*n.* [Informal] an intimate conversation

heart urchin any of an order (Spatangoida) of echinoid echinoderms with an elongated, somewhat heart-shaped shell

heart·warm·ing (härt′wôrm′iŋ) *adj.* such as to kindle a warm glow of genial feelings

heart-whole (härt′hōl′) *adj.* **1** not in love; heart-free **2** sincere; wholehearted **3** undismayed; courageous

heart·wood (härt′wood′) *n.* the hard, nonliving, older wood at the core of a tree trunk, usually dark in color and impervious to air and water; duramen: cf. SAPWOOD

heart·worm (härt′wurm′) *n.* a nematode worm (*Dirofilaria immitis*) transmitted by mosquitoes or fleas that is parasitic in the bloodstream, esp. in the heart, of dogs, cats, etc.

heart·y (härt′ē) *adj.* **heart′i·er, heart′i·est** ⟦ME *herti:* see HEART & -Y[3]⟧ **1** extremely warm and friendly; most genial or cordial [a *hearty* welcome] **2** enthusiastic; wholehearted [*hearty* cooperation] **3** strongly felt or expressed; unrestrained [a *hearty* dislike, *hearty* laughter] **4** strong and healthy [a *hearty* young farmer] **5** *a)* satisfying, nourishing, and plentiful [a *hearty* meal] *b)* needing or liking plenty of food [a *hearty* eater] —*n., pl.* **heart′ies** [Archaic] a friend; comrade; esp., a fellow sailor: usually preceded by *my*

heat (hēt) *n.* ⟦ME *hete* < OE *hætu* < base of *hat* (see HOT), akin to Ger *heiss* < IE base **kai-*, heat⟧ **1** the quality of being hot; hotness: in physics, heat is considered a form of energy existing as the result of the random motion of molecules and is the form of energy that is transferred between bodies as a result of their temperature difference **2** *a)* much hotness; great warmth [stifling *heat*] *b)* FEVER **3** degree of hotness or warmth [at low *heat*] **4** the perception of heat by the senses, resulting from contact with or nearness to something hot; sensation of hotness or warmth felt through the skin **5** hot weather or climate **6** the warming of a room, house, etc., as by a stove or furnace [his rent includes *heat*] **7** a burning sensation produced by spices, mustard, etc. **8** color or other appearance as an indication of hotness [blue *heat* in metals] **9** strong feeling or emotion; excitement, ardor, anger, zeal, etc. **10** the period or condition of excitement, intensity, stress, etc.; most violent or intense point or stage [in the *heat* of battle] **11** a single effort, round, bout, or trial; esp., any of the preliminary rounds of a race, etc., the winners of which compete in the final round **12** *a)* sexual excitement *b)* period of sexual excitement in animals; esp., estrus ☆**13** [Slang] *a)* coercion, as by intimidation *b)* great pressure, as in criminal investigation or law enforcement *c)* the police *d)* a firearm or firearms **14** [Slang] *Baseball* pitches thrown with great velocity **15** *Metallurgy a)* a single heating of metal, ore, etc. in a furnace or forge *b)* the amount processed in a single heating — *vt., vi.* **1** to make or become warm or hot **2** to make or become excited; inflame or become inflamed

heat barrier THERMAL BARRIER

heat capacity the amount of heat required to raise the temperature of a substance or system one degree, usually expressed in calories per °C

heat·ed (hēt′id) *adj.* **1** made warm or hot [a *heated* blanket] **2** provided with a HEATER (sense 1) [a *heated* garage] **3** vehement, impassioned, or angry [a *heated* dispute] —**heat′ed·ly** *adv.*

heat engine an engine for changing heat into mechanical energy, such as a steam engine or gasoline engine

heat·er (hēt′ər) *n.* **1** an apparatus for heating or warming a room, car, water, etc.; stove, furnace, radiator, etc. **2** a person whose work is to heat something **3** in an electron tube, an element set inside the cathode and heated by an electric current so that it indirectly heats the cathode to the temperature at which it will give off electrons ☆**4** [Slang] a pistol **5** [Slang] *Baseball* a fastball

heat exchanger any device, as a radiator or a condenser, for transferring heat energy to a cooler medium from a warmer one, for heating or cooling purposes

heat exhaustion a condition caused by excessive loss of salt and water, usually resulting from overexertion in a hot environment, and characterized by peripheral vascular collapse, dizziness, nausea, low body temperature, clammy skin, etc.: cf. HEATSTROKE

heath (hēth) *n.* ⟦ME *hethe* < OE *hæth*, akin to Ger *heide*, wasteland, heath < IE base **kaito-*, forested or uncultivated land > Welsh *coed*, forest⟧ **1** a tract of open wasteland, esp. in the British Isles, covered with heather, low shrubs, etc.; moor **2** any plant of the heath family; esp., any of various shrubs and plants (genera *Erica* and *Calluna*) that grow on heaths, as heather —*adj.* designating a family (Ericaceae, order Ericales) of dicotyledonous woody shrubs and small trees, including the blueberry, mountain laurel, and rhododendrons —**one's native heath** the place of one's birth or childhood

☆**heath aster** a North American wildflower (*Aster ericoides*) of the composite family, with small, stiff leaves and white flowers, growing in dry, open places; dog fennel

heath·bird (hēth′burd′) *n.* a bird living on heaths; specif., BLACK GROUSE

heath cock BLACKCOCK

hea·then (hē′thən) *n., pl.* **-thens** or **-then** ⟦ME *hethen* < OE *hæthen* < *hæth*, HEATH; like Goth *haithnō*, gentile (woman) < *haithi*, heath (hence lit., "heath dweller") a loan transl. used by ULFILAS for LL(Ec) *paganus* (see PAGAN), taken in its L sense, "a countryman, rustic" < *pagus*, the country⟧ **1** in the Old Testament, a member of any nation or people not worshiping the God of Israel **2** anyone not a Jew, Christian, or Muslim; esp., a member of a tribe, nation, etc. worshiping many gods: now chiefly a dismissive or disparaging term **3** a person regarded as irreligious, uncivilized, unenlightened, etc. —*adj.* **1** of or characteristic of heathens; pagan **2** irreligious, uncivilized, etc. —SYN. PAGAN —**hea′then·dom** *n.* —**hea′then·ish** *adj.* —**hea′then·ism′** *n.*

hea·then·ize (hē′thən īz′) *vt., vi.* **-ized′**, **-iz′ing** to make or become heathen

heath·er (heth′ər) *n.* ⟦altered (after HEATH) < ME (northern & Scot) *haddyr*, prob. < OE **hædre*, parallel with *clofre*, clover, *mædre*, madder⟧ any of various low-growing plants of the heath family; esp., a plant (*Calluna vulgaris*) common in the British Isles, with scalelike leaves and stalks of small, bell-shaped, purplish-pink flowers —*adj.* **1** like heather in color or appearance **2** *a)* muted; soft (said of colors) *b)* marked with flecks of various colors [*heather* tones] —**heath′er·y** *adj.*

heather

Heath·er (heth′ər) *n.* a feminine name

heath hen ☆an extinct New England grouse (*Tympanuchus cupido cupido*)

heath·y (hēth′ē) *adj.* of, like, or covered with heath

☆**heat index** a number expressed in degrees Fahrenheit, computed from the temperature and the relative humidity, and used as an indication of the apparent temperature as it would be felt by a person outdoors (Ex.: a temperature of 90°F and a relative humidity of 50% yield a heat index of 96°F)

heating pad a pad consisting of an electric heating element covered with fabric, for applying heat to parts of the body

☆**heat lightning** ⟦because often seen during hot summer weather⟧ distant lightning, often visible as a flicker in the atmosphere, whose thunder is inaudible

heat of fusion the amount of heat needed to melt a unit mass of a solid that has just reached the melting point

heat of vaporization the amount of heat needed to turn one gram of a liquid into a vapor, without a rise in temperature of the liquid

heat pipe a thin, sealed metal tube that efficiently transfers heat without a pump, using a fluid that vaporizes at the hot end, condenses as it reaches the cooler end, and returns to the hot end by capillary action through a wick or along tiny grooves in the wall

heat prostration HEAT EXHAUSTION

heat pump a device for cooling or warming an enclosed space by removing heat from interior air and transferring it out, or by absorbing heat from outdoor air, or from a hot-water source, and transferring it in

heat rash MILIARIA

heat shield any heat-protecting device or system, esp. an ablative coating or tiles, bonded to the surface of a reentry spacecraft

heat sink a part of a system designed to be at a lower temperature than its surroundings and used to dissipate heat from that system

heat·stroke (hēt′strōk′) *n.* a serious failure of the body's heat-regulation mechanisms resulting from excessive exposure to intense heat and characterized by high fever, dry skin, collapse, and sometimes convulsions or coma: cf. HEAT EXHAUSTION, SUNSTROKE

heat-treat (-trēt′) *vt.* to heat and cool (a metal) so as to change its ductility or other properties in a desired way

☆**heat wave** a prolonged period of unusually hot weather, typically resulting from a slowly moving air mass of relatively high temperature

heaume (hōm) *n.* ⟦Fr < OFr *helme*: see HELMET⟧ a heavy medieval helmet covering the entire head and reaching to the shoulders

heave (hēv) *vt.* **heaved** or (esp. *Naut.*) **hove, heav′ing** ⟦ME *heven* < OE *hebban*, akin to Ger *heben* (Goth *hafjan*) < IE base **kap-*, to seize, grasp > HAVE, L *capere*⟧ **1** to raise or lift, esp. with effort **2** *a)* to lift in this way and throw or cast *b)* to throw **3** to make rise or swell, as one's chest **4** to utter (a sigh, groan, etc.) with great effort or pain **5** *Geol.* to displace (a stratum or vein), as by the intersection of another stratum or vein **6** *Naut.* to raise, haul, pull, move, etc. by pulling with a rope or cable —*vi.* **1** to swell up; bulge out **2** to rise and fall rhythmically [*heaving* waves] **3** to make strenuous, spasmodic movements of the throat, chest, or stomach; specif., *a)* to retch; vomit or strain to vomit *b)* to pant; breathe hard; gasp **4** *Naut. a)* to tug or haul (*on* or *at* a cable, rope, etc.) *b)* to push (*at* a capstan to turn it) *c)* to proceed; move [a ship *hove* into sight] —*n.* **1** the act or effort of heaving **2** a throw **3** *Geol. a)* the extent of horizontal displacement caused by a fault *b)* an upward displacement of soil, rocks, etc., usually caused by frost or moisture (often called **heaving**) See also HEAVES —**heave ho!** an exclamation used when heaving or lifting something heavy, as by sailors when heaving in the anchor —**heave to 1** *Naut.* to stop forward movement, esp. by bringing the vessel's head into the wind and keeping it there **2** to stop —**heav′er** *n.*

heave-ho (hēv′hō′) *n.* ⟦see the phrase in prec.⟧ ☆[Informal] dismissal, as from a position: chiefly in the phrase **give (or get) the (old) heave-ho**

heav·en (hev′ən) *n.* ⟦ME *heven* < OE *heofon* < IE base **k̑em-*, to cover (> LL *camisia*, shirt): akin to OHG *himil* and to OS *hevan*, ON, *himinn* (dat. *hifne*), with *-fn*, *-v-n* < *-mn* by dissimilation⟧ **1** [*usually pl.*] the space surrounding or seeming to overarch the earth, in which the sun, moon, and stars appear; sky; firmament: in pl., used with *the* 2 [*often* **H-**] *a)* the abode of God, his angels, and the blessed *b)* the powers of heaven; also, God [*Heaven* help you!] 3 [*often* **H-**] a state or place of complete happiness or perfect rest, attained by the good after death 4 *a)* any place of great beauty and pleasure *b)* a state of great happiness —**move heaven and earth** to do all that can be done; exert the utmost effort, influence, etc. *USAGE*—often used in interjectional phrases of surprise, protest, etc. [for *heaven's* sake! good *heavens!*]

heav·en·ly (hev′ən lē) *adj.* ⟦ME *hevenlich* < OE *heofonlic*⟧ 1 CELESTIAL (sense 1) 2 *a)* causing or marked by great happiness, beauty, peace, etc. *b)* [Informal] very attractive, pleasing, etc. 3 *Theol.* of or in heaven; holy; divine —**heav′en·li·ness** *n.*

heav·en·ward (-wərd) *adv., adj.* ⟦ME *heveneward*: see -WARD⟧ toward heaven: also **heav′en·wards** *adv.*

heaves (hēvz) *pl.n.* [*with sing. or pl. v.*] ☆1 chronic emphysema of horses, characterized by forced breathing, coughing, heaving of the flanks, etc. 2 [Informal] a bout of vomiting Usually with *the* —**(the) dry heaves** [Informal] a bout of retching that brings up no vomit

heav·i·ly (hev′ə lē) *adv.* in a heavy manner; specif., *a)* with a heavy weight [*heavily* burdened] *b)* as if with a heavy weight; slowly; clumsily; laboriously [to rise *heavily* from one's seat] *c)* oppressively; severely [*heavily* taxed] *d)* abundantly [*heavily* populated]

heav·i·ness (hev′ē nis) *n.* a heavy quality or state

Heav·i·side layer (hev′ē sīd′) ⟦after O. *Heaviside* (1850-1925), Eng physicist⟧ E LAYER

heav·y (hev′ē) *adj.* **heav′i·er, heav′i·est** ⟦ME *hevi* < OE *hefig* (akin to OHG *hebig*) < base of *hebban* (see HEAVE) + *-ig* (see -Y³): prob. basic sense "containing something, full"⟧ 1 hard to lift or move because of great weight; weighty 2 of high specific gravity; of concentrated weight for the size 3 above the usual or defined weight: said of goods, certain animals, etc. 4 larger, greater, or more intense than usual or normal; specif., *a)* falling or striking with great force or impact [a *heavy* blow] *b)* of greater than usual quantity [a *heavy* vote] *c)* violent and intense; rough [a *heavy* sea] *d)* loud, deep, and resounding [*heavy* thunder] *e)* thick, coarse, or massive [*heavy* features] *f)* going beyond the average; to a greater than usual extent [a *heavy* drinker] *g)* prolonged and intense [*heavy* applause] *h)* weighed down [trees *heavy* with apples] 5 of great importance; serious; grave [a *heavy* responsibility] 6 hard to endure; oppressive; burdensome; distressing [*heavy* taxes] 7 hard to do or manage; difficult [*heavy* work] 8 grievous; lamentable [*heavy* sorrow] 9 burdened with sorrow; depressed [a *heavy* heart] 10 burdened with sleep or fatigue [*heavy* eyelids] 11 capable of carrying a load of great weight [a *heavy* truck] 12 characterized by density, hardness, fullness, etc. suggestive of weight; specif., *a)* hard to digest [a *heavy* meal] *b)* not leavened properly; doughy [a *heavy* cake] *c)* remaining in the atmosphere; clinging; penetrating [a *heavy* odor] *d)* overcast; cloudy; gloomy; lowering [a *heavy* sky] *e)* hard to work with or travel over because of mud, sand, clay, etc. [a *heavy* soil] 13 tedious, dull, or strained [*heavy* humor] 14 clumsy; unwieldy; physically awkward [a *heavy* gait] ☆15 steeply inclined [a *heavy* grade] 16 designating any large industry that uses massive machinery and produces raw or processed materials, as steel, basic to other industries 17 designating, of, or equipped with massive or relatively heavy weapons, armor, etc. 18 *Chem. a)* designating an isotope of greater atomic weight than the normal or most abundant isotope *b)* designating a compound containing such isotopes 19 *Theater* serious, tragic, or villainous 20 [Slang] very serious or important and, often, depressing 21 [Slang] excellent, important, serious, profound, etc. —*adv.* **heavier, heaviest** heavily: often in hyphenated compounds [*heavy*-laden] —*n., pl.* **heav′ies** 1 something heavy 2 *Theater a)* a serious, tragic, or villainous role *b)* an actor who plays such roles 3 [Slang] an influential or important person —**hang heavy** to pass tediously; drag: said of time —**heavy with child** [Old-fashioned] pregnant

SYN.—**heavy** implies relatively great density, quantity, intensity, etc. and figuratively connotes a pressing down on the mind, spirits, or senses [a *heavy* load, *heavy*-hearted]; **weighty** suggests heaviness as an absolute rather than a relative quality and figuratively connotes great importance or influence [a *weighty* problem]: **ponderous** applies to something that is very heavy because of size or bulk and figuratively connotes a labored or dull quality [a *ponderous* dissertation]; **massive** stresses largeness and solidity rather than heaviness and connotes an impressiveness due to great magnitude [*massive* structures]; **cumbersome** implies a heaviness and bulkiness that makes for awkward handling and, in extended use, connotes unwieldiness [*cumbersome* formalities] —*ANT.* **light**

heavy breathing [Informal] 1 a representation, as in a novel or film, of strong emotion or sexual passion 2 a ponderous or pompous quality, as of writing style —**heav′y-breath′ing** *adj.*

heav·y-du·ty (hev′ē dōōt′ē, -dyōōt′ē) *adj.* 1 made to withstand great strain, bad weather, etc. [*heavy-duty* work gloves] 2 [Slang] very serious or important

heav·y-foot·ed (hev′ē foot′id) *adj.* ponderous or clumsy in or as in walking; plodding

heav·y-hand·ed (-han′did) *adj.* 1 without a light touch; clumsy or tactless 2 cruel, oppressive, or tyrannical —**heav′y-hand′ed·ly** *adv.* —**heav′y-hand′ed·ness** *n.*

heav·y-heart·ed (hev′ē härt′id) *adj.* sad; depressed; despondent —**heav′y-heart′ed·ly** *adv.* —**heav′y-heart′ed·ness** *n.*

☆**heavy hitter** 1 a baseball player who hits many home runs and other extra-base hits 2 [Slang] a very important or influential person

heavy hydrogen DEUTERIUM

heav·y-lad·en (hev′ē lād′n) *adj.* 1 laden, or loaded, heavily 2 heavily burdened with care and trouble

heavy lifting [Informal] that portion of a task or job regarded as especially strenuous, burdensome, difficult, etc.

☆**heavy metal** 1 any metal or alloy having a specific gravity greater than 5.0 2 a form of rock music performed typically on guitars and drums and characterized by loud amplification, electronic distortion, shouted lyrics, etc.

heav·y·set (hev′ē set′) *adj.* having a stout or stocky build

heavy spar BARITE

heavy water water composed of heavy isotopes of hydrogen or oxygen, or of both; esp., deuterium oxide, D_2O, which is water composed of ordinary oxygen and deuterium

heav·y·weight (hev′ē wāt′) *n.* 1 a person or animal weighing much more than average 2 an athlete, in any of various sports, who is in the heaviest weight division or classification; specif., a boxer in the heaviest weight classification, typically weighing over 200 pounds (90.7 kg) ☆3 [Informal] a very intelligent, influential, or important person —*adj.* 1 heavy in weight 2 of heavyweights

Heb *abbrev.* 1 Hebrew 2 *Bible* Hebrews

heb·do·mad (heb′dō mad′, -də-) *n.* ⟦L *hebdomas* (gen. *hebdomadis*) < Gr, the number seven, week < *hebdomos*, seventh < *hepta*, SEVEN⟧ seven days; a week —**heb·dom·a·dal** (heb däm′ə dəl) *adj.*

☆**hebe** (hēb) *n.* ⟦< HEBREW⟧ [Slang] a Jew: an offensive term of hostility and contempt

He·be (hē′bē) *n.* ⟦L < Gr *Hēbē* < *hēbē*, youth⟧ *Gr. Myth.* the goddess of youth, daughter of Hera and Zeus: she is a cupbearer to the gods

He·bei (hu′bā′) province of NE China, on the gulf of Bo Hai: 78,263 sq mi (202,700 sq km); cap. Shijiazhuang

he·be·phre·ni·a (hē′bə frē′nē ə) *n.* ⟦ModL < Gr *hēbē*, youth + *phrēn*, the mind⟧ a form of schizophrenia characterized by childish or silly behavior, disorganized thinking, delusions, and hallucinations, usually beginning in adolescence —**he′be·phren′ic** (-fren′ik) *adj.*

heb·e·tate (heb′ə tāt′) *vt., vi.* **-tat′ed, -tat′ing** ⟦< L *hebetatus*, pp. of *hebetare*, to make blunt or dull < *hebes*, blunt, dull⟧ to make or become dull in feeling, spirit, etc. —*adj. Bot.* having a blunt point, as certain leaves —**heb′e·ta′tion** *n.*

he·bet·ic (hē bet′ik) *adj.* ⟦Gr *hēbētikos*, youthful < *hēbē*, youth⟧ of or happening at puberty

heb·e·tude (heb′i tōōd′, -tyōōd′) *n.* ⟦LL *hebetudo* < L *hebes* (gen. *hebetis*), blunt, dull⟧ the quality or condition of being dull or lethargic

He·bra·ic (hē brā′ik, hi-) *adj.* ⟦LL *Hebraicus* < Gr *Hebraïkos*⟧ of or characteristic of the Hebrews or their language or culture; Hebrew —**He·bra′i·cal·ly** *adv.*

He·bra·ism (hē′brā iz′əm, -bri iz′-) *n.* ⟦ModL *Hebraismus* < LGr *Hebraismos* < Gr *Hebraizein*: see fol.⟧ 1 a word, phrase, grammatical construction, etc. originating in or peculiar to Hebrew ☆2 ⟦coined by EMERSON⟧ the characteristic ethical system, moral attitude, etc. of the Hebrews —**He′bra·ist** *n.* —**He′bra·is′tic** *adj.*

He·bra·ize (-īz′) *vt., vi.* **-ized′, -iz′ing** ⟦< Gr *Hebraizein* < *Hebraios*: see fol.⟧ to make or become Hebrew in language, customs, character, etc.

He·brew (hē′brōō′) *n.* ⟦ME *Hebreu* < OFr < L *Hebraeus* < Gr *Hebraios* < Aram *ivray* < Heb *ivri*, lit., ? one from across (the Euphrates River)⟧ 1 a member of the group of Semitic peoples tracing descent from Abraham, Isaac, and Jacob; Israelite: in modern, esp. earlier, usage interchangeable with *Jew* 2 *a)* the ancient Semitic language of the Israelites, in which most of the Old Testament is written *b)* the modern form of this language, an official language of Israel —*adj.* 1 of the Hebrews or their language or culture 2 JEWISH

He·brew-Ar·a·ma·ic (-ar′ə mā′ik, -er′-) *n.* ⟦coined (*c.* 1954) by Max Weinreich (1894-1969), U.S. linguist, to render Yiddish *loshn-koydesh* & Heb *leshon-hakodesh*, lit., the language of holiness⟧ a mixture of Hebrew and Jewish Aramaic

Hebrew calendar JEWISH CALENDAR

He·brews (hē′brōōz′) *n.* a book of the New Testament, a letter of undetermined authorship to the Hebrews, traditionally ascribed to the Apostle Paul: abbrev. *He* or *Heb*

Heb·ri·des (heb′rə dēz′) group of islands off the W coast of Scotland: they are divided into the **Inner Hebrides**, nearer the mainland, & the **Outer Hebrides**: *c.* 2,800 sq mi (7,252 sq km) —**Heb′ri·de′an** (-dē′ən) *adj., n.*

He·bron (heb′rän′, hē′brən) city in the West Bank, southwest of Jerusalem: dates from Biblical times

Hec·a·te (hek′ə tē, hek′it) *n.* ⟦L < Gr *Hekatē*⟧ *Gr. Myth.* a goddess of the moon, earth, and underground realm of the dead, later regarded as the goddess of sorcery and witchcraft

hec·a·tomb (hek′ə tōm′, -tōōm′) *n.* ⟦L *hecatombe* < Gr *hekatombē* < *hekaton*, HUNDRED + *bous*, ox: see COW¹⟧ 1 in ancient Greece, any great sacrifice to the gods; specif., the slaughter of one hundred cattle at one time 2 any large-scale sacrifice or slaughter

heck (hek) *interj., n.* ⟦var. of Scot dial. *hech*, exclamation of surprise, sorrow, fatigue: Scot form of HEIGH⟧ [Informal] *euphemism for* HELL

heck·le (hek′əl) *vt.* **-led, -ling** ⟦ME *hekelin* < *hechele*: see HACKLE¹⟧ 1 HACKLE¹ 2 ⟦orig. Scot⟧ to annoy or harass (a speaker) by interrupting with questions or taunts —*n.* HACKLE¹ —*SYN.* BAIT —**heck′ler** *n.*

hec·tare (hek′ter′) *n.* ⟦Fr: see HECTO- & ARE[2]⟧ one hundred ares or 10,000 square meters or 0.01 square kilometer (11,959.9 square yards or 2.471 acres): abbrev. *ha*

hec·tic (hek′tik) *adj.* ⟦altered (after Fr or L) < ME *etik* < OFr *étique* (Fr *hectique*) < LL *hecticus* < Gr *hektikos*, habitual, hectic < *hexis*, permanent condition or habit of the body < *echein*, to have: for IE base see SCHOOL[1]⟧ **1** [Archaic] *a)* designating or of the recurrent or persistent fever accompanying wasting diseases, esp. tuberculosis *b)* of, affected with, or characteristic of a wasting disease, as tuberculosis **2** [Archaic] red or flushed, as with fever **3** characterized by confusion, rush, excitement, etc. —**hec′ti·cal·ly** *adv.*

hec·to- (hek′tō, -tə) ⟦Fr, contr < Gr *hekaton*, HUNDRED⟧ *combining form* one hundred; the factor 10^2 [*hectogram*]: also, before a vowel, **hect-**

hec·to·cot·y·lus (hek′tō kät′ə ləs) *n., pl.* **-li′** (-lī′) ⟦ModL < prec. + Gr *kotylē*, a hollow, cavity⟧ a specific arm of a male octopus, cuttlefish, or other cephalopod, which becomes modified at sexual maturity so that it can transfer sperm to the female

hec·to·gram (hek′tə gram′) *n.* ⟦Fr *hectogramme*: see HECTO- & GRAM[1]⟧ one hundred grams (3.527 ounces): abbrev. *hg*

hec·to·graph (-graf′) *n.* ⟦Ger *hektograph* < *hekto-* (< Fr *hecto-*, HECTO-) + *-graph*, -GRAPH⟧ a duplicating device by which written or typed matter is transferred to a glycerin-coated sheet of gelatin, from which many copies can be taken —**hec′to·graph′ic** *adj.*

hec·to·kil·o- (hek′tə kil′ō) ⟦HECTO- + KILO-⟧ *combining form* one hundred thousand; the factor 10^5 [*hectokilosecond*]

hec·to·li·ter (hek′tə lēt′ər) *n.* ⟦Fr *hectolitre*: see HECTO- & LITER⟧ one hundred liters (26.4179 gallons liquid measure or 2.8378 bushels dry measure): abbrev. *hl*: Brit. sp. **hec′to·li′tre**

hec·to·me·ter (-mēt′ər) *n.* ⟦Fr *hectomètre*: see HECTO- & METER[1]⟧ one hundred meters (109.361 yards): abbrev. *hm*: Brit. sp. **hec′to·me′tre**

hec·tor (hek′tər) *n.* ⟦< *Hectors*, name of a gang of rowdy young men who terrorized the streets of London in the early 18th c.: ult. after fol.⟧ a swaggering fellow; bully — *vt., vi.* to browbeat; bully —*SYN.* BAIT

Hec·tor (hek′tər) *n.* ⟦L < Gr *Hektōr*, lit., holding fast < *echein*, to hold, have: for IE base see SCHOOL[1]⟧ **1** a masculine name **2** in Homer's *Iliad*, the greatest Trojan hero, killed by Achilles to avenge the death of Patroclus: he is the eldest son of Priam and Hecuba

Hec·u·ba (hek′yo͞o bə) *n.* ⟦L < Gr *Hekabē*⟧ in Homer's *Iliad*, wife of Priam and mother of Hector, Troilus, Paris, and Cassandra

he'd (hēd) *contraction* **1** he had **2** he would

hed·dle (hed′'l) *n.* ⟦prob. (by metathesis) < ME *helde* < OE *hefeld*, weaving thread (akin to ON *hafald*) < base of *hebban*, to raise (see HEAVE) + *-eld*, instrumental suffix⟧ any of a series of parallel wires or cords in the harness of a loom, used for separating and guiding the warp threads

he·der (khā′dər) *n., pl.* ***ha·dar·im*** (khä′dä rēm′) ⟦see CHEDER⟧ a Jewish religious school for young children

hedge (hej) *n.* ⟦ME *hegge* < OE *hecg*, akin to Ger *hecke* < IE base **kagh-*, wickerwork, wickerwork pen > ON *heggr*, L *caulae*, sheepfold: basic sense "woven fence, enclosure"⟧ **1** a row of closely planted shrubs, bushes, or trees forming a boundary or fence **2** anything serving as a fence or barrier; restriction or defense **3** the act or an instance of hedging —*adj.* **1** of, in, or near a hedge **2** low, disreputable, irregular, etc. —*vt.* **hedged**, **hedg′ing** **1** to place a hedge around or along; border or bound with a hedge **2** to hinder or guard as by surrounding with a barrier: often with *in* **3** to try to avoid or lessen loss in connection with (a bet, risk, etc.) by making counterbalancing bets, investments, etc. —*vi.* **1** to hide or protect oneself, as if behind a hedge **2** to hide behind words; refuse to commit oneself or give a direct answer **3** to try to avoid or lessen loss by making counterbalancing bets, investments, etc. —**hedg′er** *n.*

☆**hedge fund** a partnership of investors who pool large sums for speculating in securities, often taking large risks, as by buying with borrowed funds or selling short

hedge·hog (hej′hôg′) *n.* ⟦HEDGE + HOG: prob. from living in hedgerows and from the hoglike snout⟧ **1** any of several small insectivores (family Erinaceidae) of the Old World, with a shaggy coat and sharp spines on the back, which bristle and form a defense when the animal curls up ☆**2** the American porcupine **3** ⟦see FOX, *n.* 4⟧ a person regarded as being of a type that tends to see things in terms of a single, overarching viewpoint or philosophy: opposed to FOX (*n.* 4) **4** *Mil.* *a)* any of several defensive obstacles *b)* any of a series of defensive fortifications capable of continued resistance after being encircled

☆**hedge·hop** (hej′häp′) *vi.* **-hopped′**, **-hop′ping** [Informal] to fly an airplane very close to the ground, as for spraying insecticide —**hedge′hop′per** *n.*

hedge hyssop a low-growing plant (*Gratiola aurea*) of the figwort family, common in wet grounds from Maine to Florida

hedge·row (hej′rō′) *n.* a row of shrubs, bushes, etc., forming a hedge

hedge sparrow a small European passerine bird (*Prunella modularis*, family Prunellidae), reddish-brown with white-tipped wings, often found in shrubbery

he·don·ic (hē dän′ik) *adj.* ⟦Gr *hēdonikos* < *hēdonē*, pleasure < base of *hēdys*, SWEET⟧ **1** having to do with pleasure **2** [Rare] of hedonism or hedonists; hedonistic

he·don·ics (hē dän′iks) *n.* ⟦< prec.⟧ the branch of psychology dealing with pleasant and unpleasant feelings

he·don·ism (hēd′'n iz′əm) *n.* ⟦< Gr *hēdonē*, pleasure (see HEDONIC) + -ISM⟧ **1** *Philos.* the ethical doctrine that pleasure, variously conceived of in terms of happiness of the individual or of society, is the principal good and the proper aim of action **2** *Psychol.* the theory that a person always acts in such a way as to seek pleasure and avoid pain **3** self-indulgent pursuit of pleasure as a way of life —**he′don·ist** *n.* —**he′do·nis′tic** *adj.* —**he′do·nis′ti·cal·ly** *adv.*

-he·dral (hē′drəl) *combining form forming adjectives* having (a specified number of) surfaces [*hexahedral*]

-he·dron (hē′drən) ⟦Gr *-edron* < *hedra*, a side, base, seat < IE base **sed-* > L *sedere*, SIT⟧ *combining form forming nouns* a geometric figure or crystal having (a specified number of) surfaces [*hexahedron*]

☆**hee·bie-jee·bies** (hē′bē jē′bēz) *pl.n.* ⟦coined by W. B. De Beck (1890-1942) in his comic strip *Barney Google*⟧ [Old Slang] a state of nervousness; jitters: with *the*

heed (hēd) *vt.* ⟦ME *heden* < OE *hedan* (< **hodjan*: akin to Ger *hüten*) < base of *hod* (see HOOD[1]) in the sense "care, keeping, protection": for IE base see HAT⟧ to pay close attention to; take careful notice of —*vi.* to pay attention —*n.* close attention; careful notice —**heed′ful** *adj.*

heed·less (hēd′lis) *adj.* not taking heed; careless; unmindful —**heed′less·ly** *adv.* —**heed′less·ness** *n.*

hee·haw (hē′hô′) *n.* ⟦echoic⟧ **1** the sound that a donkey makes; bray **2** a loud, often silly laugh like a bray —*vi.* **1** to bray **2** to laugh in a loud, often silly way; guffaw

heel[1] (hēl) *n.* ⟦ME *hele* < OE *hela*, akin to Du *hiel* < Gmc **hanhila* < **hanha* < IE base **kenk-*, leg joint, heel⟧ **1** the back part of the human foot, under the ankle and behind the instep: see CALCANEUS **2** the corresponding part of the hind foot of an animal **3** *a)* the part of a stocking, shoe, etc. that covers the heel *b)* the built-up part of a shoe or boot supporting the heel *c)* [*pl.*] women's low-cut shoes with medium to high heels **4** crushing oppressive or tyrannical power [under the *heel* of fascism] **5** anything suggesting the human heel in location, shape, or function, as the end of a loaf of bread, a rind end of cheese, the part of the palm of the hand nearest the wrist, the part of the head of a golf club nearest the shaft, the lower end of a ship's mast, or a small quantity of liquor left in a bottle ☆**6** [Informal] a despicable or unscrupulous person; cad —*vt.* **1** to furnish with a heel **2** to follow closely at the rear of **3** to touch, press, or drive forward with or as with the heel **4** to equip (a gamecock) with metal spurs ☆**5** [Informal] *a)* to provide (a person) with money (usually in the passive) *b)* to equip or arm (oneself) **6** *Golf* to hit (a ball) with the heel of the club —*vi.* **1** to follow along at the heels of someone: said of a dog **2** to move the heels rhythmically in dancing —*interj.* used in commanding a dog to follow at one's heels —**at heel** close to someone's heels; just behind —**cool one's heels** [Informal] to wait or be kept waiting for a considerable time —**dig in one's heels** *see phrase under* DIG[1] —**down at (the) heel (**or **heels) 1** with the heels of one's shoes in need of repair **2** shabby; seedy; run-down —**heel in** to cover (plant roots) temporarily with earth in preparation for planting —**kick up one's heels** to be lively or merry; have fun —**on (**or **upon) the heels of** close behind; immediately following —**out at the heel (**or **heels) 1** having holes in the heels of one's shoe(s) or sock(s) **2** shabby; seedy; run-down —**show one's (**or **a clean pair of) heels** to run away —**take to one's heels** to run away —**turn on one's heel** to turn around abruptly —**heel′less** *adj.*

heel[2] (hēl) *vi.* ⟦with assimilated *-d* < ME *helden* < OE *hieldan* (**healdjan*), to incline, slope < base of *heald*, sloping, bent < IE base **k̂el-*, to incline > (via **k̂lei-*) L *-clinare*, INCLINE⟧ to lean or tilt to one side, as a ship or boat in a high wind —*vt.* to cause (a vessel) to heel —*n.* **1** the act or an instance of heeling **2** the extent of this

heel-and-toe (hēl′ən tō′) *adj.* designating or of a walking race or jogging step in which the heel of one foot touches the ground before the toes of the other leave it

heel·ball (hēl′bôl′) *n.* ⟦orig. used by shoemakers in polishing the edges of heels and soles⟧ a ball or stick of beeswax mixed with lampblack and used in making rubbings

heeled (hēld) *adj.* **1** having a heel or heels: often used in comb. [*high-heeled* shoes] ☆**2** [Informal] *a)* having money *b)* armed, esp. with a gun

heel·er (hēl′ər) *n.* **1** one that heels ☆**2** [Informal] WARD HEELER

heel·piece (hēl′pēs′) *n.* a piece forming, affixed to, or like the heel of a shoe, etc.

heel·plate (-plāt′) *n.* a thin metal piece put on the bottom of the heel of a shoe to prevent wear

heel·tap (-tap′) *n.* **1** a lift in the heel of a shoe **2** a bit of liquor left in a glass

He·fei (hu′fā′) city in E China: capital of Anhui province

heft (heft) *n.* ⟦< base of HEAVE⟧ **1** weight; heaviness **2** importance; influence ☆**3** [Rare] the main part; bulk —*vt.* **1** to lift or heave **2** to try to determine the weight of by lifting —*vi.* to weigh

heft·y (hef′tē) *adj.* **heft′i·er**, **heft′i·est** **1** weighty; heavy **2** large and powerful **3** big or fairly big —**heft′i·ly** *adv.* —**heft′i·ness** *n.*

he·gar·i (hi ger′ē, heg′ə rē) *n.* ⟦Ar (in Sudan) *hegiri*, for *hajari*, stony⟧ any of several varieties of grain sorghums having juicy, leafy stalks and erect heads with grayish grain

He·gel (hā′gəl), **G(eorg) W(ilhelm) F(riedrich)** 1770-1831; Ger. philosopher

He·ge·li·an (hi gā′lē ən, -gē′-) *adj.* of Hegel or Hegelianism —*n.* a follower of Hegel or his philosophy

He·ge·li·an·ism (-iz′əm) *n.* the philosophy of Hegel, who held that every existent idea or fact belongs to an all-embracing mind in which each idea or situation (*thesis*) evokes its opposite (*antithesis*) and these two result in a unified whole (*synthesis*), which in turn becomes a new thesis: see also DIALECTIC (sense 3)

heg·e·mon (hej′ə män′) ***n.*** ⟦< Gr *hēgemōn*, leader: see HEGEMONY⟧ one, esp. a state or nation, having leadership or dominance over others

he·gem·o·nism (hi jem′ə niz′əm) ***n.*** the policy or practice of a nation in aggressively expanding its influence over other countries —**he·gem′o·nist′** ***n., adj.*** —**he·gem′o·nis′tic** ***adj.***

he·gem·o·ny (hi jem′ə nē, -gem′-; hej′ə mō′nē, hē′jə-) ***n., pl.*** **-nies** ⟦Gr *hēgemonia*, leadership < *hēgemōn*, leader < *hēgeisthai*, to lead, go on ahead < IE base **sāg-*, to track down > SAKE[1], SEEK⟧ leadership or dominance, esp. that of one state or nation over others —**heg·e·mon·ic** (hej′ə män′ik, heg′-; hē′jə-) ***adj.***

he·gi·ra (hi jī′rə; *also* hej′i rə) ***n.*** ⟦ML < Ar *hijrah*, lit., separation, flight, era of Muhammad < *hajara*, to leave⟧ **1** [*often* **H-**] Muhammad's flight from Mecca to Medina in 622 A.D.: the Muslim era dates from this **2** a trip or journey, esp. one made to escape a dangerous or undesirable situation

heh (hā) ***n.*** *alt. sp. of* HE[2]

Hei·deg·ger (hī′də gər), **Martin** 1889-1976; Ger. philosopher

Hei·del·berg (hīd′'l bʉrg′; *Ger* hī′dəl berkh′) city in SW Germany, in the state of Baden-Württemberg: site of a famous university (founded 1386)

Heidelberg man a type of human (*Homo heidelbergensis*) of the Lower Pleistocene, known originally from a fossil lower jaw discovered in 1907 near Heidelberg, Germany

Hei·di (hī′dē) ***n.*** a feminine name

heif·er (hef′ər) ***n.*** ⟦ME *haifre* < OE *heahfore*, lit., full-grown young ox < *heah*, high, hence full-grown (see HIGH) + *fearr*, bull, lit., young animal: see FARROW[2]⟧ a young cow, esp. one that has not yet borne a calf

Hei·fetz (hī′fits), **Ja·scha** (yä′shə) 1901-87; U.S. violinist, born in Russia

heigh (hī, hā) ***interj.*** [Archaic] used to attract notice, show pleasure, express surprise, etc.

heigh-ho (-hō′) ***interj.*** [Archaic] used variously to express mild surprise, boredom, disappointment, fatigue, etc., or used as a greeting

height (hīt) ***n.*** ⟦< earlier *highth* < ME *heighthe* < OE *hiehthu* (akin to Goth *hauhitha*) < *heah*: see HIGH & -TH[1]⟧ **1** the topmost point of anything **2** the highest limit; greatest degree; extreme; climax; culmination [the *height* of absurdity] **3** the distance from the bottom to the top **4** *a)* elevation or distance above a given level, as above the surface of the earth or sea; altitude *b)* elevation (of the sun, a star, etc.) above the horizon, measured in degrees **5** *a)* a relatively great distance from bottom to top *b)* a relatively great distance above a given level **6** [*often pl.*] a point or place considerably above most others; eminence; elevation; hill **7** [Obs.] high rank

SYN.—height refers to distance from bottom to top [a figurine four inches in *height*] or to distance above a given level [he dropped it from a *height* of ten feet]; **altitude** and **elevation** refer especially to distance above a given level (usually the surface of the earth at sea level) and generally connote great distance [the *altitude* of an airplane, the *elevation* of a mountain]; **stature** refers especially to the height of a human being standing erect [he was short in *stature*]

height·en (hīt′'n) ***vt., vi.*** ⟦< prec. + -EN⟧ **1** to bring or come to a high or higher position; raise or rise **2** to make or become larger, greater, stronger, brighter, etc.; increase; intensify —***SYN.*** INTENSIFY —**height′en·er** ***n.***

☆**height of land** a watershed

height to paper the standard height of type from face to feet, equal in the U.S. to .9186 inch

hei·li·gen·schein (hī′li gən shīn′) ***n.*** ⟦Ger, halo < *heilig*, HOLY + *schein*, light (see Ger v. at SHINE)⟧ a halolike optical phenomenon around an observer's shadow when there is a large distance between the observer and the shadow

Hei·long·jiang (hā′lo͝oŋ′jyäŋ′) province of NE China: 178,997 sq mi (463,600 sq km); cap. Harbin: former transliteration **Hei·lung·kiang** (hā′ lo͝oŋ′jyäŋ′)

Heim·dall (hām′däl′) ***n.*** ⟦ON *Heimdallr*⟧ *Norse Myth.* the watchman of Asgard, home of the gods

heim·ish (hīm′ish) ***adj.*** ⟦Yiddish⟧ *var. of* HAIMISH

☆**Heim·lich maneuver** (hīm′lik) ⟦after H. J. *Heimlich* (b. 1920), U.S. surgeon⟧ an emergency technique used to dislodge an object stuck in the windpipe: air is forced up the windpipe by applying sudden, sharp pressure to the abdomen just below the rib cage

hein (an) ***interj.*** *Fr. equiv. of* EH

Hei·ne (hī′nə), **Hein·rich** (hīn′riH) 1797-1856; Ger. poet & essayist

hei·nie (hī′nē) ***n.*** ⟦prob. < HINDER[2] + -IE⟧ [Slang] the buttocks

hei·nous (hā′nəs, hē′-) ***adj.*** ⟦ME *hainous* < OFr *hainös* (Fr *haineux*) < *haine*, hatred < *hair*, to hate < Frank **hatjan*, akin to Ger *hassen*, HATE⟧ outrageously evil or wicked; abominable [a *heinous* crime] —***SYN.*** OUTRAGEOUS —**hei′nous·ly** ***adv.*** —**hei′nous·ness** ***n.***

heir (er) ***n.*** ⟦ME < OFr < L *heres*: see HEREDITY⟧ **1** a person who inherits or is legally entitled to inherit, through the natural action of the law, another's property or title upon the other's death **2** anyone who receives property of a deceased person either by will or by law **3** a person who appears to get some trait from, or carries on in the tradition of, a predecessor

heir apparent *pl.* **heirs apparent** the heir whose right to a certain property or title cannot be denied if the heir outlives the ancestor and the ancestor dies intestate: compare HEIR PRESUMPTIVE

heir at law the heir who has the right, under the laws of intestate descent and distribution, to receive the estate of an ancestor who has died without leaving a will

heir·dom (er′dəm) ***n.*** HEIRSHIP

heir·ess (er′is) ***n.*** a female heir, esp. to great wealth

heir·loom (er′lo͞om′) ***n.*** ⟦ME *heir lome*: see HEIR & LOOM[1]⟧ **1** a piece of personal property that goes to an heir along with an estate **2** any treasured possession handed down from generation to generation —***adj.*** designating or of a type of cultivated vegetable, fruit, flower, etc. that is an older, traditional variety rather than a modern hybrid

heir presumptive *pl.* **heirs presumptive** an heir whose right to a certain property or title will be lost if someone more closely related to the ancestor is born before that ancestor dies: compare HEIR APPARENT

heir·ship (er′ship′) ***n.*** ⟦see -SHIP⟧ the position or rights of an heir; right to inheritance

Hei·sen·berg (hī′zən bərg; *Ger*, -berkh), **Wer·ner (Karl)** (ver′nər) 1901-76; Ger. theoretical & nuclear physicist

Heisenberg uncertainty principle UNCERTAINTY PRINCIPLE

hei·shi (hī′shē, hē′-) ***pl.n.*** ⟦< AmInd⟧ tiny, polished disks or beads made from the shells of clams, oysters, abalone, etc., or from semiprecious stones, and strung to form necklaces

☆**heist** (hīst) ***n.*** ⟦< HOIST⟧ [Informal] a robbery or holdup —***vt.*** **1** [Slang] to rob or steal **2** *dial. var. of* HOIST —**heist′er** ***n.***

He·jaz (he jaz′, hē-; -jäz′) region of Saudi Arabia: formerly a kingdom

he·ji·ra (hi jī′rə; *also* hej′i rə) ***n.*** *alt. sp. of* HEGIRA

Hek·a·te (hek′ə tē, hek′it) ***n.*** *alt. sp. of* HECATE

hek·to- (hek′tō, -tə) *combining form* HECTO-

Hel (hel) ***n.*** ⟦ON: see HELL⟧ *Norse Myth.* **1** Loki's daughter, goddess of death and the underworld **2** the underworld to which the dead not killed in battle are sent: cf. VALHALLA

☆**He·La cell** (hē′lə) ⟦< *He(nrietta) La(cks)*, from whose cervical cancer such cells were obtained in 1951⟧ a strain of cells derived from the first carcinoma cells to be continuously maintained in culture: still used in cancer and biological research

hé·las (ā läs′) ***interj.*** *Fr. equiv. of* ALAS

held (held) ***vt., vi.*** *pt. & pp. of* HOLD[1]

Hel·den·te·nor (hel′dən tā nôr′) ***n.*** ⟦Ger, lit., heroic tenor⟧ a robust tenor voice suited to heroic roles, as in Wagnerian opera

Hel·en (hel′ən) ***n.*** ⟦< Fr or L: Fr *Hélène* < L *Helena* < Gr *Helenē*, lit., torch⟧ a feminine name: dim. *Nell, Nellie, Nelly*; var. *Eleanor, Ellen, Helena*; equiv. Fr. *Elaine, Hélène*, It. & Sp. *Elena*

Hel·e·na[1] (hel′i nə, he lē′nə, -lā′-) ***n.*** a feminine name: dim. *Lena*: see HELEN

Hel·e·na[2] (hel′ə nə) ⟦said to be after the hometown of a settler from Minnesota⟧ capital of Mont., in the WC part

Helen of Troy *Gr. Legend* the beautiful wife of Menelaus, king of Sparta: the Trojan War begins in response to her abduction by Paris to Troy

Hel·go·land (hel′gō land′; *Ger* -länt′) island of Germany, in the North Sea: one of the North Frisian Islands: *c.* .25 sq mi (.65 sq km)

he·li-[1] (hē′li, -lə, -lē; he-) *combining form* HELIO-

hel·i-[2] (hel′i) *combining form* having to do with helicopters [*heli*-skiing]

he·li·a·cal (hi lī′ə kəl) ***adj.*** ⟦LL *Heliacus*, relating to the sun < Gr *hēliakos* < *hēlios*, HELIOS + -AL⟧ of or near the sun; solar; specif., designating the apparent rising, or setting, of a star or planet just after, or before, conjunction with the sun —**he·li′a·cal·ly** ***adv.***

he·li·an·thus (hē′lē an′thəs) ***n.*** ⟦ModL < HELI-[1] + Gr *anthos*, a flower: see ANTHO-⟧ SUNFLOWER

hel·i·cal (hel′i kəl) ***adj.*** ⟦HELIC(O)- + -AL⟧ of, or having the form of, a helix; spiral —**hel′i·cal·ly** ***adv.***

hel·i·ces (hel′i sēz′) ***n.*** *alt. pl. of* HELIX

hel·i·cline (hel′i klīn′) ***n.*** ⟦fol. + (IN)CLINE⟧ a curving ramp that ascends gradually

hel·i·co- (hel′i kō′) ⟦< Gr *helix* (gen. *helikos*): see HELIX⟧ *combining form* spiral, spiral-shaped: also, before a vowel, **hel·ic-**

hel·i·coid (hel′i koid′) ***adj.*** ⟦Gr *helikoeidēs* < *helix*, a spiral + *-eidēs*, -OID⟧ shaped like, or coiled in the form of, a spiral, as the shell of a snail or certain inflorescences: also **hel′i·coi′dal** —***n.*** *Geom.* a surface generated by the rotation of a plane or twisted curve about a fixed line so that each point of the curve traces out a circular helix with the fixed line as axis

hel·i·con (hel′i kän′, -kən) ***n.*** ⟦prob. < HELICO- + arbitrary ending: from the shape⟧ a brass instrument of the tuba family, consisting of a long, coiled tube that can be carried over the shoulder: see SOUSAPHONE

Hel·i·con (hel′i kän′, -kən) mountain group in SC Greece, on the Gulf of Corinth: in Greek mythology, the home of the Muses; highest peak, 5,735 ft (1,748 m)

hel·i·co·ni·a (hel′i kō′nē ə) ***n.*** ⟦ModL < L, fem. of *Heliconius*, of prec.⟧ any of a genus (*Heliconia*) of tropical plants of the banana family, having tall, erect leaves and spikes of flowers enclosed in brilliantly colored bracts

hel·i·cop·ter (hel′i käp′tər) ***n.*** ⟦Fr *hélicoptère*: see HELICO- & PTERO-⟧ a kind of vertical-lift aircraft, capable of hovering or moving in any direction, having a motor-driven, horizontal rotor — ***vi., vt.*** to travel or convey by helicopter

he·lic·tite (hə lik′tīt′) ***n.*** ⟦< Gr *heliktos*, rolled, twisted (akin to HELIX) + *-ite*, as in STALACTITE⟧ a thin, stony, curling cave deposit, usually of calcite, slowly formed as tiny water drops emerge from its tip and evaporate

Hel·i·go·land (hel′i gō land′) *var. of* HELGOLAND

he·li·o- (hē′lē ō, -ə) ⟦L < Gr *hēlio-* < *hēlios*, SUN[1]⟧ *combining form* sun, sunlight, light [*heliocentric, heliograph*]

he·li·o·cen·tric (hē′lē ə sen′trik) ***adj.*** ⟦prec. + -CENTRIC⟧ **1** calculated from, viewed as from, or belonging to the center of the sun **2** having or regarding the sun as the center [Copernicus's *heliocentric* model of the solar system]

he·li·o·chrome (hē′lē ə krōm′) ***n.*** ⟦HELIO- + -CHROME⟧ an early type of photograph in natural colors

He·li·o·gab·a·lus (hē′lē ə gab′ə ləs) *var. of* ELAGABALUS

he·li·o·gram (hē′lē ə gram′) ***n.*** a message sent by heliograph

he·li·o·graph (-graf′) ***n.*** ⟦HELIO- + -GRAPH⟧ **1** a permanent image formed on a glass plate by an early photographic process **2** a signaling device that uses a mirror to flash the sun's rays to a distant observer — ***vt., vi.*** to signal or communicate by heliograph —**he′li·og′ra·pher** (-äg′rə fər) ***n.*** —**he′li·o·graph′ic** ***adj.*** —**he′li·og′ra·phy** ***n.***

he·li·o·gra·vure (hē′lē ō grə vyoor′) ***n.*** ⟦Fr *héliogravure*: see HELIO- & GRAVURE⟧ *former term for* PHOTOGRAVURE

he·li·ol·a·try (hē′lē äl′ə trē) ***n.*** ⟦HELIO- + -LATRY⟧ sun worship —**he′li·ol′a·ter** ***n.***

he·li·om·e·ter (hē′lē äm′ət ər) ***n.*** ⟦Fr *héliomètre*: see HELIO- & -METER: so called because orig. used in measuring the sun's diameter⟧ an instrument formerly used for measuring the angular distance between two stars

he·li·o·pause (hē′lē ō pôz′) ***n.*** the outer boundary of the heliosphere

He·li·op·o·lis (hē′lē äp′ə lis) ⟦Gr *Hēliopolis*, lit., city of the sun < *hēlios* (see fol.) + *polis*, city⟧ **1** ancient city in the Nile delta, just north of where Cairo now stands: center for the worship of the sun god Ra **2** ancient city on the site of modern BAALBEK

He·li·os (hē′lē äs′) ***n.*** ⟦Gr *hēlios*, the sun < IE base **sāwel-*, **swel-*, **sun-*, SUN[1] > L *sol*, ON *sol*⟧ *Gr. Myth.* the sun god, son of Hyperion: later identified with Apollo

he·li·o·sphere (hē′lē ō sfir′) ***n.*** the region around the sun, extending beyond Pluto, characterized by the presence of the solar magnetic field and the solar wind

he·li·o·stat (hē′lē ō stat′) ***n.*** ⟦< ModL *heliostata*: see HELIO- & -STAT⟧ a device consisting of a mirror slowly revolved by clockwork so as to reflect the sun's rays continuously in a fixed direction

he·li·o·tax·is (hē′lē ō tak′sis) ***n.*** ⟦ModL: see HELIO- & TAXIS⟧ the positive (or negative) response of a freely moving organism toward (or away from) sunlight

he·li·o·ther·a·py (-ther′ə pē) ***n.*** ⟦HELIO- + THERAPY⟧ the treatment of disease by exposing the body to sunlight

he·li·o·trope (hē′lē ə trōp′; *also, chiefly Brit*, hel′ē ə-) ***n.*** ⟦Fr *héliotrope* < L *heliotropium* < Gr *hēliotropion* < *hēlios*, the sun (see HELIOS) + base of *trepein*, to turn (see TROPE)⟧ **1** [Obs.] a sunflower or other plant whose flowers turn to face the sun **2** any of a genus (*Heliotropium*) of plants of the borage family, with fragrant clusters of small, white or reddish-purple flowers **3** GARDEN HELIOTROPE **4** reddish purple **5** a kind of HELIOGRAPH (sense 2) used in surveying **6** BLOODSTONE —***adj.*** reddish-purple

he·li·ot·ro·pism (hē′lē ä′trə piz′əm) ***n.*** ⟦HELIO- + -TROPISM⟧ any turning or bending of a plant or sessile animal toward, or away from, light, esp. sunlight —**he′li·o·trop′ic** (-ō träp′ik) ***adj.*** —**he′li·o·trop′i·cal·ly** ***adv.***

he·li·o·type (hē′lē ō tīp′) ***n.*** ⟦HELIO- + -TYPE⟧ COLLOTYPE —**he′li·o·typ′y** ***n.***

he·li·o·zo·an (hē′lē ə zō′ən) ***n.*** ⟦< ModL *Heliozoa* (< HELIO- + -ZOA) + -AN⟧ any of a class (Heliozoa) of chiefly freshwater protozoans with slender pseudopodia arranged as rays —**he′li·o·zo′ic** (-ik) ***adj.***

hel·i·pad (hel′i pad′) ***n.*** ⟦HELI-[2] + PAD[2]⟧ a place made for use by helicopters when taking off or landing

hel·i·port (hel′i pôrt′) ***n.*** ⟦HELI-[2] + (AIR)PORT⟧ an airport for helicopters

hel·i-ski·ing (hel′i skē′iŋ) ***n.*** ⟦HELI-[2] + *skiing* (see SKI)⟧ skiing done at remote sites by skiers transported by helicopter —**hel′i-ski′er** ***n.***

he·li·um (hē′lē əm) ***n.*** ⟦ModL < Gr *hēlios*: see HELIOS⟧ a colorless, odorless chemical element, one of the noble gases, having the lowest known boiling and melting points: it is used in low-temperature work, as a diluent for oxygen, in deep-sea breathing systems, for inflating balloons, etc.: symbol, He; at. no. 2: see the periodic table of elements in the Reference Supplement

he·lix (hē′liks) ***n., pl.* he′lix·es** or **hel·i·ces** (hel′ə sēz′) ⟦L, kind of ivy, spiral < Gr, a spiral < *helissein*, to turn around < IE base **wel-*, to turn, twist > WALK⟧ **1** any spiral, as one lying in a single plane or, esp., one moving around a right circular cone or cylinder at a constant angle, as a screw or bolt thread does **2** *Anat.* the folded rim of cartilage around the outer ear **3** *Archit.* an ornamental spiral, as a volute on a Corinthian or Ionic capital **4** *Zool.* any of a genus (*Helix*) of spiral-shelled land gastropods, including the common, edible European snail (*H. pomatia*)

hell (hel) ***n.*** ⟦ME *helle* < OE *hel* (akin to Ger *hölle*, hell & ON *Hel*, the underworld goddess, HEL) < base of *helan*, to cover, hide < IE base **kel-*, to hide, cover up > L *celare*, to hide⟧ **1** [*often* **H-**] *Bible* the place where the spirits of the dead are: identified with SHEOL and HADES **2** [*often* **H-**] *a)* the abode of Satan and of all other devils and of all the damned *b)* the powers of hell or of evil **3** [*often* **H-**] a state or place of woe and anguish, arrived at by the wicked or unrepentant after death **4** any place or condition of evil, pain, disorder, cruelty, etc. **5** [Informal] *a)* any extremely disagreeable, unsettling, or punishing treatment or experience, or the cause or source of this *b)* devilish spirits or excitement [*full of hell*] —***vi.*** ☆[Slang] to live or act in a reckless or dissolute way: often with *around* —***interj.*** used to express irritation, anger, etc. —☆**a (or one) hell of a 1** [Slang] very much a: an intensifier [*a hell of a* good ale] **2** extraordinary, outrageous, terrible, etc. [*a hell of a* thing to say to one's grandparent] —**as hell** [Slang] as can be; to the highest degree; extremely —☆**be hell on** [Slang] **1** to be very difficult or painful for **2** to be very strict or severe with **3** to be very destructive or damaging to —**catch (or get) hell** [Slang] to receive a severe scolding, punishment, etc. —**for the hell of it** [Slang] for no serious reason or purpose —**give someone hell** [Informal] to scold, punish, etc. someone severely —**hell to pay** terrible results or severe penalties —**like hell** [Slang] **1** very bad; awful **2** very much **3** very fast; quickly —**to (or the) hell with** [Slang] an exclamation indicating exasperation or anger over (something)
USAGE—as profanity, *hell* is also widely used interjectionally in various combinations to express irritation, anger, etc. [*hell, no!*], and in various ways, esp. after *in* or *the*, to express surprise, disbelief, disgust, etc. [who in *hell* is he? what the *hell!*]

he'll (hēl, hil) *contraction* **1** he will **2** he shall

☆**hel·la·cious** (he lā′shəs) ***adj.*** ⟦prob. fanciful formation from HELL OF A (see HELL) + -ACIOUS⟧ [Slang] very great, bad, unbearable, etc.

Hel·lad·ic (he lad′ik) ***adj.*** designating or of the Bronze Age cultures (*c.* 3000-*c.* 1100 B.C.) of the peoples living on or around the Greek peninsula

Hel·las (hel′əs) **1** in ancient times, Greece, including the islands & colonies **2** *Gr. name for* GREECE

☆**hell·bend·er** (hel′ben′dər) ***n.*** a giant, primitive, edible salamander (*Cryptobranchus alleganiensis*, family Cryptobranchidae) with lidless eyes, found esp. in the Ohio valley

☆**hell·bent** or **hell-bent** (hel′bent′) ***adj.*** [Slang] **1** firmly resolved or recklessly determined **2** moving fast or recklessly

hell·cat (-kat′) ***n.*** an evil, spiteful, bad-tempered woman

☆**hell·div·er** (-dī′vər) ***n.*** PIED-BILLED GREBE

hel·le·bore (hel′ə bôr′) ***n.*** ⟦altered (after Gr) < ME *ellebore* < OFr < L *helleborus* < Gr *helleboros*, orig. prob. "plant eaten by fawns" < *hellos*, var. of *ellos*, fawn < base of *elaphos*, deer + *bora*, food (of beasts): for IE bases see ELK & VORACIOUS⟧ **1** any of a genus (*Helleborus*) of poisonous, winter-blooming plants of the buttercup family, with buttercuplike flowers of various colors: the rhizomes of a black European species (*H. niger*) were formerly used as a heart stimulant and cathartic **2** any of a genus (*Veratrum*) of poisonous plants of the lily family: the **white hellebore** (*V. album*) and the **false hellebore** (*V. viride*) were formerly used as cathartics, etc.

Hel·len (hel′ən) ***n.*** ⟦L < Gr *Hellēn*⟧ *Gr. Legend* the ancestor of the Hellenes, a son of Deucalion and Pyrrha

Hel·lene (hel′ēn′) ***n.*** ⟦Gr *Hellēn*⟧ a Greek

Hel·len·ic (hə len′ik, -lē′nik) ***adj.*** ⟦Gr *Hellēnikos* < *Hellēnes*, the Greeks⟧ **1** of the Hellenes; Greek **2** of the history, language, or culture of the ancient Greeks, specif. from the late 8th century B.C. to the death of Alexander the Great (323 B.C.) —***n.* 1** the language of ancient Greece **2** *former term for* GREEK (***n.*** 2)

Hel·len·ism (hel′ən iz′əm) ***n.*** ⟦Gr *Hellēnismos*, imitation of the Greeks < *Hellēnizein*, to speak Greek⟧ **1** a Greek phrase, idiom, or custom **2** the character, thought, culture, or ethical system of ancient Greece **3** adoption of the Greek language, customs, etc.

Hel·len·ist (-ist) ***n.*** ⟦Gr *Hellēnistēs*, imitator of the Greeks < *Hellēnizein*, to speak Greek⟧ **1** a non-Greek, esp. a Jew of the Hellenistic period, who adopted the Greek language, customs, etc. **2** a specialist in the study of the Classical Greek language and ancient Greek culture

Hel·len·is·tic (hel′ən is′tik) ***adj.*** **1** of or characteristic of Hellenists or Hellenism **2** of Greek history, language, and culture from the death of Alexander the Great (323 B.C.) until the death of Cleopatra (30 B.C.) —**Hel′len·is′ti·cal·ly** ***adv.***

Hel·len·ize (hel′ən īz′) ***vt., vi.* -ized′, -iz′ing** ⟦Gr *Hellēnizein* < *Hellēnes*, the Greeks⟧ to make or become Greek or Hellenistic, as in customs, ideals, form, or language —**Hel′len·i·za′tion** ***n.*** —**Hel′len·iz′er** ***n.***

☆**hell·er**[1] (hel′ər) ***n.*** ⟦HELL (*vi.*) + -ER⟧ [Slang] a person who is noisy, wild, reckless, etc.

hel·ler[2] (hel′ər) ***n., pl.* hel′ler** ⟦Ger < MHG *haller*, short for *Haller pfenninc*, penny of Hall: first coined (*c.* 1208) at Hall, Swabia⟧ **1** [Historical] a German copper coin or an Austrian bronze coin **2** *Eng. var. of* HALER or HALIER

hel·ler·i (hel′ər ī′, -ē′) ***n.*** ⟦from the species name (*Xiphophorus*) *helleri*, after C. Heller, 20th-c. aquarist⟧ SWORDTAIL

Hel·les (hel′is), **Cape** S tip of the Gallipoli Peninsula, Turkey, at the entrance to the Dardanelles

Hel·les·pont (hel′əs pänt′) ⟦Gr, lit., "sea of Helle", after *Hellē*, legendary girl who drowned there⟧ *ancient name for* DARDANELLES

hell·fire (hel′fīr′) ***n.*** ⟦ME *helle fir* < OE *hellefyr*⟧ the fire, hence punishment, of hell

hell-for-leath·er (hel′fər leth′ər) [Slang] ***adj.*** ⟦orig. with ref. to horseback riding and *leather* harness⟧ **1** with all of one's energy, will, etc.; with wholehearted or reckless determination **2** at full speed or with great speed [*a hell-for-leather chase*] —***adv.*** in a hell-for-leather manner or fashion

Hell Gate ⟦< Du *Helle Gat*, hell strait: from the whirlpools formerly there⟧ narrow channel of the East River, N.Y., between Manhattan & Queens

☆**hell·gram·mite** or **hell·gra·mite** (hel′grəm īt′) ***n.*** ⟦< ?⟧ the carnivorous, dark-brown, aquatic larva of the dobsonfly, often used as fish bait

hell·hole (hel′hōl′) ***n.*** [Informal] any extremely unpleasant place

hell·hound (-hound′) ***n.*** **1** a dog of hell, as Cerberus **2** a fiendish, evil person

☆**hel·lion** (hel′yən) ***n.*** ⟦altered (infl. by HELL) < Scot dial. *hallion*, a low fellow < ? Fr *haillon*, rag < MHG *hadel*, var. of *hader*, rag, quarrel⟧ [Informal] a person fond of deviltry; mischievous troublemaker; rascal

hell·ish (hel′ish) ***adj.*** **1** of, from, or like hell **2** devilish; fiendish **3** very unpleasant; detestable —**hell′ish·ly** ***adv.*** —**hell′ish·ness** ***n.***

Hell·man (hel′mən), **Lillian** 1905-84; U.S. playwright

hel·lo (he lō′, hel′ō′) ***interj.*** ⟦var. of HOLLO⟧ **1** used as a greeting or response, as in telephoning **2** used to attract attention **3** used to express astonishment or surprise [*hello!* what's this in my soup?] —*n., pl.* **-los′** an instance of saying or exclaiming "hello" — *vi., vt.* **-loed′**, **-lo′ing** to say or exclaim "hello" (to)

☆**hell-rais·er** (hel′rā′zər) *n.* a person who behaves recklessly, dissolutely, disruptively, etc. —**hell′-rais′ing** *n., adj.*

☆**hell·uv·a** (hel′ə və) *adj.* [Slang] *phonetic sp. of* HELL OF A (see phrase under HELL)

☆**hell week** a week during which pledges to a fraternity or sorority are subjected to hazing before initiation

helm[1] (helm) *n., vt.* ⟦ME < OE, protection, helmet, akin to Ger *helm*, helmet, OE *helmian*, to protect < IE base **kel-*, to cover, hide > HULL[1], L *celare*, to hide⟧ *archaic & old poet. var. of* HELMET

helm[2] (helm) *n.* ⟦ME *helme* < OE *helma*, akin to Ger *helm*, handle < IE **(s)kelmo-* < base **(s)kel-*, to cut > SHIELD, Gr *skallein*, to dig⟧ 1 *a)* the wheel or tiller by which a ship or boat is steered *b)* the complete steering gear, including the wheel or tiller, rudder, etc. 2 the control or leadership of an organization, government, etc. —*vt.* to guide; control; steer

hel·met (hel′mət) *n.* ⟦OFr, dim. of *helme*, helmet < Frank **helm*: for IE base see HELM[1]⟧ 1 a protective covering for the head; specif., *a)* the headpiece of ancient or medieval armor *b)* the metal head covering worn in modern warfare *c)* the rigid head covering with inner padding and often a wire face mask used in football, lacrosse, and hockey *d)* the mesh-faced mask used in fencing *e)* the headpiece of a diver's suit, equipped with air tubes, glass windows, etc. *f)* a fireman's protective hat *g)* PITH HELMET *h)* the rigid head covering worn by a motorcyclist *i)* HARD HAT 2 something suggesting such a headpiece in appearance or function, as a galea of a flower —*vt.* to cover or equip with a helmet —**hel′met·ed** *adj.*

Helm·holtz (helm′hōlts′), **Her·mann (Ludwig Ferdinand) von** (her′män fôn) 1821-94; Ger. physiologist & physicist

hel·minth (hel′minth′) *n.* ⟦Gr *helmins* (gen. *helminthos*), akin to *eilein*, to turn: for IE base see HELIX⟧ any worm or wormlike animal; esp., a worm parasite of the intestine, as the tapeworm, hookworm, or roundworm

hel·min·thi·a·sis (hel′min thī′ə sis) *n.* ⟦ModL < Gr *helminthiān*, to suffer from worms: see prec. & -IASIS⟧ a disease caused or characterized by parasitic worms in the body

hel·min·thic (hel min′thik) *adj.* 1 of, pertaining to, or caused by helminths 2 expelling or destroying helminths —*n.* a helminthic medicine; vermifuge

hel·min·thol·o·gy (hel′min thäl′ə jē) *n.* the scientific study of helminths

helms·man (helmz′mən) *n., pl.* **-men** (-mən) the person at the helm; one who steers a ship or boat

Hel·o·ise (hel′ō ēz′, hel′ō ēz′) *n.* a feminine name: see ELOISE

Hé·lo·ïse (ā lô ēz′; *E* hel′ō ēz′) 1101-64; lover &, later, wife of her teacher, Pierre Abélard

Hel·ot (hel′ət) *n.* ⟦L *Helotes, Hilotae, pl.* < Gr *Heilōtes, pl.*, taken as after *Helos*, town in Laconia whose inhabitants were enslaved by the Spartans, but < ? base of *haliskesthai*, to be captured < IE base **wel-*, to tear, injure > L *vellere*, to pluck, tear away⟧ 1 a member of the lowest class of serfs in ancient Sparta 2 [**h-**] any serf or slave

hel·ot·ism (hel′ə tiz′əm) *n.* 1 the condition of a helot; serfdom or slavery 2 *Biol.* a form of symbiosis, as among some ants, in which one species dominates and uses workers of another species

hel·ot·ry (hel′ə trē) *n.* 1 helots as a class; serfs or slaves 2 serfdom or slavery

help (help) *vt.* ⟦ME *helpen* < OE *helpan*, akin to Ger *helfen* < IE base **kelb-*, **kelp-*, to help > early Lith *sĕlbinos*, to aid⟧ 1 to make things easier or better for (a person); aid; assist; specif., *a)* to give (one in need or trouble) something necessary, as relief, succor, money, etc. [to *help* the poor] *b)* to do part of the work of; ease or share the labor of [to *help* someone lift a load] *c)* to aid in getting (*up, down, in*, etc. or *to, into, out of*, etc.) [*help* her into the house] 2 to make it easier for (something) to exist, happen, develop, improve, etc.; specif., *a)* to make more effective, larger, more intense, etc.; aid the growth of; promote [a tax to *help* the schools] *b)* to cause improvement in; remedy; alleviate; relieve [a medicine that *helps* a cold] 3 *a)* to keep from; avoid [he can't *help* coughing] *b)* to stop, prevent, change, etc. [a misfortune that can't be *helped*] 4 to serve or wait on (a customer, client, guest, etc.) —*vi.* 1 to give assistance; be cooperative, useful, or beneficial 2 to act as a waiter, clerk, servant, etc. —*n.* ⟦ME < OE < base of the v.; in U.S., sense of "servant," prob. a euphemism to avoid stigma of "serve"⟧ 1 the act of helping or a thing that helps; aid; assistance 2 relief; cure; remedy ☆3 *a)* a helper; esp., a hired helper, as a domestic servant, farmhand, etc. *b)* hired helpers; employees —*interj.* used to summon assistance, esp. urgently —**cannot help but** cannot fail to; be compelled or obliged to —**cannot help oneself** to be the victim of circumstances, a habit, etc. —**help oneself (to)** 1 to serve or provide oneself with (food, etc.) 2 [Informal] to take without asking or being given; steal or appropriate (something) —**help out** to help in getting or doing something; help —**so help me (God)** a phrase used to assert that one is making a solemn vow, sincere declaration, etc.

SYN.—**help** is the simplest and strongest of these words meaning to supply another with whatever is necessary to accomplish his or her ends or relieve his or her wants; **aid** and **assist** are somewhat more formal and weaker, **assist** esp. implying a subordinate role in the helper and less need for help [she *assisted* him in his experiments]; **succor** suggests timely help to one in distress [to *succor* a besieged city] —***ANT.*** **hinder**

help·er (hel′pər) *n.* a person or thing that helps; esp., an assisting worker who is more or less unskilled

helper T cell a type of T cell that helps coordinate the immune response, especially by activating B cells: the AIDS virus targets and destroys these T cells

help·ful (help′fəl) *adj.* giving help; of service; useful —**help′ful·ly** *adv.* —**help′ful·ness** *n.*

help·ing (hel′piŋ) *n.* 1 a giving of aid; assisting 2 a portion of food served to one person

helping verb AUXILIARY VERB

help·less (help′lis) *adj.* 1 not able to help oneself; weak 2 lacking help or protection 3 incompetent, ineffective, or powerless —**help′less·ly** *adv.* —**help′less·ness** *n.*

help·mate (help′māt′) *n.* ⟦altered < fol.⟧ a helpful companion; specif., a wife or, sometimes, a husband

help·meet (-mēt′) *n.* ⟦mistakenly read as a single word in KJV "I will make him an *help meet* for him" (Gen. 2:18): see HELP & MEET[2]⟧ [Archaic] HELPMATE

Hel·sing·borg (hel′siŋ bôr′y′) *alt. sp. of* HÄLSINGBORG

Hel·sing·ør (hel′siŋ ör′) seaport in Denmark, on the Öresund, opposite Hälsingborg, Sweden

Hel·sin·ki (hel′siŋ kē, hel siŋ′-) capital of Finland: seaport on the Gulf of Finland: Swed. name **Hel·sing·fors** (hel′siŋ fôrs′)

hel·ter-skel·ter (hel′tər skel′tər) *adv.* ⟦? arbitrary formation, suggesting confusion⟧ in haste and confusion; in a disorderly, hurried manner —*adj.* hurried and confused; disorderly —*n.* anything helter-skelter

helve (helv) *n.* ⟦ME *helfe* < OE, akin to MDu *helf*: for IE base see HALF⟧ the handle of a tool, esp. of an ax or hatchet —*vt.* **helved**, **helv′ing** to put a helve on; equip with a helve

Hel·ve·tia (hel vē′shə) 1 ancient Celtic country in central Europe, in what is now W Switzerland 2 *Latin name for* SWITZERLAND

Hel·ve·tian (-shən) *adj.* 1 of Helvetia or the Helvetii 2 Swiss —*n.* 1 a person born or living in Helvetia 2 a Swiss person

Hel·vet·ic (hel vet′ik) *adj.* [Now Rare] HELVETIAN —*n.* a Swiss Protestant; adherent of Zwingli

Hel·ve·ti·i (hel vē′shē ī′) *pl.n.* ⟦L⟧ the members of the Celtic people that lived in ancient Helvetia at the time of the rule of Julius Caesar

Hel·vé·tius (el vā syüs′; *E* hel vē′shē əs), **Claude A·dri·en** (klōd à drē an′) 1715-71; Fr. philosopher

hem[1] (hem) *n.* ⟦ME < OE, akin to MLowG *ham*, enclosed piece of land < IE base **kem-*, to compress, impede > HAMPER[1]⟧ 1 the border on a garment or piece of cloth, usually made by folding the edge and sewing it down 2 any border, edge, or margin —*vt.* **hemmed**, **hem′ming** to fold back the edge of and sew down; put a hem or hems on —**hem in (or around or about)** 1 to encircle; surround 2 to confine or restrain

hem[2] (hem) *interj., n.* (used to suggest) the sound made in clearing the throat —*vi.* **hemmed**, **hem′ming** to make this sound, as in trying to get attention or in showing doubt —**hem and haw** [Informal] 1 to grope about in speech, while searching for the right words to say 2 to be vague or indecisive

hem- (hēm, hem) *combining form* HEMO-: used before a vowel

he·ma- (hē′mə; *also* hem′ə) *combining form* HEMO-

he·ma·cy·tom·e·ter (hē′mə sī täm′ət er) *n.* ⟦prec. + CYTO- + -METER⟧ a device used to count the concentration of cells in bodily fluids, esp. the red and white cells in blood

he·mag·glu·ti·nate (hē′mə glo͞ot′'n āt′) *vt.* **-nat′ed**, **-nat′ing** ⟦HEM- + AGGLUTINATE⟧ to cause the clumping of red blood cells in —**he′mag·glu′ti·na′tion** *n.*

he·mag·glu·ti·nin (hē′mə glo͞ot′'n in) *n.* a substance, as an antibody, capable of causing hemagglutination

he·mal (hē′məl) *adj.* ⟦HEM- + -AL⟧ 1 having to do with the blood or blood vessels: also **he′ma·tal** (hē′mət əl) 2 having to do with certain structures of the body near the heart and main blood vessels

☆**he-man** (hē′man′) *n.* [Informal] a strong, virile man

he·man·gi·o·ma (hē man′jē ō′mə) *n., pl.* **-ma·ta** (-mə tə) or **-mas** a benign tumor, lesion, or birthmark consisting of dense clusters of blood vessels

he·mat- (hē′mət; *also* hem′ət) *combining form* HEMATO-: used before a vowel

he·ma·te·in (hē′mə tē′in, hē′mə tēn′) *n.* ⟦< HEMAT(OXYLIN) + -IN[1]⟧ a reddish-brown, crystalline dye, $C_{16}H_{12}O_6$, obtained from logwood extracts by oxidation and used as a stain and indicator

he·mat·ic (hē mat′ik) *adj.* ⟦Gr *haimatikos* < *haima*, blood: see HEMO-⟧ of, filled with, or colored like blood

he·ma·tin (hē′mə tin) *n.* ⟦HEMAT(O)- + -IN[1]⟧ a dark-brown or blackish hydroxide of heme, $C_{34}H_{32}N_4O_4{\cdot}FeOH$, obtained by the decomposition of hemoglobin

he·ma·tin·ic (hē′mə tin′ik) *n.* any substance that increases the amount of hemoglobin in the blood —*adj.* of or relating to hematin

he·ma·tite (hē′mə tīt′) *n.* ⟦L *haematites* < Gr *haimatitēs*, lit., bloodlike, red iron ore < *haima*, blood: see HEMO-⟧ a reddish brown to black, rhombohedral mineral, Fe_2O_3, that is a major ore of iron; ferric oxide: see RED OCHER —**he′ma·tit′ic** (-tit′ik) *adj.*

he·ma·to- (hē′mə tō; *also* hem′ə tō) ⟦< Gr *haima* (gen. *haimatos*), blood: see HEMO-⟧ *combining form* blood [*hematology*]

he·ma·to·blast (hē′mə tō blast′) *n.* ⟦prec. + -BLAST⟧ an immature blood cell —**he′ma·to·blas′tic** *adj.*

he·mat·o·crit (hi mat′ə krit) *n.* ⟦< HEMATO- + Gr *kritēs*, a judge < *krinein*, to separate: see HARVEST⟧ **1** a small centrifuge or its calibrated tube used to determine the relative volumes of blood cells and fluid in blood **2** the proportion of red blood cells to a volume of blood, as measured by a hematocrit: also **hematocrit reading**

he·ma·to·gen·e·sis (hē′mə tō jen′ə sis) *n.* HEMATOPOIESIS —**he′ma·to·gen′ic** (-jen′ik) *adj.*, **he′ma·to·ge·net′ic** (-jə net′ik)

he·ma·tog·e·nous (hē′mə täj′ə nəs) *adj.* **1** forming blood **2** spread by the bloodstream, as bacteria

he·ma·tol·o·gy (hē′mə täl′ə jē) *n.* ⟦HEMATO- + -LOGY⟧ the study of the blood, blood-forming tissues, and blood diseases —**he′ma·to·log′ic** (-tə läj′ik) *adj.*, **he′ma·to·log′i·cal** —**he′ma·tol′o·gist** *n.*

he·ma·to·ma (hē′mə tō′mə) *n., pl.* **-mas** or **-ma·ta** (-mə tə) ⟦ModL: see HEMAT(O)- & -OMA⟧ a tumorlike collection of blood, usually clotted, located outside a blood vessel

he·ma·toph·a·gous (hē′mə täf′ə gəs) *adj.* ⟦HEMATO- + -PHAGOUS⟧ feeding on blood

he·ma·to·poi·e·sis (hē′mə tō poi ē′sis, hi mat′ə-) *n.* ⟦< HEMATO- + Gr *poiēsis*, a making: see POESY⟧ the production of blood cells by the blood-forming organs —**he′ma·to·poi·et′ic** (-et′ik) *adj.*

he·ma·to·por·phy·rin (hē′mə tō pôr′fə rin, hi mat′ə-) *n.* a type of porphyrin, $C_{34}H_{38}O_6N_4$, obtained by treating hemoglobin with a strong acid: it is used in cancer research because it fluoresces under ultraviolet light and is readily absorbed by cancerous tissue

he·ma·tox·y·lin (hē′mə täk′sə lin) *n.* ⟦H(A)EMATOXYL(ON) + -IN[1]⟧ a colorless, crystalline compound, $C_{16}H_{14}O_6 \cdot 3H_2O$, extracted from logwood and used as an indicator and a stain in microscopy: when oxidized it yields hematein dye

he·mat·o·zo·on (hi mat′ə zō′än, hē′mə tə-) *n., pl.* **-zo′a** (-ə) ⟦ModL: see HEMATO- & -ZOON⟧ any parasitic animal organism in the blood —**he·mat′o·zo′ic** (-ik) *adj.*, **he·mat′o·zo′al** (-əl)

he·ma·tu·ri·a (hē′mə toor′ē ə, -tyoor′-) *n.* ⟦HEMAT(O)- + -URIA⟧ the presence of red blood cells in the urine

heme (hēm) *n.* ⟦contr. < HEMATIN⟧ the nonprotein, iron-containing pigment, $C_{34}H_{32}N_4O_4Fe$, that is a component part of hemoglobin, myoglobin, etc.

hem·el·y·tron (he mel′i trän′) *n., pl.* **-tra** (-trə) ⟦ModL < HEM(I)- + ELYTRON⟧ either of the forewings of hemipteran insects, having a thickened basal portion and a membranous end: also **hem·el′y·trum** (-trəm), *pl.* **-tra** (-trə)

hem·er·a·lo·pi·a (hem′ər ə lō′pē ə) *n.* ⟦ModL < Gr *hēmeralōps*, day blindness (< *hēmera*, day + *alaos*, blind + *ōps*, EYE) + -IA⟧ a defect in the eye in which the vision is reduced in the daylight or in bright light: cf. NYCTALOPIA —**hem′er·a·lop′ic** (-läp′ik) *adj.*

☆**Hem·i** (hem′ē) ⟦< HEMISPHERE⟧ *trademark for* a type of internal-combustion engine with somewhat hemispherical combustion chambers —*n.* [**h-**] an engine of this type

hem·i- (hem′i, -ə, -ē) ⟦Gr *hēmi-* < IE **sēmi-* > Sans *sāmi-*, L *semi-*⟧ *prefix meaning* half [*hemisphere*]

-he·mi·a (hē′mē ə) ⟦var. of -EMIA⟧ *combining form* -EMIA

he·mic (hē′mik, hem′ik) *adj.* ⟦HEM- + -IC⟧ of the blood

hem·i·cel·lu·lose (hem′i sel′yə lōs′) *n.* a polysaccharide with fewer than 150 polymer units of various sugars: it is extracted from plants, esp. woody and corn fiber, by dilute alkalies

hem·i·chor·date (-kôr′dāt′) *adj.* ⟦HEMI- + CHORDATE⟧ of or pertaining to a phylum (Hemichordata) of wormlike marine animals with visceral clefts and primitive nervous and circulatory systems —*n.* any hemichordate animal

hem·i·cra·ni·a (-krā′nē ə) *n.* ⟦LL < Gr *hēmikrania* < *hēmi-*, half + *kranion*, skull⟧ headache in only one side of the head, as in migraine

hem·i·cy·cle (hem′i sī′kəl) *n.* ⟦Fr *hémicycle* < L *hemicyclium* < Gr *hēmikyklion*: see HEMI- & CYCLE⟧ **1** a half circle **2** a semicircular room, wall, etc.

hem·i·dem·i·sem·i·qua·ver (hem′i dem′i sem′i kwā′vər) *n.* ⟦HEMI- + DEMISEMIQUAVER⟧ [Chiefly Brit.] SIXTY-FOURTH NOTE

hem·i·el·y·tron (hem′ē el′i trän′) *n. var. of* HEMELYTRON

hem·i·he·dral (hem′i hē′drəl) *adj.* ⟦HEMI- + -HEDRAL⟧ having half the number of faces required for complete symmetry: said of a crystal

hem·i·hy·drate (-hī′drāt′) *n.* a hydrate with a two-to-one ratio of molecules of substance to molecules of water

hem·i·me·tab·o·lous (-mə tab′ə ləs) *adj.* designating or of a group of insect orders in which the juvenile stages are aquatic without a pupal stage, and in which the young differ considerably from the adults: also **hem′i·met′a·bol′ic** (-met′ə bäl′ik) —**hem′i·me·tab′o·lism′** *n.*

hem·i·mor·phic (-môr′fik) *adj.* ⟦HEMI- + -MORPHIC⟧ designating a crystal with unlike faces at the ends of the same axis

hem·i·mor·phite (-môr′fīt′) *n.* ⟦Ger *hemimorphit* < *hemimorph*, hemimorphic (< *hemi-*, HEMI- + *-morph*, -MORPH) + *-it*, -ITE[1]⟧ a light-colored mineral, $Zn_4Si_2O_7(OH)_2 \cdot H_2O$, that is an ore of zinc; hydrous zinc silicate

he·min (hē′min) *n.* ⟦HEM(E) + -IN[1]⟧ a brown, crystalline chloride of heme, $C_{34}H_{32}N_4O_4FeCl$, obtained when blood is treated with glacial acetic acid and sodium chloride: its production by this reaction is evidence of the presence of blood in fluids, stains, etc.

Hem·ing·way (hem′iŋ wā′), **Ernest (Miller)** 1899-1961; U.S. novelist & short-story writer

hem·i·o·la (hem′ē ō′lə) *n.* ⟦< ML *hemiolia* < Gr *hēmiolia*, fem. of *hēmiolios*, in the ratio of one and one half to one < *hēmi-* (see HEMI-) + *holos*, whole⟧ especially in early music, time values in the relationship of three to two, as in a unit or measure divided into three beats followed by an equivalent unit divided into two beats: also **hem′i·o′li·a** (-lē ə)

hem·i·par·a·site (hem′i par′ə sīt′) *n.* **1** *Zool.* an organism that may be either free-living or parasitic; facultative parasite **2** *Bot.* a parasitic plant, as the mistletoe, which carries on some photosynthesis but obtains a portion of its food, water, or minerals from a host plant —**hem′i·par′a·sit′ic** (-sit′ik) *adj.*

hem·i·ple·gi·a (-plē′jē ə, -jə) *n.* ⟦ModL < MGr *hēmiplēgia*, paralysis: see HEMI- & -PLEGIA⟧ paralysis of one side of the body —**hem′i·ple′gic** (-jik) *adj., n.*

he·mip·ter·an (hē mip′tər ən, hə-) *n.* ⟦< ModL *Hemiptera* (see HEMI- & PTERO-) + -AN⟧ a true bug: see BUG[1] (sense 1) —**he·mip′ter·oid** *adj.* —**he·mip′ter·ous** *adj.*

hem·i·sphere (hem′i sfir′) *n.* ⟦ME *hemisperie* < L *hemisphaerium* < Gr *hēmisphairion*: see HEMI- & SPHERE⟧ **1** half of a sphere, globe, or celestial body; specif., *a)* any of the halves into which the celestial sphere is divided by either the celestial equator or the ecliptic *b)* any of the halves of the earth: the earth is divided by the equator into the N and S hemispheres and by a meridian into the E Hemisphere (containing Europe, Asia, Africa, and Australia) and the W Hemisphere (containing the Americas and Oceania) *c)* a model or map of any of these halves **2** the countries and peoples of any of the earth's hemispheres **3** an area of action, knowledge, etc. **4** either lateral half of the cerebrum or cerebellum —**hem′i·spher′i·cal** (-sfer′i kəl) *adj.*, **hem′i·spher′ic**

hem·i·sphe·roid (-sfir′oid′) *n.* a half of a spheroid

hem·i·stich (hem′i stik′) *n.* ⟦L *hemistichium* < Gr *hēmistichion* < *hēmi*, half + *stichos*, a row, line, verse: see STICH⟧ half a line of verse, esp., either half created by the chief caesura, or rhythmic pause in the middle of a line

hem·i·ter·pene (hem′i tur′pēn′) *n.* ⟦HEMI- + TERPENE⟧ any of a group of isomeric hydrocarbons with the general formula C_5H_8, as isoprene

hem·i·trope (hem′i trōp′) *adj.* ⟦Fr *hémitrope*: see HEMI- & -TROPE⟧ designating a crystal formed of two other crystals joined so that corresponding faces are directly opposed: also **hem′i·trop′ic** (-träp′ik) —*n.* such a crystal

hem·i·zy·gous (hem′i zī′gəs) *adj.* being or having a gene, esp. one on the X chromosome, that lacks an allelic complement and which therefore always expresses the trait which it carries

hem·line (hem′līn′) *n.* **1** the bottom edge, usually hemmed, of a dress, skirt, coat, etc. **2** the height of this edge above the ground

hem·lock (hem′läk′) *n.* ⟦ME *hemlok* < OE *hemlic, hymlic*, akin ? to *hymele*, hop⟧ **1** *a)* a poisonous European plant (*Conium maculatum*) of the umbel family, with compound umbels of small, white flowers and finely divided leaves; poison hemlock *b)* a poison made from this plant **2** WATER HEMLOCK **3** *a)* any of a genus (*Tsuga*) of North American and Asian evergreen trees of the pine family, with drooping branches and short needles: the bark is used in tanning *b)* the wood of such a tree

hem·mer (hem′ər) *n.* **1** a person that hems ☆**2** a sewing machine attachment for making hems

he·mo- (hē′mō, -mə; hem′ō, -ə) ⟦Gr *haimo-* < *haima*, flowing blood (replacing earlier *ear*, blood, prob. for reasons of taboo); prob. akin to OHG *seim*, thick-flowing honey < IE base **sei-*, **soi-*, to drip⟧ *combining form* blood [*hemocyte*]

he·mo·chro·ma·to·sis (hē′mə krō′mə tō′sis) *n.* ⟦prec. + CHROMAT(O)- + -OSIS⟧ a disorder of iron metabolism, characterized by a bronze-colored skin pigmentation, liver dysfunction, an excess of iron in organs, and diabetes mellitus

he·mo·cy·a·nin (hē′mō sī′ə nin) *n.* ⟦HEMO- + CYAN- + -IN[1]⟧ a blue, oxygen-carrying blood pigment containing copper, found in many arthropods and mollusks

he·mo·cyte (hē′mə sīt′) *n.* ⟦HEMO- + -CYTE⟧ a blood cell

he·mo·cy·tom·e·ter (hē′mō sī täm′ət ər) *n.* ⟦HEMO- + CYTO- + -METER⟧ *var. of* HEMACYTOMETER

he·mo·di·al·y·sis (hē′mō dī al′ə sis) *n., pl.* **-ses′** (-sēz′) DIALYSIS (sense 2)

he·mo·dy·nam·ics (hē′mō dī nam′iks) *n. Physiol.* the study of the flow of blood in the circulatory system —**he′mo·dy·nam′ic** *adj.*

he·mo·flag·el·late (hē′mō flaj′ə lāt′, -flaj′ə lit, -flə jel′it) *n.* any parasitic zooflagellate in the bloodstream

he·mo·glo·bin (hē′mə glō′bin) *n.* ⟦contr. (as if < HEMO-) < earlier *haematoglobulin*: see HEMATO- & GLOBULIN⟧ **1** the red coloring matter of the red blood corpuscles of vertebrates, a protein yielding heme and globin on hydrolysis: it carries oxygen from the lungs to the tissues, and carbon dioxide from the tissues to the lungs **2** any of various respiratory pigments found in the blood or muscle tissue of many invertebrates and in the root nodules of some plants —**he′mo·glo·bin′ic** (-glō bin′ik) *adj.* —**he′mo·glo′bi·nous** (-glō′bə nəs) *adj.*

he·mo·glo·bi·nu·ri·a (-glō′bi noor′ē ə, -nyoor′-) *n.* the presence in urine of hemoglobin free from red blood cells —**he′mo·glo′bi·nu′ric** *adj.*

he·moid (hē′moid′) *adj.* ⟦HEM(O)- + -OID⟧ like blood

he·mo·lymph (hē′mə limf′) *n.* ⟦HEMO- + LYMPH⟧ the circulating fluid in open tissue spaces of invertebrates: it may act as blood, as in arthropods, or be in addition to blood, as in earthworms

he·mol·y·sin (hi mäl′ə sin, hē′mə lī′sin) *n.* ⟦< HEMO- + Gr *lysis*, a dissolving + -IN[1]⟧ a substance formed in the blood, as by bacterial action, that causes the destruction of red corpuscles with liberation of hemoglobin

he·mol·y·sis (hi mäl′ə sis, hē′mə lī′sis) *n.* ⟦HEMO- + -LYSIS⟧ the destruction of red corpuscles with liberation of hemoglobin into the surrounding fluid —**he·mo·lyt·ic** (hē′mə lit′ik) *adj.*

he·mo·lyze (hē′mə līz′) *vi., vt.* **-lyzed′**, **-lyz′ing** to undergo, or cause to undergo, hemolysis

he·mo·phile (hē′mə fīl′) *n.* ⟦HEMO- + -PHILE⟧ a hemophilic bacterium

he·mo·phil·i·a (-fil′ē ə, -fē′lē ə) *n.* ⟦ModL: see HEMO- & -PHILIA⟧ any of several hereditary disorders, nearly always of males, in which one of the normal blood-clotting factors is deficient, causing serious internal or external hemorrhage from minor cuts and injuries: females with this defective gene are, normally, only carriers

he·mo·phil·i·ac (-fil′ē ak′) *n.* a person who has hemophilia

he·mo·phil·ic (-fil′ik) *adj.* **1** of or having hemophilia **2** growing well in a medium containing hemoglobin: said of certain bacteria

he·mop·ty·sis (hi mäp′tə sis) *n.* ⟦ModL < HEMO- + Gr *ptysis*, spitting < *ptyein*, to spit out < IE echoic base **(s)pyū-* > L *spuere*, SPEW⟧ the spitting or coughing up of blood: usually caused by bleeding in the lungs or bronchi

hem·or·rhage (hem′ə rij, hem′rij) *n.* ⟦Fr *hémorrhagie* < L *haemorrhagia* < Gr *haimorrhagia* < *haima*, blood (see HEMO-) + base of *rhēgnynai*, to break, burst⟧ the escape of large quantities of blood from a blood vessel; heavy bleeding —*vi.* **-rhaged**, **-rhag·ing** to suffer a hemorrhage —**hem′or·rhag′ic** (-ə raj′ik) *adj.*

hemorrhagic fever any of various acute viral infections, as dengue, yellow fever, or Ebola, characterized by fever, fatigue, internal bleeding, headache, etc.

hem·or·rhoid (hem′ə roid′, hem′roid′) *n.* ⟦altered (after L or Gr) < ME *emoroid(es)* < L *haemorrhoidae* < Gr *haimorrhoïdes (phlebes)*, (veins) discharging blood < *haima*, blood *haimorrhoos*, flowing with blood < (see HEMO-) + *rheein*, to flow, STREAM⟧ a painful swelling of a vein in the region of the anus, often with bleeding: *usually used in pl.* —**hem′or·rhoi′dal** *adj.*

hem·or·rhoid·ec·to·my (hem′ə roi dek′tə mē) *n., pl.* **-mies** ⟦see -ECTOMY⟧ the surgical removal of hemorrhoids

he·mo·sta·sis (hē′mə stā′sis) *n., pl.* **-ses′** (-sēz′) ⟦ModL < Gr *haimostasis*: see HEMO- & STASIS⟧ **1** the natural or surgical stoppage of bleeding **2** slowing or stoppage of the flow of blood in a vein or artery, as with a tourniquet, by clotting, etc.

he·mo·stat (hē′mə stat′) *n.* ⟦< fol.⟧ anything used to stop bleeding, specif., *a)* a clamplike instrument used in surgery *b)* a medicine that hastens clotting

he·mo·stat·ic (hē′mə stat′ik) *adj.* ⟦see HEMO- & STATIC⟧ capable of stopping the flow of blood —*n.* HEMOSTAT (sense *b*)

he·mo·tox·in (hē′mə täk′sin) *n.* a toxin capable of destroying erythrocytes —**he′mo·tox′ic** *adj.*

hemp (hemp) *n.* ⟦ME < OE *hænep* (akin to Ger *hanf*, Du *hennep*) < PGmc **hanapa-* < **kanab-*, a pre-Gmc borrowing < a (? Scythian) base > Gr *kannabis*: akin ? to Sumerian *kunibu*, hemp⟧ **1** *a)* a tall Asian herb (*Cannabis sativa*) of the hemp family, grown for the tough fiber in its stem *b)* the fiber, used to make rope, sailcloth, etc. *c)* a substance, such as marijuana, hashish, etc., made from the leaves and flowers of this plant **2** *a)* any of various plants yielding a hemplike fiber, as the sisal or Manila hemp *b)* this fiber —*adj.* designating a family (Cannabaceae, order Urticales) of dicotyledonous plants, including hops

hemp agrimony a European plant (*Eupatorium cannabinum*) of the composite family, with reddish flowers: formerly used in medicine

hemp·en (hem′pən) *adj.* [Now Rare] of, made of, or like hemp

hemp nettle any of a genus (*Galeopsis*) of European plants of the mint family; esp., a common prickly weed (*G. tetrahit*) now found in the U.S.

hemp·seed (hemp′sēd′) *n.* the seed of hemp

hem·stitch (hem′stich′) *n.* **1** an ornamental stitch, used esp. at a hem, made by pulling out several parallel threads and tying the cross threads together into small, even bunches **2** decorative needlework done with this stitch — *vt., vi.* to put a hemstitch or hemstitches (on) —**hem′stitch′er** *n.*

hemstitch

hen (hen) *n.* ⟦ME < OE *henn*, fem. of *hana*, rooster, akin to Ger *henne* (fem. of *hahn*) < IE base **kan-*, to sing, crow > L *canere*, to sing⟧ **1** the female of the domesticated chicken **2** the female of various other birds or of certain other animals, as the lobster **3** [Slang] a woman, esp. an older woman: somewhat dismissive or disparaging

He·nan (hu′nän′) province of EC China: 64,479 sq mi (167,000 sq km); cap. Zhengzhou

hen and chickens ⟦so called from fancied resemblance of the main plant and its offsets to a *hen* with *chicks* clustered around her⟧ any of various flowering plants with a dense rosette of fleshy leaves clustered at the base of the stem from which offshoots arise; specif., the common houseleek (*Sempervivum tectorum*): also **hen (**or **hens) and chicks**

hen·bane (hen′bān′) *n.* ⟦ME: see HEN & BANE⟧ a coarse, hairy, foul-smelling, poisonous plant (*Hyoscyamus niger*) of the nightshade family: it is used in medicine as a source of hyoscyamine and scopolamine

hen·bit (-bit′) *n.* ⟦HEN + BIT[2]⟧ a spreading weedy plant (*Lamium amplexicaule*) of the mint family, with rounded, opposite leaves and small, pink or lavender flowers

hence (hens) *adv.* ⟦ME *hennes* < *henne* < OE *heonan(e)*, from here + -*(e)s*, adv. gen. suffix (as in SINCE, THENCE) < IE base as in HE[1], HERE⟧ **1** from this place; away [go *hence*] **2** *a)* from this time; after now [a year *hence*] *b)* thereafter; subsequently **3** for this reason; as a result; therefore: often used as a conjunctive adverb **4** [Archaic] from this origin or source —*interj.* [Archaic] leave; go away —**hence with!** [Archaic] away with!

hence·forth (hens fôrth′, hens′fôrth′) *adv.* ⟦ME *hennesforth*: see prec. & FORTH⟧ **1** from this time on: also **hence′for′ward** (-fôr′wərd) **2** thereafter; subsequently

hench·man (hench′mən) *n., pl.* **-men** (-mən) ⟦ME *henxtman, henchemen* < OE *hengest*, stallion (see HENGIST) + *-man*: orig. sense prob. "horse attendant"⟧ **1** [Obs.] a male attendant; page or squire **2** a trusted helper or follower ☆**3** a political underling who seeks mainly to advance his own interests ☆**4** any of the followers of a criminal gang leader

hen·coop (hen′ko͞op′) *n.* a coop for poultry

hen·dec·a- (hen′dek′ə, hen dek′ə) ⟦< Gr *hendeka*, eleven < *hen*, one (< IE **sem-*, one: see SIMPLE) + *deka*, TEN⟧ *combining form* eleven

hen·dec·a·gon (hen dek′ə gän′) *n.* ⟦Fr *hendécagone*: see prec. & -GON⟧ a plane figure with eleven angles and eleven sides —**hen·de·cag·o·nal** (hen′di kag′ə nəl) *adj.*

hen·dec·a·he·dron (hen′dek′ə hē′drən) *n., pl.* **-drons** or **-dra** ⟦ModL: see HENDECA- & -HEDRON⟧ a solid figure with eleven plane surfaces —**hen′dec′a·he′dral** *adj.*

hen·dec·a·syl·lab·ic (-se lab′ik) *n.* ⟦L *hendecasyllabus* < Gr *hendekasyllabos*: see HENDECA- & SYLLABLE⟧ a line of verse having eleven syllables: also **hen′dec′a·syl′la·ble** (-sil′ə bəl) —*adj.* containing eleven syllables: said as of a line of verse

Hen·der·son (hen′dər sən) ⟦after U.S. Senator C. B. *Henderson* (1873-1954)⟧ city in SE Nev.

hen·di·a·dys (hen dī′ə dis) *n.* ⟦ML < Gr phrase *hen dia dyoin*, one (thing) by means of two⟧ a figure of speech in which two nouns joined by *and* are used instead of a noun and a modifier (Ex.: *deceit and words* for *deceitful words*)

Hen·don (hen′dən) former urban district in Middlesex, SE England: now part of Barnet

Hen·drix (hen′driks), **Jim·i** (jim′ē) (born *Johnny Allen Hendrix*) 1942-70; U.S. rock singer, composer, & guitarist

hen·e·quen (hen′i ken′, hen′i ken′) *n.* ⟦Sp *henequén, jeniquén* < Taino name in Yucatán⟧ **1** a tropical American agave (*Agave fourcroydes*) cultivated for the hard fiber of the leaves **2** the fiber, similar to sisal, used for making rope, twine, rugs, etc.

henge (henj) *n.* ⟦< (STONE)HENGE⟧ a Neolithic or Bronze Age monument of the British Isles, consisting of a circular bank or ditch enclosing, variously, stone or timber uprights, burial pits, etc.

Hen·gist (heŋ′gist) ⟦OE < *hengest*, stallion, akin to Ger *hengst* < IE base **kak-*, to leap, spurt forth⟧ died A.D. 488; Jute chief; with his brother Horsa (died 455), he is reputed to have led the first Germanic invasion of England & to have founded the kingdom of Kent

hen·house (hen′hous′) *n.* a shelter for poultry

hen·ley (hen′lē) *n.* ⟦after fol.: style based on the shirt worn by rowers in the regatta held there⟧ a knit shirt, top, etc. typically having a crew neck with a band collar, and a buttoned placket

Hen·ley (hen′lē) city in SE England, on the Thames: site of an annual rowing regatta: also **Henley-on-Thames**

hen·na (hen′ə) *n.* ⟦Ar *ḥinnā′*⟧ **1** an Old World plant (*Lawsonia inermis*) of the loosestrife family, with minute, white or red flowers having the fragrance of roses **2** a dye extracted from the leaves of this plant, often used to tint the hair auburn **3** reddish brown —*adj.* reddish-brown —*vt.* **-naed**, **-na·ing** to tint with henna

hen·ner·y (hen′ər ē) *n., pl.* **-ner·ies** a place for keeping poultry

hen·o·the·ism (hen′ō thē iz′əm, -thē′iz′-) *n.* ⟦coined (*c.* 1860) by Max MÜLLER < Gr *hen*, one (see HENDECA-) + *theos*, god⟧ belief in or worship of one god without denying the existence of others —**hen·o·the·ist** (hen′ō thē′ist) *n.* —**hen′o·the·is′tic** *adj.*

hen party [Informal] a party for women only: somewhat dismissive or disparaging

hen·peck (hen′pek′) *vt.* to nag and domineer over (one's husband) —**hen′pecked′** *adj.*

Hen·ri·cian (hen rish′ən) *adj.* ⟦< ML *Henricianus* < *Henricus*, HENRY[1]⟧ of or having to do with the reign, policies, etc. of any king named Henry, esp. Henry VIII of England

Hen·ri·et·ta (hen′rē et′ə) *n.* ⟦Fr *Henriette*, dim. of *Henri*: see HENRY[1]⟧ a feminine name: dim. *Etta, Hetty, Nettie, Netty*

☆**hen·ry** (hen′rē) *n., pl.* **-rys** or **-ries** ⟦after J. *Henry* (1797-1878), U.S. physicist⟧ *Elec.* the basic unit of electric inductance in the SI and MKS systems, equal to the inductance of a circuit in which the variation of current at the rate of one ampere per second induces an electromotive force of one volt: abbrev. *H*

Hen·ry[1] (hen′rē) *n.* ⟦Fr *Henri* < Ger *Heinrich* < OHG *Haganrih*, lit., ruler of an enclosure (< *hag-*, HAW[1], a hedging in + *rihhi*, ruler) & also altered < OHG *Heimerich*, lit., home ruler (< *heim*, HOME)⟧ a masculine name: dim. *Hal, Hank, Henny*; var. *Harry*; equiv. L. *Henricus*, Du. *Hendrik*, Fr. *Henri*, Ger. *Heinrich*, It. *Enrico*, Sp. *Enrique*; fem. *Henrietta*

Hen·ry[2] (hen′rē) **1** 1394-1460; prince of Portugal: called *Henry the Navigator* **2 Henry I** 1068-1135; king of England (1100-35): son of William the Conqueror **3 Henry II** 1133-89; king of England (1154-89): 1st Plantagenet king **4 Henry III** 1207-72; king of England (1216-72) **5 Henry III** 1551-89; king of France (1574-89) **6 Henry IV** 1050-1106; king of Germany

(1056-1105) & Holy Roman Emperor (1084-1105): dethroned **7 Henry IV** 1367-1413; king of England (1399-1413): 1st Lancastrian king: son of John of Gaunt: called *Bolingbroke* **8 Henry IV** 1553-1610; king of France (1589-1610): 1st Bourbon king: called *Henry of Navarre* **9 Henry V** 1387-1422; king of England (1413-22): defeated the French at Agincourt **10 Henry VI** 1421-71; king of England (1422-61; 1470-71) **11 Henry VII** 1457-1509; king of England (1485-1509): 1st Tudor king **12 Henry VIII** 1491-1547; king of England (1509-47): broke with the papacy and established the Church of England **13 O.** (pseud. of *William Sydney Porter*) 1862-1910; U.S. short-story writer **14 Patrick** 1736-99; Am. patriot, statesman, & orator

Hen·ry[3] (hen′rē) **1 Cape** ⟦after Prince *Henry*, son of JAMES[2]⟧ promontory in SE Va., at the entrance of Chesapeake Bay **2 Fort** Confederate fort in NW Tenn., on the Tennessee River: captured (1862) by Union forces

hent (hent) *vt.* **hent, hent′ing** ⟦ME *henten* < OE *hentan*, akin to *huntian*, HUNT⟧ [Archaic] to grasp; seize

Hen·ze (hent′sə), **Hans Wer·ner** (häns ver′nər) 1926-2012; Ger. composer

☆**hep** (hep) *adj.* ⟦< ? the drill sergeant's shout (alteration of STEP) marking time for marching troops⟧ [Slang] *var. of* HIP[4]

☆**hep·a·rin** (hep′ə rin) *n.* ⟦< Gr *hēpar*, the liver (see HEPATIC) + -IN[1]⟧ a substance found in the liver, that slows the clotting of blood: its sodium salt, taken from animals, is used in surgery and medicine

hep·a·rin·ize (-īz′) *vt.* **-ized′, -iz′ing** to treat with heparin

hep·at- (hep′ət) *combining form* HEPATO-: used before a vowel

hep·a·tec·to·my (hep′ə tek′tə mē) *n., pl.* **-mies** ⟦HEPAT(O)- + -ECTOMY⟧ the surgical removal of part or all of the liver

he·pat·ic (hi pat′ik) *adj.* ⟦L *hepaticus* < Gr *hēpatikos* < *hēpar*, the liver < IE base **jekwr̥-* > Sans *yákr̥t*, L *jecur*⟧ **1** of or affecting the liver **2** like the liver in color or shape **3** of the liverworts —*n.* LIVERWORT

he·pat·i·ca (hi pat′i kə) *n.* ⟦ModL (see prec.): in allusion to its lobed, liver-shaped leaves⟧ any of a genus (*Hepatica*) of small plants of the buttercup family, with three-lobed leaves and white, pink, blue, or purple flowers that bloom in early spring

hep·a·ti·tis (hep′ə tīt′is) *n., pl.* **-tit′i·des′** (-tit′ə dēz′) ⟦ModL < HEPAT(O)- + -ITIS⟧ inflammation of the liver, often accompanied by fever and jaundice

hepatitis A a form of hepatitis caused by an RNA virus, usually transmitted by contaminated food and water, and characterized by a shorter incubation period and milder symptoms than hepatitis B; infectious hepatitis

hepatitis B a form of hepatitis caused by a DNA virus, usually transmitted by infected blood, and characterized by a long incubation period, serious liver damage, and the sudden onset of severe fever, jaundice, abdominal pain, etc.; serum hepatitis

hepatitis C a form of hepatitis clinically similar to hepatitis B, but caused by an RNA virus

hep·a·to- (hep′ə tō′) ⟦Gr *hēpato-* < *hēpar* (gen. *hēpatos*): see HEPATIC⟧ *combining form* the liver [*hepatoblastoma*]

hep·a·tol·o·gy (hep′ə täl′ə jē) *n.* ⟦prec. + -LOGY⟧ the branch of medicine dealing with the liver, gallbladder, pancreas, etc. and their diseases —**hep′a·tol′o·gist** *n.*

hep·a·to·ma (hep′ə tō′mə) *n., pl.* **-mas** or **-ma·ta** (-mə tə) ⟦HEPAT(O)- + -OMA⟧ a cancer of the liver or from liver cells

HepB *abbrev.* hepatitis B (vaccine or vaccination)

Hep·burn (hep′burn′) **1 Audrey** (born *Audrey Kathleen Ruston*) 1929-93; Brit. film actress, born in Belgium **2 Katharine** 1909-2003; U.S. film actress

☆**hep·cat** (hep′kat′) *n.* ⟦HEP + CAT[1] (sense 9)⟧ [Old Slang] a jazz enthusiast

He·phaes·tus (hē fes′təs) *n.* ⟦Gr *Hēphaistos*⟧ *Gr. Myth.* the god of fire and the forge, son of Zeus and Hera: see VULCAN

Hep·ple·white (hep′əl hwīt′) *adj.* ⟦after George *Hepplewhite* (died 1786), Eng cabinetmaker⟧ designating or of an 18th-cent. Eng. style of furniture characterized by graceful curves and straight, slender legs

hep·ta- (hep′tə) ⟦< Gr *hepta*, SEVEN⟧ *combining form* **1** seven [*heptagon*] **2** *Chem.* having seven atoms, radicals, etc. of a (specified) substance [*heptachlor*] Also, before a vowel, **hept-**

☆**hep·ta·chlor** (hep′tə klôr′) *n.* a waxy solid, $C_{10}H_7Cl_7$, similar to chlordane, formerly used as an insecticide

hep·tad (hep′tad′) *n.* ⟦< Gr *heptas* (gen. *heptados*) < *hepta*, SEVEN⟧ a series or group of seven

hep·ta·gon (hep′tə gän′) *n.* ⟦< Gr *heptagōnos*, seven-cornered: see HEPTA- & -GON⟧ a plane figure with seven angles and seven sides —**hep·tag′o·nal** (-tag′ə nəl) *adj.*

hep·ta·he·dron (hep′tə hē′drən) *n., pl.* **-drons** or **-dra** (-drə) ⟦ModL: see HEPTA- & -HEDRON⟧ a solid figure with seven plane surfaces —**hep′ta·he′dral** *adj.*

hep·tam·er·ous (hep tam′ər əs) *adj.* ⟦HEPTA- + -MEROUS⟧ having seven parts in each whorl: said of flowers: also written **7-merous**

hep·tam·e·ter (hep tam′ət ər) *n.* ⟦HEPTA- + -METER⟧ a line of verse containing seven metrical feet or measures

hep·tane (hep′tān′) *n.* ⟦HEPT(A)- + -ANE⟧ an alkane, C_7H_{16}, existing in several isomeric forms: the normal isomer is used in standard mixtures to test octane ratings

Hep·tar·chy (hep′tär′kē), **the** ⟦HEPT(A)- + -ARCHY⟧ *a term used by historians for:* **1** the supposed confederacy of seven Anglo-Saxon kingdoms **2** the kingdoms of Anglo-Saxon England before the 9th cent. A.D.

hep·ta·stich (hep′tə stik′) *n.* ⟦HEPTA- + STICH⟧ a poem or stanza of seven lines

Hep·ta·teuch (hep′tə to͞ok′, -tyo͞ok′) *n.* ⟦LL(Ec) *Heptateuchos* < Gr(Ec) < *hepta*, SEVEN + *teuchos*, a tool, book: see PENTATEUCH⟧ the first seven books of the Bible

hep·tath·lete (hep tath′lēt′) *n.* ⟦blend of fol. & ATHLETE⟧ a participant in a heptathlon

hep·tath·lon (hep tath′län, -lən) *n.* ⟦HEPT(A)- + (DEC)ATHLON⟧ an athletic contest for women in which each contestant takes part in seven events (100-meter hurdles, shot put, high jump, 200-meter dash, long jump, javelin throw, and 800-meter run)

hep·tose (hep′tōs′) *n.* ⟦HEPT(A)- + -OSE[2]⟧ any of several isomeric monosaccharides, $C_7H_{14}O_7$

Hep·worth (hep′wurth), Dame **Barbara** 1903-75; Brit. sculptor

her[1] (hur) *pron.* ⟦ME *hir, her, hire* < OE *hire*, dat. sing. of *heo*, she, fem. of *he*, HE[1]; it replaced the orig. OE acc., *hie*, in ME⟧ *objective form of* SHE [help *her*] —*possessive pronominal adj.* of, belonging to, made by, or done by her: also used before some formal titles [*Her* Majesty]

USAGE—*her* is also used as a predicate complement with a linking verb [it's *her*] and in certain comparative constructions [he runs faster than *her*, but he's not as agile as *her*], although both usages are objected to by some

her[2] *abbrev.* heraldry

He·ra (hir′ə, her′ə, hē′rə) *n.* ⟦L < Gr *Hēra, Hērē*, lit., protectress, akin to *hērōs*, HERO⟧ *Gr. Myth.* the sister and wife of Zeus, queen of the gods, and goddess of women and marriage: identified with the Roman Juno

Her·a·cli·tus (her′ə klīt′əs) fl. *c.* 500 B.C.; Gr. philosopher

Her·a·cli·us (her′ə klī′əs, hi rak′lē əs) A.D. 575?-641; Byzantine emperor (610-641)

Her·a·kles or **Her·a·cles** (her′ə klēz′) *n. var. of* HERCULES

He·ra·kli·on or **He·ra·klei·on** (hi rak′lē ən) *var. of* IRAKLION

her·ald (her′əld) *n.* ⟦ME < OFr *heralt* < Gmc **hariwald*, army chief: see HAROLD[1]⟧ **1** [Historical] any of various officials who made proclamations, carried state messages to other sovereigns, took charge of tournaments, arranged ceremonies, etc. **2** in England, an official in charge of genealogies, coats of arms, etc.: see HERALDS' COLLEGE **3** a person who proclaims or announces significant news, etc.: often used in newspaper names **4** a person or thing that comes before to announce, or give an indication of, what follows; forerunner; harbinger —*vt.* **1** to introduce, announce, foretell, etc. **2** to publicize

he·ral·dic (hə ral′dik) *adj.* of heraldry or heralds

her·ald·ry (her′əl drē) *n., pl.* **-ries** ⟦< HERALD⟧ **1** the art or science having to do with coats of arms **2** the function of a HERALD (sense 2) **3** *a)* a coat of arms or other heraldic device *b)* coats of arms, collectively; armorial bearings **4** heraldic ceremony or pomp

Heralds' College in England, a royal corporation, appointed in 1484, in charge of granting and recording armorial emblems and coats of arms, keeping records of genealogies, etc.

Her·at (he rät′) city in NW Afghanistan

herb (urb, hurb) *n.* ⟦ME *erbe, herbe* < OFr < L *herba*, grass, herbage, herb < IE **gherdha* < base **gher-* > GRASS⟧ **1** any seed plant whose stem withers away to the ground after each season's growth, as distinguished from a tree or shrub whose woody stem lives from year to year **2** any plant used as a medicine, seasoning, or flavoring: mint, thyme, basil, and sage are herbs **3** vegetative growth; grass **4** [Slang] MARIJUANA

her·ba·ceous (hər bā′shəs, ər-) *adj.* ⟦L *herbaceus*⟧ **1** of, having the nature of, an herb or herbs, as distinguished from woody plants **2** like a green leaf in texture, color, shape, etc.

herb·age (ur′bij, hur′-) *n.* ⟦Fr: see -AGE⟧ **1** herbs collectively, esp. those used as pasturage; grass **2** the green foliage and juicy stems of herbs **3** *Law* the right of pasturing cattle on another's land

herb·al (hur′bəl, ur′-) *adj.* ⟦ML *herbalis*⟧ of herbs —*n.* a book about herbs or plants, esp. one concerned with their medicinal properties

herb·al·ist (hur′bəl ist, ur′-) *n.* **1** an author of a herbal **2** a person who grows, collects, or deals in herbs, esp. medicinal herbs

herbal tea **1** an infusion of one or more herbs, spices, fruits, or flowers, drunk usually as a hot beverage **2** the particular herbs and other ingredients that are steeped in boiling water to make such a beverage

her·bar·i·um (hər ber′ē əm, ər-) *n., pl.* **-i·ums** or **-i·a** (-ə) ⟦LL < L *herba*, HERB⟧ **1** a collection of dried plants classified, mounted, and used for botanical study **2** a room, building, case, etc. for keeping such a collection

Her·bart (her′bärt′; *E* hur′bärt′), **Jo·hann Frie·drich** (yō′hän′ frē′driH) 1776-1841; Ger. philosopher & educator

herbed (urbd, hurbd) *adj.* containing or flavored with herbs [*herbed* butter, *herbed* potatoes]

Her·bert[1] (hur′bərt) *n.* ⟦OE *Herebeorht*, lit., bright army < *here* (see HAROLD[1]) + *beorht*, BRIGHT⟧ a masculine name: dim. *Herb, Bert*

Her·bert[2] (hur′bərt) **1 George** 1593-1633; Eng. poet & clergyman **2 Victor** 1859-1924; U.S. composer & conductor, born in Ireland

her·bi·cide (hur′bə sīd′, ur′-) *n.* ⟦E or ModL *herbi-* (< L *herba*, HERB) + -CIDE⟧ any chemical substance used to kill plants, esp. weeds, or to check their growth —**her′bi·ci′dal** *adj.*

her·bi·vore (hur′bə vôr′) *n.* ⟦Fr⟧ a herbivorous animal

her·biv·o·rous (hər biv′ər əs) *adj.* ⟦< L *herba*, herb + -VOROUS⟧ feeding chiefly on plants, often, specif., on grass or leaves

herb Paris ⟦ML *herba paris*, lit. prob., herb of a pair (< L *herba*, HERB + *paris*, gen. of *par*, a pair: see PAR[1], in allusion to even number of flower parts): assoc. with PARIS[2] by folk etym.⟧ a woodland plant (*Paris quadrifolia*) of the lily family, with yellowish-green flowers, similar to the trillium, but having its leaves and flower parts in fours instead of threes

herb Robert ⟦ME *herbe robert* < ML *herba Roberti*: so named ? after *Robert*, Duke of Normandy or ? after St. *Robert*, founder of the Carthusians⟧ a weedy geranium (*Geranium robertianum*) with strong-scented compound leaves and purple to pink flowers

herb tea HERBAL TEA

herb·y (ʉr′bē, hʉr′-) *adj.* **1** of or like an herb or herbs; herbaceous **2** tasting or smelling of herbs [*herby* sausage]

Her·ce·go·vi·na (hert′sə gō vē′nə) *alt. sp. of* HERZEGOVINA

Her·cu·la·ne·um (hʉr′kyə lā′nē əm) ancient city in S Italy, at the foot of Mt. Vesuvius: buried, together with Pompeii, in a volcanic eruption (A.D. 79)

Her·cu·le·an (hər kyōō′lē ən; hʉr′kyōō lē′ən, hʉr′kyōō lē′-) *adj.* **1** of Hercules **2** [*usually* **h-**] *a)* having the great size, strength, or courage of Hercules; very powerful or courageous *b)* calling for great strength, size, or courage; very difficult to do [a *herculean* task]

Her·cu·les (hʉr′kyōō lēz′) *n.* ⟦L < Gr *Hērakleēs* < *Hēra*, HERA + *kleos*, glory⟧ **1** *Class. Myth.* the son of Zeus and Alcmene, renowned for his strength and courage, esp. as shown in his performance of twelve labors imposed on him **2** a large N constellation between Ophiuchus and Draco **3** [**h-**] any very large, strong man

☆**Her·cu·les'-club** (-klub′) *n.* ⟦in allusion to the type of club borne by Hercules, as traditionally depicted in art⟧ **1** a small, very spiny tree (*Aralia spinosa*) of the ginseng family, with clusters of small, white flowers, found in the E U.S.; devil's walking stick **2** a spiny tree or shrub (*Zanthoxylum clava-herculis*) of the rue family, native to the S U.S.; prickly ash

herd[1] (hʉrd) *n.* ⟦ME < OE *heord*, akin to Ger *herde* < IE base **kerdho-*, a row, group > Sans *śárdha*, a herd, troop⟧ **1** a number of cattle, sheep, or other animals feeding, living, or being driven together **2** *a)* any large group suggestive of this; crowd; company *b)* the common people; masses (a contemptuous term) — ***vt., vi.*** to gather together or move as a herd, group, crowd, etc. —**SYN.** GROUP

herd[2] (hʉrd) *n.* ⟦ME *herde* < OE *hierde* (akin to Ger *hirt*) < same base as prec.⟧ a herdsman: now chiefly in comb. [*cowherd, shepherd*] — ***vt., vi.*** to tend or drive as a herdsman —☆**ride herd on 1** to control a moving herd of (cattle) from horseback **2** [Informal] to keep a close or oppressive watch or control over —**herd′er** *n.*

Her·der (her′dər), **Jo·hann Gott·fried von** (yō′hän gôt′frēt fən) 1744-1803; Ger. philosopher & man of letters

☆**her·dic** (hʉr′dik) *n.* ⟦after P. *Herdic* (1824-88), U.S. inventor⟧ a low-hung public carriage of the late 19th-cent., with a back entrance and seats along the sides

☆**herd's-grass** (hʉrdz′gras′) *n.* **1** REDTOP **2** TIMOTHY

herds·man (hʉrdz′mən) *n., pl.* **-men** (-mən) a person who keeps or tends a herd —**the Herdsman** the constellation Boötes

here (hir; *often* hēr) *adv.* ⟦ME < OE *her*; akin to Ger *hier* < IE base **ko-*, **ke-*, this one > HE[1], HER[1], L *cis*, OIr *ce*⟧ **1** at or in this place: often used as an intensifier [John *here* is a talented player]: in dialectal or nonstandard use, often placed between a demonstrative pronoun and the noun it modifies [this *here* man] **2** toward, to, or into this place; hither [come *here*] **3** at this point in an action, speech, discussion, etc.; now [*here* the judge interrupted] **4** on earth; in earthly life —***interj.*** **1** used to call attention, answer a roll call, etc. **2** used to express indignation, remonstrance, etc., esp. when repeated —*n.* this place or point —**here and there** in, at, or to various places or points —**here goes!** [Informal] an exclamation used when the speaker is about to do something new, daring, disagreeable, etc. —**here's to** here's a toast to; I wish success (or joy, etc.) to —**here you are (or go)** [Informal] a phrase used to indicate or express a mild instruction to accept or take what is being offered, as when something is being handed or presented to someone —**here we go!** [Informal] an exclamation used variously, as *a)* to indicate the start of some action or endeavor *b)* to cheer on or encourage someone *c)* to express exasperation at a familiar situation or response: (also **here we go again!**) —**neither here nor there** beside the point; irrelevant —**the here and now** this place and this time; the present

here·a·bout (hir′ə bout′, hir′ə bout′) *adv.* in this general vicinity; about or near here: also **here′a·bouts′**

here·af·ter (hir af′tər) *adv.* **1** after this; from now on; in the future **2** following this: used esp. in a piece of writing, a book, etc. **3** in the state or life after death —*n.* **1** the future **2** the state or life after death

here·at (hir at′) *adv.* **1** at this time; when this occurred **2** for this reason

here·by (hir′bī′, hir bī′) *adv.* **1** by or through this; by this means **2** *obs. var. of* HEREABOUT

her·e·dit·a·ment (her′ə dit′ə mənt) *n.* ⟦ML *hereditamentum*⟧ any property that can be inherited

he·red·i·tar·i·an (hə red′i ter′ē ən) *n.* a person who accepts the theory that heredity is of overriding importance in determining individual characteristics —**he·red′i·tar′i·an·ism′** *n.*

he·red·i·tar·y (hə red′i ter′ē) *adj.* ⟦L *hereditarius* < *hereditas*: see fol.⟧ **1** *a)* of, or passed down by, inheritance from an ancestor to a legal heir; ancestral *b)* having title, right, etc. by inheritance **2** of, or passed down by, heredity; designating or of a characteristic transmitted genetically from generation to generation **3** being such because of attitudes, beliefs, etc. passed down through generations [*hereditary* allies] —**SYN.** INNATE —**he·red′i·tar′i·ly** *adv.* —**he·red′i·tar′i·ness** *n.*

he·red·i·ty (hə red′i tē) *n.* ⟦Fr *hérédité* < L *hereditas*, heirship < *heres*, heir < IE base **ĝhē-*, to be empty, leave behind > GO[1], Gr *chēres*, bereft⟧ **1** *a)* the transmission of characteristics from parent to offspring by means of genes in the chromosomes *b)* the tendency of offspring to resemble parents or ancestors through such transmission **2** all the characteristics inherited genetically by an individual

Her·e·ford[1] (hʉr′fərd) *n.* any of a breed of medium-sized beef cattle developed in Hereford, having a reddish body with a white face and belly

Her·e·ford[2] (her′ə fərd) **1** city in Hereford and Worcester, WC England, on the Wye **2** former county of England (see HEREFORD AND WORCESTER): also **Herefordshire** (-shir′)

Hereford and Worcester county in WC England, comprising the former counties of Hereford and Worcester: 1,515 sq mi (3,924 sq km)

here·in (hir in′, hir′in′) *adv.* **1** in here; in or into this place **2** in this writing **3** in this matter, detail, etc.

here·in·a·bove (hir′in ə buv′) *adv.* in the preceding part (of this document, speech, etc.): also **here′in·be·fore′** (-bə fôr′)

here·in·af·ter (-af′tər) *adv.* in the following part (of this document, speech, etc.): also **here′in·be·low′** (-bə lō′)

here·in·to (hir in′tōō, hir′in tōō′) *adv.* **1** into this place **2** into this matter, condition, etc.

here·of (hir uv′) *adv.* **1** of this **2** concerning this **3** [Obs.] from this; hence

here·on (hir′än′, hir′än) *adv.* HEREUPON

here's (hirz) *contraction* here is

he·re·si·arch (hə rez′ē ärk′, -rē′zē-) *n.* ⟦LL(Ec) *haeresiarcha* < Gr *hairesiarchēs*, leader of a school < *hairesis* (see fol.) + *-archēs*, leader < *archein*, to begin, lead⟧ the founder or head of a heresy or heretical sect

her·e·sy (her′ə sē) *n., pl.* **-sies** ⟦ME *heresie* < OFr < L *haeresis*, school of thought, sect, in LL(Ec), heresy < Gr *hairesis*, a taking, selection, school, sect, in LGr(Ec), heresy < *hairein*, to take⟧ **1** *a)* a religious belief opposed to the orthodox doctrines of a church; esp., such a belief specifically denounced by the church *b)* the rejection of a belief that is a part of church dogma **2** any opinion (in philosophy, politics, etc.) opposed to official or established views or doctrines **3** the holding of any such belief or opinion

her·e·tic (her′ə tik) *n.* ⟦ME *heretike* < MFr *hérétique* < LL(Ec) *haereticus*, of heresy, heretic < Gr *hairetikos*, able to choose, in LGr(Ec), heretical < *hairein*, to take, choose⟧ a person who professes a heresy; esp., a church member who holds beliefs opposed to church dogma —*adj.* HERETICAL

he·ret·i·cal (hə ret′i kəl) *adj.* ⟦ML *haereticalis*⟧ **1** of heresy or heretics **2** containing, characterized by, or having the nature of heresy —**he·ret′i·cal·ly** *adv.*

here·to (hir tōō′) *adv.* ⟦ME *her to*⟧ to this (document, matter, etc.) [attached *hereto*]: also **here·un·to** (hir un′tōō′, hir′un tōō′)

here·to·fore (hir′tōō fôr′, hir′tōō fôr′; -tə-) *adv.* ⟦ME *her* (see HERE) + *toforen*, before < OE *toforan*⟧ up until now; until the present; before this

here·un·der (hir un′dər, hir′un′-) *adv.* **1** under or below this (in a document, etc.) **2** under the terms stated here

here·up·on (hir′ə pän′, hir′ə pän′) *adv.* **1** immediately following this; at once **2** upon this; concerning this subject, etc.

here·with (hir with′, hir′with′) *adv.* **1** along with this **2** by this method or means

her·i·ot (her′ē ət) *n.* ⟦ME *heriet* < OE *heregeatwe*, lit., army equipment < *here*, army (see HAROLD[1]) + *geatwe*, earlier *ge-tawe*, equipment, arms < *tawian*, to prepare: see TAW[1]⟧ *Feudal Law* in England, a payment in chattels or money (orig., a restoration of arms, equipment, etc.) made to the lord from the possessions of a tenant who had died

her·it·a·ble (her′it ə bəl) *adj.* ⟦ME *heretable* < OFr *héritable*: see fol.⟧ **1** that can be inherited **2** that can inherit —**her′it·a·bil′i·ty** *n.*

her·it·age (her′ə tij) *n.* ⟦ME < OFr < *heriter* < LL(Ec) *hereditare*, to inherit < L *hereditas*: see HEREDITY⟧ **1** property that is or can be inherited **2** *a)* something handed down from one's ancestors or the past, as a characteristic, a culture, tradition, etc. *b)* the rights, burdens, or status resulting from being born in a certain time or place; birthright

SYN.—**heritage**, the most general of these words, applies either to property passed on to an heir, or to a tradition, culture, etc. passed on to a later generation; **inheritance** applies to property, a characteristic, etc. passed on to an heir; **patrimony** strictly refers to an estate inherited from one's father, but it is also used of anything passed on from an ancestor

her·i·tor (her′ə tər) *n.* ⟦ME *heriter* < OFr *heritier* < ML *hereditarius* (for L *heres*, heir) < L, HEREDITARY⟧ an inheritor, or heir

☆**herk·y-jerk·y** (hʉr′kē jʉr′kē) *adj.* ⟦redupl. of JERKY[1]⟧ [Informal] irregular, uneven, or spasmodic; not smooth or graceful

herl (hʉrl) *n.* ⟦ME *herle*: see HARL⟧ an artificial fishing fly trimmed with the barb or barbs of a feather

herm (hʉrm) *n.* ⟦< L *herma* < Gr *Hermēs*, HERMES⟧ a square pillar of stone topped by a bust or head, originally of Hermes: such pillars were used as milestones, signposts, etc. in ancient Greece: also **her·ma** (hʉr′mə), *pl.* **-mae** (-mē) or **-mai′** (-mī′)

Her·man (hʉr′mən) *n.* ⟦Ger *Hermann* < OHG *Hariman* < *heri*, army (see HAROLD[1]) + *man*, MAN⟧ a masculine name: equiv. Fr. *Armand*, Ger. *Hermann*, It. *Ermanno*

her·maph·ro·dite (hər maf′rə dīt′) *n.* ⟦altered (modeled on L or Gr) < ME *hermofrodite* < L *hermaphroditus* < Gr *hermaphroditos*, < *Hermaphroditos*, HERMAPHRODITUS⟧ **1** any of various animals, as the earthworm, possessing both male and female sexual organs **2** an individual possessing secondary sex characteristics and gonadal tissue of both the male and the female of its species **3** a plant having stamens and pistils in the same flower **4** HERMAPHRODITE BRIG —*adj.* HERMAPHRODITIC —**her·maph′ro·dit′ism′** *n.*, **her·maph′ro·dism′** (-diz′əm)

hermaphrodite brig a two-masted ship with a square-rigged foremast and a fore-and-aft-rigged mainmast

her·maph·ro·dit·ic (hər maf′rə dit′ik) ***adj.*** of, or having the nature of, a hermaphrodite: also **her·maph′ro·dit′i·cal** —**her·maph′ro·dit′i·cal·ly** ***adv.***

Her·maph·ro·di·tus (hər maf′rə dīt′əs) ***n.*** ⟦L < Gr *Hermaphroditos*⟧ *Gr. Myth.* the son of Hermes and Aphrodite: while bathing, he becomes united in a single body with a nymph

her·me·neu·tic (hur′mə no͞ot′ik, -nyo͞ot′-) ***adj.*** ⟦Gr *hermēneutikos* < *hermēneuein,* to interpret < *hermēneus,* translator⟧ of hermeneutics; interpretive: also **her′me·neu′ti·cal**

her·me·neu·tics (-iks) ***n.*** ⟦< prec.⟧ the art or science of interpretation, as of literary or religious texts

Her·mes (hur′mēz′) ***n.*** ⟦L < Gr *Hermēs*⟧ *Gr. Myth.* the god who serves as herald and messenger of the other gods, generally pictured with winged shoes and hat, carrying a caduceus: he is also the god of science, commerce, eloquence, and cunning, and guide of departed souls to Hades: identified with the Roman Mercury

Hermes Tris·me·gis·tus (tris′mə jis′təs) ⟦Gr, Thoth < *Hermēs trismegistos,* lit., Hermes the thrice greatest: the Greeks identified Thoth with Hermes⟧ legendary ancient Egyptian author of a body of esoteric writings of the 1st-3rd cent. A.D. on cosmogony, the soul, magic, etc.

her·met·ic (hər met′ik) ***adj.*** ⟦ModL *hermeticus* < L *Hermes* < Gr *Hermēs (trismegistos)*⟧ **1** [*usually* **H-**] of or derived from Hermes Trismegistus and his lore **2** [*sometimes* **H-**] *a)* magical; alchemic *b)* hard to understand; obscure **3** ⟦from use in alchemy⟧ *a)* completely sealed by fusion, soldering, etc. so as to keep air or gas from getting in or out; airtight *b)* protected from, cut off from, or impervious to outside influences: also **her·met′i·cal** —**her·met′i·cal·ly** ***adv.*** —**her·met′i·cism′** (-met′ə siz′əm) ***n.***

her·me·tism (hur′mə tiz′əm) ***n.*** the doctrines and beliefs expressed in hermetic writings

Her·mi·o·ne (hər mī′ə nē) ***n.*** *Gr. Legend* the daughter of Menelaus and Helen of Troy

her·mit (hur′mit) ***n.*** ⟦ME *hermite* < OFr < LL(Ec) *eremita* < LGr *erēmitēs,* a hermit < Gr, of the desert < *erēmos,* desolate < IE base **er-,* loose, distant, to separate > Sans **árma-* (pl.), fragments, ruins⟧ **1** a person who lives alone in a lonely or secluded spot, often from religious motives; recluse ☆**2** a spiced cookie made with nuts and raisins —**her·mit′ic** ***adj.,*** **her·mit′i·cal**

her·mit·age (hur′mə tij) ***n.*** ⟦ME < OFr: see -AGE⟧ **1** the place where a hermit lives **2** a place where a person can live away from other people; secluded retreat

Her·mi·tage[1] (er′mi täzh′) ***n.*** ⟦after *Tain-l'Hermitage,* town in SE France⟧ a full-bodied red or white wine from vineyards on the Rhone near Valence, France

Her·mi·tage[2] (er′mi täzh′, hur′mə tij) ***n.*** art museum in St. Petersburg, Russia: originally a palace

hermit crab any of various crabs (esp. family Paguridae) that have asymmetrical, soft abdomens and that live in the empty shells of certain mollusks, as snails

☆**hermit thrush** a North American thrush (*Catharus guttatus*) with a brown body, spotted breast, and reddish-brown tail

☆**hermit warbler** a common wood warbler (*Dendroica occidentalis*) of W North America, with a yellow-and-black head, a gray back, and white underparts

Her·mon (hur′mən), **Mount** mountain on the Syria-Lebanon border, in the Anti-Lebanon mountains: the southern & western slopes are under Israeli administration: 9,232 ft (2,814 m)

Her·mo·sil·lo (er′mô sē′yô) city in NW Mexico: capital of Sonora

hern (hurn) ***n.*** *archaic or dial. var. of* HERON

her·ni·a (hur′nē ə) ***n.,*** *pl.* **-ni·as** or **-ni·ae′** (-ē′, -ī′) ⟦L: for IE base see YARN⟧ the protrusion of all or part of an organ through a tear in the wall of the surrounding structure; esp., the protrusion of part of the intestine through the abdominal muscles; rupture —**her′ni·al** ***adj.***

her·ni·ate (hur′nē āt′) ***vi.*** **-at′ed, -at′ing** to protrude so as to form a hernia —**her′ni·a′tion** ***n.***

he·ro (hir′ō, hē′rō) ***n.,*** *pl.* **-roes** ⟦L *heros* < Gr *hērōs* < IE base **ser-,* to watch over, protect > Avestan *haraiti,* (he) protects, Lith *sárgas,* watchman⟧ **1** *Myth., Legend* a man of great strength and courage, favored by the gods and in part descended from them, often regarded as a demigod and worshiped after his death **2** any person, esp. a man, admired for courage, nobility, or exploits, esp. in war **3** any person, esp. a man, admired for qualities or achievements and regarded as an ideal or model **4** the central male character in a novel, play, poem, etc., with whom the reader or audience is supposed to sympathize; protagonist **5** the central figure in any important event or period, honored for outstanding qualities ☆**6** HERO SANDWICH

He·ro[1] (hir′ō, hē′rō′) ***n.*** ⟦L < Gr *Hērō*⟧ *Gr. Legend* a priestess of Aphrodite at Sestos: her lover, Leander, swims the Hellespont from Abydos every night to be with her; when he drowns in a storm, Hero throws herself into the sea

He·ro[2] (hir′ō, hē′rō) HERON

Her·od (her′əd) ⟦L *Herodes* < Gr *Hērōdēs*⟧ 73?-4 B.C.; Idumaean king of Judea (37-4): called *Herod the Great*

Herod Agrippa I 10? B.C.-A.D. 44; king of Judea (37-44); grandson of Herod (the Great)

Herod An·ti·pas (an′ti pas′, -pəs) died A.D. 40?; tetrarch of Galilee (*c.* 4 B.C.-A.D. 39): son of Herod (the Great)

He·ro·di·as (hə rō′dē əs) ***n.*** *Bible* the second wife of Herod Antipas & mother of Salome: Mark 6:17-28

He·rod·o·tus (hə räd′ə təs) 484?-425? B.C.; Gr. historian: called the *Father of History*

he·ro·ic (hi rō′ik) ***adj.*** ⟦L *heroicus* < Gr *heroikos,* of a hero < *hērōs,* HERO⟧ **1** of or characterized by men of godlike strength and courage [*the heroic* age of Greece and Rome] **2** like or characteristic of a hero or his deeds; strong, brave, noble, powerful, etc. [*heroic* conduct, a *heroic* effort] **3** of or about a hero and his deeds; epic [a *heroic* poem] **4** exalted; eloquent; high-flown [*heroic* words] **5** daring and risky, but used as a last resort [*heroic* measures] **6** *Art* larger than life-size but less than colossal [a *heroic* statue] Also **he·ro′i·cal** —***n.*** **1** [*usually pl.*] HEROIC VERSE **2** [*pl.*] heroic behavior or deeds —**he·ro′i·cal·ly** ***adv.***

heroic couplet a rhyming pair of iambic-pentameter lines, first used extensively in English by Chaucer and later developed as a syntactically complete unit, esp. by Dryden and Pope (Ex.: "In every work regard the writer's end, | Since none can compass more than they intend")

heroic verse **1** a verse form in which epic poetry is traditionally written, as dactylic hexameter in Greek or Latin, the alexandrine in French, and iambic pentameter in English **2** poetry composed in such a form

her·o·in (her′ō in) ***n.*** ⟦Ger, orig., trademark: coined (1898) by H. Dreser, Ger chemist < Gr *hērōs,* HERO + Ger *-in,* -INE[3]: ? because of euphoric effect⟧ a white, crystalline powder, an acetyl derivative of morphine, $C_{17}H_{17}NO(C_2H_3O_2)_2$: it is a very powerful, habit-forming narcotic whose manufacture and import are prohibited in the U.S.

her·o·ine (her′ō in) ***n.*** ⟦L *heroina* < Gr *hērōinē,* fem. of *hērōs,* HERO⟧ **1** a girl or woman of outstanding courage, nobility, etc., or of heroic achievements **2** the central female character in a novel, play, etc., with whom the reader or audience is supposed to sympathize

her·o·ism (her′ō iz′əm) ***n.*** ⟦Fr *héroïsme*⟧ the qualities and actions of a hero or heroine; bravery, nobility, valor, etc.

he·ro·ize (hir′ō īz′, her′-) ***vt.*** **-ized′, -iz′ing** ⟦HERO + -IZE⟧ to make a hero of; treat as a hero

her·on (her′ən) ***n.,*** *pl.* **-ons** or **-on** ⟦ME *heroun* < OFr *hairon* < Frank **heigro* (akin to OHG *heigir,* ON *hegri*) < IE **(s)ker-,* var. of base **ker-,* echoic of hoarse cry > SCREAM⟧ any of various wading birds (esp. subfamily Ardeinae) with a long neck, long legs, and a long, tapered bill, living along marshes and river banks

great blue heron

Her·on (hir′än) fl. 3d cent. A.D.; Gr. mathematician & inventor: also called **Heron of Alexandria**

her·on·ry (her′ən rē) ***n.,*** *pl.* **-ries** a place where many herons gather to breed

her·ons·bill (her′ənz bil′) ***n.*** any of a genus (*Erodium*) of plants of the geranium family, with fine leaves and yellow, white, or reddish flowers

☆**hero sandwich** a sandwich made with a long roll sliced horizontally and filled with various sliced meats, cheeses, and vegetables

hero worship great or excessive reverence or admiration for heroes or other persons —**he′ro-wor′ship** ***vt.*** —**he′ro-wor′ship·er** ***n.***

her·pes (hur′pēz′) ***n.*** ⟦L < Gr *herpēs,* lit., a creeping, herpes < *herpein,* to creep: see SERPENT⟧ any of several acute inflammatory diseases, esp. herpes simplex, caused by various herpesviruses and characterized by the eruption of small blisters on the skin and mucous membranes —**her·pet·ic** (hər pet′ik) ***adj.***

herpes sim·plex (sim′pleks′) a recurrent, incurable form of herpes usually affecting the mouth, lips, or face (type one) or the genitals (type two): the genital type is a sexually transmitted disease

her·pes·vi·rus (hur′pēz vī′rəs) ***n.*** ⟦HERPES + VIRUS⟧ any of a family (Herpesviridae) of DNA viruses variously affecting certain vertebrates and invertebrates, esp. the viruses causing herpes simplex, herpes zoster, and chickenpox in human beings

herpes zos·ter (zäs′tər) ⟦L < *herpes* + *zoster,* shingles < Gr *zōstēr,* a girdle, akin to *zōnē*: see ZONE⟧ a form of herpes that infects sensory nerves, causing pain and an eruption of blisters along the course of the affected nerve; shingles

her·pe·tol·o·gy (hur′pə täl′ə jē) ***n.*** ⟦< Gr *herpeton,* reptile (< *herpein,* to creep: see SERPENT)⟧ the branch of zoology having to do with the study of reptiles and amphibians —**her′pe·to·log′ic** (-tō läj′ik) ***adj.,*** **her′pe·to·log′i·cal** —**her′pe·tol′o·gist** ***n.***

Herr (her) ***n.,*** *pl.* **Herr·en** (her′ən) ⟦Ger; orig. compar. of *hehr,* noble, venerable, akin to OE *har,* HOAR⟧ **1** Mr.; Sir: a German title of respect **2** a man; gentleman

Her·re·ra (e re′rä), **Fran·cis·co de** (frän thēs′kô *the*) 1576?-1656?; Sp. painter: called *El Viejo* (the Elder)

Her·rick (her′ik), **Robert** 1591-1674; Eng. poet

her·ring (her′iŋ) ***n.,*** *pl.* **-rings** or **-ring** ⟦ME *hering* < OE *hæring,* akin to Ger *hering*⟧ any of various clupeid fishes; esp., a small, silvery food fish (*Clupea harengus*) of northern seas that is canned as a sardine

her·ring·bone (-bōn′) ***n.*** **1** the spine of a herring, having numerous thin, parallel bony extensions on each side similar to the barbs of a feather **2** a pattern with such a design or anything having such a pattern, as a kind of cross-stitch, a twill weave, or an arrangement of bricks **3** a method of climbing a slope on skis with the ski tips turned outward so that the tracks form a herringbone pattern —***adj.*** having the pattern of a herringbone — ***vi., vt.*** **-boned′, -bon′ing** **1** to stitch, weave, or arrange in a herringbone pattern **2** to climb (a slope) on skis, using the herringbone method

herring gull the common sea gull (*Larus argentatus*) of the Northern Hemisphere, having gray-and-white plumage and black-tipped wings

Herr·mann (hur′mən), **Bernard** 1911-75; U.S. composer of film scores

hers (hurz) ***pron.*** ⟦LME *hires, hers* < *hire, her(e)*, poss. adj. (see HER[1]) + *-s* after *his*⟧ that or those belonging to her: the possessive form of SHE, used without a following noun, often after *of* [that book is *hers*; *hers* are better; he is a friend of *hers*]

Her·schel (hur′shəl) **1** Sir **John Frederick William** 1792-1871; Eng. astronomer, chemist, & physicist: son of Sir William **2** Sir **William** (born *Friedrich Wilhelm Herschel*) 1738-1822; Eng. astronomer, born in Germany

her·self (hər self′) ***pron.*** ⟦ME *hire self* < OE *hire selfum*, dat. sing. of *hie self*: see HER[1] & SELF⟧ a form of SHE, used: *a)* as an intensifier [she said so *herself*] *b)* as a reflexive [she hurt *herself*] *c)* with the meaning "her real, true, or actual self" [she is not *herself* today] (in this construction *her* functions as an adjective and *self* as a noun, and they may be separated [*her* own sweet *self*]) *d)* [Irish] as a subject (used esp. of someone of some importance, often sarcastically) [*herself* will have her tea now]

Herst·mon·ceux (hurst′mən so͞o′) village in East Sussex, S England: site of the Royal Greenwich Observatory

her·sto·ry (hur′stə rē) ***n., pl.* -ries** ⟦HER[1] (*poss. pronominal adj.*) + (HI)STORY: intended to avoid the masc. implications of the pun "his story"/"history"⟧ history, esp. history from a feminist perspective: term used chiefly by feminists

Hert·ford·shire (här′fərd shir, härt′-) county in SE England: 633 sq mi (1,639 sq km): also called **Hert′ford** or **Herts** (härts)

Hertogenbosch *see* 'S HERTOGENBOSCH

hertz (hurts) ***n., pl.* hertz** ⟦after fol.⟧ the basic unit of frequency in the SI system, equal to one cycle per second: abbrev. *Hz*

Hertz (herts; *E* hurts), **Hein·rich Ru·dolf** (hīn′riH ro͞o′dôlf) 1857-94; Ger. physicist

Hertz·i·an waves (hert′sē ən, hurt′-) ⟦after prec., who discovered them⟧ [*sometimes* **h- w-**] radio waves or other electromagnetic radiation resulting from the oscillations of electricity in a conductor

Herz·berg (hurts′bərg), **Ger·hard** (ger′härt) 1904-99; Cdn. physicist, born in Germany

Her·ze·go·vi·na (hert′sə gō vē′nə, -gō′və nə) historical region & former duchy in the NW Balkan Peninsula: now part of Bosnia and Herzegovina —**Her′ze·go·vi′ni·an** ***adj., n.***

Herzl (her′ts′l), **The·o·dor** (tā′ô dôr′) 1860-1904; Austrian writer, born in Hungary: founder of Zionism

he's (hēz) *contraction* **1** he is **2** he has

he/she (hē′shē′, hē′ôr shē′, hē′slash′shē′) ***pron.*** he or she: used to avoid the masculine implications of the generic use of *he*

Hesh·van (khesh vän′; *E* hesh′vən) ***n.*** ⟦Heb⟧ the second month of the Jewish year: see the Jewish calendar in the Reference Supplement

He·si·od (hē′sē əd, hes′ē-) fl. 8th cent. B.C.; Gr. poet —**He′si·od′ic** (-äd′ik) ***adj.***

hes·i·tan·cy (hez′i tən sē) ***n.*** ⟦L *haesitantia*, a stammering < *haesitans*, prp. of *haesitare*⟧ hesitation or indecision; doubt: also **hes′i·tance** (-təns)

hes·i·tant (hez′i tənt) ***adj.*** ⟦L *haesitans*: see prec.⟧ hesitating or undecided; vacillating; doubtful —**SYN.** RELUCTANT —**hes′i·tant·ly** ***adv.***

hes·i·tate (hez′i tāt′) ***vi.*** **-tat′ed, -tat′ing** ⟦< L *haesitatus*, pp. of *haesitare*, to stick fast, hesitate, intens. of *haerere*, to stick, cleave < IE base **ghais-*, to be stuck, neglect > prob. Lith *gaištù*, to neglect⟧ **1** to stop because of indecision; pause or delay in acting, choosing, or deciding because of feeling unsure; waver **2** to pause; stop momentarily **3** to be reluctant; not be sure that one should: used with an infinitive [*hesitating* to ask] —**hes′i·tat′er** ***n.***, **hes′i·ta′tor** —**hes′i·tat′ing·ly** ***adv.***

hes·i·ta·tion (hez′i tā′shən) ***n.*** ⟦L *haesitatio*⟧ a hesitating or feeling hesitant; specif., *a)* uncertainty; indecision *b)* reluctance *c)* a pausing or delaying —**hes′i·ta′tive** ***adj.*** —**hes′i·ta′tive·ly** ***adv.***

Hes·per (hes′pər) ***n.*** *old poet. var. of* HESPERUS

Hes·pe·ri·a (hes pir′ē ə) ***n.*** ⟦L < Gr *Hesperia* < *hesperos*: see fol.⟧ the Western Land: the ancient Greek name for Italy and the Roman name for Spain

Hes·pe·ri·an (hes pir′ē ən) ***adj.*** ⟦< L *Hesperius* < Gr *Hesperios*, of Hesperus, western, evening < *Hesperos*, the evening star < IE **wesperos*, evening: see VESPER⟧ **1** of Hesperia **2** western; occidental **3** [Old Poet.] of the Hesperides

Hes·per·i·des (hes per′i dēz′) *Gr. Myth.* ***pl.n.***, *sing.* **Hes·per·id** (hes′pər id) the nymphs who guard the golden apples given as a wedding gift by Gaea to Hera —***n.*** the garden where the apples grow

hes·per·i·din (hes per′i din) ***n.*** ⟦< ModL *hesperidium*, orange (in allusion to the golden apples of prec.) + -IN[1]⟧ a crystalline glucoside, $C_{28}H_{34}O_{15}$, derived from flavanone and found in the peel of many citrus fruits

hes·per·id·i·um (hes′pər id′ē əm) ***n., pl.* -id′i·a** (-ə) ⟦see prec.⟧ the fruit of a citrus plant, as an orange or lemon

Hes·per·us (hes′pər əs) ***n.*** ⟦L < Gr *Hesperos*: see HESPERIAN⟧ [Literary] the evening star, esp. Venus

Hess (hes), **(Walther Richard) Rudolf** 1894-1987; Ger. Nazi leader

Hes·se[1] (hes′ə, hes), **Her·mann** (her′män) 1877-1962; Ger. novelist in Switzerland

Hesse[2] (hes, hes′ə) **1** state of central Germany: 8,152 sq mi (21,114 sq km); cap. Wiesbaden **2** former region in WC Germany, embracing various political units historically: Ger. name **Hes·sen** (hes′ən)

Hes·sian (hesh′ən) ***adj.*** of Hesse or its people —***n.*** **1** a person born or living in Hesse **2** any of the Hessian mercenaries who fought for the British in the Revolutionary War **3** [**h-**] a coarse cloth used for bags

Hessian boots knee-high, tasseled boots, introduced into England by Hessian troops in the 19th cent.

☆**Hessian fly** a small gall midge (*Mayetiola destructor*) whose larvae destroy wheat crops

hess·ite (hes′īt′) ***n.*** ⟦after G. H. *Hess* (1802-50), Swiss chemist + -ITE[1]⟧ a rare, gray, sectile mineral, Ag_2Te; silver telluride

hes·so·nite (hes′ə nīt′) ***n.*** *var. of* ESSONITE

hest (hest) ***n.*** ⟦ME, with unhistoric *-t* < OE *hæs*, command < base of *hatan*, to call, akin to Ger *heissen* < IE base **kēi-*, to set in motion > L *ciere*, Gr *kinein*⟧ [Archaic] behest; bidding; order

Hes·ter (hes′tər) ***n.*** a feminine name: see ESTHER

Hes·ti·a (hes′tē ə) ***n.*** ⟦Gr⟧ *Gr. Myth.* the goddess of the hearth: identified with the Roman Vesta

Hes·ton and I·sle·worth (hes′tən ənd ī′zəl wurth′) former municipal borough in Middlesex, England: now part of Hounslow

het (khet) ***n.*** the eighth letter of the Hebrew alphabet (ח)

he·tae·ra (hi tir′ə) ***n., pl.* -rae** (-ē) or **-ras** ⟦Gr *hetaira*, fem. of *hetairos*, companion⟧ in ancient Greece, a courtesan or concubine, usually an educated slave: also **he·tai′ra** (-tī′rə), *pl.* **-rai′** (-rī′)

he·tae·rism (hi tir′iz′əm) ***n.*** ⟦Gr *hetairismos* < *hetairizein*, to be a hetaera: see prec.⟧ **1** CONCUBINAGE **2** a system of communal marriage supposed to have been practiced among some early peoples Also **he·tai′rism′** (-tī′riz′əm)

het·er·o (het′ər ō′) ***adj., n., pl.* -os′** [Informal] *short for* HETEROSEXUAL

het·er·o- (het′ər ō′, -ə) ⟦Gr *hetero-*, other, different < *heteros*, the other (of two), earlier *hateros* < IE **sm-tero-* < base **sem-*, **sm-*, one, together > L *semper*, *simplus* + **-tero-*, expressing contrast, comparison⟧ *combining form* other, another, different [*heterosexual*]: also, before a vowel, **heter-**

het·er·o·cer·cal (het′ər ō sur′kəl) ***adj.*** ⟦< prec. + Gr *kerkos*, a tail + -AL⟧ designating, of, or having a tail fin in which the upper lobe is larger than the lower and contains the upturned end of the spinal column, as in certain fishes, esp. sharks

het·er·o·chro·mat·ic (het′ər ō krō mat′ik) ***adj.*** ⟦HETERO- + CHROMATIC⟧ **1** of, having, or consisting of different or contrasting colors; many-colored **2** of heterochromatin

het·er·o·chro·ma·tin (het′ər ō krō′mə tin) ***n.*** ⟦HETERO- + CHROMATIN⟧ *Biol.* the portion of the chromatin that stains densely and contains few or no genes: cf. EUCHROMATIN

het·er·o·chro·mo·some (het′ər ō krō′mə sōm′) ***n.*** SEX CHROMOSOME

het·er·o·clite (het′ər ə klīt′) ***adj.*** ⟦Fr *héteroclite* < LL *heteroclitus* < Gr *heteroklitos*, irregularly inflected < *hetero-* (see HETERO-) + *klinein*, to bend, INCLINE⟧ departing from the standard or norm; abnormal; anomalous: also **het′er·o·clit′ic** (-klit′ik) —***n.*** **1** *Gram.* a word, esp. a noun, inflected irregularly **2** [Rare] an anomaly

het·er·o·cy·clic (het′ər ō sī′klik, -sik′lik) ***adj.*** ⟦HETERO- + CYCLIC⟧ of or relating to certain cyclic compounds with a ring composed of atoms of carbon and some other element or elements

het·er·o·dox (het′ər ə däks′) ***adj.*** ⟦Gr(Ec) *heterodoxos* < Gr *hetero-*, HETERO- + *doxa*, opinion, akin to *dokein*, to think, seem: see DECENT⟧ departing from or opposed to the usual beliefs or established doctrines, esp. in religion; inclining toward heresy; unorthodox

het·er·o·dox·y (-däk′sē) ***n., pl.* -dox′ies** ⟦Gr *heterodoxia*⟧ **1** the quality or fact of being heterodox **2** a heterodox belief or doctrine

het·er·o·dyne (-dīn′) ***adj.*** ⟦HETERO- + DYNE⟧ designating or of the combination of two different radio frequencies to produce beats whose frequencies are equal to the sum or difference of the original frequencies —***vi.*** **-dyned′, -dyn′ing** to combine two different frequencies so as to produce beats

het·er·oe·cious (het′ər ē′shəs) ***adj.*** ⟦< HETERO- + Gr *oikia*, a house (see ECO-) + -OUS⟧ *Biol.* living as a parasite on first one species of host and then another —**het′er·oe′cism′** (-siz′əm) ***n.***

het·er·o·ga·mete (het′ər ō gam′ēt′, -gə mēt′) ***n.*** a gamete differentiated in size, structure, or activity from another with which it unites, typified by the relatively large ovum and the much smaller and more active sperm: opposed to ISOGAMETE —**het′er·o·ga·met′ic** (-gə met′ik) ***adj.***

het·er·og·a·mous (het′ər äg′ə məs) ***adj.*** **1** characterized by the uniting of heterogametes **2** characterized by reproduction in which sexual and asexual generations alternate **3** bearing flowers that are sexually different —**het′er·og′a·my** (-mē) ***n.***

het·er·o·ge·ne·ous (het′ər ə jē′nē əs) ***adj.*** ⟦ML *heterogeneus* < Gr *heterogenēs* < *hetero-*, other, HETERO- + *genos*, a race, kind: see GENUS⟧ **1** differing or opposite in structure, quality, etc.; dissimilar; incongruous; foreign **2** composed of unrelated or unlike elements or parts; varied; miscellaneous —**het·er·o·ge·ne·i·ty** (het′ər ō jə nē′ə tē) ***n., pl.* -ties** —**het′er·o·ge′ne·ous·ly** ***adv.*** —**het′er·o·ge′ne·ous·ness** ***n.***

het·er·o·gen·e·sis (het′ər ō jen′ə sis) ***n.*** ⟦HETERO- + -GENESIS⟧ ALTERNATION OF GENERATIONS —**het′er·o·ge·net′ic** (-jə net′ik) ***adj.***

het·er·og·e·nous (het′ər äj′ə nəs) ***adj.*** ⟦HETERO- + -GENOUS⟧ of different origin; not from the same source, individual, or species

het·er·og·o·ny (het′ər äg′ə nē) ***n.*** ⟦HETERO- + -GONY⟧ **1** ALTERNATION OF GENERATIONS **2** HETEROSTYLY **3** ALLOMETRY —**het′er·og′o·nous** (-nəs) ***adj.***

het·er·o·graft (het′ər ō graft′) ***n.*** XENOGRAFT

het·er·og·ra·phy (het′ər äg′rə fē) ***n.*** ⟦HETERO- + -GRAPHY⟧ **1** spelling that differs from current standard usage **2** spelling, as in modern English, in which a given letter or combination of letters does not always represent the same sound —**het·er·o·graph·ic** (het′ər ə graf′ik) *adj.*

het·er·og·y·nous (het′ər äj′ə nəs) *adj.* ⟦HETERO- + -GYNOUS⟧ having two kinds of females, reproductive and nonreproductive, as ants or bees do

het·er·ol·o·gous (het′ər äl′ə gəs) *adj.* ⟦< HETERO- + Gr *logos*, relation, word (see LOGIC) + -OUS⟧ **1** consisting of differing elements; not corresponding, as parts of different organisms or of the same organism that are unlike in structure or origin **2** *Med. a)* derived from a different species, as a graft *b)* not normal in structure, organization, etc. —**het′er·ol′o·gy** (-jē) *n.*

het·er·ol·y·sis (het′ər äl′ə sis) *n.* ⟦HETERO- + -LYSIS⟧ **1** the destruction of cells of one species by lysins or enzymes derived from cells of a different species **2** *Chem.* the breakdown of a compound into two particles with opposite charges —**het′er·o·lyt′ic** (-ō lit′ik) *adj.*

het·er·om·er·ous (het′ər äm′ər əs) *adj.* ⟦HETERO- + -MEROUS⟧ *Bot.* having a whorl or whorls with a different number of parts from that of the other whorls

het·er·o·me·tab·o·lism (het′ər ō mə tab′ə liz′əm) *n.* ⟦HETERO- + METABOLISM⟧ insect development in which the young hatch in a form very similar to the adult and then mature without a pupal stage —**het′er·o·met′a·bol′ic** (-met′ə bäl′ik) *adj.*, **het′er·o·me·tab′o·lous** (-mə tab′ə ləs)

het·er·o·mor·phic (het′ər ə môr′fik) *adj.* ⟦HETERO- + -MORPHIC⟧ **1** differing from the standard type or form **2** exhibiting different forms at various stages of development, as insects in the larval and pupal stages do Also **het′er·o·mor′phous** (-fəs) —**het′er·o·mor′phism′** *n.*

het·er·on·o·mous (het′ər än′ə məs) *adj.* ⟦< HETERO- + Gr *nomos*, law (see -NOMY) + -OUS⟧ **1** subject to another's laws or rule **2** subject to different laws of growth; differentiated or specialized, as some parts or organs are —**het′er·on′o·my** (-mē) *n.*

het·er·o·nym (het′ər ə nim′) *n.* ⟦back-form. < fol., modeled on SYNONYM⟧ a word with the same spelling as another or others, but with different meaning and pronunciation (Ex.: *tear*, a drop of water from the eye, and *tear*, to rip)

het·er·on·y·mous (het′ər än′ə məs) *adj.* ⟦Gr *heterōnymos* < *hetero*, HETERO- + *onyma*, NAME⟧ **1** of, or having the nature of, a heteronym **2** having different names: said as of a pair of correlatives [*"son" and "daughter" are heteronymous*] **3** designating or of the two crossed images of something seen when the eyes are focused at a point beyond it —**het′er·on′y·mous·ly** *adv.*

het·er·o·phile (het′ər ō fil′) *adj.* ⟦HETERO- + -PHILE⟧ designating or of a substance, as an antigen or antibody, that reacts with more than one substance: also **het′er·o·phil′** (-fil′)

het·er·oph·o·ny (het′ər äf′ə nē) *n.* ⟦HETERO- + -PHONY⟧ the playing of a passage of music with simultaneous variations in melody or rhythm by two or more performers

het·er·o·phyl·lous (het′ər ō fil′əs) *adj.* ⟦HETERO- + -PHYLLOUS⟧ growing leaves of different forms on the same stem or plant —**het′er·o·phyl′ly** *n.*

het·er·o·phyte (het′ər ō fīt′) *n.* ⟦HETERO- + -PHYTE⟧ a plant which obtains its food from other plants or animals, living or dead —**het′er·o·phyt′ic** (-fit′ik) *adj.*

het·er·o·plas·ty (het′ər ō plas′tē) *n.* ⟦HETERO- + -PLASTY⟧ plastic surgery in which tissue from one species is grafted onto another: see also HOMOPLASTIC (sense 2), AUTOPLASTY —**het′er·o′plas′tic** *adj.*

het·er·o·ploid (het′ər ō ploid′) *adj.* ⟦HETERO- + -PLOID⟧ having a chromosome number that is other than a simple multiple of the haploid number: see EUPLOID —**het′er·o·ploi′dy** *n.*

het·er·op·ter·ous (het′ər äp′tər əs) *adj.* HEMIPTEROUS

het·er·o·sex·ism (het′ər ō seks′iz′əm) *n.* ⟦< fol. + -ISM⟧ discrimination against, insensitivity toward, or prejudicial stereotyping of, homosexuals by heterosexuals —**het′er·o·sex′ist** *adj.*, *n.*

het·er·o·sex·u·al (het′ər ō sek′shōō əl) *adj.* of, characterized by, or having to do with HETEROSEXUALITY —*n.* a heterosexual individual —**het′er·o·sex′u·al·ly** *adv.*

het·er·o·sex·u·al·i·ty (-sek′shōō al′ə tē) *n.* **1** sexual desire for those of the opposite sex **2** SEXUAL ORIENTATION that is entirely or predominantly directed toward those of the opposite sex

het·er·o·sis (het′ər ō′sis) *n.* ⟦HETER(O)- + -OSIS⟧ a phenomenon resulting from hybridization, in which offspring display greater vigor, size, resistance, etc. than the parents —**het′er·ot′ic** (-ät′ik) *adj.*

het·er·o·sphere (het′ər ə sfir′) *n.* the upper of two divisions of the earth's atmosphere, above *c.* 70 km (43 mi), characterized by variation in its component gases: cf. HOMOSPHERE

het·er·os·po·rous (het′ər äs′pə rəs, het′ər ō spôr′əs) *adj. Bot.* producing more than one kind of spore; esp., producing both microspores and megaspores —**het′er·os′po·ry** *n.*

het·er·o·sty·ly (het′ər ō stī′lē) *n.* ⟦HETERO- + STYL(E) + -Y[4]⟧ the condition in which flowers on polymorphous plants have styles of different lengths, thereby encouraging cross-pollination —**het′er·o·sty′lous** *adj.*

het·er·o·thal·lic (het′ər ō thal′ik) *adj.* ⟦HETERO- + THALL(US) + -IC⟧ designating or possessing two forms of mycelia that interact as male and female in reproduction —**het′er·o·thal′lism′** *n.*

het·er·o·to·pi·a (het′ər ō tō′pē ə) *n.* ⟦ModL < HETERO- + Gr *topos*, place: see TOPIC⟧ the abnormal location of an organ, tissue, or body part: also **het′er·ot′o·py** (-ät′ə pē) —**het′er·o·top′ic** (-täp′ik) *adj.*

het·er·o·troph·ic (het′ər ə träf′ik, -trō′fik) *adj.* ⟦HETERO- + TROPHIC⟧ obtaining food from organic material only; unable to use inorganic matter to form proteins and carbohydrates: cf. AUTOTROPHIC

het·er·o·typ·ic (het′ər ō tip′ik) *adj.* ⟦HETERO- + TYPIC(AL)⟧ designating or of the first meiotic division of a germ cell: also **het′er·o·typ′i·cal**

het·er·o·zy·go·sis (het′ər ō zī gō′sis) *n.* ⟦HETERO- + ModL *zygosis* < Gr, a joining < *zygon*, YOKE⟧ **1** the condition of being a heterozygote **2** the production of a heterozygote by the union of unlike gametes

het·er·o·zy·gote (-zī′gōt′) *n.* ⟦HETERO- + ZYGOTE⟧ a plant or animal having two different alleles at a single locus on a chromosome, and hence not breeding true for the particular character involved; hybrid —**het′er·o·zy′gous** (-zī′gəs) *adj.*

heth (khet) *n. alt. sp. of* HET

het·man (het′mən) *n.*, *pl.* **-mans** ⟦Pol < Ger *hauptmann*, a captain, lit., head man < *haupt*, HEAD + *mann*, MAN⟧ a Cossack leader

☆**het up** (het) ⟦*het*, dial. pt. & pp. of HEAT⟧ [Slang] excited or angry

heu·land·ite (hyōō′lən dīt′) *n.* ⟦named (1822) after Henry *Heuland*, Eng mineralogist⟧ a semihard, lightweight, monoclinic zeolite, $(Na,Ca)_{4-6}Al_6(Al,Si)_4Si_{26}O_{72}\cdot 24H_2O$

heu·ris·tic (hyōō ris′tik) *adj.* ⟦< Ger *heuristisch* < Gr *heuriskein*, to invent, discover: see EUREKA⟧ helping to discover or learn; specif., designating a method of education or of computer programming in which the pupil or machine proceeds along empirical lines, using rules of thumb, to find solutions or answers —**heu·ris′ti·cal·ly** *adv.*

heu·ris·tics (-tiks) *pl.n.* heuristic methods or procedures —*n.* the art or practice of using heuristic methods or procedures

HEV *abbrev.* hybrid electric vehicle

hew (hyōō) *vt.* **hewed**, **hewed** or **hewn**, **hew′ing** ⟦ME *hewen* < OE *heawan*, akin to Ger *hauen*, OHG *houwan* < IE base **kāu-*, **keu-*, to hew, strike > HAY[1], L *caudex*, *codex* (see CODE), *cudere*, to beat⟧ **1** to chop or cut with an ax, knife, etc.; hack; gash **2** to make or shape by or as by cutting or chopping with an ax, etc.: often with *out* **3** to chop (a tree) with an ax so as to cause it to fall: usually with *down* —*vi.* **1** to make cutting or chopping blows with an ax, knife, etc. ☆**2** to conform or adhere (*to* a line, rule, principle, etc.) —**hew′er** *n.*

HEW *abbrev.* (Department of) Health, Education, and Welfare (1953-79)

hewn (hyōōn) *adj.* ⟦< pp. of HEW⟧ shaped or cut with an ax, knife, chisel, etc. [*hewn* stone]

☆**hex**[1] (heks) *n.* ⟦PaGer *hexe* < Ger < OHG *hagazussa*, akin to OE *hagtes*: see HAG[1]⟧ **1** [Dial.] a witch **2** *a)* a sign, spell, etc. believed to bring bad luck *b)* a jinx —*vt.* to cause to have bad luck; jinx

hex[2] (heks) *adj. short for* HEXAGONAL (sense 1) —*n. short for* HEXAGON

hex·a- (hek′sə) ⟦< Gr *hex*, SIX⟧ *combining form* six [*hexagram*]: also, before a vowel, **hex-**

hex·a·chlo·ro·eth·ane (hek′sə klôr′ō eth′ān′) *n.* ⟦prec. + CHLORO- + ETHANE⟧ a colorless, crystalline solid with a camphorlike odor, Cl_3CCCl_3, used in organic synthesis, in the manufacture of smoke-producing materials, explosives, etc., and in treating animals with liver flukes

hex·a·chlo·ro·phene (-klôr′ə fēn′) *n.* ⟦< HEXA- + CHLORO- + PHENOL⟧ a white, odorless powder, $(C_6HCl_3OH)_2CH_2$, used in medicine to destroy, or prevent the growth of, bacteria

hex·a·chord (hek′sə kôrd′) *n.* ⟦< L *hexachordos*, having six musical strings or stops < Gr: see HEXA- & CHORD[2]⟧ in medieval music, a diatonic scale of six tones, with a semitone between the third and the fourth

hex·ad (hek′sad′) *n.* ⟦LL *hexas* (gen. *hexadis*) < Gr *hexas* (gen. *hexados*), the number six < *hex*, SIX⟧ a series or group of six —**hex·ad′ic** *adj.*

hex·a·dec·i·mal (hek′sə des′ə məl) *adj.* ⟦HEXA- + DECIMAL, modeled on Gr *hexadeca*, sixteen⟧ designating or of a number system in which the base used is 16

Hex·a·em·er·on (hek′sə em′ər än′) *n.* ⟦LL(Ec) < Gr(Ec) *hexaēmeron* < Gr *hexaēmeros*, of or in six days < *hex*, SIX + *hēmera*, day⟧ [*also* **h-**] the biblical account of the Creation in the Book of Genesis

hex·a·gon (hek′sə gän′) *n.* ⟦L *hexagonum* < Gr *hexagōnon*, hexagon, neut. of *hexagōnos*, six-cornered < *hex*, SIX + *gōnia*, a corner, angle: see KNEE⟧ a plane figure with six angles and six sides

hex·ag·o·nal (hek sag′ə nəl) *adj.* ⟦ML *hexagonalis*⟧ **1** of, or having the form of, a hexagon **2** having a six-sided base or section: said of a solid figure **3** designating or of a crystal system having three axes of equal length that intersect in the same plane so as to form six 60° angles and a fourth of any length that intersects the plane of the other three at a right angle: see CRYSTAL SYSTEM —**hex·ag′o·nal·ly** *adv.*

hex·a·gram (hek′sə gram′) *n.* ⟦HEXA- + -GRAM⟧ **1** a six-pointed star formed by extending the sides of a regular hexagon, or by placing one equilateral triangle over another so that corresponding sides intersect: see also STAR OF DAVID **2** in the I Ching, a pair of trigrams

hex·a·he·dron (hek′sə hē′drən) *n.*, *pl.* **-drons** or **-dra** (-drə) ⟦ModL < Gr *hexaedron*: see HEXA- & -HEDRON⟧ a solid figure with six plane surfaces —**hex′a·he′dral** *adj.*

hex·a·hy·drate (-hī′drāt′) *n.* a hydrate with a one-to-six ratio of molecules of substance to molecules of water

hex·a·hy·dric (-hī′drik′) *adj.* containing six hydroxyl radicals [*a hexahydric alcohol*]

hex·am·er·ous (hek sam′ər əs) *adj.* ⟦HEXA- + -MEROUS⟧ having six parts in each whorl: said of flowers: also written **6-merous**

hex·am·e·ter (hek sam′ə tər) *n.* ⟦L *hexameter* < Gr *hexametros*: see HEXA- & METER[1]⟧ **1** a line of verse containing six metrical feet or measures; specif., the six-foot dactylic line of classical verse, the first four feet of which may be either dactyls or spondees, the fifth a dactyl, and the sixth a spondee or trochee **2** verse consisting of hexameters —*adj.* having six metrical feet or measures —**hex·a·met·ric** (hek′sə me′trik) *adj.*

hex·a·meth·yl·ene·tet·ra·mine (hek′sə meth′ə lēn′te′trə mēn′) *n.*

⟦HEXA- + METHYLENE + TETRA- + (A)MINE⟧ a crystalline compound, $(CH_2)_6N_4$, used in medicine for urinary tract infections and in adhesives, organic synthesis, explosives, etc.; methenamine

hex·ane (hek′sān′) *n.* ⟦HEX(A)- + -ANE⟧ any of the five colorless, volatile, liquid isomeric alkanes, C_6H_{14}

hex·an·gu·lar (hek saŋ′gyoo lər) *adj.* ⟦HEX(A)- + ANGULAR⟧ having six angles

hex·a·pla (hek′sə plə) *n.* ⟦Gr (*ta*) *hexapla*, title of Origen's edition, lit., sixfold, neut. pl. of *hexaploos*, < *hex*, SIX + base *-plo-* < IE base **pel-*, **plo-* > FOLD[1]⟧ 1 an edition presenting six texts arranged in parallel columns 2 [H-] Origen's edition of the Old Testament, presented in this manner

hex·a·pod (hek′sə päd′) *n.* ⟦< Gr *hexapous* (gen. *hexapodos*): see HEXA- & -POD⟧ INSECT (sense 1) —*adj.* having six legs, as a true insect: also **hex·ap′o·dous** (-sap′ə des)

hex·a·stich (hek′sə stik′) *n.* ⟦ModL *hexastichon* < Gr: see HEXA- & STICH⟧ a poem or stanza of six lines

Hex·a·teuch (hek′sə to͞ok′, -tyo͞ok′) *n.* ⟦Ger < Gr *hex*, SIX + *teuchos*, book, after PENTATEUCH⟧ the first six books of the Bible

hex·a·va·lent (hek′sə vā′lənt, hek′sə vā′-) *adj.* having a valence of six

hex·one (hek′sōn′) *n.* ⟦HEX(A)- + -ONE⟧ methyl isobutyl ketone, a colorless liquid, $(CH_3)_2CHCH_2COCH_3$, used as a solvent for paints, gums, and resins, in organic synthesis, etc. —*adj.* designating a group of organic bases containing six carbon atoms in each molecule, formed by the hydrolysis of proteins

hex·o·san (hek′sə san′) *n.* ⟦< fol. + -AN⟧ any of a group of polysaccharides, including starch and glycogen, that form hexoses when hydrolyzed

hex·ose (hek′sōs′) *n.* ⟦HEX(A)- + -OSE[1]⟧ any monosaccharide containing six carbon atoms in each molecule, as dextrose or fructose

☆**hex sign** any of various colorful, stylized designs traditionally painted on Pennsylvania Dutch barns and originally thought to ward off evil

hex·yl (hek′səl) *n.* ⟦HEX(A)- + -YL⟧ the monovalent radical C_6H_{13}, derived from hexane

hex·yl·res·or·cin·ol (hek′səl ri zôr′si nôl′, -nōl′) *n.* ⟦prec. + RESORCINOL⟧ a pale-yellow, crystalline substance, $C_{12}H_{18}O_2$, used as an antiseptic and germicide, esp. in treating parasitic infections

hey (hā) *interj.* ⟦ME *hei*, echoic formation akin to Ger & Du *hei*⟧ [Informal] 1 used to attract attention, to express surprise, delight, puzzlement, etc., or to preface a remark ☆2 hello

hey·day[1] (hā′dā′) *interj.* ⟦earlier *heyda* prob. < (or akin to) Ger & Dan *heida*, Du *heidaar*, hey there!: see prec.⟧ [Archaic] used to express surprise, joy, or wonder

hey·day[2] (hā′dā′) *n.* ⟦ME *hei dai*, full daylight, well on in the day < *hei*, HIGH + *dai*, DAY⟧ the time of greatest health, vigor, success, prosperity, etc.; prime

Hez·bol·lah (hez′bə lä′, hez′bə lə, hez bä′lə) *n.* ⟦Pers or Ar, lit., Party of God⟧ a militant fundamentalist-Shiite organization based in Lebanon

Hez·e·ki·ah (hez′i kī′ə) *n.* ⟦Heb *ḥizqīyāh*, lit., God strengthens⟧ *Bible* a king of Judah in the time of Isaiah: 2 Kings 18-20

hf *abbrev.* 1 half 2 high frequency: also **HF**

Hf *Chem. symbol for* hafnium

HFC *abbrev.* hydrofluorocarbon

H5N1 (āch′fīv′en′wun′) *n.* ⟦*h*(*emagglutinin*) (type) *5 n*(*euraminidase*) (type) *1*⟧ a highly contagious, often deadly type of BIRD FLU virus that is found mainly in birds and occasionally in other animals and humans

hg *abbrev.* hectogram(s)

Hg[1] *abbrev. Bible* Haggai

Hg[2] ⟦ModL *hydrargyrum* < L *hydrargyrus* < Gr *hydrargyros* < *hydōr*, WATER + *argyros*, silver⟧ *Chem. symbol for* mercury

HG *abbrev.* High German

HGH *abbrev.* human growth hormone: see GROWTH HORMONE

hgt *abbrev.* height

hgwy *abbrev.* highway

HH *abbrev.* 1 Her (or His) Highness 2 His Holiness

hhd *abbrev.* hogshead

HH.D. or **HHD** *abbrev.* Doctor of Humanities

☆**H-hour** (āch′our′) *n.* ⟦< H[1] (first letter of HOUR)⟧ ZERO HOUR

HHS *abbrev.* (Department of) Health and Human Services

☆**hi**[1] (hī) *interj.* ⟦ME *hy*, variant of *hei*, HEY⟧ [Informal] hello

hi[2] (hī) *adj. informal sp. of* HIGH

HI *abbrev.* Hawaii

Hi·a·le·ah (hī′ə lē′ə) ⟦< ? Seminole-Creek *haiyakpo hili*, lit., pretty prairie⟧ city in SE Fla.: suburb of Miami

hiatal (*or* **hiatus**) **hernia** a hernia of part of the stomach into the opening in the diaphragm through which the esophagus passes

hi·a·tus (hī āt′əs) *n.*, *pl.* **-tus·es** or **-tus** ⟦L, pp. of *hiare*, to gape < IE base **ĝhē-*, *ĝhēi-* > GAP, GASP⟧ 1 a break where a part is missing or lost, as in a manuscript; gap in a sequence; lacuna 2 any gap or interruption, as in continuity or time 3 *Phonet.* a slight pause in pronunciation between two successive vowels in adjacent words or syllables, as between the sounds represented by the successive *e*'s in *he entered* and *reenter* —**hi·a′tal** *adj.*

Hi·a·wa·tha (hī′ə wä′thə, -wô′thə) *n.* the hero of *The Song of Hiawatha*, a long narrative poem (1855) by H. W. LONGFELLOW: named for a North American Indian chief thought to have lived in the 16th cent.

hi·ba·chi (hi bä′chē) *n.*, *pl.* **-chis** ⟦Jpn < *hi*, fire + *bachi*, bowl⟧ a small, charcoal-burning grill orig. of Japanese design

hi·baku·sha (hē bäk′shä′) *n.*, *pl.* **-sha′** ⟦Jpn, lit., explosion-affected person⟧ a survivor of the atomic destruction of Hiroshima or of Nagasaki in 1945

hi·ber·nac·u·lum (hī′bər nak′yo͞o ləm) *n.*, *pl.* **-u·la** (-lə) ⟦L, winter residence < *hibernare*: see HIBERNATE⟧ any case or covering for protecting an organism during the winter, specif., *a)* a bud or bulb for protecting a plant *b)* a specially modified bud, as in some freshwater bryozoans, that can develop into a colony in the spring *c)* a structure in which a dormant animal passes the winter

hi·ber·nal (hī bur′nəl) *adj.* ⟦L *hibernalis* < *hibernus*: see fol.⟧ of or pertaining to winter; wintry

hi·ber·nate (hī′bər nāt′) *vi.* **-nat′ed**, **-nat′ing** ⟦< L *hibernatus*, pp. of *hibernare*, to pass the winter < *hibernus*, wintry < IE **ĝheimerinos* < base **ĝhei-*, winter, snow > L *hiems*, Gr *cheima*, Czech *zima*, winter⟧ to spend the winter in a dormant state: cf. ESTIVATE —**hi′ber·na′tion** *n.* —**hi′ber·na′tor** *n.*

Hi·ber·ni·a (hī bur′nē ə) ⟦L, altered < *Iverna*, *Juverna* < OCelt **Iveriu* > OIr *Ēriu*: see ERIN[1]⟧ *old poet. name for* IRELAND —**Hi·ber′ni·an** *adj.*, *n.*

Hi·ber·ni·cism (hī bur′nə siz′əm) *n.* ⟦< prec. + -IC + -ISM⟧ an Irish characteristic, custom, idiom, etc.

hi·bis·cus (hī bis′kəs; *also* hi-) *n.* ⟦ModL < L *hibiscus*, *hibiscum*, prob. < Celt⟧ any of a genus (*Hibiscus*) of plants, shrubs, and small trees of the mallow family, with large, colorful flowers

hic (hik) *interj.* ⟦echoic⟧ used to imitate the sound of a hiccup

hic·cup (hik′up′, -əp) *n.* ⟦altered < Early ModE *hikop*, *hickock*, *hicket*, of echoic orig. (as also in MDu *huckup*)⟧ 1 a sudden, involuntary contraction of the diaphragm when it begins to allow air into the lungs only to have the glottis suddenly close, producing an abrupt sound 2 [*pl.*, *sometimes with sing. v.*] a condition characterized by repeated contractions of this kind 3 [Informal] a difficulty, problem, or setback, usually a minor one; HITCH (*n.* 3) —*vi.* **-cuped′** or **-cupped′**, **-cup′ing** or **-cup′ping** to make a hiccup or hiccups —*vt.* to utter with hiccups Also sp. ⟦from assoc. with COUGH⟧ **hic′cough′**

hic ja·cet (hik′ jā′sət; -jak′ət, -yäk′ət) [L] 1 here lies: a tombstone inscription 2 an epitaph

hick (hik) [Informal] *n.* ⟦altered < RICHARD[1]⟧ an awkward, unsophisticated person regarded as typical of rural areas; yokel; hayseed: a contemptuous term —*adj.* of or like a hick or hicks

☆**hick·ey** (hik′ē) *n.*, *pl.* **-eys** or **-ies** ⟦orig. U.S. dial.⟧ 1 [Informal] any device or gadget; doohickey 2 a tool used for bending pipe 3 a coupling for electrical fixtures 4 [Informal] a pimple or pustule 5 [Slang] a bruise made on the skin from sucking, as in lovemaking

Hick·ok (hik′äk), **James Butler** 1837-76; U.S. frontier scout & marshal: called *Wild Bill Hickok*

☆**hick·o·ry** (hik′ə rē, hik′rē) *n.*, *pl.* **-ries** ⟦contr. < 17th-c. *pohickery* (Virginian term) < AmInd term recorded by Capt. John SMITH as *pawcohiccora*, product made from crushed kernels of the nut⟧ 1 any of a genus (*Carya*) of North American trees of the walnut family, with compound leaves, solid pith, and hard nuts 2 the hard, tough wood of any of these trees 3 a switch or cane as of this wood 4 the nut of any of these trees: usually **hickory nut**

hickory horned devil REGAL MOTH

hid (hid) *vt.*, *vi.* ⟦ME < OE *hydde*⟧ *pt. & alt. pp. of* HIDE[1]

hi·dal·go (hi dal′gō) *n.*, *pl.* **-gos** ⟦Sp, contr. < *hijo de algo*, son of something < *hijo*, son (< L *filius*: see FILIAL) + *de*, of + *algo*, something, possessions (< L *aliquem*)⟧ a Spanish nobleman of secondary rank, below that of a grandee

Hi·dal·go (hi dal′gō; *Sp* ē thäl′gô) state of central Mexico: 8,103 sq mi (20,987 sq km); cap. Pachuca

Hi·dat·sa (hī dät′sä′, -sə) *n.*, *pl.* **-sas′** or **-sa′** ⟦< Hidatsa *hiratsa*, willow wood lodge⟧ 1 a member of a North American Indian people now living in North Dakota; Gros Ventre (of the Missouri) 2 the Siouan language of this people

hid·den (hid′'n) *vt.*, *vi.* ⟦ME, for OE *gehydd*⟧ *alt. pp. of* HIDE[1] —*adj.* concealed; secret

☆**hid·den·ite** (hid′'n īt′) *n.* ⟦after W. E. *Hidden*, U.S. mineralogist who discovered it (1879)⟧ a rare, yellowish to emerald-green variety of spodumene, a semiprecious stone

hide[1] (hīd) *vt.* **hid**, **hid′den** or **hid**, **hid′ing** ⟦ME *hiden* < OE *hydan* < IE **(s)keudh-* (> Gr *keuthein*, to hide) < base **(s)keu-*, to cover > fol., SKY, L *cutis*, skin⟧ 1 to put or keep out of sight; secrete; conceal 2 to conceal from the knowledge of others; keep secret [to *hide* one's identity] 3 to keep from being seen by covering up, obscuring, etc. [fog *hid* the road] 4 to turn away [to *hide* one's head in shame] —*vi.* to keep oneself out of sight; conceal oneself —*n.* [Brit.] a place of concealment for an observer of wildlife, hunter, etc. —**hid′er** *n.*

SYN.—**hide**, the general word, refers to the putting of something in a place where it will not easily be seen or found [the toy was *hidden* deep in the chest]; **conceal**, a somewhat formal equivalent for **hide**, more often connotes intent [to *conceal* one's face, motives, etc.]; **secrete** and **cache** suggest a careful hiding in a secret place [they *secreted*, or *cached*, the loot in the cellar], but **cache** now often refers merely to a storing for safekeeping [let's *cache* our supplies in the cave]; **bury** implies a covering for, or as if for, concealment [to *bury* treasure; they were *buried* in the landslide] See also **skin** —***ANT.*** **reveal, expose**

hide[2] (hīd) *n.* ⟦ME < OE *hid*, akin to Ger *haut* < IE **(s)keut-* (> L *cutis*, skin, Gr *kytos*, hollow container) < base **(s)keu-*: see prec.⟧ 1 an animal skin or pelt, either raw or tanned 2 [Informal] the skin of a person —*vt.* **hid′ed**, **hid′ing** [Informal] to beat severely; flog —**neither hide nor hair** nothing whatsoever

hide[3] (hīd) *n.* ⟦ME < OE *higid* < base of *hiwan*, household (akin to OHG *hīwo*, a husband, master of a household) < IE **k̂eiwo-* (> L *civis*, citizen) < base **k̂ei-*, to lie, camp > HOME, Gr *koitos*, bed, sleep⟧ [Historical] a medieval English unit of land measure varying from 60 to 120 acres (24 to 49 hectares)

hide-and-seek (hīd′'n sēk′) ***n.*** a children's game in which one player (called "it") tries to find the other players, who have hidden: also **hide′-and-go-seek′**

hide·a·way (hīd′ə wā′) ***n.*** a place where one can hide, be secluded, etc.

hide·bound (hīd′bound′) ***adj.*** **1** having the hide tight over the bone and muscle structure of the body, as an emaciated cow **2** obstinately conservative and narrow-minded

hi-def (hī′def′) ***adj.*, *n.*** *informal var. of* HIGH-DEFINITION

hid·e·ous (hid′ē əs) ***adj.*** ⟦ME *hidous* < Anglo-Fr < OFr *hidos* < *hide, hisde*, fright⟧ horrible to see, hear, etc.; very ugly or revolting; dreadful —**hid′e·ous·ly** ***adv.*** —**hid′e·ous·ness** ***n.***

☆**hide-out** (hīd′out′) ***n.*** [Informal] a hiding place, as for gangsters

hid·ing[1] (hīd′iŋ) ***n.*** ⟦ME *huydinge*⟧ **1** *a)* the act of one that hides *b)* the condition of being hidden: usually in the phrase **in hiding** **2** a place to hide

hid·ing[2] (hīd′iŋ) ***n.*** ⟦< HIDE[2]⟧ [Informal] a severe beating; thrashing; flogging

hi·dro·sis (hī drō′sis, hi-) ***n.*, *pl.*** **-ses′** (-sēz′) ⟦ModL < Gr *hidrōsis* < *hidroun*, to perspire < *hidrōs*, SWEAT⟧ **1** perspiration; sweating; esp., excessive sweating **2** any skin condition characterized by excessive sweating

hi·drot·ic (hī drät′ik, hi-) ***adj.*** ⟦ML *hidroticus* < Gr *hidrōtikos* < *hidrōs*, sweat⟧ **1** having to do with sweat **2** causing sweat; sudorific —***n.*** a sudorific drug

hid·y-hole or **hid·ey-hole** (hī′dē hōl′) ***n.*** [Chiefly Brit.] *informal var. of* HIDEAWAY

hie (hī) ***vi.*, *vt.*** **hied**, **hie′ing** or **hy′ing** ⟦ME *hien* < OE *higian*, to strive, hasten < IE base **k̂eigh-*, fast > Russ *sigat'*, to spring⟧ [Archaic] to hurry or hasten: often reflexive

hi·e·mal (hī′i məl) ***adj.*** ⟦L *hiemalis*, of winter < *hiems*: see HIBERNATE⟧ of winter; wintry

hi·er- (hī′ər) *combining form* HIERO-: used before a vowel

hi·er·arch (hī′ər ärk′) ***n.*** ⟦ML *hierarcha* < Gr *hierarchēs*, presider over sacred rites, chief priest: see HIERO- & -ARCH⟧ the leader or chief of a religious group; high priest

hi·er·ar·chal (hī′ər är′kəl) ***adj.*** of a hierarch or a hierarchy

hi·er·ar·chi·cal (hī′ər är′ki kəl) ***adj.*** of a hierarchy: also **hi′er·ar′chic** —**hi′er·ar′chi·cal·ly** ***adv.***

hi·er·ar·chism (hī′ər är′kiz′əm) ***n.*** the principles, practices, or authority of a hierarchy —**hi′er·ar′chist** ***n.***

hi·er·ar·chy (hī′ər är′kē) ***n.*, *pl.*** **-chies** ⟦altered (modeled on Gr) < ME *ierarchie* < OFr *jerarchie* < ML(Ec) *hierarchia* < LGr(Ec), power or rule of a hierarch < Gr *hierarchēs*: see HIERARCH⟧ **1** a system of church government by priests or other clergy in graded ranks **2** the group of officials, esp. the highest officials, in such a system **3** a group of persons or things arranged in order of rank, grade, class, etc.

hi·er·at·ic (hī′ər at′ik) ***adj.*** ⟦L *hieraticus* < Gr *hieratikos*, of a priest's office, sacerdotal < *hieros*, sacred: see fol.⟧ **1** of or used by priests; priestly; sacerdotal **2** designating or of the abridged form of cursive hieroglyphic writing once used by priests of ancient Egypt Also **hi′er·at′i·cal** —**hi′er·at′i·cal·ly** ***adv.***

hi·er·o- (hī′ər ō′, -ər ə) ⟦< Gr *hieros*, sacred, holy < IE base **eis-*, to move violently, excite > Sans **iṣṇâti*, (he) sets in motion, L *ira*, IRE, ON *eisa*, to rush on⟧ *combining form* sacred, holy [*hierocracy*]

hi·er·oc·ra·cy (hī′ər äk′rə sē) ***n.*, *pl.*** **-cies** ⟦prec. + -CRACY⟧ government by priests or other clergy; a hierarchy —**hi·er·o·crat·ic** (hī′ər ō′krat′ik) ***adj.***, **hi′er·o·crat′i·cal**

hi·er·o·dule (hī′ər ō dōōl′, -dyōōl′) ***n.*** ⟦LL *hierodulus* < Gr *hierodoulos* < *hieros* (see HIERO-) + *doulos*, slave⟧ in ancient Greece, a temple slave, dedicated to the service of a god

hi·er·o·glyph (hī′ər ō glif′, hī′rə glif′) ***n.*** ⟦back-form. < fol.⟧ **1** a picture or symbol representing a word, syllable, or sound, used by the ancient Egyptians and others instead of alphabetical letters **2** a symbol, sign, etc. that is hard to understand

hi·er·o·glyph·ic (hī′ər ō′glif′ik, hī′rə glif′ik) ***adj.*** ⟦Fr *hiéroglyphique* < LL *hieroglyphicus* < Gr *hieroglyphikos* < *hieros*, sacred (see HIERO-) + *glyphein*, to carve, hollow out: see GLYPH⟧ **1** of, or having the nature of, hieroglyphics **2** written in hieroglyphs **3** hard to read or understand Also **hi′er·o′glyph′i·cal** —***n.*** **1** HIEROGLYPH **2** [*usually pl.*] a method of writing using hieroglyphs; picture writing **3** [*pl.*] writing that is hard to decipher —**hi′er·o′glyph′i·cal·ly** ***adv.***

hieroglyphics
"One cannot attain the limit of artisanship,
And there is no artisan who acquires total mastery."
Ptahhotep
2350 B.C.

hi·er·ol·o·gy (hī′ər äl′ə jē) ***n.*, *pl.*** **-gies** ⟦HIERO- + -LOGY⟧ the religious lore and literature of a people

Hi·er·on·y·mus (hī′ə rän′ə məs) *see* JEROME[2], Saint

hi·er·o·phant (hī′ər ō fant′) ***n.*** ⟦LL *hierophanta* < Gr *hierophantēs* < *hieros* (see HIERO-) + *phainein*, to show (see FANTASY)⟧ **1** in ancient Greece, a priest of a mystery cult **2** a person confidently expounding, explaining, or promoting something mysterious or obscure as though appointed to do so —**hi′er·o·phan′tic** ***adj.***

☆**hi·fa·lu·tin** (hī′fə lōōt′'n) ***adj.*** *alt. sp. of* HIGHFALUTIN

☆**hi-fi** (hī′fī′) [Informal] ***n.*** **1** HIGH FIDELITY **2** a radio, phonograph, etc. having high fidelity —***adj.*** of or having high fidelity of sound reproduction

Hi·ga·shi·o·sa·ka (hē gä′shē ō′sä kä′) city in S Honshu, Japan, east of Osaka

Hig·gin·son (hig′in sən), **Thomas Went·worth (Storrow)** (went′wurth′) 1823-1911; U.S. writer & social reformer

hig·gle (hig′əl) ***vi.*** **-gled**, **-gling** ⟦prob. weakened form of HAGGLE⟧ HAGGLE —**hig′gler** ***n.***

hig·gle·dy-pig·gle·dy (hig′əl dē′ pig′əl dē′) ***adv.*** ⟦redupl., prob. from PIG⟧ in disorder; in jumbled confusion —***adj.*** jumbled; confused

Higgs boson (higz) ⟦after P. W. Higgs (b. 1929), Brit physicist⟧ *Particle Physics* a hypothetical massive boson that binds to other subatomic particles, giving them mass: also **Higgs particle**

high (hī) ***adj.*** ⟦ME *heigh, hei, hie* < OE *heah*, akin to Ger *hoch*, Goth *hauhs* < IE **keuk-* < base **keu-*, to curve, arch > Sans *kakúd-*, peak, Russ *kuča*, heap⟧ **1** of more than normal height; lofty; tall: not used of persons **2** extending upward a (specified) distance **3** situated far above the ground or some other level **4** reaching to or done from a height [*a high* jump, a *high* dive] **5** *a)* above other persons or things in rank, position, strength, etc.; most important or powerful *b)* above other persons or things in quality, character, etc.; superior; exalted; excellent **6** grave; very serious [*high* treason] **7** greatly advanced or developed; complex: usually in the compar. [*higher* mathematics, the *higher* vertebrates] **8** main; principal; chief [a *high* priest] **9** greater in size, amount, degree, power, intensity, etc. than usual [*high* prices, *high* voltage, a *high* profile] **10** advanced to its acme or fullness; fully reached [*high* summer] **11** expensive; costly **12** luxurious and extravagant [*high* living] **13** haughty; overbearing **14** designating or producing tones made by relatively fast vibrations; acute in pitch **15** slightly tainted; having a strong smell: said of meat, esp. game **16** extremely formal or rigid in matters of ceremony, doctrine, etc. **17** excited; elated [*high* spirits] **18** far from the equator [a *high* latitude] ☆**19** designating or of that gear ratio of a motor vehicle transmission which produces the highest speed and the lowest torque **20** [Informal] *a)* drunk; inebriated *b)* under the influence of a drug **21** *Phonet.* articulated with the tongue held in a relatively elevated position in the mouth: said of certain vowels, as (ē) in *feet* —***adv.*** **1** in a high manner **2** in, at, to, or toward a high degree, level, place, position, etc. —***n.*** **1** a high degree, level, place, position, etc. ☆**2** an area of high barometric pressure ☆**3** that gear of a motor vehicle, etc. producing the greatest speed and the lowest torque **4** [Informal] a condition of euphoria induced as by drugs —**high and dry** **1** out of the reach of the water **2** alone and helpless; stranded —**high and low** everywhere —**high and mighty** [Informal] arrogant; haughty —**high on** [Informal] enthusiastic about; very interested in or impressed by —**on high** **1** up in space; high above **2** (in) heaven

☆**high·ball** (hī′bôl′) ***n.*** ⟦sense 1 < ? prec. + *ball*, bartender's slang for "whiskey glass": infl. ? by the v.⟧ **1** liquor, usually whiskey or brandy, mixed with water, soda water, ginger ale, etc. and served with ice in a tall glass **2** a railroad signal, originally a ball hung above the tracks, meaning "go ahead": sometimes used fig. —***vi.*** ⟦< *n.* 2⟧ [Slang] to proceed at great speed

high beam the brighter, long-range setting of a vehicle's headlights

☆**high·bind·er** (hī′bīn′dər) ***n.*** ⟦< ?: first recorded use in *Highbinders*, name of a New York City gang in early 19th c.⟧ [Old Slang] an unscrupulous person or a swindler; esp., a demagogic politician

high blood pressure HYPERTENSION (sense 2)

high·born (hī′bôrn′) ***adj.*** of noble birth

☆**high·boy** (hī′boi′) ***n.*** ⟦HIGH + BOY⟧ a high chest of drawers mounted on legs

high·bred (hī′bred′) ***adj.*** **1** of superior stock or breed **2** showing good breeding; cultivated

☆**high·brow** (hī′brou′) ***n.*** a person having or affecting highly cultivated, intellectual tastes; intellectual —***adj.*** of or for a highbrow Often a pejorative term

☆**high-bush cranberry** (hī′boosh′) CRANBERRY BUSH

high·chair (hī′cher′) ***n.*** a baby's chair having long legs and, usually, a tray for food

High Church a conservative party of the Anglican Church that retains various practices and much of the liturgy of the Roman Catholic Church: distinguished from LOW CHURCH —**High′-Church′** ***adj.*** —**High′-Church′man** ***n.*, *pl.*** **-men**

highboy

high-class (hī′klas′) ***adj.*** **1** of a superior class, rank, quality, etc. **2** [Informal] refined, elegant, tasteful, etc.

high comedy comedy appealing to, and reflecting the life and problems of, the upper social classes, characterized by a witty, sardonic treatment: cf. LOW COMEDY

high commissioner 1 the head of a commission; specif., the chief representative from one Commonwealth nation to another 2 COMMISSIONER (sense 4)

high-com·pres·sion (hī′kəm presh′ən) *adj.* of a modern type of internal-combustion engine designed so that the fuel mixture is compressed into a smaller cylinder space, resulting in more pressure on the pistons and more power

high-con·cept (hī′kän′sept′) *adj.* based on a simple yet striking idea, often one regarded as certain to appeal to a large audience [a *high-concept* summer movie]

high day ⟦ME *hei dai*⟧ a festival day; holiday

high-def·i·ni·tion (hī′def′ə nish′ən) *adj.* designating or of a type of broadcasting or recording, as of radio, TV, or discs, designed for greater DEFINITION (sense 7) than that of the standard type —*n.* high-definition broadcasting, recording, or reproduction Also [Informal] **high′-def′**

high-den·si·ty lipoprotein (hī′den′sə tē) HDL

☆**high-end** (hī′end′) *adj.* [Informal] 1 expensive and of very high quality [*high-end* audio equipment] 2 at, of, or for the high end of a range [a *high-end* estimate]

high-en·er·gy particle (hī′en′ər jē) an atomic or subatomic particle with energy greater than 100 MeV

high-energy physics PARTICLE PHYSICS

higher criticism the study of the authorship, dates of writing, meaning, etc. of the books of the Bible, using the techniques or findings of archaeology, literary criticism, comparative religion, etc.

higher education college or university education

☆**high·er-up** (hī′ər up′) *n.* [Informal] a person of higher rank or position

high explosive any explosive in which the combustion of the particles is so rapid as to be virtually simultaneous throughout the mass, producing a powerful explosion

☆**high·fa·lu·tin** (hī′fə lo͞ot′'n) *adj.* ⟦altered < ? *high-floating*, with intrusive vowel in mockery of excessively flowery oratorical style⟧ [Informal] ridiculously pretentious or pompous: also sp. **high′fa·lu′ting** (-lo͞ot′'n, -lo͞ot′iŋ)

high fidelity in radio, sound recording, etc., an approximately exact reproduction of sound achieved by low distortion and a wide range of reproduced frequencies, from approximately 20 to 20,000 hertz

☆**high-five** (hī′fīv′) [Informal] *n.* ⟦in ref. to the *five* fingers⟧ a slapping of the upraised, open hand of another person, as in congratulation or celebration: also **high five** —*vt.* **-fived′**, **-fiv′ing** to slap the upraised hand of

high·fli·er (hī′flī′ər) *n.* 1 a person or thing that flies high 2 a person who acts, talks, or thinks in an ambitious, extravagant, or extremist manner 3 *Finance a)* a company whose sales, profits, etc. are growing rapidly *b)* a stock whose price has risen significantly in relation to other stocks Also sp. **high′fly′er** —**high′fly′ing** *adj.*

high-flown (hī′flōn′) *adj.* 1 extravagantly ambitious or aspiring 2 high-sounding but meaningless; bombastic

high frequency any radio frequency between 3 and 30 megahertz

High German ⟦calque of Ger *hochdeutsch* (see HIGH & DEUTSCHLAND): so named because orig. spoken chiefly in the German highlands⟧ 1 the group of West Germanic dialects spoken in central and S Germany: distinguished from LOW GERMAN 2 the official and literary form of the German language, technically called *New High German*: see also OLD HIGH GERMAN, MIDDLE HIGH GERMAN

high-grade (hī′grād′) *adj.* of fine or superior quality

high ground ⟦fig.⟧ a position regarded as superior, esp. morally so: with *the*

high·hand·ed (hī′han′did) *adj.* acting or done in an overbearing or arbitrary manner —**high′hand′ed·ly** *adv.* —**high′hand′ed·ness** *n.*

☆**high hat** ⟦descriptive⟧ TOP HAT

☆**high-hat** (hī′hat′; *for v., usually* hī′hat′) *adj.* ⟦< prec.⟧ [Slang] snobbish and aloof —*n.* 1 [Slang] a snob 2 a pair of opposed cymbals mounted on a metal stand and struck together by a foot-pedal mechanism, used by drummers in jazz, rock, etc. for rhythmic accents —*vt.* **-hat′ted**, **-hat′ting** [Slang] to treat snobbishly; snub

High Holidays the period encompassing Rosh Hashana and Yom Kippur in the Jewish calendar: also **High Holy Days**

high-im·pact (hī′im′pakt′) *adj.* 1 able to withstand a relatively severe impact [*high-impact* plastic] 2 involving forceful impact

☆**high·jack** (hī′jak′) *vt. alt. sp. of* HIJACK

high jinks lively pranks; boisterous fun

high jump *Track & Field* 1 an event in which contestants take turns jumping for height over a horizontal bar set between two upright supports: the bar is gradually raised during the contest until a winner is determined 2 a jump in such an event

high·land (hī′lənd) *n.* [*often pl.*] land well above sea level; region higher than adjacent land and containing many hills or mountains —*adj.* of, in, or from such a region —**the Highlands** mountainous region occupying nearly all of the N half of Scotland

high·land·er (-lən dər) *n.* 1 a person born or living in a highland 2 [H-] *a)* a person born or living in the Highlands *b)* a soldier of a Highlands regiment

Highland fling a folk dance of the Highlands, characterized by a series of vertical springs off either foot

high-lev·el (hī′lev′əl) *adj.* 1 of or by persons of high office or rank 2 in a high office or rank 3 designating a computer language, as BASIC or FORTRAN, making use of conventional (as English) words and requiring translation by a compiler or interpreter

high life 1 the way of life of fashionable society; luxurious, extravagant way of life 2 a dance with a strong, syncopated beat, originating in W Africa: also written **high′life′** *n.*

high·light (hī′līt′) *n.* 1 *a)* a part on which light is brightest [the *highlights* on the cheeks] *b)* a part of a painting, photograph, etc. on which light is represented as brightest *c)* the representation or effect of such light in a painting, photograph, etc. (also **high light**) 2 the most important, interesting, or outstanding part, scene, etc. 3 in hairstyling, a strand of hair tinted a lighter color —*vt.* 1 to give a highlight or highlights to 2 to give prominence to; emphasize 3 to mark with a highlighter 4 to be the most outstanding in 5 to designate visually (an icon, a portion of text, etc. on a computer screen) as being selected for some operation

high·light·er (hī′līt′ər) *n.* 1 a pen, usually with a broad felt tip, for marking passages, as in a textbook 2 a cosmetic preparation for adding bright color to the eyes or cheeks

high liver one who lives in a luxurious, extravagant way

high·ly (hī′lē) *adv.* 1 [Rare] in or to a high place 2 in a high office or rank 3 in or to a high degree; very much; very; extremely 4 with high approval or esteem; favorably 5 at a high level, wage, etc.

High Mass a Mass with parts of the text sung by the celebrant rather than recited and often with added ceremony but without a deacon and subdeacon: cf. SOLEMN (HIGH) MASS

high-mind·ed (-mīn′did) *adj.* 1 [Obs.] haughty; proud; arrogant 2 having or showing high ideals, principles, etc. —**high′-mind′ed·ly** *adv.* —**high′-mind′ed·ness** *n.*

☆**high muck-a-muck** (muk′ə muk′) ⟦< Chinook jargon, plenty (of) food: first word altered by folk etym.⟧ [Slang] a person in a position of importance and authority, esp. one who is overbearing: also **high muckamuck**

☆**high muck·e·ty-muck** (muk′ə tē muk′) [Slang] *var. of* HIGH MUCK-A-MUCK

high·ness (hī′nis) *n.* 1 the quality or state of being high; height; loftiness 2 [H-] highest of the nobility: a title used in speaking to or of a member of a royal family and preceded by *Your* or by *His* or *Her*

high noon ⟦see HIGH, *adj.* 10⟧ 1 exactly noon 2 the highest point or culmination; period of great ability or power ☆3 ⟦orig. in allusion to a climactic gunfight in the film *High Noon* (1952)⟧ [*often* H- N-] a situation involving a decisive or dramatic confrontation

high-oc·tane (hī′äk′tān′) *adj.* 1 designating or of a gasoline, fuel mixture, etc. having an octane number higher than normal 2 [Informal] very energetic, powerful, or exciting

high-pitched (hī′picht′) *adj.* 1 high in pitch; shrill 2 lofty; exalted 3 showing intense feeling; agitated 4 steep in slope: said of roofs

high place in early Semitic religions, a place of usually pagan worship, located on a hill or other elevation

High Point ⟦after its location, the highest point on the N.C. Railroad⟧ city in central N.C.

high-pow·ered (hī′pou′ərd) *adj.* very powerful

☆**high-pres·sure** (hī′presh′ər) *adj.* 1 *a)* having, using, or withstanding a high or relatively high pressure *b)* having or indicating a high barometric pressure 2 using or applying forcefully persuasive or insistent methods or arguments [*high-pressure* sales techniques] —☆*vt.* **-sured**, **-sur·ing** [Informal] to urge or persuade with such methods or arguments

high-priced (hī′prīst′) *adj.* costly; expensive

high priest ⟦ME *heyge prest*⟧ 1 a chief priest; specif., the chief priest of the ancient Jewish priesthood 2 a person, esp. a man, who is a chief exponent of a philosophy, movement, etc. or an acknowledged leader, or leading expert, in some field —**high priesthood**

high priestess 1 a chief priestess, as of a religion or a cult 2 a woman who is a chief exponent of a philosophy, movement, etc. or an acknowledged leader or expert in some field

high-pro·file (hī′prō′fīl′) *adj.* having a high profile; well-known, highly publicized, etc.

high relief 1 relief in which sculptured figures, etc. project from the background by half or more than half their full natural depth 2 sculpture in high relief

☆**high-rise** (hī′rīz′) *adj.* designating or of a tall apartment house, office building, etc. of many stories —*n.* a high-rise building

high road 1 [Chiefly Brit.] a main road; highway 2 an easy or direct way 3 a course of action, position, etc. that is uninfluenced by partisanship, self-interest, vindictiveness, etc.: usually in the phrase **take the high road** Also written **high′road′** *n.*

☆**high roller** ⟦from rolling the dice in gambling⟧ [Informal] 1 a person who gambles for very high stakes 2 a person who spends or invests money freely or recklessly —**high′-roll′ing** *adj.*

high school ☆a secondary school that usually includes grades 10, 11, and 12, and sometimes grade 9 (and occasionally, esp. formerly, grades 7 and 8), and that offers academic or vocational subjects: see also JUNIOR HIGH SCHOOL, SENIOR HIGH SCHOOL —**high′-school′** *adj.* —**high schooler**, **high′-school′er** *n.*

high seas open ocean waters outside the territorial limits of any single nation

☆**high sign** a signal, often a prearranged one, given secretly, as in warning

high society fashionable, wealthy, socially prominent people and their way of life

high-sound·ing (hī′soun′diŋ) *adj.* sounding pretentious or impressive

high-spir·it·ed (hī′spir′it id) *adj.* 1 having or showing a courageous or bold spirit 2 spirited; fiery 3 merry; lively

high-step·ping (hī′step′iŋ) ***adj.*** **1** moving with the feet lifted high [*high-stepping* stallions] **2** [Informal] proud, spirited, showy, etc.

high-stick·ing (hī′stik′iŋ) ***n.*** *Ice Hockey* the illegal act of holding one's stick above a specified height and thereby making contact with an opponent or the goal: also written **high sticking**

high-strung (hī′struŋ′) ***adj.*** ⟦from the tuning of stringed instruments⟧ highly sensitive or nervous and tense

high-style (hī′stīl′) ***adj.*** of or relating to style, fashion, or design that is the most up-to-date and, often, most costly

hight (hīt) ***adj.*** ⟦ME *highte*, merging OE *hatte*, pass. pt. with *heht*, active pt. of *hatan*, to command, call: confused in sense with ME *hoten*, pp. of same v.: akin to Ger *heissen* < IE base **kēi-*, to move⟧ [Archaic] named; called [a maiden *hight* Elaine]

high table [*often* **H- T-**] [Brit.] the table, usually elevated, in the dining hall of a college or school where the head and important teachers and guests are seated

☆**high-tail** or **high·tail** (hī′tāl′) ***vi.*** ⟦in allusion to the raised tail of a startled, fleeing animal, esp. a mustang on the range⟧ [Informal] to leave or go in a hurry; scurry off: chiefly in the phrase **high-tail it**

high tea [Brit.] a meal somewhat more elaborate, and served later, than the usual tea

high tech **1** highly specialized, complex technology, as in electronics: in full **high technology** ☆**2** furnishings, fashions, etc. that in design or look suggest industrial use, as by being stark, metallic, or strictly utilitarian Also **high′-tech′** ***n.*** —**high′-tech′** ***adj.***

high-ten·sion (hī′ten′shən) ***adj.*** having, carrying, or operating under a high voltage

high-test (hī′test′) ***adj.*** **1** meeting difficult requirements **2** HIGH-OCTANE

high tide **1** the highest level to which the tide rises; high water **2** the time when the tide is at this level: see also SPRING TIDE **3** any culminating point or time

high time **1** time beyond the proper time but before it is too late; none too soon ☆**2** [Slang] a lively, exciting, enjoyable time: also **high old time**

high-toned (hī′tōnd′) ***adj.*** **1** [Now Rare] high in tone; high-pitched **2** characterized by dignity, lofty moral or intellectual quality, high principles, etc.: often used ironically or humorously ☆**3** [Informal] of or imitating the manners, attitudes, etc. of the upper classes

high-top (hī′täp′) ***adj.*** designating a sneaker or athletic shoe extending over the ankle: also written **high′top′** —**high′-tops′** ***pl.n.***

high treason treason against the ruler or government

high water **1** HIGH TIDE **2** the highest level reached by any body of water, as a river

high-wa·ter mark (hī′wôt′ər) **1** the highest level reached by a body of water in tidal flow, flood, etc. **2** the mark left after high water has receded **3** a culminating point; highest point

high·way (hī′wā′) ***n.*** ⟦ME *higewege*; see HIGH & WAY⟧ **1** any road freely open to everyone; public road: now chiefly a legal term **2** a main road; thoroughfare, specif. one maintained by a state or federal government and designed to accommodate a heavy traffic flow **3** any main route by land or water **4** a direct way to some objective

high·way·man (hī′wā mən) ***n., pl.*** **-men** (-mən) [Historical] a man, esp. one on horseback, who robbed travelers on a highway

highway patrol a police organization limited to activity on property owned or leased by a state, which controls highway traffic, investigates accidents, etc.

highway robbery ⟦fig.⟧ [Informal] any price, proposal, etc. regarded as flagrantly unfair to one side

☆**high wire** a cable or wire stretched high above the ground, on which aerialists perform; tightrope

HIH *abbrev.* Her (or His) Imperial Highness

hi-hat (hī′hat′) ***n.*** *alt. sp. of* HIGH-HAT (***n.*** 2)

Hii·u·maa (hē′o͞o mä′) island of Estonia, in the Baltic Sea: 373 sq mi (966 sq km)

hi·jab (hi jäb′) ***n.*** ⟦Ar, lit., curtain < *ḥajaba*, to cover⟧ a head covering traditionally worn in public by Muslim women

☆**hi·jack** (hī′jak′) ***vt.*** ⟦< hobo slang for robbing sleeping men < HIGH + JACK: origin obscure⟧ **1** to steal (goods in transit, a truck and its contents, etc.) by force **2** to steal such goods from (a person) by force **3** to cheat, swindle, etc. by or as by the use of force **4** to seize control forcibly of (an aircraft, bus, ship, etc.), esp. in order to go to a nonscheduled destination **5** [Informal] to seize control of [an aggressive councilman *hijacking* the proceedings] —**hi′jack′er** ***n.***

Hi·jaz (hi jaz′, hē-; -jäz′) *var. of* HEJAZ

hi·jinks or **hi-jinks** (hī′jiŋks′) ***pl.n.*** *alt. sp. of* HIGH JINKS

hike (hīk) ***vi.*** **hiked**, **hik′ing** ⟦< dial. *heik*, prob. akin to HITCH⟧ **1** to take a long, vigorous walk; tramp or march, esp. through the country, woods, etc. ☆**2** to move up out of place —***vt.*** **1** [Informal] to pull or jerk up; hoist [to *hike* up one's socks] ☆**2** [Informal] to raise (prices, etc.) ☆**3** *Football* SNAP (***vt.*** 9) —***n.*** ☆**1** a long, vigorous walk ☆**2** a moving upward; rise [a price *hike*] —**take a hike** ☆[Slang] to leave; depart: sometimes used in the imperative —**hik′er** ***n.***

hi·lar (hī′lər) ***adj.*** of or relating to a hilum

hi·lar·i·ous (hi ler′ē əs) ***adj.*** ⟦< L *hilaris, hilarus* < Gr *hilaros*, cheerful, merry (see SILLY) + -OUS⟧ **1** [Old-fashioned] noisily merry; boisterous and joyous **2** producing much laughter; very funny —**hi·lar′i·ous·ly** ***adv.*** —**hi·lar′i·ous·ness** ***n.***

hi·lar·i·ty (hi ler′i tē) ***n.*** ⟦OFr *hilarité* < L *hilaritas*⟧ the state or quality of being hilarious

Hil·a·ry (hil′ə rē) ***n.*** ⟦L *Hilarius*, lit., cheerful: see HILARIOUS⟧ a masculine and feminine name: var. *Hillary*: equiv. Fr. *Hilaire*

Hil·bert (hil′bərt; *Ger*, -bərt), **Da·vid** (*Ger* dä′vit) 1862-1943; Ger. mathematician

Hil·da (hil′də) ***n.*** ⟦Ger < Gmc **hild-*, battle, war (see HILT): often contr. of names containing base (e.g., *Hildegunde*, Brun*hilde*)⟧ a feminine name

Hil·de·gard (von Bing·en) (hil′də gärd′ vän biŋ′ən), Saint (1098-1179); Ger. nun, composer, & mystic: her day is Sept. 17

Hil·de·garde (hil′də gärd′) ***n.*** ⟦Ger < Gmc **hild-*, battle + **gard-*, to protect (see YARD²): hence, lit., battle protector⟧ a feminine name: see HILDA

hil·ding (hil′diŋ) [Archaic] ***n.*** ⟦prob. < ME *heldinge*, bending aside < *helden* (OE *hieldan*), to incline, bow⟧ a low, contemptible person —***adj.*** low and contemptible

hill (hil) ***n.*** ⟦ME < OE *hyll*, akin to MDu *hille* < IE base **kel-*, to project, rise high > L *collis*, hill, Gr *kolophōn*, peak⟧ **1** a natural elevation of the earth's surface, typically rounded and smaller than a mountain **2** [*pl.*] a chain or group of such elevations **3** a small pile, heap, or mound [an *anthill*] **4** *a)* a small mound of soil heaped over or around plants and tubers [a *hill* of potatoes] *b)* the plant or plants rooted in such a mound ☆**5** [Slang] *Baseball* the pitcher's mound: with *the* —***vt.*** **1** to shape into or like a hill **2** to cover with a HILL (sense 4*a*) —**over the hill** [Informal] **1** absent without permission; AWOL **2** in one's decline —**the Hill** ☆CAPITOL HILL —**hill′er** ***n.***

Hill (hil), **James J(erome)** 1838-1916; U.S. railroad magnate & financier, born in Canada

Hil·la·ry (hil′ər ē), Sir **Edmund (Percival)** 1919-2008; New Zealand mountain climber & explorer

☆**hill·bil·ly** (hil′bil′ē) [Informal] ***n., pl.*** **-lies** ⟦HILL + *Billy*, dim. of BILL⟧ a person who lives in or comes from the mountains or backwoods of the South, esp. from the Appalachian areas of the South: often a contemptuous term —***adj.*** of or characteristic of hillbillies [*hillbilly* music]

Hil·lel (hil′el) 60? B.C.-A.D. 10?; Jewish rabbi & scholar in Jerusalem

Hil·ling·don (hil′iŋ dən) borough of Greater London, England

hill myna an Asian myna bird (*Gracula religiosa*) with the ability to mimic human speech: often kept as a pet

hill·ock (hil′ək) ***n.*** ⟦ME *hilloc*: see HILL & -OCK⟧ a small hill; mound —**hill′ock·y** ***adj.***

☆**hill of beans** [Informal] a very small amount or value: used in negative constructions of something regarded as negligible [not worth a *hill of beans*]

hill·side (hil′sīd′) ***n.*** the side or slope of a hill

hill·top (-täp′) ***n.*** the top of a hill

hill·y (hil′ē) ***adj.*** **hill′i·er**, **hill′i·est** full of hills; rugged, uneven, and rolling —**hill′i·ness** ***n.***

hilt (hilt) ***n.*** ⟦ME *hilt* < OE, akin to ON *hjalt* < IE base **kel-*, to strike, split > L *calamitas*, harm, OE *hild*, battle⟧ the handle of a sword, dagger, tool, etc. —***vt.*** to provide a hilt for —**to the hilt** thoroughly; entirely

hi·lum (hī′ləm) ***n., pl.*** **hi′la** (-lə) ⟦ModL < L, little thing⟧ **1** HILUS **2** *Bot.* *a)* a scar on a seed, marking the place where it was attached to the seed stalk *b)* the nucleus in a starch grain

hi·lus (hī′ləs) ***n., pl.*** **hi′li′** (-lī′) ⟦ModL, var. of prec.⟧ *Anat.* a small notch, recess, or opening, as where vessels and nerves enter an organ

him (him) ***pron.*** ⟦OE *him*, dat. of *he*, he, merged in sense with *hine*, acc. of *he*⟧ *objective form of* HE¹ [help *him*; give *him* the book]

USAGE—*him* is also used as a predicate complement with a linking verb [it's *him*] and in certain comparative constructions [she runs faster than *him*, but she's not as agile as *him*], although both usages are objected to by some

HIM *abbrev.* Her (or His) Imperial Majesty

Hi·ma·la·yan (him′ə lā′ən, hi mäl′yən) ***adj.*** of the Himalayas —***n.*** **1** any of a breed of small, white, domesticated rabbit with the tail, feet, nose, and tips of the ears black **2** any of a breed of domestic cat with a stocky build, blue eyes, and a long, thick, light-colored coat shading to a darker color on the face, legs, ears, and tail: bred by crossing the Persian and the Siamese

Hi·ma·la·yas (him′ə lā′əz, hi mäl′yəz) mountain system of SC Asia, extending along the Indian-Tibetan border and through Pakistan, Nepal, & Bhutan: highest peak, Mt. Everest: also **Himalaya Mountains**

hi·mat·i·on (hi mat′ē än′, -ən) ***n., pl.*** **-mat′i·a** (-ə) ⟦Gr *himation*, dim. of *heima*, garment < *hennynai*, to clothe < IE base **wes-* > WEAR¹, L *vestis*⟧ an ancient Greek outer garment consisting of a long rectangle of cloth draped over the left shoulder and wound around the body

Him·a·vat (him′ə vat′) ***n.*** ⟦Hindi⟧ *Hindu Myth.* the personification of the Himalayas and father of Devi

Hi·me·ji (hē′me jē′) city on the S coast of Honshu, Japan, near Kobe

him/her (him′hʉr′, him′ôr hʉr′) ***pron.*** him or her: used to avoid the masculine implication of the generic use of *him*

Himm·ler (him′lər), **Hein·rich** (hīn′riH) 1900-45; Ger. Nazi leader: head of the SS & the Gestapo

him·self (him self′) ***pron.*** ⟦OE *him selfum*, dat. sing. of *he self*: see HIM & SELF⟧ a form of HE¹, used: *a)* as an intensifier [he said so *himself*] *b)* as a reflexive [he hurt *himself*] *c)* with the meaning "his real, true, or normal self" [he is not *himself* today] (in this construction *him* functions as an adjective and *self* as a noun; when they are separated, the form *his* is used [*his* own sweet *self*]) *d)* [Irish] as a subject (used esp. of someone of some importance, often sarcastically) [*himself* will have his tea now]

Him·yar·ite (him′yər īt′) *n.* ⟦< Ar *Ḥimyar*, a people of Yemen + -ITE[1]⟧ **1** a member of an ancient South Arabian people **2** an Arab descended from this people **3** the Semitic language of this people —*adj.* of the Himyarites or their language or culture: also **Him′yar·it′ic** (-rit′ik)

hin (hin) *n.* ⟦Heb *hīn*⟧ an ancient Hebrew unit of liquid measure, equal to about 1½ gallons (5.7 liters)

Hi·na·ya·na (hē′nə yä′nə, hin′ə-) *n.* ⟦Sans *hīnayāna*, lit., lesser vehicle⟧ the oldest major movement or school in Buddhism, found especially in Sri Lanka and Southeast Asia: it emphasizes the attainment of nirvana through meditation and monastic discipline

hind[1] (hīnd) *adj., superl.* **hind′most′** ⟦ME *hinde*, short for *hindan*, from behind: see HINDER[2]⟧ back; rear; posterior

hind[2] (hīnd) *n., pl.* **hinds** or **hind** ⟦ME < OE, akin to Ger *hinde* < IE base **ḱem-*, not having horns (as applied to horned animal species) > Gr *kemas*, young deer⟧ **1** the female of the red deer, in and after its third year **2** any of various groupers (genus *Epinephelus*) of the S Atlantic

hind[3] (hīnd) *n.* ⟦< ME *hine* (with unhistoric *-d*) < OE *hina*, earlier *higna*, generalized < gen. pl. of *higa*, member of a household: for base see HIDE[3]⟧ **1** in N England and Scotland, a skilled farm worker or servant **2** [Archaic] a simple or boorish peasant; rustic

Hind *abbrev.* **1** Hindi **2** Hindu **3** Hindustan **4** Hindustani

hind·brain (hīnd′brān′) *n.* **1** the hindmost part of the three primary divisions of the brain of a vertebrate embryo **2** the part of the fully developed brain evolved from this, consisting of the entire rhombencephalon, or either of its subdivisions, the metencephalon or myelencephalon

Hin·de·mith (hin′də məth; *Ger,* -mit), **Paul** 1895-1963; U.S. composer, born in Germany

Hin·den·burg (hin′dən burg′; *Ger,* -boorkh′), **Paul (Ludwig Hans Anton von Beneckendorff und) von** 1847-1934; Ger. field marshal: president of the Weimar Republic (1925-34)

hin·der[1] (hin′dər) *vt.* ⟦ME *hindren* < OE *hindrian*, lit., to keep or hold back (akin to Ger *hindern*) < base of fol.⟧ **1** to keep back; restrain; get in the way of; prevent; stop **2** to make difficult for; thwart; impede; frustrate —*vi.* to delay action; be a hindrance

SYN.*—hinder** implies a holding back of something about to begin and connotes a thwarting of progress [*hindered* by a lack of education]; **obstruct** implies a retarding of passage or progress by placing obstacles in the way [to *obstruct* the passage of a bill by a filibuster]; **block** implies the complete, but not necessarily permanent, obstruction of a passage or of progress [the road was *blocked* by a landslide]; **impede** suggests a slowing up of movement or progress by interfering with the normal action [tight garters *impede* the circulation of the blood]; **bar** implies an obstructing as if by means of a barrier [he was *barred* from the club] —ANT.*** **advance, further, help**

hind·er[2] (hīn′dər) *adj., superl.* **hind′ermost′** ⟦ME *hindre* < OE adv. *hinder*, back, behind (akin to Ger prep. *hinter*, behind) < ? base of *he* (see HE[1]) + compar. suffix *-der*, akin to Gr *-tero-*, Sans *-tara-*: the word is now taken to be the compar. of HIND[1]⟧ [Now Rare] hind; rear; posterior

hind·gut or **hind-gut** (hīnd′gut′) *n.* **1** the hindmost part of the embryonic alimentary canal, from which part of the colon is formed **2** the posterior part of the digestive tract of arthropods

Hin·di (hin′dē) *adj.* ⟦Hindi *hindī* < *Hind*: see HINDU⟧ **1** of or associated with N India **2** of Hindi —*n.* an Indo-Aryan language, the main language of India

hind·most (hīnd′mōst′) *adj.* ⟦ME: see HIND[1] & -MOST⟧ farthest back; closest to the rear; last

Hin·doo (hin′doo′) *adj., n., pl.* **-doos′** *old-fashioned sp. of* HINDU

hind·quar·ter (hīnd′kwôrt′ər) *n.* **1** either of the two hind legs and the adjoining loin of a carcass of veal, beef, lamb, etc. **2** [*pl.*] the hind part of a four-legged animal

hin·drance (hin′drəns) *n.* ⟦ME *hinderaunce*⟧ **1** the act of hindering **2** any person or thing that hinders; obstacle; impediment; obstruction —***SYN.*** OBSTACLE

hind·shank (hīnd′shaŋk′) *n.* **1** the upper part of the hind legs of cattle **2** meat from this part

☆**hind·sight** (hīnd′sīt′) *n.* **1** the rear sight of a firearm **2** ability to see, after the event, what should have been done

Hin·du (hin′doo′) *n.* ⟦Pers *Hindū* < *Hind*, India < OPers *Hindu*, India, land of the Indus < Sans *sindhu*, river, the Indus⟧ **1** [Archaic] a person born or living in India or on the Indian subcontinent **2** a follower of Hinduism —*adj.* designating or of the Hindus or Hinduism

Hin·du-Ar·a·bic numerals (-ar′ə bik′) ARABIC NUMERALS

Hin·du·ism (hin′doo iz′əm) *n.* the principal religious tradition of India, characterized by the worship of many gods, a belief in reincarnation, and the concept of karma, or the cumulative effect of all of one's actions: it is the basis of the caste system

Hindu Kush (koosh) mountain range mostly in NE Afghanistan, extending to the Karakoram in NW Kashmir: highest peak, Tirich Mir

Hin·du·stan (hin′doo stan′, -stän′) ⟦see fol.⟧ **1** kingdom in N India in the 15th & 16th cent. **2** region in N India, between the Vindhya Mountains & the Himalayas, where Hindi is spoken **3** the entire Indian subcontinent **4** *name for* the Republic of India

Hin·du·sta·ni (hin′doo stä′nē, -stan′ē) *n.* ⟦Hindi *Hindūstānī*, lit., dweller in northern India, Indian < Pers *Hindūstān*, lit., country of the Hindus < *Hindū* (see HINDU) + *stān*, a place, country⟧ a major dialect of Western Hindi, used as a lingua franca throughout N India: see also HINDI, URDU —*adj.* of Hindustan or its people, language, or culture

Hines (hīnz), **Earl (Kenneth)** 1905-83; U.S. jazz pianist & composer: also called *Earl "Fatha" Hines*

hinge (hinj) *n.* ⟦ME, earlier *henge* (vowel raised before nasal) < *hengen* (< ON *hengja*) or < *hangen*: see HANG⟧ **1** a joint or device on which a door, gate, lid, etc. swings **2** a natural joint, as of the bivalve shell of a clam or oyster **3** a thin, gummed piece of paper, folded for fastening a stamp in an album **4** anything on which matters turn or depend; cardinal point or principle; pivot —*vt.* **hinged, hing′ing** to equip with or attach by a hinge —*vi.* to hang as on a hinge; be contingent; depend [hopes *hinging* on his success]

BUTT HINGE
T-HINGE
STRAP HINGE
kinds of hinges

hinge joint a joint between bones that permits motion in only one plane, as the knee joint

☆**hink·y** (hiŋ′kē) *adj.* **hink′i·er, hink′i·est** ⟦< ? slang *hincty*, snobbish < ?⟧ [Slang] strange, weird, unusual, abnormal, suspicious, etc.

hin·ny (hin′ē) *n., pl.* **-nies** ⟦L *hinnus* < Gr *innos*, with *h-* after L *hinnire*, to whinny⟧ the hybrid offspring of a male horse and a female donkey: cf. MULE[1]

hint (hint) *n.* ⟦prob. var. of HENT⟧ **1** a slight indication of a fact, wish, etc.; indirect suggestion or piece of advice; intimation; covert allusion [they dropped *hints* that we should leave] **2** a very small amount or degree; perceptible trace [a *hint* of nutmeg] **3** [Obs.] an occasion; opportunity —*vt.* to give a hint of; suggest indirectly; intimate —*vi.* to make a hint or hints —***SYN.*** SUGGEST —**hint at** to suggest indirectly; intimate —**take a hint** to perceive and act on a hint —**hint′er** *n.*

hin·ter·land (hin′tər land′) *n.* ⟦Ger < *hinter*, back (see HINDER[2]) + *land*, LAND⟧ **1** the land or district behind that bordering on a coast or river; specif., an inland region claimed by the state that owns the coast **2** an area far from big cities and towns; backcountry

hip[1] (hip) *n.* ⟦ME *hipe* < OE *hype*, akin to Ger *hüfte* (OHG *huf*) < IE **keub-*, to bend, as at a joint (< base **keu-*, to bend, bend over) > L *cubare*, to lie, Gr *kybos*, hollow above the hips of cattle⟧ **1** *a)* the part of the human body surrounding and including the hip joint; esp., the fleshy part between the waist and the upper thigh; haunch *b)* HIP JOINT **2** the corresponding part of an animal's body **3** *Archit.* the angle formed by the meeting of two sloping sides of a roof —*vt.* **hipped, hip′ping** to make (a roof) with such an angle or angles —**on (or upon) the hip** [Rare] at a disadvantage: originally with reference to wrestling —**smite hip and thigh** ⟦cf. Judg. 15:8⟧ [Archaic] to attack unsparingly; overwhelm with or as with blows

hip[2] (hip) *n.* ⟦with Early ModE shortened vowel < ME *hepe* < OE *heope*, akin to OHG *hiufo*, OS *hiopo* < IE base **ḱeub-*, brier, thorn⟧ the fleshy false fruit of the rose, containing the achenes, or true fruits: it is rich in vitamin C

hip[3] (hip) *interj.* used in cheers [*hip, hip,* hurray!]

☆**hip**[4] (hip) *adj.* **hip′per, hip′pest** ⟦< ? HEP⟧ [Informal] **1** *a)* sophisticated; knowing; aware *b)* fashionable; stylish **2** of or associated with hipsters or hippies —**get (or be) hip to** [Slang] to become (or be) informed or knowledgeable about —**hip′ness** *n.*

hip·bone (hip′bōn′) *n.* **1** INNOMINATE BONE **2** ILIUM **3** the neck of the femur

hip boots high, usually waterproof boots that extend to the top of the legs

☆**hip hop** ⟦orig. uncert., prob. < HIP[4]⟧ **1** a form of popular music that originated among inner-city African-American youths in the 1980s, drawing on rap, funk, street sounds, and fragments of melody and rhythm borrowed from previously recorded sources **2** the culture or a fashion, dance, etc. associated with this music or its fans Also written **hip′-hop′** *n.*

hip-hug·gers (hip′hug′ərz) *n.* pants fitted very tightly around the hips, with the waistline just above the hips: also **hip huggers**

hip joint the junction between the femur and its socket in the pelvis

hip·parch (hip′ärk′) *n.* ⟦Gr *hipparchos*: see HIPPO- & -ARCH⟧ in ancient Greece, a cavalry commander

Hip·par·chus (hi pär′kəs) 2d cent. B.C.; Gr. astronomer

hipped[1] (hipt) *adj.* **1** having hips of a specified kind [*slim-hipped*] **2** having the hip dislocated: said esp. of horses, cows, etc. **3** *Archit.* having a hip or hips [a *hipped* roof]

hipped[2] (hipt) *adj.* ⟦< HYP(OCHONDRIA)⟧ **1** [Now Rare] melancholy or depressed ☆**2** [Informal] having a great, often excessive, interest; obsessed: with *on* [*hipped* on movies]

hip·pe·ty-hop or **hip·pi·ty-hop** (hip′ə tē häp′) [Informal] *adj., adv.* ⟦redupl. altered < HOP[1]⟧ with a hopping movement —*vi.* **-hopped′, -hop′ping** to move by or as if by hopping

☆**hip·pie** (hip′ē) *n.* ⟦< HIP[4] + -IE⟧ **1** any of the young people of the 1960s and 1970s who, in their alienation from conventional society, turned variously to mysticism, psychedelic drugs, communal living, etc. **2** [Slang] any person having a similar lifestyle

hip·po (hip′ō) *n., pl.* **-pos** *short for* HIPPOPOTAMUS

Hip·po (hip′ō) HIPPO REGIUS

hip·po- (hip′ō, -ə) ⟦< Gr *hippos*, a horse < IE **ekwos* > L *equus*, OE *eoh*, ON *iōr*⟧ *combining form* horse [*hippodrome*]

hip·po·cam·pus (hip′ō kam′pəs) ***n.***, *pl.* **-cam′pi** (-pī) ⟦L, sea horse < Gr *hippokampos*, hippocampus < *hippos* (see prec.) + *kampos*, sea monster⟧ **1** *Class. Myth.* a sea monster with the head and forequarters of a horse and the tail of a dolphin or fish **2** a ridge along the lower section of each lateral ventricle of the brain —**hip′po·cam′pal** ***adj.***

hip·po·cras (hip′ə kras′) ***n.*** ⟦ME *ypocras* < OFr < *Ypocras*, Hippocrates, after ML *vinum Hippocraticum*, wine of Hippocrates: from being filtered through a strainer called "Hippocrates' sleeve" (L *manica Hippocratis*)⟧ a former cordial made of wine and spices

Hip·poc·ra·tes (hi päk′rə tēz′) 460?-377? B.C.; Gr. physician: called the *Father of Medicine* —**Hip·po·crat·ic** (hip′ə krat′ik) ***adj.***

Hippocratic oath the oath generally taken by students receiving a medical degree: it is attributed to Hippocrates and sets forth an ethical code for the medical profession

Hip·po·crene (hip′ō krēn′, hip′ō krē′nē) ***n.*** ⟦L < Gr *Hippokrēnē* < *hippos* (see HIPPO-) + *krēnē*, a spring, fountain⟧ *Gr. Myth.* a fountain on Mt. Helicon, sacred to the Muses: its waters inspire poets

hip·po·drome (hip′ə drōm′) ***n.*** ⟦Fr < L *hippodromos* < Gr: see HIPPO- & -DROME⟧ **1** in ancient Greece and Rome, a course for horse races and chariot races, surrounded by tiers of seats in an oval **2** an arena or building for equestrian events, circuses, games, etc.

hip·po·griff or **hip·po·gryph** (hip′ō grif′) ***n.*** ⟦Fr *hippogriffe* < It *ippogrifo* < Gr *hippos* (see HIPPO-) + L *gryphus*, GRIFFIN⟧ a mythical monster with the hindquarters of a horse and the head and wings of a griffin

hip pointer a painful bruise or torn muscle at the upper ridge of the pelvis

Hip·pol·y·ta (hi päl′i tə) ***n.*** *Gr. Myth.* a queen of the Amazons, whose magic girdle is obtained by Hercules as one of his twelve labors: also **Hip·pol′y·te′** (-tē′)

Hip·pol·y·tus (hi päl′i təs) ***n.*** *Gr. Myth.* a son of Theseus: when he rejects the love of his stepmother, Phaedra, she turns Theseus against him by false accusations: at Theseus' request, Poseidon brings about his death

Hip·pom·e·nes (hi päm′i nēz′) ***n.*** *Gr. Myth.* the youth who wins the race against ATALANTA

hip·po·pot·a·mus (hip′ə pät′ə məs) ***n.***, *pl.* **-a·mus·es**, **-a·mi′** (-ə mī′), or **-a·mus** ⟦L < Gr *hippopotamos*, lit., river horse < *hippos* (see HIPPO-) + *potamos*, river, orig., that which goes down < IE base **pet-*, to fall, fly > FEATHER, Gr *pteryx*, wing⟧ any of a family (Hippopotamidae) of large, plant-eating, artiodactylous mammals with a heavy, thick-skinned, almost hairless body and short legs: they live chiefly in or near rivers in Africa

Hip·po Re·gi·us (hip′ō rē′jē əs) ancient city in N Africa, near modern Annaba, Algeria: capital of ancient Numidia &, later, a Roman colony

-hip·pus (hip′əs) ⟦ModL < Gr *hippos*: see HIPPO-⟧ *combining form forming nouns* horse [*eohippus*]

hip·py[1] (hip′ē) ***adj.*** **-pi·er**, **-pi·est** having wide or large hips

☆**hip·py**[2] (hip′ē) ***n.***, *pl.* **-pies** *alt. sp. of* HIPPIE

hip roof a roof with sloping ends and sides

hip-shoot·er (hip′sho͞ot′ər) ***n.*** ⟦< SHOOT FROM THE HIP (see phr. under SHOOT[1])⟧ a person who acts or talks in a rash, impetuous way: also written **hip shooter** —**hip′-shoot′ing** ***adj.***

hip·shot (hip′shät′) ***adj.*** **1** having the hip dislocated **2** having one hip lower than the other

☆**hip·ster** (hip′stər) ***n.*** **1** [Slang] a hip person **2** [Slang] BEATNIK: a term of the 1950s and early 1960s: cf. HIPPIE **3** women's panties with the top ending at the hip line

hip roof

hi·ra·ga·na (hir′ə gä′nə) ***n.*** ⟦Jpn < *hira*, plain + KANA⟧ the more widely used portion of the Japanese kana, or syllabary, having characters that are cursive

Hi·ra·ka·ta (hir′ə kät′ə) city in S Honshu, Japan, north of Osaka

Hi·ram (hī′rəm) ***n.*** ⟦Heb *ḥīrām*, prob. < *a'ḥīrām*, exalted brother⟧ a masculine name: dim. *Hi*

hir·cine (hur′sīn′, -sin) ***adj.*** ⟦L *hircinus* < *hircus*, goat < IE **gherkwo-* < **ĝhers-*, to bristle > HORRID⟧ of or like a goat; esp., smelling like a goat

hire (hīr) ***n.*** ⟦ME < OE *hyr*, wages, akin to Du *huur*, Ger *heuer*⟧ **1** the amount paid to get the services of a person or the use of a thing **2** a hiring or being hired **3** [Informal] a person who is hired; employee —***vt.*** **hired**, **hir′ing 1** to get the services of (a person) or the use of (a thing) in return for payment; employ or engage **2** to give the use of (a thing) or the services of (oneself or another) in return for payment: often with *out* **3** to pay for (work to be done) —**for hire** available for work or use in return for payment: also **on hire** —☆**hire out** to work, esp. as a laborer, for payment —**hir′a·ble** ***adj.***, **hire′a·ble** —**hir′er** ***n.***

SYN.—to **hire**, in strict usage, means to get, and **let** means to give, the use of something in return for payment, although **hire**, which is also applied to persons or their services, may be used in either sense [to *hire* a hall, a worker, etc.; rooms to *let*]; **lease** implies the letting or, in loose usage, the hiring of property (usually real property) by written contract; **rent** implies payment of a specific amount, usually at fixed intervals, for hiring or letting a house, land, or other property; **charter** implies the hiring or leasing of a bus, boat, etc.

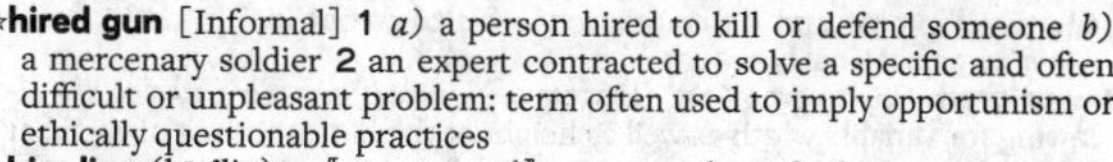

☆**hired gun** [Informal] **1** *a)* a person hired to kill or defend someone *b)* a mercenary soldier **2** an expert contracted to solve a specific and often difficult or unpleasant problem: term often used to imply opportunism or ethically questionable practices

hire·ling (hīr′liŋ) ***n.*** ⟦HIRE + -LING[1]⟧ a person who is for hire; esp., one who will follow anyone's orders for pay; mercenary —***adj.*** of or like a hireling; mercenary

hire purchase [Brit.] INSTALLMENT PLAN

☆**hiring hall** an employment office, esp. one operated by a union to place its members in jobs in the order of their applications

hi-riser (hī′rī′zər) ***n.*** a couch with two mattresses, one below the other on a separate frame, that is convertible into a double bed or two single beds

Hi·ro·hi·to (hir′ō hē′tō) 1901-89; emperor of Japan (1926-89)

Hi·ro·shi·ge (hir′ō shē′gā), **An·do** (än′dō) 1797-1858; Jpn. painter

Hi·ro·shi·ma (hir′ə shē′mə, hi rō′shi mə) seaport in SW Honshu, Japan, on the Inland Sea: largely destroyed (Aug. 6, 1945) by a U.S. atomic bomb, the first ever used in warfare

hir·sute (hur′so͞ot′, hər so͞ot′) ***adj.*** ⟦L *hirsutus* < *hirtus*, bristly, akin to *hircus*: see HIRCINE⟧ hairy; shaggy; bristly —**hir′sute′ness** ***n.***

hir·sut·ism (hur′so͞ot iz′əm, hər so͞ot′-) ***n.*** abnormally heavy hair growth

hir·u·din (hir′yo͞o din′) ***n.*** ⟦orig. a trademark: < L *hirudo*, leech + -IN[1]⟧ a substance found in the salivary glands of leeches that prevents the coagulation of blood

his (hiz) ***pron.*** ⟦ME < OE, gen. masc. & neut. of *he*⟧ that or those belonging to him: the possessive form of HE[1], used without a following noun, often after *of* [that book is *his; his* are better; I am a friend of *his*] —***possessive pronominal adj.*** of, belonging to, made by, or done by him: also used before some formal titles [*His* Grace, *His* Highness]

his/her (hiz′hur′, hiz′ôr hur′) ***possessive pronominal adj.*** his or her: used to avoid the masculine implication of the generic use of *his*

his/hers (-hurz′) ***pron.*** his or hers: used to avoid the masculine implication of the generic use of *his*

His·pa·ni·a (hi spän′yə) **1** *Latin name for* IBERIAN PENINSULA **2** *old poet. name for* SPAIN

His·pan·ic (hi span′ik) ***adj.*** ⟦L *Hispanicus*⟧ **1** Spanish or Spanish-and-Portuguese **2** of or relating to Hispanics —***n.*** a usually Spanish-speaking person of Latin American birth or descent who lives in the U.S. ➥For the *n.* and *adj.* 2, *Latino* and *Latina* are now often preferred —**His·pan′i·cism′** (-i siz′əm) ***n.*** —**His·pan′i·cist** ***n.***

His·pan·io·la (his′pən yō′lə) island in the West Indies, between Cuba & Puerto Rico: divided between Haiti & the Dominican Republic: 29,418 sq mi (76,192 sq km)

His·pan·ist (his′pə nist) ***n.*** ⟦HISPAN(IA) + -IST[1]⟧ a specialist in the study of the languages, literatures, or cultures of Spain, Portugal, or Latin America

His·pan·o (hi span′ō, -spä′nō) ***n.*** ⟦< L *Hispanus*, Spanish⟧ HISPANIC

his·pid (his′pid) ***adj.*** ⟦L *hispidus*: for IE base see HIRCINE⟧ covered with rough bristles, stiff hairs, or small spines —**his·pid′i·ty** ***n.***

hiss (his) ***vi.*** ⟦ME *hissen*, of echoic orig.⟧ **1** to make a sound like that of a prolonged *s*, as of a goose or snake when provoked or alarmed, or of escaping steam, air, etc. **2** to show dislike or disapproval by hissing —***vt.*** **1** to say or indicate by hissing **2** to show dislike or disapproval of by hissing **3** to force or drive by hissing [to *hiss* a performer off the stage] —***n.*** the act or sound of hissing —**hiss′er** ***n.***

Hiss (his), **Al·ger** (al′jər) 1904-96; U.S. public official: accused of espionage

☆**his·sy fit** (his′ē) ⟦< ? HYSTERICAL or HISS⟧ [Slang] a fit of anger: usually in the phrase **have** (or **throw**) **a hissy fit**: also **hissy** ***n.***, *pl.* **-sies**

hist[1] (st; hist *is a spelling pronun.*) ***interj.*** [Informal] used to attract attention, usually in an unobtrusive way

hist[2] *abbrev.* **1** historian **2** historical **3** history

hist- (hist) *combining form* HISTO-: used before a vowel

his·tam·i·nase (his tam′i nās′) ***n.*** ⟦fol. - + -ASE⟧ an enzyme found in the animal digestive system, capable of inactivating histamine

his·ta·mine (his′tə mēn′, -min) ***n.*** ⟦fol. - + AMINE⟧ an amine, $C_5H_9N_3$, produced by the decarboxylation of histidine and found in all organic matter: it is released by the tissues in allergic reactions, lowers the blood pressure by dilating blood vessels, stimulates gastric secretion, etc. —**his′ta·min′ic** (-min′ik) ***adj.***

his·ti·dine (his′ti dēn′, -din) ***n.*** ⟦< Gr *histion* (see fol.) + -INE[3]⟧ a nonessential amino acid, $C_3H_3N_2CH_2CH(NH)_2COOH$, that is essential for growth in infancy: see AMINO ACID

his·ti·o·cyte (his′tē ō sīt′) ***n.*** ⟦< Gr *histion*, web, dim. of *histos* (see fol.) + -CYTE⟧ a large macrophage, found in connective tissue, that participates in the body's reaction to infection and injury —**his′ti·o·cyt′ic** (-sit′ik) ***adj.***

his·to- (his′tō, -tə) ⟦< Gr *histos*, a loom, web < base of *histanai*, to set up, STAND⟧ *combining form* tissue [*histology*]

his·to·chem·is·try (his′tō kem′is trē) ***n.*** the study of the chemical components of cells and tissues —**his′to·chem′i·cal** (-i kəl) ***adj.*** —**his′to·chem′i·cal·ly** ***adv.***

his·to·com·pat·i·bil·i·ty (-kem pat′ə bil′ə tē) ***n.*** a condition of compatibility between the tissues of a graft or transplant and the tissues of the body receiving it

his·to·gen (his′tə jən) ***n.*** ⟦HISTO- + -GEN⟧ *Bot.* a group of cells, such as cambium or cork cambium, that gives rise to new tissue —**his′to·gen′ic** (-jen′ik) ***adj.***

his·to·gen·e·sis (his′tō jen′ə sis) ***n.*** ⟦HISTO- + -GENESIS⟧ the process of tissue development and differentiation —**his′to·ge·net′ic** (-jə net′ik) ***adj.*** —**his′to·ge·net′i·cal·ly** ***adv.***

his·to·gram (his′tə gram′) ***n.*** ⟦HISTO(RY) + -GRAM⟧ *Statistics* a BAR GRAPH allowing for variable width as well as height of the bars: the area of each bar is proportional to the frequency or relative frequency represented

his·tol·o·gy (his täl′ə jē) ***n.*** ⟦HISTO- + -LOGY⟧ **1** the branch of biology concerned with the microscopic study of the structure of tissues **2** the tissue structure of an organism or part, as revealed by microscopic study —**his·to·log·ic** (his′tə läj′ik) ***adj.***, **his′to·log′i·cal** —**his′to·log′i·cal·ly** ***adv.*** —**his·tol′o·gist** ***n.***

his·tol·y·sis (his täl′ə sis) ***n.*** ⟦HISTO- + -LYSIS⟧ *Biol.* the breakdown and dissolution of organic tissues —**his·to·lyt·ic** (his′tə lit′ik) ***adj.***

his·tone (his′tōn′) ***n.*** ⟦< Gr *histos* (see HISTO-) + -ONE⟧ any of a group of strongly basic, simple proteins found in the nucleus of cells and associated with DNA

his·to·pa·thol·o·gy (his′tō pə thäl′ə jē) ***n.*** ⟦HISTO- + PATHOLOGY⟧ the study of the microscopic changes in tissues caused by disease

his·to·phys·i·ol·o·gy (his′tō fiz′ē äl′ə jē) ***n.*** the branch of physiology concerned with the activity, function, etc. of bodily tissue: cf. HISTOLOGY —**his′to·phys′i·o·log′i·cal** ***adj.***

his·to·plas·mo·sis (-plaz mō′sis) ***n.*** ⟦ModL < *Histoplasma* (< HISTO- + PLASMA) + -OSIS⟧ a condition ranging from a mild infection to a severe disease, caused by a fungus (*Histoplasma capsulatum*) which may be inhaled or ingested: infections may occur in the lungs, liver, spleen, central nervous system, etc.

his·to·ri·an (his tôr′ē ən) ***n.*** ⟦MFr *historien*⟧ **1** a writer of history **2** an authority on or specialist in history

his·tor·ic (his tôr′ik, -tär′-) ***adj.*** ⟦L *historicus* < Gr *historikos*⟧ **1** having, or likely to have, lasting significance or importance [a *historic* occasion] **2** [Now Rare] HISTORICAL (senses 1-5)

his·tor·i·cal (his tôr′i kəl, -tär′-) ***adj.*** ⟦< L *historicus* + -AL⟧ **1** of or concerned with history as a science [the *historical* method] **2** providing evidence for a fact of history; serving as a source of history [a *historical* document] **3** based on or suggested by people or events of the past [a *historical* novel] **4** established by history; not legendary or fictional; factual; real **5** showing the development or evolution in proper chronological order [a *historical* account] **6** HISTORIC (sense 1) —**his·tor′i·cal·ly** ***adv.*** —**his·tor′i·cal·ness** ***n.***

historical linguistics the branch of linguistics that deals with the history and development of language

historical materialism an interpretation of history, esp. in Marxist theory, that holds that the chief determinants of society and social institutions are economic factors

historical present the present tense used for the narration of past events

historical school a school of thought, as in economics, legal philosophy, etc., maintaining that the basic facts and principles of a discipline, and their development, are to be ascertained by the study and interpretation of history

his·tor·i·cism (his tôr′i siz′əm) ***n.*** **1** a theory of history holding that the course of events is determined by unchangeable laws or cyclic patterns **2** the theory that the only true understanding of a person, society, historical period, etc. comes about through knowledge of its history **3** a reliance on historical precedents in the practice of art, architecture, music, etc. —**his·tor′i·cist** ***n., adj.***

his·to·ric·i·ty (his′tə ris′ə tē) ***n.*** the condition of having actually occurred in history; authenticity

his·tor·i·cize (his tôr′ə sīz′) ***vt.*** **-cized′**, **-ciz′ing** to make, or make seem, historical or historically real —***vi.*** to use historical materials

his·tor·i·co- (his tôr′i kō) *combining form* historical, historical and [*historicoliterary*]

his·to·ried (his′tə rēd) ***adj.*** having a history or told about in history

his·to·ri·og·ra·pher (his tôr′ē äg′rə fər) ***n.*** ⟦< OFr or LL: OFr *historiographeur* < LL *historiographus* < Gr *historiographos* < *historia* (see HISTORY) + *graphein*, to write (see GRAPHIC)⟧ **1** a historian; esp., one appointed to write the history of some institution, country, etc. **2** a specialist in historiography

his·to·ri·og·ra·phy (-fē) ***n.*** **1** the writing of history **2** HISTORY (sense 4); specif., the study of the techniques of historical research and historical writing, the methods of major historians, etc. **3** a body of historical writing —**his·to′ri·o·graph′ic** (-ə graf′ik) ***adj.***, **his·to′ri·o·graph′i·cal** —**his·to′ri·o·graph′i·cal·ly** ***adv.***

his·to·ry (his′tə rē, his′trē) ***n.***, *pl.* **-ries** ⟦ME < L *historia* < Gr, a learning by inquiry, narrative < *histōr*, knowing, learned < base of *eidenai*, to know < IE base **weid-*, to see, know > WISE[1]⟧ **1** an account of what has or might have happened, esp. in the form of a narrative, play, story, or tale **2** *a)* what has happened in the life or development of a people, country, institution, etc. *b)* a systematic account of this, usually in chronological order with an analysis and explanation *c)* the chronological story or development of a group, institution, etc. [the next election is a crucial point in our nation's *history*] **3** all recorded events of the past **4** the branch of knowledge that deals systematically with the past; a recording, analyzing, correlating, and explaining of past events **5** a known or recorded past [the strange *history* of his lost luggage] ☆**6** *a)* something that belongs to the past [the election is *history* now] *b)* [Informal] someone or something regarded as no longer important, relevant, useful, etc. **7** something important enough to be recorded, preserved, etc. **8** a scientific account of a system of natural phenomena: now rare except in NATURAL HISTORY **9** a record of a person's medical condition, treatments received, etc. [her medical *history*] —**make history** to be or do something important enough to be recorded

his·tri·on·ic (his′trē än′ik) ***adj.*** ⟦LL *histrionicus* < L *histrio*, actor; ult. of Etr orig.⟧ **1** of, or having the nature of, acting or actors **2** overacted or overacting; theatrical; artificial; affected —**his′tri·on′i·cal·ly** ***adv.***

his·tri·on·ics (-iks) ***pl.n.*** [*sometimes with sing. v.*] **1** theatricals; dramatics **2** an artificial or affected manner, display of emotion, etc.; melodramatics

hit (hit) ***vt.*** **hit**, **hit′ting** ⟦ME *hitten* < OE *hittan* < ON *hitta*, to hit upon, meet with < IE base **keid-*, to fall > Welsh *cwydd*, a fall⟧ **1** to come against, usually with force; strike [the car *hit* the tree] **2** to give a blow to; strike; knock **3** to strike so as to deliver (a blow) **4** to strike by throwing or shooting a missile at [to *hit* the target] **5** to cause to knock, bump, or strike, as in falling, moving, etc.: often with *on* or *against* [to *hit* one's head on a door] **6** to affect strongly or adversely so as to distress or harm [a town *hit* hard by floods] **7** to come upon by accident or after search; find; light upon [to *hit* the right answer] ☆**8** to arrive at (a place or point); reach; attain [stocks *hit* a new high] **9** to go to; visit [we *hit* all the art galleries in town] **10** STRIKE, ***vt.*** 8, 9, & 10 (variously) ☆**11** [Informal] to apply oneself to steadily or frequently [to *hit* the books] **12** [Slang] to demand or require of: with *for*; often with *up* [she *hit* me up for a loan] ☆**13** [Slang] to murder: said as of a hired murderer or an assassin **14** [Slang] to supply with a drug, etc. ☆**15** *Baseball a)* to get (a specified result) while batting the ball [to *hit* a double, a pop-up, etc.] *b)* to bat successfully against [to regularly *hit* southpaws] ☆**16** *Card Games* in blackjack, to deal another card to —***vi.*** **1** to give a blow or blows; strike **2** to attack suddenly **3** to knock, bump, or strike: usually with *against* **4** to come by accident or after search: with *on* or *upon* ☆**5** to ignite the combustible mixture in its cylinders: said of an internal-combustion engine ☆**6** *Baseball a)* to bat [to *hit* only against southpaws, to *hit* fourth in the lineup] *b)* to hit the ball (with a specified result) [to *hit* into a double play] —***n.*** **1** a blow, shot, etc. that strikes its mark **2** a collision of one thing with another **3** an effectively witty or sarcastic remark **4** a stroke of good fortune **5** a successful and popular song, singer, book, author, etc. ☆**6** [Slang] a murder, as by a hired murderer or an assassin **7** [Slang] a dose of a drug, a drink of alcoholic liquor, etc. **8** *Backgammon* a game won by a player after one or more of the opponent's men have been removed from the board ☆**9** *Baseball* BASE HIT **10** *Comput. a)* an instance of finding or matching particular data in a computer search *b)* an instance of being accessed: said of a website —***adj.*** [Informal] designating or of a very successful and popular movie, recording, etc. —**hit it off** [Informal] to get along well together; be congenial —**hit off** to mimic or portray briefly and well, usually in a satirical way —**hit on** [Slang] to make sexual advances to —**hit or miss** without regard to success or failure; in a haphazard or aimless way —**hit (out) at** **1** to aim a blow at; try to hit **2** to attack in words; criticize severely —**hit someone over the head** **1** to strike on the head **2** [Informal] to emphasize repeatedly or strongly to in an excessive manner —**hit the fan** [Slang] to become suddenly embarrassing, troublesome, etc.; have a strong negative effect —**hit the ground running** [Informal] to work or function vigorously and effectively from the very beginning —☆**hit the road** [Slang] to leave; go away —**hit′ta·ble** ***adj.*** —**hit′ter** ***n.***

hit-and-miss (hit′'n mis′) ***adj.*** **1** resulting in both successes and failures: said as of a series of attempts **2** HIT-OR-MISS

☆**hit-and-run** (hit′'n run′) ***adj.*** **1** involving a hitting and then escaping: used as of an automobile accident in which the driver flees from the scene **2** *Baseball* designating a prearranged play in which a runner on base starts running as the pitch is made and the batter must attempt to hit the ball to protect the runner

hitch (hich) ***vi.*** ⟦ME *hicchen*, to move jerkily < ?⟧ **1** to move jerkily; walk haltingly; limp; hobble **2** to become fastened or caught, as by becoming entangled or hooking on to something **3** to strike the feet together in moving: said of a horse ☆**4** [Slang] to hitchhike —***vt.*** **1** to move, pull, or shift with jerks [*hitch* your chair up to the table] **2** to fasten with a hook, knot, harness, etc.; unite; tie: often with *up* [to *hitch* a wagon to a tractor] **3** [Slang] to marry: usually in the passive [we got *hitched* last spring] ☆**4** [Slang] to hitchhike —***n.*** **1** a short, sudden movement or pull; tug; jerk **2** a hobble; limp **3** a hindrance; obstacle; entanglement **4** a fastening or catch; thing or part used to connect or join together [a trailer *hitch* fastened to the back of a car] ☆**5** [Slang] a ride in hitchhiking ☆**6** [Slang] a period of time served, as of military service, imprisonment, etc. **7** a kind of knot that can be easily undone, for fastening a line as to a ring or pole —**without a hitch** without a problem or setback; smoothly, easily, and successfully

Hitch·cock[1] (hich′käk) ***adj.*** ⟦after L. *Hitchcock* (1795-1852), U.S. furniture designer⟧ designating or of a style of 19th-cent. American furniture characterized by simple lines and having a black finish with stenciled designs

Hitch·cock[2] (hich′käk), Sir **Alfred (Joseph)** 1899-1980; Brit. film director, in U.S. after 1939

☆**hitch·hike** (hich′hīk′) ***vi.*** **-hiked′**, **-hik′ing** ⟦HITCH + HIKE⟧ to travel by soliciting rides from motorists along the way —***vt.*** to get (a ride) or make (one's way) in this fashion —**hitch′hik′er** ***n.***

hi-tech (hī′tek′) ***n., adj.*** *informal sp. of* HIGH-TECH

hith·er (hith′ər) ***adv.*** ⟦ME *hider* < OE (akin to Goth *hidre*, ON *hethra*) < base of *he* (see HE[1]) + *-der*, suffix as in HINDER[2]⟧ [Now Literary] to or toward this place; here —***adj.*** [Archaic] on or toward this side; nearer [the *hither* horse]

hith·er·most (hith′ər mōst′) ***adj.*** nearest

hith·er·to (hith′ər to͞o′, hith′ər to͞o′) ***adv.*** ⟦see HITHER & TO[1]⟧ **1** until this time; to now **2** [Obs.] hither

hith·er·ward (-wərd) *adv.* ⟦OE *hiderweard*: see -WARD⟧ [Rare] toward this place; hither: also **hith′er·wards**

Hit·ler (hit′lər), **Ad·olf** (ad′ôlf′, ä′dôlf′) 1889-1945; Nazi dictator of Germany (1933-45), born in Austria —**Hit·ler′i·an** (-lir′ē ən, -ler′-) *adj.*

Hit·ler·ism (-iz′əm) *n.* the fascist program, ideas, and methods of Hitler and the Nazis —**Hit′ler·ite′** (-īt′) *n., adj.*

☆**hit list** ⟦see fol.⟧ [Informal] a list of those persons, groups, programs, etc. that are to be opposed or done away with

☆**hit man** ⟦< underworld slang *hit*, murder⟧ [Informal] a man paid to kill someone; hired murderer

hit-or-miss (hit′ər mis′) *adj.* haphazard; random

☆**hit-skip** (-skip′) *adj.* HIT-AND-RUN (sense 1)

Hit·tite (hit′īt′) *n.* ⟦Heb *Ḥittī* (< Hittite *ḫatti*) + -ITE[1]⟧ **1** any of an ancient people of Asia Minor and Syria (fl. 1700-700 B.C.) **2** the language of the Hittites, now extinct and considered by most authorities to be associated with Indo-European: it is recorded in divergent cuneiform and hieroglyphic inscriptions —*adj.* of the Hittites or their language or culture

HIV (āch′ī′vē′) *n.* ⟦*h(uman) i(mmunodeficiency) v(irus)*⟧ either of two retroviruses that infect human T cells and cause AIDS

hive (hīv) *n.* ⟦ME *hyfe* < OE, akin to ON *hūfr*, ship's hull < IE **keup-* (< base **keu-*, to bend, curve) > L *cupa*, a tub⟧ **1** *a)* a box or other shelter for a colony of domesticated bees *b)* any structure made or used by a colony of bees, wasps, etc. as a nesting place *c)* a colony of bees living in a hive; swarm **2** a crowd of busy, very active people **3** a place where many people are busy or actively engaged —*vt.* **hived, hiv′ing 1** to put or gather (bees) into a hive **2** to store up (honey) in a hive **3** to store up for future use; garner —*vi.* **1** to enter a hive **2** to live together in or as in a hive —**hive off 1** to depart from a group **2** to separate from the whole [*hived off* the first graders to another playground]

hives (hīvz) *n.* ⟦orig. Scot dial.⟧ [*with sing. or pl. verb*] an allergic skin condition characterized by itching, burning, stinging, and the formation of smooth patches, or wheals, usually red; urticaria

Hiz·bol·lah (hiz′bə lä′, hez′-; hiz bä′lə, hez-) *n. var. of* HEZBOLLAH: also **Hiz·bul·lah** (hiz′bə lä′, hez′-; hiz bul′ə, hez-)

H. J. *abbrev.* ⟦L HIC JACET⟧ here lies

hl *abbrev.* hectoliter(s)

HL *abbrev.* House of Lords: also **H of L**

HLA (āch′el′ā′) *n.* ⟦*h(uman) l(eukocyte) a(ntigen)*⟧ any of certain inherited antigens present on the surface of nucleated tissue cells in humans, used in determining histocompatibility, susceptibility to certain diseases, etc.

hm *abbrev.* hectometer(s)

HM *abbrev.* **1** hazardous material **2** Her (or His) Majesty

hmm or **hm** (həm: *conventionalized pronun.*) *interj.* HEM[2]: used to signify hesitation, a question, thoughtful consideration of another person's statement, etc.

HMO (āch′em′ō′) *n., pl.* **HMO's** ⟦*h(ealth) m(aintenance) o(rganization)*⟧ a healthcare system in which an organization hires medical professionals and operates medical facilities to provide a wide range of specified services to prepaid subscribers

Hmong (muŋ) *n.* ⟦self-designation in Hmong⟧ **1** a member of a people living in highland areas of Vietnam, Laos, Thailand, and S China **2** the Tai language of this people

HMS *abbrev.* **1** Her (or His) Majesty's Service **2** Her (or His) Majesty's Ship (or Steamer)

ho[1] (hō) *interj.* ⟦ME, echoic⟧ **1** [Archaic] used to express surprise, pleasure, derision, etc. **2** used to attract attention: sometimes used after a word indicating a destination or direction [land *ho!* westward *ho!*]

ho[2] (hō) *interj.* ⟦ME < OFr⟧ *var. of* WHOA

☆**ho**[3] (hō) *n.* ⟦dial. pronun. of WHORE⟧ [Slang] WHORE: an offensive term of contempt

Ho[1] *abbrev. Bible* Hosea

Ho[2] *Chem. symbol for* holmium

☆**hoa·gie** or **hoa·gy** (hō′gē) *n., pl.* **-gies** ⟦altered < *hoggie* (< HOG): so named prob. after *Hog Island* Shipyard (Philadelphia), in the 1930s, from the sandwich's popularity among shipyard workers⟧ HERO SANDWICH

hoar (hôr) *adj.* ⟦ME *hore* < OE *har*, akin to Ger *hehr*, venerable < IE base **k̑ei-*, term for dark colors, gray, brown > HUE[1], ON *harr*, gray, old, Pol *szary*, gray⟧ **1** HOARY **2** [Obs.] moldy; stale —*n.* **1** HOARINESS **2** HOARFROST

hoard (hôrd) *n.* ⟦ME *hord* < OE, akin to Ger *hort*, Goth *huzd* < IE **keus-* < base **(s)keu-*, to cover, conceal > HIDE[1], Gr *skylos*, animal's skin⟧ a supply stored up and hidden or kept in reserve —*vi.* to accumulate and store away money, goods, or other valued items —*vt.* to accumulate and hide or keep in reserve —**hoard′er** *n.* —**hoard′ing** *n.*

hoard·ing (hôr′diŋ) *n.* ⟦< obs. *hoard*, hoarding < OFr *hourde* < Frank **hurda*, enclosure, pen: for IE base see HURDLE⟧ [Brit.] **1** a temporary wooden fence around a site of building construction or repair **2** a billboard

hoar·frost (hôr′frôst′) *n.* ⟦ME *horfrost*: see HOAR & FROST⟧ FROST (sense 3)

hoarse (hôrs) *adj.* **hoars′er, hoars′est** ⟦ME *hors, hase* < OE *has*, akin to ON *hāss*, OS *hēs*, OHG *heisi* < IE base **kai-*, heat > HOT, HEAT⟧ **1** harsh and grating in sound; sounding rough and husky **2** having a rough, husky voice, esp. temporarily as from irritation of the throat or vocal cords —**hoarse′ly** *adv.* —**hoarse′ness** *n.*

hoars·en (hôr′sən) *vt., vi.* to make or become hoarse

hoar·y (hôr′ē) *adj.* **hoar′i·er, hoar′i·est** ⟦HOAR + -Y[2]⟧ **1** white, gray, or grayish-white **2** having white or gray hair from advanced age: also **hoar′y-head′ed 3** very old; ancient —**hoar′i·ly** *adv.* —**hoar′i·ness** *n.*

☆**hoary marmot** a marmot (*Marmota caligata*) found in the mountains of NW North America

ho·at·zin (hō at′sin, wät sēn′) *n.* ⟦AmSp < Nahuatl *uatzin*⟧ a crested South American bird (*Opisthocomus hoazin*) of an order (Opisthocomiformes) with only one species: the wings of its young have claws

hoax (hōks) *n.* ⟦< ? HOCUS⟧ a trick or fraud, esp. one meant as a practical joke —*vt.* to deceive with a hoax —*SYN.* CHEAT —**hoax′er** *n.*

hob[1] (häb) *n.* ⟦? var. of HUB⟧ **1** a projecting ledge at the back or side of a fireplace, used for keeping a kettle, saucepan, etc. warm **2** a peg used as a target in quoits, etc. **3** a device for cutting teeth in a gear blank, etc.

hob[2] (häb) *n.* ⟦ME, old familiar form for ROBIN, ROBERT[1]⟧ [Brit. Dial.] **1** a rustic **2** an elf or goblin **3** [H-] Robin Goodfellow, or Puck —**play** (or **raise**) **hob with** to make trouble for; interfere with and make disordered

Ho·bart (hō′bərt, -bärt) seaport & capital of Tasmania, on the SE coast

Hob·be·ma (häb′ə mä), **Mein·dert** (mīn′dərt) 1638-1709; Du. painter

Hobbes (häbz), **Thomas** 1588-1679; Eng. social philosopher: author of *Leviathan* —**Hobbes′i·an** *adj., n.*

Hob·bism (häb′iz′əm) *n.* the philosophy of Thomas Hobbes, who held that a strong government, esp. an absolute monarchy, is needed to control clashing individual interests

hob·ble (häb′əl) *vi.* **-bled, -bling** ⟦ME *hobelen* (akin to Du *hobbelen*, Ger dial. *hobbeln*) < base of *hoppen* (see HOP[1]) + freq. suffix⟧ **1** to go unsteadily, haltingly, etc. **2** to walk lamely or awkwardly; limp —*vt.* **1** to cause to go haltingly or lamely **2** to hamper the movement of (a horse, etc.) by tying two feet together **3** to hamper; hinder —*n.* **1** an awkward, halting walk; limp **2** a rope, strap, etc. used to hobble a horse; fetter —**hob′bler** *n.*

☆**hob·ble·bush** (häb′əl boosh′) *n.* a viburnum (*Viburnum alnifolium*) with clusters of small, white flowers and red to purple berries

hob·ble·de·hoy (häb′əl dē hoi′) *n.* ⟦earlier *hoberdihoye, hobbedihoy*, prob. based on HOB[2] with cross assoc. < HOBBLE, HOBBY[1]⟧ a boy or adolescent youth, esp. one who is awkward and gawky

hobble skirt ⟦from the notion that it hinders the wearer's movements⟧ a style of woman's skirt that is long and tight below the knees, esp., such a skirt popular from 1910 to 1914

hob·by[1] (häb′ē) *n., pl.* **-bies** ⟦ME *hobi* < *hobin*, dim. of *Robert*, ROBERT[1]⟧ **1** [Archaic] a medium-sized, vigorous horse **2** HOBBYHORSE **3** ⟦< sense 2, with notions as in phrase RIDE A HOBBY⟧ something that one likes to do or study in one's spare time; favorite pastime or avocation —**ride a hobby** to be excessively devoted to one's favorite pastime or subject —**hob′by·ist** *n.*

hob·by[2] (häb′ē) *n., pl.* **-bies** ⟦ME *hobi* < OFr *hobei, hobel*, dim. of *hobe*, a hawk < Du *hobben*, to move back and forth, akin to HOP[1]⟧ a small European falcon (*Falco subbuteo*), formerly trained for hawking

hob·by·horse (häb′ē hôrs′) *n.* **1** *a)* a figure of a horse attached to the waist of a person doing a morris dance so that the person seems to be riding it *b)* such a dancer **2** a child's toy consisting of a stick with a horse's head at one end: it is straddled in a pretense of riding **3** ROCKING HORSE **4** a scheme or idea with which one is preoccupied

hob·gob·lin (häb′gäb′lin) *n.* ⟦HOB[2], sense 2 + GOBLIN⟧ **1** *Folklore* a goblin, fairy, etc. **2** anything inspiring seemingly excessive fear or dread; bogy; bugbear

hob·nail (häb′nāl′) *n.* ⟦HOB[1], sense 2 + NAIL⟧ **1** a short nail with a broad head, put on the soles of heavy shoes to prevent wear or slipping **2** one of a series of knoblike decorations, as on the edge of a glass plate —*vt.* to put hobnails on

hob·nob (häb′näb′) *adv.* ⟦earlier *habnab*, lit., to have and not have < ME *habben*, to have + *nabben* (< *ne habben*), not to have, esp. with reference to taking turns in drinking⟧ [Now Rare] at random —*vi.* **-nobbed′, -nob′bing 1** [Now Rare] to drink together **2** [Informal] to associate or mingle (*with* others, esp. famous or socially prominent people) —*n.* [Now Rare] a friendly chat

☆**ho·bo** (hō′bō) *n., pl.* **-bos** or **-boes** ⟦< ?⟧ **1** a migratory worker: so used by such workers themselves **2** a vagrant; tramp —*vi.* to travel in the manner of a hobo —*SYN.* VAGRANT

Hob·son (häb′sən), **John A(tkinson)** 1858-1940; Eng. economist

Hob·son's choice (häb′sənz) ⟦after T. *Hobson* (1544?-1631), of Cambridge, England, who owned livery stables and rented horses in strict order according to their position near the door⟧ a choice of taking what is offered or nothing at all; lack of an alternative

Ho Chi Minh (hō′ chē′ min′) (born *Nguyen That Thanh*) 1890-1969; president of North Vietnam (1954-69)

Ho Chi Minh City seaport in S Vietnam: formerly (as *Saigon*) capital of South Vietnam, 1954-76

hock[1] (häk) *n.* ⟦S Brit var. of Scot *hough* < ME *hoh*, heel < OE < Gmc **hanha*, HEEL[1], with loss of nasal as in SOFT, TOOTH⟧ **1** the joint bending backward in the hind leg of a horse, ox, etc., corresponding to the human ankle **2** the corresponding joint in the leg of a fowl —*vt.* to disable by cutting the tendons of the hock

hock[2] (häk) *n.* ⟦contr. of *hockamore*, altered < Ger *Hochheimer*⟧ [Chiefly Brit.] any white Rhine wine, originally that from Hochheim, Germany

☆**hock**[3] (häk) [Slang] *n., vt.* ⟦< Du *hok*, kennel, cage, prison⟧ PAWN[1] —**in** (or **out of**) **hock 1** in (or out of) pawn **2** in (or out of) debt

hock·ey (häk′ē) *n.* ⟦Early ModE, prob. < OFr *hoquet*, bent stick, crook, dim. of *hoc*, hook < MDu *hoec*, HOOK⟧ ☆**1** a team game played on ice, in which the players, using a long, curved stick with a flat blade (**hockey stick**) and wearing skates, try to drive a hard rubber disk (*puck*) into their opponent's goal; ice hockey **2** a similar game played on foot on a field with a small ball instead of a puck; field hockey

☆**hock·shop** (häk′shäp′) ***n.*** [Slang] PAWNSHOP

ho·cus (hō′kəs) ***vt.*** **-cused** or **-cussed**, **-cus·ing** or **-cus·sing** ⟦contr. < fol.⟧ [Archaic] **1** to play a trick on; dupe; hoax **2** to drug (a person) **3** to put drugs in (a drink)

ho·cus-po·cus (-pō′kəs) ***n.*** ⟦imitation L, prob. altered < *hax pax* (*max Deus adimax*), arbitrary magic formula attributed to medieval traveling scholars⟧ **1** meaningless words used as a formula by conjurers **2** a magician's trick or trickery; sleight of hand; legerdemain **3** any meaningless action or talk drawing attention away from some deception **4** trickery; deception — ***vt., vi.*** **-cused** or **-cussed**, **-cus·ing** or **-cus·sing** [Informal] to trick; dupe

hod (häd) ***n.*** ⟦prob. < MDu *hodde*, akin to Ger dial. *hotte*⟧ **1** a V-shaped, wooden or metal trough with a long handle, used for carrying bricks, mortar, etc. on the shoulder **2** a coal scuttle

☆**ho-dad·dy** (hō′dad′ē) ***n.***, *pl.* **-dies** ⟦< ?⟧ [Slang] one who engages in the sport of surfing or, esp., one who spends much time on beaches with surfers for vicarious excitement: also **ho′-dad′**

hod carrier a laborer who assists a bricklayer, plasterer, or mason, as by carrying bricks, mortar, etc. on a hod

hod·den (häd′′n) ***n.*** ⟦< ?⟧ [Scot.] a coarse, undyed woolen cloth: a gray variety (**hodden gray**) is made by mixing white and black fleece

Ho·dei·da (hō dā′də) seaport in Yemen, on the Red Sea

hodge·podge (häj′päj′) ***n.*** ⟦ME *hogpoch*: see HOTCHPOTCH⟧ **1** a kind of stew: now usually HOTCHPOTCH **2** any jumbled mixture; mess

Hodg·kin (häj′kin) **1** Sir **Alan Lloyd** 1914-98; Brit. biophysicist **2 Dorothy (Mary)** (born *Dorothy Mary Crowfoot*) 1910-94; Brit. chemist

Hodg·kin's disease (häj′kinz) ⟦after Dr. T. *Hodgkin* (1798-1866), Eng physician who first described it⟧ a type of lymphoma characterized by the presence of a certain kind of malignant cell: also **Hodg′kin lymphoma**

hod·o·scope (häd′ə skōp′) ***n.*** ⟦< Gr *hodos*, path (see -ODE[1]) + -SCOPE⟧ an instrument for tracing the paths of ionizing particles, as of electrons in cosmic rays

hoe (hō) ***n.*** ⟦ME *houe* < OFr < OHG *houwa* < *houwan*, to cut, HEW⟧ a tool with a thin, flat blade set across the end of a long handle, used for weeding, loosening soil, etc. — ***vt., vi.*** **hoed**, **hoe′ing** to dig, cultivate, weed, etc. with a hoe —**ho′er *n.***

☆**hoe·cake** (hō′kāk′) ***n.*** a thin bread made of cornmeal, orig. baked on a hoe at the fire

☆**hoe·down** (hō′doun′) ***n.*** ⟦prob. of black orig.; assoc. with BREAKDOWN, sense 2⟧ **1** a lively, rollicking dance, often a square dance **2** music for this **3** a party at which hoedowns are danced

Ho·fei (hu′fā′) *a former transliteration of* HEFEI

Hof·fa (häf′ə), **Jim·my** (jim′ē) (legal name *James Riddle Hoffa*) 1913-75?; U.S. labor leader

Hoff·mann (hôf′män), **E(rnst) T(heodor) A(madeus)** (born *Ernst Theodor Wilhelm Hoffmann*) 1776-1822; Ger. writer & composer

Hof·manns·thal (hôf′mäns täl′), **Hu·go von** (hōō′ gô fôn) 1874-1929; Austrian playwright & poet

garden hoe

Ho·fuf (hoo fōōf′) city in E Saudi Arabia, near the Persian Gulf

hog (hôg, häg) ***n.***, *pl.* **hogs** or, for 1 & 2, **hog** ⟦ME < OE *hogg* < ? or akin to ON *höggva*, to cut (akin to OE *heawan*, HEW), in basic sense "castrated"⟧ **1** any swine, esp. a domesticated adult (*Sus scrofa*) ready for market, or, in England, a castrated boar: see PIG (sense 1) **2** [Brit.] a young sheep not yet shorn **3** [Informal] *a)* a selfish, greedy, or gluttonous person *b)* a coarse or filthy person **4** [Slang] a large, heavy motorcycle —***vt.*** **hogged**, **hog′ging 1** *a)* to arch (the back) like a hog's *b)* to cause (a ship, keel, etc.) to be higher in the center than at the ends **2** to trim (a horse's mane) in order to make it bristly ☆**3** [Slang] to grab greedily; take all of or an unfairly large share of —***vi.*** to be higher in the center than at the ends: said of the bottom of a ship —**go (the) whole hog** [Slang] to go all the way; do or accept something fully —☆**high on (or off) the hog** [Slang] in a luxurious or costly way

☆**ho·gan** (hō′gôn′, -gän′; -gən) ***n.*** ⟦Navajo *hooghan*, house⟧ the traditional dwelling of the Navajo Indians, built of earth walls supported by timbers

Ho·gan (hō′gən), **Ben** (born *William Benjamin Hogan*) 1912-97; U.S. golfer

Ho·garth (hō′gärth), **William** 1697-1764; Eng. painter & engraver: known for his satirical pictures of 18th-cent. English life —**Ho·garth′i·an *adj.***

hog·back (hôg′bak′) ***n.*** ⟦descriptive⟧ a ridge with a sharp crest and abruptly sloping sides, often formed by the outcropping edge of steeply dipping rock strata

☆**hog cholera** an infectious viral disease of hogs, characterized by fever, loss of appetite, diarrhea, and frequently by congestion and hemorrhages in the kidneys

hog·fish (hôg′fish′) ***n.***, *pl.* **-fish′** or **-fish′es** (see FISH) ⟦orig. ? transl. of OFr *porpeis*: see PORPOISE⟧ **1** any of several fishes whose head supposedly resembles that of a hog, as a pigfish **2** a bright-red, edible wrasse (*Lachnolaimus maximus*) found off the SE coast of the U.S.

Hogg (hôg, häg), **James** 1770-1835; Scot. poet & novelist

hog·gish (hôg′ish) ***adj.*** like a hog; very selfish, greedy, coarse, or filthy —**hog′gish·ly *adv.*** —**hog′gish·ness *n.***

hog·ma·nay (häg′mə nā′) ***n.*** ⟦Anglo-Norm *hoguinané*, corrupted < OFr *aguillanneuf*, last day of the year < *aguille*, needle, point (< LL *acula*, dim. of L *acus*: see ACEROSE[1]) + *neuf*, new (< L *novus*, NEW)⟧ [Scot.] New Year's Eve, when young people go about singing and seeking gifts

☆**hog-nose snake** (hôg′nōz′) any of a genus (*Heterodon*) of small, harmless North American colubrid snakes with a flat snout and a thick body: also **hog′nosed′ snake**

☆**hog·nut** (hôg′nut′) ***n.*** PIGNUT

☆**hog peanut** a twining, leguminous vine (genus *Amphicarpaea*) native to E North America: the flowers borne near the ground develop bladdery pods underground

hogs·head (hôgz′hed′) ***n.*** ⟦ME *hoggeshede*, lit., hog's head: reason for name uncert.⟧ **1** a large barrel or cask holding from 63 to 140 gallons (*c.* 238.5 to *c.* 530 liters) **2** any of various units of liquid measure, esp. one equal to 63 gallons or *c.* 52.5 imperial gallons (*c.* 238.5 liters)

☆**hog·tie** (hôg′tī′) ***vt.*** **-tied′**, **-ty′ing** or **-tie′ing 1** to tie the four feet or the hands and feet of **2** [Informal] to make incapable of effective action, as if by tying up

hog·wash (hôg′wôsh′) ***n.*** **1** refuse fed to hogs; swill **2** useless or insincere talk, writing, etc.

hog·weed (-wēd′) ***n.*** any of various coarse weeds, as ragweed

☆**hog-wild** (hôg′wīld′) ***adj.*** [Informal] excited, enthusiastic, jubilant, angry, etc. to the point of loss of self-restraint [the crowd went *hog-wild* when the team won]: also written **hog wild**

Hoh·en·stau·fen (hō′ən shtou′fən) ***n.*** name of the ruling family of Germany (1138-1208; 1215-54) & of Sicily (1194-1268)

Hoh·en·zol·lern[1] (hō′ən tsôl′ərn; *E*, -zäl′ərn) ***n.*** name of the ruling family of Brandenburg (1415-1918), of Prussia (1701-1918), & of Germany (1871-1918)

Hoh·en·zol·lern[2] (hō′ən tsôl′ərn; *E*, -zäl′ərn) historical region of SW Germany: formerly a province of Prussia

Hoh·hot (hō′hōt′) city in N China: capital of Inner Mongolia

ho-ho (hō hō′) ***interj.*** used to suggest the sound of laughter: in traditional portrayals of Santa Claus, it is usually **ho-ho-ho**

ho-hum (hō′hum′; *for adj.* hō′hum′) ***interj.*** ⟦conventionalized representation of a yawn⟧ used to signify boredom, lack of interest, weariness, etc. —*adj.* [Informal] uninteresting; boring; tiresome

hoi pol·loi (hoi′pə loi′) ⟦Gr, lit., the many⟧ the common people; the masses: often preceded by *the*: usually patronizing or contemptuous

hoise (hoiz) ***vt.*** **hoised** or **hoist**, **hois′ing** ⟦Early ModE phonetic sp. of earlier *hyce* < Du *hijschen* < or akin to LowG *hissen*: of naut. orig.⟧ *obs. var. of* HOIST

hoi·sin sauce (hoi′sin, hoi sin′) ⟦< Chin (Cantonese) *hoi sin* (*jeung*), seafood (sauce)⟧ a dark, spicy sauce used in Chinese cooking, made of fermented rice, soy beans, vinegar, sugar, salt, and chili

hoist (hoist) ***vt.*** ⟦< HOISE + unhistoric *-t* (< ? the pp.)⟧ to raise aloft; lift or pull up, esp. by means of a cable, pulley, crane, etc. —***n.*** **1** an act of hoisting **2** an apparatus for raising heavy things; elevator; tackle **3** *Naut. a)* the perpendicular height of a sail or flag *b)* a group of signal flags displayed together on one line —**SYN.** LIFT

hoi·ty-toi·ty (hoit′ē toit′ē) ***adj.*** ⟦redupl. of obs. *hoit*, to indulge in noisy mirth⟧ haughty; arrogant; condescending

Ho·kan (hō′kən) ***n.*** ⟦< *hok*, about two, in a language or languages of this group + -AN⟧ a group of distantly related language families of the SW U.S. and Mexico, including Yuman

☆**hoke** (hōk) [Slang] ***vt.*** **hoked**, **hok′ing** ⟦< HOKUM⟧ to treat in a mawkishly sentimental, crudely comic, or artificial way: usually with *up* —***n.*** HOKUM —**hok′ey *adj.***

ho·key·po·key or **ho·ky·po·ky** (hō′kē pō′kē) ***n.*** ⟦altered ? < HOCUS-POCUS⟧ **1** [Historical] a kind of ice cream or flavored ice formerly sold by street vendors **2** a children's singing and dancing game

Hok·kai·do (hō kī′dō) one of the four main islands of Japan, north of Honshu: 32,221 sq mi (83,452 sq km); chief city, Sapporo

hok·ku (hô′kōō′) ***n.*** *var. of* HAIKU

☆**ho·kum** (hō′kəm) ***n.*** ⟦altered < HOCUS(-POCUS)⟧ [Slang] **1** trite or mawkish sentiment, crude humor, etc. used to get a quick emotional response from an audience **2** nonsense; humbug; claptrap

Ho·ku·sai (hô′koo sī′), **Ka·tsu·shi·ka** (kä′tsoo shē′kä) 1760-1849; Jpn. painter & wood engraver

Hol·arc·tic (häl ärk′tik, hōl-) ***adj.*** ⟦HOL(O)- + ARCTIC⟧ designating or of the zoogeographic region consisting of both the Nearctic and Palearctic realms

Hol·bein (hōl′bīn) **1 Hans** 1465?-1524; Ger. painter: called *the Elder* **2 Hans** 1497?-1543; Ger. portrait painter in England: son of Hans Holbein (the Elder): called *the Younger*

hold[1] (hōld) ***vt.*** **held**, **hold′ing** ⟦ME *holden* < Anglian OE *haldan* (WS *healdan*), akin to Ger *halten*, Goth *haldan*, to tend sheep < IE base **kel-*, to drive, incite to action > Gr *kelēs*, swift horse, L *celer*, swift: prob. sense development: drive (cattle, etc.) → tend → possess⟧ **1** to take and keep with the hands or arms, or by other means; grasp; clutch; seize ☆**2** to keep from going away; not let escape; detain [to *hold* the train, *hold* a prisoner] **3** to keep in a certain place or position, or in a specified condition [to *hold* one's head up] **4** to restrain or control; specif., *a)* to keep from falling; bear the weight of; support [pillars *holding* the roof] *b)* to keep from acting; keep back [*hold* your tongue] *c)* to keep from advancing or attacking *d)* to keep from getting an advantage *e)* to get and keep control of; keep from relaxing or lapsing [to *hold* someone's attention] *f)* to continue; maintain [to *hold* a course] *g)* [Informal] to sustain or satisfy for the time being [a muffin should *hold* you until supper time] ☆*h)* to keep (a letter, etc.) for delivery later *i)* to keep (a room, etc.) for use later *j)* to keep under obligation; bind [*hold* him to his word] *k)* to resist the effects of (alcoholic liquor) **5** to have and keep as one's own; have the duties, privileges, etc. of; own; possess; occupy [to *hold* shares of stock, to *hold* the office of mayor] **6** to keep against an enemy; guard; defend [*hold* the fort] **7** to have or conduct together; specif., *a)* to carry on (a meeting, conversation, etc.) *b)* to perform (a function, service, etc.) [to *hold* classes in the morning] **8** to call together or preside over [to *hold* court] **9** to have or keep within itself; have room or space for; contain [a bottle that *holds* a quart] **10** to have or keep in the mind **11** to have an opinion or belief about; believe, consider, etc. [we *hold* these truths to be self-evident] **12** *Law a)* to decide; adjudge; decree *b)* to bind by contract *c)* to possess by legal title [to *hold* a mortgage] **13** *Music* to prolong (a tone or rest) —*vi.* **1** to retain a hold, a firm contact, etc. [*hold* tight] **2** to go on being firm, loyal, etc. [to *hold* to a resolution] **3** to remain unbroken or unyielding; not give way [the rope *held*] **4** to have right or title: usually with *from* or *of* **5** to be in effect or in force; be true or valid [a rule that *holds* in any case] **6** to keep up; continue [the wind *held* from the north]; specif., *a)* to remain in the air, waiting to land [a plane *holding* over Boston] *b)* to remain on a telephone line [that line is busy—will you *hold*?] **7** [Archaic] to go no further; stop oneself; halt: usually in the imperative —*n.* **1** the act or manner of grasping or seizing; grip; specif., a way of gripping an opponent in wrestling **2** a thing to hold or hold on by **3** a thing for holding or containing something else **4** *a)* a controlling or dominating force; restraining authority [to have a firm *hold* over someone] *b)* a being aware or in control [to lose one's *hold* on life] **5** a means of confinement; prison **6** a temporary halt or delay, as to make repairs, or an order to make such a halt **7** an order reserving something **8** [Obs.] a stronghold **9** [Obs.] the act or fact of guarding, possessing, etc. **10** *Music* PAUSE (sense 4) **11** *Sports* an instance of HOLDING (*n.* 3) —**SYN.** CONTAIN —**catch hold of** to take; seize; grasp —**get (a) hold of 1** to take; seize; grasp **2** to acquire **3** to get in touch with; establish communication with —**hold back 1** to restrain **2** to refrain **3** to retain —**hold down 1** to keep down or under control; restrain ☆**2** [Informal] to have and keep (a job) **3** to limit; restrict [the rain *held down* attendance at the game] —**hold forth** ⟦cf. Phil. 2:16⟧ **1** to speak at some length; preach; lecture **2** [Now Rare] to offer; propose —**hold in 1** to keep in or back **2** to control oneself or one's impulses —**hold off 1** to keep away or at a distance **2** *a)* to repel the attack of *b)* to keep (someone) from carrying out an action **3** to delay action on a matter, as in awaiting additional information —**hold on 1** to retain one's hold **2** to continue; persist **3** [Informal] stop! wait! —**hold one's own** to maintain one's place or condition in spite of obstacles or reverses —**hold out 1** to last; endure; continue **2** to continue resistance; stand firm; not yield **3** to offer ☆**4** [Informal] to fail or refuse to give (what is to be given) —**hold out for** [Informal] to stand firm in demanding —**hold over 1** to postpone consideration of or action on **2** to keep or stay for an additional period or term ☆**3** to keep as a threat or advantage over —**hold up 1** to keep from falling; prop up **2** to show; exhibit **3** to last; endure; continue **4** to stop; delay; impede ☆**5** to stop forcibly and rob ☆**6** [Informal] to overcharge —**hold with 1** to agree or side with **2** to approve of —**lay (or take) hold of 1** to take; seize; grasp **2** to get control or possession of —**no holds barred** ⟦see *n.* 1⟧ [Informal] with no set rules or limits —**on hold 1** in a period or state of interruption or delay [the countdown was *on hold*] **2** in a state of interruption in a telephone call, as during a transfer to another line [I was *on hold* for five minutes]

hold² (hōld) *n.* ⟦altered (after prec.) < HOLE or < MDu *hol*, a hole, cave, ship's hold⟧ **1** the interior of a ship below decks, esp. below the lower deck, in which the cargo is carried **2** the compartment for cargo in an aircraft

hold·all (hōld′ôl′) *n.* [Chiefly Brit.] a large traveling case for carrying clothes, equipment, etc.: it typically has handles and a shoulder strap

hold·back (-bak′) *n.* **1** a thing that holds back; curb; check; hindrance ☆**2** a strap or iron attached to the shaft of a wagon, carriage, etc. and to the harness, to enable a horse to stop or back the vehicle

☆**hold 'em** (hōld′əm) *short for* TEXAS HOLD 'EM

hold·en (hōl′dən) *vt., vi. archaic pp. of* HOLD¹

hold·er (hōl′dər) *n.* ⟦ME *holdere*⟧ **1** a person who holds or possesses; specif., *a)* one who is legally entitled to payment of a bill, note, or check *b)* a tenant *c)* a possessor **2** a device for holding something

Höl·der·lin (höl′dər lēn′; *E* hʉr′dər lēn′, -lin), **Frie·drich** (frē′driH) 1770-1843; Ger. poet

hold·fast (hōld′fast′) *n.* **1** the act of holding fast **2** any of various devices that hold something else in place; hook, nail, clamp, etc. **3** *Bot.* a part of certain rootless plants, as some algae, used to attach the plant to a surface **4** *Zool.* an organ of a parasitic or sessile organism, specialized for attachment to a host or other object

hold·ing (hōl′diŋ) *n.* ⟦ME *holdinge*: see HOLD¹⟧ **1** land, esp. a farm, rented from another **2** [*pl.*] property owned, as stocks, bonds, or inventory; assets **3** in certain sports, the illegal use of the hands and arms to hinder the movements of an opponent **4** a decision or ruling as by a court of law

☆**holding company** a corporation organized to hold bonds or stocks of other corporations, often thereby controlling those corporations

holding pattern 1 the course an airplane takes while circling an airport waiting for clearance to land **2** any period or state in which progress is interrupted or delayed

hold·out (hōld′out′) *n.* **1** the act of holding out ☆**2** *a)* a professional athlete who refuses to play or perform until certain contract demands are met *b)* any person who resists joining in a certain action, coming to an agreement, etc.

hold·o·ver (-ō′vər) *n.* ☆a person or thing staying on from a previous period; specif., an officeholder who continues in office or an entertainer whose engagement is extended

☆**hold·up** (hōld′up′) *n.* **1** a stoppage; delay or hindrance **2** the act of stopping forcibly and robbing **3** [Informal] the act of overcharging **4** *Chem. a)* the amount of liquid retained or delayed during fractional distillation and certain types of solvent extractions *b)* the free volume between the resin particles in an ion exchange column **5** *Physics* the amount of fissionable material being processed or in storage for irradiation in a reactor cycle

hole (hōl) *n.* ⟦ME < OE *hol*, orig. neut. of adj. *holh*, hollow, akin to Ger *hohl* < IE base **kaul-*, **kul-*, hollow, hollow stalk > L *caulis*, Gr *kaulos*, stalk⟧ **1** a hollow or hollowed-out place; cavity; specif., *a)* an excavation or pit ☆*b)* a small bay or inlet; cove (often in place names) *c)* a pool or deep, relatively wide place in a stream [a swimming *hole*] *d)* an animal's burrow or lair; den **2** a small, dingy, squalid place; any dirty, badly lighted room, house, etc. **3** *a)* an opening in or through anything; break; gap [a *hole* in the wall] *b)* a tear or rent, or a place where fabric is worn away, as in a garment **4** a flaw; fault; blemish; defect [*holes* in an argument] **5** [Informal] an embarrassing situation or position; predicament **6** *Golf a)* a small, cylindrical cup sunk into a green, into which the ball is to be hit *b)* any of the distinct, numbered sections of a course, each including a tee, fairway, and green [played the fifth *hole* in par] **7** *Physics, Electronics* a vacancy in a semiconductor, crystal, etc. left by the loss or absence of an electron: in some semiconductors it acts as a carrier of a positive electric charge —*vt.* **holed, hol′ing 1** to make a hole or holes in **2** to put, hit, or drive into a hole **3** to create by making a hole [to *hole* a tunnel through a mountain] —**burn a hole in someone's pocket** to make someone eager to spend it: said humorously of money —**hole high** *Golf* at a spot on or near the green that is as far as the hole is from where the ball was hit —**hole in one** *Golf* the act of getting the ball into the hole on the shot from the tee —**hole out** *Golf* to hit the ball into the hole —**hole up** [Informal] **1** to hibernate, usually in a hole **2** to shut oneself in **3** to hide out —☆**in the hole 1** [Informal] in debt [fifty dollars *in the hole*] **2** dealt face down: said of a card or cards in stud poker —**make a hole in** to use up a sizable amount of —**pick (or poke) holes in** to pick out errors or flaws in —**the hole 1** [Slang] SOLITARY CONFINEMENT; also, a cell used for solitary confinement ☆**2** *Baseball* the area of the infield between the third baseman and the shortstop or between the second baseman and the first baseman

SYN.—hole is the general word for an open space in a thing and may suggest a depression in a surface or an opening from surface to surface [a *hole* in the ground, a *hole* in a sock]; **hollow** basically suggests an empty space within a solid body, whether or not it extends to the surface, but it may also be applied to a depressed place in a surface [a wooded *hollow*]; **cavity**, the Latin-derived equivalent of **hollow**, has special application in formal and scientific usage [the thoracic *cavity*]; an **excavation** is a hollow made in or through ground by digging [the *excavations* at Pompeii]

hole-and-corner (hōl′ən kôr′nər) *adj.* ⟦in allusion to things done in out-of-the-way places⟧ **1** kept secret, esp. to avoid blame or punishment **2** unimportant, humdrum, etc.

☆**hole card 1** *Stud Poker* a card dealt face down **2** a hidden advantage or undisclosed resource

☆**hole in the wall** [Informal] a small, dingy room, shop, etc., esp. one in a remote or unfrequented place

hole saw a hollow cylinder with teeth on the bottom edge attached by means of a bit, as to a portable electric drill, and used for cutting circles

hole·y (hōl′ē) *adj.* ⟦ME⟧ having a hole or holes

Hol·guín (ôl gēn′) city in E Cuba

-hol·ic (häl′ik) *combining form* -AHOLIC [*chocoholic*]

hol·i·day (häl′ə dā′) *n.* ⟦< ME *holidei*, with shortened first vowel < OE *hāligdæg*: see HOLY & DAY⟧ **1** HOLY DAY **2** a day of freedom from labor; day set aside for leisure and recreation **3** [*often pl.*] [Chiefly Brit.] a period of leisure or recreation; vacation **4** a day set aside by law or custom for the suspension of business, usually in commemoration of some event **5** any period of freedom from something [a weeklong sales-tax *holiday*] —*adj.* **1** suited to a holiday; merry, festive, etc. [a *holiday* atmosphere] **2** *a)* of or associated with a holiday [an extended *holiday* weekend] *b)* having to do with the year-end holidays of Thanksgiving, Christmas, Hanukkah, and New Year's [throngs of *holiday* shoppers] —*vi.* [Chiefly Brit.] to take a vacation or vacation trip

Hol·i·day (häl′ə dā′), **Billie** (born *Eleonora Fagan Holiday*) 1915-59; U.S. jazz singer: also called *Lady Day*

hol·i·day·mak·er (häl′ə dā māk′ər) *n.* [Chiefly Brit.] VACATIONER

hol·i·days (-dāz′) *adv.* during every holiday or most holidays

☆**ho·li·er-than-thou** (hō′lē ər *th*ən *th*ou′) *adj.* sanctimonious or self-righteous to an annoying degree; priggish

ho·li·ly (hō′lə lē) *adv.* ⟦ME *holiliche* < OE *haliglice*⟧ in a holy manner; piously, devoutly, or sacredly

ho·li·ness (hō′lē nis) *n.* ⟦ME *holinesse* < OE *halignesse*⟧ **1** the quality or state of being holy **2** [**H-**] a title of the pope (with *His* or *Your*)

Ho·lins·hed (häl′inz hed′, -in shed′), **Raphael** died 1580?; Eng. chronicler: also **Hol·lings·head** (häl′iŋz hed′)

ho·lism (hō′liz′əm) *n.* ⟦HOL(O)- + -ISM⟧ the view that an organic or integrated whole has an independent reality which cannot be understood simply through an understanding of its parts —**ho′list** *n.*

ho·lis·tic (hō lis′tik) *adj.* **1** of or relating to holism **2** of, concerned with, or dealing with wholes or integrated systems rather than with their parts **3**

Med. a) designating or of healthcare that takes a patient's nutritional, environmental, and psychological factors into account *b)* incorporating unconventional treatment, as, variously, folk medicine, yoga, acupuncture, massage, etc. —**ho·lis′ti·cal·ly** *adv.*

hol·la (häl′ə, hə lä′) *interj., n., vi., vt.* ⟦< Fr *holà* < *ho*, HO[1] + *là*, there < L *illac*, there⟧ *var. of* HOLLO

hol·land (häl′ənd) *n.* ⟦after HOLLAND[2], where first made⟧ a linen or cotton cloth used for clothing, window shades, etc.

Hol·land[1] (häl′ənd), **John Philip** 1840-1914; U.S. inventor, born in Ireland: developed U.S. Navy's 1st submarine

Hol·land[2] (häl′ənd) **1** former county of the Holy Roman Empire on the North Sea, now divided into two provinces (NORTH HOLLAND & SOUTH HOLLAND) of the Netherlands **2** NETHERLANDS —**Hol′land·er** *n.*

hol·lan·daise sauce (häl′ən dāz′, häl′ən dāz′) ⟦Fr *hollandaise*, fem. of *hollandais*, of prec.⟧ a creamy sauce for fish or vegetables, made of butter, egg yolks, lemon juice, etc.

Hol·lan·di·a (hä lan′dē ə) *former name for* JAYAPURA

Hol·lands (häl′əndz) *n.* ⟦Du *hollandsch* (*genever*), Dutch (gin): see GENEVA⟧ a strongly flavored gin made in the Netherlands, with the flavorings distilled in rather than added after distillation: also **Hollands** (or **Holland**) **gin**

hol·ler[1] (häl′ər) *vi., vt.* ⟦altered < HOLLO, HOLLA⟧ [Informal] to shout or yell —*n.* **1** [Informal] a shout or yell ☆**2** a working song sung by U.S. black field hands

hol·ler[2] (häl′ər) *adj., adv., n. dial. var. of* HOLLOW

hol·lo (häl′ō′, hə lō′) *interj., n., pl.* **-los′** ⟦var. of HOLLA, HALLO⟧ **1** (a shout or call) used as to attract a person's attention or to urge on hounds in hunting **2** (a shout) used to express greeting or surprise — *vi., vt.* **-loed, -lo·ing 1** to shout (at) in order to attract attention **2** to urge on (hounds) by calling out "hollo" **3** to shout or call, as in greeting

hol·low (häl′ō) *adj.* ⟦ME *holwe* < OE *holh*: see HOLE⟧ **1** having an empty space, or only air, within it; having a cavity inside; not solid **2** depressed below the surrounding surface; shaped like a cup or bowl; concave **3** deeply set; sunken [*hollow* cheeks] **4** empty or worthless; not real or meaningful [*hollow* praise] **5** hungry **6** deep-toned, dull, and muffled, as though resounding from something hollow —*adv.* in a hollow manner —*n.* **1** a hollow formation or place; cavity; hole **2** a small, sheltered valley — *vt., vi.* to make or become hollow —*SYN.* HOLE, VAIN —**beat (all) hollow** [Informal] to defeat thoroughly or surpass by far —**hollow out 1** to make hollow **2** to make by hollowing —**hol′low·ly** *adv.* —**hol′low·ness** *n.*

hol·lo·ware (häl′ō wer′) *n.* serving dishes and table accessories, esp. of silver, that are relatively hollow or concave: cf. FLATWARE: also **hol′low-ware′**

hol·low-eyed (häl′ō īd′) *adj.* having deep-set eyes or dark areas under the eyes, as from sickness or fatigue

hol·ly (häl′ē) *n., pl.* **-lies** ⟦ME *holi, holin* < OE *holegn* < IE base **kel-*, to prick > Welsh *celyn*, holly, Sans *kaṭambá-*, arrow⟧ **1** any of a genus (*Ilex*) of small trees and shrubs of the holly family, with stiff, glossy, sharp-pointed leaves and clusters of bright-red berries **2** the leaves and berries, used as Christmas decorations —*adj.* designating a family (Aquifoliaceae, order Celastrales) of dicotyledonous trees and shrubs, including the dahoon and black alder

Hol·ly (häl′ē) *n.* a feminine name

hol·ly·hock (häl′ē häk′) *n.* ⟦ME *holihoc*, lit., holy hock < OE *halig*, holy + *hoc*, mallow⟧ **1** a tall, usually biennial plant (*Alcea rosea*) of the mallow family, with palmately lobed leaves, a hairy stem, and large, showy flowers of various colors in elongated spikes **2** its flower

hollyhock

Hol·ly·wood (häl′ē wood′) ⟦HOLLY + WOOD[1]⟧ **1** section of Los Angeles, Calif., once the site of many U.S. film studios; hence, the U.S. film industry or its life, world, etc. **2** city on the SE coast of Fla.

☆**Hollywood bed** a bed consisting typically of a mattress on a box spring that rests on a metal frame or that has attached legs: it often has an upholstered headboard

holm[1] (hōm) *n.* ⟦ME < OE, sea: sense infl. by ON *holmr*, island < IE base **kel-*, to project > HILL⟧ [Brit.] **1** a small island in a river or lake, near the mainland or a larger island: used chiefly in place names **2** low, flat land by a river or stream; bottoms

holm[2] (hōm) *n.* ⟦altered < *holn*, form of ME *holin*: see HOLLY⟧ **1** HOLM OAK **2** [Dial.] HOLLY

Holmes (hōmz, hōlmz) **1 John Haynes** (hānz) 1879-1964; U.S. clergyman & reformer **2 Oliver Wen·dell** (wen′dəl) 1809-94; U.S. writer & physician **3 Oliver Wendell** 1841-1935; associate justice, U.S. Supreme Court (1902-32): son of the writer **4 Sherlock** *see* SHERLOCK HOLMES

hol·mi·um (hōl′mē əm) *n.* ⟦ModL < earlier *holmia*, so named (1879) by P. T. Cleve (see CLEVEITE), one of its discoverers, after *Holmia*, Latinized name of STOCKHOLM, his native city + -IUM⟧ a trivalent, silvery chemical element, one of the rare-earth elements: symbol, Ho; at. no. 67: see the periodic table of elements in the Reference Supplement

holm oak ⟦see HOLM[2]⟧ **1** a S European evergreen oak (*Quercus ilex*) of the beech family, with hollylike leaves **2** its wood

hol·o- (häl′ō, -ə; hō′lō, -lə) ⟦Fr < L < Gr *holos*, whole < IE base **solo-*, whole > L *salvus*, sound, safe⟧ *combining form* whole, entire [*holomorphic*]

hol·o·blas·tic (häl′ō blas′tik, hō′lō-) *adj.* ⟦prec. + -BLAST + -IC⟧ *Embryology* undergoing complete cleavage into daughter cells: said of certain ova with little yolk (*blastomeres*): cf. MEROBLASTIC

hol·o·caust (häl′ə kăst′; hō′lə kôst′, hôl′-) *n.* ⟦ME < OFr *holocauste* < LL(Ec) *holocaustum*, a whole burnt offering < Gr *holokauston* (neut. of *holokaustos*), burnt whole < *holos*, whole (see HOLO-) + *kaustos*, burnt: see CAUSTIC⟧ **1** an offering the whole of which is burned; burnt offering **2** a great or total destruction of life, specif. by fire [nuclear *holocaust*] —☆**the Holocaust** [*also* **the h-**] the systematic, genocidal destruction of over six million European Jews by the Nazis before and during WWII: the term now often includes other groups so targeted by the Nazis

Hol·o·cene (häl′ə sēn′, hō′lə-) *adj.* ⟦HOLO- + -CENE⟧ [*sometimes* **h-**] designating or of the current epoch of the Quaternary Period, characterized by a warm climate and the development of modern human culture —**the Holocene** the Holocene Epoch or its rocks: see the geologic time chart in the Reference Supplement

hol·o·crine (häl′ō krin, -krīn′, -krēn′; hō′lə-) *adj.* ⟦HOLO- + Gr *krinein*, to separate: see HARVEST⟧ designating or of a gland whose secretion results from the disintegration of the gland's cells

hol·o·en·zyme (häl′ō en′zīm′, hō′lō-) *n.* a complete enzyme, formed from an apoenzyme and a coenzyme

Hol·o·fer·nes (häl′ə fur′nēz′) *n.* a general of Nebuchadnezzar's army, killed by Judith: see JUDITH

ho·log·a·mous (hō läg′ə məs) *adj.* ⟦HOLO- + -GAMOUS⟧ having gametes essentially the same in size and form as other cells —**ho·log′a·my** (-mē) *n.*

hol·o·gram (häl′ə gram′, hō′lə-) *n.* a three-dimensional image created from, or containing the record of, an interference pattern produced by means of holography

hol·o·graph (-graf′) *adj.* ⟦Fr *holographe* < LL *holographus* < LGr *holographos* < Gr *holos*, whole (see HOLO-) + *graphein*, to write: see GRAPHIC⟧ written entirely in the handwriting of the person under whose name it appears —*n.* a holograph document, letter, etc.

hol·o·graph·ic (häl′ə graf′ik, hō′lə-) *adj.* **1** HOLOGRAPH **2** of or having to do with holography

ho·log·ra·phy (hō läg′rə fē) *n.* ⟦HOLO- + -GRAPHY⟧ a method of making three-dimensional images by splitting a laser beam into two beams and recording, as on a photographic plate, the interference patterns made when one beam passes directly from the laser to the plate and the other beam passes from the laser to the object to the plate: the image appears when the developed plate is illuminated with laser light, or in some cases with white light

hol·o·he·dral (häl′ō hē′drəl, hō′lə-) *adj.* ⟦HOLO- + -HEDRAL⟧ having the full number of planes required for complete symmetry: said of a crystal

hol·o·me·tab·o·lism (-mə tab′ə liz′əm) *n.* COMPLETE METAMORPHOSIS —**hol′o·me·tab′o·lous** *adj.*

hol·o·mor·phic (-môr′fik) *adj.* ⟦HOLO- + -MORPHIC⟧ having the two ends symmetrical in form: said of a crystal

hol·o·phras·tic (-fras′tik) *adj.* ⟦< HOLO- + Gr *phrastikos*, suited for expressing < *phrazein*, to speak⟧ expressing an entire sentence or phrase in one word

hol·o·phyt·ic (-fit′ik) *adj.* ⟦HOLO- + -PHYT(E) + -IC⟧ obtaining nutrition by photosynthesis, as do green plants and some bacteria

hol·o·plank·ton (-plaŋk′tən) *n.* an organism that is planktonic for its entire life cycle: cf. MEROPLANKTON

hol·o·thu·ri·an (-thoor′ē ən, -thyoor′-) *n.* ⟦< L *holothuria*, pl. < Gr *holothouria*, pl. of *holothourion*, kind of water polyp⟧ any of a class (Holothuroidea) of echinoderms with an elongated, flexible, wormlike body and a mouth surrounded by tentacles; sea cucumber

hol·o·type (häl′ō tīp′, hō′lə-) *n.* ⟦HOLO- + TYPE⟧ *Taxonomy* the single specimen chosen as the type of a new species or subspecies in the original description —**hol′o·typ′ic** (-tip′ik) *adj.*

hol·o·zo·ic (häl′ə zō′ik, hō′lə-) *adj.* ⟦HOLO- + ZO(O)- + -IC⟧ ingesting and using complex organic material as food, as most animals do

holp (hōlp, hōp) *vt., vi.* ⟦ME *holpe*, S Eng dial. form of fol.⟧ *archaic or dial. pt. & obs. pp. of* HELP

hol·pen (hōl′pən, hō′-) *vt., vi.* ⟦ME⟧ *archaic or dial. pp. of* HELP

hols (hälz) *pl.n.* [Brit. Informal] HOLIDAY (sense 3)

Holst (hōlst), **Gus·tav (Theodore)** (goos′täv) 1874-1934; Eng. composer

Hol·stein[1] (hōl′stēn′, hōl′stīn′) *n.* ⟦after fol., where the breed originated⟧ ☆any of a breed of large, black-and-white dairy cattle: also called **Hol′stein-Frie′sian** (-frē′zhən)

Hol·stein[2] (hōl′stīn′; *Ger* hôl′shtīn′) region of NW Germany, in the state of Schleswig-Holstein: formerly a duchy of Denmark

hol·ster (hōl′stər) *n.* ⟦Du, akin to Goth *hulistr*, a cover, ON *hulstr*, a sheath, OE *heolstor*, darkness, cover < IE base **kel-*, to conceal (> HALL, HULL[1]) + Gmc noun suffix *-stra*⟧ a contoured holder for a pistol or, sometimes, one for a rifle, usually of leather and attached to a belt, saddle, or shoulder strap —*vt.* to place in a holster

holt (hōlt) *n.* ⟦ME < OE, akin to Ger *holz*, wood < IE **kḷdos* (< base **kel-*, to strike) > Gr *klados*, young sprout⟧ [Archaic] a small woods

ho·lus-bo·lus (hō′ləs bō′ləs) *adv.* ⟦mock-Latin < WHOLE + BOLUS⟧ [Now Rare] all at once; in one lump

ho·ly (hō′lē) *adj.* **-li·er, -li·est** ⟦ME *holie* < OE *halig* (akin to Ger *heilig*) < base of OE *hal*, sound, happy, WHOLE: first used in OE as transl. of L *sacer*, *sanctus*, in the Vulg.⟧ 1 dedicated to religious use; belonging to or coming from God; consecrated; sacred 2 spiritually perfect or pure; untainted by evil or sin; sinless; saintly 3 regarded with or deserving deep respect, awe, reverence, or adoration ☆4 [Slang] very much of a: a generalized intensifier *[a holy terror]* Often used in interjectional compounds to express astonishment, emphasis, etc. *[holy cow! holy smoke!]* —*n., pl.* **-lies** a holy thing or place

SYN.—**holy** suggests that which is held in deepest religious reverence or is basically associated with a religion and, in extended use, connotes spiritual purity *[the Holy Ghost, a holy love]*; **sacred** refers to that which is set apart as holy or is dedicated to some exalted purpose and, therefore, connotes inviolability *[Parnassus was sacred to Apollo, a sacred trust]*; **consecrated** and **hallowed** describe that which has been made sacred or holy, **consecrated** in addition connoting solemn devotion or dedication *[a life consecrated to art]*, and **hallowed**, inherent or intrinsic holiness *[hallowed ground]*; **divine** suggests that which is of the nature of, is associated with, or is derived from God or a god *[the divine right of kings]*, and, in extended use, connotes supreme greatness *[the Divine Duse]* or, informally, great attractiveness —***ANT.*** **profane, unholy**

Holy Alliance an alliance formed in 1815 by the rulers of Russia, Austria, and Prussia to suppress the democratic revolutionary movement in Europe

Holy Bible BIBLE (senses 1, 2, & 3)

Holy Communion 1 the receiving of bread and wine, or either of these, consecrated in the Eucharist 2 the consecrated bread and wine, or either of these, so received 3 EUCHARIST

Holy Cross, Mount of the peak in WC Colo.: snow-filled crevices on the E face form a large cross: 13,996 ft (4,266 m)

holy day 1 a day dedicated to religious observances or to a religious festival 2 *R.C.Ch.* any of certain religious feast days on which Roman Catholics are required, as on Sundays, to attend Mass and refrain from unnecessary physical work: in full **holy day of obligation**

Holy Father a title of the pope

Holy Ghost ⟦ME *haligast*, transl. of LL(Ec) *Spiritus sanctus*⟧ HOLY SPIRIT

Holy Grail 1 GRAIL (sense 1) 2 [*often* **h- g-**] any ultimate, but elusive, goal pursued as in a quest

Holy Innocents' Day a religious feast day (Dec. 28) honoring the children slain at Herod's command: Matt. 2:16

Holy Land PALESTINE (the region)

Holy Office *R.C.Ch. former name for* The Congregation for the Doctrine of the Faith, a department of the Curia established to investigate and correct unorthodox doctrine

holy of holies ⟦transl. of Heb *qōdesh haqadōshim*⟧ 1 the innermost part of the Jewish tabernacle and Temple, where the ark of the covenant was kept 2 any most sacred place

holy orders 1 *a)* the sacrament or rite of Christian ordination *b)* the state of having received Christian ordination 2 the ranks or grades of Christian ordination; specif., in the Roman Catholic Church, those of bishop, priest, or deacon —**take holy orders** to receive Christian ordination

☆**Holy Roller** a member of any of various Christian sects that express religious emotion in an unrestrained manner during services of worship, as by shouting or falling to the floor: usually a derogatory term

Holy Roman Empire empire of WC Europe, comprising the German-speaking peoples & N Italy: begun in A.D. 800 with the papal crowning of Charlemagne as emperor or, in an alternate view, with the crowning of Otto I in 962, it lasted until Francis II (who was Francis I of Austria) resigned the title in 1806

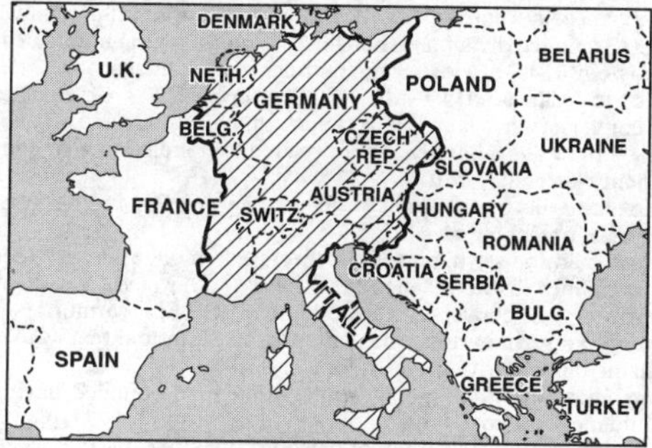

Holy Roman Empire (12th cent.)

Holy Saturday the Saturday before Easter

Holy Scripture (*or* **Scriptures**) the Bible: among Jews, the Pentateuch, the Prophets, and the Hagiographa; among Christians, the Old and New Testaments

Holy See *R.C.Ch.* the papal see; Apostolic See

Holy Spirit the spirit of God; specif. the third person of the Trinity

ho·ly·stone (hō′lē stōn′) *n.* ⟦prob. so named because the user is on his knees⟧ a large, flat piece of sandstone used for scouring a ship's wooden decks —*vt.* **-stoned′**, **-ston′ing** to scour with a holystone

Holy Synod a governing body in the Eastern Orthodox Church

Holy Thursday 1 the Thursday before Easter 2 [Now Rare] ASCENSION DAY

ho·ly·tide (hō′lē tīd′) *n.* ⟦HOLY + TIDE[1]⟧ [Obs.] a holy season; day or period of religious observance

holy war 1 a war fought on behalf of a religion or for a religious cause 2 any zealous or fanatical campaign

holy water *R.C.Ch., Eastern Orthodox Ch., etc.* water blessed by a priest and used as a sacramental

Holy Week the week before Easter

Holy Writ the Bible

hom- (hōm, häm) *combining form* HOMO-: used before a vowel

hom·age (häm′ij, äm′-) *n.* ⟦ME < OFr *hommage* < ML *hominaticum*, vassal's service, homage < L *homo*, a man: see HOMO[1]⟧ 1 [Historical] *a)* a public avowal of allegiance by a vassal to his lord *b)* an act done or thing given to show the relationship between lord and vassal 2 anything given or done to show reverence, honor, or respect: usually with *do* or *pay [to pay homage to a fallen hero]* —***SYN.*** ALLEGIANCE, HONOR

hom·ag·er (häm′i jər) *n.* a person who does homage, esp. as a vassal

☆**hom·bre**[1] (häm′brā′, äm′-) *n.* ⟦Sp < L *homo*, man: see HOMO[1]⟧ [Informal] a man; fellow

hom·bre[2] (äm′bər) *n. alt. sp. of* OMBER

hom·burg (häm′bərg) *n.* ⟦after *Homburg*, Prussia, where first made⟧ a man's felt hat with a crown dented front to back and a stiffened brim turned up slightly at the sides

home (hōm) *n.* ⟦ME < OE *hām*, akin to Ger *heim* < Gmc **haim* < IE base **kei-*, to lie, homestead > HIDE[3], Gr *keisthai*, to lie down, rest, L *civis*, townsman, ON *heimr*, home, Goth *haima*, OHG *heim*: basic sense, "place where one lies, dwelling"⟧ 1 the place where a person (or family) lives; one's dwelling place; specif., *a)* the house, apartment, etc. where one lives or is living temporarily; living quarters *b)* the region, city, state, etc. where one lives 2 the place where one was born or reared; one's own city, state, or country 3 a place thought of as home; specif., *a)* a place where one likes to be; restful or congenial place *b)* the grave 4 the members of a family as a unit; a household and its affairs *[homes broken up by divorce]* 5 an institution for the care of orphans, people who are old and helpless, etc. 6 *a)* the place that is the natural environment of an animal, plant, etc. *b)* the place where something is or has been originated, developed, etc. *[Paris is the home of fashion]* 7 *a)* in many games, the base or goal ☆*b) Baseball* HOME PLATE —*adj.* 1 of home or a home; specif., *a)* of the family, household, etc.; domestic *b)* of one's country, government, etc.; domestic (opposed to FOREIGN) *c)* of or at the center of activity or operations *[home office]* 2 *a)* designating or having to do with games played in the city, at the school, etc. where the team originates *[a team's home field]* *b)* designating or of the team playing in its own city or at its own school or facility *[white home uniforms]* 3 of or for use in the home 4 *a)* made as by or as for members of the family *[home videos]* *b)* having the qualities of something made in the home *[a restaurant serving home cooking]* —*adv.* ⟦orig. the n. as acc. of direction⟧ 1 at, to, or in the direction of home or a home 2 to the place where it must ultimately go; to the point aimed at *[to drive a nail home]* 3 to the center or heart of a matter; closely; directly; deeply —*vi.* **homed, hom′ing** 1 to go or return to one's home 2 to have a home —*vt.* to send to, put into, or provide with a home —**at home** 1 in one's own house, neighborhood, city, or country 2 as if in one's own home; comfortable; at ease; familiar 3 willing to receive visitors 4 *Sports* in the city, on the field, etc. where the team plays its HOME (*adj.* 2*a*) games —**bring something home to** 1 to impress something upon or make something clear to 2 to fasten the blame for something on (someone) —**come home** to return, as to one's home —☆**home free** [Slang] beyond the point of doubt in approaching success or victory —**home in (on)** to guide or be guided as by radar, heat, etc., to (a destination or target)

home away from home a place in which one is as comfortable as one is in one's own home

☆**home·bod·y** (hōm′bäd′ē) *n., pl.* **-bod′ies** a person mainly concerned with affairs of the home, or one who prefers to stay at home

home·bound (hōm′bound′) *adj.* 1 going home 2 confined to the home

☆**home·boy** (-boi′) *n.* [Slang] 1 a boy or man from the same town, neighborhood, etc. as oneself 2 a close male friend 3 a fellow male member of a youth gang

home·bred (-bred′) *adj.* 1 bred or reared at home; domestic; native 2 not cultivated, polished, or sophisticated; crude

home-brew (hōm′broo̅′) *n.* an alcoholic beverage, esp. beer, made at home

home-care (hōm′ker′) *adj.* providing care for young children, the elderly, convalescents, etc. in the home of the person being cared for

home·com·ing (hōm′kum′iŋ) *n.* 1 a coming or returning to one's home ☆2 in many schools, colleges, and universities, an annual celebration attended by alumni

home computer a personal computer for use in the home

Home Counties certain counties adjacent to or near London, namely Essex, Kent, Surrey, and, sometimes, Hertfordshire and Sussex

☆**home economics** the science and art of homemaking, including nutrition, clothing, budgeting, and child care: also [Informal] **home ec** (ek)

☆**home fries** raw or boiled potatoes, sliced and fried in a frying pan: also **home fried potatoes**

home from home [Brit.] HOME AWAY FROM HOME

☆**home·girl** (hōm′gurl′) *n.* [Slang] 1 a girl or woman from the same town, neighborhood, etc. as oneself 2 a close female friend 3 a fellow female member of a youth gang

home·grown or **home-grown** (hōm′grōn′) *adj.* 1 grown at home or for local consumption: said of fruits and vegetables 2 produced, developed, or appearing within a given area; native [*homegrown* musical talent]

Ho·mel (khô′mel) *var. of* GOMEL

home·land (hōm′land′, -lənd) *n.* 1 the country in which one was born or makes one's home 2 a country or region into which people of a specified group have relocated or may relocate, regarded as their ancestral land

home·less (hōm′lis) *adj.* having no home; without a permanent place of residence —☆**the homeless** those typically poor or sometimes mentally ill people who are unable to maintain a place to live and therefore often may sleep in the streets, parks, etc. —**home′less·ness** *n.*

home·like (hōm′līk′) *adj.* having qualities associated with home; comfortable, familiar, cozy, etc.

home·ly (hōm′lē) *adj.* **-li·er, -li·est** ⟦ME *homli*⟧ 1 [Obs.] *a)* of the home; domestic *b)* HOMELIKE 2 *a)* characteristic of or suitable for home or home life; simple and unpretentious or plain and everyday [*homely* virtues] *b)* not elegant or polished; crude 3 not good-looking or handsome; unattractive —**home′li·ness** *n.*

home·made (hōm′mād′) *adj.* 1 made at home or on the premises 2 as if made at home; esp., plain, simple, or crude

home·mak·er (hōm′māk′ər) *n.* a person who manages a home; esp., a housewife —**home′mak′ing** *n.*

ho·me·o- (hō′mē ō, -ə) ⟦Gr *homoio-* < *homos*, SAME⟧ *combining form* like, the same, similar [*homeomorphism*]

ho·me·o·box (hō′mē ō bäks′) *n.* any of a group of DNA sequences found in certain genes and involved in determining the development of specific organs, tissues, etc. of animal embryos

Home Office the department of government in Great Britain which supervises various domestic affairs, including immigration, law and order, and civil defense

ho·me·o·mor·phism (hō′mē ō môr′fiz′əm) *n.* ⟦HOMEO- + -MORPH + -ISM⟧ similarity in structure and form; esp., a close similarity of crystalline forms between substances of different chemical composition —**ho′me·o·mor′phous** (-fəs) *adj.*

ho·me·o·path (hō′mē ō path′) *n.* a person who practices or accepts the principles of homeopathy: also **ho′me·op′a·thist** (-äp′ə thist)

ho·me·op·a·thy (hō′mē äp′ə thē) *n.* ⟦Ger *homöopathie*, lit., likeness of feeling (see HOMEO- & -PATHY): coined (*c.* 1800) by S. HAHNEMANN⟧ a system of medical treatment based on the theory that certain diseases can be cured by giving very small doses of drugs which in a healthy person would produce symptoms like those of the disease: opposed to ALLOPATHY —**ho′me·o·path′ic** (-ə path′ik) *adj.*

☆**ho·me·o·sta·sis** (hō′mē ō stā′sis) *n.* ⟦ModL: see HOMEO- & STASIS⟧ 1 *Physiol.* the tendency to maintain, or the maintenance of, normal internal stability in an organism by coordinated responses of the organ systems that automatically compensate for environmental changes 2 any analogous maintenance of stability or equilibrium, as within a social group —**ho′me·o·stat′ic** (-stat′ik) *adj.*

ho·me·o·ther·mal (hō′mē ō thur′məl) *adj. var. of* HOMOIOTHERMAL

ho·me·o·typ·ic (-tip′ik) *adj.* ⟦HOMEO- + TYPIC(AL)⟧ designating the second division of the nuclei of germ cells in meiosis

home·own·er (hōm′ōn′ər) *n.* a person who owns the house he or she lives in —**home′own′er·ship** *n.*

home page 1 the initial or preliminary WEB PAGE of a website, providing access to the other pages 2 a WEBSITE, esp. one advertising or representing a business or individual

☆**home·place** (hōm′plās′) *n.* [Chiefly Dial.] a family home; homestead

☆**home plate** *Baseball* the base that the batter stands beside and over which the pitcher must throw the ball for a strike: it is the last base that a base runner must reach safely to score a run: see BASE[1] (*n.* 9)

home port 1 the port where a military, commercial, or cruise vessel is docked between trips or for seasonal stopovers or repairs 2 the port where a retired ship is permanently stationed

ho·mer[1] (hō′mər) *n.* ⟦Heb *ḥōmer*, homer, mound < *ḥāmar*, to surge up, swell up⟧ 1 an ancient Hebrew unit of dry measure, equal to about 6¼ bushels 2 an ancient Hebrew unit of liquid measure equal to about 58 gallons It was equivalent to the COR[1]

hom·er[2] (hōm′ər) [Informal] *n.* ☆1 HOME RUN 2 HOMING PIGEON ☆3 a radio or TV broadcaster, umpire, etc. regarded as favoring the home team —☆*vi.* to hit a home run

Ho·mer[1] (hō′mər) *n.* ⟦L *Homerus* < Gr *Homēros* < *homēros*, a pledge, hostage, one led, hence blind⟧ a masculine name

Ho·mer[2] (hō′mər) 1 semilegendary Gr. epic poet of *c.* 8th cent. B.C.: the *Iliad* & the *Odyssey* are both attributed to him 2 **Winslow** 1836-1910; U.S. painter

home range *Ecol.* the area within which an animal normally ranges in the course of a day or a season

Ho·mer·ic (hō mer′ik) *adj.* 1 of, like, or characteristic of the poet Homer, his poems, or the Greek civilization that they describe (*c.* 1200-800 B.C.) 2 [*often* **H-**] epic, large-scale, etc. [*Homeric* efforts]

Homeric laughter loud, unrestrained laughter

☆**home·room** (hōm′ro͞om′) *n.* 1 the room where a class in school meets every day to be checked for attendance, hear school announcements, etc. 2 the group of students in a specific homeroom Also **home room**

home rule the administration of the internal affairs of a country, colony, district, city, etc., granted to the citizens who live in it by a superior governing authority or state; local self-government

☆**home run** *Baseball* a base hit that allows the batter to touch all bases and score a run

☆**home-school·ing** (hōm′sko͞ol′iŋ) *n.* the practice of educating one's child in the home instead of sending him or her to a school —*adj.* of, relating to, or practicing home-schooling —**home′-school′** *vt., vi.* —**home′-school′er** *n.* —**home′-schooled′** *adj.*

home·sick (hōm′sik′) *adj.* ⟦back-form. < *homesickness*, 18th-c. rendering of Ger *heimweh*⟧ unhappy or depressed at being away from home and family; longing for home —**home′sick′ness** *n.*

home·site (hōm′sīt′) *n.* a piece of land on which a house is to be built or has been built

home·spun (hōm′spun′) *n.* 1 cloth made of yarn spun at home 2 coarse, loosely woven cloth like this —*adj.* 1 spun or made at home 2 made of homespun 3 plain; unpretentious; homely [*homespun* virtues]

☆**home·stand** (hōm′stand′) *n. Sports* any number of consecutive games played at a team's home field

home·stead (hōm′sted′) *n.* ⟦OE *hamstede*: see HOME & STEAD⟧ ☆1 a place where a family makes its home, including the land, house, and outbuildings 2 *Law* such a place occupied by the owner and his family and exempted from seizure or forced sale to meet general debts ☆3 a tract of public land (160 acres by the **Homestead Act** of 1862) granted by the U.S. government to a settler to be developed as a farm —☆*vi.* to become a settler on a homestead —☆*vt.* to settle on as a homestead

☆**home·stead·er** (-sted′ər) *n.* 1 a person who has a homestead 2 a settler who holds a homestead granted by the U.S. government

☆**homestead law** 1 a law exempting a homestead from seizure or forced sale to meet general debts 2 any law granting to settlers tracts of public land to be developed as farms 3 in certain states, any of various laws granting specific privileges or tax exemptions to homesteaders

☆**home·stretch** (hōm′strech′) *n.* 1 the part of a racetrack between the last turn and the finish line 2 the final part of any undertaking

home·town (hōm′toun′) *n.* the town, city, etc. where a person was born or grew up or where one currently lives

home truth an effectively stated, pertinent truth, esp. one that may be embarrassing or distressing

☆**home video** 1 the apparatus or technology for recording and playing videocassettes or videodiscs on a TV set in the home 2 prerecorded videocassettes or videodiscs, esp. of films, as seen on a TV set in the home

home·ward (hōm′wərd) *adv., adj.* ⟦ME *hamward* < OE *hamweard*⟧ toward home: also **home′wards** *adv.*

home·work (hōm′wurk′) *n.* 1 work, esp. piecework, done at home 2 lessons to be studied or schoolwork to be done outside the classroom ☆3 study or research in preparation for some project, activity, etc.: used mainly in the phrase **do one's homework**

home·wreck·er (hōm′rek′ər) *n.* [Informal] a person who disrupts a marriage through a romantic involvement with one of the spouses: term used esp. of a woman

home·y[1] (hōm′ē) *adj.* **hom′i·er, hom′i·est** having qualities usually associated with home; comfortable, familiar, cozy, etc. —**home′y·ness** *n.*

home·y[2] (hōm′ē) *n., pl.* **-eys** ☆[Slang] *alt. sp. of* HOMIE

hom·i·ci·dal (häm′ə sīd′'l, hō′mə-; häm′ə sīd′'l, hō′mə-) *adj.* 1 of, having the nature of, or characterized by homicide 2 having a tendency to homicide; murderous —**hom′i·ci′dal·ly** *adv.*

hom·i·cide (häm′ə sīd′, hō′mə-) *n.* 1 ⟦ME < OFr < LL *homicidium*, manslaughter, murder < L *homicida*, murderer < *homo*, a man (see HOMO[1]) + *caedere*, to cut, kill: see -CIDE⟧ any killing of one human being by another: cf. MURDER, MANSLAUGHTER 2 ⟦ME < OFr < L *homicida*⟧ a person who kills another 3 a police division responsible for investigating homicides

☆**hom·ie** (hōm′ē) *n., pl.* **-ies** [Slang] HOMEBOY OR HOMEGIRL

hom·i·let·ic (häm′ə let′ik) *adj.* ⟦LL(Ec) *homileticus* < Gr *homilētikos*, of or for conversation < *homilein*, to be in company, converse < *homilos*: see HOMILY⟧ 1 of or like a homily 2 of or related to homiletics: also **hom′i·let′i·cal** —**hom′i·let′i·cal·ly** *adv.*

hom·i·let·ics (-iks) *n.* ⟦< prec.⟧ the art of preparing and delivering sermons; art of preaching

hom·i·list (häm′ə list) *n.* one who delivers a sermon, or HOMILY (sense 1)

hom·i·ly (häm′ə lē) *n., pl.* **-lies** ⟦ME *omelye* < OFr *omelie* < LL(Ec) *homilia*, sermon < Gr, converse, instruction (in LGr(Ec), sermon) < *homilos*, assembly⟧ 1 a sermon, esp. one centering on Scriptural texts 2 a solemn, moralizing talk or writing, esp. if long or dull

hom·ing (hōm′iŋ) *adj.* 1 going home; homeward bound 2 having to do with guidance to a goal, target, etc.

homing pigeon any of a variety of pigeon trained to carry messages and to return to its home after traveling long distances: cf. RACING HOMER

hom·i·nid (häm′ə nid) *n.* ⟦< ModL *Hominidae* < L *homo* (gen. *hominis*): see HOMO[1] & -IDAE⟧ any of a family (Hominidae) of two-legged primates including all forms of humans, extinct and living

hom·i·nize (häm′ə nīz′) *vt.* **-nized′, -niz′ing** ⟦< L *homo* (gen. *hominis*): see HOMO[1] & -IZE⟧ 1 to alter (the earth, environment, etc.) to bring it into conformity with human nature or human needs 2 to further the evolutionary development of (humankind) —**hom′i·ni·za′tion** *n.*

hom·i·noid (häm′ə noid′) *n.* ⟦< ModL *Hominoidea*: see HOMO[1] & -OID⟧ a gibbon, great ape, or human: in some systems of classification, any of a superfamily (Hominoidea) of such primates —*adj.* of or like a human

☆**hom·i·ny** (häm′ə nē) ***n.*** ⟦contr. < *rockahominy* < AmInd (Algonquian), as in Virginian *rokahamen,* meal from parched corn⟧ dry corn (maize) with the hull and germ removed and often coarsely ground (**hominy grits**): it is boiled for food

hom·mage (ô mȧzh′) ***n.*** ⟦Fr⟧ homage; specif., tribute paid to an artist, writer, composer, etc., as by incorporating some characteristic idiom or style of the person in one's own work

homme moy·en sen·suel (ôm mwȧ yen sän swel′) ⟦Fr, lit., average sensual man⟧ an average man, with average tastes and appetites

ho·mo[1] (hō′mō) ***n., pl.*** **hom·in·es** (häm′ə nēz′) ⟦L, a man, human being < IE **ĝhom-* < base **ĝhthem-*, earth, ground > L *humus*, Gr *chthōn*, earth, OE *guma*, man⟧ any of a genus (*Homo*) of hominids, consisting of existing humans (*H. sapiens*) and certain extinct species of humans (*H. erectus* and *H. habilis*)

ho·mo[2] (hō′mō) ***n., pl.*** **-mos** [Slang] *short for* HOMOSEXUAL: now usually a contemptuous or disparaging term

ho·mo- (hō′mō, -mə; häm′ō, -ə) ⟦Gr *homo-* < *homos*, SAME⟧ *combining form* same, equal, like [*homograph*]

ho·mo·cer·cal (hō′mō sʉr′kəl, häm′ō-) ***adj.*** ⟦< prec. + Gr *kerkos*, a tail + -AL⟧ designating, of, or having a tail fin in which the upper and lower lobes are symmetrical and in which the spine is shortened and ends at or near the center of the base, as in most bony fishes

ho·mo·chro·mat·ic (-krō mat′ik) ***adj.*** ⟦HOMO- + CHROMATIC⟧ of, having, or consisting of a single color: also **ho′mo·chro′mous** (-krō′məs)

ho·moe·cious (hō mē′shəs) ***adj.*** ⟦< HOMO- + Gr *oikos*, house (see ECO-) + -OUS⟧ designating or of parasites that spend their entire life cycle on one species of host

ho·moe·o- (hō′mē ō, -mē ə; häm′ē ō, -ē ə) *combining form* HOMEO-

ho·mo·e·rot·i·cism (hō′mō ē rät′ə siz′əm) ***n.*** ⟦HOMO- + EROTICISM⟧ homosexual desire —**ho′mo·e·rot′ic** ***adj.***

ho·mog·a·my (hō mäg′ə mē) ***n.*** ⟦Ger *homogamie*: see HOMO- & -GAMY⟧ **1** the condition of having all flowers sexually alike **2** the condition of having stamens and pistils mature at the same time **3** inbreeding in an isolated group of individuals of the same species —**ho·mog′a·mous** (-məs) ***adj.***

☆**ho·mog·e·nate** (hə mäj′ə nāt′) ***n.*** ⟦HOMOGEN(IZE) + -ATE[2]⟧ a substance produced by homogenizing

ho·mo·ge·ne·ous (hō′mō jē′nē əs, -mə-; häm′ō-, -ə-) ***adj.*** ⟦ML *homogeneus* < Gr *homogenēs*, of the same race or kind: see HOMO- & GENUS⟧ **1** the same in structure, quality, etc.; similar or identical **2** composed of similar or identical elements or parts; uniform **3** *Math. a)* commensurable *b)* having all terms of the same dimensions or degree —**ho′mo·ge·ne′i·ty** (-jə nē′ə tē; -nā′-) ***n.*** —**ho′mo·ge′ne·ous·ly** ***adv.*** —**ho′mo·ge′ne·ous·ness** ***n.***

ho·mog·e·nize (hə mäj′ə nīz′) ***vt.*** **-nized′**, **-niz′ing** ⟦< obs. adj. *homogene*, prec. + -IZE⟧ **1** to make homogeneous **2** *a)* to make more uniform throughout in texture, mixture, quality, etc. by breaking down and blending the particles ☆*b)* to process (milk) so that the fat particles are so finely divided and emulsified that the cream does not separate on standing —**ho·mog′e·ni·za′tion** ***n.***

ho·mog·e·nous (hə mäj′ə nəs) ***adj.*** ⟦HOMO- + -GENOUS⟧ **1** having similarity in structure because of common descent **2** HOMOGENEOUS —**ho·mog′e·ny** (-nē) ***n.***

ho·mo·graft (hō′mō graft′, -mə-; häm′ō-, -ə-) ***n.*** ALLOGRAFT

hom·o·graph (häm′ə graf′, hō′mə-) ***n.*** ⟦HOMO- + -GRAPH⟧ a word with the same spelling as another or others but with a different meaning and origin and, sometimes, a different pronunciation (Ex.: *bow*, the front part of a ship; *bow*, to bend; *bow*, a decorative knot) —**hom′o·graph′ic** ***adj.***

ho·moi·o- (hō moi′ō, -ə) *combining form* HOMEO-

ho·moi·o·ther·mal (hō moi′ō thʉr′məl) ***n.*** ⟦prec. + THERMAL⟧ *Zool.* warm-blooded: also **ho·moi′o·ther′mic**

ho·moi·ou·si·an (hō′moi o͞o′sē ən) ***adj.*** ⟦LGr(Ec) *homoiousios*, of like substance < *homoios*, like (< *homos*, SAME) + *ousia*, essence < *ōn*, being: see ONTO-⟧ [*also* **H-**] *Theol.* of or holding the teaching that God the Father and God the Son are of a similar nature, not of the same nature —***n.*** [*also* **H-**] an adherent of this teaching

ho·mol·o·gate (hō mäl′ə gāt′) ***vt.*** **-gat′ed**, **-gat′ing** ⟦< ML *homologatus*, pp. of *homologare* < Gr *homologein*, to agree, assent < *homos*, SAME + *legein*, say: see LOGIC⟧ **1** to approve or countenance **2** *Civil Law* to confirm officially, as by a court of justice —**ho·mol′o·ga′tion** ***n.***

ho·mo·log·i·cal (hō′mō läj′i kəl, häm′ō-) ***adj.*** HOMOLOGOUS —**ho′mo·log′i·cal·ly** ***adv.***

ho·mol·o·gize (hō mäl′ə jīz′, hə-) ***vt.*** **-gized′**, **-giz′ing** **1** to make homologous **2** to demonstrate homology in —***vi.*** to be homologous

ho·mol·o·gous (hō mäl′ə gəs) ***adj.*** ⟦Gr *homologos*, agreeing < *homos*, SAME + *legein*, say: see LOGIC⟧ **1** corresponding in structure, position, character, etc.: opposed to HETEROLOGOUS **2** *Biol.* corresponding in basic type of structure and deriving from a common primitive origin [the wing of a bat and the foreleg of a mouse are *homologous*] **3** *Chem. a)* designating or of a series of compounds each member of which has a structure differing regularly by some increment (as a CH_2 group) from that of the adjacent members *b)* having this relation with another or other compounds of such a series *c)* designating or of a series of elements in the same group or period of the periodic table, as the halogens, actinides, etc. **4** *Immunology a)* of a serum given to and derived from the same species *b)* of a serum given to another species but for fighting the same bacterium **5** *Med.* HOMOPLASTIC (sense 2)

hom·o·lo·graph·ic (häm′ə lō′graf′ik, hō′mə lō′-) ***adj.*** ⟦altered (by assoc. with HOMO-) < *homalographic* < Gr *homalos*, even, level (akin to *homos*, SAME) + -GRAPHIC⟧ keeping the parts in proper relative size and form

homolographic projection a type of equal-area map projection

hom·o·logue or **hom·o·log** (häm′ə lôg′, hō′mə-) ***n.*** ⟦Fr < Gr *homologos*⟧ a homologous part, thing, organ, etc.

ho·mol·o·gy (hō mäl′ə jē, hə-) ***n., pl.*** **-gies** ⟦LL *homologia* < Gr: see HOMO- & -LOGY⟧ **1** the quality or state of being homologous **2** a homologous correspondence or relationship, as of animal organs, chemical compounds, etc.

ho·mol·o·sine projection (hō mäl′ə sīn′, -sēn′, -sin; hə-) ⟦< Gr *homalos* (akin to *homos*, SAME) + SINE[1]⟧ an equal-area map projection of the earth's surface that combines certain features of homolographic and sinusoidal projections so as to allow a minimum of distortion for the continents

ho·mo·mor·phism (hō′mō môr′fiz′əm, häm′ō-) ***n.*** ⟦HOMO- + -MORPH + -ISM⟧ **1** similarity in form **2** *Biol.* resemblance or similarity, without actual relationship, in structure or origin: said of organs or organisms **3** *Bot.* uniformity in shape or size, as of pistils and stamens **4** *Zool.* similarity between an insect's larva and its matured form Also **ho′mo·mor′phy** —**ho′mo·mor′phic** ***adj.***, **ho′mo·mor′phous**

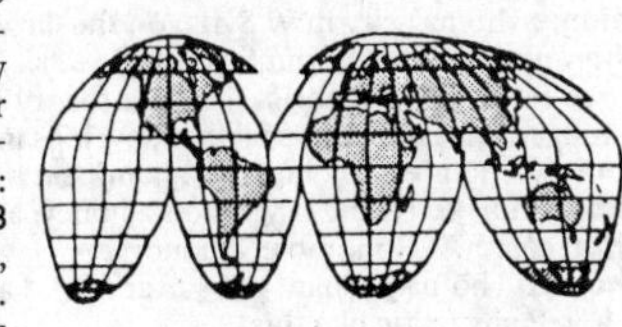

homolosine projection

hom·o·nym (häm′ə nim′) ***n.*** ⟦Fr *homonyme* < L *homonymus* < Gr *homōnymos*, having the same name < *homos*, SAME + *onyma*, NAME⟧ **1** a word with the same pronunciation as another but with a different meaning, origin, and, usually, spelling (Ex.: *bore* and *boar*); homophone **2** loosely, a homograph **3** either of two people with the same name; namesake **4** *Taxonomy* a name for a genus, species, etc. unsuitable because already used for another classification —**hom′o·nym′ic** ***adj.***

ho·mon·y·mous (hō män′i məs) ***adj.*** **1** of, or having the nature of, a homonym **2** having the same name —**ho·mon′y·my** (-mē) ***n.***

ho·mo·ou·si·an (hō′mō o͞o′sē ən) ***adj.*** ⟦LL(Ec) *homoousianus* < LGr(Ec) *homoousios*, consubstantial < *homos*, SAME + *ousia*, essence: see HOMOIOUSIAN⟧ [*also* **H-**] *Theol.* of or holding the teaching that God the Father and God the Son are of the same nature —***n.*** [*also* **H-**] an adherent of this teaching

ho·mo·phile (hō′mō fīl′, -mə-) ***n., adj.*** ⟦HOMO- + -PHILE⟧ HOMOSEXUAL

ho·mo·pho·bi·a (hō′mə fō′bē ə) ***n.*** ⟦HOMO(SEXUAL) + -PHOBIA⟧ irrational hatred or fear of homosexuals or homosexuality —**ho′mo·phobe′** (-fōb′) ***n.*** —**ho′mo·pho′bic** (-fō′bik) ***adj.***

hom·o·phone (häm′ə fōn′) ***n.*** ⟦< Gr *homophōnos*: see fol.⟧ **1** any of two or more letters or groups of letters representing the same speech sound (Ex.: *c* in *civil* and *s* in *song*) **2** HOMONYM (sense 1) —**ho·moph·o·nous** (hō mäf′ə nəs, hə-) ***adj.***

hom·o·phon·ic (häm′ə fän′ik, hō′mə-) ***adj.*** ⟦< Gr *homophōnos*, of the same sound (< *homos*, SAME + *phōnē*, sound: see PHONE[1]) + -IC⟧ **1** *Music* having one melodic line at a time, the other voices or parts serving as accompaniment **2** HOMONYMOUS —**ho·moph·o·ny** (hō mäf′ə nē) ***n., pl.*** **-nies**

ho·mo·plas·tic (hō′mō plas′tik, häm′ō-) ***adj.*** ⟦HOMO- + -PLASTIC⟧ **1** of or having to do with homoplasy **2** derived from a member of the same species: said as of a graft: see AUTOPLASTY, HETEROPLASTY —**ho′mo·plas′ti·cal·ly** ***adv.***

ho·mo·pla·sy (hō′mō plā′sē, -plas′ē) ***n.*** ⟦HOMO- + -PLASY⟧ *Biol.* correspondence between parts as a result of similarity of environment rather than common heredity: cf. HOMOGENY

ho·mo·pol·y·mer (hō′mō päl′ə mər, hä′mō-) ***n.*** a polymer consisting of a chain of identical molecules

ho·mop·ter·an (hō mäp′tər ən) ***n.*** ⟦< ModL *Homoptera*: see HOMO- & PTERO- & -AN⟧ any of an order (Homoptera) of insects with sucking mouthparts and two pairs of membranous wings of uniform thickness, as aphids, cicadas, or scale insects —***adj.*** of or relating to this order of insects

ho·mop·ter·ous (hō mäp′tər əs) ***adj.*** HOMOPTERAN

Ho·mo sa·pi·ens (hō′mō sā′pē enz′, -ənz) ⟦ModL: see HOMO[1] & SAPIENT⟧ **1** all human beings; mankind **2** a human being **3** [*usually in italics*] the scientific name for the only living species of human: see MAN (*n.* 1a)

ho·mo·sex·u·al (hō′mō sek′sho͞o əl, -mə-) ***adj.*** ⟦see HOMO-⟧ of, characterized by, or having to do with HOMOSEXUALITY —***n.*** a homosexual individual —**ho′mo·sex′u·al·ly** ***adv.***

ho·mo·sex·u·al·i·ty (-sek′sho͞o al′ə tē) ***n.*** **1** sexual desire for those of the same sex as oneself **2** SEXUAL ORIENTATION that is entirely or predominantly directed toward those of the same sex as oneself

ho·mo·sphere (hō′mō sfir′) ***n.*** the lower of two divisions of the earth's atmosphere, extending to a height of *c.* 70 km (*c.* 43 mi), characterized by a relatively constant composition of its component gases: cf. HETEROSPHERE

ho·mos·po·rous (hō mäs′pə rəs, hō′mō spôr′əs) ***adj.*** *Bot.* producing only one kind of spore

ho·mo·sty·ly (hō′mō stī′lē) ***n.*** ⟦HOMO- + STYL(E) + -Y[3]⟧ the condition in which flowers of the same species have styles of equal length: see HETEROSTYLY —**ho′mo·sty′lous** ***adj.***

ho·mo·tax·is (hō′mō tak′sis, -mə-; häm′ō-, -ə-) ***n.*** ⟦ModL < HOMO- + -TAXIS⟧ *Geol.* a similarity in the arrangement of layers, or in the fossil content, between strata of different regions not necessarily formed at the same time

ho·mo·thal·lic (-thal′ik) ***adj.*** ⟦HOMO- + THALL(US) + -IC⟧ designating or possessing a mycelium that produces two kinds of cells, which function as male and female —**ho′mo·thal′lism′** ***n.***

ho·mo·trans·plant (-trans′plant′) ***n.*** ALLOGRAFT —**ho′mo·trans′plan·ta′tion** ***n.***

ho·mo·zy·go·sis (-zī gō′sis) ***n.*** ⟦HOMO- + ModL *zygosis*: see HETEROZYGOSIS⟧ **1** the condition of being a homozygote **2** the production of a homozygote for any one pair or for several pairs of genes —**ho′mo·zy·got′ic** (-gät′ik) ***adj.***

ho·mo·zy·gote (-zī′gōt′) ***n.*** ⟦HOMO- + ZYGOTE⟧ a plant or animal having two identical alleles at a single locus on a chromosome, and hence breeding true for the particular character involved; purebred —**ho′mo·zy′gous** (-zī gəs) ***adj.***

Homs (hômz) city in W Syria, on the Orontes

ho·mun·cu·lus (hō muŋ′kyoo͞ ləs) ***n.,*** *pl.* **-li′** (-lī′) ⟦L, dim. of *homo*, man: see HOMO[1]⟧ **1** [Historical] in the theory of preformation, the minuscule, fully formed human being that develops into the fetus **2** a little man; dwarf

hom·y (hōm′ē) ***adj.*** **hom′i·er, hom′i·est** HOMEY[1] —**hom′i·ness** ***n.***

hon (hun) ***n.*** [Slang] sweet one; honey: a term of affectionate address

Hon *abbrev.* **1** Honorable **2** honorary

ho·nan (hō′nän′, -nan′) ***n.*** ⟦after fol.⟧ **1** a soft, thin silk fabric: also **honan silk 2** any fabric like this

Ho·nan (hō′nän′) *a former transliteration of* HENAN

hon·cho (hän′chō) ***n.,*** *pl.* **-chos** ⟦< Jpn *hanchō*, squad leader⟧ ☆[Slang] a person in charge; leader; chief

Hond *abbrev.* Honduras

Hon·du·ras (hän door′əs, -dyoor′-) country in Central America, with coastlines on the Pacific & the Caribbean: 43,278 sq mi (112,090 sq km); cap. Tegucigalpa —**Hon·du′ran** ***adj., n.***

hone[1] (hōn) ***n.*** ⟦ME < OE *han*, a stone, akin to ON *hein*, a hone < IE base **ko(i)-*, to sharpen, whet > L *cos*, whetstone, *cotes*, sharp rock, Gr *kōnos*, cone⟧ a fine-grained, hard stone used to sharpen cutting tools —***vt.*** **honed, hon′ing 1** to sharpen with or as with a hone **2** to develop or improve [to *hone* one's skills through practice] **3** *Mech.* to enlarge or smooth (a bore) to exact specifications with a rotating stick (**honing stone**) containing abrasive material —**hon′er** ***n.***

hone[2] (hōn) ***vi.*** **honed, hon′ing** ⟦ME *honen* < NormFr *honer* < OFr *houir*, to disgrace (< Frank **haunjan*, to scorn, insult, akin to OE *hean*, wretched) < IE base **kau-*, to humiliate > Latvian *kauns*, disgrace; sense infl. by OFr *hognier*, to grumble, prob. of echoic orig.⟧ [Dial.] **1** to yearn; long **2** to grumble; moan

Ho·neg·ger (hän′ə gər, hō′neg ər; *Fr* ô ne ger′), **Arthur** 1892-1955; Fr. composer

H1N1 (āch′wun′en′wun′) ***n.*** ⟦*h(emagglutinin)* (type) *1 n(euraminidase)* (type) *1*⟧ any of various strains of influenza virus including those that most commonly cause influenza in humans; specif., a pandemic strain originating in North America in 2009 and containing genes from swine, bird, and human influenza viruses

hon·est (än′ist) ***adj.*** ⟦ME < OFr *honeste* < L *honestus* < *honor*, honor⟧ **1** [Obs.] *a)* held in respect; honorable *b)* respectable, creditable, commendable, seemly, etc. (a generalized epithet of commendation) **2** that will not lie, cheat, or steal; truthful; trustworthy **3** *a)* showing fairness and sincerity; straightforward; free from deceit [an *honest* effort] *b)* gained or earned by fair methods, not by cheating, lying, or stealing [an *honest* living] **4** being what it seems; genuine; pure [to give *honest* measure] **5** frank and open [an *honest* face] **6** [Archaic] virtuous; chaste —***adv.*** [Informal] honestly; truly: an intensifier

hon·est·ly (-lē) ***adv.*** **1** in an honest manner **2** truly; really: used as an intensifier [*honestly*, it is so]

☆**hon·est-to-good·ness** (än′ist tə good′nis) ***adj.*** [Informal] genuine; real; authentic: also **hon′est-to-God′**

hon·es·ty (än′is tē) ***n.*** ⟦ME *honeste* < OFr *honesté* < L *honestas* < *honestus*⟧ **1** the state or quality of being honest; specif., *a)* [Obs.] honor *b)* a refraining from lying, cheating, or stealing; a being truthful, trustworthy, or upright *c)* sincerity; fairness; straightforwardness *d)* [Archaic] chastity **2** any of a genus (*Lunaria*) of plants of the crucifer family, with purple and white flowers and large, flat, oval pods; esp., a plant (*L. annua*) whose pods are used in winter bouquets

hone·wort (hōn′wurt′) ***n.*** ⟦obs. *hone*, a swelling + WORT[2]: formerly used to treat such swellings⟧ a perennial weed (*Cryptotaenia canadensis*) of the umbel family, with small, white flowers, found in shady places in the E U.S.

hon·ey (hun′ē) ***n.,*** *pl.* **-eys** ⟦ME *honi, hunig* < OE *hunig*, akin to Ger *honig* (OHG *honang*) < IE base **kenekó-*, honey-yellow > Sans *kāñcana-*, golden⟧ **1** a thick, sweet, syrupy substance that bees make as food from the nectar of flowers and store in honeycombs **2** *a)* anything like honey in texture, color, etc. *b)* sweet quality; sweetness **3** sweet one; darling; dear: usually a term of affectionate address ☆**4** [Informal] something pleasing or excellent of its kind [a *honey* of an idea] —***adj.*** **1** of or like honey **2** sweet; dear **3** yellowish-brown [*honey*-blond hair] —***vt.*** **-eyed** or **-ied, -ey·ing 1** to make sweet or pleasant as with honey **2** to speak sweetly or lovingly to **3** to flatter —***vi.*** to speak sweetly or lovingly; be very affectionate, attentive, or coaxing

honey badger ⟦so called from its habit of breaking open bees' nests in order to eat the honey: see RATEL⟧ RATEL

honey bear *name for:* **1** KINKAJOU **2** SLOTH BEAR

hon·ey·bee (hun′ē bē′) ***n.*** a bee that makes honey; esp., the common hive bee (*Apis mellifera*)

honey bucket ⟦fig. use: jocular euphemism⟧ [Slang] a bucket or container for human bodily waste, used where a toilet is not available

☆**hon·ey·bunch** (hun′ē bunch′) ***n.*** [Informal] darling; dear: used in affectionate address: also **hon′ey·bun′** (-bun′)

hon·ey·comb (hun′ē kōm′) ***n.*** ⟦ME *hunicomb* < OE *hunigcamb* < *hunig*, HONEY + *camb*, COMB[1]⟧ **1** the structure of six-sided wax cells made by bees to hold their honey or eggs **2** anything like this in structure or appearance —***vt.*** **1** to cause to have many holes like a honeycomb; riddle **2** to permeate or undermine [*honeycombed* with intrigue] —***vi.*** to become riddled with holes like a honeycomb —***adj.*** of, like, or patterned after a honeycomb: also **hon′ey·combed′**

honeycomb

hon·ey·creep·er (hun′ē krē′pər) ***n.*** **1** any of a family (Drepanididae) of brightly colored, insect-eating, Hawaiian passerine birds **2** any of various small, slender-billed passerine birds (family Emberizidae) of tropical America that feed on nectar and fruits

hon·ey·dew (hun′ē doo͞′, -dyoo͞′) ***n.*** **1** a sweet fluid, as manna, exuded from various plants **2** a sweet substance that is excreted by aphids and other juice-sucking homopteran plant insects, or secreted by certain fungi: often eaten by bees and ants ☆**3** *short for* HONEYDEW MELON

☆**honeydew melon** a type of winter melon with a smooth, whitish rind and very sweet, greenish flesh

hon·ey·eat·er (hun′ē ēt′ər) ***n.*** any of a large family (Meliphagidae) of Australasian passerine birds with a long, brushlike tongue that can be protruded to catch insects or draw nectar from flowers

hon·eyed (hun′ēd) ***adj.*** ⟦ME *honyede*⟧ **1** sweetened, covered, or filled with honey **2** sweet as honey; flattering or affectionate

hon·ey·guide (hun′ē gīd′) ***n.*** any of a family (Indicatoridae) of small, heavily built, drab-colored piciform birds of Africa, Asia, and the East Indies: they are said to lead people or animals to bees' nests in order to eat the grubs and wax they might leave behind

☆**hon·ey·lo·cust** (-lō′kəst) ***n.*** any of a genus (*Gleditsia*) of trees of the caesalpinia family, esp. a North American species (*G. triacanthos*) usually having strong, thorny branches, featherlike foliage, and large, twisted pods containing beanlike seeds and a sweet pulp

hon·ey·moon (hun′ē moo͞n′) ***n.*** ⟦as if < HONEY + MOON (? in reference to the waning of the affection of newlyweds), but ? folk etym. for ON *hjūnōttsmānathr*, lit., wedding-night month⟧ **1** the holiday or vacation spent together by a newly married couple **2** a brief period of apparent harmony in a new relationship or situation, as between political parties right after an election: also **honeymoon period** —***vi.*** to have or spend a honeymoon —**hon′ey·moon′er** ***n.***

honey pot 1 any of a caste of workers in certain species of ants, that serve as living storehouses for a honeylike material later used by the whole colony **2** a waxy honey container made by some bees, esp. bumblebees, for storing their food

hon·ey·suck·er (hun′ē suk′ər) ***n.*** **1** HONEYEATER **2** a small Australian marsupial (*Tarsipes spencerae*) with a long tongue and snout: it feeds on nectar and small insects: also **honey opossum**

hon·ey·suck·le (hun′ē suk′əl) ***n.*** ⟦ME *honisocle*, dim. (see -LE) < OE *hunigsuce* (Brit dial. *honeysuck*) < *hunig*, HONEY + *sucan*, to SUCK⟧ **1** any of a genus (*Lonicera*) of plants of the honeysuckle family, with small, fragrant flowers of red, yellow, or white **2** any of several similar plants with fragrant flowers, esp. columbine —***adj.*** designating a family (Caprifoliaceae, order Dipsacales) of dicotyledonous, mostly woody plants, including the coralberry and elder

Honey Tangerine a citrus fruit with a deep-orange pulp, formed by crossing a tangerine and a sweet orange hybrid

hong (hôŋ, häŋ) ***n.*** ⟦Chin *hōng*, a row, series, factory⟧ [Historical] in China, a warehouse or factory

Hong (häŋ, hôŋ) *Annamese name for* the RED RIVER (Vietnam)

Hong Kong or **Hong·kong** (häŋ′ käŋ′, hôŋ′kôŋ′) **1** administrative region of China (since July 1, 1997), on the South China Sea: it consists of a principal island (**Hong Kong Island**), nearby islands, Kowloon Peninsula, and an adjacent mainland area (New Territories): a former British crown colony: 421 sq mi (1,091 sq km) **2** chief city of this region; seaport on Hong Kong Island

Hong Kong

Ho·ni·a·ra (hō′nē är′ə) capital of the Solomon Islands, on Guadalcanal

hon·ied (hun′ēd) ***adj.*** *alt. sp. of* HONEYED

☆**honk** (hôŋk, häŋk) *n.* ⟦echoic⟧ **1** the call of a wild goose **2** any similar sound, as that of an automobile horn —*vi.* to make any such sound —*vt.* **1** to express by honking **2** to sound (an automobile horn) —**honk′er** *n.*

hon·kie or **hon·ky** (hôŋ′kē) *n., pl.* **-kies** ⟦< ? HUNKY[1]⟧ [Slang] a white person: a term of hostility and contempt: also sp. **hon′key**

☆**hon·ky-tonk** (hôŋ′kē tôŋk′, häŋ′kē täŋk′) *n.* ⟦< ?⟧ **1** [Old Slang] a cheap, disreputable, noisy cabaret or nightclub **2** [Slang] a bar, esp. one where country music is played —*adj.* **1** [Slang] of or like a honky-tonk; specif., cheap, loud, low-class, etc. **2** designating or of a style of piano music having a bouncy rhythm and a tinkling sound —*vi.* [Slang] to make the rounds of honky-tonks

Hon·o·lu·lu (hän′ə lo͞o′lo͞o, hō′nə-) ⟦Haw, lit., sheltered bay⟧ capital of Hawaii: seaport on the SE coast of Oahu

hon·or (än′ər) *n.* ⟦ME *honour* < OFr < L *honor, honos,* official dignity, repute, esteem⟧ **1** high regard or great respect given, received, or enjoyed; esp., *a)* glory; fame; renown *b)* good reputation; credit **2** a keen sense of right and wrong; adherence to action or principles considered right; integrity [to conduct oneself with *honor*] **3** *a)* chastity or purity *b)* reputation for chastity **4** high rank or position; distinction; dignity [the great *honor* of the presidency] **5** [**H-**] a title of respect given to certain officials, as judges: preceded by *Your* or by *His* or *Her* **6** something done or given as a token or act of respect; specif., *a)* [Obs.] a curtsy; bow *b)* a social courtesy or privilege [may I have the *honor* of this dance?] *c)* a badge, token, decoration, etc. given to a person *d)* [*pl.*] public acts or ceremonies of respect [buried with full military *honors*] *e)* [*pl.*] special distinction or credit given to students, esp. at commencement, for high academic achievement *f)* [*pl.*] an advanced course of study in place of or in addition to the regular course, for exceptional students [*Honors* English] **7** a person or thing that brings respect and fame to a school, country, etc. **8** *Bridge a)* any of the five highest cards in a suit *b)* [*pl.*] all, or any four, of the five highest cards of the trump suit or, in a notrump hand, the four aces **9** *Golf* the privilege of driving first from the tee —*vt.* **1** to respect greatly; regard highly; esteem **2** to show great respect or high regard for; treat with deference and courtesy **3** to worship (a deity) **4** to do or give something in honor of **5** *a)* to accept and pay when due [to *honor* a check] *b)* to carry out the terms of [to *honor* a treaty obligation] *c)* to accept as valid, good for credit, etc. [a store that *honors* most credit cards] **6** to make a bow to in square dancing —*adj.* of or showing honor [*honor* roll] —**do honor to 1** to show great respect for **2** to bring or cause honor to —**do the honors** to act as host or hostess, esp. by making introductions, proposing toasts, serving at table, etc. —**honor bright** [Informal] honestly; truthfully —**in honor of** as a token of respect for —**on** (or **upon**) **one's honor** staking one's good name or one's truthfulness, trustworthiness, or reliability

SYN.—**honor**, as compared here, implies popular acknowledgment of a person's right to great respect as well as any expression of such respect [in *honor* of the martyred dead]; **homage** suggests great esteem shown in praise, tributes, or obeisance [to pay *homage* to the genius of Milton]; **reverence** implies deep respect together with love [he held her memory in *reverence*]; **deference** suggests a display of courteous regard for a superior, or for one to whom respect is due, by yielding to the person's status, claims, or wishes [in *deference* to his age]

hon·or·a·ble (än′ər ə bəl) *adj.* ⟦ME *honourable* < OFr *honorable* < L *honorabilis* < *honor*⟧ **1** worthy of being honored; specif., *a)* [**H-**] of, or having a position of, high rank or worth (used as a title of courtesy for certain officials and for the children of certain British peers) [our Representative, the *Honorable* Jane Smith] *b)* noble; illustrious *c)* of good reputation; respectable **2** having or showing a sense of right and wrong; characterized by honesty and integrity; upright **3** bringing honor to the owner or doer **4** doing honor; accompanied with marks of respect [an *honorable* burial] —**hon′or·a·bil′i·ty** *n.,* **hon′or·a·ble·ness** —**hon′or·a·bly** *adv.*

honorable mention mention awarded to or for a work, performance, etc. judged to be very good but not good enough to merit a prize

hon·o·ra·ri·um (än′ə rer′ē əm) *n., pl.* **-ri·ums** or **-ri·a** (-ə) ⟦L *honorarium (donum),* honorary (gift)⟧ a payment as to a professional person for services on which no fee is set or legally obtainable

hon·or·ar·y (än′ə rer′ē) *adj.* ⟦L *honorarius,* of or conferring honor⟧ **1** given as an honor only, without the usual requirements or privileges [an *honorary* degree] **2** *a)* designating an office or position held as an honor only, without service or pay *b)* holding such a position or office *c)* recognizing academic distinction or accomplishment [an *honorary* society] **3** depending on one's honor; that cannot be legally enforced or collected: said of debts, etc. —**hon′or·ar′i·ly** *adv.*

hon·or·ee (än′ər ē′) *n.* a person receiving an honor or being honored

honor guard a ceremonial guard, as one assigned to escort a distinguished person or to accompany a casket at a funeral

hon·or·if·ic (än′ə rif′ik) *adj.* ⟦L *honorificus* < *honor* + *facere,* to make: see DO[1]⟧ conferring honor; showing respect [an *honorific* title or word]: also **hon′or·if′i·cal** —*n.* an honorific title or word —**hon′or·if′i·cal·ly** *adv.*

ho·no·ris cau·sa (ō nôr′is kou′sä, hō-) ⟦L, for the sake of honor⟧ conferred as an honor: said as of an honorary degree [a Ph.D. *honoris causa*]

honor roll a list of persons achieving distinction in some field or endeavor, specif., a list of students earning high grades

☆**honor society** a college or high-school organization for students of high academic achievement: also **honorary society**

honors of war special privileges granted to a defeated army, as that of continuing to bear arms

☆**honor system** in some schools, prisons, etc., a system whereby individuals are trusted to obey the rules, do their work, take tests, etc. without direct supervision

hon·our (än′ər) *n., vt., adj. Brit. sp. of* HONOR

Hon·shu (hän′sho͞o′) largest of the islands forming Japan: 87,992 sq mi (227,898 sq km); chief city, Tokyo

☆**hooch**[1] (ho͞och) *n.* ⟦contr. of Alaskan Ind *hoochinoo,* crude alcoholic liquor made by the *Hoochinoo* Indians (< *Hutsnuwu,* lit., grizzly bear fort)⟧ [Slang] alcoholic liquor; esp., liquor that is of low quality or that is made or obtained illegally

☆**hooch**[2] (ho͞och) *n.* ⟦< Jpn *uchi,* house⟧ [Slang, Chiefly U.S. Mil.] a place to live in; specif., a shack or thatched hut, as in Vietnam

Hooch (hōkh), **Pie·ter de** (pē′tər də) 1629?-84?; Du. painter

☆**hooch·ie-cooch·ie** (ho͞o′chē ko͞o′chē) *n. alt. sp. of* HOOTCHY-KOOTCHY

hood[1] (hood) *n.* ⟦ME < OE *hod,* akin to Ger *hut,* hat: for IE base see HAT⟧ **1** a covering for the head and neck and, sometimes, the face, worn separately or as part of a robe, cloak, or jacket [a monk's cowl is a *hood*] **2** anything resembling a hood in shape or use; specif., *a)* a fold of cloth over the back of an academic or ecclesiastical gown, judge's robe, etc., often with distinguishing colors to indicate the wearer's degree, college affiliation, etc. ☆*b)* the body panel that usually covers the engine of an automotive vehicle *c)* a protective canopy, as above a cookstove, often containing a fan, for exhausting heat, smoke, and fumes *d)* the cowl of a chimney *e)* a covering for a horse's head *f) Falconry* the covering for a falcon's head when it is not chasing game **3** *Zool. a)* a bird's crest *b)* the fold of skin near a cobra's head that expands when the snake is excited —*vt.* to cover or provide with or as with a hood

☆**hood**[2] (hood) *n.* [Informal] *short for* HOODLUM

Hood[1] (hood) **1 John Bell** 1831-79; Confederate general **2 Robin** *see* ROBIN HOOD **3 Thomas** 1799-1845; Eng. poet & humorist

Hood[2] (hood), **Mount** mountain of the Cascade Range, in N Oreg.: a peak of volcanic origin: 11,245 ft (3,427 m)

☆**'hood** (hood) *n.* [Slang] *short for* NEIGHBORHOOD: also written **hood**

-hood (hood) ⟦ME *-had, -hod* < OE *had,* order, condition, quality, rank, akin to Ger *-heit* < IE **(s)kāit-,* bright, gleaming: basic sense "appearance by which known"⟧ *suffix forming nouns* **1** state, quality, condition [*childhood*] **2** the whole group of (a specified class, profession, etc.) [*priesthood*]

hood·ed (hood′id) *adj.* **1** having or covered with a hood **2** shaped like a hood; cucullate **3** with the eyelids partly closed [*hooded* eyes] **4** *Zool. a)* having the head different in color from the body *b)* having a crest like a hood *c)* capable of expanding the skin at each side of the neck by movements of the ribs (said as of the cobra)

hooded crow a European carrion crow (*Corvus corone cornix*) with black wings, head, and tail, and a gray back and breast

hooded seal a large, dark-gray, earless seal (*Cystophora cristata*) of the N Atlantic: the male has on its head a hoodlike sac that can be inflated in displays of aggression

hood·ie (hood′ē) *n.* a sweatshirt, sweater, or other casual top having a hood and long sleeves

☆**hood·lum** (ho͞od′ləm, hood′-) *n.* ⟦prob. < Ger dial. (esp. Swiss) *hudilump,* wretch, miserable fellow < MHG *hudel,* rag, wretch + *lump,* rag, tatter, wretch⟧ **1** a wild, lawless person, often a member of a gang of criminals **2** a tough-looking young ruffian —**hood′lum·ism′** *n.*

☆**hoo·doo** (ho͞o′do͞o′) *n., pl.* **-doos′** ⟦var. of VOODOO⟧ **1** VOODOO **2** [Informal] *a)* a person or thing that causes bad luck *b)* bad luck **3** a natural rock formation of fantastic shape, esp. as found in the W U.S. —*vt.* [Slang] to cast a spell on or otherwise bring bad luck to —**hoo′doo·ism′** *n.*

hood·wink (hood′wiŋk′) *vt.* ⟦HOOD[1] + WINK⟧ **1** [Archaic] to blindfold **2** to mislead or confuse by trickery; dupe

☆**hoo·ey** (ho͞o′ē) *interj., n.* ⟦< ?⟧ [Slang] nonsense

hoof (hoof, ho͞of) *n., pl.* **hoofs** or **hooves** (ho͞ovz, hoovz) ⟦ME *hoof* < OE *hof,* akin to Ger *huf* < IE base **kapho-* > Sans *śaphá-,* hoof, claw⟧ **1** the horny covering on the feet of ungulate mammals **2** the entire foot of such an animal **3** [Slang] the human foot — *vt., vi.* **1** to kick or trample with the hoofs **2** [Informal] to walk: often with *it* **3** [Slang] to dance —☆**on the hoof** not yet butchered; alive: said of livestock

hoof-and-mouth disease (hoof′ən mouth′, ho͞of′-) *var. of* FOOT-AND-MOUTH DISEASE

hoof·beat (hoof′bēt′, ho͞of′-) *n.* the sound made by the hoof of an animal when it runs, walks, etc.

hoof·bound (-bound′) *adj.* having dryness and contraction of the hoof, which causes pain and lameness

hoofed (hooft, ho͞oft) *adj.* having hoofs; ungulate

☆**hoof·er** (hoof′ər, ho͞of′-) *n.* [Slang] a professional dancer, esp. a tap-dancer, soft-shoe dancer, etc.

Hoogh (hōkh), **Pie·ter de** (pē′tər də) *var. of* Pieter de HOOCH

Hoogh·ly (ho͞og′lē) river in E India, flowing into the Bay of Bengal: westernmost channel of the Ganges delta: *c.* 160 mi (257 km)

hoo-ha (ho͞o′hä′) *n.* ⟦echoic⟧ [Informal] a commotion, fuss, or to-do

hook (hook) *n.* ⟦ME < OE *hoc,* akin to HAKE, MDu *hoec,* ON *hakr* < IE base **keg-,* peg for hanging⟧ **1** a curved or bent piece of metal, wood, etc. used to catch, hold, or pull something; specif., *a)* a curved piece of wire or bone with a barbed end, for catching fish *b)* a curved piece of metal, wood, etc.

fastened to a wall or chain at one end, used to hang things on, raise things up, etc. *[a coat hook]* *c)* a small metal catch inserted in a loop, or eye, to fasten clothes together *d)* [Slang] *Naut.* an anchor **2** a curved metal implement for cutting grain, etc. **3** something shaped like a hook; specif., *a)* a curving cape or headland (used in place names) *[Sandy Hook]* *b)* a sharp bend in a stream **4** ⟦back-form. < HOOKER[1] (sense 3)⟧ a trap; snare **5** [Informal] something intended to attract attention or encourage involvement; specif., in popular music, a catchy, repeated phrase, verse, riff, etc. **6** *a)* the path of a hit or thrown ball that curves away to the left from a right-handed player or to the right from a left-handed player *b)* a ball that follows such a path **7** *Boxing* a short, sharp blow delivered with the arm bent at the elbow **8** *Music* FLAG[1] (sense 8) **—*vt.*** **1** to attach or fasten with or as with a hook, or a hook and eye **2** to take hold of with a hook **3** to catch with or as with a hook **4** to attack with the horns, as a bull; gore **5** to make into the shape of a hook ☆**6** to make (a rug, wall hanging, etc.) by drawing strips of yarn or cloth with a hook through a canvas or burlap backing **7** to hit or throw (a ball) in a HOOK (*n.* 6a) **8** [Informal] *a)* to tempt or attract *b)* to cause addiction to *c)* to steal; snatch **9** *Boxing* to hit with a hook **—*vi.*** **1** to curve as a hook does **2** to be fastened with a hook or hooks **3** to be caught by a hook ☆**4** [Slang] to work as a prostitute **—by hook or by crook** in any way whatever; by any means, honest or dishonest **—**☆**get the hook** [Slang] to be discharged or dismissed: from the former practice of pulling incompetent actors off the stage with a long, hooked pole **—**☆**hook, line, and sinker** [Informal] completely; altogether: orig. a fisherman's expression **—hook up** **1** to connect or attach with a hook or hooks **2** to arrange and connect the parts of (a radio, etc.) ☆**3** *a)* [Informal] to come or bring into a relationship with another, as partner, associate, spouse, etc. *b)* [Informal] to come together; meet *c)* [Slang] to have brief or casual sexual relations **—off the hook** [Informal] out of trouble, embarrassment, or a state of burdensome responsibility **—**☆**on one's own hook** [Informal] by oneself; without getting help, advice, etc.

hook·ah or **hook·a** (hook′ə, hōō′kə) ***n.*** ⟦Ar *ḥuqqa*, pipe for smoking, vase⟧ a kind of water pipe associated with the Middle East, with a long, flexible tube by means of which the smoke is drawn through water in a vase or bowl and thereby cooled

hook and eye a device for fastening clothes, etc., consisting of a small loop and a hook that catches on it

☆**hook and ladder** a fire engine that carries long ladders, hooks for tearing down ceilings, and other equipment

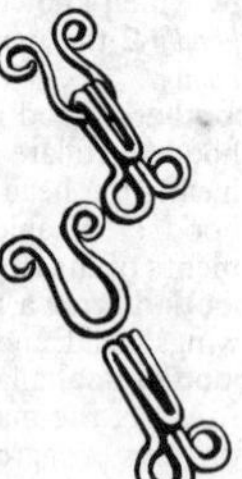

hook and eye

Hooke (hook), **Robert** 1635-1703; Eng. physicist, mathematician, & inventor

hooked (hookt) ***adj.*** **1** curved like a hook **2** having a hook or hooks ☆**3** made with a hook *[a hooked rug]* ☆**4** [Informal] *a)* addicted as to the use of a drug (often with *on*) *b)* preoccupied or obsessed with a person, fad, etc. (often with *on*) **5** [Slang] married

hook·er[1] (hook′ər) ***n.*** **1** one that hooks ☆**2** [Slang] an undiluted drink of whiskey ☆**3** ⟦orig., a resident of *Corlear's Hook*, area in New York City whose brothels were frequented by sailors⟧ [Slang] a prostitute

hook·er[2] (hook′ər) ***n.*** ⟦Du *hoeker* < MDu *hoeck-boot*, lit., hook boat: see HOOK⟧ **1** an Irish or English fishing smack with one mast **2** any old, clumsy ship

Hook·er (hook′ər) **1 Joseph** 1814-79; Union general in the Civil War **2 Richard** 1554-1600; Eng. clergyman & writer **3 Thomas** 1586?-1647; Eng. Puritan clergyman, in America after 1633

hook·nose (hook′nōz′) ***n.*** a nose curved downward somewhat like a hook; aquiline nose **—hook′nosed′** ***adj.***

☆**hook shot** *Basketball* a one-handed shot in which the extended arm is brought sideways over the head in tossing the ball toward the basket

☆**hook·up** (hook′up′) ***n.*** ⟦HOOK + UP[1]⟧ **1** the arrangement and connection of parts, circuits, etc. in a radio, telephone system, network of radio stations, etc. **2** a connection, as for water or electricity, in a trailer park or campsite **3** [Informal] an agreement or alliance, as between two governments, parties, companies, etc. **4** [Informal] a meeting, get-together, etc. **5** [Slang] a brief or casual sexual encounter

☆**hook·worm** (hook′wurm′) ***n.*** any of a superfamily (Ancylostomatoidea) of small, parasitic, intestinal nematode worms with hooks around the mouth: found esp. in tropical climates

☆**hookworm disease** a disease caused by hookworms, characterized by anemia, weakness, and abdominal pain: the larvae enter the body through the skin, usually of the bare feet; ancylostomiasis

☆**hook·y** (hook′ē) ***n.*** ⟦prob. < Du *hoeckje*, hide-and-seek < MDu *hoec* (> Du *hoek*), corner (hence, to hide around a corner): see HOOK⟧ [Informal] used only in the phrase **play hooky**, to stay away from school without permission; be a truant: also sp. **hook′ey**

hoo·li·gan (hōō′li gən) ***n.*** ⟦< ? *Hooligan* (or *Houlihan*), name of an Irish family in Southwark, London⟧ [Informal] **1** a hoodlum, esp. a young one **2** any rowdy or violent person **—hoo′li·gan·ism′** ***n.***

hoop (hōōp; *also* hoop) ***n.*** ⟦ME < OE *hop*, akin to Du *hoep*, OFris *hop*, prob. < IE **keub-* < base **keu-*, to bend, curve > Lith *kabė*, a hook⟧ **1** a circular band or ring for holding together the staves of a barrel, cask, etc. **2** anything like a hoop; specif., *a)* a large, circular band rolled along the ground by children at play *b)* any of the rings of whalebone, steel, etc. forming the framework of a hoop skirt *c)* one of a pair of small bands that hold material taut for embroidery work ☆*d)* the metal rim of the basket in basketball *e)* *Croquet* WICKET ☆**3** *[usually pl., with sing. v.]* [Slang] BASKETBALL **—*vt.*** to bind or fasten as with a hoop or hoops; encircle **—jump through hoops** ⟦by analogy with circus acts in which trained animals jump through large hoops⟧ [Informal] to do many things in order to achieve some objective, esp. things regarded as needlessly bothersome or inconvenient

☆**hoop-de-do** or **hoop-de-doo** (hōōp′dē dōō′, hoop′-) ***interj.*** [Informal] *var. of* WHOOP-DE-DO

☆**hoop·la** (hōōp′lä′, hoop′-) ***n.*** ⟦< ?⟧ [Informal] **1** great excitement; bustle **2** showy publicity; ballyhoo

hoo·poe (hōō′pōō′) ***n.*** ⟦earlier *houpe* < Fr *huppe* < L *upupa*, echoic of its cry⟧ an Old World coraciiform bird (*Upupa epops*) of a family (Upupidae) having only one species, with a long curved bill and an erectile crest

☆**hoop skirt** a skirt worn over a framework of hoops that makes the skirt flare outward

☆**hoop snake** any of several American snakes alleged in folklore to put its tail in its mouth and roll along like a hoop

☆**hoop·ster** (hōōp′stər) ***n.*** [Informal] a basketball player

hoo·ray (hoo rā′, hə-, hōō-) ***interj., n., vi., vt.*** *var. of* HURRAY

☆**hoose·gow** or **hoos·gow** (hōōs′gou′) ***n.*** ⟦< Sp *juzgado*, court of justice < pp. of *juzgar*, to judge < L *judicare* < *judex*, JUDGE⟧ [Old Slang] a jail or guardhouse

☆**Hoo·sier** (hōō′zhər) ***n.*** ⟦prob. < dial. (Cumberland) *hoozer*, something big⟧ [Informal] a person born or living in Indiana

hoop skirt

hoot[1] (hōōt) ***vi.*** ⟦ME *houten*, of echoic orig., as also in Swed, Norw *huta*⟧ **1** to utter its characteristic hollow sound: said of an owl **2** to utter a sound like this **3** to shout or cry out, esp. in scorn or disapproval **—*vt.*** **1** to express (scorn, disapproval, etc.) of by hooting **2** to drive or chase away by hooting *[to hoot an actor off the stage]* **—*n.*** **1** the sound that an owl makes **2** any sound like this **3** a loud shout or cry of scorn or disapproval ☆**4** the least bit; whit *[not worth a hoot]* **5** [Informal] a very amusing person, thing, event, etc. *[it's an old joke but a real hoot]*

hoot[2] (hōōt, ōōt) ***interj.*** ⟦? var. of prec.⟧ [Scot. or North Eng.] used to express objection, irritation, etc.: also **hoots**

☆**hootch**[1] (hōōch) ***n.*** [Slang] *alt. sp. of* HOOCH[1]

☆**hootch**[2] (hōōch) ***n.*** [Slang] *alt. sp. of* HOOCH[2]

☆**hoot·chy-koot·chy** (hōō′chē kōō′chē) ***n., pl.*** **-koot′chies** ⟦< ?⟧ a kind of erotic performance somewhat like the belly dance, as formerly performed at carnivals, etc.: also sp. **hoot′chie-koot′chie**

☆**hoot·en·an·ny** (hōōt′'n an′ē) ***n., pl.*** **-nies** ⟦orig. in sense of "dingus," "thingamajig"; a fanciful coinage⟧ an informal entertainment of folk singing, often with audience participation

hoot·er (hōōt′ər) ***n.*** **1** a person or thing that hoots ☆**2** *[pl.]* [Slang] a woman's breasts: a mildly vulgar term

hoot owl any of various owls that hoot; esp., the great horned owl

Hoo·ver[1] (hōō′vər) *trademark for* a vacuum cleaner **—*n.*** **[h-]** [Brit.] any vacuum cleaner **— *vt., vi.*** **[h-]** [Brit.] to clean with a vacuum cleaner; vacuum

Hoo·ver[2] (hōō′vər) **1 Herbert (Clark)** 1874-1964; 31st president of the U.S. (1929-33) **2 J(ohn) Edgar** 1895-1972; U.S. government official: director of the FBI (1924-72)

Hoover Dam ⟦after Pres. Herbert HOOVER[2]⟧ dam on the Colorado River, on the Ariz.-Nev. border: 726 ft (221 m) high

☆**Hoo·ver·ville** (-vil′) ***n.*** ⟦derisively, after Pres. Herbert HOOVER[2]⟧ [Informal] an area of shanties and temporary dwellings for migrants and the homeless during the Great Depression in the U.S.

hooves (hōōvz, hoovz) ***n.*** *alt. pl. of* HOOF

hop[1] (häp) ***vi.*** **hopped, hop′ping** ⟦ME *hoppen* < OE *hoppian*, akin to Ger *hüpfen* < IE **keub-* < base **keu-*, to bend, curve > HIP[1], L *cumbere*, to lie: basic sense prob. "to bend forward"⟧ **1** to make a short leap or leaps on one foot **2** to move by leaping or springing on both, or all, feet at once, as a bird, frog, etc. does **3** [Informal] *a)* to go or move briskly or in bounces *b)* to take a short, quick trip (with *up, down,* or *over*) **—*vt.*** **1** to jump over *[to hop a fence]* ☆**2** to get aboard *[to hop a train]* **3** [Informal] to fly over in an airplane **—*n.*** **1** an act or instance of hopping ☆**2** a bounce, as of a baseball **3** [Informal] a dance, esp. an informal one **4** [Informal] a short flight in an airplane **—*SYN.*** SKIP[1] **—hop on (or all over)** [Slang] to scold; reprimand **—hop to it** [Informal] to begin to do something briskly and vigorously

hop[2] (häp) ***n.*** ⟦LME *hoppe* < MDu, akin to Ger *hopfen*⟧ **1** a rough twining vine (*Humulus lupulus*) of the hemp family, having the female flowers borne in small cones covered with bladdery bracts **2** *[pl.]* the dried ripe cones of the female flowers, used for giving beer, ale, etc., a bitter taste and in medicine as a sedative ☆**3** [Slang] a narcotic drug; esp., opium **—*vt.*** **hopped, hop′ping** to flavor or treat with hops **—**☆**hop up** [Slang] **1** to stimulate by or as by a drug **2** to supercharge (an automobile engine, etc.)

-hop (häp) *combining form forming verbs* to go from one of a (specified) group or class of places or things to another or others in succession *[table-hop, job-hopping]*

hop clover any of a group of clovers with yellow flowers resembling hops when dry, esp. a species (*Trifolium agrarium*) commonly found in the NE U.S.

hope (hōp) ***n.*** ⟦ME < OE *hopa*, akin to Du *hoop*; see the v.⟧ **1** [*often pl.*] a feeling that what is wanted may happen; desire accompanied by expectation: often used in the phrase **in (the) hope (or hopes) of**, with such a feeling or desire **2** the thing that one has a hope for **3** a reason for hope **4** a person or thing on which one may base some hope **5** [Archaic] trust; reliance —***vt.*** **hoped, hop′ing** ⟦ME *hopen* < OE *hopian*, to expect, look for, akin to Ger *hoffen* < ? same IE base as HOP[1]: orig. sense (?) "to leap up in expectation"⟧ **1** to have hope; want and expect [*I hope* to be there by 5:00] **2** to want very much [*I hope* that your sick dog will recover] —***vi.*** **1** to have hope (*for*) **2** [Archaic] to trust or rely —***SYN.*** EXPECT —**hope against hope** to continue having hope though it seems baseless —**hop′er** ***n.***

Hope[1] (hōp) ***n.*** ⟦< prec.⟧ a feminine name

Hope[2] (hōp), **Bob** (born *Leslie Townes Hope*) 1903-2003; U.S. comedian & actor, born in England

☆**hope chest** a chest in which a young woman collects linen, clothing, etc. in anticipation of getting married

hope·ful (hōp′fəl) ***adj.*** ⟦ME⟧ **1** feeling or showing hope; expecting to get what one wants **2** inspiring or giving hope [*a hopeful* sign] —***n.*** a person who hopes, or seems likely, to succeed —**hope′ful·ness** ***n.***

hope·ful·ly (hōp′fəl ē) ***adv.*** **1** in a hopeful manner **2** it is to be hoped (that) [to leave early, *hopefully* by six]

Ho·pei or **Ho·peh** (hō′pā′) *a former transliteration of* HEBEI

hope·less (hōp′lis) ***adj.*** **1** without hope [*a hopeless* prisoner] **2** allowing no hope; causing despair [*a hopeless* situation] **3** impossible to solve, cure, deal with, teach, etc. —**hope′less·ly** ***adv.*** —**hope′less·ness** ***n.***

SYN.—**hopeless** means having no expectation of, or showing no sign of, a favorable outcome [*a hopeless* situation]; **despondent** implies a being in very low spirits because of a loss of hope and a sense of futility about continuing one's efforts [her rejection of his suit left him *despondent*]; **despairing** implies utter loss of hope and may suggest the extreme dejection that results [the *despairing* lover spoke of suicide]; **desperate** implies such despair as makes one resort to extreme measures [hunger makes men *desperate*] —***ANT.*** **hopeful, optimistic**

☆**hop·head** (häp′hed′) ***n.*** ⟦HOP[2], ***n.*** 3 + HEAD, ***n.*** 22⟧ [Slang] a drug addict

hop hornbeam **1** any of a genus (*Ostrya*) of North American trees of the birch family, with gray bark and hoplike cones **2** the hard wood of this tree, often used in tool handles

☆**Ho·pi** (hō′pē) ***n.*** ⟦Hopi *Hópitu*, lit., good, peaceful⟧ **1** *pl.* **-pis** or **-pi** a member of a North American Indian people living in NE Arizona **2** the Uto-Aztecan language of this people —***adj.*** of the Hopis or their language or culture

Hopkins (häp′kinz) **1** Sir **Frederick Gow·land** (gou′lənd) 1861-1947; Eng. biochemist **2 Gerard Man·ley** (man′lē) 1844-89; Eng. poet & Jesuit priest **3 Johns** 1795-1873; U.S. financier & philanthropist **4 Mark** 1802-87; U.S. educator

Hop·kin·son (häp′kin sən), **Francis** 1737-91; Am. jurist & poet: signer of the Declaration of Independence

hop·lite (häp′līt′) ***n.*** ⟦Gr *hoplitēs* < *hoplon*, a tool < *hepein*, to prepare, care for < IE base **sep-*, to concern oneself with > Sans *sápati*, (he) woos, cultivates, L *sepelire*, to bury⟧ a heavily armed foot soldier of ancient Greece

hop-o'-my-thumb (häp′ō mī thum′) ***n.*** ⟦earlier *hop on my thombe* < HOP[1]⟧ [Archaic or Literary] a very small person

hop·per (häp′ər) ***n.*** ⟦ME *hoppere*⟧ **1** a person or thing that hops **2** any hopping insect, esp. a grasshopper **3** ⟦so called from making material "hop"⟧ a box, tank, rail car, etc., often funnel-shaped, from which the contents can be emptied slowly and evenly [the *hopper* of an automatic coal stoker] ☆**4** a freight car with a bottom that opens to unload freight: in full **hopper car** **5** a box into which legislative bills are dropped for introduction, assignment to committees, etc.: often used fig.

Hop·per (häp′ər), **Edward** 1882-1967; U.S. painter

hop·ping (häp′iŋ) [Informal] ***adj.*** very busy or active —***adv.*** very agitatedly or violently: chiefly in the phrase **hopping mad**, extremely angry

hop·ple (häp′əl) ***n., vt.*** **-pled, -pling** HOBBLE

hop·py (häp′ē) ***adj.*** **-pi·er, -pi·est** having a flavor or aroma rich in hops: said of beer or ale

☆**hop·sack·ing** (häp′sak′iŋ) ***n.*** ⟦lit., sacking for hops⟧ **1** a coarse material for bags, made of jute or hemp **2** a sturdy fabric somewhat simulating this, made from cotton, wool, linen, or synthetic fiber and used for suits, coats, etc. Also **hop′sack′**

hop·scotch (häp′skäch′) ***n.*** ⟦HOP[1] + SCOTCH[1]⟧ a children's game in which a player tosses a small, flat object, as a stone, into one section after another of a figure drawn on the ground, hopping from section to section to pick up the object after each toss —***vi.*** to move or travel on an indirect course, making many stops

hor *abbrev.* **1** horizon **2** horizontal

ho·ra (hō′rə, hôr′ə) ***n.*** ⟦ModHeb *hōrāh* < Romanian *horă* < Turk *hora*⟧ **1** a lively Romanian and Israeli folk dance performed in a circle **2** music for this dance

Hor·ace[1] (hôr′is, här′-) ***n.*** ⟦< L *Horatius*: see HORATIO⟧ a masculine name: see HORATIO

Hor·ace[2] (hôr′is, här′-) (L. name *Quintus Horatius Flaccus*) 65-8 B.C.; Rom. poet: known for his odes

Hor·ae (hō′rē′, hôr′ē) ***pl.n.*** ⟦L < Gr *Hōrai*⟧ *Gr. Myth.* HOURS

ho·ra·ry (hō′rə rē, hôr′ə-) ***adj.*** ⟦ML *horarius* < L *hora*, HOUR⟧ **1** of or indicating an hour or hours **2** occurring once every hour; hourly

Ho·ra·tian (hō rā′shən, -shē ən; hə-) ***adj.*** ⟦L *Horatianus* < *Horatius*, Horace⟧ of, like, or characteristic of Horace or his poetry

Ho·ra·tio (hō rā′shō, -shē ō′; hə-) ***n.*** ⟦altered (modeled on L) < It *Orazio* < L *Horatius*, name of a Roman gens⟧ a masculine name: var. *Horace*

Horatio Alger *see* ALGER, Horatio

Ho·ra·tius (hō rā′shəs, -shē əs; hə-) ***n.*** *Rom. Legend* a hero who defends a bridge over the Tiber against the Etruscans

horde (hôrd) ***n.*** ⟦Fr < Ger, earlier *horda* < Pol < Turk *ordū*, a camp < Tatar *urdu*, a camp, lit., something erected < *urmak*, to pitch (a camp)⟧ **1** a nomadic tribe or clan of Mongols **2** any wandering tribe or group **3** a large, moving crowd or throng; swarm —***vi.*** **hord′ed, hord′ing** to form or gather in a horde —***SYN.*** CROWD[1]

Ho·reb (hō′reb, hôr′eb) ***n.*** *Bible* a mountain usually identified with Mt. Sinai: Ex. 3:1

hore·hound (hôr′hound′) ***n.*** ⟦ME *horehune* < OE *harhune* < *har*, white, HOAR + *hune*, horehound⟧ **1** a bitter herb (*Marrubium vulgare*) of the mint family, with white, downy leaves **2** a bitter juice extracted from its leaves, stems, or flowers and used in medicines and confections **3** cough medicine or candy made with this juice **4** any of various other mints

ho·ri·zon (hə rī′zən) ***n.*** ⟦altered (after L) < ME *orizont* < OFr *orizonte* < L *horizon* < Gr *horizōn* (*kyklos*), the bounding (circle), horizon < prp. of *horizein*, to bound, limit < *horos*, boundary, limit, akin to L *urvus*, city boundary, orig., furrow around city⟧ **1** *a)* the distant line where the sky appears to meet the surface of the earth *b)* a similar line observed from the surface of the moon, etc. **2** [*usually pl.*] the limit or extent of one's outlook, experience, interest, knowledge, etc. [travel broadens one's *horizons*] **3** *Archaeol.* an archaeological level or an area of culture as indicated by surviving artifacts **4** *Astron.* the great circle on the celestial sphere perpendicular to the line from the observer's zenith to the nadir: see also EVENT HORIZON **5** *Geol.* a layer of soil or rock identified by physical characteristics, particular fossils, etc. —**on the horizon** in the foreseeable future; impending, looming, destined, etc.

hor·i·zon·tal (hôr′i zänt′'l) ***adj.*** ⟦ModL *horizontalis* < L *horizon* (gen. *horizontis*): see prec.⟧ **1** of or near the horizon: now chiefly in technical usage [*horizontal* parallax] **2** *a)* parallel to the plane of the horizon; not vertical *b)* placed, operating, or acting chiefly in a direction parallel to the horizon **3** flat and even; level **4** at, or made up of elements at, the same levels of industrial production and distribution, or of status —***n.*** **1** a horizontal line, plane, etc. **2** position parallel to the horizon —**hor′i·zon′tal′i·ty** (-zän tal′ə tē) ***n.*** —**hor′i·zon′tal·ly** ***adv.***

horizontal bar **1** a metal bar fixed in a horizontal position approximately nine feet above the floor for use as in gymnastics **2** an event in gymnastics in which a routine is performed on a horizontal bar

horizontal union CRAFT UNION

hor·mone (hôr′mōn′) ***n.*** ⟦< Gr *hormōn*, prp. of *horman*, to stimulate, excite < *hormē*, impulse < IE base **ser-*, to stream > Sans *sará-*, fluid, L *serum*, whey⟧ **1** a substance formed in some organ of the body, as the adrenal glands, the pituitary, etc., and carried by a bodily fluid to another organ or tissue, where it has a specific effect **2** a similar substance produced in a plant, as an auxin **3** a synthetic substance produced to have similar effects to an animal or plant hormone **4** [*pl.*] loosely, the human sex hormones as they affect mood, personality, etc. —**hor·mo′nal** (-mō′nəl) ***adj.***, **hor·mon′ic** (-män′ik)

Hor·muz (hôr mo͞oz′, hôr′məz), **Strait of** strait joining the Persian Gulf & the Gulf of Oman, between Arabia & Iran

horn (hôrn) ***n.*** ⟦ME < OE, akin to Ger < IE base **k̂er-*, upper part of the body, head > L *cornu*, Gr *keras*⟧ **1** *a)* a hard, hollow, bony or keratinous, permanent projection that grows on the head of various hoofed animals, esp. bovid ruminants *b)* an antler **2** anything that protrudes naturally from the head of an animal, as one of the tentacles of a snail, a tuft of feathers on certain birds, etc. **3** [*usually pl.*] a horn or antler figuratively attributed to a cuckold **4** *a)* the hard, smooth, keratinous substance that forms the horns, nails, beaks, hoofs, or shells of various animals *b)* any substance like this in appearance, texture, etc. **5** *a)* a container made by hollowing out a horn [a powder *horn*] *b)* a drink contained in a horn **6** CORNUCOPIA **7** anything shaped like or suggesting a horn; specif., *a)* a peninsula or cape *b)* either end of a crescent *c)* the pointed part of an anvil ☆*d)* a projection above the pommel of a cowboy's saddle **8** *a)* an instrument made of horn and sounded by blowing, as the shofar *b)* any brass instrument; specif., FRENCH HORN ☆*c)* *Jazz* any wind instrument **9** a device with a kind of blaring sound for signaling or warning **10** *Bible* an emblem of glory, strength, or honor **11** *Electronics* *a)* a horn-shaped speaker *b)* a horn-shaped antenna **12** *Geol.* a jagged mountain peak resulting from the erosion of several cirques, as the Matterhorn in the Alps —***vt.*** **1** to strike, butt, or gore with the horns **2**

horn (French horn)

to furnish with horns **3** [Archaic] to cuckold —***adj.*** made of horn *[horn-*rimmed glasses*]* —☆**around the horn** ⟦prob. in allusion to sailing around Cape HORN⟧ *Baseball* (thrown) from third base to second to first in trying for a double play —☆**blow one's own horn** [Informal] to praise oneself; boast —☆**horn in (on)** [Informal] to intrude or meddle (in) —**lock horns** ☆to have a disagreement or conflict —**on the horns of a dilemma** having to make a choice between two things, both unpleasant —**pull** (or **draw** or **haul**) **in one's horns 1** to hold oneself back; restrain one's impulses or efforts **2** to back down; become less dogmatic, positive, zealous, etc. —**the horn** ☆[Informal] the telephone —**horn′less** ***adj.*** —**horn′like′** ***adj.***

Horn (hôrn), **Cape** cape on an island (**Horn Island**) in Tierra del Fuego, Chile: southernmost point of South America

horn·beam (hôrn′bēm′) ***n.*** ⟦HORN + BEAM⟧ **1** any of a genus (*Carpinus*) of small, hardy trees of the birch family, with smooth, gray bark and drooping catkins with flat, papery bracts around a greenish nut **2** the very hard, white wood of this tree, which takes a hornlike polish

horn·bill (-bil′) ***n.*** any of a family (Bucerotidae) of large, tropical, Old World coraciiform birds with partly united toes and a huge, curved bill, often with a bony protuberance

horn·blende (hôrn′blend′) ***n.*** ⟦Ger: see HORN & BLENDE⟧ a hard, heavy, dark-colored, monoclinic mineral, one of the amphiboles, $(Ca,Na)_{2-3}(Mg,Fe,Al)_5(Al,Si)_8O_{22}(OH)_2$

horn·book (hôrn′bo͝ok′) ***n.*** **1** a sheet of parchment with the alphabet, a table of numbers, etc. on it, mounted on a small board with a handle and protected by a thin, transparent plate of horn: it was formerly used as a child's primer **2** an elementary treatise

horned (hôrnd; *occas.* hôr′nid) ***adj.*** **1** having a horn or horns: often in hyphenated compounds *[*two-*horned]* **2** having a hornlike projection **3** [Archaic] cuckolded

horned owl any of several owls having two projecting tufts of feathers on the head

☆**horned pout** a bullhead catfish, esp. any of a brown species (*Ictalurus nebulosus*) of the E U.S.: also **horn pout**

☆**horned toad** any of a genus (*Phrynosoma*) of small, scaly, insect-eating iguanas with a flattened body, short tail, and hornlike spines: also called **horned lizard**

horned viper a poisonous N African viper (*Cerastes cornutus*) with a hornlike spine above each eye

hor·net (hôr′nit) ***n.*** ⟦ME *harnette* < OE *hyrnet*, akin to Ger *hornisse* < IE base **k̂er-* (see HORN) > L *crabro*, hornet⟧ any of several large social wasps (family Vespidae), strikingly colored yellow and black

hornet's nest a situation fraught with trouble, hostility, risk, etc.

horn·fels (hôrn′felz′) ***n.***, *pl.* **-fels′** ⟦Ger, horn rock < *horn*, HORN + *fels*, rock: see FELL[5]⟧ a fine-grained metamorphic rock usually formed at shallow depths

☆**horn fly** a muscid fly (*Haematobia irritans*) that is a pest on cattle and sucks blood, esp. at the base of the horns

horn·ist (hôr′nist) ***n.*** a person who plays the French horn

hor·ni·to (hôr nēt′ō, ôr-) ***n.***, *pl.* **-tos** ⟦Sp, dim. of *horno*, oven < L *furnus*: see FURNACE⟧ a small, domed mound built up from clots of molten lava ejected from an underlying volcanic tube

horn-mad (hôrn′mad′) ***adj.*** **1** maddened enough to gore: said of horned animals **2** enraged; furious

Horn of Africa easternmost part of NE Africa, on the Gulf of Aden and the Indian Ocean, including Eritrea, Djibouti, Ethiopia, & Somalia

horn of plenty CORNUCOPIA

horn·pipe (hôrn′pīp′) ***n.*** ⟦ME⟧ **1** an obsolete wind instrument with a bell and mouthpiece made of horn **2** *a)* a lively dance to the music of the hornpipe, formerly popular with sailors *b)* music for this

horn-rimmed (hôrn′rimd′) ***adj.*** having horn-rims: said as of eyeglasses

horn-rims (-rimz′) ***pl.n.*** **1** a frame for eyeglasses made of HORN (***n.*** 4) or of a material made to resemble this **2** eyeglasses with such a frame

horn silver CERARGYRITE

horn·stone (hôrn′stōn′) ***n.*** ⟦transl. of Ger *hornstein*: so named from its appearance⟧ [Obs.] flint, chert, etc.

☆**horn·swog·gle** (hôrn′swäg′əl) ***vt.*** **-gled, -gling** ⟦fanciful coinage⟧ [Slang] to swindle or hoax; trick

horn·tail (hôrn′tāl′) ***n.*** any of a family (Siricidae) of hymenopteran insects, whose adult female has a horny, taillike extension for depositing eggs in tree trunks, in which the larvae burrow

☆**horn·worm** (-wurm′) ***n.*** the caterpillar of various hawk moths, with a horny growth on the last segment

horn·wort (hôrn′wurt′) ***n.*** ⟦after ModL *Ceratophyllum*: see CERATO- & -PHYLL⟧ any of a genus (*Ceratophyllum*) of long, rootless waterlilies of the hornwort family submerged in lakes and slow-moving streams and having whorls of finely divided leaves —***adj.*** designating a family (Ceratophyllaceae) of dicotyledonous, rapidly growing waterlilies

horn·y (hôr′nē) ***adj.*** **horn′i·er, horn′i·est** ⟦ME⟧ **1** of, like, or made of horn **2** having horns **3** toughened and calloused *[horny* hands*]* **4** ⟦< *horn*, erect penis⟧ [Slang] *a)* sexually excited *b)* easily aroused sexually *c)* yearning for or desiring sex —**horn′i·ness** ***n.***

ho·ro·loge (hôr′ə lōj′, -läj′) ***n.*** ⟦ME < OFr < L *horologium* < Gr *hōrologion* < *hōra*, HOUR + *legein*, to say: see LOGIC⟧ a timepiece; clock, hourglass, sundial, etc.

hor·o·log·ic (hôr′ə läj′ik) ***adj.*** ⟦L *horologicus*⟧ of horology or horologes: also **hor′o·log′i·cal**

ho·rol·o·gist (hō räl′ə jist) ***n.*** an expert in horology; maker of or dealer in timepieces: also **ho·rol′o·ger**

Hor·o·log·i·um (hôr′ə lō′jē əm) ***n.*** ⟦L, a clock: see HOROLOGE⟧ a S constellation near Eridanus: essentially a large area with few bright objects

ho·rol·o·gy (hō räl′ə jē) ***n.*** ⟦< Gr *hōra*, HOUR + -LOGY⟧ the science or art of measuring time or making timepieces

hor·o·scope (hôr′ə skōp′) ***n.*** ⟦Fr < L *horoscopus* < Gr *hōroskopos*, observer of the hour of birth < *hōra*, HOUR + *skopos*, watcher, by metathesis < IE **spokos* < base **spek-*, to SPY⟧ **1** the position of the planets and stars with relation to one another at a given time, esp. at the time of a person's birth, regarded in astrology as influencing or determining one's destiny **2** a chart of the zodiacal signs and the positions of the planets, etc. **3** a forecast based on such a chart, usually a set of twelve predictions for the twelve signs of the zodiac —**hor′o·scop′ic** (-skäp′ik) ***adj.*** —**ho·ros·co·py** (hō räs′kə pē) ***n.***

Hor·o·witz (hôr′ə wits, här′-), **Vladimir** 1903-89; U.S. pianist, born in Russia

hor·ren·dous (hô ren′dəs, hə-) ***adj.*** ⟦L *horrendus* < prp. of *horrere*: see HORRID⟧ horrible; frightful —**hor·ren′dous·ly** ***adv.***

hor·rent (hôr′ənt) ***adj.*** ⟦L *horrens* (gen. *horrentis*), prp. of *horrere*: see HORRID⟧ [Archaic] **1** bristly or bristling **2** horrified

hor·ri·ble (hôr′ə bəl, här′-) ***adj.*** ⟦ME < OFr < L *horribilis* < *horrere*: see HORRID⟧ **1** causing a feeling of horror; terrible; dreadful; frightful **2** [Informal] very bad, ugly, shocking, unpleasant, etc.

hor·ri·bly (hôr′ə blē, här′-) ***adv.*** **1** in a horrible manner **2** to a horrible degree **3** [Informal] very; extremely

hor·rid (hôr′id, här′-) ***adj.*** ⟦L *horridus* < *horrere*, to bristle, shake, be afraid < IE base **ĝhers-*, to bristle > GORSE⟧ **1** [Archaic] bristling; shaggy; rough **2** causing a feeling of horror; terrible; revolting **3** very bad, ugly, unpleasant, etc. —**hor′rid·ly** ***adv.*** —**hor′rid·ness** ***n.***

hor·rif·ic (hô rif′ik, hə-) ***adj.*** ⟦Fr *horrifique* < L *horrificus* < *horrere*, to bristle (see prec.) + *facere*, to make (see DO[1])⟧ horrifying; horrible

hor·ri·fy (hôr′ə fī′, här′-) ***vt.*** **-fied′, -fy′ing** ⟦L *horrificare* < *horrificus*: see prec.⟧ **1** to cause to feel horror **2** to shock or disgust —***SYN.*** DISMAY —**hor′ri·fi·ca′tion** ***n.***

hor·rip·i·late (hô rip′ə lāt′) ***vt.*** **-lat′ed, -lat′ing** ⟦< L *horripilatus*, pp. of *horripilare*, to bristle with hairs < *horrere*, to bristle (see HORRID) + *pilus*, hair⟧ to cause horripilation of —***vi.*** to experience horripilation; bristle

hor·rip·i·la·tion (hô rip′ə lā′shən) ***n.*** ⟦LL *horripilatio*: see prec.⟧ the erection of hair of the head or body, as from fear, disease, or cold; goose bumps

hor·ror (hôr′ər, här′-) ***n.*** ⟦ME *horrour* < OFr < L *horror* < *horrere*, to bristle: see HORRID⟧ **1** [Obs.] a shuddering **2** the strong feeling caused by something frightful or shocking; shuddering fear and disgust; terror and repugnance **3** strong dislike or aversion; loathing **4** the quality of causing horror **5** something that causes horror **6** a genre of fiction, films, comic books, etc. characterized by the depiction of frightening events and, variously, ghosts, vampires, monsters, etc. **7** [Informal] something very bad, ugly, disagreeable, etc. —***adj.*** of the horror genre *[*a matinee of *horror* movies*]* —***SYN.*** FEAR —**the horrors** [Informal] a fit of extreme nervousness, panic, depression, revulsion, etc.

hor·ror-struck (hôr′ər struk′) ***adj.*** struck with horror; horrified: also **hor′ror-strick′en** (-strik′ən)

Hor·sa (hôr′sə) ⟦OE: see HORSE⟧ *see* HENGIST

hors con·cours (ôr kōn ko͞or′) ⟦Fr⟧ [Literary] unmatched; peerless

hors de com·bat (ôr də kōn bä′) ⟦Fr, out of combat⟧ put out of military action, as by injury: often used fig.

hors d'oeuvre (ôr′durv′; *Fr* ôr dë′vr′) *pl.* **hors d'oeuvres** (durvz′) or Fr. ***hors d'oeuvre*** (dë′vr′) ⟦Fr, lit., outside of work < *hors*, outside (< L *foris*) + *de*, of (see DE-) + *oeuvre*, work (< L *opera*, works)⟧ a small portion of a tasty food served as an appetizer before a meal or as at a cocktail party

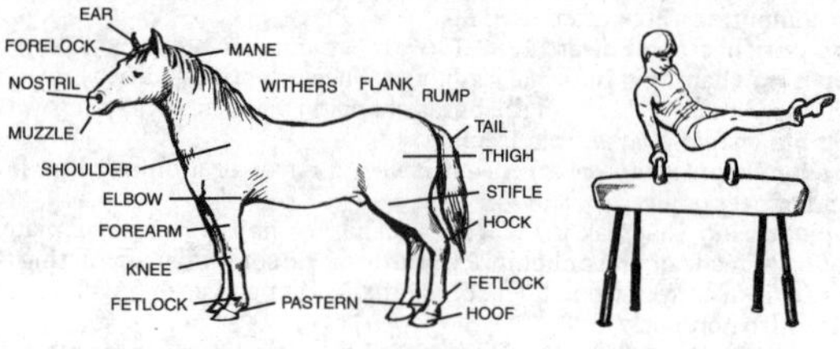

horse (sense 1) pommel horse

horse (hôrs) ***n.***, *pl.* **hors′es** or **horse** ⟦ME *hors* < OE *hors, hros*, akin to Ger *ross* (OHG *hros*), prob. < IE base **(s)ker-*, to leap (or < ? **k̂ers-*, to run > L *cursus*)⟧ **1** a domesticated or wild, perissodactylous mammal (*Equus caballus*), raised in many breeds, having a large body and head, four usually long, thin legs, and a long, flowing tail: horses have been ridden, used to pull loads, etc. since ancient times **2** the full-grown male of the horse; gelding or stallion **3** anything like a horse in that a person sits, rides, or is carried on it **4** a device, esp. a frame with legs, to support something; specif., *a)* SAWHORSE *b)* a clotheshorse **5** a man regarded as resembling a horse, as in having great strength or endurance **6** [Informal] *Chess* a knight ☆**7** [Informal] PONY (sense 5) **8** [Slang] *a)* HORSEPOWER (sense

2) *b)* [*pl.*] HORSEPOWER (sense 3) ☆*c)* HEROIN **9** *Gym.* a padded block on legs, used for vaulting events: see POMMEL HORSE **10** [*with pl. v.*] [Brit.] *Mil.* mounted troops; cavalry **11** *Mining* a mass of earth or rock inside a vein or coal seam —***vt.* horsed, hors′ing 1** to supply with a horse or horses; put on horseback **2** [Informal] to shove; push —***vi.*** to mount or go on horseback —***adj.* 1** of a horse or horses **2** mounted on horses **3** large, strong, or coarse of its kind [*horse* mackerel] —☆**back the wrong horse 1** to bet on a horse that loses the race **2** to choose or support the losing side —**beat** (or **flog**) **a dead horse** [Informal] to argue an issue that is already settled —**from the horse's mouth** [Informal] from the original or authoritative source of information —☆**hold one's horses** [Informal] to curb one's impatience —☆**horse around** [Slang] **1** to engage in horseplay **2** to spend time in pointless or trifling activity —**horse of another** (or **a different**) **color** an entirely different matter —**on one's high horse** [Informal] acting in an arrogant, haughty, or disdainful manner —**to horse!** get on your horse! mount!

☆**horse-and-bug·gy** (hôrs′ən bug′ē) ***adj.* 1** of the period in which the horse-drawn buggy was a common mode of transportation **2** old-fashioned; outmoded

horse·back (hôrs′bak′) ***n.* 1** the back of a horse ☆**2** a low, sharp ridge; hog-back — ***adv., adj.*** on horseback

☆**horse·car** (hôrs′kär′) ***n.* 1** a streetcar drawn by horses **2** a car for transporting horses

horse chestnut 1 any of a genus (*Aesculus*) of shrubs and trees of the horse-chestnut family, including buckeyes; esp., a tree (*A. hippocastanum*) with large, palmately compound leaves, clusters of white flowers, and glossy, brown seeds **2** a seed of this tree

horse-chest·nut (hôrs′ches′nut) ***adj.*** ⟦transl. of obs. botanical L *Castanea equina*: reason for name uncert.⟧ designating a family (Hippocastanaceae, order Sapindales) of dicotyledonous trees, including the horse chestnuts

horse·feath·ers (-feth′ərs) ***n., interj.*** [Slang] nonsense

horse·flesh (-flesh′) ***n.* 1** the flesh of the horse, esp. when used as food **2** horses collectively

horse·fly (-flī′) ***n., pl.* -flies′** ⟦ME *hors fleege*⟧ **1** any of a number of large dipterous flies (family Tabanidae), the female of which sucks the blood of horses, cattle, etc. **2** any of various other dipterous flies that bite or infest horses, esp. any of a family (Gasterophilidae) of botflies

☆**horse gentian** any of a genus (*Triosteum*) of coarse, weedy plants of the honeysuckle family, with opposite leaves, inconspicuous flowers, and leathery, orange fruit

Horse Guard a special cavalry brigade assigned to the British royal household

horse·hair (hôrs′her′) ***n.*** ⟦ME *horsher*⟧ **1** any of the hairs from the mane or tail of a horse **2** a growth of these hairs **3** a stiff fabric made from horsehair; haircloth —***adj.* 1** of horsehair **2** covered or stuffed with horsehair

horsehair worm GORDIAN WORM

horse·hide (-hīd′) ***n.* 1** the hide of a horse **2** leather made from this ☆**3** ⟦because baseballs were formerly covered in this type of leather⟧ [Informal] a baseball

horse latitudes ⟦said to be so named because horses being transported to the West Indies often would be thrown overboard from becalmed sailing vessels because of water shortages⟧ either of two belts over the oceans at *c.* 30°-35° north and south latitude, characterized by calms, light wind, high barometric pressure, and hot, dry weather

horse·laugh (hôrs′laf′) ***n.*** a loud, boisterous, usually derisive laugh; guffaw

horse·leech (-lēch′) ***n.* 1** a large North American leech (*Haemopis marmoratis*) that is said to attach itself to the mouth of a horse while it is drinking **2** ⟦see LEECH[1]⟧ [Archaic] a veterinarian

horse·less (hôrs′lis) ***adj.* 1** without a horse **2** not requiring a horse; self-propelled: the automobile was formerly called a *horseless carriage*

horse mackerel 1 any of various large tuna **2** any of various jack fishes (genus *Trachurus*) having a bony plate along the entire lateral line

horse·man (hôrs′mən) ***n., pl.* -men** (-mən) ⟦ME *horsman*⟧ **1** a man who rides on horseback **2** a man skilled in the riding, managing, or care of horses

horse·man·ship (hôrs′mən ship′) ***n.*** skill in, or the art of, riding, managing, or training horses

horse·mint (hôrs′mint′) ***n.*** ⟦ME *horsminte*⟧ ☆any of a genus (*Monarda*) of North American plants of the mint family, with heads of showy flowers, usually red or purplish

☆**horse nettle** a weed (*Solanum carolinense*) of the nightshade family, with yellow prickles, white or bluish flowers, and yellow berries

☆**horse opera** ⟦so called prob. in allusion to its melodramatic narrative style⟧ [Slang] a film or TV western

horse pistol [Historical] any large pistol of a kind formerly carried by horsemen

horse·play (hôrs′plā′) ***n.*** rough, boisterous play

horse·play·er (hôrs′plā′ər) ***n.*** ⟦< PLAY (*vt.* 5b)⟧ one who is in the habit of betting on horses in horse races

horse·pow·er (hôrs′pou′ər) ***n.*** ⟦first adopted by James WATT⟧ **1** the power exerted by a horse in pulling **2** *pl.* **-pow′er** a basic unit of power in the FPS system, equal to the power needed to raise a weight of 550 pounds a distance of 1 foot in 1 second or a weight of 33,000 pounds a distance of 1 foot in 1 minute (746 watts or 42.41 British thermal units per minute): used esp. for measuring the power of motors or engines: abbrev. *hp* **3** [Informal] effective power [my computer doesn't have enough *horsepower* to crunch those numbers]

horse·pow·er-hour (-our′) ***n.*** a unit of work equal to 1,980,000 foot-pounds

horse·pox (hôrs′päks′) ***n.*** a highly contagious viral skin disease of horses, characterized by fever and poxlike lesions on the mouth, leg, etc.

horse race 1 a race for horses, usually, specif., one for horses ridden by jockeys over an oval track, with organized betting on the outcome **2** a close, highly competitive contest, as in an election

horse·rad·ish (-rad′ish) ***n.* 1** a plant (*Armoracia lapathifolia*) of the crucifer family, grown for its pungent, white, fleshy root **2** a relish made of the grated root

☆**horse sense** [Informal] common sense

horse·shit (hôrs′shit′, hôr′-) [Slang] ***n.* 1** horse excrement **2** foolish or exaggerated talk or behavior; nonsense —***interj.*** nonsense Somewhat vulgar

horse·shoe (hôrs′sho͞o′, hôr′-) ***n.*** ⟦ME *horscho*, contr. of *horsis sho*⟧ **1** a flat, U-shaped metal plate nailed to the bottom of a horse's hoof to protect the foot **2** anything shaped like this **3** [*pl., with sing. v.*] a game in which players take turns tossing horseshoes first at one stake and then at another driven into the ground forty feet apart, the object being to encircle the stake or to come closer to the stake than one's opponent does —***vt.* -shoed′, -shoe′ing** to fit with a horseshoe or horseshoes —**horse′sho′er *n.***

horseshoe arch an arch shaped like a horseshoe

☆**horseshoe crab** any of an order (Xiphosura, class Merostomata) of sea arthropods shaped like the base of a horse's foot and having a long, spinelike tail

☆**horse's neck** an iced drink consisting of ginger ale or ginger ale and soda water, garnished with lemon, and sometimes containing an alcoholic liquor

horse·tail (hôrs′tāl′) ***n.* 1** a horse's tail **2** ⟦descriptive⟧ any of the only surviving genus (*Equisetum*) of a division (Equisetophyta) of plants having hollow, jointed stems, with scalelike leaves at the joints and spores borne in terminal cones; scouring rush

☆**horse trade** [Informal] any bargaining session marked by shrewd calculation by each side —**horse′-trade′ *vi.* -trad′ed, -trad′ing —horse′-trad′er *n.***

☆**horse·weed** (hôrs′wēd′) ***n.* 1** a common weed (*Conyza canadensis*) of the composite family, with a wandlike stem and a panicle of many small, greenish-white flower heads **2** any of various other weeds

horse·whip (-hwip′) ***n.*** a whip for driving or managing horses —***vt.* -whipped′, -whip′ping** to lash or beat with a horsewhip

horse·wom·an (-wo͝om′ən) ***n., pl.* -wom′en** (-wim′in) **1** a woman who rides on horseback **2** a woman skilled in the riding or managing of horses

horst (hôrst) ***n.*** ⟦Ger, orig., thicket, prob. < IE **kuṛs-to-* < base **kuṛs-*, thicket, tree > OIr *crann*, thicket⟧ *Geol.* a raised, usually elongated, rock mass between two faults

hors·y (hôr′sē) ***adj.* hors′i·er, hors′i·est 1** of, like, or suggesting a horse; esp., having large features and a big body that looks strong but awkward **2** *a)* connected with or fond of horses, fox-hunting, or horse racing *b)* having the manners, attitudes, etc. of people who are fond of horses, hunting, etc. Also sp. **hors′ey —hors′i·ly *adv.* —hors′i·ness *n.***

hort *abbrev.* **1** horticultural **2** horticulture

hor·ta·to·ry (hôr′tə tôr′ē) ***adj.*** ⟦LL(Ec) *hortatorius* < pp. of L *hortari*, to incite, encourage, freq. of *horiri*, to urge, encourage < IE base **ĝher-*, to desire > YEARN, Gr *charis*⟧ **1** serving to encourage or urge to good deeds **2** exhorting; giving advice Also **hor′ta·tive** (-tiv)

Hor·tense[1] (hôr′tens′) ***n.*** ⟦Fr < L *Hortensia*, fem. of *Hortensius*, name of a Roman gens⟧ a feminine name

Hor·tense[2] (hor′tens′; *Fr* ôr täns′) (born *Hortense de Beauharnais*) 1783-1837; queen of Holland (1806-10): wife of Louis Bonaparte

hor·ti·cul·ture (hôr′tə kul′chər) ***n.*** ⟦< L *hortus*, a garden (< IE base **ĝher-*, to enclose > Gr *chortos*, farmyard, Welsh *garth*, fold) + *cultura*: see CULTURE⟧ the art or science of growing flowers, fruits, vegetables, and shrubs, esp. in gardens or orchards —**hor′ti·cul′tur·al *adj.* —hor′ti·cul′tur·ist *n.*, hor′ti·cul′tur·al·ist**

Ho·rus (hō′rəs) ***n.*** ⟦L < Gr *Hōros* < Egypt *Ḥeru*, hawk⟧ *Egypt. Myth.* the sun god, represented as having the head of a hawk: the son of Osiris and Isis

Hos *abbrev. Bible* Hosea

ho·san·na (hō zan′ə, -zä′nə) ***n., interj.*** ⟦ME *osanna* < OE < LL(Ec) < Gr(Ec) *hōsanna* < Heb *hōshīʿāh nnā*, lit., save, we pray⟧ (an exclamation) used to give praise to God

hose (hōz) ***n., pl.* hose** or, for 3, **hos′es** ⟦ME < OE *hosa*, leg covering, akin to Ger *hose* < IE **(s)kéus-* < base **(s)keu-*, to conceal, hide > SKY⟧ **1** [Historical] a tightfitting outer garment worn by men, covering the hips, legs, and feet, or extending only to the knees or ankles, and attached to the doublet by cords or ribbons (called *points*) **2** [*pl.*] *a)* stockings or pantyhose *b)* socks **3** ⟦prob. infl. by Du *hoos*, water pipe, of same origin⟧ *a)* a flexible tube used to convey fluids, esp. water from a hydrant or faucet *b)* such a tube equipped with a nozzle and attachments —***vt.* hosed, hos′ing 1** to put water on with a hose; sprinkle or drench with a hose: often with *down* ☆**2** [Slang] to beat as with a hose ☆**3** [Slang] to cheat; deceive; trick

Ho·se·a (hō zē′ə, -zā′ə) ***n.*** ⟦Heb *hōshēaʿ*, lit., salvation⟧ *Bible* **1** a Hebrew prophet of the 8th cent. B.C. **2** the book of his writings Abbrev. *Hos* or *Ho*

ho·sel (hō′zəl) ***n.*** ⟦dim. of HOSE, as used in the dial. sense, "a covering or sheath"⟧ the socket-like part of the head of a golf club, to which the shaft is attached

ho·sen (hō′zən) ***n.*** *archaic pl. of* HOSE (*n.* 1 & 2)

hos·er (hōz′ər) ***n.*** ⟦prob. < HOSE in slang sense, "penis" + -ER⟧ [Cdn. Slang] a boorish, unsophisticated man

ho·sier (hō′zhər) ***n.*** ⟦ME < *hose,* HOSE⟧ **1** a person who makes or sells hosiery **2** [Brit.] HABERDASHER

ho·sier·y (hō′zhər ē) ***n.*** ⟦< prec.⟧ **1** hose; stockings and socks **2** [Chiefly Brit.] hose and knitted or woven underwear

hosp *abbrev.* hospital

hos·pice (häs′pis) ***n.*** ⟦Fr < L *hospitium,* hospitality, inn, lodging < *hospes,* host, guest < **hostipots* < *hostis,* stranger, enemy < IE base **ghostis,* stranger, guest (> GUEST, OSlav *gospodi*) + **potis,* master: see DESPOT⟧ **1** a place of shelter for travelers, esp. such a shelter maintained by monks **2** a home for the sick or poor **3** *a)* a homelike facility to provide supportive care for terminally ill patients *b)* such care, often when provided in a patient's home, a nursing home, etc. (also **hospice care**)

hos·pi·ta·ble (häs′pit ə bəl, häs pit′-) ***adj.*** ⟦MFr < ML *hospitabilis* < *hospitare,* to receive as a guest < *hospes:* see prec.⟧ **1** *a)* friendly, kind, and solicitous toward guests *b)* prompted by or associated with friendliness and solicitude toward guests [a *hospitable* act] **2** favoring the health, growth, comfort, etc. of new arrivals; not adverse [a *hospitable* climate] **3** receptive or open, as to new ideas —**hos′pi·ta·bly** ***adv.***

hos·pi·tal (häs′pit′'l) ***n.*** ⟦ME < OFr < LL *hospitale,* a house, inn < L (*cubiculum*) *hospitale,* guest (room), neut. of *hospitalis,* of a guest < *hospes:* see HOSPICE⟧ **1** [Obs.] *a)* a place of shelter and rest for travelers, etc. *b)* a charitable institution for providing and caring for the aged, infirm, orphaned, etc. (now only in names) **2** an institution providing medical, surgical, or psychiatric testing and treatment for people who are ill, injured, pregnant, etc. on an inpatient, outpatient, or emergency care basis: often involved with public health programs, research, medical education, etc.: in British English, usually without an article when preceded by a preposition **3** a clinic providing surgical or emergency medical care for domesticated animals, esp. pets **4** a repair shop for dolls, clocks, or other small items

hospital corners neat, secure corners made by tucking in bedclothes at the foot with a double fold

Hos·pi·tal·er or **Hos·pi·tal·ler** (häs′pit′'l ər) ***n.*** ⟦ME < OFr *hospitalier* < ML < *hospitalarius* < LL *hospitale*⟧ [*occas.* **h-**] a member of a religious military society (Knights of Malta) organized during the Middle Ages to care for the sick and needy

Hos·pi·ta·let (ôs′pē tä let′) city in NE Spain: suburb of Barcelona

☆**hos·pi·tal·ist** (häs′pit′l ist) ***n.*** a doctor who specializes in treating inpatients

hos·pi·tal·i·ty (häs′pi tal′ə tē) ***n., pl.* -ties** ⟦L *hospitalitas* < *hospitalis:* see HOSPITAL⟧ the act, practice, or quality of being hospitable; solicitous entertainment of guests

hospitality suite a suite or room, as in a hotel during a convention, rented by a corporation or organization as a place for potential clients or members to socialize, view sample products, etc.

hos·pi·tal·i·za·tion (häs′pit′l i zā′shən) ***n.*** **1** a hospitalizing or being hospitalized ☆**2** insurance providing for payment of hospital expenses for the insured and, usually, members of the immediate family: in full **hospitalization insurance**

hos·pi·tal·ize (häs′pit′l īz′) ***vt.* -ized′, -iz′ing** to send to, put in, or admit to a hospital

host[1] (hōst) ***n.*** ⟦ME *hoste* < OFr *hoiste* < ML(Ec) *hostia,* consecrated host < L, animal sacrificed, prob. < *hostire,* to recompense, requite⟧ **1** a wafer of the bread used in a Eucharistic service **2** [**H-**] a consecrated Eucharistic wafer

host[2] (hōst) ***n.*** ⟦ME *hoste* < OFr, host, guest < L *hospes* (gen. *hospitis*): see HOSPICE⟧ **1** one who entertains guests either at home or elsewhere **2** a person who keeps an inn or hotel; innkeeper **3** an organization, municipality, etc. providing the site and services for a competition or event [Berlin was *host* to the 1936 summer Olympics] **4** *a)* any organism on or in which a parasitic organism lives for nourishment or protection *b)* an individual, esp. an embryo, into which a graft is inserted **5** *Comput. a)* the main or central computer in a network *b)* a server that stores Web pages and makes them available on the World Wide Web *c)* a company that provides customers with such a server and related services for maintaining a website: see also WEB HOSTING **6** *Radio, TV a)* the person who conducts a program that features conversation, interviews, etc. *b)* the emcee of a game show — ***vi., vt.*** to act as host or hostess (for)

host[3] (hōst) ***n.*** ⟦ME < OFr < ML *hostis,* army, hostile force < L: see HOSPICE⟧ **1** an army **2** a multitude; great number —***SYN.*** CROWD[1]

hos·ta (häs′tə, hō′stə) ***n.*** ⟦after N. *Host* (1761-1834), Austrian physician & botanist⟧ PLANTAIN LILY

hos·tage (häs′tij) ***n.*** ⟦ME < OFr < *hoste:* see HOST[2]⟧ **1** a person given as a pledge, or taken prisoner as by an enemy or terrorist, until certain conditions are met **2** [Obs.] the state of being a hostage —***SYN.*** PLEDGE

hos·tel (häs′təl) ***n.*** ⟦ME < OFr < LL *hospitale:* see HOSPITAL⟧ an inn; hostelry; specif., YOUTH HOSTEL —***vi.* -teled** or **-telled, -tel·ing** or **-tel·ling** to stop at hostels when traveling

hos·tel·er (-ər) ***n.*** ⟦ME < OFr *hostelier*⟧ **1** [Archaic] an innkeeper **2** a traveler who stops at hostels Also sp. **hos′tel·ler**

hos·tel·ry (häs′təl rē) ***n., pl.* -ries** ⟦ME *hostellerie* < OFr < *hostel:* see HOSTEL⟧ a lodging place; inn; hotel

hostel school any of the boarding schools operated by the Canadian government for Inuit and North American Indian children

host·ess (hōs′tis) ***n.*** ⟦ME < OFr *hostesse,* fem. of *hoste,* HOST[2]⟧ **1** a woman who entertains guests either at home or elsewhere; sometimes, the wife of a host **2** a woman innkeeper or the wife of an innkeeper **3** *a)* a woman whose work is seeing that guests or travelers are comfortable, as in a lodge *b)* a woman employed in a restaurant to supervise serving, often in charge of reservations and of seating patrons *c)* a woman who serves as a paid partner at a public dance hall — ***vi., vt.*** to act as hostess (for)

hos·tile (häs′təl; *chiefly Brit,* -tīl′) ***adj.*** ⟦L *hostilis* < *hostis,* enemy: see HOSPICE⟧ **1** of or characteristic of an enemy; warlike **2** having or showing ill will; unfriendly; antagonistic **3** not hospitable or compatible; adverse **4** *Finance* designating or of a takeover of a corporation against the wishes of its management —***n.*** a hostile person —**hos′tile·ly** ***adv.***

hos·til·i·ty (häs til′ə tē) ***n., pl.* -ties** ⟦Fr *hostilité* < LL *hostilitas* < L *hostilis,* prec.⟧ **1** a feeling of enmity, ill will, unfriendliness, etc.; antagonism **2** *a)* an expression of enmity and ill will; hostile act *b)* [*pl.*] open acts of war; warfare —***SYN.*** ENMITY

hos·tler (häs′lər, äs′-) ***n.*** ⟦contr. of HOSTELER⟧ **1** a person who takes care of horses at an inn, stable, etc.; groom ☆**2** a person who services a truck or a railroad engine at the end of a run **3** [Obs.] an innkeeper

hot (hät) ***adj.* hot′ter, hot′test** ⟦ME < OE *hat,* akin to Ger *heiss,* Goth *heito,* fever < IE base **kai-,* heat > Lith *kaistù,* to become hot⟧ **1** *a)* having a high temperature, esp. one that is higher than that of the human body *b)* characterized by a relatively or abnormally high temperature; very warm *c)* feeling uncomfortably overheated **2** producing a burning sensation, as in the mouth, throat, etc. [*hot* pepper] **3** full of or characterized by any very strong feeling, or by intense activity, speed, excitement, etc.; specif., *a)* impetuous; fiery; excitable [a *hot* temper] *b)* violent; raging; angry [a *hot* battle, *hot* words] *c)* full of enthusiasm; eagerly intent; ardent *d)* inflamed with sexual desire; lustful *e)* very controversial *f)* [Informal] very lucky or effective [a *hot* streak in gambling] **4** *a)* following or pressing closely [in *hot* pursuit] *b)* close to what is being sought (said of the seeker) ☆**5** as if heated by friction; specif., *a)* electrically charged, esp. with a current of high voltage [a *hot* wire] *b)* highly radioactive **6** designating or of color that is bright and intense [*hot* pink] **7** [Informal] that has not had time to lose heat, freshness, currency, etc.; specif., *a)* recently issued or announced [*hot* news] *b)* just arrived [*hot* from the front] *c)* fresh; clear; intense; strong [a *hot* scent] ☆*d)* recent and from an inside source [a *hot* tip] *e)* currently very popular [a *hot* recording] ☆**8** [Informal] thrown or batted hard or with great speed: said of a ball ☆**9** [Slang] *a)* recently stolen *b)* contraband *c)* sought by the police *d)* dangerous or risky for use as a hiding place **10** [Slang] *a)* excellent, good, funny, etc. (a general term of approval) *b)* very skillful or successful *c)* sexually attractive or exciting ☆**11** *Jazz* designating or of highly emotional music or playing characterized by exciting rhythmic and tonal effects and an insistent, driving beat —***adv.* hot′ter, hot′test** in a hot manner; hotly —**(all) hot and bothered** [Slang] flustered, excited, etc. —**hot under the collar** [Informal] extremely angry or provoked —**make it hot for** [Informal] to make things troublesome and uncomfortable for —**hot′ly** ***adv.*** —**hot′ness** ***n.***

hot air ☆[Informal] empty or pretentious talk or writing

hot-and-sour soup (hät′ən sour′) a spicy Chinese soup made with pork, chicken, beans, vinegar, etc., served hot

hot·bed (hät′bed′) ***n.*** **1** a bed of earth covered with glass and heated by manure, electricity, etc. for forcing plants **2** any place that fosters rapid growth or extensive activity

hot·blood·ed (-blud′id) ***adj.*** easily excited; excitable; ardent, reckless, etc.

☆**hot·box** (hät′bäks′) ***n.*** an overheated bearing on an axle or shaft

☆**hot button** [Informal] an idea, subject, issue, etc. that evokes strong feelings —**hot′-but′ton** ***adj.***

☆**hot·cake** (hät′kāk′) ***n.*** PANCAKE: also written **hot cake** —**sell like hotcakes** [Informal] to be sold rapidly and in large quantities

hot cell a protected enclosure, usually made of concrete and having shielded windows and manipulators operated by remote control, used to handle radioactive materials, as for processing or testing

hotch·pot (häch′pät′) ***n.*** ⟦ME *hochepot* < OFr, stew < *hocher,* to shake (< Frank **hottisōn,* akin to LowG *hotzen* < IE base **kwet-,* to shake > L *quatere*) + *pot,* POT[1]⟧ *Eng. Law* a pooling of property of different persons for equal redistribution

hotch·potch (häch′päch′) ***n.*** ⟦< prec.⟧ **1** a thick stew of various meats and vegetables **2** *a)* [Brit.] HODGEPODGE *b)* HOTCHPOT

☆**hot comb** a comblike device that is heated, usually electrically, and used to straighten or style the hair

hot cross bun a bun marked with a cross, usually of frosting, on top: traditionally eaten during Lent

☆**hot dog** ⟦orig. (?) so named (*c.* 1900) by T. A. Dorgan (died 1929), U.S. cartoonist, prob. in allusion to popular notion that the sausage was made of *dog* meat⟧ **1** a frankfurter, esp. one served hot in a long, soft roll, with mustard, relish, etc. **2** [Slang] an exclamation used to express delight

☆**hot-dog** (hät′dôg′) ***vi.* -dogged′, -dog′ging** ⟦< prec.⟧ [Slang] to perform, esp. in sports, so as to attract attention; show off —***n.*** [Slang] a person who hot-dogs; showoff —***adj.*** [Informal] designating a form of freestyle skiing or surfing that involves acrobatics Also **hot′dog′** —**hot′-dog′ger** ***n.***

ho·tel (hō tel′) ***n.*** ⟦Fr *hôtel* < OFr *hostel,* HOSTEL⟧ **1** a commercial establishment providing lodging and, usually, meals and other services for the public, esp. travelers **2** in France, the mansion of a person of wealth or rank

hô·tel de ville (ō tel də vēl′) ⟦Fr⟧ a city hall; town hall

ho·tel·ier (hō tel′yər, -yā′; ōt′l yā′, ôt-) ***n.*** ⟦Fr *hôtelier* < OFr: see HOTEL & -IER⟧ an owner or manager of a hotel
hot flash the sensation of a wave of heat passing over the body, specif. as experienced by women during menopause
hot·foot (hät′foot′) ***adv.*** ⟦ME *hot fot*⟧ [Informal] in great haste —☆***vi.*** [Informal] to hurry; hasten —☆***n.***, *pl.* **-foots′** the prank of secretly inserting a match between the sole and upper of a victim's shoe and then lighting it —☆**hotfoot it** [Informal] to hurry
hot·head (-hed′) ***n.*** [Informal] a hotheaded person
hot·head·ed (-hed′id) ***adj.*** **1** quick-tempered; easily made angry **2** hasty; rash —**hot′head′ed·ly** ***adv.*** —**hot′head′ed·ness** ***n.***
hot·house (hät′hous′) ***n.*** a building made mainly of glass, artificially heated for growing plants; greenhouse —***adj.*** **1** grown in a hothouse **2** needing very careful treatment, as if grown in a hothouse; delicate
☆**hot·line** (hät′līn′) ***n.*** **1** a means of direct communication for use in emergency or crisis; specif., a direct telephone line between government leaders **2** a telephone line to a social service agency, as a suicide prevention center Sometimes written **hot line**
hot pad **1** a small pad, usually quilted, knitted, etc., on which to set a hot dish at the table during a meal **2** POTHOLDER Also **hot′pad′** ***n.***
hot pants **1** very short, closefitting shorts **2** underpants, a bikini bottom, etc. designed to resemble these shorts ☆**3** [Slang] strong sexual desire: usually in the phrase **get** (or **have**) **hot pants for**
hot pepper **1** any of various pungent peppers: see CAPSICUM (sense 1) **2** a plant on which these grow
hot plate a small, portable device for cooking food, usually with only one or two gas or electric burners: also written **hot′plate′** ***n.***
hot pot **1** [Chiefly Brit.] meat or fish and potatoes cooked together in a tightly covered pot **2** MONGOLIAN HOT POT
hot potato ☆[Informal] a troubling or seemingly insoluble problem, issue, etc. that no one wants to handle
hot-press (hät′pres′) ***vt.*** to exert heat and pressure on (metals, paper, etc.) with a press, as for producing a smooth surface, imparting a gloss, etc. —***n.*** a machine for doing this
☆**hot rod** [Slang] an automobile, usually an old one stripped of extraneous parts, adjusted or rebuilt for quick acceleration and great speed
☆**hot-rod·der** (-räd′ər) ***n.*** [Slang] a person who drives hot rods —**hot′-rod′ding** (-räd′iŋ) ***n.***
☆**hots** (häts) ***n.*** [Slang] strong sexual desire: with *the*
☆**hot seat** **1** [Slang] ELECTRIC CHAIR **2** [Informal] any difficult position subjecting a person to harassment, criticism, or stress With *the*
hot·shot (hät′shät′) ***n.*** [Slang] ☆**1** a person regarded by others or personally as an expert in some activity or as very important, aggressive, or skillful: often used ironically and attributively ☆**2** a fast freight train Also written **hot shot** or **hot-shot**
☆**hot spot** **1** [Informal] an area of actual or potential trouble or violence **2** [Informal] *a)* a lively, popular place for entertainment or socializing *b)* any place regarded as a center for a specified activity or interest [a bird-watching *hot spot*] **3** an area of especially intense heat or radiation **4** *Comput.* a building, business, or locality where wireless access to the internet is provided or is available: see also WI-FI Often sp. **hot′spot′** ***n.***
hot spring a spring of naturally heated groundwater
Hot Springs city in central Ark., adjoining a national park: the park has 47 hot mineral springs
hot·spur (hät′spur′) ***n.*** ⟦nickname of Sir Henry PERCY²: see, e.g., Shakespeare's *Henry IV*⟧ a rash, hotheaded person
hot-tem·pered (hät′tem′pərd) ***adj.*** having a fiery temper; easily made angry
Hot·ten·tot (hät′'n tät′) ***n.*** ⟦Afrik, lit., *hot & tot*, echoic of click consonants characteristic of the language⟧ **1** a member of a nomadic pastoral people of SW Africa **2** the Khoisan language of this people —***adj.*** of the Hottentots or their language or culture
☆**hot·tie** (hät′ē) ***n.*** ⟦< HOT, *adj.* 10c⟧ [Slang] a person who is sexually attractive
☆**hot tub** a large tub for hot water, originally made of wood but now having a plastic liner, jets for circulating the water, and built-in ledges for seating, in which several people can soak and relax together
hot-walk·er (hät′wôk′ər) ***n.*** a person whose job is walking racehorses after races, workouts, etc. to allow them to cool off gradually
hot war actual warfare: opposed to COLD WAR
hot water [Informal] trouble; difficulty: preceded by *in, into*, etc.
☆**hot-wire** (hät′wīr′) ***vt.*** **-wired′**, **-wir′ing** [Informal] to start the engine of (an automobile, boat, etc.) without a key, as by crossing ignition wires
hou·dah (hou′də) ***n.*** *alt. sp. of* HOWDAH
Hou·dan (ho͞o′dan′) ***n.*** ⟦Fr, after *Houdan*, town in NC France⟧ any of a breed of medium-sized domestic chicken with five toes and white or black-and-white feathers
Hou·din·i (ho͞o dē′nē), **Harry** (born *Ehrich Weiss*) 1874-1926; U.S. stage magician & escape artist
Hou·don (o͞o dōn′; *E* ho͞o′dän), **Jean An·toine** (zhän än twȧn′) 1741-1828; Fr. sculptor
hound¹ (hound) ***n.*** ⟦ME < OE *hund*, a dog (generic term), akin to Ger *hund* < IE base **kwon-*, dog > CYNIC, Gr *kyōn*, L *canis*: sense 1*a* shows specialization, accompanied by generalization of OE *docga*: see DOG⟧ **1** *a)* any of several breeds of hunting dog that find game either by scenting and tracking, as the beagle, bloodhound, and foxhound, or by sighting followed by swift pursuit, as the borzoi, deerhound, and greyhound *b)* any dog, especially a member of one of the hunting breeds, with drooping ears, a deep-throated bark, and a keen sense of smell: also **hound dog** **2** a contemptible person ☆**3** [Slang] a devotee, fan, or collector [an autograph *hound*] —***vt.*** **1** to hunt or chase with or as with hounds; chase or follow continually; nag [to *hound* a debtor] **2** to urge on; incite as to pursuit —**SYN.** BAIT —**follow the** (or **ride to**) **hounds** to hunt a fox, etc. on horseback with hounds
hound² (hound) ***n.*** ⟦< ME *houn* < ON *hūnn*, knob (< IE base **keu-*, to swell, arch > L *cavus*, hollow), with unhistoric *-d*, infl. by prec.⟧ **1** either of two projections at the masthead of a sailing vessel for supporting the trestle-trees and the upper parts of the lower rigging **2** a horizontal bar in the running gear of a wagon, cart, etc., for strengthening the connection of various parts
hound's-tongue (houndz′tuŋ′) ***n.*** any of a genus (*Cynoglossum*) of weedy plants of the borage family, with white, blue, or reddish flowers and hairy, tongue-shaped leaves
hounds·tooth (check) (-to͞oth′) a pattern of broken checks, used in woven material for jackets, shirts, etc.: also written **hound's-tooth (check)**
Houns·low (hounz′lō) borough of Greater London, England
hour (our) ***n.*** ⟦ME < OFr *hore* < L *hora* < Gr *hōra*, hour, time, period, season < IE base **yē-*, year, summer (< **ei-*, to go) > YEAR⟧ **1** *a)* a division of time, one of the twenty-four parts of a day; sixty minutes *b)* one of the twelve points on a clock, watch, etc. marking the beginning or end of such a division [the ninth *hour*] **2** a point or period of time; specif., *a)* a fixed point or period of time for a particular activity, occasion, etc. [the dinner *hour*] *b)* an indefinite period of time of a specified kind [his finest *hour*] *c)* [*pl.*] a period fixed for work, receiving patients, etc. [office *hours* from 2 to 5] *d)* [*pl.*] the usual times for getting up or going to bed [to keep late *hours*] **3** *a)* the time of day as indicated by a timepiece [the *hour* is 4:30 A.M.] *b)* [*pl.*] the time of day as reckoned in MILITARY TIME (used following the four-digit numeral) [departure is scheduled for 0100 *hours*] **4** a measure of the distance usually covered in an hour [two *hours* from New York to Philadelphia by rail] **5** *Astron.* a sidereal hour; angular unit equaling 15° measured along the celestial equator **6** *Eccles.* a canonical hour or the prayers said at that time: see BREVIARY ☆**7** *Educ.* a class session of approximately one hour: typically used in determining a unit of academic credit —**after hours** after the regular hours for business, school, etc. —**bottom** (or **top**) **of the hour** *see* BOTTOM OF THE HOUR, TOP OF THE HOUR —**hour after hour** every hour or for many successive hours —**hour by hour** each hour —**of the hour** most prominent at this time —**one's hour** the time of one's death —**on the hour** at the beginning of any or each of the twenty-four divisions of the day; at noon, 1:00, 2:00, etc. [news is broadcast every hour *on the hour*]
hour angle *Astron.* the angle formed at the pole, or its arc on the celestial equator, between the hour circle of a celestial object and the observer's celestial meridian measured in hours, minutes, etc.: it represents the elapsed time since the object passed directly over the observer
hour circle *Astron.* any great circle of the celestial sphere which passes through the celestial poles and is therefore perpendicular to the celestial equator
hour·glass (our′glas′) ***n.*** an instrument for measuring time by the trickling of sand, mercury, water, etc. through a small opening from one glass bulb to another below it, in a fixed period of time, esp. one hour —***adj.*** shaped like an hourglass [her *hourglass* figure]

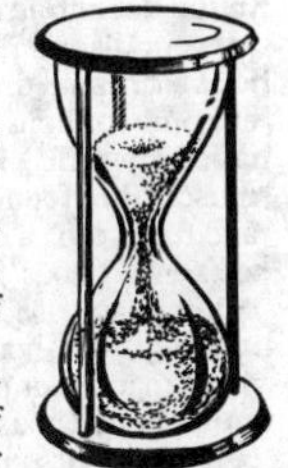
hourglass

hour hand the short hand of an analog clock or watch, which indicates the hours and moves around the dial once every twelve hours
hou·ri (ho͞o′rē, hou′-) ***n.***, *pl.* **-ris** ⟦Fr < Pers *ḥūri* < Ar *ḥūrīyah*, black-eyed woman, ult. < *ḥawira*, to be dark-eyed⟧ **1** in Muslim belief, any of the beautiful nymphs of the Muslim Paradise **2** a seductively beautiful woman
hour·ly (our′lē) ***adj.*** **1** done, taken, or happening every hour **2** completed or happening in the course of an hour [the *hourly* output] **3** reckoned by the hour [*hourly* wage] **4** frequent or continual [to live in *hourly* dread] —***adv.*** **1** once an hour; every hour **2** with frequency
Hours (ourz) ***pl.n.*** ⟦L *Horae*, pl. of *hora*; Gr *Hōrai*, pl. of *hōra*: see HOUR⟧ *Gr. Myth.* the goddesses of the seasons, justice, order, etc.
house (hous; *for v.* houz) ***n.***, *pl.* **hous·es** (hou′ziz, -siz) ⟦ME *hous* < OE *hus*, akin to Ger *haus* (OHG *hūs*) < IE **(s)keus-* < base **(s)keu-*, to cover, conceal > SKY⟧ **1** a building for human beings to live in; specif., *a)* the building or part of a building occupied by one family or tenant; dwelling place *b)* [Brit.] a college in a university *c)* an inn; tavern; hotel *d)* a building where a group of people live as a unit [a fraternity *house*] *e)* a monastery, convent, or similar religious establishment ☆*f)* [Informal] a brothel **2** the people, esp. members of a family, who live together in a house, considered as a unit; household **3** [*often* **H-**] a family as including kin, ancestors, and descendants, esp. a royal or noble family [the *House* of Tudor] **4** something regarded as a house; place that provides shelter, living space, etc.; specif., *a)* the habitation of certain animals, as the shell of a mollusk *b)* a building or shelter where animals are kept [the monkey *house* in a zoo] *c)* a building where things are kept when not in use [a carriage *house*] **5** any place where something is thought of as living, resting, etc. **6** *a)* a theater *b)* the audience in a theater **7** *a)* a place of

business *b)* a business firm; commercial establishment [a publishing *house*] *c)* a building where people meet for a particular activity or pursuit [a *house* of worship, a *house* of prostitution] ☆8 the management of a gambling establishment 9 [*often* H-] *a)* the building or rooms where a legislature or branch of a legislature meets *b)* a legislative assembly or governing body ☆10 HOUSE MUSIC 11 *Astrol.* *a)* any of the twelve parts into which the heavens are divided by great circles through the north and south points of the horizon *b)* a sign of the zodiac considered as the seat of a planet's greatest influence —*adj.* 1 designating or of a salad dressing, type of wine, etc. featured at a particular bar or restaurant 2 trained, housebroken, etc. so that it can be kept in a house or apartment [a *house* cat] 3 of or pertaining to a house or household [a *house* servant] 4 of or pertaining to a particular business establishment, specif., *a)* of or pertaining to a publishing house [an article edited in accord with *house* style] ☆*b)* of or pertaining to the management of a gambling establishment [a *house* limit on bets] —*vt.* **housed, hous′ing** 1 to provide, or serve as, a house or lodgings for 2 to store in a house 3 to cover, harbor, or shelter by or as if by putting into a house 4 *Archit., Mech.* to insert into a housing —*vi.* 1 to take shelter 2 to reside; live —**bring down the house** [Informal] to receive enthusiastic applause from the audience —**clean house** 1 to clean and put a home in order ☆2 [Informal] to get rid of all unwanted things, undesirable conditions, etc. —**keep house** to take care of the affairs of a home; run a household —**like a house on fire (or afire)** with speed and vigor —☆**on the house** given free, at the expense of the establishment —**play house** to pretend in child's play to be grown-up people with the customary household duties —**set (or put) one's house in order** to put one's affairs in order —**the House** 1 HOUSE OF COMMONS 2 HOUSE OF REPRESENTATIVES —**the man of the house** the male head of a household

house arrest detention, often under guard, of an arrested person in that person's own home, in a hospital, etc.

house·boat (hous′bōt′) *n.* a large, flat-bottomed boat with a superstructure resembling a house, usually moored and used as a residence

house·bound (hous′bound′) *adj.* confined to one's home, as by an illness

house·boy (-boi′) *n.* HOUSEMAN (sense 1)

house·break (-brāk′) *vt.* **-broke′, -bro′ken, -break′ing** ⟦back-form. < HOUSEBROKEN⟧ to cause to be housebroken

house·break·ing (-brāk′iŋ) *n.* a BREAKING AND ENTERING into another's house to commit theft or some other felony —**house′break′er** *n.*

house·bro·ken (-brō′kən) *adj.* 1 trained to defecate and urinate outdoors or in a special place indoors so that it can live in a house: said of a pet dog, cat, etc. 2 made docile and conventional

house call a visit to the home of a patient, as by a doctor, or of a client, as by a businessperson, for professional purposes

house·carl (hous′kärl′) *n.* ⟦Late OE *huscarl* < ON *hūskarl*, lit., houseman: see HOUSE & CHURL⟧ a member of the bodyguard or household troops of a Danish or English king or nobleman in late Anglo-Saxon times

☆**house·clean·ing** (hous′klēn′iŋ) *n.* 1 the cleaning of the furniture, floors, woodwork, etc. of a house 2 ⟦see the phrase CLEAN HOUSE (at HOUSE)⟧ a getting rid of superfluous things, unwanted personnel, undesirable conditions, etc. —**house′clean′** *vi., vt.*

☆**house·coat** (hous′kōt′) *n.* a woman's garment, typically long and loose, for casual wear at home

house detective a private detective working as for a hotel or large store to prevent disorderly conduct, theft, etc.

house·dress (-dres′) *n.* any fairly cheap dress, as of printed cotton, worn at home for housework, etc.

house·fly (-flī′) *n., pl.* **-flies′** any of a genus (*Musca*) of disease-carrying muscid flies found in and around houses, and feeding on garbage, manure, and food; esp., a common worldwide species (*M. domestica*)

house·ful (hous′fool′) *n.* as much or as many as a house will hold or accommodate [a *houseful* of guests]

house·guest (hous′gest′) *n.* a person who stays overnight for at least one night in another person's home

house·hold (hous′hōld′) *n.* ⟦ME *houshold*: see HOUSE & HOLD[1], *n.*⟧ 1 the person or persons who live in one house, apartment, etc.; variously, one person or a group, esp. a family 2 the home and its affairs —*adj.* 1 of a household or home; domestic [*household* chores] 2 *a)* common; ordinary *b)* known to almost everyone; very familiar [the incident made him a *household* name overnight]

☆**household arts** HOME ECONOMICS

house·hold·er (-hōl′dər) *n.* ⟦ME *housholdere*⟧ a person who owns or maintains a house, apartment, etc. alone or as head of the household or family

household word a common word, saying, name, or thing that is familiar to nearly everyone

☆**house·hus·band** (hous′huz′bənd) *n.* ⟦modeled on HOUSEWIFE⟧ a married man whose principal occupation is managing a household and taking care of domestic affairs

house·keep·er (-kēp′ər) *n.* a person who manages a household; esp., a woman hired to do this

house·keep·ing (-kēp′iŋ) *n.* 1 the work of a housekeeper 2 the department or staff at a hotel or motel responsible for cleaning guest rooms and public areas, changing linens, etc. 3 internal management of affairs, as of a business

hou·sel (hou′zəl) [Obs.] *n.* ⟦ME < OE *husel*, akin to Goth *hunsl*, a sacrifice < Gmc **kun-s-lo* < IE base **k̑wen-*, to sanctify⟧ EUCHARIST —*vt.* to give the Eucharist to

house·leek (hous′lēk′) *n.* ⟦ME *houslek*: see HOUSE & LEEK⟧ SEMPERVIVUM

house·lights (hous′līts′) *pl.n.* the lights that illuminate the part of a theater where the audience is seated

house·maid (-mād′) *n.* a female servant who does housework

housemaid's knee inflammation and swelling of the bursa in the knee, caused by trauma or excessive kneeling; bursitis of the knee

house·man (-mən, -man′) *n., pl.* **-men** (-mən, -men′) 1 a man employed to do cleaning or other routine work as in a house or hotel 2 [Brit.] INTERN (*n.* 1)

house·mas·ter (hous′mas′tər) *n.* a male faculty member serving as resident director of a boys' dormitory at a preparatory school

house·mate (-māt′) *n.* a person who shares a house, apartment, condominium, etc. with another person

house·moth·er (-muth′ər) *n.* a woman who has charge of a group living together, as in a dormitory or sorority house, and serves as chaperone and, often, housekeeper

☆**house music** ⟦named after *Warehouse*, a dance club in Chicago where it originated⟧ a kind of synthesized electronic dance music with heavily syncopated rhythms, very low-pitched bass tones, and lyrics in a rap style

☆**House of Burgesses** the lower house of the colonial legislature of Virginia

house of cards ⟦in ref. to the pastime of erecting simple structures by balancing playing cards on edge⟧ any flimsy structure, plan, etc.

House of Commons the lower house of the legislature of Great Britain or Canada

house of correction a place of short-term confinement for persons convicted of minor offenses and regarded as capable of being reformed

House of Delegates ☆the lower house of the legislature of Maryland, Virginia, or West Virginia

House of Keys the lower, elective house of the legislature of the Isle of Man

House of Lords the upper house of the legislature of Great Britain, made up of the nobility and high-ranking clergy

☆**House of Representatives** the lower house of the legislature of the U.S., certain other countries, and most of the states of the U.S.

☆**house organ** a periodical published by a business firm for distribution among its employees, affiliates, etc.

house party 1 [Now Rare] the entertainment of guests overnight or for a few days in a home 2 an informal party at someone's home, as for social entertainment, political discussion, or viewing a televised event

house physician a resident physician of a hospital, hotel, etc.: also **house doctor**

house·plant (hous′plant′) *n.* a plant that is grown indoors, primarily for decoration

house-proud (hous′proud′) *adj.* proud of, or preoccupied with, one's house, its appearance, fine or expensive furnishings, etc.

☆**house-rais·ing** (hous′rā′ziŋ) *n.* a gathering of the members of a rural community to help build a neighbor's house or its framework

house·room (hous′ro͞om′) *n.* room or available space in a house; accommodation

house sale a sale of used or unwanted household articles and other possessions, usually held within a house, often by a person who is moving to another dwelling

house·sit (hous′sit′) *vi.* **-sat′, -sit′ting** to stay in a residence and care for it while its usual residents are absent —**house′sit′ter** *n.*

house sparrow ENGLISH SPARROW

house·top (-täp′) *n.* the top of a house; roof —**from the housetops** publicly and widely

house·wares (-werz′) *pl.n.* articles for household use; often, specif., cooking utensils

house·warm·ing (hous′wôr′miŋ) *n.* a party given by or for someone moving into a new home

house·wife (hous′wīf′; *for 2, usually* huz′if) *n., pl.* **house·wives** (hous′wīvz′; *for 2, usually* huz′ivz) ⟦ME *houswif, huswif*⟧ 1 a married woman whose principal occupation is managing a household and taking care of domestic affairs 2 a small sewing kit

house·wife·ly (-wīf′lē) *adj.* of or characteristic of a good housewife; thrifty, orderly, and managing well —*adv.* in the manner of a good housewife

house·wif·er·y (-wīf′ər ē; *Brit* -wif′ər ē) *n.* the work or function of a housewife; housekeeping

house·work (-wurk′) *n.* the work involved in housekeeping, such as cleaning, cooking, and laundering

hous·ing[1] (hou′ziŋ) *n.* ⟦ME *husing*⟧ 1 the act of providing shelter or lodging 2 shelter or lodging; accommodation in houses, apartments, etc.: often used attributively [the *housing* crisis] 3 houses collectively 4 a shelter; covering 5 *Carpentry* a space or recess made in a piece of wood so that another piece can be inserted 6 *Mech.* a frame, box, etc. for containing some part, mechanism, etc. 7 *Naut.* the part of the mast below the main deck

hous·ing[2] (hou′ziŋ) *n.* ⟦< ME *house, houce*, housing < OFr *houce* < Frank **hulfti*: for IE base see HOLSTER⟧ 1 [*often pl.*] *a)* an ornamental covering draped over a horse or other animal *b)* a decorative saddlecloth 2 [*pl.*] trappings; ornamentation

housing estate [Brit.] a housing development: see DEVELOPMENT (sense 4)

Hous·man (hous′mən), **A(lfred) E(dward)** 1859-1936; Eng. poet & classical scholar

Hous·ton[1] (hyo͞os′tən), **Sam(uel)** 1793-1863; U.S. general & statesman

Hous·ton² (hyōōs′tən) ⟦after prec.⟧ city in SE Tex.: port on a ship canal connected with the Gulf of Mexico

☆**hous·to·ni·a** (hōōs tō′nē ə) ***n.*** ⟦ModL, after W. *Houston* (1695-1733), Eng botanist⟧ any of a genus (*Houstonia*) of small North American plants of the madder family, with blue, white, or purple flowers, as the bluet

Hou·yhn·hnm (hōō in′əm, hwin′əm) ***n.*** ⟦coined by Jonathan SWIFT to suggest a horse's *whinny*⟧ in Swift's *Gulliver's Travels*, any of a race of horses with reasoning power and human virtues: see also YAHOO

HOV *abbrev.* high-occupancy vehicle

hove (hōv) ***vt., vi.*** *alt. pt. & pp. of* HEAVE

hov·el (huv′əl, häv′-) ***n.*** ⟦ME < ?⟧ **1** a low, open shed as for sheltering animals or storing supplies or equipment **2** any small, miserable dwelling; hut —***vt.*** **-eled** or **-elled**, **-el·ing** or **-el·ling** to shelter in a hovel

hov·er (huv′ər, häv′-) ***vi.*** ⟦ME *hoveren*, freq. of *hoven*, to stay (suspended)⟧ **1** to stay suspended or flutter in the air near one place **2** to linger or wait close by, esp. in an overprotective, insistent, or anxious way **3** to be in an uncertain condition; waver (*between*) —***n.*** the act of hovering —**hov′er·er** ***n.***

hov·er·craft (huv′ər kraft′) ***n.*** ⟦prec. + (AIR)CRAFT⟧ a vehicle which travels across land or water just above a cushion of air provided by a downward jet, as from its engines and propellers

how¹ (hou) ***adv.*** ⟦ME *hwu, hu* < OE, akin to OHG *hweo* (Ger *wie*), Goth *hwai-wa* < IE interrogative base **kwo-*, **kwe-* > WHY, WHO, L *quo*, Sans *kā*⟧ **1** in what manner or way; by what means **2** in what state or condition **3** for what reason or purpose; why [*how* is it that you don't know?] **4** by what name **5** with what meaning; to what effect **6** to what extent, degree, amount, etc. **7** at what price ☆**8** [Informal] what: usually a request to repeat something said *How* is also used in exclamations and as an intensifier —***conj.*** **1** the manner or way in which [show us *how* you did it] **2** the state or condition in which [ask him *how* he's been] **3** the extent, degree, amount, etc. to which [do you know *how* I despise you?] **4** in whatever manner or way [judge him *how* you will] **5** [Informal] that [he told us *how* he was happy about it] —***n.*** the way of doing; manner; method —☆**and how!** [Informal] I agree! certainly! —**how about something (**or **someone)?** [Informal] what is your wish, opinion, or information concerning something (or someone)? —**how about that!** [Informal] isn't that interesting! —**how come?** [Informal] how is it that? why? —**how do you do?** how is your health?: a conventionalized expression used in greeting a person or upon being introduced —**how now?** [Archaic] what is the meaning of this? —**how so?** how is it so? why? —**how then? 1** what is the meaning of this? **2** how else?

☆**how**² (hou) ***interj.*** ⟦prob. orig. from an exclamation in a Siouan language, as heard by missionaries or explorers⟧ hello: a greeting attributed to, and still used, with humorous intent, in imitation of, American Indians

How·ard¹ (hou′ərd) ***n.*** ⟦< the surname *Howard*⟧ a masculine name: dim. *Howie*

How·ard² (hou′ərd) **1 Catherine** 1520?-42; 5th wife of Henry VIII of England: beheaded **2 Henry** *see* SURREY¹

how·be·it (hou bē′it) ***adv.*** ⟦HOW¹ + BE + IT¹⟧ [Archaic] however it may be; nevertheless —***conj.*** [Obs.] although

how·dah (hou′də) ***n.*** ⟦Anglo-Ind < Hindi *hauda* < Ar *haudaj*⟧ a seat, esp. with a canopy and railing, for riding on the back of an elephant or camel

how-do-you-do or **how-d'ye-do** (hou′ də yə dōō′, houd′ yə dōō′) ***n.*** ⟦< the greeting HOW DO YOU DO? (see phrase at HOW¹)⟧ [Informal] an annoying or awkward situation: usually preceded by *fine, pretty, nice*, etc.: also **how-de-do** (hou′dē dōō′)

how·dy (hou′dē) ***interj.*** ⟦contr. of HOW DO YOU DO? (see phrase at HOW¹)⟧ [Informal or Dial.] hello

Howe (hou) **1 Elias** 1819-67; U.S. inventor of a sewing machine **2 Julia Ward** 1819-1910; U.S. social reformer & poet **3** Sir **William** 5th Viscount Howe 1729-1814; commander in chief of Brit. forces in the American Revolution (1775-78)

How·ells (hou′əlz), **William Dean** 1837-1920; U.S. novelist, critic, & editor

how·ev·er (hou ev′ər) ***adv.*** ⟦ME *hou-ever*⟧ **1** no matter how; in whatever manner **2** to whatever degree or extent **3** by what means [*however* did he escape?]: intensive form of HOW¹ **4** nevertheless; yet; in spite of that; all the same: often used as a conjunctive adverb —***conj.*** [Obs.] although: also [Old Poet.] **how·e'er′** (-er′)

how·itz·er (hou′it sər) ***n.*** ⟦Du *houvietser* < 15th-c. Ger *haufenitz* < Czech *houfnice*, howitzer, orig., a sling⟧ a short cannon, larger than a mortar, firing shells in a high trajectory

howl (houl) ***vi.*** ⟦ME *hulen*, akin to Ger *heulen* < IE echoic base **kāu-* > Sans *kāuti*, (it) cries, OHG *hūwila*, owl⟧ **1** to utter the long, loud, wailing cry of wolves, dogs, etc. **2** to utter a similar cry of pain, anger, grief, etc. **3** to make a sound like this [the wind *howls*] **4** to shout or laugh in scorn, mirth, etc. —***vt.*** **1** to utter with a howl or howls **2** to drive or effect by howling —***n.*** **1** a long, loud, wailing cry of a wolf, dog, etc. **2** any similar sound **3** [Informal] something hilarious —**howl down** to drown out with shouts of scorn or anger —**someone's night to howl** someone's time for unrestrained pleasure [it was *his night to howl*]

howl·er (-ər) ***n.*** **1** a person or thing that howls **2** HOWLER MONKEY **3** [Informal, Chiefly Brit.] a ludicrous blunder

howler monkey any of a genus (*Alouatta*, family Cebidae) of large New World monkeys with a loud, howling cry and a long, prehensile tail: occasionally called **howling monkey**

howl·et (hou′lit) ***n.*** ⟦ME *howlat*, akin? to Fr *hulotte* < OFr *huler*, to howl < L *ululare*, to howl: see ULULATE⟧ [Archaic] an owl

howl·ing (houl′iŋ) ***adj.*** **1** that howls **2** mournful; dreary **3** [Slang] great; tremendous [*a howling* success]

How·rah (hou′rə) city in S West Bengal, India, on the Hooghly River, opposite Kolkata

how's (houz) *contraction* **1** how is **2** how has **3** how does

how·so·ev·er (hou′sō ev′ər) ***adv.*** **1** to whatever degree or extent **2** by whatever means; in whatever manner

☆**how-to** (hou′tōō′) ***adj.*** [Informal] giving elementary instruction in some handicraft, hobby, etc. [*a how-to* book]

hoy¹ (hoi) ***n.*** ⟦ME *hoye* < MDu *hoei*, var. of *hoede*⟧ **1** a former type of small, fore-and-aft-rigged vessel resembling a sloop **2** a heavy barge

hoy² (hoi) ***interj., n.*** ⟦ME⟧ (used as) a cry to attract attention, drive hogs, etc.

hoy·a (hoi′ə) ***n.*** ⟦after T. *Hoy* (1750-1822), Brit botanist & gardener⟧ any of a genus (*Hoya*) of tropical evergreen shrubs of the milkweed family; esp., a vine (*H. carnosa*) with waxy, star-shaped, white-and-pink flowers

hoy·den (hoid′'n) ***n.*** ⟦Early ModE, a rude fellow < ? Du *heiden*, akin to OE *hæthen*, HEATHEN⟧ a bold, boisterous girl; tomboy —***adj.*** bold and boisterous; tomboyish —**hoy′den·ish** ***adj.***

Hoyle (hoil) ***n.*** a book of rules and instructions for indoor games, esp. card games, originally compiled by Edmond Hoyle (1672-1769), English authority on card games and chess —**according to Hoyle** according to the rules and regulations; in the prescribed, fair, or correct way

HP *abbrev.* **1** high-powered **2** high pressure **3** ⟦Brit⟧ hire purchase **4** horsepower: usually written **hp**

HPV *abbrev.* human papillomavirus

HQ or **hq** *abbrev.* headquarters

hr *abbrev.* hour

HR *abbrev.* **1** Home Rule **2** *Baseball* home run(s) **3** House of Representatives **4** human resources

Hra·dec Krá·lo·vé (hrä′dets krä′lô ve) city in the N Czech Republic: in a battle at nearby Sadová (1866), the Prussians defeated the Austrians

HRH *abbrev.* Her (or His) Royal Highness

Hrolf (räl**f**, rôlf) *var. of* ROLLO

HRT *abbrev.* hormone replacement therapy: therapy for replacing or replenishing certain female sex hormones as during menopause or after a hysterectomy

hryv·ni·a (hriv′nē ə) ***n.*** ⟦Ukrainian⟧ the basic monetary unit of Ukraine: see the table of monetary units in the Reference Supplement

Hs *Chem. symbol for* hassium

HS *abbrev.* high school

h.s. *abbrev.* ⟦L *hora somni*⟧ *Pharmacy* bedtime

Hsia·men (shyä′mun′) *a former transliteration of* XIAMEN

HSM *abbrev.* Her (or His) Serene Majesty

HST *abbrev.* Hawaiian-Aleutian Standard Time

ht *abbrev.* **1** heat **2** height **3** high tension

HT *abbrev. Pharmacy* hypertension

HTLV (āch′tē′el′vē′) ***n.*** ⟦*h(uman) T(-cell) l(ymphotropic) v(irus)*⟧ any of a group of retroviruses that invade T cells, including the HIV retroviruses that cause AIDS

HTML *abbrev.* Hypertext Markup Language

http *abbrev.* hypertext transfer protocol: an abbreviation indicating that the address that follows is on the World Wide Web

https *abbrev.* hypertext transfer protocol secure: an abbreviation indicating that the address that follows is on the World Wide Web and that access is to be encrypted for security

HUAC (hōō′ak′, hyōō′-) *abbrev.* House Un-American Activities Committee

Huang (hwäŋ) river in N China, flowing from Tibet into the Gulf of Bo Hai: *c.* 3,395 mi (5,464 km): sometimes called **Huang He** (hwäŋ′ hu′)

Huang Hai (hwäŋ′ hī′) *Chin. name for* YELLOW SEA

☆**hua·ra·ches** (wə rä′chēz, hə-) ***pl.n.*** ⟦pl. of MexSp *huarache*⟧ flat sandals whose uppers are made of straps or woven leather strips

Huás·car (wäs′kär) 1495?-1533; Inca king of Peru, deposed by his half brother Atahualpa

Huas·ca·rán (wäs′kä rän′) mountain of the Andes, in WC Peru: 22,205 ft (6,768 m)

Huas·tec (wäs tek′, wäs′tek′) ***n.*** ⟦MexSp *huasteco* < Nahuatl *kʷešte:kaλ*, of uncert. orig.⟧ **1** a member of an Amerindian people living in N Veracruz state and adjacent regions of Mexico **2** the Mayan language of this people

hub (hub) ***n.*** ⟦prob. ult. < IE base **keu-*, to bend, mound, boss⟧ **1** the center part of a wheel, etc.; the part fastened to the axle, or turning on it **2** a center of interest, importance, or activity **3** an airport that serves as a central connecting point through which many flights of a particular airline are routed —☆**the Hub** name for BOSTON, Mass.

☆**hub·ba-hub·ba** (hub′ə hub′ə) ***interj.*** ⟦< ?⟧ [Old Slang] used to express approval, enthusiasm, etc., esp. to or about an attractive woman

☆**Hub·bard squash** (hub′ərd) a hard winter squash with a green or yellow rind and firm, yellow flesh

Hub·ble (hub′əl), **Edwin (Powell)** 1889-1953; U.S. astronomer

hub·ble-bub·ble (hub′əl bub′əl) ***n.*** ⟦echoic⟧ **1** a tobacco pipe in which the smoke is drawn through water, causing a bubbling sound; simple type of hookah **2** a bubbling sound **3** hubbub

☆**Hubble constant** a ratio expressing the rate at which the universe is expanding, the so-called constant in Hubble's law, equal to the velocity of a receding galaxy divided by its distance from the earth: symbol, H_0

Hubble effect ⟦after Edwin HUBBLE, who discovered it⟧ REDSHIFT

Hubble's law the law, formulated by Edwin Hubble, that the velocities of distant galaxies moving away from the earth are directly proportional to their distance from the earth: cf. REDSHIFT

hub·bub (hub′bub′, hu′-) ***n.*** ⟦prob. < Celt, as in Gael *ubub*, exclamation of aversion⟧ a confused sound of many voices; uproar; tumult —***SYN.*** NOISE

hub·by (hub′ē) ***n., pl.*** **-bies** [Informal] a husband

hub·cap (hub′kap′) ***n.*** a tightfitting cap over the hub and lug nuts of a wheel, esp. of an automobile; wheel cover

Hu·bei (ho͞o′bā′) province in EC China: 72,394 sq mi (187,500 sq km); cap. Wuhan

Hu·bert (hyo͞o′bərt) ***n.*** ⟦Fr < OHG *Huguberht*, lit., bright (in) spirit < *hugu*, mind, spirit + *beraht*, BRIGHT⟧ a masculine name: equiv. It. *Uberto*

Hu·bli-Dhar·war (ho͝ob′lē där′wär′) city in SW India

hu·bris (hyo͞o′bris; *also* ho͞o′-) ***n.*** ⟦Gr *hybris* < IE base **ud-*, up (> OUT) + **gwerī-*, heavy: basic sense prob. "to rush at impetuously"⟧ wanton insolence or arrogance resulting from excessive pride or from passion —**hu·bris′tic** ***adj.***

huck·a·back (huk′ə bak′) ***n.*** ⟦< ?⟧ a coarse linen or cotton cloth with a rough surface, used for toweling: also **huck** (huk)

huck·le (huk′əl) ***n.*** ⟦dim. (see -LE) of obs. *huck* in same sense: ? akin to ON *hūka*, to crouch < IE base **keu-*, to bend⟧ [Archaic] the hip or haunch

☆**huck·le·ber·ry** (huk′əl ber′ē) ***n., pl.*** **-ries** ⟦prob. altered < HURTLEBERRY⟧ **1** any of a genus (*Gaylussacia*) of plants of the heath family, having dark-blue berries with ten large seeds **2** the fruit of any of these shrubs **3** loosely, a blueberry

huck·le·bone (huk′əl bōn′) ***n.*** ⟦see HUCKLE⟧ [Archaic] **1** the hipbone **2** the anklebone; talus

huck·ster (huk′stər) ***n.*** ⟦ME *hokestere* < MDu *hoekster* < *hoeken*, to peddle, akin to Ger *hökern*: see HAWKER[1]⟧ **1** a peddler or hawker of wares, esp. of fruits, vegetables, etc. **2** an aggressive or haggling merchant, esp. one who uses questionable methods ☆**3** [Informal] a person engaged in advertising, esp. for the mass media —***vt.*** **1** to peddle or sell **2** to sell or advertise in an aggressive, questionable way —**huck′ster·ism′** ***n.***

HUD (ăch′yo͞o′dē′, hud) ***abbrev.*** **1** (Department of) Housing and Urban Development **2** head-up display

hud·dle (hud′'l) ***vi.*** **-dled, -dling** ⟦orig. (16th c.), to put out of sight < ? or akin to ME *hudel*, var. of *hidel*, a hiding place < OE *hydel* < *hydan*, HIDE[1]⟧ **1** to crowd, push, or nestle close together, as cows do in a storm **2** to draw the limbs close to the body, as from cold [*to huddle under a blanket*] ☆**3** [Informal] to hold a private, informal conference ☆**4** *Football* to gather in a huddle —***vt.*** **1** to crowd close together **2** to hunch or draw (oneself) up **3** to do, put, or make hastily and carelessly **4** to push or thrust in a hurried or disordered manner —***n.*** **1** a confused crowd or heap of persons or things **2** confusion; muddle; jumble ☆**3** [Informal] a private, informal conference ☆**4** *Football* a grouping of a team behind the line of scrimmage to receive signals before a play

Hu·di·bras·tic (hyo͞o′di bras′tik) ***adj.*** like, or in the style of, Samuel Butler's *Hudibras*, a mock-heroic satirical poem (1663-78) in iambic-tetrameter and rhyming couplets, ridiculing the Puritans

Hud·son[1] (hud′sən) **1 Henry** died 1611; Eng. explorer, esp. of the waters about NE North America **2 W(illiam) H(enry)** 1841-1922; Eng. naturalist & writer

Hud·son[2] (hud′sən) ⟦after Henry HUDSON[1]⟧ river in E N.Y., flowing southward into Upper New York Bay: *c.* 315 mi (507 km)

Hudson Bay ⟦after Henry HUDSON[1]⟧ inland sea in NE Canada; arm of the Atlantic: *c.* 281,900 sq mi (730,118 sq km)

Hudson River school ⟦after the HUDSON[2] *River*, depicted in many works of the earlier members of this group⟧ a group of U.S. landscape painters of the 19th cent., including Thomas Cole and Albert Bierstadt

Hudson seal muskrat fur processed to resemble seal

Hudson Strait ⟦after Henry HUDSON[1]⟧ strait in NE Canada, connecting Hudson Bay with the Atlantic: *c.* 430 mi (692 km) long; 37-120 mi (60-193 km) wide

hue[1] (hyo͞o) ***n.*** ⟦ME *hewe* < OE *heow*, akin to Goth *hiwi*, appearance, form < IE **ki-wo* < base **kei-*, (dark-)colored > OE *hæwen*, blue, *har*, HOAR⟧ **1** [Obs.] general appearance; aspect **2** color; esp., the distinctive characteristics of a given color that enable it to be assigned a position in the spectrum **3** a particular shade or tint of a given color —***SYN.*** COLOR

hue[2] (hyo͞o) ***n.*** ⟦ME *hu* < OFr, a warning interj.⟧ a shouting; outcry: now only in HUE AND CRY (see phrase below) —**hue and cry** ⟦Anglo-Norm *hu e cri*⟧ **1** [Historical] *a)* a loud shout or cry by those pursuing a felon: all who heard were obliged to join in the pursuit *b)* the pursuit itself **2** any loud outcry or clamor

Hue (hwā, wā) city in central Vietnam, on the South China Sea

hued (hyo͞od) ***adj.*** ⟦ME *hewed*, pp. of *heowien*, to color < OE *heowian* < *heow*: see HUE[1]⟧ having some (specified) shade or intensity of color or a (specified) number of colors: used mainly in hyphenated compounds [*rosy-hued, many-hued*]

☆**hue·vos ran·che·ros** (wā′vōs ran cher′ōs) ⟦MexSp, eggs in ranch or country style < pl. of *huevo*, egg + pl. of *ranchero* (in adjectival use): see RANCHERO⟧ fried eggs with a creole sauce, a Mexican dish popular in the U.S.

huff (huf) ***vt.*** ⟦echoic⟧ **1** [Obs.] to blow, swell, or puff up **2** to treat insolently; bully; hector **3** to make angry; offend ☆**4** [Slang] to inhale (an aerosol, solvent, glue, etc.) for the intoxicating or euphoric affects —***vi.*** **1** to blow; puff **2** to become angry; take offense **3** [Obs.] to swell with pride or arrogance ☆**4** [Slang] to inhale something for the intoxicating or euphoric affects —***n.*** a condition of smoldering anger or resentment —**huff′er** ***n.*** —**huff′ing** ***n.***

huff·ish (huf′ish) ***adj.*** ⟦prec. + -ISH⟧ **1** peevish; petulant; sulky **2** [Obs.] inclined to be arrogant —**huff′ish·ly** ***adv.*** —**huff′ish·ness** ***n.***

huff·y (huf′ē) ***adj.*** **huff′i·er, huff′i·est** **1** easily offended; touchy **2** angered or offended —**huff′i·ly** ***adv.*** —**huff′i·ness** ***n.***

Hu·fuf (ho͝o fo͞of′) *alt. sp. of* HOFUF

hug (hug) ***vt.*** **hugged, hug′ging** ⟦prob. via dial. < ON *hugga*, to comfort, console⟧ **1** to put the arms around and hold closely; esp., to embrace tightly and affectionately **2** to squeeze tightly between the forelegs, as a bear does **3** to cling to or cherish (a belief, opinion, etc.) **4** to keep close to [*to hug the shoreline in sailing*] —***vi.*** to clasp or embrace each other closely —***n.*** **1** a close, affectionate embrace **2** a tight clasp or hold with the arms, as in wrestling **3** a bear's squeeze —**hug′ga·ble** ***adj.*** —**hug′ger** ***n.***

huge (hyo͞oj, yo͞oj) ***adj.*** **hug′er, hug′est** ⟦ME < OFr *ahuge, ahoge*, prob. < *a*, to + *hoge*, hill < ON *haugr*: for IE base see HIGH⟧ **1** very large; gigantic; immense **2** very great, important, powerful, extensive, etc. **3** [Informal] extremely popular, successful, etc. —***SYN.*** ENORMOUS —**huge′ly** ***adv.*** —**huge′ness** ***n.***

hug·ger·mug·ger (hug′ər mug′ər) ***n.*** ⟦earlier also *hokermoker*, apparently rhyming comp. based on ME *mokeren*, to hoard, conceal > the basic sense, "secrecy"⟧ **1** a confusion; muddle; jumble **2** [Archaic] secrecy —***adj.*** **1** confused; muddled; jumbled **2** [Archaic] secret —***adv.*** **1** in a confused or jumbled manner **2** [Archaic] secretly —***vi.*** to behave in a secretive or confused way

Hug·gins (hug′inz), Sir **William** 1824-1910; Eng. astronomer

Hugh (hyo͞o) ***n.*** a masculine name: var. *Hugo*

Hugh Capet *see* CAPET, Hugh

Hughes (hyo͞oz) **1 Charles Evans** 1862-1948; U.S. statesman: chief justice of the U.S. (1930-41) **2 Howard (Robard)** 1905-75; U.S. businessman **3 (James) Lang·ston** (laŋ′stən) 1902-67; U.S. poet & writer **4 Ted** (born *Edward James Hughes*) 1930-98; Eng. poet: poet laureate (1984-98)

Hu·go[1] (hyo͞o′gō) ***n.*** a masculine name: see HUGH

Hu·go[2], **Vic·tor (Marie)** (vēk tôr′) 1802-85; Fr. poet, novelist, & playwright

Hu·gue·not (hyo͞o′gə nät′, -nō′) ***n.*** ⟦MFr, orig., supporter of group in Geneva opposing annexation to Savoy: altered (after *Hugues* Besançon, leader of the group) < earlier *eidgnot* < Ger *eidgenosse*, a confederate, ally: name later applied to Protestants in reference to the Calvinist Reformation in Geneva⟧ any French Protestant of the 16th or 17th cent.

huh (hu, hun) ***interj.*** [Informal] **1** used to express contempt, surprise, etc. **2** used to ask a question See also HUNH

Hu·he·hot (ho͞o′hā′hōt′) *a former transliteration of* HOHHOT

☆**hui·pil** (wē pēl′) ***n.*** ⟦AmSp < Nahuatl⟧ a loose, boxy, often colorfully embroidered blouse worn as by Indian women of Mexico and Guatemala

☆**hui·sa·che** (wē sä′chē′, -chā′) ***n.*** ⟦AmSp < Nahuatl *wiša:čin* < *huitztli*, a spine + *izachi*, plentiful⟧ a spiny plant (*Acacia farnesiana*) of the mimosa family, native to Tex. and Mexico, with fragrant yellow flowers used in perfumery

Hui·zing·a (hī′ziŋ ə, hoi′-), **Jo·han** (yō hän′) 1872-1945; Du. historian

hu·la (ho͞o′lə) ***n.*** ⟦Haw⟧ a native Hawaiian dance marked by flowing, pantomimic gestures and a swaying of the hips: also **hu′la-hu′la**

☆**hula hoop** a hoop like a Hula-Hoop

☆**Hu·la-Hoop** (ho͞o′lə ho͞op′) ⟦< HULA + HOOP⟧ *trademark for* a lightweight hoop twirled around the body in play or exercise by rotating the hips

hulk (hulk) ***n.*** ⟦ME < OE *hulc* < ML *hulcus* < Gr *holkas*, towed vessel < IE **solkos*, a pull, something dragged < base **selk-*, to pull > Gr *hēlkein*, to pull, OE *sulh*, a plow⟧ **1** *a)* [Archaic] any ship *b)* a big, unwieldy ship **2** *a)* the hull of an old, dismantled ship *b)* such a ship used for storage in a port or, earlier, as a prison **3** a big, clumsy person or thing —***vi.*** **1** to rise bulkily: usually with *up* **2** [Dial.] to slouch or lounge about in a heavy, clumsy manner

hulk·ing (hul′kiŋ) ***adj.*** large, heavy, and often unwieldy or clumsy: also **hulk′y** (-kē)

hull[1] (hul) ***n.*** ⟦ME *hule* < OE *hulu*, akin to Ger *hülle*, covering: for IE base see HALL⟧ **1** the outer covering of a seed or fruit, as the husk of grain, pod of a pea, shell of a nut, etc. **2** the calyx of some fruits, as the raspberry **3** any outer covering —***vt.*** to take the hull or hulls off (a seed or fruit) —**hull′er** ***n.***

hull[2] (hul) ***n.*** ⟦special use of prec., prob. infl. by Du *hol*, ship's hold⟧ **1** the frame or body of a ship, excluding the masts, rigging, superstructure, etc. **2** *a)* the main body of an airship *b)* the watertight frame or main body of a flying boat, amphibious plane or vehicle, hydrofoil, etc., on which it floats when in the water —***vt.*** to pierce the hull of (a ship) with a shell, torpedo, etc. —**hull down** far enough away so that the hull is below the horizon and only the masts, stacks, etc. are visible

Hull[1] (hul), **Cor·dell** (kôr′del) 1871-1955; U.S. statesman: secretary of state (1933-44)

Hull[2] (hul) **1** seaport in NE England, on the Humber estuary: officially *Kingston upon Hull* **2** ⟦after district in Yorkshire, England⟧ former city in SW Quebec, Canada, now part of Gatineau

hul·la·ba·loo (hul′ə bə lo͞o′) ***n.*** ⟦echoic redupl. based on HULLO⟧ loud noise and confusion; hubbub

Hull-House (hul′hous′) ⟦after C. J. Hull (1820-89), U.S. real estate developer for whom it was built and whose heir leased it to Jane Addams⟧ a social settlement house founded in Chicago in 1889 by Jane Addams: usually written **Hull House**

hul·lo (hə lō′) *interj., n., vi., vt. var. of* HELLO

hum[1] (hum) *vi.* **hummed, hum′ming** ⟦ME *hummen,* of echoic orig., as in Ger *hummel,* bumblebee, MDu *hommeln,* hum⟧ **1** to make a low, continuous, murmuring sound like that of a bee or a motor **2** to sing with the lips closed, not producing words **3** to give forth a confused, droning sound [a room *humming* with voices] **4** [Informal] to be busy or full of activity —*vt.* **1** to sing (a tune, etc.) with the lips closed **2** to produce an effect on by humming [to *hum* a child to sleep] —*n.* **1** the act of humming **2** a continuous, murmuring sound —**hum′mer** *n.*

hum[2] (həm: *conventionalized pronun.*) *interj., n.* HEM[2] —*vi.* **hummed, hum′ming** HEM[2]

hu·man (hyo͞o′mən, yo͞o′-) *adj.* ⟦ME *humayne* < OFr *humaine* < L *humanus,* akin to *homo,* a man: see HOMO[1]⟧ **1** *a)* of, belonging to, or typical of mankind (*Homo sapiens*) [the *human* race] *b)* of or having to do with hominids in general [*human* fossils from the Pliocene] **2** consisting of or produced by people [*human* society] **3** having or showing qualities, as rationality or fallibility, viewed as distinctive of people [a *human* act, a *human* failing] —*n.* a person: the compound **human being** is still preferred by some —**hu′man·ness** *n.*

human chorionic gonadotropin HCG

hu·mane (hyo͞o mān′, yo͞o-) *adj.* ⟦earlier var. of HUMAN, now usually assoc. directly with L *humanus*⟧ **1** having what are considered the best qualities of human beings; kind, tender, merciful, sympathetic, etc. **2** civilizing; humanizing [*humane* learning] —**hu·mane′ly** *adv.* —**hu·mane′ness** *n.*

humane society an organization promoting the humane treatment of animals

☆**human growth hormone** GROWTH HORMONE (sense 1)

human immunodeficiency virus HIV

hu·man·ism (hyo͞o′mə niz′əm, yo͞o′-) *n.* **1** the quality of being human; human nature **2** any system of thought or action based on the nature, interests, and ideals of humanity; specif., a modern, nontheistic, rationalist movement that holds that humanity is capable of self-fulfillment, ethical conduct, etc. without recourse to supernaturalism **3** the study of the humanities **4** [*often* **H-**] the intellectual and cultural secular movement that stemmed from the study of classical literature and culture during the Middle Ages and was one of the factors giving rise to the Renaissance

hu·man·ist (-nist) *n.* ⟦< Fr *humaniste* < It *umanista* (coined by L. ARIOSTO) < *umano,* a human < L *humanus,* HUMAN⟧ **1** a student of human nature and human affairs **2** a student of the humanities **3** an adherent of any system of humanism **4** [**H-**] a follower of Humanism —*adj.* of humanism or the humanities —**hu′man·is′tic** *adj.* —**hu′man·is′ti·cal·ly** *adv.*

hu·man·i·tar·i·an (hyo͞o man′ə ter′ē ən, yo͞o-) *n.* **1** a person devoted to promoting the welfare of humanity, esp. through the elimination of pain and suffering; philanthropist **2** an adherent of HUMANITARIANISM (sense 2) —*adj.* **1** helping humanity **2** of humanitarianism —***SYN.*** PHILANTHROPIC

hu·man·i·tar·i·an·ism (-iz′əm) *n.* **1** the beliefs or actions of a HUMANITARIAN (sense 1) **2** *Ethics a)* the doctrine that humanity's chief or only obligations are to its temporal welfare *b)* the doctrine that a human being is capable of perfection without divine aid

hu·man·i·ty (hyo͞o man′ə tē, yo͞o-) *n., pl.* **-ties** ⟦ME *humanite* < OFr < L *humanitas*⟧ **1** the fact or quality of being human; human nature **2** [*pl.*] human qualities or characteristics, esp. those considered desirable **3** the human race; mankind; people **4** the fact or quality of being humane; kindness, mercy, sympathy, etc. —**the humanities 1** languages and literature, esp. those of the classical Greeks and Romans **2** the branches of learning concerned with human thought and relations, as distinguished from the sciences: literature, philosophy, history, etc.

hu·man·ize (hyo͞o′mə nīz′, yo͞o′-) *vt.* **-ized′, -iz′ing 1** to make human; give a human nature or character to **2** to make humane; make kind, merciful, considerate, etc.; civilize; refine —*vi.* to become human or humane —**hu′man·i·za′tion** *n.* —**hu′man·iz′er** *n.*

hu·man·kind (hyo͞o′mən kīnd′, yo͞o′-) *n.* the human race; mankind

hu·man·ly (hyo͞o′mən lē, yo͞o′-) *adv.* **1** in a human manner **2** within human ability or knowledge **3** from a human viewpoint

human nature 1 the common qualities of all human beings **2** *Sociology* the pattern of responses inculcated by the tradition of the social group

hu·man·oid (hyo͞o′mə noid′, yo͞o′-) *adj.* ⟦HUMAN + -OID⟧ nearly human, as in appearance or behavior —*n.* **1** a nearly human creature; specif., any of the earliest ancestors of modern man **2** in science fiction, *a)* an alien that physically resembles a human being *b)* ANDROID

human papillomavirus any of a group of papillomaviruses causing cutaneous warts and lesions of the oral, anal, and genital mucous membranes in human beings

human potential movement a movement in psychology that includes group therapy, encounter therapy, primal therapy, etc., is based mainly on Freudian and Gestalt psychology, and is aimed at self-realization

human resources a department, in a company or institution, responsible for personnel records, company benefits, hiring and training of employees, etc.; personnel department

human rights rights, as the right to organize politically or worship freely, thought of as belonging inherently to each human being and not to be taken away or interfered with by arbitrary or repressive government action

Hum·ber (hum′bər) estuary in NE England, formed by the Ouse & Trent rivers: *c.* 40 mi (64 km) long

Hum·ber·side (-sīd′) former county in NE England, on the Humber estuary & the North Sea: now divided into several administrative units

hum·ble (hum′bəl) *adj.* **-bler, -blest** ⟦ME < OFr < L *humilis,* low, small, slight, akin to *humus,* soil, earth: see HUMUS[1]⟧ **1** having or showing a consciousness of one's defects or shortcomings; not overly proud; not self-assertive; modest **2** low in condition, rank, or position; lowly; unpretentious [a *humble* home] —*vt.* **-bled, -bling 1** to lower in condition, rank, or position; abase **2** to lower in pride; make modest or humble in mind —***SYN.*** DEGRADE —**hum′ble·ness** *n.* —**hum′bler** *n.* —**hum′bly** *adv.*

hum·ble·bee (hum′bəl bē′) *n.* ⟦ME *humbylbee* < *humblen,* to hum, akin to *hummen* (see HUM[1]) + *bee,* BEE[1]⟧ [Now Chiefly Dial. or Literary] BUMBLEBEE

humble pie ⟦earlier *umble pie* < *umbles,* entrails of a deer < ME *noumbles:* see NUMBLES⟧ [Historical] a pie made of the inner parts of a deer, served to the servants after a hunt —**eat humble pie** to undergo humiliation, esp. that of admitting one's error and apologizing

Hum·boldt (ho͝om′bôlt′; *E* hum′bōlt′), Baron **(Friedrich Heinrich) Al·ex·an·der von** (ä′lek sän′dər fôn) 1769-1859; Ger. scientist, explorer, & writer

Humboldt current ⟦after prec.⟧ the cold ocean current flowing north along the coasts of Chile and Peru

hum·bug (hum′bug′) *n.* ⟦18th-c. slang: orig. reference uncert.⟧ **1** *a)* something made or done to cheat or deceive; fraud; sham; hoax *b)* misleading, dishonest, or empty talk; nonsense **2** a person who is not what he or she claims to be; impostor **3** a spirit of trickery, deception, etc. **4** [Brit.] a striped hard candy —*vt.* **-bugged′, -bug′ging** to dupe; deceive —*interj.* nonsense —**hum′bug′ger** *n.* —**hum′bug′ger·y** *n.*

☆**hum·ding·er** (hum′diŋ′ər) *n.* ⟦fanciful coinage⟧ [Slang] a person or thing considered excellent or otherwise remarkable of its kind

hum·drum (hum′drum′) *adj.* ⟦echoic extension (infl. by DRUM[1]) of HUM[1]⟧ lacking variety; dull; monotonous; boring —*n.* humdrum talk, routine, etc.; monotony

Hume (hyo͞om), **David** 1711-76; Scot. philosopher & historian

hu·mec·tant (hyo͞o mek′tənt) *n.* ⟦< L *humectans,* var. of *umectans,* prp. of *humectare,* to moisten < *umectus,* moist < *umere,* to be moist: see HUMOR⟧ a substance, as glycerol, added or applied to another to help it retain moisture

hu·mer·al (hyo͞o′mər əl) *adj.* ⟦ModL *humeralis* < L *humerus*⟧ **1** of or near the humerus **2** of or near the shoulder or shoulders

humeral veil *Eccles.* a long, narrow piece of cloth, usually of silk, worn over the shoulders and covering the hands as of a priest holding the monstrance at Benediction

hu·mer·us (hyo͞o′mər əs) *n., pl.* **-mer·i′** (-ī) ⟦L *humerus, umerus,* the shoulder, upper arm < IE **om(e)sos,* the shoulder > Sans *áṁsa-,* Gr *ōmos*⟧ the bone of the upper arm or forelimb, extending from the shoulder to the elbow

hu·mic (hyo͞o′mik) *adj.* of or derived from humus

humic acid a brown powder consisting of organic acids, derived from humus

hu·mid (hyo͞o′mid, yo͞o′-) *adj.* ⟦Fr *humide* < L *humidus* < *humere,* altered (after *humus*) < *umere,* to be moist: see HUMOR⟧ full of water vapor; damp; moist —***SYN.*** WET

hu·mid·i·fi·er (hyo͞o mid′ə fī′ər, yo͞o-) *n.* a device or appliance for humidifying indoor air

hu·mid·i·fy (-fī′) *vt.* **-fied′, -fy′ing** to add moisture to (the air, etc.) —**hu·mid′i·fi·ca′tion** *n.*

☆**hu·mid·i·stat** (-stat′) *n.* ⟦< fol. + -STAT⟧ an automatic device for controlling the extent to which a humidifier or dehumidifier modifies the relative humidity

hu·mid·i·ty (-tē) *n., pl.* **-ties** ⟦ME *humydite* < OFr *humidite* < LL *humiditas* < L *humidus:* see HUMID⟧ **1** moistness; dampness **2** the amount or degree of moisture in the air: see ABSOLUTE HUMIDITY, RELATIVE HUMIDITY

☆**hu·mi·dor** (hyo͞o′mə dôr′) *n.* ⟦HUMID + -OR⟧ a case, jar, etc. designed for storing cigars, pipe tobacco, etc. and keeping them properly moist

hu·mil·i·ate (hyo͞o mil′ē āt′, yo͞o-) *vt.* **-at′ed, -at′ing** ⟦< LL *humiliatus,* pp. of *humiliare,* to humiliate < L *humilis,* HUMBLE⟧ to hurt the pride or dignity of by causing to be or seem foolish or contemptible; mortify —***SYN.*** ASHAMED, DEGRADE —**hu·mil′i·a′tion** *n.*

hu·mil·i·ty (hyo͞o mil′ə tē, yo͞o-) *n.* ⟦ME *humilite* < OFr < L *humilitas*⟧ the state or quality of being humble; absence of vanity or excessive pride

hum·ma·ble (hum′ə bəl) *adj.* suitable for being hummed, esp. because catchy or melodious [a *hummable* tune]

hum·mer (hum′ər) *n.* **1** a person or thing that hums ☆**2** HUMMINGBIRD ☆**3** [Slang] *Baseball* FASTBALL

hum·ming (hum′iŋ) *adj.* **1** that buzzes, drones, or hums **2** [Informal] full of activity; lively; brisk

☆**hum·ming·bird** (hum′iŋ burd′) *n.* any of a large family (Trochilidae, order Apodiformes) of very small, brightly colored New World birds with a long, slender bill for feeding on nectar, and narrow wings that vibrate rapidly, often with a humming sound

hum·mock (hum′ək) *n.* ⟦orig. naut. < ?⟧ **1** a low, rounded hill; knoll; hillock **2** a ridge or rise in an ice field ☆**3** a tract of fertile, heavily wooded land, higher than a surrounding marshy area —☆**hum′mock·y** *adj.*

ruby-throated hummingbird

hum·mus (hum′əs, ho͝om′əs) *n.* ⟦Turk *humus*⟧ a Middle Eastern dish, a paste of mashed chickpeas, tahini, garlic, etc., eaten, often with pita bread, as an appetizer

☆**hu·mon·gous** (hyo͞o mäŋ′gəs, -muŋ′-) *adj.* ⟦prob. blend & alteration of HUGE & MONSTROUS⟧ [Informal] of enormous size or extent; very large or great

hu·mor (hyo͞o′mər, yo͞o′-) *n.* ⟦ME < OFr < L *humor, umor*, moisture, fluid, akin to *umere*, to be moist < IE base **wegw-, *ugw-*, moist, moisten > WAKE[2], Gr *hygros*, moist, fluid, Du *wak*, wet⟧ **1** *a)* [Obs.] any fluid or juice of an animal or plant *b)* [Historical] any of the four fluids (**cardinal humors**) formerly considered responsible for one's health and disposition: blood, phlegm, choler, or melancholy **2** *a)* a person's disposition or temperament *b)* a mood; state of mind **3** whim; fancy; caprice **4** the quality that makes something seem funny, amusing, or ludicrous; comicality **5** *a)* the ability to perceive, appreciate, or express what is funny, amusing, or ludicrous *b)* the expression of this in speech, writing, or action **6** *Physiol.* any of certain fluids or fluidlike substances of the body [the aqueous *humor*] —*vt.* **1** to comply with the mood or whim of (another); indulge **2** to act in agreement with the nature of; adapt oneself to —*SYN.* INDULGE, MOOD[1], WIT[1] —**out of humor** not in a good mood; cross; disagreeable —**hu′mor·less** *adj.*

hu·mor·al (hyo͞o′mər əl) *adj.* ⟦ModL (Paracelsus) *humoralis* < L *humor*⟧ of or relating to the humors of the body

hu·mor·esque (hyo͞o′mər esk′) *n.* ⟦Ger *humoreske* < *humor* (see HUMOR, *n.* 3) + *-eske*, -ESQUE⟧ a light, fanciful or playful musical composition; capriccio

hu·mor·ist (hyo͞o′mər ist, yo͞o′-) *n.* ⟦HUMOR + -IST[1]⟧ **1** [Archaic] a person with a good sense of humor **2** a person skilled in the expression of humor; esp., a professional writer or teller of amusing stories, jokes, etc. —**hu′mor·is′tic** *adj.*

hu·mor·ous (hyo͞o′mər əs, yo͞o′-) *adj.* ⟦HUMOR + -OUS; sense 2 < Fr *humoreux* (< L); sense 3 < L *humorosus*⟧ **1** having or expressing humor; funny; amusing; comical **2** [Archaic] whimsical; capricious **3** [Obs.] *a)* moist *b)* humoral —*SYN.* WITTY —**hu′mor·ous·ly** *adv.*

hu·mour (hyo͞o′mər) *n., vt. Brit. sp. of* HUMOR

hump (hump) *n.* ⟦< or akin to LowG *humpe*, thick piece < IE **kumb-* (< base **keu-*, to bend, curve) > HIP[1], Sans *kumba-*, thick end (of a bone), Gr *kymbē*, a bowl⟧ **1** a rounded, protruding lump, specif., *a)* such a lump resulting from kyphosis *b)* the fleshy mass on the back of a camel **2** a hummock; mound **3** [Brit. Informal] a fit of melancholy: with *the* —*vt.* **1** to hunch; arch [the cat *humped* its back] **2** [Brit. & Austral. Informal] to carry on the back **3** [Slang] to have sexual intercourse with: somewhat vulgar —☆*vi.* [Slang] **1** to exert oneself **2** to hurry —☆**over the hump** [Informal] over the worst or most difficult part

hump·back (hump′bak′) *n.* **1** a humped, deformed back; kyphosis **2** HUNCHBACK (sense 2) ☆**3** a large rorqual whale (*Megaptera novaeangliae*) with long flippers and a raised, rounded back ☆**4** a male pink salmon at the time it travels up rivers to spawn —**hump′backed′** *adj.*

☆**hump day** [Informal] Wednesday, regarded as the middle of the workweek

humped (humpt) *adj.* having a hump; humpbacked

Hum·per·dinck (ho͝om′pər diŋk′; *E* hum′pər-), **Eng·el·bert** (eŋ′gəl bert′; *E*, -burt′) 1854-1921; Ger. composer

humph (humf: *conventionalized pronun.*) *n., interj.* (a snorting or grunting sound) used to express doubt, disdain, disgust, etc.

Hum·phrey (hum′frē) *n.* ⟦OE *Hunfrith* < Gmc **hun*, strength + OE *frith*, peace⟧ a masculine name: equiv. Ger. *Humfried*, It. *Onfredo*

Hump·ty Dump·ty (hump′tē dump′tē) a short, squat character in an old nursery rhyme, a personification of an egg, who fell from a wall and broke into pieces

hump·y (hum′pē) *adj.* **hump′i·er, hump′i·est** **1** having humps **2** like a hump

hu·mus[1] (hyo͞o′məs, yo͞o′-) *n.* ⟦L, earth, ground, soil < IE **ĝhom-*: see HOMO[1]⟧ a brown or black substance resulting from the partial decay of plant and animal matter; organic part of the soil

hum·us[2] (hum′əs, ho͝om′əs) *n. alt. sp. of* HUMMUS

Hum·vee (hum′vē′) ⟦modified acronym < the phr. *high-mobility multipurpose vehicle*⟧ *trademark for* a four-wheel-drive, all-purpose vehicle, successor to the jeep, used by U.S. armed forces

Hun (hun) *n.* ⟦OE *Hune* < LL *Hunni* (pl.), prob. < orig. local name > Chin *Hiong-nu, Han*⟧ **1** a member of a warlike Asian people that, led by Attila and others, invaded E and central Europe in the 4th and 5th cent. A.D. **2** [*often* **h-**] any savage or destructive person; vandal: term of contempt applied to German soldiers, esp. in WWI

Hu·nan (ho͞o′nän′) province of SE China: 81,274 sq mi (210,499 sq km); cap. Changsha

hunch (hunch) *vt.* ⟦< ?⟧ to draw (one's body, etc.) up so as to form a hump; arch into a hump —*vi.* **1** to move forward jerkily; push; shove **2** to sit or stand with the back arched —*n.* **1** a hump **2** a chunk; lump; hunk ☆**3** ⟦from the superstition that touching a *hunchback* brings good luck⟧ a guess or feeling not based on known facts; premonition or suspicion

hunch·back (hunch′bak′) *n.* **1** HUMPBACK (sense 1) **2** a person having a humped back —**hunch′backed′** *adj.*

hun·dred (hun′drəd; *often*, -dərd) *n.* ⟦ME < OE, akin to OS *hunderod*, ON *hundrath* < PGmc base **hund-*, 100 (< IE base **kmto-* > Gr *hekaton*, L *centum*: see CENT[1], SATEM) + **rath-*, to count (> Goth *-rathjan*) < IE base **rē-*: see READ[1]⟧ **1** the cardinal number next above ninety-nine; ten times ten; 100; C **2** a former division of an English county: orig., probably, 100 hides of land **3** a similar division in the early U.S., now only in Delaware —*adj.* ten times ten

Hundred Days the period from Napoleon's recapture of power, after his escape from Elba, to his final defeat, roughly March 20 to June 28, 1815

hun·dred·fold (-fōld′) *adj.* ⟦HUNDRED + -FOLD⟧ having a hundred times as much or as many —*adv.* a hundred times as much or as many: with *a* (or, British, *an*) —*n.* a number or an amount a hundred times as great

hun·dredth (hun′drədth) *adj.* ⟦HUNDRED + -TH[2]⟧ **1** preceded by ninety-nine others in a series; 100th **2** designating any of the hundred equal parts of something —*n.* **1** the one following the ninety-ninth **2** any of the hundred equal parts of something; $\frac{1}{100}$ —*adv.* in the hundredth place, rank, group, etc.

hun·dred·weight (hun′drəd wāt′) *n., pl.* **-weight′** or sometimes **-weights′** **1** a unit of weight, equal to 100 pounds avoirdupois (45.3592 kilograms): the British hundredweight equals 112 pounds avoirdupois (50.8023 kilograms) **2** a unit of weight, equal to 100 pounds troy (37.3242 kilograms) Symbol, cwt

Hundred Years' War a series of English-French wars (1337 to 1453), in which England lost all its possessions in France except Calais (lost to France in 1558)

hung (huŋ) *vt., vi. pt. & pp. of* HANG (*alt. pt. & pp. for vt.* 3 & *vi.* 5) —*adj.* [Slang] WELL-HUNG: a somewhat vulgar usage —☆**hung over** [Informal] suffering from a hangover —☆**hung up (on)** [Slang] **1** emotionally disturbed (by); neurotic, repressed, etc. **2** baffled, frustrated, stymied, etc. (by) **3** addicted or committed (to), or obsessed (by)

Hung *abbrev.* **1** Hungarian **2** Hungary

Hun·gar·i·an (huŋ ger′ē ən, hun-) *n.* **1** a person born or living in Hungary **2** the Finno-Ugric language spoken in Hungary; Magyar —*adj.* of Hungary or its people, language, or culture

Hun·ga·ry (huŋ′gə rē) country in SC Europe: 35,919 sq mi (93,030 sq km); cap. Budapest: Hung. name MAGYARORSZÁG

hun·ger (huŋ′gər) *n.* ⟦ME < OE *hungor*, akin to Ger *hunger* < IE base **kenk-*, to burn, dry up > Lith *kankà*, pain⟧ **1** *a)* the discomfort, pain, or weakness caused by a need for food *b)* famine; starvation **2** a desire, need, or appetite for food **3** any strong desire; craving —*vi.* **1** to feel hunger; be hungry; need food **2** to have a strong desire; crave: with *for* or *after* —*vt.* [Rare] to subject to hunger; starve

hunger center a place where food is collected and distributed to the needy

hunger strike a form of protest in which a prisoner or demonstrator refuses to eat until certain demands are met

hung jury ⟦see HANG (*vt.* 11)⟧ a jury that is unable to arrive at a verdict; deadlocked jury

hun·gry (huŋ′grē) *adj.* **-gri·er, -gri·est** ⟦ME < OE *hungrig*⟧ **1** feeling, having, or showing hunger; specif., *a)* wanting or needing food *b)* craving; eager [*hungry* for praise] **2** [Rare] producing hunger **3** not fertile; barren: said of soil —**hun′gri·ly** (-grə lē) *adv.* —**hun′gri·ness** *n.*

hunh (hun) *interj.* [Informal] **1** used to ask a question **2** used to express anger, contempt, etc.: a snorting sound See also HUH

hunk (huŋk) *n.* ⟦Fl *hunke*⟧ [Informal] **1** a large piece, lump, or slice of bread, meat, etc.; chunk **2** a sexually attractive man, esp. one who is large and well-built

hun·ker (huŋ′kər) *vi.* ⟦orig. dial., prob. < or akin to Faroese *hokna*, to crouch < ON *hokra*, to creep < IE **keuk-* (< base **keu-*, to bend) > Sans *čúčim*, to cower⟧ to settle down on one's haunches; squat or crouch: usually with *down* —*n.* [*pl.*] haunches —**hunker down** [Informal] to make preparations, as to defend oneself or take on a difficult task

Hunk·pa·pa (huŋk′pä′pə) *n., pl.* **-pas, -pa** a member of a North American Indian people that is a subgroup of the Tetons

hunks (huŋks) *n., pl.* **hunks** ⟦< ?⟧ [Now Rare] a stingy, disagreeable, surly person

hun·ky[1] (huŋ′kē) *n., pl.* **-kies** ⟦? altered < HUNGARIAN⟧ [*often* **H-**] [Slang] a person from EC Europe or of Hungarian or Slavic extraction: a somewhat offensive term of hostility and contempt: also sp. **hun′kie, hun′key**

hunk·y[2] (huŋ′kē) *adj.* **-i·er, -i·est** [Slang] of, like, or characteristic of a HUNK (sense 2)

☆**hun·ky-do·ry** (huŋ′kē dôr′ē) *adj.* ⟦*hunky* (< U.S. local *hunk*, goal, home, as in the game of tag, hence safe place, all right < Du *honk*, a post, station, goal) + *-dory* < ?⟧ [Slang] all right; fine

Hun·nish (hun′ish) *adj.* **1** of, like, or characteristic of the Huns **2** barbarous; savage and destructive

hunt (hunt) *vt.* ⟦ME *hunten* < OE *huntian*, prob. < base of *hentan*, to seize < ? IE **kend-*, var. of **kent-* > Goth *(fra)hinthan*, to seize: see HAND⟧ **1** to go out to kill or catch (game) for food or sport **2** to search eagerly or carefully for; try to find **3** *a)* to pursue; chase; drive *b)* to hound; harry; persecute **4** *a)* to go through (a woods, fields, etc.) in pursuit of game *b)* to search (a place) carefully **5** to use (dogs or horses) in chasing game —*vi.* **1** to go out after game; take part in the chase **2** to search; seek **3** in bell ringing, to change the order of bells in a HUNT (*n.* 5) —*n.* **1** the act of hunting; the chase **2** a group of people who hunt together **3** a district covered in hunting **4** a search **5** in bell ringing, a series of regularly varying sequences in ringing a group of from five to twelve bells —**hunt down** **1** to pursue until successful in catching or killing **2** to search for until successful in finding —**hunt up** **1** to hunt for; search for **2** to find by searching —**in the hunt** [Informal] having a chance to win a competition

hunt-and-peck (hunt′'n pek′) *n.* [Informal] a method of typing while looking at the keyboard, typically using only the forefingers to press the keys: cf. TOUCH SYSTEM

hunt·er (hunt′ər) ***n.*** ⟦ME *huntere*⟧ **1** a person or animal that hunts **2** a dog trained for hunting **3** a horse trained to carry a rider over open country, as in fox hunting **4** a watch with a hunting case

hunt·er-gath·er·er (-gath′ər ər) ***n.*** *Anthrop.* a member of a culture that supplies its food by hunting game and gathering berries, roots, etc. rather than by raising crops or livestock

hunter green a dark, slightly yellowish, green

hunter's moon the full moon after the harvest moon

hunt·ing (hunt′iŋ) ***n.*** ⟦ME < OE *huntung*⟧ **1** the act of a person or animal that hunts **2** a periodic oscillation of the rotor of a synchronous electrical machine about its average position **3** a periodic oscillation in the controlled function of any feedback control system, as a thermostat, caused by fluctuation in the control system **4** any similar fluctuation, as of a control surface, compass, indicator, etc. —***adj.*** of or for hunting

hunting case ⟦so named from use by fox hunters⟧ a watchcase with a hinged cover to protect the crystal

Hun·ting·don·shire (hunt′iŋ dən shir′) former county of EC England, now part of Cambridgeshire: also **Hun′ting·don**

hunting horn a signaling horn used during a hunt

☆**hunting knife** a large, sharp knife used by hunters to skin and cut up game

Hun·ting·ton (hunt′iŋ tən) **1 Col·lis Potter** (käl′is) 1821-1900; U.S. railroad magnate **2 Samuel** 1731-96; Am. statesman: signer of the Declaration of Independence

Huntington Beach ⟦after H. E. *Huntington* (1850-1927), U.S. financier⟧ city in SW Calif.: suburb of Los Angeles

☆**Huntington's disease** ⟦after G. *Huntington* (1851-1916), U.S. physician⟧ a progressive hereditary chorea, accompanied by increasing mental deterioration: sometimes called **Hun·ting·ton's chorea**

hunt·ress (hun′tris) ***n.*** a woman or girl who hunts

Hunts (hunts) Huntingdonshire

hunts·man (hunts′mən) ***n.***, *pl.* **-men** (-mən) **1** a person, esp. a man, who hunts **2** the manager of a hunt, in charge of the hounds

hunt's-up (hunts up′) ***n.*** ⟦contr. < *the hunt is up* (i.e., the hunt is starting)⟧ a rousing tune played on a hunting horn to get the hunters out

Hunts·ville (hunts′vil) ⟦after J. *Hunt*, its first settler (1805)⟧ city in N Ala.

Hu·nya·di (hoo′nyä dē), **Já·nos** (yä′nôsh) 1387-1456; Hung. general & national hero: also sp. **Hu′nya·dy**

Hu·on pine (hyo͞o′än′) ⟦after the *Huon* River in Tasmania⟧ a large Tasmanian tree (*Dacrydium franklinii*) of the podocarp family, with scalelike leaves and fragrant, soft wood used for furniture

hup (hup) ***interj.*** ⟦prob. alt. of ONE⟧ used to call out a cadence as for marching

Hu·pa (ho͞o′pä′, -pə) ***n.*** ⟦< name for this people in Yurok, the language of a neighboring Indian people⟧ **1** a member of a North American Indian people of NW California **2** the Athabaskan language of this people

Hu·peh or **Hu·pei** (ho͞o′bā′, -pā′) *a former transliteration of* HUBEI

hup·pah (kho͞o′pə, -pä) ***n.*** *alt. sp. of* CHUPPAH

hur·dle (hurd′'l) ***n.*** ⟦ME *hirdel* < OE *hyrdel* < Gmc base **hurd-*, wickerwork, hurdle, akin to *hyrd*, door, Frank **hurda*, a pen, fold < IE base **kert-*, to plait, twist together > L *cratis* (see CRATE), Gr *kyrtos*, bird cage⟧ **1** [Chiefly Brit.] a portable frame made of interlaced twigs, etc., used as a temporary fence or enclosure **2** [Historical] a kind of frame or sled on which prisoners in England were drawn through the streets to execution **3** any of a series of framelike barriers over which horses or runners must leap in a special race (the **hurdles**) **4** a difficulty to be overcome; obstacle —***vt.*** **-dled**, **-dling** **1** to enclose or fence off with hurdles **2** to jump over (a barrier), as in a race **3** to overcome (an obstacle) —**hur′dler** ***n.***

hurdles

hur·dy-gur·dy (hur′dē gur′dē) ***n.***, *pl.* **-gur′dies** ⟦prob. echoic⟧ **1** an early instrument shaped like a lute or viol but played by turning a crank attached to a rosined wheel that causes the strings to vibrate **2** popularly, a barrel organ

hurl (hurl) ***vt.*** ⟦ME *hurlen*, prob. of ON echoic orig. as in Dan *hurle*, to whir, Norw *hurla*, to buzz⟧ **1** to throw or fling with force or violence **2** to cast down; overthrow **3** to utter vehemently [*to hurl insults*] ☆**4** [Informal] *Baseball* to pitch —***vi.*** **1** to throw or fling something **2** to move with force or violence; rush ☆**3** [Informal] *Baseball* to pitch **4** [Slang] to vomit —***n.*** a hurling —**SYN.** THROW —**hurl′er** ***n.***

hurl·ing (hur′liŋ) ***n.*** ⟦< prec.⟧ an Irish game resembling field hockey

hurl·y (hur′lē) ***n.*** ⟦< HURL⟧ [Archaic] uproar; turmoil

hurl·y-burl·y (hur′lē bur′lē) ***n.***, *pl.* **-burl′ies** ⟦prob. extended < prec.⟧ a turmoil; uproar; hubbub; confusion —***adj.*** disorderly and confused

Hu·ron[1] (hyoor′än′, -ən) ***n.***, *pl.* **-rons′** or **-ron′** ⟦Fr *huron*, coarse fellow, ruffian < *hure*, unkempt head⟧ **1** a member of a confederation of North American Indian peoples that lived between Georgian Bay and Lake Ontario, Canada, now living in Oklahoma and Quebec **2** the Iroquoian language of this people

Hu·ron[2] (hyoor′än′, -ən), **Lake** second largest of the Great Lakes, between Mich. & Ontario, Canada: 23,000 sq mi (59,570 sq km)

hur·rah (hə rä′, -rô′) ***interj.*** ⟦ult. of echoic orig.⟧ HURRAY —***n.*** **1** an instance of shouting "hurrah" **2** excitement, tumult, commotion, etc. —***vi., vt.*** to shout "hurrah" (for); cheer

hur·ray (-rā′) ***interj.*** ⟦< prec.⟧ used to express joy, triumph, approval, etc.: a shout used as in cheering —***n.*** an instance of shouting "hurray" —***vi., vt.*** to shout "hurray" (for); cheer

Hur·ri·an (hoor′ē ən) ***n.*** **1** any of an ancient people of N Mesopotamia and E Syria (fl. 1600-1300 B.C.) **2** the extinct non-Indo-European language of the Hurrians —***adj.*** of the Hurrians or their language or culture

hur·ri·cane (hur′ə kān′, -kən) ***n.*** ⟦Sp *huracán* < WInd (Taino) *huracan*⟧ **1** a violent tropical cyclone with winds moving at 74 or more miles per hour, often accompanied by torrential rains, and originating usually in the West Indian region: winds of hurricane force sometimes occur in the absence of a hurricane system: see the Saffir-Simpson Hurricane Damage Potential Scale in the Reference Supplement **2** anything like a hurricane in force and speed

☆**hurricane deck** the upper deck of a passenger ship, esp. of a river steamer

hurricane lamp **1** an oil lamp or candlestick with a tall glass chimney to keep the flame from being blown out **2** an electric lamp in imitation of this

hur·ried (hur′ēd) ***adj.*** done or acting in a hurry; rushed or rushing; hasty —**hur′ried·ly** (-ēd lē, -id-) ***adv.*** —**hur′ried·ness** ***n.***

hur·ry (hur′ē) ***vt.*** **-ried**, **-ry·ing** ⟦prob. < echoic base seen in HURL or ? in ON *hurra*, to whir, whirl around⟧ **1** to cause to move or act more rapidly or too rapidly; drive, move, send, force, or carry with haste **2** to cause to occur or be done more rapidly or too rapidly; accelerate the preparation or completion of; urge on **3** to urge or cause to act soon or too soon —***vi.*** to move or act with haste; move faster than is comfortable or natural —***n.*** **1** a hurrying or being hurried; rush; urgency **2** eagerness to do, act, go, etc. quickly —**SYN.** HASTE —**hurry it up** [Slang] to do or carry out with speed or promptness —**hurry up** [Informal] to act with speed or promptness —**in a hurry** **1** very rapidly; in a rush **2** eager to do, act, etc. [*in a hurry* to graduate and find a job] —**hur′ri·er** ***n.***

hur·ry-scur·ry or **hur·ry-skur·ry** (-skur′ē) ***n.*** ⟦redupl. of prec.⟧ an agitated, confused rushing about; disorderly confusion —***vi.*** **-ried**, **-ry·ing** to hurry and scurry about; act hurriedly and confusedly —***adj.*** hurried and confused —***adv.*** in a hurried, confused manner

hurst (hurst) ***n.*** ⟦ME < OE *hyrst*, hillock, wooded mound, prob. < IE **kurs-to-*, thicket: see HORST⟧ **1** a hillock, knoll, or mound **2** a grove or wooded hillock Now usually in place names [*Sandhurst*]

Hurs·ton (hurs′tən), **Zor·a Neale** (zôr′ə nēl) 1891-1960; U.S. writer

hurt (hurt) ***vt.*** **hurt**, **hurt′ing** ⟦ME *hurten*, to knock, hurt < OFr *hurter*, to push, thrust, hit, prob. < Frank **hurt*, a thrust, blow (as by a ram); akin to ON *hrūtr*, a ram⟧ **1** to cause physical pain or injury to; wound **2** to harm or damage in some way; be bad for **3** to cause mental distress or pain to; wound the feelings of; offend —***vi.*** **1** to cause injury, damage, or pain **2** to give or have the sensation of pain; be sore [*a leg that hurts*] **3** to be a source of inconvenience, difficulty, or trouble —***n.*** **1** the act or an instance of hurting; pain, injury, or wound **2** harm, wrong, or damage **3** something that wounds the feelings —***adj.*** injured; damaged —**SYN.** INJURE

hurt·ful (hurt′fəl) ***adj.*** causing hurt; specif., wounding the feelings [*hurtful remarks*] —**hurt′ful·ly** ***adv.*** —**hurt′ful·ness** ***n.***

hur·tle (hurt′'l) ***vi.*** **-tled**, **-tling** ⟦ME *hurtlen*, freq. of ME *hurten*: see HURT⟧ **1** [Archaic] to dash (*against* or *together*) with great force or crushing impact; collide **2** to move swiftly and with great force —***vt.*** to throw, shoot, or fling with great force; hurl —***n.*** [Old Poet.] the act of hurtling; collision; clash

hur·tle·ber·ry (hurt′'l ber′ē) ***n.***, *pl.* **-ries** ⟦ME *hurtilberye* < OE *horte*, a whortleberry (+ *-il* suffix) + ME *berie*, BERRY⟧ **1** WHORTLEBERRY ☆**2** HUCKLEBERRY

hurt·less (hurt′lis) ***adj.*** **1** causing no hurt; harmless **2** [Archaic] unhurt

Hus (hoos, hus), **Jan** (yän) 1369?-1415; Bohemian religious reformer and martyr, burned as a heretic

hus·band (huz′bənd) ***n.*** ⟦ME *husbonde*, householder, husband < Late OE *husbonda* < ON *hūsbondi*, lit., householder < *hūs*, HOUSE + *bondi*, freeholder, yeoman < earlier *būandi*, prp. of *būa*, to dwell: see BONDAGE⟧ **1** *a)* a man with reference to the person to whom he is married *b)* any married man **2** [Archaic] a manager, as of a household —***vt.*** **1** to manage economically; conserve **2** [Archaic] to provide with a husband or become the husband of; marry **3** [Archaic] to cultivate (soil or plants)

hus·band·man (huz′bənd mən) ***n.***, *pl.* **-men** (-mən) ⟦ME: see prec.⟧ [Archaic] a farmer

hus·band·ry (huz′bən drē) ***n.*** ⟦ME *husbonderie*: see HUSBAND⟧ **1** [Archaic] management of domestic affairs, resources, etc. **2** careful, thrifty management; thrift; frugality **3** the science or art of farming: see ANIMAL HUSBANDRY

hush (hush) ***vt.*** ⟦ME *huschen* < *huscht*, quiet (mistaken as pp.): of echoic orig.⟧ **1** to stop from making noise; make quiet or silent **2** to soothe; calm; lull —***vi.*** to stop making noise; be or become quiet or silent —***adj.*** [Archaic] silent; hushed —***n.*** absence of noise or a cessation of noise; quiet; silence —***interj.*** be silent —**hush up** **1** to keep quiet **2** to keep from being told; suppress the report or discussion of

hush·a·by (hush′ə bī′) ***interj.*** ⟦see prec. & LULLABY⟧ [Archaic] HUSH: a word used to quiet an infant

hush-hush (hush′hush′) ***adj.*** ⟦redupl. of HUSH (***interj.***)⟧ [Informal] very secret; most confidential

Hu Shih (ho͞o′ shē′, shē′) 1891-1962; Chin. diplomat, philosopher, & writer

hush money money paid to a person to keep him or her from telling something

Hush Puppies *trademark for* a kind of shoe with soft leather or suede uppers

☆**hush puppy** ⟦< ?⟧ a small ball of fried cornmeal dough

husk (husk) ***n.*** ⟦ME *huske,* prob. < MDu *huuskijn,* dim. of *huus,* HOUSE⟧ **1** the dry outer covering of various fruits or seeds, as of an ear of corn **2** the dry, rough, or useless outside covering of anything —***vt.*** to remove the husk or husks from —**husk′er** ***n.***

☆**husk·ing (bee)** (hus′kiŋ) CORNHUSKING (sense 2)

☆**husk-to·ma·to** (husk′tə māt′ō) ***n.,*** *pl.* **-toes** GROUND-CHERRY

hus·ky[1] (hus′kē) ***n.,*** *pl.* **-kies** ⟦shortened < a 19th-c. var. of ESKIMO⟧ [*also* **H-**] a dog of any of several breeds for pulling sleds in the Arctic; esp., the SIBERIAN HUSKY

husk·y[2] (hus′kē) ***adj.*** **husk′i·er, husk′i·est** **1** *a)* full of, containing, or consisting of husks *b)* like a husk **2** sounding deep and hoarse; rough [*a husky voice*] ☆**3** ⟦with reference to the toughness of a HUSK⟧ big and strong; robust; burly **4** wide in girth in proportion to height: often used to denote a width of boys' garments —☆***n.,*** *pl.* **husk′ies** [Informal] a husky person —**husk′i·ly** ***adv.*** —**husk′i·ness** ***n.***

Huss (hus, ho͝os), **John** *Eng. name for* Jan HUS

hus·sar (ho͝o zär′, hə-) ***n.*** ⟦Hung *huszár,* orig., highwayman < Serb *husar, gusar* < It *corsaro:* see CORSAIR⟧ **1** a member of the light cavalry of Hungary, formed in the 15th c. **2** a member of any European regiment of light-armed cavalry, usually with brilliant dress uniforms

Hus·sein (ho͞o sān′) **1 Hussein I** 1935-99; king of Jordan (1952-99) **2 Saddam** (sä däm′, sä′däm′) 1937-2006; president of Iraq (1979-2003)

Hus·serl (ho͝os′ərl), **Edmund** 1859-1938; Ger. philosopher

Huss·ite (hus′īt′) ***n.*** a follower of John Huss —***adj.*** of John Huss or his religious beliefs

hus·sy (huz′ē, hus′-) ***n.,*** *pl.* **-sies** ⟦contr. < ME *huswif,* housewife⟧ **1** a woman of low morals **2** an impudent girl or young woman **3** [Dial.] a small sewing kit

hus·tings (hus′tiŋz) ***pl.n.*** ⟦ME *husting* < OE < ON *hūsthing,* lit., house council < *hūs,* a house + *thing,* assembly (see THING[1]): orig., a lord's household assembly as distinct from a general assembly⟧ [*usually with sing. v.*] **1** [Obs.] *a)* a deliberative assembly *b)* a court held in various English cities and still occasionally in London *c)* the platform in London Guildhall where such a court was formerly held *d)* the temporary platform where candidates for Parliament formerly stood for nomination and spoke **2** the proceedings at an election **3** any place where political campaign speeches are made **4** the route followed by a campaigner for political office

hus·tle (hus′əl) ***vt.*** **-tled, -tling** ⟦Du *hutseln, husselen,* to shake up (coins, lots), freq. of MDu *hutsen,* to shake⟧ **1** to push or knock about; shove or jostle in a rude, rough manner **2** to force in a rough, hurried manner [*to hustle a rowdy customer out of a bar*] ☆**3** [Informal] to cause to be done, prepared, sent, etc. quickly or too quickly; hurry ☆**4** [Slang] to get, sell, victimize, etc. by aggressive, often dishonest means —***vi.*** **1** to push one's way; move hurriedly **2** [Informal] to work or act rapidly or energetically ☆**3** [Slang] *a)* to obtain money by aggressive or dishonest means *b)* to work as a prostitute —***n.*** **1** the act of hustling; esp., rough jostling or shoving ☆**2** [Informal] energetic action or effort; drive ☆**3** [Slang] a way of making money, esp. a dishonest way

hus·tler (hus′lər) ***n.*** a person who hustles; specif., *a)* [Slang] one who obtains money dishonestly *b)* [Slang] PROSTITUTE (***n.*** 1)

Hus·ton (hyo͞o′stən, yo͞o′-), **John** 1906-87; U.S. film director

hut (hut) ***n.*** ⟦Fr *hutte* < MHG *hütte* < OHG *hutta:* for IE base see HIDE[1]⟧ a little house or cabin of the plainest or crudest kind — ***vt., vi.*** **hut′ted, hut′ting** to shelter or be sheltered in or as in a hut or huts

hutch (huch) ***n.*** ⟦ME *hucche* < OFr *huche,* bin, kneading trough < ML *hutica,* a chest⟧ **1** a bin, chest, or box for storage ☆**2** a cabinet with open shelves, designed to rest upon a low cupboard, dresser, etc. **3** a pen or coop for small animals [*a rabbit hutch*] **4** a hut **5** a mining trough for washing ore **6** a car or truck for carrying ore out of a mine —***vt.*** to store or put in or as in a hutch

Hutch·ins (huch′inz), **Robert May·nard** (mā′nərd) 1899-1977; U.S. educator

Hutch·in·son (huch′in sən) **1 Anne** (born *Anne Marbury*) 1591?-1643; Am. religious leader, born in England: a founder of Rhode Island **2 Thomas** 1711-80; colonial governor of Mass. (1771-74)

hut·ment (hut′mənt) ***n.*** ⟦HUT + -MENT⟧ a hut or group of huts, as in an army camp

☆**Hut·ter·ite** (hut′ər īt′) ***n.*** ⟦after J. *Hutter,* 16th-c. Austrian religious reformer + -ITE[1]⟧ a member of a Protestant denomination, Anabaptist in origins and originally from Moravia, who live communally in the Dakotas, Montana, and Alberta, Canada, with beliefs and customs much like those of the Mennonites

Hu·tu (ho͞o′to͞o′) ***n.,*** *pl.* **Hu′tus′, Ba·hu′tu′** (bə-), or **Hu′tu′** ⟦< name in a local Bantu language⟧ a member of a Bantu people of Burundi and Rwanda —***adj.*** of the Hutus or their culture

☆**hutz·pah** (ho͝ots′pə, kho͝ots′-; -pä) ***n.*** *alt. sp. of* CHUTZPAH

Hux·ley (huks′lē) **1 Al·dous (Leonard)** (ôl′dəs) 1894-1963; Eng. novelist & essayist, in the U.S. after *c.* 1935 **2** Sir **Andrew Fielding** 1917-2012; Brit. biophysicist: half-brother of Aldous & Julian **3** Sir **Julian (Sorrell)** 1887-1975; Eng. biologist & writer: brother of Aldous **4 Thomas Henry** 1825-95; Eng. biologist & writer: grandfather of Aldous, Julian, & Andrew

Huy·gens or **Huy·ghens** (hī′gənz; *Du* hoi′gəns), **Christian** 1629-95; Du. physicist, mathematician, & astronomer

huz·zah or **huz·za** (hə zä′, -zô′) ***interj., n., vi., vt.*** ⟦echoic⟧ *archaic var. of* HURRAH

HV *abbrev.* high voltage

HVAC *abbrev.* heating, ventilating, and air conditioning

hwan (hwän) ***n.,*** *pl.* **hwan** ⟦Kor⟧ WON[3]

Hwang Hai (hwäŋ′ hī′) *Chin. name for* YELLOW SEA

Hwang Ho (hwäŋ′ hō′) *a former transliteration of* HUANG HE (see HUANG)

hwy *abbrev.* highway

hy·a·cinth (hī′ə sinth′) ***n.*** ⟦L *hyacinthus* < Gr *hyakinthos,* wild hyacinth, bluebell, blue larkspur, hence a blue gem⟧ **1** *a)* among the ancients, a blue gem, probably the sapphire *b)* any of the reddish-orange or brownish varieties of zircon or certain other minerals, used as a semiprecious stone **2** *a)* any of a genus (*Hyacinthus*) of plants of the lily family, with narrow channeled leaves and spikes of fragrant, bell-shaped flowers in white, yellow, red, blue, or purple *b)* the bulb of any of these plants *c)* the flower **3** a bluish purple —**hy′a·cin′thine** (-sin′thin, -thīn′) ***adj.***

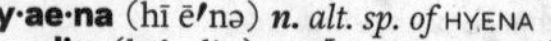

hyacinth (sense 2)

Hy·a·cin·thus (hī′ə sin′thəs) ***n.*** ⟦L < Gr *Hyakinthos,* lit., prec.⟧ *Gr. Myth.* a youth loved and accidentally slain by Apollo, who causes a hyacinth to grow from his blood

Hy·a·des (hī′ə dēz′) ***pl.n.*** ⟦L *Hyades* < Gr⟧ **1** *Gr. Myth.* daughters of Atlas, placed in the sky by Zeus: as stars they were thought to be bringers of rain **2** [*often with sing. v.*] *Astron.* an open cluster of more than 200 stars in the constellation Taurus, whose five brightest members form a V near Aldebaran

hy·ae·na (hī ē′nə) ***n.*** *alt. sp. of* HYENA

hy·a·lin (hī′ə lin) ***n.*** ⟦HYAL(O)- + -IN[1]⟧ any of various glassy translucent substances, esp. such a substance occurring normally in vertebrate cartilage

hy·a·line (hī′ə lin, -lēn′, -līn′) ***adj.*** ⟦LL *hyalinus* < Gr *hyalinos,* glassy < *hyalos,* glass⟧ **1** transparent as glass; glassy **2** of or relating to hyalin —***n.*** anything transparent or glassy, as a smooth sea or clear sky

hyaline membrane disease a respiratory disease of newborn, esp. premature, infants, characterized by an abnormal membrane of protein lining the alveoli of the lungs

hy·a·lite (hī′ə līt′) ***n.*** ⟦< fol. + -ITE[1]⟧ a colorless, transparent or translucent variety of opal

hy·a·lo- (hī′ə lō′, -lə; hī al′ō, -ə) ⟦< Gr *hyalos,* glass⟧ *combining form* glass, glassy, transparent [*hyaloplasm*]: also, before a vowel, **hyal-**

hy·al·o·gen (hī al′ə jən) ***n.*** ⟦prec. + -GEN⟧ any of the various insoluble, mucoidlike substances found in animal tissue and producing hyalins upon hydrolysis

hy·a·loid (hī′ə loid′) ***adj.*** ⟦Gr *hyaloeidēs* < *hyalos,* glass + *eidos,* appearance: see -OID⟧ HYALINE

hyaloid membrane a delicate membrane containing the vitreous humor of the eye

hy·a·lo·plasm (hī′ə lō plaz′əm) ***n.*** ⟦HYALO- + -PLASM⟧ the basic substance of the protoplasm of a cell: it is clear and fluid, as distinguished from the granular and reticulate parts

hy·a·lu·ron·ic acid (hī′ə lo͞o rän′ik) ⟦< HYAL(O)- + Gr *ouron,* URINE + -IC⟧ a highly viscous mucopolysaccharide that holds cells together, lubricates bodily tissue, and blocks the spread of microorganisms: it is found in the skin, the vitreous humor of the eye, and the synovial fluid of the joints

hy·a·lu·ron·i·dase (-rän′i dās′) ***n.*** ⟦< prec. + -ID(E) + -ASE⟧ an enzyme that inactivates hyaluronic acid by breaking down its polymeric structure, thus promoting the diffusion of substances through tissues: found in sperm cells, certain venoms and bacteria, etc.

hy·brid (hī′brid) ***n.*** ⟦L *hybrida,* offspring of mixed parentage⟧ **1** the offspring produced by crossing two individuals of unlike genetic constitution; specif., the offspring of two animals or plants of different races, varieties, species, etc. **2** anything of mixed origin, unlike parts, etc. **3** any automotive vehicle powered by an internal-combustion engine and another power-producing system, that is designed to save fuel; specif., such a vehicle with several large, rechargeable batteries used to help power a computer-controlled electric motor that is activated in specific situations to assist, or substitute for, the main engine **4** *Linguis.* a word made up of elements originally from different languages —***adj.*** of, or having the nature of, a hybrid —**hy′brid·ism′** ***n.,*** **hy·brid′i·ty**

hy·brid·ize (hī′bri dīz′) ***vi., vt.*** **-ized′, -iz′ing** to produce or cause to produce hybrids; crossbreed —**hy′brid·i·za′tion** ***n.*** —**hy′brid·iz′er** ***n.***

hy·brid·o·ma (hī′bri dō′mə) ***n.*** ⟦HYBRID + (MYEL)OMA⟧ a tissue culture consisting of cancer cells fused to lymphocytes to mass-produce a specific antibody

hybrid tea any of a popular group of rose varieties having desirable characteristics, as fragrance, colors, etc.: created by crossing the tea rose with certain hybrid roses

hybrid vigor HETEROSIS

hy·da·thode (hī′də thōd′) ***n.*** ⟦Ger < Gr *hydōr* (gen. *hydatos*), WATER + *ho-*

dos, way: see -ODE[1]⟧ a specialized microscopic pore or stoma on the leaves of many plants, through which water may be excreted

hy·da·tid (-tid′) ***n.*** ⟦Gr *hydatis* (gen. *hydatidos*), watery vesicle < base of *hydōr*, WATER⟧ a cyst containing watery fluid and the larvae of certain tapeworms (esp. genus *Echinococcus*), found in the bodily tissue, esp. the liver, of many animals —***adj.*** of or like such a cyst

Hyde (hīd) **1 Douglas** 1860-1949; Ir. statesman & writer: president of Eire (1938-45) **2 Edward** *see* CLARENDON, 1st Earl of **3 Mr.** *see* JEKYLL[1], Dr.

Hyde Park 1 public park in London, noted for the public discussions on current issues that take place there **2** ⟦after the London park⟧ village in SE N.Y., on the Hudson: site of the estate & burial place of Franklin D. Roosevelt

Hy·der·a·bad (hī′dər ə bad′, -bäd′; hī′drə-) **1** city in SC India: capital of Andhra Pradesh state **2** city in S Pakistan, on the Indus River **3** former state of SC India

hydr- *combining form* HYDRO-: used before a vowel

Hy·dra (hī′drə) ***n.***, *pl.* for 3 & 4 **Hy′dras** ⟦ME *ydre* (< OFr < L), *ydra* < L *Hydra* < Gr, water serpent, akin to *hydōr*, WATER⟧ **1** *Gr. Myth.* the nine-headed serpent slain by Hercules as one of his twelve labors: when any one of its heads is cut off, it is replaced by two others **2** a long S constellation between Cancer and Libra: the largest constellation **3** [**h-**] any persistent or ever-increasing evil with many sources and causes **4** [**h-**] any of a family (Hydridae) of small, freshwater, solitary hydroids having a dominant soft-bodied polyp stage

hy·drac·id (hī dras′id) ***n.*** ⟦HYDR(O)- + ACID⟧ an acid, as hydrochloric acid, that does not contain oxygen

hy·dran·gea (hī drān′jə, -dran′-) ***n.*** ⟦ModL < HYDR(O)- + Gr *angeion*, vessel⟧ any of a genus (*Hydrangea*) of shrubs or vines of the saxifrage family, with opposite leaves and large, showy clusters of blue, white, or pink flowers, often sterile

☆**hy·drant** (hī′drənt) ***n.*** ⟦< Gr *hydōr*, WATER⟧ **1** a large discharge pipe with a valve for drawing water from a water main; specif., a fireplug **2** [Dial.] a faucet

hy·dranth (hī′dranth′) ***n.*** ⟦< HYDR(O)- + Gr *anthos*, a flower: see ANTHO-⟧ *Zool.* any of the feeding individuals (*zooids*) of a hydroid colony

hy·dras·tine (hī dras′tēn′, -tin) ***n.*** ⟦ModL *Hydrastis*, name of the genus of herbs (< Gr *hydōr*, WATER) + -INE[3]⟧ a bitter, crystalline alkaloid, $C_{21}H_{21}NO_6$, extracted from the rootstock of the goldenseal

hy·dras·tis (hī dras′tis) ***n.*** ⟦see prec.⟧ the rhizome and roots of the goldenseal, containing hydrastine: formerly much used in medicine

hy·drate (hī′drāt′) ***n.*** ⟦HYDR(O)- + -ATE[1]⟧ a compound formed by the chemical combination of water and some other substance in a definite molecular ratio [plaster of Paris, $2CaSO_4 \cdot H_2O$, is a *hydrate*] —***vi., vt.* -drat′ed, -drat′ing 1** to become or cause to become a hydrate **2** to combine with water **3** to moisturize (the skin) **4** to drink water or other liquid or administer a liquid to (a patient) in an effort to prevent or treat dehydration —**hy·dra′tion *n.*** —**hy′dra′tor *n.***

hy·drau·lic (hī drô′lik, -drä′-) ***adj.*** ⟦Fr *hydraulique* < L *hydraulicus* < Gr *hydraulikos*, of a water organ (musical instrument played by means of water) < *hydraulis*, water organ < *hydōr*, WATER + *aulos*, tube, pipe < IE base **aulos* > (with metathesis) L *alvus*, the belly⟧ **1** of hydraulics **2** operated by the movement and force of liquid; specif., operated by the pressure created when a liquid is forced through an aperture, tube, etc. [*hydraulic* brakes] **3** setting or hardening under water [*hydraulic* mortar] —**hy·drau′li·cal·ly *adv.***

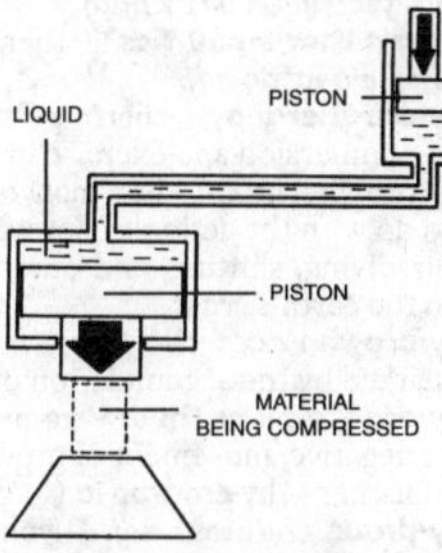

LIQUID
PISTON
PISTON
MATERIAL BEING COMPRESSED

hydraulic press

hydraulic ram a device for delivering a small portion of a flowing liquid to a higher elevation by using the momentum of the flowing liquid as the energy source

hy·drau·lics (hī drô′liks, -drä′-) ***n.*** ⟦formed < HYDRAULIC, as in names of other sciences and areas of study: see -ICS⟧ the branch of physics having to do with the mechanical properties of water and other liquids in motion and with the application of these properties in engineering

hy·dra·zide (hī′drə zīd′) ***n.*** ⟦< fol. + -IDE⟧ any of several derivatives of hydrazine in which at least one of the hydrogens has been replaced by an acyl group

hy·dra·zine (hī′drə zēn′, -zin) ***n.*** ⟦HYDR(O)- + AZINE⟧ a colorless, corrosive, liquid base, H_2NNH_2, used as a jet and rocket fuel, a reducing agent, antioxidant, etc.

hy·dra·zo·ate (hī′drə zō′āt′) ***n.*** any salt of hydrazoic acid

hy·dra·zo·ic acid (-zō′ik) ⟦HYDR(O)- + AZO- + -IC⟧ a colorless, volatile, poisonous acid, NHN:N, used in the manufacture of explosives

hy·dric (hī′drik) ***adj.*** ⟦HYDR(O)- + -IC⟧ of or containing hydrogen

-hy·dric (hī′drik) ⟦see prec.⟧ *combining form* having (a specified number of) hydroxyl radicals or replaceable hydrogen atoms in the molecule [*monohydric*]

hy·dride (hī′drīd′) ***n.*** ⟦HYDR(O)- + -IDE⟧ a binary inorganic compound containing hydrogen

hy·dri·od·ic acid (hī′drē äd′ik) ⟦HYDR(O)- + IODIC⟧ a strong acid that is a water solution of the gas hydrogen iodide, HI

hy·dro[1] (hī′drō) ***n.***, *pl.* **-dros** [Brit. Informal] a place, such as a spa, where people can receive hydropathic treatments

hy·dro[2] (hī′drō) [Cdn.] ***n.*** **1** hydroelectric power **2** *pl.* **-dros** a hydroelectric power plant —***adj.*** hydroelectric

hy·dro- (hī′drō, -drə) ⟦< Gr *hydōr*, WATER⟧ *combining form* **1** water [*hydrostatics, hydrometer*] **2** containing hydrogen [*hydrocyanic* acid]

hy·dro·bro·mic acid (hī′drō brō′mik) ⟦prec. + BROMIC⟧ a strong acid that is a water solution of the gas hydrogen bromide, HBr

hy·dro·car·bon (hī′drə kär′bən, hī′drə kär′bən) ***n.*** any compound containing only hydrogen and carbon, as benzene or methane

hy·dro·cele (hī′drə sēl′) ***n.*** ⟦L < Gr *hydrokēlē* < *hydōr*, WATER + *kēlē*, tumor: see -CELE⟧ a collection of watery fluid in a cavity of the body, esp. in the scrotum or along the spermatic cord

hy·dro·ceph·a·lus (hī′drə sef′ə ləs) ***n.*** ⟦ModL < Gr *hydrokephalon* < *hydōr*, WATER + *kephalē*, head: see CEPHALIC⟧ a condition characterized by an abnormal increase in the amount of fluid in the cranium, esp. in young children, causing enlargement of the head and deterioration of the brain: also **hy′dro·ceph′a·ly** (-lē) —**hy′dro·ce·phal′ic** (-sə fal′ik) ***adj., n.*** —**hy′dro·ceph′a·lous** (-ləs) ***adj.***

hy·dro·chlo·ric acid (hī′drə klôr′ik) ⟦< HYDRO- + CHLORIC⟧ a strong, highly corrosive acid that is a water solution of the gas hydrogen chloride, HCl: it is widely used in ore processing, for cleaning metals, as a reagent, etc.

hy·dro·chlo·ride (-klôr′īd′) ***n.*** ⟦HYDRO- + CHLORIDE⟧ a compound, such as amidol, of hydrochloric acid and an organic base

hy·dro·chlor·o·fluor·o·car·bon (hī′drə klôr′ō flôr′ə kär′bən, -floor′-) ***n.*** any of various inert compounds containing carbon, fluorine, hydrogen, and chlorine: used as a propellant, refrigerant, etc. and considered less damaging to the atmosphere than chlorofluorocarbons

hy·dro·col·loid (-käl′oid′) ***n.*** any of several substances, as gum arabic or agar, that form gels with water and are mostly used to thicken or smooth food products

☆**hy·dro·cor·ti·sone** (-kôrt′ə sōn′, -zōn′) ***n.*** the principal carbohydrate-regulating corticosteroid, $C_{21}H_{30}O_5$, in humans, with effects similar to those of cortisone

hy·dro·crack·ing (hī′drə krak′iŋ) ***n.*** ⟦HYDRO- (sense 2) + CRACKING[2]⟧ a modern, highly efficient petroleum cracking process designed to maximize the production of auto and jet fuels: under great pressure, but at a relatively low temperature, heavy hydrocarbons combine with hydrogen and solid catalysts to produce saturated light distillates, gasoline, etc. —**hy′dro·crack′ *vt.*** —**hy′dro·crack′er *n.***

hy·dro·cy·an·ic acid (hī′drō sī an′ik) a weak, highly poisonous acid, HCN, that is a colorless liquid with the odor of bitter almonds: it is used as a fumigant, as a poison gas, in metallurgy, etc.

hy·dro·dy·nam·ic (hī′drō dī nam′ik) ***adj.*** **1** having to do with hydrodynamics **2** of, derived from, or operated by, the action of fluids in motion —**hy′dro′dy·nam′i·cal·ly *adv.***

hy·dro·dy·nam·ics (-dī nam′iks) ***n.*** the branch of physics having to do with the motion and action of fluids

hy·dro·e·lec·tric (hī′drō ē lek′trik) ***adj.*** producing, or having to do with the production of, electricity by water power —**hy′dro·e·lec′tric′i·ty *n.***

hy·dro·fluor·ic acid (-flôr′ik, -floor′ik) ⟦HYDRO- + FLUOR(INE) + -IC⟧ a strong, fuming acid that is a water solution of the gas, or liquid, hydrogen fluoride (H_6F_6, H_4F_4, H_2F_2, or HF, depending on the temperature): it reacts with silicates and is used in etching glass

hy·dro·fluo·ro·car·bon (-flôr′ə kär′bən, -floor′-) ***n.*** ⟦HYDRO- + FLUOROCARBON⟧ a halocarbon containing hydrogen, fluorine, and carbon: used as an alternative to chlorofluorocarbons as being less harmful to the atmosphere

hy·dro·foil (hī′drə foil′) ***n.*** ⟦HYDRO- + (AIR)FOIL⟧ **1** any of the winglike structures attached to the hull of some watercraft: at certain speeds the hull lifts clear of the water and the craft skims along on the hydrofoils **2** a craft with hydrofoils

hy·dro·form·ing (-fôrm′iŋ) ***n.*** a process for converting alkenes of low octane numbers into high-octane fuels by applying temperatures and pressures in the presence of hydrogen and a catalyst

hy·dro·gas·i·fi·ca·tion (hī′drō gas′i fi kā′shən) ***n.*** a high-temperature, high-pressure process for producing liquid or gaseous fuels from fine particles of coal and hydrogen gas

hy·dro·gen (hī′drə jən) ***n.*** ⟦Fr *hydrogène* (see HYDRO- & -GEN): coined (1787) by L. B. Guyton de Morveau (1737-1816), Fr chemist, in reference to the generation of water from the combustion of hydrogen⟧ a flammable, colorless, odorless, gaseous chemical element, the lightest of all known substances: symbol, H; at. no. 1: see the periodic table of elements in the Reference Supplement —**hy·drog·e·nous** (hī dräj′ə nəs) ***adj.***

hy·drog·e·nate (hī dräj′ə nāt′, hī′drə jə-) ***vt.* -nat′ed, -nat′ing** to combine with, treat with, or expose to the action of, hydrogen; specif., to produce a saturated fat or trans fat by treating (an unsaturated fat) with hydrogen —**hy·drog′e·na′tion *n.***

☆**hydrogen bomb** an extremely destructive nuclear bomb in which an initial atomic bomb explosion creates the necessary intense heat and pressure to start a nuclear fusion explosion of the heavy isotopes of hydrogen (deuterium and tritium); H-bomb

hydrogen bond a weak chemical bond formed through a hydrogen atom, esp. if bridging two similar electronegative atoms or groups from two different molecules

hydrogen ion 1 the positively charged nucleus of hydrogen, H^+, without its electron 2 HYDRONIUM ION

hy·drog·e·nize (hī'dräj'ə nīz', hī'drə jə-) *vt.* **-nized', -niz'ing** HYDROGENATE

hydrogen peroxide a colorless, syrupy liquid, H_2O_2, often used in dilute, unstable solutions as a bleaching or disinfecting agent, and in more concentrated form as a rocket fuel, in the production of foam rubber, etc.

hydrogen sulfide a flammable, poisonous gas, H_2S, with the characteristic odor of rotten eggs, widely used as a reagent in analytical chemistry

hy·dro·ge·ol·o·gy (hī'drō jē äl'ə jē) *n.* a branch of hydrology dealing with underground water and related surface water —**hy'dro·ge'o·log'i·cal** (-ə läj'i kəl) *adj.* —**hy'dro·ge·ol'o·gist** (-jist) *n.*

hy·drog·ra·phy (hī dräg'rə fē) *n.* ⟦Fr *hydrographie*: see HYDRO- & -GRAPHY⟧ 1 the study, description, and mapping of oceans, lakes, and rivers, esp. with reference to their navigational and commercial uses 2 the oceans, lakes, rivers, etc. of a region, esp. as dealt with on a map or in a survey, treatise, etc. —**hy·drog'ra·pher** *n.* —**hy·dro·graph·ic** (hī'drō graf'ik) *adj.*, **hy'dro·graph'i·cal**

hy·droid (hī'droid') *adj.* ⟦HYDR(A) + -OID⟧ 1 like a hydra or polyp 2 of or related to an order (Hydroida) of hydrozoans, including the hydras and many colonial marine species —*n.* any hydroid hydrozoan

hy·dro·ki·net·ic (hī'drō ki net'ik) *adj.* of the motions of fluids or the forces producing or influencing such motions —**hy'dro·ki·net'i·cal·ly** *adv.*

hy·dro·ki·net·ics (-iks) *n.* the branch of physics having to do with fluids in motion

hy·dro·lase (hī'drō lās', -lāz') *n.* any of a class of enzymes that act as catalysts in chemical reactions involving hydrolysis

hydrologic cycle WATER CYCLE

hy·drol·o·gy (hī dräl'ə jē) *n.* ⟦ModL *hydrologia*: see HYDRO- & -LOGY⟧ the science dealing with the waters of the earth, their distribution on the surface and underground, and the cycle involving evaporation, precipitation, flow to the seas, etc. —**hy·dro·log·ic** (hī'drə läj'ik) *adj.*, **hy'dro·log'i·cal** —**hy·drol'o·gist** *n.*

hy·drol·y·sate (hī dräl'ə sāt', -zāt') *n.* a product resulting from hydrolysis: also **hy·drol'y·zate'** (-zāt')

hy·drol·y·sis (hī dräl'ə sis) *n., pl.* **-ses'** (-sēz') ⟦HYDRO- + -LYSIS⟧ a chemical reaction in which a substance reacts with water so as to be changed into one or more other substances, as a starch into glucose, natural fats into glycerol and fatty acids, or a salt into a weak acid or a weak base —**hy·dro·lyt·ic** (hī'drō lit'ik) *adj.*

hy·dro·lyte (hī'drə līt') *n.* any substance undergoing hydrolysis

hy·dro·lyze (-līz') *vt., vi.* **-lyzed', -lyz'ing** to undergo or cause to undergo hydrolysis —**hy'dro·lyz'a·ble** *adj.*

hy·dro·mag·net·ics (hī'drō mag net'iks) *n.* MAGNETOHYDRODYNAMICS —**hy'dro·mag·net'ic** *adj.*

hy·dro·man·cy (hī'drō man'sē) *n.* ⟦ME *idromancie* < OFr *ydromancie* < L *hydromantia* < Gr *hydromanteia*: see HYDRO- & -MANCY⟧ divination by the observation of water —**hy'dro·man'cer** (-sər) *n.*

hy·dro·me·chan·ics (hī'drō mə kan'iks) *n.* the branch of physics having to do with the laws governing the motion and equilibrium of fluids —**hy'dro·me·chan'i·cal** *adj.*

hy·dro·me·du·sa (-mə dōō'sə, -dyōō'-; -zə) *n., pl.* **-sae** (-sē) ⟦ModL: see HYDRO- & MEDUSA⟧ a jellyfish (*medusa*) formed from a bud produced asexually on a hydroid

hy·dro·mel (hī'drə mel') *n.* ⟦ME *ydromel* (prob. via OFr *ydromelle*) < L *hydromeli* < Gr < *hydōr*, WATER + *meli*, honey: see MILDEW⟧ a mixture of honey and water that becomes mead when fermented

hy·dro·met·al·lur·gy (hī'drō met''l ur'jē) *n.* the recovery of metals from ores by a liquid process, as by leaching the ore with an acid

hy·dro·me·te·or (-mēt'ē ər) *n.* any type of condensation or frost formed from atmospheric water vapor, as rain, snow, fog, dew, etc.: opposed to LITHOMETEOR

hy·drom·e·ter (hī dräm'ət ər) *n.* ⟦HYDRO- + -METER⟧ an instrument for measuring the specific gravity of liquids: it is a graduated, weighted tube that sinks in a liquid up to the point determined by the density of that liquid —**hy·dro·met·ric** (hī'drō me'trik, -drə-) *adj.*, **hy'dro·met'ri·cal** —**hy·drom'e·try** *n.*

hy·dro·mor·phic (hī'drə môr'fik) *adj. Bot.* having properties of structure adapted to growth wholly or partially in water

hy·dron·ic (hī drän'ik) *adj.* of or having to do with a system of heating or cooling by means of the forced circulation of liquids or vapors through a set of pipes

hy·dro·ni·um ion (hī drō'nē əm) ⟦HYDR(O)- + -ONIUM⟧ the positively charged ion H_3O^+ of any acid in a water solution

hy·drop·a·thy (hī dräp'ə thē) *n.* ⟦HYDRO- + -PATHY⟧ a method of treatment that attempts to cure all illnesses by the use of water, including saunas, enemas, the consumption of mineral water, and various forms of HYDROTHERAPY (sense 2) —**hy·dro·path·ic** (hī'drə path'ik) *adj.* —**hy·drop'a·thist** *n.*

hy·dro·phane (hī'drə fān') *n.* ⟦HYDRO- + -PHANE⟧ an opaque variety of opal that becomes translucent or transparent when wet —**hy·droph·a·nous** (hī dräf'ə nəs) *adj.*

hy·dro·phil·ic (hī'drə fil'ik) *adj.* ⟦HYDRO- + -PHIL(IA) + -IC⟧ capable of uniting with or taking up water: also **hy'dro·phile'** (-fīl')

hy·droph·i·lous (hī dräf'ə ləs) *adj.* ⟦HYDRO- + -PHILOUS⟧ 1 HYDROPHYTIC 2 requiring the presence of water for fertilization

hy·dro·pho·bi·a (hī'drə fō'bē ə) *n.* ⟦LL < Gr *hydrophobia*: see HYDRO- & -PHOBIA⟧ 1 an abnormal fear of water 2 ⟦from the symptomatic inability to swallow liquids⟧ *old-fashioned term for* RABIES

hy·dro·pho·bic (-fō'bik) *adj.* 1 of or having hydrophobia 2 not capable of uniting with or absorbing water Also **hy'dro·phobe'** (-fōb')

hy·dro·phone (hī'drə fōn') *n.* ⟦HYDRO- + -PHONE⟧ an instrument for detecting, and registering the distance and direction of, sound transmitted through water

hy·dro·phyte (-fīt') *n.* ⟦HYDRO- + -PHYTE⟧ any plant growing only in water or very wet earth —**hy'dro·phyt'ic** (-fit'ik) *adj.*

☆**hy·dro·plane** (hī'drə plān') *n.* ⟦HYDRO- + PLANE[4]⟧ 1 a small, light motorboat with a flat bottom rising in steps to the stern so that it can skim along the water's surface at high speeds 2 SEAPLANE 3 an attachment for an airplane that enables it to glide along on the water 4 a horizontal rudder used to submerge or raise a submarine —*vi.* **-planed', -plan'ing** 1 to drive or ride in a hydroplane 2 to skim along on a film of liquid without touching the surface beneath, as vehicle tires on a wet road

☆**hy·dro·pon·ics** (hī'drə pän'iks) *n.* ⟦HYDRO- + (GEO)PON(IC) + -ICS⟧ 1 the science of growing plants in nutrient-rich solutions or moist inert material, instead of in soil 2 cultivation of plants using this method —**hy'dro·pon'ic** *adj.* —**hy'dro·pon'i·cal·ly** *adv.* —**hy'dro·pon'i·cist** (-ə sist) *n.*, **hy·drop·o·nist** (hī dräp'ə nist)

hy·dro·pow·er (hī'drō pou'ər, -drə-) *n.* hydroelectric power

hy·drops (hī'dräps') *n.* ⟦< Gr *hydrōps*: see DROPSY⟧ accumulation of fluid within an organ or tissue —**hy·drop'ic** *adj.*

hy·dro·qui·none (hī'drō kwi nōn', -kwin'ōn') *n.* ⟦HYDRO- + QUINONE⟧ a white, crystalline substance, $C_6H_4(OH)_2$, used in photographic developers, dyes, paints, etc. and in medicine to remove pigmentation from the skin: also **hy'dro·quin'ol** (-kwin'ôl, -ōl)

hy·dro·scope (hī'drə skōp') *n.* ⟦HYDRO- + -SCOPE⟧ a device like a periscope, for viewing things at some distance below the surface of water

hy·dro·ski (hī'drə skē') *n.* an elongated planing surface, similar to a snow ski, allowing an aircraft to take off or land on water, snow, etc.

hy·dro·sol (hī'drə sôl', -säl', -sōl') *n.* ⟦HYDRO- + SOL(UTION)⟧ a DISPERSE SYSTEM in which water is the disperse medium

hy·dro·space (hī'drə spās') *n.* the ocean waters and ocean depths of the earth, esp. as a realm to be explored and investigated scientifically; inner space

hy·dro·sphere (hī'drə sfir') *n.* ⟦HYDRO- + -SPHERE⟧ all the water on the surface of the earth, including oceans, lakes, glaciers, etc.: water vapor, clouds, etc. may be considered part of the atmosphere or of the hydrosphere

hy·dro·stat·ics (hī'drə stat'iks) *n.* ⟦< Fr *hydrostatique* < ModL *hydrostaticus*: see HYDRO- & STATIC⟧ the branch of physics having to do with the pressure and equilibrium of water and other liquids; statics of liquids —**hy'dro·stat'ic** *adj.*, **hy'dro·stat'i·cal** —**hy'dro·stat'i·cal·ly** *adv.*

hy·dro·sul·fide (-sul'fīd') *n.* MERCAPTAN

hy·dro·tax·is (hī'drō tak'sis) *n.* ⟦HYDRO- + -TAXIS⟧ the positive (or negative) response of a freely moving organism to (or away from) water —**hy'dro·tac'tic** (-tak'tik) *adj.*

hy·dro·ther·a·peu·tics (-ther'ə pyōōt'iks) *n.* HYDROTHERAPY —**hy'dro·ther'a·peu'tic** *adj.*

hy·dro·ther·a·py (-ther'ə pē) *n.* 1 HYDROPATHY 2 physical therapy involving immersion and exercise in water, as in a pool or whirlpool

hy·dro·ther·mal (-thur'məl) *adj.* having to do with hot water; esp., having to do with the action of hot water in producing minerals and springs or in dissolving, shifting, and otherwise changing the distribution of minerals in the earth's crust

hy·dro·tho·rax (-thôr'aks') *n.* ⟦ModL: see HYDRO- & THORAX⟧ a condition marked by the accumulation of watery fluid in the pleural cavity

hy·drot·ro·pism (hī drä'trə piz'əm) *n.* ⟦HYDRO- + -TROPISM⟧ the positive, or negative, movement or growth, as of a plant root, toward, or away from, moisture —**hy·dro·trop·ic** (hī'drə träp'ik) *adj.*

hy·drous (hī'drəs) *adj.* ⟦HYDR(O)- + -OUS⟧ containing water, esp. water of crystallization or hydration: said as of certain minerals and chemical compounds

hy·drox·ide (hī dräk'sīd') *n.* ⟦HYDR(O)- + OXIDE⟧ a compound consisting of an element or radical combined with the hydroxyl radical

hydroxide ion the negatively charged ion OH^- of any base in a water solution

hy·drox·y (hī dräk'sē) *adj.* containing or related to hydroxyl

hy·drox·y- (hī dräk'sē, -sə) *combining form* hydroxyl [*hydroxybutyric* acid]: also, before a vowel, **hydrox-**

hydroxy acid an organic acid, as lactic acid, in which both the hydroxyl and carboxyl radicals occur

hy·drox·y·bu·tyr·ic acid (hī dräk'sē byōō tir'ik, -dräk'sə-) any of three isomeric acids, $CH_3CH(OH)CH_2COOH$: the beta isomer is found in the urine of diabetics

hy·drox·y·ke·tone (-kē'tōn') *n.* a ketone containing the hydroxyl radical

hy·drox·yl (hī dräk'səl) *n.* ⟦HYDR(O)- + OX(YGEN) + -YL⟧ the monovalent radical OH, present in all hydroxides —**hy'drox·yl'ic** (-sil'ik) *adj.*

hy·drox·yl·a·mine (hī dräk'səl ə mēn') *n.* ⟦prec. + AMINE⟧ a colorless, crystalline base, NH_2OH, used as a reducing agent

hy·drox·yl·ate (hī dräk'sə lāt') *vt.* **-at'ed, -at'ing** to introduce the hydroxyl group into (a compound) —**hy·drox'yl·a'tion** *n.*

hydroxyl ion HYDROXIDE ION

hy·drox·y·pro·line (hī dräk′sə prō′lēn′, -lin) ***n.*** a nonessential amino acid, HOC_4H_7NCOOH, found in connective tissue, esp. collagens

hy·dro·zo·an (hī′drə zō′ən) ***adj.*** ⟦< ModL *Hydrozoa* < HYDRA + ZO- + -AN⟧ of a class (Hydrozoa) of cnidarians having a saclike body consisting of two layers of cells, and a mouth that opens directly into the body cavity —***n.*** any animal of this class, as a hydroid or Portuguese man-of-war

Hy·drus (hī′drəs) ***n.*** ⟦L < Gr *hydros*, water snake, akin to *hydōr*, WATER⟧ a S constellation near the celestial pole

hy·e·na (hī ē′nə) ***n.*** ⟦L *hyaena* < Gr *hyaina*, hyena, lit., sow (so called from its hoglike mane) < *hys*, a hog (+ *-aina*, fem. suffix) < IE base **sū-*, hog > SWINE⟧ any of various wolflike carnivores (family Hyaenidae) of Africa and Asia, with powerful jaws, a bristly mane, short hind legs, and a characteristic shrill cry suggestive of laughter: hyenas are hunters and scavengers

hy·e·to- (hī′ə tō, -tə) ⟦< Gr *hyetos*, rain < *hyein*, to rain < IE base **seu-*, juice, moisture, rain > L *sugere*, SUCK⟧ *combining form* rain, rainfall [*hyetograph*]: also, before a vowel, **hyet-**

hy·e·to·graph (hī′ə tə graf′) ***n.*** ⟦prec. + -GRAPH⟧ a chart showing the distribution of rainfall over a particular period of time or a particular area

hy·e·tog·ra·phy (hī′ə täg′rə fē) ***n.*** ⟦HYETO- + -GRAPHY⟧ the branch of meteorology having to do with the geographical distribution and annual variation of rainfall —**hy·e·to·graph·ic** (hī′ə tə graf′ik) ***adj.*, hy′e·to·graph′i·cal**

Hy·ge·ia (hī jē′ə) ***n.*** ⟦L *Hygea* < Gr *Hygeia*, *Hygieia* < *hygiēs*: see fol.⟧ *Gr. Myth.* the goddess of health

hy·giene (hī′jēn′) ***n.*** ⟦Fr *hygiène* < Gr *hygieinē* (*technē*), (art) of health < *hygiēs*, healthy, sound < IE **su-gwiyēs*, living well < base **su-*, well (> Sans *su-*, well) + base **gwei-*, to live > Gr *bios*, life, L *vivus*, living⟧ **1** the science of health and its maintenance; system of principles for the preservation of health and prevention of disease **2** sanitary practices; cleanliness [*personal hygiene*]

hy·gien·ic (hī jen′ik, -jē′nik; *occas.* hī′jē en′ik) ***adj.*** **1** of hygiene or health **2** promoting health; healthful; sanitary —**hy′gien′i·cal·ly** ***adv.***

hy·gien·ics (-iks) ***n.*** ⟦formed < prec., as in names of other sciences and areas of study: see -ICS⟧ the science of health; hygiene

hy·gien·ist (hī jē′nist, -jen′ist) ***n.*** **1** an expert in hygiene **2** *short for* DENTAL HYGIENIST

hy·gro- (hī′grō, -grə) ⟦< Gr *hygros*, wet, moist: see HUMOR⟧ *combining form* wet, moisture [*hygrometer*]: also, before a vowel, **hygr-**

hy·gro·graph (hī′grō graf′, -grə-) ***n.*** a hygrometer for continuously recording atmospheric humidity

hy·grom·e·ter (hī gräm′ət ər) ***n.*** ⟦Fr *hygromètre*: see HYGRO- & -METER⟧ any of various instruments for measuring the absolute or relative amount of moisture in the air —**hy·gro·met·ric** (hī′grō me′trik, -grə-) ***adj.*** —**hy·grom′e·try** (-trē) ***n.***

hy·gro·phyte (hī′grō fīt′, -grə-) ***n.*** ⟦HYGRO- + -PHYTE⟧ HYDROPHYTE

hy·gro·scop·ic (hī′grō skäp′ik, -grə-) ***adj.*** ⟦< *hygroscope*, early instrument for detecting change in humidity (< HYGRO- + -SCOPE) + -IC⟧ **1** attracting or absorbing moisture from the air **2** changed or altered by the absorption of moisture Cf. DELIQUESCE (sense 3) —**hy′gro·scop′i·cal·ly** ***adv.*** —**hy′gro·sco·pic′i·ty** (-skō pis′ə tē, -skə-) ***n.***

hy·gro·ther·mo·graph (-thur′mə graf′) ***n.*** ⟦HYGRO- + THERMOGRAPH⟧ an instrument that measures and records atmospheric humidity and temperature on the same graph

hy·ing (hī′iŋ) ***vi.*, *vt.*** *alt. prp. of* HIE

Hyk·sos (hik′sōs, -säs) ***pl.n.*** ⟦Gr *Hyksōs* < Egypt *Hiq shasu*, chief of the nomadic tribes⟧ foreign (prob. Semitic) kings of Egypt (*c.* 1700-*c.* 1550 B.C.), traditionally considered to have formed the XVth & XVIth dynasties

hy·la (hī′lə) ***n.*** ⟦ModL < Gr *hylē*, wood⟧ any of a large genus (*Hyla*) of tree frogs, as the spring peeper

hy·lo- (hī′lō, -lə) ⟦< Gr *hylē*, wood, matter⟧ *combining form* **1** wood [*hylophagous*] **2** matter, substance [*hylozoism*] Also, before a vowel, **hyl-**

hy·loph·a·gous (hī läf′ə gəs) ***adj.*** ⟦prec. + -PHAGOUS⟧ feeding on wood, as some insects do

hy·lo·zo·ism (hī′lō zō′iz′əm, -lə-) ***n.*** ⟦< HYLO- + Gr *zōē*, life (see BIO-) + -ISM⟧ the doctrine that all matter has life, or that life is inseparable from matter —**hy′lo·zo′ist** ***n.*** —**hy′lo·zo·is′tic** ***adj.***

hy·men (hī′mən) ***n.*** ⟦Gr *hymēn*, membrane < IE **syumen-*, ligature < base **siw-* > SEW⟧ the thin mucous membrane that closes part or sometimes all of the opening of the vagina; maidenhead: an intact hymen is traditionally associated with virginity —**hy′men·al** ***adj.***

Hy·men (hī′mən) ***n.*** ⟦L < Gr *Hymēn*: see prec.⟧ **1** *Gr. Myth.* the god of marriage **2** [**h-**] [Old Poet.] a wedding song or poem

hy·me·ne·al (hī′mə nē′əl) ***adj.*** ⟦< L *hymenaeus* < Gr *hymenaios* (see prec.) + -AL⟧ [Literary] of marriage —***n.*** [Old Poet.] **1** a wedding song **2** [*pl.*] a marriage

hy·me·ni·um (hī mē′nē əm) ***n.*, *pl.*** **-ni·a** (-ə) or **-ni·ums** ⟦ModL: see HYMEN & -IUM⟧ a superficial layer of spore-producing cells in fungi —**hy·me′ni·al** ***adj.***

hy·me·nop·ter·an (hī′mə näp′tər ən) ***n.*** ⟦< ModL < Gr *hymenopteros*, membrane-winged < *hymēn*, membrane (see HYMEN) + *pteron*, a wing (see PTERO-) + -AN⟧ any of a large, highly specialized order (Hymenoptera) of insects, including wasps, bees, and ants, having complete metamorphosis and often living in social colonies: the insect has a biting or sucking mouth and, when winged, four membranous wings —***adj.*** of or belonging to the hymenopterans: also **hy′me·nop′ter·ous**

Hy·met·tus (hī met′əs) mountain range in EC Greece, near Athens: highest peak, 3,367 ft (1,026 m)

hymn (him) ***n.*** ⟦ME *ymen* < OE *ymen* & OFr *ymne*, both < LL (Ec) *hymnus* < Gr *hymnos*, a hymn, festive song, ode⟧ **1** a song in praise or honor of God, a god, or gods **2** any song of praise or glorification —***vt.*** to express or praise in a hymn —***vi.*** to sing a hymn

hym·nal (him′nəl) ***n.*** ⟦ME *hymnale* < ML < L *hymnus*⟧ a collection of religious hymns: also **hymn′book′** or **hym′na·ry** (-nə rē) *pl.* **-ries** —***adj.*** of hymns

hym·nist (him′nist) ***n.*** a composer of hymns

hym·no·dy (him′nə dē) ***n.*** ⟦ML *hymnodia* < Gr *hymnoidia*: see HYMN & ODE⟧ **1** the singing of hymns **2** hymns collectively **3** HYMNOLOGY (senses 1 & 2) —**hym′no·dist** ***n.***

hym·nol·o·gy (him näl′ə jē) ***n.*** ⟦ML *hymnologia*, praise in song < Gr: see HYMN & -LOGY⟧ **1** the study of hymns, their history, use, etc. **2** the writing or composition of hymns **3** HYMNODY (sense 2) —**hym·nol′o·gist** ***n.***

hy·oid (hī′oid′) ***adj.*** ⟦Fr *hyoïde* < ModL *hyoides* < Gr *hyoeidēs*, shaped like the letter υ (upsilon) < *hy*, upsilon + *-eidēs*, -OID⟧ designating or of a bone or bones supporting the tongue at its base: U-shaped in humans —***n.*** the hyoid bone or bones

hy·o·scine (hī′ə sēn′, -sin) ***n.*** ⟦< L *hyoscyamus* (see fol.) + -INE[3]⟧ SCOPOLAMINE

hy·os·cy·a·mine (hī′ə sī′ə mēn′, -min) ***n.*** ⟦< L *hyoscyamus*, henbane (< Gr *hyoskyamos* < *hys*, pig (see HYENA) + *kyamos*, bean) + -INE[3]⟧ a colorless, crystalline, very poisonous alkaloid, $C_{17}H_{23}NO_3$, obtained from henbane and other plants of the nightshade family: it is used in medicine as a sedative, antispasmodic, etc.

hyp *abbrev.* **1** hypothesis **2** hypothetical

hyp- (hip, hīp) *prefix* HYPO-: used before a vowel

hyp·a·byss·al (hip′ə bis′əl) ***adj.*** ⟦HYP(O)- + ABYSSAL⟧ *Geol.* designating or of igneous rocks solidified at moderate depths, generally as sills or dikes

hy·pae·thral (hi pē′thrəl, hī-) ***adj.*** ⟦< L *hypaethrus*, uncovered, in the open air (< Gr *hypaithros* < *hypo-*, HYPO- + *aithēr*, ether, clear sky: see ETHER) + -AL⟧ open to the sky; roofless: said of classical buildings and courts

hy·pan·thi·um (hi pan′thē əm, hī-) ***n.*, *pl.*** **-thi·a** (-ə) ⟦ModL: see HYPO- & ANTHO- & -IUM⟧ an enlarged cup or rim of tissue in flowers, as of the rose family, which supports the sepals, petals, and stamens —**hy·pan′thi·al** ***adj.***

☆**hype[1]** (hīp) [Slang] ***n.*** **1** *short for* HYPODERMIC **2** a drug addict —***vt.*** **hyped, hyp′ing** to stimulate or enliven by or as by the injection of a drug: usually in pp. with *up* [a *hyped*-up fanatic]

hype[2] (hīp) [Informal] ***n.*** ⟦< ? HYPERBOLE, infl. by verb sense of prec.⟧ **1** deception or fraud **2** extravagant or excessive promotion —***vt.*** **hyped, hyp′ing 1** to deceive or con **2** to promote in a sensational way

hy·per (hī′pər) ***adj.*** ⟦shortened < HYPERACTIVE⟧ [Informal] high-strung; keyed up

hy·per- (hī′pər) ⟦Gr *hyper-* < *hyper*, over, above, concerning: see SUPER[2]⟧ *prefix* **1** over, above, more than the normal, excessive [*hypercritical, hyperopia*] **2** existing in a space of four or more dimensions [*hyperplane*] **3** *Chem. former term for* PER- [*hyperoxide*]

hy·per·a·cid·i·ty (hī′pər ə sid′ə tē) ***n.*** excessive acidity, as of the gastric juice —**hy′per·ac′id** (-as′id) ***adj.***

hy·per·ac·tive (hī′pər ak′tiv) ***adj.*** **1** extremely, esp. abnormally, active **2** designating or having a condition characterized by excessive activity and excitability, esp. in children: cf. ATTENTION DEFICIT (HYPERACTIVITY) DISORDER —**hy′per·ac·tiv′i·ty** (-ak tiv′ə tē) ***n.***

hy·per·bar·ic (-bar′ik) ***adj.*** ⟦HYPER- + BARIC⟧ **1** of or having a pressure or specific gravity greater than that within the bodily tissues or fluids **2** designating or of a pressurized, usually oxygenated chamber, used in the treatment of various diseases and conditions

hy·per·bo·la (hī pur′bə lə) ***n.*, *pl.*** **-las** or **-lae′** (-lē) ⟦ModL < Gr *hyperbolē*, a throwing beyond, excess < *hyperballein*, to throw beyond < *hyper-* (see HYPER-) + *ballein*, to throw (see BALL[1])⟧ *Geom.* the path of a point that moves so that the difference of its distances from two fixed points, the foci, is constant; curve formed by the section of a cone cut by a plane more steeply inclined than the side of the cone

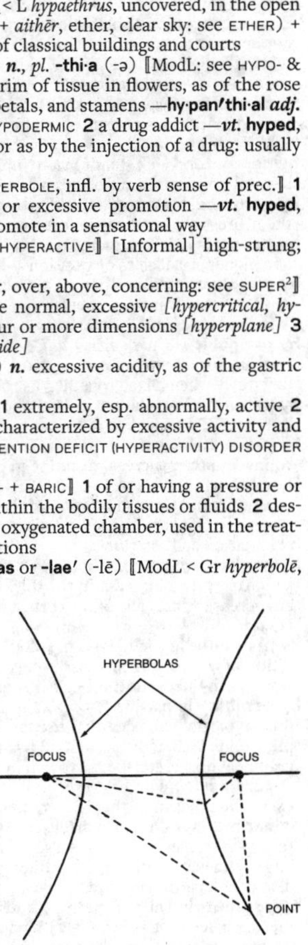

HYPERBOLAS
FOCUS
FOCUS
POINT

hyperbolas

hy·per·bo·le (hī pur′bə lē) ***n.*** ⟦L < Gr: see prec.⟧ exaggeration for effect and not meant to be taken literally (Ex: He's as strong as an ox.)

hy·per·bol·ic (hī′pər bäl′ik) ***adj.*** ⟦LL *hyperbolicus* < Gr *hyperbolikos* < *hyperbolē*: see HYPERBOLA⟧ **1** of, having the nature of, or using hyperbole; exaggerated or exaggerating **2** of, or having the form of, a hyperbola **3** designating or of any of a set of six functions (**hyperbolic sine, hyperbolic cosine**, etc.) related to the hyperbola in a manner similar to that by which the trigonometric functions are related to the circle Also **hy′per·bol′i·cal** —**hy′per·bol′i·cal·ly** ***adv.***

hy·per·bo·lism (hī pur′bə liz′əm) ***n.*** **1** the use of hyperbole **2** a hyperbolic statement

hy·per·bo·lize (hī pur′bə līz′) *vt., vi.* **-lized′**, **-liz′ing** to express with or use hyperbole

hy·per·bo·loid (hī pur′bə loid′) *n. Geom.* **1** a solid often formed by rotating a hyperbola around either main axis: its plane sections are hyperbolas, ellipses, or circles **2** the surface of such a solid

hy·per·bo·re·an (hī′pər bôr′ē ən, -bə rē′ən) *adj.* ⟦LL *Hyperboreanus* < L *Hyperboreus* < Gr *hyperboreos*, beyond the north wind < *hyper-* (see HYPER-) + *boreas*, north wind: see BOREAS⟧ **1** of the far north **2** very cold; frigid **3** [**H-**] of the Hyperboreans —*n.* **1** [**H-**] *Gr. Myth.* an inhabitant of a northern region of sunshine and everlasting spring, beyond the north wind **2** a person of a far northern region

hy·per·cat·a·lec·tic (-kat′ə lek′tik) *adj.* ⟦LL *hypercatalecticus* < Gr *hyperkatalēktikos*: see HYPER- & CATALECTIC⟧ having one or more extra syllables following the last regular measure: said of a line of verse

hy·per·charge (hī′pər chärj′) *n.* ⟦< *hyperonic charge* < HYPERON + -IC⟧ *Physics* a characteristic of a group of elementary particles: it is a number equal to twice the average charge of the group divided by the elementary charge

hy·per·cho·les·ter·ol·e·mi·a (hī′pər kə les′tər ôl ē′mē ə) *n.* ⟦see -EMIA⟧ the presence of excessive cholesterol in the blood —**hy′per·cho·les′ter·ol·e′mic** *adj.*

hy·per·cor·rec·tion (hī′pər kə rek′shən) *n. Linguis.* a nonstandard usage resulting from an overly conscious effort to avoid a grammatical error, as in the case of personal pronouns (Ex.: "between you and I")

hy·per·crit·ic (hī′pər krit′ik) *n.* a hypercritical person

hy·per·crit·i·cal (hī′pər krit′i kəl) *adj.* too critical; too severe in judgment; hard to please —*SYN.* CRITICAL —**hy′per·crit′i·cal·ly** *adv.* —**hy′per·crit′i·cism′** *n.*

hy·per·du·li·a (hī′pər do͞o lī′ə, -dyo͞o-) *n.* ⟦HYPER- + DULIA⟧ *R.C.Ch.* special veneration of the Virgin Mary: distinguished from DULIA, LATRIA

hy·per·e·mi·a (-ē′mē ə) *n.* ⟦ModL: see HYPER- & -EMIA⟧ an increased blood flow or congestion of blood in an organ, tissue, etc.

hy·per·es·the·sia (-es thē′zhə) *n.* ⟦ModL: see HYPER- & ESTHESIA⟧ an abnormally high sensitivity of the skin or some sense organ: opposed to HYPOESTHESIA —**hy′per·es·thet′ic** (-es thet′ik) *adj.*

hy·per·eu·tec·tic (-yo͞o tek′tik) *adj.* containing more of the secondary component than is present in a eutectic solution or alloy —**hy′per·eu·tec′toid** (-toid) *adj.*

hy·per·ex·tend (-ek stend′) *vt.* to injure (a knee, elbow, etc.) by bending it beyond its normal limit of extension —**hy′per·ex·ten′sion** *n.*

hy·per·fo·cal distance (-fō′kəl) the distance from a photographic lens to the nearest object that is in focus when the lens is focused at infinity

hy·per·ga·my (hī pur′gə mē) *n.* ⟦HYPER- + -GAMY⟧ marriage with a person of a higher social class or position —**hy·per′ga·mous** *adj.*

hy·per·gly·ce·mi·a (hī′pər glī sē′mē ə) *n.* ⟦ModL < HYPER- + Gr *glykys*, sweet + -EMIA⟧ an abnormally high concentration of sugar in the blood —**hy′per·gly·ce′mic** (-mik) *adj.*

hy·per·gol·ic (hī′pər gäl′ik) *adj.* ⟦< Ger *hypergol*, a hypergolic liquid fuel (< *hyp-*, for HYPER- + Gr *ergon*, work + L *oleum*, OIL) + -IC⟧ igniting spontaneously when mixed together, as rocket fuel and oxidizer combinations

hy·per·in·fla·tion (hī′pər in flā′shən) *n.* economic inflation that is particularly severe or extensive —**hy′per·in·fla′tion·ar·y** *adj.*

hy·per·in·su·lin·ism (-in′sə lin iz′əm) *n.* chronic excessive secretion of insulin from the pancreas, resulting in persistent hypoglycemia

Hy·pe·ri·on (hī pir′ē ən) *n.* ⟦L < Gr *Hyperiōn*⟧ **1** *Gr. Myth. a)* a Titan, son of Uranus and Gaea, and father of the sun god Helios *b)* Helios himself **2** a small, irregularly shaped satellite of Saturn having an unusual shifting orientation and rotation

hy·per·ker·a·to·sis (hī′pər ker′ə tō′sis) *n., pl.* **-ses′** (-sēz′) ⟦HYPER- + KERATOSIS⟧ **1** an increase in the thickness of the horny layer of the skin **2** an increase of the cells of the cornea of the eye —**hy′per·ker′a·tot′ic** (-tät′ik) *adj.*

hy·per·ki·ne·sis (-ki nē′sis) *n.* ⟦ModL < HYPER- + Gr *kinēsis*, motion⟧ a condition of abnormally increased muscular movement: also **hy′per·ki·ne′sia** (-zhə) —**hy′per·ki·net′ic** (-net′ik) *adj.*

hy·per·link (hī′pər liŋk′; *for v., also* hī′pər liŋk′) *Comput. n.* a hypertext link, typically embedded in text and appearing as an underlined word, phrase, or Web address, that allows ready access to a related document, graphical image, etc. —*vt.* **1** to join by a hyperlink **2** to install hyperlinks in

hy·per·lip·i·de·mi·a (hī′pər li′pi dē′mē ə) *n.* ⟦see -EMIA⟧ the presence of excessive lipids in the blood —**hy′per·lip′i·de′mic** *adj.*

hy·per·mar·ket (hī′pər mär′kit) *n.* ⟦transl. of Fr *hypermarché*, formed after *supermarché*, SUPERMARKET: see HYPER- & MARKET⟧ [Chiefly Brit.] a very large retail store offering the products of a supermarket and the merchandise of a department store

hy·per·met·ric (hī′pər me′trik) *Prosody adj.* ⟦< Gr *hypermetros*, beyond measure: see HYPER- & METRIC⟧ having an extra syllable or syllables: also **hy′per·met′ri·cal** —*n.* a hypermetric line of verse

hy·per·me·tro·pi·a (-mi trō′pē ə) *n.* ⟦ModL < Gr *hypermetros*, beyond measure (see HYPER- & METRIC) + -OPIA⟧ HYPEROPIA —**hy′per·me·trop′ic** (-träp′ik) *adj.*

hy·perm·ne·sia (hī′pərm nē′zhə) *n.* ⟦ModL: see HYPER- & AMNESIA⟧ abnormally sharp memory or vivid recall, seen in certain mental disorders —**hy′perm·ne′sic** (-zik, -sik) *adj.*

hy·per·on (hī′pər än′) *n.* ⟦HYPER- + (BARY)ON⟧ *Particle Physics* an unstable baryon that is more massive than a neutron

hy·per·o·pi·a (hī′pər ō′pē ə) *n.* ⟦HYPER- + -OPIA⟧ abnormal vision in which the rays of light are focused behind the retina, so that distant objects are seen more clearly than near ones; farsightedness —**hy′per·op′ic** (-äp′ik) *adj.*

hy·per·os·to·sis (-äs tō′sis) *n., pl.* **-ses′** (-sēz′) ⟦ModL < HYPER- + OSTOSIS⟧ an abnormal increase or thickening of bone tissue —**hy′per·os·tot′ic** (-tät′ik) *adj.*

hy·per·par·a·site (hī′pər par′ə sīt′) *n.* a parasitic organism living on or in another parasite

hy·per·pi·tu·i·ta·rism (-pi to͞o′i tə riz′əm, -tyo͞o′-) *n.* **1** excessive activity of the pituitary gland, esp. of its anterior lobe **2** a condition resulting from this, as gigantism —**hy′per·pi·tu′i·tar′y** (-ter′ē) *adj.*

hy·per·plane (hī′pər plān′) *n. Math.* an analogue of a plane in a space of four or more dimensions

hy·per·pla·si·a (hī′pər plā′zhə) *n.* ⟦ModL < HYPER- + -PLASIA⟧ an abnormal increase in the number of cells composing a tissue or organ —**hy′per·plas′tic** (-plas′tik) *adj.*

hy·per·ploid (hī′pər ploid′) *adj.* having one or more chromosomes in addition to the characteristic euploid number of chromosomes: cf. HYPOPLOID

hy·per·pne·a (hī′pərp nē′ə, -pər nē′ə) *n.* ⟦ModL < HYPER- + Gr *pnoē*, breathing < *pnein*, to breathe: see PNEUMA⟧ abnormally rapid breathing; panting —**hy′per·pne′ic** *adj.*

hy·per·py·rex·i·a (hī′pər pī rek′sē ə) *n.* ⟦ModL < HYPER- + PYREXIA⟧ a very high fever —**hy′per·py·ret′ic** (-ret′ik) *adj.*

hy·per·sen·si·tive (hī′pər sen′sə tiv) *adj.* abnormally or excessively sensitive —**hy′per·sen′si·tiv′i·ty** *n.*

hy·per·sex·u·al (-sek′sho͞o əl) *adj.* having an unusually great sexual drive —**hy′per·sex′u·al′i·ty** *n.*

hy·per·son·ic (-sän′ik) *adj.* designating, of, or traveling at a speed equal to five times the speed of sound or greater: see also SONIC

hy·per·space (hī′pər spās′) *n.* **1** *Math.* space of four or more dimensions **2** any theoretical or fictional space, dimension, location, etc. thought of as affording preternatural or surreal experiences or capabilities

hy·per·sthene (hī′pər sthēn′) *n.* ⟦altered (modeled on Gr) < Fr *hyperstène*: coined (1803) by R.-J. Haüy (1743-1822), Fr mineralogist < Gr *hyper-*, HYPER- + *sthenos*, strength⟧ a dark-colored variety, $(Mg,Fe)SiO_3$, of enstatite, containing a large amount of iron; magnesium iron silicate —**hy′per·sthen′ic** (-sthen′ik) *adj.*

hy·per·ten·sion (hī′pər ten′shən) *n.* **1** any abnormally high tension **2** abnormally high blood pressure, or a disease of which this is the chief sign —**hy′per·ten′sive** *adj., n.*

hy·per·text (hī′pər tekst′) *n. Comput.* information stored in a computer and specially organized so that related items, as in separate documents, are linked together and can be readily accessed

hy·per·ther·mi·a (hī′pər thur′mē ə) *n.* ⟦< HYPER- + Gr *thermē*, heat: see WARM⟧ hyperpyrexia, esp. if induced to combat an illness: also **hy′per·ther′my**

hy·per·thy·roid (hī′pər thī′roid′) *adj.* of, characterized by, or having hyperthyroidism —*n.* a hyperthyroid person

hy·per·thy·roid·ism (-thī′roid iz′əm) *n.* **1** excessive activity of the thyroid gland **2** the disorder resulting from this or from taking too much thyroid extract, characterized by loss of weight, nervousness, a rapid pulse, etc.

hy·per·ton·ic (hī′pər tän′ik) *adj.* **1** having abnormally high tension or tone, esp. of the muscles **2** having an osmotic pressure higher than that of an isotonic solution

hy·per·tro·phy (hī pur′trə fē) *n.* ⟦ModL: see HYPER- & -TROPHY⟧ a considerable increase in the size of an organ or tissue, caused by enlargement of its cellular components — *vi., vt.* **-phied**, **-phy·ing** to undergo or cause to undergo hypertrophy —**hy·per·troph·ic** (hī′pər träf′ik, -trō′fik) *adj.*

hy·per·ven·ti·la·tion (hī′pər vent′′l ā′shən) *n.* extremely rapid or deep breathing that may cause dizziness, fainting, etc. as a result of a rapid loss of carbon dioxide —**hy′per·ven′ti·late′** (-āt′) *vi., vt.* **-lat′ed**, **-lat′ing**

hy·per·vi·ta·mi·no·sis (-vīt′ə mi nō′sis) *n., pl.* **-ses** (-sēz) a disorder resulting from excessive dosage with one or more vitamins

hy·pe·thral (hi pē′thrəl, hī-) *adj. alt. sp. of* HYPAETHRAL

hy·pha (hī′fə) *n., pl.* **-phae** (-fē) ⟦ModL < Gr *hyphē*, a web < IE base **webh-* > WEAVE⟧ any of the threadlike parts making up the mycelium of a fungus —**hy′phal** *adj.*

hy·phen (hī′fən) *n.* ⟦LL < Gr *hyphen* (for *hyph' hen*), a hyphen, lit., under one, together, in one < *hypo-*, under + *hen*, neut. acc. of *heis*, one: for IE base see SAME⟧ a mark (-) used between the parts of a compound word or the syllables of a divided word, as at the end of a line —*vt.* HYPHENATE

hy·phen·ate (hī′fə nāt′; *for adj.*, -nit, -nāt′) *vt.* **-at′ed**, **-at′ing** **1** to connect or separate by a hyphen **2** to write or print with a hyphen —*adj.* hyphenated —*n.* ⟦< the use of *hyphens* to separate job titles⟧ a person who has more than one job or function, as in the film industry [a producer-director-writer is a Hollywood *hyphenate*] —**hy′phen·a′tion** *n.*

hy·phen·at·ed (-nāt′əd) *adj.* **1** connected or separated with a hyphen ☆**2** of or pertaining to a citizen of a country who is identified with the ethnic group or nationality of his or her forebears and, typically, designated by a hyphenated compound [*hyphenated* Americans, such as Chinese-Americans, Polish-Americans, etc.]

hyp·na·gog·ic (hip′nə gäj′ik) *adj.* ⟦fol. + -AGOG(UE) + -IC⟧ **1** causing sleep; soporific **2** designating or of the state intermediate between wakefulness and sleep [*hypnagogic* fantasies] Also sp. **hyp′no·gog′ic**

hyp·no- (hip′nō, -nə) ⟦< Gr *hypnos*, sleep < IE **supnos* < base **swep-*, to sleep > L *sopire*, to lull to sleep, OE *swefan*, to sleep⟧ *combining form* **1** sleep [*hypnology*] **2** hypnotism [*hypnotherapy*] Also, before a vowel, **hypn-**

hyp·no·a·nal·y·sis (hip′nō ə nal′ə sis) ***n.*** the use of hypnosis or hypnotic drugs in combination with psychoanalytic techniques

hyp·no·gen·e·sis (hip′nō jen′ə sis) ***n.*** ⟦ModL < HYPNO- + -GENESIS⟧ the inducing of sleep or hypnosis —**hyp′no·gen′ic** (-jen′ik) ***adj.***, **hyp′no·ge·net′ic** (-jə net′ik)

hyp·noid (hip′noid′) ***adj.*** resembling sleep or hypnosis: also **hyp·noid′al**

hyp·nol·o·gy (hip näl′ə jē) ***n.*** ⟦HYPNO- + -LOGY⟧ the science dealing with sleep and hypnotism: now a nontechnical term

hyp·no·pom·pic (hip′nō päm′pik) ***adj.*** ⟦HYPNO- + Gr *pompē*, procession (see POMP) + -IC⟧ designating or of the state intermediate between sleep and complete wakefulness [*hypnopompic* visions]

Hyp·nos (hip′näs′) ***n.*** ⟦Gr *Hypnos* < *hypnos*: see HYPNO-⟧ *Gr. Myth.* the god of sleep, identified with the Roman Somnus

hyp·no·sis (hip nō′sis) ***n.***, *pl.* **-ses′** (-sēz′) ⟦ModL: see HYPNO- & -OSIS⟧ **1** a trancelike condition usually induced by another person, in which the subject is in a state of altered consciousness and responds, with certain limitations, to the suggestions of the hypnotist **2** HYPNOTISM

hyp·no·ther·a·py (hip′nō ther′ə pē) ***n.*** the use of hypnotism in treating illness, dependency, etc. —**hyp′no·ther′a·pist *n.***

hyp·not·ic (hip nät′ik) ***adj.*** ⟦Fr or LL: Fr *hypnotique* < LL *hypnoticus* < Gr *hypnōtikos*, tending to sleep < *hypnos*: see HYPNO-⟧ **1** causing sleep; soporific **2** of, characterized by, having the nature of, or inducing hypnosis **3** easily hypnotized —***n.*** **1** any agent causing sleep; soporific **2** a hypnotized person or one easily hypnotized —**hyp·not′i·cal·ly *adv.***

hyp·no·tism (hip′nə tiz′əm) ***n.*** **1** the act or practice of inducing hypnosis **2** the science of hypnosis

hyp·no·tist (-tist) ***n.*** a person who induces hypnosis

hyp·no·tize (-tīz′) ***vt.*** **-tized′**, **-tiz′ing** **1** to put into a state of hypnosis **2** to affect or influence by or as if by hypnotism; spellbind —**hyp′no·tiz′a·ble *adj.***

Hyp·nus (hip′nəs) ***n.*** *var. of* HYPNOS

hy·po[1] (hī′pō) ***n.***, *pl.* **-pos** (-pōz) [Informal] *short for:* ☆**1** HYPODERMIC **2** HYPOCHONDRIAC —☆***vt.*** **-poed**, **-po·ing** [Slang] to boost, stimulate, etc. by or as if by a hypodermic injection

hy·po[2] (hī′pō) ***n.*** SODIUM THIOSULFATE

hy·po- (hī′pō, -pə; hip′ō, -ə) ⟦Gr *hypo-* < *hypo*, under, less than: see UP[1]⟧ *prefix* **1** under, beneath, below [*hypodermic*] **2** less than, subordinated to [*hypotaxis*] **3** *Chem.* having a lower state of oxidation [*hypophosphorous* acid]

hy·po·al·ler·gen·ic (hī′pō al′ər jen′ik) ***adj.*** less likely to cause an allergic reaction than other comparable preparations or goods: said of cosmetics, clothing, pillows, etc.

hy·po·blast (hī′pō blast′, hip′ō-) ***n.*** ⟦HYPO- + -BLAST⟧ the endoderm of a gastrula —**hy′po·blas′tic *adj.***

hy·po·caust (hī′pō kôst′, hip′ō-) ***n.*** ⟦L *hypocaustum* < Gr *hypokauston* < *hypokaiein*, to heat by applying fire below < *hypo-* (see HYPO-) + *kaiein*, to burn⟧ a space below the floor in some ancient Roman buildings, into which hot air was piped to warm the rooms

hy·po·cen·ter (hī′pō sen′tər, -pə-) ***n.*** **1** the focus point of an earthquake **2** GROUND ZERO

hy·po·chlo·rite (hī′pō klôr′īt′) ***n.*** a salt of hypochlorous acid containing the monovalent negative radical ClO

hy·po·chlo·rous acid (-klôr′əs) ⟦< HYPO- + CHLOROUS, as in Fr *hypochloreux*⟧ a weak, unstable acid, HClO, known only in solution and used as a bleaching and oxidizing agent

hy·po·chon·dri·a (hī′pə kän′drē ə) ***n.*** ⟦ModL < LL, pl., abdomen (the supposed seat of the condition) < pl. of Gr *hypochondrion*, soft part of the body below the cartilage of the breastbone < *hypo-* (see HYPO-) + *chondros*, cartilage, by dissimilation < *-chrondros* < IE **ghren-* < base **gher-*, to pulverize, rub hard > GRIND, GROUND[1]⟧ abnormal anxiety over one's health, often with imagined symptoms and severe melancholy

hy·po·chon·dri·ac (hī′pə kän′drē ak′) ***adj.*** ⟦Fr *hypocondriaque* < Gr *hypochondriacus*⟧ **1** designating or of the region of the hypochondrium **2** of or having hypochondria —***n.*** a person who has hypochondria —**hy′po·chon·dri′a·cal** (-kän drī′ə kəl; -kən-) ***adj.*** —**hy′po·chon·dri′a·cal·ly *adv.***

hy·po·chon·dri·a·sis (-kän drī′ə sis, -kən-) ***n.*** HYPOCHONDRIA: term preferred in medicine

hy·po·chon·dri·um (hī′pō kän′drē əm, hip′ō-) ***n.***, *pl.* **-dri·a** (-ə) ⟦ModL: see HYPOCHONDRIA⟧ either of the upper lateral abdominal regions containing the lower ribs

hy·po·co·ris·tic (hī′pō kə ris′tik, hip′ō-) ***adj.*** ⟦< Gr *hypokoristikos* < *hypokorizesthai*, to call by endearing names < *hypo-* (see HYPO-) + *korizesthai*, to pet < *korē*, girl < IE base **ker-*, to grow > CEREAL⟧ of or being a pet name or a diminutive or term of endearment —**hy·poc·o·rism** (hī päk′ə riz′əm) ***n.***

hy·po·cot·yl (hī′pō kät′'l, hip′ō-) ***n.*** ⟦HYPO- + COTYL(EDON)⟧ the part of the axis, or stem, below the cotyledons in the embryo of a plant

hy·poc·ri·sy (hi päk′rə sē) ***n.***, *pl.* **-sies** ⟦ME *ipocrisie* < OFr < L *hypocrisis*, mimicry (in LL(Ec), pretended sanctity) < Gr *hypokrisis*, acting a part (in LXX and N.T., hypocrisy) < *hypokrinesthai*, to play a part < *hypo-*, HYPO- + *krinesthai*, to dispute < *krinein*, to separate: see HARVEST⟧ a pretending to be what one is not, or to feel what one does not feel; esp., a pretense of virtue, piety, etc.

hyp·o·crite (hip′ə krit′) ***n.*** ⟦ME *ipocrite* < OFr < L *hypocrita*, stage actor (in LL(Ec), hypocrite) < Gr *hypokritēs*, an actor (in LXX & N.T., a pretender, hypocrite) < *hypokrinesthai*: see prec.⟧ a person who pretends to be what he or she is not; specif., one who pretends to be pious, virtuous, etc. without really being so —**hyp′o·crit′i·cal** (-krit′i kəl) ***adj.*** —**hyp′o·crit′i·cal·ly *adv.***

hy·po·cy·cloid (hī′pō sī′kloid′, -pə-; *also* hip′ō-, hip′ə-) ***n.*** ⟦HYPO- + CYCLOID⟧ *Geom.* the curve traced by a point on the circumference of an epicycle that rolls around the inside of a fixed circle: cf. EPICYCLOID

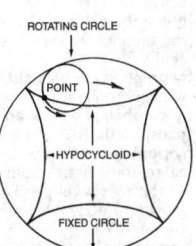

ROTATING CIRCLE
POINT
HYPOCYCLOID
FIXED CIRCLE

hypocycloid

hy·po·derm (hī′pō durm′, -pə-; hip′ō-, -ə-) ***n.*** ⟦ModL: see HYPO- & DERMA[1]⟧ HYPODERMIS: also **hy′po·der′ma** (-dur′mə)

hy·po·der·mal (hī′pō dur′məl, -pə-; hip′ō-, -ə-) ***adj.*** **1** of the hypodermis **2** lying under the epidermis

hy·po·der·mic (hī′pə dur′mik) ***adj.*** ⟦HYPODERM + -IC⟧ **1** of the parts under the skin **2** injected under the skin **3** of the hypodermis **4** [Rare] stimulating or exciting, as though resulting from a hypodermic injection —***n.*** **1** HYPODERMIC INJECTION **2** HYPODERMIC SYRINGE —**hy′po·der′mi·cal·ly *adv.***

hypodermic injection the injection of a medicine or drug under the skin

hypodermic syringe a piston syringe attached to a hollow metal needle (**hypodermic needle**) and used for giving hypodermic injections

hy·po·der·mis (hī′pō dur′mis, -pə-; hip′ō-, -ə-) ***n.*** ⟦ModL: see HYPO- & DERMIS⟧ **1** *Bot.* a specialized layer of cells, as for support or water storage, lying immediately beneath the epidermis of a plant organ **2** *Zool.* a layer of cells that lies beneath, and secretes, the cuticle of annelids, arthropods, etc.

hy·po·es·the·si·a (hī′pō es thē′zhə, -zhē ə, -zē ə) ***n.*** ⟦HYPO- + ESTHESIA⟧ an abnormally low sensitivity of the skin or some other organ: opposed to HYPERESTHESIA —**hy′po·es·thet′ic** (-thet′ik) ***adj.***

hy·po·eu·tec·tic (hī′pō yo͞o tek′tik, hip′ō-) ***adj.*** containing less of the secondary component than is present in a eutectic solution or alloy —**hy′po·eu·tec′toid *adj.***

hy·po·gas·tri·um (hī′pō gas′trē əm, hip′ō-) ***n.***, *pl.* **-tri·a** (-ə) ⟦ModL < Gr *hypogastrion*, lower belly, neut. of *hypogastrios*, abdominal < *hypo-*, HYPO- + *gastēr*, the belly: see GASTRO-⟧ the lower, middle region of the abdomen —**hy′po·gas′tric *adj.***

hy·po·ge·al (hī′pō jē′əl, hip′ō-) ***adj.*** ⟦< LL *hypogeus*, underground (< Gr *hypogaios* < *hypo-*, under + *gē*, earth) + -AL⟧ **1** of, or occurring in, the region below the surface of the earth **2** *a)* *Bot.* growing or maturing underground, as peanuts or truffles (said esp. of cotyledons) *b)* *Zool.* burrowing, living, or developing beneath the ground, as certain insect larvae: see EPIGEAL Also **hy′po·ge′an**

hy·po·gene (hī′pō jēn′, hip′ō-) ***adj.*** ⟦HYPO- + Gr *-genēs*: see -GEN⟧ *Geol.* **1** produced or formed within the earth, as plutonic and metamorphic rocks **2** designating minerals or ore deposits formed by waters ascending from great depths

hy·pog·e·nous (hī päj′ə nəs, hi-) ***adj.*** ⟦HYPO- + -GENOUS⟧ growing on the lower surface of something, as spores on the underside of some fern leaves: see EPIGENOUS

hy·po·ge·ous (hī′pō jē′əs, hip′ō-) ***adj.*** HYPOGEAL

hy·po·ge·um (-jē′əm) ***n.***, *pl.* **-ge′a** (-ə) ⟦L < Gr *hypogaios*: see HYPOGEAL⟧ an underground cellar, vault, tomb, etc.

hy·po·geu·si·a (hī′pō gyo͞o′sē ə, -jo͞o′-) ***n.*** ⟦< HYPO- + Gr *geusis*, taste + -IA⟧ a disease characterized by a decreased ability to taste and, sometimes, to smell: associated with a zinc deficiency

hy·po·glos·sal (hī′pō gläs′əl, -glôs′-; hip′ō-) ***adj.*** ⟦HYPO- + GLOSSAL⟧ **1** under the tongue **2** designating or of the motor nerves of the tongue —***n.*** a hypoglossal nerve

hy·po·gly·ce·mi·a (-glī sē′mē ə) ***n.*** ⟦ModL < HYPO- + Gr *glykys*, sweet + -EMIA⟧ an abnormally low concentration of sugar in the blood —**hy′po·gly·ce′mic** (-mik) ***adj.***

hy·pog·na·thous (hī päg′nə thəs, hi-) ***adj.*** ⟦HYPO- + -GNATHOUS⟧ having a protruding lower jaw

hy·pog·y·nous (hī päj′ə nəs, hi-) ***adj.*** ⟦HYPO- + -GYNOUS⟧ designating petals, sepals, and stamens that are attached to the receptacle, below and free from the pistil, as in a tulip: see PERIGYNOUS, EPIGYNOUS —**hy·pog′y·ny** (-nē) ***n.***

hy·poid gear (hī′poid′) ⟦< *hyp*(*erbol*)*oid*(*al*) < HYPERBOL(A) + -OID + -AL⟧ a curved-tooth bevel gear in a system in which the axis of the driving shaft does not intersect with the axis of the driven shaft

hy·po·ki·ne·sis (hī′pō ki nē′sis) ***n.*** ⟦ModL < HYPO- + Gr *kinēsis*, motion < *kinein*, to move: see CITE⟧ a condition of abnormally diminished muscular movement: also **hy′po·ki·ne′sia** (-zhə) —**hy′po·ki·net′ic** (-net′ik) ***adj.***

☆**hy·po·lim·ni·on** (-lim′nē än′, -ən) ***n.*** ⟦ModL < HYPO- + Gr *limnion*, dim. of *limnē*, a pool of standing water⟧ an unfrozen lake's cold, lowermost, stagnant layer of oxygen-poor water that is below the thermocline: see EPILIMNION

hy·po·ma·ni·a (hī′pō mā′nē ə, -mān′yə; hip′ō-) ***n.*** ⟦HYPO- + -MANIA⟧ a mild form of mania, specif. of the manic phase of bipolar affective disorder —**hy′po·man′ic** (-man′ik) ***adj.***

hy·po·nas·ty (hī′pō nas′tē, hip′ō-) ***n.*** ⟦< HYPO- + -NASTY⟧ *Bot.* the condition in which an organ, as a leaf, turns upward because of the more rapid growth of the bottom layers of cells: opposed to EPINASTY —**hy′po·nas′tic *adj.***

hy·po·phos·phate (hī′pō fäs′fāt′, -pə-) ***n.*** **1** a salt of hypophosphoric acid containing any of several negative radicals, monovalent HP_2O_6, divalent $H_2P_2O_6$, trivalent $H_3P_2O_6$, or tetravalent P_2O_6 **2** an uncharged ester of this acid

hy·po·phos·phite (-fäs′fīt′) ***n.*** **1** a salt of hypophosphorous acid containing the monovalent negative radical H_2PO_2 **2** an uncharged ester of this acid

hy·po·phos·phor·ic acid (hī′pō fäs fôr′ik, -pə-) an acid, $H_4P_2O_6$, obtained when phosphorus is slowly oxidized in moist air

hy·po·phos·pho·rous acid (hī′pō fäs′fə rəs, -pə-) a monobasic acid of phosphorus, H_3PO_2: it is a strong reducing agent

hy·poph·y·sec·to·my (hī päf′ə sek′tə mē, hī′pə fə-) ***n., pl.*** **-mies** the surgical removal of the pituitary gland

hy·poph·y·sis (hī päf′ə sis, hi-) ***n., pl.*** **-ses′** (-sēz) ⟦ModL < Gr, undergrowth, process < *hypophyein* < *hypo-*, under + *phyein*, to grow: see BE⟧ PITUITARY GLAND

hy·po·pi·tu·i·ta·rism (hī′pō pi to͞o′i tə riz′əm, -tyo͞o′-) ***n.*** **1** deficient activity of the pituitary gland, esp. of its anterior lobe **2** the condition resulting from this, characterized by decreased growth in children or decreased activity of the gonads, thyroid gland, or adrenal glands —**hy′po·pi·tu′i·tar′y** (-ter′ē) ***adj.***

hy·po·pla·si·a (hī′pō plā′zhə) ***n.*** ⟦ModL < HYPO- + -PLASIA⟧ a condition of decreased or arrested growth of an undeveloped organ or tissue of the body —**hy′po·plas′tic** (-plas′tik) ***adj.***

hy·po·ploid (hī′pə ploid′) ***adj.*** having one or more fewer chromosomes than the characteristic euploid number of chromosomes: cf. HYPERPLOID

hy·po·sen·si·tize (hī′pō sen′sə tīz′) ***vt.*** **-tized′**, **-tiz′ing** ⟦HYPO- + SENSITIZE⟧ to treat with frequent, small injections of an antigen so as to decrease the symptoms of an allergy to that antigen —**hy′po·sen′si·ti·za′tion** ***n.***

hy·pos·ta·sis (hī päs′tə sis, hi-) ***n., pl.*** **-ses′** (-sēz′) ⟦Gr, a supporting, foundation < *hyphistanai*, to set under, pass, stand under < *hypo-*, under (see HYPO-) + *histanai*, to STAND, cause to stand⟧ **1** the masking or suppression of a gene by another gene that is not its allele **2** *Med. a)* a deposit or sediment *b)* a settling of blood in the lower parts of the body as a result of a slowing down of the blood flow **3** *Philos.* the underlying, essential nature of a thing **4** *Christian Theol. a)* the unique nature of the one God *b)* any of the three persons of the Trinity, each person having the divine nature fully and equally *c)* the union of the wholly divine nature and of a wholly human nature in the one person of Jesus Christ (in full **hypostatic union**) —**hy·po·stat·ic** (hī′pō stat′ik, -pə-) ***adj.***

hy·pos·ta·tize (hī päs′tə tīz′) ***vt.*** **-tized′**, **-tiz′ing** ⟦< Gr *hypostatos* (< *hyphistanai*: see prec.) + -IZE⟧ to think of (a concept, abstraction, etc.) as having real, objective existence —**hy·pos′ta·ti·za′tion** ***n.***

hyp·o·style (hī′pō stīl′, hip′ō-) ***adj.*** ⟦Gr *hypostylos*, resting on pillars < *hypo-*, under + *stylos*, a pillar: see HYPO- & STEER[1]⟧ having a roof supported by rows of pillars or columns —***n.*** a hypostyle structure

hy·po·tax·is (hī′pō tak′sis, hip′ō-) ***n.*** ⟦ModL < Gr, submission: see HYPO- & -TAXIS⟧ *Gram.* the placing of one clause or construction in a dependent relationship to another, as by the use of a conjunction: cf. PARATAXIS —**hy′po·tac′tic** (-tak′tik) ***adj.***

hy·po·ten·sion (hī′pō ten′shən) ***n.*** abnormally low blood pressure —**hy′po·ten′sive** ***adj.***

hy·pot·e·nuse (hī pät′′n o͞os′, -yo͞os′) ***n.*** ⟦L *hypotenusa* < Gr *hypoteinousa*, lit., subtending, properly fem. of prp. of *hypoteinein*, to subtend, stretch under < *hypo-*, under (see HYPO-) + *teinein*, to stretch: see HYPO- & THIN⟧ the longest side of a right triangle, located opposite the right angle: sometimes **hy·poth′e·nuse** (-päth′i-)

hy·po·thal·a·mus (hī′pō thal′ə məs) ***n., pl.*** **-mi′** (-mī′) ⟦ModL: see HYPO- & THALAMUS⟧ the part of the diencephalon in the brain that forms the floor of the third ventricle and regulates many basic bodily functions, as the regulation of temperature —**hy′po·tha·lam′ic** (-thə lam′ik) ***adj.***

hy·poth·ec (hī päth′ek′, -ik; hi-) ***n.*** ⟦Fr *hypothèque* < LL *hypotheca*, a pledge, security < Gr *hypothēkē*, something put under (obligation), pledge < *hypotithenai*, to put under, pledge: see HYPOTHESIS⟧ *Civil Law* security or right given to a creditor over a debtor's property without transfer of possession or title

hy·poth·e·cate (hī päth′i kāt′, hi-) ***vt.*** **-cat′ed**, **-cat′ing** ⟦< ML *hypothecatus*, pp. of *hypothecare*, to hypothecate < LL *hypotheca*: see prec.⟧ **1** to pledge (property) to another as security without transferring possession or title **2** HYPOTHESIZE —**hy·poth′e·ca′tion** ***n.*** —**hy·poth′e·ca′tor** ***n.***

hy·po·ther·mal (hī′pō thur′məl, -pə-) ***adj.*** **1** tepid or lukewarm **2** of or characterized by hypothermia **3** produced in a temperature range of 300°C to 500°C: said of certain mineral deposits

hy·po·ther·mi·a (-thur′mē ə) ***n.*** ⟦ModL < HYPO- + Gr *thermē*, heat: see WARM⟧ a subnormal body temperature

hy·poth·e·sis (hī päth′ə sis, hi-) ***n., pl.*** **-ses′** (-sēz′) ⟦Gr, groundwork, foundation, supposition < *hypotithenai*, to place under < *hypo-*, under + *tithenai*, to place: see HYPO- & DO[1]⟧ an unproved theory, proposition, supposition, etc. tentatively accepted to explain certain facts or (**working hypothesis**) to provide a basis for further investigation, argument, etc. —***SYN.*** THEORY

hy·poth·e·size (hī päth′ə sīz′, hi-) ***vi.*** **-sized′**, **-siz′ing** to make a hypothesis —***vt.*** to assume; suppose

hy·po·thet·i·cal (hī′pə thet′i kəl) ***adj.*** ⟦< Gr *hypothetikos* (< *hypothesis*) + -AL⟧ **1** based on, involving, or having the nature of a hypothesis; assumed; supposed **2** given to the use of hypotheses [*a hypothetical mind*] **3** *Logic* CONDITIONAL Also **hy′po·thet′ic** —***n.*** a hypothetical statement, idea, circumstance, etc. —**hy′po·thet′i·cal·ly** ***adv.***

hy·po·thy·roid (hī′pō thī′roid′) ***adj.*** of, characterized by, or having hypothyroidism —***n.*** a hypothyroid person

hy·po·thy·roid·ism (-thī′roid iz′əm) ***n.*** **1** deficient activity of the thyroid gland **2** the disorder resulting from this, characterized by a retarded rate of metabolism and resulting sluggishness, puffiness, etc.

hy·po·ton·ic (hī′pō tän′ik, -pə-) ***adj.*** **1** having abnormally low tension or tone, esp. of the muscles **2** having an osmotic pressure lower than that of an isotonic solution —**hy′po·to·nic′i·ty** (-tə nis′ə tē) ***n.***

hy·po·xan·thine (-zan′thēn′, -thin) ***n.*** a nitrogenous compound, $C_5H_4N_4O$, formed in the body from the breakdown of nucleic acids

hy·pox·i·a (hī päk′sē ə, hi-) ***n.*** ⟦ModL: see HYPO- & OXY-[1] & -IA⟧ an abnormal condition resulting from a decrease in the oxygen supplied to or utilized by bodily tissue —**hy·pox′ic** ***adj.***

hyp·so- (hip′sō, -sə) ⟦< Gr *hypsos*, height < IE **ups-*, high < base **upo-*: see UP[1]⟧ *combining form* height, high [*hypsometer*]: also, before a vowel, **hyps-**

hyp·sog·ra·phy (hip säg′rə fē) ***n.*** ⟦prec. + -GRAPHY⟧ **1** the science of measuring the configuration of land or underwater surfaces with respect to a datum plane, as sea level **2** the configuration of such surfaces; topographic relief **3** the representation or description of relief features on a map or chart, as by tints, hachures, etc. **4** HYPSOMETRY —**hyp′so·graph′ic** (-sə graf′ik) ***adj.***

hyp·som·e·ter (-säm′ət ər) ***n.*** ⟦HYPSO- + -METER⟧ **1** a device for determining height above sea level by measuring atmospheric pressure as indicated by the boiling point of water **2** any of several instruments for measuring heights of trees by triangulation

hyp·som·e·try (-säm′ə trē) ***n.*** ⟦HYPSO- + -METRY⟧ the measurement of surface elevations above any level reference plane, esp. sea level —**hyp·so·met·ric** (hip′sə me′trik) ***adj.***

hy·ra·coid (hī′rə koid′) ***n.*** ⟦< ModL *Hyracoidea*: see fol. & -OID⟧ HYRAX —***adj.*** designating or of the hyraxes

hy·rax (hī′raks′) ***n., pl.*** **-rax′es** or **-ra·ces′** (-rə sēz′) ⟦ModL < Gr, shrew mouse < IE base **swer-*, to hum, buzz > SWARM[1]⟧ any of an order (Hyracoidea) of small, rodentlike mammals of Africa and SW Asia that feed on plants and live in rocky areas (genus *Procavia*) or in trees (genera *Dendrohyrax* and *Heterohyrax*)

Hyr·ca·ni·a (hər kā′nē ə) province of the ancient Persian & Macedonian empires, on the S & SE coast of the Caspian Sea —**Hyr·ca′ni·an** ***adj., n.***

hy·son (hī′sən) ***n.*** ⟦Chin *hsi-tchun*, lit., blooming spring, first crop⟧ a variety of Chinese green tea: the early crop is called **young hyson**, and the inferior leaves are called **hyson skin**

hys·sop (his′əp) ***n.*** ⟦ME *isope* < OE & OFr *ysope* < L *hyssopus* < Gr *hyssōpos*, *hyssōpon* < Heb *ēzōbh*⟧ **1** *a)* a fragrant herb (*Hyssopus officinalis*) of the mint family, usually with blue flowers, having leaves used in folk medicine as a tonic, stimulant, etc. *b)* its flower ☆**2** any of several American plants of various families **3** *Bible* a plant whose twigs were used for sprinkling in certain ancient Jewish rites

hys·ter·ec·to·my (his′tər ek′tə mē) ***n., pl.*** **-mies** ⟦HYSTER(O)- + -ECTOMY⟧ surgical removal of all or part of the uterus

hys·ter·e·sis (his′tər ē′sis) ***n.*** ⟦ModL < Gr *hysterēsis*, a deficiency < *hysterein*, to be behind, come short < *hysteros*, later, behind < IE **udteros*, compar. of base **ud-*, up > OUT⟧ *Physics* a lag of effect when the forces acting on a body are changed, as a lag in magnetization (**magnetic hysteresis**) of a ferromagnetic substance when the magnetizing force is changed —**hys′ter·et′ic** (-et′ik) ***adj.***

hys·te·ri·a (hi ster′ē ə, -stir′-) ***n.*** ⟦ModL < fol. + -IA⟧ **1** a psychiatric condition variously characterized by emotional excitability, excessive anxiety, sensory and motor disturbances, or the unconscious simulation of organic disorders, such as blindness, deafness, etc. **2** any outbreak of wild, uncontrolled excitement or feeling, such as fits of laughing and crying —***SYN.*** MANIA

hys·ter·ic (hi ster′ik) ***adj.*** ⟦L *hystericus* < Gr *hysterikos*, suffering in the womb, hysterical < *hystera*, uterus: from the notion that women are hysterical more often than men⟧ HYSTERICAL —***n.*** **1** [*usually pl., occas. with sing. v.*] a hysterical fit; HYSTERIA (sense 2) **2** a person subject to hysteria

hys·ter·i·cal (hi ster′i kəl) ***adj.*** ⟦prec. + -AL⟧ **1** of or characteristic of hysteria **2** *a)* like or suggestive of hysteria; emotionally uncontrolled and wild *b)* extremely comical **3** having or subject to hysteria —**hys·ter′i·cal·ly** ***adv.***

hys·ter·o- (his′tər ō, -ə) ⟦< Gr *hystera*, uterus, womb⟧ *combining form* **1** uterus, womb [*hysterotomy*] **2** hysteria, hysteria and [*hysterogenic*] Also, before a vowel, **hyster-**

hys·ter·oid (his′tər oid′) ***adj.*** ⟦prec. + -OID⟧ resembling hysteria

hys·ter·on pro·te·ron (his′tər än′ prät′ər än′) ⟦LL < Gr *hysteron*, neut. of *hysteros*, latter + *proteron*, neut. of *proteros*, earlier⟧ a figure of speech in which the logical order of ideas is reversed (Ex.: "I die, I faint, I fail")

hys·ter·ot·o·my (his′tər ät′ə mē) ***n., pl.*** **-mies** ⟦HYSTERO- + -TOMY⟧ incision of the uterus, as in a cesarean section

hys·tri·co·mor·phic (his′tri kō môr′fik) ***adj.*** ⟦< ModL *Hystricomorpha* < L *hystrix*, porcupine (< Gr) + Gr *morphē*, form + -IC⟧ designating or of a suborder (Hystricomorpha) of rodents, including the porcupines and chinchillas

Hz or **hz** *abbrev.* hertz

I

i¹ or **I** (ī) *n., pl.* **i's, I's 1** the ninth letter of the English alphabet: via Latin from the Greek *iota,* a modification of the Phoenician (Semitic *yodh,* a hand): this letter, first dotted in the 11th cent., was not distinguished from *j* until the 17th cent. **2** any of the speech sounds that this letter represents, as, in English, the vowel (i) of *pick,* (ē) of *pique,* or (ī) of *pike,* or, when it is unstressed, (ə) as in *sanity,* or the semivowel (y) in *boil* **3** a type or impression for *i* or *I* **4** the ninth in a sequence or group **5** an object shaped like I or I —*adj.* **1** of *i* or *I* **2** ninth in a sequence or group **3** shaped like I or I

i² (ī) *n.* **1** a Roman numeral for 1: see I¹ (sense 1) **2** *Astron.* the inclination of a planet's orbit to some reference plane, as the ecliptic

i³ *abbrev.* **1** interest **2** intransitive **3** island(s) **4** isle(s)

i⁴ *Math. symbol* $\sqrt{-1}$, the square root of negative one: usually printed in italic type

I¹ (ī) *n.* **1** the Roman numeral for 1: placed after another Roman numeral, it adds one unit (e.g., VI = 6), and placed before a greater Roman numeral, it subtracts one unit (e.g., IV = 4) **2** *Educ.* a grade indicating incompletion of assigned work; an incomplete

I² (ī) *pron., pl.* **we** ⟦ME *i, ich, ih* < OE *ic,* akin to Ger *ich,* Goth *ik* < IE base **êgom,* orig. prob. neut. n. meaning "(my) presence here" > L *ego,* Gr *egō,* Sans *ahám*⟧ the person speaking or writing: personal pronoun in the first person singular: *I* is the nominative form, *me* the objective, *mine* the possessive, and *myself* the reflexive and intensive; *my* is the possessive pronominal adjective —*n., pl.* **I's** the ego; the self

I³ *abbrev.* **1** Imperator **2** *Dentistry* incisor **3** Independent **4** interstate **5** Island(s) **6** Isle(s) **7** *Physics* moment of inertia

I⁴ 1 *Physics symbol* electric current **2** *Chem. symbol for* iodine

i- (i) *prefix* [Archaic] Y- *[iwis]*

-i- (i, ə) *infix* forming compound words: a connective vowel originally used for combining Latin elements only, but now used freely

IA or **Ia** *abbrev.* Iowa

-i·a (ē ə, yə) ⟦for 1, 2, 7 (& sometimes 4), L *-ia* & Gr *-ia* < *-i-,* thematic vowel + *-a,* noun suffix of 1st declension; for 3, 5, 6 (& sometimes 4), L *-ia* & Gr *-ia,* neut. pl. ending of L nouns in *-ium* & Gr nouns in *-ion; -i-,* thematic vowel + *-a,* suffix⟧ *suffix forming nouns* **1** name of a country *[India]* **2** name of a disease *[pneumonia]* **3** name of an ancient Greek or Roman festival *[Lupercalia]* **4** any of certain words formed in Greek or Latin and carried over into English *[militia]* **5** the English plural of any of certain Greek or Latin words *[paraphernalia]* **6** *Bot.* generic name of any of certain plants *[Zinnia]* **7** *Zool.* name of any of certain classes, orders, etc. *[Reptilia]*

IAEA *abbrev.* International Atomic Energy Agency

I·a·go (ē ä′gō) *n. see* OTHELLO

-i·al (ē əl, yəl, əl) ⟦L *-ialis, -iale*⟧ *suffix* -AL (senses 1 & 2) *[magisterial, jovial, artificial]*

i·amb (ī′amb′, -am′) *n.* ⟦Fr *iambe* < L *iambus* < Gr *iambos*⟧ a metrical foot consisting, in Greek and Latin verse, of one short syllable followed by one long one, or, as in English verse, of one unaccented syllable followed by one accented one (Ex.: "Tŏ stríve, tŏ séek, tŏ fínd, ănd nót tŏ yíeld")

i·am·bic (ī am′bik) *adj.* ⟦< Fr or L: Fr *iambique* < L *iambicus* < Gr *iambikos*⟧ of or made up of iambs —*n.* **1** an iamb **2** [*usually pl.*] an iambic line of poetry

i·am·bus (ī am′bəs) *n., pl.* **-bus·es** or **-bi′** (-bī′) ⟦L⟧ IAMB

I·an (ē′ən) *n.* ⟦Gael, var. of JOHN¹⟧ a masculine name: var. *Iain:* see JOHN¹

-i·an (ē ən, yən, ən) ⟦Fr or L: Fr *-ien* < L *-ianus* < -I- stem ending + *-anus:* see -AN⟧ *suffix* -AN *[Jeffersonian, reptilian]*

-i·an·a (ē an′ə) *suffix* -ANA

I·a·pe·tus (ī ä′pə təs, ē-) *n.* ⟦L < Gr *Iapetos,* name of a Titan in Gr myth., son of Uranus and Gaea⟧ a satellite of Saturn having an extreme contrast of low and high reflectiveness on its leading and trailing sides

IAS *abbrev.* indicated airspeed

Ia·şi (yäsh, yä′shē) city in NE Romania

-i·a·sis (ī′ə sis) ⟦ModL < Gr *-iasis*⟧ *suffix* **1** process or condition **2** pathological or morbid condition *[hypochondriasis]*

i·at·ric (ī a′trik′) *adj.* ⟦Gr *iatrikos* < *iatros,* physician < *iasthai,* to cure, heal⟧ of medicine or medical doctors; medical or medicinal: also **i·at′ri·cal**

-i·at·rics (ē a′triks′) ⟦see prec.⟧ *combining form* medical treatment *[pediatrics]*

i·at·ro- (ī a′trō, ē ä′-; -trə) ⟦Gr *iatro-* < *iatros:* see IATRIC⟧ *combining form* medicine, medical, medicinal *[iatrogenic]*

i·at·ro·gen·ic (ī a′trə jen′ik) *adj.* ⟦prec. + -GENIC⟧ caused by medical treatment: said esp. of symptoms, ailments, or disorders induced by drugs or surgery

-i·a·try (ī′ə trē) ⟦ModL *-iatria* < Gr *iatreia,* healing⟧ *combining form* medical treatment *[podiatry, psychiatry]*

IAU *abbrev.* **1** International Association of Universities **2** International Astronomical Union

ib. *abbrev.* IBID.

I·ba·dan (ē bä′dän′) city in SW Nigeria

Ibáñez *see* BLASCO IBÁÑEZ, Vicente

I-beam (ī′bēm′) *n.* a steel beam which in cross section has the shape of an I

I·be·ri·a (ī bir′ē ə) ⟦L⟧ **1** ancient region in the S Caucasus, in what is now Georgia **2** IBERIAN PENINSULA

I·be·ri·an (-ē ən) *adj.* **1** of ancient Iberia in the Caucasus or its people, language, or culture **2** of the Iberian Peninsula in ancient times or its people, language, or culture —*n.* **1** *a)* a member of an ancient people of the S Caucasus, believed to be the ancestors of the Georgians *b)* the language of this people **2** *a)* a member of an ancient people of the Iberian Peninsula *b)* the language of this people **3** a person born or living in the Iberian Peninsula

Iberian Peninsula peninsula in SW Europe, comprising Spain & Portugal

Iberville *see* D'IBERVILLE

i·bex (ī′beks′) *n., pl.* **i′bex′es, i·bi·ces** (ī′bə sēz′, ib′ə-), or **i′bex′** ⟦L, prob. < IE word in an Alpine language, signifying "climber," akin to IVY⟧ any of various Old World wild goats: the male has large, backward-curved horns

ibex

Ib·i·bi·o (ib′ə bē′ō) *n.* **1** *pl.* **-bi′os** or **-bi′o** a member of a people of SE Nigeria **2** the Niger-Congo language of this people

ibid. *abbrev.* ⟦L *ibidem*⟧ in the same place: used in referring again to the book, page, etc. cited just before

-i·bil·i·ty (ə bil′ə tē) ⟦L *-ibilitas* < -I-, thematic vowel + *-bilitas:* see -ABILITY⟧ *suffix forming nouns* -ABILITY *[sensibility]* Corresponds to -IBLE

i·bis (ī′bis) *n., pl.* **i′bis·es** or **i′bis** ⟦L < Gr < Egypt *hb*⟧ any of several large wading birds (family Threskiornithidae) with long legs and a long, slender, curved bill, found chiefly in tropical regions, as the sacred ibis of the Nile (*Threskiornis aethiopica*)

I·bi·zan hound (i bē′zən) ⟦after *Ibiza,* one of the BALEARIC ISLANDS⟧ any of a breed of tall, slender dog whose ancestry can be traced to ancient Egypt, characterized by a long, narrow head and a short or wire-haired coat, usually of white and reddish brown

-i·ble (i bəl, ə bəl) ⟦L *-ibilis*⟧ *suffix* -ABLE: used to form adjectives derived directly from Latin verbs ending in *-ire* or *-ere [divisible, legible]*

ibn- (ib ən) ⟦Ar⟧ *prefix* son of: used in many hyphenated Arabic surnames

Ibn Rushd (ib′ən ro͝osht′) *Ar. name for* AVERROËS

Ibn Sin·a (ib′ən sin′ə) *Ar. name for* AVICENNA

☆**I·bo** (ē′bō′) *n.* ⟦< Ibo *Igbo,* self-designation⟧ **1** *pl.* **I′bos′** or **I′bo′** a member of a people of SE Nigeria **2** the Kwa language of this people

i·bo·ga·ine (ī′bō gā′ēn′, -in; ī bō′gā ēn′, i bō′-) *n.* ⟦Fr *ibogaïne* < *iboga,* species name < name in a language of C Africa⟧ an alkaloid, $C_{20}H_{26}N_2O$, extracted from a tropical African shrub (*Tabernanthe iboga*) of the dogbane family: may cause hallucinations, paralysis, etc.

IBS *abbrev.* irritable bowel syndrome

Ib·sen (ib′sən), **Hen·rik** (hen′rik) 1828-1906; Norw. playwright & poet —**Ib·se·ni·an** (ib sē′nē ən) *adj.* —**Ib′sen·ism′** *n.*

i·bu·pro·fen (ī′byo͞o prō′fən) *n.* ⟦ISO- + BUTYL + PROPIONIC ACID + *-fen* (altered < PHENYL), < components of the chemical name⟧ a nonsteroidal, anti-inflammatory drug, $C_{13}H_{18}O_2$, used for reducing fever and relieving pain, esp. arthritic pain

IC (ī′sē′) *n.* INTEGRATED CIRCUIT

-ic (ik) ⟦< Fr or LGr; Fr *-ique* < L *-icus* < Gr *-ikos:* akin to Ger *-isch,* OE *-ig:* see -Y³⟧ *suffix* **1** *forming adjectives a)* of, having to do with *[volcanic] b)* like, having the nature of, characteristic of *[angelic] c)* produced by, caused by *[anaerobic] d)* producing, causing *[analgesic] e)* consisting of, containing, forming *[dactylic] f)* having, showing, affected by *[lethargic] g) Chem.* of or derived from *[benzoic, citric] h) Chem.* having a higher valence than is indicated by the suffix -OUS *[nitric, phosphoric]* **2** ⟦< ME or L or Gr: ME *-ike* < L *-icus* < Gr *-ikos:* from substantive use of respective adjectives⟧ *forming nouns* a person or thing: *a)* having, showing, affected by *[hysteric, paraplegic]* *b)* supporting, adhering to *[Gnostic]* *c)* belonging to, characteristic of *[cynic, Philippic]* *d)* derived from *[patronymic]* *e)* producing, causing *[hypnotic]* *f)* affecting *[stomachic]*

I·çá (ē sä′) *Brazilian name for* PUTUMAYO

-i·cal (i kəl, ə kəl) ⟦LL *-icalis* < *-icus*, -IC + *-alis*, -AL⟧ *suffix* -IC: adjectives formed with *-ical* sometimes have special or differentiated meanings that the corresponding *-ic* forms do not have *[historical, economical]*

ICAO *abbrev.* International Civil Aviation Organization

I·car·i·a (ī ker′ē ə, i-) Greek island in the Aegean Sea, southwest of Samos: 99 sq mi (256 sq km)

I·car·i·an (-ən) *adj.* ⟦L *Icarius* < Gr *Ikarios*, of ICARUS⟧ **1** of, like, or characteristic of Icarus **2** too daring; foolhardy; rash

Icarian Sea *former name for* the S part of the Aegean Sea, between the Cyclades & Asia Minor

Ic·a·rus (ik′ə rəs; *occas.* ī′kə-) *n.* ⟦L < Gr *Ikaros*⟧ *Gr. Myth.* the son of Daedalus: escaping from Crete by flying with wings made by Daedalus, Icarus flies so high that the sun's heat melts the wax by which his wings are fastened, and he falls to his death in the sea

ICBM (ī′sē′bē′em′) *n.* an intercontinental ballistic missile

ICC *abbrev.* Interstate Commerce Commission

ice (īs) *n.* ⟦ME *is* < OE *īs*, akin to Ger *eis* (OHG *īs*), Dan *is*, ON *iss* < IE base **eis*, **ein-* > Avestan *isu-*, icy, OSlav *inej*, snow flurry⟧ **1** the glassy, brittle, crystalline form of water made solid by cold; frozen water **2** a piece, layer, or sheet of this **3** anything like frozen water in appearance, structure, etc. **4** coldness in manner or attitude **5** *a)* a frozen dessert, usually made of water, fruit juice, egg white, and sugar *b)* [Brit.] ice cream **6** [Slang] a diamond or diamonds ☆**7** [Slang] *a)* the illegal profit made in ticket scalping, as through extra payment by ticket brokers to theater management *b)* any money paid in bribes or graft —*vt.* **iced, ic′ing 1** to change into ice; freeze **2** to cover with ice; apply ice to **3** to cool by putting ice on, in, or around **4** to cover (cake, etc.) with icing ☆**5** [Slang] to kill **6** *Ice Hockey* to shoot (the puck) from defensive to offensive territory —*vi.* to freeze: often with *up* or *over* —**break the ice** [Informal] **1** to make a start by getting over initial difficulties **2** to make a start toward getting better acquainted —☆**cut no ice** [Informal] to have no influence or effect —☆**on ice 1** [Slang] in readiness, reserve, or safekeeping **2** in abeyance **3** with success or victory ensured —**on thin ice** [Informal] in a risky, dangerous situation

Ice *abbrev.* **1** Iceland **2** Icelandic

-ice (is, əs) ⟦ME *-ice, -ise, -is* < OFr *-ice* < L *-itius*, masc., *-itia*, fem., *-itium*, neut.⟧ *suffix* condition, state, or quality of *[justice, malice]*

ice age a time of extensive glaciation covering vast areas of the earth, esp., any of several such times during the Pleistocene Epoch —**the Ice Age** the Pleistocene Epoch

ice ax an axlike mountain-climbing tool having a pick and an adz at opposite ends of the head, and a spike at the bottom of the handle

ice bag a bag, as of rubber, for holding ice, applied to the body to reduce a swelling, ease pain, etc.

ice·berg (īs′burg′) *n.* ⟦prob. via Du *ijsberg*, lit., ice mountain < Scand, as in Dan *isbjerg* < *is*, ICE + *bjerg*, mountain⟧ a great mass of ice broken off from a glacier and floating in the sea —**tip of the iceberg** ⟦from the fact that most of an iceberg is submerged and thus unseen⟧ a small difficulty, problem, misdeed, etc. that is thought to be only a part of one much larger in scope

☆**iceberg lettuce** variety of lettuce with crisp, medium-green leaves tightly folded into a round, compact head

ice·blink (īs′bliŋk′) *n.* ⟦ICE + BLINK, transl. of Du *ijsblink* or Dan *isblink*⟧ a bright reflection of sunlight, esp. in polar regions, on the bottom of a low cloud, caused by ice on a distant expanse of water or land: cf. SNOWBLINK

ice·boat (-bōt′) *n.* a light, boatlike frame, often triangular, mounted on runners and designed to be propelled, as by a sail, over frozen lakes, rivers, etc.

ice·bound (-bound′) *adj.* **1** held fast by ice: said as of a boat **2** made inaccessible by ice: said as of a port

☆**ice·box** (īs′bäks′) *n.* **1** a cabinet, box, or room with ice in it for keeping foods, etc., cold **2** [Old-fashioned] a similar cabinet or room operating by mechanical refrigeration

☆**ice·break·er** (-brāk′ər) *n.* **1** a sturdy, powerful vessel designed to cut channels through heavy ice **2** a wedgelike structure for protecting a bridge pier, dock, etc. from floating ice **3** anything serving to lessen formality or break down social reserve

ice bucket a cylindrical container for holding ice cubes; often, specif., such a container in which a bottle of wine may be placed to chill it or to keep it chilled

ice cap a dome-shaped mass of glacial ice that spreads slowly out in all directions from a center

ice-cold (īs′kōld′) *adj.* very cold *[an ice-cold drink]*

☆**ice cream** ⟦orig., *iced cream*⟧ a rich, sweet, creamy frozen food made from variously flavored cream and milk products churned or stirred to a smooth consistency during the freezing process and often containing gelatin, eggs, fruits, nuts, etc. —**ice′-cream′** *adj.*

ice dancing the sport of figure skating, usually in pairs, using movements adapted especially from ballroom dance

iced tea brewed tea served chilled, often with sugar or lemon

ice·fall (īs′fôl′) *n.* ☆**1** a jumbled mass of pulverized ice broken from the terminus of a glacier at the edge of a mountain shelf **2** that part of a valley glacier descending an unusually steep slope where the ice is broken by crevasses

ice field 1 an extensive mass of thick ice, esp. in a highland area, which may feed valley glaciers at its borders **2** an extensive area of floating sea ice, specif. an area more than 8 km (5 mi) across

ice fishing fishing on a frozen lake or stream through a hole in the ice

ice floe 1 ICE FIELD (sense 2) **2** a single piece, large or small, of floating sea ice

ice foot ⟦ICE + FOOT, transl. of Dan *isfod*⟧ a fringe of sea ice frozen to the shore in polar regions

ice hockey *see* HOCKEY (sense 1)

ice·house (īs′hous′) *n.* **1** a building where ice is stored **2** a place where ice is manufactured

Ice·land (īs′lənd) **1** island in the North Atlantic, southeast of Greenland **2** country including this island & a few small nearby islands: settled by Norwegians in 9th cent. A.D.; united with Norway (1262), with Denmark (1380); became an independent kingdom with a common sovereign with Denmark (1918), and an independent republic (1944): 39,769 sq mi (103,000 sq km); cap. Reykjavik —**Ice′land·er** *n.*

Ice·lan·dic (īs lan′dik) *adj.* of Iceland or its people, language, or culture —*n.* the North Germanic language spoken in Iceland

Iceland moss an arctic lichen (*Cetraria islandica*) sometimes used as a food and in folk medicine

Iceland poppy an arctic poppy (*Papaver nudicaule*) with fragrant, nodding flowers, cultivated in gardens

Iceland spar a transparent, colorless calcite, found esp. in Iceland: it is used by opticians for making double-refracting prisms

ice·man (īs′man′, -mən) *n., pl.* **-men′** (-men′, -mən) ☆a person who sells or delivers ice

☆**ice milk** frozen dessert like ice cream, but with a lower butterfat content

ice needle *Meteorol.* a long, thin, light ice crystal that falls slowly through the air

I·ce·ni (ī sē′nī′, -nē′) *pl.n.* ⟦L⟧ an ancient British people that, led by Queen Boadicea, rebelled against the Romans in A.D. 60 —**I·ce′ni·an** (-nē ən) *adj.*

☆**ice pack 1** PACK ICE **2** an ice bag, folded cloth, etc. filled with crushed ice and applied to the body, as to reduce a swelling or ease pain

☆**ice pick** a sharply pointed metal tool used to chop ice into small pieces

ice plant a succulent Old World plant (*Mesembryanthemum crystallinum*) of the carpetweed family, having thick leaves covered with thin, glistening cells that look like ice crystals

ice road a temporary, unpaved road plowed in winter across ice or frozen ground

ice sheet a thick layer of ice covering an extensive area for a long period, as in an ice age

ice shelf a thick mass of glacial ice extending along a polar shore, often resting on the bottom near the shore with the seaward edge afloat: it may protrude hundreds of miles out to sea

ice skate a SKATE[1] (sense 1) for gliding on ice —**ice′-skate′** *vi.* **-skat′ed, -skat′ing** —**ice skater**

☆**ice storm** a storm in which freezing rain falls and forms a glaze on surfaces

ice tea *var. of* ICED TEA

ice water 1 melted ice **2** water chilled as with ice

IC 4-A *abbrev.* Intercollegiate Association of Amateur Athletes of America

ICFTU *abbrev.* International Confederation of Free Trade Unions

Ich·a·bod (ik′ə bäd′) *n.* ⟦Heb *Ī-khābhōdh*, lit. (according to popular etym.), inglorious: orig. meaning uncert.⟧ a masculine name

I·chi·ka·wa (ē chē′kä wä′) city in SE Honshu, Japan, east of Tokyo

I Ching (ē′chiŋ′, ē′jiŋ′) ⟦Chin *yi jing*, usually transl. in E as "Book of Changes"⟧ an ancient Chinese book of divination, consisting of 64 symbolic hexagrams used to foretell the future and indicate wise courses of action: see also TRIGRAM (sense 2)

I·chi·no·mi·ya (ē′chē nō′mē yä′) city in SE Honshu, Japan, northwest of Nagoya

ich·neu·mon (ik no͞o′mən, -nyo͞o′-) *n.* ⟦L < Gr *ichneumōn*, ichneumon, lit., tracker < *ichneuein*, to track out, hunt after < *ichnos*, a track, footprint (from its supposed practice of locating and destroying crocodile eggs)⟧ **1** the Egyptian mongoose (*Herpestes ichneumon*) **2** ICHNEUMON FLY

ichneumon fly any of a large family (Ichneumonidae) of hymenopteran insects whose larvae live as parasites in or on other insect larvae: also **ichneumon wasp**

ich·nite (ik′nīt′) *n.* ⟦fol. + -ITE[1]⟧ a fossil footprint: also **ich′no·lite′** (-nō līt′)

ich·no- (ik′nō, -nə) ⟦< Gr *ichnos*, footprint⟧ *combining form* track, footprint, trace *[ichnology]*: also, before a vowel, **ichn-**

ich·nog·ra·phy (ik näg′rə fē) *n.* ⟦< Fr or L; Fr *ichnographie* < L *ichnographia* < Gr, a tracing out, ground plan: see prec. & -GRAPHY⟧ **1** FLOOR PLAN **2** the art of drawing floor plans

ich·nol·o·gy (ik näl′ə jē) *n.* ⟦ICHNO- + -LOGY⟧ the scientific study of fossil footprints —**ich′no·log′i·cal** *adj.*

i·chor (ī′kôr′, ī′kər) *n.* **1** ⟦Gr *ichōr*⟧ *Gr. Myth.* the ethereal fluid flowing instead of blood in the veins of the gods **2** ⟦ModL < Gr⟧ a thin, acrid, watery discharge from a wound or sore —**i′chor·ous** (-kər əs) *adj.*

ich·thy·ic (ik′thē ik) *adj.* ⟦fol. + -IC⟧ of or characteristic of a fish or fishes

ich·thy·o- (ik′thē ō, -ə) ⟦Gr < *ichthys*, a fish, akin to Lith *žuvìs*, Arm *jukn*, fish⟧ *combining form* fish *[ichthyology]*: also, before a vowel, **ich·thy-**

ich·thy·o·lite (ik′thē ō līt′, -thē ə-) *n.* ⟦ModL: see prec. & -LITE⟧ a fossil of a fish

ich·thy·ol·o·gy (ik′thē äl′ə jē) *n.* ⟦ModL *ichthyologia*: see ICHTHYO- & -LOGY⟧ the branch of zoology having to do with the study of fish —**ich′thy·o·log′i·cal** (-ə läj′i kəl) *adj.*, **ich′thy·o·log′ic** —**ich′thy·ol′o·gist** *n.*

ich·thy·oph·a·gous (ik′thē äf′ə gəs) ***adj.*** ⟦Gr *ichthyophagos*: see ICHTHYO- & -PHAGOUS⟧ feeding on fish; fish-eating —**ich′thy·oph′a·gy** (-jē) ***n.***

ich·thy·or·nis (ik′thē ôr′nis) ***n.*** ⟦ModL < ICHTHYO- + Gr *ornis*, bird⟧ any of a genus (*Ichthyornis*) of extinct birds of the Late Cretaceous, somewhat like a gull

ich·thy·o·saur (ik′thē ō sôr′, -thē ə-) ***n.*** ⟦< ModL < ICHTHYO- + -SAUR⟧ any of an extinct order (Ichthyosauria) of marine reptiles of the Mesozoic Era, which had a fishlike body, four paddle-shaped flippers, and a dolphinlike head: also **ich′thy·o·sau′rus** —**ich′thy·o·sau′ri·an** (-sôr′ē ən) ***adj.***

ich·thy·o·sis (ik′thē ō′sis) ***n.*** ⟦ModL: see ICHTHY(O)- & -OSIS⟧ a congenital, hereditary skin disease characterized by roughening and thickening of the horny layer of the skin, producing dryness and scaling —**ich′thy·ot′ic** (-ät′ ik) ***adj.***

-i·cian (ish′ən) ⟦Fr -*icien*: see -IC & -IAN⟧ *suffix* a person engaged in, skilled in, or specializing in (a specified field) [*phonetician*]

i·ci·cle (ī′sik′əl, -sə kəl) ***n.*** ⟦ME *isikel* < OE *īsgicel* (akin to ON *isjökull*) < *īs*, ICE + *gicel*, piece of ice, icicle (Brit dial. *ickle*), akin to ON *jökull*, icicle, glacier, *jaki*, lump of ice < IE base **yeg-*, ice > MIr *aig*, Welsh *iā*, ice, Cornish *yeyn*, cold⟧ a tapering, pointed, hanging piece of ice, formed by the freezing of dripping or falling water —**i′ci′cled** ***adj.***

i·ci·ly (ī′sə lē) ***adv.*** in an icy manner; very coldly

i·ci·ness (ī′sē nis) ***n.*** the quality or state of being icy

ic·ing[1] (ī′siŋ) ***n.*** ⟦< ICE, in earlier use, to cover a cake with a hard coating of sugar + -ING: prob. so named from the resemblance of this coating to a layer of ice⟧ a mixture variously of sugar, butter, flavoring, water or other liquid, egg whites, etc. for covering a cake or pastries; frosting —**icing on the cake** any additional benefit or value beyond what is needed or expected

ic·ing[2] (ī′siŋ) ***n.*** ⟦< ICE (*vt.* 6)⟧ *Ice Hockey* an infraction in which a player in the defensive half of the rink hits the puck past the opponent's goal line but not into the net

ICJ *abbrev.* International Court of Justice

ick (ik) ***interj.*** [Slang] used to express disgust, horror, etc.

-ick (ik) *suffix former sp. of* -IC [*magick*]

☆**ick·y** (ik′ē) ***adj.*** **ick′i·er, ick′i·est** ⟦baby talk, short for STICKY⟧ [Slang] **1** unpleasantly sticky or gluey **2** cloyingly sweet or sentimental **3** very distasteful; disgusting —**ick′i·ly** ***adv.*** —**ick′i·ness** ***n.***

i·con (ī′kän′) ***n.*** ⟦L < Gr *eikōn*, an image, figure (in LGr, sacred image) < IE base **weik-*, to resemble > Lith *į-vykti*, to happen, become true⟧ **1** *a)* an image; figure; representation *b)* any of various stylized figures, as displayed on a microcomputer screen, representing available functions or resources **2** *Eastern Orthodox Ch.* an image or picture of Jesus, Mary, a saint, etc., venerated as sacred; specif., such an image painted on a wooden panel **3** any person or thing that is revered **4** someone or something regarded as embodying the essential characteristics of an era, group, etc.

i·con- (ī′kän′) *combining form* ICONO-: used before a vowel

i·con·ic (ī kän′ik) ***adj.*** ⟦LL *iconicus* < Gr *eikonikos* < *eikōn*, an image: see ICON⟧ **1** of, or having the nature of, an icon **2** done in a fixed or conventional style: said of certain statues and busts

I·co·ni·um (ī kō′nē əm) *Latin name for* KONYA

i·con·o- (ī kän′ō, -ə) ⟦< Gr *eikōn*, a figure, image: see ICON⟧ *combining form* image, likeness, figure [*iconolatry*]

i·con·o·clasm (ī kän′ə klaz′əm) ***n.*** ⟦< prec. + Gr *klasma*, a breaking < *klaein*: see fol.⟧ the actions or beliefs of an iconoclast

i·con·o·clast (ī kän′ə klast′) ***n.*** ⟦ML *iconoclastes* < MGr *eikonoklastēs* < LGr *eikōn* (see ICON) + *klaein*, to break: for IE base see CALAMITY⟧ **1** one opposed to the religious use of images or advocating the destruction of such images **2** one who attacks and seeks to destroy widely accepted ideas, beliefs, etc. —**i·con′o·clas′tic** ***adj.***

i·co·nog·ra·phy (ī′kə näg′rə fē) ***n.*** ⟦ML *iconographia* < Gr *eikonographia*, a sketch, description: see ICONO- & -GRAPHY⟧ **1** the art of representing or illustrating by pictures, figures, images, etc. **2** the study of symbols, themes, and subject matter in the visual arts **3** *pl.* **-phies** icons collectively; esp., any system, use, or collection of symbols or images of a particular artist, artistic or historical period, religious tradition, etc. [Hindu *iconography*, the *iconography* of William Blake] **4** ICONOLOGY (sense 1) —**i′co·nog′ra·pher** ***n.*** —**i·con·o·graph·ic** (ī kän′ə graf′ik) ***adj.***, **i·con′o·graph′i·cal**

i·co·nol·a·try (ī′kə näl′ə trē) ***n.*** ⟦ICONO- + -LATRY⟧ the worship of images —**i′co·nol′a·ter** ***n.***

i·co·nol·o·gy (ī′kə näl′ə jē) ***n.*** ⟦ICONO- + -LOGY⟧ **1** the study of the meaning of works of visual art through the analysis of subject matter, symbolism and imagery, style and medium, and historical context **2** ICONOGRAPHY (senses 1-3) —**i·con·o·log·i·cal** (ī kän′ə läj′i kəl) ***adj.*** —**i′co·nol′o·gist** ***n.***

☆**i·con·o·scope** (ī kän′ə skōp′) ***n.*** ⟦ICONO- + -SCOPE⟧ a television camera electron tube, consisting of a vacuum tube enclosing a photosensitive plate on which the image is projected, and of an electron gun that scans the image with a narrow focused beam

i·co·nos·ta·sis (ī′kə näs′tə sis) ***n.***, *pl.* **-ses′** (-sēz′) ⟦ModGr(Ec) *eikonostasis* < Gr *eikōn*, an image + *stasis*, a standing < *histanai*, to STAND⟧ *Eastern Orthodox Ch.* a partition or screen, decorated with icons, separating the sanctuary from the rest of the church: also **i·con·o·stas** (ī kän′ə stas′)

i·co·sa·he·dron (ī′kō sə hē′drən) ***n.***, *pl.* **-he′dra** (-drə) or **-drons** ⟦Gr *eikosaedron*: see fol. & -HEDRON⟧ a solid figure with twenty plane surfaces —**i′co·sa·he′dral** ***adj.***

i·co·si- (ī′kō sē, -sə) ⟦Gr *eikosi-* < *eikosi*, twenty < IE **wikmti*, twenty < **wi-*, two + **dḷemt-* < base **dekṃ*, TEN⟧ *combining form* twenty: also **i′co·sa-** (-sə) or, before a vowel, **icos-**

ICRC *abbrev.* International Committee of the Red Cross

-ics (iks) ⟦-IC + -S (pl.): used as transl. of Gr -*ika* (L -*ica*), neut. pl. of -*ikos* (L -*icus*)⟧ *suffix forming nouns* **1** [*usually with sing. v.*] art, science, study [*mathematics*] **2** [*usually with sing. v.*] system [*hydroponics*] **3** [*usually with pl. v.*] activities, practices [*politics*] **4** [*usually with pl. v.*] qualities, properties [*atmospherics*]

ic·ter·ic (ik ter′ik) ***adj.*** ⟦L *ictericus* < Gr *ikterikos* < *ikteros*, jaundice⟧ relating to or having jaundice

ic·ter·us (ik′tər əs) ***n.*** ⟦ModL < Gr *ikteros*, jaundice⟧ JAUNDICE

Ic·ti·nus (ik tī′nəs) 5th cent. B.C.; Gr. architect who designed the Parthenon

ic·tus (ik′təs) ***n.***, *pl.* **-tus·es** or **-tus** ⟦L, a blow, stroke, metrical stress < pp. of *icere*, to strike, hit, beat < IE base **aik-*, **ik-*, spear, to strike with a sharp weapon > Gr *aichmē*, a spear⟧ **1** rhythmic or metrical stress, or accent **2** *Med.* a convulsion, stroke, or sudden attack

ICU *abbrev.* intensive care unit: see INTENSIVE (*adj.* 3)

i·cy (ī′sē) ***adj.*** **i′ci·er, i′ci·est** ⟦ME *isy* < OE *isig*⟧ **1** having much ice; full of or covered with ice **2** of or like ice; specif., *a)* slippery *b)* very cold; frigid **3** cold in manner or attitude; unfriendly

id (id) ***n.*** ⟦ModL < L, it, neut. sing. of *is*, he: used as transl. of Ger *es*, it⟧ *Psychoanalysis* that part of the psyche which is regarded as the reservoir of the instinctual drives and the source of psychic energy: it is dominated by the pleasure principle and irrational wishing, and its impulses are controlled through the development of the ego and superego

Id or **Ida** *abbrev.* Idaho

ID[1] (ī′dē′) [Informal] ***n.***, *pl.* **ID's** or **IDs** **1** identification ☆**2** a card (**ID card**) or document, as a birth certificate, that serves to identify a person, prove one's age, etc. —***adj.*** of or for identification [an *ID* card] —***vt.*** **ID'd** or **IDed**, **ID'ing** or **IDing** to identify Also written **I.D.**

ID[2] *abbrev.* **1** Idaho **2** identification **3** Intelligence Department **4** INTELLIGENT DESIGN

id. *abbrev.* ⟦L *idem*⟧ the same

-id (id, əd) *suffix* **1** ⟦< L -*is*, pl. -*ides* < Gr -*is*, pl. -*idēs*, patronymic suffix⟧ a thing belonging to or connected with; specif., *a)* *Astron.* a meteor that seems to radiate from a (specified) constellation [*Leonid*] *b)* *Biol.* a particle or body [*energid*] *c)* *Med.* an allergic reaction of the skin to (specified) bacteria, fungi, etc. in the body **2** ⟦< ModL -*idae*: see -IDAE⟧ an animal or plant belonging to a (specified) group [*ephemerid*] **3** *Chem.* -IDE

I'd (īd) *contraction* **1** I had **2** I would **3** I should

I·da[1] (ī′də) ***n.*** ⟦ML < OHG: akin ? to ON *Ithunn*, goddess of youth⟧ a feminine name

I·da[2] (ī′də), **Mount** **1** highest mountain in Crete, in the central part: 8,058 ft (2,456 m) **2** mountain in NW Asia Minor, in ancient Phrygia & Mysia near the site of Troy: *c.* 5,800 ft (1,768 m): Turk. name KAZDAĞI

-i·dae (i dē′) ⟦ModL, pl. of L -*ides* < Gr -*idēs*, patronymic suffix⟧ *suffix* forming the scientific names of zoological families [*Canidae* is the name of the canine family]

I·da·ho[1] (ī′də hō′) ***n.*** ⟦after fol., where principally grown⟧ a type of large, oblong white potato with a high starch content, grown chiefly in Idaho and used mainly for baking: in full **Idaho potato**

I·da·ho[2] (ī′də hō′) ⟦name said to be a Native American word but in fact invented by a local businessman, who orig. suggested it (1860) for the Colo. Territory; later given (1863) to territory that became the state of Idaho; possibly < a similar word in Shoshonean or Kiowa⟧ Mountain State of the NW U.S.: admitted 1890; 82,747 sq mi (214,314 sq km); cap. Boise: abbrev. *ID*, *Id*, or *Ida*

I·da·ho·an (ī′də hō′ən) ***adj.*** of Idaho: usually used in the predicate —***n.*** a person born or living in Idaho

-ide (īd, id) ⟦< (OX)IDE⟧ *Chem. suffix* **1** forming the second word in the name of a binary compound: added to part of the name of the nonmetallic or electronegative element or radical [sodium *chloride*, potassium *hydroxide*] **2** forming the name of any of certain classes of related compounds [*glucoside*]

i·de·a (ī dē′ə) ***n.*** ⟦L < Gr, form or appearance of a thing as opposed to its reality < IE **widswo-* < base **weid-*, to see, know > L *videre*, to see, Gr *idein*, to see, OE *witan*, to know⟧ **1** something one thinks, knows, or imagines; a thought; mental conception or image; notion **2** an opinion or belief **3** a plan; scheme; project; intention; aim **4** a hazy perception; vague impression; fanciful notion; inkling **5** meaning or significance **6** *Music* a theme or figure **7** *Philos.* according to Plato, any of the unchanging, eternal, intelligible models or archetypes of which all material things are only imperfect imitations and from which their existence derives: in modern philosophy, used variously to mean the immediate object of thought, absolute truth, etc.

SYN.—**idea**, the most general of these terms, may be applied to anything existing in the mind as an object of knowledge or thought; **concept** refers to a generalized idea of a class of objects, based on knowledge of particular instances of the class [his *concept* of a republic]; **conception**, often equivalent to **concept**, specifically refers to something conceived in the mind, or imagined [my *conception* of how the role should be played]; **thought** is used of any idea, whether or not expressed, that occurs to the mind in reasoning or contemplation [she rarely speaks her *thoughts*]; **notion** implies vagueness or incomplete intention [I had a *notion* to go]; **impression** also implies vagueness of an idea provoked by some external stimulus [I have the *impression* that she's unhappy]

i·de·al (ī dē′əl, -dēl′; ī′dē′əl, -dēl′) ***adj.*** ⟦Fr *idéal* < LL *idealis,* existing in idea, ideal < L *idea:* see prec.⟧ **1** existing as an idea, model, or archetype; consisting of ideas: see IDEA (sense 7) **2** thought of as perfect or as a perfect model; exactly as one would wish; of a perfect kind **3** of, or having the nature of, an idea or conception; identifying or illustrating an idea or conception; conceptual **4** existing only in the mind as an image, fancy, or concept; visionary; imaginary **5** *Philos.* of idealism; idealistic —***n.*** **1** *a)* a conception of something in its most excellent or perfect form *b)* a person or thing regarded as fulfilling this conception; perfect model **2** something that exists only in the mind **3** a goal or principle, esp. one of a noble character

i·de·al·ism (ī dē′əl iz′əm) ***n.*** ⟦Fr *idéalisme* or Ger *idealismus*⟧ **1** behavior or thought based on a conception of things as they should be or as one would wish them to be; idealization **2** a striving to achieve one's ideals **3** imaginative treatment in art that seeks to show the artist's or author's conception of perfection; representation of imagined types, or ideals: cf. REALISM (sense 2) **4** *Philos.* any of various theories which hold that: *a)* things exist only as ideas in the mind rather than as material objects independent of the mind (cf. REALISM, sense 3) *b)* things in the material world are actually manifestations of an independent realm of unchanging, immaterial models or forms (cf. MATERIALISM, sense 1*a*)

i·de·al·ist (ī dē′əl ist) ***n.*** **1** *a)* a person whose behavior or thought is based on ideals *b)* one who follows his or her ideals to the point of impracticality; visionary or dreamer **2** an adherent or practitioner of idealism in art or philosophy —***adj.*** IDEALISTIC

i·de·al·is·tic (ī′dē ə lis′tik, ī dē′ə-) ***adj.*** **1** of or characteristic of an idealist **2** of, characterized by, or based on idealism —**i′de·al·is′ti·cal·ly *adv.***

i·de·al·i·ty (ī′dē al′ə tē) ***n.*** **1** the state or quality of being ideal or of existing only in the mind **2** *pl.* **-ties** something that is only ideal and has no reality

i·de·al·ize (ī dē′əl īz′) ***vt.* -ized′, -iz′ing** **1** to make ideal; think of or represent as ideal **2** to regard or show as perfect or more nearly perfect than is true —***vi.*** **1** to form an ideal or ideals **2** to represent things in the manner of an idealist —**i·de′al·i·za′tion *n.*** —**i·de′al·iz′er *n.***

i·de·al·ly (ī dē′əl ē) ***adv.*** **1** in accordance with an ideal or ideals; in an ideal manner; perfectly **2** in supposing the perfect or best option or outcome [*ideally,* they'll let us stay the weekend]

ideal point a point at infinity usually thought of as being infinitely distant from the other points of a geometric system

i·de·ate (ī′dē āt′, ī dē′āt′) ***vt., vi.* -at′ed, -at′ing** ⟦see IDEA & -ATE[1]⟧ to form an idea (of); imagine or conceive

i·de·a·tion (ī′dē ā′shən) ***n.*** ⟦ML *ideatio*⟧ the formation or conception of ideas by the mind —**i′de·a′tion·al *adj.***

i·dée fixe (ē dā fēks′) ⟦Fr⟧ a fixed idea; obsession

i·dée re·çue (ē dā rə sü′) ⟦Fr, lit., received idea⟧ a generally accepted idea; convention; commonplace

i·dem (ī′dem′, ē′-) ***pron.*** ⟦L: see IDENTITY⟧ the same as mentioned

i·den·tic (ī den′tik, i-) ***adj.*** ⟦ML *identicus* < LL *identitas:* see IDENTITY⟧ identical; esp., having exactly the same wording, form, etc.: said of diplomatic messages or action by two or more governments

i·den·ti·cal (ī den′ti kəl) ***adj.*** ⟦prec. + -AL⟧ **1** the very same **2** exactly alike or equal: often followed by *with* or *to* **3** designating twins, always of the same sex, developed from a single fertilized ovum and very much alike in physical appearance: cf. FRATERNAL (sense 3) —**SYN.** SAME —**i·den′ti·cal·ly *adv.***

identical proposition *Logic* a proposition whose subject and predicate are identical in content and extent (Ex.: that which is mortal is not immortal)

i·den·ti·fi·ca·tion (ī den′tə fi kā′shən) ***n.*** ⟦Fr⟧ **1** an identifying or being identified **2** something, esp. a card or document, serving to establish the identity of someone or something [a driver's license is accepted as *identification*] **3** *Psychoanalysis* a mainly unconscious process by which a person formulates a mental image of another person and then thinks, feels, and acts in a way which resembles this image

i·den·ti·fy (ī den′tə fī′) ***vt.* -fied′, -fy′ing** ⟦LL *identificare*⟧ **1** to make identical; consider or treat as the same [to *identify* one's interests with another's] **2** to recognize as being, or show to be, the very person or thing known, described, or claimed; fix the identity of [to *identify* a biological specimen] **3** to connect, associate, or involve closely [to *identify* a person with a school of thought] **4** *Psychoanalysis* to make an identification of (oneself) with someone else: often used absolutely —***vi.*** **1** to put oneself in another's place, so as to understand and share the other's thoughts, feelings, problems, etc.; sympathize or empathize (*with*) **2** to regard oneself as being of a (specified) kind or class: with *as:* [they *identify* as working-class Americans] —**i·den′ti·fi′a·ble *adj.*** —**i·den′ti·fi′a·bly *adv.*** —**i·den′ti·fi′er *n.***

i·den·ti·kit (ī den′tə kit′) ***adj.*** ⟦< *Identi-Kit,* trademark for a set of transparencies depicting types of noses, eyes, etc. that can be combined variously to form a composite face < IDENTI(FICATION) + KIT[1]⟧ like or suggesting a composite picture, as of traits or qualities arbitrarily put together to form a type [an *identikit* lawyer]

i·den·ti·ty (ī den′tə tē) ***n., pl.* -ties** ⟦Fr *identité* < LL *identitas,* coined (prob. infl. by LL *essentitas,* essence) < L *idem,* the same, akin to Sans *idám,* the same < IE base **e-,* **ei-,* he, that > Sans *ayám,* OIr *ē,* Goth *is,* he⟧ **1** the condition or fact of being the same or exactly alike; sameness; oneness [groups united by *identity* of interests] **2** *a)* the condition or fact of being a specific person or thing; individuality *b)* the characteristics and qualities of a person, considered collectively and regarded as essential to that person's self-awareness *c)* the condition of being the same as a person or thing described or claimed *d)* a person's financial and legal individuality, as dependent upon such personal information as a Social Security number, bank-account numbers, PINs, etc. **3** *Math.* an equation which is true for all permissible sets of values of the variables which appear in it: Ex.: $x^2 - y^2 = (x + y)\ (x - y)$

☆**identity crisis** ⟦coined by E. Erikson (1902-94), U.S. psychoanalyst⟧ the condition of being uncertain of one's feelings about oneself, esp. with regard to character, goals, and origins, occurring esp. in adolescence

identity element an element of a mathematical system that does not change the other elements in the system when it operates on them: zero is the identity element for addition $(x + 0 = x)$ and one is the identity element for multiplication $(y \times 1 = y)$

identity politics political activity, views, etc. based on identification with an interest group, esp. one organized around racial, gender, or ethnic identity

identity theft the unauthorized use of private information concerning some person, to engage fraudulently in activities under that person's name

id·e·o- (id′ē ō′, -ə; ī′dē ō′, -ə) ⟦< Fr or Gr: Fr *idéo-* < Gr *idea*⟧ *combining form* idea [*ideology*]

id·e·o·gram (id′ē ō gram′, -ē ə-; ī′dē-) ***n.*** ⟦prec. + -GRAM⟧ **1** a graphic symbol representing an object or concept without expressing, as in a phonetic system, the sounds that form its name **2** a symbol representing a concept rather than a word: 5, +, ÷ are all ideograms Also **id′e·o·graph′**

id·e·o·graph·ic (id′ē ō graf′ik, -ē ə-; ī′dē-) ***adj.*** of, or having the nature of, an ideogram or ideography: also **id′e·o·graph′i·cal**

id·e·og·ra·phy (id′ē äg′rə fē, ī′dē-) ***n.*** the use of ideograms; representation of objects or ideas by graphic symbols

id·e·o·logue (id′ē ə lôg′, ī′dē-) ***n.*** ⟦Fr *idéologue,* back-form. < *idéologie:* see fol.⟧ a zealous exponent or advocate of a specified ideology

i·de·ol·o·gy (ī′dē äl′ə jē, id′ē-) ***n., pl.* -gies** ⟦Fr *idéologie:* see IDEO- & -LOGY⟧ **1** [Archaic] the philosophical study of the nature and origin of ideas **2** [Rare] thinking or theorizing that is of an idealistic, abstract, or impractical nature; fanciful speculation **3** the doctrines, opinions, or way of thinking of an individual, class, etc.; specif., the body of ideas on which a particular political, economic, or social system is based —**i′de·o·log′i·cal *adj.*, i′de·o·log′ic** —**i′de·o·log′ical·ly *adv.*** —**i′de·ol′o·gist *n.*** —**i′de·ol′o·gize′ *vt.* -gized′, -giz′ing**

id·e·o·mo·tor (id′ē ō′mōt′ər, -ē ə-; ī′dē-) ***adj.*** ⟦IDEO- + MOTOR⟧ *Psychol.* designating or of an unconscious bodily movement made in response to an idea

id·e·o·phone (id′ē ō fōn′, -ē ə-; ī′dē-) ***n.*** ⟦IDEO- + PHONE[1]⟧ *Linguis.* a form that conveys an idea or impression, as in certain African languages, by means of a sound, often reduplicated, that suggests an action, quality, manner, etc.

ides (īdz) ***pl.n.*** ⟦Fr < L *idus*⟧ [*often with sing. v.*] [*sometimes* **I-**] in the ancient Roman calendar, the 15th day of March, May, July, or October, or the 13th of the other months

id est (id est) ⟦L⟧ that is (to say)

id·i·o- (id′ē ō, -ə) ⟦Gr *idio-* < *idios,* one's own < IE **swedyos* < base **swe-,* poss. > L *suus,* his, her, one's, OE *swæs,* beloved, own⟧ *combining form* one's own, personal, distinct [*idiomorphic*]

id·i·o·blast (id′ē ō blast′) ***n.*** ⟦prec. + -BLAST⟧ a specialized plant cell, usually thick-walled and without chlorophyll, occurring isolated among other cells of different type

id·i·o·cy (id′ē ə sē) ***n.*** ⟦IDIO(T) + -CY⟧ **1** the state of being an idiot **2** behavior like that of an idiot; great foolishness or stupidity **3** *pl.* **-cies** an idiotic act or remark

id·i·o·lect (id′ē ə lekt′) ***n.*** ⟦IDIO- + (DIA)LECT⟧ *Linguis.* the dialect of an individual

id·i·om (id′ē əm) ***n.*** ⟦< Fr & LL: Fr *idiome* < LL *idioma* < Gr *idiōma,* peculiarity, idiom < *idios:* see IDIO-⟧ **1** the language or dialect of a people, region, class, etc. **2** the usual way in which the words of a particular language are joined together to express thought **3** a phrase, construction, or expression that is recognized as a unit in the usage of a given language and either differs from the usual syntactic patterns or has a meaning that differs from the literal meaning of its parts taken together (Ex.: not a word did she say; she heard it straight from the horse's mouth) **4** the style of expression characteristic of an individual [the *idiom* of Hemingway] **5** a characteristic style, as in art or music

id·i·o·mat·ic (id′ē ə mat′ik) ***adj.*** ⟦Gr *idiōmatikos,* peculiar, characteristic⟧ **1** characteristic of a particular language **2** using or having many idioms **3** of, or having the nature of, an idiom or idioms —**id′i·o·mat′i·cal·ly *adv.***

id·i·o·mor·phic (id′ē ə môr′fik) ***adj.*** ⟦IDIO- + -MORPHIC⟧ **1** having its own proper form **2** *Mineralogy* having the normal faces characteristic of a particular mineral: said of crystals in rock that have developed without interference

id·i·o·path·ic (-path′ik) ***adj.*** ⟦< Gr *idiopatheia,* feeling for oneself alone (see IDIO- & -PATHY) + -IC⟧ designating or of a disease whose cause is unknown or uncertain —**id′i·op′a·thy** (-äp′ə thē) ***n., pl.* -thies**

id·i·o·plasm (-plaz′əm) ***n.*** ⟦IDIO- + -PLASM⟧ the chromatin in a cell regarded as the part of the cell transmitting hereditary qualities: cf. TROPHOPLASM

id·i·o·syn·cra·sy (id′ē ō siŋ′krə sē, -sin′-) ***n., pl.* -sies** ⟦Gr *idiosynkrasia* < *idio-,* one's own, peculiar (see IDIO-) + *synkrasis,* a mixing together, tempering < *synkerannynai,* to mix together < *syn-,* together + *kerannynai,* to mix < IE **k̑ere-,* to mix > RARE[3], Ger *rühren,* to stir⟧ **1** the temperament or mental constitution peculiar to a person or group **2** any personal peculiarity, mannerism, etc. **3** an individual reaction to a drug, food, etc. that is different from the reaction of most people —**id′i·o·syn·crat′ic** (-sin krat′ik) ***adj.*** —**id′i·o·syn·crat′i·cal·ly *adv.***

SYN.—**idiosyncrasy** refers to any personal mannerism or peculiarity and connotes strong individuality [the *idiosyncrasies* of a writer's style]; **eccentricity** implies considerable deviation from what is normal or customary and connotes whimsicality or even mental aberration [his *eccentricity* of wearing overshoes in the summer]

id·i·ot (id′ē ət) ***n.*** ⟦ME *idiote* < OFr < L *idiota*, ignorant and common person < Gr *idiōtēs*, layman, ignorant person < *idios*, one's own, peculiar: see IDIO-⟧ **1** [Obs.] a disabled person mentally equal or inferior to a child two years old: see MENTAL RETARDATION **2** a very foolish or stupid person

☆**idiot board (*or* card)** [Slang] a board, placard, etc. bearing the lines to be spoken by a television performer, used in prompting

idiot box [Slang] television or a television set

id·i·ot·ic (id′ē ät′ik) ***adj.*** ⟦L *idioticus*, uneducated, ignorant < Gr *idiōtikos*, private, peculiar, rude⟧ of, having the nature of, or characteristic of an idiot; very foolish or stupid —**id′i·ot′i·cal·ly** ***adv.***

id·i·ot·ism (id′ē ət iz′əm) ***n.*** ⟦Fr *idiotisme*: see IDIOT & -ISM⟧ **1** [Archaic] IDIOCY **2** [Obs.] IDIOM

idiot light [Informal] any of various lights on an instrument panel or dashboard that remind or warn the operator or driver of something

id·i·ot sa·vant (id′ē ət sə vänt′, -vant′; -sav′ənt; *Fr* ē dyō sȧ vän′) *pl.* **id′i·ot sa·vants′** or Fr. ***i·di·ots sa·vants*** (ē dyō sȧ vän′) ⟦Fr, lit., wise idiot⟧ *former term for* SAVANT (sense 2)

i·dle (īd′'l) ***adj.*** **i′dler, i′dlest** ⟦ME *idel* < OE, empty, akin to Ger *eitel*, vain, empty < ? IE base **ai-dh*, to burn, shine: basic sense, either "only apparent, seeming" or "burned out"⟧ **1** *a)* having no value, use, or significance; worthless; useless [*idle* talk] *b)* vain; futile; pointless [an *idle* wish] **2** baseless; unfounded [*idle* rumors] **3** *a)* unemployed; not busy *b)* inactive; not in use [*idle* machines] *c)* not filled with activity [*idle* hours] **4** not inclined to work; lazy **5** designating certain parts of a fuel system that set an engine's idling speed —***vi.*** **i′dled, i′dling** ⟦< the *adj.*: parallel with OE *idlian*, to come to nothing, be useless⟧ **1** to move slowly or aimlessly; loaf **2** to spend time unprofitably; be unemployed or inactive **3** to operate without transmitting power: said as of a motor vehicle's engine while the vehicle is not moving —***vt.*** **1** to waste; squander: usually with *away* [to *idle* away one's youth] **2** to cause (a motor, etc.) to idle **3** to cause to be inactive or unemployed —***n.*** the state or act of idling [an engine at *idle*] —*SYN.* LOITER, VAIN —**i′dle·ness** ***n.*** —**i′dly** ***adv.***

i·dler (īd′lər, īd′'l ər) ***n.*** **1** a person who wastes time and does no work; lazy person **2** a gear placed between two others to transfer motion from one to the other without changing their direction or speed: also **idler gear** (or **wheel**) or **idle wheel** **3** a pulley riding loosely on a shaft, pressing against a belt to guide it or take up the slack: also **idler pulley**

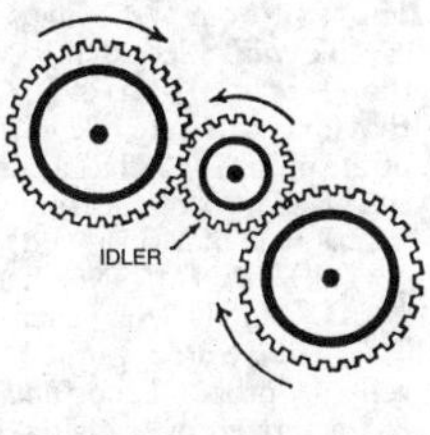

i·dlesse (īd′les′) ***n.*** ⟦< IDLE + -ESS: a pseudo-archaic coinage⟧ [Old Poet.] idleness; indolence

I·do (ē′dō) ***n.*** ⟦an Esperanto affix used as a complete word, meaning "offspring"⟧ an invented language based on Esperanto, constructed *c.* 1907 by French logician Louis de Beaufront and proposed for use as an international auxiliary language

i·do·crase (ī′dō krās′, id′ō-) ***n.*** ⟦Fr < Gr *eidos*, form (see -OID) + *krasis*, mixture⟧ VESUVIANITE

i·dol (īd′'l) ***n.*** ⟦ME *idole* < OFr < L *idolum*, an image, form, specter, apparition (in LL(Ec), idol) < Gr *eidōlon*, an image, phantom (in LGr(Ec), idol) < *eidos*, form: see -OID⟧ **1** an image of a god, used as an object or instrument of worship **2** in monotheistic belief, any heathen deity **3** any object of ardent or excessive devotion or admiration [a pop-music *idol*] **4** a false notion or idea that causes errors in thinking or reasoning **5** [Archaic] anything that has no substance but can be seen, as an image in a mirror **6** [Obs.] *a)* any image or effigy *b)* an impostor

i·dol·a·ter (ī däl′ə tər) ***n.*** ⟦ME *idolatre* < OFr < LL(Ec) *idololatres* < LGr(Ec) *eidōlolatrēs* < Gr *eidōlon* (see prec.) + *latris*, hired servant < *latron*, wages: see LARCENY⟧ **1** a person who worships an idol or idols **2** a devoted admirer; adorer

i·dol·a·trize (ī däl′ə trīz′) ***vt., vi.*** **-trized′, -triz′ing** to worship in the manner of an idolater

i·dol·a·trous (ī däl′ə trəs) ***adj.*** **1** of, or having the nature of, idolatry **2** worshiping an idol or idols **3** having or showing excessive admiration or devotion —**i·dol′a·trous·ly** ***adv.*** —**i·dol′a·trous·ness** ***n.***

i·dol·a·try (ī däl′ə trē) ***n.***, *pl.* **-tries** ⟦ME *idolatrie* < OFr < LL(Ec) *idolatria* < Gr(N.T.) *eidōlolatreia*: see IDOLATER⟧ **1** worship of idols **2** excessive devotion to or reverence for some person or thing

i·dol·ism (īd′'l iz′əm) ***n.*** **1** IDOLATRY **2** [Archaic] a fallacious notion; false reasoning

i·dol·ize (īd′'l īz′) ***vt.*** **-ized′, -iz′ing** **1** to make an idol of **2** to love or admire excessively; adore —***vi.*** to worship idols —**i′dol·i·za′tion** ***n.***

I·dom·e·neus (ī däm′i no͞os′, -nyo͞os′) ***n.*** *Gr. Legend* a king of Crete and leader of his subjects against Troy in the Trojan War

Id·u·mae·a or **Id·u·me·a** (id′yo͞o mē′ə, ī′jo͞o-; ī′dyo͞o-, ī′jo͞o-) *Gr. name for* EDOM[2] —**Id′u·mae′an** ***adj., n.***, **Id′u·me′an**

I·dun (ē′do͞on′) ***n.*** *Norse Myth.* the goddess of spring, keeper of the golden apples of youth, and wife of Bragi: also **I·du·na** (ē′do͞o nä′)

i·dyll or **i·dyl** (īd′'l; *Brit* id′'l) ***n.*** ⟦L *idyllium* < Gr *eidyllion*, dim. of *eidos*, a form, figure, image: see -OID⟧ **1** a short poem or prose work describing a simple, peaceful scene of rural or pastoral life **2** a scene or incident suitable for such a work **3** a narrative poem somewhat like a short epic [Tennyson's "*Idylls* of the King"] **4** *Music* a simple, pastoral composition

i·dyl·lic (ī dil′ik) ***adj.*** **1** of, or having the nature of, an idyll **2** pleasing and simple; pastoral or picturesque **3** romantic —**i·dyl′li·cal·ly** ***adv.***

i·dyll·ist (īd′'l ist) ***n.*** a writer or composer of idylls

IE *abbrev.* Indo-European

-ie (ē) ⟦earlier form of -Y[1]: revitalized in contr. MOVIE⟧ *suffix forming nouns* **1** small or little (person or thing specified): often used to express affection [*doggie, lassie*] **2** *a)* one that is as specified [*softie*] *b)* one connected with [*groupie, townie, roadie*]

i.e. *abbrev.* ⟦L *id est*⟧ that is (to say)

IEA *abbrev.* International Energy Agency

IED *abbrev.* improvised explosive device

IEEE (ī′trip′əl ē′) *abbrev.* Institute of Electrical and Electronics Engineers

Ie·per (ē′pər) *Fl. name for* YPRES

-i·er (ē′ər, yər; ir, ər) ⟦< various sources: (1) ME < OFr < L *-arius*; (2) Fr < OFr as in 1, with the primary stress in E on the suffix; (3) ME var. of -ER; (4) ME < -I- ending of prec. stem + *-er*⟧ *suffix forming nouns* a person concerned with (a specified action or thing) [*furrier, bombardier, glazier*]

if[1] (if) ***conj.*** ⟦ME < OE *gif*, akin to Ger *ob* (OHG *oba, ibu*, Goth *ibai*): ult. source uncert.⟧ **1** on condition that; in case; supposing [*if* I come, I'll see him; *if* I were you, I wouldn't do that] **2** allowing that; granting that [*if* she was there, I didn't see her] **3** even though or though perhaps [an engaging, *if* clumsy, story line] **4** though maybe not even [an athlete with few, *if* any, peers] **5** whether: used to introduce an indirect question [ask him *if* he knows her] ➥*If* is also used to introduce an exclamation expressing a wish or regret [*if* only I had known!] or surprise, annoyance, etc. [well, *if* that isn't the most ridiculous thing!] —***n.*** **1** a supposition or speculation **2** a condition or qualification [a clause filled with *ifs*]

if[2] *abbrev.* **1** *Baseball* infield **2** intermediate frequency

IFC *abbrev.* International Finance Corporation

I·fe (ē′fā′) city in SW Nigeria, near Ibadan

IFF *abbrev.* Identification, Friend or Foe: an electronic system for recognition of friendly aircraft, ships, etc.

if·fy (if′ē) ***adj.*** **-fi·er, -fi·est** [see IF[1] & -Y[2]] [Informal] not definite; containing doubtful elements; dependent upon varying conditions [an *iffy* situation]

If·ni (ēf′nē) region of SW Morocco: formerly a Spanish province

I formation ⟦so named because *I*-shaped on the field, with the players positioned one behind the other⟧ *Football* an offensive formation with the tailback behind the fullback and the fullback behind the quarterback

IFR *abbrev.* Instrument Flight Rules

IG *abbrev.* **1** imperial gallon **2** Inspector General

Ig·bo (ig′bō′) ***n.*** *var. of* IBO

Ig·dra·sil (ig′drə sil′) ***n.*** *alt. sp. of* YGDRASIL

ig·loo (ig′lo͞o′) ***n.***, *pl.* **-loos′** ⟦Esk *igdlu*, snow house⟧ **1** an Eskimo house or hut, usually dome-shaped and built of blocks of packed snow **2** any dome-shaped building, esp. one used for storage

ign *abbrev.* **1** ignition **2** ⟦L *ignotus*, pp. of *ignoscere* < *i-* (for *in-*), not + *gnoscere*, KNOW⟧ unknown

Ig·na·tius (ig nā′shəs), Saint (A.D. 50?-110?); Christian martyr & bishop of Antioch: his day is Oct. 17

Ignatius (of) Loyola, Saint (born *Iñigo López de Recalde*) (1491-1556); Sp. priest: founder of the Society of Jesus (Jesuit order): his day is July 31

ig·ne·ous (ig′nē əs) ***adj.*** ⟦L *igneus* < *ignis*, a fire < IE base **egnis* > Sans *agníḥ*, fire, Lith *ugnìs*⟧ **1** of, containing, or having the nature of, fire; fiery **2** produced by the action of fire; specif., formed by volcanic action or intense heat, as intrusive or extrusive rock solidified from molten magma or lava

ig·nes·cent (ig nes′ənt) ***adj.*** ⟦L *ignescens*, prp. of *ignescere*, to take fire, burn < *ignis*: see prec.⟧ **1** bursting into flame **2** giving off sparks when struck with steel —***n.*** an ignescent substance

ig·nis fat·u·us (ig′nis fach′o͞o əs) *pl.* ***ig·nes fat·u·i*** (ig′nēz fach′o͞o ī′) ⟦ML < L *ignis*, a fire + *fatuus*, foolish⟧ **1** a light seen at night moving over swamps or marshy places, believed to be caused by the combustion of gases arising from decaying organic matter: popularly called *will-o'-the-wisp* **2** a deceptive hope, goal, or influence; delusion

ig·nite (ig nīt′) ***vt.*** **-nit′ed, -nit′ing** ⟦< L *ignitus*, pp. of *ignire*, to set on fire < *ignis*: see IGNEOUS⟧ **1** to set fire to; cause to burn **2** to heat to a great degree; make glow with heat **3** to arouse the feelings of; excite —***vi.*** to catch on fire; start burning —**ig·nit′a·ble** ***adj.***, **ig·nit′i·ble** —**ig·nit′er** ***n.***, **ig·ni′tor**

ig·ni·tion (ig nish′ən) ***n.*** ⟦ModL (Paracelsus) *ignitio* < L *ignitus*: see prec.⟧ **1** a setting on fire or catching on fire **2** the means by which a thing is ignited **3** in an internal-combustion engine, *a)* the igniting of the explosive mixture in the cylinder *b)* the system for doing this; often, specif., its key-operated switch **4** *Chem.* the heating of a compound or mixture to the point of complete combustion, complete chemical change, or complete removal of volatile material —***adj.*** designating certain parts of an engine causing ignition

ig·ni·tron (ig nī′trän′) ***n.*** ⟦IGNI(TE) + (ELEC)TRON⟧ a type of mercury-arc rectifier tube having a mercury-pool cathode and a single graphite anode: when a current is passed through an igniter rod into the pool, the mercury vapor is ionized and an arc starts between the cathode and anode: used in resistance welders, the control equipment for much high-energy research apparatus, etc.

ig·no·ble (ig nō′bəl) ***adj.*** ⟦MFr < L *ignobilis,* unknown, obscure < *in-,* not + *nobilis* (OL *gnobilis*), known: see NOBLE⟧ **1** not noble in birth or position; of the common people **2** not noble in character or quality; dishonorable; base; mean —***SYN.*** BASE[2] —**ig·no′ble·ness** ***n.*** —**ig·no′bly** ***adv.***

ig·no·min·i·ous (ig′nə min′ē əs) ***adj.*** ⟦Fr *ignominieux* < L *ignominiosus*⟧ **1** characterized by or bringing on ignominy; shameful; dishonorable; disgraceful **2** contemptible; despicable **3** degrading; humiliating —**ig′no·min′i·ous·ly** ***adv.*** —**ig′no·min′i·ous·ness** ***n.***

ig·no·min·y (ig′nə min′ē) ***n.*** ⟦Fr *ignominie* < L *ignominia* < *in-,* no, not + *nomen,* NAME⟧ **1** loss of one's reputation; shame and dishonor; infamy **2** *pl.* **-min′ies** disgraceful, shameful, or contemptible quality, behavior, or act

ig·no·ra·mus (ig′nə rā′məs, -ram′əs) ***n., pl.*** **-mus·es** ⟦< the name of a lawyer in Geo. Ruggle's play *Ignoramus* (1615); L, lit., we take no notice (a legal term formerly written on a bill of indictment by a grand jury that finds it to be not a true bill)⟧ an ignorant and stupid person

ig·no·rance (ig′nə rəns) ***n.*** ⟦OFr < L *ignorantia*⟧ **1** the condition or quality of being ignorant; lack of knowledge, education, etc. **2** unawareness (*of*)

ig·no·rant (ig′nə rənt) ***adj.*** ⟦OFr < L *ignorans,* prp. of *ignorare:* see IGNORE⟧ **1** *a)* having little knowledge, education, or experience; uneducated; inexperienced *b)* lacking knowledge (*in* a particular area or matter) **2** caused by or showing lack of knowledge or education **3** unaware (*of*) —**ig′no·rant·ly** ***adv.***

SYN.—**ignorant** implies a lack of knowledge, either generally [*an ignorant* man] or on some particular subject [*ignorant* of the reason for their quarrel]; **illiterate** implies a failure to conform to some standard of knowledge, esp. in an inability to read or write; **unlettered**, sometimes a milder term for **illiterate**, often implies unfamiliarity with fine literature [although a graduate engineer, he is relatively *unlettered*]; **uneducated** and **untutored** imply a lack of formal or systematic education, as of that acquired in schools [his brilliant, though *uneducated* mind]; **unlearned** suggests a lack of learning, either generally or in some specific subject [*unlearned* in science] —**ANT. educated, learned**

ig·no·ra·ti·o e·len·chi (ig′nō rä′tē ō′ ā leŋ′kē′) ⟦L, ignorance of the refutation⟧ *Logic* a fallacious argument in which the conclusion reached or proposition proved is irrelevant to the matter at hand

ig·nore (ig nôr′) ***vt.*** **-nored′, -nor′ing** ⟦Fr *ignorer* < L *ignorare,* to have no knowledge of, ignore < *in-,* not + base of *gnarus,* knowing < IE base **ĝnā-, *ĝnō-,* KNOW⟧ **1** to disregard deliberately; pay no attention to; refuse to consider **2** *Law* to reject (a bill of indictment) for lack of evidence —***SYN.*** NEGLECT —**ig·nor′er** ***n.***

I·go·rot (ē′gō rōt′, ig′ə-) ***n.*** ⟦Sp *Igorrote,* prob. < *Igolot,* name used in certain older records: of Tagalog orig.⟧ **1** *pl.* **-rots′** or **-rot′** a member of any of several indigenous peoples of the highlands of N Luzon, in the Philippines **2** any of the Austronesian languages of these peoples

I·graine (ē grān′) ***n.*** ⟦akin ? to OFr *Iguerne* < ? Celt⟧ *Arthurian Legend* the mother of King Arthur

I·gua·çú (ē′gwä sōō′) river in S Brazil, flowing into the Paraná River on the border of NE Argentina: *c.* 800 mi (1,287 km): contains **Iguaçú Falls**, *c.* 2.5 mi (4 km) wide, comprising more than 200 cataracts averaging 200 ft (61 m) in height: also sp. **I′gua·zú′** or **I′guas·sú′**

i·gua·na (i gwä′nə, ē-) ***n.*** ⟦Sp < native SAm (Arawak) *iuana*⟧ any of a large family (Iguanidae) of mostly American tree, ground, or marine lizards; esp., any of a genus (*Iguana*) of large, tropical American lizards that feed on insects or vegetation and have a row of spines from neck to tail

i·guan·o·don (i gwan′ə dän′, ē-) ***n.*** ⟦ModL < prec. + -ODON(T)⟧ any of a genus (*Iguanodon*) of very large, herbivorous, two-footed ornithopod dinosaurs: also **i·guan′o·dont′** (-dänt′)

IGY *abbrev.* International Geophysical Year (July 1, 1957 – December 31, 1958): a period of international earth-science research

IH *abbrev.* Indo-Hittite

ihp *abbrev.* indicated horsepower

ih·ram (ē räm′) ***n.*** ⟦Ar *iḥrām,* a prohibiting < *ḥarama,* to forbid⟧ **1** a costume worn by Muslim pilgrims to Mecca, consisting of one piece of white cotton around the waist and hips and another over the shoulder **2** the restrictions and rules that must be observed by a pilgrim so dressed

IHS *abbrev.* ⟦< L miscopying of Gr ΙΗΣ, for which the proper L form would be IES⟧ a contraction derived from the Greek word ΙΗΣΟΥΣ, Jesus, used as a symbol or monogram: later misunderstood as a Latin abbreviation I.H.S. and expanded variously as *Iesus Hominum Salvator,* Jesus, Savior of Men; *In Hoc Signo (Vinces),* in this sign (thou shalt conquer); *In Hac (Cruce) Salus,* in this (cross) salvation

IJs·sel (ī′səl) river in the E Netherlands, flowing from the Rhine north into the IJsselmeer: 72 mi (116 km): also sp. **Ijs′sel** or **Ij′sel**

IJs·sel·meer (-mer′) shallow freshwater lake in N & central Netherlands: formerly part of the Zuider Zee, until cut off by a dam (1932): also sp. **Ijs′sel·meer′** or **Ij′sel·meer′**

I·ka·rí·a (ē′kä rē′ä) *Gr. name for* ICARIA

i·kat (ē′kät′) ***n.*** ⟦Malay, lit., to tie, fasten⟧ **1** a weaving technique, orig. of Asia, in which a pattern is created from tie-dyed thread **2** a fabric made by this technique

i·ke·ba·na (ē′ke bä′nä) ***n.*** ⟦Jpn⟧ the Japanese art of arranging cut flowers

Ikh·na·ton (ik nät′'n) died 1362? B.C.; king of Egypt (as *Amenhotep IV,* 1376?-62?) & religious reformer

i·kon (ī′kän′) ***n.*** *alt. sp. of* ICON

IL *abbrev.* Illinois

il- (il) *prefix* **1** IN-[1] [*illuminate*] **2** IN-[2] [*illiterate*] Used before *l*

-il (il) *suffix* -ILE [*civil, fossil*]

ILA *abbrev.* International Longshoremen's Association

i·lang-i·lang (ē′läŋ′ē′läŋ′) ***n.*** *alt. sp. of* YLANG-YLANG

-ile (il, əl, ′l, īl) ⟦< Fr or L: Fr *-il, ile* < L *-ilis*⟧ *suffix forming adjectives* of, having to do with, that can be, like, suitable for [*docile, missile*]

il·e·ac (il′ē ak′) ***adj.*** of or having to do with the ileum: also **il′e·al** (-əl)

Île-de-France (ēl də fräns′) **1** historical region of NC France, surrounding Paris **2** metropolitan region of modern France, in the same general area: 4,638 sq mi (12,012 sq km); chief city, Paris

Île du Dia·ble (ēl dü dyȧ′bl′) *Fr. name for* DEVIL'S ISLAND

il·e·i·tis (il′ē īt′is) ***n.*** inflammation of the ileum

il·e·o- (il′ē ō, -ə) *combining form* **1** ileum [*ileostomy*] **2** ileum and Also, before a vowel, **il·e-**

il·e·os·to·my (il′ē äs′tə mē) ***n.*** the surgical operation of making an opening in the ileum

il·e·um (il′ē əm) ***n., pl.*** **il′e·a** (-ə) ⟦ModL < L, flank, groin (var. of *ilium, ile*): form prob. infl. by *ileus* (see fol.) < ?⟧ the lowest part of the small intestine, opening into the large intestine

il·e·us (il′ē əs) ***n.*** ⟦ModL < L *ileus, ileos* < Gr *eileos,* colic, altered (infl. by *eilein,* to twist) < *eilyos* < *eilyein,* to envelop, creep along < IE **wel-,* to turn, roll > WALK⟧ an abnormal condition caused by paralysis or obstruction of the intestines and resulting in the failure of intestinal contents to pass through properly

i·lex (ī′leks′) ***n.*** ⟦L, holm oak⟧ **1** HOLLY **2** HOLM OAK

ILGWU *abbrev.* International Ladies' Garment Workers' Union

il·i·ac (il′ē ak′) ***adj.*** ⟦LL *iliacus,* relating to colic < L *ileus* (see ILEUS), but with meaning as if < L *ileum*⟧ of or near the ilium

Il·i·ad (il′ē əd) ***n.*** ⟦L *Ilias* (gen. *Iliadis*) < Gr *Ilias (poiēsis),* (poem) concerning Troy < *Ilios,* Ilium, Troy⟧ a long Greek epic poem, ascribed to Homer, dealing with events near the end of the Trojan War

Il·i·am·na (il′ē am′nə) ⟦< Esk: named for a mythical great fish of the lake⟧ lake in SW Alas., at the base of the Alaska Peninsula: 1,000 sq mi (2,590 sq km)

il·i·o- (il′ē ō, -ə) *combining form* **1** ilium **2** iliac and

-il·i·ty (il′i tē, il′ə-) *suffix forming nouns* the quality of being (as specified) [*civility*]: corresponds to -ILE, -IL

il·i·um (il′ē əm) ***n., pl.*** **il′i·a** (-ə) ⟦ModL: see ILEUM⟧ the flat, uppermost portion of the three sections of the innominate bone

Il·i·um (il′ē əm) ⟦see ILIAD⟧ *Latin name for* TROY

ilk[1] (ilk) ***adj.*** ⟦Scot dial. < ME *ilke* < OE *ilca,* same; prob. < **ī-līca* < *ī-,* lit., the + *-līca,* like: see LIKE[1]⟧ [Obs.] same; like —***n.*** kind; sort; class: only in **of that** (or **his, her,** etc.) **ilk**, of the same sort or class: from a misunderstanding of the phrase *of that ilk* as used in Scotland to mean "of the same name (as the place he owns or from which he comes)" [MacDonald *of that ilk* (i.e., MacDonald of MacDonald)] and often used disparagingly

ilk[2] (ilk) ***adj.*** ⟦ME, Northern & Midlands var. of *ilch, œlch* < OE *ælc:* see EACH⟧ [Chiefly Scot.] each; every: also **il·ka** (il′kə)

ill[1] (il) ***adj.*** **worse, worst** ⟦ME < ON *illr* (replacing OE *yfel,* evil, in many senses): prob. < Gmc **ilhila* < IE base **elk-,* hungry, bad > OIr *elc,* bad⟧ **1** characterized by, causing, or tending to cause harm or evil; specif., *a)* morally bad or wrong; evil [a person of *ill* repute] *b)* causing pain, hardship, etc.; adverse [*ill* fortune] *c)* not kind or friendly; harsh; cruel [*ill* will] *d)* promising trouble; unfavorable; unfortunate; unpropitious [an *ill* omen] **2** not healthy, normal, or well; having a disease; sick; indisposed **3** not according to rule, custom, desirability, etc.; faulty; imperfect [*ill* breeding] —***n.*** **1** evil or misfortune **2** anything causing harm, trouble, wrong, pain, unhappiness, etc. —***adv.*** **worse, worst** **1** in an ill manner; specif., *a)* badly; wrongly; improperly; imperfectly [*ill*-gotten gains] *b)* harshly; cruelly; unkindly [to speak *ill* of someone] *c)* [Now Rare] with annoyance or offense [he took her remarks *ill*] **2** with difficulty; scarcely [they can *ill* afford to refuse] —***SYN.*** BAD[1], SICK[1] —**ill at ease** uneasy; uncomfortable

ill[2] *abbrev.* **1** illustrated **2** illustration **3** illustrator

Ill *abbrev.* Illinois

I'll (īl) *contraction* **1** I will **2** I shall

ill-ad·vised (il′əd vīzd′) ***adj.*** showing or resulting from a lack of sound advice or careful consideration; unwise —**ill′-ad·vis′ed·ly** (-vī′zid lē) ***adv.***

I·llam·pu (ē yäm′pōō′) mountain of the Andes, in WC Bolivia: highest peak, *c.* 21,500 ft (6,553 m)

il·la·tion (i lā′shən) ***n.*** ⟦LL *illatio* < L *illatis* < *illatus* (used as pp. of *inferre,* to bring in) < *in-,* in + *latus* (used as pp. of *ferre,* to bring) < earlier **tlatus* < IE **tḷtós* < base **tel-,* to lift, bear > L *tolerare* (see TOLERATE), Gr *tlēnai,* to bear⟧ **1** the act of drawing a conclusion or making an inference **2** the conclusion drawn; inference

il·la·tive (il′ə tiv, i lāt′iv) ***adj.*** ⟦L *illativus:* see prec.⟧ **1** expressing or introducing an inference: said of such words as *therefore* **2** of, or having the nature of, an illation; inferential —***n.*** **1** an illative word or phrase **2** an illation or inference —**il′la·tive·ly** ***adv.***

ill-be·ing (il′bē′iŋ) ***n.*** an unhealthy, unhappy, or unprosperous condition

ill-bod·ing (-bōd′iŋ) ***adj.*** boding evil; ominous

ill-bred (-bred′) ***adj.*** badly brought up; lacking good manners; rude; impolite

ill-con·ceived (-kən sēvd′) ***adj.*** not properly conceived or thought out; poorly planned

ill-con·sid·ered (-kən sid′ərd) ***adj.*** not properly considered; not suitable or wise

ill-de·fined (-dē fīnd′) *adj.* poorly defined; not clear or definite

ill-dis·posed (-di spōzd′) *adj.* 1 having a bad disposition; malicious or malevolent 2 unfriendly, unkindly, or unfavorable (*toward*) or unreceptive (*to*)

il·le·gal (i lē′gəl) *adj.* ⟦< Fr *illégal* or ML *illegalis*: see IN-[2] & LEGAL⟧ 1 prohibited by law; against the law; unlawful; illicit 2 not authorized or sanctioned, as by rules —*n.* an alien who has entered a country illegally: considered an insulting term by some —**il·le·gal·i·ty** (il′lē gal′ə tē) *n., pl.* **-ties** —**il·le′gal·ly** *adv.*

il·le·gal·ize (-gə līz′) *vt.* **-ized′**, **-iz′ing** to make illegal or unlawful

il·leg·i·ble (i lej′ə bəl) *adj.* ⟦< IN-[2] + LEGIBLE⟧ very difficult or impossible to read because badly written or printed, faded, etc. —**il·leg′i·bil′i·ty** *n.* —**il·leg′i·bly** *adv.*

il·le·git·i·ma·cy (il′ə jit′ə mə sē) *n., pl.* **-cies** ⟦< fol. + -CY⟧ the fact, condition, or quality of being illegitimate

il·le·git·i·mate (il′ə jit′ə mət) *adj.* ⟦< ML *illegitimatus*, pp. of *illegitimare*, to make illegitimate < L *illegitimus*, not lawful: see IN-[2] & LEGITIMATE⟧ 1 born of parents not married to each other 2 incorrectly deduced: not logical [an *illegitimate* conclusion] 3 contrary to law or rules; illegal; unlawful 4 not in keeping with accepted usage: said of words or phrases —**il′le·git′i·mate·ly** *adv.*

ill-e·quipped (il′ē kwipt′) *adj.* not properly equipped; poorly prepared

ill fame bad reputation —**house of ill fame** a house of prostitution; brothel

ill-fat·ed (il′fāt′id) *adj.* 1 having or certain to have an evil fate or unlucky end 2 causing misfortune; unlucky

ill-fa·vored (-fā′vərd) *adj.* 1 of unpleasant or evil appearance; ugly 2 unpleasant; offensive

ill-found·ed (-foun′did) *adj.* not supported by facts or sound reasons

ill-got·ten (-gät′'n) *adj.* obtained by evil, unlawful, or dishonest means [*ill-gotten* gains]

ill humor a disagreeable, cross, or sullen mood or state of mind —**ill′-hu′mored** *adj.* —**ill′-hu′mored·ly** *adv.*

il·lib·er·al (i lib′ər əl) *adj.* ⟦Fr *illibéral* < L *illiberalis*: see IN-[2] & LIBERAL⟧ 1 [Archaic] lacking a liberal education; without culture; unrefined 2 intolerant; bigoted; narrow-minded 3 not generous; stingy —**il·lib′er·al·ism′** (-iz′əm) *n.*, **il·lib′er·al′i·ty** (-ər al′i tē) —**il·lib′er·al·ly** *adv.*

il·lic·it (i lis′it) *adj.* ⟦Fr *illicite* < L *illicitus*, not allowed: see IN-[2] & LICIT⟧ not allowed by law, custom, rule, etc.; unlawful; improper; prohibited; unauthorized —**il·lic′it·ly** *adv.* —**il·lic′it·ness** *n.*

I·lli·ma·ni (ē′yē mä′nē) mountain of the Andes, in WC Bolivia: *c.* 21,200 ft (6,462 m)

il·lim·it·a·ble (i lim′i tə bəl) *adj.* ⟦< IN-[2] + LIMITABLE⟧ without limit or bounds; immeasurable —**il·lim′it·a·bil′i·ty** *n.*, **il·lim′it·a·ble·ness** —**il·lim′it·a·bly** *adv.*

☆**il·lin·i·um** (i lin′ē əm) *n.* ⟦ModL: so named (1926) by J. A. Harris & B. S. Hopkins, U.S. chemists, after the University of ILLINOIS[2] (site of early research on the element) + -IUM⟧ *former name for* PROMETHIUM

Il·li·nois[1] (il′ə noi′; *occas.*, -noiz′) *n.* ⟦Fr, earlier also *Ilinoués* < name in an unidentified Algonquian language; ? orig. meaning, ordinary speaker⟧ 1 *pl.* **Il′li·nois′** a member of a confederacy of North American Indian peoples that lived in N Illinois, S Wisconsin, and parts of Iowa and Missouri 2 the Algonquian language of this people

Il·li·nois[2] (il′ə noi′; *occas.*, -noiz′) ⟦after prec.⟧ 1 Midwestern state of the U.S.: admitted 1818; 55,584 sq mi (143,961 sq km); cap. Springfield: abbrev. *IL* or *Ill* 2 river in Ill., flowing from southwest of Chicago into the Mississippi, near St. Louis: *c.* 273 mi (439 km)

Il·li·nois·an (-noi′ən; *occas.*, -noi′zən) *adj.* of the state of Illinois: usually used in the predicate —*n.* a person born or living in Illinois

il·liq·uid (i lik′wid) *adj.* ⟦IL- (var. of IN-[2]) + LIQUID⟧ 1 not readily convertible into cash 2 characterized by an insufficiency of cash —**il·li·quid·i·ty** (il′i kwid′i tē) *n.*

☆**il·lite** (il′īt′) *n.* ⟦< ILL(INOIS) + -ITE[1]⟧ any of a group of micalike clay minerals usually consisting of interlayered muscovite and montmorillonite

il·lit·er·a·cy (i lit′ər ə sē) *n.* 1 the state or quality of being illiterate; lack of education or culture; esp., an inability to read or write 2 *pl.* **-cies** a mistake (in writing or speaking) suggesting poor or inadequate education

il·lit·er·ate (i lit′ər it) *adj.* ⟦L *illiteratus*, unlettered: see IN-[2] & LITERATE⟧ 1 ignorant; uneducated; esp., not knowing how to read or write 2 having or showing limited knowledge, experience, or culture, esp. in some particular field [musically *illiterate*] 3 violating accepted usage in language [an *illiterate* sentence] —*n.* an illiterate person; esp., a person who does not know how to read or write —*SYN.* IGNORANT —**il·lit′er·ate·ly** *adv.*

ill-look·ing (il′look′iŋ) *adj.* 1 unattractive; ugly 2 of evil or sinister appearance

ill-man·nered (-man′ərd) *adj.* having or showing bad manners; rude; impolite —*SYN.* RUDE

ill nature an unpleasant, disagreeable, or mean disposition —**ill-na·tured** (il′nā′chərd) *adj.* —**ill′-na′tured·ly** *adv.*

ill·ness (il′nis) *n.* 1 the condition of being ill, or in poor health; sickness; disease 2 [Obs.] wickedness

il·lo·cu·tion·ar·y (il′ə kyōō′shə ner′ē) *adj.* of or having to do with that aspect of an utterance which relates to the speaker's intention as distinct from what is actually said or the effect on a listener

il·log·ic (i läj′ik) *n.* 1 the quality of being illogical 2 thought or reasoning that is illogical

il·log·i·cal (i läj′i kəl) *adj.* ⟦< IN-[2] + LOGICAL⟧ not logical or reasonable; using, based on, or caused by faulty reasoning —**il·log′i·cal′i·ty** (-kal′i tē) *n.*, **il·log′i·cal·ness** —**il·log′i·cal·ly** *adv.*

ill-o·mened (il′ō′mənd) *adj.* having bad omens; ill-fated; inauspicious

ill-pre·pared (-prē pard′) *adj.* not properly prepared; poorly prepared

ill repute bad reputation —**house of ill repute** a house of prostitution; brothel

ill-sort·ed (-sôrt′id) *adj.* badly matched [an *ill-sorted* pair]

ill-spent (-spent′) *adj.* misspent; spent wastefully

ill-starred (-stärd′) *adj.* ⟦< astrological notion of being born or conceived under an evil star⟧ unlucky or doomed to disaster

ill-suit·ed (-sōōt′id) *adj.* not suited or appropriate

ill-tem·pered (-tem′pərd) *adj.* having or showing a bad temper; quarrelsome; sullen; irritable

ill-timed (-tīmd′) *adj.* coming or done at the wrong time; inopportune [an *ill-timed* remark]

ill-treat (-trēt′) *vt.* to treat unkindly, cruelly, or unfairly; harm; abuse; maltreat —**ill′-treat′ment** *n.*

il·lume (i lōōm′) *vt.* **-lumed′**, **-lum′ing** [Old Poet.] to illuminate

il·lu·mi·nance (i lōō′mə nəns) *n. Physics* ILLUMINATION (sense 2)

il·lu·mi·nant (i lōō′mə nənt) *adj.* ⟦L *illuminans*, prp. of *illuminare*⟧ giving light; illuminating —*n.* something that illuminates, or gives light

il·lu·mi·nate (i lōō′mə nāt′) *vt.* **-nat′ed**, **-nat′ing** ⟦< L *illuminatus*, pp. of *illuminare*, to light up < *in-*, in + *luminare*, to light < *lumen* (gen. *luminis*), a light < IE **leuksmen* < base **leuk-*: see ILLUSTRATE⟧ 1 *a)* to give light to; light up *b)* to brighten; animate 2 *a)* to make clear; explain; elucidate *b)* to inform; instruct; enlighten 3 to make illustrious, glorious, or famous 4 to decorate with lights 5 *a)* to decorate (an initial letter or word) with designs, tracings, etc. of gold, silver, or bright colors *b)* to decorate (a manuscript, page border, etc.) with such initial letters, miniature pictures, etc. —*adj.* 1 made bright with light 2 enlightened in mind or spirit —*n.* [Archaic] a person who has or claims to have special knowledge —**il·lu′mi·na·ble** (-nə bəl) *adj.*

il·lu·mi·na·ti (i lōō′mə nät′ē) *pl.n.* ⟦It (or ModL) < L, pl. of *illuminatus*: see prec.⟧ 1 *sing.* **-to** (-ō) people who have or profess to have special intellectual or spiritual enlightenment 2 [**I-**] any of various societies, sects, etc., historical or conjectured, of such people: such groups are usually secret and, often specif., thought to wield a furtive influence as over world affairs: usually with *the*

il·lu·mi·na·tion (i lōō′mə nā′shən) *n.* ⟦ME *illumynacyon* < OFr *illumination* < LL *illuminatio*⟧ 1 an illuminating or being illuminated; specif., *a)* a lighting up; supplying of light *b)* clarification; explanation *c)* enlightenment; instruction *d)* decoration with lights *e)* decoration of manuscripts with designs, colors, etc. 2 *Physics* the intensity of light per unit of area 3 the designs, tracings, etc. used in decorating manuscripts 4 decorative lighting, as for a city

il·lu·mi·na·tive (i lōō′mə nāt′iv, -nə tiv) *adj.* ⟦ML *illuminativus*⟧ illuminating or tending to illuminate

il·lu·mi·na·tor (i lōō′mə nāt′ər) *n.* ⟦LL(Ec), an enlightener⟧ a person or thing that illuminates; specif., *a)* any apparatus or device for giving, concentrating, or reflecting light *b)* one who decorates manuscripts, etc.

il·lu·mine (i lōō′mən) *vt.* **-mined**, **-min·ing** ⟦ME *illuminen* < OFr *illuminer* < L *illuminare*⟧ to illuminate; light up

il·lu·min·ism (i lōō′mə niz′əm) *n.* [*often* **I-**] the doctrines or claims of any of the Illuminati —**il·lu′min·ist** *n.*

illus *abbrev.* 1 illustrated 2 illustration 3 illustrator

ill-us·age (il′yōō′sij) *n.* unfair, unkind, or cruel treatment; abuse: also written **ill usage**

ill-use (il′yōōz′; *for n.*, -yōōs′) *vt.* **-used′**, **-us′ing** to treat unfairly, unkindly, or cruelly; use badly; abuse —*n.* ILL-USAGE

il·lu·sion (i lōō′zhən) *n.* ⟦ME *illusioun* < OFr *illusion* < L *illusio*, a mocking (in LL(Ec), deceit, illusion) < *illusus*, pp. of *illudere*, to mock, play with < *in-*, on + *ludere*, to play: see LUDICROUS⟧ 1 a false idea or conception; belief or opinion not in accord with the facts 2 *a)* an unreal, deceptive, or misleading appearance or image [a large mirror giving the *illusion* of space in a small room] *b)* a trick, as one designed or performed by a stage magician, appearing to defy ordinary physical laws 3 *a)* a false perception, conception, or interpretation of what one sees, where one is, etc. *b)* the misleading image resulting in such a false impression 4 HALLUCINATION 5 a delicate, gauzy silk tulle used for veils, etc. —*SYN.* DELUSION —**il·lu′sion·al** *adj.*, **il·lu′sion·ar′y**

il·lu·sion·ism (-iz′əm) *n.* the use of illusions in art —**il·lu′sion·is′tic** *adj.*

il·lu·sion·ist (-ist) *n.* 1 a person subject to illusions, or false impressions; visionary 2 an entertainer, as a magician or conjurer, who performs sleight-of-hand tricks or other illusions 3 an artist who employs illusionism

il·lu·sive (i lōō′siv) *adj.* illusory; unreal —**il·lu′sive·ly** *adv.* —**il·lu′sive·ness** *n.*

il·lu·so·ry (i lōō′sə rē, -zə-) *adj.* producing, based on, or having the nature of, illusion; deceptive; unreal —**il·lu′so·ri·ly** *adv.* —**il·lu′so·ri·ness** *n.*

il·lus·trate (il′ə strāt′; *also* i lus′trāt′) *vt.* **-trat′ed**, **-trat′ing** ⟦< L *illustratus*, pp. of *illustrare*, to light up, illuminate < *in-*, in + *lustrare*, to illuminate < *lustrum*: see LUSTRUM⟧ 1 *a)* to make clear; explain *b)* to make clear or easily understood by examples, comparisons, etc.; exemplify 2 *a)* to furnish (books, etc.) with explanatory or decorative drawings, designs, or pictures *b)* to explain or decorate (said as of pictorial illustrations, diagrams, etc.) 3 [Obs.] *a)* to make luminous; illuminate *b)* to enlighten *c)* to make bright; adorn *d)* to make illustrious —*vi.* to offer an example for clarification

il·lus·tra·tion (il′ə strā′shən) *n.* ⟦ME *illustracione* < OFr *illustration* < L *illustratio*⟧ **1** an illustrating or being illustrated **2** an example, story, analogy, etc. used to help explain or make something clear **3** a picture, design, diagram, etc. used to decorate or explain something —**SYN.** INSTANCE —**il′lus·tra′tion·al** *adj.*

il·lus·tra·tive (i lus′trə tiv, il′ə strāt′iv) *adj.* ⟦ML(Ec) *illustrativus*⟧ serving as an illustration or example —**il·lus′tra·tive·ly** *adv.*

il·lus·tra·tor (il′ə strāt′ər; *also* i lus′trāt′ər) *n.* ⟦LL(Ec), an enlightener⟧ a person or thing that illustrates; esp., an artist who makes illustrations for books, magazines, etc.

il·lus·tri·ous (i lus′trē əs) *adj.* ⟦< L *illustris*, clear, conspicuous, distinguished (back-form. < *illustrare*: see ILLUSTRATE) + -OUS⟧ **1** [Obs.] *a)* lustrous; shining; bright *b)* very clear; evident **2** very distinguished; famous; eminent; outstanding —**SYN.** FAMOUS —**il·lus′tri·ous·ly** *adv.* —**il·lus′tri·ous·ness** *n.*

il·lu·vi·al (i lo͞o′vē əl) *adj.* of or relating to illuvium or illuviation

il·lu·vi·ate (i lo͞o′vē āt′) *vi.* **-at′ed, -at′ing** to be subjected to illuviation

il·lu·vi·a·tion (i lo͞o′vē ā′shən) *n.* ⟦see fol. & -ATION⟧ the accumulation in an underlying soil layer of materials, as colloids or soluble salts, that have been leached out of an upper layer

il·lu·vi·um (i lo͞o′vē əm) *n., pl.* **-vi·ums** or **-vi·a** (-ə) ⟦ModL < IL- + (AL)LUVIUM⟧ soil materials which have been leached from an upper layer of soil and deposited in a lower layer

ill will unfriendly feeling; hostility; hate; malice

ill-wish·er (il′wish′ər) *n.* a person who wishes evil or misfortune to another

ill·y (il′lē) *adv.* [Now Dial.] badly; ill

Il·lyr·i·a (i lir′ē ə) ancient region along the E coast of the Adriatic —**Il·lyr′ic** (-lir′ik) *adj.*

Il·lyr·i·an (i lir′ē ən) *adj.* of Illyria or its people, language, or culture —*n.* **1** a person born or living in Illyria **2** the extinct language or languages of the Illyrians, generally regarded as a distinct branch of the Indo-European family

Il·lyr·i·cum (-i kəm) Roman province including Illyria; later, Roman prefecture including much of the Balkan Peninsula & some of the area north of the Adriatic

il·men·ite (il′mən īt′) *n.* ⟦Ger *ilmenit*, after the *Ilmen* Mts. in the southern Urals + *-it*, -ITE[1]⟧ a hard, dark brown or black, rhombohedral mineral, $FeTiO_3$, an oxide of iron and titanium

ILO *abbrev.* International Labor Organization

I·lo·ca·no (ē′lō kä′nō) *n.* **1** *pl.* **-nos** or **-no** a member of a people of N Luzon **2** the Austronesian language of this people

I·lo·i·lo (ē′lō ē′lō) seaport on S Panay, in the Philippines

ILS *abbrev.* instrument landing system

IM *abbrev.* **1** instant message **2** instant messaging

im- (im) *prefix* **1** IN-[1] *[imbibe]* **2** IN-[2] *[immaterial]* Used before *b*, *m*, or *p*

I'm (īm) *contraction* I am

im·age (im′ij) *n.* ⟦OFr < *imagene* < L *imaginem*, acc. of *imago*, imitation, copy, image, akin to *aemulus*: see EMULATE⟧ **1** *a)* a representation or likeness of a person or thing, as in a drawing, painting, photograph, or sculpture *b) Bible* a sculptured figure used as an idol **2** the visual impression of something, produced variously as by reflection from a mirror, refraction through a lens, electromagnetic or ultrasound scanning, etc. **3** a person or thing very much like another; copy; counterpart; likeness *[she is the very image of her mother]* **4** *a)* a mental picture of something; conception; idea; impression ☆*b)* the concept of a person, product, institution, etc. held by the general public, often one deliberately created or modified by publicity, advertising, or propaganda **5** a type; typical example; symbol; embodiment *[he is the very image of laziness]* **6** a vivid representation; graphic description *[a drama that is the image of life]* **7** a figure of speech; esp., a metaphor or simile **8** *Psychoanalysis* a conception of a person, as of a parent, usually idealized, fashioned in the unconscious and remaining there; imago —*vt.* **-aged, -ag·ing** ⟦< the *n.*; also < Fr *imager* < the n.⟧ **1** to make a representation or imitation of; portray, delineate, etc. **2** to reflect; mirror **3** to picture in the mind; imagine **4** to be a symbol or type of **5** to describe graphically, vividly, or with figures of speech —**im′ag·er** *n.*

im·age-mak·er (im′ij māk′ər) *n.* HANDLER (sense *c*)

☆**image orthicon** *Electronics* a television camera tube of high sensitivity that combines an image converter, an orthicon, and an electron-multiplier amplifier

im·age·ry (im′ij rē, -ər ē) *n., pl.* **-ries** ⟦ME *imagerie* < OFr⟧ **1** [Now Rare] images generally; esp., statues **2** mental images, as produced by memory or imagination **3** descriptions and figures of speech **4** IMAGING

i·mag·i·na·ble (i maj′i nə bəl) *adj.* ⟦ME *ymaginable* < LL *imaginabilis*⟧ that can be imagined —**i·mag′i·na·bly** *adv.*

i·mag·i·nal[1] (i maj′i nəl) *adj.* of or having to do with the imagination or mental images

i·mag·i·nal[2] (i maj′i nəl) *adj. Entomology* of, or pertaining to, an IMAGO (sense 1)

i·mag·i·nar·y (i maj′i ner′ē) *adj.* ⟦L *imaginarius*⟧ **1** existing only in the imagination; fanciful; unreal **2** *Math.* designating or of the square root of a negative quantity, or of a complex number that is not real —**i·mag′i·nar′i·ly** *adv.* —**i·mag′i·nar′i·ness** *n.*

imaginary number a complex number in the form $a + bi$ where b is not zero: when a is zero, it is a **pure imaginary number**

imaginary part the coefficient of the square root of negative one in a complex number as 5 in $(3 + 5i)$: formerly, this coefficient multiplied by i was considered the imaginary part

imaginary unit the square root of negative one; $\sqrt{-1}$: abbrev. *i*

i·mag·i·na·tion (i maj′i nā′shən) *n.* ⟦ME *ymaginacioun* < OFr *imagination* < L *imaginatio* < pp. of *imaginari*: see IMAGINE⟧ **1** *a)* the act or power of forming mental images of what is not actually present *b)* the act or power of creating mental images of what has never been actually experienced, or of creating new images or ideas by combining previous experiences; creative power **2** anything imagined; mental image; creation of the mind; fancy **3** a foolish notion; empty fancy **4** the ability to understand and appreciate imaginative creations of others, esp. works of art and literature **5** resourcefulness in dealing with new or unusual experiences **6** [Obs.] an evil plan or scheme

i·mag·i·na·tive (i maj′i nə tiv, -nāt′iv) *adj.* ⟦ME *imaginatif* < OFr < ML *imaginativus*⟧ **1** having, using, or showing imagination; having great creative powers **2** given to imagining **3** of or resulting from imagination *[imaginative literature]* —**i·mag′i·na·tive·ly** *adv.* —**i·mag′i·na·tive·ness** *n.*

i·mag·ine (i maj′in) *vt.* **-ined, -in·ing** ⟦ME *imaginen* < OFr *imaginer* < L *imaginari* < *imago*, a likeness, IMAGE⟧ **1** to make a mental image of; form an idea or notion of; conceive in the mind; create by the imagination **2** to suppose; guess; think —*vi.* **1** to use the imagination **2** to suppose; guess; think

im·ag·ing (im′ij iŋ) *n.* the act or process of recording or producing an image, esp. by electronic means, as in radar, ultrasound, CT scan, computer graphics, etc., as for scientific research, medical diagnosis, or filmmaking

im·ag·ism (im′ə jiz′əm) *n.* ⟦after *Des Imagistes*, title of the first anthology of imagist poetry (1913)⟧ a movement in modern poetry (*c.* 1909-17), characterized by the use of precise, concrete images, free verse, and suggestion rather than complete statement —**im′ag·ist** *n., adj.* —**im′ag·is′tic** *adj.*

i·ma·go (i mā′gō, -mä′-) *n., pl.* **-goes, -gos,** or **i·mag·i·nes** (i maj′i nēz′) ⟦ModL, special use (by LINNAEUS) of L, an IMAGE, likeness⟧ **1** an insect in its final, adult, reproductive stage, generally having wings **2** *Psychoanalysis* IMAGE (*n.* 8)

i·mam (i mäm′, ē′mäm′) *n.* ⟦Ar *imām*, a guide, leader < *amma*, to walk before, precede⟧ **1** the leader of prayer in a Muslim mosque **2** [*often* **I-**] any of various kinds of Muslim leader or ruler: often used as a title

i·mam·ate (-āt′) *n.* ⟦see -ATE[2]⟧ **1** the territory ruled by an imam **2** the office or function of an imam

i·ma·ret (i mä′ret′) *n.* ⟦Turk *'imāret* < Ar *'imāra(t)*, building⟧ in Turkey, an inn or hospice

im·bal·ance (im bal′əns) *n.* lack of balance, as in proportion, force, functioning, etc.

im·be·cile (im′bə sil, -səl; *Brit*, -sēl′, -sīl′) *n.* ⟦Fr *imbécile* < L *imbecilis, imbecillus*, feeble, weak, prob. < *in-*, without + *baculus*, staff (see BACILLUS): hence "without support"⟧ **1** [Obs.] a disabled person mentally equal to a child between three and eight years old: see MENTAL RETARDATION **2** a very foolish or stupid person —*adj.* very foolish or stupid: also **im′be·cil′ic** (-sil′ik)

im·be·cil·i·ty (im′bə sil′ə tē) *n., pl.* **-ties** ⟦Fr *imbécillité* < L *imbecillitas*⟧ **1** the state of being an imbecile **2** behavior like that of an imbecile; great foolishness or stupidity **3** an imbecile act or remark

im·bed (im bed′) *vt. var. of* EMBED

im·bibe (im bīb′) *vt.* **-bibed′, -bib′ing** ⟦ME *enbiben* < L *imbibere* < *in-*, in + *bibere*, to drink < **pibere* < IE **pi-*, **pō-*, to drink > Sans *pāti*, (he) drinks, L *potare*⟧ **1** *a)* to drink (esp. alcoholic liquor) *b)* to take in with the senses; drink in **2** *a)* to absorb (moisture) *b)* to inhale **3** to take in with the mind —*vi.* to drink, esp. alcoholic liquor —**im·bib′er** *n.*

im·bi·bi·tion (im′bi bish′ən) *n.* ⟦LME: see prec. & -ITION⟧ the absorption or adsorption of water by certain colloids, as in seeds, with resultant swelling of the tissues

im·bit·ter (im bit′ər) *vt. var. of* EMBITTER

im·bri·cate (im′bri kit; *also, and for v. always*, -kāt′) *adj.* ⟦LL *imbricatus*, pp. of L *imbricare*, to cover with gutter tiles < *imbrax*, gutter tile < *imber*, rain < IE base **m̥bh-*, var. of **nebh-*, moist, water > Gr *nephos*, cloud, Ger *nebel*, fog⟧ **1** overlapping evenly, as tiles or fish scales do **2** ornamented with overlapping scales or a pattern like this —*vt.* **-cat′ed, -cat′ing** to place (tiles, shingles, etc.) in overlapping order —*vi.* to overlap —**im′bri·cate·ly** *adv.*

im·bri·ca·tion (im′bri kā′shən) *n.* ⟦see prec.⟧ **1** an overlapping, as of tiles or scales **2** an ornamental pattern like or suggesting this

im·bro·glio (im brōl′yō) *n., pl.* **-glios** ⟦It < *imbrogliare*, to embroil < or akin to MFr *embrouiller*: see EN-[1] & BROIL[2]⟧ **1** [Rare] a confused heap **2** an involved and confusing situation; state of confusion and complication **3** a confused misunderstanding or disagreement

im·brue (im bro͞o′) *vt.* **-brued′, -bru′ing** ⟦ME *enbrewen* < OFr *embreuver*, to moisten < VL **imbiberare*, for L *imbibere*: see IMBIBE⟧ to wet, soak, or stain, esp. with blood

im·brute (im bro͞ot′) *vt., vi.* **-brut′ed, -brut′ing** ⟦IM- + BRUTE⟧ to make or become brutal

im·bue (im byo͞o′) *vt.* **-bued′, -bu′ing** ⟦L *imbuere*, to wet, soak⟧ **1** [Rare] to fill with moisture; saturate **2** to fill with color; dye; tinge **3** to permeate or inspire (*with* principles, ideas, emotions, etc.)

IMF *abbrev.* International Monetary Fund

im·id·az·ole (im′id az′ōl′, im id′ə zōl′) *n.* ⟦fol. + AZOLE⟧ a colorless, heterocyclic, crystalline base, $C_3H_4N_2$

im·ide (im′īd′, -id) *n.* ⟦arbitrary alteration of AMIDE⟧ an organic compound having the divalent radical NH combined with two acid radicals

im·i·do (im′i dō′, i mē′dō′) *adj.* of an imide or imides

i·mid·o- (i mē′dō, -də; im′i dō′, -də) ⟦< IMIDE⟧ *combining form* of or containing the divalent radical NH combined with two acid radicals: also, before a vowel, **i·mid-**

i·mine (i mēn′; im′ēn′, -in) ***n.*** ⟦arbitrary alteration of AMINE⟧ a compound containing the divalent radical NH united to alkyl or other nonacid radicals

im·i·no (i mē′nō, im′i nō′) ***adj.*** of an imine or imines

i·mi·no- (i mē′nō, -nə; im′i nō′, -nə) ⟦< IMINE⟧ *combining form* of or containing the divalent radical NH united to alkyl or other nonacidic radicals: also, before a vowel, **imin-**

i·mip·ra·mine (i mi′prə mēn′) ***n.*** ⟦IMI(DE) + PR(OPYL) + AMINE⟧ a white, crystalline powder, $C_{19}H_{24}N_2$, used as an antidepressant

imit. *abbrev.* **1** imitation **2** imitative

im·i·tate (im′i tāt′) ***vt.*** **-tat′ed, -tat′ing** ⟦< L *imitatus*, pp. of *imitari*, to imitate, akin to *aemulus*: see EMULATE⟧ **1** to seek to follow the example of; take as one's model or pattern **2** to act the same as; impersonate; mimic **3** to reproduce in form, color, etc.; make a duplicate or copy of **4** to be or become like in appearance; resemble [glass made to *imitate* diamonds] —**im′i·ta·ble** (-tə bəl) ***adj.*** —**im′i·ta′tor *n.***

SYN.—imitate implies the following of something as an example or model but does not necessarily connote exact correspondence with the original [the child *imitates* the father's mannerisms]; **copy** implies as nearly exact imitation or reproduction as is possible [to *copy* a painting]; **mimic** suggests close imitation, often in fun [to *mimic* the speech peculiarities of another]; **mock** implies imitation with the intent to deride or affront [to *mock* the teacher to her face]; **ape** implies close imitation either in mimicry or in servile emulation [she *aped* the fashions of the court ladies]

im·i·ta·tion (im′i tā′shən) ***n.*** ⟦L *imitatio*⟧ **1** the act of imitating **2** *a)* the result or product of imitating; artificial likeness; copy *b)* a counterfeit **3** *Biol.* MIMICRY (sense 2) **4** *Music* the repetition in close succession of a theme or theme fragment in a different voice: used often as a technique of counterpoint **5** *Philos. a)* in Platonism, the process wherein sensible objects imperfectly embody unchanging, immaterial models or archetypes *b)* in Aristotelianism, artistic portrayal not as literal copying but as representation of the essential nature of something —***adj.*** made to resemble something specified, usually something superior or genuine; not real; sham; bogus [*imitation* leather]

im·i·ta·tive (im′i tāt′iv; *also*, -i tə tiv′) ***adj.*** ⟦LL *imitativus*⟧ **1** formed from a model; reproducing the qualities of an original or another **2** given to imitating; inclined to imitate others **3** not genuine or real; imitation **4** approximating in sound the thing or action signified; echoic: said of such words as *hiss, ripple, clang* —**im′i·ta′tive·ly *adv.*** —**im′i·ta′tive·ness *n.***

im·mac·u·late (i mak′yə lit) ***adj.*** ⟦ME < L *immaculatus* < *in-*, not + *maculatus*, pp. of *maculare*, to spot, soil < *macula*, a spot, prob. < IE base **smē-*, to smear > SMITE⟧ **1** perfectly clean; without a spot or stain; unsoiled **2** perfectly correct; without a flaw, fault, or error **3** pure; innocent; without sin **4** *Biol.* of a solid color, without marks or spots —**im·mac′u·late·ly *adv.*** —**im·mac′u·late·ness *n.*, im·mac′u·la·cy** (-lə sē)

Immaculate Conception *R.C.Ch.* the doctrine that the Virgin Mary, though conceived naturally, was from the moment of conception free from original sin: compare VIRGIN BIRTH

im·mane (i mān′) ***adj.*** ⟦L *immanis* < *in-*, not + *manus*, good < IE base **ma-*, good > OIr *maith*, good⟧ [Archaic] **1** huge; immense **2** cruel or brutal

im·ma·nent (im′ə nənt) ***adj.*** ⟦LL *immanens*, prp. of *immanere*, to remain in or near < *in-*, in + *manere*, to remain: see MANOR⟧ **1** living, remaining, or operating within; inherent **2** *Theol.* present throughout the universe: said of God: distinguished from TRANSCENDENT —**im′ma·nence *n.*, im′ma·nen·cy** —**im′ma·nent·ly *adv.***

im·ma·nent·ism (-iz′əm) ***n.*** *Theol.* the theory that God pervades the universe

Im·man·u·el (i man′yoo͞ el′, -əl) ***n.*** ⟦Heb *ʻimmānūēl* < *ʻim*, with + *ānū*, us + *ēl*, God, hence, lit., God with us⟧ **1** a masculine name: var. *Emmanuel, Manuel* **2** a name given by Isaiah to the Messiah of his prophecy (Isa. 7:14), later identified with Jesus Christ (Matt. 1:23)

im·ma·te·ri·al (im′ə tir′ē əl) ***adj.*** ⟦ME *immateriel* < LL *immaterialis*: see IN-[2] & MATERIAL⟧ **1** not consisting of matter; incorporeal; spiritual **2** that does not matter; not pertinent; unimportant —**im′ma·te′ri·al′i·ty** (-al′ə tē) ***n.***, *pl.* **-ties** —**im′ma·te′ri·al·ly *adv.***

im·ma·te·ri·al·ism (-iz′əm) ***n.*** the theory or doctrine that material things exist only as mental perceptions or ideas —**im′ma·te′ri·al·ist *n.***

im·ma·te·ri·al·ize (im′ə tir′ē əl īz′) ***vt.*** **-ized′, -iz′ing** to make immaterial

im·ma·ture (im′ə toor′, -choor′, -tyoor′) ***adj.*** ⟦L *immaturus*⟧ **1** not mature or ripe; not completely grown or developed **2** not finished or perfected; incomplete **3** lacking the emotional maturity, sense of responsibility, etc. characteristic of an adult, or of others one's own age **4** *Geol.* worn down only slightly by erosion, as a land surface having steeply entrenched stream valleys that lack well-developed flood plains —**im′ma·ture′ly *adv.*** —**im′ma·tu′ri·ty *n.*, im′ma·ture′ness**

im·meas·ur·a·ble (i mezh′ər ə bəl) ***adj.*** that cannot be measured; boundless: often used hyperbolically —**im·meas′ur·a·bil′i·ty *n.*, im·meas′ur·a·ble·ness** —**im·meas′ur·a·bly *adv.***

im·me·di·a·cy (i mē′dē ə sē) ***n.***, *pl.* **-cies** the quality or condition of being immediate; esp., direct pertinence or relevance to the present time, place, purpose, etc.

im·me·di·ate (i mē′dē it) ***adj.*** ⟦LL *immediatus*: see IN-[2] & MEDIATE⟧ **1** having nothing coming between; with no intermediary; specif., *a)* not separated in space; in direct contact; closest; nearest *b)* close by; near [*immediate* neighbors] *c)* not separated in time; acting or happening at once; without delay; instant **2** of the present time **3** next in order, succession, etc.; next in line **4** directly or closely related [one's *immediate* family] **5** directly affecting; direct; firsthand [an *immediate* cause] **6** understood or perceived directly or intuitively [an *immediate* inference] —**im·me′di·ate·ness *n.***

immediate constituent any of the meaningful hierarchical components into which a complex linguistic structure may be directly divided and which may in turn be subdivided

im·me·di·ate·ly (-lē) ***adv.*** in an immediate manner; specif., *a)* without intervening agency or cause; directly *b)* without delay; at once; instantly —***conj.*** [Chiefly Brit.] at the very moment that; as soon as [return *immediately* you are done]

im·med·i·ca·ble (i med′i kə bəl) ***adj.*** ⟦L *immedicabilis*: see IN-[2] & MEDICABLE⟧ that cannot be healed; incurable

Im·mel·mann (turn) (im′əl mən; *also*, -män′) ⟦after M. *Immelmann* (1890-1916), Ger ace⟧ a maneuver in which an airplane is half looped to an upside-down position and then half rolled back to normal, upright flight: used to gain altitude while reversing direction

im·me·mo·ri·al (im′ə môr′ē əl) ***adj.*** ⟦ML *immemorialis*: see IN-[2] & MEMORIAL⟧ extending back beyond memory or record; ancient —**im′me·mo′ri·al·ly *adv.***

im·mense (i mens′) ***adj.*** ⟦Fr < L *immensus* < *in-*, not + *mensus*, pp. of *metiri*, to MEASURE⟧ **1** [Obs.] unmeasured; limitless; infinite **2** very large; vast; huge **3** [Old Slang] very good; excellent —**SYN.** ENORMOUS —**im·mense′ly *adv.*** —**im·mense′ness *n.***

im·men·si·ty (i men′sə tē) ***n.***, *pl.* **-ties** ⟦Fr *immensité* < L *immensitas*⟧ the state or quality of being immense; specif., *a)* great size or limitless extent *b)* infinite space or being

im·men·su·ra·ble (i men′shər ə bəl) ***adj.*** ⟦< Fr or LL: Fr *immensurable* < LL *immensurabilis*: see IN-[2] & MENSURABLE⟧ IMMEASURABLE

im·merge (i murj′) ***vt.*** **-merged′, -merg′ing** ⟦L *immergere*: see fol.⟧ *archaic var. of* IMMERSE —***vi.*** to plunge or disappear, as in a liquid —**im·mer′gence *n.***

im·merse (i murs′) ***vt.*** **-mersed′, -mers′ing** ⟦< L *immersus*, pp. of *immergere*, to dip, plunge into: see IN-[1] & MERGE⟧ **1** to plunge, drop, or dip into or as if into a liquid, esp. so as to cover completely **2** to baptize by submerging in water **3** to absorb deeply; engross [*immersed* in study]

im·mersed (i murst′) ***adj.*** **1** plunged into or as if into a liquid **2** baptized by immersion **3** *Biol.* embedded in another organ **4** *Bot.* growing completely under water

im·mers·i·ble (i mur′sə bəl) ***adj.*** ☆that can be immersed in water without harm, as some electrical appliances

im·mer·sion (i mur′zhən, -shən) ***n.*** ⟦LL(Ec) *immersio*⟧ **1** an immersing or being immersed **2** baptism by immersing **3** [Now Rare] *Astron.* occultation or eclipse

immersion heater an electric coil or rod that heats water while directly immersed in it

im·mesh (i mesh′) ***vt.*** *archaic var. of* ENMESH

☆**im·mi·grant** (im′ə grənt) ***n.*** ⟦< L *immigrans*, prp.⟧ **1** a person who immigrates **2** a plant or animal that has recently appeared for the first time in a locality —***adj.*** **1** of or relating to immigrants **2** immigrating —**SYN.** ALIEN

im·mi·grate (im′ə grāt′) ***vi.*** **-grat′ed, -grat′ing** ⟦< L *immigratus*, pp. of *immigrare*, to go or remove into: see IN-[1] & MIGRATE⟧ to come into a new country, region, or environment, esp. in order to settle there: opposed to EMIGRATE —***vt.*** to bring in as an immigrant —**SYN.** MIGRATE

im·mi·gra·tion (im′ə grā′shən) ***n.*** **1** an act or instance of immigrating **2** the number of immigrants entering a country or region during a specified period

im·mi·nence (im′ə nəns) ***n.*** ⟦L *imminentia*⟧ **1** the quality or fact of being imminent: sometimes **im′mi·nen·cy** **2** something imminent; esp., impending evil, danger, etc.

im·mi·nent (im′ə nənt) ***adj.*** ⟦L *imminens*, prp. of *imminere*, to project over, threaten < *in-*, on + *minere*, to project: see MENACE⟧ likely to happen without delay; impending; often, specif., threatening, looming, etc. [*imminent* danger] —**im′mi·nent·ly *adv.***

im·mis·ci·ble (i mis′ə bəl) ***adj.*** ⟦< IN-[2] + MISCIBLE⟧ that cannot be mixed, as oil and water —**im·mis′ci·bil′i·ty *n.*** —**im·mis′ci·bly *adv.***

im·mis·er·a·tion (i miz′ər ā′shən) ***n.*** a making or becoming miserable, as through impoverishment: also **im·mis′er·i·za′tion** (-i zā′shən)

im·mit·i·ga·ble (i mit′i gə bəl) ***adj.*** ⟦LL *immitigabilis*: see IN-[2] & MITIGATE⟧ that cannot be mitigated

im·mix (i miks′) ***vt., vi.*** ⟦back-form. < obs. *immixt*, mixed in with (< L *immixtus*, pp. of *immiscere* < *in-*, in + *miscere*, to MIX), taken as Eng pp.⟧ to mix thoroughly —**im·mix′ture** (-chər) ***n.***

im·mo·bile (i mō′bəl) ***adj.*** ⟦ME *inmobill* < OFr *immobile* < L *immobilis*: see IN-[2] & MOBILE⟧ **1** not movable; firmly set or placed; stable **2** not moving or changing; motionless —**im′mo·bil′i·ty *n.***

im·mo·bi·lize (-bə līz′) ***vt.*** **-lized′, -liz′ing** ⟦Fr *immobiliser*⟧ **1** to make immobile; prevent the movement of; keep in place **2** to prevent the movement of (a limb or joint) with splints or a cast —**im·mo′bi·li·za′tion *n.***

im·mod·er·ate (i mäd′ər it) ***adj.*** ⟦ME < L *immoderatus*⟧ not moderate; without restraint; unreasonable, excessive, etc. —**SYN.** EXCESSIVE —**im·mod′er·ate·ly *adv.*** —**im·mod′er·a′tion *n.*, im·mod′er·ate·ness**, or **im·mod′er·a·cy** (-ə sē)

im·mod·est (i mäd′ist) ***adj.*** ⟦L *immodestus*, excessive, immoderate: see IN-[2] & MODEST⟧ not modest; specif., *a)* not decorous; indecent *b)* not shy or humble; bold; forward —**im·mod′est·ly *adv.*** —**im·mod′es·ty *n.***

im·mo·late (im′ə lāt′) *vt.* **-lat′ed, -lat′ing** ⟦< L *immolatus*, pp. of *immolare*, to sprinkle a victim with sacrificial meal < *in-*, on + *mola*, MEAL[2]⟧ **1** to sacrifice; esp., to offer or kill as a sacrifice **2** to kill or destroy, as by burning —**im′mo·la′tion** *n.* —**im′mo·la′tor** *n.*

im·mor·al (i môr′əl) *adj.* ⟦< IN-[2] + MORAL⟧ **1** not in conformity with accepted principles of right and wrong behavior, specif., depraved **2** not in conformity with the accepted standards of proper sexual behavior, specif., unchaste or lewd —**im·mor′al·ly** *adv.*

im·mor·al·ist (-ist) *n.* an immoral person; specif., one who advocates immorality

im·mo·ral·i·ty (im′ôr al′i tē, im′ō ral′-) *n.* **1** the state or quality of being immoral **2** immoral behavior **3** *pl.* **-ties** an immoral act or practice; vice

im·mor·tal (i môrt′'l) *adj.* ⟦ME < L *immortalis*: see IN-[2] & MORTAL⟧ **1** not mortal; everlasting **2** of or relating to immortality **3** lasting a long time; enduring **4** having lasting fame [an *immortal* poet] —*n.* an immortal being; specif., *a)* [*pl.*] the ancient Greek or Roman gods *b)* a person having lasting fame —**im·mor·tal·i·ty** (im′ôr tal′i tē) *n.* —**im·mor′tal·ly** *adv.*

im·mor·tal·ize (i môrt′'l īz′) *vt.* **-ized′, -iz′ing** to make immortal; esp., to give lasting fame to —**im·mor′tal·i·za′tion** *n.* —**im·mor′tal·iz′er** *n.*

im·mor·telle (im′ôr tel′) *n.* ⟦Fr fem. of *immortel*, IMMORTAL⟧ EVERLASTING (*n.* 2)

im·mo·tile (i mōt′'l) *adj.* not motile; unable to move

im·mov·a·ble (i mo͞ov′ə bəl) *adj.* ⟦ME *immouable*⟧ **1** that cannot be moved; firmly fixed; not capable of movement **2** not moving; immobile; motionless; stationary **3** that cannot be changed; unyielding; steadfast **4** unemotional; impassive —*n.* [*pl.*] *Law* immovable objects or property, as land, buildings, etc. —**im·mov′a·bil′i·ty** *n.*, **im·mov′a·ble·ness** —**im·mov′a·bly** *adv.*

im·mune (i myo͞on′) *adj.* ⟦ME *immuin* < L *immunis*, free from public service, exempt < *in-*, without + *munia*, duties, functions < IE **moini-*: see COMMON⟧ **1** protected against something disagreeable or harmful **2** not susceptible to some specified disease because of the presence of the specific antibodies **3** of or relating to immunity or the immune system —*n.* an immune person

immune body ANTIBODY

immune response a biological response involving the natural production of antibodies, macrophages, etc. as in reaction to the presence in the body of bacteria, a poison, or a transplanted organ: also called **immune reaction**

immune system the system that protects the body from disease by producing antibodies

im·mu·ni·ty (i myo͞on′ə tē) *n.*, *pl.* **-ties** ⟦ME *ynmunite* < OFr *immunité* < L *immunitas*, freedom from public service < *immunis*: see IMMUNE⟧ **1** exemption or freedom from something burdensome or otherwise unpleasant; specif., legal exemption as from criminal prosecution or civil suit [a foreign ambassador with diplomatic *immunity*] **2** resistance to or protection against a specified disease; power to resist infection, esp. as a result of antibody formation —*SYN.* EXEMPTION

im·mu·nize (im′yo͞o nīz′, -yə-) *vt.* **-nized′, -niz′ing** to give immunity to, as by inoculation —**im′mu·ni·za′tion** *n.*

im·mu·no- (im′yə nō, i myo͞o′nō) *combining form* immune, immunity [*immunology*]

im·mu·no·as·say (im′yə nō as′ā, i myo͞o′nō-) *n.* ⟦prec. + ASSAY⟧ a technique for analyzing, and measuring the concentration of, antibodies, hormones, etc. in the body, used in diagnosing disease, detecting the presence of a tumor or drug, etc.

im·mu·no·chem·is·try (-kem′is trē) *n.* the study of the chemical reactions and phenomena of immunity —**im′mu·no·chem′i·cal** *adj.*

im·mu·no·com·pe·tent (-käm′pə tənt) *adj.* able to have a normal immune response —**im′mu·no·com′pe·tence** *n.*

im·mu·no·com·pro·mised (-käm′prə mīzd′) *adj.* having a weakened or otherwise impaired immune system

im·mu·no·cy·to·chem·is·try (-sīt′ō kem′is trē) *n.* the branch of immunochemistry dealing with cells and cellular activity —**im′mu·no·cy′to·chem′i·cal** *adj.*

im·mu·no·de·fi·cien·cy (-dē fish′ən sē) *n.* a condition in which the ability of the immune system to produce antibodies is impaired

im·mu·no·fluo·res·cence (-flô res′əns) *n.* a technique for locating specific antigens in tissues, using a special microscope with ultraviolet light and antibodies labeled with fluorescent dyes —**im′mu·no·fluo·res′cent** *adj.*

im·mu·no·ge·net·ics (-jə net′iks) *n.* the branch of genetics dealing with inherited differences in antigens or antibody responses

im·mu·no·gen·ic (-jen′ik) *adj.* producing an immune response —**im′mu·no·gen′i·cal·ly** *adv.*

im·mu·no·glob·u·lin (-gläb′yə lin) *n.* a globulin protein that participates in the immune reaction as the antibody for a specific antigen

☆**im·mu·nol·o·gy** (im′yo͞o näl′ə jē) *n.* ⟦IMMUNO- + -LOGY⟧ the branch of science dealing with *a)* antigens and antibodies, esp. concerning immunity to some infections *b)* cellular immune mechanisms, as in the rejection of foreign tissues —**im′mu·no·log′i·cal** (-nō läj′i kəl) *adj.*, **im′mu·no·log′ic** —**im′mu·no·log′i·cal·ly** *adv.* —**im′mu·nol′o·gist** *n.*

im·mu·no·re·ac·tion (im′yə nō rē ak′shən, i myo͞o′nō-) *n.* the reaction between an antigen and its antibody

im·mu·no·sup·pres·sion (-sə presh′ən) *n.* the inactivation of a specific antibody by various agents, thus permitting the acceptance of a foreign substance, as a transplant, by an organism —**im′mu·no·sup·pres′sant** *adj.*, **im′mu·no·sup·pres′sive**

im·mu·no·ther·a·py (-ther′ə pē) *n.* **1** the treatment of disease or infection by immunization **2** the process of immunosuppression

im·mure (i myoor′) *vt.* **-mured′, -mur′ing** ⟦< OFr or ML: OFr *emmurrer* < ML *immurare* < L *in-*, in + *murus*, wall: see MERE[3]⟧ **1** to shut up within or as within walls; imprison, confine, or seclude **2** to entomb in a wall —**im·mure′ment** *n.*

im·mu·ta·ble (i myo͞ot′ə bəl) *adj.* ⟦ME < L *immutabilis*: see IN-[2] & MUTABLE⟧ never changing or varying; unchangeable —**im·mu′ta·bil′i·ty** *n.*, **im·mu′ta·ble·ness** —**im·mu′ta·bly** *adv.*

Im·o·gen (im′ə jen′) *n.* ⟦first recorded in Shakespeare's *Cymbeline* (First Folio): ? misprint for Holinshed's *Innogen*⟧ a feminine name: also **Im′o·gene′** (-jēn′)

imp[1] (imp) *n.* ⟦ME *impe* < OE *impa* < *impian*, to graft in, akin to OHG *impfōn* < VL **imputare* (< *im-*, in + *putare*, to prune), transl. of Gr *emphyteyein*, to engraft < *emphyta*, scion < *em-*, in + *phyton*, growth: see -PHYTE⟧ **1** [Obs.] *a)* a shoot or graft *b)* a child; offspring **2** a devil's offspring; young demon **3** a mischievous child —*vt.* ⟦ME *impen* < OE *impian*⟧ *Falconry* to repair (the wing or tail of a falcon) by grafting on (feathers)

imp[2] *abbrev.* **1** imperative **2** imperfect **3** imperial **4** impersonal **5** import **6** importer **7** imprimatur

im·pact (im pakt′, im′pakt′; *for n.* im′pakt′) *vt.* ⟦< L *impactus*, pp. of *impingere*, to press firmly together: see IMPINGE⟧ **1** to force tightly together; pack; wedge **2** to affect: a usage still objected to by some —*vi.* **1** to hit with force **2** to have an effect: usually with *on*: a usage still objected to by some —*n.* **1** a striking together; violent contact; collision **2** the force of a collision; shock **3** the power of an event, idea, etc. to produce changes, move the feelings, etc. —**im·pac′tion** *n.*

im·pact·ed (im pak′tid) *adj.* **1** pressed tightly together; driven firmly in; wedged in; esp., firmly lodged in the jaw: said of a tooth unable to erupt properly because of its abnormal position, lack of space, etc. ☆**2** financially or otherwise strained by heavy demand on public services, as schools: said esp. of areas having a high population density or a large proportion of federal employees living on nontaxable federal property such as a military base

im·pac·tive (im pak′tiv) *adj.* of or having an impact

im·pair (im per′) *vt.* ⟦ME *empeiren* < OFr *empeirer* < VL **impejorare* < L *in-*, intens. + LL *pejorare*, to make worse: see PEJORATIVE⟧ to make worse, less, weaker, etc.; reduce an ability or function —*SYN.* INJURE —**im·pair′ment** *n.*

im·paired (im perd′) *adj.* disabled; handicapped: often used in comb. [visually *impaired*]

im·pa·la (im pä′lə, -pal′ə) *n.*, *pl.* **-la** or **-las** ⟦Zulu⟧ a medium-sized, reddish antelope (*Aepyceros melampus*) of central and S Africa

im·pale (im pāl′) *vt.* **-paled′, -pal′ing** ⟦Fr *empaler* < ML *impalare* < L *in-*, on + *palus*, a stake, POLE[1]⟧ **1** *a)* to pierce through with, or fix on, something pointed; transfix *b)* to punish or torture by fixing on a stake **2** to make helpless, as if fixed on a stake [*impaled* by her glance] **3** *Heraldry* to join (two coats of arms) side by side on one shield —**im·pale′ment** *n.* —**im·pal′er** *n.*

im·pal·pa·ble (im pal′pə bəl) *adj.* ⟦Fr < ML *impalpabilis*: see IN-[2] & PALPABLE⟧ **1** that cannot be felt by touching **2** too slight or subtle to be grasped easily by the mind —**im·pal′pa·bil′i·ty** *n.* —**im·pal′pa·bly** *adv.*

im·pa·na·tion (im′pə nā′shən) *n.* ⟦ML *impanatio* < pp. of *impanare*, to embody in bread < L *in-*, in + *panis*, bread: see FOOD⟧ *Theol.* the doctrine that the body and blood of Christ are present in the bread and wine of the Eucharist after consecration but without change in the substance of the bread and wine: cf. TRANSUBSTANTIATION

im·pan·el (im pan′əl) *vt.* **-eled** or **-elled, -el·ing** or **-el·ling** **1** to enter the name or names of on a jury list **2** to choose (a jury) from such a list —**im·pan′el·ment** *n.*

im·part (im pärt′) *vt.* ⟦ME *imparten* < OFr *empartir* < L *impartire*: see IN-[1] & PART[2]⟧ **1** to give a share or portion of **2** to make known; tell; reveal —**im·part′a·ble** *adj.* —**im′par·ta′tion** *n.* —**im·part′er** *n.*

im·par·tial (im pär′shəl) *adj.* ⟦< IN-[2] + PARTIAL⟧ favoring no one side or party more than another; without prejudice or bias; fair; just —*SYN.* FAIR[1] —**im·par′ti·al′i·ty** (-shē al′ə tē) *n.* —**im·par′tial·ly** *adv.*

im·part·i·ble (im pärt′ə bəl) *adj.* ⟦LL *impartibilis*: see IN-[2] & PARTIBLE⟧ that cannot be partitioned or divided; indivisible: said of an estate —**im·part′i·bly** *adv.* —**im·part′i·bil′i·ty** *n.*

im·pass·a·ble (im pas′ə bəl) *adj.* that cannot be passed, crossed, or traveled over [a highway made *impassable* by flooding] —**im·pass′a·bil′i·ty** *n.* —**im·pass′a·bly** *adv.*

im·passe (im′pas′, im pas′) *n.* ⟦Fr: see IN-[2] & PASS[3]⟧ **1** a passage open only at one end; blind alley **2** a situation offering no escape, as a difficulty without solution, an argument where no agreement is possible, etc.

im·pas·si·ble (im pas′ə bəl) *adj.* ⟦ME < OFr < LL(Ec) *impassibilis*: see IN-[2] & PASSIBLE⟧ **1** that cannot feel pain; incapable of suffering **2** that cannot be injured; invulnerable **3** that cannot be moved emotionally; unfeeling —**im·pas′si·bil′i·ty** *n.* —**im·pas′si·bly** *adv.*

im·pas·sion (im pash′ən) *vt.* ⟦It *impassionare*⟧ to fill with passion; arouse emotionally

im·pas·sioned (-ənd) *adj.* filled with passion; having or showing strong feeling; passionate; fiery; ardent —*SYN.* PASSIONATE —**im·pas′sioned·ly** *adv.*

im·pas·sive (im pas′iv) *adj.* ⟦< IN-[2] + PASSIVE⟧ **1** not feeling pain; not liable to suffering; insensible **2** not feeling or showing emotion; placid; calm —**im·pas′sive·ly** (im′pə siv′ə tē) *adv.* —**im·pas·siv·i·ty** (im′pa siv′i tē) *n.*, **im·pas′sive·ness**

SYN.—impassive means not having or showing any feeling or emotion, although it does not necessarily connote an incapability of being affected [his *impassive* face did not betray his anguish]; **apathetic** stresses an indifference or listlessness from which one cannot easily be stirred to feeling [an *apathetic* electorate]; **stoical** implies an austere indifference to pleasure or pain and specifically suggests the ability to endure suffering without flinching [he received the bad news with *stoic* calm]; **stolid** suggests dullness, obtuseness, or stupidity in one who is not easily moved or excited; **phlegmatic** is applied to one who by temperament is not easily disconcerted or aroused

im·paste (im pāst′) *vt.* **-past′ed, -past′ing** ⟦It *impastare* < *in-* (see IN-[1]) + *pasta*, PASTE⟧ 1 to enclose or crust over with or as with paste 2 to make a paste or crust of 3 to apply a thick coat as of paint to

im·pas·to (im päs′tō, -pas′-) *n.* ⟦It < *impastare*: see prec.⟧ 1 painting in which the paint is laid thickly on the canvas 2 paint so laid on

im·pa·tience (im pā′shəns) *n.* ⟦ME *impacience* < OFr < L *impatientia*⟧ lack of patience; specif., *a)* annoyance because of delay, opposition, etc. *b)* restless eagerness to do something, go somewhere, etc.

im·pa·ti·ens (im pā′shē enz′, -shənz-) *n.* ⟦ModL < L (see fol.): so named because the seedpods burst at the slightest touch⟧ any of a genus (*Impatiens*) of plants of the balsam family, with spurred flowers and pods that burst and scatter their seeds when ripe

im·pa·tient (im pā′shənt) *adj.* ⟦ME *impacient* < OFr < L *impatiens*: see IN-[2] & PATIENT⟧ feeling or showing a lack of patience; specif., *a)* feeling or showing annoyance because of delay, opposition, etc. *b)* feeling or showing restless eagerness to do something, go somewhere, etc. —**impatient of** not willing to bear or tolerate —**im·pa′tient·ly** *adv.*

im·peach (im pēch′) *vt.* ⟦ME *empechen* < OFr *empechier*, to hinder < LL *impedicare*, to fetter, entangle < L *in-*, in + *pedica*, a fetter < *pes*, FOOT⟧ 1 to challenge or discredit (a person's honor, reputation, etc.) 2 *a)* to formally charge (a public official) with malfeasance in office *b)* loosely, to remove from office (a public official so charged) —*n.* [Obs.] a challenge or accusation —**SYN.** ACCUSE —**im·peach′ment** *n.*

im·peach·a·ble (im pēch′ə bəl) *adj.* 1 liable to be impeached 2 making one liable to be impeached [an *impeachable* act] —**im·peach′a·bil′i·ty** *n.*

im·pec·ca·ble (im pek′ə bəl) *adj.* ⟦L *impeccabilis* < *in-*, not + *peccare*, to sin⟧ 1 not liable to sin, incapable of wrongdoing 2 without defect or error; faultless; flawless —**im·pec′ca·bil′i·ty** *n.* —**im·pec′ca·bly** *adv.*

im·pe·cu·ni·ous (im′pi kyo͞o′nē əs) *adj.* ⟦< IN-[2] + obs. *pecunious*, rich < ME < OFr *pécunieux* < L *pecuniosus*, wealthy < *pecunia*, money: see PECUNIARY⟧ having no money; poor; penniless —**SYN.** POOR —**im′pe·cu′ni·os′i·ty** (-äs′i tē) *n.*, **im′pe·cu′ni·ous·ness** —**im′pe·cu′ni·ous·ly** *adv.*

im·ped·ance (im pēd′′ns) *n.* ⟦< fol. + -ANCE⟧ 1 the total opposition offered by an electric circuit to the flow of an alternating current of a single frequency: it is a combination of resistance and reactance and is measured in ohms: the reciprocal of admittance: symbol, Z 2 the ratio of the force per unit area to the volume displacement of a given surface across which sound is being transmitted

im·pede (im pēd′) *vt.* **-ped′ed, -ped′ing** ⟦L *impedire*, to entangle, ensnare, lit., to hold the feet < *in-*, in + *pes* (gen. *pedis*), FOOT⟧ to bar or hinder the progress of; obstruct or delay —**SYN.** HINDER[1] —**im·ped′er** *n.*

im·ped·i·ment (im ped′ə mənt) *n.* ⟦ME < L *impedimentum*, hindrance⟧ 1 [Now Rare] an impeding or being impeded; obstruction 2 anything that impedes; specif., *a)* a speech defect; stutter, lisp, stammer, etc. (in full **speech impediment**) *b)* anything preventing the making of a legal contract, esp. of a marriage contract *c)* *R.C.Ch.* anything making marriage or ordination invalid or illicit —**SYN.** OBSTACLE

im·ped·i·men·ta (im ped′ə men′tə) *pl.n.* ⟦L, pl. of *impedimentum*: see prec.⟧ things hindering progress, as on a trip; esp., baggage, supplies, or equipment, as those carried along with an army

im·pel (im pel′) *vt.* **-pelled′, -pel′ling** ⟦ME *impellen* < L *impellere* < *in-*, in + *pellere*, to drive < IE base **pel-*, to push into motion, drive > FELT⟧ 1 to push, drive, or move forward; propel 2 to force, compel, or urge; incite; constrain —**im·pel′lent** *adj., n.*

im·pel·ler (im pel′ər) *n.* any person or thing that impels, as the rotorlike part in a water pump

im·pend (im pend′) *vi.* ⟦L *impendere*, to overhang, threaten < *in-*, in + *pendere*, to hang, prob. < IE base **(s)pen(d)-*, to pull, stretch > SPIN⟧ 1 [Now Rare] to hang or be suspended (*over*) 2 *a)* to be about to happen; be imminent *b)* to threaten —**im·pend′ing** *adj.*

im·pen·e·tra·ble (im pen′i trə bəl) *adj.* ⟦ME *inpenetrable* < Fr *impénétrable* < L *impenetrabilis*⟧ 1 that cannot be penetrated or passed through [an *impenetrable* jungle] 2 that cannot be solved or understood; unfathomable; inscrutable 3 unreceptive to ideas, impressions, influences, etc. 4 *Physics* having that property of matter by which two bodies are prevented from occupying the same space at the same time —**im·pen′e·tra·bil′i·ty** *n.* —**im·pen′e·tra·bly** *adv.*

im·pen·i·tent (im pen′ə tənt) *adj.* ⟦LL(Ec) *impaenitens*⟧ without regret, shame, or remorse; unrepentant —*n.* an impenitent person —**im·pen′i·tence** *n.*, **im·pen′i·ten·cy** —**im·pen′i·tent·ly** *adv.*

imper *abbrev.* imperative

im·per·a·tive (im per′ə tiv) *adj.* ⟦LL *imperativus*, commanding < pp. of L *imperare*, to command: see EMPEROR⟧ 1 having the nature of, or indicating, power or authority; commanding [an *imperative* gesture] 2 absolutely necessary; urgent; compelling [it is *imperative* that I go] 3 *Gram.* designating or of the mood of a verb that expresses a command, strong request, or exhortation —*n.* 1 a binding or compelling rule, duty, requirement, etc. 2 a command; order 3 *Gram. a)* the imperative mood *b)* a verb in this mood —**im·per′a·tive·ly** *adv.* —**im·per′a·tive·ness** *n.*

im·pe·ra·tor (im′pə rā′tôr′, -rä′-; -tər) *n.* ⟦L, commander in chief: see EMPEROR⟧ in ancient Rome, a title of honor given originally to generals and later to emperors —**im·per·a·to·ri·al** (im pir′ə tôr′ē əl) *adj.*

im·per·cep·ti·ble (im′pər sep′tə bəl) *adj.* ⟦Fr < ML *imperceptibilis*: see IN-[2] & PERCEPTIBLE⟧ not plain or distinct to the senses or the mind; esp., so slight, gradual, subtle, etc. as not to be easily perceived —**im′per·cep′ti·bil′i·ty** *n.* —**im′per·cep′ti·bly** *adv.*

im·per·cep·tive (im′pər sep′tiv) *adj.* not perceptive; lacking perception —**im′per·cep′tive·ness** *n.*

im·per·cip·i·ent (-sip′ē ənt) *adj.* IMPERCEPTIVE —**im′per·cip′i·ence** *n.*

imperf *abbrev.* imperfect

im·per·fect (im pʉr′fikt) *adj.* ⟦ME *inperfit* < OFr *imparfit* < L *imperfectus*: see IN-[2] & PERFECT⟧ 1 not finished or complete; lacking in something 2 not perfect; having a defect, fault, or error 3 *Gram.* in certain inflected languages, designating or of the tense of a verb that indicates a past action or state as uncompleted, continuous, customary, or going on at the same time as another: "was writing" and "used to write" are English forms corresponding to the imperfect tense in such languages 4 *Music* designating an interval of a major or minor third or sixth —*n.* 1 the imperfect tense 2 a verb in this tense —**im·per′fect·ly** *adv.* —**im·per′fect·ness** *n.*

imperfect flower a unisexual flower with only stamens or only pistils

imperfect fungus any of a subdivision (Deuteromycotina) of fungi for which no sexual stage of reproduction is known

im·per·fec·tion (im′pər fek′shən) *n.* ⟦ME *imperfeccioun* < OFr *imperfection* < LL *imperfectio*⟧ 1 the quality or condition of being imperfect 2 a shortcoming; defect; fault; blemish —**SYN.** DEFECT

im·per·fec·tive (im′pər fek′tiv) *adj. Gram.* designating or of an aspect of verbs, as in Russian, expressing continuing or incomplete action or making no reference to completion —*n.* 1 the imperfective aspect 2 a verb in this aspect

im·per·fo·rate (im pʉr′fə rit, -rāt′) *adj.* ⟦< IN-[2] + PERFORATE⟧ 1 having no holes or openings; unpierced 2 having a straight edge without perforations: said of a postage stamp, etc. 3 *Anat.* lacking the normal opening Also **im·per′fo·rat′ed** —*n.* an imperforate stamp —**im·per′fo·ra′tion** *n.*

im·pe·ri·al (im pir′ē əl) *adj.* ⟦OFr < L *imperialis* < *imperium*, EMPIRE⟧ 1 of an empire 2 of a country having control or sovereignty over other countries or colonies 3 of, or having the rank of, an emperor or empress 4 having supreme authority; sovereign 5 *a)* majestic; august *b)* imperious 6 of great size or superior quality 7 *a)* of or pertaining to the Commonwealth *b)* according to the standard of weights and measures set by British law and used in Great Britain, Canada, and some other countries —*n.* 1 [I-] a supporter or a soldier of any of the Holy Roman emperors 2 the roof or top of a coach, or a luggage case carried on it 3 an article of great size or superior quality 4 a size of writing paper measuring 23 by 31 inches (in England, 22 by 30 or 32 inches) ☆5 ⟦after the emperor Louis Napoleon, who set this fashion⟧ a pointed tuft of beard on the lower lip and chin —**im·pe′ri·al·ly** *adv.*

imperial gallon the standard British gallon, equal to 4.54596 liters or *c.* 1.2 U.S. gallons

im·pe·ri·al·ism (im pir′ē əl iz′əm) *n.* 1 imperial state, authority, or system of government 2 the policy and practice of forming and maintaining an empire in seeking to control raw materials and world markets by the conquest of other countries, the establishment of colonies, etc. 3 the policy and practice of seeking to dominate the economic or political affairs of underdeveloped areas or weaker countries —**im·pe′ri·al·ist** *n., adj.* —**im·pe′ri·al·is′tic** *adj.* —**im·pe′ri·al·is′ti·cal·ly** *adv.*

☆**imperial moth** a large American moth (*Eacles imperialis*) having yellow wings with purple markings

Imperial Valley a rich agricultural region in S Calif. & N Baja California, reclaimed from the Colorado Desert

im·per·il (im per′əl) *vt.* **-iled** or **-illed**, **-il·ing** or **-il·ling** to put in peril; endanger —**im·per′il·ment** *n.*

im·pe·ri·ous (im pir′ē əs) *adj.* ⟦L *imperiosus* < *imperium*, EMPIRE⟧ 1 overbearing, arrogant, domineering, etc. 2 urgent; imperative —**SYN.** MASTERFUL —**im·pe′ri·ous·ly** *adv.* —**im·pe′ri·ous·ness** *n.*

im·per·ish·a·ble (im per′ish ə bəl) *adj.* not perishable; that will not die or decay; indestructible; immortal —**im·per′ish·a·bil′i·ty** *n.* —**im·per′ish·a·bly** *adv.*

im·pe·ri·um (im pir′ē əm) *n., pl.* **-ri·a** (-ə) ⟦L: see EMPIRE⟧ 1 supreme power; absolute authority or rule; imperial sovereignty 2 *Law* the right of a state to use force in maintaining the law

im·per·ma·nent (im pʉr′mə nənt) *adj.* not permanent; not lasting; fleeting; temporary —**im·per′ma·nence** *n.*, **im·per′ma·nen·cy** —**im·per′ma·nent·ly** *adv.*

im·per·me·a·ble (im pʉr′mē ə bəl) *adj.* ⟦LL *impermeabilis*⟧ not permeable; not permitting fluids to pass through it; impenetrable —**im·per′me·a·bil′i·ty** *n.* —**im·per′me·a·bly** *adv.*

im·per·mis·si·ble (im′pər mis′ə bəl) *adj.* not permissible —**im′per·mis′si·bil′i·ty** *n.*

im·per·son·al (im pʉr′sə nəl) *adj.* ⟦LL *impersonalis*⟧ 1 not personal; specif., *a)* without connection or reference to any particular person [an *impersonal* comment] *b)* not existing as a person [an *impersonal* force] 2 not showing human feelings, esp. sympathy or warmth [don't be so cold and *impersonal*] **3** *Gram.* *a)* designating or of a verb occurring only in the third person singular: in English, either with no explicit subject (Ex.: *methinks* all is lost) or with *it* as the indefinite subject (Ex.: it *snowed* all night) *b)* indefinite (said of pronouns) —*n.* an impersonal verb or pronoun —**im·per'son·al'i·ty** (-nal'i tē) *n.* —**im·per'son·al·ly** *adv.*

im·per·son·al·ize (im pʉr'sə nə līz') *vt.* **-ized', -iz'ing** to make impersonal

im·per·son·ate (im pʉr'sə nāt') *vt.* **-at'ed, -at'ing 1** [Now Rare] to represent in the form of a person; personify; embody **2** to act the part of; specif., *a)* to mimic the appearance, manner, etc. of (a person) for purposes of entertainment *b)* to pretend to be for purposes of fraud [to *impersonate* an officer] —**im·per'son·a'tion** *n.* —**im·per'son·a'tor** *n.*

im·per·ti·nence (im pʉrt''n əns) [Fr] *n.* **1** the quality or fact of being impertinent; specif., *a)* lack of pertinence; irrelevance *b)* insolence; impudence **2** an impertinent act, remark, etc. Also **im·per'ti·nen·cy**, *pl.* **-cies**

im·per·ti·nent (im pʉrt''n ənt) *adj.* [OFr < LL *impertinens*] **1** not pertinent or suitable **2** not showing proper respect or manners; insolent; impudent —**im·per'ti·nent·ly** *adv.*

SYN.—**impertinent** implies a forwardness of speech or action that is disrespectful and oversteps the bounds of propriety or courtesy; **impudent** implies a shameless or brazen impertinence; **insolent** implies defiant disrespect as displayed in openly insulting and contemptuous speech or behavior; **saucy** implies a flippancy and provocative levity toward one to whom respect should be shown

im·per·turb·a·ble (im'pər tʉr'bə bəl) *adj.* [LL *imperturbabilis*: see IN-[2], PERTURB, -ABLE] that cannot be disconcerted, disturbed, or excited; impassive —**im'per·turb'a·bil'i·ty** *n.* —**im'per·turb'a·bly** *adv.*

im·per·vi·ous (im pʉr'vē əs) *adj.* [L *impervius*: see IN-[2] & PERVIOUS] **1** incapable of being passed through or penetrated [a fabric *impervious* to moisture] **2** *a)* not affected by [a garden chair *impervious* to the elements] *b)* able to withstand; not susceptible [polar bears *impervious* to the cold, a poet *impervious* to criticism]: with *to* —**im·per'vi·ous·ly** *adv.* —**im·per'vi·ous·ness** *n.*

im·pe·ti·go (im'pə tī'gō) *n.* [L < *impetere*, to attack: see IMPETUS] any of certain skin diseases characterized by the eruption of pustules, esp., a contagious disease of this kind, caused by staphylococci and streptococci —**im'pe·tig'i·nous** (-tij'ə nəs) *adj.*

im·pe·trate (im'pə trāt') *vt.* **-trat'ed, -trat'ing** [< L *impetratus*, pp. of *impetrare*, to accomplish < *in-*, intens. + *patrare*, to accomplish < *pater*, FATHER] **1** to get by request or entreaty **2** [Rare] to implore; beseech —**im'pe·tra'tion** *n.*

im·pet·u·os·i·ty (im pech'ōō äs'i tē) *n.* [MFr *impétuosité* < LL *impetuositas* < L *impetuosus*] **1** the quality of being impetuous **2** *pl.* **-ties** an impetuous action or feeling

im·pet·u·ous (im pech'ōō əs) *adj.* [ME *impetuouse* < OFr *impetueuse* < L *impetuosus* < *impetus*: see fol.] **1** [Now Rare] moving with great force or violence; having great impetus; rushing; furious [*impetuous* winds] **2** acting or done suddenly with little thought; rash; impulsive —**SYN.** SUDDEN —**im·pet'u·ous·ly** *adv.* —**im·pet'u·ous·ness** *n.*

im·pe·tus (im'pə təs) *n.*, *pl.* **-tus·es** [L < *impetere*, to rush upon < *in-*, in + *petere*, to rush at: see FEATHER] **1** the force with which a body moves against resistance, resulting from its mass and the velocity at which it is set in motion **2** anything that stimulates activity; driving force or motive; incentive; impulse

impf *abbrev.* imperfect

imp gal *abbrev.* imperial gallon(s)

Imp·hal (imp'hul') city in NE India: capital of Manipur state

im·pi·e·ty (im pī'ə tē) *n.* [ME *impietie* < OFr or L: OFr *impiété* < L *impietas*] **1** a lack of piety; specif., *a)* lack of reverence for God *b)* lack of respect or dutifulness, as toward a parent **2** *pl.* **-ties** an impious act or remark

im·pinge (im pinj') *vi.* **-pinged', -ping'ing** [L *impingere* < *in-*, in + *pangere*, to strike: see FANG] **1** *a)* to strike, hit, or dash (*on*, *upon*, or *against* something) *b)* to touch (*on* or *upon*); have an effect [an idea that *impinges* on one's mind] **2** to make inroads or encroach (*on* or *upon* the property or rights of another) —**im·pinge'ment** *n.* —**im·ping'er** *n.*

im·pi·ous (im'pē əs) *adj.* [L *impius*] not pious; specif., *a)* lacking reverence for God *b)* lacking respect or dutifulness, as toward a parent —**im'pi·ous·ly** *adv.* —**im'pi·ous·ness** *n.*

imp·ish (im'pish) *adj.* of or like an imp; mischievous —**imp'ish·ly** *adv.* —**imp'ish·ness** *n.*

im·plac·a·ble (im plak'ə bəl, -plā'kə-) *adj.* [Fr < L *implacabilis*] **1** not placable; that cannot be appeased or pacified; relentless; inexorable **2** [Rare] that cannot be eased, lessened, or allayed —**SYN.** INFLEXIBLE —**im·plac'a·bil'i·ty** *n.* —**im·plac'a·bly** *adv.*

im·pla·cen·tal (im'plə sent''l) *adj.* [< IN-[1] + PLACENTAL] APLACENTAL: also **im'pla·cen'tate'** (-sen'tāt')

im·plant (im plant'; *for n.* im'plant') *vt.* [Fr *implanter*: see IN-[1] & PLANT] **1** to plant firmly or deeply; embed **2** to fix firmly in the mind; instill; inculcate **3** *Dentistry, Med.* to insert (an organ, prosthetic device, living tissue, etc.) within the body —*n.* *Dentistry, Med.* an implanted organ, device, etc. —**im·plant'a·ble** (-plant'ə bəl) *adj.* —**im'plan·ta'tion** (-plan tā'shən) *n.*

im·plau·si·ble (im plô'zə bəl) *adj.* not plausible; not credible —**im·plau'si·bil'i·ty** *n.*, *pl.* **-ties** —**im·plau'si·bly** *adv.*

im·plead (im plēd') *vt., vi.* [ME *enpleden* < Anglo-Fr *enpleder* < OFr *emplaidier*: see IN-[1] & PLEAD] **1** to prosecute or sue in a law court **2** to bring into an action by impleader

im·plead·er (-ər) *n.* a legal procedure by which a defendant brings into an action a new party who may be liable for all or part of the plaintiff's claim against the defendant

im·ple·ment (im'plə mənt; *for v.*, -ment') *n.* [ME < LL *implementum*, a filling up < L *implere*, to fill up < *in-*, in + *plere*, to fill: see FULL[1]] **1** any article or device used or needed in a given activity; tool, instrument, utensil, etc. **2** any thing or person used as a means to some end —*vt.* **1** to carry into effect; fulfill; accomplish **2** to provide the means for the carrying out of; give practical effect to **3** to provide with implements —**im'ple·men'tal** *adj.* —**im'ple·men·ta'tion** (-mən tā'shən) *n.* —**im'ple·ment'er** *n.*, **im'ple·men'tor**

SYN.—**implement** applies to any device used to carry on some work or effect some purpose [agricultural *implements*]; **tool** is commonly applied to manual implements such as are used in carpentry, plumbing, etc.; **instrument** specifically implies use for delicate work or for scientific or artistic purposes [surgical *instruments*] and may also be applied, as are **tool** and **implement**, to a thing or person serving as a means to an end; **appliance** specifically suggests a mechanical or power-driven device, esp. one for household use; **utensil** is used of any implement or container for domestic use, esp. a pot, pan, etc.

im·pli·cate (im'pli kāt') *vt.* **-cat'ed, -cat'ing** [< L *implicatus*, pp. of *implicare*, to enfold, involve: see IMPLY] **1** *a)* to show to have a connection with a crime, fault, etc.; involve *b)* to show to be involved or concerned **2** [Rare] to imply **3** [Archaic] to twist or fold together; intertwine; entangle —**im'pli·ca'tive** *adj.* —**im'pli·ca'tive·ly** *adv.*

im·pli·ca·tion (im'pli kā'shən) *n.* [ME *implicacioun* < L *implicatio*] **1** an implicating or being implicated **2** an implying or being implied **3** *a)* something implied, from which an inference may be drawn *b)* *Logic* a formal relationship between two propositions such that if the first is true then the second is necessarily or logically true

im·plic·it (im plis'it) *adj.* [L *implicitus*, pp. of *implicare*: see IMPLY] **1** suggested or to be understood though not plainly expressed; implied: distinguished from EXPLICIT **2** necessarily or naturally involved though not plainly apparent or expressed; essentially a part or condition; inherent **3** without reservation or doubt; unquestioning; absolute **4** [Obs.] implicated; entangled —**im·plic'it·ly** *adv.* —**im·plic'it·ness** *n.*

implicit function the mathematical rule or function which permits computation of one variable directly from another when an equation relating both variables is given (Ex.: y is an *implicit function* of x in the equation $x + y^3 + 2x^2y + xy = 0$): compare EXPLICIT FUNCTION

im·plied (im plīd') *adj.* involved, suggested, or understood without being openly or directly expressed

im·plode (im plōd') *vt.* **-plod'ed, -plod'ing** [< IN-[1] + (EX)PLODE] **1** to cause to burst or collapse inward **2** *Phonet.* to articulate by implosion —*vi.* to burst or collapse inward

im·plore (im plôr') *vt.* **-plored', -plor'ing** [L *implorare*, to beseech, entreat < *in-*, intens. + *plorare*, to cry out, weep] **1** to ask or beg earnestly for **2** to ask or beg (a person) to do something; entreat —**SYN.** BEG —**im·plor'ing·ly** *adv.*

im·plo·sion (im plō'zhən) *n.* [< IN-[1] + (EX)PLOSION] the act or an instance of imploding; specif., in phonetics, the sudden rush of air into the pharynx that occurs in the articulation of certain stops found esp. in some African languages: see CLICK (*n.* 5)

im·plo·sive (im plō'siv) *Phonet.* *adj.* formed by implosion —*n.* an implosive sound or consonant —**im·plo'sive·ly** *adv.*

im·ply (im plī') *vt.* **-plied', -ply'ing** [ME *implien* < OFr *emplier* < L *implicare*, to involve, entangle < *in-*, in + *plicare*, to fold: see PLY[1]] **1** to have as a necessary part, condition, or effect; contain, include, or involve naturally or necessarily [drama *implies* conflict] **2** to indicate indirectly or by allusion; hint; suggest; intimate [an attitude *implying* boredom] **3** [Obs.] to enfold; entangle —**SYN.** SUGGEST

im·po·lite (im'pə līt') *adj.* [L *impolitus*, unpolished] not polite; ill-mannered; discourteous —**SYN.** RUDE —**im'po·lite'ly** *adv.* —**im'po·lite'ness** *n.*

im·pol·i·tic (im päl'ə tik') *adj.* not politic; unwise; injudicious; inexpedient —**im·pol'i·tic·ly** *adv.*

im·pon·der·a·ble (im pän'dər ə bəl) *adj.* not ponderable; specif., *a)* that cannot be weighed or measured *b)* that cannot be conclusively determined or explained —*n.* anything imponderable —**im·pon'der·a·bil'i·ty** *n.* —**im·pon'der·a·bly** *adv.*

im·port (im pôrt', im'pôrt'; *for n.* im'pôrt') *vt.* [ME *importen* < L *importare*, to bring in, introduce < *in-*, in + *portare*, to carry (see FARE); *vt.* 2 & 3 < ML *importare*, to imply, mean, be of importance < L] **1** *a)* to bring in from the outside; introduce *b)* to bring (goods) from another country or countries, esp. for purposes of sale **2** to mean; signify [an action that *imports* trouble] **3** [Archaic] to be of importance to; concern —*n.* **1** the act or business of importing (goods) **2** something imported **3** meaning; signification **4** importance —*adj.* of or for importing or imports —**im·port'a·ble** *adj.* —**im·port'er** *n.*

im·por·tance (im pôrt''ns) *n.* [MFr < OIt *importanza*] **1** the state or quality of being important; significance; consequence **2** [Obs.] *a)* a matter or consequence *b)* import, or meaning *c)* importunity

SYN.—**importance**, the broadest of these terms, implies great worth, meaning, influence, etc. [news of *importance*]; **consequence**, often interchangeable with the preceding, more specifically suggests importance with regard to outcome or result [a disagreement of no *consequence*]; **moment** expresses this same idea of importance in effect with somewhat stronger force [affairs of great *moment*]; **weight** implies an estimation of the relative importance of something [his word carries great *weight* with us]; **significance** implies an importance or momentousness because of a special meaning that may or may not be immediately apparent [an event of *significance*]

im·por·tant (im pôrt′'nt) ***adj.*** ⟦Fr < OIt *importante* < ML *importans*, prp. of *importare*: see IMPORT⟧ **1** meaning a great deal; having much significance, consequence, or value **2** having, or acting as if having, power, authority, influence, high position, etc.

im·por·tant·ly (-lē) ***adv.*** **1** in an important or, often, self-important way or manner **2** it is important to note (that) [he left and, more *importantly*, never came back]

im·por·ta·tion (im′pôr tā′shən) ***n.*** **1** an importing or being imported **2** something imported

im·por·tu·nate (im pôr′chə nit) ***adj.*** ⟦< L *importunus* (see fol.) + -ATE[1]⟧ **1** urgent or persistent in asking or demanding; insistent; refusing to be denied; annoyingly urgent or persistent **2** [Obs.] troublesome —**im·por′tu·nate·ly *adv.*** —**im·por′tu·nate·ness *n.***

im·por·tune (im′pôr to͞on′, -tyo͞on′; -pər-; im pôr′tyo͞on′, -cho͞on′) ***vt.*** **-tuned′, -tun′ing** ⟦Fr *importuner* < the adj.⟧ **1** to trouble with requests or demands; urge or entreat persistently or repeatedly **2** [Archaic] to ask for urgently; demand **3** [Obs.] to trouble; annoy —***vi.*** to make urgent requests or demands —***adj.*** ⟦ME < OFr *importun* < L *importunus*, unsuitable, troublesome < *in-*, not + *(op)portunus*: see OPPORTUNE⟧ *rare var. of* IMPORTUNATE —***SYN.*** BEG, URGE —**im′por·tune′ly *adv.*** —**im′por·tun′er *n.***

im·por·tu·ni·ty (-to͞on′i tē; -tyo͞on′-) ***n., pl.*** **-ties** ⟦Fr *importunité* < L *importunitas*⟧ an importuning or being importunate; persistence in requesting or demanding

im·pose (im pōz′) ***vt.*** **-posed′, -pos′ing** ⟦Fr, altered by assoc. with *poser* (see POSE[1]) < L *imponere*, to place upon < *in-*, on + *ponere*: see POSITION⟧ **1** to place or set (a burden, tax, fine, etc. *on* or *upon*) as by authority **2** to force (oneself, one's presence or will, etc.) on another or others without right or invitation; obtrude **3** to pass off; foist, esp. by deception [to *impose* false cures on unsuspecting patients] **4** to arrange (pages of type or plates) in a frame in the proper order of printing **5** [Archaic] to place; put; deposit **6** to lay (the hands) on, as in ordaining —**impose on** (or **upon**) **1** to take advantage of; put to some trouble or use unfairly for one's own benefit **2** to cheat or defraud —**im·pos′er *n.***

im·pos·ing (im pō′ziŋ) ***adj.*** making a strong impression because of great size, strength, dignity, etc.; impressive —***SYN.*** GRAND —**im·pos′ing·ly *adv.***

im·po·si·tion (im′pə zish′ən) ***n.*** ⟦OFr < L *impositio*, a laying upon, application⟧ **1** an imposing or imposing on; specif., *a)* the forcing of oneself, one's presence or will, etc. on another or others without right or invitation *b)* a taking advantage of friendship, etc. *c)* the laying on of hands, as in ordaining **2** something imposed; specif., *a)* a tax, fine, etc. *b)* an unjust burden or requirement *c)* a deception; fraud **3** the arrangement of type pages or plates in the proper order of printing

im·pos·si·bil·i·ty (im päs′ə bil′i tē) ***n.*** ⟦OFr *impossibilite* < LL *impossibilitas*⟧ **1** the fact or quality of being impossible **2** *pl.* **-ties** something impossible

im·pos·si·ble (im päs′ə bəl) ***adj.*** ⟦OFr < L *impossibilis*: see IN-[2] & POSSIBLE⟧ **1** not capable of being, being done, or happening **2** not capable of being done easily or conveniently **3** not capable of being endured, used, agreed to, etc. because disagreeable or unsuitable [an *impossible* task, an *impossible* request] —**im·pos′si·ble·ness *n.*** —**im·pos′si·bly *adv.***

im·post[1] (im′pōst′) ***n.*** ⟦OFr < ML *impostus* < L *impositus*, pp. of *imponere*: see IMPOSE⟧ **1** a tax; esp., a duty on imported goods **2** *Horse Racing* the weight assigned to a horse in a handicap race —☆***vt.*** to classify (imported goods) in order to assess the proper taxes

im·post[2] (im′pōst′) ***n.*** ⟦Fr *imposte* < It *imposta* < L *impositus*: see prec.⟧ the top part of a pillar, pier, or wall supporting an arch

im·pos·tor or **im·post·er** (im päs′tər) ***n.*** ⟦Fr *imposteur* < LL *impostor* < pp. of L *imponere*: see IMPOSE⟧ a person who pretends to be someone or something that he or she is not, as to deceive or cheat others —***SYN.*** QUACK[2]

im·pos·ture (im päs′chər) ***n.*** ⟦Fr < LL *impostura*⟧ the act or practice of an impostor; fraud; deception

im·po·tence (im′pə təns) ***n.*** ⟦OFr < L *impotentia*⟧ the quality or condition of being impotent: also **im′po·ten·cy**, *pl.* **-cies**

im·po·tent (im′pə tənt) ***adj.*** ⟦OFr < L *impotens*: see IN-[2] & POTENT⟧ **1** lacking physical strength; weak **2** ineffective, powerless, or helpless [*impotent* rage] **3** unable to engage in sexual intercourse, esp. because of an inability to have or sustain an erection: said of a male —***SYN.*** STERILE —**im′po·tent·ly *adv.***

im·pound (im pound′) ***vt.*** **1** to shut up (an animal) in a pound **2** to take and hold (a document, funds, a vehicle, etc.) in legal custody **3** to gather and enclose (water) for irrigation, etc. —**im·pound′ment *n.***

im·pov·er·ish (im päv′ər ish, -päv′rish) ***vt.*** ⟦ME *empoverishen* < extended stem of OFr *empovrir* < *em-* (< L *in-*, in) + *povre* < L *pauper*, POOR⟧ **1** to make poor; reduce to poverty **2** to deprive of strength, resources, etc. —***SYN.*** POOR —**im·pov′er·ish·ment *n.***

im·pow·er (im pou′ər) ***vt.*** *var. of* EMPOWER

im·prac·ti·ca·ble (im prak′ti kə bəl) ***adj.*** ⟦< IN-[2] + PRACTICABLE⟧ **1** not capable of being carried out in practice [an *impracticable* plan] **2** not capable of being used [an *impracticable* road] **3** [Archaic] not capable of being managed or dealt with; intractable [an *impracticable* person] —**im·prac′ti·ca·bil′i·ty *n.***, **im·prac′ti·ca·ble·ness** —**im·prac′ti·ca·bly *adv.***

im·prac·ti·cal (im prak′ti kəl) ***adj.*** not practical; specif., *a)* not workable or useful; impracticable *b)* not handling practical matters well *c)* given to theorizing; idealistic —**im·prac′ti·cal′i·ty** (-kal′ə tē) ***n.***, **im·prac′ti·cal·ness** —**im·prac′ti·cal·ly *adv.***

im·pre·cate (im′pri kāt′) ***vt., vi.*** **-cat′ed, -cat′ing** ⟦< L *imprecatus*, pp. of *imprecari*, to invoke, pray to < *in-*, in, on + *precari*, to PRAY⟧ [Rare] to invoke (evil) upon (someone); curse —**im′pre·ca′tor *n.***

im·pre·ca·tion (im′pri kā′shən) ***n.*** ⟦L *imprecatio*⟧ **1** the act of imprecating evil, etc. on someone **2** a curse [muttering *imprecations* as he worked] —**im′pre·ca·to′ry** (-kə tôr′ē) ***adj.***

im·pre·cise (im′pri sīs′) ***adj.*** not precise, exact, or definite; vague —**im′pre·cise′ly *adv.*** —**im′pre·ci′sion** (-sizh′ən) ***n.***

im·preg·na·ble[1] (im preg′nə bəl) ***adj.*** ⟦ME *imprenable* < OFr: see IN-[2] & PREGNABLE⟧ **1** not capable of being captured or entered by force **2** unshakable; unyielding; firm [an *impregnable* belief] —**im·preg′na·bil′i·ty *n.*** —**im·preg′na·bly *adv.***

im·preg·na·ble[2] (im preg′nə bəl) ***adj.*** ⟦fol. + -ABLE⟧ that can be impregnated

im·preg·nate (im preg′nāt′; *for adj.*, -nit, -nāt′) ***vt.*** **-nat′ed, -nat′ing** ⟦< LL *impraegnatus*, pp. of *impraegnare*, to make pregnant < L *in-*, in + *praegnans*, PREGNANT⟧ **1** to fertilize (an ovum) **2** to make pregnant **3** to fertilize (land); make fruitful **4** to fill or saturate; cause to be permeated [clothing *impregnated* with smoke] **5** to indoctrinate or imbue (*with* ideas, feelings, principles, etc.) —***adj.*** [Archaic] impregnated —***SYN.*** SOAK —**im′preg·na′tion *n.*** —**im·preg′na′tor *n.***

im·pre·sa (im prā′zä) ***n.*** ⟦It: see fol.⟧ [Historical] a design, device, or heraldic emblem, typically one bearing a motto

im·pre·sa·ri·o (im′prə sä′rē ō, -ser′ē-) ***n., pl.*** **-ri·os** ⟦It < *impresa*, enterprise < *imprendere*, to undertake < VL **imprehendere*: see EMPRISE⟧ the organizer, manager, or director of an opera or ballet company, concert series, etc.

im·pre·scrip·ti·ble (im′pri skrip′tə bəl) ***adj.*** ⟦Fr: see IN-[2] & PRESCRIPTIBLE⟧ **1** that cannot rightfully be taken away, lost, or revoked; inviolable **2** *Law* not subject to PRESCRIPTION (*n.* 5) —**im′pre·scrip′ti·bly *adv.***

im·press[1] (im pres′; *for n.* im′pres′) ***vt.*** ⟦< IN-[1] + PRESS[2]⟧ **1** to force (a person) into service, esp. into military or naval service **2** to levy, seize, or requisition (money, property, etc.), as for military use —***n.*** IMPRESSMENT

im·press[2] (im pres′; *for n.* im′pres′) ***vt.*** ⟦ME *impressen* < L *impressus*, pp. of *imprimere*: see IMPRINT⟧ **1** to use pressure on so as to leave a mark [to *impress* clay with a die] **2** to mark by using pressure; stamp; imprint **3** to apply with pressure [to *impress* a die into clay] **4** *a)* to have a marked effect on the mind or emotions of *b)* to arouse the interest or approval of **5** to implant firmly in the mind or fix in the memory: with *on* or *upon* **6** *Elec.* to apply (a voltage or current) to a circuit or device, as from a generator —***n.*** **1** the act of impressing **2** any mark, imprint, etc. made by pressure; stamp; impression **3** a distinctive quality or effect produced by some strong influence —***SYN.*** AFFECT[1]

im·press·i·ble (im pres′ə bəl) ***adj.*** ⟦ML *impressibilis*⟧ that can be impressed; impressionable —**im·press′i·bil′i·ty *n.*** —**im·press′i·bly *adv.***

im·pres·sion (im presh′ən) ***n.*** ⟦ME *impressioun* < OFr *impression* < L *impressio*⟧ **1** the act of impressing **2** a result or effect of impressing; specif., *a)* a mark, imprint, etc. made by physical pressure *b)* an effect produced, as on the mind or senses, by some force or influence *c)* the effect produced by any effort or activity [hard cleaning made little *impression* on the stain] **3** a notion, feeling, or recollection, esp. a vague one **4** a first or single coat of paint or color **5** an imitation or mimicking intended as a caricature or amusing impersonation **6** *Dentistry* *a)* the imprint of the teeth and surrounding tissues in wax, plaster, etc., used as a mold in making dentures *b)* the mold used to make an inlay **7** *Printing* *a)* the pressing or pressure of type or plates as on paper; printing *b)* a printed copy *c)* all the copies printed in a single operation from a set of unaltered type or plates —***SYN.*** IDEA —**im·pres′sion·al *adj.***

im·pres·sion·a·ble (im presh′ən ə bəl) ***adj.*** ⟦Fr⟧ easily affected by impressions; esp., capable of being influenced intellectually, emotionally, or morally; sensitive —**im·pres′sion·a·bil′i·ty *n.*** —**im·pres′sion·a·bly *adv.***

im·pres·sion·ism (im presh′ən iz′əm) ***n.*** ⟦< Fr *impressionisme*, coined (1874) by Louis Leroy, Fr art critic, in adverse reaction to a Monet painting entitled "Impression, sunrise"⟧ [*often* **I-**] a theory and school of painting exemplified chiefly by Monet, Pissarro, and Sisley, but also by Manet, Renoir, etc., whose chief aim is to capture a momentary glimpse of a subject, esp. to reproduce the changing effects of light by applying paint to canvas in short strokes of pure color: the term has been extended to literature (as in the fiction of Stephen Crane and Virginia Woolf and in imagist poetry) and to music (as by Debussy and Ravel), in which the artist seeks to render impressions and moods by various characteristic devices

im·pres·sion·ist (-ist) ***n.*** **1** [*often* **I-**] a painter, writer, or composer whose work exhibits the characteristics of impressionism **2** an entertainer who does impressions, or impersonations —***adj.*** [*often* **I-**] of impressionism or impressionists

im·pres·sion·is·tic (im presh′ən is′tik) ***adj.*** **1** IMPRESSIONIST **2** conveying a quick or overall impression —**im·pres′sion·is′ti·cal·ly *adv.***

im·pres·sive (im pres′iv) ***adj.*** having or tending to have a strong effect on the mind or emotions; eliciting wonder or admiration —**im·pres′sive·ly *adv.*** —**im·pres′sive·ness *n.***

im·press·ment (im pres′mənt) ***n.*** ⟦IMPRESS¹ + -MENT⟧ the practice or act of impressing men or property into service, esp. into military or naval service

im·prest (im′prest′) ***n.*** ⟦It *impresto,* a loan < *(dare) in prestito,* (to give) in loan < *in,* in + *prestito,* a loan < *prestare,* to lend < L *praestare,* to become surety for, lit., to stand before < *prae-,* before + *stare,* to STAND⟧ a loan or advance of money, as from government funds —***adj.*** *Accounting* designating a fund, as of petty cash, that is replenished in exactly the amount expended from it

im·pri·ma·tur (im′pri mät′ər, -māt′-; im prim′ə tur′) ***n.*** ⟦ModL, lit., let it be printed, 3d pers. sing., pres. subjunc. pass., of L *imprimere:* see IMPRINT⟧ **1** *a)* license or permission to publish or print a book, article, etc. *b) R.C.Ch.* such permission granted by a bishop **2** any sanction or approval

im·pri·mis (im prē′mis, -prī′-) ***adv.*** ⟦ME *inprimis* < L *in primis,* lit., among the first < *in,* among + *primis,* abl. pl. of *primus,* first: see PRIME⟧ in the first place; to begin with

im·print (im print′; *for n.* im′print′) ***vt.*** ⟦ME *emprenten* < OFr *empreinter* < *empreinte,* an imprint < pp. of *empreindre* < L *imprimere* < *in-,* on + *premere,* to PRESS¹⟧ **1** to mark by or as by pressing or stamping; impress [to *imprint* a paper with a seal] **2** to make (a mark or impression) by pressing **3** to press or apply [to *imprint* a kiss on someone's forehead] **4** to implant firmly in the mind or fix in the memory: with *on* [a sight *imprinted* forever on her memory] —***vi.*** *Psychol.* to learn by means of IMPRINTING —***n.*** **1** a mark made by imprinting **2** a lasting effect or characteristic result [the *imprint* of starvation] **3** *a)* a note on a book's title page or its reverse or at the end of the book, giving the publisher's or printer's name, time and place of publication, etc. *b)* the name of a publishing company *c)* a brand name under which books are published

im·print·ing (im print′iŋ) ***n.*** *Psychol.* a learning mechanism operating very early in the life of an animal, in which a particular stimulus immediately establishes an irreversible behavior pattern with reference to the same stimulus in the future

im·pris·on (im priz′ən) ***vt.*** **1** to put or keep in prison; jail **2** to restrict, limit, or confine in any way —**im·pris′on·ment *n.***

im·prob·a·ble (im präb′ə bəl) ***adj.*** ⟦L *improbabilis*⟧ not probable; not likely to happen or be true; unlikely —**im′prob·a·bil′i·ty *n.,*** *pl.* **-ties** —**im·prob′a·bly *adv.***

im·pro·bi·ty (im prō′bi tē) ***n.,*** *pl.* **-ties** ⟦ME *improbite* < L *improbitas*⟧ lack of probity; dishonesty

im·promp·tu (im prämp′to͞o′) ***adj., adv.*** ⟦Fr < L *in promptu,* in readiness < *in,* in + *promptu,* abl. of *promptus,* readiness < *promptus,* brought out, ready, PROMPT⟧ without preparation or advance thought; offhand —***n.*** an impromptu speech, performance, etc.

SYN.—**impromptu** is applied to that which is spoken, made, or done on the spur of the moment to suit the occasion and stresses spontaneity; **extemporaneous, extempore** (more commonly used as an adverb), and **extemporary** may express the same idea but are now more often used of a speech that has received some preparation, but has not been written out or memorized; **improvised** applies to something composed or devised without any preparation and, with reference to things other than music, suggests the ingenious use of whatever is at hand to fill an unforeseen and immediate need

im·prop·er (im präp′ər) ***adj.*** ⟦OFr *impropre* < L *improprius:* see IN-² & PROPER⟧ **1** not suitable for or consistent with the purpose or circumstances; poorly adapted; unfit **2** not in accordance with the truth, fact, or rule; wrong; incorrect **3** contrary to good taste or decency; indecorous —**im·prop′er·ly *adv.*** —**im·prop′er·ness *n.***

SYN.—**improper,** the word of broadest application in this list, refers to anything that is not proper or suitable, esp. to that which does not conform to conventional standards; **unseemly** applies to that which is improper or inappropriate to the particular situation [her *unseemly* laughter at the funeral]; **unbecoming** applies to that which is inappropriate to a certain kind of person, his character, etc. [his rigid views are most *unbecoming* in a teacher]; **indecorous** refers to that which violates propriety or good taste in behavior, speech, etc. [his *indecorous* interruption of a private conversation]; **indelicate** implies a lack of propriety or tact and connotes immodesty or coarseness [an *indelicate* anecdote]; **indecent** is used of that which is regarded as highly offensive to morals or modesty [*indecent* exposure] —*ANT.* **proper, decorous**

improper fraction a fraction in which the denominator is less than the numerator (Ex.: 5/3)

im·pro·pri·ate (im prō′prē āt′; *for adj., usually,* -it) ***vt.*** **-at′ed, -at′ing** ⟦< ML(Ec) *impropriatus,* pp. of ML *impropriare,* to take as one's own < L *in,* in + *proprius,* one's own⟧ [Historical] to transfer (church income or property) to private individuals or corporations —**im·pro′pri·a′tion *n.*** —**im·pro′pri·a′tor *n.***

im·pro·pri·e·ty (im′prə prī′ə tē) ***n.,*** *pl.* **-ties** ⟦< MFr *impropriété* or < L *improprietas:* see IN-² & PROPRIETY⟧ **1** the quality of being improper **2** improper action or behavior **3** an improper or unacceptable use of a word or phrase (Ex.: "borrow" for "lend"): see also BARBARISM, SOLECISM

im·prov (im′präv′) [Informal] ***n.*** **1** improvisation; specif., a skit or act in which the actors improvise a situation **2** the art or technique of doing such improvisations —***adj.*** relating to or doing improvisation [an *improv* course, an *improv* theater]

im·prove (im pro͞ov′) ***vt.*** **-proved′, -prov′ing** ⟦earlier *improw* < Anglo-Fr *emprower* < *en-,* in + *prou,* gain, advantage < LL *prode,* advantage (backform. < L *prodesse,* to be of advantage): see PRO-² & IS¹⟧ **1** [Now Rare] to use profitably or to good advantage [to *improve* one's leisure by studying] **2** to raise to a better quality or condition; make better ☆**3** to make (land or structures) more valuable by cultivation, construction, etc. —***vi.*** to become better in quality or condition —**improve on** (or **upon**) to do or make better than, as by additions or changes —**im·prov′a·bil′i·ty *n.*** —**im·prov′a·ble *adj.*** —**im·prov′er *n.***

SYN.—**improve** and **better** both imply a correcting or advancing of something that is not in itself necessarily bad, the former by supplying a lack or want [to *improve* a method] and the latter by seeking something more satisfying [he's left his job to *better* himself]; **ameliorate** implies a bad, oppressive, or intolerable condition to begin with [to *ameliorate* the lot of the poor] —*ANT.* **worsen, impair**

im·prove·ment (im pro͞ov′mənt) ***n.*** ⟦Anglo-Fr *emprowement*⟧ **1** an improving or being improved; esp., *a)* betterment *b)* an increase in value or in excellence of quality or condition *c)* [Now Rare] profitable use **2** *a)* an addition or change that improves something *b)* a person or thing representing a higher degree of excellence **3** a change or addition to land or real property, as a sewer, fence, etc., that makes it more valuable or desirable

im·prov·i·dent (im präv′ə dənt) ***adj.*** ⟦< L *improvidus* < *in-,* not + *providus,* foreseeing, cautious + *providere:* see PROVIDE⟧ failing to provide for the future; lacking foresight, thrift, etc. —**im·prov′i·dence *n.*** —**im·prov′i·dent·ly *adv.***

im·prov·i·sa·tion (im präv′i zā′shən, im′prə vi-) ***n.*** **1** the act of improvising **2** something improvised —**im·prov′i·sa′tion·al *adj.***

im·prov·i·sa·to·ri·al (im präv′i zə tôr′ē əl) ***adj.*** of, or having the nature of, an improviser or improvisation: also **im·pro·vi·sa·to·ry** (im′prə vī′zə tôr′ē)

im·pro·vise (im′prə vīz′) ***vt., vi.*** **-vised′, -vis′ing** ⟦Fr *improviser* < It *improvvisare* < *improvviso,* unprepared < L *improvisus,* unforeseen < *in-,* not + *provisus,* pp. of *providere,* to foresee, anticipate: see PROVIDE⟧ **1** to compose, or simultaneously compose and perform, on the spur of the moment and without any preparation; extemporize **2** *a)* to bring about, make, or do on the spur of the moment [to *improvise* a solution to a problem] *b)* to make, provide, or do with the tools and materials at hand, usually to fill an unforeseen and immediate need [to *improvise* a bed out of leaves] —*SYN.* IMPROMPTU —**im′pro·vis′er *n.,*** **im′pro·vi′sor,** or **im·prov′i·sa′tor** (-präv′i zāt′ər)

im·pru·dent (im pro͞od′′nt) ***adj.*** ⟦ME < L *imprudens:* see IN-² & PRUDENT⟧ not prudent; without thought of the consequences; lacking in judgment or caution; rash; indiscreet —**im·pru′dence *n.*** —**im·pru′dent·ly *adv.***

im·pu·dence (im′pyo͞o dəns) ***n.*** ⟦OFr < L *impudentia*⟧ **1** the quality of being impudent **2** impudent speech or behavior: also **im′pu·den·cy,** *pl.* **-cies**

im·pu·dent (im′pyo͞o dənt) ***adj.*** ⟦ME < L *impudens* < *in-,* not + *pudens,* modest, orig. prp. of *pudere,* to feel shame⟧ shamelessly bold or disrespectful; insolent —*SYN.* IMPERTINENT —**im′pu·dent·ly *adv.***

im·pu·dic·i·ty (im′pyo͞o dis′i tē) ***n.*** ⟦Fr *impudicité* < LL **impudicitas,* for L *impudicitia* < *impudicus* < *in-,* not + *pudicus,* modest⟧ immodesty; shamelessness

im·pugn (im pyo͞on′) ***vt.*** ⟦ME *impugnen* < OFr *impugner* < L *impugnare* < *in-,* on, against + *pugnare,* to fight: see PUGNACIOUS⟧ **1** [Obs.] to attack physically **2** to attack by argument or criticism; oppose or challenge as false or questionable —*SYN.* DENY —**im·pugn′a·ble *adj.*** —**im·pug·na·tion** (im′pəg nā′shən) ***n.*** —**im·pugn′er *n.***

im·pu·is·sance (im pyo͞o′i səns, -pwis′əns; im′pyo͞o is′əns) ***n.*** ⟦Fr: see IN-² & PUISSANCE⟧ lack of power; weakness —**im·pu′is·sant *adj.***

im·pulse (im′puls′) ***n.*** ⟦L *impulsus* < pp. of *impellere:* see IMPEL⟧ **1** *a)* an impelling, or driving forward with sudden force *b)* an impelling force; sudden, driving force; push; thrust; impetus *c)* the motion or effect caused by such a force **2** *a)* incitement to action arising from a state of mind or some external stimulus *b)* a sudden inclination to act, usually without premeditation (often used attributively) [an *impulse* purchase] *c)* a motive or tendency coming from within [prompted by an *impulse* of curiosity] **3** *Elec.* a momentary surge in one direction of voltage or current **4** *Mech.* the change in momentum effected by a force, measured by multiplying the average value of the force by the time during which it acts **5** *Physiol.* the progressive wave of excitation over a muscle or nerve fiber, which causes or inhibits activity in the body

impulse turbine a kind of turbine having rotor blades so shaped that the force of jets of fluid striking against the blades moves the wheel, without pressure drop occurring across the blades

im·pul·sion (im pul′shən) ***n.*** ⟦L *impulsio* < *impulsus,* IMPULSE⟧ **1** an impelling or being impelled **2** an impelling force **3** movement or tendency to move resulting from this force; impetus **4** IMPULSE (senses 2*a* & *c*)

im·pul·sive (im pul′siv) ***adj.*** ⟦< MFr or ML: MFr *impulsif* < ML *impulsivus* < L *impulsus,* IMPULSE⟧ **1** impelling; driving forward **2** *a)* acting or likely to act on impulse [an *impulsive* person] *b)* produced by or resulting from a sudden impulse [an *impulsive* remark] **3** *Mech.* acting briefly and as a result of impulse —*SYN.* SPONTANEOUS —**im·pul′sive·ly *adv.*** —**im·pul′sive·ness *n.***

im·pu·ni·ty (im pyo͞o′ni tē) ***n.*** ⟦Fr *impunité* < L *impunitas* < *impunis,* free from punishment < *in-,* without + *poena,* punishment: see PAIN⟧ freedom or exemption from punishment, penalty, or harm —*SYN.* EXEMPTION

im·pure (im pyoor′) ***adj.*** ⟦L *impurus*⟧ not pure; specif., *a)* unclean;

dirty *b)* unclean according to religious ritual; defiled *c)* obscene; unchaste *d)* mixed with foreign matter; adulterated *e)* mixed so as to lack purity in color, tone, style, etc. —**im·pure′ly** *adv.* —**im·pure′ness** *n.*

im·pu·ri·ty (im pyoor′ə tē) *n.* ⟦OFr *impurité* < L *impuritas*⟧ **1** the state or quality of being impure **2** *pl.* **-ties** *a)* an impure thing or element *b)* something, as foreign matter or a pollutant, that renders something else impure

im·put·a·ble (im pyōōt′ə bəl) *adj.* ⟦ML *imputabilis*⟧ that can be imputed; ascribable —**im·put′a·bil′i·ty** *n.* —**im·put′a·bly** *adv.*

im·pute (im pyōōt′) *vt.* **-put′ed**, **-put′ing** ⟦ME *imputen* < OFr *imputer* < L *imputare* < *in-*, in, to + *putare*, to estimate, think, orig., to prune, cleanse: see PURE⟧ **1** to attribute (esp. a fault or misconduct) to another; ascribe **2** *Theol.* to ascribe (the goodness or guilt of one person) to another as well —*SYN.* ASCRIBE —**im′pu·ta′tion** (-pyōō tā′shən) *n.* —**im·put′a·tive** (-pyōōt′ə tiv) *adj.*

impv *abbrev.* imperative

in¹ (in) *prep.* ⟦ME < OE, akin to Ger *in* < IE base **en-* > Gr *en*, L *in* (OL *en*), OIr *in*, OSlav *on-*, Sans *an-*⟧ **1** contained or enclosed by; inside; within [*in* the room, *in* the envelope] **2** wearing; clothed by [to dress *in* one's best] **3** during the course of [done *in* a day] **4** at or before the end of [return *in* an hour] **5** perceptible to (one of the senses) [the town is *in* sight; he told a lie *in* my hearing] **6** limited by the scope of [*in* my opinion] **7** *a)* being a member of or worker at [*in* the navy, *in* business] *b)* being a student at [she's *in* college] *c)* being an inmate of [to be *in* prison] **8** out of a group or set of [one *in* ten will fail] **9** amidst; surrounded by [*in* a storm, *in* total darkness] **10** affected by (a specified state or condition); having [he's *in* trouble; they were *in* tears] **11** engaged or occupied by (an activity or process) [*in* a search for truth, deep *in* thought] **12** with regard to; as concerns [weak *in* faith, to vary *in* size, six feet two *in* height] **13** so as to form; arranged to produce the form or shape of [hair done *in* curls, funeral cars moving *in* a line] **14** with; by; using [to paint *in* oils, written *in* English, sculpture done *in* wood] **15** because of; for [to cry *in* pain] **16** by way of; for the purpose of [do this *in* my defense] **17** as a part of the capacity or function of; belonging to [he didn't have it *in* him to cheat; can you find it *in* yourself to forgive her?] **18** into [break it *in* two; come *in* the house]: when the idea of motion from outside to inside is intended, *into* is generally preferred **19** living or located at [vacationing *in* Venice] ➥*In* expresses inclusion with relation to space, place, time, state, circumstances, manner, quality, substance, a class, a whole, etc. —*adv.* **1** from a point outside to one inside [to invite visitors *in*] **2** to or toward a certain place or direction [he flies *in* today, they live ten miles *in*] **3** at or inside one's home, office, etc. [forced to stay *in* for the day] **4** *a)* so as to be contained by a certain space or condition *b)* so as to be in office or power **5** so as to be agreeing or involved [he fell *in* with our plans] **6** so as to form a part [mix *in* the cream] —*adj.* **1** that is successful or in power [the *in* group] **2** inner; inside **3** coming or going inside or inward [the *in* door, the *in* boat] **4** completed, gathered, counted, etc. [the votes are *in*] **5** [Informal] profiting to the extent of [to be *in* $100] **6** [Informal] currently smart, popular, fashionable, etc. [an *in* place to go] **7** [Informal] known to, or able to be understood by, only a certain group of people; INSIDE (*adj.* 4) [an *in* reference between friends] ☆**8** [Informal] considered certain to succeed —*n.* **1** a person, group, etc. that is in power, in office, or in a favored position: *usually used in pl.* ☆**2** [Informal] special influence or favor; pull —*vt.* **inned**, **in′ning** [Dial., Chiefly Brit.] **1** to collect; gather in [we must *in* the hay before it rains] **2** to enclose —**come in** *Golf* to play the last nine holes of an 18-hole golf course —**have it in for** [Informal] to hold a grudge against —**in and out of** recurrently or frequently situated in, engaged in, or experiencing [*in and out of* the hospital, trouble, etc.] —**in for** certain to have or get (usually an unpleasant experience) —**in on** [Informal] having a share or part of —**ins and outs** **1** all the complex physical details of a place **2** all the details and intricacies —**in that** because; since —**in with** associated with as a partner, friend, etc.

NOTE—this dictionary enters many Latin phrases beginning with the word *in*; look for them alphabetically

in² *abbrev.* inch(es)

In¹ *abbrev.* Indiana

In² *Chem. symbol for* indium

IN *abbrev.* Indiana

in-¹ (in) ⟦< the prep. IN¹; also ME < OE *inn* & MFr *in-* or OFr *en-* < L *in-* < *in*: see IN¹⟧ *prefix* in, into, within, on, toward: also used as an intensifier in some words of Latin origin [*inbreed, infer, induct, instigate*]: it becomes *il-* before *l*; *im-* before *b*, *m*, or *p*; and *ir-* before *r*

in-² (in) ⟦ME < OFr & ML < L < IE **n̥-*, initial negative particle, var. of **ne*, **nē-* > NO¹, L *ne-*⟧ *prefix* no, not, without, non- [*insignificant*]: it becomes *il-* before *l*; *im-* before *b*, *m*, or *p*; and *ir-* before *r*

-in¹ (in) ⟦see -INE³⟧ *suffix forming nouns* **1** a neutral carbohydrate [*inulin*] **2** a glycoside [*amygdalin*] **3** a protein [*albumin*] **4** a glyceride [*palmitin*] **5** an enzyme [*rennin*] **6** an antibiotic [*streptomycin*] **7** an alkaloid or a nitrogenous base [*codein*]: an infrequent variant of -INE³ **8** a pharmaceutical preparation [*chrysarobin*] **9** a commercial product, material, or mixture [*algin*] **10** an antigen [*tuberculin*] Cf. -INE³

-in² (in) ⟦< SIT-IN⟧ *combining form* any of various mass actions or gatherings of a (specified) type, as a political demonstration or a form of entertainment [*pray-in, be-in*]

-i·na (ē′nə) ⟦L, fem. of *-inus*⟧ *suffix* forming feminine names, titles, occupational designations, etc. [*Christina, czarina, ballerina*]

in·a·bil·i·ty (in′ə bil′i tē) *n.* ⟦ME *inabilite*: see IN-² & ABILITY⟧ the quality or state of being unable; lack of ability, capacity, means, or power

in ab·sen·tia (in′ ab sen′shə, -sen′shē ə) ⟦L, lit., in absence⟧ although not present [to receive a college degree *in absentia*]

in·ac·ces·si·ble (in′ak ses′ə bəl) *adj.* ⟦Fr < LL *inaccessibilis*⟧ not accessible; specif., *a)* impossible to reach or enter *b)* that cannot be seen, talked to, influenced, etc.; inapproachable *c)* not obtainable —**in′ac·ces′si·bil′i·ty** *n.* —**in′ac·ces′si·bly** *adv.*

in·ac·cu·ra·cy (in ak′yər ə sē) *n.* **1** the quality of being inaccurate; lack of accuracy **2** *pl.* **-cies** an error or mistake

in·ac·cu·rate (in ak′yər it) *adj.* not accurate; not correct; not exact; in error —**in·ac′cu·rate·ly** *adv.*

in·ac·tion (in ak′shən) *n.* absence of action or motion; inertness or idleness

in·ac·ti·vate (in ak′tə vāt′) *vt.* **-vat′ed**, **-vat′ing** **1** to make inactive **2** *Biochem.* to destroy the activity of (a substance) by heat, pH, etc. —**in·ac′ti·va′tion** *n.* —**in·ac′ti·va′tor** *n.*

in·ac·tive (in ak′tiv) *adj.* **1** not active or moving **2** not inclined to act; idle; dull; sluggish **3** not in use or force; not functioning **4** not in active service in the armed forces **5** not affecting the plane of polarized light: said of some isomers of certain optically active crystalline substances **6** chemically inert —**in·ac′tive·ly** *adv.* —**in′ac·tiv′i·ty** *n.*

in·ad·e·qua·cy (in ad′i kwə sē) *n.*, *pl.* **-cies** quality, state, or instance of being inadequate

in·ad·e·quate (in ad′i kwət) *adj.* not adequate; not sufficient; not equal to what is required —**in·ad′e·quate·ly** *adv.* —**in·ad′e·quate·ness** *n.*

in·ad·mis·si·ble (in′ad mis′ə bəl, -əd-) *adj.* not admissible; not to be allowed, accepted, granted, or conceded [evidence that is ruled *inadmissible*] —**in′ad·mis′si·bil′i·ty** *n.* —**in′ad·mis′si·bly** *adv.*

in·ad·vert·ence (in′ad vurt′'ns, -əd-) *n.* ⟦ML *inadvertentia*: see IN-² & ADVERTENCE⟧ **1** the quality of being inadvertent **2** an instance of this; oversight; mistake Also **in′ad·vert′en·cy**, *pl.* **-cies**

in·ad·vert·ent (in′ad vurt′'nt, -əd-) *adj.* ⟦prob. back-form. < prec.⟧ due to oversight; unintentional —**in′ad·vert′ent·ly** *adv.*

in·ad·vis·a·ble (in′ad vī′zə bəl, -əd-) *adj.* not advisable; not wise or prudent —**in′ad·vis′a·bil′i·ty** *n.*

-i·nae (ī′nē) ⟦ModL, fem. pl. of adj. in *-inus* (in agreement with understood *bestiae*, animals) < L⟧ *suffix* forming the scientific names of zoological subfamilies [*Ardeinae* is the name of a heron subfamily]

in ae·ter·num (in ē tur′nəm, -ī ter′nōōm) ⟦L, to eternity⟧ forever

in·al·ien·a·ble (in āl′yən ə bəl) *adj.* ⟦Fr *inaliénable*: see IN-² & ALIENABLE⟧ that may not be taken away or transferred [*inalienable* rights] —**in·al′ien·a·bil′i·ty** *n.* —**in·al′ien·a·bly** *adv.*

USAGE—see the usage note at UNALIENABLE

in·al·ter·a·ble (in ôl′tər ə bəl) *adj.* ⟦ML *inalterabilis*⟧ that cannot be altered; unchangeable —**in·al′ter·a·bil′i·ty** *n.* —**in·al′ter·a·bly** *adv.*

in·am·o·ra·ta (in am′ə rät′ə, -rāt′ə) *n.* ⟦It, fem. of *in(n)amorato*, lover, orig. pp. of *in(n)amorare*, to fall in love < *in-* (see IN-¹) + *amore* < L *amor*, love⟧ a woman in relation to the person who loves her; female sweetheart or lover

in·ane (in ān′) *adj.* ⟦L *inanis*, empty, void⟧ lacking sense or meaning; foolish; silly —*n.* [Obs.] the void of infinite space —**in·ane′ly** *adv.*

in·an·i·mate (in an′ə mit) *adj.* ⟦LL *inanimatus*⟧ **1** not animate; not endowed with (animal) life **2** not animated; dull; spiritless —*SYN.* DEAD —**in·an′i·mate·ly** *adv.* —**in·an′i·mate·ness** *n.*, **in·an′i·ma′tion**

in·a·ni·tion (in′ə nish′ən) *n.* ⟦ME *inanicioun* < OFr *inanition* < LL *inanitio* < L *inanitus*, pp. of *inanire*, to empty < *inanis*, inane⟧ emptiness; specif., *a)* exhaustion from lack of food or an inability to assimilate it *b)* lack of strength or spirit

in·an·i·ty (in an′i tē) *n.* ⟦Fr *inanité* < L *inanitas*, emptiness⟧ **1** [Archaic] emptiness **2** lack of sense or meaning; silliness **3** *pl.* **-ties** something inane; senseless or silly act, remark, etc.

in·ap·par·ent (in′ə per′ənt) *adj.* not apparent

in·ap·peas·a·ble (in′ə pē′zə bəl) *adj.* not to be appeased

in·ap·pe·tence (in ap′ə təns) *n.* ⟦IN-² + APPETENCE⟧ *Med.*, *Vet.Med.* lack or loss of appetite —**in·ap′pe·tent** *adj.*

in·ap·pli·ca·ble (in ap′li kə bəl, in′ə plik′ə-) *adj.* not applicable; not suitable; inappropriate —**in′ap·pli·ca·bil′i·ty** *n.* —**in·ap′pli·ca·bly** *adv.*

in·ap·po·site (in ap′ə zit) *adj.* not apposite; irrelevant or unsuitable —**in·ap′po·site·ly** *adv.* —**in·ap′po·site·ness** *n.*

in·ap·pre·ci·a·ble (in′ə prē′shə bəl, -shē ə bəl) *adj.* ⟦IN-² + APPRECIABLE⟧ too small or insignificant to be observed or have any value; negligible —**in′ap·pre′ci·a·bly** *adv.*

in·ap·pre·ci·a·tive (in′ə prē′shə tiv) *adj.* not feeling or showing appreciation —**in′ap·pre′ci·a·tive·ly** *adv.* —**in′ap·pre′ci·a·tive·ness** *n.*

in·ap·pre·hen·si·ble (in ap′rē hen′sə bəl) *adj.* that cannot be apprehended, or understood

in·ap·pre·hen·sion (-hen′shən) *n.* lack of apprehension

in·ap·proach·a·ble (in′ə prōch′ə bəl) *adj.* that cannot be approached —**in′ap·proach′a·bil′i·ty** *n.*

in·ap·pro·pri·ate (in′ə prō′prē it) *adj.* not appropriate; not suitable, fitting, or proper —**in′ap·pro′pri·ate·ly** *adv.* —**in′ap·pro′pri·ate·ness** *n.*

in·apt (in apt′) *adj.* not apt; not suitable; inappropriate —**in·apt′i·tude′** (-ap′tə tōōd′, -tyōōd′) *n.* —**in·apt′ly** *adv.* —**in·apt′ness** *n.*

in·arch (in ärch′) *vt.* ⟦IN-¹ + ARCH¹, v.⟧ to graft (a plant) by uniting a shoot to another plant while both are growing on their own roots

in·ar·tic·u·late (in′är tik′yo͞o lit, -yə-) ***adj.*** ⟦LL *inarticulatus*: see IN-[2] & ARTICULATE⟧ **1** produced without the normal articulation of understandable speech: said of vocal sounds [an *inarticulate* cry] **2** *a)* not able to speak, as because of strong emotion; mute *b)* not able to speak understandably, effectively, or coherently **3** not expressed or not able to be expressed [*inarticulate* passion] **4** *Zool.* without joints, segments, hinges, or valves —**in′ar·tic′u·late·ly** ***adv.*** —**in′ar·tic′u·late·ness** ***n.***, **in′ar·tic′u·la·cy**

in·ar·ti·fi·cial (in′är tə fish′əl) ***adj.*** [Now Rare] **1** not artificial; natural **2** inartistic; unskillful **3** unaffected; simple

in·ar·tis·tic (in′är tis′tik) ***adj.*** not artistic; specif., *a)* not conforming to the standards or principles of art *b)* lacking artistic taste or skill —**in′ar·tis′ti·cal·ly** ***adv.***

in·as·much as (in′əz much′ az′) **1** seeing that; since; because **2** to the extent that

in·at·ten·tion (in′ə ten′shən) ***n.*** failure to pay attention; heedlessness; negligence

in·at·ten·tive (in′ə ten′tiv) ***adj.*** not attentive; heedless; negligent —***SYN.*** ABSENT-MINDED —**in′at·ten′tive·ly** ***adv.*** —**in′at·ten′tive·ness** ***n.***

in·au·di·ble (in ôd′ə bəl) ***adj.*** ⟦LL *inaudibilis*⟧ not audible; that cannot be heard or be distinctly heard —**in′au′di·bil′i·ty** ***n.*** —**in·au′di·bly** ***adv.***

in·au·gu·ral (in ô′gyə rəl, -gə-) ***adj.*** ⟦Fr⟧ **1** of an inauguration **2** that begins a series; first —***n.*** ☆**1** a speech made at an inauguration ☆**2** an inauguration

in·au·gu·rate (in ô′gyə rāt′, -gə-) ***vt.*** **-rat′ed**, **-rat′ing** ⟦< L *inauguratus*, pp. of *inaugurare*, to practice augury; to consecrate (a person in office) by augury: see IN-[1] & AUGUR⟧ **1** to induct (an official) into office with a formal ceremony **2** to make a formal beginning of; start [to *inaugurate* a new policy] **3** to celebrate formally the first public use of; dedicate [to *inaugurate* a new library] —***SYN.*** BEGIN —**in·au′gu·ra′tion** ***n.*** —**in·au′gu·ra′tor** ***n.***

☆**Inauguration Day** the day on which a president of the U.S. is inaugurated: Jan. 20 (before 1934, March 4) of the year following the election

in·aus·pi·cious (in′ô spish′əs) ***adj.*** not auspicious; unfavorable; unlucky; ill-omened —**in′aus·pi′cious·ly** ***adv.*** —**in′aus·pi′cious·ness** ***n.***

in·au·then·tic (in′ô then′tik) ***adj.*** not authentic

in·board (in′bôrd′) ***adv.***, ***adj.*** ⟦< *in board*: see BOARD⟧ **1** inside the hull or bulwarks of, or toward the center of, a ship or boat **2** close or closer to the fuselage or hull of an aircraft **3** *Mech.* toward the inside —***n.*** a boat with the motor mounted inboard

in·born (in′bôrn′) ***adj.*** ⟦OE *inboren*⟧ **1** present in the organism at birth; innate; not acquired **2** hereditary; inherited —***SYN.*** INNATE

in·bound (in′bound′) ***adj.*** **1** traveling or going inward **2** *Basketball* INBOUNDS — ***vt.***, ***vi.*** *Basketball* to put (the ball) in play onto the court from out of bounds

in·bounds (in′boundz′) ***adj.*** *Basketball* of or relating to putting the ball in play onto the court from out of bounds [an *inbounds* pass]

inbounds line *Football* either of two lines (appearing as *hash marks*) extending along the field inside and parallel to the sidelines: see HASH MARK

☆**in-box** (in′bäks′) ***n.*** **1** a box or tray, as on an office worker's desk, into which new memos, mail, etc. are placed: also written **in box** **2** a folder, as in email software, in which received or unread messages are automatically stored: also written **inbox**

in·breathe (in′brēth′) ***vt.*** **-breathed′**, **-breath′ing** ⟦ME *inbrethen* (see IN-[1] & BREATHE), after L *inspirare*⟧ [Rare] **1** to inhale **2** to inspire

in·bred (in′bred′) ***adj.*** ⟦pp. of fol.⟧ **1** innate or deeply instilled **2** *a)* bred from closely related parents *b)* resulting from physical inbreeding [*inbred* traits] **3** resulting from narrow or limited associations [a small town with *inbred* political ideas] —***SYN.*** INNATE

in·breed (in′brēd′) ***vt.*** **-bred′**, **-breed′ing** **1** [Rare] to form or develop within **2** to breed by continual mating of individuals of the same or closely related stocks —***vi.*** to engage in such breeding —**in′breed′ing** ***n.***

in·built (in′bilt′) ***adj.*** [Chiefly Brit.] BUILT-IN

inc (*for 5, now often* iŋk) ***abbrev.*** **1** inclosure **2** including **3** inclusive **4** income **5** incorporated: also ☆**Inc.** **6** increase

In·ca (iŋ′kə) ***n.***, *pl.* **-cas** or **-ca** ⟦Sp < Quechua, prince of the royal family⟧ **1** a member of a group of Quechuan or related Indian peoples that dominated ancient Peru until the Spanish conquest: the Incas had a highly developed civilization **2** a ruler or member of the ruling family of these peoples, specif., the emperor —**In′can** ***adj.***

in·cal·cu·la·ble (in kal′kyo͞o lə bəl, -kyə-) ***adj.*** **1** that cannot be calculated; too great or too many to be counted **2** too uncertain to be counted on; unpredictable —**in·cal′cu·la·bil′i·ty** ***n.*** —**in·cal′cu·la·bly** ***adv.***

in·can·desce (in′kən des′) ***vi.***, ***vt.*** **-desced′**, **-desc′ing** ⟦L *incandescere*⟧ to become or make incandescent

in·can·des·cent (in′kən des′ənt) ***adj.*** ⟦L *incandescens*, prp. of *incandescere*: see IN-[1] & CANDESCENT⟧ **1** glowing with intense heat; red-hot or, esp., white-hot **2** very bright; shining brilliantly; gleaming **3** of or having to do with lighting by means of incandescent lamps —***n.*** INCANDESCENT LAMP —**in′can·des′cence** ***n.*** —**in′can·des′cent·ly** ***adv.***

incandescent lamp a lamp in which the light is produced by a filament of conducting material contained in a vacuum and heated to incandescence by an electric current: also **incandescent bulb**

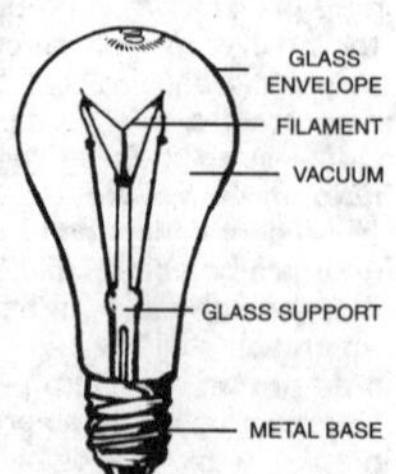

incandescent lamp

in·can·ta·tion (in′kan tā′shən, -kən-) ***n.*** ⟦ME *incantacion* < OFr *incantation* < LL *incantatio* < pp. of L *incantare* < *in-* (intens.) + *cantare*: see CHANT⟧ **1** the chanting of words or formulas that are believed to cast a spell or perform other magic **2** words or a formula so chanted —**in′can·ta′tion·al** ***adj.***

in·can·ta·to·ry (in kan′tə tôr′ē) ***adj.*** **1** of or like a chant or incantation **2** producing an effect like that of an incantation; hypnotic, dreamlike, etc.

in·ca·pa·ble (in kā′pə bəl) ***adj.*** ⟦LL *incapabilis*⟧ not capable; specif., *a)* lacking the necessary ability, competence, strength, etc. *b)* not legally qualified or eligible —**incapable of** **1** not allowing or admitting; not able to accept or experience [*incapable* of change] **2** lacking the ability or fitness for [*incapable* of subtlety] **3** not legally qualified for —**in′ca·pa·bil′i·ty** ***n.***, **in·ca′pa·ble·ness** —**in·ca′pa·bly** ***adv.***

in·ca·pac·i·tate (in′kə pas′ə tāt′) ***vt.*** **-tat′ed**, **-tat′ing** ⟦fol. + -ATE[1]⟧ **1** to make unable or unfit; esp., to make incapable of normal activity; disable **2** *Law* to make ineligible; disqualify —**in′ca·pac′i·ta′tion** ***n.***

in·ca·pac·i·ty (in′kə pas′i tē) ***n.*** ⟦Fr *incapacité* < ML *incapacitas*⟧ **1** lack of capacity, power, or fitness; disability **2** legal ineligibility or disqualification

In·cap·a·ri·na (in kap′ə rē′nə) ***n.*** ⟦*INCAP* (acronym for Institute of Nutrition in Central America and Panama) + (F)ARINA⟧ a low-cost protein food made of corn and soy flours, yeast, etc. and used, esp. in Latin America, in preventing protein deficiency disease

in·cap·su·late (in kap′sə lāt′) ***vt.*** **-lat′ed**, **-lat′ing** *var. of* ENCAPSULATE

in·car·cer·ate (in kär′sər āt′) ***vt.*** **-at′ed**, **-at′ing** ⟦< ML *incarceratus*, pp. of *incarcerare*, to imprison < L *in*, in + *carcer*, prison⟧ **1** to imprison; jail **2** to shut up; confine —**in·car′cer·a′tion** ***n.*** —**in·car′cer·a′tor** ***n.***

in·car·di·nate (in kärd′'n āt′) ***vt.*** **-nat′ed**, **-nat′ing** ⟦< pp. of ML *incardinare*: see IN-[1] & CARDINAL⟧ *R.C.Ch.* to attach (a cleric) to a particular diocese —**in·car′di·na′tion** ***n.***

in·car·na·dine (in kär′nə dīn′, -din, -dēn′) ***adj.*** ⟦Fr *incarnadin* < It *incarnatino* < *incarnato* < LL(Ec) *incarnatus*: see fol.⟧ **1** flesh-colored; pink **2** red; esp., blood-red —***n.*** the color of either flesh or blood —***vt.*** **-dined′**, **-din′ing** to make incarnadine

in·car·nate (in kär′nit, -nāt′; *for v.*, -nāt′) ***adj.*** ⟦ME < LL(Ec) *incarnatus*, pp. of *incarnari*, to be made flesh < L *in-*, in + *caro* (gen. *carnis*), flesh: see CARNAL⟧ **1** endowed with a body, esp. a human body; in bodily form **2** being a living example of; personified [evil *incarnate*] **3** *a)* flesh-colored; pink *b)* red; rosy —***vt.*** **-nat′ed**, **-nat′ing** **1** to provide with flesh or a body; embody **2** to give actual form to; make real **3** to be the type or embodiment of [to *incarnate* the frontier spirit]

in·car·na·tion (in′kär nā′shən) ***n.*** ⟦ME *incarnacion* < OFr *incarnatiun* < LL(Ec) *incarnatio* < pp. of *incarnari*: see prec.⟧ **1** endowment with a human body; appearance in human form **2** any person or animal serving as the embodiment of a god or spirit **3** any person or thing serving as the type or embodiment of a quality or concept [the *incarnation* of courage] —**the Incarnation** *Christian Theol.* the taking on of a human body by the second person of the Trinity; the joining of the divine and the human in Jesus Christ

in·case (in kās′) ***vt.*** **-cased′**, **-cas′ing** *var. of* ENCASE

in·cau·tion (in kô′shən) ***n.*** lack of caution

in·cau·tious (in kô′shəs) ***adj.*** not cautious; not careful or prudent; reckless; rash —**in·cau′tious·ly** ***adv.*** —**in·cau′tious·ness** ***n.***

in·cen·di·ar·y (in sen′dē er′ē; *also*, -dē ər ē) ***adj.*** ⟦L *incendiarius*, setting on fire, an incendiary < *incendium*, a fire < *incendere*: see fol.⟧ **1** having to do with the willful destruction of property by fire **2** causing or designed to cause fires, as certain substances, bombs, etc. **3** willfully stirring up strife, riot, rebellion, etc. —***n.***, *pl.* **-ar′ies** **1** a person who willfully destroys property by fire **2** a person who willfully stirs up strife, riot, rebellion, etc. **3** an incendiary bomb, substance, etc. —**in·cen′di·a·rism′** (-dē ə riz′əm) ***n.***

in·cense[1] (in′sens′) ***n.*** ⟦ME *encens* < OFr < LL *incensum*, incense < neut. of L *incensus*, pp. of *incendere*, to kindle, inflame < *in-*, in, on + *candere*, to burn, shine: see CANDESCENT⟧ **1** any of various substances, as gums or resins, producing a pleasant odor when burned: used in some religious ceremonies **2** the smoke or fragrance from such a substance **3** any pleasant odor **4** pleasing attention, praise, or admiration —***vt.*** **-censed′**, **-cens′ing** **1** to make fragrant with or as with incense; perfume **2** to burn or offer incense to —***vi.*** to burn incense

in·cense[2] (in sens′) ***vt.*** **-censed′**, **-cens′ing** ⟦ME *encensen* < OFr *incenser* < L *incensus*: see prec.⟧ to make very angry; fill with wrath; enrage —**in·cense′ment** ***n.***

☆**incense cedar** a large, W North American tree (*Calocedrus decurrens*) of the cypress family with reddish bark and flattened, scalelike leaves

in·cen·tive (in sent′iv) ***adj.*** ⟦ME < LL *incentivum* < neut. pp. of L *incinere*, to sing < *in-*, in, on + *canere*, to sing: see CHANT⟧ stimulating one to take action, work harder, etc.; encouraging, motivating, etc. —***n.*** something that stimulates one to take action, work harder, etc.; stimulus

in·cen·tiv·ize (in sen′tə vīz′) ***vt.*** **-ized′**, **-iz′ing** to provide an incentive or incentives for —**in·cen′tiv·i·za′tion** ***n.***

in·cept (in sept′) ***vt.*** ⟦L *inceptare*, to begin, freq. of *incipere*: see INCIPIENT⟧ **1** [Obs.] to begin or undertake **2** to take in; receive; specif., to ingest (food particles) —***vi.*** [Brit. Archaic] to receive a master's or doctor's degree at a university

in·cep·tion (in sep′shən) ***n.*** ⟦L *inceptio* < *inceptus*, pp. of *incipere*: see INCIPIENT⟧ the beginning of something; start; commencement —***SYN.*** ORIGIN

in·cep·tive (in sep′tiv) ***adj.*** ⟦OFr *inceptif* < LL *inceptivus* < L *inceptus*: see prec.⟧ **1** beginning; introductory; initial **2** *Gram.* expressing the beginning of an action —***n.*** an inceptive verb or form, as in Latin —**in·cep′tive·ly** ***adv.***

in·cer·ti·tude (in surt′ə to͞od′, -tyo͞od′) ***n.*** ⟦Fr < ML *incertitudo*: see IN-² + CERTITUDE⟧ **1** an uncertain state of mind; doubt **2** an uncertain state of affairs; insecurity

in·ces·sant (in ses′ənt) ***adj.*** ⟦Early ModE < LL *incessans* < L *in-*, not + *cessans*, prp. of *cessare*, to CEASE⟧ never ceasing; continuing or being repeated without stopping or in a way that seems endless; constant —***SYN.*** CONTINUAL —**in·ces′san·cy *n.*, in·ces′sant·ness —in·ces′sant·ly *adv.***

in·cest (in′sest′) ***n.*** ⟦ME < L *incestum*, moral sin, incest, neut. of *incestus*, unchaste < *in-*, not + *castus*, chaste: see CASTE⟧ **1** sexual intercourse between persons too closely related to marry legally **2** sexual molestation of a child or adolescent by a relative, esp. by a parent or other adult relative

in·ces·tu·ous (in ses′tyo͞o əs, -cho͞o-) ***adj.*** ⟦LL *incestuosus*⟧ **1** guilty of incest **2** of, or having the nature of, incest **3** designating or characterized by a relationship of exceptional closeness or interrelation, often one regarded as unproductive, unseemly, etc. [an *incestuous* community of expatriates] —**in·ces′tu·ous·ly *adv.* —in·ces′tu·ous·ness *n.***

inch¹ (inch) ***n.*** ⟦ME *inche* < OE *ynce* < L *uncia*, twelfth part, inch, OUNCE¹⟧ **1** a unit of length in the FPS system, equal to 1⁄12 foot (2.54 cm): symbol, ″: abbrev. *in* **2** a fall (of rain, snow, etc.) equal to the amount that would cover a surface to the depth of one inch **3** a unit of pressure as measured by a barometer or manometer, traditionally equal to the pressure balanced by the weight on a one-inch column of liquid in the instrument **4** a very small amount, degree, or distance; trifle; bit — ***vt., vi.*** to move by inches or degrees; move very slowly —**every inch** in all respects; thoroughly [he's *every inch* a gentleman] —**inch by inch** gradually; slowly; by degrees: also **by inches** —**within an inch of** very close to; almost to —**within an inch of one's life** almost to the point of death: often used hyperbolically

inch² (inch) ***n.*** ⟦ME < Gael *innis*, island⟧ in Scotland and Ireland, an isolated piece of land, as a small island or hill

In·cheon (in′chän′) seaport in NW South Korea, on the Yellow Sea

inch·meal (inch′mēl′) ***adv.*** ⟦INCH¹ + -MEAL⟧ gradually; inch by inch: also **by inchmeal**

in·cho·ate (in kō′it, -āt′) ***adj.*** ⟦L *inchoatus, incohatus*, pp. of *inchoare, incohare*, to begin, orig. rural term "hitch up, harness" < *in-*, in + *cohum*, the strap from plow beam to yoke < IE base **kagh-*, to hold, enclose > HEDGE⟧ **1** just begun; in the early stages; incipient; rudimentary **2** not yet clearly or completely formed or organized; disordered **3** *Law* not yet completed or made effective; pending —**in·cho′ate·ly *adv.* —in·cho′ate·ness *n.***

in·cho·a·tion (in′kō ā′shən) ***n.*** ⟦L *incohatio*: see prec.⟧ a beginning; early stage

in·cho·a·tive (in kō′ə tiv) ***adj.*** ⟦LL *incohativus*⟧ **1** [Rare] INCHOATE (sense 1) **2** *Gram.* expressing the beginning of an action; inceptive, as, in English, through the use of the auxiliary *get* (Ex.: "we got going early") —***n.*** an inchoative verb or phrase

In·chon (in′chän′) *alt. sp. of* INCHEON

☆**inch·worm** (inch′wurm′) ***n.*** MEASURING WORM

in·ci·dence (in′sə dəns) ***n.*** ⟦ME (North) < OFr < LL *incidentia*⟧ **1** the act, fact, or manner of falling upon or influencing **2** the degree or range of occurrence or effect; extent of influence **3** [Informal] an individual or particular occurrence or happening; instance or occasion [several *incidences* of the disease in our village] **4** *Geom.* partial coincidence between two figures, as of a line and a point contained in it **5** *Physics a)* the falling of a line, or a ray of light, projectile, etc. moving in a line, on a surface *b)* the direction of such falling See also ANGLE OF INCIDENCE

in·ci·dent (in′sə dənt) ***adj.*** ⟦OFr < ML < prp. of L *incidere*, to fall upon < *in-*, on + *cadere*, to fall: see CASE¹⟧ **1** likely to happen as a result or concomitant; incidental (*to*) [the cares *incident* to parenthood] **2** falling upon, striking, or affecting [*incident* rays] **3** *Law* dependent upon or involved in something else —***n.*** ⟦ME *incydente*⟧ **1** something that happens; happening; occurrence **2** something that happens as a result of or in connection with something more important; minor event or episode, specif. one in a novel, play, etc. **3** *a)* an apparently minor conflict, disturbance, etc., as between persons, states, etc., that may have serious results *b)* a minor public disturbance, fracas, etc. **4** *Law* something incident to something else —***SYN.*** OCCURRENCE

in·ci·den·tal (in′sə dent′'l) ***adj.*** ⟦ML *incidentalis*⟧ **1** *a)* happening as a result of or in connection with something more important; casual [*incidental* benefits] *b)* likely to happen as a result or concomitant (with *to*) [troubles *incidental* to divorce] **2** secondary or minor, but usually associated [*incidental* expenses] **3** happening by chance; accidental —***n.*** **1** something incidental **2** [*pl.*] miscellaneous or minor items or expenses —***SYN.*** ACCIDENTAL

in·ci·den·tal·ly (in′sə dent′'l ē, -dent′lē) ***adv.*** **1** in an incidental manner; as something less important but associated **2** as a new but related point; by the way

incidental music music played in connection with the presentation of a play, film, poem, etc. in order to heighten the mood or effect on the audience

in·cin·er·ate (in sin′ər āt′) ***vt., vi.*** **-at′ed, -at′ing** ⟦< ML *incineratus*, pp. of *incinerare*, to burn to ashes < L *in*, in, to + *cinis* (gen. *cineris*), ashes < IE **kenis* < base **ken-*, to scratch, rub > Gr *konis*, dust, ashes⟧ to burn to ashes; burn up; cremate —**in·cin′er·a′tion *n.***

in·cin·er·a·tor (-ər āt′ər) ***n.*** a person or thing that incinerates; esp., a furnace or other device for incinerating trash

in·cip·i·ent (in sip′ē ənt) ***adj.*** ⟦L *incipiens*, prp. of *incipere*, to begin, lit., take up < *in-*, in, on + *capere*, to take: see HAVE⟧ in the first stage of existence; just beginning to exist or to come to notice [an *incipient* illness] —**in·cip′i·ence *n.*, in·cip′i·en·cy,** *pl.* **-cies —in·cip′i·ent·ly *adv.***

in·ci·pit (in′si pit′, iŋ kip′it) ***v.*** ⟦L⟧ (here) begins: a word sometimes placed at the beginning of a medieval manuscript —***n.*** the beginning of something; specif., the first words of a medieval manuscript

in·cise (in sīz′) ***vt.*** **-cised′, -cis′ing** ⟦Fr *inciser* < L *incisus*, pp. of *incidere*, to cut into < *in-*, into + *caedere*, to cut: see -CIDE⟧ to cut into with a sharp tool; specif., to cut (designs, inscriptions, etc.) into (a surface); engrave; carve

in·cised (-sīzd′) ***adj.*** **1** *a)* cut into *b)* engraved or carved *c)* made by cutting into with a sharp tool **2** having the edges deeply notched, as a leaf

in·ci·sion (in sizh′ən) ***n.*** ⟦OFr < L *incisio*⟧ **1** the act or result of incising; cut; gash **2** a deep notch, as in the edge of a leaf **3** *Surgery* a cut made into tissue or an organ

in·ci·sive (in sī′siv) ***adj.*** ⟦ML *incisivus* < L *incisus*: see INCISE⟧ **1** cutting into **2** sharp; keen; penetrating; acute [an *incisive* mind] **3** of the incisors —**in·ci′sive·ly *adv.* —in·ci′sive·ness *n.***

SYN.—**incisive** is applied to speech or writing that seems to penetrate directly to the heart of the matter, resulting in a clear and unambiguous statement [an *incisive* criticism]; **trenchant** implies clean-cut expression that results in sharply defined categories, differences, etc. [a *trenchant* analysis]; **cutting** implies incisive qualities but also connotes such harshness or sarcasm as to hurt the feelings [his *cutting* remark about her inefficiency]; **biting** implies a caustic or stinging quality that makes a deep impression on the mind [Swift's *biting* satire]

in·ci·sor (in sī′zər) ***n.*** ⟦ModL < L *incisus* (see INCISE) + -OR⟧ a cutting tooth; any of the front teeth between the canines in either jaw: in humans there are eight incisors

in·cite (in sīt′) ***vt.*** **-cit′ed, -cit′ing** ⟦ME *inciten* < OFr *inciter* < L *incitare* < *in-*, in, on + *citare*, to set in motion, urge: see CITE⟧ to urge to action; stir up; rouse —**in·cite′ment *n.*, in·ci·ta·tion** (in′sə tā′shən, -sī-) —**in·cit′er *n.***

SYN.—**incite** implies an urging or stimulating to action, either in a favorable or unfavorable sense [*incited* to achievement by rivalry]; **instigate** always implies responsibility for initiating the action and usually connotes a bad or evil purpose [who *instigated* the fight?]; **arouse**, in this connection, means little more than a bringing into being or action [it *aroused* my suspicions]; **foment** suggests continued incitement over an extended period of time [the unjust taxes *fomented* rebellion] —***ANT.*** **restrain, inhibit**

in·ci·vil·i·ty (in′sə vil′i tē) ***n.*** ⟦Fr *incivilité* < LL *incivilitas* < L *incivilis*, impolite: see IN-² & CIVIL⟧ **1** a lack of courtesy or politeness; rudeness **2** *pl.* **-ties** a rude or discourteous act

incl *abbrev.* **1** inclosure **2** including **3** inclusive

in·clem·ent (in klem′ənt, in′klem′ənt) ***adj.*** ⟦L *inclemens*: see IN-² & CLEMENT⟧ **1** rough; severe; stormy [*inclement* weather] **2** lacking mercy or leniency; harsh —**in·clem′en·cy *n.*,** *pl.* **-cies —in·clem′ent·ly *adv.***

in·clin·a·ble (in klīn′ə bəl) ***adj.*** **1** *a)* having an inclination or tendency *b)* favorably disposed **2** that can be inclined

in·cli·na·tion (in′klə nā′shən) ***n.*** ⟦OFr < L *inclinatio* < pp. of *inclinare*, fol.⟧ **1** the act of bending, leaning, or sloping; esp., a bowing or nodding **2** an inclined surface or plane; slope; incline; slant **3** the extent or degree of incline from a horizontal or vertical position, course, etc. **4** the difference in direction of two lines, planes, or surfaces as measured by the angle between them; specif., a property of a line in a plane, being the angle measured from the positive portion of the x-axis to the line in question **5** *a)* a particular disposition or bent of mind; bias; tendency [an *inclination* to talk] *b)* a liking or preference **6** any action, practice, or thing, toward which one is inclined —**in′cli·na′tion·al *adj.***

SYN.—**inclination** refers to a more or less vague mental disposition toward some action, practice, or thing [he had an *inclination* to refuse the offer]; **leaning** suggests a general inclination toward something but implies only the direction of attraction and not the final choice [Dr. Green had always had a *leaning* toward the study of law]; **bent** and **propensity** imply a natural or inherent inclination, the latter also connoting an almost uncontrollable attraction [she has a *bent* for art; he has a *propensity* for getting into trouble]; **proclivity** suggests a strong tendency as a result of habit, often, specif., toward something bad or wrong [a *proclivity* to falsehood]

in·cline (in klīn′; *for n., usually* in′klīn′) ***vi.*** **-clined′, -clin′ing** ⟦ME *enclinen* < OFr *encliner* < L *inclinare* < *in-*, on, to + *clinare*, to LEAN¹⟧ **1** to deviate from a horizontal or vertical position, course, etc.; lean; slope; slant **2** to bend or bow the body or head **3** *a)* to have a particular disposition or bent of mind, will, etc. *b)* to have a tendency or preference [he *inclines* toward a drier wine] —***vt.*** **1** to cause to lean, slope, slant, etc.; bend **2** to bend or bow (the body or head) **3** to give a tendency to; make willing; dispose; influence —***n.*** an inclined plane or surface; slope; grade; slant —**incline one's ear** to pay heed; listen willingly —**in·clin′er *n.***

in·clined (in klīnd′; *for 2, also* in′klīnd′) ***adj.*** **1** having an inclination; specif., *a)* at or on a slant; sloping; leaning *b)* disposed; willing; tending **2** forming an angle with another line, plane, or body

inclined plane

inclined plane a plane surface set at any angle other than a right angle against a horizontal surface: it is a simple machine that increases mechanical advantage but requires a longer working distance

in·cli·nom·e·ter (in′kli näm′ət ər, -klī-) *n.* ⟦< INCLINE + -O- + -METER⟧ **1** DIP NEEDLE **2** CLINOMETER **3** an instrument that measures the inclination of an axis of an airplane or ship in relation to the horizontal

in·close (in klōz′) *vt.* **-closed′, -clos′ing** *var. of* ENCLOSE

in·clo·sure (in klō′zhər) *n. var. of* ENCLOSURE

in·clude (in klo͞od′) *vt.* **-clud′ed, -clud′ing** ⟦ME *includen* < L *includere* < *in-*, in + *claudere*, to shut, CLOSE[1]⟧ **1** [Archaic] to shut up or in; enclose **2** to have as part of a whole; contain; comprise [the price *includes* sales tax] **3** to consider as part of a whole; take into account **4** to make part of a whole; put into a total, category, etc. [to be *included* as a candidate] —**in·clud′a·ble** *adj.*, **in·clud′i·ble**

SYN.—**include** implies a containing as part of a whole; **comprise**, in discriminating use, means to consist of and takes as its object the various parts that make up the whole [his library *comprises* 2,000 volumes and *includes* many first editions]; **comprehend** suggests that the object is contained within the total scope or range of the subject, sometimes by implication [the word "beauty" *comprehends* various concepts]; **embrace** stresses the variety of objects comprehended [he had *embraced* a number of hobbies]; **involve** implies inclusion of an object because of its connection with the subject as a consequence or antecedent [acceptance of the office *involves* responsibilities] —*ANT.* **exclude**

in·clud·ed (-id) *adj.* **1** enclosed, contained, or involved **2** *Bot.* with stamens and pistils wholly contained within the petals, sheath, etc.

in·clud·ing (-iŋ) *prep.* involving, containing, or comprising

in·clu·sion (in klo͞o′zhən) *n.* ⟦L *inclusio* < *inclusus*, pp. of *includere*: see INCLUDE⟧ **1** an including or being included **2** something included; specif., *a)* a solid, liquid, or gaseous foreign substance encased in mineral or rock *b)* *Biol.* a separate body, as a grain of starch, within the protoplasm of a cell

inclusion body any of various small particles of nonliving or foreign material occurring in tissue cells, as a pigment or secretion granule, a microsome, or a virus

in·clu·sive (in klo͞o′siv; *also*, -ziv) *adj.* ⟦LL *inclusivus* < L *inclusus*, pp. of *includere*⟧ **1** including or tending to include; esp., taking everything into account; reckoning everything **2** including the terms, limits, or extremes mentioned [ten days, from April third to the twelfth *inclusive*] —**inclusive of** including; taking into account —**in·clu′sive·ly** *adv.* —**in·clu′sive·ness** *n.*

in·co·er·ci·ble (in′kō ʉr′sə bəl) *adj.* that cannot be coerced

in·cog·ni·ta (in′käg nē′tə, in käg′ni tə) *adj., adv., n.* INCOGNITO: used of a woman or girl

in·cog·ni·to (in′käg nē′tō′, in käg′ni tō′) *adj., adv.* ⟦It < L *incognitus*, unknown < *in-*, not + *cognitus*: see COGNITION⟧ with true identity unrevealed or disguised; under an assumed name, rank, etc. —*n., pl.* **-tos′ 1** a person who is incognito **2** *a)* the state of being incognito *b)* the disguise assumed —*SYN.* PSEUDONYM

in·cog·ni·zant (in käg′nə zənt, -kän′ə-) *adj.* not cognizant (*of*); unaware (*of*) —**in·cog′ni·zance** *n.*

in·co·her·ence (in′kō hir′əns, -her′-) *n.* **1** lack of coherence; the quality or state of being incoherent **2** incoherent speech, thought, etc. Also **in′co·her′en·cy**, *pl.* **-cies**

in·co·her·ent (in′kō hir′ənt, -her′-) *adj.* not coherent; specif., *a)* lacking cohesion; not sticking together *b)* not logically connected; disjointed; rambling *c)* characterized by incoherent speech, thought, etc. —**in′co·her′ent·ly** *adv.*

in·com·bus·ti·ble (in′kəm bus′tə bəl) *adj.* ⟦ME < ML *incombustibilis*⟧ not combustible; that cannot be burned; fireproof —*n.* an incombustible substance —**in′com·bus′ti·bil′i·ty** *n.*

in·come (in′kum′) *n.* ⟦ME: see IN[1] & COME⟧ **1** [Archaic] the act or an instance of coming in **2** the money or other gain received, esp. in a given period, by an individual, corporation, etc. for labor or services or from property, investments, operations, etc.

income statement a financial statement that summarizes the various transactions of a business during a specified period, showing the net profit or loss; profit and loss statement

income tax a tax on income or on that part of income which exceeds a certain amount

in·com·ing (in′kum′iŋ) *adj.* ⟦ME < *incomen*, to come in < OE *incuman*⟧ coming in or about to come in [the *incoming* tide, the *incoming* mayor] —*n.* **1** an act or instance of coming in **2** [*usually pl.*] income

in·com·men·su·ra·ble (in′kə men′sho͝or ə bəl, -sər-) *adj.* ⟦LL *incommensurabilis*: see IN-[2] & COMMENSURABLE⟧ **1** that cannot be measured or compared by the same standard or measure; without a common standard of comparison **2** not worthy of comparison [a statement *incommensurable* with truth] **3** not being integral multiples of the same number or quantity: said of two or more numbers or quantities, as 2 and $\sqrt{3}$ —*n.* an incommensurable thing, quantity, etc. —**in′com·men′su·ra·bil′i·ty** *n.* —**in′com·men′su·ra·bly** *adv.*

in·com·men·su·rate (in′kə men′sho͝or it, -sər-) *adj.* not commensurate; specif., *a)* not proportionate; not adequate [a supply *incommensurate* to the demand] *b)* INCOMMENSURABLE (*adj.* 1) —**in′com·men′su·rate·ly** *adv.*

in·com·mode (in′kə mōd′) *vt.* **-mod′ed, -mod′ing** ⟦Fr *incommoder* < L *incommodare* < *incommodus*, inconvenient < *in-*, not + *commodus*, convenient: see COMMODE⟧ to bother; inconvenience

in·com·mo·di·ous (in′kə mō′dē əs) *adj.* ⟦IN-[2] + COMMODIOUS⟧ **1** causing inconvenience; uncomfortable; troublesome **2** inconveniently small, narrow, etc. —**in′com·mo′di·ous·ly** *adv.* —**in′com·mo′di·ous·ness** *n.*

in·com·mod·i·ty (in′kə mäd′i tē) *n., pl.* **-ties** ⟦ME *incommodite* < OFr *incommodité* < L *incommoditas*: see INCOMMODE⟧ [Archaic] inconvenience; disadvantage; discomfort

in·com·mu·ni·ca·ble (in′kə myo͞o′ni kə bəl) *adj.* ⟦LL *incommunicabilis*⟧ that cannot be communicated or told —**in′com·mu′ni·ca·bil′i·ty** *n.* —**in′com·mu′ni·ca·bly** *adv.*

☆**in·com·mu·ni·ca·do** (in′kə myo͞o′ni kä′dō) *adj., adv.* ⟦Sp *incomunicado* < pp. of *incomunicar*, to isolate, cut off from communication < *in-* (< L *in-*, IN-[2]) + *comunicar* < L *communicare*, to COMMUNICATE⟧ **1** without a means of communicating **2** in isolation or seclusion [a prisoner held *incommunicado*, a celebrity living *incommunicado*] **3** not willing to communicate with others

in·com·mu·ni·ca·tive (in′kə myo͞o′ni kāt′iv, -ni kə tiv) *adj.* not communicative; reserved; taciturn

in·com·mut·a·ble (in′kə myo͞ot′ə bəl) *adj.* ⟦ME < L *incommutabilis*: see IN-[2] & COMMUTABLE⟧ that cannot be changed or exchanged —**in′com·mut′a·bil′i·ty** *n.* —**in′com·mut′a·bly** *adv.*

in·com·pa·ra·ble (in käm′pə rə bəl; *occas.* in′kəm par′ə bəl) *adj.* ⟦OFr < L *incomparabilis*⟧ that cannot be compared; specif., *a)* having no common basis of comparison; incommensurable *b)* beyond comparison; unequaled; matchless [*incomparable* skill] —**in·com′pa·ra·bil′i·ty** *n.* —**in·com′pa·ra·bly** *adv.*

in·com·pat·i·ble (in′kəm pat′ə bəl) *adj.* ⟦ML *incompatibilis*⟧ **1** not compatible; specif., *a)* not able to exist in harmony or agreement *b)* not going, or getting along, well together; incongruous, conflicting, discordant, etc. (often followed by *with*) **2** that cannot be held at one time by the same person: said of positions, ranks, etc. **3** *Logic* *a)* that cannot both be true at the same time (said of propositions) *b)* not predicable of the same subject without contradiction (said of terms) **4** *Math.* logically contradictory: said of equations or other statements **5** *Med., Pharmacy* not suitable for being mixed or used together: said of substances having an undesirable action on each other or, when mixed, on the body —*n.* an incompatible person or thing: *usually used in pl.* —**in·com′pat′i·bil′i·ty** *n., pl.* **-ties** —**in·com′pat′i·bly** *adv.*

in·com·pe·tent (in käm′pə tənt) *adj.* ⟦Fr *incompétent* < LL *incompetens*: see IN-[2] & COMPETENT⟧ **1** without adequate ability, knowledge, fitness, etc.; failing to meet requirements; incapable; unskillful **2** not legally qualified **3** lacking strength and sufficient flexibility to transmit pressure, thus breaking or flowing under stress: said of rock structures —*n.* an incompetent person; esp., one who is mentally deficient —**in·com′pe·tence** *n.*, **in·com′pe·ten·cy**, *pl.* **-cies** —**in·com′pe·tent·ly** *adv.*

in·com·plete (in′kəm plēt′) *adj.* ⟦ME *incompleet* < LL *incompletus*: see IN-[2] & COMPLETE⟧ **1** lacking a part or parts; not whole; not full **2** unfinished; not concluded **3** not perfect; not thorough ☆**4** *Football* not successfully executed: said of a forward pass —*n.* *Educ.* *a)* incompletion of assigned work in a course *b)* a grade or mark (usually "I") indicating incompletion of assigned work —**in′com·plete′ly** *adv.* —**in′com·plete′ness** *n.* —**in′com·ple′tion** *n.*

in·com·pli·ant (in′kəm plī′ənt) *adj.* not compliant; not yielding; not pliant —**in′com·pli′ance** *n.* —**in′com·pli′ant·ly** *adv.*

in·com·pre·hen·si·ble (in käm′prē hen′sə bəl, -pri-) *adj.* ⟦ME < OFr or L: OFr *incompréhensible* < L *incomprehensibilis*⟧ **1** not comprehensible; that cannot be understood; obscure or unintelligible **2** [Archaic] illimitable —**in·com′pre·hen′si·bil′i·ty** *n.* —**in·com′pre·hen′si·bly** *adv.*

in·com·pre·hen·sion (in käm′prē hen′shən, -pri-) *n.* lack of comprehension; inability to understand

in·com·pre·hen·sive (-siv) *adj.* not inclusive; including little —**in·com′pre·hen′sive·ly** *adv.*

in·com·press·i·ble (in′kəm pres′ə bəl) *adj.* that cannot be compressed —**in′com·press′i·bil′i·ty** *n.*

in·com·put·a·ble (in′kəm pyo͞ot′ə bəl) *adj.* that cannot be computed —**in′com·put′a·bly** *adv.*

in·con·ceiv·a·ble (in′kən sēv′ə bəl) *adj.* that cannot be conceived; that cannot be thought of, understood, imagined, or believed —**in′con·ceiv′a·bil′i·ty** *n.*, **in′con·ceiv′a·ble·ness** —**in′con·ceiv′a·bly** *adv.*

in·con·cin·ni·ty (in′kən sin′ə tē) *n., pl.* **-ties** ⟦< L *inconcinnitas*, absurdity, incongruity⟧ lack of harmony, proportion, or elegance, esp. in writing style

in·con·clu·sive (in′kən klo͞o′siv) *adj.* not conclusive or final; not leading to a definite result —**in′con·clu′sive·ly** *adv.* —**in′con·clu′sive·ness** *n.*

in·con·den·sa·ble or **in·con·den·si·ble** (in′kən den′sə bəl) *adj.* that cannot be condensed —**in′con·den′sa·bil′i·ty** *n.*, **in′con·den′si·bil′i·ty**

in·con·dite (in kän′dīt′, -dit) *adj.* ⟦L *inconditus* < *in-*, not + *conditus*, pp. of *condere*, to put together: see RECONDITE⟧ [Rare] **1** poorly constructed: said of literary works **2** lacking refinement; crude

in·con·form·i·ty (in′kən fôrm′ə tē) *n.* ⟦ML *inconformitas*⟧ lack of conformity; nonconformity

in·con·gru·ent (in′käŋ′gro͞o ənt) *adj.* ⟦L *incongruens*⟧ not congruent —**in·con′gru·ence** *n.* —**in·con′gru·ent·ly** *adv.*

in·con·gru·i·ty (in′kän gro͞o′i tē, -kən-) *n.* ⟦ML *incongruitas* < L *incongruus*⟧ **1** the condition, quality, or fact of being incongruous; specif., *a)* lack of harmony or agreement *b)* lack of fitness or appropriateness **2** *pl.* **-ties** something incongruous

in·con·gru·ous (in käŋ′gro͞o əs, -kän′-) *adj.* ⟦L *incongruus*⟧ not congruous; specif., *a)* lacking harmony or agreement; incompatible *b)* having inconsistent or inharmonious parts, elements, etc. *c)* not corresponding to what is right, proper, or reasonable; unsuitable; inappropriate —**in·con′gru·ous·ly** *adv.*

in·con·nu (in′kə no͞o′) *n., pl.* **-nus′** or **-nu′** ⟦Fr, an unknown, stranger⟧ a large, oily, freshwater trout (*Stenodus leucichthys*) of NW North America and NE Asia

in·con·sec·u·tive (in′kən sek′yo͞o tiv, -yə-) *adj.* not consecutive

in·con·se·quent (in kän′si kwent′, -kwənt) *adj.* ⟦L *inconsequens*⟧ not consequent; specif., *a)* not following as a result *b)* not following as a logical inference or conclusion; irrelevant *c)* not proceeding in logical sequence; characterized by lack of logic —**in·con′se·quence′** *n.* —**in·con′se·quent′ly** *adv.*

in·con·se·quen·tial (in kän′si kwen′shəl) *adj.* **1** inconsequent; illogical **2** of no consequence; unimportant; trivial —*n.* something inconsequential —**in·con′se·quen′ti·al′i·ty** (-shē al′ə tē) *n.* —**in·con′se·quen′tial·ly** *adv.*

in·con·sid·er·a·ble (in′kən sid′ər ə bəl) *adj.* not worth consideration; unimportant; trivial; small —**in′con·sid′er·a·ble·ness** *n.* —**in′con·sid′er·a·bly** *adv.*

in·con·sid·er·ate (in′kən sid′ər it) *adj.* ⟦ME, ill-considered < L *inconsideratus*⟧ without thought or consideration for others; thoughtless; heedless —**in′con·sid′er·ate·ly** *adv.* —**in′con·sid′er·ate·ness** *n.*, **in′con·sid′er·a′tion** (-ər ā′shən)

in·con·sis·ten·cy (in′kən sis′tən sē) *n.* **1** the quality or state of being inconsistent **2** *pl.* **-cies** an inconsistent act, remark, etc.

in·con·sis·tent (in′kən sis′tənt) *adj.* not consistent; specif., *a)* not in agreement, harmony, or accord; incompatible [acts *inconsistent* with belief] *b)* not uniform; self-contradictory [*inconsistent* testimony] *c)* not always holding to the same principles or practice; changeable —**in′con·sis′tent·ly** *adv.*

inconsistent equations two or more equations impossible to satisfy by any one set of values for the variables (Ex.: $x + y = 1$ and $x + y = 2$)

in·con·sol·a·ble (in′kən sōl′ə bəl) *adj.* ⟦L *inconsolabilis*⟧ that cannot be consoled; disconsolate; brokenhearted —**in′con·sol′a·bil′i·ty** *n.*, **in′con·sol′a·ble·ness** —**in′con·sol′a·bly** *adv.*

in·con·so·nant (in kän′sə nənt) *adj.* ⟦L *inconsonans*⟧ not consonant; not in harmony or agreement; discordant —**in·con′so·nance** *n.* —**in·con′so·nant·ly** *adv.*

in·con·spic·u·ous (in′kən spik′yo͞o əs) *adj.* ⟦L *inconspicuus*⟧ not conspicuous; hard to see or perceive; attracting little attention; not striking —**in′con·spic′u·ous·ly** *adv.* —**in′con·spic′u·ous·ness** *n.*

in·con·stant (in kän′stənt) *adj.* ⟦OFr < L *inconstans*⟧ not constant; changeable; specif., *a)* not remaining firm in mind or purpose *b)* unsteady in affections or loyalties; fickle *c)* not uniform in nature, value, etc.; irregular; variable —**in·con′stan·cy** *n.* —**in·con′stant·ly** *adv.*

SYN.—**inconstant** implies an inherent tendency to change or a lack of steadfastness [an *inconstant* lover]; **fickle** suggests an even greater instability or readiness to change, especially in affection [spurned by a *fickle* public]; **capricious** implies an instability or irregularity that seems to be the product of whim or erratic impulse [a *capricious* climate]; **unstable,** in this connection, applies to one who is emotionally unsettled or variable [an *unstable* person laughs and cries easily] —**ANT. constant, reliable**

in·con·sum·a·ble (in′kən so͞o′mə bəl, -syo͞o′-) *adj.* that cannot be consumed

in·con·test·a·ble (in′kən tes′tə bəl) *adj.* ⟦Fr < *in-*, IN-[2] + *contestable* < *contester*, CONTEST⟧ not to be contested; indisputable; unquestionable —**in′con·test′a·bil′i·ty** *n.* —**in′con·test′a·bly** *adv.*

in·con·ti·nent[1] (in känt′'n ənt) *adj.* ⟦OFr < L *incontinens*: see IN-[2] & CONTINENT⟧ **1** *a)* without self-restraint, esp. in regard to sexual activity *b)* unrestrained **2** without the normal ability to restrain a particular natural discharge, as of urine, from the body —**in·con′ti·nence** *n.* —**in·con′ti·nent·ly** *adv.*

in·con·ti·nent[2] (in känt′'n ənt) *adv.* ⟦OFr < L *in continenti (tempore)*, in continuous (time): see CONTINENT⟧ [Archaic] immediately; without delay

in·con·trol·la·ble (in′kən trōl′ə bəl) *adj.* [Archaic] that cannot be controlled; uncontrollable

in·con·tro·vert·i·ble (in kän′trə vurt′ə bəl) *adj.* that cannot be controverted; not disputable or debatable; undeniable —**in·con′tro·vert′i·bil′i·ty** *n.* —**in·con′tro·vert′i·bly** *adv.*

in·con·ven·ience (in′kən vēn′yəns) *n.* ⟦OFr < LL *inconvenientia*⟧ **1** the quality or state of being inconvenient; lack of comfort, ease, etc.; bother; trouble **2** anything inconvenient Also **in′con·ven′ien·cy** (-yən sē), *pl.* **-cies** —*vt.* **-ienced, -ienc·ing** to cause inconvenience to; cause trouble or bother to; incommode

in·con·ven·ient (in′kən vēn′yənt) *adj.* ⟦OFr < L *inconveniens*⟧ not convenient; specif., *a)* not favorable to one's comfort; difficult to do, use, or get to; causing trouble or bother; unhandy *b)* [Obs.] not appropriate —**in′con·ven′ient·ly** *adv.*

in·con·vert·i·ble (in′kən vurt′ə bəl) *adj.* ⟦LL(Ec) *inconvertibilis*⟧ that cannot be converted; that cannot be changed or exchanged [paper money that is *inconvertible* into silver] —**in′con·vert′i·bil′i·ty** *n.*

in·con·vin·ci·ble (in′kən vin′sə bəl) *adj.* ⟦LL(Ec) *inconvincibilis*⟧ that cannot be convinced

in·co·or·di·nate (in′kō ôrd′'n it) *adj.* not coordinate

in·co·or·di·na·tion (in′kō ôrd′'n ā′shən) *n.* lack of coordination; esp., inability to achieve the harmonious action of muscles necessary to perform complex movements

incorp *abbrev.* incorporated

in·cor·po·ra·ble (in kôr′pə rə bəl) *adj.* that can be incorporated

in·cor·po·rate[1] (in kôr′pə rit; *for v.*, -pə rāt′) *adj.* ⟦ME *incorporat* < LL *incorporatus*, pp. of *incorporare*: see IN-[1] & CORPORATE⟧ INCORPORATED —*vt.* **-rat′ed, -rat′ing** ⟦ME *incorporaten*⟧ **1** to combine or join with something already formed; make part of another thing; include; embody **2** to bring together into a single whole; merge **3** to admit into a corporation or association as a member **4** to form (individuals or units) into a legally organized group that acts as one individual; form into a corporation **5** to give substantial, material, or physical form to —*vi.* **1** to unite or combine into a single whole; be combined or merged **2** to form a corporation —**in·cor′po·ra′tion** *n.* —**in·cor·po·ra·tive** (in kôr′pə rāt′iv, -rə tiv) *adj.*

in·cor·po·rate[2] (in kôr′pə rit, -rāt′) *adj.* ⟦L *incorporatus*: see IN-[2] & CORPORATE⟧ [Archaic] INCORPOREAL

in·cor·po·rat·ed (in kôr′pə rāt′id) *adj.* **1** combined into one body or unit; united **2** organized as a legal corporation [an *incorporated* town]

in·cor·po·ra·tor (in kôr′pə rāt′ər) *n.* **1** a person who incorporates **2** any of the original members of a corporation, whose names appear in its charter

in·cor·po·re·al (in′kôr pôr′ē əl) *adj.* ⟦L *incorporeus* (see fol.) + -AL⟧ **1** not consisting of matter; without material body or substance **2** of spirits or angels **3** *Law* without physical existence in itself but belonging as a right to a material thing or property: said of a patent, copyright, etc. —**in′cor·po′re·al·ly** *adv.*

in·cor·po·re·i·ty (in′kôr pə rē′ə tē) *n.* ⟦ML *incorporeitas* < L *incorporeus* < *in-*, IN-[2] + *corporeus*, CORPOREAL⟧ **1** the quality or state of being incorporeal **2** *pl.* **-ties** an incorporeal entity or attribute

in·cor·rect (in′kə rekt′) *adj.* ⟦ME < L *incorrectus*⟧ not correct; specif., *a)* improper *b)* untrue; inaccurate; wrong; faulty —**in′cor·rect′ly** *adv.* —**in′cor·rect′ness** *n.*

in·cor·ri·gi·ble (in kôr′ə jə bəl, -kär′-) *adj.* ⟦ME *incorygibile* < OFr < LL *incorrigibilis*⟧ not corrigible; that cannot be corrected, improved, or reformed, esp. because firmly established, as a habit, or because set in bad habits, as a child —*n.* an incorrigible person —**in·cor′ri·gi·bil′i·ty** *n.*, **in·cor′ri·gi·ble·ness** —**in·cor′ri·gi·bly** *adv.*

in·cor·rupt (in′kə rupt′) *adj.* ⟦ME *incorrupte* < L *incorruptus*⟧ not corrupt; specif., *a)* [Obs.] uncontaminated; not rotten *b)* morally sound; not depraved, evil, impure, or perverted *c)* not taking bribes; upright; honest *d)* containing no errors, alterations, or foreign admixtures (said of texts, languages, etc.)

in·cor·rupt·i·ble (-rup′tə bəl) *adj.* ⟦ME *incorruptyble* < LL (Ec) *incorruptibilis*⟧ **1** that cannot be corrupted, esp. morally **2** not liable to physical decay —**in′cor·rupt′i·bil′i·ty** *n.* —**in′cor·rupt′i·bly** *adv.*

in·cor·rup·tion (in′kə rup′shən) *n.* ⟦LL(Ec) *incorruptio*⟧ [Archaic] the quality or state of being INCORRUPTIBLE (sense 2)

incr *abbrev.* **1** increase **2** increment

in·cras·sate (in kras′āt′) *adj.* ⟦< L *incrassatus*, pp. of *incrassare*, to make thick < *in-*, in + *crassare*, to thicken < *crassus*, thick: see CRASS⟧ *Biol.* thickened; swollen —**in′cras·sa′tion** *n.*

in·crease (in krēs′, in′krēs′; *for n.* in′krēs′, in krēs′) *vi.* **-creased′, -creas′ing** ⟦ME *encresen* < OFr *encreistre* < L *increscere* < *in-*, in, on + *crescere*, to grow: see CRESCENT⟧ **1** to become greater in size, amount, degree, etc.; grow **2** to become greater in numbers by producing offspring; multiply; propagate —*vt.* to cause to become greater in size, amount, degree, etc.; add to; augment —*n.* ⟦ME *encrese*⟧ **1** an increasing or becoming increased; specif., *a)* growth, enlargement, etc. *b)* [Archaic] multiplication, as of offspring **2** the result or amount of an increasing [a population *increase* of 10%] —**on the increase** increasing —**in·creas′a·ble** *adj.* —**in·creas′er** *n.*

SYN.—**increase**, the general word in this list, means to make or become greater in size, amount, degree, etc. [to *increase* one's weight, one's power, debts, etc.]; **enlarge** specifically implies a making or becoming greater in size, volume, extent, etc. [to *enlarge* a house, a business, etc.]; **augment**, a more formal word, generally implies increase by addition, often of something that is already of a considerable size, amount, etc. [to *augment* one's income]; **multiply** suggests increase in number, specif. by procreation [rabbits *multiply* rapidly] —**ANT. decrease, diminish, lessen**

in·creas·ing·ly (in krēs′iŋ lē) *adv.* more and more; to an ever-increasing degree

in·cre·ate (in′krē āt′, in′krē āt′) *adj.* ⟦ME < LL *increatus*⟧ not created: said of divine beings or attributes

in·cred·i·ble (in kred′ə bəl) *adj.* ⟦L *incredibilis*⟧ **1** not credible; unbelievable **2** seeming too unusual or improbable to be possible **3** [Informal] wonderful, impressive, extraordinary, etc. —**in·cred′i·bil′i·ty** *n.* —**in·cred′i·bly** *adv.*

in·cre·du·li·ty (in′krə do͞o′lə tē, -dyo͞o′-) *n.* ⟦ME *incredulite* < OFr *incrédulité* < L *incredulitas*: see IN-[2] & CREDULITY⟧ unwillingness or inability to believe; doubt; skepticism —**SYN.** UNBELIEF

in·cred·u·lous (in krej′o͝o ləs) *adj.* ⟦L *incredulus*: see IN-[2] & CREDULOUS⟧ **1** unwilling or unable to believe; doubting; skeptical **2** showing doubt or disbelief [an *incredulous* look] —**in·cred′u·lous·ly** *adv.*

in·cre·ment (in′krə mənt, iŋ′-) *n.* ⟦ME < L *incrementum* < base of *increscere*, to INCREASE⟧ **1** the fact of becoming greater or larger; increase; gain; growth **2** *a)* an increase, usually small, often one of a series *b)* the amount of increase [an annual *increment* of $300 in salary] **3** *Math.* the quantity, usually small, by which a variable increases or is increased: a negative increment results in a decrease —**in′cre·men′tal** (-ment′'l) ***adj.***

in·crim·i·nate (in krim′i nāt′) ***vt.*** **-nat′ed, -nat′ing** ⟦< ML *incriminatus*, pp. of *incriminare*: see IN-[1] & CRIMINATE⟧ **1** to charge with a crime; accuse **2** to involve in, or make appear guilty of, a crime or fault —**in·crim′i·na′tion** ***n.*** —**in·crim′i·na·to′ry** (-nə tôr′ē) ***adj.***

in·cross (in′krôs′) ***n.*** an organism formed by close inbreeding within a stock —***vt.*** INBREED (sense 2)

in·crust (in krust′) ***vt., vi.*** *var. of* ENCRUST —**in·crus·ta·tion** (in′krus tā′shən) ***n.***

in·cu·bate (in′kyə bāt′, iŋ′-) ***vt.*** **-bat′ed, -bat′ing** ⟦< L *incubatus*, pp. of *incubare*, to lie in or upon < *in-*, IN-[1] + *cubare*, to lie: see CUBE[1]⟧ **1** to sit on and hatch (eggs) **2** to keep (eggs, embryos, bacteria, etc.) in a favorable environment for hatching or developing **3** to cause to develop or take form, as by thought or planning —***vi.*** **1** to go through the process of incubation **2** to develop or take form, esp. gradually

in·cu·ba·tion (in′kyə bā′shən, iŋ′-) ***n.*** ⟦L *incubatio*⟧ **1** an incubating or being incubated **2** the phase in the development of a disease between the infection and the first appearance of symptoms —**in′cu·ba′tion·al** ***adj.*** —**in′cu·ba′tive** ***adj.***

in·cu·ba·tor (in′kyə bāt′ər, iŋ′-) ***n.*** a person or thing that incubates; specif., *a)* an artificially heated container for hatching eggs *b)* an apparatus in which a premature baby is kept for a period, in which temperature, etc. can be controlled *c)* an apparatus for growing microbial or cell cultures under controlled conditions

in·cu·bus (in′kyə bəs, iŋ′-) ***n., pl.*** **-bus·es** or **-bi′** (-bī′) ⟦ME < LL, nightmare (in ML, demon supposed to cause nightmares) < L *incubare*: see INCUBATE⟧ **1** *Folklore* an evil spirit or demon who has sexual intercourse with sleeping women: cf. SUCCUBUS **2** a nightmare **3** anything oppressive; burden

in·cu·des (in kyo͞o′dēz′) ***n. pl. of*** INCUS

in·cul·cate (in kul′kāt′, in′kul kāt′) ***vt.*** **-cat′ed, -cat′ing** ⟦< L *inculcatus*, pp. of *inculcare*, to tread in, tread down < *in-*, in, on + *calcare*, to trample underfoot < *calx*, heel: see CALCAR⟧ to impress upon the mind by frequent repetition or persistent urging —**in′cul·ca′tion** ***n.*** —**in·cul′ca′tor** ***n.***

in·culp·a·ble (in kul′pə bəl) ***adj.*** ⟦LL *inculpabilis*⟧ not culpable; free from blame or guilt

in·cul·pate (in kul′pāt′, in′kul pāt′) ***vt.*** **-pat′ed, -pat′ing** ⟦< ML *inculpatus*, pp. of *inculpare*, to blame < L *in*, in, on + *culpa*, fault, blame⟧ INCRIMINATE —**in′cul·pa′tion** ***n.*** —**in·cul′pa·to′ry** (-pə tôr′ē) ***adj.***

in·cult (in kult′) ***adj.*** ⟦L *incultus*: see IN-[2] & CULT⟧ [Rare] **1** uncultivated: said of land **2** lacking culture; unrefined

in·cum·ben·cy (in kum′bən sē) ***n., pl.*** **-cies** **1** the quality or condition of being incumbent **2** something incumbent, as a duty or obligation **3** *a)* the holding and administering of a position; esp., the holding of a church benefice *b)* tenure of office

in·cum·bent (in kum′bənt) ***adj.*** ⟦L *incumbens*, prp. of *incumbere*, to recline or rest on < *in-*, on + *cubare*, to lie down: see CUBE[1]⟧ **1** lying, resting, or pressing with its weight on something else **2** currently in office —***n.*** the holder of an office or benefice —**incumbent on (**or **upon)** depending upon as a duty or obligation

in·cum·ber (in kum′bər) ***vt.*** *var. of* ENCUMBER

in·cum·brance (in kum′brəns) ***n.*** *var. of* ENCUMBRANCE

in·cu·nab·u·la (in′kyo͞o nab′yo͞o lə, -yə lə) ***pl.n., sing.*** **-u·lum** (-ləm) or **in·cun·a·ble** (in kyo͞o′nə bəl) ⟦L, neut. pl., swaddling clothes, infancy, origin < *in-*, in + *cunabula*, neut. pl., a cradle, dim. of *cunae*, fem. pl., a cradle < IE **koinā*, bed < base **kei-*, to lie down > HOME⟧ books produced in the early years of printing, esp. those printed before 1500 —**in′cu·nab′u·lar** ***adj.***

in·cur (in kur′) ***vt.*** **-curred′, -cur′ring** ⟦ME *incurren* < L *incurrere*, to run into or toward, attack < *in-*, in, toward + *currere*, to run: see CURRENT⟧ **1** to come into or acquire (something undesirable) [*to incur* a debt] **2** to bring upon oneself [*to incur* someone's wrath]

in·cur·a·ble (in kyoor′ə bəl) ***adj.*** ⟦OFr < LL *incurabilis*⟧ not curable; that cannot be remedied or corrected —***n.*** a person having an incurable disease or disorder —**in·cur′a·bil′i·ty** ***n.*** —**in·cur′a·bly** ***adv.***

in·cu·ri·ous (in kyoor′ē əs) ***adj.*** ⟦L *incuriosus*⟧ not curious; not eager to find out; uninterested; indifferent —***SYN.*** INDIFFERENT —**in·cu·ri·os·i·ty** (in′kyoor′ē äs′ə tē) ***n.***, **in·cu′ri·ous·ness** —**in·cu′ri·ous·ly** ***adv.***

in·cur·rence (in kur′əns) ***n.*** the act of incurring

in·cur·rent (in kur′ənt) ***adj.*** ⟦L *incurrens*, prp. of *incurrere*: see INCUR⟧ flowing in; esp., characterized by the flowing in of water [the *incurrent* canals of a sponge]

in·cur·sion (in kur′zhən; -shən) ***n.*** ⟦ME < L *incursio* < *incurrere*: see INCUR⟧ **1** a running in or coming in, esp. when undesired; inroad **2** a sudden, brief invasion or raid —**in·cur′sive** (-siv) ***adj.***

in·cur·vate (in kur′vit, -vāt′; in′kər-; *for v.* in kur′vāt′, in′kər-) ***adj.*** ⟦L *incurvatus*, pp. of *incurvare*: see fol.⟧ bent or curving inward — ***vt., vi.*** **-vat′ed, -vat′ing** to bend or curve inward —**in′cur·va′tion** ***n.*** —**in·cur′va·ture** (-və chər) ***n.***

in·curve (in kurv′, in′kurv′; *for n.* in′kurv′) ***vt., vi.*** **-curved′, -curv′ing** ⟦L *incurvare* < *in-*, IN-[1] + *curvare*, to CURVE⟧ to curve inward —***n.*** an act or instance of incurving

in·cus (iŋ′kəs) ***n., pl.*** **in·cu·des** (in kyo͞o′dēz′) ⟦ModL < L, anvil < *incusus*: see fol.⟧ the central one of the three small bones in the middle ear: it is shaped somewhat like an anvil

in·cuse (in kyo͞oz′, -kyo͞os′) ***adj.*** ⟦L *incusus*, pp. of *incudere*, to forge with a hammer < *in-*, in, on + *cudere*, to strike, hit: see HEW⟧ hammered or stamped in: said of the design on a coin —***n.*** such a design

ind *abbrev.* **1** independent **2** index **3** indicative **4** indigo **5** industrial

Ind[1] (ind) ⟦ME & OFr *Inde* < L *India*⟧ **1** [Old Poet.] India **2** [Obs.] the Indies

Ind[2] *abbrev.* **1** India **2** Indian **3** Indiana **4** Indies

in d. *abbrev.* ⟦L *in dies*⟧ *Pharmacy* daily

in·da·ba (in dä′bä′) ***n.*** ⟦Zulu *in-daba*, subject, matter⟧ a council or conference, esp. between or with indigenous peoples of South Africa

in·da·mine (in′də mēn′, -min) ***n.*** ⟦IND(IGO) + AMINE⟧ any of a group of blue or blue-green organic dyes containing the NH group; esp., phenylene blue, $NH{:}C_6H_4{:}N{\cdot}C_6H_4{\cdot}NH_2$

in·debt·ed (in det′id) ***adj.*** ⟦ME *endetted* < OFr *endeté*, pp. of *endetter* < *en-* (L *in-*) + *dette*: see DEBT⟧ **1** in debt or under legal obligation to repay something received **2** owing gratitude, as for a favor received

in·debt·ed·ness (-nis) ***n.*** **1** the state of being indebted **2** the amount owed; all one's debts

in·de·cen·cy (in dē′sən sē) ***n.*** ⟦L *indecentia*⟧ **1** the state or quality of being indecent; lack of modesty, taste, or propriety **2** *pl.* **-cies** an indecent act, statement, etc.

in·de·cent (in dē′sənt) ***adj.*** ⟦< Fr or L: Fr *indécent* < L *indecens*⟧ not decent; specif., *a)* not proper and fitting; unseemly; improper *b)* morally offensive; obscene —***SYN.*** IMPROPER —**in·de′cent·ly** ***adv.***

in·de·cid·u·ous (in′dē sij′o͞o əs) ***adj.*** not deciduous

in·de·ci·pher·a·ble (in′dē sī′fər ə bəl, -di-) ***adj.*** that cannot be deciphered; illegible —**in′de·ci′pher·a·bil′i·ty** ***n.***

in·de·ci·sion (in′dē sizh′ən, -di-) ***n.*** ⟦Fr *indécision* < *indécis*, undecided < ML *indecisus*⟧ lack of decision; inability to decide or tendency to change the mind frequently; hesitation or vacillation

in·de·ci·sive (in′dē sī′siv, -di-) ***adj.*** **1** not decisive; not conclusive or final **2** characterized by indecision; hesitating or vacillating —**in′de·ci′sive·ly** ***adv.*** —**in′de·ci′sive·ness** ***n.***

in·de·clin·a·ble (in′dē klīn′ə bəl, -di-) ***adj.*** *Gram.* not declinable; having no case inflections

in·de·com·pos·a·ble (in′dē′kəm pō′zə bəl) ***adj.*** that cannot be decomposed

in·dec·o·rous (in dek′ə rəs) ***adj.*** ⟦L *indecorus*⟧ not decorous; lacking decorum, propriety, good taste, etc.; unseemly —***SYN.*** IMPROPER —**in·dec′o·rous·ly** ***adv.*** —**in·dec′o·rous·ness** ***n.***

in·de·co·rum (in′di kôr′əm) ***n.*** ⟦L, neut. of *indecorus*⟧ **1** lack of decorum; lack of propriety, good taste, etc. **2** indecorous conduct, speech, etc.

in·deed (in dēd′) ***adv.*** ⟦ME *indede*: see IN[1], ***prep.*** & DEED⟧ certainly; truly; admittedly: often used for emphasis or confirmation [it is *indeed* warm] or, in questions, to seek confirmation [did she *indeed* tell you that?] —***interj.*** used to express surprise, doubt, sarcasm, irony, etc.

indef *abbrev.* indefinite

in·de·fat·i·ga·ble (in′di fat′i gə bəl) ***adj.*** ⟦MFr *indéfatigable* < L *indefatigabilis* < *in-*, not + *defatigare*, to tire out, weary: see DE- & FATIGUE⟧ that cannot be tired out; not yielding to fatigue; untiring —**in′de·fat′i·ga·bil′i·ty** ***n.*** —**in′de·fat′i·ga·bly** ***adv.***

in·de·fea·si·ble (in′dē fē′zə bəl, -di-) ***adj.*** not defeasible; that cannot be undone or made void —**in′de·fea′si·bil′i·ty** ***n.*** —**in′de·fea′si·bly** ***adv.***

in·de·fect·i·ble (in′dē fek′tə bəl, -di-) ***adj.*** ⟦IN-[2] + DEFECT + -IBLE⟧ **1** not likely to fail, decay, become imperfect, etc. **2** without a fault or blemish; perfect —**in′de·fect′i·bil′i·ty** ***n.*** —**in′de·fect′i·bly** ***adv.***

in·de·fen·si·ble (in′dē fen′sə bəl, -di-) ***adj.*** **1** that cannot be defended or protected **2** that cannot be justified or excused; inexcusable —**in′de·fen′si·bil′i·ty** ***n.*** —**in′de·fen′si·bly** ***adv.***

in·de·fin·a·ble (in′dē fīn′ə bəl, -di-) ***adj.*** ⟦ML *indeffinabilis*⟧ that cannot be defined —**in′de·fin′a·bil′i·ty** ***n.*** —**in′de·fin′a·bly** ***adv.***

in·def·i·nite (in def′ə nit) ***adj.*** ⟦L *indefinitus*⟧ not definite; specif., *a)* having no exact limits or having no limits at all *b)* not precise or clear in meaning; vague *c)* not sharp or clear in outline; blurred; indistinct *d)* not sure or positive; uncertain *e) Bot.* of no fixed number, or too many to count (said of the stamens, etc. of certain flowers) *f) Gram.* not limiting or specifying; not referring to a specific or previously identified person, thing, etc. ["a" and "an" are *indefinite* articles; "any" is an *indefinite* pronoun] —**in·def′i·nite·ness** ***n.***

indefinite integral *Math.* any function which when differentiated yields a specified function

in·def·i·nite·ly (in def′ə nit lē) ***adv.*** in an indefinite manner; specif., without a foreseeable end or limit

in·de·his·cent (in′dē his′ənt) ***adj.*** not dehiscent; not opening at maturity to discharge its seeds [*indehiscent* fruits] —**in′de·his′cence** ***n.***

in·del·i·ble (in del′ə bəl) ***adj.*** ⟦L *indelibilis* < *in-*, not + *delibilis*, perishable < *delere*, to destroy: see DELETE⟧ **1** that cannot be erased, blotted out, eliminated, etc.; permanent; lasting **2** leaving a lasting mark [*indelible* ink] —**in·del′i·bil′i·ty** ***n.*** —**in·del′i·bly** ***adv.***

in·del·i·ca·cy (in del′i kə sē) ***n.*** **1** the quality of being indelicate **2** *pl.* **-cies** something indelicate

in·del·i·cate (in del′i kit) ***adj.*** not delicate; coarse; crude; rough; esp., lacking, or offensive to, propriety or modesty; gross —***SYN.*** COARSE, IMPROPER —**in·del′i·cate·ly** ***adv.*** —**in·del′i·cate·ness** ***n.***

in·dem·ni·fi·ca·tion (in dem′ni fi kā′shən) ***n.*** **1** an indemnifying or being indemnified **2** something that indemnifies; recompense —***SYN.*** REPARATION

in·dem·ni·fy (in dem′ni fī′) ***vt.*** **-fied′, -fy′ing** ⟦< L *indemnis*, unhurt < *in-*, not + *damnum*, hurt, harm, damage (see DAMN) + -FY⟧ **1** to protect against or keep free from loss, damage, etc.; insure **2** *a)* to repay for what has been lost or damaged; compensate for a loss, etc.; reimburse *b)* to redeem or make good (a loss) —**SYN.** PAY[1] —**in·dem′ni·fi′er** *n.*

in·dem·ni·ty (in dem′ni tē) *n., pl.* **-ties** ⟦Fr *indemnité* < LL *indemnitas* < L *indemnis*: see prec.⟧ **1** protection or insurance against loss, damage, etc. **2** legal exemption from penalties or liabilities incurred by one's actions **3** repayment or reimbursement for loss, damage, etc.; compensation

in·de·mon·stra·ble (in′di män′strə bəl; in dem′ən-) *adj.* ⟦LL *indemonstrabilis*⟧ not demonstrable; that cannot be proved

in·dene (in′dēn′) *n.* ⟦IND(OLE) + -ENE⟧ a colorless, oily hydrocarbon, C_9H_8, obtained from coal tar and used in the manufacture of synthetic resins

in·dent[1] (in dent′; *for n.* in′dent′, in dent′) *vt.* ⟦ME *endenten* < OFr *endenter* or ML *indentare*, both < L *in*, in + *dens*, TOOTH⟧ **1** *a)* to cut toothlike points into (an edge or border); notch; also, to join by mating notches *b)* to make jagged or zigzag in outline **2** to sever (a written contract, etc.) along an irregular line, so that the parts may be identified **3** to write out (a contract, etc.) in duplicate **4** to bind (a servant or apprentice) by indenture **5** to place (the first line of a paragraph, an entire paragraph, a column of figures, etc.) some number of spaces away from the regular margin **6** [Brit.] *Business* to order by an INDENT[1] (*n.* 4) —*vi.* **1** to create a starting point some number of spaces away from the margin; make an indentation **2** to draw up an order or requisition in duplicate or triplicate —*n.* **1** a notch or cut in an edge **2** an indenture, or written contract **3** *a)* a starting point some number of spaces away from the margin; indentation *b)* an indented line, paragraph, etc. **4** [Brit.] *Business* an order form used in foreign trade and usually drawn up in duplicate or triplicate; specif., *a)* any order for foreign merchandise *b)* an export order to buy certain goods at stated terms

in·dent[2] (in dent′; *for n.* in′dent′, in dent′) *vt.* ⟦IN-[1] + DENT[1]⟧ **1** to make a dent, or slight hollow, in **2** to apply (a mark, etc.) with pressure; impress; stamp in —*n.* a dent, or indentation

in·den·ta·tion (in′den tā′shən) *n.* ⟦INDENT[1] or prec. + -ATION⟧ **1** an indenting or being indented **2** a result of indenting; specif., *a)* a notch, cut, or inlet on a coastline, etc. *b)* a dent, or slight hollow *c)* an empty or blank space preceding an indent

in·den·tion (in den′shən) *n.* ⟦INDENT[1] or INDENT[2] + -ION⟧ **1** an act of indenting or the state of being indented **2** an empty or blank space left by this **3** *a)* a dent, or slight hollow *b)* the making of a dent

in·den·ture (in den′chər) *n.* ⟦ME *endenture* < OFr & < ML *indentura*: see INDENT[1]⟧ **1** [Now Rare] INDENTATION **2** a written contract or agreement: originally, it was in duplicate, the two copies having correspondingly notched edges for identification **3** [*often pl.*] a contract binding a person to work for another for a given length of time, as an apprentice to a master, or an immigrant to service in a colony **4** an official, authenticated list, inventory, etc. **5** *Finance* a document containing the terms under which bonds are issued —*vt.* **-tured, -tur·ing 1** to bind by indenture **2** [Archaic] INDENT[2]

in·de·pend·ence (in′dē pen′dəns, -di-) *n.* ⟦ML *independentia*⟧ **1** the state or quality of being independent; freedom from the influence, control, or determination of another or others **2** [Now Rare] an income sufficient for a livelihood

In·de·pend·ence (in′dē pen′dəns, -di-) ⟦in honor of Andrew JACKSON[1] in allusion to his *independence* of character⟧ city in W Mo.: suburb of Kansas City

☆**Independence Day** a legal holiday in the U.S., celebrated on July 4, the anniversary of the adoption of the Declaration of Independence in 1776

Independence Hall building in Philadelphia, Pa., where the Declaration of Independence was proclaimed: see also LIBERTY BELL

in·de·pend·en·cy (in′dē pen′dən sē, -di-) *n., pl.* **-cies 1** INDEPENDENCE **2** [I-] the church polity of the Independents **3** an independent nation, province, etc.

in·de·pend·ent (in′dē pen′dənt, -di-) *adj.* ⟦ML *independens*: see IN-[2] & DEPENDENT⟧ **1** free from the influence, control, or determination of another or others; specif., *a)* free from the rule of another; controlling or governing oneself; self-governing *b)* free from influence, persuasion, or bias; objective [an *independent* observer] *c)* relying only on oneself or one's own abilities, judgment, etc.; self-confident; self-reliant [*independent* in his thinking] *d)* not adhering to any political party or organization [an *independent* voter] *e)* not connected or related to another, to each other, or to a group; separate [an *independent* grocer] **2** *a)* not depending on another or others, esp. for financial support *b)* large enough to enable one to live without working (said of an income, a fortune, etc.) *c)* having such an income, fortune, etc. and, hence, not needing to work for a living **3** [I-] of or having to do with Independents —*n.* **1** a person, company, etc. that is independent, as in thinking, action, or practice ☆**2** [*often* I-] a voter who is not an adherent of or registered with any political party **3** [I-] a member of a religious and political movement of the 17th cent. in England that advocated self-sufficiency of each local Christian church: the movement led to the organization of Congregationalists and Baptists —**independent of** apart from; regardless of —**in′de·pend′ent·ly** *adv.*

independent clause *Gram.* a clause that can function syntactically as a complete sentence and that conveys a complete meaning; main clause (Ex.: *She will visit us* if she can.): distinguished from DEPENDENT CLAUSE

independent school a private school, not open to or controlled by the public, esp., one that is nonreligious and supported mainly by tuition and private funds

independent variable *Math.* a variable whose value may be determined freely without reference to other variables

in-depth (in′depth′) *adj.* carefully worked out, detailed, profound, thorough, etc. [an *in-depth* study]

in·de·scrib·a·ble (in′di skrīb′ə bəl) *adj.* that cannot be described; beyond the power of description —**in′de·scrib′a·bil′i·ty** *n.* —**in′de·scrib′a·bly** *adv.*

in·de·struct·i·ble (in′di struk′tə bəl) *adj.* not destructible; that cannot be destroyed —**in′de·struct′i·bil′i·ty** *n.* —**in′de·struct′i·bly** *adv.*

in·de·ter·mi·na·ble (in′dē tʉr′mi nə bəl, -di-) *adj.* ⟦LL *indeterminabilis*⟧ not determinable; specif., *a)* that cannot be decided or settled *b)* that cannot be definitely learned or ascertained —**in′de·ter′mi·na·ble·ness** *n.* —**in′de·ter′mi·na·bly** *adv.*

in·de·ter·mi·na·cy (in′dē tʉr′mi nə sē, -di-) *n.* the state or quality of being indeterminate

indeterminacy principle UNCERTAINTY PRINCIPLE

in·de·ter·mi·nate (in′dē tʉr′mi nit, -di-) *adj.* ⟦LL *indeterminatus*⟧ **1** not determinate; specif., *a)* inexact in its limits, nature, etc.; indefinite; uncertain; vague [an *indeterminate* amount] *b)* not yet settled, concluded, or known; doubtful or inconclusive **2** *Bot.* RACEMOSE —**in′de·ter′mi·nate·ly** *adv.* —**in′de·ter′mi·nate·ness** *n.*

indeterminate cleavage *Zool.* the division of an egg into cells, each of which has the potential of developing into a complete organism: cf. TWINNING (sense 1)

in·de·ter·mi·na·tion (in′dē tʉr′mi nā′shən, -di-) *n.* **1** lack of determination **2** an indeterminate state or quality

in·de·ter·min·ism (in′dē tʉr′mi niz′əm, -di-) *n.* ⟦IN-[2] + DETERMINISM⟧ **1** the doctrine that the will is free or to some degree free in that one's actions and choices are not altogether the necessary result of a sequence of causes **2** the quality or condition of being indeterminate —**in′de·ter′min·ist** *n., adj.* —**in′de·ter′min·is′tic** *adj.*

in·dex (in′deks′) *n., pl.* **-dex′es** or **-di·ces′** (-di sēz′) ⟦L, informer, that which points out < *indicare*, INDICATE⟧ **1** *short for* INDEX FINGER **2** a pointer or indicator, as the needle on a dial **3** a thing that points out; indication; sign; representation [performance is an *index* of ability] **4** *a)* an alphabetical list of contents, as names or subjects; specif., such a list, together with the page numbers where they appear in the text, usually placed at the end of a book or other publication *b)* THUMB INDEX *c)* a list describing the items of a collection and where they may be found; catalog [a library *index*] *d)* [I-] INDEX LIBRORUM PROHIBITORUM *e)* [I-] INDEX EXPURGATORIUS *f)* a periodical that lists books according to subject, with publishing information and summary of contents **5** *a)* the relation or ratio of one amount or dimension to another, or the formula expressing this relation [cranial *index*] *b)* a number used to measure change in prices, wages, employment, production, etc.: it shows percentage variation from an arbitrary standard, usually 100, representing the status at some earlier time (in full **index number**) **6** *Math.* *a)* EXPONENT (sense 3) *b)* a subscript *c)* an integer or symbol placed above and to the left of a radical (Ex.: $\sqrt[3]{8}$, $\sqrt[n]{x}$) **7** *Printing* a sign ☞ calling attention to something; fist —*vt.* **1** *a)* to make an index of or for *b)* to include in an index *c)* to supply with a thumb index **2** to be an index, or sign, of **3** to adjust (wages, interest rates, etc.) automatically to changes in the cost of living —**in·dex′a·ble** *adj.*, **in·dex′i·ble** —**in′dex′er** *n.*

in·dex·a·tion (in′dek sā′shən) *n.* the practice of indexing wages, interest rates, etc.

index card a small card, often 3 inches by 5 inches or 4 inches by 6 inches, used in preparing an index or card file, for recording notes, etc.

In·dex Ex·pur·ga·to·ri·us (in′deks′ eks po͝or′gä tō′rē o͞os′) ⟦ModL, expurgatory index⟧ [Historical] a list of books that the Roman Catholic Church forbade its members to read unless certain passages condemned as dangerous to faith or morals were deleted or changed

index finger ⟦from its being used in pointing⟧ the finger next to the thumb; forefinger

index fossil any fossil of wide geographical distribution and a short range in time, used to correlate and date rock strata and their associated fossils

index fund a mutual fund that invests in the stocks used to compute a particular stock-market index, thus tying its performance to that index

in·dex·i·cal (in dek′si kəl) *Linguis., Logic n.* a word or expression whose reference may vary from speaker to speaker: some indexicals are "I," "this," "now," and "here" —*adj.* of, having to do with, or serving as an indexical —**in·dex′i·cal′i·ty** *n.*

In·dex Li·bro·rum Pro·hi·bi·to·rum (in′deks′ lē brō′ro͞om′ prō hib′ē tō′ro͞om′) ⟦ModL, index of prohibited books⟧ [Historical] a list of books that the Roman Catholic Church forbade its members to read (except by special permission) because the books were judged to be dangerous to faith or morals

index of refraction the ratio of the sine of the angle of incidence to the sine of the angle of refraction for a ray of light crossing from one medium into another

In·di·a (in′dē ə) ⟦L < Gr < *Indos*, the INDUS[2] < OPers *Hindu*, India: see HINDU⟧ **1** region in S Asia, south of the Himalayas, including a large peninsula between the Arabian Sea & the Bay of Bengal: it contains the republic of India, Pakistan, Bangladesh, Nepal, & Bhutan **2** republic in the central & S part of this region: established by the British Parliament (1947), it became a republic in 1950: member of the Commonwealth: 1,269,346 sq mi (3,287,590 sq km); cap. New Delhi: see also JAMMU AND KASHMIR **3** INDIAN EMPIRE

India ink **1** a black pigment, as of specially prepared lampblack, or carbon black, mixed with a gelatinous substance and dried into cakes or sticks **2** a liquid ink made from this, used in writing, drawing, etc.

In·di·a·man (in′dē ə mən) *n., pl.* **-men** ⟦see MAN, *n.* 10⟧ [Historical] a large merchant ship sailing regularly between England and India

In·di·an (in′dē ən) *adj.* ⟦LL *Indianus* < L *India*⟧ **1** *a)* of India or its peoples, languages, or cultures *b)* of the East Indies or their peoples or cultures **2** of American Indians or their languages or cultures; Native American **3** of a type used or made by Indians ☆**4** made of maize, or Indian corn —*n.* **1** a person born or living in India or the East Indies **2** ⟦so named by early explorers of the New World, who believed they had reached INDIA⟧ AMERICAN INDIAN; Native American **3** popularly, any of the languages spoken by American Indian peoples

In·di·an·a (in′dē an′ə) ⟦ModL, land of the Indians: see prec.⟧ Midwestern state of the U.S.: admitted 1816; 35,867 sq mi (92,895 sq km); cap. Indianapolis: abbrev. *IN, In,* or *Ind*

☆**Indian agent** [Historical] in the U.S. or Canada, an official representing the government in dealings with native peoples, as on reservations

In·di·an·an (in′dē an′ən) *adj.* of Indiana: usually used in the predicate —*n.* a person born or living in Indiana Also **In′di·an′i·an** (-an′ē ən)

In·di·an·ap·o·lis (in′dē ə nap′ə lis) ⟦INDIANA + Gr *polis,* city: see POLIS⟧ capital of Ind., in the central part

☆**Indian bread** ⟦< INDIAN (*adj.* 2)⟧ **1** bread made from cornmeal **2** TUCKAHOE

☆**Indian club** ⟦< INDIAN (*adj.* 1a)⟧ a bottle-shaped club of wood, metal, etc. swung in the hand for exercise

☆**Indian corn** ⟦< INDIAN (*adj.* 2)⟧ **1** CORN[1] (sense 3) **2** [Informal] any primitive corn having ears with kernels of various colors, often used for decoration in autumn

Indian Desert THAR DESERT

Indian elephant *see* ELEPHANT

Indian Empire territories in & near India, under British control: dissolved in 1947

☆**Indian file** SINGLE FILE: from the notion that American Indians walked along a trail in this manner

☆**Indian giver** a person who gives something and then asks for it back: from the notion that a North American Indian expected an equivalent in return when giving something: now regarded by many as an offensive term

☆**Indian hemp** ⟦< INDIAN (*adj.* 2)⟧ **1** a perennial American plant (*Apocynum cannabium*) of the dogbane family, with a medicinal root and a tough bark once used in rope making by the Indians **2** HEMP (sense 1)

Indian licorice ⟦< INDIAN (*adj.* 2)⟧ JEQUIRITY (sense 2)

Indian mallow ⟦< INDIAN (*adj.* 1a)⟧ a tall weed (*Abutilon theophrasti*) of the mallow family, with small, yellow flowers and large, heart-shaped, velvety leaves

☆**Indian meal** ⟦< INDIAN (*adj.* 2)⟧ meal made from corn (maize); cornmeal

Indian Ocean ocean south of Asia, between Africa & Australia: 28,350,500 sq mi (73,427,511 sq km)

☆**Indian paintbrush** ⟦< INDIAN (*adj.* 2)⟧ any of a large genus (*Castilleja*) of plants of the figwort family, with brilliantly colored orange or red flowers and red or yellow upper leaves

☆**Indian pipe** ⟦< INDIAN (*adj.* 2): from the resemblance of the flower and its stem to a long-stemmed tobacco *pipe*⟧ a leafless, fleshy, white, saprophytic plant (*Monotropa uniflora*) of the heath family, native to the forests of the Northern Hemisphere: its unbranched, erect stalks each bear a single, nodding, white flower

☆**Indian pudding** ⟦< INDIAN (*adj.* 2)⟧ a cornmeal pudding made with milk, molasses, etc.

Indian red **1** ⟦< INDIAN (*adj.* 1a)⟧ a yellowish-red ocher, originally from an island in the Persian Gulf, used in early times as a pigment ☆**2** ⟦< INDIAN (*adj.* 2)⟧ an impure native iron oxide used by North American Indians as a reddish war paint, and by early American painters

☆**Indian sign** ⟦< INDIAN (*adj.* 2)⟧ a hex or jinx: chiefly in the phrase **have** (or **put**) **the Indian sign on**

Indian States and Agencies [Historical] the group of partly independent states and agencies of British India

☆**Indian summer** ⟦< INDIAN (*adj.* 2): reason for name obscure⟧ **1** a period of mild, warm, hazy weather following the first frosts of late autumn **2** the final period, as of a person's life, regarded as tranquil, serene, etc.

Indian Territory [Historical] territory (1834-90) of the S U.S., reserved for Amerindian peoples: now a part of Oklahoma

☆**Indian tobacco** ⟦< INDIAN (*adj.* 2)⟧ a poisonous annual plant (*Lobelia inflata*) of the bellflower family, common over the E U.S., with inflated pods and with light-blue flowers in slender spikes

☆**Indian turnip** ⟦< INDIAN (*adj.* 2)⟧ the jack-in-the-pulpit or its root

☆**Indian wrestling** ⟦< INDIAN (*adj.* 2)⟧ **1** ARM-WRESTLING **2** a contest in which two standing persons, each placing a foot alongside the other's corresponding foot and grasping a hand of the other, try to force each other off balance —**In′di·an-wres′tle** *vi., vt.* **-tled, -tling**

India paper ⟦after INDIA in generalized sense "Far East"⟧ **1** a thin, absorbent paper made in China and Japan from vegetable fiber, used in taking proofs from engraved plates **2** a thin, strong, opaque paper used for printing Bibles, dictionaries, etc.: often called *Bible paper*

India (*or* **india**) **rubber** crude, natural rubber obtained from latex; caoutchouc —**In′di·a-rub′ber** *adj.*

indic *abbrev.* **1** indicative **2** indicator

In·dic (in′dik) *adj.* ⟦L *Indicus* < Gr *Indikos*⟧ **1** of India; Indian **2** INDO-ARYAN —*n.* INDO-ARYAN (sense 1)

in·di·can (in′di kan′) *n.* ⟦< L *indicum,* INDIGO + -AN⟧ **1** a glucoside, $C_{14}H_{17}NO_6$, that is found in a natural state in the indigo plant: it is converted by water and oxygen into indigo **2** an indigo-forming substance, $C_8H_6NOSO_2OH$, the potassium salt of which is present in animal urine

in·di·cant (in′di kənt) *adj.* ⟦L *indicans*⟧ indicating; pointing out —*n.* something that indicates or points out

in·di·cate (in′di kāt′) *vt.* **-cat′ed, -cat′ing** ⟦< L *indicatus,* pp. of *indicare,* to indicate, show < *in-,* in, to + *dicare,* to point out, declare: see DICTION⟧ **1** to direct attention to; point to or point out; show **2** to be or give a sign, token, or indication of; signify; betoken [fever *indicates* illness] **3** to show the need for; call for; make necessary [a fabric for which dry cleaning is *indicated*] **4** *Med.* to point to as the advisable treatment [bed rest is *indicated*] **5** to express briefly or generally [to *indicate* guidelines for action]

in·di·ca·tion (in′di kā′shən) *n.* ⟦L *indicatio*⟧ **1** the act of indicating **2** something that indicates, points out, or signifies; sign **3** something that is indicated as necessary **4** the amount or degree registered by an indicator

in·dic·a·tive (in dik′ə tiv) *adj.* ⟦Fr *indicatif* < L *indicativus*⟧ **1** giving an indication, suggestion, or intimation; showing; signifying [a look *indicative* of joy]: also **in·dic·a·to·ry** (in′di kə tôr′ē, in dik′ə-) **2** designating or of the mood of a verb used to identify an act, state, or occurrence as actual, or to ask a question of fact: cf. SUBJUNCTIVE, IMPERATIVE —*n.* **1** the indicative mood **2** a verb in this mood —**in·dic′a·tive·ly** *adv.*

in·di·ca·tor (in′di kāt′ər) *n.* **1** a person or thing that indicates; specif., *a)* any device, as a gauge, dial, register, or pointer, that measures or records and visibly indicates *b)* an apparatus that diagrams the varying fluid pressure of an engine in operation **2** any of various substances used to indicate the acidity or alkalinity of a solution, the beginning or end of a chemical reaction, the presence of certain substances, etc., by changes in color **3** a statistic, as the unemployment rate, used to measure economic or social conditions **4** *Ecol.* a species of plant or animal, or a community, whose occurrence serves as evidence that certain environmental conditions exist

in·di·ces (in′di sēz′) *n. alt. pl. of* INDEX

in·di·cia (in dish′ə, -ē ə) *pl.n., sing.* **-cium** (-əm, -ē əm) ⟦L, pl. of *indicium,* a notice, information < *index* (gen. *indicis*): see INDEX⟧ **1** characteristic marks or tokens ☆**2** printed designs or legends on mail signifying that postage has been paid

in·dict (in dīt′) *vt.* ⟦altered (infl. by L) < ME *enditen,* to write down, accuse < Anglo-L *indictare* < LL **indictare* < L *in,* against + *dictare:* see DICTATE⟧ to charge with the commission of a crime; esp., to make a formal accusation against on the basis of positive legal evidence: usually said of the action of a grand jury —*SYN.* ACCUSE —**in′dict·ee′** *n.* —**in·dict′er** *n.,* **in·dict′or**

in·dict·a·ble (-ə bəl) *adj.* ⟦ME *enditable*⟧ **1** that should be indicted **2** making indictment possible: said as of a criminal offense

in·dic·tion (in dik′shən) *n.* ⟦ME *indictioun* < L *indictio* < pp. of *indicere,* to declare, announce < *in-,* in + *dicere,* to say, tell: see DICTION⟧ **1** the edict of a Roman emperor, fixing the tax valuation of property for each fifteen-year period **2** the tax levied or this valuation

in·dict·ment (in dīt′mənt) *n.* ⟦ME & Anglo-Fr *enditement*⟧ **1** an indicting or being indicted; charge; accusation **2** *Law* a formal written accusation charging one or more persons with the commission of a crime, presented by a grand jury to the court when the jury has found, after examining the evidence presented, that there is a valid case

in·die (in′dē) *n.* ⟦IND(EPENDENT) + -IE⟧ a company smaller than and independent of the major companies in a particular field, esp., such a company producing and distributing recorded music or films —*adj.* of or produced by an indie

In·dies (in′dēz′) **1** EAST INDIES **2** WEST INDIES

in·dif·fer·ence (in dif′ər əns, -dif′rəns) *n.* ⟦Fr < L *indifferentia*⟧ the quality, state, or fact of being indifferent; specif., *a)* lack of concern, interest, or feeling; apathy *b)* lack of importance, meaning, or worth Also [Archaic] **in·dif′fer·en·cy**

in·dif·fer·ent (in dif′ər ənt, -dif′rənt) *adj.* ⟦OFr < L *indifferens:* see IN-[2] & DIFFERENT⟧ **1** having or showing no partiality, bias, or preference; neutral **2** having or showing no interest, concern, or feeling; uninterested, apathetic, or unmoved **3** of no consequence or importance; immaterial **4** not particularly good or bad, large or small, right or wrong, etc.; fair, average, etc. **5** not really good; rather poor or bad **6** neutral in quality, as a chemical, magnet, etc.; inactive: chiefly in scientific use **7** capable of developing in various ways, as the cells of an embryo that are not yet specialized; undifferentiated —**in·dif′fer·ent·ly** *adv.*

SYN.—**indifferent** implies either apathy or neutrality, esp. with reference to choice [to remain *indifferent* in a dispute]; **unconcerned** implies a lack of concern, solicitude, or anxiety, as because of callousness, ingenuousness, etc. [to remain *unconcerned* in a time of danger]; **incurious** suggests a lack of interest or curiosity [*incurious* about the details]; **detached** implies an impartiality or aloofness resulting from a lack of emotional involvement in a situation [he viewed the struggle with *detached* interest]; **disinterested** strictly implies a commendable impartiality resulting from a lack of selfish motive or a lack of desire for personal gain [a *disinterested* journalist], but it is now often used to mean indifferent or not interested

in·dif·fer·ent·ism (in dif′ər ən tiz′əm, -dif′rən-) *n.* the state of being indifferent; esp., *a)* systematic indifference to religion *b)* the belief that all religions have equal validity —**in·dif′fer·ent·ist** *n.*

in·di·gence (in′di jəns) *n.* ⟦OFr < L *indigentia*⟧ the condition of being indigent: also **in′di·gen·cy** —*SYN.* POVERTY

in·di·gene (in′di jēn′) ***n.*** ⟦Fr *indigène* < L *indigena* < OL *indu* (L *in*), in + *gignere*, to be born: see GENUS⟧ a native or indigenous person, animal, or plant: also **in′di·gen** (-jən)

in·dig·e·nous (in dij′ə nəs) ***adj.*** ⟦LL *indigenus* < L *indegena*: see prec.⟧ **1** existing, growing, or produced naturally in a region or country; native [*indigenous* plant, *indigenous* to Florida] **2** innate; inherent; inborn —**SYN.** NATIVE —**in·dig′e·nous·ly** ***adv.*** —**in·dig′e·nous·ness** ***n.***

in·di·gent (in′di jənt) ***adj.*** ⟦ME *indygent* < OFr < L *indigens*, prp. of *indegere*, to be in need < OL *indu* (L *in*), in + *egere*, to need < IE base **eg-*, lack > ON *ekla*⟧ **1** in poverty; poor; needy; destitute **2** [Archaic] lacking; destitute (*of*) —***n.*** an indigent person —**SYN.** POOR —**in′di·gent·ly** ***adv.***

in·di·gest·ed (in′di jes′tid, -dī-) ***adj.*** ⟦IN-[2] + DIGEST + -ED⟧ [Archaic] **1** not well considered or thought out **2** confused; chaotic **3** not digested; undigested

in·di·gest·i·ble (in′di jes′tə bəl, -dī-) ***adj.*** ⟦L *indigestibilis*⟧ **1** that cannot be digested **2** not easily digested —**in′di·gest′i·bil′i·ty** ***n.***

in·di·ges·tion (in di jes′chən, -dī-) ***n.*** ⟦Fr < LL *indigestio*⟧ **1** *a)* the condition of impaired digestion *b)* an instance of improper digestion **2** discomfort associated with this

in·di·ges·tive (-jes′tiv) ***adj.*** having or characterized by indigestion

in·dign (in dīn′) ***adj.*** ⟦Fr *indigne* < L *indignus* < *in-*, not + *dignus*, worthy: see DIGNITY⟧ [Obs. or Old Poet.] **1** undeserving; unworthy **2** disgraceful

in·dig·nant (in dig′nənt) ***adj.*** ⟦L *indignans*, prp. of *indignari*, to consider as unworthy or improper, be displeased at < *in-*, not + *dignari*, to deem worthy < *dignus*, worthy: see DIGNITY⟧ feeling or expressing anger or scorn, esp. at unjust, mean, or ungrateful action or treatment —**in·dig′nant·ly** ***adv.***

in·dig·na·tion (in′dig nā′shən) ***n.*** ⟦ME *indignacion* < OFr < L *indignatio* < pp. of *indignari*: see prec.⟧ anger or scorn that is a reaction to injustice, ingratitude, or meanness; righteous anger —**SYN.** ANGER

in·dig·ni·ty (in dig′nə tē) ***n.*** ⟦L *indignitas*, unworthiness, vileness: see IN-[2] & DIGNITY⟧ **1** *pl.* **-ties** something that humiliates, insults, or injures the dignity or self-respect; affront **2** the quality of being humiliating, insulting, etc.

in·di·go (in′di gō′) ***n.***, *pl.* **-gos′** or **-goes′** ⟦Sp < L *indicum* < Gr *indikon* (*pharmakon*), lit., Indian (dye) < *Indikos*, Indian < *India*, INDIA⟧ **1** a blue dye, $C_{16}H_{10}N_2O_2$, obtained from certain plants, esp. a plant (*Indigofera tinctoria*) native to India, or made synthetically, usually from aniline **2** any of a genus (*Indigofera*) of plants of the pea family that yield indigo **3** a deep violet-blue color, designated by Newton as one of the seven prismatic or primary colors —***adj.*** of this color

indigo blue **1** INDIGOTIN **2** INDIGO (sense 3) —**in′di·go′-blue′** ***adj.***

☆**indigo bunting** a small bunting (*Passerina cyanea*) native to the E U.S.: the male is indigo-blue

in·di·goid (in′di goid′) ***adj.*** ⟦INDIG(O) + -OID⟧ of a class of dyes that produce a color resembling indigo and contain the chromophoric group C:OC:CC:O —***n.*** a dye of this class

☆**indigo snake** a large, smooth, harmless, colubrid snake (*Drymarchon corais*) found in lowlands from S.C. to Tex.

in·dig·o·tin (in dig′ə tin, in′di gō′tin) ***n.*** ⟦INDIGO + *-t-* + -IN[1]⟧ a dark-blue powder, $C_{16}H_{10}N_2O_2$, with a coppery luster, the coloring matter and chief ingredient in indigo dye

in·di·rect (in′də rekt′; *occas.*, -dī-) ***adj.*** ⟦ME < ML *indirectus*⟧ not direct; specif., *a)* not straight; deviating; roundabout *b)* not straight to the point, or to the person or thing aimed at [an *indirect* reply] *c)* not straightforward; not fair and open; dishonest [*indirect* dealing] *d)* not immediate; secondary [an *indirect* result] —**in′di·rect′ly** ***adv.*** —**in′di·rect′ness** ***n.***

indirect discourse statement of what a person said, without quoting the exact words (Ex.: She said that she could not go.)

in·di·rec·tion (in′də rek′shən; *occas.*, -dī-) ***n.*** ⟦< INDIRECT, by analogy with DIRECTION⟧ **1** roundabout act, procedure, or means **2** deceit; dishonesty **3** lack of direction or purpose

indirect lighting lighting reflected, as from a ceiling, or diffused so as to provide an even illumination without glare or shadows

indirect object *Gram.* the word or words denoting the person or thing indirectly affected by the action of the verb: it generally names the person or thing to which something is given or for which something is done (Ex.: *him* in "give *him* the ball," "do *him* a favor")

indirect tax any tax levied during the production, importation, etc. of goods that is included in the ultimate sale price and is thus in effect paid by the consumer

in·dis·cern·i·ble (in′di sʉrn′ə bəl, -zʉrn′-) ***adj.*** ⟦LL *indiscernibilis*⟧ that cannot be discerned; imperceptible —**in′dis·cern′i·bly** ***adv.***

in·dis·ci·pline (in dis′ə plin′) ***n.*** lack of discipline

in·dis·creet (in′di skrēt′) ***adj.*** ⟦ME *indiscrete* < L *indiscretus*, unseparated (in LL & ML, careless, indiscreet): see IN-[2] & DISCREET⟧ not discreet; lacking prudence, as in speech or action —**in′dis·creet′ly** ***adv.*** —**in′dis·creet′ness** ***n.***

in·dis·crete (in′di skrēt′) ***adj.*** ⟦L *indiscretus*: see prec.⟧ not discrete; not separate or separated into distinct parts —**in′dis·crete′ly** ***adv.*** —**in′dis·crete′ness** ***n.***

in·dis·cre·tion (in′di skresh′ən) ***n.*** ⟦ME *indiscrecyone* < OFr *indiscrétion* < LL *indiscretio*⟧ **1** lack of discretion, or good judgment; imprudence **2** an indiscreet act or remark

in·dis·crim·i·nate (in′di skrim′i nit) ***adj.*** **1** not based on careful selection or a discerning taste; confused, random, or promiscuous **2** not discriminating; not making careful choices or distinctions —**in′dis·crim′i·nate·ly** ***adv.***

in·dis·crim·i·na·tion (in′di skrim′i nā′shən) ***n.*** the condition of being indiscriminate; lack of discrimination —**in′dis·crim′i·na′tive** ***adj.***

in·dis·pen·sa·ble (in′di spen′sə bəl) ***adj.*** **1** that cannot be dispensed with or neglected **2** that cannot be omitted; absolutely necessary or required —***n.*** an indispensable person or thing —**SYN.** ESSENTIAL —**in′dis·pen′sa·bil′i·ty** ***n.*** —**in′dis·pen′sa·bly** ***adv.***

in·dis·pose (in′di spōz′) ***vt.*** **-posed′**, **-pos′ing** ⟦prob. back-form. < INDISPOSED⟧ **1** to make unfit or unable; disqualify **2** to make unwilling or disinclined **3** to make slightly ill

in·dis·posed (in′di spōzd′) ***adj.*** ⟦ME *indisposid* < *in-*, IN-[2] + pp. of *disposen*, DISPOSE⟧ **1** slightly ill **2** unwilling; disinclined **3** [Informal] otherwise occupied; busy, unavailable, etc. —**SYN.** SICK[1]

in·dis·po·si·tion (in′dis pə zish′ən) ***n.*** **1** a slight illness **2** unwillingness; disinclination

in·dis·pu·ta·ble (in′di spyo͞ot′ə bəl, in dis′pyo͞ot ə bəl) ***adj.*** ⟦LL *indisputabilis*⟧ that cannot be disputed or doubted; unquestionable —**in·dis′pu′ta·bil′i·ty** ***n.*** —**in·dis′put′a·bly** ***adv.***

in·dis·sol·u·ble (in′di säl′yo͞o bəl) ***adj.*** ⟦L *indissolubilis*⟧ that cannot be dissolved, decomposed, broken, or destroyed; firm, stable, lasting, permanent, etc. —**in′dis·sol′u·bil′i·ty** ***n.*** —**in′dis·sol′u·bly** ***adv.***

in·dis·tinct (in′di stiŋkt′) ***adj.*** ⟦L *indistinctus*⟧ not distinct; specif., *a)* not seen, heard, or perceived clearly; faint; dim; obscure *b)* not separate or separable; not clearly marked off; not plainly defined —**in′dis·tinct′ly** ***adv.*** —**in′dis·tinct′ness** ***n.***

in·dis·tinc·tive (in′di stiŋk′tiv) ***adj.*** **1** not distinctive; lacking distinction **2** making no distinction; incapable of distinguishing —**in′dis·tinc′tive·ly** ***adv.***

in·dis·tin·guish·a·ble (in′di stiŋ′gwish ə bəl) ***adj.*** **1** that cannot be distinguished as being different or separate **2** that cannot be discerned or recognized; imperceptible —**in′dis·tin′guish·a·bly** ***adv.***

in·dite (in dīt′) ***vt.*** **-dit′ed**, **-dit′ing** ⟦ME *enditen* < OFr *enditer* < LL **indictare*: see INDICT⟧ [Archaic] **1** to express or describe in prose or verse **2** to put in writing; compose and write —**in·dite′ment** ***n.*** —**in·dit′er** ***n.***

in·di·um (in′dē əm) ***n.*** ⟦ModL: so named (1863) by F. Reich (1799-1882) & H. T. Richter (1824-98), Ger metallurgists < L *indicum*, INDIGO + -IUM, because of the two indigo lines in its spectrum⟧ a rare metallic chemical element, soft, ductile, and silver-white, occurring in some zinc ores and used in producing bearings and various alloys that melt at relatively low temperatures: symbol, In; at. no. 49: see the periodic table of elements in the Reference Supplement

in·di·vid·u·al (in′də vij′o͞o əl; -vij′əl) ***adj.*** ⟦ML *individualis* < L *individuus* (< *in-*, IN-[2] + *dividuus*, divisible < *dividere*, to DIVIDE) + -AL⟧ **1** [Obs.] not divisible; not separable **2** existing as a single, separate thing or being; single; separate; particular **3** of, for, or by a single person or thing **4** relating to or characteristic of a single person or thing **5** distinguished from others by special characteristics; of a unique or striking character [an *individual* style] —***n.*** **1** a single thing, being, or organism, esp., when regarded as a member of a class, species, group, etc. **2** a person —**SYN.** CHARACTERISTIC

in·di·vid·u·al·ism (in′də vij′o͞o əl iz′əm) ***n.*** ⟦Fr *individualisme*⟧ **1** individual character; individuality **2** an individual peculiarity **3** the doctrine that individual freedom in economic enterprise should not be restricted by governmental or social regulation; laissez faire **4** the doctrine that the state exists for the individual and not the individual for the state **5** the doctrine that self-interest is the proper goal of all human actions; egoism **6** *a)* action based on any of these doctrines *b)* the leading of one's life in one's own way without conforming to prevailing patterns —**in′di·vid′u·al·ist** ***n.***, ***adj.*** —**in′di·vid′u·al·is′tic** ***adj.***

in·di·vid·u·al·i·ty (in′də vij′o͞o al′ə tē) ***n.***, *pl.* **-ties** ⟦ML *individualitas*⟧ **1** *a)* the sum of the characteristics or qualities that set one person or thing apart from others; individual character *b)* personal identity; personality **2** the quality or condition of being individual, or different from others [houses in the suburbs often have no *individuality*] **3** a single person or thing; individual **4** [Obs.] indivisibility

in·di·vid·u·al·ize (in′də vij′o͞o əl īz′) ***vt.*** **-ized′**, **-iz′ing** **1** to make individual; mark as different from other persons or things **2** to suit to the use, taste, requirements, etc. of a particular individual **3** to consider individually; particularize —**in′di·vid′u·al·i·za′tion** ***n.***

in·di·vid·u·al·ly (in′də vij′o͞o əl ē, -vij′əl ē) ***adv.*** **1** as an individual or individuals rather than as a group; one at a time; separately; singly **2** as an individual with special characteristics; personally **3** in a way showing individual characteristics; distinctively

in·di·vid·u·ate (in′də vij′o͞o āt′) ***vt.*** **-at′ed**, **-at′ing** ⟦< ML *individuatus*, pp. of *individuare* < L *individuus*: see INDIVIDUAL⟧ **1** to make individual or distinct; specif., to differentiate from others of the same species or kind **2** to form into an individual; develop as a separate organic unit —**in′di·vid′u·a′tion** ***n.***

in·di·vis·i·ble (in′də viz′ə bəl) ***adj.*** ⟦ME *indyvysible* < LL *indivisibilis*: see IN-[2] & DIVISIBLE⟧ **1** that cannot be divided **2** *Math.* that cannot be divided by a specific number or quantity without leaving a remainder —***n.*** anything indivisible —**in′di·vis′i·bil′i·ty** ***n.*** —**in′di·vis′i·bly** ***adv.***

In·do- (in′dō) ⟦Gr < *Indos*: see INDIA⟧ *combining form* **1** India or the East Indies **2** India and **3** Indo-European [*Indo*-Hittite]

In·do-Ar·y·an (in′dō ar′ē ən, -er′-) ***n.*** ⟦prec. + ARYAN⟧ **1** a group of languages making up the Indic branch, Indo-Iranian subfamily, of the Indo-European language family, including Hindi, Bengali, Urdu, and most of the other languages of N India, Pakistan, and Bangladesh **2** [Rare] a native speaker of any of these languages —***adj.*** designating or of Indo-Aryan

In·do·chi·na (in′dō chī′nə) 1 large peninsula south of China, including Laos, Cambodia, Myanmar, Thailand, Vietnam, & the Malay Peninsula 2 E part of this peninsula, formerly under French control, consisting of Laos, Cambodia, & Vietnam

Indochina

In·do·chi·nese or **In·do-Chi·nese** (in′dō chī nēz′) *adj.* 1 of Indochina or its peoples, languages, or cultures 2 SINO-TIBETAN: term now seldom used —*n., pl.* **-nese′** a person born or living in Indochina

in·doc·ile (in däs′əl) *adj.* ⟦Fr < L *indocilis*⟧ not docile; difficult to manage or discipline —**in·do·cil·i·ty** (in′dō sil′ə tē) *n.*

in·doc·tri·nate (in däk′trə nāt′) *vt.* **-nat′ed, -nat′ing** ⟦prob. (after ML *doctrinatus*, pp. of *doctrinare*, to instruct < L *doctrina*) < ME *endoctrinen* < OFr *endoctriner*: see IN-[1] & DOCTRINE⟧ 1 to instruct in, or imbue with, doctrines, theories, or beliefs, as of a sect 2 to instruct; teach —**in·doc′tri·na′tion** *n.* —**in·doc′tri·na′tor** *n.*

In·do-Eu·ro·pe·an (in′dō yoor′ə pē′ən) *adj.* designating or of a family of languages that includes most of those spoken in Europe and many of those spoken in SW Asia and India —*n.* 1 the Indo-European family of languages: its principal branches are Albanian, Anatolian, Armenian, Baltic, Celtic, Germanic, Greek, Indic, Iranian (often grouped with Indic as the Indo-Iranian subfamily), Italic, Slavic, and Tocharian 2 the hypothetical language, reconstructed by modern linguists, from which these languages are thought to have descended: in this sense, *Proto-Indo-European* is now the preferred term 3 *a)* a member of a people that speaks an Indo-European language *b)* a hypothetical speaker of Proto-Indo-European Abbrev. *IE*

In·do-Ger·man·ic (-jər man′ik) *adj., n.* ⟦transl. of Ger *Indogermanisch*⟧ [Old-fashioned] INDO-EUROPEAN (*adj.* & *n.* 1-2)

In·do-Hit·tite (-hi′tīt′) *n.* 1 according to one theory, the language family comprising the Indo-European and Anatolian languages: most scholars now believe Anatolian to be a branch of Indo-European 2 the hypothetical parent language from which the Indo-European and Anatolian languages descended

In·do-I·ra·ni·an (-i rā′nē ən) *adj.* designating or of a subfamily of the Indo-European language family that includes the Indic and Iranian branches —*n.* the hypothetical parent language from which all Indic and Iranian languages have descended

in·dole (in′dōl′) *n.* ⟦< INDIGO + PHENOL⟧ a white, crystalline compound, C_8H_7N, obtained from indigo and other sources and formed as a product of the intestinal putrefaction of proteins: it is used in perfumery, as a reagent, etc.

in·dole·a·ce·tic acid (in′dōl′ə sēt′ik) a plant hormone, $C_{10}H_9NO_2$, that promotes the growth of plants and roots

in·dole·bu·tyr·ic acid (-byoo tir′ik) a plant hormone, $C_{12}H_{13}NO_2$, that promotes the growth of roots

in·do·lent (in′də lənt) *adj.* ⟦< LL *indolens* < L *in-*, not + *dolens*, prp. of *dolere*, to feel pain: see DOLEFUL⟧ 1 disliking or avoiding work; lazy; idle 2 *Med.* *a)* causing little or no pain [an *indolent* cyst] *b)* slow to heal [an *indolent* ulcer] *c)* inactive or slowly developing [an *indolent* tumor] —**in′do·lence** *n.* —**in′do·lent·ly** *adv.*

in·do·meth·a·cin (in′dō meth′ə sin) *n.* ⟦INDO(LE) + METH(YL) + AC(ETIC ACID) + -IN[1]⟧ a nonsteroidal, anti-inflammatory drug, $C_{19}H_{16}ClNO_4$, used for reducing fever and relieving pain, esp. in the treatment of arthritis

in·dom·i·ta·ble (in däm′i tə bəl) *adj.* ⟦LL *indomitabilis* < L *indomitus*, untamed < *in-*, not + *domitus*, pp. of *domitare*, to tame, intens. < *domare*, to TAME⟧ not easily discouraged, defeated, or subdued; unyielding; unconquerable —**in·dom′i·ta·bil′i·ty** *n.*, **in·dom′i·ta·ble·ness** —**in·dom′i·ta·bly** *adv.*

In·do·ne·sia (in′də nē′zhə, -shə) republic in the Malay Archipelago, consisting of Java, Sumatra, W New Guinea, most of Borneo, & many smaller nearby islands: formerly, until 1945, the Netherlands East Indies, an overseas territory of the Netherlands: became fully independent in 1949: 741,100 sq mi (1,919,440 sq km); cap. Jakarta

In·do·ne·sian (-zhən, -shən) *n.* 1 a person born or living in Indonesia 2 [Now Rare] a member of any of the indigenous peoples of Indonesia and the Philippines, esp. as opposed to Negritos or Papuans 3 the official language of Indonesia, a variety of the Malay language 4 [Obs.] the western branch of the Austronesian language family, including Indonesian, Tagalog, Javanese, etc. —*adj.* of Indonesia or its people, language, or culture

in·door (in′dôr′) *adj.* ⟦for earlier *within-door*⟧ 1 of the inside of a house or building 2 living, belonging, or carried on within a house or building

in·doors (in′dôrz′, in dôrz′) *adv.* ⟦< earlier WITHINDOORS⟧ in or into a house or other building

in·do·phe·nol (in′dō fē′nôl′, -nōl′) *n.* ⟦IND(IG)O + PHENOL⟧ any of a series of synthetic blue dyes derived from the oxidation of mixtures of phenols and diamines, used for dyeing wool and cotton

In·dore (in dôr′) 1 city in central India 2 former state of central India

in·dorse (in dôrs′) *vt.* **-dorsed′, -dors′ing** ⟦var. of ENDORSE, after ML *indorsare*⟧ *var. of* ENDORSE

in·dox·yl (in däk′səl) *n.* ⟦IND(IGO) + (HYDR)OXYL⟧ a compound, C_8H_7NO, produced by the hydrolysis of indican and synthesized by several methods: it is important in the synthesis of indigo

In·dra (in′drə) *n.* ⟦Sans⟧ the chief god of the early Hindu religion, associated with rain and thunderbolts

in·draft (in′draft′) *n.* 1 a drawing in; inward pull or attraction 2 an inward flow, stream, or current, esp. of air or water Brit. sp. **in′draught′**

in·drawn (in′drôn′) *adj.* 1 drawn in 2 introspective; reserved; withdrawn

in·dri (in′drē) *n.* ⟦Fr < Malagasy *indry*, behold!: erroneously taken for the name of the animal⟧ any of a family (Indriidae) of herbivorous prosimian primates of Madagascar with large eyes and slightly opposable thumbs

in·du·bi·ta·ble (in doo′bi tə bəl, -dyoo′-) *adj.* ⟦L *indubitabilis*: see IN-[2] & DUBITABLE⟧ that cannot be doubted; unquestionable —**in·du′bi·ta·bly** *adv.*

in·duce (in doos′, -dyoos′) *vt.* **-duced′, -duc′ing** ⟦ME *enducen* < L *inducere* < *in-*, in + *ducere*, to lead: see DUCT⟧ 1 to lead on to some action, condition, belief, etc.; prevail on; persuade 2 to bring on; bring about; cause; effect [to *induce* vomiting with an emetic] 3 to draw (a general rule or conclusion) from particular facts; infer by induction 4 *Physics* to bring about (an electric or magnetic effect) in a body by exposing it to the influence or variation of a field of force —**in·duc′er** *n.* —**in·duc′i·ble** *adj.*

in·duce·ment (in doos′mənt, -dyoos′-) *n.* 1 an inducing or being induced 2 anything that induces; motive; incentive 3 *Law* *a)* an explanatory introduction in a pleading *b)* the benefit which a party is to receive for entering into a contract

in·duct (in dukt′) *vt.* ⟦ME *inducten* < L *inductus*, pp. of *inducere*: see INDUCE⟧ 1 [Obs.] to bring or lead in 2 to place in a benefice or official position with formality or ceremony; install 3 *a)* to bring formally into a society or organization; initiate *b)* to provide with knowledge or experience of something, esp. something not open to all [*inducting* them into the secrets of the trade] ☆*c)* to enroll (esp. a draftee) in the armed forces

in·duct·ance (in duk′təns) *n.* ⟦prec. + -ANCE⟧ 1 the property of an electric circuit by which a varying current in it produces a varying magnetic field that induces voltages in the same circuit or in a nearby circuit: it is measured in henrys: symbol, L 2 the capacity of an electric circuit for producing a counter electromotive force when the current changes

☆**in·duct·ee** (in′duk tē′) *n.* a person inducted or being inducted, specif. into the armed forces

in·duc·tile (in duk′til) *adj.* not ductile; not malleable, pliant, etc. —**in′duc·til′i·ty** (-til′ə tē) *n.*

in·duc·tion (in duk′shən) *n.* ⟦OFr < L *inductio*⟧ 1 an inducting or being inducted; installation, initiation, etc. 2 [Archaic] an introduction; preface or prelude 3 an inducing, or bringing about 4 a bringing forward of separate facts or instances, esp. so as to prove a general statement 5 *Embryology* the influence of one tissue upon the development of adjacent tissue, as by the diffusion of a chemical substance to nearby tissue 6 *Logic* reasoning from particular facts or individual cases to a general conclusion; also, a conclusion reached by such reasoning: distinguished from DEDUCTION 7 *Math.* a method of proving a theorem which holds true for all whole numbers greater than or equal to some first number, by demonstrating that it holds true for the first number and by showing that, if it holds true for all the subsequent numbers preceding a given number, then it must hold for the next following number: in full **mathematical induction** 8 *Physics* *a)* the act or process by which an electric or magnetic effect is produced in an electrical conductor or magnetizable body when it is exposed to the influence or variation of a field of force *b)* the transference of the explosive mixture of air and fuel from the carburetor to the cylinder of an internal-combustion engine

induction coil an apparatus made up of two magnetically coupled coils in a circuit in which interruptions of the direct-current supply to one coil produce a high-voltage alternating current in the other

induction heating the heating of a conducting material by means of electric current induced by an externally applied, varying electromagnetic field

in·duc·tive (in duk′tiv) *adj.* ⟦LL *inductivus*⟧ 1 [Rare] inducing; leading on 2 of, or proceeding by methods of, logical induction [*inductive* reasoning] 3 produced by induction 4 of inductance or electrical or magnetic induction 5 [Rare] introductory 6 *Physiol.* producing a change or response in an organism —**in·duc′tive·ly** *adv.*

in·duc·tor (in duk′tər) *n.* ⟦L, one who stirs up, lit., one who leads or brings in⟧ 1 a person who inducts 2 *Chem.* a substance that speeds up a slow chemical reaction 3 *Elec.* a device designed primarily to introduce inductance into an electric circuit

in·due (in doo′, -dyoo′) *vt.* **-dued′, -du′ing** ⟦L *induere*, to put on, dress oneself < OL *indu* (L *in*), in, on + base < IE **eu-*, to put on > EXUVIAE⟧ *var. of* ENDUE

in·dulge (in dulj′) *vt.* **-dulged′, -dulg′ing** ⟦L *indulgere*, to be kind to, yield to < *in-* + base prob. akin to Gr *dolichos*, long & Goth *tulgus*, firm⟧ 1 to yield to or satisfy (a desire); give oneself up to [to *indulge* a craving for sweets] 2 to gratify the wishes of; be very lenient with; humor 3 [Archaic] to grant as a kindness, favor, or privilege —*vi.* to give way to one's own desires; indulge oneself (*in* something) —**in·dulg′er** *n.*

SYN.—**indulge** implies a yielding to the wishes or desires of oneself or another, as because of a weak will or an amiable nature; **humor** suggests compliance with the mood or whim of another [they *humored* the dying man]; **pamper** implies overindulgence or excessive gratification; **spoil** emphasizes the harm done to the personality or character by overindulgence or excessive attention [grandparents often *spoil* children]; **baby** suggests the sort of pampering and devoted care lavished on infants and connotes a potential loss of self-reliance [because he was sickly, his mother continued to *baby* him] **—ANT. discipline, restrain**

in·dul·gence (in dul′jəns) ***n.*** ⟦OFr < L *indulgentia*⟧ **1** an indulging or being indulgent **2** a thing indulged in **3** the act of indulging oneself, or giving way to one's own desires **4** a favor or privilege **5** *Business* an extension of time to make payment on a bill or note, granted as a favor **6** [*sometimes* **I-**] *Eng. History* the grant of certain religious liberties to Dissenters and Roman Catholics by Charles II and James II **7** *R.C.Ch.* a partial or complete remission, under conditions specified by the Church, of divine temporal punishment that may otherwise still be due for sin committed but forgiven —***vt.*** **-genced**, **-genc·ing** *R.C.Ch.* to attach an indulgence to

in·dul·gent (in dul′jənt) ***adj.*** ⟦L *indulgens*⟧ indulging or inclined to indulge; kind or lenient, often to excess —**in·dul′gent·ly** ***adv.***

in·du·line (in′do͞o lēn′, -lin; -dyo͞o-) ***n.*** ⟦INDIGO) + -UL(E) + -INE[3]⟧ any of a series of blue or black azine dyes

in·dult (in′dult′) ***n.*** ⟦< ML(Ec) *indultum* < LL, indulgence, favor < neut. of L *indultus*, pp. of *indulgere*, INDULGE⟧ *R.C.Ch.* a privilege or special permission granted by the pope to bishops and others to do something otherwise prohibited by the general law of the Church

in·du·pli·cate (in do͞o′pli kit, -dyo͞o′-) ***adj.*** ⟦IN-[1] + DUPLICATE⟧ having the edges folded or rolled in, but not overlapping: said of the arrangement of leaves in a leaf bud or of the calyx or corolla in a flower bud

in·du·rate (in′do͞o rāt′, -dyo͞o-) ***vt.*** **-rat′ed**, **-rat′ing** ⟦< L *induratus*, pp. of *indurare*, to make hard < *in-*, in + *durare*, to harden < *durus*, hard: see DURABLE⟧ **1** to make hard; harden **2** to make callous, unfeeling, or stubborn **3** to cause to be firmly established —***vi.*** to become indurated —***adj.*** **1** [Now Rare] hardened **2** made callous, unfeeling, or stubborn —**in′du·ra′tion** ***n.*** —**in′du·ra′tive** ***adj.***

In·dus[1] (in′dəs) ***n.*** ⟦L, an INDIAN: so named by J. Bayer (1572-1625), Ger astronomer, with ref. to the American Indian⟧ a S constellation between Pavo and Grus

In·dus[2] (in′dəs) river in S Asia, rising in SW Tibet and flowing west across Jammu and Kashmir, India, then southwest through Pakistan into the Arabian Sea: *c.* 1,900 mi (3,058 km)

in·du·si·um (in do͞o′zē əm, -dyo͞o′-; -zhē-) ***n.***, *pl.* **-si·a** (-ə) ⟦ModL < L, undergarment, tunic; assoc. with *induere*, to put on (see INDUE), but prob. < Gr *endysis*, dress, clothing < *endyein*, to go into, put on⟧ **1** *Anat., Zool.* *a)* any covering membrane, as the amnion *b)* a case enclosing an insect larva or pupa **2** *Bot.* *a)* a membranous outgrowth of the leaf epidermis in certain ferns, covering the sporangia *b)* the annulus of certain fungi —**in·du′si·al** (-əl) ***adj.***

in·dus·tri·al (in dus′trē əl) ***adj.*** ⟦< Fr & ML: Fr *industriel* < ML *industrialis*⟧ **1** having the nature of or characterized by industries **2** of, connected with, or resulting from industries **3** working in industries **4** of or concerned with people working in industries **5** for use by industries: said of products **6** designating or of a form of music characterized by pulsating rhythms, fragmented vocal lines, and distorted electronic sounds including sound effects —***n.*** **1** a stock, bond, etc. of an industrial corporation or enterprise: *usually used in pl.* **2** [Rare] a person working in industry —**in·dus′tri·al·ly** ***adv.***

industrial archaeology the study of the history of technology based on the discovery, examination, and sometimes preservation, of the buildings, machinery, etc. of earlier industrial activity —**industrial archaeologist**

industrial arts the mechanical and technical skills used in industry, esp. as a subject for study in schools

industrial disease OCCUPATIONAL DISEASE

in·dus·tri·al·ism (in dus′trē əl iz′əm) ***n.*** social and economic organization characterized by large industries, machine production, concentration of workers in cities, etc.

in·dus·tri·al·ist (-ist) ***n.*** a person who owns, controls, or has an important position in the management of an industrial enterprise

in·dus·tri·al·ize (-īz′) ***vt.*** **-ized′**, **-iz′ing** **1** to make industrial; establish or develop industrialism in **2** to organize as an industry —***vi.*** to become industrial —**in·dus′tri·al·i·za′tion** ***n.***

☆**industrial park** a landscaped area zoned for industrial and office use, typically located in a suburb or on the outskirts of a city

industrial policy any national policy of government intervention or participation in private industry, as for the purpose of protecting domestic companies and jobs from foreign competition

industrial relations relations between industrial employers and their employees

Industrial Revolution [*often* **i- r-**] the change in social and economic organization resulting from the replacement of hand tools by machine and power tools and the development of factories and large-scale industrial production: applied to this development in England from about 1760 and to later changes in other countries

industrial school **1** a school where industrial arts are taught **2** such a school to which neglected or delinquent youths are sent for rehabilitation

in·dus·tri·al-strength (-streŋkth′) ***adj.*** so strong, durable, etc. as to be suitable for industrial use: often used hyperbolically, as in the marketing of household products, or humorously

industrial union a labor union to which all workers in a given industry may belong, regardless of occupation or trade: distinguished from CRAFT UNION

in·dus·tri·o- (in dus′trē ō′) *combining form* industrial, industrial and [*industrio*-economic]

in·dus·tri·ous (in dus′trē əs) ***adj.*** ⟦< Fr or L: Fr *industrieux* < L *industriosus* < *industria*: see fol.⟧ **1** [Obs.] skillful or clever **2** characterized by earnest, steady effort; hardworking; diligent **—SYN.** BUSY —**in·dus′tri·ous·ly** ***adv.*** —**in·dus′tri·ous·ness** ***n.***

in·dus·try (in′dəs trē) ***n.***, *pl.* **-tries** ⟦LME < MFr *industrie* < L *industria* < *industrius*, active, industrious < **indo-struus* < OL *endo* (> L *in*) + *struere*, to pile up, arrange: see STREW⟧ **1** [Obs.] *a)* skill or cleverness *b)* the application of this **2** earnest, steady effort; constant diligence in or application to work **3** systematic work; habitual employment **4** *a)* any particular branch of productive, esp. manufacturing, enterprise [the paper *industry*] *b)* any large-scale business activity [the tourist *industry*] **5** *a)* manufacturing productive enterprises collectively, esp. as distinguished from agriculture *b)* the owners and managers of industry **—SYN.** BUSINESS

in·dwell (in′dwel′, in dwel′) ***vi.***, ***vt.*** **-dwelt′**, **-dwell′ing** ⟦ME *indwellen*: used by John WYCLIFFE to transl. L *inhabitare*⟧ to dwell (in); reside (within): said of an animating spirit or essential element —**in′dwell′er** ***n.***

Indy[1], **Vincent d′** *see* D′INDY

In·dy[2] (in′dē) *informal name for* INDIANAPOLIS

-ine[1] (īn, in, ēn, ən) ⟦Fr *-in*, *-ine* < L *-inus*, masc., *-ina*, fem., *-inum*, neut. < Gr *-inos*: also directly < L for modern scientific words⟧ *suffix forming adjectives* of, having the nature of, like [*aquiline, crystalline*]

-ine[2] (in, ən) ⟦Fr < L *-ina*, suffix of fem. abstract nouns⟧ *suffix* forming abstract nouns [*discipline, doctrine*]

-ine[3] (ēn, in, īn, ən) ⟦arbitrary use of L *-inus*, masc., *-ina*, fem., n. & adj. ending⟧ *suffix forming nouns* **1** a chemical of any of certain groups, as *a)* a halogen [*iodine*] *b)* an alkaloid or a nitrogenous base [*morphine*] *c)* any of certain hydrides [*stibine*] *d)* an amino acid [*alanine*] **2** any of certain commercial products [*Vaseline*] Cf. -IN[1]

in·e·bri·ant (in ē′brē ənt) ***adj.***, ***n.*** ⟦L *inebrians*, prp. of *inebriare*⟧ INTOXICANT

in·e·bri·ate (in ē′brē āt′; *for adj.* & *n.*, -it, -āt′) ***vt.*** **-at′ed**, **-at′ing** ⟦< L *inebriatus*, pp. of *inebriare*, to intoxicate < *in-*, intens. + *ebriare*, to make drunk < *ebrius*, drunk⟧ **1** to make drunk; intoxicate **2** to excite; exhilarate —***adj.*** drunk; intoxicated —***n.*** a drunken person, esp. a drunkard —**in·e′bri·a′tion** ***n.***

in·e·bri·at·ed (-āt′id) ***adj.*** drunk; intoxicated **—SYN.** DRUNK

in·e·bri·e·ty (in′ē brī′ə tē) ***n.*** drunkenness; intoxication

in·ed·i·ble (in ed′ə bəl) ***adj.*** not edible; not fit to be eaten —**in′ed·i·bil′i·ty** ***n.***

in·é·dit (ēn ā dē′) ***n.***, *pl.* ***in·é·dits′*** (-dē′) ⟦Fr⟧ unpublished writing: *usually used in pl.*

in·ed·it·ed (in ed′it id) ***adj.*** [Now Rare] **1** unpublished **2** not edited

in·ed·u·ca·ble (in ej′ə kə bəl) ***adj.*** thought to be incapable of being educated

in·ef·fa·ble (in ef′ə bəl) ***adj.*** ⟦ME < MFr < L *ineffabilis* < *in-*, not + *effabilis*, utterable < *effari*, to speak out < *ex-*, out + *fari*, to speak: see FAME⟧ **1** too overwhelming to be expressed or described in words; inexpressible [*ineffable* beauty] **2** too awesome or sacred to be spoken [God's *ineffable* name] —**in′ef·fa·bil′i·ty** ***n.***, **in·ef′fa·ble·ness** —**in·ef′fa·bly** ***adv.***

in·ef·face·a·ble (in′e fās′ə bəl, -i fās′-) ***adj.*** that cannot be effaced; impossible to wipe out or erase; indelible —**in′ef·face′a·bil′i·ty** ***n.*** —**in′ef·face′a·bly** ***adv.***

in·ef·fec·tive (in′e fek′tiv, -i fek′-) ***adj.*** **1** not effective; not producing the desired effect; ineffectual [an *ineffective* plan] **2** not capable of performing satisfactorily; incompetent; inefficient [an *ineffective* mayor] —**in′ef·fec′tive·ly** ***adv.*** —**in′ef·fec′tive·ness** ***n.***

in·ef·fec·tu·al (in′e fek′cho͞o əl, -i fek′-) ***adj.*** not effectual; not producing or not able to produce the desired effect —**in′ef·fec′tu·al′i·ty** (-al′ə tē) ***n.***, **in′ef·fec′tu·al·ness** —**in′ef·fec′tu·al·ly** ***adv.***

in·ef·fi·ca·cious (in′ef i kā′shəs) ***adj.*** not efficacious; unable to produce the desired effect [an *inefficacious* medicine] —**in′ef·fi·ca′cious·ly** ***adv.*** —**in′ef·fi·ca′cious·ness** ***n.***

in·ef·fi·ca·cy (in ef′i kə sē) ***n.*** ⟦LL *inefficacia*⟧ lack of efficacy; inability to produce the desired effect

in·ef·fi·cient (in′e fish′ənt, -i fish′-) ***adj.*** not efficient; specif., *a)* not producing the desired effect with a minimum use of energy, time, etc.; ineffective *b)* lacking the necessary ability; unskilled; incompetent —**in′ef·fi′cien·cy** ***n.*** —**in′ef·fi′cient·ly** ***adv.***

in·e·las·tic (in′ē las′tik, -i las′-) ***adj.*** **1** not elastic; inflexible, rigid, unyielding, unadaptable, etc. **2** *Econ.* not responding to changes in price: said of the demand for, or supply of, particular goods or services —**in·e·las·tic·i·ty** (in′ē′las tis′ə tē) ***n.***

inelastic collision *Physics* a collision process whereby part of the total kinetic energy of the system is converted into a different form of energy, such as radiant energy

in·el·e·gance (in el′ə gəns) ***n.*** lack of elegance

in·el·e·gant (in el′ə gənt) ***adj.*** ⟦Fr *inélégant* < L *inelegans*⟧ not elegant; lacking refinement, good taste, grace, etc.; coarse; crude —**in·el′e·gant·ly** ***adv.***

in·el·i·gi·ble (in el′i jə bəl) ***adj.*** ⟦ML *ineligibilis*⟧ not eligible; specif., *a)* not legally or morally qualified *b)* not fit to be chosen *c)* not suitable —***n.*** an ineligible person —**in·el′i·gi·bil′i·ty** ***n.*** —**in·el′i·gi·bly** ***adv.***

in·el·o·quent (in el′ə kwənt) ***adj.*** not eloquent; not fluent, forceful, and persuasive —**in·el′o·quence** ***n.*** —**in·el′o·quent·ly** ***adv.***

in·e·luc·ta·ble (in′i luk′tə bəl) ***adj.*** ⟦L *ineluctabilis* < *in-*, not + *eluctabilis*, that can be resisted by struggling < *eluctari*, to struggle < *ex-*, out + *luctari*, to struggle < IE base **leug-*, to bend > LOCK[1], Gr *lygos*, supple twig⟧ not to be avoided or escaped; certain; inevitable *[ineluctable* fate*]* **—in′e·luc′ta·bil′i·ty** *n.* **—in′e·luc′ta·bly** *adv.*

in·ept (in ept′) *adj.* ⟦Fr *inepte* < L *ineptus* < *in-*, not + *aptus*, suitable, APT[1]⟧ **1** not suitable to the purpose; unfit **2** wrong in a foolish and awkward way *[inept* praise*]* **3** *a)* clumsy or bungling *b)* inefficient **—SYN.** AWKWARD **—in·ept′ly** *adv.* **—in·ept′ness** *n.*

in·ep·ti·tude (in ep′tə to͞od′, -tyo͞od′) *n.* ⟦L *ineptitudo*⟧ **1** the quality or condition of being inept **2** an inept act, remark, etc.

in·e·qual·i·ty (in′ē kwôl′ə tē, -kwäl′-; -in′i-) *n., pl.* **-ties** ⟦ME *inequalitie* < MFr *inequalité* < L *inaequalitas*⟧ **1** the quality of being unequal; lack of equality **2** an instance of lack of equality; specif., *a)* a difference or variation in size, amount, rank, quality, social position, etc. *b)* an unevenness in surface; lack of levelness *c)* a lack of proper proportion; unequal distribution **3** *Math.* the relation between two unequal quantities, or an expression of this relationship: Ex.: $a \neq b$ (a is not equal to b), $3a > 2b$ (3a is greater than 2b)

in·eq·ui·ta·ble (in ek′wit ə bəl) *adj.* not equitable; unfair; unjust **—in·eq′ui·ta·bly** *adv.*

in·eq·ui·ty (in ek′wit ē) *n.* ⟦IN-[2] + EQUITY⟧ **1** lack of justice; unfairness **2** *pl.* **-ties** an instance of this

in·e·qui·valve (in ē′kwi valv′) *adj.* having the two valves of the shell unequal, as an oyster

in·e·rad·i·ca·ble (in′ē rad′i kə bəl, -i rad′-) *adj.* that cannot be eradicated **—in′e·rad′i·ca·bly** *adv.*

in·er·ra·ble (in er′ə bəl, -ʉr′-) *adj.* ⟦L *inerrabilis*⟧ not erring; infallible **—in·er′ra·bil′i·ty** *n.*

in·er·rant (in er′ənt, -ʉr′-) *adj.* ⟦L *inerrans*, not wandering, fixed: see IN-[2] & ERRANT⟧ not erring; making no mistakes; infallible **—in·er′ran·cy** *n.*

in·ert (in ʉrt′) *adj.* ⟦L *iners*, without skill or art, idle < *in-*, not + *ars* (gen. *artis*), skill, ART[3])⟧ **1** having inertia; without power to move, act, or resist **2** tending to be physically or mentally inactive; dull; slow **3** having or exhibiting little or no activity, esp. chemical activity *[inert* matter in a fertilizer, an *inert* gas*]* **—in·ert′ly** *adv.* **—in·ert′ness** *n.*

in·er·ti·a (in ʉr′shə, -shē ə) *n.* ⟦L, lack of art or skill, ignorance < *iners*: see prec.⟧ **1** *Physics* the tendency of matter to remain at rest if at rest, or, if moving, to keep moving in the same direction, unless affected by some outside force **2** a tendency to remain in a fixed condition without change; disinclination to move or act **—in·er′tial** *adj.*

inertial guidance (or **navigation)** a self-contained, automatic guidance system composed of gyroscopes, accelerometers, and computers and used to control rockets, airplanes, submarines, etc.: it continuously measures acceleration, calculates the present speed and position, and compares this to an assigned course

in·es·cap·a·ble (in′e skāp′ə bəl, -i skāp′-) *adj.* that cannot be escaped or avoided; inevitable **—in′es·cap′a·bil′i·ty** *n.* **—in′es·cap′a·bly** *adv.*

in es·se (in es′ē, -es′ā) ⟦L⟧ in being; in actual existence: opposed to IN POSSE

in·es·sen·tial (in′e sen′shəl, -i sen′-) *adj.* **1** [Rare] without essence or existence; immaterial **2** not essential; not really necessary or important; unessential **—*n.*** something inessential

in·es·ti·ma·ble (in es′tə mə bəl) *adj.* ⟦OFr < L *inaestimabilis*⟧ that cannot be estimated or measured; esp., too great or valuable to be properly measured or appreciated; invaluable **—in·es′ti·ma·bly** *adv.*

in·ev·i·ta·ble (in ev′i tə bəl) *adj.* ⟦ME < L *inevitabilis*: see IN-[2] & EVITABLE⟧ that cannot be avoided or evaded; certain to happen **—*n.*** that which is inevitable: often preceded by *the* **—in·ev′i·ta·bil′i·ty** *n.* **—in·ev′i·ta·bly** *adv.*

in·ex·act (in′eg zakt′, -ig-) *adj.* not exact; not accurate or precise **—in·ex·ac′ti·tude** (-zak′tə to͞od′, -tyo͞od′) *n.*, **in′ex·act′ness —in′ex·act′ly** *adv.*

in·ex·cus·a·ble (in′ek skyo͞o′zə bəl, -ik-) *adj.* that cannot or should not be excused; unpardonable; unjustifiable **—in′ex·cus′a·bil′i·ty** *n.* **—in′ex·cus′a·bly** *adv.*

in·ex·er·tion (in′eg zʉr′shən, -ig-) *n.* lack of exertion; failure to exert oneself

in·ex·haust·i·ble (in′eg zôs′tə bəl, -ig-) *adj.* that cannot be exhausted; specif., *a)* that cannot be used up or emptied *b)* that cannot be tired out; tireless **—in′ex·haust′i·bil′i·ty** *n.* **—in′ex·haust′i·bly** *adv.*

in·ex·ist·ent (in′eg zis′tənt, -ig-) *adj.* ⟦LL *inexistens*⟧ not existent; not having being **—in′ex·ist′ence** *n.*

in·ex·o·ra·ble (in ek′sə rə bəl) *adj.* ⟦L *inexorabilis*: see IN-[2] & EXORABLE⟧ **1** that cannot be moved or influenced by persuasion or entreaty; unrelenting **2** that cannot be altered, checked, etc. *[their inexorable* fate*]* **—in·ex′o·ra·bil′i·ty** *n.* **—in·ex′o·ra·bly** *adv.*

in·ex·pe·di·ent (in′ek spē′dē ənt, -ik-) *adj.* not expedient; not suitable or practicable for a given situation; inadvisable, unwise, etc. **—in′ex·pe′di·ence** *n.*, **in′ex·pe′di·en·cy —in′ex·pe′di·ent·ly** *adv.*

in·ex·pen·sive (in′ek spen′siv, -ik-) *adj.* not expensive; costing relatively little; low-priced; cheap **—SYN.** CHEAP **—in′ex·pen′sive·ly** *adv.* **—in′ex·pen′sive·ness** *n.*

in·ex·pe·ri·ence (in′ek spir′ē əns, -ik-) *n.* ⟦Fr *inexpérience* < LL *inexperientia*⟧ lack of experience or of the knowledge or skill resulting from experience **—in′ex·pe′ri·enced** *adj.*

in·ex·pert (in ek′spərt; in′ek spʉrt′, -ik-) *adj.* ⟦ME < MFr < L *inexpertus*⟧ not expert; unskillful; amateurish **—in·ex′pert·ly** *adv.* **—in·ex′pert·ness** *n.*

in·ex·pi·a·ble (in eks′pē ə bəl) *adj.* ⟦L *inexpiabilis*⟧ **1** that cannot be expiated or atoned for *[*an *inexpiable* sin*]* **2** [Archaic] that cannot be appeased; implacable **—in·ex′pi·a·bly** *adv.*

in·ex·plain·a·ble (in′ek splān′ə bəl, -ik-) *adj.* that cannot be explained; inexplicable **—in′ex·plain′a·bly** *adv.*

in·ex·pli·ca·ble (in eks′pli kə bəl; *often* in′ek splik′ə bəl, -ik-) *adj.* ⟦Fr < L *inexplicabilis*⟧ not explicable; that cannot be explained, understood, or accounted for **—in·ex′pli·ca·bil′i·ty** *n.* **—in·ex′pli·ca·bly** *adv.*

in·ex·plic·it (in′eks plis′it, -ik splis′-) *adj.* ⟦L *inexplicitus*⟧ not explicit; vague; indefinite; general **—in′ex·plic′it·ly** *adv.* **—in′ex·plic′it·ness** *n.*

in·ex·press·i·ble (in′eks pres′ə bəl, -ik spres′-) *adj.* that cannot be expressed; indescribable or unutterable **—in′ex·press′i·bil′i·ty** *n.*, **in′ex·press′i·ble·ness —in′ex·press′i·bly** *adv.*

in·ex·pres·sive (in′eks pres′iv, -ik spres′-) *adj.* **1** [Archaic] INEXPRESSIBLE **2** not expressive; displaying no expression **—in′ex·pres′sive·ly** *adv.* **—in′ex·pres′sive·ness** *n.*

in·ex·pug·na·ble (in′eks pug′nə bəl, -ik spug′-) *adj.* ⟦LME < MFr < L *inexpugnabilis* < *in-*, not + *expugnabilis*, that can be taken by storm < *expugnare*, to take by storm < *ex-*, intens. + *pugnare*, to fight: see PUGNACIOUS⟧ that cannot be defeated by force; unconquerable; unyielding

in·ex·ten·si·ble (in′ek sten′sə bəl, -ik-) *adj.* not extensible

in ex·ten·so (in eks ten′sō) ⟦L⟧ at full length

in·ex·tin·guish·a·ble (in′ek stiŋ′gwish ə bəl, -ik-) *adj.* not extinguishable; that cannot be quenched, put out, or stopped **—in′ex·tin′guish·a·bly** *adv.*

in·ex·tir·pa·ble (in eks′tər pə bəl; in′eks tʉr′-, -ik stʉr′-) *adj.* ⟦L *inextirpabilis*⟧ that cannot be extirpated, or rooted out

in ex·tre·mis (in′ eks trē′mis) ⟦L, in extremity⟧ at the point of death

in·ex·tric·a·ble (in′ek strik′ə bəl, in eks′tri kə bəl) *adj.* ⟦L *inextricabilis* < *in-*, IN-[2] + *extricabilis*⟧ **1** that one cannot extricate oneself from **2** that cannot be disentangled or untied **—in′ex·tri·ca·bil′i·ty** *n.* **—in′ex·tric′a·bly** *adv.*

I·nez (ē nez′, ī-; ē′nez′, ī′-) *n.* ⟦Sp⟧ a feminine name: see AGNES[1]

inf *abbrev.* **1** ⟦L *infra*⟧ below **2** infantry **3** infinitive **4** information

INF *abbrev.* intermediate(-range) nuclear forces

in·fal·li·ble (in fal′ə bəl) *adj.* ⟦ML *infallibilis*: see IN-[2] & FALLIBLE⟧ **1** incapable of error; never wrong **2** not liable to fail, go wrong, make a mistake, etc.; dependable; reliable; sure **3** *R.C.Ch.* incapable of error in setting forth doctrine on faith and morals: said esp. of the pope speaking ex cathedra **—*n.*** an infallible person or thing **—in·fal′li·bil′i·ty** *n.* **—in·fal′li·bly** *adv.*

in·fa·mous (in′fə məs) *adj.* ⟦ME < OFr *infameux* < ML *infamosus* < L *infamis*: see IN-[2] & FAMOUS⟧ **1** having a very bad reputation; notorious; in disgrace or dishonor **2** causing or deserving a bad reputation; scandalous; outrageous **3** *Law* *a)* punishable by imprisonment in a penitentiary (said of certain crimes, usually felonies) *b)* guilty of such a crime **—in′fa·mous·ly** *adv.*

in·fa·my (in′fə mē) *n., pl.* **-mies** ⟦ME *infamye* < OFr *infamie* < L *infamia* < *infamis*: see prec.⟧ **1** very bad reputation; notoriety; disgrace; dishonor **2** the quality of being infamous; great wickedness **3** an infamous act **4** *Law* loss of character and of certain civil rights sustained by a person convicted of an infamous crime

in·fan·cy (in′fən sē) *n., pl.* **-cies** ⟦LME < L *infantia*⟧ **1** the state or period of being an infant; babyhood; very early childhood **2** the beginning or earliest stage of anything **3** *Law* the state or period of being a minor; period before the age of legal majority, usually eighteen; minority

in·fant (in′fənt) *n.* ⟦ME *infaunt* < OFr *enfant* < L *infans* (gen. *infantis*), child < adj., not yet speaking < *in-*, not + *fans*, prp. of *fari*, to speak: see FAME⟧ **1** a very young child; baby: often used of certain nonhuman animals *[*a chimpanzee *infant]* **2** a person in the state of legal infancy; minor **—*adj.*** **1** of or for infants or infancy **2** in a very early stage

in·fan·ta (in fan′tə, -fän′-) *n.* ⟦Sp & Port, fem. of *infante*: see fol.⟧ [Historical] **1** any daughter of a king of Spain or Portugal **2** the wife of an infante

in·fan·te (in fan′tā′, -fän′-) *n.* ⟦Sp & Port < L *infans*: see INFANT⟧ [Historical] any son of a king of Spain or Portugal except the heir to the throne

in·fan·ti·cide (in fan′tə sīd′) *n.* ⟦Fr < LL *infanticidium* < *infanticidia*, one who kills an infant: see INFANT & -CIDE⟧ **1** the murder of a baby **2** ⟦Fr < LL *infanticida*⟧ a person guilty of this

in·fan·tile (in′fən tīl′, -til) *adj.* ⟦L *infantilis*⟧ **1** of or having to do with infants or infancy **2** like, suitable for, or characteristic of an infant; babyish; childish or childlike; immature **3** in the earliest stage of development

infantile paralysis POLIOMYELITIS

in·fan·til·ism (in fan′ti liz′əm; *also* in′fən-) *n.* **1** immature or childish behavior **2** *Psychol.* any abnormal state in which childish behavior or childlike traits persist into adult life: marked by INTELLECTUAL DISABILITY and stunted growth and by failure to mature sexually

in·fan·til·ize (in fan′təl īz′) *vt.* **-lized′**, **-liz′ing** **1** to treat (a child or adult) like an infant or baby **2** to keep in a dependent, infantile stage of development **—in·fan′til·i·za′tion** *n.*

in·fan·tine (in′fən tīn′; *also*, -tēn′, -tin) *adj.* ⟦Fr *infantin, enfantin*⟧ *archaic var. of* INFANTILE

in·fan·try (in′fən trē) *n., pl.* **-tries** ⟦Fr *infanterie* < It *infanteria* < *infante*, very young person, knight's page, foot soldier < L *infans*: see INFANT⟧ **1** foot soldiers collectively; esp., that branch of an army consisting of soldiers trained and equipped to fight chiefly on foot **2** [**I-**] a (designated) infantry regiment *[*the 274th *Infantry]*

in·fan·try·man (-mən) *n. pl.* **-men** (-mən) a soldier in the infantry

infant school [Brit.] a school for children aged five to seven

in·farct (in färkt′) *n.* ⟦ML *infarctus*, for L *infartus*, pp. of *infarcire* < *in-*, in + *farcire*, to stuff: see FARCE⟧ an area of dying or dead tissue resulting from inadequate blood flow through blood vessels normally supplying the part

in·farc·tion (in färk′shən) *n.* **1** the development of an infarct **2** INFARCT

in·fare (in′far′) ***n.*** ⟦ME *infer*, entrance < OE *infær* < *inn*, IN-[1] + *fær*, a going < *faran*, a going < *faran*: see FARE⟧ [Dial.] a reception or dinner party after a wedding, usually on the day after

in·fat·u·ate (in fach′o͞o āt′) ***vt.* -at′ed, -at′ing** ⟦< L *infatuatus*, pp. of *infatuare*, to make a fool of < *in-*, intens. + *fatuus*, foolish: see FATUOUS⟧ **1** to make foolish; cause to lose sound judgment **2** to inspire with foolish or shallow love or affection —***adj.*** infatuated —***n.*** a person who is infatuated

in·fat·u·at·ed (-id) ***adj.*** **1** lacking sound judgment; foolish **2** completely carried away by foolish or shallow love or affection —**in·fat′u·at′ed·ly** ***adv.***

in·fat·u·a·tion (in fach′o͞o ā′shən) ***n.*** ⟦LL *infatuatio*⟧ an infatuating or being infatuated —***SYN.*** LOVE

in·fau·na (in′fô′nə) ***n.*** ⟦ModL < Dan *ifauna*: see IN-[1] & FAUNA⟧ the animals burrowing into marine or freshwater sediment: cf. EPIFAUNA

in·fea·si·ble (in fē′zə bəl) ***adj.*** not feasible; not easily done; impracticable —**in·fea′si·bil′i·ty** ***n.***

in·fect (in fekt′) ***vt.*** ⟦ME *infecten* < MFr *infecter* < L *infectus*, pp. of *inficere*, to put or dip into, tinge, stain < *in-*, in + *facere*, to DO[1]⟧ **1** to contaminate with a disease-producing organism or matter **2** to cause to become diseased by bringing into contact with such an organism or matter **3** to invade (an individual, organ, tissue, etc.): said of a pathogenic organism **4** to affect or imbue with feelings, beliefs, etc. that are regarded as negative or harmful **5** *Comput.* to invade for the purpose of disrupting the functioning of: said of a virus, worm, etc. —**in·fec′tor** ***n.***

in·fec·tion (in fek′shən) ***n.*** ⟦ME *infeccioun* < OFr *infection* < LL *infectio*⟧ **1** an infecting; specif., *a)* the act of causing to become diseased *b)* the act of affecting with feelings or beliefs regarded as negative or harmful **2** the fact or state of being infected, esp. by the presence in the body of bacteria, protozoans, viruses, or other parasites **3** something that results from infecting or being infected; specif., *a)* a disease resulting from INFECTION (sense 2) *b)* a feeling, belief, influence, etc. transmitted from one person to another and regarded as negative or harmful **4** anything that infects

in·fec·tious (in fek′shəs) ***adj.*** **1** likely to cause infection **2** designating a disease that can be communicated by INFECTION (sense 2) **3** tending to spread or to affect others; catching [an *infectious* laugh] **4** [Obs.] infected with disease —**in·fec′tious·ly** ***adv.*** —**in·fec′tious·ness** ***n.***

infectious hepatitis HEPATITIS A

infectious mononucleosis an acute disease, esp. of young people, characterized by fever, swollen lymph nodes, sore throat, and abnormalities of the lymphocytes: it is caused by the Epstein-Barr virus

in·fec·tive (in fek′tiv) ***adj.*** ⟦ME *infectif* < OFr < L *infectivus*⟧ likely to cause infection; infectious —**in′fec·tiv′i·ty** ***n.***

in·fe·cund (in fē′kənd, -fek′ənd) ***adj.*** ⟦ME *infecunde* < L *infecundus*⟧ not fecund; not fertile; barren —**in·fe·cun·di·ty** (in′fē kun′də tē, -fi-) ***n.***

in·fe·lic·i·tous (in′fə lis′ə təs) ***adj.*** not felicitous; unfortunate or unsuitable —**in′fe·lic′i·tous·ly** ***adv.***

in·fe·lic·i·ty (in′fə lis′ə tē) ***n.*** ⟦L *infelicitas* < *infelix*, unfortunate: see IN-[2] & FELICITY⟧ **1** the quality or condition of being infelicitous **2** *pl.* **-ties** something infelicitous; unsuitable or inapt remark, action, etc.

in·fer (in fur′) ***vt.* -ferred′, -fer′ring** ⟦L *inferre*, to bring or carry in, infer < *in-*, in + *ferre*, to carry, BEAR[1]⟧ **1** [Obs.] to bring on or about; cause; induce **2** to conclude or decide from something known or assumed; derive by reasoning; draw as a conclusion **3** to indicate indirectly; imply: in this sense, still regarded as a loose usage by many —***vi.*** to draw inferences —**in·fer′a·ble** ***adj.*** —**in·fer′rer** ***n.***

SYN.**—infer** suggests the arriving at a decision or opinion by reasoning from known facts or evidence [from your smile, I *infer* that you're pleased]; **deduce**, in strict discrimination, implies inference from a general principle by logical reasoning [Aristotle's findings in physics are *deduced* from his metaphysical theory]; **conclude** strictly implies an inference that is the final logical result in a process of reasoning [I must, therefore, *conclude* that you are wrong]; **judge** stresses the careful checking and weighing of premises and evidence, in arriving at a conclusion; **gather** is an informal substitute for **infer** or **conclude** [I *gather* that you don't care]

in·fer·ence (in′fər əns) ***n.*** ⟦ML *inferentia*⟧ **1** an act or the process of inferring **2** a conclusion or opinion arrived at by inferring

in·fer·en·tial (in′fər en′shəl) ***adj.*** ⟦< ML *inferentia* + -AL⟧ based on or having to do with inference —**in′fer·en′tial·ly** ***adv.***

in·fe·ri·or (in fir′ē ər) ***adj.*** ⟦ME < L, compar. of *inferus*, low, below < IE **n̥dheros* < base **n̥dhos*, UNDER⟧ **1** lower in space; placed lower down **2** low or lower in order, status, rank, etc.; subordinate **3** lower in quality or value than: with *to* **4** poor in quality; below average **5** *Anat.* located below or directed downward **6** *Astron.* designating or of planets between the earth and the sun **7** *Bot.* having the sepals, petals, and stamens attached at the apex: said of the ovary of an epigynous flower **8** *Printing* placed below the type line (Ex.: 2 in NO_2) —***n.*** an inferior person or thing —**in·fe′ri·or′i·ty** (-ôr′ə tē, -är′-) ***n.*** —**in·fe′ri·or·ly** ***adv.***

inferiority complex **1** *Psychol.* a neurotic condition resulting from various feelings of inferiority, such as derive from real or imagined physical or social inadequacy, and often manifested through overcompensation in excessive aggressiveness, a domineering attitude, etc. **2** popularly, any feeling of inferiority, inadequacy, etc.: cf. SUPERIORITY COMPLEX

in·fer·nal (in fur′nəl) ***adj.*** ⟦OFr < LL *infernalis* < L *infernus*, underground, lower, infernal < *inferus*: see INFERIOR⟧ **1** *a)* of the ancient mythological world of the dead *b)* of hell **2** hellish; diabolic; fiendish; inhuman **3** [Informal] hateful; outrageous —**in·fer′nal·ly** ***adv.***

infernal machine *former name for*: **1** a booby trap **2** a time bomb

in·fer·no (in fur′nō) ***n.***, *pl.* **-nos** ⟦It < L *infernus*: see INFERNAL⟧ **1** hell or any place suggesting hell, usually characterized by great heat or flames **2** [**I-**] that section of Dante's *Divine Comedy* which describes hell and the sufferings of the damned

in·fe·ro·an·te·ri·or (in′fə rō′an tir′ē ər) ***adj.*** ⟦< comb. form *infero-* (< L *inferus*: see INFERIOR) + ANTERIOR⟧ lying below and in front

in·fer·tile (in furt′'l) ***adj.*** ⟦MFr < L *infertilis*⟧ **1** not fertile; not productive; barren **2** not fertilized: said of an egg —***SYN.*** STERILE —**in·fer·til·i·ty** (in′fər til′ə tē) ***n.***

in·fest (in fest′) ***vt.*** ⟦Fr *infester* < L *infestare*, to attack, trouble < *infestus*, hostile < *in-*, in + IE base **dhers-*, to be bold, attack > DARE⟧ **1** to overrun or inhabit in large numbers, usually so as to be harmful or bothersome; swarm in or over **2** to be parasitic in or on (a host) —**in′fes·ta′tion** ***n.*** —**in·fest′er** ***n.***

in·feu·da·tion (in′fyo͞o dā′shən) ***n.*** ⟦ML *infeudatio* < pp. of *infeudare*, to enfeoff < *in-*, in + *feodum*: see FEUD[2]⟧ in feudal law, the granting of an estate in fee; enfeoffment

in·fib·u·la·tion (in fib′yo͞o lā′shən) ***n.*** the practice, as in some areas of North Africa, of sewing up most of the opening to the vagina, esp. of unmarried girls, to prevent sexual intercourse

in·fi·del (in′fə del′, -dəl) ***n.*** ⟦ME < MFr *infidèle* < L *infidelis*, unfaithful (in LL(Ec), unbelieving) < *in-*, IN-[2] + *fidelis*: see FIDELITY⟧ **1** a person who does not believe in a particular religion, esp. the prevailing religion; specif., *a)* [Chiefly Historical] among Christians, a non-Christian *b)* among Muslims, a non-Muslim: now often a disparaging term, but still used descriptively as within historical contexts **2** a person who holds no religious belief **3** a person who does not accept some particular theory, belief, etc. —***adj.*** **1** that is an infidel; unbelieving **2** of infidels —***SYN.*** ATHEIST

in·fi·del·i·ty (in′fə del′ə tē) ***n.*** ⟦L *infidelitas* < *infidelis*: see prec.⟧ **1** the fact or state of being an infidel **2** unfaithfulness or disloyalty to another; esp., adultery **3** *pl.* **-ties** an unfaithful or disloyal act

in·field (in′fēld′) ***n.*** ⟦IN[1], *adv.* + FIELD⟧ **1** the land of a farm nearest the farmhouse ☆**2** *a)* the square area enclosed by the four base lines on a baseball field *b)* the infielders collectively, or the area covered by them ☆**3** the area inside a racetrack or running track: field events of a track meet are often held on it Distinguished from OUTFIELD

☆**in·field·er** (in′fēl′dər) ***n.*** *Baseball* a player whose defensive position is in the infield; shortstop, first baseman, second baseman, or third baseman: the pitcher and the catcher are considered infielders when fielding the ball

in·fight·ing (in′fīt′iŋ) ***n.*** **1** fighting, esp. boxing, at close range **2** intense competition or conflict, often bitterly personal, as within an organization or group —**in′fight′er** ***n.***

in·fill (in′fil′) ***adj.*** of or having to do with the filling in of remaining available space [an *infill* housing project uptown]

in·fil·trate (in′fil trāt′, in fil′trāt′) ***vi., vt.* -trat′ed, -trat′ing** ⟦IN-[1] + FILTRATE⟧ **1** to pass, or cause (a fluid, cell, etc.) to pass, through small gaps or openings; filter **2** to pass through, as in filtering **3** to pass, or cause (individual troops) to pass, through weak places in the enemy's lines in order to attack the enemy's flanks or rear **4** to penetrate, or cause to penetrate (a region or group) gradually or stealthily, so as to attack or to seize control from within —***n.*** something that infiltrates —**in′fil·tra′tion** ***n.*** —**in′fil·tra′tive** ***adj.*** —**in′fil·tra′tor** ***n.***

infin *abbrev.* infinitive

in·fi·nite (in′fə nit) ***adj.*** ⟦ME < L *infinitus*: see IN-[2] & FINITE⟧ **1** lacking limits or bounds; extending beyond measure or comprehension: without beginning or end; endless **2** very great; vast; immense **3** *a)* *Math.* indefinitely large; greater than any finite number however large *b)* capable of being put into one-to-one correspondence with a part of itself [*infinite* set] —***n.*** something infinite, as space or time —**the Infinite (Being)** God —**in′fi·nite·ly** ***adv.*** —**in′fi·nite·ness** ***n.***

in·fin·i·tes·i·mal (in′fin i tes′i məl, -tez′-) ***adj.*** ⟦ModL *infinitesimus* < L *infinitus* (see prec.), infl. by *centesimus*, hundredth < *centum*, HUNDRED⟧ **1** too small to be measured **2** *Math.* of or pertaining to an infinitesimal —***n.*** **1** an infinitesimal quantity **2** *Math.* a variable that approaches zero as a limit —**in′fin·i·tes′i·mal·ly** ***adv.***

infinitesimal calculus the combined methods of mathematical analysis of DIFFERENTIAL CALCULUS and INTEGRAL CALCULUS

in·fin·i·tive (in fin′i tiv) ***adj.*** ⟦LL *infinitivus* < L *infinitivus (modus)*, lit., unlimited (mood) < *infinitus* (see INFINITE): so named because it is not limited to any person, number, or tense⟧ *Gram.* of or connected with an infinitive [an *infinitive* phrase] —***n.*** *Gram.* the form of a verb that expresses existence or action without reference to person, number, or tense and that can function grammatically as a noun, adjective, or adverb: in English, it is usually the form of the first person singular present preceded by the marker *to* (Ex.: *to go, to think*) or by another verb form (Ex.: can he *speak?* make him *try*) —**in·fin′i·ti′val** (-tī′vəl) ***adj.***

in·fin·i·tude (in fin′i to͞od′, -tyo͞od′) ***n.*** ⟦< L *infinitus*, INFINITE, prob. infl. by MAGNITUDE⟧ **1** the quality of being infinite **2** an infinite quantity, number, or extent

in·fin·i·ty (in fin′i tē) ***n.***, *pl.* **-ties** ⟦ME *infinite* < OFr *infinité* < L *infinitas*⟧ **1** the quality of being infinite **2** anything infinite; endless or unlimited space, time, distance, quantity, etc. **3** an indefinitely large number or amount **4** *Geom.* an ideal point or location thought of as being infinitely distant from the origin or base point of the space being considered **5** *Math.* an ideal number thought of as the numerical value of an infinite quantity: symbol, ∞

6 *Photog.* *a)* a distance so far from a camera that rays of light reflected from a subject there may be regarded as parallel *b)* a setting for such a distance on a focusing scale —**to infinity** without limit or end

in·firm (in furm′) *adj.* ⟦ME < L *infirmus*⟧ **1** not firm or strong physically; weak; feeble, as from old age **2** not firm in mind or purpose; not resolute; vacillating **3** not stable, firm, or sound; frail; shaky, as a structure **4** not secure or valid [an *infirm* title to property] —*SYN.* WEAK —**in·firm′ly** *adv.* —**in·firm′ness** *n.*

in·fir·ma·ry (in fur′mə rē) *n., pl.* **-ries** ⟦ML *infirmaria, infirmarium* < L *infirmus*⟧ a place for the care of the sick, injured, or infirm; esp., a building or room, as in a school, that serves as a hospital or dispensary

in·fir·mi·ty (in fur′mə tē) *n.* ⟦ME *infirmite* < L *infirmitas*⟧ **1** the quality or state of being infirm; feebleness; weakness **2** *pl.* **-ties** an instance of this; specif., *a)* a physical weakness or defect; frailty or ailment, as from old age *b)* a moral weakness; defect

in·fix (in fiks′, in′fiks′; *for n.* in′fiks′) *vt.* ⟦< L *infixus*, pp. of *infigere*, to fix or drive in: see IN-[1] & FIX⟧ **1** to fasten or set firmly in or on, esp. by inserting or piercing **2** to fix firmly in the mind; instill; implant **3** to place (an infix) within a word —*n.* *Linguis.* a morpheme that is added within a word (Ex.: *-o-* in *gemology*)

infl. *abbrev.* **1** influence **2** influenced

in fla·gran·te de·lic·to (in flə grän′tā de lik′tō′, -gran′tē də-) ⟦L, lit., during the blazing of the crime⟧ **1** in the very act of committing the offense; red-handed **2** while engaged in sexual activity, often, specif., in illicit or perverse sexual activity Also **in flagrante**

in·flame (in flame′) *vt.* **-flamed′**, **-flam′ing** ⟦ME *enflamen* < OFr *enflammer* < L *inflammare*: see IN-[1] & FLAME⟧ **1** to set on fire **2** to arouse passion, desire, or violence in; excite intensely, as with anger **3** to increase the intensity of (passion, desire, violence, etc.) **4** to cause inflammation in (some organ or tissue) —*vi.* **1** to become roused, excited, stimulated, etc. **2** to catch fire **3** to become hot, feverish, swollen, red, sore, etc. —**in·flam′er** *n.*

in·flam·ma·ble (in flam′ə bəl) *adj.* ⟦Fr < ML *inflammabilis* < L *inflammare*: see prec.⟧ **1** FLAMMABLE **2** easily roused, provoked, or excited —*n.* anything flammable —**in·flam′ma·bil′i·ty** *n.*, **in·flam′ma·ble·ness** —**in·flam′ma·bly** *adv.*

in·flam·ma·tion (in′flə mā′shən) *n.* ⟦Fr < L *inflammatio*⟧ **1** the act of inflaming **2** the state of being inflamed; specif., a condition of some part of the body that is a reaction to injury, infection, irritation, etc., and is characterized by varied combinations of redness, pain, heat, swelling, and loss of function

in·flam·ma·to·ry (in flam′ə tôr′ē) *adj.* ⟦< L *inflammatus*, pp. of *inflammare* (see IN-[1] & FLAME) + -ORY⟧ **1** rousing or likely to rouse excitement, anger, violence, rioting, etc. [an *inflammatory* speech] **2** *Med.* of, caused by, or characterized by inflammation

in·flat·a·ble (in flāt′ə bəl) *adj.* that can be inflated —*n.* something inflatable; specif., a boat made of rubber, plastic, etc. that must be inflated before it is used

in·flate (in flāt′) *vt.* **-flat′ed**, **-flat′ing** ⟦< L *inflatus*, pp. of *inflare*, to blow into, inflate < *in-*, in + *flare*, to BLOW[1]⟧ **1** to blow full or swell out as with air or gas; distend; expand; dilate **2** to raise in spirits; make proud or elated **3** to increase or raise beyond what is normal or valid **4** to cause inflation of (money, credit, etc.) —*vi.* to become inflated; swell: opposed to DEFLATE —*SYN.* EXPAND —**in·flat′er** *n.*, **in·fla′tor**

in·flat·ed (-id) *adj.* **1** puffed out; swollen **2** pompous; bombastic; highflown **3** increased or raised beyond what is normal or valid **4** characterized or caused by inflation

in·fla·tion (in flā′shən) *n.* ⟦ME *inflacioun* < L *inflatio*⟧ **1** an inflating or being inflated ☆**2** *Econ.* *a)* increase in the amount of money and credit in relation to the supply of goods and services *b)* condition resulting from this, characterized by a general increase in price levels, specif. an excessive or persistent increase, leading to a decline in purchasing power

in·fla·tion·ar·y (in flā′shə ner′ē) *adj.* of, causing, or characterized by inflation

☆**inflationary spiral** a continuous and accelerating rise in the prices of goods and services, sustained as by the interaction of wages and costs

in·fla·tion·ism (in flā′shən iz′əm) *n.* the advocacy or promotion of monetary inflation —**in·fla′tion·ist** *adj., n.*

in·flect (in flekt′) *vt.* ⟦ME *inflecten* < L *inflectere* < *in-*, in + *flectere*, to bend⟧ **1** to turn, bend, or curve, usually inward **2** to vary or change the tone or pitch of (the voice); modulate **3** *Gram.* to change the form of (a word) by inflection, as in conjugating or declining —*vi.* to be changed by inflection —**in·flec′tive** *adj.*

in·flec·tion (in flek′shən) *n.* ⟦L *inflexio* < *inflexus*, pp. of *inflectere*: see prec.⟧ **1** a turning, bending, or curving **2** a turn, bend, or curve **3** any change in tone or pitch of the voice; modulation [to signal a question by a rising *inflection*] **4** a change of a curve or arc from convex to concave or the reverse **5** *Gram.* *a)* the change of form by which some words indicate certain grammatical relationships, as number, case, gender, or tense *b)* an inflected form *c)* an inflectional element, as those bound forms used in English to form the plural and possessive case of nouns (ship*s*, ship*'s*) and the past tense and third person singular, present indicative, of verbs (he shipp*ed*, he ship*s*)

in·flec·tion·al (in flek′shə nəl) *adj.* **1** of, having, or expressing grammatical inflection [an *inflectional* suffix] **2** characterized by the use of inflection to express grammatical relations [Greek and Latin are *inflectional* languages] —**in·flec′tion·al·ly** *adv.*

in·flexed (in flekst′, in′flekst′) *adj.* ⟦< L *inflexus* (see INFLECT) + -ED⟧ *Biol.* bent sharply downward or inward; turned toward the axis

in·flex·i·ble (in flek′sə bəl) *adj.* ⟦ME < L *inflexibilis*: see IN-[2] & FLEXIBLE⟧ **1** that cannot be bent or curved; stiff; rigid **2** firm in mind or purpose; stubborn; unyielding; unshakable **3** that cannot be changed; fixed; unalterable [an *inflexible* rule] —**in·flex′i·bil′i·ty** *n.*, **in·flex′i·ble·ness** —**in·flex′i·bly** *adv.*

SYN.—**inflexible** implies an unyielding or unshakable firmness in mind or purpose, sometimes connoting stubbornness [his *inflexible* attitude]; **adamant** implies a firm or unbreakable resolve that remains unaffected by temptation or pleading [*adamant* to her entreaties]; **implacable** suggests the impossibility of pacifying or appeasing [*implacable* in his hatred]; **obdurate** implies a hardheartedness that is not easily moved to pity, sympathy, or forgiveness [her *obdurate* refusal to help] —*ANT.* **flexible, compliant**

in·flex·ion (in flek′shən) *n.* *Brit. sp. of* INFLECTION

in·flict (in flikt′) *vt.* ⟦< L *inflictus*, pp. of *infligere*, to strike or beat against < *in-*, on, against + *fligere*, to strike < IE base **bhlīg-*, to strike > Welsh *blif*, catapult⟧ **1** to give or cause (pain, wounds, etc.) by or as by striking; cause to be borne **2** to impose (a punishment, disagreeable task, etc.) *on* or *upon* —**in·flict′er** *n.*, **in·flic′tor** —**in·flic′tive** *adj.*

in·flic·tion (in flik′shən) *n.* ⟦LL *inflictio*⟧ **1** the act of inflicting **2** something inflicted, as punishment

in-flight (in′flīt′) *adj.* done, occurring, shown, etc. while the aircraft is in flight [*in-flight* movies]

in·flo·res·cence (in′flō res′əns, -flô-; -flə-) *n.* ⟦ModL *inflorescentia* < LL *inflorescens*, prp. of *inflorescere*, to begin to blossom: see IN-[1] & FLORESCENCE⟧ *Bot.* **1** the producing of blossoms; flowering **2** the arrangement of flowers on a stem or axis **3** a flower cluster on a common axis **4** flowers collectively **5** a solitary flower, regarded as a reduced cluster —**in′flo·res′cent** *adj.*

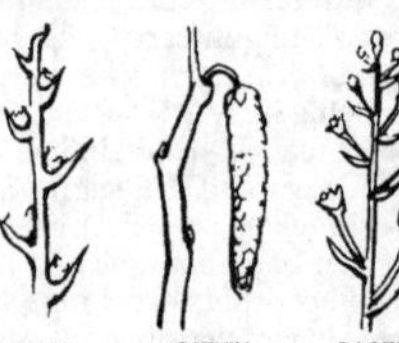

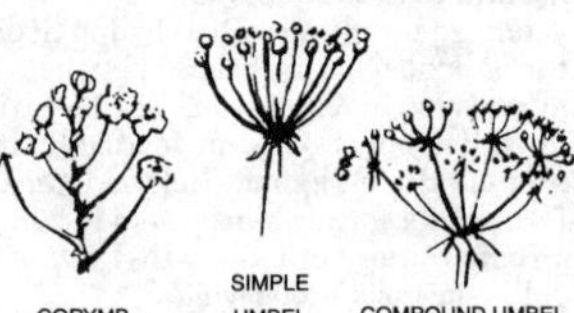

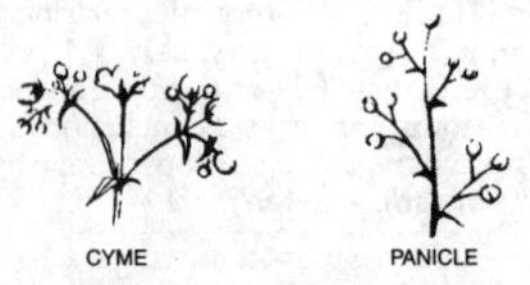

types of inflorescence

in·flow (in′flō′) *n.* **1** a flowing in or into **2** anything that flows in

in·flu·ence (in′flo͞o əns, in flo͞o′əns) *n.* ⟦OFr < ML *influentia*, a flowing in < L *influens*, prp. of *influere*, to flow in < *-in*, in + *fluere*, to flow: see FLUCTUATE⟧ **1** *Astrol.* the flowing of an ethereal fluid or power from the stars, affecting people's character and actions **2** *a)* the power of persons or things to affect others, seen only in its effects *b)* the action or effect of such power **3** the ability of a person or group to produce effects indirectly by means of power based on wealth, high position, etc. **4** a person, group, or thing that has influence **5** *Elec.* the effect of an external field —*vt.* **-enced**, **-enc·ing** to exert or have influence on; have an effect on the nature, behavior, development, action, or thought of —**under the influence** (while) having one's judgment, motor skills, etc. affected by the use of alcohol or a drug

SYN.—**influence** implies the power of persons or things (whether or not exerted consciously or overtly) to affect others [he owed his position to political *influence*]; **authority** implies the power to command acceptance, belief, obedience, etc., based on strength of character, expertness of knowledge, etc. [a statement made on good *authority*]; **prestige** implies the power to command esteem or admiration, based on brilliance of achievement or outstanding superiority; **weight** implies influence that is more or less preponderant in its effect [he threw his *weight* to the opposition] See also **affect**

in·flu·ent (in′flo͞o ənt) *adj.* ⟦L *influens*: see prec.⟧ flowing in —*n.* **1** anything flowing in, as a tributary **2** an organism that has important interactions within an ecological community, but is not a dominant

in·flu·en·tial (in′flo͞o en′shəl) *adj.* ⟦ML *influentialis*⟧ having or exerting influence, esp. great influence; powerful; effective —**in′flu·en′tial·ly** *adv.*

in·flu·en·za (in′flo͞o en′zə) *n.* ⟦It, lit., an influence (because attributed by astrologers to the influence of the stars) < ML *influentia*: see INFLUENCE⟧ **1** an acute, contagious, infectious disease, caused by any of various viruses and characterized by inflammation of the respiratory tract, fever, and muscular pain **2** any of various viral diseases of domestic animals, characterized by inflammation of the respiratory tract —**in′flu·en′zal** *adj.*

in·flux (in′fluks′) *n.* ⟦Fr < LL *influxus* < pp. of L *influere*: see INFLUENCE⟧ **1** *a)* a flowing in; inflow, as of a liquid, gas, etc. *b)* a continual coming in of persons or things [an *influx* of customers] **2** the point where a body of water, as a river, joins another body of water

in·fo (in′fō) ***n.*** [Slang] *short for* INFORMATION (senses 1, 2, & 3)

in·fo·graph·ics (in′fō graf′iks) ***n.*** ⟦< *information graphics*⟧ the informal presentation of quantitative information in a vivid, convenient way, as by means of graphs, tables, maps, etc. that incorporate illustrations and designs —**in′fo·graph′ic** ***adj., n.***

in·fold (in fōld′) ***vt. var. of*** ENFOLD

☆**in·fo·mer·cial** (in′fō mʉr′shəl) ***n.*** ⟦INFO(RMATION) + (COM)MERCIAL; or < earlier *informercial*, formed similarly⟧ a long TV commercial, often made to resemble a talk-show, educational demonstration, interview, etc.

in·form[1] (in fôrm′) ***vt.*** ⟦ME *informen* < OFr *enformer* < L *informare*: see IN-[1] & FORM⟧ **1** *a)* [Obs.] to give form to *b)* to give character to; be the formative principle of *c)* to give or inspire with some specific quality or character **2** [Rare] to form or shape (the mind); teach; instruct **3** to give knowledge of something to; tell; acquaint with a fact, etc. —***vi.*** **1** to give information **2** to give information laying blame or accusation upon another —***SYN.*** NOTIFY

in·form[2] (in fôrm′) ***adj.*** ⟦Fr *informe* < L *informis*⟧ [Archaic] without form

in·for·mal (in fôr′məl) ***adj.*** not formal; specif., *a)* not according to prescribed or fixed customs, rules, ceremonies, etc. *b)* casual, easy, unceremonious, or relaxed *c)* designed for use or wear on everyday occasions *d)* not requiring formal dress *e)* designating or of the words, phrases, and idioms characteristic of speech or writing that is casual, ordinary, unceremonious, etc.; colloquial: the label [Informal] is used throughout this dictionary in this sense —**in·for′mal·ly** ***adv.***

in·for·mal·i·ty (in′fôr mal′ə tē) ***n.*** **1** the quality or state of being informal **2** *pl.* **-ties** an informal act

in·form·ant (in fôr′mənt) ***n.*** ⟦< L *informans*, prp. of *informare*, to inform⟧ a person who gives, or serves as a source of, information; specif., *a)* a native speaker of a language whose pronunciations, usages, etc. are studied and recorded by linguists *b)* INFORMER

in for·ma pau·pe·ris (in fôr′mə pô′pə ris) ⟦L, in the manner of a pauper⟧ *Law* without being liable to pay court fees, as because of poverty

in·for·ma·tion (in′fər mā′shən) ***n.*** ⟦ME *informacioun* < OFr *information* < L *informatio*, a representation, outline, sketch⟧ **1** an informing or being informed [*for your information*, water accounts for about 60% of an adult's weight] **2** something told; news; intelligence; word **3** knowledge acquired in any manner; facts; data; learning; lore **4** a person or agency answering questions as a service to others **5** in information theory and computer science, a precise measure of the information content of a message, measured in bits and ranging from zero when the entire message is known in advance to some maximum when nothing is known of its content **6** any data that can be stored in and retrieved from a computer **7** *Law* an accusation, under oath, of a criminal offense, not by indictment of a grand jury, but by a public officer, such as a prosecutor —**in′for·ma′tion·al** ***adj.***

SYN.—**information** applies to data that are gathered in any way, as by reading, observation, hearsay, etc. and does not necessarily connote validity [inaccurate *information*]; **knowledge** applies to any body of facts gathered by study, observation, etc. and to the ideas inferred from these facts, and connotes an understanding of what is known [man's *knowledge* of the universe]; **learning** is knowledge acquired by study, especially in languages, literature, philosophy, etc.; **erudition** implies profound or abstruse learning beyond the comprehension of most people; **wisdom** implies superior judgment and understanding based on broad knowledge

information science the science dealing with the efficient collection, storage, and retrieval of information

information superhighway **1** the INTERNET or other extensive computer network **2** a hypothetical electronic communications network encompassing computer networks, television, telephones, etc. Often **information highway**

information technology the branch of technology dealing with the practical, esp. the business and industrial, uses of computer and telecommunication systems

information theory the study of processes of communication and the transmission of messages; specif., the study of the information content of messages and of the probabilistic measurement of signal recognition in the presence of interference, noise, etc.

in·form·a·tive (in fôr′mə tiv) ***adj.*** ⟦ML *informativus* < L *informatus*, pp. of *informare*: see INFORM[1]⟧ giving information; educational; instructive: also **in·form′a·to′ry** —**in·form′a·tive·ly** ***adv.***

in·formed (in fôrmd′) ***adj.*** having or based on much information, knowledge, or education

informed consent consent, normally written, to surgery, experimental treatment, etc., given as by a patient after having been informed of the potential medical risks

in·form·er (in fôr′mər) ***n.*** a person who secretly accuses, or gives evidence against, another, often for a reward

☆**in·fo·tain·ment** (in′fō tān′mənt) ***n.*** ⟦< INFO(RMATION) + (ENTER)TAINMENT⟧ television programming of news and information, as about celebrities, presented in a dramatic or sensational style

in·fra- (in′frə) ⟦< L adv. & prep. *infra*, below: see UNDER⟧ *prefix* below; beneath [*infrared*]

in·fract (in frakt′) ***vt.*** ⟦< L *infractus*, pp. of *infringere*: see INFRINGE⟧ [Rare] to break or violate (a law, pledge, etc.) —**in·frac′tor** ***n.***

in·frac·tion (in frak′shən) ***n.*** ⟦L *infractio*: see prec.⟧ a breaking of a law, pact, etc.; violation; infringement

in·fra dig (in′frə dig′) ⟦< L *infra dig(nitatem)*⟧ [Informal] beneath one's dignity

in·fra·lap·sar·i·an (in′frə lap ser′ē ən) ***n.*** ⟦< INFRA- + L *lapsus*, a fall (see LAPSE) + -ARIAN⟧ any of a group of Calvinists who held that God's plan of salvation for some people followed and was a consequence of the fall of humankind from grace: opposed to SUPRALAPSARIAN —***adj.*** of this doctrine —**in′fra·lap·sar′i·an·ism′** ***n.***

in·fran·gi·ble (in fran′jə bəl) ***adj.*** ⟦MFr: see IN-[2] & FRANGIBLE⟧ **1** that cannot be broken or separated **2** that cannot be violated or infringed —**in·fran′gi·bil′i·ty** ***n.***, **in·fran′gi·ble·ness** —**in·fran′gi·bly** ***adv.***

in·fra·red (in′frə red′, in′frə red′) ***adj.*** designating or of those invisible rays just beyond the red end of the visible spectrum: their waves are longer than those of the spectrum colors but shorter than radio waves, and have a penetrating heating effect: used in cooking, photography, etc.

in·fra·son·ic (in′frə sän′ik) ***adj.*** ⟦INFRA- + SONIC⟧ designating or of a frequency of mechanical vibrations below the range audible to the human ear, i.e., below *c.* sixteen vibrations per second

in·fra·spe·cif·ic (in′frə spə sif′ik) ***adj.*** *Taxonomy* of or pertaining to any taxon or category within a species, as a subspecies

in·fra·struc·ture (in′frə struk′chər) ***n.*** ⟦INFRA- + STRUCTURE⟧ a substructure or underlying foundation; esp., the basic installations and facilities on which the continuance and growth of a community, state, etc. depend, as roads, schools, power plants, transportation and communication systems, etc. —**in′fra·struc′tur·al** ***adj.***

in·fre·quent (in frē′kwənt) ***adj.*** ⟦L *infrequens*⟧ not frequent; happening seldom or at long intervals; rare; uncommon —**in·fre′quen·cy** ***n.***, **in·fre′quence** —**in·fre′quent·ly** ***adv.***

in·fringe (in frinj′) ***vt.*** **-fringed′**, **-fring′ing** ⟦L *infringere*, to break off, break, impair, violate < *in-*, in + *frangere*, to BREAK⟧ to break (a law or agreement); fail to observe the terms of; violate —***SYN.*** TRESPASS —**infringe on** (or **upon**) to break in on; encroach or trespass on [to *infringe on* their right to privacy] —**in·fringe′ment** ***n.***

in·fun·dib·u·lar (in′fun dib′yo͞o lər) ***adj.*** **1** shaped like a funnel **2** of or having an infundibulum Also **in·fun·dib·u·late** (in′fun dib′yo͞o lət)

in·fun·dib·u·lum (-ləm) ***n.***, *pl.* **-la** (-lə) ⟦ModL < L, a funnel < *infundere*: see INFUSE⟧ *Anat.* any of various funnel-shaped organs or passages, as *a)* the extension of the third ventricle of the brain to the pituitary gland *b)* the calyx of a kidney *c)* the ovarian end of a fallopian tube

in·fu·ri·ate (in fyoor′ē āt′; *for adj.*, -it, -āt′) ***vt.*** **-at′ed**, **-at′ing** ⟦< ML *infuriatus*, pp. of *infuriare*, to enrage < L *in-*, in + *furiare*, to enrage < *furia*, rage, FURY⟧ to cause to become very angry; enrage —***adj.*** [Archaic] furious; very angry; enraged —**in·fu′ri·at′ing·ly** ***adv.*** —**in·fu′ri·a′tion** ***n.***

in·fus·cate (in fus′kit, -kāt′) ***adj.*** ⟦L *infuscatus*, pp. of *infuscare*, to make dark, obscure < *in-*, in + *fuscare*, to darken < *fuscus*, dark < IE base **dhus-*: see OBFUSCATE⟧ darkened or tinged with brown: said as of the wings of an insect: also **in·fus′cat′ed** (-kāt′id)

in·fuse (in fyo͞oz′) ***vt.*** **-fused′**, **-fus′ing** ⟦ME *infusen* < L *infusus*, pp. of *infundere*, to pour in < *in-*, in + *fundere*, to pour: see FOUND[2]⟧ **1** [Obs.] to pour (a liquid) in, into, or upon **2** to put (a substance) into [butter *infused* with garlic] **3** to put (a quality, idea, etc.) into, as if by pouring; instill; impart **4** to fill (*with* a quality, feeling, etc.); imbue; inspire **5** to steep or soak (tea leaves, etc.) so as to extract flavor or other qualities —**in·fus′er** ***n.***

in·fu·si·ble (in fyo͞o′zə bəl) ***adj.*** **1** ⟦IN-[2] + FUSIBLE⟧ that cannot be fused or melted **2** ⟦< L **infusibilis*, part. of *infundere*: see prec.⟧ allowing or capable of infusion —**in·fu′si·bil′i·ty** ***n.***

in·fu·sion (in fyo͞o′zhən) ***n.*** ⟦< Fr or L: Fr *infusion* < L *infusio*⟧ **1** the act or process of infusing **2** something infused; tincture; admixture **3** the liquid extract that results from steeping a substance in water **4** *Med.* the introduction of a solution into the body, specif. into a vein

in·fu·sion·ism (-iz′əm) ***n.*** *Theol.* the doctrine that the preexisting human soul enters the body by divine infusion at conception or birth

in·fu·sive (in fyo͞o′siv) ***adj.*** tending or able to infuse

in·fu·so·ri·al (in′fyo͞o sôr′ē əl) ***adj.*** of, consisting of, containing, or having the nature of, infusorians

in·fu·so·ri·an (-ən) ***n.*** ⟦< ModL (*animalcula infusoria*), neut. pl. of *infusorius*, pertaining to infusions (< L *infusus*: see INFUSE) + -AN⟧ **1** any of a former large group (Infusoria) of microscopic animals found in infusions of decayed organic matter and in stagnant water **2** any of a former class (Infusoria) of protozoans found in most water, characterized by cilia which permit free movement, as paramecia or stentors —***adj.*** of this group or class

-ing (iŋ) ⟦ME *-ing, -yng*, orig. *-end, -and, -ind* < OE *-ende*, suffix of prp. of verbs⟧ *suffix* **1** forming the present participle of verbs [*hearing, noticing*] **2** ⟦ME *-ing, -yng* < OE *-ung*⟧ *forming verbal nouns: a)* the act or an instance of (a specified verb) [*talking, digging*] *b)* something produced by the action of (a specified verb) [*a painting*] *c)* something that does the action of (a specified verb) [*a covering* for her head] *d)* material used for (a specified thing) [*blanketing, carpeting*] *e)* an act or process involving (a specified thing) (added to verbs or, sometimes, nouns) **3** ⟦ME < OE⟧ *forming nouns* a person or thing of a (specified) kind or origin: sometimes used with diminutive force [*atheling, farthing*]

in·gath·er (in′gath′ər, in gath′ər) ***vt., vi.*** **1** to assemble or draw together **2** [Archaic] to harvest —**in′gath′er·ing** ***n.***

Inge (iŋ), **William** 1913-73; U.S. playwright

in·gem·i·nate (in jem′ə nāt′) ***vt.*** **-nat′ed**, **-nat′ing** ⟦< L *ingeminatus*, pp. of *ingeminare*, to redouble, repeat: see IN-[1] & GEMINATE⟧ [Now Rare] to stress or make more forceful by repeating —**in·gem′i·na′tion** ***n.***

in·gen·ious (in jēn′yəs) *adj.* ⟦LME < MFr *ingenieux* < L *ingeniosus*, of good capacity, gifted with genius, ingenious < *ingenium*, innate quality, ability < *in-*, in + *gignere*: see GENUS⟧ **1** [Obs.] having genius; having great mental ability **2** clever, resourceful, original, and inventive **3** made or done in a clever or original way —**SYN.** CLEVER —**in·gen′ious·ly** *adv.* —**in·gen′ious·ness** *n.*

in·gé·nue or **in·ge·nue** (an′zhə no͞o′, än′-; -jə-) *n.* ⟦Fr, fem. of *ingénu* < L *ingenuus*, INGENUOUS⟧ **1** an innocent, inexperienced, unworldly young woman **2** *Theater a)* the role of such a character *b)* an actress playing such a role or roles

in·ge·nu·i·ty (in′jə no͞o′ə tē, -nyo͞o′-) *n.* ⟦L *ingenuitas* < *ingenuus* (see fol.): sense 1 infl. by assoc. with INGENIOUS⟧ **1** [Obs.] the quality of being ingenuous **2** the quality of being ingenious; cleverness, originality, skill, etc. **3** *pl.* **-ties** an ingenious device, stratagem, etc.

in·gen·u·ous (in jen′yo͞o əs) *adj.* ⟦L *ingenuus*, native, inborn, freeborn, noble, frank < *ingignere*, to engender < *in-*, in + *gignere*, to produce: see GENUS⟧ **1** [Obs.] of noble birth or nature **2** frank; open; candid **3** simple; artless; naive; without guile —**SYN.** NAIVE —**in·gen′u·ous·ly** *adv.* —**in·gen′u·ous·ness** *n.*

In·ger·soll (iŋ′gər sôl′, -səl), **Robert Green** 1833-99; U.S. lawyer & lecturer: exponent of agnosticism

in·gest (in jest′) *vt.* ⟦< L *ingestus*, pp. of *ingerere*, to carry, put into < *in-*, into + *gerere*, to carry⟧ to take (food, drugs, etc.) into the body, as by swallowing, inhaling, or absorbing —**in·ges′tion** *n.* —**in·ges′tive** *adj.*

in·ges·ta (in jes′tə) *pl.n.* ⟦L, neut. pl. of *ingestus*: see prec.⟧ things ingested: sometimes used fig.

in·gle (iŋ′gəl) *n.* ⟦Scot < Gael *aingeal*, fire⟧ [Brit. Dial.] **1** a fire or blaze, esp. on a hearth **2** a fireplace

in·gle·nook (iŋ′gəl no͝ok′) *n.* [Chiefly Brit.] a corner by a fireplace; chimney corner: also written **ingle nook**

In·gle·wood (iŋ′gəl wo͝od′) ⟦after the hometown in Canada of a relative of one of the promoters⟧ city in SW Calif.: suburb of Los Angeles

in·glo·ri·ous (in glôr′ē əs) *adj.* ⟦L *ingloriosus*: see IN-[2] & GLORIOUS⟧ **1** not giving, receiving, or deserving glory; shameful; disgraceful; dishonorable **2** [Now Rare] without glory; not famous; little-known —**in·glo′ri·ous·ly** *adv.* —**in·glo′ri·ous·ness** *n.*

in·go·ing (in′gō′iŋ) *adj.* going in; entering

in·got (iŋ′gət) *n.* ⟦ME < MFr *lingot* (with faulty separation of *l-*, as if *l′*, for *le*, the) < OFr, prob. < *lingo*, var. of *lengo*, tongue (< L *lingua*: see LANGUAGE): from the elongated form⟧ **1** [Obs.] a mold for casting metal into a bar **2** a mass of metal cast into a bar or other convenient shape

ingot iron a ductile, rust-resistant, highly purified steel with an impurity level below 0.15%

in·graft (in graft′) *vt. var. of* ENGRAFT

in·grain (in grān′, in′grān′; *for adj.* in′grān′; *for n.* in′grān′) *vt.* ⟦see ENGRAIN⟧ **1** to dye in the fiber before manufacture **2** to work into the fiber; infuse deeply: chiefly in a fig. sense, and in the pp. —*adj.* **1** dyed in the fiber, before manufacture; thoroughly dyed **2** made of fiber or yarn dyed before weaving: said of rugs, carpeting, etc. **3** deeply infused —*n.* yarn, fiber, carpeting, etc. dyed before manufacture

in·grained (in′grānd′, -grānd′) *adj.* **1** *a)* worked into the fiber *b)* firmly fixed or established [*ingrained* principles] **2** inveterate; thoroughgoing [an *ingrained* liar]

in·grate (in′grāt′) *adj.* ⟦ME *ingrat* < OFr < L *ingratus*, unpleasant, ungrateful < *in-*, not + *gratus*, grateful: see GRACE⟧ [Obs.] ungrateful —*n.* an ungrateful person

in·gra·ti·ate (in grā′shē āt′) *vt.* **-at′ed**, **-at′ing** ⟦prob. via It *ingratiare* (now *ingraziare*) < L phr. *in gratiam*, for the favor of < *in-*, in + *gratia*, favor, GRACE⟧ to make acceptable; esp., to bring (oneself) into another's favor or good graces by conscious effort —**in·gra′ti·at′ing** *adj.* —**in·gra′ti·at′ing·ly** *adv.* —**in·gra′ti·a′tion** *n.* —**in·gra′ti·a·to′ry** (-ə tôr′ē) *adj.*

in·grat·i·tude (in grat′i to͞od′, -tyo͞od′) *n.* ⟦OFr < LL *ingratitudo*: see INGRATE⟧ lack of gratitude; ungratefulness

in·gra·ves·cent (in′grə ves′ənt) *adj.* ⟦L *ingravescens*, prp. of *ingravescere*, to become heavier, grow worse < *in-*, IN-[1] + *gravis*, heavy, severe, GRAVE[1]⟧ [Now Rare] becoming more and more severe, as a disease or symptom

in·gre·di·ent (in grē′dē ənt) *n.* ⟦ME < L *ingrediens*, prp. of *ingredi*: see INGRESS⟧ **1** any of the things that a mixture is made of **2** a component part, or constituent, of anything —**SYN.** ELEMENT

In·gres (an′gr′), **Jean Au·guste Do·mi·nique** (zhän ô güst′ dô mē nēk′) 1780-1867; Fr. painter

in·gress (in′gres′) *n.* ⟦ME < L *ingressus*, pp. of *ingredi*, to step into, enter < *in-*, into + *gradi*, to go: see GRADE⟧ **1** the act of entering: also **in·gres·sion** (in gresh′ən) **2** the right or permission to enter **3** a place or means of entering; entrance

in·gres·sive (in gres′iv) *adj.* ⟦ML *ingressivus*⟧ **1** having to do with ingress **2** *Gram.* INCEPTIVE

Ing·rid (iŋ′grid) *n.* ⟦< Scand; ult < ON *Ingvi*, name of a Gmc god + *rida*, ride⟧ a feminine name

in-group (in′gro͞op′) *n.* any group of people with common interests that give them a sense of solidarity and exclusivity as regards all nonmembers

in·grow·ing (in′grō′iŋ) *adj.* growing within, inward, or into; esp., growing into the flesh [an *ingrowing* hair]

in·grown (in′grōn′) *adj.* **1** grown within, inward, or into; esp., grown into the flesh: said as of a toenail that curves under at the sides **2** inborn; native; innate

in·growth (in′grōth′) *n.* **1** a growing inward **2** something ingrowing or ingrown

in·gui·nal (iŋ′gwi nəl) *adj.* ⟦L *inguinalis* < *inguen* (gen. *inguinis*), the groin < IE base **ngwēn-* > OIce *økkr*, tumor, Gr *adēn*, gland⟧ of or near the groin

in·gulf (in gulf′) *vt. var. of* ENGULF

in·gur·gi·tate (in gur′jə tāt′) *vt., vi.* **-tat′ed**, **-tat′ing** ⟦< L *ingurgitatus*, pp. of *ingurgitare*, to pour in like a flood, guzzle: see IN-[1] & GURGITATION⟧ to swallow up greedily or in large amounts; gulp; gorge; guzzle —**in·gur′gi·ta′tion** *n.*

INH *abbrev.* ⟦*i(so)n(icotinic) h(ydrazide)*⟧ isoniazid

in·hab·it (in hab′it) *vt.* ⟦ME *enhabiten* < OFr *enhabiter* < L *inhabitare* < *in-*, in + *habitare*, to dwell < *habitus*: see HABIT⟧ to dwell or live in (a region, house, etc.); occupy —*vi.* [Archaic] to dwell; live —**in·hab′it·a·bil′i·ty** *n.* —**in·hab′it·a·ble** *adj.* —**in·hab′it·er** *n.*

in·hab·it·an·cy (in hab′i tən sē) *n., pl.* **-cies** **1** an inhabiting or being inhabited **2** place of residence; home; dwelling Also [Obs.] **in·hab′it·ance**

in·hab·it·ant (in hab′i tənt) *n.* ⟦ME *inhabitaunt* < OFr *inhabitant* < L *inhabitans*, prp. of *inhabitare*⟧ a person or animal that inhabits some specified region, dwelling, etc.; permanent resident

in·hab·i·ta·tion (in hab′i tā′shən) *n.* ⟦ME *inhabitacioun* < LL *inhabitatio*⟧ an inhabiting or being inhabited

in·hab·it·ed (in hab′it id) *adj.* having inhabitants; lived in; occupied

in·hal·ant (in hāl′ənt) *adj.* ⟦< L *inhalans*, prp. of *inhalare*⟧ used in inhalation; inhaling —*n.* a medicine or other substance to be inhaled as a vapor

in·ha·la·tion (in′hə lā′shən) *n.* ⟦< pp. of L *inhalare*⟧ **1** the act or an instance of inhaling **2** INHALANT

☆**in·ha·la·tor** (in′hə lāt′ər) *n.* **1** INHALER (sense 3) **2** RESPIRATOR (sense 2)

in·hale (in hāl′, in′hāl′) *vt.* **-haled′**, **-hal′ing** ⟦L *inhalare* < *in-*, in + *halare*, to breathe: see EXHALE⟧ **1** to draw (air, vapor, etc.) into the lungs; breathe in **2** [Informal] to consume rapidly or voraciously [to *inhale* one's dinner] —*vi.* **1** to draw air, vapor, etc. into the lungs **2** to draw tobacco smoke into the lungs when smoking

in·hal·er (in hāl′ər) *n.* **1** a person who inhales **2** RESPIRATOR (sense 1) **3** a device for administering medicine in the form of a vapor by inhalation

in·har·mon·ic (in′här män′ik) *adj.* not harmonic; out of harmony; discordant

in·har·mo·ni·ous (in′här mō′nē əs) *adj.* not harmonious; discordant, in conflict, etc. —**in′har·mo′ni·ous·ly** *adv.* —**in′har·mo′ni·ous·ness** *n.*

in·har·mo·ny (in här′mə nē) *n.* lack of harmony; discord; conflict

in·haul (in′hôl′) *n. Naut.* a rope used to haul in something, specif. the corner of a sail

in·here (in hir′) *vi.* **-hered′**, **-her′ing** ⟦L *inhaerere*, to stick in, adhere to < *in-*, in + *haerere*, to stick⟧ to be inherent; exist as a quality, characteristic, or right (*in*); be intrinsic

in·her·ence (in hir′əns, -her′-) *n.* ⟦ME *inhaerentia*⟧ **1** the fact or state of inhering or being inherent **2** *Philos.* the relation of an attribute to its subject —**in·her′en·cy** (-ən sē) *n.*

in·her·ent (-ənt) *adj.* ⟦L *inhaerens*, prp. of *inhaerere*: see INHERE⟧ existing in someone or something as a natural and inseparable quality, characteristic, or right; intrinsic; innate; basic —**in·her′ent·ly** *adv.*

in·her·it (in her′it) *vt.* ⟦ME *enheriten* < OFr *enheriter* < LL *inhereditare*, to appoint as heir, inherit < L *in*, in + *heres*, HEIR⟧ **1** [Obs.] to transfer property to (an heir) **2** *a)* to receive (an ancestor's property, title, etc.) by the laws of inheritance upon the ancestor's death *b)* to receive (property) by bequest **3** to receive as if by inheritance from a predecessor **4** to have (certain characteristics) by heredity —*vi.* to receive an inheritance; become an heir —**in·her′i·tor** *n.*

in·her·it·a·ble (in her′it ə bəl) *adj.* ⟦ME *enheritable* < Anglo-Fr < OFr⟧ **1** capable of inheriting; having the rights of an heir **2** capable of being inherited —**in·her′it·a·bil′i·ty** *n.*, **in·her′it·a·ble·ness**

in·her·it·ance (in her′i təns) *n.* ⟦ME *inheritauns* < Anglo-Fr & OFr *enheritance*⟧ **1** the action of inheriting **2** something inherited or to be inherited; legacy; bequest **3** ownership by virtue of birthright; right to inherit **4** anything received as if by inheritance from a predecessor **5** any characteristic passed on by heredity —**SYN.** HERITAGE

inheritance tax **1** a tax levied on persons who inherit property, typically a percentage of the value of the inheritance received **2** loosely, an estate tax

in·he·sion (in hē′zhən) *n.* ⟦LL *inhaesio* < pp. of L *inhaerere*: see INHERE⟧ [Rare] INHERENCE

in·hib·in (in hib′in) *n.* a protein-based hormone, produced in small quantities in the testes and ovaries, that inhibits the secretion of FOLLICLE-STIMULATING HORMONE

in·hib·it (in hib′it) *vt.* ⟦< L *inhibitus*, pp. of *inhibere*, to hold back, restrain, curb < *in-*, in, on + *habere*, to have, hold: see HABIT⟧ **1** to hold back or keep from some action, feeling, etc.; check or repress **2** *Eccles.* to prohibit; forbid —**SYN.** RESTRAIN —**in·hib′i·tive** *adj.*, **in·hib′i·to′ry** (-i tôr′ē)

in·hi·bi·tion (in′hi bish′ən, in′i-) *n.* ⟦ME *inhibicion* < OFr < L *inhibitio*⟧ **1** an inhibiting or being inhibited **2** anything that inhibits, esp., a mental or psychological process that restrains or suppresses an action, emotion, or thought

in·hib·i·tor (in hib′it ər) *n.* a person or thing that inhibits; esp., any substance that slows or prevents a chemical or organic reaction: also sp. **in·hib′it·er**

in·ho·mo·ge·ne·ous (in′hō′mō jē′nē əs, -mə-) *adj.* not homogeneous

in·hos·pi·ta·ble (in häs′pit ə bəl, in′häs pit′-) *adj.* ⟦ML *inhospitabilis*⟧ **1** not hospitable; not offering hospitality **2** not offering protection, shelter, etc.; barren; forbidding [an *inhospitable* climate] —**in·hos′pi·ta·ble·ness** *n.* —**in·hos′pi·ta·bly** *adv.*

in·hos·pi·tal·i·ty (in′häs pi tal′ə tē) *n.* lack of hospitality; inhospitable treatment

in-house (in′hous′) *adj.* originating within an organization, company, etc., rather than brought in from outside —*adv.* at or within an organization, company, etc. rather than outside it

in·hu·man (in hyo͞o′mən) *adj.* ⟦LME *inhumayn* < MFr *inhumain* < L *inhumanus*⟧ 1 not human 2 not having the qualities considered normal to or for human beings; unfeeling, heartless, cruel, barbarous, etc. —SYN. CRUEL —**in·hu′man·ly** *adv.*

in·hu·mane (in′hyo͞o mān′) *adj.* ⟦IN-[2] + HUMANE⟧ not humane; unmoved by the suffering of others; cruel, brutal, unkind, etc. —**in′hu·mane′ly** *adv.*

in·hu·man·i·ty (in′hyo͞o man′ə tē) *n.* ⟦LME *inhumanite* < MFr < L *inhumanitas*⟧ 1 the quality or condition of being inhuman or inhumane 2 *pl.* **-ties** an inhuman or inhumane act or remark

in·hume (in hyo͞om′) *vt.* **-humed′, -hum′ing** ⟦Fr *inhumer* < L *inhumare* < *in-*, in + *humus*, earth: see HUMUS[2]⟧ to bury (a dead body); inter —**in′hu·ma′tion** *n.*

in·im·i·cal (i nim′i kəl) *adj.* ⟦LL *inimicalis* < L *inimicus*, hostile, ENEMY⟧ 1 like an enemy; hostile; unfriendly 2 in opposition; adverse; unfavorable [laws *inimical* to freedom] —**in·im′i·cal·ly** *adv.*

in·im·i·ta·ble (i nim′i tə bəl) *adj.* ⟦L *inimitabilis*: see IN-[2] & IMITABLE⟧ that cannot be imitated or matched; too good to be equaled or copied —**in·im′i·ta·bil′i·ty** *n.*, **in·im′i·ta·ble·ness** —**in·im′i·ta·bly** *adv.*

in·i·on (in′ē ən, -än′) *n.* ⟦ModL < Gr, the back of the head < *is* (gen. *inos*), sinew, muscle, lit., strength, akin to L *vis*, strength < IE **wis-* < base **wei-*, to strive forward, > L *via*⟧ the bulging part at the rear of the human skull

in·iq·ui·tous (i nik′wi təs) *adj.* showing iniquity; wicked; unjust —**in·iq′ui·tous·ly** *adv.* —**in·iq′ui·tous·ness** *n.*

in·iq·ui·ty (i nik′wi tē) *n.* ⟦ME *iniquite* < OFr *iniquité* < L *iniquitas* < *iniquus*, unequal < *in-*, not + *aequus*, EQUAL⟧ 1 lack of righteousness or justice; wickedness 2 *pl.* **-ties** a wicked, unjust, or unrighteous act

init *abbrev.* initial

in·i·tial (i nish′əl) *adj.* ⟦< Fr or L: Fr < L *initialis* < *initium*, a beginning < *inire*, to go into, enter upon, begin < *in-*, into, in + *ire*, to go < IE base **ei-* > Goth *iddja*⟧ having to do with, indicating, or occurring at the beginning [the *initial* stage of a disease, the *initial* letter of a word] —*n.* 1 a capital, or uppercase, letter; specif., *a)* an extra-large capital letter at the start of a printed paragraph, chapter, etc. *b)* the first letter of a name, specif. when used in place of that name 2 *Biol.* a primordial cell that determines the basic pattern of derived tissues; specif., a meristematic cell —*vt.* **-tialed** or **-tialled**, **-tial·ing** or **-tial·ling** to mark or sign with an initial or initials

in·i·tial·ism (i nish′əl iz′əm) *n.* an acronym or abbreviation formed from initial letters, specif., one pronounced using the letters' names rather than phonetically (Ex.: CD, DNA, FBI)

in·i·tial·ize (i nish′əl īz′) *vt.* **-ized′, -iz′ing** *Comput.* to prepare for use by renewing the settings, clearing memory, etc. —**in·i′tial·i·za′tion** *n.*

in·i·tial·ly (i nish′əl ē) *adv.* at the beginning; at first

in·i·ti·ate (i nish′ē āt′; *for adj. & n.* i nish′ē it, -āt′ *or, occas.* i nish′it) *vt.* **-at′ed, -at′ing** ⟦< L *initiatus*, pp. of *initiare*, to enter upon, initiate < *initium*: see INITIAL⟧ 1 to bring into practice or use; introduce by first doing or using; start [to *initiate* a new course of studies] 2 to teach the fundamentals of some subject to; help to begin doing something [to *initiate* someone into the game of chess] 3 to admit as a member into a fraternity, club, etc., as with customary practices or ceremonies —*adj.* 1 initiated 2 [Archaic] just begun —*n.* a person who has recently been, or is about to be, initiated —SYN. BEGIN —**in·i′ti·a′tor** *n.*

in·i·ti·a·tion (i nish′ē ā′shən) *n.* ⟦L *initiatio*⟧ 1 an initiating or being initiated 2 the ceremony or conventions by which a person is initiated into a fraternity, club, etc.

in·i·tia·tive (i nish′ə tiv, -ē ə tiv) *adj.* ⟦ML *initiativus*⟧ of, or having the nature of, initiation; introductory; initial —*n.* 1 the action of taking the first step or making the first move; responsibility for beginning or originating 2 the characteristic of originating new ideas or methods; ability to think and act without being urged; enterprise 3 *a)* the right of a legislature to introduce new legislation on some specified matter *b)* the right of a group of citizens to introduce a matter for legislation either to the legislature or directly to the voters *c)* the procedure by which such matters are introduced, usually by a petition signed by a specified percentage of the voters

in·i·ti·a·to·ry (i nish′ē ə tôr ē, i nish′ə-) *adj.* 1 beginning; introductory; initial 2 of or used in an initiation

in·ject (in jekt′) *vt.* ⟦< L *injectus*, pp. of *injicere*, to throw, cast, or put in < *in-*, in + *jacere*, to throw: see JET[1]⟧ 1 to force or drive (a fluid) into some passage, cavity, or chamber; esp., to introduce or force (a liquid) into some part of the body by means of a syringe, hypodermic needle, etc. 2 to fill by, or subject to, injection 3 to introduce (a missing feature, quality, etc.) [to *inject* a note of humor into a story] 4 to interject (a remark, opinion, etc.) as into a discussion —**in·ject′a·ble** *adj.*

in·jec·tion (in jek′shən) *n.* ⟦L *injectio*⟧ 1 an act or instance of injecting 2 something injected; esp., *a)* a liquid injected into the body *b)* a fuel under pressure forced into a combustion chamber

injection molding a method of shaping certain materials, as thermoplastic substances, by forcing the heated, syrupy resin into water-chilled molds for cooling and setting —**in·jec′tion-mold′ed** *adj.*

in·jec·tor (in jek′tər) *n.* a person or thing that injects, as a device for injecting pressurized fuel into a combustion chamber or for injecting water into a steam boiler

in-joke (in′jōk′) *n.* a joke, typically a humorous allusion, meant to be appreciated only by insiders

in·ju·di·cious (in′jo͞o dish′əs) *adj.* ⟦IN-[2] + JUDICIOUS⟧ showing poor judgment; not discreet or wise —**in′ju·di′cious·ly** *adv.* —**in′ju·di′cious·ness** *n.*

in·junc·tion (in juŋk′shən) *n.* ⟦LL *injunctio* < pp. of L *injungere*, to ENJOIN⟧ 1 an enjoining; bidding; command 2 something enjoined; command; order 3 a writ or order from a court prohibiting a person or group from carrying out a given action, or ordering a given action to be done —**in·junc′tive** *adj.*

in·jure (in′jər) *vt.* **-jured, -jur·ing** ⟦altered < earlier *injury*, to harm < LME *injurien* < MFr *injurier* < L *injuriari* < *injuria*: see INJURY⟧ 1 to do physical harm or damage to; hurt 2 to offend (one's feelings, pride, etc.); wound 3 to weaken or otherwise cause a loss in value to (a business, reputation, etc.) 4 to be unjust to; wrong —**in′jur·er** *n.*

SYN.—**injure** implies the marring of the appearance, health, soundness, etc. of a person or thing [*injured* pride]; **harm** more strongly suggests the pain or distress caused [he wouldn't *harm* a fly]; **damage** stresses the loss, as in value, usefulness, etc., resulting from an injury [*damaged* goods]; **hurt** implies a wounding physically or emotionally or a causing of any kind of harm or damage [the rumors *hurt* his business]; to **impair** something is to cause it to deteriorate in quality or to lessen in value, strength, etc. [*impaired* hearing]; **spoil** implies such serious impairment of a thing as to destroy its value, usefulness, etc. [the canned food was *spoiled*]

in·ju·ri·ous (in jo͝or′ē əs) *adj.* ⟦LME *iniuryous* < MFr *injurieux* < L *injuriosus*⟧ 1 injuring or likely to cause injury; harmful 2 offensive or abusive; slanderous or libelous —**in·ju′ri·ous·ly** *adv.* —**in·ju′ri·ous·ness** *n.*

in·ju·ry (in′jə rē) *n.*, *pl.* **-ries** ⟦ME *iniurie* < L *injuria* < *injurius*, wrongful, unjust < *in-*, not + *jus* (gen. *juris*), right, justice: see JUST[1]⟧ 1 physical harm or damage to a person, property, etc. 2 an injurious act; specif., *a)* an offense against a person's feelings, dignity, etc. *b)* loss in value inflicted on a business, reputation, etc. *c)* a violation of rights; wrong 3 [Obs.] an insult

in·jus·tice (in jus′tis) *n.* ⟦OFr < L *injustitia*⟧ 1 the quality of being unjust or unfair; lack of justice 2 an unjust act; injury

ink (iŋk) *n.* ⟦ME *enke* < OFr *enque* < LL *encaustum* < Gr *enkauston*, purple or red ink < *enkaustos*, burned in < *enkaiein*, to burn in < *en-*, in + *kaiein*, to burn < IE base **kai-* > HEAT⟧ 1 a colored liquid used for writing, drawing, etc. 2 a sticky, colored paste used in printing; printer's ink 3 [Slang] publicity, esp. in newspapers 4 a dark, liquid secretion ejected by cuttlefish, octopuses, and squid to confuse or inhibit a predator —*vt.* 1 to cover with ink; spread ink on 2 to mark, write, sign, draw, or color with ink: often with *in* 3 [Informal] to sign one's name to

☆**ink·ber·ry** (iŋk′ber′ē) *n.*, *pl.* **-ries** 1 an evergreen holly (*Ilex glabra*) with shiny, leathery leaves, native to E North America 2 its dark-purple fruit 3 POKEWEED

ink·blot (iŋk′blät′) *n.* 1 a blot of ink 2 any of a standard series of irregular patterns made by blots of ink and used in psychological testing: see RORSCHACH TEST

ink·er (iŋ′kər) *n.* 1 a person or thing that inks 2 *Printing* a roller for spreading ink on type

ink·horn (iŋk′hôrn′) *n.* a small container made of horn or other material, formerly used to hold ink —*adj.* pedantic; bookish [an *inkhorn* term]

ink·jet (iŋk′jet′) *adj.* designating or of a printing process in which jets of ink are broken up into electrostatically charged droplets that are propelled onto paper to form printed characters

in·kle (iŋ′kəl) *n.* ⟦< ? obs. Du *inckel* (Du *enkel*), single (with reference to the narrow width)⟧ [Now Rare] 1 a kind of braided linen tape 2 the thread or yarn from which this is made

ink·ling (iŋk′liŋ) *n.* ⟦ME *ingkiling* < *inclen*, to give an inkling of⟧ 1 an indirect suggestion; slight indication; hint 2 a vague idea or notion; suspicion

ink·stand (iŋk′stand′) *n.* 1 a small stand holding an inkwell, pens, etc. 2 INKWELL

ink·well (iŋk′wel′) *n.* a container for holding ink, usually set into the top of a desk, inkstand, etc.

☆**ink·wood** (-wo͝od′) *n.* a tropical tree (*Exothea paniculata*) of the soapberry family found in Florida and the West Indies, having dark, hard wood used for pilings, fence posts, etc.

ink·y (iŋ′kē) *adj.* **ink′i·er, ink′i·est** 1 like ink in color; dark; black 2 colored, marked, stained, or covered with ink —**ink′i·ness** *n.*

inky cap any of several mushrooms (genus *Coprinus*) whose cap liquefies and forms an inky material

in·laid (in′lād′, in lād′) *vt. pt. & pp. of* INLAY —*adj.* 1 set in pieces into a surface of another material so as to form a smooth surface [a pine table with an *inlaid* walnut design] 2 decorated with a surface made in this way [an *inlaid* floor]

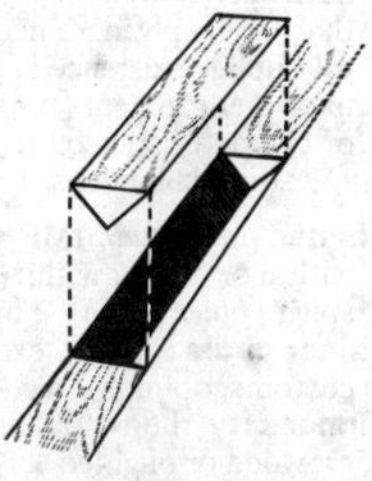
inlaid wood

in·land (in′lənd; *for n. & adv.*, -land′, -lənd) *adj.* ⟦IN-[1] + LAND⟧ 1 of, located in, or confined to the interior of a country or region; away from the coast or border 2 [Brit.] carried on or operating within a country; domestic —*n.* ⟦ME < OE *in-lande*⟧ the interior of a country or region; inland areas —*adv.* into or toward the interior; away from the coast or border

in·land·er (in′lən dər, -lan′-) ***n.*** a person living inland

☆**Inland Passage** INSIDE PASSAGE

Inland Sea arm of the Pacific surrounded by the Japanese islands of Honshu, Shikoku, & Kyushu

in-law (in′lô′) ***n.*** ⟦back-form. < MOTHER-IN-LAW, FATHER-IN-LAW, etc.⟧ [Informal] a relative by marriage

-in-law (in lô′) *combining form* being a (specified type of relative) by marriage, not by descent in the same family line

in·lay (in′lā′, in lā′; *for n.* in′lā′) ***vt.* -laid′, -lay′ing** ⟦IN-^{1} & LAY^1⟧ **1** *a)* to set (pieces of wood, metal, etc.) into a surface to make a design that is typically level with the surface *b)* to decorate with such pieces **2** to fit or insert (an illustration) into a mat **3** to add extra silver to (silver-plated objects) —***n.*** **1** inlaid decoration or material **2** a filling for a tooth made from a mold of the prepared cavity and then cemented into place —**in′lay′er *n.***

in·let (in′let′, in let′; *for n.* in′let′, -lət) ***vt.* -let′, -let′ting** ⟦ME *inletan*: see IN-^{1} & LET^1⟧ to inlay or insert —***n.*** ⟦ME *inlate* < the v.⟧ **1** *a)* a narrow strip of water extending into a body of land from a river, lake, ocean, etc.; small bay or creek *b)* a narrow strip of water between islands *c)* a stream, river, etc. that flows into a larger body of water, as a lake or pond **2** the act of letting something in **3** an entrance, opening, or passage **4** something inlaid or inserted

in·li·er (in′lī′ər) ***n.*** ⟦< IN-^{1} + LIE^1 + -ER⟧ an outcrop area of older rocks entirely surrounded by younger rocks

in-line skate (in′līn′) a kind of roller skate having wheels arranged in a line from toe to heel, rather than in pairs: typically for use outdoors on smooth, paved lanes —**in-line skating**

in-line skate

in loc. cit. *abbrev.* ⟦L *in loco citato*⟧ in the place cited

in lo·co pa·ren·tis (in lō′kō′ pə ren′tis) ⟦L⟧ in the place of a parent, or of a parent's authority

in·ly (in′lē) ***adv.*** ⟦ME *inliche* < OE *inlice*: see IN-^{1} & -LY^2⟧ [Old Poet.] **1** inwardly **2** intimately

in·mate (in′māt′) ***n.*** ⟦IN-^{1} + MATE^1⟧ **1** [Archaic] a person living with others in the same building **2** a person confined in a prison or mental institution

in me·di·as res (in mā′dē äs′ räs′, -res′) ⟦L, into the midst of things⟧ in the middle of the action rather than at the beginning, as in commencing a classical epic

in me·mo·ri·am (in′ mə môr′ē əm) ⟦L⟧ in memory (of): used on tombstones, in obituary notices, etc.

in-mi·grant (in′mī′grənt) ***adj.*** coming in from another region of the same country *[in-migrant* workers*]* —***n.*** an in-migrant person or animal —**in′-mi′grate′ *vi.* -grat′ed, -grat′ing** —**in′-mi·gra′tion *n.***

in·most (in′mōst′) ***adj.*** ⟦ME *innemest* < OE: see IN-^{1} & -MOST⟧ **1** located farthest within **2** most intimate or secret; innermost *[inmost* thoughts*]*

inn (in) ***n.*** ⟦ME *yn* < OE *inn* (akin to ON *inni*) < adv. *inn, inne,* within: see IN^1⟧ **1** [Obs.] any dwelling or lodging **2** *a)* an establishment or building providing lodging and, usually, food and drink for travelers; hotel or motel, esp. one in the country or along a highway *b)* a restaurant or tavern (now usually only in the names of such places) **3** [Brit. Historical] any of various houses in London providing lodging for students: see INNS OF COURT — ***vt., vi.*** [Archaic] to lodge at an inn

Inn (in) river flowing from E Switzerland across W Austria & SE Bavaria into the Danube: *c.* 320 mi (515 km)

in·nards (in′ərdz) ***pl.n.*** ⟦altered < INWARDS⟧ [Informal or Dial.] **1** the internal organs of the body; viscera; entrails **2** the inner parts of anything

in·nate (i nāt′, in′āt′) ***adj.*** ⟦L *innatus*, pp. of *innasci*, to be born in, originate in < *in-*, in + *nasci*, to be born: see NATURE⟧ **1** *a)* existing naturally rather than acquired; that seems to have been in one from birth *[innate* talent*]* *b)* existing as an inherent attribute *[*the *innate* humor of a situation*]* **2** *Bot.* borne at the apex of the support, as an anther —**in·nate′ly *adv.*** —**in·nate′ness *n.***

SYN.—**innate** and **inborn** are often interchangeable, but **innate** has more extensive connotations, describing that which belongs to something as part of its nature or constitution, and **inborn**, the simpler term, more specifically suggesting qualities so much a part of one's nature as to seem to have been born in or with one *[inborn* modesty*]*; **inbred** refers to qualities that are deeply ingrained by breeding *[*an *inbred* love of learning*]*; **congenital** implies existence at or from one's birth, specifically as a result of prenatal environment *[congenital* blindness*]*; **hereditary** implies acquirement of characteristics by transmission genetically from parents or ancestors *[hereditary* blondness*]*

in·ner (in′ər) ***adj.*** ⟦ME < OE *innerra*, compar. of *inne*, within, IN^1⟧ **1** located within or farther within; interior; internal *[inner* organs*]* **2** of the mind or spirit *[inner* peace*]* **3** more intimate, central, or secret *[inner* emotions*]*

inner circle a small, exclusive group of people who control or influence customs, opinion, etc.

☆**inner city** the sections of a large city in or near its center, esp. when crowded or blighted

☆**in·ner-di·rect·ed** (in′ər də rek′tid) ***adj.*** guided by or concerned with goals or ideals determined by oneself rather than by others

inner ear the part of the ear in the temporal bone consisting of the semicircular canals, vestibule, and cochlea

Inner Hebrides *see* HEBRIDES

Inner Light in Quaker belief, the presence of God in each human soul, serving as a guiding influence

inner man one's spiritual being; mind or soul

Inner Mongolia autonomous region of NE China, south & southeast of Mongolia: 454,635 sq mi (1,177,500 sq km); cap. Hohhot: in full **Inner Mongolian Autonomous Region**

in·ner·most (in′ər mōst′) ***adj.*** ⟦< INMOST, infl. by INNER⟧ **1** located farthest within **2** most intimate or secret

inner planet any of the four planets with an orbit inside the asteroid belt; Mercury, Venus, Earth, or Mars

in·ner-ring (in′ər riŋ′) ***adj.*** designating or of a suburb that borders on a large city, often characterized as being older, less affluent, etc. than suburbs located farther from the center of the city

in·ner·sole (in′ər sōl′) ***n.*** INSOLE

☆**inner space** any space deep within, as contrasted with outer space; specif., *a)* the spiritual world within a person *b)* the sea or depths of the sea

in·ner·spring mattress (in′ər spriŋ′) a mattress with built-in coil springs

Inner Temple *see* INNS OF COURT

inner tube a rubber tube used, esp. formerly, in a pneumatic tire: see TIRE^2

in·ner·vate (i nʉr′vāt′, in′ər vāt′) ***vt.* -vat′ed, -vat′ing** ⟦< IN-^{1} + NERVE + -ATE^1⟧ *Med.* **1** to supply (a part of the body) with nerves **2** to stimulate (a nerve, muscle, etc.) to movement or action —**in′ner·va′tion *n.***

In·ness (in′is), **George** 1825-94; U.S. painter

in·ning (in′iŋ) ***n.*** ⟦IN^1 + -ING⟧ **1** *[pl. for Cricket, with sing. or pl. v.] Baseball, Cricket a)* the period of play in which a team has a turn at bat, completed in baseball by three outs and in cricket by ten outs *b)* a numbered round of play in which both teams have a turn at bat: a baseball game normally consists of nine innings, and a cricket game of two innings **2** *[often pl.]* [Informal] the period of or opportunity for action, expression, exercise of authority, etc. *[*the election gave him his *innings]*

inn·keep·er (in′kēp′ər) ***n.*** the proprietor or manager of an inn: a somewhat dated term

in·no·cence (in′ə səns) ***n.*** ⟦OFr < L *innocentia*⟧ **1** the quality or state of being innocent; specif., *a)* freedom from sin or moral wrong *b)* freedom from legal guilt *c)* freedom from guile or cunning; simplicity *d)* lack of sophistication; naiveté *e)* ignorance or inexperience, specif. with regard to sex ☆**2** BLUET — [Archaic] **in′no·cen·cy** (-sən sē) ***n.***

in·no·cent (in′ə sənt) ***adj.*** ⟦OFr < L *innocens* < *in-*, not + *nocens*, prp. of *nocere*, to do wrong to: see NECRO-⟧ **1** free from sin, evil, or guilt; specif., *a)* doing or thinking nothing morally wrong; pure *b)* not guilty of a specific crime or offense; guiltless *c)* free from harmful intent or effect *[*an *innocent* mistake*]* *d)* not malignant; benign *[*an *innocent* tumor*]* **2** *a)* knowing no evil *b)* without guile or cunning; artless; simple *c)* naive *d)* ignorant or inexperienced, specif. with regard to sex **3** totally lacking: with *of [innocent* of adornment*]* —***n.*** **1** a person knowing no evil or sin, such as a child **2** a very naive or simple-minded person —**the (Holy) Innocents** *Bible* those children of Bethlehem slaughtered by King Herod: Matt. 2:16 —**in′no·cent·ly *adv.***

In·no·cent (in′ə sənt) **1** Saint **Innocent I** (died A.D. 417); pope (401-417): his day is July 28 **2 Innocent II** (born *Gregorio Papareschi*) died 1143; pope (1130-43) **3 Innocent III** (born *Lotario de' Conti de' Segni*) 1161?-1216; pope (1198-1216) **4 Innocent IV** (born *Sinibaldo de' Fieschi*) died 1254; pope (1243-54) **5 Innocent XI** (born *Benedetto Odeschalchi*) 1611-89; pope (1676-89)

in·noc·u·ous (i näk′yoo əs) ***adj.*** ⟦L *innocuus* < *in-*, not + *nocuus*, harmful < *nocere*, to harm, injure: see NECRO-⟧ **1** that does not injure or harm; harmless *[*an *innocuous* insect*]* **2** not controversial, offensive, or stimulating; dull and uninspiring *[*an *innocuous* speech*]* —**in·noc′u·ous·ly *adv.*** —**in·noc′u·ous·ness *n.***

in·nom·i·nate (i näm′ə nit) ***adj.*** ⟦LL *innominatus*: see IN-^{2} & NOMINATE⟧ **1** not named; anonymous **2** having no specific name

innominate bone either of the two large, irregular bones that, together with the sacrum and coccyx, make up the pelvis: it is formed of three bones, the ilium, ischium, and pubis, which become fused in the adult

in·no·vate (in′ə vāt′, in′ō-) ***vi.* -vat′ed, -vat′ing** ⟦< L *innovatus*, pp. of *innovare*, to renew < *in-*, in + *novare*, to renew, alter < *novus*, NEW⟧ to introduce new methods, devices, etc. —***vt.*** to bring in as an innovation —**in′no·va′tive *adj.*, in·no·va·to·ry** (in′ə və tôr′ē) —**in′no·va′tor *n.***

in·no·va·tion (in′ə vā′shən, in′ō-) ***n.*** ⟦LL *innovatio*⟧ **1** the act or process of innovating **2** something newly introduced; new method, custom, device, etc. —**in′no·va′tion·al *adj.***

in·nox·ious (i näk′shəs) ***adj.*** ⟦L *innoxius*⟧ not noxious; harmless; innocuous

Inns·bruck (inz′brook′; *Ger* ins′brook′) city in the Tirol region, W Austria, on the Inn River

Inns of Court ⟦see INN, 3⟧ **1** the four legal societies in London having the exclusive right to admit persons to practice at the bar **2** the four groups of buildings (*Gray's Inn, Lincoln's Inn, Inner Temple,* and *Middle Temple*) belonging to these societies

in·nu·en·do (in′yoo en′dō) ***n.***, *pl.* **-does** or **-dos** ⟦L, by nodding to, abl. of ger. of *innuere*, to nod to, hint < *in-*, in + *-nuere*, to nod < IE base *neu-, to jerk, beckon, nod > Sans *návatē*, (he) turns, L *numen*, a nod⟧ **1** *Law* explanatory material, set forth in the complaint in an action for libel or slander, explaining the expressions alleged to be libelous or slanderous **2** an indirect remark, gesture, or reference, usually implying something derogatory; insinuation

in·nu·mer·a·ble (i no͞o′mer ə bəl, -nyo͞o′-) ***adj.*** ⟦ME < L *innumerabilis:* see IN-[2] & NUMERABLE⟧ too numerous to be counted; countless: often used hyperbolically: also [Old Poet.] **in·nu′mer·ous —in·nu′mer·a·bil′i·ty *n.*, in·nu′mer·a·ble·ness —in·nu′mer·a·bly *adv.***

in·nu·mer·ate (-mər it) ***adj.*** [Chiefly Brit.] not numerate; lacking the knowledge needed to deal with scientific, esp. mathematical, concepts **—in·nu′mer·a·cy** (-mər ə sē) ***n.***

in·ob·serv·ance (in′əb zʉr′vəns) ***n.*** **1** lack of attention; disregard **2** failure to observe a custom, rule, etc. **—in′ob·serv′ant *adj.***

in·oc·u·la·ble (i näk′yə lə bəl) ***adj.*** ⟦< INOCULATE + -ABLE⟧ **1** that can be communicated by inoculation **2** that can be infected with a disease by inoculation **3** that may be used in inoculation **—in·oc′u·la·bil′i·ty *n.***

in·oc·u·lant (i näk′yə lənt) ***n.*** INOCULUM

in·oc·u·late (i näk′yə lāt′) ***vt.*** **-lat′ed, -lat′ing** ⟦ME *enoculaten* < L *inoculatus*, pp. of *inoculare*, to engraft a bud in another plant < *in-*, in + *oculus*, a bud, EYE⟧ **1** *a)* to inject a serum, vaccine, etc. into (a living organism), esp. in order to create immunity *b)* to communicate (a disease) in this way **2** to put or implant microorganisms into (soil, a culture medium, etc.) to develop a culture, stimulate growth, fix nitrogen, etc. **3** to introduce ideas, etc. into the mind of; imbue **—in·oc′u·la′tive** (-lāt′iv; -lə tiv) ***adj.* —in·oc′u·la′tor *n.***

in·oc·u·la·tion (i näk′yə lā′shən) ***n.*** ⟦L *inoculatio*⟧ the act or process of inoculating; esp., *a)* the injection of a disease agent into an animal or plant, usually to cause a mild form of the disease and build up immunity to it *b)* the putting of bacteria, serum, etc. into soil, a culture medium, etc.

in·oc·u·lum (i näk′yo͞o ləm, -yə-) ***n.***, *pl.* **-u·la** or **-lums** ⟦ModL⟧ material used in an inoculation, as bacteria; inoculant

in·o·dor·ous (in ō′dər əs) ***adj.*** not odorous; odorless

in·of·fen·sive (in′ə fen′siv) ***adj.*** not offensive; not objectionable; causing no harm, discomfort, or annoyance **—in′of·fen′sive·ly *adv.* —in′of·fen′sive·ness *n.***

in·of·fi·cious (in′ə fish′əs) ***adj.*** ⟦L *inofficiosus*, undutiful: see IN-[2] & OFFICIOUS⟧ *Law* showing neglect of moral duty: said esp. of a will that unreasonably deprives an heir of a just inheritance

I·nö·nü (ē nö nü′), **Is·met** (is met′) 1884-1973; Turk. statesman: president of Turkey (1938-50): prime minister (1923-24; 1925-37; 1961-65)

in·op·er·a·ble (in äp′ər ə bəl) ***adj.*** not operable; specif., *a)* that will not practicably allow of surgical operation *[an inoperable cancer]* *b)* inoperative

in·op·er·a·tive (in äp′ər ə tiv, -ər āt′iv) ***adj.*** not operative; not working; not functioning; without effect

in·o·per·cu·late (in′ō pʉr′kyo͞o lit) ***adj.*** ⟦IN-[2] + OPERCULATE⟧ *Bot.* lacking a definite, separable lid, as some spore cases

in·op·por·tune (in äp′ər to͞on′, -tyo͞on′) ***adj.*** ⟦L *inopportunus*⟧ not opportune; coming or happening at a poor time; not appropriate **—in·op′por·tune′ly *adv.* —in·op′por·tune′ness *n.***

in·or·di·nate (in ôrd′'n it) ***adj.*** ⟦ME *inordinat* < L *inordinatus* < *in-*, IN-[2] + *ordinatus*, pp. of *ordinare*, to arrange: see ORDAIN⟧ **1** disordered; not regulated **2** lacking restraint or moderation; too great or too many; immoderate **—*SYN.*** EXCESSIVE **—in·or′di·nate·ly *adv.* —in·or′di·nate·ness *n.***

in·or·gan·ic (in′ôr gan′ik) ***adj.*** not organic; specif., *a)* designating or composed of matter that is not animal or vegetable; not having the organized structure of living things *b)* lacking design, relation, and coordination of parts *c)* designating or of any chemical compound not classified as organic: most inorganic compounds do not contain carbon and are derived from mineral sources *d)* designating or of the branch of chemistry dealing with these compounds **—in′or·gan′i·cal·ly *adv.***

in·os·cu·late (in äs′kyo͞o lāt′) ***vt., vi.*** **-lat′ed, -lat′ing** ⟦IN-[1] + OSCULATE⟧ **1** *a)* to join together by openings at the ends (said of arteries, ducts, etc.) *b)* to intertwine (said of vines, etc.) **2** to join, blend, or unite intimately **—in·os′cu·la′tion *n.***

in·o·si·tol (i nō′sə tôl′, -tōl′, -täl′) ***n.*** ⟦< Gr *is* (gen. *inos*), muscle, fiber, strength (see INION) + -IT(E) + -OL[1]⟧ a sweet crystalline alcohol, $C_6H_6(OH)_6$, existing in nine isomeric forms and found in both plant and animal tissues, esp. the form found in the vitamin B complex that may have some effect on cholesterol metabolism: also **in·o·site** (in′ō sīt′)

in·pa·tient (in′pā′shənt) ***n.*** a patient who is lodged and fed in a hospital, clinic, etc. while receiving treatment **—*adj.*** of or serving inpatients

in per·pe·tu·um (in′ pʉr pet′yo͞o əm) ⟦L⟧ forever

in per·so·nam (in′ pər sō′nəm) ⟦L, lit., against the person⟧ *Law* designating an action or judgment against a person, as distinguished from one against a thing, as property *(in rem)*

in pet·to (ēn pet′tō) ⟦It, in the breast⟧ *R.C.Ch.* secretly; not revealed: said of cardinals appointed by the pope but not named in consistory

in-phase (in′fāz′) ***adj.*** *Elec., Physics* being of the same phase

in pos·se (in pä′sē, -pä′sā) ⟦L⟧ in possibility; only potentially: opposed to IN ESSE

in pro·pri·a per·so·na (in prō′prē ə pər sō′nə) ⟦L⟧ in one's own person or right

in·put (in′po͝ot′) ***n.*** **1** the act of putting in **2** what is put in; specif., *a)* the amount of money, material, effort, etc. put into a project or process; investment *b)* electric current, voltage, or power put into a circuit, machine, etc. *c)* data or programs entered or to be entered into a computer for processing *d)* any offered information, as an opinion or advice **3** a terminal connection for receiving electric power or signals **—*vt.* -put′** or **-put′ted, -put′ting** to enter (data) into a computer **—*adj.*** of or relating to computer input **—in′put′ter *n.***

in·quest (in′kwest′) ***n.*** ⟦ME *enqueste* < OFr < VL **inquaesita*, fem. pp. of **inquaerere:* see INQUIRE⟧ **1** a judicial inquiry, as a coroner's investigation of a death **2** the jury or group holding such an inquiry **3** the verdict of such an inquiry

in·qui·e·tude (in kwī′ə to͞od′, -tyo͞od′) ***n.*** ⟦ME < MFr *inquiétude* < LL *inquietudo* < L *inquietus*, restless: see IN-[2] & QUIET⟧ restlessness; uneasiness

in·qui·line (in′kwə līn′, -lin) ***n.*** ⟦L *inquilinus*, inhabitant < *in-*, in + stem of *colere*, to till, dwell: see CULT⟧ an animal, usually an insect, that lives in the nest or abode of another, with or without harm to the host: cf. COMMENSAL **—in′qui·lin·ism′** (-lin iz′əm) ***n.***

in·quire (in kwīr′) ***vi.*** **-quired′, -quir′ing** ⟦ME *enqueren* < OFr *enquerre* < VL **inquaerere*, for L *inquirere* < *in-*, into + *quaerere*, to seek⟧ **1** to seek information; ask a question or questions **2** to carry out an examination or investigation: usually with *into* **—*vt.*** to seek information about *[to inquire the way]* **—*SYN.*** ASK **—inquire after** to pay respects by asking about the health of **—inquire for 1** to ask to see (someone) **2** to try to get by asking **—in·quir′er *n.* —in·quir′ing·ly *adv.***

in·quir·y (in′kwər ē, in kwīr′ē, in′kwīr′ē) ***n.***, *pl.* **-quir·ies** ⟦earlier *enquery* < ME *enquere*⟧ **1** the act of inquiring **2** an investigation or examination **3** a question; query

in·qui·si·tion (in′kwə zish′ən) ***n.*** ⟦ME *inquicisioun* < OFr *inquisition* < L *inquisitio* < *inquisitus*, pp. of *inquirere*⟧ **1** the act of inquiring; investigation **2** [**I-**] [Historical] *a)* a general tribunal established by the Roman Catholic Church in the 13th cent. for the discovery and suppression of heresy and the punishment of heretics; often, specif., SPANISH INQUISITION *b)* the activities of this tribunal **3** *a)* any harsh or arbitrary suppression or punishment of dissidents or nonconformists *b)* any severe or intensive questioning **4** *Law* *a)* an inquest or any judicial inquiry *b)* the written finding of such an inquiry **—in′qui·si′tion·al *adj.***

in·qui·si·tion·ist (-ist) ***n.*** INQUISITOR

in·quis·i·tive (in kwiz′ə tiv) ***adj.*** ⟦ME *enquesitif* < OFr *inquisitif* < LL *inquisitivus* < L *inquisitus*, pp. of *inquirere:* see INQUIRE⟧ **1** inclined to ask many questions or seek information; eager to learn **2** asking more questions than is necessary or proper; prying **—*SYN.*** CURIOUS **—in·quis′i·tive·ly *adv.* —in·quis′i·tive·ness *n.***

in·quis·i·tor (in kwiz′ə tər) ***n.*** ⟦OFr *inquisiteur* < L *inquisitor* < *inquisitus*, pp.: see INQUIRE⟧ **1** an official whose work is examining, or making an inquisition **2** any harsh or prying questioner **3** [**I-**] [Historical] an official of the Inquisition

in·quis·i·to·ri·al (in kwiz′ə tôr′ē əl) ***adj.*** ⟦< ML *inquisitorius*⟧ **1** of or like an inquisitor or inquisition **2** inquisitive; prying **—in·quis′i·to′ri·al·ly *adv.***

in re (in rē′, in rā′) ⟦L⟧ in the matter (of); concerning

in rem (in rem′) ⟦L, lit., against the thing⟧ *Law* designating an action or judgment against a thing, as property, as distinguished from one against a person *(in personam)*

-in-res·i·dence (in rez′i dəns) *combining form* appointed to work at, and usually residing at, a given institution, as a college, for a certain period *[the English Department's poet-in-residence]*

INRI *abbrev.* ⟦L *I(esus) N(azarenus,) R(ex) I(udaeorum)*⟧ *Bible* Jesus of Nazareth, King of the Jews: the inscription placed above Christ's head during the crucifixion: cf. Luke 23:38

in·road (in′rōd′) ***n.*** ⟦IN-[1] + ROAD (in obs. sense of "riding")⟧ **1** a sudden invasion or raid **2** any advance; esp., an intrusion or encroachment: *usually used in pl.*

in·rush (in′rush′) ***n.*** a rushing in; inflow; influx

ins *abbrev.* **1** inches **2** insulated **3** insurance

INS *abbrev.* Immigration and Naturalization Service

in sae·cu·la sae·cu·lo·rum (in sä′ko͞o lä′ sä′ko͞o lō ro͝om′) ⟦L, into ages of ages⟧ for ever and ever; for eternity

in·sal·i·va·tion (in sal′ə vā′shən) ***n.*** ⟦IN-[1] + SALIVATION⟧ the mixing of food with saliva in chewing

in·sa·lu·bri·ous (in′sə lo͞o′brē əs) ***adj.*** ⟦< L *insalubris* + -OUS⟧ not salubrious; not healthful; unwholesome **—in′sa·lu′bri·ty** (-brə tē) ***n.***

in·sane (in sān′) ***adj.*** ⟦L *insanus*⟧ **1** not sane; mentally ill or deranged; demented; mad: now a nontechnical term except in legal usage: see INSANITY ☆**2** of or for insane people *[an insane asylum]* **3** [Informal] very foolish, excessive, fantastic, etc. **—in·sane′ly *adv.***

in·san·i·tar·y (in san′ə ter′ē) ***adj.*** UNSANITARY

in·san·i·ty (in san′ə tē) ***n.***, *pl.* **-ties** ⟦L *insanitas* < *insanus*⟧ **1** the state of being insane; mental illness or derangement: no longer a technical term in medicine **2** *Law* any form or degree of mental derangement or unsoundness of mind, permanent or temporary, that makes a person incapable of what is regarded legally as normal, rational conduct or judgment **3** great folly; extreme senselessness

***SYN.*—insanity**, current in popular and legal language but not used technically in medicine (see definition above), implies mental derangement in one who formerly had mental health; **lunacy** specifically suggests periodic spells of insanity, but is now most commonly used in its extended sense of extreme folly; **dementia** is the general term for an acquired mental disorder, now generally one of organic origin, as distinguished from *amentia* (congenital mental deficiency); **psychosis** is the psychiatric term for any of various specialized mental disorders, functional or organic, in which the personality is seriously disorganized —*ANT.* **sanity**

in·sa·tia·ble (in sā′shə bəl, -shē ə-) ***adj.*** ⟦see IN-² & SATIATE⟧ constantly wanting more; that cannot be satisfied or appeased —**in·sa′tia·bil′i·ty** ***n.***, **in·sa′tia·ble·ness** —**in·sa′tia·bly** ***adv.***

in·sa·tiate (in sā′shət; -shē ət, -āt′) ***adj.*** ⟦L *insatiatus*⟧ never satisfied; insatiable —**in·sa′tiate·ly** ***adv.*** —**in·sa′tiate·ness** ***n.***

in·scape (in′skāp′) ***n.*** ⟦coined by G. M. HOPKINS < ? IN¹ (*adv.*) + *scape* (< LANDSCAPE)⟧ the essential quality of a thing, place, person, etc., esp. as expressed in an artistic work

in·scribe (in skrīb′) ***vt.*** **-scribed′**, **-scrib′ing** ⟦L *inscribere*: see IN-¹ & SCRIBE⟧ **1** *a)* to write, mark, or engrave (words, symbols, etc.) on some surface *b)* to write on, mark, or engrave (a surface) **2** to add the name of (someone) to a list; enroll **3** *a)* to dedicate (a book, song, etc.) briefly and informally *b)* to write a short, signed message in (a book, etc. one is presenting as a gift) **4** to fix or impress deeply or lastingly in the mind, memory, etc. **5** *Geom.* to draw (a figure) inside another figure so that their boundaries touch at as many points as possible —**in·scrib′er** ***n.***

in·scrip·tion (in skrip′shən) ***n.*** ⟦ME *inscripcioun* < L *inscriptio* < *inscriptus*, pp. of *inscribere*⟧ **1** the act of inscribing **2** something inscribed or engraved, as on a coin or monument **3** *a)* a brief or informal dedication in a book, etc. *b)* a short, signed message written in a book, etc. one is presenting as a gift —**in·scrip′tive** ***adj.***, **in·scrip′tion·al**

in·scru·ta·ble (in skrōōt′ə bəl) ***adj.*** ⟦ME < LL(Ec) *inscrutabilis* < L *in-*, not + *scrutari*, to search carefully, examine: see SCRUTINY⟧ that cannot be easily understood; completely obscure or mysterious; unfathomable; enigmatic —*SYN.* MYSTERIOUS —**in·scru′ta·bil′i·ty** ***n.*** —**in·scru′ta·bly** ***adv.***

in·seam (in′sēm′) ***n.*** an inner seam; specif., either seam extending down from the crotch seam to the bottom of a trouser leg

in·sect (in′sekt′) ***n.*** ⟦< L *insectum (animale)*, lit., notched (animal), neut. of pp. of *insecare*, to cut into < *in-*, in + *secare*, to cut (see SAW²): from the segmented bodies: cf. ENTOMO-⟧ **1** any of a large class (Insecta) of small arthropod animals, including beetles, bees, flies, wasps, and mosquitoes, characterized in the adult state by division of the body into head, thorax, and abdomen, by three pairs of legs on the thorax, and, usually, by two pairs of membranous wings **2** popularly, any small arthropod, usually wingless, including spiders, centipedes, pill bugs, and mites **3** an unimportant or contemptible person

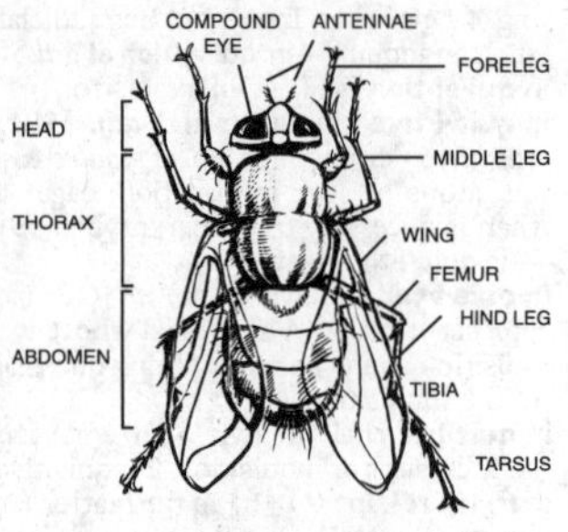

insect (housefly)

in·sec·tar·i·um (in′sek ter′ē əm) ***n.***, *pl.* **-i·a** (-ə) ⟦ModL⟧ a place where insects are raised, esp. for study: also **in·sec·ta·ry** (in sek′tə rē, in′sek′-; in′sek ter′ē) *pl.* **-ta·ries**

in·sec·ti·cide (in sek′tə sīd′) ***n.*** ⟦< INSECT + -CIDE⟧ any substance used to kill insects —**in·sec′ti·ci′dal** ***adj.***

☆**in·sec·ti·fuge** (in sek′tə fyōōj′) ***n.*** any substance used to repel or drive away insects

in·sec·tile (in sek′təl) ***adj.*** **1** of or like an insect: also **in·sec·ti·val** (in′sek tī′vəl) **2** consisting of insects

in·sec·ti·vore (in sek′tə vôr′) ***n.*** ⟦Fr < ModL *insectivorus*: see fol.⟧ **1** any of an order (Insectivora) of generally small, primitive mammals, as moles, shrews, or hedgehogs, that are active mainly at night and that feed principally on insects **2** any animal or plant that feeds on insects

in·sec·tiv·o·rous (in′sek tiv′ə rəs) ***adj.*** ⟦ModL *insectivorus*: see INSECT & -VOROUS⟧ feeding chiefly on insects

in·se·cure (in′si kyoor′) ***adj.*** ⟦ML *insecurus*⟧ not secure; specif., *a)* not safe from danger *b)* not confident; filled with anxieties; apprehensive *c)* not firm or dependable; unreliable —**in′se·cure′ly** ***adv.*** —**in′se·cu′ri·ty** ***n.***, *pl.* **-ties**

in·sel·berg (in′səl burg′, -zəl-) ***n.***, *pl.* **-bergs′** or **-ber′ge** (-bur′gə) ⟦Ger < *insel*, island + *berg*, mountain⟧ an isolated rocky hill or mountain rising above a peneplain in a hot, dry region: cf. MONADNOCK

in·sem·i·nate (in sem′ə nāt′) ***vt.*** **-nat′ed**, **-nat′ing** ⟦< L *inseminatus*, pp. of *inseminare*, to sow in < *in-*, in + *seminare*, to sow < *semen*, seed: see SEMEN⟧ **1** [Archaic] to sow seeds in **2** to impregnate by sexual intercourse or by artificially injecting semen **3** to implant (ideas, etc.) in (the mind, etc.) —**in·sem′i·na′tion** ***n.*** —**in·sem′i·na·tor** ***n.***

in·sen·sate (in sen′sāt′, -sit) ***adj.*** ⟦LL(Ec) *insensatus*, irrational < L *in-*, IN-² + *sensatus*, gifted with sense < *sensus*, SENSE⟧ **1** lacking sensation; not feeling, or not capable of feeling, sensation; inanimate **2** without sense or reason; foolish; stupid **3** lacking sensibility; without regard or feeling for others; cold; insensitive —**in·sen′sate′ly** ***adv.*** —**in·sen′sate′ness** ***n.***

in·sen·si·ble (in sen′sə bəl) ***adj.*** ⟦OFr < L *insensibilis*: see IN-² & SENSIBLE⟧ **1** lacking sensation; not having the power to perceive with the senses **2** having lost sensation; unconscious **3** not recognizing or realizing; unaware; indifferent **4** not responsive emotionally; without feeling **5** so small, slight, or gradual as to be virtually imperceptible **6** not intelligible; without meaning: now chiefly in legal use **7** [Obs.] senseless; stupid —**in·sen′si·bil′i·ty** ***n.*** —**in·sen′si·bly** ***adv.***

in·sen·si·tive (in sen′sə tiv) ***adj.*** **1** not sensitive; esp., incapable of being impressed, influenced, or affected; having little or no reaction (*to*) **2** having or showing a lack of concern for the feelings of others; tactless —**in·sen′si·tive·ly** ***adv.*** —**in·sen′si·tiv′i·ty** ***n.***, **in·sen′si·tive·ness**

in·sen·tient (in sen′shənt, -shē ənt) ***adj.*** not sentient; without life, consciousness, or perception —**in·sen′tience** ***n.***

in·sep·a·ra·ble (in sep′ə rə bəl, -sep′rə-) ***adj.*** not separable; that cannot be separated or parted: often used hyperbolically [*inseparable* friends] —***n.*** inseparable persons or things —**in·sep′a·ra·bil′i·ty** ***n.***, **in·sep′a·ra·ble·ness** —**in·sep′a·ra·bly** ***adv.***

in·sert (in surt′; *for n.* in′surt′) ***vt.*** ⟦< L *insertus*, pp. of *inserere* < *in-*, in + *serere*, to join⟧ to put or fit (something) into something else; put in; introduce —***n.*** anything inserted or for insertion; esp., an extra leaf or section inserted, as in a publication

in·sert·ed (in surt′id) ***adj.*** *Biol.* joined by natural growth

in·ser·tion (in sur′shən) ***n.*** ⟦L *insertio*⟧ **1** an inserting or being inserted **2** something inserted; specif., *a)* a piece of lace or embroidery that can be set into a piece of cloth for ornamentation *b)* a single placement of an advertisement, as in a newspaper **3** *Anat.* the point of attachment of a muscle to the part that it moves

☆**in-ser·vice** (in′sur′vis) ***adj.*** **1** designating or of training, as through special courses, workshops, etc., given to employees in connection with their work **2** while employed [an *in-service* withdrawal from 401k savings]

in·ses·so·ri·al (in′se sôr′ē əl) ***adj.*** ⟦< ModL *Insessores*, pl., perching birds < L *insessor*, occupant, lit., one who sits in or on < *insidere* (see INSIDIOUS) + -IAL⟧ *Ornithology* **1** adapted for perching, as a bird's foot or claw **2** perching frequently or habitually

in·set (in set′, in′set′; *for n.* in′set′) ***vt.*** **-set′**, **-set′ting** ⟦ME *insetten* < OE *insettan*, to set in, appoint < *in-*, in + *settan*, to SET⟧ to set into something; insert —***n.*** something set in; insert; specif., *a)* a smaller picture or map set within the border of a larger one *b)* a piece of material set into a garment

in·shal·lah (in′shä lä′, in shä′lä) ***interj.*** ⟦Ar⟧ if Allah is willing; please God

in·shore (in′shôr′, in shôr′) ***adv., adj.*** **1** in toward the shore **2** near the shore —**inshore of** nearer than (something else) to the shore

in·side (in′sīd′, in′sīd′, in sīd′) ***n.*** **1** the part lying within; inner side, surface, or part; interior **2** the part closest to something specified or implied, as the part of a sidewalk closest to the buildings **3** [*pl.*] [Informal] the internal organs of the body, as the stomach and intestines —***adj.*** **1** on or in the inside; internal **2** of or suited for the inside **3** working or used indoors; indoor ☆**4** known only to insiders; secret or private [the *inside* story] **5** *Baseball* passing between home plate and the batter: said of a pitch —***adv.*** **1** on or to the inside; within **2** indoors —***prep.*** **1** in or to the inside or inner part of **2** within the limits of [*inside* an hour] —☆**inside of** in less than (a specified time or distance); within the space of —**inside out** **1** with the inside or the inner surface on the outside; reversed [a sweater turned *inside out*] **2** [Informal] thoroughly; completely [to know a subject *inside out*] —**on the inside** ☆**1** in a position allowing access to secret information, special advantage or favor, etc. **2** in one's inner thoughts or feelings

inside job [Informal] a crime committed by, or with the aid of, a person employed or trusted by the victim

☆**Inside Passage** protected sea route along the W coast of North America, from Seattle, Wash., to the N part of the Alas. panhandle: the route uses channels and straits between islands and the mainland: *c.* 950 mi (1,529 km) long

in·sid·er (in′sīd′ər, in sīd′ər) ***n.*** **1** a person inside a given place or group **2** a person having or likely to have secret or confidential information

insider trading the buying or selling of a company's stock by one who has access to information not made public: trading based on such information is typically illegal

☆**inside track** **1** the inner, shorter way around an oval racetrack **2** [Informal] a favorable position or advantage

in·sid·i·ous (in sid′ē əs) ***adj.*** ⟦L *insidiosus* < *insidiae*, an ambush, plot < *insidere*, to sit in or on, lie in wait for < *in-*, in + *sedere*, to SIT⟧ **1** characterized by treachery or slyness; crafty; wily **2** working harm in a slow or subtle manner; hence, more dangerous than seems evident [an *insidious* disease] —**in·sid′i·ous·ly** ***adv.*** —**in·sid′i·ous·ness** ***n.***

in·sight (in′sīt′) ***n.*** ⟦ME *insiht*: see IN-¹ & SIGHT⟧ **1** the ability to see and understand clearly the inner nature of things, esp. by intuition **2** a clear understanding of the inner nature of some specific thing **3** *a)* *Psychol.* awareness of one's own mental attitudes and behavior *b)* *Psychiatry* recognition of one's own mental disorder

in·sight·ful (in sīt′fəl; in′sīt′-) ***adj.*** having or showing insight —**in·sight′ful·ly** ***adv.***

in·sig·ni·a (in sig′nē ə) ***pl.n.***, *sing.* **in·sig′ne** (-nē) ⟦L, pl. of *insigne*, neut. of *insignis*, distinguished by a mark < *in-*, in + *signum*, a mark, SIGN⟧ badges, emblems, or other distinguishing marks, as of rank, membership, etc. —*sing.n.*, *pl.* **in·sig′ni·as** such a badge, emblem, etc.

in·sig·nif·i·cant (in′sig nif′i kənt) ***adj.*** ⟦IN-² + SIGNIFICANT⟧ **1** having little or no meaning **2** having little or no importance; trivial **3** small; unimposing **4** low in position, character, etc.; mean —**in′sig·nif′i·cance** ***n.***, **in′sig·nif′i·can·cy** —**in′sig·nif′i·cant·ly** ***adv.***

in·sin·cere (in′sin sir′) ***adj.*** ⟦L *insincerus*⟧ not sincere; deceptive or hypocritical; not to be trusted —**in′sin·cere′ly** ***adv.***

in·sin·cer·i·ty (in′sin ser′ə tē) *n.* 1 the quality of being insincere 2 *pl.* **-ties** an insincere act, remark, etc.

in·sin·u·ate (in sin′yo͞o āt′) *vt.* **-at′ed, -at′ing** ⟦< L *insinuatus*, pp. of *insinuare*, to introduce by windings and turnings, insinuate < *in-*, in + *sinus*, curved surface⟧ 1 to introduce or work into gradually, indirectly, and artfully [to *insinuate* oneself into another's favor] 2 to hint or suggest indirectly; imply —*vi.* to make insinuations —*SYN.* SUGGEST —**in·sin′u·at′ing·ly** *adv.* —**in·sin′u·a′tive** *adj.* —**in·sin′u·a′tor** *n.*

in·sin·u·a·tion (in sin′yo͞o ā′shən) *n.* ⟦L *insinuatio*⟧ 1 the act of insinuating 2 something insinuated; specif., *a)* a sly hint or suggestion, esp. against someone *b)* action or remark intended to win favor

in·sip·id (in sip′id) *adj.* ⟦< Fr & LL: Fr *insipide* < LL *insipidus* < L *in-*, not + *sapidus*, savory < *sapere*, to taste: see SAPIENT⟧ 1 without flavor; tasteless 2 not exciting or interesting; dull; lifeless —**in′si·pid′i·ty** *n.*, *pl.* **-ties** —**in·sip′id·ly** *adv.* —**in·sip′id·ness** *n.*

SYN.—**insipid** implies a lack of taste or flavor and is, hence, figuratively applied to anything that is lifeless, dull, etc. [*insipid* table talk]; **vapid** and **flat** apply to that which once had, but has since lost, freshness, sharpness, tang, zest, etc. [the *vapid*, or *flat*, epigrams that had once so delighted him]; **banal** is used of that which is so trite or hackneyed as to seem highly vapid or flat [her *banal* compliments] —*ANT.* **zestful, spicy, pungent**

in·sist (in sist′) *vi.* ⟦MFr *insister* < L *insistere*, to stand on, pursue diligently, persist < *in-*, in, on + *sistere*, to stand, redupl. of *stare*, STAND⟧ to take and maintain a stand or make a firm demand: often with *on* or *upon* —*vt.* 1 to demand strongly 2 to declare firmly or persistently —**in·sist′er** *n.* —**in·sist′ing·ly** *adv.*

in·sist·ence (in sis′təns) *n.* 1 the quality of being insistent 2 the act or an instance of insisting Also **in·sist′en·cy**

in·sist·ent (-tənt) *adj.* ⟦L *insistens*⟧ 1 insisting or demanding; persistent in demands or assertions 2 compelling the attention [an *insistent* rhythm] —**in·sist′ent·ly** *adv.*

in si·tu (in sī′to͞o′, -sit′o͞o′) ⟦L⟧ in position; in its original place

in·snare (in sner′) *vt.* **-snared′, -snar′ing** *var. of* ENSNARE

in·so·bri·e·ty (in′sō brī′ə tē, -sə-) *n.* lack of sobriety; intemperance, esp. in drinking

in·so·far (in′sō fär′) *adv.* to such a degree or extent; in so far: usually with *as* [*insofar* as one can tell]

in·so·late (in′sō lāt′) *vt.* **-lat′ed, -lat′ing** ⟦< L *insolatus*, pp. of *insolare*, to expose to the sun < *in-*, in + *sol*, the SUN[1]⟧ to expose to the rays of the sun so as to dry, bleach, etc.

in·so·la·tion (in′sō lā′shən) *n.* ⟦L *insolatio*⟧ 1 the act or an instance of insolating 2 the treatment of disease by exposure to the sun's rays 3 SUNSTROKE 4 *Meteorol.* *a)* radiation from the sun received by a surface, esp. the earth's surface *b)* the rate of such radiation per unit of surface

in·sole (in′sōl′) *n.* 1 the inside sole of a shoe 2 an extra, removable inside sole put in for comfort

in·so·lent (in′sə lənt) *adj.* ⟦ME < L *insolens* < *in-*, IN-[2] + *solens*, prp. of *solere*, to be accustomed⟧ 1 boldly disrespectful in speech or behavior; impertinent; impudent 2 [Now Rare] arrogantly contemptuous; overbearing —*SYN.* IMPERTINENT, PROUD —**in′so·lence** *n.* —**in′so·lent·ly** *adv.*

in·sol·u·ble (in säl′yə bəl) *adj.* ⟦ME *insolible* < L *insolubilis*⟧ 1 that cannot be solved; unsolvable 2 that cannot be dissolved; not soluble —**in·sol′u·bil′i·ty** *n.*, **in·sol′u·ble·ness** —**in·sol′u·bly** *adv.*

in·solv·a·ble (in säl′və bəl, -sôl′-) *adj.* INSOLUBLE (sense 1)

in·sol·ven·cy (in säl′vən sē, -sôl′-) *n.*, *pl.* **-cies** the state or an instance of being insolvent; bankruptcy

in·sol·vent (in säl′vənt, -sôl′-) *adj.* 1 not solvent; unable to pay debts as they become due; bankrupt 2 not enough to pay all debts [an *insolvent* inheritance] 3 of insolvents or insolvency —*n.* an insolvent person

in·som·ni·a (in säm′nē ə) *n.* ⟦L < *insomnis*, sleepless < *in-*, IN-[2] + *somnus*, sleep: see SOMNOLENT⟧ abnormally prolonged inability to sleep, esp. when chronic —**in·som′ni·ac′** (-ak′) *n.*, *adj.*

in·so·much (in′sō much′) *adv.* 1 to such a degree or extent; so: with *that* 2 inasmuch (*as*)

in·sou·ci·ant (in so͞o′sē ənt, -shənt) *adj.* ⟦Fr < *in-*, not + *souciant*, prp. of *soucier*, to regard, care < L *sollicitare*: see SOLICIT⟧ casually or smugly indifferent; nonchalant —**in·sou′ci·ance** *n.* —**in·sou′ci·ant·ly** *adv.*

in·soul (in sōl′) *vt.* *var. of* ENSOUL

in·sourc·ing (in′sôrs′iŋ) *n.* ⟦IN-[1] + (OUT)SOURCING⟧ the practice of subcontracting work to another company under the same general ownership

insp *abbrev.* inspector

in·span (in span′) *vt.*, *vi.* **-spanned′, -span′ning** ⟦Afrik < Du *inspannen*: see IN-[1] & SPAN[1]⟧ [South Afr.] to harness or yoke (animals) to a wagon, etc.

in·spect (in spekt′) *vt.* ⟦L *inspectare*, freq. < *inspectus*, pp. of *inspicere*, to look into, examine < *in-*, in, at + *specere*, to look at: see SPY⟧ 1 to look at carefully; examine critically, esp. in order to detect flaws or errors 2 to examine or review (troops, etc.) officially —*SYN.* SCRUTINIZE —**in·spec′tive** *n.*

in·spec·tion (in spek′shən) *n.* ⟦OFr < L *inspectio* < *inspectus*: see prec.⟧ 1 critical examination 2 official examination or review, as of troops

in·spec·tor (in spek′tər) *n.* 1 a person who inspects; official examiner; overseer 2 an officer on a police force, ranking next below a superintendent or police chief 3 a fire department officer in charge of prevention of fires, as in public buildings —**in′spec·to′ri·al** (-tôr′ē əl) *adj.*, **in·spec′to·ral** —**in·spec′tor·ship′** *n.*

in·spec·tor·ate (-it, -āt′) *n.* 1 the position or duties of an inspector 2 inspectors collectively 3 the district supervised by an inspector

inspector general *pl.* **inspectors general** an official, as of a government department, whose responsibility is to investigate and report on that department

in·sphere (in sfir′) *vt.* **-sphered′, -spher′ing** *var. of* ENSPHERE

in·spi·ra·tion (in′spə rā′shən) *n.* ⟦ME *inspiracioun* < OFr *inspiration* < LL *inspiratio*⟧ 1 a breathing in, as of air into the lungs; inhaling 2 an inspiring or being inspired mentally, emotionally, or spiritually 3 *a)* an inspiring influence; any stimulus to creative thought or action *b)* an inspired idea, action, etc. 4 a prompting of something to be written or said 5 *Theol.* a divine influence upon human beings, as that resulting in the writing of the Scriptures

in·spi·ra·tion·al (-shə nəl) *adj.* 1 of or giving inspiration; inspiring 2 produced, influenced, or stimulated by inspiration; inspired —**in′spi·ra′tion·al·ly** *adv.*

in·spir·a·to·ry (in spīr′ə tôr′ē) *adj.* ⟦< L *inspiratus*, pp. of *inspirare* (see fol.) + -ORY⟧ of, for, or characterized by inspiration, or inhalation

in·spire (in spīr′) *vt.* **-spired′, -spir′ing** ⟦ME *inspiren* < OFr *inspirer* < L *inspirare* < *in-*, in, on + *spirare*, to breathe: see SPIRIT⟧ 1 [Obs.] *a)* to breathe or blow upon or into *b)* to infuse (life, etc. *into*) by breathing 2 to draw (air) into the lungs; inhale 3 to have an animating effect upon; influence or impel; esp., to stimulate or impel to some creative or effective effort 4 to cause, guide, communicate, or motivate as by divine or spiritual influence 5 to arouse or produce (a thought or feeling) [kindness *inspires* love] 6 to affect with a specified feeling or thought [to *inspire* someone with fear] 7 to occasion, cause, or produce 8 to prompt, or cause to be written or said, by influence [to *inspire* a rumor] —*vi.* 1 to inhale 2 to give inspiration —**in·spir′a·ble** *adj.* —**in·spir′er** *n.* —**in·spir′ing** *adj.*

in·spired (in spīrd′) *adj.* extraordinarily creative, as if resulting from or influenced by inspiration [an actor's *inspired* performance]

in·spir·it (in spir′it) *vt.* to put spirit into; give life or courage to; cheer; exhilarate

in·spis·sate (in spis′āt′) *vt.*, *vi.* **-sat′ed, -sat′ing** ⟦< LL *inspissatus*, thick < L *in-*, in + *spissatus*, pp. of *spissare*, to thicken < *spissus*, thick < IE base **spei-*, to flourish, grow fat > SPEED, Ger *speck*, bacon⟧ to thicken, as by evaporation; condense —**in′spis·sa′tion** *n.* —**in′spis·sa′tor** *n.*

inst *abbrev.* 1 INSTANT (*adv.* 2) 2 institute 3 institution 4 instrumental

in·sta·bil·i·ty (in′stə bil′ə tē) *n.* 1 lack of stability; unstableness; specif., *a)* lack of firmness or steadiness *b)* lack of determination; irresolution 2 tendency to behave or react violently or erratically [the *instability* of a chemical compound, emotional *instability*]

in·sta·ble (in stā′bəl) *adj.* ⟦L *instabilis*⟧ *var. of* UNSTABLE

in·stall or **in·stal** (in stôl′) *vt.* **-stalled′, -stall′ing** ⟦ML(Ec) *installare* < *in-*, in + *stallum* < OHG *stal*, a place, seat, STALL[1]⟧ 1 to place in an office, rank, etc., with formality or ceremony 2 to establish in a place or condition; settle [to *install* oneself in a deck chair] 3 to fix in position for use [to *install* new fixtures] —**in·stall′er** *n.*

in·stal·la·tion (in′stə lā′shən) *n.* ⟦ML(Ec) *installatio*⟧ 1 an installing or being installed 2 something installed; specif., a complete mechanical apparatus fixed in position for use [a heating *installation*] 3 any military post, camp, base, etc. 4 a work of art requiring construction or elaborate setting up at its exhibition site: an installation typically makes use of a variety of media and often includes nontraditional media, as projected images or taped sounds

in·stall·ment[1] (in stôl′mənt) *n.* ⟦altered (infl. by INSTALL) < *estallment* < *estall*, to arrange payments for < OFr *estaler*, to stop, fix < *estal*, a halt, place < OHG *stal*: see STALL[1]⟧ 1 any of the parts of a debt or other sum of money to be paid at regular times over a specified period 2 any of several parts, as of a serial story, appearing at intervals

in·stall·ment[2] (in stôl′mənt) *n.* ⟦INSTALL + -MENT⟧ an installing or being installed; installation

☆**installment plan** a credit system by which debts, as for purchased articles, are paid in installments

in·stal·ment (in stôl′mənt) *n.* *alt. sp. of:* 1 INSTALLMENT[1] 2 INSTALLMENT[2]

in·stance (in′stəns) *n.* ⟦ME *instaunce* < OFr *instance* < L *instantia*, a standing upon or near, being present < *instans*: see INSTANT⟧ 1 an example; case; illustration 2 a step in proceeding; occasion or case [in the first *instance*] 3 [Archaic] an urgent plea; persistent solicitation 4 [Obs.] a motive; cause 5 [Obs.] a token or sign 6 *Law* a process or proceeding in a court; suit —*vt.* **-stanced, -stanc·ing** 1 to show by means of an instance; exemplify 2 to use as an example; cite —**at the instance of** at the suggestion or instigation of —**for instance** as an example; by way of illustration

SYN.—**instance** refers to a person, thing, or event that is adduced to prove or support a general statement [here is just one *instance* of his sincerity]; **case** is applied to any happening or condition that demonstrates the general existence or an occurrence of something [a *case* of mistaken identity]; **example** is applied to something that is cited as typical of the members of its group [his novel is an *example* of Romantic literature]; **illustration** is used of an instance or example that helps to explain or clarify something [this sentence is an *illustration* of the use of a word]

in·stan·cy (in′stən sē) *n.* ⟦L *instantia*⟧ [Archaic] the quality or condition of being instant; specif., urgency

in·stant (in′stənt) *adj.* ⟦LME < MFr < L *instans*, prp. of *instare*, to stand upon or near, press < *in-*, in, upon + *stare*, to STAND⟧ 1 soon to happen; imminent 2 without delay; immediate [to demand *instant* obedience] 3 designating a food or beverage in readily soluble, concentrated, or precooked form, that can be prepared quickly, as by adding water 4 [Archaic] urgent; pressing 5 [Archaic] present; current —*adv.* 1 [Old Poet.] at once; instantly 2 [Old-fashioned] (in the) present (month) [yours of the 13th (day) *instant* received]: cf. PROXIMO, ULTIMO —*n.* 1 a point or very short space of time; moment 2 a particular moment —**on the instant** without delay —**the instant** as soon as

in·stan·ta·ne·ous (in′stən tā′nē əs) *adj.* ⟦ML *instantaneus*⟧ 1 done, made, or happening in an instant 2 done or made without delay; immediate [an *instantaneous* reply] 3 existing at a particular instant —**in′stan·ta′ne·ous·ly** *adv.* —**in′stan·ta′ne·ous·ness** *n.*

in·stan·ter (in stan′tər) *adv.* ⟦L, earnestly, pressingly < *instans*: see INSTANT⟧ *Law* without delay; immediately

in·stan·ti·ate (in stan′shē āt′) *vt.* **-at′ed, -at′ing** ⟦< L *instantia*, INSTANCE + -ATE[1]⟧ to represent as or by a concrete example —**in·stan′ti·a′tion** *n.*

in·stant·ly (in′stənt lē) *adv.* 1 in an instant; without delay; immediately 2 [Archaic] urgently; pressingly —*conj.* [Brit.] as soon as; the instant that [I came *instantly* I saw the need]

instant messaging an online service enabling subscribers to CHAT[1] (*vi.* 2) with one another: cf. CHAT ROOM —**instant message**

☆**instant replay** playback, as during a live broadcast of a sporting event, of a just-recorded play, often in slow motion

in·star (in′stär′) *n.* ⟦ModL < L, a shape, form < *instare*: see INSTANT⟧ any of the various stages of an insect or other arthropod between molts

in·state (in stāt′) *vt.* **-stat′ed, -stat′ing** ⟦IN-[1] + STATE⟧ 1 to put in a particular status, position, or rank; install 2 [Obs.] to endow; invest (*with*)

in sta·tu quo (in stā′tōō kwō′, -stä′-) ⟦L, in the state in which⟧ in the existing, or same, condition

in·stau·ra·tion (in′stô rā′shən) *n.* ⟦L *instauratio* < *instauratus*, pp. of *instaurare*, to renew, repeat: see STORE⟧ the act of restoring; repair or renewal

in·stead (in sted′) *adv.* ⟦IN[1] + STEAD⟧ in place of the person or thing mentioned: as an alternative or substitute [to feel like crying, but to laugh *instead*] —**instead of** in place of

in·step (in′step′) *n.* ⟦prob. IN-[1] + STEP⟧ 1 the top surface of the foot, between the ankle and the toes 2 the part of a shoe or stocking that covers this 3 the front part of the hind leg of a horse, between the hock and the pastern joint

in·sti·gate (in′stə gāt′) *vt.* **-gat′ed, -gat′ing** ⟦< L *instigatus*, pp. of *instigare*, to stimulate, incite < *in-*, IN-[1] + *-stigare*, to prick: for IE base see STICK⟧ 1 to urge on, spur on, or incite to some action, esp. to some evil [to *instigate* others to rebel] 2 to cause by inciting; foment [to *instigate* a rebellion] —*SYN.* INCITE —**in′sti·ga′tion** *n.* —**in′sti·ga′tive** *adj.* —**in′sti·ga′tor** *n.*

in·still or **in·stil** (in stil′) *vt.* **-stilled′, -still′ing** ⟦MFr *instiller* < L *instillare* < *in-*, in + *stillare*, to drop < *stilla*, a drop⟧ 1 to put in drop by drop 2 to put (an idea, principle, feeling, etc.) *in* or *into* little by little; impart gradually —**in′stil·la′tion** *n.* —**in·still′er** *n.* —**in·still′ment** *n.*, **in·stil′ment**

in·stinct (in′stiŋkt′; *for adj.* in stiŋkt′, in′stiŋkt′) *n.* ⟦< L *instinctus*, pp. of *instinguere*, to impel, instigate < *in-*, in + **stinguere*, to prick: for IE base see STICK⟧ 1 (an) inborn tendency to behave in a way characteristic of a species; natural, unlearned, predictable response to stimuli [suckling is an *instinct* in mammals] 2 a natural or acquired tendency, aptitude, or talent; bent; knack; gift [an *instinct* for doing the right thing] 3 *Psychoanalysis* a primal psychic force or drive, as fear, love, or anger; specif., in Freudian analysis, either the life instinct (*Eros*) or the death instinct (*Thanatos*) —*adj.* filled or charged (*with*) [a look *instinct* with pity] —**in·stinc·tu·al** (in stiŋk′chōō əl) *adj.*

in·stinc·tive (in stiŋk′tiv) *adj.* 1 of, or having the nature of, instinct 2 prompted or done by or as if by instinct —*SYN.* SPONTANEOUS —**in·stinc′tive·ly** *adv.* —**in·stinc′tive·ness** *n.*

in·sti·tute (in′stə tōōt′, -tyōōt′) *vt.* **-tut′ed, -tut′ing** ⟦< L *institutus*, pp. of *instituere*, to set up, erect, construct < *in-*, in, on + *statuere*, to cause to stand, set up, place: see STATUTE⟧ 1 to set up; establish; found; introduce 2 to start; initiate [to *institute* a search] 3 to install in office, esp. as a minister in a church or parish —*n.* ⟦L *institutum*, arrangement, plan < the v.⟧ something instituted; specif., *a)* an established principle, law, custom, or usage *b)* [*pl.*] a summary or digest of established principles, esp. in law *c)* an organization for the promotion of art, science, education, etc. *d)* a school specializing in art, music, etc. ☆*e)* a college or university specializing in technical subjects *f)* an institution for advanced study, research, and instruction in a restricted field ☆*g)* a short teaching program established for a group concerned with some special field of work *h)* INSTITUTION (sense 3) —**in′sti·tut′er** *n.*, **in′sti·tu′tor**

in·sti·tu·tion (in′stə tōō′shən, -tyōō′-) *n.* ⟦ME *institucion* < OFr < L *institutio*⟧ 1 an instituting or being instituted; establishment 2 an established law, custom, practice, system, etc. 3 *a)* an organization, society, or corporation having a public purpose, as a school, church, bank, hospital, etc. *b)* the building housing such an organization; often, specif., such a place where persons are kept or confined, as a mental hospital, nursing home, prison, etc. 4 a person or thing long established in a place

in·sti·tu·tion·al (-shə nəl) *adj.* 1 of, characteristic of, or having the nature of, an institution, specif. as in being standardized, impersonal, dreary, etc. 2 of or to institutions, rather than individuals [*institutional* sales] 3 designating advertising that is intended primarily to gain prestige and goodwill rather than immediate sales —**in′sti·tu′tion·al·ly** *adv.*

in·sti·tu·tion·al·ism (-iz′əm) *n.* 1 a belief in the usefulness or sanctity of established institutions 2 the care of the poor, homeless, or others needing assistance by or in public institutions 3 the nature of such care, regarded as impersonal, standardized, etc. —**in′sti·tu′tion·al·ist** *adj.*

in·sti·tu·tion·al·ize (-īz′) *vt.* **-ized′, -iz′ing** 1 to make into or consider as an institution 2 to place in an institution, as for treatment or detention —**in′sti·tu′tion·al·i·za′tion** *n.*

in·sti·tu·tion·ar·y (in′stə tōō′shə ner′ē, -tyōō′-) *adj.* 1 of legal institutes 2 of institutions; institutional

in·sti·tu·tive (in′stə tōōt′iv, -tyōōt′-) *adj.* instituting or tending to institute; of institution

instr *abbrev.* 1 instructor 2 instrument 3 instrumental

in·struct (in strukt′) *vt.* ⟦ME *instructen* < L *instructus*, pp. of *instruere*, to pile upon, put in order, erect < *in-*, in, upon + *struere*, to pile up, arrange, build: see STREW⟧ 1 to communicate knowledge to; teach; educate 2 to give facts or information to on a particular matter; inform or guide [the judge *instructs* the jury] 3 to order or direct [to *instruct* a visitor to wait at the door] —*SYN.* COMMAND, TEACH

in·struc·tion (in struk′shən) *n.* ⟦ME *instruccioun* < OFr *instruccion* < L *instructio*⟧ 1 the act of instructing; education 2 *a)* knowledge, information, etc. given or taught *b)* any teaching, lesson, rule, or precept 3 *a)* a command or order *b)* any of the sequence of steps to be followed, as in doing, using, or operating something (*usually used in pl.*) *c)* a sequence of bits specifying an operation to be performed by a computer —**in·struc′tion·al** *adj.*

in·struc·tive (in struk′tiv) *adj.* ⟦ML *instructivus*⟧ serving to instruct; giving useful knowledge or information —**in·struc′tive·ly** *adv.* —**in·struc′tive·ness** *n.*

in·struc·tor (in struk′tər) *n.* ⟦ME *instructour* < Anglo-Fr < L *instructor*, a preparer (in ML, teacher)⟧ 1 a person who instructs; teacher ☆2 a college teacher ranking below an assistant professor —**in·struc′tor·ship′** *n.*

in·struc·tress (-tris) *n.* [Now Rare] a female instructor: see -ESS

in·stru·ment (in′strə mənt) *n.* ⟦OFr < L *instrumentum*, a tool or tools, stock, furniture, dress < *instruere*: see INSTRUCT⟧ 1 *a)* a thing by means of which something is done; means *b)* a person used by another to bring something about 2 a tool or implement, esp. one used for delicate work or for scientific or artistic purposes 3 any of various devices for indicating or measuring conditions, performance, position, direction, etc. or, sometimes, for controlling operations, as in an aircraft 4 any of various devices designed or used to produce musical sound, as a piano, drum, violin, oboe, etc. 5 *Law* a formal document, as a deed, contract, etc. 6 *Finance* a written order or promise to pay a sum of money [a negotiable *instrument*] —*adj. Aeron.* of or having to do with INSTRUMENT FLYING —*vt.* 1 to provide with instruments 2 *Music* to arrange (a composition) for instruments; orchestrate —*SYN.* IMPLEMENT

in·stru·men·tal (in′strə ment′'l) *adj.* ⟦ME < MFr < ML *instrumentalis*⟧ 1 serving as a means; helpful (*in* bringing something about) 2 of or performed with an instrument or tool 3 of, performed on, or written for a musical instrument or instruments 4 of or in keeping with instrumentalism 5 *Gram.* designating, of, or in the case of nouns, pronouns, or adjectives expressing means or agency —*n.* 1 a composition for a musical instrument or instruments 2 *Gram.* *a)* the instrumental case: this case is expressed by inflection in Old English, Sanskrit, Russian, etc., and in English with the prepositions *by* or *with* (Ex.: OE ðȳ spere, "by the spear, with the spear") *b)* a word or phrase in this case —**in′stru·men′tal·ly** *adv.*

in·stru·men·tal·ism (-iz′əm) *n.* *Philos.* the pragmatic doctrine that ideas are plans for action serving as instruments to alter the environment, and that their validity is tested by their effectiveness

in·stru·men·tal·ist (-ist) *n.* 1 a person who performs on a musical instrument 2 a person who believes in instrumentalism —*adj.* of or in keeping with instrumentalism

in·stru·men·tal·i·ty (in′strə men′tal′ə tē) *n.*, *pl.* **-ties** 1 the condition, quality, or fact of being instrumental, or serving as a means 2 a means or agency

in·stru·men·ta·tion (-tā′shən) *n.* 1 the composition or arrangement of music for instruments; orchestration 2 the act of developing, using, or equipping with, instruments, esp. scientific instruments 3 the instruments used, as in a mechanical apparatus or in a particular musical score, band, etc. 4 INSTRUMENTALITY (sense 2)

instrument flying the flying of an aircraft by the use of instruments only: distinguished from CONTACT FLYING

instrument landing a landing made using only the instruments of the aircraft and electronic or radio signals from the ground

instrument panel a panel or board with instruments, gauges, etc. mounted on it, as in an automobile or airplane

in·sub·or·di·nate (in′sə bôrd′'n it) *adj.* ⟦IN-[2] + SUBORDINATE⟧ not submitting to authority; intractable, insolent, disobedient, etc. —*n.* an insubordinate person —**in′sub·or′di·nate·ly** *adv.* —**in′sub·or′di·na′tion** *n.*

in·sub·stan·tial (in′səb stan′shəl) *adj.* ⟦ML *insubstantialis*⟧ not substantial; specif., *a)* not real; imaginary *b)* not solid or firm; weak or flimsy —**in′sub·stan′ti·al′i·ty** (-shē al′ə tē) *n.*

in·suf·fer·a·ble (in suf′ər ə bəl) *adj.* not sufferable; intolerable; unbearable —**in·suf′fer·a·bly** *adv.*

in·suf·fi·cien·cy (in′sə fish′ən sē) *n.*, *pl.* **-cies** ⟦LL *insufficientia*⟧ 1 lack of sufficiency; deficiency; inadequacy: also [Rare] **in′suf·fi′cience** (-əns) 2 inability or failure of an organ or tissue to perform its normal function: said esp. of a heart valve or heart muscle

in·suf·fi·cient (in′sə fish′ənt) *adj.* ⟦LL *insufficiens*⟧ not sufficient; not enough; inadequate —**in′suf·fi′cient·ly** *adv.*

in·suf·flate (in suf′lāt′, in′sə flāt′) *vt.* **-flat′ed, -flat′ing** ⟦< L *insufflatus*, pp. of *insufflare*, to blow or breathe into < *in-*, in + *sufflare*, to blow from below < *sub-*, under + *flare*, to BLOW[1]⟧ **1** to blow or breathe into or on **2** *Med.* to blow (a powder, vapor, air, etc.) into a cavity of the body —**in′suf·fla′tion** *n.* —**in′suf·fla′tor** *n.*

in·su·la (in′sə lə, -syə-) *n., pl.* **-lae′** (-lē′) ⟦L, island: see ISLE⟧ a small interior lobe of the cerebral cortex associated with various functions, as emotional response, perception, and motor control: in full **insular cortex**

in·su·lar (in′sə lər, -syə-) *adj.* ⟦L *insularis* < *insula*, island: see ISLE⟧ **1** of, or having the form of, an island **2** living or situated on an island **3** like an island; detached; isolated **4** narrow-minded, illiberal, or provincial **5** *Med. a)* characterized by isolated spots *b)* of the islets of Langerhans or other islands of tissue *c)* of the insula —**in·su·lar·i·ty** (-ler′ə tə) *n.*, **in′su·lar·ism′** —**in′su·lar·ly** *adv.*

in·su·late (in′sə lāt′, -syə-) *vt.* **-lat′ed, -lat′ing** ⟦< L *insulatus*, made like an island < *insula*, ISLE⟧ **1** to set apart; detach from the rest; isolate **2** to separate or cover with a nonconducting material in order to prevent the passage or leakage of electricity, heat, sound, radioactive particles, etc.

in·su·la·tion (in′sə lā′shən, -syə-) *n.* **1** an insulating or being insulated **2** any material used to insulate

in·su·la·tor (in′sə lāt′ər, -syə-) *n.* anything that insulates; specif., *a)* a nonconductor of electricity, heat, or sound *b)* a device, as of glass or porcelain, for insulating and supporting electric wires

in·su·lin (in′sə lin) *n.* ⟦< L *insula*, island (see ISLE) + -IN[1]: in allusion to the islets of Langerhans⟧ **1** a protein hormone secreted by the islets of Langerhans, in the pancreas, which helps the body use sugar and other carbohydrates **2** a preparation extracted from the pancreas of sheep, oxen, etc. and used hypodermically in the treatment of diabetes mellitus

insulin shock the abnormal condition caused by an overdose or excess secretion of insulin, resulting in a sudden reduction in the sugar content of the blood: it is characterized by tremors, cold sweat, convulsions, and coma

in·sult (in sult′; *for n.* in′sult′) *vt.* ⟦MFr *insulter* < L *insultare*, to leap upon, scoff at, insult < *in-*, in, on + *saltare*, freq. of *salire*, to leap: see SALIENT⟧ **1** to treat or speak to with scorn, insolence, or great disrespect; subject to treatment, a remark, etc. that hurts or is meant to hurt the feelings or pride **2** [Obs.] to attack; assail —*vi.* [Archaic] to behave arrogantly —*n.* **1** an insulting act, remark, etc.; affront; indignity **2** [Archaic] an attack; assault **3** *Med. a)* damage or injury to tissues or organs of the body *b)* anything that causes this —**SYN.** OFFEND —**in·sult′er** *n.* —**in·sult′ing** *adj.* —**in·sult′ing·ly** *adv.*

in·su·per·a·ble (in so͞o′pər ə bəl, -syo͞o′-) *adj.* ⟦ME < L *insuperabilis*⟧ not superable; that cannot be overcome or passed over; insurmountable —**in·su′per·a·bil′i·ty** *n.* —**in·su′per·a·bly** *adv.*

in·sup·port·a·ble (in′sə pôrt′ə bəl) *adj.* ⟦LL(Ec) *insupportabilis*⟧ not supportable; specif., *a)* intolerable; unbearable; unendurable *b)* incapable of being upheld, proved, etc. [*insupportable* charges] —**in′sup·port′a·bly** *adv.*

in·sup·press·i·ble (in′sə pres′ə bəl) *adj.* not suppressible; that cannot be suppressed —**in′sup·press′i·bly** *adv.*

in·sur·ance (in sho͝or′əns) *n.* ⟦earlier *ensurance* < OFr *enseurance*: see ENSURE⟧ **1** an insuring or being insured against loss **2** *a)* a system of protection against loss in which a number of individuals agree to pay certain sums (*premiums*) periodically for a guarantee that they will be compensated under stipulated conditions for any specified loss by fire, accident, death, etc. *b)* a contract guaranteeing such protection (usually called **insurance policy**: see POLICY[2], sense 1) *c)* the premium specified for such a contract **3** the amount for which life, property, etc. is insured **4** the business of insuring against loss

in·sure (in sho͝or′) *vt.* **-sured′, -sur′ing** ⟦ME *ensuren*: see ENSURE⟧ **1** to contract to be paid or to pay money in the case of loss of (life, property, etc.); take out or issue insurance on (something or someone) **2** to make sure or certain; guarantee; ensure [measures to *insure* accuracy] **3** to make safe; protect; ensure [safety devices to *insure* workers against accidents] —*vi.* to give or take out insurance —**in·sur′a·bil′i·ty** *n.* —**in·sur′a·ble** *adj.*

in·sured (in sho͝ord′) *n.* a person whose life, property, etc. is insured against loss

in·sur·er (in sho͝or′ər) *n.* a person or company that insures others against loss or damage; underwriter

in·sur·gence (in sʉr′jəns) *n.* a rising in revolt; uprising; insurrection

in·sur·gen·cy (in sʉr′jən sē) *n.* **1** the quality, state, or fact of being insurgent **2** *pl.* **-cies** INSURGENCE

in·sur·gent (in sʉr′jənt) *adj.* ⟦L *insurgens*, prp. of *insurgere*, to rise up (against) < *in-*, in, upon + *surgere*, to rise: see SURGE⟧ rising up against established authority; rebellious; specif., *a)* designating or of a revolt or rebellion not well enough organized to be recognized in international law as belligerency *b)* designating or of a faction in revolt against the leadership of a political party —*n.* a person engaged in insurgent activity —**in·sur′gent·ly** *adv.*

in·sur·mount·a·ble (in′sər mount′ə bəl) *adj.* not surmountable; that cannot be passed over or overcome; insuperable —**in′sur·mount′a·bil′i·ty** *n.* —**in′sur·mount′a·bly** *adv.*

in·sur·rec·tion (in′sə rek′shən) *n.* ⟦LME < MFr < LL *insurrectio* < pp. of L *insurgere*: see INSURGENT⟧ a rising up against established authority; rebellion; revolt —**in′sur·rec′tion·al** *adj.* —**in′sur·rec′tion·ist** *n., adj.*, **in′sur·rec′tion·ar′y**, *pl.* **-ar′ies**

in·sus·cep·ti·ble (in′sə sep′tə bəl) *adj.* not susceptible (*to* or *of*); not easily affected or influenced —**in′sus·cep′ti·bil′i·ty** *n.* —**in′sus·cep′ti·bly** *adv.*

int *abbrev.* **1** interest **2** interim **3** interior **4** interjection **5** internal **6** international **7** intransitive

Int *abbrev. Football* interception: sometimes written **int** or **INT**

.int *abbrev. Comput.* international: a domain name

in·tact (in takt′) *adj.* ⟦ME *intacte* < L *intactus* < *in-*, not + *tactus*, pp. of *tangere*, to touch: see TACT⟧ with nothing missing or injured; kept or left whole; sound; entire; unimpaired —**SYN.** COMPLETE —**in·tact′ness** *n.*

in·ta·glio (in tal′yō′, -täl′-; *also*, -täg′lē ō′, -tag′-) *n., pl.* **-glios′** ⟦It < *intagliare*, to cut in, engrave < *in-*, in + *tagliare*, to cut < LL *taliare*: see TAILOR⟧ **1** a design or figure carved, incised, or engraved into a hard material so that it is below the surface **2** something, as a gem or stone, ornamented with such a design or figure: opposed to CAMEO **3** the art or process of making such designs or figures **4** a method of printing in which lines forming an image are cut into a metal plate and the incised lines then filled with ink: when a sheet of paper is pressed against the surface of the plate a PRINT (*n.* 8) of the image is formed on the paper **5** a die cut to produce a design in relief —*vt.* **-glioed′, -glio′ing** to engrave, carve, etc. in intaglio

in·take (in′tāk′) *n.* **1** the act or process of taking in **2** the amount or thing taken in **3** the place at which a fluid is taken into a pipe, channel, etc. **4** a narrowing; an abrupt lessening in breadth **5** *Mech.* the amount of energy taken in **6** *Mining* an air shaft

in·tan·gi·ble (in tan′jə bəl) *adj.* ⟦ML *intangibilis*: see IN-[2] & TANGIBLE⟧ **1** that cannot be touched; incorporeal; impalpable **2** designating or of any of certain business assets, esp. goodwill, that have no material being but have monetary value **3** that cannot be easily defined, formulated, or grasped; vague —*n.* something intangible; specif., a quality, as of character, that is desirable but cannot be measured: *often used in pl.* [the rookie quarterback displays leadership and is unruffled—*intangibles* necessary for success] —**in·tan′gi·bil′i·ty** *n., pl.* **-ties** —**in·tan′gi·bly** *adv.*

in·tar·si·a (in tär′sē ə) *n.* ⟦It *intarsio* < *intarsiare*, to inlay, incrust < *in-*, in + Ar *tarṣīʿ*, inlay work < *raṣṣaʿa*, to inlay⟧ a style of decorative inlay, involving a mosaic of usually wood pieces

in·te·ger (in′tə jər) *n.* ⟦L, untouched, whole, entire < *in-*, not + base of *tangere*, to touch: see TACT⟧ **1** anything complete in itself; entity; whole **2** any positive or negative whole number or zero: see also RATIONAL (sense 4*a*)

in·te·gra·ble (in′tə grə bəl) *adj.* that can be integrated

in·te·gral (in′tə grəl; *often, for adj. 1-3*, in teg′rəl) *adj.* ⟦LL *integralis* < L *integer*: see INTEGER⟧ **1** necessary for completeness; essential [an *integral* part] **2** whole or complete **3** made up of parts forming a whole **4** *Math. a)* of or having to do with an integer or integers; not fractional *b)* of or having to do with integrals or integration —*n.* **1** a whole **2** *Math. a)* the result of integrating a fraction (cf. DEFINITE INTEGRAL, INDEFINITE INTEGRAL) *b)* a solution of a differential equation —**in′te·gral′i·ty** (-gral′ə tē) *n.* —**in′te·gral·ly** *adv.*

integral calculus the branch of higher mathematics that deals with integration and its use in finding volumes, areas, equations of curves, solutions of differential equations, etc.

in·te·grand (in′tə grand′) *n.* ⟦< L *integrandus*, ger. of *integrare*: see INTEGRATE⟧ *Math.* the function or expression to be integrated

in·te·grant (-grənt) *adj.* ⟦L *integrans*, prp. of *integrare*: see fol.⟧ integral —*n.* an integral part; constituent

in·te·grate (in′tə grāt′) *vt.* **-grat′ed, -grat′ing** ⟦< L *integratus*, pp. of *integrare*, to make whole, renew < *integer*: see INTEGER⟧ **1** to make whole or complete by adding or bringing together parts **2** to put or bring (parts) together into a whole; unify **3** to give or indicate the whole, sum, or total of ☆**4** *a)* to remove the legal and social barriers imposing segregation upon (a group, specif. a racial group) so as to permit free and equal association *b)* to abolish segregation in; desegregate (a school, neighborhood, etc.) **5** *Math. a)* to calculate the integral or integrals of (a function, equation, etc.) *b)* to perform the process of integration upon **6** *Psychol.* to cause to undergo integration —*vi.* to become integrated —**in′te·gra′tive** *adj.*

integrated circuit an electronic circuit containing many interconnected amplifying devices and circuit elements formed on a single body, or chip, of semiconductor material

in·te·gra·tion (in′tə grā′shən) *n.* ⟦L *integratio*⟧ **1** an integrating or being integrated ☆**2** the bringing of different racial or ethnic groups into free and equal association **3** *Math.* the process of finding an integral when given a quantity or function that is the derivative or differential of that integral **4** *Psychol.* the organization of various traits, feelings, attitudes, etc. into one harmonious personality —**in′te·gra′tion·al** *adj.*

☆**in·te·gra·tion·ist** (-ist) *n.* a person who advocates integration or desegregation —*adj.* believing in or advocating integration

in·te·gra·tor (in′tə grāt′ər) *n.* **1** a person or thing that integrates **2** a mechanical device for calculating integrals

in·teg·ri·ty (in teg′rə tē) *n.* ⟦LME *integrite* < L *integritas* < *integer*: see INTEGER⟧ **1** the quality or state of being complete; unbroken condition; wholeness; entirety **2** the quality or state of being unimpaired; perfect condition; soundness **3** the quality or state of being of sound moral principle; uprightness, honesty, and sincerity

in·teg·u·ment (in teg′yo͞o mənt, -yə-) *n.* ⟦L *integumentum*, a covering < *integere*, to cover < *in-*, in, upon + *tegere*, to cover: see THATCH⟧ a natural outer covering of the body or of a plant, including skin, shell, hide, husk, or rind —**in·teg′u·men′ta·ry** (-men′tər ē) *adj.*

☆**in·tel** (in′tel′) ***n.*** ⟦< INTEL(LIGENCE), ***n.*** 3⟧ secret information, specif. when gathered for military purposes

in·tel·lect (in′tə lekt′) ***n.*** ⟦ME < L *intellectus*, a perceiving, understanding < pp. of *intellegere, intelligere*, to perceive, understand < *inter-*, between, among + *legere*, to gather, pick, choose: see LOGIC⟧ **1** the ability to reason or understand or to perceive relationships, differences, etc.; power of thought; mind **2** great mental ability; high intelligence **3** *a)* a mind or intelligence, esp. a superior one *b)* a person of high intelligence *c)* minds or intelligent persons, collectively —**in′tel·lec′tive** ***adj.***

in·tel·lec·tion (in′tə lek′shən) ***n.*** ⟦ME *intelleccioun* < ML *intellectio*⟧ **1** the process of using the intellect; thinking; cognition **2** an act of the intellect; a thought or perception

in·tel·lec·tu·al (in′tə lek′cho͞o əl) ***adj.*** ⟦ME < LL *intellectualis*⟧ **1** of or pertaining to the intellect **2** appealing to the intellect **3** *a)* requiring or involving the intellect *b)* inclined toward activities that involve the intellect **4** guided by the intellect rather than by feelings **5** having or showing a high degree of intellect; having superior reasoning powers —***n.*** **1** a person with intellectual interests or tastes **2** a person engaged in intellectual work **3** a member of the intelligentsia —**SYN.** INTELLIGENT —**in′tel·lec′tu·al′i·ty** (-cho͞o al′ə tē) ***n.*** —**in′tel·lec′tu·al·ly** ***adv.***

intellectual disability a condition, typically present from infancy, characterized by cognitive impairment resulting in difficulty in carrying out the functions of normal daily life: it can result from any of various causes: now the preferred technical term (see also the note at MENTAL RETARDATION)

in·tel·lec·tu·al·ism (-iz′əm) ***n.*** **1** the quality of being intellectual; devotion to intellectual pursuits **2** *Philos.* RATIONALISM (sense 2) —**in′tel·lec′tu·al·ist** ***n.*** —**in′tel·lec′tu·al·is′tic** ***adj.***

in·tel·lec·tu·al·ize (-īz′) ***vt.*** **-ized′, -iz′ing** **1** to make intellectual; give an intellectual quality to **2** to examine or interpret rationally, often without proper regard for emotional considerations —***vi.*** to reason; think —**in′tel·lec′tu·al·i·za′tion** ***n.***

intellectual property something produced by the mind, of which the ownership or right to use may be legally protected by a copyright, patent, trademark, etc.

in·tel·li·gence (in tel′ə jəns) ***n.*** ⟦OFr < L *intelligentia*, perception, discernment < *intelligens*, prp. of *intelligere*: see INTELLECT⟧ **1** *a)* the ability to learn or understand from experience; ability to acquire and retain knowledge; mental ability *b)* the ability to respond quickly and effectively to a new situation; use of the faculty of reason in solving problems, directing conduct, etc. *c)* *Psychol.* measured success in using these abilities to perform certain tasks *d)* generally, any degree of keenness of mind, cleverness, shrewdness, etc. **2** news or information **3** *a)* the gathering of secret information, as for military or police purposes *b)* such information *c)* the persons or agency employed at gathering it **4** an intelligent spirit or being —**in·tel′li·gen′tial** (-jen′shəl) ***adj.***

☆**intelligence quotient** *see* IQ

in·tel·li·genc·er (in tel′ə jən sər) ***n.*** [Archaic] a person who supplies news or information; esp., a spy or secret agent

intelligence test a standardized series of problems intended to test the relative intelligence of an individual

in·tel·li·gent (in tel′ə jənt) ***adj.*** ⟦L *intelligens*, prp. of *intelligere*: see INTELLECT⟧ **1** having or using intelligence; rational **2** having or showing an alert mind or high intelligence; bright, perceptive, informed, clever, wise, etc. **3** capable of some independent functioning because equipped with a microprocessor or computer [an *intelligent* missile]: cf. DUMB (sense 9) **4** [Archaic] aware (*of* something) —**in·tel′li·gent·ly** ***adv.***

SYN.—**intelligent** implies the ability to learn or understand from experience or to respond successfully to a new experience; **clever** implies quickness in learning or understanding, but sometimes connotes a lack of thoroughness or depth; **alert** emphasizes quickness in sizing up a situation; **bright** and **smart** are somewhat informal, less precise equivalents for any of the preceding; **brilliant** implies an unusually high degree of intelligence; **intellectual** suggests keen intelligence coupled with interest and ability in the more advanced fields of knowledge —***ANT.*** **stupid, dull**

intelligent design the concept that the order and complexity seen in nature must be the result of a rational design, as by God, and that natural processes such as evolution are insufficient to account for them entirely

in·tel·li·gent·si·a (in tel′ə jent′sē ə; *esp. formerly*, -gent′-) ***pl.n.*** ⟦Russ *intelligencija* < L *intelligentia*: see INTELLIGENCE⟧ [*also with sing. v.*] those persons regarded as, or regarding themselves as, the educated and enlightened class; intellectuals collectively: often with *the*

in·tel·li·gi·ble (in tel′i jə bəl) ***adj.*** ⟦ME < L *intelligibilis* < *intelligere*: see INTELLECT⟧ **1** that can be understood; clear; comprehensible **2** understandable by the intellect only, not by the senses —**in·tel′li·gi·bil′i·ty** ***n.*** —**in·tel′li·gi·bly** ***adv.***

in·tem·per·ance (in tem′pər əns, -prəns) ***n.*** **1** a lack of temperance or restraint; immoderation **2** excessive drinking of alcoholic liquor

in·tem·per·ate (in tem′pər it, -prit) ***adj.*** ⟦L *intemperatus*⟧ **1** not temperate; specif., *a)* not moderate; lacking restraint; excessive *b)* severe or violent; inclement [an *intemperate* wind] **2** drinking too much alcoholic liquor —**in·tem′per·ate·ly** ***adv.***

in·tend (in tend′) ***vt.*** ⟦ME *entenden* < OFr *entendre* < L *intendere*, to stretch out for, aim at < *in-*, in, at + *tendere*, to stretch: see THIN⟧ **1** to have in mind as a purpose; plan **2** to mean (something) to be or be used (*for*); design; destine [a cake *intended* for the party] **3** to mean or signify **4** [Archaic] to direct or turn (the mind, eyes, thoughts, etc.) **5** *Law* to construe or interpret legally —***vi.*** to have a purpose or intention —**in·tend′er** ***n.***

SYN.—**intend** implies a having in mind of something to be done, said, etc. [I *intended* to write you]; **mean**, a more general word, does not connote so clearly a specific, deliberate purpose [he always *means* well]; **design** suggests careful planning in order to bring about a particular result [their delay was *designed* to forestall suspicion]; **propose** implies a clear declaration, openly or to oneself, of one's intention [I *propose* to speak for an hour]; **purpose** adds to **propose** a connotation of strong determination to effect one's intention [he *purposes* to become a doctor]

in·tend·an·cy (-dən sē) ***n.***, *pl.* **-cies** **1** the position or duties of an intendant **2** intendants collectively **3** the district supervised by an intendant: also sp. **in·tend′en·cy**, *pl.* **-cies**

in·tend·ant (in ten′dənt) ***n.*** ⟦Fr *intendant* or Sp *intendente*, both < L *intendens*, prp. of *intendere*: see INTEND⟧ a director, manager of a public business, superintendent, etc.: term applied to certain foreign officials, as to the supervisors of any of certain districts in Spanish America

in·tend·ed (in ten′did) ***adj.*** **1** meant; planned **2** prospective; future [one's *intended* wife] —***n.*** [Informal] one's fiancé or fiancée

in·tend·ing (-diŋ) ***adj.*** prospective; future

in·tend·ment (in tend′mənt) ***n.*** ⟦ME *entendement* < OFr: see INTEND⟧ the true and correct meaning or intention, as of law

intens *abbrev.* intensive

in·tense (in tens′) ***adj.*** ⟦ME < MFr < L *intensus*, pp. of *intendere*: see INTEND⟧ **1** occurring or existing in a high degree; very strong; violent, extreme, sharp, vivid, etc. [an *intense* light] **2** strained to the utmost; strenuous; earnest; fervent; zealous [*intense* thought] **3** having or showing strong emotion, firm purpose, great seriousness, etc. **4** characterized by much action, emotion, etc. —**in·tense′ly** ***adv.*** —**in·tense′ness** ***n.***

in·ten·si·fi·er (in ten′sə fī′ər) ***n.*** **1** something that intensifies **2** *Gram.* an intensive word, prefix, etc. **3** *Photog.* any of several solutions used to increase the printing density of a negative

in·ten·si·fy (in ten′sə fī′) ***vt.*** **-fied′, -fy′ing** **1** to make intense or more intense; increase; strengthen **2** *Photog.* to make (a film, etc.) more dense or opaque by treating with an intensifier —***vi.*** to become intense or increase in intensity —**in·ten′si·fi·ca′tion** ***n.***

SYN.—**intensify** implies an increasing in the degree of force, vehemence, vividness, etc. [his absence only *intensified* her longing]; **aggravate** implies a making more serious, unbearable, etc. and connotes something that is unpleasant or troublesome in itself [your insolence only *aggravates* the offense]; to **heighten** is to make greater, stronger, more vivid, etc. so as to raise above the ordinary or commonplace [the film's score served to *heighten* the dramatic effect]; **enhance** implies the addition of something so as to make more attractive or desirable [she used cosmetics to *enhance* her beauty] —***ANT.*** **diminish, mitigate**

in·ten·sion (in ten′shən) ***n.*** ⟦L *intensio* < *intensus*, pp. of *intendere*: see INTEND⟧ **1** [Archaic] intentness; determination **2** [Archaic] intensity or degree of intensity **3** *Logic* the properties possessed by all the objects in a term's extension; connotation: cf. EXTENSION (sense 11) —**in·ten′sion·al** ***adj.***

in·ten·si·ty (in ten′sə tē) ***n.***, *pl.* **-ties** ⟦ML *intensitas*⟧ **1** the quality of being intense; specif., *a)* extreme degree of anything *b)* great energy or vehemence of emotion, thought, or activity **2** degree or extent; relative strength, magnitude, vigor, etc. **3** SATURATION (sense 2) **4** *Physics* the amount of force or energy of heat, light, sound, electric current, etc. per unit area, volume, charge, etc.

in·ten·sive (in ten′siv) ***adj.*** ⟦ML *intensious* < L *intensus*: see INTENSE & -IVE⟧ **1** increasing or causing to increase in degree or amount **2** of or characterized by intensity; thorough, profound, and intense; concentrated or exhaustive **3** designating care of an especially attentive nature given to critically ill hospital patients, typically in a special ward (**intensive care unit**) **4** *Agric.* designating a system of farming which aims at the increase of yield per acre by using increased labor, capital, etc.: see EXTENSIVE (sense 4) **5** *Gram.* giving force or emphasis; emphasizing ["very" in "the very same man" is an *intensive* adverb] —***n.*** **1** anything that intensifies **2** an intensive word, prefix, etc. —**in·ten′sive·ly** ***adv.*** —**in·ten′sive·ness** ***n.***

-in·ten·sive (in ten′siv) *combining form* intensively using, requiring large amounts of, or concentrating within itself large amounts of (a specified thing) [labor-*intensive*]

in·tent (in tent′; *for n., also* in′tent′) ***adj.*** ⟦< L *intentus*, var. pp. of *intendere*: see INTEND⟧ **1** firmly directed or fixed; earnest; intense [an *intent* look] **2** *a)* having the mind or attention firmly directed or fixed; engrossed [*intent* on his studies] *b)* strongly resolved [*intent* on going] —***n.*** ⟦ME *entente, intente* < OFr *entente* & ML *intentus*, both < L *intentus*, a stretching out < pp. of *intendere*: see ***adj.***⟧ **1** an act or instance of intending **2** something intended; specif., *a)* a purpose; object; aim *b)* meaning or import **3** *Law* one's mental attitude, including purpose, will, determination, etc., at the time of doing an act —**SYN.** INTENTION —**for** (or **to**) **all intents and purposes** in almost every respect; practically; virtually —**in·tent′ly** ***adv.*** —**in·tent′ness** ***n.***

in·ten·tion (in ten′shən) ***n.*** ⟦ME *entencioun* < OFr *entencion* < L *intentio* < pp. of *intendere*⟧ **1** the act or fact of intending; determination to do a specified thing or act in a specified manner **2** *a)* anything intended or planned; aim, end, or purpose *b)* [*pl.*] [Old-fashioned] purpose in regard to marriage 3 [Rare] meaning or import 4 *Philos.* the direction or orientation of the mind toward an object 5 *Surgery* the manner or process by which a wound heals: the three degrees (*first, second,* and *third intention*) are distinguished by the relative amounts and types of granulation that occur

SYN.—**intention** is the general word implying a having something in mind as a plan or design, or referring to the plan had in mind; **intent**, a somewhat formal term now largely in legal usage, connotes more deliberation [assault with *intent* to kill]; **purpose** connotes still greater resolution in the plan [my *purpose* in writing you]; **aim** refers to a specific intention and connotes a directing of all efforts toward this [his *aim* is to become a doctor]; **goal** suggests laborious effort in striving to attain something [the presidency was the *goal* of his ambition]; **end** emphasizes the final result one hopes to achieve as distinct from the process of achieving it [does a desirable *end* justify the use of immoral means?]; **object** is used of an end that is the direct result of a need or desire [the *object* of the discussion was to arouse controversy]; **objective** refers to a specific end that is capable of being reached [her immediate *objective* is to pass the course]

in·ten·tion·al (in ten′shə nəl) *adj.* ⟦ML *intentionalis*⟧ 1 having to do with intention or purpose 2 done purposely; intended —**SYN.** VOLUNTARY —**in·ten′tion·al′i·ty** *n.* —**in·ten′tion·al·ly** *adv.*

in·ten·tioned (in ten′shənd) *adj.* having (specified) intentions: often in hyphenated compounds [well-*intentioned*]

in·ter (in tur′) *vt.* **-terred′**, **-ter′ring** ⟦ME *enteren* < OFr *enterrer* < VL **in-terrare*, to put in the earth < L *in*, in + *terra*, earth: see THRUST⟧ to put (a dead body) into a grave or tomb; bury

in·ter- (in′tər) ⟦L < *inter*, between, among < IE **enter*, **n̥ter* (compar. of base **en*, in) > OFr *entre-*, Sans *antár*, within, OE *under*, Ger *unter*, among, Gr *enteron*, intestine⟧ *prefix* 1 between or among: the second element of the compound is singular in form [*interstate*] 2 with or on each other (or one another), together, mutual, reciprocal, mutually, reciprocally [*interact*]

in·ter·act (in′tər akt′) *vi.* 1 to act on one another; act reciprocally 2 to deal, work, etc. *with* someone or something [a politician who *interacts* well with members of the media]

in·ter·act·ant (-ak′tənt) *n.* any of the elements involved in an interaction; specif., any of the substances involved in a chemical reaction

in·ter·ac·tion (-ak′shən) *n.* 1 action on each other; reciprocal action or effect 2 a dealing, working, etc. together or with another —**in′ter·ac′tion·al** *adj.*

in·ter·ac·tive (-ak′tiv) *adj.* 1 acting on one another; reciprocally active 2 designating or of programming or electronic equipment, as for TV, videodiscs, etc., which allows viewers to participate, as by making a response, influencing the pace of the action, etc. 3 *Comput.* of or involving a mode of operation in which there is a continual exchange of information between the computer and the user

in·ter·a·gen·cy (in′tər ā′jən sē) *adj.* of or having to do with two or more governmental agencies

in·ter a·li·a (in′tər ä′lē ə) ⟦L⟧ among other things

in·ter a·li·os (in′tər ä′lē ōs′) ⟦L⟧ among other persons

in·ter-A·mer·i·can (in′tər ə mer′i kən) *adj.* between or among nations of the Americas

in·ter·a·tom·ic (in′tər ə täm′ik) *adj.* of or having to do with the space between atoms

in·ter·bank (in′tər baŋk′) *adj.* between or among banks [*interbank* lending]

in·ter·brain (in′tər brān′) *n.* DIENCEPHALON

in·ter·breed (in′tər brēd′, in′tər brēd′) *vt., vi.* **-bred′**, **-breed′ing** HYBRIDIZE

in·ter·ca·lar·y (in tur′kə ler′ē) *adj.* ⟦L *intercalarius, intercalaris* < *intercalare*: see fol.⟧ 1 added to the calendar: said of a day, month, etc. inserted in a calendar year to make it correspond to the solar year 2 having such a day, month, etc. added: said of a year 3 interpolated or inserted

in·ter·ca·late (in tur′kə lāt′) *vt.* **-lat′ed**, **-lat′ing** ⟦< L *intercalatus*, pp. of *intercalare*, to insert < *inter-*, between + *calare*, to call, proclaim: for IE base see CLAMOR⟧ 1 to insert (an intercalary day, month, etc.) 2 to interpolate or insert —**in·ter′ca·la′tion** *n.*

in·ter·cede (in′tər sēd′) *vi.* **-ced′ed**, **-ced′ing** ⟦L *intercedere* < *inter-*, between + *cedere*, to go: see CEDE⟧ 1 to plead or make a request in behalf of another or others [to *intercede* with the authorities for the prisoner] 2 to intervene for the purpose of producing agreement; mediate 3 *R.C.Ch., Eastern Orthodox Ch., etc.* to make a supplication to God in behalf of someone: said of a saint so petitioned in prayer

in·ter·cel·lu·lar (in′tər sel′yoo lər) *adj.* located between or among cells

in·ter·cept (in′tər sept′; *for n.* in′tər sept′) *vt.* ⟦< L *interceptus*, pp. of *intercipere*, to take between, interrupt < *inter-*, between + *capere*, to take: see HAVE⟧ 1 to seize or stop on the way, before arrival at the intended place; stop or interrupt the course of; cut off 2 [Now Rare] *a)* to stop, hinder, or prevent *b)* to cut off communication with, sight of, etc. 3 *Football a)* to catch (a pass) as an interception *b)* to catch an interception thrown by (an offensive player) 4 *Math.* to cut off, mark off, or bound between two points, lines, or planes —*n.* 1 *a)* the act of intercepting *b)* the fact or condition of being intercepted 2 a message intercepted during electronic or radio transmission 3 *Math.* the part of a line, plane, etc. intercepted 4 *Mil.* the act of intercepting an enemy force, esp. enemy aircraft —**in′ter·cep′tive** *adj.*

in·ter·cep·tion (in′tər sep′shən) *n.* 1 the act or an instance of intercepting 2 *Football* a play in which a defensive player catches a pass thrown by an offensive player

in·ter·cep·tor (in′tər sep′tər) *n.* a person or thing that intercepts; esp., a fast-climbing fighter jet or a surface-to-air missile: also sp. **in′ter·cept′er**

in·ter·ces·sion (in′tər sesh′ən) *n.* ⟦L *intercessio* < *intercessus*, pp. of *intercedere*⟧ the act of interceding; mediation, pleading, or prayer in behalf of another or others —**in′ter·ces′sion·al** *adj.*

in·ter·ces·sor (in′tər ses′ər, in′tər ses′ər) *n.* ⟦ME *intercessour* < L *intercessor*⟧ one who intercedes —**in′ter·ces′so·ry** *adj.*

in·ter·change (in′tər chānj′; *for n.* in′tər chānj′) *vt.* **-changed′**, **-chang′ing** ⟦ME *entrechangen* < OFr *entrechangier*: see INTER- & CHANGE⟧ 1 to give and take mutually; exchange [to *interchange* ideas] 2 to put (each of two things) in the other's place 3 to alternate; cause to follow in succession [to *interchange* work with play] —*vi.* to change places with each other —*n.* 1 the act or an instance of interchanging 2 a junction, as a cloverleaf, which allows movement of traffic between highways on different levels

in·ter·change·a·ble (in′tər chān′jə bəl) *adj.* ⟦OFr *entrechangeable*⟧ that can be interchanged; esp., that can be put or used in place of each other —**in′ter·change′a·bil′i·ty** *n.* —**in′ter·change′a·bly** *adv.*

in·ter·cit·y (in′tər sit′ē) *adj.* between cities [*intercity* trains]

in·ter·clav·i·cle (in′tər klav′i kəl) *n.* a bone lying between the tips of the clavicles and on the sternum in certain vertebrates —**in′ter·cla·vic′u·lar** (-klə vik′yoo lər) *adj.*

in·ter·coast·al (in′tər kōs′təl) *adj.* 1 existing or taking place between seacoasts 2 designating or having to do with a waterway that connects ports along a coast

in·ter·col·le·giate (in′tər kə lē′jit) *adj.* between or among colleges and universities

in·ter·co·lum·ni·a·tion (-kə lum′nē ā′shən) *n.* 1 the space between two columns, measured from their axes 2 a system for spacing a series of columns

in·ter·com (in′tər käm′) *n.* a radio or telephone intercommunication system, as between rooms of a building

in·ter·com·mu·ni·cate (in′tər kə myoo′ni kāt′) *vt., vi.* **-cat′ed**, **-cat′ing** to communicate with or to each other or one another —**in′ter·com·mu′ni·ca′tion** *n.*

in·ter·com·mun·ion (-kə myoon′yən) *n.* mutual communion, as among religious groups

in·ter·con·nect (in′tər kə nekt′) *vt., vi.* to connect or be connected with one another —**in′ter·con·nec′tion** *n.* —**in′ter·con′nec·tiv′i·ty** *n.*

in·ter·con·ti·nen·tal (in′tər känt″n ent′'l) *adj.* 1 between or among continents 2 able to travel from one continent to another, as a plane, rocket-launched missile, etc.

in·ter·cos·tal (in′tər käs′təl, -kôs′-) *adj.* between the ribs —*n.* an intercostal muscle, etc. —**in′ter·cos′tal·ly** *adv.*

in·ter·course (in′tər kôrs′) *n.* ⟦ME *entercours* < OFr *entrecours* < L *intercursus*: see INTER- & COURSE⟧ 1 communication or dealings between or among people, countries, etc.; interchange of products, services, ideas, feelings, etc. 2 *a)* SEXUAL INTERCOURSE *b)* any other sexual act involving insertion of the penis [anal *intercourse*]

in·ter·crop (in′tər kräp′, in′tər kräp′; *for n.* in′tər kräp′) *vt., vi.* **-cropped′**, **-crop′ping** to grow a crop with (another crop) in the same field, as in alternate rows —*n.* any such crop

in·ter·cross (in′tər krôs′, in′tər krôs′; *for n.* in′tər krôs′) *vt., vi.* HYBRIDIZE —*n.* HYBRID (sense 1)

in·ter·cul·tur·al (in′tər kul′chər əl) *adj.* between or among people of different cultures

in·ter·cur·rent (-kur′ənt) *adj.* ⟦L *intercurrens*, prp. of *intercurrere*: see INTER- & CURRENT⟧ 1 running between; intervening 2 *Med.* occurring during another disease and modifying it —**in′ter·cur′rent·ly** *adv.*

in·ter·cut (in′tər kut′) *vt., vi.* **-cut′**, **-cut′ting** *Film, TV* to interrupt (a scene, sequence, etc.) by inserting (a shot, sequence, etc.), sometimes repeatedly

in·ter·de·nom·i·na·tion·al (in′tər dē näm′ə nā′shən əl, -di-) *adj.* between, among, or involving different religious denominations

in·ter·den·tal (in′tər dent′'l) *adj.* 1 situated between the teeth 2 *Phonet.* articulated with the tip of the tongue between the upper and lower teeth, as (th) and (*th*) —*n.* an interdental consonant

in·ter·de·part·men·tal (-dē′pärt ment′'l) *adj.* between or among departments —**in′ter·de′part′men′tal·ly** *adv.*

in·ter·de·pend·ence (in′tər dē pen′dəns, -di-) *n.* dependence on each other or one another; mutual dependence: also **in′ter·de·pend′en·cy**, *pl.* **-cies** —**in′ter·de·pend′ent** *adj.* —**in′ter·de·pend′ent·ly** *adv.*

in·ter·dict (in′tər dikt′; *for n.* in′tər dikt′) *vt.* ⟦altered (infl. by L *interdictus*) < ME *entrediten* < n. *entredit*: see **n.** below⟧ 1 to prohibit (an action) or prohibit the use of (a thing); forbid with authority 2 to restrain from doing or using something 3 *Mil.* to impede or hinder (the enemy) or isolate (an area, route, etc.) by firepower or bombing 4 *R.C.Ch.* to exclude (a person, parish, etc.) from certain acts, sacraments, or privileges —*n.* ⟦altered (infl. by L) < ME *entredit* < OFr < L *interdictum* < pp. of *interdicere*, to forbid, prohibit, lit., to speak between < *inter-* (see INTER-) + *dicere*, to speak (see DICTION)⟧ 1 an official prohibition or restraint 2 *R.C.Ch.* an interdicting of a person, parish, etc. —**SYN.** FORBID —**in′ter·dic′tion** *n.* —**in′ter·dic′tor** *n.* —**in′ter·dic′to·ry** *adj.*, **in′ter·dic′tive**

in·ter·dig·i·tate (in′tər dij′i tāt′) *vi.* **-tat′ed**, **-tat′ing** to interlock like the fingers of folded hands —**in′ter·dig′i·ta′tion** *n.*

in·ter·dis·ci·pli·nar·y (-dis′ə pli ner′ē) *adj.* involving, or joining, two or more disciplines, or branches of learning [the *interdisciplinary* approach of the psychohistorian]

in·ter·est (in′trist; in′tər est′, -əst) ***n.*** ⟦ME *interesse* < ML usury, compensation (in L, to be between, be different, interest < *inter-*, between + *esse*, to be: see IS[1]): altered, infl. by OFr *interest* < L, it interests, concerns, 3d pers. sing., pres. indic., of *interesse*⟧ **1** a right or claim to something **2** *a)* a share or participation in something *b)* something, as a business, in which one participates or has a share *c)* a personal connection or involvement which might be thought to compromise one's impartiality in carrying out one's official duties (usually in **declare an interest**) **3** [*often pl.*] advantage; welfare; benefit **4** [*usually pl.*] a group of people having a common concern or dominant power in some industry, occupation, cause, etc. [the steel *interests*] **5** personal influence **6** *a)* a feeling of intentness, concern, or curiosity about something [an *interest* in politics] *b)* the power of causing this feeling [books of *interest* to children] *c)* something causing this feeling [the Lake District is an *interest* of literary scholars] **7** importance; consequence [a matter of little *interest*] **8** *a)* money paid for the use of money, as on a loan *b)* the rate of such payment, expressed as a percentage per unit of time **9** any increase over what is owed [to repay kindness with *interest*] —***vt.*** ⟦prob. < ME *interessed* < *interesse* + *-ed*⟧ **1** to involve the interest, or concern, of; have an effect upon **2** to cause to have an interest or take part in [can I *interest* you in a drink before dinner?] **3** to excite the attention or curiosity of —**in the interest (or interests) of** for the sake of

in·terest·ed (in′tris tid, in′tər es′tid) ***adj.*** **1** having an interest or share; concerned **2** influenced by personal interest; biased or prejudiced **3** feeling or showing interest or curiosity —**in′terest·ed·ly** ***adv.*** —**in′terest·ed·ness** ***n.***

interest group an organized group active in supporting and advancing a particular cause or goal: see also SPECIAL INTEREST

in·terest·ing (in′tris tiŋ, in′tər es′tiŋ) ***adj.*** exciting curiosity or attention; of interest —**in′terest·ing·ly** ***adv.***

in·ter·eth·nic (in′tər eth′nik) ***adj.*** between, among, or involving members of two or more ethnic groups [*interethnic* marriage]

in·ter·face (in′tər fās′) ***n.*** **1** a plane forming the common boundary between two parts of matter or space **2** a point or means of interaction between two systems, disciplines, groups, etc. **3** *Comput.* a point or means of interaction between two or more systems, components of a computer system, or the system and a user — ***vt., vi.*** **-faced′**, **-fac′ing** **1** to sew material (**interfacing**) between the outer fabric and the facing of (a collar, lapel, etc.) so as to give body or to prevent stretching **2** to interact with (another system, discipline, group, etc.)

in·ter·fa·cial (in′tər fā′shəl) ***adj.*** **1** of or having to do with an interface **2** designating the angle between any two faces of a crystal or a crystal form

in·ter·faith (in′tər fāth′) ***adj.*** between or involving persons adhering to different religions [an *interfaith* council]

in·ter·fere (in′tər fir′) ***vi.*** **-fered′**, **-fer′ing** ⟦OFr *(s')entreferir*, to strike (each other) < *entre-*, INTER- + *férir* < L *ferire*, to strike < IE base **bher-* > BORE[1]⟧ **1** to knock one foot or leg against the other: said of a horse **2** to come into collision or opposition; clash; conflict **3** *a)* to come in or between for some purpose; intervene *b)* to meddle **4** *Law* to claim priority for an invention, as when two or more applications for its patent are pending **5** *Physics* to affect each other by interference: said of two waves or streams of vibration **6** *Radio, TV, etc.* to create interference in reception **7** *Sports* to be guilty of interference —**interfere with** to hinder —**in′ter·fer′er** ***n.***

in·ter·fer·ence (in′tər fir′əns) ***n.*** **1** an act or instance of interfering **2** something that interferes ☆**3** *a)* *Football* the legal blocking of opposing players in order to clear the way for the ball carrier; also, the player or players who do such blocking *b)* *Sports* the illegal hindering of an opposing player, specif., in football, of an opponent who is trying to catch a pass **4** *Physics* the mutual action of two waves of the same frequency, as of sound, light, etc., in reinforcing or neutralizing each other according to their relative phases on meeting **5** *Radio, TV, etc.* *a)* static, unwanted signals, etc., producing a distortion as of sounds or images and preventing good reception *b)* such distorted reception —☆**run interference (for)** **1** *Football* to accompany (the ball carrier) in order to block opposing players **2** [Informal] to interfere or intervene in behalf of someone else —**in′ter·fe·ren′tial** (-fə ren′shəl) ***adj.***

in·ter·fer·om·e·ter (in′tər fir äm′ət ər) ***n.*** ⟦INTERFER(E) + -O- + -METER⟧ an instrument for measuring wavelengths of light and very small distances and thicknesses, for determining indices of refraction, and for analyzing small parts of a spectrum by means of the interference phenomena of light —**in′ter·fer′o·met′ric** (-fir′ə me′trik) ***adj.*** —**in′ter·fer·om′e·try** ***n.***

in·ter·fer·on (in′tər fir′än′) ***n.*** ⟦INTERFER(E) + *-on*, arbitrary suffix⟧ a cellular protein produced in response to infection by a virus and acting to inhibit viral growth

in·ter·fer·tile (in′tər furt′'l) ***adj.*** able to interbreed, or hybridize —**in′ter·fer·til′i·ty** (-fər til′ə tē) ***n.***

in·ter·file (in′tər fil′) ***vt.*** **-filed′**, **-fil′ing** to place (papers, etc.) in order in a file or organized set; esp., to combine two or more such organized sets

in·ter·fluve (in′tər flo͞ov′) ***n.*** ⟦< INTER- + L *fluvius*, river⟧ the land between two streams or river valleys

in·ter·fold (in′tər fōld′, in′tər fōld′) ***vt., vi.*** to fold together or inside one another

in·ter·fuse (in′tər fyo͞oz′) ***vt.*** **-fused′**, **-fus′ing** ⟦< L *interfusus*, pp. of *interfundere*, to pour between: see INTER- & FOUND[3]⟧ **1** to combine by mixing, blending, or fusing together **2** to cause to pass into or through a substance; infuse **3** to spread itself through; pervade —***vi.*** to fuse; blend —**in′ter·fu′sion** ***n.***

in·ter·ga·lac·tic (in′tər gə lak′tik) ***adj.*** existing or occurring between or among galaxies

in·ter·gen·er·a·tion·al (-jen′ə rā′shə nəl) ***adj.*** of or involving persons of different generations, as parents and children

in·ter·gla·cial (-glā′shəl) ***adj.*** formed or occurring between two glacial epochs

in·ter·gov·ern·men·tal (-guv′ərn ment′'l) ***adj.*** **1** of, between, or involving different levels of government, as the federal level and the state level **2** of, between, or involving the governments of different nations [Interpol is an *intergovernmental* organization]

in·ter·grade (in′tər grād′; *for n.* in′tər grād′) ***vi.*** **-grad′ed**, **-grad′ing** to pass into another form or kind by a series of intermediate grades —***n.*** an intermediate grade; transitional form —**in′ter·gra·da′tion** (-grā dā′shən, -grə-) ***n.***

in·ter·group (in′tər gro͞op′) ***adj.*** between, among, or involving different groups, specif. different social, ethnic, or racial groups

in·ter·im (in′tər im) ***n.*** ⟦L, meanwhile < *inter*: see INTER-⟧ the period of time between; meantime —***adj.*** for or during an interim; temporary; provisional [an *interim* council] —**SYN.** TEMPORARY

in·te·ri·or (in tir′ē ər) ***adj.*** ⟦ME < MFr < L, compar. of *inter*, between: see INTER-⟧ **1** situated within; on the inside; inner **2** away from the coast, border, or frontier; inland **3** of the internal, or domestic, affairs of a country **4** of the inner nature of a person or thing; private, secret, etc. —***n.*** **1** the interior part of anything; specif., *a)* the inside of a room or building *b)* the inland part of a country or region *c)* the inner nature of a person or thing **2** a picture, view, etc. of the inside of a room or building **3** the internal, or domestic, affairs of a country [the U.S. Department of the *Interior*] —**in·te′ri·or·ly** ***adv.***

interior angle **1** any of the four angles formed on the inside of two straight lines when crossed by a transversal **2** the angle formed inside a polygon by two adjacent sides

interior decoration the act, art, or business of decorating and furnishing the interiors of houses, rooms, offices, etc. —**interior decorator**

interior design the act, art, or business of planning and carrying out the design for the interiors of houses, rooms, offices, etc., sometimes including interior decoration —**interior designer**

in·te·ri·or·i·ty (in tir′ē ôr′ə tē) ***n.*** inward or inner quality, character, nature, etc.

in·te·ri·or·ize (in tir′ē ər īz′) ***vt.*** **-ized′**, **-iz′ing** to make (a concept, value, etc.) part of one's inner nature —**in·te′ri·or·i·za′tion** ***n.***

interior monologue a narrative technique or passage which suggests a character's stream of consciousness

interj *abbrev.* interjection

in·ter·ject (in′tər jekt′) ***vt.*** ⟦< L *interjectus*, pp. of *interjicere*, to throw between < *inter-*, between + *jacere*, to throw: see JET[1]⟧ to throw in between; interrupt with; insert; interpose [to *interject* a question] —**in′ter·jec′tor** ***n.***

in·ter·jec·tion (in′tər jek′shən) ***n.*** ⟦ME *interjeccioun* < MFr *interjection* < L *interjectio*⟧ **1** the act of interjecting **2** something interjected, as a word or phrase **3** *Gram.* *a)* a word, esp. an exclamation, inserted into an utterance without grammatical connection to it (Ex.: ah! I declare!) *b)* any of a class of words used independently in this way (Ex.: ouch! well! pow! arf!)

in·ter·jec·tion·al (-jek′shə nəl) ***adj.*** **1** of, or having the nature of, an interjection **2** interjected **3** containing an interjection Also **in′ter·jec′to·ry** —**in′ter·jec′tion·al·ly** ***adv.***

in·ter·knit (in′tər nit′) ***vt., vi.*** **-knit′ted** or **-knit′**, **-knit′ting** to knit together; intertwine

in·ter·lace (-lās′) ***vt., vi.*** **-laced′**, **-lac′ing** ⟦ME *entrelacen* < OFr *entrelacier*: see INTER- & LACE⟧ **1** to unite by passing over and under each other; weave together **2** to connect intricately —**in′ter·lace′ment** ***n.***

In·ter·lak·en (in′tər lä′kən) resort town in the Bernese Alps, central Switzerland, on the Aar River

in·ter·lam·i·nate (in′tər lam′ə nāt′) ***vt.*** **-nat′ed**, **-nat′ing** **1** to put between laminae **2** to place in alternate laminae —**in′ter·lam′i·na′tion** ***n.***

in·ter·lard (-lärd′) ***vt.*** ⟦MFr *entrelarder*: see INTER- & LARD⟧ **1** to insert strips or pieces of fat, bacon, etc. in (meat to be cooked) **2** to intersperse; diversify [to *interlard* a lecture with quotations] **3** *a)* to mix together *b)* to be intermixed in (said of things)

in·ter·lay (in′tər lā′) ***vt.*** **-laid′** (-lād′), **-lay′ing** to lay or put between or among —**in′ter·lay′er** ***n.***

in·ter·leaf (in′tər lēf′) ***n.***, *pl.* **-leaves′** (-lēvz′) a leaf, usually blank, bound between the other leaves of a book, for notes, etc.

in·ter·league (in′tər lēg′) ***adj.*** between or among leagues

in·ter·leave (in′tər lēv′) ***vt.*** **-leaved′**, **-leav′ing** **1** to put an interleaf or interleaves in **2** to insert (something) at intervals into (something else) [an essay *interleaved* with Scripture quotations]

in·ter·leu·kin (in′tər lo͞o′kin) ***n.*** ⟦INTER- + LEUK(OCYTE) + -IN[1]⟧ **1** any of a closely related family of polypeptides, derived from many cell types, that stimulate several components of the inflammatory response, including fever; lymphocyte activating factor: in full **interleukin-1** **2** a glycoprotein lymphocyte product that stimulates the growth of T cells and is used experimentally in cancer therapy; T cell growth factor: in full **interleukin-2**

in·ter·line[1] (in′tər līn′, in′tər līn′) ***vt.*** **-lined′**, **-lin′ing** ⟦ME *enterlynen* < ML *interlineare*: see INTER- & LINE[2]⟧ **1** to write or print between the lines of (a text, document, etc.) **2** to insert between the lines [to *interline* notes on pages] Also **in'ter·lin'e·ate'** (-lin'ē āt') **-at'ed, -at'ing** —***adj.*** of, relating to, or using more than one transportation line or system —**in'ter·lin'e·a'tion** ***n.***

in·ter·line[2] (in'tər līn', in'tər līn') ***vt.*** **-lined', -lin'ing** ⟦INTER- + LINE[2]⟧ to put an inner lining between the outer material and the ordinary lining of (a garment)

in·ter·lin·e·ar (in'tər lin'ē ər) ***adj.*** ⟦ME *interlineare* < ML *interlinearis*⟧ **1** written or printed between the lines [*interlinear* notes] ☆**2** having the same text in different languages printed in alternate lines [an *interlinear* Bible] Also **in'ter·lin'e·al**

in·ter·lin·ing (in'tər lī'niŋ) ***n.*** **1** an inner lining put between the outer material and the ordinary lining of a garment **2** any fabric used to make such an inner lining

in·ter·link (in'tər liŋk') ***vt.*** to link together —**in'ter·link'age** ***n.***

in·ter·lock (in'tər läk', in'tər läk'; *for n.* in'tər läk') ***vt., vi.*** **1** to lock together; join with one another **2** to connect or be connected so that neither part can be operated independently —***n.*** **1** the condition of being interlocked **2** a device or arrangement by means of which the functioning of one part is controlled by the functioning of another, as for safety

interlocking directorates boards of directors having some members in common, so that the corporations concerned are more or less under the same control

in·ter·lo·cu·tion (in'tər lō kyo͞o'shən) ***n.*** ⟦L *interlocutio* < pp. of *interloqui*, to speak between < *inter-*, INTER- + *loqui*, to speak⟧ talk between two or more people; conversation; dialogue

in·ter·loc·u·tor (in'tər läk'yo͞o tər, -yə-; *for 2 often*, -läk'ət ər) ***n.*** ⟦< pp. of L *interloqui*: see prec.⟧ **1** a person taking part in a conversation or dialogue ☆**2** [Historical] an entertainer in a minstrel show who served as master of ceremonies and as a foil for the end men

in·ter·loc·u·to·ry (in'tər läk'yo͞o tôr'ē, -yə-) ***adj.*** ⟦ML(Ec) *interlocutorius*: see INTERLOCUTION⟧ **1** of, having the nature of, or occurring in dialogue; conversational **2** interjected [*interlocutory* wit] **3** *Law* pronounced during the course of a suit, pending final decision; not final [an *interlocutory* divorce decree]

in·ter·lope (in'tər lōp') ***vi.*** **-loped', -lop'ing** ⟦prob. back-form. < fol.⟧ **1** [Archaic] to intrude on another's trading rights or privileges **2** to intrude or meddle in others' affairs —***SYN.*** INTRUDE

in·ter·lop·er (in'tər lō'pər) ***n.*** ⟦INTER- + *-loper* < *landloper*, a vagrant < Du < *land*, LAND + *loper*, a runner < *lopen*, to run: see LEAP⟧ **1** [Archaic] *a)* an unauthorized trading vessel in areas assigned to monopolies or chartered companies *b)* any unauthorized trader **2** a person who meddles in others' affairs

in·ter·lude (in'tər lo͞od') ***n.*** ⟦ME *enterlude* < OFr *entrelude* < ML *interludium* < L *inter*, between + *ludus*, play: see LUDICROUS⟧ **1** [Historical] a short, humorous play presented between the parts of a miracle play or morality play **2** a short play of a sort popular in the Tudor period, either farcical or moralistic in tone and with a plot typically derived from French farce or the morality play **3** any performance between the acts of a play **4** instrumental music played between the parts of a song, liturgy, play, etc. **5** *a)* anything that fills time between two events *b)* intervening time or, rarely, space

in·ter·lu·nar (in'tər lo͞o'nər) ***adj.*** ⟦prob. < MFr *interlunaire*: see INTER- & LUNAR⟧ of the period of time each month when the moon cannot be seen because it is in or near conjunction with the sun

in·ter·mar·riage (in'tər mar'ij) ***n.*** **1** marriage between persons of different clans, tribes, races, religions, castes, etc. **2** marriage between closely related persons

in·ter·mar·ry (in'tər mar'ē) ***vi.*** **-ried, -ry·ing** **1** to become connected by or unite in marriage: said of persons of different clans, tribes, races, religions, castes, etc. **2** to marry: said of closely related persons

in·ter·med·dle (in'tər med''l) ***vi.*** **-dled, -dling** ⟦ME *entremedlen* < Anglo-Fr *entremedler*: see INTER- & MEDDLE⟧ to meddle in the affairs of others, esp. to do so officiously —**in'ter·med'dler** ***n.***

in·ter·me·di·ar·y (in'tər mē'dē er'ē, -dē ər ē) ***adj.*** ⟦Fr *intermédiaire* < L *intermedius*: see fol. + -ARY⟧ **1** acting between two persons; acting as mediator **2** being or happening between; intermediate —***n., pl.*** **-ar'ies** **1** a go-between; mediator **2** any medium, means, or agency **3** an intermediate form, phase, etc.

in·ter·me·di·ate (in'tər mē'dē it; *for v.*, -dē āt') ***adj.*** ⟦ML *intermediatus* < L *intermedius* < *inter-*, between + *medius*, middle: see MID[1]⟧ **1** being or happening between two things, places, stages, etc.; in the middle **2** designating or of an automobile larger than a compact but smaller than the standard size —***n.*** **1** anything intermediate **2** INTERMEDIARY **3** an intermediate automobile **4** *Chem.* a substance obtained as a necessary intermediate stage between the original material and the final product —***vi.*** **-at'ed, -at'ing** to mediate —**in'ter·me'di·ate·ly** ***adv.*** —**in'ter·me'di·ate·ness** ***n.***, **in'ter·me'di·a·cy** —**in'ter·me'di·a'tion** ***n.*** —**in'ter·me'di·a'tor** ***n.***

intermediate frequency *Radio* in superheterodyne reception, a frequency resulting from combining the incoming signal with a locally produced signal for amplification prior to detection

intermediate host the organism on or in which a parasite lives during an immature stage

intermediate (vector) boson *Particle Physics* WEAKON

in·ter·me·din (in'tər mēd''n) ***n.*** ⟦< L (*pars*) *intermedia*, intermediate (lobe) + -IN[1]⟧ a hormone produced by the intermediate lobe of the pituitary gland in certain vertebrates, that influences the activity of pigment cells

in·ter·ment (in tʉr'mənt) ***n.*** the act of interring; burial

in·ter·mez·zo (in'tər met'sō', -med'zō') ***n., pl.*** **-zos'** or **-zi'** (-sē', -zē') ⟦It < L *intermedius*: see INTERMEDIATE⟧ **1** a short, light dramatic, musical, or ballet entertainment between the acts of a play or opera **2** *Music a)* a short movement connecting the main parts of a composition *b)* any of certain short instrumental pieces similar to this

in·ter·mi·na·ble (in tʉr'mi nə bəl) ***adj.*** ⟦OFr < LL *interminabilis*: see IN-[2] & TERMINABLE⟧ without, or apparently without, end; lasting, or seeming to last, forever; endless —**in·ter'mi·na·bly** ***adv.***

in·ter·min·gle (in'tər miŋ'gəl) ***vt., vi.*** **-gled, -gling** to mix together; mingle; blend

in·ter·mis·sion (in'tər mish'ən) ***n.*** ⟦L *intermissio* < *intermissus*, pp. of *intermittere*⟧ **1** an intermitting or being intermitted; interruption **2** an interval of time between periods of activity; extended pause, as between acts of a play —**in'ter·mis'sive** (-mis'iv) ***adj.***

in·ter·mit (in'tər mit') ***vt., vi.*** **-mit'ted, -mit'ting** ⟦L *intermittere* < *inter-* + *mittere*: see INTER- & MISSION⟧ to stop for a time; cease at intervals; make or be intermittent; discontinue

in·ter·mit·tent (in'tər mit''nt) ***adj.*** ⟦L *intermittens*, prp. of *intermittere*: see prec.⟧ stopping and starting at intervals; pausing from time to time; periodic —**in'ter·mit'tence** ***n.***, **in'ter·mit'ten·cy** —**in'ter·mit'tent·ly** ***adv.***

SYN.—**intermittent** and **recurrent** both apply to something that stops and starts, or disappears and reappears, from time to time, but the former usually stresses the breaks or pauses, and the latter, the repetition or return [an *intermittent* fever, *recurrent* attacks of the hives]; **periodic** refers to something that recurs at more or less regular intervals [*periodic* economic crises]; **alternate** is usually used of two recurrent things that follow each other in regular order [a life of *alternate* sorrow and joy] —***ANT.*** **continued, continuous**

intermittent current *Elec.* a direct current interrupted at regular or irregular intervals

intermittent fever a fever characterized by periodic intervals when the body temperature returns to normal

in·ter·mix (in'tər miks') ***vt., vi.*** to mix together; blend

in·ter·mix·ture (-miks'chər) ***n.*** **1** an intermixing or being intermixed **2** a mixture **3** an added ingredient; admixture

in·ter·mod·al (in'tər mōd''l) ***adj.*** of or pertaining to the conveyance of freight or passengers by more than one carrier or mode of transportation in a single journey

in·ter·mo·lec·u·lar (in'tər mō lek'yo͞o lər, -mə-) ***adj.*** having activity between or among molecules: cf. INTRAMOLECULAR

☆**in·ter·mon·tane** (in'tər män'tān', -män tān') ***adj.*** ⟦< INTER + L *montanus*, of a mountain < *mons* (gen. *montis*), MOUNTAIN⟧ between or among mountains: also **in·ter·moun·tain** (in'tər mount''n, in'tər mount''n)

in·tern (in'tʉrn'; *for vt.* in tʉrn', in'tʉrn') ☆***n.*** ⟦Fr *interne*, resident within < L *internus*, inward: see fol.⟧ **1** a doctor serving an apprenticeship as an assistant resident in a hospital generally just after graduation from medical school: cf. EXTERN **2** a person, esp. a student, participating in a program of temporary, supervised work in a particular field in order to gain practical experience —☆***vi.*** to serve as an intern —***vt.*** to detain or confine (foreign persons, ships, etc.), as during a war

in·ter·nal (in tʉr'nəl) ***adj.*** ⟦ML *internalis* < L *internus*, inward, internal, akin to *inter*: see INTER-⟧ **1** of or having to do with the inside; inner **2** to be taken inside the body [*internal* remedies] **3** having to do with the inner nature of a thing; intrinsic [*internal* evidence] **4** having to do with the inner being; subjective **5** having to do with the domestic affairs of a country [*internal* revenue] **6** *a) Anat.* situated toward the inside of the body or closer to its center *b)* existing or occurring inside the body or a body part —***n.*** [*pl.*] innards; entrails —**in'ter·nal'i·ty** (-nal'ə tē) ***n.*** —**in·ter'nal·ly** ***adv.***

in·ter·nal-com·bus·tion engine (-kəm bus'chən) an engine, as in an automobile, motorboat, or lawn mower, that obtains its power from heat and pressure produced by the combustion of a fuel-and-air mixture inside one or more closed chambers or cylinders

internal ear INNER EAR

internal exile the condition or a period of enforced removal from one's home or community to another place, usually remote, within the same country

in·ter·nal·ize (in tʉr'nəl īz') ***vt.*** **-ized', -iz'ing** to make internal; interiorize; specif., to make (others', esp. the prevailing, attitudes, ideas, norms, etc.) a part of one's own patterns of thinking —**in·ter'nal·i·za'tion** ***n.***

internal medicine the branch of medicine that deals with the diagnosis and nonsurgical treatment of diseases

internal respiration **1** the exchange of oxygen and carbon dioxide between the blood or lymph and the tissue cells **2** the metabolic consumption of oxygen and the production of carbon dioxide in the protoplasm of cells

☆**internal revenue** governmental income from taxes on income, profits, amusements, luxuries, etc.

internal rhyme *Poetry* rhyme involving a word or words not at the end of a line

internal secretion a substance secreted directly into the blood, as by an endocrine gland; hormone

internat *abbrev.* international

in·ter·na·tion·al (in'tər nash'ə nəl; *for n. 2 also*, -nash'ə nal', -näl') ***adj.*** **1**

between or among nations [an *international* treaty] 2 concerned with the relations between nations [an *international* court] 3 for the use of all nations [*international* waters] 4 of, for, or by people in various nations 5 of or having to do with activities or operations carried on in countries other than the home country [*international* sales] —*n.* 1 a person associated with two different countries, as a resident alien 2 *a)* an international group *b)* [I-] any of several international socialist organizations existing variously from 1864 on —**in′ter·na′tion·al′i·ty** *n.* —**in′ter·na′tion·al·ly** *adv.*

international candle CANDLE (*n.* 3b)

International Court of Justice the principal judicial body of the United Nations, seated at The Hague: it settles legal disputes between member states and issues advisory opinions on various legal questions submitted to it

international date line [*often* I- D- L-] an imaginary line running north and south through the Pacific Ocean, largely along the 180th meridian: there is a 24-hour time difference between a point just west and one just east of the line, so that when it is Sunday just west of the line, it is Saturday just east of it

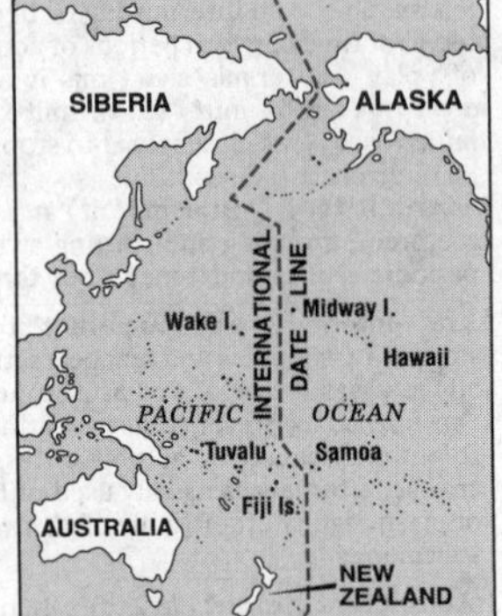

international date line

In·ter·na·tio·nale (in′tər nash′ə nal′, -näl′; *Fr* an ter nȧ syô nȧl′) *n.* ⟦Fr⟧ a revolutionary socialist hymn written in France in 1871

in·ter·na·tion·al·ism (in′tər nash′ə nəl iz′əm) *n.* 1 the principle or policy of international cooperation for the common good 2 international character, quality, etc.

in·ter·na·tion·al·ist (-ist) *n.* 1 a person who believes in internationalism 2 a specialist in international law and relations

in·ter·na·tion·al·ize (-īz′) *vt.* **-ized′**, **-iz′ing** 1 to make international 2 to bring under international control —**in′ter·na′tion·al·i·za′tion** *n.*

international law the rules generally observed and regarded as binding in the relations between nations

International Monetary Fund an international organization, established by the United Nations, to promote monetary cooperation, international trade, and exchange stability and to help equalize balance of payments by allowing members to draw from its fund

International Phonetic Alphabet a standard, internationally recognized set of symbols, each uniquely representing a human speech sound: abbrev. *IPA*

international pitch (since 1939) CONCERT PITCH (sense 2)

International Style 1 a style of modern architecture characterized by boxlike structure, little or no decoration, and smooth, flat surfaces of stone, concrete, glass, etc. 2 a style of painting of the 14th and 15th cent., characterized by realistic detail and the effect of light on the subject

International System of Units *see* SI

☆**in·terne** (in′turn′) *n. alt. sp. of* INTERN

in·ter·ne·cine (in′tər nē′sin, -sēn′; *chiefly Brit*, -nē′sīn′) *adj.* ⟦L *internecinus* < *internecare*, to kill, destroy < *inter-*, between + *necare*, to kill: see NECRO-⟧ 1 [Now Rare] full of slaughter or destruction 2 deadly or harmful to both sides of a group involved in a conflict, as a civil war; mutually destructive or harmful 3 of or involving conflict within a group

in·tern·ee (in′turn′ē′) *n.* ⟦INTERN (*vt.*) + -EE[1]⟧ a person interned as a prisoner of war or enemy alien

in·ter·net (in′tər net′) *n.* ⟦INTER- + NET(WORK)⟧ [*often* I-] the international computer network made up of thousands of smaller business, academic, and governmental networks and used extensively as an information resource: usually with *the*

in·ter·neu·ron (in′tər no͞o′rän′, -nyo͞o′-; -no͝or′än′, -nyo͝or′-) *n.* any of various nerve cells connecting sensory and motor neurons in the brain and spinal cord

☆**in·tern·ist** (in′tur′nist, in tur′nist) *n.* a doctor who specializes in INTERNAL MEDICINE

in·tern·ment (in turn′mənt) *n.* an interning or being interned

in·ter·node (in′tər nōd′) *n.* ⟦L *internodium*⟧ 1 *Anat., Zool.* the part between two nodes, as a segment of a nerve fiber 2 *Bot.* the section of a plant between two successive nodes or joints —**in′ter·nod′al** *adj.*

in·ter nos (in′tər nōs′) ⟦L⟧ between (or among) ourselves

☆**in·tern·ship** (in′turn′ship′, in turn′-) *n.* 1 the position of an intern 2 the period of service as an intern

in·ter·nu·cle·ar (in′tər no͞o′klē ər, -nyo͞o′-) *adj.* of or having to do with the space between the nuclei of atoms or cells

in·ter·nun·cial (in′tər nun′shəl, -sē əl) *adj.* ⟦see fol.⟧ 1 of or having to do with an internuncio 2 of or having to do with an interneuron

in·ter·nun·cio (in′tər nun′shō′, -shē ō′; -sē ō′; -no͞on′tsē ō′) *n., pl.* **-cios′** ⟦It *internunzio* < L *internuntius*: see INTER- & NUNCIO⟧ 1 a messenger; envoy 2 a papal representative ranking below a nuncio

in·ter·o·ce·an·ic (-ō′shē an′ik) *adj.* between or connecting oceans

in·ter·o·cep·tor (in′tər ō sep′tər) *n.* ⟦ModL: see INTERNAL & RECEPTOR⟧ an efferent nerve terminal or internal sensory receptor that responds to the internal organs, muscles, blood vessels, and the ear labyrinth —**in′ter·o·cep′tive** *adj.*

in·ter·of·fice (in′tər ôf′is, in′tər ôf′is) *adj.* between or among the offices within an organization

in·ter·op·er·a·bil·i·ty (in′tər äp′ər ə bil′ə tē) *n.* the ability of a system or component to function effectively with other systems or components —**in′ter·op′er·a·ble** *adj.*

in·ter·pel·late (in′tər pel′āt′, in tur′pə lāt′) *vt.* **-lat′ed**, **-lat′ing** ⟦< L *interpellatus*, pp. of *interpellare*, to interrupt in speaking < *inter-*, between + *-pellare* < *pellere*, to drive, urge: see FELT[1]⟧ to question (someone) formally: a form of political challenge to members of the administration in legislative bodies of certain countries —**in′ter·pel′lant** *adj., n.* —**in′ter·pel′la′tor** *n.*

in·ter·pel·la·tion (in′tər pə lā′shən; *also* in tur′pə lā′shən) *n.* ⟦L *interpellatio*⟧ the act of interpellating; formal calling to account of a cabinet minister, etc. by a legislative body

in·ter·pen·e·trate (in′tər pen′ə trāt′) *vt.* **-trat′ed**, **-trat′ing** 1 to penetrate thoroughly; pervade; permeate 2 to penetrate (each other) reciprocally or mutually —*vi.* 1 to penetrate each other 2 to penetrate between parts, etc. —**in′ter·pen′e·tra′tion** *n.* —**in′ter·pen′e·tra′tive** *adj.*

in·ter·per·son·al (in′tər pur′sə nəl) *adj.* of or involving relations between persons —**in′ter·per′son·al·ly** *adv.*

in·ter·phase (in′tər fāz′) *n.* the stage of a cell between mitotic divisions

☆**in·ter·phone** (in′tər fōn′) *n.* an intercommunication telephone system, as between departments of an office

in·ter·plan·e·tar·y (in′tər plan′ə ter′ē) *adj.* 1 between planets 2 within the solar system but outside the atmosphere of any planet or the sun

in·ter·play (in′tər plā′; *for v.* in′tər plā′, in′tər plā′) *n.* action, effect, or influence on each other or one another; interaction —*vi.* to exert influence reciprocally

in·ter·plead (in′tər plēd′) *vi.* **-plead′ed** or **-plead′** (-pled′) or **-pled′**, **-plead′ing** ⟦Anglo-Fr *entrepleder*: see INTER- & PLEAD⟧ *Law* to initiate an interpleader

in·ter·plead·er (-ər) *n.* ⟦< Anglo-Fr *entrepleder*, to interplead: substantive use of inf.⟧ a legal procedure by which two or more parties claiming the same money or property may be compelled to resolve the dispute among themselves in a single action rather than proceeding individually against the party holding the disputed money or property

In·ter·pol (in′tər pōl′) *n.* ⟦*inter(national) pol(ice)*⟧ an international police organization with headquarters in Lyon, France: it coordinates the police activities of participating nations against international criminals: full name *International Criminal Police Organization*

in·ter·po·late (in tur′pə lāt′) *vt.* **-lat′ed**, **-lat′ing** ⟦< L *interpolatus*, pp. of *interpolare*, to polish, dress up, corrupt < *interpolis*, altered by furbishing, repaired < *inter-*, between + *polire*, to POLISH⟧ 1 to alter, enlarge, or corrupt (a book or manuscript, etc.) by putting in new words, subject matter, etc. 2 to insert between or among others; specif., to insert (a word or words) in a text 3 *Math.* to estimate (a missing functional value) by taking a weighted average of known functional values at neighboring points, as in estimating a specific, missing intermediate value on a table, esp. a logarithmic or trigonometric table —*vi.* to make interpolations —**in·ter′po·lat′er** *n.*, **in·ter′po·la′tor** —**in·ter′po·la′tion** *n.* —**in·ter′po·la′tive** *adj.*

in·ter·pose (in′tər pōz′, in′tər pōz′) *vt.* **-posed′**, **-pos′ing** ⟦Fr *interposer*, altered (infl. by *poser*: see POSE[1]) < L *interpositus*, pp. of *interponere*, to set between < *inter-*, between + *ponere*, to put, place: see POSITION⟧ 1 to place or put between; insert 2 to introduce by way of intervention; put forward as interference 3 to introduce (a remark, opinion, etc.) into a conversation, debate, etc.; put in as an interruption —*vi.* 1 to be or come between 2 to intervene or mediate 3 to interrupt —**in′ter·pos′al** *n.* —**in′ter·pos′er** *n.*

in·ter·po·si·tion (in′tər pə zish′ən) *n.* ⟦ME *interposicioun* < OFr *interposicion* < L *interpositio* < pp. of *interponere*: see prec.⟧ 1 an interposing or being interposed 2 a thing interposed ☆3 the disputed doctrine that a state may reject a federal mandate that it considers to be encroaching on its rights

in·ter·pret (in tur′prət, -pət) *vt.* ⟦ME *interpreten* < MFr *intepréter* < L *interpretari* < *interpres*, agent between two parties, broker, interpreter⟧ 1 to explain the meaning of; make understandable [to *interpret* a poem] 2 to translate (esp. oral remarks) 3 to have or show one's own understanding of the meaning of; construe [to *interpret* someone's silence as contempt] 4 to bring out the meaning of; esp., to give one's own conception of (a work of art), as in performance or criticism 5 to translate (a program in a high-level language) into machine language and execute it, statement by statement: said of an interpreter program —*vi.* to act as an interpreter; explain or translate —*SYN.* EXPLAIN —**in·ter′pret·a·ble** *adj.*

in·ter·pre·ta·tion (in tur′prə tā′shən, -pə-) *n.* ⟦ME *interpretacioun* < OFr *entrepretation* < L *interpretatio*⟧ 1 the act or result of interpreting; explanation, meaning, translation, exposition, etc. 2 the expression of a person's conception of a work of art, a topic, etc. through acting, playing, writing, criticizing, etc. [the pianist's *interpretation* of a Bach sonata] —**in·ter′pre·ta′tion·al** *adj.*

in·ter·pre·ta·tive (in tur′prə tāt′iv, -tə tiv) *adj.* ⟦ML *interpretativus*⟧ INTERPRETIVE —**in·ter′pre·ta′tive·ly** *adv.*

in·ter·pret·er (in tur′prə tər, -pə-) *n.* ⟦ME *interpretour* < Anglo-Fr < OFr *interpreteur* < LL(Ec) *interpretator*⟧ 1 a person who interprets; specif., a person whose work is translating a foreign language orally, as in a conversation between people speaking different languages 2 a computer program that translates and executes, statement by statement, a program written in a high-level language

in·ter·pre·tive (-prə tiv) *adj.* 1 that interprets; explanatory 2 designed to offer educational guidance at or to a park, museum, etc. [a park's *interpretive* trail has labeled trees and flowers] —**in·ter′pre·tive·ly** *adv.*

interpretive dance a form of modern dance characterized by expressive, often exaggerated, and usually improvised movements intended to suggest a particular emotion or represent a story or situation

in·ter·ra·cial (in′tər rā′shəl) *adj.* between, among, or involving members of different races: also **in′ter·race′**

in·ter·ra·di·al (in′tər rā′dē əl) *adj.* situated between rays or radii —**in′ter·ra′di·al·ly** *adv.*

in·ter·reg·num (in′tər reg′nəm) *n., pl.* **-reg′nums** or **-reg′na** (-nə) ⟦L < *inter-*, between + *regnum*, REIGN⟧ 1 an interval between two successive reigns, when the state has no sovereign 2 a suspension of governmental or administrative functions; period without the usual ruler, governor, etc. 3 any break in a series or in a continuity; interval

in·ter·re·late (in′tər rē lāt′, -ri-) *vt., vi.* **-lat′ed, -lat′ing** to make, be, or become mutually related —**in′ter·re·lat′ed** *adj.*

in·ter·re·la·tion (-rē lā′shən) *n.* [*often pl.*] mutual relationship; interconnection —**in′ter·re·la′tion·ship** *n.*

in·ter·re·li·gious (in′tər ri lij′əs) *adj.* between or among religions, religious denominations, or sects

in·ter·rex (in′tər reks′) *n., pl.* **in′ter·re′ges′** (-rē′jēz′) ⟦L < *inter-*, between + *rex* (gen. *regis*), king: see REGAL⟧ a person acting as ruler during an interregnum

☆**in·ter·ro·bang** (in ter′ə baŋ′) *n.* ⟦INTERRO(GATION MARK) + *bang*, proofreaders' term for exclamation mark: see BANG[1] (*n.* 3)⟧ a punctuation mark (‽), a combination of a question mark and an exclamation point, used to express incredulity, disbelief, etc.

in·ter·ro·gate (in ter′ə gāt′) *vt.* **-gat′ed, -gat′ing** ⟦< L *interrogatus*, pp. of *interrogare*, to ask < *inter-*, between + *rogare*, to ask: see ROGATION⟧ to ask questions of formally or closely, in examining [to *interrogate* a witness] —*vi.* to ask questions —**SYN.** ASK

in·ter·ro·ga·tion (in ter′ə gā′shən) *n.* ⟦ME *interrogacion* < MFr *interrogation* < L *interrogatio*⟧ 1 an interrogating or being interrogated; examination 2 a question 3 [Now Rare] *short for* INTERROGATION MARK

interrogation mark (*or* point) QUESTION MARK

in·ter·rog·a·tive (in′tə räg′ə tiv) *adj.* ⟦LL *interrogativus*: see INTERROGATE⟧ 1 asking, or having the form of, a question 2 used in a question —*n.* an interrogative word or expression (Ex.: what? where?) —**in′ter·rog′a·tive·ly** *adv.*

in·ter·ro·ga·tor (in ter′ə gāt′ər) *n.* 1 a person who interrogates; questioner 2 a radio or radar transmitter whose signals actuate a transponder or a beacon

in·ter·rog·a·to·ry (in′tə räg′ə tôr′ē) *adj.* ⟦LL *interrogatorius*⟧ expressing or implying a question —*n. pl.* **-ries** a formal question or set of questions; specif., a written question or set of questions to be answered in writing under oath as by a witness in a lawsuit

in·ter·rupt (in′tə rupt′) *vt.* ⟦ME *interrupten* < L *interruptus*, pp. of *interrumpere*, to break apart, break off < *inter-*, between + *rumpere*, to break: see RUPTURE⟧ 1 *a)* to break into or in upon (a discussion, train of thought, etc.) *b)* to break in upon (a person) who is speaking, working, etc.; stop or hinder 2 to make a break in the continuity of; cut off; obstruct —*vi.* to make an interruption, esp. in another's speech, action, etc. —**in′ter·rup′tive** *adj.*

in·ter·rupt·ed (-id) *adj.* 1 broken by interruption; not continuous 2 *Bot.* asymmetrical; irregular: said of parts not equally spaced on a stem

interrupted screw a screw having the thread interrupted by a slot or slots to enable it to be locked or released by a partial turn

in·ter·rupt·er (-ər) *n.* 1 a person or thing that interrupts 2 *Elec.* a mechanism for intermittently opening and closing a circuit Also sp. **in′ter·rup′tor**

in·ter·rup·tion (in′tə rup′shən) *n.* ⟦ME *interrupcion* < OFr < L *interruptio*⟧ 1 an interrupting or being interrupted 2 anything that interrupts 3 the interval during which something is interrupted; intermission

in·ter·scho·las·tic (in′tər skə las′tik) *adj.* between or among schools [an *interscholastic* debate]

in·ter se (in′tər sā′, -sē′) [L] between (or among) themselves

in·ter·sect (in′tər sekt′) *vt.* ⟦< L *intersectus*, pp. of *intersecare*, to cut between, cut off < *inter-*, between + *secare*, to cut: see SAW[2]⟧ to divide into two parts by passing through or across; cut across [a river *intersects* the plain] —*vi.* to cross each other [lines *intersecting* to form right angles]

in·ter·sec·tion (in′tər sek′shən, in′tər sek′shən) *n.* ⟦L *intersectio*⟧ 1 the act of intersecting 2 a place of intersecting; specif., *a)* the point or line where two lines or surfaces meet or cross *b)* the place where two or more roads meet or, esp., cross 3 *Math.* the set containing all the points common to two or more given sets

in·ter·sec·tion·al (in′tər sek′shə nəl) *adj.* 1 ⟦prec. + -AL⟧ of or forming an intersection 2 ⟦INTER- + SECTION + -AL⟧ between sections or regions [*intersectional* football games]

in·ter·serv·ice (in′tər sʉr′vis, in′tər sʉr′-) *adj.* between or among branches of the armed forces

☆**in·ter·ses·sion** (in′tər sesh′ən) *n.* a short session, usually a month long, between regular sessions of a college year, in which the student concentrates on a specialized project —**in′ter·ses′sion·al** *adj.*

in·ter·sex (in′tər seks′) *n. Biol.* an individual having anatomical characteristics that are neither typically male nor typically female

in·ter·sex·u·al (in′tər sek′sho͞o əl) *adj.* 1 between the sexes [*intersexual* rivalry] 2 of, or having the characteristics of, an intersex —**in′ter·sex′u·al′i·ty** *n.*

in·ter·space (in′tər spās′; *for v.* in′tər spās′, in′tər spās′) *n.* a space between —*vt.* **-spaced′, -spac′ing** 1 to make spaces between 2 to fill spaces between

in·ter·spe·cif·ic (in′tər spə sif′ik) *adj.* between species

in·ter·sperse (in′tər spʉrs′) *vt.* **-spersed′, -spers′ing** ⟦< L *interspersus*, pp. of *interspergere* < *inter-*, among + *spargere*, to scatter: see SPARK[1]⟧ 1 to scatter among other things; put here and there or at intervals 2 to decorate or diversify with things scattered here and there —**in′ter·sper′sal** *adj.* —**in′ter·sper′sion** (-spʉr′shən, -zhən) *n.*

in·ter·sta·di·al (in′tər stā′dē əl) *adj.* of a relatively warm period during a glacial epoch, when glaciers temporarily stop or retreat

☆**in·ter·state** (in′tər stāt′) *adj.* between or among states, esp. states of the U.S. [*interstate* commerce] —*n.* one of a network of U.S. highways connecting the 48 contiguous states

in·ter·stel·lar (in′tər stel′ər, in′tər stel′ər) *adj.* ⟦INTER- + STELLAR⟧ between or among the stars [*interstellar* space]

in·ter·stice (in tʉr′stis) *n., pl.* **-sti·ces** (-stə siz, -sēz′) ⟦Fr < LL *interstitium* < *inter-*, between + *sistere*, to set, redupl. of *stare*, to STAND⟧ a small or narrow space between things or parts; crevice: *usually used in pl.*

in·ter·sti·tial (in′tər stish′əl) *adj.* 1 of, forming, or occurring in interstices 2 *Anat.* situated between the cellular components of an organ or structure —**in′ter·sti′tial·ly** *adv.*

in·ter·tes·ta·men·tal (in′tər tes′tə ment′'l) *adj.* of or pertaining to the period of Jewish literature between the writing of the last books of the Hebrew Bible (*c.* 200 B.C.) and the writing of the books of the Christian New Testament (*c.* A.D. 100)

in·ter·tex·tu·al (in′tər teks′cho͞o əl) *adj.* of or having to do with the links between one literary work and another or others, as those formed by allusions —**in′ter·tex′tu·al′i·ty** (-cho͞o al′ə tē) *n.* —**in′ter·tex′tu·al·ly** *adv.*

in·ter·tex·ture (-teks′chər) *n.* ⟦< L *intertextus*, pp. of *intertexere*, to interweave (see INTER- & TEXTURE) + -URE⟧ 1 the act or process of interweaving 2 something formed by interweaving

in·ter·tid·al (-tīd′'l) *adj.* of or pertaining to a shore zone bounded by the levels of low and high tide

in·ter·ti·tle (in′tər tīt′'l) *n.* one or more lines of dialogue or narration appearing between shots of action, as in a silent film

in·ter·trib·al (-trī′bəl) *adj.* between or among tribes

in·ter·trop·i·cal (-träp′i kəl) *adj.* within or between the tropics

in·ter·twine (in′tər twīn′, in′tər twīn′) *vt., vi.* **-twined′, -twin′ing** to twine together; intertwist

in·ter·twist (-twist′) *vt., vi.* to twist together

☆**in·ter·ur·ban** (-ʉr′bən) *adj.* ⟦INTER- + URBAN⟧ between cities or towns [an *interurban* train] —*n.* an interurban railway, train, etc.

in·ter·val (in′tər vəl) *n.* ⟦ME *enterval, intervalle* < OFr < L *intervallum*, lit., space between two palisades or walls < *inter-*, between + *vallum*, palisade, WALL⟧ 1 a space between two things; gap; distance 2 *a)* a period of time between two events, points of time, etc.; intervening period *b)* [Brit.] INTERMISSION (sense 2) 3 the extent of difference between two qualities, conditions, etc. ☆4 INTERVALE 5 *Math.* the set containing all numbers between two given numbers: it may include one, both, or neither end point 6 *Music* the difference in pitch between two tones —**at intervals** 1 once in a while 2 here and there —**in′ter·val′lic** (-val′ik) *adj.*

☆**in·ter·vale** (in′tər vāl′) *n.* ⟦blend of prec. & VALE[1]⟧ [Chiefly New England] BOTTOMLAND: sometimes called **intervale land**

in·ter·vene (in′tər vēn′) *vi.* **-vened′, -ven′ing** ⟦L *intervenire* < *inter-*, between + *venire*, to COME⟧ 1 to come, be, or lie between 2 to take place between two events, points of time, etc. 3 to come or be in between as something unnecessary or irrelevant 4 to come between as an influence, as in order to modify, settle, or hinder some action, argument, etc. 5 *Law* to come in as a third party to a suit, to protect one's own interests —**in′ter·ven′er** *n.* or *Law* **in′ter·ve′nor**

in·ter·ven·ient (-vēn′yənt) *adj.* ⟦L *interveniens*, prp.⟧ intervening —*n.* an intervening person or thing

in·ter·ven·tion (in′tər ven′shən) *n.* ⟦LL *interventio* < L *intervenire*⟧ 1 the act of intervening 2 any interference in the affairs of others, esp. by one country in the affairs of another 3 an organized confronting of a person who has a serious problem, as an addiction to drugs or alcohol, by friends and family assembled to urge rehabilitation, etc. —**in′ter·ven′tion·al** *adj.*

in·ter·ven·tion·ist (-ist) *n.* one who favors or practices intervention, esp. in international affairs —*adj.* 1 of intervention or interventionists 2 favoring or practicing intervention —**in′ter·ven′tion·ism′** *n.*

in·ter·ver·te·bral (-vʉrt′ə brəl) *adj.* between the vertebrae —**in′ter·ver′te·bral·ly** *adv.*

intervertebral disk a disk of fibrous cartilage between adjacent vertebral surfaces

in·ter·view (in′tər vyo͞o′) *n.* ⟦Fr *entrevue*: see INTER- & VIEW⟧ 1 a meeting of people face to face, as for evaluating a job applicant ☆2 *a)* a meeting in which a person is asked about personal views, activities, etc., as by a newspaper reporter or a pollster *b)* a published, taped, or filmed account of such a meeting —*vt.* ☆to conduct an interview with —☆*vi.* 1 to conduct an interview [*interviewing* three applicants today] 2 to undergo an interview: usually with *with* [*interviewing* with several law firms] —**in′ter·view·ee′** *n.* —**in′ter·view′er** *n.*

in·ter vi·vos (in′tər vī′vōs′, -vē′vōs′) ⟦L, among the living⟧ *Law* from one living person to another or others [a gift made *inter vivos*, *inter vivos* trusts]

in·ter·vo·cal·ic (in′tər vō kal′ik) *adj. Phonet.* immediately preceded by and followed by a vowel: said of a consonant

in·ter·war (in′tər wôr′) ***adj.*** happening in or designating a period between two wars, specif. the period between WWI and WWII

in·ter·weave (in′tər wēv′, in′tər wēv′) ***vt., vi.*** **-wove′, -wo′ven, -weav′ing 1** to weave together; interlace **2** to connect closely or intricately; intermingle; blend

in·tes·ta·cy (in tes′tə sē) ***n.*** the fact or state of dying intestate

in·tes·tate (in tes′tāt′, -tit) ***adj.*** ⟦ME < L *intestatus* < *in-*, not + *testatus*, pp. of *testari*, to make a will: see TESTAMENT⟧ **1** having made no will **2** not disposed of by a will —***n.*** a person who has died intestate

in·tes·tin·al (in tes′tə nəl) ***adj.*** of, in, or affecting the intestines —**in·tes′ti·nal·ly** ***adv.***

☆**intestinal fortitude** ⟦orig. a euphemism for "guts" (see GUT, ***n.*** *7a*)⟧ courage and perseverance

in·tes·tine (in tes′tən) ***adj.*** ⟦L *intestinus*, inward, internal < *intus*, within, akin to Gr *entos* < IE **entos* < base **en*, in⟧ [Archaic] internal, with regard to a country or community; domestic; civil —***n.*** ⟦L *intestinum*, neut. sing. of *intestinus*⟧ [*usually pl.*] the lower part of the alimentary canal, extending from the stomach to the anus and consisting of the small intestine and the large intestine; bowels

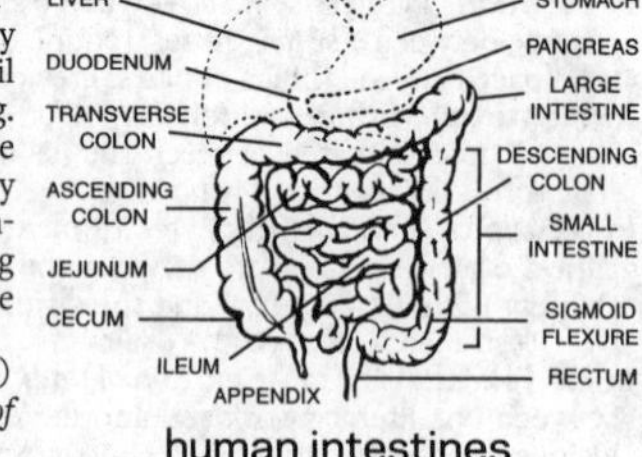

human intestines

in·thrall or **in·thral** (in thrôl′) ***vt.*** **-thralled′, -thrall′ing** *var. of* ENTHRALL

in·ti·fa·da (in′tə fä′də) ***n.*** ⟦Ar *intifāḍa*, lit., a shudder, shaking off < *nafaḍa*, to shake⟧ an uprising; specif., either of two insurrections (1987-93, 2000-05) of Palestinian Arabs against Israeli military forces in the occupied territories of the Gaza Strip and the West Bank of the Jordan: also sp. **in′ti·fa′deh**

in·ti·ma (in′tə mə) ***n., pl.*** **-mae′** (-mē′) or **-mas** ⟦ModL < fem. of L *intimus*: see INTIMATE⟧ the innermost living membrane of an organ or other part, as of an artery, vein, or lymphatic, or of an insect's trachea —**in′ti·mal** ***adj.***

in·ti·ma·cy (in′tə mə sē) ***n., pl.*** **-cies 1** the state or fact of being intimate; intimate association; familiarity **2** *a)* an intimate act *b)* [*usually pl.*] sexual intercourse

in·ti·mate (in′tə mət; *for v.*, -māt′) ***adj.*** ⟦altered (infl. by the v.) < earlier *intime* < Fr < L *intimus*, superl. of *intus*, within: see INTESTINE⟧ **1** pertaining to the inmost character of a thing; fundamental [the *intimate* structure of the atom] **2** most private or personal [one's *intimate* feelings] **3** closely acquainted or associated; very familiar [an *intimate* friend] **4** promoting a feeling of privacy, coziness, romance, etc. [an *intimate* nightclub] **5** *a)* resulting from careful study or investigation; thorough [an *intimate* knowledge of French] *b)* very close [an *intimate* acquaintance with the facts] **6** having sexual relations —***n.*** an intimate friend or companion —***vt.*** **-mat′ed, -mat′ing** ⟦< L *intimatus*, pp. of *intimare*, to announce < *intimus*⟧ **1** [Archaic] to make known formally; announce **2** to make known indirectly; hint or imply —***SYN.*** FAMILIAR, SUGGEST —**in′ti·mate·ly** ***adv.*** —**in′ti·mate·ness** ***n.***

intimate apparel LINGERIE (sense 2)

in·ti·ma·tion (in′tə mā′shən) ***n.*** ⟦ME *intimacion* < OFr *intimation* < LL *intimatio*⟧ **1** the act of intimating **2** a formal announcement or declaration: now chiefly in law **3** a hint; indirect suggestion

in·time (an tēm′) ***adj.*** ⟦Fr⟧ INTIMATE (esp. sense 4)

in·tim·i·date (in tim′ə dāt′) ***vt.*** **-dat′ed, -dat′ing** ⟦< ML *intimidatus*, pp. of *intimidare*, to make afraid < L *in-*, in + *timidus*, afraid, TIMID⟧ **1** to make timid; make afraid; daunt; cow **2** to force or deter with threats or violence —**in·tim′i·da′tion** ***n.*** —**in·tim′i·da′tor** ***n.***

in·ti·mism (in′tə miz′əm) ***n.*** ⟦Fr *intimisme* < *intime*, INTIMATE⟧ [*often* **I-**] a style of impressionist painting depicting interior domestic settings and subjects rather than landscapes —**in′ti·mist** ***n., adj.***

in·tinc·tion (in tiŋk′shən) ***n.*** ⟦LL(Ec) *intinctio*, a dipping in, baptizing < L *intinctus*, pp. of *intingere*, to dip in < *in-*, + *tingere*, to dye, TINGE⟧ the act of dipping the Eucharistic bread into the consecrated wine, so that the communicant receives both together

in·tine (in′tin′, -tēn′, -tīn′) ***n.*** ⟦Ger < L *intus*, within + Ger *-ine*, -INE[3]⟧ ENDOSPORE (sense 2)

in·ti·tle (in tīt′'l) ***vt.*** **-tled, -tling** *var. of* ENTITLE

in·tit·ule (in tit′yo͞ol′) ***vt.*** **-uled, -ul·ing** ⟦ME *intitulen* < OFr *intituler* < LL *intitulare*, to ENTITLE⟧ [Chiefly Brit.] to entitle (a legislative act, etc.)

intl or **intnl** *abbrev.* international

in·to (in′to͞o, -to͝o, -tə; in to͞o′) ***prep.*** ⟦ME < OE: see IN[1] & TO[1]⟧ **1** from the outside to the inside of; to the midst or depths of [walked *into* the house, jumped *into* the lake] **2** advancing or continuing to the midst of (a period of time) [dancing far *into* the night] **3** to the form, substance, or condition of [turned *into* a swan, divided *into* parts] **4** so as to strike; against [to bump *into* a door] **5** to the work or activity of [to go *into* teaching] **6** in the direction of [the road leads *into* town] ☆**7** [Informal] involved in, interested in, or concerned with [*into* yoga] **8** *Arith.* considered as a divisor of [3 *into* 21 is 7]

in·tol·er·a·ble (in täl′ər ə bəl) ***adj.*** ⟦ME *intollerable* < L *intolerabilis*⟧ not tolerable; unbearable; too severe, painful, cruel, etc. to be endured —**in·tol′er·a·bil′i·ty** ***n.***, **in·tol′er·a·ble·ness** —**in·tol′er·a·bly** ***adv.***

in·tol·er·ance (in täl′ər əns) ***n.*** ⟦L *intolerantia*⟧ **1** lack of tolerance, esp. of others' opinions, beliefs, etc.; bigotry **2** a sensitivity to some food, medicine, etc.

in·tol·er·ant (in täl′ər ənt) ***adj.*** ⟦L *intolerans*⟧ **1** not tolerant; unwilling to tolerate others' opinions, beliefs, etc. or persons of other races, background, etc.; bigoted; illiberal **2** unable to digest normally (a particular food, food additive, etc.): often in comb. [lactose-*intolerant*] —**intolerant of** not able or willing to tolerate —**in·tol′er·ant·ly** ***adv.*** —**in·tol′er·ant·ness** ***n.***

in·to·nate (in′tō nāt′, -tə-) ***vt.*** **-nat′ed, -nat′ing** INTONE

in·to·na·tion (in′tō nā′shən, -tə-) ***n.*** ⟦ML *intonatio* < *intonare*: see INTONE⟧ **1** the act of intoning **2** the quality of singing or playing tones in or out of tune with regard to a given standard of pitch **3** *a)* the opening words of a Gregorian chant *b)* the singing of these **4** *Linguis.* *a)* the system of significant levels and variations in pitch sequences within an utterance *b)* the type of pitch used at the end of a spoken sentence or phrase [to ask a question with a rising *intonation*] —**in′to·na′tion·al** ***adj.***

intonation pattern *Linguis.* the sequence or arrangement of pitch levels occurring in an utterance

in·tone (in tōn′) ***vt.*** **-toned′, -ton′ing** ⟦ME *entonen* < OFr *entoner* < ML *intonare*: see IN-[1] & TONE⟧ **1** to utter or recite in a singing tone or in prolonged monotones; chant **2** to give a particular intonation to **3** to sing or recite the opening phrase of (a chant, canticle, etc.) —***vi.*** to speak or recite in a singing tone or in prolonged monotones; chant —**in·ton′er** ***n.***

in to·to (in tō′tō) ⟦L⟧ in the whole; as a whole

in·tox·i·cant (in täk′si kənt) ***n.*** ⟦< ML *intoxicans*, prp. of *intoxicare*⟧ something that intoxicates; esp., alcoholic liquor —***adj.*** that intoxicates; intoxicating

in·tox·i·cate (in täk′si kāt′) ***vt.*** **-cat′ed, -cat′ing** ⟦< ML *intoxicatus*, pp. of *intoxicare*, to poison, drug < L *in-*, in + *toxicare*, to smear with poison < *toxicum*, poison: see TOXIC⟧ **1** to affect the nervous system of, so as to cause a loss of control; make drunk; stupefy; inebriate: said of alcoholic liquor or a drug **2** to excite to a point beyond self-control; make wild with excitement or happiness **3** *Med.* to poison or have a poisonous effect on —***SYN.*** DRUNK

in·tox·i·ca·tion (in täk′si kā′shən) ***n.*** **1** an intoxicating or becoming intoxicated; specif., *a)* a making or becoming drunk *b)* *Med.* a poisoning or becoming poisoned, as by a drug, serum, etc. **2** a feeling of wild excitement; rapture; frenzy

intr *abbrev.* intransitive

in·tra- (in′trə) ⟦L *intra-* < *tra*, within, inside < **intera*, akin to *interior, inter*: see INTER-⟧ *prefix* within, inside [*intramural, intravenous*]

in·tra·cel·lu·lar (in′trə sel′yo͞o lər) ***adj.*** *Biol.* existing or occurring within a cell

☆**in·tra·cit·y** (in′trə sit′ē, in′trə sit′ē) ***adj.*** existing or occurring within a large municipality, often, specif., the inner city

In·tra·coast·al Waterway (in′trə kōs′təl) waterway for small craft extending in two sections from Boston, Mass., to Brownsville, Tex.: it consists of natural and artificial channels within the U.S. coastline except for a stretch of open water along the W Fla. coast: 2,500 to 3,000 mi (4,023 to 4,828 km) long

in·tra·cra·ni·al (in′trə krā′nē əl) ***adj.*** existing or occurring within the cranium [*intracranial* pressure]

in·trac·ta·ble (in trak′tə bəl) ***adj.*** ⟦L *intractabilis*⟧ not tractable; specif., *a)* hard to manage; unruly or stubborn *b)* hard to work, manipulate, cure, treat, etc. —**in·trac′ta·bil′i·ty** ***n.***, **in·trac′ta·ble·ness** —**in·trac′ta·bly** ***adv.***

in·tra·cu·ta·ne·ous (in′trə kyo͞o tā′nē əs) ***adj.*** INTRADERMAL

in·tra·day (in′trə dā′) ***adj.*** of or within a day or session [*intraday* trading on the stock market]

in·tra·der·mal (in′trə dʉr′məl) ***adj.*** within the skin or between the layers of the skin

in·tra·dos (in trā′däs′) ***n.*** ⟦Fr < L *intra*, within + Fr *dos* < L *dorsum*, the back⟧ *Archit.* the inside curve or surface of an arch or vault

in·tra·ga·lac·tic (in′trə gə lak′tik) ***adj.*** located or occurring within a galaxy

in·tra·mo·lec·u·lar (in′trə mō lek′yə lər) ***adj.*** acting, existing, or taking place within a molecule: cf. INTERMOLECULAR —**in′tra·mo·lec′u·lar·ly** ***adv.***

in·tra·mu·ral (-myo͝or′əl) ***adj.*** ⟦INTRA- + MURAL⟧ **1** within the walls or limits of a city, college, etc. **2** between or among members of the same school, college, etc. [*intramural* athletics] **3** *Anat.* within the substance of the walls of an organ —**in′tra·mu′ral·ly** ***adv.***

in·tra·mus·cu·lar (-mus′kyə lər) ***adj.*** located or injected within the substance of a muscle —**in′tra·mus′cu·lar·ly** ***adv.***

in·tra·net (in′trə net′) ***n.*** ⟦INTRA- + NET[1] (***n.*** 7), after INTERNET⟧ a private computer network using internet technology, in which access is restricted to members of a particular organization, company, &c.

intrans *abbrev.* intransitive

in·tran·si·gent (in tran′sə jənt, -zə-) ***adj.*** ⟦Fr *intransigeant* < Sp *intransigente* < L *in-*, IN-[2] + *transigens*, prp. of *transigere*, to come to a settlement, TRANSACT⟧ **1** refusing to compromise or come to an agreement; uncompromising **2** that cannot be reconciled —***n.*** a person who is intransigent, esp. in politics —**in·tran′si·gence** ***n.***, **in·tran′si·gen·cy** —**in·tran′si·gent·ly** ***adv.***

in·tran·si·tive (in tran′sə tiv, -zə-) ***adj.*** ⟦LL *intransitivus*⟧ **1** not transitive **2** *Gram.* designating a verb that does not require a direct object —***n.*** an intransitive verb —**in·tran′si·tive·ly** ***adv.*** —**in·tran′si·tiv′i·ty** ***n.***, **in·tran′si·tive·ness**

in·tra·oc·u·lar (in′trə äk′yo͞o lər) ***adj.*** located within, or surgically implanted into, an eyeball [*intraocular* pressure, *intraocular* lens]

in·tra·par·ty (in′trə pär′tē) ***adj.*** within a political party

in·tra·per·son·al (in′trə pur′sə nəl) ***adj.*** existing or occurring within one person's mind or self

☆**in·tra·pre·neur** (in′trə prə no͝or′) ***n.*** a person in a corporation who is given the freedom and resources to initiate products, business ventures, etc. —**in′tra·pre·neur′i·al** ***adj.*** —**in′tra·pre·neur′ship** ***n.***

in·tra·psy·chic (in′trə sī′kik) ***adj.*** existing or occurring within the mind or psyche: also **in′tra·psy′chi·cal** —**in′tra·psy′chi·cal·ly** ***adv.***

in·tra·spe·cif·ic (-spə sif′ik) ***adj.*** within a single species

☆**in·tra·state** (-stāt′) ***adj.*** within a state; esp., within a state of the U.S.

in·tra·tel·lu·ric (-te lo͝or′ik) ***adj.*** ⟦INTRA- + TELLURIC[2], modeled on Ger *intratellurisch*⟧ **1** formed, located, or occurring deep inside the earth: used esp. to refer to the minerals of igneous rocks before eruption or to phenocrysts formed before the ground mass solidified **2** designating or of the period of crystallization of a magma before extrusion as a lava

in·tra·u·ter·ine (-yo͞ot′ər in) ***adj.*** within the uterus

☆**intrauterine (contraceptive) device** any of various devices, as a coil or loop of plastic, inserted in the uterus as a contraceptive

in·trav·a·sa·tion (in trav′ə sā′shən) ***n.*** ⟦INTRA- + (EXTRA)VASATION⟧ the entry of a foreign substance into a blood or lymph vessel

in·tra·vas·cu·lar (in′trə vas′kyo͞o lər) ***adj.*** *Anat.* in, or directly into, a vessel, esp. a blood vessel [an *intravascular* injection] —**in′tra·vas′cu·lar·ly** ***adv.***

in·tra·ve·nous (in′trə vē′nəs) ***adj.*** ⟦INTRA- + VENOUS⟧ in, or directly into, a vein or veins [an *intravenous* injection] —**in′tra·ve′nous·ly** ***adv.***

in·tra·zon·al (-zō′nəl) ***adj.*** designating or of a soil whose characteristics indicate the dominance of local conditions, such as topography or parent material, over the ordinary effects of climate and vegetation

in·treat (in trēt′) ***vt., vi.*** *archaic var. of* ENTREAT

in·trench (in trench′) ***vt., vi.*** *var. of* ENTRENCH

in·trep·id (in trep′id) ***adj.*** ⟦L *intrepidus* < *in-*, not + *trepidus*, alarmed, anxious: see TREPIDATION⟧ not afraid; bold; fearless; dauntless —*SYN.* BRAVE —**in′tre·pid′i·ty** (-trə pid′ə tē) ***n.***, **in·trep′id·ness** —**in·trep′id·ly** ***adv.***

Int Rev *abbrev.* Internal Revenue

in·tri·ca·cy (in′tri kə sē) ***n.*** **1** the quality or state of being intricate; complexity **2** *pl.* **-cies** something intricate; involved matter, proceeding, etc.

in·tri·cate (in′tri kit) ***adj.*** ⟦L *intricatus*, pp. of *intricare*, to entangle, perplex, embarrass < *in-*, in + *tricae*, vexations: see TRICK⟧ **1** hard to follow or understand because full of puzzling parts, details, or relationships [an *intricate* problem] **2** full of elaborate detail [an *intricate* filigree] —*SYN.* COMPLEX —**in′tri·cate·ly** ***adv.*** —**in′tri·cate·ness** ***n.***

in·tri·gant (in′tri gənt; *Fr* an trē gän′) ***n.***, *pl.* **-gants** (-gənts; *Fr*, -gän′) ⟦Fr < It *intrigante* < *intrigare*, to fol.⟧ a person given to or involved in intrigue: also sp. **in′tri·guant**

in·trigue (in trēg′; *for n., also* in′trēg′) ***vi.*** **-trigued′**, **-trigu′ing** ⟦Fr *intriguer* < It *intrigare* < L *intricare*: see INTRICATE⟧ **1** to carry on a secret love affair **2** to plot or scheme secretly or underhandedly —***vt.*** **1** to bring on, or get, by secret or underhanded plotting **2** to excite the interest or curiosity of; fascinate [the puzzle *intrigued* her] **3** [Archaic] to trick or perplex **4** [Obs.] to entangle —***n.*** **1** an intriguing; secret or underhanded plotting **2** a secret or underhanded plot or scheme; machination **3** a secret love affair —*SYN.* PLOT —**in·trigu′er** ***n.***

in·trigu·ing (in trē′giŋ) ***adj.*** exciting interest or curiosity; fascinating —**in·trigu′ing·ly** ***adv.***

in·trin·sic (in trin′sik, -zik) ***adj.*** ⟦LME *intrinsique* < MFr *intrinsèque* < LL *intrinsecus*, inward < L, inwardly < *intra-*, within (see INTRA-) + *secus*, following: see EXTRINSIC⟧ **1** belonging to the real nature of a thing; not dependent on external circumstances; essential; inherent **2** *Anat.* located within, or exclusively of, a part Opposed to EXTRINSIC Also [Archaic] **in·trin′si·cal** —**in·trin′si·cal′i·ty** ***n.*** —**in·trin′si·cal·ly** ***adv.***

intrinsic factor a substance secreted by the stomach which permits the absorption of vitamin B_{12} in the intestines, thus preventing pernicious anemia

in·tro[1] (in′trō) [Informal] ***n.*** *short for* INTRODUCTION —***adj.*** *short for* INTRODUCTORY

intro[2] or **introd** *abbrev.* **1** introduction **2** introductory

in·tro- (in′trō, -trə) ⟦L *intro-* < *intro*, inwardly, on the inside < **intero*, akin to *inter*: see INTER-⟧ *prefix* into, within, inward [*introvert*]

in·tro·duce (in′trə do͞os′, -dyo͞os′) ***vt.*** **-duced′**, **-duc′ing** ⟦L *introducere* < *intro-* (see prec.) + *ducere*, to lead: see DUCT⟧ **1** to lead or bring into a given place or position; conduct in **2** to put in or within; insert [to *introduce* an electric wire into a conduit] **3** to bring or add as a new feature into some action, composition, etc. [to *introduce* a humorous note in a speech] **4** to bring into use, knowledge, or fashion; make popular or common; institute [space science has *introduced* many new words] ☆**5** to offer (a new product) for sale **6** *a)* to make acquainted; present (*to* another or others or to one another) [please *introduce* me to your friend] *b)* to present (a person) to society, a court, the general public, etc. *c)* to present (a performer) for a public appearance, as on stage or television *d)* to give knowledge or experience of [to *introduce* a freshman to campus life] **7** to bring forward; bring to notice formally [to *introduce* a bill into Congress] **8** to start; open; begin [to *introduce* a talk with an anecdote] —**in′tro·duc′er** ***n.***

in·tro·duc·tion (-duk′shən) ***n.*** ⟦ME *introduccion* < MFr *introduction* < L *introductio*⟧ **1** an introducing or being introduced **2** anything introduced, or brought into use, knowledge, or fashion **3** anything that introduces, or prepares the way for; specif., *a)* the preliminary section of a book, often having material considered essential to an understanding of the main text *b)* the preliminary part of a speech, treatise, etc. *c)* an opening section of a musical composition *d)* a preliminary guide or text **4** the formal presentation of one person to another, to an audience, to society, etc.

SYN.—**introduction**, in strict usage, refers to the preliminary section of a book, etc. that explains and leads into the subject proper; **preface** refers to a statement preliminary to a book, written by the author or editor and explaining the purpose, plan, or preparation of the work; the preface may also include acknowledgments for help or for permissions granted for use of previously published material; **foreword** is a brief preface written typically by someone other than the author; **preamble** refers to a formal, but usually brief, introduction to a constitution, treaty, etc.; **prologue** applies to the preliminary section as of a play or poem, serving as an introduction and, in the play, frequently spoken by one of the characters —*ANT.* **conclusion, epilogue**

in·tro·duc·to·ry (-duk′tə rē) ***adj.*** ⟦L *introductorius*⟧ used or serving as an introduction; preliminary: also **in′tro·duc′tive** —**in′tro·duc′to·ri·ly** ***adv.***

in·tro·gres·sion (-gresh′ən) ***n.*** ⟦INTRO- + (DI)GRESSION⟧ the infiltration of genes from the gene pool of one species into that of another —**in′tro·gres′sive** (-gres′iv) ***adj.***

in·tro·it (in trō′it, in′troit′) ***n.*** ⟦ME *introite* < MFr < L *introitus*, a going in, entrance (in LL(Ec), Introit of the Mass) < *introire* < *intro-*, INTRO- + *ire*, to go: see EXIT⟧ **1** a psalm or hymn sung or played at the opening of a Christian worship service **2** [**I-**] *R.C.Ch.* the first variable part of the Mass, consisting typically of one or more psalm verses

in·tro·ject (in′trə jekt′) ***vt.*** ⟦INTRO- + (PRO)JECT(ION)⟧ *Psychoanalysis* to incorporate unconsciously into the psyche (a mental image of an object, person, etc.) and focus aggressive energy upon this image rather than upon the object itself —**in′tro·jec′tion** ***n.***

in·tro·mit (-mit′) ***vt.*** **-mit′ted**, **-mit′ting** ⟦L *intromittere* < *intro-*, INTRO- + *mittere*, to send: see MISSION⟧ **1** to cause to enter; put in; insert **2** to allow to enter; admit —**in′tro·mis′sion** (-mish′ən) ***n.*** —**in′tro·mit′tent** ***adj.***

☆**in·tron** (in′trän′) ***n.*** ⟦coined (1978) by W. Gilbert, U.S. molecular biologist < INTRA- (because within the gene) + *-on*, as in OPERON⟧ an intervening sequence in the eukaryote genetic code, interrupting protein formation

in·trorse (in trôrs′, in′trôrs′) ***adj.*** ⟦L *introrsus*, contr. of *introversus*: see INTRO- & VERSE⟧ *Bot.* facing inward, or toward the center: opposed to EXTRORSE —**in·trorse′ly** ***adv.***

in·tro·spect (in′trə spekt′) ***vt., vi.*** ⟦L *introspectare*, freq. < *introspectus*, pp. of *introspicere*, to look within < *intro-*, INTRO- + *specere*, to see: see SPY⟧ [Rare] to look into (one's own mind, feeling, etc.)

in·tro·spec·tion (-spek′shən) ***n.*** a looking into one's own mind, feelings, etc.; observation and analysis of oneself —**in′tro·spec′tive** ***adj.*** —**in′tro·spec′tive·ly** ***adv.*** —**in′tro·spec′tive·ness** ***n.***

in·tro·ver·sion (-vur′zhən, -shən) ***n.*** ⟦ModL *introversio*, coined by C. G. JUNG < *intro-*, INTRO- + *versio*: see VERSION⟧ **1** an introverting or being introverted **2** *Psychol.* an attitude in which one directs one's interest to one's own experiences and feelings rather than to external objects or other persons **3** a tendency to be introspective and socially retiring Opposed to EXTROVERSION —**in′tro·ver′sive** ***adj.*** —**in′tro·ver′sive·ly** ***adv.***

in·tro·vert (in′trə vurt′; *for v., also* in′trə vurt′) ***vt.*** ⟦ModL *introvertere* < L *intro-*, INTRO- + *vertere*, to turn: see VERSE⟧ **1** to direct (one's interest, mind, or attention) upon oneself; introspect **2** to bend (something) inward **3** *Zool.* to draw (a tubular organ or part) inward upon itself, commonly by invagination —***vi.*** to practice introversion; become introverted —***n.*** **1** a thing, esp. a tubular organ or part, that can be introverted **2** *a)* *Psychol.* someone characterized by INTROVERSION (sense 2) *b)* someone characterized by a tendency to be introspective and socially retiring: opposed to EXTROVERT —***adj.*** INTROVERTED

in·tro·vert·ed (-id) ***adj.*** **1** *Psychol.* characterized by INTROVERSION (sense 2) **2** introspective and socially retiring Opposed to EXTROVERTED

in·trude (in tro͞od′) ***vt.*** **-trud′ed**, **-trud′ing** ⟦L *intrudere* < *in-*, in + *trudere*, to thrust, push: see THREAT⟧ **1** to push or force (something *in* or *upon*) **2** to force (oneself or one's thoughts) upon others without being asked or welcomed **3** *Geol.* to force (liquid magma, etc.) into or between solid rocks —***vi.*** **1** to intrude oneself or itself **2** to enter or appear in a manner regarded as disruptive, inappropriate, or unwelcome —**in·trud′er** ***n.***

SYN.—**intrude** implies the forcing of oneself or something upon another without invitation, permission, or welcome [to *intrude* upon another's privacy]; **obtrude** connotes even more strongly the distractive nature or the undesirability of the invasion [side issues keep *obtruding*]; **interlope** implies an intrusion upon the rights or privileges of another to the disadvantage or harm of the latter [the *interloping* merchants have ruined our trade]; **butt in (or into)** (at BUTT[2]) is an informal term implying intrusion in a meddling or officious way [stop *butting into* my business] See also **trespass**

in·tru·sion (in tro͞o′zhən) ***n.*** ⟦ME < OFr < ML *intrusio* < L *intrusus*: see fol.⟧ **1** *a)* the act of intruding *b)* *Law* the illegal entering upon another's property without right to possession *c)* *Law* INVASION OF PRIVACY **2** *Geol.* *a)* the invasion, as of liquid magma, into or between solid rock *b)* the body of rock resulting from such invasion

in·tru·sive (-siv) ***adj.*** ⟦< L *intrusus*, pp. of *intrudere* (see INTRUDE) + -IVE⟧ **1** intruding or tending to intrude; constituting intrusion **2** *Geol.* designating or of igneous rock formed from magma that hardened while still within the earth, moon, etc.: cf. EXTRUSIVE (sense 2) 3 *Phonet.* present or added in speech although not represented originally in spelling or accounted for otherwise etymologically (Ex.: the *d* added to OE *spinel* to form *spindle*): see also EPENTHESIS —**in·tru′sive·ly** *adv.* —**in·tru′sive·ness** *n.*

in·trust (in trust′) *vt.* ENTRUST

in·tu·bate (in′to͞o bāt′, -tyo͞o-) *vt.* **-bat′ed, -bat′ing** ⟦IN-[1] + TUB(E) + -ATE[1]⟧ to insert a tube into (an orifice or hollow organ, as the larynx) for the administration of gases or to admit air —**in′tu·ba′tion** *n.*

in·tu·it (in to͞o′it, -tyo͞o′-; in′to͞o wit) *vt., vi.* ⟦< L *intuitus*⟧ to know or learn by intuition —**in·tu′it·a·ble** *adj.*

in·tu·i·tion (in′to͞o ish′ən, -tyo͞o-) *n.* ⟦LL < L *intuitus*, pp. of *intueri*, to look at, regard < *in-*, in + *tueri*, to look at, view⟧ 1 *a)* the direct knowing or learning of something without the conscious use of reasoning; immediate understanding *b)* something known or learned in this way 2 the ability to perceive or know things without conscious reasoning —**in′tu·i′tion·al** *adj.* —**in′tu·i′tion·al·ly** *adv.*

in·tu·i·tion·ism (-iz′əm) *n.* 1 *Philos.* the doctrine that things and principles are truly apprehended by intuition 2 *Ethics* the doctrine that fundamental moral principles or the rightness of acts is apprehended by intuition —**in′tu·i′tion·ist** *adj., n.*

in·tu·i·tive (in to͞o′i tiv, -tyo͞o′-) *adj.* ⟦ML *intuitivus* < L *intuitus*⟧ 1 having to do with intuition 2 having, or perceiving by, intuition 3 that is or can be perceived by intuition or common sense [an *intuitive* truth] —*n.* a person who is supposedly sensitive to forces beyond the physical world; psychic —**in·tu′i·tive·ly** *adv.* —**in·tu′i·tive·ness** *n.*

in·tu·mesce (in′to͞o mes′, -tyo͞o-) *vi.* **-mesced′, -mesc′ing** ⟦L *intumescere*: see IN-[1] & TUMESCENT⟧ to swell, enlarge, expand, or bubble up, as with heat

in·tu·mes·cence (-mes′əns) *n.* ⟦Fr⟧ 1 an intumescing or being intumesced 2 a swollen or enlarged organ or mass, as a tumor; swelling —**in′tu·mes′cent** *adj.*

in·tus·sus·cept (in′tə sə sept′) *vt.* ⟦< L *intus*, within + *susceptus*, pp. of *suscipere*: see fol.⟧ to receive within itself or into another part; specif., to telescope (one section of the intestines) into another; invaginate

in·tus·sus·cep·tion (in′tə sə sep′shən) *n.* ⟦< L *intus*, within (see INTESTINE) + *susceptio*, a taking up < pp. of *suscipere*, to take up: see SUSCEPTIBLE⟧ 1 an intussuscepting or being intussuscepted 2 the process of taking in food or other foreign matter and interposing the tiny particles among those already present in the cell walls —**in′tus·sus·cep′tive** *adj.*

in·twine (in twīn′) *vt., vi.* **-twined′, -twin′ing** *var. of* ENTWINE

In·u·it (in′o͞o it, -yo͞o-) *n., pl.* **-it** or **-its** ⟦Esk *inuit*, pl. of *inuk*, person, man⟧ 1 a member of a group of Eskimos of N North America, inhabiting areas from Greenland and E Canada to Alaska 2 the language of this people, belonging to the Eskimo-Aleut language family 3 ESKIMO (*n.* 1): in this sense, *Inuit* is now the preferred term in Canada

I·nuk·ti·tut (i no͝ok′ti to͞ot′) *n.* a group of Eskimo languages spoken in the eastern and central parts of arctic Canada

in·u·lase (in′yo͞o lās′) *n.* ⟦< fol. + -ASE⟧ an enzyme that converts inulin into fructose

in·u·lin (-lin) *n.* ⟦< ModL *Inula*, genus of plants (< L *inula*, ELECAMPANE) + -IN[1]⟧ a white, starchlike polysaccharide which yields fructose, and glucose when hydrolyzed: found in the roots and tubers of many composite plants

in·unc·tion (in uŋk′shən) *n.* ⟦L *inunctio*: see IN-[1] & UNCTION⟧ 1 the act of rubbing ointment, liniment, etc. into the skin 2 an ointment, liniment, etc.

in·un·dant (in un′dənt) *adj.* ⟦L *inundans*, prp. of *inundare*: see fol.⟧ overflowing or inundating

in·un·date (in′ən dāt′) *vt.* **-dat′ed, -dat′ing** ⟦< L *inundatus*, pp. of *inundare*, to overflow < *in-*, in, on + *undare*, to move in waves, flood < *unda*, a wave: see WATER⟧ 1 to cover or engulf with a flood; deluge 2 to overwhelm with a rush or great amount of anything —**in′un·da′tion** *n.* —**in′un·da′tor** *n.* —**in·un·da·to·ry** (in un′də tôr′ē) *adj.*

I·nu·pi·aq (i no͞o′pē ak′, -nyo͞o′-) *n.* the language of the Inupiat, spoken in N Alaska and in Canada and Greenland —*adj.* of this language

I·nu·pi·at (i no͞o′pē at′, -nyo͞o′-) *n., pl.* **-at′, -ats′** a member of an Eskimo people of N Alaska —*adj.* of this people or their culture

in·ur·bane (in′ər bān′) *adj.* ⟦L *inurbanus*⟧ not urbane; crude; unpolished —**in′ur·ban′i·ty** (-ban′ə tē) *n.*

in·ure (in yoor′, i noor′) *vt.* **-ured′, -ur′ing** ⟦ME (in pp. *enured*) < *in ure*, in practice < *in*, in + *ure*, practice, work < OFr *eure*, *ovre* < L *opera*, work: see OPERA[1]⟧ to make accustomed to something difficult, painful, etc.; habituate —*vi.* to come into use or take effect [sick pay *inures* from the first day of illness] —**in·ure′ment** *n.*

in·urn (in urn′) *vt.* 1 to put (ashes of the dead) into an urn 2 to bury; entomb —**in·urn′ment** *n.*

in u·ter·o (in yo͞ot′ər ō) ⟦L⟧ in, within, or while inside the uterus

in·u·tile (in yo͞ot′'l) *adj.* ⟦ME < MFr < L *inutilis* < *in-*, IN-[2] + *utilis*, useful: see UTILITY⟧ useless; unprofitable —**in·u·til·i·ty** (in′yo͞o til′ə tē) *n.*

In·u·vik (i no͞o′vik) 1 region of Northwest Territories, Canada 2 town in this region

inv *abbrev.* 1 invented 2 inventor 3 invoice

inv. *abbrev.* ⟦L *invenit*⟧ he (or she) designed it

in va·cu·o (in vak′yo͞o ō′) ⟦L⟧ 1 in a vacuum 2 without or disregarding context, circumstances, etc.

in·vade (in vād′) *vt.* **-vad′ed, -vad′ing** ⟦ME *invaden* < L *invadere* < *in-*, in + *vadere*, to come, go: see WADE⟧ 1 to enter forcibly or hostilely; come into as an enemy 2 to crowd into; throng [tourists *invading* the beaches] 3 to intrude upon; infringe; violate [to *invade* someone's privacy] 4 to enter and spread through with harmful effects [a body *invaded* by pathogens] —*vi.* to make an invasion —*SYN.* TRESPASS —**in·vad′er** *n.*

in·vag·i·nate (in vaj′ə nāt′) *vt.* **-nat′ed, -nat′ing** ⟦< ML *invaginatus*, pp. of *invaginare* < L *in-*, in + *vagina*, a sheath⟧ 1 to place or receive into a sheath 2 INTUSSUSCEPT —*vi.* 1 to become invaginated 2 to grow inward to form a hollow or cavity, as in the formation of a gastrula —**in·vag′i·na′tion** *n.*

in·va·lid[1] (in′və lid; *chiefly Brit*, -lēd′) *adj.* ⟦Fr *invalide* < L *invalidus*, feeble: see IN-[2] & VALID⟧ 1 not well; weak and sickly; infirm 2 of or for invalids [an *invalid* home] —*n.* a weak, sickly person; esp., one who is chronically ill or disabled —*vt.* 1 to make invalid; disable or weaken 2 [Chiefly Brit.] to remove (a soldier, sailor, etc.) from active duty or from a combat zone because of injury or illness

in·val·id[2] (in val′id) *adj.* ⟦L *invalidus*⟧ not valid; having no force; null or void —**in·va·lid·i·ty** (in′və lid′ə tē) *n.* —**in·val′id·ly** *adv.*

in·val·i·date (in val′ə dāt′) *vt.* **-dat′ed, -dat′ing** ⟦prec. + -ATE[1]⟧ to make invalid; deprive of legal force —**in·val′i·da′tion** *n.* —**in·val′i·da′tor** *n.*

in·va·lid·ism (in′və lid iz′əm) *n.* the state of being an invalid; chronic ill health or disability

in·val·u·a·ble (in val′yə bəl, in val′yo͞o ə bəl) *adj.* extremely valuable; having value too great to measure; priceless —*SYN.* COSTLY —**in·val′u·a·ble·ness** *n.* —**in·val′u·a·bly** *adv.*

In·var (in′vär′) ⟦abbrev. < fol.⟧ *trademark for* a steel alloy containing approximately 36% nickel, used for making precision instruments and thermostatic elements because of its low coefficient of thermal expansion —*n.* [i-] this substance

in·var·i·a·ble (in ver′ē ə bəl) *adj.* ⟦ML *invariabilis*⟧ not variable; not changing; constant; uniform —*n.* an invariable quantity; constant —**in·var′i·a·bil′i·ty** *n.*, **in·var′i·a·ble·ness** —**in·var′i·a·bly** *adv.*

in·var·i·ant (in ver′ē ənt) *adj.* not varying; constant; specif., having the nature of an invariant —*n.* *Math.* an entity that is unchanged by a given transformation —**in·var′i·ance** *n.*

in·va·sion (in vā′zhən) *n.* ⟦MFr < LL *invasio* < L *invasus*, pp. of *invadere*⟧ an invading or being invaded; specif., *a)* an entering or being entered by an attacking military force *b)* an intrusion or infringement *c)* the onset, appearance, or spread of something

invasion of privacy *Law* a wrongful intrusion into, or exposure of, one's private affairs such as to cause humiliation or mental suffering to a person of average sensibilities

in·va·sive (in vā′siv) *adj.* 1 of or having to do with invasion or an invasion [an *invasive* military force] 2 spreading beyond its native range [*invasive* wildflowers] 3 *Med.* *a)* tending to spread into healthy tissue [an *invasive* tumor] *b)* penetrating into the body [an *invasive* diagnostic instrument]

in·vec·tive (in vek′tiv) *adj.* ⟦ME *invectiff* < MFr *invectif* < LL *invectivus* < L *invectus*, pp. of *invehere*: see fol.⟧ inveighing; using, inclined to use, or characterized by strong verbal abuse —*n.* 1 a violent verbal attack; strong criticism, insults, curses, etc.; vituperation 2 an abusive term, insult, curse, etc. —**in·vec′tive·ly** *adv.* —**in·vec′tive·ness** *n.*

in·veigh (in vā′) *vi.* ⟦ME *invehen* < L *invehi*, to assail, attack with words, pass. of *invehere*, to bring in < *in-*, in, to + *vehere*, to carry: see VEHEMENT⟧ to make a violent verbal attack; talk or write bitterly (*against*); rail —**in·veigh′er** *n.*

in·vei·gle (in vā′gəl, -vē′-) *vt.* **-gled, -gling** ⟦LME *invegelen*, altered (after IN-[1]) < MFr *aveugler*, to blind, delude < *aveugle*, blind < LL **aboculus*, blind < L *ab*, from + *oculus*, an EYE⟧ to lead on with deception; entice or trick into doing or giving something, going somewhere, etc. —*SYN.* LURE —**in·vei′gle·ment** *n.* —**in·vei′gler** *n.*

in·vent (in vent′) *vt.* ⟦ME *inventen* < L *inventus*, pp. of *invenire*, to come upon, meet with, discover < *in-*, in, on + *venire*, to COME⟧ 1 to think up; devise or fabricate in the mind [to *invent* excuses] 2 to think out or produce (a new device, process, etc.); originate, as by experiment; devise for the first time 3 [Archaic] to find; discover

in·ven·tion (in ven′shən) *n.* ⟦ME *inuencioun* < OFr *invencion* < L *inventio*⟧ 1 an inventing or being invented 2 the power of inventing; ingenuity or creativity 3 something invented; specif., *a)* something thought up or mentally fabricated; esp., a falsehood *b)* something originated by experiment, etc.; new device or contrivance 4 *Music* a short composition, usually for a keyboard instrument, developing a single short motif in counterpoint; esp., any of a group of these by J. S. Bach

in·ven·tive (-tiv) *adj.* ⟦ME *inventif* < ML *inventivus*⟧ 1 of or characterized by invention [*inventive* powers] 2 skilled in inventing; creative [an *inventive* person] —**in·ven′tive·ly** *adv.* —**in·ven′tive·ness** *n.*

in·ven·tor (-tər) *n.* a person who invents; esp., one who devises a new contrivance, method, etc.

in·ven·to·ry (in′vən tôr′ē) *n., pl.* **-ries** ⟦ML *inventorium* < LL *inventarium* < L *inventus*: see INVENT⟧ 1 an itemized list or catalog of goods, property, etc.; esp., such a list made annually of the stock, or goods, of a business 2 the store of goods, etc. that are or may be so listed; stock 3 any detailed list 4 the act of making such a list —*vt.* **-ried, -ry·ing** 1 to make an inventory of 2 to place on an inventory —*SYN.* LIST[1] —**take inventory** 1 to make an inventory of stock, or goods, on hand 2 to make an appraisal, as of one's skills or personal characteristics —**in′ven·to′ri·al** *adj.* —**in′ven·to′ri·al·ly** *adv.*

in·ve·rac·i·ty (in′və ras′ə tē) *n.* lack of veracity; untruthfulness

In·ver·ness (in′vər nes′) 1 former county & former district of N Scotland: also, for the county, **In′ver·ness′-shire** (-shir) 2 burgh at the head of Moray Firth

in·verse (in vurs′, in′vurs′) *adj.* ⟦L *inversus*, pp. of *invertere*⟧ 1 inverted;

reversed in order or relation; directly opposite **2** *Math.* designating or of an operation which, when applied after a specific operation, cancels it [subtraction is the *inverse* operation of addition] —*n.* **1** any inverse thing; direct opposite **2** *Math.* *a)* the result of an inversion *b)* the result obtained after dividing 1 by the given number; reciprocal [the *inverse* of x is 1/x] —**in·verse′ly** *adv.*

inverse function the function obtained by expressing the independent variable of another function in terms of the dependent variable which is then regarded as an independent variable

inverse square law *Physics* a general principle of light, sound, gravity, etc. in which the intensity of energy coming from a given point varies inversely with the square of the distance from that point (Ex.: as the distance from a point increases from 1 to 2 to 3 units, the intensity will correspondingly decrease from 1 to ¼ to ⅑)

in·ver·sion (in vʉr′zhən, -shən) *n.* ⟦L *inversio* < *inversus*, pp. of *invertere*⟧ **1** an inverting or being inverted **2** something inverted; reversal **3** *Chem.* *a)* a chemical change in which an optically active substance is converted into another substance having no effect, or the opposite rotatory effects, on the plane of polarization *b)* the conversion of an isomeric compound to its opposite **4** *Gram., Rhetoric* a reversal of the normal order of words in a sentence (Ex.: "said he" for "he said") **5** *Math.* *a)* the process of using an opposite rule or method *b)* an interchange of the terms of a ratio **6** *Meteorol.* an atmospheric condition in which the normal properties of layers of air are reversed; esp., a temperature reversal in which a layer of warm air traps cooler air near the surface of the earth, preventing the normal rising of surface air **7** *Music* *a)* the reversal of the position of the tones in an interval or chord, as by raising the lower tone by an octave *b)* the recurrence of a theme, fugue subject, motive, or figure in identical intervals and note values, but consistently in the opposite direction **8** *Phonet.* a position of the tongue in which the tip is turned upward and backward **9** *Psychiatry* HOMOSEXUALITY: term now seldom used —**in·ver′sive** *adj.*

in·vert (in vʉrt′; *for adj. & n.,* in′vʉrt′) *vt.* ⟦L *invertere* < *in-*, in, to, toward + *vertere*, to turn: see VERSE⟧ **1** to turn upside down **2** to change to the direct opposite; reverse the order, position, direction, etc. of **3** to subject to inversion (in various senses) **4** *Math.* to divide 1 by (a given quantity) —*adj. Chem.* inverted [*invert* sugar] —*n.* **1** an inverted person or thing **2** *Psychiatry* HOMOSEXUAL: term now seldom used —**in·vert′ible** *adj.*

in·vert·ase (in vʉr′tās′) *n.* ⟦prec. + -ASE⟧ SUCRASE

in·ver·te·brate (in vʉr′tə brit, -brāt′) *adj.* ⟦ModL *invertebratus*⟧ **1** not vertebrate; having no backbone, or spinal column **2** of invertebrates **3** having no moral backbone; lacking courage, resolution, etc. —*n.* any animal without a backbone, or spinal column; any animal other than a fish, amphibian, reptile, bird, or mammal

inverted comma [Brit.] a single QUOTATION MARK (' or ')

inverted mordent *see* MORDENT

in·vert·er (in vʉrt′ər) *n. Elec.* a device for transforming direct current into alternating current: cf. CONVERTER (sense *b*)

invert sugar a mixture of dextrose and levulose in approximately equal proportions, found in fruits and produced artificially by the hydrolysis of sucrose

in·vest (in vest′) *vt.* ⟦L *investire* < *in-*, in + *vestire*, to clothe < *vestis*, clothing: see VEST⟧ **1** to clothe; array; adorn **2** *a)* to cover, surround, or envelop like, or as if with, a garment [fog *invests* the city] *b)* to endow with qualities, attributes, etc. **3** to install in office with ceremony **4** to furnish with power, privilege, or authority **5** [Rare] to vest or settle (a power or right) in a person, legislative body, etc. **6** to put (money) into business, real estate, stocks, bonds, etc. for the purpose of obtaining an income or profit **7** to spend (time, effort, etc.) with the expectation of some satisfaction **8** *Mil.* to hem in or besiege (a town, port, enemy, etc.) —*vi.* **1** to invest money; make an investment **2** to make a commitment to something or someone: with *in*: usually in the pp. [volunteers who are *invested* in the charitable project] —**in·vest′a·ble** *adj.*, **in·vest′i·ble** —**in·ves′tor** *n.*

in·ves·ti·gate (in ves′tə gāt′) *vt.* **-gat′ed**, **-gat′ing** ⟦< L *investigatus*, pp. of *investigare*, to trace out < *in-*, in + *vestigare*, to track < *vestigium*, a track⟧ to search into so as to learn the facts; inquire into systematically —*vi.* to make an investigation —**in·ves′ti·ga·ble** (-gə bəl) *adj.*

in·ves·ti·ga·tion (in ves′tə gā′shən) *n.* ⟦ME *investigacioun* < MFr < L *investigatio*⟧ **1** an investigating or being investigated **2** a careful search or examination; systematic inquiry —**in·ves′ti·ga′tion·al** *adj.*

in·ves·ti·ga·tive (in ves′tə gāt′iv, -gə tiv) *adj.* ⟦ML *investigativus*⟧ **1** of or characterized by investigation **2** inclined to investigate Also **in·ves′ti·ga·to′ry** (-gə tôr′ē)

in·ves·ti·ga·tor (in ves′tə gāt′ər) *n.* a person who gathers confidential information and conducts an investigation for an individual or company; private detective: also **private investigator**

in·ves·ti·tive (in ves′tə tiv) *adj.* ⟦< L *investitus*, pp. (see INVEST) + -IVE⟧ **1** that invests or can invest authority, etc. **2** of such investing

in·ves·ti·ture (-chər) *n.* ⟦ME < ML *investitura* < L *investire*⟧ **1** a formal investing as with an office, power, or authority, often with appropriate symbols or robes **2** anything that clothes or covers; vesture **3** *Feudal Law* ceremonial transfer of land to a tenant

in·vest·ment (in vest′mənt) *n.* **1** an investing or being invested **2** an outer covering **3** INVESTITURE (sense 1) **4** *a)* the investing of money *b)* the amount invested *c)* anything in which money is or may be invested

investment bank (*or* banker) a firm which underwrites and markets issues of stocks, bonds, etc., often in association with other such firms

investment company (*or* trust) a company or trust that invests in diverse securities with funds obtained through the sale of its own shares: see also CLOSED-END, OPEN-END (sense 1)

in·vet·er·ate (in vet′ər it) *adj.* ⟦L *inveteratus*, pp. of *inveterare*, to make or become old < *in-*, in + *vetus*, old: see VETERAN⟧ **1** firmly established over a long period; of long standing; deep-rooted **2** settled in a habit, practice, prejudice, etc.; habitual —***SYN.*** CHRONIC —**in·vet′er·a·cy** *n.* —**in·vet′er·ate·ly** *adv.*

in·vi·a·ble (in vī′ə bəl) *adj.* not viable; unable to live and develop normally —**in·vi′a·bil′i·ty** *n.*

in·vid·i·ous (in vid′ē əs) *adj.* ⟦L *invidiosus* < *invidia*: see ENVY⟧ **1** *a)* such as to excite ill will, odium, or envy; giving offense *b)* giving offense by discriminating unfairly [*invidious* comparisons] **2** [Obs.] envious —**in·vid′i·ous·ly** *adv.* —**in·vid′i·ous·ness** *n.*

in·vig·i·late (in vij′ə lāt′) *vi., vt.* **-lat′ed**, **-lat′ing** ⟦< L *invigilatus*, pp. of *invigilare* < *in-*, in, on + *vigilare*, to watch: see VIGIL⟧ [Brit.] to keep watch (over); esp., to monitor (students) during a written examination —**in·vig′i·la′tion** *n.* —**in·vig′i·la′tor** *n.*

in·vig·or·ate (in vig′ər āt′) *vt.* **-at′ed**, **-at′ing** ⟦IN-[1] + VIGOR + -ATE[1]⟧ to give vigor to; fill with energy; enliven —***SYN.*** ANIMATE —**in·vig′or·a′tion** *n.* —**in·vig′or·a′tive** *adj.* —**in·vig′or·a′tor** *n.*

in·vin·ci·ble (in vin′sə bəl) *adj.* ⟦ME *invyncyble* < MFr *invincible* < L *invincibilis*: see IN-[2] & VINCIBLE⟧ that cannot be overcome; unconquerable —**in·vin′ci·bil′i·ty** *n.*, **in·vin′ci·ble·ness** —**in·vin′ci·bly** *adv.*

in vi·no ve·ri·tas (in vē′nō ver′i täs′) ⟦L, lit., in wine there is truth: a quotation from Pliny the Elder⟧ one's true thoughts and nature are revealed when one drinks wine

in·vi·o·la·ble (in vī′ə lə bəl) *adj.* ⟦MFr < L *inviolabilis*⟧ **1** not to be violated; not to be profaned or injured; sacred [an *inviolable* promise] **2** that cannot be violated; indestructible [the *inviolable* heavens] —**in·vi′o·la·bil′i·ty** *n.* —**in·vi′o·la·bly** *adv.*

in·vi·o·late (in vī′ə lit, -lāt′) *adj.* ⟦ME < L *inviolatus*: see IN-[2] & VIOLATE⟧ not violated; kept sacred or unbroken —**in·vi′o·la·cy** (-lə sē) *n.*, **in·vi′o·late·ness** —**in·vi′o·late·ly** *adv.*

in·vis·cid (in vis′id) *adj.* ⟦IN-[2] + VISCID⟧ **1** having no viscosity **2** of or having to do with a fluid having no viscosity

in·vis·i·ble (in viz′ə bəl) *adj.* ⟦OFr < L *invisibilis*⟧ **1** not visible; that cannot be seen **2** out of sight; not apparent **3** too small or too faint to be seen; imperceptible **4** kept hidden [*invisible* assets] —*n.* an invisible thing or being —**the Invisible 1** God **2** the unseen world —**in·vis′i·bil′i·ty** *n.*, **in·vis′i·ble·ness** —**in·vis′i·bly** *adv.*

invisible ink a colorless ink that cannot be seen on paper until it is treated with heat, vapor, or a chemical

in·vi·ta·tion (in′və tā′shən) *n.* ⟦L *invitatio* < pp. of *invitare*⟧ **1** an inviting to come somewhere or do something **2** the message or note used in inviting **3** enticement or allurement

in·vi·ta·tion·al (-shə nəl) *adj.* participated in only by those invited [an *invitational* tennis tournament] —*n.* an invitational event

in·vi·ta·to·ry (in vīt′ə tôr′ē) *adj.* ⟦LL *invitatorius*⟧ containing an invitation —*n., pl.* **-ries** a form of invitation used in worship as a call to prayer or praise; esp., Ps. 95 (94 in the Douay)

in·vite (in vīt′; *for n.* in′vīt′) *vt.* **-vit′ed**, **-vit′ing** ⟦Fr *inviter* < L *invitare* < *in-*, IN-[1] + ? IE base *wei-, to go directly toward, chase after > L *via* & OE *wæthan*, to hunt⟧ **1** to ask courteously to come somewhere or do something; request the presence or participation of **2** to make a request for [to *invite* questions] **3** to tend to bring on; give occasion for [action that *invites* scandal] **4** to tempt; allure; entice —*n.* [Informal] an invitation —***SYN.*** CALL —**in′vit·ee′** *n.* —**in·vit′er** *n.*

in·vit·ing (in vīt′iŋ) *adj.* tempting, alluring, welcoming, etc.

in vi·tro (in vē′trō′) ⟦L, lit., in glass⟧ outside or isolated from the living organism and in a test tube or other artificial environment [*in vitro* fertilization]

in vi·vo (in vī′vō, in vē′vō) ⟦L, lit., in one that is living⟧ occurring within the living organism

in·vo·cate (in′və kāt′) *vt., vi.* **-cat′ed**, **-cat′ing** ⟦< L *invocatus*, pp. of *invocare*: see INVOKE⟧ [Rare] to speak or ask in invocation

in·vo·ca·tion (in′və kā′shən) *n.* ⟦OFr < L *invocatio* < pp. of *invocare*: see INVOKE⟧ **1** the act of calling on God, a god, a saint, the Muses, etc. for blessing, help, inspiration, support, or the like **2** *a)* a formal prayer used in invoking, as at the beginning of a church service *b)* a formal plea for aid from a Muse, god, etc., at the beginning of an epic or similar poem **3** *a)* a conjuring of evil spirits *b)* an incantation used in conjuring —**in′vo·ca′tion·al** *adj.* —**in·voc′a·to′ry** (-väk′ə tôr′ē) *adj.*

in·voice (in′vois′) *n.* ⟦prob. orig. pl. of ME *envoie*, a message: see ENVOY[1]⟧ an itemized list of goods shipped or services rendered, stating quantities, prices, fees, shipping charges, etc.; bill —*vt.* **-voiced′**, **-voic′ing** to present an invoice for or to

in·voke (in vōk′) *vt.* **-voked′**, **-vok′ing** ⟦ME *invoken* < MFr *invoquer* < L *invocare* < *in-*, in, on + *vocare*, to call < *vox*, VOICE⟧ **1** to call on (God, a god, a saint, the Muses, etc.) for blessing, help, inspiration, support, etc. **2** to resort to or put into use (a law, ruling, penalty, etc.) as pertinent [to *invoke* an article of the UN Charter] **3** to call forth; cause **4** to summon (evil spirits) by incantation; conjure **5** to ask solemnly for; beg for; implore [to *invoke* aid] —**in·vok′er** *n.*

in·vol·u·cel (in väl′yoo sel′) *n.* ⟦ModL *involucellum*, dim. < L *involucrum*⟧ a secondary involucre; ring of small leaves, or bracts, at the base of each segment of a cluster —**in·vol′u·cel′late** (-sel′it) *adj.*

in·vo·lu·crate (in′vō lo͞o′krit, -krāt′; -və-) *adj.* having an involucre

in·vo·lu·cre (in′vō lo͞o′kər, -və-) ***n.*** ⟦Fr < L *involucrum*, wrapper, case, envelope < *involvere*: see INVOLVE⟧ 1 *Anat.* a membranous covering or envelope 2 *Bot.* a ring of small leaves, or bracts, at the base of a flower, flower cluster, or fruit: involucres are found in all plants of the composite family Also **in′vo·lu′crum** (-krəm), *pl.* **-cra** (-krə) —**in′vo·lu′cral** (-krəl) ***adj.***

in·vol·un·tar·y (in väl′ən ter′ē) ***adj.*** ⟦LL *involuntarius*⟧ not voluntary; specif., *a)* not done of one's own free will; not done by choice *b)* unintentional; accidental *c)* not consciously controlled; automatic [sneezing is *involuntary*] —***SYN.*** SPONTANEOUS —**in·vol′un·tar′i·ly** ***adv.*** —**in·vol′un·tar′i·ness** ***n.***

in·vo·lute (in′və lo͞ot′) ***adj.*** ⟦L *involutus*, pp. of *involvere*, INVOLVE⟧ 1 intricate; involved 2 rolled up or curled in a spiral; having whorls wound closely around the axis [*involute* shells] 3 *Bot.* rolled inward at the edges [*involute* leaves] —***n.*** *Math. a)* the curve traced by any point of a taut string when it is wound upon or unwound from a fixed curve on the same plane with it *b)* the locus of any fixed point on a moving tangent which rolls, but does not slide on a curve: correlative to EVOLUTE —***vi.*** **-lut′ed, -lut′ing** to become involute or undergo involution

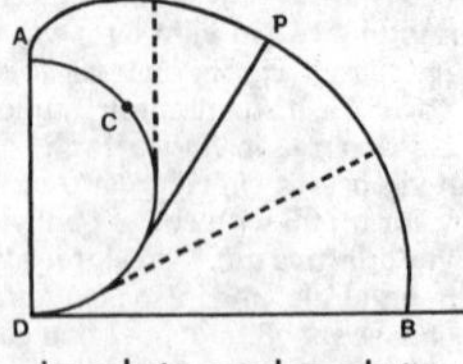

involute and evolute
(involute, curve APB; evolute, curve ACD)

in·vo·lu·tion (in′və lo͞o′shən) ***n.*** ⟦L *involutio* < *involutus*, pp. of *involvere*⟧ 1 an entanglement, complication, or intricacy 2 *Anat.* the process of rolling or curling inward, as in the formation of a gastrula 3 *Biol.* a retrograde or degenerative change 4 *Gram.* an involved construction, esp. one created by a clause interposed between a subject and its predicate 5 *Math.* the raising of a quantity to any given power 6 *Med. a)* the return of an organ to its normal size after distention, as of the uterus after childbirth *b)* a decline in the normal functions of the human body or of an organ occurring with age, as the changes taking place at menopause —**in′vo·lu′tion·al** ***adj.*** —**in′vo·lu′tion·ar′y** ***adj.***

in·volve (in välv′, -vôlv′) ***vt.*** **-volved′, -volv′ing** ⟦ME *involven* < L *involvere* < *in-*, in + *volvere*, to roll: see WALK⟧ 1 [Archaic] to enfold or envelop as in a wrapping [fog *involved* the shoreline] 2 [Obs.] to wind spirally; coil 3 to make intricate, tangled, or complicated 4 to entangle in trouble, difficulty, danger, etc.; implicate 5 to draw or hold within itself; include [a riot that soon *involved* thousands] 6 to include by necessity; entail; require [a project *involving* years of work] 7 to relate to or affect [the matter *involves* his honor] 8 to make busy; employ; occupy [*involved* the class in research] —***SYN.*** INCLUDE —**in·volve′ment** ***n.***

in·volved (-välvd′, -vôlvd′) ***adj.*** 1 not easily understood; intricate; complicated 2 implicated, affected, or committed 3 having a close emotional, and often sexual, relationship *with* —***SYN.*** COMPLEX

in·vul·ner·a·ble (in vul′nər ə bəl) ***adj.*** ⟦L *invulnerabilis*⟧ not vulnerable; specif., *a)* that cannot be wounded or injured *b)* proof against attack; unassailable —**in·vul′ner·a·bil′i·ty** ***n.*** —**in·vul′ner·a·bly** ***adv.***

in·ward (in′wərd) ***adj.*** ⟦ME *inneward* < OE *inweard, inneweard*: see IN-[1] & -WARD⟧ 1 situated within; being on the inside; internal 2 of or belonging to the inner nature of a person; mental or spiritual 3 directed toward the inside; ingoing [the *inward* pull of a centrifuge] 4 *a)* intuitive; empathetic [an *inward* understanding of the poetic mind] *b)* subtle [a delicate *inward* lyricism] *c)* intimate (*with*) [the play invites the audience to be *inward* with the character] *d)* introspective [an obsession with *inward* consciousness] *e)* withdrawn; reticent [a shy and *inward* person] —***n.*** the inside; inward part —***adv.*** 1 toward the inside, interior, or center 2 into the mind, thoughts, or soul

in·ward·ly (-lē) ***adv.*** ⟦ME *inwardlich* < OE *inweardlic*: see prec. & -LY[2]⟧ 1 in or on the inside; internally 2 in the mind or spirit [*inwardly* resentful] 3 toward the inside

in·ward·ness (-nis) ***n.*** ⟦ME *inwardnesse*⟧ 1 the inner nature, essence, or meaning 2 the quality or state of being inward 3 depth of thought; insight and sensitivity 4 intimacy; familiarity (*with*) 5 introspection 6 reticence

in·wards (in′wərdz) ***adv.*** *var. of* INWARD

in·weave (in wēv′, in′wēv′) ***vt.*** **-wove′** (-wōv′), **-wo′ven** (-wō′vən) or **-wove′, -weav′ing** to weave in; interweave

in·wrap (in rap′) ***vt.*** **-wrapped′, -wrap′ping** *var. of* ENWRAP

in·wrought (in rôt′, in′rôt′) ***adj.*** ⟦IN-[1] + WROUGHT⟧ 1 *a)* worked or woven into a fabric (said of a pattern, etc.) *b)* [Archaic] having a decoration worked in 2 closely blended with other things

in-your-face (in′yoor′fās′) ***adj.*** ⟦prob. < BE (*or* GET) IN SOMEONE'S FACE (see phr. under FACE)⟧ [Slang] done, expressed, or presented in a bold, direct, and often aggressive way; confrontational, assertive, daring, etc. [an *in-your-face* conversational manner]

i·o (ī′ō′) ***n.*** *see* IO MOTH

I·o[1] (ī′ō′; *for 2, also* ē′ō′) ***n.*** ⟦L < Gr *Iō*⟧ 1 *Gr. Myth.* a maiden loved by Zeus and changed into a heifer by jealous Hera or, in some tales, by Zeus to protect her 2 the third largest satellite of Jupiter: discovered in 1610 by Galileo and found in 1979 to be volcanically active

Io[2] *Chem. symbol for* ionium

I/O *abbrev.* input/output

IOC *abbrev.* International Olympic Committee

i·o·date (ī′ə dāt′) ***vt.*** **-dat′ed, -dat′ing** ⟦IOD(O)- + -ATE[2]⟧ to treat with iodine —***n.*** any salt of iodic acid —**i′o·da′tion** ***n.***

i·od·ic (ī äd′ik) ***adj.*** designating, of, or containing iodine, esp. pentavalent iodine

iodic acid a colorless or white, crystalline powder, HIO_3, that is a relatively strong acid: used as an analytical reagent and oxidizing agent

i·o·dide (ī′ə dīd′) ***n.*** ⟦IOD(O)- + -IDE⟧ a compound of iodine with another element, as in sodium iodide, NaI, or with a radical, as in methyl iodide, CH_3I

i·o·di·nate (ī′ə di nāt′) ***vt.*** **-nat′ed, -nat′ing** to treat or cause to combine with iodine —**i′o·di·na′tion** ***n.***

i·o·dine (ī′ə dīn′, -din; *Brit & among chemists*, -dēn′) ***n.*** ⟦Fr *iode*, iodine (< Gr *iōdēs*, violetlike < *ion*, a violet + *eidos*, form: see -OID) + -INE[3]⟧ 1 a nonmetallic chemical element, one of the halogens, consisting of grayish-black crystals that volatilize into a violet-colored vapor: used as an antiseptic, in the manufacture of dyes, in photography, etc.: symbol, I; at. no. 53: a radioactive isotope (**iodine-131**) is used esp. in the diagnosis and treatment of thyroid function, in internal radiation therapy, and as a tracer: see the periodic table of elements in the Reference Supplement 2 tincture of iodine, used as an antiseptic

i·o·dism (ī′ə diz′əm) ***n.*** ⟦IOD(O)- + -ISM⟧ a disease caused by excessive exposure to iodine

i·o·dize (-dīz′) ***vt.*** **-dized′, -diz′ing** ⟦IOD(O)- + -IZE⟧ to treat (a wound, substance, photographic plate, etc.) with iodine or an iodide —**i′o·di·za′tion** ***n.***

iodized salt common table salt to which a small amount of sodium iodide or potassium iodide has been added

i·o·do- (ī ō′də, ī′ə də) ⟦< Fr *iode*, IODINE⟧ *combining form* iodine or a compound of iodine [*iodoform*]: also, before a vowel, **iod-**

i·o·do·form (ī ō′də fôrm′) ***n.*** ⟦prec. + FORM(YL)⟧ a yellowish, crystalline compound of iodine, CHI_3, used as an antiseptic in surgical dressings

i·o·dom·e·try (ī′ə däm′ə trē) ***n.*** ⟦IODO- + -METRY⟧ quantitative determination of iodine, or of substances that will react with it or liberate it, by volumetric analytical methods —**i′o·do′met′ric** (-dō′me′trik) ***adj.***

i·o·do·pro·tein (ī′ō də prō′tēn′) ***n.*** a protein that contains iodine

i·o·dop·sin (ī′ə däp′sin) ***n.*** ⟦< IOD(O)- + Gr *opsis*, sight (< *ōps*, EYE) + -IN[1]⟧ a photosensitive, violet-colored protein pigment found in the cones of the retinas of animals that have color vision: see OPSIN

i·o·dous (ī ō′dəs, ī′ə dəs) ***adj.*** ⟦IOD(O)- + -OUS⟧ 1 of or containing iodine 2 designating or of a chemical compound containing trivalent iodine

I of M or **I.O.M.** *abbrev.* Isle of Man

i·o·lite (ī′ə līt′) ***n.*** ⟦altered (infl. by -LITE) < Ger *iolith* < Gr *ion*, violet + *lithos*, stone⟧ CORDIERITE

☆**i·o moth** (ī′ō′) ⟦after IO[1], sense 1⟧ a large, yellowish, North American moth (*Automeris io*) with an eyelike spot on each hind wing: its caterpillar has poisonous, stinging hairs

i·on (ī′ən, -än′) ***n.*** ⟦arbitrary use (by Michael FARADAY) of Gr *ion*, neut. of *iōn*, prp. of *ienai*, to go < IE base *wei-, to go, chase after > L *via*, way⟧ an atom or group of atoms with an electrical charge resulting from the loss or gain of one or more electrons during chemical reactions: the loss of electrons results in a positively charged ion (*cation*), the gain of electrons in a negatively charged ion (*anion*)

-ion (ən) ⟦< Fr or L: Fr *-ion* < L *-io*, nom., (gen. *-ionis*)⟧ *suffix forming nouns* 1 the act or condition of [*retrospection*] 2 the result of [*retroaction*]

☆**ion engine** a reaction engine, as for space vehicles, that uses for propulsion a stream of ionized atoms or molecules, accelerated by an electrostatic field

Io·nes·co (yə nes′kō, ē′ə-), **Eugene** 1912-94; Fr. playwright, born in Romania

ion exchange a chemical process whereby ions are reversibly transferred between an insoluble solid, such as a resin, and a fluid mixture, usually an aqueous solution: widely used in water softening, in recovering metals from waste solutions, etc.

I·o·ni·a (ī ō′nē ə) ancient region in W Asia Minor, including a coastal strip & the islands of Samos & Khíos: colonized by the Greeks in the 11th cent. B.C.

I·o·ni·an (-nē ən) ***adj.*** 1 of Ionia or its people or culture 2 of an ancient Greek people that settled in E Greece and in Ionia —***n.*** an Ionian Greek

Ionian Islands group of islands along the W coast of Greece, on the Ionian Sea: 891 sq mi (2,308 sq km)

Ionian Sea section of the Mediterranean, between Greece, Sicily, & the S part of the Italian peninsula

i·on·ic (ī än′ik) ***adj.*** of, or being in the form of, an ion or ions

I·on·ic (ī än′ik) ***adj.*** ⟦L *Ionicus* < Gr *Iōnikos*⟧ 1 of Ionia or its people or culture; Ionian 2 of Ionic (the language variety) 3 designating or of a classical (Greek or Roman) order of architecture, distinguished by ornamental scrolls (spiral volutes) on the capitals 4 of the Ionic of Greek and Latin prosody —***n.*** 1 *Gr. & Latin Prosody a)* either of two feet consisting of four syllables, the first two long and the second two short or the first two short and the second two long *b)* verse or meter of such feet 2 the variety of the ancient Greek language spoken in Ionia, closely related to that of ancient Attica

ionic bond the chemical bond between two oppositely charged ions formed when one atom transfers electrons to another atom, as in the formation of sodium chloride; electrovalent bond: see COVALENT BOND

i·o·ni·um (ī ō′nē əm) ***n.*** ⟦ION + -IUM⟧ a radioactive isotope of thorium having a mass number of 230 and a half-life of 8×10^4 years

ionization chamber any of various devices, as a closed vessel containing a suitable gas, for determining the intensity of X-rays or the disintegration rate of a radioactive material, by measuring the current flow between oppositely charged electrodes in the gas

i·on·ize (ī′ə nīz′) ***vt., vi.*** **-ized′, -iz′ing** to change or be changed into ions;

dissociate into ions, as a salt dissolved in water, or become electrically charged, as a gas under the influence of radiation or electric discharge —i′on·i·za′tion *n.* —i′on·iz′er *n.*

i·on·o·gen (ī än′ə jən) *n.* ⟦< ION + -O- + -GEN⟧ a substance that can be ionized or that produces ions —i·on′o·gen′ic *adj.*

i·o·none (ī′ə nōn′) *n.* ⟦Gr *ion,* violet + -ONE⟧ a colorless liquid, $C_{13}H_{20}O$, made from citral and acetone and used in perfume manufacture for its violetlike odor

i·on·o·phore (ī än′ə fôr′) *n.* any of a group of compounds that transport, across a plasma membrane, ions which are not able to cross by themselves; esp., any of certain antibiotics, as valinomycin

i·on·o·sonde (ī än′ə sänd′) *n.* ⟦< ION + -O- + (RADIO)SONDE⟧ a pulse radar device operated at a frequency that can be varied from 1 to 25 megahertz: used to measure the height, thickness, etc. of ionospheric layers

i·on·o·sphere (ī än′ə sfir′) *n.* ⟦< ION + -O- + SPHERE⟧ the outer part of the earth's atmosphere, beginning at an altitude of *c.* 55 km (*c.* 34 mi) and extending to the highest parts of the atmosphere: it contains several regions that consist of a series of constantly changing layers characterized by an appreciable electron and ion content: see D REGION, E REGION, F REGION —i·on′o·spher′ic *adj.*

i·on·to·pho·re·sis (ī än′tō fə rē′sis) *n.* ⟦ModL < *ionto-,* ion, ionic (< Gr *iont-, iōn:* see ION) + Gr *phorēsis,* a being carried < *phērein,* BEAR[1]⟧ a medical technique in which an electric current is used to drive ions of chemicals through the skin and into the bodily tissues —i·on′to·pho·ret′ic (-ret′ik) *adj.*

IOOF *abbrev.* Independent Order of Odd Fellows

i·o·ta (ī ōt′ə) *n.* ⟦Gr *iōta* < Sem, as in Heb *yōdh*⟧ 1 the ninth letter of the Greek alphabet (Ι, ι) 2 a very small quantity; jot

i·o·ta·cism (-siz′əm) *n.* ⟦LL *iotacismus* < Gr *iōtakismos*⟧ 1 in Greek, excessive use of the letter *iota* 2 a change, esp. in Greek, of other vowel sounds to the sound (ē) represented by this letter

IOU (ī′ō′yo͞o′) *n., pl.* **IOU's** ⟦for *I owe you*⟧ an informally written, signed acknowledgment of a specified debt, characteristically bearing the letters *IOU*

-ious (ē əs, yəs, əs) ⟦< -I-, thematic vowel or stem ending + -OUS, for Fr *-ieux* & L *-ius*⟧ *suffix* 1 *forming adjectives* having, characterized by *[furious]* 2 forming adjectives corresponding to nouns ending in -ION *[rebellious, religious]*

I·o·wa[1] (ī′ə wə, -wā′) *n.* ⟦< Fr *ayoés,* earlier *aiou[h]ouea,* etc., prob. via Illinois < Dakota *ayúxba,* ? lit., the sleepy ones⟧ 1 *pl.* **-wa** or **-was** a member of a North American Indian people previously living in Iowa and Missouri and now living in Nebraska, Kansas, and Oklahoma 2 the Siouan language of this people, closely related to Missouri

I·o·wa[2] (ī′ə wə) ⟦after prec.⟧ 1 Midwestern state of the NC U.S.: admitted 1846; 55,869 sq mi (144,701 sq km); cap. Des Moines: abbrev. *IA* or *Ia* 2 river flowing from N Iowa southeast into the Mississippi: *c.* 300 mi (483 km)

Iowa City city in E Iowa

I·o·wan (ī′ə wən) *adj.* of the state of Iowa: usually used in the predicate —*n.* a person born or living in Iowa

ip or **IP** *abbrev. Baseball* innings pitched

IP *abbrev.* internet protocol

IPA *abbrev.* International Phonetic Alphabet

IPCC *abbrev.* Intergovernmental Panel on Climate Change

☆**ip·e·cac** (ip′i kak′) *n.* ⟦contr. < Port *ipecacuanha* < Tupí *ipe-kaa-guéne*⟧ 1 the dried root of a tropical South American plant (*Cephaëlis ipecacuanha*) of the madder family, that yields emetine and other alkaloids 2 a preparation from the dried roots, used to induce vomiting 3 any of several plant roots used in a similar way Also **i·pe·ca·cu·a·nha** (ip′i ka′ko͞o an′yə)

Iph·i·ge·ni·a (if′ə jə nī′ə) *n.* ⟦L < Gr *Iphigeneia*⟧ *Gr. Myth.* a daughter of Agamemnon, offered by him as a sacrifice to Artemis and, in some versions, saved by the goddess, who makes her a priestess

ipm *abbrev.* inches per minute

IPO *abbrev. Finance* initial public offering

I·poh (ē′pō) city in Perak, NW Malaysia

ip·o·moe·a (ip′ə mē′ə, ī′pō-) *n.* ⟦ModL < Gr *ips* (gen. *ipos*), a worm + *homoios,* like: see SAME⟧ any of a genus (*Ipomoea*) of twining or creeping plants of the morning-glory family, with funnel-shaped flowers and heart-shaped or lobed leaves, including the morning glory and the sweet potato

I-prop·o·si·tion (ī′präp′ə zish′ən) *n. Logic* a particular, affirmative proposition

ips *abbrev.* inches per second

ip·se dix·it (ip′sā dik′sit, -sē-) ⟦L, he himself has said (it)⟧ an arbitrary or dogmatic statement

ip·si·lat·er·al (ip′sə lat′ər əl) *adj.* ⟦< L *ipse,* self + LATERAL⟧ on or affecting the same side of the body

ip·sis·si·ma ver·ba (ip sis′i mə ver′bə, -vʉr′-) ⟦L⟧ the very words (of a person being quoted)

ip·so fac·to (ip′sō fak′tō) ⟦L⟧ by that very fact

ip·so ju·re (ip′sō jo͝or′ē, -jo͝or′ā) ⟦L⟧ by the law itself

Ips·wich (ips′wich) river port in E England; county seat of Suffolk

IQ (ī′kyo͞o′) *n., pl.* **IQ's** ⟦< I(NTELLIGENCE) Q(UOTIENT)⟧ 1 *Psychol.* a number indicating a person's relative level of intelligence: it is the mental age (as shown by intelligence tests) multiplied by 100 and divided by the chronological age 2 figuratively, the extent of a person's knowledge within a given field *[a homeowner's financial IQ]*

i.q. *abbrev.* ⟦L *idem quod*⟧ the same as

I·qa·lu·it (ē kä′lo͞o it) capital of Nunavut, Canada, in the E part

I·qui·que (ē kē′ke) seaport in N Chile

I·qui·tos (ē kē′tôs) river port in NE Peru, on the Amazon

ir or **i-r** *abbrev.* infrared

Ir[1] *abbrev.* 1 Iran 2 Iranian 3 Ireland 4 Irish

Ir[2] *Chem. symbol for* iridium

IR *abbrev. Sports* injured reserve

ir- (ir) *prefix* 1 IN-[1] *[irrigate]* 2 IN-[2] *[irresponsible]* Used before *r*

I·ra (ī′rə) *n.* ⟦Heb *'īrā,* lit., watchful⟧ a masculine name

IRA[1] (ī′är′ā′, ī′rə) ☆*n., pl.* **IRA's** ⟦*I(ndividual) R(etirement) A(ccount)*⟧ a self-funded retirement account for which certain deferrals and exemptions from federal taxation are allowed: in a **Traditional IRA**, annual contributions may be deductible from taxable income, in a **Roth IRA** (rôth), withdrawals after retirement are tax-free

IRA[2] (ī′är′ā′) *abbrev.* Irish Republican Army

I·rak·li·on (ē räk′lē ôn′) seaport & capital of Crete, on the N coast

I·ran[1] (i ran′, i rän′) 1 country in SW Asia, between the Caspian Sea & the Persian Gulf: formerly an empire, it became an Islamic republic in 1979: 636,296 sq mi (1,648,000 sq km); cap. Tehran: former name PERSIA 2 **Plateau of** plateau extending from the Tigris River to the Indus River, mostly in Iran & Afghanistan

Iran[2] *abbrev.* Iranian

I·ra·ni (ē rä′nē, i-) *adj., n.* IRANIAN

I·ra·ni·an (i rā′nē ən, -rä′-; *occas.* ī-) *adj.* 1 of Iran or its people, language, or culture 2 of the Iranian branch of Indo-European —*n.* 1 a member of the people of Iran; Persian 2 the group of languages making up the Iranian branch, Indo-Iranian subfamily, of the Indo-European language family, including languages now spoken in the Plateau of Iran and a small area of the Caucasus: among the extant languages of the group are Farsi (Persian), Kurdish, and Pashto

I·raq (i räk′, i rak′) country in SW Asia, at the head of the Persian Gulf, coinciding more or less with ancient Mesopotamia: formerly a kingdom, it became a republic in 1958: 168,754 sq mi (437,072 sq km); cap. Baghdad

I·ra·qi (i rä′kē, -rak′ē) *n., pl.* **-qis** a person born or living in Iraq —*adj.* of Iraq or its people, language, or culture

i·ras·ci·ble (i ras′ə bəl) *adj.* ⟦ME *irascibel* < MFr < LL *irascibilis* < L *irasci:* see fol.⟧ 1 easily angered; quick-tempered 2 showing or resulting from a quick temper or a fit of anger *[an irascible reply]* —**SYN.** IRRITABLE —i·ras′ci·bil′i·ty *n.*, i·ras′ci·ble·ness —i·ras′ci·bly *adv.*

i·rate (ī rāt′, ī′rāt′) *adj.* ⟦L *iratus* < *irasci,* to be angry < *ira,* IRE⟧ angry; wrathful; incensed —i·rate′ly *adv.* —i·rate′ness *n.*

Ir·bil (ʉr′bil) city in N Iraq, on the site of ancient ARBELA

IRBM *abbrev.* intermediate-range ballistic missile

ire (īr) *n.* ⟦OFr < L *ira* < IE base **eis-,* to move quickly, violently > Gr *oima,* stormy attack, ON *eisa,* to rush on⟧ anger; wrath —**SYN.** ANGER —ire′ful *adj.* —ire′ful·ly *adv.*

Ire *abbrev.* Ireland

Ire·land (īr′lənd) ⟦OE *Īrland* < *Īra-land:* see IRISH⟧ 1 island of the British Isles, west of Great Britain: 32,595 sq mi (84,421 sq km) 2 republic comprising the S provinces of this island & three counties of Ulster province: established as a republic in 1922, it was a member of the Commonwealth until 1949: 27,135 sq mi (70,280 sq km); cap. Dublin: cf. NORTHERN IRELAND: in full **Republic of Ireland**

I·rene (*for 1,* ī rēn′ *or, esp. Brit,* ī rē′nē; *for 2,* ī rē′nē) *n.* ⟦< Fr or L: Fr *Irène* < L *Irene* < Gr *Eirēnē,* lit., peace⟧ 1 a feminine name 2 *Gr. Myth.* the goddess of peace, daughter of Zeus and Themis: identified with the Roman Pax

i·ren·ic (ī ren′ik, ī rē′nik) *adj.* ⟦Gr *eirēnikos* < *eirēnē,* peace⟧ promoting peace; peaceful; pacific: also **i·ren′i·cal** —i·ren′i·cal·ly *adv.*

i·ren·ics (ī ren′iks, ī rē′niks) *n.* ⟦see prec. & -ICS⟧ *Christianity* the doctrine or practice of promoting peace and reconciliation among Christian churches and sects

Ir·i·an (ir′ē än′) *Indonesian name for* NEW GUINEA

i·rid (ī′rid) *n.* ⟦see IRIS⟧ a plant of the iris family

ir·i·dec·to·my (ir′i dek′tə mē, ī′ri-) *n., pl.* **-mies** ⟦IRID(O)- + -ECTOMY⟧ the surgical removal of part of the iris of the eye

ir·i·des (ir′i dēz′, ī′ri-) *n. alt. pl. of* IRIS

ir·i·des·cent (ir′i des′ənt) *adj.* ⟦< L *iris,* rainbow < Gr, rainbow (see IRIS) + -ESCENT⟧ having or showing shifting changes in color or an interplay of rainbowlike colors, as when seen from different angles —ir′i·des′cence *n.* —ir′i·des′cent·ly *adv.*

i·rid·ic (ī rid′ik, i-) *adj.* 1 of or containing iridium 2 designating or of a chemical compound containing tetravalent iridium 3 of the iris of the eye

i·rid·i·um (i rid′ē əm) *n.* ⟦ModL: so named (1804) by S. Tennant (1761-1815), Eng chemist < Gr *iris* (gen. *iridos*), IRIS, because its salts have varied colors; + -IUM⟧ a white, extremely dense, brittle, corrosion-resistant chemical element, one of the platinum metals: alloys of iridium are used in electrodes, pen points, crucibles, etc.: symbol, Ir; at. no. 77: see the periodic table of elements in the Reference Supplement

ir·i·do- (ir′i dō′, ī′ri-) ⟦< ModL *iris:* see IRIS⟧ *combining form* the iris (of the eye) *[iridoparalysis]*: also, before a vowel, **irid-**

ir·i·dos·mine (ir′i däz′min, -mēn′) *n.* ⟦< IRIDIUM + OSMIUM⟧ a native alloy of iridium and osmium containing small amounts of other metals of the platinum group: it crystallizes in the hexagonal system: also **ir′i·dos′mi·um** (-mē əm)

i·ris (ī′ris) *n., pl.* **i′ris·es;** also for 3, **ir·i·des** (ir′i dēz′, ī′ri-); also for 4 & 5, **i′ris** ⟦LME < L < Gr *iris* (gen. *iridos*) < IE **wir-* (> WIRE) < base **wei-,* to turn, bend⟧ **1** a rainbow **2** a rainbowlike show or play of colors **3** the round, pigmented membrane surrounding the pupil of the eye, having muscles that adjust the size of the pupil to regulate the amount of light entering the eye **4** any of a large genus (*Iris*) of perennial plants of the iris family, with sword-shaped leaves and conspicuous flowers composed of three petals and three drooping sepals of widely varying color **5** the flower of these plants —*adj.* designating a family (Iridaceae, order Liliales) of monocotyledonous plants, including crocuses and gladioluses

I·ris (ī′ris) ***n.*** ⟦L < Gr *Iris*: see prec.⟧ **1** a feminine name **2** *Gr. Myth.* the goddess of the rainbow: in the *Iliad*, she is the messenger of the gods

iris diaphragm a device consisting of thin, overlapping metal blades that can be adjusted to form an aperture of varying size for camera lenses, etc.

I·rish (ī′rish) ***adj.*** ⟦ME < OE *Irisc* < *Iras*, the Irish < OIr *Eriu*, Ireland > EIRE⟧ of Ireland or its people, language, or culture —***n.*** **1** the Celtic language spoken in Ireland **2** the variety of English spoken in Ireland **3** [Informal] temper: chiefly in **get someone's Irish up**, to arouse someone's temper —**the Irish** the people of Ireland

Irish bull BULL[3]

Irish coffee brewed coffee containing Irish whiskey and topped with cream or whipped cream

Irish Free State *former name* (1922-37) *for* IRELAND (the republic)

Irish Gaelic IRISH (*n.* 1)

I·rish·ism (ī′rish iz′əm) ***n.*** **1** a word, phrase, grammatical construction, or other feature originating among or peculiar to the Irish **2** an Irish custom, belief, etc.

I·rish·man (ī′rish mən) ***n.***, *pl.* **-men** (-mən) a person, esp. a man, born or living in Ireland

Irish moss CARRAGEEN

Irish potato the common white potato: so called because extensively cultivated in Ireland

Irish Republican Army **1** a paramilitary organization formed in 1919 to fight for Irish independence from England **2** either of the two branches (Official and Provisional) of a similar, present-day organization seeking Northern Ireland's independence from the United Kingdom

I·rish·ry (ī′rish rē) ***n.***, *pl.* **I′rish·ry** **1** a custom, characteristic, or folkway of the Irish people **2** a word, phrase, grammatical construction, or other feature originating in or peculiar to English as it is spoken in Ireland **3** a group of people of Irish descent; esp., the people of Ireland

Irish Sea arm of the Atlantic between Ireland & Great Britain

Irish setter any of a breed of setter with a silky, reddish-brown coat

Irish stew a stew of meat, originally mutton, with potatoes, onions, and other vegetables

Irish terrier any of a breed of terrier with a long head and a dense, wiry coat of a solid color, often red or reddish: traditionally the tail is docked

Irish water spaniel any of a breed of spaniel with a liver-colored coat of dense ringlets, a topknot, and a ratlike tail, often used as a retriever of waterfowl

Irish whiskey whiskey distilled in Ireland from a mixture of malted barley and small amounts of other grains

Irish wolfhound any of a breed of very large, heavy, powerful dog with a dense, rough coat and bushy brows

I·rish·wom·an (ī′rish woom′ən) ***n.***, *pl.* **-wom′en** (-wim′in) a woman born or living in Ireland

i·ri·tis (ī rīt′is) ***n.*** ⟦ModL: see IRIS & -ITIS⟧ inflammation of the iris of the eye —**i·rit′ic** (-rit′ik) ***adj.***

irk (ʉrk) ***vt.*** ⟦ME *irken*, to loathe, be weary of, akin to northern & N Midland adj. *irk*, *yrk*, weary, troubled < ? ON *yrkja*, to WORK⟧ to annoy, disgust, irritate, tire out, etc. —***SYN.*** ANNOY

irk·some (ʉrk′səm) ***adj.*** ⟦ME *irksum*: see prec. & -SOME[1]⟧ that tends to irk; tiresome or annoying —**irk′some·ly** ***adv.*** —**irk′some·ness** ***n.***

Ir·kutsk (ir ko͞otsk′) city in S Asian Russia, near Lake Baikal

Ir·ma (ʉr′mə) ***n.*** ⟦Ger, orig. contr. of *Irmenberta, Irmintrud, Irmgard*, etc. < OHG *Irmin*, cognomen of the Gmc war god Tiu⟧ a feminine name

i·ron (ī′ərn) ***n.*** ⟦ME *iren* < OE (chiefly poetic & prob. dissimilated), var. of *isern, isen* akin to Goth *eisarn*) < Gmc **īsarna*, akin to early Celt **isarno*, prob. via Illyrian **eisarno-* < IE base **eis-*, to move vigorously; strong, holy (> IRE): orig. sense prob. "the strong metal" (in contrast to the softer bronze)⟧ **1** a white, malleable, ductile, metallic chemical element that can be readily magnetized, rusts rapidly in moist or salty air, and is vital to plant and animal life: it is the most common of all metals, and its alloys, as steel, are extensively used: symbol, Fe; at. no. 26: see the periodic table of elements in the Reference Supplement **2** any tool, implement, device, apparatus, etc. made of iron, as *a)* a hand-held device with a handle and flat, smooth underside, used, when heated, for pressing clothes or cloth *b)* BRANDING IRON **3** [*pl.*] iron shackles or chains **4** firm strength; power **5** [Old Slang] a pistol **6** *Golf* any of a set of numbered clubs with metal heads having various lofts; specif., the **number 2 iron** with little loft, used chiefly for relatively long fairway shots; the **number 5 iron** with medium loft; and the **number 9 iron** with much loft, used chiefly for short, lofted shots to the green **7** *Med.* a tonic or other preparation containing iron —***adj.*** **1** of or consisting of iron **2** like iron, as *a)* firm; unyielding [an *iron* will] *b)* capable of great endurance; strong [an *iron* constitution] **3** cruel; merciless —***vt.*** **1** to furnish or cover with iron **2** to shackle (a prisoner) with irons **3** to press (clothes or cloth) smooth or flat with a hot iron —***vi.*** to iron clothes or cloth —**have many** (or **several**, etc.) **irons in the fire** to have or be engaged in many (or several, etc.) activities, enterprises, or the like —**in irons** **1** shackled with irons **2** *Naut.* headed into the wind with no way on: said of a sailing vessel that has failed to come about —☆**iron out** [Informal] to smooth out; eliminate —**strike while the iron is hot** to act at the opportune time

Iron Age **1** a phase of many human cultures, often following a Bronze Age, characterized by the introduction and development of iron tools and weapons; specif., in Europe beginning *c.* 1000 B.C. **2** *Class. Myth.* the last and worst age of the world, characterized by wickedness, selfishness, and degeneracy

i·ron·bark (ī′ərn bärk′) ***n.*** **1** any of several Australian eucalyptus trees (genus *Eucalyptus*) with hard wood and hard, gray bark **2** the wood of any of these trees

i·ron·bound (-bound′) ***adj.*** **1** bound with iron **2** hard; rigid; unyielding; inflexible **3** edged with rocks or cliffs, as a coast

i·ron·clad (-klad′) ***adj.*** **1** covered or protected with iron **2** difficult to change or break [an *ironclad* lease] —***n.*** a warship of the 19th cent. armored with thick iron plates

iron curtain ⟦prob. calque of Ger *eiserner vorhang*, as used by Joseph Goebbels: popularized by Winston Churchill in a speech (1946)⟧ **1** [*often* **I- C-**] a barrier of secrecy and censorship regarded as isolating the Soviet Union and other countries in its sphere: often with *the* **2** a similar barrier to information in other regions

i·ron·er (ī′ər nər) ***n.*** one that irons; esp., a mangle

i·ron-fist·ed (ī′ərn fis′tid) ***adj.*** ruthlessly autocratic; despotic and brutal

iron gray a dark to medium gray like that of freshly broken cast iron —**i′ron-gray′** ***adj.***

iron hand firm, rigorous, severe control —**i′ron·hand′ed** ***adj.***

i·ron·heart·ed (ī′ərn härt′id) ***adj.*** unfeeling; cruel

☆**iron horse** [Old Informal] a locomotive

i·ron·ic (ī rän′ik) ***adj.*** ⟦L *ironicus* < Gr *eirōnikos* < *eirōneia*: see IRONY[1]⟧ **1** meaning the contrary of what is expressed **2** using, or given to the use of, irony **3** having the quality of irony; directly opposite to what is or might be expected **4** marked by coincidence or by a curious or striking juxtaposition of events: regarded by many as a loose usage Also **i·ron′i·cal** —***SYN.*** SARCASTIC —**i·ron′i·cal·ly** ***adv.***

i·ron·ing (ī′ər niŋ) ***n.*** **1** the act or process of pressing cloth or clothes smooth or flat with a hot iron **2** cloth or clothes that are to be ironed or have been ironed

ironing board (*or* **table**) a cloth-covered board or stand on which clothes are ironed

i·ron·ist (ī′rə nist) ***n.*** a writer or speaker noted for using irony frequently

☆**iron lung** a large metal respirator that encloses all of the body but the head, used for maintaining artificial respiration

iron maiden [*also* **I- M-**] [Historical] an instrument of torture consisting of a large case having the general contour of a person, with sharp spikes inside

i·ron·man (ī′ərn man′) ***n.***, *pl.* **-men′** (-men′) a man having great physical strength and endurance

i·ron·mas·ter (ī′ərn mas′tər) ***n.*** a manufacturer of iron

i·ron·mon·ger (-muŋ′gər) ***n.*** ⟦ME *irenmonger*: see IRON & MONGER⟧ [Brit.] a dealer in hardware —**i′ron·mon′ger·y** ***n.***

iron oxide any oxide of iron, esp. ferric oxide or ferrous oxide

iron pyrites PYRITE

I·ron·sides (ī′ərn sīdz′) ***n.*** **1** *name for* Oliver CROMWELL **2** *a)* the regiment that Cromwell led in the English Civil War *b)* his entire army

i·ron·smith (ī′ərn smith′) ***n.*** an ironworker or blacksmith

i·ron·stone (-stōn′) ***n.*** **1** any rock rich in iron **2** a hard variety of white ceramic ware

i·ron·ware (-wer′) ***n.*** articles, esp. tools and utensils, made of iron

i·ron·weed (-wēd′) ***n.*** ⟦so named from its hard stem⟧ any of a genus (*Vernonia*) of perennial plants of the composite family, with clusters of small, tubular, purple flowers

i·ron·wood (-wood′) ***n.*** **1** any of various trees, esp. hornbeam and hop hornbeam, with extremely hard, heavy wood **2** the wood of an ironwood

i·ron·work (-wʉrk′) ***n.*** articles or parts made of iron

i·ron·work·er (-wʉr′kər) ***n.*** **1** a person who makes iron or articles of iron **2** a worker who builds the framework of steel bridges, skyscrapers, etc.

i·ron·works (-wʉrks′) ***pl.n.*** [*often with sing. v.*] a place where iron is smelted or heavy iron goods are made

i·ro·ny[1] (ī′rə nē, ī′ər nē) ***n.***, *pl.* **-nies** ⟦Fr *ironie* < L *ironia* < Gr *eirōneia* < *eirōn*, dissembler in speech < *eirein*, to speak < IE base **wer-*, to speak > WORD⟧ **1** *a)* a method of humorous or subtly sarcastic expression in which the intended meaning of the words is the direct opposite of their usual sense [the *irony* of calling a stupid plan "clever"] *b)* an instance of this **2** the contrast, as in a play, between what a character thinks the truth is, as revealed in a speech or action, and what an audience or reader knows the truth to be: often **dramatic irony** **3** a combination of circumstances or a result that is the opposite of what is or might be expected or considered appropriate [an *irony* that the firehouse burned] **4** *a)* a cool, detached attitude of mind, characterized by recognition of the incongruities and complexities of experience *b)* the expression of such an attitude in a literary work **5** the feigning of ignorance as a tactic in argument: usually **Socratic irony** (after Socrates' use of this tactic in Plato's *Dialogues*) —***SYN.*** WIT[1]

i·ron·y[2] (ī′ər nē) ***adj.*** of, like, or containing iron

☆**Ir·o·quoi·an** (ir′ə kwoi′ən) ***n.*** ⟦< fol. + -AN: coined (1891) by J. W.

Powell]] 1 a family of North American Indian languages including Oneida, Mohawk, Huron, Tuscarora, and Cherokee 2 a member of any of the peoples speaking these languages —*adj.* designating or of these languages or the peoples that speak them

Ir·o·quois (ir′ə kwoi′) *n.* [[Fr, prob. < an Algonquian language]] 1 *pl.* **-quois′** (-kwoi′, -kwoiz′) a member of a confederation of Iroquoian Indian peoples that lived in upstate New York and included the Senecas, Cayugas, Onondagas, Oneidas, Mohawks, and (after 1723) the Tuscaroras: their descendants live in New York, Ontario, Quebec, and Oklahoma: see FIVE NATIONS 2 any of the languages spoken by the Iroquois —*adj.* of the Iroquois or their languages or cultures

ir·ra·di·ance (i rā′dē əns) *n.* 1 an irradiating; radiance 2 the amount of light or other radiant energy striking a given area of a surface; illumination —**ir·ra′di·ant** *adj.*

ir·ra·di·ate (-āt′; *for adj., usually,* -it) *vt.* **-at′ed, -at′ing** [[< L *irradiatus,* pp. of *irradiare,* to beam upon, illumine: see IN-[1] & RADIATE]] 1 to shine or throw light upon; light up; make bright 2 to make clear; illuminate intellectually; enlighten 3 to radiate; diffuse; spread; give out 4 to expose to or treat by exposing to X-rays, ultraviolet rays, radium, or some other form of radiant energy 5 to heat with radiant energy —*vi.* 1 to emit rays; shine 2 to become radiant —*adj.* lighted up; irradiated —**ir·ra′di·a′tive** *adj.* —**ir·ra′di·a′tor** *n.*

ir·ra·di·a·tion (i rā′dē ā′shən) *n.* [[Fr < ML *irradiatio*]] 1 an irradiating or being irradiated; esp., *a)* exposure to radiation *b)* emission of radiant energy 2 IRRADIANCE (sense 2) 3 *Optics* the apparent enlargement of a brightly lighted object seen against a dark background

ir·ra·tion·al (i rash′ə nəl) *adj.* [[ME < L *irrationalis:* see IN-[2] & RATIONAL]] 1 lacking the power to reason 2 contrary to reason or rationality; senseless; unreasonable; absurd 3 *Math.* designating a real number not expressible as an integer or as a quotient of two integers: $\sqrt{3}$ and pi are irrational numbers: cf. RATIONAL (sense 4*a*) —**ir·ra′tion·al′i·ty** (-ə nal′ə tē) *n., pl.* **-ties** —**ir·ra′tion·al·ly** *adv.*

SYN.—**irrational** implies mental unsoundness or may be used to stress the utterly illogical nature of that which is directly contrary to reason [*an irrational belief that everybody was his enemy*]; **unreasonable** implies bad judgment, willfulness, prejudice, etc. as responsible for that which is not justified by reason [*unreasonable demands*] —ANT. **rational, reasonable**

ir·ra·tion·al·ism (-iz′əm) *n.* irrational thought, belief, or action —**ir·ra′tion·al·ist** *n., adj.*

Ir·ra·wad·dy (ir′ə wä′dē, -wô′-) river flowing from N Myanmar south into the Andaman Sea: *c.* 1,000 mi (1,609 km)

ir·real (i rēl′) *adj.* [[IR- (var. of IN-[2]) + REAL[1]]] not real —**ir′re·al′i·ty** *n.*

ir·re·claim·a·ble (ir′i klām′ə bəl) *adj.* that cannot be reclaimed —**ir′re·claim′a·bil′i·ty** *n.* —**ir′re·claim′a·bly** *adv.*

ir·rec·on·cil·a·ble (i rek′ən sīl′ə bəl) *adj.* that cannot be reconciled; that cannot be brought into agreement; incompatible, conflicting, or inconsistent —*n.* 1 a person who is irreconcilable and refuses to make any compromise 2 [*pl.*] ideas, beliefs, etc. that cannot be brought into agreement with each other —**ir·rec′on·cil′a·bil′i·ty** *n.* —**ir·rec′on·cil′a·bly** *adv.*

ir·re·cov·er·a·ble (ir′i kuv′ər ə bəl) *adj.* that cannot be recovered, rectified, or remedied; irretrievable —**ir′re·cov′er·a·bly** *adv.*

ir·re·cu·sa·ble (ir′i kyo͞o′zə bəl) *adj.* [[< Fr or LL: Fr *irrécusable* < LL *irrecusabilis* < *in-,* IN-[2] + *recusabilis,* that should be rejected < L *recusare,* to refuse: see RECUSANT]] that cannot be refused or rejected —**ir′re·cu′sa·bly** *adv.*

ir·re·deem·a·ble (ir′i dēm′ə bəl) *adj.* [[see IN-[2] & REDEEMABLE]] 1 that cannot be bought back ☆2 that cannot be converted into coin, as certain kinds of paper money 3 that cannot be reformed, saved, salvaged, etc.; hopeless —**ir′re·deem′a·bly** *adv.*

ir·re·den·tist (ir′i den′tist) *n.* [[It *irredentista* < (*Italia*) *irredenta,* unredeemed (Italy) < L *in-,* not + *redemptus:* see REDEMPTION]] 1 [*usually* **I-**] [Historical] any member of an Italian political party, organized in 1878, seeking to recover for Italy adjacent regions inhabited largely by Italians but under foreign control 2 any person who advocates a similar policy about territory formerly a part of that person's country —**ir′re·den′tism′** *n.*

ir·re·duc·i·ble (ir′i do͞os′ə bəl, -dyo͞os′-) *adj.* that cannot be reduced —**ir′re·duc′i·bil′i·ty** *n.* —**ir′re·duc′i·bly** *adv.*

ir·ref·ra·ga·ble (i ref′rə gə bəl) *adj.* [[LL *irrefragabilis* < L *in-,* IN-[2] + *refragari,* to oppose < *re-,* against + (*suf*)*fragari:* see SUFFRAGAN]] that cannot be refuted; indisputable —**ir·ref′ra·ga·bil′i·ty** *n.* —**ir·ref′ra·ga·bly** *adv.*

ir·re·fran·gi·ble (ir′i fran′jə bəl) *adj.* [[IR- + REFRANGIBLE]] 1 that cannot be broken or violated 2 that cannot be refracted —**ir′re·fran′gi·bly** *adv.*

ir·ref·u·ta·ble (i ref′yo͞o tə bəl, ir′i fyo͞ot′ə bəl) *adj.* [[LL *irrefutabilis*]] that cannot be refuted or disproved —**ir·ref′u·ta·bil′i·ty** *n.* —**ir·ref′u·ta·bly** *adv.*

irreg *abbrev.* irregular

☆**ir·re·gard·less** (ir′i gärd′lis) *adj., adv.* REGARDLESS: a nonstandard var. often used for humorous effect

ir·reg·u·lar (i reg′yə lər) *adj.* [[ME < OFr *irregulier* < ML *irregularis:* see IN-[2] & REGULAR]] 1 not conforming to established rule, method, usage, standard, etc.; out of the ordinary; anomalous 2 not conforming to legal or moral requirements; lawless; disorderly 3 not straight or even; not symmetrical; not uniform in shape, design, or proportion 4 uneven in occurrence or succession; variable or erratic ☆5 having minor flaws or imperfections: said of merchandise 6 not defecating at more or less fixed intervals or times; experiencing constipation 7 *Bot.* not uniform in shape, size, etc., as the petals of a flower 8 *Gram.* not inflected in the usual way ["go" is an *irregular* verb] 9 *Mil.* not belonging to the regularly established army —*n.* 1 a person or thing that is irregular 2 a soldier who belongs to an irregular military force ☆3 [*usually pl.*] irregular merchandise —**ir·reg′u·lar′i·ty** *n., pl.* **-ties** —**ir·reg′u·lar·ly** *adv.*

SYN.—**irregular** implies deviation from the customary or established rule, procedure, etc. [*irregular* conduct]; **abnormal** and **anomalous** imply deviation from the normal condition or from the ordinary type, **abnormal** stressing atypical form or character [a man of *abnormal* height], and **anomalous,** an exceptional condition or circumstance [in the *anomalous* position of a leader without followers]; **unnatural** applies to that which is contrary to the order of nature or to natural laws [an *unnatural* appetite for chalk] —ANT. **regular, normal, natural**

ir·rel·a·tive (i rel′ə tiv) *adj.* unrelated or irrelevant —**ir·rel′a·tive·ly** *adv.*

ir·rel·e·vant (i rel′ə vənt) *adj.* not relevant; not pertinent; not to the point; not relating to the subject —**ir·rel′e·vance** *n.,* **ir·rel′e·van·cy,** *pl.* **-cies** —**ir·rel′e·vant·ly** *adv.*

ir·re·li·gious (ir′i lij′əs) *adj.* [[L *irreligiosus*]] 1 not religious; adhering to no particular religious belief 2 indifferent or hostile to religion 3 not in accord with religious principles; profane; impious —**ir′re·li′gion** (-ən) *n.* —**ir′re·li′gion·ist** *n.* —**ir′re·li′gious·ly** *adv.*

ir·rem·e·a·ble (i rem′ē ə bəl, -rē′mē-) *adj.* [[L *irremeabilis* < *-in-,* not + *remeabilis,* returning < *remeare,* to go back < *re-,* back + *meare,* to go < IE base **mei-,* to go, wander]] [Archaic] from which there is no return

ir·re·me·di·a·ble (ir′i mē′dē ə bəl) *adj.* [[L *irremediabilis*]] that cannot be remedied or corrected; incurable or irreparable —**ir′re·me′di·a·ble·ness** *n.* —**ir′re·me′di·a·bly** *adv.*

ir·re·mis·si·ble (ir′i mis′ə bəl) *adj.* [[ME < OFr *irrémissible* < L *irremissibilis*]] not remissible; specif., *a)* that cannot be excused or pardoned *b)* that cannot be shirked —**ir′re·mis′si·bly** *adv.*

ir·re·mov·a·ble (ir′i mo͞o′və bəl) *adj.* not removable —**ir′re·mov′a·bil′i·ty** *n.* —**ir′re·mov′a·bly** *adv.*

ir·rep·a·ra·ble (i rep′ə rə bəl) *adj.* [[ME *irreperable* < OFr *irréparable* < L *irreparabilis*]] not reparable; that cannot be repaired, mended, remedied, etc. —**ir·rep′a·ra·bil′i·ty** *n.* —**ir·rep′a·ra·bly** *adv.*

ir·re·peal·a·ble (ir′i pēl′ə bəl) *adj.* not repealable

ir·re·place·a·ble (-plās′ə bəl) *adj.* not replaceable

ir·re·press·i·ble (-pres′ə bəl) *adj.* that cannot be repressed or restrained —**ir′re·press′i·bil′i·ty** *n.* —**ir′re·press′i·bly** *adv.*

ir·re·proach·a·ble (-prō′chə bəl) *adj.* [[Fr *irréprochable*]] not reproachable; beyond reproach; blameless; faultless —**ir′re·proach′a·bil′i·ty** *n.,* **ir′re·proach′a·ble·ness** —**ir′re·proach′a·bly** *adv.*

ir·re·sist·i·ble (-zis′tə bəl) *adj.* [[LL *irresistibilis*]] too strong, fascinating, compelling, etc. to be resisted or withstood —**ir′re·sist′i·bil′i·ty** *n.,* **ir′re·sist′i·ble·ness** —**ir′re·sist′i·bly** *adv.*

ir·re·sol·u·ble (ir′i zäl′yə bəl) *adj.* [[L *irresolubilis*]] that cannot be resolved; insoluble

ir·res·o·lute (i rez′ə lo͞ot′) *adj.* [[L *irresolutus*]] not resolute; wavering in decision, purpose, or opinion; indecisive; vacillating —**ir·res′o·lute′ly** *adv.* —**ir·res′o·lute′ness** *n.* —**ir·res′o·lu′tion** *n.*

ir·re·solv·a·ble (ir′i zäl′və bəl) *adj.* 1 that cannot be resolved into elements or parts 2 that cannot be solved

ir·re·spec·tive (-spek′tiv) *adj.* [[IR- + RESPECTIVE]] [Rare] showing disregard for persons or consequences —**irrespective of** regardless of; independent of; notwithstanding —**ir′re·spec′tive·ly** *adv.*

ir·re·spir·a·ble (ir′i spīr′ə bəl, i res′pər ə-) *adj.* [[Fr < LL *irrespirabilis:* see IN-[2] & RESPIRE]] not suitable to be breathed

ir·re·spon·si·ble (ir′i spän′sə bəl) *adj.* not responsible; specif., *a)* not liable to be called to account for actions *b)* lacking a sense of responsibility; unreliable, shiftless, etc. *c)* said or done as by an irresponsible person —*n.* an irresponsible person —**ir′re·spon′si·bil′i·ty** *n.,* **ir′re·spon′si·ble·ness** —**ir′re·spon′si·bly** *adv.*

ir·re·spon·sive (-siv) *adj.* not responsive —**ir′re·spon′sive·ness** *n.*

ir·re·triev·a·ble (-trēv′ə bəl) *adj.* that cannot be retrieved, recovered, restored, or recalled —**ir′re·triev′a·bil′i·ty** *n.* —**ir′re·triev′a·bly** *adv.*

ir·rev·er·ence (i rev′ər əns) *n.* [[ME < L *irreverentia*]] 1 lack of reverence; disrespect 2 an act or statement showing this 3 the condition of not being treated with reverence —**ir·rev′er·ent** *adj.* —**ir·rev′er·ent·ly** *adv.*

ir·re·vers·i·ble (ir′i vur′sə bəl) *adj.* not reversible; specif., *a)* that cannot be repealed, annulled, or undone *b)* that cannot be turned inside out, run backward, etc. —**ir′re·vers′i·bil′i·ty** *n.* —**ir′re·vers′i·bly** *adv.*

ir·rev·o·ca·ble (i rev′ə kə bəl) *adj.* [[ME < MFr *irrévocable* < L *irrevocabilis*]] that cannot be revoked, recalled, or undone; unalterable —**ir·rev′o·ca·bil′i·ty** *n.,* **ir·rev′o·ca·ble·ness** —**ir·rev′o·ca·bly** *adv.*

ir·ri·ga·ble (ir′i gə bəl) *adj.* that can be irrigated

ir·ri·gate (ir′ə gāt′) *vt.* **-gat′ed, -gat′ing** [[< L *irrigatus,* pp. of *irrigare,* to bring water to or upon < *in-,* in, to, upon + *rigare,* to water, moisten: see RAIN]] 1 to refresh by or as by watering 2 to supply (land) with water by means of ditches or artificial channels or by sprinklers 3 *Med.* to wash out or flush (a cavity, wound, etc.) with water or other fluid —**ir′ri·ga′tion** *n.* —**ir′ri·ga′tive** *adj.* —**ir′ri·ga′tor** *n.*

ir·ri·ta·ble (ir′i tə bəl) *adj.* [[L *irritabilis* < *irritare,* to IRRITATE]] 1 easily annoyed or provoked 2 in an ill humor; bad-tempered; peevish 3 *Med.* excessively or pathologically sensitive to a stimulus 4 *Physiol.* able to respond to a stimulus —**ir′ri·ta·bil′i·ty** *n.,* **ir′ri·ta·ble·ness** —**ir′ri·ta·bly** *adv.*

SYN.—**irritable** implies quick excitability to annoyance or anger, usually resulting from emotional tension, restlessness, physical indisposition, etc.; **irascible** and **choleric** are applied to persons who are hot-tempered and can be roused to a fit of anger at the slightest irritation; **splenetic** suggests a peevish moroseness in one quick to vent malice or spite; **touchy** applies to one who is acutely irritable or sensitive and is too easily offended; **cranky** and **cross** suggest moods in which one cannot be easily pleased or satisfied, **cranky** because of stubborn notions or whims, and **cross** because of ill humor

irritable bowel syndrome a chronic gastrointestinal ailment lacking a specific known cause, characterized by abdominal pain, cramps, and diarrhea: abbrev. *IBS*

ir·ri·tant (ir′i tənt) *adj.* ⟦L *irritans*, prp. of *irritare*⟧ causing irritation or inflammation —*n.* something that causes irritation —**ir′ri·tan·cy** *n.*, **ir′ri·tance**

ir·ri·tate (ir′i tāt′) *vt.* **-tat′ed**, **-tat′ing** ⟦< L *irritatus*, pp. of *irritare*, to excite, stimulate, irritate < *ir-*, in- + IE base **erei-*, to excite, agitate > ROAM⟧ **1** to excite to anger; provoke; annoy; exasperate **2** to cause (an organ or part of the body) to be inflamed or sore **3** *Physiol.* to excite (an organ, muscle, etc.) to a characteristic action or function by a stimulus —**ir′ri·tat′ing·ly** *adv.*

SYN.—**irritate**, the broadest in scope of these terms, may suggest temporary superficial impatience, or constant annoyance in, or an outburst of anger from, the person stirred to feeling [their smugness *irritated* him]; to **provoke** is to arouse strong annoyance or resentment, or, sometimes, vindictive anger [*provoked* by an insult]; **nettle** implies irritation that stings or piques rather than infuriates [sly, *nettling* remarks]; **exasperate** implies intense irritation such as exhausts one's patience or makes one lose one's self-control [*exasperating* impudence]; **peeve**, an informal word, means to cause to be annoyed, cross, or fretful [he seems *peeved* about something]

ir·ri·ta·tion (ir′i tā′shən) *n.* ⟦L *irritatio*⟧ **1** the act or process of irritating **2** the fact or condition of being irritated **3** something that irritates **4** *Med.* an excessive response to stimulation in an organ or body part; specif., a condition of soreness or inflammation

ir·ri·ta·tive (ir′i tāt′iv) *adj.* **1** causing irritation **2** accompanied or caused by irritation

ir·rupt (i rupt′) *vi.* ⟦< L *irruptus*, pp. of *irrumpere*, to break in: see IN-[1] & RUPTURE⟧ **1** to burst suddenly or violently (*into*) **2** *Ecol.* to increase abruptly in size of population —**ir·rup′tion** *n.* —**ir·rup′tive** *adj.*

IRS *abbrev.* Internal Revenue Service

Ir·tysh (ir tish′) river in central Asia, flowing from NW China northwestward into the Ob: *c.* 1,850 mi (2,977 km): also sp. **Ir·tish′**

Ir·vine (ʉr′vīn′) ⟦after the *Irvine* Company, the developers⟧ city in SW Calif.: suburb of Los Angeles

Ir·ving[1] (ʉr′viŋ) *n.* ⟦< N Brit surname *Irving*, prob. orig. a place name⟧ a masculine name

Ir·ving[2] (ʉr′viŋ) **1** Sir **Henry** (born *John Henry Brodribb*) 1838-1905; Eng. actor & theatrical manager **2 Washington** 1783-1859; U.S. writer

Ir·ving[3] (ʉr′viŋ) ⟦prob. an arbitrary selection⟧ city in NW Tex.: suburb of Dallas

Ir·win (ʉr′win) *n.* a masculine name: see ERWIN

is[1] (iz) *vi.* ⟦ME < OE, akin to Ger *ist* < IE **esti* (> Sans *ásti*, Gr *esti*, L *est*) < base **es-*, to be + *-*ti*, prob. orig. an enclitic pron.⟧ *3d pers. sing., pres. indic., of* BE

is[2] *abbrev.* **1** island(s) **2** isle(s)

is- (īs) *combining form* ISO-: used before a vowel

Isa or **Is** *abbrev. Bible* Isaiah

I·saac (ī′zək) *n.* ⟦LL(Ec) *Isaacus* < Gr(Ec) *Isaak* < Heb *yitshāq*, lit., laughter: see Gen. 17:17⟧ **1** a masculine name: dim. *Ike* **2** *Bible* one of the patriarchs, son of Abraham and Sarah, and father of Jacob and Esau: Gen. 21:3

Is·a·bel (iz′ə bel′) *n.* ⟦Sp, prob. an alteration of *Elizabeth*⟧ a feminine name: dim. *Bel*; var. *Isabelle, Isabella*

Is·a·bel·la[1] (iz′ə bel′ə) *n.* ⟦It⟧ a feminine name: dim. *Bella*: see ISABEL

Is·a·bel·la[2] (iz′ə bel′ə) **1 Isabella I** 1451-1504; wife of Ferdinand V & queen of Castile (1474-1504): supported Columbus in his expedition: called **Isabella of Castile 2 Isabella II** 1830-1904; queen of Spain (1833-68): deposed

Is·a·belle (iz′ə bel′) *n.* ⟦Fr⟧ a feminine name: dim. *Belle*: see ISABEL

is·a·cous·tic (ī′sə ko͞os′tik) *adj.* ⟦IS- + ACOUSTIC⟧ of or having to do with equal intensity of sound

Is·a·dor·a (iz′ə dôr′ə) *n.* ⟦var. of Gr *Isidōra*: see ISIDORE⟧ a feminine name: see ISIDORE

i·sa·gog·ics (ī′sə gäj′iks) *n.* ⟦< L *isagogic* < Gr *eisagōgikos* < *eisagōgē*, introduction < *eisagein*, to lead in, introduce < *eis-*, into + *agein*, to lead: see ACT[1]⟧ introductory study; esp., the study of the literary history of the Bible, considered as introductory to the study of Bible interpretation —**i′sa·gog′ic** *adj.*

I·sa·iah (ī zā′ə; *chiefly Brit*, -zī-) *n.* ⟦LL(Ec) *Isaias* < Gr(Ec) *Ēsaias* < Heb *yĕsha ʻyah*, lit., God is salvation⟧ **1** a masculine name **2** *Bible a)* a Hebrew prophet of the 8th cent. B.C. *b)* the book containing his teachings (abbrev. *Is* or *Isa*)

is·al·lo·bar (īs al′ō bär′, -al′ə-) *n.* ⟦< IS- + ALLO- + (ISO)BAR⟧ a line on a weather map connecting places having an equal change of barometric pressure over a given period

i·sa·tin (ī′sə tin) *n.* ⟦< L *isatis*, variety of herb (< Gr *isatis*, woad) + -IN[1]⟧ a reddish-orange, crystalline compound, $C_8H_5NO_2$, produced by the oxidation of indigo and used in making dyes

-i·sa·tion (ī zā′shən, i-, ə-) *suffix chiefly Brit. sp. of* -IZATION

ISBN *abbrev.* International Standard Book Number

Is·car·i·ot (is ker′ē ət) *n.* ⟦LL(Ec) *Iscariota* < Gr(Ec) *Iskariōtēs* < ? Heb *īsh-qĕrīyōth*, man of Kerioth (town in Palestine)⟧ *see* JUDAS (sense 1)

is·che·mi·a (is kē′mē ə) *n.* ⟦ModL < Gr *ischaimos*, stanching blood (< *ischein*, to hold + *haima*, blood: see SCHEME & HEMO-) + -IA⟧ a lack of blood supply in an organ or tissue —**is·che′mic** *adj.*

is·chi·um (is′kē əm) *n.*, *pl.* **-chi·a** (-ə) ⟦L < Gr *ischion*, hip, hip joint⟧ the lowermost of the three sections of the innominate bone; bone on which the body rests when sitting —**is′chi·al** *adj.*, **is′chi·at′ic**, or **is′chi·ad′ic**

ISDN *abbrev.* integrated services digital network

-ise (īz) *suffix chiefly Brit. sp. of* -IZE

I·seult (i so͞olt′) *n.* ⟦Fr⟧ *var. of* ISOLDE

Is·fa·han (is′fä hän′) *var. of* ESFAHÁN

-ish (ish) *suffix* **1** ⟦ME < OE *-isc*, akin to Ger *-isch*, L *-iscus*, Gr *-iskos*⟧ *forming adjectives a)* of or belonging to (a specified nation or people) [*Spanish, Irish*] *b)* like or characteristic of [*devilish, boyish*] *c)* tending to be or verging on being (a specified person or thing) [*knavish*] *d)* somewhat, rather [*tallish, bluish*] *e)* [Informal] approximately, about [*thirtyish*, or about thirty years old] **2** ⟦ME *-ishen, -ischen, -issen* < OFr *-iss-, -is-*, stem element in pres. tense < L *-isc-*, in inceptive verbs⟧ *forming verbs*: it was generalized from certain verbs of French origin [*finish, cherish, punish*]

Ish·er·wood (ish′ər wood), **Christopher (William Bradshaw)** 1904-86; Brit. writer

Ish·ma·el (ish′mā əl) *n.* ⟦LL(Ec) *Ismaël* < Heb *yishmāʻēl*, lit., God hears⟧ **1** the son of Abraham and Hagar: he and his mother were made outcasts: Gen. 21:9-21 **2** an outcast

Ish·ma·el·ite (-īt′) *n.* **1** a descendant of Ishmael, the traditional progenitor of Arab peoples **2** an outcast —**Ish′ma·el·it′ish** *adj.*

Ish·tar (ish′tär′) *n.* ⟦Assyr-Bab < Akkadian, var. of *Ash-dar*: see ASHTORETH⟧ *Bab. & Assyr. Myth.* the goddess of love, fertility, and war

Is·i·dore or **Is·i·dor** (iz′ə dôr′) *n.* ⟦< Ger *Isdor* or Fr *Isidore*, both < L *Isidorus* < Gr *Isidōros* < *Isis* + *dōron*, gift; hence, lit., gift of Isis⟧ a masculine name: dim. *Izzy*; var. *Isadore, Isador*; fem. *Isadora*

Isidore of Seville, Saint (L. *Isidorus Hispalensis*) (A.D. 560?-636); Sp. bishop & scholar: his day is April 4

i·sin·glass (ī′zin glas′, -ziŋ-) *n.* ⟦prob. altered < MDu *huizenblas*, lit., sturgeon bladder < *huizen*, sturgeon + *blas*, bladder⟧ **1** a form of gelatin prepared from the internal membranes of fish bladders: it is used as a clarifying agent and adhesive **2** mica, esp. in the form of thin, transparent sheets of muscovite

I·sis[1] (ī′sis) *n.* ⟦L < Gr⟧ *Egypt. Myth.* the goddess of fertility, sister and wife of Osiris, typically represented with a cow's horns surrounding a solar (or lunar) disk

I·sis[2] (ī′sis) *local & literary name for* the THAMES, esp. at, & west of, Oxford

Is·ken·de·run (is ken′də ro͞on′) seaport in S Turkey, on the Mediterranean

isl *abbrev.* **1** island **2** isle

Is·lam (is′läm′, iz′-; -ləm, -lam′; is läm′, iz-) *n.* ⟦Ar *islām*, lit., submission (to God's will) < *salama*, to be resigned⟧ **1** the Muslim religion, a monotheistic religion in which the supreme deity is Allah and the chief prophet and founder is Muhammad **2** Muslims collectively **3** all the lands in which the Muslim religion predominates —**Is·lam′ic** *adj.*

Is·lam·a·bad (is läm′ə bäd′) capital of Pakistan, in the NE part, near Rawalpindi

Is·lam·i·cist (is läm′ə sist, iz-; -lam′-) *n.* **1** a student of Islam **2** *var. of* ISLAMIST —*adj. var. of* ISLAMIST

Is·lam·ism (is′ləm iz′əm, iz′-) *n.* a movement advocating the social and political establishment of Islamic fundamentalism

Is·lam·ist (iz läm′ist, is-; -lam′-; iz′ləm ist) *n.* an advocate or supporter of Islamism —*adj.* of or pertaining to Islamists, their political and social goals, etc.

Is·lam·ize (is′ləm īz′, iz′-) *vt.*, *vi.* **-ized′**, **-iz′ing** to convert or conform to, or bring within, Islam: also **Is·lam′i·cize′**, **-cized′**, **-ciz′ing** —**Is′lam·i·za′tion** *n.*, **Is·lam′i·ci·za′tion**

is·land (ī′lənd) *n.* ⟦< ME *iland* (respelled by assoc. with unrelated ISLE) < OE *igland, iegland*, lit., island land & *ealand*, lit., water land < *ig, ieg*, isle (akin to Ger *aue*, ON *ey* < PGmc **aujo*, akin to **ahwo*) & *ea*, water < PGmc **ahwo*, water < IE **akwa* > L *aqua*: see LAND⟧ **1** a land mass not as large as a continent, surrounded by water **2** anything like an island in position or isolation; specif., *a)* a structure above the flight deck of an aircraft carrier containing the bridge, radar, etc. *b)* a counter which stands alone as in the central area of a kitchen *c)* any of the elevated areas of a service station, having a bank of gasoline pumps [a self-service *island*] **3** *short for: a)* TRAFFIC ISLAND *b)* SAFETY ISLAND (see SAFETY ZONE) **4** *Anat.* a tissue or cluster of cells differing from surrounding tissue in formation, etc. —*vt.* **1** to make into or like an island; isolate **2** to intersperse with or as with islands [a prairie *islanded* with wooded tracts]

is·land·er (ī′lən dər) *n.* a person born or living on an island

islands of Lang·er·hans (läŋ′ər hänz′) *see* ISLETS OF LANGERHANS

Islands of the Blessed *Class. Myth.* the islands of bliss in the Western Ocean, where heroes are sent after death

island universe *former term for* EXTERNAL GALAXY

isle (īl) *n.* ⟦ME *ile* < OFr *ile*, earlier *isle* < ML *isla*, contr. < L *insula* < ? (*terra*) *in salo,* (land) in the sea < *salum,* sea: the form *isle* became general in the Renaissance, infl. by L *insula*⟧ an island, esp., a small island: poetic except as part of a place name

Isle of France ÎLE-DE-FRANCE

Isle Roy·ale (roi′əl) ⟦Fr, lit., royal island⟧ island of Mich., in N Lake Superior

is·let (ī′lit) ***n.*** ⟦OFr, dim. of *isle,* ISLE⟧ **1** a very small ISLAND (***n.*** 1) **2** *Anat.* a small ISLAND (***n.*** 4)

islets (*or* islands) of Lang·er·hans (läŋ′ər hänz′) ⟦after P. *Langerhans* (1847-88), Ger histologist⟧ irregular groups of endocrine cells in the pancreas that produce the hormone insulin: their degeneration may cause diabetes mellitus

Is·ling·ton (iz′liŋ tən) borough of N Greater London, England

ism (iz′əm) ***n.*** ⟦< fol.⟧ a doctrine, theory, system, etc., esp. one whose name ends in *-ism*: a somewhat dismissive term

-ism (iz′əm) ⟦ME *-isme* < OFr & L *-isma* (< Gr) & *-ismus* (< Gr *-ismos*): orig. suffix of action or of state, forming nouns from verbs in L *-izare,* Gr *-izein*⟧ *suffix forming nouns* **1** the act, practice, or result of *[terrorism]* **2** the condition or state of being *[pauperism]* **3** action, conduct, or qualities characteristic of *[patriotism]* **4** the doctrine, school, theory, or principle of *[cubism, socialism]* **5** devotion to *[nationalism]* **6** an instance, example, or peculiarity of *[Gallicism, witticism]* **7** an abnormal condition caused by *[alcoholism]* **8** belief, attitudes, actions, or conduct characterized by prejudice or bigotry related to *[ageism, classism, sexism]*

Is·ma·i·li·a (is′mä ē lē′ä) city in NE Egypt

Is·ma·il·i·an (is′mā il′ē ən) ***n.*** any member of a Shiite sect of Muslims holding that the office of imam should have gone to the descendant of Jafar's elder son Ismail (died A.D. 760) when Jafar, the sixth imam, died in A.D. 765: also **Is′ma·e′li·an** (-mä ē′lē-)

is·n't (iz′ənt) *contraction* is not

ISO *service mark* International Organization for Standardization

i·so- (ī′sō, -sə) ⟦< Gr *isos,* equal⟧ *combining form* **1** equal, similar, alike, identical *[isomorph]* **2** isomeric *[isoalloxazine]*

i·so·ag·glu·ti·na·tion (ī′sō ə glo͞ot′'n ā′shən) ***n.*** the clumping of the red blood cells of an individual by the blood serum of another member of the same species

i·so·ag·glu·ti·nin (-ə glo͞ot′'n in) ***n.*** ⟦ISO- + AGGLUTININ⟧ a substance in the blood that causes isoagglutination

i·so·al·lox·a·zine (-ə läks′ə zēn′) ***n.*** ⟦ISO- + *alloxazine* < Ger *alloxan* (< *all(antoin)* + *ox(alsäure)* + *-an,* -ANE) + AZINE⟧ FLAVIN (sense 1)

i·so·bar (ī′sō bär′, -sə-) ***n.*** ⟦< ISO- + Gr *baros,* weight⟧ **1** a line on a map connecting points having equal barometric pressure at a given reference altitude, commonly sea level, over a given period or at a given time **2** any atom that has the same atomic weight (or mass number) as another atom but a different atomic number (Ex.: carbon-14 and nitrogen-14) **—i′so·bar′ic** (-bar′ik) ***adj.***

isobars
(figures in millibars)

i·so·bath (-bath′) ***n.*** ⟦< ISO- + Gr *bathos,* depth⟧ a contour line on a map connecting points of equal depth in a body of water or below the earth's surface **—i′so·bath′ic *adj.***

iso·bu·tyl (-byo͞ot′'l) ***n. see*** BUTYL

i·so·bu·tyl·ene (-byo͞ot′'l ēn′) ***n.*** a colorless, volatile liquid, $(CH_3)_2C{:}CH_2$, obtained from gases in petroleum cracking: it polymerizes readily and is used in making synthetic rubber and resins: also **i′so·bu′tene′** (-byo͞o′tēn′)

i·so·cheim (ī′sō kīm′, -sə-) ***n.*** ⟦< ISO- + Gr *cheima,* winter: see HIBERNATE⟧ a line on a map connecting points on the earth's surface that have the same mean winter temperature **—i′so·chei′mal *adj.***

i·so·chor or **i·so·chore** (ī′sō kôr′, -sə-) ***n.*** ⟦< ISO- + Gr *chōra,* a place < IE base **ĝhē(i)-,* to be empty > OE *gad,* lack⟧ *Physics* a line on a graph representing the parallel changes in pressure and temperature of something whose volume remains constant **—i′so·chor′ic *adj.***

i·so·chro·mat·ic (ī′sō krō mat′ik, -sə-) ***adj.*** ⟦ISO- + CHROMATIC⟧ **1** *Optics* having the same color: said of lines or curves in figures formed by interfering light waves from biaxial crystals **2** ORTHOCHROMATIC

i·soch·ro·nal (ī säk′rə nəl) ***adj.*** ⟦< ModL *isochronus* < Gr *isochronos* < *isos,* equal + *chronos,* time + -AL⟧ **1** equal in length of time **2** occurring at equal intervals of time Also **i·soch′ro·nous —i·soch′ro·nal·ly *adv.* —i·soch′ro·nism′ *n.***

i·so·chrone (ī′sō krōn′, -sə-) ***n.*** ⟦< Gr *isochronos*: see prec.⟧ a line, as on a chart or map, connecting points that have the same value at the same time: also **i′so·chron′** (-krän′)

i·soch·ro·ous (ī säk′rō əs) ***adj.*** ⟦ISO- + -CHROOUS⟧ having the same color in every part

i·so·cli·nal (ī′sō klī′nəl, -sə-) ***adj.*** ⟦< ISO- + Gr *klinein,* to slope (see LEAN[1]) + -AL⟧ **1** of similar or equal inclination or dip **2** connecting or showing points on the earth's surface having equal magnetic inclination or dip *[isoclinal* lines on a map*]* **3** *Geol.* dipping in the same direction: said of strata Also **i′so·clin′ic** (-klin′ik) **—*n.*** an isoclinal line **—i′so·cli′nal·ly *adv.***

i·so·cline (ī′sō klīn′, -sə-) ***n.*** ⟦see prec.⟧ **1** an anticline or syncline so compressed that the strata on both sides of the axis dip with equal inclination in the same direction **2** an isoclinal line

I·soc·ra·tes (ī säk′rə tēz′) 436-338 B.C.; Athenian orator & rhetorician

i·so·cy·a·nate (ī′sō sī′ə nāt′, ī′sə-) ***n.*** ⟦see fol. & -ATE[2]⟧ any of various compounds containing the group N:C:O, used in making resins and adhesives

i·so·cy·a·nine (-nēn′, -nin) ***n.*** ⟦ISO- + CYANINE⟧ any of a group of quinoline dyes used in sensitizing photographic plates and films

i·so·cy·clic (-sī′klik, -sik′lik) ***adj.*** ⟦ISO- + CYCLIC⟧ consisting of or being a ring of atoms of the same element

i·so·di·a·met·ric (-dī′ə me′trik) ***adj.*** *Bot.* having equal diameters or axes, as certain cells

i·so·di·mor·phism (-dī môr′fiz′əm) ***n.*** a similarity of crystalline structure between the two forms of two dimorphous substances **—i′so·di·mor′phous** (-fəs) ***adj.***

i·so·dose (ī′sō dōs′, -sə-) ***adj.*** designating or of points representing equal doses of radiation

i·so·dy·nam·ic (ī′sō dī nam′ik, -sə-) ***adj.*** **1** of or having equal force **2** connecting or showing points on the earth's surface having equal magnetic intensity *[isodynamic* lines on a map*]*

i·so·e·lec·tric point (-ē lek′trik) the point, or pH value, at which a substance is neutral or has zero electric potential

i·so·e·lec·tron·ic (-ə lek trän′ik) ***adj.*** designating or of any of two or more atoms which have the same number of electrons around the nucleus and similar spectral and physical properties **—i′so·e′lec′tron′i·cal·ly *adv.***

i·so·en·zyme (ī′sō en′zīm) ***n.*** an enzyme reacting the same as another enzyme but having a slightly different composition; isozyme

i·so·fla·vone (ī′sō flā′vōn′) ***n.*** an estrogen-like compound, an isomer of flavone, found in soybeans and used to reduce cholesterol levels, maintain bone health, etc.

i·so·ga·mete (-gam′ēt′, -gə mēt′) ***n.*** a gamete not differentiated in size, structure, or function from another with which it unites: found in some protozoans, fungi, etc.: opposed to HETEROGAMETE **—i′so·ga·met′ic** (-gə met′ik) ***adj.***

i·sog·a·my (ī säg′ə mē) ***n.*** ⟦ISO- + -GAMY⟧ reproduction by the uniting of isogametes **—i·sog′a·mous** (-məs) ***adj.***

i·sog·e·nous (ī säj′ə nəs) ***adj.*** ⟦ISO- + -GENOUS⟧ *Biol.* of the same origin; genetically uniform **—i·sog′e·ny** (-nē) ***n.***

i·so·ge·o·therm (ī′sō jē′ō thurm′) ***n.*** ⟦< ISO- + GEO- + Gr *thermē,* heat: see WARM⟧ an imaginary line or curved plane connecting points beneath the earth's surface that have the same average temperature **—i′so·ge′o·ther′mal *adj.***

i·so·gloss (ī′sō glôs′, -sə-) ***n.*** ⟦< ISO- + Gr *glōssa,* tongue, speech: see GLOSS[2]⟧ *Linguis.* **1** a line of demarcation between regions differing in a particular feature of language, as on a point of pronunciation, vocabulary, etc. **2** such a line indicated on a map

i·so·gon·ic (ī′sō gän′ik, -sə-) ***adj.*** ⟦ISO- + -GON + -IC⟧ **1** of or having equal angles **2** connecting or showing points on the earth's surface having the same magnetic declination *[isogonic* lines on a map*]* **3** of or having to do with isogony Also **i·sog·o·nal** (ī säg′ə nəl) **—*n.*** an isogonic line

i·sog·o·ny (ī säg′ə nē) ***n.*** ⟦ISO- + -GONY⟧ equivalent growth of parts of an organism so that size remains proportionate to the whole

i·so·gram (ī′sō gram′, -sə-) ***n.*** ⟦ISO- + -GRAM⟧ a line on a particular surface, as on a map, that represents a constant or equal value of a given quantity

i·so·hel (ī′sō hel′, -sə-) ***n.*** ⟦< ISO- + Gr *helios,* SUN[1]⟧ a line on a map connecting points having equal hours of sunshine in a standard period of time

i·so·hy·et (ī′sō hī′ət, -sə-) ***n.*** ⟦< ISO- + Gr *hyetos,* rain: see HYETO-⟧ a line on a map connecting points having equal amounts of precipitation during a given time period or for a particular storm **—i′so·hy′et·al *adj.***

i·so·late (ī′sə lāt′; *for n., usually,* -lit) ***vt.* -lat′ed, -lat′ing** ⟦back-form. < fol.⟧ **1** to set apart from others; place alone **2** *Chem.* to separate (an element or compound) in pure form from substances with which it is combined or mixed **3** *Med.* to place or keep (a patient) apart from others to prevent the spread of infection **4** *Microbiol.* to grow a pure culture of (a microbe), usually as individual colonies on a solid medium **—*adj.*** of or relating to someone or something that is set apart **—*n.*** **1** a person or group that is set apart **2** *Psychol., Sociology* a person who is separated from normal social activity, as through choice, rejection, psychological problems, etc. **—i′so·la·ble** (-lə bəl) ***adj.* —i′so·la′tor *n.***

i·so·lat·ed (ī′sə lāt′əd) ***adj.*** ⟦< It *isolato,* pp. of *isolare,* to set apart, isolate < *isola,* island < L *insula*: see ISLE⟧ **1** set apart; separate; solitary *[an isolated* lighthouse*]* **2** *a)* having little or no social contact *b)* having little in common with one's associates, family, etc. **3** not occurring or happening regularly or frequently; rare *[an isolated* instance of violence*]*

isolated point a separated or distant point of a set of points, as in graphing certain equations (e.g. $y^2 = x^{2(x-1)}$ has many solutions that graphically form a curve but has one solution (0,0) that is isolated from this curve)

i·so·la·tion (ī′sə lā′shən) ***n.*** ⟦Fr⟧ an isolating or being isolated **—SYN.** SOLITUDE

☆**i·so·la·tion·ist** (-ist) ***n.*** a person who believes in or advocates isolation; specif., one who opposes the involvement of his or her own country in international alliances, agreements, etc. **—*adj.*** of isolationists or their policy **—i′so·la′tion·ism′ *n.***

I·sol·de (i sōl′də, i sōld′; *Ger* ē zôl′də) ***n.*** ⟦Ger < OFr *Isolt, Iseut* < OHG *Isold,* prob. < *is,* ice + *waltan,* to rule, WIELD⟧ *Medieval Legend* **1** the Irish princess betrothed to King Mark of Cornwall and loved by Tristram **2** the daughter of the king of Brittany, married to Tristram See TRISTRAM Also **I·solt** (i sōlt′)

☆**I·so·lette** (ī′sə let′) ⟦arbitrary blend of ISOLATE & BASSINET⟧ *trademark for* a kind of incubator for premature babies —*n.* [*usually* **i-**] such an incubator

i·so·leu·cine (ī′sə lo͞o′sēn′, -sin) *n.* ⟦ISO- + LEUCINE⟧ an essential amino acid, $CH_3CH_2CH(CH_3)CH(NH_2)COOH$, an isomer of leucine, found in small amounts in most proteins: see AMINO ACID

i·so·line (ī′sō līn′, -sə-) *n.* ISOGRAM

i·sol·o·gous (ī säl′ə gəs) *adj.* ⟦ISO- + (HOMO)LOGOUS⟧ 1 designating or of any of two or more chemical compounds of similar structure but consisting of different atoms of the same valence and usually of the same periodic group 2 designating or of a series formed by such compounds —**i′so·logue′** *n.*, **i′so·log′** (-sə lôg′)

i·so·mag·net·ic (ī′sō mag net′ik) *adj.* 1 of equal magnetic force 2 connecting or showing points on the earth's surface having the same magnetic intensity [*isomagnetic* lines on a map] —*n.* an isomagnetic line

i·so·mer (ī′sə mər) *n.* ⟦< Gr *isomerēs*, equally divided < *isos*, equal + *meros*, a part: see MERIT⟧ 1 *Chem.* any of two or more chemical compounds having the same constituent elements in the same proportion by weight but differing in physical or chemical properties because of differences in the structure of their molecules 2 *Physics* any of two or more nuclei possessing the same number of neutrons and protons, but existing in different energy states, and thus having different radioactive properties —**i′so·mer′ic** (-mer′ik) *adj.* —**i′so·mer′i·cal·ly** *adv.*

i·som·er·ase (ī säm′ər āz′, -ās′) *n.* any of a class of enzymes that act as catalysts in chemical reactions in which certain compounds are converted into their isomers

i·som·er·ism (ī säm′ər iz′əm) *n.* the state or relation of isomers

i·som·er·ous (-əs) *adj.* ⟦ISO- + -MEROUS⟧ 1 having the same number of parts, markings, etc. 2 *Bot.* having the same number of parts in each whorl 3 ISOMERIC

i·so·met·ric (ī′sə met′rik) *adj.* ⟦< Gr *isometros* < *isos*, equal + *metron*, measure (see METER[1]) + -IC⟧ 1 of, indicating, or having equality of measure 2 CUBIC (sense 3) 3 of or having to do with isometrics —*n.* 1 a line, as on a chart, indicating changes of pressure or temperature at constant volume 2 [*pl.*] a method of physical exercise in which one set of muscles is tensed, for a period of seconds, in opposition to another set of muscles or to an immovable object Also **i′so·met′ri·cal** —**i′so·met′ri·cal·ly** *adv.*

isometric projection a type of AXONOMETRIC PROJECTION in which the object is shown with its three principal axes all equally tilted from the plane of viewing, with two of them usually tilted 30 degrees upward from the horizontal

i·so·me·tro·pi·a (ī′sō mə trō′pē ə, -sə-) *n.* ⟦ModL < ISO- + Gr *metron*, measure (see METER[1]) + -OPIA⟧ the condition of being equal in refraction: said of the two eyes

i·som·e·try (ī säm′ə trē) *n.* ⟦ISO- + -METRY⟧ 1 equality of measure 2 *Geog.* equality of height above sea level

i·so·morph (ī′sō môrf′, -sə-) *n.* ⟦ISO- + -MORPH⟧ an organism, substance, or structure that exhibits isomorphism

i·so·mor·phic (ī′sō môr′fik, -sə-) *adj.* 1 having similar or identical structure or form 2 *Biol., Chem.* showing isomorphism Also **i′so·mor′phous** (-fəs)

i·so·mor·phism (-fiz′əm) *n.* ⟦< prec. + -ISM⟧ 1 *Biol.* a similarity in appearance or structure of organisms belonging to different species or races 2 *Chem.* an identity or close similarity in the crystalline form of substances usually containing different elements but having similar composition 3 *Math.* a one-to-one correspondence between two mathematical systems, sets, etc. that preserves the basic operations, as the correspondence between binary numbers and decimal numbers, each a set of real numbers

☆**i·so·ni·a·zid** (ī′sō nī′ə zid′, -sə-) *n.* ⟦ISO- + NI(COTINIC) + (HYDR)AZ(INE) + -ID⟧ an antibacterial drug, $C_6H_7N_3O$, used in treating and preventing tuberculosis

i·son·o·my (ī sän′ə mē) *n.* ⟦Gr *isonomia*: see ISO- & -NOMY⟧ equality of laws, rights, or privileges

i·so·oc·tane (ī′sō äk′tān, -sə-) *n.* ⟦ISO- + OCTANE⟧ a liquid hydrocarbon, $(CH_3)_2CHCH_2C(CH_3)_3$, occurring in petroleum and used in octane rating standards

i·so·pi·es·tic (ī′sō pī es′tik, -sə-) *adj.* ⟦< ISO- + Gr *piestos*, compressible < *piezein*: see PIEZO-⟧ indicating equal pressure —*n.* ISOBAR

i·so·pleth (ī′sō pleth′, -sə-) *n.* ⟦< Gr *isoplēthēs*, equal in number or quantity < *isos*, equal + *plēthos*, number, quantity⟧ the line connecting points on a graph or map that have equal or corresponding values with regard to certain variables

i·so·pod (-päd′) *n.* ⟦< ModL < ISO- + -POD⟧ any of an order (Isopoda) of mostly aquatic malacostracan crustaceans with a flat, oval body and seven pairs of walking legs of similar size and form, each pair attached to a segment of the thorax —*adj.* of an isopod or the isopods Also **i·sop·o·dan** (ī säp′ə dən)

i·so·prene (-prēn′) *n.* ⟦coined (1860) by C. G. Williams (1829-1910), Brit chemist < ISO- + PR(OPYL) + -ENE⟧ a colorless, volatile liquid, $CH_2{:}C(CH_3)CH{:}CH_2$, prepared by the dry distillation of raw rubber or synthetically: when heated with sodium or certain other substances, it polymerizes to form a substance closely resembling natural rubber

i·so·pro·pyl (ī′sə prō′pəl) *n.* ⟦ISO- + PROPYL⟧ the monovalent radical $(CH_3)_2CH$, an isomer of the monovalent propyl radical C_3H_7

isopropyl alcohol a colorless, volatile, flammable, poisonous liquid, $CH_3CHOHCH_3$, that mixes readily with alcohol, water, or ether: it is derived from propylene and used in antifreezes, antiseptics, etc. and as a solvent: also called **i·so·pro·pa·nol** (ī′sə prō′pə nôl′, -nōl′)

i·sos·ce·les (ī säs′ə lēz′) *adj.* ⟦LL < Gr *isoskelēs* < *isos*, equal + *skelos*, a leg < IE base *(*s*)*kel-*, to bend > L *calx*, heel *coluber*, serpent⟧ *Geom.* designating a figure, esp. a triangle, with two equal sides

i·so·seis·mal (ī′sō sīz′məl, -sīs′-) *adj.* ⟦< ISO- + Gr *seismos*, earthquake (see SEISMIC) + -AL⟧ 1 of equal intensity: said of earthquake shocks 2 connecting or showing points of such equal intensity on the earth's surface [*isoseismal* lines on a map] —*n.* an isoseismal line Also **i′so·seis′mic**

is·os·mot·ic (is′äs mät′ik) *adj.* ⟦IS(O)- + OSMOTIC⟧ ISOTONIC (sense 2)

i·so·spin (ī′sō spin′, -sə-) *n.* *Particle Physics* a quantum number used to distinguish the various states of electrical charge of a subatomic particle

i·sos·ta·sy (ī säs′tə sē) *n.* ⟦< ISO- + Gr *stasis*, a standing still: see STASIS⟧ 1 a condition in which there is equal pressure on every side 2 *Geol.* approximate equilibrium in large, equal areas of the earth's crust, preserved by the action of gravity upon the different substances in the crust in proportion to their densities —**i·so·stat·ic** (ī′sō stat′ik, -sə-) *adj.* —**i′so·stat′i·cal·ly** *adv.*

i·so·there (ī′sō thir′, -sə-) *n.* ⟦Fr *isothère* < *iso-* (see ISO-) + Gr *theros*, summer (see WARM)⟧ a line on a map connecting points on the earth's surface that have the same mean summer temperature

i·so·therm (-thurm′) *n.* ⟦Fr *isotherme* < *iso-*, ISO- + Gr *thermē*, heat < *thermos*, hot: see WARM⟧ 1 a line on a map connecting points on the earth's surface having the same mean temperature or the same temperature at a given time 2 a line representing changes of volume or pressure at constant temperature —**i′so·ther′mic** *adj.*

i·so·ther·mal (ī′sə thur′məl) *adj.* ⟦Fr *isotherme* (see prec.) + -AL⟧ 1 of or indicating equality or constancy of temperature 2 of or indicating changes of volume or pressure at constant temperature [an *isothermal* line] 3 of an isotherm or isotherms —*n.* ISOTHERM —**i′so·ther′mal·ly** *adv.*

i·so·tone (ī′sə tōn′) *n.* ⟦ISO- + TONE⟧ any atom with the same number of neutrons as another atom but a different atomic number

i·so·ton·ic (ī′sō tän′ik, -sə-) *adj.* ⟦< Gr *isotonos* (< *isos*, equal + *tonos*, a stretching: see TONE) + -IC⟧ 1 having equal tension 2 having the same osmotic pressure; esp., designating or of a salt solution having the same osmotic pressure as blood —**i′so·ton′i·cal·ly** *adv.* —**i′so·to·nic′i·ty** (-tə nis′ə tē) *n.*

i·so·tope (ī′sə tōp′) *n.* ⟦coined by F. SODDY < ISO- + Gr *topos*, place: see TOPIC⟧ any of two or more forms of an element having the same or very closely related chemical properties and the same atomic number but different atomic weights (or mass numbers) [U-235, U-238, and U-239 are three *isotopes* of uranium] —**i′so·top′ic** (-täp′ik, -tō′pik) *adj.* —**i′so·top′i·cal·ly** *adv.* —**i·sot·o·py** (ī sät′ə pē, īs′ə tō′pē) *n.*

isotopic spin ISOSPIN

i·so·trop·ic (ī′sō träp′ik, -trō′pik; -sə-) *adj.* ⟦ISO- + -TROPIC⟧ having physical properties, as conductivity, elasticity, etc., that are the same regardless of the direction of measurement: also **i·sot·ro·pous** (ī sä′trə pəs) —**i·sot′ro·py** (-pē) *n.*

i·so·zyme (ī′sō zīm′) *n.* ISOENZYME

☆**ISP** (ī′es′pē′) *n.*, *pl.* **ISPs** ⟦*i*(*nternet*) *s*(*ervice*) *p*(*rovider*)⟧ a company that provides subscribers with access to the internet

Isr *abbrev.* 1 Israel 2 Israeli

Is·ra·el¹ (iz′rē əl, -rā-; iz′rəl) *n.* ⟦OFr < LL(Ec) < Gr *Israēl* < Heb *yisrael*, lit., contender with God < *sara*, to wrestle + *el*, God⟧ 1 a masculine name: dim. *Izzy* 2 *Bible* Jacob: so named after wrestling with the angel: Gen. 32:28 3 the Jewish people, as descendants of Jacob

Is·ra·el² (iz′rē əl, -rā-; iz′rəl) 1 ancient land of the Hebrews at the SE end of the Mediterranean 2 kingdom in the N part of this region, formed (10th cent. B.C.) by the ten tribes of Israel that broke with Judah & Benjamin 3 country between the Mediterranean Sea & Jordan: established (1948) as a Jewish state according to the United Nations plan (1947) partitioning Palestine into Arab and Jewish states: 8,019 sq mi (20,770 sq km); cap. Jerusalem

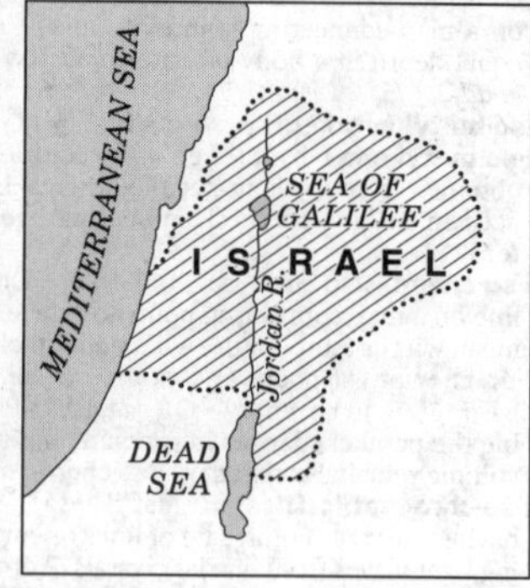

Israel (8th cent. B.C.)

Is·rae·li (iz rā′lē) *n.* ⟦ModHeb *yisreeli* < Heb: see ISRAEL¹⟧ a person born or living in modern Israel —*adj.* of modern Israel or its people or culture

Is·ra·el·ite (iz′rē ə līt′, -rā-; iz′rə līt′) *n.* ⟦ME < LL(Ec) *Israelita* < Gr *Israēlitēs*⟧ a member of the people of ancient Israel or their descendants; Hebrew —*adj.* of ancient Israel or the Israelites

Is·sa·char (is′ə kär′) *n.* 1 Jacob's ninth son, whose mother was Leah: Gen. 30:18 2 the tribe of Israel descended from him: Num. 1:28

☆**is·sei** (ē′sā′) *n.*, *pl.* **-sei′** or **-seis′** ⟦Jpn, lit., first generation⟧ [*also* **I-**] a Japanese immigrant to North America, esp. one coming to the U.S. after 1907 and ineligible until 1952 to become a U.S. citizen: cf. KIBEI, NISEI, SANSEI

ISSN *abbrev.* International Standard Serial Number

is·su·a·ble (ish′o͞o ə bəl) *adj.* **1** that can issue or be issued **2** that can be disputed, debated, or raised, as an issue at law —**is′su·a·bly** *adv.*

☆**is·su·ance** (ish′o͞o əns) *n.* an issuing; issue

is·su·ant (-ənt) *adj.* ⟦orig., issuing or rising⟧ *Heraldry* having only the upper part visible [a lion *issuant*]

is·sue (ish′o͞o; *chiefly Brit* is′yo͞o) *n.* ⟦OFr pp. of *issir*, to go out < L *exire* < *ex-*, out + *ire*, to go: see YEAR⟧ **1** an outgoing; outflow; passing out **2** [Archaic] a way out; exit; outlet **3** a result; consequence; upshot **4** offspring; a child or children **5** profits from lands, estates, or fines; produce; proceeds **6** a point, matter, or question to be disputed or decided **7** a sending or giving out; putting forth **8** the thing or set of things issued; all that is put forth and circulated at one time [the July *issue* of a magazine, an *issue* of bonds] **9** *Med. a)* a discharge of blood, pus, etc. *b)* an incision or artificial ulcer for the discharge of pus **10** [Informal] a problem or difficulty, esp. one of a psychological or emotional nature: *usually used in pl.* —*vi.* **-sued**, **-su·ing** **1** to go, come, pass, or flow out; emerge **2** to be descended; be born **3** to be derived or result (*from* a cause) **4** to end or result (*in* an effect or consequence) **5** to come as revenue; accrue **6** to be printed or published; be put forth and circulated —*vt.* **1** to let out; discharge **2** to give or deal out; distribute [to *issue* supplies] **3** to print or publish; put forth and circulate; give out publicly or officially [to *issue* commemorative stamps] —*SYN.* EFFECT, RISE —**at issue** **1** in dispute or under discussion: also, esp. in law, **in issue** **2** at variance; in disagreement —**join issue** **1** to enter into conflict, argument, etc. with another or each other **2** to join in submitting an issue for decision at law —**take issue** to disagree; differ —**is′su·er** *n.*

Is·sus (is′əs) ancient town in Cilicia, in SE Asia Minor: site of a battle (333 B.C.) in which Alexander the Great defeated Darius III of Persia

Is·syk Kul (is′ik ko͝ol′) mountain lake in E Kyrgyzstan: *c.* 2,400 sq mi (6,216 sq km): also written **Issyk-Kul**

-ist[1] (ist, əst) ⟦ME *-iste* < OFr < L *-ista* < Gr *-istēs* < verbs ending in *-izein*⟧ *suffix forming nouns* **1** a person who does, makes, or practices (the thing specified): many words so formed correspond to verbs ending in -IZE or nouns ending in -ISM [*moralist, satirist*] **2** a person skilled in or occupied with; an expert in [*druggist, violinist*] **3** an adherent of or believer in [*anarchist*] **4** a person having or displaying prejudice related to [*ageist*]: see -ISM (sense 8)

-ist[2] (ist, əst) *suffix* forming adjectives corresponding to nouns ending in -ISM or -IST[1] [*Darwinist, escapist, ageist*]

Is·tan·bul (is′tan bo͞ol′, -tän-; -bo͞ol′; *Turk* is täm′bo͞ol) ⟦altered < ModGr *'s ten poli* < Gr *eis tēn polin*, lit., into the city⟧ seaport in NW Turkey, on both sides of the Bosporus: former name CONSTANTINOPLE; ancient name BYZANTIUM

isth *abbrev.* isthmus

isth·mi·an (is′mē ən) *adj.* ⟦< L *isthmius* (Gr *isthmios* < *isthmos*: see fol.) + -AN⟧ **1** of an isthmus **2** [**I-**] *a)* of the Isthmus of Panama *b)* of the Isthmus of Corinth or the games held there in ancient times —*n.* a person born or living on an isthmus

isth·mus (is′məs) *n., pl.* **-mus·es** or **-mi′** (-mī′) ⟦L < Gr *isthmos*, a neck, narrow passage, isthmus⟧ **1** a narrow strip of land having water at each side and connecting two larger bodies of land **2** *Anat. a)* a narrow strip of tissue connecting two larger parts of an organ [the *isthmus* of the thyroid] *b)* a narrow passage between two larger cavities [the *isthmus* of the fallopian tubes]

-is·tic (is′tik) ⟦MFr *-istique* < L *-isticus* < Gr *-istikos*: also formed in E < -IST[1] + -IC⟧ *suffix forming adjectives* of or relating to an action, practice, doctrine, quality, etc., or to a person involved in or with it [*realistic, artistic*]: also **-is′ti·cal**

is·tle (ist′lē) *n.* ⟦< AmSp *ixtle* < Nahuatl *i:ƛi*⟧ a fiber obtained from certain tropical American plants, as various agaves: used for cordage, nets, baskets, etc.

Is·tri·a (is′trē ə) peninsula in W Slovenia & Croatia, projecting into the N Adriatic, formerly including part of the area around Trieste: also **Istrian Peninsula** —**Is′tri·an** *adj., n.*

it[1] (it) *pron.* ⟦ME *hit, it* < OE *hit*, akin to Du *het*, Goth *hita*, this: IE base as in HE[1]: basic sense "this one"⟧ *1 pl.* **they** the animal or thing previously mentioned or under discussion: neuter personal pronoun in the third person singular: *it* is the nominative and objective form, *its* the possessive, and *itself* the reflexive and intensive; *its* is the possessive pronominal adjective **2** *it* is also used as: *a)* the subject of an impersonal verb without reference to agent [*it* is snowing] *b)* the grammatical subject of a clause of which the actual subject is another clause or phrase following [*it* is clear that he wants to go] *c)* an object of indefinite sense in certain idiomatic expressions [to lord *it* over someone]; often, specif., an unpleasant consequence [now you're in for *it;* let him have *it*] *d)* the antecedent of a relative pronoun from which it is separated by a predicate [*it* is your support that we want] *e)* a term of reference to something indefinite but understood, as the state of affairs [*it's* all right—I didn't hurt myself] ☆*f)* [Informal] an emphatic predicate pronoun referring to the person, thing, situation, etc. which is considered ultimate, final, or perfect [zero hour is here: this is *it!*] —*n.* **1** the player in a game who must do some essential thing, as the one in a game of tag who must try to catch another **2** [Informal] any of various attractive personal qualities, as charm, charisma, or sex appeal —**do it** [Informal] to engage in sexual intercourse —☆**with it** [Slang] alert, informed, or hip

it[2] *abbrev.* italic(s)

It *abbrev.* **1** Italian **2** Italy

IT *abbrev.* information technology

ita or **ITA** *abbrev.* initial teaching alphabet

it·a·col·u·mite (it′ə käl′yo͞o mīt′) *n.* ⟦after *Itacolumi*, mountain in Brazil, where found⟧ a type of fine-grained sandstone deposited in flexible layers

it·a·con·ic acid (it′ə kän′ik) ⟦arbitrary transposition of constituents of *aconitic* (< ACONITE + -IC)⟧ a white crystalline material, CH_2:C(COOH) CH_2 COOH, prepared by the fermentation of sugar with a special mold: it is used in making resins and plasticizers

ital *abbrev.* italic(s)

Ital *abbrev.* **1** Italian **2** Italy

I·tal·ia (ē täl′yä) *It. name for* ITALY

I·tal·ian (i tal′yən) *adj.* ⟦ME < L *Italianus* < *Italia*⟧ of Italy or its people, language, or culture —*n.* **1** a person born or living in Italy **2** the Romance language spoken in Italy

I·tal·ian·ate (-yə nit, -yə nāt′) *adj.* ⟦It *Italianato*⟧ Italian in quality, appearance, or character

Italian dressing a strongly flavored vinaigrette for salads, containing garlic, oregano, red peppers, etc.

Italian East Africa former It. colony in E Africa, consisting of Ethiopia, Eritrea, & Italian Somaliland

Italian greyhound any of a breed of toy dog very similar to the greyhound, but much smaller in size and more slender

I·tal·ian·ism (-yə niz′əm) *n.* **1** a word, phrase, grammatical construction, or other feature originating in or peculiar to Italian **2** an Italian custom, belief, etc. **3** Italian spirit, quality, etc. **4** fondness for Italian customs, ideas, etc.

I·tal·ian·ize (-yə nīz′) *vt., vi.* **-ized′**, **-iz′ing** ⟦Fr *italianiser*⟧ to make or become Italian in quality, appearance, character, etc. —**I·tal′ian·i·za′tion** *n.*

Italian provincial designating or of a style of rural, Italian furniture of the 18th and 19th cent., with straight lines and simple decoration, usually of fruitwood or mahogany

Italian Somaliland former Italian colony on the E coast of Africa: merged with British Somaliland to form Somalia

Italian sonnet PETRARCHAN SONNET

i·tal·ic (i tal′ik, ī-) *adj.* ⟦see fol.: so called because first used in an Italian edition of Virgil (1501)⟧ designating or of a type in which the characters slant upward to the right, used variously, as to emphasize words, indicate foreign words, set off book titles, etc. (Ex.: *this is italic type*) —*n.* **1** an italic letter or other character **2** [*usually pl., sometimes with sing. v.*] italic type or print

I·tal·ic (i tal′ik, ī-) *n.* ⟦L *Italicus*⟧ a branch of the Indo-European language family, including Latin, Oscan, Umbrian, and other languages of ancient Italy, as well as Latin's descendants, the Romance languages —*adj.* **1** of these languages **2** of ancient Italy or its peoples or cultures

I·tal·i·cism (i tal′ə siz′əm) *n.* ITALIANISM (sense 1)

i·tal·i·cize (i tal′ə sīz′, ī-) *vt.* **-cized′**, **-ciz′ing** **1** to print in italics **2** to underscore (handwritten or typed matter) with a single line to indicate that it is to be printed in italics —**i·tal′i·ci·za′tion** *n.*

I·tal·o- (it′ə lō, i tal′ō) *combining form* Italian, Italian and [*Italo*-American]

It·a·ly (it′'l ē) ⟦L *Italia*, altered, prob. by Greeks living in S Italy < earlier (prob. Oscan) *Vitelíú*; orig. used only of the SW point of the peninsula⟧ country in S Europe, mostly on a peninsula extending into the Mediterranean & including Sicily, Sardinia, and numerous other islands: formerly a kingdom created by the unification of various Italian monarchies & states (1861), it became a republic in 1946: 116,306 sq mi (301,230 sq km); cap. Rome: It. name ITALIA

I·tas·ca (i tas′kə), **Lake** ⟦coined by H. R. SCHOOLCRAFT < L *(ver)itas*, truth + *ca(put)*, head, in ref. to other alleged sources⟧ lake in NW Minn., a source of the Mississippi: *c.* 2 sq mi (5.2 sq km)

itch (ich) *vi.* ⟦ME *yicchen, icchen* < OE *giccan*, akin to Ger *jucken*⟧ **1** to feel or cause an irritating sensation on the skin that makes one want to scratch the affected part **2** to have a restless desire or hankering —*vt.* **1** to make itch **2** to irritate or annoy **3** [Informal] SCRATCH —*n.* **1** an irritating sensation on the skin that makes one want to scratch the affected part **2** a restless desire; hankering [an *itch* to travel] —**the itch** [Informal] any of various skin disorders accompanied by severe irritation of the skin, as scabies

itch·y (ich′ē) *adj.* **itch′i·er**, **itch′i·est** like, feeling, or causing an itch —**itch′i·ly** *adv.* —**itch′i·ness** *n.*

it'd *contraction* **1** it would **2** it had

-ite[1] (īt) ⟦ME < OFr or L or Gr: OFr *-ite* < L *-ita*, *-ites* < Gr *-itēs*, fem. *-itis*⟧ *suffix forming nouns* **1** a native, inhabitant, or citizen of [*Brooklynite*] **2** a descendant from or offspring of [*Israelite*] **3** an adherent of, believer in, or member of: often disparaging [*laborite, Luddite*] **4** a product, esp. a commercially manufactured one [*Lucite, dynamite, vulcanite*] **5** a fossil [*ammonite*] **6** a part of a body or bodily organ [*somite*] **7** ⟦Fr, arbitrary alteration of *-ate*, -ATE[2]⟧ a salt or ester of an acid whose name ends in -OUS [*nitrite, sulfite*] **8** a (specified) mineral or rock [*anthracite, dolomite*]

-ite[2] (īt; it) ⟦L *-itus*, ending of some past participles⟧ *suffix* forming adjectives, nouns, and verbs [*finite*]

i·tem (īt′əm) *adv.* ⟦ME < L < *ita*, so, thus⟧ [Old-fashioned] used before each article in a series being enumerated —*n.* **1** an article; unit; separate thing; particular; entry in an account [an *item* of clothing] **2** a bit of news or information, specif. when in a newspaper [an *item* of interest] **3** [Slang] a couple identified publicly as sweethearts or lovers [John and Joan are an *item*] —*vt.* [Archaic] ITEMIZE

☆**i·tem·ize** (-īz′) *vt.* **-ized′**, **-iz′ing** **1** to specify the items of; set down, item by item [to *itemize* a bill of purchases] 2 to specify (the individual items in a group or list) [to *itemize* deductions on one's tax return] —**i'tem·i·za'tion** *n.*

☆**item veto** LINE-ITEM VETO

I·té·nez (ē tā'nes) *Bolivian name for* GUAPORÉ

it·er·ate (it'ər āt') *vt.* **-at'ed, -at'ing** ⟦< L *iteratus,* pp. of *iterare,* to repeat < *iterum,* again < **iterus,* compar. of **i-,* pron. stem > *is, ea, id,* he, she, it, *ita,* thus⟧ to utter or do again or repeatedly —*SYN.* REPEAT

it·er·a·tion (it'ər ā'shən) *n.* ⟦ME < L *iteratio*⟧ 1 an iterating or being iterated; repetition 2 something iterated Also **it'er·ance** (-ər əns)

it·er·a·tive (it'ər āt'iv, -ər ə tiv) *adj.* ⟦ME < MFr *itératif* < L *iteratus*⟧ 1 repetitious; repeating or repeated 2 *Gram.* FREQUENTATIVE

Ith·a·ca (ith'ə kə) one of the Ionian Islands, off the W coast of Greece: legendary home of Odysseus: 37 sq mi (96 sq km): Gr. name **I·thá·ki** (ē thä'kē) —**Ith'a·can** *adj., n.*

ith·y·phal·lic (ith'i fal'ik) *adj.* ⟦L *ithyphallicus* < Gr *ithyphallikos* < *ithyphallos,* erect phallus < *ithys,* straight (< IE base **sīdh-,* to go directly toward > Sans *sādhú-,* straight) + *phallos,* PHALLUS⟧ 1 of the phallus carried in the rites of Bacchus 2 lewd; lascivious 3 in the meter of the Bacchic hymns

i·tin·er·an·cy (ī tin'ər ən sē, i-) *n.* 1 *a)* an itinerating, or traveling from place to place *b)* the state of being itinerant 2 a group of itinerant preachers or judges 3 official work requiring constant travel from place to place or frequent change of residence, as preaching or presiding over courts in a circuit Also **i·tin'er·a·cy** (-ə sē)

i·tin·er·ant (-ənt) *adj.* ⟦LL *itinerans,* prp. of *itinerari,* to travel < L *iter* (gen. *itineris*), a walk, journey < base of *ire,* to go: see YEAR⟧ traveling from place to place or on a circuit —*n.* a person who travels from place to place —**i·tin'er·ant·ly** *adv.*

SYN.—**itinerant** applies to persons whose work or profession requires them to travel from place to place [*itinerant* laborers, an *itinerant* preacher]; **ambulatory** specifically implies ability to walk about [an *ambulatory* patient]; **peripatetic** implies a walking or moving about in carrying on some activity and is applied humorously to persons who are always on the go; **nomadic** is applied to tribes or groups of people who have no permanent home, but move about constantly in search of food for themselves, pasture for the animals they herd, etc.; **vagrant** is applied to individuals, specif. hobos or tramps, who wander about without a fixed home, and implies shiftlessness, disorderliness, etc.

i·tin·er·ar·y (ī tin'ər er'ē, i-) *adj.* ⟦LL *itinerarius* < *itinerans:* see prec.⟧ of traveling, journeys, routes, or roads —*n., pl.* **-ar'ies** ⟦LL *itinerarium,* neut. of *itinerarius*⟧ 1 a route 2 a record of a journey 3 a guidebook for travelers 4 a detailed outline for a proposed journey

i·tin·er·ate (-ər āt') *vi.* **-at'ed, -at'ing** ⟦< LL *itineratus,* pp. of *itinerari:* see ITINERANT⟧ to travel from place to place or on a circuit —**i·tin'er·a'tion** *n.*

-i·tion (ish'ən) ⟦< Fr or L: Fr *-ition* < L *-itio* (gen. *-itionis*) < -I-, thematic vowel + *-tio* (gen. *-tionis*)⟧ *see* -ATION *suffix forming nouns*

-i·tious (ish'əs) ⟦L *-icius, -itius*⟧ *suffix forming adjectives* of, having the nature of, characterized by: used in forming adjectives corresponding to nouns ending in -ITION [*nutritious, seditious*]

-i·tis (īt'is, -əs) ⟦ModL < L < Gr *-itis,* orig. fem. of adjectives ending in *-itēs,* used to modify *nosos,* disease (later understood, but omitted)⟧ *suffix* 1 inflammatory disease or inflammation of (a specified part or organ) [*neuritis, bronchitis*] 2 addiction to, or weariness resulting from preoccupation with: used in nonce words [*golfitis*]

it'll (it''l) *contraction* 1 it will 2 it shall

ITO *abbrev.* International Trade Organization

-i·tol (i tôl', -tōl', -täl') ⟦< -ITE[1] + -OL[1]⟧ *suffix forming nouns* any of certain alcohols with more than one hydroxyl group [*mannitol*]

its (its) *pron.* ⟦Early ModE analogical formation < *it* + *'s;* written *it's* until early 19th c.: the ME & OE form was *his*⟧ that or those belonging to it: the possessive form of IT[1], used without a following noun —***possessive pronominal adj.*** of, belonging to, made by, or done by it

it's (its) *contraction* 1 it is 2 it has

it·self (it self') *pron.* a form of IT[1], used: *a)* as an intensifier [the work *itself* is easy] *b)* as a reflexive [the dog bit *itself*] *c)* with the meaning "its real, true, or normal self" [the bird is not *itself* today] (in this construction, *it* functions as an adjective and *self* as a noun; when they are separated, the form *its* is used) [*its* own sweet *self*]

it·ty-bit·ty (it'ē bit'ē) *adj.* ⟦baby talk alteration < *little bit*⟧ [Informal] very small; tiny: a facetious imitation of child's talk: also **it·sy-bit·sy** (it'sē bit'sē)

-i·ty (ə tē, i-) ⟦ME *-ite* < OFr or L: OFr *ité* < L *-itas* < -I-, ending of stem, or thematic vowel + *-tas,* -TY[1]⟧ *suffix* state, character, or condition of being ____, or an instance of any of these [*chastity, possibility*]

IU or **iu** *abbrev.* international unit(s)

IUCD *abbrev.* intrauterine contraceptive device

IUD (ī'yo͞o'dē') *n., pl.* **IUDs** INTRAUTERINE (CONTRACEPTIVE) DEVICE

-i·um (ē əm, yəm) ⟦ModL < L, ending of certain neuter nouns⟧ *suffix* 1 *a)* forming Modern Latin names for chemical elements [*sodium*] *b)* forming the names of certain positive ions [*ammonium, carbonium*] 2 forming the names of certain biological structures [*conidium, syncytium*]

IUPAC (*often* ī'yo͞o pak') *abbrev.* International Union of Pure and Applied Chemistry

IV[1] (ī'vē') *n., pl.* **IVs** ⟦< I(NTRA)V(ENOUS)⟧ *Med.* 1 a procedure in which a hypodermic needle inserted into a vein provides a continuous supply of blood plasma, nutrients, or medicine directly to the bloodstream 2 the apparatus used in such a procedure, typically consisting of a bag or bottle containing the fluid, which flows through plastic tubing to the needle

IV[2] *abbrev.* intravenous(ly)

I·van[1] (ī'vən, i vän') *n.* ⟦Russ < Gr *Iōannēs:* see JOHN[1]⟧ a masculine name

I·van[2] (ī'vən, i vän') 1 **Ivan III** 1440-1505; grand duke of Muscovy (1462-1505): called *the Great* 2 **Ivan IV** 1530-84; grand duke of Muscovy (1533-84) & 1st czar of Russia (1547-84): called *the Terrible*

I·va·no·vo (ē vä'nô vô) city in central European Russia

-ive (iv) ⟦ME < OFr *-if,* fem. *-ive* < L *-ivus*⟧ *suffix* 1 of, relating to, belonging to, having the nature or quality of [*sportive*] 2 tending to, given to [*retrospective*]

I've (īv) *contraction* I have

Ives (īvz) 1 **Charles Edward** 1874-1954; U.S. composer 2 **J(ames) M(erritt)** *see* CURRIER AND IVES —**Ives'i·an** *adj.*

IVF *abbrev.* in vitro fertilization

i·vied (ī'vēd) *adj.* covered or overgrown with ivy

i·vo·ry (ī'vər ē, ī'vrē) *n., pl.* **-ries** ⟦ME < OFr *yvoire* < L *eboreus* (adj.) < *ebur* (gen. *eboris*), ivory < Egypt *3bw,* elephant, ivory⟧ 1 the hard, white substance, a form of dentin, that makes up the tusks of elephants, walruses, etc. 2 *a)* dentin in any form *b)* any substance like ivory in appearance, use, etc. 3 the color of ivory; creamy white 4 a tusk of an elephant, walrus, etc. 5 [*pl.*] things made of ivory 6 [*pl.*] [Slang] things resembling or suggesting ivory; specif., *a)* piano keys *b)* teeth *c)* dice *d)* billiard balls —***adj.*** 1 of, made of, or like ivory 2 creamy-white —**tickle the ivories** [Slang] to play the piano: a jocular usage

☆**i·vo·ry-billed woodpecker** (-bild') a large, white-billed, black-and-white woodpecker (*Campephilus principalis*) formerly found in the SE U.S. and Cuba: it is possibly extinct

ivory black a fine black pigment made from burnt ivory

Ivory Coast 1 country in WC Africa, on the Gulf of Guinea, west of Ghana: formerly a French territory, it became independent in 1960: 124,503 sq mi (322,460 sq km); cap. Yamoussoukro 2 [Historical] the African coast in this region —**I·vor·i·an** (ī vôr'ē ən, i-) *adj., n.* or ⟦see CÔTE D'IVOIRE⟧ **I·voir'i·an**

ivory nut VEGETABLE IVORY (sense 1)

ivory tower ⟦transl. of Fr *tour d'ivoire,* first used by C. A. SAINTE-BEUVE with ref. to the poet A. V. de VIGNY⟧ a condition or place, as academia, regarded as isolated or withdrawn from the practical affairs of society

i·vy (ī'vē) *n., pl.* **i'vies** ⟦ME *ivi* < OE *ifig, ifegn,* akin to Ger *efeu* (OHG *ebawi, ebah*): orig. sense prob. "climber"⟧ 1 a climbing vine (*Hedera helix*) of the ginseng family, with a woody stem and evergreen leaves, grown as ornamentation on buildings, walls, etc. 2 any of various similar climbing plants, as ground ivy or poison ivy —***adj.*** ☆[*usually* **I-**] of or characteristic of the Ivy League

I·vy (ī'vē) *n.* ⟦< prec.⟧ a feminine name

☆**Ivy League** ⟦< the fact that many of the buildings are traditionally ivy-covered⟧ a group of colleges in the NE U.S. forming a league for intercollegiate sports: often used to describe the fashions, standards, attitudes, etc. associated with their students —**Ivy Leaguer**

I·wa·ki (i wäk'ē) city in NE Honshu, Japan, northeast of Tokyo

i·wis (i wis') *adv.* ⟦ME < OE *gewiss* (akin to Ger), certain(ly) < *ge-,* + *wiss,* certain: for IE base see WISE[2]⟧ [Obs.] certainly; assuredly

I·wo (ē'wō) city in SW Nigeria

I·wo Ji·ma (ē'wō jē'mə, ē'wə) small island of the Volcano Islands in the W Pacific: captured from the Japanese by U.S. forces in WWII (1945); returned to Japan (1968): *c.* 8 sq mi (20.7 sq km): Jpn. name **I·wo To** (ē'wō tō')

☆**IWW** *abbrev.* Industrial Workers of the World

ix·i·a (ik'sē ə) *n.* ⟦ModL < Gr *ixos,* birdlime: from the viscid nature of some of the species⟧ any of a genus (*Ixia*) of South African plants of the iris family, with grasslike leaves and funnel-shaped flowers

Ix·i·on (iks'ī än', -ən) *n.* ⟦L < Gr *Ixiōn*⟧ *Gr. Myth.* a Thessalian king who is bound to a revolving wheel in Tartarus because he sought the love of Hera

☆**ix·nay** (iks'nā') *adv., interj.* ⟦pig Latin for NIX[2]⟧ [Old Slang] NIX[2]

ix·o·ra (iks'ə rə) *n.* ⟦ModL, after *Iśvara,* Hindu deity⟧ any of a genus (*Ixora*) of tropical evergreen plants of the madder family, with showy flowers

Ix·ta·ci·huatl (ēs'tä sē'wät'l) volcanic mountain in central Mexico, southeast of Mexico City: 17,343 ft (5,286 m): also sp. **Ix'tac·ci'huatl** or **Iz'tac·ci'huatl**

ix·tle (ikst'lē, ist'-) *n. var. of* ISTLE

I·yar (ē yär', ē'yär) *n.* ⟦Heb⟧ the eighth month of the Jewish year: see the Jewish calendar in the Reference Supplement

-i·za·tion (ə zā'shən, ī-) *suffix forming nouns* the act, process, or result of making or doing [*realization*]

-ize (īz) ⟦ME *-isen* < OFr *-iser* < LL *-izare* < Gr *-izein*⟧ *suffix forming verbs* 1 to cause to be or become; make conform with or resemble; make [*democratize, Americanize*] 2 to become, become like, or change into [*crystallize*] 3 to subject to, treat with, or combine with [*oxidize, galvanize*] 4 to engage in; act in a (specified) way [*soliloquize, theorize*]

I·zhevsk (i zhefsk') city in EC European Russia

Iz·mir (iz mir') seaport in W Turkey, on the Aegean Sea: former name SMYRNA

Iz·mit (iz mit') city in NW Turkey, on an inlet of the Sea of Marmara

iz·zard (iz'ərd) *n.* ⟦earlier *ezed, ezod,* var. of ZED⟧ [Now Chiefly Dial.] the letter Z

j¹ or J (jā) ***n.**, pl.* **j's, J's 1** the tenth letter of the English alphabet: formerly a variant of *I, i,* in the 17th cent. it became established as a consonant only, as in *Julius,* originally spelled *Iulius* **2** any of the speech sounds that this letter represents, as, in English, the *j* of *joy* **3** a type or impression for *j* or J **4** the tenth in a sequence or group **5** an object shaped like J —***adj.*** **1** of *j* or J **2** tenth in a sequence or group **3** shaped like J

j² (jā) ***n.*** *Physics* the imaginary number $\sqrt{-1}$

J *abbrev.* **1** January **2** *Physics* joule **3** Judge **4** July **5** June **6** Justice

ja (yä) ***adv., interj.*** ⟦Ger⟧ yes

Ja *abbrev.* January

JA *abbrev.* **1** Judge Advocate **2** Junior Achievement

J/A or **j/a** *abbrev.* joint account

jab (jab) ***vt., vi.*** **jabbed, jab′bing** ⟦var. of JOB²⟧ **1** to poke or thrust, as with a sharp instrument **2** to punch with short, straight blows —***n.*** a quick thrust, blow, or punch

Ja·bal·pur (jub′əl po͝or′) city in central India

jab·ber (jab′ər) ***vi., vt.*** ⟦LME *jaberen:* prob. echoic⟧ to speak or say quickly, incoherently, or nonsensically; chatter; gibber —***n.*** fast, incoherent, nonsensical talk; gibberish —**jab′ber·er *n.***

jab·ber·wock·y (-wäk′ē) ***n.*** ⟦after *Jabberwocky* (< prec. + ?), nonsense poem by Lewis CARROLL⟧ meaningless syllables that seem to make sense; gibberish

jab·i·ru (jab′ə ro͞o′) ***n.*** ⟦Port < Tupí *jabirú*⟧ any of various large wading storks, esp. a tropical American species (*Jabiru mycteria*)

jab·o·ran·di (jab′ə ran′dē) ***n.*** ⟦Port < Tupí⟧ the dried leaflets of various South American plants (genus *Pilocarpus*) of the rue family, that yield the alkaloid pilocarpine

ja·bot (zha bō′) ***n.*** ⟦Fr, bird's crop⟧ a trimming or frill, as of lace, attached to the neck or front of a blouse, bodice, or shirt

☆**ja·cal** (hä käl′) ***n.**, pl.* **-cal′es** (-kä′läs) or **-cals′** ⟦AmSp < Nahuatl *xacalli,* contr. < *xamitl calli,* adobe house⟧ a hut in Mexico and the Southwest, with walls of close-set wooden stakes plastered with mud and roofed with straw, rushes, etc.

jac·a·mar (jak′ə mär′) ***n.*** ⟦Fr < Tupí name⟧ any of a family (Galbulidae) of tropical forest piciform birds of South and Central America that feed on insects

ja·ça·na or **ja·ca·na** (zhä′sə nä′) ***n.*** ⟦Port < Tupí *jasana*⟧ any of a family (Jacanidae) of tropical and subtropical shorebirds with long toes that enable them to walk on the floating leaves of water plants; esp., a species (*Jacana spinosa*) native to Mexico

jac·a·ran·da (jak′ə ran′də) ***n.*** ⟦ModL < Port < native (Tupí) name in Brazil⟧ any of a genus (*Jacaranda*) of tropical American trees of the bignonia family, with finely divided foliage and large clusters of lavender flowers, often grown in the S U.S.

j'ac·cuse (zhä küz′) ***n.*** ⟦Fr, I accuse: phrase made famous by Émile Zola in a public letter attacking irregularities in the DREYFUS trial⟧ any strong denunciation: usually printed in italic type

ja·cinth (jā′sinth, jas′inth) ***n.*** ⟦ME *jacinte* < OFr *iacinte* < L *hyacinthus:* see HYACINTH⟧ **1** HYACINTH (sense 1*b*) **2** reddish orange

jack (jak) ***n.**, pl.* for 7, 8, 9, 10 **jacks** or **jack** ⟦ME *Jacke, Jake* < OFr *Jaque, Jaques* < LL(Ec) *Jacobus,* JACOB⟧ **1** [**J-**] *nickname for* JOHN¹ **2** [*often* **J-**] *a)* [Obs.] a common fellow or boy assistant *b)* a man or boy; fellow (sometimes used as a slang form of address) *c)* [Now Rare] a sailor; jack-tar ☆*d)* a lumberjack *e)* a jack-of-all-trades **3** *a)* BOOTJACK *b)* MONTEREY JACK *c)* SMOKEJACK **4** a fruit-flavored alcoholic liquor, as applejack **5** ⟦prob. < JACK (*n.* 2*b*), as used of devices that take the place of a person or reduce human labor⟧ any of various machines used to lift, hoist, or move something heavy a short distance [*hydraulic jack,* automobile *jack*] **6** a wooden bar attached to each key of a harpsichord, etc. that raises the plectrum when the key is depressed **7** a male donkey; jackass ☆**8** *short for* JACK RABBIT **9** any of various birds, as a jackdaw **10** *a)* any of a tropical, marine family (Carangidae) of predatory, silvery, percoid, game and food fishes with widely forked tails, including the pompanos and yellowtails *b)* JACKFISH ☆**11** [Old Slang] money **12** *Elec.* a plug-in receptacle used to make electrical contact **13** *Games a)* a playing card with a conventionalized picture of a royal male servant or soldier on it; knave *b)* a small ball used as the center mark in lawn bowling *c)* any of the small stones or six-pronged metal pieces used in playing JACKS ☆**14** *Hunting* a torch or light used to attract fish or game at night **15** *Naut.* a small flag usually flown on a ship's bow to show nationality, often, specif., UNION JACK —***vt.*** **1** to raise by means of a jack ☆**2** to hunt or fish for with a light —***adj.*** male: of some animals —**every man jack** every man; everyone —☆**jack around** [Slang] **1** to spend time in useless activity **2** to trifle or meddle (*with*) **3** to harass, treat with contempt, etc. —**jack off** [Slang] to masturbate: used chiefly of males —**jack up 1** to raise by means of a jack ☆**2** [Informal] to raise (prices, salaries, etc.) ☆**3** [Informal] *a)* to reproach for misbehavior or neglect *b)* to encourage to perform one's duty

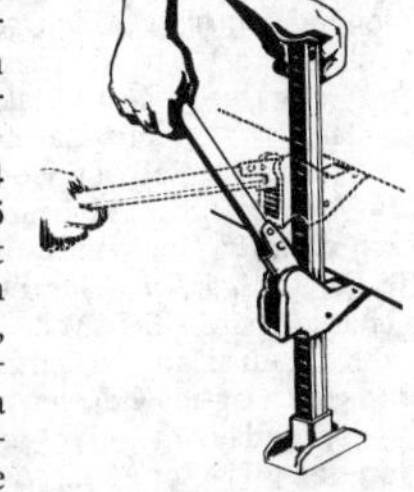
automobile jack

jack- (jak) ⟦see prec.⟧ *combining form* **1** male [*jackass*] **2** large or strong [*jackboot*] **3** boy; fellow: used in hyphenated compounds [*jack-in-the-box*]

jack·al (jak′əl, -ôl′) ***n.**, pl.* **-als** or **-al** ⟦Turk *chaqāl* < Pers *shagāl* < Sans *śṛgālá*⟧ **1** any of several wild dogs of Asia and N Africa, mostly yellowish-gray and smaller than the wolf: they often hunt prey in packs, generally at night, and also eat carrion and certain plants **2** a person who does dishonest or humiliating tasks for another: from the notion that the jackal hunts game for the lion and eats the leavings **3** a cheat or swindler

jack·a·napes (jak′ə nāps′) ***n.*** ⟦ME *Jac Napes,* nickname of William de la Pole, Duke of Suffolk (1396-1450), whose badge was a clog and a chain like a tame ape's⟧ **1** [Archaic] a monkey **2** a conceited, insolent, presumptuous fellow **3** a pert, mischievous child

jack·a·roo (jak′ə ro͞o′) ***n.*** [Austral.] *alt. sp. of* JACKEROO

jack·ass (jak′as′) ***n.*** ⟦JACK- + ASS¹⟧ **1** a male donkey **2** a stupid or foolish person; nitwit

☆**jack bean** a tropical plant (*Canavalia ensiformis*) of the pea family, often grown in S U.S. for forage and its edible seeds

jack·boot (-bo͞ot′) ***n.*** ⟦JACK- + BOOT¹⟧ a heavy, sturdy military boot that reaches above the knee

jack·boot·ed (-bo͞ot′id) ***adj.*** **1** wearing jackboots **2** severely oppressive, esp. in a brutal or cruel way

jack cheese [*occas.* **J- c-**] MONTEREY JACK

jack·daw (-dô′) ***n.*** ⟦JACK- + DAW¹⟧ **1** a small European crow (*Corvus monedula*) with a gray nape **2** any of various birds, as a large-tailed grackle (*Quiscalus mexicanus*)

jack·e·roo (jak′ə ro͞o′) ***n.*** ⟦blend of JACK (*n.* 2*b*) & KANGAROO⟧ [Austral.] an inexperienced apprentice working on a sheep or cattle ranch

jack·et (jak′it) ***n.*** ⟦ME *jaket* < OFr *jaquette,* dim. of *jaque* < Sp *jaco* < Ar *shakk*⟧ **1** a coat extending to the waist or hips, usually with long sleeves **2** an outer coating or covering; specif., *a)* DUST JACKET ☆*b)* a cardboard holder for a phonograph record *c)* the metal casing of a bullet *d)* the insulating casing on a pipe or boiler *e) Cooking* the skin of a potato ☆*f)* a folder or envelope for holding letters or documents **3** *short for* SPORT JACKET —***vt.*** **1** to put a jacket, or coat, on **2** to cover with a casing, wrapper, etc.

jacket crown a type of artificial, tooth-colored dental crown made of acrylic or porcelain

jack·fish (jak′fish′) ***n.**, pl.* **-fish′** or **-fish′es** (see FISH) ⟦JACK- + FISH⟧ any of various fishes; esp., the northern pike

Jack Frost frost or cold weather personified

jack·fruit (-fro͞ot′) ***n.*** ⟦JACK- + FRUIT⟧ **1** an East Indian tree (*Artocarpus integrifolia*) of the mulberry family, like the breadfruit **2** its large, heavy fruit, containing edible seeds **3** its yellow, fine-grained wood

☆**jack·ham·mer** (-ham′ər) ***n.*** ⟦JACK- + HAMMER⟧ a portable type of pneumatic hammer, used for breaking up concrete, rock, etc.

jack-in-the-box (jak′in *thə* bäks′) ***n.**, pl.* **-box′es** a toy consisting of a box from which a little figure on a spring jumps up when the lid is lifted: also **jack′-in-a-box′**

☆**jack-in-the-pul·pit** (-po͝ol′pit) ***n.**, pl.* **-pits** ⟦descriptive of its appearance: see JACK (*n.* 1)⟧ [*also* **J-**] an American plant (*Arisaema triphyllum*) of the arum family, with a flower spike partly arched over by a hoodlike covering

jack-in-the-pulpit

Jack Ketch (kech′) ⟦after a famous Eng public executioner (died 1686)⟧ [Brit.] an official hangman

☆**jack·knife** (jak′nīf′) *n., pl.* **-knives′** (-nīvz′) ⟦JACK- + KNIFE⟧ **1** a large pocketknife **2** a dive in which the diver keeps his knees unbent, touches his feet with his hands, and then straightens out just before plunging into the water —*vt.* **-knifed′**, **-knif′ing 1** to cut with a jackknife **2** to cause to jackknife —*vi.* **1** to bend at the middle as in a jackknife dive **2** to turn on its hitch so as to form a sharp angle: said as of a tractor-trailer after a driving accident

☆**jack·leg** (-leg′, -lāg′) *adj.* ⟦JACK, *n.* 2*e* + (BLACK)LEG⟧ **1** *a)* not properly trained or qualified; incompetent *b)* MAKESHIFT **2** unprofessional, unscrupulous, or dishonest —*n.* a jackleg person or thing

jack·light (-līt′) *n.* ⟦JACK (*n.* 14) + LIGHT[1]⟧ JACK (*n.* 14) —*vt.* JACK (*vt.* 2)

jack mackerel a marine food fish (*Trachurus symmetricus*) of the jack family, found in schools from British Columbia to Baja California

jack-of-all-trades (jak′əv ôl trādz′) *n., pl.* **jacks′-of-all-trades′** [*often* **J-**] **1** a person who can do many kinds of work acceptably **2** a handyman

jack-o'-lan·tern (jak′ə lant′ərn) *n., pl.* **-terns 1** [Archaic] IGNIS FATUUS (sense 1) **2** a hollow pumpkin cut to look like a face and usually illuminated inside as by a candle, used as a decoration at Halloween

☆**jack pine** a pine (*Pinus banksiana*) of Canada and N U.S., having short needles in pairs and many woody cones

☆**jack·pot** (jak′pät′) *n.* ⟦JACK, *n.* 13*a* + POT[4]⟧ **1** a pot in a poker game made up of accumulated stakes, which can be played for only when some player has a pair of jacks or better with which to open **2** any cumulative stakes or highest prize, as in a slot machine —**hit the jackpot** [Slang] **1** to win the jackpot **2** to attain the highest success or reward

☆**jack rabbit** ⟦JACK(ASS) + RABBIT: so named because of its long ears⟧ any of several large hares (genus *Lepus*) of W North America, with long ears and strong hind legs

☆**jack·roll** (jak′rōl′) *vt.* [Slang] ROLL (*vt.* 14) —**jack′roll′er** *n.*

Jack Russell terrier ⟦after John (*Jack*) *Russell* (1795–1883), Eng clergyman who developed this breed⟧ any of a breed of terrier with short hair and a mottled brown and white coat: also **Jack Russell**

jacks (jaks) *n.* ⟦< JACKSTONE⟧ a children's game in which pebbles or small, six-pronged metal pieces are tossed and picked up in various ways, esp. while bouncing a small ball

jack·screw (jak′skro͞o′) *n.* ⟦JACK (*n.* 5) + SCREW⟧ a machine used to raise heavy things a short distance, operated by turning a screwlike shaft

☆**jack·smelt** (jak′smelt′) *n.* ⟦JACK + SMELT⟧ a common silverside fish (*Atherinopsis californiensis*) of Pacific waters

jack·snipe (-snīp′) *n., pl.* **-snipes′** or **-snipe′** ⟦JACK- + SNIPE⟧ **1** a small snipe (*Lymnocryptes minimus*) of the Old World **2** any of several similar American birds, as the pectoral sandpiper

Jack·son[1] (jak′sən) **1 Andrew** 1767-1845; U.S. general: 7th president of the U.S. (1829-37): also called *Old Hickory* **2 Robert H(oughwout)** 1892-1954; associate justice, U.S. Supreme Court (1941-54) **3 Thomas Jonathan** 1824-63: Confederate general in the Civil War: called *Stonewall Jackson*

Jack·son[2] (jak′sən) ⟦after Andrew JACKSON[1]⟧ capital of Miss., in the SW part, on the Pearl River

Jack·so·ni·an (jak sō′nē ən) *adj.* of or relating to Andrew Jackson or his policies —*n.* a follower of Jackson

Jack·son·ville (jak′sən vil′) ⟦after Andrew JACKSON[1]⟧ port in NE Fla., on the St. Johns River

jack·stay (jak′stā′) *n.* ⟦JACK- + STAY[1]⟧ **1** a rope or rod along a ship's yard, to which the edge of a sail is fastened **2** a rope or rod that runs up and down a ship's mast, along which the yard moves when being hoisted or lowered

jack·stone (-stōn′) *n.* ⟦< dial. *checkstone, chackstone* < *check, chuck,* pebble⟧ **1** JACK (*n.* 13*c*) **2** [*pl., with sing. v.*] JACKS

jack·straw (-strô′) *n.* **1** ⟦JACK + STRAW⟧ [Obs.] STRAW MAN (sense 2) **2** ⟦JACK- + STRAW⟧ a narrow strip of wood, plastic, etc. used in a game (**jackstraws**) played by tossing a number of such strips into a jumbled heap and trying to remove them one at a time without moving any of the others

jack-tar (-tär′) *n.* ⟦JACK + TAR[2]⟧ [*often* **J-**] [Old Brit. Informal] a sailor

Jack the Ripper name given to the notorious, unidentified murderer of at least six London prostitutes in 1888

Ja·cob (jā′kəb) *n.* ⟦LL(Ec) *Jacobus* < Gr *Iakōbos* < Heb *Ja'aqob,* Jacob, lit., seizing by the heel of (cf. Gen. 25:26)⟧ **1** a masculine name: dim. *Jake, Jack;* var. *James;* equiv. Fr. *Jacques,* It. *Giácomo* **2** *Bible* a son of Isaac, twin brother of Esau, and the father of the founders of the twelve tribes of Israel: also called *Israel:* Gen. 25:24-34

Jac·o·be·an (jak′ə bē′ən) *adj.* ⟦< ModL *Jacobaeus* < *Jacobus,* L form of the name of James I (see JACK) + -AN⟧ **1** of James I of England **2** of the period in England when he was king (1603-25) —*n.* a poet or other person of this period

Ja·co·bi·an (jə kō′bē ən) *n.* ⟦after Karl G. J. *Jakobi* (1804-51), Ger mathematician⟧ *Math.* a determinant whose elements are the first, partial derivatives of a finite number of functions of the same number of variables, with the elements in each row being the derivatives of the same function with respect to each of the variables

Jac·o·bin (jak′ə bin) *n.* ⟦MFr < ML *Jacobinus* < LL(Ec) *Jacobus:* see JACK⟧ **1** a French Dominican friar: the Dominicans were established in a convent at the Church of St. Jacques in Paris **2** any member of a society of radical democrats in France during the Revolution of 1789: their meetings were held in the Jacobin friars' convent **3** an extreme political radical —*adj.* of the Jacobins or their policies: also **Jac′o·bin′ic** or **Jac′o·bin′i·cal** —**Jac′o·bin·ism′** *n.*

Jac·o·bite (jak′ə bīt′) *n.* ⟦< LL(Ec) *Jacobus:* see JACK⟧ a supporter of James II of England after his abdication, or of the claims of his son or his son's descendants to the throne —**Jac′o·bit′ic** (-bit′ik) *adj.*, **Jac′o·bit′i·cal**

Jacob's ladder 1 *Bible* the ladder from earth to heaven that Jacob saw in a dream: Gen. 28:12 **2** a portable ladder used on ships and having, typically, wooden rungs and rope or wire sides **3** any of several plants (genus *Polemonium*) of the phlox family, with pinnately compound leaves and small, blue, bell-shaped flowers **4** CARRION FLOWER (sense 1)

Ja·cob·son's organ (jā′kəb sənz) ⟦after L. *Jacobson* (1783-1843), Dan surgeon⟧ VOMERONASAL ORGAN

Jacob's rod ASPHODEL (sense 1)

Ja·co·bus (jə kō′bəs) *n.* ⟦see JACOBEAN⟧ UNITE[2]

jac·o·net (jak′ə net′) *n.* ⟦Urdu *jagannāthī,* after *Jagannāth* (now Puri), town in India, where it was manufactured⟧ any of various lightweight cotton cloths, often glazed, used for clothing, bandages, etc.

Jac·quard (jak′ärd, jə kärd′) *n.* ⟦after J. M. *Jacquard* (1752-1834), Fr inventor⟧ **1** *a)* a loom with an endless belt of cards punched with holes arranged to produce a figured weave (also **Jacquard loom**) *b)* the distinctive mechanism of this loom **2** *a)* the weave made (also **Jacquard weave**) *b)* [*usually* **j-**] a fabric with such a weave

Jac·que·line (jak′wə lin, jak′ə-) *n.* ⟦Fr, fem. of *Jacques* < OFr *Jaques:* see JACK⟧ a feminine name: dim. *Jackie, Jacky*

Jac·que·rie (zhäk rē′) *n.* ⟦Fr < *Jacques Bonhomme,* nobles' epithet for "peasant"⟧ **1** the French peasants' revolt of 1358 **2** [*often* **j-**] any peasants' revolt

jac·ta·tion (jak tā′shən) *n.* ⟦L *jactatio,* a throwing, boasting < *jactare:* see JET[1]⟧ **1** [Rare] the act of bragging **2** *Med.* JACTITATION (sense 3)

jac·ti·ta·tion (jak′ti tā′shən) *n.* ⟦ML *jactitatio* < L *jactitare,* to utter, tell in public < *jactare,* to throw: see JET[1]⟧ **1** the act of bragging **2** *Law* a false boast or false statement that causes harm to another person **3** *Med.* restless tossing or jerking of the body in severe illness

☆**Ja·cuz·zi** (jə ko͞o′zē) ⟦after *Jacuzzi,* U.S. family who developed it⟧ *trademark for* a kind of whirlpool bath —*n.* [*occas.* **j-**] a bath of this type

jade[1] (jād) *n.* ⟦Fr < Sp (*piedra de*) *ijada,* (stone of) the side, loin < VL **iliata* < L *ilia,* pl. of *ileum* (see ILEUM): from the notion that it cured pains in the side⟧ **1** any of various hard greenish gems used in jewelry and artistic carvings, including jadeite and nephrite **2** a green color of medium hue —*adj.* **1** made of jade **2** green like jade

jade[2] (jād) *n.* ⟦ME, prob. via Anglo-Fr < ON *jalda,* a mare < Finn⟧ **1** a horse, esp. a worn-out, worthless one **2** *a)* a loose or disreputable woman *b)* [Now Rare] a saucy, pert young woman — *vt., vi.* **jad′ed, jad′ing** to make or become tired, weary, or worn-out —**jad′ish** *adj.*

jad·ed (jād′id) *adj.* ⟦pp. of prec.⟧ **1** tired; worn-out; wearied **2** dulled or satiated, as from overindulgence **3** made apathetic, insensitive, or embittered by experience, esp. in a particular environment or situation [*jaded* by his years in politics] —**jad′ed·ly** *adv.* —**jad′ed·ness** *n.*

jade·ite (jād′īt′) *n.* ⟦JAD(E) + -ITE[1]⟧ a translucent, usually greenish, mineral, sodium aluminum iron silicate, $Na(Al,Fe)Si_2O_6$, of the pyroxene group, found only in metamorphic rock, esp. in Myanmar: it is the most precious type of jade

jade plant a thick-leaved plant (*Crassula argentea*) of the orpine family, native to S Africa and Asia

Ja·dot·ville (zhä dō vēl′) *former name for* LIKASI

jae·ger (yā′gər; *for 2, also,* jā′-) *n.* **1** JÄGER **2** any of a genus (*Stercorarius,* family Stercorariidae) of shorebirds which force other, weaker birds to leave or give up their prey

Ja·el (jā′əl) *n.* ⟦Heb *yāel,* lit., mountain goat⟧ *Bible* the woman who killed Sisera by hammering a tent peg through his head while he slept: Judg. 4:17-22

Jaf·fa (yäf′ə, jaf′ə) seaport in central Israel: since 1950, incorporated with Tel Aviv

Jaff·na (jaf′nə) seaport in N Sri Lanka

jag[1] (jag) *n.* ⟦ME *jagge,* projecting point < ?⟧ **1** a sharp, toothlike projection or similar indentation **2** [Archaic] a notch or pointed tear, as in cloth —*vt.* **jagged, jag′ging** ⟦ME *jaggen, joggen* < the n.⟧ **1** to cut jags in; notch or pink (cloth, etc.) **2** to cut unevenly; tear raggedly

jag[2] (jag) *n.* ⟦< ?⟧ **1** [Dial.] a small load or amount, as of wood or hay **2** [Slang] *a)* an intoxicated condition due to liquor or drugs *b)* a drinking spree *c)* a period of uncontrolled activity [a crying *jag*]

JAG *abbrev.* Judge Advocate General

Jag·an·nath (jug′ə nät′, -nôt′) *n.* JUGGERNAUT (sense 1)

jä·ger (yā′gər) *n.* ⟦Ger, huntsman < *jagen,* to hunt < ? IE base **yagh-,* to chase, desire > Sans *yahú-,* restless⟧ **1** a hunter **2** [*often* **J-**] a rifleman in the old Austrian and German armies **3** JAEGER

jag·ged (jag′id) *adj.* having sharp projecting points; notched or ragged —**jag′ged·ly** *adv.* —**jag′ged·ness** *n.*

jag·ger·y (jag′ər ē) *n.* ⟦Anglo-Ind < Hindi *jāgri* < Sans *śarkarā,* SUGAR⟧ a dark, crude sugar from the sap of certain palm trees

jag·gy (jag′ē) *adj.* **-gi·er, -gi·est** jagged; notched

jag·uar (jag′wär′; *Brit* jag′yo͞o är′) *n., pl.* **-uars′** or **-uar′** ⟦Port < Tupí *jaguara*⟧ the largest New World predatory cat (*Panthera onca*), yellowish with black spots, found from SW U.S. to Argentina: cf. LEOPARD (*n.* 1)

jag·ua·run·di (jag′wə run′dē, jä′gwə-) *n.* ⟦AmSp & Port < Tupí⟧ a small wildcat (*Herpailurus yagouaroundi*) of tropical and subtropical America, with a slender body and a long tail: also sp. **jag′ua·ron′di**

Jah·veh or **Jah·ve** (yä′ve) *n.* ⟦see YAHWEH⟧ JEHOVAH: also **Jah·weh** or **Jah·we** (yä′we, -wā)

jai a·lai (hī′lī′, hī′ə lī′) ⟦Sp < Basque *jai*, celebration + *alai*, merry⟧ a game like handball, popular in Latin America: it is played with a curved basket (*cesta*) fastened to the arm, for catching the ball and hurling it against the wall

jail (jāl) *n.* ⟦ME *jaile, gaile* < OFr *jaole, gaole*, a cage, prison < LL *caveola*, dim. of L *cavea*, CAGE⟧ **1** a building for the confinement of people who are awaiting trial or who have been convicted of minor offenses **2** imprisonment —*vt.* to put or keep in or as in jail

☆**jail·bait** (jāl′bāt′) *n.* [Slang] a young woman, considered a potential sexual partner, who has not reached the age of consent

jail·bird (-burd′) *n.* [Informal] **1** a prisoner or former prisoner in a jail **2** a person often put in jail; habitual lawbreaker

☆**jail·break** (-brāk′) *n.* a breaking out of jail by force

jail delivery **1** [Historical] *Eng. Law* a procedure for clearing a jail by which all prisoners are tried and either convicted or released **2** [Archaic] in the U.S., a criminal court **3** [Archaic] an escape or liberation of prisoners by force

jail·er or **jail·or** (-ər) *n.* a person in charge of a jail or of prisoners

☆**jail·house** (jāl′hous′) *n.* JAIL (*n.* 1)

☆**jailhouse lawyer** [Slang] a prison inmate who has learned enough about legal procedures while incarcerated to seek release or sentence reduction and, often, to counsel other inmates in doing so

Jain (jīn) *n.* ⟦Hindi *Jaina* < Sans *jina*, saint < base *ji*, to conquer⟧ a believer in Jainism —*adj.* of the Jains or their religion Also **Jai·na** (jī′nə) or **Jain′ist**

Jain·ism (jīn′iz′əm) *n.* a religion of India, founded in the 6th cent. B.C.: it emphasizes asceticism, nonviolence, and reverence for all living things

Jai·pur (jī′poor′) city in NW India: capital of Rajasthan state

Ja·kar·ta (jə kär′tə) capital of Indonesia, on the NW coast of Java

☆**jake** (jāk) *adj.* ⟦prob. < *Jake*, abbrev. of JACOB: sense development unknown⟧ [Slang] just right; satisfactory

jakes (jāks) *n.* ⟦< *Jacques* (see JACK): cf. JOHN[1]⟧ [Now Chiefly Dial.] an outdoor toilet; privy

Ja·kob·son (jā′kəb sən), **Roman (Osipovič)** 1896-1982; U.S. linguist, born in Russia

jal·ap (jal′əp) *n.* ⟦Fr < Sp *jalapa*, after fol., whence it is imported⟧ **1** the dried root of a Mexican vine (*Ipomoea purga*) of the morning-glory family, formerly used as a purgative **2** a resin obtained from this root **3** the plant bearing this root **4** any of several other plants with similar roots

Ja·la·pa (hä lä′pä) city in E Mexico: capital of Veracruz state: in full **Jalapa En·rí·quez** (en rē′kes)

☆**ja·la·pe·ño** (hä′lə pān′yō; *also* -pēn′yō, -pē′nō) *n., pl.* **-ños** ⟦< MexSp *chile jalapeño*, lit., chili (pepper) of prec.⟧ a kind of chili, or hot pepper, that is small, dark green, and very hot: it is used esp. in Mexican cooking: also **jalapeño pepper**

jal·a·pin (jal′ə pin) *n.* a glycoside, $C_{34}H_{56}O_{16}$, contained in jalap

Ja·lis·co (hä lēs′kô) state of W Mexico, on the Pacific: 30,941 sq mi (80,137 sq km); cap. Guadalajara

☆**ja·lop·y** (jə läp′ē) *n., pl.* **-lop′ies** ⟦earlier *jaloupy* < ?⟧ [Slang] an old, ramshackle automobile

jal·ou·sie (jal′ə sē′; *Brit* zhal′oo zē′) *n.* ⟦Fr < It *gelosia*, lit., JEALOUSY: prob. so named from permitting one to see without being seen⟧ a window, shade, or door formed of overlapping, horizontal slats, or louvers, of wood, metal, or glass, that can be adjusted to regulate the air or light coming between them

jam[1] (jam) *vt.* **jammed**, **jam′ming** ⟦< ?⟧ **1** to squeeze or wedge into or through a confined space **2** *a)* to bruise or crush *b)* to force (a thumb, toe, etc.) back against its joint so as to cause impaction **3** to push, shove, or crowd **4** to pack full or tight **5** to fill or block (a passageway, river, etc.) by crowding or squeezing in **6** *a)* to wedge or make stick to prevent movement *b)* to put out of order by such jamming [*to jam a rifle*] **7** to make (radio broadcasts, radar signals, etc.) unintelligible, as by sending out other signals on the same wavelength ☆**8** [Slang] *Basketball* STUFF (*vt.* 9) —*vi.* **1** *a)* to become wedged or stuck fast *b)* to become unworkable through such jamming of parts **2** to push against one another in a confined space ☆**3** [Informal] to improvise freely, esp. in a jam session —*n.* **1** a jamming or being jammed **2** a group of persons or things so close together as to jam a passageway, etc. [*a traffic jam*] ☆**3** [Informal] a difficult situation; predicament ☆**4** [Informal] JAM SESSION ☆**5** [Slang] *Basketball* STUFF (*n.* 11)

jam[2] (jam) *n.* ⟦< ? prec.⟧ a food made by boiling fruit with sugar to a thick mixture: cf. PRESERVE, JELLY

Jam *abbrev.* Jamaica

Ja·mai·ca (jə mā′kə) country on an island in the West Indies, south of Cuba: a former colony, it became independent & a member of the Commonwealth (1962): 4,244 sq mi (10,991 sq km); cap. Kingston —**Ja·mai′can** *adj., n.*

Jamaica rum a dark, full-bodied rum with a heavy aroma

jamb (jam) *n.* ⟦ME *jambe* < OFr, a leg, shank, pier, side post of a door: see GAMB⟧ **1** a side post or piece of a framed opening, as for a door, window, or fireplace **2** a pillar of ore

☆**jam·ba·lay·a** (jum′bə lī′ə, jam′-) *n.* ⟦AmFr (Louisiana) < Prov *jambalaia*⟧ **1** a Creole stew made of rice and shrimp, oysters, crabs, ham, chicken, etc., with spices and, often, vegetables **2** any jumbled mixture

jam·beau (jam′bō′) *n., pl.* **-beaux′** (-bōz′) ⟦ME < OFr *jambe*: see JAMB⟧ GREAVE

☆**jam·bo·ree** (jam′bə rē′) *n.* ⟦< ?⟧ **1** *a)* a boisterous party or noisy revel *b)* a gathering or celebration, with planned entertainment **2** a national or international assembly of Boy Scouts

James[1] (jāmz) *n.* ⟦ME < OFr < LL(Ec) *Jacomus*, later form of *Jacobus*: see JACOB⟧ **1** a masculine name: dim. *Jamie, Jim, Jimmy*; fem. *Jamie*: see JACOB **2** *Bible a)* one of the twelve Apostles, Zebedee's son and brother of John: his day is July 25 (also **Saint James the Greater**) *b)* one of the twelve Apostles, Alphaeus's son: his day is May 3 (also **Saint James the Less**) *c)* a brother of Jesus: Gal. 1:19; also, a book of the New Testament sometimes ascribed to him (abbrev. *Jas* or *Jm*)

James[2] (jāmz) **1 James I** 1566-1625; king of England (1603-25) & (as **James VI**) king of Scotland (1567-1625): son of Mary, Queen of Scots **2 James II** 1633-1701; king of England & (as **James VII**) king of Scotland (1685-88): deposed: son of Charles I **3 Henry** 1811-82; U.S. writer on religion & philosophy: father of Henry & William **4 Henry** 1843-1916; U.S. novelist, in England after 1876: son of Henry and brother of William **5 Jesse (Woodson)** 1847-82; U.S. outlaw **6 M(ontague) R(hodes)** 1862-1936; Eng. medieval scholar & writer of horror stories **7 William** 1842-1910; U.S. psychologist & philosopher: exponent of pragmatism: son of Henry

James[3] (jāmz) **1** river in Va., flowing from the W part southeast into Chesapeake Bay: 340 mi (547 km) **2** river in E N.Dak. & E S.Dak., flowing south into the Missouri: 710 mi (1,143 km)

James Bay arm of Hudson Bay, extending south into NE Ontario & NW Quebec: *c.* 275 mi (443 km) long

James Bond (bänd) the dashing Brit. spy in a series of stories by Ian FLEMING[2]

James Edward *see* STUART[2], James Francis Edward

James·i·an (jām′zē ən) *adj.* of or characteristic of Henry James or of his brother William

James·town (jāmz′toun′) ⟦after JAMES I⟧ **1** former village near the mouth of the James River, Va.: the 1st permanent English colonial settlement in America (1607) **2** capital of St. Helena

jam·mies (jam′ēz) *pl.n.* ⟦(contr. < PAJAMAS) + -IE (sense 1)⟧ [Informal] PAJAMAS

Jam·mu (jum′oo) **1** city in SW Jammu and Kashmir, India: winter capital of the state **2** former kingdom in N India: merged with Kashmir in 1846

Jammu and Kashmir state of N India: its control is disputed by Pakistan, which claims 30,476 sq mi (78,933 sq km) in the NW part; NE border areas in Indian territory (16,500 sq mi; 42,735 sq km) are claimed by China; total area, 85,806 sq mi (222,237 sq km); caps. Srinagar and Jammu

Jam·na·gar (jäm nug′ər) city in W Gujarat state, W India

☆**jam-packed** (jam′pakt′) *adj.* [Informal] tightly packed; crammed

jams (jamz) *pl.n.* ⟦< (PA)JAM(A)S⟧ baggy, knee-length shorts, usually brightly colored, for casual wear

☆**jam session** an informal gathering of musicians, esp. jazz musicians, to play improvised music or to improvise together, usually on tunes they all know

Jam·shed·pur (jum′shed poor′) city in SE Bihar, NE India

Jam·shid or **Jam·shyd** (jam shēd′) *n.* ⟦Pers⟧ *Pers. Myth.* the king of the peris: because he boasts that he is immortal, he has to live as a human being on earth

Jan *abbrev.* January

Ja·ná·ček (yä′nə chek′), **Le·oš** (le′ôsh) 1854-1928; Czech composer

Jane (jān) *n.* ⟦Fr *Jeanne* < ML *Joanna*: see JOANNA⟧ **1** a feminine name: dim. *Janet, Jenny* ☆**2** [**j-**] [Slang] a girl or woman

Jane Doe *see* DOE

Jan·et (jan′it) *n.* a feminine name: dim. *Jan*: see JANE

jan·gle (jaŋ′gəl) *vi.* **-gled**, **-gling** ⟦ME *janglen* < OFr *jangler*, to jangle, prattle, prob. < Frank **jangelon*, to jeer⟧ **1** to quarrel or argue noisily **2** to make a harsh sound, inharmonious sound, as of a bell out of tune —*vt.* **1** to utter in a harsh, inharmonious manner **2** to cause to make a harsh sound **3** to irritate very much [*to jangle someone's nerves*] —*n.* **1** noisy or annoying talk **2** noisy quarrel or arguing **3** a harsh sound; discordant ringing —**jan′gler** *n.*

Jan·ice (jan′is) *n.* ⟦< JANE, JANET⟧ a feminine name: dim. *Jan*

Ja·ni·na (yä′nē nä′) *Serb. name for* IOANNINA

jan·is·sar·y (jan′i ser′ē) *n., pl.* **-sar′ies** ⟦Fr *janissaire* < It *giannizzero* < Turk *yeniçeri*, lit., new troops < *yeñi*, new + *çeri*, soldiery⟧ [*often* **J-**] **1** a soldier (orig. a slave) in the Turkish sultan's guard, established in the 14th cent. and abolished in 1826 **2** any Turkish soldier **3** any very loyal or submissive follower or supporter Also **jan′i·zar′y** (-zer′ē), *pl.* **-zar′ies**

jan·i·tor (jan′i tər) *n.* ⟦L, doorkeeper < *janua*, door < *janus*, arched passageway: see JANUS⟧ **1** [Now Rare] a doorman or doorkeeper **2** the custodian of a building, who maintains the heating system, does routine repairs, general cleaning, etc. —**jan′i·to′ri·al** (-i tôr′ē əl) *adj.*

Jan May·en (yän mī′ən) Norwegian island in the Arctic Ocean, between Greenland & N Norway: site of a meteorological station: 144 sq mi (373 sq km)

Jan·sen (yän′sən; *E* jan′sən), **Cor·ne·lis** (kôr nä′lis) (L. name *Jansenius*) 1585-1638; Du. Rom. Catholic theologian

Jan·sen·ism (jan′sən iz′əm) *n.* a set of rigorous, unorthodox, predestinarian doctrines held by Cornelis Jansen —**Jan′sen·ist** *n., adj.* —**Jan′sen·is′tic** *adj.*

Jan·u·ar·y (jan′yo͞o er′ē) *n., pl.* **-ar′ies** ⟦ME *Janyuere* < L *Januarius (mensis)*, (the month) of fol., to whom it was sacred⟧ the first month of the year, having 31 days: abbrev. *Jan, Ja*, or *J*

Ja·nus (jā′nəs) *n.* ⟦L, lit., gate, arched passageway < IE base **yă*-, var. of **ei*-, to go > YEAR⟧ 1 *Rom. Myth.* the god who is guardian of portals and patron of beginnings and endings: he is shown as having two faces, one in front, the other at the back of his head 2 a small satellite of Saturn

Ja·nus-faced (-fāst′) *adj.* two-faced; deceiving

Jap[1] (jap) *adj., n.* [Slang] *short for* JAPANESE: now a term of hostility and contempt

Jap[2] *abbrev.* 1 Japan 2 Japanese

☆**JAP** (jap) *n.* ⟦*J(ewish-)A(merican) P(rincess)*⟧ a young, upper-middle-class Jewish woman thought of as being materialistic, spoiled, self-indulgent, etc.: a term of ridicule or mild contempt

ja·pan (jə pan′) *n.* ⟦orig. produced in fol.⟧ 1 a lacquer or varnish giving a hard, glossy finish 2 a liquid mixture used as a paint drier: also **japan drier** 3 objects decorated and lacquered in the Japanese style —*vt.* **-panned′, -pan′ning** to varnish or lacquer with or as with japan

Ja·pan (jə pan′) 1 island country in the Pacific, off the E coast of Asia, including Hokkaido, Honshu, Kyushu, Shikoku, & many smaller islands: 145,883 sq mi (377,835 sq km); cap. Tokyo: Jpn. names NIHON, NIPPON 2 **Sea of** arm of the Pacific, between Japan & E Asia: 391,100 sq mi (1,012,945 sq km)

☆**Japan clover** an annual plant (*Lespedeza striata*) of the pea family, grown for hay and foliage in the SW U.S.

Japan Current a fast, warm ocean current flowing northeast from the Philippine Sea east of Taiwan: it moves along the southern coast of Japan

Jap·a·nese (jap′ə nēz′, -nēs′) *adj.* of Japan or its people, language, or culture —*n.* 1 *pl.* **-nese′** a person born or living in Japan 2 the language spoken in Japan, believed by some scholars to be distantly related to Korean

Japanese andromeda ⟦see ANDROMEDA⟧ an evergreen plant (*Pieris japonica*) of the heath family, with drooping racemes of bell-shaped, white flowers

☆**Japanese beetle** a shiny, green-and-brown scarab beetle (*Popillia japonica*), orig. from Japan, which eats leaves, fruits, grasses, and roses and is damaging to crops

Japanese bobtail any of a breed of domestic cat, originating in Japan, with a very short, fluffy tail, and a soft, silky coat often in three colors, white, black, and red

Japanese Chin (chin) any of a breed of toy dog with a long, silky, usually black-and-white coat, a very short muzzle, and a tail that curls over the back: formerly called *Japanese spaniel*

Japanese iris any of several tall, beardless irises with showy flowers, esp. a species (*Iris kaempferi*) commonly cultivated in gardens

Japanese ivy BOSTON IVY

Japanese lantern CHINESE LANTERN

☆**Japanese oyster** a large, edible oyster (*Ostrea gigas*) native to Japan but introduced in the Puget Sound region

☆**Japanese persimmon** 1 an Asian persimmon (*Diospyros kaki*), bearing large, soft, edible, red or orange-colored fruit 2 its fruit

☆**Japanese plum** a cultivated plum tree (*Prunus salicina*) with yellow or reddish fruits, native to China

Japanese quince 1 a spiny plant (*Chaenomeles lagenaria*) of the rose family, with pink or red flowers and hard, fragrant, greenish-yellow fruit 2 the fruit

Japanese spurge a trailing pachysandra (*Pachysandra terminalis*) used as a ground cover

Jap·a·nesque (jap′ə nesk′) *adj.* of Japanese style

Japan wax a white, waxy fat obtained from the fruit of several Asian sumacs (esp. *Toxicodendron verniciflua* and *T. succedanea*), used in lubricants, polishes, etc.

jape (jāp) *vi.* **japed, jap′ing** ⟦ME *japen* < OFr *japer*, to howl, of echoic orig.⟧ 1 to joke; jest 2 to play tricks —*vt.* [Now Rare] 1 to make fun of; mock 2 to play tricks on; fool —*n.* 1 a joke or jest 2 a trick —**jap′er** *n.* —**jap′er·y** *n., pl.* **-er·ies**

Ja·pheth (jā′feth′) *n.* ⟦LL(Ec) < Gr(Ec) < Heb *yepheth*, lit., enlargement: cf. Gen. 9:27⟧ *Bible* the youngest of Noah's three sons: Gen. 5:32

Ja·phet·ic (jə fet′ik) *adj.* 1 of or from Japheth 2 [Archaic] INDO-EUROPEAN (*adj.*)

ja·po·nais·e·rie (jap′ə nez rē′, -nez′ə rē; *Fr* zhȧ pô nez rē′) *n.* ⟦Fr < *japonais*, JAPANESE + *-erie*, -ERY⟧ [*also in italics*] 1 an ornate style of Western art, design, etc. employing Japanese motifs 2 articles, designs, etc. in this style

ja·pon·i·ca (jə pän′i kə) *n.* ⟦ModL, fem. of *Japonicus*, of Japan < *Japonia*, Japan < Fr *Japon*⟧ any of various trees, shrubs, or plants associated with the Far East, as a camellia or the Japanese quince

Ja·pu·rá (zhä′po͝o rä′) river in S Colombia & NW Brazil, flowing southeast into the Amazon: *c.* 1,750 mi (2,816 km)

Ja·ques (jā′kwēz) *n.* ⟦OFr: see JACK⟧ a cynically philosophical nobleman in Shakespeare's *As You Like It*

Jaques-Dal·croze (zhäk dȧl krōz′), **É·mile** (ā mēl′) 1865-1950; Swiss composer: originated eurythmics

jar[1] (jär) *vi.* **jarred, jar′ring** ⟦ult. echoic⟧ 1 to make a harsh sound or a discord; grate 2 to have a harsh, irritating effect (*on* one) 3 to shake or vibrate from a sudden impact 4 to clash, disagree, or quarrel sharply —*vt.* 1 to make vibrate or shake by sudden impact 2 to cause to give a harsh or discordant sound 3 to jolt or shock —*n.* 1 a harsh, grating sound; discord 2 a vibration due to a sudden impact 3 a jolt or shock 4 a sharp clash, disagreement, or quarrel

jar[2] (jär) *n.* ⟦ME *jarre* < Fr *jarre* < OProv or Sp *jarra* < Ar *jarrah*, earthen water container⟧ 1 a container made of glass, stone, earthenware, etc., usually cylindrical, with a large opening and no spout: some jars have handles 2 as much as a jar will hold: also **jar′ful′** (-fo͝ol′)

jar[3] (jär) *n.* ⟦see AJAR[1]⟧ [Archaic] a turn: now only in the phrase **on the jar**, ajar; partly open

jar·di·niere (jär′də nir′; *Fr* zhȧr dē nyer′) *n.* ⟦Fr *jardinière*, a flower stand, orig. fem. of *jardinier*, gardener < *jardin*, GARDEN⟧ 1 an ornamental bowl, pot, or stand for flowers or plants 2 a garnish for meats, made up of different kinds of vegetables cooked separately and cut into pieces

Jar·ed (jar′id) *n.* ⟦LL(Ec) < Gr(Ec) < Heb *yeredh*, lit., descent: cf. Gen. 5:15⟧ a masculine name

jar·gon[1] (jär′gən) *n.* ⟦ME < MFr, a chattering (of birds): ult. of echoic orig.⟧ 1 incoherent speech; gibberish 2 a language or dialect unknown to one so that it seems incomprehensible or outlandish 3 a mixed or hybrid language or dialect; esp., pidgin 4 the specialized vocabulary and idioms of those in the same work, profession, etc., as of sportswriters or social workers: a somewhat derogatory term, often implying unintelligibility: see SLANG 5 speech or writing full of long, unfamiliar, or roundabout words or phrases —*vi.* JARGONIZE —**SYN.** DIALECT —**jar′gon·is′tic** *adj.*

jar·gon[2] (jär′gän′) *n.* ⟦Fr < It *giargone* < Ar *zarqūn*: see ZIRCON⟧ a colorless or smoky variety of zircon: also called **jar·goon′** (-go͞on′)

jar·gon·ize (jär′gən īz′) *vi.* **-ized′, -iz′ing** to talk or write in jargon —*vt.* to express in jargon

☆**jar·head** (jär′hed′) *n.* ⟦ult. < slang term, mule⟧ [Slang] a member of the U.S. Marine Corps

jarl (yärl) *n.* ⟦ON, akin to OE *eorl*: see EARL⟧ in early Scandinavia, a chieftain or nobleman

Jarls·berg (yärlz′burg′) ⟦after *Jarlsberg*, town in Norway⟧ *trademark for* a mild, buttery Norwegian cheese with large holes —*n.* [*sometimes* **j-**] this cheese: also **Jarlsberg cheese**

jar·o·vize (yär′ə vīz′) *vt.* **-vized′, -viz′ing** ⟦< Russ *yar'*, spring grain + -IZE⟧ VERNALIZE

jar·rah (jer′ə, jar′ə) *n.* 1 a tall eucalyptus (*Eucalyptus marginata*) usually found in the forests of W Australia 2 the hard, reddish wood of this tree, used for construction, furniture, etc.

Jar·ry (zhȧ rē′), **Alfred** 1873-1907; Fr. playwright

Jas *abbrev.* 1 James 2 *Bible* (The Letter of) James

jas·mine (jaz′min, jas′-) *n.* ⟦Fr *jasmin* < Ar *yās(a)mīn* < Pers *yāsamīn*⟧ 1 any of a genus (*Jasminum*) of tropical and subtropical plants of the olive family, with fragrant flowers of yellow, red, or white, used in perfumes or for scenting tea 2 any of several other similar plants with fragrant flowers, as yellow jasmine 3 pale yellow Often sp. **jas′min**

Ja·son (jā′sən) *n.* ⟦L *Iāson* < Gr, lit., healer⟧ 1 a masculine name 2 *Gr. Myth.* a prince who leads the Argonauts, and, with Medea's help, gets the Golden Fleece

jas·per (jas′pər) *n.* ⟦ME *jaspre* < MFr < L *iaspis* < Gr, a green precious stone, prob. akin to Heb *yāšpeh*⟧ 1 a type of chert quartz that is usually reddish due to the presence of hematite 2 *Bible* a precious stone, probably an opaque green quartz 3 a kind of porcelain developed by Wedgwood, having a dull surface in green, blue, etc., with raised designs, usually in white

Jas·per (jas′pər) *n.* ⟦OFr *Jaspar* < ?⟧ a masculine name: equiv. Fr. *Gaspard*, Ger. *Kasper*, Sp. *Gaspar*

Jas·pers (yäs′pərz), **Karl** 1883-1969; Ger. philosopher

jas·pi·lite (jas′pə līt′) *n.* ⟦< Gr *iaspis*, JASPER + -LITE⟧ a metamorphic rock consisting primarily of alternating bands of red jasper and hematite

jas·sid (jas′id) *n.* ⟦< ModL *Jassidae* < L *Iassus*, ancient town on the coast of Caria + ModL *-idae*, -IDAE⟧ LEAFHOPPER

Jas·sy (yä′sē) *var. of* IAŞI

Jat (jät, jôt) *n.* ⟦Hindi⟧ a member of an agricultural people of N India and Pakistan

ja·to or **JATO** (jā′tō) *n.* ⟦*j(et)-a(ssisted) t(ake)o(ff)*⟧ an airplane takeoff assisted by a jet-producing unit or units, usually small, solid-propellant rockets

jaun·dice (jôn′dis) *n.* ⟦ME *jaundis* < OFr *jaunisse* < *jaune*, yellow < L *galbinus*, greenish yellow < *galbus*, yellow, prob. via Celt **galbos* < IE base **ghel*-, YELLOW⟧ 1 *a)* a condition in which the eyeballs, the skin, and the urine become abnormally yellowish as a result of increased amounts of bile pigments in the blood *b)* popularly, a disease causing this condition, as hepatitis 2 a bitter or prejudiced state of mind, caused by jealousy, envy, etc. —*vt.* **-diced, -dic·ing** 1 to cause to have jaundice 2 to make bitter or prejudiced through jealousy, envy, etc.

jaunt (jônt) *vi.* ⟦< ?⟧ to take a short trip for pleasure —*n.* such a trip; excursion —**SYN.** TRIP

jaunting car a light, topless, two-wheeled cart used esp. in 19th-cent. Ireland, with seats on both sides

jaun·ty (jôn′tē) *adj.* **-ti·er, -ti·est** ⟦earlier *janty, genty* < Fr *gentil*, genteel: see GENTLE⟧ 1 in fashion; stylish; chic 2 lighthearted and merry; sprightly; perky —**jaun′ti·ly** *adv.* —**jaun′ti·ness** *n.*

Jau·rès (zhô res′), **Jean Lé·on** (zhän lā ōn′) 1859-1914; Fr. Socialist leader & journalist: assassinated

Jav *abbrev.* 1 Java 2 Javanese

Ja·va[1] (jä′və, jav′ə) *n.* 1 any of a breed of domestic chicken developed in the U.S. from Asian stock, having black or mottled black plumage ☆2 a kind of coffee grown on Java and nearby islands ☆3 [j-] [Slang] coffee

Ja·va[2] (jä′və, jav′ə) large island of Indonesia, southeast of Sumatra: 49,255 sq mi (127,569 sq km)

Java man a type of early human (*Homo erectus erectus*) known from fossil remains found in Java and thought to be from the Lower Pleistocene: see SOLO MAN

Jav·a·nese (jä′və nēz′, -nēs′; jav′ə-) *adj.* of Java or its people, language, or culture —*n.* 1 *pl.* **-nese′** a person born or living on Java; esp., a member of a group of peoples occupying the main part of Java 2 the Western Austronesian language of these peoples

Java Sea part of the Pacific, between Java & Borneo: *c.* 600 mi (966 km) long

Java sparrow a white, pink, and gray SE Asian passerine finch (*Padda oryzivora*, family Estrildidae) widely kept as a cage bird

jav·e·lin (jav′lin, jav′ə lin) *n.* ⟦MFr *javeline,* fem. dim. < *javelot,* a spear, prob. < Gaul **gabalaccos* < IE base **ghabh(o)lo-,* forked branch, fork > OE *gafol,* Ger *gabel*⟧ 1 a light spear for throwing 2 *a)* a pointed wooden or metal shaft, about 8½ ft long, thrown for distance as a test of strength and skill *b)* the throwing of the javelin as a field event in track and field meets: in full **javelin throw**

☆**jav·e·li·na** (hä′və lē′nə) *n.* ⟦Sp *jabalina,* wild sow, fem. of *jabalí,* boar < Ar *(khinzīr) jabalī,* lit., mountain (pig) < *jabal,* mountain⟧ PECCARY

Ja·velle (*or* **Ja·vel**) **water** (zhə vel′) ⟦after *Javel,* former Fr village (now part of Paris), where it was made⟧ a solution of sodium hypochlorite, NaOCl, in water, used as a bleaching agent or disinfectant

jaw (jô) *n.* ⟦ME *jowe* < OFr *joue,* cheek⟧ 1 *a)* either of the two bones or bony parts that hold the teeth and frame the mouth in most vertebrates: the mandible (**lower jaw**) is usually hinged and movable, the maxilla (**upper jaw**) is usually not *b)* the lower of these bony parts, or the portion of the face covering it 2 any of various analogous biting structures of invertebrates 3 [*pl.*] the mouth 4 either of two mechanical parts that open and close to grip or crush something, as in a monkey wrench or vise 5 [*pl.*] the narrow entrance of a canyon, valley, strait, etc. 6 [*pl.*] something grasping or imminent [the *jaws* of death] 7 [Old Slang] a talk —*vi.* [Slang] to talk, esp. in a boring or abusive way —*vt.* [Old Slang] to scold or reprove, esp. repeatedly

Ja·wa (jä′və) *Indonesian name for* JAVA[2]

jaw·bone (jô′bōn′) *n.* a bone of a jaw, esp. of the lower jaw —☆*vt., vi.* **-boned′**, **-bon′ing** [Informal] 1 to talk (to) or converse (with), esp. at length 2 to speak forcefully or threateningly (to or about) [the President *jawboned* against price increases]

jaw·break·er (-brāk′ər) *n.* 1 a machine with jaws for crushing rocks, ore, etc. ☆2 a hard, usually round candy 3 [Slang] a word that is hard to pronounce

jaw-drop·ping (jô′dräp′iŋ) *adj.* ⟦< the facial expression assoc. with surprise⟧ [Informal] causing wonder or amazement; astounding, stunning, overwhelming, etc. —**jaw′-drop′ping·ly** *adv.*

jaw harp JEW'S-HARP: also **jaw's harp** or **jaws' harp**

jaw·less fish (-lis) any of a class (Agnatha) of fishes with a cartilaginous skeleton, an eel-like body, and a circular, sucking mouth lacking jaws, consisting of the lampreys and hagfishes

Jaws of Life ⟦so named from snatching accident victims from the "jaws of death": see JAW (*n.* 6)⟧ *trademark for* a pneumatic, pincerlike tool that is inserted into the body of a wrecked vehicle to pry sections of it apart: used esp. to free people trapped inside

Jax·ar·tes (jak särt′ēz′) *ancient name for* SYR DARYA

jay[1] (jā) *n.* ⟦ME < OFr *gai* < LL *gaius,* a jay, prob. echoic, but sp. infl. by the L proper name *Gaius*⟧ 1 any of several corvids, usually strikingly colored birds, as the **Eurasian jay** (*Garrulus glandarius*) or the blue jay 2 [Informal] a foolish or talkative person

jay[2] (jā) *n.* ⟦< J(OINT), *n.* 6: phonetic sp. of name of initial letter⟧ [Slang] JOINT (*n.* 6)

Jay (jā), **John** 1745-1829; Am. statesman: 1st chief justice of the U.S. (1789-95)

Ja·ya·pu·ra (jä′yə po͝or′ə) seaport & capital of Papua, Indonesia, on the NE Pacific coast

jay·bird (jā′burd′) *n. dial. var. of* JAY[1]

☆**Jay·cee** (jā′sē′) *n.* ⟦< *j(unior) c(hamber)*⟧ a member of a junior chamber of commerce

☆**jay·hawk·er** (jā′hôk′ər) *n.* ⟦< ?⟧ 1 an abolitionist guerrilla of Missouri and Kansas in Civil War days 2 a robber, raider, or plunderer 3 [J-] [Informal] a person born or living in Kansas: also **Jay′hawk′**

☆**jay·vee** (jā′vē′) *n.* ⟦< *j(unior) v(arsity)*⟧ a member of a junior varsity team

☆**jay·walk** (jā′wôk′) *vi.* ⟦JAY[1], *n.* 2 + WALK⟧ to walk in or across a street without obeying traffic rules and signals, esp. at other than proper crossing places —**jay′walk′er** *n.* —**jay′walk′ing** *n.*

☆**jazz** (jaz) *n.* ⟦etym. uncert.: < ? Creole patois *jass,* sexual term applied to the Congo dances (New Orleans)⟧ 1 a kind of music, originally improvised but now also arranged, characterized by syncopation, rubato, usually heavily accented rhythms, dissonances, individualized melodic variations, and unusual tonal effects on the trumpet, trombone, clarinet, saxophone, etc.: it originated with Southern blacks in the late 19th cent.: see also SWING, BOP[2] 2 [Slang] a quality reminiscent of jazz music; lively spirit 3 [Slang] remarks, acts, concepts, etc. regarded as hypocritical, tiresome, trite, pretentious, etc. [the same old *jazz*] —*adj.* of, in, like, or having to do with jazz —*vt.* 1 to speed up 2 [Slang] to fill with jazz qualities; make exciting or elaborate; enliven or embellish: usually with *up* —*vi.* [Slang] to move or behave in a lively or carefree way —**and all that jazz** [Informal] and so forth; et cetera

☆**Jazz Age** ⟦< ? phr. attributed to F. Scott FITZGERALD⟧ a period of U.S. history in the 1920s noted for general prosperity, financial speculation, Prohibition, the emergence of organized crime, profound social, cultural, and literary change, and the influence of jazz

☆**jazz·bo** (jaz′bō′) *n.* [Old Slang] a jazz devotee or a jazz musician or performer, esp. one thought of as being very serious, committed, skilled, etc.

☆**jazz·er** (jaz′ər) *n.* [Slang] a jazz musician

☆**jazz·man** (jaz′man′) *n., pl.* **-men′** (-men′) a jazz musician, esp. a male one

☆**jazz-rock** (-räk′) *n.* a style of popular music that combines jazz improvisation with rock rhythms

☆**jazz·y** (jaz′ē) *adj.* **jazz′i·er**, **jazz′i·est** 1 characterized by the qualities of jazz music, often, specif., the more superficial and showy qualities 2 [Slang] lively, bright, showy, etc. —**jazz′i·ly** *adv.* —**jazz′i·ness** *n.*

Jb *abbrev. Bible* Job

JB *abbrev.* Jerusalem Bible

J-bar (jā′bär′) *n.* a J-shaped hook suspended from the moving cable of a ski lift, used to pull a skier uphill

JC or **J.C.** *abbrev.* 1 Jesus Christ 2 Julius Caesar 3 jurisconsult

JCD or **J.C.D.** *abbrev.* 1 ⟦L *Juris Canonici Doctor*⟧ Doctor of Canon Law 2 ⟦L *Juris Civilis Doctor*⟧ Doctor of Civil Law

JCS *abbrev.* Joint Chiefs of Staff

jct *abbrev.* junction

J-curve (jā′kurv′) *n.* ⟦descriptive of its shape on a graph⟧ a curve which, in some economic theories, indicates that a decline in the value of a nation's currency initially causes an increase, and then a decrease, in that nation's balance-of-trade deficit

Jd *abbrev. Bible* Jude

JD *abbrev.* 1 ⟦L *Jurum Doctor*⟧ Doctor of Laws: also **J.D.** ☆2 juvenile delinquent: also **jd**

JDL *abbrev.* Jewish Defense League

Jdt *abbrev. Bible* Judith

Je *abbrev.* June

jeal·ous (jel′əs) *adj.* ⟦ME *jelous* < OFr *gelos* < ML *zelosus:* see ZEAL⟧ 1 very watchful or careful in guarding or keeping [*jealous* of one's rights] 2 *a)* resentfully suspicious of a rival or a rival's influence [a husband *jealous* of other men] *b)* resentfully envious *c)* resulting from such feelings [a *jealous* rage] 3 [Archaic] requiring exclusive loyalty ["for I the Lord your God am a *jealous* God"] —**jeal′ous·ly** *adv.* —**jeal′ous·ness** *n.*

jeal·ous·y (jel′əs ē) *n.* ⟦ME *jalousie* < OFr *gelosie* < *gelos:* see prec.⟧ 1 the quality or condition of being jealous 2 *pl.* **-ous·ies** an instance of this; jealous feeling

jean (jēn) *n.* ⟦< ME *Gene (fustian),* (fustian) of Genoa < OFr *Janne* < ML *Janua* < L *Genua,* Genoa⟧ 1 a durable cotton cloth in a twill weave, used for work clothes and casual wear 2 [*pl.*] trousers of this material, often blue, or of denim, flannel, etc.

Jean (zhän; *for 2,* jēn) *n.* 1 *Fr. var. of* JOHN[1] 2 a feminine name: var. *Jeanne:* see JOANNA

Jeanne (jēn) *n.* a feminine name: dim. *Jeannette:* see JOANNA

Jeanne d'Arc (zhån dårk) *Fr. name for* JOAN OF ARC

Jean·nette (jə net′) *n.* a feminine name: dim. *Nettie, Netty:* see JEANNE

Jeans (jēnz), Sir **James (Hopwood)** 1877-1946; Eng. mathematician, physicist, astronomer, & writer

je·bel (jeb′əl) *n.* ⟦Ar⟧ a hill or mountain: often used in Arabic place names

Jebel Druze (dro͞oz) region in S Syria, on the N Jordanian border, inhabited by the Druses: 2,584 sq mi (6,693 sq km): also **Jebel ed Druz** (ed dro͞oz)

Jebel Mu·sa (mo͞o′sə) mountain in N Morocco, opposite Gibraltar: *c.* 2,700 ft (823 m): cf. PILLARS OF HERCULES

Jed·dah (jed′ə) *var. of* JIDDA: also sp. **Jed′da**

☆**jeep** (jēp) *n.* ⟦orig. military slang, after a creature (Eugene the *Jeep*) with extraordinary powers, in comic strip by E. C. Segar (1894-1938): later assoc. with *G.P.,* abbrev. for General Purpose Car⟧ a small, rugged automotive vehicle with a ¼-ton capacity and a four-wheel drive, used by U.S. armed forces in WWII — [J-] *trademark for* a similar vehicle for civilian use

☆**jee·pers** (jē′pərz) *interj.* ⟦euphemistic alteration of JESUS[2]⟧ [Slang] used to express surprise or as a mild oath: also [Old Slang] **jeepers creepers**

jeer (jir) *vi., vt.* ⟦? altered < CHEER⟧ to make fun of (a person or thing) in a rude, sarcastic manner; mock; taunt; scoff (at) —*n.* a jeering cry or remark; sarcastic or derisive comment —**jeer′er** *n.* —**jeer′ing·ly** *adv.*

jeez (jēz) *interj.* ⟦euphemism for JESUS[2]⟧ [Slang] used variously to express surprise, anger, annoyance, etc.

Jef·fers (jef′ərz), **(John) Robinson** 1887-1962; U.S. poet

Jef·fer·son (jef′ər sən), **Thomas** 1743-1826; Am. statesman: 3d president of the U.S. (1801-09): drew up the Declaration of Independence

Jefferson City ⟦after prec.⟧ capital of Mo., on the Missouri River

☆**Jef·fer·so·ni·an** (jef′ər sō′nē ən) *adj.* of or characteristic of Thomas Jefferson or his democratic principles —*n.* a follower of Thomas Jefferson —**Jef′fer·so′ni·an·ism′** *n.*

Jeff·rey (jef′rē) *n.* a masculine name: dim. *Jeff:* see GEOFFREY

Jeffrey pine ⟦after John *Jeffrey,* 19th-c. Scot botanist⟧ a pine (*Pinus jeffreyi*) native to Oregon and California, resembling the ponderosa pine and having similar wood

jeg·gings (jeg′iŋz, -inz) *pl.n.* ⟦blend of JEAN & *leggings* (see LEGGING)⟧ women's stretch pants that fit like long leggings, made with a denimlike fabric

je·had (jē häd′) *n. alt. sp. of* JIHAD

Je·hol (jə hōl′) former province of NE China: divided (1955) between Hebei & Liaoning provinces & Inner Mongolia

Je·hosh·a·phat (ji häsh′ə fat′, -häs′-) *n.* ⟦Heb *yehōshāphāt,* lit., God has judged⟧ *Bible* a king of Judah in the 9th cent. B.C.: 2 Chron. 17-21

Je·ho·vah (ji hō′və) *n.* ⟦modern transliteration of the Tetragrammaton YHWH; the vowels appear through arbitrary transference of the vowel points of *Adōnāi,* my Lord: see YAHWEH⟧ *name for* God (in some translations of the Old Testament): see TETRAGRAMMATON

☆**Jehovah's Witnesses** ⟦name adopted after Isa. 43:10, "Ye are my witnesses"⟧ a millenarian, actively proselytizing Christian sect founded by Charles T. Russell (1852-1916)

Je·ho·vist (ji hō′vist) *n.* YAHWIST

Je·hu (jē′ho͞o′, -hyo͞o′) *n.* ⟦Heb⟧ **1** *Bible* a king of Israel in the 9th cent. B.C., described as a furious charioteer: 2 Kings 9 **2** [**j-**] [Now Rare] *a)* a driver of a cab or coach *b)* a fast, reckless driver

je·june (ji jo͞on′) *adj.* ⟦L *jejunus,* empty, dry, barren⟧ **1** not nourishing; barren **2** not interesting or satisfying; dull or empty **3** ⟦? by confusion with JUVENILE⟧ not mature; childish —**je·june′ly** *adv.* —**je·june′ness** *n.*

je·ju·nec·to·my (jē′jo͞o nek′tə mē) *n., pl.* **-mies** ⟦JEJUN(UM) + -ECTOMY⟧ the surgical removal of all or part of the jejunum

je·ju·nos·to·my (-näs′tə mē) *n., pl.* **-mies** ⟦fol. + -O- + -STOMY⟧ the surgical operation of making an artificial opening into the jejunum

je·ju·num (jē jo͞o′nəm, jə-) *n., pl.* **je·ju′na** (-nə) ⟦ML < neut. of L *jejunus,* empty: it was formerly thought to be empty after death⟧ the middle part of the small intestine, between the duodenum and the ileum —**je·ju′nal** *adj.*

Je·kyll[1] (jek′əl; *occas., and prob. Stevenson's intended pronun.,* jē′kəl), **Dr.** a kind doctor in R. L. Stevenson's story *The Strange Case of Dr. Jekyll and Mr. Hyde,* who develops drugs that enable him to transform himself into a vicious brute named Mr. Hyde and back again

Je·kyll[2] (jē′kəl; *also* jek′əl), **Gertrude** 1843-1932; Eng. landscape architect

☆**jell** (jel) *vi., vt.* ⟦back-form. < JELLY⟧ **1** *a)* to become or cause to become jelly *b)* to become or cause to become somewhat firm, as gelatin does; set **2** [Informal] to take or cause to take definite form; crystallize [*plans that haven't jelled yet*] —*n.* [Dial.] JELLY

Jel·li·coe (jel′i kō′), **John Rush·worth** (rush′wʉrth′) 1st Earl Jellicoe 1859-1935; Eng. admiral

jel·lies (jel′ēz) *pl.n.* ⟦so called prob. from their bright colors and translucence, in allusion to JELLY (*n.* 1)⟧ inexpensive sandals made of usually translucent molded plastic: occasionally **jelly shoes**

jel·li·fy (jel′ə fī′) *vt., vi.* **-fied′**, **-fy′ing** [Rare] to change into jelly —**jel′li·fi·ca′tion** *n.*

☆**jell·o** (jel′ō) *n.* ⟦< *Jell-O,* a trademark for such a gelatin⟧ a flavored gelatin eaten as a dessert or used in molded salads

jel·ly (jel′ē) *n., pl.* **-lies** ⟦ME *gely* < OFr *gelée,* a frost, jelly < fem. pp. of *geler* < L *gelare,* to freeze: see GELATIN⟧ **1** a soft, partially transparent, semisolid food resulting from the cooling of fruit juice boiled with sugar, or of meat juice cooked down **2** any substance like this; gelatinous substance —*vt.* **-lied**, **-ly·ing** **1** to make into jelly **2** to coat, fill, or serve with jelly —*vi.* to become jelly —**jel′ly·like′** *adj.*

☆**jelly bean** a small, bean-shaped candy with a soft, jellylike center and a hard sugar coating: also written **jel′ly·bean′** *n.*

jel·ly·fish (-fish′) *n., pl.* **-fish′** or **-fish′es** (see FISH) **1** any of various free-swimming, mostly marine cnidarians (esp. class Scyphozoa) with a body made up largely of jellylike substance and shaped like an umbrella: it has long, hanging tentacles with stinging cells on them **2** [Informal] a weak-willed person

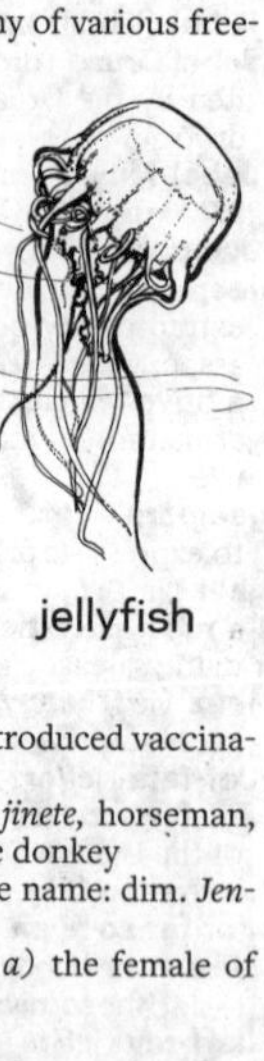

jel·ly·roll (-rōl′) *n.* a kind of cake consisting of a thin sheet of spongecake that has been spread with jelly and rolled into a spiral

Je·mi·ma (jə mī′mə) *n.* ⟦Heb *yemīmāh,* lit., a dove⟧ a feminine name

jem·my (jem′ē) *n., pl.* **-mies** ⟦< dim. of JAMES[1]⟧ [Brit.] **1** JIMMY **2** a sheep's head used for food

Je·na (yā′nä′) city in central Germany, in the state of Thuringia: site of a battle (1806) in which the Prussian forces were routed by Napoleon

jellyfish

je ne sais quoi (zhən sā kwä′) ⟦Fr, I do not know what⟧ a quality that is hard to describe or express

Jen·ghiz Khan (jeŋ′gis) *var. of* GENGHIS KHAN

Jen·ner (jen′ər) **1 Edward** 1749-1823; Eng. physician: introduced vaccination **2** Sir **William** 1815-98; Eng. physician

jen·net (jen′et′, -it) *n.* ⟦ME *genett* < MFr *genette* < Sp *jinete,* horseman, mounted soldier < Ar *Zenāta,* a tribe of Barbary⟧ a female donkey

Jen·ni·fer (jen′i fər) *n.* ⟦altered < GUINEVERE⟧ a feminine name: dim. *Jennie, Jenny*

jen·ny (jen′ē) *n., pl.* **-nies** ⟦< fol.⟧ **1** SPINNING JENNY **2** *a)* the female of some birds [*a jenny wren*] *b)* a female donkey

Jen·ny (jen′ē) *n.* a feminine name: see JANE, JENNIFER

jeop·ard (jep′ərd) *vt.* ⟦ME *jeuparten,* back-form. < *jeuparti,* JEOPARDY⟧ *now rare var. of* JEOPARDIZE

jeop·ard·ize (jep′ər dīz′) *vt.* **-ized′**, **-iz′ing** to put in jeopardy; risk loss, damage, or failure of; endanger

jeop·ard·y (-dē) *n., pl.* **-ard·ies** ⟦ME *jeuparti* < OFr *jeu parti,* lit., a divided game, game with even chances < ML *jocus partitus,* an even chance, alternative < L *jocus,* a game, JOKE + pp. of *partire,* to divide: see PART[2]⟧ **1** great danger; peril [*to have one's life in jeopardy*] **2** *Law* exposure to conviction and punishment; situation of an accused person on trial for a crime —**SYN.** DANGER

Jeph·thah (jef′thə) *n.* ⟦Heb *Yiphtáh,* lit., God opens⟧ *Bible* a judge who sacrificed his daughter in fulfillment of a vow: Judg. 11:30-40

je·quir·i·ty (ji kwir′ə tē) *n., pl.* **-ties** ⟦Fr *Jéquirity* < Tupí-Guaraní⟧ **1** any of the poisonous, red and black seeds of a tropical, climbing plant (*Abrus precatorius*) of the pea family, used for beads and, formerly, as a weight: also **jequirity bean** **2** the plant it grows on

Jer *abbrev. Bible* Jeremiah

jer·bo·a (jər bō′ə) *n.* ⟦Ar *yarbū'*⟧ any of a family (Dipodidae) of small, nocturnal, leaping rodents of N Africa and Asia, with very long hind legs

jer·e·mi·ad (jer′ə mī′ad′, -əd) *n.* ⟦Fr *jérémiade* < *Jérémie,* Jeremiah: see fol.⟧ **1** a long lamentation or complaint: in allusion to the *Lamentations of Jeremiah* **2** a long, scolding speech, sermon, etc. expressing disapproval or warning of disaster

Jer·e·mi·ah (-ə) *n.* ⟦LL(Ec) *Jeremias* < Gr(Ec) *Hieremias* < Heb *yirmeyāh,* lit., the Lord loosens (i.e., from the womb)⟧ **1** a masculine name: dim. *Jerry;* var. *Jeremy* **2** *Bible a)* a Hebrew prophet of the 7th and 6th cent. B.C. *b)* the book containing his prophecies (abbrev. *Jer* or *Jr*) **3** a person pessimistic about the future

Jer·e·my (jer′ə mē) *n.* a masculine name: see JEREMIAH

Je·rez de la Fron·te·ra (he reth′ *the* lä frôn te′rä) city in SW Spain, near Cadiz: noted for the sherry made there: also **Jerez**

Jer·i·cho (jer′i kō′) city in the West Bank, just north of the Dead Sea: site of an ancient Canaanite city whose walls, according to the Bible, were miraculously destroyed when trumpets were sounded: Josh. 6

jerk[1] (jʉrk) *vt.* ⟦var. of archaic *yerk* < ?⟧ **1** to pull, twist, push, thrust, or throw with a sudden, sharp movement ☆**2** [Old Informal] to make and serve (ice cream sodas) —*vi.* **1** to move with a jerk or in jerks **2** to twitch —*n.* **1** a sharp, abrupt movement; quick pull, twist, push, etc. **2** a sudden muscular contraction caused by a reflex action ☆**3** [Slang] a person regarded as disagreeable, contemptible, etc., esp. as the result of foolish or mean behavior **4** *Weight Lifting* a lift in which the barbell is raised upward from shoulder level with the arms completely extended: see CLEAN AND JERK —☆**jerk off** [Slang] to masturbate: used chiefly of males: somewhat vulgar —**jerk out** to utter sharply and abruptly

jerk[2] (jʉrk) *vt.* ⟦altered (after prec.) < JERKY[2]⟧ to preserve (meat) by slicing into strips and drying, esp. originally in the sun —*n.* **1** JERKY[2] **2** a marinade consisting of habanero peppers, onions, vinegar, allspice, thyme, cinammon, etc., used in Jamaican cooking —*adj.* marinated with JERK[2] (sense 2) and barbecued [*jerk chicken, pork, etc.*]

jer·kin (jʉr′kin) *n.* ⟦< ?⟧ a short, closefitting jacket, often sleeveless, or a vest, of a kind worn in the 16th and 17th cent.

☆**jerk-off** (jʉrk′ôf′) [Slang] *adj.* **1** of or having to do with masturbation: somewhat vulgar **2** obnoxious, stupid, contemptible, etc.: mildly vulgar —*n.* JERK[1] (*n.* 3): mildly vulgar

☆**jerk·wa·ter** (jʉrk′wôt′ər) *n.* ⟦JERK[1] + WATER: prob. in reference to pulling the valve on the water tank to fill the engine boiler⟧ [Historical] a train on an early branch railroad —*adj.* [Informal] being or appropriate to a small, remote, unimportant community or region [*a jerkwater town*]

jerk·y[1] (jʉr′kē) *adj.* **jerk′i·er**, **jerk′i·est** **1** characterized or moving by jerks; making sudden starts and stops or spasmodic movements ☆**2** [Slang] foolish, mean, contemptible, etc. —**jerk′i·ly** *adv.* —**jerk′i·ness** *n.*

☆**jer·ky**[2] (jʉr′kē) *n.* ⟦Sp *charquí:* see CHARQUI⟧ meat, esp. beef, that has been sliced into strips and dried: cf. JERK[2] (*vt.*)

Jer·o·bo·am (jer′ə bō′əm) *n.* ⟦Heb *yārobh'ām,* lit., prob., the people increases⟧ **1** *Bible* the first king of Israel: 1 Kings 11:26-14:20 **2** [*usually* **j-**] *Winemaking* a wine bottle, esp. one for champagne, holding about 3 liters, or about twice as much as a magnum

Je·rome[1] (jə rōm′, jer′əm) *n.* ⟦Fr *Jérôme* < L *Hieronymus* < Gr *Hierōnymos* < *hieros,* holy (see HIERO-) + *onyma,* NAME⟧ a masculine name: dim. *Jerry*

Je·rome[2] (jə rōm′), Saint (born *Eusebius Hieronymus Sophronius*) (A.D. 340?-420); monk & church scholar, born in Pannonia: author of the Vulgate: his day is Sept. 30

Jer·ry (jer′ē) *n.* a masculine name: see GERALD, GERARD, JEREMIAH, JEROME[1]

jer·ry-built (jer′ē bilt′) *adj.* ⟦< prec. (as an old generalized epithet, esp. of belittlement: cf. JACK), prob. reinforced by JURY[2]⟧ built poorly, of cheap materials

jer·ry·can (jer′ē kan′) *n.* ⟦< *jerry,* short for *jeroboam* + CAN[2]⟧ a large, flat can for holding liquids, esp. gasoline: also **jerry can** or **jer′ri·can′**

jer·sey (jʉr′zē) *n., pl.* **-seys** ⟦after JERSEY[2]: orig. used of worsted garments made on Jersey from locally produced wool⟧ **1** a soft, elastic, knitted cloth **2** a closefitting pullover sweater or shirt worn by athletes, sailors, etc. **3** any closefitting, knitted upper garment

Jer·sey[1] (jʉr′zē) *n., pl.* **-seys** any of a breed of small dairy cattle, originally from Jersey, often light red or fawn in color: its milk has a high butterfat content

Jer·sey[2] (jʉr′zē) **1** largest of the Channel Islands of the United Kingdom,

15 mi (24 km) from the coast of France: 45 sq mi (117 sq km) **2** *informal name for* NEW JERSEY

Jersey City ⟦after NEW JERSEY⟧ city in NE N.J., across the Hudson from New York City

Je·ru·sa·lem (jə ro͞o′zə ləm, -sə-; -lem) capital of Israel (the country) in the central part: divided (1948-67) between Israel & Jordan: since 1967 Israel holds entire city and environs —**Je·ru′sa·lem·ite′** *n.*

Jerusalem artichoke ⟦altered, after prec., by folk etym. < GIRASOL⟧ **1** a tall North American sunflower (*Helianthus tuberosus*) of the composite family, with potatolike tubers used as a vegetable **2** such a tuber

Jerusalem Bible a Roman Catholic version of the Bible published in 1966, translated from the French *La Bible de Jérusalem*, produced by Dominican scholars in Jerusalem (1956): abbrev. *JB*

☆**Jerusalem cherry** either of two bushy plants (*Solanum pseudo-capsicum* or *S. capsicastrum*) of the nightshade family, with small, star-shaped, white flowers and orange to red berries, grown widely as ornamentals

☆**Jerusalem cricket** any of a family (Stenopelmatidae) of burrowing, wingless, long-horned crickets common in dry regions of W U.S.

Jerusalem oak an aromatic Eurasian goosefoot (*Chenopodium botrys*) occurring as a weed in N U.S. and Canada

Jerusalem thorn **1** a leguminous, tropical American tree (*Parkinsonia aculeata*) having compound leaves and yellow, fragrant flowers: used for hedges **2** CHRIST'S-THORN

Jer·vis Bay (jär′vis) inlet of the Pacific, on the SE coast of New South Wales, Australia: peninsula on its S shore is a detached part of Australian Capital Territory

Jes·per·sen (yes′pər sən, jes′-), **(Jens) Otto (Harry)** 1860-1943; Dan. linguist, noted for his studies of English

jess (jes) *n.* ⟦ME *ges* < OFr *gies, gets,* pl. (see JET[1]): from its use in letting a hawk fly⟧ a strap for fastening around a falcon's leg, with a ring at one end for attaching a leash: also sp. **jesse** —*vt.* to fasten jesses on

Jes·sa·mine (jes′ə min) *n.* ⟦< MFr *jessemin,* JASMINE⟧ **1** [**j-**] JASMINE **2** a feminine name

Jes·se (jes′ē) *n.* ⟦Heb *yīshai*⟧ **1** a masculine name: dim. *Jess* **2** *Bible* the father of David: 1 Sam. 16

Jes·sel·ton (jes′əl tən) *former name for* KOTA KINABALU

Jes·si·ca (jes′i kə) *n.* a feminine name: dim. *Jessie*

Jes·sie (jes′ē) *n.* a feminine name: see JESSICA

jest (jest) *n.* ⟦ME *geste* < OFr, an exploit, tale of exploits < L *gesta,* neut. pl. pp. of *gerere,* to perform, carry out⟧ **1** [Obs.] a notable deed **2** a mocking or bantering remark; jibe; taunt **3** a joke; witticism **4** a lighthearted action or mood; fun; joking **5** something to be laughed at or joked about —*vi.* **1** to jeer; mock **2** to be playful in speech and actions; joke

jest·er (jes′tər) *n.* a person who jests; esp., a professional fool employed by a medieval ruler for amusement

Je·su (jē′zo͞o, -so͞o; jā′-, yā′-) *n. archaic var. of* JESUS[2]

Jes·u·it (jezh′o͞o it; jez′yo͞o-, jez′o͞o-) *n.* ⟦ModL *Jesuita* < LL(Ec) *Iesus,* JESUS[2] + *-ita,* -ITE[1]⟧ **1** a member of the Society of Jesus, a Roman Catholic religious order for men, founded by Ignatius Loyola in 1534 **2** [**j-**] a crafty schemer; cunning dissembler: hostile term, as used by anti-Jesuits and anti-Catholics —**Jes′u·it′ic** *adj.,* **Jes′u·it′i·cal** —**Jes′u·it′i·cal·ly** *adv.*

Jes·u·it·ism (-it iz′əm) *n.* **1** the teachings or practice of the Jesuits **2** [**j-**] craftiness; duplicity; intrigue: hostile term, as used by anti-Jesuits and anti-Catholics Also **Jes′u·it·ry** (-i trē)

Je·sus[1] (jē′zəz, -zəs; *Sp* hā zo͞os′) *n.* ⟦LL(Ec) *Iesus* < Gr(Ec) *Iēsous* < Heb *yēshū'a,* contr. of *yehōshū'a* (JOSHUA), help of Jehovah < *yāh,* Jehovah + *hōshia,* to help⟧ a masculine name

Je·sus[2] (jē′zəz, -zes) **1** *c.* 8-4 B.C.-A.D. 29? (see CHRISTIAN ERA); founder of the Christian religion: name used interjectionally to express, variously, surprise, wonder, annoyance, etc.: see also CHRIST[2]: also called **Jesus Christ** or **Jesus of Nazareth** **2** fl. early 2d cent. B.C.; author of *Ecclesiasticus,* a book of the O.T. apocrypha

jet[1] (jet) *vt., vi.* **jet′ted, jet′ting** ⟦< MFr *jeter,* to throw < OFr < VL **jectare,* for L *jactare,* freq. of *jacere,* to throw < IE base **yē-,* to throw, do > Gr *hienai,* to set in motion, throw, send⟧ **1** to spout, gush, or shoot out in a stream, as liquid or gas **2** to travel or convey by jet airplane —*n.* ⟦ME < OFr *get, giet,* a throw, spurt < L *jactus,* a throw, cast⟧ **1** a stream of liquid or gas emitted or forced out, as from a spout **2** a spout or nozzle for emitting a stream of water or gas **3** a jet-propelled airplane: in full **jet airplane** (or **plane**) —*adj.* **1** jet-propelled **2** of or having to do with jet propulsion or jet-propelled aircraft [the *jet* age]

jet[2] (jet) *n.* ⟦ME *get* < OFr *jaiet* < L *gagates* < Gr *gagatēs,* jet, after *Gagas,* town and river in Lycia, Asia Minor⟧ **1** a hard, black variety of lignite, which takes a high polish: sometimes used in jewelry: also called **jet coal** **2** a deep, lustrous black —*adj.* **1** made of jet **2** black like jet

jet·bead (jet′bēd′) *n.* a cultivated Japanese shrub (*Rhodotypos tetrapetala*) of the rose family, having white, four-petaled flowers and four shiny, black, beadlike fruits

jet-black (-blak′) *adj.* glossy black, like jet

je·té (zhə tā′) *n.* ⟦Fr, pp. of *jeter,* to throw⟧ *Ballet* a leap from one foot to the other, made with a kicking movement of the leg

jet engine an engine for aircraft, ships, etc., operating on the principle of jet propulsion

jet lag a disruption of circadian rhythms, associated with high-speed travel by jet airplane to distant time zones —**jet′-lagged′** *adj.*

jet·lin·er (jet′līn′ər) *n.* ⟦JET[1] + LINER[1]⟧ a commercial jet aircraft for carrying passengers or cargo

je·ton (zhə tōn′) *n.* ⟦Fr < MFr < OFr *jeter,* to calculate, lit., to throw: see JET[1]⟧ a metal disk or counter, now used, as in some European countries, for operating a pay telephone, etc.

jet·pack (jet′pak′) *n.* a backpack powered by jets, used especially to enable an astronaut to maneuver independently during a spacewalk

jet·port (jet′pôrt′) *n.* ⟦JET[1] + (AIR)PORT⟧ a large commercial airport with long runways designed for use by jetliners

jet-pro·pelled (-prə peld′) *adj.* driven by jet propulsion

jet propulsion a method of propelling airplanes, boats, etc. that uses the reaction force created when compressed outside air and hot exhaust gases are forced through a jet nozzle

jet·sam (jet′səm) *n.* ⟦var. of JETTISON⟧ **1** that part of the cargo or equipment thrown overboard to lighten a ship in danger: see FLOTSAM **2** such material washed ashore **3** discarded things

☆**jet set** a social set of rich, fashionable people who frequently travel, often by jet, for business or pleasure —**jet′-set′ter** *n.*

Jet Ski *trademark for* a watercraft built like a motorcycle that is propelled by a jet of water — [**j- s-**] any such watercraft

☆**jet stream** **1** any of several bands of high-velocity winds moving from west to east around the earth at altitudes from *c.* 12 to 16 km (*c.* 8 to 10 mi) **2** the stream of exhaust from any reaction engine: also written **jet′stream′** *n.*

jet·ti·son (jet′ə sən, -zən) *n.* ⟦ME *jetteson* < Anglo-Fr *getteson* < OFr *getaison,* a throwing, jetsam < L *jactatio,* a throwing < *jactare,* to throw: see JET[1]⟧ **1** a throwing overboard of goods to lighten a ship, airplane, etc. in an emergency **2** JETSAM —*vt.* **1** to throw (goods) overboard **2** to discard (something) as useless or a burden

jet·ty[1] (jet′ē) *n., pl.* **-ties** ⟦ME *gete* < OFr *jetée,* jetty, orig. pp. of *jeter*: see JET[1]⟧ **1** a kind of wall built out into the water to restrain currents, protect a harbor or pier, etc. **2** a landing pier **3** an overhanging part of a building —*vi.* **-tied, -ty·ing** to project, or jut out

jet·ty[2] (jet′ē) *adj.* **-ti·er, -ti·est** very black, like jet

Jet·way (jet′wā′) *trademark for* a tunnel-like, enclosed walkway that can be adjusted to connect an airport boarding area and the doorway of an aircraft —*n.* [*usually* **j-**] any such walkway

jeu (zhö) *n., pl.* ***jeux*** (zhö) ⟦Fr⟧ a game; diversion

jeu de mots (zhöd mō′) *pl.* ***jeux de mots*** (zhöd mō′) ⟦Fr⟧ a play on words; pun

jeu d'es·prit (zhö des prē′) *pl.* ***jeux d'es·prit*** (zhö) ⟦Fr, lit., play of intellect⟧ a clever, witty turn of phrase, piece of writing, etc.

jeune fille (zhën fē′y′) *pl.* ***jeunes filles*** (zhën fē′y′) ⟦Fr⟧ a young girl

jeu·nesse (zhë nes′) *n.* ⟦Fr⟧ **1** the time of one's youth **2** young people

jew (jo͞o) [Slang] *vt.* ⟦< fol., by assoc. with occupation of Jews as moneylenders in Middle Ages⟧ to swindle; cheat; gyp —**jew someone down** to get or bargain for better terms from someone in a business transaction, esp. in a petty or niggardly way

USAGE—an offensive term of contempt

Jew (jo͞o) *n.* ⟦ME < OFr *Giu, Juiu* < L *Judaeus* < Gr *Ioudaios* < Heb *yehūdī,* member of the tribe or kingdom of Judah: see JUDAH[1]⟧ **1** a person descended, or regarded as descended, from the ancient Hebrews of Biblical times **2** a person whose religion is Judaism —*adj.* [*also* **j-**] [Slang] JEWISH: used before the noun it modifies: a hostile or contemptuous usage See also HEBREW

jew·el (jo͞o′əl) *n.* ⟦ME < OFr *joel* < *jeu,* a game, trifle < L *jocus,* a trifle, JOKE⟧ **1** a valuable ring, pin, necklace, etc., esp. one set with a gem or gems **2** a precious stone; gem **3** any person or thing that is very precious or valuable **4** a small gem or hard, gemlike bit, used as one of the bearings in a watch —*vt.* **-eled** or **-elled, -el·ing** or **-el·ling** to decorate or set with jewels

jewel box a thin rectangular plastic case with a hinged cover, for holding a compact disc

jew·el·er or **jew·el·ler** (jo͞o′əl ər, jo͞ol′ər) *n.* ⟦ME *jueler* < OFr *joieleor* < *joel*: see JEWEL⟧ a person who makes, deals in, or repairs jewelry, watches, etc.

jew·ell·ery (jo͞o′əl rē, jo͞ol′rē) *n. chiefly Brit. sp. of* JEWELRY

jewel neckline a plain, slightly rounded neckline without a collar, as on a dress or sweater: also **jewel neck**

jew·el·ry (jo͞o′əl rē, jo͞ol′rē) *n.* ornaments such as rings, brooches, bracelets, etc., collectively

jewel tone any deep or vivid color suggestive of that of a gemstone; ruby, emerald, sapphire, amethyst, etc.

☆**jew·el·weed** (jo͞o′əl wēd′) *n.* any of a number of plants (genus *Impatiens*) of the balsam family, bearing yellow or orange-yellow flowers with short spurs, and seedpods that split at the touch when ripe

Jew·ess (jo͞o′is) *n.* a Jewish woman or girl

USAGE—now mostly a disparaging term, but still used descriptively within historical contexts [a young *Jewess* making her way in Victorian society]: see also -ESS

Jew·ett (jo͞o′it), **Sarah Orne** (ôrn) 1849-1909; U.S. writer

jew·fish (jo͞o′fish′) *n., pl.* **-fish′** or **-fish′es** (see FISH) ⟦orig. uncert.⟧ any of several large fish found in warm seas; esp., the GOLIATH GROUPER

Jew·ish (jo͞o′ish) *adj.* of or having to do with Jews or Judaism —*n.* loosely, Yiddish —**Jew′ish·ly** *adv.* —**Jew′ish·ness** *n.*

Jewish calendar a calendar used by the Jews in calculating Jewish history, holidays, etc., based on the lunar month and reckoned from 3761 B.C., the traditional date of the Creation: see the Jewish calendar in the Reference Supplement

Jew·ry (jo͞o′rē) *n., pl.* **-ries** ⟦ME *jewerie* < OFr *juerie* < *Giu:* see JEW⟧ **1** [Historical] a district inhabited only or mainly by Jews; ghetto **2** Jewish people collectively [*American Jewry*]

jew's-harp or **jews'-harp** (jo͞oz′härp′) *n.* ⟦earlier *Jew's trump,* altered (by assoc. with JEW) < Du *jeugdtromp,* child's trumpet < *jeugd,* YOUTH (confused in Eng with ME *Judeu,* Jew) + *tromp,* trumpet < OFr *trompe:* see TRUMP[2]⟧ a small musical instrument consisting of a lyre-shaped metal frame held between the teeth and played by plucking a projecting bent piece with the finger: it produces twanging tones

Jez·e·bel (jez′ə bel′, -bəl) *n.* ⟦Heb *'Izebhel*⟧ **1** *Bible* the wicked woman who married Ahab, king of Israel: 1 Kings 21:5-23; 2 Kings 9:30-37 **2** [*also* **j-**] any woman regarded as wicked, shameless, licentious, etc.

Jez·re·el (jez rē′əl, -rēl′) **1** ancient town in N Israel, on the plain of Esdraelon **2 Plain of** ESDRAELON

JFK *abbrev.* John Fitzgerald Kennedy

jg or **JG** *abbrev. U.S. Navy* junior grade

Jg *abbrev. Bible* Judges

Jgs *abbrev. Bible* Judges

Jhan·si (jän′sē) city in S Uttar Pradesh, N India

Jhe·lum (jā′ləm) river in India, flowing from the Himalayas in Kashmir through Pakistan into the Chenab: *c.* 480 mi (772 km)

JHS *abbrev.* Jesus: see IHS

JHVH or **JHWH** *see* TETRAGRAMMATON

Ji·ang·su (jē äŋ′so͞o′) province of SE China: 39,460 sq mi (102,201 sq km); cap. Nanjing

Ji·ang·xi (-shē′) province of SE China: 63,630 sq mi (164,801 sq km); cap. Nanchang

jib[1] (jib) *n.* ⟦prob. < GIBBET⟧ **1** the projecting arm of a crane **2** the boom of a derrick

jib[2] (jib) *vi., vt.* **jibbed, jib′bing** ⟦< Dan *gibbe,* to shift from one side to the other, jibe, akin to Du *gijpen* < IE *ĝheib-* < base **ghe-,* to yawn > GAPE⟧ *Naut.* to jibe (a sail or boom) —*n.* ⟦Dan *gib:* so named because it jibs: see the *vi., vt.*⟧ a triangular sail secured to a stay forward of the mast or foremast —**cut of one's jib** [Informal] one's appearance or way of dressing

jib[3] (jib) *vi.* **jibbed, jib′bing** ⟦prob. < prec.⟧ **1** to stop and refuse to go forward; balk **2** to start or shy (*at* something) —*n.* ⟦prob. < *vi.*⟧ an animal that jibs, as a horse —**jib′ber** *n.*

jí·ba·ro (hē′vä rô′, -bä-) *n., pl.* **-ros′** (-rôs′) ⟦AmSp⟧ a peasant or farm worker, esp. in Puerto Rico

jib·ber-jab·ber (jib′ər jab′ər) *n., vi.* ⟦GIBBER + JABBER⟧ [Informal] JABBER

jib boom a spar fixed to and extending beyond the bowsprit of a ship, used in securing a jib or other headsail: also written **jib′boom′** (-bo͞om′) *n.*

jibe[1] (jīb) *vi.* **jibed, jib′ing** ⟦< Du *gijpen,* to shift over (of sails), orig., to gasp for air: see JIB[2]⟧ **1** to shift from one side of a ship to the other when the stern passes across a following or quartering wind: said of a fore-and-aft sail or its boom **2** to change the course of a ship so that the sails shift thus: cf. TACK (*vi.* 1*a*) **3** [Informal] to be in harmony, agreement, or accord: often with *with* [accounts that don't *jibe*] —*vt. Naut.* to cause to jibe —*n.* an act of jibing

jibe[2] (jīb) *vi., vt.,* **jibed, jib′ing,** *n. alt. sp. of* GIBE —**jib′er** *n.*

☆**ji·ca·ma** (hē′kə mə) *n.* ⟦MexSp *jícama* < Nahuatl⟧ the large, white, fleshy root of a Mexican vine, eaten raw or cooked

Jid·da (jid′ə) seaport in W Saudi Arabia, on the Red Sea

jif·fy (jif′ē) *n., pl.* **-fies** ⟦18th-c. slang < ?⟧ [Informal] a very short time; instant [*done in a jiffy*]: also **jiff**

jig[1] (jig) *n.* ⟦prob. < MFr *giguer,* to gambol, dance < *gigue,* a fiddle < MHG *giga* (akin to ON *gigja*) < OHG **gigan* (> Ger dial. *geigen*), to move back and forth⟧ **1** *a)* a fast, springy sort of dance, usually in triple time *b)* the music for such a dance **2** any of various fishing lures that are jiggled up and down in the water **3** any of several mechanical devices operated in a jerky manner, as a sieve for separating ores, a pounding machine, or a drill **4** a device, often with metal surfaces, used as a guide for a tool or as a template — *vi., vt.* **jigged, jig′ging** ⟦< ? *giguer:* see the *n.*⟧ **1** to dance or perform (a jig) or to dance in jig style **2** to move jerkily and quickly up and down or to and fro **3** to use a jig (on) in working **4** to fish or catch (a fish) with a jig —☆**in jig time** [Informal] very quickly —☆**the jig is up** [Slang] that ends it; all chances for success are gone: said of a risky or improper activity

jig[2] (jig) *n.* ⟦orig. uncert.⟧ [Slang] BLACK (*n.* 5): a hostile and offensive term: also **jig·a·boo** (jig′ə bo͞o′)

jig·ger[1] (jig′ər) *n.* ☆*var. of* CHIGGER

jig·ger[2] (jig′ər) *n.* **1** a person who jigs ☆**2** *a)* a small cup or glass used to measure liquor, containing usually 1½ fluid ounces *b)* the quantity of liquor in a jigger **3** any device or contraption whose name does not occur to one; gadget **4** JIG[1] (*n.* 2) **5** *Mech. a)* any of several devices that operate with a jerky, reciprocating motion *b)* a device used in making ceramic ware that consists of a rotating molded plaster form that shapes clay into a number of identical plates, bowls, etc. **6** *Naut. a)* a small tackle, as for hoisting *b)* the smaller, aftermost sail of a yawl or ketch *c)* JIGGERMAST —*vt.* to adjust, alter, rearrange, or manipulate [*to jigger the financial records*]

jig·ger·mast (-mast′) *n.* **1** the small mast in the stern of a yawl or ketch **2** the mast nearest the stern in a ship with four masts

jig·ger·y-pok·er·y (jig′ər ē pōk′ər ē) *n.* ⟦altered < Scot *joukery-paukery,* rhyming slang < IE **joukerie,* trickery < **joukere,* a cheater < **jouk,* a dodge, dart < ?⟧ [Informal, Chiefly Brit.] trickery or deception; hanky-panky

jig·gle (jig′əl) *vt., vi.* **-gled, -gling** ⟦dim. or freq. of JIG[1], v.⟧ to move in a succession of quick, slight jerks; rock lightly —*n.* a jiggling movement

jig·gly (jig′lē) *adj.* moving or tending to move with a jiggle; unsteady

☆**jig·saw** (jig′sô′) *n.* ⟦JIG[1], v. + SAW[1]⟧ an electric saw with a narrow blade set in a frame, that moves with an up-and-down motion for cutting curves or ornamental patterns: also **jig saw** —*vt.* to cut or form with a jigsaw

☆**jigsaw puzzle** a puzzle consisting of a picture, typically with a cardboard backing, that has been cut up into irregularly shaped pieces which must be put together again to re-form the picture

ji·had (jē häd′) *n.* ⟦Ar *jihād,* a struggle, contest⟧ **1** a war by Muslims against unbelievers or enemies of Islam, carried out as a religious duty **2** a fanatical campaign for or against an idea, etc. —**ji·had′ist** *adj., n.,* **ji·had′i** (-ē)

Ji·lin (jē′lin′) **1** province of NE China: 72,201 sq mi (187,000 sq km); cap. Changchun **2** city in this province, on the Songhua River

Jill (jil) *n.* ⟦var. of GILL[3]⟧ **1** a feminine name **2** [*often* **j-**] [Chiefly Literary] a girl or woman; esp., a female sweetheart

☆**jil·lion** (jil′yən) *n.* ⟦arbitrary coinage, modeled on MILLION⟧ [Informal] an indefinite but very large number

jilt (jilt) *n.* ⟦< *jillet,* dim. of JILL⟧ [Now Rare] a woman who rejects a lover or suitor after accepting or encouraging him —*vt.* to reject or cast off (a previously accepted lover, etc.)

Jim (jim) *n. nickname for* JAMES[1]

☆**Jim Crow** ⟦name of an early black minstrel song⟧ [*also* **j- c-**] traditional, institutionalized discrimination against or segregation of blacks, esp. in the S U.S. —**Jim′-Crow′** *adj.* —**Jim Crow′ism′**

☆**jim-dan·dy** (jim′dan′dē) [Old Informal] *n.* ⟦JIM (used as an intens.) + DANDY⟧ an excellent or very pleasing person or thing —*adj.* excellent; very pleasing

Ji·mé·nez (hē me′neth), **Juan Ra·món** (hwän rä môn′) 1881-1958; Sp. poet, in the Americas after 1937

jim·jams (jim′jamz′) *pl.n.* ⟦arbitrary echoic formation⟧ [Slang] **1** delirium tremens **2** a nervous feeling; jitters: usually with *the*

jim·mies (jim′ēz) *pl.n.* [Informal] particles for sprinkling on something, as in decorating it; specif., particles of chocolate for sprinkling on ice-cream cones

Jim·my (jim′ē) *n.* **1** *nickname for* JAMES[1]: also **Jim′mie** **2** *pl.* **-mies** [**j-**] a short crowbar, used as by burglars to pry open windows, etc. —☆*vt.* **-mied, -my·ing** [**j-**] to use a jimmy on; pry open with a jimmy or similar tool

☆**jim·son weed** (jim′sən) ⟦altered < *Jamestown weed,* after JAMESTOWN, Va.⟧ a poisonous annual weed (*Datura stramonium*) of the nightshade family, with foul-smelling leaves, prickly fruit, and white or purplish, trumpet-shaped flowers: also **jimp′son weed** (jimp′-)

Ji·nan (jē′nän′) city in NE China; capital of Shandong province

jin·gle (jiŋ′gəl) *vi.* **-gled, -gling** ⟦ME *gingelen,* prob. echoic⟧ **1** to make a succession of light, ringing sounds, as small bells or bits of metal striking together; tinkle **2** to have obvious, easy rhythm, simple repetitions of sound, etc., as some poetry and music —*vt.* to cause to jingle —*n.* **1** a jingling sound **2** a brief verse or song that jingles, as in an advertisement —**jin′gly** *adj.*

jin·go (jiŋ′gō) *n., pl.* **-goes** ⟦< phr. *by jingo* in the refrain of a patriotic Brit music-hall song (1878): orig. ? euphemism for JESUS[2]⟧ a person who boasts of his or her patriotism and favors an aggressive, threatening, warlike foreign policy; chauvinist —*adj.* of jingoes; jingoistic —**by jingo!** [Informal] an exclamation used to indicate strong assertion, surprise, etc. —**jin′go·ism′** *n., adj.* —**jin′go·ist** *n.* —**jin′go·is′tic** *adj.* —**jin′go·is′ti·cal·ly** *adv.*

jink (jiŋk) [Chiefly Brit.] *vi.* ⟦< ?⟧ to move swiftly or with sudden turns, as in dodging a pursuer —*n.* an eluding, as by a quick, sudden turn

jinn (jin) *n., pl.* **jinns** or **jinn** ⟦see JINNI⟧ *Muslim Folklore* a supernatural being that can take human or animal form and influence human affairs

Jin·nah (ji′nä, jin′ə), **Mohammed Ali** 1876-1948; Indian statesman: 1st governor general of Pakistan (1947-48)

jin·ni (ji nē′, jin′ē) *n., pl.* **jinn** ⟦Ar *jinnī,* pl. *jinn*⟧ *var. of* JINN

jin·riki·sha (jin rik′shô′, -shä′) *n.* ⟦Jpn < *jin,* a man + *riki,* power + *sha,* carriage⟧ RICKSHAW (sense 1): also sp. **jin·rick′sha′** or **jin·rik′sha′**

☆**jinx** (jiŋks) [Informal] *n.* ⟦earlier *jynx* < L *iynx* < Gr, the wryneck (bird used in black magic)⟧ **1** a person or thing believed to bring bad luck **2** a spell or period of bad luck —*vt.* to bring bad luck to

Jin·zhou (jin′jō′) city in Liaoning province, NE China, at the head of Bo Hai

ji·pi·ja·pa (hē′pē hä′pə) *n.* ⟦Sp, after *Jipijapa,* place in Ecuador⟧ **1** a Central and South American plant (*Carludovica palmata*) of a family (Cyclanthaceae, order Cyclanthales) of monocotyledonous perennials, whose leaves yield a flexible, durable straw used for hats **2** this straw **3** a Panama hat

jism (jiz′əm) *n.* [Vulgar Slang] SEMEN

☆**jit·ney** (jit′nē) *n., pl.* **-neys** ⟦*c.* 1903 < ? Fr *jeton,* JETON⟧ **1** [Old Slang] a five-cent coin; nickel **2** a small bus or a car, esp. one traveling a regular route, that carries passengers for a low fare, originally five cents

☆**jit·ter** (jit′ər) *n.* ⟦< ?⟧ **1** an unsteady condition in which there are many small, rapid movements **2** uneven fluctuations in a video or audio signal, causing distortion —*vi.* **1** to be unsteady with many small, rapid movements **2** [Informal] to be nervous; have the jitters; fidget —**the jitters** [Informal] a very uneasy, nervous feeling; the fidgets

☆**jit·ter·bug** (-bug′) *n.* ⟦prec. + BUG[1]⟧ **1** a dance for couples, esp. in the late 1930s and early 1940s, involving fast, acrobatic movements to swing music **2** [Old Informal] a dancer of the jitterbug ***—vi.* -bugged′, -bug′ging** to dance the jitterbug

☆**jit·ter·y** (jit′ər ē) ***adj.*** [Informal] having the jitters

jiu·jit·su (jo͞o jit′so͞o′) ***n.*** *var. of* JUJITSU: also **jiu·jut′su′** (-jut′-, -jo͝ot′-)

Jí·va·ro (hē′vä rō′) ***n.*** ⟦AmSp *Jíbaro,* prob. altered < self-designation in Jívaro⟧ **1** *pl.* **-ros′** or **-ro′** a member of a South American Indian people living in S Ecuador and N Peru **2** the language of this people

☆**jive¹** (jīv) ***vt., vi.* jived, jiv′ing** ⟦altered < JIBE²: sense development, to taunt → banter → improvise → swing (music)⟧ [Slang] to speak (to) in a way that is exaggerated, insincere, flippant, etc., esp. in trying to fool or mislead ***—n.*** **1** [Slang] talk used in jiving someone **2** *former term for* JAZZ *or* SWING (*c.* 1930-45) ***—adj.*** [Slang] insincere, misleading, fake, fraudulent, etc.: also **jive′ass′** (-as′)

jive² (jīv) ***vi.* jived, jiv′ing** *var. of* JIBE¹ (sense 3)

jiz·ya or **jiz·yah** (jēz′yə) ***n.*** ⟦Ar *jizya* < Syriac *gzītā,* poll tax⟧ under traditional sharia law, a poll tax levied on non-Muslim subjects of an Islamic state

Jl *abbrev.* **1** *Bible* Joel **2** July

Jm *abbrev. Bible* James

Jn *abbrev. Bible* John

Jnr *abbrev.* [Brit.] Junior

jo (jō) ***n.,*** *pl.* **joes** ⟦var. of JOY⟧ [Scot.] a sweetheart

Jo·ab (jō′ab′) ***n.*** ⟦LL(Ec) < Gr(Ec) *Iōab* < Heb *yō'ābh,* lit., Yahweh is (his) father⟧ *Bible* the commander of David's army: 2 Sam. 10:7

Joan (jōn) ***n.*** a feminine name: see JOANNA

Jo·an·na (jō an′ə) ***n.*** ⟦ML, fem. of *Joannes:* see JOHN¹⟧ a feminine name: var. *Joan, Jane, Jean, Joanne;* equiv. L. & Ger. *Johanna,* Fr. *Jeanne,* It. *Giovanna,* Sp. *Juana*

Jo·anne (jō an′) ***n.*** a feminine name: var. *Joann:* see JOANNA

Joan of Arc (ärk) (Fr. name *Jeanne d'Arc*) 1412-31; Fr. heroine: defeated the English at Orléans (1429): burned at the stake for witchcraft: called the *Maid of Orléans:* also **Saint Joan of Arc**

Jo·ão Pes·so·a (zho͞o oun′ pə sō′ə) city in NE Brazil; capital of Paraíba state

job¹ (jäb) ***n.*** ⟦< ?⟧ **1** a specific piece of work, as in one's trade, or done by agreement for pay **2** anything one has to do; task; chore; duty **3** the thing or material being worked on **4** *a)* the action of doing a task, duty, or piece of work *b)* a result or product of such action [*a used car with a new paint job*] ☆**5** a position of employment; situation; work **6** [Informal] a criminal act or deed, as a theft, etc. **7** [Informal] any happening, affair, matter, object, etc. **8** [Slang] cosmetic surgery performed on a (specified) body part [*a nose job, boob job*] **9** [Chiefly Brit.] a thing done supposedly in the public interest but actually for private gain ***—adj.*** hired or done by the job: see also JOB LOT ***—vi.* jobbed, job′bing 1** to do odd jobs **2** to act as a jobber or broker **3** [Chiefly Brit.] to do public or official business dishonestly for private gain ***—vt.* 1** to buy and sell (goods) as wholesaler; handle as middleman **2** to let or sublet (work, contracts, etc.) **3** to hire or let for hire, as a horse or carriage **4** [Slang] to deceive; trick; cheat **5** [Chiefly Brit.] to transact (public business) dishonestly for private gain **—*SYN.*** POSITION, TASK **—odd jobs** miscellaneous tasks or pieces of work **—on the job 1** (while) working at one's job **2** [Slang] attentive to one's task or duty

job² (jäb) ***n., vt., vi.* jobbed, job′bing** ⟦ME *jobben,* to peck⟧ *dial. var. of* JAB

Job (jōb) ***n.*** ⟦LL(Ec) < Gr(Ec) *Iōb* < Heb *'Iyyōbh*⟧ *Bible* **1** a man who endured much suffering but did not lose his faith in God **2** the book telling of him: abbrev. *Jb*

☆**job action** any concerted disruption or cessation of work by employees in an attempt to force the granting of certain demands

☆**job analysis** a study of a specific job, or of all jobs, in an enterprise with respect to operations involved, working conditions, qualifications required, etc.

job·ber (jäb′ər) ***n.*** **1** a person who jobs; esp., one who buys goods in quantity from manufacturers or importers and sells them to dealers; wholesaler; middleman **2** a person who works by the job; also, one who does piecework **3** [Brit.] a person who deals in stock-exchange securities: distinguished from BROKER

job·ber·y (jäb′ər ē) ***n.*** ⟦see JOB¹, *vi.* 3⟧ [Chiefly Brit.] the carrying on of public or official business dishonestly for private gain

Job Corps a U.S. government program for training underprivileged youth for employment

☆**job·hold·er** (jäb′hōl′dər) ***n.*** a person who has a steady job; specif., a government employee

job·less (jäb′lis) ***adj.*** **1** without a job; unemployed **2** having to do with the unemployed **—the jobless** those who are unemployed **—job′less·ness *n.***

job lot 1 an assortment of goods for sale as one quantity **2** any random assortment, esp. when of inferior quality

Jobs (jäbz), **Steve** (legal name *Steven Paul Jobs*) 1955-2011; U.S. inventor & computer-industry executive

Job's comforter a person who aggravates one's misery while attempting or pretending to comfort: see Job 16:1-5

Job's-tears (jōbz′tirz′) ***n.*** ⟦see JOB⟧ a coarse, annual tropical grass (*Coix lacryma-jobi*) which bears hard, beadlike structures (modified leaves) containing edible grains ***—pl.n.*** the beadlike structures, often used ornamentally

Jo·cas·ta (jō kas′tə) ***n.*** ⟦L < Gr *Iokastē*⟧ *Gr. Myth.* the queen who unwittingly marries her own son, Oedipus, and kills herself when she finds out

Joc·e·lyn or **Joc·e·lin** (jäs′ə lin, jäs′lin) ***n.*** ⟦OFr *Joscelin* < OHG *Gauzelen,* dim. < *Gauta,* a Goth⟧ a feminine name

jock¹ (jäk) ***n.*** **1** *short for* JOCKSTRAP **2** [Slang] an athlete, esp. a male athlete

☆**jock²** (jäk) ***n.*** *short for:* **1** JOCKEY **2** [Slang] *a)* DISC JOCKEY *b)* VJ

☆**jock·ette** (jäk′et′) ***n.*** [Informal] a woman JOCKEY (sense 1)

jock·ey (jäk′ē) ***n.,*** *pl.* **-eys** ⟦< *Jocky, Jockie,* northern Eng and Scot form of *Jacky,* dim. of JACK⟧ **1** a person whose work is riding horses in races ☆**2** [Slang] one who operates a specified vehicle, machine, etc. ***— vt., vi.* -eyed, -ey·ing 1** to ride (a horse) in a race **2** to cheat; trick; swindle **3** *a)* to maneuver for position or advantage *b)* to bring about by such maneuvering ☆**4** [Slang] to be the operator, pilot, etc. (of)

jockey shorts ⟦< *Jockey,* a trademark⟧ [*often* **J- s-**] boys' or men's closefitting knit undershorts, as of cotton, with an elastic waistband

☆**jock itch** [Informal] a skin infection in the genital area caused by a fungus; tinea cruris

☆**jock·strap** (jäk′strap′) ***n.*** ⟦slang *jock,* penis + STRAP⟧ [Informal] ATHLETIC SUPPORTER

jo·cose (jō kōs′) ***adj.*** ⟦L *jocosus* < *jocus,* a jest, JOKE⟧ joking or playful; humorous **—*SYN.*** WITTY **—jo·cose′ly *adv.* —jo·cose′ness *n.***

jo·cos·i·ty (jō käs′ə tē) ***n.*** ⟦ML *iocositas*⟧ **1** the quality or state of being jocose **2** *pl.* **-ties** a jocose action or remark

joc·u·lar (jäk′yə lər) ***adj.*** ⟦L *jocularis* < *joculus,* dim. of *jocus,* JOKE⟧ **1** joking; humorous; full of fun **2** said as a joke **—*SYN.*** WITTY **—joc′u·lar′i·ty** (-lar′ə tē) ***n.,*** *pl.* **-ties —joc′u·lar·ly *adv.***

joc·und (jäk′ənd, jō′kənd) ***adj.*** ⟦ME < OFr *jocond* < LL *jocundus* (altered by assoc. with L *jocus,* JOKE) < L *jucundus,* pleasant < *juvare,* to help⟧ cheerful; genial **—jo·cun·di·ty** (jō kun′də tē) ***n.,*** *pl.* **-ties —joc′und·ly *adv.***

jodh·pur (jäd′pər) ***n.*** ⟦after fol., where the breeches first became popular⟧ **1** [*pl.*] riding breeches made loose and full above the knees and tight from the knees to the ankles **2** a boot high enough to cover the ankle, with an adjustable buckle and strap, or an elastic insert, at the side

Jodh·pur (jōd′po͝or′, jäd′-) **1** city in NW India **2** former state of NW India

Jo·di or **Jo·dy** (jō′dē) ***n.*** a feminine and masculine name

Joe (jō) ***n.*** **1** *nickname for* JOSEPH¹ ☆**2** [*often* **j-**] [Slang] fellow; guy ☆**3** [**j-**] [Slang] coffee

Joe Blow [Slang] **1** *personification of* an average, ordinary man **2** a name used to refer to a man whose name is not known or whose typicalness is being emphasized

Jo·el (jō′əl, -el′) ***n.*** ⟦LL(Ec) < Gr(Ec) *Iōēl* < Heb *yō'ēl,* lit., the Lord is God⟧ **1** a masculine name **2** *Bible a)* a Hebrew prophet, probably of the 5th cent. B.C. *b)* the book of his preachings (abbrev. *Jl*)

☆**joe-pye weed** (jō′pī′) ⟦< ? the name of an Indian doctor said to have used the plant as medicine⟧ any of a number of perennial American plants (genus *Eupatorium*) of the composite family, with whorled leaves and clusters of rayless, pinkish or purple flower heads

jo·ey (jō′ē) ***n.*** ⟦< *joè,* name in a language of Australia⟧ **1** a young kangaroo **2** [Austral.] any young animal

Jof·fre (zhôf′r′), **Jo·seph Jacques Cé·saire** (zhō zef′ zhäk sā zer′) 1852-1931; Fr. general: commander in chief of French forces in WWI

jog¹ (jäg) ***vt.* jogged, jog′ging** ⟦ME *joggen,* to spur (a horse), var. of *jaggen,* to JAG¹⟧ **1** *a)* to give a little shake, shove, or jerk to *b)* to nudge **2** to stir or revive (a person's memory) **3** to cause to jog ***—vi.* 1** to move along at a slow, steady, jolting pace or trot; specif., to engage in jogging as a form of exercise **2** to go (*on* or *along*) in a steady, slow, heavy manner ***—n.* 1** a little shake, shove, or nudge **2** a slow, steady, jolting motion or trot **3** an act or instance of jogging **—jog′ger *n.***

jog² (jäg) ***n.*** ⟦var. of JAG¹⟧ **1** a projecting or notched part, esp. one at right angles, in a surface or line **2** a sharp, temporary change of direction, as in a road or one's course ***—vi.* jogged, jog′ging** to form or make a jog [*turn left where the road jogs*]

jog·ging (jäg′iŋ) ***n.*** the practice of trotting at a slow, steady pace for some distance as a form of exercise

jog·gle¹ (jäg′əl) ***vt., vi.* -gled, -gling** ⟦freq. of JOG¹⟧ to shake or jolt slightly ***—n.*** a slight jolt

jog·gle² (jäg′əl) ***n.*** ⟦< JOG²⟧ **1** *a)* a joint between two surfaces of wood, stone, etc. made by cutting a notch in one and making a projection in the other to fit into it so as to prevent slippage *b)* a notch or projection for such a joint **2** DOWEL ***—vt.* -gled, -gling** to join by joggles

joggle post 1 a post made of pieces joined by joggles **2** a king post with shoulders to receive the feet of struts

Jog·ja·kar·ta (jäg′yə kärt′ə) *var. of* YOGYAKARTA

jog trot 1 a slow, steady trot **2** a routine, monotonous, or leisurely way of doing something

Jo·han·na (jō han′ə) ***n.*** a feminine name: see JOANNA

jo·han·nes (jō han′ēz′) ***n.,*** *pl.* **-nes** ⟦< ML *Johannes* for *John* V, king of Portugal (1706-50), who first issued them⟧ a Portuguese gold coin of the 18th and 19th cent.

Jo·han·nes·burg (jō han′is burg′, -hän′-) capital of Gauteng province, South Africa

Jo·han·nine (jō han′in, -īn′) ***adj.*** ⟦< ML *Johannes* (see JOHN¹) + -INE¹⟧ of or characteristic of the Apostle and Evangelist John or of the books of the New Testament attributed to him

john (jän) ***n.*** [Slang] **1** a toilet ☆**2** *a)* any man, esp. one who is an easy mark *b)* a customer of a prostitute

John¹ (jän) ***n.*** ⟦ME *Jon* < OFr *Johan, Jehan, Jan* < ML *Johannes* < LL(Ec) *Joannes* < Gr(Ec) *Iōannēs* < Heb *yōhānān,* contr. < *yehōhānān,* lit., Yahweh is gracious⟧ **1** a masculine name: dim. *Jack, Johnnie, Johnny;* equiv. Fr. *Jean,* Ger. *Hans, Johann, Johannes,* Ir. *Sean, Shane, Shawn,* It. *Giovanni,*

Pol. *Jan*, Russ. *Ivan*, Scot. *Iain, Ian, Jock*, Sp. *Juan*, Welsh *Evan*; fem. *Jane, Jean, Jeanne, Joan, Joanna, Joanne, Johanna* **2** *Bible a)* one of the twelve Apostles and one of the four Evangelists, to whom are ascribed the fourth Gospel, the three Letters of John, and the Book of Revelation: his day is Dec. 27 (also **Saint John the Divine**) *b)* the fourth book of the New Testament (abbrev. *Jn*) *c)* any of the three Letters of John *d)* JOHN THE BAPTIST

John[2] (jän) **1** (called *John Lackland*) 1167?-1216; king of England (1199-1216): forced by his barons to sign the Magna Carta: son of Henry II **2 John III** (born *John Sobieski*) 1624-96; king of Poland (1674-96) **3 John XXIII** (born *Angelo Giuseppe Roncalli*) 1881-1963; pope (1958-63) **4 Augustus (Edwin)** 1879-1961; Eng. painter

John Barleycorn *personification of* corn liquor, malt liquor, etc.

☆**john·boat** (jän′bōt′) *n.* a flat-bottomed boat with square ends, used on inland waters as for fishing

John Bull ⟦title character in John Arbuthnot's *History of John Bull* (1712)⟧ *personification of* England or an Englishman

John Doe *see* DOE

John Do·ry (dôr′ē) *pl.* **John Do′rys** ⟦JOHN[1] + DORY[2]⟧ any of various bony fishes (order Zeiformes); esp., *a)* an edible, marine, European fish (*Zeus faber*) with a yellow-ringed black spot on each side of its flat body *b)* a similar silvery fish (*Zenopsis conchifera*) of the W Atlantic

☆**John Hancock** [Informal] a person's signature: so called because John Hancock's signature on the Declaration of Independence is large and bold

☆**John Henry[1]** [Informal] one's signature

☆**John Henry[2]** *American Folklore* the hero, usually depicted as black, of an American ballad, who died after a contest pitting his strength with a sledge hammer against that of a steam drill

john·ny (jän′ē) *n., pl.* **-nies** ⟦< ? fol.: see JACKET⟧ ☆a short muslin gown with short sleeves and a back opening that is closed with ties, worn as by hospital patients

John·ny or **John·nie** (jän′ē) *n.* ⟦cf. JACK⟧ **1** *nickname for* JOHN[1] **2** *pl.* **-nies** [Informal, Chiefly Brit.] any man or boy

☆**john·ny·cake** (jän′ē kāk′) *n.* ⟦altered (by assoc. with prec. & CAKE) < north Eng dial *jannock, johnnick*, a bread of oatmeal or wheat flour < ME *janok* (< ? *Jan*, var. of *Jo(h)n*)⟧ **1** a kind of thin, flat, corn bread baked on a griddle **2** any corn bread

☆**John·ny-come-late·ly** (-kum′lāt′lē) *n., pl.* **-lies** [Informal] one who is late or recent in arriving at a place, position, or viewpoint

☆**John·ny-jump-up** (-jump′up′) *n.* **1** WILD PANSY **2** DAFFODIL **3** any of various American violets

☆**Johnny on the spot** [Informal] a person who is ready and at hand whenever needed: also written **John′ny-on-the-spot′** *n.*

☆**Johnny Reb** (reb) ⟦JOHNNY + REB(EL)⟧ *personification of* a Confederate soldier

John of Gaunt (gônt) Duke of Lancaster 1340-99; founder of the house of Lancaster: son of Edward III

John of the Cross, Saint (born *Juan de Yepes y Álvarez*) (1542-91); Sp. monk & mystic: his day is Nov. 24

John Paul 1 John Paul I (born *Albino Luciani*) 1912-78; pope (1978) **2 John Paul II** (born *Karol Wojtyła*) 1920-2005; pope (1978-2005)

☆**John Q. Public** *personification of* an ordinary or average citizen, esp. of the U.S.

Johns (jänz), **Jasper** 1930- ; U.S. painter, sculptor, & printmaker

John·son (jän′sən) **1 Andrew** 1808-75; 17th president of the U.S. (1865-69) **2 James Wel·don** (wel′dən) 1871-1938; U.S. writer & diplomat **3 Lyndon Baines** (lin′dən bānz′) 1908-73; 36th president of the U.S. (1963-69) **4 Philip Cor·tel·you** (kôr tel′yo͞o′) 1906-2005; U.S. architect **5 Robert (Leroy)** 1911-38; U.S. blues guitarist, singer, & composer **6 Samuel** 1709-84; Eng. lexicographer, writer, & critic: known as *Dr. Johnson*

☆**Johnson grass** a forage and pasture grass (*Sorghum halepense*), widespread in the S U.S., often as a weed

John·so·ni·an (jän sō′nē ən) *adj.* of, like, or characteristic of Samuel Johnson or his style

☆**Johnson noise** ⟦after J. B. *Johnson*, 20th-c. U.S. physicist⟧ thermal background noise in a radio receiver

Johns·ton (jänz′tən) **1 Albert Sidney** 1803-62; Confederate general **2 Joseph Eggleston** 1807-91; Confederate general

John the Baptist *Bible* the forerunner and baptizer of Jesus: he was killed by Herod: Matt. 3

Jo·hore (jə hôr′) state of Malaysia, at the tip of the Malay Peninsula: 7,330 sq mi (18,985 sq km)

joie de vi·vre (zhwȧd vē′vr′) ⟦Fr⟧ (the) joy of living; high spirits, exuberance, etc.

join (join) *vt.* ⟦ME *joinen* < OFr *joindre* < L *jungere*, to bind together, YOKE⟧ **1** to put or bring together; connect; fasten **2** to make into one; unite [*join* forces, *join* people in marriage] **3** to become a part or member of; enter into association with [to *join* a club] **4** to go to and combine with [the path *joins* the highway] **5** *a)* to enter into the company of; accompany [*join* us later] *b)* to participate or take part with [they *join* me in congratulating you] **6** [Informal] to adjoin **7** *Geom.* to connect with a straight line or curve —*vi.* **1** to come together; meet **2** *a)* to enter into association *b)* to become a member of a group or organization: often with *up* **3** to participate (*in* a conversation, singing, an activity, etc.) —*n.* a place of joining; joint —**join battle** to start fighting or competing —**join′a·ble** *adj.*

SYN.—**join** is the general term implying a bringing or coming together of two or more things and may suggest direct contact, affiliation, etc.; **combine** implies a mingling together of things, often with a loss of distinction of elements that completely merge with one another [to *combine* milk and water]; **unite** implies a joining or combining of things to form a single whole [the *United* States]; **connect** implies attachment by some fastening or relationship [roads *connected* by a bridge, the duties *connected* with a job]; **link** stresses firmness of a connection [*linked* together in a common cause]; **associate** implies a joining with another or others as a companion, partner, etc. and, in extended use, suggests a connection made in the mind [to *associate* Freud's name with psychoanalysis]; **consolidate** implies a merger of distinct and separate units into a single whole for resulting compactness, strength, efficiency, etc. [to *consolidate* one's debts] —*ANT.* **separate, part**

join·der (join′dər) *n.* ⟦OFr *joindre*, use of inf. as n.: see prec.⟧ **1** a joining; act of meeting or coming together **2** *Law a)* a joining of causes *b)* a joining of parties as plaintiffs or defendants *c)* a uniting on facts or procedure *d)* an accepting of an issue offered

join·er (join′ər) *n.* ⟦ME *joinour* < OFr *joignour* < *joindre*: see JOIN⟧ **1** a person or thing that joins **2** a worker who constructs and finishes interior woodwork, as doors, molding, or stairs ☆**3** [Informal] a person given to joining various organizations

join·er·y (-ər ē) *n.* the work or skill of a joiner

joint (joint) *n.* ⟦OFr < L *junctus*, pp. of *jungere*, to join, YOKE⟧ **1** a place or part where two things or parts are joined **2** the way in which two things are joined at such a part **3** one of the parts or sections of a jointed whole **4** a large cut of meat with the bone still in it, as for a roast ☆**5** [Slang] *a)* a cheap bar, nightclub, etc. *b)* any house, building, etc. *c)* a prison ☆**6** [Slang] a marijuana cigarette **7** *Anat. a)* a place or part where two bones or corresponding structures are joined, usually so that they can move *b)* the way in which they are joined **8** *Bot.* a point where a branch or leaf grows out of the stem **9** *Geol.* a fracture in a rock mass, along which displacement has not occurred —*adj.* ⟦OFr *joint, jointe*, pp. of *joindre*: see JOIN⟧ **1** joined as to time; concurrent **2** common to two or more persons, governments, etc. as to ownership or action [a *joint* declaration, *joint* property, *joint* custody] **3** sharing with someone else [a *joint* owner] —*vt.* **1** to connect by a joint or joints **2** to give a joint or joints to **3** to prepare (a board or stave) for joining to another **4** to cut (meat) into joints; separate at the joints —**out of joint 1** not in place at the joint; dislocated **2** disordered or disorganized **3** inappropriate

joint account a bank account in the name of two or more persons, each of whom may withdraw funds

☆**Joint Chiefs of Staff** a group within the Department of Defense, consisting of the Chief of Staff of the Army, the Chief of Naval Operations, the Chief of Staff of the Air Force, the Commandant of the Marine Corps, a director, and a chairman

☆**joint committee** a committee with members from both houses of a bicameral legislature, or from two or more organizations

joint·ed (joint′id) *adj.* having joints

joint·er (joint′ər) *n.* **1** a person or machine that joints **2** a long plane used in jointing boards **3** a triangular device with an edge, fastened to a plow beam **4** a tool for finishing mortar joints, as of brickwork

joint·ly (joint′lē) *adv.* in a joint manner; together

☆**joint resolution** a resolution passed by both houses of a bicameral legislature: it has the force of a law if signed by the chief executive or passed over his veto

joint·ress (join′tris) *n.* a woman who has a jointure

joint return a single income tax return filed by a married couple, combining their individual incomes

joint stock stock or capital held in a common fund

joint-stock company (joint′stäk′) a business firm with a joint stock, owned by the stockholders in shares which each may sell or transfer independently

joint tenancy ownership of property by two or more persons, each having an undivided interest in the entire property and SURVIVORSHIP (sense 2) —**joint tenant**

join·ture (join′chər) *n.* ⟦< OFr < L *junctura*, a joining < *jungere*: see YOKE⟧ **1** [Now Rare] an act or instance of joining **2** *Law a)* an arrangement by which a husband grants real property to his wife for her use after his death *b)* the property thus settled; widow's portion *c)* [Obs.] the holding of property jointly

☆**joint·weed** (joint′wēd′) *n.* a plant (*Polygonella articulata*) of the buckwheat family, with threadlike leaves, jointed stems, and clusters of small, white flowers

joint·worm (-wurm′) *n.* ☆the larva of a genus (*Harmolita*, family Eurytomidae) of small wasps which attack grain stems and cause galls to form in the joints

Join·ville (zhwan vēl′), **Jean de** (zhän də) 1224?-1317; Fr. chronicler

joist (joist) *n.* ⟦ME *giste* < OFr, a bed, couch, beam < *gesir*, to lie < L *jacere*, to lie, throw: see JET[1]⟧ any of the parallel planks or beams that hold up the planks of a floor or the laths of a ceiling —*vt.* to provide with joists

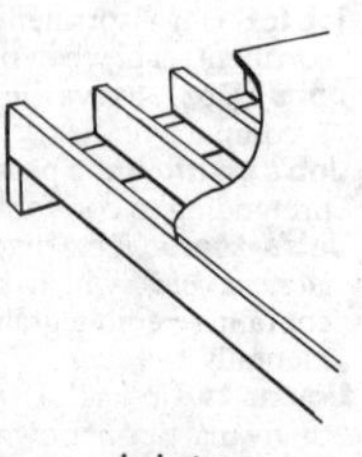

joists

jo·jo·ba (hō hō′bə) ***n.*** ⟦Sp⟧ an evergreen desert shrub (*Simmondsia californica*) of the box family, found in Mexico and the SW U.S., with a seed (**jojoba bean**) containing an odorless, colorless liquid wax (**jojoba oil**) used in cosmetics, lubricants, etc.

joke (jōk) ***n.*** ⟦L *jocus,* a joke, game < IE base **jek-,* to speak > OHG *jehan*⟧ **1** anything said or done to arouse laughter; specif., *a)* a funny anecdote with a punchline *b)* an amusing trick played on someone **2** the humorous element in a situation **3** a thing done or said merely in fun **4** a person or thing to be laughed at, not to be taken seriously, because absurd, ridiculous, etc. —***vi.*** **joked, jok′ing** ⟦< the *n.* or L *jocari,* to joke⟧ **1** to tell or play jokes **2** to say or do something as a joke; jest —***vt.*** **1** [Now Rare] to make fun of; make (a person) the object of jokes or teasing **2** to bring to a specified condition by joking —**no joke** a serious matter —**jok′ing·ly** ***adv.***

jok·er (jōk′ər) ***n.*** **1** a person who jokes ☆**2** a cunningly worded provision put into a law, legal document, etc. to make it different from what it seems to be ☆**3** any hidden, unsuspected difficulty ☆**4** an extra playing card, usually with a conventionalized picture of a court jester on it, used in some games as the highest trump or as a wild card **5** [Slang] a person, fellow, etc.; esp., one deserving contempt, as because of being foolish, inept, or disagreeable

joke·ster (jōk′stər) ***n.*** ⟦see -STER⟧ JOKER (*n.* 1)

jok·ey (jōk′ē) ***adj.*** amusing; comical or lighthearted; humorous: also **jok′y** —**jok′i·ly** ***adv.*** —**jok′i·ness** ***n.***

Jok·ja·kar·ta (jäk′yə kärt′ə) *var. of* YOGYAKARTA

jo·lie laide (zhô lē led′) ⟦Fr, lit., pretty ugly woman⟧ a girl or woman oddly attractive though not conventionally beautiful

Jo·li·et¹ or **Jol·li·et** (jō′lē et′, jō′lē et′; *Fr* zhô lye′), **Louis** 1645-1700; Fr.-Cdn. explorer of the Mississippi

Jo·li·et² (jō′lē et′, jō′lē et′) ⟦after prec.⟧ city in NE Ill.

Jo·liot-Cu·rie (zhô lyō kü rē′) **1 (Jean) Fré·dé·ric** (frā dā rēk′) (born *Jean Frédéric Joliot*) 1900-58; Fr. nuclear physicist **2 I·rène** (ē ren′) (born *Irène Curie*) 1897-1956; Fr. nuclear physicist: wife of Frédéric & daughter of Pierre & Marie Curie

jol·li·fy (jäl′ə fī′) ***vt., vi.*** **-fied′, -fy′ing** [Informal] to make or be jolly or merry —**jol′li·fi·ca′tion** ***n.***

jol·li·ty (jäl′ə tē) ***n.*** ⟦ME *jolite* < OFr < *joli:* see fol.⟧ **1** the quality or state of being jolly; fun; gaiety **2** *pl.* **-ties** [Brit.] a jolly occasion; party

jol·ly (jäl′ē) ***adj.*** **-li·er, -li·est** ⟦ME *joli* < OFr, prob. < ON *jol,* YULE⟧ **1** full of high spirits and good humor; merry **2** [Informal] enjoyable; pleasant —***adv.*** **-li·er, -li·est** [Brit. Informal] very; altogether — ***vt., vi.*** **-lied, -ly·ing** [Informal] ☆to try to make (a person) feel good or agreeable, as by coaxing or flattering: often with *along* —***n., pl.*** **-lies** [Brit. Informal] a British marine —**get one's jollies** [Slang] to have fun or get pleasure; often, specif., from that which is cheap or disreputable —**jol′li·ly** ***adv.*** —**jol′li·ness** ***n.***

jolly boat ⟦< MDu *jolle,* yawl + BOAT⟧ a sailing vessel's small boat, usually carried on the stern

Jolly Roger ⟦JOLLY + *Roger,* pirate flag < ROGER¹⟧ [Historical] a black flag of pirates, with white skull and crossbones

Jo·lo (hō lō′, hō′lō′) island in the Philippines, southwest of Mindanao: largest island in Sulu Archipelago: 345 sq mi (894 sq km)

jolt (jōlt) ***vt.*** ⟦earlier *jot,* to jog, bump, of echoic orig: prob. infl. by obs. *jowl,* to strike⟧ **1** to shake up or jar, as with a bumpy ride or sharp blow **2** to shock or surprise —***vi.*** to move along in a bumpy, jerky manner —***n.*** **1** a sudden jerk or shake, as from a blow **2** a shock or surprise ☆**3** a drink of liquor neat —**jolt′ing·ly** ***adv.*** —**jolt′y** ***adj.***

Jo·nah (jō′nə) ***n.*** ⟦LL(Ec) *Jonas* < Gr(Ec) *Iōnas* < Heb *jōnāh,* lit., a dove⟧ **1** a masculine name: var. *Jonas* **2** *Bible a)* a Hebrew prophet: thrown overboard in a storm sent because he had disobeyed God, he was swallowed by a big fish, but three days later was cast up on the shore unharmed *b)* the book telling Jonah's story (abbrev. **Jon**) **3** any person said to bring bad luck by being present

☆**Jonah crab** a large, reddish, edible crab (*Cancer borealis*) of the NE coast of North America

Jon·a·than (jän′ə thən) ***n.*** ⟦Heb *yonāthān,* contr. < *yehonāthān,* lit., Yahweh has given⟧ **1** a masculine name: dim. *Jon* **2** *Bible* Saul's oldest son, a close friend of David: 1 Sam. 18-20 ☆**3** BROTHER JONATHAN ☆**4** a late fall variety of apple

jones (jōnz) ***n.*** ⟦< slang term *jones,* thing⟧ [*often* **J-**] [Slang] **1** an addiction to a drug, specif. to heroin **2** any strong or compulsive craving

Jones (jōnz) **1 Howard Mum·ford** (mum′fərd) 1892-1980; U.S. educator & critic **2 In·i·go** (in′i gō′) 1573-1652; Eng. architect & stage designer **3 John Paul** (born *John Paul*) 1747-92; Am. naval officer in the Revolutionary War, born in Scotland

jon·gleur (jäŋ′glər; *Fr* zhōn glër′) ***n.*** ⟦Fr < OFr *jogleor:* see JUGGLER⟧ a wandering minstrel in medieval France and England, who entertained by reciting or singing

Jon·quière (zhōn kyer′) ⟦after J. P. Taffanel, Marquis de la Jonquière (1685-1752), gov. of New France (1749-52)⟧ *see* SAGUENAY (sense 1)

jon·quil (jäŋ′kwil, jän′-) ***n.*** ⟦Fr *jonquille* < Sp *junquillo,* dim. of *junco,* a reed < L *juncus,* a rush < IE base **yoini-,* rush > MIr *ain,* rush, ON *einir,* juniper⟧ **1** *a)* a species of narcissus (*Narcissus jonquilla*) having relatively small yellow flowers with a very short crown, and long, slender leaves *b)* its bulb or flower **2** loosely, any narcissus

Jon·son (jän′sən), **Ben** 1572?-1637; Eng. dramatist & poet —**Jon·so·ni·an** (jän sō′nē ən) ***adj.***

Jop·lin (jäp′lin), **Scott** 1868-1917; U.S. ragtime pianist & composer

Jop·pa (jäp′ə) *ancient name for* JAFFA

Jor·daens (yôr′däns′), **Ja·cob** (yä′kôp) 1593-1678; Fl. painter

Jor·dan¹ (jôrd′′n) ***n.*** ⟦after the JORDAN³, from the practice, among Crusaders and pilgrims, of bringing back water from the river for baptizing their children⟧ a masculine and feminine name

Jor·dan² (jôrd′′n), **David Starr** (stär) 1851-1931; U.S. educator & naturalist

Jor·dan³ (jôrd′′n) **1** river in the Near East, flowing from the Anti-Lebanon mountains south through the Sea of Galilee, through Jordan, into the Dead Sea: 200 mi (322 km) **2** country in the Near East, east of Israel: 35,637 sq mi (92,300 sq km); cap. Amman —**Jor·da·ni·an** (jôr dā′nē ən) ***adj., n.***

Jordan almond ⟦altered (by assoc. with the proper name *Jordan*) < ME *jardyne almaunde* < OFr *jardin,* garden + ME *almande,* ALMOND: i.e., a cultivated almond⟧ **1** a variety of large Spanish almond **2** a confection consisting of such an almond with a smooth, hard sugar coating, often variously colored

jo·rum (jō′rəm, jôr′əm) ***n.*** ⟦prob. after *Joram* (2 Sam. 8:10), bringer of silver vessels < Heb *Yōrām*⟧ **1** a large drinking bowl **2** the amount of liquor that it holds

Jos *abbrev.* **1** Joseph **2** *Bible* Joshua **3** Josiah

Jo·seph¹ (jō′zəf, -səf) ***n.*** ⟦LL(Ec) < Gr(Ec) *Iōsēph* < Heb *yōsēph,* lit., may he add: see Gen. 30:24⟧ **1** a masculine name: dim. *Joe, Joey;* equiv. L. *Josephus,* It. *Giuseppe,* Sp. *José;* fem. *Josepha, Josephine* **2** *Bible a)* Jacob's eleventh son, whose mother was Rachel: Joseph was sold into slavery in Egypt by his jealous brothers but became a high official there: Gen. 30:22-24; 37; 45 *b)* the husband of Mary, mother of Jesus: Matt. 1:18-25: his day is March 19 (also called **Saint Joseph**) **3** ⟦see JOSEPH'S COAT⟧ a woman's long riding coat, with a cape, worn in the 18th cent.

Jo·seph² (jō′zef, -səf) 1840?-1904; Nez Percé Indian chief

Jo·se·phine¹ (jō′zə fēn′, -sə-) ***n.*** ⟦Fr *Joséphine* < *Joseph:* see JOSEPH¹⟧ a feminine name: dim. *Jo, Josie;* var. *Josepha*

Jo·se·phine² (jō′zə fēn′, -sə-) 1763-1814; wife of Napoleon (1796-1809) & empress of France (1804-09): wife (1779-94) of Vicomte *Alexandre de Beauharnais* (1760-94), Fr. army officer

Joseph of Arimathea *Bible* a wealthy disciple who provided a tomb for Jesus' body: Matt. 27:57-60

☆**Joseph's coat** ⟦with ref. to *Joseph's coat* (*of many colors*), Gen. 37:3, as rendered in the KJV: see JOSEPH¹ (*n. 2a*)⟧ an ornamental species of pigweed (*Amaranthus tricolor*) having red, yellow, and green upper leaves

Jo·seph·son junction (jō′zef sən, -səf-) ⟦after Brian *Josephson* (b. 1940), Brit physicist⟧ a low-power, high-speed electronic switching device consisting of a thin insulator between two superconducting metals: it operates at a temperature near absolute zero

Jo·se·phus (jō sē′fəs), **(Flavius)** A.D. 37-95?; Jewish historian who wrote works on Jewish history

josh (jäsh) [Informal] ***vt., vi.*** ⟦< ?⟧ to ridicule in a good-humored way; tease jokingly —***n.*** good-humored joking —**josh′er** ***n.*** —**josh′ing·ly** ***adv.***

Josh·u·a (jäsh′yōō ə, jäsh′ōō ə) ***n.*** ⟦Heb *yehōshū'a,* lit., help of Jehovah: see JESUS²⟧ **1** a masculine name: dim. *Josh* **2** *Bible a)* Moses' successor, who led the Israelites into the Promised Land *b)* the book telling about him (abbrev. *Josh, Jos, or Js*)

☆**Joshua tree** ⟦? Mormon coinage on the fancied resemblance of the angular branches to the arms of prec. leading the Israelites⟧ a tree (*Yucca brevifolia*) of the agave family, found in the SW U.S. and characterized by branches that are extended grotesquely like upraised arms and by dagger-shaped, spine-tipped leaves

Jo·si·ah (jō sī′ə, -zī′ə) ***n.*** ⟦Heb *yōshīyāh,* lit., the Lord supports⟧ *Bible* a king of Judah in the 7th cent. B.C.: 2 Kings 22, 23: abbrev. *Jos*

Jos·quin des Prez (*or* Des·prez) (zhôs kan′ dā prā′) 1440?-1521; Fr. composer

joss (jôs, jäs) ***n.*** ⟦PidE < Port *deos* < L *deus,* a god: see DEITY⟧ a figure of a traditional Chinese deity

joss house a traditional Chinese temple

joss stick a thin stick of dried paste made of fragrant wood dust, burned originally by the Chinese as incense

jos·tle (jäs′əl) ***vt., vi.*** **-tled, -tling** ⟦earlier *justle,* freq. < ME *justen:* see JOUST⟧ **1** to bump or push, as in a crowd; elbow or shove roughly **2** to push (one's way) by shoving or bumping **3** to come or bring into close contact **4** to contend (*with* someone *for* something) —***n.*** the act of jostling; rough bump or shove —**jos′tler** ***n.***

jot (jät) ***n.*** ⟦L *iota* < Gr *iōta,* the letter *i,* the smallest letter (hence, very small thing): see IOTA⟧ a trifling amount; the smallest bit —***vt.*** **jot′ted, jot′ting** ⟦prob. < the *n.*⟧ to make a brief, quick note of: usually with *down* —**jot′ter** ***n.***

jo·ta (hō′tə) ***n.*** ⟦Sp < OSp *sota* < *sotar,* to dance < L *saltare,* to leap: see SALTANT⟧ a Spanish dance in 3/4 time performed by a man and woman to the rhythm of castanets

jot·ting (jät′iŋ) ***n.*** [*often pl.*] a short note jotted down

Jo·tunn or **Jo·tun** (yô′toon′) ***n.*** ⟦ON *jǫtunn,* akin to OE *eoten,* a giant < IE base **ed-,* to eat: hence, orig., glutton or ? man-eater⟧ *Norse Myth.* any of the giants

Jo·tunn·heim or **Jo·tun·heim** (-hām′) ***n.*** ⟦ON *jǫtunheimar,* pl. < *jǫtunn* (see prec.) + *heimr,* HOME⟧ *Norse Myth.* the home of the giants

jou·al (zhōō äl′) ***n.*** ⟦Fr < a dial. pronun. of *cheval,* horse⟧ *name for* any of various dialects of Canadian French: orig., and still sometimes, a derogatory term, used esp. for those dialects that diverge most widely from standard speech

joule (jo͞ol; *occas.* joul) ***n.*** ⟦after fol.⟧ *Physics* the basic unit of energy or work in the SI & MKS systems, equal to the amount of work done by a force of one newton acting through a distance of one meter: abbrev. *J*

Joule (jo͞ol), **James Prescott** 1818-89; Eng. physicist

jounce (jouns) ***vt., vi.*** **jounced, jounc′ing** ⟦ME *jounsen* < ?⟧ to shake, jolt, or bounce, as in riding —***n.*** a bounce or jolt —**jounc′y** ***adj.***

jour *abbrev.* **1** journal **2** journeyman

jour·nal (jʉr′nəl) ***n.*** ⟦ME, book containing forms of worship for the day hours (Little Hours) < OFr, lit., daily < L *diurnalis* < *dies,* day (see DEITY): sense 3 prob. via It *giornale,* of same orig.⟧ **1** *a)* a daily record of happenings, as a diary *b)* a collection of one's thoughts or observations, written over time as on a particular topic or as a creative exercise **2** a record of the transactions of a legislature, club, etc. **3** a daily newspaper: often used in newspaper titles **4** any newspaper or periodical, as one dealing with scientific or professional matters **5** *Bookkeeping a)* DAYBOOK *b)* a book of original entry, used in the double-entry system, for recording all transactions, in the order in which they occur, with an indication of the special accounts to which they belong **6** ⟦orig. Scot⟧ *Mech.* the part of a rotary axle or shaft that turns in a bearing —***vi.*** to keep a JOURNAL (***n.*** 1)

journal box *Mech.* a casing or housing for a journal

jour·nal·ese (jʉr′nəl ēz′) ***n.*** a facile or sensational style, with many clichés, regarded as typical of many newspapers, magazines, etc.

jour·nal·ing (jʉr′nəl iŋ) ***n.*** the keeping of a JOURNAL (***n.*** 1*b*)

jour·nal·ism (jʉr′nəl iz′əm) ***n.*** ⟦Fr *journalisme* < *journal:* see JOURNAL⟧ **1** the work of gathering, writing, editing, and publishing or disseminating news, as through newspapers and magazines or by radio and television **2** journalistic writing **3** newspapers and magazines collectively

jour·nal·ist (-ist) ***n.*** **1** a person whose occupation is journalism; reporter, news editor, etc. **2** a person who keeps a journal or diary

jour·nal·is·tic (jʉr′nəl is′tik) ***adj.*** of or characteristic of journalists or journalism —**jour′nal·is′ti·cal′ly** ***adv.***

jour·nal·ize (jʉr′nəl īz′) ***vt., vi.*** **-ized′, -iz′ing** to record (transactions, daily events, etc.) in a journal

jour·ney (jʉr′nē) ***n., pl.*** **-neys** ⟦ME *journee* < OFr < VL **diurnata,* day's journey, day's work < LL *diurnum,* a daily portion < L *diurnus,* daily < *dies,* day: see DEITY⟧ **1** the act or an instance of traveling from one place to another; trip **2** any course or passage from one stage or experience to another —***vi.*** **-neyed, -ney·ing** to go on a trip; travel [*to journey through France on a motorbike*] —**SYN.** TRIP —**jour′ney·er** ***n.***

jour·ney·man (-mən) ***n., pl.*** **-men** (-mən) ⟦ME < *journee* (see prec.), in sense "day's work" + *man*⟧ **1** *a)* [Obs.] a worker for a daily wage *b)* a worker who has served an apprenticeship and is therefore qualified to work at a specified trade **2** any sound, experienced, but not brilliant craftsman or performer

jour·ney·work (-wʉrk′) ***n.*** work of a journeyman

joust (joust; *occas.* just) ***n.*** ⟦ME *jouste* < OFr < *jouster:* see the ***vi.***⟧ **1** a combat or contest with lances, as between two medieval knights on horseback; esp., such a formal combat as part of a tournament **2** [*pl.*] a tournament —***vi.*** ⟦ME *justen* < OFr *jouster, juster* < VL **juxtare,* to approach, tilt < L *juxta:* see JUXTA-⟧ to engage in a joust

Jove (jōv) ***n.*** ⟦< L *Jovis* (used as gen. of *Juppiter,* JUPITER) < OL *Jovis* (gen. *Jovis*) < IE **diwes,* gen. of **dyēus* (> Gr *Zeus*) < base **dei-,* to gleam, shine > DEITY⟧ JUPITER, the Roman god —**by Jove!** an exclamation used to express astonishment, emphasis, etc.

jo·vi·al (jō′vē əl) ***adj.*** ⟦Fr < LL *Jovialis,* of Jupiter < L *Jovis:* see prec.⟧ **1** [**J-**] JOVIAN **2** full of hearty, playful good humor; genial and cheerful: from the astrological notion that people born under the sign of Jupiter are joyful —**jo′vi·al′i·ty** (-al′ə tē) ***n.*** —**jo′vi·al·ly** ***adv.***

Jo·vi·an (jō′vē ən) ***adj.*** **1** of or like Jove (the god Jupiter); majestic **2** of the planet Jupiter **3** of or referring to the four large, gaseous planets of the solar system, specif. Jupiter, Saturn, Uranus, and Neptune: cf. TERRESTRIAL (sense 6)

Jow·ett (jou′it, jō′-), **Benjamin** 1817-93; Eng. classical scholar & translator of Plato and others

jowl[1] (joul; *occas.* jōl) ***n.*** ⟦ME *chavel* < OE *ceafl,* jaw, cheek, akin to ON *kjoptr,* MHG *kivel* < IE base **ĝebh-,* jaw, mouth > OIr *gop,* mouth, Czech *žábra,* gill (of fish)⟧ **1** a jawbone or jaw; esp., the lower jaw with the chin and cheeks **2** the cheek **3** the meat of a hog's cheek

jowl[2] (joul; *occas.* jōl) ***n.*** ⟦ME *cholle* < OE *ceole,* throat, akin to Ger *kehle* < IE base **gel-,* to swallow > OIr *gaile,* stomach⟧ **1** [*usually pl.*] the fleshy hanging part under the lower jaw **2** *a)* the dewlap of cattle *b)* the wattle of fowl **3** the head and adjacent parts of a fish —**jowl′y** ***adj.***

joy (joi) ***n.*** ⟦ME *joie* < OFr < LL *gaudia,* orig. pl. of L *gaudium,* joy < IE base **gāu-,* to rejoice > Gr *gēthein,* to rejoice, MIr *gūaire,* noble⟧ **1** a very glad feeling; happiness; great pleasure; delight **2** anything causing such feeling **3** the expression or showing of such feeling —***vi.*** to be full of joy; rejoice —***vt.*** [Archaic] **1** to make joyful **2** to enjoy —**SYN.** PLEASURE

Joy (joi) ***n.*** a feminine name

joy·ance (joi′əns) ***n.*** [Archaic] joy; rejoicing

Joyce[1] (jois) ***n.*** ⟦< older *Jocosa* < L *jocosa,* fem. of *jocosus,* JOCOSE⟧ a feminine and masculine name

Joyce[2] (jois), **James (Augustine Aloysius)** 1882-1941; Ir. novelist —**Joyc·e·an** (joi′sē ən) ***adj.***

joy·ful (joi′fəl) ***adj.*** feeling, expressing, or causing joy; glad; happy —**SYN.** HAPPY —**joy′ful·ly** ***adv.*** —**joy′ful·ness** ***n.***

joy·less (joi′lis) ***adj.*** without joy; sullen, gloomy, dreary, etc. —**joy′less·ly** ***adv.*** —**joy′less·ness** ***n.***

joy·ous (joi′əs) ***adj.*** ⟦ME < OFr *joios* < *joie,* JOY⟧ full of joy; happy; glad —**SYN.** HAPPY —**joy′ous·ly** ***adv.*** —**joy′ous·ness** ***n.***

joy-pop (joi′päp′) ***vi.*** **-popped′, -pop′ping** [Slang] to inject a narcotic drug under the skin, esp. in small quantities and infrequently —**joy′-pop′per** ***n.***

☆**joy·ride** (joi′rīd′) ***n.*** [Informal] an automobile ride merely for pleasure, often at a reckless speed and often, specif., in a stolen car —**joy′rid′er** ***n.*** —**joy′rid′ing** ***n.***

joy·stick (joi′stik′) ***n.*** **1** [Slang] the control stick of an airplane **2** *Comput.* a manual device connected as to a video game, with a control lever that can be tilted in various directions to move the cursor or part of the display

JP *abbrev.* Justice of the Peace

J particle *Particle Physics* a short-lived, relatively massive meson having no charge and a mass *c.* 6,060 times that of an electron: it is the combination of a charmed quark and its antiparticle

Jpn *abbrev.* **1** Japan **2** Japanese

Jr *abbrev.* **1** *Bible* Jeremiah **2** Junior: also **jr**

Js *abbrev. Bible* Joshua

JSD or **J.S.D** *abbrev.* Doctor of the Science of Laws

Jth *abbrev. Bible* Judith

Ju *abbrev.* June

Juan (hwän, wän) ***n.*** ⟦Sp, var. of JOHN[1]⟧ a masculine name: fem. *Juana*

Juan de Fu·ca Strait (wän′ də fo͞o′kə, -fyo͞o′kə) ⟦after *Juan de Fuca,* a sailor, who reputedly discovered it for Spain (1592)⟧ strait between Vancouver Island and NW Wash.: *c.* 100 mi (161 km) long: also called **Strait of Juan de Fuca**

Juan Fer·nán·dez Islands (hwän′ fer nan′dez) group of three islands in the South Pacific, *c.* 400 mi (644 km) west of, & belonging to, Chile: *c.* 69 sq mi (179 sq km)

Juá·rez[1] (hwä′res, -rez), **Be·ni·to Pa·blo** (be nē′tô pä′blô) 1806-72; Mex. statesman: president of Mexico (1861-65; 1867-72)

Juá·rez[2] (hwä′res, -rez) CIUDAD JUÁREZ

☆**ju·ba** (jo͞o′bə) ***n.*** ⟦< Zulu, lit., to kick about⟧ a kind of dance characterized by a lively rhythm marked by clapping the hands, popular among blacks on 19th-cent. Southern plantations

Ju·ba (jo͞o′bə) **1** river in Africa, flowing from S Ethiopia south through Somalia into the Indian Ocean: *c.* 1,000 mi (1,609 km): also sp. **Jub′ba** **2** capital of South Sudan, on the White Nile

Ju·bal (jo͞o′bəl) ***n.*** ⟦Heb *yūbhāl*⟧ *Bible* one of Cain's descendants, a musician or inventor of musical instruments: Gen. 4:19-21

jub·bah (jo͝ob′ə) ***n.*** ⟦Ar⟧ a long outer garment worn by both men and women in some Muslim countries

ju·bi·lant (jo͞o′bə lənt) ***adj.*** ⟦L *jubilans,* prp. of *jubilare:* see JUBILATE⟧ joyful and triumphant; elated; rejoicing —**ju′bi·lance** ***n.*** —**ju′bi·lant·ly** ***adv.***

ju·bi·lar·i·an (jo͞o′bə ler′ē ən) ***n.*** one celebrating an anniversary, esp. the 50th or 25th, as of entering a religious order

ju·bi·late (jo͞o′bə lāt′) ***vi.*** **-lat′ed, -lat′ing** ⟦< L *jubilatus,* pp. of *jubilare,* to shout for joy < *jubilum,* wild shout < IE base **yu-,* an outcry, especially of rejoicing > YOWL⟧ to rejoice, as in triumph; exult

Ju·bi·la·te (yo͞o′bē lä′tā′; *E* jo͞o′bi lā′tē) ***n.*** ⟦L, pl. imper. of *jubilare:* see prec.⟧ *Bible* the 100th Psalm (99th in the Vulgate version), beginning (in the Vulgate) "*Jubilate deo*", "Make a joyful noise to the Lord" (RSV)

ju·bi·la·tion (jo͞o′bə lā′shən) ***n.*** **1** a jubilating or a being jubilant **2** a happy celebration, as of victory

ju·bi·lee (jo͞o′bə lē′, jo͞o′bə lē′) ***n.*** ⟦ME < OFr *jubile* < LL(Ec) *jubilaeus* < Gr(Ec) *iōbēlaios* < Heb *yōbēl,* a ram, ram's horn used as a trumpet to announce the sabbatical year: infl. by L *jubilum:* see JUBILATE⟧ **1** *Jewish History* a year-long celebration held every fifty years in which all bondmen were freed, mortgaged lands were restored to the original owners, and land was left fallow: Lev. 25:8-17 **2** *a)* an anniversary, esp. a 50th or 25th anniversary *b)* a celebration of this **3** a time or occasion of rejoicing **4** jubilation; rejoicing **5** *R.C.Ch.* a year proclaimed as a solemn time for gaining a plenary indulgence and for receiving absolution, on certain conditions: an **ordinary jubilee** occurs every twenty-five years

Jud *abbrev.* Judaism

Ju·dah[1] (jo͞o′də) ***n.*** ⟦Heb *yehūdhāh,* lit., praised⟧ **1** a masculine name: dim. *Jude;* fem. *Judith* **2** *Bible a)* Jacob's fourth son, whose mother was Leah: Gen. 29:35 *b)* the tribe descended from him, the strongest of the twelve tribes of Israel: Num. 1:26

Ju·dah[2] (jo͞o′də) the kingdom in the S part of Palestine formed by the tribes of Judah and Benjamin after they broke with the other ten tribes: 1 Kings 11:31; 12: 17-21

Ju·da·ic (jo͞o dā′ik) ***adj.*** ⟦L *Judaicus* < Gr *Ioudaikos* < *Ioudaios:* see JEW⟧ **1** of Judah **2** of the Jews or Judaism; Jewish —**Ju·da′i·cal·ly** ***adv.***

Ju·da·i·ca (-i kə) ***n.*** ⟦ModL < L *Judaicus,* prec.⟧ **1** books, papers, objects, data, etc. having to do with Jews or Judaism **2** a collection of such materials

Ju·da·ism (jo͞o′dā iz′əm, -dē-, -də-) ***n.*** ⟦ME *Judaisme* < LL(Ec) *Judaismus* < Gr(Ec) *Ioudaismos* < *Ioudaios:* see JEW⟧ **1** the Jewish religion, a monotheistic religion based on the laws and teachings of the Holy Scripture and the Talmud **2** the Jewish way of life; observance of Jewish morality, traditions, ceremonies, etc. **3** Jews collectively; Jewry —**Ju′da·ist** ***n.*** —**Ju′da·is′tic** ***adj.***

Ju·da·ize (-īz′) ***vi.*** **-ized′**, **-iz′ing** ⟦LL(Ec) *Judaizare* < Gr(Ec) *Ioudaizein* < *Ioudaios:* see JEW⟧ to conform to Jewish morality, traditions, etc. ***—vt.*** to bring into conformity with Judaism **—Ju′da·i·za′tion *n.***

Ju·das (jo͞o′dəs) ***n.*** ⟦ME < LL(Ec) < Gr(Ec) *Ioudas* < Heb *yehūdhāh,* JUDAH[1]⟧ **1** *Bible* Judas Iscariot, the disciple who betrayed Jesus: Matt. 26:14, 48 **2** *Bible* Jude, the Apostle **3** *Bible* a brother of Jesus and James: Mark 6:3; Matt. 13:55 **4** a traitor or betrayer **5** [*usually* **j-**] *Archit.* a peephole or small window, as in the door of a prison cell: in full **judas window (**or **hole)**

Judas Maccabaeus *see* MACCABAEUS, Judas

Judas tree ⟦from the legend that Judas Iscariot hanged himself on one⟧ CERCIS

jud·der (jud′ər) ***vi.*** ⟦altered < ? SHUDDER⟧ [Brit.] to shake, wobble, or vibrate

Jude (jo͞od) ***n.*** **1** a masculine name: see JUDAH[1] **2** *Bible a)* one of the twelve Apostles: his day is Oct. 28 (also called *Judas,* **Saint Jude**) *b)* a book of the New Testament, the Letter of Jude (abbrev. *Jd*) *c)* its author, perhaps the Judas called Jesus' brother See JUDAS

Ju·de·a (jo͞o dē′ə) ancient region of S Palestine under Persian, Greek, & Roman rule, corresponding roughly to the Biblical Judah **—Ju·de′an *adj., n.***

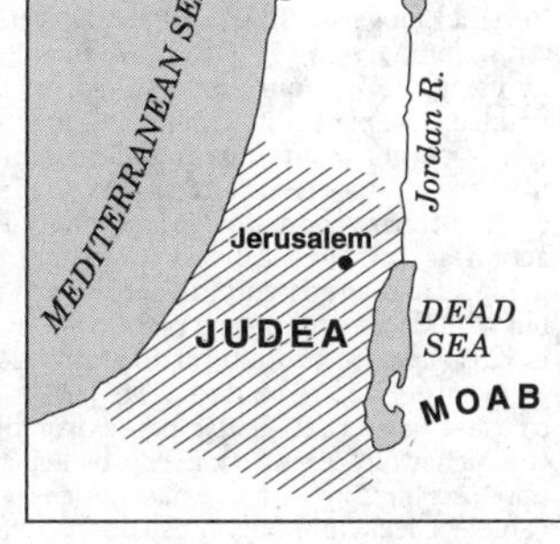

Judea (1st cent. A.D.)

Ju·de·o- (jo͞o dā′ō, -dē′-; jo͞o′ dē ō′) *combining form* **1** Judaic; Jewish **2** Jewish and [*Judeo-Christian*]

Ju·de·o-Chris·tian (jo͞o dā′ ō kris′chən, -dē′-) ***adj.*** having to do with or characteristic of both Judaism and Christianity

Ju·dez·mo (jo͞o dez′mō) ***n.*** ⟦Judezmo *judezmo,* lit., Jewishness, Jewish way of life; akin to Sp *judaísmo,* Judaism⟧ a language derived from Old Spanish, formerly the chief language of Sephardic Jews: it is written in the Hebrew alphabet and contains vocabulary borrowings from various languages, including Hebrew, Portuguese, and Turkish: see also LADINO ***—adj.*** of or in this language

Judg *abbrev. Bible* Judges

judge (juj) ***n.*** ⟦ME *juge* < OFr < L *judex,* a judge, lit., one who points out the right < *jus,* law + *dicere,* to say, point out: see JURY[1] & DICTION⟧ **1** an elected or appointed public official with authority to hear and decide cases in a court of law **2** a person designated to determine the winner in a contest, settle a controversy, etc. **3** a person qualified to give an opinion or decide on the relative worth of anything [a good *judge* of music] **4** *Jewish History* any of the governing leaders of the Israelites after Joshua and before the time of the kings **— *vt., vi.* judged, judg′ing** ⟦ME *juggen* < OFr *juger, jugier* < L *judicare,* to judge, declare the law < *judex:* see the ***n.***⟧ **1** to hear and pass judgment on (persons or cases) in a court of law **2** to determine the winner of (a contest) or settle (a controversy) **3** to decree **4** to form an idea, opinion, or estimate about (any matter) **5** to criticize or censure **6** to think or suppose **7** *Jewish History* to govern **—judg′er *n.***

SYN.—judge is applied to one who, by the authority vested in him or her by expertness of knowledge, is qualified to settle a controversy or decide on the relative merit of things [a *judge* of a beauty contest]; **arbiter** emphasizes the authoritativeness of decision of one whose judgment in a particular matter is considered indisputable [an *arbiter* of the social graces]; **referee** and **umpire** both apply to a person to whom anything is referred for decision or settlement [a *referee* in bankruptcy] and, in sports, to officials charged with the regulation of a contest, ruling on the plays in a game, etc. [a *referee* in boxing, basketball, etc., an *umpire* in baseball, cricket, etc.] See also **infer**

judge advocate *pl.* **judge advocates** a military legal officer; esp., an officer designated to act as prosecutor at a court-martial

judge advocate general *pl.* **judge advocates general** ☆the head officer of the legal section in the U.S. Army, Navy, or Air Force

judge-made (juj′mād′) ***adj.*** made by judges or by their decisions, often, specif., through judicial interpretation which is thought of as circumventing legislative intent

judge·ment (juj′mənt) ***n.*** *chiefly Brit. sp. of* JUDGMENT

Judg·es (juj′iz) ***n.*** a book of the Bible telling the history of the Jews from the death of Joshua to the birth of Samuel: abbrev. *Judg, Jg, Jgs,* or *Jud*

judge·ship (juj′ship′) ***n.*** the position, functions, or term of office of a judge

judg·mat·ic (juj mat′ik) ***adj.*** ⟦< JUDG(E) + (DOG)MATIC⟧ [Informal] discerning; judicious: also **judg·mat′i·cal**

judg·ment (juj′mənt) ***n.*** ⟦ME *jugement* < OFr < ML *judicamentum* < L *judicare:* see JUDGE, ***vt., vi.***⟧ **1** the act of judging; deciding **2** a legal decision; order, decree, or sentence given by a judge or law court **3** *a)* a debt or other obligation resulting from a court order *b)* a document recording this obligation **4** a misfortune looked on as a punishment from God **5** an opinion or estimate **6** criticism or censure **7** the ability to come to opinions about things; power of comparing and deciding; understanding; good sense **8** *Bible* justice; right **9** [**J-**] *short for* LAST JUDGMENT

judg·men·tal (juj ment′'l) ***adj.*** **1** of or having to do with the exercise of judgment **2** making or tending to make judgments as to value, importance, etc., often specif., judgments considered to be lacking in tolerance, compassion, objectivity, etc.

judgment call a ruling or decision on a matter that is, typically, not straightforward but that depends upon the judgment or evaluation of someone, as an umpire

Judgment Day *Theol.* the time of God's final judgment of all people; end of the world; doomsday

ju·di·ca·ble (jo͞o′di kə bəl) ***adj.*** ⟦LL *judicabilis* < L *judicatus,* pp. of *judicare:* see JUDGE, ***vt., vi.***⟧ **1** that can be judged **2** liable to be judged

ju·di·ca·tive (-kāt′iv, -kə tiv) ***adj.*** ⟦< L *judicatus,* pp. of *judicare* (see prec.) + -IVE⟧ judging; judicial

ju·di·ca·to·ry (-kə tôr′ē) ***adj.*** ⟦LL(Ec) *judicatorius* < L *judicatus:* see prec.⟧ having to do with administering justice; judging ***—n.,*** *pl.* **-ries** ⟦LL *judicatorium*⟧ **1** a court of law; tribunal **2** the system of administration of justice **3** law courts collectively

ju·di·ca·ture (-kə chər) ***n.*** ⟦MFr < ML *judicatura* < L *judicare:* see JUDGE, ***vt., vi.***⟧ **1** the administering of justice **2** the position, functions, or legal power of a judge **3** the extent of legal power of a judge or court of law; jurisdiction **4** a court of law **5** judges or courts of law collectively

ju·di·cial (jo͞o dish′əl) ***adj.*** ⟦OFr < L *judicialis* < *judex:* see JUDGE⟧ **1** of judges, law courts, or their functions **2** allowed, enforced, or set by order of a judge or law court **3** administering justice **4** like or befitting a judge **5** carefully considering the facts, arguments, etc., and reasoning to a decision; fair; unbiased **—ju·di′cial·ly *adv.***

ju·di·ci·ar·y (jo͞o dish′ē er′ē; -dish′ər ē, -ē ə rē) ***adj.*** ⟦L *judiciarius* < *judicium,* judgment, court of justice < *judex:* see JUDGE⟧ of judges, law courts, or their functions ***—n.,*** *pl.* **-ar′ies 1** the part of government whose work is the administration of justice **2** a system of law courts **3** judges collectively

ju·di·cious (-dish′əs) ***adj.*** ⟦Fr *judicieux* < L *judicium,* judgment < *judex:* see JUDGE⟧ having, applying, or showing sound judgment; wise and careful **—ju·di′cious·ly *adv.* —ju·di′cious·ness *n.***

Ju·dith (jo͞o′dith) ***n.*** ⟦LL(Ec) < Gr(Ec) *Ioudith* < Heb *yehūdhīth,* fem. of *yehūdhāh,* JUDAH[1]⟧ **1** a feminine name: dim. *Judy* **2** *a)* a Jewish woman who saved her people by killing Holofernes *b)* a book of the Apocrypha telling her story (abbrev. *Jdh, Jdt, Jth* or *Jud*)

ju·do (jo͞o′dō) ***n.*** ⟦Jpn *jūdo* < *jū,* soft + *dō,* way⟧ a form of jujitsu developed as a sport and as a means of self-defense without the use of weapons

ju·do·ka (jo͞o′dō kä′) ***n.*** ⟦Jpn < *jūdō* (see prec.) + *-ká,* expert⟧ one who performs, or is expert in, judo

Ju·dy (jo͞o′dē) ***n.*** **1** a feminine name: see JUDITH **2** Punch's wife in a PUNCH-AND-JUDY SHOW

jug[1] (jug) ***n.*** ⟦echoic⟧ a sound meant to imitate a nightingale's note ***—vi.*** **jugged, jug′ging** to make a nightingale's sound or a sound imitating this

jug[2] (jug) ***n.*** ⟦apparently a pet form of JUDITH or JOAN⟧ **1** *a)* a container for liquids, usually large and deep with a small opening at the top and a handle *b)* the contents of such a container **2** [Slang] a jail **3** [Slang] a bottle of whiskey ***—vt.*** **jugged, jug′ging 1** to put into a jug **2** to stew (esp. hare) in a covered earthenware container **3** [Slang] to jail **—jug′ful′** (-fo͝ol′) ***n.***

ju·gal (jo͞o′gəl) ***adj.*** ⟦L *jugalis* < *jugum,* a YOKE: cf. ZYGOMA⟧ designating or of a bone of the upper cheek

ju·gate (jo͞o′git, -gāt′) ***adj.*** ⟦L *jugatus,* pp. of *jugare,* to yoke, connect < *jugum,* YOKE⟧ *Biol.* paired or connected

☆**jug band** ⟦< the *jug,* used as a musical instrument⟧ a kind of small band consisting of string instruments, as guitars or mandolins, with harmonicas, kazoos, and such household items as a washtub and washboard for percussion and an empty jug that produces bass notes when the performer blows across its mouth

jug-eared (jug′ird′) ***adj.*** [Informal] having ears (**jug ears**) that stick out from the head, resembling the way that a handle sticks out from a jug

Jug·ger·naut (jug′ər nôt′) ***n.*** ⟦altered < Hindi *Jagannāth* < Sans *Jagannātha,* lord of the world < *jagat,* world + *nātha,* lord⟧ **1** an incarnation of the Hindu god Vishnu, whose idol, it was formerly supposed, so excited his worshipers when it was hauled along on a large car during religious rites that they threw themselves under the wheels and were crushed **2** [*usually* **j-**] anything that exacts blind devotion or terrible sacrifice **3** [*usually* **j-**] any relentless, destructive, irresistible force

jug·gle (jug′əl) ***vt.*** **-gled, -gling** ⟦ME *jogelen* < OFr *jogler,* to juggle, play false < ML *jogulari,* to play, entertain < L *joculari,* to joke < *joculus,* dim. of *jocus,* JOKE⟧ **1** to perform skillful tricks of sleight of hand with (balls, knives, etc.) as by keeping a number of them in the air continuously **2** to make several awkward attempts to catch or hold (a ball, etc.) **3** to manage, often resourcefully, (various tasks or responsibilities) at the same time **4** to manipulate or practice trickery on so as to deceive or cheat [to *juggle* figures so as to show a profit] ***—vi.*** to toss up a number of balls, knives, etc. and keep them continuously in the air ***—n.*** **1** an act of juggling **2** a clever trick or deception **—jug·gler** (jug′lər) ***n.***

jug·gler·y (jug′lər ē) ***n.,*** *pl.* **-gler·ies** ⟦ME *jugelri* < OFr *jogelerie*⟧ **1** the art or act of juggling; sleight of hand **2** trickery; deception

☆**jug·head** (jug′hed′) ***n.*** [Slang] a foolish or stupid person

Ju·go·sla·vi·a (yo͞o′gō slä′vē ə) *alt. sp. of* YUGOSLAVIA **—Ju′go·slav′** (-släv′) ***adj., n.,*** **Ju′go·sla′vi·an —Ju′go·slav′ic *adj.***

jug·u·lar (jug′yo͞o lər, -yə-) ***adj.*** ⟦LL *jugularis* < L *jugulum,* collarbone, neck, throat, dim. of *jugum*, a YOKE⟧ **1** of the neck or throat **2** of a jugular vein **3** *Zool.* of or having ventral fins in front of the pectoral, under the throat —***n.*** JUGULAR VEIN —**go for the jugular** [Informal] to be utterly ruthless with an opponent or competitor

jugular vein either of two large veins in the neck carrying blood back from the head to the heart

ju·gu·late (jo͞o′gyo͞o lāt′, -gyə-) ***vt.*** **-lat′ed, -lat′ing** ⟦L *jugulatus*, pp. of *jugulare* < *jugulum:* see JUGULAR⟧ **1** [Now Rare] to kill by cutting the throat **2** *Med.* to use extreme measures in arresting (a disease)

ju·gum (jo͞o′gəm) ***n., pl.*** **-ga** (-gə) or **-gums** ⟦ModL < L, YOKE⟧ a special process on the forewings of some insects by means of which the forewings and hind wings are hooked together during flight

Ju·gur·tha (jo͞o gur′thə) died 104 B.C.; king of Numidia (112?-104 B.C.)

jug wine inexpensive wine sold in jugs or large bottles

juice (jo͞os) ***n.*** ⟦ME *juis* < OFr *jus* < L, broth, juice < IE **yūs-* < base **yeu-*, to mix > Gr *zyme*, leaven⟧ **1** *a)* the liquid part of a plant, fruit, or vegetable *b)* the liquid part of a fruit or vegetable, used as a beverage [tomato *juice*] **2** a liquid in or from animal tissue [gastric *juice*, meat *juices*] **3** the essence of anything **4** [Informal] energy; vitality ☆**5** [Slang] *a)* electricity *b)* gasoline, oil, or any liquid fuel ☆**6** [Slang] alcoholic liquor: often with *the* ☆**7** [Slang] exorbitant interest charged on a loan **8** [Slang] power or influence —***vt.*** **juiced, juic′ing** ☆**1** to extract juice from ☆**2** [Informal] to add power, vigor, energy, etc. or interest, excitement, etc. to: usually with *up* —***vi.*** [Slang] to drink alcoholic beverages, esp. to excess —**juice′less** ***adj.***

juiced (jo͞ost) ***adj.*** [Slang] drunk; intoxicated

☆**juice·head** (jo͞os′hed′) ***n.*** [Slang] a drunkard or alcoholic

☆**juic·er** (jo͞o′sər) ***n.*** **1** a device or appliance for extracting juice from fruits and vegetables **2** [Slang] an excessive drinker of alcoholic beverages

juic·y (jo͞o′sē) ***adj.*** **juic′i·er, juic′i·est** **1** full of juice; containing much juice; succulent **2** [Informal] full of interest, as a racy story or bit of gossip; piquant; spicy **3** [Informal] highly profitable [a *juicy* contract] —**juic′i·ly** ***adv.*** —**juic′i·ness** ***n.***

ju·jit·su (jo͞o jit′so͞o′) ***n.*** ⟦Jpn *jū-jutsu*, lit., soft art < *jū*, soft, pliant + *jutsu*, art⟧ a Japanese system of wrestling in which knowledge of anatomy and the principle of leverage are applied so that the strength and weight of an opponent are used against him or her

ju·ju[1] (jo͞o′jo͞o′) ***n.*** ⟦Hausa, an evil spirit, fetish⟧ **1** a magic charm or fetish used by some West African peoples **2** magic or sorcery associated with such peoples

ju·ju[2] (jo͞o′jo͞o′) ***n.*** ⟦? after the sound of a tambourine used when playing the characteristic rhythm of this music⟧ a popular dance music that originated in Nigeria, characterized by repetitive, complex rhythms and chanted vocals that create a hypnotic effect

ju·jube (jo͞o′jo͞ob′; *for 3, often* jo͞o′jo͞o bē′) ***n.*** ⟦Fr < ML *jujuba* < L *zizyphum* < Gr *zizyphon*⟧ **1** the edible, datelike fruit of any of several trees and shrubs (genus *Zizyphus*) of the buckthorn family, growing in warm climates **2** a tree or shrub bearing this fruit **3** a jellylike, fruit-flavored lozenge or a gumdrop

ju·jut·su (jo͞o jit′so͞o′, -jut′-) ***n.*** *var. of* JUJITSU

☆**juke** (jo͞ok) ⟦orig. uncert.⟧ [Slang] *Sports* ***vt.*** **juked, juk′ing** to outmaneuver by a feint or other deceptive movement —***vi.*** to outmaneuver someone in such a manner

☆**juke·box** (jo͞ok′bäks′) ***n.*** ⟦Gullah *juke*, wicked, disorderly (as in *juke-house*, house of prostitution), of WAfr orig.⟧ **1** a coin-operated player of recorded music, used in restaurants, bars, etc.: a record, disc, etc. is chosen by pushing a button **2** any device for playing CDs, accessing CD-ROMs, etc., in which one of several discs may be selected for use Also written **juke box**

☆**juke joint** [Slang] a small, inexpensive tavern or roadhouse with a JUKEBOX (sense 1) playing music for dancing

Jul *abbrev.* July

ju·lep (jo͞o′ləp) ***n.*** ⟦ME < MFr < Ar *julāb* < Pers *gulāb* < *gul*, rose + *āb*, water⟧ ☆**1** MINT JULEP **2** a mixture of water with syrup or sugar, as for drinking along with, or after taking, medicine

Jules (jo͞olz) ***n.*** a masculine name: see JULIUS

Jul·ia (jo͞ol′yə, jo͞o′lē ə) ***n.*** ⟦L, fem. of *Julius*: see JULIUS⟧ a feminine name: dim. *Juliet*; var. *Julie*; equiv. Fr. & Ger. *Julie*, It. *Giulia*

Jul·ian[1] (jo͞ol′yən, jo͞o′lē ən) ***n.*** ⟦L *Julianus* < *Julius:* see JULIUS⟧ a masculine name: dim. *Jule*; equiv. Fr. *Julien*, It. *Giuliano*; fem. *Juliana*

Jul·ian[2] (jo͞ol′yən, jo͞o′lē ən) (L. name *Flavius Claudius Julianus*) A.D. 331-363; Rom. general: emperor of Rome (361-363): called *Julian the Apostate*

Ju·li·an·a (jo͞o′lē an′ə) ***n.*** ⟦L, fem. of *Julianus*, JULIAN[1]⟧ a feminine name: equiv. Fr. *Julienne*, It. *Giuliana*

Julian Alps SE range of the Alps, mostly in Slovenia: highest peak, 9,395 ft (2,864 m)

Julian calendar the calendar introduced by Julius Caesar in 46 B.C., in which the ordinary year had 365 days: the months were the same as in the Gregorian, or New Style, calendar now used

Jul·ie (jo͞o′lē) ***n.*** a feminine name: see JULIA

ju·li·enne (jo͞o′lē en′; *Fr* zhü lyen′) ***n.*** ⟦Fr, prob. < *Julienne*, JULIANA[1]; reason for name unknown⟧ a clear soup containing vegetables cut into strips or bits —***adj.*** cut into short, thin strips: said of vegetables, cheese, etc. —***vt.*** **-enned′, -en′ning** to cut (vegetables, cheese, etc.) into short, thin strips

Ju·li·et (jo͞o′lē et′, -it; jo͞o′lē et′; jo͞ol′yit) ***n.*** ⟦Fr *Juliette*, dim. < L *Julia*⟧ **1** a feminine name: see JULIA **2** the heroine of Shakespeare's tragedy *Romeo and Juliet*: see ROMEO

Juliet cap ⟦after the Shakespeare character prec.: type of cap once common in the role's costume⟧ a woman's small, brimless cap, worn usually on the back of the head: often the base for a bridal veil

Jul·ius (jo͞ol′yəs, jo͞o′lē əs) ***n.*** ⟦L, name of a Roman gens⟧ a masculine name: dim. *Jule, Julie*; equiv. Fr. *Jules*, It. *Giulio*, Sp. *Julio*; fem. *Julia*

Julius II (born *Giuliano della Rovere*) 1443-1513; pope (1503-13)

Julius Caesar *see* CAESAR[2], (Gaius) Julius

Jul·lun·dur (jul′ən dər) city in N Punjab, NW India

Ju·ly (joo lī′, jo͞o-, jə-) ***n., pl.*** **-lys′** or **-lies′** ⟦ME *Julie* < Anglo-Fr < L *Julius* < *mensis Julius*, the month of Julius CAESAR[2]⟧ the seventh month of the year, having 31 days: abbrev. *Jul, Jl, Jy*, or *J*

jum·ble[1] (jum′bəl) ***n.*** ⟦< ? OFr *jumel, gemel* (Fr *jumeau*), twin: see GIMBAL⟧ a kind of thin, sugared cookie shaped like a ring: also sp. **jum′bal**

jum·ble[2] (jum′bəl) ***vt.*** **-bled, -bling** ⟦? blend of JUMP + TUMBLE⟧ **1** to mix in a confused, disorderly heap **2** to confuse mentally —***vi.*** to be jumbled —***n.*** **1** a confused mixture or heap **2** a muddle **3** [Brit.] RUMMAGE SALE: in full **jumble sale** —***SYN.*** CONFUSION

☆**jum·bo** (jum′bō) ***n., pl.*** **-bos** ⟦< Gullah *jamba*, elephant; of Afr orig.: reinforced by P. T. BARNUM's use of it for his famous elephant, *Jumbo*⟧ a very large person, animal, or thing —***adj.*** very large; larger than usual of its kind [a *jumbo* jet airliner]

Jum·na (jum′nə) river in N India, flowing from the Himalayas southwest into the Ganges in SE Uttar Pradesh state: 860 mi (1,384 km)

jump (jump) ***vi.*** ⟦< ?⟧ **1** to move oneself suddenly from the ground, etc. by using the leg muscles; leap; spring **2** to be moved with a jerk; bob; bounce **3** to parachute from an aircraft **4** to move, act, or react energetically or eagerly: often with *at* **5** to move suddenly and involuntarily, as from fright, surprise, etc. **6** to pass suddenly from one thing or topic to another **7** to rise suddenly [prices have *jumped*] **8** to break in continuity of action, as a film image, because of faulty alignment of the film **9** [Slang] to be lively and animated [the party was *jumping*] **10** *Bridge* to make a jump bid ☆**11** *Checkers* to move a piece over an opponent's piece, thus capturing it **12** *Comput.* to continue at an instruction in another part of the program by means of a JUMP (***n.*** 13) —***vt.*** **1** *a)* to leap over *b)* to pass over; skip **2** to cause to leap [to *jump* a horse over a fence] ☆**3** to advance (a person) to a higher rank or position, esp. by bypassing intervening ranks ☆**4** to leap upon; spring aboard **5** to cause (prices, etc.) to rise suddenly ☆**6** to bypass (an electrical component, esp. a weak battery on a vehicle) **7** [Informal] to attack suddenly as from hiding **8** [Informal] to react to prematurely, in anticipation [to *jump* a traffic light] ☆**9** [Slang] to leave suddenly or without permission [to *jump* town, *jump* ship] **10** *Bridge* to raise (the bid) by making a jump bid ☆**11** *Checkers* to capture (an opponent's piece) by jumping **12** *Journalism* to continue (a story) on another page —***n.*** **1** a jumping; leap; bound; spring **2** a distance jumped **3** a descent from an aircraft by parachute **4** a thing to be jumped over or from, as on a ski jump **5** a sudden transition **6** a sudden rise, as in prices **7** a sudden, nervous start or jerk; twitch ☆**8** [Informal] JUMP-START (***n.*** 1) **9** [*pl.*] [Slang] chorea; also, delirium tremens: usually with *the* **10** *Athletics* a contest in jumping [the high *jump*, the long *jump*] **11** *Bridge* JUMP BID ☆**12** *Checkers* a move by which an opponent's piece is jumped and captured **13** *Comput.* a program instruction that causes an instruction in another part of the program to be the next executed **14** *Journalism* a line telling on, or from, what page a story is continued: also **jump line** —☆***adj.*** **1** designating or of a style of jazz music characterized by recurrent short riffs and a strong, fast beat **2** of or for parachuting or paratroops —☆**get (or have) the jump on** [Informal] to get (or have) an earlier start than and thus have an advantage over —☆**jump a claim** to seize mining rights or land claimed by someone else —**jump at** [Informal] to accept hastily and eagerly —☆**jump bail** [Informal] to forfeit one's bail by fleeing —☆**jump in with both feet** to enter into an activity or venture wholeheartedly —**jump off** [Mil. Slang] to start an attack —**jump on (or all over)** [Slang] to scold; censure severely —☆**jump rope** to exercise or play a game with a jump-rope —☆**jump the track (or tracks)** to go suddenly off the rails —**jump to conclusions** to make a hasty judgment

☆**jump ball** *Basketball* a ball tossed by the referee between two opposing players who must tip it to a teammate, as in beginning play

jump bid *Bridge* a bid that is higher than is necessary to surpass the previous bid

jump-cut (jump′kut′) *Film* ***n.*** an abrupt change from one shot, scene, or sequence to another, caused by the absence of transitional action, effects, etc. —***vi.*** **-cut′, -cut′ting** to make or use a jump-cut

jump drive *Comput.* a FLASH DRIVE that plugs into a USB port

jumped-up (jumpt′up′) ***adj.*** [Brit. Informal] having recently gained wealth, power, success, etc. and regarded as behaving presumptuously, aggressively, etc.

jump·er[1] (jum′pər) ***n.*** **1** a person, animal, or thing that jumps ☆**2** a kind of sled **3** a short wire to close a break in, or cut out part of, a circuit, or to make a temporary electrical connection ☆**4** *Basketball* JUMP SHOT **5** *Mining* a boring tool that operates with an up-and-down jumping motion

jump·er[2] (jum′pər) ***n.*** ⟦< earlier dial. *jump*, short coat, prob. altered (infl. by JUMP) < Fr *jupe* (? via Sp *aljuba*,

jumper[2] (sense 2)

Moorish garment) < Ar *al jubbah* < *al*, the + *jubbah*, JUBBAH⟧ 1 a loose jacket or blouse; specif., *a)* one worn by workmen to protect clothing *b)* one with a wide collar hanging down in back, worn by sailors 2 a sleeveless, collarless dress for wearing over a blouse or sweater ☆3 [*pl.*] rompers: see ROMPER (sense 2)

jumper cables ⟦< JUMPER¹ (*n.* 3)⟧ a pair of long, thick, insulated electrical wires with large, clamplike terminals: used to start a motor vehicle's engine by connecting its dead battery to a live battery

☆**jumping bean** the seed of any of several Mexican plants (esp. genus *Sebastiana*) of the spurge family, containing the larva of a small moth (*Cydia saltitans*), which by its movements makes the seed jump or roll about

jumping gene *nontechnical term for* TRANSPOSON

jumping jack 1 a child's toy consisting of a little jointed figure made to jump or dance by pulling a string or pushing an attached stick 2 a form of exercise in which one jumps from a standing position, with the feet together and the arms at the sides, to a position in which the feet are apart and the hands touch overhead, and then jumps back again: *usually used in pl.*

☆**jumping mouse** any of various small North American and Asian rodents (family Zapodidae) with large hind legs and a long tail

☆**jump·ing-off place** (jum′piŋ ôf′) 1 any isolated or remote place regarded as the outmost limit of human habitation 2 the starting point for a trip or venture

jump jet [Slang, Chiefly Mil.] a jet fighter, often used on aircraft carriers, that can take off and land with little or no runway space: cf. V/STOL: sometimes written **jump′-jet′** *n.*

jump·off (jump′ôf′) *n. Sports* an extra round of competitive jumping added at the end of regular competition to break a tie, as in certain equestrian events: also written **jump-off**

☆**jump-rope** (jump′rōp′) *n.* 1 a length of rope, usually with handles on each end, that is swung over the head and then under the feet as one jumps 2 a child's game or an exercise using such a rope: also written **jump rope**

☆**jump seat** a small folding seat, as one behind the front seat of a limousine, taxi, etc.

☆**jump shot** *Basketball* a shot in which the player jumps up and shoots the ball at the top of the jump

☆**jump-start** (jump′stärt′) *vt.* 1 to start (the engine of a motor vehicle) by using jumper cables, or by pushing the vehicle and then suddenly releasing the clutch when the vehicle has begun to roll 2 [Informal] to start or start up, energize, revive, etc. [a plan to *jump-start* the economy] —*n.* 1 the act of jump-starting an engine 2 [Informal] a quick start, recovery, etc.

☆**jump·suit** (jump′so͞ot′) *n.* 1 a coverall worn by paratroops, garage mechanics, etc. 2 a lounging outfit somewhat like this

jump·y (jum′pē) *adj.* **jump′i·er**, **jump′i·est** 1 moving in jumps, jerks, or abrupt variations 2 easily startled 3 nervous or apprehensive —**jump′i·ly** *adv.* —**jump′i·ness** *n.*

Jun *abbrev.* 1 June 2 junior: also **jun**

junc *abbrev.* junction

jun·co (juŋ′kō) *n., pl.* **-cos** ⟦ModL < Sp *junco*, a rush < L *juncus*: see JONQUIL⟧ ☆any of a genus (*Junco*, family Emberizidae) of passerine birds of North America with a gray or black head and white outer tail feathers

junc·tion (juŋk′shən) *n.* ⟦L *junctio* < *jungere*, to JOIN⟧ 1 a joining or being joined 2 a place or point of joining or crossing, as of highways or railroads 3 an interface between materials having different characteristics, as the pn junction in a semiconductor or the boundary between two metals in a thermocouple —**junc′tion·al** *adj.*

junc·ture (juŋk′chər) *n.* ⟦L *junctura* < *jungere*, to JOIN⟧ 1 a joining or being joined 2 a point or line of joining or connection; joint, as of two bones, or seam 3 a point of time 4 a particular or critical moment in the development of events; crisis 5 a state of affairs 6 *Linguis.* the transition from one speech sound to the next, either within a word, as between (t) and (r) in *nitrate* (**close juncture**), or marking the boundaries between words, as between (t) and (r) in *night rate* (**open juncture**)

June (jo͞on) *n.* ⟦OFr < L *Junius* < *mensis Junius*, the month of *Juno*⟧ 1 a feminine name 2 the sixth month of the year, having 30 days: abbrev. *Jun, Ju, Je*, or *J*

Ju·neau (jo͞o′nō) ⟦after Cdn prospector J. *Juneau* (1836-99)⟧ capital of Alas.: seaport on the SE coast

☆**June·ber·ry** (jo͞on′ber′ē) *n., pl.* **-ries** 1 any of a genus (*Amelanchier*) of trees and shrubs of the rose family, with white flowers, small, purple-black fruits, and simple leaves 2 the fruit

June bug ☆1 any of several large scarab beetles (genus *Phyllophaga*) appearing in May or June in the N U.S.: also **June beetle** ☆2 FIGEATER

Jung (yooŋ), **Carl Gus·tav** (goos′täf′) 1875-1961; Swiss psychologist & psychiatrist —**Jung′i·an** *adj., n.*

Jung·gar Pen·di (zhooŋ′gär′ pen′dē) region in N Xinjiang, China, between the Tian Shan & the Altai Mountains

jun·gle (juŋ′gəl) *n.* ⟦Hindi *jangal*, desert forest, jungle < Sans *jaṅgala*, wasteland, desert⟧ 1 land in a wet, tropical region, usually with large trees, dense underbrush, and a hot climate 2 any confused, tangled growth, collection, etc. 3 a form of electronic dance music originating in England in the early 1990s, that blends elements of hip hop, reggae, techno, and house music, emphasizing fast tempos, heavy, elongated bass beats, and highly syncopated, complicated breakbeats and rhythms ☆4 [Old Slang] a hobos' camp ☆5 [Slang] a place or situation in which people engage in ruthless competition or in a struggle for survival —**jun′gly** *adj.*

jungle fever any of several diseases of tropical regions; esp., a severe malarial fever of the East Indies

jungle fowl any of several Asian gallinaceous birds (genus *Gallus*, family Phasianidae), having combs and throat wattles: the red Indian species (*G. gallus*) is regarded as the ancestor of the present-day domestic chicken

☆**jungle gym** an apparatus for playgrounds, consisting of bars, ladders, etc. for children to climb on

jun·ior (jo͞on′yər) *adj.* ⟦L, contr. of *juvenior*, compar. of *juvenis*, YOUNG⟧ 1 the younger: written *Jr.* after the name of a son who bears exactly the same name as his father: opposed to SENIOR 2 of more recent position or lower status [a *junior* partner, a *junior* lien] 3 of later date 4 made up of younger members ☆5 of or for juniors in a high school or college —*n.* 1 a younger person 2 a person of lower standing or rank ☆3 a student in the next-to-last year of college or the eleventh grade in high school ☆4 a size and style of clothing designed for teens and young women, cut to fit smaller in the bust and hips than regular women's clothing —**be someone's junior** to be younger than someone

☆**junior college** a school offering courses for two years beyond high school, either as the first two years of a standard four-year college program or as a complete career-training program resulting in a certificate or an associate degree

junior featherweight a boxer between a bantamweight and a featherweight, with a maximum weight of 122 pounds (55.34 kg)

junior flyweight a boxer with the maximum weight of 108 pounds (48.99 kg)

☆**junior high school** a school intermediate between elementary school and senior high school: it usually includes grades 7, 8, and 9: see MIDDLE SCHOOL

jun·ior·i·ty (jo͞on yôr′ə tē) *n.* the quality or state of being junior, as in age or rank

☆**Junior League** any of the local branches of the Association of Junior Leagues, Inc., whose members are women, often typically of leisure and the upper social class, trained for volunteer work in community-service projects

junior lightweight a boxer between a featherweight and a lightweight, with a maximum weight of 130 pounds (58.99 kg)

junior middleweight a boxer between a welterweight and a middleweight, with a maximum weight of 154 pounds (69.85 kg)

☆**junior miss** 1 a girl in her early teens 2 JUNIOR (*n.* 4)

☆**junior varsity** a team that represents a school, college, etc. on a level just below the varsity team in games or contests

junior welterweight a boxer between a lightweight and a welterweight, with a maximum weight of 140 pounds (63.50 kg)

ju·ni·per (jo͞o′ni pər) *n.* ⟦ME *junipur* < L *juniperus* < IE base **yoini-*, reed (> JONQUIL) + unexplained second element⟧ 1 any of a genus (*Juniperus*) of evergreen shrubs or trees of the cypress family, with needlelike or scalelike foliage, aromatic wood, and berrylike cones that yield an oil used for flavoring gin and formerly in medicine ☆2 any of several similar trees grown for ornament 3 RETEM

junk¹ (juŋk) *n.* ⟦ME *jonk* < ? *jonk*, reed < OFr *jonc* < L *juncus*, a rush: see JONQUIL⟧ 1 [Obs.] old cable or rope used for making oakum, mats, etc. 2 old metal, glass, paper, rags, etc., parts of which may be salvageable for reuse 3 [Informal] useless or worthless stuff; trash; rubbish ☆4 [Slang] a narcotic drug; esp., heroin 5 [Slang] *Baseball* low-velocity pitches, esp. slow curve balls —*vt.* ☆[Informal] to throw away as worthless or get rid of by selling as junk; discard; scrap —**junk′y** *adj.* **junk′i·er**, **junk′i·est**

junk² (juŋk) *n.* ⟦Fr *jonque* < Port *junco* < Jav *jong* < Malay *adjong*⟧ a Chinese or Japanese flat-bottomed ship with a high stern and lugsails or lateen sails

junk²

junk bond [Informal] a corporate bond with a relatively high yield that reflects the heightened investment risk associated with the bond's issuer

☆**junk DNA** ⟦coined (1972) by Susumu Ohno (1928-2000), U.S. geneticist⟧ that portion of an organism's DNA that is not directly involved in protein production and has no known function

☆**junk·er** (juŋ′kər) *n.* ⟦< JUNK¹, *vt.*⟧ [Slang] an old, dilapidated car or truck

Jun·ker (yooŋ′kər) *n.* ⟦Ger < MHG *junc herre*, young nobleman < OHG *jung*, YOUNG + *herro*, lord: see HOAR⟧ [Historical] 1 a member of the privileged, militaristic landowning class in Germany; Prussian aristocrat 2 a German military officer, esp. one who is autocratic, illiberal, etc.

jun·ket (juŋ′kit) *n.* ⟦ME *joncate* < ML **juncata*, a sweetmeat, cream cheese < L *juncus*, a rush (see JONQUIL): because orig. brought to market in rush baskets⟧ 1 milk sweetened, flavored, and thickened into curd with rennet 2 a feast or picnic 3 a pleasure trip ☆4 an excursion, as by a public official, paid for out of public funds —*vi.* to go on a junket or excursion, esp. one paid for out of public funds —*vt.* to entertain at a feast —☆**jun·ket·eer** (juŋ′ki tir′) *n.*, **jun·ket·er** (juŋ′kit ər)

☆**junk food** food, esp. snack food, having little nutritional value and processed as with chemical additives

☆**junk·ie** or **junk·y** (juŋ′kē) *n., pl.* **junk′ies** ⟦< JUNK¹, *n.* 4⟧ [Slang] 1 a narcotics addict, esp. one addicted to heroin **2** a person who is addicted to a specified interest, activity, food, etc. [a TV *junkie*]

☆**junk jewelry** [Informal] inexpensive costume jewelry

☆**junk mail** advertisements, solicitations, etc. mailed in large quantities

☆**junk·man** (juŋk′man′) ***n.***, *pl.* **-men′** (-men′) a dealer in old metal, glass, paper, rags, etc.: also **junk dealer**

☆**junk·yard** (-yärd′) ***n.*** a place where old metal, paper, etc. is kept, sorted, and sold, or where old cars are junked

Ju·no (jo͞o′nō) ***n.*** ⟦L⟧ *Rom. Myth.* the sister and wife of Jupiter, queen of the gods, and goddess of marriage: identified with the Greek Hera

Ju·no·esque (jo͞o′nō esk′) ***adj.*** ⟦after prec.⟧ tall, with a mature, shapely figure: said of a woman

jun·ta (ho͝on′tə, jun′-, jo͝on′-) ***n.*** ⟦Sp < L *juncta,* fem. of *junctus,* pp. of *jungere,* to JOIN⟧ **1** an assembly or council; esp., a Spanish or Latin American legislative or administrative body **2** a group of political intriguers; esp., such a group, of military men in power after a coup d'état: also **jun·to** (jun′tō), *pl.* **-tos**

Ju·pi·ter (jo͞o′pit ər) ***n.*** ⟦L *Juppiter,* orig. a voc. < bases of *Jovis,* JOVE & *pater,* FATHER⟧ **1** *Rom. Myth.* the chief deity, god of thunder and the skies: identified with the Greek Zeus **2** the largest planet of the solar system and the fifth in distance from the sun: it has a ring composed of microscopic dustlike particles: diameter, *c.* 142,980 km (*c.* 88,850 mi); period of revolution, 11.86 earth years; period of rotation, 9.92 hours; 64 satellites; symbol, ♃

Jupiter Plu·vi·us (plo͞o′vē əs) ⟦L, lit., Jupiter who brings rain: *pluvius,* rainy < *pluere,* to rain: see PLUVIAL⟧ Jupiter regarded as the giver of rain

ju·pon (jo͞o′pän′, jo͞o pän′; *Fr* zhü pōn′) ***n.*** ⟦ME *jopon* < OFr *jupon* < *jupe:* see JUMPER[2]⟧ a medieval jacket or tunic worn over or under armor

ju·ra (jo͝or′ə, yo͝or′ə, yo͞o′rä′) ***n.*** ⟦L⟧ *pl. of* JUS

Ju·ra[1] (jo͝or′ə), **the** the Jurassic Period or its rocks

Ju·ra[2] (jo͝or′ə) **1** canton in W Switzerland: 323 sq mi (837 sq km) **2** mountain range along the Swiss-French border: highest peak, 5,652 ft (1,723 m): also called **Jura Mountains**

ju·ral (jo͝or′əl) ***adj.*** ⟦< L *jus* (gen. *juris*), right, law (see JURY[1]) + -AL⟧ **1** of law; legal **2** relating to natural rights and duties —**ju′ral·ly** ***adv.***

Ju·ras·sic (jo͞o ras′ik, jo͝o-) ***adj.*** ⟦Fr *jurassique,* after JURA MOUNTAINS⟧ [*sometimes* **j-**] designating or of the second geologic period of the Mesozoic Era, characterized by the breakup of Laurasia and Gondwana and the development of giant dinosaurs and the first birds —**the Jurassic** the Jurassic Period or its rocks: see the geologic time chart in the Reference Supplement

ju·rat (jo͝or′at′) ***n.*** ⟦Fr < ML *juratus,* lit., one sworn < L *juratus,* pp. of *jurare:* see JURY[1]⟧ **1** a municipal officer or magistrate in certain French towns and the Channel Islands **2** ⟦< L *juratum,* neut. pp. of *jurare*⟧ *Law* a statement or certification added to an affidavit, telling when, before whom, and, sometimes, where the affidavit was made

ju·ra·to·ry (jo͝or′ə tôr′ē) ***adj.*** ⟦LL *juratorius* < L *jurator,* sworn witness < *jurare:* see JURY[1]⟧ of or expressed in an oath

ju·rel (ho͞o rel′) ***n.*** ⟦Sp, ult. < Gr *sauros,* horse mackerel: see SAURY⟧ any of various edible jack fishes (esp. genus *Caranx*) having narrow bodies

ju·rid·i·cal (jo͞o rid′i kəl, jo͝o-) ***adj.*** ⟦L *juridicus* < *jus* (gen. *juris*), law (see JURY[1]) + *dicere,* to point out, declare (see DICTION) + -AL⟧ of judicial proceedings, jurisprudence, or law: also **ju·rid′ic** —**ju·rid′i·cal·ly** ***adv.***

juridical days the days on which courts are in session

ju·ried (jo͝or′ēd) ***adj.*** designating or of a competition, exhibition, etc. in which the winners or participants have been selected by a JURY[1] (sense 2)

ju·ris·con·sult (jo͝or′is kän′səlt) ***n.*** ⟦L *jurisconsultus,* lawyer < *jus* (gen. *juris*), law + *consultus:* see CONSULT⟧ JURIST

ju·ris·dic·tion (jo͝or′is dik′shən) ***n.*** ⟦ME *jurisdiccioun,* altered (infl. by L) < OFr *juridiction* < L *jurisdictio,* administration of the law < *jus* (gen. *juris*), law + *dictio:* see JURY[1] & DICTION⟧ **1** the administering of justice; authority or legal power to hear and decide cases **2** authority or power in general **3** a sphere of authority **4** the territorial range of authority **5** a law court or system of law courts —***SYN.*** POWER —**ju′ris·dic′tion·al** ***adj.*** —**ju′ris·dic′tion·al·ly** ***adv.***

ju·ris·pru·dence (jo͝or′is pro͞od′'ns) ***n.*** ⟦L *jurisprudentia* < *jus,* law (see JURY[1]) + *prudentia,* a foreseeing, knowledge, skill: see PRUDENT⟧ **1** the science or philosophy of law **2** a part or division of law [medical *jurisprudence*] —**ju′ris·pru·den′tial** (-pro͞o den′shəl) ***adj.*** —**ju′ris·pru·den′tial·ly** ***adv.***

ju·ris·pru·dent (-pro͞od′'nt) ***n.*** ⟦Fr, back-form. < *jurisprudence:* see prec.⟧ a student of jurisprudence; jurist —***adj.*** skilled in the law

ju·rist (jo͝or′ist) ***n.*** ⟦ME *juriste* < MFr < ML *jurista* < L *jus,* law: see JURY[1]⟧ **1** an expert in law; scholar or writer in the field of law **2** JUDGE (***n.*** 1)

ju·ris·tic (jo͞o ris′tik, jo͝o-) ***adj.*** of jurists or jurisprudence; having to do with law; legal —**ju·ris′ti·cal·ly** ***adv.***

ju·ror (jo͝or′ər, -ôr′) ***n.*** ⟦ME *jurour* < Anglo-Fr < OFr *jureor* < L *jurator,* taker of an oath < *jurare,* to swear: see JURY[1]⟧ **1** a member of a jury or jury panel **2** a person taking an oath, as of allegiance

Ju·ruá (zho͞or wä′) river flowing from the Andes in Peru northeast across NW Brazil into the Amazon: *c.* 1,200 mi (1,931 km)

ju·ry[1] (jo͝or′ē) ***n.***, *pl.* **-ries** ⟦ME *jure* < Anglo-Fr *juree* < OFr, oath, judicial inquest < ML *jurata,* a jury, properly fem. pp. of L *jurare,* to take an oath, swear < *jus* (gen. *juris*), law < IE **yewos,* fixed rule > OIr *huisse,* just⟧ **1** a group of people sworn to hear the evidence and inquire into the facts in a law case, and to give a decision in accordance with their findings **2** a group of people, often experts, selected to decide the winners or participants in a competition, exhibition, etc.

ju·ry[2] (jo͝or′ē) ***adj.*** ⟦< ?⟧ *Naut.* for temporary or emergency use; makeshift [a *jury* mast, *jury* rig]

ju·ry-rigged (-rigd′) ***adj.*** ⟦see prec.⟧ rigged for temporary or emergency use

jus (jus, yo͝os, yo͞os) ***n.***, *pl.* **ju·ra** (jo͝or′ə, yo͝or′ə, yo͞o′rä′) ⟦L: see JURY[1]⟧ **1** *a)* law; the whole body of law *b)* a particular system of law **2** a legal principle, right, or power

Jus or **Just** *abbrev.* Justice

jus ci·vi·le (jus′ siv′ə lē, jus′ sə vil′ē) ⟦L⟧ CIVIL LAW

jus gen·ti·um (jen′shē əm) ⟦L, law of nations⟧ **1** *Rom. Law* the laws common to all people as distinguished from those applying only to Roman citizens **2** INTERNATIONAL LAW

jus na·tu·rae (nə to͝or′ē) ⟦L, law of nature⟧ law of nature; natural law: also ***jus na·tu·ra·le*** (na′to͞o rä′lē)

jus san·gui·nis (saŋ′gwi nis) ⟦L, lit., right of blood⟧ a right which entitles one to citizenship of a nation of which one's natural parents are citizens

jus·sive (jus′iv) ***adj.*** ⟦< L *jussus,* a command (< *jubere,* to command < IE **yeu-dh-,* to be in violent movement, fight > Sans *yúdh-,* fighter) + -IVE⟧ *Gram.* expressing a command —***n.*** a jussive word, form, case, or mood

jus so·li (jus′ sō′lī′) ⟦L, right of land⟧ a right which entitles one to citizenship of a nation in which one was born

just[1] (just) ***adj.*** ⟦ME < OFr *juste* < L *justus,* lawful, rightful, proper < *jus,* right, law: see JURY[1]⟧ **1** right or fair; equitable; impartial [a *just* decision] **2** righteous; upright [a *just* man] **3** deserved; merited [*just* praise] **4** legally right; lawful; rightful **5** proper, fitting, etc. [a *just* balance of colors] **6** well-founded; reasonable [a *just* suspicion] **7** correct or true [a *just* report] **8** accurate; exact [a *just* measure] —***adv.*** **1** neither more nor less than; precisely; exactly [*just* one o'clock] **2** almost at the point of; nearly [*just* preparing to leave] **3** no more than; only [*just* a taste, *just* teasing you] **4** by a very small amount; barely [to *just* miss a train] **5** a very short time ago [she has *just* left] **6** immediately [*just* east of the church] **7** [Informal] quite; really [to feel *just* fine] —***SYN.*** FAIR[1] —**just about** [Informal] almost; nearly —**just now** a moment ago —☆**just the same** [Informal] nevertheless —**just′ness** ***n.***

just[2] (just) ***n.***, ***vi.*** JOUST

jus·tice (jus′tis) ***n.*** ⟦OFr < L *justitia* < *justus:* see JUST[1]⟧ **1** the quality of being righteous; rectitude **2** impartiality; fairness **3** the quality of being right or correct **4** sound reason; rightfulness; validity **5** reward or penalty as deserved; just deserts **6** *a)* the use of authority and power to uphold what is right, just, or lawful *b)* [**J-**] the personification of this, usually a blindfolded goddess holding scales and a sword **7** the administration of law; procedure of a law court **8** *a)* JUDGE (***n.*** 1) *b)* JUSTICE OF THE PEACE —**bring to justice** to cause (a wrongdoer) to be tried in court and duly punished —**do justice to** **1** to treat fitly or fairly **2** to treat with due appreciation; enjoy properly —**do oneself justice** **1** to do something in a manner worthy of one's ability **2** to be fair to oneself

justice of the peace in some states, a magistrate with jurisdiction over a small district, authorized to decide minor cases, commit persons to trial in a higher court, perform marriages, etc.

jus·tice·ship (-ship′) ***n.*** the position, functions, or term of office of a justice

jus·ti·ci·a·ble (jus tish′ē ə bəl) ***adj.*** ⟦Anglo-Fr < OFr < *justice:* see JUSTICE⟧ **1** liable for trial in court **2** subject to court jurisdiction

jus·ti·ci·ar (-ər) ***n.*** JUSTICIARY (***n.*** 1 & 2)

jus·ti·ci·ar·y (-er′ē) ***n.***, *pl.* **-ar′ies** ⟦ME < ML *justitiarius* < L *justitia:* see JUSTICE⟧ **1** the chief political and judicial officer under the Norman and early Plantagenet kings **2** [Archaic] one who administers justice, as a judge **3** the jurisdiction of a justiciary —***adj.*** relating to the administration of justice or the office of a judge

jus·ti·fi·a·ble (jus′tə fī′ə bəl, jus′tə fī′ə bəl) ***adj.*** ⟦Fr < *justifier:* see JUSTIFY⟧ that can be justified; demonstrably just, right, or reasonable —**jus′ti·fi′a·bil′i·ty** ***n.*** —**jus′ti·fi′a·bly** ***adv.***

jus·ti·fi·ca·tion (jus′tə fi kā′shən) ***n.*** ⟦ME *justificacioun* < OFr *justification* < LL *justificatio* < *justificare:* see JUSTIFY⟧ **1** a justifying or being justified **2** a fact that justifies or vindicates **3** *Christian Theol.* the state or condition, necessary for salvation, of being blameless or absolved of the guilt of sin **4** *Printing* the adjustment of printed lines by proper spacing

jus·tif·i·ca·to·ry (jəs tif′i kə tôr′ē; jus′tə fə kāt′ə rē) ***adj.*** ⟦< LL *justificatus,* justified, pp. of *justificare* (see fol.) + -ORY⟧ justifying; serving to uphold or vindicate: also **jus·ti·fi·ca·tive** (jus′tə fi kāt′iv)

jus·ti·fy (jus′tə fī′) ***vt.*** **-fied′**, **-fy′ing** ⟦ME *justifien* < OFr *justifier* < LL (chiefly Ec.) *justificare,* to act justly toward, justify < L *justus,* JUST[1] + *-ficare* < *facere,* to DO[1]⟧ **1** to show to be just, right, or in accord with reason; vindicate **2** to supply good or lawful grounds for; warrant **3** *Christian Theol.* to free from blame; declare guiltless; absolve **4** *Printing* to adjust (characters in printed lines) by spacing so that the lines will end evenly at the margin —***vi.*** **1** *Law a)* to show an adequate reason for something done *b)* to prove qualified as surety **2** *Printing* to fit; be in line or flush: said as of printed lines —**jus′ti·fi′er** ***n.***

Jus·tin[1] (jus′tin) ***n.*** ⟦L *Justinus* < *justus:* see JUST[1]⟧ a masculine name: var. *Justus;* fem. *Justina*

Jus·tin[2] (jus′tin), Saint (A.D. 100?-165?); Christian apologist & martyr, born in Samaria: his day is June 1: called *Justin Martyr*

Jus·ti·na (jus tē′nə, -tī′-) ***n.*** ⟦L, fem. of *Justinus:* see JUSTIN[1]⟧ a feminine name: dim. *Tina;* var. *Justine*

Jus·tin·i·an I (jus tin′ē ən) (L. name *Flavius Ancius Justinianus*) A.D. 483-565; Byzantine emperor (527-565): known for the codification of Roman law (**Justinian code**): called *the Great*

jus·tle (jus′əl) ***vt., vi.,* jus′tled, jus′tling,** ***n. var. of*** JOSTLE

just·ly (just′lē) ***adv.*** **1** in a just manner **2** rightly **3** deservedly

jut (jut) ***vi., vt.* jut′ted, jut′ting** ⟦prob. var. of JET[1]⟧ to stick out; project —***n.*** a part that juts

jute (jo͞ot) ***n.*** ⟦Hindi *jhuto* < Sans *jūta,* matted hair, *jata,* braid of hair, fibrous roots⟧ **1** a strong, glossy fiber used for making burlap, sacks, mats, rope, etc. **2** either of two S Asian plants (*Corchorus capsularis* and *C. olitorius*) of the linden family, which yield this fiber

Jute (jo͞ot) ***n.*** ⟦< ME *Jutes,* pl. < ML *Jutae* or OE *Iotas* < ON *Iōtar*⟧ a member of an ancient Germanic people that lived in Jutland: Jutes invaded SE England in the 5th cent. A.D., settling in what became Kent —**Jut′ish** ***adj.***

Jut·land (jut′lənd) peninsula of N Europe that forms the mainland of Denmark & the N part of the German state of Schleswig-Holstein

juv *abbrev.* juvenile

Ju·ve·nal (jo͞o′və nəl) (L. name *Decimus Junius Juvenalis*) A.D. 60?-140; Rom. satirical poet

ju·ve·nes·cent (jo͞o′və nes′ənt) ***adj.*** ⟦L *juvenescens,* prp. of *juvenescere,* to become young < *juvenis,* YOUNG⟧ becoming young; growing youthful —**ju′ve·nes′cence** ***n.***

ju·ve·nile (jo͞o′və nīl′, -nəl) ***adj.*** ⟦L *juvenilis* < *juvenis,* YOUNG⟧ **1** *a)* young or youthful *b)* immature or childish **2** of, characteristic of, or suitable for children or young persons **3** *Geol.* emanating from the interior of the earth for the first time: said of gas, water, etc. —***n.*** **1** a young person; child or youth **2** an actor who plays youthful roles ☆**3** a book for young people **4** a two-year-old race horse **5** *Biol.* a young plant or animal differing variously in form, features, etc. from the adult —***SYN.*** YOUNG

☆**juvenile court** a law court for cases involving young persons under a specified age, usually 18 years

juvenile delinquency behavior by young persons of not more than a specified age, usually 18 years, that is antisocial or in violation of the law —**juvenile delinquent**

juvenile diabetes TYPE 1 DIABETES

juvenile hall DETENTION HOME

juvenile hormone a hormone secreted by insects that regulates growth and metamorphosis and which must be absent for the emergence of an adult: used to inhibit insect growth, as for preventing insect reproduction

ju·ve·nil·i·a (jo͞o′və nil′ē ə) ***pl.n.*** ⟦L, neut. pl. of *juvenilis,* JUVENILE⟧ **1** writings, paintings, etc. done by an author, artist, etc. in his or her youth **2** books for children

ju·ve·nil·i·ty (jo͞o′və nil′i tē) ***n.*** ⟦L *juvenilitas*⟧ **1** the quality or state of being juvenile **2** *pl.* **-ties** a childish action, manner, etc.

☆**ju·vy** (jo͞o′vē) ***n., pl.* ju′vies** ⟦JUV(ENILE) + -Y[1]⟧ [Slang] **1** JUVENILE DELINQUENT **2** a reformatory or juvenile hall **3** JUVENILE COURT Also sp. **ju′vie,** *pl.* **ju′vies**

jux·ta- (juks′tə) ⟦Fr < L *juxta,* near, beside < IE *yugistos, superl. of base *yug-, closely connected, var. of *yeug- > YOKE⟧ *combining form* near, beside, close by [*juxtapose*]

jux·ta·pose (juks′tə pōz′, juks′tə pōz′) ***vt.*** **-posed′, -pos′ing** ⟦Fr *juxtaposer*: see prec. & POSE[1]⟧ to put side by side or close together —**jux′ta·po·si′tion** ***n.***

☆**JV** *abbrev.* junior varsity

JWB *abbrev.* Jewish Welfare Board

JWV *abbrev.* Jewish War Veterans

Jy *abbrev.* July

Jyl·land (yül′län) *Dan. name for* JUTLAND

k[1] or **K** (kā) *n., pl.* **k's, K's** **1** the eleventh letter of the English alphabet: from the Greek *kappa,* a borrowing from the Phoenician **2** any of the speech sounds that this letter represents, as, in English, the (k) of *kept* **3** a type or impression for *k* or *K* **4** the eleventh in a sequence or group **5** an object shaped like K —*adj.* **1** of *k* or *K* **2** eleventh in a sequence or group **3** shaped like K

k[2] *abbrev.* **1** karat (carat) **2** kilo- **3** kilogram **4** kilometer **5** kopeck(s)

k[3] *symbol* Boltzmann constant

K[1] (kā) *n.* ⟦< KILO-⟧ **1** *Comput.* KILOBYTE **2** [Informal] a thousand dollars [she earns 40K now]

K[2] *abbrev.* **1** karat (carat) **2** kathode (cathode) **3** *Physics* Kelvin **4** *Football* kicker: sometimes written **k** **5** kilobyte(s) **6** kilometer(s) **7** kindergarten **8** *Chess* king **9** *Bible* Kings **10** knit **11** kosher: prepared according to kashrut ☆**12** ⟦< *(struc)k (out)*⟧ *Baseball* strikeout **13** *Comput.* the number 1,024, or 2^{10} **14** *Music* a prefix to the numbers of the works of W. A. Mozart as indexed in the catalog of his works compiled by L. Köchel (1800-77), Austrian musicologist

K[3] **1** *Elec. symbol* capacity **2** ⟦ModL *kalium* < Ar *(al-)qali:* see ALKALI⟧ *Chem. symbol for* potassium

ka (kä) *n.* ⟦Egypt *k'*⟧ in ancient Egyptian religion, the soul, regarded as dwelling in a person's body or in an image

Ka or **ka** *abbrev.* kathode (cathode)

Kaa·ba (kä′bə, kä′ə bə) *n.* ⟦Ar *ka'ba,* lit., square building < *ka'b,* a cube⟧ the sacred Muslim shrine, a square stone structure in the Great Mosque at Mecca, toward which believers turn when praying: it contains a black stone venerated as holy

kab (kab) *n. alt. sp. of* CAB[2]

Kab·ba·lah (kə bä′lə, kab′ə lə) *n.* ⟦< ML *cabbala:* see CABALA⟧ a Jewish mystical movement and form of mystical theology based on a symbolic interpretation of the Scriptures: it flourished from the end of the 12th cent.: also sp. **Ka·ba′la** or **Kab·ba′la**

kab·ba·list (kä′bə list, kab′ə-) *n.* an adherent or student of KABBALAH

kab·ba·lis·tic (kä′bə lis′tik, kab′ə-) *adj.* of or having to do with KABBALAH or kabbalists

ka·bob (kə bäb′) *n. alt. sp. of* KEBAB

ka·boom (kə bo͞om′) *interj., n.* ⟦echoic⟧ (used to suggest) the sound of an explosion

Ka·bu·ki (kä bo͞o′kē, kə-) *n.* ⟦Jpn, nominal form of *kabuku,* to be divergent, to deviate: in ref. to the early evaluation of this drama form⟧ [*also* **k-**] a form of Japanese drama dating from the 17th cent.: it is based on popular themes, with male and female roles performed by men only, chiefly in formalized pantomime, dance, and song

Ka·bul (kä′bo͝ol′) capital of Afghanistan, in the NE part

Ka·byle (kə bīl′, -bēl′) *n.* ⟦Fr < Ar *qabā'il,* pl. of *qabīla,* tribe⟧ **1** a member of any of a group of Berber peoples in Algeria and Tunisia **2** the variety of Berber spoken by these peoples

☆**ka·chi·na** (kə chē′nə) *n., pl.* **-nas** or **-na** ⟦Hopi *ķacína* < Keresan: cf. Santa Ana Keresan *kâcina*⟧ **1** in Pueblo folklore, a beneficent spirit, either a minor deity or the spirit of an ancestor **2** *a)* a male dancer impersonating such a spirit *b)* the mask worn by the dancer **3** a small, wooden doll representing such a spirit

kad·dish (käd′ish) *n.* ⟦Aram *kadish,* lit., holy, akin to Heb *kadosh,* holy < root *kdš,* sanctify⟧ *Judaism* **1** a prayer in praise of God, recited as part of the daily service **2** another form of this prayer, recited by mourners

Ka·desh (kā′desh′) oasis in the desert, south of Palestine: Gen. 14:7, 16:14; Num. 32:8; Deut. 1:46, 2:14

ka·di (kä′dē, kā′-) *n. alt. sp. of* CADI

kaf (käf, kôf) *n.* ⟦Heb⟧ the eleventh letter of the Hebrew alphabet (כ, ך): in a text containing points, this letter written with a dot is designated *kaf;* without a dot it is *khaf*

☆**kaf·fee·klatsch** (kä′fā kläch′, kô′fē klach′) *n.* ⟦Ger < *kaffee,* COFFEE + *klatsch,* gossip, of echoic orig.⟧ [*also* **K-**] an informal gathering for drinking coffee and talking: also written **kaffee klatsch**

Kaf·fir (kaf′ər) *n.* ⟦Ar *kāfir,* infidel < prp. of *kafara,* to be irreligious⟧ **1** *a)* a member of any of several Bantu-speaking peoples of S Africa *b)* XHOSA: in these senses, regarded as contemptuous **2** [**k-**] *alt. sp. of* KAFIR **3** [*usually* **k-**] [South Afr.] a black African: a contemptuous term

kaf·fi·yeh (kə fē′ə) *n.* ⟦Ar *kaffiya,* var. of *kūfiya,* prob. < LL *cofea,* COIF⟧ a headdress worn by Arabs as a protection against dust and heat: it is a large square of cotton cloth, draped and folded, and held in place by a cord wound about the head: also sp. **kaf·fi′yah**

kaf·ir (kaf′ər) *n.* ⟦Ar *kāfir:* see KAFFIR⟧ **1** a sorghum (*Sorghum bicolor* var. *caffrorum*) with juicy stalks and slender, cylindrical seed heads, grown in dry regions for grain and fodder: also **kafir corn** **2** [**K-**] *alt. sp. of* KAFFIR

Kaf·ka (käf′kə), **Franz** (fränts) 1883-1924; Austrian-Czech writer

Kaf·ka·esque (käf′kə esk′) *adj.* of, characteristic of, or like the writings of Kafka; specif., surreal, nightmarish, confusingly complex, etc.

kaf·tan (kaf′tən, -tan′; käf tän′) *n. alt. sp. of* CAFTAN

Ka·gan (kā′gən), **E·le·na** (ē lā′nə) 1960- ; associate justice, U.S. Supreme Court (2010-

Ka·ga·wa (kä′gä wä′), **To·yo·hi·ko** (tō′yō hē′kō) 1888-1960; Jpn. social reformer & writer

Ka·go·shi·ma (kä′gō shē′mä) seaport on the S coast of Kyushu, Japan

Kah·lo (kä′lō), **Fri·da** (frē′də) (born *Magdalena Carmen Frida Kahlo y Calderon*) 1907-54; Mex. painter: wife of Diego Rivera

Kah·lu·a (kə lo͞o′ə) *trademark for* a sweet, coffee-flavored liqueur

☆**Kahn test** (kän) ⟦after R. L. *Kahn* (1887-1979), U.S. immunologist⟧ a modified form of the Wassermann test for the diagnosis of syphilis

Ka·ho·o·la·we (kä hō′ō lä′wā, -vā) ⟦Haw *Ka-ho'olawe,* lit., the carrying away (by currents)⟧ one of the Hawaiian Islands, southwest of Maui: 45 sq mi (117 sq km)

ka·hu·na (kə ho͞o′nə) *n.* ⟦Haw⟧ **1** in traditional Hawaiian society, a person with specialized knowledge of ritual, agriculture, navigation, sorcery, etc. **2** [Slang] any person or thing having larger-than-life power, authority, or repute: a hyperbolic and humorous usage: usually in the phrase **the big kahuna**

Kai·e·teur Falls (kī′ə to͝or′) waterfall in WC Guyana: 741 ft (226 m)

kail (kāl) *n. alt. sp. of* KALE

kai·nite (kī′nīt′, kā′-) *n.* ⟦Ger *kainit* < Gr *kainos,* new < IE base **ken-,* to sprout forth > L *(re)cens,* RECENT⟧ a usually whitish, soft mineral, $MgSO_4 \cdot KCl \cdot 3H_2O$, used in fertilizers and as a source of potassium and magnesium

Kair·ouan (ker wän′) a city in NE Tunisia: a holy city of the Muslims

kai·ser (kī′zər) *n.* ⟦ME *caiser,* prob. via ON *keisari,* akin to OFris *keisar,* OHG *keisar* < Goth *kaisar,* ult. < L *Caesar,* family name of first Roman emperors; reinforced, esp. in senses *b* & *c,* by Ger *kaiser*⟧ [*often* **K-**] the title of: *a)* the rulers of the Holy Roman Empire, 962-1806 *b)* the rulers of Austria, 1804-1918 *c)* the rulers of Germany, 1871-1918

Kai·ser (kī′zər), **Henry J(ohn)** 1882-1967; U.S. industrialist

kaiser roll ⟦partial transl. of Ger *kaisersemmel,* kaiser bun: prob. named for its large size & crownlike shape⟧ a large, round roll with a hard crust, used for sandwiches

ka·ka (kä′kə) *n.* ⟦Maori *kākā* < *kā,* to screech⟧ a brownish New Zealand parrot (*Nestor meridionalis*) often kept as a pet

ka·ka·po (kä′kä pō′) *n., pl.* **-pos′** ⟦Maori < *kākā,* parrot + *pō,* night⟧ a flightless, nocturnal parrot (*Strigops habroptilus*) of New Zealand having a green body with brown and yellow markings: it is an endangered species

ka·ke·mo·no (kä′kə mō′nō) *n., pl.* **-nos** ⟦Jpn < *kake,* to hang + *mono,* thing⟧ a Japanese hanging or scroll of silk or paper with an inscription or picture on it and rollers at the top and bottom

ka·ki (kä′kē) *n., pl.* **-kis** ⟦Jpn⟧ JAPANESE PERSIMMON

kal *abbrev.* kalends (calends)

Ka·laal·lit Nu·naat (kə lä′lit no͞o nät′) ⟦Inuktitut *Kalaallit,* self-designation + *nunaat,* country⟧ *local name for* GREENLAND

ka·la a·zar (kä′lä ä zär′) ⟦Hindi *kālā-āzār,* lit., black disease⟧ an infectious disease, a type of leishmaniasis, that occurs in subtropical or tropical areas, caused by a protozoan parasite (*Leishmania donovani*) transmitted by sand flies (esp. genus *Phlebotomus*), and characterized by an enlarged spleen and liver, irregular fever, anemia, etc.: also written **ka′la-a·zar′** *n.*

Ka·la·ha·ri (kä′lä hä′rē) desert plateau in S Africa, mostly in Botswana: *c.* 350,000 sq mi (906,497 sq km)

Kal·a·ma·zoo (kal′ə mə zo͞o′) ⟦< *(Ke-)Kalamazoo,* name of nearby river; lit., ? smoke, ? boiling water in an Algonquian language, prob. because of its many springs⟧ city in SW Mich.

kal·an·cho·e (kal′an kō′ē) *n.* any of a genus (*Kalanchoe*) of succulent perennial plants of the orpine family; esp., a species (*K. blossfeldiana*) with small red flowers that can be induced to bloom in December for Christmas

Ka·lash·ni·kov (kə läsh′ni kôf′) *n.* ⟦after M. *Kalashnikov* (1919–2013), Soviet arms designer⟧ any of various assault rifles or submachine guns, originally of Soviet design, including, specif., the AK-47

Ka·lat (kə lät′) division of Baluchistan, Pakistan: former state of British India

Kalb, Johann *see* DE KALB, Johann

kale (kāl) *n.* ⟦Scot *kale, kail,* var. of COLE⟧ **1** a hardy vegetable (*Brassica oleracea* var. *acephala*) of the crucifer family, with loose, spreading, curled leaves that do not form a head **2** [Scot.] *a)* any cabbage or greens *b)* a broth made of cabbage or other greens ☆**3** [Slang] money; esp., paper money

ka·lei·do·scope (kə lī′də skōp′) *n.* ⟦< Gr *kalos,* beautiful + *eidos,* form (see -OID) + -SCOPE⟧ **1** a tubular device containing loose bits of colored glass, plastic, etc. reflected by mirrors so that various symmetrical patterns appear when the tube is held to the eye and rotated **2** anything that constantly changes, as in color and pattern —**ka·lei′do·scop′ic** (-skäp′ik) *adj.* —**ka·lei′do·scop′i·cal·ly** *adv.*

kal·ends (kal′əndz) *pl.n.* [*sometimes* **K-**] *alt. sp. of* CALENDS

Ka·le·va·la (kä′lə vä′lä) *n.* ⟦Finn < *kaleva,* personal name + *-la,* abode, hence, lit., land of Kaleva⟧ a Finnish epic poem in trochaic alliterative verse, compiled in the early 19th cent. from orally transmitted folklore and poetry

Kal·gan (käl gän′) *former name for* ZHANGJIAKOU

Ka·li (kä′lē) *n.* a Hindu goddess viewed both as destroying life and as giving it

Ka·li·da·sa (kä′lē dä′sä) fl. 5th cent. A.D.; Hindu poet & dramatist

ka·lif or **ka·liph** (kā′lif, kal′if; kə lēf′) *n. alt. sp. of* CALIPH

Ka·li·man·tan (kä′lē män′tän′) S part of the island of Borneo, belonging to Indonesia: 208,286 sq mi (539,459 sq km); chief city, Banjarmasin

ka·lim·ba (kə lim′bə) *n.* ⟦of Afr orig., prob. from a word in Shona (a Bantu language)⟧ a musical instrument similar to the mbira, but usually smaller and with fewer keys

Ka·li·nin (kä lē′nin) *name* (1931-90) *for* TVER

Ka·li·nin·grad (-grät′) city in W European Russia, on the Baltic Sea: part of an exclave surrounded by Poland & Lithuania

Ka·lisz (kä′lish) city in central Poland: one of the oldest Polish towns

kal·li·kre·in (kal′i krē′in) *n.* ⟦< Gr *kallikreas,* pancreas < *kallos,* beauty + *kreas,* flesh⟧ any of a group of proteolytic enzymes in the blood, urine, etc. that release a kinin from various globulins

☆**kal·mi·a** (kal′mē ə) *n.* ⟦ModL, after P. *Kalm* (1715-1779), Swed botanist⟧ any of a genus (*Kalmia*) of North American evergreen shrubs of the heath family, as the mountain laurel, with flowers of white or rose

Kal·muck or **Kal·muk** (kal′muk′) *n.* ⟦prob. of Mongolian orig.⟧ **1** a member of a group of Mongolian peoples living chiefly in the lower Volga region and N Xinjiang **2** the Mongolian language of these peoples Also **Kal′myk** (-mik)

ka·long (kä′lôŋ′) *n.* ⟦prob. via Malay < Javanese *kalong*⟧ FLYING FOX

kal·pak (kal′pak′) *n. alt. sp. of* CALPAC

kal·so·mine (kal′sə mīn′, -min) *n., vt.* **-mined′, -min′ing** *alt. sp. of* CALCIMINE

Ka·lu·ga (kə lo͞o′gə) city in WC European Russia, on the Oka

Ka·ma[1] (kä′mə) *n.* ⟦Sans *kāma,* desire, love, god of love < IE **kama-* < base **ka-,* to desire > WHORE, L *carus,* dear⟧ *Hindu Myth.* the god of love

Ka·ma[2] (kä′mə) river in European Russia, flowing from the Urals southwest into the Volga: 1,262 mi (2,031 km)

Ka·ma·ku·ra (käm′ə ko͝or′ə) city in SE Honshu, Japan, southeast of Yokohama: site of Daibutsu, the great bronze figure of Buddha (cast 1252)

ka·ma·la (kə mä′lə, kam′ə lə) *n.* ⟦Sans⟧ **1** an East Indian tree (*Mallotus philippinensis*) of the spurge family **2** a powder obtained from its seed pods, used as the base of an orange dye and, formerly, as a vermifuge

Ka·ma Su·tra (kä′mə so͞o′trə) ⟦Sans *kāmasūtra* < *kāma,* love (see KAMA[1]) + *sūtra,* thread, guideline (see SUTRA)⟧ a Hindu religious treatise written *c.* A.D. 400, that deals with pleasure, love, and sexuality: also written **Ka′ma·su′tra** *n.*

Kam·chat·ka (käm chät′kə) peninsula in NE Siberia, between the Sea of Okhotsk & the Bering Sea: *c.* 750 mi (1,207 km) long; 140,000 sq mi (362,599 sq km)

kame (kām) *n.* ⟦north Brit dial. var. of COOMB⟧ a hill or short, steep ridge of stratified sand or gravel deposited at the edge of a melting glacier

Ka·me·ha·me·ha I (kä mā′hä mā′hä) 1758?-1819; 1st king of the Hawaiian Islands (1810-19): called *the Great*

Ka·mensk-U·ral·ski (kä′minsk o͞o räl′skē) city in W Asian Russia, in the Urals

ka·mi (kä′mē) *n., pl.* **-mi** ⟦Jpn, deity, god⟧ in Shinto, a divine power or aura, often identified with one or more deities or ancestors

ka·mi·ka·ze (kä′mə kä′zē) *adj.* ⟦Jpn, lit., divine wind < *kami,* god + *kaze,* the wind⟧ **1** of or pertaining to a suicide attack by a Japanese airplane pilot in WWII **2** [Informal] very reckless, suicidal, etc. —*n.* **1** the pilot or airplane in a kamikaze attack **2** [Informal] a person who acts recklessly

Kam·pa·la (käm pä′lə) capital of Uganda, in the S part near Lake Victoria

kam·pong (käm′pôŋ′) *n.* ⟦Malay: see COMPOUND[2]⟧ a small Malay village or cluster of huts

Kam·pu·che·a (kam′po͞o chē′ə) *see* CAMBODIA —**Kam′pu·che′an** *adj., n.*

kam·seen (kam sēn′) *n. var. of* KHAMSIN: also **kam·sin** (kam′sin)

Kan *abbrev.* Kansas

ka·na (kä′nə, -nä) *n.* ⟦Jpn⟧ **1** the portion of the Japanese writing system that is a syllabary **2** *pl.* **-na** any of the characters in this syllabary

Ka·na·ka (kə nak′ə, -nä′kə; kan′ə kə) *n.* ⟦Haw, man < Proto-Polynesian **tangata,* man, person⟧ **1** a Hawaiian **2** a person born in the South Sea Islands

USAGE—this is a neutral term in Hawaiian, but is derogatory as used in English

Ka·na·ra (kä′nə rə, kə nä′rə) region of SW India

Ka·na·rese (kä′nə rēz′, -rēs′) *adj.* of Kanara or its people, language or culture —*n.* **1** *pl.* **-rese′** any of a group of Kannada-speaking peoples living chiefly in Kanara **2** KANNADA

Ka·na·za·wa (kä′nə zä′wə) city in WC Honshu, Japan, on the Sea of Japan

kan·ban (kän′bän′) *n.* ⟦Jpn, sign, card < Chin: with reference to the sign a worker displays at a workstation when a supply of parts is about to run out⟧ a method or system of arranging to have parts, raw materials, etc. delivered just as they are needed in the manufacturing process

Kan·chen·jun·ga (kän′chən jo͝oŋ′gə) mountain in the E Himalayas, on the Nepal-Sikkim border: 3d highest mountain in the world: 28,168 ft (8,586 m)

Kan·da·har (kän′də här′) city in S Afghanistan

Kan·din·sky (kan din′skē), **Was·si·li** (or **Va·si·li**) (vas′ə lē′) 1866-1944; Russ. painter in Germany & France

Kan·dy (kan′dē, kän′-) city in central Sri Lanka

kan·ga·roo (kaŋ′gə ro͞o′) *n., pl.* **-roos′** or **-roo′** ⟦said (by James COOK[1]) to be the name in a language of NE Australia⟧ any of various leaping, plant-eating marsupials (family Macropodidae) native to Australia and neighboring islands, with short forelegs, strong, large hind legs, and a long, thick tail: the female has a ventral pouch, or marsupium, for her young

☆**kangaroo court** ⟦said to be so named because its justice progresses by leaps and bounds⟧ [Informal] **1** an unauthorized, irregular court, usually disregarding normal legal procedure, as one in a frontier region **2** any tribunal in which judgment is rendered arbitrarily or unfairly

kangaroo rat ☆**1** any of a genus (*Dipodomys,* family Heteromyidae) of small, long-legged, jumping, mouselike rodents living in desert regions of the SW U.S. and Mexico **2** RAT KANGAROO

kan·ji (kän′jē) *n.* ⟦Jpn < *kan,* Chinese + *ji,* character, letter⟧ **1** the portion of the Japanese writing system whose characters are based on Chinese ideographs **2** *pl.* **-ji** any of these characters

Kan·na·da (kä′nə də) *n.* ⟦Kannada *Kannaḍa*⟧ the Dravidian language spoken in Mysore and adjacent districts of S India

Ka·no (kä′nō) city in N Nigeria

Kan·pur (kän′po͝or′) city in N India, on the Ganges, in Uttar Pradesh

Kans *abbrev.* Kansas

Kan·san (kan′zən) *adj.* of the state of Kansas: usually used in the predicate —*n.* a person born or living in Kansas

Kan·sas (kan′zəs) ⟦Fr *kansa* (prob. via Illinois) < a Siouan name⟧ **1** Midwestern state of the NC U.S.: admitted 1861; 81,815 sq mi (211,900 sq km); cap. Topeka: abbrev. *KS* or *Kans* **2** river in NE Kans., flowing east into the Missouri at Kansas City: *c.* 170 mi (274 km)

Kansas City ⟦after prec.⟧ **1** city in W Mo., on the Missouri River **2** city in NE Kans., on the Missouri & Kansas rivers, opposite Kansas City, Mo.

Kan·su (gän′so͞o′) *a former transliteration of* GANSU

Kant (känt, kant), **Immanuel** 1724-1804; Ger. philosopher

Kant·i·an (kän′tē ən, kan′-) *adj.* of or having to do with Kant or Kantianism —*n.* a follower of Kant or Kantianism

Kant·i·an·ism (-iz′əm) *n.* the philosophy of Kant, who held that the content of knowledge comes a posteriori from sense perception, but that its form is determined by a priori categories of the mind: he also declared that God, freedom, and immortality, although they cannot be proved or disproved, are necessary postulates of a rational morality

Ka·nu·ri (kä no͝or′ē) *n.* **1** *pl.* **-ris** or **-ri** a member of a Muslim people of N Nigeria and adjacent regions **2** the Nilo-Saharan language of this people

Kao·hsiung (kou′shoo͝ŋ′) seaport on the SW coast of Taiwan

ka·o·lin (kā′ə lin) *n.* ⟦Fr < Chin *kao-ling* (lit., high mountain), name of the hill in Jiangxi Province where it was found⟧ a fine white clay used in making porcelain, as a filler in textiles, paper, rubber, etc., and in medicine in the treatment of diarrhea

ka·o·lin·ite (-lə nīt′) *n.* a colorless or white, soft mineral, hydrous aluminum silicate, $Al_2Si_2O_5(OH)_4$, that is the main constituent of kaolin

ka·on (kā′än′) *n.* ⟦*ka* (for the letter *K*) + (MES)ON⟧ *Particle Physics* any of four short-lived mesons that are positive, negative, or neutral and have a mass of 495 MeV/c^2 (about 970 times that of an electron)

ka·pell·meis·ter (kə pel′mīs′tər) *n.* ⟦Ger, lit., choir master < *kapelle,* choir < It *capella,* a company of musicians (orig. CHAPEL, hence the choir or orchestra in a court chapel) + Ger *meister,* a master⟧ **1** [**K-**] [Historical] the conductor of a choir or orchestra in a court chapel to a German or Austrian court **2** in German-speaking countries, the director of a choir, chamber orchestra, etc.

kaph (käf, kôf) *n. alt. sp. of* KAF

Ka·pi·tsa (kä′pi tsä′), **Pyotr L(eonidovich)** (pyôtr) 1894-1984; Russian nuclear physicist

ka·pok (kā′päk′) *n.* ⟦Malay⟧ **1** the silky fibers around the seeds of any of several silk-cotton trees, esp. a ceiba (*Ceiba pentandra*): used for stuffing mattresses, life preservers, sleeping bags, etc. **2** CEIBA (sense 1): also **kapok tree**

Ka·po·si's sarcoma (kə pō′zēz′, -sēz′; kap′ə zēz′, -sēz′) ⟦after M. K. *Kaposi* (1837-1902), Hung dermatologist⟧ a malignant tumor, usually of the skin, appearing primarily in persons with an immunological deficiency

kap·pa (kap′ə) *n.* ⟦Gr < Sem, as in Heb *kaph*⟧ the tenth letter of the Greek alphabet (Κ, κ)

Kap·ton (kap′tän′) *trademark for* a strong, lightweight plastic resistant to high temperatures, used primarily by the aerospace industry to make thin sheets of insulation

ka·put (kə po͝ot′, -po͞ot′) *adj.* ⟦Ger *kaputt,* lost, ruined, broken < Fr *(faire) capot,* to lose all tricks (as in piquet) < *capster,* to capsize⟧ [Slang] ruined, destroyed, defeated, etc. [*the toaster is kaput*]

Ka·ra·chi (kə rä′chē) capital of Sind province, Pakistan, on the Arabian Sea: former (1947-59) capital of Pakistan

Ka·ra·de·niz Bo·ğa·zi (kä′rä deŋ ēz′ bō′gä zē′) *Turk. name for* BOSPORUS

Ka·ra·fu·to (kä′rä fo͞o′tō) *Jpn. name for* SAKHALIN

Ka·ra·gan·da (kä′rə gän′də) city in EC Kazakhstan

Ka·ra·ite (kā′rə īt′) *n.* ⟦< Heb *karaim,* readers of the Scriptures (< *kara,* to read + *-im,* pl. suffix) + -ITE[1]⟧ a member of a Jewish sect, established in the Middle East in the 8th cent., rejecting the Talmud and acknowledging only the Bible as the authority in religion —**Ka′ra·ism′** *n.*

Ka·ra·jan (kär′ə yän′), **Herbert von** 1908-89; Austrian orchestra conductor

Ka·ra-Kal·pak (kä rä′ käl päk′) *n.* ⟦Turkic < *kara,* black + *kalpak,* hat: reason for name unknown⟧ **1** a member of a people living mainly in Uzbekistan **2** the Turkic language of this people

Ka·ra·ko·ram (kä′rä kôr′əm, kar′ə-) mountain range in SC Asia between Xinjiang, China, and N Kashmir, India, extending *c.* 300 mi (483 km) to the Pamirs: NW extension of the Himalayas: highest peak, GODWIN AUSTEN

kar·a·kul (kar′ə kul′, -kəl) *n.* ⟦Russ *karakul′,* astrakhan (the fur) < Turkic *qara köl,* lit., dark lake: common place name in central Asia⟧ **1** any of a breed of medium-sized sheep native to central Asia, having long, drooping ears, long legs, and a broad, fat tail **2** the tightly curled, lustrous fur made from the fleece of its newborn lambs: in this sense commonly sp. *caracul*

Ka·ra Kum (kä rä′ ko͞om′; *E* kar′ə) desert in Turkmenistan, east of the Caspian Sea: *c.* 135,000 sq mi (349,649 sq km)

ka·ra·o·ke (kar′ē ō′kē, ker′-) *n.* ⟦< Jpn *kara,* empty + *oke,* ult. < E *orchestra*⟧ a form of entertainment in which patrons, as in a bar, take turns singing popular songs into a microphone accompanied by prerecorded music played on a special device, with the lyrics displayed on a screen

Ka·ra Sea (kä′rə) arm of the Arctic Ocean, between Novaya Zemlya & NW Siberia

kar·at (kar′ət) *n.* ⟦var. of CARAT⟧ one 24th part: a measure of the relative amount of pure gold combined with an alloy

ka·ra·te (kə rät′ē) *n.* ⟦Jpn < *kara,* empty + *te,* hand⟧ a Japanese system of self-defense characterized chiefly by sharp, quick blows delivered with the hands and feet —**ka·ra′te·ist** *n.*

ka·rat·e·ka (kə rä′tə kə) *n., pl.* **-e·ka** or **-e·kas** ⟦Jpn < *karate* (see prec.) + *-ka,* expert⟧ one who performs, or is expert in, karate

Ka·re·li·a (kə rēl′yə; *Russ* kä rē′lē ä) region in N Europe between the Gulf of Finland and the White Sea, constituting an autonomous republic of Russia: 66,564 sq mi (172,400 sq km)

Ka·re·li·an (kə rēl′yən, -rē′lē ən) *adj.* ⟦< prec. < Finn *karja,* livestock + *-la,* suffix of place⟧ of Karelia or its people, language, or culture —*n.* **1** a member of a people living in Karelia and E Finland **2** the Finno-Ugric language of this people

Karelian Isthmus isthmus in Karelia, NW Russia, between the Gulf of Finland & Lake Ladoga: 90 mi (145 km) long

Ka·ren[1] (kə ren′) *n.* ⟦Burmese *kayin,* name of one of the peoples⟧ **1** *pl.* **-rens′** or **-ren′** a member of a group of peoples of S and SE Myanmar and of Thailand **2** their Sino-Tibetan language

Kar·en[2] (kar′ən) *n.* a feminine name: see CATHERINE[1]

Ka·ri·ba Dam (kə rē′bə) dam on the Zambezi River, on the Zambian-Zimbabwean border: 420 ft (128 m) high: it has created a lake (**Kariba Lake**), 2,000 sq mi (5,180 sq km)

Karl (kärl) *n.* a masculine name: see CHARLES[1]

Karl-Marx-Stadt (kärl′märks′shtät′) *name* (1953-90) *for* CHEMNITZ

Kar·loff (kär′lôf), **Boris** (born *William Henry Pratt*) 1887-1969; U.S. film actor, born in England

Kar·lo·vy Var·y (kär′lô vē vä′rē) city in the W Czech Republic: famous for its hot springs

Karls·bad (kärls′bät; *E* kärlz′bad) *Ger. name for* KARLOVY VARY

Karls·ruh·e (-ro͞o ə; *E,* -ro͞o ə) city in SW Germany, on the Rhine, in the state of Baden-Württemberg

kar·ma (kär′mə, kur′-) *n.* ⟦Sans, a deed, act, fate < IE base **kwer-,* to make, form > Welsh *pryd,* shape, time⟧ **1** *Buddhism, Hinduism* the totality of a person's actions in any one of the successive states of that person's existence, thought of as determining the fate of the next stage **2** loosely, fate; destiny —**kar′mic** *adj.*

Kar·nak (kär′nak′) village in S Egypt, on the Nile: site of ancient Thebes

Kärn·ten (kern′tən) *Ger. name for* CARINTHIA

ka·ross (kə räs′) *n.* ⟦Afrik *karos*⟧ in S Africa, a cape, blanket, or rug made of animal skins

kar·roo (kə ro͞o′, ka-) *n., pl.* **-roos′** ⟦Hottentot *karo*⟧ a dry tableland, esp. one in S Africa: also sp. **ka·roo′**, *pl.* **-roos′** —**the Great Karroo** karroo in S South Africa: *c.* 350 mi (563 km) long & 2,000 to 3,000 ft (610 to 914 m) high

karst (kärst) *n.* ⟦Ger < *Karst,* Ger name for the hinterland of Trieste, altered < Slovenian *Kras*⟧ a region made up of porous limestone containing deep fissures and sinkholes and characterized by underground caves and streams

kart (kärt) *n.* ⟦arbitrary alteration of CART⟧ ☆**1** any of various small, wheeled vehicles with or without a motor: so used chiefly as part of certain trademarked names ☆**2** a small, flat, 4-wheeled, motorized vehicle seating one person: used for recreation and in special racing events (**kart′ing**)

Kart·ve·li·an (kärt vē′lē ən) *n.* ⟦ult. < a Georgian word, self-designation of the Georgian people⟧ the South Caucasian language family, whose principal member is Georgian: see CAUCASIAN (*adj.* 3)

kar·y·o- (kar′ē ō, -ə) ⟦ModL < Gr *karyon,* a nut, kernel < IE base **kar-,* HARD⟧ *combining form* **1** nut, kernel **2** *Biol.* the nucleus of a cell [*karyolymph*]

kar·y·og·a·my (kar′ē äg′ə mē) *n.* ⟦prec. + -GAMY⟧ the fusion of the nuclei of two gametes, as in fertilization

kar·y·o·ki·ne·sis (kar′ē ō ki nē′sis) *n.* ⟦KARYO- + Gr *kinēsis,* motion⟧ MITOSIS —**kar′y·o·ki·net′ic** (-net′ik) *adj.*

kar·y·ol·o·gy (kar′ē äl′ə jē) *n.* ⟦KARYO- + -LOGY⟧ the branch of cytology dealing with the functions and structures of the cell nucleus and, esp., of the chromosomes

kar·y·o·lymph (kar′ē ō limf′) *n.* ⟦KARYO- + LYMPH⟧ a colorless, watery liquid found inside the nucleus of a cell

kar·y·o·plasm (-plaz′əm) *n.* ⟦KARYO- + PLASM⟧ NUCLEOPLASM —**kar′y·o·plas′mic** (-plaz′mik) *adj.*

kar·y·o·some (-sōm′) *n.* ⟦KARYO- + -SOME[3]⟧ *Biol.* **1** an aggregation of chromatin in a resting nucleus **2** the nucleus of a cell

kar·y·o·tin (kar′ē ō′tin) *n.* ⟦KARYO- + (CHROMA)TIN⟧ CHROMATIN

kar·y·o·type (kar′ē ə tīp′) *n.* ⟦KARYO- (sense 2) + -TYPE (sense 1)⟧ the general appearance, including size, number, and shape, of the set of somatic chromosomes —*vt.* **-typed′**, **-typ′ing** to analyze and determine (a karyotype) —**kar′y·o·typ′ic** (-tip′ik) *adj.*, **kar′y·o·typ′i·cal**

kar·y·o·typ·ing (-tīp′iŋ) *n.* the procedure or technique used to karyotype a set of chromosomes

Ka·sai (kä sī′) river in SC Africa, flowing from Angola northwest into the Congo River: *c.* 1,100 mi (1,770 km)

kas·bah or **Kas·bah** (käz′bä′) *n. alt. sp. of* CASBAH

ka·sha (kä′shə) *n.* ⟦Russ *kaša,* porridge, partly via Yiddish⟧ cracked buckwheat, wheat, etc. cooked until soft and served variously as a porridge, with meat, etc.

ka·sher (kä′shər) *adj., n., vt. var. of* KOSHER

Kash·mir (kash′mir, kash mir′) **1** region in S Asia, between Afghanistan & Tibet: since 1846, part of Jammu and Kashmir **2** JAMMU AND KASHMIR **3 Vale of** valley of the Jhelum River, in W Kashmir —**Kash·mir′i·an** *adj., n.*

Kash·mir·i (kash mir′ē) *n.* **1** the Indo-Aryan language spoken in Kashmir **2** *pl.* **-mir′is** or **-mir′i** a person born or living in Kashmir

kash·rut or **kash·ruth** (käsh ro͞ot′, käsh′ro͞ot′) *n.* **1** the dietary regulations of Judaism: see KOSHER **2** the state of being in compliance with such regulations

Ka·shu·bi·an (ka sho͞o′bē ən) *n.* the variety of Polish spoken in N Poland near Gdańsk

Kas·sel (käs′əl) city in central Germany, in the state of Hesse

kat (kät) *n. alt. sp. of* KHAT

kat·a- (kat′ə) *prefix* CATA-: also, before a vowel, **kat-**

kat·a·bat·ic (kat′ə bat′ik) *adj.* ⟦< Gr *katabatikos* < *katabainein,* to go down < *kata-* (see CATA-) + *bainein* (see ANABASIS)⟧ moving downward: said of air currents or winds

ka·ta·ka·na (kä′tə kä′nə) *n.* ⟦Jpn < *kata,* side + KANA⟧ the portion of the Japanese kana, or syllabary, whose characters are angular in form: it is used esp. for foreign words

Kate (kāt) *n.* a feminine name: dim. *Katie:* see CATHERINE[1], KATHERINE

ka·tha·rev·ou·sa (kä′thä rev′o͞o sä′) *n.* ⟦ModGr, lit., being pure⟧ the form of Modern Greek that conforms to classical Greek usage

ka·thar·sis (kə thär′sis) *n. alt. sp. of* CATHARSIS

Kath·er·ine or **Kath·a·rine** (kath′ə rin, kath′rin) *n.* a feminine name: dim. *Kate, Kathy, Kay, Kit, Kitty:* see CATHERINE[1]

Kath·leen (kath′lēn, kath lēn′) *n.* ⟦Ir⟧ a feminine name: see CATHERINE[1]

Kath·man·du (kät′män do͞o′) capital of Nepal, in the central part: sometimes sp. **Kat′man·du′**

Kath·ryn (kath′rin) *n.* a feminine name: see KATHERINE

Kath·y (kath′ē) *n.* a feminine name: see CATHERINE[1], KATHERINE

kat·i·on (kat′ī′ən) *n. alt. sp. of* CATION

Ka·to·wi·ce (kä′tô vē′tse) city in S Poland

Kat·rine (ka′trin, kä′-), **Loch** lake in central Scotland: scene of Scott's *Lady of the Lake:* 8 mi (12.9 km) long

Kat·te·gat (kat′i gat′) strait between SW Sweden & E Jutland, Denmark: *c.* 150 mi (241 km) long

☆**ka·ty·did** (kāt′ē did′) *n.* ⟦echoic of the sound made by the males⟧ any of several large, green orthopteran insects (esp. family Tettigoniidae) having long, slender antennae and long hind legs: the male has highly developed stridulating organs on the forewings, that produce a shrill sound

☆**katz·en·jam·mer** (kats′ən jam′ər) *n.* ⟦Ger < *katze,* CAT[1] + *jammer,* woe < OHG *jamar,* orig. adj., sad, akin to OE *geomor,* miserable: sense 1 infl. by U.S. cartoon strip (*The Katzenjammer Kids*), originated (1897) by R. Dirks⟧ **1** a farcical quality; travesty **2** a bewildering hodgepodge or distressing confusion **3** a severe headache, esp. as part of a hangover

Ka·u·a·i (kä′o͞o ä′ē, kou′ī′) ⟦< Haw, prob. desert⟧ one of the Hawaiian Islands, northwest of Oahu: 552 sq mi (1,430 sq km)

Kauf·man (kôf′mən), **George S(imon)** 1889-1961; U.S. playwright

Kau·nas (kou′näs′) city in SC Lithuania, on the Neman River

kau·ri (kou′rē) *n.* ⟦Maori⟧ **1** a tall evergreen tree (*Agathis australis*) of the pine family, growing in New Zealand **2** its wood **3** a resin (**kauri resin, kauri gum**) from this tree, often found as a fossil, used in varnishes, adhesives, and linoleum

ka·va (kä′və, -vä′) *n.* ⟦< Polynesian, prob. Tongan < Proto-Polynesian **kawa*⟧ **1** a plant (*Piper methysticum*) of the pepper family, with an aromatic odor: its roots and rhizomes have narcotic properties **2** an intoxicating drink made from the roots, for use in certain rituals Also **ka′va·ka′va**

Ka·vir Desert (kə vir′) DASHT-E-KAVIR

Ka·wa·ba·ta (kä′wä bä′tä), **Ya·su·na·ri** (yä′so͞o nä′rē) 1899-1972; Jpn. writer

Ka·wa·gu·chi (kä′wä go͞o′chē) city in E Honshu, Japan, north of Tokyo

ka·wai·i (kə wə e′) ***adj.*** ⟦Jpn⟧ in Japanese popular culture, characterized by or emphasizing the quality of prettiness or cuteness —***n.*** this quality

Ka·wa·sa·ki (kä′wä sä′kē) city in central Honshu, Japan, on Tokyo Bay

Kawasaki syndrome ⟦after T. *Kawasaki*, 20th-c. Jpn pediatrician⟧ a syndrome, usually afflicting children, characterized by high fever, swollen lymph nodes in the neck, rashes, irritated eyes and mucous membranes, etc. with possible damage to the cardiovascular system: also called **Kawasaki disease**

Kay[1] (kā) *n.* **1** a feminine name: see KATHERINE **2** a masculine name

Kay[2] (kā), **Sir** *Arthurian Legend* a knight of the Round Table, the boastful and rude seneschal and foster brother of King Arthur

kay·ak (kī′ak′) *n.* ⟦Esk⟧ **1** an Eskimo canoe made of skins completely covering a wooden frame except for an opening in the middle for the paddler **2** any similarly designed canoe for one or two paddlers, made of canvas, plastic, fiberglass, etc. —*vi.* to paddle, or go in, a kayak —**kay′ak′er** *n.*

kayak

☆**kay·o** (kā′ō′) [Slang] *vt.* **-oed′**, **-o′ing** ⟦phonetic sp. of KO⟧ *Boxing* to knock out —*n., pl.* **kay′os′** *Boxing* a knockout

Kay·se·ri (kī′se rē′) city in central Turkey

ka·za·chok (kä′zä chôk′) *n., pl.* **-zach·ki′** (-zäch kē′) ⟦Russ < *Kazak*, Cossack⟧ a vigorous Russian folk dance in which a man alternately kicks out each leg from a squatting position

Ka·zakh or **Ka·zak** (kä zäk′) *n.* **1** a member of a people living chiefly in Kazakhstan and adjacent parts of China **2** the Turkic language of this people

Kazakh Soviet Socialist Republic a republic of the U.S.S.R.: now KAZAKHSTAN

Ka·zakh·stan (kä′zäk stän′) **1** KAZAKH SOVIET SOCIALIST REPUBLIC **2** country in W Asia: became independent upon the breakup of the U.S.S.R. (1991): 1,049,155 sq mi (2,717,300 sq km); cap. Astana: formerly, *Kazakh Soviet Socialist Republic*

Ka·zan[1] (kä zän′, kä zan′), **E·li·a** (ē′lē ə, ēl′yə, e lē′ə) (born *Elias Kazanjoglou*) 1909-2003; U.S. theater & film director, born in Turkey

Ka·zan[2] (kä zän′; *Russ* kȧ zän′y′) city in W Russia, on the Volga

Ka·zan·tza·kis (kä′zän dzä′kēs′), **Ni·kos** (nē′kôs) 1885-1957; Gr. novelist

ka·zat·sky or **ka·zat·ski** (kə zät′skē) *n., pl.* **-skies** *var. of* KAZACHOK

Kaz·bek (käz bek′) volcanic mountain in the central Caucasus, N Georgia: 16,558 ft (5,047 m)

Kaz·da·ği (käz′dä gē′) *Turk. name for* Mount IDA[2]

☆**ka·zoo** (kə zo͞o′) *n., pl.* **-zoos′** ⟦echoic⟧ a toy musical instrument consisting of a small, open tube with a top hole covered by a membrane, as of paper, that vibrates to give a buzzing quality to tones hummed through the tube

kb *abbrev.* **1** kilobar(s) **2** kilobase(s)

Kb *abbrev.* kilobit(s)

KB *abbrev.* **1** kilobyte(s) **2** King's Bench **3** *Chess* king's bishop **4** Knight Bachelor

k·bar (kā′bär′) *n. short for* KILOBAR

KBE *abbrev.* Knight Commander of (the Order of) the British Empire

Kbps *abbrev.* kilobits per second

kc *abbrev.* kilocycle(s)

KC *abbrev.* **1** Kansas City: also **K.C. 2** King's Counsel **3** Knight Commander **4** Knight(s) of Columbus

kcal *abbrev.* kilocalorie(s)

KCB *abbrev.* Knight Commander of (the Order of) the Bath

Kčs *abbrev.* koruna(s)

KCVO *abbrev.* Knight Commander of the (Royal) Victorian Order

KD or **kd** *abbrev. Commerce* knocked down (not assembled)

ke·a (kā′ə, kē′ə) *n.* ⟦Maori⟧ a large, brownish-green mountain parrot (*Nestor notabilis*) of New Zealand

Ke·a (kā′ä) island of the NW Cyclades, Greece, in the Aegean Sea: 50 sq mi (129 sq km)

Kean (kēn), **Edmund** 1787-1833; Eng. actor

Kea·ton (kēt′'n), **Bus·ter** (bus′tər) (born *Joseph Frank Keaton*) 1895-1966; U.S. comic film actor

Keats (kēts), **John** 1795-1821; Eng. poet

ke·bab or **ke·bob** (kə bäb′) *n.* ⟦Ar *kabāb*⟧ **1** a small piece of marinated meat used as for shish kebab **2** [*often pl.*] SHISH KEBAB

keb·buck or **keb·bock** (keb′ək) *n.* ⟦ME *cabok* < Gael *ceapag*, a cheese, wheel⟧ [Scot.] a cheese

Ke·ble (kē′bəl), **John** 1792-1866; Eng. Anglican clergyman & poet: a founder of the Oxford movement

keck (kek) *vi.* ⟦echoic⟧ **1** to retch or heave, as if about to vomit **2** to feel or show great disgust

Kecs·ke·mét (kech′ke māt′) city in central Hungary

Ke·dah (kā′dä) state of Malaysia, in NW Peninsular Malaysia, bordering on Thailand: 3,639 sq mi (9,425 sq km)

kedge (kej) *vt.* **kedged**, **kedg′ing** ⟦ME *caggen*, to fasten < ?⟧ to move (a ship) by hauling on a rope fastened to an anchor that has been dropped some distance from it —*vi.* **1** to move a ship by kedging it **2** to move by being kedged —*n.* a light anchor, used esp. in kedging a ship: also **kedge anchor**

kedg·er·ee (kej′ər ē) *n.* ⟦Hindi *khichri* < Sans *khiccā*, mixture⟧ **1** an Indian dish of lentils, rice, and, sometimes, fish **2** a traditional British breakfast dish, a mixture of fish, rice, hard-boiled eggs, etc.

Ke·dron (kē′drən) *alt. sp. of* KIDRON

ke·ef (kē ef′) *n. var. of* KEF

keek (kēk) *vi.* ⟦ME *kiken*, prob. < MDu or MLowG *kīken*⟧ [Scot. or North Eng.] to peep; spy

keel[1] (kēl) *n.* ⟦ME *kele* < ON *kjǫlr* < Gmc **kelu-* < IE base **gel-*, to swallow > L *gula*, throat⟧ **1** the chief timber or steel piece extending along the entire length of the bottom of a boat or ship and supporting the frame: it sometimes protrudes beneath the hull **2** [Old Poet.] a ship **3** anything resembling a ship's keel **4** the assembly of beams, girders, etc. at the bottom of a rigid or semirigid airship to prevent sagging or buckling **5** *Biol.* a ridgelike part — *vt., vi.* to turn over on its side so as to turn up the keel or bottom —☆**keel over 1** to turn over or upside down; upset; capsize **2** to fall over suddenly, as in a faint —**on an even keel 1** in or keeping an upright, level position **2** steady, stable, etc.

keel[2] (kēl) *n.* ⟦ME *kele* < MDu *kiel*, boat < Gmc **keula* < IE **geul-*, rounded vessel > Sans *gōlā*, ball, round jug⟧ **1** a flat-bottomed ship; esp., a low, flat-bottomed coal barge or lighter, used on the Tyne **2** *a)* a barge load of coal *b)* a British unit of weight for coal, equal to 21.1 long tons

keel[3] (kēl) *vt.* ⟦ME *kelen* < OE *celan* (akin to Ger *kühlen*) < base of *col*, COOL⟧ [Now Dial.] to cool (a hot liquid) as by stirring

keel[4] (kēl) *n.* ⟦prob. < Ir or Gael *cīl*, ruddle⟧ a red stain used for marking lumber, etc.; ruddle

☆**keel·boat** (kēl′bōt′) *n.* a large, shallow freight boat with a keel, formerly used on the Mississippi, Missouri, etc.

keel·haul (-hôl′) *vt.* ⟦Du *kielhalen* < *kiel* < MDu, boat (see KEEL[2]) + ODu *halen*, to HAUL⟧ **1** to haul (a person) down through the water on one side of a ship, under the keel, and up on the other side as a punishment or torture **2** to scold or rebuke harshly

Kee·ling Islands (kē′liŋ) COCOS ISLANDS

keel·son (kel′sən, kēl′-) *n.* ⟦prob. via Du *kolsem* < Dan *kjølsvin*, altered (infl. by *svin*, swine) < *kjølsvill* < *kjøl*, KEEL[1] + *sville*, SILL⟧ a longitudinal beam or set of timbers or metal plates fastened inside the hull of a ship along the keel to add structural strength

Kee·lung (kē′lo͝oŋ′) seaport in N Taiwan

keen[1] (kēn) *adj.* ⟦ME *kene* < OE *cene*, wise, learned, akin to Ger *kühn*, bold < IE base **ĝen-*, to KNOW: the principal senses spring from the basic notion "capable"⟧ **1** having a sharp edge or point; that can cut well [*a keen* knife, a *keen* edge] **2** sharp or cutting in force; piercing [*a keen* appetite, a *keen* wind] **3** sharp and quick in seeing, hearing, thinking, etc.; acute [*keen* eyes, a *keen* intelligence] **4** sharp-witted; mentally acute; shrewd **5** eager; enthusiastic; much interested: often with *about, on*, etc. **6** strongly felt or perceived; intense; strong [*keen* desire, a *keen* scent] ☆**7** [Slang] good, fine, etc.: a generalized term of approval —**SYN.** EAGER[1], SHARP —**keen′ly** *adv.* —**keen′ness** *n.*

keen[2] (kēn) *n.* ⟦Ir *caoine* < *caoinim*, I wail⟧ [Irish] a wailing for the dead; dirge —*vi.* **1** [Irish] to lament or wail for the dead **2** to make a wailing, shrill, or mournful sound suggestive of a keen —*vt.* to utter in a wailing tone —**SYN.** CRY

keep (kēp) *vt.* **kept**, **keep′ing** ⟦ME *kepen* < OE *cœpan*, to behold, watch out for, lay hold of, akin to MLowG *kapen*, ON *kopa*, to stare at < ? IE base **ĝab-*, to look at or for⟧ **1** to observe or pay regard to; specif., *a)* to observe with due or prescribed acts, ceremonies, etc.; celebrate or solemnize [to *keep* the Sabbath] *b)* to fulfill (a promise, etc.) *c)* to follow or adhere to (a routine, diet, etc.) *d)* to go on maintaining [to *keep* pace] *e)* [Archaic] to attend (church, etc.) regularly **2** to take care of, or have and take care or charge of; specif., *a)* to protect; guard; defend *b)* to look after; watch over; tend *c)* to raise (livestock) *d)* to maintain in good order or condition; preserve *e)* to supply with food, shelter, etc.; provide for; support *f)* to supply with food or lodging for pay [to *keep* boarders] *g)* to have or maintain in one's service or for one's use [to *keep* servants] *h)* to set down regularly in writing; maintain (a continuous written record) [to *keep* an account of sales] *i)* to make regular entries in; maintain a continuous record of transactions, accounts, or happenings in [to *keep* books of account, to *keep* a diary] *j)* to carry on; conduct; manage **3** to maintain, or cause to stay or continue, in a specified condition, position, etc. [to *keep* an engine running] **4** to have or hold; specif., *a)* to have or hold for future use or for a long time *b)* to have regularly in stock for sale **5** to have or hold and not let go; specif., *a)* to hold in custody; prevent from escaping *b)* to prevent from leaving; detain *c)* to hold back; restrain [to *keep* someone from talking] *d)* to withhold *e)* to conceal; not tell (a secret, etc.) *f)* to continue to have or hold; not lose or give up *g)* to stay in or at; not leave (a path, course, or place) —*vi.* **1** to stay or continue in a specified condition, position, etc. **2** to continue; go on; persevere or persist: often with *on* [to *keep* on talking] **3** to hold oneself back; refrain [to *keep* from telling someone] **4** to stay in good condition; not become spoiled, sour, stale, etc.; last **5** to require no immediate attention [a task that will *keep* until tomorrow] ☆6 [Informal] to continue in session [will school *keep* all day?] 7 [Now Rare] to reside; live; stay —*n.* 1 [Obs.] care, charge, or custody 2 *a)* the strongest, innermost part or central tower of a medieval castle; donjon *b)* a stronghold; fort; castle 3 [Rare] a keeping or being kept 4 what is needed to maintain a person or animal; food and shelter; support; livelihood —*SYN.* CELEBRATE —☆**for keeps** [Informal] 1 with the agreement that the winner will keep what he or she wins 2 forever; permanently —**keep at** to continue doing, practicing, etc.; persist in (an activity) —**keep in with** [Informal] to remain on good terms with —**keep to** 1 to persevere in 2 to avoid swerving from; adhere to 3 to remain in —**keep to oneself** 1 to avoid the company of others 2 to treat (information, etc.) as confidential; not tell —**keep up** 1 to maintain in good order or condition 2 to continue; not stop or end 3 to maintain the pace; not lag behind 4 to remain informed about: with *on* or *with* —**keep up with** to go or do as fast as; stay even with —**keep up with the Joneses** to strive to get all the material things one's neighbors or associates have

keep·er (kēp′ər) *n.* 1 a person or thing that keeps; specif., *a)* a guard, as of prisoners or animals *b)* a guardian or protector *c)* [Chiefly Brit.] a curator *d)* a custodian; caretaker *e)* [Brit.] a gamekeeper *f)* any of several devices for keeping something in place, as a clasp *g)* something that keeps or lasts (well or poorly) 2 [Informal] something worth keeping, as a fish large enough for a fisherman to keep legally ☆3 *Football* a play in which the quarterback takes the ball from the center and runs with it

keep·ing (-iŋ) *n.* 1 observance (of a rule, holiday, promise, etc.) 2 care; custody; charge 3 maintenance or means of maintenance; keep 4 the condition in which something is kept 5 reservation for future use; preservation —**in keeping with** in conformity or accord with

keep·sake (-sāk′) *n.* something kept, or to be kept, for the sake of, or in memory of, the giver, an event, etc.; memento

kees·hond (kās′hônt′, kēs′-; -hund′) *n., pl.* **-honds′** or **-hond′en** (-hônt″n, -hun′dən) ⟦Du < *Kees,* nickname for *Cornelis,* CORNELIUS + *hond,* dog⟧ any of a breed of medium-sized dog with a thick, gray-and-black coat of long, straight hair, a foxlike head with small, pointed ears, and a tail that curls over the back

☆**kees·ter** (kēs′tər) *n. alt. sp. of* KEISTER

☆**keet** (kēt) *n.* ⟦echoic⟧ a young guinea fowl

Kee·wa·tin[1] (kē wät′'n) *adj. Geol.* designating or of a series of Archean rocks that make up the Canadian Shield

Kee·wa·tin[2] (kē wät′'n) ⟦coined < Cree *kiiweetin,* the north, north wind, lit., the wind that comes back < *kiiwee-,* come back + *-tin,* wind⟧ region of Nunavut, Canada

kef (kāf) *n.* ⟦Ar *kaif,* well-being⟧ 1 a dreamy condition 2 a substance, as Indian hemp, smoked to produce this condition

Ke·fal·li·ni·a (kä′fä lē nē′ä) *Gr. name for* CEPHALONIA

kef·fi·yeh (kə fē′ə) *n. var. of* KAFFIYEH: also sp. **kef·fi′yah**

ke·fir (kef′ər, ke fir′, kē′fər) *n.* ⟦Russ < word in a Caucasian language⟧ a thick, sour beverage fermented from cow's milk and usually containing a small amount of alcohol

keg (keg) *n.* ⟦ME *cagge* < or akin to ON *kaggi,* keg < IE base **ĝegh-,* a branch, stake > E dial *cag,* stump⟧ 1 a small barrel, usually one holding less than ten gallons 2 a unit of weight for nails, equal to 100 pounds

☆**keg·ler** (keg′lər) *n.* ⟦Ger < *kegel,* (nine)pin, (ten)pin < OHG *kegil,* a post, stake, dim. of base akin to prec.⟧ [Informal] a person who bowls; bowler

keg·ling (keg′liŋ) *n.* ⟦see prec.⟧ the game of bowling

☆**keg party** a boisterous party, attended as by college students, at which beer in kegs is served: also [Slang] **keg·ger** (keg′ər) *n.*

kei·ret·su (kī ret′so͞o) *n., pl.* **-su** (-so͞o) ⟦Jpn⟧ in Japan, an association of corporations joined by reciprocal shareholder arrangements or by agreements among the members to deal exclusively or preferentially among themselves

☆**keis·ter** (kēs′tər) *n.* ⟦prob. < Ger *kiste,* chest, case, (slang) rump < OHG < L *cista,* CHEST⟧ [Slang] 1 a satchel, suitcase, etc. 2 the buttocks; rump

Keith (kēth) *n.* ⟦Scot < base in Gael, the wind⟧ a masculine name

Ke·lan·tan (kə län′tän′) state of Malaysia, in NE Peninsular Malaysia, bordering on Thailand: 5,770 sq mi (14,944 sq km)

☆**kel·ep** (kel′əp) *n.* ⟦native name in Guatemala⟧ a Central American stinging ant (*Ectatomma tuberculatum*)

Kel·ler (kel′ər), **Helen (Adams)** 1880-1968; U.S. writer & lecturer: blind and deaf from infancy, she was taught to speak and read

Kel·ly[1] (kel′ē) *n.* a feminine and masculine name: var. **Kelley**

Kel·ly[2] (kel′ē), **Gene** (born *Eugene Curran Kelly*) 1912-96; U.S. dancer, choreographer, & film actor

Kelly green [*also* **k- g-**] a bright yellowish-green color

ke·loid (kē′loid′) *n.* ⟦Fr *kéloïde, chéloïde* < Gr *chēlē,* crab's claw (see CHELA) + *-oeidēs,* -OID⟧ an excessive growth of scar tissue on the skin —**ke·loi′dal** *adj.*

Ke·low·na (kə lō′nə) ⟦< ? AmInd⟧ city in S British Columbia, Canada

kelp (kelp) *n.* ⟦ME *culp*⟧ 1 any of an order (Laminariales) of large, coarse, brown algae 2 ashes of seaweed, from which iodine is obtained

kel·pie[1] or **kel·py** (kel′pē) *n., pl.* **-pies** ⟦Scot < ? Gael *calpa,* colt⟧ *Celt. Folklore* a water spirit, supposed to take the form of a horse and drown people

kel·pie[2] (kel′pē) *n.* ⟦after *Kelpie,* one of the first dogs of this breed⟧ any of a breed of medium-sized sheepdog with erect ears, a pointed muzzle, and a thick coat of black, tan, red, etc.: first bred in Australia from the collie and wild dingo

kel·son (kel′sən) *n. var. of* KEELSON

Kelt (kelt) *n. var. of* CELT[1] —**Kelt′ic** *adj., n.*

Kel·thane (kel′thān′) *trademark for* a pesticide sprayed on agricultural and ornamental plants to eliminate mites

Kel·vin[1] (kel′vin) *adj.* ⟦after fol.⟧ designating or of a scale of thermodynamic temperature measured from absolute zero (-273.16°C): the formula for converting Celsius to Kelvin is °K=°C + 273.16 —*n.* [**k-**] a basic unit of temperature on this scale, equal to one degree Celsius: abbrev. *K*

Kel·vin[2] (kel′vin), 1st Baron (*William Thomson*) 1824-1907; Brit. physicist & mathematician

Ke·mal A·ta·türk (ke mäl′ ät ä turk′) 1881-1938; Turk. general: 1st president of Turkey (1923-38): also called *Mustafa Kemal* or *Kemal Pasha*

Ke·me·ro·vo (kem′ə rō vō′, -və) city in SC Russia, in the Kuznetsk Basin

Kem·pis (kem′pis), **Thomas à** (born *Thomas Hamerken* or *Hammerlein*) 1380?-1471; Ger. monk & scholar

kempt (kempt) *adj.* ⟦ME, combed: in mod. use, back-form. < UNKEMPT⟧ neat; tidy; well-groomed

ken (ken) *vt.* **kenned, ken′ning** ⟦ME *kennen* < OE *cennan,* lit., to cause to know < **kannjan* < base of CAN[1], akin to Ger *kennen,* ON *kenna,* to know⟧ 1 [Scot.] to know 2 [Archaic] to see; look at; descry 3 [Now Chiefly Dial.] to recognize —*vi.* [Scot.] to know (*of* or *about*) —*n.* ⟦< the *v.*⟧ 1 [Rare] range of vision 2 mental perception; range of knowledge [that is beyond my *ken*]

ke·naf (kə naf′) *n.* ⟦Pers, akin to *kanab,* HEMP⟧ 1 a tropical Asian plant (*Hibiscus cannabinus*) of the mallow family, grown for its fiber, which is similar to jute 2 this fiber

Ke·nai Peninsula (kē′nī′) peninsula in S Alas. between Cook Inlet & the main body of the Gulf of Alaska: *c.* 150 mi (241 km) long: site of one the world's largest ice fields

kench (kench) *n.* ⟦? var. of Brit dial. *canch*⟧ a box or bin in which fish or skins are salted

Ken·dal (green) (ken′dəl) ⟦after *Kendal,* city in England, where orig. made⟧ 1 a coarse, green woolen cloth 2 its color

ken·do (ken′dō) *n.* ⟦Jpn < SinoJpn *ken,* sword + *dō,* way⟧ stylized swordplay in which bamboo swords are used: a Japanese sport

Ken·il·worth (ken′əl wurth′) town in Warwickshire, England, near Coventry: site of the ruins of a major castle celebrated by Sir Walter Scott in his novel *Kenilworth*

Ken·nan (ken′ən), **George F(rost)** 1904-2005; U.S. diplomat & historian

Ken·ne·bec (ken′ə bek′) ⟦E Abenaki *kinəpekw* < *kin-,* large + *əpekw,* body of water⟧ river in W Me., flowing into the Atlantic: *c.* 150 mi (241 km)

Ken·ne·dy[1] (ken′ə dē) **1 Anthony M(cLeod)** 1936- ; associate justice, U.S. Supreme Court (1988-) **2 John F(itzgerald)** 1917-63; 35th president of the U.S. (1961-63): assassinated **3 Joseph (Patrick)** 1888-1969; U.S. businessman & diplomat: father of John & Robert **4 Robert F(rancis)** 1925-68; U.S. lawyer & political leader: assassinated

Ken·ne·dy[2] (ken′ə dē), **Cape** ⟦after Pres. John F. KENNEDY[1]⟧ *name* (1963-73) *for* Cape CANAVERAL

ken·nel[1] (ken′əl) *n.* ⟦ME *kenel,* prob. via NormFr < OFr *chenil* < VL **canile* < L *canis,* a dog: see CANINE⟧ 1 a doghouse 2 [*often pl.*] a place where dogs are bred or kept 3 a pack of dogs —*vt.* **-neled** or **-nelled, -nel·ing** or **-nel·ling** to place or keep in a kennel —*vi.* to live or take shelter in a kennel

ken·nel[2] (ken′əl) *n.* ⟦ME *canel* < OFr *canel, chanel,* CHANNEL[1]⟧ [Archaic] an open drain or sewer; gutter

Ken·nel·ly-Heav·i·side layer (ken′əl ē hev′ē sīd′) ⟦after A. *Kennelly* (1861-1939), U.S. electrical engineer & O. *Heaviside* (1850-1925), Eng physicist⟧ E LAYER

Ken·ne·saw Mountain (ken′ə sô′) ⟦prob. < Cherokee; meaning unknown⟧ mountain in NW Ga.: scene of an unsuccessful attack by Sherman on Confederate forces (1864): 1,800 ft (549 m)

Ken·neth (ken′əth) *n.* ⟦Scot < Gael *Caioneach,* lit., handsome⟧ a masculine name: dim. *Ken, Kenny*

ken·ning (ken′iŋ) *n.* ⟦ME: see KEN⟧ 1 [Scot.] *a)* knowledge or recognition *b)* a tiny quantity; trace 2 ⟦ON, symbol < *kenna:* see KEN⟧ in early Germanic, as Old English, poetry, a metaphorical name, usually a compound, for something (Ex.: "whale-path" for *sea*)

☆**ke·no** (kē′nō) *n.* ⟦< Fr *quine,* five winning numbers < L *quini,* five each < *quinque,* FIVE⟧ a gambling game resembling bingo

Ke·no·sha (kə nō′shə) ⟦prob. ult. < Ojibwa *ginoozhe,* northern pike⟧ city in SE Wis., on Lake Michigan

ke·no·sis (kə nō′sis) *n.* ⟦Gr *kenōsis,* an emptying < *kenos,* empty⟧ *Christian Theol.* the voluntary self-abasement of the second person of the Trinity in becoming human —**ke·not′ic** (-nät′ik) *adj.*

Ken·sing·ton and Chel·sea (ken′ziŋ tən ənd chel′sē) borough of W Greater London, England

Kent[1] (kent) **1 James** 1763-1847; U.S. jurist **2 Rock·well** (räk′wel′) 1882-1971; U.S. artist

Kent[2] (kent) county in SE England: formerly, an Anglo-Saxon kingdom (6th-9th cent. A.D.): 1,442 sq mi (3,735 sq km)

ken·te cloth (ken′tā, -tə) ⟦< Twi *kente,* cloth⟧ a fabric made esp. in Ghana, woven in strips of brightly patterned bands interspersed with bands of black

Kent·ish (ken′tish) *adj.* of Kent or its people or language —*n.* the English dialect spoken in Kent, esp. in its Old English and Middle English stages

kent·ledge (kent′lij) *n.* ⟦Fr *quintelage* < *quintal,* QUINTAL + *-age:* see -AGE⟧ pig iron used as permanent ballast in a ship

Ken·tuck·i·an (kən tuk′ē ən) *adj.* of Kentucky: usually used in the predicate —*n.* a person born or living in Kentucky

Ken·tuck·y (kən tuk′ē) ⟦earlier (18th c.) *Kentucke* (River), of Iroquois or Shawnee orig.⟧ **1** state of the EC U.S.: admitted 1792; 39,728 sq mi (102,896 sq km); cap. Frankfort: abbrev. *KY* or *Ky* **2** river in E Ky., flowing northwest into the Ohio: 259 mi (417 km)

Kentucky bluegrass a bluegrass (*Poa pratensis*) native to Eurasia, now widely grown in the U.S. as a lawn and pasture grass

☆**Kentucky coffee tree** a large tree (*Gymnocladus dioica*) of the caesalpinia family, with brown, curved pods containing seeds sometimes used as a substitute for coffee: it is native to the E U.S.

☆**Kentucky Derby** an annual horse race run at Churchill Downs in Louisville, Kentucky

Kentucky Lake ⟦after the state⟧ reservoir in SW Ky. & W Tenn., on the Tennessee River: 247 sq mi (640 sq km); 184 mi (296 km) long

Ken·ya (ken′yə, kēn′-) **1** country in EC Africa, on the Indian Ocean: formerly a British crown colony & protectorate, it became independent & a member of the Commonwealth (1963): 224,962 sq mi (582,650 sq km); cap. Nairobi **2 Mount** volcanic mountain in central Kenya: 17,040 ft (5,194 m) —**Ken′yan** *adj., n.*

☆**Ke·ogh plan** (kē′ō) ⟦after Eugene J. *Keogh* (1907-89), U.S. Congressman⟧ a retirement plan for self-employed persons and for the owners and employees of unincorporated businesses, similar to an IRA: see IRA[1] (Individual Retirement Account)

Ke·os (kā′äs′) *var. of* KEA

kep·i (kep′ē, kā′pē) *n., pl.* **kep′is** ⟦Fr *képi* < Ger dial. *käppi,* dim. of *kappe,* a cap < OHG *kappa* < LL *cappa:* see CAP[1]⟧ a cap with a flat, round top and stiff visor, worn by French soldiers

Kep·ler (kep′lər), **Jo·han·nes** (yô hän′əs) 1571-1630; Ger. astronomer & mathematician —**Kep·ler·i·an** (kep lir′ē ən, -ler′-) *adj.*

kept (kept) *vt., vi. pt. & pp. of* KEEP —*adj.* financially supported as, or in the manner of, a MISTRESS (sense 4*a*): often a dismissive or contemptuous term

☆**ker-** (kər) ⟦echoic⟧ *prefix* forming words suggesting a thump, thud, explosion, etc.: used as a humorous intensifier [*kerplunk, kerflooey*]

ke·ram·ic (kə ram′ik) *adj. var. of* CERAMIC

ker·a·tec·to·my (ker′ə tek′tə mē) *n., pl.* **-mies** ⟦KERAT(O)- + -ECTOMY⟧ the surgical removal of part or all of the cornea

ker·a·tin (ker′ə tin) *n.* ⟦KERAT(O)- + -IN[1]⟧ a tough, fibrous, insoluble protein forming the principal matter of hair, nails, horn, etc. —**ke·rat·i·nous** (kə rat′'n əs) *adj.,* **ke·rat′i·noid′** (-oid′)

ker·a·tin·ize (ker′ə tin īz′) *vt.* **-ized′**, **-iz′ing** to form or develop keratin —**ker′a·tin′i·za′tion** *n.*

ker·a·ti·tis (ker′ə tīt′is) *n.* ⟦fol. + -ITIS⟧ inflammation of the cornea

ker·a·to- (ker′ə tō′, -tə) ⟦< Gr *keras* (gen. *keratos*), HORN: see also CERATO-⟧ *combining form* **1** horn, hornlike, horny tissue [*keratogenous*] **2** the cornea [*keratotomy*] Also, before a vowel, **kerat-**

ke·ra·to·co·nus (ker′ə tō′kō′nəs) *n.* ⟦prec. + L *conus,* CONE⟧ an abnormal conical bulging of a cornea causing impaired vision or blindness: thought to be an inherited disorder

ker·a·tog·e·nous (ker′ə täj′ə nəs) *adj.* ⟦KERATO- + -GENOUS⟧ causing the growth of horny tissue

ker·a·toid (ker′ə toid′) *adj.* ⟦Gr *keratoeidēs:* see KERATO- & -OID⟧ hornlike; horny

ker·a·to·plas·ty (ker′ə tō plas′tē) *n., pl.* **-ties** ⟦KERATO- + -PLASTY⟧ the surgical operation of grafting new corneal tissue onto an eye

ker·a·tose (ker′ə tōs′) *adj.* ⟦KERAT(O)- + -OSE[2]⟧ **1** horny **2** having horny material in the skeleton, as certain sponges and some other invertebrates

ker·a·to·sis (ker′ə tō′sis) *n., pl.* **-ses′** (-sēz′) ⟦ModL < KERAT(O)- + -OSIS⟧ **1** a horny growth of the skin, as a wart **2** any disease characterized by horny growths

ker·a·tot·o·my (ker′ə tät′ə mē) *n., pl.* **-mies** ⟦KERATO- + -TOMY⟧ surgical incision of the cornea

kerb (kurb) *n. Brit. sp. of* CURB (*n.* 5, 6, & *vt.* 3)

Kerch (kerch) seaport in W Crimea, on a strait (**Kerch Strait**) connecting the Black Sea & the Sea of Azov

ker·chief (kur′chif) *n.* ⟦ME *kerchef, coverchef* < OFr *covrechef* < *covrir,* to COVER + *chef,* the head: see CHIEF⟧ **1** a piece of cloth, usually square, worn over the head or around the neck **2** a handkerchief —**ker′chiefed** (-chift) *adj.*

Ke·ren·sky (kə ren′skē), **Alexander** (born *Aleksandr Fyodorovich Kerensky*) 1881-1970; Russ. revolutionary leader: prime minister of Russia (July-Nov., 1917), overthrown by the Bolshevik Revolution: in the U.S. after 1940

Ke·res (kā′res′) *n.* ⟦Sp *Queres* < a Tanoan language⟧ **1** *pl.* **Ke′res′** a member of any of seven Indian pueblos in N.Mex., mostly on the Rio Grande **2** a family of languages, comprising the seven languages or dialects spoken by the Keres: also **Ker·e·san** (ker′ə sən)

kerf (kurf) *n.* ⟦ME < OE *cyrf* (akin to ON *kurfr,* a cutting, chip) < pp. base of *ceorfan,* to CARVE⟧ the cut or channel made by a saw —*vt.* to make a kerf or kerfs in

ker·fuf·fle (kər fuf′əl) *n.* [Informal, Chiefly Brit.] disorder; uproar; confusion

Ker·gue·len Islands (kur′gə lən) group of French islands in the S Indian Ocean, consisting of one large island & over 200 small ones: 2,786 sq mi (7,216 sq km)

Kér·ki·ra (ker′kē rä) *Gr. name for* CORFU

Ker·man[1] (kər män′, ker-) *n.* KIRMAN

Ker·man[2] (ker män′) city in SE Iran

Ker·man·shah (ker′män shä′) *former name for* BAKHTARAN

ker·mes (kur′mēz′) *n.* ⟦Fr *kermès* < Ar & Pers *qirmiz:* see CARMINE⟧ **1** the dried bodies of the females of certain soft scale insects (genus *Kermes*), used for making a purple-red dye **2** this dye **3** a small, evergreen Mediterranean oak (*Quercus coccifera*) on which the kermes insects are found: also **kermes oak**

ker·mis or **ker·mess** (kur′mis) *n.* ⟦Du *kermis,* orig. *kerkmis* < *kerk,* CHURCH + *mis,* MASS[1]: orig. the feast day of the local patron saint, hence, a fair or carnival held on that day⟧ **1** in the Netherlands, Belgium, etc., an outdoor fair or carnival ☆**2** any somewhat similar fair or entertainment, held usually for charity

kern[1] (kurn) *n.* ⟦Fr *carne,* projecting angle, hinge < dial. form of OFr *charne,* a hinge, corner, edge < L *cardo* (gen. *cardinis*), a hinge: see CARDINAL⟧ that part of the face of a printed character which projects beyond the body —*vt.* to put a kern on (a printed character)

kern[2] or **kerne** (kurn) *n.* ⟦ME *kerne* < OIr *ceitern,* band of soldiers, soldier; akin to Gael *ceathairne,* common people⟧ **1** [Archaic] a medieval Irish or Scottish foot soldier armed with light weapons **2** an Irish peasant

Kern (kurn), **Jerome (David)** 1885-1945; U.S. composer of musicals

ker·nel (kur′nəl) *n.* ⟦ME < OE *cyrnel* < base of *corn,* seed (see CORN[1]) + *-el,* dim. suffix⟧ **1** a grain or seed, as of corn, wheat, etc. **2** the inner, softer part of a nut, fruit pit, etc. **3** the central, most important part of something; core; essence —*vt.* **-neled** or **-nelled**, **-nel·ing** or **-nel·ling** to enclose as a kernel

☆**kern·ite** (kur′nīt′) *n.* ⟦after *Kern* County, Calif., where mined + -ITE[1]⟧ a colorless, soft, monoclinic mineral, hydrous sodium borate, $Na_2B_4O_7{\cdot}4H_2O$, that is an important ore of boron

ker·o·gen (ker′ə jən) *n.* ⟦< Gr *kēros,* wax + -GEN⟧ solid bituminous material in some shales, which yields petroleum when heated

☆**ker·o·sene** (ker′ə sēn′, ker′ə sēn′) *n.* ⟦Gr *kēros,* wax + -ENE⟧ a thin oil distilled from petroleum or shale oil, used as a fuel, solvent, illuminant, etc.; coal oil: also, esp. in scientific and industrial usage, sp. **ker′o·sine′**

Ker·ou·ac (ker′o͞o ak′), **Jack** (born *Jean Louis Kerouac*) 1922-69; U.S. writer

ker·plunk (kər pluŋk′) *interj., n.* ⟦echoic⟧ (used to suggest) the sound of something heavy falling or dropping with a thud —*adv.* with or as with such a sound [I tripped and fell *kerplunk*] — *vi., vt.* to fall or drop heavily or with a thud

ker·ri·a (ker′ē ə) *n.* ⟦ModL, after William *Kerr,* Brit horticulturist (died 1814)⟧ any of a genus (*Kerria*) of Chinese plants of the rose family, esp. an ornamental species (*K. japonica*) with slender, green twigs and bright yellow, often double flowers

Ker·ry (ker′ē) county in Munster province, SW Ireland: 1,815 sq mi (4,701 sq km)

Kerry blue terrier ⟦after prec., place of orig.⟧ any of a breed of terrier with a long, narrow head, a dense, wavy, grayish-blue coat, and an erect tail that traditionally is docked

ker·sey (kur′zē) *n., pl.* **-seys** ⟦ME, after *Kersey,* village in Suffolk, England⟧ a coarse, lightweight woolen cloth, usually ribbed and with a cotton warp

ker·sey·mere (-mir′) *n.* ⟦altered (infl. by prec.) < CASSIMERE⟧ a fine woolen cloth in a twill weave

ke·ryg·ma (kə rig′mə) *n.* ⟦Gr(Ec) *kērygma,* preaching < Gr, a proclamation < *kēryssein,* to proclaim < *kēryx,* a herald < IE base **kar-,* to praise loudly > OE *hrothor,* joy⟧ *Christian Theol.* **1** preaching of the Gospel **2** emphasis on the essence and spirit of the Gospel, as in preaching, catechesis, etc. —**ker·yg·mat·ic** (ker′ig mat′ik) *adj.*

kes·trel (kes′trəl) *n.* ⟦ME *castrel* < OFr *cresserelle, quercerelle:* orig. echoic of its call⟧ **1** either of two small, reddish-gray European falcons (*Falco tinnunculus* or *F. naumanni*) that can hover in the air **2** AMERICAN KESTREL

ke·ta·mine hydrochloride (kēt′ə mēn′) ⟦< KETO- + AMINE⟧ a powerful anesthetic, $C_{13}H_{16}ClNO{\cdot}HCl$, used in surgery

ketch (kech) *n.* ⟦ME *cache* < *cacchen,* to CATCH: orig. used of fishing vessels⟧ a small, two-masted sailing vessel rigged fore and aft, with the mizzenmast somewhat shorter than the mainmast and located forward of the rudderpost: distinguished from YAWL

ketch·up (kech′əp) *n.* ⟦? via Malay *kēchap,* a fish sauce < Chin *ke-tsiap*⟧ a sauce for meat, fish, etc.; esp., a thick sauce (**tomato ketchup**) made of tomatoes flavored with onion, salt, sugar, etc.

ke·tene (kē′tēn′) *n.* ⟦fol. + -ENE⟧ **1** a colorless, toxic gas, $H_2C{:}CO$, with a penetrating odor, made by passing acetone or acetic acid through hot metal tubes: used esp. as an acetylating agent **2** any of a series of related organic compounds containing the C:CO group

ke·to- (kēt′ō, -ə) *combining form* ketone, of ketones [*ketogenesis*]: also, before a vowel, **ket-**

ke·to·gen·e·sis (kēt′ō jen′ə sis) *n.* ⟦prec. + -GENESIS⟧ the formation of ketones, such as acetone, in the body as a result of the incomplete oxidation of organic compounds such as fatty acids or carbohydrates —**ke′to·gen′ic** *adj.*

ke·tol (kē′tôl′, -tōl′) *n.* ⟦KET(O)- + -OL[1]⟧ any of a group of organic compounds containing a ketone group and an alcohol group in the molecule

ke·tone (-tōn′) *n.* ⟦Ger *keton,* arbitrary var. of Fr *acétone:* see ACETONE⟧ an organic chemical compound containing the carbonyl group, CO, in combination with two hydrocarbon radicals

ketone body any of three related compounds, including acetone, found in the blood and urine when there is excessive oxidation of fatty acids by the liver, as during starvation or pregnancy, or in diabetes

ke·to·ne·mi·a (kēt′ō nē′mē ə) ***n.*** ⟦KETON(E) + -EMIA⟧ an excess of ketone bodies in the blood

ke·to·nu·ri·a (-noor′ē ə, -nyoor′-) ***n.*** ⟦KETON(E) + -URIA⟧ an excess of ketone bodies in the urine

ke·tose (kē′tōs′) ***n.*** ⟦KET(O)- + -OSE[1]⟧ a sugar that contains a ketone group in the molecule

ke·to·sis (kē tō′sis) ***n.*** ⟦ModL < KET(O)- + -OSIS⟧ a condition in which there is excessive formation of ketones in the body

ke·to·ster·oid (kēt′ō stir′oid′, -ster′-) ***n.*** a steroid containing a ketone group in the molecule

Ket·ter·ing (ket′ər iŋ), **Charles Franklin** 1876-1958; U.S. electrical engineer & inventor

ket·tle (ket′'l) ***n.*** ⟦ME *ketel* < ON *ketill,* akin to OE *cetel,* Ger *kessel,* Goth *katils,* early Gmc loanword < L *catillus,* dim. of *catinus,* container for food⟧ **1** a metal container for boiling or cooking things; pot **2** a teakettle **3** a kettledrum **4** *Geol. a)* a depression in glacial drift remaining after the melting of an isolated mass of buried ice *b)* a kettle-shaped hole in rock, gravel, etc.: also **kettle hole**

ket·tle·drum (-drum′) ***n.*** ⟦so named from its shape⟧ a percussion instrument consisting of a hollow hemisphere of copper or brass and a parchment top that can be tightened or loosened to change the pitch; timpano

kettledrum

kettle of fish **1** a difficult or embarrassing situation **2** a matter to be dealt with

keV or **kev** (kev) *abbrev.* ⟦*k(ilo-)e(lectron-)v(olts)*⟧ one thousand electron volts

kev·el (kev′əl) ***n.*** ⟦ME *keuil* < NormFr *keville* (Fr *cheville*) < L *clavicula,* small key (in LL, a bar, bolt for a door), dim. of *clavis,* key: see CLOSE[2]⟧ *Naut.* a bitt or large cleat for securing heavy lines

Kev·in (kev′in) ***n.*** ⟦Ir *Caomghin* < OIr *Coemgen,* lit., comely birth⟧ a masculine name

Kev·lar (kev′lär′) ⟦arbitrary coinage⟧ *trademark for* an aramid fiber used in making bulletproof vests, boat hulls, airplane parts, etc.

Kew (kyoo) parish in NE Surrey, England: now part of the Greater London borough of Richmond: site of the Royal Botanic Gardens (**Kew Gardens**)

☆**Kew·pie** (kyoo′pē) ⟦altered < CUPID⟧ *trademark for* a chubby, rosy-faced doll with its hair in a topknot —***n.*** [**k-**] KEWPIE DOLL

kewpie doll ⟦< prec.⟧ a doll like a Kewpie

key[1] (kē) ***n.,*** *pl.* **keys** ⟦ME *keye* < OE *cæge,* akin to OFris *kei, kēia,* to secure, guard⟧ **1** an instrument, usually of metal, for moving the bolt of a lock and thus locking or unlocking something **2** any of several instruments or mechanical devices resembling or suggesting this in form or use; specif., *a)* a device to turn a bolt, etc. [a skate *key,* a watch *key*] *b)* a pin, bolt, wedge, cotter, or similar device put into a hole or space to lock or hold parts together *c)* something that completes or holds together the parts of another thing, as the keystone of an arch or a roughened surface forming a secure base for plaster *d)* any of a set of levers, or the disks, buttons, etc. connected to them, pressed down in operating a piano, accordion, clarinet, typewriter, linotype, word processor, etc. *e)* a device for opening or closing an electric circuit *f)* a small metal piece for fastening a wheel, pulley, etc. to a shaft *g)* a key-shaped emblem presented as an honor [the *key* to the city] **3** something regarded as like a key in opening or closing a way, revealing or concealing, etc.; specif., *a)* a place so located as to give access to or control of a region [Vicksburg was the *key* to the lower Mississippi] *b)* a thing that explains or solves something else, as a book of answers, the explanations on a map, the code to a system of pronunciation, etc. *c)* a controlling or essential person or thing **4** tone of voice; pitch **5** *a)* tone or style of thought or expression [in a cheerful *key*] *b)* relative intensity of feeling [low-*key* remarks on a volatile subject] **6** the tone of a picture with regard to lightness or darkness or intensity of color ☆**7** ⟦< KEYHOLE, because orig. shaped somewhat like an old-fashioned keyhole, a vertical slot opening out at the top into a wider, rounded hole⟧ *Basketball* either of the marked or painted areas on the court near each basket, extending from the end line to the top of the circle that surrounds the foul line **8** *Biol.* an arrangement or listing of the significant characteristics of a group of organisms, used as a guide for taxonomic identification **9** *Bot.* KEY FRUIT **10** *Comput.* a field in a record, used to uniquely identify that record **11** *Music a)* [Obs.] the keynote of a scale *b)* a system of related notes or tones based on and named after a certain note (*keynote, tonic*) and forming a given scale; tonality *c)* the main tonality of a composition —***adj.*** controlling; essential; important [a *key* position] —***vt.*** **keyed, key′ing 1** to fasten or lock with a key or wedge **2** to furnish with a key; specif., *a)* to put the keystone in (an arch) *b)* to provide with an explanatory key **3** to regulate the tone or pitch of **4** to bring into harmony or accord **5** KEYBOARD —**key in** to input (data) by means of a keyboard or keypad —**key (in) on** to focus one's attention, effort, etc. on [the teacher *keyed in on* the final chapter] —**key up** to make tense or excited, as in anticipation

key[2] (kē) ***n.,*** *pl.* **keys** ⟦Sp *cayo*: sp. infl. by prec. & earlier *key* (quay)⟧ a reef or low island

key[3] (kē) ***n.*** ⟦< pronun. of 1st syllable of Sp *kilogramo,* kilogram⟧ [Slang] a kilogram (of marijuana or a narcotic drug)

Key (kē), **Francis Scott** 1779-1843; U.S. lawyer: wrote "The Star-Spangled Banner"

key·board (kē′bôrd′) ***n.*** **1** the row or rows of keys of a piano, typewriter, linotype, computer terminal, etc. **2** a musical instrument with a keyboard; esp., an electronic piano, synthesizer, etc. as employed in a rock or jazz group —☆***vt., vi.*** **1** to set (type) using a keyboard typesetting machine **2** to write or input by means of a keyboard —**key′board′er** ***n.***

key·board·ist (-ist) ***n.*** a performer on a keyboard instrument

key·chain (-chān′) ***n.*** a small chain or strap for holding keys, a fob, etc.

☆**key club** a private nightclub, restaurant, or cafe, to which each member has a key

keyed (kēd) ***adj.*** **1** having keys, as some musical instruments **2** reinforced with a key or keystone **3** pitched in a specific key **4** adjusted so as to conform [a speech *keyed* to the mood of the voters]

key fruit a dry, winged fruit, as of the maple, ash, or elm, containing the seed or seeds; samara

key·hole (kē′hōl′) ***n.*** an opening (in a lock) into which a key is inserted

keyhole saw ⟦from being used to cut out *keyholes* and other small shapes⟧ a handsaw with a narrow, tapering blade for cutting small circles, curves, etc.

Key Lar·go (lär′gō) ⟦Sp *Cayo Largo,* lit., long islet⟧ largest island of the Florida Keys: *c.* 40 sq mi (104 sq km)

Key lime a small, tart lime originally grown widely in the Florida Keys

Key lime pie ⟦orig. made in the FLORIDA KEYS with the juice of the prec.⟧ [*also* **k-**] a custardlike pie with a light, tart filling made traditionally with condensed milk and lime juice

key money money paid covertly, and usually illegally, by a prospective tenant, as to a landlord, to increase the likelihood of being able to lease an apartment in an area where housing is scarce

Keynes (kānz), **John Maynard** 1st Baron Keynes 1883-1946; Eng. economist & writer

Keynes·i·an (kān′zē ən) ***adj.*** designating, of, or in accord with the economic theories of Keynes and his followers, which hold that full employment and a stable economy depend on the continued governmental stimulation of spending and investment through adjustment of interest rates and tax rates, deficit financing, etc. —***n.*** an adherent of these theories —**Keynes′i·an·ism′** ***n.***

key·note (kē′nōt′) ***n.*** **1** TONIC (*n.* 3) **2** the basic idea or ruling principle, as of a speech or policy —☆***vt.*** **-not′ed, -not′ing 1** to give the keynote of **2** to deliver the keynote address at —☆**key′not′er** ***n.***

☆**keynote address** a speech, as at a political convention, that sets forth the main ideas of a policy or platform: often **keynote speech**

keynote speaker a person who delivers a keynote addresss

key·pad (kē′pad′) ***n.*** the set of keys or push buttons on a computer keyboard, telephone, TV remote control, etc., used to perform certain functions

key punch a machine, operated from a keyboard, used to record data by punching holes in cards that can then be fed into machines for sorting, accounting, etc.

key ring a metal ring for holding keys, a fob, etc.

key signature *Music* a music notation indicating the key of a piece or section by means of sharps or flats positioned on the staff: the opening or predominant key of a piece is indicated directly after the opening clef

key·stone (kē′stōn′) ***n.*** **1** the central, topmost voussoir of an arch, popularly thought of as especially holding the others in place **2** that one of a number of associated parts or things that supports or holds together the others; main part or principle

☆**Key·stone** (kē′stōn′) ***adj.*** ⟦after *Keystone* Comedy Co., the film producers⟧ designating, of, or like the slapstick comedy of a series of silent films featuring a bungling, inept squad of policemen (**Keystone Kops** or **Keystone Cops**) in wild chases, etc.

Keystone State *name for* PENNSYLVANIA: from its central position among the 13 original colonies

key·stroke (kē′strōk′) ***n.*** any of the individual strokes made in operating a keyboard, as of a computer terminal

key·way (-wā′) ***n.*** *Lockmaking* **1** a groove or slot cut in a shaft, hub, etc. to hold the key **2** the keyhole in a lock for a flat key

Key West ⟦< Sp *Cayo Hueso,* island of bones, from the human bones found there; also infl. by folk etym., because it is the farthest *west*⟧ **1** westernmost island of the Florida Keys: *c.* 4 mi (6.4 km) long **2** seaport on this island: southernmost city in the continental U.S.

key·word (kē′wurd′) ***n.*** a word or phrase submitted to a SEARCH ENGINE in an effort to locate relevant documents or websites

kg *abbrev.* **1** keg(s) **2** kilogram(s)

KG *abbrev.* Knight of (the Order of) the Garter

KGB or **K.G.B.** *abbrev.* ⟦Russ < *Komitet Gosudarstvennoj Bezopasnosti,* Committee of State Security⟧ the security police and intelligence agency (1954-91) of the Soviet Union

Kgs *abbrev. Bible* Kings

Kha·ba·rovsk (kä bä′rôfsk′) **1** territory in E Siberia: 304,480 sq mi (788,600 sq km) **2** capital of this territory, on the Amur River

Kha·cha·tu·ri·an (kach′ə toor′ē ən, kä′chə-), **A·ram** (ar′əm) 1903-78; Soviet composer

Kha·da·fy (kə dä′fē) *alt. sp. of* QADDAFI

khad·dar (käd′ər) ***n.*** ⟦Hindi *khādī*⟧ homespun cotton cloth made in India: also **kha·di** (käd′ē)

khaf (khäf, khôf) ***n.*** ⟦Heb⟧ *see* KAF

kha·ki (kak′ē, kä′kē) ***adj.*** ⟦Hindi *khākī,* dusty, dust-colored < Pers *khāk,* dust, earth⟧ 1 dull yellowish-brown 2 made of khaki (cloth) —*n., pl.* **-kis** 1 a dull yellowish-brown color 2 strong, twilled cloth of this color, used esp. for military uniforms 3 [*often pl.*] a khaki uniform or pair of trousers

kha·lif (kā′lif) *n. var. of* CALIPH

Khal·kha (kal′kə) *n.* 1 a member of a people of Mongolia 2 the Mongolian language of this people, the official language of Mongolia

Khal·ki·di·ki (khäl′ki thē′kē) *Gr. name for* CHALCIDICE

kham·sin (kam′sin, kam sēn′) *n.* ⟦Ar *khamsīn* < *khamsūn*, fifty: so named for the fifty days the wind blows⟧ a hot south wind from the Sahara that blows in the Near East, esp. Egypt, from late March until early May

khan[1] (kän, kan) *n.* ⟦ME *c(h)aan* (sp. *khan* since 19th c.) < OFr *chan* or ML *canus* < Turkic *khān*, lord, prince < Mongolian *qan, qaγan*⟧ 1 a title given to Genghis Khan and his successors, who ruled Mongolian and Turkic tribes of central Asia and dominated most of Asia during the Middle Ages 2 a title given to various officials and dignitaries in Iran, Afghanistan, etc.

khan[2] (kän, kan) *n.* ⟦Ar *khān*⟧ in Turkey and some other Asian countries, a public inn; caravansary

khan·ate (kän′āt′, kan′-) *n.* the area ruled over by a khan

kha·pra beetle (kä′prə) ⟦Hindi *khaprā*, lit., destroyer, akin to Sans *kṣayati*, (he) destroys < IE **gwhthei(e)-*, to swindle, destroy > Gr *phthiein*, to waste away⟧ a dermestid beetle (*Trogoderma granarium*) native to S and Southeast Asia, now a destructive grain pest in much of the world

Kha·rag·pur (kar′əg poor′) city in SW West Bengal, India

Khar·kov (kär′kôf′) city in NE Ukraine

Khar·toum (kär to͞om′) capital of Sudan, on the Nile

khat (kät) *n.* ⟦Ar *qāt*⟧ a plant (*Catha edulis*) of the staff-tree family, found in Africa and Arabia: the fresh leaf is chewed for its stimulating effects or used in tea

Khayyám, Omar *see* OMAR KHAYYÁM

khe·dive (kə dēv′) *n.* ⟦Fr *khédive* < Turk *hıdiv* < Pers *khidīw*, prince, ruler⟧ the title of the Turkish viceroys of Egypt, from 1867 to 1914

Kher·son (ker sôn′) port in S Ukraine, on the Dnieper near its mouth

kheth (khet) *n.* HET

Khí·os (kē′ôs′) Greek island in the Aegean, off the W coast of Turkey

Khi·va (kē′və) former khanate in central Asia

Khmer (kə mer′) *n.* ⟦< the Khmer name⟧ 1 a member of a people of Cambodia that had a highly developed civilization that reached its peak in the 12th cent. 2 the Mon-Khmer language of this people, also spoken in NE Thailand and S Vietnam

Khmer Rouge (ro͞ozh) ⟦prec. + Fr *rouge*, red⟧ the Communist regime that ruled Cambodia (1975-79) after its guerrilla force overthrew the government: under POL POT it was characterized by brutal repression

Khoi·san (koi′sän′) *n.* a family of S African languages including Nama, Bushman, and Kung: an important phonological characteristic of these languages is the presence of a group of consonants known as *clicks* (see CLICK, *n.* 5) —*adj.* designating or of this language family

Kho·mei·ni (kō mān′ē, kə-), Ayatollah **Ru·hol·la (Mussaui)** (ro͞o hō′lə) 1900-89; fundamentalist religious leader of Iran (1979-89)

Kho·ra·na (kə rän′ə), **H(ar) Go·bind** (gō′bind′) 1922-2011; U.S. biochemist, born in India

khoum (ko͞om) *n.* ⟦< Ar *khums*, one fifth⟧ a monetary unit of Mauritania, equal to 1/5 of an ouguiya

Kho·war (kō′wär′) *n.* an Indo-Iranian language of NW Pakistan

Khru·shchev (kro͞o′shôf′), **Ni·ki·ta (Sergeyevich)** (ni kē′tä) 1894-1971; premier of the U.S.S.R. (1958-64)

Khu·fu (ko͞o′fo͞o′) fl. *c.* 2650 B.C.; king of Egypt, of the IVth dynasty: builder of the largest of the Great Pyramids

Khy·ber Pass (kī′bər) mountain pass in a range of the Hindu Kush, between Afghanistan & Pakistan: *c.* 33 mi (53 km) long

kHz *abbrev.* kilohertz

Ki *abbrev. Bible* Kings

KIA *abbrev.* killed in action

ki·ang (kē aŋ′) *n.* ⟦< Tibetan *rkyaṅ*⟧ a wild ass (*Equus hemionus kiang*) found in Tibet and Mongolia

Kiang·si (jē äŋ′sē′) *a former transliteration of* JIANGXI

Kiang·su (-so͞o′) *a former transliteration of* JIANGSU

kib·be or **kib·beh** (kib′ē, -ə) *n.* ⟦Ar *kubba*⟧ a Near Eastern dish of finely ground lamb mixed with wheat and pine nuts and baked, or sometimes eaten raw

kib·ble (kib′əl) *vt.* **-bled, -bling** ⟦< ?⟧ to grind or form into coarse particles or bits —*n.* meal, prepared dog food, etc. in this form

kib·butz (ki bo͞ots′, -boots′) *n., pl.* **kib·but·zim** (kē′bo͞o tsēm′) ⟦ModHeb⟧ an Israeli collective settlement, esp. a collective farm

kib·butz·nik (-nik) *n.* ⟦see -NIK⟧ a member of a kibbutz

kibe (kīb) *n.* ⟦ME, prob. < Welsh *cibi*⟧ [Archaic] a chapped or ulcerated chilblain, esp. on the heel

☆**ki·bei** (kē′bā′) *n., pl.* **-bei′** or **-beis′** ⟦Jpn < SinoJpn *ki*, return + *bei*, America, U.S.A.⟧ [*also* **K-**] a native U.S. citizen born of immigrant Japanese parents but educated largely in Japan: cf. ISSEI, NISEI, SANSEI

☆**kib·itz** (kib′its) *vi.* [Informal] to act as a kibitzer

☆**kib·itz·er** (kib′it sər) *n.* ⟦Yiddish < colloq. Ger *kiebitzen*, to look on (at cards) < *kiebitz*, meddlesome onlooker, orig., plover, of echoic orig.⟧ [Informal] 1 an onlooker at a card or chess game, etc., esp. one who volunteers advice 2 a giver of unwanted advice or meddler in others' affairs

kib·lah (kib′lä) *n.* ⟦Ar *qibla*, something placed opposite < *qabala*, to be opposite⟧ the direction of the Kaaba in Mecca, toward which Muslims turn when praying

ki·bosh (kī′bäsh′, ki bäsh′) *n.* ⟦earlier also *kyebosh* < ? Ir *cie bais*, lit., cap of death: infl. in Eng by assoc. with BOSH[1]⟧ [Slang] a thing that stops (something else): now usually in **put the kibosh on**, to put an end to; squelch or veto

kick[1] (kik) *vi.* ⟦ME *kiken* < ?⟧ 1 to strike out with the foot or feet, as in anger, or in swimming, dancing, etc. 2 to spring back suddenly, as a gun when fired; recoil 3 to bounce or ricochet, often in a way that is unexpected or seemingly erratic [*his tee shot kicked off to the right*] 4 [Informal] to object strongly; complain; grumble 5 *Football* to kick the ball —*vt.* 1 to strike or shove suddenly with the foot or feet 2 to drive or move (a ball, etc.) by striking with the foot 3 to make or force (one's way, etc.) by kicking 4 to score (a goal or point in football) by kicking ☆5 [Slang] *a)* to stop taking (a narcotic drug) *b)* to get rid of (a habit) —*n.* 1 a blow with or thrust of the foot 2 a method of kicking 3 a sudden, sharp thrust or jolt, as the recoil of a gun when fired 4 a sudden burst of speed by a runner toward the end of a race ☆5 [Informal] an objection; complaint ☆6 [Informal] a stimulating or intoxicating effect, as of alcoholic liquor ☆7 [*often pl.*] [Informal] pleasure; esp., pleasurable excitement 8 [Old Slang] a pocket 9 *Football a)* the act of kicking the ball *b)* the kicked ball *c)* the distance that it travels *d)* one's turn at kicking —☆**kick around (or about)** [Informal] 1 to treat roughly 2 to move from place to place 3 to lie about unnoticed or forgotten 4 to think about or discuss informally —**kick ass** [Slang] 1 to use power or authority, as to force others into achieving a goal or goals 2 to punish, treat roughly, etc. —**kick back** ☆1 [Informal] to recoil suddenly and in an unexpected way ☆2 [Informal] to give back (money) as a kickback ☆3 [Slang] *a)* to lean or lie back *b)* to relax or rest —**kick down** to shift to a lower gear —☆**kick in** 1 [Slang] to pay (one's share) 2 [Informal] to take effect —**kick off** 1 to put a football into play with a kickoff ☆2 [Informal] to start (a campaign, etc.) ☆3 [Slang] to die 4 [Slang] to depart; leave —**kick on** [Informal] to begin operating —☆**kick oneself** to blame oneself severely —**kick out** 1 [Informal] to get rid of; expel; dismiss 2 *Football* to make a kick out of bounds —**kick over** to start up; turn over: said of an internal-combustion engine —**kick the can (or it) down the road** [Informal] to put off doing something unpleasant or burdensome until a future time; procrastinate —**kick up** 1 to raise by kicking 2 [Informal] to make or cause (trouble, confusion, etc.) —**kick upstairs** [Informal] to promote to a nominally higher level so as to be rid of on a lower, but more effective, level, as in a corporation —☆**on a kick** [Slang] currently enthusiastic about a particular activity

kick[2] (kik) *n.* ⟦prob. < prec.⟧ an indentation at the bottom of a glass bottle, which reduces its capacity

☆**Kick·a·poo** (kik′ə po͞o′) *n.* ⟦< Kickapoo *kiikaapoa* < ?⟧ 1 *pl.* **-poos′** or **-poo′** a member of a North American Indian people formerly living in N Illinois and S Wisconsin, now living in Kansas, Oklahoma, and N Mexico 2 the Algonquian language of this people

☆**kick-ass** (kik′as′) *adj.* [Slang] 1 having a strong effect on someone or something; forceful; powerful 2 exceptionally good; spectacular, impressive, etc.

☆**kick·back** (-bak′) *n.* [Informal] 1 a sharp, violent reaction 2 *a)* a giving back of a portion of money received as payment, often as a result of coercion or an illicit agreement *b)* the money so returned

kick·ball (-bôl′) *n.* ☆a children's game with the general rules of baseball, but using a large ball that is kicked rather than batted

kick·board (-bôrd′) *n.* a floating board used in swimming, usually by a beginner, to assist in keeping the head up while practicing the flutter kick

kick·box·ing (-bäk′siŋ) *n.* a martial art incorporating the techniques of karate and boxing: often written **kick-boxing** or **kick boxing**

kick·er (-ər) *n.* 1 one that kicks 2 [Informal] an outboard motor 3 [Slang] *a)* a surprise ending, ironic twist, etc. *b)* a hidden, unsuspected point or difficulty

kick·off (-ôf′) *n.* ☆1 *Football* a placekick that puts the ball into play at the beginning of each half or after a touchdown or field goal ☆2 a beginning, as of a campaign or drive

kick pleat ⟦so named prob. because it provides room for the leg to move forward⟧ a double, inverted pleat at the bottom of a woman's skirt, dress, coat, etc. to allow for ease of movement

kick·shaw (kik′shô′) *n.* ⟦earlier *kickshaws*, altered (by folk etym.) < Fr *quelque chose*, something⟧ 1 a fancy food or dish; delicacy; tidbit 2 a trinket; trifle; gewgaw

☆**kick·stand** (kik′stand′) *n.* a pivoting metal bar or pair of bars attached to the frame of a bicycle or motorcycle: it holds the stationary cycle upright when kicked down into a vertical position

kick-start (kik′stärt′) *vt.* 1 to start (a motor, motorcycle, etc.) by means of a lever attached to a pedal that one pushes sharply downward with the foot 2 [Informal] to start, energize, revive, etc.

kick·up (kik′up′) *n.* [Informal] a fuss; row

kick·y (kik′ē) *adj.* **kick′i·er, kick′i·est** [Slang] 1 fashionable; stylish 2 stimulating; exciting

kid (kid) *n.* ⟦ME *kide*, prob. < Anglo-N, akin to ON *kith*, Dan & Swed *kid*, Ger *kitze*⟧ 1 a young goat or, occasionally, antelope 2 its flesh, used as a food 3 leather made from the skin of young goats, used for gloves, shoes, etc. 4 [*pl.*] gloves or shoes made of this leather 5 [Informal] a child or young person —*adj.* 1 made of kidskin ☆2 [Informal] younger [*my kid sister*] — *vt., vi.* **kid′ded, kid′ding** 1 to give birth to (a kid or kids): said of goats or antelopes **2** [Informal] *a)* to deceive or fool (someone) in a playful way *b)* to tease or ridicule (someone) playfully —**kid around** [Informal] to engage in joking, horseplay, etc. —**no kidding!** [Informal] I can hardly believe it!: an exclamation of doubt or surprise —**kid′der** *n.* —**kid′like′** *adj.*, **kid′dish**

Kidd (kid), Captain **(William)** 1645?-1701; Brit. privateer & pirate, born in Scotland: hanged

Kid·der·min·ster (kid′ər min′stər) *n.* a kind of ingrain or reversible carpet, originally made at Kidderminster, England

kid·die or **kid·dy** (kid′ē) [Informal] *n., pl.* **-dies** ⟦dim. of KID, *n.* 5⟧ a child —*adj.* of or for children [*a kiddie* park]

kid·do (kid′ō) *n.* [Informal] a term of affectionate address: sometimes mildly patronizing

kid·dush (kid′oosh, ki dōōsh′) *n.* ⟦TalmudHeb *kidush,* sanctification < root *kdš*: see KADDISH⟧ *Judaism* a prayer recited over wine or bread on the eve of or on the day of the Sabbath or of a festival so as to set the day apart as holy

kid gloves soft, smooth gloves made of kidskin —☆**handle with kid gloves** [Informal] to treat with care, tact, etc.

kid·nap (kid′nap′) *vt.* **-napped′** or **-naped′**, **-nap′ping** or **-nap′ing** ⟦KID, *n.* 5 + dial. *nap:* see NAB⟧ **1** to steal (a child) **2** to seize and hold or carry off (a person) against that person's will, by force or fraud, often for ransom —**kid′nap′per** *n.*, **kid′nap′er**

kid·ney (kid′nē) *n., pl.* **-neys** ⟦ME *kidenei* < ?⟧ **1** either of a pair of glandular organs in the upper abdominal cavity of vertebrates, which separate water and waste products of metabolism from the blood and excrete them as urine through the bladder **2** the kidney of an animal, used as food **3** *a)* disposition; temperament *b)* class; kind; sort [persons of the wrong *kidney*]

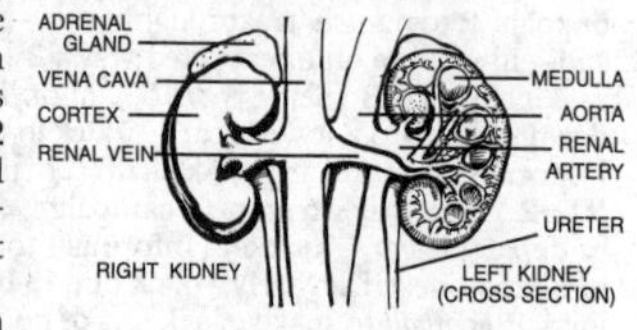

human kidneys

kidney bean ⟦so named from its shape⟧ **1** the seed of the common garden bean, esp. the large, reddish seed of some varieties, eaten as a vegetable **2** the common garden bean plant (*Phaseolus vulgaris*)

kidney stone a hard mineral deposit sometimes formed in the kidney from phosphates, urates, etc.; renal calculus

Ki·dron (kē′drən, kī′-, ki′-) **1** valley in Jordan, east of Jerusalem **2** brook in this valley, flowing to the Dead Sea

kid·skin (kid′skin′) *n.* leather from the skin of young goats, used for gloves, shoes, etc.

kid stuff [Informal] **1** something appropriate for children only **2** something very easy to do, make, etc.

Kiel (kēl) seaport in N Germany, on the Kiel Canal: capital of the state of Schleswig-Holstein

kiel·ba·sa (kēl bä′sə, kil-; kə bä′-) *n., pl.* **-si** (-sē) or **-sas** ⟦Pol⟧ a type of Polish smoked sausage, flavored with garlic, etc.

Kiel Canal canal in N Germany, connecting the North Sea & the Baltic Sea: 61 mi (98 km)

Kiel·ce (kyel′sə) city in S Poland

kier (kir) *n.* ⟦prob. < ON *ker,* tub, akin to MLowG *kar,* Goth *kas,* tub, keg⟧ a large vat to hold cloth for bleaching, boiling, etc.

Kier·ke·gaard (kir′kə gärd′, -gôr′), **Sø·ren (Aabye)** (sö′rən) 1813-55; Dan. philosopher & theologian

kie·sel·guhr or **kie·sel·gur** (kē′zəl goor′) *n.* ⟦Ger < *kiesel,* flint + *guhr, gur,* earthy sediment < *gären,* to ferment⟧ DIATOMITE

kie·ser·ite (kē′zər īt′) *n.* ⟦Ger *kieserit,* after D. G. *Kieser* (1779-1862), Ger scientist⟧ a white, monoclinic mineral, $MgSO_4{\cdot}H_2O$, used as a source of sulfuric acid and magnesium; hydrous magnesium sulfate

Ki·ev (kē′ef′, -ev′) *Russ. name for* KYIV —**Ki′ev′an** (-ən) *n., adj.*

kif or **kief** (kif, kēf) *n. var. of* KEF

Ki·ga·li (ki gä′lē) capital of Rwanda, in the central part

kike (kīk) *n.* ⟦orig. uncert.⟧ [Slang] a Jew: a hostile and offensive term

Ki·kon·go (kē käŋ′gō) *n. var. of* KONGO (sense 2)

Ki·ku·yu (kē kōō′yōō) *n.* **1** *pl.* **-yus** or **-yu** a member of an agricultural people of Kenya **2** the Bantu language of this people

Ki·lau·e·a (kē′lou ā′ə) ⟦< Haw, lit., spewing⟧ active volcanic crater on the slope of Mauna Loa, Hawaii: *c.* 8 mi (13 km) in circumference

Kil·dare (kil der′) county in Leinster province, E Ireland: 654 sq mi (1,694 sq km)

kil·der·kin (kil′dər kin) *n.* ⟦ME *kylderkin,* altered < MDu *kinderkin,* quarter tun, dim. < *kintal* < ML *quintale:* see QUINTAL⟧ **1** a cask **2** an English unit of liquid measure of about 18 imperial gallons

ki·lim (ki lēm′) *n.* ⟦Turk < Pers *kilīm*⟧ [*sometimes* **K-**] a patterned, reversible wool rug in a flat weave, produced in Turkey, other parts of the Middle East, and some parts of E Europe: also **kilim rug**

Kil·i·man·ja·ro (kil′ə män jär′ō) mountain in NE Tanzania: highest mountain in Africa: 19,340 ft (5,895 m)

Kil·ken·ny (kil ken′ē) county in Leinster province, E Ireland: 796 sq mi (2,062 sq km)

kill¹ (kil) *vt.* ⟦ME *kullen, killen* < ? OE **cyllan,* special late phonetic development of *cwellan,* to kill: see QUELL⟧ **1** to cause the death of; make die **2** *a)* to destroy the vital or active qualities of *b)* to destroy; put an end to; ruin **3** to prevent the passage of (legislation); defeat or veto **4** to spend (time) on matters of little or no importance ☆**5** *a)* to cause (an engine, etc.) to stop; turn off *b)* to turn off (a light, esp. a theater spotlight) *c)* to muffle (sound) ☆**6** to prevent publication of [to *kill* a newspaper story] **7** to spoil the effect of; destroy by contrast: said of colors, etc. **8** [Informal] to overcome with laughter, chagrin, pleasure, surprise, etc. **9** [Informal] to cause to feel great pain or discomfort **10** [Informal] to tire out; exhaust ☆**11** [Slang] to drink the last, or all, of (a bottle of liquor, etc.); finish off ☆**12** *Printing* to mark as not to be used; score out; cancel **13** *Tennis, etc.* to return (the ball) with such force that it cannot be returned —*vi.* **1** to destroy life **2** to be killed [plants that *kill* easily] —*n.* **1** an act or instance of killing **2** an animal or animals killed **3** an enemy plane, ship, etc. destroyed —**go (in) for the kill** to make a strong or aggressive effort to win or succeed —**in at the kill 1** present when the hunted animal is killed **2** present at the end or climax of some action —**to kill** [Informal] to make a strongly desirable impression [dressed *to kill*]: see also FIT TO KILL at FIT¹

SYN.—**kill** is the general word in this list, meaning to cause the death of in any way, and may be applied to persons, animals, or plants; **slay,** now largely a literary word, implies deliberate and violent killing; **murder** applies to an unlawful and malicious or premeditated killing; **assassinate** implies specifically the sudden killing of a politically important person, often by someone hired or delegated to do this; **execute** denotes a killing in accordance with a legally imposed sentence; **dispatch** suggests a killing by direct action, such as shooting, and emphasizes speed or promptness

☆**kill²** (kil) *n.* ⟦Du *kil* < MDu *kille,* akin to ON *kīll,* inlet⟧ a stream; channel; creek: used esp. in place names

Kil·lar·ney (ki lär′nē) **1** town in central Kerry county, SW Ireland **2 Lakes of** three lakes near this town

☆**kill·deer** (kil′dir′) *n., pl.* **-deers′** or **-deer′** ⟦echoic of its cry⟧ a medium-sized North American plover (*Charadrius vociferus*) with a high, piercing cry, that nests in open fields, on beaches, etc.: also **kill·dee** (kil′dē′)

Kil·leen (ki lēn′) ⟦after F. P. *Killeen* (1838-1924), official of the Santa Fe Railroad & early settler⟧ city in central Tex., north of Austin

kill·er (kil′ər) *n.* **1** a person, animal, or thing that kills, esp. one that kills habitually or wantonly **2** KILLER WHALE **3** [Slang] something devastating, difficult, hard to cope with, etc. **4** [Slang] an extremely successful, impressive, exciting, etc. person or thing —*adj.* **1** that kills or has the potential for killing [*a killer* storm] **2** [Slang] very difficult, hard to cope with, etc. **3** [Slang] successful, impressive, exciting, etc.

☆**killer bee** ⟦after the notion that in a swarm this bee attacks unusually aggressively⟧ AFRICANIZED BEE

killer cell any of various cells that destroy germs, infected cells, etc.; esp., a lymphocyte (**killer T cell**) that destroys infected or cancerous cells by releasing proteins that damage the cell membranes of the target cells

killer instinct a tendency to be ruthless and single-minded in dealing with opponents

killer satellite an orbiting satellite that can be maneuvered to approach a target satellite and destroy it by exploding

killer whale a very large, mostly black dolphin (*Orcinus orca*) with white patches, that hunts in large packs and preys on large fish, seals, and whales

☆**kill fee** a fee paid to a freelance writer for material written on assignment but not used

kil·lick (kil′ik) *n.* ⟦New England dial.⟧ a small anchor; often, an anchor weighted with or using a stone: also **kil′lock** (-ək)

Kil·lie·cran·kie (kil′ē kraŋ′kē) mountain pass in the Grampians, central Scotland: *c.* 1.5 mi (2.4 km) long

☆**kil·li·fish** (kil′i fish′) *n., pl.* **-fish′** or **-fish′es** (see FISH) ⟦*killie,* killifish (< KILL² + -IE) + FISH⟧ any of a family (Cyprinodontidae, order Atheriniformes) of small, freshwater bony fishes used in mosquito control and as bait: also **kil′lie** (-ē), *pl.* **-lies**

kill·ing (kil′iŋ) *adj.* **1** causing, or able to cause, death; destructive; deadly **2** exhausting; fatiguing **3** [Informal] very funny or comical —*n.* **1** the act or an instance of murder, destruction, etc. ☆**2** [Informal] a sudden, great profit or success [to make a *killing* in the stock market] —**kill′ing·ly** *adv.*

kill·joy (kil′joi′) *n.* a person who destroys or lessens other people's enjoyment: also written **kill-joy**

Kil·mer (kil′mər), **(Alfred) Joyce** 1886-1918; U.S. poet

kiln (kil, kiln) *n.* ⟦ME *kylne* < OE *cylne* < L *culina,* cookstove, kitchen⟧ a furnace or oven for drying, burning, or baking something, as bricks, grain, or pottery —*vt.* to dry, burn, or bake in a kiln

kiln-dry (-drī′) *vt.* **-dried′**, **-dry′ing** to dry in a kiln

ki·lo (kē′lō, kil′ō) *n., pl.* **-los** ⟦Fr: abbreviated form⟧ KILOGRAM

kil·o- (kil′ō, -ə) ⟦Fr < Gr *chilioi,* thousand < IE base **ĝheslo-,* thousand⟧ *combining form* one thousand; the factor 10^3 [*kilogram*]

kil·o·bar (kil′ō bär′, kil′ə-) *n.* one thousand bars: abbrev. *kb*

ki·lo·base (kil′ə bās′) *n.* a unit of length equal to the length of 1000 base pairs of a nucleic acid

kil·o·bit (kil′ə bit′) *n.* ⟦KILO- + BIT⁴⟧ **1** a unit of storage capacity in a computer system, equal to 1,024 (2^{10}) bits **2** loosely, one thousand bits

kil·o·byte (-bīt′) *n.* **1** a unit of storage capacity in a computer system, equal to 1,024 (2^{10}) bytes **2** loosely, one thousand bytes Abbrev. *KB*

kil·o·cal·o·rie (kil′ō kal′ə rē, kil′ə-) *n.* CALORIE (sense 2)

kil·o·cy·cle (-sī′kəl) *n. former term for* KILOHERTZ

kil·o·gram (-gram′) ***n.*** ⟦Fr *kilogramme:* see KILO- & GRAM[1]⟧ one thousand grams (2.204623 pounds avoirdupois): abbrev. *kg:* see GRAM[1]

kil·o·gram-me·ter (-gram′mēt′ər) ***n.*** a unit of energy or work, being the amount needed to raise one kilogram one meter: it is equal to 7.2334 foot-pounds: also [Chiefly Brit.] **kil′o·gram′-me′tre**

kil·o·hertz (-hurts′, -herts′) ***n., pl.*** **-hertz′** one thousand hertz: abbrev. *kHz*

kil·o·li·ter (-lēt′ər) ***n.*** ⟦Fr *kilolitre:* see KILO- & LITER⟧ one thousand liters, or one cubic meter (264.179 gallons or 1.31 cubic yards): abbrev. *kl:* Brit. sp. **kil′o·li′tre**

kil·o·me·ter (kə läm′ət ər, kil′ə mēt′ər) ***n.*** ⟦Fr *kilomètre:* see KILO- & METER[1]⟧ one thousand meters (3,280.84 feet or 0.6214 miles): abbrev. *km:* Brit. sp. **kil·o·me·tre** —**kil·o·met·ric** (kil′ə me′trik) ***adj.***

kil·o·par·sec (kil′ō pär′sek′, kil′ə-) ***n.*** one thousand parsecs or 3,262 light-years: abbrev. *kpc*

kil·o·ton (-tun′) ***n.*** the explosive force of one thousand tons of TNT: a unit for measuring the power of thermonuclear weapons: abbrev. *kT*

kil·o·volt (-vōlt′) ***n.*** one thousand volts: abbrev. *kV*

kil·o·volt-am·pere (-am′pir′) ***n.*** one thousand volt-amperes: abbrev. *kVA*

kil·o·watt (kil′ō wät′, kil′ə-) ***n.*** one thousand watts: abbrev. *kW*

kil·o·watt-hour (-our) ***n.*** a unit of electrical energy or work, equal to the power supplied by one kilowatt for one hour: abbrev. *kWh*

kilt (kilt) ***vt.*** ⟦ME (northern) *kilten,* prob. < Scand, as in ON *kilting,* a skirt, *kjalta,* lap⟧ **1** [Scot.] to tuck up (a skirt, etc.) **2** to pleat **3** to provide a kilt for —***n.*** a pleated skirt reaching to the knees; esp., the tartan skirt worn sometimes by men of the Scottish Highlands

kil·ter (kil′tər) ***n.*** ⟦< ?⟧ [Informal] good condition; proper order: now chiefly in **out of kilter**

kilt·ie (kil′tē) ***n.*** **1** a flap of fringed and, sometimes, perforated leather extending from and folding back over the top end of the vamp of a shoe **2** a shoe with such a flap

Kim·ber·ley (kim′bər lē) capital of Northern Cape province, South Africa: diamond-mining center

kim·ber·lite (kim′bər līt′) ***n.*** ⟦< prec. + -ITE[1]⟧ a kind of peridotite which sometimes contains diamonds

Kim·ber·ly (kim′bər lē) ***n.*** a feminine name: dim. *Kim, Kimmy;* var. *Kimberley*

kim·chi or **kim·chee** (kim′chē) ***n.*** ⟦Kor⟧ a spicy Korean dish consisting of pickled cabbage, peppers, garlic, etc.

ki·mo·no (kə mō′nə, -nō′) ***n., pl.*** **-nos** ⟦Jpn *ki* (< *kiru,* to wear) + *mono,* thing⟧ **1** a robe with wide sleeves and a sash, part of the traditional costume of Japanese men and women **2** a loose dressing gown

kin (kin) ***n.*** ⟦ME *kyn* < OE *cynn,* akin to Du *kunne,* Goth *kuni,* ON *kyn* < Gmc **kunja-* < IE base **ĝen-,* to produce: see GENUS⟧ one's family; relatives; kinfolk; kindred —***adj.*** related, as by blood: used only in the predicate [*she is kin* to my brother-in-law] —**of kin** related

-kin (kin) ⟦ME < MDu *-ken, -kijn,* dim. suffix, akin to Ger *-chen*⟧ *suffix forming nouns* little (specified person or thing) [*lambkin*]

ki·na (kē′nə) ***n.*** ⟦Papuan, a crescent-shaped piece of shell money⟧ the basic monetary unit of Papua New Guinea: see the table of monetary units in the Reference Supplement

Kin·a·ba·lu (kin′ə bə lo͞o′) mountain in NW Sabah: highest peak on Borneo: 13,455 ft (4,101 m)

kin·aes·the·si·a (kin′es thē′zhə) ***n.*** *alt. sp. of* KINESTHESIA: also **kin′aes·the′sis** (-sis) —**kin′aes·thet′ic** (-thet′ik) ***adj.***

ki·nase (kī′nās′, kin′ās′) ***n.*** ⟦KIN(ETIC) + -ASE⟧ an enzyme capable of activating a zymogen or one causing the transfer of the terminal phosphate group, generally from ATP, to a receiving molecule

Kin·car·dine (kin kär′din) former county of E Scotland: also **Kin·car′dine·shire′** (-shir′, -shər)

kind (kīnd) ***n.*** ⟦ME *kynd* < OE *cynd,* akin to Ger *kind,* child, ON *kundr,* son < IE **ĝnti-* (> L *natio,* NATION) < base **ĝen-:* see GENUS⟧ **1** [Archaic] *a)* origin *b)* nature *c)* manner; way **2** a natural group or division: sometimes used in compounds [*humankind*] **3** essential character **4** sort; variety; class —***adj.*** ⟦ME *kynde* < OE *gecynde*⟧ **1** sympathetic, friendly, gentle, tenderhearted, generous, etc. **2** cordial [*kind* regards] **3** [Archaic] loving; affectionate **4** [Obs.] natural; native —**after one's (or its) kind** [Archaic] in agreement with one's (or its) nature —**all kinds of** [Informal] many or much [*all kinds of* money] —**in kind 1** in goods or produce instead of money **2** with something like that received; in the same way —**kind of** [Informal] somewhat; rather; almost —**of a kind 1** of the same kind; alike **2** of poor quality; mediocre [entertainment *of a kind*]

SYN.—**kind** implies the possession of sympathetic or generous qualities, either habitually or specifically, or is applied to actions manifesting these [he is *kind* only to his mother, your *kind* remarks]; **kindly** usually implies a characteristic nature or general disposition marked by such qualities [his *kindly* old uncle]; **benign** suggests a mild or kindly nature and is applied especially to a gracious superior [a *benign* employer]; **benevolent** implies a charitable or altruistic inclination to do good [his *benevolent* interest in orphans] —***ANT.*** **unkind, unfeeling, cruel**

kind·a (kīnd′ə) ***adv.*** *phonetic sp. of* KIND OF (in informal pronunciation) (see phrase under KIND)

kin·der·gar·ten (kin′dər gärt′′n) ***n.*** ⟦Ger, lit., children's garden, coined (1840) by F. FROEBEL < *kinder,* gen. pl. of *kind,* child (see KIND) + *garten,* GARDEN⟧ a school or class for young children, usually four to six years old, that prepares them for first grade and that develops basic skills and social behavior by games, exercises, music, simple handicrafts, etc. —**kin′der·gart′ner *n.*, kin′der·gar′ten·er** (-gärt′nər)

kind·heart·ed (kīnd′härt′id) ***adj.*** having or resulting from a kind heart; sympathetic; kindly —**kind′heart′ed·ly *adv.*** —**kind′heart′ed·ness *n.***

kin·dle[1] (kin′dəl) ***vt.*** **-dled, -dling** ⟦ME *kindlen,* freq. < ON *kynda,* to set on fire, akin to MHG *künten*⟧ **1** to set on fire; ignite **2** to light (a fire) **3** to arouse or excite (interest, feelings, etc.) **4** to cause to light up; make bright —***vi.*** **1** to catch fire **2** to become excited **3** to become bright [eyes *kindling* with joy] —**kin′dler *n.***

kin·dle[2] (kin′dəl) ***vt., vi.*** **-dled, -dling** ⟦ME *kindlen:* see KIND, ***n.***⟧ [Dial.] to give birth to (young)

kind·less (kīnd′lis) ***adj.*** **1** [Rare] lacking kindness **2** [Obs.] lacking natural feeling; unnatural

kin·dling (kind′liŋ) ***n.*** ⟦ME: see KINDLE[1]⟧ bits of dry wood or other easily lighted material for starting a fire

kind·ly (kīnd′lē) ***adj.*** **-li·er, -li·est** ⟦ME *cyndelich* < OE *(ge)cyndelic,* natural < *cynd(e):* see KIND⟧ **1** kind; gracious; benign **2** agreeable; pleasant [a *kindly* climate] **3** [Archaic] natural; native; innate —***adv.*** **-li·er, -li·est 1** in a kind, gracious manner **2** agreeably; favorably **3** as a courtesy; please [*kindly* shut the door]: see note at PLEASE **4** [Obs.] naturally: now only in **take kindly to,** *a)* to be naturally attracted to *b)* to accept willingly —***SYN.*** KIND —**thank kindly** to thank heartily —**kind′li·ness *n.***

kind·ness (-nis) ***n.*** ⟦ME *kyndeness*⟧ **1** the state, quality, or habit of being kind **2** a kind act or kindly treatment **3** [Archaic] kind feeling; affection; goodwill

kin·dred (kin′drid) ***n.*** ⟦with intrusive *-d-* < ME *kinreden* < OE *cynn,* KIN + *rœden,* state, condition, akin to *rœdan,* READ[1]⟧ **1** [Archaic] kinship **2** family or relatives; kin; kinfolk —***adj.*** **1** [Archaic] related by birth or common origin **2** of like nature; similar [*kindred* spirits] —***SYN.*** RELATED

kine (kīn) ***pl.n.*** ⟦ME *kin,* double pl. of *cou* (< OE *cy,* pl. of *cu,* COW[1]) + *(-e)n*⟧ [Archaic] cows; cattle

kin·e·mat·ics (kin′ə mat′iks) ***n.*** ⟦Fr *cinématique* < Gr *kinēma* (gen. *kinēmatos*), motion < *kinein,* to move (see CITE) + -ICS⟧ the branch of mechanics that deals with motion in the abstract, without reference to the force or mass —**kin′e·mat′ic *adj.*, kin′e·mat′i·cal**

☆**kin·e·scope** (kin′ə skōp′) ***n.*** ⟦KINE(TO)- + -SCOPE⟧ **1** PICTURE TUBE **2** a recording made on film of images from a television camera, esp. such a recording of a live broadcast of a television program

ki·ne·sics (ki nē′siks, kī-; -ziks) ***n.*** ⟦< Gr *kinēsis* (see fol.) + -ICS⟧ the study of bodily movements, facial expressions, etc. as ways of communication or as accompaniments to speech —**ki·ne′sic *adj.***

ki·ne·si·ol·o·gy (ki nē′sē äl′ə jē, kī-; -zē-) ***n.*** ⟦< Gr *kinēsis,* motion < *kinein,* to move (see CITE) + -LOGY⟧ the science or study of human muscular movements, esp. as applied in physical education

ki·ne·sis (ki nē′sis, kī-) ***n., pl.*** **-ses′** (-sēz′) ⟦ModL < Gr *kinēsis,* motion: see prec.⟧ *Physiol.* physical movement, esp. involuntary random movement resulting from a particular stimulus: distinguished from TAXIS (sense 2)

kin·es·the·si·a (kin′is thē′zhə, -zhē ə) ***n.*** ⟦ModL < Gr *kinein,* to move (see CITE) + *aisthēsis,* perception: for IE base see AESTHETIC⟧ the sensation of position, movement, tension, etc. of parts of the body, perceived through nerve-end organs in muscles, tendons, and joints: also **kin′es·the′sis** (-sis) —**kin′es·thet′ic** (-thet′ik) ***adj.***

ki·net·ic (ki net′ik) ***adj.*** ⟦Gr *kinētikos* < *kinētos,* movable < *kinein,* to move: see CITE⟧ **1** of or caused by motion **2** energetic or dynamic

kinetic art an art style, esp. in sculpture or assemblage, involving the use of moving, often motorized, parts, shifting lights, sounds, etc.

kinetic energy the energy of a body that results from its motion

ki·net·ics (-iks) ***n.*** ⟦< KINETIC⟧ DYNAMICS (sense 1)

kinetic theory the theory that the minute particles of all matter are in constant motion and that the temperature of a substance is dependent on the velocity of this motion, increased motion being accompanied by increased temperature: according to the **kinetic theory of gases,** the elasticity, diffusion, pressure, and other physical properties of a gas are due to the rapid motion in straight lines of its molecules, to their collisions against each other and the walls of the container, to weak cohesive forces between molecules, etc.

☆**ki·ne·tin** (kī′nə tin) ***n.*** ⟦KINET(IC) + -IN[1]⟧ a substance, $C_{10}H_9N_5O$, found in many plants, that regulates growth by inducing cell division and cell differentiation

ki·net·o- (ki net′ō, -nēt′-; -ə) ⟦< Gr *kinētos:* see KINETIC⟧ *combining form* moving, motion [*kinetoplast*]

ki·net·o·chore (ki net′ə kôr′, -nēt′-) ***n.*** ⟦< prec. + Gr *chōros,* a place⟧ CENTROMERE

ki·net·o·plast (ki net′ə plast′, -nēt′-) ***n.*** ⟦KINETO- + -PLAST⟧ a cytoplasmic structure lying at the base of the flagellum in many flagellated protists

kin·folk (kin′fōk′) ***pl.n.*** relatives; family; kin; kindred: also **kin′folks′**

king (kiŋ) ***n.*** ⟦ME < OE *cyning,* akin to ON *konungr,* OHG *kuning* < Gmc **kuningaz* < **kunja-,* KIN + *-ing-,* belonging to: prob. basic sense, either "head of a kin" or "son of noble kin"⟧ **1** a male ruler of a nation or state usually called a kingdom; male sovereign, limited or absolute; monarch **2** *a)* a man who is supreme or highly successful in some field [an oil *king*] *b)* something supreme in its class **3** a playing card with a conventionalized picture of a king on it **4** *Checkers* a piece that has been crowned and can thus move backward as well as forward **5**

Chess the chief piece, which can move one square in any direction: see CHECKMATE —*adj.* chief (in size, importance, etc.): often in comb. —*vt.* CROWN (*vt.* 8) —**the Three Kings** the three learned men from the East who came bearing gifts to the infant Jesus (Matt. 2:1-13): see MAGI (sense 2)

King (kiŋ) **1 (William Lyon) Mackenzie** 1874-1950; Cdn. statesman: prime minister (1921-26; 1926-30; 1935-48) **2 Martin Luther, Jr.** 1929-68; U.S. clergyman & leader in the civil rights movement: assassinated

king·bird (kiŋ′burd′) *n.* ☆any of several aggressive tyrant flycatchers (genus *Tyrannus*) of the U.S. and Canada

king·bolt (-bōlt′) *n.* any main bolt; esp., one that acts as a vertical pivot for a turning vehicle, as that connecting the front axle of a wagon, etc., or the truck of a railroad car, with the body

King Charles's head ⟦in allusion to a character's obsession with the head of Charles I of England (beheaded 1649) in the novel *David Copperfield* (1850) by Charles DICKENS⟧ a fixed idea; personal obsession

King Charles spaniel a variety of English toy spaniel with a black-and-tan coat: made fashionable by Charles II of England

king cobra a large, very poisonous snake (*Ophiophagus hannah*) native to Southeast Asia and the Philippines; hamadryad

☆**king crab 1** a very large, edible spider crab (*Paralithodes camtschatica*) of the N Pacific **2** HORSESHOE CRAB

king·craft (-kraft′) *n.* the art of ruling as a monarch

king·cup (-kup′) *n.* BUTTERCUP

king·dom (kiŋ′dəm) *n.* ⟦ME < OE *cyningdom:* see KING & -DOM⟧ **1** [Obs.] the position, rank, or power of a king **2** a government or country headed by a king or queen; monarchy **3** a realm; domain; sphere [the *kingdom* of poetry] **4** any of the three great divisions into which all natural objects have been classified (the animal, vegetable, and mineral kingdoms) **5** the spiritual realm of God **6** *Biol.* a major category in the classification of animals, plants, etc., ranking above a phylum or division: in some systems it ranks below a domain or superkingdom: the Latinized kingdom names are capitalized but not italicized (Ex.: Monera, monerans)

kingdom come ⟦< "Thy kingdom come," in the LORD'S PRAYER⟧ the hereafter; heaven

king·fish (kiŋ′fish′) *n.* **1** *pl.* **-fish′** or **-fish′es** (see FISH) any of various large food fishes found along the Atlantic or Pacific coast, esp. certain drums ☆**2** [Informal] a person with absolute power in a group

king·fish·er (-fish′ər) *n.* ⟦ME *kyngys fyschare,* lit., king's fisher⟧ any of a family (Alcedinidae) of coraciiform birds, usually having bright coloration, a large, crested head, a large, strong beak, and a short tail: most species dive for fish

King James Version AUTHORIZED VERSION

King Lear (lir) **1** a tragedy by Shakespeare (*c.* 1606) **2** its main character, whose division of his kingdom between his older daughters, Goneril and Regan, and disinheritance of his youngest, Cordelia, lead to civil strife and his own insanity and death

king·let (kiŋ′lit) *n.* ⟦see -LET⟧ **1** a petty, unimportant king **2** any of several small Old World warblers (genus *Regulus*) with a bright-colored crown, as the **golden-crowned kinglet** (*R. satrapa*) of North America: see WARBLER (sense 3)

king·ly (-lē) *adj.* **-li·er, -li·est** ⟦ME⟧ of, like, or fit for a king or kings; royal; regal; noble —**king′li·ness** *n.*

king·mak·er (-māk′ər) *n.* a politically powerful person who is instrumental in getting candidates into office

king-of-arms (-əv ärmz′) *n.* in Great Britain, any of the chief officers who decide questions of heraldry

king of beasts *name for* a lion

king·pin (-pin′) *n.* **1** a vertical pin attached to some axles to serve as the axis for a wheel spindle, so that the wheel may be turned for steering **2** the headpin or the center pin in bowling, tenpins, etc. ☆**3** [Informal] the main or essential person or thing

king post *Carpentry* a vertical supporting post between the apex of a triangular truss and the base, or tie beam, as at the ridge of a roof: cf. QUEEN POST

Kings (kiŋz) *n. Bible* **1** either of two books (1 Kings, 2 Kings) which give the history of the reigns of the Jewish kings after David: abbrev. *K, Kgs, Ki* **2** in the Douay Bible, any of four books called 1 & 2 Samuel and 1 & 2 Kings in other versions

☆**king salmon** CHINOOK SALMON

King's (*or* **Queen's) Bench** ⟦so called because the sovereign used to sit in court on a raised bench⟧ *Eng. Law* **1** [Historical] the supreme court of common law **2** one of the three divisions of the High Court of Justice

king's blue COBALT BLUE

King's (*or* **Queen's) Counsel** a barrister appointed to be counsel of the British Crown

King's (*or* **Queen's) English** standard or accepted (esp. British) English usage in speech or writing: so called from the notion of royal sanction: with *the*

King's (*or* **Queen's) evidence** *Eng. Law* STATE'S EVIDENCE

king's evil ⟦transl. of ML *regius morbus:* from the notion that a king's touch could cure it⟧ [Obs.] SCROFULA

king·ship (kiŋ′ship′) *n.* **1** the position, rank, dignity, or dominion of a king **2** the rule of a king **3** [**K-**] majesty: a title sometimes used (with *his*) in referring to a king

☆**king-size** (-sīz′) *adj.* larger than the regular kind [a *king-size* bed is 76 by 80 in]: also **king′-sized′**

☆**king·snake** (-snāk′) *n.* any of several large, harmless, New World colubrid snakes (genus *Lampropeltis*) found esp. in SW U.S. and N Mexico: also written **king snake**

Kings·ton (kiŋz′tən, kiŋ′stən) **1** seaport & capital of Jamaica, on the SE coast **2** ⟦orig., *King's Town* (1784), in honor of George III⟧ port in SE Ontario, Canada, at the outlet of Lake Ontario into the St. Lawrence

Kingston upon Hull HULL[2] (in England)

Kingston upon Thames borough of SW Greater London, England

Kings·town (kiŋz′toun′) capital of St. Vincent and the Grenadines

king's yellow ORPIMENT

king·wood (kiŋ′wood′) *n.* **1** a hard, fine-grained, violet-tinted wood from a Brazilian tree (*Dalbergia cearensis*) of the pea family **2** the tree

ki·nin (kī′nin) *n.* ⟦< KIN(ETIC) + -IN[1]⟧ a powerful, short-lived peptide that lowers blood pressure, increases vascular permeability, dilates blood vessels, causes smooth muscle to contract, and triggers pain

kink (kiŋk) *n.* ⟦< Scand, as in Swed & Dan *kink,* akin to MLowG *kinke,* Du *kink*⟧ **1** a short twist, curl, or bend in a thread, rope, hair, wire, etc. **2** a painful muscle spasm or cramp in the neck, back, etc.; crick ☆**3** *a)* a mental twist; odd notion; whim; eccentricity *b)* a quirk; peculiarity **4** a difficulty or defect in a plan or process — *vi., vt.* to form or cause to form a kink or kinks

kin·ka·jou (kiŋ′kə jo͞o′) *n.* ⟦Fr, earlier *quincajou,* (properly, wolverine, misapplied by the Comte de BUFFON) < a crossing of Ojibwa *gwiinwa'aage* & Montagnais *kwaahkwaacheew:* see CARCAJOU⟧ a nocturnal, tree-dwelling carnivore (*Potos flavus*) of Central and South America of the same family (Procyonidae) as the raccoon, with soft, yellowish-brown fur, large eyes, and a long prehensile tail

kink·y (kiŋ′kē) *adj.* **kink′i·er, kink′i·est** ☆**1** full of kinks; tightly curled [*kinky* hair] **2** [Slang] weird, bizarre, eccentric, peculiar, etc.; specif., sexually abnormal or perverse —**kink′i·ness** *n.*

☆**kin·ni·ki·nick** or **kin·ni·ki·nic** (kin′i ki nik′) *n.* ⟦earlier *killikinnick* < Delaware dialect *kələk'ənī'k'an,* lit., mixture⟧ **1** a mixture, as of tobacco and dried sumac leaves, bark, etc., formerly smoked by certain American Indians and some pioneers **2** any of the plants used for such a mixture

ki·no (kē′nō) *n.* ⟦< Mande name in W Africa⟧ a dark-red or reddish-brown gum obtained from certain leguminous tropical plants (esp. *Pterocarpus marsupium*): used in varnishes, as an astringent in medicine, etc.

Kin·ross (kin rôs′) former county of EC Scotland: also **Kin·ross′-shire** (-shir)

Kin·sey (kin′zē), **Alfred Charles** 1894-1956; U.S. zoologist: studied human sexual behavior in the U.S.

kins·folk (kinz′fōk′) *pl.n.* ⟦< KIN + FOLK, after KINSMAN⟧ *former form of* KINFOLK

Kin·sha·sa (kēn shä′sä) capital of the Democratic Republic of the Congo, in the W part, on the Congo River

kin·ship (kin′ship′) *n.* ⟦see KIN & -SHIP⟧ **1** family relationship **2** relationship; close connection

kins·man (kinz′mən) *n., pl.* **-men** (-mən) ⟦ME *kynnesman* < *kynnes-,* gen. sing. of *kyn* (see KIN) + *man*⟧ a relative; esp., a male relative

kins·wom·an (-woom′ən) *n., pl.* **-wom′en** (-wim′in) a female relative

ki·osk (kē′äsk′, kē äsk′) *n.* ⟦Fr *kiosque* < Turk *köşk* < Pers *kūshk,* palace⟧ **1** in Turkey and Persia, a summerhouse or pavilion of open construction **2** a somewhat similar small structure open at one or more sides, used as a newsstand, bandstand, entrance to a subway, etc. **3** any of various unmanned, free-standing structures housing, variously, interactive terminals, video monitors, etc., located in retail stores or other public places for the use of customers, the general public, etc.

Kio·to (kē ō′tō) *alt. sp. of* KYOTO

Ki·o·wa (kī′ō wä′, -ə wə) *n.* ⟦Sp *Caygua* < Kiowa *kɔ́ygú*⟧ **1** *pl.* **-was′** or **-wa′** a member of a North American Indian people formerly living in Colorado, Oklahoma, and other W states, and now living in Oklahoma **2** the Tanoan language of this people

kip[1] (kip) *n.* ⟦earlier *kyppe,* prob. < MDu *kip* (in sense 2)⟧ **1** the untanned hide of a calf, lamb, or other young or small animal **2** a set of such hides

kip[2] (kip) *n.* ⟦< or akin to Dan *kippe,* low alehouse⟧ [Slang, Chiefly Brit.] **1** a rooming house **2** a bed **3** sleep —*vi.* **kipped, kip′ping** [Slang, Chiefly Brit.] to sleep

kip[3] (kip) *n., pl.* **kips** or **kip** ⟦Thai⟧ the basic monetary unit of Laos: see the table of monetary units in the Reference Supplement

kip[4] (kip) *n.* ⟦KI(LO)- + P(OUND)⟧ a unit of weight equal to 1,000 pounds

Kip·ling (kip′liŋ), **(Joseph) Rud·yard** (rud′yərd) 1865-1936; Eng. writer, born in India

kip·pa or **kip·pah** (ki pä′) *n., pl.* **-pot′** (-pōt′) ⟦Heb *kipah*⟧ a traditional skullcap worn by Orthodox Jewish men and boys: often Conservative and sometimes Reform Jewish males wear it at worship: also sp. **ki·pa′** or **ki·pah′**, *pl.* **-pot′**

kip·per (kip′ər) *vt.* ⟦< ? the *n.*⟧ to cure (herring, salmon, etc.) by cleaning, salting, and drying or smoking —*n.* ⟦ME *kypre* < OE *cypera* < ? *coper,* copper (from the color)⟧ **1** a male salmon or sea trout during or shortly after the spawning season **2** a kippered herring, salmon, etc.

kir (kir) *n.* [*also* **K-**] an aperitif consisting of dry white wine and a small amount of cassis

Kirch·hoff (kirH′hôf′), **Gus·tav Ro·bert** (goos′täf′ rō′bert′) 1824-87; Ger. physicist

Kirch·ner (kirk′nər; *Ger* kirH′nər), **Ernst Lud·wig** (ernst lo͞ot′viH) 1880-1938; Ger. painter & sculptor

Kir·ghiz (kir gēz′) ***n.*** ⟦orig. uncert.⟧ **1** *pl.* **-ghiz′** or **-ghiz′es** a member of a people living chiefly in Kyrgyzstan and adjacent areas **2** the Turkic language of this people Also sp. **Kir·giz′**

Kir·ghi·zi·a (kir gē′zhə, -zhē ə) KIRGHIZ SOVIET SOCIALIST REPUBLIC —**Kir·ghi′zi·an** ***adj., n.***

Kirghiz Soviet Socialist Republic a republic of the U.S.S.R.: now KYRGYZSTAN

Kir·i·bati (kir′ə bas′, -bäs′, -bus′) country consisting principally of three groups of atolls in the WC Pacific, east of the Solomon Islands: formerly a British territory, it became independent & a member of the Commonwealth (1979): 313 sq mi (811 sq km); cap. Tarawa

Ki·rik·ka·le (kə rik′ə lā′) city in central Turkey

Ki·rin (kē′rin′) *a former transliteration of* JILIN

Ki·riti·mati (kə ris′məs) island in the central Pacific, in the country of Kiribati: 150 sq mi (388 sq km)

kirk (kʉrk; *Scot* kirk) ***n.*** ⟦Scot < ME *kirke* < OE *cirice* (infl. by ON *kirkja*): see CHURCH⟧ [Scot. or North Eng.] a church —**the Kirk** the Presbyterian Church of Scotland

Kirk·cal·dy (kər kô′dē, -kôl′dē) seaport in E Scotland, on the Firth of Forth

Kirk·cud·bright (kər ko͞o′brē) former county of SW Scotland: also **Kirk·cud′bright·shire′** (-shir′, -shər)

Kir·li·an photography (kir′lē ən) ⟦after S. *Kirlian*, its Soviet developer (1939)⟧ a method of capturing on a photographic plate an image of what is thought by some to be an aura of energy that emanates from animals and plants and that undergoes changes in accordance with physiological or emotional changes

Kir·man (kər män′, kir-) ***n.*** ⟦after KERMAN[2], where produced⟧ a Persian rug or carpet having an elaborate design in rich, muted colors

kir·mess (kʉr′mis) ***n.*** *var. of* KERMIS

Ki·rov (kē′rôf′) city in NC European Russia

Ki·rov·a·bad (kē rō′və bad′) *name* (1935-89) *for* GYANDZHA: also used before 1804

Ki·rov·o·grad (-grad′) city in SC Ukraine

kirsch (kirsh) ***n.*** ⟦< Ger *kirschwasser* < *kirsche*, cherry (akin to OE *cirse* < Gmc **kirissa* < L *cerasus*, CHERRY) + *wasser*, WATER⟧ a colorless alcoholic drink distilled from the fermented juice of black cherries: sometimes **kirsch′was′ser** (-väs′ər)

kir·tle (kʉrt′'l) ***n.*** ⟦ME *kirtel* < OE *cyrtel* (akin to ON *kyrtill*) < Gmc **kurt-*, short (< L *curtus:* see CURT) + *-el*, dim. suffix⟧ [Archaic] **1** a man's tunic or coat **2** a woman's dress or skirt

Ki·san·ga·ni (kē′sän gä′nē) city in the NE Democratic Republic of the Congo, on the upper Congo River

Kish (kish) ancient Sumerian city on the Euphrates in what is now central Iraq: fl. *c.* 4000 B.C.

Ki·shi·nev (kish′ə nev′, -nef′) *former name for* CHIŞINAU

kish·ke (kish′kə) ***n.*** ⟦Yiddish, shortened < *gefilte kishke*, lit., stuffed intestine < Russ *kiška* or Pol *kiszka*, intestine⟧ beef casing stuffed with matzo meal or bread crumbs, flour, onions, etc. and then steamed and roasted: also sp. **kish′ka**

Kis·lev (kis′lef) ***n.*** ⟦Heb⟧ the third month of the Jewish year: see the Jewish calendar in the Reference Supplement

kis·met (kiz′met, kis′-) ***n.*** ⟦Turk *kısmet* < Ar *qisma(t)*, a portion, lot, fate < *qasama*, to divide⟧ fate; destiny

kiss (kis) ***vt.*** ⟦ME *kissen* < OE *cyssan*, akin to Ger *küssen* < IE base **kus-*, prob. echoic⟧ **1** to give a kiss to (a person or thing); touch or caress with the lips **2** to touch lightly or gently [the bowling ball just *kissed* the pin] —***vi.*** **1** to give a kiss to one another on the lips **2** to touch one another lightly —***n.*** ⟦ME *kisse* < the v., replacing *cosse* < OE *coss*⟧ **1** a touch or caress with the lips, often with some pressure and suction, as an act of affection, desire, greeting, etc. **2** a light, gentle touch or slight contact **3** *a)* any of various candies *b)* a baked confection of egg white and sugar —**kiss ass** [Slang] to be obsequious or fawning, as to gain an advantage or approval: somewhat vulgar —**kiss goodbye 1** to kiss in taking leave ☆**2** [Informal] to give up all hope of getting, recovering, realizing, etc. —**kiss off** [Slang] to dismiss rudely or contemptuously —☆**kiss up** [Slang] to try to gain favor by acting servilely; fawn: often with *to* [*to kiss up* to the judge] —**kiss′a·ble** ***adj.***

kiss-and-tell (kis′ən tel′) ***adj.*** [Informal] revealing personal or confidential information, as about a well-known person, gained from the author's close relationship with that person [a *kiss-and-tell* memoir]

kiss·er (-ər) ***n.*** **1** a person who kisses, esp. one who kisses in a (specified) way [a good *kisser*] **2** [Slang] *a)* the mouth or lips *b)* the face

☆**kissing bug** CONENOSE

☆**kissing cousin** [Informal] **1** a distant relative known well enough to greet with a friendly kiss **2** someone or something closely akin to another

kissing disease ⟦because transmitted primarily via saliva⟧ [Informal] *popular term for* INFECTIOUS MONONUCLEOSIS

Kis·sin·ger (kis′ən jər), **Henry (Alfred)** 1923- ; U.S. secretary of state (1973-77), born in Germany

☆**kiss of death** ⟦in allusion to the *kiss* with which Judas betrayed Jesus: Matt. 26:48-50⟧ an action or quality, often seemingly helpful, which is actually harmful or ruinous

☆**kiss-off** (-ôf′) ***n.*** [Slang] dismissal, esp. when rude or contemptuous

kiss of life [Chiefly Brit.] mouth-to-mouth resuscitation

kiss of peace SIGN OF PEACE: though still sometimes used, *kiss of peace* is now mainly applied in historical contexts

☆**kiss·y** (kis′ē) ***adj.*** [Slang] **1** inclined to kiss; affectionately demonstrative **2** inviting kissing [*kissy* lips]

☆**kiss·y-face** (-fās′) ***n.*** [Slang] an engaging in kissing, caressing, etc. —**play kissy-face** to engage in kissing, caressing, etc., esp. overtly or publicly

kist[1] (kist) ***n.*** ⟦ME *kiste* < ON *kista*, akin to Ger *kiste* < L *cista:* see CHEST⟧ [Chiefly Scot. or North Eng.] a chest, box, or locker

kist[2] (kist) ***n.*** CIST

Kist·na (kist′nə) *former name for* KRISHNA[2]

Ki·swa·hi·li (kē′swä hē′lē) ***n.*** SWAHILI (sense 2)

kit[1] (kit) ***n.*** ⟦ME *kyt* < MDu *kitte*, container made of hooped staves⟧ **1** [Brit. Dial.] a small wooden tub or bucket for holding fish, butter, etc. **2** *a)* personal equipment, esp. as packed for travel *b)* a set of tools or implements *c)* equipment for some particular activity, sport, etc. [a first-aid *kit*, a salesman's *kit*] *d)* a set containing a number of parts to be assembled [a model airplane *kit*] **3** a box, bag, or other container for carrying such parts, equipment, or tools **4** [Informal] lot; collection: now chiefly in ☆**the whole kit and caboodle**, everybody or everything —***vt.*** **kit′ted, kit′ting** [Chiefly Brit.] to provide with what is needed for a given task or situation; equip: usually with *out* or *up*

kit[2] (kit) ***n.*** KITTEN

kit[3] (kit) ***n.*** ⟦Early ModE: abbrev. < ? CITHARA⟧ a tiny fiddle used by 16th- through 18th-cent. dancing masters

Kit (kit) ***n.*** **1** a masculine name: see CHRISTOPHER[1] **2** a feminine name: see CATHERINE[1], KATHERINE

Ki·ta·kyu·shu (kē′tä kyo͞o′sho͞o) seaport on the N coast of Kyushu, Japan

kitch·en (kich′ən) ***n.*** ⟦ME *kychene* < OE *cycene* < VL *cocina, cucina:* see CUISINE⟧ **1** a room or place or the equipment for the preparation and cooking of food **2** a staff that cooks and serves food

kitchen cabinet 1 a cabinet or cupboard in a kitchen ☆**2** [*often* **K- C-**] *a)* the group of unofficial advisors on whom President Jackson relied *b)* any similar group on whom a governmental head relies

Kitch·e·ner[1] (kich′ə nər), **(Horatio) Herbert** 1st Earl Kitchener of Khartoum 1850-1916; Brit. military officer & statesman, born in Ireland

Kitch·e·ner[2] (kich′ə nər) ⟦after prec.⟧ city in SE Ontario, Canada

☆**kitch·en·ette** or **kitch·en·et** (kich′ən et′) ***n.*** a small, compact kitchen, as in some apartments

kitchen garden a garden in which vegetables and, sometimes, fruit are grown, usually for home use

kitchen midden ⟦transl. of Dan *køkkenmødding:* see MIDDEN⟧ a mound of shells, animal bones, and other accumulated refuse discarded by a prehistoric settlement, esp. from the Mesolithic period

☆**kitchen police 1** soldiers detailed to assist the cooks in an army kitchen **2** this duty; KP

kitch·en-sink (kich′ən siŋk′) ***adj.*** **1** ⟦< common expression, *everything but the kitchen sink*, everything possible included without discrimination⟧ showing a lack of discriminating thought or careful planning; random; indiscriminate [a sitcom with a *kitchen-sink* series of subplots] **2** ⟦from use of the *kitchen sink* as a symbol of drab and unpleasant aspects of domesticity⟧ [Chiefly Brit.] portraying life, esp. domestic situations, with realism that emphasizes the negative or sordid aspects

kitch·en·ware (-wer′) ***n.*** utensils used in the kitchen; pots, pans, etc.

kite (kīt) ***n.*** ⟦ME < OE *cyta*, akin to MLowG *kuten*, to gossip < IE echoic base **gou-*, to scream > Gr *goan*, to moan⟧ **1** any of various accipitrine birds with long, pointed wings and, usually, a forked tail: they prey esp. on insects, reptiles, and small mammals **2** [Chiefly Brit.] a greedy, grasping person **3** a light frame, usually of wood, covered with paper, cloth, or plastic, to be flown in the wind at the end of a string **4** [*pl.*] the topmost sails of a ship, for use in a light breeze **5** a bad check or similar fictitious or worthless financial instrument used to raise money or maintain credit temporarily —***vi.*** **kit′ed, kit′ing 1** [Informal] *a)* to fly like a kite; soar *b)* to move lightly and rapidly **2** to get money or credit by using bad checks, etc. —***vt.*** to issue (a bad check, etc.) as a kite —☆**go fly a kite!** go away and stop being a bother!

kith (kith) ***n.*** ⟦ME < OE *cyth*, earlier *cyththu* < base of *cuth*, known: see UNCOUTH⟧ friends, acquaintances, or neighbors: now only in **kith and kin**, *a)* friends, acquaintances, and relatives *b)* relatives

kithe (kīth) ***vt., vi.*** **kithed, kith′ing** ⟦ME *kithen* < OE *cythan*, akin to *cunnan*, to know: see CAN[1]⟧ [Scot. or North Eng.] to make or become known

Ki·tik·me·ot (ki tik′mē ät′) region of Nunavut, Canada: formerly part of the Northwest Territories

kitsch (kich) ***n.*** ⟦Ger, gaudy trash < dial. *kitschen*, to smear⟧ art, writing, etc. of a shallow kind, calculated to have popular appeal —**kitsch′y** ***adj.*** —**kitsch′i·ness** ***n.***

kit·ten (kit′'n) ***n.*** ⟦ME *kitoun* < OFr *chitoun*, var. of *chaton*, dim. of *chat*, CAT[1]⟧ a young cat: occasionally applied to the young of some other small animals — ***vi., vt.*** to give birth to (kittens)

kit·ten·ish (-ish) ***adj.*** like a kitten; playful; frisky; often, playfully coy —**kit′ten·ish·ly** ***adv.*** —**kit′ten·ish·ness** ***n.***

kit·ti·wake (kit′i wāk′) ***n., pl.*** **-wakes′** or **-wake′** ⟦echoic of its cry⟧ any of a genus (*Rissa*) of small gulls of the northern oceans, that nest in cliffs and have a short or rudimentary hind toe

kit·tle (kit′'l) ***vt.*** **-tled, -tling** ⟦LME < *kytylle* < ON *kitla*, akin to Ger *kitzeln*, prob. echoic in orig.⟧ [Scot.] 1 to tickle 2 to puzzle —*adj.* [Scot.] hard to deal with; ticklish; skittish

kit·ty¹ (kit′ē) *n., pl.* **-ties** [Informal] a cat, esp. a kitten: orig. a child's term

kit·ty² (kit′ē) *n., pl.* **-ties** ⟦prob. < KIT¹⟧ 1 in poker, *a)* the stakes or pot *b)* a pool formed from part of the winnings, to pay for refreshments, etc. 2 money pooled for some particular purpose 3 WIDOW (*n.* 2)

Kit·ty (kit′ē) *n.* a feminine name: see CATHERINE¹, KATHERINE

kit·ty-cor·nered (kit′ē kôr′nərd) *adj., adv.* CATER-CORNERED: also **kit′ty-cor′ner**

Kitty Hawk ⟦< ? Algonquian language⟧ village on the Outer Banks of N.C., near where the first controlled & sustained airplane flight was made by Orville & Wilbur Wright in 1903

☆**kitty litter** ⟦< *Kitty Litter,* former trademark⟧ LITTER (*n.* 4)

☆**ki·va** (kē′və) *n.* ⟦Hopi⟧ in a Pueblo Indian dwelling, a large room used for religious and other purposes

Ki·vu (kē′vo͞o′), **Lake** lake in EC Africa, on the border of the Democratic Republic of the Congo & Rwanda: *c.* 1,100 sq mi (2,849 sq km)

☆**Ki·wa·nis** (ki wä′nis) *n.* ⟦< ? AmInd language⟧ an international service club of business and professional men and women —**Ki·wa′ni·an** (-nē ən) *adj., n.*

ki·wi (kē′wē) *n., pl.* **-wis** ⟦Maori: echoic of its cry⟧ 1 any of an order (Apterygiformes) of tailless New Zealand birds, with undeveloped wings, hairlike feathers, and a long, slender bill: it feeds chiefly on insects and worms 2 [*also* **K-**] the brown, hairy, egg-shaped fruit, with a sweet, edible, green pulp, of a vine (*Actinidia chinensis*) of a family (Actinidiaceae, order Theales) of dicotyledonous tropical trees, shrubs, and vines 3 [**K-**] [Informal] a New Zealander

Ki·zil (ki zil′) river in NC Turkey, flowing into the Black Sea: *c.* 700 mi (1,127 km): also **Kizil Ir·mak** (ir mäk′) or **Ki·zil′ir·mak′**

KJV *abbrev.* King James Version (of the Bible)

KKK *abbrev.* Ku Klux Klan

KKt *abbrev. Chess* king's knight

kl *abbrev.* kiloliter(s)

Klai·pe·da (klī′pi də) seaport in W Lithuania, on the Baltic

Kla·math¹ (klam′əth) *n.* ⟦< ?⟧ 1 *pl.* **-maths** or **-math** a member of a North American Indian people living in S Oregon 2 the language of this people: it is believed to be a member of the Penutian family

Kla·math² (klam′əth) ⟦< ?⟧ river flowing from S Oreg. southwest across NW Calif., into the Pacific: *c.* 250 mi (402 km)

☆**Klan** (klan) *n.* 1 *short for* KU KLUX KLAN 2 any chapter of the Ku Klux Klan —**Klans′man** *n., pl.* **-men**

klatch or **klatsch** (kläch, klach) *n.* ⟦Ger *klatsch,* gossip; of echoic orig.⟧ [Informal] an informal gathering, as for conversation

☆**klav·ern** (klav′ərn) *n.* ⟦blend of KLAN & CAVERN⟧ a local branch of the Ku Klux Klan

☆**klax·on** (klaks′ən) *n.* ⟦< *Klaxon,* former trademark, arbitrary coinage based on Gr *klaxein,* to shout, scream < IE base **kel-* > CLAMOR⟧ [*also* **K-**] a kind of electric horn with a loud, shrill sound

Klee (klā), **Paul** 1879-1940; Swiss abstract painter

☆**Klee·nex** (klē′neks′) ⟦arbitrary alteration < CLEAN + *-ex,* arbitrary suffix⟧ *trademark for* soft tissue paper used as a handkerchief, etc. —*n.* [*occas.* **k-**] a piece of such paper

☆**kleig light** (klēg) *alt. sp. of* KLIEG LIGHT

Klein (klīn), **Melanie** 1882-1960; Brit. psychoanalyst, born in Austria

Kleist (klīst), **(Bernd) Hein·rich Wil·helm von** (hīn′riH vil′helm′ fôn) 1777-1811; Ger. playwright

Klem·per·er (klem′pər ər), **Otto** 1885-1973; Ger. orchestra conductor

klepht (kleft) *n.* ⟦ModGr *klephtēs,* robber < Gr *kleptēs:* see KLEPTOMANIA⟧ 1 a member of the Greek patriot bands who held out after the Turkish conquest of Greece in the 15th cent. 2 a brigand

klep·toc·ra·cy (klep täk′rə sē) *n., pl.* **-cies** ⟦< *klept-* (see fol. + -O- + -CRACY⟧ a corrupt political regime characterized by widespread theft of its nation's wealth and resources —**klep′to·crat′** (-tə krat′) *n.* —**klep′to·crat′ic** *adj.*

klep·to·ma·ni·a (klep′tō mā′nē ə, -tə-) *n.* ⟦ModL < Gr *kleptēs,* thief (< IE base **klep-,* to hide, steal > L *clepere,* Goth *hlifan,* to steal) + -MANIA⟧ an abnormal, persistent impulse or tendency to steal, not prompted by need —**klep′to·ma′ni·ac′** *n., adj.*

klez·mer (klez′mər) *n., pl.* **-mers** or **klez·mo·rim** (klez môr′əm′, klez′mə rēm′) ⟦Yiddish < Heb *klezmer* < *kley zemer,* musical instruments⟧ 1 *a)* [Historical] an itinerant musician who performed at Jewish weddings and holiday celebrations in E Europe *b)* a musician who performs klezmer music 2 klezmer music —*adj.* designating or of a kind of E European Jewish folk music, typically performed by a small band consisting of a violin, clarinet, mandolin, accordion, etc. and accompanying Yiddish vocals

☆**klieg light** (klēg) ⟦after its inventors, Anton *Kliegl* (1872-1927) and his brother John (1869-1959), U.S. lighting engineers⟧ a very bright, hot arc light used to light film sets

Klimt (klimt), **Gus·tav** (goos′täf′) 1862-1918; Austrian painter

Kline (klīn), **Franz** 1910-62; U.S. painter

☆**Kline·fel·ter's syndrome** (klīn′fel′tərz) ⟦after H. *Klinefelter* (1912-90), U.S. physician⟧ a congenital disorder of males, caused by the presence of an extra X chromosome and characterized by small testicles and sterility

☆**Kline test** (klīn) ⟦after B. S. *Kline* (1886-1968), U.S. pathologist⟧ a modified form of the Kahn test for the diagnosis of syphilis

klip·spring·er (klip′spriŋ′ər) *n., pl.* **-ers** or **-er** ⟦Afrik < Du *klip,* a rock, cliff + *springer,* springer⟧ a small, agile mountain antelope (*Oreotragus oreotragus*) of S and E Africa

Klon·dike (klän′dīk′) ⟦Athabaskan < ?⟧ 1 river in W Yukon Territory, Canada, flowing west into the Yukon River: *c.* 100 mi (161 km) 2 gold-mining region surrounding this river: site of a gold rush (1897-98): usually used with *the*

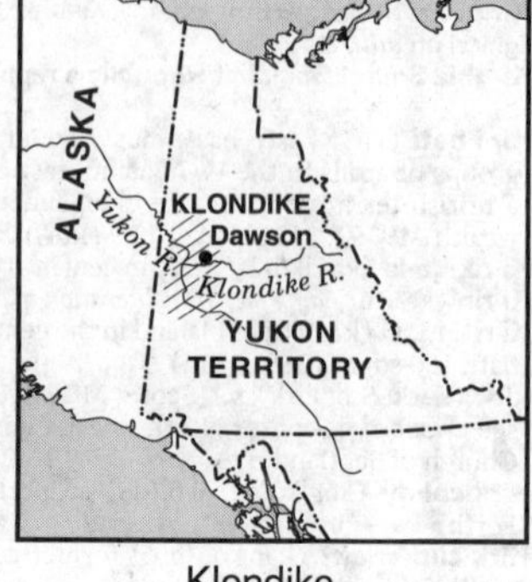

Klondike

kloof (klo͞of) *n.* ⟦Afrik < Du *klooven,* to cleave, akin to CLEAVE¹⟧ [South Afr.] a deep, narrow valley; gorge

kluge or **kludge** (klo͞oj, kluj) *n.* [Slang] 1 a piece of computer hardware or software, or a computer system, that is clumsily designed or improvised from mismatched parts 2 any poorly designed device or system

☆**klutz** (kluts) *n.* ⟦< Yiddish *klots,* lit., wooden block, beam < MHG; akin to CLEAT, CLOD⟧ [Informal] 1 a clumsy, awkward person 2 a stupid or dull person —**klutz′y** *adj.* **klutz′i·er, klutz′i·est** —**klutz′i·ness** *n.*

klys·tron (klīs′trən, klis′-; -trän′) *n.* ⟦< Gr *klys-* (see CLYSTER) + (ELEC)TRON⟧ an electron tube that uses electric fields and resonant cavities to bunch electrons from a uniform stream, used as an oscillator, amplifier, etc. in ultrahigh frequency circuits, and esp. as a generator and amplifier of microwaves

km *abbrev.* kilometer(s)

K meson *Particle Physics* KAON: also written **K′-mes′on** *n.*

kn *abbrev. Naut.* knot(s)

knack (nak) *n.* ⟦ME *knak,* sharp blow: see KNOCK⟧ 1 *a)* a trick; device *b)* a clever expedient or way of doing something 2 ability to do something easily; particular skill 3 [Archaic] a knickknack; trinket; trifle —*SYN.* TALENT

knack·er (nak′ər) *n.* ⟦Early ModE, harness maker < ON *hnakker,* saddle, neck, akin to OE *hnecca,* NECK⟧ [Brit.] 1 a person who buys and slaughters worn-out horses and sells their flesh as dog's meat, etc. 2 a person who buys and wrecks old houses, etc. and sells their materials

knack·ered (nak′ərd) *adj.* ⟦< pp. of slang *knacker,* to kill, castrate, wear out, prob. < prec.⟧ [Brit. Slang] very tired; exhausted

knack·wurst (näk′wurst′, -woorst′) *n.* ⟦Ger < *knacken,* to crack, burst (prob. ult. akin to IE base **gneuĝ-,* > KNOCK) + *wurst,* sausage⟧ a thick, highly seasoned sausage

knap¹ (nap) [Brit. Dial.] *vt., vi.* **knapped, knap′ping** ⟦LME *knappen,* akin to Du, to snap, eat < IE **gnebh-:* for base see KNEAD⟧ 1 to knock, rap, or snap 2 to break or shape (stones or flints) by a quick, hard blow 3 to bite sharply; snap —*n.* a knock; rap

knap² (nap) *n.* ⟦ME < OE *cnæp,* top, knob, button, akin to ON *knappr* < IE **gnebh-:* see prec.⟧ [Chiefly Dial.] 1 the top of a hill; summit 2 a hillock

knap·sack (nap′sak′) *n.* ⟦Du *knapzak* < *knappen* (see KNAP¹) + *zak,* a SACK¹⟧ a bag or case of leather, canvas, nylon, etc. worn on the back, as by soldiers or hikers, for carrying equipment or supplies

knap·weed (nap′wēd′) *n.* ⟦earlier *knopweed:* see KNOP & WEED¹⟧ any of several weedy plants (genus *Centaurea*) of the composite family; esp., a hardy perennial (*C. nigra*) with heads of rose-purple flowers

knar (när) *n.* ⟦ME *knarre* < or akin to LowG *knarre,* Du *knar,* a stump, knob, knot < IE **gner-:* for base see KNEAD⟧ a knot in wood; esp., a bark-covered bulge on a tree trunk or root —**knarred** *adj.*

knave (nāv) *n.* ⟦ME *knaue* < OE *cnafa,* boy, male child, akin to Ger *knabe*⟧ 1 [Archaic] *a)* a serving boy or male servant *b)* a man of humble birth or status 2 a dishonest, deceitful person; tricky rascal; rogue 3 JACK (*n.* 13*a*)

knav·er·y (nāv′ər ē) *n., pl.* **-er·ies** 1 behavior or an act characteristic of a knave; rascality; dishonesty 2 [Obs.] roguishness; mischievous quality

knav·ish (-ish) *adj.* like or characteristic of a knave; esp., dishonest; tricky —**knav′ish·ly** *adv.* —**knav′ish·ness** *n.*

knead (nēd) *vt.* ⟦ME *kneden* < OE *cnedan,* akin to Ger *kneten* < IE **gnet-,* to press together < base **gen-,* to form into a ball, pinch, compress > KNOT¹, KNOB⟧ 1 to mix and work (dough, clay, etc.) into a pliable mass by folding over, pressing, and squeezing, usually with the hands 2 to press, rub, or squeeze with the hands; massage 3 to make or form by or as if by kneading —**knead′er** *n.*

knee (nē) *n.* ⟦ME *kne* < OE *cneow,* akin to Ger *knie* < IE base **ĝeneu-* > Sans *jā́nu,* Gr *gony, gonia,* L *genu,* a knee⟧ 1 *a)* the joint between the thigh and the lower part of the human leg *b)* the front part of the leg at this joint 2 a joint regarded as corresponding or similar to the human knee, as a joint in the leg of a quadruped or bird 3 anything resembling or suggesting a knee, esp. a bent knee; specif., *a)* a bent piece of wood used as a brace *b)* a protuberant, woody growth on certain trees 4 the part of a stocking, trouser leg, etc. that covers the knee —*vt.* **kneed, knee′ing** 1 to hit or touch with the knee 2 *Carpentry* to fasten with a KNEE (sense 3*a*) or knees —**bring someone to his (or her) knees** to force someone to submit or give in —☆**take a knee** [Informal] to kneel on one knee, as to rest or pray [players *took a knee* for a pre-game prayer]

knee breeches BREECHES (sense 1)

knee·cap (-kap′) *n.* PATELLA —*vt.* **-capped′**, **-cap′ping** to maim by shooting or drilling the kneecap, often as an act of terrorism

knee-deep (-dēp′) *adj.* **1** sunk to the knees [standing *knee-deep* in water] **2** so deep as to reach to the knees [*knee-deep* mud] **3** very much involved or concerned

knee-high (-hī′) *adj.* so high, long, or tall as to reach to the knees

knee·hole (-hōl′) *n.* a space for the knees, as below a desk

knee jerk PATELLAR REFLEX

☆**knee-jerk** (-jurk′) *adj.* ⟦< prec.⟧ [Informal] designating, characterized by, or reacting with a response regarded as automatic and predictable

kneel (nēl) *vi.* **knelt** or **kneeled**, **kneel′ing** ⟦ME *knelen* < OE *cneowlian* < *cneow*, KNEE⟧ to rest on a knee or the knees

kneel·er (nēl′ər) *n.* **1** a person who kneels **2** *a)* a cushion or stool for kneeling upon *b)* a low, often cushioned, support that worshipers in a church, chapel, etc. can fold down and kneel upon

knee·pad (nē′pad′) *n.* a pad worn to protect the knee, as by a hockey player

knee·piece (-pēs′) *n.* a piece of armor to protect the knee

☆**knee·sies** (nē′zēz′) *n.* [Informal] the act of pressing one's knees against another person's in an amorous way, as under a dining table: usually in the phrase **play kneesies (with)**, to engage in this act (with)

☆**knee-slap·per** (nē′slap′ər) *n.* ⟦from the common gesture accompanying laughter⟧ [Informal] a very funny joke, anecdote, etc.: also written **knee slapper**

knee sock a sock that covers at least part of the calf or extends to just below the knee: also written **knee′sock′** *n.*

knell (nel) *vi.* ⟦ME *knyllen* & (with echoic vowel change) *knellen* < OE *cnyllan*, akin to MHG *(er)knellen*: prob. echoic⟧ **1** to ring in a slow, solemn way; toll **2** to sound ominously or mournfully —*vt.* to call or announce by or as by a knell —*n.* **1** the sound of a bell, esp. of a bell rung slowly, as at a funeral **2** an omen of death, failure, etc.

knelt (nelt) *vi. alt. pt. and pp. of* KNEEL

Knes·set (k′nes′et) *n.* ⟦ModHeb *keneset*, lit., assembly, gathering < *kanas*, to assemble⟧ the unicameral legislature of Israel

knew (no͞o, nyo͞o) *vt., vi. pt. of* KNOW

☆**Knick·er·bock·er** (nik′ər bäk′ər) *n.* ⟦after Diedrich *Knickerbocker*, fictitious Du author of Washington Irving's *History of New York* (1809)⟧ **1** a descendant of the early Dutch settlers of New York **2** any New Yorker **3** [**k-**] [*pl.*] KNICKERS (sense 1), as those worn by Dutch settlers of New York

knick·ers (nik′ərz) *pl.n.* ⟦contr. < prec.⟧ **1** short, loose trousers gathered at, or just below, the knees **2** *a)* [Chiefly Brit.] a bloomerlike undergarment worn by women or girls *b)* [Brit.] panties

knick·knack (nik′nak′) *n.* ⟦redupl. of KNACK⟧ a small ornamental article or contrivance; trinket

knife (nīf) *n., pl.* **knives** ⟦ME *knif* < OE *cnif*, akin to Ger *kneif*, ON *knīfr* < IE **gneibh-* (> Lith *gnaibis*, a pinching): for base see KNEAD⟧ **1** a cutting or stabbing instrument with a sharp blade, single-edged or double-edged, set in a handle **2** a cutting blade, as in a machine —*vt.* **knifed**, **knif′ing** **1** to cut or stab with a knife ☆**2** [Informal] to use underhanded methods in order to hurt, defeat, or betray —☆*vi.* to pass into or through something quickly, like a sharp knife —☆**under the knife** [Informal] undergoing surgery —**knife′like′** *adj.*

knife-edge (nīf′ej′) *n.* **1** the edge of a knife **2** any very sharp edge **3** a metal wedge whose fine edge serves as the fulcrum for a scale beam, pendulum, etc.

knife pleat one of a series of pleats that are sharply folded —**knife′-pleat′ed** *adj.*

knife switch an electrical switch in which the hinged contact blade is pressed down between the contact clips

knight (nīt) *n.* ⟦ME *kniht* < OE *cniht*, boy, retainer, akin to Ger *knecht*, lad, servant < IE **gnegh-*: for base see KNEAD⟧ **1** in the Middle Ages, *a)* a military servant of a king or other feudal superior; tenant holding land on condition that he serve his superior as a mounted man-at-arms *b)* later, a man, usually one of high birth, who after serving as page and squire was formally raised to special military rank and pledged to chivalrous conduct **2** in Great Britain, a man who for some achievement is given honorary nonhereditary rank next below a baronet, entitling him to use *Sir* before his given name **3** an ancient Roman, Athenian, etc. whose status is regarded as equivalent to that of a knight **4** [*usually* **K-**] a member of any order or society that officially calls its members *knights* **5** [Old Poet.] *a)* a lady's devoted champion or attendant *b)* a devoted follower of some cause, person, etc. **6** *Chess* a piece usually shaped like a horse's head: it is moved two squares, whether occupied or unoccupied, in any vertical or horizontal direction, and then one square to the side —*vt.* to make (a man) a knight

knight bachelor *pl.* **knights bachelors** or **knights bachelor** a member of the oldest and lowest rank of British knights

knight-er·rant (nīt′er′ənt) *n., pl.* **knights′-er′rant** **1** a medieval knight wandering in search of adventures, esp. ones allowing him to redress wrongs or show his prowess **2** a chivalrous or quixotic person

knight-er·rant·ry (-er′ən trē) *n., pl.* **-ries** **1** the behavior or action of a knight-errant **2** quixotic behavior

knight·hood (-hood′) *n.* **1** the rank or status of a knight: see also DAME (sense 3*b*) **2** the profession or vocation of a knight **3** knightly conduct **4** knights collectively

knight·ly (-lē) *adj.* **1** of, characteristic of, like, or befitting a knight; chivalrous, brave, etc. **2** consisting of knights —*adv.* [Archaic] in a knightly manner —**knight′li·ness** *n.*

☆**Knights of Columbus** a fraternal and benevolent society of Roman Catholic men, founded in 1882

Knights of Malta *see* HOSPITALER

☆**Knights of Pythias** a fraternal and benevolent society founded in 1864

Knight Templar **1** *pl.* **Knights Templars** a member of a military and religious order established among the Crusaders about 1118 **2** *pl.* **Knights Templar** a member of a certain order of Masons

K-9 or **K9** (kā′nīn′) *abbrev.* ⟦phonetic pun on *canine*⟧ canine: informal except in law-enforcement or military use [a police *K-9* unit]

knish (k′nish) *n.* ⟦Yiddish, variously < Pol *knysz* & Ukrainian *knyš*, etc.⟧ a piece of thin rolled dough folded over a filling, as of mashed potatoes or chopped meat, and baked or fried

knit (nit) *vt.* **knit′ted** or **knit**, **knit′ting** ⟦ME *knitten* < OE *cnyttan* (akin to Ger *knütten*, to tie (fishing) nets) < base of *cnotta*, KNOT[1]⟧ **1** to make (cloth or a garment) by interconnecting loops of yarn or thread in rows of stitches by means of a pair of special needles or a machine **2** *a)* to form into cloth in this way rather than by weaving *b)* to form (one or more stitches of the basic type) ["K2, P2" means "*knit* two stitches, purl 2 stitches"] **3** to join together closely and firmly; unite **4** to draw (the brows) together; contract in wrinkles **5** [Now Chiefly Dial.] to tie or fasten in or with a knot —*vi.* **1** *a)* to make cloth or a garment by knitting yarn or thread *b)* to produce a basic stitch or stitches **2** *a)* to become joined together closely and firmly *b)* to become whole or intact, as a broken bone **3** to become contracted into a frown: said of the eyebrows —*n.* cloth or a garment made by knitting —**knit′ter** *n.*

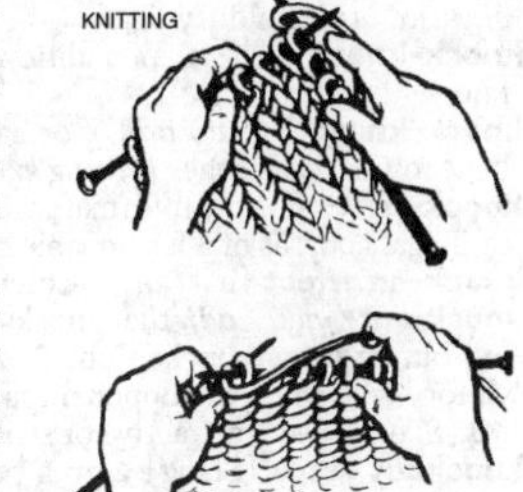

knit·ting (nit′iŋ) *n.* **1** the action of a person or thing that knits **2** knitted work

knitting needle an eyeless, usually long, needle of metal, bone, plastic, etc., with a blunt point at one or both ends, used in pairs in knitting by hand

knit·wear (-wer′) *n.* clothing made by knitting

knives (nīvz) *n. pl. of* KNIFE

knob (näb) *n.* ⟦ME *knobbe* < or akin to Du, a knot, knob, bud < IE **gn-eu-bh* < base **gen-*: see KNEAD⟧ **1** a rounded lump or protuberance **2** *a)* a handle, usually round, of a door, drawer, etc. *b)* a similar device which is turned to control operations of electronic or electrical equipment, as a radio or TV receiver **3** a rounded hill or mountain; knoll —**with knobs on** [Slang, Chiefly Brit.] in an extreme or more emphatic way —**knobbed** *adj.*

knob·bly (näb′lē) *adj.* **-bli·er**, **-bli·est** ⟦< archaic *knobble*, dim. of prec. + -Y[2]⟧ having or covered with lumps or knobs; knotty

knob·by (näb′ē) *adj.* **-bi·er**, **-bi·est** **1** covered with knobs **2** like a knob —**knob′bi·ness** *n.*

knob·ker·rie (-ker′ē) *n.* ⟦Afrik *knopkirie* < Du *knobbe*, KNOB + Hottentot *kirri*, a club⟧ a short club with a knobbed end, used by some South African tribes as a weapon

knock (näk) *vi.* ⟦ME *knokken* < OE *cnocian*, akin to ON *knoka*, MHG *knochen*, to press < echoic base > KNACK⟧ **1** to strike a blow or blows with the fist or some hard object; esp., to rap on a door **2** to bump; collide; clash **3** to make a thumping, pounding, or rattling noise: said of an engine, etc. ☆**4** [Informal] to find fault; criticize adversely ☆**5** in gin rummy, to end a deal by exposing one's hand and showing a surplus of not more than ten points in unmatched cards —*vt.* **1** to hit; strike **2** to make by hitting or striking [to *knock* a hole in a wall] ☆**3** [Informal] to find fault with; criticize adversely —*n.* **1** the act of knocking **2** a hit; sharp or resounding blow; rap, as on a door **3** a thumping or rattling noise in an engine, etc., as because of faulty combustion ☆**4** [Informal] an adverse criticism **5** [Informal] a misfortune or trouble [the school of hard *knocks*] —**knock about** (or **around**) [Informal] **1** to wander about; roam **2** to treat roughly —**knock back** [Informal] to gulp down (an alcoholic drink) —**knock down** **1** to hit so as to cause to fall ☆**2** to take apart for convenience in shipping **3** *a)* to sell at auction *b)* to indicate the sale of (an article) at an auction, as by a blow of the auctioneer's hammer **4** [Slang] to earn as pay —☆**knock it off!** [Slang] stop doing that! —**knock off** **1** [Informal] *a)* to stop working *b)* to leave off (work) **2** [Informal] to deduct **3** [Informal] to do; accomplish ☆**4** [Slang] to kill, overcome, etc. ☆**5** [Slang] to make a knockoff of —☆**knock oneself out** [Informal] to make great efforts; exhaust oneself —**knock out** **1** *Boxing* to defeat (an opponent) by knocking to the ground so that it is not possible to rise before an official count of ten **2** *a)* to make unconscious *b)* to make exhausted; tire out **3** to defeat, destroy, etc. **4** [Informal] to do; make; specif., to compose or write casually or with careless haste **5** [Slang] to overwhelm with excited delight; thrill —☆**knock out of the box** ⟦in allusion to the pitcher's *box*, the area formerly marked around the pitching rubber⟧ [Slang] *Baseball* to make so many hits against (an opposing pitcher) as to cause the pitcher's removal —**knock over** ☆[Slang] to burglarize or rob —**knock together** **1** to cause to collide **2** to make or compose hastily or crudely —**knock up 1** [Brit. Informal] *a)* to tire out; exhaust *b)* to wake (someone), as by knocking at the door ☆**2** [Slang] to make pregnant

knock·a·bout (-ə bout′) ***n.*** ☆**1** a small, single-masted sailing vessel with a mainsail and jib, but no bowsprit **2** something suitable for knockabout use —***adj.*** **1** rough; noisy; boisterous **2** made or suitable for knocking about or rough use

knock·down (-doun′) ***adj.*** **1** so severe as to knock down; overwhelming ☆**2** made so as to be easily taken apart [a *knockdown* table] —***n.*** **1** a knocking down; felling **2** a blow, stroke, etc. that knocks one down

☆**knock-down-, drag-out** (näk′doun′ drag′out′) [Informal] **1** characterized by great violence, harshness, animosity, etc. [a *knock-down, drag-out* argument] **2** an extremely harsh or violent fight, argument, etc.

knocked down ☆not assembled: said of furniture, etc.

knock·er (-ər) ***n.*** **1** a person or thing that knocks; specif., *a)* a small metal ring, hammer, etc. attached by a hinge to a door, for use in knocking for admittance ☆*b)* [Informal] a faultfinder **2** [Slang] a woman's breast: *usually used in pl.*: mildly vulgar

knock-knee (-nē′) ***n.*** a condition in which the legs bend inward at the knees

knock-kneed (-nēd′) ***adj.*** of or having knock-knee —***adv.*** with the knees bent toward each other [sitting *knock-kneed* on a stool]

☆**knock·off** (-ôf′) ***n.*** [Informal] a copy or imitation; esp., an inexpensive or illegal copy, as of a fashionable clothing design: also written **knock-off**

knock-on effect (näk′än′) [Chiefly Brit.] a subsidiary or indirect effect

knock·out (-out′) ***adj.*** that knocks out: said of a blow, etc. —***n.*** **1** a knocking out or being knocked out **2** *a)* a blow that knocks out *b) Boxing* a victory won when the opponent is knocked out (cf. TECHNICAL KNOCKOUT) ☆**3** [Slang] a very attractive or striking person or thing

☆**knockout drops** [Slang] a drug put into a drink to cause the drinker to become stupefied or unconscious

knock·wurst (näk′wurst′, -woorst′) ***n.*** *alt. sp. of* KNACKWURST

knoll[1] (nōl) ***n.*** ⟦ME < OE *cnoll,* akin to Ger *knollen,* lump, clod: for IE base see KNOT[1]⟧ a hillock; mound

knoll[2] (nōl) ***vi., vt., n.*** *archaic or dial. var. of* KNELL

knop (näp) ***n.*** ⟦ME *knoppe;* prob. < ON *knappr* or MDu *cnoppe;* akin to KNOB⟧ a knob; esp., a knoblike ornament

Knos·sos (näs′əs) ancient city in N Crete, near modern Iraklion: center of ancient Minoan civilization

knot[1] (nät) ***n.*** ⟦ME *knotte* < OE *cnotta,* akin to Du *knot,* Swed *knut,* Ger *knoten* < IE **gn-eu-t* < base **gen-,* to press together > KNOB, KNEAD⟧ **1** a lump or knob in a thread, cord, etc., formed by passing one free end through a loop and drawing it tight, or by a tangle drawn tight **2** a fastening made by intertwining or tying together pieces of string, cord, rope, etc. **3** an ornamental bow of ribbon or twist of braid; cockade; epaulet **4** a small group or cluster **5** something that ties or fastens closely or intricately; bond of union; esp., the bond of marriage **6** a problem; difficulty; entanglement **7** a knotlike part; node or lump [a *knot* in a tense muscle]; specif., *a)* a hard lump on a tree where a branch grows out *b)* a cross section of such a lump, appearing as cross-grained in a board or log *c)* a joint on a plant stem where two leaves grow out *d)* any of several fungal diseases of trees, in which abnormal protuberances appear **8** *Naut. a)* [Historical] any of the knots tied at regular intervals in a line used in measuring a ship's speed *b)* a unit of speed of one nautical mile (6,076.12 feet or 1,852 meters) an hour (abbrev. *kn* or *kt*) [to average a speed of 10 *knots*] *c)* loosely, NAUTICAL MILE —***vt.*** **knot′ted, knot′ting 1** to tie, fasten, or intertwine in or with a knot or knots; make a knot or knots in **2** to tie or unite closely or intricately; entangle **3** to make (fringe) by tying knots —***vi.*** **1** to form a knot or knots; become entangled **2** to make knots for fringe —**tie the knot** [Informal] to get married

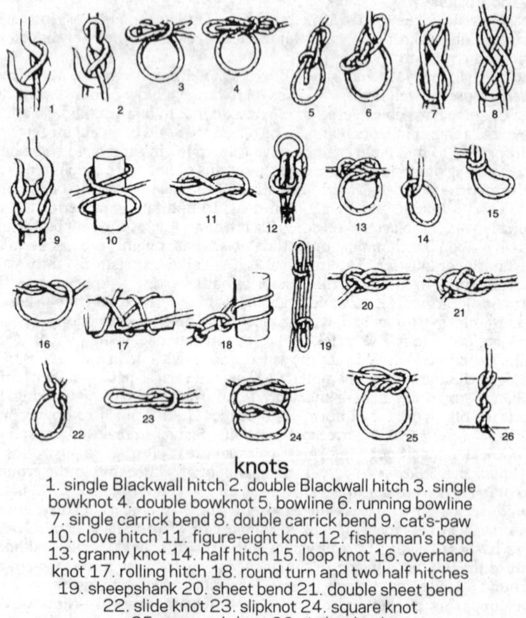

knots

1. single Blackwall hitch 2. double Blackwall hitch 3. single bowknot 4. double bowknot 5. bowline 6. running bowline 7. single carrick bend 8. double carrick bend 9. cat's-paw 10. clove hitch 11. figure-eight knot 12. fisherman's bend 13. granny knot 14. half hitch 15. loop knot 16. overhand knot 17. rolling hitch 18. round turn and two half hitches 19. sheepshank 20. sheet bend 21. double sheet bend 22. slide knot 23. slipknot 24. square knot 25. surgeon's knot 26. timber hitch

knot[2] (nät) ***n.*** ⟦rare ME *knotte* < ?⟧ any of various sandpipers (genus *Calidris*); esp., a large, migratory species (*C. canutus*) that breeds in arctic regions

knot·grass (nät′gras′) ***n.*** **1** any of several weedy plants (genus *Polygonum*) of the buckwheat family; esp., a common weed (*P. aviculare*) with slender stems, narrow leaves, and small axillary flowers: often called **knot′weed′** (-wēd′) ☆**2** a creeping grass (*Paspalum distichum*) growing in wet places in the S U.S.

knot·hole (-hōl′) ***n.*** a hole in a board, etc. where a knot has fallen out

knot·ted (-id) ***adj.*** **1** tied or fastened in or with a knot or knots **2** having or full of knots **3** tangled; intricate **4** puzzling; knotty

knot·ter (-ər) ***n.*** **1** a person or thing that ties knots **2** a remover of knots

knot·ting (-iŋ) ***n.*** fringe made of knotted threads

knot·ty (-ē) ***adj.*** **-ti·er, -ti·est** ⟦ME⟧ **1** having or full of knots [a *knotty* board] **2** hard to solve or explain; puzzling [a *knotty* problem] —**knot′ti·ness** ***n.***

☆**knotty pine** pine wood cut and finished to emphasize the decorative quality of the knots, used for some interior finishing and furniture

knout (nout) ***n.*** ⟦Russ *knut* < Swed, a KNOT[1]⟧ a leather whip formerly used in Russia to flog criminals —***vt.*** to flog with a knout

know (nō) ***vt.*** **knew, known, know′ing** ⟦ME *knowen* < OE *cnawan,* akin to OHG *-cnāhan* < IE base **ĝen-, *ĝnō-,* to know, apprehend > CAN[1], KEN, L *gnoscere,* to know, Gr *gignōskein*⟧ **1** to have a clear perception or understanding of; be sure of or well informed about [to *know* the facts] **2** to be aware or cognizant of; have perceived or learned [to *know* that one is loved] **3** to have a firm mental grasp of; have securely in the memory [to *know* the multiplication tables] **4** *a)* to be acquainted or familiar with [I *knew* him well] *b)* to experience [she has *known* both pleasure and pain] **5** to have understanding of or skill in as a result of study or experience [to *know* music] **6** to recognize [I'd *know* that face anywhere] **7** to recognize as distinct; distinguish [to *know* right from wrong] **8** [Archaic] to have sexual intercourse with —***vi.*** **1** to have knowledge **2** to be sure, informed, or aware —**in the know** [Informal] having confidential information —**know better** to be aware that one could or should act better or think more correctly —**know best** to be the best guide, authority, etc. —☆**know from** *see* FROM (sense 11) —☆**you know** [Informal] you understand: a phrase used in conversational pauses —☆**what do you know!** [Informal] an exclamation of surprise —**know′a·ble** ***adj.*** —**know′er** ***n.***

☆**know-how** (nō′hou′) ***n.*** [Informal] knowledge of how to do something well; technical skill

know·ing (-iŋ) ***adj.*** **1** having knowledge or information **2** shrewd; clever **3** implying shrewd understanding or possession of secret or inside information [a *knowing* look] **4** deliberate; intentional —***n.*** awareness or familiarity —**know′ing·ly** ***adv.*** —**know′ing·ness** ***n.***

know-it-all (-it ôl′) [Informal] ***adj.*** pretending or claiming to know much about almost everything —***n.*** a know-it-all person

knowl·edge (näl′ij) ***n.*** ⟦ME *knoweleche,* acknowledgment, confession < Late OE *cnawlæc* < *cnawan* (see KNOW) + *-læc* < *lācan,* to play, give, move about⟧ **1** the act, fact, or state of knowing; specif., *a)* acquaintance or familiarity (with a fact, place, etc.) *b)* awareness *c)* understanding **2** acquaintance with facts; range of information, awareness, or understanding **3** all that has been perceived or grasped by the mind; learning; enlightenment **4** the body of facts, principles, etc. acquired through human experience and thought **5** [Archaic] carnal knowledge: see CARNAL —***SYN.*** INFORMATION —**to (the best of) one's knowledge** as far as one knows; within the range of one's information

knowl·edge·a·ble (-ə bəl) ***adj.*** having or showing knowledge or intelligence —**knowl′edge·a·bil′i·ty** ***n.,*** **knowl′edge·a·ble·ness** —**knowl′edge·a·bly** ***adv.***

known (nōn) ***vt., vi.*** *pp. of* KNOW —***adj.*** **1** within one's knowledge, understanding, etc.; familiar **2** recognized, proven, etc. [a *known* expert, a *known* theory] —***n.*** a known person or thing

know-noth·ing (nō′nuth′iŋ) ***n.*** **1** an ignorant person; ignoramus **2** [Rare] an agnostic **3** [**Know-Nothing**] a member of a secret political party in the U.S. in the 1850s with a program of keeping out of public office anyone not a native-born American: so called because members professed ignorance of the party's activities

known quantity an algebraic quantity whose value is given: usually represented by an early letter of the alphabet, as *a, b,* or *c*

Knox (näks), **John** 1514?-72; Scot. Protestant clergyman & religious reformer

Knox·ville (näks′vil′) ⟦after Gen. Henry *Knox* (1750-1806), 1st secretary of war⟧ city in E Tenn., on the Tennessee River

Knt *abbrev.* Knight

knuck·le (nuk′əl) ***n.*** ⟦ME *knokyl* < or akin to MDu & MLowG *knokel,* dim. of *knoke,* bone < IE **gneuĝ-*: for IE base see KNOT[1]⟧ **1** *a)* a joint of the finger;

esp., the joint connecting a finger to the rest of the hand *b)* the rounded knob formed by the bones at such a joint **2** the knee or hock joint and nearby parts of a pig or other animal, used as food **3** something resembling a knuckle, as any of the projecting, cylindrical parts through which a pin is passed to form a hinge ☆**4** [*pl.*] BRASS KNUCKLES **5** *Archit.* the central joint in a gambrel or curb roof —***vt.* -led, -ling** to strike, press, or touch with the knuckles —☆**knuckle down 1** to rest the knuckles on the ground in shooting a marble **2** [Informal] to work energetically or seriously —**knuckle under** [Informal] to yield; give in

☆**knuckle ball** *Baseball* a slow pitch without spin thrown with the first knuckles, or the nails, of the middle two or three fingers pressed against the ball: also called **knuck′ler** (-lər) ***n.***

knuck·le·bone (-bōn′) ***n.*** **1** any bone of a human knuckle **2** *a)* an animal's limb bone with a rounded knob at the joint end *b)* the knob

☆**knuck·le-dust·er** (-dus′tər) ***n.*** BRASS KNUCKLES

☆**knuck·le·head** (-hed′) ***n.*** [Informal] a stupid person; fool

knuckle joint 1 any articulation, or point of movement, between two bones forming a knuckle **2** a hinged joint formed by a knuckle on one part that fits between two knuckles on another part

knur (nur) ***n.*** ⟦ME *knorre* < or akin to MDu & MLowG < IE *gner- < base *gen- > KNOT[1]⟧ a knot, as on the trunk or branch of a tree

knurl (nurl) ***n.*** ⟦prob. blend of prec. + GNARL[1]⟧ **1** a knot, knob, nodule, etc. **2** any of a series of small beads or ridges, as along the edge of a coin or on a dial **3** [Scot.] a short, thickset person —***vt.*** to make knurls on; mill —**knurled** ***adj.***

knurl·y (-ē) ***adj.* knurl′i·er, knurl′i·est** full of knurls, as wood; gnarled

Knut (k′no͞ot) *see* CANUTE

☆**KO** (kā′ō′) [Slang] ***vt.* KO'd, KO'ing** ⟦*k(nock) o(ut)*⟧ *Boxing* to knock out —***n.*, *pl.* KO's** *Boxing* a knockout Also written **K.O.** or **k.o.**

ko·a (kō′ə) ***n.*** ⟦Haw < Proto-Polynesian **toa*, tree⟧ a Hawaiian acacia tree (*Acacia koa*) valued for its wood, used in building and cabinetmaking, and its bark, used in tanning

ko·a·la (kō ä′lə) ***n.*** ⟦< *külla*, native name in Australia⟧ an Australian, tailless, tree-dwelling animal that is the only species (*Phascolarctos cinereus*) of a family (Phascolarctidae) of marsupials with thick, gray fur, sharp claws, and large, tufted ears: it resembles a small bear and feeds exclusively on eucalyptus leaves and buds: popularly called **koala bear**

ko·an (kō′än′) ***n.*, *pl.* ko′ans′, ko′an′** ⟦Jpn < *kō*, public + *an*, (a matter for) investigation, consideration⟧ in Zen Buddhism, a verbal puzzle put to a student as a means to enlightenment

kob (käb) ***n.*** ⟦< name in a Niger-Congo language, as in Wolof *koba*⟧ an orange-red antelope (*Kobus kob*) of SE Africa

Ko·ba·rid (kō′bä rēd′) *Slovenian name for* CAPORETTO

Ko·be (kō′bā′; *E* kō′bē) seaport on the S coast of Honshu, Japan, on the Inland Sea

Kø·ben·havn (kö′bən houn′) *Dan. name for* COPENHAGEN

Ko·blenz (kō′blents′) city in W Germany, on the Rhine, in the state of Rhineland-Palatinate

kob·o (käb′ō) ***n.*, *pl.* kob′o** ⟦altered < COPPER[1], referring to a penny⟧ a monetary unit of Nigeria, equal to 1/100 of a naira

ko·bold (kō′bôld′, -bäld′) ***n.*** ⟦Ger < MHG *kobolt*, a household spirit < *kobe*, a hut (akin to COVE[1]) + *-olt* < ? *walten*, to rule (see WIELD) or *holde*, spirit⟧ *Gmc. Folklore* **1** a helpful or mischievous sprite in households **2** a gnome in mines and other underground places

Koch (kōk; *Ger* kôkh), **Robert** 1843-1910; Ger. bacteriologist & physician

Ko·chi (kō′chē) seaport in S Shikoku, Japan

Ko·dály (kō dī′), **Zol·tán** (zôl′tän′) 1882-1967; Hung. composer

Ko·di·ak (kō′dē ak′) ⟦< Russ < ? native name meaning "island"⟧ island off the SW coast of Alas., in the Gulf of Alaska: 5,363 sq mi (13,890 sq km)

Kodiak bear [*sometimes* **k- b-**] the largest brown bear (*Ursus arctos middendorffi*), found on Kodiak Island and in adjacent areas: it can attain a weight of 780 kg (*c.* 1,700 lb)

ko·el (kō′əl) ***n.*** ⟦Hindi < Sans *kokila:* orig. echoic⟧ any of various large cuckoos (genus *Eudynamys*) of India, the East Indies, and Australia

Koest·ler (kest′lər), **Arthur** 1905-83; Brit. writer & philosopher, born in Hungary

K of C *abbrev.* Knight (or Knights) of Columbus

K of P *abbrev.* Knight (or Knights) of Pythias

Ko·hel·eth (kō hel′eth) ***n.*** ⟦Heb *qōheleth:* see ECCLESIASTES⟧ ECCLESIASTES; also, its author, traditionally identified with Solomon

Koh·i·noor or **Koh-i-noor** (kō′i noor′) ***n.*** ⟦Pers *kōh-i-nūr*, lit., mountain of light⟧ a famous large Indian diamond, now one of the British crown jewels

kohl (kōl) ***n.*** ⟦Ar *kuḥl*, antimony > ALCOHOL⟧ a cosmetic preparation, as powdered antimony sulfide, used, esp. in certain Eastern countries, for eye makeup

kohlrabi

kohl·ra·bi (kōl rä′bē) ***n.*, *pl.* -bies** ⟦Ger, altered (infl. by *kohl*, cabbage) < It *cavoli rape*, pl. of *cavolo rapa*, cole rape < L *caulis* (> COLE) + *rapa*, turnip⟧ a garden vegetable (*Brassica oleracea* var. *gongylodes*) of the crucifer family, similar to cabbage: the edible part is a bulbous portion of the stem just above the ground

koi (koi) ***n.*, *pl.* koi, kois** ⟦Jpn⟧ a large, colorful variety of carp (*Cyprinus carpio*) bred mostly in Japan for display in ornamental ponds

koi·ne (koi nā′; koi′nā′, -nē′) ***n.*** ⟦Gr (*hē*) *koinē* (*dialektos*), (the) common (dialect) < *koinos:* see COENO-⟧ **1** [*also* **K-**] the language used throughout the Greek world, from Syria to Gaul, during the Hellenistic and Roman periods: its spoken form consisted of colloquial Attic, supplemented by borrowings from other dialects: the New Testament is written in koine **2** any regional dialect or language that has become the common language of a larger area

ko·kan·ee (kō kan′ē) ***n.*, *pl.* -ees** or **-ee** ⟦prob. after *Kokanee* Creek, stream in British Columbia⟧ any landlocked population of the sockeye salmon of W North America

Ko·ko Nor (kō′kō nôr′) *another name for* QINGHAI (the lake)

Ko·kosch·ka (kō kôsh′kə), **Os·kar** (äs′kər) 1886-1980; Brit. painter, born in Austria

kok-sa·ghyz or **kok-sa·gyz** (kōk′sa gēz′) ***n.*** ⟦Russ *kok-sagyz* < Turkic, lit., gum (or tar or rubber) root⟧ a dandelion (*Taraxacum kok-saghyz*) grown in Russia, Turkmenistan, etc. for the rubber obtained from its roots

ko·la (kō′lə) ***n.*** COLA[1] (sense 1)

kola nut the seed of the cola

Ko·la Peninsula (kō′lə) peninsula in NW Russia, between the White & Barents seas: *c.* 40,000 sq mi (103,600 sq km)

kol·bas·i or **kol·bas·si** (kōl bä′sē) ***n.*** *var. of* KIELBASA

Kol·ha·pur (kōl′hä po͝or′) city in S Maharashtra, W India

ko·lin·sky (kə lin′skē, kō-) ***n.*, *pl.* -skies** ⟦Russ *kolinskij*, after *Kola*, district in N Russia⟧ **1** any of several weasels of Asia, esp. a Russian species (*Mustela siberica*) **2** the brown fur of a kolinsky

Kol·ka·ta (kôl kut′ə) seaport in NE India, on the Hooghly River: capital of West Bengal state: formerly *Calcutta*

kol·khoz (käl kôz′) ***n.*, *pl.* -khoz′y** (-kô′zē) ⟦Russ *kolxoz* < *kol*(*lektivnoe*), collective + *xoz*(*jajstvo*), household, farm⟧ a Soviet collective farm

Koll·witz (kôl′vits′), **Kä·the** (kā′tə) (born *Käthe Schmidt*) 1867-1945; Ger. painter, etcher, & lithographer

Köln (köln) *Ger. name for* COLOGNE

Kol Nid·re (kōl nē′drā, nid′rə; *Heb* kôl′nē drā′) ⟦Heb-Aram *kol-nidre*, all (our) vows: opening words of prayer < Aram *kol*, all + *nidre*, vows, pl. of *neder*, vow < root *ndr*, to vow⟧ *Judaism* **1** a prayer recited or chanted in synagogues on the eve of Yom Kippur, declaring a release from vows, specifically religious vows, that were made unintentionally or under duress **2** the traditional melody associated with this prayer

ko·lo (kō′lō) ***n.*, *pl.* -los** ⟦Serb < OSlav, wheel < IE base **kwel-*, to turn > WHEEL⟧ a Serbian folk dance performed in a circle

Ko·ly·ma (kä′lē mä′) river in far E Russia, flowing north into the East Siberian Sea: *c.* 1,500 mi (2,414 km): also sp. **Ko′li·ma′**

Ko·mo·do dragon (kə mō′dō) ⟦after *Komodo* Island, Indonesia⟧ a giant, flesh-eating monitor lizard (*Varanus komodoensis*) of SE Asian jungles: it is the largest living lizard, reaching a length of *c.* 3.5 m (11.5 ft)

ko·mon·dor (kō′mən dôr′, käm′ən-) ***n.*, *pl.* -dors′** or **-do′rok** (-dôr′ək) ⟦Hung < Turkic⟧ any of a breed of large, powerful dog with a dense, white coat that forms itself into cords which hang freely: long bred in Hungary to guard herds and flocks

Kom·so·mol (käm′sə môl′) ***n.*** ⟦Russ < *Kom*(*munističeskij*) *So*(*juz*) *Mol*(*odeži*), Communist League of Youth⟧ the Communist organization for youth in the Soviet Union

Kom·so·molsk-on-A·mur (käm′sə môlsk′ än′ ä moor′) city in SE Russia, on the Amur River

Kon·go (käŋ′gō) ***n.*** **1** *pl.* **-gos** or **-go** a member of an African people of N Angola and the SW Democratic Republic of the Congo **2** the Bantu language of this people

Kö·nig·grätz (kö′niH grets′) *former (Ger.) name for* HRADEC KRÁLOVÉ

Kö·nigs·berg (-niHs berk′) *former (Ger.) name for* KALININGRAD

konk (käŋk, kôŋk) ***n.*, *vt.*** [Slang] *alt. sp. of* CONK[1]

Kon·ya (kôn′yä) city in SW Turkey

koo·doo (ko͞o′do͞o′) ***n.*, *pl.* -doos′** or **-doo′** *alt. sp. of* KUDU

☆**kook** (ko͞ok) ***n.*** ⟦prob. contr. < CUCKOO⟧ [Informal] a person regarded as eccentric, crazy, etc.

kook·a·bur·ra (kook′ə bur′ə, -bu′rə) ***n.*** ⟦< native name in Australia⟧ an Australian kingfisher (*Dacelo gigas*) with an abrupt, harsh cry suggestive of loud laughter

☆**kook·y** or **kook·ie** (ko͞o′kē) ***adj.* kook′i·er, kook′i·est** [Informal] of or characteristic of a kook; eccentric, crazy, etc. —**kook′i·ness *n.***

☆**Kool-Aid** (ko͞ol′ād′) ⟦orig. sp. *Kool-Ade* < *kool* (prob. altered < COOL) + *-ade* (as in LEMONADE)⟧ *trademark for:* **1** a kind of sweet, fruit-flavored drink **2** a powdered mix to be combined with water to make this drink —**drink the Kool-Aid** ⟦in ref. to the death (1978) of more than 900 U.S. citizens, members of Jonestown, a settlement in N Guyana, who consumed a fruit-flavored beverage laced with cyanide, as ordered by the group's leader⟧ [Informal] to devote oneself blindly or unreasonably to a cause, ideology, leader, etc.

Kooning, Willem de *see* DE KOONING, Willem

Koo·te·nay[1] (ko͞ot′′n ā′) ***n.*** ⟦see fol.⟧ *alt. sp. of* KUTENAI

Koo·te·nay[2] (ko͞ot′′n ā′) ⟦< a native name < ?⟧ **1** river flowing from SE British Columbia through Mont. & Ida. into Kootenay Lake, thence into the Columbia River: 407 mi (655 km): also, in the U.S., sp. **Kootenai 2** elongated lake in the valley of this river, SE British Columbia: 168 sq mi (435 sq km)

kop[1] (käp) *n.* ⟦Afrik < Du *kop*, head: see COP[1]⟧ [South Afr.] a hill or mountain

kop[2] *abbrev.* kopeck

ko·peck or **ko·pek** (kō′pek′) *n.* ⟦Russ *kopejka* < *kop'e*, a lance: so named from the lance held by the czar pictured on the coin⟧ **1** a monetary unit of various countries, equal to 1/100 of a ruble: abbrev. *k* or *kop* **2** a monetary unit of Azerbaijan, equal to 1/100 of a manat

koph (kôf) *n.* ⟦Heb *qōph*⟧ the nineteenth letter of the Hebrew alphabet (ק)

ko·piy·ka (kō pē′kə) *n.* ⟦Ukrainian, KOPECK⟧ a monetary unit of Ukraine, equal to 1/100 of a hryvnia

kop·je (käp′ē) *n.* ⟦Afrik, dim. of *kop:* see KOP[1]⟧ [South Afr.] a small hill; hillock

kor (kôr) *n.* ⟦Heb *kōr*⟧ HOMER[1]

Kor *abbrev.* **1** Korea **2** Korean

Ko·ran (kə ran′, -rän′; kôr′an′, -än′) *n.* ⟦Ar *qur'ān* lit., book, reading, recitation < *qara'a*, to read⟧ the sacred book of Islam: in Muslim belief, it contains revelations made to Muhammad by Allah: the form QURAN is now preferred in many contexts —**Ko·ran′ic** *adj.*

ko·rat (kō rät′, kôr′ät′) *n.* ⟦after the *Khorat* (or *Korat*) Plateau, NE Thailand⟧ any of a breed of domestic cat with a glossy, silver-blue coat and large, round, greenish eyes

Kor·do·fan (kôr′də fän′) former administrative region of central Sudan, west & south of Khartoum

Kor·do·fan·i·an (kôr′də fan′ē ən) *n.* ⟦< prec.⟧ a subfamily of the Niger-Kordofanian family of languages

Ko·re·a (kə rē′ə, kô-) peninsula & country in E Asia, extending south from NE China: divided (1948) into *a)* **Korean People's Democratic Republic** (**North Korea**) occupying the N half of the peninsula: 46,541 sq mi (120,540 sq km); cap. Pyongyang, and *b)* **Republic of Korea** (**South Korea**) occupying the S half of the peninsula: 38,023 sq mi (98,480 sq km); cap. Seoul

Ko·re·an (-ən) *adj.* of Korea or its people, language, or culture —*n.* **1** a person born or living in Korea **2** the language spoken in Korea: believed by some scholars to be distantly related to Japanese, although no clear relationship to any language has been established

Korean War the war (1950-53) between the Korean People's Democratic Republic (North Korea) and the Republic of Korea (South Korea), which ended in an inconclusive cease-fire: the U.S. and other United Nations member nations participated on the side of South Korea

Korea Strait strait between Korea & Japan, connecting the Sea of Japan & the East China Sea: *c.* 110 mi (177 km) wide

Ko·rin·thos (kô′rēn thôs′) *Gr. name for modern* CORINTH

Ko·ri·ya·ma (kôr′ē yäm′ə) city in NC Honshu, Japan

Korn·berg (kôrn′burg′), **Arthur** 1918-2007; U.S. biochemist

Ko·ror (kô′rôr′) island & capital of Palau

Kor·sa·koff's psychosis (*or* syndrome) (kôr′sə kôfs′) ⟦after S. S. *Korsakoff* (1854-1900), Russ neurologist⟧ a severe mental disorder caused by damage to the nervous system from alcohol, vitamin deficiencies, etc. and characterized by neuritis, memory loss, disorientation, etc.

ko·ru·na (kô′ro͞o nə) *n., pl.* **ko′ru·nas** or **ko′run′** (-ro͞on′) ⟦Czech, lit., crown < L *corona:* see CROWN⟧ **1** the basic monetary unit of the Czech Republic: see the table of monetary units in the Reference Supplement **2** the former basic monetary unit of Slovakia, superseded (2009) by the EURO

Kor·zyb·ski (kôr zip′skē), **Alfred (Habdank)** 1879-1950; U.S. semanticist, born in Poland

kos (kōs) *n., pl.* **kos** ⟦Hindi < Sans *krósa-*, lit., a shout (hence, lit., shouting distance) < IE **krauk-* < base **ker-* > L *corvus,* RAVEN[1]⟧ in India, a unit of linear measure varying from 1.5 to 3 miles

Kos (käs, kôs) Greek island in the Dodecanese, off the SW coast of Turkey: *c.* 111 sq mi (287 sq km)

Kos·ci·usz·ko[1] (käs′ē us′kō; *Pol* kôsh cho͞osh′kô), **Thaddeus** (born *Tadeusz Andrzej Bonawentura Kościuszko*) 1746-1817; Pol. patriot & general: served in the Am. army in the American Revolution: also sp. **Kos′ci·us′ko**

Kos·ci·usz·ko[2] (kä′zē us′kō), **Mount** ⟦after prec.⟧ mountain of the Australian Alps, in SE New South Wales: highest peak in Australia: 7,316 ft (2,230 m): also sp. **Kos′ci·us′ko**

ko·sher (kō′shər; *for v., usually* käsh′ər) *adj.* ⟦Yiddish < Heb *kasher*, fit, proper < root *kšr*, to be appropriate⟧ **1** *Judaism a)* clean or fit to eat according to the dietary laws: Lev. 11 *b)* serving or dealing with food prepared according to such laws [*a kosher* kitchen] **2** loosely, prepared according to traditional Jewish recipes [*kosher* pickles]: see also KOSHER STYLE ☆**3** [Slang] all right, proper, correct, etc. —*n.* kosher food —*vt.* to make kosher —**keep kosher** to observe the Jewish dietary laws

kosher salt common salt in crystals larger than those of table salt

☆**kosher style** **1** designating or of food prepared according to traditional Jewish recipes but not strictly according to kashrut **2** serving such food [*a kosher style* deli]

Ko·ši·ce (kô′shē tse) city in E Slovakia

Ko·so·vo (kō′sə vō′, kä′-, kô′-) province of S Serbia: declared its independence (2008): 4,203 sq mi (10,886 sq km); cap. Pristina —**Ko′so·var′** (-vär′) *adj., n.*

Kos·suth (käs′o͞oth′, kä so͞oth′; *Hung* kô′sho͞ot), **Louis** (Hung. name *Lajos Kossuth*) 1802-94; Hung. patriot & statesman

Ko·stro·ma (kä′strō mä′) city in WC Russia, on the Volga

Ko·sy·gin (kə sē′gin), **A·lek·sei Ni·ko·la·e·vich** (ä′lyik sā′ nē′kô lä′yi vich′) 1904-80; Russ. statesman: premier of the U.S.S.R. (1964-80)

Ko·ta Kin·a·ba·lu (kōt′ə kin′ə bə lo͞o′) seaport in N Borneo: capital of Sabah, Malaysia

ko·to (kō′tō) *n.* ⟦Jpn, a generic term for zitherlike stringed instruments⟧ a Japanese musical instrument of the zither family, with a rectangular body and seven to thirteen waxed silk strings

kou·miss (ko͞o′mis) *n. alt. sp. of* KUMISS (sense 2)

kou·ros (ko͞o′rôs) *n., pl.* **-roi** (-roi) ⟦Gr, dial. form of *koros*, boy, youth⟧ a statue of a nude male youth in a standing position, from the archaic period of Greek art (620-500 B.C.)

Kous·se·vitz·ky (ko͞o′sə vit′skē), **Serge** (surj, serzh) (born *Sergey Aleksandrovich Kusevitsky*) 1874-1951; U.S. orchestra conductor, born in Russia

Ko·var (kō′vär′) *trademark for* an alloy that consists mostly of iron, nickel, and cobalt, and has the same heat expansion properties as heat-resistant glass: it is usually fused to glass to form a gas seal

Kov·no (kôv′nô) *Russ. name for* KAUNAS

Kow·loon (kou′lo͞on′) **1** peninsula in SE China, opposite Hong Kong island & part of Hong Kong region: 3 sq mi (7.8 sq km) **2** city on this peninsula

kow·tow (kou′tou′) *n.* ⟦Chin *k'o-t'ou*, lit., bump head⟧ the act of kneeling and touching the ground with the forehead to show great deference, submissive respect, homage, etc., as formerly in China —*vi.* **1** to perform a kowtow **2** to show servile respect (*to*)

Ko·zhi·kode (kō′zhi kōd′) *another name for* CALICUT

KP *abbrev.* kitchen police

kpc *abbrev.* kiloparsec(s)

kph *abbrev.* kilometers per hour

kr *abbrev.* **1** krona **2** KRONE[2]

Kr *Chem. symbol for* krypton

KR *abbrev. Chess* king's rook

Kra (krä), **Isthmus of** narrow strip of land connecting the Malay Peninsula with the Indochinese peninsula

kraal (kräl, krôl) *n.* ⟦Afrik, village, pen, enclosure < Port *curral*, pen for cattle; akin to Sp *corral*, CORRAL⟧ **1** a traditional South African village, typically of huts surrounded by a stockade **2** a fenced enclosure for cattle or sheep in South Africa; pen —*vt.* to shut up in a kraal

Krafft-E·bing (kraft′ā′biŋ, kräft′-), Baron **Richard von** 1840-1902; Ger. neurologist

kraft (kraft, kräft) *n.* ⟦< Ger, strength: see CRAFT⟧ strong wrapping paper, usually brown, made from wood pulp prepared with a sodium sulfate solution: also **kraft paper**

krait (krīt) *n.* ⟦Hindi *karait*⟧ any of a genus (*Bungarus*) of SC and SE Asian elapine snakes that are generally black or dark brown with tan or yellow bands

Kra·ka·tau (krä′kä tou′) small island & volcano of Indonesia, between Java & Sumatra: site of a massive eruption (1883): 2,667 ft (813 m): also **Kra′ka·to′a** (-tō′ə)

kra·ken (krä′kən) *n.* ⟦Norw⟧ a legendary sea monster of northern seas

Kra·ków (krä′kou′, krā′-; *Pol* krä′ko͝of) city in S Poland, on the Vistula

Kra·ma·torsk (kräm′ə tôrsk′) city in E Ukraine

Kras·no·dar (kräs′nō där′) **1** territory in SW Russia, in the N Caucasus: 29,300 sq mi (75,887 sq km) **2** capital of this territory, on the Kuban River

Kras·no·yarsk (kräs′nō yärsk′) **1** territory in SC Russia: 903,400 sq mi (2,339,797 sq km) **2** capital of this territory, on the Yenisei River

kra·ter (krāt′ər, krä ter′) *n.* ⟦Gr *kratēr:* see CRATER⟧ an ancient Greek jar with a broad body, a wide neck, and two handles, used for mixing water and wine

☆**K ration** ⟦after Ancel *K*(*eys*) (1904-2004), Am physiologist; altered < C RATION⟧ a compactly packaged meal for emergency use in the field by military personnel in World War II

kraut (krout) *n.* ⟦Ger, cabbage⟧ **1** [Informal] *short for* SAUERKRAUT ☆**2** [Slang] a German or a person of German ancestry: a derogatory term

Krebs cycle (krebz) ⟦after H. A. *Krebs* (1900-81), Brit biochemist⟧ a cyclic series of biochemical reactions, usually in the mitochondria, that represents the final common pathway in all aerobic organisms for the oxidation of amino acids, fats, and carbohydrates, and that converts the citric acid, etc. from food into carbon dioxide and ATP

KREEP (krēp) *n.* ⟦*K* (symbol for potassium) + *r*(*are-*)*e*(*arth*) *e*(*lements*) + *p*(*hosphorus*)⟧ a type of basaltic lunar rock rich in potassium, phosphorus, etc.

Kre·feld (krā′felt′) city in W Germany, on the Rhine, in the state of North Rhine-Westphalia

Kreis·ler (krīs′lər), **Fritz** (frits) (born *Friedrich Kreisler*) 1875-1962; U.S. violinist & composer, born in Austria

Kre·men·chug (krem′ən cho͞ok′, -cho͞og′) city in EC Ukraine

krem·lin (krem′lin) *n.* ⟦Fr < Russ *kreml'*⟧ in Russia, the citadel of a city —**the Kremlin** **1** the citadel of Moscow, in which some government offices of the Soviet Union were located: it now contains some offices of the Russian government **2** the government of the Soviet Union or, now, Russia

Krem·lin·ol·o·gy (krem′lin äl′ə jē) *n.* ⟦prec. + -OLOGY⟧ the study and analysis, as based on intelligence, of the internal and foreign policies of the Soviet Union or modern Russia —**Krem′lin·ol′o·gist** *n.*

☆**krep·lach** (krep′läkh′) *pl.n.* ⟦Yiddish *kreplech*, pl. of *krepel* < MHG (dial.) *kreppel*, var. of *krepfel*, dim. of *krapfe*, fritter < OHG *krapfo*, lit., a hook: for IE base see CRADLE⟧ small casings of dough filled with ground meat or cheese, etc., boiled, and served usually in soup

Kre·te (krē′tē) *ancient Gr. name for* CRETE

kreut·zer or **kreu·zer** (kroit′sər) *n.* ⟦Ger *kreuzer* < *kreuz*, a cross: so called because the coin had the figure of a cross on it]] a former small, copper coin of Germany and Austria

krieg·spiel (krēg′spēl′, -shpēl′) *n.* [[Ger *kriegsspiel* < *kriegs* (gen. of *krieg,* war) + *spiel,* game]] a game for teaching military tactics by the use of small figures representing troops, tanks, etc. moved about as on a large map

Kriem·hild (krēm′hilt′) *n.* [[Ger < MHG *Kriemhilt* < Gmc **grim-,* a mask (akin to Frank **grima:* see GRIMACE) + **hild-,* battle (akin to HILT)]] in the *Nibelungenlied,* the wife of Siegfried and sister of Gunther: see also GUDRUN

krill (kril) *n., pl.* **krill** [[Norw *kril,* young fry (of fish)]] any of an order (Euphausiacea) of small, pelagic, shrimplike malacostracan crustaceans, the main food of baleen whales

Krim (krim) *Russ. name for* CRIMEA

krim·mer (krim′ər) *n.* [[Ger < prec.]] a grayish, tightly curled fur made from the pelts of Crimean lambs

kris (krēs) *n.* [[Malay *keris*]] a traditional Malay double-edged dagger, often, specif., one having a wavy blade

Krish·na[1] (krish′nə) *n.* [[Sans *kṛṣṇa,* lit., black < IE base **kers-,* black, dark]] an important Hindu god, an incarnation of Vishnu, second god of the Hindu trinity —**Krish′na·ism′** *n.*

Krish·na[2] (krish′nə) river in S India, flowing from the Western Ghats eastward into the Bay of Bengal: *c.* 800 mi (1,287 km)

☆**Kriss Krin·gle** (kris′ kriŋ′gəl) [[Ger *Christkindl* < *Christ,* Christ + *kindl,* dim. of *kind,* child]] SANTA CLAUS

Kris·ten (kris′tən) *n.* a feminine name: dim. *Kris;* var. *Kristin*

Krí·ti (krē′tē) *modern Gr. name for* CRETE

Kri·voi Rog (kri voi′ rôg′) city in SC Ukraine

Krogh (krôg), **(Schack) August Steen·berg** (stēn′bərg) 1874-1949; Dan. physiologist

kro·na (krō′nə) *n., pl.* **kro′nor′** (-nôr′) [[Swed < L *corona,* CROWN]] the basic monetary unit of Sweden: see the table of monetary units in the Reference Supplement

kró·na (krō′nə) *n., pl.* **kró′nur** (-nər) [[Ice < L *corona,* CROWN]] the basic monetary unit of Iceland: see the table of monetary units in the Reference Supplement

kro·ne[1] (krō′nə) *n., pl.* **kro′nen** (-nən) [[Ger < L *corona,* CROWN]] **1** a former German gold coin **2** a former monetary unit or a silver coin of Austria

kro·ne[2] (krō′nə) *n., pl.* **kro′ner** (-nər) [[Dan < L *corona,* CROWN]] the basic monetary unit of Denmark and Norway: see the table of monetary units in the Reference Supplement

Kron·shtadt (krun shtät′) city & naval fortress on an island in NW Russia, on the Gulf of Finland: Ger. **Kron·stadt** (krôn′shtät′)

kroon (krōn) *n., pl.* **kroon′i** (krō′nē) [[Estonian]] the former monetary unit of Estonia

Kro·pot·kin (krô pôt′kin; *E* krə pät′kin), Prince **Pëtr A·lek·se·ye·vich** (pyô̂tr ä′lyik sä′yi vich′) 1842-1921; Russ. anarchist & writer

Kru·ger (kro͞o′gər), **Paul** (born *Stephanus Johannes Paulus Kruger*) 1825-1904; South African statesman: president of the South African Republic (1883-1900)

Kru·ger·rand (kro͞o′gə rand′) *n.* [[after prec. + RAND[2]]] a gold coin of South Africa, often bought for investment

☆**krul·ler** (krul′ər) *n. alt. sp. of* CRULLER

krumm·horn or **krum·horn** (kro͝om′hôrn′, krum′-) *n. var. of* CRUMHORN

Krung Thep (kro͝oŋ′ täp′) *Thai name for* BANGKOK

Krupp (krup; *Ger* kro͝op) *n.* name of a family of Ger. steel & munitions manufacturers in the 19th & 20th cent.

kryp·ton (krip′tän′) *n.* [[ModL: so named (1898) by Sir William RAMSAY and M. W. Travers (1872-1961), Brit chemists, its discoverers < Gr *krypton,* neut. of *kryptos,* hidden (see CRYPT), in ref. to their difficulty in isolating it]] a rare, gaseous chemical element, one of the noble gases, present in very small quantities in air: basically inert, it reacts with fluorine and some other elements under special conditions: symbol, Kr; at. no. 36: see the periodic table of elements in the Reference Supplement

KS *abbrev.* Kansas

Kshat·ri·ya (kə shat′rē yə) *n.* [[Sans *kṣatriya* < *kṣatra,* rule]] a member of the military Hindu caste, next below the Brahmans

☆**K Street** a street in downtown Washington, D.C., on which many lobbyists have offices: term often used to refer to such lobbyists collectively

kt *abbrev.* **1** karat(s) **2** kiloton(s) **3** knot(s)

Kt *abbrev.* **1** Knight **2** *Chess* knight

KT *abbrev.* **1** Knight of (the Order of) the Thistle **2** Knight (or Knights) Templar

K2 (kā′to͞o′) [[so designated because it was the second mountain in the KARAKORAM range to have its height measured]] GODWIN AUSTEN

Ku *Chem. symbol for* kurchatovium

Kua·la Lum·pur (kwä′lə lo͝om po͝or′) capital of Malaysia, in SW Peninsular Malaysia

Kuang-chou (kwäŋ′jō′) *var. of* GUANGZHOU

Ku·ban (ko͞o ban′; *Russ* ko͞o bän′y′) river in the N Caucasus, flowing northwest into the Sea of Azov: *c.* 570 mi (917 km)

Ku·blai Khan (ko͞o′blə, -blī) 1216?-94; Mongol emperor of China (1260?-94): founder of the Mongol dynasty: grandson of Genghis Khan: also **Ku·bla Khan** (ko͞o′blə)

Ku·brick (ko͞o′brik, kyo͞o′-), **Stanley** 1928-99; U.S. film director, in England after 1961

ku·chen (ko͞o′kən, -khən) *n.* [[Ger, cake: see CAKE]] a German coffeecake, made of yeast dough covered with sugar and spices, and often containing raisins, nuts, etc.

Ku·ching (ko͞o′chiŋ) seaport & capital of Sarawak, Malaysia

ku·do (ko͞o′dō′, kyo͞o′-) *n., pl.* **-dos′** (-dōz′) [[back-form. < fol., erroneously interpreted as a pl.]] an expression of credit or praise for an achievement: a common usage objected to by many [he received many *kudos* for his charity work]: cf. KUDOS

ku·dos (ko͞o′dōs′, kyo͞o′-; -däs′) *n.* [[Gr *kydos,* glory, fame < IE **kud-* < base **keu-,* to pay attention to, HEAR]] credit or praise for an achievement; glory; fame [the performance earned her much *kudos*]: cf. KUDO

ku·du (ko͞o′do͞o′) *n., pl.* **-dus′** or **-du′** [[Hottentot]] either of two large, grayish-brown African antelopes (genus *Tragelaphus*), with narrow, white stripes across the back and long, twisted horns

☆**kud·zu** (ko͝od′zo͞o′) *n.* [[Jpn]] a fast-growing, hairy perennial vine (*Pueraria lobata*) of the pea family, with large, three-part leaves: sometimes planted in the South for soil stabilization or forage

Ku·fic (ko͞o′fik, kyo͞o′-) *adj.* [[after *Kufa* (Ar *al-Kūfa*), town on the Euphrates, south of Babylon + -IC]] designating or of a form of the Arabic alphabet having mostly angular letters

ku·gel (ko͞o′gəl) *n.* [[Yiddish *kugl* < MHG *kugel,* ball]] a crusty baked pudding made as of potatoes or noodles

Kuhn (ko͞on), **Thomas S(amuel)** 1922-96; U.S. historian & philosopher of science

Kui·by·shev (kwē′bi shef′) *name* (1935-91) *for* SAMARA

Kui·per belt (kī′pər) [[after G. P. *Kuiper* (1905-73), U.S. astronomer]] a belt of icy debris orbiting in the outer solar system in the same plane as the planets, thought to be the source of many short-period comets

☆**Ku Klux** (ko͞o′ kluks′, kyo͞o′-) [[< Gr *kyklos,* a circle (see CYCLE): prob. suggested by *Kuklos Adelphōn,* a S college fraternity (1812-66)]] *short for* KU KLUX KLAN

☆**Ku Klux·er** (ko͞o′ kluks′ər, kyo͞o′-) a member of the Ku Klux Klan: also **Ku Klux**

☆**Ku Klux Klan** (ko͞o′ kluks′ klan′, kyo͞o′-) [[KU KLUX + *klan,* arbitrary sp. for CLAN]] **1** a secret society of white men founded in the S States after the Civil War to reestablish and maintain white supremacy **2** a secret society organized in Atlanta, Georgia, in 1915 as "the Invisible Empire, Knights of the Ku Klux Klan": it is anti-black, anti-Semitic, anti-Catholic, etc., and uses terrorist methods

kuk·ri (ko͝ok′rē) *n.* [[Hindi]] a long, curved knife used as a weapon by the Gurkhas of Nepal

ku·lak (ko͞o läk′, ko͞o′läk′) *n.* [[Russ, lit., fist, hence, tightwad < ?]] any of a class of well-to-do peasant farmers in Russia who opposed the Soviet collectivization of the land

Kul·tur (ko͝ol to͞or′) [[Ger, lit., culture]] *n.* civilization: specif., the highly systematized social organization of Hohenzollern or Nazi Germany: now usually ironic in application, with reference to chauvinism, militarism, etc.

Kul·tur·kampf (-kämpf′) *n.* [[Ger < prec. + *kampf,* a battle]] **1** the late 19th-cent. struggle between the Roman Catholic Church and the German government over control of education, civil marriage, etc. **2** [*also* **k-**] [*usually not in italics*] any prolonged conflict over values, beliefs, etc.

Ku·ma·mo·to (ko͞o′mä mō′tō) city in W Kyushu, Japan

Ku·mas·i (ko͞o mä′sē) city in SC Ghana: capital of Ashanti region

Ku·may·ry (ko͞o mä′rē) city in NW Armenia

ku·miss (ko͞o′mis) *n.* [[Ger < Russ *kumys* < Turkic *qumis, qımız*]] **1** mare's or camel's milk fermented and used as a drink by Tatar nomads of Asia **2** a similar drink made from cow's milk, used in certain special diets

küm·mel (kim′əl; *Ger* küm′əl) *n.* [[Ger, caraway < OHG *kumil, kumin* < L *cuminum:* see CUMIN]] a colorless liqueur flavored with caraway seeds, anise, cumin, etc.

kum·quat (kum′kwät′) *n.* [[Cantonese *kam-kwat* < Mandarin *chin-chü,* lit., golden orange]] **1** an orange-colored, oval fruit about the size of a small plum, with a sour pulp and a sweet rind, used in preserves and confections **2** a tree (genus *Fortunella*) of the rue family that bears this fruit

Kun (ko͞on), **Bé·la** (bā′lä) 1886-1937?; Hung. Communist leader

ku·na (ko͞o′nə, kyo͞o′nə) *n., pl.* **-na** [[Serbo-Croatian, lit., marten: from former use of the animal's fur as currency]] the basic monetary unit of Croatia: see the table of monetary units in the Reference Supplement

kun·da·li·ni (ko͞on′dä lē′nē) *n.* [[< Sans *kuṇḍalinī,* lit., coiled, snake]] *Hinduism* a cosmic or divine energy in human beings located at the base of the spine and released upward by means of yogic techniques

Kung or **!Kung** (ko͝oŋ) *n.* **1** *pl.* **Kung, !Kung** a member of a people of S Africa living in the Kalahari **2** the Khoisan language of this people

kung fu (kuŋ′fo͞o′, ko͝oŋ′-) [[< Chin *ch'uan-fa,* lit., boxing principles]] a Chinese system of self-defense, like karate but emphasizing circular rather than linear movements

K'ung Fu-tzu (ko͝oŋ′ fo͞o′dzu′) *Chin. name for* CONFUCIUS

Kun·lun Mountains (ko͞on′lo͞on′) mountain system in W China, between Tibet & Xinjiang: highest peak, *c.* 25,300 ft (7,711 m)

Kun·ming (ko͞on′miŋ′) city in S China: capital of Yunnan province

☆**kunz·ite** (ko͝onts′īt′) *n.* [[after G. F. *Kunz* (1856-1932), U.S. gem expert + -ITE[1]]] a pinkish or lilac-colored, transparent variety of spodumene, used as a gem

Kuo·min·tang (kwō′min taŋ′; *Chin* gwō′min′däŋ′) *n.* [[Mandarin *kuo,* nation(alist) + *min,* people('s) + *tang,* party]] the ruling party in Taiwan under Chiang Kai-shek and his successors (1949-2000), originally a revolutionary party of China that split with, and was defeated by, the Communists

Ku·ra (ko͝o rä′) river flowing from NE Turkey west across Transcaucasia, into the Caspian Sea: *c.* 940 mi (1,513 km)

Ku·ra·shi·ki (ko͝o rä′shē kē) city in SW Honshu, Japan

kur·cha·to·vi·um (kur′chə tō′vē əm) ***n.*** ⟦ModL, after I. V. *Kurchatov* (1903–60), Soviet nuclear physicist⟧ RUTHERFORDIUM: symbol, Ku: the name for this element originally proposed by Russian scientists

Kurd (kurd) ***n.*** ⟦< Kurdish: a self-designation⟧ a member of an Islamic people living chiefly in Kurdistan and the S Caucasus

Kurd·ish (kur′dish) ***n.*** the Iranian language spoken by the Kurds —***adj.*** of the Kurds or their language or culture

Kur·dis·tan (kur′di stan′, -stän′) region in SW Asia inhabited chiefly by Kurds, occupying SE Turkey, N Iraq, & NW Iran

Ku·re (ko͞o′rä′) seaport in SW Honshu, Japan

Kur·gan (ko͝or gän′) city in SW Siberian Russia

Ku·ril (*or* Ku·rile) Islands (ko͞o′ril, ko͝o rēl′) chain of islands belonging to Russia, between N Hokkaido, Japan, and Kamchatka Peninsula: formerly Japanese (1875-1945): *c.* 6,000 sq mi (15,540 sq km)

Kur·land (ko͝or′lənd) historical name for a region in W Latvia: see KURZEME

Ku·ro·sa·wa (ko͞o′rō sä′wä), **A·ki·ra** (ä kē′rä) 1910-98; Jpn. film director

Ku·ro·shi·o (ko͝o rō′shē ō′) JAPAN CURRENT

kur·ra·jong (kur′ə jôŋ′) ***n.*** ⟦< native name in Australia⟧ any of several Australian trees and shrubs; esp., a bottletree (*Brachychiton populneum*) yielding fibers used for weaving nets, mats, etc.

Kursk (ko͞orsk) city in SW Russia, near the Ukrainian border

Kurt (kurt) ***n.*** a masculine name: var. *Curt*

kur·ta (kurt′ə) ***n.*** **1** a knee-length, collarless shirt worn over pajamas by men in India **2** a woman's dress resembling this shirt

kur·to·sis (kər tō′sis) ***n.*** ⟦< Gr *kyrtōsis*, a bulging, convexity < *kyrtos*, curved: for IE base see CURVE⟧ the degree of peakedness of the graph of a statistical distribution, indicative of the concentration around the mean

ku·ru (ko͞o′ro͞o′) ***n.*** ⟦< native name in New Guinea⟧ a degenerative disease of the central nervous system, found among certain aborigines of the eastern highlands of New Guinea

ku·ruş (ko͝o ro͞osh′) ***n.***, *pl.* **-ruş′** ⟦Turk⟧ a monetary unit of Turkey equivalent to 1⁄100 of a lira

Kur·ze·me (ko͝or′ze mə) state of Latvia: it occupies the historical region of KURLAND

Kush (ko͝osh, kush) *alt. sp. of* CUSH

Kush·it·ic (ko͝osh it′ik, kush-) ***adj., n.*** *alt. sp. of* CUSHITIC

Kus·ko·kwim (kus′kə kwim′) ⟦< Esk⟧ river in SW Alas., flowing from the Alaska Range southwest into the Bering Sea: 550 mi (885 km)

Kutch (kuch) **1** former state of W India, on the Arabian Sea: now part of the state of Gujarat **2 Rann of** (run əv) large salt marsh in W India & S Pakistan: *c.* 9,000 sq mi (23,310 sq km)

Ku·te·nai or **Ku·te·nay** (ko͞ot′'n ā′) ***n.*** **1** a member of a North American Indian people living in the Rocky Mountains in Montana, Idaho, and British Columbia **2** the language of this people: no relationship with any other language has been clearly established

Ku·tu·zov (kə to͞o′zôf′, -zôv′), **Mi·kha·il I·la·ri·o·no·vich** (mē′khä ēl′ ē′lä rē ô nô′vich′) 1745-1813; Russ. field marshal: defeated Napoleon at Smolensk (1812)

ku·vasz (ko͞o′väs′) ***n.***, *pl.* **-va·szok′** (-vä sôk′) ⟦Hung < Turk *kavas*, guard⟧ any of a breed of large, sturdily built dog with a white coat, long and wavy on the back and legs, originally used to herd sheep and as a guard dog

Ku·wait (ko͞o wāt′) **1** independent Arab state in E Arabia, at the head of the Persian Gulf between Iraq & Saudi Arabia: 6,880 sq mi (17,820 sq km) **2** its capital, a seaport on the Persian Gulf —**Ku·wai′ti** (-wāt′ē) ***adj., n.***

Kuyp (koip), **Aelbert** *alt. sp. of* Aelbert CUYP

Kuz·nets (kuz′nets′), **Simon** 1901-85; U.S. economist, born in Russia

Kuz·netsk Basin (ko͞oz netsk′) industrial & coal-mining region in SC Asian Russia, including the cities of Kemerovo, Prokopyevsk, and Novokuznetsk: *c.* 10,000 sq mi (25,900 sq km)

kV or **kv** *abbrev.* kilovolt(s)

kvass or **kvas** (kväs′) ***n.*** ⟦Russ *kvas* < IE **kwātso-* < base **kwat-*, to ferment > L *caseus*, CHEESE[1]⟧ a Russian fermented drink made from rye, barley, rye bread, etc. and often flavored

kvell (kvel′) ***vi.*** ⟦Yiddish⟧ [Informal] to exclaim joyfully or proudly, esp. in boasting of the achievements of a family member

☆**kvetch** (kvech′) [Slang] ***vi.*** ⟦< Yiddish *kvechen* < Ger *quetschen*, to pinch, squeeze < MHG *quetsen* < IE base **gwedh-*, to injure, destroy⟧ **1** to be urgent or insistent; press; strain **2** to complain in a nagging or whining way —***n.*** a person who kvetches: also **kvetch′er**

kW or **kw** *abbrev.* kilowatt(s)

Kwa (kwä) ***adj.*** designating or of a branch of the Niger-Congo subfamily of languages, spoken in W Africa in a coastal belt extending from Liberia to Nigeria and including Akan, Ewe, Yoruba, and Ibo —***n.*** this group of languages

kwa·cha (kwä′chä′) ***n.***, *pl.* **kwa′cha′** ⟦lit., dawn, in a Bantu language of Zambia: in allusion to the word's use by the independence movement as a cry for the "dawn of freedom"⟧ the basic monetary unit of: *a)* Malawi *b)* Zambia: see the table of monetary units in the Reference Supplement

Kwa·ja·lein (kwä′jə län′) atoll in the W Pacific, in the Marshall Islands: *c.* 6 sq mi (15.5 sq km)

Kwa·ki·u·tl (kwä′kē o͞ot′'l) ***n.*** ⟦< name in Kwakiutl, lit., beach at the north end of the river⟧ **1** a member of a North American Indian people of British Columbia, noted esp. for elaborate potlatches **2** the Wakashan language of this people

Kwang·chow (kwäŋ′chō′; *Chin* gwäŋ′jō′) *a former transliteration of* GUANGZHOU

Kwang·ju (gwäŋ′jo͞o′) *a former transliteration of* GWANGJU

Kwang·si (gwäŋ′sē′) *a former transliteration of* GUANGXI

Kwang·tung (kwaŋ′to͝oŋ′; *Chin* gwäŋ′do͝oŋ′) *a former transliteration of* GUANGDONG

kwan·za (kwän′zä) ***n.***, *pl.* **kwan′zas** ⟦after the *Cuanza* River, in Angola⟧ the basic monetary unit of Angola: see the table of monetary units in the Reference Supplement

☆**Kwan·zaa** (kwän′zä) ***n.*** ⟦coined (1966) by M. Ron Karenga, U.S. academic < Swahili *matunda ya kwanza*, first fruits (of harvest)⟧ an African-American cultural festival observed from Dec. 26 through Jan. 1: also sp. **Kwan′za**

kwa·shi·or·kor (kwä′shē ôr′kôr′) ***n.*** ⟦< name in a Kwa language of Ghana⟧ a severe disease of young children, caused by chronic deficiency of protein and calories in the diet and characterized by stunted growth, edema, and a protuberant belly

Kwa·Zu·lu-Na·tal (kwä zo͞o′lo͞o nə tal′) province of W South Africa: 35,591 sq mi (92,180 sq km); cap. Pietermaritzburg

Kwei·chow (kwā′chou′; *Chin* gwā′jō′) *a former transliteration of* GUIZHOU

Kwei·lin (kwā′lin′; *Chin* gwā′lin′) *a former transliteration of* GUILIN

Kwei·yang (kwā′yäŋ′; *Chin* gwā′yäŋ′) *a former transliteration of* GUIYANG

kWh *abbrev.* kilowatt-hour(s): sometimes written **kwh** or **kW-h**

KY or **Ky** *abbrev.* Kentucky

☆**ky·ack** (kī′ak′) ***n.*** ⟦< ?⟧ [West] a kind of packsack consisting of two sack-like containers swung on either side of a packsaddle

ky·ak (kī′ak′) ***n.*** *alt. sp. of* KAYAK

ky·a·nite (kī′ə nīt′) ***n.*** ⟦alt. sp. of CYANITE⟧ a bluish silicate of aluminum, Al_2SiO_5, that forms in long, thin, bladed crystals that are found in metamorphic rocks

ky·an·ize (-nīz′) ***vt.*** **-ized′**, **-iz′ing** ⟦after J. H. *Kyan* (1774-1850), Ir inventor⟧ to make (wood) resistant to decay by treatment with a solution of mercuric chloride

kyat (kyät) ***n.*** ⟦< Burmese⟧ the basic monetary unit of Myanmar: see the table of monetary units in the Reference Supplement

Kyd (kid), **Thomas** 1558-94; Eng. dramatist

Ky·iv (kē′yo͞o) capital of Ukraine, on the Dnieper: Russ. name KIEV

Kyle (kīl) ***n.*** a masculine and feminine name

ky·lix (kī′liks′, kil′iks′) ***n.***, *pl.* **ky·li·kes** (kī′li kēz′, kil′i-) ⟦Gr *kylix* < IE base *(*s*)*kel-*, cup > L *calix*⟧ a lavishly decorated, ancient Greek two-handled drinking cup with a stem and a wide, shallow bowl

ky·mo·gram (kī′mō gram′, -mə-) ***n.*** the chart produced by a kymograph

ky·mo·graph (-graf′) ***n.*** ⟦< Gr *kyma*, a wave (see CYME) + -GRAPH⟧ an apparatus consisting of a rotating drum for recording wavelike motions, variations, or modulations, such as muscular contractions —**ky′mo·graph′ic** ***adj.*** —**ky·mog·ra·phy** (kī mäg′rə fē) ***n.***

Kym·ric (kim′rik) ***adj., n.*** *var. of* CYMRIC

Kym·ry or **Kym·ri** (-rē) ***pl.n.*** *var. of* CYMRY

Ky·nar (kī′när′) *trademark for* a hard, white polyvinylidene fluoride resin that resists chemicals and heat, used in pipes, pumps, etc.

Kyong·song (kyôŋ′sôŋ′) *former Kor. name for* SEOUL

Kyo·to (kē ō′tō) city in S Honshu, Japan: former capital of Japan (794-1869)

ky·pho·sis (kī fō′sis) ***n.*** ⟦ModL < Gr *kyphōsis* < *kyphos*, a hump, hunch < IE **keubh-* < base **keu-*, to bend, arch > HIP[1], HUMP⟧ abnormal curvature of the spine resulting in a hump —**ky·phot′ic** (-fät′ik) ***adj.***

Kyr·gyz·stan (kir′gi stan′) country in SC Asia: became independent upon the breakup of the U.S.S.R. (1991): 76,641 sq mi (198,500 sq km); cap. Bishkek: formerly, *Kirghiz Soviet Socialist Republic*

Kyr·i·e (e·le·i·son) (kir′ē ā′ ā lā′ē sōn′) ⟦Gr(Ec) *Kyrie eleēson*, Lord, have mercy (upon us): see Ps. 123:3, Matt. 15:22⟧ **1** an invocation or response used in several Christian liturgies; specif., a regular part of the Roman Catholic Mass **2** a musical setting of this

Ky·the·ra (kē′thi rä′) *Gr. name for* CYTHERA

Kyu·shu (kyo͞o′sho͞o′, kē o͞o′sho͞o) one of the four main islands of Japan, south of Honshu: 16,276 sq mi (42,155 sq km); chief city, Nagasaki

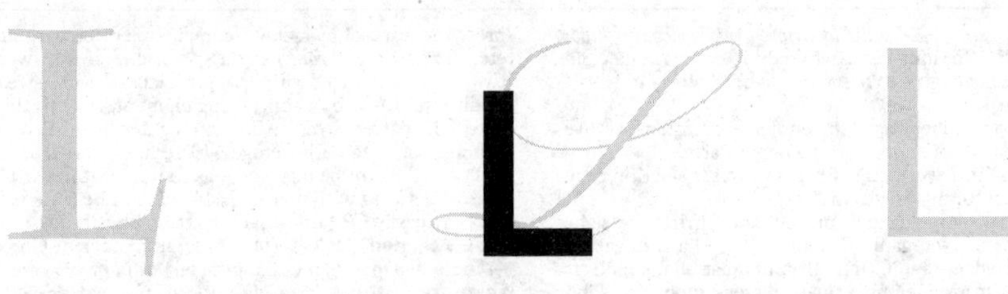

l[1] or **L** (el) ***n.,*** *pl.* **l's, L's 1** the twelfth letter of the English alphabet: from the Greek *lambda,* a borrowing from the Phoenician **2** any of the speech sounds that this letter represents, as, in English, the (l) of *love* **3** a type or impression for *l* or *L* **4** the twelfth in a sequence or group **5** an object shaped like L —***adj.*** **1** of *l* or *L* **2** twelfth in a sequence or group **3** shaped like L

l[2] *abbrev.* **1** land **2** large **3** latitude **4** law **5** leaf **6** league **7** left **8** length **9** line **10** link **11** lira; lire **12** liter(s) **13** long **14** loss(es)

L[1] (el) ***n.,*** *pl.* **L's** ☆**1** an extension of a building that gives the whole a shape resembling L; ell **2** a Roman numeral for 50: with a superior bar ($\bar{L}$), 50,000 ☆**3** ⟦for *el,* short for ELEVATED⟧ an elevated railroad

L[2] *abbrev.* **1** lake **2** lambert(s) **3** large **4** *Physics* latent heat **5** Latin **6** left **7** length **8** *Football* lineman: sometimes written **l 9** lira; lire **10** liter(s) **11** lobby **12** longitude **13** loss(es) **14** low **15** *Rom. History* Lucius (the praenomen)

L[3] *symbol* **1** Avogadro constant **2** *Elec.* inductance **3** ⟦L *libra,* pl. *librae*⟧ [*sometimes* **l-**] [Brit.] pound(s) sterling: now usually £

l- *prefix Chem.* levorotatory: usually printed in italic type [*l-limonene*] or symbolized by a minus sign (−)

L- *prefix Chem.* having an asymmetrical, left-handed spatial arrangement of atoms: usually printed as a small capital [L-glucose]

la[1] (lä, lô) ***interj.*** ⟦see LO[1]⟧ [Now Chiefly Dial.] oh; look: an exclamation expressing surprise or providing emphasis

la[2] (lä) ***n.*** ⟦ME < ML < *labii,* word of a Latin hymn: see GAMUT⟧ *Music* a syllable representing the sixth tone of the diatonic scale: see SOLFEGGIO

La[1] *abbrev.* **1** *Bible* Lamentations **2** Louisiana

La[2] *Chem. symbol for* lanthanum

LA *abbrev.* **1** Los Angeles: also **L.A. 2** Louisiana

laa·ger (lä′gər) [South Afr.] ***n.*** ⟦Afrik < Ger *lager,* Du *leger,* a camp: see LAIR⟧ a temporary camp within an encircling barricade of wagons, etc. —***vt.*** to form into a laager —***vi.*** to camp in a laager

Laa·land (lô′län) *var. of* LOLLAND

laa·ri (lä′rē) ***n.,*** *pl.* **-ri** ⟦< Pers⟧ a monetary unit of the Maldives, equal to 1⁄100 of a rufiyaa

lab (lab) ***n.*** *short for* LABORATORY

Lab[1] (lab) ***n.*** *short for* LABRADOR RETRIEVER

Lab[2] *abbrev.* Labrador

La·ban (lā′bən) ***n.*** ⟦Heb *lavan,* lit., white⟧ *Bible* the father of Rachel and Leah: Gen. 29:16

La·ba·no·ta·tion (lä′bə nō tā′shən) ***n.*** ⟦after R. *Laban* (1879–1958), Hung dance theoretician, choreographer, & teacher + (N)OTATION⟧ a system using symbols for recording and choreographing the movements of dancers

lab·a·rum (lab′ə rəm) ***n.,*** *pl.* **-ra** (-rə) ⟦LL (> LGr *labaron*) < ?⟧ the royal cavalry standard carried before the Roman emperors in war, esp. that first carried by Constantine, bearing the first two letters (XP) of the Greek *Christos* (Christ)

lab·da·num (lab′də nəm) ***n.*** ⟦ML, altered < L *ladanum* < Gr *ladanon* < *lēdon,* mastic < Ar *lādan* < Pers⟧ a dark resin obtained from various cistus shrubs, used in perfumery

La·be (lä′be) *Czech name for* the ELBE

lab·e·fac·tion (lab′ə fak′shən) ***n.*** ⟦< L *labefactus,* pp. of *labefacere,* to cause to totter < *labare,* to totter (see LAP[1]) + *facere,* to make: see DO[1]⟧ [Rare] a weakening, ruining, etc.; downfall; deterioration

la·bel (lā′bəl) ***n.*** ⟦OFr, a rag, strip < Frank **labba,* akin to OHG *lappa,* a rag, shred: for IE base see LAP[1]⟧ **1** [Archaic] *a)* a narrow band of cloth, etc.; fillet *b)* a narrow strip of ribbon attached to a document to hold the seal **2** a card, strip of paper, etc. marked and attached to an object to indicate its nature, contents, ownership, destination, etc. **3** a descriptive word or phrase applied to a person, group, theory, etc. as a convenient generalized classification ☆**4** an identifying brand, as of a company producing recorded music **5** *a)* a company producing and distributing prerecorded discs, tapes, etc. *b)* such a tape, disc, etc. **6** TRACER (*n.* 4) **7** *Archit.* a projecting molding over a door, window, etc. **8** *Heraldry* a horizontal bar with several dependent points, on the coat of arms of an eldest son —***vt.*** **-beled** or **-belled, -bel·ing** or **-bel·ling 1** to attach a label to; mark with a label **2** to classify as; call or describe, specif. in a way that stereotypes **3** *a)* to differentiate (an element, atom, etc.) by introducing a radioactive isotope or an isotope of unusual mass that may be readily traced through a complex process *b)* to incorporate a labeled element into (a molecule, compound, material, etc.) —**la′bel·er** ***n.,*** **la′bel·ler**

la·bel·lum (lə bel′əm) ***n.,*** *pl.* **-la** (-ə) ⟦ModL < L, dim. of *labrum,* lip, akin to *labium:* see LIP⟧ the lowest of the three petals forming the corolla of an orchid, usually larger than the other two petals, and often spurred

la·bi·a (lā′bē ə) ***n.*** **1** *pl. of* LABIUM **2** *short for: a)* LABIA MAJORA *b)* LABIA MINORA

la·bi·al (-əl) ***adj.*** ⟦ML *labialis* < L *labium,* LIP⟧ **1** of the labia, or lips **2** *Phonet.* articulated with one or both lips, as (f), (b), and (ü) —***n.*** **1** FLUE PIPE **2** a labial sound —**la′bi·al·ly** ***adv.***

la·bi·al·ize (-īz′) ***vt.*** **-ized′, -iz′ing** ⟦prec. + -IZE⟧ **1** to pronounce (a sound or sounds) by using the lips, sometimes excessively **2** to round (a vowel) —**la′bi·al·i·za′tion** ***n.***

labia ma·jo·ra (mə jôr′ə) ⟦ModL, lit., greater lips⟧ the outer folds of skin of the vulva, one on either side

labia mi·no·ra (mi nôr′ə) ⟦ModL, lit., lesser lips⟧ the two folds of mucous membrane within the labia majora

la·bi·ate (lā′bē it, -āt′) ***adj.*** ⟦ModL *labiatus* < L *labium,* LIP⟧ **1** formed or functioning like a lip **2** having a lip or lips; lipped **3** *Bot. a)* having the calyx or corolla so divided that one part overlaps the other like a lip *b)* of or pertaining to the mint family —***n.*** a plant of the mint family

la·bile (lā′bəl, -bīl′) ***adj.*** ⟦L *labilis* < *labi,* to slip, fall: see LAP[1]⟧ liable to change; unstable [*labile* chemical compounds] —**la·bil·i·ty** (lā bil′i tē) ***n.***

la·bi·o- (lā′bē ō, -ə) ⟦< L *labium,* LIP⟧ *combining form* **1** the lips **2** the lips and [*labiodental*]

la·bi·o·den·tal (lā′bē ō dent′'l) ***adj.*** ⟦prec. + DENTAL⟧ *Phonet.* articulated with the lower lip against the upper front teeth, as (f) and (v) —***n.*** a labiodental sound

la·bi·o·na·sal (-nā′zəl) ***adj.*** ⟦LABIO- + NASAL⟧ *Phonet.* articulated with the lips but having nasal resonance, as (m) —***n.*** a labionasal sound

la·bi·o·ve·lar (-vē′lər) ***adj.*** ⟦LABIO- + VELAR⟧ *Phonet.* articulated with the lips rounded and the back of the tongue against or near the velum, or soft palate, as (w) —***n.*** a labiovelar sound

la·bi·um (lā′bē əm) ***n.,*** *pl.* **-bi·a** (-ə) ⟦L, LIP⟧ a lip or liplike organ; esp., *a)* the lower, liplike part of the corolla of certain flowers *b)* the lower lip of an insect, formed by the fusion of the second maxillae

la·bor (lā′bər) ***n.*** ⟦OFr < L, labor, orig., hardship, pain, prob. < base of *labi,* to slip, totter: see LAP[1]⟧ **1** physical or mental exertion; work; toil **2** a specific task; piece of work **3** *a)* all wage-earning workers as a group (distinguished from CAPITAL[1] OR MANAGEMENT) *b)* all manual workers whose work is characterized largely by physical exertion **4** labor unions collectively **5** the work accomplished by, or the role in production of, all workers, esp. workers for wages **6** [**L-**] Labor Party **7** *Med.* the process or period of childbirth; parturition; esp., the muscular contractions of giving birth —***vi.*** ⟦ME *laboren* < OFr *laborer* < L *laborare* < the n.⟧ **1** to work; toil **2** to work hard; exert oneself to get or do something; strive **3** *a)* to move slowly and with difficulty [the car *labored* up the hill] *b)* to pitch and roll heavily [the ship *labored* in the rough sea] **4** to be afflicted or burdened with a liability or limitation (with *under*) [to *labor* under a delusion] **5** to undergo, and suffer the pains of, childbirth —***vt.*** ⟦earlier *elabour* < Fr *élaborer:* see ELABORATE⟧ to spend too much time and effort on; belabor [to *labor* a point]

lab·ora·to·ry (lab′rə tôr′ē; *occas.* lab′ər ə tôr′ē; *Brit* lə bôr′ə trē) ***n.,*** *pl.* **-ries** ⟦ML *laboratorium* < L *laborare:* see prec.⟧ **1** a room, building, etc. for scientific experimentation or research **2** a place for preparing chemicals, drugs, etc. ☆**3** a place where theories, techniques, and methods, as in education or social studies, are tested, analyzed, demonstrated, etc. **4** a room, often containing special equipment and materials, in which students work to enhance skills, remedy deficiencies, etc. in a particular subject, as a foreign language **5** a class period during which students perform experiments or work in a laboratory —***adj.*** of or performed in, or as in, a laboratory

labor camp 1 a camp for confining political prisoners, prisoners of war, dissidents, etc., who are forced to perform physical labor **2** a camp or other housing for migrant farm workers

☆**Labor Day** in the U.S. & Canada, the first Monday in September, a legal holiday in honor of working people

la·bored (lā′bərd) ***adj.*** made or done with great effort; not effortless and natural; strained

la·bor·er (lā′bər ər) ***n.*** ⟦ME < OFr *laboreor* < *laborer:* see LABOR⟧ **1** a person who labors; esp., a wage-earning worker whose work is largely hard physical labor **2** an unskilled or semiskilled worker who brings materials to, and does preparatory work for, skilled workers in a trade [mason's *laborer*]

la·bor-in·ten·sive (-in ten′siv) ***adj.*** **1** requiring a large labor force and a relatively small investment in capital goods [a *labor-intensive* industry or plant] **2** requiring a great deal of work or effort

la·bo·ri·ous (lə bôr′ē əs) *adj.* ⟦ME < OFr *laborios* < L *laboriosus* < *labor,* LABOR⟧ 1 involving or calling for much hard work; difficult 2 [Archaic] industrious; hardworking 3 LABORED —**SYN.** HARD —**la·bo′ri·ous·ly** *adv.* —**la·bo′ri·ous·ness** *n.*

☆**la·bor·ite** (lā′bər īt′) *n.* 1 a member or supporter of a labor union or movement 2 [*usually* **L-**] a member or supporter of a Labor Party

labor of love ⟦see 1 Thess. 1:3⟧ work done for personal satisfaction or altruistic reasons rather than for material gain

labor party 1 a political party organized to protect and further the rights of workers, or one dominated by organized labor 2 [**L- P-**] any of various national parties so organized, as that in Great Britain, Australia, Israel, etc.

la·bor-sav·ing (lā′bər sāv′iŋ) *adj.* eliminating or lessening physical labor [*labor-saving* appliances]

☆**labor union** an association of workers to promote and protect the welfare, interests, and rights of its members, primarily by collective bargaining

la·bour (lā′bər) *n., vi., vt. Brit. sp. of* LABOR

la·bour·ite (-īt′) *n. Brit. sp. of* LABORITE

la·bra (lā′brə, lab′rə) *n. pl. of* LABRUM

lab·ra·doo·dle (lab′rə do͞od′'l) *n.* ⟦< fol. + POODLE⟧ a dog crossbred from a Labrador retriever and a poodle

Lab·ra·dor[1] (lab′rə dôr′) *n.* [*also* **l-**] LABRADOR RETRIEVER

Lab·ra·dor[2] (lab′rə dôr′) ⟦prob. < Port *lavrador,* landholder, for 15th-c. Port explorer João Fernandes, a landholder in the Azores: the name was first applied to Greenland⟧ 1 region along the Atlantic coast of NE Canada, constituting the mainland part of the province of Newfoundland and Labrador: 112,826 sq mi (292,218 sq km) 2 large peninsula between the Atlantic & Hudson Bay, containing Quebec & Labrador (the region) —**Lab′ra·dor′e·an** *adj., n.,* **Lab′ra·dor′i·an** (-ē ən)

Labrador Current icy arctic current flowing south from Baffin Bay past Labrador into the Gulf Stream

lab·ra·dor·ite (lab′rə dôr īt′, lab′rə dôr′-) *n.* ⟦after LABRADOR[2], where specimens have been found⟧ a variety of plagioclase with dark, iridescent colors

Labrador retriever ⟦after LABRADOR[2] (in Newfoundland), where first bred⟧ any of a breed of medium-sized retriever with a muscular build, a short, dense coat of a solid color (black, yellow, or dark brown), and a tapering tail, very thick at the base

la·bret (lā′bret) *n.* ⟦dim. of L *labrum,* lip⟧ an ornament of wood, bone, etc. worn, as by some South American Indians, in a hole pierced through the lip

la·brum (lā′brəm, lab′rəm) *n., pl.* **la·bra** (lā′brə, lab′rə) ⟦ModL < L, lip⟧ a lip or liplike edge; esp., the upper or front lip of insects and other arthropods

la·brus·ca (lə brus′kə) *adj.* ⟦ModL (*Vitis*) *labrusca,* lit., wild (vine), species name given by LINNAEUS < L *labrusca,* wild vine⟧ designating or of the FOX GRAPE

La Bru·yère (lä′ bro͞o yer′; *Fr* lȧ brü yer′), **Jean de** (zhän də) 1645-96; Fr. essayist & moralist

La·bu·an (lä′bo͞o än′) island of Malaysia, off the NW coast of Sabah: 35 sq mi (91 sq km)

la·bur·num (lə bur′nəm) *n.* ⟦ModL < L⟧ any of a genus (*Laburnum*) of small, poisonous trees and shrubs of the pea family, with three-part leaves and drooping racemes of yellow flowers

lab·y·rinth (lab′ə rinth′) *n.* ⟦ME *laborintus* (altered by folk etym. by assoc. with L *labor,* LABOR + *intus,* into) < L *labyrinthus* < Gr *labyrinthos,* of pre-Hellenic orig.⟧ 1 a structure consisting of an intricate network of winding passages bordered as by walls or hedges; specif., such a structure designed for prayer and meditation: technically, a labyrinth (unlike a *maze*) contains no dead ends and consists of a single path leading to a center: cf. MAZE (*n.* 1) 2 a complicated, perplexing arrangement, course of affairs, etc. 3 *Anat.* the inner ear: see EAR[1] 4 [**L-**] *Gr. Myth.* the labyrinthine structure built by Daedalus for King Minos of Crete, to house the Minotaur

lab·y·rin·thine (lab′ə rin′thin, -thēn′, -thīn′) *adj.* 1 of or constituting a labyrinth 2 like a labyrinth; intricate; complicated; puzzling: also **lab′y·rin′thi·an** (-thē ən) or **lab′y·rin′thic**

lab·y·rin·thi·tis (lab′ə rin thīt′is) *n.* inflammation of the inner ear, often accompanied by an impaired sense of balance

lac (lak) *n.* ⟦Hindi *lākh* < Sans *lākṣā,* var. of *rākṣā,* prob. < IE base **reg-,* to color (> Gr *regma,* colored material); in part via Fr *laque* < OProv *laca* < Ar *lakk* < Pers *lak,* of same orig.⟧ 1 a resinous substance secreted by various scale insects, esp. a species (*Laccifer lacca*) of India, that live on certain fig, soapberry, and acacia trees: when melted, strained, and rehardened, it forms shellac 2 *alt. sp. of* LAKH

La·can (lȧ kän′), **Jacques** (zhȧk) 1901-81; Fr. structuralist & psychoanalytic theorist

Lac·ca·dive Islands (lak′ə dīv′) group of islands in the Arabian Sea, off the SW coast of India: part of Lakshadweep territory

lac·co·lith (lak′ə lith′) *n.* ⟦< Gr *lakkos,* a cistern + -LITH⟧ a dome-shaped, irregular formation of intrusive igneous rock found between layers of sedimentary rock: cf. BATHOLITH

lace (lās) *n.* ⟦ME *las* < OFr *las, laz* < L *laqueus,* a noose, snare, trap < IE base **lēk-* > OE *læla,* a whip⟧ 1 a string, ribbon, etc. used to draw together and fasten the parts of a shoe, corset, etc. by being drawn through eyelets or over hooks 2 an ornamental braid of gold or silver, for trimming uniforms, hats, etc. 3 a fine netting or openwork fabric of cotton, polyester, etc., woven in ornamental designs —*vt.* **laced, lac′ing** ⟦ME *lacen, lasen* < OFr *lacier* < L *laqueare,* to ensnare, entangle < the n.⟧ 1 to draw the ends of (a garment, shoe, etc.) together and fasten with a lace: often with *up* 2 to compress the waist of by lacing a corset, etc.: often with *up* 3 to pass (a cord, etc.) in and out *through* eyelets, fabric, etc. 4 to weave together; intertwine 5 to ornament with or as with lace 6 *a)* to streak, as with color *b)* to diversify, as with a contrasting element 7 *a)* to thrash; whip *b)* to hit hard [the batter *laced* the ball into center field] 8 *a)* to add a dash of alcoholic liquor to (a beverage) *b)* to add a small amount of a substance to (something to be ingested), as to render it flavorful, potent, toxic, etc. [brownies *laced* with marijuana] —*vi.* 1 to be fastened with a lace [shoes that *lace* easily] 2 [Informal] to attack physically or verbally: with *into*

Lac·e·dae·mon (las′ə dē′mən) region in ancient Greece including Sparta —**Lac′e·dae·mo′ni·an** (-di mō′nē ən) *adj., n.*

lac·er·ate (las′ər āt′; *for adj.,* -it, -āt′) *vt.* **-at′ed, -at′ing** ⟦< L *laceratus,* pp. of *lacerare,* to tear < *lacer,* lacerated < IE base **lēk-,* to tear > Gr *lakis,* a tatter⟧ 1 to tear jaggedly; mangle (something soft, as flesh) 2 to wound or hurt (someone's feelings, etc.) deeply; distress —*adj.* 1 torn; mangled 2 *Bot.* having jagged edges —**lac′er·a·ble** (-ər ə bəl) *adj.*

lac·er·a·tion (las′ər ā′shən) *n.* ⟦L *laceratio*⟧ 1 the act or an instance of lacerating 2 the result of lacerating; jagged tear or wound

La·cer·ta (lə surt′ə) *n.* ⟦L: see LIZARD⟧ a N constellation in the Milky Way, between Cygnus and Andromeda

la·cer·til·i·an (las′ər til′ē ən) *n., adj.* ⟦< ModL *Lacertilia* < L *lacertus, lacerta* (see LIZARD) + -AN⟧ SAURIAN

lace·wing (lās′wiŋ′) *n.* any of various families of neuropteran insects with four delicate, gauzy wings: the larvae feed on aphids and other insect pests

lace·work (-wurk′) *n.* lace, or any openwork decoration like lace

La·chaise (lȧ shez′), **Gas·ton** (gȧs tōn′) 1882-1935; U.S. sculptor, born in France

lach·es (lach′iz) *n.* ⟦ME *lachesse* < OFr *laschesse* < *lasche,* lax, negligent < VL **lascus,* metathetic for L *laxus,* LAX⟧ *Law* failure to do the required thing at the proper time (e.g., inexcusable delay in enforcing a claim)

Lach·e·sis (lak′i sis) *n.* ⟦L < Gr *lachesis,* lit., lot < *lanchanein,* to obtain by lot or fate, happen⟧ *Class. Myth.* that one of the three Fates who determines the length of the thread of life

La·chine (lə shēn′) ⟦< Fr *Chine,* CHINA: derisive name applied to the land grant of explorer LA SALLE, in allusion to his failure to find a westward passage to China⟧ borough of Montreal

lach·ry·mal (lak′ri məl) *adj.* ⟦ML *lacrimalis* < L *lacrima,* TEAR[2]⟧ 1 of, characterized by, or producing tears 2 *alt. sp. of* LACRIMAL (sense 1) —*n. var. of* LACHRYMATORY

lach·ry·ma·tor (lak′ri māt′ər) *n.* ⟦< L *lacrima,* TEAR[2] + -ATOR⟧ a substance, as tear gas, that irritates the eyes and produces tears

lach·ry·ma·to·ry (-mə tôr′ē) *n., pl.* **-ries** ⟦ML *lacrimatorium,* neut. of *lacrimatorius,* of tears < L *lacrima,* TEAR[2]⟧ any of various small vases found in ancient Roman sepulchers, formerly supposed to have been used to catch the tears of mourners —*adj.* of, causing, or producing tears

lach·ry·mose (-mōs′) *adj.* ⟦L *lacrimosus* < *lacrima,* TEAR[2]⟧ 1 inclined to shed many tears; tearful 2 causing tears; sad [a *lachrymose* tale] —**lach′ry·mose′ly** *adv.*

lac·i·ly (lās′ə lē) *adv.* in a lacy manner or pattern

lac·i·ness (lās′ē nis) *n.* a lacy quality or state

lac·ing (lās′iŋ) *n.* 1 the act of a person who laces 2 a thrashing; beating 3 a cord or lace, as a shoelace 4 gold or silver braid used to trim a uniform, etc. 5 a small amount, as of liquor or a flavoring, added to something

la·cin·i·ate (lə sin′ē it, -āt′) *adj.* ⟦< L *lacinia,* a flap (akin to *lacer:* see LACERATE) + -ATE[1]⟧ 1 having a fringe; fringed 2 *Bot.* cut deeply into narrow, jagged segments Also **la·cin′i·at′ed** (-āt′id) —**la·cin′i·a′tion** *n.*

lack (lak) *n.* ⟦early ME *lac* < or akin to MLowG & MDu *lak,* lack: for IE base see LEAK⟧ 1 the fact or condition of not having enough; shortage; deficiency 2 the fact or condition of not having any; complete absence 3 the thing that is lacking or needed —*vi.* ⟦ME *lacen* < MDu *laken,* to be wanting⟧ 1 to be wanting or missing; show a deficiency 2 *a)* to be short (with *in, for,* or, now rarely, *of*) *b)* to be in need —*vt.* 1 to be deficient in or entirely without 2 to fall short by [*lacking* one ounce of being a pound] 3 [Obs.] to need; require

SYN.—**lack** implies an absence or insufficiency of something essential or desired [she *lacks* experience]; **want** (in this sense, chiefly British) and **need** stress the urgency of supplying what is lacking [this matter *needs,* or *wants,* immediate attention]; **require** emphasizes, even more strongly, imperative need, connoting that what is needed is indispensable [his work *requires* great powers of concentration] —**ANT. have, possess**

lack- (lak) *combining form* lacking [*lackluster*]

lack·a·dai·si·cal (lak′ə dā′zi kəl) *adj.* ⟦< *lackadaisy,* altered (infl. by DAISY) < fol.⟧ showing lack of interest or spirit; listless; languid —**lack′a·dai′si·cal·ly** *adv.*

lack·a·day (lak′ə dā′) *interj.* ⟦contr. < ALACKADAY⟧ [Archaic] ALACK

lack·ey (lak′ē) *n., pl.* **-eys** ⟦Fr *laquais,* a lackey, soldier < Catalan *alacay* < Sp *lacayo,* lackey, footman < OSp *alcayaz* < Ar *al qā′id:* see ALCAIDE⟧ 1 a male servant of low rank, usually in some sort of livery or uniform 2 a follower who carries out another's orders like a servant; toady —*vt., vi.* **-eyed, -ey·ing** [Now Rare] to serve as a lackey

lack·lus·ter (lak′lus′tər) *adj.* 1 lacking brightness; dull [*lackluster* eyes] 2 lacking energy or vitality; boring, unimaginative, etc. [a *lackluster* performance] Also [Chiefly Brit.] **lack′lus′tre**

La·clos (lȧ klō′), **(Pierre Ambroise François) Cho·der·los de** (shō der lō′ də) 1741-1803; Fr. novelist

La·co·ni·a (lə kō′nē ə) **1** ancient country on the SE coast of the Peloponnesus, Greece: dominated by the city of Sparta **2** department of modern Greece in the same general area: also sp. **Lakonia** —**La·co′ni·an** *adj., n.*

la·con·ic (lə kän′ik) *adj.* ⟦L *Laconicus* < Gr *Lakōnikos*, Laconian < *Lakōn*, a Laconian, Spartan⟧ brief or terse in speech or expression; using few words —*SYN.* CONCISE —**la·con′i·cal·ly** *adv.*

lac·o·nism (lak′ə niz′əm) *n.* ⟦Gr *Lakōnismos* < *Lakōnizein*, to imitate the Laconians⟧ **1** brevity of speech or expression **2** a laconic speech or expression Also **la·con·i·cism** (lə kän′i siz′əm)

La Co·ru·ña (lä′ kō ro͞o′nyä) seaport in NW Spain, on the Atlantic

lac·quer (lak′ər) *n.* ⟦Fr *laquer*, earlier *lacre* < Port < *laca*, gum lac < Hindi *lākh*: see LAC⟧ **1** a coating substance consisting of resinous materials, as cellulose esters or ethers, shellac, or gum or alkyd resins, dissolved in ethyl alcohol or another solvent that evaporates rapidly on application, leaving a tough, adherent film: pigments are often added to form **lacquer enamels** **2** a resinous varnish obtained from certain Chinese and Japanese trees (esp. *Toxicodendron verniciflutum*) of the cashew family, used to give a hard, smooth, highly polished finish to wood **3** a decorative article or articles made of wood and coated with this lacquer: in full **lac′quer·ware′** or **lac′quer·work′** —*vt.* to coat with or as with lacquer —**lac′quer·er** *n.*

lac·ri·mal (lak′ri məl) *adj.* **1** *Anat.* designating, of, or near the glands that secrete tears **2** *alt. sp. of* LACHRYMAL (sense 1)

lac·ri·ma·tion (lak′ri mā′shən) *n.* ⟦L *lacrimatio*, a weeping < pp. of *lacrimare*, to weep < *lacrima*, TEAR[2]⟧ normal or excessive secretion or shedding of tears

lac·ri·ma·tor (lak′ri māt′ər) *n. alt. sp. of* LACHRYMATOR

lac·ri·ma·to·ry (-mə tôr′ē) *adj., n., pl.* **-ries** *alt. sp. of* LACHRYMATORY

la·crosse (lə krôs′) *n.* ⟦CdnFr < Fr *la*, the + *crosse*, a crutch, hockey stick < ML *crucia*: see CROSIER⟧ a game, similar to field hockey, in which two teams of ten men or twelve women each, using long-handled, pouched rackets, try to throw a small rubber ball into the opponents' goal: the game was first played by North American Indians

lacrosse player

lact- (lakt) *combining form* LACTO-: used before a vowel

lac·tam (lak′tam′) *n.* ⟦LACT(ONE) + AM(INO)⟧ any of a group of organic cyclic compounds containing the NHCO group in the ring, formed by the elimination of water from the amino and carboxyl groups; inner anhydride of an amino acid

lac·tase (lak′tās′) *n.* ⟦LACT(O)- + (DIAST)ASE⟧ an enzyme, present in certain yeasts and in the intestines of animals, which splits lactose into glucose and galactose

lac·tate (-tāt′) *vi.* **-tat′ed**, **-tat′ing** ⟦< L *lactatus*, pp. of *lactare*, secrete milk, suckle < *lac*: see LACTO-⟧ to secrete milk —*n.* **1** a salt of lactic acid containing the monovalent, negative radical $C_3H_5O_3$ **2** an uncharged ester of lactic acid

lac·ta·tion (lak tā′shən) *n.* ⟦LL *lactatio*: see prec.⟧ **1** the secretion of milk by a mammary gland **2** the period during which milk is secreted **3** the suckling of young —**lac·ta′tion·al** *adj.*

lac·te·al (lak′tē əl) *adj.* ⟦< L *lacteus*, milky < *lac* (see LACTO-) + -AL⟧ **1** of or like milk; milky **2** containing or carrying chyle, the milky fluid that is a product of digestion —*n.* any of the lymphatic vessels that take up this fluid from the small intestine and carry it to the thoracic duct

lac·tes·cent (lak tes′ənt) *adj.* ⟦L *lactescens*, prp. of *lactescere*, to turn into milk < *lactare*: see LACTATE⟧ **1** becoming milky **2** of a milky appearance **3** *a)* secreting milk *b)* forming or exuding a milky fluid (said of certain plants) —**lac·tes′cence** *n.*

lac·tic (lak′tik) *adj.* ⟦Fr *lactique*: see LACTO- & -IC⟧ of or obtained from milk

lactic acid a yellowish or clear, syrupy organic acid, $CH_3CHOHCOOH$, produced by the fermentation of lactose when milk sours or from sucrose and some other carbohydrates by the action of certain microorganisms: used in tanning leather, as a preservative, in the formation of plasticizers, etc.

lac·tif·er·ous (lak tif′ər əs) *adj.* ⟦LL *lactifer* < L *lac* (see fol.) + *ferre*, to BEAR[1] + -OUS⟧ **1** yielding or conveying milk **2** forming a milky fluid

lac·to- (lak′tō, -tə) ⟦< L *lac* (gen. *lactis*), milk < IE base **glak-* > GALACTIC⟧ *combining form* **1** milk [*lactometer*] **2** *Chem.* lactic acid or lactate [*lactobacillus*]

lac·to·ba·cil·lus (lak′tō bə sil′əs) *n., pl.* **-cil′li′** (-ī′) ⟦ModL < prec. + BACILLUS⟧ any of a genus (*Lactobacillus*) of bacteria that ferment milk, carbohydrates, etc., producing lactic acid and carbon dioxide: found as saprophytes or as parasites in the mouth, intestinal tract, and vagina of humans and other mammals

lac·to·fla·vin (-flā′vin) *n.* ⟦LACTO- + FLAVIN⟧ RIBOFLAVIN

lac·to·gen·ic (-jen′ik) *adj.* ⟦LACTO- + -GENIC⟧ capable of inducing milk secretion [*lactogenic* hormone]

lac·tom·e·ter (lak täm′ət ər) *n.* ⟦LACTO- + -METER⟧ a hydrometer for determining the specific gravity, and hence the richness, of milk

lac·tone (lak′tōn′) *n.* ⟦LACT(O)- + -ONE⟧ any of a group of organic cyclic esters formed by the elimination of a molecule of water from the OH and COOH groups of a molecule of a hydroxy acid

lac·to·pro·tein (lak′tō prō′tēn′, -prōt′ē in) *n.* any of the proteins found in milk

lac·tose (lak′tōs′) *n.* ⟦LACT(O)- + -OSE[1]⟧ a white, crystalline disaccharide found in milk and prepared by evaporation of the whey, leaving the crystallized sugar: used in infant foods, medicine, etc.

la·cu·na (lə kyo͞o′nə) *n., pl.* **-nas** or **-nae** (-nē) ⟦L, a ditch, hole, pool < *lacus*: see LAKE[1]⟧ **1** a space where something has been omitted or has come out; gap; hiatus; esp., a missing portion in a manuscript, text, etc. **2** *Anat., Biol.* a space, cavity, or depression; specif., any of the very small cavities in bone that are filled with bone cells

la·cu·nar (-nər) *adj.* of or having a lacuna or lacunas: also **la·cu′nal** (-nəl) —*n., pl.* **la·cu′nars** or **lac·u·nar·i·a** (lak′yo͞o ner′ē ə) ⟦L < *lacuna*: see prec.⟧ *Archit.* **1** a ceiling made up of sunken panels **2** a sunken panel in such a ceiling

la·cu·nose (-nōs′) *adj.* ⟦L *lacunosus*⟧ full of lacunas

la·cus·trine (lə kus′trin) *adj.* ⟦< Fr *lacustre* < L *lacus*, LAKE[1]⟧ **1** of or having to do with a lake or lakes **2** found or formed in lakes

lac·y (lās′ē) *adj.* **lac′i·er**, **lac′i·est** **1** of lace **2** like lace; having a delicate open pattern

lad (lad) *n.* ⟦ME *ladde* < ?⟧ **1** a boy or youth **2** [Informal] any man; fellow: familiar or endearing term

lad·a·num (lad′ə nəm) *n.* ⟦L⟧ *var. of* LABDANUM

lad·der (lad′ər) *n.* ⟦ME < OE *hlæder*, akin to Ger *leiter* < IE base **klei-*, to incline, LEAN[1]⟧ **1** *a)* a framework consisting of two parallel sidepieces connected by a series of rungs or crosspieces on which a person steps in climbing up or down *b)* *Naut.* any staircase or vertical set of steps **2** anything by means of which a person climbs or rises **3** a rising series of steps, stages, or levels [the *ladder* of success] **4** [Chiefly Brit.] a run as in a stocking —*vt., vi.* [Chiefly Brit.] to have or cause to have a ladder, or run

lad·der-back chair (lad′ər bak′) a chair with a back of two upright posts connected by horizontal slats

ladder stitch an embroidery stitch with parallel crossbars in a ladderlike design

ladder truck HOOK AND LADDER

lad·die (lad′ē) *n.* ⟦Scot, dim. of LAD⟧ [Chiefly Scot.] a young lad

lade (lād) *vt., vi.* **lad′ed**, **lad′ed** or **lad′en**, **lad′ing** ⟦ME *laden* < OE *hladan*, akin to Ger *laden* < IE base **klā-*, to set down, lay, place > LADLE, OSlav *klasti*, to load⟧ [Archaic] **1** to load **2** to dip or draw out (water, etc.) with a ladle; bail; ladle

lad·en[1] (lād′'n) *adj.* **1** loaded **2** burdened; afflicted [*laden* with sorrow]

lad·en[2] (lād′'n) *vt.* [Now Chiefly Literary] to load or burden [*ladened* with gifts]

-lad·en (lād′'n) *combining form* filled, covered, permeated, or burdened with [flower-*laden*, metaphor-*laden*, doom-*laden*]

la-di-da (lä′dē dä′) [Informal] *adj.* ⟦imitation of affected speech⟧ affected in speech, manners, etc.; pretentiously refined —*n.* **1** a la-di-da person **2** affected speech or behavior —*interj.* used to express derision in response to affectation, foppishness, etc. Also sp. **la-de-da**

ladies' room [*also* **L- r-**] a restroom for women, with washbasins and toilets

la·dies'-tress·es (lā′dēz tres′iz) *n.* any of a genus (*Spiranthes*) of wild orchids with small, white flowers arranged spirally on spikes

La·din (lə dēn′) *n.* ⟦Rhaeto-Romanic < L *Latinus*, Latin⟧ **1** the dialect of Rhaeto-Romance spoken in NE Italy and SE Switzerland **2** a native speaker of this dialect

lad·ing (lād′iŋ) *n.* ⟦LME: see LADE⟧ **1** the act of one that lades **2** a load; cargo; freight

la·di·no (lə dē′nō, -dī′-) *n.* ⟦prob. < It *Ladino*, of the Ladin-speaking area of the Tirol and Grisons < L *Latinus*, LATIN⟧ a large, vigorous strain of the white clover, often grown as a forage crop

La·di·no (lə dē′nō) *n.* **1** ⟦Judezmo *ladino* < Medieval Sp, Latin < L *latinus*⟧ JUDEZMO, specif. the earlier, literary variety of Judezmo, used chiefly for translating sacred Jewish texts **2** *pl.* **-nos** ⟦AmSp⟧ in Spanish America, a person of mixed ancestry

la·dle (lād′'l) *n.* ⟦ME *ladel* < OE *hlædel*, a ladle: see LADE⟧ **1** a long-handled spoon with a relatively large, deep bowl, for dipping out liquids **2** any similar device, as a large container for carrying and pouring molten metal —*vt.* **-dled**, **-dling** **1** to dip out or serve with or as with a ladle **2** to lift out and carry in a ladle **3** to distribute generously: with *out* —**la′dle·ful′** *n., pl.* **-fuls′** —**lad′ler** *n.*

La·do·ga (lä′dô gä′), **Lake** lake in NW Russia, near the Finnish border: largest lake in Europe: *c.* 7,000 sq mi (18,130 sq km)

la·drone (lə drōn′) *n.* ⟦Sp *ladrón* < L *latro*, hired servant, mercenary, freebooter: see LARCENY⟧ in Spanish-speaking regions of the U.S., a robber or bandit

la·dy (lād′ē) *n., pl.* **-dies** ⟦ME *lavedi* < OE *hlæfdige*, lady, mistress < *hlaf*, LOAF[1] + *-dige* < *dæge*, (bread) kneader < IE base **dheigh-*: see DOUGH⟧ **1** the mistress of a household: now obs. except in the phrase **the lady of the house** **2** a woman who has the rights, rule, or authority of a lord **3** a woman of high social position **4** a woman who is polite, refined, and well-mannered **5** any woman: as a form of address, generally regarded as a polite term when used in the pl. [welcome, *ladies* and gentlemen] and as informal when used in the sing. [hey, *lady*, move your car!] **6** [Old-fashioned] a woman with reference to the man who is her devoted attendant, lover, etc. **7** [**L-**] in Great Britain, *a)* the title of respect given to a marchioness, countess, viscountess, or baroness; to the daughter of a duke, marquis, or earl; or to the wife of a baronet, knight, or holder of the courtesy title *Lord* *b)* this title as a form of address for a woman holding the title *Lady*, now used only by servants, salespeople, etc. (preceded by *My*) 8 [**L-**] the Virgin Mary: usually with *Our* 9 [Informal] a MISTRESS (sense 4) or GIRLFRIEND (sense 1), esp. one who is cohabiting —*adj.* [Informal] being an adult female [a *lady* barber] —*SYN.* WOMAN —**the Ladies'** (or **Ladies**) [*also* **the l-**] [Informal, Chiefly Brit.] LADIES' ROOM

la·dy·bird (beetle) (-burd') ⟦short for *Our Lady's bird*⟧ LADYBUG: also **lady beetle**

Lady Bountiful ⟦after a character in Farquhar's comedy *The Beaux' Stratagem* (1707)⟧ a charitable woman, esp. one who gives ostentatiously: a humorous or sarcastic usage

la·dy·bug (-bug') *n.* ⟦see LADYBIRD⟧ any of a family (Coccinellidae) of small, roundish beetles with spotted backs, usually brightly colored: they feed chiefly on insect pests and their eggs

Lady chapel ⟦< *Our Lady* (or *Lady's*) *Chapel*⟧ a chapel, as in a cathedral or parish church, dedicated to the Virgin Mary

Lady Day ⟦< *Our Lady Day*⟧ *Brit. name for* THE ANNUNCIATION (sense 2) (see phrase at ANNUNCIATION)

la·dy·fin·ger (-fiŋ'gər) *n.* a small spongecake with a rounded, elongated shape

la·dy·fish (-fish') *n., pl.* **-fish'** or **-fish'es** (see FISH) any of various fishes; esp., a tropical tenpounder (*Elops saurus*)

la·dy-in-wait·ing (-in wāt'iŋ) *n., pl.* **la'dies-in-wait'ing** a lady of the court attending, or waiting upon, a queen or princess

lady killer [Informal] a man considered particularly attractive or seductive by women, typically such a man who aggressively seeks to seduce women: also written **la'dy·kill'er** *n.*

la·dy·like (-līk') *adj.* like, characteristic of, or suitable for a lady; refined; well-bred —*SYN.* FEMALE

la·dy·love (-luv') *n.* [Old-fashioned] a female sweetheart

Lady Luck *personification of* luck or fortune

lady of the evening a prostitute: also **lady of the night**

Lady of the Lake *Arthurian Legend* an enchantress who gives Arthur his sword, Excalibur: sometimes identified with VIVIAN

la·dy·ship (lād'ē ship') *n.* 1 the rank or position of a Lady 2 [*usually* **L-**] a title used in speaking to or of a woman holding the rank of Lady: preceded by *Your* or *Her*

lady's (*or* **ladies'**) **man** a man who is very fond of the company of women and who, because of his charm, attentiveness, and flirtatiousness, is very attractive to them

lady's room [*also* **L- r-**] LADIES' ROOM

la·dy's-slip·per (lād'ēz slip'ər) *n.* 1 CYPRIPEDIUM 2 any of various cultivated orchids whose flowers somewhat resemble a slipper Also **la'dy-slip'per**

la·dy's-smock (lād'ēz smäk') *n.* CUCKOOFLOWER (sense 1)

☆**la·dy's-thumb** (-thum') *n.* an annual plant (*Polygonum persicaria*) of the buckwheat family, with dense spikes of pinkish or purplish flowers

la·dy's-tress·es (-tres'iz) *n. alt. sp. of* LADIES'-TRESSES

lae·o·trop·ic (lē'ō träp'ik) *adj.* ⟦< Gr *laios*, left (see LEVO-) + -TROPIC⟧ spiraling to the left if viewed from the side: said as of the sinistral whorls in some gastropod shells: opposed to DEXIOTROPIC

La·er·tes (lā ur'tēz', -er'-) *n.* ⟦L < Gr *Laertēs*⟧ 1 *Gr. Myth.* the father of Odysseus 2 in Shakespeare's *Hamlet*, the brother of Ophelia

la·e·trile (lā'ə tril') *n.* ⟦*lae(vorotatory glycosidic ni)trile*⟧ any of several organic compounds derived chiefly from apricot kernels, used by some unorthodox practitioners to treat cancer

lae·vo- (lē'vō, -və) *combining form* LEVO-

La Farge (lə färzh', färj'), **John** 1835-1910; U.S. artist

La·fa·yette[1] (lä'fē et', -fā-; laf'ē-; *Fr* lȧ fȧ yet'), Marquis **de** (born *Marie Joseph Paul Yves Roch Gilbert du Motier*) 1757-1834; Fr. military officer & statesman: a general (1777-81) in the Continental army during the American Revolution

La·fa·yette[2] (laf'ē et; lä'fē-, -fā-; lə fā'it) ⟦after prec.⟧ city in SC La.

La Fa·yette (lä'fē et', -fā-; laf'ē-; *Fr* lȧ fȧ yet'), Comtesse **de** (born *Marie Madeleine Pioche de La Vergne*) 1634-93; Fr. novelist

☆**Laf·fer Curve** (laf'ər) ⟦after A. *Laffer* (b. 1940), U.S. economist, its originator⟧ [*also* **L- c-**] a graph illustrating a theory which maintains that increasing tax rates beyond a certain point causes a reduction in government revenues by discouraging production and investment

La·fitte (lȧ fēt'), **Jean** (zhän) 1780?-1826?; Fr. pirate in the Gulf of Mexico: also sp. **Laffite**

La Fol·lette (lə fäl'it), **Robert Marion** 1855-1925; U.S. legislator, reformer, & Progressive Party leader

La Fon·taine (lä' fän tān'; *Fr* lȧ fōn ten'), **Jean de** (zhän də) 1621-95; Fr. poet & writer of fables

lag[1] (lag) *vi.* **lagged, lag'ging** ⟦? akin to obs. Dan *lakke*, to go slowly⟧ 1 *a)* to fall, move, or stay behind; loiter; linger *b)* to move or develop more slowly than expected, desired, etc.; be retarded in motion, development, etc. 2 to become gradually less intense, strong, etc.; wane; flag 3 in the game of marbles, to toss a marble toward a line marked on the ground to determine the order of play 4 *Billiards* to strike the cue ball so that it rebounds from the far rail to stop as close as possible to the near rail or the string line: done to decide the order of play —*n.* 1 a falling behind or being retarded in motion, development, etc. 2 the amount of such falling behind; interval between two related events, processes, etc. 3 a lagging, as in billiards and marbles 4 [Archaic] one that lags, or is last

lag[2] (lag) *n.* ⟦prob. < Scand, as in Swed *lagg*, barrel stave < IE base **leu-*, to cut off > L *luere*, to cleanse, purge⟧ a strip of insulating material used for covering boilers, cylinders, etc. —*vt.* **lagged, lag'ging** to cover with insulating material

lag[3] (lag) [Slang, Chiefly Brit.] *vt.* **lagged, lag'ging** ⟦< ?⟧ 1 to imprison 2 to arrest —*n.* 1 a convict or ex-convict: often **old lag** 2 a term of imprisonment

lag·an (lag'ən) *n.* ⟦< OFr, goods washed up by the sea < ? base of ON *leggja*, to lie⟧ *Maritime Law* goods cast overboard, as in a storm, with a buoy attached to identify the owner

lag bolt LAG SCREW

Lag b'O·mer (läg' bō'mər) ⟦Heb *lag b'ōmer*, 33d (day) of the omer (the count of 49 days from the second day of Passover to the first day of Shabuoth)⟧ a Jewish holiday observed on the 18th day of Iyar

☆**la·ger** (lä'gər) *n.* ⟦Ger *lagerbier*, lit., store beer < *lager*, storehouse (akin to OE *leger*: see LAIR) + *bier*, BEER⟧ a type of beer stored at a low temperature for aging after it has been brewed: often **lager beer**

La·ger·kvist (lä'gər kvist'; *Swed* lä'gər kvist'), **Pär (Fabian)** (par) 1891-1974; Swed. poet, novelist, & playwright

La·ger·löf (lä'gər luf'), **Sel·ma (Ottiliana Lovisa)** (sel'mä) 1858-1940; Swed. novelist

lag·gard (lag'ərd) *n.* ⟦< LAG[1] + -ARD⟧ a slow person, esp. one who is always falling behind; loiterer —*adj.* slow or late in doing things; falling behind —**lag'gard·ly** *adv., adj.*

lag·ger (lag'ər) *n.* a person or thing that lags

lag·ging (lag'iŋ) *n.* ⟦< LAG[2] + -ING⟧ 1 thermal insulation for wrapping around pipes, boilers, etc. 2 a wood framework to support an arch while it is being built 3 *Mining* planks or timber used to prevent rocks from falling in a shaft or drift

☆**la·gniappe** or **la·gnappe** (lan yap', lan'yap') *n.* ⟦Creole < Fr *la*, the + Sp *ñapa*, lagniappe < Quechuan *yapa*⟧ 1 [Chiefly South] a small present given to a customer with a purchase 2 a gratuity or the like

lag·o·morph (lag'ə môrf') *n.* ⟦< Gr *lagōs*, hare + -MORPH⟧ any of an order (Lagomorpha) of plant-eating mammals characterized by a short tail and two pairs of upper incisors, one behind the other, and consisting of the rabbits, hares, and pikas —**lag'o·mor'phic** *adj.*

la·goon (lə go͞on') *n.* ⟦< Fr *lagune* & It *laguna* < L *lacuna*: see LACUNA⟧ 1 a shallow lake or pond, esp. one connected with a larger body of water 2 the area of water enclosed by a circular coral reef, or atoll 3 an area of shallow salt water separated from the sea by sand dunes

La·gos (lā'gäs', -gəs, -gōs') seaport in Nigeria, on the Bight of Benin: former capital

La·grange (lȧ gränzh), Comte **Jo·seph Louis de** (zhō zef lwē' də) 1736-1813; Fr. mathematician & astronomer

lag screw a wood screw with a boltlike head

La Guar·di·a (lə gwär'dē ə), **Fi·o·rel·lo H(enry)** (fē'ə rel'ō) 1882-1947; U.S. political leader: mayor of New York (1934-45)

la·har (lä'här', lä här') *n.* ⟦Javanese⟧ 1 a mudflow down the side of a volcano, containing pieces of hardened lava, ash, etc. 2 the deposit of such a mudflow

lah-di-dah or **lah-de-dah** (lä'dē dä') *adj., n., interj. alt. sp. of* LA-DI-DA

La·hore (lə hôr') city in NE Pakistan

la·ic (lā'ik) *adj.* ⟦LL(Ec) *laicus*, not priestly < Gr *laikos* < *laos*, the people⟧ of the laity; secular; lay: also **la'i·cal** (-ə kəl) —*n.* a layman —**la·i'ci·ty** *n.*

la·i·cism (lā'ə siz'əm) *n.* policy and principles opposing clericalism and restricting political influence and power to the laity

la·i·cize (-sīz') *vt.* **-cized', -ciz'ing** ⟦LAIC + -IZE⟧ 1 to reduce (a cleric) to the lay state; make a layman of 2 to remove clerical influence from; restrict to laymen; secularize —**la'i·ci·za'tion** *n.*

laid (lād) *vt., vi. pt. & pp. of* LAY[1] —**get laid** [Slang] to have sexual intercourse: somewhat vulgar

☆**laid-back** (lād'bak') *adj.* [Informal] relaxed, calm, easygoing, etc.; not frenetic, hurried, or forced

laid paper paper having evenly spaced parallel lines watermarked in it

laigh (lākh) *adj., adv.* [Scot.] low

lain (lān) *vi. pp. of* LIE[1]

Laing (laŋ), **R(onald) D(avid)** 1927-89; Brit. psychiatrist

lair (ler) *n.* ⟦ME *lier* < OE *leger*, lit., lying place, hence bed, couch (in Du, a camp) < Gmc base (**leg-*) of *licgan*, to LIE[1]⟧ 1 a bed or resting place of a wild animal; den 2 any place of refuge or for hiding —*vi.* to go to, rest in, or have a lair

laird (lerd; *Scot* lārd) *n.* ⟦Scot form of LORD⟧ in Scotland, a landowner, esp. a wealthy one —**laird'ly** *adj.*

lais·sez faire (les'ā fer', lez'-) ⟦Fr, lit., let (people) do (as they please)⟧ the policy or practice of letting people act without interference or direction; noninterference; specif., the policy of letting the owners of industry and business fix the rules of competition, the conditions of labor, etc. as they please, without governmental regulation or control: also sp. **lais'ser faire'** —**lais'sez-faire'** *adj.*

lais·sez-pas·ser (le sā pȧ sā') *n.* ⟦Fr, let (someone) pass⟧ a pass authorizing access to a place, travel in a country, etc.

la·i·ty (lā'i tē) *n., pl.* **-ties** ⟦LAY[3] + -ITY⟧ 1 all the people not included among the clergy; laymen collectively 2 all the people not belonging to a given profession

La·ius (lā'yəs) *n.* ⟦L < Gr *Laios*⟧ *Gr. Myth.* a king of Thebes and the father of OEDIPUS

lake[1] (lāk) *n.* ⟦ME < OE *lacu* & OFr *lac*, both < L *lacus*, a basin, lake < IE base *laku-, accumulation of water, pond, lake > LOCH, OE *lagu*, water, sea⟧ **1** an inland body of usually fresh water, larger than a pool or pond, generally formed by some obstruction in the course of flowing water **2** a pool of oil or other liquid

lake² (lāk) ***n.*** ⟦Fr *laque*: see LAC⟧ **1** *a)* a dark-red pigment prepared from cochineal *b)* its color **2** an insoluble coloring compound precipitated from a solution of a dye by adding a metallic salt, which acts as a mordant: used in applying dyes to cloth and in making paints, printing inks, etc.

Lake (lāk), **Simon** 1866-1945; U.S. engineer & naval architect

Lake Charles ⟦after *Charles* A. Sallier (1776?-1834?), an early settler⟧ city in SW La.

Lake District (*or* Country) lake & mountain region in Cumbria county, NW England: see CUMBERLAND, WESTMORLAND, LANCASHIRE

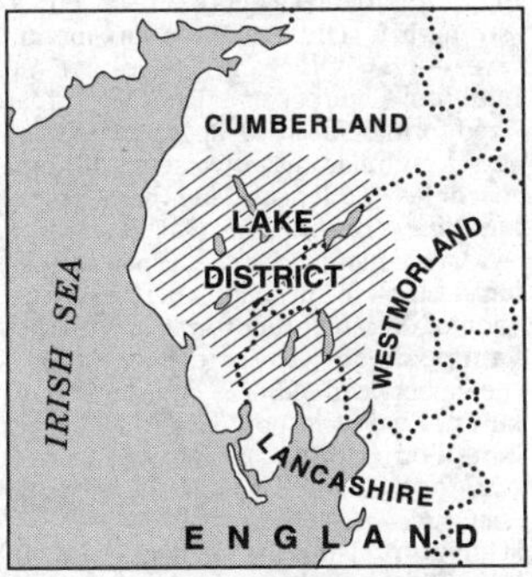

lake dwelling a dwelling built on wooden piles rising above the surface of a lake or marshy land; esp., such a structure built in prehistoric times —**lake dweller**

☆**lake-ef·fect** (lāk′ə fekt′) ***adj.*** caused or greatly influenced by the moist air above a large lake [*lake-effect* storms near Chicago]

lake·front (lāk′frunt′) ***n.*** the land along the shore of a lake —***adj.*** near, at, or of the lakefront [a *lakefront* stadium]

☆**lake herring** a trout (*Coregonus artedii*) of the Great Lakes

Lake·land terrier (lāk′lənd) ⟦after the LAKE DISTRICT, where orig. bred⟧ any of a breed of terrier with a long head, a square build, and a dense, wiry coat

Lake District
(former county boundaries)

Lake of the Woods ⟦descriptive⟧ lake in N Minn. & in Ontario & Manitoba, Canada: 1,485 sq mi (3,846 sq km)

Lake poets the English poets Wordsworth, Coleridge, and Southey, who lived in the Lake District

☆**lak·er** (lāk′ər) ***n.*** **1** a fish, esp. a trout, found in lakes **2** a ship operating on lakes, esp. the Great Lakes

lake·shore (lāk′shôr′) ***n., adj.*** LAKEFRONT: also **lake′side′**

lake trout ☆**1** a large gray trout (*Salvelinus namaycush*) of deep lakes of the N U.S. and Canada **2** any of several other species of trout found in lakes

Lake·wood (lāk′wood′) ⟦descriptive⟧ city in NC Colo.: suburb of Denver

lakh (lak) ***n.*** ⟦Hindi *lākh* < Sans *lakṣa*⟧ in India and Pakistan, *a)* the sum of 100,000 (said specifically of rupees) *b)* any indefinitely large number

La·ko·ta (lə kōt′ə) ***n.*** ⟦self-designation in Lakota⟧ **1** *pl.* **-tas** or **-ta** a member of the westernmost branch of the Dakotas **2** the group of dialects of Dakota spoken by the Lakotas

Lak·shad·weep (luk shäd′wēp′) territory of India comprising the Laccadive, Minicoy, and Amindivi islands: 12.4 sq mi (32 sq km)

lak·y (lāk′ē) ***adj.*** of the dark-red color of the pigment LAKE²

La La·gu·na (lä lə gōō′nə) city in Tenerife, Canary Islands

☆**la-la land** (lä′lä′) ⟦after ? fol.⟧ a fanciful, impractical state of mind: also written **LaLa Land**

☆**La-La Land** (lä′lä′) ⟦redupl. of *La* < LA (abbrev. of *Los Angeles*); infl. ? by *la-la*, conventional song refrain⟧ *name for* Los Angeles: often used to symbolize the entertainment industry centered there: often written **lala land**

☆**la·la·pa·loo·za** or **lal·la·pa·loo·za** (läl′ə pə lōō′zə) ***n.*** [Slang] *alt. sp. of* LOLLAPALOOZA

la·lique (la lēk′, lä-; *Fr* lȧ-) ***n.*** ⟦after R. *Lalique* (1860-1945), Fr jeweler & designer⟧ [*also* **L-**] an art nouveau style of cut glass or crystal with figures of animals, flowers, etc. in relief

Lal·lan (lal′ən) ***adj.*** [Scot.] of the Lowlands of Scotland

Lal·lans (lal′ənz) ***n.*** the English dialect of the Scottish Lowlands, esp. in its written form: also **Lal′lan**

lal·la·tion (la lā′shən) ***n.*** ⟦< pp. of L *lallare*, to sing a lullaby⟧ LAMBDACISM

☆**lal·ly·gag** (lä′lē gag′) ***vi.*** **-gagged′**, **-gag′ging** [Informal] *alt. sp. of* LOLLYGAG

La·lo (lȧ lō′), **É·douard (Victor Antoine)** (ā dwȧr′) 1823-92; Fr. composer

lam¹ (lam) ***vt., vi.*** **lammed**, **lam′ming** ⟦< Scand, as in ON *lemja*, lit., to lame: see LAME¹⟧ [Old Slang] to beat; hit; strike

☆**lam²** (lam) [Slang] ***n.*** ⟦< ? prec.: cf. slang *beat it!*⟧ headlong flight, usually to escape punishment for a crime —***vi.*** **lammed**, **lam′ming** to flee; escape —**on the lam** in flight, as from the police —**take it on the lam** to make a getaway; escape

Lam *abbrev. Bible* Lamentations

la·ma (lä′mə) ***n.*** ⟦Tibetan *blama* (with silent *b*), a chief, high priest⟧ a priest or monk in Lamaism: cf. DALAI LAMA

La·ma·ism (lä′mə iz′əm) ***n.*** a form of Buddhism practiced in Tibet and Mongolia, characterized by elaborate ritual and a strong hierarchal organization —**La′ma·ist** ***adj., n.*** —**La′ma·is′tic** ***adj.***

La·marck (lə märk′; *Fr* lȧ mȧrk′), Chevalier **de** (born *Jean Baptiste Pierre Antoine de Monet*) 1744-1829; Fr. naturalist: see LAMARCKISM

La·marck·i·an (lə märk′ē ən) ***adj.*** of or according to Lamarckism —***n.*** an adherent of Lamarckism

La·marck·ism (lə märk′iz′əm) ***n.*** a theory of organic evolution advanced by Lamarck that claimed acquired characters can be inherited: sometimes **La·marck′i·an·ism′**

La·mar·tine (lam′ər tēn′; *Fr* lȧ mȧr tēn′), **Al·phonse Ma·rie Louis de (Prat de)** (ȧl fōns mȧ rē lwē′ də) 1790-1869; Fr. poet

la·ma·ser·y (lä′mə ser′ē) ***n.***, *pl.* **-ser′ies** a monastery of lamas

La·maze (lə mäz′) ***n.*** ⟦after F. *Lamaze* (1891-1957), Fr physician who developed it⟧ a training program in NATURAL CHILDBIRTH, emphasizing breathing control and relaxation during labor together with the presence and encouraging assistance of the father

lamb (lam) ***n.*** ⟦ME < OE, akin to Ger *lamm* (OHG *lamb*) < IE **lonbhos* (< base **el-*: see ELK) > Goth *lamb*⟧ **1** a young sheep **2** the flesh of a young sheep, used as food **3** lambskin **4** a gentle or innocent person, particularly a child **5** a loved person; dear **6** a person easily tricked or outwitted, as an inexperienced speculator —***vi.*** to give birth: said of a ewe —**the Lamb** Jesus

Lamb (lam) **1 Charles** (pen name *Elia*) 1775-1834; Eng. essayist & critic **2 Mary (Ann)** 1764-1847; Eng. writer: sister of Charles

lam·ba·da (läm bä′də) ***n.*** a lively dance for couples, originally of South America, with sensuous movements of the lower body

lam·baste (lam bāst′, -bast′) ***vt.*** **-bast′ed**, **-bast′ing** ⟦LAM¹ + BASTE³⟧ [Informal] **1** to beat soundly; thrash **2** to scold or denounce severely Also sp. **lam·bast′**

lamb·da (lam′də) ***n.*** ⟦Gr < Sem, as in Heb *lāmedh*, LAMED⟧ **1** the eleventh letter of the Greek alphabet (Λ, λ) **2** *Particle Physics* an uncharged hyperon with a mass of *c.* 1,115.68 MeV/c, which is *c.* 2,183 times the mass of an electron: it decays very rapidly, usually into a nucleon and a pion: sometimes called **lambda particle** or **lambda hyperon**

lamb·da·cism (lam′də siz′əm) ***n.*** ⟦LL *lambdacismus* < Gr *lambdakismos* < *lambdakizein*, to pronounce *l* imperfectly < *lambda*, prec.⟧ **1** substitution of the sound (l) for another sound, esp. (r) **2** substitution of another sound, esp. (r), for (l)

lamb·doid (-doid′) ***adj.*** ⟦Gr *lambdoeidēs*: see LAMBDA & -OID⟧ shaped like the Greek lambda (λ); specif., designating the suture that connects the occipital and the parietal bones of the skull

lam·bent (lam′bənt) ***adj.*** ⟦L *lambens*, prp. of *lambere*, to lick, lap < IE base **lab-* > LAP²⟧ **1** playing lightly over a surface; flickering: said of a flame, etc. **2** giving off a soft glow [a *lambent* sky] **3** playing lightly and gracefully over a subject: said of wit, humor, etc. —**lam′ben·cy** ***n.*** —**lam′bent·ly** ***adv.***

lam·bert (lam′bərt) ***n.*** ⟦after J. H. *Lambert* (1728-77), Ger mathematician, physicist, & philosopher⟧ the basic unit of luminance in the CGS system, equal to the brightness of an ideal surface that radiates or reflects light at the rate of one lumen per square centimeter (929.023 foot-candles or 10,000 lux or $1/\pi$ candela per square centimeter): abbrev. *L*

Lam·bert (conformal conic) projection (lam′bərt) ⟦see prec.⟧ a map projection in which all meridians are represented by straight lines radiating from a common point outside the mapped area and the parallels are represented by arcs or circles whose center is this same common point: this projection may have one or two standard parallels that maintain exact scale, while the scale varies along the meridians, and, since the meridians and parallels intersect at right angles, angles between locations on the surface of the earth are correctly shown

Lam·beth (lam′bəth) borough of S Greater London, England: site of the official residence (**Lambeth Palace**) of the archbishops of Canterbury since 1197

lam·bic (lam′bik) ***n.*** ⟦Fr < Dutch *lambiek*, *lambik* < ? alteration of *Lembeek*, name of a village near Brussels⟧ a beer of Belgian origin, made from malted barley and unmalted wheat, that is fermented by naturally occurring airborne yeast and often flavored with fruit

lamb·ing (lam′iŋ) ***n.*** the period when lambs are born on a farm, ranch, etc.

lamb·kill (lam′kil′) ***n.*** ☆SHEEP LAUREL

lamb·kin (lam′kin) ***n.*** a little lamb: sometimes applied to a child or young person as a term of affection

lamb·like (-līk′) ***adj.*** like, or having qualities attributed to, a lamb; gentle, meek, innocent, etc.

Lamb of God Jesus: so called by analogy with the paschal lamb: John 1:29, 36

lam·bre·quin (lam′brə kin′, -bər-) ***n.*** ⟦Fr < Du **lamperkin* < *lamper*, a veil + *-ken*, -KIN⟧ **1** a fabric covering for a knight's helmet ☆**2** a drapery hanging from a shelf or covering the upper part of a window or doorway

Lam·brus·co (läm brōōs′kō, lam-; -brōōs′-) ***n.*** ⟦It, name of grape from which it is made < L *labruscum*, fruit of the wild vine: see LABRUSCA⟧ [*sometimes* **l-**] a red wine, usually sparkling, from N Italy

lamb·skin (lam′skin′) ***n.*** **1** the skin of a lamb, esp. with the fleece left on it **2** leather or parchment made from the skin of a lamb

lamb's-quar·ters (lamz′kwôrt′ərz) ***n.*** an annual weed (*Chenopodium album*) of the goosefoot family, with whitened or mealy leaves and dense clusters of small green flowers: the leaves are edible

lambs·wool (lamz′wool′) ***n.*** **1** very soft wool shorn from lambs **2** a soft, lightweight, resilient yarn or fabric made of this wool, used for making high-quality sweaters, scarves, blankets, etc. Sometimes written **lamb's wool**

lame¹ (lām) ***adj.*** ⟦ME < OE *lama*, akin to Ger *lahm*, ON *lami* < IE base **lem-*, to break > Russ *lomat′*, to break⟧ **1** crippled; disabled; esp., having an injured leg or foot that makes one limp **2** stiff and very painful [a *lame* back] **3** [Informal] weak, unconvincing, inadequate, etc. [a *lame* excuse]

☆4 [Slang] inept, ineffectual, pathetic, etc. —*vt.* **lamed, lam′ing** to make lame ➥Sense 4 is often, and sense 3 and the phrase are now sometimes, regarded as offensive —**the lame** those who are crippled by an injured or deformed leg or foot —**lame′ly** *adv.* —**lame′ness** *n.*

lame[2] (lām; *Fr* läm) *n.* ⟦Fr < L *lamina*: see LAMINA⟧ **1** a thin metal plate **2** [*pl.*] the thin, overlapping metal plates in a piece of armor

la·mé (la mā′, lä-) *n.* ⟦Fr, laminated < *lame*: see prec.⟧ a fabric of silk, wool, or cotton interwoven with metallic threads, as of gold or silver

lame·brain (lām′brān′) *n.* [Informal] a slow-witted or stupid person; dolt; numskull —**lame′brained′** *adj.*

la·med (lä′mid) *n.* ⟦Heb *lāmedh*, lit., a whip or club⟧ the twelfth letter of the Hebrew alphabet (ל)

lame duck 1 a disabled, ineffectual, or helpless person or thing ☆**2** *a)* an elected official whose term extends beyond the time of the election at which he or she was not reelected *b)* an elected official near the end of his or her term who is not seeking reelection and is therefore regarded as having little remaining influence

la·mel·la (lə mel′ə) *n., pl.* **-lae** (-ē) or **-las** ⟦L, dim. of *lamina*: see LAMINA⟧ a thin, platelike part, layer, organ, or structure; specif., *a)* one of the layers of bone around a Haversian canal *b)* one of the two plates forming a gill in bivalve mollusks *c)* the gill of an agaric, as a mushroom *d) Cytology* MIDDLE LAMELLA —**la·mel′lar** *adj.*

lam·el·late (lam′ə lāt′, lə mel′āt′) *adj.* ⟦ModL *lamellatus*⟧ **1** having, consisting of, arranged in, or resembling a lamella or lamellae **2** LAMELLIFORM Also **lam′el·lat′ed**

la·mel·li- (lə mel′i, -mel′ə) *combining form* of, like, or consisting of a lamella or lamellae *[lamelliform]*

la·mel·li·branch (lə mel′i braŋk′) *n.* ⟦< ModL *Lamellibranchia*, the class name: see prec. & BRANCHIAE⟧ BIVALVE —*adj.* designating or of a bivalve mollusk: also **la·mel′li·bran′chi·ate** (-braŋ′kē it, -āt′)

la·mel·li·form (-fôrm′) *adj.* having the form of a lamella

la·ment (lə ment′) *vi.* ⟦Fr *lamenter* < L *lamentari* < *lamentum*, a mourning, wailing < IE echoic base **lā-* > Arm *lam*, I weep⟧ to feel deep sorrow or express it as by weeping or wailing; mourn; grieve —*vt.* **1** to feel or express deep sorrow for; mourn or grieve for **2** to regret deeply —*n.* **1** an outward expression of sorrow; lamentation; wail **2** a literary or musical composition, as an elegy or dirge, mourning some death or calamity

la·ment·a·ble (lə men′tə bəl, lam′ən tə bəl) *adj.* ⟦ME < MFr < L *lamentabilis*⟧ **1** to be lamented; grievous; deplorable; distressing **2** [Now Rare] expressing sorrow; mournful —**la·ment′a·bly** *adv.*

lam·en·ta·tion (lam′ən tā′shən) *n.* the act of lamenting; outward expression of grief; esp., a weeping or wailing

Lam·en·ta·tions (-shənz) *n.* ⟦LL(Ec) *Lamentationes*, transl. in Vulg. for Gr *thrēnoi*, in LXX⟧ *Bible* a book traditionally ascribed to Jeremiah, lamenting the destruction of Jerusalem: abbrev. *La, Lam*, or *Lm*

la·ment·ed (lə ment′id) *adj.* mourned for: usually said of someone dead —**la·ment′ed·ly** *adv.*

la·mi·a (lā′mē ə) *n.* ⟦ME *lamya* < L *lamia* < Gr; akin to *lamos*, abyss < IE base **lem-*, with gaping mouth > L *lemures*, ghosts (see LEMUR), Welsh *llef*, voice⟧ **1** *Class. Myth.* any of a class of monsters, half woman and half serpent, supposed to lure people, esp. children, in order to suck their blood **2** *Folklore* a female demon or vampire

lam·i·na (lam′i nə) *n., pl.* **-nae′** (-nē′) or **-nas** ⟦L, thin piece of metal or wood < ? IE **(s)tlamen*, a spreading out < base **stel-*, to spread⟧ **1** a thin flake, scale, or layer, as of metal or animal tissue **2** the flat, expanded part of a leaf; blade, as distinguished from the petiole

lam·i·na·ble (lam′i nə bəl) *adj.* that can be laminated

lam·i·nar (lam′i nər) *adj.* composed of, arranged in, or like laminae: also **lam′i·nal** (-nəl)

laminar flow the regular, continuous, smooth movement of a fluid

lam·i·nar·i·a (lam′i ner′ē ə) *n.* ⟦ModL < L *lamina*: see LAMINA⟧ any of a genus (*Laminaria*) of marine kelp having fluted, ribbonlike blades attached at one end to a stalk and holdfast

lam·i·nate (lam′i nāt′; *for adj. & n.*, -nit, -nāt′) *vt.* **-nat′ed, -nat′ing** ⟦< ModL *laminatus* < L *lamina*: see LAMINA⟧ **1** to form or press into a thin sheet or layer **2** to separate into laminae **3** to cover with or bond to one or more thin layers, as of clear plastic **4** to make by building up in layers —*vi.* to split into laminae —*adj.* LAMINATED —*n.* something made by laminating —**lam′i·na′tor** *n.*

lam·i·nat·ed (-nāt′id) *adj.* **1** composed of or built in thin sheets or layers, as of fabric, wood, plastic, etc., that have been bonded or pressed together, sometimes under heat **2** covered with a thin protective layer, as of clear plastic

lam·i·na·tion (lam′i nā′shən) *n.* **1** a laminating or being laminated **2** a laminated structure; something built up in layers **3** a thin layer

lam·i·nec·to·my (lam′i nek′tə mē) *n., pl.* **-mies** ⟦LAMIN(A) + -ECTOMY⟧ the surgical removal of all or part of the bony arch of a spinal vertebra

lam·i·nin (lam′i nin) *n.* ⟦LAMIN(A) + -IN[1]⟧ *Biochem.* a large glycoprotein that binds epithelial cells to connective tissue

lam·i·ni·tis (lam′i nīt′is) *n.* ⟦ModL: see -ITIS⟧ an inflammation of laminae in a horse's hoof

Lam·mas (lam′əs) *n.* ⟦ME *lammasse* < OE *hlammæsse*, for *hlafmæsse*, lit., loaf mass, bread feast: see LOAF[1] & MASS[1]⟧ **1** a harvest festival formerly held in England on Aug. 1, when bread baked from the first crop of wheat was consecrated at Mass **2** this day (**Lammas Day**) or this time (**Lam′mas·tide′**) of the year

lam·mer·gei·er or **lam·mer·gey·er** (lam′ər gī′ər) *n.* ⟦Ger *lämmergeier* < *lämmer*, pl. of *lamm*, LAMB + *geier*, vulture, akin to *gier*, greed < IE base **ghī-*, var. of *ghē-* > GAPE⟧ a very large Old World vulture (*Gypaetus barbatus*) with grayish-black plumage streaked with white and a tuft of bristles over the nostrils and under the bill; bearded vulture

L'A·mour (lə moor′), **Louis** (born *Louis Dearborn LaMoore*) 1908-88; U.S. writer of westerns

lamp (lamp) *n.* ⟦ME *lampe* < OFr < VL *lampade* < L *lampas* (gen. *lampadis*) < Gr < *lampein*, to shine < IE base **lap-* > Latvian *lāpa*, torch⟧ **1** a container with a wick for burning oil, alcohol, etc. to produce light or heat: the wick is often enclosed in a glass tube or chimney, to protect the flame **2** a gas jet, lightbulb, etc. for producing light or heat **3** a holder, stand, or frame, often decorative and typically including a lampshade, for supporting such a gas jet or for holding a lightbulb **4** a source of knowledge, wisdom, or spiritual strength **5** [Old Poet.] the sun, moon, a star, etc. **6** [*pl.*] [Old Slang] the eyes —*vt.* ☆[Old Slang] to look at

lam·pas[1] (lam′pəs) *n.* ⟦Fr < OFr, throat: ? akin to *lamper*, to guzzle (nasalized form of *laper*, to lap), prob. < Gmc **lapian* < IE echoic base **lab-*: see LAP[2]⟧ an inflammatory disease of horses, in which the roof of the mouth becomes swollen: also **lam′pers** (-pərz)

lam·pas[2] (lam′pəs) *n.* ⟦ME *laumpas*, prob. < MDu *lampers*⟧ woven cloth with ornamental designs, esp. a silk cloth like damask

lamp·black (lamp′blak′) *n.* fine soot produced by the incomplete combustion of oils and other forms of carbon: used as a pigment in paint, ink, etc.

Lam·pe·du·sa (läm′pə do͞os′ə, -do͞oz′ə) Italian island in the Mediterranean, between Malta & Tunisia: 8 sq mi (21 sq km)

lam·per eel (lam′pər) ⟦Eng dial. *lamper*, var. of LAMPREY⟧ LAMPREY

lam·pi·on (lam′pē ən) *n.* ⟦Fr < It *lampione* < *lampa*, a lamp < OFr *lampe*, LAMP⟧ a small oil lamp, usually with a colored glass chimney, formerly used as for a carriage light

lamp·light (lamp′līt′) *n.* light given off by a lamp

lamp·light·er (-līt′ər) *n.* **1** [Historical] a person whose work is lighting and extinguishing gas street lamps ☆**2** a roll of paper, a wood splinter, etc. used to light lamps

lam·poon (lam po͞on′) *n.* ⟦Fr *lampon* < *lampons*, let us drink (refrain in a drinking song) < *lamper*, to guzzle: see LAMPAS[1]⟧ a piece of satirical writing, usually attacking or ridiculing someone —*vt.* to attack or ridicule by means of a lampoon —**SYN.** CARICATURE —**lam·poon′er** *n.*, **lam·poon′ist** —**lam·poon′er·y** *n.*

lamp·post (lamp′pōst′) *n.* a post supporting a street lamp

lam·prey (lam′prē) *n., pl.* **-preys** ⟦ME *lampreie* < OFr < ML *lampreda*⟧ any of an order (Petromyzoniformes) of jawless fishes with a funnel-shaped mouth surrounded by rasping teeth with which it bores into the flesh of other fishes to suck their blood

lamp·shade (lamp′shād′) *n.* a partial, often decorative cover on a lamp, designed to direct or diffuse the light given off by the bulb or flame

lamp shell ⟦from its resemblance to an ancient Roman oil lamp⟧ any of various brachiopods

LAN (lan) *n.* LOCAL AREA NETWORK

☆**la·na·i** (lə nä′ē, lə nī′; lä-) *n.* ⟦Haw *lānai*⟧ a veranda or open-sided living room of a kind found in Hawaii

La·na·i (lä nä′ē, lə nī′; lə-) ⟦Haw *Lā-na'i*, lit., day of conquest < Proto-Polynesian **la'ā*, day + **ngaki*, conquer⟧ one of the Hawaiian Islands, west of Maui: 141 sq mi (365 sq km)

Lan·ark (lan′ərk) former county of SC Scotland: also **Lan′ark·shire′** (-shir′, -shər)

la·nate (lā′nāt′) *adj.* ⟦L *lanatus*, woolly < *lana*, WOOL⟧ *Biol.* having a woolly or hairy covering or appearance

Lan·ca·shire (laŋ′kə shir′) county on the NW coast of England: 1,185 sq mi (3,069 sq km)

Lan·cas·ter (laŋ′kə stər; *for 3 & 4 also*, laŋ′kas′tər) **1** city in NW England; county seat of Lancashire **2** LANCASHIRE **3** ⟦prob. after a railroad official⟧ city in SW Calif.: suburb of Los Angeles

Lan·cas·tri·an (laŋ kas′trē ən) *adj.* **1** of the English royal house of Lancaster **2** of Lancaster or Lancashire or its people —*n.* **1** a member or follower of the house of Lancaster, esp. in the Wars of the Roses **2** a person born or living in Lancaster or Lancashire

lance (lans, läns) *n.* ⟦OFr < L *lancea*, light spear, lance, orig. Spanish lance < Celt⟧ **1** a thrusting weapon consisting of a long wooden shaft with a sharp metal spearhead **2** LANCER **3** any sharp instrument resembling a lance, as a fish spear **4** a surgical lancet —*vt.* **lanced, lanc′ing 1** to attack or pierce with or as with a lance **2** to cut open (a boil, etc.) with or as with a lancet

lance corporal ⟦< obs. *lance(-pesade)*, lance corporal (< MFr *lance pessade*, infantry officer under the rank of corporal < It *lancia spezzata*, lit., broken lance) + CORPORAL[1]⟧ **1** *Brit. Army* a private acting temporarily as a corporal ☆**2** *U.S. Marine Corps* an enlisted person ranking below a corporal and above a private first class

lance·let (lans′lit) *n.* ⟦LANCE + -LET⟧ CEPHALOCHORDATE

Lan·ce·lot (län′sə lät′, -lət) *n.* ⟦OFr, double dim. < *Lance* < OHG *Lanzo*, lit., landed < *lant*, land⟧ *Arthurian Legend* the most celebrated of the Knights of the Round Table, and the lover of Guinevere

lan·ce·o·late (lan′sē ə lit, -lāt′) *adj.* ⟦LL *lanceolatus* < *lanceola*, dim. of L *lancea*: see LANCE⟧ narrow and tapering like the head of a lance, as certain leaves

lanc·er (lan′sər) *n.* ⟦Fr *lancier* < LL *lancearius*⟧ **1** a cavalry soldier armed with a lance **2** a member of a cavalry regiment that was originally or traditionally armed with lances

lanc·ers (lan′sərz) *n.* ⟦< prec.⟧ 1 a 19th-cent. quadrille 2 music for this
lan·cet (lan′sit) *n.* ⟦ME *lancettis*, pl. < OFr *lancette*, dim. of *lance*, LANCE⟧ 1 a small, pointed surgical knife, usually two-edged, used for making small incisions, skin punctures, etc. 2 *a)* LANCET ARCH *b)* LANCET WINDOW
lancet arch *Archit.* a narrow, sharply pointed arch
lan·cet·ed (-id) *adj.* having lancet arches or windows
lancet window a tall, narrow window having a lancet arch

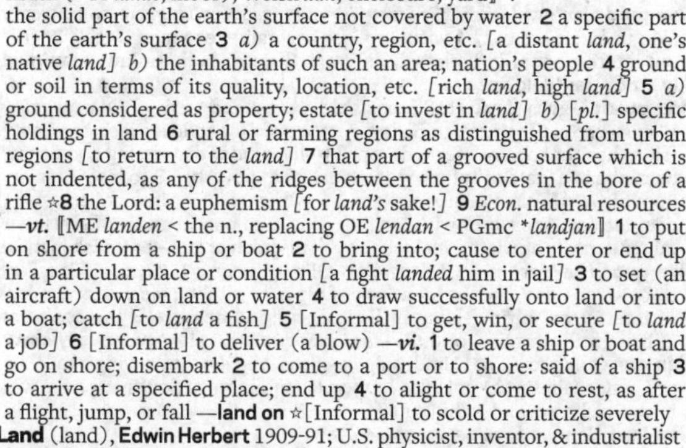
window with lancet arch

lance·wood (lans′wood′) *n.* 1 a tough, elastic wood used for shafts, fishing rods, billiard cues, etc. 2 any of various tropical trees yielding such wood; esp., a tree (*Oxandra lanceolata*) of the custard-apple family
Lan·chow (lan′chou′; *Chin* län′jō′) *a former transliteration of* LANZHOU
lan·ci·form (lan′si fôrm′) *adj.* ⟦< LANCE + -FORM⟧ narrow and pointed, like the head of a lance
lan·ci·nate (-nāt′) *vt.* **-nat′ed, -nat′ing** ⟦< L *lancinatus*, pp. of *lancinare*, to tear, akin to *lacer*: see LACERATE⟧ to stab, pierce, or tear: now rare except in medical use [*a lancinating* pain]
land (land) *n.* ⟦ME < OE, akin to OHG *lant* < IE base **lendh-*, unoccupied land, heath, steppe > Bret *lann*, heath (> Fr *lande*, moor), Welsh *llan*, enclosure, yard⟧ 1 the solid part of the earth's surface not covered by water 2 a specific part of the earth's surface 3 *a)* a country, region, etc. [a distant *land*, one's native *land*] *b)* the inhabitants of such an area; nation's people 4 ground or soil in terms of its quality, location, etc. [rich *land*, high *land*] 5 *a)* ground considered as property; estate [to invest in *land*] *b)* [*pl.*] specific holdings in land 6 rural or farming regions as distinguished from urban regions [to return to the *land*] 7 that part of a grooved surface which is not indented, as any of the ridges between the grooves in the bore of a rifle ☆8 the Lord: a euphemism [for *land's* sake!] 9 *Econ.* natural resources —*vt.* ⟦ME *landen* < the n., replacing OE *lendan* < PGmc **landjan*⟧ 1 to put on shore from a ship or boat 2 to bring into; cause to enter or end up in a particular place or condition [a fight *landed* him in jail] 3 to set (an aircraft) down on land or water 4 to draw successfully onto land or into a boat; catch [to *land* a fish] 5 [Informal] to get, win, or secure [to *land* a job] 6 [Informal] to deliver (a blow) —*vi.* 1 to leave a ship or boat and go on shore; disembark 2 to come to a port or to shore: said of a ship 3 to arrive at a specified place; end up 4 to alight or come to rest, as after a flight, jump, or fall —**land on** ☆[Informal] to scold or criticize severely
Land (land), **Edwin Herbert** 1909-91; U.S. physicist, inventor, & industrialist
-land (land, lənd) *combining form* 1 a kind or quality of land [*grassland, highland*] 2 a particular place or realm [*England, dreamland*]
lan·dau (lan′dô′, -dou′) *n.* ⟦after *Landau*, town in SW Germany where orig. made⟧ 1 a four-wheeled covered carriage with the top in two sections, either of which can be lowered independently 2 a former style of automobile with a top whose back could be folded down
Lan·dau (län′dou′), **Lev (Davidovich)** (lyef) 1908-68; Soviet theoretical physicist
lan·dau·let or **lan·dau·lette** (lan′də let′) *n.* 1 a small LANDAU (sense 1) 2 an early type of automobile with a folding hood over the rear seat
land bank ☆1 a bank primarily financing transactions in real estate, specif. farmland 2 *a)* an accumulation of real estate held for future development, use, or sale *b)* a private or public organization holding such real estate —**land banking**
land breeze a breeze blowing seaward from the land
land contract a contract in which a purchaser of real estate, upon making an initial payment, agrees to pay the seller stipulated amounts at specified intervals until the total purchase price is paid, at which time the seller transfers his interest in the property
land·ed (lan′did) *adj.* 1 owning land [*landed* gentry] 2 consisting of, or having the nature of, land or real estate [a *landed* estate]
landed immigrant [Cdn.] an immigrant who has been admitted to Canada as a permanent resident
land·er (lan′dər) *n.* a spacecraft designed to separate from an orbiting spacecraft and make a soft landing on a planet, moon, etc.
land·fall (land′fôl′) *n.* 1 a sighting of land from a ship at sea 2 the land sighted 3 a landing by ship or airplane
land·fill (-fil′) *n.* 1 disposal of garbage, rubbish, etc. by burying it under soil or earth 2 a place used for this purpose 3 garbage, rubbish, etc. so disposed of
land·form (-fôrm′) *n.* any topographic feature on the earth's surface, as a plain, valley, hill, etc., caused by erosion, sedimentation, or movement
☆**land-grab·ber** (-grab′ər) *n.* a person who gets possession of land unfairly or fraudulently —**land′-grab′bing** *n.*
☆**land grant** an appropriation of public land by the government for a railroad, state college, etc.
☆**land-grant** (-grant′) *adj.* designating any of a number of colleges and universities originally given federal aid, esp. by land grants, on condition that they offer instruction in agriculture and the mechanical arts: they are now supported by the individual states with supplementary federal funds
land·grave (-grāv′) *n.* ⟦Ger *landgraf* < *land*, LAND + *graf*, a count⟧ 1 in medieval Germany, a count having jurisdiction over a specified territory 2 later, the title of any of certain German princes —**land′gra′vi·ate** (-grā′vē it) *n.*
land·hold·er (-hōl′dər) *n.* an owner or occupant of land —**land′hold′ing** *adj., n.*
land·ing (lan′diŋ) *n.* 1 the act of coming to shore or of going or putting ashore 2 a place where a ship or boat takes on or unloads cargo or passengers 3 a platform at the end of a flight of stairs 4 the act of alighting, or coming to the ground, as after a flight, jump, or fall
landing craft any of various naval craft designed to bring troops and equipment close to shore during amphibious operations
landing field a field provided with a smooth surface to enable airplanes to land and take off easily
landing gear the system of related parts on an aircraft or spacecraft used for support or mobility on land or water, including wheels, pontoons, shock absorbers, etc.
landing net a small, baglike net attached to a long handle, for taking a hooked fish from the water
landing strip AIRSTRIP
land·la·dy (land′lād′ē) *n., pl.* **-dies** ⟦after LANDLORD⟧ 1 a woman who rents or leases land, houses, apartments, etc. to others 2 a woman who rents rooms to lodgers 3 [Brit.] a woman who operates a pub
land·less (land′lis) *adj.* not owning land
land·line (-līn′) *n.* 1 a telephone system network connected by wires and cables underground or on poles 2 any individual telephone line in such a wired network 3 a telephone connected to such a line Also written **land line**
land·locked (-läkt′) *adj.* 1 entirely or almost entirely surrounded by land, as a bay or a country 2 cut off from the sea and confined to fresh water by a geographical barrier [*landlocked* salmon]
land·lord (-lôrd′) *n.* ⟦ME *londelorde* < OE *landhlaford*: see LAND & LORD⟧ 1 a person, company, etc. that rents or leases land, houses, apartments, etc. to others 2 a man who rents rooms to lodgers 3 [Brit.] a man who operates a pub
land·lord·ism (-lôrd′iz′əm) *n.* the economic system under which land is privately owned and rented as to tenant farmers
land·lub·ber (-lub′ər) *n.* ⟦LAND + LUBBER⟧ a person who has had little experience at sea and is therefore awkward aboard a ship: a sailor's term of contempt
land·mark (-märk′) *n.* 1 any fixed object used to mark the boundary of a piece of land 2 any prominent feature of the landscape, as a tree or building, serving to identify a particular locality 3 an event, discovery, etc. considered as a high point or turning point in the history or development of something —*vt.* to designate (a building, site, etc.) as a landmark, esp. an official historic landmark —**land′mark′ing** *n.*
land·mass (-mas′) *n.* a very large area of land; esp., a continent
land measure 1 a system of square measure for finding the area of a piece of land 2 any unit of measurement in such a system, as an acre, hectare, etc.
land mine an explosive charge hidden under the surface of the ground and detonated as by pressure upon it
☆**land office** a government office that handles and records the sales and transfers of public lands
☆**land-of·fice business** (land′ôf′is) ⟦with ref. to Western U.S. land offices in the 19th c.⟧ [Informal] a booming business
Land of Nod (näd) 1 *Bible* the country to which Cain journeyed after slaying Abel: Gen. 4:16 2 ⟦< pun based on NOD (*vi.* 2)⟧ [**l- of N-**] the imaginary realm of sleep and dreams
Land of Promise PROMISED LAND
Land of the Rising Sun ⟦transl. of *Nihon koku* (see NIHON)⟧ *name for* JAPAN
Lan·dor (lan′dər, -dôr′), **Walter Savage** 1775-1864; Eng. writer & poet
land·own·er (land′ōn′ər) *n.* a person who owns land —**land′own′er·ship′** *n.* —**land′own′ing** *adj., n.*
Lan·dow·ska (län dôf′skä), **Wan·da** (vän′dä) 1879-1959; U.S. harpsichordist, born in Poland
☆**land plaster** finely ground gypsum, used as a fertilizer
☆**land-poor** (land′poor′) *adj.* owning land, often much land, but poor, or lacking ready money, because of high taxes on the land, its low yield, etc.
land rail CORNCRAKE
land reform the redistribution of agricultural land by breaking up large landholdings and apportioning shares to small farmers, peasants, etc.
Land·sat (land′sat′) *n.* ⟦LAND + SAT(ELLITE)⟧ any of a system of U.S. satellites for gathering and transmitting data about the earth's natural resources, topography, etc.
land·scape (land′skāp′) *n.* ⟦17th-c. art borrowing (cf. EASEL, LAY FIGURE) < Du *landschap* < *land*, land + *-schap*, -SHIP: earlier also *landskip*, akin to OE *landscipe*, Ger *landschaft*⟧ 1 a picture representing a section of natural, inland scenery, as of prairie, woodland, mountains, etc. 2 the branch of painting, photography, etc. dealing with such pictures 3 an expanse of natural scenery considered in terms of its visual effect 4 the conditions prevailing in a particular time, place, institution, etc. [the political *landscape* of postwar Britain] —*vt.* **-scaped′, -scap′ing** to change the natural features of (a plot of ground) so as to make it more attractive, as by adding a lawn, trees, bushes, etc. —*vi.* to work as a landscape architect or gardener —**land′scap′er** *n.*
☆**landscape architecture** the art or profession of planning or changing the natural scenery of a place for a desired purpose or effect —**landscape architect**
landscape gardening the art or work of placing or arranging lawns, trees,

bushes, etc. on a plot of ground to make it more attractive —**landscape gardener**

land·scap·ist (-skăp′ist) ***n.*** a painter of landscapes

Land·seer (land′sir), Sir **Edwin Henry** 1802-73; Eng. painter & sculptor, esp. of animal subjects

Land's End cape in Cornwall at the southwesternmost point of England: also written **Lands End**

land·side (land′sīd′) ***n.*** the flat side of a plow, which is turned toward the soil not yet broken up

land·skip (-skip′) ***n.*** *obs. var. of* LANDSCAPE

lands·leit (länts′līt′) ***pl.n.***, *sing.* **lands′man** (-mən) ⟦Yiddish⟧ fellow Jews; sometimes, specif., those from the same town or village in Europe as oneself

☆**land·slide** (land′slīd′) ***n.*** **1** the sliding of a mass of loosened rocks or earth down a hillside or slope **2** the mass of loosened material sliding down **3** an overwhelming majority of votes for one candidate or party in an election **4** any overwhelming victory

land·slip (-slip′) ***n.*** [Chiefly Brit.] LANDSLIDE (senses 1 & 2)

Lands·mål (länts′môl) ***n.*** ⟦Norw < *land,* country + *mål,* language⟧ *former name for* NYNORSK

lands·man (landz′mən) ***n.***, *pl.* **-men** (-mən) **1** a person who lives on land: distinguished from SEAMAN **2** ⟦partly via Yiddish < MHG *lantsman,* for earlier *lantman* < OHG < *lant,* LAND + *man,* MAN⟧ a fellow countryman; compatriot

Land·stei·ner (land′stī′nər; *Ger* länt′shtī′nər), **Karl** 1868-1943; U.S. pathologist & immunologist, born in Austria

land·ward (land′wərd) ***adv.*** toward the land: also **land′wards** —***adj.*** situated or facing toward the land

land wind a wind blowing seaward from the land

lane[1] (lān) ***n.*** ⟦ME < OE *lanu,* akin to Du *laan* < ? IE base **elā-,* to be in motion, go⟧ **1** a narrow way between hedges, walls, buildings, etc.; narrow country road or city street **2** any narrow way, as an opening in a crowd of people **3** *a)* a path or route designated, as for reasons of safety, for ships or aircraft ☆*b)* a marked strip of road wide enough for a single line of cars, trucks, etc. **4** any of the parallel courses marked off for contestants in a race **5** *Basketball* FREE THROW LANE **6** *Bowling a)* a long, narrow strip of highly polished wood, along which the balls are rolled; alley *b)* [*usually pl.*] a bowling establishment

lane[2] (lān) ***adj.*** *Scot. var. of* LONE

lang *abbrev.* language

Lang (laŋ) **1 Andrew** 1844-1912; Scot. writer **2 Fritz** (born *Friedrich Christian Anton Lang*) 1890-1976; U.S. film director, born in Austria

lang·bein·ite (laŋ′bīn īt′) ***n.*** ⟦Ger *langbeinit,* after A. Langbein, 19th-c. Ger chemist who identified it + *-it,* -ITE[1]⟧ a mineral, $K_2Mg_2(SO_4)_3$, that is often found in salt deposits as a natural sulfate of potassium and magnesium, used as a source of potash

Langerhans islets (*or* **islands)** ISLETS OF LANGERHANS

Lang·land (laŋ′lənd), **William** 1330?-1400?; Eng. poet

Lang·lauf (läŋ′louf′) ***n.*** ⟦Ger < *lang,* LONG[1] + *lauf,* a course < *laufen,* to run⟧ *Skiing* a cross-country run —***Lang′läuf′er*** (-loi′fər) ***n.***

lang·ley (laŋ′lē) ***n.***, *pl.* **-leys** ⟦after S. P. LANGLEY⟧ a unit for measuring solar radiation, equal to one small calorie per square centimeter

Lang·ley (laŋ′lē) **1 Samuel Pier·pont** (pir′pänt′) 1834-1906; U.S. astronomer, physicist, & pioneer in airplane construction **2 William** *var. of* William LANGLAND

Lang·muir (laŋ′myoor′), **Irving** 1881-1957; U.S. chemist

Lan·go·bard (laŋ′gō bärd′) ***n.*** LOMBARD (*n.* 2)

Lan·go·bar·dic (laŋ′gō bär′dik) ***adj.*** of the Lombards or their language or culture —***n.*** the West Germanic language of the Lombards

lan·go·sti·no (laŋ′gə stē′nō) ***n.*** ⟦Sp⟧ *var. of* LANGOUSTINE

lan·gouste (län gōōst′) ***n.*** ⟦Fr⟧ SPINY LOBSTER

lan·gous·tine (läŋ′goo stēn′, laŋ′-; -gə-; *Fr* län gōō stēn′) ***n.*** ⟦Fr, dim. of prec.⟧ any of several edible decapod crustaceans, esp. a small lobster of the North Atlantic

lan·grage or **lan·gridge** (laŋ′grij) ***n.*** ⟦< ?⟧ [Historical] a type of irregularly shaped shot used in naval battles to damage rigging and sails: also **lan′grel** (-grəl)

lang·syne (laŋ′sīn′, -zīn′) ***adv.*** ⟦Scot < *lang,* LONG[1] + *syne,* since, contr. < *sithen,* SINCE⟧ [Scot.] long since; long ago —***n.*** [Scot.] the long ago; bygone days Also written **lang syne**

Lang·try (laŋ′trē), **Lil·lie** (lil′ē) (born *Emily Charlotte Le Breton*) 1852-1929; Eng. actress

lan·guage (laŋ′gwij) ***n.*** ⟦ME < OFr *langage* < *langue,* tongue < L *lingua,* tongue, language, altered (by assoc. with *lingere,* to lick) < OL *dingua* < IE **dn̥ĝhwa* > OE *tunge,* TONGUE⟧ **1** *a)* human speech *b)* [Archaic] the ability to communicate by this means *c)* a system of vocal sounds and combinations of such sounds to which meaning is attributed, used for the expression or communication of thoughts and feelings *d)* the written representation of such a system **2** *a)* any means of expressing or communicating, as gestures, signs, or animal sounds [body *language*] *b)* a special set of symbols, letters, numerals, rules, etc. used for the transmission of information, as in a computer **3** all the vocal sounds, words, and ways of combining them common to a particular nation, tribe, or other speech community [the French *language*] **4** the particular form or manner of selecting and combining words characteristic of a person, group, or profession; form or style of expression in words [the *language* of teenagers] **5** the study of language in general or of some particular language or languages; linguistics **6** [Informal] coarse or obscene words and expressions —**speak the same (**or **someone's) language** to have the same beliefs, attitudes, etc. (as another)

language arts *Educ.* language-related subjects such as grammar, composition, literature, creative writing, and foreign languages

language laboratory a classroom in which students learning a foreign language can practice sound and word patterns individually or under supervision with the aid of audio equipment, etc.: also **language lab**

Langue·doc (läng dôk′) historical region of S France, between the E Pyrenees & the lower Rhone

langue d'oc (läng dôk′) ⟦Fr, lit., language of *oc* (< Prov, yes < L *hoc,* this thing): from characteristic use of *oc* for affirmation (in contrast to LANGUE D'OÏL)⟧ a group of French dialects spoken in medieval S France and surviving in Provençal

Langue·doc-Rous·sil·lon (läng dôk rōō sē yōn′) metropolitan region of France incorporating part of the Languedoc region and the Roussillon: 10,570 sq mi (27,376 sq km); chief city, Montpellier

langue d'o·ïl (läng dô ēl′) ⟦Fr, lit., language of *oïl* (< OFr, yes < LL *hoc illi* < L *hoc,* this + *ille,* that): from characteristic use of *oïl* (Fr *oui*) for affirmation: cf. LANGUE D'OC⟧ a group of French dialects spoken in most of central and N France in the Middle Ages: it is the Old French from which modern French is derived

lan·guet or **lan·guette** (laŋ′gwit) ***n.*** ⟦ME < MFr, dim. of OFr *langue:* see LANGUAGE⟧ a thing or part resembling the tongue in shape or use

lan·guid (laŋ′gwid) ***adj.*** ⟦Fr *languide* < L *languidus* < *languere,* to be weary, akin to *laxus:* see LAX⟧ **1** without vigor or vitality; drooping; weak **2** without interest or spirit; listless; indifferent **3** sluggish; dull; slow —**lan′guid·ly** ***adv.*** —**lan′guid·ness** ***n.***

lan·guish (-gwish) ***vi.*** ⟦ME *languishen* < extended stem of OFr *languir* < L *languescere* < *languere,* to be weary: see prec.⟧ **1** to lose vigor or vitality; fail in health; become weak; droop **2** to live under distressing conditions; continue in a state of suffering [to *languish* in poverty] **3** to lose intensity, impetus, enthusiastic support, etc. [a bill *languishing* in a congressional committee] **4** to suffer with longing; pine **5** to put on an air of sentimental tenderness or wistful melancholy —**lan′guish·er** ***n.*** —**lan′guish·ment** ***n.***

lan·guor (laŋ′gər) ***n.*** ⟦ME *langour* < OFr *langueur* < L *languor* < *languere,* to be weary: see LANGUID⟧ **1** a lack of vigor or vitality; weakness **2** a lack of interest or spirit; feeling of listlessness; indifference **3** the condition of being still, sluggish, or dull —**lan′guor·ous** ***adj.*** —**lan′guor·ous·ly** ***adv.***

lan·gur (luŋ′goor′) ***n.*** ⟦Hindi *laṅgūr* < Sans *lāṅgūlin,* lit., having a tail⟧ any of a genus (*Presbytis*) of lanky, long-tailed monkeys of Southeast Asia, with bushy eyebrows and a chin tuft

lan·iard (lan′yərd) ***n.*** *alt. sp. of* LANYARD

la·ni·ar·y (lā′nē er′ē, lan′ē-) ***adj.*** ⟦L *laniarius,* of a butcher < *lanius,* a butcher, of Etr orig.⟧ adapted for tearing; canine: said of teeth

La·nier (lə nir′), **Sidney** 1842-81; U.S. poet

La Ni·ña (lä nē′nyä) ⟦Sp, fem. of EL NIÑO⟧ periodic, significant cooling of the surface waters of the equatorial Pacific Ocean, which causes abnormal weather patterns: cf. EL NIÑO

lank (laŋk) ***adj.*** ⟦ME < OE *hlanc,* slim, flexible < IE base **kleng-,* to bend, wind > Ger *lenken,* to bend, ON *hlekkr,* a ring⟧ **1** *a)* slender or lean *b)* gaunt or meager **2** hanging straight and limp; not curly: said of hair —**lank′ly** ***adv.*** —**lank′ness** ***n.***

lank·y (laŋ′kē) ***adj.*** **lank′i·er, lank′i·est** ⟦prec. + -Y[2]⟧ tall and lean, or long and slender: often used to suggest awkwardness in appearance or gait —**lank′i·ly** ***adv.*** —**lank′i·ness** ***n.***

lan·ner (lan′ər) ***n.*** ⟦ME *lanere* < MFr *lanier* < VL **lanarius,* type of falcon < L *laniarius:* see LANIARY⟧ a falcon (*Falco biarmicus*) of the Mediterranean region, specif. the female used in falconry

lan·ner·et (lan′ər et′) ***n.*** ⟦ME *lanerette* < MFr *laneret,* dim.⟧ the male of the lanner: it is smaller than the female

lan·o·lin (lan′ə lin) ***n.*** ⟦< L *lana,* WOOL + *oleum,* oil + -IN[1]⟧ a fatty substance obtained from sheep wool and used as a base for ointments, cosmetics, etc.: also **lan′o·line** (-lin, -lēn′)

Lan·sing (lan′siŋ) ⟦ult. after J. *Lansing* (1751-1829?), Am jurist⟧ capital of Mich., in the SC part

lan·ta·na (lan tā′nə, -tä′-) ***n.*** ⟦ModL < It dial., viburnum < Gaul < IE base **lento-,* lithe, flexible > LINDEN, L *lentus*⟧ any of a genus (*Lantana*) of shrubby plants of the verbena family, growing in tropical and subtropical America and often cultivated as pot plants

lan·tern (lan′tərn) ***n.*** ⟦ME < OFr *lanterne* < L *lanterna* < Gr *lamptēr* < *lampein,* to shine: see LAMP⟧ **1** a transparent or translucent case for holding a light and protecting it from wind and weather: it usually has a handle on its framework so that it can be carried **2** the room containing the lamp at the top of a lighthouse **3** an open or windowed structure on the roof of a building or in the upper part of a tower or the like, to admit light or air **4** *short for* MAGIC LANTERN

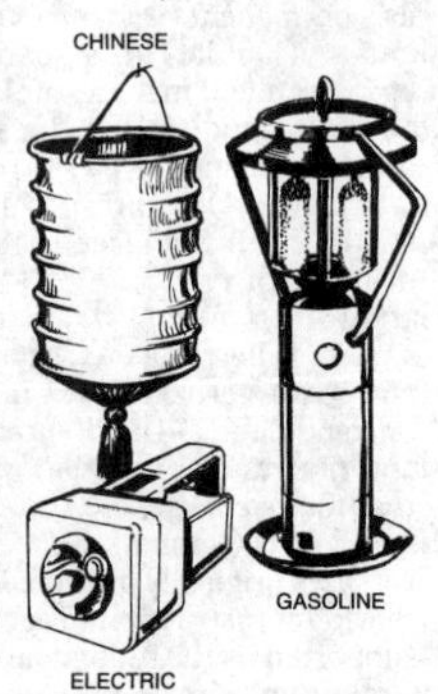

lanterns

lan·tern·fish (-fish′) ***n.***, *pl.* **-fish′** or **-fish′es** (see FISH) ⟦so named from its light-producing organs⟧ any of a family (Myctophidae) of deep-sea bony fishes (order Myctophiformes) with a large mouth, large eyes, and luminescent organs along each side of the body: also written **lantern fish**

lantern fly any of various large, brightly colored South American homopteran insects (family Fulgoridae) having a long head with a hollow part formerly thought to emit light

lantern jaw ⟦from resemblance to the early lantern with long sides of thin, concave horn⟧ **1** a projecting lower jaw **2** [*pl.*] long, thin jaws, with sunken cheeks, that give the face a lean, gaunt appearance —**lan′tern-jawed′** *adj.*

lantern pinion (*or* **wheel**) an old type of gear consisting of two circular disks connected by projecting bars around their edges

lantern slide a photographic slide for projection, as, originally, by a magic lantern

lantern tree a Chilean tree (*Crinodendron hookerianum*) of a family (Elaeocarpaceae, order Malvales) of tropical dicotyledonous trees and shrubs having leathery, elliptical leaves and hanging red flowers, sometimes grown in the far S U.S. as an ornamental

lan·tha·nide (lan′thə nīd′) *n.* any of the rare-earth elements (**lanthanide series**): see the periodic table of elements in the Reference Supplement: sometimes called **lan′tha·noid′** (-noid′) or **lan′tha·non′** (-nän′)

lan·tha·num (-nəm) *n.* ⟦ModL: so named (1839) by C. G. Mosander, Swed chemist (see ERBIUM) < *lanthana*, lanthanum oxide, lit., the hidden one < Gr *lanthanein*, to be hidden (see LATENT): it had previously been undetected in the mineral cerite⟧ a soft, malleable, silvery chemical element, one of the rare-earth elements and the first member of the lanthanide series: symbol, La; at. no. 57: see the periodic table of elements in the Reference Supplement

lant·horn (lan′tərn) *n.* ⟦altered by folk etym. < LANTERN, by assoc. with HORN, material once used for the sides⟧ *archaic var. of* LANTERN

la·nu·go (lə no͞o′gō, -nyo͞o′-) *n.* ⟦L, down < *lana*, WOOL⟧ the soft, downy hair covering the human fetus —**la·nu′gi·nous** (-ji nəs) *adj.*, **la·nu′gi·nose′** (-ji nōs′)

lan·yard (lan′yərd) *n.* ⟦altered (infl. by YARD[1]) < ME *lanyer* < MFr *laniere* < OFr *lasniere* < *lasne*, noose, earlier *nasle* < Frank **nastila*, a cord, lace, dim. of Gmc **nast-* < IE base **ned-* > L *nodus*, knot⟧ **1** a short rope or cord used on board ship for holding or fastening something **2** a cord worn around the neck, as by sailors, from which to hang something, as a knife, whistle, etc. **3** a cord with attached hook, for firing certain types of cannon

Lan·zhou (län′jō′) city in NC China, on the Huang; capital of Gansu

La·o (lä′ō) *adj., n., pl.* **La′o** or **La′os** LAOTIAN

La·oc·o·ön (lā äk′ō än′) *n.* ⟦L < Gr *Laokoōn*⟧ *Gr. Myth.* a priest of Troy who, with his two sons, is destroyed by two huge sea serpents after he warns the Trojans against the wooden horse

La·od·i·ce·a (lā äd′i sē′ə, lā′ə də-) **1** ancient city in Phrygia, SW Asia Minor **2** *ancient name for* LATAKIA[2] (the seaport)

La·od·i·ce·an (-ən) *adj.* **1** of Laodicea **2** indifferent or lukewarm in religion: an allusion to the early Christians of LAODICEA (city in Phrygia): Rev. 3:14-16 **3** indifferent or lukewarm about any subject —*n.* **1** a person born or living in Laodicea **2** one who is indifferent or lukewarm, esp. in religion

Laoigh·is (lā′ish) county in Leinster province, central Ireland: 664 sq mi (1,720 sq km): also sp. **Lao′is**

La·om·e·don (lā äm′ə dän′) *n.* ⟦L < Gr *Laomedōn*⟧ *Gr. Myth.* father of Priam and founder of Troy

La·os (lä′ōs, lous) country in the NW part of the Indochinese peninsula: formerly a French protectorate, it became an independent kingdom (1949) & a republic (1975): 91,429 sq mi (236,800 sq km); cap. Vientiane

La·o·tian (lā ō′shən, lä-) *adj.* of Laos or its people, language, or culture —*n.* **1** a person born or living in Laos; specif., a member of a Buddhist Tai people **2** the Tai language of this people

Lao·tzu (lou′dzo͞o′) 6th cent. B.C.; Chin. philosopher: reputed founder of Taoism: also sp. **Lao′-tze′**, **Lao′zi′**, or **Lao′-tsze′** (-dzo͞o′)

lap[1] (lap) *n.* ⟦ME *lappe* < OE *læppa*, fold or hanging part of a garment, skin; akin to Ger *lappen* < IE base **leb-*, *lāb-*, to hang down > L *labare*, to totter, *labi*, to fall, sink, *lapsus*, a fall⟧ **1** [Now Rare] the loose lower part of a garment, which may be doubled or folded over; skirt of a coat or gown **2** the front part of the skirt when it is held up to form a hollow place in which things can be carried **3** *a)* the front part from the waist to the knees of a person in a sitting position *b)* the part of the clothing covering this **4** anything hollow like a lap, as a valley **5** that in which a person or thing rests or is cared for, sheltered, or coddled **6** *a)* a part extending over another part; overlapping part *b)* such extension; overlapping *c)* amount or place of this **7** a turn or loop, as of a rope around a post **8** a rotating disk for cutting and polishing glass, gems, etc. **9** *a)* one complete circuit around a racetrack, in a race consisting of more than one *b)* one part or stage of an extended project **10** the act or condition of lapping —*vt.* **lapped, lap′ping** ⟦ME *lappen* < the *n.*⟧ **1** to fold (*over* or *on*) **2** to wrap; enfold **3** to hold in or as in the lap; envelop [*lapped* in luxury] **4** to place partly upon something else [to *lap* one board over another] **5** to lie partly upon; overlap [one shingle *laps* the other] **6** to cut or polish (glass, gems, etc.) with a lap **7** to get a lap ahead of (an opponent) in a race —*vi.* **1** to be folded [rough edges must *lap* under] **2** to lie partly upon something or upon one another; overlap **3** to project beyond something in space, or extend beyond something in time: with *over* —**drop** (or **dump**, etc.) **into someone's lap** [Informal] to cause to be someone's property or responsibility —**in the lap of luxury** surrounded by luxury —**in the lap of the gods** beyond human control or power

lap[2] (lap) *vi., vt.* **lapped, lap′ping** ⟦ME *lapen* < OE *lapian*, akin to MDu *lapen*, OHG *laffan*, to lick < IE echoic base **lab-*, to lick > L *lambere*⟧ **1** to drink (a liquid) by dipping it up with the tongue in the manner of a dog **2** to move or strike gently with a light splashing sound: said of waves, etc. —*n.* **1** the act of lapping **2** the sound of lapping **3** something that is, or is intended to be, lapped up —**lap up 1** to take up (liquid or liquid food) by lapping **2** [Informal] to eat or drink greedily **3** [Informal] *a)* to accept with enthusiasm *b)* to believe too readily —**lap′per** *n.*

lap·a·ro- (lap′ə rō′, -rə) ⟦< Gr *lapara*, the flank < *laparos*, weak, thin < IE base **lep-*, to peel off: see LEPER⟧ *combining form* the flank, the abdominal wall [*laparotomy*]: also, before a vowel, **lapar-**

lap·a·ro·scope (lap′ə rō skōp′) *n.* ⟦prec. + -SCOPE⟧ a fiber-optic instrument introduced surgically into the abdomen for examining visually the abdominal or pelvic organs —**lap′a·ro·scop′ic** (-skäp′ik) *adj.*

lap·a·ros·co·py (lap′ə räs′kə pē) *n.* the use of a laparoscope in a medical examination or in any of various surgical procedures

lap·a·rot·o·my (lap′ə rät′ə mē) *n., pl.* **-mies** ⟦LAPARO- + -TOMY⟧ a surgical incision into the abdomen

La Paz (lä päs′; *E* lə päz′) ⟦Sp, lit., the peace⟧ **1** city in W Bolivia: seat of government (cf. SUCRE[2]) **2** seaport in NW Mexico, on the Gulf of California: capital of Baja California Sur

☆**lap·board** (lap′bôrd′) *n.* a flat board placed on or over the lap and used as a table or desk

lap dance an erotic performance in which a nude or nearly nude exotic dancer (**lap dancer**) moves about on the lap of a clothed customer —**lap dancing**

lap dissolve *Film, TV* a dissolving view in which a new scene is blended in with a scene being faded out, as by lapping two exposures on one film or two images on a TV screen

lap dog 1 a pet dog small enough to be held in the lap, often, specif., one that is pampered **2** a fawning or submissive person Also written **lap′dog′** *n.*

la·pel (lə pel′) *n.* ⟦dim. of LAP[1]⟧ either of the front parts of a coat, jacket, etc. folded back on the chest, forming a continuation of the collar

lap·ful (lap′fo͝ol′) *n., pl.* **-fuls′** as much as a lap can hold

lap·i·dar·i·an (lap′ə der′ē ən) *adj.* LAPIDARY

lap·i·dar·y (lap′ə der′ē) *n., pl.* **-dar′ies** ⟦ME *lapidarie* < LL *lapidarius* < L, of stones < *lapis* (gen. *lapidis*), a stone, akin to Gr *lepas*, ult. ? < IE base **lep-*: see LEPER⟧ **1** a person who cuts, polishes, and engraves precious stones **2** an expert in precious stones; collector of or dealer in gems —*adj.* ⟦L *lapidarius*⟧ **1** of or connected with the art of cutting and engraving precious stones **2** engraved on stone **3** short, precise, and elegant, like an inscription on a monument

la·pid·i·fy (lə pid′ə fī′) *vt., vi.* **-fied′, -fy′ing** ⟦Fr *lapidifier* < ML *lapidificare* < L *lapis* (gen. *lapidis*), a stone + *facere*, to make: see DO[1]⟧ to turn into stone —**la·pid′i·fi·ca′tion** *n.*

la·pil·lus (lə pil′əs) *n., pl.* **-pil′li′** (-ī′) ⟦L, dim. of *lapis*, stone⟧ a small fragment of igneous rock, up to the size of a walnut, ejected from a volcano

lap·in (lap′in; *Fr* lȧ pan′) *n.* ⟦Fr, rabbit < *lapereau* < or akin to Port *laparo*, of Iberian-Balearic orig.⟧ rabbit fur, generally dyed in imitation of more valuable skins

la·pis[1] (lā′pis, lap′is) *n., pl.* ***la·pi·des*** (lā′pi dēz′, lap′i-) ⟦L⟧ stone: term used esp. in chemistry

lap·is[2] (lap′is) *n. short for* LAPIS LAZULI

lapis laz·u·li (laz′yo͞o lī′, lazh′-; -lē′) ⟦ModL < L *lapis*, a stone + ML *lazuli*, gen. of *lazulus*, azure < Ar *lāzaward*: see AZURE⟧ **1** an azure-blue, opaque semiprecious stone, a mixture of lazurite and various other minerals **2** its color

lap joint *Carpentry, etc.* a joint made by lapping one piece or part over another and fastening them together: also **lapped joint** —**lap′-joint′** *vt.*

La·place (lȧ plȧs′), Marquis **Pierre Si·mon de** (pyer sē mōn′ də) 1749-1827; Fr. mathematician & astronomer

Lap·land (lap′land′) region of N Europe, including the N parts of Norway, Sweden, & Finland, & the NW extremity of European Russia, inhabited by the Lapps

La Pla·ta (lä plä′tä) seaport in E Argentina, on the Río de la Plata, southeast of Buenos Aires

lap joint

Lapp (lap) *n.* ⟦Swed⟧ **1** a member of a people living in Lapland: also **Lap′land′er 2** the Finnic language of this people: also **Lap′pish** For those in this ethnic group, SAMI is the preferred term

lap·pet (lap′it) *n.* ⟦dim. of LAP[1]⟧ **1** a loose flap or fold of a garment or head covering **2** any fleshy or membranous part hanging loosely or in a fold, as the dewlap of a cow, the lobe of the ear, etc.

☆**lap robe** a small blanket laid over the lap and knees for warmth

Lap·sang (lap′saŋ′) *adj.* designating a fine variety of souchong tea with a smoky flavor

lapse (laps) *n.* ⟦L *lapsus*, a fall: see LAP[1]⟧ **1** a slip of the tongue, pen, or memory; small error or failing **2** *a)* a falling away from a moral standard; moral slip *b)* a falling or slipping into a lower or worse condition, esp. for a short time **3** a falling away from one's belief or faith **4** a gliding or passing away, as of time or of anything continuously flowing **5** *Law a)* the termination or forfeiture of a right or privilege through disuse, through failure of some contingency, or through failure to meet stated obligations within a stated time *b)* the failure of a bequest or devise to take effect because of the death of the person who was to receive it —*vi.* **lapsed, laps′ing** ⟦L *lapsare* < *labi*: see LAP[1]⟧ **1** to slip or fall; esp., to slip into a specified state [to *lapse* into a coma] **2** to slip or deviate from a higher standard or fall into (former) erroneous ways; backslide **3** to stop practicing one's religion; lose or abandon one's faith: often in the pp. [a *lapsed* Catholic] **4** to pass away; elapse: said of time **5** to come to an end; stop or expire [my subscription *lapsed*] **6** to become forfeit or void because of failure to pay the premium at the stipulated time: said of an insurance policy **7** *Law* to pass to another proprietor by reason of negligence or death —*vt.* to make forfeit or void by not meeting standards —**laps′i·ble** *adj.*, **laps′a·ble** —**laps′er** *n.*

lapse rate the rate of decrease of an atmospheric variable, usually temperature, with increase of altitude

lap·strake (lap′strāk′) *adj.* ⟦LAP[1] + STRAKE⟧ built with the planks of the hull overlapping: said of a boat: also ☆**lap′streak′** (-strēk′)

lap·sus (lap′səs, läp′so͝os) *n.* ⟦L⟧ a slip; error; lapse

lapsus ca·la·mi (kal′ə mī′, kä′lä mē′) ⟦L⟧ a slip of the pen

lapsus lin·guae (liŋ′gwē′, -gwī′) ⟦L⟧ a slip of the tongue

Lap·tev Sea (läp′tef′, -tev′) arm of the Arctic Ocean, between the New Siberian Islands & the Taimyr Peninsula

lap·top (lap′täp′) *n.* a microcomputer small and light enough to sit on the user's lap and containing, in a single unit, a keyboard, LCD screen, microprocessor, and, usually, a rechargeable battery

La·pu·ta (lə pyo͞ot′ə) *n.* in Swift's *Gulliver's Travels*, a flying island inhabited by impractical, visionary philosophers who engage in various absurd activities —**La·pu′tan** *adj., n.*

lap·wing (lap′wiŋ′) *n.* ⟦ME *lapwinge*, altered (by folk etym., by assoc. with *lappe*, LAP[1] & *wing*, WING) < OE *hleapewince* < *hleapan*, to LEAP + *wince* < *wincian* (see WINK): prob. so called from its irregular flight⟧ any of a genus (*Vanellus*) of black-and-white plovers; esp., an Old World crested species (*V. vanellus*) with broad, rounded wings, noted for spectacular aerial displays

lar (lär) *n. sing. of* LARES

Lar·a·mie (lar′ə mē) ⟦after J. *Laramie* (died *c.* 1821), trapper & explorer⟧ city in SE Wyo.

lar·board (lär′bərd, -bôrd′) [Old-fashioned] *n.* ⟦ME *laddeborde*, orig. lading side < OE *hladan*, to lade + *bord*, side: sp. infl. by STARBOARD⟧ PORT[4] —*adj.* PORT[4] (*adj.* 1)

lar·ce·ny (lär′sə nē) *n., pl.* **-nies** ⟦ME < Anglo-Fr *larcin* < OFr *larrecin* < L *latrocinium* < *latrocinari*, to rob, plunder < *latro*, mercenary soldier, robber < Gr **latrōn* < *latron*, wages, pay < IE **lēi-*, to possess, acquire > OE *læs*, landed property⟧ *Law* the taking of personal property without consent and with the intention of permanently depriving the owner of it; theft: in some states of the U.S., and formerly in England, larceny in which the value of the property equals or exceeds a specified amount is *grand larceny*, and larceny involving lesser amounts is *petit* (or *petty*) *larceny* —*SYN.* THEFT —**lar′ce·nist** *n.*, [Archaic] **lar′ce·ner** —**lar′ce·nous** *adj.* —**lar′ce·nous·ly** *adv.*

larch (lärch) *n.* ⟦early modern Ger *larche* (Ger *lärche*) < L *larix*⟧ **1** any of a genus (*Larix*) of trees of the pine family, found in cold and temperate regions of the Northern Hemisphere, bearing cones and needlelike leaves that are shed annually **2** the tough wood of this tree

lard (lärd) *n.* ⟦OFr < L *lardum*, bacon fat, lard < IE base **lai-*, fat > Gr *larinos*, fattened, fat, L *largus*, large⟧ **1** the soft, white solid made by melting down and clarifying the fat of hogs, esp. the inner abdominal fat **2** [Informal] excess fat on the human body —*vt.* ⟦ME *larden* < OFr *larder*⟧ **1** to cover or smear with lard or other fat; grease **2** to put strips of fat pork, bacon, etc. over, or into slits in (meat or poultry) before cooking; interlard **3** to add to; embellish; garnish [a talk *larded* with jokes] —**lard′y** *adj.* **lard′i·er, lard′i·est**

lard·er (lär′dər) *n.* ⟦ME < OFr *lardier*, orig., storehouse for bacon < ML *lardarium* < L *lardum*, prec.⟧ **1** a place where the food supplies of a household are kept; pantry **2** a supply of food; provisions

larder beetle a small, mostly black dermestid beetle (*Dermestes lardarius*) whose larvae feed on dead animal matter, cheese, etc.

Lard·ner (lärd′nər), **Ring(gold Wilmer)** 1885-1933; U.S. journalist & writer of short stories

lar·don (lärd′'n) *n.* ⟦ME < MFr < *lard*, LARD⟧ a strip of bacon or pork used to lard meat: also **lar·doon** (lär do͞on′)

La·re·do (lə rā′dō) ⟦after *Laredo*, town in Spain⟧ city in S Tex., on the Rio Grande

la·res (lā′rēz′) *pl.n., sing.* **lar** (lär) ⟦L, pl. of *lar* < ? IE base **las-*, greedy, wanton > LUST⟧ in ancient Rome, guardian spirits, esp. the deified spirits of ancestors, who watch over the households of their descendants

lares and penates **1** the household gods of the ancient Romans: see LARES, PENATES **2** the treasured belongings of a family or household

lar·gan·do (lär gän′dō) *adj., adv.* ⟦It⟧ *Musical Direction var. of* ALLARGANDO

large (lärj) *adj.* **larg′er, larg′est** ⟦OFr < L *largus*: see LARD⟧ **1** [Archaic] liberal; generous **2** big; great; specif., *a)* taking up much space; bulky *b)* enclosing much space; spacious [a *large* office] *c)* of great extent or amount [a large sum] **3** big as compared with others of its kind; of more than usual or average size, extent, or amount **4** comprehensive; far-reaching [to have *large* views on a subject] **5** pompous or exaggerated [*large* talk] **6** operating on a big scale [a *large* manufacturer] **7** *Naut.* favorable; specif., quartering: said of a wind —*adv.* **larg′er, larg′est** **1** in a large way; so as to be large [to write *large*] **2** *Naut.* with a favoring wind, specif. one on the quarter —*n.* liberty: now only in the phrase AT LARGE (see phrase below) —**at large** **1** free; not confined; not in jail **2** fully; in complete detail **3** in general; taken altogether ☆**4** representing an entire state or other district rather than only one of its subdivisions: often in hyphenated compounds [a congressman *at large*] **5** covering any area or many areas; not covering any specific area: often in hyphenated compounds [a critic *at large*] —**large′ness** *n.*

SYN.—**large, big,** and **great** are often interchangeable when meaning of more than usual size, extent, etc. [a *large, big,* or *great* oak], but in strict discrimination, **large** is used with reference to dimensions or quantity [a *large* studio, amount, etc.], **big**, to bulk, weight, or extent [a *big* baby, *big* business], and **great**, to size or extent that is impressive, imposing, surprising, etc. [a *great* river, success, etc.] —*ANT.* **small, little**

large calorie CALORIE (sense 2)

large·heart·ed (lärj′härt′id) *adj.* generous; kindly

large intestine the relatively large section of the intestines of vertebrates, between the small intestine and the anus, including the cecum, colon, and rectum

large·ly (-lē) *adv.* **1** much; in great amounts **2** for the most part; mainly

large-mind·ed (-mīn′did) *adj.* liberal in one's views; broad-minded —**large′-mind′ed·ness** *n.*

☆**large·mouth (black) bass** (lärj′mouth′) a black bass (*Micropterus salmoides*) found in warm, sluggish waters

larg·er-than-life (lär′jər *th*an′līf′) *adj.* greater, grander, etc. than normally encountered; exceeding normal bounds: a hyperbolic use

large-scale (lärj′skāl′) *adj.* **1** drawn to a large scale: said of a map, etc. **2** of wide scope; over a large area; extensive [*large-scale* business operations]

large-scale integration LSI

lar·gesse (lär jes′, lär′jis) *n.* ⟦ME *largesse* < OFr < *large*, LARGE⟧ **1** generous giving, as from a patron **2** a gift or gifts given in a generous, or sometimes showy or patronizing, way **3** nobility of spirit Often sp. **lar·gess′**

lar·ghet·to (lär get′ō) [*also in italics*] *Music adj., adv.* ⟦It < *largo*: see LARGO⟧ relatively slow(ly), but faster than largo: often used as a musical direction —*n., pl.* **-tos** a larghetto movement or passage

larg·ish (lär′jish) *adj.* rather large

lar·go (lär′gō) [*also in italics*] *Music adj., adv.* ⟦It, large, slow < L *largus*, large: see LARD⟧ (in a) slow and stately (manner): often used as a musical direction —*n., pl.* **-gos** a largo movement or passage

la·ri (lä′rē) *n., pl.* **-ri** or **-ris** ⟦< Pers⟧ the basic monetary unit of the country of Georgia: see the table of monetary units in the Reference Supplement

☆**lar·i·at** (lar′ē ət) *n.* ⟦Sp *la reata* < *la*, the + *reata*, a rope < *reatar*, to tie (horses) in single file, orig., retie < *re-*, RE- + *atar*, to tie < L *aptare* < *aptus*: see APT[1]⟧ **1** a rope used for tethering grazing horses, etc. **2** LASSO —*vt.* to tie or catch with a lariat

lar·ine (lar′in, -īn′) *adj.* ⟦< ModL *Larinae*, name of the subfamily < LL(Ec) *larus*, a ravenous sea bird < Gr *laros* < IE echoic base **lā-*: see LAMENT⟧ **1** designating or of a suborder (Lari) of seabirds, including gulls, skuas, and skimmers **2** of or like a gull

La·ri·sa (lə ris′ə, lä′rē sə) city in E Thessaly, Greece: also sp. **La·ris′sa**

La·ris·sa (lə ris′ə, lə rē′sə) *n.* ⟦< ? prec.⟧ a feminine name: var. *Larisa*

lark[1] (lärk) *n.* ⟦ME *lark, laverke* < OE *laferce*, older *læwerce*, akin to Ger *lerche* (OHG *lērahha*), ON *lævirki* (Dan *lerke*)⟧ **1** any of a large family (Alaudidae) of chiefly Old World passerine birds, including the skylark and horned lark **2** any of various birds from other families, as the meadowlark

lark[2] (lärk) *vi.* ⟦? alteration (infl. by prec.) of northern dial. *lake* < ME *laike*, to play < ON *leika* & OE *lacan*, akin to Goth *laikan*, to hop, leap < IE base **leig-*, **loig-*, to hop > Sans *rējatē*, (he) hops, quivers⟧ to play or frolic; have a merry time —*n.* **1** a frolic or spree **2** a merry prank —**on a lark** impulsively; without forethought: often implying a carefree or playful attitude —**lark′er** *n.* —**lark′ish** *adj.*, **lark′y**

Lar·kin (lär′kin), **Philip (Arthur)** 1922-85; Brit. poet

lark·spur (lärk′spur′) *n.* DELPHINIUM

La Roche·fou·cauld (lȧ rôsh fo͞o kō′), Duc **Fran·çois de** (frän swȧ′ də) 1613-80; Fr. moralist & writer of maxims

La Ro·chelle (lȧ rô shel′) seaport in W France, on the Bay of Biscay

La·rousse (lȧ ro͞os′; *E* lə ro͞os′), **Pierre A·tha·nase** (pyer ȧ tȧ näz′) 1817-75; Fr. lexicographer & grammarian

lar·ri·gan (ler′i gən) *n.* ⟦of Cdn orig. < ?⟧ a high moccasin made of oiled leather, worn by woodsmen

lar·ri·kin (lar′i kin) *n.* ⟦ult. < ? LARK[2]⟧ [Slang, Chiefly Austral.] a hoodlum or rowdy, esp. a young one

lar·rup (lar′əp) *vt.* ⟦East Anglian dial., prob., with intrusive vowel, for **lerp*, **larp* < or akin to Du *larpen*, to thrash⟧ [Informal or Dial.] to whip; flog; beat

Lar·ry (lar′ē) *n.* a masculine name: see LAURENCE

lar·va (lär′və) *n., pl.* **-vae′** (-vē′) or **-vas** ⟦L, ghost, specter, akin to *lar*, household spirit: see LARES⟧ the early, free-living, immature form of any animal that changes structurally when it becomes an adult, usually by a complex metamorphosis [the caterpillar is the *larva* of the butterfly; the tadpole is the *larva* of the frog] —**lar′val** *adj.*

lar·vi·cide (-vi sīd′) *n.* ⟦< prec. + -CIDE⟧ a substance used to kill harmful larvae —**lar′vi·ci′dal** *adj.*

la·ryn·ge·al (lə rin′jē əl, -jəl) *adj.* 1 of, in, or near the larynx 2 used for treating the larynx 3 *Phonet.* articulated in, or by constriction of, the larynx —*n.* a laryngeal sound

lar·yn·gec·to·my (lar′in jek′tə mē) *n., pl.* **-mies** ⟦LARYNG(O)- + -ECTOMY⟧ the surgical removal of all or part of the larynx

lar·yn·gi·tis (lar′in jīt′is) *n.* ⟦ModL < fol. + -ITIS⟧ an inflammation of the larynx, often characterized by a temporary loss of voice —**lar′yn·git′ic** (-jit′ik) *adj.*

la·ryn·go- (lə riŋ′gō, -gə) ⟦< Gr *larynx* (gen. *laryngos*), LARYNX⟧ *combining form* 1 larynx *[laryngoscope]* 2 larynx and Also, before a vowel, **la·ryng/-**

lar·yn·gol·o·gy (lar′in gäl′ə jē) *n.* the branch of medicine having to do with diseases of the larynx and adjacent parts —**lar′yn·gol′o·gist** *n.*

la·ryn·go·phar·ynx (lə riŋ′gō far′iŋks) *n., pl.* **-phar′yn·ges′** (-far′in jēz′) or **-phar′ynx·es** the lower part of the pharynx, extending from the upper tip of the epiglottis to the larynx and esophagus:: cf. OROPHARYNX, NASOPHARYNX —**la·ryn′go·phar·yn′ge·al** (-fə rin′jē əl) *adj.*

la·ryn·go·scope (lə riŋ′gə skōp′) *n.* ⟦LARYNGO- + -SCOPE⟧ an instrument for examining the interior of the larynx

lar·yn·gos·co·py (lar′in gäs′kə pē) *n.* examination of the larynx by means of a laryngoscope —**la·ryn·go·scop·ic** (lə riŋ′gō skäp′ik, -gə-) *adj.*, **la·ryn′go·scop′i·cal**

lar·ynx (lar′iŋks) *n., pl.* **lar′ynx·es** or **la·ryn·ges** (lə rin′jēz′) ⟦ModL < Gr⟧ 1 the structure of muscle and cartilage at the upper end of the human trachea, containing the vocal cords and serving as the organ of voice 2 a similar structure in most other vertebrates

la·sa·gna (lə zän′yə, -sän′-) *n.* ⟦It (pl. *lasagne*) < VL **lasania*, a kind of noodle < L *lasanum*, a pot < Gr *lasanon*, pot with feet, trivet⟧ 1 pasta in wide, flat strips 2 a dish consisting of this pasta baked with alternating layers of, typically, tomato sauce, ground meat, and cheese Also sp. **la·sa′gne**

La·Salle (lə sal′; *Fr* lȧ sȧl′) ⟦after fol.⟧ borough of Montreal

La Salle (lə sal′; *Fr* lȧ sȧl′), Sieur **(René-)Rob·ert (Cavelier de)** (räb′ərt; *Fr* rô ber′) 1643-87; Fr. explorer in North America

las·car (las′kər) *n.* ⟦Hindi *lashkar*, army, camp < Pers, army < Ar *al-ʿaskar*, army⟧ [Historical] an Indian or East Indian sailor, employed on European ships

Las Ca·sas (läs kä′səs), **Bar·to·lo·mé de** (bär tō lō mā′ dā) 1474-1566; Sp. missionary & historian in the Americas

Las·caux (las kō′) cave in the Dordogne region, SW France, containing Upper Paleolithic paintings and engravings

las·civ·i·ous (lə siv′ē əs) *adj.* ⟦ME *lascyuyous* < ML *lasciviosus* < LL < L *lascivia*, wantonness < *lascivus*: see LUST⟧ 1 characterized by or expressing lust or lewdness; wanton 2 tending to excite lustful desires —**las·civ′i·ous·ly** *adv.* —**las·civ′i·ous·ness** *n.*

Las Cru·ces (läs kroo͞′sis) ⟦Sp, lit., the crosses: prob. from crosses marking an early burial spot⟧ city in S N.Mex., on the Rio Grande

lase (lāz) *vi.* **lased, las′ing** ⟦back-form. < fol.⟧ to emit laser light

☆**la·ser** (lā′zər) *n.* ⟦*l(ight) a(mplification by) s(timulated) e(mission of) r(adiation)*⟧ a device containing a substance the majority of whose atoms or molecules can be put into an excited energy state, allowing the substance to emit coherent light of a precise wavelength in an intense, narrow beam

la·ser·disc (-disk′) *n.* a videodisc on which audio and video signals are recorded in the form of microscopic pits, which are read by a laser beam: also **la′ser·disk′**, **laser disc**, or **laser disk**

laser printer a computer printer that uses a laser beam to reproduce images or text on a photosensitive drum to which toner is applied

lash[1] (lash) *n.* ⟦ME *lassche* < the v.⟧ 1 a whip, esp. the flexible striking part as distinguished from the handle 2 a stroke with or as with a whip; switch 3 a sharp, censuring or rebuking remark 4 an eyelash —*vt.* ⟦ME *laschen* < ?⟧ 1 to strike or drive with or as with a lash; flog 2 to swing or move quickly or angrily; switch [the cat *lashed* her tail] 3 to strike with great force; dash against [waves *lashed* the cliffs] 4 to attack violently in words; censure or rebuke 5 to incite by appealing to the emotions [to *lash* a crowd into a frenzy of anger] —*vi.* 1 to move quickly or violently; switch 2 to make strokes with or as with a whip —**lash out** 1 to strike out violently 2 to speak angrily or in bitter criticism —**lash′er** *n.*

lash[2] (lash) *vt.* ⟦ME *lashen* < OFr *lachier*, var. of *lacier*: see LACE⟧ to fasten or tie with a rope, etc.

lash·ing[1] (lash′iŋ) *n.* 1 the act of a person or thing that lashes; specif., *a)* a whipping *b)* a strong rebuke 2 [*pl.*] [Informal, Chiefly Brit.] a large amount; lots

lash·ing[2] (-iŋ) *n.* 1 the act of fastening or tying with a rope, etc. 2 a rope, etc. so used

lash-up (lash′up′) *n.* ⟦< *lash up*, to fasten < LASH[2] + UP[1]⟧ [Informal] 1 a temporary or improvised contrivance; expedient 2 any arrangement or setup

LASIK (lā′sik, -zik) *n.* ⟦*las(er-assisted) i(n situ) k(eratomileusis)* < ModL *keratomileusis*, a cutting of the cornea < KERATO- + Gr *(s)mileusis*, carving < *smilē*, a knife; see IN SITU⟧ a type of eye surgery used to correct faulty vision: a thin, outer layer of the cornea is cut open and folded back temporarily so that the inner layer can be reshaped with an excimer laser: often written **La′sik**

Las·ki (las′kē), **Harold J(oseph)** 1893-1950; Eng. political scientist & socialist leader

Las Pal·mas (läs päl′məs) seaport in the Canary Islands

L-as·par·a·gin·ase (el′as par′ə ji nās′, -as′pər aj′i-; -nāz′) *n.* ⟦L(EVOROTATORY) + ASPARAGIN(E) + -ASE⟧ an enzyme that destroys asparagine, a nonessential amino acid needed as a nutrient by rapidly growing cells: used in treating leukemia

La Spe·zi·a (lä spāt′sē ä) seaport in NW Italy, on the Ligurian Sea

lass (las) *n.* ⟦north ME *lasce, lasse*: prob. < Anglo-N **lasqa* < ON *lǫskr*, weak, idle < IE **lēid-*, var. of base **lēi-* > LATE, LET[1]⟧ 1 a young woman; girl 2 a sweetheart 3 [Scot.] a girl servant; maid

Las·sa fe·ver (läs′ə) ⟦after *Lassa*, village in E Nigeria, where first detected⟧ an acute viral disease endemic to W Africa, characterized by high fever and inflammation of various body parts

Las·salle (lə sal′; *Ger* lä säl′), **Ferdinand** 1825-64; Ger. socialist & writer

las·sie (las′ē) *n.* ⟦dim. of LASS⟧ [Scot.] a young woman; girl

las·si·tude (las′i to͞od′, -tyo͞od′) *n.* ⟦Fr < L *lassitudo* < *lassus*, faint, weary: see LATE⟧ a state or feeling of being tired and listless; weariness; languor

☆**las·so** (las′ō, -o͞o; *for v., also* la sō′, -so͞o′) *n., pl.* **-sos** or **-soes** ⟦Sp *lazo* < L *laqueus*, noose, snare: see LACE⟧ a long rope or leather thong with a sliding noose at one end, used to catch cattle or wild horses —*vt.* **-soed, -so·ing** to catch with or as with a lasso —**las′so·er** *n.*

last[1] (last, läst) *adj.* ⟦ME *laste*, earlier *latest, latst* < OE *latost*, superl. of adj. *læt*, adv. *late*: see LATE⟧ 1 *alt. superl. of* LATE 2 being or coming after all others in place; farthest from the first; hindmost 3 coming after all others in time; farthest from the beginning; latest 4 only remaining [took the *last* chocolate in the box] 5 directly before the present [*last* month] 6 farthest from what is expected; least likely [he would be the *last* person to suspect anything] 7 utmost; greatest 8 coming after all others in importance; lowest in rank 9 newest [the *last* thing in hats] 10 conclusive; authoritative [the *last* word in scientific research] 11 individual: used as an intensive [to spend every *last* cent] —*adv.* 1 *alt. superl. of* LATE 2 after all others; at the end 3 most recently 4 finally; in conclusion —*n.* 1 someone or something which comes last [Elizabeth I was the *last* of the Tudor monarchs] 2 the final or concluding part; end [friends to the *last*] —**at (long) last** after a long time; finally —**at the last minute** (or **moment, second,** etc.) at the latest possible time or opportunity; just before it is too late —**see** (or **hear,** etc.) **the last of** to see (or hear, etc.) for the last time

last[2] (last, läst) *vi.* ⟦ME *lasten* < OE *læstan*, akin to Ger *leisten*, vt., to perform, carry out, Goth *laistjan*, lit., to follow in the track of < IE base **leis-*, a track, spoor > L *lira*, furrow (see LEARN): sense development: to follow → to go on, continue⟧ 1 to remain in existence or operation; continue; go on; endure 2 to remain in good condition; wear well 3 to continue unconsumed, unspent, etc. [enough food to *last* for a month] —*vt.* to continue or endure throughout: often with *out* [doubtful whether he can *last* (out) the training period] —**SYN.** CONTINUE —**last′er** *n.*

last[3] (last, läst) *n.* ⟦ME *laste* < OE *læst*, a boot, *læste*, shoemaker's last < base of *last*, footstep, track, furrow < same base as prec.⟧ a block or form shaped like a person's foot, on which shoes are made or repaired —*vt.* to form with a last —**stick to one's last** 1 to keep to one's own work 2 to mind one's own business —**last′er** *n.*

last call 1 the signal or announcement, as by a bartender, calling for final drink orders before the bar closes 2 the time such an announcement is made [downtown taverns have a *last call* of 1 A.M.]

last-ditch (last′dich′) *adj.* ⟦as in phr. (*to die in the*) *last ditch*⟧ made, done, used, etc. in a final, often desperate act of resistance or opposition

☆**last hurrah** a final attempt or appearance, as in politics

last·ing (las′tiŋ) *adj.* that lasts a long time; enduring; durable [a *lasting* peace] —*n.* 1 a strong twilled cloth 2 [Archaic] endurance —**last′ing·ly** *adv.* —**last′ing·ness** *n.*

Last Judgment *Theol.* 1 the final judgment of humanity at the end of the world 2 the time of this judgment

last·ly (last′lē) *adv.* in conclusion; finally

last-min·ute (last′min′it) *adj.* occurring at the latest possible time or opportunity [a *last-minute* decision]

last name SURNAME

last quarter 1 the time of month between second half-moon and new moon 2 the phase of the moon after the waning gibbous when only the left half of its face, as viewed from the Northern Hemisphere, reflects sunlight to the earth

last rites 1 final rites and prayers for a dead person 2 sacraments administered to a person near death

last straw ⟦from the *last straw* that breaks the back of the overburdened camel in the fable⟧ the last of a sequence of annoyances or troubles that results in a breakdown, loss of patience, etc.: with *the*

Last Supper the last supper eaten by Jesus with his disciples before the Crucifixion, as related in the New Testament

last word 1 *a)* the final word or speech, regarded as settling the argument *b)* final authority 2 something regarded as perfect or definitive 3 [Informal] the very latest style

Las Ve·gas (läs vā′gəs) ⟦Sp, the plains or meadows⟧ city in SE Nev.

lat *abbrev.* latitude

Lat *abbrev.* 1 Latin 2 Latvia 3 Latvian

La·ta·ki·a[1] (lät′ə kē′ə, lat′-) *n.* a fine grade of highly aromatic Turkish smoking tobacco, produced near the port of Latakia, Syria

La·ta·ki·a[2] (lät′ə kē′ə, lat′-) 1 seaport in W Syria, on the Mediterranean 2 coastal region of NW Syria, bordering on the Mediterranean

latch (lach) *n.* ⟦ME *lacche* < *lacchen*, to seize, catch hold of < OE *læccan* < IE base **(s)lagw-*, to grasp, seize > Gr *lazesthai*, to take, *lambanein*, to seize⟧ 1 a fastening for a door or gate, esp. one capable of being worked from either side by means of a lever and consisting of a bar that drops into a notch in a piece attached to the doorjamb or gatepost **2** a spring lock on a door; specif., a NIGHT LATCH **3** a fastening for a window, etc. —*vt., vi.* to fasten or close with a latch —☆**latch on to** (or **onto**) [Informal] **1** to seize or grasp **2** to comprehend or embrace (an idea, etc.) **3** to attach oneself to in a manner regarded as assertive, presumptuous, etc. [tried to *latch on to* her big sister's circle of friends] —**on the latch** fastened by the LATCH (sense 1) but not locked or bolted

latch·et (lach′it) *n.* ⟦ME *lachet* < OFr, dial. var. of *lacet*, dim. of *laz*: see LACE⟧ [Archaic] a strap or lace for fastening a sandal or shoe to the foot

latch·key (lach′kē′) *n.* a key for drawing back or unfastening the latch of a door, esp. of an outer door, from the outside —*adj.* ⟦from the door key carried by such a child⟧ designating, of, or having to do with a child or children who receive no supervision at home after school hours, because their parents are away working

latch·string (-striŋ′) *n.* a cord fastened to the bar of a latch and passed through a hole in the door so that the latch can be raised from the outside

late (lāt) *adj.* **lat′er** or **lat′ter**, **lat′est** or **last** ⟦ME < OE *læt*, slow, sluggish, tardy, akin to Du *laat*, Ger *lass*, slow, lazy < IE **lēid* < base **lēi-*, to neglect, let go > LET[1], L *lassus*, weak⟧ **1** happening, coming, etc. after the usual, proper, or expected time; tardy; behindhand **2** *a)* happening, being, continuing, etc. far on in the day, night, year, etc. [the *late* afternoon, a *late* party] *b)* happening, being, continuing, etc. toward the end; far advanced in a period, development, etc. [the *late* Middle Ages] **3** happening, appearing, etc. just prior to the present time; recent [a *late* news bulletin] **4** having been so recently but not now [our *late* allies] **5** having recently died —*adv.* **lat′er**, **lat′est** or **last** ⟦ME < OE < base of the adj.⟧ **1** after the usual, proper, or expected time; tardily **2** at or until an advanced time of the day, night, year, etc. **3** toward the end of a given period, development, etc. **4** recently; lately [as *late* as yesterday] —**SYN.** DEAD —**late on** [Chiefly Brit.] at a late stage; near the end —**of late** lately —**late′ness** *n.*

late bloomer a person who matures, achieves proficiency in some field or skill, etc. later than such a person is normally expected to

late·com·er (lāt′kum′ər) *n.* one that arrives or comes late

la·teen (la tēn′, lə-) *adj.* ⟦Fr *latine* < *(voile) latine*, Latin (sail) < fem. of L *Latinus*, LATIN⟧ designating or of a triangular, fore-and-aft-rigged sail attached to a long yard suspended obliquely from a short mast: now used chiefly on Mediterranean vessels —*n.* a lateen-rigged vessel: also **la·teen′er**

la·teen-rigged (-rigd′) *adj.* having a lateen sail or sails

Late Greek the Greek language of the period after classical Greek: term applied chiefly to the written language seen in patristic writings and texts from *c.* A.D. 200-600

late·ish (lāt′ish) *adj., adv. alt. sp. of* LATISH

Late Latin the Latin language of the period after classical Latin, seen chiefly in late Western Roman Empire and patristic writings from *c.* A.D. 200-600

late·ly (lāt′lē) *adv.* recently; a short while ago

La Tène (lä ten′) ⟦name of the site of such a find on Lake of Neuchâtel⟧ designating or of a Celtic Iron Age culture (*c.* 400-*c.* 15 B.C.) of central Europe, characterized by decorations in bronze, gold, and enamel on weapons, utensils, ornaments, etc.

la·tent (lāt′'nt) *adj.* ⟦L *latens*, prp. of *latere*, to lie hidden, lurk < IE **lāidh-* < base **lā-*, to be hidden > ON *lōmr*, deception, Gr *lēthē*, forgetfulness, *lanthanein*, to be hidden⟧ **1** present but invisible or inactive; lying hidden and undeveloped within a person or thing, as a quality, power, or talent **2** *Biol.* dormant but capable of normal development under the best conditions: said of buds, spores, cocoons, etc. **3** *Psychol.* unconsciously but not actively so [a *latent* homosexual] —*n.* a fingerprint found on an object as at the scene of a crime —**la′ten·cy** *n.* —**la′tent·ly** *adv.*

SYN.—latent applies to that which exists but is as yet concealed or unrevealed [his *latent* ability]; **potential** applies to that which exists in an undeveloped state but which can be brought to development in the normal course of events [a *potential* concert pianist]; **dormant** suggests a lack of visible activity, as of something asleep [a *dormant* volcano]; **quiescent** implies a stopping of activity, usually only temporarily [the raging sea had become *quiescent*] —**ANT. active, actual, operative**

latent ambiguity *Law* uncertainty existing where language employed in an instrument is clear and appears to have but one meaning, yet outside evidence makes it capable of more than one meaning: see PATENT AMBIGUITY

latent heat the heat liberated or absorbed by a substance as it changes phase at a constant temperature and pressure

latent period **1** the interval in the course of a disease between infection and the first appearance of the symptoms; incubation period **2** the interval between a stimulus and its response

lat·er (lāt′ər) *adj. alt. compar. of* LATE —*adv.* at a later time; after some time; subsequently —**later on** subsequently

lat·er·ad (lat′ər ad′) *adv.* ⟦< L *later(alis)* < gen. of *latus*, side (see fol.) + -AD[2]⟧ *Anat.* toward the side

lat·er·al (lat′ər əl) *adj.* ⟦L *lateralis* < *latus* (gen. *lateris*), a side, prob. akin to *latus*, broad < IE **stlā-to-* < base **stel-*, to spread out > Arm *lain*, broad⟧ **1** of, at, from, on, or toward the side; sideways [*lateral* movement] **2** not involving a significant change in prestige, income, etc.; being neither a promotion nor a demotion [an employee's *lateral* move to another job within the company] **3** characterized by an unconventional or innovative line of reasoning [*lateral* thinking]: opposed to LINEAR (sense 6*b*) **4** *Bot.* growing on the side of a stem or branch [a *lateral* bud] **5** *Phonet.* articulated by partial blockage of the air passage with the tongue in such a way that breath escapes along one or both sides of the tongue —*n.* **1** anything located, done, etc. to the side; lateral part, growth, branch, etc. ☆**2** *Football* a short pass parallel to the goal line or in a slightly backward direction: in full **lateral pass** **3** *Mining* a drift off to the side of and parallel to a main drift **4** *Phonet.* a lateral sound, as (l) —*vt., vi.* *Football* to pass (the ball) as a LATERAL (*n.* 2) —**lat′er·al·ly** *adv.*

lat·er·al·i·za·tion (lat′ər ə li zā′shən) *n.* the control of some physical or mental function by one side of the body or either hemisphere of the brain

lateral line a row of sensory organs along each side of the head and body in fishes and a few amphibians, for detecting vibrations, currents, etc.

lateral moraine *see* MORAINE

Lat·er·an (lat′ər ən) *n.* ⟦< L *Lateranus*, pl. *Laterani*, name of the Roman family (the *Plautii Laterani*) whose palace once occupied the same site⟧ **1** the church of St. John Lateran, the cathedral of the pope as bishop of Rome **2** the palace, now a museum, adjoining this church

lat·er·ite (lat′ər īt′) *n.* ⟦L *later*, brick, tile (prob. akin to *latus*, broad: see LATERAL) + -ITE[1]⟧ *Geol.* a red, residual soil containing large amounts of aluminum and ferric hydroxides, formed by the decomposition of many kinds of rocks, and found esp. in well-drained tropical rain forests —**lat′er·it′ic** (-it′ik) *adj.*

lat·er·i·za·tion (lat′ər i zā′shən) *n.* the process by which rock is converted into laterite —**lat′er·ize′** (-ər īz′) *vt.* **-ized′**, **-iz′ing**

lat·est (lāt′ist) *adj., adv.* **1** *alt. superl. of* LATE **2** most recent; newest **3** [Archaic] last —**at the latest** no later than (the time specified) —**the latest** the most recent, or the currently fashionable, thing, development, etc.

la·tex (lā′teks′) *n., pl.* **lat·i·ces** (lat′i sēz′) or **la′tex′es** ⟦L *latex* (gen. *laticis*), a fluid, liquid < Gr *latax*, a drop, wine lees < IE base **lat-*, wet > MIr *laith*, beer⟧ **1** a milky liquid containing resins, proteins, etc., present in certain plants and trees, as the rubber tree, milkweed, and poppy: used esp. as the basis of rubber **2** a suspension in water of particles of natural or synthetic rubber or plastic: used in rubber goods, adhesives, paints, etc.

lath (lath, läth) *n., pl.* **laths** (lathz, laths, läthz, läths) ⟦ME *lathe* (< OE **læthth*, akin to OHG *latta*) & *latte* (< OE *lætt*, akin to ON *latto*)⟧ **1** any of the thin, narrow strips of wood used in lattices or nailed to two-by-fours, rafters, etc. as a foundation for plaster, tiles, etc. **2** any foundation for plaster, as wire screening or expanded metal **3** laths collectively, esp. when used as a base for plaster —*vt.* to cover with laths

lathe (lāth) *n.* ⟦ME *lath*, turning lathe, supporting stand, prob. < MDu *lade* in the same senses (> Dan *dreielad*, turning lathe): for IE base see LADE⟧ a machine for shaping an article of wood, metal, etc. by holding and turning it rapidly against the edge of a cutting or abrading tool —*vt.* **lathed**, **lath′ing** to shape on a lathe

lath·er (lath′ər) *n.* ⟦ME < OE *leathor*, washing soda or soap, akin to ON *lauthr*, washing soda, foam < IE **loutro-* < base **lou-*, to LAVE⟧ **1** the foam or froth formed by soap or other detergent in water **2** foamy sweat, as that on a racehorse ☆**3** [Slang] an excited or agitated state —*vt.* **1** to cover with lather **2** [Informal] to flog soundly —*vi.* to form, or become covered with, lather

lath·er·y (-ər ē) *adj.* made of, covered with, or capable of forming lather

la·thi (lä′tē) *n.* ⟦Hindi⟧ in India, a heavy stick of bamboo and iron, used as a club esp. by police

lath·ing (lath′iŋ) *n.* **1** laths collectively, esp. when serving as a base for plaster **2** the putting up of laths on walls, ceilings, etc.

lath·y·rism (lath′ə riz′əm) *n.* a painful, poisoned condition caused by the ingestion of certain peas (esp. genus *Lathyrus*) and characterized by paralysis of the legs, hyperesthesia, etc.

lat·i·cif·er·ous (lat′ə sif′ər əs) *adj.* ⟦see LATEX & -FEROUS⟧ producing, containing, or secreting latex

lat·i·fun·di·um (lat′ə fun′dē əm) *n., pl.* **-di·a** (-ə) ⟦L < *latus*, broad (see LATERAL) + *fundus*, estate, orig., bottom: see FOUND[2]⟧ a large landed estate, typically owned by an absentee landlord and worked by serfs, as in some Latin American countries

lat·i·go (lat′i gō′) *n., pl.* **-gos′**, **-goes′** ⟦Sp *látigo*⟧ a wide leather strap on a saddle, used to tighten the cinch around a horse

Lat·i·mer (lat′ə mər), **Hugh** 1485?-1555; Eng. Protestant bishop & religious reformer: burned at the stake

lat·i·mer·i·a (lat′ə mir′ē ə) *n.* ⟦ModL *Latimeria*, after Marjorie Courtenay-*Latimer* (1907-2004), South African museum curator who participated in identification of the fish, which was believed to be extinct⟧ a deep-sea coelacanth fish (*Latimeria chalumnae*) with large, circular scales and six of its seven fins lobelike: discovered in 1938 and found only near the Comoro Islands

Lat·in (lat′'n) *adj.* ⟦L *Latinus* < *Latium*, Latium (in which Rome was included), orig. ? "flat land" < IE **tletiom* < base **(s)tel-*, to spread out > L *latus*, broad⟧ **1** of ancient Latium or its people **2** of ancient Rome or its people **3** of or in the language of ancient Latium and ancient Rome **4** *a)* designating or of the languages derived from Latin, the peoples that speak them, or their countries or cultures *b)* of or relating to Latin Americans **5** of the Roman Catholic Church, esp. as distinguished from the Eastern Church —*n.* **1** a person born or living in ancient Latium or ancient Rome **2** the Italic language of ancient Latium and ancient Rome: see also OLD LATIN, VULGAR LATIN, LATE LATIN, LOW LATIN, MEDIEVAL LATIN, MODERN LATIN **3** a person whose language is derived from Latin, as a Spaniard, Italian, or Latin American **4** a Roman Catholic: so called esp. by Eastern Christians

☆**La·ti·na** (la tē′nə, lə-) *n.* ⟦AmSp, fem. of LATINO⟧ [*sometimes* **l-**] **1** a Latin

American woman or girl **2** a usually Spanish-speaking woman or girl of Latin American birth or descent who lives in the U.S. —*adj.* of, relating to, or characteristic of Latinas

USAGE—for *n.* 2 and the *adj.*, now often preferred to *Hispanic*

Latin alphabet the alphabet used for writing in Latin by the ancient Romans, from which most modern European alphabets are derived: it consisted of 23 letters (*J*, *U*, and *W* were added later)

Latin America that part of the Western Hemisphere south of the U.S., in Mexico, Central America, the West Indies, & South America, where Spanish, Portuguese, & French are the official languages —**Latin American**

Lat·in·ate (-āt′, -it) *adj.* of, derived from, or similar to Latin

Latin Church WESTERN CHURCH (sense 2)

Latin cross a plain, right-angled cross having the vertical bar longer

Lat·in·ism (lat′'n iz′əm) *n.* **1** a word, phrase, grammatical construction, or other feature originating in or peculiar to Latin **2** a Latin quality

Lat·in·ist (-ist) *n.* a specialist in the study of the Latin language or of Roman culture

La·tin·i·ty (la tin′i tē) *n.* ⟦L *latinitas*⟧ **1** the use or knowledge of Latin **2** a way of speaking or writing Latin **3** a writing quality characterized by a style, vocabulary, etc. influenced by Latin or classical Latin writing

Lat·in·ize (lat′'n īz′) *vt.* **-ized′**, **-iz′ing** ⟦LL *latinizare*, to translate into Latin < L *Latinus*, LATIN⟧ **1** [Archaic] to translate into Latin **2** to give Latin form or characteristics to **3** to transliterate into the Latin alphabet; Romanize **4** to bring into conformity with the rites, practices, etc. of the Roman Catholic Church —*vi.* to use Latin expressions, forms, etc. —**Lat′in·i·za′tion** *n.* —**Lat′in·iz′er** *n.*

☆**La·ti·no** (la tē′nō, lə-) *n., pl.* **-nos** ⟦AmSp < Sp, lit., Latin < L *Latinus*, LATIN⟧ [*sometimes* **l-**] **1** a Latin American **2** a usually Spanish-speaking person of Latin American birth or descent who lives in the U.S. —*adj.* of, relating to, or characteristic of Latinos [*Latino* music]

USAGE—for *n.* 2 and the *adj.*, now often preferred to *Hispanic*

Latin Quarter section of Paris, south of the Seine, where many artists and students live

Latin Rite **1** the liturgy and other rites of the Catholic Church as authorized for use in Rome and generally throughout the Western Church **2** WESTERN CHURCH (sense 2)

Latin square any square array of numbers, letters, etc. so arranged that every element occurs exactly once in each row and in each column

lat·ish (lāt′ish) *adj., adv.* somewhat late

la·tis·si·mus dor·si (lä tis′i məs dôr′sī, dôr′sē) *pl.* **la·tis′si·mi dor′si** (lä tis′i mē-) ⟦ModL (*musculus*) *latissimus dorsi*, broadest (muscle) of the back⟧ either of the large, wide, triangular muscles, one on each side of the back, connecting the lower and central spine with the arm: it helps rotate, extend, and adduct the arm

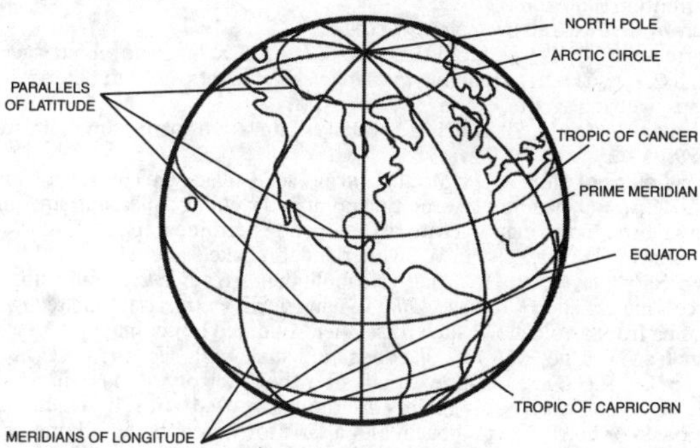

lines of latitude and longitude

lat·i·tude (lat′ə to͞od′, -tyo͞od′) *n.* ⟦OFr < L *latitudo* < *latus*, wide: see LATERAL⟧ **1** [Rare] breadth; width **2** extent; scope; range of applicability **3** freedom from narrow restrictions; freedom of opinion, conduct, or action **4** *see* ASTRONOMICAL LATITUDE, CELESTIAL LATITUDE **5** *Geog. a)* angular distance, measured in degrees, north or south from the equator [a ship at forty degrees north *latitude*] *b)* a region or place as determined by such measurement Cf. LONGITUDE —**lat′i·tu′di·nal** *adj.* —**lat′i·tu′di·nal·ly** *adv.*

lat·i·tu·di·nar·i·an (lat′ə to͞o′də ner′ē ən, -tyo͞o′-) *adj.* ⟦< L *latitudo* (gen. *latitudinis*): see prec. & -ARIAN⟧ liberal in one's views; permitting free thought, esp. in religious matters; very tolerant —*n.* a person who has very liberal views and, in religion, is tolerant of a wide variety of doctrines and forms of worship —**lat′i·tu′di·nar′i·an·ism′** *n.*

La·tium (lā′shəm, -shē əm) ⟦L: see LATIN⟧ **1** region of central Italy, on the Tyrrhenian Sea: 6,644 sq mi (17,208 sq km); chief city, Rome: It. name LAZIO **2** ancient country in the part of this region southeast of Rome

lat·ke (lät′kə) *n.* ⟦Yiddish < Russ *latka*, a patch⟧ a fried cake made of grated potatoes mixed with beaten eggs, flour, and, usually, onions and seasonings

La Tour (lȧ to͝or′), **Georges de** (zhôrzh də) 1593-1652; Fr. painter

la·tri·a (lə trī′ə) *n.* ⟦LL(Ec) < Gr(Ec) *latreia* < Gr, hired service < *latreuein*, to serve, worship < *latris*, hired servant: for IE base see LARCENY⟧ *R.C.Ch.* that worship which is due to God alone: distinguished from DULIA, HYPERDULIA

la·trine (lə trēn′) *n.* ⟦Fr < L *latrina*, contr. of *lavatrina*, bath < *lavare*, to wash: see LAVE⟧ a toilet, privy, etc. for the use of a large number of people, as in an army camp

La·trobe (lə trōb′), **Benjamin Henry** 1764-1820; U.S. architect, born in England

-la·try (lə trē) ⟦Gr(Ec) *-latreia* < *latreia*: see LATRIA⟧ *combining form* worship of or excessive devotion to [*bibliolatry*, *demonolatry*]

Latium (4th cent. B.C.)

lats[1] (lats) *pl.n.* [Slang] latissimus dorsi muscles, esp. of a bodybuilder or weight lifter

lats[2] (läts) *n., pl.* **lat·i** (lät′ē) ⟦Latvian⟧ the former monetary unit of Latvia

lat·te (lä′tā) *n.* ⟦It⟧ espresso coffee mixed with steamed milk

lat·ten (lat′'n) *n.* ⟦ME *laton* < OFr < Ar *lātūn*, copper⟧ **1** brass or a brasslike alloy hammered into thin sheets, formerly used for making church vessels **2** any metal, esp. tin, in thin sheets

lat·ter (lat′ər) *adj.* ⟦ME *lattre* < OE *lætra*, compar. of *læt*: it represents the orig. compar. form; LATER is a new formation⟧ **1** *alt. compar. of* LATE **2** *a)* later; more recent *b)* nearer the end or close [the *latter* part of May] **3** last mentioned of two: often used absolutely (with *the*) [Jack and Bill are twins, but the *latter* is shorter than the former]: opposed to FORMER[1] (sense 2)

lat·ter-day (-dā′) *adj.* of recent or present time; modern

☆**Lat·ter-day Saint** *see* MORMON

lat·ter·ly (lat′ər lē) *adv.* lately; of late; recently

lat·tice (lat′is) *n.* ⟦ME *latis* < OFr *lattis* < *latte* < MHG < OHG *latta*: see LATH⟧ **1** an openwork structure of crossed strips or bars of wood, metal, etc. used as a screen, support, etc. **2** something resembling or suggesting such a structure **3** a door, gate, shutter, trellis, etc. formed of such a structure **4** *Physics a)* a three-dimensional pattern of points in space, as of atoms or groups of atoms in a solid or crystal *b)* SPACE LATTICE *c)* the arrangement in a geometric pattern of fissionable and nonfissionable material in a nuclear reactor —*vt.* **-ticed**, **-tic·ing** **1** to arrange like a lattice; make a lattice of **2** to furnish or cover with a lattice or latticework —**lat′tice·like′** *adj.*

lat·tice·work (-wurk′) *n.* **1** a lattice **2** lattices collectively; trelliswork Also **lat′tic·ing**

lat·ti·ci·nio (lat′ə chēn′yō) *n.* ⟦It, lit., food prepared with milk < LL *lacticinium* < L *lac*, milk: see GALACTIC⟧ **1** opaque white glass, often used in threads for a decorative pattern on glassware **2** this type of glassware

Lat·ti·more (lat′ə môr′), **Richmond (Alexander)** 1906-84; U.S. scholar, translator, & poet

Latv *abbrev.* **1** Latvia **2** Latvian

Lat·vi·a (lat′vē ə) country in N Europe, on the Baltic Sea: from 1940 to 1991 it was a republic of the U.S.S.R.: 24,938 sq mi (64,589 sq km); cap. Riga: formerly, **Latvian Soviet Socialist Republic**

Lat·vi·an (-ən) *n.* **1** a person born or living in Latvia **2** the Baltic language spoken in Latvia —*adj.* of Latvia or its people, language, or culture

laud (lôd) *n.* ⟦ME *laude* < OFr < ML(Ec) *laudes*, pl. < L *laus* (gen. *laudis*), glory, praise < ? IE echoic base **lēu-* > OE *leoth*, Ger *lied*, song⟧ **1** [Archaic] praise **2** [*often* **L-**] [*pl., usually with sing. v.*] the service of dawn which constitutes the second (or, when said together with matins, the first) of the canonical hours and includes psalms of praise; morning prayer —*vt.* ⟦ME *lauden* < L *laudare* < the n.⟧ to praise; extol —*SYN.* PRAISE

Laud (lôd), **William** 1573-1645; Eng. prelate: archbishop of Canterbury (1633-45): executed

laud·a·ble (lôd′ə bəl) *adj.* ⟦L *laudabilis*⟧ worthy of being lauded —**laud′a·bil′i·ty** *n.*, **laud′a·ble·ness** —**laud′a·bly** *adv.*

lau·da·num (lôd′'n əm) *n.* ⟦ModL, altered use (by PARACELSUS) of ML var. of *ladanum*: see LABDANUM⟧ a solution of opium in alcohol: formerly taken as a painkiller and once popular as a narcotic

lau·da·tion (lô dā′shən) *n.* ⟦L *laudatio*⟧ a lauding or being lauded

laud·a·to·ry (lôd′ə tôr′ē) *adj.* ⟦LL *laudatorius* < L *laudare*: see LAUD⟧ expressing praise; eulogistic; commendatory: also **laud′a·tive**

laugh (laf) *vi.* ⟦ME *laughen* < OE *hleahhan*, akin to Ger *lachen* (OHG *hlahhan*) < IE base **klēg-*, to cry out, sound > Gr *klangē*, L *clangor*⟧ **1** to make the explosive sounds of the voice, and the characteristic movements of the features and body, that express mirth, amusement, ridicule, etc. **2** to be amused **3** to feel or suggest joyousness; appear bright and merry [*laughing* eyes] —*vt.* **1** to express or say with laughter **2** to bring about, effect, or cause to be by means of laughter [to *laugh* oneself hoarse] —*n.* **1** the act or sound of laughing **2** anything that provokes or is fit to provoke laughter **3** [*pl.*] [Informal] mere diversion or pleasure —**have the last laugh** to win or prevail ultimately, after apparent defeat and discomfiture —**laugh at** **1** to be amused by **2** to make fun of; ridicule; deride **3** to be indifferent to or contemptuous of; disregard —**laugh away** to get rid of (something unpleasant or embarrassing) by laughter —**laugh down** to silence or suppress by laughing —**laugh up** (or **in**) **one's sleeve** to laugh secretly or inwardly —**laugh off** to reject or dismiss from consideration as by laughter or ridicule —**laugh on** (or **out of**) **the other** (or **wrong**) **side of one's face** (or **mouth**) to undergo a change in mood from joy to sorrow, from amusement to annoyance, etc. —**no laughing matter** a serious matter —**laugh'er** *n.*

SYN.—**laugh** is the general word for the sounds or exhalation made in expressing mirth, amusement, etc.; **chuckle** implies soft laughter in low tones, expressive of mild amusement or inward satisfaction; **giggle** and **titter** both refer to a half-suppressed laugh consisting of a series of rapid, high-pitched sounds, suggesting embarrassment, silliness, etc., but **titter** is also used of a laugh of mild amusement suppressed in affected politeness; **snicker** is used of a sly, half-suppressed laugh, as at another's discomfiture or a bawdy story; **guffaw** refers to loud, coarse laughter

laugh·a·ble (laf'ə bəl) *adj.* **1** of such a nature as to cause laughter; amusing **2** so ridiculous as to deserve laughter or scorn; ludicrous —SYN. FUNNY —**laugh'a·ble·ness** *n.* —**laugh'a·bly** *adv.*

laugh·er (laf'ər) *n.* **1** one that laughs ☆**2** [Informal] a contest won by a wide margin; easy victory

laugh·ing (laf'iŋ) *adj.* **1** that laughs or makes a sound like laughter [a *laughing* brook] **2** uttered with laughter [a *laughing* remark] —*n.* laughter —**laugh'ing·ly** *adv.*

laughing gas nitrous oxide used as an anesthetic: so called from the laughter and exhilaration that inhaling it may induce

laughing jackass KOOKABURRA

laugh·ing·stock (laf'iŋ stäk') *n.* an object of ridicule; butt

laugh·ter (laf'tər) *n.* ⟦ME < OE *hleahtor* (akin to Ger *gelächter*) < base of *hleahhan*, to LAUGH⟧ **1** the action of laughing or the sound resulting **2** an indication of mirth or amusement [with *laughter* in her eyes] **3** [Archaic] a matter for or cause of laughter

laugh track recorded laughter, applause, etc. added to a soundtrack, as of a TV program, to simulate the responses of a studio audience

launce (lôns, lans, läns) *n.* ⟦prob. < LANCE, from its shape⟧ SAND LANCE

launch[1] (lônch) *vt.* ⟦ME *launchen* < OFr *lanchier* < LL(Ec) *lanceare*, to wield a lance < L *lancea*, LANCE⟧ **1** to hurl, discharge, or send off (a weapon, blow, etc.) **2** to send forth with some force [to *launch* a plane by catapult] **3** to cause (a newly built vessel) to slide from the land into the water; set afloat **4** to set in operation; start, inaugurate, etc. [to *launch* an attack, *launch* a new ad campaign] **5** to start (a person) on some course or career —*vi.* **1** to put to sea: often with *out* or *forth* **2** to start on some new course or enterprise: often with *out* or *forth* **3** to throw oneself (*into*) with vigor; rush; plunge [to *launch* into a tirade] —*n.* the act or process of launching —*adj.* designating or of vehicles, facilities, sites, etc. used in the launching of spacecraft or missiles

launch[2] (lônch) *n.* ⟦Sp or Port *lancha* < ? Malay *lancharan* < *lanchar*, swift⟧ **1** [Historical] the largest boat carried by a warship **2** an open, or partly enclosed, motorboat

launch·er (lôn'chər) *n.* **1** a catapult **2** *a)* a device, attached to a rifle, for shooting grenades *b)* a weapon, as an RPG, for shooting grenades: in full **grenade launcher** **3** a device or structure that provides initial guidance to a self-propelled missile, spacecraft, etc. or that catapults an airplane from a flight deck

launching pad **1** LAUNCHPAD (sense 1) **2** [Informal] a place, thing, situation, etc. serving as the starting point or providing the impetus for something else

launch·pad (lônch'pad') *n.* **1** the platform from which a rocket, guided missile, etc. is launched **2** [Informal] LAUNCHING PAD (sense 2) Also written **launch pad**

launch vehicle any system, usually a rocket, designed to launch a spacecraft or other payload

launch window the period of time during which a missile, spacecraft, etc. must be launched so that it can arrive at a desired location at a specific time

laun·der (lôn'dər) *n.* ⟦ME, contr. < *lavender*, washerwoman < OFr *lavandier* < ML *lavandarius* < LL *lavandaria*, things to be washed < L *lavandus*, ger. of L *lavare*, to wash: see LAVE⟧ a water trough, esp. one used in mining for washing dirt from the ore —*vt.* **1** to wash, or wash and iron (clothes, etc.) **2** to exchange or invest (money) in such a way as to conceal that it came from an illegal or improper source **3** to make (something improper or offensive) seem less so —*vi.* **1** to withstand washing [a fabric that *launders* well] **2** to do laundry —**laun'der·er** *n.* —**laun'der·ing** *n.*

☆**laun·der·ette** (lôn'dər et') *n.* ⟦< *Launderette*, former service mark⟧ a self-service laundry: also [Chiefly Brit.] **laun·drette** (lôn dret')

laun·dress (lôn'dris) *n.* a woman whose work is washing clothes, ironing, etc.; washerwoman

☆**laun·dro·mat** (lôn'drə mat') *n.* ⟦< *Laundromat*, a former service mark < a trademark for a brand of automatic washing machine⟧ a self-service laundry: also **laun·der·mat** (lôn'dər mat')

laun·dry (lôn'drē) *n., pl.* **-dries** ⟦ME *lavenderie* < OFr < *lavandier*: see LAUNDER⟧ **1** [Rare] the act or process of laundering **2** *a)* a room with facilities for laundering *b)* a commercial establishment providing laundering service *c)* a commercial establishment providing self-service laundering facilities; laundromat **3** clothes, linens, etc. that have been, or are about to be, laundered **4** a place or process for laundering money that has been illegally or improperly obtained

laundry list [Informal] any lengthy list of items, esp. one regarded as including too much and not being selective enough [a *laundry list* of complaints]

laun·dry·man (-man', -mən) *n., pl.* **-men'** (-men', -mən) a man who works in or for a laundry, esp. one who collects and delivers clothes, etc. for laundering service

laun·dry·wom·an (-wʊom'ən) *n., pl.* **-wom'en** (-wim'in) LAUNDRESS

Lau·ra (lôr'ə) *n.* ⟦prob. short for *Laurencia*, fem. of LAURENCE⟧ a feminine name: dim. *Laurie*; var. *Loretta, Lori, Lorinda*

Lau·ra·sia (lô rā'zhə, -shə) ⟦LAUR(ENTIAN) + (EUR)ASIA⟧ the Mesozoic landmass in the Northern Hemisphere that included what are now North America and Eurasia: it and Gondwana were the result of the splitting of Pangea

lau·re·ate (lôr'ē it; *for v.*, -āt') *adj.* ⟦ME < L *laureatus* < *laurea* (*corona*), laurel (wreath), fem. of *laureus*, of laurel < *laurus*, laurel⟧ **1** woven of sprigs of laurel: said of a crown or wreath **2** crowned with a laurel wreath as a mark of honor or distinction **3** worthy of honor; distinguished; preeminent, esp. among poets —*n.* **1** a person on whom honor or distinction is conferred **2** POET LAUREATE —*vt.* **-at'ed**, **-at'ing** [Archaic] **1** to honor or confer distinction upon **2** to appoint to the position of poet laureate —**lau're·ate·ship'** *n.*

lau·rel (lôr'əl) *n.* ⟦ME *laurer, lorel* < OFr *lorier* < L *laurus*⟧ **1** any of a genus (*Laurus*) of evergreen trees or shrubs of the laurel family, native to S Europe and widely cultivated in the U.S., with large, glossy, aromatic leaves, greenish-yellow flowers, and black berries: see BAY LEAF **2** the foliage of this tree, esp. as woven into wreaths such as those used by the ancient Greeks to crown the victors in various contests or by the ancient Romans to signify military success **3** [*pl.*] *a)* fame; honor *b)* victory **4** any of various trees and shrubs resembling the true laurel, as the mountain laurel, cherry laurel, or California laurel —*adj.* designating a family (Lauraceae, order Laurales) of dicotyledonous shrubs and trees, including the sassafras, cinnamon, and camphor —*vt.* **-reled** or **-relled**, **-rel·ing** or **-rel·ling** **1** to crown with laurel **2** to honor —**look to one's laurels** to beware of having one's achievements surpassed —**rest on one's laurels** to be satisfied with what one has already achieved

Lau·rel (lôr'əl), **Stan(ley)** (born *Arthur Stanley Jefferson*) 1890-1965; U.S. film comedian, born in England: teamed with Oliver HARDY

Lau·rence (lôr'əns) *n.* ⟦L *Laurentius*, prob. < *Laurentum*, town in Latium < ? *laurus*, laurel⟧ a masculine name: dim. *Larry*; var. *Lawrence*; equiv. Fr. *Laurent*, Ger. *Lorenz*, It. & Sp. *Lorenzo*; fem. *Laura*

Lau·ren·tian (lô ren'shən) *adj.* ⟦< L *laurentius*, Lawrence + -AN⟧ **1** of or relating to the St. Lawrence River **2** designating or of a series of rocks of the Precambrian system in E Canada

Laurentian Mountains mountain range in S Quebec, Canada, extending along the St. Lawrence River valley: highest peak, 3,905 ft (1,190 m): also **Laurentian Highlands**

Laurentian Plateau CANADIAN SHIELD

lau·ric acid (lôr'ik) ⟦< ModL *Laurus* < L *laurus*, LAUREL + -IC⟧ a fatty acid, $CH_3(CH_2)_{10}COOH$, occurring in many vegetable fats, used in detergents, soaps, wetting agents, etc.

Lau·ri·er (lôr'ē ā'), Sir **Wilfrid** 1841-1919; Cdn. statesman: prime minister (1896-1911)

lau·ryl alcohol (lôr'əl) ⟦< ModL *Laurus* (see LAURIC ACID) + -YL⟧ a white solid, $C_{12}H_{26}O$, having a low melting point and yielding a pleasant-smelling liquid: used in the manufacture of detergents, perfumes, etc.

Lau·sanne (lō zan') city in W Switzerland, on Lake Geneva

la·va (lä'və, lav'ə) *n.* ⟦It < dial. (Neapolitan) *lave* < L *labes*, a fall, subsidence < *labi*, to slide < IE base **lāb-*, to hang down > LAP[1], LIP⟧ **1** melted rock issuing from a volcano **2** such rock when solidified by cooling

la·va·bo (lə vä'bō, -vā'-) *n., pl.* **-boes** ⟦L, I shall wash < *lavare*: see LAVE⟧ **1** [*often* **L-**] *R.C.Ch.* *a)* a short ritual, after the Offertory of Mass, in which the celebrant washes his fingers *b)* the basin used (in full **lavabo dish** (or **basin** or **bowl**)) **2** *a)* a basin and a tank for water above it, hung on a wall *b)* a wall planter resembling this

la·vage (lə väzh', lav'ij) *n.* ⟦Fr < *laver* < L *lavare*, to wash: see LAVE⟧ *Med.* the washing out of an organ, as the stomach, intestinal tract, or sinuses

La·val[1] (là vȧl'; *E* lə val'), **Pierre** (pyer) 1883-1945; Fr. politician: premier of France (1931-32; 1935-36): executed for treason

La·val[2] (là vȧl'; *E* lə val') ⟦after François de *Laval* (1623-1708), 1st bishop of Quebec⟧ city in SW Quebec, Canada, on an island just northwest of Montreal

lava lamp ⟦so called because the swirling motions resemble a flow of *lava*⟧ a vertical cylindrical lamp containing a thick liquid mixed with masses of a colored waxy substance: a lightbulb at the lamp's base generates heat that causes the waxy masses to rise and circulate in random swirling motions

la·va-la·va (lä'və lä'və) *n.* ⟦Samoan⟧ a loincloth or skirt of printed cloth, traditionally worn by men and women of the South Sea islands

lav·a·lier or **lav·a·liere** (lav'ə lir', lä'və-) *n.* ⟦Fr *lavallière*, kind of tie, after Duchesse de *La Vallière* (1644-1710), mistress of Louis XIV⟧ an ornament hanging from a chain, worn around the neck: also **la'val·lière'**

lavalier microphone

—adj. designating or of a type of very small microphone formerly hung on a cord around the neck, but now usually attached to the clothing with a clip

la·va·tion (la vā′shən) *n.* ⟦L *lavatio* < *lavare*, to wash: see LAVE⟧ LAVAGE

lav·a·to·ry (lav′ə tôr′ē) *n., pl.* **-ries** ⟦LL *lavatorium* < L *lavare*, to wash: see fol.⟧ **1** [Now Rare] a bowl or basin, esp. one with faucets and drainage, for washing the face and hands; washbowl **2** *a)* a room equipped with a washbowl and flush toilet *b)* [Chiefly Brit.] a flush toilet

lave (lāv) *vt.* **laved, lav′ing** ⟦ME *laven* < OE & OFr: OE *lafian* (akin to MDu *laven*, OHG *labon*) < L *lavare*; OFr *laver* < L *lavare* < IE base **lou-*, to wash > LATHER, LYE⟧ [Old Poet.] **1** to wash or bathe **2** to flow along or against **3** to dip or pour with or as with a ladle *—vi.* to wash or bathe

lav·en·der (lav′ən dər) *n.* ⟦ME < Anglo-Fr *lavendre* < ML *lavandria*, akin to *lavendula* (> Ger *lavendel*) < L *lavare*, to wash (see prec.): from use as bath perfume⟧ **1** any of a genus (*Lavandula*) of fragrant European plants of the mint family, having spikes of pale-purplish flowers and yielding an aromatic oil (**oil of lavender**) **2** the dried flowers, leaves, and stalks of this plant, used to fill sachets and to perfume clothes, linens, etc. **3** a pale purple *—adj.* **1** pale-purple ☆**2** [Informal] of or having to do with homosexuals or homosexuality *—vt.* to perfume with lavender

lavender water a perfume or toilet water made from flowers of the lavender plant

la·ver¹ (lā′vər) *n.* ⟦ME *lavour* < OFr *laveoir* < L *lavatorium* < *lavare*, to wash: see LAVE⟧ **1** [Archaic] *a)* a large basin to wash in *b)* water or any cleansing liquid **2** a large basin used for ceremonial washing by priests of the ancient Jewish Temple

la·ver² (lā′vər) *n.* ⟦L, water plant⟧ any of various large, edible, ribbonlike seaweeds

La·vin·i·a (lə vin′ē ə, -vin′yə) *n.* ⟦L⟧ a feminine name: var. *Lavina*

lav·ish (lav′ish) *adj.* ⟦< ME *lavas*, abundance < MFr < OFr *lavasse*, torrent of rain, prob. < *laver*, to wash: see LAVE⟧ **1** very generous or liberal in giving or spending, often extravagantly so; prodigal **2** characterized by abundance, luxuriance, splendor, etc. [a *lavish* wedding reception] *—vt.* to give or spend generously or liberally [to *lavish* time and money on pets] **—*SYN.*** PROFUSE **—lav′ish·ly** *adv.* **—lav′ish·ness** *n.*

La·voi·sier (lȧ vwȧ zyā′; *E* lə vwä′zē ā′), **An·toine Lau·rent** (än twȧn lō rän′) 1743-94; Fr. chemist: guillotined

law (lô) *n.* ⟦ME *lawe* < OE *lagu* < Anglo-Norm **lagu*, akin to ON *lǫg*, pl. of *lag*, something laid down or settled < IE base **legh-*, to lie down > LIE¹⟧ **1** *a)* all the rules of conduct established and enforced by the authority, legislation, or custom of a given community, state, or other group (often with *the*) *b)* any one of such rules **2** the condition existing when obedience to such rules is general [to establish *law* and order] **3** the branch of knowledge dealing with such rules; jurisprudence **4** the system of courts in which such rules are referred to in defending one's rights, securing justice, etc. [to resort to *law* to settle a matter] **5** all such rules having to do with a particular sphere of human activity [business *law*] **6** common law, as distinguished from equity **7** the profession of lawyers, judges, etc.: often with *the* **8** *a)* a sequence of events in nature or in human activities that has been observed to occur with unvarying uniformity under the same conditions (often **law of nature**) *b)* the formulation in words of such a sequence [the *law* of gravitation, the *law* of diminishing returns] **9** any rule or principle expected to be observed [the *laws* of health, a *law* of grammar] **10** inherent tendency; instinct [the *law* of self-preservation] **11** *Eccles. a)* a divine commandment *b)* all divine commandments collectively **12** *Math., Logic, etc.* a general principle to which all applicable cases must conform [the *laws* of exponents] **13** [Brit.] *Sports* an allowance in distance or time as in a race; handicap *— vi., vt.* [Informal or Dial.] to take legal action (against) **—lay down the law 1** to give explicit orders in an authoritative manner **2** to give a scolding (*to*) **—read law** to study to become a lawyer **—the Law 1** the Mosaic law, or the part of the Jewish Scriptures containing it; specif., the Pentateuch ☆**2** [**the l-**] [Informal] a policeman or the police

***SYN.*—law**, in its specific application, implies prescription and enforcement by a ruling authority [the *law* of the land]; a **rule** may not be authoritatively enforced, but it is generally observed in the interests of order, uniformity, etc. [the *rules* of golf]; **regulation** refers to a rule of a group or organization, enforced by authority [military *regulations*]; a **statute** is a law enacted by a legislative body; an **ordinance** is a local, generally municipal, law; a **canon** is, strictly, a law of a church, but the term is also used of any rule or principle regarded as true or in conformity with good usage [the *canons* of taste] See also **theory**

law-a·bid·ing (lô′ə bīd′iŋ) *adj.* characterized by lawful behavior

law·book (-bo͝ok′) *n.* a book containing or discussing laws, esp. one used as a textbook by law students

law·break·er (-brāk′ər) *n.* a person who violates the law **—law′break′ing** *adj., n.*

law court a court for administering justice under the law

law French NORMAN FRENCH (sense 2)

law·ful (lô′fəl) *adj.* **1** in conformity with the principles of the law; permitted by law [a *lawful* act]: see also LEGAL (sense 2) **2** recognized by or established by law; just or valid [*lawful* debts] **3** obeying the law; law-abiding **—*SYN.*** LEGAL **—law′ful·ly** *adv.* **—law′ful·ness** *n.*

law·giv·er (-giv′ər) *n.* a person who draws up, introduces, or enacts a code of laws for a nation or people

law·less (-lis) *adj.* **1** without law; not regulated by the authority of law [a *lawless* city] **2** not in conformity with law; illegal [*lawless* practices] **3** not obeying the law; unruly; disorderly **—law′less·ly** *adv.* **—law′less·ness** *n.*

law·mak·er (-māk′ər) *n.* a person who makes or helps to make laws; esp., a member of a legislature; legislator **—law′mak′ing** *adj., n.*

law·man (-mən) *n., pl.* **-men** (-mən) a law officer; esp., a marshal, sheriff, constable, etc.

law merchant [Historical] the body of customary laws regulating trade and commerce that developed in medieval Europe

lawn¹ (lôn) *n.* ⟦ME *launde* < OFr, heath < Bret *lann*, heath, country: see LAND⟧ **1** land covered with grass kept closely mowed, esp. in front of or around a house **2** the grass itself [to mow the *lawn*] **3** [Archaic] an open space in a forest; glade **—lawn′y** *adj.*

lawn² (lôn) *n.* ⟦ME *lawne*, for *laune lynen*, Laon linen, after *Laon*, city in France, where made⟧ a fine, sheer cloth of linen or cotton, used for blouses, curtains, etc. **—lawn′y** *adj.*

lawn bowling a game played on a smooth lawn with wooden balls, which are rolled to stop as near as possible to a target ball (the *jack*)

lawn mower a hand-propelled or power-driven machine for cutting the grass of a lawn

lawn tennis *see* TENNIS

law of averages the popularly held supposition that a possible event can be expected to occur with a frequency at or near its probability

law of mass action the law that the rate of a chemical reaction is directly proportional to the concentrations of the reactants

Law of Moses MOSAIC LAW

law of nations INTERNATIONAL LAW

Law·rence¹ (lôr′əns, lär′-) *n.* a masculine name: see LAURENCE

Law·rence² (lôr′əns, lär′-) **1 D(avid) H(erbert)** 1885-1930; Eng. novelist & poet **2 Ernest O(rlando)** 1901-58; U.S. physicist **3 Gertrude** (born *Gertrud Alexandra Dagmar Lawrence Klasen*) 1898-1952; Eng. actress **4 T(homas) E(dward)** (changed name, 1927, to *Thomas Edward Shaw*) 1888-1935; Brit. soldier & writer: called **Lawrence of Arabia 5** Sir **Thomas** 1769-1830; Eng. portrait painter

☆**law·ren·ci·um** (lô ren′sē əm) *n.* ⟦ModL, after E. O. LAWRENCE² (who invented the cyclotron) + -IUM⟧ a radioactive, metallic chemical element, the last member of the actinide series: originally produced by bombarding californium with boron nuclei: symbol, Lr; at. no. 103: see the periodic table of elements in the Reference Supplement

Law·son (lô′sən) *adj.* ⟦after T. W. *Lawson* (1857-1925), U.S. financier, for whom designed⟧ designating or of a style of overstuffed sofa or chair with straight lines and a low back higher than the arms, which are square or rolled

law·suit (lô′so͞ot′) *n.* SUIT (*n.* 5)

law·yer (lô′yər) *n.* ⟦ME *lawyere*: see LAW & -IER⟧ a person who has been trained in the law, esp. one whose profession is advising others in matters of law or representing them in lawsuits *—vi.* to work as a lawyer **—lawyer up** [Slang] **1** to secure the services of a lawyer or legal team **2** to make aggressive use of legal tactics with a lawyer or legal team **—law′yer·ly** *adj.*

***SYN.*—lawyer** is the general term for a person trained in the law and authorized to advise or represent others in legal matters; **counselor** and its British equivalent, **barrister**, refer to a lawyer who conducts cases in court; **attorney**, usually, and its British equivalent, **solicitor**, always, refer to a lawyer legally empowered to act for a client, as in drawing up a contract or will, settling property, etc.; **counsel**, often equivalent to **counselor**, is frequently used collectively for a group of counselors

law·yer·ing (-iŋ) *n.* the profession of being a lawyer; the practice of law

lax (laks) *adj.* ⟦ME < L *laxus* < IE base **(s)lēg-*, loose, lax > SLACK¹⟧ **1** *a)* loose; emptying easily (said of the bowels) *b)* having lax bowels **2** slack; of a loose texture; not rigid or tight **3** not strict or exact; careless [*lax* morals] **4** *Bot.* loose; open: said of a flower cluster **5** *Phonet.* articulated with the jaw and tongue muscles relatively relaxed: said of certain vowels, as (e) and (i): opposed to TENSE¹ *—n.* a lax vowel **—*SYN.*** REMISS **—lax′ly** *adv.* **—lax′ness** *n.*

LAX¹ (laks) *n.* ⟦< LA(CROSSE), with *X* substituting for *crosse*, as if equiv. to CROSS⟧ [Informal] LACROSSE: also written **lax**

LAX² *symbol* Los Angeles International Airport

lax·a·tion (lak sā′shən) *n.* ⟦ME *laxacion* < L *laxatio*⟧ the act or process of making or being made lax

lax·a·tive (lak′sə tiv) *adj.* ⟦ME *laxatif* < OFr < ML *laxativus* < LL, mitigating < pp. of L *laxare*, to relax, slacken < *laxus*: see LAX⟧ tending to make lax; specif., making the bowels loose, as in relieving constipation *—n.* any laxative medicine or substance; mild cathartic **—*SYN.*** PHYSIC

lax·i·ty (lak′si tē) *n.* ⟦Fr *laxité* < L *laxitas*⟧ the quality or condition of being lax; looseness

Lax·ness (läks′nes), **Hall·dór (Kiljan)** (häl′dôr) (born *Halldór Gudjonsson*) 1902-98; Icelandic novelist

lay¹ (lā) *vt.* **laid, lay′ing** ⟦ME *leyen*, new formation < 3d pers. sing. of earlier *leggen* < OE *lecgan*, lit., to make lie (akin to Goth *lagjan*, Ger *legen*) < pt. base of OE *licgan*, to LIE¹⟧ **1** to cause to come down or fall with force; knock down, as from an erect position [a blow *laid* him low] **2** to cause to lie; place or put so as to be in a resting or recumbent position; deposit: often with *on* or *in* [*lay* the pen on the desk] **3** *a)* to put down or place (bricks, carpeting, etc.) in the correct position or way for a specific purpose *b)* to cause to be situated in a particular place or condition [the film's first scene is *laid* in France] *c)* to establish or prepare as a basis or for use [to *lay* the groundwork] *d)* to arrange the fuel in a fireplace for (a fire) **4** to place; put;

set: esp. of something abstract [to *lay* emphasis on accuracy] **5** to produce and deposit (an egg or eggs): said of a bird, reptile, etc. **6** *a)* to cause to subside or settle [*lay* the dust] *b)* to allay, suppress, overcome, or appease [to *lay* a ghost, *lay* one's fears] **7** to press or smooth down [to *lay* the nap of cloth] **8** to bet (a specified sum, etc.) **9** to impose or place (a tax, penalty, etc. *on* or *upon*) **10** to work out; devise [to *lay* plans] **11** to prepare (a table) for a meal; set with silverware, plates, etc. **12** to advance, present, or assert [to *lay* claim to property, to *lay* a matter before the voters] **13** to attribute; ascribe; charge; impute [to *lay* the blame on someone] **14** to arrange and twist together (strands) so as to form (rope, yarn, etc.) ☆**15** [Slang] to have sexual intercourse with: somewhat vulgar **16** *Mil.* to aim (a gun) by adjusting its direction and elevation —*vi.* **1** to lay an egg or eggs **2** to bet; wager **3** to lie; recline: a dialectal or nonstandard usage: see usage note below **4** [Dial.] to get ready; plan [*laying* to rob a store] **5** *Naut.* to go; proceed [all hands, *lay* aft to the fantail!] —*n.* **1** the way or position in which something is situated or arranged [the *lay* of the land] ☆**2** a share in the profits of some enterprise, esp. of a whaling expedition **3** the direction or amount of twist of the strands of a rope, cable, etc. ☆**4** [Informal] terms of employment, a sale, etc. **5** [Slang] *a)* an instance of sexual intercourse [a quick *lay*] *b)* a partner in sexual intercourse, esp. the female partner [a good *lay*]: somewhat vulgar **6** [Slang, Chiefly Brit.] one's occupation, esp. as a criminal —**lay about one** to deliver blows on all sides; strike out in every direction —**lay a course 1** *Naut.* to proceed in a certain direction without the need for tacking **2** to make plans to do something —**lay aside 1** to put to one side; lay out of the way **2** to save; lay away —**lay away 1** to set aside for future use; save ☆**2** to set (merchandise) aside for future delivery ☆**3** to bury: usually in the passive —**lay by 1** to save; lay away **2** [Dial.] ☆*a)* to cultivate (a crop) for the last time *b)* to harvest and store (a crop or crops) —**lay down 1** to sacrifice or give up (one's life) **2** to assert or declare emphatically **3** to bet; wager **4** to store away, as wine in a cellar —**lay for** [Informal] to be waiting to attack —**lay in** to get and store away —**lay into** [Informal] **1** to attack and hit repeatedly; beat **2** to attack with words; scold —**lay it on (thick)** [Informal] **1** to exaggerate or overdo **2** to express praise effusively —**lay low** *see the phrase under* LOW[1] —**lay off 1** to put (a garment, etc.) aside ☆**2** to put (an employee) out of work, esp. temporarily **3** to mark off the boundaries of ☆**4** [Slang] *a)* to cease *b)* to stop criticizing, teasing, etc. *c)* to stop for a rest **5** [Slang] to transfer part of (a bet) to another bookmaker so as to minimize risk: said of a bookmaker —**lay on 1** to spread on **2** to attack with force; strike repeatedly —**lay oneself open** to expose oneself to attack, blame, etc. —**lay open 1** to open up; cut open **2** to expose; uncover —**lay out 1** to spend **2** to arrange according to a plan **3** to spread out (clothes, equipment, etc.) ready for wear, inspection, etc. **4** to make (a corpse) ready for burial and for viewing, as at a wake **5** [Slang] to knock down or make unconscious **6** [Slang] to scold or censure (someone) —**lay over** ☆to stop a while in a place during a journey before going on —**lay something on someone** [Slang] **1** to tell something to someone **2** to give something to someone —**lay to 1** to attribute to; credit to or blame on **2** to apply oneself with vigor **3** *Naut.* *a)* to check a ship's forward motion, esp. by bringing the bow into the wind *b)* to lie more or less stationary with the bow to the wind (now usually *lie to*) —**lay to rest** to bury; inter —**lay up 1** to store for future use; hoard **2** to disable; confine to bed or the sickroom [*laid up* with the flu] **3** to take (a ship) out of operation, as by putting into a dry dock for repairs

USAGE—**lay**[1] and its inflections (**laid, laying**), meaning placing *something else* down, are commonly confused with **lie**[1] and its inflections (**lay, lain, lying**), meaning being or putting *oneself* in a resting or reclining position

lay[2] (lā) *vi. pt. of* LIE[1]

lay[3] (lā) *adj.* ⟦ME *lai* < OFr < LL(Ec) *laicus*, lay, not priestly < Gr *laikos* < *laos*, the people⟧ **1** of or consisting of the laity, or ordinary people, as distinguished from the clergy **2** not belonging to or connected with a given profession; nonprofessional [a legal handbook for *lay* readers]

lay[4] (lā) *n.* ⟦ME *lai* < OFr < Bret **laid*, song, akin to Ir *laod*⟧ **1** a short poem, esp. a narrative poem, orig. for singing as by a medieval minstrel **2** [Obs.] a song or melody

lay·a·bout (lā′ə bout′) *n.* [Brit. Informal] a loafer; bum

Lay·a·mon (lā′ə mən, lī′-) fl. *c.* 1200; Eng. poet and chronicler

lay analyst a psychoanalyst who is not a medical doctor

lay·a·way (lā′ə wā′) *n.* **1** a method of buying in which a deposit is made on something that is then set aside for delivery only after it is paid for in full, as by monthly payments **2** the state of an item thus set aside: chiefly in the phrase **in layaway**

lay brother *Eccles.* a member of a clerical religious order or congregation who is not a priest or a clerical student

lay-by (-bī′) *n.* **1** a widened section of a stream, canal, etc. where vessels can lay over or pass **2** a railroad siding **3** [Brit.] a widened section as along a highway, for emergency parking

lay day ⟦short for *delay day*⟧ *Commerce* any of the days allowed for loading or unloading a ship without payment of extra charge

lay·er (lā′ər) *n.* **1** a person or thing that lays **2** a single thickness, coat, fold, or stratum **3** a shoot or twig (of a living plant) bent down and partly covered with earth so that it may take root —*vi.* to form layers —*vt.* **1** to grow (a plant) by means of a LAYER (*n.* 3) **2** to arrange in or as if in layers **3** to trim and style (hair) to hang in layers

lay·er·age (lā′ər ij) *n.* the growing of plants by layering

☆**layer cake** a cake made in two or more layers, with icing, preserves, etc. between them

lay·ette (lā et′) *n.* ⟦Fr, dim. of *laie*, packing box, drawer < Fl *laeye* < MDu *lade*, a chest, trunk < Gmc **hlatho-*, container < base of LADE⟧ a complete outfit for a newborn baby, including clothes, bedding, and accessories

lay figure ⟦earlier *layman* < Du *leeman* < MDu *led*, limb, joint, akin to OE *lith*, limb + *man*, man⟧ **1** an artist's jointed model of the human form, on which drapery is arranged to get the proper effect **2** a person who is a mere puppet or a nonentity

lay·man (lā′mən) *n., pl.* **-men** (-mən) ⟦LAY[3] + MAN⟧ **1** a member of the laity; person not a member of the clergy **2** a person not belonging to or skilled in a given profession [a medical textbook not for the *layman*]

☆**lay·off** (lā′ôf′) *n.* ⟦< phr. LAY OFF (see LAY[1])⟧ the act of laying off; esp., temporary unemployment, or the period of this

lay of the land 1 the arrangement of the natural features of an area **2** the existing state or disposition of affairs

☆**lay·out** (lā′out′) *n.* **1** the act or process of laying something out **2** the manner in which anything is laid out; arrangement; specif., the plan or makeup of a newspaper, book page, advertisement, etc. **3** the thing laid out **4** the art or process of arranging type, illustrations, etc. in an advertisement, newspaper, etc. **5** an outfit or set, as of tools **6** [Informal] a residence, factory, etc., esp. when large and complex

☆**lay·o·ver** (-ō′vər) *n.* ⟦< phr. LAYOVER (see LAY[1])⟧ a stopping for a while in some place during a journey

lay·per·son (lā′pur′sən) *n.* a layman

lay reader READER (sense 2)

lay·up (-up′) *n.* ☆*Basketball* a type of shot made from just under the basket and, typically, off the backboard

lay·wom·an (lā′woom′ən) *n., pl.* **-wom′en** (-wim′in) **1** a woman of the laity; woman not a nun, not a member of the clergy, etc. **2** a woman not belonging to or skilled in a given profession

la·zar (lā′zər, laz′ər) *n.* ⟦ME < ML *lazarus*, leper < LL(Ec) *Lazarus* < Gr(Ec) *Lazaros*, LAZARUS[1]⟧ [Archaic] an impoverished, diseased, esp. leprous, person

laz·a·ret·to (laz′ə ret′ō) *n., pl.* **-tos** ⟦It < Venetian *lazareto, nazareto*, after Venetian church of Santa Madonna di *Nazaret*, used as a plague hospital during the 15th c.; initial *l-* by assoc. with *lazzaro*, leper: see prec.⟧ **1** [Historical] a public hospital for poor people having contagious diseases, esp. for lepers **2** a building or ship used as a quarantine station **3** a storage space below deck in the stern of a ship or boat Also, and for 3 usually, **laz·a·rette** or **laz·a·ret** (laz′ə ret′)

Laz·a·rus[1] (laz′ə rəs) *n.* ⟦LL(Ec) < Gr(Ec) *Lazaros* < Heb *el'azar*, lit., God has helped⟧ *Bible* **1** the brother of Mary and Martha, raised from the dead by Jesus: John 11 **2** the diseased beggar in Jesus' parable of the rich man and the beggar: Luke 16:19-31

Laz·a·rus[2] (laz′ə rəs), **Emma** 1849-87; U.S. poet

laze (lāz) *vi.* **lazed, laz′ing** ⟦back-form. < LAZY⟧ to be lazy or idle; loaf —*vt.* to spend (time, etc.) in idleness: often with *away* —*n.* an act or instance of lazing

La·zi·o (lä′tsē ō) *It. name for* LATIUM (the region)

laz·u·lite (laz′yə līt′, lazh′-) *n.* ⟦Ger *lazulith*, altered (infl. by ML *lazulum*, azure + Gr *lithos*, stone) < earlier *lazurstein* < ML *lazur* (see AZURE) + *stein*, STONE⟧ a hard, glassy, bright blue, monoclinic mineral, (Mg,Fe) $Al_2(PO_4)_2(OH)_2$, used sometimes as a gem; hydrous magnesium-iron aluminum phosphate

laz·u·rite (laz′yə rīt′, lazh′-) *n.* ⟦< ML *lazur* < Ar *lāzaward*, AZURE⟧ a very rare, hard, bluish, crystalline mineral, $(Na,Ca)_7(Al,Si)_{12}(O,S)_{24}[SO_4,Cl_2(OH)_2]_2$, that is the main component of lapis lazuli

la·zy (lā′zē) *adj.* **-zi·er, -zi·est** ⟦Early ModE, prob. < MLowG or MDu, as in MLowG *lasich*, slack, loose < IE **les-*, slack, tired, akin to base **lēi-*: see LATE⟧ **1** not eager or willing to work or exert oneself; indolent; slothful **2** slow and heavy; sluggish [a *lazy* river] **3** characterized by idleness, relaxation, etc. [a *lazy* day] ☆**4** designating or of a letter or figure placed on its side in a livestock brand — *vi., vt.* **-zied, -zy·ing** LAZE —**la′zi·ly** *adv.* —**la′zi·ness** *n.*

la·zy·bones (-bōnz′) *n.* [Informal] a lazy person

☆**Lazy Susan** a rotating tray placed at the center of a dining table, from which one can help oneself to food

lazy tongs tongs made with a series of crossed, jointed bars, that can be extended to pick up or deposit small objects at a distance

lb *symbol* ⟦abbrev. of LIBRA (*n.* 1)⟧ pound(s): also, for the plural, **lbs**

LB *abbrev.* **1** ⟦L *Lit(t)erarum Baccalaureus*⟧ Bachelor of Letters; Bachelor of Literature: also **L.B.** **2** *Football* linebacker: sometimes written **lb**

LBJ *abbrev.* Lyndon Baines Johnson

LBO (el′bē′ō′) *n., pl.* **LBOs** LEVERAGED BUYOUT

lc *abbrev. Printing* lowercase

LC *abbrev.* **1** Lance Corporal **2** Library of Congress

L/C or **l/c** *abbrev.* letter of credit

LC- *prefix U.S. Navy* landing craft: additional letters indicate type, as **LCV**, Landing Craft Vehicle

l.c. *abbrev.* ⟦L *loco citato*⟧ in the place cited

lcd or **LCD** *abbrev.* least (or lowest) common denominator

LCD (el′sē′dē′) *n.* ⟦*l(iquid-)c(rystal) d(isplay)*⟧ a type of low-power, electronic device displaying text or images, as on the screens of digital watches, cell phones, or computer monitors, using a pattern of tiny, sealed capsules which contain a transparent liquid crystal to which an electric field is applied: cf. LED

LCDR *abbrev.* Lieutenant Commander

l'cha·im (lə khä′yim) ***interj.*** ⟦Heb⟧ to life: used as a toast: also sp. ***l'chay'im***
lcm or **LCM** *abbrev.* least (or lowest) common multiple
LCpl *abbrev.* Lance Corporal
LCSW *abbrev.* Licensed Clinical Social Worker
LD *abbrev.* **1** learning disability **2** learning-disabled
LDC *abbrev.* less-developed country
LDL (el′dē′əl′) ***n.*** ⟦< LOW-DENSITY LIPOPROTEIN⟧ a lipoprotein that carries cholesterol in the blood to the cell tissues and that in excess is believed to increase the risk of coronary artery disease: cf. HDL
L-do·pa (el′dō′pə) ***n.*** ⟦L- + DOPA⟧ *see* DOPA
Ldp. *abbrev.* **1** Ladyship **2** Lordship
LDPE *abbrev.* low-density polyethylene
LDS *abbrev.* **1** Latter-day Saints **2** Licentiate in Dental Surgery
-le (əl, ′l) *suffix* **1** ⟦ME v. suffix *-len* < OE *-lian*⟧ forming verbs denoting repeated action, esp. of a small or trivial kind *[babble, sparkle]* **2** ⟦ME n. suffix *-el, -le* < OE *-ol, -ul, -el*⟧ forming nouns, orig. usually with a diminutive sense *[icicle, thimble]* **3** ⟦ME adj. suffix *-el* < OE *-ol*⟧ forming adjectives, esp. from verb stems *[brittle]*
lea[1] (lē) ***n.*** ⟦ME *leye* < OE *leah*, orig., open ground in a wood, akin to Du *-loo* (in Waterloo), Ger *-loh*, grove < IE base **leuk-*, to light > LIGHT[1] & L *lucus*, grove, orig., clearing, glade⟧ **1** [Old Poet.] a meadow or grassy field **2** LEY (sense 2)
lea[2] (lē) ***n.*** ⟦ME *lee*, prob. taken as sing. of *leese* < OFr *lesse*: see LEASH⟧ a measure of yarn varying from 80 to 300 yards, according to the kind of yarn (usually 80 yards for wool, 120 yards for silk and cotton, 300 yards for linen)
leach[1] (lēch) ***vt.*** ⟦prob. < OE *leccan*, to water, irrigate, orig. a caus. form of base akin to ON *leka*: see LEAK⟧ **1** to cause (a liquid) to filter down through some material **2** to subject to the washing action of a filtering liquid [wood ashes are *leached* to extract lye] **3** to extract (a soluble substance) from some material by causing water to filter down through the material [lye is *leached* from wood ashes] —***vi.*** **1** to lose soluble matter as a result of the filtering through of water [soil that has *leached* badly] **2** to dissolve and be washed away —***n.*** **1** the action of leaching **2** a sievelike container used in leaching **3** LEACHATE —**leach′a·ble** ***adj.*** —**leach′er** ***n.***
leach[2] (lēch) ***n.*** *alt. sp. of* LEECH[2]
leach·ate (lē′chāt′) ***n.*** a solution obtained by leaching
☆**leach·y** (lē′chē) ***adj.*** ⟦LEACH[1] + -Y[2]⟧ porous, as soil
Lea·cock (lē′käk′), **Stephen (Butler)** 1869-1944; Cdn. humorist & economist, born in England
lead[1] (lēd) ***vt.*** **led, lead′ing** ⟦ME *leden* < OE *lædan*, caus. of *lithan*, to travel, go, akin to Ger *leiten*: for IE base see LOAD⟧ **1** *a)* to show the way to, or direct the course of, by going before or along with; conduct; guide *b)* to show (the way) in this manner *c)* to mark the way for [lights to *lead* you there] **2** to guide, or cause to follow one, by physical contact, holding the hand, pulling a rope, etc. [to *lead* a horse by the bridle] **3** to conduct (water, steam, rope, etc.) in a certain direction, channel, or the like **4** *a)* to guide or direct, as by persuasion or influence, to a course of action or thought [to *lead* pupils to think clearly] *b)* to cause; prompt [trouble that *led* him to drink] **5** to be the head of; specif., *a)* to proceed at the front of (a parade, etc.) *b)* to act as chief officer of; command the operations of (a military unit) *c)* to direct operations of (an expedition, etc.) *d)* to direct, conduct, or serve as the leader or conductor of (an orchestra, ballet, etc.) **6** *a)* to be the first or foremost among; be at the head of [to *lead* one's class in grades] *b)* to be ahead of by a specified margin **7** *a)* to live; spend; pass [to *lead* a hard life] *b)* to cause to live or spend [to *lead* someone a dog's life] **8** to aim a rifle, throw a ball, etc. just ahead of (a moving target or receiver) **9** *Card Games* to begin the play with (a specified card or suit); lay down as the first card or suit of a hand or round **10** *Law* to put a LEADING QUESTION to (a witness) —***vi.*** **1** to show the way by going before or along; act as guide **2** to be led; submit to being led: said esp. of a horse **3** to be or form a way (*to, from, under,* etc.); tend in a certain direction; go **4** to come, or bring one, as a result: with *to* [one thing *led* to another, a cold can *lead* to pneumonia] **5** to be or go first; act as leader ☆**6** *Boxing* to aim a first blow or a blow designed to test an opponent's defense [to *lead* with a right jab] **7** *Card Games* to play the first card of a hand or round —***n.*** **1** the part of director or leader; leadership [to take the *lead* in a project] **2** example [follow my *lead*] **3** *a)* first or front place; precedence [the horse in the *lead*] *b)* the amount or distance that one is ahead [to hold a safe *lead*] **4** LEASH (sense 1) **5** anything that serves as a clue or that leads one to an objective **6** information that directs a salesperson to a potential customer, a source of new business, etc. **7** a long, narrow, navigable passage in an ice pack or ice field **8** *a)* the most important news story, as in a newspaper or telecast *b)* the opening words or paragraph of a news story, containing all the essential facts ☆**9** *Baseball* a position taken by a base runner a short distance from his or her base in the direction of the next ☆**10** *Boxing* the act of leading, or the blow used **11** *Card Games* the act or right of playing first, as in a hand, or the card or suit played **12** *Elec.* a wire carrying current between two points in a circuit, between devices, etc. ☆**13** *Mining* a stratum of ore; lode, ledge, or vein **14** *Music* the leading part or main melody in a harmonic composition **15** *Naut.* the course of a rope **16** *Film, Theater* *a)* the principal role, or a main role, in a play or other production *b)* the actor or actress who plays such a role —***adj.*** acting as leader or being the leader [the *lead* horse, the *lead* runner in a race] —**lead off** **1** to begin; start ☆**2** *Baseball* *a)* to be the first batter in the lineup or of an INNING (sense 1*a*) *b)* to take a LEAD[1] (***n.*** 9) —**lead on** **1** to conduct further **2** to lure or tempt **3** [Informal] to mislead regarding one's intentions —**lead someone a merry chase** to cause someone trouble by luring into a vain pursuit —**lead up to** **1** to prepare the way for **2** to approach (a subject) in a subtle or indirect way —**lead with one's chin** [Informal] to act so imprudently as to invite disaster
lead[2] (led) ***n.*** ⟦ME *lede* < OE *lead*, akin to Du *lood*, Ger *lot*, plummet, prob. < Celt (as in MIr *luaide*, lead) < IE **ploud-*, **pleud-* < **pleu-*, to flow < base **pel-*, to flow, pour > L *pluere*, to rain, OIr *lu-*, to move⟧ **1** a heavy, soft, malleable, bluish-gray metallic chemical element used in batteries and in numerous alloys and compounds: symbol, Pb; at. no. 82: see the periodic table of elements in the Reference Supplement **2** anything made of this metal; specif., *a)* a weight for measuring depth of water at sea, in a harbor, etc.: it is attached to a line and tossed over the side of a ship *b)* any of the strips of lead used to hold the individual panes in ornamental windows (*usually used in pl.*) *c)* [*pl.*] [Brit.] sheets of lead used for covering a roof *d)* *Printing* a thin strip of type metal inserted to increase the space between lines of type **3** bullets **4** ⟦short for BLACK LEAD⟧ a thin stick of graphite, used in pencils —***adj.*** made of or containing lead —***vt.*** **1** to cover, line, weight, or fasten with lead or leads **2** *Ceramics* to glaze (pottery) with a glaze made primarily of lead **3** *Printing* to increase the space between (lines of type), as by inserting thin strips of type metal —☆**get the lead out** [Slang] to act with more speed or promptness; hurry up
lead acetate a poisonous, colorless, crystalline compound, $Pb(C_2H_3O_2)_2 \cdot 3H_2O$, used in making varnishes and paints
lead arsenate a very poisonous, colorless, crystalline compound, $Pb_3(AsO_4)_2$, used as an insecticide or herbicide
lead colic a form of lead poisoning causing abdominal pain
lead crystal (led) bright LEAD GLASS having a high index of refraction, used for crystalware
lead·ed (led′əd) ***adj.*** containing lead or a lead compound [*leaded* gasoline, *leaded* glass]
lead·en (led′'n) ***adj.*** **1** made of lead **2** having the inert heaviness of lead; hard to move or lift **3** sluggish; dull; heavy in action, feeling, etc. **4** depressed; dispirited; gloomy **5** of a dull gray —**lead′en·ly** ***adv.*** —**lead′en·ness** ***n.***
lead·er (lēd′ər) ***n.*** ⟦ME *leder* < OE *lœder* < *lœdan*: see LEAD[1]⟧ **1** a person or thing that leads; directing, commanding, or guiding head, as of a group or activity **2** a horse harnessed before all others in the same hitch or as one of the two horses in the foremost span **3** a pipe for carrying fluid; specif., *a)* DOWNSPOUT *b)* a hot-air duct in a heating system **4** a tendon **5** a section of blank film or recording tape at the beginning of a reel, for use in threading, etc. ☆**6** a featured article of trade, esp. one offered at an attractively low price: cf. LOSS LEADER **7** *Bot.* the central or dominant stem of a plant, esp. of a tree ☆**8** *Fishing* a short piece of catgut, nylon, etc. used to attach the hook or lure to the fish line **9** *Journalism* LEADING ARTICLE **10** *Music* *a)* a conductor, esp. of a dance band *b)* the main performer in an instrumental or vocal section, generally given the solo passages **11** *Naut.* FAIR-LEAD **12** [*pl.*] *Printing* dots, dashes, etc. in a line, used to direct the eye across the page, as in a table of contents —**lead′er·less** ***adj.***
lead·er board (lēd′ər) a scoreboard listing the contestants who are currently leading a golf tournament, auto race, etc.
lead·er·ship (-ship′) ***n.*** **1** the position or guidance of a leader **2** the ability to lead **3** the leaders of a group
lead-foot (led′foot′) ***n.*** **1** a person who walks slowly and ploddingly ☆**2** ⟦from the notion that a heavy foot depresses the accelerator⟧ [Informal] a motorist who drives faster than is safe or legal; speeder —**lead′-foot′ed** ***adj.***
lead glass (led) glass that contains lead oxide
lead-in (lēd′in′) ***n.*** **1** the wire leading from an aerial or antenna to a receiver or transmitter **2** an introduction —***adj.*** that is a lead-in
lead·ing[1] (led′iŋ) ***n.*** **1** a covering or being covered with lead **2** strips or sheets of lead, collectively **3** *Printing* *a)* strips of LEAD[2] (***n.*** 2*d*) *b)* the space between lines of type
lead·ing[2] (lēd′iŋ) ***n.*** the action of one that leads; guidance; direction; leadership —***adj.*** **1** that leads; guiding **2** principal; chief **3** of or playing the lead in a play, film, etc. —***SYN.*** CHIEF
lead·ing article (lēd′iŋ) the principal article or, esp. in England, editorial in a newspaper
lead·ing edge (lēd′iŋ) **1** *Aeron.* the front edge of a propeller blade or airfoil ☆**2** a position of leadership, as in cultural or technological advances
lead·ing lady (lēd′iŋ) *Film, Theater* **1** the actress playing the principal female role **2** an actress cast in such roles
lead·ing light (lēd′iŋ) an important or influential member of a club, community, etc.
lead·ing man (lēd′iŋ) *Film, Theater* **1** the actor playing the principal male role **2** an actor cast in such roles
lead·ing question (lēd′iŋ) a question put in such a way as to suggest the answer sought
lead·ing strings (lēd′iŋ) **1** strings or straps formerly used to guide and support a young child learning to walk **2** a condition of childlike dependence or restricting guidance: usually in the phr. **in leading strings (to)**
lead·ing tone (lēd′iŋ) *Music* the seventh tone of a scale, a half tone below the tonic
lead line (led) *Naut.* a line with a lead weight at one end, used for measuring the depth of water
lead·off (lēd′ôf′) ***n.*** the first in a series of actions, moves, etc. —***adj.*** ☆*Baseball* designating or of the first batter in a lineup or of an INNING (sense 1*a*)

lead pencil (led) ⟦< LEAD², *n.* 4: see PLUMBAGO⟧ a pencil consisting of a slender stick of graphite encased in wood, etc.

☆**lead-pipe cinch** (led′pīp′) ⟦prob. < slang *lead-pipe*, complete, absolute⟧ [Slang] **1** a thing very easy to do **2** a sure thing; certainty

☆**lead·plant** (led′plant′) *n.* a small, leguminous, American plant (*Amorpha canescens*) thought by early miners to indicate lead deposits

lead poisoning (led) an acute or chronic poisoning caused by the absorption of lead or any of its salts into the body: various symptoms include headache, dizziness, anemia, muscular cramps, or paralysis

leads·man (ledz′mən) *n., pl.* **-men** (-mən) *Naut.* a man who uses a lead line to take soundings

lead tetraethyl TETRAETHYL LEAD

lead time (lēd) *Manufacturing* the period of time between the decision to make a product and the beginning of actual production

lead·wort (led′wurt′) *n.* ⟦LEAD² + WORT²⟧ any of several shrubby plants (genus *Plumbago*) of a family (Plumbaginaceae, order Plumbaginales) of dicotyledonous plants grown for their ornamental white, blue, or red flowers, esp. in warm climates

lead·y (led′ē) *adj.* resembling lead; leaden

leaf (lēf) *n., pl.* **leaves** ⟦ME *lefe* < OE *leaf*, akin to Du *loof*, Ger *laub* < IE base **leubh-*, to peel off, pull off > Lith *lupù*, to skin, pare off⟧ **1** any of the flat, thin, expanded organs, usually green, growing laterally from the stem or twig of a plant: it usually consists of a broad blade, a petiole, or stalk, and stipules and is involved in the processes of photosynthesis and transpiration **2** in popular usage, *a)* the blade of a leaf *b)* a petal **3** leaves collectively [choice tobacco *leaf*] **4** a design resembling a leaf, used as an ornament in architecture **5** a sheet of paper, esp. as part of a book, with a page on each side **6** *a)* a very thin sheet of metal; lamina *b)* such sheets collectively [covered with gold *leaf*] **7** *a)* a hinged section of a table top, forming an extension when raised into place *b)* a board inserted into a table top to expand its surface area **8** a flat, hinged or movable part of a folding door, shutter, etc. ☆**9** one of a number of metal strips laid one upon another to make a leaf spring —*vi.* **1** to put forth or bear leaves: often with *out* **2** to turn the pages of a book, etc., esp. so as to glance quickly (*through*) —*vt.* turn the pages of —**in leaf** having leaves grown; with foliage —**turn over a new leaf** to make a new start —**leaf′less** *adj.* —**leaf′like′** *adj.*

leaf forms

leaf·age (lēf′ij) *n.* leaves collectively; foliage

leaf bud a bud from which only stems and leaves develop: cf. FLOWER BUD, MIXED BUD

leaf fat fat built up in layers around the kidneys of a hog, used in making lard

☆**leaf·hop·per** (lēf′häp′ər) *n.* any of a family (Cicadellidae) of homopteran insects that leap from one plant to another, sucking the juices and often transmitting plant diseases

leaf insect any of a family (Phylliidae, order Phasmatoptera) of sluggish, winged insects that resemble leaves

leaf lard the highest grade of lard, made from LEAF FAT

leaf·let (lēf′lit) *n.* **1** one of the divisions of a compound leaf **2** a small or young leaf **3** a separate sheet of printed matter, often folded but not stitched — *vt., vi.* **-let·ed** or **-let·ted**, **-let·ing** or **-let·ting** to distribute leaflets to (people in public places) —**leaf·let·eer** (lēf′lə tir′) *n.*, **leaf′let·er**

leaf lettuce lettuce with relatively flat leaves arranged in loose, open bunches

leaf miner any of various insect larvae, esp. of small moths and flies, that burrow into and eat the soft tissues of leaves and green stems

leaf mold **1** a rich soil consisting largely of decayed leaves **2** a mold that forms on leaves

leaf spot any of various plant diseases characterized by lesions in the form of spots on the leaves

☆**leaf spring** a SPRING (*n.* 3) built up of strips of metal

leaf·stalk (-stôk′) *n.* the slender, usually cylindrical portion of a leaf, which supports the blade and is attached to the stem; petiole

leaf·y (lēf′ē) *adj.* **leaf′i·er**, **leaf′i·est** **1** of, covered with, consisting of, or like a leaf or leaves **2** having many leaves **3** having broad leaves or consisting mainly of such leaves [spinach is a *leafy* vegetable] —**leaf′i·ness** *n.*

league¹ (lēg) *n.* ⟦ME *ligg* < OFr *ligue* < It *liga* < *legare*, to bind < L *ligare*: see LIGATURE⟧ **1** a compact or covenant made by nations, groups, or individuals for promoting common interests, assuring mutual protection, etc. **2** an association or alliance of individuals, groups, or nations formed by such a covenant **3** *Sports* a group of teams organized to compete against one another ☆**4** [Informal] a level of quality; class [the best and worst students were not in the same *league*] — *vt., vi.* **leagued**, **leagu′ing** to form into a league —*SYN.* ALLIANCE —**in league** associated for a common purpose; allied —☆**out of someone's league** [Informal] so superior to someone as to seem unattainable or unapproachable [the prettiest girls were always *out of his league*]

league² (lēg) *n.* ⟦ME *lege* < OFr *legue* < LL *leuga, leuca*, Gallic mile < Celt **leuca* > OE *leowe*, mile⟧ **1** a unit of linear measure varying in different times and countries: in English-speaking countries it is usually about 3 statute miles or 3 nautical miles ☆**2** [Historical] a land measure in parts of the U.S. that were formerly Mexican, equal to about 4,400 acres

League of Nations an association of nations (1920-46), established to promote international cooperation and peace: it was succeeded by the United Nations

lea·guer¹ (lē′gər) *n.* ⟦Du *leger*, a camp, bed: see LAIR⟧ [Archaic] **1** a siege **2** *a)* a besieging army *b)* its camp —*vt.* [Obs.] to besiege; beleaguer

leagu·er² (lē′gər) *n.* a member of a league

Le·ah (lē′ə, lā′ə) *n.* ⟦Heb *Lē'āh*, gazelle⟧ **1** a feminine name **2** *Bible* the elder of the sisters who were wives of Jacob: Gen. 29:13-30

leak (lēk) *vi.* ⟦ME *leken* < ON *leka*, to drip < IE base **leg-*, to drip, trickle, LACK, OIr *legaim*, (I) dissolve, Welsh *llaith*, damp⟧ **1** to let a fluid substance out or in accidentally [the kettle *leaks*; the boat *leaks*] **2** to enter, or escape accidentally from, an object or container: often with *in* or *out* **3** to become known little by little, by accident, carelessness, or treachery [the truth *leaked* out] —*vt.* **1** to permit (water, air, light, radiation, etc.) to pass accidentally in or out; allow to leak **2** to allow (secret or confidential information) to become known —*n.* **1** an accidental hole or crack that lets something out or in **2** any means of escape for something that ought not to be let out, lost, etc. **3** the fact of leaking; leakage **4** a disclosure of secret or confidential information; specif., an ostensibly accidental disclosure by a government official to the news media, actually intended to produce an effect: in full **news leak** **5** *a)* a loss of electrical current through faulty insulation *b)* the point or path where this occurs **6** [Slang] the act of urinating: usually in the phrase **take a leak**

leak·age (lēk′ij) *n.* **1** an act or instance of leaking; leak **2** something that leaks in or out **3** the amount that leaks in or out

leak·er (-ər) *n.* a person or thing that leaks; specif., a person who leaks secret or private information

Lea·key (lē′kē) **1 Louis (Seymour Bazett)** 1903-72; Brit. paleontologist, born in Kenya **2 Mary (Douglas)** (born *Mary Douglas Nicol*) 1913-96; Brit. paleontologist: wife of Louis

leak·proof (lēk′pro͞of′) *adj.* that will not leak: said of a container, sealing device, etc.

leak·y (lēk′ē) *adj.* **leak′i·er**, **leak′i·est** allowing the accidental entrance or escape of a fluid substance; having a leak or leaks —**leak′i·ness** *n.*

leal (lēl) *adj.* ⟦north Brit dial. & Scot < ME *lele* < OFr < L *legalis*: see LEGAL, LOYAL⟧ [Now Chiefly Scot.] loyal; true —**leal′ly** *adv.*

lean¹ (lēn) *vi.* **leaned** or [Chiefly Brit.] **leant**, **lean′ing** ⟦ME *lenen* < OE *hlinian*, to lean, *hlænan*, to cause to lean, akin to Ger *lehnen* < IE base **k̂lei-*, to incline, lean > Gr *klinein*, L *clinare*⟧ **1** to bend or deviate from an upright position; stand at a slant; incline **2** to bend or incline the body so as to rest part of one's weight upon or against something [he *leaned* on the desk] **3** to depend for encouragement, aid, etc.; rely (*on* or *upon*) **4** to have a particular mental inclination; tend (*toward* or *to* a certain opinion, attitude, etc.) —*vt.* to cause to lean [to *lean* one's head back; *lean* the ladder against the house] —*n.* the act or condition of leaning; inclination; slant —☆**lean on** [Informal] to pressure, as by using influence or through intimidation —**lean′er** *n.*

lean² (lēn) *adj.* ⟦ME *lene* < OE *hlæne*, prob. akin to prec., in sense "leaning, drooping," hence "thin, slender"⟧ **1** with little flesh or fat; thin; spare **2** containing little or no fat: said of meat **3** lacking in richness, profit, productivity, etc.; meager **4** deficient in some quality or substance [a *lean* mixture in the carburetor] **5** characterized by brevity, incisiveness, directness, etc. [a *lean* writing style] **6** characterized by economy and efficiency achieved as by eliminating waste, cutting labor costs, shortening lead times, etc. —*n.* meat containing little or no fat —**lean′ly** *adv.* —**lean′ness** *n.*

Lean (lēn), Sir **David** 1908-91; Brit. film director

Le·an·der (lē an′dər) *n.* ⟦L < Gr *Leiandros* < ? *leōn*, lion + *anēr* (gen. *andros*), a man: see ANDRO-⟧ *Gr. Legend* the lover of HERO[1]

lean·ing (lēn′iŋ) *n.* **1** the act of a person or thing that leans **2** a tendency; inclination; penchant; predilection —*SYN.* INCLINATION

Leaning Tower of Pisa bell tower in Pisa, Italy, which leans approximately 4° from the vertical

leant (lent) *vi., vt.* [Chiefly Brit.] *pt. & pp. of* LEAN[1]

lean-to (lēn′to͞o′) *n., pl.* **-tos′** **1** a roof with a single slope, its upper edge abutting a wall or building **2** a shed with a one-slope roof, the upper end of the rafters resting against an external support, such as trees or the wall of a building **3** a structure, as the wing of a building, whose roof is a lean-to —*adj.* having or characterized by such construction

leap (lēp) *vi.* **leaped, leapt** (lept, lēpt), or **lept** (lept), **leap′ing** ⟦ME *lepen* < OE *hleapan*, akin to MDu *lopen*, Ger *laufen*⟧ **1** to move oneself suddenly from the ground, etc. by using one's leg muscles; jump; spring **2** to move suddenly or swiftly, as if by jumping; bound **3** to accept eagerly something offered: with *at* [to *leap* at a chance] —*vt.* **1** to pass over by a jump **2** to cause or force to leap [to *leap* a horse over a wall] —*n.* **1** the act of leaping; jump; spring **2** the distance covered in a jump **3** a place that is, or is to be, leapt over or from **4** a sudden transition —**by leaps and bounds** with very rapid progress —**leap in the dark** an act that is risky because its consequences cannot be foreseen —**leap′er** *n.*

leap day the additional day in a LEAP YEAR; Feb. 29

leap·frog (lēp′frôg′) *n.* a children's game in which players crouch on hands and knees in a line, with each player taking a turn vaulting with legs spread wide over the others from behind, one at a time —*vi.* **-frogged′**, **-frog′ging** **1** to jump in or as if in leapfrog; skip (*over*) **2** to move or progress in jumps or stages —*vt.* **1** to jump or skip over, as in leapfrog **2** to overtake and go beyond [a business *leapfrogging* the competition]

leap year ⟦so called prob. because after Feb. 29 in such a year, a given date advances by two days of the week, not one as in other years, thus *leaping* over the usual day⟧ a year of 366 days in the Gregorian calendar, occurring every fourth year: the additional day, Feb. 29, makes up for the time lost annually when the approximate 365¼-day cycle is computed as 365 days: a leap year is a year whose number is exactly divisible by 4, or, in case of the final year of a century, by 400

Lear[1] (lir) *n. see* KING LEAR

Lear[2] (lir), **Edward** 1812-88; Eng. humorist, illustrator, & painter

learn (lʉrn) *vt.* **learned** or [Chiefly Brit.] **learnt, learn′ing** ⟦ME *lernen*, to learn, teach < OE *leornian* (akin to Ger *lernen*) < WGmc **liznōn* (akin to Goth *laisjan*, to teach) < IE base **leis-*, track, furrow > L *lira*, furrow⟧ **1** to get knowledge of (a subject) or skill in (an art, trade, etc.) by study, experience, instruction, etc. **2** to come to know [to *learn* what happened] **3** to come to know how [to *learn* to swim] **4** to fix in the mind; memorize **5** to acquire as a habit or attitude [to *learn* humility] **6** to teach: now dialectal or otherwise nonstandard —*vi.* **1** to gain knowledge or skill **2** to be informed; hear (*of* or *about*) —**learn′a·ble** *adj.* —**learn′er** *n.*

SYN.—**learn**, as considered here, implies a finding out of something without conscious effort [I *learned* of their marriage from a friend]; **ascertain** implies a finding out with certainty as by careful inquiry, experimentation, or research [I *ascertained* the firm's credit rating]; **determine** stresses intention to establish the facts exactly, often so as to settle something in doubt [to *determine* the exact denotation of a word]; **discover** implies a finding out, by chance, exploration, etc., of something already existing or known to others [to *discover* a conspiracy, a star, etc.]; **unearth**, in its figurative sense, implies a bringing to light, as by diligent search, of something that has been concealed, lost, or forgotten [to *unearth* old documents]

learn·ed (lʉr′nid; *for 3*, lʉrnd) *adj.* ⟦orig. pp. of prec. in obs. sense, "to teach"⟧ **1** *a)* having or showing much learning; well-informed; erudite *b)* having or showing much learning in some special field [a *learned* doctor] **2** of or characterized by scholarship, study, and learning [a *learned* society] **3** acquired by study, experience, etc. [a *learned* response] —**learn′ed·ly** *adv.* —**learn′ed·ness** *n.*

learn·ing (lʉr′niŋ) *n.* ⟦ME *lerning* < OE *leornung* < *leornian*, to LEARN⟧ **1** the acquiring of knowledge or skill **2** acquired knowledge or skill; esp., much knowledge in a special field —*SYN.* INFORMATION

learning curve **1** the time required to learn certain information, acquire certain skills, etc. **2** the rate of progress in such learning represented on or as if represented on a graph

learning disability any of several conditions, believed to involve the nervous system, which interfere with mastering a skill such as reading or writing

learn·ing-dis·a·bled (-dis ā′bəld) *adj.* having a learning disability

lear·y (lir′ē) *adj.* **lear′i·er, lear′i·est** *informal sp. of* LEERY (sense 2)

lease (lēs) *n.* ⟦ME *leas* < Anglo-Fr *les* < OFr *lais* < *laissier*: see LEASH⟧ **1** a contract by which one party (landlord, or lessor) gives to another (tenant, or lessee) the use and possession of lands, buildings, property, etc. for a specified time and for fixed payments **2** the period of time for which such a contract is in force [a two-year *lease*] **3** the property that is leased —*vt.* **leased, leas′ing** ⟦Anglo-Fr *lesser* < OFr *laissier*⟧ **1** to give by a lease; let **2** to get by a lease; take a lease on —*SYN.* HIRE —**new lease on life** another chance to lead a happy life, be successful, etc. because of a new turn of events: also [Brit.] **new lease of life** —**leas′a·ble** *adj.* —**leas′er** *n.*

lease-back (lēs′bak′) *n.* an arrangement by which an owner sells a property and simultaneously obtains a lease for its continued use: also called **sale and lease-back**

lease·hold (-hōld′) *n.* **1** the act or condition of holding by lease **2** lands, buildings, etc. held by lease —*adj.* held by lease —**lease′hold′er** *n.*

leash (lēsh) *n.* ⟦ME *lese* < OFr *lesse*, length of cord, leash < *laissier*, to let, permit < *laxare*, to lighten, relieve < *laxus*, loose: see LAX⟧ **1** a cord, strap, etc. by which a dog or other animal is held in check **2** *Hunting* a set of three, as of hounds; brace and a half —*vt.* **1** to attach a leash to **2** to check or control by or as by a leash —**hold in leash** to control; curb; restrain —**strain at the leash** to be impatient to have freedom from restraint

leas·ing (lēz′iŋ) *n.* ⟦ME *lesinge* < OE *leasung*, falsehood < *leasian*, to lie < *leas*, lacking, false < base of *leosan*, to LOSE⟧ [Obs.] lying, lies, or a lie

least (lēst) *adj.* ⟦ME *lest* < OE *læsest*, *læst*, superl. of *læssa*, LESS⟧ **1** *alt. superl. of* LITTLE **2** smallest or slightest in size, degree, importance, etc. [the *least* movement] **3** *Biol.* very small: used in names of species or varieties [*least* flycatcher] —*adv.* **1** *superl. of* LITTLE **2** in the smallest degree —*n.* the smallest in size, amount, importance, etc. —**at least** **1** at the very lowest figure or amount; with no less **2** at any rate; in any event; anyhow Also **at the (very) least** —**not in the least** not at all

least common denominator the least common multiple of the denominators of two or more fractions

least common multiple the smallest positive whole number that is exactly divisible by two or more given whole numbers [the *least common multiple* of 4, 5, and 10 is 20]

☆**least flycatcher** a small, gray tyrant flycatcher (*Empidonax minimus*) common in N North America

least squares a statistical method used to find the curve that most closely approximates a set of data: it is based on minimizing the sum of the squares of the differences between expected and observed values of the data

least·ways (lēst′wāz′) *adv.* ⟦< phr. *at the least ways*, at least⟧ [Dial. or Informal] leastwise; anyway

least·wise (-wīz′) *adv.* [Informal] at least; anyway

leath·er (leth′ər) *n.* ⟦ME *lether* < OE *lether-*, akin to Ger *leder*, ON *lethr*, MHG *leder* < Gmc **lethra* < ? or akin ? to Celt base as in OIr *lethar*, Welsh *lledr*⟧ **1** a material consisting of animal skin prepared for use by removing any hair and tanning **2** any of various articles or parts made of this material **3** the flap of a dog's ear —*adj.* **1** of or made of leather **2** ⟦< the *leather* attire often associated with sadomasochism⟧ of or having to do with sadomasochists, esp. homosexual sadomasochists —*vt.* **1** to cover or furnish with leather **2** [Informal] to whip or thrash with or as with a leather strap

leath·er·back (-bak′) *n.* the only species (*Dermochelys coriacea*) of a family (Dermochelyidae) of tropical sea turtles, covered with a tough, leathery upper shell: it is the largest living turtle, weighing up to *c.* 725 kg (*c.* 1,600 lb)

leather bar ⟦see LEATHER, *adj.* 2⟧ a bar frequented by gays, often sadomasochists, dressed typically in leather garments

Leath·er·ette (leth′ər et′) *n.* [*also* **l-**] imitation leather made of paper, cloth, vinyl, etc.

leath·ern (leth′ərn) *adj.* ⟦ME *letherne* < OE *letheren*⟧ **1** made or consisting of leather **2** like leather

leath·er·neck (leth′ər nek′) *n.* ⟦from the leather lining that was part of the collar of the Marine uniform⟧ ☆[Slang] a U.S. Marine

☆**leath·er·wood** (-wood′) *n.* a small North American tree (*Dirca palustris*) of the mezereum family, with a tough, flexible bark used by Indian peoples for making rope

leath·er·y (-ē) *adj.* like leather in appearance or texture —**leath′er·i·ness** *n.*

leave[1] (lēv) *vt.* **left, leav′ing** ⟦ME *leven* < OE *læfan*, lit., to let remain (< base of *laf*, remnant, what remains), akin to (*be*)*lifan*, to remain, Ger *bleiben*, OHG *belīban* < IE **leip-*, to smear with grease, stick to < base **lei-*, viscous, sticky > L *limus*: see LIME[1]⟧ **1** to cause or allow to remain; not take away [to *leave* some of the food for latecomers] **2** to make, place, deposit, etc., and cause to remain behind one [to *leave* one's calling card] **3** to have remaining after one [the deceased *leaves* a widow] **4** to bequeath [to *leave* a fortune to charity] **5** to let be in the care of; entrust: with *to* or *up to* [to *leave* a decision to another] **6** to give as a remainder by subtraction [ten minus two *leaves* eight] **7** to reject [take it or *leave* it] **8** to go away from [to *leave* the house] **9** to let stay or cause to be in a certain condition [the flood *left* them homeless] **10** to give up; abandon; forsake **11** to stop living in, working for, or belonging to ➥*Leave* is also used dialectally in place of LET[1], in the sense "allow or permit (to)" [*leave* it be; *leave* go of the handle] or, in suggestions or commands, as an auxiliary where standard English would use *let us* or *let's* [*leave us* rest awhile] —*vi.* to go away, depart, or set out —**leave alone** *see the phrase under* ALONE —**leave off** **1** to stop; cease **2** to stop doing, using, or wearing —**leave out** **1** to omit **2** to ignore —**leave well enough alone** *see the phrase under* ALONE —**leav′er** *n.*

leave[2] (lēv) *n.* ⟦ME *leve* < OE *leaf*, permission, akin to obs. Ger *laube*, permission, *erlauben*, to allow, permit < IE base **leubh-*, to like, desire > LIEF, LOVE, L *libido*⟧ **1** permission **2** *a)* permission to be absent from duty or work, esp. such permission given to personnel in the armed services *b)* the period for which such permission is granted —**beg leave** to ask permission —**by your leave** **1** with your permission: now mainly a formal usage **2** [Informal, Chiefly Brit.] an apology or a request for permission: used mainly in negative constructions [he left abruptly, without so much as a *by your leave*]: sometimes sp. **by-your-leave** —**on leave** absent from duty with permission —**take leave of** to say goodbye to —**take one's leave** to go away; depart

leave[3] (lēv) *vi.* **leaved, leav′ing** ⟦ME *leven* < *lefe*, LEAF⟧ to put forth, or bear, leaves; leaf

leaved (lēvd) *adj.* having leaves: usually in hyphenated compounds

leav·en (lev′ən) ***n.*** ⟦ME *levein* < OFr *levain* < VL **levamen* (in L, alleviation) < L *levare*, to make light, relieve, raise: see LEVER⟧ **1** *a)* a small piece of fermenting dough put aside to be used for producing fermentation in a fresh batch of dough *b)* LEAVENING (sense 1) **2** LEAVENING (sense 2) **—*vt.*** **1** to make (batter or dough) rise before or during baking by means of a leavening agent **2** to spread through, causing a gradual change

leav·en·ing (-iŋ) ***n.*** **1** a substance used to make baked goods rise by the formation of gas, esp. carbon dioxide, in the batter or dough, as baking powder, yeast, etc.: also **leavening agent** **2** any influence spreading through something and working on it to bring about a gradual change **3** a causing to be leavened

Leav·en·worth (lev′ən wurth′) ⟦ult. after U.S. Army Col. H. *Leavenworth* (1783-1834)⟧ city in NE Kans., on the Missouri River: site of a federal prison

leave of absence **1** permission to be absent from work or duty, usually for an extended period of time **2** such a period

leaves (lēvz) ***n. pl. of*** LEAF

leave-tak·ing (lēv′tāk′iŋ) ***n.*** the act of taking leave, or saying goodbye

leav·ings (lēv′iŋz) ***pl.n.*** ⟦< LEAVE[1]⟧ things left over; leftovers, remnants, refuse, etc.

Lea·vis (lē′vis), **F(rank) R(aymond)** 1895-1978; Eng. literary critic

leav·y (lē′vē) ***adj.*** *archaic var. of* LEAFY

Leb *abbrev.* Lebanon

Leb·a·non (leb′ə nän′, -nən) **1** country in SW Asia, at the E end of the Mediterranean: formerly a French mandate, it became independent after elections (1944): 4,015 sq mi (10,400 sq km); cap. Beirut **2** mountain range extending nearly the entire length of Lebanon: highest peak, 10,131 ft (3,088 m): also **Lebanon Mountains** **—Leb′a·nese′** (-nēz′, -nēs′) ***adj., n.***, *pl.* **-nese′**

Le·bens·raum (lā′bəns roum′) ***n.*** ⟦Ger, lit., living space⟧ territory for political and economic expansion: term used by Hitler as a euphemism for German expansionism

Leb·ku·chen (lāp′ko͞o′khən) ***n.***, *pl.* **-chen** ⟦Ger < MHG *lebekuoche* < *lebe*, loaf, akin to *leip* (< OHG *leib, hlaib*), LOAF[1]) + MHG *kuoche*, cake > Ger *kuchen*: see CAKE⟧ a chewy cookie made with honey, spices, nuts, and candied fruits

Le·brun (lə brën′), **Charles** (shärl) 1619-90; Fr. historical painter: also **Le Brun**

lech (lech) [Slang] ***vi.*** to behave like a lecher; lust (*for, after*, etc.) **—*n.*** **1** a lecherous desire **2** LECHER

lech·er (lech′ər) ***n.*** ⟦ME *lechoure* < OFr *lecheur* < *lechier*, to live a debauched life, lit., lick < Frank **lekkon*, akin to Ger *lecken*, to LICK⟧ a man who indulges in lechery

lech·er·ous (lech′ər əs) ***adj.*** ⟦ME < OFr *lecheros*⟧ given to, characterized by, or stimulating to lechery **—lech′er·ous·ly *adv.*** **—lech′er·ous·ness *n.***

lech·er·y (lech′ər ē) ***n.*** ⟦ME *lecherie* < OFr < *lecheur*, LECHER⟧ unrestrained, excessive indulgence of sexual desires; gross sensuality; lewdness

lec·i·thin (les′ə thin) ***n.*** ⟦< Gr *lekithos*, yolk of an egg + -IN[1]⟧ any of several phosphatides found in nerve tissue, blood, milk, egg yolk, soybeans, corn, etc.: used in medicine, foods, cosmetics, etc. as a wetting, emulsifying, and penetrating agent

lec·i·thin·ase (-thi nās′) ***n.*** ⟦prec. + -ASE⟧ any of a group of enzymes that hydrolyze lecithin

Leck·y (lek′ē), **William Edward Hart·pole** (härt′pōl′) 1838-1903; Brit. historian, born in Ireland

Le·conte de Lisle (lə kōnt də lēl′), **Charles Ma·rie (René)** (shárl má rē′) 1818-94; Fr. poet

Le Cor·bu·sier (lə kôr bü zyā′) (pseud. of *Charles-Édouard Jeanneret-Gris*) 1887-1965; Fr. architect, born in Switzerland

lect *abbrev.* **1** lecture **2** lecturer

-lect (lekt) ⟦(DIA)LECT⟧ *combining form* a variety within a language

lec·tern (lek′tərn) ***n.*** ⟦ME *lectorne*, altered (infl. by L forms) < earlier *lettrun* < OFr < ML *lectrum* < L *lectus*, pp. of *legere*, to read: see LOGIC⟧ **1** a reading desk in a church, esp. such a desk from which a part of the Scriptures is read in a church service **2** a stand for holding the notes, written speech, etc., as of a lecturer

lec·tin (lek′tin) ***n.*** ⟦coined (1954) < L *lectus*, pp. of *legere*, to select + -IN[1]⟧ any of several proteins, found in plants and animals, that bind to specific sugar molecules, as on cancer or red blood cells

lec·tion (lek′shən) ***n.*** ⟦L *lectio* < *lectus*: see prec.⟧ **1** [Now Rare] the version in a particular text of a certain passage **2** a selection, as of Scripture, forming part of a religious service; lesson

lec·tion·ar·y (-shə ner′ē) ***n.***, *pl.* **-ar′ies** ⟦ML(Ec) *lectionarium*: see prec. & -ARY⟧ a sequence or list of lections to be read in church services during the year

lec·tor (lek′tər) ***n.*** ⟦LME < L, reader (in ML(Ec), church officer) < *lectus*: see LECTERN⟧ **1** a person who reads the Scripture lessons in a church service **2** *Eccles.* that one of the MINOR ORDERS whose special function is to read the Scriptures (except the Gospel) at worship services **3** a college or university lecturer, esp. in Europe

lectern

lec·ture (lek′chər) ***n.*** ⟦ME, act of reading < ML *lectura* < pp. of L *legere*, to read: see LOGIC⟧ **1** *a)* an informative talk given as before an audience or class and usually prepared beforehand *b)* the text of such a talk **2** a lengthy rebuke or scolding **—*vi.*** **-tured**, **-tur·ing** to give a lecture or lectures **—*vt.*** to give a lecture to **—*SYN.*** SPEECH

lec·tur·er (-ər) ***n.*** a person who gives lectures, esp. by profession or in connection with teaching duties: sometimes used as an academic title for one who teaches at a college or university but does not have the rank or tenure of a regular faculty member

lec·ture·ship (-ship′) ***n.*** **1** the position or rank of a lecturer **2** a series of lectures or the foundation supporting such a series

lec·y·this (les′i this) ***adj.*** ⟦< *Lecythis*, genus name < Gr *lēkythos*, flask or bottle for oil⟧ designating a family (Lecythidaceae, order Lecythidales) of dicotyledonous tropical shrubs and trees, including the Brazil nut and anchovy pear

led (led) ***vt., vi. pt. & pp. of*** LEAD[1]

☆**LED** (el′ē′dē′) ***n.*** ⟦*l(ight-)e(mitting) d(iode)*⟧ a semiconductor diode that emits light when voltage is applied: used in electric lighting, alphanumeric displays, as on digital watches, etc.: cf. LCD

Le·da (lē′də) ***n.*** ⟦L < Gr *Lēda*⟧ *Gr. Myth.* a queen of Sparta and the wife of Tyndareus: she is the mother (variously by Tyndareus and by Zeus, who visited her in the form of a swan) of Clytemnestra, Helen of Troy, and Castor and Pollux

Led·bet·ter (led′bet′ər), **Hud·die (William)** (hud′ē) 1888-1949; U.S. blues singer: called *Leadbelly*

Led·er·berg (led′ər burg′, lā′dər-), **Joshua** 1925-2008; U.S. geneticist

le·der·ho·sen (lā′dər hō′zən) ***n.*** ⟦Ger < MHG *lederhose* < *leder*, LEATHER + *hose*, pants: see HOSE⟧ traditional short leather pants worn with suspenders by men and boys in the Alps

ledge (lej) ***n.*** ⟦ME *legge*, prob. < base of *leggen*, to LAY[1]⟧ **1** a shelflike projection [*a window ledge*] **2** *a)* a projecting ridge of rocks *b)* such a ridge under the surface of the water near the shore **3** *Mining* a vein **—ledg′y *adj.***

ledg·er (lej′ər) ***n.*** ⟦ME *legger*, prob. < ME *leggen* or *liggen* after MDu *ligger*: see LAY[1], LIE[1]⟧ **1** a large, flat stone placed over a tomb **2** *a)* a large, horizontal timber in a scaffold *b)* LEDGER BOARD (sense 1) **3** ⟦< ME sense "large volume kept in one place in church"⟧ *Bookkeeping* the book of final entry, used, in a double-entry system, for recording all debits and credits, as by transfer from a journal, according to the accounts to which they belong

ledger board **1** a board attached to studding to help support the joists **2** a board forming the top rail as of a fence

ledger line ⟦< ? LEDGER (*n.* 2*a*), from being a horizontal "support" for, or a place to "hang," the note⟧ *Music* a short line written above or below the staff, for notes beyond the range of the staff

lee (lē) ***n.*** ⟦ME *le* < OE *hleo*, shelter, akin to ON *hle*, Du *lij*, Ger *lee* (in sense 3) < IE **kleu-* < base **k̑el-*, warm > L *calere*, to be warm⟧ **1** shelter; protection **2** a sheltered place, esp. one on that side of anything away from the wind **3** *Naut.* the side or direction away from the wind **—*adj.*** **1** designating, of, or on the side sheltered or away from the wind ☆**2** facing or located in the direction toward which a glacier moves: opposed to STOSS

Lee[1] (lē) ***n.*** ⟦var. of LEIGH; also short for LEROY⟧ a masculine and feminine name

Lee[2] (lē) **1 Ann** 1736-84; Eng. mystic: founder of the Shakers in America (1776) **2 Charles** 1731-82; Am. general in the Revolutionary War, born in England **3 Henry** 1756-1818; Am. general in the Revolutionary War & statesman: called *Light-Horse Harry Lee* **4 Richard Henry** 1732-94; Am. Revolutionary statesman: signer of the Declaration of Independence: cousin of Henry **5 Robert E(dward)** 1807-70; commander in chief of the Confederate army in the Civil War: son of Henry

lee·board (lē′bôrd′) ***n.*** a large, flat board or piece of metal let down into the water on the lee side of a sailboat to lessen its leeward drift

leech[1] (lēch) ***n.*** ⟦ME *leche* < OE *lœce*, akin to OHG *lāhhi*, Goth *lēkeis*, magician, healer, OE *lacnian*, to heal, prob. < IE base **leĝ-*, collect, gather together > L *lex* (see LEGAL); sense 2 is supposedly the same word (from use in medicine), but OE (Kentish) *lyce*, ME *liche*, MDu *lieke* suggest a different word assimilated by folk etym.⟧ **1** [Archaic] a physician **2** any of a subclass (Hirudinea) of mostly flattened, annelid worms living in water or wet earth and having a well-developed sucker at each end: most are bloodsuckers, and one species (*Hirudo medicinalis*) has been used in medicine, esp. in former times, to bleed patients **3** a person who clings to another to gain some personal advantage; parasite **—*vt.*** **1** [Obs.] to heal **2** to apply leeches to; bleed with leeches **3** to cling to (another) as a parasite; drain dry **—*vi.*** to act as a parasite: often with *onto*

leech[2] (lēch) ***n.*** ⟦LME *lyche*, akin to ON *lik* < Du *lijk*, boltrope < IE base **leiĝ-*, to bind, fasten > L *ligare*, to tie⟧ **1** the after edge of a fore-and-aft sail **2** either of the vertical edges of a square sail

Leeds (lēdz) city in N England, in West Yorkshire

leek (lēk) ***n.*** ⟦ME *lek* < OE *leac*, akin to Ger *lauch* < ? IE base **leug-*, to bend > L *luxus*, excess: so named ? from its outward-bent leaves⟧ any of various perennial, onionlike, wild or garden vegetables (genus *Allium*, esp. *A. porrum*) of the lily family, having a small bulb with a cylindrical stem, and broad, flat, folded leaves: used in soups, sauces, etc.

leer (lir) ***n.*** ⟦< ME *lere*, cheek < OE *hleor*: in sense "look over one's cheek, look askance"⟧ a sly, sidelong look showing salaciousness, malicious triumph, etc. **—*vi.*** to look with a leer **—leer′ing·ly *adv.***

leer·y (lir′ē) ***adj.*** **leer′i·er**, **leer′i·est** ⟦prob. < ME *lere* (var. of *lore*, LORE[1]) + -Y[3]: current sense infl. by prec.⟧ **1** [Obs.] knowing ☆**2** on one's guard; wary; suspicious

lees (lēz) ***pl.n.*** ⟦pl. of *lee* (obs. in sing.) < ME *lie* < OFr < ML *lia* < Gaul **liga*, akin to OIr *lige*, a bed, layer < IE base **legh-* > LIE[1]⟧ dregs or sediment, as of fermenting wine

Lee's Birthday Jan. 19, Robert E. Lee's birthday, a legal holiday in several Southern states

lee shore the shore on the lee side of a ship; shore toward which the wind is blowing and driving a ship

leet (lēt) *n.* ⟦ME & Anglo-Fr *lete*, akin ? to OE *læth*, land division, esp. in southeast England⟧ [Historical] in England, a manorial court or its jurisdiction

lee tide a leeward tide: in full **leeward tidal current**

Leeu·war·den (lā′vär′dən) city in N Netherlands: capital of Friesland province

Leeu·wen·hoek (lā′vən ho͝ok′), **An·ton van** (än′tôn vän) 1632-1723; Du. naturalist & pioneer in microscopy

lee·ward (lē′wərd′; *naut.* lo͞o′ərd) *adj.* **1** in the direction toward which the wind blows **2** on the lee side —*n.* the side or direction away from the wind —*adv.* toward the lee; away from the wind Opposed to WINDWARD

Lee·ward Islands (lē′wərd) **1** N group of islands in the Lesser Antilles of the West Indies, extending from Puerto Rico southeast to the Windward Islands **2** former British colony in this group (dissolved 1962), now separate countries or territories

lee·way (lē′wā′) *n.* **1** the leeward drift of a ship or aircraft from the course being steered **2** [Informal] *a)* margin of time, money, etc. *b)* room for freedom of action

left[1] (left) *adj.* ⟦ME (Kentish) var. of *lift* < OE *lyft*, weak, akin to EFris *luf*, weak⟧ **1** *a)* designating or of that side of one's body which is toward the west when one faces north, the side of the less-used hand in most people *b)* designating or of the corresponding side of anything *c)* closer to the left side of a person directly before and facing the thing mentioned or understood [the top *left* drawer of a desk] **2** of the side or bank of a river on the left of a person facing downstream **3** of the political LEFT[1] (*n.* 4); communist, socialist, liberal, etc. —*n.* **1** *a)* all or part of the left side *b)* what is on the left side *c)* a direction or location on the left side (often with *the*) *d)* a turn toward the left side ☆**2** *Baseball short for* LEFT FIELD **3** *Boxing a)* the left hand *b)* a blow delivered with the left hand **4** ⟦from the arrangement of seats of the various parties in some European legislatures⟧ [*often* **L-**] *Politics* a liberal or radical position, esp. one varying from moderate socialism to communism, or a party or group advocating this: often with *the* —*adv.* on or toward the left hand or side —*SYN.* LIBERAL —**have two left feet** to be very clumsy, specif., to be a clumsy dancer

left[2] (left) *vt., vi. pt. & pp. of* LEAVE[1] —**left over** remaining

Left Bank ⟦see LEFT[1], *adj.* 2⟧ district in Paris on the S bank of the Seine, associated with artists, bohemians, etc.

left brain the left cerebral hemisphere of the human brain, which includes areas associated with logical thinking, numerical calculation, and language skills: popularly regarded as the center of rational thought —**left′-brain′** *adj.* —**left′-brained′** *adj.*

Left Coast ⟦so called because it is at the *left* side of a map of the U.S.⟧ [*also* **l- c-**] the part of the U.S. near the Pacific coast; esp., California: a humorous usage alluding to left-wing political views supposed to be prevalent there

☆**left field** *Baseball* **1** the area in the outfield behind the third baseman and shortstop **2** the defensive position of the outfielder (**left fielder**) who plays there **3** [Informal] a position or source regarded as unconventional, irrational, unexpected, etc.: in such phrases as **out in left field** or **out of left field**

left-hand (left′hand′) *adj.* **1** being on or directed toward the left **2** of, for, or with the left hand

left-hand·ed (-han′did) *adj.* **1** using the left hand more skillfully than, and in preference to, the right **2** done with the left hand **3** clumsy; awkward **4** designating an insincere or ambiguous compliment; BACKHANDED (sense 2) **5** MORGANATIC: from the custom of having the groom give his left hand to the bride at such a wedding **6** made for use with the left hand or by left-handed people **7** turning from right to left; worked by counterclockwise motion **8** designating one who swings a bat, club, etc. rightward **9** having an asymmetrical molecular or crystal structure that is conventionally viewed as having certain components on the left side: said of an isomer that is the mirror image of one that is right-handed —*adv.* **1** with the left hand [to write *left-handed*] **2** in such a way that the bat, club, etc. swings rightward —**left′-hand′ed·ly** *adv.* —**left′-hand′ed·ness** *n.* —**left′-hand′er** *n.*

left heart the half of the heart containing the left ventricle and left atrium, which supply oxygenated blood to all parts of the body

left·ish (left′ish) *adj.* inclined to be leftist or a leftist

left·ist (-ist) *n.* a person whose political position is of the LEFT[1] (*n.* 4), esp., a communist or socialist —*adj.* liberal or radical —*SYN.* LIBERAL —**left′ism′** *n.*

☆**left·o·ver** (-ō′vər) *n.* **1** something left over **2** [*usually pl.*] food left over from one meal and, often, eaten at a later meal —*adj.* remaining unused, uneaten, etc.

left·ward (-wərd) *adv., adj.* on or toward the left: also **left′wards** *adv.*

left wing ⟦see LEFT[1], *n.* 4⟧ the more liberal or radical section of a political party, group, etc. —**left′-wing′** *adj.* —**left′-wing′er** *n.*

☆**left·y** (lef′tē) *n., pl.* **left′ies** [Slang] **1** a left-handed person **2** LEFTIST

leg[1] (leg, lāg) *n.* ⟦ME < ON *leggr*, a leg, limb < IE base **lek-*, limb > L *lacertus*, muscle, *lacerta*, lizard⟧ **1** one of the parts of the body by means of which animals stand and walk, specif., in human beings, *a)* one of the lower limbs *b)* *Anat.* the part of either lower limb from the knee to the foot **2** a cut of meat consisting of the leg or its lower part **3** the part of slacks, a stocking, etc. that covers the leg **4** anything that resembles a leg in shape or use; specif., *a)* a bar or pole used as a support or prop *b)* any of the supports of a piece of furniture *c)* any of the branches of a forked or jointed object **5** the run made by a sailing vessel on one tack **6** any of the stages of a journey or other course **7** [*pl.*] [Slang] a sustained ability to attract audiences: said as of a film **8** *Cricket* that part of the field which lies to the left and back of the batsman **9** *Math.* either of the sides of a triangle other than its base or, in a right triangle, other than its hypotenuse —*vi.* **legged**, **leg′ging** [Informal] to walk or run: chiefly in the phr. **leg it** —**get up on one's hind legs** [Informal] to become assertive, belligerent, etc. —**not have a leg to stand on** [Informal] to have absolutely no defense, excuse, or justification —**on one's (or its) last legs** [Informal] not far from exhaustion, death, breakdown, etc. —**pull someone's leg** [Informal] to tease or fool someone, esp. in a playful manner —**shake a leg** [Slang] **1** to hurry **2** to dance —**stretch one's legs** to walk, esp. after sitting a long time —**take to one's legs** to run away —**leg′less** *adj.*

leg[2] *abbrev.* **1** legal **2** legato **3** legislative **4** legislature

leg·a·cy (leg′ə sē) *n., pl.* **-cies** ⟦ME *legacie* < OFr < ML *legatia* < L *legatus*: see LEGATE⟧ **1** money or property left to someone by a will; bequest **2** anything handed down from, or as from, an ancestor ☆**3** a student applying or admitted to a college or university who is a relative of an alumnus —*adj.* being or having to do with something, esp. something outdated or otherwise undesirable, that is carried over from a previous system, business operation, etc.

le·gal (lē′gəl) *adj.* ⟦MFr *légal* < L *legalis* < *lex* (gen. *legis*), law, prob. < IE base **leĝ-*, to collect > L *legere*, Gr *legein*, to collect⟧ **1** of, created by, based upon, or authorized by law **2** in conformity with the positive rules of law; permitted by law [a *legal* act] **3** that can be enforced in a court of law [*legal* rights] **4** of or applicable to lawyers [*legal* ethics] **5** in terms of the law [a *legal* offense] **6** [Informal] at or above the statutory age at which one may, variously, consent to sexual intercourse, purchase alcoholic beverages, etc. —**le′gal·ly** *adv.*

SYN.—**legal** implies literal connection or conformity with statute or common law or its administration [*legal* rights]; **lawful**, a more general word, may suggest conformity to the principle rather than to the letter of the law or may broadly refer to that which is not contrary to the law [a *lawful* but shady enterprise]; **legitimate** implies legality of a claim to a title or right [a *legitimate* heir] or accordance with what is sanctioned or accepted as lawful, reasonable, etc. [a *legitimate* argument]; **licit** implies strict conformity to the law, especially in trade, commerce, or personal relations [*licit* marriage] —*ANT.* **illegal, unlawful, illicit**

legal age **1** the age at which a person acquires full legal rights and responsibilities; majority **2** the age at which a person acquires legally a particular right or obligation [the *legal age* for buying alcoholic beverages]

☆**legal cap** ⟦< *cap*, shortened < *cap-paper*, a size or kind of writing paper: see FOOLSCAP⟧ writing paper used by lawyers for documents, 8½ by 13 or 14 inches, folded at the top and with a ruled margin

☆**legal eagle** [Slang] a lawyer, esp. one regarded as highly skilled or ambitious

le·gal·ese (lē′gəl ēz′) *n.* the technical and often arcane legal terminology and forms used in deeds, contracts, etc.

☆**legal holiday** a holiday set by statute, during which government and, usually, business affairs are suspended, schools and courts are closed, etc.

le·gal·ism (lē′gəl iz′əm) *n.* **1** strict, often too strict and literal, adherence to law or to a code **2** *Theol.* the doctrine of salvation by good works —**le′gal·ist** *n.* —**le′gal·is′tic** *adj.* —**le′gal·is′ti·cal·ly** *adv.*

le·gal·i·ty (li gal′ə tē) *n., pl.* **-ties** ⟦ML *legalitas*⟧ **1** quality, condition, or instance of being legal or lawful **2** [*pl.*] legal aspects

le·gal·ize (lē′gəl īz′) *vt.* **-ized′**, **-iz′ing** to make legal or lawful —**le′gal·i·za′tion** *n.*

legal limit the point at or above which a person is deemed to be too intoxicated to operate a motor vehicle legally, expressed as a specified percentage of alcohol in the blood

legal list a list of securities and other investments that insurance companies, pension funds, etc. are legally permitted to hold

☆**legal pad** a writing pad of yellow or white, lined paper the size of legal cap or slightly smaller

☆**legal reserve** the funds that a bank, insurance company, etc. is required by law to maintain as reserves

☆**legal separation** an agreement by which a husband and wife live apart but are not divorced

☆**le·gal-size** (lē′gəl sīz′) *adj.* **1** designating or for paper of the size used for a legal pad **2** designating an envelope approximately 4 by 9½ inches Also **le′gal-sized′**

legal tender money that may be legally offered in payment of an obligation and that a creditor must accept

Le·ga·nés (le′gä nes′) city in central Spain: suburb of Madrid

leg·ate (leg′it) *n.* ⟦ME < OFr *legat* < L *legatus*, pp. of *legare*, to send as ambassador < *lex*, law: see LEGAL⟧ **1** an envoy or ambassador **2** *Rom. History* the governor of a province, or his deputy —**leg′ate·ship′** *n.* —**leg′a·tine′** (-ə tēn′) *adj.*

leg·a·tee (leg′ə tē′) *n.* ⟦< L *legatus*, pp. of *legare*, to bequeath, appoint (see prec.) + -EE[1]⟧ one to whom a legacy is bequeathed

le·ga·tion (li gā′shən) *n.* ⟦ME *legacion* < OFr < L *legatio*⟧ **1** *a)* the act of sending a legate on a mission *b)* the mission **2** *a)* a diplomatic minister and staff collectively, representing their government in a foreign country and ranking just below an embassy *b)* the residence or offices of such a legation *c)* the position or authority of such a legation

le·ga·to (li gät′ō) *[also in italics]* *Music adj., adv.* ⟦It, lit., tied, bound < pp. of *legare*, to tie < L *ligare*: see LEECH[2]⟧ in a smooth, even style, with no noticeable interruption between the notes: often used as a musical direction: cf. STACCATO —*n.* a passage to be played legato

le·ga·tor (li gāt′ər) *n.* one who bequeaths legacies; testator

leg bye *Cricket* a run scored for a ball that touches the batsman on any part of the body except the hand

leg·end (lej′ənd) *n.* ⟦ME *legende* < OFr < ML *legenda*, things to read, neut. pl. of L *legendus*, ger. of *legere*, to read: see LOGIC⟧ **1** *a)* a story handed down for generations among a people and popularly believed to have a historical basis, although not verifiable (cf. MYTH[1]) *b)* all such stories belonging to a particular group of people *[famous in Irish legend]* **2** *a)* a notable person whose deeds or exploits are much talked about in his or her own time *b)* the stories of his or her exploits **3** an inscription on a coin, coat of arms, etc. **4** a title, brief description, or key accompanying an illustration or map

leg·end·ar·y (lej′ən der′ē) *adj.* **1** of, based on, or presented in legends **2** *a)* remarkable; extraordinary *b)* well-known; famous —***SYN.*** FICTITIOUS

Le·gen·dre (lə zhän′dr′), **A·dri·en Ma·rie** (å drē an må rē′) 1752-1833; Fr. mathematician

leg·end·ry (lej′ən drē) *n.* legends collectively

Lé·ger (lā zhā′) **1 A·lex·is Saint-Lé·ger** (å lek sē san lā zhā′) *see* SAINT-JOHN PERSE **2 Fer·nand** (fer nän′) 1881-1955; Fr. painter

leg·er·de·main (lej′ər di mān′) *n.* ⟦ME < MFr *leger de main*, lit., light of hand < *leger* (< LL **levarius* < L *levis*, LIGHT[2]) + *de* (< L *de*, of, from) + *main* < L *manus*, hand⟧ **1** sleight of hand; skill of a stage magician **2** trickery of any sort; deceit

leg·er line (lej′ər) [Chiefly Brit.] LEDGER LINE

le·ges (lē′jēz′, lā′gās′) *n.* ⟦L⟧ *pl. of* LEX[1]

-leg·ged (leg′id, legd; lā′gid, lāgd) *combining form* having (a specified number or kind of) legs *[long-legged, four-legged]*

leg·gie·ro (le jer′ō) *adj., adv.* ⟦It *leggero*, light⟧ *Musical Direction* (in a) light, nimble, or graceful (manner)

leg·ging (leg′iŋ, -in; lā′giŋ, -gin) *n.* **1** a covering of canvas, leather, etc. for protecting the leg below the knee **2** *[pl.]* a child's outer garment with legs, worn in cold weather **3** *[pl.]* a tightfitting garment like tights but without feet, varying in length from the ankle to just above the knee

leg·gy (leg′ē, lā′gē) *adj.* **-gi·er**, **-gi·est** **1** having long and awkward legs *[a leggy colt]* **2** [Informal] having long, well-shaped legs *[a leggy chorus girl]* **3** [Informal] having long, spindly stems with leaves far apart *[leggy plants]* —**leg′gi·ness** *n.*

leg·horn (leg′hôrn′, leg′ərn; lāg′hôrn′) *n.* ⟦after fol.⟧ **1** *[sometimes* **L-***]* any of a breed of small, domestic chicken with white feathers, originating in the Mediterranean region: the prevalent egg-producing breed in the U.S. **2** *a)* a plaiting made of an Italian wheat straw, cut green and bleached when dry *b)* a hat, typically broad-brimmed, made of this straw

Leg·horn (leg′hôrn′, -ərn) ⟦altered by folk etym. < It *Livorno*⟧ seaport in Tuscany, W Italy, on the Ligurian Sea: It. name LIVORNO

leg·i·ble (lej′ə bəl) *adj.* ⟦ME (northern) *legeable* < LL *legibilis* < L *legere*, to read: see LOGIC⟧ **1** that can be read or deciphered **2** that can be read or deciphered easily —**leg′i·bil′i·ty** *n.* —**leg′i·bly** *adv.*

le·gion (lē′jən) *n.* ⟦OFr < L *legio* < *legere*, to choose: see LOGIC⟧ **1** *Rom. History* a military division varying at times from 3,000 to 6,000 foot soldiers, with additional cavalrymen **2** a large group of soldiers; army **3** a large number; multitude *[a legion of admirers]* **4** [**L-**] *short for* AMERICAN LEGION, Foreign Legion, etc. —*adj.* numerous; many: used in the predicate *[her honors were legion]*

le·gion·ar·y (-er′ē) *adj.* ⟦L *legionarius*⟧ of or constituting a legion or legions —*n., pl.* **-ar′ies** a member of a legion

legionary ant ARMY ANT

le·gion·naire (lē′jə ner′) *n.* ⟦Fr *légionnaire* < L *legionarius*⟧ **1** a member of a legion **2** *[often* **L-***]* a member of the American Legion, Foreign Legion, etc.

☆**Legionnaires' disease** ⟦< prec.: from the first recognized outbreak of the illness at an American Legion convention in 1976⟧ an acute respiratory infection, often resulting in pneumonia, caused by bacteria (*Legionella pneumophila*) that may contaminate water or soil

Legion of Honor **1** a French honorary society founded in 1802 by Napoleon for recognition of distinguished military or civil service **2** the decoration given to those receiving such recognition

☆**Legion of Merit** a U.S. decoration awarded to members of the armed forces of the U.S. or of foreign nations for exceptionally meritorious conduct

legis *abbrev.* **1** legislation **2** legislative **3** legislature

leg·is·late (lej′is lāt′) *vi.* **-lat′ed**, **-lat′ing** ⟦back-form. < LEGISLATOR⟧ to make or pass a law or laws —*vt.* to cause to be, become, go, etc. by making laws

leg·is·la·tion (lej′is lā′shən) *n.* ⟦LL *legislatio* < L *lex* (gen. *legis*), law (see LEGAL) + *latio*, a bringing, proposing < *latus*, pp. of *ferre*, to bring, BEAR[1]⟧ **1** the act or process of making a law or laws **2** the law or laws made

leg·is·la·tive (lej′is lāt′iv) *adj.* **1** of legislation *[legislative powers]* ☆**2** of a legislature or its members *[legislative party whip]* **3** having the power to make laws *[a legislative assembly]* **4** brought about or enforced by legislation —*n.* the lawmaking branch of a government; legislature —**leg′is·la′tive·ly** *adv.*

leg·is·la·tor (-lāt′ər, -lā′tôr′) *n.* ⟦L *legis lator*, lit., a proposer of a law: for bases see LEGISLATION⟧ a member of a legislative assembly; lawmaker

leg·is·la·ture (-lā′chər) *n.* ⟦see prec. & -URE⟧ a body of persons given the responsibility and power to make laws for a country or state; specif., the lawmaking body of a U.S. state, corresponding to the U.S. Congress

le·gist (lē′jist) *n.* ⟦LME < MFr *legiste* < ML *legista* < L *lex*, law: see LEGAL⟧ a person who has special knowledge of the law, or of some branch of it

le·git (lə jit′) *adj.* [Informal] legitimate

le·git·i·ma·cy (lə jit′ə mə sē) *n.* the quality or state of being legitimate

le·git·i·mate (lə jit′ə mət; *for v.*, -māt′) *adj.* ⟦ML *legitimatus*, pp. of *legitimare*, to make lawful < L *legitimus*, lawful < *lex*: see LEGAL⟧ **1** conceived or born of parents legally married to each other **2** *a)* sanctioned by law or custom; lawful *[a legitimate claim]* *b)* conforming to or abiding by the law **3** ruling by the rights of heredity *[a legitimate king]* **4** *a)* reasonable; logically correct *[a legitimate inference]* *b)* justifiable or justified **5** conforming to or in accordance with established rules, standards, principles **6** *Theater* designating or of professionally produced stage plays, as distinguished from films, vaudeville, etc. *[an actor of the legitimate stage]* —*vt.* **-mat′ed**, **-mat′ing** LEGITIMIZE —***SYN.*** LEGAL —**le·git′i·mate·ly** *adv.* —**le·git′i·ma′tion** *n.*

le·git·i·ma·tize (lə jit′ə mə tīz′) *vt.* **-tized′**, **-tiz′ing** LEGITIMIZE

le·git·i·mist (lə jit′ə mist) *n.* ⟦Fr *légitimiste*⟧ a supporter of someone claiming a throne on the right of heredity —*adj.* having to do with support for such a claimant —**le·git′i·mism′** *n.*

le·git·i·mize (lə jit′ə mīz′) *vt.* **-mized′**, **-miz′ing** **1** to make or declare legitimate; specif., *a)* to make lawful; give legal force or status to *b)* to give official or formal sanction to; authorize *c)* to give the status of a legitimate child to (one born out of wedlock) **2** to make seem just, right, or reasonable; justify —**le·git′i·mi·za′tion** (-mə zā′shən, -mī′-) *n.*

☆**leg·man** (leg′man′, lāg′-) *n., pl.* **-men′** (-men′) **1** a news reporter who gathers information at the scene of events or at various sources, usually transmitting it to an office or news room for editing **2** a person who runs errands or gathers information to assist someone in an office

Leg·o (lā′gō, leg′ō) *n., pl.* **Leg′os** ⟦< *LEGO*, a trademark for such blocks and related products < Dan *Le(g) go(dt)*, play well⟧ any of a set of small, plastic, interlocking building blocks used as a construction toy

leg-of-mut·ton (leg′əv mut′'n, lāg′-) *adj.* shaped somewhat like a leg of mutton; specif., designating a sleeve that puffs out toward the shoulder

le·gong (lā′gôŋ′) *n.* ⟦Balinese⟧ a traditional Balinese dance, performed by two young girls

Legree, **Simon** *see* SIMON LEGREE

leg·room (leg′ro͞om′) *n.* adequate space for the legs while one is seated, as in a car or theater seat

leg·ume (leg′yo͞om′, li gyo͞om′) *n.* ⟦Fr *légume*, vegetable < L *legumen*, lit., anything that can be gathered < *legere*, to gather: see LOGIC⟧ **1** any of an order (Fabales) of dicotyledonous herbs, shrubs, and trees, including the peas, beans, mimosas, and the Kentucky coffee tree, with usually compound leaves, flowers having a single carpel, and fruit that is a dry pod splitting along two sutures: many legumes are nitrogen-fixing and often are used as green manure and for forage **2** the pod or seed of some members of this order, used for food

le·gu·mi·nous (lə gyo͞o′mə nəs) *adj.* **1** of, having the nature of, or bearing a legume or legumes **2** of the order of plants bearing legumes

leg up [Informal] **1** assistance; help; specif., a boosting, as of a rider onto a horse **2** an advantage; lead *[to get a leg up on the competition]* Also **leg′-up′** *n.*

leg warmers a set of coverings, typically knitted, for the legs, worn for warmth or, as by dancers rehearsing, to prevent leg cramps

☆**leg·work** (leg′wurk′, lāg′-) *n.* [Informal] routine work that is necessary to a job, as that of a news reporter, involving, typically, walking or driving from place to place, away from the office

Le·hár (lā′här′), **Franz** (fränts) 1870-1948; Hung. composer of operettas

Le Ha·vre (lə häv′rə, -ər; *Fr* lə å′vr′) seaport in NW France, on the English Channel

Le·high (lē′hī′) ⟦< ? Algonquian⟧ river in E Pa., flowing into the Delaware: *c.* 120 mi (193 km)

le·hu·a (lā ho͞o′ä) *n.* ⟦Haw⟧ **1** a tropical tree (*Metrosideros collina*) of the myrtle family, with clusters of bright-red flowers and hard, durable wood: it grows in Hawaii and other Pacific islands **2** its wood **3** its flower

lei[1] (lā, lā′ē) *n., pl.* **leis** ⟦Haw⟧ in Hawaii, a wreath of flowers and leaves, generally worn about the neck

lei[2] (lā) *n. pl. of* LEU

Leib·niz (līp′nits′, līb′-), Baron **Gott·fried Wil·helm von** (gôt′frēt′ vil′helm′ fôn) (born *Gottfried Wilhelm Leibnütz*) 1646-1716; Ger. philosopher & mathematician: also sp. **Leib′nitz′**

Leices·ter[1] (les′tər) *n.* any of a breed of large sheep with long, coarse wool, and, usually, a wedge-shaped face, originally developed in Leicestershire

Leices·ter[2] (les′tər), Earl of (*Robert Dudley*) 1532?-88; Eng. courtier & general: favorite of Elizabeth I

Leices·ter[3] (les′tər) city in central England; county seat of Leicestershire

Leices·ter·shire (-shir′, -shər) county in central England: 985 sq mi (2,551 sq km)

Lei·den (līd′'n) city in W Netherlands

Leif (lēf, lāf, lāv) *n.* ⟦ON *Leifr*, lit., descendant < base of *leifa*; akin to OE *læfan*, LEAVE[1]⟧ a masculine name

Leif Ericson *alt. sp. of* Leif ERIKSON

Leigh (lē) *n.* ⟦< surname *Leigh* < ME *leye*: see LEA[1]⟧ a masculine and feminine name; var. *Lee*

Lein·ster (len′stər) province of E Ireland: 7,578 sq mi (19,627 sq km)

Leip·zig (līp′sig, -siH) city in E Germany, in the state of Saxony

leish·ma·ni·a·sis (lēsh′mə nī′ə sis) ***n.*** ⟦ModL < *Leishmania*, after Sir W. B. *Leishman* (1865-1926), Scot bacteriologist⟧ any of several infectious diseases, esp. kala azar, caused by protozoan parasites (genus *Leishmania*)

leis·ter (lēs′tər) ***n.*** ⟦< Scand, as in ON *ljoster* < *ljosta*, to strike < IE base **leu-*, to cut off > Gr *lyein*, to loosen, dissolve⟧ a kind of fish spear, usually with three prongs —***vt.*** to spear (fish) with a leister

lei·sure (lē′zhər, lezh′ər) ***n.*** ⟦ME *leiser* < OFr *leisir*, substantive use of inf., to be permitted < L *licere* < IE base **leik-*, to offer for sale, bargain⟧ free, unoccupied time, as for indulging in rest, recreation, etc. —***adj.*** **1** free and unoccupied; spare [*leisure* time] **2** wealthy, with much leisure for recreation [the *leisure* class]: also **lei′sured 3** done or used during one's leisure [*leisure* activities, *leisure* wear] —**at leisure 1** having free or spare time **2** with no hurry **3** not occupied or engaged —**at one's leisure** when one has the time or opportunity

lei·sure·ly (-lē) ***adj.*** characterized by or having leisure; without haste; deliberate; slow [to make a *leisurely* inspection of a place] —***adv.*** in an unhurried manner

☆**leisure suit** a man's suit, popular in the 1970s, designed for casual wear, having the jacket styled like a shirt, typically with a button front, and usually worn without a necktie

leit·mo·tif or **leit·mo·tiv** (līt′mō tēf′) ***n.*** ⟦Ger *leitmotiv* < *leiten*, to LEAD[1] + *motiv*, MOTIVE⟧ **1** a short, recurring musical phrase or theme, esp. as used in Wagnerian opera to represent a given character, emotion, etc. **2** a dominant theme or underlying pattern

Lei·trim (lē′trəm) county in Connacht province, in the N part of the Republic of Ireland: 589 sq mi (1,526 sq km)

Leix (lāsh, lēsh) *var. of* LAOIGHIS

Lei·zhou (lā′jō′) peninsula in Guangdong province, SE China, opposite Hainan island: *c.* 90 mi (145 km) long

lek[1] (lek) ***n.*** ⟦Albanian⟧ the basic monetary unit of Albania: see the table of monetary units in the Reference Supplement

lek[2] (lek) ***n.*** ⟦ult. < Swed⟧ an area where certain male animals, as the male of the prairie chicken, gather to perform their courtship displays

lek·var (lek′vär′) ***n.*** ⟦Hung⟧ a sweet purée of cooked plums or prunes, used chiefly as a filling in pastries

Le·ly (lē′lē, lā′-), Sir **Peter** (born *Peter van der Faes*) 1618-80; Du. portrait painter in England

☆**LEM** (lem) ***n.***, *pl.* **LEMs** a lunar excursion module, the manned spacecraft that landed on the moon

lem·an (lem′ən, lē′mən) ***n.*** ⟦ME *lemman, lefman* < *lef*, dear (see LIEF) + *man*⟧ [Archaic] a sweetheart or lover (man or woman); esp., a mistress

Le·man (lē′mən), **Lake** Lake GENEVA: Fr. name **Lac Lé·man** (lȧk lā män′)

Le Mans (lə män′) city in W France

lem·ma[1] (lem′ə) ***n.***, *pl.* **-mas** or **-ma·ta** (-ə tə) ⟦L < Gr *lēmma*, something taken or received, something taken for granted < *lambanein*, to seize, assume < IE base **(s)lagw-*, to grasp > LATCH⟧ **1** a proposition proved, or sometimes assumed, to be true and used in proving a theorem **2** the subject of a composition, gloss, or note, esp. when used as a heading **3** a term glossed in a list

lem·ma[2] (lem′ə) ***n.*** ⟦Gr, a husk < base of *lepein*, to peel: see LEPER⟧ the outer or lower of the two bracts or scales surrounding the flower of a grass

lem·ming (lem′iŋ) ***n.***, *pl.* **-mings** or **-ming** ⟦Dan < ON *lœmingi*, lemming, orig., prob. "barker" < IE echoic base **lā-* > L *latrare*, to bark, *lamentum*, LAMENT⟧ any of various small, mostly arctic rodents (family Cricetidae) resembling mice but having short tails and fur-covered feet: some species (esp. genus *Lemmus*) undertake mass migrations at peaks of population growth

lem·nis·cus (lem nis′kəs) ***n.***, *pl.* **-nis′ci** (-nis′ī) ⟦ModL < L, hanging ribbon < Gr *lēmniskos*, ribbon⟧ a band of sensory nerve fibers in the central nervous system, usually terminating in the thalamus

Lem·nos (lem′näs′, -nōs′) Greek island in the N Aegean: 184 sq mi (477 sq km)

lem·on (lem′ən) ***n.*** ⟦ME *lymon* < MFr *limon* < Ar *laimūn* < Pers *līmūn*⟧ **1** a small, egg-shaped, edible citrus fruit with a yellow rind and a juicy, sour pulp, rich in ascorbic acid **2** the small, spiny, semitropical evergreen citrus tree (*Citrus limon*) bearing this fruit **3** any of various shades of yellow; specif., *a)* pale yellow *b)* bright yellow *c)* greenish yellow: also **lemon yellow** ☆**4** [Informal] *a)* something, esp. a manufactured article, that is defective or imperfect *b)* an inadequate person —***adj.*** **1** having the color of a lemon; pale to bright yellow **2** made with or from lemons **3** having a flavor more or less like that of lemons —**lem′on·y** ***adj.***

lem·on·ade (lem′ən ād′) ***n.*** ⟦Fr *limonade*⟧ a drink made of lemon juice, sweetening, and water

lemon balm a perennial mint (*Melissa officinalis*) with white or yellowish flowers and aromatic leaves: used in flavoring food, liqueurs, and medicines

☆**lemon butter 1** a spread made of butter flavored with lemon **2** a sauce of melted butter, lemon juice, and seasoning, used on fish, vegetables, etc.: also **lemon butter sauce**

lemon drop a small, hard, lemon-flavored candy

lemon grass any of various tall, lemon-scented grasses (genus *Cymbopogon*, esp. *C. citratus*) used as a flavoring in SE Asian cooking: also written **lem′on·grass′** ***n.***

☆**lemon law** ⟦< LEMON (*n.* 4*a*)⟧ [Informal] a statute providing legal recourse to consumers who purchase products, esp. motor vehicles, that prove to be seriously defective

lemon verbena a Chilean shrub (*Aloysia triphylla*) of the verbena family, with white flowers and whorls of narrow, lemon-scented leaves

lem·pi·ra (lem pir′ə) ***n.***, *pl.* **-ras** ⟦AmSp, after *Lempira* (1499-1537), Honduran chieftain who organized resistance to the Spanish invaders⟧ the basic monetary unit of Honduras: see the table of monetary units in the Reference Supplement

le·mur (lē′mər) ***n.*** ⟦< L *lemures*, ghosts, specters (akin to Gr *lamia*: see LAMIA): so called from its nocturnal habits⟧ any of a family (Lemuridae) of prosimian primates with large eyes, a long tail, a pointed muzzle, and soft, woolly fur: they are mostly tree-dwelling and nocturnal, and are found only in Madagascar and the Comoro Islands

lem·u·res (lem′yoo rēz′) ***pl.n.*** ⟦L: see prec.⟧ *Rom. Myth.* evil, night-walking spirits of the dead

Le·na[1] (lē′nə, lā′-) ***n.*** a feminine name: var. *Lina*: see HELENA[1], MAGDALENE

Le·na[2] (lē′nə, lā′-) river in EC Siberian Russia, rising near Lake Baikal and flowing northeast into the Laptev Sea: *c.* 2,734 mi (4,400 km)

Len·a·pe (len′ə pē′) ***n.***, *pl.* **-pe′** ⟦short for Lenape *Leni-lenape*, lit., real man < *leni*, real + *lenape*, man⟧ DELAWARE[1] (***n.*** 1 & 2)

lend (lend) ***vt.*** **lent**, **lend′ing** ⟦< ME *lenen* (with unhistoric *-d* < pt.) < OE *lænan* < *læn*, a LOAN⟧ **1** to let another use or have (a thing) temporarily and on condition that it, or the equivalent, be returned **2** to let out (money) at interest **3** to give; impart [a fire *lends* cheer to a room] —***vi.*** to make a loan or loans —**lend itself** (or **oneself**) **to** to be adapted to, useful for, or open to —**lend′a·ble** ***adj.*** —**lend′er** ***n.***

lending library (or **department**) CIRCULATING LIBRARY

☆**lend-lease** (lend′lēs′) ***n.*** in WWII, material aid in the form of munitions, tools, food, etc. granted by the U.S. to certain of its allies —**lend′-lease′** ***vt.*** **-leased′**, **-leas′ing**

L'En·fant (län fän′), **Pierre Charles** (pyer shȧrl′) 1754-1825; Fr. engineer & architect who served in the Am. Revolutionary army & drew up plans for Washington, D.C.

length (leŋkth, leŋth) ***n.*** ⟦ME < OE *lengthu* < base of *lang*, LONG[1] + -TH[1]⟧ **1** the measure of how long a thing is; measurement of anything from end to end; the greatest of the two or three dimensions of anything **2** extent in space; distance anything extends **3** extent in time; duration **4** a long stretch or extent **5** the quality, state, or fact of being long **6** a piece or stretch of something; specif., a piece of a certain or standardized measure [a *length* of stove pipe] **7** a unit of measure consisting of the length of an object or animal competing in a race [to win a boat race by two *lengths*] **8** *Phonet. a)* the duration of the pronunciation of a vowel [the *i* in *bride* has greater *length* than the *i* in *bright*] *b)* popularly, the quality of a vowel **9** *Prosody* syllabic quantity —**at full length** stretched out; completely extended —**at length 1** after a long time; finally **2** *a)* in great detail *b)* for a long time —**go to any lengths** (or **length**) to do whatever is necessary; scruple at nothing

-length (leŋkth, leŋth) *combining form forming adjectives* of a (specified) length, of such length as to reach a (specified) point or part [*full-length*]

length·en (leŋk′thən, leŋ′-) ***vt., vi.*** to make or become longer —***SYN.*** EXTEND —**length′en·er** ***n.***

length·wise (leŋkth′wīz′, leŋ′-) ***adv., adj.*** in the direction of the length: also, for *adv.*, **length′ways′** (-wāz′)

☆**length·y** (leŋk′thē, leŋ′-) ***adj.*** **length′i·er**, **length′i·est** having length; long; esp., too long, or so long as to be tiresome [a *lengthy* voyage, a *lengthy* sermon] —**length′i·ly** ***adv.*** —**length′i·ness** ***n.***

le·ni·en·cy (lē′nē ən sē, lēn′yən sē) ***n.***, *pl.* **-cies 1** the quality or condition of being lenient **2** lenient treatment, as in disciplining or sentencing Also **le·ni·ence** (lēn′yəns, lē′nē əns) —***SYN.*** MERCY

le·ni·ent (lē′nē ənt, lēn′yənt) ***adj.*** ⟦L *leniens*, prp. of *lenire*, to soften, alleviate < *lenis*, smooth, soft, mild < IE base **lēi-*: see LATE⟧ **1** not harsh or severe in disciplining, punishing, judging, etc.; mild; merciful; clement **2** [Archaic] soothing —**le′ni·ent·ly** ***adv.***

Len·i-Len·a·pe (len′ē len′ə pē′) ***n.*** *var. of* LENAPE

Len·in (len′in; *Russ* lye′nyin), **V(ladimir) I(lyich)** (orig., surname *Ulyanov*; formerly often referred to in error as *Nikolai Lenin*) 1870-1924; Russ. leader of the Communist revolution of 1917: premier of the U.S.S.R. (1917-24)

Le·nin·a·kan (len′in ə kän′) *name* (1924-90) *for* KUMAYRY

Len·in·grad (len′in grad′) *name* (1924-91) *for* ST. PETERSBURG (Russia)

Len·in·ism (len′in iz′əm) ***n.*** the communist theories, doctrines, policies, and methods of Lenin, including esp. his theory of the dictatorship of the proletariat and analysis of imperialism: a development of Marxism —**Len′in·ist** ***n., adj.***

Lenin Peak mountain located on the border between Kyrgyzstan & Tajikistan: *c.* 23,400 ft (7,132 m)

le·nis (lē′nis, lā′-) ***adj.*** ⟦L, smooth, soft, mild: see LENIENT⟧ *Phonet.* articulated with little muscle tension and little or no aspiration, as (b) and (d) —***n.*** a lenis sound Opposed to FORTIS

len·i·tive (len′ə tiv) ***adj.*** ⟦< ML *lenitivus* < L *lenitus*, pp. of *lenire*, to soften: see LENIENT⟧ soothing or assuaging; lessening pain or distress —***n.*** anything that soothes; esp., a lenitive medicine

len·i·ty (len′ə tē) ***n.*** ⟦OFr *lenité* < L *lenitas* < *lenis*, mild: see LENIENT⟧ **1** the quality or condition of being lenient; mildness; gentleness; mercifulness **2** *pl.* **-ties** a lenient act

le·no (lē′nō) ***n.*** ⟦Fr *linon* < *lin*, flax: see LINEN⟧ **1** a type of weave in which the warp yarns are paired and twisted **2** a soft, meshed fabric of this weave

Le·nore (lə nôr′) ***n.*** a feminine name: see LEONORA

lens (lenz) ***n.*** ⟦L, lentil: from the resemblance to the shape of a lentil⟧ **1** *a)* a piece of glass, or other transparent substance, with two curved surfaces, or one plane and one curved, regularly bringing together or spreading rays of light passing through it: a lens or combination of lenses is used in optical instruments, eyeglasses, etc. to form an image *b)* a combination of two or more such pieces **2** any of various devices used to focus microwaves, electrons, or sound waves **3** *Anat.* a transparent, biconvex body situated between the iris and the vitreous humor of the eye: it focuses upon the retina light rays entering the pupil —***vt.*** [Informal] **1** to photograph **2** to make a film of

BICONVEX PLANO-CONVEX POSITIVE MENISCUS
BICONCAVE PLANO-CONCAVE NEGATIVE MENISCUS

lenses

lent (lent) ***vt., vi. pt. & pp. of*** LEND

Lent (lent) ***n.*** ⟦ME *lenten* < OE *lengten*, the spring < Gmc **langat-tin* < base of LONG[1] + **tina-*, day < IE base **dei-*, to shine > L *dies*, day: from the lengthening of the days in the spring; akin to Ger *lenz*, spring⟧ **1** the period of forty weekdays from Ash Wednesday to Easter, observed variously in Christian churches by fasting and penitence **2** in the Middle Ages, the period from Martinmas (November 11) to Christmas: in full **St. Martin's Lent**

len·ta·men·te (len′tə men′tā) ***adv.*** ⟦It < *lento*, LENTO⟧ *Musical Direction* slowly

len·tan·do (len tän′dō) ***adj., adv.*** ⟦It < *lentare*, to make slow < *lento*, LENTO⟧ *Musical Direction* slowing down gradually

Lent·en (lent′'n) ***adj.*** ⟦ME *lenten* < OE *lengten*, full form of LENT: now felt as LENT + -EN⟧ [*also* **l-**] of, connected with, or suitable for Lent

len·tic (len′tik) ***adj.*** ⟦< L *lentus*, slow (see LITHE) + -IC⟧ *Ecol.* designating, of, or living in a freshwater habitat characterized by slowly moving water that is, hence, easily polluted: cf. LOTIC

len·ti·cel (len′ti sel′) ***n.*** ⟦ModL *lenticella*, dim. < L *lens* (gen. *lentis*), lentil⟧ a spongy area in the bark of a woody plant, serving as a pore to permit the exchange of gases between the stem and the atmosphere —**len′ti·cel′late** (-sel′it) ***adj.***

len·tic·u·lar (len tik′yoo lər) ***adj.*** ⟦L *lenticularis* < *lenticula*: see LENTIL⟧ **1** shaped like a lentil or biconvex lens **2** of a lens **3** of the lens of the eye **4** designating or of a projection screen made up of a series of small cylindrical lenses set on the surface: the screen is very bright over a wide angle of viewing

len·tic·u·late (-lāt′) ***vt.*** **-lat′ed, -lat′ing** to emboss lenticules on the base side of (a film) in order to produce, with a special color filter, pictures in natural color —**len·tic′u·la′tion** ***n.***

len·ti·cule (len′ti kyool′) ***n.*** ⟦< L *lenticula*: see LENTIL⟧ any of the microscopic lenses lenticulated on a film

len·tig·i·nous (len tij′ə nəs) ***adj.*** ⟦L *lentiginosus* < *lentigo*: see fol.⟧ **1** of lentigo **2** freckled Also **len·tig′i·nose′** (-nōs′)

len·ti·go (-tī′gō) ***n., pl.*** **len·tig′i·nes′** (-tij′ə nēz′) ⟦L < *lens*, lentil⟧ a frecklelike spot on the skin that often appears during or after middle age

len·til (lent′'l) ***n.*** ⟦ME < OFr *lentille* < L *lenticula*, dim. of *lens*, lentil⟧ **1** an Old World plant (*Lens culinaris*) of the pea family with small, edible seeds shaped like biconvex lenses **2** the seed of this plant

len·tis·si·mo (len tis′ə mō′) ***adj., adv.*** ⟦It, superl. of *lento*: see LENTO⟧ *Musical Direction* very slow(ly)

len·ti·vi·rus (len′ti vī′rəs) ***n.*** ⟦ModL < L *lentus*, slow + VIRUS⟧ any of a genus (*Lentivirus*) of retroviruses that have a slow but persistent rate of replication and cause various chronic, progressive diseases in hoofed animals, esp. sheep

len·to (len′tō) [*also in italics*] *Music* ***adj., adv.*** ⟦It, slow < L *lentus*, pliant, lasting, slow: see LITHE⟧ slow(ly): often used as a musical direction —***n.*** a passage to be performed lento

len·toid (len′toid′) ***adj.*** ⟦< L *lens* (gen. *lentis*): see LENS & -OID⟧ lens-shaped

Le·o[1] (lē′ō) ***n.*** **1** ⟦L: see LION⟧ a masculine name: var. *Leon*; fem. *Leona* **2** a N constellation between Cancer and Virgo, containing the bright star Regulus; the Lion **3** the fifth sign of the zodiac, entered by the sun about July 21: also called *the Lion* **4** a person born under this sign

Le·o[2] (lē′ō) **1** Saint **Leo I** A.D. (400?-461); pope (440-461): his day is Nov 10 **2** Saint **Leo III** (died A.D. 816); pope (795-816): his day is June 12 **3** **Leo XIII** 1810-1903; pope (1878-1903)

Leo Minor ⟦L, lit., the Lesser Lion⟧ a small N constellation between Leo and Ursa Major

Le·on (lē′än′) ***n.*** a masculine name: see LEO[1]

Le·ón (le ôn′) **1** region in NW Spain: from the 10th cent., a kingdom which united with Castile (1037-1157), separated (1157-1230), and permanently united with Castile (1230) **2** city in this region **3** city in central Mexico, in Guanajuato state: in full **León de los Al·da·mas** (de lôs äl dä′mäs) **4** city in W Nicaragua

Le·o·na (lē ō′nə) ***n.*** a feminine name: see LEO[1]

Leon·ard (len′ərd) ***n.*** ⟦Fr *Léonard* < OFr *Leonard* < OHG **Lewenhart*, lit., strong as a lion < *lewo*, lion (< L *leo*: see LION) + *hart*, strong, HARD⟧ a masculine name: dim. *Len, Lenny*

Le·o·nar·desque (lē′ō när desk′) ***adj.*** resembling Leonardo da Vinci or his style of painting

Leonardo da Vinci *see* DA VINCI, Leonardo

Le·on·ca·val·lo (le ôn′kä väl′lô), **Rug·gie·ro** (roo̅d je′rô) 1858-1919; It. operatic composer

le·one (lē ōn′) ***n.*** ⟦< SIERRA LEONE⟧ the basic monetary unit of Sierra Leone: see the table of monetary units in the Reference Supplement

Le·on·i·das (lē än′ə dəs) died 480 B.C.; king of Sparta (491?-480): defeated & killed by the Persians at Thermopylae

Le·o·nids (lē′ə nidz′) ***pl.n.*** ⟦Fr < L *Leo* (gen. *Leonis*): see LEO[1] & -ID⟧ the meteor showers visible annually about November 16: they appear to radiate from the constellation Leo: also **Le·on·i·des** (lē än′i dēz′) —**Le′o·nid′** ***adj.***

le·o·nine (lē′ə nīn′) ***adj.*** ⟦ME < OFr *leonin* < L *leoninus* < *leo*, LION⟧ of, characteristic of, or like a lion

Le·o·no·ra (lē′ə nôr′ə) ***n.*** a feminine name: dim. *Nora*; var. *Lenora, Lenore, Leonore*: see ELEANOR

Le·o·nore (lē′ə nôr′) ***n.*** a feminine name: see LEONORA

Le·ont·ief (lē änt′yef), **Was·si·ly** (vas′ə lē) 1906-99; U.S. economist, born in Russia

leop·ard (lep′ərd) ***n., pl.*** **-ards** or **-ard** ⟦ME *leoparde* < OFr *leupart* < LL *leopardus* < Gr *leopardos* < *leōn*, lion + *pardos*, pard, panther⟧ **1** any of various large, ferocious cats, including the jaguar and snow leopard, esp. a species (*Panthera pardus*) of Africa and S Asia usually having a tawny coat spotted with black **2** *Heraldry* a lion represented in side view, with one foreleg raised and the head facing the viewer

leop·ard·ess (lep′ər dəs) ***n.*** a female leopard

Le·o·par·di (le′ô pär′dē), Conte **Gia·co·mo** (jä′kô mô) 1798-1837; It. poet

Le·o·pold[1] (lē′ə pōld′) ***n.*** ⟦Ger < OHG *Liutbalt* < *liut*, people (orig., prob., free man, akin to OE *leod*, man, king) + *balt*, strong, BOLD⟧ a masculine name

Le·o·pold[2] (lē′ə pōld′) **1 Leopold I** 1640-1705; emperor of the Holy Roman Empire (1658-1705) **2 Leopold I** 1790-1865; king of Belgium (1831-65) **3 Leopold II** 1747-92; emperor of the Holy Roman Empire (1790-92): son of Maria Theresa **4 Leopold II** 1835-1909; king of Belgium (1865-1909): son of Leopold I **5 Leopold III** 1901-83; king of Belgium (1934-51): abdicated: son of Albert I

Lé·o·pold·ville (lē′ə pōld vil′; lā-) *former name for* KINSHASA

☆**le·o·tard** (lē′ə tärd′) ***n.*** ⟦after J. *Léotard*, 19th-c. Fr aerial performer⟧ a one-piece, tightfitting, sleeved or sleeveless garment that covers, usually, only the torso: it is worn by acrobats, dancers, etc.: see also UNITARD, TIGHTS

Le·pan·to (li pan′tō, -pän′-), **Gulf of** *former name for* Gulf of CORINTH: site of naval battle (**Battle of Lepanto**, 1571) in which the European powers defeated Turkey

lep·er (lep′ər) ***n.*** ⟦ME *lepre*, leprosy < OFr < LL *lepra* (L *leprae*, pl.) < Gr < *lepros*, rough, scaly < *lepein*, to peel < IE base **lep-*, to peel off, scale > OE *læfer*, rush, reed⟧ **1** a person having leprosy **2** a person to be shunned or ostracized, as because of the danger of moral contamination

lep·i·do- (lep′ə dō) ⟦< Gr *lepis* (gen. *lepidos*), a scale < *lepein*: see prec.⟧ *combining form* scaly: also, before a vowel, **lep′id-**

le·pid·o·lite (li pid′ə līt′, lep′i dō līt′) ***n.*** ⟦prec. + -LITE⟧ mica that contains lithium, commonly occurring in scaly masses of rose, lilac, or gray color

lep·i·dop·ter·an (lep′ə däp′tər ən) ***n.*** ⟦< ModL *Lepidoptera* (see LEPIDO- & -PTEROUS) + -AN⟧ any of a large order (Lepidoptera) of insects, consisting of the butterflies and moths, characterized by two pairs of broad, membranous wings covered with very fine scales, often brightly colored: the larvae are caterpillars —**lep′i·dop′ter·ous** ***adj.***

lep·i·dop·ter·ist (-ist) ***n.*** a specialist in the study of lepidopteran insects —**lep·i·dop·ter·ol·o·gy** ***n.***

lep·i·do·si·ren (lep′ə dō sī′rən) ***n.*** ⟦ModL < LEPIDO- + SIREN⟧ any of a genus (*Lepidosiren*) of lungfishes with an eel-like form, found in swamps and stagnant waters of the South American tropics

lep·i·dote (lep′i dōt′) ***adj.*** ⟦Gr *lepidōtos* < *lepis* (gen. *lepidos*), a scale: see LEPIDO-⟧ *Biol.* covered with small flakes, scales, or scalelike hairs; scurfy

Lep·i·dus (lep′ə dəs), **(Marcus Aemilius)** died 13 B.C.; Rom. triumvir (43-36 B.C.), with Antony & Octavian

Le·pon·tine Alps (li pän′tin) division of the W Alps between Switzerland & Italy: highest peak, 11,684 ft (3,561 m)

lep·o·rid (lep′ə rid) ***n., pl.*** **le·por·i·dae** (li pôr′i dē′) ⟦< ModL *Leporidae* < L *lepus* (gen. *leporis*) hare, of Iberian-Balearic orig. > Gr *leberis*, Fr *lapin*⟧ any of a family (Leporidae) of lagomorphic mammals, consisting of the hares and rabbits —***adj.*** of this family

lep·o·rine (lep′ə rīn′, -rin) ***adj.*** ⟦L *leporinus* < *lepus*: see prec.⟧ of or like a hare or hares

lep·re·chaun (lep′rə kôn′, -kän′) ***n.*** ⟦Ir *lupracān* < OIr *luchorpan* < *lu*, little + *corpān*, dim. of *corp*, body < L *corpus*, body: see CORPUS⟧ *Ir. Folklore* a fairy in the form of a little old man who can reveal a buried crock of gold to anyone who catches him

lep·ro·sa·ri·um (lep′rə ser′ē əm) ***n., pl.*** **-ri·ums** or **-ri·a** (-ə) ⟦LEPROS(Y) + (SANIT)ARIUM⟧ a hospital or colony for leprosy patients

lep·rose (lep′rōs′) ***adj.*** ⟦LL *leprosus*: see LEPROUS⟧ *Biol.* scaly; scurfy

lep·ro·sy (lep′rə sē) ***n.*** ⟦ME *leprūsē* < *leprus, lepros*: see fol.⟧ a progressive infectious disease caused by a bacterium (*Mycobacterium leprae*) that attacks the skin, flesh, nerves, etc.; it is characterized by nodules, ulcers, white scaly scabs, deformities, and the eventual loss of sensation, and is apparently communicated only after long and close contact

lep·rous (-rəs) *adj.* ⟦ME *lepros* < OFr < LL *leprosus* < *lepra:* see LEPER⟧ **1** of or like leprosy **2** having leprosy **3** LEPROSE

-lep·sy (lep′sē) ⟦ModL *-lepsia* < Gr *-lēpsia* < *lēpsis*, an attack < base of *lambanein*, to seize: see LEMMA[1]⟧ *combining form* a fit, attack, seizure [*narcolepsy*]: also **-lep′si·a** (-sē ə)

lept (lept) *vi., vt. alt. pt. of* LEAP

lep·to- (lep′tō, -tə) ⟦Gr *lepto-* < *leptos*, thin: see LEPTON[1]⟧ *combining form* thin, fine, slender [*leptodactylous*]: also, before a vowel, **lept-**

lep·to·ceph·a·lus (lep′tō sef′ə ləs) *n., pl.* **-li′** (-lī′) ⟦ModL: see prec. & -CEPHALOUS⟧ the marine, ribbonlike larva of tarpons, bonefishes, and eels

lep·to·dac·ty·lous (-dak′tə ləs) *adj.* ⟦LEPTO- + DACTYL + -OUS⟧ having slender toes, as some birds

lep·ton[1] (lep′tän′) *n., pl.* **lep′ta** (-tə) ⟦Gr < *leptos*, thin, small < *lepein*, to peel: see LEPER⟧ **1** a small coin of ancient Greece **2** a former monetary unit of modern Greece, equal to $\frac{1}{100}$ of a drachma

lep·ton[2] (lep′tän′) *n.* ⟦LEPT(O)- + -ON⟧ *Particle Physics* any of a class of fermions subject to the weak interaction but not the strong interaction, as the electron, neutrino, muon, or tau particle —**lep·ton′ic** *adj.*

lep·to·spi·ro·sis (lep′tō spī rō′sis) *n.* ⟦ModL < *Leptospira* (< LEPTO- + L *spira:* see SPIRE[1]) + -OSIS⟧ any of several systemic infections of humans and domestic animals caused by a genus (*Leptospira*) of spirochetes found in sewage and natural waters, and involving variously the eyes, liver, kidneys, etc. —**lep′to·spi′ral** (-spī′rəl) *adj.*

Le·pus (lē′pəs) *n.* ⟦L, the Hare: see LEPORID⟧ a S constellation between Eridanus and Canis Major

Lé·ri·da (lā′rē dä′) city in NE Spain

Ler·mon·tov (ler′män tôf′), **Mi·kha·il Yur·ie·vich** (mē khä ēl′ yoor′yə vich′) 1814-41; Russ. poet & novelist

Le·roy (lə roi′, lē′roi′) *n.* ⟦< Fr *le roi*, the king⟧ a masculine name: also written **LeRoy**

les (lez) *n.* [Slang] *short for* LESBIAN: a term of contempt

Le·sage (lə säzh′), **A·lain Re·né** (à lan rə nā′) 1668-1747; Fr. novelist & dramatist: also written **Le Sage**

les·bi·an (lez′bē ən) *adj.* ⟦L *Lesbius* < Gr *Lesbios*⟧ **1** [**L-**] of Lesbos or its people or culture **2** ⟦from the eroticism or homosexuality attributed to Sappho and her followers on Lesbos⟧ [*sometimes* **L-**] of homosexuality between women —*n.* **1** [**L-**] a person born or living on Lesbos **2** [*sometimes* **L-**] a homosexual woman —**les′bi·an·ism′** *n.*

les·bo (lez′bō′) *adj., n., pl.* **-bos′** [Slang] LESBIAN: a term of contempt

Les·bos (lez′bäs, -bəs) Greek island in the Aegean, off the coast of Asia Minor: *c.* 630 sq mi (1,632 sq km)

lèse-ma·jest·é (lez′ma′zhes tā′, -maj′is tē) *n.* ⟦Fr < L *laesa majestas* < *laesa*, fem. of *laesus* (see fol.) + *majestas*, MAJESTY⟧ **1** a crime against the sovereign; offense against a ruler's dignity as head of the state; treason **2** any insolent or slighting behavior toward a person to whom deference is due Also **lese′ maj′es·ty** (-maj′is tē)

le·sion (lē′zhən) *n.* ⟦ME < MFr < L *laesio* < *laesus*, pp. of *laedere*, to harm, injure⟧ **1** an injury; hurt; damage **2** an injury or other change in an organ or tissue of the body tending to result in impairment or loss of function

Les·lie (lez′lē, les′-) *n.* ⟦< a surname (orig. place name) said to be < *less lee (lea)*, i.e., smaller meadow, dell⟧ **1** a masculine name: dim. *Les* **2** a feminine name: var. *Lesley*

Le·sot·ho (le sōō′tōō, le sō′tō) country in SE Africa, surrounded by South Africa: formerly the British protectorate of *Basutoland*, it became an independent member of the Commonwealth in 1966: 11,720 sq mi (30,355 sq km); cap. Maseru

☆**les·pe·de·za** (les′pə dē′zə) *n.* ⟦ModL *Lespedeza*, based on erroneous reading of the name of V. M. de *Céspedes*, 18th-c. Sp governor of E Florida⟧ any of a genus (*Lespedeza*) of annual or perennial plants of the pea family, cultivated for forage, hay, soil improvement, etc.

less (les) *adj.* ⟦ME *les* < OE *læs*, adv. *læssa*, adj. (used as compar. of *lytel*, LITTLE), akin to OFris *les* < IE **leis-* < base **lei-*, to diminish, meager > LITTLE⟧ **1** *alt. compar. of* LITTLE **2** not so much; smaller in size or amount [to drink *less* milk, take *less* time] **3** fewer [in *less* than 25 words] —*adv.* **1** *compar. of* LITTLE **2** to a smaller extent [*less* likely to succeed] —*n.* a smaller amount —*prep.* with the deduction of; minus [earned about $5,000, *less* taxes; thirty *less* ten is twenty] —**less and less** to a decreasing degree; decreasingly —**much** (or **still**) **less** to an even smaller degree or extent [she won't even talk to him, *much less* work with him] —**no less** phrase used to express mild surprise at the high degree or quality of something or someone [she was an actual princess, *no less*] —**no less than** phrase used to introduce someone or something of some importance or significance [*no less* a dignitary *than* the governor himself led the parade]

USAGE—although the use of *less* instead of *fewer* with plural nouns is very old, it is objected to by some, esp. immediately preceding a plural noun [*less* coins in his pocket]

-less (lis, ləs) ⟦ME *-les, -leas* < OE *-leas* < *leas*, free, loose, akin to *losian*, LOSE⟧ *suffix forming adjectives* **1** without, lacking [*pitiless, valueless*] **2** not able or apt to [*relentless, tireless, reckless*] **3** not able or apt to be ____ed [*dauntless*]

les·see (les ē′) *n.* ⟦ME < Anglo-Fr < OFr *lessé*, pp. of *lesser* < OFr *laissier:* see LEASE & -EE[1]⟧ a person to whom property is leased; tenant

less·en (les′ən) *vt.* **1** to make less; decrease **2** [Archaic] to belittle; minimize; disparage —*vi.* to become less —*SYN.* DECREASE

Les·seps (les′əps; *Fr* le seps′), Vicomte **Fer·di·nand Ma·rie de** (fer dē nän mȧ rē′ də) 1805-94; Fr. engineer & diplomat: promoter & planner of the Suez Canal

less·er (les′ər) *adj.* ⟦LESS + -ER⟧ **1** *alt. compar. of* LITTLE **2** smaller, less, or less important —*adv.* less

Lesser Antilles group of islands in the West Indies, southeast of Puerto Rico, including the Leeward Islands, the Windward Islands, & the islands off the N coast of Venezuela

lesser celandine CELANDINE (sense 2)

lesser omentum *see* OMENTUM

lesser panda ⟦see PANDA⟧ a small, reddish Himalayan carnivore (*Ailurus fulgens*) of the same family (Procyonidae) as the raccoon, with a long, ringed tail

lesser yellowlegs *see* YELLOWLEGS

Les·sing (les′iŋ), **Gott·hold E·phra·im** (gôt′hôlt′ ā′frä im′) 1729-81; Ger. dramatist & critic

les·son (les′ən) *n.* ⟦ME *lessoun* < OFr *leçon* < L *lectio*, a reading, hence text, lesson < pp. of *legere*, to read: see LOGIC⟧ **1** something to be learned; specif., *a)* an exercise or assignment that a student is to prepare or learn within a given time; unit of instruction *b)* the instruction given during one class or instruction period *c)* something that needs to be learned (or the event through which it is learned) for the sake of one's safety, well-being, etc. *d)* [*pl.*] course of instruction [music *lessons*] **2** a selection, as of Scripture, forming part of a religious service; lection **3** a rebuke; reproof —*vt.* [Now Rare] **1** to give a lesson to **2** to rebuke; reprove

les·sor (les′ôr′, les ôr′) *n.* ⟦Anglo-Fr < *lesser:* see LEASE⟧ a person who gives a lease; landlord

lest (lest) *conj.* ⟦ME *leste* < OE *the læste* < *thy læs the*, lit., by the less that < *thy*, instrumental of *thæt*, pron. + *læs* (see LESS) + *the*, particle⟧ **1** for fear that; in case; so that . . . not [speak low *lest* you be overheard] **2** [Archaic] that: used only after a word or words expressing fear [afraid *lest* he should fail us]

Les·ter (les′tər) *n.* ⟦orig. surname < LEICESTER[3]⟧ a masculine name: dim. *Les*

let[1] (let) *vt.* **let, let′ting** ⟦ME *leten* < OE *lætan*, to leave behind, akin to Ger *lassen* < IE **lēd-* < base **lēi-*, to neglect, leave behind > LATE, L *letum*, death⟧ **1** to leave; forsake; abandon: now only in phrases **let alone** or **let be**, to refrain from bothering, disturbing, touching, etc. **2** *a)* to give the use of (a house, room, etc.) to a tenant in return for rent; rent; hire out *b)* to give out (work), assign (a contract), etc. **3** to allow or cause to escape; cause to flow or come out, as by shedding, emitting, etc. [to *let* blood] **4** to allow to pass, come, or go [*let* me in] **5** to allow; permit: followed by an infinitive, normally without *to* [*let* me help], or by an adverb, etc. with the verb itself unexpressed [*let* me up] **6** to cause to; make: usually with *know* or *hear* [*let* me hear from you] ➥When used in commands, suggestions, or dares with a noun or pronoun as object, *let* serves as an auxiliary [*let* us give generously; just *let* him make one false move] —*vi.* to be rented or leased [house to *let*] —**let alone** *see vt.* 1 *above & see the phrase under* ALONE —**let down 1** to lower **2** to slow up; relax; slacken **3** to disappoint or fail —**let off 1** to give forth (steam, etc.) **2** to excuse from work for a short time **3** to deal leniently with; release with light punishment or none —**let on** [Informal] **1** to indicate one's awareness of a fact **2** to pretend —**let out 1** to allow to flow, run, etc. away; release **2** to give forth; emit **3** to lease or rent out **4** to reveal (a secret, etc.) **5** to make a garment larger by reducing (the seams, hem, etc.) **6** to cut (fur pelts) into strips that are then sewn together to achieve suppleness, attractive shading, etc. ☆**7** to dismiss or release (attendees, detainees, etc.) [school *lets out* at 3:00 P.M.] —**let someone have it** [Informal] to attack, hit, shoot, strongly rebuke, etc. someone —**let up 1** to slacken; relax **2** to cease —☆**let up on** [Informal] to stop dealing harshly or severely with —**let well enough alone** *see the phrase under* ALONE

SYN.—**let** may imply positive consent but more often stresses the offering of no opposition or resistance, sometimes connoting negligence, lack of power, etc. [don't *let* this happen again]; **allow** and **permit** imply power or authority to give or deny consent, **allow** connoting a refraining from the enforcement of usual requirements [honor students were *allowed* to miss the examinations], and **permit** more positively suggesting formal consent or authorization [he was *permitted* to talk to the prisoner]; **suffer**, now somewhat rare in this sense, is closely synonymous with **allow** and may connote passive consent or reluctant tolerance See also **hire**

let[2] (let) *vt.* **let′ted** or **let, let′ting** ⟦ME *letten* < OE *lettan*, to hinder, lit., to make late (akin to Goth *latjan*, to delay) < base of *læt*, LATE⟧ [Archaic] to hinder; obstruct; prevent —*n.* **1** an obstacle or impediment: used in the legal phrase **without let or hindrance** **2** *Tennis, etc.* a serve which does not count, specif. one that lands in the correct segment of the opposing player's side of the court after hitting the net

-let (lit) ⟦ME < MFr *-el* (< L *-ellus*) + *-et*, both dim. suffixes⟧ *suffix forming nouns* **1** small [*piglet, starlet*] **2** a small object worn as a band on (a specified part of the body) [*armlet*]

letch (lech) *vi., n. alt. sp. of* LECH

let·down (let′doun′) *n.* **1** a slowing up or feeling of dejection, as after great excitement, effort, etc. **2** the gliding descent of an airplane as it prepares to land **3** a disappointment or disillusionment

le·thal (lē′thəl) *adj.* ⟦L *letalis, lethalis* < *letum*, death: see LET[1]⟧ causing or capable of causing death; fatal or deadly —*SYN.* FATAL —**le·thal′i·ty** (-thal′i tē) *n.* —**le′thal·ly** *adv.*

lethal gene a gene that causes death during some immature stage in the development of an organism: also **lethal factor**

lethal injection a hypodermic injection that causes or is capable of causing death, esp., such an injection used to administer the death penalty

le·thar·gic (li thär′jik) ***adj.*** ⟦ME *litargik* < L *lethargicus* < Gr *lēthargikos*⟧ **1** of or producing lethargy **2** having lethargy; abnormally drowsy or dull, sluggish, etc. —**le·thar′gi·cal·ly** ***adv.***

leth·ar·gy (leth′ər jē) ***n.*** ⟦ME *litarge* < OFr < LL *lethargia* < Gr *lēthargia* < *lēthargos*, forgetful < *lēthē* (see fol.) + *argos*, idle < *a-*, not + *ergon*, WORK⟧ **1** a condition of abnormal drowsiness or torpor **2** a great lack of energy; sluggishness, dullness, apathy, etc.

Le·the (lē′thē) ***n.*** ⟦L < Gr *lēthē*, forgetfulness, oblivion: see LATENT⟧ **1** *Class. Myth.* the river of forgetfulness, flowing through Hades, whose water produces loss of memory in those who drink of it **2** oblivion; forgetfulness —**Le·the·an** (lē thē′ən, lē′thē ən) ***adj.***

Le·ti·tia (li tish′ə) ***n.*** ⟦< L *laetitia*, gladness < *laetus*, joyful, glad⟧ a feminine name: dim. *Letty*

let's (lets) *contraction* let us (as an auxiliary): see LET[1]

Lett (let) ***n.*** ⟦Ger *Lette* < Latvian *Latvi*⟧ LATVIAN (***n.*** 1)

let·ted (let′id) ***vt.*** *alt. pt. & pp. of* LET[2]

let·ter[1] (let′ər) ***n.*** ⟦ME *lettre* < OFr < L *littera*, letter of the alphabet, (in pl.) a letter, epistle⟧ **1** a written or printed symbol employed to represent a speech sound or sounds; character in an alphabet: in some languages, as English, some words contain letters that are no longer sounded **2** a written or printed message to a person or group, usually sent by mail in an envelope **3** an official document giving certain authorities or privileges: *usually used in pl.* **4** [*pl.*] *a)* literature generally *b)* learning; knowledge, esp. of literature **5** the strict interpretation of the literal meaning, or the literal meaning itself; exact wording [*the letter of the law*] ☆**6** a cloth representation of the first letter of the name of a school or college, awarded and worn for superior performance in sports, etc. **7** *Printing a)* a type, impression, or photographic reproduction of a character of the alphabet *b)* a particular style of type —***vt.*** **1** to make hand-printed letters on; mark with letters [*to letter a poster*] **2** to set down in hand-printed letters [*to letter one's name*] —***vi.*** **1** to make hand-printed letters ☆**2** [Informal] to earn a school letter as in a sport —**to the letter** just as written or directed; precisely —**let′ter·er** ***n.***

let·ter[2] (let′ər) ***n.*** a person who lets, or rents out, property

letter bomb a small explosive device, as one used by terrorists, designed to be mailed in an envelope

let·ter·box (let′ər bäks′) ***n.*** ⟦< fol.⟧ a video format designed to display the widescreen image of a film on a traditional-width video screen, by means of dark bands above and below the image —***adj.*** telecast or recorded for playback using such a format: also **let′ter·boxed′**

letter box MAILBOX (sense 1)

letter carrier a postal employee who delivers mail

let·tered (let′ərd) ***adj.*** **1** able to read and write; literate **2** very well educated; learned **3** inscribed or marked with letters

let·ter·head (let′ər hed′) ***n.*** **1** the name, address, etc. of a person or firm printed as a heading on a sheet of letter paper **2** a sheet of letter paper with such a heading printed on it

let·ter·ing (-iŋ) ***n.*** the process of putting letters on something by inscribing, printing, painting, engraving, etc., or the letters so made

☆**let·ter·man** (-man′) ***n.***, *pl.* **-men′** (-men′) a student who has won a school letter, as for proficiency in a sport

letter of advice a letter notifying its recipient of something relating to a commercial transaction, as one notifying a buyer that goods have been shipped

letter of credit a letter from a bank asking that the holder of the letter be allowed to draw specified sums of money from other banks or agencies, to be charged to the account of the writer of the letter

letter opener a knifelike tool for slitting open sealed envelopes

let·ter-per·fect (-pur′fikt) ***adj.*** **1** correct in all its letters, or in every respect **2** knowing one's lesson, theatrical role, etc. perfectly

let·ter·press (-pres′) ***n.*** **1** *a)* the method of printing from raised surfaces, as set type (cf. OFFSET) *b)* matter printed by this method **2** [Chiefly Brit.] reading matter, as distinguished from illustrations

let·ter-qual·i·ty (-kwôl′i tē) ***adj.*** of or producing printed characters similar in quality and clarity to typewritten characters

letters of administration *Law* a document issued by the probate court or some officer who has authority, directing a person to administer the goods or property of a dead person

letters (*or* letter) of credence a formal document which a country's diplomatic representative carries as credentials to a foreign government: also **letters credential**

letters (*or* letter) of marque a former government document authorizing an individual to make reprisals on the subjects of an enemy nation, specif. to arm a ship and capture enemy merchant ships and cargo: also **letters (**or **letter) of marque and reprisal**

letters patent (let′ərz pat′'nt) a document granting a patent: see PATENT

letters testamentary *Law* a document issued by the probate court or some officer who has authority, directing the person named as executor in a will to act in that capacity

Let·tish (let′ish) ***n.*** LATVIAN (***n.*** 2) —***adj.*** LATVIAN

let·tre de ca·chet (le tr′ də kä shā′) *pl.* **let·tres de ca·chet′** (le tr′ də-) ⟦Fr⟧ a sealed letter; esp., in France before the Revolution, a letter containing a royal warrant for the imprisonment without trial of a specified person

let·tuce (let′əs) ***n.*** ⟦ME *letuse* < OFr *laitues*, pl. of *laitue* < L *lactuca* < *lac* (gen. *lactis*), milk (see GALACTIC): from its milky juice⟧ **1** any of a genus (*Lactuca*) of hardy, annual composite plants; specif., a plant (*L. sativa*) grown for its crisp, succulent, green leaves **2** the leaves of such a plant, much used in salads **3** [Slang] paper money

☆**let·up** (let′up′) ***n.*** ⟦< phr. *let up*⟧ [Informal] **1** a slackening or lessening, as of effort **2** a stop or pause

le·u (le′oo) ***n.***, *pl.* **lei** (lā) ⟦Romanian, lit., lion < L *leo*, LION⟧ the basic monetary unit of Romania and Moldova: see the table of monetary units in the Reference Supplement

leu·cine (lo͞o′sēn′, -sin) ***n.*** ⟦< Gr *leukos*, white (see LIGHT[1]) + -INE[3]⟧ an essential amino acid, $(CH_3)_2CHCH_2CH(NH_2)COOH$, produced by the hydrolysis of proteins by pancreatic enzymes during digestion and by the putrefaction of nitrogenous organic matter: see AMINO ACID

leu·cite (-sīt′) ***n.*** ⟦Ger *leucit*, now *leuzit* (< Gr *leukos*, white: see LIGHT[1]) + *-it*, -ITE[1]⟧ a white or gray mineral, $KAlSi_2O_6$, found in potassium-rich igneous rocks; potassium aluminum silicate

leu·co- (lo͞o′kō, -kə) ⟦< Gr *leukos*, white⟧ *combining form* **1** white, weakly colored, or colorless [*leucoplast*] **2** leukocyte Also, before a vowel, **leuc-**

leu·co·plast (lo͞o′kō plast′) ***n.*** ⟦prec. + -PLAST⟧ any of the colorless plastids found in the protoplasm of vegetable cells, in which starch forms in the absence of light

leu·ka·phe·re·sis (lo͞o′kə fe rē′sis) ***n.*** ⟦LEUK(O)- + APHERESIS⟧ apheresis that separates certain leukocytes from the blood

leu·ke·mi·a (lo͞o kē′mē ə) ***n.*** ⟦ModL: see LEUCO- & -EMIA⟧ any of a group of cancerous diseases of the blood-forming organs, resulting in an abnormal increase in the production of leukocytes, often accompanied by anemia and enlargement of the lymph nodes, spleen, and liver: also sp. **leu·kae′mi·a** —**leu·ke′mic** (-mik) ***adj.*** —**leu·ke′moid′** (-moid′) ***adj.***

leu·ko- (lo͞o′kō, -kə) ⟦< Gr *leukos*, white⟧ *combining form* LEUCO-: now often the preferred form in medical and biological usage: also, before a vowel, **leuk-**

leu·ko·cyte (lo͞o′kō sīt′, -kə-) ***n.*** ⟦see LEUCO- & -CYTE⟧ any of the small, colorless nucleated cells in the blood, lymph, and tissues, which are important in the body's defenses against infection, including granular types such as neutrophils, eosinophils, and basophils, and nongranular types such as lymphocytes and monocytes; white blood cell —**leu′ko·cyt′ic** (-sit′ik) ***adj.*** —**leu′ko·cy′toid′** (-sī′toid′) ***adj.***

leu·ko·cy·to·blast (lo͞o′kō sīt′ō blast′, -kə-; -sīt′ə-) ***n.*** ⟦see LEUCO- & CYTO- & BLAST⟧ the precursor cell to a mature leukocyte —**leu′ko·cy′to·blas′tic** (-sīt′ō blas′tik, -sīt′ə-) ***adj.***

leu·ko·cy·to·sis (-sī tō′sis) ***n.*** ⟦ModL < LEUKOCYTE + -OSIS⟧ an increase in the number of leukocytes in the blood: it is a normal response to pregnancy and is found in certain cases of poisoning or inflammation and in many infections —**leu′ko·cy·tot′ic** (-tät′ik) ***adj.***

leu·ko·der·ma (-dur′mə) ***n.*** ⟦ModL: see LEUCO- & -DERM⟧ an often congenital lack of pigmentation in areas of the skin, resulting in white patches

leu·ko·ma (lo͞o kō′mə) ***n.*** ⟦ModL < Gr *leukōma* < *leukos*, white: see LIGHT[1] & -OMA⟧ a dense, white opacity of the cornea, caused by injury or inflammation

leu·ko·pe·ni·a (lo͞o′kō pē′nē ə, -kə-) ***n.*** ⟦ModL < LEUKO- (var. of LEUCO-) + Gr *penia*, poverty⟧ a decrease below normal in the number of leukocytes in the blood —**leu′ko·pe′nic** ***adj.***

leu·ko·pla·ki·a (lo͞o′kō plā′kē ə, lo͞o′kə-) ***n.*** ⟦< LEUKO- (var. of LEUCO-) + Gr *plax* (gen. *plakos*), flat object (see PLACENTA) + -IA⟧ a disease, sometimes precancerous, characterized by thick, white patches covering the tongue, gums, etc.

leu·ko·poi·e·sis (-poi ē′sis) ***n.*** ⟦ModL < Gr *leukos*, white + *poiēsis*, a making: see LEUCO- & POESY⟧ the process of forming leukocytes —**leu′ko·poi·et′ic** (-et′ik) ***adj.***

leu·kor·rhe·a (lo͞o′kə rē′ə) ***n.*** ⟦ModL: see LEUCO- + -RRHEA⟧ an abnormal, whitish discharge from the vagina —**leu′kor·rhe′al** ***adj.***

leu·kot·o·my (loo kät′ə mē) ***n.***, *pl.* **-mies** ⟦LEUKO- (var. of LEUCO-), for the white matter of the brain + -TOMY⟧ LOBOTOMY

leu·ko·tri·ene (lo͞o′kō trī′ēn′, -kə-) ***n.*** ⟦LEUKO- (var. of LEUCO-) + TRI- + -ENE: it contains three double bonds⟧ any of a group of compounds similar to the prostaglandins, which are released in the body when various cells are stimulated as by pollen, and cause constriction of air passages, swelling, and inflammation, as in asthma and rheumatoid arthritis

lev (lef) ***n.***, *pl.* **le·va** (le′və) ⟦Bulg, lit., lion < OSlav *livu*, ult. < Gr *leōn*, lion⟧ the basic monetary unit of Bulgaria: see the table of monetary units in the Reference Supplement

Lev *abbrev. Bible* Leviticus

lev- (lev) *combining form* LEVO-: used before a vowel

Le·val·loi·si·an (lev′ə loi′zē ən) ***adj.*** ⟦after fol. where such tools were found⟧ designating or of a middle Paleolithic culture, characterized by the production of flake tools

Le·val·lois-Per·ret (lə väl lwä pe re′) city in NC France, on the Seine: suburb of Paris

le·vant[1] (lə vant′) ***vi.*** ⟦prob. < Sp *levantar*, to start suddenly (as game), lit., to rise, ult. < L *levare*, to raise: see LEVER⟧ [Brit., Old-fashioned] to abscond, as to avoid paying one's debts

le·vant[2] (lə vant′, -vänt′) ***n.*** LEVANT MOROCCO

Le·vant (lə vant′, -vänt′) ⟦Fr *levant* < It *levante* (< L *levans*, rising, raising, prp. of *levare,* to raise: see LEVER⟧: applied to the East, from the "rising" of the sun⟧ region on the E Mediterranean, including all countries bordering the sea between Greece & Egypt: usually used with *the*

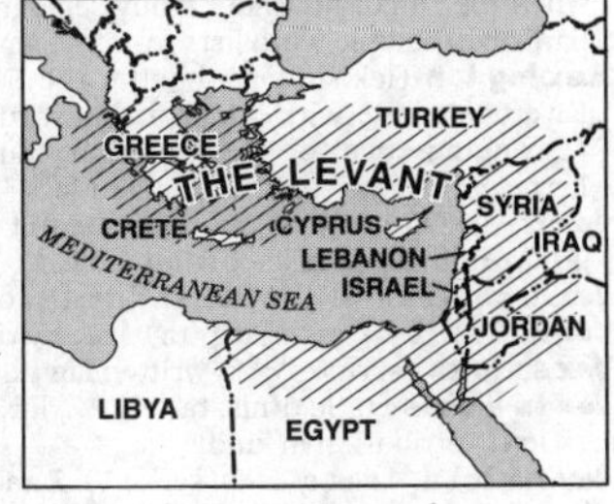

The Levant

le·vant·er[1] (lə van′tər, -vän′-) ***n.*** ⟦LEVANT[2] + -ER⟧ **1** a strong wind that blows over the Mediterranean area from the east **2** [**L-**] LEVANTINE (sense 1)

le·vant·er[2] (lə van′tər) ***n.*** [Brit., Old-fashioned] one who absconds, leaving unpaid debts

Le·van·tine (li van′tin, -vän′-; lev′ən tīn′) ***adj.*** ⟦Fr *levantin*⟧ of the Levant —***n.*** **1** a person born or living in the Levant **2** [**l-**] a strong, twilled silk cloth

Levant morocco a fine morocco leather with a large, irregular grain, used esp. in bookbinding

le·va·tor (lə vāt′ər) ***n., pl.*** **lev·a·to·res** (lev′ə tôr′ēz′) or **le·va′tors** ⟦ModL < pp. of L *levare,* to raise: see LEVER⟧ **1** a muscle that raises a limb or other part of the body **2** a surgical instrument for lifting depressed fragments of bone in a skull fracture

☆**lev·ee**[1] (lev′ē) ***n.*** ⟦Fr *levée,* fem. pp. of OFr *lever,* to raise: see LEVER⟧ **1** an embankment built alongside a river to prevent high water from flooding bordering land **2** a landing place, as a pier, on the bank of a river **3** a low ridge of earth around a field to be irrigated —***vt.*** **lev′eed, lev′ee·ing** to build a levee along

lev·ee[2] (lev′ē; lə vē′, -vā′) ***n.*** ⟦Fr *levé,* for OFr *lever,* substantival use of inf., to raise, *se lever,* to rise: see prec.⟧ **1** [Historical] a morning reception held by a sovereign or person of high rank upon arising **2** any formal or stylish reception **3** [Brit.] a reception held in the afternoon by the king or his representative, attended only by men

lev·el (lev′əl) ***n.*** ⟦OFr *livel* < VL **libellus* < L *libella,* dim. of *libra,* a balance, level, weight⟧ **1** an instrument for determining, or adjusting a surface to, an even horizontal plane: the traditional level has a clear tube partly filled with liquid so as to leave an air bubble that moves to the exact center of the tube when the instrument is on an even horizontal plane; often there is another such tube which indicates when the instrument is perpendicular to the horizontal **2** *a)* SURVEYOR'S LEVEL *b)* a measuring of differences in elevation with this instrument **3** *a)* a horizontal plane or line; esp., such a plane taken as a basis for the measurement of elevation [*sea level*] *b)* the height, or altitude, of such a plane **4** a relatively flat and even area of land or other surface; horizontal area **5** the same horizontal plane [*to keep the tops of pictures on a level*] **6** usual or normal position with reference to a certain height [*water seeks its level*] **7** position, elevation, or rank considered as one of the planes in a scale of values [*levels of income*] **8** a horizontal drift or gallery in a mine **9** the degree of concentration, as of a substance in a fluid **10** any of a series of stages, as in a computer game, each presenting a more difficult challenge over the previous stage **11** *Physics* the ratio of a quantity's magnitude to an arbitrarily selected magnitude —***adj.*** **1** having no part higher than any other; perfectly flat and even; conforming to the surface of still water **2** conforming to the plane of the horizon; not sloping **3** being of the same height or being in the same plane; even (*with*) **4** even with the top of the container; not heaping [*a level teaspoonful*] **5** *a)* equal in importance, rank, degree, etc. *b)* conforming to a specified level or rank [*high-level negotiations*] *c)* equally advanced in development *d)* even or uniform in tone, color, pitch, volume, rate, etc. **6** *a)* not having or showing sudden differences or inequalities; well-balanced; equable *b)* not excited or disturbed; calm or steady **7** paid or to be paid in equal amounts over a period of time ☆**8** [Slang] honest; straight —***adv.*** so as to be level; so as to be flat, even, in line, etc. —***vt.*** **-eled** or **-elled, -el·ing** or **-el·ling 1** to make level; specif., *a)* to make perfectly horizontal by means of a level *b)* to make flat and even *c)* to equalize in height, rank, quality, etc. (often with *down* or *up*) *d)* to make even in tone, color, pitch, etc. **2** to knock to the ground; demolish; lay low [*the storm leveled one section of town*] **3** to aim (a gun, etc.) for firing **4** to aim or direct **5** *Surveying* to determine the differences in altitude in (a plot of ground) —***vi.*** **1** to aim a gun, etc. (*at*) **2** to bring people or things to an equal rank, condition, etc.: usually with *down* or *up* ☆**3** [Informal] to be frank and honest (*with* someone) —**find one's (or its) level** to reach one's (or its) proper or natural place according to one's (or its) qualities, capacity, etc. —**level off 1** to make flat and even **2** to become horizontal, as an airplane in flight: also **level out 3** to become stable or constant —**one's level best** [Informal] the best one can do —☆**on the level** [Informal] honest(ly) and fair(ly) —**lev′el·ly** ***adv.*** —**lev′el·ness** ***n.***

level (*n.* 1)

SYN.—**level** is applied to a surface that is parallel to, or conforms with, the horizon; **flat** implies the absence, to any marked degree, of depressions or elevations in a surface, in whatever direction it lies; **plane** describes a real or imaginary surface that is absolutely flat and wholly contains every straight line joining any two points lying in it; **even** is applied to a surface that is uniformly level or flat, or to a surface that is in the same plane with, or in a plane parallel to, another; a **smooth** surface has no roughness or projections, often as a result of wear, planing, polishing, etc.

level crossing [Brit.] GRADE CROSSING

lev·el·er (lev′əl ər) ***n.*** **1** one that levels **2** a person who wishes to abolish political and social inequalities **3** [**L-**] a member of an English party that arose among radical Parliamentarians (*c.* 1646) and advocated the establishment of a more democratic government Also sp. **lev′el·ler**

☆**lev·el·head·ed** (lev′əl hed′id) ***adj.*** having or showing an even temper and sound judgment; sensible —**lev′el·head′ed·ly** ***adv.*** —**lev′el·head′ed·ness** ***n.***

leveling rod (or staff) *Surveying* a graduated rod used in determining the difference in elevation between two points

lev·er (lev′ər, lē′vər) ***n.*** ⟦OFr *leveour* < *lever,* to raise < L *levare* < *levis,* light: see LIGHT[2]⟧ **1** a bar used as a pry **2** a means to an end **3** *Mech.* a device consisting of a bar turning about a fixed point, the fulcrum, using power or force applied at a second point to lift or sustain a weight at a third point; hence, any handle or the like used to operate something —***vt.*** **1** to move, lift, etc. with or as with a lever **2** to use as a lever

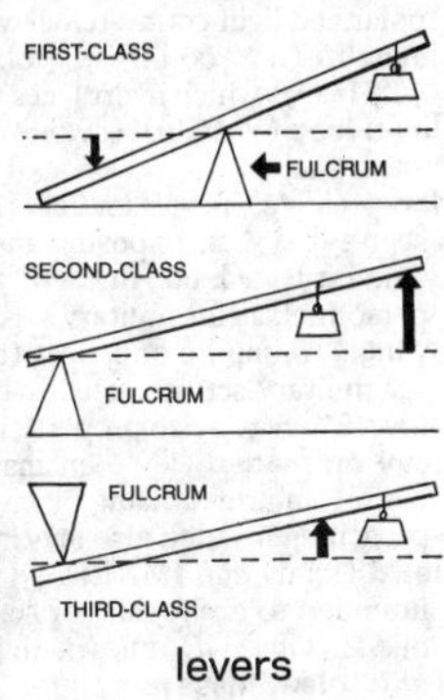

levers

lev·er·age (lev′ər ij, lev′rij; lē′vər ij, lēv′rij) ***n.*** **1** the action of a lever **2** the increased force resulting from this **3** power to effect change; specif., strategic means of accomplishing some purpose **4** *Finance a)* use of borrowed funds to improve one's ability to speculate *b)* funds or credit obtained in this way —***vt.*** **-aged, -ag·ing 1** *Finance a)* to borrow against (one's assets) in order to speculate *b)* to increase the debt of (a business) in this way [*a firm that is heavily leveraged*] **2** to make strategic use of (something) to accomplish some purpose; exploit

leveraged buyout the acquisition of a corporation, using mostly borrowed funds which are secured by the assets of the corporation being acquired

lev·er·et (lev′ər it) ***n.*** ⟦LME < MFr *levrette,* dim. of *levre,* hare < L *lepus* (gen. *leporis*): see LEPORID⟧ an immature hare

Le·vi[1] (lē′vī′) ***n.*** ⟦Heb, *lēwī,* lit., joining⟧ **1** a masculine name: dim. *Lev* **2** *Bible* the third son of Jacob and Leah: Gen. 29:34: see also LEVITE

Lev·i[2] (lev′ē), **Pri·mo (Michele)** (prē′mō) 1919-87; It. writer

lev·i·a·ble (lev′ē ə bəl) ***adj.*** **1** that can be levied upon; taxable; assessable **2** that can be levied

le·vi·a·than (lə vī′ə thən) ***n.*** ⟦ME < LL(Ec) < Heb *liwyāthān* < base akin to Akkadian *lawū,* to surround, Ar *liyatu,* snake⟧ [*often* **L-**] **1** *Bible* a sea monster, variously thought of as a reptile or a whale **2** anything huge or very powerful

lev·i·er (lev′ē ər) ***n.*** a person who levies taxes, fines, tributes, etc.

lev·i·gate (lev′i gāt′) ***vt.*** **-gat′ed, -gat′ing** ⟦< L *levigatus,* pp. of *levigare,* to make smooth, polish < *levis,* smooth (see LIME[1]) + *agere,* to make (see ACT[1])⟧ **1** to grind to a fine, smooth powder **2** to separate the fine particles of (a substance) from its coarse particles by grinding it in water: the coarse particles settle to the bottom first, leaving the fine particles suspended

lev·in (lev′in) ***n.*** ⟦ME *levene,* ult. < IE base **leuk-,* to shine > LIGHT[1]⟧ [Old Poet.] lightning

lev·i·rate (lev′ə rit, -rāt′; lē′və-) ***n.*** ⟦L *levir,* husband's brother, brother-in-law (< **daiwer* < IE **dāiwēr* > Sans *dēvár,* Gr *daēr,* OE *tacor*) + -ATE[2]⟧ a custom of the Jews in Biblical times by which a dead man's brother was obligated to marry the widow if there were no sons: Deut. 25:5-10 —**lev′i·rat′ic** (-ə rat′ik) ***adj.,*** **lev′i·rat′i·cal**

Lé·vis (lā vē′) ⟦after F.-G. de *Lévis* (1719-87), Fr duke & marshal, commander of Fr troops in Canada after the death of Montcalm at Quebec⟧ city in S Quebec, Canada, near Quebec City

☆**Le·vi's** (lē′vīz′) ⟦after *Levi* Strauss, U.S. manufacturer (1829-1902) who first made them in San Francisco (*c.* 1850)⟧ *trademark for* closefitting trousers of heavy denim, reinforced at the seams, etc. with small copper rivets —***pl.n.*** such trousers: also written **Le′vis** or **le′vis**

Lé·vi-Strauss (lā′vē strous′), **Claude** 1908-2009; Fr. social anthropologist, born in Belgium

lev·i·tate (lev′ə tāt′) ***vt.*** **-tat′ed, -tat′ing** ⟦< L *levis,* LIGHT[2] by analogy with GRAVITATE⟧ to cause to rise and float in the air —***vi.*** to rise and float in the air because of, or as if because of, lightness and buoyancy —**lev′i·ta′tor** ***n.***

lev·i·ta·tion (lev′ə tā′shən) ***n.*** **1** a levitating or being levitated **2** the illusion, as by a stage magician, of raising and keeping a heavy body in the air with little or no physical support

Le·vite (lē′vīt′) ***n.*** ⟦LL(Ec) *Levites* < Gr(Ec) *Leuitēs* < Heb *lēwī:* see LEVI[1]⟧ *Bible* any member of the tribe of Levi, chosen to assist the priests in the Temple: Num. 18:6

Le·vit·i·cal (lə vit′i kəl) ***adj.*** ⟦< LL(Ec) *Leviticus* + -AL⟧ **1** of the Levites **2** of Leviticus or its laws

Le·vit·i·cus (-kəs) *n.* ⟦LL(Ec) *Leviticus (liber)* < Gr(Ec) *Leuitikon (biblion)*, lit., the Levitical (book)⟧ the third book of the Pentateuch in the Bible, containing the laws relating to priests and Levites: abbrev. *Lev* or *Lv*

Lev·it·town (lev′it toun′) ⟦after *Levitt* & Sons, Inc., builders of planned towns⟧ town in SE N.Y., on Long Island

lev·i·ty (lev′ə tē) *n., pl.* **-ties** ⟦OFr *levité* < L *levitas* < *levis*, LIGHT²⟧ **1** [Rare] lightness of weight; buoyancy **2** lightness or gaiety of disposition, conduct, or speech; esp., improper or unbecoming gaiety or flippancy; lack of seriousness; frivolity **3** fickleness; instability

Lev·kás (lef käs′) one of the Ionian Islands, in the Ionian Sea, off the W coast of Greece: 117 sq mi (303 sq km)

le·vo- (lē′vō, -və) ⟦< L *laevus*, left < earlier **laiwos* < IE **laiwos* (> Gr *laios*) < base **(e)lei-*, to bend, curve > EL(BOW)⟧ *combining form* **1** toward or on the left-hand side *[levorotatory]* **2** *Chem.* levorotatory *[levulose]*

le·vo·ro·ta·tion (-rō tā′shən) *n.* ⟦prec. + ROTATION⟧ rotation to the left; counterclockwise rotation: usually said of the plane of polarization of light

le·vo·ro·ta·to·ry (-rōt′ə tôr′ē) *adj.* ⟦LEVO- + ROTATORY⟧ **1** turning or circling to the left, in a counterclockwise direction **2** that turns the plane of polarized light counterclockwise: said as of certain crystals

lev·u·lin (lev′yoo lin) *n.* ⟦fol. + -IN¹⟧ a colorless, starchlike carbohydrate ($C_6H_{10}O_5$) which hydrolyzes to form levulose

lev·u·lose (-lōs′) *n.* ⟦LEV(O)- + -UL(E) + -OSE²: so called because levorotatory⟧ FRUCTOSE

lev·y (lev′ē) *n., pl.* **lev′ies** ⟦ME *levee* < MFr, fem. pp. of *lever*, to raise: see LEVER⟧ **1** an imposing and collecting of a tax or other payment **2** an amount levied; tax, fine, etc. **3** *a)* the enlistment, usually compulsory, of personnel, as for military service *b)* a group so enlisted —*vt.* **lev′ied, lev′y·ing 1** to impose or collect (a tax, tribute, fine, etc.) **2** to enlist (troops) for military service, usually by force **3** to wage (war) —*vi.* **1** to make a levy **2** *Law* to seize property in order to satisfy a judgment: often with *on*

levy en masse (lev′ē en mas′, -än mäs′) ⟦partial transl. of Fr *levée en masse*⟧ an armed rising by civilians in a territory in order to resist an approaching invader: also **levy in mass**

lewd (lood) *adj.* ⟦ME *lewed* < OE *læwede*, lay, unlearned < ?⟧ **1** showing, or intended to excite, lust or sexual desire, esp. in an offensive way; lascivious **2** [Obs.] *a)* unlearned; ignorant *b)* unprincipled; vicious —**lewd′ly** *adv.* —**lewd′ness** *n.*

lew·is (lo͞o′is) *n.* ⟦prob. < the name *Lewis*⟧ a device for hoisting blocks of stone, consisting of a dovetailed iron tenon made in sections that fit into a mortise cut into the stone

Lew·is¹ (lo͞o′is) *n.* a masculine name: dim. *Lew, Lewie*: see LOUIS¹

Lew·is² (lo͞o′is) **1 C(ecil) Day** *see* DAY-LEWIS **2 C(live) S(taples)** 1898-1963; Brit. writer, born in Ireland **3 John L(lewellyn)** 1880-1969; U.S. labor leader **4 Mer·iweth·er** (mer′ē weth′ər) 1774-1809; Am. explorer: co-leader of the Lewis & Clark expedition (1804-06) to the Northwest **5 Sinclair** (sin kler′, siŋ′kler′) 1885-1951; U.S. novelist **6 (Percy) Wynd·ham** (win′dəm) 1884-1957; Brit. writer & painter, born in the U.S.

Lew·i·sham (lo͞o′i shəm, -səm) borough of SE Greater London, England

☆**lew·is·ite** (lo͞o′is īt′) *n.* ⟦after W. L. *Lewis* (1878-1943), U.S. chemist⟧ a pale-yellow, odorless arsenical compound, $ClCH{=}CHAsCl_2$, used as a blistering poison gas

Lewis with Harris northernmost island of the Outer Hebrides, Scotland, consisting of a larger N part (**Lewis**) & a S part (**Harris**): part of the Western Isles administrative division: *c.* 825 sq mi (2,137 sq km): also called **Lewis and Harris**

lex¹ (leks) *n., pl.* **le·ges** (lē′jēz′, lā′gās′) ⟦L: see LEGAL⟧ law

lex² *abbrev.* lexicon

☆**Lex·an** (lek′san′) *trademark for* a polycarbonate resin, used in molded products, as a substitute for glass, etc.

lex·eme (lek′sēm′) *n.* ⟦< Gr *lexis*, word (see LEXICON) + -EME⟧ *Linguis.* a word or stem that is a meaningful unit in a language and coincides with the abstract unit underlying a given set of inflected forms —**lex′em′ic** (-ē′mik) *adj.*

lex·i·cal (lek′si kəl) *adj.* ⟦ModL *lexicalis* < Gr *lexikon*, LEXICON⟧ **1** of a vocabulary, or stock of words, as that of a language; specif., of words as isolated items of vocabulary rather than elements in a grammatical structure **2** of, or having the nature of, a lexicon or lexicography

lexical meaning the meaning of a BASE¹ (*n.* 15) in a paradigm, apart from any meaning it may acquire as part of a sentence (Ex.: the meaning of *walk* in the conjugations *walks/walked/walking*)

lexicog *abbrev.* **1** lexicographer **2** lexicographic **3** lexicography

lex·i·cog·ra·pher (lek′sə käg′rə fər) *n.* ⟦LGr *lexikographos* < Gr *lexikon*, LEXICON + *graphein*, to write: see GRAPHIC⟧ a person who writes, compiles, or edits a dictionary

lex·i·cog·ra·phy (lek′sə käg′rə fē) *n.* ⟦< Gr *lexikon*, LEXICON + -GRAPHY⟧ the act, process, art, or work of writing, compiling, or editing a dictionary or dictionaries —**lex·i·co·graph·ic** (lek′si kə graf′ik) *adj.*, **lex′i·co·graph′i·cal** —**lex′i·co·graph′i·cal·ly** *adv.*

lex·i·col·o·gy (-käl′ə jē) *n.* ⟦< Gr *lexikon*, fol. + -LOGY⟧ the study of the meanings and origins of words —**lex′i·co·log′i·cal** (-kə läj′i kəl) *adj.* —**lex′i·col′o·gist** *n.*

lex·i·con (lek′si kän′) *n.* ⟦Gr *lexikon*, neut. of *lexikos*, of words < *lexis*, saying, phrase, word < *legein*: see LOGIC⟧ **1** a dictionary, esp. of an ancient language **2** the special vocabulary of a particular author, field of study, etc. **3** a record or inventory *[a notable case in the lexicon of subversion]* **4** *Linguis.* the total stock of morphemes in a language

lex·i·co·sta·tis·tics (lek′si kō′stə tis′tiks) *n.* ⟦< Gr *lexikon*, prec. + STATISTICS (*n.*)⟧ a technique used in GLOTTOCHRONOLOGY to determine the time when the languages under study separated, based on the statistical comparison of sample word lists from the languages

Lex·ing·ton (lek′siŋ tən) **1** ⟦after the Boston suburb⟧ city in NC Ky., in Fayette county, with which it constitutes a metropolitan government (**Lexington-Fayette**) **2** ⟦after Robt. Sutton (1661-1723), 2d Baron of *Lexington*⟧ suburb of Boston, in E Mass.: see CONCORD² (town in Mass.)

lex·is (lek′sis) *n.* ⟦see LEXICON⟧ the full vocabulary of a language, or of a group, individual, field of study, etc.

lex lo·ci (leks lō′sī′, -lō′kē) ⟦L⟧ the law of the place

lex non scrip·ta (nän skrip′tə) ⟦L, unwritten law⟧ COMMON LAW

lex scrip·ta (skrip′tə) ⟦L, written law⟧ STATUTE LAW

lex ta·li·o·nis (tā′lē ō′nis, tal′ē-) ⟦L, lit., the law of retaliation: see LEX¹ & TALION⟧ retribution in kind

ley (lā, lē) *n.* **1** *var. of* LEA¹ (sense 1) **2** an arable field being used temporarily as a pasture for grazing animals

Leyden¹, Lucas van *see* LUCAS VAN LEYDEN

Ley·den² (līd′'n) *alt. sp. of* LEIDEN

Leyden jar (*or* vial) (līd′'n; *also*, lād′'n) ⟦after LEIDEN, where invented⟧ a condenser for static electricity, consisting of a glass jar with a coat of tinfoil outside and inside and a metal rod connecting with the inner lining and passing through the lid

ley-line (lā′līn′, lē′-) *n.* ⟦< LEY (*n.* 1)⟧ any of various imaginary lines along which certain ancient, man-made structures are thought by some to have been aligned

Ley·te (lāt′ē; *Sp* lā′tā) island of EC Philippines, between Luzon & Mindanao: 2,785 sq mi (7,213 sq km)

lez (lez) *n.* [Slang] a lesbian: a term of contempt: also **lez′zie** or **lez′zy**, *pl.* **-zies**

lf *abbrev.* **1** *Baseball a)* left field *b)* left fielder: also **LF 2** *Printing* lightface **3** low frequency: also **LF**

lg *abbrev.* large

LG *abbrev.* Low German

LGBT *abbrev.* lesbian, gay, bisexual, and transgender

LGr *abbrev.* Late Greek

lgth *abbrev.* length

LH *abbrev.* **1** left hand: also **lh 2** luteinizing hormone

Lha·sa (lä′sə) capital of Tibet, China, in the SE part: it is a Buddhist holy city

Lhasa ap·so (äp′sō, ap′-) *pl.* **-sos** ⟦prec. + Tibet *apso*, sentinel⟧ any of a Tibetan breed of small dog with dense, straight hair that hangs over the eyes and a tail that curls over the back

LHD or **L.H.D.** *abbrev.* ⟦L *Litterarum Humaniorum Doctor*⟧ Doctor of Human Letters; Doctor of the Humanities: an honorary degree

LHeb *abbrev.* Late Hebrew

li (lē) *n., pl.* **li** [Chin] a Chinese unit of linear measure, equal to about one third of a mile (.52 kilometer)

Li *Chem. symbol for* lithium

LI *abbrev.* Long Island

li·a·bil·i·ty (lī′ə bil′ə tē) *n., pl.* **-ties 1** the state of being liable **2** anything for which a person is liable **3** *Accounting a)* a debt of a person or business, as a note payable or a long-term debenture *b)* an account on a balance sheet showing this **4** something that works to one's disadvantage

li·a·ble (lī′ə bəl; *often, esp. for 3*, lī′bəl) *adj.* ⟦prob. via Anglo-Fr < OFr *lier*, to bind < L *ligare*, to bind (see LIGATURE) + -ABLE⟧ **1** legally bound or obligated, as to make good any loss or damage that occurs in a transaction; responsible **2** likely or prone to have, suffer from, etc.; exposed to or subject to *[liable to attacks of gout]* **3** subject to the possibility of; likely (*to* do, have, get, etc. something unpleasant or unwanted) *[liable to cause hard feelings, liable to get worse]* —*SYN.* LIKELY

li·aise (lē āz′) *vi.* **-aised′, -ais′ing** ⟦back-form. < fol.⟧ **1** to establish a liaison *with* another group or entity **2** to act as a liaison

li·ai·son (*for 1, 2, & 4*, lē ā′zän′, -zən; lē′ə zän′, lā′-; *for 3*, lē′ā zōn′, -zōn′, -zän′) *n.* ⟦Fr < OFr < L *ligato* < *ligare*, to bind: see LIGATURE⟧ **1** a linking up or connecting of two or more separate entities or of the parts, as military units, of a whole so that they can work together effectively **2** an illicit love affair **3** in spoken French, the linking of words, under certain conditions, by pronouncing the final consonant, ordinarily silent, of one word as though it were the initial consonant of the following word (Ex.: the phrase *chez elle* is pronounced shā zel′) **4** a person who functions as a connection or go-between, as between persons or groups

li·a·na (lē ä′nə, -an′ə) *n.* ⟦NormFr *liane* < Fr *lierne, liorne*, altered (by assoc. with *lier*, to bind) < *viorne* < L *viburnum*, VIBURNUM⟧ any luxuriantly growing, woody, tropical vine that roots in the ground and climbs, as around tree trunks: also **li·ane′** (-än′, -an′)

Li·ao·dong (lē ou′dooŋ′) peninsula in Liaoning province, NE China, extending into the Yellow Sea

Li·ao He (lē ou′hu′) river in NE China, flowing from Inner Mongolia west & south into the Yellow Sea: *c.* 900 mi (1,448 km)

Li·ao·ning (lē ou′niŋ′) province of NE China: 58,301 sq mi (151,000 sq km); cap. Shenyang

Li·ao·yang (lē ou′yäŋ′) city in central Liaoning province, NE China

li·ar (lī ər) *n.* ⟦ME *lier* < OE *leogere* < base of *leogan* (akin to OHG *liugari*): see LIE²⟧ a person who tells lies

Li·ard (lē′ärd′, lē är′) river in W Canada, flowing from S Yukon Territory in a SE direction to British Columbia, then north & east into the Mackenzie River: 755 mi (1,215 km)

liar dice a gambling game in which the throw of five dice by each player is concealed from the opponent and bluffing is permitted: also **liar's dice**

Li·as (lī′əs) ***n.*** ⟦ME *lyas* < OFr *liois* (Fr *liais*), kind of limestone < ? Gmc, as in MHG *leie,* stone⟧ a series of rocks, the oldest or lowest part of the Jurassic System, noted for its fossils

Li·as·sic (lī as′ik, lē-) ***adj.*** of or pertaining to the Lias series

lib[1] (lib) ***n.*** [Informal] *short for* LIBERATION (sense 2)

lib[2] *abbrev.* **1** librarian **2** library

Lib *abbrev.* **1** Liberal **2** Liberia **3** Libya

lib. *abbrev.* ⟦L *liber*⟧ book

li·ba·tion (lī bā′shən) ***n.*** ⟦ME *libacioun* < L *libatio* < *libare,* to taste, pour out < IE base **lei-,* to pour > Gr *leibein*⟧ **1** the ritual of pouring out wine or oil upon the ground as a sacrifice to a god **2** the liquid so poured out **3** an alcoholic drink or the act of drinking: used humorously —**li·ba′tion·al** ***adj.***

☆**lib·ber** (lib′ər) ***n.*** ⟦< LIB[1] + -ER⟧ [Informal] a person who advocates the securing of equal social and economic rights for some group, specif. for women: often a dismissive term

Lib·by (lib′ē), **W(illard) F(rank)** 1908-80; U.S. chemist

li·bel (lī′bəl) ***n.*** ⟦ME, little book < OFr < L *libellus,* little book, writing, lampoon, dim. of *liber,* a book: see LIBRARY⟧ **1** *a)* any false and malicious written or printed statement, or any sign, picture, or effigy, tending to expose a person to public ridicule, hatred, or contempt or to injure a person's reputation *b)* act of publishing or displaying publicly such a thing **2** anything that gives an unflattering or damaging picture of the subject with which it is dealing **3** in ecclesiastical law and formerly in maritime law, a written statement containing the plaintiff's grievances; initial pleading —***vt.*** **-beled** or **-belled, -bel·ing** or **-bel·ling 1** to publish or make a libel against **2** to give an unflattering or damaging picture of **3** to bring suit against by presenting a LIBEL (***n.*** 3)

li·bel·ant or **li·bel·lant** (lī′bəl ənt) ***n.*** a person who sues by filing a LIBEL (***n.*** 3)

li·bel·ee or **li·bel·lee** (lī′bəl ē′) ***n.*** the person in a suit against whom a LIBEL (***n.*** 3) has been filed

li·bel·er or **li·bel·ler** (lī′bəl ər) ***n.*** a person who commits libel

li·bel·ous or **li·bel·lous** (-əs) ***adj.*** **1** of the nature of, or involving, libel or a libel **2** given to writing and publishing libels; defamatory —**li′bel·ous·ly** ***adv.***, **li′bel·lous·ly**

li·ber (lī′bər, lē′ber′) ***n.***, *pl.* ***li·bri*** (lī′brē′, lē′-) ⟦L: see LIBRARY⟧ a book; esp., a book of public records, as of mortgages or deeds

lib·er·al (lib′ər əl, lib′rəl) ***adj.*** ⟦OFr < L *liberalis* < *liber,* free < IE base **leudhero-,* belonging to the people, free < base **leudh-,* to grow up, rise > Ger *leute,* people, OE *leodan,* to grow⟧ **1** suitable for a freeman; not restricted: now only in LIBERAL ARTS, LIBERAL EDUCATION, etc. **2** giving freely; generous **3** large or plentiful; ample; abundant *[a liberal reward]* ☆**4** not restricted to the literal meaning; not strict *[a liberal interpretation of the Bible]* **5** tolerant of views differing from one's own; broad-minded; specif., not orthodox **6** of democratic or republican forms of government, as distinguished from monarchies, aristocracies, etc. **7** *a)* favoring reform or progress in a particular social or cultural setting, as in religion, education, etc. *b)* favoring ongoing political reform, promoting in recent times, variously, labor unions, the welfare state, environmentalism, etc.; progressive **8** [**L-**] designating or of a political party upholding liberal principles, esp. such a party in England or Canada **9** [Obs.] excessively free or indecorous in behavior; licentious —***n.*** **1** a person who is LIBERAL (***adj.*** 7) or who favors liberalism **2** [**L-**] a member of a Liberal political party —**lib′er·al·ly** ***adv.*** —**lib′er·al·ness** ***n.***

SYN.—**liberal** implies tolerance of others' views as well as open-mindedness to ideas that challenge tradition, established institutions, etc.; **progressive**, a relative term opposed to *reactionary* or *conservative,* is applied to persons favoring progress and reform in politics, education, etc. and connotes an inclination to more direct action than **liberal**; **advanced** specifically implies a being ahead of the times, as in science, the arts, philosophy, etc.; **radical** implies a favoring of fundamental or extreme change, specifically of the social structure; **left** or **leftist**, originally referring to the position in legislatures of the seats occupied by parties holding such views, implies political liberalism or radicalism

liberal arts ⟦transl. of L *artes liberales,* lit., arts befitting a freeman: so named in contrast to *artes serviles,* lower (lit., servile) arts, and because open to study only by freemen (L *liberi*); in later use understood as "arts becoming a gentleman"⟧ **1** [Historical] the subjects in the TRIVIUM and QUADRIVIUM **2** the subjects of an academic college course, including literature, philosophy, languages, history, and, usually, survey courses of the sciences, as distinguished from professional or technical subjects: sometimes referred to as *arts,* as in *Bachelor of Arts*

liberal education an education mainly in the liberal arts, providing the student with a broad cultural background rather than with training in any specific profession

lib·er·al·ism (-iz′əm) ***n.*** the quality or state of being liberal; specif., *a)* a political philosophy advocating personal freedom for the individual, democratic forms of government, continual reform in political and social institutions, etc. *b)* the advocating of LIBERAL (***adj.*** 7) reforms *c)* a movement in Protestantism advocating a broad interpretation of the Bible, freedom from rigid doctrine and authoritarianism, etc.

lib·er·al·i·ty (lib′ər al′i tē) ***n.*** ⟦ME *liberalite* < OFr < L *liberalitas*⟧ the quality or state of being liberal; specif., *a)* willingness to give or share freely; generosity *b)* absence of narrowness or prejudice in thinking; broad-mindedness

lib·er·al·ize (lib′ər əl īz′, lib′rəl īz′) ***vt., vi.*** **-ized′, -iz′ing** to make or become liberal —**lib′er·al·i·za′tion** ***n.*** —**lib′er·al·iz′er** ***n.***

lib·er·ate (lib′ər āt′) ***vt.*** **-at′ed, -at′ing** ⟦< L *liberatus,* pp. of *liberare,* to set free, release < *liber,* free: see LIBERAL⟧ **1** to release from slavery, oppression, enemy occupation, etc. **2** [Slang] to steal or loot, esp. from a defeated enemy in wartime **3** *Chem.* to free from combination in a compound —*SYN.* FREE

lib·er·a·tion (lib′ər ā′shən) ***n.*** **1** a liberating or being liberated ☆**2** the securing of equal social and economic rights *[women's liberation movement]* —**lib′er·a′tion·ist** ***n.***

liberation theology ⟦Sp *teología de la liberación* < the title of a book (1971) by G. Gutiérrez, Peruvian theologian⟧ a Christian theology incorporating Marxist theory and seeking to liberate people, esp. of the Third World, from economic or political oppression

lib·er·a·tor (lib′ər āt′ər) ***n.*** a person who liberates; esp., one who frees a country from an enemy or tyranny

Li·be·rec (lē′bə rets′) city in the N Czech Republic

Li·ber·i·a (lī bir′ē ə) country on the W coast of Africa: founded (1821) by the American Colonization Society as settlement for freed U.S. slaves; established as an independent republic in 1847: 43,000 sq mi (111,370 sq km): cap. Monrovia —**Li·ber′i·an** ***adj., n.***

lib·er·tar·i·an (lib′ər ter′ē ən) ***n.*** ⟦LIBERT(Y) + -ARIAN⟧ **1** a person who believes in the doctrine of the freedom of the will **2** a person who believes in full individual freedom of thought, expression, and action ☆**3** [**L-**] *a)* a U.S. political party stressing libertarian principles, as protection of the rights of the individual and minimization of the role of government *b)* a member of this party —***adj.*** **1** of or upholding libertarian principles ☆**2** [**L-**] of, belonging to, or characteristic of the Libertarian Party —**lib′er·tar′i·an·ism′** ***n.***

li·ber·té, é·ga·li·té, fra·ter·ni·té (lē ber tā′ ā gȧ lē tā′ frȧ ter nē tā′) ⟦Fr⟧ liberty, equality, fraternity: the motto of the French Revolution of 1789

lib·er·tine (lib′ər tēn′, -tin) ***n.*** ⟦ME *libertyn* < L *libertinus* < *libertus,* freedman < *liber,* free: see LIBERAL⟧ **1** in ancient Rome, a person who had been freed from slavery **2** ⟦prob. via Fr *libertin*⟧ a person, esp. a man, who leads an unrestrained, sexually immoral life; rake **3** [Archaic] a freethinker —***adj.*** morally unrestrained; licentious —**lib′er·tin·ism′** ***n.***, **lib′er·tin′age**

lib·er·ty (lib′ər tē) ***n.***, *pl.* **-ties** ⟦ME & OFr *liberte* < L *libertas* < *liber,* free: see LIBERAL⟧ **1** freedom or release from slavery, imprisonment, captivity, or any other form of arbitrary control **2** the sum of rights and exemptions possessed in common by the people of a community, state, etc.: see also CIVIL LIBERTIES, POLITICAL LIBERTY **3** a particular right, franchise, or exemption from compulsion **4** a too free, too familiar, or impertinent action or attitude **5** the limits within which a certain amount of freedom may be exercised *[to have the liberty of the third floor]* **6** *a)* permission given to a sailor to go ashore; specif., in the U.S. Navy, permission given to an enlisted person to be absent from duty for a period ordinarily of 48 hours or less *b)* the period of time given **7** *Philos.* freedom to choose; freedom from compulsion or constraint —*SYN.* FREEDOM —**at liberty 1** not confined; free **2** permitted (to do or say something); allowed **3** not busy or in use —**take liberties 1** to be too familiar or impertinent in action or speech: often used with *with* **2** to deal (*with* facts, data, etc.) in a distorting way

☆**Liberty Bell** the bell of Independence Hall in Philadelphia, rung on July 8, 1776, to proclaim the independence of the U.S.: it cracked in 1835

liberty cap a soft, closefitting cap without a visor, adopted by the French Revolutionists as a symbol of liberty

Liberty Island island in SE N.Y., in New York Bay: site of the Statue of Liberty: *c.* 10 acres or 0.015 sq mi (0.038 sq km)

li·bid·i·nal (li bid′'n əl) ***adj.*** of the libido

li·bid·i·nous (-əs) ***adj.*** ⟦ME *lybidynous* < L *libidinosus* < *libido*: see fol.⟧ full of or characterized by lust; lewd; lascivious —**li·bid′i·nous·ly** ***adv.*** —**li·bid′i·nous·ness** ***n.***

li·bi·do (li bē′dō) ***n.***, *pl.* **-dos** ⟦ModL < L, pleasure, wantonness < *libet, lubet,* it pleases: for IE base see LOVE⟧ **1** the sexual urge or instinct **2** *Psychoanalysis* instinctive psychic energy, specif. sexual energy, manifested variously at different stages of personality development

LIBOR (lī′bôr′) ***n.*** ⟦*L(ondon) i(nter)b(ank) o(ffered) r(ate)*⟧ the interest rate at which banks make short-term loans to one another: also written **Li′bor′**

li·bra (lī′brə; *also, and for 3 always,* lē′-) ***n.***, *pl.* **-brae′** (-brē′) ⟦ME < L⟧ **1** *obs. term for* POUND[1]: the abbreviation for the unit of measure, *lb.*, derives from this word and the symbol for the Brit. monetary unit, £, derives from its first letter **2** an ancient Roman unit of weight, equal to about 12 ounces **3** ⟦Sp: cf. POUND[1]⟧ *a)* a former gold coin of Peru *b)* a unit of weight in Spain, and various Latin American countries, equal to about one pound

Li·bra (lē′brə, lī′-) ***n.*** ⟦L, a balance⟧ **1** a S constellation between Virgo and Scorpius; the Scales; the Balance **2** the seventh sign of the zodiac, entered by the sun about September 23: also called *the Scales* **3** a person born under this sign: also **Li′bran**

li·brar·i·an (lī brer′ē ən) ***n.*** ⟦< L *librarius* + -AN⟧ **1** a person in charge of a library **2** a library worker trained in library science —**li·brar′i·an·ship′** ***n.***

li·brar·y (lī′brer′ē, -brər ē; *also, though usually regarded as nonstandard,* lī′

ber′ē) *n., pl.* **-brar′ies** ⟦ME *librarie* < OFr < *libraire*, copyist < L *librarius, n.*, transcriber of books, *adj.*, of books < *liber*, a book, orig. inner bark or rind of a tree (which was written on) < IE base **leubh-*, to peel off > LEAF, Gr *lepein*, to strip off rind⟧ **1** *a)* a collection of books, periodicals, musical scores, music and film recordings, etc., esp. a large, systematically arranged collection for reading or reference *b)* a room or building where such a collection is kept **2** a public or private institution in charge of the care and circulation of such a collection **3** a set or series of books issued in a single format by a publishing house **4** any collection of things that is organized for a particular purpose [a software *library*]

Library of Congress the national library in Washington, D.C., established in 1800 by the U.S. Congress for the use of its members: it is now one of the largest public reference libraries in the world

☆**library science** the study of library organization and management

li·bra·tion (lī brā′shən) *n.* ⟦L *libratio* < *libratus*, pp. of *librare*, to weigh, balance < *libra*, a balance⟧ *Astron.* a slight, apparent rocking motion of the moon as seen from the earth, allowing approximately 59% of the moon's surface to be visible —**li′bra·to′ry** (-brə tôr′ē) *adj.*

li·bret·tist (li bret′ist) *n.* a writer of librettos or of a libretto

li·bret·to (li bret′ō) *n., pl.* **-tos** or **-ti** (-ē) ⟦It, dim. of *libro* (< L *liber*), a book: see LIBRARY⟧ **1** the words, or text, of an opera, oratorio, or other long choral work **2** a book containing these words

Li·bre·ville (lē′brə vēl′) capital of Gabon: seaport on the Gulf of Guinea

li·bri (lī′brē′, lē′-) *n.* ⟦L⟧ *pl. of* LIBER

li·bri·form (lī′brə fôrm′) *adj.* ⟦L *liber* (gen. *libri*), inner bark of a tree (see LIBRARY) + -FORM⟧ *Bot.* designating or of wood fibers which are elongated and have simple pits

☆**Lib·ri·um** (lib′rē əm) ⟦arbitrary coinage < Fr *libre*, free (< L *liber*: see LIBERTY) + -IUM⟧ *trademark for* a tranquilizing drug: see CHLORDIAZEPOXIDE

Lib·y·a (lib′ē ə, lib′yə) **1** ancient Greek & Roman name of N Africa, west of Egypt **2** country in N Africa, on the Mediterranean: under Turkish domination from the 16th cent.; occupied by Italy (1911-43); placed under British and French military rule, it became an independent kingdom (1951) and a republic (1969): 679,362 sq mi (1,759,540 sq km); cap. Tripoli

Lib·y·an (lib′ē ən, lib′yən) *adj.* of Libya or its people or culture —*n.* **1** a person born or living in Libya **2** the earliest form of the Berber language as found in inscriptions in ancient Libya

Libyan Desert E part of the Sahara, in Libya, Sudan, & Egypt west of the Nile

lice (līs) *n. pl. of* LOUSE

li·cense (lī′səns) *n.* ⟦OFr < L *licentia* < *licens*, prp. of *licere*, to be permitted: see LEISURE⟧ **1** *a)* formal permission to do something; esp., authorization by law to do some specified thing [*license* to marry, practice medicine, hunt, etc.] *b)* a document, printed tag, permit, etc. indicating that such permission has been granted **2** *a)* freedom to deviate from strict conduct, rule, or practice, generally permitted by common consent [poetic *license*] *b)* an instance of such deviation **3** excessive, undisciplined freedom, constituting an abuse of liberty Brit. sp. **li′cence** —*vt.* **-censed, -cens·ing** to give license or a license to or for; permit formally —***SYN.*** AUTHORIZE, FREEDOM —**li′cens·a·ble** *adj.*

licensed practical nurse *see* PRACTICAL NURSE: also (in Calif. & Tex.) **licensed vocational nurse**

li·cen·see (lī′sən sē′) *n.* a person to whom a license is granted

☆**license plate** a numbered or lettered metal tag displayed on a motor vehicle, indicating that the vehicle has been registered with the state or country and may be driven on public streets and highways

li·cens·er (lī′sən sər) *n.* a person with authority to grant licenses: also sp. *Law* **li′cen·sor**

li·cen·sure (lī′sən shoor′) *n.* the act or practice of granting licenses as for practicing a profession

li·cen·ti·ate (lī sen′shē it, -āt′; -shət) *n.* ⟦ME *licenciat* < ML *licentiatus*, pp. of *licentiare*, to license < L *licentia*: see LICENSE⟧ **1** a person licensed to practice a specified profession **2** in certain European and Canadian universities, an academic degree between that of bachelor and that of doctor —**li·cen′ti·ate·ship′** *n.*

li·cen·tious (lī sen′shəs) *adj.* ⟦L *licentiosus* < *licentia*: see LICENSE⟧ **1** [Rare] disregarding accepted rules and standards **2** morally unrestrained, esp. in sexual activity; lascivious —**li·cen′tious·ly** *adv.* —**li·cen′tious·ness** *n.*

lich (lich) *n.* ⟦ME < OE *lic*, akin to Ger *leiche*, corpse < IE base **lig-*, figure, shape, similar, like > LIKE²⟧ [Now Brit. Dial.] a dead body

li·chee (lē′chē′) *n. alt. sp. of* LITCHI

li·chen (lī′kən) *n.* ⟦L < Gr *leichēn*, prob. < *leichein*, to LICK⟧ **1** any of various small plants composed of a particular fungus and a particular alga (or blue-green alga) growing in an intimate symbiotic association and forming a dual plant, commonly adhering in colored patches or spongelike branches to rock, wood, soil, etc. **2** any of various skin diseases characterized by papules and enlarged skin markings —*vt.* to cover with lichens —**li′chen·ous** *adj.*, **li′chen·ose′** (-ōs′)

li·chen·ol·o·gy (lī′kən äl′ə jē) *n.* the study of lichens

lich gate (lich′) ⟦see LICH⟧ [Brit.] a roofed gate at the entrance to a churchyard, where a coffin can be set down to await the arrival of the clergyman

licht (likht) *adj., adv., n., vi., vt. Scot. var. of:* **1** LIGHT¹ **2** LIGHT²

Lich·ten·stein (lik′tən stīn′, -stēn′), **Roy (Fox)** 1923-97; U.S. painter

lic·it (lis′it) *adj.* ⟦ME *lycite* < L *licitus*, pp. of *licere*, to be permitted: see LEISURE⟧ permitted; lawful —***SYN.*** LEGAL —**lic′it·ly** *adv.* —**lic′it·ness** *n.*

lick (lik) *vt.* ⟦ME *licken* < OE *liccian*, akin to Ger *lecken* < IE base **leiĝh-*, to lick > Gr *leichein*, L *ligurrire*, to lick, *lingere*, to lick up⟧ **1** to pass the tongue over [to *lick* one's lips] **2** to bring into a certain condition by passing the tongue over [to *lick* one's fingers clean] **3** to pass lightly over like a tongue [flames *licking* the logs] **4** [Informal] *a)* to whip; thrash *b)* to overcome, vanquish, or control —*vi.* to move lightly and quickly, as a flame [waves *licking* about her feet] —*n.* **1** the act or an instance of licking with the tongue **2** a small quantity **3** *short for* SALT LICK **4** [Informal] *a)* a sharp blow *b)* a short, rapid burst of activity, often careless, as in cleaning up, etc. (also **lick and a promise**) *c)* a fast pace; spurt of speed; clip ☆**5** [Slang] a phrase of jazz music, esp. an interpolated improvisation **6** [*often pl.*] [Slang] chance; turn [to get one's *licks* in] —**lick into shape** ⟦from an old belief that bear cubs were born formless and their parents had to shape them by licking them⟧ [Informal] to bring into proper condition by careful, persistent work —**lick one's chops** [Informal] to anticipate something eagerly —**lick one's wounds** to withdraw physically or emotionally after experiencing failure, humiliation, or disappointment, as to collect or console oneself —**lick up** to consume as by licking or lapping

lick·er·ish (lik′ər ish) *adj.* ⟦altered < *lickerous* < ME *lykerous* < Anglo-Fr form of OFr *lecheros*⟧ **1** [Now Rare] *a)* lecherous; lustful; lewd *b)* greedy or eager, esp. to eat or taste **2** [Obs.] tempting the appetite

☆**lick·e·ty-split** (lik′ə tē split′) *adv.* ⟦fanciful formation based on LICK, *n.* 4c⟧ [Informal] at great speed

lick·ing (lik′iŋ) *n.* **1** the act of a person or thing that licks **2** [Informal] *a)* a whipping *b)* a defeat

lick·spit·tle (-spit′'l) *n.* ⟦LICK, *v.* + SPITTLE⟧ a servile flatterer; toady

lic·o·rice (lik′ə rish, lik′rish; *occas.* lik′ə ris) *n.* ⟦ME *licorys* < OFr *licorece* < LL *liquiritia*, altered (by assoc. with *liquor*: see LIQUOR) < L *glycyrrhiza* < Gr *glykys*, sweet (see GLYCERIN) + *rhiza*, ROOT¹⟧ **1** a European perennial plant (*Glycyrrhiza glabra*) of the pea family, with spikes of blue flowers and short, flat pods **2** the dried root of this plant or the black extract made from it, used in medicine, esp. as a vehicle and a diluting agent, or as a flavoring **3** candy flavored with this extract or otherwise made to resemble it in taste

lic·tor (lik′tər) *n.* ⟦ME (Wycliffe) *littour* < L *lictor* < base of *ligare* (see LIGAMENT), in allusion to the fasces⟧ in ancient Rome, any of a group of minor officials who carried the fasces and cleared the way for the chief magistrates

lid (lid) *n.* ⟦ME < OE *hlid* (akin to Ger *-lid* in *augenlid*, eyelid) < base seen in OE *hlidan*, to cover < IE base **k̂lei-*, to LEAN¹⟧ **1** a movable cover, hinged or unattached, as for a box, trunk, pot, etc.; top **2** *short for* EYELID ☆**3** [Informal] a curb or restraint [to put a *lid* on illegal gambling] **4** [Slang] a cap, hat, etc. **5** [Slang] a small package of marijuana, usually about an ounce **6** *Bot.* loosely, an operculum

li·dar (lī′där′) *n.* ⟦LI(GHT) + (RA)DAR⟧ a meteorological instrument using transmitted and reflected laser light, for detecting atmospheric particles, as pollutants, and determining their elevation, concentration, etc.

lid·ded (lid′id) *adj.* **1** covered with or as with a lid **2** having (a specified kind of) eyelids [heavy-*lidded*]

lid·less (lid′lis) *adj.* **1** without a lid **2** without eyelids **3** [Old Poet.] not closed; watchful: said of the eyes

li·do (lē′dō) *n.* ⟦after *Lido*, island in NE Italy⟧ a resort at a beach

li·do·caine (lī′dō kān′, -də-) *n.* ⟦(*diethylaminoacetoxy*)*lid*(*ide*) + (C)OCAINE⟧ a synthetic crystalline compound, $C_{14}H_{22}N_2O$, used esp. in the form of its hydrochloride as a local anesthetic and to control irregularity in the heartbeat

lie¹ (lī) *vi.* **lay, lain, ly′ing** ⟦ME *lien* < 2d & 3d pers. sing. of earlier *liggen* < OE *licgan*, to lie, akin to Ger *liegen* < IE base **legh-*, to lie, lay oneself down > L *lectus* & Gr *lēchos*, bed, *lōchos*, lair⟧ **1** to be or put oneself in a reclining position along a relatively horizontal surface: often with *down* **2** to be in a more or less horizontal position on some supporting surface: said of inanimate things **3** to be or remain in a specified condition [motives that *lie* hidden] **4** to be situated [Canada *lies* to the north] **5** to extend; stretch [the road that *lies* before us] **6** to be; exist; be found [the love that *lies* in her eyes] **7** to be buried or entombed **8** [Archaic] to stay overnight or for a short while; lodge **9** [Archaic] to have sexual intercourse (*with*) **10** *Law* to be maintainable or admissible [an action that will not *lie*] —*vt. Golf* to have, on the hole being played, a score of [after her approach shot, she *lies* three on the ninth hole] —*n.* **1** the way in which something is situated or arranged; lay **2** an animal's lair or resting place **3** [Brit.] a period of resting **4** *Golf* the relative situation of a ball with reference to the advantage it offers the player [a good *lie*] —☆**lie down on the job** [Informal] to put forth considerably less than one's best efforts —**lie in** [Old-fashioned] to be in confinement for childbirth —**lie low** *see the phrase under* LOW¹ —**lie off** *Naut.* to stay at a distance from shore or another ship —☆**lie over** to stay and wait until some future time —**lie to** *Naut.* to lie more or less stationary with the bow to the wind —**take lying down** [Informal] to submit to (punishment, a wrong, etc.) without protest

USAGE—See usage note at LAY¹

lie² (lī) *vi.* **lied, ly′ing** ⟦ME *lien* < OE *leogan*, akin to Ger *lügen* (Goth *liugan*) < IE base **leugh-*, to tell lies > Lith *lūgoti*, to ask⟧ **1** *a)* to make a statement that one knows is false, esp. with intent to deceive *b)* to make such statements habitually **2** to give a false impression; be deceptive [statistics can *lie*] —*vt.* to bring, put, accomplish, etc. by lying [to *lie* his way into political office] —*n.* **1** a false statement or action, esp. one made with intent to deceive **2** anything that gives or is meant to give a false impression —**give**

the lie to 1 to charge with telling a lie 2 to prove to be false; belie —**lie in one's throat** (or **in** or **through one's teeth**) to tell a foul or outrageous lie

SYN.—**lie** is the simple direct word meaning to make a deliberately false statement; **prevaricate** strictly means to quibble or confuse the issue in order to evade the truth, but it is loosely used as a formal or affected substitute for **lie**; **equivocate** implies the deliberate use of ambiguity in order to deceive or mislead; **fabricate** suggests the invention of a false story, excuse, etc. intended to deceive and is, hence, sometimes used as a somewhat softer equivalent for **lie**; **fib** implies the telling of a falsehood about something unimportant and is sometimes a euphemism for **lie**

Lie (lē), **Tryg·ve (Halvdan)** (trig′və) 1896-1968; Norw. statesman: 1st secretary-general of the United Nations (1946-53)

Lieb·frau·milch (lēb′frou milk′; *Ger* lēp′frou milH′) ***n.*** ⟦Ger contr. < *Liebfrauenmilch*, orig. jocular formation (after *Liebfrauenstift*, monastery of our dear lady, i.e., the Virgin Mary) < *lieb*, dear + *frauen*, obs. gen. of *frau*, lady + *milch*, MILK: the wine was first produced at the monastery in WORMS⟧ a variety of white Rhine wine

Lie·big (lē′biH), Baron **Jus·tus von** (yo͞os′to͝os fôn) 1803-73; Ger. chemist

Lieb·knecht (lēp′k′neHt′), **Karl** (kärl) 1871-1919; Ger. socialist leader

Liech·ten·stein (lik′tən stīn′; *Ger* liH′tən shtīn′) country in WC Europe, on the Rhine: a principality: 62 sq mi (160 sq km); cap. Vaduz —**Liech′ten·stein′er** ***n.***

lied (lēd) ***n., pl.*** **lied·er** (lē′dər) ⟦Ger: see LAUD⟧ a German song, esp. a German ART SONG of a lyrical nature

☆**Lie·der·kranz** (lē′dər kränts′, -krants′) ⟦Ger, lit., garland of songs (see prec.): after a N.Y. choral society⟧ *trademark for* a soft cheese having a strong odor and flavor

☆**lie detector** a polygraph used on persons suspected of lying: it records certain physiological changes assumed to occur when the subject lies in answering questions

lief (lēf) ***adj.*** ⟦ME *lef* < OE *leof*, beloved, dear, akin to Ger *lieb* < IE base **leubh-* > LOVE⟧ [Archaic] 1 valued; dear; beloved 2 willing —***adv.*** willingly; gladly: only in **would** (or **had**) **as lief**

liege (lēj) ***adj.*** ⟦OFr, prob. < Frank base akin to OHG *ledig*, free, but infl. by L *ligare*, to bind⟧ 1 *Feudal Law* *a)* entitled to the service and allegiance of his vassals [a *liege* lord] *b)* bound to give service and allegiance to the lord [*liege* subjects] 2 loyal; faithful —***n.*** *Feudal Law* 1 a lord or sovereign 2 a subject or vassal

Li·ège (lē ezh′, -āzh′; *Fr* lyezh) 1 province of E Belgium: 1,491 sq mi (3,862 sq km) 2 its capital, on the Meuse River

liege·man (lēj′mən) ***n., pl.*** **-men** (-mən) 1 a vassal 2 a loyal follower Also written **liege man**

lien (lēn, lē′ən) ***n.*** ⟦Fr < L *ligamen*, a band < *ligare*, to bind, tie: see LIGATURE⟧ *Law* a claim on the property of another as security for the payment of a just debt

lie of the land [Chiefly Brit.] LAY OF THE LAND

li·er (lī′ər) ***n.*** one who lies (reclines)

li·erne (lē urn′) ***n.*** ⟦Fr: see LIANA⟧ *Archit.* a short rib used in Gothic vaulting to connect the bosses and intersections of the main ribs

lieu (lo͞o) ***n.*** ⟦ME *liue* < OFr *lieu* < L *locus*, place: see LOCUS⟧ place: now chiefly in the phrase **in lieu of**, in place of; instead of

Lieut *abbrev.* Lieutenant

lieu·ten·ant (lo͞o ten′ənt; *Brit & Cdn* lef ten′-) ***n.*** ⟦ME *lutenand*, *luftenand* < MFr < *lieu* (see LIEU) + *tenant*, holding, prp. of *tenir*, to hold < L *tenere*, to hold: see THIN⟧ 1 a person who acts for a superior, as during the latter's absence; aide; deputy 2 an officer ranking below a captain as in a police or fire department 3 *U.S. Mil.* a title used in addressing a first lieutenant or second lieutenant: see also FIRST LIEUTENANT, SECOND LIEUTENANT 4 *U.S. Navy* an officer ranking above a lieutenant junior grade and below a lieutenant commander —**lieu·ten′an·cy** (-ən sē) ***n., pl.*** **-cies**

lieutenant colonel *U.S. Mil.* an officer ranking above a major and below a colonel

lieutenant commander *U.S. Navy* an officer ranking above a lieutenant and below a commander

lieutenant general *U.S. Mil.* an officer, with an insignia of three stars, ranking above a major general and below a general

lieutenant governor 1 an elected official of a U.S. state who ranks below the governor and substitutes for the governor in case of the latter's absence or death 2 the official head of the government of a Canadian province, appointed by the governor general: also **lieu·ten′ant-gov′er·nor** ***n.***

lieutenant junior grade *U.S. Navy* an officer ranking above an ensign and below a lieutenant

life (līf) ***n., pl.*** **lives** ⟦ME < OE *līf*, akin to ON *líf*, life, Ger *leib*, body < IE base **leibh-*, to LIVE[1]⟧ 1 that property or quality of plants and animals that distinguishes them from inorganic matter or dead organisms; specif., the cellular biochemical activity or processes of an organism, as the ingestion of nutrients, the storage and use of energy, the excretion of wastes, growth, reproduction, etc. 2 this activity, or the state of possessing this property [brought back to *life*] 3 a living being, esp. a human being [the *lives* lost in wars] 4 living things collectively, often of a specified kind [plant *life*] 5 the time a person or thing is alive or exists, or a specific portion of such time [his early *life*] 6 a sentence of imprisonment for the rest of one's life 7 one's manner of living [a *life* of ease] 8 the activities of a given time or in a given setting, and the people who take part in them [military *life*] 9 lives considered together as belonging to a certain class or type [high *life*] 10 *a)* an individual's animate existence *b)* an account of this; biography *c)* a specific aspect of an individual's activities [her love *life*] 11 the existence of the soul [eternal *life*] 12 something essential to the continued existence of something else [freedom of speech is the *life* of democracy] 13 the source of vigor or liveliness [the *life* of the party] 14 vigor; liveliness; animation; vivacity 15 the period of flourishing, usefulness, etc.; period during which anything lasts [fads have a short *life*] 16 another chance 17 *Fine Arts* *a)* a lifelike quality or appearance *b)* representation from living models [a class in *life*] —***adj.*** 1 for a lifetime [given a *life* sentence] 2 of or relating to the property of life [*life* processes] 3 using live models [a *life* class in painting] —**a matter of life and death** 1 something whose outcome determines whether a person lives or dies 2 any extremely important matter —**as large** (or **big**) **as life** 1 LIFE-SIZE 2 [Informal] in actual fact; truly —**bring to life** 1 to bring back to consciousness 2 to make lively or lifelike; animate —**come to life** 1 to recover consciousness 2 to become lively or animated —**for dear life** to, or as if to, save one's life; with a desperate intensity —**for life** 1 for the duration of one's life 2 in order to save one's life —**for the life of me** [Informal] even though my life were at stake on it; by any means: used in negative expressions —**from life** from a living model —☆**not on your life** [Informal] by no means; certainly not —**see life** to have a wide variety of social experiences —**take a** (or **someone's**) **life** to kill (someone) —**take one's** (**own**) **life** to commit suicide —☆**the life** or **the Life** [Slang] prostitution as a trade —☆**the life of Riley** [Informal] a carefree or luxurious way of living —**to the life** like the living original; exactly —**true to life** corresponding to what happens or exists in real life; true to reality or to common experience

life-and-death (līf′ən deth′) ***adj.*** *var. of* LIFE-OR-DEATH

life belt a life preserver in the form of a belt

life·blood (-blud′) ***n.*** 1 the blood necessary to life 2 a vital element or animating influence

life·boat (-bōt′) ***n.*** 1 a strong, seaworthy boat kept in readiness on shore for use in rescuing people in danger of drowning 2 one of the small boats carried by a ship for use if the ship must be abandoned

life buoy a life preserver in the shape of a ring

life-care (līf′ker′) ***adj.*** designating or of a residential community or facility for elderly people that is designed to provide an apartment, meals, nursing care, etc. for the duration of the resident's life

life cycle 1 the series of developmental changes in form undergone by a particular type of organism from its earliest stage to the recurrence of the same stage in the next generation 2 any series of changes like this

life expectancy the statistically probable length of time that a typical individual can be expected to live

life force *Eng. term for* ÉLAN VITAL

life-form (līf′ôrm′) ***n.*** a particular type of organism, specif. one that is unusual, alien, or newly discovered: often written **life form**

life-giv·ing (-giv′iŋ) ***adj.*** 1 that gives or can give life 2 strengthening; refreshing; inspiring

life·guard (-gärd′) ***n.*** ☆an expert swimmer employed as at a beach or pool to prevent drownings

Life Guards ⟦earlier also *liefguard*, prob. after Ger *leibgarde*, bodyguard < *leib*, body (see LIFE) + *garde* (see GUARD)⟧ a special unit of cavalry which serves as part of the ceremonial guard for the British sovereign

life history 1 the history of the changes undergone by an organism in development from the egg, spore, etc. to its death in maturity 2 one series of such changes 3 the story of a person's life

life insurance insurance in which a stipulated sum is paid to the beneficiary or beneficiaries at the death of the insured, or, if specified, to the insured at a certain age

life interest interest (in property) that is payable during a person's lifetime, but which cannot be passed on to another at death

life jacket (*or* **vest**) a life preserver in the form of a sleeveless jacket or vest

life·less (līf′lis) ***adj.*** 1 without life; specif., *a)* that never had life; inanimate *b)* that no longer has life; dead *c)* having no living beings [a *lifeless* planet] 2 dull; listless —**SYN.** DEAD —**life′less·ly** ***adv.*** —**life′less·ness** ***n.***

life·like (-līk′) ***adj.*** 1 resembling that of actual life [*lifelike* dialogue in the film] 2 closely resembling a real person or thing [a *lifelike* portrait]

life·line (-līn′) ***n.*** 1 a rope or line for saving life, as one thrown to a person in the water 2 any rope strung along or above a vessel's weather deck to provide a handhold as in rough weather 3 the rope by means of which a diver is raised and lowered, used by the diver for signaling 4 *Palmistry* a line in the palm of the hand, curving about the base of the thumb, that reveals facts about a person's life 5 a commercial, esp. maritime, route of great importance 6 a route that is the only one over which supplies can be transported to a certain place 7 someone or something called upon in time of need

life list a listing of all the different species of birds sighted by a birder, as over a lifetime

life·long (-lôŋ′) ***adj.*** lasting or not changing during one's whole life [a *lifelong* love]

☆**life net** a strong net used as by firefighters to catch people jumping from a burning building

life-or-death (līf′ôr deth′) ***adj.*** 1 having death as a possible result [a *life-or-death* struggle] 2 so extremely important as to be crucial [a *life-or-death* decision]

life preserver 1 a buoyant device for saving a person from drowning by keeping the body afloat, as a ring or sleeveless jacket of canvas-covered cork or kapok 2 [Chiefly Brit.] BLACKJACK (sense 3)

lif·er (līf′ər) *n.* [Slang] **1** a person sentenced to imprisonment for life **2** a person whose working life is spent in one occupation or profession, esp. in the armed forces

life raft a small raft, now usually inflatable, for use as an emergency craft at sea

☆**life·sav·er** (-sāv′ər) *n.* **1** a person or thing that saves people from drowning, as a lifeguard **2** [Informal] a person or thing that gives aid in time of need

☆**life·sav·ing** (-sāv′iŋ) *adj.* designed for or connected with the saving of human life —*n.* the saving of human life, esp. through the prevention of drowning

life science any of various sciences, as botany or zoology, dealing with living organisms and their life processes —**life scientist**

life-size (-sīz′) *adj.* of the same size as the person or thing represented: said of a picture, sculpture, etc.: also **life′-sized′**

life span **1** LIFETIME (*n.* 1) **2** the longest period of time that a typical individual can be expected to live Also written **life′span′** *n.*

☆**life·style** (līf′stīl′) *n.* the consistent, integrated way of life of an individual as typified by his or her manner, attitudes, possessions, etc.: also written **life style** —*adj.* of or having to do with a lifestyle or lifestyles; specif., of or promoting a healthy, fashionable, or affluent lifestyle

life-sup·port (līf′sə pôrt′) *adj.* **1** *Engineering* designating or of any system that enables normal living in space, under water, etc. **2** *Med.* designating or of any device or system, usually connected directly to a patient, that can take over for a vital bodily organ or function that is failing or has failed —*n.* a life-support system or device

life table MORTALITY TABLE

life·time (-tīm′) *n.* **1** the period of time that someone lives, or that something lasts, functions, or is in effect **2** a very long time [made to last a *lifetime*] —*adj.* lasting for such a period [a *lifetime* job]

life·work (-wurk′) *n.* the work to which a person's life is devoted; most important work of one's life

life zone any of a series of biogeographic zones into which a continent, region, etc. is divided by both latitude and altitude on the basis of the characteristic animal and plant life in a zone

☆**LIFO** (lī′fō′) *n.* ⟦*l(ast) i(n), f(irst) o(ut)*⟧ a method of valuing inventories in which items sold or used are priced at the cost of the most recent acquisitions and those remaining are valued at the cost of earliest acquisitions: cf. FIFO

lift (lift) *vt.* ⟦ME *liften* < ON *lypta* < *lopt*, air, akin to OE *lyft*, Ger *luft*, Du *lucht*⟧ **1** to bring up to a higher position; raise **2** to pick up and move or set [*lift* the box down from the shelf] **3** to hold up; support high in the air **4** to raise in rank, condition, dignity, spirits, etc.; bring to a higher level; elevate; exalt **5** to pay off (a mortgage, debt, etc.) **6** to end (a blockade, siege, etc.) by withdrawing forces **7** to revoke or rescind (a ban or order) **8** to loosen and remove (bulbs, seedlings, or root crops) from the soil **9** to take an imprint of (a fingerprint) from a surface **10** [Informal] to remove from its proper place; esp., to plagiarize [to *lift* a passage from another writer] **11** [Informal] to steal **12** to reduce the sagging of (the face, breasts, etc.) by means of cosmetic surgery **13** to transport, esp. by aircraft **14** *Golf* to pick (a ball) up, as from an unplayable position **15** *Mil.* to change the direction of or cease (fire) —*vi.* **1** to exert strength in raising or trying to raise something **2** to rise and vanish; be dispelled [the fog *lifted*] **3** to become raised or elevated; go up **4** to stop for a time —*n.* **1** a lifting, raising, or rising; upward movement **2** the amount lifted at one time **3** *a)* the distance through which something is lifted *b)* the extent of rise or elevation **4** lifting power or influence **5** elevation of spirits or mood **6** elevated position or carriage, as of the neck, head, etc. **7** [Informal] a ride in the direction in which one is going **8** help of any kind **9** a swell or rise in the ground **10** the means by which a person or thing is lifted; specif., *a)* a layer as of leather placed inside a shoe to increase the wearer's height *b)* [Brit.] ELEVATOR *c)* any of various devices used to transport people up or down a slope [a ski *lift*] *d)* a device for lifting an automobile for repairs **11** *Aeron.* the component of total air force acting on a body, as on an airfoil or wing, that is perpendicular to the direction of flight and exerted, normally, in an upward direction **12** *Mining* a set of pumps in a mine —**lift up one's voice** ⟦as in Isa. 24:14, 52:8, Luke 17:12, etc.⟧ [Literary] to raise the voice, now, esp., as in song or in jubilation, praise, etc. —**lift′er** *n.*

SYN.—**lift**, in its general literal sense, implies the use of some effort in bringing something up to a higher position [help me *lift* the box]; **raise**, often interchangeable with **lift**, specifically implies a bringing into an upright position by lifting one end [to *raise* a flagpole]; **elevate** is now a less frequent synonym for **lift** or **raise** [the balloon had been *elevated* 500 feet]; **rear** is a literary equivalent of **raise** [the giant trees *reared* their branches to the sky]; **hoist** implies the lifting of something heavy, usually by some mechanical means, as a block and tackle, crane, etc. [to *hoist* bales of cotton into a ship]; **boost** implies a lifting by or as by a push from behind or below [*boost* me into the tree]. All these terms are used figuratively to imply a bringing into a higher or better state [to *lift*, or *hoist*, one's spirits, to *raise* one's hopes, to *elevate* one's mind, to *rear* children, to *boost* sales] —*ANT.* **lower**

---

lift·gate (lift′gāt′) *n.* **1** a door or window on the back of a station wagon, hatchback, etc. that swings upward **2** a motorized platform on the back of a truck used to lift or lower heavy items

☆**lift·ing body** (lift′iŋ) a vehicle combining features of aircraft and spacecraft, designed for reentry into the atmosphere, flight at high altitudes, and the ability to land itself

☆**lift·off** (-ôf′) *n.* **1** the initial vertical takeoff of a rocket, helicopter, etc. **2** the moment at which this occurs Also written **lift-off**

lift pump a suction pump that raises a column of liquid to the level of a spout out of which the liquid runs of its own accord: cf. FORCE PUMP

lig·a·ment (lig′ə mənt) *n.* ⟦L *ligamentum* < *ligare*, to tie, bind: see LIGATURE⟧ **1** a bond or tie connecting one thing with another **2** *Anat.* a band of tough tissue connecting bones or holding organs in place

li·gan (lī′gən) *n. var. of* LAGAN

lig·and (lig′ənd, lī′gənd) *n.* ⟦< L *ligandum*, ger. of *ligare*, to bind: see LIGATURE⟧ an atom, group, ion, radical, or molecule which forms a coordination complex with a central atom or ion

li·gase (lī′gās′, -gāz′) *n.* ⟦< L *ligare* (see LIGATURE) + -ASE⟧ any of a class of enzymes that act as catalysts in chemical reactions in which molecules are linked together, as in the synthesis and repair of DNA or in the formation of recombinant DNA

li·gate (lī′gāt′) *vt.* **-gat′ed, -gat′ing** ⟦< L *ligatus*, pp. of *ligare*, to bind, tie: see fol.⟧ *Surgery* to tie or bind (a bleeding artery, etc.) with a ligature —**li·ga′tion** *n.*

lig·a·ture (lig′ə chər) *n.* ⟦ME < MFr < LL *ligatura* < pp. of L *ligare*, to bind < IE base **leiĝ-*, to bind > MLowG *līk*, a tie, MHG *geleich*, joint, Alb *lidhe*, a bond⟧ **1** a tying or binding together **2** a thing used in tying or binding together **3** *a)* a written or printed character containing two or more letters united, as *œ, fl, th* *b)* a curved line connecting such letters in writing **4** *Music* *a)* in medieval mensural notation, a symbol representing two or more notes *b)* a curved line joining two or more notes in a tie or slur *c)* the notes so connected **5** *Surgery* a thread or wire used to tie up an artery, etc. —*vt.* **-tured, -tur·ing** to tie or bind together with a ligature; ligate

li·ger (lī′gər) *n.* ⟦LI(ON) + (TI)GER⟧ the hybrid offspring of a male lion and a female tiger

Li·ge·ti (lē′gä tē), **György (Sándor)** (jôrj) 1923-2006; Hungarian composer

light¹ (līt) *n.* ⟦ME *liht* < OE *lēoht*, akin to Ger *licht* < IE base **leuk-*, to shine, bright > Gr *leukos*, white, L *lux* & *lumen*, light, *lucere*, to shine, *luna*, moon, Welsh *llug*, gleam⟧ **1** *a)* the form of electromagnetic radiation that acts upon the retina of the eye, optic nerve, etc., making sight possible: this energy is transmitted in a vacuum at a velocity of 299,792,458 meters per second (*c.* 186,000 miles per second) *b)* a form of radiant energy similar to this, but not acting on the normal retina, as ultraviolet and infrared radiation **2** the rate of flow of light radiation with respect to the sense of sight: it is measured in *lumens* **3** the sensation that light stimulates in the organs of sight **4** brightness; illumination, often of a specified kind [the dim *light* of a candle] **5** a source of light, as the sun, a lamp, a lightbulb, etc. **6** TRAFFIC LIGHT **7** the light from the sun; daylight or dawn **8** a thing by means of which something can be started burning [a *light* for a cigar] **9** a windowpane, specif., any of the segments of a mullioned window **10** mental illumination; knowledge or information; enlightenment [to shed *light* on a past event] **11** spiritual inspiration **12** public knowledge or view [to bring new facts to *light*] **13** the way in which something is seen; aspect [presented in a favorable *light*] **14** facial expression showing a mental or emotional state [a *light* of recognition in his eyes] **15** a person whose brilliant record makes him or her an example for others; outstanding figure [one of the shining *lights* of the school] **16** *a)* the quality suggesting light created in a painting, drawing, etc., esp. in certain areas *b)* such an area —*adj.* ⟦ME *liht* < OE *leoht*⟧ **1** having light; not dark; bright **2** pale in color; not bright [a *light* blue color] —*vt.* **light′ed** or **lit**, **light′ing** ⟦ME *lighten* < OE *lihtan*⟧ **1** to set on fire; ignite [to *light* a bonfire] **2** to cause to give off light [to *light* a lamp] **3** to give light to; furnish with light; illuminate [lamps *light* the streets] **4** to brighten; animate **5** to show the way to by giving light [a beacon *lights* the ships to harbor] —*vi.* **1** to catch fire [the fuse *lighted* at once] **2** to be lighted; brighten: usually with *up* —**according to one's lights** as one's opinions, information, or standards may direct —**in (the) light of** with knowledge of; considering —**light up** **1** to make or become light **2** to make or become bright, cheerful, etc. **3** [Informal] to begin smoking (a cigar, etc.) —**out like a light** [Informal] unconscious or fast asleep —**see the light (of day)** **1** to come into existence **2** to come to public view ☆**3** to come to understand —**stand in one's own light** to harm one's reputation by acting unwisely —**strike a light** to make a flame, as with a match —**under the lights** at night: said of an outdoor event, as a football or baseball game, illuminated by electric lighting

light² (līt) *adj.* ⟦ME < OE *lēoht*, akin to Ger *leicht*, Du *licht* < IE **lengwhto-* < base **legwh-*, light in movement and weight > L *levis*, Gr *elaphros*⟧ **1** having little weight; not heavy **2** having little weight for its size; of low specific gravity **3** below the usual or defined weight [a *light* coin] **4** less than usual or normal in amount, extent, intensity, force, etc.; specif., *a)* striking or making contact with little force or impact [a *light* blow] *b)* of less than the usual quantity or density [a *light* voter turnout, a *light* rain] *c)* not thick, coarse, or massive; delicate and graceful in structure [*light* tracery] *d)* not violent or intense; mild [a *light* wind] *e)* soft, muted, or muffled [a *light* sound] *f)* not prolonged or intense [*light* applause] *g)* not deep; easily disturbed [a *light* sleep] **5** of little importance; not serious or profound [*light* conversation] **6** easy to bear; not burdensome [a *light* tax] **7** easy to do; not difficult [*light* housekeeping] **8** not burdened with grief or sorrow; happy; buoyant [*light* spirits] **9** of a flighty nature; frivolous; capricious **10** loose in morals; wanton **11** dizzy; giddy **12** of an amusing or nonserious nature [*light* reading] **13** containing little alcohol [*light* wine] **14** containing fewer calories than others of its kind [*light* beer] **15** characterized by qualities suggestive of little weight; not dense, hard, full, etc.; specif., *a)* not as full as usual; moderate [a *light* meal] *b)* easy to digest *c)* well leavened; soft and spongy [a *light* cake] *d)* loose in consistency; easily crumbled; porous [*light* sand] **16** moving with ease and nimbleness [*light* on one's feet] **17** able to carry little weight or cargo [a *light* vehicle] **18** unstressed or slightly stressed: said of a syllable in phonetics, prosody, etc. **19** designating or of an industry equipped with relatively light machinery and producing relatively small products **20** designating, of, or equipped with weapons, armor, ships, etc. of a relatively small size or light weight **21** [Informal] *a)* lacking personnel; short-handed *b)* owing (a specified sum) to the pot in a poker game [*light* fifty cents] —*adv.* **1** LIGHTLY **2** with little luggage, cargo, etc. [to travel *light*] —*vi.* **light′ed** or **lit**, **light′ing** ⟦ME *lihten* < OE *līhtan*: also aphetic for ALIGHT[1]⟧ **1** [Now Dial.] to get down from a horse or vehicle; dismount; alight **2** to come to rest after traveling through the air [ducks *lighting* on the pond] **3** to come or happen (*on* or *upon*) by chance **4** to fall or strike suddenly, as a blow —**light in the head 1** dizzy; giddy **2** simple; foolish —☆**light into** [Informal] **1** to attack **2** to scold; berate —☆**light out** [Informal] to depart suddenly —**make light of** to treat as trifling or unimportant; pay little or no attention to —**light′ish** *adj.*

light adaptation the automatic adaptive response of the eye as it accommodates itself to brighter light

light air a wind whose speed is 1 to 3 miles per hour: see the Beaufort scale in the Reference Supplement

light-armed (līt′ärmd′) *adj.* bearing light weapons

☆**light bread** [Chiefly South] bread made of wheat flour with yeast as a leavening agent

light breeze *Meteorol.* a wind whose speed is 4 to 7 miles per hour: see the Beaufort scale in the Reference Supplement

light·bulb (līt′bulb′) *n.* any device, consisting of a filament, gas, etc. within a glass bulb or tube, for producing artificial light by means of an electric current; specif., an INCANDESCENT LAMP: often used metaphorically for a moment of illumination, recognition, etc.

light-e·mit·ting diode (līt′ē mit′iŋ, -ə mit′-) LED

light·en[1] (līt′'n) *vt.* ⟦ME *lightnen*⟧ **1** to make light or bright; illuminate **2** to make light or pale **3** to cause to flash in or as in lightning: with *out* or *forth* **4** [Archaic] to give knowledge to; enlighten —*vi.* **1** to become light; grow brighter **2** to shine brightly; flash **3** to give off flashes of lightning —*SYN.* RELIEVE —**light′en·er** *n.*

light·en[2] (līt′'n) *vt.* ⟦ME *lihtnen*⟧ **1** *a)* to make lighter in weight *b)* to make less heavy; reduce the load of **2** to make less severe, harsh, or troublesome **3** to make more cheerful; gladden —*vi.* **1** to become lighter in weight **2** to become more cheerful —**lighten up** [Informal] to become less serious, angry, worried, concerned, etc.; take it easy —**light′en·er** *n.*

light·er[1] (līt′ər) *n.* a person or thing, as a mechanical or electrical device, that lights something or starts it burning [a cigarette *lighter*, charcoal *lighter*]

light·er[2] (līt′ər) *n.* ⟦LME < MDu *lichter* < *lichten*, to make light, unload < *licht*, LIGHT[2]⟧ a large, open barge used chiefly to load or unload ships anchored in a harbor —*vt., vi.* to transport (goods) in a lighter

light·er·age (-ər ij) *n.* **1** the loading or unloading of a ship, or transportation of goods, by means of a lighter, or barge **2** the charge for this

light·er-than-air (līt′ər *th*an er′) *adj.* designating or of an airship or a balloon designed to be aloft by means of a gas, as hydrogen or helium, that is lighter than air

light·face (līt′fās′) *n.* a printing type having thin, light lines —*adj.* set or printed in lightface: also **light′faced′**

light·fast (līt′fast′) *adj.* that will not fade because of exposure to light —**light′fast′ness** *n.*

light-fin·gered (līt′fiŋ′gərd) *adj.* **1** having a light, delicate touch **2** *a)* skillful at stealing, esp. by picking pockets *b)* thievish —**light′-fin′gered·ness** *n.*

light-foot·ed (-foot′id) *adj.* stepping lightly and gracefully; nimble of foot: also [Old Poet.] **light′-foot′** —**light′-foot′ed·ly** *adv.* —**light′-foot′ed·ness** *n.*

light guide a hair-thin, fiber-optic cable: also written **light′guide′** *n.*

light-hand·ed (-han′did) *adj.* **1** having a light, delicate touch **2** having little to carry

light·head·ed (-hed′id) *adj.* **1** mentally confused or feeling giddy; dizzy **2** not sensible; flighty; frivolous —**light′head′ed·ly** *adv.* —**light′head′ed·ness** *n.*

light·heart·ed (-härt′id) *adj.* free from care; cheerful; carefree —**light′heart′ed·ly** *adv.* —**light′heart′ed·ness** *n.*

☆**light heavyweight** a boxer between a super middleweight and a cruiserweight, with a maximum weight of 175 pounds (79.38 kg)

light horse light-armed cavalry —**light′-horse′man** (-hôrs′mən) *n., pl.* **-men** (-mən)

light·house (līt′hous′) *n.* a tower marking some place that is dangerous or important to navigation: typically a very bright light is beamed from its top and often it is equipped with foghorns, sirens, etc., by which ships are guided or warned

light·ing (līt′iŋ) *n.* **1** a giving light or being lighted; illumination; ignition **2** the distribution of light and shade, as in a painting **3** *a)* the art, practice, or manner of using and arranging lights on a stage, film or TV set, etc. *b)* these lights collectively

light·ly (līt′lē) *adv.* **1** with little weight, pressure, or motion; gently **2** to a small degree or amount [to spend *lightly*] **3** nimbly; deftly **4** cheerfully; merrily **5** *a)* with indifference or neglect *b)* so as to slight **6** with little or no reason **7** with little or no punishment [to let someone off *lightly*] **8** [Obs.] with ease; readily —**take lightly** to regard or treat as unimportant, slight, easy, etc.

light meter EXPOSURE METER

light-mind·ed (līt′mīn′did) *adj.* not serious; frivolous —**light′-mind′ed·ly** *adv.* —**light′-mind′ed·ness** *n.*

light·ness[1] (līt′nis) *n.* **1** the state, quality, or intensity of lighting; brightness **2** *a)* the state of being nearer to white than to black; paleness *b)* the relative amount of light reflected by an object ranging from black to white or colorless

light·ness[2] (līt′nis) *n.* **1** the state of being light, not heavy **2** mildness, nimbleness, delicacy, cheerfulness, lack of seriousness, etc.

light·ning (līt′niŋ) *n.* ⟦ME *lightninge* < *lightnen*, to LIGHTEN[1]⟧ **1** a flash, or series of flashes, of light in the sky caused by the discharge of atmospheric electricity from one cloud to another or between a cloud and the earth **2** such a discharge of electricity —*vi.* to give off such a discharge —*adj.* like lightning, as in being rapid or instantaneous [a cat's *lightning* reflexes]

☆**lightning arrester** a device that protects electronic or electrical equipment from lightning by diverting any surges of high-voltage electricity caused by atmospheric discharges to a ground

☆**lightning bug** (*or* **beetle**) FIREFLY

☆**lightning rod 1** a tall metal pole placed high on a structure, as a building or tower, and attached to a ground so as to attract lightning and protect the structure from damage **2** a person or thing that attracts controversy, strong feelings, etc. and diverts them from some other potential object or target

light opera a short, comic musical play; operetta

☆**light pen** a hand-held, pen-shaped electronic device used to scan images, draw lines, designate points, etc. as on a computer video screen

light pollution unwanted light in the night sky, as from city lights, that makes it more difficult for astronomers to see and photograph celestial objects

light·proof (līt′pro͞of′) *adj.* that does not admit light

light quantum PHOTON

light reaction the photochemical phase of photosynthesis, in which light energy is converted and stored biochemically in the form of ATP: cf. DARK REACTION

lights (līts) *pl.n.* ⟦ME *lihtes* < *liht*, LIGHT[2]: so called from being lighter in weight than the rest of the body: cf. LUNG⟧ [Dial.] the lungs of animals, as sheep, hogs, or cattle, used as food

light·ship (līt′ship′) *n.* a ship moored in a place dangerous or important to navigation and bearing a light or lights and foghorns, sirens, etc. by which ships are warned or guided

☆**light show** a display of moving, changing patterns of colored light, images, etc. projected as in a darkened auditorium, often as an accompaniment to rock music

light·some[1] (līt′səm) *adj.* ⟦ME *lihtsum*: see LIGHT[2] & -SOME[1]⟧ **1** nimble, buoyant, graceful, or lively **2** lighthearted; cheerful or merry **3** not serious; frivolous

light·some[2] (līt′səm) *adj.* ⟦ME *lyghtesum*: see LIGHT[1] & -SOME[1]⟧ [Archaic] **1** giving light; luminous **2** well-lighted; bright

lights out 1 a signal, as in a military camp, etc., to extinguish lights at bedtime **2** bedtime **3** [Slang] of or giving an overmastering performance [their pitcher was *lights out* in the final innings]

light-struck (līt′struk′) *adj. Photog.* damaged or fogged by being exposed to light accidentally

light verse VERSE (*n.* 2*a*) characterized by humor and a lightness of tone

light·wave (līt′wāv′) *adj.* of or designating a communications system, equipment, etc. using fiber optics

light·weight (līt′wāt′) *n.* **1** one below normal weight **2** a boxer between a junior lightweight and a junior welterweight, with a maximum weight of 135 pounds (61.24 kg) ☆**3** [Informal] a person of limited influence, intelligence, or competence —*adj.* **1** light in weight **2** of lightweights **3** not serious or profound; not deep; insignificant, shallow, etc.

light whiskey ☆a light-colored, mild whiskey aged in new or used casks for not less than four years

light·wood (-wood′) *n.* [Chiefly South] **1** very dry wood ☆**2** ⟦LIGHT[1] (*n.* or *vt.*) + WOOD[1]⟧ dry, resinous pine wood that burns readily with a bright light

light-year (-yir′) *n.* **1** *Astron.* a unit of distance equal to the distance that light travels in a vacuum in one year, *c.* 9,460,000,000,000 km (5,880,000,000,000 mi): abbrev. *lt-yr* or *ly*: cf. PARSEC **2** a very great distance, amount of time, etc.: *usually used in pl.* [*light-years* ahead in basic research] Also written **light year**

lign·al·oes (lī nal′ōz, lig-) *n.* ⟦ME *ligne aloes* < OFr *lignaloë* < ML *lignum aloës*, wood of aloe: see fol. & ALOE⟧ the resinous wood of various tropical trees containing an oil used in perfumes, soaps, foods, etc.

lig·ne·ous (lig′nē əs) *adj.* ⟦L *ligneus* < *lignum*, wood < **legnom*, collected wood < base of *legere*, to collect: see LOGIC⟧ of, or having the nature of, wood; woody

lig·ni- (lig′ni, -nə) ⟦< L *lignum*: see prec.⟧ *combining form* wood [*lignify*]: also **ligno-** (-nō, -nə) or, before a vowel, **lign-**

lig·ni·fy (lig′ni fī′) *vt.* **-fied′**, **-fy′ing** ⟦prec. + -FY⟧ to make into wood —*vi.* to become wood or like wood as a result of the depositing of lignin in the cell walls —**lig′ni·fi·ca′tion** *n.*

lig·nin (lig′nin) ***n.*** ⟦LIGN(I)- + -IN[1]⟧ an amorphous, cellulose-like substance which acts as a binder for the cellulose fibers in wood and certain plants and adds strength and stiffness to the cell walls

lig·nite (lig′nīt′) ***n.*** ⟦Fr: see LIGNEOUS & -ITE[1]⟧ a usually soft, brownish-black coal in which the texture of the original wood can often still be seen: in the process of coalification it represents the intermediate stage in density and amount of carbon between peat and bituminous coal —**lig·nit′ic** (-nit′ik) ***adj.***

lig·no·cel·lu·lose (lig′nō sel′yo͞o lōs′) ***n.*** ⟦LIGNO- (var. of LIGNI-) + CELLULOSE⟧ any of several combinations of lignin and hemicellulose, forming the essential part of woody tissue —**lig′no·cel′lu·lo′sic** (-lō′sik) ***adj.***

lig·num vi·tae (lig′nəm vīt′ē, -vēt′ī) ⟦ModL < L *lignum*, wood (see LIGNEOUS) + *vitae*, gen. of *vita*, life: see BIO-⟧ **1** GUAIACUM (sense 1) **2** *Commerce* the very hard wood of the guaiacum, used in marine and machine bearings, casters, pulleys, etc.

lig·ro·in (lig′rō in) ***n.*** ⟦arbitrary coinage, prob. < Gr *liguros*, clear + -IN[1]⟧ a mixture of hydrocarbons, a colorless, flammable liquid, obtained in the fractional distillation of petroleum and used as a motor fuel and as a solvent for fats and oils in dry cleaning, etc.

lig·u·la (lig′yo͞o lə) ***n.***, *pl.* **-lae′** (-lē′) or **-las** ⟦see LIGULE⟧ *Zool.* a structure containing typically the terminal lobes of the labium of an insect

lig·u·late (-lit, -lāt′) ***adj.*** **1** of or having ligules **2** shaped like a strap

lig·ule (lig′yo͞ol) ***n.*** ⟦L *ligula*, a spoon, tongue of a shoe, shoe strap < IE base **leiǧh-*, to lick > MIr *liag*, LICK: infl. by assoc. with L *lingua*, tongue, *ligare*, to bind⟧ **1** a strap-shaped corolla in the flowers of certain composite plants **2** a thin membrane attached to a leaf of grass at the point where the blade meets the leaf sheath **3** any of various similar appendages on other plants

lig·ure (lig′yoor) ***n.*** ⟦LL(Ec) *ligurius* < Gr(Ec) *ligyrion*⟧ *Bible* one of the twelve precious stones in the breastplate of the Jewish high priest, thought to be yellow HYACINTH (sense 1*b*): Ex. 28:19

Li·gu·ri·a (li gyoor′ē ə) region of NW Italy, on the Ligurian Sea: 2,093 sq mi (5,421 sq km); chief city, Genoa —**Li·gu′ri·an** ***adj., n.***

Ligurian Sea part of the Mediterranean, between Corsica & NW Italy

lik·a·ble (līk′ə bəl) ***adj.*** having qualities that inspire liking; easy to like because attractive, pleasant, genial, etc. —**lik′a·ble·ness** ***n.***, **lik′a·bil′i·ty**

Li·ka·si (li käs′ē) city in the SE Democratic Republic of the Congo

like[1] (līk) ***adj.*** ⟦ME *lik*, aphetic for *ilik* < OE *gelic*, similar, equal, lit., of the same form or shape, akin to Ger *gleich* < PGmc **galīka-* < **ga-*, prefix of uncert. meaning + **līka*, body, (ON *līk*, Goth *leik*, OE *lic*): for IE base see LICH⟧ **1** having almost or exactly the same qualities, characteristics, etc.; similar; equal [*a cup of sugar and a like amount of flour*] **2** [Rare] alike **3** [Dial.] likely —***adv.*** [Informal] likely [*like as not, he is already there*] —***prep.*** **1** similar to; somewhat resembling [*she is like a bird*] **2** in a manner characteristic of; similarly to [*she sings like a bird*] **3** in accord with the nature of; characteristic of [*it's not like her to sleep late*] **4** in the mood for; desirous of [*to feel like sleeping*] **5** indicative or prophetic of [*that sounds like fun; it looks like a clear day tomorrow*] **6** as for example [*great dramatists like Sophocles and Shakespeare*] ➥*Like* was originally an adjective in ***prep.*** senses 1, 3, 5, and an adverb in sense 2, and is still considered so by conservative grammarians —***conj.*** [Informal] **1** in the way that; as [*it was just like you said*] **2** as if [*it looks like he is late*] —***n.*** a person or thing regarded as the equal or counterpart of another or of the person or thing being discussed [*I've never met her like*] —***interj.*** [Informal] inserted into spoken sentences before or after a word, phrase, or clause, apparently without meaning or syntactic function, but possibly for emphasis [*it's, like, hot*] —**and the like** and so forth; et cetera —**be like** [Slang] to say, think, or feel [*so I'm like, "We have to be there on time," and he's like all nervous*] —**like anything** [Informal] very much; exceedingly —**(as) like as not** most likely; probably —**like blazes (**or **crazy** or **the devil, mad,** etc.**)** [Informal] with furious energy, speed, etc. —**like to** [Dial.] nearly; almost [*he like to broke the door down*] —**more like it** [Informal] closer to being what is wanted or needed —**nothing like** not at all like; completely different from —**something like** almost like; about —**the like** others of the same kind —**the like (**or **likes) of** [Informal] any person or thing of a type like

like[2] (līk) ***vi.*** **liked**, **lik′ing** ⟦ME *liken* < OE *lician* (akin to Goth *leikan*) < base of *lic*, body, form (see prec.): sense development: to be of like form → be like → be suited to → be pleasing to⟧ **1** [Obs.] to please **2** to be so inclined; choose [*leave whenever you like*] —***vt.*** **1** to have a taste or fondness for; be pleased with; have a preference for; enjoy **2** to want or wish [*I would like to see him*] **3** [Informal] to favor and support as the probable winner [*I like Chicago in the World Series*] —***n.*** [*pl.*] preferences, tastes, or affections —**lik′er** ***n.***

-like (līk) ⟦< LIKE[1]⟧ *suffix* **1** *forming adjectives* like, characteristic of, suitable for [*doglike, manlike, homelike*] **2** *forming adverbs* in the manner of [*coward-like*] Words formed with *-like* are sometimes hyphenated and are always hyphenated when three *l's* fall together [*bull-like*]

like·a·ble (līk′ə bəl) ***adj.*** *alt. sp. of* LIKABLE

like·li·hood (līk′lē hood′) ***n.*** ⟦ME *liklihode*: see fol. & -HOOD⟧ **1** the fact of being likely to happen; probability **2** something that is likely to happen

like·ly (līk′lē) ***adj.*** **-li·er**, **-li·est** ⟦ME *likly*, prob. aphetic < OE *geliclic* (or < ? ON *likligr*): see LIKE[1] & -LY[1]⟧ **1** apparently true to the facts; credible; probable [*a likely cause*]: often used to express skepticism [*a likely story!*] **2** seeming as if it would happen or might happen; reasonably to be expected; apparently destined [*it is likely to rain*] **3** such as will probably be satisfactory or rewarding; suitable [*a likely choice for the job*] **4** having good prospects; promising [*a likely lad*] **5** [Dial.] attractive; agreeable —***adv.*** **-li·er**, **-li·est** probably [*she will very likely go*]

SYN.—**likely** suggests probability or an eventuality that can reasonably be expected [*he's not likely to win*]; **liable** and **apt** are loosely or informally used equivalents of **likely**, but in strict discrimination, **liable** implies exposure or susceptibility to something undesirable [*you're liable to be killed if you play with firearms*] and **apt** suggests a natural or habitual inclination or tendency [*such people are always apt to be fearful*]; **prone** also suggests a propensity or predisposition to something that seems almost inevitable [*she's prone to have accidents*] —*ANT.* **unlikely, indisposed**

like-mind·ed (līk′mīn′did) ***adj.*** having the same opinions, tastes, etc.; agreeing mentally —**like′-mind′ed·ly** ***adv.*** —**like′-mind′ed·ness** ***n.***

lik·en (līk′ən) ***vt.*** to represent or describe as being like, or similar (*to*); compare

like·ness (līk′nis) ***n.*** **1** the state or quality of being like; similarity **2** (the same) form or shape; semblance [*Zeus appeared in the likeness of a swan*] **3** something that is like; copy, portrait, etc.

SYN.—**likeness** implies close correspondence in appearance, qualities, nature, etc. [*his remarkable likeness to his brother*]; **similarity** suggests only partial correspondence [*your problem bears a certain similarity to mine*]; **resemblance** usually implies correspondence in appearance or in superficial aspects [*the resemblance between a diamond and zircon*]; **analogy** refers to a correspondence between attributes or circumstances of things that are basically unlike [*the analogy between a calculating machine and the human brain*] —*ANT.* **unlikeness, difference**

like·wise (līk′wīz′) ***adv.*** ⟦short for *in like wise*⟧ **1** in the same manner **2** also; too; moreover

lik·ing (līk′iŋ) ***n.*** ⟦ME < OE *licung* < *lician*: see LIKE[2]⟧ **1** fondness; affection **2** preference or taste [*not to my liking*]

li·ku·ta (lē ko͞o′tä) ***n.***, *pl.* **ma·ku′ta** (mä-) ⟦Kongo⟧ a monetary unit of the Democratic Republic of the Congo, equal to $\frac{1}{100}$ of a zaire

li·lac (lī′lak′, -läk′, -lək) ***n.*** ⟦Fr (now *lilas*) < Ar *līlak* < Pers *līlak, nīlak*, bluish < *nīl*, indigo < Sans *nila*, dark blue, indigo⟧ **1** any of a genus (*Syringa*) of hardy shrubs or trees of the olive family, with large clusters of tiny, fragrant flowers ranging in color from white, through many shades of lavender, to deep crimson **2** the flower of this plant **3** pale purple —***adj.*** of a pale-purple color

li·lan·gen·i (li′läŋ gen′ē) ***n.***, *pl.* **em′a·lan·gen′i** (em′ə-) ⟦< name in a local Bantu language, lit., royal⟧ the basic monetary unit of Swaziland: see the table of monetary units in the Reference Supplement

lil·ied (lil′ēd) ***adj.*** [Old Poet.] decorated or covered with lilies

Lil·ith (lil′ith) ***n.*** ⟦Heb *līlīth* < Assyr-Bab *lilītu*, lit., of the night⟧ **1** in ancient Semitic folklore, a female demon or vampire that lives in desolate places **2** *Jewish Folklore a)* the first wife of Adam, before the creation of Eve *b)* a night witch who menaces infants

Li·li·u·o·ka·la·ni (li lē′o͞o ō′kä lä′nē), **Lydia Ka·me·ke·ha** (kä′mā kā′hä) 1838-1917; queen of the Hawaiian Islands (1891-93)

Lille (lēl) city in N France

Lil·li·an (lil′ē ən) ***n.*** ⟦earlier *Lilion*, prob. < L *lilium*, lily⟧ a feminine name: dim. *Lil, Lilly, Lily*; var. *Lilian*

Lil·li·put (lil′ə put′, -pət) ***n.*** in Swift's *Gulliver's Travels*, a land inhabited by tiny people about six inches tall

Lil·li·pu·tian (lil′ə pyo͞o′shən) ***adj.*** **1** of Lilliput or its people **2** very small; tiny **3** narrow-minded; petty —***n.*** **1** an inhabitant of Lilliput **2** a very small person **3** a narrow-minded person

Li·long·we (li lôŋ′wā) capital of Malawi, in the W part

lilt (lilt) ***vt., vi.*** ⟦ME *lilten, lulten*, prob. of echoic orig.⟧ to sing, speak, play, or move with a light, graceful rhythm or swing —***n.*** **1** a merry song or tune with a light, swingy, and graceful rhythm **2** a light and graceful rhythm or movement —**lilt′ing** ***adj.*** —**lilt′ing·ly** ***adv.***

lil·y (lil′ē) ***n.***, *pl.* **lil′ies** ⟦ME *lilie* < OE < L *lilium*⟧ **1** any of a large genus (*Lilium*) of perennial plants of the lily family, grown from a bulb and having typically trumpet-shaped flowers, white or colored **2** the flower or the bulb of any of these plants **3** any of several plants similar to the true lily, as the waterlily **4** the flower of any of these plants **5** the heraldic fleur-de-lis, as in the royal arms of France —***adj.*** **1** designating a family (Liliaceae, order Liliales) of monocotyledonous, usually herbaceous, plants, including the tulips, hyacinths, onions, and asparagus **2** like a lily, as in whiteness, delicacy, etc.

Lil·y (lil′ē) ***n.*** ⟦dim. of *Lillian* or < prec.⟧ a feminine name

lil·y-liv·ered (lil′ē liv′ərd) ***adj.*** ⟦first recorded in SHAKESPEARE's *Macbeth*, V, iii (1605): see WHITE-LIVERED⟧ cowardly; timid

lily of the valley *pl.* **lilies of the valley** ⟦transl. of LL(Ec) *lilium convallium* in S. of Sol. 2:1 (Vulg)⟧ a perennial plant (*Convallaria majalis*) of the lily family, that grows in the shade and has a single pair of basal, oblong leaves and a single leafless raceme of very fragrant, small, white, bell-shaped flowers

☆**lily pad** one of the large, flat, floating leaves of the waterlily

lil·y-white (-hwīt′, -wīt′) ***adj.*** **1** white as a lily **2** innocent and pure; unsullied: often used sarcastically ☆**3** made up entirely or predominantly of white people: usually used disparagingly to connote discrimination against or segregation from nonwhites, esp. blacks

lily of the valley

LIM *abbrev.* linear (induction) motor

Li·ma (lē′mə) capital of Peru, in the WC part

li·ma bean (lī′mə) ⟦after prec.: from being native to tropical America⟧ [*also* **L- b-**] **1** a common variety of bean (*Phaseolus limensis*), with creamy flowers and broad pods **2** the broad, flat, nutritious seed of this plant

lim·a·cine (lim′ə sīn′, lī′mə-; -sin) *adj.* ⟦ModL *limacinus* < L *limax* (gen. *limacis*), a slug < IE **leimāk*, snail (> Gr *leimax*) < base *(*s*)*lei-*, SLIME⟧ of or like slugs or shell-less snails: also **li·mac·i·form** (lī mas′ə fôrm′)

limb[1] (lim) *n.* ⟦with unhistoric *-b* < ME *lim* < OE, akin to ON *limr*, limb < IE base *(*e*)*lei-*, to bend > EL(BOW)⟧ **1** a part that extends from the trunk of a body, as an arm, leg, or wing **2** a large branch of a tree **3** any projecting part forming an outgrowth or extension from a larger body **4** a person or thing regarded as a branch, part, agent, or representative [*a policeman is a limb of the law*] **5** [Old Informal] a naughty child —*vt.* [Rare] to dismember; disjoint —☆**out on a limb** [Informal] in a precarious or vulnerable position or situation —**limb′less** *adj.*

limb[2] (lim) *n.* ⟦Fr *limbe*, orig., limbo < ML(Ec) *limbus* < L: see LIMBO[1]⟧ **1** a border, margin, or edge **2** *Astron.* the apparent outer edge of a celestial object **3** *Bot.* the spreading outer portion of the corolla of certain flowers

lim·bate (lim′bāt′) *adj.* ⟦LL *limbatus* < L *limbus*: see LIMBO[1]⟧ having a distinct border or edging, as of a color different from the main part of a plant

limbed (limd) *adj.* having (a specified number or kind of) limbs [*straight-limbed, four-limbed*]

lim·ber[1] (lim′bər) *adj.* ⟦< ? LIMB[1]⟧ **1** easily bent; flexible; pliant **2** able to bend the body easily; supple; lithe —*vt.* to make limber [*to limber the fingers*] —*vi.* to make oneself limber, as by exercises: usually with *up* —**lim′ber·ness** *n.*

lim·ber[2] (lim′bər) *n.* ⟦ME *lymour* < ? ML *limonarius*, of the shaft of a cart < *limo*, shaft < ?⟧ the two-wheeled, detachable front part of a gun carriage, usually supporting an ammunition chest — *vt., vi.* to attach the limber to (a gun carriage), as in preparing to move off: often with *up*

lim·bers (lim′bərz) *pl.n.* ⟦prob. < Fr *lumière*, a hole, aperture, lit., light < VL *luminaria*, orig. pl. of L *luminare*, a light, window: see LUMINARY⟧ *Naut.* holes in the lower part of a vessel's frames to allow bilge water to drain to the pump

lim·bic system (lim′bik) ⟦< Fr *limbique* < L *limbus*, an edge, border: see fol.⟧ a primitive part of the brain near the brain stem, thought to control emotions, behavior, smell, etc.

lim·bo[1] (lim′bō) *n., pl.* for 2 & 3 **lim′bos** ⟦ME < L, abl. of *limbus*, edge, border (in *in limbo*, in or on the border) < IE *(*s*)*lemb-*, to hand down: see LIMP[1]⟧ **1** [*usually* **L-**] in some Christian theologies, the eternal abode or state, neither heaven nor hell, of the souls of infants or others dying in original sin but free of grievous personal sin, or, before the coming of Christ, the temporary abode or state of all holy souls after death **2** any intermediate, indeterminate state **3** a place or condition of confinement, neglect, or oblivion

lim·bo[2] (lim′bō) *n., pl.* **-bos** ⟦prob. altered < LIMBER[1]⟧ a dance, originated in the West Indies, in which the dancers bend from the knees as far back as possible to pass beneath a horizontal bar that is set lower and lower

Lim·burg (lim′burg′) **1** province of NE Belgium: 935 sq mi (2,422 sq km); cap. Hasselt: also **Limbourg** (*Fr* lan bo͞or′) **2** province of SE Netherlands: 848 sq mi (2,196 sq km); cap. Maastricht **3** former duchy occupying the general area of these two provinces

Lim·burg·er (cheese) (lim′bur′gər) a semisoft cheese of whole milk, with a strong odor and flavor, made originally in Limburg, Belgium: also **Lim′burg′ (cheese)**

lim·bus (lim′bəs) *n., pl.* **-bi′** (-bī′) ⟦L: see LIMBO[1]⟧ a distinct border or edging, as of a bodily organ or structure

lime[1] (līm) *n.* ⟦ME < OE *līm*, akin to Ger *leim* < IE base *(*s*)*lei-*, SLIME, wet and sticky, to smooth over > Gr *leios*, smooth, L *limus*, slime, mud, *linere*, to smear, *levis*, smooth, OE *lam*, clay⟧ **1** *short for* BIRDLIME **2** a white substance, calcium oxide, CaO, obtained by the action of heat on limestone, shells, and other material containing calcium carbonate, and used in making mortar and cement, and, when hydrated, in neutralizing acid soil **3** a calcareous deposit from water inside pipes, pans, etc. —*vt.* **limed, lim′ing 1** to cement **2** to smear with birdlime **3** to catch with or as with birdlime **4** to apply lime to; treat with lime

lime[2] (līm) *n.* ⟦Fr < Prov *limo* < Ar *līmah* < *līm*, citrus fruit > LEMON⟧ **1** a small, lemon-shaped, greenish-yellow citrus fruit with a juicy, sour pulp, rich in ascorbic acid **2** the small, thorny, semitropical citrus tree (*Citrus aurantifolia*) that it grows on, originally native to S Asia **3** greenish yellow —*adj.* **1** made with or of limes **2** having a flavor like that of limes **3** greenish-yellow

lime[3] (līm) *n.* ⟦< earlier *line* < ME *lind*: see LINDEN⟧ LINDEN

☆**lime·ade** (līm′ād′) *n.* a drink made of lime juice, sweetening, and water

lime burner a person who burns limestone, shells, etc. to make lime

Lime·house (līm′hous′) district in the E London borough of Tower Hamlets, on the Thames: former Chinese quarter

lime·kiln (līm′kil′, -kiln′) *n.* a furnace in which limestone, shells, etc. are reduced to lime by burning

lime·light (-līt′) *n.* ⟦< LIME[1] (*n.* 2)⟧ **1** a brilliant light created by the incandescence of lime (calcium oxide), formerly used in theaters to throw an intense beam of light upon a particular part of the stage, a certain actor, etc. **2** the part of a stage where a limelight or spotlight is cast **3** a prominent or conspicuous position before the public

li·men (lī′mən) *n., pl.* **li′mens** or **lim·i·na** (lim′i nə) ⟦L *limen* (gen. *liminis*), threshold, akin to *limes*, border, frontier: used as transl. of Ger *schwelle*⟧ *Physiol., Psychol.* THRESHOLD

lim·er·ick (lim′ər ik, lim′rik) *n.* ⟦prob. < Ir refrain containing the name: see fol.⟧ a nonsense poem of five anapestic lines, now often bawdy, usually with the rhyme scheme aabba, the first, second, and fifth lines having three stresses, the third and fourth having two: the form was popularized by Edward Lear (Ex.: There was a young lady named Harris, | Whom nothing could ever embarrass | Till the bath salts one day | In the tub where she lay | Turned out to be plaster of Paris)

Lim·er·ick (lim′ər ik, lim′rik) **1** county in SW Ireland, in Munster province: 1,037 sq mi (2,686 sq km) **2** its county seat

lime·stone (līm′stōn′) *n.* a sedimentary rock consisting mainly of calcium carbonate, often composed of the organic remains of sea animals, as mollusks, corals, etc., and used as building stone, a source of lime, etc.: when crystallized by heat and pressure it becomes marble

lime sulfur solution made by boiling together sulfur, water, and lime: used as an insecticide and fungicide

lime twig 1 a twig smeared with birdlime to snare birds **2** any kind of snare

lime·wa·ter (līm′wôt′er) *n.* a solution of calcium hydroxide in water, used to neutralize acids and to absorb carbon dioxide from the air

☆**lim·ey** (līm′ē) [Slang] *n.* ⟦from the LIME[2] juice formerly served to the crew on British ships to prevent scurvy⟧ **1** an English sailor or, sometimes, soldier **2** an Englishman —*adj.* British

li·mic·o·line (lī mik′ə līn′, -lin) *adj.* ⟦< LL *limicola*, mud dweller < L *limus*, mud (see LIME[1]) + *colere*, to dwell (see CULT) + -INE[1]⟧ inhabiting the shore; specif., designating or of a shorebird

li·mic·o·lous (-ləs) *adj.* ⟦< L *limicola* (see prec.) + -OUS⟧ living in mud

lim·i·nal (lim′i nəl, lī′mi-) *adj.* **1** *Physiol., Psychol.* of or at the limen, or threshold **2** at a boundary or transitional point between two conditions, stages in a process, ways of life, etc. —**lim′i·nal′i·ty** *n.*

lim·it (lim′it) *n.* ⟦OFr *limite* < L *limes* (gen. *limitis*), border, frontier⟧ **1** the point, line, or edge where something ends or must end; boundary or border beyond which something ceases to be or to be possible **2** [*pl.*] bounds; boundary lines **3** the greatest number or amount allowed [*to catch the limit for a day of trout fishing*] **4** the maximum amount which may be bet, or by which a bet may be raised, at one time, as in poker **5** LEGAL LIMIT **6** *Math.* a fixed quantity or value which a varying quantity is regarded as approaching indefinitely —*vt.* ⟦ME *limiten* < OFr *limiter* < L *limitare*⟧ to confine within bounds; set a limit to; restrict; curb —**the limit** ☆[Informal] any person or thing regarded as unbearable, remarkable, etc. to an extreme degree —**lim′it·a·ble** *adj.* —**lim′it·er** *n.*

SYN.—**limit** implies the prescribing of a point in space, time, or extent, beyond which it is impossible or forbidden to go [*limit your response to 25 words*]; **bound** implies an enclosing in boundaries or borders [*a meadow bounded by hills*]; **restrict** implies a boundary that completely encloses and connotes a restraining within these bounds [*the soldier was restricted to the camp area*]; **circumscribe** emphasizes more strongly the cutting off or isolation of that which is within the bounds [*he leads the circumscribed life of a monk*]; **confine** stresses the restraint or hampering of enclosing limits [*confined in jail*] —*ANT.* **widen, expand**

lim·i·tar·y (lim′i ter′ē) *adj.* ⟦L *limitaris*⟧ **1** [Now Rare] serving as a limit or boundary **2** [Archaic] limited; restricted

lim·i·ta·tion (lim′i tā′shən) *n.* ⟦ME *limitacioun* < OFr *limitacion* < L *limitatio*⟧ **1** a limiting or being limited **2** something that limits, as some factor in makeup which restricts the scope of a person's activity or accomplishment; qualification **3** *Law* a period of time, fixed by statute, during which legal action can be brought, as for settling a claim

lim·i·ta·tive (lim′i tāt′iv) *adj.* ⟦Fr *limitatif* < ML *limitativus*⟧ limiting; restrictive

lim·it·ed (lim′it id) *adj.* **1** *a)* confined within bounds; restricted *b)* circumscribed or narrow in scope or extent *c)* brief; very short [*a limited time*] ☆**2** accommodating a restricted number of passengers, making fewer stops than on the regular runs, and often charging extra fare: said of a train, bus, etc. **3** exercising governmental powers under constitutional restrictions; not having absolute power [*a limited monarchy*] **4** *a)* of or designating a partnership in which the liability of certain of its partners is limited to the amount of their individual investments *b)* [Chiefly Brit.] designating a company in which the liability of its shareholders is similarly restricted —☆*n.* a limited train, bus, etc. —**lim′it·ed·ly** *adv.* —**lim′it·ed·ness** *n.*

limited access highway EXPRESSWAY

limited edition 1 a special, finely bound edition of a book, of which only a predetermined number of copies are printed ☆**2** a set of collectible items, as of dolls, plates, coins, etc., of which only a given number are made

lim·it·ing (lim′it iŋ) *adj.* **1** that limits **2** *Gram.* designating or of any of a class of adjectives that limit or specify the range of application of the noun modified (Ex.: *this, several, any*)

limiting factor an environmental factor that limits the growth or activities of an organism or that restricts the size of a population or its geographical range

lim·it·less (-lis) *adj.* without limits; unbounded; vast; infinite —**lim′it·less·ly** *adv.* —**lim′it·less·ness** *n.*

li·miv·o·rous (lī miv′ə rəs) *adj.* ⟦< L *limus*, mud, slime (see LIME[1]) + -VOROUS⟧ eating mud or earth for the organic matter in it, as earthworms do

limn (lim) *vt.* **limned, limn·ing** (lim′iŋ, -niŋ) ⟦ME *limnen,* contr. < *luminen,* for *enluminen* < OFr *enluminer* < L *illuminare,* ILLUMINATE⟧ **1** to paint or draw **2** to portray in words; describe **3** to outline or highlight **4** [Obs.] to illuminate (manuscripts) —**limn·er** (lim′ər, -nər) *n.*

lim·net·ic (lim net′ik) *adj.* ⟦< Gr *limnē,* marsh (see fol.) + E *-etic* < L or Gr: L *-eticus* < Gr *-etikos,* adj. suffix⟧ designating, of, or living in the open waters of lakes, away from shore vegetation

lim·nol·o·gy (lim näl′ə jē) *n.* ⟦< Gr *limnē,* marsh, akin to *leimōn* (see LIMONITE) + -LOGY⟧ the science that deals with the physical, chemical, and biological properties and features of fresh waters, esp. lakes and ponds —**lim′no·log′i·cal** (-nə läj′i kəl) *adj.* —**lim·nol′o·gist** *n.*

☆**lim·o** (lim′ō) *n., pl.* **lim′os** [Informal] LIMOUSINE

Li·moges[1] (lē mōzh′; *Fr* lē mȏzh′) *n.* fine porcelain made in Limoges, France: also **Limoges ware**

Li·moges[2] (lē mōzh′; *Fr* lē mȏzh′) city in WC France

lim·o·nene (lim′ə nēn′) *n.* ⟦< ModL *Limonum* (< Fr *limon,* LEMON) + -ENE⟧ any of three isomeric terpenes, $C_{10}H_{16}$, present in lemon peel, orange oil, pine needles, peppermint, etc.

li·mo·nite (lī′mə nīt′) *n.* ⟦< Gr *leimōn,* meadow, orig., low ground (for IE base see LIMB[1]) + -ITE[1]⟧ a brownish, amorphous mineral mixture of several iron oxides, esp. goethite, used as a coloring agent: sometimes an ore of iron: cf. YELLOW OCHER —**li′mo·nit′ic** (-nit′ik) *adj.*

Li·mou·sin (lē mo͞o zan′) **1** historical region of WC France, west of Auvergne **2** metropolitan region of modern France in the same general area: 6,541 sq mi (16,941 sq km); chief city, Limoges

lim·ou·sine (lim′ə zēn′, lim′ə zēn′) *n.* ⟦Fr, lit., cloak, cape: from the costume worn in prec.⟧ **1** a former kind of automobile with a closed compartment seating three or more passengers and the top extended forward over the driver's seat **2** any large, luxurious sedan, esp. one driven by a chauffeur and with a glass partition separating the driver and passengers ☆**3** a buslike sedan used to carry passengers to or from an airport, train station, etc.

☆**limousine liberal** a wealthy person who supports liberal political causes while enjoying a lifestyle regarded as contrary to such values or removed from the practical concerns of the average person

limp[1] (limp) *vi.* ⟦ME *lympen* < OE *limpan,* to befall, occur (in a specialized sense, "to walk lamely"), akin to MHG *limpfen,* to walk with a limp, OHG *limfan,* to befall, happen < IE *(*s*)*lemb-* < base **leb-,* to hang down, be limp > SLUMP, MHG *lumpe,* rag, L *labor, limbus*⟧ **1** to walk with or as with a lame or partially disabled leg or foot **2** to move or proceed unevenly, jerkily, or laboriously, as because of being impaired, defective, damaged, etc. —*n.* a halting gait or lameness in walking —**limp′er** *n.* —**limp′ing·ly** *adv.*

limp[2] (limp) *adj.* ⟦< base of prec., akin to MHG *lampen,* to hang limply⟧ **1** lacking or having lost stiffness or body; flaccid, drooping, wilted, etc. **2** lacking firmness, energy, or vigor **3** flexible, as the binding of some books —**limp′ly** *adv.* —**limp′ness** *n.*

limp·et (lim′pit) *n.* ⟦ME *lempet* < OE *lempedu* < ML *lempreda,* limpet, LAMPREY⟧ a gastropod mollusk of various families, mostly marine, with a single, low, cone-shaped shell and a thick, fleshy foot, by means of which it clings to rocks, timbers, etc.

lim·pid (lim′pid) *adj.* ⟦Fr *limpide* < L *limpidus,* altered (? from *liquidus,* LIQUID) < OL *limpa, lumpa,* water: see LYMPH⟧ **1** perfectly clear; transparent; not cloudy or turbid [*limpid* waters] **2** characterized by clarity and elegant simplicity [*limpid* prose] —**lim·pid′i·ty** *n.,* **lim′pid·ness** —**lim′pid·ly** *adv.*

☆**limp·kin** (limp′kin) *n.* ⟦LIMP[1] + -KIN: from its walk⟧ a gruiform bird (*Aramus guarauna*) of a family (Aramidae) with only one species, found in Florida, Central America, the West Indies, and South America

Lim·po·po (lim pō′pō) river in SE Africa, flowing from Northern Transvaal, South Africa, across Mozambique into the Indian Ocean: *c.* 1,000 mi (1,609 km)

limp·sy or **limp·sey** (limp′sē) *adj.* **-si·er, -si·est** [Dial.] limp, as from exhaustion or weakness

limp-wrist·ed (limp′ris′təd) *adj.* [Informal] **1** effeminate: a term of mild contempt **2** weak; soft; ineffectual

lim·u·lus (lim′yo͞o ləs) *n., pl.* **-li′** (-lī′) ⟦ModL < L *limulus,* dim. of *limus,* oblique + -OID⟧ HORSESHOE CRAB

lim·y (līm′ē) *adj.* **lim′i·er, lim′i·est** **1** covered with, consisting of, or like birdlime; sticky **2** of, like, or containing lime —**lim′i·ness** *n.*

lin·ac (lin′ak′) *n. short for* LINEAR ACCELERATOR

lin·age (līn′ij) *n.* **1** the number of written or printed lines on a page or in an article, advertisement, etc. **2** payment based on the number of lines produced by a writer

lin·al·o·ol (lin al′ō ôl′, -al′ə ōl′; lin′ə lo͞ol′) *n.* ⟦< MexSp *linaloa,* an aromatic Mexican wood (< Sp *lináloe* < ML *lignum aloës:* see LIGNALOES) + -OL[1]⟧ a terpene alcohol, $C_{10}H_{17}OH$, in several essential oils, used in perfumery

linch·pin (linch′pin′) *n.* ⟦ME *lynspin* < *lyns* (< OE *lynis,* linchpin, akin to Ger *lünse* < IE base *(*e*)*lei-* to bend > ELL[2], Sans *āṇīh,* linchpin) + *pin,* PIN⟧ **1** a pin that goes through the end of an axle outside the wheel to keep the wheel from coming off **2** anything or anyone regarded as crucial or essential

Lin·coln[1] (liŋ′kən) *n.* a breed of sheep with long wool: originally from Lincolnshire

Lin·coln[2] (liŋ′kən), **Abraham** 1809-65; 16th president of the U.S. (1861-65): assassinated —☆**Lin·coln·esque** (liŋ′kən esk′) *adj.* —☆**Lin·coln·i·an** (liŋ kō′nē ən) *adj.*

Lin·coln[3] (liŋ′kən) **1** ⟦after prec.⟧ capital of Nebr., in the SE part **2** LINCOLNSHIRE

Lin·coln·i·an·a (liŋ kō′nē an′ə, -än′ə) *pl.n.* books, papers, objects, etc. having to do with Abraham Lincoln

Lin·coln·shire (liŋ′kən shir′, -shər) county in NE England, on the North Sea: 2,286 sq mi (5,921 sq km)

Lincoln's Inn *see* INNS OF COURT

☆**lin·co·my·cin** (liŋ′kō mī′sin) *n.* ⟦(*Streptomyces*) *linco*(*lnensis*), the bacterium from which it is derived (orig. isolated from soil collected near LINCOLN[3], Nebr.) + MYC(O)- + -IN[1]⟧ an antibiotic drug, $C_{18}H_{34}N_2O_6S$, used in the treatment of various bacterial diseases, esp. those resistant to penicillin, and in treating persons with an allergy to penicillin

Lind (lind), **Jenny** (born *Johanna Maria Lind*) 1820-87; Swed. soprano: called the *Swedish Nightingale*

Lin·da (lin′də) *n.* a feminine name: var. *Lynda:* see BELINDA

lin·dane (lin′dān′) *n.* ⟦after T. van der *Linden,* 20th-c. Du chemist + -ANE⟧ an isomeric form of benzene hexachloride, used as an insecticide

Lind·bergh (lind′burg′), **Charles (Augustus)** 1902-74; U.S. aviator: made first nonstop solo flight from New York to Paris (1927)

lin·den (lin′dən) *n.* ⟦ME, adj. < OE < *lind,* linden, akin to Ger *linde:* popularized as n. via Ger *linden,* pl. of *linde:* prob. < IE base **lento-,* flexible, yielding > LITHE⟧ BASSWOOD —*adj.* designating a family (Tiliaceae) of chiefly tropical, dicotyledonous trees (order Malvales), including the jutes

Lind·say[1] (lin′zē, lind′-) *n.* a feminine or masculine name: var. *Lindsey*

Lind·say[2] (lin′zē, lind′-), **(Nicholas) Va·chel** (vā′chəl) 1879-1931; U.S. poet

☆**Lin·dy Hop** (lin′dē) ⟦so named from the transatlantic "*hop*" of Charles LINDBERGH (nicknamed "Lucky *Lindy*")⟧ [*also* **l- h-**] a lively dance for couples, popular in the early 1930s: also **Lin′dy** *n.*

line[1] (līn) *n.* ⟦ME form merging OE, a cord, with OFr *ligne* (both < L *linea,* lit., linen thread, n. use of fem. of *lineus,* of flax < *linum,* flax)⟧ **1** *a)* a cord, rope, wire, string, or the like *b)* a long, fine, strong cord with a hook, sinker, leader, etc., used in fishing *c)* a clothesline *d)* a cord, steel tape, etc. used in measuring or leveling *e)* a rope, hawser, or cable used on a ship *f)* a rein (*usually used in pl.*) ☆**2** *a)* a wire or wires connecting a telephone or telegraph system *b)* a system of such wires *c)* effective contact between telephones *d)* a telephone extension [call me on *line* 9] **3** any wire, pipe, system of pipes or wires, etc. for conducting water, gas, electricity, etc. **4** a very thin, threadlike mark; specif., *a)* a long, thin mark made by a pencil, pen, chalk, etc. *b)* a similar mark cut in a hard surface, as by engraving *c)* a thin crease in the palm or on the face **5** a mark made on the ground in certain sports; specif., *a)* any of the straight, narrow marks dividing or bounding a football field, tennis court, etc. (often used in comb.) [*sideline*] *b)* a mark indicating a starting point, a limit not to be crossed, or a point which must be reached or passed (often used fig.) [a remark that crosses the *line* of good taste] ☆**6** a border or boundary [the state *line*] **7** a division between conditions, qualities, classes, etc.; limit; demarcation **8** [*pl.*] outline; contour; lineament [built along modern *lines*] **9** [*pl.*] [Archaic] lot in life; one's fate **10** [*usually pl.*] a plan of construction; plan of making or doing **11** a row or series of persons or things of a particular kind; specif., *a)* a row of written or printed characters extending across or part way across a page *b)* a single row of words or characters making up a unit of poetry, often of a specified number of feet ☆*c)* a row of persons waiting in turn to buy something, enter a theater, etc.; queue *d)* an ASSEMBLY LINE or a similar arrangement for the packing, shipping, etc. of merchandise **12** a connected series of persons or things following each other in time or place; succession [a *line* of Democratic presidents] **13** LINEAGE[1] **14** the descendants of a common ancestor or of a particular breed ☆**15** *a)* a transportation system or service consisting of regular trips by buses, ships, etc. between two or more points ☆*b)* a company operating such a system *c)* one branch or division of such a system [the main *line* of a railroad] *d)* a single track of a railroad **16** the course or direction anything moving takes; path [the *line* of fire] **17** *a)* a course of conduct, action, explanation, etc. [the *line* of an argument, taking a hard *line* with juvenile delinquents] *b)* a course of movement **18** a person's trade or occupation [what's his *line?*] ☆**19** a stock of goods of a particular type, often with reference to quality, quantity, variety, etc. **20** the field of one's special knowledge, interest, or ability **21** *a)* [*pl.*] all the dialogue in a play, film, etc.; esp., the dialogue of any single character *b)* any bit of dialogue in a play, film, etc. ☆**22** the odds given by a bookmaker on the contestants in a race, game, etc. **23** [Informal] a short letter, note, or card [drop me a *line*] **24** [Informal] a source or piece of information [a *line* on a bargain] **25** [Informal] persuasive or flattering talk that is insincere **26** [Slang] a small quantity of cocaine sniffed at one time **27** [Brit.] a stock, supply, display, etc., as of literary or artistic qualities, methods, or techniques [a nice *line* in irony] **28** [*pl.*] [Chiefly Brit.] a marriage certificate: in full **marriage lines** ☆**29** *Basketball* short for FREE THROW LINE: see FREE THROW **30** *Bridge* the horizontal line on a score sheet below which are recorded points that count toward a game and above which, all other points ☆**31** *Football a) short for* LINE OF SCRIMMAGE *b)* the players arranged in a row on either side of the line of scrimmage at the start of each play **32** *Geog.* an imaginary circle of the earth or of the celestial sphere, as the equator or the equinoctial circle **33** *Hockey* the two wings and the center playing together **34** *Math.* a continuous series of points, or the path of a moving point, thought of as having length but not breadth, specif., such a series or path when perfectly straight **35** *Mil.* *a)* a formation of ships, troops, etc. in which elements are abreast of each other *b)* the area or position in closest contact with the enemy during combat *c)* the troops in this area *d)* the officers in immediate command of fighting ships or combat troops ☆*e)* the combatant branches of the army as distinguished from the supporting branches and the staff **36** *Music* any of the long parallel marks forming the staff **37** *TV* a scanning line —*vt.* **lined, lin′ing 1** to mark with lines **2** to draw or trace with or as with lines **3** to bring or cause to come into a straight row or into conformity; bring into alignment: often with *up* **4** to form a line along [elms *line* the streets] **5** to place objects along the edge of [*line* the walk with flowers] ☆**6** *Baseball* to hit (a pitched ball) in a line drive —*vi.* **1** to form a line: usually with *up* ☆**2** *Baseball* to hit a line drive —*adj.* of or having to do with the managing of departments, operations, etc. which are involved directly in producing income, as in production or sales as distinguished from those involved in routine internal functions —**all along the line 1** everywhere **2** at every turn of events —**bring (or come or get) into line** to bring (or come) into a straight row or into conformity; bring (or come) into alignment —**down the line** completely; entirely —**draw the (or a) line** to set a limit —☆**get a line on** [Informal] to find out about —**hard lines** [Brit. Slang] misfortune; bad luck —☆**hit the line 1** *Football* to try to carry the ball through the opposing line **2** to try boldly or firmly to do something —**hold the line** to stand firm; not permit a breakthrough or retreat: often used fig. —**in line 1** in a straight row; in alignment **2** in agreement or conformity **3** behaving properly or as required **4** in a row or in some other sequence, awaiting a turn as to be served or to be allowed to proceed —**in line for** being considered for [*in line for* a promotion] —**in the line of duty** in or during the performance of authorized or prescribed duty, esp. military duty —**lay (or put) it on the line** [Informal] **1** to put up or pay money; pay up **2** to speak frankly and in detail **3** to stake (one's reputation, etc.) on something: usually with the object of the verb explicitly stated —**line out** ☆**1** *Baseball* to be put out by hitting a line drive that is caught by a fielder **2** to sing or utter forcefully, loudly, or emphatically [to *line out* a song] —**line up 1** to form a line **2** to bring into a line **3** to organize effectively, secure a pledge of support from, etc. **4** to take a position (*against* a competitor or rival) —**on a line** in the same plane; level —**on line 1** in or into active use or production [the new plant came *on line* this year] **2** IN LINE (sense 4) (see phrase above) —**on the line 1** at great risk **2** at a critical juncture, as between success and failure or life and death —**out of line 1** not in a straight line; not in alignment **2** not in agreement or conformity **3** [Informal] impertinent, insubordinate, etc. —**read between the lines** to discover a hidden meaning or purpose in something written, said, or done —**the end of the line** ⟦in allusion to the last stop on a railway or trolley *line*⟧ the point beyond which there can be no further progress; finish; conclusion —**lin′a·ble** *adj.*, **line′a·ble**

line[2] (līn) *vt.* **lined, lin′ing** ⟦ME *lynen* < *lin*, long-fiber flax, linen cloth < OE, ult. < L *linum*, flax: from use of linen to line clothes⟧ **1** to put a layer or lining of a different material on the inside of **2** to be used as a lining in [cloth *lined* the trunk] **3** to fill; stuff: now chiefly in **line one's pockets**, to make money, esp. greedily or unethically

lin·e·age[1] (lin′ē ij) *n.* ⟦ME *linage* < OFr *lignage* < *ligne*: see LINE[1]⟧ **1** direct descent from an ancestor **2** ancestry; family; stock **3** descendants from a common ancestor

line·age[2] (līn′ij) *n. alt. sp. of* LINAGE

lin·e·al (lin′ē əl) *adj.* ⟦OFr *linéal* < LL *linealis* < L *linea*: see LINE[1]⟧ **1** in the direct line of descent from an ancestor **2** hereditary **3** of or composed of lines; linear —**lin′e·al′i·ty** (-al′ə tē) *n.* —**lin′e·al·ly** *adv.*

lin·e·a·ment (lin′ē ə mənt) *n.* ⟦ME *liniamente* < L *lineamentum* < *lineare*, to fashion to a straight line < *linea*, LINE[1]⟧ **1** any of the features of the body, usually of the face, esp. with regard to its outline **2** a distinctive feature or characteristic **3** any extensive, linear surface feature on a planet, as a fault line, that indicates the nature of the underlying crust *Usually used in pl.* —**lin′e·a·men′tal** *adj.*

lin·e·ar (lin′ē ər) *adj.* ⟦L *linearis*⟧ **1** of or relating to a line or lines **2** made of or using lines [*linear* design] **3** in relation to length only; extended in a line **4** designating or of a style of art in which forms are sharply delineated and line is emphasized over color, light and shadow, etc. **5** having an effect or giving a response directly proportional to stimulus, force, or input: used esp. of electronic devices **6** *a)* characterized by a straightforward, sequential approach or strategy [a *linear* narrative] *b)* characterized by a conventional or predictable line of reasoning [*linear* thinking] (opposed to LATERAL, *adj.* 3) **7** narrow and uniform in width, as the leaves of grasses **8** *Chem.* having the basic structure of a straight chain **9** *Math.* of or involving terms of a linear equation —**lin′e·ar·ly** *adv.*

Linear A a Minoan script that was in use on Crete earlier than LINEAR B and has not yet been deciphered

linear accelerator a high-energy accelerator in which charged particles are given electrostatic acceleration in a straight line at periodic intervals as they pass between metal tubes along the flight path

linear algebra the algebra of vectors and matrices, as distinct from the ordinary algebra of real numbers and the abstract algebra of unspecified entities

Linear B a Minoan syllabic script inscribed on clay tablets discovered at Knossos, Crete, deciphered and found to contain an archaic form of Greek

linear equation an algebraic equation whose variable quantity or quantities are in the first power only and whose graph is a straight line (Ex.: $2x + 3y - 5 = 0$)

linear (induction) motor an electric motor that produces thrust in a direct line by means of the interaction of a moving magnetic field and the current induced by that field: distinguished from the rotary motion produced by a rotary engine

lin·e·ar·i·ty (lin′ē ar′ə tē) *n., pl.* **-ties 1** the quality or state of being linear **2** *Electronics a)* the extent to which any signal modification process, as detection, is accomplished without amplitude distortion *b)* the fidelity with which a televised image is reproduced as determined by the extent to which there is a uniform distribution of the picture elements on the screen **3** *Physics* the extent to which any effect is exactly proportional to its cause

lin·e·ar·ize (lin′ē ər īz′) *vt.* **-ized′, -iz′ing** to give a linear form to —**lin′e·ar·i·za′tion** *n.*

linear measure 1 measurement of length, as distinguished from volume, weight, etc. **2** a system of measuring length, in which 12 inches = 1 foot or one in which 100 centimeters = 1 meter: see the table of weights and measures in the Reference Supplement

linear perspective *see* PERSPECTIVE

linear programming *Math.* a procedure for minimizing or maximizing a linear function of several variables, subject to a finite number of linear restrictions on these variables

lin·e·ate (lin′ē it, -āt′) *adj.* ⟦L *lineatus*, pp. of *lineare*: see LINEAMENT⟧ having or marked with lines; streaked

lin·e·a·tion (lin′ē ā′shən) *n.* ⟦ME *lyneacion* < L *lineatio*⟧ **1** *a)* a marking with lines *b)* a system or series of lines **2** a division into lines **3** any linear structure in a rock, as the ripple marks in a sedimentary rock

☆**line·back·er** (līn′bak′ər) *n. Football* a defensive player positioned behind the defensive linemen

☆**line breeding** the producing of desired characteristics in animals by inbreeding through several successive generations —**line′-breed′** *vt.* **-bred′, -breed′ing**

line dance a kind of partnerless dance in which the dancers stand side by side in a line or lines and perform, in unison, a series of set, often complex, steps to various kinds of popular music

line drawing a drawing done entirely in lines, from which a cut (**line cut**) can be photoengraved for printing

☆**line drive** *Baseball* a hard-hit ball that travels close to, and nearly parallel with, the ground

line engraving 1 a kind of engraving in which the effect is produced by lines of varying thickness and nearness to each other **2** a plate engraved in this way **3** a print from such a plate

Line Islands (līn) group of coral atolls in the central Pacific, south of Hawaii: most are now part of Kiribati

line item a specific item, esp., an amount listed separately, in a budget, appropriation bill, etc.

☆**line-i·tem veto** (līn′īt′əm) executive power to reject a section of a bill, esp. one containing specific appropriations, without vetoing the entire bill

line judge 1 *Football* an official who makes rulings regarding play along the line of scrimmage and who keeps the official time of the game: see HEAD LINESMAN **2** *Tennis, Volleyball, etc.* a linesman

line·man (līn′mən) *n., pl.* **-men** (-mən) **1** a person who carries a surveying line, tape, or chain **2** a person whose work is setting up and repairing telephone lines, electric power lines, etc. ☆**3** *Football* a player on the line of scrimmage, whose primary role is blocking or tackling

lin·en (lin′ən) *n.* ⟦ME < OE (akin to Ger *leinen*) < *lin*, flax: see LINE[2]⟧ **1** yarn, thread, or cloth made of flax **2** [*often pl.*] things made of linen, or of cotton, etc., as tablecloths, sheets, shirts, etc.: cf. BED LINEN, TABLE LINEN **3** fine stationery orig. made from linen rags —*adj.* **1** spun from flax [*linen* thread] **2** made of linen

linen closet a closet with shelves for sheets, towels, table linen, etc.

line of battle troops, ships, etc. drawn up to fight

line of credit 1 a declaration by a bank that it will extend credit to a borrower up to a specified maximum amount **2** the maximum amount so specified

line officer 1 *Mil.* a commissioned officer in charge of combat troops ☆**2** *U.S. Navy* a commissioned officer eligible to command a ship at sea

line of fire 1 the course of a bullet, shell, etc. that has been, or is to be, fired **2** a position open to attack of any kind

line of force a line in a field of electrical or magnetic force that indicates the direction taken by the force at any point

☆**line of scrimmage** *Football* an imaginary line, parallel to the goal lines, on which the ball rests at the start of each play and on either side of which the teams line up

line of sight 1 an imaginary straight line joining the center of the eye of the observer with the object viewed **2** *Radio, TV* the straight path from a transmitting antenna to the horizon, representing the normal range of high-frequency wave propagation Also **line of vision**

lin·e·o·late (lin′ē ə lāt′) *adj.* ⟦ModL *lineolatus* < L *lineola*, dim. of *linea*: see LINE[1]⟧ *Biol.* marked with fine, usually parallel, lines

line printer a high-speed computer printer that prints an entire line at a time, rather than single characters

lin·er[1] (līn′ər) *n.* **1** a person or thing that traces lines or stripes ☆**2** a steamship, passenger airplane, etc. in regular service for a specific line ☆**3** [Informal] *Baseball* LINE DRIVE **4** a cosmetic applied in a fine line, as along the eyelid or, in the theater, to accentuate a natural line in the face

lin·er[2] (līn′ər) *n.* **1** a person who makes or attaches linings **2** a lining or something that suggests a lining by fitting inside something else [a helmet *liner*] ☆**3** the covering, originally the SLEEVE (*n.* 3) and later, usually, the JACKET (*n.* 2*b*), of a long-playing record

lin·er·board (līn′ər bôrd′) *n.* sturdy cardboard, used as for the smooth facing layers of corrugated containerboard

☆**liner notes** information about a recording, as on the back of a long-playing record JACKET (*n.* 2*b*) or in a booklet in a CD case

line score ⟦so called because presented in a horizontal table⟧ a brief listing of the final score and major statistical totals of a game, esp. a baseball game: cf. BOX SCORE

lines·man (līnz′mən) *n., pl.* **-men** (-mən) **1** LINEMAN (senses 1 & 2) **2** *Football* HEAD LINESMAN **3** *Soccer, Tennis, etc.* an official who has the responsibility to make decisions along a sideline, goal line, etc., as in reporting whether the ball is inside or outside the line

line spectrum 1 a spectrum that consists of narrow, brightly colored, parallel lines on a dark background, emitted by a low-pressurized glowing gas: used to determine the chemical composition of a gas, star, etc. **2** a spectrum that consists of narrow, dark, parallel lines on a brightly colored background, produced from a hot light source surrounded by cooler gases that absorb and thus remove certain wavelengths: used to determine the chemical composition of a gas, star, etc.

line squall a strong sudden wind along a line of windstorms or thunderstorms

☆**line storm** EQUINOCTIAL (*n.* 2)

lines·wom·an (līnz′wo͝om′ən) *n., pl.* **-wom′en** (-wim′in) *Soccer, Tennis, etc.* a female official who has the responsibility to make decisions along a sideline, goal line, etc., as in reporting whether the ball is inside or outside the line

☆**line·up** (līn′up′) *n.* an arrangement of persons or things in or as in a line; specif., *a)* a group of people lined up by police and shown to a witness, in attempting to identify a suspect *b)* a schedule of television programs *c)* *Sports* a list of the players, often including their numbers and positions, who participate in a game; esp., in baseball, a list of the players in the exact order in which they will bat

ling[1] (liŋ) *n., pl.* **ling** or **lings** ⟦ME *lenge*, akin to MDu *lange*, ON *langa* < base of LONG[1]: so named from its shape⟧ any of several edible gadoid fishes mostly of the N Atlantic

ling[2] (liŋ) *n.* ⟦ME < ON *lyng* < IE base **lenk-*, to bend > -LING[2]⟧ HEATHER

ling[3] *abbrev.* linguistics

-ling[1] (liŋ) ⟦ME < OE, combining the bases of -LE + -ING⟧ *suffix forming nouns* **1** small or young (person or thing specified) *[duckling]* **2** one in relation to a (specified) thing, esp. in seeming subordinate, unimportant, or contemptible *[hireling, earthling, groundling]*

-ling[2] (liŋ) ⟦ME *-linge* < OE *-ling, -lang* < IE base **lenk-*, to bend > Latvian *lùnkans*, flexible⟧ *suffix forming adverbs* [Now Chiefly Dial.] in a (specified) manner, condition, or direction; to a (specified) extent *[darkling]*

Lin·ga·la (liŋ gä′lə) *n.* a Bantu language used as a lingua franca in the W part of the Democratic Republic of the Congo

lin·gam (liŋ′gəm) *n.* ⟦Sans, lit., token, symbol⟧ the phallic symbol used in the worship of the Hindu god Siva: cf. YONI: also **lin′ga**

ling·cod (liŋ′käd′) *n., pl.* **-cod′** or **-cods′** ⟦LING[1] + COD[1]⟧ ☆a large greenling fish (*Ophiodon elongatus*) of the N Pacific

lin·ger (liŋ′gər) *vi.* ⟦North ME *lengeren*, freq. of *lengen*, to delay, stay < OE *lengan*, to lengthen, delay < base of *lang*, LONG[1]⟧ **1** to continue to stay, esp. from a reluctance to leave *[lingering at the door]* **2** to pause or dwell (*over* or *on* something) in contemplation, deliberation, enjoyment, etc. *[to linger over a favorite passage in a novel]* **3** to continue to live or exist although very close to death or the end **4** to be unnecessarily slow in doing something; delay; loiter —*vt.* to spend (a period of time) idly, slowly, etc. —*SYN.* STAY[3] —**lin′ger·er** *n.* —**lin′ger·ing** *adj.* —**lin′ger·ing·ly** *adv.*

lin·ge·rie (län′zhə rā′, lôn′-; -rē′) *n.* ⟦Fr < *linge*, linen < L *lineus*, linen < *linum*, flax, linen⟧ **1** [Obs.] articles made of linen **2** women's underwear and nightclothes of silk, nylon, lace, etc.

lin·go (liŋ′gō) *n., pl.* **-goes** ⟦Prov *lingo, lengo* < L *lingua*, tongue: see LANGUAGE⟧ [Informal] language; esp., a dialect, jargon, or special vocabulary that one is not familiar with: often a humorous or disparaging term —*SYN.* DIALECT

☆**ling·on·ber·ry** (liŋ′ən ber′ē) *n., pl.* **-ries** ⟦< Swed *lingon*, lingonberry (akin to ON *lyng*, heather: see LING[2]) + BERRY⟧ COWBERRY

lin·gua (liŋ′gwə) *n., pl.* **-guae** (-gwē) ⟦L: see LANGUAGE⟧ a tongue or an organ resembling a tongue, as the proboscis of a butterfly or moth

lin·gua fran·ca (liŋ′gwə fraŋ′kə) *pl.* **lin′gua fran′cas** or ⟦ModL⟧ **lin·guae fran·cae** (liŋ′gwē fraŋ′kē) ⟦It, lit., Frankish language⟧ **1** a hybrid language based on Italian, with Spanish, French, Greek, and Arabic elements, spoken, esp. formerly, in certain Mediterranean ports **2** *a)* a language used for communication between different peoples, as English in global commerce, or Swahili in C Africa *b)* a hybrid language used for this purpose, as pidgin English **3** something that is like a common language

lin·gual (liŋ′gwəl) *adj.* ⟦ME < ML *lingualis* < L *lingua*: see LANGUAGE⟧ **1** of the tongue **2** of language or languages **3** *Phonet.* articulated with the tongue, as (l) and (t): not widely used as a technical term —*n. Phonet.* a lingual sound: not widely used as a technical term —**lin′gual·ly** *adv.*

lin·gui·ca or **lin·gui·ça** (liŋ gwē′sə) *n.* ⟦Port⟧ a highly seasoned Portuguese pork sausage containing much garlic: also sp. **lin·gui′sa**

lin·gui·ne (liŋ gwē′nē) *n.* ⟦It, pl. of *linguina*, dim. of *lingua*, tongue (< L: see LANGUAGE)⟧ pasta in thin, flat, narrow strips, often served with seafood sauces: also sp. **lin·gui′ni**

lin·guist (liŋ′gwist) *n.* ⟦< L *lingua* (see LANGUAGE) + -IST[1]⟧ **1** a specialist in linguistics: cf. PHILOLOGIST **2** loosely, POLYGLOT (*n.* 1)

lin·guis·tic (liŋ gwis′tik) *adj.* **1** of language **2** of linguistics —**lin·guis′ti·cal·ly** *adv.*

linguistic atlas a book of maps charting the geographical distribution of linguistic forms and usages

linguistic form a meaningful unit of speech, as a morpheme, word, phrase, sentence, etc.

linguistic geography the branch of linguistics studying the geographical distribution of linguistic forms and usages —**linguistic geographer**

lin·guis·tics (liŋ gwis′tiks) *n.* ⟦< LINGUISTIC⟧ **1** the science of language, including phonetics, phonology, morphology, syntax, and semantics: sometimes subdivided into *descriptive, historical, comparative, theoretical,* and *geographical linguistics*: often **general linguistics 2** the study of the structure, development, etc. of a particular language and its relationship to other languages *[English linguistics]*

linguistic stock 1 a parent language and all the languages and dialects derived from it **2** all the native speakers of any of these languages or dialects

lin·gu·late (liŋ′gyo͞o lit, -lāt′) *adj.* ⟦L *lingulatus* < *lingula*, dim. of *lingua*, the tongue: see LANGUAGE⟧ shaped like a tongue; linguiform

lin·i·ment (lin′ə mənt) *n.* ⟦ME *lynyment* < LL *linimentum* < L *linere*, to smear: see LIME[1]⟧ a medicated liquid to be rubbed on the skin for soothing sore, sprained, or inflamed areas

li·nin (lī′nin) *n.* ⟦< L *linum*, flax + -IN[1]⟧ the achromatic substance constituting the netlike structure connecting granules of chromatin in a cell nucleus

lin·ing (līn′iŋ) *n.* ⟦see LINE[2] & -ING⟧ **1** the act or process of covering the inner surface of something **2** the material used or suitable for this purpose

link[1] (liŋk) *n.* ⟦ME *linke* < Scand, as in ON *hlekkr*, Dan *lænke*, Swed *länk*, in same senses, akin to OE *hlence*, link of a chain, coat of mail < base of *hlencan*, to twist < IE base **kleng-*, to bend, wind > LANK⟧ **1** any of the series of rings or loops making up a chain **2** any section of a chainlike series; specif., *a)* one of the cylindrical portions of sausage formed by tying off at intervals a long tube of stuffed CASING (sense 2*a*) *b)* a point or stage in a series of circumstances *[a weak link in the evidence]* **3** CUFF LINK **4** anything serving to connect or tie *[a link with the past]* **5** *a)* one division ($\frac{1}{100}$) of a surveyor's, or Gunter's, chain, equal to 7.92 inches (20.117 centimeters) *b)* one division ($\frac{1}{100}$) of an engineer's chain, equal to 1 foot (30.48 centimeters) **6** *Chem.* BOND[1] (sense 8) **7** *Comput.* HYPERLINK **8** *Elec.* the part of a fuse that melts when the current becomes too strong **9** *Mech.* a short connecting rod for transmitting power or motion **10** *Radio, TV* a radio unit for transmitting sound or picture between specific stations —*vt., vi.* to join together with or as with a link or links —*SYN.* JOIN —**link′er** *n.*

link[2] (liŋk) *n.* ⟦prob. < ML *linchinus*, var. of *lichinus*, a lamp < L *lychnus*, a light < Gr *lychnos*, a lamp < IE **luksnos* < base **leuk-*, to shine, LIGHT[1]⟧ a torch made of tow and pitch

link·age (liŋk′ij) *n.* **1** a linking or being linked **2** a series or system of links, slides, cranks, wheels, or gears for transmitting power or motion **3** *Biol.* the tendency of some genes to remain together and act as a unit (**linkage group**) in inheritance, generally in the same chromosome **4** *Chem. a)* BOND[1] (sense 8) *b)* the type of bonding between various atoms or groups in a molecule **5** *Elec.* the product of the number of lines of magnetic flux times the number of turns in the coil surrounding it: it is used to measure the voltage that is induced by magnetic flux

link·boy (liŋk′boi′) *n.* [Historical] a boy or man hired to carry a link, or torch, to light a person's way at night: also **link′man** (-mən), *pl.* **-men** (-mən)

linking verb a verb (such as *be, appear, seem, become*) that functions chiefly as a connection between a subject and a predicate complement; copula

link motion a valve gear that reverses the motion in steam engines: it operates by a slotted bar linked with the eccentric rods

Lin·kö·ping (lin′shö′piŋ) city in SE Sweden

links (liŋks) *pl.n.* ⟦OE *hlincas*, pl. of *hlinc*, a slope, akin to *hlence*: see LINK[1]⟧ **1** [Scot.] a stretch of rolling, sandy land, esp. along a seashore **2** GOLF COURSE

link·up (liŋk′up′) *n.* **1** a joining together of two objects, factions, interests, etc. **2** any connection made to enable electronic communication *[a TV broadcast via satellite linkup]*

link·work (liŋk′wurk′) *n.* **1** anything made in links, as a chain **2** a gear system operating by links

Lin·lith·gow (lin lith′gō) *former name for* WEST LOTHIAN

linn (lin) *n.* ⟦< OE *hlynn*, torrent, confused with Gael *linne*, a pond: orig., noise, roar < *hlynnan*, to resound < IE **k(e)len-* < base **kel-*, to cry out > L *clamor*⟧ [Scot.] **1** *a)* a waterfall *b)* a pool of water at its base **2** a steep ravine

Lin·nae·an or **Lin·ne·an** (li nē′ən, -nā′-) *adj.* of Linnaeus; esp., designating or of his system of classifying plants and animals by using a double name, the first word naming the genus, and the second the species

Lin·nae·us (li nē′əs, -nā′-), **Car·o·lus** (kar′ə ləs) (Latinized form of *Karl von Linné*) 1707-78; Swed. botanist: considered the founder of the binomial nomenclature that is the basis of modern taxonomy

lin·net (lin′it) *n.* ⟦ME *linet* < OFr *linette* < *lin*, flax (< L *linum*): so called because it feeds on flaxseed⟧ either of two small, variously colored finches, an Old World species (*Acanthis cannabina*) or a New World species (*Carpodacus mexicanus*)

li·no (lī′nō) *n.* [Slang, Chiefly Brit.] *short for* LINOLEUM

li·no·cut (lī′nō kut′, -nə-) *n.* ⟦LINO(LEUM) + CUT⟧ **1** a design cut into the surface of a block of linoleum **2** a print made from this

li·no·le·ate (li nō′lē āt′) *n.* ⟦< fol. + -ATE[2]⟧ a salt or ester of linoleic acid

lin·o·le·ic acid (lin′ō lē′ik, li nō′lē ik) ⟦< L *linum*, flax + OLEIC⟧ an unsaturated fatty acid, $C_{17}H_{31}COOH$, found as a glyceryl ester in linseed oil and other fats and oils: used as a drying agent and in soaps, foods, etc. and considered essential in animal diets

lin·o·le·nate (lin′ō lē′nat′, -len′āt′) ***n.*** ⟦< fol. + -ATE²⟧ a salt or ester of linolenic acid

lin·o·le·nic acid (lin′ō lē′nik, -len′ik) ⟦< LINOL(EIC ACID) + -EN(E) + -IC⟧ an unsaturated fatty acid, $C_{17}H_{29}COOH$, found as a glyceryl ester in fats and oils: used in drying oils, varnishes, resins, paints, etc. and considered essential in animal diets

li·no·le·um (li nō′lē əm) ***n.*** ⟦coined (1863) by F. Walton, Eng manufacturer < L *linum*, flax + *oleum*, OIL⟧ **1** a hard, smooth, washable floor covering **2** any floor covering similar to linoleum

☆**li·no·type** (līn′ə tīp′) ***n.*** ⟦< *Linotype*, former trademark < *line of type*⟧ [*also* **L-**] **1** a typesetting machine that casts an entire line of type in one bar, or slug: it is operated from a keyboard **2** matter set in this way —***vt., vi.*** **-typed′**, **-typ′ing** to set (matter) with this machine —**li′no·typ′ist** ***n.***, **li′no·typ′er**

lin·sang (lin′saŋ′) ***n.*** ⟦Javanese *liṅsaṅ, wliṅsaṅ*⟧ any of several small, long-tailed, catlike carnivores (family Viverridae) found in the Old World tropics

lin·seed (lin′sēd′) ***n.*** ⟦ME *linsed* < OE *linsæd* < *lin*, flax (see LINE²) + *sæd*, SEED⟧ the seed of flax; flaxseed

linseed oil a yellowish oil extracted from flaxseed, and used, because of its drying qualities, in making oil paints, printer's ink, linoleum, etc.

lin·sey-wool·sey (lin′zē wool′zē) ***n.***, *pl.* **-wool′seys** ⟦ME *linsy wolsye* < *lin*, linen (see LINE²) + *wolle*, WOOL + jingling suffix⟧ **1** a coarse cloth made of linen and wool, or cotton and wool: also **lin′sey** **2** [Obs.] an incongruous mixture; jumble

lin·stock (lin′stäk′) ***n.*** ⟦altered (by assoc. with fol., used as tinder) < Du *lontstok* < *lont*, a match, lunt + *stok*, a stick⟧ [Historical] a long stick used to hold a lighted match for firing a cannon

lint (lint) ***n.*** ⟦ME *linnet*, prob. < *lin*, linen: see LINE²⟧ **1** scraped and softened linen formerly used as a dressing for wounds **2** cotton fiber used to make yarn **3** the waste cotton remaining after ginning **4** bits of thread, ravelings, or fluff from cloth or yarn, specif., such fluff caught by a removable screen in a clothes dryer —***vi.*** to give off lint or fluff —**lint′less** ***adj.*** —**lint′y** ***adj.*** **lint′i·er**, **lint′i·est**

lin·tel (lin′təl) ***n.*** ⟦OFr < VL **limitellus*, for *limitaris*, altered (by assoc. with L *limes*, gen. *limitis*, border, frontier) < L *liminaris*, of a threshold or lintel < *limen*: see LIMEN⟧ the horizontal crosspiece over an opening, as a door or window, usually carrying the weight of the structure above it

☆**lint·er** (lin′tər) ***n.*** **1** a machine for removing the short, fuzzy fibers which remain stuck to cotton seeds after ginning **2** [*pl.*] these fibers, used in making cotton batting, guncotton, etc.

lint·white (lint′hwīt′, -wīt′) ***n.*** ⟦ME *lynkwhitte*, altered < OE *lynetuige*, lit., flax-plucker < *lin* (see LINE²) + *-twige* < or akin to *twiccian*: see TWITCH⟧ LINNET

lin·y (līn′ē) ***adj.*** **lin′i·er**, **lin′i·est** **1** like a line; thin **2** marked with, or full of, lines or streaks

Linz (lints) city in N Austria, on the Danube

Lin·zer torte (lin′zər tôrt′) *pl.* **Linzer tortes** (tôrts) ⟦< Ger < *Linzer*, of prec. + *torte*, TORTE⟧ [*sometimes* **l- t-**] a rich Austrian pastry consisting of a filling of raspberry jam and a bottom crust and lattice top of a spiced ground-almond dough: also Ger. **Lin·zer·tor·te** (lints′ər tôr′tə) ***n.***, *pl.* **-tor′ten** (-tôr′tən)

li·on (lī′ən) ***n.***, *pl.* **li′ons** or **li′on** ⟦OFr < L *leo* (gen. *leonis*) < Gr *leōn* (gen. *leontos*)⟧ **1** a large, powerful cat (*Panthera leo*), found in Africa and SW Asia, with a tawny coat, a tufted tail, and, in the adult male, a shaggy mane: in folklore and fable the lion is king of beasts **2** a person of great courage or strength **3** a prominent person who is in demand socially; celebrity **4** [*pl.*] LIONS CLUB —**beard the lion (in his den)** to approach, oppose, etc. an influential or feared person, as in a place where that person has the advantage —**the Lion** Leo, the constellation and fifth sign of the zodiac

Li·o·nel (lī′ə nəl, -nel′) ***n.*** ⟦OFr, dim. of *lion*, prec.⟧ a masculine name

li·on·ess (lī′ə nəs) ***n.*** a female lion

li·on·heart·ed (lī′ən härt′id) ***adj.*** very brave

li·on·ize (lī′ə nīz′) ***vt.*** **-ized′**, **-iz′ing** ⟦LION + -IZE⟧ **1** to treat as a celebrity **2** [Brit.] to visit the interesting sights of (a place) —**li′on·i·za′tion** ***n.*** —**li′on·iz′er** ***n.***

Lions (lī′ənz), **Gulf of (the)** part of the Mediterranean, on the S coast of France, between Toulon & Spain: Fr. name **Golfe du Li·on** (gôlf dü lyōn′)

Lions Club any of the local branches of The International Association of Lions Clubs, an organization of community-service clubs primarily dedicated to serving the blind or visually impaired

lion's share ⟦from Aesop's fable in which the *lion* takes all the spoils of a joint hunt⟧ the whole thing or, now usually, the biggest and best portion

lip (lip) ***n.*** ⟦ME *lippe* < OE *lippa*, akin to MDu *lippe* < IE base **leb-*, to hang loosely, lip > L *labes*, a falling, *labium*, lip⟧ **1** either of the two fleshy folds forming the edges of the mouth **2** anything like a lip, as in structure or in being an edge, rim, or margin; specif., *a)* the edge of a wound *b)* the projecting rim of a pitcher, cup, etc. *c)* the edge of the mouthpiece of a wind instrument *d)* the edge on either side of the sound-producing opening of an organ flue pipe *e)* the cutting edge of any of certain tools *f) Anat.* LABIUM *g) Bot.* a lip-shaped corolla, calyx, or petal, as in a mint or an orchid *h)* LABELLUM **3** the position and use of the lips in playing a wind instrument; embouchure **4** [Slang] impertinent or insolent talk —***vt.*** **lipped**, **lip′ping** **1** to touch with the lips; specif., *a)* to place the lips in the proper position for playing (a wind instrument) *b)* [Archaic] to kiss **2** *Golf* to come just to the edge of (the cup): said of the ball —***adj.*** **1** *Phonet.* articulated with a lip or the lips; labial: not widely used as a technical term [*a lip consonant*] **2** of or for the lips **3** from the lips only; spoken, but insincere —**bite one's lip** to keep back one's anger, annoyance, etc. —**hang on the lips of** to listen to with close attention —☆**keep a stiff upper lip** to bear pain or distress bravely or stoically —**one's lips are sealed** one is determined to keep a secret or keep quiet —**smack one's lips** to express great satisfaction in anticipating or remembering something pleasant —**lip′less** ***adj.***

li·pa (lē′pə) ***n.***, *pl.* **-pa** or **-pas** ⟦Serbo-Croatian⟧ a monetary unit of Croatia, equal to 1⁄100 of a kuna

Li·pa·ri Islands (lip′ə rē) group of volcanic islands of Italy in the Tyrrhenian Sea, northeast of Sicily: 34 sq mi (88 sq km)

li·pase (lī′pās′, lip′ās′) ***n.*** ⟦LIP(O)- + -ASE⟧ any of a group of enzymes, esp. from the pancreas, that aid in digestion by hydrolyzing fats into fatty acids and glycerol

Lip·chitz (lip′shits′), **Jacques** (zhäk) (born *Chaim Jacob Lipchitz*) 1891-1973; U.S. sculptor, born in Lithuania

li·pec·to·my (li pek′tə mē) ***n.***, *pl.* **-mies** ⟦LIP(O)- + -ECTOMY⟧ surgical removal of fatty tissue from under the skin

Li·petsk (lē′petsk′) city in SW European Russia

lip gloss a transparent, sometimes colored cosmetic ointment applied to the lips as a moisturizer and to give a shiny appearance

lip·id (lip′id) ***n.*** ⟦LIP(O)- + -ID⟧ any of a group of organic compounds consisting of the fats and of other substances of similar properties: they are insoluble in water, soluble in fat solvents and alcohol, and greasy to the touch, and are important constituents of living cells: also **lip·ide** (lip′īd′, -id)

Lip·iz·zan·er (lip′it sän′ər, lip′ə zän′-) ***n.*** ⟦Ger, after *Lipizza*, the imperial Austrian stud farm, near TRIESTE⟧ any of a breed of medium-sized, stocky horse, usually white when mature, used esp. in dressage and jumping exhibitions

lip liner a cosmetic applied in a fine line on or around the edge of the lips to define the mouth: also written **lip′lin′er** ***n.***

Li Po (lē′bō′, lē′pō′) A.D. 701-762; Chin. poet

lip·o- (lip′ō, -ə; lī′pō, -pə) ⟦< Gr *lipos*, fat < IE **leip-*: see LEAVE¹⟧ *combining form* fat or fatty [*lipolysis*]: also, before a vowel, **lip-**

lip·o·fus·cin (lip′ō fus′in, lī′pō-) ***n.*** ⟦< prec. + L *fuscus*, dark: see OBFUSCATE⟧ any of a group of fatty pigments that are found in various tissue cells and are associated with aging

lip·oid (lip′oid′, lī′poid′) ***adj.*** ⟦LIP(O)- + -OID⟧ *Biochem., Chem.* resembling fat: also **li·poi·dal** (li poid′'l, lī-) —***n.*** LIPID

li·pol·y·sis (li päl′ə sis, lī-) ***n.*** ⟦ModL: see LIPO- & -LYSIS⟧ the decomposition of fat, as during digestion

li·po·ma (li pō′mə, lī-) ***n.***, *pl.* **-ma·ta** (-tə) or **-mas** ⟦ModL: see LIP(O)- & -OMA⟧ a benign tumor made up of fat tissue —**li·pom′a·tous** (-päm′ə təs) ***adj.***

lip·o·phil·ic (lip′ō fil′ik, lip′ə-; lī′pō-, -pə-) ***adj.*** ⟦LIPO- + -PHIL(E) + -IC⟧ having a strong attraction for fats

lip·o·pol·y·sac·cha·ride (lip′ō pä′lē sak′ə rīd′, lī′pō-) ***n.*** *Biochem.* a large molecule that contains a polysaccharide and a lipid, found especially in cell membranes

lip·o·pro·tein (-prō′tēn′, -prō′tē in) ***n.*** any of a group of proteins combined with a lipid, found as in blood plasma or egg yolk

lip·o·some (lip′ə sōm′, lī′pə-) ***n.*** ⟦LIPO- + -SOME³⟧ ☆a synthetic, microscopic globule consisting of layers of lipids encapsulating certain substances (as enzymes or drugs): used to introduce these substances into a cell or specified tissue

lip·o·suc·tion (lip′ō suk′shən; lī′pō-, lī′pə-) ***n.*** ⟦LIPO- + SUCTION⟧ lipectomy by means of suction through a small incision in the skin

lip·o·trop·ic (lip′ō träp′ik, lip′ə-; lī′pō-, -pə-) ***adj.*** ⟦LIPO- + -TROPIC⟧ regulating or reducing the accumulation of fat in the body or its organs

lip·o·tro·pin (-trō′pin) ***n.*** a hormone made in the pituitary gland, that stimulates release of fatty acids from adipose tissue: its amino acid sequence includes an endorphin

Lip·pe (lip′ə) region in W Germany, in the state of North Rhine-Westphalia: formerly a principality

lipped (lipt) ***adj.*** **1** having a lip or lips (of a specified kind): often used in compounds [*tight-lipped*] **2** having a spoutlike projection in the rim: said of a pitcher, cup, etc. **3** LABIATE

☆**Lip·pes loop** (lip′is) ⟦after J. Lippes (b. 1924), U.S. physician who designed it⟧ a polyethylene, intrauterine contraceptive device, shaped like a double S

Lip·pi (lip′ē; *It* lēp′pē) **1 Fi·lip·pi·no** (fē′lēp pē′nô) 1457?-1504; Florentine painter **2 Fra Fi·lip·po** (fē lēp′pô) 1406?-69; Florentine painter: father of Filippino: also called **Fra Lip·po Lip·pi** (frä lip′ō lip′ē)

Lip·pi·zan·er (lip′it sän′ər, lip′ə zän′-) ***n.*** *alt. sp. of* LIPIZZANER

Lipp·mann (lip′mən), **Walter** 1889-1974; U.S. journalist

lip·py (lip′ē) ***adj.*** **-pi·er**, **-pi·est** [Slang] impudent, brash, or insolent —**lip′pi·ness** ***n.***

lip-read (lip′rēd′) ***vt., vi.*** **-read′** (-red′), **-read′ing** to recognize (a speaker's words) by lip reading —**lip reader**

lip reading the act or skill of recognizing a speaker's words by watching his or her lip movements: it is taught esp. to the deaf

Lips·comb (lips′kəm), **William Nunn, Jr.** (nun) 1919-2011; U.S. chemist

lip service insincere expression of respect, loyalty, support, etc.: often in the phrase **pay lip service to**

☆**lip·stick** (lip′stik′) ***n.*** a small stick of cosmetic paste, set in a case, for coloring the lips

lip-sync or **lip-synch** (lip′siŋk′) ***vt., vi.*** ⟦< *lip sync(hronization)*⟧ to synchronize one's lip movements with (recorded speaking or singing), to give the appearance of an actual performance —***n.*** the act or process of lip-syncing

liq *abbrev.* **1** liquid **2** liquor

li·quate (lī′kwāt′) ***vt.*** **-quat′ed, -quat′ing** ⟦< L *liquatus,* pp. of *liquare,* to melt, akin to *liquere:* see LIQUID⟧ *Metallurgy* to heat (a metal, etc.) in order to separate a fusible substance from one less fusible —**li·qua′tion** ***n.***

liq·ue·fa·cient (lik′wi fā′shənt) ***adj.*** ⟦< L *liquefaciens,* prp. of *liquefacere:* see LIQUID & -FACIENT⟧ that liquefies, or causes to become liquid —***n.*** something that causes liquefaction

liq·ue·fac·tion (-fak′shən) ***n.*** a liquefying or being liquefied

liquefied petroleum gas a compressed or liquefied gas, generally a mixture of propane, propylene, butane, and butylene obtained as a byproduct from petroleum refining: used as a domestic or industrial fuel and in certain organic syntheses

liq·ue·fy (lik′wi fī′) ***vt., vi.*** **-fied′, -fy′ing** ⟦Fr *liquefier* < L *liquefacere:* see LIQUID & -FY⟧ to make or become liquid —***SYN.*** MELT —**liq′ue·fi′a·ble** ***adj.*** —**liq′ue·fi′er** ***n.***

li·ques·cent (li kwes′ənt) ***adj.*** ⟦L *liquescens,* prp. of *liquescere,* to become liquid < *liquere:* see LIQUID⟧ becoming liquid; melting —**li·ques′cence** ***n.***

li·queur (li kur′, -koor′, -kyoor′) ***n.*** ⟦Fr⟧ any of certain strong, sweet, syrupy alcoholic liquors, variously flavored

liq·uid (lik′wid) ***adj.*** ⟦OFr *liquide* < L *liquidus* < *liquere,* to be liquid, prob. < IE base **wlikw-,* wet > Welsh *gwlyb,* moist⟧ **1** readily flowing; fluid; specif., having its molecules moving freely with respect to each other so as to flow readily, unlike a solid, but because of cohesive forces not expanding indefinitely like a gas **2** clear; limpid *[liquid* eyes*]* **3** flowing smoothly and musically, gracefully, etc. *[liquid* verse*]* **4** in cash or readily convertible into cash *[liquid* assets*]* **5** *Phonet.* articulated without friction and capable of being prolonged like a vowel, as (l) and (r) —***n.*** **1** a liquid substance **2** a liquid sound —**liq′uid·ness** ***n.*** —**liq′uid·ly** ***adv.***

liquid air air brought to a liquid state by being subjected to great pressure and then cooled by its own expansion to a temperature below the boiling point of its main constituents, nitrogen and oxygen: it is used as a refrigerant

liq·uid·am·bar (lik′wid am′bər) ***n.*** ⟦ModL < L *liquidus* (see LIQUID) + Ar *ʿanbar* (see AMBER)⟧ **1** any of a genus (*Liquidambar*) of trees of the witch hazel family, found in Asia and North America, esp. the SWEET GUM **2** the balsam from such a tree

liq·ui·date (lik′wi dāt′) ***vt.*** **-dat′ed, -dat′ing** ⟦< ML *liquidatus,* pp. of *liquidare,* to make liquid or clear < L *liquidus,* LIQUID⟧ **1** to settle by agreement or legal process the amount of (indebtedness, damages, etc.) **2** to settle the accounts of (a bankrupt business firm) by apportioning assets and debts **3** to pay or settle (a debt) **4** to convert (holdings or assets) into cash **5** to dispose of or get rid of, as by killing —***vi.*** to liquidate debts, accounts, etc.

liq·ui·da·tion (lik′wi dā′shən) ***n.*** a liquidating or being liquidated —**go into liquidation** to close one's business by collecting assets and settling all debts

liq·ui·da·tor (lik′wi dāt′ər) ***n.*** a person who liquidates, esp. one legally appointed to liquidate a company

liquid crystal a liquid in which nearby molecules have a fixed orientation with respect to each other: such liquids may exhibit some properties of crystals

liquid crystal display LCD

liquid diet a diet restricted to liquids and, sometimes, certain semisolid foods, as custards, gelatin, etc.

li·quid·i·ty (li kwid′i tē) ***n.*** **1** the quality or state of being liquid **2** *Finance a)* the ability of a business to meet obligations without disposing of its fixed assets *b)* the ability of a market to absorb buying and selling without producing undue price fluctuations

liq·uid·ize (lik′wid īz′) ***vt.*** **-ized′, -iz′ing** to cause to become liquid

liquid measure **1** the measurement of liquids **2** a system of measuring liquids in which 4 gills = 1 pint, 2 pints = 1 quart, 4 quarts = 1 gallon: see the table of weights and measures in the Reference Supplement

liquid oxygen the light-bluish liquid form of oxygen produced by fractionation of liquid air and used as an oxidizer in liquid-fueled rockets: oxygen is often stored in this form, which boils at −183°C

liq·ui·fy (lik′wi fī′) ***vt., vi.*** **-fied′, -fy′ing** *alt. sp. of* LIQUEFY

liq·uor (lik′ər) ***n.*** ⟦altered (infl. by L) < ME *licour* < OFr *licor* < L *liquor,* akin to *liquere:* see LIQUID⟧ **1** any liquid or juice *[*meat *liquor]* **2** an alcoholic drink, esp. one made by distillation, as whiskey or rum **3** *Pharmacy* a solution of some substance in water — ***vt., vi.*** [Informal] to drink or cause to drink alcoholic liquor, esp. to the point of intoxication: now usually with *up*

liq·uo·rice (lik′ə ris, -rish) ***n.*** *chiefly Brit. var. of* LICORICE

li·ra (lir′ə) ***n., pl.*** **li′re;** also, and for 2 always, **li′ras** ⟦It < L *libra,* a balance, pound⟧ **1** the former basic monetary unit of: *a)* Italy, San Marino, and Vatican City, superseded in 2002 by the EURO *b)* Malta, superseded in 2008 by the EURO **2** the basic monetary unit of Turkey: see the table of monetary units in the Reference Supplement

lir·i·pipe (lir′ə pīp′) ***n.*** ⟦ML *liripipium* < ?⟧ in early academic costume, a long tail to a hood

Li·sa (lē′sə, -zə) ***n.*** a feminine name: see ELIZABETH[1]

Lis·bon (liz′bən) capital of Portugal: seaport on the Tagus estuary: Port. name **Lis·bo·a** (lēzh bô′ə)

li·sen·te (li sen′tē) ***n. pl. of*** SENTE

lisle (līl) ***n.*** ⟦after *Lisle,* earlier sp. of LILLE, where orig. made⟧ **1** a fine, hard, extra-strong cotton thread: in full **lisle thread** **2** a fabric, or stockings, gloves, etc., knit or woven of lisle —***adj.*** made of lisle

Lisle *see* LECONTE DE LISLE and ROUGET DE LISLE

lisp (lisp) ***vi.*** ⟦ME *lyspen,* earlier *wlispen* < OE *-wlyspian* < *wlisp, wlips,* a lisping, akin to Ger *lispeln,* MLowG *wlispen, wilspen,* of echoic orig.⟧ **1** to substitute the sounds (th) and (*th*) for the sounds of *s* and *z,* as from a speech defect or as an affectation (Ex.: pronouncing *sing* as though it were *thing*) **2** to speak imperfectly or like a child —***vt.*** to utter with a lisp or in an imperfect or childlike way —***n.*** **1** the act or speech defect of lisping **2** the sound of lisping —**lisp′er** ***n.*** —**lisp′ing·ly** ***adv.***

lis pen·dens (lis pen′denz) ⟦L⟧ *Law* a pending suit: a lis pendens involves the legal doctrine that a court acquires jurisdiction over property involved in a suit

lis·some or **lis·som** (lis′əm) ***adj.*** ⟦altered < LITHESOME⟧ bending or moving gracefully or with ease and lightness; lithe, supple, limber, agile, etc. —**lis′some·ly** ***adv.,*** **lis′som·ly** —**lis′some·ness** ***n.,*** **lis′som·ness**

list[1] (list) ***n.*** ⟦ME *liste,* merging < OE, a hem, border & Anglo-Fr < OFr < Gmc **lista,* akin to Ger *leiste* < IE base **leizd-,* edge, border > L *lira,* line, furrow, Alb *leth,* the raised border of a plot of ground, wall⟧ **1** [Obs.] a narrow strip or border; specif., *a)* a strip of cloth *b)* a stripe of color *c)* a boundary **2** *a)* a narrow strip of wood, esp. sapwood, trimmed from the edge of a board *b)* LISTEL **3** the selvage of cloth **4** ⟦from the idea of a narrow slip of paper⟧ a series of names, words, numbers, etc. set forth in order; catalog, roll, etc. ☆**5** a ridge of earth between two furrows **6** LIST PRICE ➥See also LISTS —***vt.*** **1** [Obs.] to edge with, or arrange in, stripes or bands **2** *a)* to set forth (a series of names, items, etc.) in order *b)* to enter (a name, item, etc.) in a list, directory, catalog, etc. ☆**3** to plow (ground) or plant (corn) with a lister **4** to trim a strip of wood, esp. sapwood, from the edge of (a board) **5** *Finance* to admit (a stock, option, etc.) for trading on an exchange —***vi.*** ☆**1** to plow with a lister **2** to be listed for sale, as in a catalog (at the price specified) **3** [Archaic] to enlist in the armed forces

SYN.—**list,** the broadest in scope of these terms, applies to a series of items of any kind, no matter what the arrangement or purpose; **catalog** implies methodical arrangement, usually alphabetical, and is used of lists of articles for sale or on exhibit, of library card files, etc.; an **inventory** is an itemized list of goods, property, etc., especially one made annually in business; a **register** is a book, etc. in which names, events, or other items are formally or officially recorded *[a register* of voters*]*; a **roll** is an official list of the members of an organization, especially as used for checking attendance

list[2] (list) [Archaic] ***vt.*** ⟦ME *listen* < OE *lystan* < base of *lust,* desire, appetite: see LUST⟧ to be pleasing to; suit —***vi.*** to wish; like; choose —***n.*** a craving, desire, or inclination

list[3] (list) ***vt., vi.*** ⟦prob. specialized use of prec.⟧ to tilt to one side, as a ship —***n.*** a tilting or inclining to one side

list[4] (list) ***vt., vi.*** ⟦ME *listen* < OE *hlystan* < base of *hlyst,* hearing, akin to Ger *lauschen,* dial. *laustern* < IE base **k̑leu-,* to hear > L *cluere,* to be called⟧ [Archaic] to listen (to)

lis·tel (lis′təl) ***n.*** ⟦Fr < It *listello,* dim. of *lista,* a border, strip < Gmc **lista:* see LIST[1]⟧ *Archit.* a narrow molding or band; fillet

lis·ten (lis′ən) ***vi.*** ⟦ME *listnen,* felt as freq. of *listen* (see LIST[4]) < OE *hlysnan* (akin to MHG *lüsenen*)⟧ **1** to make a conscious effort to hear; attend closely, so as to hear **2** to pay close attention; take advice —***vt.*** [Archaic] to pay attention to by listening; hear —***n.*** the act of listening —☆**listen in** **1** to listen to the conversation of others; esp., to eavesdrop **2** to listen to a broadcast —☆**listen up!** [Informal] listen carefully! give me your attention! —**lis′ten·er** ***n.***

lis·ten·a·ble (-ə bəl) ***adj.*** that can be listened to, esp. with pleasure

lis·ten·ing post (lis′ən iŋ) **1** *Mil.* an advanced, concealed position near the enemy's lines, for detecting the enemy's movements by listening **2** any strategic position or center for securing information or intelligence

list·er[1] (lis′tər) ***n.*** ⟦LIST[1], ***vt.*** 3 + -ER⟧ ☆a plow with a double moldboard, which heaps the earth on both sides of the furrow: it is sometimes combined with a drill that plants seed at the same time

list·er[2] (lis′tər) ***n.*** a person who compiles a list or lists

Lis·ter (lis′tər), **Joseph** 1st Baron Lister of Lyme Regis 1827-1912; Eng. surgeon: introduced antiseptic surgery

lis·te·ri·a (lis tir′ē ə) ***n.*** ⟦after prec.⟧ any of a genus (*Listeria,* esp. *L. monocytogenes*) of small, Gram-positive, rod-shaped bacteria that cause listeriosis, sometimes found in dairy products and raw meat

lis·te·ri·o·sis (lis tir′ē ō′sis) ***n., pl.*** **-ses′** (-sēz′) ⟦see prec.⟧ any of various infections in animals and occas. humans, caused by listeria and often associated with encephalitis, meningitis, etc.

list·ing (lis′tiŋ) ***n.*** **1** the act of making a list **2** an entry in a list, as in a directory, a real-estate broker's record of property for sale, etc. **3** a list

list·less (list′lis) ***adj.*** ⟦LIST[2] + -LESS⟧ **1** having no interest in what is going on about one, as a result of illness, weariness, dejection, etc.; spiritless; languid **2** characterized by such a feeling —**list′less·ly** ***adv.*** —**list′less·ness** ***n.***

list price retail price as given in a list or catalog, variously discounted in sales to dealers

lists (lists) ***pl.n.*** ⟦ME *listes,* specialized use of *liste,* border, hedging, boundary (see LIST[1]), prob. infl. by OFr *lisse* (Fr *lice*) in same sense < Frank **listia*

< Gmc **lista,* LIST[1]] **1** *a)* in the Middle Ages, a high fence of stakes enclosing the area for a tournament *b)* this area itself or the tournament held there **2** any place or realm of combat, conflict, etc. —**enter the lists** to enter a contest or struggle

LISW *abbrev.* Licensed Independent Social Worker

Liszt (list), **Franz** (fränts) 1811-86; Hung. composer & pianist —**Liszt′i·an** *adj.*

lit[1] (lit) *vt., vi. alt. pt. & pp. of* LIGHT[1]

lit[2] (lit) *vi. alt. pt. & pp. of* LIGHT[2]

lit[3] (lit) *n.* [*also* **L-**] [Informal] *short for* LITERATURE

lit[4] *abbrev.* **1** liter(s) **2** literally **3** literary **4** literature

Li Tai Po (lē′ tī′ bō′) LI PO

lit·a·ny (lit′′n ē) *n., pl.* **-nies** ⟦ME *letanie* < OFr < LL(Ec) *litania* < Gr(Ec) *litaneia* < Gr *litanos,* pleading < *litē,* a request⟧ **1** a series of fixed invocations and responses, used as a prayer **2** any recital or account regarded as repetitive or long-winded

li·tas (lē′täs) *n., pl.* **-tas** ⟦Lith⟧ the former basic monetary unit of Lithuania: superseded in 2015 by the EURO

LitB or **Lit.B.** *abbrev. see* LITTB

li·tchi (lē′chē′) *n.* ⟦Chin *li-chih*⟧ **1** a Chinese evergreen tree (*Litchi chinensis*) of the soapberry family, cultivated in warm climates for its fruit **2** its fruit, usually eaten as a dried or preserved nut (**litchi nut**): it consists of a single seed surrounded by a sweet, edible, raisinlike pulp, enclosed in a rough, papery shell

lit crit (lit′krit′) [Informal] literary criticism

LitD or **Lit.D.** *abbrev. see* LITTD

lite (līt) *adj. informal sp. of:* **1** LIGHT[2] (*adj.* 14): often used in brand names **2** LIGHT[2] (*adj.* 5): often used postpositively

-lite (līt) ⟦Fr, for *-lithe:* see -LITH⟧ *combining form* stone: used in the names of minerals, rocks, and fossils [*chrysolite, cryolite*]

li·ter (lēt′ər) *n.* ⟦Fr *litre* < *litron,* obs. unit of measure < ML *litra* < Gr, a pound⟧ the basic unit of volume or capacity in the metric system, equal to 33.76 fluid ounces or 1.0567 liquid quarts (0.9081 dry quarts or 61.0237 cubic inches); the volume of one cubic decimeter or one kilogram of water at its maximum density at 4°C: abbrev. *l* or L

lit·er·a·cy (lit′ər ə sē) *n.* the state or quality of being literate; specif., *a)* ability to read and write *b)* knowledgeability or capability (in a specified field) [computer *literacy*]

lit·er·al (lit′ər əl) *adj.* ⟦ME *litterall* < MFr *litteral* < LL *litteralis* < L *littera,* LETTER[1]⟧ **1** of, involving, or expressed by a letter or letters of the alphabet [*literal* notation] **2** following or representing the exact words of the original; word-for-word [a *literal* translation] **3** *a)* based on the actual words in their ordinary meaning; not figurative or symbolic [the *literal* meaning of a passage] *b)* giving the actual denotation of the word (said of the senses of words) *c)* giving the original or earlier meaning of a word; etymological [the *literal* meaning of *ponder* is "to weigh"] **4** *a)* habitually interpreting statements or words according to their actual denotation; prosaic; matter-of-fact [a *literal* mind] *b)* having a literal mind; lacking imagination **5** real; not going beyond the actual facts; accurate; unvarnished [the *literal* truth] **6** being so in fact but not in name; virtual [the chairman is a *literal* tyrant] —*n.* [Chiefly Brit.] a typographical error —**lit′er·al·ness** *n.*

lit·er·al·ism (-iz′əm) *n.* **1** the tendency or disposition to take words, statements, etc. in their literal sense **2** thoroughgoing realism in art —**lit′er·al·ist** *n.* —**lit′er·al·is′tic** *adj.*

lit·er·al·i·ty (lit′ər al′ə tē) *n., pl.* **-ties 1** the state or quality of being literal **2** a literal meaning or interpretation

lit·er·al·ize (lit′ər əl īz′) *vt.* **-ized′, -iz′ing 1** to make (a translation, etc.) literal **2** to interpret according to the literal sense —**lit′er·al·i·za′tion** *n.*

lit·er·al·ly (lit′ər əl ē) *adv.* in a literal manner or sense; specif., *a)* word for word; not imaginatively, figuratively, or freely [to translate a passage *literally*] *b)* actually; in fact [the house *literally* burned to the ground] (now often used as an intensive to modify a word or phrase that itself is being used fig. [she *literally* flew into the room]: this latter usage is objected to by some)

lit·er·ar·y (lit′ər er′ē) *adj.* ⟦L *litterarius* < *littera,* LETTER[1]⟧ **1** *a)* of, having the nature of, or dealing with literature *b)* of or having to do with books or writing [*literary* agents] **2** characterized by the more formal, balanced, and polished language of literature rather than the informal language of speech **3** *a)* familiar with or versed in literature *b)* making literature a profession —**lit′er·ar′i·ness** *n.*

lit·er·ate (lit′ər it) *adj.* ⟦ME *litterate* < L *litteratus* < *littera,* LETTER[1]⟧ **1** able to read and write **2** well-educated; having or showing extensive knowledge, learning, or culture **3** [Now Rare] versed in literature **4** knowledgeable or capable (in a specified field) [economically *literate*] —*n.* a literate person —**lit′er·ate·ly** *adv.*

lit·e·ra·ti (lit′ə rät′ē) *pl.n.* ⟦It < L *litterati,* learned, pl. of *litteratus:* see prec.⟧ scholarly or learned people, specif. those whose work is in the field of literature

lit·e·ra·tim (-rāt′im, -rät′-) *adv.* ⟦ML < L *littera,* LETTER[1]⟧ letter for letter; literally

lit·er·a·ture (lit′ər ə chər, li′trə-) *n.* ⟦ME *litterature* < OFr < L *litteratura* < *littera,* LETTER[1]⟧ **1** the profession of an author; production of writings, esp. of imaginative prose, verse, etc. **2** *a)* all writings in prose or verse, esp. those of an imaginative or critical character, without regard to their excellence: often distinguished from scientific writing, news reporting, etc. *b)* all of such writings considered as having permanent value, excellence of form, great emotional effect, etc. *c)* all the writings of a particular time, country, region, etc., specif. those regarded as having lasting value because of their beauty, imagination, etc. [American *literature*] *d)* all the writings dealing with a particular subject [the medical *literature*] **3** all the compositions for a specific musical instrument, voice, or ensemble **4** printed matter of any kind, as advertising, campaign leaflets, etc. **5** [Archaic] acquaintance with books; literary knowledge

lith *abbrev.* **1** lithograph **2** lithography

Lith *abbrev.* **1** Lithuania **2** Lithuanian

-lith (lith) ⟦Fr *-lithe* < Gr *lithos,* stone⟧ *combining form* stone [*eolith, megalith*]

lith·arge (lith′ärj′, li thärj′) *n.* ⟦OFr *litarge* < L *lithargyrus* < Gr *lithargyros,* spume or foam of silver < *lithos,* a stone + *argyros,* silver⟧ an oxide of lead, PbO, used in storage batteries, ceramic cements, paints, etc.

lithe (līth) *adj.* **lith′er, lith′est** ⟦ME < OE *lithe,* soft, mild, akin to OHG *lindi* < IE base **lento-,* flexible, bendable > LINDEN, L *lentus,* pliant, flexible⟧ bending easily; flexible; supple; limber; lissome: also **lithe′some** (-səm) —**lithe′ly** *adv.* —**lithe′ness** *n.*

lith·i·a (lith′ē ə) *n.* ⟦ModL < earlier *lithion* < Gr *litheion,* neut. of *litheois,* stony < *lithos,* stone + -IA: so named in reference to its mineral orig.⟧ lithium oxide, Li_2O, a white, crystalline compound

li·thi·a·sis (li thī′ə sis) *n.* ⟦ModL < Gr *lithos,* stone + -IASIS⟧ the formation of calculi, or mineral concretions, within the body

lithia water mineral water containing lithium salts

lith·ic (lith′ik) *adj.* ⟦Gr *lithikos* < *lithos,* a stone⟧ **1** of stone **2** *Chem.* of lithium **3** *Med.* of calculi

-lith·ic (lith′ik) *combining form* of a (specified) period of the STONE AGE [*Neolithic, Paleolithic*]

lith·i·fy (lith′ə fī′) *vt.* **-fied′, -fy′ing** ⟦< Gr *lithos,* a stone + -I- + -FY⟧ to change (esp. sediment) into rock —*vi.* to become rock —**lith′i·fi·ca′tion** (-fi kā′shən) *n.*

lith·i·um (lith′ē əm) *n.* ⟦ModL: name coined (1818) by BERZELIUS < LITHIA + -IUM⟧ **1** a soft, silver-white, metallic chemical element, one of the alkali metals and the lightest metal: used in thermonuclear explosives, in metallurgy, etc.: symbol, Li; at. no. 3: see the periodic table of elements in the Reference Supplement **2** any of various antidepressants containing lithium, esp. lithium carbonate

lithium carbonate a white, powdery salt, Li_2CO_3, used in the manufacture of glass, ceramics, dyes, etc. and in psychiatry to treat bipolar affective disorder

lith·o[1] (lith′ō) *n., pl.* **-os** *short for* LITHOGRAPH — *vt., vi.* **-oed, -o·ing**

litho[2] *abbrev.* **1** lithograph **2** lithography

lith·o- (lith′ō, -ə) ⟦< Gr *lithos,* a stone⟧ *combining form* stone, rock, calculus [*lithosphere, lithography, lithotomy*]: also, before a vowel, **lith-**

lith·o·graph (lith′ə graf′) *n.* a print made by lithography — *vi., vt.* to make (prints or copies) by this process —**li·thog·ra·pher** (li thäg′rə fər) *n.*

li·thog·ra·phy (li thäg′rə fē) *n.* ⟦LITHO- + -GRAPHY⟧ the art or process of printing from a flat stone or metal plate by a method based on the repulsion between grease and water: the design is put on the surface with a greasy material, and then water and printing ink are successively applied; the greasy parts, which repel water, absorb the ink, but the wet parts do not —**lith·o·graph·ic** (lith′ə graf′ik) *adj.* —**lith′o·graph′i·cal·ly** *adv.*

li·thol·o·gy (li thäl′ə jē) *n.* ⟦LITHO- + -LOGY⟧ **1** the scientific study of rocks, usually with the unaided eye or with little magnification **2** loosely, the structure and composition of a rock formation —**lith·o·log·ic** (lith′ə läj′ik) *adj.*, **lith′o·log′i·cal** —**lith′o·log′i·cal·ly** *adv.*

lith·o·marge (lith′ə märj′) *n.* ⟦< LITHO- + L *marga,* MARL[1]⟧ a smooth, closely packed variety of kaolin

lith·o·phyte (lith′ə fīt′) *n.* ⟦LITHO- + -PHYTE⟧ a plant that grows on rock surfaces —**lith′o·phyt′ic** (-fit′ik) *adj.*

lith·o·pone (-pōn′) *n.* ⟦< LITHO- + Gr *ponos,* work, product of work⟧ a white pigment made by mixing barium sulfate with zinc sulfide, used in paints, linoleum, etc.

lith·o·sphere (-sfir′) *n.* ⟦LITHO- + -SPHERE⟧ the solid, rocky part of the earth; earth's crust

li·thot·o·my (li thät′ə mē) *n., pl.* **-mies** ⟦LL *lithotomia* < Gr: see LITHO- & -TOMY⟧ *Surgery* the surgical removal of a calculus, or mineral concretion —**lith·o·tom·ic** (lith′ə täm′ik) *adj.*

lith·o·trip·sy (lith′ə trip′sē) *n., pl.* **-sies** a noninvasive medical procedure in which ultrasound generated by a machine (**lith′o·trip′ter** or **lith′o·trip′tor**) pulverizes kidney stones or gallstones into small pieces that can be excreted

li·thot·ri·ty (li thä′trə tē) *n., pl.* **-ties** ⟦< LITHO- + L *tritus,* pp. of *terere,* to grind, rub: see THROW⟧ the process of crushing a calculus in the bladder into very small pieces so that it can be eliminated in the urine

Lith·u·a·ni·a (lith′o͞o ā′nē ə, lith′ə wā′-) country in N Europe, on the Baltic Sea: from 1940 to 1991 it was a republic of the U.S.S.R.: 25,174 sq mi (65,200 sq km); cap. Vilnius: formerly, **Lithuanian Soviet Socialist Republic**

Lith·u·a·ni·an (-ən) *adj.* of Lithuania or its people, language, or culture —*n.* **1** a person born or living in Lithuania **2** the Baltic language spoken in Lithuania

lit·i·ga·ble (lit′i gə bəl) *adj.* that gives cause for litigation, or a lawsuit; actionable

lit·i·gant (lit′i gənt) *adj.* ⟦Fr < L *litigans*⟧ [Rare] engaged in litigation —*n.* a party to a lawsuit

lit·i·gate (-gāt′) *vt.* **-gat′ed, -gat′ing** ⟦< L *litigatus*, pp. of *litigare*, to dispute, carry on a suit < *lis* (gen. *litis*), dispute + *agere*, to do: see ACT[1]⟧ to contest in a lawsuit —*vi.* to carry on a lawsuit —**lit′i·ga′tor** *n.*

lit·i·ga·tion (lit′i gā′shən) *n.* ⟦LL *litigatio*⟧ **1** the act or process of carrying on a lawsuit **2** a lawsuit

li·ti·gious (li tij′əs) *adj.* ⟦ME < MFr *litigieux* < L *litigiosus* < *litigium*, strife < *litigare*: see LITIGATE⟧ **1** *a)* given to carrying on lawsuits *b)* quarrelsome **2** disputable at law **3** of lawsuits —**li·ti′gious·ly** *adv.* —**li·ti′gious·ness** *n.*

lit·mus (lit′məs) *n.* ⟦ON *litmose*, lichen used in dyeing < *litr*, color (akin to Goth *wlits*, face < IE **wltu-*, appearance < base **wel-*, to see > L *voltus*, expression, Welsh *gweled*, to see) + *mosi*, MOSS⟧ a purple coloring matter obtained from various lichens and used as an acid-base indicator in chemical analysis: it turns blue in bases and red in acids

litmus paper absorbent paper treated with litmus and used as an acid-base indicator

litmus test **1** a test using litmus, esp. litmus paper, to determine whether a solution is an acid or a base **2** any factor regarded as the decisive criterion in assessing the quality or authenticity of someone or something

li·to·tes (lī′tə tēz′, lī tōt′ēz) *n.* ⟦Gr *litotēs* < *litos*, smooth, simple, plain, akin to *leios*: see LIME[1]⟧ understatement for effect, esp. such understatement in which something is expressed by a negation of the contrary (Ex.: not a few regrets) —**li·tot·ic** (lī tät′ik) *adj.*

li·tre (lēt′ər) *n. Brit. sp. of* LITER

LittB or **Litt.B.** *abbrev.* ⟦L *Lit(t)erarum Baccalaureus*⟧ Bachelor of Letters; Bachelor of Literature

LittD or **Litt.D.** *abbrev.* ⟦L *Lit(t)erarum Doctor*⟧ Doctor of Letters; Doctor of Literature

lit·ten (lit′'n) *adj.* ⟦extended < LIT⟧ [Archaic] lighted

lit·ter (lit′ər) *n.* ⟦ME *litere* < OFr *litiere* < ML *literia, lectaria* < L *lectus*, a couch: see LIE[1]⟧ **1** [Historical] a framework set on poles for transporting dignitaries, etc., having a canopied couch and typically carried by servants **2** a stretcher for carrying the sick or wounded **3** straw, hay, leaves, etc. used as bedding for animals, as a protective covering for plants, etc. **4** an absorbent granular or pelletized material used to cover the bottom of a receptacle (**litter box**) into which a domestic pet, esp. a cat, is trained to urinate and defecate **5** the young borne at one time by a dog, cat, or other animal which normally bears several young at a delivery **6** things lying about in disorder, esp., bits of rubbish scattered about **7** untidiness; disorder **8** *Forestry* the surface layer of the forest floor, in which the leaves are slightly decomposed —*vt.* **1** to supply with a bed, covering, etc. of straw, hay, or the like **2** to bring forth (a number of young) at one time: said of certain animals **3** to make messy with things scattered about **4** to scatter about carelessly —*vi.* to bear a litter of young —**the pick of the litter** the best or most desirable puppy, kitten, etc. of a single litter: often used fig.

lit·té·ra·teur (lit′ər ə tur′; *Fr* lē tä rȧ tër′) *n.* ⟦Fr⟧ a literary man; man of letters: also written **litterateur**

lit·ter·bag (lit′ər bag′) *n.* a small bag, as one kept in an automobile, for the disposal of trash

☆**lit·ter·bug** (lit′ər bug′) *n.* [Informal] a person who litters highways or other public places with waste paper, garbage, etc.

lit·ter·mate (-māt′) *n.* an offspring in relation to another or others in its litter

lit·ter·y (lit′ər ē) *adj.* covered with litter; untidy

lit·tle (lit′'l) *adj.* **lit′tler** or **less** or **less′er, lit′tlest** or **least** ⟦ME *littel* < OE *lytel* (akin to Ger dial. *lützel*) < base of *lyt*, small (< IE base **leud-*, to stoop > Welsh *lludded*, fatigue), infl. by ON *litill*, small (akin to Goth *leitils*) < IE base **lei-*, to decline, be lean > LESS⟧ **1** small in size; not big, large, or great **2** small in amount, number, or degree; not much **3** short in duration or distance; brief; not long **4** small in importance or power [the rights of the *little* man] **5** small in force, intensity, etc.; weak **6** trivial; trifling **7** lacking in breadth of vision; narrow-minded; illiberal [a *little* mind] **8** small and quite young: said of children or animals **9** younger [her *little* brother] ➥Sometimes used with implications of pleasing or endearing qualities [bless your *little* heart] Also used in the names of certain neighborhoods, sections of town, etc. that are populated by people from (a specified place) who have largely maintained their ethnic customs and traditions [the *Little* Italy section of Manhattan] —*adv.* **less, least** **1** in a small degree; to a slight extent; only slightly; not much **2** not in the least [he *little* suspects the plot] —*n.* **1** *a)* small amount, degree, etc. (often used with *a* and having adverbial force) [a *little* crazy] *b)* not much [*little* will be done about it] **2** a short time or distance —**SYN.** SMALL —**in little** on a small scale; in miniature —**little by little** by slow degrees or small amounts; gradually —**make little of** to treat as not very important; depreciate —**not a little** very much; very —**some little** a considerable amount or extent of [stayed for *some little* time] —**lit′tle·ness** *n.*

Little America five operational bases established by the Admiral Byrd expeditions, on the Ross Ice Shelf, Antarctica

Little Bear, the the constellation Ursa Minor

Little Bighorn river in N Wyo., flowing north into the Bighorn in S Mont.: *c.* 90 mi (145 km): in a battle near here (**Battle of the Little Bighorn,** 1876) George Custer's troops attacked Dakota and Cheyenne Indians and were annihilated

little black book ⟦from the characteristic design⟧ [Informal] a personal address book, esp. one containing the names of companions considered available for dating

Little Corporal *name for* Napoleon BONAPARTE[2]

Little Diomede *see* DIOMEDE ISLANDS

☆**Little Dipper, the** a dipper-shaped group of stars in the constellation Ursa Minor

little finger the finger farthest from the thumb; smallest finger —**twist** (or **wrap**) **around one's little finger** to influence or control (another) with ease

Little Hours *R.C.Ch.* the canonical hours of prime, terce, sext, and none

Little John *Eng. Legend* a member of Robin Hood's band

little leaf a disease of stone fruits, apples, grapes, etc. caused by a deficiency of zinc and characterized by crinkled, small leaves and yellowing of the tips of new growth

☆**Little League** *service mark for* a league of baseball teams for youngsters and teenagers —**Little Leaguer**

little magazine a noncommercial magazine of limited circulation, often, specif., one publishing experimental poetry or fiction

Little Missouri river in the NW U.S., flowing from NE Wyo. into the Missouri in N.Dak.: 560 mi (901 km)

☆**lit·tle·neck** (lit′'l nek′) *n.* ⟦after *Little Neck*, Long Island⟧ the young of the quahog, a round, thick-shelled clam, usually eaten raw: also **littleneck clam**

Little Office *R.C.Ch.* a short office patterned after a longer one of the breviary, used esp. in private devotion

little people **1** *Folklore* small, humanlike imaginary beings, as fairies, elves, dwarfs, or leprechauns **2** *sing.* **little person** people who are abnormally undersized —**SYN.** DWARF

Little Rock ⟦after a rocky promontory in the river⟧ capital of Ark., on the Arkansas River

little slam *Bridge* SMALL SLAM

Little St. Bernard Pass mountain pass in the Graian Alps, between France & Italy: 7,178 ft (2,188 m) high

little theater **1** a small theater, usually noncommercial and amateur, that produces experimental drama directed at a limited audience **2** drama produced by such theaters

little toe the small toe on the outside of the foot

little woman, the ☆[Informal] one's wife: now a humorously patronizing term

lit·to·ral (lit′ə rəl) *adj.* ⟦L *litoralis* < *litus* (gen. *litoris*), seashore, coast, prob. < IE **leitos* < base **lei-*, to flow > Welsh *lli*, sea, flood⟧ **1** of, on, or along the shore, esp. a seashore **2** designating or of the intertidal ecological zone along the shore —*n.* a region along the shore

li·tur·gi·cal (lə tur′ji kəl) *adj.* ⟦< Gr *leitourgikos* + -AL⟧ of or pertaining to liturgy in general or to the liturgy of a particular church or religion [*liturgical* vestments, a *liturgical* calendar] —**li·tur′gi·cal·ly** *adv.*

li·tur·gics (-jiks) *n.* the study of LITURGY (sense 1)

lit·ur·gist (lit′ər jist) *n.* **1** a person who uses, or advocates the use of, a liturgy **2** a specialist in liturgies

lit·ur·gy (-jē) *n., pl.* **-gies** ⟦Fr *liturgie* < ML(Ec) *liturgia* < Gr *leitourgia*, public service to the gods (in LXX & N.T., ministry of priests), ult. < *leōs, laos*, people + *ergon*, WORK⟧ **1** prescribed forms or ritual for public worship in any of various religions or churches **2** the Eucharistic service, esp. (DIVINE LITURGY) in the Eastern Orthodox Church

Liturgy of the Hours *R.C.Ch.* a revision (promulgated in 1970) of the arrangement and texts of the Divine Office

liv·a·ble (liv′ə bəl) *adj.* **1** fit or pleasant to live in; habitable: said of a city, house, room, etc. **2** that can be lived through; endurable: said of life or of a specified sort of existence **3** agreeable to live with: often used in comb. with *with*: said of a person —**liv′a·bil′i·ty** *n.*, **liv′a·ble·ness**

live[1] (liv) *vi.* **lived, liv′ing** ⟦ME *liven* < OE *libban* (akin to ON *lifa*, Goth *liban*, Ger *leben*) < IE **lib(h)s-* < base **leibh-*, to live⟧ **1** to be alive; have life **2** *a)* to remain alive *b)* to last; endure **3** *a)* to pass one's life in a specified manner [to *live* happily] *b)* to regulate or conduct one's life [to *live* by a strict moral code] **4** to enjoy a full and varied life [he really knows how to *live*] **5** *a)* to maintain life; support oneself [to *live* on a pension] *b)* to be dependent for a living (with *off*) **6** to feed; subsist; depend *on* or have as one's usual food [to *live* on fruits and nuts] **7** to make one's dwelling; reside **8** to remain in human memory [men's good deeds *live* after them] —*vt.* **1** to practice or carry out in one's life [to *live* one's faith] **2** to spend; pass [to *live* a useful life] **3** to act (a role in a play) very convincingly or feelingly —**live and let live** to do as one wishes and let other people do the same; be tolerant —**live something down** [Informal] to succeed in making others forget the memory or shame of (one's fault, misdeed, etc.) —**live high** to live in luxury —**live in** to live at the place where one is in domestic service —**live it up** [Informal] **1** to have a joyous or merry time **2** to indulge in pleasures, extravagances, etc. that one usually forgoes —**live out** **1** to live until the end of; last through ☆**2** to sleep away from the place where one is in domestic service —**live together** to dwell with each other; specif., to cohabit —**live up to** to live or act in accordance with (certain ideals, promises, expectations, etc.) —**live well** **1** to live in luxury **2** to lead a virtuous life —**live with** **1** to dwell with; be a lodger at the home of **2** to cohabit with **3** to tolerate; bear; endure —**where one lives** [Slang] in a sensitive or vulnerable area

live[2] (līv) *adj.* ⟦aphetic for ALIVE⟧ **1** having life; not dead **2** of the living state or living beings **3** having positive qualities, as of warmth, vigor, vitality, brightness, brilliance, etc. [a *live* organization, a *live* color] ☆**4** of immediate or present interest [a *live* issue] **5** *a)* still burning or glowing [a *live* spark] *b)* not extinct [a *live* volcano] **6** not yet burned: said of a match **7** charged for explosion; unexploded [a *live* shell] **8** carrying an electric current [a *live* wire] **9** in the native state; not quarried or mined [*live* rocks] **10** having resilience or elasticity [a *live* rubber ball] **11** fresh; pure: said of the air **12** *a)* involving an appearance or performance in person, rather than a filmed or recorded one; transmitted during the actual performance [a *live* broadcast] *b)* recorded at a public performance **13** *Mech.* imparting motion or power **14** *Printing* set up ready to be printed **15** *Sports* in play [a *live* ball] —*adv.* in, from, or at an actual or public performance [recorded *live* at a nightclub]

live·a·ble (liv′ə bəl) *adj. alt. sp. of* LIVABLE

live-ac·tion (līv′ak′shən) *adj.* of or involving the direct filming of actors, sets, etc., as distinguished from animation

live·bear·er (līv′ber′ər) *n.* any of a family (Poeciliidae, order Atheriniformes) of small, tropical, American, freshwater bony fishes that bear live young rather than lay eggs, as the guppy, swordtail, and molly: commonly kept as aquarium fishes

live center (līv) the center in the revolving spindle of a lathe or other machine on which work is turned

-lived (līvd, livd) ⟦< ME *lyved*: see LIFE & -ED⟧ *combining form* having (a specified kind or duration of) life [long-*lived*]

live-for·ev·er (liv′fər ev′ər) *n.* SEDUM

☆**live-in** (liv′in′) *adj.* **1** living at the place where one is employed, esp. in domestic service [a *live-in* housekeeper] **2** [Informal] designating a person who lives at the residence of his or her sexual partner without being married [a *live-in* girlfriend] —*n.* [Informal] a live-in person

live·li·hood (līv′lē hood′) *n.* ⟦ME *livelode* < OE *liflad*, course of life < *lif*, LIFE + *lad*, course (see LOAD): form altered by assoc. with LIVELY & -HOOD⟧ means of living or of supporting life; subsistence

live load (līv) *Engineering* any load not constant in its application, as the moving traffic carried by a bridge or other structure in addition to its own weight: opposed to DEAD LOAD

live·long (liv′lôŋ′) *adj.* ⟦ME *lefe longe*, lit., lief long (see LIEF): the first word is merely intens.: altered by assoc. with LIVE[1]⟧ whole; entire [the *livelong* day]

live·ly (līv′lē) *adj.* **-li·er, -li·est** ⟦ME *liflich* < OE *liflic*: see LIFE & -LY[1]⟧ **1** full of life; active; vigorous **2** full of spirit; exciting; animated [a *lively* debate] **3** showing or inspiring liveliness; cheerful **4** moving quickly and lightly, as a dance **5** brisk [a *lively* breeze] **6** vivid; keen; intense [*lively* colors] ☆**7** bounding back with, or having, great resilience [a *lively* tennis ball] —*adv.* **-li·er, -li·est** in a lively manner —**live′li·ness** *n.*

SYN.—**lively** implies being full of life and energy and suggests an active or vigorous quality in something [a *lively* dance, talk, etc.]; **animated** is applied to that which is made alive or bright and suggests a spirited quality [an *animated* face, discussion, etc.]; **vivacious** and, more emphatically, **sprightly** suggest buoyancy of spirit or sparkling brightness [a *vivacious* manner, a *sprightly* tune]; **merry** suggests lightheartedness and unrestrained good spirits [a *merry* laugh, *merry* festivities] —*ANT.* **dull**

liv·en (līv′ən) *vt., vi.* ⟦< LIVE[2] + -EN⟧ to make or become lively or merry; cheer: often with *up* —**liv′en·er** *n.*

☆**live oak** (līv) **1** any of several American oaks; esp., *a)* a wide-spreading, evergreen oak (*Quercus virginiana*) native to the SE U.S. *b)* a large evergreen oak (*Quercus agrifolia*) native to California **2** the hard wood of these trees, used in shipbuilding and other construction

liv·er[1] (liv′ər) *n.* ⟦ME *livere* < OE *lifer*, akin to Ger *leber* < ? IE base **leip-*, to smear with fat > Gr *liparos*, fat⟧ **1** the largest glandular organ in vertebrate animals, located in the upper or anterior part of the abdomen: it secretes bile, has an important function in the storage and metabolism of carbohydrates, fats, and proteins, and helps detoxify many poisonous substances that may be ingested **2** loosely, a similar organ or tissue in invertebrate animals **3** the liver of cattle, fowl, etc., used as food **4** the reddish-brown color of liver **5** [Archaic] the liver thought of as the seat of emotion or desire

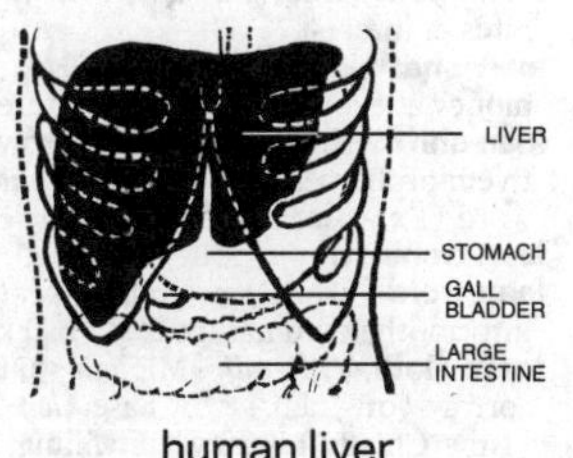

human liver

liv·er[2] (liv′ər) *n.* a person who lives (in a specified way or place) [a clean *liver*]

liver extract an extract consisting of the water-soluble, nonprotein constituents of fresh mammalian liver, that can promote the formation of blood cells

liver fluke any of various trematodes (esp. *Clonorchis sinensis*) that in the adult stage live as parasites in the liver of various vertebrates, including humans

liv·er·ied (liv′ər ēd) *adj.* wearing a livery

liv·er·ish (liv′ər ish) *adj.* [Informal] **1** having a disordered liver; bilious **2** having a sour disposition; peevish; cross —**liv′er·ish·ness** *n.*

☆**liv·er·leaf** (liv′ər lēf′) *n.* HEPATICA

liv·er·mo·ri·um (liv′ər môr′ē əm) *n.* ⟦after the Lawrence *Livermore* National Laboratory in *Livermore*, Calif.⟧ a radioactive, metallic chemical element: a transactinide produced by bombarding curium with calcium ions: symbol, Lv; at. no. 116: see the periodic table of chemical elements in the Reference Supplement

Liv·er·pool (liv′ər po͞ol′) seaport in NW England, in Merseyside, on the Mersey estuary

Liv·er·pud·li·an (liv′ər pud′lē ən) *adj.* ⟦< *Liverpuddle*, jocular alteration of prec. + -IAN⟧ of Liverpool or its people —*n.* a person born or living in Liverpool

liver spot ⟦formerly attributed to faulty functioning of the *liver*⟧ a yellowish-brown, red, or black spot or patch on the skin

liv·er·wort (liv′ər wurt′) *n.* ⟦ME: see LIVER[1] & WORT[2]: so called from having liver-shaped parts⟧ any of two classes (Hepaticopsida and Anthocerotopsida) of bryophytes, often forming dense, green, mosslike mats on logs, rocks, or soil in moist places

☆**liv·er·wurst** (liv′ər wurst′) *n.* ⟦partial transl. of Ger *leberwurst* < *leber*, LIVER[1] + *wurst*, sausage⟧ a sausage containing ground liver: also called **liver sausage**

liv·er·y (liv′ər ē) *n., pl.* **-er·ies** ⟦ME, allowance of food, gift of clothes to a servant, thing delivered < OFr *livree*, pp. of *livrer*, to deliver < L *liberare*, to LIBERATE⟧ **1** an identifying uniform such as was formerly worn by feudal retainers or is now worn by servants or those in some particular group, trade, etc. **2** the people wearing such uniforms **3** characteristic dress or appearance **4** *a)* the keeping and feeding of horses for a fixed charge *b)* the keeping of horses, vehicles, or both, for hire ☆*c)* LIVERY STABLE ☆**5** a place where boats can be rented **6** [Historical] *Eng. Law* the legal delivery of property, esp. landed property, into the hands of the new owner

livery company any of the London city companies that grew out of earlier trade guilds, characterized by distinctive ceremonial dress

liv·er·y·man (-mən) *n., pl.* **-men** (-mən) **1** [Obs.] a liveried servant **2** a member of a livery company **3** a person who owns or works in a livery stable

livery stable a stable where horses and carriages can be had for hire, or where horses are kept for a fixed charge

lives (līvz) *n. pl. of* LIFE

☆**live steam** (līv) steam that comes directly from the boiler before its expansion in work, as distinguished from exhaust steam

live·stock (līv′stäk′) *n.* [*with sing. or pl. v.*] domestic animals kept for use on a ranch or farm and raised for sale and profit

live wire (līv) ⟦see LIVE[2], *adj.* 8⟧ **1** a wire carrying an electric current ☆**2** [Informal] a person who is energetic, impulsive, etc.

liv·id (liv′id) *adj.* ⟦< Fr or L: Fr *livide* < L *lividus*, akin to *livere*, to be black and blue < IE **(s)līwos-* < base **(s)li-*, bluish > SLOE, OSlav *sliva*, plum⟧ **1** discolored by a bruise; black-and-blue **2** *a)* grayish-blue; lead-colored *b)* pallid; ashen *c)* dark red in the face; flushed [*livid* with rage] **3** very angry; enraged —*SYN.* PALE[1] —**li·vid·i·ty** (li vid′i tē) *n.*, **liv′id·ness**

liv·ing (liv′iŋ) *adj.* **1** alive; having life; not dead **2** full of vigor; in active operation or use [a *living* institution] **3** of persons alive [within *living* memory] **4** in its natural state or place, or having its natural force, motion, etc. [hewn from the *living* rock, a *living* stream] **5** still spoken and undergoing changes [a *living* language] **6** true to reality; lifelike [a portrait that is her *living* image] **7** of life or the sustaining of life [*living* conditions] **8** suited for social and recreational activities in a house [the *living* area] **9** presented in person before a live audience [*living* theater] **10** [Informal] very [scared the *living* daylights out of me] —*n.* **1** the state of being alive **2** the means of sustaining life; livelihood [to work for a *living*] **3** manner of existence [the standard of *living*] **4** in England, a church benefice —**the living** those who are still alive

SYN.—**living** and **alive**, the latter usually a predicate adjective, are the simple, basic terms for organisms having life or existence, **living** figuratively connoting continued existence or activity [a *living* faith] and **alive**, full force or vigor [prejudices kept *alive* by ignorance]; **animate**, opposed to *inanimate*, is applied to living organisms as distinguished from lifeless ones or inorganic objects; **animated** is applied to inanimate things to which life or, in extended use, motion has been imparted [*animated* cartoons]; **vital** is applied to that which is essential to organic life [*vital* functions] or to the energy, force, etc. manifested by living things

living death a life of unrelieved misery

living room ☆a room in a home, with sofas, chairs, etc., used for social activities, entertaining guests, etc.: also written **liv′ing·room′** *n.*

Liv·ing·ston (liv′iŋ stən), **Robert R(obert)** 1746-1813; Am. statesman; helped draft the Declaration of Independence

Liv·ing·stone (liv′iŋ stən), **David** 1813-73; Scot. missionary & explorer in Africa

living wage a wage sufficient to meet an employee's basic needs

☆**living will** ⟦see WILL[1], *n.* 5⟧ a legal document expressing one's intentions regarding future healthcare, life-support, resuscitation, etc. in the event that one becomes incapable of giving informed consent

Li·vo·ni·a (li vō′nē ə) former province (1783-1918) of Russia, on the Gulf of Riga: divided (1918) between Latvia & Estonia —**Li·vo′ni·an** *adj., n.*

Li·vor·no (lə vôr′nō; *It* lē vôr′nô) *It. name for* LEGHORN

li·vre (lē′vər; *Fr* lē′vr′) *n.* ⟦Fr < L *libra*, a pound⟧ a former French money of account (discontinued in the late 18th cent.), orig. equivalent in value to a pound of silver

Liv·y (liv′ē) (L. name *Titus Livius*) 59 B.C.-A.D. 17; Rom. historian

lix·iv·i·ate (lik siv′ē āt′) *vt.* **-at′ed, -at′ing** ⟦see fol. & -ATE[1]⟧ LEACH[1] —**lix·iv′i·a′tion** *n.*

lix·iv·i·um (lik siv′ē əm) *n., pl.* **-i·ums** or **-i·a** (-ə) ⟦LL < L *lixivius*, made into lye < *lix*, ashes, lye, akin to *liquere*: see LIQUID⟧ a solution, as lye, obtained by leaching

liz·ard (liz′ərd) ***n.*** ⟦ME *lesard* < OFr < L *lacerta*, lizard: see LEG[1]⟧ **1** any of a suborder (Sauria, order Squamata) of reptiles characterized typically by a long slender body and tail, scaly skin, and four legs: most species live in hot, dry regions, as the gecko, horned toad, chameleon, and iguana **2** loosely, any of various similar reptiles or other animals, as alligators or salamanders

liz·ard·fish (-fish′) ***n., pl.*** **-fish′** or **-fish′es** (see FISH) any of a family (Synodontidae) of small, brightly colored, marine bony fishes (order Myctophiformes) with a slender body, lizardlike head, and large mouth: often written **lizard fish**

Lizard Head (*or* **Point**) promontory at the tip of a peninsula (**The Lizard**) in SW Cornwall, England: southernmost point of Great Britain

Lju·blj·a·na (lo͞o′blē ä′nä′, lyo͞o′-) capital of Slovenia, in the central part

Lk *abbrev.* **1** Lake **2** *Bible* Luke

ll *abbrev.* lines

LL *abbrev.* **1** Late Latin **2** Low Latin

-'ll (əl) *suffix* will or shall: used in contractions [*she'll* sing; *I'll* go; *what'll* we do?]

lla·ma (lä′mə) ***n., pl.*** **-mas** or **-ma** ⟦Sp < Quechua⟧ **1** any of a genus (*Lama*, family Camelidae) of South American ruminants without humps, including the alpaca, guanaco, and vicuña, esp., a domesticated species (*L. glama glama*) used as a beast of burden and as a source of wool, meat, and milk **2** cloth made from the woolly hair of this animal

lla·no (lä′nō; *Sp* yä′nô) ***n., pl.*** **-nos** (-nōz; *Sp*, -nôs) ⟦Sp < L *planus*, plain, PLANE[1]⟧ any of the level, grassy plains covering large areas of N South America, SW U.S., etc.

Lla·no Es·ta·ca·do (lä′nō es′tə kä′dō) ⟦Sp, lit., staked plain⟧ extensive high plain in W Tex. & SE N.Mex.: S extension of the Great Plains: *c.* 40,000 sq mi (103,600 sq km)

LLB or **LL.B.** *abbrev.* ⟦L *Legum Baccalaureus*⟧ Bachelor of Laws

LLC *abbrev.* limited liability company

LLD or **LL.D.** *abbrev.* ⟦L *Legum Doctor*⟧ Doctor of Laws

Llew·el·lyn (lo͞o el′in) ***n.*** ⟦Welsh *Llewelyn*, lit., prob., lionlike⟧ a masculine name: var. *Llewelyn*

LLM or **LL.M.** *abbrev.* ⟦L *Legum Magister*⟧ Master of Laws

Lloyd (loid) ***n.*** ⟦Welsh *Llwyd*, lit., gray⟧ a masculine name

Lloyd George, **David** 1st Earl Lloyd-George of Dwyfor 1863-1945; Brit. statesman: prime minister (1916-22)

Lloyd's (of London) (loidz) ⟦after *Lloyd's* coffeehouse, meeting place of the orig. assoc.⟧ an association of insurance underwriters in London formed in the early 18th cent. to subscribe marine insurance policies: it now handles many kinds of insurance

LLP *abbrev.* limited liability partnership

lm *abbrev.* lumen

Lm *abbrev. Bible* Lamentations

LM *abbrev.* **1** Licentiate in Medicine **2** Lord Mayor

Ln *abbrev.* Lane

LNG (el′en′jē′) ***n.*** liquefied natural gas: natural gas cooled and compressed into a liquid for shipment in pressurized containers

lo[1] (lō) ***interj.*** ⟦ME < OE *la*⟧ [Archaic] look; see: now mainly in the phrase **lo and behold**

lo[2] (lō) ***adj.*** *informal sp. of* LOW[1]

loach (lōch) ***n.*** ⟦ME *loche* < OFr⟧ any of a family (Cobitidae, order Cypriniformes) of small, bottom-dwelling, freshwater, bony fishes with barbels around the mouth

load (lōd) ***n.*** ⟦ME *lode* < OE *lad*, a course, way, journey < Gmc **laidō*, way < IE base **leit(h)-*, to go, leave > LEAD[1], ON *litha*, Goth *galeithan*, to go: sense infl. by ME *laden*, LADE⟧ **1** something carried or to be carried at one time or in one trip; burden; cargo **2** the amount that can be or usually is carried: a measure of weight or quantity varying with the type of conveyance, often used in comb. [a *carload* of coal] **3** something carried with difficulty; specif., *a)* a heavy burden or weight *b)* a great mental or spiritual burden [a *load* off one's mind] **4** the weight that a structure bears or the stresses that are put upon it **5** a single charge, as of powder and bullets, for a firearm ☆**6** the amount of work carried by or assigned to a person, group, etc. [the course *load* of a student, the *caseload* of a social worker] **7** [*often pl.*] [Informal] a great amount or number [*loads* of friends] **8** *Elec. a)* the amount of power delivered by a generator, motor, etc. or carried by a circuit *b)* a device to which this power is delivered **9** *Finance* an amount, expressed as a percentage of the NET ASSET VALUE, added to the price of some mutual fund shares to cover sales commissions and other marketing costs **10** *Mech.* the rate at which work is done by an engine, etc.; specif., the external resistance offered to an engine by the machine that it is operating —***vt.*** **1** to put something to be carried into or upon; esp., to fill or cover with as much as can be carried [to *load* a wagon with wheat] **2** to put into or upon a carrier [to *load* coal into a truck] **3** to weigh down with or as with a heavy load; burden; oppress **4** to supply in large quantities; give much of something to [to *load* a person with honors, a novel *loaded* with suspense] **5** to put ammunition into (a firearm, etc.) **6** to put (a roll of film or a plate) into (a camera) **7** to add weight to, esp. so as to make one end or one side heavier [dice fraudulently *loaded* to fall with a certain face up] **8** to add extra or excessive costs, profits, etc. to [to *load* an expense account] **9** to add (an adulterant, filler, etc.) to **10** to phrase (a question, etc.) so as to elicit a desired answer or reaction ☆**11** *Baseball* to have or cause to have runners on (first, second, and third bases) **12** *Comput.* to transfer (a program or data) into main memory from a disk, tape, etc. —***vi.*** **1** to put a charge of ammunition into a firearm **2** to receive a charge of ammunition [mortars that *load* at the muzzle] **3** to put on, receive, or take on passengers, goods, fuel, etc. [the bus is *loading* now] —☆**get a load of** [Slang] **1** to listen to or hear **2** to look at or see —**have a load on** [Slang] to be intoxicated —**load′er** ***n.***

load displacement the displacement of a completely loaded ship

load·ed (lōd′id) ***adj.*** **1** carrying a load **2** filled, charged, weighted, etc. (as indicated by various senses of LOAD, ***vt., vi.***) **3** [Slang] under the influence of liquor or drugs ☆**4** [Slang] well supplied with money or riches **5** [Informal] well equipped with accessories or features —☆**loaded for bear** ⟦in allusion to a gun *loaded* with ammunition appropriate for hunting large game⟧ [Slang] **1** ready for a fight or conflict **2** very well prepared or equipped

load factor *Elec.* the ratio of average load to greatest load

load·ing (-iŋ) ***n.*** **1** the act of one that loads **2** the thing with which something is loaded **3** the part of an insurance premium added by the insurer to cover expenses, increase surplus, etc. **4** LOAD (***n.*** 9) **5** WING LOADING

loading coil a coil placed in an electric circuit, as of a telephone cable, to increase its inductance

load line any of the lines on the hull of a merchant ship showing the depths to which it may legally be loaded under various circumstances

load·star (lōd′stär′) ***n.*** *alt. sp. of* LODESTAR

load·stone (lōd′stōn′) ***n.*** *alt. sp. of* LODESTONE

loaf[1] (lōf) ***n., pl.*** **loaves** (lōvz) ⟦ME *lof* < OE *hlaf*, akin to Ger *laib*, OHG *hlaib*, ON *hleifr*, Goth *hlaifs*⟧ **1** a portion of bread baked in one piece, commonly of oblong shape and in a size convenient for table use **2** any mass of food shaped somewhat like a loaf of bread and baked [*meatloaf*] **3** LUMP[1] (***n.*** *2b*) **4** [Brit. Slang] head or brain

☆**loaf**[2] (lōf) ***vi.*** ⟦prob. back-form. < fol.⟧ to spend time idly; loiter or lounge about; idle, dawdle, etc. —***vt.*** to spend (time) idly: often with *away*

☆**loaf·er** (lōf′ər) ***n.*** **1** ⟦prob. contr. < *land-loafer* < Ger *landläufer*, a vagabond (akin to Du *landlooper*, obs. E *landloper*) < land, LAND + *laufen*, to run: see LEAP⟧ a person who loafs; lounger; idler **2** ⟦< *Loafer*, former trademark⟧ a moccasinlike shoe for informal wear

loam (lōm) ***n.*** ⟦ME *lome* < OE *lam*: see LIME[1]⟧ **1** a rich soil composed of clay, sand, and some organic matter **2** a mixture of moistened clay, sand, and some organic matter, as straw, used in plastering, making foundry molds, etc. **3** popularly, any rich, dark soil —***vt.*** to fill or cover with loam —**loam′y** ***adj.*** **loam′i·er**, **loam′i·est**

loan (lōn) ***n.*** ⟦ME *lone* < ON *lān* (akin to OE *læn*, lending, loan, *lænan*, to lend) < IE base **leikw-*, to leave behind > L *linquere*, Gr *leipen*, Sans *riṅákti*, (he) leaves⟧ **1** the act of lending, esp. for short-term use [the *loan* of a pen] **2** something lent; esp., a sum of money lent, often for a specified period and repayable with interest — ***vt., vi.*** to lend —**on loan** lent for temporary use or service to another by the owner, regular employer, etc.

loan·a·ble (lōn′ə bəl) ***adj.*** designating or of funds which are available for making loans, often, specif., to governments and large corporations in the financial markets

loan collection a collection of pictures, curios, etc. lent for temporary public exhibition

loan·er (-ər) ***n.*** **1** a person who loans something **2** an automobile, TV, etc. lent in place of one left for repair

☆**loan shark** [Informal] a person who lends money at exorbitant or illegal rates of interest

☆**loan-shark·ing** (lōn′shär′kiŋ) ***n.*** [Informal] the practice of lending money at exorbitant or illegal interest rates

loan·shift (-shift′) ***n.*** a word borrowed from another language in which native morphemes have replaced some of the original ones in the borrowed word (Ex.: SMEARCASE < Ger *Schmierkäse*)

loan translation CALQUE

loan·word (-wurd′) ***n.*** ⟦infl. by Ger *lehnwort*⟧ a word of one language taken into another and naturalized (Ex.: KINDERGARTEN < Ger; CHAUFFEUR < Fr)

loath (lōth, lōth) ***adj.*** ⟦ME *loth* < OE *lath*, hostile, hateful, akin to Ger *leid*, sorrow (orig. adj.) < IE base **leit-*, to detest, abhor > Gr *aleitēs*, sinner⟧ [Now Chiefly Literary] unwilling; reluctant: usually followed by an infinitive [to be *loath* to depart] —***SYN.*** RELUCTANT —**nothing loath** not reluctant(ly); willing(ly)

loathe (lōth) ***vt.*** **loathed**, **loath′ing** ⟦ME *lothen* < OE *lathian*, to be hateful < base of *lath*: see prec.⟧ to feel intense dislike, disgust, or hatred for; abhor; detest —***SYN.*** HATE —**loath′er** ***n.***

loath·ing (-iŋ) ***n.*** ⟦ME *lothynge*⟧ intense dislike, disgust, or hatred; abhorrence —***SYN.*** AVERSION

loath·ly[1] (lōth′lē, lōth′-) ***adv.*** ⟦ME *lothlie* < OE *lathlice*: see LOATH & -LY[2]⟧ [Rare] unwillingly; reluctantly

loath·ly[2] (lōth′lē) ***adj.*** ⟦ME *lothely* < OE *lathlice*: see LOATHE & -LY[1]⟧ *old poet. var. of* LOATHSOME

loath·some (lōth′səm, lōth′-) ***adj.*** ⟦ME *lothsum*⟧ causing loathing; disgusting; abhorrent; detestable —**loath′some·ly** ***adv.*** —**loath′some·ness** ***n.***

loaves (lōvz) ***n.*** *pl. of* LOAF[1]

lob (läb) ***n.*** ⟦ME *lobbe-* (in *lobbe-keling*, large codfish), heavy, thick, akin to OE *lobbe*, spider, EFris, MLowG *lobbe*, hanging lump of flesh, OHG *luppa*, lumpy mass < IE base *(*s*)*leubh-*, to hang loosely > SLOVEN⟧ **1** [Brit. Dial.] a big, slow, clumsy person **2** a soft underhand toss **3** *Tennis* a stroke in which the ball is sent high into the air, usually so as to drop into the back of the opponent's court —*vt.* **lobbed, lob′bing** to throw, toss, etc. in a high curve —*vi.* 1 to move heavily and clumsily: often with *along* 2 to lob a ball —**lob′ber** *n.*

Lo·ba·chev·ski (lō′bə chef′skē), **Ni·ko·lai I·va·no·vich** (nē kô lī′ ē vä′nô vich) 1793-1856; Russ. mathematician

lo·bar (lō′bər, -bär′) *adj.* ⟦ModL *lobaris*⟧ of a lobe or lobes [*lobar* pneumonia]

lo·bate (-bāt′) *adj.* ⟦ModL *lobatus*⟧ having or formed into a lobe or lobes

lo·ba·tion (lō bā′shən) *n.* 1 the condition of having lobes 2 the process of forming lobes 3 a lobe

lob·by (läb′ē) *n., pl.* **-bies** ⟦LL *lobia*: see LODGE⟧ 1 a hall or large anteroom, as a waiting room or vestibule of an apartment house, hotel, theater, etc. 2 a large hall adjacent to the assembly hall of a legislature and open to the public ☆3 a group of lobbyists representing the same special interest [the oil *lobby*] —☆*vi.* **-bied, -by·ing** ⟦from the practice of meeting with legislators in the LOBBY (*n.* 2)⟧ 1 to work as a lobbyist 2 to make an effort to influence someone on a particular matter: often with *for* or *against* —☆*vt.* 1 to attempt to influence the decision or policy of (someone, esp. a public official) as or in the manner of a lobbyist 2 to attempt to influence the passage of (a measure) by acting as a lobbyist

☆**lob·by·ist** (-ist) *n.* a person, acting for a special-interest group, who tries to influence the decisions of legislators or government administrators —**lob′by·ism′** *n.*

lobe (lōb) *n.* ⟦Fr < LL *lobus* < Gr *lobos* < IE base *lob-, var. of *leb-, to hang down > LAP[1], SLEEP⟧ a rounded projecting part; specif., *a)* the fleshy lower part of the human ear *b)* any of the main divisions of an organ separated by fissures, etc. [a *lobe* of the brain, lung, or liver] *c)* any of the major divisions of a simple leaf that is not divided completely to the midrib or base

lo·bec·to·my (lō bek′tə mē) *n., pl.* **-mies** ⟦prec. + -ECTOMY⟧ the surgical removal of a lobe, as of a lung

lobed (lōbd) *adj.* 1 LOBATE 2 having major divisions which extend almost to the base or center, as the leaves of oaks or maples

lobe-fin (lōb′fin′) *n.* any of a subclass (Sarcopterygii) of bony fishes having thick, limblike, paired fins, including the lungfishes and the coelacanth

lo·be·li·a (lō bēl′yə, -bē′lē ə) *n.* ⟦ModL, after *Lobelius*, Latinized name of Matthias de L'*Obel* (1538-1616), Fl botanist⟧ any of a genus (*Lobelia*) of annual or perennial plants of the bellflower family, having white, blue, or red flowers of very irregular shape

lo·be·line (lō′bə lēn′, -lin) *n.* ⟦< ModL *Lobelia* (see prec.) + -INE[3]⟧ a yellow, crystalline alkaloid, $C_{22}H_{27}NO_2$, related to nicotine, used in medicine and in products that help smokers quit smoking

lob·lol·ly (läb′läl′ē) *n., pl.* **-lies** ⟦16th-c., prob. < dial. *lob*, to bubble, boil + dial. *lolly*, broth, soup⟧ 1 [Dial.] a thick gruel ☆2 [Dial.] a mudhole; muddy puddle 3 *a)* a common pine (*Pinus taeda*) of the SE U.S., having long needles borne in pairs or threes *b)* the wood of this tree: also **loblolly pine**

☆**loblolly bay** an evergreen tree (*Gordonia lasianthus*) of the tea family, found in the SE U.S. and having large, white, fragrant flowers

☆**lo·bo** (lō′bō) *n., pl.* **-bos** ⟦Sp < L *lupus*, WOLF⟧ GRAY WOLF

lo·bot·o·mize (lō bät′ə mīz′, lə-) *vt.* **-mized′, -miz′ing** 1 to perform a lobotomy on 2 to cause to behave in a machinelike way, as without vitality, emotion, or independent thought: usually in the pp.

lo·bot·o·my (-bät′ə mē) *n., pl.* **-mies** ⟦< LOBE + -TOMY⟧ a surgical operation in which a lobe of the brain, esp. the frontal lobe of the cerebrum, is cut into or across: once a treatment for psychoses

lob·scouse (läb′skous′) *n.* ⟦*lob* (as in LOBLOLLY) + *scouse* < ?⟧ a traditional sailor's stew, originating in Germany, of meat, vegetables, and hardtack

lob·ster (läb′stər) *n., pl.* **-sters** or **-ster** ⟦ME < OE *loppestre, lopustre* < *loppe*, spider (from the external resemblance: see LOB) + *-estre*: see -STER⟧ 1 any of various families (esp. Nephropidae) of marine, bottom-dwelling decapods with compound eyes, long antennae, and usually the first pair of legs modified into large, powerful pincers: lobsters are greenish or dark gray in color when alive, but turn bright red when boiled 2 the flesh of these animals used as food —*vi.* to fish for lobsters —**lob′ster·ing** *n.*

lobster

lob·ster·man (-mən) *n., pl.* **-men** (-mən) a person who catches lobsters for a living

lobster pot a basketlike trap for catching lobsters

☆**lobster shift** (*or* **trick**) ⟦orig. uncert.⟧ [Informal] the night shift of a newspaper staff, or now of any working force

lobster tail the flesh of the tail of any of various crustaceans, esp. the crayfish, prepared as food, often by broiling in the shell

lobster ther·mi·dor (thur′mə dôr′) ⟦see THERMIDOR⟧ a dish consisting of lobster flesh, mushrooms, etc. in a thick, creamy sauce, browned and served in half of a lobster shell

lob·ule (läb′yo͞ol′) *n.* ⟦ModL *lobulus*, dim.⟧ 1 a small lobe 2 a subdivision of a lobe —**lob′u·lar** (-yo͞o lər) *adj.* —**lob′u·late′** (-lāt′) *adj.*

lob·worm (läb′wurm′) *n.* LUGWORM

loc. *abbrev.* locative

lo·cal (lō′kəl) *adj.* ⟦ME *locall* < OFr *local* < LL *localis* < L *locus*, a place < IE *stlokos < base *stel-, to set up, stand, location > STALK[1], STALL[1], STILL[1], Gr *stellein*, to put⟧ 1 relating to place 2 of, characteristic of, or confined to a particular place or district [items of *local* interest] 3 not broad; restricted; narrow [*local* outlook] 4 of or for a particular part or specific area of the body; not general ☆5 making all stops along its run [a *local* bus] 6 *Comput.* occurring or located on-site: opposed to REMOTE (*adj.* 9) 7 [Chiefly Brit.] of or relating to specific portions or details of a literary text, as distinguished from its overall structure, themes, style, etc. —*n.* ☆1 a local train, bus, etc. ☆2 a newspaper item of local interest only ☆3 a chapter or branch of a labor union 4 [Informal] a resident of a particular place [the town *locals* are friendly enough] 5 [Brit. Informal] a neighborhood pub 6 an anesthetic that numbs only a small area of the body, allowing the patient to remain conscious during minor surgery, a biopsy, etc.: cf. GENERAL (*n.* 5): in full **local anesthetic**

lo·cal (lō′kal′) *adj.* [Informal] *alt. sp. of* LOW-CAL

local anesthesia *see* ANESTHESIA (sense 2)

local anesthetic *see* LOCAL (*n.* 6)

local area network a computer NETWORK (sense 3*a*) within a small area or within a common environment, as one within a building or one connecting offices on separate floors

local color behavior, speech, etc. characteristic of a certain region or time, depicted in a novel, play, etc. to add a feeling of authenticity

lo·cale (lō kal′) *n.* ⟦OFr *local*⟧ a place or locality, esp. with reference to events or circumstances connected with it, often as a setting for a story, play, etc.

local government 1 government of the affairs of a town, district, etc. by the people living there 2 the people chosen to administer this government

Local Group, the the cluster of neighboring galaxies that includes Andromeda, the Magellanic Clouds, and the Milky Way

lo·cal·ism (lō′kəl iz′əm) *n.* 1 a way of acting characteristic of one locality; local custom, practice, or mannerism 2 a word, meaning, expression, pronunciation, etc. peculiar to one locality 3 fondness for a particular locality 4 narrow outlook; provincialism —**lo′cal·is′tic** *adj.*

lo·cal·ite (lō′kəl īt′) *n.* ⟦see -ITE[1]⟧ a resident of a particular place

lo·cal·i·ty (lō kal′ə tē) *n., pl.* **-ties** ⟦Fr *localité* < LL *localitis*: see LOCAL⟧ 1 position with regard to surrounding objects, landmarks, etc. [a sense of *locality*] 2 a place; district; neighborhood

lo·cal·ize (lō′kə līz′) *vt.* **-ized′, -iz′ing** 1 to make local; limit or confine to a particular place, area, or locality 2 to determine the specific local origin of, as a tradition 3 to concentrate in one area, esp. of the body —**lo′cal·iz′a·ble** *adj.* —**lo′cal·i·za′tion** *n.*

lo·cal·iz·er (-lī′zər) *n.* a directional radio beam sent from the beginning of the runway and used to align an incoming airplane

lo·cal·ly (lō′kəl ē) *adv.* 1 in a local way; with respect to place 2 within a given area or areas [the damage done by a tornado *locally*]

local option the right of determining by a vote of the residents whether something, as the sale of intoxicating liquors, shall be permitted in their locality

Lo·car·no (lō kär′nō) town in S Switzerland, on Lake Maggiore: site of peace conference (1925)

lo·cate (lō′kāt′, lō kāt′) *vt.* **-cat′ed, -cat′ing** ⟦< L *locatus*, pp. of *locare*, to place < *locus*: see LOCAL⟧ 1 to mark off or designate the site of (a mining claim, etc.) 2 to establish in a certain place [offices *located* downtown] 3 to discover the position of after a search [to *locate* a lost object] 4 to show the position of [to *locate* Guam on a map] 5 to assign to a particular place, function, occupation, etc. —*vi.* ☆[Informal] to make one's home or headquarters; settle [to *locate* in Boston] —**lo′cat′er** *n.*, **lo′ca′tor**

lo·ca·tion (lō kā′shən) *n.* ⟦L *locatio*⟧ 1 a locating or being located 2 position in space; place where a factory, house, etc. is or is to be; situation 3 an area marked off or designated for a specific purpose ☆4 *Film* an outdoor set or setting, away from the studio, where scenes are filmed: chiefly in **on location** —**lo·ca′tion·al** *adj.*

loc·a·tive (läk′ə tiv) *Gram. adj.* ⟦< L *locatus* (see LOCATE) + -IVE, by assoc. with VOCATIVE⟧ designating, of, or in the case indicating place at which or in which, as in Latin, Greek, Sanskrit, etc. —*n.* 1 the locative case 2 a word in the locative case

loc. cit. *abbrev.* ⟦L *loco citato*⟧ in the place cited

loch (läk, läkh) *n.* ⟦ME *louch* < Gael & OIr: for IE base see LAKE[1]⟧ [Scot.] 1 a lake 2 an arm of the sea, esp. when narrow and nearly surrounded by land

lo·chi·a (lō′kē ə, läk′ē ə) *n.* ⟦ModL < Gr, neut. pl. of *lochios*, of childbirth < IE *loghos, bed < base *legh-, to LIE[1]⟧ the uterine discharge from the vagina that occurs for several days after childbirth

Loch Ness monster *see* NESS, Loch

lo·ci (lō′sī′) *n. pl. of* LOCUS

lock[1] (läk) *n.* ⟦ME < OE *loc*, a bolt, bar, enclosure, prison, akin to Ger *loch*, a hole, ON *lok*, a lid, prob. < IE base *leug-, to bend > Gr *lygos*, supple twig, L *luctari*, to struggle⟧ 1 a mechanical device furnished with a bolt and usually a spring, for fastening a door, strongbox, etc. by means of a key or combination 2 anything that fastens something else and prevents it from opening, turning, etc. 3 a locking together; jam 4 an enclosed part of a canal, waterway, etc. equipped with gates so that the level of the water can be changed to raise or lower boats from one level to another 5 the mechanism of a firearm used to explode the ammunition charge; gunlock 6 AIR LOCK (sense 1) 7 [Slang] a certainty; sure thing [our team is a *lock* to win the title] 8 *Wrestling* a hold in which a part of the opponent's body is firmly gripped: often in comb. [*headlock*] —*vt.* 1 to fasten (a door, trunk, etc.) by means of a lock **2** to keep from going in or out by or as by means of a lock; shut (*up, in* or *out*); confine [*locked* in jail] **3** to fit closely; link; intertwine [to *lock* arms] **4** to embrace tightly **5** to jam or force together so as to make immovable [*locked* gears, *locked* brakes] **6** to put in a fixed position [a throttle *locked* in the idle position] **7** to make (a bid, etc.) firm, definite, or final: with *in* ☆**8** to equip (a canal, etc.) with a lock or locks **9** to move or pass (a ship) through a lock **10** *Printing* to fasten (type elements) in a chase or on the bed of a press by means of quoins: often with *up* ***—vi.*** **1** to become locked **2** to be capable of being locked **3** to intertwine or interlock; link together **4** to close tightly and firmly [the dog's jaws *locked* on its prey] **5** to jam, as gears **6** to pass through the locks of a canal **—have a lock on** [Slang] to be sure of winning, gaining, or controlling [the other party *has a lock on* that Senate seat] **—lock away** to store or safeguard in a locked box, container, etc. **—locked in** displaying total concentration **—lock on (or onto)** to track and automatically follow (a target), as by radar **—lock out 1** to shut out by or as by locking the door against **2** to keep (workers) from a place of employment in seeking to force terms upon them **—lock, stock, and barrel** ⟦with reference to the main parts of a gun⟧ [Informal] completely; entirely **—lock up 1** to fasten the doors of (a house, etc.) by means of locks **2** to enclose or store in a locked container **3** to put in jail **4** to make certain to have the result one wants [to have an election *locked up*] **—under lock and key** locked up; safely put away

lock² (läk) ***n.*** ⟦ME *lokke* < OE *loc* (akin to Ger *locke*): basic sense "a bend, twist": IE base as in prec.⟧ **1** a curl, tress, or ringlet of hair **2** [*pl.*] [Old Poet.] the hair of the head **3** a tuft of wool, cotton, etc.

lock·age (läk′ij) ***n.*** **1** *a)* the act of moving a ship through a lock or locks *b)* the charge for such a service **2** a system of canal locks

lock·box (läk′bäks′) ***n.*** **1** a box with a lock, used for securing items of value, as a safe-deposit box, a strongbox, a post-office box, etc. **2** an electronic device which can block designated cable TV channels to prevent viewing by unauthorized persons Also written **lock box**

lock·down (läk′doun′) ***n.*** **1** an emergency security procedure in which prison inmates are locked in their cells and denied the usual privileges of dining, showering, etc. outside of them **2** any emergency security procedure in which authorities prohibit persons from leaving a building, compound, etc.

Locke (läk) **1 David Ross** *see* NASBY, Petroleum V. **2 John** 1632-1704; Eng. empirical philosopher

Lock·e·an (läk′ē ən) ***adj.*** of John Locke or his philosophy

lock·er (läk′ər) ***n.*** **1** a person or thing that locks **2** *a)* a chest, closet, compartment, drawer, etc., usually of metal, which can be fastened with a lock, esp. such a container for individual or specified use ☆*b)* FOOTLOCKER ☆**3** a large compartment, as one rented in a cold-storage plant, for freezing and storing foods at or below 0°F

☆**locker room** a room equipped with lockers, as at a gymnasium, swimming pool, factory, etc., for storing one's clothes and equipment

lock·et (läk′it) ***n.*** ⟦OFr *loquet*, dim of *loc*, a latch, lock < Frank **lok*, akin to OE *loc*, LOCK¹⟧ a small, hinged, ornamental case of gold, silver, etc., for holding a picture, lock of hair, etc.: it is usually worn suspended from a necklace or chain

lock·jaw (läk′jô′) ***n.*** ⟦short for earlier *locked jaw*⟧ *nontechnical term for:* **1** TRISMUS **2** TETANUS (sense 1)

lock·mak·er (-māk′ər) ***n.*** a locksmith **—lock′mak′ing *n.***

lock·mas·ter (-mas′tər) ***n.*** one in charge of a canal lock

lock·nut (-nut′) ***n.*** **1** a thin nut screwed typically onto or above an ordinary nut to prevent the latter from working loose **2** any of various nuts specially designed to resist loosening Also written **lock nut**

lock·out (-out′) ***n.*** the refusal by an employer to allow employees to come in to work until agreement is reached, as on contract terms

lock·smith (-smith′) ***n.*** a person whose work is making or repairing locks and making keys

lock·step (-step′) ***n.*** **1** a way of marching in such close file that the corresponding legs of the marchers must keep step precisely **2** a condition or relationship in which one rigidly conforms to the actions of another [interest rates in *lockstep* with inflation] ***—adj.*** inflexibly conforming or conformist [*lockstep* adherence to party ideology]

lock stitch the typical sewing-machine stitch formed by the interlocking of two threads

lock·up (-up′) ***n.*** **1** the act of locking up **2** a being locked up, as in jail **3** a jail

☆**lo·co** (lō′kō) ***n.*** ⟦MexSp < Sp, mad < L *ulucus*, owl, akin to *ulula*, OWL⟧ **1** LOCOWEED **2** LOCO DISEASE ***—vt.* -coed, -co·ing 1** to poison with locoweed **2** [Slang] to craze Usually in the pp. ***—adj.*** [Slang] crazy; demented

lo·co- (lō′kō, -kə) ⟦< L *loco*, abl. of *locus*, place: see LOCAL⟧ *combining form* from place to place [*locomotion*]

lo·co ci·ta·to (lō′kō sī tāt′ō, -si tät′ō) ⟦L⟧ in the place cited or quoted: referring to a previously cited passage

☆**loco disease** (lō′kō) a nervous disease of horses, sheep, and cattle caused by locoweed poison: also **lo·co·ism** (lō′kō iz′əm) ***n.***

☆**lo·co·fo·co** (lō′kō fō′kō) ***n.,*** *pl.* **-cos** ⟦coined (*c.* 1834) after LOCO(MOTIVE), interpreted as "self-(moving)" + It *fuoco*, fire < L *focus*: see FOCUS; sense 2 from the use of such matches in Tammany Hall, Oct. 22, 1835, by one faction to restore lights extinguished by another⟧ **1** [Historical] a cigar or match ignited by friction **2** [**L-**] [Historical] *a)* a faction of the Democratic Party in New York (*c.* 1835) *b)* a member of this faction **3** [Archaic] any Democrat

lo·co·mo·bile (lō′kə mō bēl′) ***n.*** ⟦< a make of automobile < adj., self-propelled < *loco-* (see prec.) + MOBILE⟧ ☆[Historical] an early, steam-powered automobile

lo·co·mo·tion (-mō′shən) ***n.*** ⟦LOCO- + MOTION⟧ motion, or the power of moving, from one place to another

lo·co·mo·tive (-mōt′iv) ***adj.*** ⟦< LOCO- + LL *motivus*, moving⟧ **1** of locomotion **2** moving or capable of moving from one place to another; not stationary **3** designating or of engines that move under their own power [*locomotive* design] ***—n.*** an engine that can move about by its own power; esp., an electric, steam, or diesel engine on wheels, designed to push or pull a railroad train

lo·co·mo·tor (lō′kə mōt′ər, lō′kə mōt′ər) ***n.*** ⟦LOCO- + L *motor*, mover⟧ a machine or organism with power of locomotion ***—adj.*** of or relating to locomotion **—lo′co·mo′to·ry *adj.***

locomotor ataxia TABES DORSALIS

☆**lo·co·weed** (lō′kō wēd′) ***n.*** any of several perennial plants (genera *Astragalus* and *Oxytropis*) of the pea family, which are common in W North America and cause the loco disease of cattle, sheep, and esp. horses

Lo·cris (lō′kris) region of ancient Greece, north of the Gulf of Corinth **—Lo·cri·an** (lō′krē ən, lôk′rē-) ***adj., n.***

loc·u·lar (läk′yoo lər, -yə-) ***adj.*** *Biol.* of, having the nature of, or consisting of loculi, or cavities: also **loc′u·late** (-lit, -lāt′)

loc·u·li·ci·dal (läk′yoo li sīd′'l) ***adj.*** ⟦< fol. + *-i-* + -CIDAL⟧ *Bot.* splitting open along the midribs of the carpels of which it is formed: said of a capsule

loc·u·lus (läk′yoo ləs, -yə-) ***n.,*** *pl.* **-li′** (-lī′) ⟦ModL < L, dim. of *locus*, place: see LOCAL⟧ any small cavity or chamber in plant or animal tissue: also **loc′ule′** (-yool′)

☆**lo·cum te·nens** (lō′kəm tē′nənz) ⟦ML, lit., holding the place < L *locum*, acc. of *locus*, a place (see LOCAL) + *tenens*, prp. of *tenere*, to hold: see THIN⟧ [Chiefly Brit.] a person taking another's place for the time being; temporary substitute, as for a doctor or a member of the clergy: also **lo′cum *n.***

lo·cus (lō′kəs) ***n.,*** *pl.* **lo·ci** (lō′sī′) ⟦L: see LOCAL⟧ **1** a place: typically a technical usage **2** *Genetics* the position on a chromosome occupied by a particular gene **3** *Math. a)* any system of points, lines, etc. which satisfies one or more given conditions *b)* a line, plane, etc. every point of which satisfies a given condition and which contains no point that does not satisfy this condition

lo·cus clas·si·cus (lō′kəs klas′i kəs) *pl.* ***lo·ci clas·si·ci*** (lō′sī′ klas′i sī′) ⟦L⟧ a passage typically or frequently cited as authoritative in illustrating a certain point or subject

lo·cus in quo (lō′kəs in kwō′) ⟦L, lit., the place in which⟧ the very place

lo·cust (lō′kəst) ***n.*** ⟦ME < L *locusta*, prob. akin to *lacerta*, LIZARD⟧ **1** any of various large grasshoppers; specif., a migratory grasshopper often traveling in great swarms and causing extensive damage to vegetation **2** SEVENTEEN-YEAR LOCUST **3** *a)* a spiny tree (*Robinia pseudoacacia*) of the pea family, native to the E or central U.S. and having long, pendulous racemes of fragrant white flowers (also called **black locust** or **yellow locust**) *b)* the yellowish, hard, durable wood of this tree **4** any honeylocust **5** CAROB (sense 1)

lo·cu·tion (lō kyoo′shən) ***n.*** ⟦ME *locucion* < L *locutio*, a speaking < pp. of *loqui*, to speak⟧ **1** a word, phrase, or expression **2** a particular style of speech; phraseology

lode (lōd) ***n.*** ⟦var. of LOAD (ME *lode* < OE *lad*) retaining etym. senses "course, way"⟧ *Mining* **1** a vein containing important quantities of metallic ore and filling a well-defined fissure in the rock **2** any flat deposit of valuable ore separated from the adjoining rock by definite boundaries **3** any abundant or rich source

lo·den (lōd′'n) ***n.*** ⟦Ger < MHG *lode* < OHG *lodo*, coarse cloth, akin to OE *lotha*, cloak < IE base **(s)leu-*, to hang loosely > SLOUCH, SLEET⟧ **1** a fulled, waterproof wool cloth with a short pile, used for coats **2** a dark olive green often used for this cloth: also **loden green**

lode·star (lōd′stär′) ***n.*** ⟦ME *lodesterre*: see LODE & STAR⟧ **1** a star by which one directs one's course; esp., the North Star **2** a guiding principle or ideal

lode·stone (-stōn′) ***n.*** ⟦LODE + STONE⟧ **1** any strongly magnetized rock, esp. one containing magnetite **2** something that attracts as with magnetic force

lodge (läj) ***n.*** ⟦ME *loge*, hut, masons' workshop (> sense 2) < OFr, summer house, arbor (> LOGE) < LL *lobia* < Gmc **laubja*, sheltered place, leafy arbor (> OHG *louba*, upper roof, porch, leafy cover): for IE base see LEAF⟧ **1** *a)* a small house, esp. one for a servant or one for use during a special season [a caretaker's *lodge*, hunting *lodge*] *b)* a resort hotel or motel **2** *a)* the meeting place of a local chapter, as of a fraternal organization *b)* such a local chapter **3** the den or typical lair of certain wild animals, esp. beavers ☆**4** *a)* the traditional hut or tent of an American Indian *b)* those living in it ***—vt.* lodged, lodg′ing** ⟦ME *loggen* < OFr *logier* (> Fr *loger*)⟧ **1** to provide with a place of temporary residence; house **2** to rent rooms to; take as a paying guest **3** to serve as a temporary dwelling for **4** to serve as a container for **5** to place or deposit for safekeeping **6** to put or send into a place or position by shooting, thrusting, etc.; place; land: with *in* [to *lodge* an arrow in a target] **7** to bring (an accusation, complaint, etc.) before legal authorities **8** to confer (powers) upon: with *in* **9** to beat down (growing crops), as rain ***—vi.*** **1** to live in a certain place for a time **2** to live (*with* another or *in* another's home) as a paying guest **3** to come to rest or be placed and remain firmly fixed: with *in* [a chicken bone *lodged* in the cat's throat]

Lodge (läj), **Henry Cabot** 1850-1924; U.S. senator (1893-1924)

lodge·pole (pine) (läj′pōl′) **1** a Rocky Mountain pine (*Pinus contorta*) used for lumber, poles, etc. **2** its wood

lodg·er (läj′ər) ***n.*** a person or thing that lodges; esp., one who lives in a rented room in another's home

lodg·ing (-iŋ) ***n.*** ⟦ME *loggyng*: see LODGE, ***vt.***⟧ **1** the act of one that lodges **2** a place to live in, esp. temporarily; quarters **3** [*pl.*] a room or rooms rented in a private home

lodging house ROOMING HOUSE

lodg·ment (-mənt) ***n.*** ⟦Fr *logement*⟧ **1** a lodging or being lodged **2** a lodging place **3** an accumulation of deposited material, often in the nature of an obstruction **4** *Mil.* a foothold gained in territory held by the enemy Also sp. **lodge′ment**

Lo·di (lō′dē) city in Lombardy, NW Italy: scene of Napoleon's defeat of the Austrians (1796)

lod·i·cule (läd′i kyo͞ol′) ***n.*** ⟦L *lodicula*, a small coverlet, dim. of *lodix*, a coverlet⟧ one of the usually two minute, flat or fleshy outgrowths at the base of the flower of a grass, that swell up at flowering, assisting the escape of anthers and stigmas

Łódź (lo͞oj, lo͝oj) city in central Poland

Loeb (lōb), **Jacques** (zhäk) 1859-1924; U.S. physiologist & biologist, born in Germany

lo·ess (lō′es′; *also* les, lus) ***n.*** ⟦Ger *löss*, arbitrary use of dial. *lösch*, loose < base of *lösen*, to loosen: for IE base see LOSE⟧ a fine-grained, yellowish-brown, extremely fertile loam deposited mainly by the wind and found widely in North America, Asia, and Europe —**lo·ess·i·al** (lō es′ē əl) ***adj.***

Loe·wy (lō′ē), **Raymond (Fernand)** 1893-1986; U.S. industrial designer, born in France

Lo·fo·ten Islands (lō′fo͞ot′'n) group of Norwegian islands within the Arctic Circle, off the NW coast of Norway: *c.* 550 sq mi (1,424 sq km)

loft (lôft, läft) ***n.*** ⟦ME *lofte* < Late OE *loft* < ON *lopt*, upper room, air, sky (akin to OE *lyft*, air, sky) < IE base **leup-*, **leubh-*, to peel off > LEAF⟧ **1** *a)* an attic or atticlike space, usually not partitioned off into rooms, immediately below the roof of a house, barn, etc. ☆*b)* any of the upper stories of a warehouse or factory; now often, specif., a dwelling space, artist's studio, etc. on an upper story of a converted warehouse or factory **2** a gallery [the choir *loft* in a church] **3** *a)* the slope given to the face of a golf club to aid in knocking the ball in a high curve *b)* the height attained by hitting or throwing a ball in a high curve —***vt.*** **1** to store in a loft **2** *a)* to hit or throw (a golf ball, baseball, etc.) into the air in a high curve *b)* to throw (a bowling ball) so that it strikes the alley sharply some distance past the foul line —***vi.*** to loft a ball —**loft′er** ***n.***

loft bed a bed raised, as on supports, high enough overhead to allow the use of the floor area below for various purposes, as for part of a living room

Lof·ting (lôf′tiŋ), **Hugh (John)** 1886-1947; U.S. writer & illustrator, esp. of children's books, born in England

loft·y (lôf′tē, läf′-) ***adj.*** **loft′i·er**, **loft′i·est** **1** very high [a *lofty* peak in the Alps] **2** elevated; noble; sublime **3** haughty; arrogant —**loft′i·ly** ***adv.*** —**loft′i·ness** ***n.***

log[1] (lôg, läg) ***n.*** ⟦ME *logge*, prob. < or akin to ON *lāg* (Dan *laag*), felled tree < base of *liggia*, to lie, akin to OE *licgan*, to LIE[1]⟧ **1** a section of the trunk or of a large branch of a felled tree, either in its natural state or cut up for use in building, as firewood, etc. **2** something made or prepared in the shape of a cylinder [a cheese *log*] **3** ⟦because orig. a quadrant of WOOD[1]⟧ any of various devices for measuring the speed of a ship **4** a daily record of a ship's speed, progress, etc. and of the events in its voyage, kept in a logbook **5** *a)* a similar record of an aircraft's flight *b)* a record of a pilot's flying time, experience, etc. **6** any record of progress or occurrences, as on a journey, in an experiment, etc. **7** a book in which a log is kept, specif. a log of a ship's voyage or an aircraft's flight; logbook —***adj.*** made of a log or logs —***vt.*** **logged**, **log′ging** **1** to saw (trees) into logs ☆**2** to cut down the trees of (a region) for use as lumber or logs **3** to enter or record in a log **4** to sail or fly (a specified distance) **5** to be credited with a record of (certain accomplishments) —☆***vi.*** to cut down trees and transport the logs to a sawmill —**log on (or off)** to enter the necessary information to begin (or end) a session on a computer terminal, PC, etc.

log[2] (lôg, läg) ***n.*** *short for* LOGARITHM

-log (lôg, läg) *combining form* -LOGUE

Lo·gan (lō′gən), **Mount** ⟦after Sir W. E. *Logan* (1798-1875), Cdn geologist⟧ mountain in the St. Elias range, SW Yukon Territory, Canada: highest mountain in Canada: 19,850 ft (6,050 m)

☆**lo·gan·ber·ry** (lō′gən ber′ē) ***n.***, *pl.* **-ries** ⟦after Judge J. H. *Logan* (1841-1928), who developed it (1881)⟧ **1** a hybrid bramble (*Rubus loganobaccus*) of the rose family, developed from the blackberry and the red raspberry and extensively grown for its fruit **2** the highly acid, purplish-red fruit of this shrub

lo·ga·ni·a (lō gā′nē ə, -gān′yə) ***adj.*** ⟦ModL, after J. *Logan* (1674-1751), Ir botanist + -IA⟧ designating a family (Loganiaceae, order Gentianales) of chiefly tropical and subtropical, often poisonous dicotyledonous plants, including buddleia, nux vomica, and gelsemium

log·a·rithm (lôg′ə rith′əm, läg′-) ***n.*** ⟦ModL *logarithmus* < Gr *logos*, a word, proportion, ratio (see LOGIC) + *arithmos*, number (see ARITHMETIC)⟧ *Math.* the exponent expressing the power to which a fixed number (the *base*) must be raised in order to produce a given number (the *antilogarithm*): logarithms computed to the base 10 are often used for shortening mathematical calculations —**log′a·rith′mic** ***adj.*** —**log′a·rith′mi·cal·ly** ***adv.***

log·book (lôg′bo͝ok′) ***n.*** a book in which a log, or record, is kept, specif. a log of a ship's voyage or an aircraft's flight; LOG[1] (***n.*** 7)

loge (lōzh) ***n.*** ⟦OFr: see LODGE⟧ **1** a BOX[1] (***n.*** 6) in a theater **2** the forward section of a mezzanine or balcony in a theater, set off by an aisle or railing **3** a privately owned or leased luxury unit in a stadium or arena, resembling a living room or hotel room, as for entertaining guests while watching a sporting or other event

☆**log·ger** (lôg′ər) ***n.*** a person whose work is logging; lumberjack

log·ger·head (lôg′ər hed′, läg′-) ***n.*** ⟦dial. *logger*, heavy block of wood (< LOG[1]) + HEAD⟧ **1** [Historical] a long-handled tool with a ball, or bulb, at the end, used when heated to melt tar, heat liquids, etc. **2** any of a genus (*Caretta*, family Cheloniidae) of sea turtles with a hard shell and a large head: also **loggerhead turtle** **3** [Dial.] a stupid fellow; blockhead —**at loggerheads** ⟦< sense 1, ? when used as a weapon⟧ in disagreement; quarreling

☆**loggerhead shrike** a common North American shrike (*Lanius ludovicianus*), white below with black markings on the upper parts

log·gia (lä′jə, lô′-; -jē ə) ***n.*** ⟦It < OFr *loge*: see LODGE⟧ an arcaded or roofed gallery built into or projecting from the side of a building, esp. one overlooking an open court

loggia

☆**log·ging** (lôg′iŋ) ***n.*** the occupation of cutting down trees, cutting them into logs, and transporting the logs to a sawmill

lo·gi·a (lō′gē ə, lä′-) ***pl.n.***, *sing.* **lo′gi·on′** (-än′) ⟦Gr, pl., sayings < *logos*, a word: see fol.⟧ **1** maxims attributed to a religious leader **2** [**L-**] AGRAPHA

log·ic (läj′ik) ***n.*** ⟦ME *logike* < OFr *logique* < L *logica* < Gr *logikē* (*technē*), logical (art) < *logikos*, of speaking or reasoning < *logos*, a word, reckoning, thought < *legein*, to speak, choose, read < IE base **leĝ-*, to gather > L *legere*, to collect, OE *lœce*, LEECH[1]⟧ **1** *a)* the branch of philosophy dealing with correct reasoning, describing relationships among propositions in terms of implication, contradiction, contrariety, conversion, etc. *b)* a particular system of such relationships [Aristotelian *logic*]: see also FORMAL LOGIC, SYMBOLIC LOGIC **2** correct reasoning; valid induction or deduction [the lack of *logic* in his scheme] **3** way of reasoning, whether correct or incorrect [to use faulty *logic*] **4** the system of principles underlying any art or science **5** necessary connection or outcome, as through the working of cause and effect [the *logic* of events] **6** the systematized interconnection of switching functions, circuits, or devices, as in electronic computers

log·i·cal (läj′i kəl) ***adj.*** ⟦ML *logicalis*⟧ **1** of or used in the science of logic **2** according to the principles of logic, or correct reasoning **3** necessary or to be expected because of what has gone before; that follows as reasonable **4** using, or accustomed to using, correct reasoning —**log′i·cal′i·ty** (-kal′i tē) ***n.***, **log′i·cal·ness** —**log′i·cal·ly** ***adv.***

-log·i·cal (läj′i kəl) ⟦< Gr -*logikos* (< *logikos*: see LOGIC) + -AL⟧ *combining form forming adjectives* of or relating to the science, doctrine, or theory of: also **-log·ic**

logical positivism a movement in philosophy which tests all statements by reference to sense experience or the structure of language and is concerned with the unification of the sciences through a common logical language: also called **logical empiricism**

lo·gi·cian (lō jish′ən) ***n.*** an expert in logic

lo·gis·tic[1] (lō jis′tik) ***adj.*** of logistics: also **lo·gis′ti·cal** —**lo·gis′ti·cal·ly** ***adv.***

lo·gis·tic[2] (lō jis′tik) ***adj.*** ⟦ML *logisticus* < Gr *logistikos*, skilled in calculation < *logizesthai*, to calculate < *logos*, a word: see LOGIC⟧ *Math., Statistics* designating or of an S-shaped curve representing an exponential function, used in population studies, etc. —**lo·gis′ti·cal·ly** ***adv.***

lo·gis·tics (-tiks) ***n.*** ⟦Fr *logistique* < *logis*, lodgings (< *loger*, to quarter: see LODGE): form as if < ML *logisticus*: see prec.⟧ [*with sing. or pl. v.*] **1** the branch of military science having to do with procuring, maintaining, and transporting materiel, personnel, and facilities **2** the managing of the details of an undertaking

☆**log·jam** (lôg′jam′) ***n.*** **1** an obstacle formed by logs jamming together in a stream **2** an accumulation of unfinished work, unresolved problems, etc.; backlog **3** a deadlock or impasse

log·o (lō′gō; *occas.* lä′gō) ***n.*** a distinctive symbol, colophon, signature, trademark, newspaper nameplate, etc., as for a company or brand

Lo·go (lō′gō) ***n.*** ⟦< Gr *logos*: see LOGIC⟧ a simplified computer language designed esp. for teaching school children about computer programming: also written **LOGO**

log·o- (lôg′ō, -ə; läg′-) ⟦Gr < *logos*: see LOGIC⟧ *combining form* word, speech, discourse [*logogram*]

log·o·gram (lôg′ō gram′, lôg′ə-) ***n.*** ⟦prec. + -GRAM⟧ a letter, character, or symbol used to represent an entire word (Ex.: $ for *dollar*): also **log′o·graph′** (-graf′) —**log′o·gram·mat′ic** (-grə mat′ik) ***adj.***

lo·gog·ra·phy (lō gäg′rə fē) ***n.*** ⟦Gr *logographia*, writing of speeches, office of official recorder in a law court: see LOGO- & -GRAPHY⟧ the use of logotypes in printing

log·o·griph (lôg′ō grif′, lôg′ə-) ***n.*** ⟦LOGO- + Gr *griphos*, fishing basket, riddle, prob. < IE **grebh-* > CRIB⟧ a word puzzle, as an anagram

lo·gom·a·chy (lō gäm′ə kē) ***n.***, *pl.* **-chies** ⟦Gr *logomachia* < *logos*, a word (see LOGIC) + -*machia*, -MACHY⟧ strife or contention in words only, or an argument about words

log·or·rhe·a (lôg′ə rē′ə) ***n.*** ⟦ModL: see LOGO- & -RRHEA⟧ excessive talkativeness, esp. when incoherent and uncontrollable —**log′or·rhe′ic** (-ik) ***adj.***

Lo·gos (lō′gōs′, lô′-, lä′-; -gôs′, -gäs′) ***n.*** ⟦L *logos* < Gr, a word: see LOGIC⟧ **1** [*sometimes* **l-**] in classical Greek philosophy, reason regarded as constituting the controlling principle of the universe and as being manifested by speech **2** *Christian Theol.* the eternal thought or word of God, made incarnate in Jesus Christ: John 1

log·o·type (lôg′ə tīp′, läg′-) ***n.*** ⟦LOGO- + -TYPE⟧ **1** *Typography* a single type body or matrix containing a short, often-used set of letters, or word, as *an, qu*: cf. LIGATURE **2** LOGO

☆**log·roll** (lôg′rōl′) ***vi.*** ⟦back-form. < fol.⟧ to take part in logrolling —***vt.*** to get passage of (a bill) by logrolling —**log′roll′er** ***n.***

☆**log·roll·ing** (-rōl′iŋ) ***n.*** **1** the act of rolling logs, as when a group of neighbors help to clear off land by rolling logs into some spot for burning, etc. **2** *a)* an exchange of help or favors *b)* *Politics* mutual aid among politicians, as by reciprocal voting for each other's bills **3** BIRLING

Lo·gro·ño (lə grōn′yō) city in N Spain

-logue (lôg, läg) ⟦Fr < L *-logus* < Gr *-logos* < *logos*: see LOGIC⟧ *combining form* **1** a (specified kind of) speaking or writing [*Decalogue*] **2** a student or scholar (in a specified field) [*Sinologue*]

log·wood (lôg′wood′) ***n.*** ⟦so called from being imported in logs⟧ **1** the hard, brownish-red wood of a tropical tree (*Haematoxylon campechianum*) of the caesalpinia family, native to Central America and the West Indies: it is a source of hematoxylin and other dyes **2** *a)* this tree, having thorny branches and small, yellow flowers *b)* a dye extracted from the wood of this tree

☆**lo·gy** (lō′gē) ***adj.*** **-gi·er, -gi·est** ⟦< ? Du *log*, heavy, dull⟧ dull or sluggish, as from overeating —**lo′gi·ness** ***n.***

-lo·gy (lə jē) ⟦ME *-logie* < OFr < L *-logia* < Gr < *logos*, word: see LOGIC⟧ *combining form* **1** a (specified kind of) speaking [*eulogy*] **2** the science, doctrine, or theory of [*biology, theology*]

Lo·hen·grin (lō′ən grin′) ***n.*** *Gmc. Legend* a knight of the Holy Grail, son of Parsifal

loin (loin) ***n.*** ⟦ME *loine* < OFr *loigne* < VL **lumbea* < L *lumbus*: see LUMBAR⟧ **1** [*usually pl.*] the lower part of the back on either side of the backbone between the hipbones and the ribs **2** the front part of the hindquarters of beef, lamb, mutton, veal, etc. with the flank removed **3** [*pl.*] the hips and the lower abdomen regarded as a part of the body to be clothed or as the region of strength and procreative power —**gird (up) one's loins** to get ready to do something difficult or strenuous

loin·cloth (-klôth′) ***n.*** a cloth worn about the loins, specif. as the only garment as by some peoples in warm climates

Loire (lə wär′; *Fr* lwȧr) river flowing from S France north & west into the Bay of Biscay: 625 mi (1,006 km)

Lo·is (lō′is) ***n.*** ⟦LL(Ec) < Gr(Ec) *Lōis*: see 2 Tim. 1:5⟧ a feminine name

loi·ter (loit′ər) ***vi.*** ⟦ME *loitren* < MDu *loteren* (Du *leuteren*, to dawdle), akin to OE *loddere*, beggar < IE base **(s)leu-*, to hang loosely > SLEET, SLUR⟧ **1** to linger in an aimless way; spend time idly: often with *about* **2** to walk or move slowly and indolently, with frequent stops and pauses; often, specif., to linger aimlessly in a public place —***vt.*** to spend (time) idly [*loitered* away the day] —**loi′ter·er** ***n.***

SYN.—**loiter** implies aimlessness or slowness of movement and may suggest a wasting of time in lingering or lagging [to *loiter* around street corners]; **dawdle** implies a wasting of time over trifles or a frittering away of time that makes for slow progress [to *dawdle* over a cup of tea]; **dally** suggests a spending of time in trifling or frivolous pursuits; **idle** suggests habitual avoidance of work, or inactivity, indolence, etc. [to *idle* away the hours]

Lo·ki (lō′kē) ***n.*** ⟦ON, lit., destroyer < IE base **leug-*, to break > Sans *rugṇá-*, broken⟧ *Norse Myth.* the god who constantly creates discord and mischief

Lo·li·ta (lō lēt′ə) ***n.*** ⟦after title character in *Lolita*, novel (1955) by V. NABOKOV⟧ a pubescent girl who is sexually precocious

loll (läl) ***vi.*** ⟦ME *lollen* < MDu, to mumble, doze, of echoic orig.⟧ **1** to lean or lounge about in a relaxed or lazy manner **2** to hang in a relaxed manner; droop [the dog's tongue *lolled* out] —***vt.*** to let droop or hang loosely —**loll′er** ***n.***

Lol·land (lä′lənd; *Dan* lôl′ȧn) island of Denmark, in the Baltic Sea, south of Zealand: 479 sq mi (1,241 sq km)

☆**lol·la·pa·loo·za** or **lol·la·pa·loo·sa** (läl′ə pə lo͞o′zə) ***n.*** ⟦< ?⟧ [Slang] something or someone very striking or exceptional

Lol·lard (lä′lərd) ***n.*** ⟦ME < MDu *lollaerd*, lit., mutterer (of prayers, psalms) < *lollen*: see LOLL⟧ any of the followers of John Wycliffe in 14th- and 15th-cent. England

lol·li·pop or **lol·ly·pop** (lä′lē päp′) ***n.*** ⟦child's term: prob. after dial. *lolly*, the tongue + *pop*⟧ a piece of hard candy fixed to the end of a small stick; sucker

lol·lop (lä′ləp) ***vi.*** ⟦extended < LOLL, prob. by assoc. with GALLOP⟧ [Chiefly Brit.] **1** to lounge about; loll **2** to move in a clumsy or relaxed way, bobbing up and down or from side to side

lol·ly (lä′lē) ***n.***, *pl.* **-lies** ⟦contr. < LOLLYPOP⟧ [Brit. Slang] **1** money **2** piece of hard candy

☆**lol·ly·gag** (lä′lē gag′) ***vi.*** **-gagged′, -gag′ging** ⟦var. of *lallygag* < ?⟧ [Informal] to waste time in trifling or aimless activity; fool around

Lo·mas (lō′mäs′) city in E Argentina: suburb of Buenos Aires: in full **Lomas de Za·mo·ra** (lō′mäz′ də zə mōr′ə, -môr-)

Lo·max (lō′maks′), **Alan** 1915-2002; U.S. scholar of folk music

Lom·bard (läm′bärd′, -bərd) ***n.*** ⟦ME *Lumbarde* < ML *Lombardus* < L *Langobardus* < Gmc **lango-*, LONG¹ + **barda*, BEARD⟧ **1** a person born or living in Lombardy **2** a member of an ancient Germanic people that settled in the Po Valley **3** ⟦from the activity of the medieval Lombards as pawnbrokers⟧ a banker or moneylender —***adj.*** of Lombardy or the Lombards —**Lom·bar′dic** (-bär′dik) ***adj.***

Lom·bar·dy (läm′bər dē) ⟦the region was invaded and settled by Lombards in the 6th c. A.D.⟧ region of N Italy, on the Swiss border: 9,213 sq mi (23,862 sq km); chief city, Milan: It. name **Lom·bar·dia** (lôm bär′dyä)

Lombardy poplar a tall, slender poplar (*Populus nigra*), with upward-curving branches

Lom·bok (läm bäk′) island of Indonesia, between Bali & Sumbawa: 2,098 sq mi (5,434 sq km)

Lom·bro·so (lôm brô′sô), **Ce·sa·re** (che′zä re) 1836-1909; It. physician & criminologist

Lo·mé (lô mā′) capital of Togo: seaport on the Bight of Benin

lo mein (lō′mān′) a Chinese dish made of soft noodles combined variously with meat, vegetables, and seasonings

lo·ment (lō′ment′) ***n.*** ⟦ModL < L *lomentum*, bean meal < pp. of *lavare*, to wash (see LAVE): Roman women used it in a cosmetic wash⟧ a legume fruit that separates at its constrictions into one-seeded segments when ripe

Lo·mond (lō′mənd), **Loch** lake in WC Scotland: *c.* 24 mi (39 km) long

☆**Lo·mo·til** (lō′mə til′) ⟦contr. < LO(W) + MOTIL(ITY)⟧ *trademark for* a drug, $C_{30}H_{32}N_2O_2$·HCl, related to meperidine and used in treating diarrhea

Lon·don¹ (lun′dən), **Jack** (born *John Griffith London*) 1876-1916; U.S. novelist & short-story writer

Lon·don² (lun′dən) **1** capital of England, the United Kingdom, & the Commonwealth, consisting of the City of London & 32 boroughs; port on the Thames: 610 sq mi (1,580 sq km): officially called **Greater London** **2** ⟦after the city in England⟧ city in SE Ontario, Canada **3 City of** historic center of London, England, with its ancient boundaries: 1.05 sq mi (2.7 sq km)

☆**London broil** a boneless cut of beef, as of the flank, that is marinated, then broiled, and served in thin slices cut usually on a diagonal

Lon·don·der·ry (-der′ē) **1** former county of NW Northern Ireland: *c.* 801 sq mi (2,075 sq km) **2** district in NW Northern Ireland, in the E part of the former county: 149 sq mi (387 sq km) **3** seaport in this district, on an inlet of the Atlantic Ocean

lone (lōn) ***adj.*** ⟦ME, aphetic < *alone*⟧ **1** by oneself; alone; solitary **2** [Archaic] unmarried or widowed **3** *a)* standing apart from others of its kind; isolated *b)* [Old Poet.] unfrequented (said of places) —*SYN.* ALONE —**lone′ness** ***n.***

lone hand **1** a hand, esp. in euchre, played without using a partner's hand **2** a person who manages any activity without help **3** a position different from that taken by one's friends, associates, etc.

lone·ly (lōn′lē) ***adj.*** **-li·er, -li·est** **1** alone; solitary **2** *a)* standing apart from others of its kind; isolated *b)* unfrequented or uninhabited **3** unhappy at being alone; longing for friends, company, etc. **4** causing such a feeling —*SYN.* ALONE —**lone′li·ly** ***adv.*** —**lone′li·ness** ***n.***

lone·ly-hearts (-härts′) ***adj.*** of or having to do with single persons who are looking for companionship [a *lonely-hearts* newspaper column]

☆**lon·er** (lōn′ər) ***n.*** one who prefers to be independent of others, as by living or working alone

lone·some (lōn′səm) ***adj.*** **1** having or causing a lonely feeling **2** unfrequented; desolate —***n.*** [Informal] self; own: in such phrases as **on (or all by) one's lonesome** —*SYN.* ALONE —**lone′some·ly** ***adv.*** —**lone′some·ness** ***n.***

Lone Star State ⟦from the single *star* on its flag⟧ *name for* TEXAS

☆**lone wolf** LONER

long¹ (lôŋ) ***adj.*** ⟦ME < OE, akin to Ger *lang* < Gmc **lango-* > ON *langr*, Goth *laggs*: ? akin to L *longus*⟧ **1** measuring much from end to end in space or from beginning to end in time; not short or brief **2** measured from end to end rather than from side to side [the *long* dimension] **3** of a specified extent in length [a foot *long*] **4** of greater than usual or standard length, height, quantity, etc. [a *long* game, a *long* window, a *long* ton] **5** containing many items or members: said of a series, list, etc. **6** overextended in length **7** taking too much time; tedious; slow **8** extending to what is distant in space or time; far-reaching [a *long* view of the matter] **9** large; big [the *long* odds of 100 to 1, to take a *long* chance] **10** having an abundance of: with *of* or *on* [*long* on excuses] **11** designating a historical period considered in terms of a greater duration than technically would be ascribed to it [the *long* 19th century" (1789-1914) extends from the French Revolution to WWI]: cf. SHORT (***adj.*** 12) ☆**12** *Finance* holding a commodity or security in anticipation of a rise in price **13** *a)* *Phonet.* of relatively long duration (said of a speech sound) *b)* popularly, diphthongized [the *long a* in "pain"] (opposed to SHORT, ***adj.*** 14*b*) **14** *Prosody* *a)* requiring a relatively long time to pronounce (said of syllables in quantitative verse) *b)* stressed (said of syllables in accentual verse) —***adv.*** **1** for a long time **2** for the duration of; from the beginning to the end [all day *long*]: often used in comb. to form adjectives [a *monthlong* celebration, a decades-*long* war] **3** at a much earlier or a much later time than the time indicated; remotely [to stay *long* after midnight] —***n.*** **1** a variation of clothing size longer than the average for that size **2** [*pl.*] long pants **3** a signal, syllable, etc. of long duration **4** a long time [it won't take *long* to finish the work] —**as (or so) long as** **1** of the same length as **2** during the time that **3** seeing that; since **4** provided that —**before long** soon —**long live (someone)!** may (someone) live a long time! [*long live* the king!]: often used fig. [*long live* freedom!] —**no longer** not up to this or that time; not still [*no longer* interested in sports] —**the long and (the) short of** the whole story of in a few words; gist or point of

long[2] (lôŋ) ***vi.*** ⟦ME *longen* < OE *langian* (akin to Ger *langen*, to reach, extend) < base of *lang*: see prec.⟧ to feel a strong yearning; wish earnestly *[to long to go home, to long for affection]*

long[3] (lôŋ) ***vi.*** ⟦ME *longen* < OE *langian*, to belong⟧ [Archaic] to be fitting or appropriate

long[4] *abbrev.* longitude

Long (lôŋ), **Hu·ey (Pierce)** (hyo͞o′ē) 1893-1935; U.S. political leader: assassinated: called *(the) Kingfish*

long·an (läŋ′gən) ***n.*** ⟦Cantonese *long-yan*, lit., dragon's eye: in allusion to the white pulp of the fresh fruit surrounding a single seed⟧ **1** an Asian tree (*Euphoria longana*) of the soapberry family, bearing an edible fruit resembling a small litchi **2** this fruit

lon·ga·nim·i·ty (lôŋ′gə nim′ə tē) ***n.*** ⟦LL *longanimitas* < L *longus*, LONG[1] + *animus*, mind: see ANIMAL⟧ patient endurance of injuries; forbearance

Long Beach ⟦descriptive⟧ seaport in SW Calif., on the Pacific

long·board (lông′bôrd′) ***n.*** **1** a long skateboard, used especially for riding at high speeds over long distances **2** a long surfboard, usually over eight feet in length —**long′board′er** ***n.*** —**long′board′ing** ***n.***

long·boat (lôŋ′bōt′) ***n.*** the largest boat carried on a merchant sailing ship

long·bow (-bō′) ***n.*** a large bow drawn by hand for shooting a long, feathered arrow —**draw (or pull) the longbow** to exaggerate in telling something

long·cloth (-klôth′) ***n.*** ⟦so called because made in *long* pieces⟧ a soft cotton fabric of fine quality

long-day (-dā′) ***adj.*** *Bot.* maturing and blooming under long periods of light and short periods of darkness

☆**long distance** long-distance telephone service

☆**long-dis·tance** (-dis′təns) ***adj.*** **1** to or from a distant place or places *[long-distance telephone calls]* **2** that covers a long distance *[a long-distance runner]* —***adv.*** by long-distance telephone service

long division the process of dividing a number by another number containing, ordinarily, two or more figures, and of putting the steps down in full

long dozen thirteen

long-drawn-out (lôŋ′drôn′out′) ***adj.*** continuing for a long or very long time; prolonged: also **long′-drawn′**

longe (lunj) ***n.*** ⟦Fr, back-form. < *allonge*, extension < *allonger* < LL *elongare*: see ELONGATE⟧ **1** a long rope fastened to a horse's head and held by the trainer, who causes the horse to move around in a circle **2** the use of the longe in training horses —***vt.*** **longed**, **longe′ing** or **long′ing** to put (a horse) through its paces, using a longe

lon·ge·ron (län′jə rän′, -rən) ***n.*** ⟦Fr⟧ a main structural member along the length of an airplane fuselage, nacelle, etc.

lon·gev·i·ty (län jev′ə tē, lôn-) ***n.*** ⟦L *longaevitas* < *longaevus*: see fol.⟧ **1** *a)* long life; great span of life *b)* the length or duration of a life or lives **2** length of time spent in service, employment, etc.

long face a glum, sad, or disconsolate facial expression —**long-faced** (lôŋ′fāst′) ***adj.***

Long·fel·low (lôŋ′fel′ō), **Henry Wads·worth** (wädz′wurth′) 1807-82; U.S. poet

Long·ford (lôŋ′fərd) county in Leinster province, central Ireland: 403 sq mi (1,044 sq km)

☆**long green** [Old Slang] PAPER MONEY

☆**long·hair** (lôŋ′her′) ***n.*** **1** a domestic cat with fur made up of relatively long hairs **2** [Informal] *a)* an intellectual; specif., a longhair musician *b)* a person, esp. a male, with long hair; specif., a HIPPIE: sometimes used disparagingly —***adj.*** [Informal] designating or of intellectuals or their tastes; specif., playing or preferring classical music rather than jazz or popular tunes: sometimes used disparagingly: also **long′haired′**

long·hand (-hand′) ***n.*** ordinary handwriting, in which the words are written out in full, as distinguished from shorthand or typing

long·head (-hed′) ***n.*** a dolichocephalic person

long-head·ed (-hed′id) ***adj.*** **1** DOLICHOCEPHALIC **2** having much foresight, good sense, or shrewdness; sagacious Also written **long′head′ed**

long·horn (-hôrn′) ***n.*** **1** any of a breed of cattle with long horns, raised in great numbers in the Southwest in the 19th cent. and later crossed with English stock to create improved beef and dairy breeds ☆**2** a mild, typically orange-colored Cheddar cheese, shaped during manufacture in long, cylindrical molds: in full **longhorn cheese**

long-horned beetle (lôŋ′hôrnd′) any of a family (Cerambycidae) of slender beetles having very long antennae and wood-eating larvae

long-horned grasshopper any of a family (Tettigoniidae) of greenish grasshoppers with long antennae

long·house (lôŋ′hous′) ***n.*** any of various long, communal dwellings, as that common until the 19th cent. among the Iroquoian peoples of NE North America: also written **long house**

long hundredweight the British hundredweight: see HUNDREDWEIGHT

lon·gi- (län′ji, -jə) ⟦L < *longus*, long⟧ *combining form* long *[longicorn]*

lon·gi·corn (län′ji kôrn′) ***adj.*** ⟦< prec. + L *cornu*, HORN⟧ having long feelers, or antennae, as the long-horned beetles

☆**long·ies** (lôŋ′ēz) ***pl.n.*** [Informal] LONG JOHNS

long·ing (lôŋ′iŋ) ***n.*** ⟦see LONG[2]⟧ strong desire; yearning —***adj.*** feeling or showing a yearning —**long′ing·ly** ***adv.***

Lon·gi·nus (län jī′nəs) A.D. 213?-273; Gr. Platonic philosopher & rhetorician

long·ish (lôŋ′ish) ***adj.*** somewhat long

Long Island ⟦descriptive⟧ island in SE N.Y. between Long Island Sound & the Atlantic: 1,411 sq mi (3,654 sq km)

☆**Long Island iced tea** ⟦after *Long Island*, New York, the location of a nightclub where it was first served⟧ an iced cocktail made with vodka, gin, tequila, rum, triple sec, sweetener mixed with lime or lemon juice, and cola

Long Island Sound arm of the Atlantic, between N Long Island & S Conn.: *c.* 100 mi (161 km) long

lon·gi·tude (län′jə to͞od′, -tyo͞od′; lôŋ′-) ***n.*** ⟦ME < L *longitudo* < *longus*, LONG[1]⟧ **1** length **2** distance east or west on the earth's surface, measured as an arc of the equator (in degrees up to 180° or by the difference in time) between the meridian passing through a particular place and a standard or prime meridian, usually the one passing through Greenwich, England **3** *Astron. see* CELESTIAL LONGITUDE

lon·gi·tu·di·nal (län′jə to͞od′'n əl, -tyo͞od′-; lôŋ′-) ***adj.*** ⟦ML *longitudinalis*⟧ **1** of or in length **2** running or placed lengthwise: opposed to TRANSVERSE **3** of longitude **4** designating or of studies dealing with the development of an individual or group over a period of years —**lon′gi·tu′di·nal·ly** ***adv.***

☆**long johns** [Informal] long underwear

long jump *Track & Field* **1** an event in which contestants take turns jumping for distance, after a running start, usually into a long pit of sand **2** a jump in such an event

☆**long·leaf pine** (lôŋ′lēf′) a pine (*Pinus palustris*) native to the S U.S., having very long needles and valued for its hard, heavy wood

long-lived (lôŋ′livd′, -līvd′) ***adj.*** ⟦orig. < LONG[1] ***(adj.)*** + *live*, form of LIFE + -ED (sense 3); later understood also as < LONG[1] ***(adv.)*** + -LIVED⟧ having or tending to have a long life span or existence

long measure LINEAR MEASURE

☆**long moss** ⟦descriptive⟧ SPANISH MOSS

Lon·go·bard (läŋ′gō bärd′) ***n.***, *pl.* **-bards′** or **Lon′go·bar′di** (-bär′dē) ⟦LL *Longobardus* < L *Langobardus*: see LOMBARD⟧ LOMBARD (***n.*** 2) —**Lon′go·bar′dic** ***adj.***

Long Parliament the English Parliament that met in 1640, was expelled by Cromwell in 1653, reconvened briefly in 1659, and was dissolved in 1660

long pig ⟦calque of the Maori and Polynesian term⟧ [Historical] human flesh or a human body as food for cannibals

long-play·ing (lôŋ′plā′iŋ) ***adj.*** designating or of a phonograph record having microgrooves, for playing at 33⅓ revolutions per minute

long-range (lôŋ′rānj′) ***adj.*** **1** designating or of a gun, aircraft, missile, etc. that has a range of great distance **2** looking far into the future *[long-range plans]*

long-run (-run′) ***adj.*** extending over a long time

long·shore (-shôr′) ***adj.*** ⟦aphetic for ALONGSHORE⟧ existing, occurring, working, etc. along the shore or waterfront

long·shore·man (-shôr′mən) ***n.***, *pl.* **-men** (-mən) ⟦prec. + MAN⟧ a person whose work is loading and unloading ships; stevedore

long shot **1** *a)* in betting, a choice that has only a slight chance of winning and, hence, carries great odds *b)* [Informal] any venture with only a slight chance of success, but offering great rewards if successful **2** *Film, TV* a scene shot with or as with the camera at some distance from the subject or action —☆**not by a long shot** [Informal] absolutely not; by no means

long·sight·ed (lôŋ′sīt′id) ***adj.*** FARSIGHTED —**long′sight′ed·ly** ***adv.*** —**long′sight′ed·ness** ***n.***

long·some (-səm) ***adj.*** ⟦ME *langsum* < OE < *lang*, LONG[1] + *-sum*, -SOME[1]⟧ [Dial.] lengthy; overly long; tedious

Longs Peak (lôŋz) ⟦after S. H. *Long* (1784-1864), U.S. engineer⟧ peak of the Rocky Mountains, in NC Colo.: 14,255 ft (4,345 m)

☆**long·spur** (lôŋ′spʉr′) ***n.*** ⟦LONG[1] + SPUR⟧ any of a genus (*Calcarius*, family Emberizidae) of northern passerine birds distinguished by their long hind claws

long-stand·ing (-stan′diŋ) ***adj.*** having continued for a long time *[a long-standing custom]*: also written **long′stand′ing**

Long·street (lôŋ′strēt′), **James** 1821-1904; Confederate general in the Civil War

long-suf·fer·ing (-suf′ər iŋ) ***adj.*** bearing injuries, insults, trouble, etc. patiently for a long time —***n.*** long and patient endurance of injuries, insults, trouble, etc.: also [Archaic] **long′-suf′fer·ance** —**long′-suf′fer·ing·ly** ***adv.***

long suit **1** *Card Games* the suit in which a player holds the most cards **2** something at which one excels

long-term (-tʉrm′) ***adj.*** **1** for or extending over a long time **2** designating or of a bond, capital gain, etc. that involves a relatively long period of time for maturity, repayment, amortization, etc. or for computing tax liability **3** designating memory involving facts and events over a long period of time or over a lifetime —***adv.*** over or for a long period of time

long·time (-tīm′) ***adj.*** as such over a long period of time *[a longtime companion]*

long ton *see* TON[1] (sense 2): abbrev. *lt*

longue dur·ée (lôŋ dü rā′) ⟦Fr, long duration: popularized by F. BRAUDEL⟧ an approach from the ANNALES school of Fr. historians, concentrating on long-term conditions and gradual change rather than relatively brief political and military events

Lon·gueuil (lôŋ gāl′; *Fr* lōn gë′y′) ⟦after Charles Le Moyne de *Longueuil* (1626-85), Fr colonist⟧ city in S Quebec, Canada, on the St. Lawrence: suburb of Montreal

lon·gueur (lôŋ gʉr′; *Fr* lōn gër′) ***n.*** ⟦Fr⟧ **1** a long, boring section, as in a novel, musical work, etc. **2** a tedious stretch of time

long underwear underwear worn for keeping warm, often having full-length sleeves and legs fitting snugly at the wrists and ankles

long-waist·ed (lôŋ′wās′tid) *adj.* unusually long between shoulders and waistline; with a low waistline

long wave a radio wave that is longer than those used in commercial broadcasting, usually one longer than 1,000 meters and below 300 kilohertz in frequency —**long′-wave′** *adj.*

long·ways (-wāz′) *adv.* LENGTHWISE

long-wind·ed (-win′did) *adj.* **1** capable of considerable exertion without getting out of breath **2** *a)* speaking or writing at great, often tiresome length *b)* tiresomely long (said of a speech, writing, etc.) —**long′-wind′ed·ly** *adv.* —**long′-wind′ed·ness** *n.*

long·wise (-wīz′) *adv.* LENGTHWISE

lon·gyi (loȯŋ′gē, luŋ′-) *n.* ⟦Hindi & Pers *lungī*⟧ in India, Burma, etc., a long, traditional garment like a sarong, worn tied about the waist

loo[1] (lo͞o) [Historical] *n.* ⟦contr. < *lanterloo* < Fr *lanturelu*, name of the game, orig. fanciful word in refrain of a 17th-c. song⟧ a card game played for a pool made up of stakes and forfeits —*vt.* to cause to pay a forfeit at loo

loo[2] (lo͞o) *n.* ⟦< Fr *lieux*, short for *les lieux d'aisances*, toilets, lit., places of conveniences⟧ [Brit. Informal] a toilet

loo·by (lo͞o′bē) *n., pl.* **-bies** ⟦ME *loby*, prob. akin to LOB, LUBBER⟧ [Chiefly Dial.] a big, clumsy fellow; lout

loo·fah (lo͞o′fə) *n.* ⟦< ModL *Luffa*, genus name of this gourd < Ar *lūfah*, *lūf*⟧ **1** DISHCLOTH GOURD **2** the fibrous, vascular skeleton of the pod of a dishcloth gourd, used as a sponge

☆**loo·ie** or **loo·ey** (lo͞o′ē) *n.* [Mil. Slang] a lieutenant

look (loȯk) *vi.* ⟦ME *loken* < OE *locian*, akin to OS *lōkōn*, OHG *luogēn* (Ger dial. *lugen*), to spy after, look for⟧ **1** to make use of the sense of sight; see **2** *a)* to direct one's eyes in order to see *b)* to direct one's attention mentally upon something **3** to try to see or find something; search **4** to appear to be; seem [*to look sick*]: esp. in Brit. usage, often used with a predicate n. [*he looked a perfect fool*] **5** to be facing or turned in a specified direction —*vt.* **1** to direct one's eyes on [*to look someone in the face*] **2** to express by one's looks, or appearance [*to look one's disgust*] **3** [Rare] to bring to a certain condition by looking **4** to have an appearance that is suitable for or in accord with [*the fat actor looked the part; you don't look your age*] **5** to expect: with an infinitive object [*they look to succeed with our help*] —*n.* **1** the act of looking; glance **2** outward impression; appearance; aspect [*the look of a beggar*] **3** [Informal] [*pl.*] *a)* appearance; the way something seems to be [*from the looks of things*] *b)* personal appearance, esp. of a pleasing nature [*to have looks and youth*] —*interj.* **1** direct your eyes and attention to this; see **2** pay attention: also **look here** —*SYN.* APPEARANCE —**it looks like 1** it seems that there will be [*it looks like rain*] **2** [Informal] it seems as if —**look after** to take care of; watch over —**look alive (or sharp)** [Informal] to be alert; act or move quickly: usually in the imperative —**look back** to recall the past; recollect —**look down on (or upon) 1** to regard as an inferior **2** to regard with contempt; despise —**look for 1** to search or hunt for **2** to expect; anticipate —**look forward to** to anticipate, esp. eagerly —**look in (on)** to pay a brief visit (to) —**look into** to examine carefully; investigate —**look on 1** to be an observer or spectator **2** to consider; regard (*as*) [*they looked on her as a born leader*] —**look (like) oneself** to appear to be in normal health, spirits, etc. —**look out** to be on the watch; be careful —**look out for 1** to be wary about **2** [Informal] to take care of —**look over** to examine; inspect —**look the other way** to ignore something troublesome or disagreeable —**look to 1** to take care of; give attention to **2** to rely upon; resort to **3** to look forward to; expect —**look up 1** to search for in a book of reference, etc. **2** [Informal] to pay a visit to; call on **3** [Informal] to get better; improve —**look up and down 1** to search everywhere **2** to examine with an appraising eye; scrutinize —**look upon** to think of (*as*); consider [*to look upon housework as boring*] —**look up to** to regard with great respect

look-a·like (loȯk′ə līk′) *n.* a person or thing that resembles or is made to resemble another, esp. another that is famous, prestigious, etc.

look·er (-ər) *n.* **1** a person who looks ☆**2** [Slang] a handsome person; esp., a pretty woman

look·er-on (loȯk′ər än′) *n., pl.* **look′ers-on′** an observer or spectator; onlooker

look-in (loȯk′in′) *n.* **1** a quick glance **2** a brief visit **3** [Brit. Informal] an opportunity to participate or succeed

looking glass a (glass) mirror

look·ing-glass (loȯk′iŋ glas′) *adj.* ⟦in allusion to *Through the Looking-Glass* by Lewis CARROLL, in which Alice passes through a mirror and enters a world that is illogical and unpredictable⟧ counter to logic, common sense, or ordinary expectations; topsy-turvy [*the looking-glass world of Cold War propaganda*]

look·out (loȯk′out′) *n.* **1** an alert, careful watching for someone or something **2** a place for keeping watch, esp. a high place affording an extensive view **3** a person detailed to watch; sentry **4** [Chiefly Brit.] outlook, esp. for the future **5** [Informal] concern; worry [*that's your lookout, not mine*]

Lookout Mountain ⟦descriptive⟧ mountain ridge in Tenn., Ga., & Ala.: the section near Chattanooga was the site of a Civil War battle (1863) in which Union forces defeated the Confederates: highest point, 2,125 ft (648 m)

look-say method (loȯk′sā′) a method of teaching beginners to read by memorizing and recognizing whole words, rather than by associating letters with sounds: cf. PHONICS (sense 2): also **look-and-say method** (loȯk′ ənd sā′)

look-see (loȯk′sē′) *n.* [Informal] a quick look or inspection

loom[1] (lo͞om) *n.* ⟦ME *lome* < OE (*ge*)*loma*, tool, utensil⟧ **1** a machine for weaving thread or yarn into cloth **2** the art of weaving: usually with *the* —*vt.* to weave on a loom

loom[2] (lo͞om) *vi.* ⟦earlier *lome, loam* < ?⟧ to appear, take shape, or come in sight indistinctly as through a mist, esp. in a large, portentous, or threatening form: often with *up* [*the peak loomed up before us*]: also used fig. [*the specter of war loomed ahead*] —*n.* a looming appearance, as of a ship in the fog

loom[3] (lo͞om) *n.* [Brit. Dial.] LOON[1]

loom[4] (lo͞om) *n.* ⟦ON *hlumr*⟧ the part of an oar or paddle between the handle and the blade

LOOM *abbrev.* Loyal Order of Moose

loon[1] (lo͞on) *n.* ⟦altered (by assoc. with fol.) < earlier *loom* < ON *lomr* < IE echoic base **lā-* > L *latrare*, to bark⟧ any of an order (Gaviiformes) of fish-eating diving birds, with a sharp bill and webbed feet, found mainly in subarctic regions: noted for its weird cry

loon[2] (lo͞on) *n.* ⟦Scot *lown, loun* < ME *lowen* < ? or akin to MDu *loen*⟧ **1** a clumsy, stupid person **2** a crazy person **3** [Scot.] a boy **4** [Archaic] a rogue

☆**loon·ey-tunes** (lo͞o′nē to͞onz′) *adj.* ⟦after *Looney Tunes*, trademark for a series of animated cartoons⟧ [Slang] crazy; demented: also sp. **loon′y-tunes′**

loon·ie (lo͞o′nē) *n.* ⟦after the LOON[1] depicted on the reverse⟧ [Cdn.] **1** the Canadian one-dollar coin **2** the Canadian dollar

loon·y (lo͞o′nē) [Slang] *adj.* **loon′i·er, loon′i·est** ⟦< LUNATIC⟧ crazy; demented —*n., pl.* **loon′ies** a loony person Also sp. **loon′ey**, *pl.* **-eys**

loony bin [Slang] an institution for hospitalizing the mentally ill

loop[1] (lo͞op) *n.* ⟦ME *loup* < Anglo-N forms corresponding to ON *hlaup*, a leap, *hlaupa*, to run (akin to LEAP) > Dan *løbe(knude)*, lit., running (knot)⟧ **1** *a)* the more or less circular figure formed by a line, thread, wire, etc. that curves back to cross itself *b)* a noose *c)* anything having or forming this figure [*the loop of a written l*] **2** a sharp bend, as in a mountain road, which almost comes back upon itself **3** a ring-shaped fastening or ornament [*loops for a belt*] **4** a plastic intrauterine contraceptive device: usually with *the* **5** a segment of film or magnetic tape joined end to end to form a continuous strip for endless repetition in mixing or dubbing sound **6** a system consisting of a series of operations or activities in which each depends on the outcome of the previous one; esp., such a system in which the result of a later operation affects an earlier operation, providing continuous feedback **7** *Aeron.* an airplane maneuver describing a vertical circle in the air **8** *Comput.* a sequence of program instructions that are repeatedly executed until certain conditions are reached **9** *Elec.* a complete circuit **10** *Physics* the part of a vibrating string, air column, etc. between the nodes; antinode —*vt.* **1** to make a loop or loops in or of **2** to wrap around one or more times [*loop the wire around the post*] **3** to fasten with a loop or loops [*to loop curtains back*] **4** to dub in or rerecord dialogue or other sound into (a film) **5** *Elec.* to join (conductors) so as to complete a circuit —*vi.* **1** to form into a loop or loops **2** to progress as a measuring worm does by alternately straightening the body and drawing it up into a loop **3** *Aeron.* to perform a loop or loops —**in (or out of) the loop** within (or not within) a particular exclusive group, often one that has influence, information, etc.; being (or not being) an insider —☆**knock (or throw) for a loop** [Slang] to shock, amaze, confuse, etc. —**loop the loop** to describe a vertical loop in the air: said as of an airplane or amusement-park ride —☆**the Loop** the main business district and a major shopping district in downtown Chicago

loop[2] (lo͞op) *n.* ⟦ME *loupe*, prob. < MDu *lupen*, to peer⟧ [Archaic] a narrow opening or loophole

loop antenna *Radio* a coil of large diameter, used as an antenna, esp. in direction-finding equipment and in radio receivers

☆**looped** (lo͞opt) *adj.* [Slang] intoxicated; drunk

loop·er (lo͞o′pər) *n.* **1** a person or thing that makes loops **2** ⟦so called from its way of moving: see LOOP[1], *vi.* 2⟧ *Zool.* MEASURING WORM

loop·hole (lo͞op′hōl′) *n.* ⟦LOOP[2] + HOLE⟧ **1** a hole or narrow slit in the wall of a fort, etc., for looking or shooting through **2** a means of escape; esp., a means of evading or escaping an obligation, enforcement of a law or contract, etc.

loop knot a knot tied in a double rope so that a loop extends beyond it

loop of Hen·le (hen′lē) *pl.* **loops of Henle** ⟦after F. G. J. *Henle* (1809-85), Ger pathologist⟧ the long U-shaped section of a nephron in the kidney, where urine is formed

loop stitch any sewing stitch formed of connected loops

loop·y (lo͞o′pē) *adj.* **-i·er, -i·est** [Slang] **1** slightly crazy **2** confused; befuddled

loose (lo͞os) *adj.* **loos′er, loos′est** ⟦ME *lous* < ON *lauss*, akin to Ger *los*, OE *leas*: see -LESS⟧ **1** not confined or restrained; free; unbound **2** moving freely; not contained in a special holder, package, binding, etc. [*loose salt, loose change in one's pocket*] **3** readily available; not put away under lock and key [*loose cash*] **4** not firmly fastened down, on, or in [*a loose tooth, a loose wheel*] **5** not taut; slack **6** not tight; giving enough room [*loose clothing*] **7** not compact or compactly constructed [*loose soil, a loose frame*] **8** not restrained; irresponsible [*loose talk*] **9** not precise or close; inexact [*a loose translation*] **10** sexually immoral or promiscuous **11** *a)* not strained or hard [*a loose cough*] *b)* moving freely or excessively [*loose bowels*] **12** [Informal] relaxed; easy; unconstrained **13** *Sports* not in the possession of either team [*a foul committed while the basketball was loose*] —*adv.* **loos′**

er, loos′est loosely; in a loose manner —*vt.* **loosed, loos′ing 1** to make loose; loosen; specif., *a)* to set free; unbind *b)* to free from an obligation or responsibility; absolve **2** to let fly; release [to *loose* an arrow into the air] —**break loose 1** to free oneself by force **2** to shake off restraint —**cast loose 1** to untie or unfasten **2** to set free —**let loose (with)** to set free or give out; release —**on the loose 1** not confined or bound; free **2** [Informal] having fun in a free, unrestrained manner —**set (or turn) loose** to make free; release —**loose′ly** *adv.* —**loose′ness** *n.*

loose cannon ⟦by analogy with a cannon on an old warship that had come loose from its mounting and was rolling around dangerously⟧ a careless, uncontrollable person whose words or actions cause embarrassment or harm to others

loose ends ⟦from the ends of a spliced rope⟧ final, relatively minor matters still to be taken care of —**at loose ends** ⟦orig., naut., with reference to rope⟧ **1** in an unsettled, disorganized, or confused condition **2** without anything definite to do **3** unemployed

loose·fit·ting (-fit′iŋ) *adj.* fitting loosely: used esp. of clothing

loose-joint·ed (lo͞os′joint′id) *adj.* **1** having loose joints **2** moving freely and flexibly; limber —**loose′-joint′ed·ly** *adv.* —**loose′-joint′ed·ness** *n.*

loose-leaf (lo͞os′lēf′) *adj.* ⟦see LEAF, *n.* 5⟧ designating or of writing paper sold in separate sheets, rather than bound or as a tablet

loose-limbed (-limd′) *adj.* **1** having flexible and limber arms and legs [a *loose-limbed* gymnast] **2** characterized by loose, supple movement of the arms and legs [a *loose-limbed* vaudeville dancer]

loos·en (lo͞os′ən) *vt., vi.* to make or become loose or looser; specif., *a)* to free from confinement or restraint; unbind, unfasten, etc. *b)* to make less taut, less compact, etc. —☆**loosen up** [Informal] **1** to talk freely **2** to relax —**loos′en·er** *n.*

loose sentence a sentence in which the main clause, containing the essential information, comes first, followed by subordinate parts, modifiers, etc., as in some complex sentences: cf. PERIODIC SENTENCE

loose smut any of various diseases of cereal grasses caused by smut fungi (esp. genus *Ustilago*) that cover the plant with dustlike masses of spores

loose·strife (lo͞os′strīf′) *n.* ⟦LOOSE, V. + STRIFE: used as transl. of L *lysimachia* < Gr *lysimacheios*, understood as "ending strife" < *lyein*, to loosen, solve (see LYSIS) + *machē*, battle: from its assumed soothing properties, but prob. after *Lysimachia*, city in Thrace, or *Lysimachos*, king of Thrace, its founder⟧ **1** any of a genus (*Lysimachia*) of plants of the primrose family, with leafy stems and loose spikes of white, rose, or yellow flowers **2** any of a genus (*Lythrum*) of plants of the loosestrife family, esp. **purple loosestrife** (*L. salicaria*) with spikes of purple flowers —*adj.* designating a family (Lythraceae, order Myrtales) of chiefly tropical dicotyledonous plants, including henna

loose-tongued (lo͞os′tuŋd′) *adj.* talking too much; careless or irresponsible in speech

loos·ey-goos·ey (lo͞o′sē go͞o′sē) [Informal] *adj.* ⟦redupl. based on slang phr. *loose as a goose*⟧ relaxed, easy, or unconstrained —*adv.* in a loose, relaxed way

loot (lo͞ot) *n.* ⟦Hindi *lūt* < Sans *luṇṭ*, to rob⟧ **1** goods stolen or taken by force, as from a captured enemy city in wartime or by rioters or a corrupt official; plunder, spoils, etc. **2** the act of looting **3** [Slang] *a)* money *b)* items of value; esp., gifts received —*vt.* **1** to plunder; strip of valuables; despoil **2** to take or carry off as plunder **3** to burglarize or steal, as during a riot or natural diaster —*vi.* to engage in plundering or burglary, as during a riot or natural disaster —*SYN.* SPOIL —**loot′er** *n.*

lop[1] (läp) *vt.* **lopped, lop′ping** ⟦ME *loppen* < OE *loppian*, prob. < Scand (as in Norw *loppa*) < IE **leub-*, to peel off, break off, var. of base **leubh-* > LEAF⟧ **1** to trim (a tree, etc.) by cutting off branches, twigs, or stems **2** to remove by or as by cutting off: usually with *off* —*n.* something lopped off —**lop′per** *n.*

lop[2] (läp) *vi.* **lopped, lop′ping** ⟦prob. akin to LOB⟧ **1** to hang down loosely **2** to move in a halting way —*adj.* hanging down loosely

lope (lōp) *vi.* **loped, lop′ing** ⟦ME *lopen* < ON *hlaupa*, to leap, run (or MDu *lopen*): see LEAP⟧ to move along easily, with a long, swinging stride or in an easy canter —*vt.* to cause to lope —*n.* a long, easy, swinging stride —**lop′er** *n.*

lop-eared (läp′ird′) *adj.* having ears that droop or hang down

Lope de Vega *see* VEGA[2], Lope de

lo·pho·phore (-fôr′) *n.* ⟦< Gr *lophos*, crest, tuft + -PHORE⟧ a usually horseshoe-shaped ring of ciliated tentacles around the mouth of certain aquatic animals, as in brachiopods

lop·py (läp′ə) *adj.* **-pi·er, -pi·est** hanging down loosely; drooping

lop·sid·ed (-sīd′id) *adj.* **1** noticeably heavier, bigger, or lower on one side; not symmetrical **2** not balanced; uneven —**lop′sid′ed·ly** *adv.* —**lop′sid′ed·ness** *n.*

loq. *abbrev.* ⟦L *loquitur*⟧ he (or she) speaks

lo·qua·cious (lō kwā′shəs) *adj.* ⟦< L *loquax* (gen. *loquacis*) < *loqui*, to speak + -OUS⟧ very talkative; fond of talking —*SYN.* TALKATIVE —**lo·qua′cious·ly** *adv.* —**lo·qua′cious·ness** *n.*

lo·quac·i·ty (lō kwas′ə tē) *n.* ⟦L *loquacitas* < *loquax*: see prec.⟧ talkativeness, esp. when excessive

lo·quat (lō′kwät′, -kwat′) *n.* ⟦< Chin (Canton dial.) *lō kwat*, lit., rush orange⟧ **1** a small evergreen tree (*Eriobotrya japonica*) of the rose family, native to China and Japan **2** the small, yellow, edible, plumlike fruit of this tree

lo·ral (lôr′əl) *adj.* of or having to do with the LORE[2] of a bird, fish, or snake

Lor·an (lôr′an′) *n.* ⟦< *Lo(ng) Ra(nge) N(avigation)*⟧ [*also* **l-**] a navigation system for determining the position of a ship or aircraft by means of the time interval between radio signals received from two or more known stations

Lorca, Federico García *see* GARCÍA LORCA, Federico

lord (lôrd) *n.* ⟦ME < OE *hlaford* < earlier *hlafweard* < *hlaf* (see LOAF[1]) + *weard* (see WARD): basic sense, "loaf keeper" (i.e., one who feeds dependents): some senses infl. by use as transl. of L *dominus*⟧ **1** a person having great power and authority; ruler; master **2** the owner and head of a feudal estate **3** [**L-**] *a)* God (with *the* except in direct address) *b)* Jesus Christ (often with *Our*) **4** in Great Britain *a)* a nobleman holding the rank of baron, viscount, earl, or marquess; member of the House of Lords *b)* a man who by courtesy or because of his office is given the title of Lord, as a bishop, a younger son of a duke or marquess, or a Lord Mayor **5** [**L-**] in Great Britain, the title of a lord, variously used (Ex.: as Earl of Leicester, John Doe would be called *Lord* Leicester; as a baron, John, *Lord* Doe; as a younger son of a marquess or duke, *Lord* John Doe) **6** [**L-**] this title as a form of address for a judge, bishop, or nobleman: preceded by *My* —*interj.* [*often* **L-**] used to express surprise or irritation —*vi.* to act like a lord; rule: chiefly in the phrase **lord it (over)**, to act in an overbearing, dictatorial manner (toward) —*vt.* [Archaic] to make a lord of —**the Lords** the House of Lords in the British Parliament

Lord (High) Chancellor the privy councilor in Great Britain who presides over the House of Lords and is head of the judiciary

lord·ling (lôrd′liŋ) *n.* ⟦ME: see LORD & -LING[1]⟧ an unimportant or minor lord: usually contemptuous

lord·ly (-lē) *adj.* **-li·er, -li·est** ⟦ME < OE *hlafordlic*⟧ of, like, characteristic of, or suitable to a lord; specif., *a)* noble; grand *b)* haughty; overbearing —*adv.* **-li·er, -li·est** in the manner of a lord —**lord′li·ness** *n.*

Lord Mayor the title of the mayor of London and of the mayor of any of several other British cities

Lord of hosts ⟦see, e.g., 1 Sam. 17:45⟧ Jehovah; God

Lord of Misrule [Historical] in England, a person presiding over revels and games, as at Christmas

lor·do·sis (lôr dō′sis) *n.* ⟦ModL < Gr *lordōsis* < *lordos*, bent backward < IE base **lerd-*, to make crooked > Gael *lorcach*, with a lame foot⟧ forward curvature of the spine, producing a hollow in the back —**lor·dot′ic** (-dät′ik) *adj.*

Lord's Day ⟦transl. of LL(Ec) *dies Dominica* < Gr(Ec) *hē kyriakē hēmera* (see Rev. 1:10): from being the day of the resurrection of Christ⟧ [*sometimes* **L- d-**] Sunday, the Christian Sabbath: with *the*

lord·ship (lôrd′ship′) *n.* ⟦OE *hlafordscipe*: see -SHIP⟧ **1** the rank or authority of a lord **2** rule; dominion **3** the territory of a lord **4** [*often* **L-**] a title used in speaking to or of a lord: preceded by *Your* or *His*

Lord's Prayer the prayer beginning "Our Father", which Jesus taught his disciples: Matt. 6:9-13

lords spiritual the archbishops and bishops who are members of the British House of Lords

Lord's Supper 1 LAST SUPPER **2** EUCHARIST: term used by certain Protestant denominations

lords temporal those members of the British House of Lords who are not members of the clergy

lore[1] (lôr) *n.* ⟦ME < OE *lar*, learning, teaching, akin to Ger *lehre*, teaching: see LEARN⟧ **1** [Archaic] *a)* a teaching or being taught; instruction *b)* something taught **2** knowledge or learning; specif., all the knowledge of a particular group or having to do with a particular subject, esp. that of a traditional nature

lore[2] (lôr) *n.* ⟦ModL *lorum* < L, thong < IE **wloro-* < base **wel-* > Gr *eulēra*, reins⟧ the space between the eye and the upper edge of the bill of a bird or between the eye and the nostril of a snake or fish

Lor·e·lei (lôr′ə lī′) *n.* ⟦Ger, altered by C. Brentano (1778-1842), Ger poet, after *Lurlei*, name of the rock (prob. lit., "ambush cliff") < MHG *luren*, to watch, LOWER[2] + *lei*, a cliff, rock⟧ *Gmc. Folklore* a siren whose singing on a rock in the Rhine lures sailors to shipwreck on the reefs: originally a character in literature

Lo·rentz (lô′rents), **Hen·drik An·toon** (hen′drik än′tōn) 1853-1928; Du. physicist

Lo·renz (lô′rents), **Kon·rad (Zacharias)** (kôn′rät) 1903-89; Austrian ethologist

Lo·ren·zo (lô ren′zō, lə-) *n.* a masculine name: see LAURENCE

Lo·ret·ta (lô ret′ə, lə-) *n.* a feminine name: see LAURA

lor·gnette (lôr nyet′) *n.* ⟦Fr < *lorgner*, to spy, peep < OFr *lorgne*, squinting⟧ **1** eyeglasses attached to a handle **2** opera glasses similarly mounted

lor·gnon (lôr nyōn′) *n.* ⟦Fr < *lorgner*: see prec.⟧ **1** a single or double eyeglass, as a monocle or pince-nez **2** LORGNETTE

Lo·ri (lôr′ē) *n.* a feminine name: see LAURA

lo·ri·ca (lō rī′kə, lə-) *n., pl.* **-cae** (-sē) ⟦L, orig., corselet of thongs < *lorum*, a thong: see LORE[2]⟧ **1** the cuirass worn by a soldier of ancient Rome **2** a hard, protective shell or other covering around certain invertebrates —**lor·i·cate** (lôr′i kāt′, -kət) *adj.*, **lor′i·cat′ed**

lor·i·keet (lôr′i kēt′) *n.* ⟦< LORY + (PARA)KEET⟧ any of several small, brightly colored parakeets native to Australia and the East Indies with a lorylike tongue for feeding on nectar

Lo·rin·da (lô rin′də, lə-) *n.* a feminine name: see LAURA

lo·ris (lō′ris, lôr′is) *n.* ⟦ModL < Fr, special use (by BUFFON) of Du *loeres* <

loer, a clown] any of various small, slow-moving, large-eyed Asian prosimians (family Lorisidae) that live in trees and are active at night

lorn (lôrn) ***adj.*** ⟦ME < OE *loren*, pp. of *leosan* (see LOSE): the change of *s* to *r* is due to VERNER'S LAW⟧ **1** [Obs.] lost, ruined, or undone **2** [Old Poet.] forsaken, forlorn, bereft, or desolate

Lor·na (lôr′nə) ***n.*** ⟦apparently coined by R. D. Blackmore (1825-1900), Eng novelist, for the title character of his novel *Lorna Doone* (1869) < title of the Marquess of *Lorne*: see LOUISE[2]⟧ a feminine name

Lorrain, Claude *see* CLAUDE LORRAIN

Lor·raine[1] (lô rān′) ***n.*** ⟦Fr⟧ a feminine name

Lor·raine[2] (lô ren′) **1** historical region of NE France: see ALSACE-LORRAINE **2** metropolitan region of modern France in the same general area: 9,092 sq mi (23,548 sq km); chief city, Nancy —**Cross of Lorraine** a Latin cross with a second, usually longer horizontal bar beneath the first

lor·ry (lôr′ē) ***n., pl.*** **-ries** ⟦prob. < dial. *lurry, lorry*, to tug, pull⟧ **1** a low, flat wagon without sides **2** any of various trucks fitted to run on rails **3** [Brit.] a motor truck

lo·ry (lō′rē, lôr′ē) ***n., pl.*** **-ries** ⟦Malay *lūrī*⟧ any of several small, brightly colored, short-tailed parrots, native to Australia and the East Indies with a fringed, brushlike tip of the tongue for feeding on soft fruits and nectar

Los Al·a·mos (lôs al′ə mōs′, läs) ⟦Sp, lit., the poplars⟧ town in NC N.Mex., near Santa Fe: site of nuclear energy facility where the atomic bomb was developed

Los An·ge·les (lôs an′jə ləs, läs-; -lēz; -aŋ′gə-) ⟦Sp, short for *Reina de los Ángeles*, lit., Queen of the Angels⟧ city & seaport on the SW coast of Calif. —**Los An·ge·le·no** (an′jə lē′nō)

lose (lo͞oz) ***vt.*** **lost, los′ing** ⟦ME *losen, lesen*, merging OE *losian*, to lose, be lost (< *los*, LOSS) + *leosan*, to lose, akin to OHG *(vir)liosan*, Goth *(fra) liusan* < IE base **leu-*, to cut off, separate > Gr *lyein*, to dissolve; L *luere*, to loose, release (from debt)⟧ **1** *a)* to bring to ruin or destruction [a ship *lost* in the storm] *b)* *Theol.* to incur the damnation of [to *lose* one's soul] **2** to become unable to find; mislay [to *lose* one's keys] **3** *a)* to have taken from one by negligence, accident, death, removal, separation, etc.; suffer the loss of; be deprived of *b)* to suffer the miscarriage or stillbirth of (a baby) **4** to get rid of (something undesirable) [to *lose* unwanted weight] **5** to fail to keep or maintain [to *lose* one's temper, to *lose* speed] **6** *a)* to fail to see, hear, or understand [she did not *lose* a word of his speech] *b)* to fail to keep in sight, mind, or existence **7** to fail to have, get, take advantage of, etc.; miss [to *lose* one's chance] **8** to fail to win or gain [to *lose* a game] **9** to cause the loss of [it *lost* him his job] **10** to cause to go astray, become bewildered, etc. **11** to wander from and not be able to find (one's way, the right track, etc.) **12** to fail or be unable to make proper use of; waste [to *lose* time] **13** to leave behind; outdistance **14** to engross or preoccupy: usually in the passive [to be *lost* in reverie] **15** to go slower by [a watch that *loses* two minutes a day] —***vi.*** **1** to undergo or suffer loss **2** to be defeated in a contest, etc. **3** to be slow: said of a clock, etc. —**lose it** [Informal] **1** to fail to maintain one's composure, as by an outburst of anger, laughter, etc. **2** to suffer temporary or permanent diminution of one's ability, skill, etc. [the pitcher *lost it* in the sixth inning] —**lose oneself** **1** to lose one's way; go astray; become bewildered **2** to become absorbed [to *lose oneself* in a good novel] **3** to disappear from view or notice —☆**lose out** [Informal] to fail; be unsuccessful —☆**lose out on** [Informal] to fail to win, gain, or take advantage of —**los′a·ble** ***adj.***

lo·sel (lō′zəl, lo͞o′-) [Now Chiefly Dial.] ***n.*** ⟦ME *losel, lorel* < *losen*, pp. of *lesen*, prec.⟧ a worthless person —***adj.*** worthless

los·er (lo͞o′zər) ***n.*** **1** *a)* one that loses *b)* [Informal] one that seems doomed to lose; esp., an ineffectual person who habitually fails or is easily victimized **2** a person who reacts to loss or defeat in a specified way [a poor *loser*] **3** [Slang] a person who has been imprisoned for crime a (specified) number of times [a three-time *loser*]

los·ing (-ziŋ) ***n.*** **1** the act of one that loses **2** [*pl.*] losses by gambling —***adj.*** **1** that loses [a *losing* team] **2** resulting in loss [a *losing* proposition]

loss (lôs, läs) ***n.*** ⟦ME *los* < pp. of *losen, lesen*, to LOSE⟧ **1** a losing or being lost **2** an instance of this **3** the damage, trouble, disadvantage, deprivation, etc. caused by losing something **4** the person, thing, or amount lost **5** any reduction, lessening, etc. [a *loss* of strength, power, etc.] **6** any reduction of heat energy, electrical energy, etc. in a system, esp. the reduction of power, voltage, or current in a circuit due to the resistance of the components **7** *Insurance a)* death, injury, damage, etc. that is the basis for a valid claim for indemnity under the terms of an insurance policy *b)* the amount paid by the insurer on this basis **8** *Mil. a)* the losing of military personnel in combat by death, injury, or capture *b)* [*pl.*] those lost in this way *c)* [*pl.*] ships, aircraft, etc. lost in battle —**at a loss** **1** in an uncertain or perplexed state; puzzled **2** so as to lose money [to operate a business *at a loss*] **3** not able to; uncertain how to: followed by an infinitive [he was *at a loss* to explain the missing funds] —**at a loss for words** temporarily unable to speak or to articulate one's feelings or thoughts, as from surprise or deep emotion

☆**loss leader** any article that a store sells cheaply or below cost in order to attract customers

loss·less (lôs′lis, läs′-) ***adj.*** ⟦used orig. with regard to dissipation of electrical or electromagnetic energy⟧ designating or of a format for compressing digital files, as of sound or images, without any loss of data: contrasted with LOSSY

loss ratio the ratio between the losses incurred and the premiums earned by an insurance company during a specified time

loss·y (lôs′ē, läs′ē) ***adj.*** ⟦used orig. with regard to dissipation of electrical or electromagnetic energy⟧ designating or of a format for compressing digital files, as of sound or images, that involves some loss of data: contrasted with LOSSLESS

lost (lôst, läst) ***vt., vi. pt. & pp. of*** LOSE —***adj.*** **1** *a)* destroyed or ruined physically or morally *b)* *Theol.* damned; reprobate **2** not to be found; missing **3** no longer held or possessed; parted with **4** no longer seen, heard, or known [a person *lost* in a crowd] **5** not gained or won; attended with defeat **6** having wandered from the way; uncertain as to one's location **7** bewildered or ill at ease **8** not spent profitably or usefully; wasted **9** spent away from one's place of work, as because of illness [to make up *lost* time] —☆**get lost!** [Slang] go away! —**lost in** absorbed in; engrossed in —**lost on** without effect on; failing to influence [his sarcastic tone was not *lost on* me] —**lost to** **1** no longer in the possession or enjoyment of **2** no longer available to **3** having no sense of (shame, right, etc.); insensible to

lost cause an undertaking or movement that has failed or is certain to fail

lost motion the difference in the rate of motion of driving and driven parts of a machine, due to faulty fittings, etc.

Lost Pleiad, the *see* PLEIADES

lost tribes the ten tribes of Israel carried off into Assyrian captivity about 722 B.C.: 2 Kings 17:6

lost-wax process (lôst′waks′) a method of casting in which a wax form is encased in a heat-resistant material, as clay, that is hardened and then heated to melt and drain away the wax, producing a mold into which molten material is poured: used in casting dental plates, metal sculpture, etc.

lot (lät) ***n.*** ⟦ME < OE *hlot*, akin to Ger *los*, Du *lot*, ON *hlutr*, Goth *hlauts* < IE base **klēu-*, a hook, forked branch > CLOSE[2], L *clavis*, key⟧ **1** *a)* an object used in deciding a matter by chance, a number of these being placed in a container and then drawn or cast out at random one by one *b)* the use of such an object or objects in determining a matter [to choose men by *lot*] *c)* the decision or choice arrived at by this means, regarded as the verdict of chance *d)* what a person receives as the result of such a decision; share **2** one's portion in life; fortune [her unhappy *lot*] **3** a plot of ground; specif., ☆*a)* a subdivision of a block in a town or city ☆*b)* a parcel of land in a cemetery **4** *a)* a number of persons or things regarded as a group *b)* a quantity of material processed or manufactured at the same time **5** [*often pl.*] [Informal] a great number or amount [a *lot* of cars, *lots* of money] **6** [Informal] sort (of person or persons) [they're a bad *lot*] ☆**7** *Film* a studio with the surrounding area belonging to it; specif., the area used for outdoor filming —***vt.*** **lot′ted, lot′ting** **1** to divide into lots **2** [Rare] to allot —***vi.*** to draw or cast lots —**SYN.** FATE —**a lot** a great deal; very much: considered somewhat informal by some [*a lot* happier]: also [Informal] **a whole lot** [*a whole lot* nicer] —**cast (or throw) in one's lot with** to take one's chances in association with; share the fortune of —**draw (or cast) lots** to decide an issue by using lots —**the lot** [Informal] the whole of a quantity or number [a dollar apiece, or ten for *the lot*]

Lot[1] (lät) ***n.*** ⟦Heb *Lōṭ*⟧ *Bible* Abraham's nephew, who, warned by two angels, fled from the doomed city of Sodom: his wife looked back to see the destruction and was turned into a pillar of salt: Gen. 19:1-26

Lot[2] (lôt) river in S France, flowing west into the Garonne: *c.* 300 mi (483 km)

lo·ta or **lo·tah** (lō′tə) ***n.*** ⟦Hindi *loṭā*⟧ in India, a globe-shaped water pot, usually of brass

loth (lōth, lōth) ***adj. alt. sp. of*** LOATH

Lo·thar·i·o (lō ther′ē ō′, -thär′-) ***n., pl.*** **-i·os′** ⟦name of young rake in Nicholas Rowe's play *The Fair Penitent* (1703)⟧ [*often* **l-**] [Chiefly Literary] a seducer of women

Lo·thi·an (lō′thē ən, -thē-) former administrative region of SE Scotland, which included Edinburgh & the former districts of East Lothian, Midlothian, & West Lothian

lo·ti (lō′tē) ***n., pl.*** **ma·lo·ti** (mə lō′tē) ⟦Sotho⟧ the basic monetary unit of Lesotho: see the table of monetary units in the Reference Supplement

Lo·ti (lô tē′), **Pierre** (pseud. of *Louis Marie Julien Viaud*) 1850-1923; Fr. novelist

lo·tic (lōt′ik) ***adj.*** ⟦< L *lotus*, a washing (< *lautus*, pp. of *lavare*, to wash: see LAVE) + -IC⟧ *Ecol.* designating, of, or living in a freshwater habitat characterized by swiftly moving water: cf. LENTIC

lo·tion (lō′shən) ***n.*** ⟦ME *loscion* < L *lotio* (gen. *lotionis*) < *lotus*: see prec.⟧ a liquid preparation used, as on the skin, for cleansing, soothing, healing, etc.

lo·tos (lōt′əs) ***n. alt. sp. of*** LOTUS (sense 1)

lots (läts) ***adv.*** [Informal] a great deal; very much [feeling *lots* more relaxed since our vacation] —***pl.n.*** *see* LOT (***n.*** 5)

lot·sa (läts′ə) ***adv.*** [Informal] *phonetic sp. of an informal pronun. of* lots of

lotte (lôt) ***n.*** ⟦Fr⟧ [*also in roman type*] MONKFISH

lot·ter·y (lät′ər ē) ***n., pl.*** **-ter·ies** ⟦MFr *loterie* < MDu *loterije* < *lot*, LOT⟧ **1** a game of chance in which people buy numbered tickets, and prizes are given to those whose numbers are drawn by lot: often sponsored by a state or organization as a means of raising funds **2** any undertaking that involves chance selections, as by the drawing of lots [military draft *lottery*]

Lot·tie or **Lot·ty** (lät′ē) ***n.*** a feminine name: see CHARLOTTE[1]

lot·to (lät′ō) ***n.*** ⟦It < Fr *lot* < MDu: see LOT⟧ a game, esp. a lottery, resembling bingo

lo·tus (lōt′əs) ***n.*** ⟦L < Gr *lōtos* < Heb *lōṭ*⟧ **1** *Gr. Legend a)* a fruit inducing a dreamy languor and forgetfulness *b)* the plant bearing this fruit, variously supposed to be the date, the jujube, etc. **2** any of various waterlilies, esp. the **white lotus** (*Nymphaea lotus*), once sacred in Egypt, or the pink or white Asian lotus (*Nelumbo nucifera*), used as a religious symbol in Hinduism and Buddhism **3** a representation of any of these plants in ancient, esp. Egyptian, sculpture and architecture **4** any of a genus (*Lotus*) of plants of the pea family, with irregular, pinnate leaves and yellow, purple, or white flowers

lo·tus-eat·er (-ēt′ər) ***n.*** in the *Odyssey*, one of a people who ate the fruit of the lotus and consequently became indolent, dreamy, and forgetful of duty

lotus land **1** the land of the lotus-eaters, or any fabulous, dreamlike setting **2** [Slang] Hollywood and its film industry, thought of as glittery and alluring, not like the real world: also **Lo′tus·land′**

lotus position ⟦so named from perceived resemblance to the blossom of the LOTUS (***n.*** 2)⟧ in yoga, an erect sitting posture with the legs crossed and with each foot, sole upturned, resting on the upper thigh of the opposite leg

louche (lo͞osh) ***adj.*** ⟦Fr, lit., squinting < L *lusca*, fem. of *luscus*, one-eyed⟧ [*also in italics*] **1** morally loose or questionable **2** slightly decadent in style or behavior

loud (loud) ***adj.*** ⟦ME < OE *hlud*, akin to Ger *laut* < IE base **k̂leu-*, to hear, listen > L *cluere*, to be spoken of, esteemed⟧ **1** striking with force on the organs of hearing; strongly audible: said of sound **2** making a sound or sounds of great intensity [*a loud bell*] **3** noisy **4** clamorous; emphatic; insistent [*loud denials*] **5** [Informal] too vivid; flashy [*a loud Hawaiian shirt*] **6** [Informal] unrefined; vulgar **7** [Dial.] strong or offensive, as in smell —***adv.*** in a loud manner —**out loud** with the normal voice; not silently; aloud —**loud′ish** ***adj.*** —**loud′ly** ***adv.*** —**loud′ness** ***n.***

loud·en (loud′'n) ***vt., vi.*** to make or become loud or louder

loud·hail·er (loud′hāl′ər) ***n.*** [Chiefly Brit.] BULLHORN

loud·mouthed (-mouthd′, -moutht′) ***adj.*** in the habit of talking in a loud, irritating, or indiscreet manner —**loud′mouth′** ***n.***

loud·speak·er (-spēk′ər) ***n.*** SPEAKER (sense 2)

☆**Lou Gehrig's disease** ⟦after *Lou* GEHRIG, who died of the disease⟧ AMYOTROPHIC LATERAL SCLEROSIS: also **Lou Gehrig disease**

lough (läkh) ***n.*** ⟦ME, prob. < Gael & OIr *loch*, LOCH⟧ **1** a lake **2** an arm of the sea

lou·is (lo͞o′ē) ***n.***, *pl.* **lou′is** (-ēz) LOUIS D'OR

Lou·is¹ (lo͞o′is, lo͞o′ē) ***n.*** ⟦Fr < OFr *Loeis*; prob. via ML *Ludovicus* < OHG *Hludowig* < Gmc base **hluda-*, famous (< base of LOUD) + **wiga-*, war, hence, lit., famous in war; in the form *Lewis*, sometimes an adaptation of Welsh *Llewelyn*⟧ a masculine name: dim. *Lou, Louie*; var. *Lewis*; equiv. L. *Ludovicus*, Ger. *Ludwig*, It. *Luigi*, Sp. *Luis*, Welsh *Llewellyn, Llewelyn*; fem. *Louisa, Louise*

Lou·is² (lo͞o′ē; *Fr* lwē; *for 12*, lo͞o′is) **1 Louis I** A.D. 778-840; king of France & emperor of the Holy Roman Empire (814-840): son & successor of Charlemagne **2 Louis II de Bourbon** *see* CONDÉ, Prince de **3 Louis IX** 1214-70; king of France (1226-70): canonized as **Saint Louis**, his day is Aug. 25 **4 Louis XI** 1423-83; king of France (1461-83): son of Charles VII **5 Louis XII** 1462-1515; king of France (1498-1515) **6 Louis XIII** 1601-43; king of France (1610-43): son of Henry IV **7 Louis XIV** 1638-1715; king of France (1643-1715): his reign encompassed a period of flourishing Fr. culture: son of Louis XIII: called *the Sun King* **8 Louis XV** 1710-74; king of France (1715-74): great-grandson of Louis XIV **9 Louis XVI** 1754-93; king of France (1774-92): reign marked by the French Revolution: guillotined: grandson of Louis XV **10 Louis XVII** 1785-95; titular king of France (1793-95): son of Louis XVI **11 Louis XVIII** 1755-1824; king of France (1814-15; 1815-24): brother of Louis XVI **12 Joe** (born *Joseph Louis Barrow*) 1914-81; U.S. boxer: world heavyweight champion (1937-49)

Lou·i·sa (lo͞o ē′zə) ***n.*** a feminine name: see LOUIS¹

lou·is d'or (lo͞o′ē dôr′) ⟦Fr, lit., gold louis: orig. after LOUIS XIII⟧ **1** an old French gold coin of varying value, issued during the reigns of Louis XIII through Louis XVI **2** a later French gold coin worth 20 francs

Lou·ise¹ (lo͞o ēz′) ***n.*** ⟦Fr, fem. of LOUIS¹⟧ a feminine name: dim. *Lou, Lulu*; var. *Eloise*

Lou·ise² (lo͞o ēz′), **Lake** ⟦after Princess *Louise* Caroline Alberta (1848-1939), daughter of Queen VICTORIA² & wife of the Marquess of Lorne (1845-1914), Cdn Governor General (1878-83)⟧ small lake in SW Alberta, Canada

Lou·i·si·an·a (lo͞o ē′zē an′ə, lo͞o′ə zē-, lo͞o′zē-) ⟦Fr *La Louisianne*, name for the Mississippi Valley, after LOUIS XIV⟧ state of the S U.S., on the Gulf of Mexico: admitted 1812; 43,562 sq mi (112,825 sq km); cap. Baton Rouge: abbrev. *LA* or *La*

Louisiana Purchase

Louisiana Purchase land bought by the U.S. from France in 1803 for $15,000,000: it extended from the Mississippi to the Rocky Mountains & from the Gulf of Mexico to Canada

Lou·i·si·an·i·an (-an′ē ən) ***adj.*** of Louisiana: usually used in the predicate —***n.*** a person born or living in Louisiana Also **Lou·i′si·an′an** (-an′ən)

Louis Napoleon (born *Charles Louis Napoléon Bonaparte*) 1808-73; president of France (1848-52) &, as *Napoleon III*, emperor (1852-70): deposed: nephew of Napoleon I

Louis Phi·lippe (fi lēp′) 1773-1850; king of France (1830-48): abdicated in the Revolution of 1848: son of the Duc d'Orléans: called *the Citizen King*: see ORLÉANS¹

Louis Qua·torze (ka tôrz′) ⟦< Fr *quatorze*, lit., fourteen⟧ designating or of the style of furniture, architecture, etc. of the time of Louis XIV of France, characterized by massive, baroque forms and lavish ornamentation

Louis Quinze (kanz) ⟦< Fr *quinze*, lit., fifteen⟧ designating or of the style of furniture, architecture, etc. of the time of Louis XV of France, characterized by rococo treatment with emphasis on curved lines and highly decorative forms based on shells, flowers, etc.

Louis Seize (sez) ⟦< Fr *seize*, lit., sixteen⟧ designating or of the style of furniture, architecture, etc. of the time of Louis XVI of France, characterized by a return to straight lines, symmetry, and classic ornamental details

Louis Treize (trez) ⟦< Fr *treize*, lit., thirteen⟧ designating or of the style of furniture, architecture, etc. of the time of Louis XIII of France, characterized by Renaissance forms, rich inlays, etc.

Lou·is·ville (lo͞o′ə vəl, lo͞o′ē vil) ⟦after LOUIS XVI⟧ city in N Ky., on the Ohio River

lounge (lounj) ***vi.*** **lounged**, **loung′ing** ⟦15th-c. Scot dial. < ? *lungis*, laggard, lout < OFr *longis* < L *Longinus*, Apocryphal name of the soldier who lanced the crucified Jesus in the side: sense infl. in OFr by assoc. with *longe*, long, slow < L *longus*, LONG¹⟧ **1** to stand, move, sit, lie, etc. in a relaxed or lazy way; loll **2** to spend time in idleness [*they lounge around on street corners, wasting their lives*] —***vt.*** to spend by lounging [*to lounge the summer away*] —***n.*** **1** an act or time of lounging **2** [Archaic] a lounging gait or stroll **3** *a)* a room, as in a hotel or theater, where guests or patrons may go to relax, socialize, smoke, etc. *b)* COCKTAIL LOUNGE **4** a couch or sofa, esp. a backless one with a headrest at one end —**loung′er** ***n.***

☆**lounge car** a railroad car where passengers may lounge in comfortable chairs and obtain refreshments

☆**lounge lizard** [Slang] an indolent, pleasure-seeking person, esp. a man, who frequents lounges, nightclubs, etc. where rich people or socialites gather

lounge·wear (lounj′wer′) ***n.*** comfortable, loose-fitting clothing for casual wear, esp. at home

loup¹ (loup, lōp, lo͞op) [Scot.] ***vi., vt., n.*** ⟦ME, akin to *leap, hleap*: see LEAP⟧ LEAP

loup² (lo͞o) ***n.*** ⟦Fr < *loup (de mer)*, wolf (of the sea)⟧ a European sea bass: also called **loup de mer** (lo͞od mer′)

loupe (lo͞op) ***n.*** ⟦Fr < MFr, gem of imperfect transparency, shapeless iron lump, prob. < or akin to OHG *luppa*, lumpy mass: see LOB⟧ any of various types of small, high-powered magnifying lens held or worn close to the eye, used by jewelers

loup-ga·rou (lo͞o gȧ ro͞o′) ***n.***, *pl.* **loups-ga·rous** (lo͞o gȧ ro͞o′) ⟦Fr < *loup*, wolf (< L *lupus*) + *garou*, werewolf < OFr *garolf* < Frank **werwulf*, akin to OE *werwulf*, WEREWOLF⟧ WEREWOLF

lour (lour) ***vi., n.*** *var. of* LOWER²: the preferred Brit. sp.

Lou·ren·ço Mar·ques (lō ren′sō mär′kes; *Port* lô ren′soo mär′kezh) *former name for* MAPUTO

louse (lous; *for v., also* louz) ***n.***, *pl.* **lice** and, for 4, **lous′es** ⟦ME *lous* < OE *lus* (pl. *lys*), akin to Ger *laus* < IE **lūs* > Welsh *lleuen*, Bret *laouen*⟧ **1** *a)* any of an order (Anoplura) of small, flat, wingless insects with sucking mouthparts, parasitic on the skin or hair of humans and some other mammals; esp., the human **body louse** (*Pediculus humanus corporis*) and **head louse** (*P. h. capitis*) *b)* any of various arthropods that suck blood or juice from other animals or plants **2** BIRD LOUSE **3** any of various other small insects, arachnids, and crustaceans that are not parasitic, as the book louse or wood louse **4** [Informal] a person regarded as mean, contemptible, etc. —***vt.*** **loused**, **lous′ing** [Archaic] to delouse —☆**louse up** [Slang] to botch; spoil; ruin

louse·wort (lous′wurt′) ***n.*** ⟦so named from former belief that sheep feeding on the plants became infested with vermin⟧ any of a genus (*Pedicularis*) of perennial plants of the figwort family, with pinnately divided leaves and spiked clusters of yellow, rose, or purple flowers

lous·y (lou′zē) ***adj.*** **lous′i·er**, **lous′i·est** **1** infested with lice **2** covered with specks: said of silk **3** [Informal] dirty, disgusting, or contemptible ☆**4** [Informal] poor; inferior: a generalized epithet of disapproval ☆**5** [Slang] well supplied or oversupplied (*with*) —**lous′i·ly** ***adv.*** —**lous′i·ness** ***n.***

lout¹ (lout) ***n.*** ⟦prob. < or akin to ME *lutien*, to lurk < OE *lutian*, akin to *lutan*: see fol.⟧ an awkward, ill-mannered person; boor —**lout′ish** ***adj.*** —**lout′ish·ly** ***adv.*** —**lout′ish·ness** ***n.***

lout² (lout) ***vi., vt.*** ⟦ME *louten* < OE *lutan*: for IE base see LITTLE⟧ [Now Chiefly Dial.] to bow or curtsy; stoop

Louth (louth) county in Leinster province, E Ireland: 317 sq mi (821 sq km)

Lou·vain (lo͞o van′; *E* lo͞o vān′) *Fr. name for* LEUVEN

lou·ver (lo͞o′vər) ***n.*** ⟦ME *luver* < MFr *lover* < MDu *love*, gallery (in a theater), akin to OHG *louba*: see LODGE⟧ **1** an open turret or lantern on the roof of a medieval building **2** *a)* a window or opening furnished with a series of overlapping, horizontal slats arranged so as to admit light and air but shed rainwater outward *b)* any of these slats (also **louver board**) *c)* any similar arrangement of slats or fins, often adjustable, used to control ventilation, light intensity, etc. **3** a ventilating slit Also sp. **lou′vre** —**lou′vered** ***adj.***

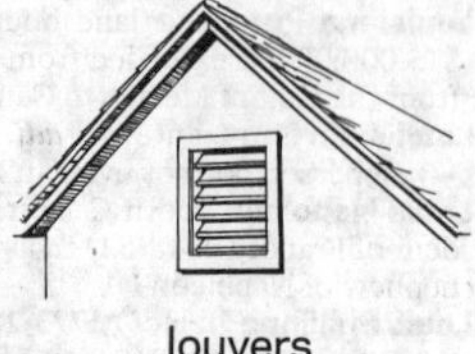
louvers

L'Ouverture *see* TOUSSAINT L'OUVERTURE

Lou·vre (lo͞o′vrə, lo͞ov; *Fr* lo͞o′vr′) ***n.*** national museum of art in Paris, on the Seine: converted from a royal palace in the 18th cent.

lov·a·ble (luv′ə bəl) ***adj.*** inspiring love; easily loved; endearing: also sp. **love′a·ble** —**lov′a·bil′i·ty** ***n.***, **lov′a·ble·ness** —**lov′a·bly** ***adv.***

lov·age (luv′ij) ***n.*** ⟦ME *loveache*, altered (by assoc. with *love*, LOVE & *ache*, ACHE) < OFr *levesche* < LL *levisticum* for L *ligusticum*, lovage, plant native to Liguria < *Ligusticus*, Ligurian, after *Liguria*, country in Cisalpine Gaul⟧ a European plant (*Levisticum officinale*) of the umbel family, sometimes used as a potherb and formerly as a home medicine

lo·va·stat·in (lō′və stat′'n, lō′və stat′'n) ***n.*** **1** a white, crystalline powder, $C_{24}H_{36}O_5$ **2** a drug made of this powder, used to reduce the levels of LDL and cholesterol in the blood

lov·at (luv′ət) ***n.*** ⟦prob. after *Lovat*, locality in the shire of INVERNESS⟧ a variegated color, chiefly green, with shades of blue, gray, etc., characteristic of some tweeds

love (luv) ***n.*** ⟦ME < OE *lufu*, akin to OHG *luba*, Goth *lubo* < IE base **leubh-*, to be fond of, desire > LIBIDO, LIEF, LUST⟧ **1** a deep and tender feeling of affection for or attachment or devotion to a person or persons **2** an expression of one's love or affection [give Mary my *love*] **3** a feeling of brotherhood and good will toward other people **4** *a)* strong liking for or interest in something [a *love* of music] *b)* the object of such liking **5** *a)* a strong, usually passionate, affection of one person for another, based in part on sexual attraction *b)* the person who is the object of such an affection; sweetheart; lover **6** *a)* sexual passion *b)* sexual intercourse **7** ⟦< phr. *play for love*, i.e., play for no stakes⟧ *Tennis* a score of zero **8** *Theol.* *a)* God's tender regard and concern for all human beings *b)* devotion to and desire for God as the supreme good, that all human beings have **9** [**L-**] *Myth.* *a)* Cupid, or Eros, as the god of love *b)* [Rare] Venus —***vt.* loved, lov′ing 1** to feel love for **2** to show love for by embracing, fondling, kissing, etc. **3** to delight in; take pleasure in [to *love* books] **4** to gain benefit from [a plant that *loves* shade] —***vi.*** to feel the emotion of love; be in love —**fall in love (with)** to begin to feel love, esp. romantic love, (for) —**for love** as a favor or for pleasure; without payment —**for the love of 1** for the sake of; with loving regard for **2** a mild exclamation of surprise, exasperation, etc., used in the phrases **for the love of God** (or **Christ, Pete**, etc.) —**in love (with)** feeling love, esp. romantic love, (for); enamored (of) —**make love 1** [Old-fashioned] to woo; court **2** to embrace, kiss, etc. as lovers do **3** to have sexual intercourse —**no love lost between** no liking or affection existing between —**not for love or money** not under any conditions

SYN.—**love** implies intense fondness or deep devotion and may apply to various relationships or objects [sexual *love*, brotherly *love*, *love* of one's work, etc.]; **affection** suggests warm, tender feelings, usually not as powerful or deep as those implied by **love** [he has no *affection* for cats]; **attachment** implies connection by ties of affection, attraction, devotion, etc. and may be felt for inanimate things as well as for people [an *attachment* to an old pair of jeans]; **infatuation** implies a foolish or unreasoning passion or affection, often a transient one [an elderly man's *infatuation* for a much younger woman]

love affair 1 an amorous or romantic relationship or episode between two people not married to each other **2** an intense or eager interest in something

love apple ⟦transl. of Fr *pomme d'amour*, Ger *liebesapfel*, calques of It *pomo d'amore*, folk etym. for earlier It *pomo dei Mori*, lit., apple of the Moors⟧ [Archaic] the tomato

☆**love beads** a long strand of colorful beads worn by both men and women, esp. in the 1960s and 1970s, as a symbol of the counterculture

love·bird (luv′burd′) ***n.*** any of various small parrots, esp. of an African genus (*Agapornis*), often kept as cage birds: the mates appear to be greatly attached to each other

love bite a bruise made on the skin by sucking, as in lovemaking

☆**love·bug** (luv′bug′) ***n.*** ⟦so called because they mate in midair and remain coupled as they swarm⟧ a small, mostly black, dipterous fly (*Plecia nearctica*) of the SE U.S.: they swarm in large numbers in May and September, causing a nuisance to motorists

love child an illegitimate child: a euphemism

Love·craft (luv′kraft′), **H(oward) P(hillips)** 1890-1937; U.S. writer of horror stories

love feast 1 *a)* among the early Christians, a meal eaten together as a symbol of brotherhood *b)* a modern gathering imitating this ☆**2** any gathering characterized by friendliness and good feeling

love game ⟦see LOVE (*n.* 7)⟧ a game, as in tennis, in which the losing player or team scores no points

☆**love handles** [Informal] bulges of fat at the sides of the waist

love-hate (luv′hāt′) ***adj.*** characterized simultaneously by feelings of love and hate [a *love-hate* relationship]

☆**love-in** (luv′in′) ***n.*** **1** an outdoor gathering or demonstration that is a public display or expression of love, unity, etc., as of hippies in the 1960s **2** a display of consensus or unanimity, often staged or forced, or a gathering of persons putting on such a display

love-in-a-mist (luv′in′ə mist′) ***n.*** an annual European plant (*Nigella damascena*) of the buttercup family, with finely cut leaves and blue or white flowers: also **love′-in′-the-mist′** (*-thə* mist′)

love knot TRUELOVE KNOT

Love·lace (luv′lās′), **Richard** 1618-57; Eng. poet

love·less (luv′lis) ***adj.*** without love; specif., *a)* feeling no love *b)* receiving no love; unloved —**love′less·ly** ***adv.***

love letter a letter expressing amorous feelings, written by someone as to his or her sweetheart

love-lies-bleed·ing (-līz′blēd′iŋ) ***n.*** an amaranth (*Amaranthus caudatus*) with drooping spikes of small, red flowers

love life that part of one's life having to do with amorous or sexual relationships

Lov·ell (luv′əl), Sir **(Alfred Charles) Bernard** 1913-2012; Eng. astronomer

love·lock (luv′läk′) ***n.*** a lock of hair lying apart from the rest of the hair; specif., such a long lock as formerly worn by courtiers

love·lorn (-lôrn′) ***adj.*** ⟦see LORN⟧ deserted by or pining for one's sweetheart; pining from love

love·ly (luv′lē) ***adj.* -li·er, -li·est** ⟦ME *luvelich* < OE *luflic*⟧ having those qualities that inspire love, affection, or admiration; specif., *a)* beautiful; exquisite *b)* morally or spiritually attractive; gracious *c)* [Informal] very pleasant or enjoyable [a *lovely* party] —***n.***, ***pl.* -lies** [Informal] a lovely person or thing; esp., a beautiful young woman —**SYN.** BEAUTIFUL —**love′li·ly** ***adv.*** —**love′li·ness** ***n.***

love·mak·ing (luv′māk′iŋ) ***n.*** the act of making love; specif., *a)* embracing, kissing, etc. *b)* sexual intercourse

love match a marriage for love only, not for wealth, status, etc.

love nest [Informal] a place where newlyweds, sweethearts, etc. reside or spend time alone together

love potion *Folklore* a drink intended to arouse love or passion in or for a certain person

lov·er (luv′ər) ***n.*** **1** a person who greatly enjoys something or has great affection for something [a *lover* of fine wine] **2** a person who loves sexually or romantically; specif., *a)* either partner in a sexual relationship of any kind *b)* either partner in an adulterous or otherwise illicit sexual relationship *c)* [Old-fashioned] the illicit male sexual partner of a married woman *d)* a person with regard to his or her degree of sexual skill, responsiveness, etc. **3** [*pl.*] a couple in love with each other or in a sexual relationship with each other —**lov′er·ly** ***adj., adv.***

lovers' lane any secluded place frequented by young couples so as to engage in lovemaking in their parked vehicles

love seat 1 a double chair or small sofa seating two persons **2** TÊTE-À-TÊTE (*n.* 2)

love set ⟦see LOVE (*n.* 7)⟧ *Tennis* a set in which the loser wins no games

love·sick (luv′sik′) ***adj.*** **1** exhibiting variously the moodiness, absentmindedness, etc. traditionally regarded as resulting from a strong romantic infatuation **2** expressive of such a condition [a *lovesick* song] —**love′sick′ness** ***n.***

love·some (-səm) ***adj.*** [Chiefly Literary] lovely, lovable, etc.

lov·ey-dov·ey (luv′ē duv′ē) ***adj.*** ⟦LOVE + -Y[2] + DOVE + -Y[2]⟧ [Slang] very affectionate, amorous, or sentimental

lov·ing (luv′iŋ) ***adj.*** **1** feeling love; devoted **2** expressing love [a *loving* act] —**lov′ing·ly** ***adv.*** —**lov′ing·ness** ***n.***

loving cup a large drinking cup of silver, etc., with two or more large handles by which it was formerly passed from guest to guest at banquets: now often given as a trophy in sports and games

lov·ing·kind·ness (-kīnd′nis) ***n.*** ⟦earlier *loving kindness*: first use by Miles COVERDALE (1535)⟧ kindness or affectionate behavior resulting from or expressing love

low[1] (lō) ***adj.*** ⟦ME *lah* < ON *lagr*, akin to MDu *lage*, MLowG *lœge* < IE base **legh-*, LIE[1]⟧ **1** *a)* of little height or elevation; not high or tall *b)* relatively close to the ground [*low* clouds] **2** depressed below the surrounding surface or normal elevation [*low* land] **3** of little depth; shallow [the river is *low* this time of year] **4** of little quantity, degree, intensity, value, etc. [a *low* cost, *low* water pressure, a *low* profile] **5** of less than normal height, elevation, depth, quantity, degree, power, etc. **6** below others in order, position, rating, etc. [*low* man on the team, *low* marks] **7** near the horizon [the sun was *low* in the west] **8** near the equator [a *low* latitude] **9** cut so as to expose the neck or part of the shoulders, chest, or back; décolleté [a dress with a *low* neckline] **10** deep; profound [a *low* bow] **11** lacking energy; enfeebled; weak **12** depressed in spirits; melancholy **13** not of high rank; humble; plebeian [a man of *low* origin] **14** vulgar; coarse; debased; undignified **15** mean; despicable; contemptible [a *low* trick] **16** poor; slight; unfavorable [to have a *low* opinion of someone] **17** containing less than a normal amount of some usual element [*low* in calories, *low*-salt diet] **18** not advanced in evolution, development, complexity, etc.; inferior [a *low* form of plant life] **19** relatively recent [a manuscript of a *low* date] ☆**20**

designating or of that gear ratio of a motor vehicle transmission which produces the lowest speed and the greatest torque **21** not well supplied with; short of: with *on [low* on ammunition*]* **22** of little intensity; not loud: said of a sound **23** designating or producing tones made by relatively slow vibrations; deep in pitch **24** [Informal] not having any or much money; short of ready cash **25** *Phonet.* articulated with the tongue held relatively low in the mouth: said of certain vowels (Ex.: ä in *far*) ***—adv.*** **1** in, at, to, or toward a low degree, level, place, position, etc. *[*hit them *low]* **2** in a low manner **3** quietly; softly *[*speak *low]* **4** with a deep pitch ***—n.*** something low; specif., ☆*a)* that gear of a motor vehicle, etc., producing the lowest speed and the greatest torque: also, an arrangement similar to this in an automatic transmission *b)* a low degree, level, place, position, etc. ☆*c) Meteorol.* an area of low barometric pressure **—*SYN.*** BASE² **—lay low 1** to cause to fall by hitting **2** to overcome or kill **—lie low** ☆**1** to keep oneself hidden or inconspicuous ☆**2** to wait patiently for an opportunity **—low′ness *n.***

low² (lō) ***vi.*** ⟦ME *lowen* < OE *hlowan*, akin to ON *hloa*, to roar < IE base **kel-*, to cry > L *clamor*⟧ to make the characteristic vocal sound of a cow; moo ***—vt.*** to express by lowing ***—n.*** the characteristic sound of a cow

low³ (lō) ***n., vi.*** ⟦ME *loghe* < ON *logi*, akin to MHG *lohe*, flame: for IE base see LIGHT¹⟧ [Scot. or North Eng.] flame or blaze

Low (lō) **1** Sir **David** 1891-1963; Brit. political cartoonist, born in New Zealand **2 Juliette** (born *Juliette Gordon*) 1860-1927; U.S. founder of the Girl Scouts

☆**low·ball** (lō′bôl′) ***vt.*** **1** to give an understated price, estimate, etc. to (someone), esp. without intending to honor it **2** to so understate (a price, etc.) ***—adj.*** of or having to do with prices, estimates, fares, etc. that are kept very low, esp. so as to take away sales from competitors **—low′ball′ing *n.***

low beam the dimmer, shorter-range setting of a vehicle's headlights

low blood pressure HYPOTENSION

low blow 1 a blow below the belt, illegal in boxing ☆**2** [Informal] an unsportsmanlike or unfair action, attack, etc.

low·born (lō′bôrn′) ***adj.*** of humble birth

low·boy (-boi′) ***n.*** ⟦LOW¹ + BOY⟧ ☆a chest of drawers mounted on short legs to about the height of a table

low·bred (-bred′) ***adj.*** **1** of inferior stock or breed **2** ill-mannered; vulgar; crude; coarse

☆**low·brow** (-brou′) ***n.*** a person regarded as having low or uncultivated tastes ***—adj.*** of or for a lowbrow

☆**low-cal** (lō′kal′) ***adj.*** [Informal] having a low caloric value *[low-cal* salad dressing*]*

Low Church a liberal, evangelical party of the Anglican Church that attaches relatively little importance to traditional rituals and doctrines: distinguished from HIGH CHURCH **—Low′-Church′ *adj.***

low-class (lō′klas′) ***adj.*** [Informal] vulgar, coarse, or undignified

low comedy a comedy that gets its effect mainly from action and situation, as burlesque, farce, slapstick, and horseplay, rather than from witty dialogue and characterization: cf. HIGH COMEDY

low-cost (-kôst′) ***adj.*** available at a low cost

Low Countries ⟦so named because they contain much land that is at or slightly below sea level⟧ the Netherlands, Belgium, & Luxembourg

low-cut (lō′kut′) ***adj.*** having the material forming the neckline cut low so as to reveal more flesh or, often, specif., more cleavage than usual *[*a *low-cut* evening gown*]*

low-den·si·ty lipoprotein (lō′den′sə tē) LDL

☆**low·down** (lō′doun′; *for adj.*, -doun′) ***n.*** [Slang] the true, pertinent facts; esp., secret or inside information: with *the* ***—adj.*** [Informal] **1** mean; contemptible **2** depressed; blue *[*feeling *lowdown]* **3** *Jazz* earthy; funky *[*a *lowdown* blues*]*

Low·ell¹ (lō′əl) **1 Abbott Lawrence** 1856-1943; U.S. educator **2 Amy** 1874-1925; U.S. poet & critic: sister of Abbott **3 James Russell** 1819-91; U.S. poet, essayist, & editor **4 Percival** 1855-1916; U.S. astronomer: brother of Abbott & Amy **5 Robert (Traill Spence, Jr.)** 1917-77; U.S. poet

Low·ell² (lō′əl) ⟦after F. C. *Lowell* (1775-1817), Am industrialist⟧ city in NE Mass.

low-end (lō′end′) ***adj.*** [Informal] **1** *a)* inexpensive and of a very low quality *b)* having only the basic features, without options or extras **2** at, of, or for the low end of a range *[*a *low-end* estimate*]*

low·er¹ (lō′ər) ***adj.*** ⟦compar. of LOW¹⟧ **1** in a place or on a level below another *[lower* lip*]* **2** inferior in rank, authority, or dignity *[*the *lower* classes*]* **3** less in quantity, degree, value, intensity, etc. **4** being farther south, closer to a shore or to the mouth of a river, or below land of higher elevation **5** [**L-**] *Archaeol., Geol.* earlier: used of a division of a period *[Lower* Devonian, *Lower* Paleolithic*]* ***—n.*** [Informal] ☆**1** a lower berth, as in a Pullman car **2** [*pl.*] the lower teeth or dentures ***—vt.*** **1** to let or put down *[lower* the window sash*]* **2** to reduce in height, elevation, amount, value, etc. *[*to *lower* prices*]* **3** to weaken or lessen *[*a disease that *lowers* one's resistance to further infection*]* **4** to bring down in respect, dignity, etc.; demean *[*to *lower* oneself by accepting a bribe*]* **5** to reduce (a sound) in volume or pitch ***—vi.*** to become lower; sink, fall, become reduced, etc.

low·er² (lou′ər) ***vi.*** ⟦ME *louren*, akin to LURK, Ger *lauern*, to lurk, MHG *luren*, to watch⟧ **1** to scowl or frown **2** to appear dark and threatening ***—n.*** a frowning or threatening look

lower bound *Math.* a number that is less than or equal to every number in a set

Lower California BAJA CALIFORNIA

Lower Canada *former name* (1791-1841) *for* QUEBEC

low·er·case (lō′ər kās′) ***n.*** ⟦from their being kept traditionally in the *lower case* (of two cases of type)⟧ small-letter type or writing used in printing, as distinguished from capital letters (*uppercase*): see SMALL LETTER ***—adj.*** designating, of, or in lowercase; small ***—vt.* -cased′, -cas′ing** to print in or change to lowercase

lower class the social class below the middle class; working class **—low′er-class′ *adj.***

☆**low·er·class·man** (-klas′mən) ***n., pl.* -men** (-mən) a student in the freshman or sophomore class of a high school or college

lower criticism textual criticism of the Scriptures

lower forty-eight the forty-eight conterminous states of the United States: a term used mainly by Alaskans: usually written **lower 48**

lower house [*often* **L- H-**] in a legislature having two branches, that branch which is usually larger and more representative, as the House of Representatives of the U.S. Congress

low·er·ing (lou′ər iŋ) ***adj.*** ⟦prp. of LOWER²⟧ **1** scowling; frowning darkly **2** dark, as if about to rain or snow; overcast *[*a *lowering* sky*]* **—low′er·ing·ly *adv.***

low·er·most (lō′ər mōst′) ***adj.*** below all others; lowest

Lower Saxony state of NW Germany, on the North Sea: 18,382 sq mi (47,609 sq km); cap. Hanover

Lower Silurian *former name for* ORDOVICIAN

lower world 1 NETHERWORLD **2** the earth

low·er·y (lou′ər ē) ***adj.*** ⟦see LOWER² & -Y²⟧ dark and cloudy

lowest common denominator 1 LEAST COMMON DENOMINATOR **2** *a)* that part of a group made up of those with the lowest level of taste, education, sophistication, etc. *b)* that which is accepted, understood, appreciated, etc. by them

lowest common multiple LEAST COMMON MULTIPLE

Lowes·toft¹ (lōs′tôft) ***n.*** a variety of porcelain formerly made in Lowestoft, England

Lowes·toft² (lōs′tôft) city in Suffolk, E England, on the North Sea

low frequency any radio frequency between 30 and 300 kilohertz

Low German ⟦calque of Ger *niederdeutsch* (see NETHER & DEUTSCHLAND): so named because orig. spoken chiefly in the Ger lowlands⟧ **1** PLATTDEUTSCH **2** the West Germanic languages, except for High German, of the Germanic branch of Indo-European, represented by Old Low Franconian, Old Saxon, Old Frisian, and Old English, and their later stages, including Dutch, Plattdeutsch, English, and Frisian: distinguished from HIGH GERMAN

low-grade (lō′grād′) ***adj.*** **1** of inferior quality or value **2** of little degree *[*a *low-grade* fever*]*

low-key (-kē′) ***adj.*** of low intensity, tone, etc.; subdued or restrained: also **low′-keyed′**

low·land (lō′lənd, -land′) ***n.*** land that is below the level of the surrounding land ***—adj.*** of, in, or from such a region **—the Lowlands** lowland region of SC Scotland, south & east of the Highlands **—low′land·er *n.*, Low′land·er**

Low Latin nonclassical Latin, esp. in the medieval period

low-lev·el (lō′lev′əl) ***adj.*** **1** of or by persons of low office or rank **2** in a low office or rank **3** designating a computer language based on machine language and requiring translation by an assembler

low·life (-līf′) [Informal] ***n.*** **1** *pl.* **-lifes′** a vulgar, coarse, or undignified person: also **low′lif′er 2** lowlifes collectively or their milieu ***—adj.*** of or characteristic of a lowlife; low-class

low·light (lō′līt′) ***n.*** ⟦LOW¹ + LIGHT¹: formed on the pattern of HIGHLIGHT⟧ [Informal] the part, as of a performance or event, which is the least interesting or the most inept, ridiculous, etc.: used somewhat humorously in opposition to *highlight*

low·ly (lō′lē) ***adj.* -li·er, -li·est 1** of or suited to a low position or rank **2** humble; meek **3** ordinary; commonplace ***—adv.* -li·er, -li·est 1** humbly; meekly **2** in a low manner, position, etc. **3** low in sound; softly; gently **—low′li·ness *n.***

low-ly·ing (lō′lī′iŋ) ***adj.*** **1** having little or no elevation above a surface or level, esp. ground level or sea level *[low-lying* hills, *low-lying* flood plains*]* **2** lying below the usual altitude or level *[low-lying* clouds*]*

Low Mass *former term for* a Mass of simple ceremony, the texts being recited, not sung, by the celebrant

low-mind·ed (-mīn′did) ***adj.*** having or showing a coarse, vulgar mind **—low′-mind′ed·ly *adv.* —low′-mind′ed·ness *n.***

low-necked (-nekt′) ***adj.*** having a low neckline; décolleté: said of a dress, etc.: also **low′-neck′**

low-pitched (-picht′) ***adj.*** **1** having a low tone or a low range of tone *[*a *low-pitched* voice*]* **2** having little pitch, or slope: said of a roof **3** of low intensity; subdued

low-pres·sure (-presh′ər) ***adj.*** **1** *a)* having or using a low or relatively low pressure *b)* having or indicating a low barometric pressure **2** not energetic or forceful

low-priced (-prīst′) ***adj.*** costing relatively little

low-pro·file (-prō′fīl′) ***adj.*** having a low PROFILE (*n.* 4); characterized by a lack of prominence or the avoiding of publicity

low-proof (-pro͞of′) ***adj.*** low in alcohol content

low relief BAS-RELIEF

low-rent (lō′rent′) ***adj.*** **1** designating or of a district, neighborhood, etc. characterized by poor or working-class residents **2** of, for, or like persons lacking education, refinement, etc.; lowbrow; coarse **3** [Informal] inferior to others of its kind; second-rate, cheap, etc. [a *low-rent* version of *Romeo and Juliet*]

☆**low·rid·er** or **low-rid·er** (lō′rīd′ər) *n.* [Informal] **1** a car modified with a lowered suspension, so that the body is very close to the road, used for cruising slowly **2** the driver, or a passenger, in such a car

☆**low-rise** (-rīz′) *adj.* **1** designating or of a building, esp. an apartment house, having only a few stories **2** designating pants cut so that the waistband sits at or below the pelvis

Low·ry (lou′rē), **(Clarence) Malcolm** 1909-57; Brit. writer

low-spir·it·ed (-spir′it id) *adj.* in low spirits; sad; depressed

Low Sunday the first Sunday after Easter

low-tech (lō′tek′) *adj.* **1** not involving specialized, complex technology: in full **low′-tech·nol′o·gy** ☆**2** of or having to do with businesses, systems, etc. using such technology

low-ten·sion (-ten′shən) *adj.* having, carrying, or operating under a low voltage

low-test (lō′test′) *adj.* vaporizing at a relatively high temperature: said of gasoline with a low octane number

low tide **1** the lowest level reached by the ebbing tide **2** the time when the tide is at this level: see also NEAP[1] **3** the lowest point reached by anything

low water **1** water at its lowest level, as in a stream **2** LOW TIDE

low-wa·ter mark (-wôt′ər) **1** a mark showing low water **2** the lowest point reached by anything

lox[1] (läks) *n.* ⟦via Yiddish < Ger *lachs*, salmon, akin to OE *leax*, salmon, Tocharian *lakṣi*, fish < IE **lak̆sos*, salmon < base **lak-*, speckled⟧ a variety of salty smoked salmon

lox[2] (läks) *n.* ⟦L(IQUID) OX(YGEN)⟧ liquid oxygen, esp. when used in rockets: also written **LOX**

loy·al (loi′əl) *adj.* ⟦Fr < OFr *loial, leial* < L *legalis*: see LEGAL⟧ **1** faithful to the constituted authority of one's country **2** faithful to those persons, ideals, etc. that one is under obligation to defend, support, or be true to **3** relating to or indicating loyalty —*SYN.* FAITHFUL —**loy′al·ly** *adv.*

loy·al·ist (-ist) *n.* **1** a person who is loyal; esp., one who supports the country's established government during times of revolt ☆**2** [*usually* **L-**] in the American Revolution, a colonist who was loyal to the British government **3** [**L-**] in the Spanish Civil War, one who remained loyal to the Republic, opposing Franco's revolt —*adj.* [*often* **L-**] of loyalists or Loyalists —**loy′al·ism′** *n.*

loy·al·ty (-tē) *n.* ⟦ME *loyaulte* < OFr *loialte*⟧ **1** quality, state, or instance of being loyal **2** *pl.* **-ties** an obligation of support and faithfulness to a person, government, cause, duty, etc. —*SYN.* ALLEGIANCE

loyalty card a small card issued by a business to a customer, for keeping track of that customer's participation in a LOYALTY PROGRAM

loyalty program a promotional program as of a retail business, airline, or restaurant, that rewards regular customers: typically, each purchase is assigned a point value, with accumulated points entitling a customer to free or discounted merchandise or services

Lo·yang (lō′yän′) *a former transliteration of* LUOYANG

Loy·o·la (loi ō′lə) *see* IGNATIUS (OF) LOYOLA

loz·enge (läz′ənj) *n.* ⟦ME *losenge* < OFr, prob. < Gaul **lausa*, stone slab: from the shape⟧ **1** a plane figure with four equal sides and two obtuse angles; diamond **2** a cough drop or small piece of hard candy, at one time made in a diamond shape

☆**LP**[1] (el′pē′) *n.* ⟦*L(ong) P(laying)*⟧ a phonograph record having microgrooves, for playing at 33⅓ revolutions per minute

LP[2] *abbrev.* **1** limited partnership **2** low pressure

LPG *abbrev.* liquefied petroleum gas

LPGA *service mark* Ladies Professional Golf Association

lpm or **LPM** *abbrev. Comput.* lines per minute

LPN (el′pē′en′) *n., pl.* **LPNs** licensed practical nurse: see PRACTICAL NURSE

Lr *Chem. symbol for* lawrencium

LS- *prefix U.S. Navy* landing ship: additional letters indicate type, as **LST**, Landing Ship-Tank

l.s. *abbrev.* ⟦L *locus sigilla*⟧ place of the seal

LSAT (*often* el′sat′) *trademark* Law School Admission Test

LSD (el′es′dē′) *n.* ⟦*l(y)s(ergic acid) d(iethylamide)*⟧ a crystalline compound, $C_{15}H_{15}N_2CON(C_2H_5)_2$, an amide of lysergic acid, used in the study of schizophrenia and other mental disorders and as a psychedelic drug: it produces hallucinations, delusions, etc. resembling those occurring in a psychotic state: also **LSD 25**

L.S.D., l.s.d., *or* **£.s.d.** *symbol* ⟦abbrev. of L *librae, solidi, denarii*; for £, see LIBRA (*n.* 1)⟧ pounds, shillings, pence

LSI (el′es′ī′) *n.* ⟦*l(arge-)s(cale) i(ntegration)*⟧ a complex integrated circuit, esp. one having between 100 and 5,000 transistors or other electronic components: cf. VLSI

LSW *abbrev.* Licensed Social Worker

lt *abbrev.* **1** local time **2** long ton

Lt *abbrev.* Lieutenant

LTC or **Lt Col** *abbrev.* Lieutenant Colonel

Lt Comdr *abbrev.* Lieutenant Commander

Ltd or **ltd** *abbrev.* limited

LTG or **Lt Gen** *abbrev.* Lieutenant General

Lt Gov *abbrev.* Lieutenant Governor

LTJG *abbrev.* Lieutenant, junior grade

lt-yr *abbrev. Astron.* light-year(s)

Lu *Chem. symbol for* lutetium

Lu·a·la·ba (lo͞o′ə lä′bə) upper course of the Congo, rising in the SE Democratic Republic of the Congo & flowing north

Lu·an·da (lo͞o än′də, -an′-) seaport & capital of Angola, on the Atlantic

lu·au (lo͞o′ou′) *n.* ⟦Haw⟧ a traditional Hawaiian feast, usually with entertainment

Lu·ba (lo͞o′bä′) *n.* **1** *pl.* **-bas′** or **-ba′** a member of a people of the S Democratic Republic of the Congo **2** the Bantu language of this people, used as a lingua franca in the Democratic Republic of the Congo

Lu·ba·vitch·er (lo͞o bäv′ə chər, lo͞o′bə vich′ər) *n.* ⟦after *Lubavitch*, town in Belorussia to which the group's headquarters was moved in 1820⟧ a member of a Hasidic group (**Lubavitch**) that emphasizes outreach services directed at nonobservant and unaffiliated Jews

lub·ber (lub′ər) [Archaic] *n.* ⟦ME *lobre* < *lobbe-*: see LOB⟧ **1** a big, slow, clumsy person **2** an inexperienced, clumsy sailor; landlubber —*adj.* big and clumsy —**lub′ber·li·ness** *n.* —**lub′ber·ly** *adj., adv.*

☆**lubber grasshopper** a flightless grasshopper (*Romalea microptera*) of the SE U.S., with a large, dark-brown body and clumsy movements

lubber's line a fixed mark or line on a compass, aligned with the bow of a ship (or aircraft) and used as by the helmsman in steering a course: also **lubber line**

Lub·bock (lub′ək) ⟦after T. S. *Lubbock*, Confederate officer⟧ city in NW Tex.

☆**lube** (lo͞ob) *n.* ⟦contr. < *lubricating (oil)*⟧ **1** a lubricating oil for machinery: also **lube oil** **2** [Informal] a lubrication —*vt.* **lubed, lub′ing** [Informal] to lubricate

Lü·beck (lo͞o′bek′; *Ger* lü′bek′) city & port in N Germany, in the state of Schleswig-Holstein

Lub·lin (lo͞o′blin; *Pol* lo͞o′blēn′) city in SE Poland

lu·bri·cant (lo͞o′bri kənt) *adj.* ⟦L *lubricans*, prp. of *lubricare*: see fol.⟧ reducing friction by providing a smooth film as a covering over parts that move against each other; lubricating —*n.* a substance for reducing friction in this way, as oil or grease

lu·bri·cate (-kāt′) *vt.* **-cat′ed, -cat′ing** ⟦< L *lubricatus*, pp. of *lubricare*, to make smooth or slippery < *lubricus*, smooth, slippery < IE base **sleub-*, to slide, slip > SLIP[3], SLEEVE⟧ **1** to make slippery or smooth **2** to apply a lubricant to —*vi.* to serve as a lubricant —**lu′bri·ca′tion** *n.* —**lu′bri·ca′tive** *adj.*

lu·bri·ca·tor (-kāt′ər) *n.* a person or thing that lubricates; specif., *a)* a lubricant *b)* an oil cup or similar device for supplying a lubricant to machinery

lu·bric·i·ty (lo͞o bris′i tē) *n., pl.* **-ties** ⟦Fr *lubricité* < LL *lubricitas*⟧ **1** slipperiness; smoothness; esp., effectiveness as a lubricant as indicated by this quality **2** trickiness; shiftiness **3** lewdness —**lu·bri′cious** (-brish′əs) *adj.*, **lu′bri·cous** (-bri kəs)

Lu·bum·ba·shi (lo͞o′bo͝om bä′shē) city in the SE Democratic Republic of the Congo, near the Zambian border

Lu·can[1] (lo͞o′kən) *adj.* ⟦< L *Lūcas*, Luke + -AN⟧ of or characteristic of the Evangelist Luke or the book of the New Testament attributed to him

Lu·can[2] (lo͞o′kən) (L. name *Marcus Annaeus Lucanus*) A.D. 39-65; Rom. poet, born in Spain

Lu·ca·ni·a (lo͞o kā′nē ə) **1** ancient district in S Italy, now in the Italian region of BASILICATA **2 Mount** mountain in the St. Elias range, SW Yukon Territory, Canada: 17,150 ft (5,227 m)

lu·carne (lo͞o′kärn′) *n.* ⟦Fr, altered (by assoc. with OFr *luiserne*, lantern: see LUCERNE) < OFr *lucanne* < ? Frank **lukinna*, a lamp, dim. < **luk-*: for IE base see LIGHT[1]⟧ a dormer window

Lu·cas van Ley·den (lo͞o′käs′ vän līd′′n) (born *Lucas Jacobsz*) 1494-1533; Du. painter & etcher

Luc·ca (lo͞o′kä′) city in Tuscany, W Italy

luce (lo͞os) *n.* ⟦ME < OFr *lus* < L *lucius*, kind of fish⟧ the PIKE[3], esp. when full-grown

Luce (lo͞os), **Henry Robinson** 1898-1967; U.S. editor & publisher

lu·cent (lo͞o′sənt) *adj.* ⟦L *lucens*, prp. of *lucere*, to shine: see LIGHT[1]⟧ **1** giving off light; shining **2** translucent or clear —**lu′cen·cy** *n.* —**lu′cent·ly** *adv.*

lu·cerne or **lu·cern** (lo͞o surn′) *n.* ⟦Fr *luzerne* < Prov *luzerno*, lit., glowworm < Prov *luzerna*, lamp, ult. < L *lucerna*, lamp < *lucere* (see LIGHT[1]): so named because of the shiny seeds⟧ [Chiefly Brit.] ALFALFA

Lu·cerne (lo͞o surn′; *Fr* lü sern′) **1** canton in central Switzerland: 576 sq mi (1,492 sq km) **2** its capital **3 Lake of** lake in central Switzerland: 44 sq mi (114 sq km)

Lu·chow (lo͞o′jō′) *a former transliteration of* LUZHOU

Lu·ci·a (lo͞o chē′ə, -ä, -sē′ə; lo͞o′sē ə, -shē ə, -shə) *n.* ⟦It < L: see LUCIUS, LUCY[1]⟧ a feminine name: see LUCIUS, LUCY[1]

Lu·cian (lo͞o′shən) ⟦L *Lucianus*, lit., of Lucius⟧ fl. 2d cent. A.D.; Gr. satirist, born in Syria

lu·cid (lo͞o′sid) *adj.* ⟦L *lucidus* < *lucere*, to shine: see LIGHT[1]⟧ **1** [Old Poet.] bright; shining **2** transparent **3** designating an interval of sanity in a mental disorder **4** clear to the mind; readily understood [*lucid* instructions] **5** clearheaded; rational [a *lucid* thinker] —**lu·cid′i·ty** *n.*, **lu′cid·ness** —**lu′cid·ly** *adv.*

Lu·ci·fer (lo͞o′sə fər) *n.* ⟦ME < OE < L, morning star (in ML, Satan), lit., light-bringing < *lux* (gen. *lucis*), LIGHT[1] + *ferre*, to BEAR[1]⟧ **1** [Old Poet.] the planet Venus when it is the morning star **2** *Theol.* SATAN; specif., in Christian theology, Satan as leader of the fallen angels: he was an angel of light until he revolted against God and, with the others, was cast into hell **3** [**l-**] an early type of friction match

lu·cif·er·ase (lo͞o sif′ər ās′) ***n.*** ⟦fol. + -ASE⟧ an oxidizing enzyme that acts with LUCIFERIN to produce light

lu·cif·er·in (-ər in) ***n.*** ⟦L *lucifer* (see LUCIFER) + -IN[1]⟧ a substance in luminescent organisms, as fireflies, that produces light by combining with oxygen in the presence of luciferase

lu·cif·er·ous (-ər əs) ***adj.*** ⟦L *lucifer* (see LUCIFER) + -OUS⟧ [Now Rare] providing light or mental insight

Lu·cille (lo͞o sēl′) ***n.*** a feminine name: see LUCY[1]

Lu·ci·na (lo͞o sī′nə) ***n. Rom. Myth.*** the goddess of childbirth: variously identified with Juno and Diana

Lu·cin·da (lo͞o sin′də) ***n.*** a feminine name: see LUCY[1]

☆**Lu·cite** (lo͞o′sīt′) ⟦< L *lux* (gen. *lucis*), LIGHT[1] + -ITE[1]⟧ *trademark for* an acrylic resin or plastic that is cast or molded into transparent or translucent sheets, rods, etc. —***n.*** [*also* **l-**] this resin, or a resin like it

Lu·cius (lo͞o′shəs) ***n.*** ⟦L < *lux*, LIGHT[1]⟧ a masculine name: fem. *Lucia*

luck (luk) ***n.*** ⟦ME *lucke*, prob. < MDu *luk*, contr. < *gelucke* < ODu **gilukki* (> Ger *glück*, fortune, good luck) < ? IE base **leug-*, to bend (> LEEK, LOCK[1]): basic sense "what bends together," hence, "what occurs, what is fitting, lucky occurrence"⟧ **1** the chance happening of events with respect to how they affect someone; fortune; fate **2** *a)* good fortune as the result of chance [success is based on hard work and a bit of *luck*] *b)* success; favorable outcome [an experienced gardener should have great *luck* growing annuals] **3** an object, action, etc. believed to bring or portend good or bad fortune [seeing a black cat is bad *luck*] —***vi.*** [Informal] to be lucky enough to come (*into, on, through,* etc.) —**down on one's luck** [Informal] in misfortune; unlucky —**in luck** fortunate; lucky —☆**luck out** [Slang] to have things turn out favorably for one; be lucky —**out of luck** unfortunate; unlucky —☆**press** (or **push**) **one's luck** [Informal] to take unnecessary risks in an already favorable situation —**try one's luck** to try to do something without being sure of the outcome —**worse luck** [Informal] unfortunately

luck·less (luk′lis) ***adj.*** having no good luck; unlucky —**luck′less·ly** ***adv.*** —**luck′less·ness** ***n.***

Luck·now (luk′nou′) city in N India: capital of Uttar Pradesh

luck·y (luk′ē) ***adj.*** **luck′i·er, luck′i·est 1** having good luck; fortunate **2** happening or resulting fortunately [a *lucky* change] **3** believed to bring good luck [a *lucky* coin] —☆**get lucky** [Slang] to have sexual intercourse —**luck′i·ly** ***adv.*** —**luck′i·ness** ***n.***

lucky dip [Brit.] GRAB BAG

lu·cra·tive (lo͞o′krə tiv) ***adj.*** ⟦ME *lucratif* < L *lucrativus* < pp. of *lucrari*, to gain < *lucrum*: see fol.⟧ producing wealth or profit; profitable; remunerative [a *lucrative* investment] —**lu′cra·tive·ly** ***adv.*** —**lu′cra·tive·ness** ***n.***

lu·cre (lo͞o′kər) ***n.*** ⟦ME < L *lucrum*, gain, riches < IE base **lāu-*, to capture > Sans *lōtram*, booty, OE *lean*, OHG *lon*, reward⟧ riches; money: now chiefly in a humorously derogatory sense, as in **filthy lucre** (cf. 1 Tim. 3:3)

Lu·cre·ti·a (lo͞o krē′shə, -shē ə) ***n.*** ⟦L, fem. of *Lucretius* < ? *lucrum*: see prec.⟧ a feminine name: equiv. Fr. *Lucrèce*, It. *Lucrezia*

Lu·cre·ti·us (lo͞o krē′shəs, -shē əs) (born *Titus Lucretius Carus*) 96?-55? B.C.; Rom. poet & Epicurean philosopher

lu·cu·brate (lo͞o′kə brāt′, -kyo͞o-) ***vi.*** **-brat′ed, -brat′ing** ⟦< L *lucubratus*, pp. of *lucubrare*, to work by candlelight < *lux* (gen. *lucis*), LIGHT[1]⟧ **1** to work, study, or write laboriously, esp. late at night **2** to write in a scholarly manner —**lu′cu·bra′tor** ***n.***

lu·cu·bra·tion (lo͞o′kə brā′shən, -kyo͞o-) ***n.*** ⟦L *lucubratio* < prec.⟧ **1** the act of lucubrating; laborious work, study, or writing, esp. that done late at night **2** something produced by such study, etc.; esp., a learned or carefully elaborated work **3** [*often pl.*] any literary composition: humorous usage suggesting pedantry

lu·cu·lent (lo͞o′kyo͞o lənt) ***adj.*** ⟦ME < L *luculentus* < *lux* (gen. *lucis*), LIGHT[1]⟧ **1** [Rare] bright; shining **2** clear to the understanding; lucid —**lu′cu·lent·ly** ***adv.***

Lu·cul·lus (lo͞o kul′əs), **(Lucius Lucinius)** 110?-57? B.C.; Rom. general & consul: proverbial for his wealth & luxurious banquets —**Lu·cul′lan** (-ən) ***adj.***, **Lu·cul′li·an** (-ē ən)

Lu·cy[1] (lo͞o′sē) ***n.*** ⟦prob. via Fr *Lucie* < L *Lucia* fem. of *Lucius*: see LUCIUS⟧ a feminine name: var. *Lucille, Lucinda*; equiv. It. & Sp. *Lucia*

Lu·cy[2] (lo͞o′sē), Saint (died A.D. 303?); It. martyr: her day is Dec. 13

☆**Lucy Ston·er** (stōn′ər) ⟦see STONE, Lucy⟧ [Old-fashioned] one who advocates that married women use only their maiden names

Lü·da (lo͞o′dä) urban complex in NE China, at the tip of the Liaodong Peninsula: it consists of the seaports of Dalian (formerly *Dairen*) & Lüshun (formerly *Port Arthur*)

Lud·dite (lud′īt′) ***n.*** ⟦said to be after a Ned *Lud*, feebleminded man who smashed two frames belonging to a Leicestershire employer (*c.* 1779)⟧ **1** any of a group of workers in England (1811-16) who smashed new labor-saving textile machinery in protest against unemployment and reduced wages **2** a person opposed in principle to technological change: a pejorative term —***adj.*** of or relating to Luddites

lude (lo͞od) ***n.*** ⟦< QUAALUDE⟧ [Slang] a methaqualone pill

Lu·dhi·a·na (lo͞o′dē ä′nə) city in central Punjab, NW India

☆**lu·dic** (lo͞o′dik) ***adj.*** ⟦Fr *ludique* < L *ludus*: see fol.⟧ characterized by playful behavior or a playful outlook

lu·di·crous (lo͞o′di krəs) ***adj.*** ⟦L *ludicrus* < *ludus*, a play, game < IE base **leid-*, to play, tease > Gr *loidorein*, to rail at, rebuke⟧ so absurd, ridiculous, or exaggerated as to cause or merit laughter —***SYN.*** ABSURD —**lu′di·crous·ly** ***adv.*** —**lu′di·crous·ness** ***n.***

Lud·wigs·ha·fen (lo͝od′vigz hä′fən) city in SW Germany, on the Rhine, in the state of Rhineland-Palatinate

lu·es (lo͞o′ēz′) ***n.*** ⟦ModL < L, a plague, decay < *luere*, to flow: see LOSE⟧ SYPHILIS —**lu·et′ic** (-et′ik) ***adj.***

luff (luf) ***n.*** ⟦ME *lof* < ODu *loef*, weather side (of a ship), auxiliary oar for steering, akin to ON *lōfi*, palm of the hand < IE base **lēp-*, **lōp-*, flat object, flat hand > OHG *lappo*, flat hand, rudder blade, Russ *lopata*, a shovel, rudder blade⟧ **1** the act of sailing close or closer to the wind **2** the forward edge of a fore-and-aft sail —***vi.*** **1** to turn the bow of a ship toward the wind; sail close or closer to the wind **2** to flutter: said of a sail, as on a boat that is heading too close to the wind **3** to raise or lower the jib of a crane

luf·fa (lo͞o′fə, luf′ə) ***n.*** *var. of* LOOFAH

luft·mensch (lo͝oft′mensh′) ***n.***, *pl.* ***-mensch′en*** (-men′shən) ⟦Yiddish < Ger *luft*, air (see fol.) + *mensch*, person⟧ an impractical, unrealistic person

Luft·waf·fe (lo͝oft′vä′fə) ***n.*** ⟦Ger < *luft*, air (akin to OE *lyft*, air & ON *lopt*: see LOFT) + *waffe*, WEAPON⟧ the air force of *a)* Nazi Germany *b)* the Federal Republic of Germany

lug[1] (lug) ***vt.*** **lugged, lug′ging** ⟦ME *luggen*, prob. < Scand, as in Swed *lugga*, to pull, lit., pull by the hair < *lugg*, forelock⟧ **1** to carry or drag laboriously (something heavy) [to *lug* a crate upstairs] **2** [Informal] to bring or introduce with some effort, awkwardness, etc. [you needn't *lug* my name into your argument] —***vi.*** ☆*Horse Racing* to veer slightly from a direct course [the favorite *lugged* in toward the rail] —***n.*** ⟦< ?⟧ **1** [Scot.] an ear **2** an earlike projection by which a thing is held or supported **3** a loop on the side of a harness through which the shaft passes **4** any of the heavy bolts which extend out from an axle hub or a disc brake, used with a nut (**lug nut**) to mount a wheel **5** a shallow box for shipping fruit or produce **6** any of a series of raised or projecting areas as on an automobile tire or the sole of a boot, for increasing traction ☆**7** [Slang] money exacted for political purposes: chiefly in **put the lug on**, to exact a contribution from **8** [Slang] a fellow, esp. a large, awkward fellow **9** [Archaic] the act of lugging

lug[2] (lug) ***n.*** *short for* LUGSAIL

lug[3] (lug) ***n.*** ⟦< ?⟧ *short for* LUGWORM

Lu·ga·no (lo͞o gä′nō), **Lake** lake on the Swiss-Italian border: *c.* 20 sq mi (52 sq km)

Lu·gansk (lo͞o gänsk′) city in E Ukraine, in the Donets Basin: see VOROSHILOVGRAD

luge (lo͞ozh) ***n.*** ⟦Fr < dial. (esp. in Savoy and Switzerland), prob. ult. < Gaul⟧ **1** a small racing sled on which one or two riders lie face up with the feet forward **2** the winter sport of racing on a luge —***vi.*** **luged, luge′ing** to race with such a sled —**lug′er** ***n.***

Lu·ger (lo͞o′gər) ⟦Ger⟧ *trademark for* a German automatic pistol —***n.*** [*often* **l-**] this pistol

lug·gage (lug′ij) ***n.*** ⟦< LUG[1] + -AGE⟧ suitcases, valises, trunks, etc.; baggage

lug·ger (lug′ər) ***n.*** a small vessel equipped with a lugsail or lugsails

lug·sail (lug′sāl′; *naut.*, -səl) ***n.*** ⟦< ? LUG[1], with reference to hauling sail around the mast in changing course⟧ a four-sided sail with the upper edge supported by a yard that is fastened obliquely to the mast

lu·gu·bri·ous (lə go͞o′brē əs, -gyo͞o′-) ***adj.*** ⟦L *lugubris* < *lugere*, to mourn (< IE base **leuǧ-*, **leug-*, to break > Welsh *llwyth*, burden) + -OUS⟧ very sad or mournful, esp. in a way that seems exaggerated or ridiculous —**lu·gu′bri·ous·ly** ***adv.*** —**lu·gu′bri·ous·ness** ***n.***

lug·worm (lug′wurm′) ***n.*** ⟦LUG[3] + WORM⟧ any of a family (Arenicolidae) of polychaetous worms that burrow into sandy seashores and are used for bait

Lui·chow (lə wē′jō′) *a former transliteration of* LEIZHOU

Luik (loik) *Fl. name for* LIÈGE

Lu·kács (lo͞o′käch′), **György (Szegedi von)** (jôrj) (born *György Bernát Löwinger*) 1885-1971; Hung. Marxist philosopher & literary critic

Luke (lo͞ok) ***n.*** ⟦LL(Ec) *Lucas* < Gr(Ec) *Loukas*, prob. contr. of *Loukanos*⟧ **1** a masculine name **2** *Bible a)* one of the four Evangelists, a physician and companion of the Apostle Paul and the reputed author of the third Gospel and the Acts of the Apostles: his day is Oct. 18 (also **Saint Luke**) *b)* the third book of the New Testament, telling the story of Jesus' life (abbrev. *Lk* or *Lu*)

luke·warm (lo͞ok′wôrm′) ***adj.*** ⟦ME *luke warme* < *luke*, tepid (akin to LowG *luk*, Du *leuk*, tepid < IE **ǩleu-* < base **ǩel-*, warm > OE *hleowe*, tepid, L *calere*, to be warm) + *warm*, WARM⟧ **1** barely or moderately warm: said of liquids **2** not very warm or enthusiastic [*lukewarm* praise] —**luke′warm′ly** ***adv.*** —**luke′warm′ness** ***n.***

lull (lul) ***vt.*** ⟦ME *lullen*, of echoic orig.⟧ **1** to calm or soothe by gentle sound or motion: chiefly in **lull to sleep** **2** to bring into a specified condition by soothing and reassuring [to *lull* people into a false sense of security] **3** to make less intense; quiet; allay [to *lull* someone's fears] —***vi.*** to become calm —***n.*** a short period of quiet or of comparative calm, lessened activity, etc.

lull·a·by (lul′ə bī′) ***n.***, *pl.* **-bies′** ⟦< *lulla* (< ME), echoic + *-by*, as in BYE-BYE⟧ **1** a song for lulling a baby to sleep **2** music based on or like this —***vt.*** **-bied′, -by′ing** to lull with or as with a lullaby

Lul·ly (lü lē′), **Jean Bap·tiste** (zhän bȧ tēst′) (born *Giovanni Battista Lulli*) 1632-87; Fr. composer, chiefly of operas, born in Italy

Lu·lu (lo͞o′lo͞o) ***n.*** **1** a feminine name: see LOUISE[1] ☆**2** [**l-**] [Slang] someone or something that is remarkable; now, specif., someone or something that is remarkably complex, difficult, frustrating, etc. ☆**3** [**l-**] [Slang] a fixed allowance given in lieu of payment for itemized expenses

lum (lum) ***n.*** ⟦< ?⟧ [Scot. or North Eng.] a chimney

lu·ma (lo͞o′mə) *n., pl.* **-ma** or **-mas** ⟦Arm⟧ a former monetary unit of Armenia, equal to 1/100 of a dram

lum·ba·go (lum bā′gō) *n.* ⟦L < *lumbus*, loin: see fol.⟧ rheumatic pain in the lumbar region; backache, esp. in the lower part of the back

lum·bar (lum′bär′, -bər) *adj.* ⟦ModL *lumbaris* < L *lumbus*, loin < IE **lond-hwos* < base **lendh-* > OE *lendenu*, loins⟧ of or near the loins; specif., designating or of the vertebrae, nerves, arteries, etc. in the part of the back just below the thoracic region

lum·ber[1] (lum′bər) *n.* ⟦< ? LOMBARD: orig., pawnbroker's shop or storeroom, hence pawned articles in storage, hence stored articles, hence lumber⟧ **1** [Brit.] miscellaneous discarded household articles, furniture, etc. stored away or taking up room ☆**2** timber sawed into beams, planks, boards, etc. of sizes convenient for building or carpentry —*vt.* **1** *a)* to fill or obstruct with useless articles or rubbish; clutter *b)* [Brit. Informal] to encumber or burden (often with *with*) ☆**2** to remove (timber) from (an area) for use as lumber —☆*vi.* to cut down timber and saw it into lumber —☆**lum′ber·er** *n.*

lum·ber[2] (lum′bər) *vi.* ⟦ME *lomeren* < ? Scand, as in Swed *lomra*, to resound, *loma*, to walk heavily⟧ **1** to move heavily, clumsily, and, often, noisily [tanks *lumbering* up a slope] **2** to rumble

lum·ber·ing[1] (lum′bər iŋ) *n.* ☆the work or business of cutting down trees and preparing lumber

lum·ber·ing[2] (lum′bər iŋ) *adj.* **1** moving heavily, clumsily, or noisily **2** rumbling —**lum′ber·ing·ly** *adv.*

☆**lum·ber·jack** (lum′bər jak′) *n.* **1** LOGGER **2** an earlier type of short, woolen or leather coat or jacket, of a kind worn by lumberjacks: also called **lumber jacket**

☆**lum·ber·man** (-mən) *n., pl.* **-men** (-mən) **1** [Now Rare] LOGGER **2** a person who deals in lumber

☆**lum·ber·yard** (-yärd′) *n.* a place where lumber is kept for sale

lum·bo- (lum′bō, -bə) ⟦< L *lumbus*, loin: see LUMBAR⟧ *combining form* **1** loin **2** lumbar, lumbar and [*lumbovertebral*]

lum·bri·ca·lis (lum′bri kā′lis) *n., pl.* **-ca′les′** (-kā′lēz′) ⟦ModL < L *lumbricus*, intestinal worm, earthworm: from the shape of the muscles⟧ any of four small muscles in the palm of the hand and in the sole of the foot: also **lum′bri·cal** (-kəl)

lum·bri·coid (lum′bri koid′) *adj.* ⟦< L *lumbricus* (see prec.) + -OID⟧ resembling an earthworm

lu·men (lo͞o′mən) *n., pl.* **-mens** or **-mi·na** (-mi nə) ⟦ModL < L, LIGHT[1]⟧ **1** the basic unit used to measure the flow of light in the SI system, equal to the amount of light emitted through a solid angle of one steradian by a light source with the intensity of one candela (0.0015 watt): abbrev. *lm* **2** the bore of a hollow needle, catheter, etc. **3** *Anat.* the passage within a tubular organ

lu·mi·naire (lo͞o′mə ner′) *n.* ⟦Fr, light, lighting < LL(Ec) *luminare*, a light, lamp: see LUMINARY⟧ a floodlight fixture, with a lamp, reflector, etc.

lu·mi·nance (lo͞o′mə nəns) *n.* ⟦< L *lumen* (gen. *luminis*), LIGHT[1] + -ANCE⟧ **1** the quality or state of being luminous **2** a measure of the brightness of a luminous surface, measured in candelas per unit area **3** that component of a video signal that carries information about brightness

☆**lu·mi·nar·i·a** (lo͞o′mə ner′ē ə) *n., pl.* **-i·as** a traditional Christmas ornament in Mexico and the SW U.S., consisting of a candle in an open, sand-filled paper bag: typically several of these are placed in a row outdoors and lighted as on Christmas Eve

lu·mi·nar·y (lo͞o′mə ner′ē) *n., pl.* **-nar′ies** ⟦OFr *luminarie* < LL(Ec) *luminarium* < L *luminare*: see ILLUMINATE⟧ **1** a body that shines, such as the sun or moon **2** *a)* a person who sheds light on some subject or enlightens mankind; famous intellectual *b)* any well-known or celebrated person

lu·mi·nesce (lo͞o′mə nes′) *vi.* **-nesced′**, **-nesc′ing** ⟦back-form. < LUMINESCENT⟧ to be or become luminescent

lu·mi·nes·cence (lo͞o′mə nes′əns) *n.* ⟦< L *lumen*, LIGHT[1] + -ESCENCE⟧ any giving off of light caused by the absorption of radiant or corpuscular energy and not by incandescence; any cold light; specif., fluorescence or phosphorescence occurring in various chemical, biological, electrical, etc. processes at relatively low temperatures

lu·mi·nes·cent (-ənt) *adj.* ⟦< L *lumen*, LIGHT[1] + -ESCENT⟧ of, exhibiting, or capable of exhibiting luminescence

lu·mi·nif·er·ous (lo͞o′mə nif′ər əs) *adj.* ⟦< L *lumen*, LIGHT[1] + -FEROUS⟧ giving off or transmitting light

lu·mi·nos·i·ty (-näs′ə tē) *n.* ⟦ML *luminositas*⟧ **1** the quality or condition of being luminous **2** *pl.* **-ties** something luminous **3** brightness

lu·mi·nous (lo͞o′mə nəs) *adj.* ⟦ME < L *luminosus* < *lumen*, LIGHT[1]⟧ **1** giving off light; shining; bright **2** filled with light; illuminated **3** glowing in the dark, as paint with a phosphor in it **4** clear; readily understood **5** intellectually brilliant —*SYN.* BRIGHT —**lu′mi·nous·ly** *adv.* —**lu′mi·nous·ness** *n.*

luminous energy LIGHT[1] (sense 1*a*)

luminous flux the flow of light measured in lumens

lum·mox (lum′əks) *n.* ⟦< ?⟧ [Informal] a clumsy, stupid person

lump[1] (lump) *n.* ⟦ME *lompe, lumpe*, akin ? to Dan *lompe*, a mass, lump, Swed dial. *lump*, a block, stump, MHG *lumpe*, rag: see LIMP[1]⟧ **1** a solid mass of no special shape, esp. one small enough to be taken up in the hand; hunk **2** *a)* a small cube or oblong piece *b)* such a cube or piece made of sugar crystals bound together with sugar syrup **3** a swelling or protuberance, as one caused by a blow or formed by a tumor or cyst **4** *a)* [Obs.] aggregate or collection *b)* a great mass, amount, number, etc. **5** a dull, clodlike person ☆**6** [*pl.*] [Informal] hard blows, punishment, criticism, or the like: usually in **get** (or **take**) **one's lumps** or **give someone his** (or **her**) **lumps** —*adj.* forming or formed into a lump or lumps [*lump* sugar] —*vt.* **1** to put together in a lump or lumps **2** to treat or deal with in a mass, or include in one group **3** to make lumps in —*vi.* **1** to become lumpy **2** to move heavily and laboriously: usually with *along* —**in the lump** in the mass or aggregate; all together —**lump in one's throat** a tight feeling in the throat, as from restrained emotion

lump[2] (lump) *vt.* ⟦Early ModE, to look sour < ? prec., but infl. by GRUMP, MUMP⟧ ☆[Informal] *in the phrase* **(like it or) lump it**, to (willingly or) unwillingly have to put up with something disagreeable

☆**lum·pec·to·my** (lum pek′tə mē) *n., pl.* **-mies** ⟦LUMP[1] + -ECTOMY⟧ the surgical removal of a breast tumor with minimum removal of adjacent normal tissues

lum·pen (loom′pən; *E* lum′-) *adj.* ⟦shortened < *lumpenproletariat* < Ger, lowest level of the proletariat: coined (1850) by Karl Marx < *lumpen-*, trashy (< *lump*, scoundrel, ragamuffin, lit., rag < MHG *lumpe*: see LIMP[1]) + *proletariat*, PROLETARIAT⟧ designating or of persons or groups regarded as belonging to a low or contemptible segment of their class or kind because of their unproductiveness, shiftlessness, alienation, etc. —*n., pl.* **lum·pen** such a person or group

lump·er (lum′pər) *n.* ⟦LUMP[1], *vt.* + -ER⟧ a laborer who helps to load and unload ships; longshoreman

lump·fish (lump′fish′) *n., pl.* **-fish′** or **-fish′es** (see FISH) ⟦prob. so called from the bony tubercles⟧ any of several sluggish, marine percoid fishes (family Cyclopteridae), esp. a large N Atlantic species (*Cyclopterus lumpus*), usually having a heavy body with hard spines, lumps, and a powerful ventral sucker: also called **lump′suck′er**

lump·ish (lum′pish) *adj.* **1** like a lump **2** heavy, clumsy, dull, stupid, etc. —**lump′ish·ly** *adv.* —**lump′ish·ness** *n.*

lump sum a gross, or total, sum paid at one time

lump·y (lum′pē) *adj.* **lump′i·er**, **lump′i·est** **1** full of lumps [*lumpy* pudding] **2** covered with lumps; having an uneven surface **3** rough: said of water **4** like a lump; heavy; clumsy —**lump′i·ly** *adv.* —**lump′i·ness** *n.*

☆**lumpy jaw** ACTINOMYCOSIS

Lu·na (lo͞o′nə) *n.* ⟦ME < L, the moon: see LIGHT[1]⟧ **1** *Rom. Myth.* the goddess of the moon: identified with the Greek Selene **2** the moon personified **3** [ML] *Alchemy* silver

lu·na·cy (lo͞o′nə sē) *n.* ⟦LUNA(TIC) + -CY⟧ **1** *a)* [Obs.] intermittent insanity, formerly supposed to change in intensity with the phases of the moon *b)* mental unsoundness; insanity **2** *pl.* **-cies** great folly or a foolish act —*SYN.* INSANITY

☆**lu·na moth** (lo͞o′nə) ⟦so named from the crescent-shaped markings on the wings⟧ a large, North American moth (*Actias luna*) with crescent-marked, pastel-green wings, the hind pair of which end in elongated tails

lu·nar (lo͞o′nər) *adj.* ⟦L *lunaris* < *luna*, the moon: see LIGHT[1]⟧ **1** of or on the moon **2** like the moon; specif., *a)* pale; pallid *b)* round or crescent-shaped **3** measured by the moon's revolutions [a *lunar* year] **4** [Rare] of or containing silver

lunar caustic fused silver nitrate, used in medicine for cauterizing

lunar eclipse *see* ECLIPSE (*n.* 1)

lunar (excursion) module the component of the Apollo spacecraft used to carry astronauts to the moon's surface and return them to the command and service modules in lunar orbit

lunar month *see* MONTH (sense 3)

lunar rover an open, electric-powered, four-wheeled vehicle used by astronauts to explore the surface of the moon

lunar year *see* YEAR (sense 4)

lu·nate (lo͞o′nāt′, -nit) *adj.* ⟦L *lunatus*, pp. of *lunare*, to bend like a half-moon < *luna*, the moon: see LIGHT[1]⟧ crescent-shaped: also **lu′nat′ed** —**lu′nate′ly** *adv.*

lu·na·tic (lo͞o′nə tik) *adj.* ⟦ME *lunatik* < OFr *lunatique* < LL *lunaticus*, moon-struck, crazy < L *luna*, the moon: see LIGHT[1]⟧ **1** suffering from lunacy; insane **2** of or characterized by lunacy **3** of or for insane persons **4** utterly foolish —*n.* an insane person

USAGE—the term is seldom used now except in hyperbolic extension

☆**lunatic fringe** that minority considered fanatical, foolishly extremist, etc. in a political, social, religious, or other movement

lu·na·tion (lo͞o nā′shən) *n.* ⟦ME *lunacyon* < ML *lunatio* < L *luna*, the moon: see LIGHT[1]⟧ LUNAR MONTH

lunch (lunch) *n.* ⟦earlier, a piece, thick piece < ?; first appears as rendering of Sp *lonja*, slice of ham, which it formerly paralleled in pronun.⟧ **1** any light meal; esp., the regular midday meal between breakfast and dinner **2** the food prepared for such a meal **3** LUNCHTIME —*vi.* to eat lunch —*vt.* to provide lunch for —**out to lunch** [Slang] **1** inattentive, distracted, etc. **2** eccentric or insane —**lunch′er** *n.*

lunch·box (lunch′bäks′) *n.* a small, lightweight container used to carry meals from home to school or work: also written **lunch box**

lunch·eon (lun′chən) *n.* ⟦earlier *lunchion, lunshin* < LUNCH, prob. after dial. *nuncheon*, a snack, lunch < ME *nonachenche*, lit., noon drink⟧ a lunch; esp., a formal lunch with others

☆**lunch·eon·ette** (lun′chən et′) *n.* ⟦see -ETTE⟧ a place where light lunches are served

lunch·meat (lunch′mēt′) *n.* meat processed in loaves, sausages, etc. and ready to eat: also **luncheon meat**

☆**lunch·room** (lunch′ro͞om′) *n.* **1** a restaurant where light, quick meals, as lunches, are served **2** a room in an office, school, etc. where lunches, usually brought in, may be eaten

lunch·time (lunch′tīm′) *n.* the midday period during which lunch is typically eaten

Lun·dy's Lane (lun′dēz) ⟦< ?⟧ road near Niagara Falls, Ontario, Canada: site of an indecisive battle (1814) between British & American forces

lune[1] (lo͞on) *n.* ⟦Fr < L *luna*, the moon: see LIGHT[1]⟧ a crescent-shaped figure on a plane or spherical surface

lune[2] (lo͞on) *n.* ⟦var. of *loyn* < OFr *loigne* < ML *longia* < L *longus*, LONG[1]⟧ *Falconry* a leash for a hawk

lu·nette (lo͞o net′) *n.* ⟦Fr, dim. of *lune*, the moon: see LUNE[1]⟧ **1** a crescent-shaped figure or object **2** a crescent-shaped opening in a vaulted roof to admit light **3** a semicircular space, often containing a windowpane or a mural, above a door or window **4** *Mil.* a projecting fieldwork consisting of two faces and two flanks

Lu·né·ville (lü nā vēl′) city in NE France: treaty signed here (1801) between France & Austria

lung (luŋ) *n.* ⟦ME *lunge* < OE *lungen*, akin to Ger *lunge* < IE base **legwh-*, light in weight and movement: the lungs were so named because of their lightness: see LIGHTS⟧ **1** either of the two spongelike respiratory organs in the thorax of air-breathing vertebrates, that oxygenate the blood and remove carbon dioxide from it **2** any analogous organ in invertebrates —**at the top of one's lungs** in one's loudest voice

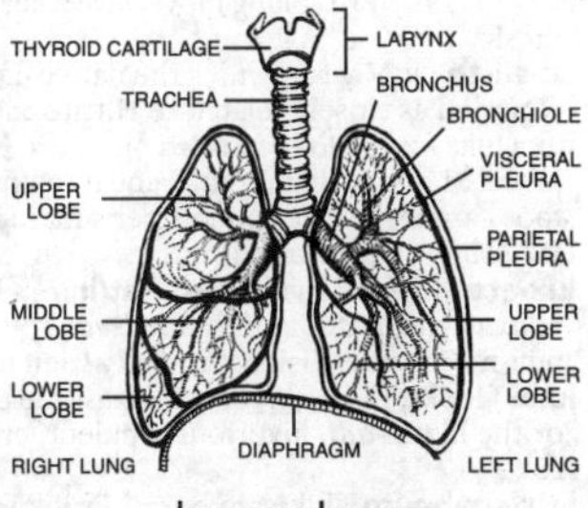

human lungs

lunge[1] (lunj) *n.* ⟦contr. < *allonge* < Fr, lit., a lengthening < *allonger*, to lengthen, thrust < *a-* (< L *ad*), to + *long* < L *longus*, LONG[1]⟧ **1** a sudden thrust with a sword or other weapon **2** a sudden plunge forward —*vi.* **lunged, lung′ing** ⟦< the *n.*⟧ to make a lunge or move with a lunge —*vt.* to cause to lunge; thrust with a lunge —**lung′er** *n.*

lunge[2] (lunj) *n., vt.* **lunged, lung′ing** *var. of* LONGE

lung·er (luŋ′ər) *n.* [Old Slang] a person who has tuberculosis of the lungs

lung·fish (luŋ′fish′) *n., pl.* **-fish′** or **-fish′es** (see FISH) any of two orders (Ceratodiformes and Lepidosireniformes) of lobefins having lungs as well as gills

lun·gi (lo͝oŋ′gē, luŋ′-) *n. alt. sp. of* LONGYI

lung·wort (luŋ′wurt′) *n.* ⟦ME *longwort* < OE *lungenwyrt* (see LUNG & WORT[2]): from a fancied resemblance to human lungs⟧ any of various plants formerly used in treating lung diseases; esp., any of a genus (*Pulmonaria*) of European plants of the borage family, with large, spotted leaves and clusters of blue or purple flowers

lu·ni- (lo͞o′ni, -nə) ⟦< L *luna*, the moon: see LIGHT[1]⟧ *combining form* **1** moon [*lunitidal*] **2** moon and [*lunisolar*]

lu·ni·so·lar (lo͞o′ni sō′lər) *adj.* ⟦prec. + SOLAR⟧ involving the mutual relationship or combined attraction of the moon and sun [*lunisolar tides*]

lu·ni·tid·al (-tīd′'l) *adj.* ⟦LUNI- + TIDAL⟧ of a tide or tidal movement caused by the moon's attraction

lunitidal interval the interval by which the lunar high tide lags behind the transit of the moon

☆**lunk·er** (luŋk′ər) *n.* ⟦< ?⟧ [Informal] a big fish

☆**lunk·head** (luŋk′hed′) *n.* ⟦prob. echoic alteration of LUMP[1] (after HUNK) + HEAD⟧ [Informal] a stupid person: also **lunk** —**lunk′head′ed** *adj.*

Lunt (lunt), **Alfred** 1893-1977; U.S. actor: see also FONTANNE, Lynn

lu·nu·la (lo͞on′yə lə) *n., pl.* **-lae′** (-lē′) ⟦ModL < L, dim. of *luna*, the moon: see LIGHT[1]⟧ any structure or marking in the shape of a crescent, as the whitish half-moon at the base of a fingernail: also **lu·nule** (lo͞on′yo͞ol′) —**lu′nu·lar** *adj.*

lu·nu·late (-lit, -lāt′) *adj.* ⟦< L *lunula* (see prec.) + -ATE[1]⟧ **1** crescent-shaped **2** having crescent-shaped markings Also **lu′nu·lat′ed**

Luo·yang (lə wō′yäŋ′) city in Henan province, EC China, near the Huang

Lu·per·ca·li·a (lo͞o′pər kā′lē ə) *n., pl.* **-li·as** or **-li·a** ⟦L < adj. *Lupercalis* < *Lupercus*, a pastoral god sometimes identified with Faunus < *lupus*, a wolf: orig. meaning obscure⟧ an ancient Roman festival with fertility rites, held Feb. 15: also **Lu′per·cal′** (-kal′) —**Lu′per·ca′li·an** *adj.*

lu·pine[1] (lo͞o′pin) *n.* ⟦ME *lupyne* < L *lupinus* < *lupus*, WOLF: reason for name uncert.⟧ **1** any of a genus (*Lupinus*) of plants of the pea family, with palmately compound leaves, racemes of white, rose, yellow, or blue flowers, and pods containing beanlike seeds: used for forage, green manure, etc. **2** the seed of the European lupine (*Lupinus albus*), used in some parts of Europe as food

lu·pine[2] (lo͞o′pīn′) *adj.* ⟦L *lupinus* < *lupus*, WOLF⟧ **1** of a wolf or wolves **2** wolflike; fierce; ravenous

lu·pu·lin (lo͞o′pyo͞o lin) *n.* ⟦< ModL *lupulus*, the hop (dim. of L *lupus*, hop plant, apparently identical to *lupus*, WOLF) + -IN[1]⟧ a bitter resinous powder obtained from the strobiles of hops, formerly used in medicine as a sedative

lu·pus (lo͞o′pəs) *n.* ⟦ModL < L, WOLF: from the idea of eating into the flesh⟧ any of various diseases with skin lesions, esp. systemic LUPUS ERYTHEMATOSUS

Lu·pus (lo͞o′pəs) *n.* ⟦L, WOLF⟧ a S constellation near the Milky Way between Centaurus and Scorpius

lupus er·y·the·ma·to·sus (er′ə thē′mə tō′səs, -them′ə-) ⟦ModL, lit., erythematous lupus: see ERYTHEMA⟧ a usually chronic inflammatory disease in which immunological reactions cause abnormalities of blood vessels and connective tissue: the systemic form commonly involves the joints, kidneys, nervous system, and skin, while the discoid form produces a chronic skin disease characterized by red scaly patches that tend to produce scars

lupus vul·gar·is (vul gar′is, -ger′-) ⟦ModL, lit., common lupus: see VULGAR⟧ tuberculosis of the skin, characterized by the appearance of red-dish-brown nodules that tend to ulcerate and form scars

lurch[1] (lurch) *vi.* ⟦< ?⟧ **1** to roll, pitch, or sway suddenly forward or to one side **2** to stagger —*n.* ⟦earlier *lee-lurch* < ?⟧ a lurching movement; sudden rolling, pitching, etc.

lurch[2] (lurch) *vi.* ⟦ME *lorchen*, var. of LURK⟧ [Obs.] to remain furtively near a place; lurk —*vt.* **1** [Archaic] to prevent (a person) from getting his fair share of something **2** [Obs.] to get by cheating, robbing, tricking, etc. —*n.* [Obs.] the act of lurching —**lie at** (or **on**) **the lurch** [Archaic] to lie in wait

lurch[3] (lurch) *n.* ⟦Fr *lourche*, name of a 16th-c. game like backgammon, prob. < OFr, duped < MDu *lurz*, left (hand), hence unlucky, akin to MHG *lërz*, left, *lürzen*, to deceive⟧ [Archaic] a situation in certain card games, in which the winner has more than double the score of the loser —**leave someone in the lurch** [Informal] to leave someone in a difficult situation; leave someone in trouble and needing help

lurch·er (lur′chər) *n.* **1** a person that lurches, or lurks **2** a thief; poacher **3** [Brit.] a crossbred dog trained to hunt silently: used by poachers

lur·dan or **lur·dane** (lur′dən) [Archaic] *n.* ⟦ME *lurdan* < OFr *lourdin* < *lourd*, heavy, dull, stupid, prob. < VL **lurdus* < L *luridus*, LURID⟧ a lazy, dull person —*adj.* lazy and dull

lure (loor) *n.* ⟦ME < MFr *leurre* < OFr *loirre*, prob. < Frank or Goth **lōthr*, akin to MDu *loder*, lure, OE *lathian*, to invite⟧ **1** a device consisting of a bunch of feathers on the end of a long cord, often baited with food: it is used in falconry to recall the hawk **2** *a)* the power of attracting, tempting, or enticing [the *lure* of the stage] *b)* anything that so attracts or tempts **3** a bait for animals; esp., an artificial one used in fishing —*vt.* **lured, lur′ing 1** to recall (a falcon) with a lure **2** to attract, tempt, or entice: often with *on* —**lur′er** *n.*

SYN.—**lure** suggests an irresistible force, as desire, greed, curiosity, etc., in attracting someone, esp. to something harmful or evil [*lured* on by false hopes]; **entice** implies a crafty or skillful luring [he *enticed* the squirrel to eat from his hand]; **inveigle** suggests the use of deception or cajolery in enticing someone [they *inveigled* him with false promises]; **decoy** implies the use of deceptive appearances in luring into a trap [artificial birds are used to *decoy* wild ducks]; **beguile** suggests the use of subtly alluring devices in leading someone on [*beguiled* by her sweet words]; **tempt** suggests the influence of a powerful attraction that tends to overcome scruples or judgment [I'm *tempted* to accept your offer]; **seduce** implies enticement to a wrongful or unlawful act, especially to loss of chastity —***ANT.*** **repel**

☆**Lur·ex** (loor′eks′) *n.* ⟦former trademark: arbitrary coinage, based on prec. + *-ex*, suffix of trade names⟧ [*also* **l-**] a thread of aluminum coated with plastic, or fabric made of such thread

lu·rid (loor′id) *adj.* ⟦L *luridus*, pale yellow, ghastly⟧ **1** [Rare] deathly pale; wan **2** glowing through a haze, as flames enveloped by smoke **3** *a)* vivid in a harsh or shocking way; startling; sensational *b)* characterized by violent passion or crime [a *lurid* tale] —**lu′rid·ly** *adv.* —**lu′rid·ness** *n.*

lurk (lurk) *vi.* ⟦ME *lurken*, akin to *louren* (see LOWER[2]), Norw *lurka*, to sneak off⟧ **1** to stay hidden, ready to spring out, attack, etc.; lie in wait **2** to exist undiscovered or unobserved; be present as a latent or not readily apparent threat **3** to move furtively

Lu·sa·ka (lo͞o sä′kä) capital of Zambia, in the central part

Lu·sa·tia (lo͞o sā′shə, -shē ə) region in E Germany & SW Poland

Lu·sa·tian (-shən) *n.* **1** a member of an old Slavic people formerly living in the historical region of Lusatia, and now living in an enclave in E Germany, south of Berlin; Sorb; Wend **2** the West Slavic language of this people —*adj.* of the Lusatians or their language or culture

lus·cious (lush′əs) *adj.* ⟦ME *lucius*, prob. var. of *licious*, aphetic form of DELICIOUS, infl. by *lusch*, fol.⟧ **1** highly gratifying to taste or smell, esp. because of a rich sweetness; delicious **2** *a)* delighting any of the senses *b)* having a strong sensual appeal; voluptuous **3** [Archaic] sickeningly sweet or full-flavored; cloying —**lus′cious·ly** *adv.* —**lus′cious·ness** *n.*

lush[1] (lush) *adj.* ⟦ME *lusch*, ? echoic var. of *lassch*, soft, flaccid < OFr *lasche*, lax, loose < *laschier*, to loosen < LL **lascare* < **lascus*, altered by metathesis < L *laxus*, LAX⟧ **1** tender and full of juice **2** of luxuriant growth [*lush* vegetation] **3** characterized by a rich growth of vegetation [*lush* fields] **4** characterized by richness, abundance, or extravagance, as in ornamentation, invention, etc., often tending to excess [*lush* writing] —***SYN.*** PROFUSE —**lush′ly** *adv.* —**lush′ness** *n.*

lush[2] (lush) *n.* ⟦< ? prec., in sense "full of juice"⟧ **1** [Old Slang] alcoholic liquor **2** [Informal] a person who drinks liquor habitually and to excess; esp., an alcoholic — *vi., vt.* [Slang] to drink (liquor)

Lü·shun (lo͞o′sho͝on′) seaport in Liaoning province, NE China: see LÜDA

Lu·si·ta·ni·a (lo͞o′sə tā′nē ə) ancient Roman province in the Iberian Peninsula, corresponding to most of modern Portugal & part of W Spain

lust (lust) *n.* ⟦ME < OE, pleasure, delight, appetite, akin to Ger *lust*, pleasure < IE base **las-*, to be eager > L *lascivus*, wanton, *larva*, specter, ghost:

sexual senses in E chiefly < rendering Vulg. *concupiscentia carnis* (1 John 2:16) as "lusts of the flesh"] **1** a desire to gratify the senses; bodily appetite **2** *a)* sexual desire *b)* excessive sexual desire, esp. as seeking unrestrained gratification **3** *a)* overmastering desire [*a lust for power*] *b)* intense enthusiasm; zest **4** [Obs.] *a)* pleasure *b)* inclination —*vi.* to feel an intense desire, esp. sexual desire: often with *after* or *for*

lus·ter[1] (lus′tər) *n.* ⟦Fr *lustre* < It *lustro* < *lustrare* < L, to light, illumine < *lustrum*, LUSTRUM⟧ **1** the quality, condition, or fact of shining by reflected light; gloss; sheen **2** brightness; radiance; brilliance **3** *a)* radiant beauty *b)* great fame or distinction; glory **4** *a)* any of the glass pendants on a chandelier or candlestick *b)* a chandelier, etc. adorned with such pendants **5** a substance used to give luster to an object **6** a glossy fabric of cotton and wool **7** the reflecting quality and brilliance of the surface of a mineral **8** a metallic, sometimes iridescent, appearance given to pottery by a glaze —*vt.* **1** to give a lustrous finish or gloss to **2** to add glory or fame to —*vi.* to be or become lustrous —**lus′ter·less** *adj.*

lus·ter[2] (lus′tər) *n.* LUSTRUM (sense 2)

lus·ter·ware (lus′tər wer′) *n.* highly glazed earthenware decorated by the application of metallic oxides to the glaze

lust·ful (lust′fəl) *adj.* **1** filled with or characterized by lust **2** [Archaic] lusty; vigorous —**lust′ful·ly** *adv.* —**lust′ful·ness** *n.*

lust·i·hood (lus′tē hood′) *n.* [Archaic] lustiness

lus·tral (lus′trəl) *adj.* ⟦L *lustralis* < *lustrum*, LUSTRUM⟧ **1** of, used in, or connected with ceremonial purification **2** [Rare] of a lustrum, or five-year period

lus·trate (lus′trāt′) *vt.* **-trat′ed**, **-trat′ing** ⟦< L *lustratus*, pp. of *lustrare*, to purify by means of a propitiatory sacrifice: see LUSTRUM⟧ to purify by means of certain ceremonies —**lus·tra′tion** *n.*

lus·tre (lus′tər) *n., vt., vi.* **-tred**, **-tring** *chiefly Brit. sp. of* LUSTER[1], LUSTER[2]

lus·tre·ware (-wer′) *n. chiefly Brit. sp. of* LUSTERWARE

lus·tring (lus′triŋ) *n.* ⟦Fr *lustrine* < It *lustrino* < *lustro*, LUSTER[1]⟧ *var. of* LUTESTRING

lus·trous (lus′trəs) *adj.* having luster; shining; bright; glorious —*SYN.* BRIGHT —**lus′trous·ly** *adv.* —**lus′trous·ness** *n.*

lus·trum (lus′trəm) *n., pl.* **-trums** or **-tra** (-trə) ⟦L, orig., prob. illumination < IE **leukstrom*, illumination < base **leuk-*, to light, shine > LIGHT[1]⟧ **1** in ancient Rome, a purification of all the people by means of ceremonies held every five years, after the census **2** a five-year period

lust·y (lus′tē) *adj.* **lust′i·er**, **lust′i·est** full of vigor; strong, robust, hearty, etc. —**lust′i·ly** *adv.* —**lust′i·ness** *n.*

lu·sus na·tu·rae (lo͞o′səs nə toor′ē, -toor′ī) ⟦L⟧ a sport of nature; freak of nature

lu·ta·nist (lo͞ot′'n ist) *n.* ⟦ML *lutanista* < *lutana*, a lute < MFr *lut*, LUTE[1]⟧ *alt. sp. of* LUTENIST

Lut Desert (lo͞ot) DASHT-E-LUT

lute[1] (lo͞ot) *n.* ⟦ME < MFr *lut* < OFr *leüt* < Prov *läut* < Ar *al-ʿūd*, lit., the wood⟧ an old stringed instrument related to the guitar, with a body shaped like half a pear and six to thirteen strings stretched along the fretted neck, which is often bent to form a sharp angle — *vi., vt.* **lut′ed**, **lut′ing** to play (on) a lute

lute[2] (lo͞ot) *n.* ⟦OFr *lut* < L *lutum*, mud, clay < IE base **leu-*, dirt > Gr *lyma*, filth, OIr *loth*, dirt⟧ a clayey cement used to keep the joints of pipes from leaking and as a sealing agent generally —*vt.* **lut′ed**, **lut′ing** to seal with lute

lu·te·al (lo͞ot′ē əl) *adj.* of or pertaining to the corpus luteum

lu·te·ci·um (lo͞o tē′shē əm) *n. former sp. of* LUTETIUM

lu·te·fisk (lo͞ot′ə fisk′) *n.* ⟦Norw < *lute*, to soak in lye (< *lut*, lye) + *fisk*, fish⟧ a Scandinavian dish consisting of dried cod that has been softened by soaking in a lye solution, rinsed, and then boiled

lu·te·in (lo͞ot′ē in) *n.* ⟦< (CORPUS) LUTE(UM) + -IN[1]⟧ **1** XANTHOPHYLL **2** a preparation of dried and powdered corpus luteum

lu·te·in·ize (-īz′) *vt.* **-ized′**, **-iz′ing** to stimulate the production of the corpus luteum in —*vi.* to become part of the corpus luteum —**lu′te·in·i·za′tion** *n.*

luteinizing hormone a hormone, secreted by the anterior lobe of the pituitary gland, that stimulates ovulation, the development of interstitial tissue, the secretion of testosterone in the testes of males, and the development of the corpus luteum with its subsequent secretion of progesterone in females

lu·te·nist (lo͞ot′'n ist) *n.* a lute player

lu·te·o·lin (lo͞ot′ē ə lin) *n.* ⟦Fr *lutéoline* < ModL (*Reseda*) *luteola*, lit., yellowish (reseda) < L *luteolus*, yellowish, dim. of *luteus*: see fol.⟧ a yellow crystalline compound, $C_{15}H_{10}O_6$, extracted from weld

lu·te·ous (lo͞ot′ē əs) *adj.* ⟦L *luteus*, golden-yellow < *lutum*, weed used in dyeing yellow, akin to *luridus*, LURID⟧ golden-yellow tinged with green

lute·string (lo͞ot′striŋ′) *n.* ⟦altered (by assoc. with LUTE[1]) < LUSTRING⟧ a glossy silk cloth, formerly used for women's apparel

Lu·te·tia (lo͞o tē′shə) *Latin name for* PARIS[2]

lu·te·ti·um (lo͞o tē′shē əm) *n.* ⟦ModL < *lutetia*, lutetium oxide (< L *Lutetia*: see prec.) + -IUM: so named by G. Urbain (1872-1938), Fr chemist, after his native city⟧ a soft, silvery-white chemical element, one of the rare-earth elements and the last member of the lanthanide series: symbol, Lu; at. no. 71: see the periodic table of elements in the Reference Supplement

Luth *abbrev.* Lutheran

Lu·ther[1] (lo͞o′thər) *n.* ⟦MHG < OHG *Chlothar, Hludher* < Gmc base **hluda-*, famous (akin to LOUD) + OHG *hari*, army, host: hence, lit., famous fighter⟧ a masculine name

Lu·ther[2] (lo͞o′thər), **Martin** 1483-1546; Ger. theologian & translator of the Bible: leader of the Protestant Reformation in Germany

Lu·ther·an (-ən) *adj.* **1** of Martin Luther **2** of his doctrines, esp. justification by faith **3** designating or of the Protestant denomination founded by Luther —*n.* any member of a Lutheran Church —**Lu′ther·an·ism′** *n.*

lu·thern (lo͞o′thərn) *n.* ⟦altered < ? Fr *lucarne*⟧ a dormer window: see DORMER

lu·thi·er (lo͞ot′ē ər) *n.* ⟦Fr < *luth*, lute (< OFr *leüt*, LUTE[1]) + *-ier*, -ER⟧ a maker of stringed instruments, originally of lutes

lut·ing (lo͞ot′iŋ) *n.* LUTE[2]

lut·ist (lo͞ot′ist) *n.* **1** LUTENIST **2** a maker of lutes

Lu·ton (lo͞ot′'n) city in Bedfordshire, SC England

Lu·tu·li (lə to͞o′lē), **Albert (John Mvumbi)** 1898-1967; South African political leader, born in Zimbabwe: also **Lu·thu′li** (-tho͞o′-)

Lut·yens (lut′yənz, luch′ənz), Sir **Edwin (Landseer)** 1869-1944; Eng. architect

Lutz (luts) *n., pl.* **Lutz′es** [*also* **l-**] *Figure Skating* a jump in which the skater takes off from one skate, does one full turn in the air, and lands on the other skate: cf. AXEL

luv (luv) *n.* [Brit. Slang] love; sweetheart; lover: a term of affectionate address

Lu·wi·an (lo͞o′wē ən) *n.* ⟦< the native name⟧ an extinct Anatolian language regarded as closely related to Hittite: also **Lu·vi·an** (lo͞o′vē ən)

lux (luks) *n., pl.* **lux** or **lux′es** ⟦L, LIGHT[1]⟧ *Physics* a basic unit of illumination in the SI and MKS systems, equal to one lumen per square meter (0.0929 foot-candles or one candela per square meter): abbrev. *lx*

Lux *abbrev.* Luxembourg

lux·ate (luk′sāt′) *vt.* **-at′ed**, **-at′ing** ⟦< L *luxatus*, pp. of *luxare*, to dislocate < *luxus*, dislocated < IE base **leug-*, to bend > LOCK[1], Gr *loxos*, slanting⟧ to put out of joint; dislocate —**lux·a′tion** *n.*

luxe (looks, luks) *n.* ⟦Fr < L *luxus*: see LUXURY⟧ richness, elegance, luxury, or the like —*adj.* luxurious, opulent, etc. and very expensive See also DE-LUXE

Lux·em·bourg (luk′səm burg′; *Fr* lük sän bo͞or′) **1** grand duchy in W Europe, bounded by Belgium, Germany, & France: 998 sq mi (2,586 sq km) **2** its capital, in the S part **3** province of S Belgium: 1,715 sq mi (4,442 sq km): also **Luxemburg** —**Lux′em·bourg′er** *n.*, **Lux′em·burg′er** —**Lux′em·bourg′i·an** *adj.*, **Lux′em·burg′i·an**

Lux·em·burg (luk′səm burg′; *Ger* lo͝ok′səm bo͝ork′), **Rosa** 1870?-1919; Ger. socialist leader, born in Poland

Lux·or (luk′sôr, look′-) city in S Egypt, on the Nile, near the ruins of ancient Thebes

lux·u·ri·ant (lug zhoor′ē ənt, luk shoor′-) *adj.* ⟦L *luxurians*, prp. of *luxuriare*: see fol.⟧ **1** [Rare] very productive; fertile [*luxuriant soil*] **2** growing with vigor and in great abundance; lush; teeming **3** characterized by richness and extravagance, as in ornamentation, invention, etc., often tending to excess [*a luxuriant imagination*] **4** LUXURIOUS (sense 2) —*SYN.* PROFUSE —**lux·u′ri·ance** *n.*, **lux·u′ri·an·cy** —**lux·u′ri·ant·ly** *adv.*

lux·u·ri·ate (-āt′) *vi.* **-at′ed**, **-at′ing** ⟦< L *luxuriatus*, pp. of *luxuriare*, to be too fruitful, be rank < *luxuria*, LUXURY⟧ **1** to grow with vigor and in great abundance **2** to expand or develop greatly **3** to live in great luxury **4** to take great pleasure; revel (*in*) —**lux·u′ri·a′tion** *n.*

lux·u·ri·ous (-əs) *adj.* ⟦OFr *luxurius* < L *luxuriosus*⟧ **1** fond of or indulging in luxury **2** constituting or contributing to luxury; splendid, rich, comfortable, etc. —*SYN.* SENSUOUS —**lux·u′ri·ous·ly** *adv.* —**lux·u′ri·ous·ness** *n.*

lux·u·ry (luk′shə rē, -shoor ē; lug′zhə rē, -zhoor ē) *n., pl.* **-ries** ⟦ME *luxurie* < OFr < L *luxuria* < *luxus*, extravagance, luxury, excess, prob. identical in orig. with *luxus*, dislocated: see LUXATE⟧ **1** the use and enjoyment of the best and most costly things that offer the most physical comfort and satisfaction **2** anything contributing to such enjoyment, usually something considered unnecessary to life and health **3** *a)* the unusual intellectual or emotional pleasure or comfort derived from some specified thing [*to give in to the luxury of tears*] *b)* something producing such pleasure or comfort —*adj.* characterized by luxury

Lu·zern (lo͞ot sern′) *Ger. name for* LUCERNE

Lu·zhou (lo͞o′jō′) city in Sichuan province, SC China, on the Chang

Lu·zon (lo͞o zän′) main island of the Philippines: 40,420 sq mi (104,687 sq km); chief city, Manila

lv *abbrev.* leave(s)

Lv[1] *abbrev. Bible* Leviticus

Lv[2] *Chem. symbol for* livermorium

Lviv (l′vēf′) city in W Ukraine: Russ. name **Lvov** (l′vôf′)

LVN *abbrev.* licensed vocational nurse

Lw *Chem. symbol for* lawrencium

lwei (lə wā′) *n., pl.* **lweis** ⟦after a tributary of the Cuanza River: see KWANZA⟧ a monetary unit of Angola, equal to 1⁄100 of a kwanza

Lwów (l′vo͞of′) *Pol. name for* LVIV

LWV *abbrev.* League of Women Voters

lx *abbrev.* lux

LXX *symbol* ⟦Rom. numeral for 70⟧ SEPTUAGINT

ly *abbrev. Astron.* light-year(s)

-ly[1] (lē) ⟦ME < OE *-lic* < Gmc **lika-*, body > LIKE[1]⟧ *suffix forming adjectives* **1** like, characteristic of, suitable to [*manly, godly, deadly*] **2** happening (once) every (specified period of time) [*hourly, monthly*]

-ly[2] (lē) ⟦ME < OE *-lice* < *-lic*⟧ *suffix forming adverbs* **1** in a (specified) manner or direction, to a (specified) extent, in or at a (specified) time or place *[haply, inwardly, merely]* **2** in the (specified) order *[firstly, thirdly]*

Ly·all·pur (lī′əl po͝or′) *former name for* FAISALABAD

ly·ase (lī′ās′, -āz′) ***n.*** ⟦LY(SIS) + -ASE⟧ any of a class of enzymes that act as catalysts in chemical reactions involving double bonds

ly·can·thrope (lī′kən thrōp′, lī kan′-) ***n.*** ⟦< ModL *lycanthropus* < Gr *lykanthrōpos* < *lykos*, WOLF + *anthrōpos*, a man: see ANTHROPO-⟧ WEREWOLF

ly·can·thro·py (lī kan′thrə pē) ***n.*** ⟦ModL *lycanthropia* < Gr *lykanthrōpia*: see prec.⟧ **1** [Archaic] a mental disorder in which one imagines oneself to be a beast, esp. a wolf **2** *Folklore* transformation of a person into a wolf or werewolf —**ly·can·throp·ic** (lī′kən thräp′ik) ***adj.***

ly·cée (lē sā′) ***n.**, pl.* **-*cées′*** (-sā′) ⟦Fr < L *lyceum*: see LYCEUM⟧ in France, a secondary school maintained by the government for preparing students for a university

ly·ce·um (lī sē′əm) ***n.*** ⟦after the fol. in Athens⟧ **1** a hall where public lectures or discussions are held **2** an organization presenting public lectures, concerts, etc. **3** LYCÉE

Ly·ce·um (lī sē′əm) ⟦L < Gr *Lykeion*, the Lyceum: so called from the neighboring temple of *Apollōn Lykeios*⟧ the grove at Athens where Aristotle taught

ly·chee (lē′chē′) ***n.*** *alt. sp. of* LITCHI

lych gate (lich) *alt. sp. of* LICH GATE

lych·nis (lik′nis) ***n.*** ⟦ModL < L, a fiery red rose < Gr *lychnos*, lamp < IE base **leuk-* > LIGHT[1]⟧ any of a genus (*Lychnis*) of plants of the pink family, with red, pink, or white flowers

Ly·cia (lish′ə, -ē ə) ancient country in SW Asia Minor, on the Mediterranean: came under Persian and Syrian rule; annexed as a province by Rome (1st cent. A.D.)

Ly·ci·an (-ən) ***adj.*** of Lycia or its people, language, or culture —***n.*** **1** a person born or living in Lycia **2** the language spoken by the Lycians, an extinct Anatolian language

ly·co·pene (lī′kō pēn′) ***n.*** ⟦< *lycop(in)*, earlier name (< ModL *Lycopersicon*, genus name of the tomato < Gr *lykos*, wolf + *persikos*, peach) + -ENE⟧ *Biochem.* a red, crystalline, carotenoid pigment, $C_{40}H_{56}$, that acts as an antioxidant: found in tomatoes, carrots, etc.

ly·co·pod (lī′kō päd′) ***n.*** ⟦see fol.⟧ any of a division (Lycopodiophyta) of living or fossil vascular plants with small leaves having a single vascular strand, and spores produced in cones at the tips of the stems or in leaf axils, including lycopodiums, selaginellas, and quillworts; club moss

ly·co·po·di·um (lī′kō pō′dē əm) ***n.*** ⟦ModL < Gr *lykos*, WOLF + -PODIUM⟧ **1** any of a genus (*Lycopodium*) of usually creeping, often evergreen, lycopods popular as Christmas decorations **2** the flammable yellow powder found in the spore cases of these plants, used in making fireworks and in medicine

☆**Ly·cra** (lī′krə) *trademark for* a spandex fiber or fabric used in underwear, swimwear, athletic apparel, etc. —***n.*** [*sometimes* **l-**] a fiber or fabric like this

Ly·cur·gus (lī kur′gəs) semilegendary Spartan lawgiver of about the 9th cent. B.C.

lydd·ite (lid′īt′) ***n.*** ⟦after *Lydd*, village in KENT[2] (where first made and tested) + -ITE[1]⟧ a powerful explosive containing picric acid, used in shells

Lyd·gate (lid′gāt, -git), **John** 1370?-1450?; Eng. poet

Lyd·i·a[1] (lid′ē ə) ***n.*** ⟦LL(Ec) < Gr(Ec), orig. fem. of Gr *Lydios*, Lydian: see Acts 16:14⟧ a feminine name

Lyd·i·a[2] (lid′ē ə) ancient kingdom in W Asia Minor: fl. 7th-6th cent. B.C.; conquered by Persians and absorbed into Persian Empire (6th cent. B.C.)

Lyd·i·an (-ən) ***adj.*** **1** of Lydia or its people, language, or culture **2** *a)* soft; gentle; effeminate *b)* voluptuous; sensual —***n.*** **1** a person born or living in Lydia **2** the language spoken by the Lydians, an extinct Anatolian language

lye (lī) ***n.*** ⟦ME *lie* < OE *leag*, akin to Ger *lauge* < IE base **lou-*, to LAVE⟧ **1** [Obs.] a strong, alkaline solution obtained by leaching wood ashes **2** any strongly alkaline substance, usually sodium or potassium hydroxide, used in cleaning, making soap, etc. **3** any substance obtained by leaching

Ly·ell (lī′əl), Sir **Charles** 1797-1875; Brit. geologist

ly·gus bug (lī′gəs) ⟦ModL⟧ any of a genus (*Lygus*, family Miridae) of hemipterous bugs, including many that damage plants

ly·ing[1] (lī′iŋ) ***vi.*** *prp. of* LIE[1]

ly·ing[2] (lī′iŋ) ***vt., vi.*** *prp. of* LIE[2] —***adj.*** false; not truthful —***n.*** the telling of a lie or lies —***SYN.*** DISHONEST

ly·ing-in (-in′) [Old-fashioned] ***n.*** **1** the situation (often, traditionally, involving confinement to bed) of a woman during the process of giving birth **2** the time needed for this, often including time before labor begins and after delivery —***adj.*** of or for childbirth [*a lying-in hospital*]

Lyle (līl) ***n.*** ⟦< Brit place name & surname⟧ a masculine name

Lyl·y (lil′ē), **John** 1554?-1606; Eng. writer & dramatist

Lyme disease (līm) ⟦after *Lyme*, Conn., town where it first was identified (1975)⟧ an acute, recurrent, inflammatory disease caused by a spirochete (*Borrelia burgdorferi*) transmitted by certain ticks (esp. *Ixodes dammini*), characterized at first by a skin rash, headache, fever, etc. and later by arthritis, neurological damage, and cardiac abnormalities

lymph (limf) ***n.*** ⟦L *lympha*, spring water, altered (infl. by Gr *nymphē*: see NYMPH) < OL *limpa, lumpa*, orig. < ? Gr *nymphē*⟧ **1** [Archaic] a spring of clear water **2** a clear, yellowish fluid resembling blood plasma, found in intercellular spaces and in the lymphatic vessels of vertebrates **3** any of various colorless liquids similar to this; esp., the clear liquid given off from inflamed bodily tissues

lymph- (limf) *combining form* LYMPHO-: used before a vowel

lym·phad·e·ni·tis (lim fad″n īt′is) ***n.*** ⟦ModL < prec. + ADEN- + -ITIS⟧ inflammation of the lymph nodes

lym·phad·e·nop·a·thy (lim fad′ə näp′ə thē) ***n.**, pl.* **-thies** **1** swollen lymph nodes **2** any disease of the lymph nodes

lym·phan·gi·al (lim fan′jē əl) ***adj.*** ⟦< LYMPH- + Gr *angeion*, vessel + -AL⟧ of the lymphatic vessels

lym·phan·gi·o·gram (lim fan′jē ə gram′) ***n.*** an X-ray picture produced by lymphangiography

lym·phan·gi·og·ra·phy (lim fan′jē äg′rə fē) ***n.*** ⟦LYMPH(O)- + ANGIOGRAPHY⟧ the process of making X-ray pictures of lymph vessels and lymph nodes after first injecting a radiopaque substance —**lym·phan·gi·o·graph·ic** (lim fan′jē ə graf′ik) ***adj.***

lym·phan·gi·tis (lim′fən jīt′is) ***n.*** ⟦ModL < LYMPHANGIAL + -ITIS⟧ inflammation of the lymphatic vessels

lym·phat·ic (lim fat′ik) ***adj.*** ⟦ModL *lymphaticus* < L *lympha*: see LYMPH & -ATIC⟧ **1** of, containing, or conveying lymph **2** of, or caused by improper functioning of, the lymph nodes **3** sluggish; without energy: a sluggish condition was formerly thought to be due to too much lymph in the body —***n.*** a lymphatic vessel

lymphatic system the network of small vessels, lymph nodes, etc., that collects lymph and returns it to the bloodstream mainly through the thoracic duct: this system also includes the bone marrow, spleen, and thymus

lymph node any of the many small, compact structures located throughout the lymphatic system, that produce lymphocytes, collect and eliminate foreign bacteria and viruses, etc.: sometimes called **lymph gland**

lym·pho- (lim′fō, -fə) *combining form* **1** lymph **2** the lymphatics [*lymphocyte*]

lym·pho·blast (lim′fō blast′) ***n.*** ⟦prec. + -BLAST⟧ a primitive cell that is a precursor of a lymphocyte

lym·pho·cyte (lim′fō sīt′) ***n.*** ⟦LYMPHO- + -CYTE⟧ a nongranular variety of leukocyte formed in lymphatic tissue, important in the synthesis of antibodies: see B CELL —**lym′pho·cyt′ic** (-sit′ik) ***adj.***

lym·pho·cy·to·sis (lim′fō sī tō′sis) ***n.*** ⟦ModL: see prec. + -OSIS⟧ a condition characterized by an increase in the number of lymphocytes in the blood, as in acute or chronic infection —**lym′pho·cy·tot′ic** (-tät′ik) ***adj.***

lym·pho·gran·u·lo·ma (ve·ne·re·um) (-gran′yo͞o lō′mə və nir′ē əm) ⟦LYMPHO- + GRANULOMA + L *venereum*, of sexual love < *venus* (see VENEREAL)⟧ a sexually transmitted disease caused by a bacterium (*Chlamydia trichomatis*), often causing swelling of lymph nodes in the groin

lymph·oid (lim′foid′) ***adj.*** ⟦LYMPH- + -OID⟧ of or like lymph or the tissue of the lymph nodes

lym·pho·kine (lim′fō kīn′) ***n.*** ⟦LYMPHO- + *-kine* < Gr *kinein*, to move⟧ any of various soluble proteins, as interferon, that are secreted by T cells interacting with an antigen and that help fight infection

lym·pho·ma (lim fō′mə) ***n.*** ⟦LYMPH- + -OMA⟧ **1** a type of cancer characterized by swollen lymph nodes and by malignant tumors that arise in, and are spread through, the lymphatic system: see also HODGKIN'S DISEASE, NON-HODGKIN'S LYMPHOMA **2** such a tumor

lym·pho·poi·e·sis (lim′fō poi ē′sis) ***n.*** ⟦ModL < LYMPHO- + Gr *poiesis*: see POESY⟧ the production of lymphocytes

☆**lynch** (linch) ***vt.*** ⟦< LYNCH LAW⟧ to murder (an accused person) by mob action and without lawful trial, esp. by hanging —**lynch′er** ***n.*** —**lynch′ing** ***n.***

Lynch·burg (linch′burg′) ⟦after J. *Lynch*, reputed founder⟧ city in central Va., on the James River

☆**lynch law** ⟦formerly *Lynch's law*, after Capt. W. *Lynch* (1742-1820), member of a vigilance committee in Pittsylvania, Virginia (1780)⟧ the lawless practice of killing by lynching

lynch·pin (linch′pin′) ***n.*** *alt. sp. of* LINCHPIN

Lynn (lin) ***n.*** ⟦prob. < Brit place name *Lynn* < Celt, as in Welsh *llyn*, a lake⟧ **1** a masculine name **2** a feminine name: var. *Lynne*

lynx (liŋks) ***n.*** ⟦ME < L < Gr *lynx*; prob. so named from its shining eyes: see LIGHT[1]⟧ **1** *pl.* **lynx′es** or **lynx** any of a genus (*Lynx*) of wildcats found throughout the Northern Hemisphere and characterized by a ruff on each side of the face, relatively long legs, a short tail, long, usually tufted ears, and keen vision, as the bobcat or Canada lynx of North America **2** the long, silky, tawny fur of the lynx **3** [**L**] a N constellation between Auriga and Ursa Major

lynx-eyed (liŋks′īd′) ***adj.*** having very keen sight

Ly·on[1] (lī′ən), **Mary** 1797-1849; U.S. educator

Lyon[2] (lyōn) city in EC France, at the juncture of the Rhone & Saône rivers

Ly·on·nais (lē ô ne′) historical region of SE central France

ly·on·naise (lī′ə nāz′, lē′-) ***adj.*** ⟦Fr, fem. of *Lyonnais*, of LYON[2]⟧ prepared with finely sliced onions; esp., designating potatoes prepared with fried onions

Ly·on·nesse (lī′ə nes′) ***n.*** ⟦OFr *Leonois*, earlier *Loonois*, ult., after ? *Lothian*, former division of Scotland⟧ *Arthurian Legend* a region in SW England, apparently near Cornwall, supposed to have sunk beneath the sea

Ly·ons (lē ōn′, lī′ənz) *Eng. name for* LYON[2]

ly·o·phil·ic (lī′ō fil′ik) ***adj.*** ⟦*lyo-* < Gr *lyein*, to loose (see LOSE) + -PHIL + -IC⟧ having a strong affinity for, and stabilized by, the liquid dispersing medium: said of a colloidal material: also **ly′o·phile′** (-fīl′)

ly·oph·i·lize (lī äf′ə līz′) ***vt.*** **-lized′**, **-liz′ing** ⟦see prec. & -IZE⟧ to freeze-dry (esp. biologicals) —**ly·oph′i·li·za′tion** ***n.***

ly·o·pho·bic (lī′ō fō′bik) ***adj.*** ⟦*lyo-* (see LYOPHILIC) + -PHOB(E) + -IC⟧ having little affinity for the liquid dispersing medium: said of a colloidal material

Ly·ra (lī′rə) *n.* ⟦L < Gr: see LYRE⟧ a N constellation between Hercules and Cygnus, containing the bright star Vega; the Harp; the Lyre

ly·rate (lī′rāt′) *adj.* ⟦ModL *lyratus*⟧ shaped like or suggestive of a lyre: also **ly′rat′ed**

lyre (līr) *n.* ⟦ME *lire* < L *lyra* < Gr⟧ a small stringed instrument of the harp family, used by the ancient Greeks to accompany singers and reciters —**the Lyre** the constellation Lyra

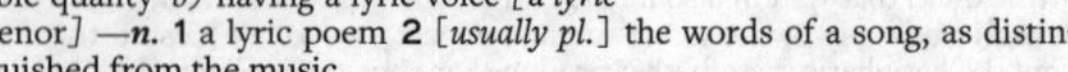
lyre

lyre·bird (līr′burd′) *n.* any of a family (Menuridae) of Australian passerine birds: the long tail feathers of the male resemble a lyre when spread

lyr·ic (lir′ik) *adj.* ⟦< Fr or L: Fr *lyrique* < L *lyricus* < Gr *lyrikos*⟧ **1** of a lyre **2** suitable for singing, as to the accompaniment of a lyre; songlike; specif., designating poetry or a poem mainly expressing the poet's emotions and feelings: sonnets, elegies, odes, hymns, etc. are lyric poems **3** writing or having written lyric poetry **4** LYRICAL (sense 2) **5** *Music a)* characterized by a relatively high compass and a light, flexible quality *b)* having a lyric voice *[a lyric tenor]* —*n.* **1** a lyric poem **2** [*usually pl.*] the words of a song, as distinguished from the music

lyr·i·cal (lir′i kəl) *adj.* **1** LYRIC **2** characterized by or expressing rapture or great enthusiasm *[a lyrical account of her trip]* —**lyr′i·cal·ly** *adv.*

lyr·i·cism (lir′ə siz′əm) *n.* **1** lyric quality, style, or character *[lyricism in the Romantic poets]* **2** emotional and poetic expression of enthusiasm, etc.

lyr·i·cist (-sist) *n.* a writer of lyrics, esp. lyrics for popular songs

ly·ri·form (lī′rə fôrm′) *adj.* shaped like a lyre

lyr·ism (lir′iz′əm; *for 2* lir′iz′əm) *n.* ⟦Fr *lyrisme* < Gr *lyrismos*⟧ **1** the act of playing on a lyre **2** LYRICISM

lyr·ist (lir′ist; *for 2 & 3* lir′ist) *n.* ⟦L *lyristes* < Gr *lyristēs* < *lyrizein,* to play on a lyre⟧ **1** a player on a lyre **2** a lyric poet **3** LYRICIST

Lys (lēs) river in N France & W Belgium, flowing northwest into the Scheldt: *c.* 130 mi (209 km)

Ly·san·der (lī san′dər) died 395 B.C.; Spartan naval and military commander

lyse (līs, līz) *vt., vi.* **lysed, lys′ing** ⟦back-form. < LYSIS⟧ to cause or undergo lysis

-lyse (līz) *combining form chiefly Brit. sp. of* -LYZE

Ly·sen·ko·ism (lī seŋ′kō iz′əm) *n.* ⟦after T. D. *Lysenko* (1898-1976), Soviet agronomist who promoted it⟧ a repudiated doctrine, officially imposed for a time by the Soviet government, based on the belief that characteristics acquired through environmental changes can be transmitted by heredity: term often used fig. to indicate any official or governmental promotion of pseudoscience

ly·ser·gic acid (lī sur′jik) ⟦< fol. + ERG(OT) + -IC⟧ a monobasic acid, $C_{16}H_{16}N_2O_2$, extracted from ergot alkaloids or synthesized: see LSD

ly·si- (lī′si, -sə; lis′i, -ə) ⟦ModL < Gr *lysi-* < *lysis:* see LYSIS⟧ *combining form* freeing, loosening, dissolving *[lysimeter]*: also, before a vowel, **lys-**

Ly·sim·a·chus (lī sim′ə kəs) 355?-281 B.C.; Macedonian general: ruler of Thrace (323-281)

ly·sim·e·ter (lī sim′ət ər) *n.* ⟦LYSI- + -METER⟧ a device for determining the solubility of substances

ly·sin (lī′sin) *n.* ⟦LYS(I)- + -IN[1]⟧ any antibody capable of dissolving bacteria, blood corpuscles, etc.

ly·sine (lī′sēn′) *n.* ⟦LYS(I)- + -INE[3]⟧ an essential amino acid, $NH_2(CH_2)_4CH(NH_2)COOH$, obtained synthetically or by the hydrolysis of certain proteins in digestion: see AMINO ACID

Ly·sip·pus (lī sip′əs) 360?-316? B.C.; Gr. sculptor

ly·sis (lī′sis) *n.* ⟦ModL < Gr, a loosening, dissolving: see LOSE⟧ **1** the process of cell destruction through the action of specific lysins **2** the gradual ending of disease symptoms

-ly·sis (lə sis, li-) ⟦< Gr *lysis:* see prec.⟧ *combining form* a loosening, dissolution, dissolving, destruction *[catalysis, electrolysis]*

ly·sog·e·ny (lī säj′ə nē) *n.* a dormant viral infection of bacteria in which the genetic material of a virus combines with that of a host bacterium —**ly·so·gen·ic** (lī′sō jen′ik) *adj.*

Ly·sol (lī′sôl) ⟦< Gr *lysis* (see LYSIS) + *-ol,* suffix in some product names⟧ *trademark for* a liquid or spray disinfectant

ly·so·some (lī′sə sōm′) *n.* ⟦*lyso-,* pertaining to dissolving < Gr *lysis* (see LYSIS) + -SOME[3]⟧ a particle in the cytoplasm of cells containing a number of digestive enzymes capable of breaking down most of the constituents of living matter —**ly′so·so′mal** *adj.*

ly·so·zyme (lī′sə zīm′) *n.* ⟦see prec. & ZYME⟧ an enzyme present in egg white, tears, saliva, etc. that can kill certain bacteria by dissolving the cell walls

-lyte[1] (līt) ⟦< Gr *lytos* < *lyein:* see LOSE⟧ *combining form* a substance subjected to a process of decomposition (specified by the corresponding noun ending in -LYSIS) *[electrolyte]*

-lyte[2] (līt) *combining form* -LITE

lyt·ic (lit′ik) *adj.* ⟦see fol.⟧ **1** of a lysin **2** of or causing lysis

-lyt·ic (lit′ik) ⟦Gr *-lytikos* < *lytikos,* able to loose: see LYSIS⟧ *combining form forming adjectives* **1** of, relating to, or causing (a specified kind of) dissolution or decomposition **2** *Biochem.* undergoing hydrolysis by enzymes

lyt·ta (lit′ə) *n., pl.* **-tae** (-ē) ⟦ModL < L < Gr *lytta, lyssa* (lit., madness), thought to be a worm under a dog's tongue causing rabies⟧ a band of cartilage lying along the underside of the tongue of dogs and certain other carnivores

Lytton *see* BULWER-LYTTON

-lyze (līz) ⟦Fr *-lyser* < nouns ending in *-lyse* (< Gr *-lysis:* see LYSIS) + *-er,* inf. ending⟧ *combining form forming verbs* to dissolve, decompose, etc. by a (specified) means *[electrolyze]*

M

m[1] or **M** (em) ***n.***, *pl.* **m's, M's 1** the thirteenth letter of the English alphabet: from the Greek *mu*, derived ultimately from the Phoenician **2** any of the speech sounds that this letter represents, as, in English, the (m) of *milk* or *stratagem* **3** a type or impression for *m* or *M* **4** the thirteenth in a sequence or group **5** *Printing* an em (Example: a "☆ dash" is a dash that is one em long) **6** an object shaped like M —***adj.* 1** of *m* or *M* **2** thirteenth in a sequence or group **3** shaped like M

m[2] *abbrev.* **1** male **2** manual **3** mark (a coin) **4** married **5** masculine **6** *Physics a)* mass *b)* modulus **7** medium **8** meridian **9** meter(s) **10** mile(s) **11** mill(s) **12** milli- **13** million(s) **14** minim **15** minute(s) **16** month **17** moon **18** morning **19** ⟦see M[2] (sense 20)⟧ noon *[a.m., p.m.]*

M[1] (em) ***n.*** a Roman numeral for 1,000: with a superior bar ($\bar{M}$), 1,000,000

M[2] *abbrev.* **1** *Bible* Maccabees **2** male **3** Manitoba **4** March **5** *Rom. History* Marcus (the praenomen) **6** mark (a coin) **7** Marquis **8** married **9** May **10** medieval **11** medium **12** mega- **13** *Astron.* Messier catalog **14** *Chem.* metal **15** *Music* mezzo **16** *Physics* momentum **17** Monday **18** Monsieur **19** *Elec.* mutual inductance **20** ⟦L *meridies*⟧ noon *[A.M., P.M.]*

m- *prefix Chem.* META- (sense 6*d*): usually italicized and hyphenated in chemical names

-'m *suffix* am: used in contractions, sometimes very informally *[I'm* here; *how'm* I doing?*]*

M'- (mə) *prefix* MAC- *[M'Donald]*

ma (mä) ***n.*** [Informal] MOTHER[1] (***n.*** 1 & 2)

mA or **ma** *abbrev.* milliampere(s)

MA *abbrev.* **1** Massachusetts **2** ⟦L *Magister Artium*⟧ Master of Arts: also **M.A. 3** Military Academy

ma'am (mam, mäm) ***n.*** [Informal] madam: used in direct address

Maas (mäs) *Du. name for* the MEUSE

Maa·sai (mä sī′) ***n.*** *alt. sp. of* MASAI

Maas·tricht (mäs′triHt) city in SE Netherlands, on the Maas River: a treaty signed here in 1991 led to the establishment of the EUROPEAN UNION

Mab (mab) ***n.*** *see* QUEEN MAB

Ma·bel (mā′bəl) ***n.*** ⟦< *Amabel* < L *amabilis,* lovable < *amare,* to love⟧ a feminine name

mac (mak) ***n.*** [Informal, Chiefly Brit.] MACKINTOSH (sense 1)

Mac (mak) ***n.*** ⟦< fol., MC-[1]⟧ [Slang] fellow: used as a general term of address for a man or boy

Mac- (mak, mək, mə) ⟦< Ir & Gael *mac,* son < OCelt **makkos,* akin to **makwos,* son > OWelsh *map,* Welsh *mab, ap,* son: see MAIDEN⟧ *prefix* son of: used in Scottish and Irish family names *[MacDonald]*: this form and its variants *Mc-, M^c-, M'-* are often grouped together when names are alphabetized

ma·ca·bre (mə käb′rə, mə käb′, -kä′bər) ***adj.*** ⟦Fr < OFr *(danse) Macabré,* (dance) of death, prob. altered < ML *(Chorea) Machabaeorum,* lit., dance of the Maccabees (see MACCABEES): semantic connection obscure⟧ grim and horrible; gruesome; ghastly: also **ma·ca′ber** (-kä′bər)

mac·ad·am (mə kad′əm) ***n.*** ⟦after John L. *McAdam* (1756-1836), Scot engineer⟧ **1** small broken stones used in making roads; esp., such stones combined with a binder such as tar or asphalt **2** macadamized pavement

mac·a·dam·i·a nut (mak′ə dā′mē ə) ⟦ModL *Macadamia,* after John *Macadam* (died 1865), Scot chemist in Australia⟧ a spherical, hard-shelled, edible nut from an Australian tree *(Macadamia ternifolia)* of the protea family, cultivated in Hawaii

mac·ad·am·ize (mə kad′ə mīz′) ***vt.*** **-ized′, -iz′ing 1** to make (a road) by rolling successive layers of macadam on a dry earth roadbed **2** to repair or cover (a road) with macadam

Ma·cao (mə kou′) **1** administrative zone of China, consisting of a peninsula & two small adjacent islands at the mouth of the Zhu River, west of Hong Kong: formerly under Portuguese administration: 10.5 sq mi (27.3 sq km) **2** its capital, a seaport coextensive with the peninsula —**Mac·a·nese** (mak′ə nēz′) ***n.***, *pl.* **-nese′**

Ma·ca·pá (mak′ə pä′) seaport in N Brazil, on the Amazon delta: capital of Amapá state

ma·caque (mə käk′) ***n.*** ⟦Fr < Port *macaco,* monkey⟧ any of a genus *(Macaca)* of monkeys of Asia, Africa, and the East Indies, with a long or short tail that is not prehensile, including the rhesus monkey and Barbary ape

mac·a·ro·ni (mak′ə rō′nē) ***n.*** ⟦It *maccaroni, maccheroni,* pl. of *maccherone* < LGr *makaria,* food of broth and barley groats, sacrificial cake made from such mixture, lit., blessed (cake) < Gr, bliss < *makar,* blessed⟧ **1** pasta in the form of tubes or in various other shapes, often baked with cheese, ground meat, etc. **2** *pl.* **-nies** an English dandy in the 18th cent. who affected foreign mannerisms and fashions

mac·a·ron·ic (-rän′ik) ***adj.*** ⟦Fr *macaronique* < It *maccaronico* < *maccaroni,* lit., macaroni: see prec.⟧ involving or characterized by a mixture of languages; esp., designating or of burlesque verse in which real or coined words from two or more languages are mixed, or words of a modern language are given Latin case endings and mixed with Latin words —***n.*** macaronic verse: *usually used in pl.*

mac·a·roon (mak′ə ro͞on′) ***n.*** ⟦Fr *macaron* < It *maccaroni,* MACARONI⟧ a small, chewy cookie made chiefly of egg white, crushed almonds or coconut, and sugar

Mac·Ar·thur (mak är′thər, mək-), **Douglas** 1880-1964; U.S. general: commander in chief of Allied forces in the SW Pacific, WWII

Ma·cas·sar (mə kas′ər) *alt. sp. of* MAKASSAR

Ma·cau (mə kou′) *Port. sp. of* MACAO

Ma·cau·lay (mə kô′lē) **1** Dame **(Emilie) Rose** 1881-1958; Eng. novelist **2 Thomas Bab·ing·ton** (bab′iŋ tən) 1st Baron Macaulay of Rothley 1800-59; Eng. historian, essayist, & statesman

ma·caw (mə kô′) ***n.*** ⟦Port *macao,* prob. < Brazilian (Tupí) native name⟧ any of a group of large, bright-colored, long-tailed, harsh-voiced parrots (esp. genus *Ara*) of Central and South America

Mac·beth (mək beth′, mak-) ***n.*** **1** a tragedy (1606?) by Shakespeare **2** its title character, who, goaded by his ruthlessly ambitious wife, murders the king to gain the crown for himself

Macc *abbrev. Bible* Maccabees

Mac·ca·bae·us (mak′ə bē′əs), **Judas** died 161 B.C.; Jewish patriot & military leader

Mac·ca·be·an (mak′ə bē′ən) ***adj.*** of Judas Maccabaeus or the Maccabees

Mac·ca·bees (mak′ə bēz′) ***n.*** ⟦LL(Ec) *Machabaei,* pl. of *Machabaeus,* surname of Judas < Gr(Ec) *Makkabaios* < ? Aram *maqqābā,* hammer: hence, lit., the hammerer⟧ **1** family of Jewish patriots who, under Judas Maccabaeus, headed a successful revolt against the Syrians (175-164 B.C.) & ruled Palestine until 37 B.C. **2** *Bible* two books of the Old Testament Apocrypha that tell of this revolt: abbrev. *M, Macc,* or *Mc*

mac·ca·boy (mak′ə boi′) ***n.*** ⟦Fr *macouba,* after *Macouba,* district in Martinique where made⟧ a kind of snuff, usually rose-scented: also sp. **mac′co·boy′**

Mac·Diar·mid (mək dur′mid), **Hugh** (pseud. of *Christopher Murray Grieve*) 1892-1978; Scot. poet

Mac·don·ald (mək dän′əld), Sir **John Alexander** 1815-91; Cdn. statesman, born in Scotland

Mac·Don·ald (mək dän′əld), **(James) Ram·say** (ram′zē) 1866-1937; Brit. statesman & Labour Party leader: prime minister (1924; 1929-35)

Mac·Dow·ell (mək dou′əl), **Edward Alexander** 1860-1908; U.S. composer

mace[1] (mās) ***n.*** ⟦ME < OFr *masse* < VL **mattea,* a club < L **matea* < IE base **mat-,* a hoe, club > MATTOCK⟧ **1** *a)* a heavy medieval war club, often with a spiked, metal head *b)* any similar weapon **2** *a)* a staff used as a symbol of authority by certain officials *b)* MACEBEARER

mace[2] (mās) ***n.*** ⟦ME, assumed as sing. of *macis,* mace < OFr < ML, prob. scribal error for L *macir* < Gr *makir,* a fragrant resin from India⟧ a spice, usually ground, made from the dried outer covering of the nutmeg seed

Mace (mās) ⟦< MACE[1]⟧ *trademark for* a chemical compound, prepared for use in aerosol containers, that has the combined effect of a tear gas and a nerve gas, temporarily stunning its victims —***n.*** *[often* **m-***]* such a compound, or a container of it —***vt.*** **Maced, Mac′ing** *[often* **m-***]* to spray with Mace

mace·bear·er (mās′ber′ər) ***n.*** a person who carries a MACE[1] (sense 2*a*) in ceremonial processions

ma·cé·doine (mas′i dwän′; *Fr* mȧ sā dwȧn′) ***n.*** ⟦Fr, lit., Macedonia: ? referring to mixture of many different peoples there⟧ **1** a mixture of diced fruits or vegetables served as a cocktail, salad, garnish, etc. **2** a medley

Mac·e·don (mas′ə dän′) ancient Macedonia

Mac·e·do·ni·a (mas′ə dō′nē ə, -dōn′yə) **1** ancient kingdom in SE Europe: now a region divided among Greece, the country of Macedonia, & Bulgaria **2** country in the Balkan Peninsula: formerly (1946-91) a constituent republic of Yugoslavia: 9,781 sq mi (25,333 sq km); cap. Skopje

Mac·e·do·ni·an (-dō′nē ən, -dōn′yən) ***adj.*** of Macedonia or its ancient or modern people, language, or culture —***n.* 1** a person born or living in Macedonia **2** the Indo-European language of the ancient Macedonians, believed to be akin either to Greek or to Illyrian **3** the South Slavic language of modern Macedonia and adjoining regions

Ma·ce·ió (mä′sā yô′) seaport in NE Brazil, on the Atlantic: capital of Alagoas state

mac·er (mā′sər) ***n.*** ⟦ME < OFr *massier* < *masse:* see MACE[1] & -ER⟧ a mace-bearer, esp. one who is an official in a Scottish court

mac·er·ate (mas′ər āt′) ***vt.*** **-at′ed, -at′ing** ⟦< L *maceratus,* pp. of *macerare,* to make soft or tender, weaken, harass < IE base **māk-,* to knead > Latvian *màcu,* to squeeze⟧ **1** to soften and break down into component parts by soaking in liquid for some time **2** to soften and break down (food) in the digestive system **3** to steep (fruit or vegetables) as in wine or liquor **4** loosely, to break, tear, chop, etc. into bits **5** to cause to waste away or grow thin —***vi.*** to undergo maceration; waste away; grow thin —**mac′er·a′tion** ***n.*** —**mac′er·a′tor** ***n.***

Mac·Guf·fin (mə guf′in) ***n.*** ⟦coined by A. HITCHCOCK[2], ? ult. from a joke involving the Scot surname *MacGuffin* (variously sp.)⟧ something that serves as the impetus for the plot of a thriller, but that is of little further significance *[the book's MacGuffin, in this case a bit of microfilm, is sought by both hero and villain]*

mach *abbrev.* **1** machine **2** machinery **3** machinist

Mach (mäk) ***n.*** *short for* MACH NUMBER

mâche or **mache** (mäsh; *Fr* mȧsh) ***n.*** ⟦Fr⟧ CORN SALAD

mach·er (mä′khər) ***n.*** ⟦Ger (chiefly via Yiddish) < *machen,* to make, do⟧ [Slang] **1** a person who gets things done, makes things happen, etc. **2** a person with power and influence Sometimes used derisively

ma·che·te (mə shet′ē, -chet′ē) ***n.*** ⟦Sp < *macho,* hammer, ax < L *marculus,* dim. of *marcus,* hammer⟧ **1** a large, heavy-bladed knife used for cutting down sugar cane, dense underbrush, etc., esp. in Central and South America **2** a small Pacific tenpounder fish (*Elops affinis*) sometimes found in fresh waters

Mach·i·a·vel·li (mak′ē ə vel′ē, mäk′-), **Nic·co·lò (di Bernardo)** (nē′kô lô′) 1469-1527; Florentine statesman & writer

Mach·i·a·vel·li·an (mak′ē ə vel′ē ən, mäk′-; -vel′yən) ***adj.*** **1** of Machiavelli **2** of, like, or characterized by the political principles and methods of expediency, craftiness, and duplicity set forth in Machiavelli's book, *The Prince;* crafty, deceitful, etc. —***n.*** a follower of such principles and methods —**Mach′i·a·vel′li·an·ism′** ***n.***

ma·chic·o·late (mə chik′ə lāt′) ***vt.*** **-lat′ed, -lat′ing** ⟦< ML *machicolatus,* pp. of *machicolare* < MFr *machicoler* < **machicol,* machicolation < Prov *machacol* < *macar,* to crush, beat (< VL **maccare,* to crush) + *col,* neck: from use of machicolations for dropping stones, etc.⟧ to put machicolations in (a parapet, etc.)

ma·chic·o·la·tion (mə chik′ə lā′shən) ***n.*** ⟦< prec.⟧ **1** a defensive opening in the floor of a projecting gallery or parapet, between supports or corbels, or in the roof over an entrance, through which hot liquids, heavy stones, etc. could be dropped upon attackers, etc. **2** a gallery, parapet, etc. with such openings

Ma·chi·da (mä chē′dä, mä′chē′dä′) city in SE Honshu, Japan, near Tokyo

mach·i·nate (mak′ə nāt′, mash′-) ***vi., vt.*** **-nat′ed, -nat′ing** ⟦< L *machinatus,* pp. of *machinari,* to devise, plan, plot < *machina,* MACHINE⟧ to devise, plan, or plot artfully, esp. with evil intent —**mach′i·na′tor** ***n.***

mach·i·na·tion (mak′ə nā′shən, mash′-) ***n.*** ⟦ME *machinacion* < L *machinatio*⟧ **1** [Rare] the act of machinating **2** an artful or secret plot or scheme, esp. one with evil intent: *usually used in pl.* —**SYN.** PLOT

ma·chine (mə shēn′) ***n.*** ⟦Fr < L *machina* < Gr *mēchanē,* a machine, engine < *mēchos,* a contrivance < IE base **magh-,* to be able, help > MAY[1], MIGHT[2]⟧ **1** [Now Rare] a structure or built-up fabric of any kind **2** [Old-fashioned] a vehicle, as an automobile, bicycle, etc. **3** *a)* a structure consisting of a framework and various fixed and moving parts, for doing some kind of work; mechanism *[a sewing machine]* *b)* any device thought of as functioning in such a way, as an electronic computer or a device for automatically answering telephone calls *c)* a VENDING MACHINE for a specified article, product, etc. *[a postage stamp machine]* **4** *a)* a person or organization regarded as acting in a machinelike way, variously, highly efficient, impersonal, lacking spontaneity, etc. *b)* a complex organization coordinated to function in a smooth, effective way *[the military machine]* ☆**5** *a)* the members of a political party or group who control policy and confer patronage *b)* the party organization generally **6** a device or apparatus, as in the ancient theater, for producing stage effects **7** [Archaic] a literary device for dramatic effect, as a supernatural agent or force introduced into a poem **8** *Mech.* a device, as a lever or pulley, that transmits, or changes the application of, energy —***adj.*** **1** of or for a machine or machines **2** made or done by machinery **3** standardized; stereotyped —***vt.*** **-chined′, -chin′ing** to make, shape, finish, etc. by machinery —**ma·chin′a·ble** ***adj.***

machine bolt a large bolt with a square or hexagonal head, and threads on the lower part for use with a nut

☆**machine gun** an automatic gun, usually mounted and with a cooling apparatus, designed to fire a rapid and continuous stream of bullets —**ma·chine′-gun′** ***vt.*** **-gunned′, -gun′ning**

machine language a computer language, entirely in binary digits representing instructions and information, used directly by a computer without translation

ma·chine-read·a·ble (mə shēn′rēd′ə bəl) ***adj.*** in a form that can be scanned or otherwise accessed directly by a computer

ma·chin·er·y (mə shēn′ər ē, -shēn′rē) ***n., pl.*** **-er·ies** **1** machines collectively **2** the working parts of a machine **3** any combination of things or persons by which something is kept in action or a desired result is obtained *[the machinery of government]* **4** apparatus used to produce stage effects **5** [Archaic] literary devices involving the introduction of supernatural beings or forces, as in epic poetry

machine screw a small screw designed for fastening metal parts having tapped holes

☆**machine shop** a workshop, factory, or part of a factory for making or repairing machines or machine parts

machine tool an automatic or semiautomatic power-driven tool, as an electric lathe, punch press, drill, or planer: machine tools are used in making machines or machine parts —**ma·chine′-tool′** ***adj., vt.***

ma·chin·ist (mə shēn′ist) ***n.*** **1** a person who makes or repairs machinery **2** a worker skilled in using machine tools **3** a worker who operates a machine

☆**machinist's mate** *U.S. Navy* a petty officer trained to operate, repair, etc. ships' engines

ma·chis·mo (mə chēz′mō; -kēz′-, -kiz′-, -chiz′-) ***n.*** ⟦Sp < *macho* (see MACHO) + *-ismo,* -ISM⟧ overly assertive or exaggerated masculinity, esp. as characterized by a show of virility, domination of women, etc.

Mach·me·ter (mäk′mēt′ər) ***n.*** ⟦see fol. & -METER⟧ an aircraft instrument that measures airspeed by comparing it to the speed of sound

Mach number (mäk) ⟦after E. *Mach* (1838-1916), Austrian physicist⟧ [*also* **m- n-**] a number representing the ratio of the speed of an object to the speed of sound in the surrounding medium, as air, through which the object is moving

ma·cho (mä′chō) ***n., pl.*** **-chos** ⟦Sp < Port, ult. < L *masculus,* MASCULINE⟧ **1** an overly assertive, virile, and domineering man **2** MACHISMO —***adj.*** exhibiting or characterized by machismo; overly aggressive, virile, domineering, etc.

ma·chree (mə krē′, mə khrē′) ***n.*** ⟦< Ir *mo,* my + *croidhe* (OIr *cride*), HEART⟧ literally, my heart: Anglo-Irish term of endearment *[Mother machree]*

Ma·chu Pic·chu (mä′cho͞o pēk′cho͞o) site of ruins of an ancient Incan city in SC Peru

-ma·chy (mə kē) ⟦< Gr *machē,* a battle⟧ *combining form* struggle or contest *[theomachy]*

mac·in·tosh (mak′in täsh′) ***n.*** *alt. sp. of* MACKINTOSH

mack (mak) ***n.*** [Informal] MACKINTOSH (sense 1)

Mac·ken·zie[1] (mə ken′zē) **1** Sir **Alexander** 1763?-1820; Cdn. explorer, born in Scotland **2 William Ly·on** (lī′ən) 1795-1861; Cdn. journalist & insurgent leader, born in Scotland

Mac·ken·zie[2] (mə ken′zē) ⟦after Sir Alexander MACKENZIE[1]⟧ **1** river in W Northwest Territories, Canada, flowing from the Great Slave Lake northwest into the Beaufort Sea: 1,079 mi (1,738 km) **2** former district of Northwest Territories, Canada

mack·er·el (mak′ər əl, mak′rəl) ***n., pl.*** **-el** or **-els** ⟦ME *makerel* < OFr *maquerel* < ?⟧ any of various scombroid fishes; esp., an edible fish (*Scomber scombrus*) of the North Atlantic, that has a greenish, blue-striped back and a silvery belly

mackerel shark any of a family (Lamnidae) of large, partly warm-blooded sharks, including the porbeagle, mako, and white sharks

mackerel sky ⟦from resemblance to streaks on a mackerel's back⟧ a sky covered with rows of small, fleecy, cirrocumulus or altocumulus clouds

Mack·i·nac (mak′ə nô′) ⟦see fol.⟧ **1** small island in the Straits of Mackinac: 6 sq mi (15.5 sq km): formerly a center of trade with the Indians of the Northwest **2 Straits of** channel connecting Lake Huron & Lake Michigan, separating the upper & lower peninsulas of Mich.: *c.* 4 mi (6.4 km) wide

Mack·i·naw (mak′ə nô′) ***adj.*** ⟦CdnFr *Mackinac* < Ojibwa *mitchimakinak,* large turtle⟧ **1** of or from Mackinac Island, formerly a center of trade with the Indians of the Northwest **2** of or made of a heavy, napped woolen cloth, often plaid —***n.*** [*usually* **m-**] **1** MACKINAW BLANKET **2** MACKINAW BOAT **3** MACKINAW COAT

Mackinaw blanket a thick woolen blanket, often woven in bars of bright colors, formerly much used by Indians, lumbermen, etc. in the American Northwest

Mackinaw boat a small boat for sailing or rowing with pointed bow and stern, formerly used on and around the upper Great Lakes

Mackinaw coat a short, double-breasted coat made of heavy woolen cloth, usually plaid

mack·in·tosh (mak′in täsh′) ***n.*** ⟦after C. *Macintosh* (1766-1843), Scot inventor⟧ **1** a waterproof outer coat; raincoat **2** the fabric used for this, orig. made by cementing layers of cloth with rubber

mack·le (mak′əl) *Printing* ***n.*** ⟦Fr *macule* < L *macula,* a spot, stain⟧ **1** a blot or blur **2** a blurred sheet — ***vt., vi.*** **-led, -ling** to print blurred or double; blur

ma·cle (mak′əl) ***n.*** ⟦Fr < OFr *mascle,* prob. < ODu *maske,* MESH⟧ a twin crystal, as of a diamond

Mac·Leish (mə klēsh′), **Archibald** 1892-1982; U.S. poet

Mac·leod (mə kloud′), **J(ohn) J(ames) R(ickard)** 1876-1935; Scot. physiologist: co-discoverer of insulin

Mac·Ma·hon (mȧk mȧ ōn′), Comte **Ma·rie Ed·mé Pa·trice Mau·rice de** (mȧ rē′ ed mā′ pȧ trēs′ mô rēs′ də) Duc de Magenta 1808-93; marshal of France: president of France (1873-79)

Mac·mil·lan (mak mil′ən, mək-), **(Maurice) Harold** 1894-1986; Eng. statesman: prime minister (1957-63)

Mac·Mil·lan (mak mil′ən, mək-), **Donald Bax·ter** (bak′stər) 1874-1970; U.S. arctic explorer

Mac·Neice (mək nēs′), **(Frederick) Louis** 1907-63; Brit. poet, born in Ireland

Ma·con (mā′kən) ⟦after N. *Macon* (1758-1837), N.C. patriot⟧ city in central Ga.

Mâ·con (mä kōn′) ***n.*** any of several white or red wines produced in or near the city of Mâcon in S Burgundy, France

Mac·pher·son (mək fur′sən), **James** 1736-96; Scot. poet: see OSSIAN

☆**Mac·Pher·son strut** (mək fir′sən, -fur′-) ⟦after E. *MacPherson*, U.S. engineer who designed it *c.* 1950⟧ an assembly functioning as a STRUT (*n.* 2) in the suspension system of a motor vehicle, that combines a shock absorber inside a coil spring

Mac·quar·ie (mə kwôr′ē, -kwär′-) river in SE Australia, flowing northwest into the Darling: *c.* 600 mi (966 km)

mac·ra·mé (mak′rə mā′) *n.* ⟦Fr < It *macrame* < Turk *makrama*, napkin < Ar *miqramah*, a veil⟧ **1** the technique or art of knotting lengths of cord or thread into decorative patterns **2** a kind of coarse lace or fringe produced in this way, used as a belt, necklace, wall hanging, edging, etc. —*adj.* made of or by macramé [a *macramé* bracelet] Also written **macrame**

mac·ro[1] (mak′rō) *adj.* ⟦see MACRO-⟧ **1** broad, general, or comprehensive in coverage, outlook, etc. or large in scale, effect, etc. [*macro* issues bringing together disparate factions] **2** *short for:* *a)* macrobiotic *b)* macroeconomic **3** of or for macrophotography [a *macro* lens]

mac·ro[2] (mak′rō) *n., pl.* **-ros** ⟦MACRO(INSTRUCTION)⟧ a single computer instruction that represents a given sequence of instructions; macroinstruction

mac·ro- (mak′rō, -rə) ⟦< Gr *makros*, long < IE **mak̑rós* < base **māk-*, long, slender > L *macer*, MEAGER⟧ *combining form* long (in extent or duration), large, enlarged or elongated (in a specified part) [*macrocyte, macrocephaly*]: also, before a vowel, **macr-**

mac·ro·bi·ot·ics (mak′rō bī ät′iks) *n.* ⟦see prec. & -BIOTIC⟧ a dietary regimen consisting mainly of grains and vegetables and based on traditional Chinese principles of physical and emotional balance —**mac′ro·bi·ot′ic** *adj.*

mac·ro·ceph·a·ly (mak′rō sef′ə lē) *n.* ⟦MACRO- + -CEPHALY⟧ a condition in which the head or cranial capacity is abnormally large: opposed to MICROCEPHALY —**mac′ro·ceph′a·lous** *adj.*, **mac′ro·ce·phal′ic** (-sə fal′ik)

mac·ro·cli·mate (mak′rō klī′mət, -rə-) *n.* ⟦MACRO- + CLIMATE⟧ the general climate over a large geographical area —**mac′ro·cli·mat′ic** (-klī mat′ik) *adj.*

mac·ro·cosm (-käz′əm) *n.* ⟦Fr *macrocosme* < ML *macrocosmus:* see MACRO- & COSMOS⟧ **1** the great world; the universe **2** any large, complex entity Opposed to MICROCOSM —**mac′ro·cos′mic** (-käz′mik) *adj.*

mac·ro·cy·clic (mak′rō sīk′lik, -sik′lik) *adj.* **1** *Bot.* of or having to do with an organism that has a complex life cycle **2** *Chem.* of or having to do with a molecule that has a complex ring structure with at least fifteen atoms

mac·ro·cyst (mak′rō sist′, -rə-) *n.* ⟦MACRO- + CYST⟧ a large or enlarged cyst; esp., an encysted mass of cytoplasm with many nuclei in a slime mold

mac·ro·cyte (-sīt′) *n.* ⟦MACRO- + -CYTE⟧ an abnormally large red blood corpuscle occurring esp. in pernicious anemia —**mac′ro·cyt′ic** (-sit′ik) *adj.*

mac·ro·dont (-dänt′) *adj.* having large teeth

mac·ro·ec·o·nom·ics (mak′rō ek′ə näm′iks, -ē′kə-) *n.* a branch of economics dealing with all the forces at work in an economy or with the interrelationship of large sectors, as in employment or income —**mac′ro·ec′o·nom′ic** *adj.*

mac·ro·ev·o·lu·tion (-ev′ə lo͞o′shən) *n.* large-scale and long-range evolution involving the appearance of new genera, families, etc. of organisms

mac·ro·ga·mete (-gam′ēt′, -ga mēt′) *n.* ⟦MACRO- + GAMETE⟧ the larger of two conjugating cells in heterogamous sexual reproduction, considered to be female

mac·ro·in·struc·tion (mak′rō in struk′shən) *n.* MACRO[2]

mac·ro·mere (mak′rō mir′) *n.* ⟦MACRO- + -MERE⟧ one of the large cells produced by unequal cell division during the early embryonic development of many animals, as mollusks

mac·ro·mol·e·cule (mak′rō mäl′ə kyo͞ol′) *n.* a very large molecule, as a protein or polymer molecule, composed of hundreds of thousands of atoms: also **mac′ro·mole′** (-mōl′) —**mac′ro·mo·lec′u·lar** (-mō lek′yo͞o lər) *adj.*

ma·cron (mā′krən, -krän′) *n.* ⟦Gr *makron*, neut. of *makros*, long: see MACRO-⟧ a short, straight mark (¯) placed over a vowel to indicate that it is long or is to be pronounced in a certain way

mac·ro·nu·cle·us (mak′rō no͞o′klē əs) *n.* the larger of two types of nuclei present in the cells of ciliated protozoans —**mac′ro·nu′cle·ar** *adj.*

mac·ro·nu·tri·ent (-no͞o′trē ənt) *n.* ⟦MACRO- + NUTRIENT⟧ any of the chemical elements, as carbon, required in relatively large quantities for plant growth

mac·ro·phage (mak′rō fāj′) *n.* ⟦MACRO- + -PHAGE⟧ *Immunology* any of various large, phagocytic cells in connective tissue, lymphatic tissue, bone marrow, etc. of vertebrates —**mac′ro·phag′ic** (-faj′ik) *adj.*

mac·ro·pho·tog·ra·phy (mak′rō fə täg′rə fē) *n.* extreme close-up photography, usually producing an image of an object that is larger than the object itself

ma·crop·ter·ous (ma kräp′tər əs) *adj.* ⟦MACRO- + -PTEROUS⟧ having unusually large wings or fins

mac·ro·scop·ic (mak′rō skäp′ik) *adj.* ⟦MACRO- + -SCOP(E) + -IC⟧ **1** visible to the naked eye: opposed to MICROSCOPIC **2** having to do with large groups or units Also **mac′ro·scop′i·cal** (-i kəl)

mac·ro·spo·ran·gi·um (mak′rō spə ran′jē əm) *n., pl.* **-gi·a** (-ə) MEGASPORANGIUM

mac·ro·spore (mak′rō spôr′) *n.* ⟦MACRO- + SPORE⟧ MEGASPORE

ma·cru·ran (mə kro͝or′ən) *n.* ⟦< ModL *macrura* (< MACRO- + Gr *oura*, tail) + -AN⟧ any of various decapods with large abdomens, including the lobsters and shrimps —**ma·cru′rous** *adj.*

mac·u·la (mak′yə lə) *n., pl.* **-lae′** (-lē′) or **-las** ⟦L, a spot, stain⟧ **1** a spot, stain, blotch, etc.; esp., a discolored spot on the skin **2** *short for* MACULA LUTEA —**mac′u·lar** *adj.*

macula lu·te·a (lo͞ot′ē ə) ⟦ModL, lit., luteous spot⟧ an area of especially keen vision on the retina

macular degeneration an eye disorder in which the macula lutea gradually deteriorates, resulting in blurred vision, blind spots, etc.

mac·u·late (mak′yə lāt′; *for adj.*, -lit) *vt.* **-lat′ed, -lat′ing** ⟦ME *maculaten* < L *maculatus*, pp. of *maculare*, to spot, speckle < *macula*, a spot, stain⟧ [Archaic] to spot; stain; blemish; defile —*adj.* **1** spotted; blotched **2** defiled; impure

mac·u·la·tion (mak′yə lā′shən) *n.* ⟦L *maculatio:* see prec.⟧ **1** [Archaic] a spotting or being spotted **2** a spot; blemish **3** the pattern of spots on an animal or plant

mac·ule (mak′yo͞ol′) *n.* ⟦ME⟧ MACULA

ma·cum·ba (mə ko͞om′bə) *n.* ⟦BrazPort⟧ a religious cult in Brazil, combining beliefs and practices of African origin, similar to those of VOODOO (*n.* 1), with elements of Roman Catholicism and indigenous religions

mad (mad) *adj.* **mad′der, mad′dest** ⟦ME *madd*, aphetic < OE *gemæd*, pp. of *(ge)mædan*, to make mad, akin to Goth *gamaiths*, crippled, OS *gimēd*, foolish < IE **mait-* < base **mai-*, to hew, cut off > Goth *maitan*, to hew, Gr *mitylos*, dehorned⟧ **1** mentally ill; insane **2** wildly excited or disorderly; frenzied; frantic [*mad* with fear] **3** showing or resulting from lack of reason; foolish and rash; unwise [a *mad* scheme] **4** blindly and foolishly enthusiastic or fond; infatuated [to be *mad* about clothes] **5** wildly amusing; hilarious [a *mad* comedy] **6** having rabies [a *mad* dog] **7** *a)* angry or provoked (often with *at*) *b)* showing or expressing anger — *vt., vi.* **mad′ded, mad′ding** [Archaic] to madden —*n.* an angry or sullen mood or fit —**have a mad on** [Informal] to be angry —**mad as a hatter** (or **March hare**) completely crazy

MAD (mad) *n.* ⟦*m(utual) a(ssured) d(estruction)*⟧ the theory that the possession of equally devastating nuclear weapons by superpowers will deter each from attacking another or its allies

Mad·a·gas·car (mad′ə gas′kər) **1** large island in the Indian Ocean, off the SE coast of Africa **2** country comprising this island and nearby islands: discovered by the Portuguese (1500), it became a French protectorate (1895) & colony (1896), & a republic (*Malagasy Republic*) of the French Community; it became fully independent (1960); since 1975, the **Democratic Republic of Madagascar**: 226,657 sq mi (587,040 sq km); cap. Antananarivo —**Mad′a·gas′can** *adj., n.*

mad·am (mad′əm) *n., pl.* **mad′ams**; for 1, usually **mes·dames** (mā däm′, -dam′) ⟦Fr *madame*, orig. *ma dame* < L *mea domina*, my lady: see DAME⟧ **1** a polite term of address to a woman, specif., *a)* [**M-**] one used in the salutation of a formal letter [Dear *Madam*] *b)* [**M-**] one used before the title of an office or position [*Madam* President] **2** the mistress of a household ☆**3** a woman in charge of a brothel

ma·dame (mə däm′, -dam′; mad′əm; *Fr* mȧ dȧm′) *n., pl.* **mes·dames** (mā däm′, -dam′; *Fr* mā dȧm′) ⟦Fr: see prec.⟧ a married woman: French title equivalent to *Mrs.*: used in English as a title of respect for a distinguished woman or generally for any foreign married woman: abbrev. *Mme, Mdme*

mad·cap (mad′kap′) *n.* ⟦MAD + CAP[1], fig. for head⟧ a reckless, impulsive, or uninhibited person, orig. esp. a girl —*adj.* reckless, uninhibited, or zany [*madcap* pranks]

mad cow disease a progressive, degenerative brain disease of adult cows, thought to be caused by an infectious agent in their food: see also BSE

MADD (mad) *abbrev.* Mothers Against Drunk Driving

mad·den (mad′′n) *vt., vi.* to make or become mad; make or become insane, angry, frustrated, etc. —**mad′den·ing** *adj.* —**mad′den·ing·ly** *adv.*

mad·der[1] (mad′ər) *n.* ⟦ME *mader* < OE *mædere*, akin to ON *mathra*, Norw *modra* < IE base **modhro-*, dye plant > Czech *modrý*, blue⟧ **1** any of a genus (*Rubia*) of plants of the madder family, with petals fused to form a funnel-shaped corolla; esp., a perennial vine (*R. tinctorum*) with panicles of small, yellow flowers **2** *a)* the red root of this vine *b)* a red dye made from this: see also ALIZARIN **3** bright red; crimson —*adj.* designating a family (Rubiaceae, order Rubiales) of chiefly tropical, dicotyledonous herbs, shrubs, and trees, including bedstraw, bluet, coffee, and cinchona

mad·der[2] (mad′ər) *adj. compar. of* MAD

mad·ding (mad′iŋ) *adj.* [Literary] **1** raving; frenzied: now usually in the phrase **far from the madding crowd**, in a remote or secluded place: orig. in allusion to Thomas Gray's "Elegy Written in a Country Churchyard" (1751) and Thomas Hardy's novel *Far from the Madding Crowd* (1874) **2** maddening; making mad

mad·dish (mad′ish) *adj.* somewhat mad

made (mād) *vt., vi. pt. & pp. of* MAKE[1] —*adj.* **1** constructed; shaped; formed; manufactured [a well-*made* play, Swiss-*made* knife] **2** produced artificially [*made* ground, from filling in a swamp] **3** invented; contrived [a *made* word] **4** [Now Rare] prepared from various ingredients [a *made* dish] **5** sure of success [a *made* man] —☆**have (got) it made** [Informal] to be assured of success, prosperity, contentment, etc.

Ma·deir·a[1] (mə dir′ə) *n.* any of several fortified wines, ranging from pale to amber and dry to sweet, made chiefly on Madeira

Ma·deir·a[2] (mə dir′ə) **1** group of Portuguese islands in the Atlantic, off the W coast of Morocco: 310 sq mi (803 sq km); chief city, Funchal **2** largest island of this group: 288 sq mi (746 sq km) **3** river in NW Brazil, flowing northeast into the Amazon: *c.* 2,100 mi (3,380 km)

mad·e·leine (mad′′l in) *n.* ⟦Fr, ? after *Madeleine* Paulmier, 19th-c. Fr cook⟧ a type of small, rich cake baked in a shell-shaped mold

Mad·e·line (mad′'l in, -īn′) *n.* ⟦Fr *Madeleine* < LL(Ec) *Magdalene*: see MAGDALENE⟧ a feminine name: var. *Madelyn*: see MAGDALENE

ma·de·moi·selle (mad′ə mə zel′, mam zel′; *Fr* mȧd mwȧ zel′) *n., pl.* **ma′de·moi·selles′** or, for 1 and 2, Fr. ***mes·de·moi·selles*** (mād mwȧ zəl′) ⟦Fr < *ma*, my + *demoiselle*, young lady < OFr *dameisele*: see DAMSEL⟧ **1** an unmarried woman or girl: French title equivalent to *Miss*: abbrev. *Mlle* or *Mdlle* **2** a French governess **3** SILVER PERCH (sense 1)

mad·er·ize (mad′ər īz′) *vi.* **-ized′**, **-iz′ing** ⟦Fr *madériser* < *Madère*, MADEIRA[1]⟧ to turn brown usually from improper storage: said of white wine —**mad′er·i·za′tion** *n.*

Ma·de·ro (mə der′ō; *Sp* mä *thā*′rô), **Fran·cis·co In·da·le·cio** (frän sēs′kô ēn′dä le′syô) 1873-1913; Mex. revolutionary & statesman: president of Mexico (1911-13)

made-to-or·der (mād′tə ôr′dər) *adj.* **1** made to conform to the customer's specifications or measurements; custom-made **2** perfectly suitable or conformable

made-up (-up′) *adj.* **1** put together; arranged [*a made-up* page of type] **2** invented; fabricated; false [*a made-up* story] **3** with cosmetics applied

Madge (maj) *n.* a feminine name: see MARGARET

mad·house (mad′hous′) *n.* **1** a former kind of institution for the confinement of the mentally ill **2** [Informal] an insane asylum **3** any place of turmoil, noise, and confusion

Mad·i·son[1] (mad′ə sən) **1 Dol·ley** (or, incorrectly, **Dol·ly**) (däl′ē) (born *Dorothea Payne*) 1768-1849; wife of James **2 James** 1751-1836; 4th president of the U.S. (1809-17)

Mad·i·son[2] (mad′ə sən) ⟦after James MADISON[1]⟧ capital of Wis., in the SC part

Madison Avenue 1 a street in New York City, regarded as the center of the U.S. advertising industry ☆**2** this industry, its practices, its influence, etc.

☆**Mad·i·so·ni·an** (mad′ə sō′nē ən) *adj.* of or characteristic of James Madison or his federalist principles

mad·ly (mad′lē) *adv.* **1** insanely **2** wildly; furiously **3** foolishly

mad·man (mad′man′, -mən) *n., pl.* **-men′** (-men′, -mən) a person, esp. a man, who is demented or insane; lunatic; maniac

mad money 1 [Old-fashioned] a small amount of money carried by a woman for emergencies, as on a date to enable her to get home alone if she wishes **2** money saved for minor purchases, often specif. for spending frivolously

mad·ness (mad′nis) *n.* **1** dementia; insanity; lunacy **2** great anger **3** great folly **4** wild excitement **5** [Archaic] rabies

ma·don·na (mə dän′ə) *n.* ⟦It, my lady < *ma*, my (< L *mea*) + *donna*, lady (< L *domina*, see DAME)⟧ **1** a former Italian title for a woman, equivalent to *madam* **2** [**M-**] Mary, mother of Jesus: usually with *the* **3** [**M-**] a picture or statue of Mary

☆**Madonna lily** ⟦the flower is a symbol of purity traditionally assoc. with the *Madonna*⟧ a hardy lily (*Lilium candidum*) with white flowers

ma·dras (ma′drəs; mə dras′, -dräs′) *n.* ⟦after fol.⟧ **1** a fine, tightly woven cotton cloth, usually striped or plaid, used for shirts, dresses, etc. **2** a durable silk cloth, usually striped **3** a figured cotton or rayon cloth in leno weave, used for draperies **4** a large, bright-colored kerchief of silk or cotton —*adj.* made of madras

Ma·dras (mə dras′, -dräs′; mad′rəs, mäd′-) **1** *former name for* TAMIL NADU **2** *former name for* CHENNAI

ma·dras·sa (mə dras′ə, -drä′sə) *n.* ⟦Ar *madrasa* < *darasa*, to study⟧ a college or school for the study of Islam, often affiliated with a mosque: also sp. **ma·dras′a** or **ma·dras′ah**

ma·dre[1] (mä′*thre*; *E* -drā) *n., pl.* **-dres** (-*thres*; *E* -drāz) ⟦Sp⟧ mother

ma·dre[2] (mä′drā) *n., pl.* **-dri** (-drē) ⟦It⟧ mother

Ma·dre de Dios (mä′dre de dyôs′) river in SE Peru & N Bolivia, flowing east into the Beni: *c.* 700 mi (1,127 km)

mad·re·pore (ma′drə pôr′) *n.* ⟦Fr *madrépore* < It *madrepora*, lit., motherstone (from its rapid production) < *madre* (< L *mater*, MOTHER[1]) + *poro*, a pore < L *porus*, PORE[2]⟧ STONY CORAL —**mad′re·por′ic** *adj.*, **mad′re·po′ri·an**

mad·re·por·ite (ma′drə pôr′īt′) *n.* ⟦prec. + -ITE[1]⟧ a porous calcareous plate in most echinoderms, through which seawater enters the water-vascular system: see STARFISH, illus.

Ma·drid (mə drid′; *Sp* mä *thrēth*′) capital of Spain, in the central part —**Mad·ri·le·ni·an** (mad′rə le′nē ən) *adj., n.* —**Ma·dri·le·ño** (mä′drə lā′nyō′) *n.*

mad·ri·gal (ma′dri gəl) *n.* ⟦It *madrigale* < ?⟧ **1** a short poem, usually a love poem, which can be set to music **2** a PART SONG, esp. an often contrapuntal song popular in the 15th, 16th, and 17th cent. —**mad′ri·gal·ist** *n.*

ma·dri·lène (ma′drə len′; *Fr* mȧ drē len′) *n.* ⟦Fr *(consommé) Madrilène*, Madrid (consommé) < Sp *Madrileño*, of Madrid⟧ a consommé made with tomatoes

☆**ma·dro·ño** (mə drō′nyō) *n., pl.* **-ños** ⟦Sp < *maduro*: see MADURO⟧ an evergreen tree (*Arbutus menziesii*) of the heath family, with smooth, red bark, leathery, oval leaves, and edible, red berries, native to W North America: also **ma·dro′ne** (-nə) or **ma·dro′ña** (-nyə)

Ma·du·ra (mä door′ä) island of Indonesia, just off the NE coast of Java: 2,042 sq mi (5,289 sq km): see JAVA[2] —**Mad·u·rese** (mad′ə rēz′, mäj′-) *adj., n., pl.* **-rese′**

Ma·du·rai (mä də rī′) city in S India, in the state of Tamil Nadu

ma·du·ro (mə door′ō) *adj.* ⟦Sp, mature < L *maturus*, MATURE⟧ designating or of a cigar that has a dark-brown wrapper leaf —*n.* such a cigar

mad·wom·an (mad′woom′ən) *n., pl.* **-wom′en** (-wim′in) a demented or insane woman

mad·wort (-wurt′) *n.* ⟦MAD + WORT[2]; once a supposed remedy for rabies⟧ ALYSSUM

mae (mā) *adj., n., adv. Scot. var. of* MORE

Mae (mā) *n.* a feminine name: see MARY[1]

Mae·an·der (mē an′dər) *ancient name for* the MENDERES (river in W Turkey)

Ma·e·ba·shi (mä′yə bäsh′ē, mē bäsh′ē) city in central Honshu, Japan

Mae·ce·nas[1] (mī sē′nəs, mi-) *n.* ⟦after fol.⟧ any wealthy, generous patron, esp. of literature or art

Mae·ce·nas[2] (mī sē′nəs, mi-), **(Gaius Cilnius)** 70?-8 B.C.; Rom. statesman & patron of Horace & Virgil

Mael·strom (māl′strəm) *n.* ⟦17th-c. Du (now *maalstroom*) < *malen*, to grind, whirl round (akin to Ger *mahlen*: see MILL[1]) + *stroom*, a stream: first applied by 16th-c. Du geographers⟧ **1** a famous strong, swirling tidal current off the W coast of Norway, hazardous to safe navigation **2** [**m-**] any large or violent whirlpool **3** [**m-**] a violently confused or dangerously agitated state of mind, emotion, affairs, etc.

mae·nad (mē′nad′) *n.* ⟦L *Maenas* (gen. *Maenadis*) < Gr *mainas* (gen. *mainados*) < *mainesthai*, to rave < IE **mnā-*, var. of base **men-*, to think > MIND⟧ **1** [*often* **M-**] a female votary of Dionysus, who took part in the wild, orgiastic rites that characterized his worship; bacchante **2** a frenzied or raging woman —**mae·nad·ic** (mē nad′ik) *adj.*

maes·to·so (mī stō′sō; *It* mä′ə stô′sô) *adj., adv.* ⟦It, majestic < *maestà*, majesty < L *majestas*: see MAJESTY⟧ [*also in italics*] *Musical Direction* with majesty or dignity

maes·tro (mīs′trō, mä es′trō) *n., pl.* **-tros** or **-tri** (-trē) ⟦It < L *magister*, MASTER⟧ a master in any art; esp., a great composer, conductor, or teacher of music

Mae·ter·linck (māt′ər liŋk′, met′-), Count **Maurice** 1862-1949; Belgian playwright, essayist, & poet

Mae West (mā′west′) ⟦after *Mae West* (1892-1980), buxom U.S. actress⟧ an inflatable life jacket for use as by aviators downed at sea

Maf·e·king (mäf′ə kiŋ) *former sp. of* MAFIKENG

maf·fick (maf′ik) *vi.* ⟦back-form. < prec., where unrestrained celebration marked the successful Brit stand against the Boers (1900)⟧ [Chiefly Brit.] to celebrate in an exuberant, unrestrained manner

Ma·fi·a (mä′fē ə) *n.* ⟦< It (Sicilian), name for a Sicilian secret society⟧ **1** in the U.S. and elsewhere, a secret society, of Italian origin, engaged in such illegal activities as gambling, prostitution, and illicit trade in narcotics **2** [**m-**] [Informal] any group engaged in organized crime [the Russian *mafia*] **3** [**m-**] any exclusive, dominating group

maf·ic (maf′ik) *adj.* ⟦MA(GNESIUM) + L *f(errum)*, iron + -IC⟧ *Geol.* of or pertaining to igneous rocks that are rich in dark-colored minerals and that contain magnesium and iron and a comparatively low level of silica

Maf·i·keng (mäf′ə kiŋ) city in N South Africa, near the border of Botswana: scene of famous siege of British garrison by the Boers, lasting 217 days

Ma·fi·o·so (mä′fē ō′sō) *n., pl.* **-si** (-sē) ⟦It⟧ **1** [*also* **m-**] a member of the Mafia **2** [**m-**] a member of any mafia

mag[1] (mag) *n. short for:* **1** MAGNETO **2** [Slang] MAGAZINE (*n.* 5) **3** MAG WHEEL

mag[2] *abbrev.* **1** magazine **2** magnetism **3** magnitude

Ma·gal·la·nes (mä′gä yä′nes) *former name for* PUNTA ARENAS

mag·a·zine (mag′ə zēn′, mag′ə zēn′) *n.* ⟦Fr *magasin* < OFr *magazin* < It *magazzino* < Ar *makhāzin*, pl. of *makhzan*, a storehouse, granary < *khazana*, to store up⟧ **1** [Archaic] a place of storage, as a warehouse, storehouse, or military supply depot **2** a space in which ammunition and explosives are stored, as a building or room in a fort, or a section of a warship **3** a supply chamber, as a space in or container on a rifle or pistol from which cartridges are fed, or a space in or container on a camera from which a protected roll of film is fed **4** the things kept in a magazine, as munitions or supplies **5** ⟦from being a "storehouse" of information⟧ *a)* a publication, usually with a paper cover and sometimes illustrated, that appears at regular intervals and contains stories, articles, etc. by various writers and, usually, advertisements *b)* a newspaper section similar to this *c)* an online version of a printed magazine ☆**6** a television program, appearing regularly, with brief informational segments

Mag·da·le·na (mäg′dä le′nä) river in W Colombia, flowing north into the Caribbean Sea: *c.* 1,000 mi (1,609 km)

Mag·da·lene (mag′də lən, -lin, -lēn′; *also, for* 2, mag′ də lē′nə) *n.* ⟦LL(Ec) < Gr(Ec) *Magdalēne*, lit., of Magdala, after *Magdala*, town on the Sea of Galilee⟧ **1** a feminine name: dim. *Lena*; var. *Madeline*, *Madelyn* **2** *Bible* Mary Magdalene: Luke 8:2 (identified with the repentant woman in Luke 7:37) **3** [**m-**] [Archaic] a reformed and repentant prostitute **4** [**m-**] [Brit. Historical] a reformatory for prostitutes Also **Mag′da·len** (-lən)

Mag·da·le·ni·an (mag′də lē′nē ən) *adj.* ⟦Fr *magdalénien*, after *La Madeleine*, rock shelter in SW France, where many of the artifacts were found⟧ designating or of an Upper Paleolithic culture characterized by cave art, bone engraving, and tools of polished stone and bone

Mag·de·burg (mäg′də boorkh; *E* mag′də burg′) city & port in E Germany, on the Elbe: capital of Saxony-Anhalt

mage (māj) *n.* ⟦Fr < L *magus*: see MAGI⟧ [Archaic] **1** a magician or wizard **2** a man of great learning

Ma·gel·lan[1] (mə jel′ən), **Ferdinand** 1480?-1521; Port. navigator in the service of Spain: discovered the Strait of Magellan & the Philippine Islands —**Mag·el·lan·ic** (maj′ə lan′ik) *adj.*

Ma·gel·lan[2] (mə jel′ən), **Strait of** channel between the South American mainland & Tierra del Fuego: *c.* 350 mi (563 km) long

Magellanic Cloud ⟦after F. MAGELLAN[1]⟧ *Astron.* either of two irregular galaxies visible to the naked eye in the S constellations Dorado, Mensa, and Tucana: they are the nearest external galaxies to the Milky Way

Strait of Magellan

Ma·gen Da·vid (mä gän′ dä vēd′, mô′gən dô′vid) ⟦Heb⟧ STAR OF DAVID

ma·gen·ta (mə jen′tə) *n.* ⟦after *Magenta,* town in Italy: so called because discovered about the time (1859) of the battle fought there⟧ **1** FUCHSIN **2** purplish red —*adj.* purplish-red

Mag·gie (mag′ē) *n.* a feminine name: see MARGARET

Mag·gio·re (mə jôr′ē; *It* mäd jô′re), **Lake** lake in NW Italy & S Switzerland: 82 sq mi (212 sq km)

mag·got (mag′ət) *n.* ⟦ME *magotte,* prob. < earlier *mathek,* flesh worm < ON *mathkr* or OE *matha,* a worm, maggot: see MAWKISH⟧ **1** a wormlike insect larva, as the legless larva of the housefly: often found in decaying matter **2** [Archaic] an odd notion; whim —**mag′got·y** *adj.*

Ma·ghreb (mu′grəb) NW Africa, chiefly Morocco, Algeria, & Tunisia: the Arabic name

Ma·gi (mā′jī′) *pl.n., sing.* **Ma′gus** (-gəs) ⟦L, pl. of *magus* < Gr *magos* < OPers *magus* (or Iran *magu-*), member of a priestly caste, magician < IE base **magh-,* to be able > MIGHT[2], L *machina*⟧ **1** [**m-**] members of a priestly caste of ancient Media and Persia **2** the learned astrologers from the East (in later tradition, three in number: *Balthasar, Gaspar,* and *Melchior*) who came bearing gifts to the infant Jesus: Matt. 2:1-13 —**Ma′gi·an** (-jē ən) *adj., n.*

mag·ic (maj′ik) *n.* ⟦ME *magike* < OFr *magique* < L *magice* < Gr *magikē (technē),* magic (art), sorcery < *magikos,* of the Magi: see prec.⟧ **1** *a)* the use of spells, charms, and rituals in seeking to cause or control events or to govern certain natural or supernatural forces; occultism *b)* such spells, charms, etc. **2** any mysterious, seemingly inexplicable, or extraordinary power or quality [the *magic* of love] **3** the art or performing skill of producing baffling effects or illusions by sleight of hand, concealed apparatus, etc. —*adj.* ⟦L *magicus* < Gr *magikos*⟧ **1** of, produced by, used in, or using magic **2** producing extraordinary results, as if by magic or supernatural means —*vt.* **-icked, -ick·ing 1** to cause, change, make, etc. by or as if by magic **2** to make disappear by or as if by magic: with *away*

SYN.—**magic** is the general term for any of the supposed arts of producing marvelous effects by supernatural or occult power and is figuratively applied to any extraordinary, seemingly inexplicable power; **sorcery** implies magic in which spells are cast or charms are used, usually for a harmful or sinister purpose; **witchcraft** (used esp. of women) and **wizardry** (used esp. of men) imply the possession of supernatural power by compact with evil spirits, **witchcraft** figuratively suggesting the use of womanly wiles, and **wizardry,** remarkable skill, cleverness, etc.

mag·i·cal (maj′i kəl) *adj.* MAGIC (esp. *adj.* 2) —**mag′i·cal·ly** *adv.*

magic bullet any remedy, esp. a medication, regarded as having thorough or wide-ranging effectiveness

magic carpet in Middle Eastern folklore, a rug capable of conveying persons through the air

ma·gi·cian (mə jish′ən) *n.* ⟦ME *magicien* < OFr⟧ an expert in magic; specif., *a)* a sorcerer; wizard *b)* a performer skilled in sleight of hand, illusions, etc.

magic lantern an early type of projector for showing still pictures from transparent slides

Magic Marker *trademark for* a pen holding colored, waterproof ink that is applied through a felt tip, used for writing, drawing, etc. — [*sometimes* **m-**] a pen of this type

magic realism ⟦Ger *magischer realismus,* first used with ref. to a style of painting⟧ a style in 20th-cent. literature and art that depicts fantastic or magical characters or occurrences in an otherwise realistic presentation: also **magical realism**

magic square a square TABLE (*n.* 4*b*) with a numeral in each cell, so devised that the sums of the numerals in each column, row, or main diagonal are always equal

Ma·gi·not line (mazh′ə nō′) ⟦after A. *Maginot* (1877-1932), Fr minister of war⟧ a system of heavy fortifications built before WWII on the E frontier of France: it failed to prevent invasion by the Nazi armies

mag·is·te·ri·al (maj′is tir′ē əl) *adj.* ⟦ML *magisterialis* < LL *magisterius* < L *magister,* a MASTER⟧ **1** of or suitable for a magistrate or master **2** showing or having the skill or knowledge of a master; expert **3** authoritative; official **4** domineering; pompous —*SYN.* MASTERFUL —**mag′is·te′ri·al·ly** *adv.*

mag·is·te·ri·um (maj′is tir′ē əm) *n.* ⟦L < *magister,* MASTER⟧ the authority, office, and power to teach true doctrine by divine guidance, held by the Roman Catholic Church to have been given to itself alone by divine commission; also, the doctrine so taught

mag·is·tra·cy (maj′is trə sē) *n., pl.* **-cies 1** the position, office, function, or term of a magistrate **2** magistrates collectively **3** the district under a magistrate; magistrate's jurisdiction

mag·is·tral (-trəl) *adj.* ⟦L *magistralis*⟧ **1** [Rare] magisterial; authoritative **2** [Archaic] from a specific prepared prescription: said of medicines

mag·is·trate (-trāt′, -trit) *n.* ⟦ME < L *magistratus* < *magister,* MASTER⟧ **1** a civil officer empowered to administer the law: the President of the U.S. is sometimes called *chief magistrate* **2** a minor official with limited judicial powers, as a justice of the peace or judge of a police court —**mag′is·trate′ship′** *n.*

Mag·le·mo·se·an or **Mag·le·mo·si·an** (mag′lə mō′sē ən) *adj.* ⟦after *Maglemose,* bog in Denmark⟧ designating or of a Mesolithic lake or bog culture of N Europe characterized by microliths

mag·lev (mag′lev′) *adj.* ⟦< *mag(netic) lev(itation)*⟧ of or having to do with a railroad system using magnets to float a swiftly moving train above its tracks

mag·ma (mag′mə) *n.* ⟦L, the dregs of an unguent < Gr < *massein,* to knead < IE base **menk-,* to knead, crush > MINGLE⟧ **1** a pasty mixture of crude mineral or organic matter **2** liquid or molten rock deep in the earth, which on cooling solidifies to produce igneous rock **3** *Pharmacy* a suspension of precipitated matter in a watery substance —**mag·mat′ic** (-mat′ik) *adj.*

Mag·na Car·ta (*or* **Char·ta**) (mag′nə kär′tə) ⟦ML, lit., great charter⟧ the great charter that King John of England was forced by the English barons to grant at Runnymede (June 15, 1215), traditionally interpreted as guaranteeing certain civil and political liberties

mag·na cum lau·de (mäg′nä koom lou′de, mag′nə kum lô′dē) ⟦L, lit., with great praise⟧ phrase signifying high academic distinction upon graduating from a college or university: see also CUM LAUDE, SUMMA CUM LAUDE

Mag·na Grae·ci·a (mag′nə grē′shē ə) ancient Greek colonies in S Italy

mag·na·nim·i·ty (mag′nə nim′ə tē) *n.* ⟦ME *magnanimite*⟧ **1** the quality or state of being magnanimous **2** *pl.* **-ties** a magnanimous act

mag·nan·i·mous (mag nan′ə məs) *adj.* ⟦L *magnanimus* < *magnus,* great (see MAGNI-) + *animus,* mind, soul (see ANIMAL)⟧ noble in mind; esp., generous in overlooking injury or insult; rising above pettiness or meanness —**mag·nan′i·mous·ly** *adv.*

mag·nate (mag′nāt′, -nit) *n.* ⟦ME < LL *magnas* (pl. *magnates*), great man < L *magnus,* great: see MAGNI-⟧ a very important and influential person in business or industry

mag·ne·sia (mag nē′zhə, -shə) *n.* ⟦ModL *magnesia (alba),* lit., (white) magnesia (in contrast to ML *magnesia,* a black mineral < LGr *magnēsia* < *Magnēsia,* fol.): term substituted by F. Hoffmann (1660-1742), Ger physician, for ModL *magnes carneus,* lit., flesh-magnet (see MAGNET & CARNAL): so named from clinging to the lips⟧ **1** magnesium oxide, MgO, a white, tasteless powder, used as a mild laxative and antacid, and as an insulating substance, in firebrick, etc. **2** hydrated magnesium carbonate, also used as a laxative —**mag·ne′sian** *adj.,* **mag·ne′sic** (-sik)

Mag·ne·sia (mag nē′zhə, -shə) *ancient name for* MANISA

mag·ne·site (mag′nə sīt′) *n.* a light-colored, semihard mineral, magnesium carbonate, $MgCO_3$, used widely in industry as a source of magnesium and carbon dioxide

mag·ne·si·um (mag nē′zē əm, -zhē əm, -zhəm) *n.* ⟦ModL < MAGNESIA⟧ a lightweight, silver-white, malleable and ductile, metallic chemical element, one of the alkaline-earth metals, used in making several alloys and, because it burns with a hot, white light, in photographic flashbulbs, incendiary bombs, etc.: symbol, Mg; at. no. 12: see the periodic table of elements in the Reference Supplement

mag·net (mag′nit) *n.* ⟦ME *magnete* < OFr < L *magnes* (gen. *magnetis*) < Gr *Magnētis (lithos),* (stone) of MAGNESIA⟧ **1** any piece of certain, esp. ferromagnetic, material, as iron, that produces a MAGNETIC FIELD, thereby attracting ferromagnetic materials and attracting or repelling other magnets: this property may be permanent or temporarily induced: see also ELECTROMAGNET **2** a person or thing that attracts or collects as if by magnetism

mag·net·ic (mag net′ik) *adj.* ⟦ModL *magneticus* < L *magnes,* prec. + *-icus,* -IC⟧ **1** having the properties of a magnet [*magnetic* needle] **2** of, producing, caused by, or operating by magnetism **3** of the earth's magnetism [the *magnetic* poles] **4** that is or can be magnetized **5** powerfully attractive: said of a person, personality, etc. —**mag·net′i·cal·ly** *adv.*

magnetic amplifier a sensitive device that controls the flow of an alternating current by applying a weak signal to the windings of its magnetic core

magnetic axis the straight line joining the two poles of a magnet, as the poles of the earth

☆**magnetic bottle** *Physics* a geometric configuration whose extent is outlined by magnetic lines of force that will confine a hot plasma, and, in thermonuclear reactors, keep it away from the walls of the chambers

magnetic bubble *see* BUBBLE MEMORY

magnetic circuit a closed path, usually of magnetic material, that confines the magnetic flux

magnetic compass a COMPASS (*n.* 5) that works by the action of the earth's magnetic field, as on a MAGNETIC NEEDLE

magnetic course an airplane's course measured clockwise in degrees from the direction of magnetic north

magnetic declination (*or* deviation) DECLINATION (sense 3)

magnetic disk *Comput.* DISK (sense 6)

magnetic equator an imaginary line around the earth near the equator, where the lines of force of the earth's magnetic field are parallel with the surface of the earth and where a magnetic needle will consequently not dip

magnetic field a physical field that arises from an electric charge in motion, producing a force on a moving electric charge

magnetic flux the component of a magnetic field perpendicular to an area multiplied by the size of that area; a measure of the number of magnetic field lines passing through the area: it is measured in maxwells or webers: symbol, Φ

magnetic flux density the magnetic flux per unit area perpendicular to the direction of the magnetic force: it is measured in teslas or gausses: symbol, B

magnetic field
E, direction of electron flow;
F, direction of magnetic field

magnetic force the repelling or attracting force between a magnet and a ferromagnetic material, between a magnet and a current-carrying conductor, etc.

magnetic induction 1 MAGNETIC FLUX DENSITY 2 the process by which a substance becomes magnetized

magnetic meridian a continuous line on the earth's surface connecting the north and south magnetic poles

magnetic mine a naval mine designed to explode when the metal hull of a ship passing near it deflects a magnetic needle, closing an electric circuit and thus detonating the charge

magnetic moment 1 a measure of the strength of a localized source of magnetic field 2 a moment of electrons and nuclear particles caused by the intrinsic spin of a particle and the orbital motion of a particle, as around a nucleus

magnetic monopole MONOPOLE

magnetic needle a slender bar of magnetized steel which, when mounted so as to swing freely on a pivot, will point along the line of the magnetic meridian toward the magnetic poles, approximately north and south: it is the essential part of a magnetic compass

magnetic north the direction toward which a MAGNETIC NEEDLE points: see also MAGNETIC POLE

magnetic pickup a phonograph pickup in which a part of the stylus assembly vibrates in a magnetic field between two coils, thus inducing current in the coils

magnetic pole 1 either pole of a magnet, where the magnetic lines of force seem to be concentrated 2 either point on the earth's surface toward which the needle of a magnetic compass points: the north and south magnetic poles do not precisely coincide with the geographical poles

magnetic recording the recording of electrical signals by means of changes in areas of magnetization on a tape, wire, or disc: used for recording sound, video material, digital computer data, etc.

mag·net·ics (mag net′iks) ***n.*** the branch of physics dealing with magnets and magnetic phenomena

magnetic storm a worldwide disturbance of the earth's magnetic field, caused by solar flares and sunspots

magnetic tape a thin plastic ribbon coated with a suspension of ferromagnetic iron oxide particles, used as a storage medium for magnetic recording

magnetic wire a fine wire of a ferromagnetic alloy, used as a storage medium for magnetic recording

mag·net·ism (mag′nə tiz′əm) ***n.*** 1 the property, quality, or condition of being magnetic 2 the force to which this is due 3 the branch of physics dealing with magnets and magnetic phenomena; magnetics 4 power to attract; personal charm or allure 5 *former term for* HYPNOTISM

mag·net·ite (mag′nə tīt′) ***n.*** ⟦Ger *magnetit:* see MAGNET & -ITE[1]⟧ a black, hard, magnetic mineral, (Fe,Mg)Fe_2O_4, that is a major ore of iron: cf. LODESTONE (sense 1)

mag·net·ize (mag′nə tīz′) ***vt.*** **-ized′**, **-iz′ing** 1 to make into a magnet; give magnetic properties to (steel, iron, etc.) 2 [Archaic] HYPNOTIZE (sense 1) 3 to attract or charm (a person), often in an almost hypnotic way —***vi.*** to become magnetic —**mag′net·iz′a·ble** ***adj.*** —**mag′net·i·za′tion** ***n.*** —**mag′net·iz′er** ***n.***

mag·ne·to (mag nēt′ō) ***n.***, *pl.* **-tos** ⟦see MAGNET⟧ an electric generator in which one or more permanent magnets produce the magnetic field; esp., a small machine of this sort connected with and run by an internal-combustion engine, used to generate the electric current providing a spark for the ignition

mag·ne·to- (mag nēt′ō, -net′-; -ə) ⟦see MAGNET⟧ *combining form* 1 magnetism, magnetic force [*magnetometer*] 2 magnetoelectric [*magnetohydrodynamics*]

mag·ne·to·e·lec·tric (-ō ē lek′trik) ***adj.*** designating or of electricity produced by changing magnetic fields in the vicinity of electric conductors —**mag·ne′to·e′lec′tric′i·ty** (-tris′ə tē) ***n.***

mag·ne·to·hy·dro·dy·nam·ics (-hī′drō dī nam′iks) ***n.*** ⟦MAGNETO- + HYDRODYNAMICS⟧ the science that deals with the interaction of a magnetic field with an electrically conducting fluid, as a liquid metal or an ionized gas —**mag·ne′to·hy′dro·dy·nam′ic** ***adj.***

mag·ne·tom·e·ter (mag′nə täm′ət ər) ***n.*** ⟦MAGNETO- + -METER⟧ 1 an instrument for measuring the intensity of magnetic forces, esp. of the earth's magnetic field 2 an instrument for detecting the presence of magnetic materials by their influence on the local magnetic field: often used to screen for weapons at airports, etc. —**mag·ne·to·met·ric** (mag nēt′ō met′rik, -net′-) ***adj.*** —**mag′ne·tom′e·try** (-ə trē) ***n.***

mag·ne·to·mo·tive (mag nēt′ō mōt′iv, -net′ō-) ***adj.*** ⟦MAGNETO- + -MOTIVE⟧ designating or of a force that gives rise to magnetic flux

mag·ne·ton (mag′nə tän′) ***n.*** ⟦Fr: see MAGNET & -ON⟧ a unit of the magnitude of the magnetic moment of atoms or other particles

mag·ne·to·pause (mag nēt′ō pôz′, -nēt′ə-) ***n.*** the outer boundary of a magnetosphere that separates a planet's magnetic field from interplanetary space

mag·ne·to·re·sist·ance (mag nēt′ō ri zis′təns, -net′ō-) ***n.*** ⟦MAGNETO- + RESISTANCE⟧ a change in the electrical resistance of a substance in the presence of a magnetic field

mag·ne·to·sphere (mag nēt′ō sfir′, -nēt′ə-; -net′-) ***n.*** ⟦MAGNETO- + -SPHERE⟧ that region surrounding a planet in which the planet's magnetic field is stronger than the interplanetary field: the solar wind gives it a cometlike shape with the tail extending from the night side of the planet for vast distances —**mag·ne′to·spher′ic** (-sfer′ik, -sfir′-) ***adj.***

mag·ne·to·stric·tion (-strik′shən) ***n.*** ⟦MAGNETO- + (CON)STRICTION⟧ a small variation in the size of a ferromagnetic material when subjected to an applied magnetic field —**mag·ne′to·stric′tive** ***adj.***

mag·ne·to·tax·is (mag nēt′ō tak′sis) ***n.*** ⟦MAGNETO- + -TAXIS (sense 2)⟧ the movement of an organism, as certain marine bacteria, in response to a magnetic field —**mag·ne′to·tac′tic** (-tak′tik) ***adj.***

mag·ne·tron (mag′nə trän′) ***n.*** ⟦MAGNE(T) + (ELEC)TRON⟧ an electron tube in which the flow of electrons from the cathode to one or more anodes is controlled by an externally applied magnetic field: used to generate alternating currents at microwave frequencies

☆**magnet school** a public school which offers innovative courses, specialized training, etc. in order to attract students from a broad region

mag·ni- (mag′ni, -nə) ⟦< L *magnus,* great, big < IE base **meĝ(h)-* > MUCH, Sans *mahā-,* Gr *megas,* big⟧ *combining form* great, big, large [*magnificence*]

mag·nif·ic (mag nif′ik) ***adj.*** ⟦ME *magnyfyque* < OFr *magnifique* < L *magnificus*⟧ [Archaic] 1 magnificent 2 imposing in size, dignity, etc. 3 *a)* pompous *b)* grandiloquent 4 eulogistic Also **mag·nif′i·cal**

Mag·nif·i·cat (mag nif′i kat′, män yif′i-; -kät′) ***n.*** ⟦L⟧ 1 the hymn of the Virgin Mary in Luke 1:46-55, beginning (in Latin) *Magnificat anima mea Dominum,* "My soul magnifies the Lord" 2 any musical setting for this 3 [**m-**] any song, poem, or hymn of praise

mag·ni·fi·ca·tion (mag′nə fi kā′shən) ***n.*** ⟦LL *magnificatio*⟧ 1 a magnifying or being magnified 2 the power of magnifying 3 a magnified image, model, or representation

mag·nif·i·cence (mag nif′ə səns) ***n.*** ⟦OFr < L *magnificentia* < *magnificus,* noble < *magnus,* great (see MAGNI-) + *facere,* to DO[1]⟧ richness and splendor, as of furnishings, color, dress, etc.; stately or imposing beauty

mag·nif·i·cent (mag nif′ə sənt) ***adj.*** ⟦OFr < LL *magnificens:* see prec.⟧ 1 beautiful in a grand or stately way; rich or sumptuous, as in construction, decoration, form, etc. 2 exalted: said of ideas, etc., and also of some former rulers, as Lorenzo the *Magnificent* 3 exceptionally good; excellent —***SYN.*** GRAND —**mag·nif′i·cent·ly** ***adv.***

mag·nif·i·co (mag nif′i kō′) ***n.***, *pl.* **-coes′** or **-cos′** ⟦It < L *magnificus:* see MAGNIFICENCE⟧ 1 a nobleman of Renaissance Venice 2 a person of high rank or great importance

mag·ni·fi·er (mag′nə fī′ər) ***n.*** 1 a person who magnifies 2 a thing that magnifies; specif., a lens or combination of lenses for magnifying

mag·ni·fy (mag′nə fī′) ***vt.*** **-fied′**, **-fy′ing** ⟦ME *magnifien* < OFr *magnifier* < L *magnificare,* to make much of, esteem highly, LL(Ec), to worship < *magnus,* great (see MAGNI-) + *facere,* to make, DO[1]⟧ 1 to make greater in size, status, degree, etc.; enlarge or strengthen 2 to cause to seem greater, more important, etc. than is really so; exaggerate [*to magnify* one's sufferings] 3 to cause to seem or appear larger than is really so; increase the apparent size of, esp. by means of a lens or lenses 4 [Archaic] to glorify; praise; extol —***vi.*** to have the power of increasing the apparent size of an object, as a microscope or telescope does

magnifying glass a lens or combination of lenses that increases the apparent size of an object seen through it

mag·nil·o·quent (mag nil′ə kwənt) ***adj.*** ⟦prob. back-form. < *magniloquence* < L *magniloquentia* < *magniloquus,* speaking in a lofty style < *magnus,* great (see MAGNI-) + *loqui,* to speak⟧ 1 lofty, pompous, or grandiose in speech or style of expression 2 boastful or bombastic —**mag·nil′o·quence** ***n.*** —**mag·nil′o·quent·ly** ***adv.***

Mag·ni·to·gorsk (mäg′ni tō gôrsk′) city in SW Russia, on the Ural River

mag·ni·tude (mag′nə to͞od′, -tyo͞od′) ***n.*** ⟦L *magnitudo* < *magnus,* great: see MAGNI-⟧ 1 greatness, specif. *a)* of size *b)* of extent *c)* of importance or influence *d)* [Obs.] of character 2 *a)* size or measurable quantity [the *magnitude* of a velocity] *b)* loudness (of sound) *c)* importance or influence 3 *Astron.* a number representing the apparent brightness of a celestial body: originally a number in a scale of values 1-6 and applied only to objects (excluding the sun and moon) visible to the naked eye, with the brightest stars at *c.* 1.5 (1 is the *first magnitude*) and stars at *c.* 6 (*sixth magnitude*) being barely visible, the scale now includes the sun (at −26.7) and moon (*c.* −12.7 when full) as well as the faintest objects visible telescopically (*c.* 36): each increase of one magnitude represents an increase of 2.512 times the brightness: see also ABSOLUTE MAGNITUDE 4 *Geol.* a measure of the amount of energy released by an earthquake: see RICHTER SCALE 5

Math. a number given to a quantity for purposes of comparison with other quantities of the same class —**of the first magnitude** of the greatest importance

☆**mag·no·li·a** (mag nō′lē ə, -nōl′yə) ***n.*** ⟦ModL, after P. *Magnol* (1638-1715), Fr botanist⟧ **1** any of a genus (*Magnolia*) of trees or shrubs of the magnolia family, with large, fragrant flowers of white, pink, or purple **2** the flower —***adj.*** designating a family (Magnoliaceae, order Magnoliales) of dicotyledonous trees, shrubs, and, sometimes, vines, including the cucumber tree and the tulip tree

magnolia tree and flower

mag·num (mag′nəm) ***n.*** ⟦L, neut. sing. of *magnus,* great: see MAGNI-⟧ **1** a wine bottle holding about 1.5 liters, about twice as much as the usual bottle ☆**2** [*usually* **M-**] a firearm, esp. a revolver, designed to fire magnum cartridges —***adj.*** of or pertaining to a cartridge having more explosive force than an ordinary cartridge of its size would

mag·num o·pus (mag′nəm ō′pəs) ⟦L⟧ **1** a great work, esp. of art or literature; masterpiece **2** a person's greatest work or undertaking

Magog ***n.*** *see* GOG AND MAGOG

mag·pie (mag′pī′) ***n.*** ⟦< *Mag,* dim. of MARGARET + PIE³⟧ **1** any of several jaylike corvids characterized by black-and-white coloring, a long, tapering tail, and a habit of noisy chattering **2** a person who chatters **3** a person who collects odds and ends

Ma·gritte (mȧ grēt′), **Re·né (François Ghislain)** (rə nā′) 1898-1967; Belgian painter

mag·uey (mag′wā′; *Sp* mä ge′ē) ***n.*** ⟦Sp < Taino⟧ **1** any of a number of fleshy-leaved, fiber-yielding agaves of the SW U.S., Mexico, and Central America; esp., the century plant and species used in making rope, pulque, and tequila **2** any of several other plants (genus *Furcraea*) of the same family **3** any of several kinds of tough fibers from these plants

Ma·gus (mā′gəs) ***n., pl.*** **-gi′** (-jī′) ⟦ME < L: see MAGI⟧ **1** [*also* **m-**] one of the Magi or magi **2** [**m-**] a sorcerer or astrologer

mag wheel ⟦short for *magnesium (alloy) wheel*⟧ a shiny, lightweight wheel for motor vehicles, having a decorative, symmetrical pattern of holes or spokes around the hub

Mag·yar (mag′yär′; *Hung* môd′yär) ***n.*** ⟦Hung⟧ **1** a member of the people constituting the main ethnic group in Hungary **2** the Ugric language of this people; Hungarian —***adj.*** of the Magyars or their language or culture

Ma·gyar·or·szág (môd′yär ôr′säg) *Hung. name for* HUNGARY

Ma·ha·bha·ra·ta (mə hä′bä′rə tə) ***n.*** ⟦Sans *Mahābhārata,* lit., the great story⟧ one of the two great epics of India, written in Sanskrit about 200 B.C.: cf. RAMAYANA

Ma·hal·la el Ku·bra (mä hä′lä el ko͞o′brä) city in N Egypt, in the Nile delta

ma·ha·ra·jah or **ma·ha·ra·ja** (mä′hə rä′jə) ***n.*** ⟦Sans *mahārājā* < *mahā,* great (see MAGNI-) + *rājā,* king: see REGAL⟧ [Historical] in India, a prince, specif. one ruling any of the chief states

ma·ha·ra·ni or **ma·ha·ra·nee** (-nē) ***n.*** ⟦Hindi *mahārānī* < *mahā,* great (< Sans: see MAGNI-) + *rānī,* queen⟧ [Historical] in India, *a)* the wife of a maharajah *b)* a princess ruling any of the chief states

Ma·ha·rash·tra (mə hä′räsh′trə) state of W India: 118,809 sq mi (307,714 sq km); cap. Mumbai

ma·ha·ri·shi (mä′hə rish′ē) ***n.*** ⟦Hindi *mahārishi* < *mahā,* great + *ṛshi,* sage⟧ a Hindu teacher of mysticism

ma·hat·ma (mə hat′mə, -hät′-) ***n.*** ⟦Sans *mahātman* < *mahā,* great (see MAGNI-) + *ātman,* ATMAN⟧ in India, any of a class of wise and holy persons held in special regard or reverence: Mohandas Gandhi was called *Mahatma*

Ma·ha·ya·na (mä′hə yä′nə) ***n.*** ⟦Sans *mahāyāna,* lit., greater vehicle⟧ a major movement or school in Buddhism: it emphasizes acts of virtue and compassion rather than asceticism and contemplation

Mah·di (mä′dē) ***n.*** ⟦Ar *mahdīy,* one guided aright < *hadā,* to lead aright⟧ a Muslim messianic leader; esp., such a leader and prophet expected by Muslims to appear on earth before the world ends —**Mah′dism′** (-diz′əm) ***n.*** —**Mah′dist** ***n.***

Ma·hé (mä hā′) chief island of the Seychelles, in the Indian Ocean: 59 sq mi (153 sq km)

☆**Ma·hi·can** (mə hē′kən) ***n.*** ⟦self-designation⟧ **1** *pl.* **-cans** or **-can** a member of a North American Indian people that lived chiefly in the upper Hudson Valley **2** the Algonquian language of this people —***adj.*** of the Mahicans or their language or culture

ma·hi-ma·hi (mä′hē mä′hē) ***n., pl.*** **ma′hi-ma′hi** ⟦Haw⟧ the DOLPHIN (sense 2) fish: also written **ma′hi·ma′hi** or **mahi mahi**

mah-jongg or **mah·jong** (mä′jôŋ′, -jäŋ′, -zhôŋ′, -zhäŋ′) ***n.*** ⟦< dial. form of Chin *ma-ch'iao,* lit., house sparrow, a figure on one of the tiles⟧ a game of Chinese origin played with 136 or 144 pieces called *tiles:* the object is to accumulate winning sets of these tiles

Mah·ler (mä′lər), **Gus·tav** (goos′täf′) 1860-1911; Austrian composer & conductor —**Mah·le·ri·an** (mä ler′ē ən) ***adj.***

mahl·stick (mäl′stik′, môl′-) ***n.*** ⟦Du *maalstok* < *malen,* to paint (< *mal,* a spot, akin to OE *mal:* see MOLE¹) + *stok,* STICK⟧ a long, lightweight stick used by painters to rest and steady the brush hand while at work

ma·hog·a·ny (mə häg′ə nē, -hôg′-) ***n., pl.*** **-nies** ⟦earlier *mohogeney* < ?⟧ **1** *a)* any of a genus (*Swietenia*) of tropical trees of the mahogany family, with dark, heavy heartwood *b)* the wood of any of these trees; esp., the hard, reddish-brown to yellow wood of a tropical American tree (*S. mahogani*), valued for furniture, interior finishing, and cabinetwork **2** *a)* any of various trees of this family having similar wood, as any of several African trees (genus *Khaya*) *b)* any of various trees of other families having similar wood, as a Philippine mahogany or certain eucalyptus trees *c)* the wood of any of these trees **3** reddish brown —***adj.*** **1** designating a family (Meliaceae, order Sapindales) of chiefly tropical, dicotyledonous plants, including baywood and chinaberry **2** made of mahogany **3** reddish-brown

Ma·hom·et (mə häm′it) *var. of* MUHAMMAD —**Ma·hom′et·an** ***adj., n.***

☆**ma·ho·ni·a** (mə hō′nē ə) ***n.*** ⟦ModL, after B. *McMahon* (1775?-1816), Am botanist⟧ any of a genus (*Mahonia*) of low evergreen shrubs of the barberry family, with clusters of yellow flowers followed by blue berries

Ma·hound (mə hound′, -ho͞ond′) ***n.*** ⟦ME *Mahun* < OFr *Mahon,* contr. < *Mahomet*⟧ **1** *archaic var. of* MUHAMMAD **2** [Scot.] the Devil

ma·hout (mə hout′) ***n.*** ⟦Hindi *mahāut, mahāvat* < Sans *mahāmātra,* lit., great in measure (hence, high officer) < *mahā,* great (see MAGNI-) + *mātrā,* measure: see METER¹⟧ in India and the East Indies, an elephant driver or keeper

Mah·rat·ta (mə rät′ə) ***n.*** *var. of* MARATHA

Mah·rat·ti or **Mah·ra·ti** (-ē) ***n.*** *var. of* MARATHI

mah·zor (mäkh′zər, mäkh zôr′) ***n., pl.*** **-zors** or **mah·zo·rim** (mäkh zô rēm′, -zôr′im) ⟦Yiddish *makhzer* < MHeb *machazor,* lit., cycle < root *ḥzr,* to return⟧ the Jewish prayer book that contains the liturgy for festivals and holy days: cf. SIDDUR

Ma·ia (mā′ə, mī′ə) ***n.*** ⟦Gr, lit., mother < *ma,* baby talk for *mētēr,* MOTHER¹⟧ **1** *Gr. Myth.* one of the Pleiades, mother of Hermes by Zeus **2** ⟦L, fem. of *Maius,* a deity (lit., ? he who brings increase, or the great one) < *Magnus* (see MAGNI-): later confused with Gr *Maia*⟧ *Rom. Myth.* an earth goddess, sometimes identified with the Greek Maia: the month of May was named in her honor

maid (mād) ***n.*** ⟦ME *maide,* contr. < *maiden*⟧ **1** *a)* [Now Chiefly Literary] a girl or young unmarried woman *b)* [Obs.] a virgin **2** [Now Rare] OLD MAID **3** a girl or woman servant: often in compounds [*barmaid, housemaid*] —**the Maid** *name for* JOAN OF ARC

Mai·da·nek (mī′də nek′) *alt. sp. of* MAJDANEK

maid·en (mād′'n) ***n.*** ⟦ME < OE *mægden,* dim. < base of *mægeth,* maid, virgin, akin to Goth *magaths,* OHG *magad* < IE base **maghu-,* youngster, unmarried > OIr *macc,* son, MAC-⟧ **1** [Now Chiefly Literary] *a)* a girl or young unmarried woman *b)* a virgin **2** a race horse that has never won a race **3** [**M-**] a device like the guillotine, formerly used in Scotland for beheading criminals **4** *Cricket* an over in which no runs are scored: in full **maiden over** —***adj.*** **1** of, characteristic of, or suitable for a maiden **2** *a)* unmarried *b)* virgin: now used only of older women [*a maiden aunt*] **3** inexperienced; untried; unused; new; fresh **4** first or earliest; inaugural [*a maiden speech, maiden voyage*] **5** *a)* never having won a race [*a maiden horse*] *b)* for such horses [*a maiden race*]

maid·en·hair (-her′) ***n.*** any of a genus (*Adiantum*) of ferns with delicate fronds and slender black stalks: also **maidenhair fern**

maidenhair tree GINKGO

maid·en·head (-hed′) ***n.*** **1** [Archaic] maidenhood; virginity **2** the hymen

maid·en·hood (-hood′) ***n.*** ⟦ME *maidenhod* < OE *mægdenhad:* see MAIDEN & -HOOD⟧ [Now Chiefly Literary] the state or time of being a maiden: also [Archaic] **maid′hood′**

maid·en·ly (-lē) ***adj.*** [Now Chiefly Literary] **1** of a maiden or maidenhood **2** like or characteristic of a maiden; modest, gentle, etc. —**maid′en·li·ness** ***n.***

maiden name the surname that a married woman had before marrying: now used chiefly with regard to a woman who has adopted her husband's surname

Maid Marian **1** a character in old May Day festivities and morris dances **2** *Eng. Legend* Robin Hood's sweetheart

maid of honor ☆**1** an unmarried woman acting as chief attendant to the bride at a wedding: cf. MATRON OF HONOR **2** an unmarried woman, usually of noble birth, attending a queen or princess

Maid of Orléans *name for* JOAN OF ARC

maid·ser·vant (mād′sur′vənt) ***n.*** a girl or woman servant

Maid·stone (mād′stən, -stōn′) city in SE England; county seat of Kent

mai·eu·tic (mā yo͞ot′ik) ***adj.*** ⟦Gr *maieutikos* < *maia,* midwife, orig., mother: see MAIA⟧ designating or of the Socratic method of helping a person to bring forth and become aware of latent ideas or memories

mail¹ (māl) ***n.*** ⟦ME *male* < OFr < MHG *malhe,* a traveling bag < OHG *malaha,* wallet⟧ **1** *a)* [Now Scot.] a bag or piece of baggage *b)* [Archaic] a bag or packet of letters, etc. to be transported by post **2** *a)* letters, papers, packages, etc. handled, transported, and delivered by the post office or other delivery service ☆*b)* letters, papers, etc. received or sent by a person, company, etc. **3** the system of collection, transportation, and delivery of letters, packages, etc.; postal system: also called **the mails** **4** the collection or delivery of letters, packages, etc. at a certain time [*late for the morning mail*] **5** [Chiefly Brit.] a vehicle for mail **6** *Comput.* EMAIL —***adj.*** of mail; esp., *a)* carrying, or used in the handling of, mail *b)* designating a person, or boat, train, etc. that transports letters, packages, etc. —***vt.*** ☆to send by mail, as by putting into a mailbox; post —**mail′a·bil′i·ty** ***n.*** —**mail′a·ble** ***adj.***

mail[2] (māl) ***n.*** ⟦ME *maile* < OFr *maille,* a link, mesh < L *macula,* a spot, mesh of a net⟧ **1** flexible body armor made of small, overlapping metal rings, loops of chain, or scales **2** the hard protective covering of some animals, as turtles —***vt.*** to cover or protect with or as with mail —**mailed** ***adj.***

suit of mail

mail[3] (māl) ***n.*** ⟦ME *male,* rent, tribute: see BLACKMAIL⟧ [Chiefly Scot.] rent or payment of any kind

mail·bag (māl′bag′) ***n.*** **1** a bag, as of leather, used for deliveries by a mail carrier: also **mail pouch** **2** a heavy canvas bag in which mail is transported: also written **mail sack**

mail·box (-bäks′) ***n.*** ☆**1** a box or compartment into which mail is put when delivered, as at one's home ☆**2** a box, as on a street corner, into which mail is put for collection **3** *Comput.* the part of an electronic mail system that stores incoming messages for a particular user Also written **mail box**

☆**mail carrier** a postal employee whose work is delivering mail; letter carrier

mail drop **1** a receptacle or slot into which mail is put for collection **2** a location or an address used for sending or receiving mail, often for secrecy or for illicit purposes

mailed fist ⟦calque of Ger *eiserne faust:* see MAIL[2]⟧ the use or threat of force, as between nations

☆**mail·er** (mā′lər) ***n.*** **1** a person who addresses and mails letters, packages, etc. **2** an envelope or container in which something is to be mailed **3** an advertising leaflet for mailing out

Mai·ler (mā′lər), **Norman** 1923-2007; U.S. writer

Mail·gram (māl′gram′) *trademark for* a telegram delivered by the postal service with the regular mail —***n.*** [*also* **m-**] such a telegram

mail·ing[1] (mā′liŋ) ***n.*** ⟦see MAIL[3] & -ING⟧ [Scot.] a farm that is rented; also, the rent paid for it

☆**mail·ing**[2] (mā′liŋ) ***n.*** **1** *a)* the action of sending (something) by mail *b)* anything sent by mail **2** a batch of mail dispatched by a mailer at one time

☆**mailing list** a list of members, contributors, or potential buyers to whom literature or advertisements are mailed

mailing tube a pasteboard cylinder in which printed matter or fragile objects are inserted for mailing

Mail·lol (mȧ yôl′), **A·ris·tide** (ȧ rēs tēd′) 1861-1944; Fr. sculptor

mail·lot (mä yō′, mī′ō′, mī ō′) ***n.*** ⟦Fr, dim. < *maille,* knitted material, lit., mail: see MAIL[2]⟧ **1** a swimsuit; esp., a one-piece swimsuit for women **2** a one-piece garment like this, worn by gymnasts, etc.

mail·man (māl′man′, -mən) ***n., pl.*** **-men′** (-men′, -mən) a man who is a MAIL CARRIER

☆**mail order** an order for goods to be sent by mail —**mail′-or′der** ***adj.***

☆**mail-order house** a business establishment that takes mail orders and sends goods by mail

mail·room (māl′ro͞om′) ***n.*** a room or office, as in a business or organization, in which incoming and outgoing mail is processed, sorted, etc.

maim (mām) ***vt.*** ⟦ME *maymen* < OFr *mahaigner, mayner*⟧ to deprive of the use of some necessary part of the body; cripple; mutilate; disable —***n.*** ⟦ME *mayme, maheym* < OFr *mahaing, main*⟧ [Obs.] an injury causing the loss or crippling of some necessary part of the body; mutilation; disablement: see MAYHEM —**maim′er** ***n.***

SYN.—**maim** implies an injuring of a person's body so as to deprive him or her of some member or its use [*maimed* in an auto accident]; to **cripple** is to cause to be legless, armless, or lame in any member [*crippled* by rheumatism]; to **mutilate** is to remove or severely damage a part of a person or thing essential to the completeness of that person or thing [a speech *mutilated* by censors]; **mangle** implies mutilation or disfigurement by or as by repeated tearing, hacking, or crushing [his arm was *mangled* in the press]; to **disable** is to make incapable of normal physical activity, as by crippling [*disabled* war veterans]

Mai·mon·i·des (mī män′ə dēz′), **Moses** (born *Moses ben Maimon*) 1135-1204; Sp. rabbi, physician, & philosopher, in Egypt

main (mān) ***n.*** ⟦ME < OE *mægen,* akin to ON *magn:* see MIGHT[2]⟧ **1** physical strength; force; power: now only in **with might and main,** with all one's strength **2** ⟦< the ***adj.***⟧ the principal or most important part or point: usually in the phrase **in the main,** mostly, chiefly **3** a principal pipe, conduit, or line in a distribution system for water, gas, electricity, etc. **4** [Old Poet.] the high, or open, sea; ocean **5** [Archaic] the mainland: see SPANISH MAIN **6** [Obs.] any broad expanse **7** *Naut. short for: a)* MAINMAST *b)* MAINSAIL —***adj.*** ⟦ME *mayn* < OE *mægen-* (in comp.) & ON *meginn,* strong⟧ **1** [Obs.] strong; powerful **2** chief in size, extent, importance, etc.; principal; leading; specif., designating a large central unit on which subsidiaries or branches depend [the *main* post office] **3** of, near, or connected with the mainmast or mainsail **4** [Brit. Dial.] remarkable; considerable **5** [Obs.] designating a broad expanse of land, sea, or space —***SYN.*** CHIEF —**by main force (or strength)** by sheer force (or strength)

Main (mīn; *E* mān) ⟦Ger < Gaul *Moenus* < IE **moin-,* river name < base **mei-,* to go, wander > L *meare,* to go⟧ river in SW Germany, flowing west into the Rhine at Mainz: 307 mi (494 km)

main chance, the [Informal] one's own advantage or self-interest

main clause *Gram.* INDEPENDENT CLAUSE

main deck the principal deck of a ship, usually the topmost complete deck

☆**main drag** [Slang] the principal street of a city or town

Maine (mān; *for 2, Fr* men) **1** ⟦orig. after *Maine,* region in NW France, but later interpreted as signifying its status as the *main* part of the New England region⟧ New England state of the U.S.: admitted 1820; 30,862 sq mi (79,931 sq km); cap. Augusta: abbrev. *ME* or *Me* **2** historical region of NW France, south of Normandy

Maine coon (cat) any of a breed of domestic cat, thought to have been developed in Maine, with a thick, smooth, silky coat and a bushy tail

Main·er (mā′nər) ***n.*** a person born or living in Maine

main·frame (mān′frām′) ***n.*** a relatively powerful computer designed for multitasking, to which several smaller computers, terminals, etc. may be connected

main·land (mān′land′, -lənd) ***n.*** the principal land or largest part of a continent or country, as distinguished from a relatively small island or peninsula —**main′land′er** ***n.***

Main·land (mān′land′, -lənd) **1** chief island of Japan: see HONSHU **2** largest of the Orkney Islands: *c.* 190 sq mi (492 sq km) **3** largest of the Shetland Islands: 407 sq mi (1,054 sq km)

main·line (-līn′) ***n.*** the principal road, course, etc. —***adj.*** having a principal, prominent, or moderate position or status —☆***vt.*** **-lined′, -lin′ing** [Slang] to inject (a narcotic drug) directly into a large vein —**main′lin′er** ***n.***

main·ly (-lē) ***adv.*** chiefly; principally; in the main

main·mast (mān′mast′; *naut.,* -məst) ***n.*** the principal mast of a vessel: in a schooner, brig, bark, etc., the mast second from the bow; in a ketch or yawl, the larger mast nearer the bow

main memory the primary memory of a computer: it is random-access and stores the programs and data while they are being processed

main·sail (mān′sāl′; *naut.,* -səl) ***n.*** **1** in a square-rigged vessel, the sail set from the main yard **2** in a fore-and-aft-rigged vessel, the large sail set from the after side of the mainmast

main·sheet (-shēt′) ***n.*** a sheet, or line, controlling the angle at which the mainsail is set

main·spring (-spriŋ′) ***n.*** **1** the principal spring in a clock, watch, or other mechanism; driving spring, whose steady uncoiling keeps the mechanism running **2** the chief motive or cause

main·stay (-stā′) ***n.*** **1** a stay, or line, extending forward from the mainmast, supporting it and holding it in position **2** a chief support

☆**main stem** [Slang] **1** MAIN DRAG **2** MAINLINE (***n.***)

main·stream (-strēm′) ***n.*** **1** the middle of a stream, where the current is strongest **2** the part of something considered to be the most active, productive, lively, busy, etc. [the *mainstream* of life] **3** a major or prevailing trend, as of thought, action, literature, or music ☆**4** *Jazz* a style of playing that evolved in the 1950s, based on rhythmic and harmonic elements of swing modified slightly by those of bop —***vt.*** **1** to cause to undergo mainstreaming **2** to bring into the mainstream, as of employment, the economy, or politics

main·stream·ing (main′stream′iŋ) ***n.*** the placement of disabled people into regular school classes, workplaces, etc.

☆**Main Street** **1** the principal street of any small town **2** ⟦term popularized by Sinclair LEWIS[2] in his novel *Main Street* (1920)⟧ the typical inhabitants of a small town, regarded as provincial and conservative **3** ordinary citizens and the places in which they live and work [an economic upheaval felt from Wall Street to *Main Street*]

main·tain (mān tān′) ***vt.*** ⟦ME *mainteinen* < OFr *maintenir* < ML *manutenere* < L *manu tenere,* to hold in the hand < *manu,* abl. of *manus,* hand + *tenere,* to hold: see MANUAL & TENANT⟧ **1** to keep or keep up; continue in or with; carry on **2** *a)* to keep in existence or continuance [food *maintains* life] *b)* to keep in a certain condition or position, esp. of efficiency, good repair, etc.; preserve [to *maintain* roads] **3** to keep or hold (a place, position, etc.) against attack; defend **4** *a)* to uphold or defend, as by argument; affirm *b)* to declare in a positive way; assert **5** to support by aid, influence, protection, etc. **6** to support by providing means of existence; bear the expenses of [to *maintain* a family] —***SYN.*** SUPPORT —**main·tain′a·ble** ***adj.*** —**main·tain′er** ***n.***

main·te·nance (mānt′'n əns) ***n.*** ⟦ME *maintenaunce* < OFr *maintenance*⟧ **1** a maintaining or being maintained; upkeep, support, defense, etc.; specif., the work of keeping a building, machinery, etc. in good repair **2** a department or the personnel responsible for keeping a building, etc. in good repair **3** means of support or sustenance; livelihood [a job that barely provides a *maintenance*] **4** *Law* the act of interfering unlawfully in a suit between others by helping either party, as by giving money, to carry it on

Mainte·non (mant nōn′), Marquise **de** (born *Françoise d' Aubigné*) 1635-1719; 2d wife of Louis XIV

main·top (mān′täp′) ***n.*** a platform at the head of the bottommost section of the mainmast

main-top·mast (mān′täp′mast′; *naut.,* -məst) ***n.*** the section of the mainmast just above the bottommost section

main-top·sail (-sāl′; *naut.,* -səl) ***n.*** the sail set on the main-topmast above the mainsail

main yard the lowest yard on the mainmast, from which the mainsail is set

Mainz (mīnts) city in W Germany, on the Rhine: capital of the state of Rhineland-Palatinate

mai·son·ette (mā′zə net′) ***n.*** ⟦Fr, dim. of *maison,* house < L *mansio:* see MANSION⟧ **1** a small house; cottage **2** an apartment, esp. a duplex apartment

maist (māst) ***adj.*** [Scot.] most

mai tai (mī′ tī′) ⟦Tahitian, lit., good⟧ [*often* **M- T-**] a cocktail made with rum and fruit juices, often garnished with pineapple or other fruit or with a tiny orchid

mai·ta·ke (mī täk′ē) *n.* ⟦Jpn, lit., dancing mushroom: from its whorled appearance⟧ an edible mushroom (*Grifola frondosa*), native to Japan and parts of North America, growing in overlapping clusters and used also in traditional Asian medicine

Mait·land (māt′lənd), **Frederic William** 1850-1906; Eng. legal historian & jurist

mai·tre d' (māt′ər dē′) *pl.* **mai′tre d's′** ⟦< fol.⟧ a headwaiter, as of an upscale restaurant

maî·tre d'hô·tel (me tr' dô tel′) *pl.* ***maî·tres d'hô·tel′*** (me tr′-) ⟦Fr, lit., master of the house⟧ **1** a butler or steward; major-domo **2** a hotel manager **3** a headwaiter **4** with a sauce of melted butter, parsley, and lemon juice or vinegar

maize (māz) *n.* ⟦Sp *maíz* < WInd (Taino) *mahiz*⟧ **1** *chiefly Brit. name for* CORN[1] (*n.* 3) **2** the color of ripe corn; yellow

Maj *abbrev.* Major

Maj·da·nek (mī′də nek′) Nazi concentration camp & extermination center in E Poland, near Lublin

ma·jes·tic (mə jes′tik) *adj.* having or characterized by majesty; very grand or dignified: also **ma·jes′ti·cal** —*SYN.* GRAND —**ma·jes′ti·cal·ly** *adv.*

maj·es·ty (maj′is tē) *n., pl.* **-ties** ⟦ME *maiesty* < OFr *majesté* < L *majestas* < base of *major,* compar. of *magnus,* great: see MAGNI-⟧ **1** *a)* the dignity or power of a sovereign *b)* sovereign power [the *majesty* of the law] **2** [**M-**] a title used in speaking to or of a sovereign, preceded by *Your* or by *His* or *Her* **3** grandeur or stateliness

Maj Gen *abbrev.* Major General

ma·jol·i·ca (mə jäl′i kə) *n.* ⟦It *maiolica* < *Maiolica,* MAJORCA, where orig. produced⟧ **1** a variety of Italian pottery, enameled, glazed, and richly colored and decorated **2** pottery like this

ma·jor (mā′jər) *adj.* ⟦ME *maiour* < L *major,* compar. of *magnus,* great: see MAGNI-⟧ **1** *a)* greater in size, amount, number, or extent *b)* greater in importance or rank **2** of full legal age **3** constituting the majority: said of a part, etc. ☆**4** *Educ.* of or having to do with a field of study in which a student specializes and receives a degree **5** *Music a)* designating an imperfect interval greater than the corresponding minor by a semitone *b)* characterized by major intervals, scales, etc. [in a *major* key] *c)* designating a triad having intervals of a major third between the lower two pitches, and a minor third between the upper two pitches *d)* based on the scale pattern of the major mode (see MAJOR SCALE) —*vi.* ☆*Educ.* to pursue a major subject or field of study; specialize [to *major* in physics] —*n.* **1** ⟦< the *adj.*⟧ a superior in some class or group **2** ⟦Fr⟧ *U.S. Mil.* an officer ranking above a captain and below a lieutenant colonel ☆**3** *Educ. a)* a major subject or field of study *b)* a student specializing in a specified subject [a music *major*] **4** *Law* a person who has reached full legal age **5** *Music* a major interval, key, etc. —**the Majors** ☆[Informal] *Baseball* the Major Leagues

major axis *Geom.* the longer axis of an ellipse, that passes through both focus points: see also MINOR AXIS

Ma·jor·ca (mə jôr′kə, -yôr′-) island of Spain, largest of the Balearic Islands: 1,405 sq mi (3,639 sq km); chief city, Palma: Sp. name MALLORCA —**Ma·jor·can** (-jôr kən, -yôr-) *adj., n.*

ma·jor-do·mo (mā′jər dō′mō) *n., pl.* **-mos** ⟦Sp *mayordomo* or It *maggiordomo* < LL *major domus* < L *major,* greater (see MAJOR) + gen. of *domus,* house⟧ the chief steward of a great, royal, or noble household

☆**ma·jor·ette** (mā′jər et′) *n. short for* DRUM MAJORETTE

major general *pl.* **major generals** *U.S. Mil.* an officer, with the insignia of two stars, ranking above a brigadier general and below a lieutenant general

ma·jor·i·tar·i·an (mə jôr′ə ter′ē ən) *adj.* ⟦fol. + -ARIAN⟧ of or decided by the majority —*n.* an advocate of majoritarian rule —**ma·jor′i·tar′i·an·ism′** *n.*

ma·jor·i·ty (mə jôr′ə tē, -jär′-) *n., pl.* **-ties** ⟦Fr *majorité* < ML *majoritas* < L *major:* see MAJOR⟧ **1** [*also with pl. v.*] the greater part or larger number; more than half of a total ☆**2** the number by which the votes cast for the candidate, bill, etc. receiving more than half of the votes, exceed the remaining votes (Ex.: if candidate A gets 100 votes, candidate B, 50, and candidate C, 30, A has a majority of 20): cf. PLURALITY (sense 4) **3** the group, party, or faction with more than half of the votes **4** the condition or time of having reached full legal age, with full legal rights and responsibilities **5** [Obs.] the state or quality of being greater **6** *Mil.* the rank or position of a major

☆**major league** a principal league in a professional sport —**the Major Leagues** the two main leagues of professional baseball clubs in the U.S., the National League and the American League —**ma′jor-leagu′er** *n.*

☆**ma·jor-league** (mā′jər lēg′) *adj.* **1** of or pertaining to a major league or the Major Leagues **2** [Slang] great in extent, importance, impressiveness, etc.

major mode *Music* a MODE (*n.* 6c) predominantly using the intervals of the major scale

major orders the Christian clergy orders of deacon, priest, and bishop

major premise in a syllogism, the premise that contains the major term

Major Prophets **1** the longer books of prophecy in the Bible, attributed to the prophets Ezekiel, Isaiah, and Jeremiah **2** those prophets

major scale *Music* any of the diatonic scales having the eight tones succeeding by whole tones but with a semitone between the third and fourth and between the seventh and eighth tones: there are twelve major scales, one in each key

major seminary *R.C.Ch.* a seminary offering typically the final six years of training for the priesthood

major suit *Bridge* spades or hearts: so called from their higher value

major term in a syllogism, the predicate of the conclusion

Ma·ju·ro Atoll (mə joor′ō) coral atoll in the WC Pacific, near the equator: capital of the Marshall Islands: 3.7 sq mi (9.7 sq km)

ma·jus·cule (mə jus′kyool′, maj′əs-) *n.* ⟦Fr < L *majuscula (littera),* somewhat larger (letter), dim. < *major:* see MAJOR⟧ **1** a large letter, capital or uncial, as in medieval manuscripts **2** writing in which such letters are used —*adj.* of, written in, or like a majuscule Cf. MINUSCULE —**ma·jus′cu·lar** *adj.*

Ma·kas·sar (mə kas′ər) *former name for* UJUNG PANDANG

make[1] (māk) *vt.* **made, mak′ing** ⟦ME *maken* < OE *macian,* akin to Ger *machen* < IE base **maĝ-,* to knead, press, stretch > MASON, Gr *magis,* kneaded mass, paste, dough, *mageus,* kneader⟧ **1** to bring into being; specif., *a)* to form by shaping or putting parts or ingredients together, physically or mentally; build, construct, fabricate, fashion, create, compose, devise, formulate, etc. *b)* to fit or destine, as if by fashioning (*in the pp.*) [two lovers who were *made* for each other, a singer *made* for stardom] *c)* to cause; bring about; produce [to *make* corrections] *d)* to bring together materials for and start [to *make* a fire] *e)* to cause to be available; provide [to *make* change for a ten-dollar bill, to *make* room] *f)* to present for consideration [to *make* a suggestion] **2** to bring into a specified condition; specif., *a)* to cause to be or become, as by election or appointment [*make* her director] *b)* to cause to seem [the portrait *makes* him an old man]: sometimes used reflexively [*make* yourself comfortable] **3** to prepare by arranging the sheets, blankets, etc.: said of a bed **4** *a)* to amount to; form as a total [two pints *make* a quart] *b)* to count as; constitute [this *makes* his fifth bestseller] **5** to turn out to be; have, or prove to have, the essential qualities of [to *make* a fine leader] **6** to set up; establish [to *make* rules] **7** *a)* to get or acquire, as by one's behavior [to *make* friends] *b)* to get by earning, investing, etc. [to *make* a fortune] **8** to cause the success of [that venture *made* her] **9** to understand or regard as the meaning (*of*) [what do you *make* of the poem?] **10** to estimate to be; regard as [I *make* the distance about 500 miles] **11** *a)* to do or perform (a specified action); execute; accomplish [to *make* a quick turn] *b)* to engage in; carry on [to *make* war] **12** to deliver (a speech) or utter (remarks, etc.) **13** to cause or force: followed by an infinitive without *to* [*make* the machine work, *make* him behave] **14** *a)* to arrive at; reach [the ship *made* port] *b)* to arrive at in time [to *make* a train] **15** to go or travel; traverse [to *make* 500 miles the first day, to *make* 90 miles an hour] **16** [Informal] to succeed in getting membership in, a position on, the status of, recognition in, etc. [to *make* the team, to *make* the headlines] ☆**17** [Slang] to succeed in becoming the lover of; seduce **18** [Slang] to identify or recognize **19** [Slang] to induct, for one's lifetime, into the Mafia: usually used as a participial adj. [a *made* man] **20** [Archaic] to shut (a door) tight **21** *Card Games a)* to win (tricks) or fulfill (one's bid) *b)* to take a trick with (a specified card) *c)* to shuffle (the cards) **22** *Elec.* to close (a circuit); effect (a contact) **23** *Games* to score, get as a score, or execute so as to score [to *make* a shot in basketball] **24** *Law* to perform, execute, or sign (a legal document) —*vi.* **1** to start (to do something) [she *made* to go] **2** to tend, extend, or point (*to, toward,* etc.) **3** to behave in a specified manner: with a following adjective [*make* bold, *make* merry, etc.] **4** to cause something to be in a specified condition [*make* ready, *make* fast, etc.] **5** to increase in depth or volume; rise or accumulate, as tide, snow, water in a ship, etc. **6** to mature: said of hay, etc. —*n.* **1** the act or process of making; esp., manufacture **2** the amount made; output, esp. of manufacture **3** the way in which something is made; style; build **4** type, sort, or brand: with reference to the maker or to the place, time, etc. of making [a foreign *make* of car] **5** disposition; character; nature [a man of this *make*] **6** [Slang] the act or process of identifying a person, taking fingerprints, etc. in police work [run a *make* on a suspect] **7** *Elec.* the closing of a circuit by making contact —**make a fool (or an ass, etc.) of** to cause to seem a fool (or an ass, etc.) —**make after** [Informal] to chase or follow —**make a meal on (or of)** to eat as a meal —**make as if (or as though)** [Informal] to behave as if —**make away with** **1** to steal **2** to get rid of **3** to eat all of **4** to kill —**make believe** to pretend; act a part —☆**make someone's day** [Informal] to give pleasure that will be the high point of someone's day —**make do** to get along, or manage, with what is available —**make for** **1** to head for; go toward **2** to charge at; attack **3** to tend toward; help effect —☆**make good** [Informal] **1** to give or do something as a substitute for; repay or replace **2** to fulfill **3** to succeed in doing; accomplish **4** to be successful **5** to prove —**make it** **1** [Informal] to accomplish a goal or achieve success ☆**2** [Slang] to have sexual intercourse (*with*) —☆**make like** [Slang] to imitate; impersonate —**make something of** **1** to find a use for **2** to treat as of great importance ☆**3** [Informal] to make an issue of —**make off** to go away; run away —**make off with** to steal —**make or break** to cause the success or failure of —**make out** **1** to see or hear with some difficulty but clearly enough to understand **2** to understand **3** to write out **4** to fill out (as a blank form) **5** to show or prove to be **6** to try to show, affirm, or imply to be **7** to succeed; get along ☆**8** [Slang] *a)* to kiss and caress as lovers *b)* to have sexual intercourse —**make over** **1** to change; renovate **2** to transfer the ownership of by or as by signing a legal document **3** [Informal] to be demonstrative toward or about —**make up** **1** to put together; compose; compound **2** to form; constitute **3** to invent; create **4** to complete by providing what is lacking **5** to compensate (*for*) **6** to arrange **7** *a)* to become friendly again after a disagreement or quarrel *b)* to settle (an argument or differences) in a friendly manner **8** *a)* to put on what is required for a role in a play, as a costume, wig, greasepaint, powder, etc. *b)* to put cosmetics on **9** to select and arrange type, illustrations, etc. for (a book, magazine, page, etc.) ☆10 *Educ.* to take again (an examination or course that one has failed) or to take (an examination that one has missed) —**make up one's mind** to come to a decision —**make up to** [Informal] to flatter, or try to be agreeable to, in order to become friendly with or to be in (someone's) good graces —**make with** [Slang] 1 to use, or do something with, in the way indicated or implied 2 to produce or supply [to *make with* the jokes] —☆**on the make** [Slang] 1 trying to succeed financially, socially, etc., esp. in an aggressive way 2 seeking a lover —**put the make on** [Slang] to make sexual advances to —**make′a·ble** *adj.*, **mak′a·ble**

NOTE—*make* is used widely and variously in idiomatic phrases, many of which are entered in this dictionary under the key word, as *make fun of, make the grade,* and *make hay*

SYN.—**make** is the general term meaning to bring into being and may imply a producing of something physically or mentally; **form** suggests a definite contour, structure, or design in the thing made; **shape** suggests the imparting of a specific form as by molding, cutting, hammering, etc.; **fashion** implies inventiveness, cleverness of design, the use of skill, etc.; **construct** implies a putting of parts together systematically according to some design; **manufacture** implies a producing from raw materials, now especially by machinery and on a large scale; **fabricate** implies a building or manufacturing, often by assembling standardized parts, and, in extended use, connotes fictitious invention

make[2] (māk) *n.* ⟦ME < OE *gemaca* (akin to Ger *gemach,* fitting, suitable) < base of *macian:* see prec.⟧ [Archaic] 1 an equal; peer 2 a mate, companion, or spouse

make-be·lieve (māk′bə lēv′) *n.* a pretending, as in children's play —*adj.* pretended; feigned; sham

make·fast (-fast′) *n.* a buoy, post, pile, etc. to which a boat is fastened

make·o·ver (māk′ō′vər) *n.* 1 a making over; change; renovation 2 a transformation in a person's appearance made by altering clothing, makeup, hairstyle, etc., esp. as a service performed by a consultant

mak·er (-ər) *n.* 1 a person or thing that makes (in various senses): often used in compounds [*steelmaker, cabinetmaker*] 2 [Archaic] a poet 3 a person who executes, as by signing, a check, contract, etc.; specif., a person who signs a promissory note 4 [**M-**] God —**meet one's Maker** to die

make·read·y (-red′ē) *n.* ☆*Printing* the final adjustment of the printing surfaces on a press by the use of leveling devices, overlays, underlays, etc.

make·shift (-shift′) *n.* a thing that will do for a while as a substitute; temporary expedient —*adj.* that will do for a while as a substitute —***SYN.*** RESOURCE

make·up or **make-up** (-up′) *n.* 1 the way in which something is put together; composition; construction 2 nature; disposition; constitution [to have a stolid *makeup*] 3 *a)* the way in which an actor is made up for a role, as with a costume, wig, greasepaint, powder, etc. *b)* the costumes, wigs, greasepaint, etc. so used 4 *a)* cosmetics generally; blush, lipstick, mascara, etc. *b)* the way in which these are applied or worn 5 the arrangement of type, illustrations, etc. in a book, newspaper, page, etc. ☆6 [Informal] a special test that a student takes to make up for a test missed or failed —*adj.* of or for making up

make·weight (-wāt′) *n.* 1 anything added to a scale to complete the required weight 2 an unimportant person or thing added to make up some lack

☆**make-work** (-wurk′) *adj., n.* (designating) a job, project, or assignment that serves no useful purpose other than to give an otherwise idle or unemployed person something to do

Ma·key·ev·ka (mä kā′yif kä′) city in SE Ukraine, in the Donets Basin

Ma·khach·ka·la (mə käch′kə lä′) city & seaport of SW Russia, on the Caspian Sea

ma·ki·mo·no (mä′ki mō′nō) *n.* ⟦Jpn⟧ a Japanese art scroll with pictures or calligraphy, intended to be held in the hands and unrolled from right to left while being examined

mak·ing (māk′iŋ) *n.* 1 the act of one that makes or the process of being made; formation, construction, creation, production, composition, manufacture, development, performance, etc. 2 the cause or means of success or advancement [an experience that will be the *making* of him] 3 *a)* something made *b)* the quantity made at one time 4 [*pl.*] *a)* the material or qualities needed for the making or development of something [to have the *makings* of a good doctor] ☆*b)* [Informal] tobacco and paper for making one's own cigarettes (usually preceded by *the*)

-making (māk′iŋ) *combining form forming adjectives* [Chiefly Brit.] creating a (specified) state or condition [shy-*making*, angry-*making*]

Mak·kah (mäk′ə) *Ar. name for* MECCA[2]

ma·ko (mä′kō, mā′-) *n., pl.* **-kos** ⟦Maori⟧ a large, swift, dangerous mackerel shark (genus *Isurus*)

Ma·ku·a (mä ko͞o′ä) *n.* 1 *pl.* **-ku′as** or **-ku′a** a member of a people of N Mozambique and adjacent areas of Tanzania 2 the Bantu language of this people

ma·ku·ta (mä ko͞o′tä) *n. pl. of* LIKUTA

Mal *abbrev.* 1 *Bible* Malachi 2 Malay 3 Malayan 4 Malaysia 5 Malaysian

mal- (mal) ⟦Fr < L *male-* < *male,* badly, *malus,* bad, evil⟧ *prefix* bad or badly, wrong, ill [*maladroit*]

Mal·a·bar Coast (mal′ə bär′) coastal region in SW India on the Arabian Sea, extending from Cape Comorin to Goa & inland to the Western Ghats: *c.* 450 mi (725 km) long: also **Malabar**

Ma·la·bo (mä lä′bō) capital of Equatorial Guinea: seaport on Bioko

mal·ab·sorp·tion (mal′əb sôrp′shən, -zôrp-) *n.* the poor absorption of nutrients by the alimentary canal

Ma·lac·ca (mə lak′ə) 1 state of Malaysia in W Peninsular Malaysia, on the Strait of Malacca: 637 sq mi (1,650 sq km) 2 seaport in this state: its capital 3 **Strait of** strait between Sumatra & the Malay Peninsula: *c.* 500 mi (805 km) long

Malacca cane ⟦after prec.⟧ a lightweight walking stick of rattan, often mottled brown

Mal·a·chi (mal′ə kī′) *n.* ⟦Heb *mal'ākhī,* lit., my messenger⟧ *Bible* 1 a Hebrew prophet of the 5th cent. B.C. 2 the book containing prophecies attributed to him: abbrev. *Mal* or *Mi*

mal·a·chite (mal′ə kīt′) *n.* ⟦ME *melochites* < L *molochites* < Gr *molochitēs,* a stone (? malachite) < *malachē, molochē,* mallow (its color is like that of mallow leaves): < ? Heb *malluaḥ,* a lettuce-like plant > L *malva,* MALLOW⟧ a bright green, monoclinic mineral, copper carbonate, $Cu_2CO_3(OH)_2$, that is an ore of copper and is used as a gem and to make ornamental objects

mal·a·co- (mal′ə kō′, -kə) ⟦< Gr *malakos,* soft < IE **mlāk-* < base **mel-,* to crush, grind > MILL[1]⟧ *combining form* 1 soft 2 mollusks [*malacology*]

mal·a·col·o·gy (mal′ə käl′ə jē) *n.* ⟦Fr *malacologie:* see prec. & -LOGY⟧ the branch of zoology dealing with mollusks

mal·a·cos·tra·can (mal′ə käs′trə kən) *adj.* ⟦< ModL *Malacostraca* < Gr *malakostrakos,* soft-shelled < *malakos,* soft (see MALACO-) + *ostrakon,* shell + -AN⟧ of a large class (Malacostraca) of highly evolved crustaceans typically consisting of 19 segments, including the decapods, krill, and isopods: also **mal′a·cos′tra·cous** (-kəs) —*n.* such a crustacean

mal·ad·ap·ta·tion (mal′ad əp tā′shən) *n.* inadequate or faulty adaptation —**mal′a·dap′tive** (-ə dap′tiv) *adj.*

mal·a·dapt·ed (mal′ə dap′tid) *adj.* not suited or properly adapted (to a function, situation, etc.)

mal·ad·just·ed (mal′ə jus′tid) *adj.* poorly adjusted, esp. to the environment; specif., unable to adjust properly to the stresses, etc. of daily life —**mal′ad·just′ment** *n.*

mal·ad·jus·tive (-tiv) *adj.* not leading to proper adjustment

mal·ad·min·is·ter (-ad min′is tər) *vt.* to administer badly; conduct (as public affairs) corruptly or inefficiently —**mal′ad·min′is·tra′tion** (-ə strā′shən) *n.*

mal·a·droit (mal′ə droit′) *adj.* ⟦Fr: see MAL- & ADROIT⟧ awkward; clumsy; bungling —***SYN.*** AWKWARD —**mal′a·droit′ly** *adv.* —**mal′a·droit′ness** *n.*

mal·a·dy (mal′ə dē) *n., pl.* **-dies** ⟦ME *maladie* < OFr < *malade,* sick < VL *male habitus,* badly kept, out of condition: see MAL- & HABIT⟧ a disease; illness; sickness: often used fig. —***SYN.*** DISEASE

Mal·a·ga (mal′ə gə) *n.* ⟦after fol.⟧ 1 a large, white, oval table grape, grown esp. in California 2 any of several fortified wines made originally in Málaga

Má·la·ga (mä′lä gä′; *E* mal′ə gə) seaport in S Spain, on the Mediterranean

Mal·a·gas·y (mal′ə gas′ē) *n., pl.* **-gas′y** or **-gas′ies** ⟦< native name, var. of the base *Madagas-* in MADAGASCAR⟧ 1 a person born or living in Madagascar 2 the Austronesian language spoken by the Malagasy —*adj.* of the Malagasy or their language or culture

Malagasy Republic *former name for* MADAGASCAR (the country)

mal·a·gue·na (mal′ə gān′yə) *n.* ⟦Sp *malagueña,* orig. fem. of *malagueño,* of MÁLAGA⟧ any of several Spanish folk tunes or dances, esp. one like the fandango

ma·laise (ma lāz′, mə-; -lez′) *n.* ⟦Fr < *mal,* bad (see MAL-) + *aise,* EASE⟧ 1 a vague feeling of physical discomfort or uneasiness, as early in an illness 2 any vague feeling of uneasiness, often, specif., one that is pervasive in a community

Mal·a·mud (mal′ə məd), **Bernard** 1914-86; U.S. writer

☆**mal·a·mute** (mal′ə myo͞ot′) *n.* ⟦< Inuit *malimiut,* name of the Inuit people living on the coast of NW Alaska that developed the breed⟧ ALASKAN MALAMUTE

mal·an·ders (mal′ən dərz) *pl.n.* ⟦ME *malawnder* < MFr *malandre* < L *malandria,* blisters or pustules on the neck, esp. of horses⟧ a variety of eczema around the knee of a horse's foreleg: see SALLENDERS

Ma·lang (mä läŋ′) city in E Java, Indonesia

☆**ma·lan·ga** (mə laŋ′gə) *n.* ⟦AmSp < ?⟧ YAUTIA

mal·a·pert (mal′ə purt′) [Archaic] *adj.* ⟦OFr < *mal,* badly (see MAL-) + *apert,* var. of *espert,* experienced, deft (see EXPERT): infl. by *apert,* open, bold (< L *apertus:* see APERTURE)⟧ saucy; impudent; pert —*n.* a saucy, impudent person —**mal′a·pert′ly** *adv.*

mal·ap·por·tion (mal′ə pôr′shən) *vt.* to apportion improperly or unfairly (voting districts, a legislature, etc.) —**mal′ap·por′tion·ment** *n.*

mal·a·prop (mal′ə präp′) *adj.* ⟦after Mrs. *Malaprop,* a character in SHERIDAN's play *The Rivals,* who makes ludicrous blunders in her use of words⟧ using or characterized by malapropisms: also **mal′a·prop′i·an** (-ē ən) —*n.* MALAPROPISM (sense 2)

mal·a·prop·ism (mal′ə präp′iz′əm) *n.* ⟦< prec. + -ISM⟧ 1 ludicrous misuse of words, esp. through confusion caused by resemblance in sound 2 an instance of this (Ex.: *progeny* for *prodigy*)

mal·ap·ro·pos (mal′ap rə pō′) *adj.* ⟦Fr *mal à propos:* see MAL- & APROPOS⟧ at an awkward or improper time or place; inopportune; inappropriate —*adv.* in an inopportune or inappropriate manner

ma·lar (mā′lər) *adj.* ⟦ModL < L *mala,* the cheek⟧ of the cheek, cheekbone, or side of the head —*n.* the cheekbone

Mäl·ar (mel′är) lake in SE Sweden: 440 sq mi (1,140 sq km): Swed. name **Mäl·ar·en** (mel′ä rən)

ma·lar·i·a (mə ler′ē ə) *n.* ⟦It, contr. < *mala aria,* bad air: see MAL- & ARIA⟧ 1

[Archaic] unwholesome or poisonous air, as from marshy ground; miasma **2** ⟦from the former notion that it was caused by the bad air of swamps⟧ an infectious disease, generally intermittent and recurrent, caused by any of various protozoans (genus *Plasmodium*) that are parasitic in the red blood corpuscles and are transmitted to humans by the bite of an infected anopheles mosquito: it is characterized by severe chills and fever —**ma·lar′i·al** ***adj.***, **ma·lar′i·an**, or **ma·lar′i·ous**

☆**ma·lar·key** or **ma·lar·ky** (mə lär′kē) ***n.*** ⟦< ?⟧ [Slang] insincere, meaningless, or deliberately misleading talk; nonsense

mal·ate (mal′āt′, mā′lāt′) ***n.*** a salt or ester of malic acid

☆**mal·a·thi·on** (mal′ə thī′än′, -ən) ***n.*** ⟦< MAL(IC) A(CID) + THION(IC)⟧ an organic phosphate, $C_{10}H_{19}O_6S_2P$, of relatively low toxicity for mammals, used as an insecticide

Ma·la·tya (mä′lä tyä′) city in EC Turkey

Ma·la·wi (mə lou′ē) **1** country in SE Africa, on Lake Malawi: a former British protectorate, it became independent & a member of the Commonwealth in 1964; a republic since 1966: 45,745 sq mi (118,480 sq km); cap. Lilongwe **2 Lake** lake in SE central Africa bounded by Malawi, Tanzania, & Mozambique: *c.* 11,150 sq mi (28,878 sq km) —**Ma·la′wi·an** ***adj., n.***

Ma·lay (mā′lā′, mə lā′) ***n.*** ⟦Malay *melaya* < ?⟧ **1** a member of a large group of indigenous peoples of the Malay Peninsula, the Malay Archipelago, and nearby islands **2** the Western Austronesian family of languages of these peoples, including the official languages of Malaysia and Indonesia —***adj.*** of the Malays or their language or culture

Ma·lay·a (mə lā′ə) **1** MALAY PENINSULA **2 Federation of** former federation of states on the S end of the Malay Peninsula: formerly a British colony, it became independent & a member of the Commonwealth (1957); since 1963 a territory of Malaysia called PENINSULAR MALAYSIA: see MALAYSIA

Mal·a·ya·lam (mal′ə yä′ləm) ***n.*** ⟦Malayalam *malayālam*⟧ a Dravidian language spoken on the Malabar Coast of SW India

Ma·lay·an (mə lā′ən) ***adj.*** *var. of* MALAY —***n.*** any of a breed of domestic cat related to the Burmese, differing only in the color of the coat, which is solid but in any of several lighter shades

Malay Archipelago large group of islands between Southeast Asia & Australia, including Indonesia, the Philippines, &, sometimes, New Guinea

Ma·lay·o- (mə lā′ō) *combining form* Malay and

Ma·lay·o-Pol·y·ne·sian (mə lā′ō päl′ə nē′zhən, -shən) ***n., adj.*** AUSTRONESIAN

Malay Peninsula peninsula in Southeast Asia, extending from Singapore to the Isthmus of Kra: it includes Peninsular Malaysia & part of Thailand: *c.* 700 mi (1,127 km) long

Ma·lay·sia (mə lā′zhə, -shə) **1** MALAY ARCHIPELAGO **2** country in Southeast Asia: a union (1963) of the former Federation of MALAYA, Sabah, Sarawak, & Singapore (which seceded in 1965 to become an independent nation); member of the Commonwealth: 127,317 sq mi (329,750 sq km); cap. Kuala Lumpur —**Ma·lay′sian** ***adj., n.***

Mal·colm (mal′kəm) ***n.*** ⟦Celt *Maolcolm,* lit., servant of Saint COLUMBA[2]⟧ a masculine name

Malcolm X (eks) (born *Malcolm Little*) 1925-65; U.S. political activist & leader in the Nation of Islam organization: assassinated

mal·con·tent (mal′kən tent′) ***adj.*** ⟦OFr: see MAL- & CONTENT[1]⟧ discontented, dissatisfied, or rebellious: applied esp. to critics of the government —***n.*** a discontented, dissatisfied, or rebellious person, esp. one who is habitually so

mal de mer (màl də mer′) ⟦Fr⟧ seasickness

mal·de·vel·op·ment (mal′di vel′əp mənt) ***n.*** MALFORMATION —**mal′de·vel′oped** ***adj.***

mal·dis·tri·bu·tion (mal′dis trə byo͞o′shən) ***n.*** inadequate or faulty distribution, as of wealth or income among people

Mal·dives (môl′dīvz′) country on a group of islands in the Indian Ocean, southwest of Sri Lanka: a former sultanate under British protection, it became independent in 1965, a republic in 1968, & a member of the Commonwealth in 1982: 116 sq mi (300 sq km); cap. Malé —**Mal·div·i·an** (môl div′ē ən) ***adj., n.***

male (māl) ***adj.*** ⟦ME < OFr *male, masle* < L *masculus* < *mas* (gen. *maris*), a male, man⟧ **1** designating or of the sex that fertilizes the ovum of the female and begets offspring: biological symbol, ♂: cf. FEMALE **2** of, characteristic of, or suitable for members of this sex; masculine; virile **3** consisting of men or boys **4** designating or having a part shaped to fit into a corresponding hollow part (called *female*): said of pipe fittings, electric plugs, etc. **5** *Bot. a)* having stamens or antheridia, but no carpels, archegonia, or oogonia *b)* designating or of a reproductive structure or part producing spermatozoids that can fertilize the female eggs —***n.*** **1** a male person; man or boy **2** a male animal or plant —**male′ness** ***n.***

SYN.—male is the basic term applied to members of the sex that is biologically distinguished from the female sex and is used of animals and plants as well as of human beings; **masculine** is applied to qualities, such as strength and vigor, traditionally ascribed to men, or to things appropriate to men; **manly** suggests the noble qualities, such as courage and independence, that a culture ideally associates with a man who has maturity of character; **mannish**, used chiefly of women, is most often used derogatorily and implies the possession or adoption of the traits and manners thought to be more appropriate to a man; **virile** stresses qualities such as robustness, vigor, and, specif., sexual potency, that belong to a physically mature man

Ma·lé (mä′lā) chief island & capital of the Maldives: also **Ma·le** (mä′lē)

Ma·le·bo Pool (mä lā′bō) broad, lakelike expansion of the Congo River between the Democratic Republic of the Congo & the Republic of the Congo: *c.* 116 sq mi (300 sq km)

Male·branche (mȧl bränsh′, mȧ lə-), **Ni·co·las (de)** (nē kō̂ lä′) 1638-1715; Fr. philosopher

☆**male chauvinist pig** [Slang] a man who is perceived as approving of an inferior status for women in society: a disparaging term

mal·e·dict (mal′ə dikt′) [Archaic] ***adj.*** ⟦L *maledictus,* pp. of *maledicere:* see fol.⟧ accursed; hateful —***vt.*** to curse

mal·e·dic·tion (mal′ə dik′shən) ***n.*** ⟦ME *malediccioun* < OFr *malediction* < LL(Ec) *maledictio* < L, abuse, reviling: see MAL- & DICTION⟧ **1** a calling down of evil on someone; curse **2** evil talk about someone; slander —**mal′e·dic′to·ry** ***adj.***

mal·e·fac·tion (mal′ə fak′shən) ***n.*** ⟦LL *malefactio* < pp. of *malefacere:* see fol.⟧ wrongdoing; crime

mal·e·fac·tor (mal′ə fak′tər) ***n.*** ⟦L < pp. of *malefacere* < *male,* evil (see MAL-) + *facere,* to DO[1]⟧ an evildoer or criminal

male fern a fern (*Dryopteris filix-mas*) of the Northern Hemisphere: source of an oleoresin used to expel tapeworms

ma·lef·ic (mə lef′ik) ***adj.*** ⟦L *maleficus* < *malefacere:* see MALEFACTOR⟧ causing disaster; harmful; evil

ma·lef·i·cent (mə lef′ə sənt) ***adj.*** ⟦back-form. < *maleficence* < L *maleficentia* < *maleficus:* see prec.⟧ harmful; hurtful; evil —**ma·lef′i·cence** ***n.***

ma·le·ic acid (mə lē′ik) ⟦< Fr *maléique,* altered (1834) by T. J. Pelouze (1807-67), Fr chemist < *malique,* MALIC (ACID), to indicate a relationship between the two acids⟧ a colorless, crystalline, poisonous acid, HOOCCH: CHCOOH, an isomer of fumaric acid, used in organic syntheses, in textile dyeing, etc.

maleic hydrazide a slightly soluble solid, $C_4H_4N_2O_2$, used to inhibit plant growth, to stop the sprouting of vegetables in storage, etc.

☆**mal·e·mute** or **mal·e·miut** (mal′ə myo͞ot′) ***n.*** *alt. sp. of* MALAMUTE

mal·en·ten·du (mȧ län tän dü′) ***adj.*** ⟦Fr⟧ misunderstood; poorly conceived —***n.*** a misunderstanding

male-pat·tern baldness (māl′pat′ərn) inherited baldness characterized by the loss of hair from the front and top of the head: see also ALOPECIA: often written **male pattern baldness**

male-pattern baldness

ma·lev·o·lence (mə lev′ə ləns) ***n.*** ⟦ME *malyvolence* < OFr *malivolence* < L *malevolentia*⟧ the quality or state of being malevolent; malice; spitefulness; ill will

ma·lev·o·lent (-lənt) ***adj.*** ⟦OFr *malivolent* < L *malevolens* (gen. *malevolentis*) < *male,* evil (see MAL-) + *volens,* prp. of *velle,* to wish: see WILL[2]⟧ wishing evil or harm to others; having or showing ill will; malicious —**ma·lev′o·lent·ly** ***adv.***

mal·fea·sance (mal fē′zəns) ***n.*** ⟦obs. Fr *malfaisance* < *malfaisant* < *mal,* evil (see MAL-) + *faisant,* prp. of *faire* < L *facere,* to DO[1]⟧ wrongdoing or misconduct, esp. by a public official; commission of an act that is positively unlawful: distinguished from MISFEASANCE, NONFEASANCE —**mal·fea′sant** ***adj.***

mal·for·ma·tion (mal′fôr mā′shən) ***n.*** faulty, irregular, or abnormal formation or structure of a body or part —**mal·formed′** (-fôrmd′) ***adj.***

mal·func·tion (mal fuŋk′shən) ***vi.*** ⟦MAL- + FUNCTION⟧ to fail to function as it should —***n.*** the act or an instance of malfunctioning

Ma·li (mä′lē) country in W Africa, south & east of Mauritania: a former French territory (FRENCH SUDAN), it joined the French Community as the autonomous *Sudanese Republic* (1958); it joined with Senegal to form the **Mali Federation** (1959); union dissolved & full independence proclaimed (1960): 478,767 sq mi (1,240,000 sq km); cap. Bamako

Mal·i·bu (mal′ə bo͞o′) ⟦< native name for the region⟧ city in SW Calif., on the Pacific

mal·ic acid (mal′ik, mā′lik) ⟦Fr *acide malique* < L *malum,* apple < Gr *mēlon*⟧ a crystalline acid, $COOHCH_2CH(OH)COOH$, occurring in apples and other fruits

mal·ice (mal′is) ***n.*** ⟦OFr < L *malitia* < *malus,* bad: see MAL-⟧ **1** active ill will; desire to harm another or to do mischief; spite **2** *Law* evil intent; state of mind shown by intention to do, or intentional doing of, something unlawful —**malice aforethought (**or **prepense)** a deliberate intention and plan to do something unlawful, as murder

ma·li·cious (mə lish′əs) ***adj.*** ⟦ME < OFr *malicios* < L *malitiosus* < *malitia:* see prec.⟧ having, showing, or caused by malice; spiteful; intentionally mischievous or harmful —**ma·li′cious·ly** ***adv.*** —**ma·li′cious·ness** ***n.***

malicious mischief the willful destruction of another's property

ma·lign (mə līn′) ***vt.*** ⟦ME *malignen* < OFr *malignier,* to plot, deceive < LL *malignare* < LL *malignus,* wicked, malicious < *male,* ill (see MAL-) + base of *genus,* born: see GENUS⟧ to speak evil of; defame; slander; traduce —***adj.*** **1** showing ill will; malicious **2** evil; baleful [*a malign* influence] **3** very harmful; malignant —**SYN.** SINISTER —**ma·lign′er** ***n.***

ma·lig·nan·cy (mə lig′nən sē) ***n.*** **1** the quality or condition of being malignant: also **ma·lig′nance** **2** *pl.* **-cies** a malignant tumor

ma·lig·nant (-nənt) ***adj.*** ⟦LL *malignans* (gen. *malignantis*), prp. of *malignare:* see MALIGN⟧ **1** having an evil influence; malign **2** wishing evil; very malevolent or malicious **3** very harmful, dangerous, or virulent **4** *a)* causing or likely to cause death *b)* not benign; specif., cancerous **5** [Obs.]

malcontent; rebellious; disaffected —*n.* [Archaic] a malcontent —**ma·lig′nant·ly** *adv.*

ma·lig·ni·ty (-nə tē) *n.* ⟦ME *malignitee* < OFr *malignité* < L *malignitas:* see MALIGN⟧ 1 persistent, intense ill will or desire to harm others; great malice 2 the quality of being very harmful or dangerous; malignancy 3 *pl.* **-ties** a malignant act, event, or feeling

☆**ma·li·hi·ni** (mä′lə hē′nē) *n.* ⟦Haw⟧ a newcomer to Hawaii

ma·lines (mə lēn′; *Fr* må lēn′) *n.* ⟦Fr, after fol.⟧ 1 MECHLIN[2] 2 a thin, somewhat stiff, silk net used in dressmaking, etc.: also sp. **ma·line′**

Ma·lines (må lēn′) *Fr. name for* MECHELEN

ma·lin·ger (mə liŋ′gər) *vi.* ⟦< Fr *malingre,* sickly, infirm < *mal,* bad (see MAL-) + ? OFr *heingre,* lean, haggard⟧ to pretend to be ill or otherwise incapacitated in order to escape duty or work; shirk —**ma·lin′ger·er** *n.*

Ma·lin·ke (mä′liŋ kā′) *n.* 1 *pl.* **-kes′** or **-ke′** a member of a Mande people of WC Africa 2 the Mande language of this people

Ma·li·now·ski (mä′lə nôf′skē), **Bro·ni·slaw (Kaspar)** (brô′nə släf′) 1884-1942; U.S. anthropologist, born in Poland

mal·i·son (mal′ə zən, -sən) *n.* ⟦ME < OFr *maleison* < L *maledictio:* see MALEDICTION⟧ [Archaic] a curse

mal·kin (mô′kin) *n.* ⟦ME *malkyn,* orig. dim. of *Malde,* Maud, dim. of *Matilda*⟧ [Archaic or Brit. Dial.] 1 a slovenly or sluttish woman 2 a mop 3 a scarecrow 4 a hare 5 a cat

mall (môl, mäl) *n.* ⟦var. of MAUL, esp. assoc. in 17th c. with (PALL)-MALL⟧ 1 [Historical] *a)* a large, heavy mallet, used to strike the ball in the game of pall-mall *b)* ⟦< PALL-MALL⟧ the game itself *c)* a lane or alley where the game was played 2 a shaded walk or public promenade ☆3 *a)* a street for pedestrians only, with shops on each side, and often with decorative plantings, benches, etc. *b)* a completely enclosed, air-conditioned shopping center like this 4 a median strip: see MEDIAN (*n.* 3)

mal·lard (mal′ərd) *n., pl.* **-lards** or **-lard** ⟦ME < OFr *malart* < **maslart* < *masle:* see MALE⟧ the common wild duck (*Anas platyrhynchos*), from which the domestic duck is descended: the male has a green or bluish-black head, a thin band of white around the neck, and a rusty breast

Mal·lar·mé (må lår mā′), **Sté·phane** (stā fån′) 1842-98; Fr. symbolist poet

mal·le·a·ble (mal′ē ə bəl) *adj.* ⟦ME *malliable* < ML *malleabilis* < L *malleare,* to beat with a hammer < *malleus,* a hammer < IE base **mel-,* to grind, beat > MILL[1]⟧ 1 that can be hammered, pounded, or pressed into various shapes without breaking: said of metals 2 capable of being changed, molded, trained, etc.; adaptable —SYN. PLIABLE —**mal′le·a·bil′i·ty** *n.,* **mal′le·a·ble·ness**

malleable iron cast iron made from pig iron by long heating at a high temperature and slow cooling: it is especially strong and malleable: also **malleable cast iron**

mal·lee (mal′ē) *n.* ⟦native name in Australia⟧ 1 any of several shrubby species of Australian eucalyptus (as *Eucalyptus dumosa* and *E. oleosa*) 2 in Australia, dense thicket formed by such plants

mal·le·muck (mal′ə muk′) *n.* ⟦Du *mallemok* < *mal,* foolish + *mok,* a gull⟧ any of the large, docile, tubenose ocean birds

mal·le·o·lus (mə lē′ə ləs) *n., pl.* **-li′** (-lī′) ⟦L, dim. of *malleus,* a hammer: see MALLEABLE⟧ the rounded, bony protuberance on each side of the ankle joint —**mal·le′o·lar** *adj.*

mal·let (mal′it) *n.* ⟦ME *malyet* < MFr *maillet,* dim. of *mail* < OFr *maile:* see MAUL⟧ 1 a kind of hammer, usually with a heavy wooden head and a short handle, for driving a chisel, etc. 2 *a)* a long-handled hammer with a cylindrical wooden head, used in playing croquet *b)* a similar instrument, but with a longer, flexible handle, used in playing polo 3 a small, light hammer, usually with a felt-covered head, used for playing a vibraphone, xylophone, etc.

mal·le·us (mal′ē əs) *n., pl.* **-le·i′** (-ē ī′) ⟦L, a hammer: see MALLEABLE⟧ the largest and outermost of the three small bones in the middle ear of mammals, shaped somewhat like a hammer

☆**mall·ing** (môl′iŋ, mäl′-) *n.* [Informal] 1 ⟦prob. partially a pun on *mauling*⟧ the construction of indoor shopping malls: often used to suggest an undesirable proliferation of such malls 2 the act or an instance of shopping or spending time at a shopping mall

Ma·llor·ca (mäl yôr′kä, mä-) *Sp. name for* MAJORCA

mal·low (mal′ō) *n.* ⟦ME *malwe* < OE *mealuwe* < L *malva* (> Ger *malve,* Fr *mauve*): see MALACHITE⟧ 1 any of a genus (*Malva*) of plants of the mallow family, with dissected or lobed leaves 2 any of various other plants of the mallow family, as the marsh mallow or rose mallow —*adj.* designating a family (Malvaceae, order Malvales) of dicotyledonous plants, including the hollyhock, cotton, marsh mallow, and okra, typically having large, showy flowers with many stamens borne on a tube, and a sticky juice in their stems, leaves, and roots

mallow rose ROSE MALLOW

mall rat [Slang] a young person who loiters about shopping malls

malm (mäm) *n.* ⟦ME *malme* < OE *mealm-,* sand, akin to Goth *malma,* sand, ON *malmr,* ore < IE base **mel-,* to grind > MILL[1]⟧ 1 [Brit.] *a)* a soft, crumbly, grayish-white limestone *b)* a soft, chalky loam formed from this 2 a mixture of clay and chalk used in making bricks

Malmes·bur·y (mämz′bər ē, -brē), **William of** *see* WILLIAM OF MALMESBURY

Malm·ö (mälm′ö; *E* mal′mō) seaport in S Sweden, on the Öresund

malm·sey (mäm′zē) *n.* ⟦ME *malmesey* < ML *malmasia* < *Malmasia* < Gr *Monembasia,* Monemvasia, or Malvasia, small town on the coast of Laconia, Greece, formerly noted for exporting wine⟧ 1 the darkest and sweetest type of Madeira 2 the white grape from which this is made 3 any other wine made from this grape

mal·nour·ished (mal nʉr′isht) *adj.* improperly nourished

mal·nu·tri·tion (mal′no͞o trish′ən) *n.* inadequate nutrition; poor nourishment resulting from insufficient food, improper diet, etc.

mal·oc·clu·sion (-ə klo͞o′zhən) *n.* improper meeting of the upper and lower teeth; faulty occlusion

mal·o·dor (mal ō′dər) *n.* a bad odor; stench

mal·o·dor·ous (-ō′dər əs) *adj.* having a bad odor; stinking —**mal·o′dor·ous·ly** *adv.* —**mal·o′dor·ous·ness** *n.*

Ma·lone (mə lōn′), **Edmund (or Edmond)** 1741-1812; Ir. literary critic & editor of Shakespeare's works

ma·lo·nic acid (mə lō′nik, -län′ik) ⟦Fr *malonique,* altered < *malique:* see MALIC ACID⟧ a crystalline, dibasic acid, $HOOCCH_2COOH$, obtained from malic acid by oxidation and used in synthesizing barbiturates

Mal·o·ry (mal′ə rē), Sir **Thomas** died 1471?; Eng. writer: author of *Morte Darthur,* the first comprehensive prose account in English of the Arthurian legend

ma·lo·ti (mə lo͞o′tē) *n. pl. of* LOTI

Mal·pi·ghi (mäl pē′gē), **Mar·cel·lo** (mär chel′lô) 1628-94; It. physiologist & pioneer in microscopic anatomy —**Mal·pigh·i·an** (mal pig′ē ən) *adj.*

mal·pigh·i·a (mal pig′ē ə) *adj.* ⟦after prec.⟧ designating a family (Malpighiaceae, order Polygalales) of dicotyledonous tropical trees, shrubs, and vines

Malpighian body (*or* corpuscle) 1 any nodule of lymphatic tissue in the spleen 2 any of a number of small masses of blood vessels in the kidney, enclosed by a capsule that is an enlargement of the end of a tubule through which urine passes

Malpighian layer the soft, lowest layer of the epidermis, from which the outer layers are formed

Malpighian tubules a group of small, tubular, excretory and water-regulating glands that open into the hind part of the alimentary canal in most insects and spiders

mal·po·si·tion (mal′pə zish′ən) *n.* faulty or abnormal position, esp. of the fetus in the uterus

mal·prac·tice (mal prak′tis) *n.* 1 injurious or unprofessional treatment or culpable neglect of a patient by a physician or surgeon 2 misconduct or improper practice in any professional or official position —**mal′prac·ti′tion·er** (-tish′ən ər) *n.*

Mal·raux (mål rō′), **An·dré** (än drā′) 1901-76; Fr. writer & art historian

malt (môlt) *n.* ⟦ME *malte* < OE *mealt,* akin to Ger *malz* < IE **mel-d,* soft < base **mel-,* to crush, grind > MELT, MILL[1]⟧ 1 barley or other grain softened by soaking in water until it sprouts and then kiln-dried: used for brewing and distilling certain alcoholic beverages or liquors 2 a beverage or liquor made from malt, esp. beer, ale, or the like ☆3 [Informal] MALTED MILK —*adj.* made with malt —*vt.* 1 to change (barley, etc.) into malt or something maltlike 2 to treat or prepare (milk, etc.) with malt or malt extract —*vi.* 1 to be changed into malt or something maltlike 2 to change barley, etc. into malt

Mal·ta (môl′tə) 1 country on a group of islands in the Mediterranean, south of Sicily: a former British colony, it became independent & a member of the Commonwealth (1964): 122 sq mi (316 sq km); cap. Valletta 2 main island of this group: 95 sq mi (246 sq km)

Malta fever ⟦so named because prevalent in Malta and nearby areas⟧ UNDULANT FEVER

malt·ase (môl′tās′) *n.* ⟦MALT + -ASE⟧ an enzyme found in the small intestine, in yeast, etc., that hydrolyzes maltose into glucose

☆**malt·ed milk** (môlt′id) 1 a powdered preparation of dried milk and malted cereals 2 a drink made by mixing this with milk and, usually, ice cream and flavoring: also **malted** *n.*

Mal·tese (môl tēz′, -tēs′; *for adj., also* môl′tēz′, -tēs′) *adj.* 1 of Malta or its people, language, or culture 2 of the medieval Knights of Malta —*n.* 1 *pl.* **-tese′** a person born or living in Malta 2 the Semitic language spoken in Malta, closely related to Arabic, strongly influenced by Italian, and written in the Latin alphabet 3 *pl.* **-tese′** *a)* any of a breed of toy dog with a coat of long, silky, white hair that hangs nearly to the ground and with a tail that curls over the back *b)* any of a variety of shorthaired domestic cat with bluish-gray fur

Maltese cross ⟦from its use as an emblem by the medieval Knights of *Malta:* see HOSPITALER⟧ 1 a cross whose arms look like arrowheads pointing inward 2 a perennial garden flower (*Lychnis chalcedonica*) of the pink family, having brilliant-red flowers with five heart-shaped lobes

malt extract a sticky, sugary substance obtained from malt soaked in water: it is used as a medicinal food

mal·tha (mal′thə) *n.* ⟦L < Gr, mixture of wax and pitch < IE **meldh-,* become soft < base **mel-,* to grind > MILL[1]⟧ 1 any of several black, semisolid bitumens between petroleum and asphalt in consistency 2 any of several natural, viscous hydrocarbon mixtures, as ozocerite

Mal·thus (mal′thəs), **Thomas Robert** 1766-1834; Eng. economist

Mal·thu·sian (mal tho͞o′zhən, -zē ən) *adj.* of Malthus and his theory that the world population tends to increase faster than the food supply with inevitable disastrous results unless natural restrictions, such as war, famine, and disease, reduce the population or the increase is checked by moral restraint —**Mal·thu′sian·ism′** *n.*

malt liquor beer, ale, or the like made from malt by fermentation

malt·ose (môl′tōs′) *n.* ⟦MALT + -OSE[2]⟧ a white, crystalline, dextrorotatory disaccharide obtained by the action of the diastase of malt on starch

mal·treat (mal trēt′) *vt.* ⟦Fr *maltraiter:* see MAL- & TREAT⟧ to treat roughly or unkindly; abuse —**mal·treat′ment** *n.*

malt·ster (môlt′stər) ***n.*** one who makes or sells malt

malt sugar MALTOSE

malt·y (môl′tē) ***adj.*** **malt′i·er, malt′i·est** of, like, or containing malt

Ma·lu·ku (mə lo͞o′ko͞o) *Indonesian name for* MOLUCCAS

mal·va·si·a (mal′və sē′ə) ***n.*** ⟦It: see MALMSEY⟧ MALMSEY —**mal′va·si′an** ***adj.***

Mal·vern Hill (mal′vərn) ⟦after *Malvern Hills,* England⟧ plateau near Richmond, Va.: site of a battle (1862) of the Civil War in which Union troops repulsed Confederate attacks but withdrew the next day

mal·ver·sa·tion (mal′vər sā′shən) ***n.*** ⟦Fr < *malverser,* to commit malpractices < L *male,* badly (see MAL-) + *versari,* to turn, occupy oneself < *versus* (see VERSE)⟧ *Law* corrupt conduct or fraudulent practices, as in public office

Mal·vi·nas (mäl vē′näs) *Sp. (specif., Argentine) name for* FALKLAND ISLANDS

mal·ware (mal′wer′) ***n.*** ⟦*mal*(*icious soft*)*ware*⟧ any unauthorized program or set of instructions, as a virus, worm, or Trojan horse, designed to disrupt the normal functioning of a computer

ma·ma (mä′mə; *for 1, also* mə mä′) ***n.*** ⟦like L *mamma,* mother, Sans *mā,* Gr *mammē* < baby talk⟧ **1** [Informal] MOTHER[1] ☆**2** [Slang] a woman

ma·ma·li·ga (mä′mä lē′gə) ***n.*** ⟦Romanian *mămăligă*⟧ a traditional Romanian porridge of cornmeal

ma·ma's boy (mä′məz) [Informal] a boy or man regarded as unduly attached or submissive to his mother

mam·ba (mäm′bə) ***n.*** ⟦Zulu *imamba*⟧ any of a genus (*Dendroaspis*) of extremely poisonous, elapine, African tree snakes similar to the cobras but not hooded; esp., a long, green E African snake (*D. angusticeps*)

☆**mam·bo** (mäm′bō) ***n.,*** *pl.* **-bos** ⟦AmSp: musicians' slang term equivalent to "riff"⟧ **1** a rhythmic musical form, of Caribbean origin, in 4/4 syncopated time with a heavy accent on the second and fourth beats **2** a ballroom dance to such music —***vi.*** to dance the mambo

Mam·e·luke (mam′ə lo͞ok′) ***n.*** ⟦obs Fr *mameluk* < Ar *mamlūk,* slave, lit., one possessed < *malaka,* to possess⟧ **1** a member of a military caste, orig. made up of slaves, that ruled in Egypt from 1250 until 1517 and remained powerful until 1811 **2** [**m-**] in Muslim countries, a slave Also **Mam·luk** (mam′lo͞ok′)

ma·mey (mä mā′, -mē′) ***n.*** *alt. sp. of* MAMMEE

mam·ma[1] (mä′mə, mə mä′) ***n.*** *alt. sp. of* MAMA

mam·ma[2] (mam′ə) ***n.,*** *pl.* **-mae** (-ē) ⟦L, breast, prob. identical with prec.: see also MAMA⟧ a gland for secreting milk, present in the female of all mammals; mammary gland: it is rudimentary in the male

mam·mal (mam′əl) ***n.*** ⟦< ModL *Mammalia* < LL *mammalis,* of the breasts < L *mamma:* see prec.⟧ any of a large class (Mammalia) of warmblooded, usually hairy vertebrates whose offspring are fed with milk secreted by the female mammary glands —**mam·ma·li·an** (mə mā′lē ən, -mal′yən; ma-) ***adj., n.***

mam·mal·o·gy (mə mal′ə jē, ma-) ***n.*** the branch of zoology dealing with mammals —**mam·mal′o·gist** ***n.***

mam·ma·plas·ty (mam′ə plas′tē) ***n.*** ⟦MAMMA[2] + -PLASTY⟧ plastic surgery to alter the size or shape of the breasts

mam·ma·ry (mam′ə rē) ***adj.*** designating or of the milk-secreting glands; of the mammae —***n.,*** *pl.* **-ries** [Informal] a female breast

mam·mee (mä mā′, -mē′) ***n.*** ⟦Sp *mamey* < Taino⟧ **1** *a)* any of a genus (*Mammea*) of West Indian trees of the St. Johnswort family; specif., a tall, tropical, American tree (*M. americana*) bearing a large, russet, apricot-flavored fruit (also **mammee apple**) *b)* the fruit **2** MARMALADE TREE Also sp. **mam·mey′**

mam·mif·er·ous (ma mif′ər əs, mə-) ***adj.*** ⟦see -FEROUS⟧ having mammae, or breasts

mam·mil·la (ma mil′ə, mə-) ***n.,*** *pl.* **-lae** (-ē) ⟦L *mam(m)illa,* dim. of *mamma:* see MAMMA[2]⟧ **1** a nipple **2** any nipple-shaped or breast-shaped protuberance —**mam·mil·lar·y** (mam′ə ler′ē) ***adj.***

mam·mil·late (mam′ə lāt′) ***adj.*** **1** having mammillae **2** nipple-shaped Also **mam′mil·lat′ed** —**mam′mil·la′tion** ***n.***

mam·mock (mam′ək) [Now Chiefly Dial.] ***n.*** ⟦< ?⟧ a fragment; shred; scrap —***vt.*** to break or tear into fragments or shreds

mam·mo·gram (mam′ə gram′) ***n.*** ⟦< MAMMA[2] + -O- + -GRAM⟧ an X-ray obtained by mammography

mam·mog·ra·phy (mə mäg′rə fē, ma-) ***n.*** ⟦< MAMMA[2] + -GRAPHY⟧ an X-ray technique for the detection of breast tumors

mam·mon (mam′ən) ***n.*** ⟦ME *mammon(as)* < LL(Ec) < Gr(Ec) *mammōnas* (see Matt. 6:24) < Aram *māmōnā,* riches, prob. < *mā'mon,* that which is made secure or deposited < *'amān,* to trust⟧ [*often* **M-**] riches regarded as an object of worship and greedy pursuit; wealth or material gain as an evil, more or less deified —**mam′mon·ism′** ***n.***

mam·moth (mam′əth) ***n.*** ⟦altered < Russ *mamont, mamot* < ?⟧ any of a genus (*Mammuthus*) of extinct elephants with a hairy skin and long tusks curving upward: remains have been found in North America, Europe, and Asia: cf. MASTODON —☆***adj.*** very big; huge; enormous —***SYN.*** ENORMOUS

mam·my (mam′ē) ***n.,*** *pl.* **-mies** ⟦dial. var. of MAMA⟧ [Chiefly Dial.] **1** *child's term for* MOTHER[1] ☆**2** [Historical] a black woman responsible for the care of white children, esp. in the South

mammy wagon (*or* bus) ⟦< ?⟧ a small, open, brightly decorated bus or truck used for public transportation in W Africa

Ma·mo·ré (mä′mô *re*′) river in NC Bolivia, flowing north to join the Beni & form the Madeira: *c.* 1,200 mi (1,931 km)

man (man) ***n.,*** *pl.* **men** (men) ⟦ME < OE *mann,* akin to Ger *mann,* Goth *manna* < IE base **manu-* (> Sans *mánu-,* Russ *muž*); ? akin to IE **men-,* to think > MIND⟧ **1** a human being; person; specif., *a)* a hominid (*Homo sapiens*) having an opposable thumb, the ability to make and use specialized tools, articulate speech, and a highly developed brain with the faculty of abstract thought: the only living hominid *b)* any extinct hominid, as Neanderthal man **2** the human race; mankind: used without *the* or *a* **3** *a)* an adult male human being *b)* sometimes, a boy **4** *a)* an adult male servant, follower, attendant, or subordinate *b)* a male employee; workman *c)* [*usually pl.*] a soldier, sailor, etc.; esp., one of the rank and file *d)* [Archaic] a vassal **5** *a)* a husband *b)* a male lover **6** a person with qualities conventionally regarded as manly, such as strength, courage, etc. **7** a player on a team **8** any of the pieces used in chess, checkers, etc. **9** [Slang] a man or boy; fellow: used in direct address **10** *Naut.* a ship: used in compounds [*man*-of-war, *merchantman*] —***vt.*** **manned, man′ning 1** to furnish with a labor force for work, defense, etc. [to *man* a ship] **2** to take assigned places in, on, or at for work or defense [*man* the guns!] **3** to strengthen; brace; fortify; nerve [to *man* oneself for an ordeal] **4** *Falconry* to tame or accustom (a hawk) to the presence of men —***interj.*** [Slang] **1** used to provide emphasis **2** used in a neutral way to preface or resume one's remarks —***adj.*** male —**as a (or one) man** in unison; unanimously —**be one's own man** to be free and independent —**man and boy** first as a boy and then as a man; since childhood —☆**the Man** [Slang] **1** the person having power or authority over one; esp., as orig. used by U.S. blacks, a white man or white men collectively **2** *a)* a policeman *b)* the police —**to a man** with no one as an exception; everyone

Man[1] (man), **Isle of** one of the British Isles, between Northern Ireland & England: 221 sq mi (572 sq km); cap. Douglas

Man[2] *abbrev.* **1** Manila (paper) **2** Manitoba

-man (mən, man) *combining form* man or person of a (specified) kind, in a (specified) activity, etc.: now often replaced by -PERSON or -WOMAN to avoid the masculine implication: pl. form -MEN

ma·na (mä′nä) ***n.*** ⟦native Polynesian term⟧ in some indigenous beliefs, as in Polynesia, a dynamic supernatural power or influence dwelling in and flowing from certain individuals, spirits, or things and capable of producing great good or evil

man about town a worldly man who spends much time in fashionable restaurants, clubs, etc.

man·a·cle (man′ə kəl) ***n.*** ⟦ME *manicle* < OFr < L *manicula,* dim. of *manus,* hand: see MANUAL⟧ **1** a handcuff; fetter or shackle for the hand **2** any restraint *Usually used in pl.* —***vt.*** **-cled, -cling 1** to put handcuffs on; fetter **2** to restrain; hamper

man·age (man′ij) ***vt.*** **-aged, -ag·ing** ⟦It *maneggiare* < *mano,* hand < L *manus:* see MANUAL⟧ **1** [Obs.] to train (a horse) in its paces; cause to do the exercises of the manège **2** to control the movement or behavior of; handle **3** to have charge of; direct; administer [to *manage* a household] **4** [Rare] to use carefully; husband **5** to get (a person) to do what one wishes, esp. by skill, tact, flattery, etc. **6** to bring about by contriving; succeed in accomplishing: often used ironically [he *managed* to make a mess of it] —***vi.*** **1** to conduct or direct affairs; carry on business **2** to find ways to go on functioning; get along somehow; succeed in handling matters —***n.*** ⟦It *maneggio* < *maneggiare:* infl. by Fr *ménage:* see MÉNAGE⟧ [Archaic] MANÈGE —***SYN.*** CONDUCT

man·age·a·ble (man′ij ə bəl) ***adj.*** that can be managed; controllable, tractable, contrivable, etc. —**man′age·a·bil′i·ty** ***n.,*** **man′age·a·ble·ness** —**man′age·a·bly** ***adv.***

managed care any healthcare plan or system, as an HMO or PPO, in which limitations are placed on the fees charged by member physicians and facilities

managed currency a currency regulated by various governmental agencies through procedures that alter the amount of money in circulation so as to control credit, the price structure, etc.

man·age·ment (man′ij mənt) ***n.*** **1** the act, art, or manner of managing, or handling, controlling, directing, etc. **2** skillful managing; careful, tactful treatment **3** skill in managing; executive ability **4** *a)* the person or persons managing a business, institution, etc. *b)* such persons collectively, regarded as a distinct social group, often as opposed to LABOR (*n.* 3*a* or 4)

man·ag·er (man′ij ər) ***n.*** a person who manages; esp., *a)* one who manages a business, institution, etc. *b)* one who manages affairs or expenditures, as of a household, a client (as an entertainer or athlete), an athletic team, etc. ☆*c)* *Baseball* the person in overall charge of a team and its strategy during games, practice sessions, etc. *d)* in a school or college, a student in charge of the equipment and records of a team under the supervision of a coach —**man′ag·er·ship′** ***n.***

man·ag·er·ess (man′i jə ris) ***n.*** a female manager: see -ESS

man·a·ge·ri·al (man′ə jir′ē əl) ***adj.*** **1** of, like, or characteristic of a manager **2** of management —**man′a·ge′ri·al·ism′** ***n.*** —**man′a·ge′ri·al·ly** ***adv.***

☆**managing editor** an editor having certain supervisory responsibilities over the editorial staff of a publication or publisher

Ma·na·gua (mä nä′gwä) **1** capital of Nicaragua, in the W part, on Lake Managua **2 Lake** lake in W Nicaragua: *c.* 390 sq mi (1,010 sq km)

man·a·kin (man′ə kin) ***n.*** ⟦var. of MANIKIN⟧ **1** any of a family (Pipridae) of brightly colored, small passerine birds of Central and South America, with short beaks **2** *alt. sp. of* MANIKIN

Ma·na·ma (mə nam′ə) capital of Bahrain, in the N part

ma·ña·na (mə nyä′nə) ***n.*** ⟦Sp < VL **maneana* < L (*cras*) *mane,* (tomorrow) morning, orig. loc. of *manis,* good (in sense "in good time"), akin to *ma-*

nus, good < IE base *mā, good, early > L *maturus,* ripe, mature⟧ tomorrow —*adv.* 1 tomorrow 2 at an unspecified time in the future

Ma·nas·sas (mə nas′əs) ⟦< ?⟧ city in NE Va., near Bull Run: site of two Civil War battles in which Union forces were defeated

Ma·nas·seh (mə nas′ə) *n.* ⟦Heb *mĕnaṣṣeh,* lit., causing to forget⟧ 1 *Bible* the elder son of Joseph: Gen. 41:52 2 the tribe of Israel descended from him: Num. 1:34 3 a king of Judah in the 7th cent. B.C. 2 Kings 21:1-18 4 PRAYER OF MANASSES

ma·nat (mə nät′) *n.* ⟦Azerbaijani & Turkmen name⟧ the basic monetary unit of Azerbaijan and Turkmenistan: see the table of monetary units in the Reference Supplement

man-at-arms (man′at ärmz′) *n., pl.* **men′-at-arms′** (men′-) a soldier; esp., a heavily armed medieval soldier on horseback

man·a·tee (man′ə tē′, man′ə tē′) *n.* ⟦Sp *manatí* < name in a Carib language⟧ any of a family (Trichechidae) of sirenians living in shallow tropical waters near the coasts of North and South America and W Africa

Ma·naus (mä nous′) city in NW Brazil, on the Negro River: capital of Amazonas state

☆**man cave** a recreation room furnished primarily for use by a man or men: a humorous usage

Man·ches·ter (man′ches′tər, -chi stər) 1 city & port in NW England, connected by canal (**Manchester Ship Canal**), 35 mi (56 km) long, with the Irish Sea 2 GREATER MANCHESTER 3 ⟦after Eng city⟧ city in S N.H., on the Merrimack River

Manchester terrier any of a breed of terrier, orig. bred in Manchester, England, with a short, glossy coat, black with tan markings: the two varieties (*standard* and *toy*) differ mainly in size

man·chet (man′chət) *n.* ⟦ME *manchete* < *maine* (same sense), aphetic < OFr *paindemaine* < L *panis dominicus,* lit., lord's bread + *chet* < Anglo-Fr, wheat bread of lower quality < ?⟧ [Archaic] a roll or small loaf of white bread made of the finest wheat flour

man-child (man′chīld′) *n., pl.* **men-chil·dren** (men′chil′drən) [Archaic] a male child; boy; son

man·chi·neel (man′chə nēl′) *n.* ⟦Fr *mancenille* < Sp *manzanilla,* dim. of *manzana,* apple < L *matianum (pomum),* (apple) of *Matius,* Roman author of a cookery manual⟧ 1 a tropical American tree (*Hippomane mancinella*) of the spurge family, with a milky, irritant juice and plumlike, poisonous fruit 2 its wood

Man·chu (man cho͞o′, man′cho͞o′) *n.* ⟦Manchu, lit., pure⟧ 1 *pl.* **-chus′** or **-chu′** a member of a people of Manchuria: the Manchus conquered China in 1643-44 and set up a dynasty that ruled until 1912 2 the Tungusic language of this people —*adj.* of the Manchus or their language or culture

Man·chu·kuo (man cho͞o′kwō) former country (1932-45), a Japanese puppet state consisting mainly of Manchuria

Man·chu·ri·a (man choor′ē ə) region & former administrative division of NE China coextensive with the provinces of Heilongjiang, Jilin, & Liaoning, & the NE section of Inner Mongolia —**Man·chu′ri·an** *adj., n.*

man·ci·ple (man′sə pəl) *n.* ⟦ME < OFr *manciple, mancipe* < ML *mancipium,* office of a purchaser < L, legal purchase, possession < *manceps,* buyer, contractor < *manus,* a hand + base of *capere,* to take: see MANUAL & HAVE⟧ a steward or buyer of provisions, as for an English college, a monastery, etc.

Man·cu·ni·an (man kyo͞o′nē ən) *adj.* ⟦< ML *Mancunium,* Manchester < Celt *Mancenion*⟧ of Manchester, England —*n.* a person born or living in Manchester, England

-man·cy (man′sē) ⟦ME < OFr *-mancie* < LL *-mantia* < Gr *manteia,* divination < *mantis,* prophet: see MANTIS⟧ *combining form* divination [*chiromancy*]

M&A *abbrev.* mergers and acquisitions

Man·dae·an (man dē′ən) *n., adj. alt. sp. of* MANDEAN

man·da·la (mun′də lə, mən däl′ə) *n.* ⟦Sans *maṇḍala,* a circle⟧ *Buddhism, Hinduism* a circular design containing concentric geometric forms, images of deities, etc. and symbolizing the universe, totality, or wholeness

Man·da·lay (man′də lā′, man′də lā′) city in central Myanmar, on the Irrawaddy River

man·da·mus (man dā′məs) *n.* ⟦L, we command, 1st pers. pl., pres. indic., of *mandare:* see MANDATE⟧ *Law* a writ commanding that a specified thing be done, issued by a higher court to a lower one, or to a private or municipal corporation, government agency, official, etc.

☆**Man·dan** (man′dan) *n.* ⟦Fr *Mandanes, Mantanes,* pl., perhaps ult. < Dakota *mawáta^{n}na*⟧ 1 *pl.* **-dans** or **-dan** a member of a North American Indian people of North Dakota 2 the Siouan language of this people

man·da·rin (man′də rin) *n.* ⟦Port *mandarim,* altered (infl. by *mandar,* to command < L *mandare:* see MANDATE) < Hindi *mantrī,* minister of state < Sans *mantrin,* counselor < *mantár-,* thinker < IE base **men-,* to think > MIND, Gr *mentōr,* Sans *mantra*⟧ 1 in the Chinese Empire, a member of any of the nine ranks of high officials, each rank distinguished by a characteristic jeweled button worn on the cap 2 a member of any elite group; leading intellectual, political figure, etc., sometimes one who is pompous, arbitrary, etc. 3 [M-] the most widely spoken language of China, comprising a variety of dialects 4 *a)* a small, sweet orange with loose rind (in full **mandarin orange**) *b)* the orange tree (*Citrus reticulata*) on which it grows 5 a deep-orange color —*adj.* 1 designating or of a woman's dress in a Chinese style, often characterized by a narrow, closefitting, stand-up collar parted in the front 2 characterized by a highly formal, self-conscious, and subtle use of language —**man′da·rin·ism′** *n.*

man·da·rin·ate (-āt′) *n.* 1 the office or position of a mandarin 2 rule by mandarins 3 a governing group of mandarins

mandarin duck a bright-colored, crested, Asian duck (*Aix galericulata*), sometimes domesticated

man·date (man′dāt′) *n.* ⟦L *mandatum,* neut. pp. of *mandare,* lit., to put into one's hand, command, entrust < *manus,* a hand + *dare,* to give: see MANUAL & DATE[1]⟧ 1 an authoritative order or command, esp. a written one 2 [Historical] *a)* a commission from the League of Nations to a country to administer some region, colony, etc. (cf. TRUSTEESHIP, sense 2) *b)* the area so administered (cf. TRUST TERRITORY) 3 the wishes of constituents expressed to a representative, legislature, etc., as through an election and regarded as an order 4 *Law a)* an order from a higher court or official to a lower one: a **mandate on remission** is a mandate from an appellate court to the lower court, communicating its decision in a case appealed *b)* in English law, a bailment of personal property with no consideration *c)* in Roman law, a commission or contract by which a person undertakes to do something for another, without recompense but with indemnity against loss *d)* any contract of agency —*vt.* **-dat′ed, -dat′ing** 1 to assign (a region, etc.) as a mandate 2 to require as by law; make mandatory —**man′da′tor** *n.*

man·da·to·ry (man′də tôr′ē) *adj.* ⟦LL *mandatorius*⟧ 1 of, having the nature of, or containing a mandate 2 authoritatively commanded or required; obligatory 3 having received a mandate over some territory —*n., pl.* **-ries** a country assigned to administer a mandate Also **man′da·tar′y** (-ter′ē) —**man′da·to′ri·ly** *adv.*

Man·de (män′dā′, -dē′) *n.* 1 *pl.* **-des′** or **-de′** a member of a group of peoples of W Africa, including the Malinkes, Mendes, Susus, etc. 2 a group of Congo languages spoken by these peoples —*adj.* of the Mandes or their languages or cultures

Man·de·an (man dē′ən) *n.* ⟦< Mandean *mandayyā,* lit., having knowledge (used as transl. of Gr *gnōstikoi,* Gnostics) < *mandā,* knowledge + -AN⟧ 1 a member of an ancient Gnostic sect still extant in S Iraq 2 the Eastern Aramaic dialect used in the writings of the Mandeans: it was spoken along the Euphrates from the 7th to the 9th cent. A.D. —*adj.* 1 of the Mandeans, their doctrines, etc. 2 of Mandean

Man·de·la (man del′ə), **Nelson (Rolihlahla)** 1918-2013; president of South Africa (1994-99); leader in the anti-apartheid movement

☆**Man·del·brot** (man′dəl brōt′) *adj.* ⟦after B. *Mandelbrot* (1924-2010), U.S. mathematician, born in Poland⟧ *Math.* designating or of any of various sets of points used in the study of chaos to generate fractals

Man·del·stam (man′dəl stam′; *Russ* mun′dyil shtäm′), **O·sip** (ôs′yip) 1891-1938; Russ. poet

Man·de·ville (man′də vil′), Sir **John** 14th cent.; putative English author of a romanticized book of travels

man·di·ble (man′də bəl) *n.* ⟦OFr < LL *mandibula* < *mandibulum,* a jaw < L *mandere,* to chew < IE base **menth-,* to chew > MOUTH⟧ the jaw; specif., *a)* the lower jaw of a vertebrate *b)* either of a pair of biting jaws of an insect or other arthropod *c)* either jaw of a beaked animal, as a cephalopod —**man·dib′u·lar** (-dib′yo͞o lər) *adj.*

man·dib·u·late (man dib′yo͞o lit, -lāt′) *adj.* 1 having a mandible or mandibles, as some insects 2 adapted for chewing —*n.* a mandibulate insect

Man·din·go (man diŋ′gō) *n., pl.* **-gos, -goes,** or **-go** ⟦< the native name⟧ MANDE

Man·din·ka (man diŋ′kə) *n., pl.* **-ka** or **-kas** MALINKE

man·do·lin (man′də lin′, man′də lin) *n.* ⟦Fr *mandoline* < It *mandolino,* dim. of *mandola, mandora* < LL *pandura,* kind of lute < LGr *pandoura,* prob. < Ar *ṭanbur*⟧ a musical instrument of the lute family, with four to six pairs of strings stretched over a fretted neck and a deep, rounded sound box: it is played with a plectrum, which is moved rapidly back and forth to give a tremolo effect —**man′do·lin′ist** *n.*

man·do·line (män′də lēn′, män′də lēn′) *n.* ⟦Fr: from its general shape (see prec.)⟧ a utensil consisting of an adjustable blade within a frame along which food is slid for even slicing

man·drag·o·ra (man drag′ə rə) *n.* [Literary] MANDRAKE (senses 1 & 2)

man·drake (man′drāk′) *n.* ⟦ME *mondrake,* altered by folk etym. (by assoc. with *man* + *drake,* dragon) < *mandrag(g)e* < OE *mandragora* < LL < L *mandragoras* < Gr⟧ 1 a poisonous plant (*Mandragora officinarum*) of the nightshade family, found in Mediterranean regions: it has purple or white flowers and a thick root, often forked, formerly used in medicine for its narcotic and emetic properties 2 the root, formerly thought to have magic powers because of its fancied resemblance to the human form ☆3 MAY APPLE

man·drel or **man·dril** (man′drəl) *n.* ⟦earlier *manderil;* prob. < Fr *mandrin* < Prov *mandre,* spindle, winch, beam (of a balance) < L *mamphur,* a bow drill < IE base **menth-,* to twirl > ON *mǫndull,* handle of a quern⟧ 1 a metal spindle or bar, often tapered, inserted into a lathe center to support work while it is being machined or turned 2 a metal rod or bar used as a core around which metal, wire, glass, etc. is cast, molded, forged, or shaped

man·drill (man′dril) *n.* ⟦MAN + DRILL[4]⟧ a large, fierce, strong baboon (*Mandrillus sphinx*) of W Africa: the male has blue and scarlet patches on the face and rump

man·du·cate (man′do͞o kāt′, -dyo͞o-) *vt.* **-cat′ed, -cat′ing** ⟦< L *manducatus,* pp. of *manducare:* see MANGER⟧ [Rare] to chew; masticate —**man′du·ca′tion** *n.* —**man′du·ca·to′ry** (-kə tôr′ē) *adj.*

Man·dy (man′dē) *n.* a feminine name: see AMANDA, MIRANDA[1]

mane (mān) *n.* ⟦ME < OE *manu,* akin to Ger *mähne* < IE **mono-,* neck (> Sans *mányā,* nape of the neck, Welsh *mwn,* neck), prob. < base **men-,* to project > MENACE⟧ 1 the long hair growing from the top or sides of the neck of certain animals, as the horse or lion **2** long, thick human hair —**maned** *adj.* —**mane′less** *adj.*

man-eat·er (man′ēt′ər) *n.* **1** a cannibal **2** an animal that eats, or is reputed to eat, human flesh, as a shark, lion, or tiger —**man′-eat′ing** *adj.*

ma·nège or **ma·nege** (ma nezh′, -nāzh′; mə-) *n.* ⟦Fr < It *maneggio:* see MANAGE⟧ **1** the art of riding and training horses; horsemanship **2** the paces and exercises of a trained horse **3** a school for training horses and teaching riders; riding academy

ma·nes (mā′nēz′) [*often* **M-**] *pl.n.* ⟦ME < L < IE base **mā-*, good: see MAÑANA⟧ in ancient Roman belief, the deified souls of the dead, esp. of dead ancestors —*n.* the soul or spirit of a dead person

Ma·nes (mā′nēz′) *var. of* MANI

Ma·net (ma nā′), **É·douard** (ā dwȧr′) 1832-83; Fr. impressionist painter

ma·neu·ver (mə no͞o′vər, -nyo͞o′-) *n.* ⟦Fr *manœuvre,* orig., hand labor < VL *manuopera* < L *manu operare,* to work by hand < *manus,* a hand (see MANUAL) + *opera,* pl. of *opus,* a work: see OPUS⟧ **1** a planned and controlled tactical or strategic movement of troops, warships, aircraft, etc. **2** [*pl.*] large-scale practice movements and exercises of troops, warships, aircraft, etc. under simulated battle conditions **3** any skillful change of movement or direction in driving or controlling a vehicle or craft; specif., *a)* any change of aircraft movement executed by the pilot *b)* a series of aircraft movements executed by the pilot according to a specific pattern, as a roll, a loop, etc. **4** any movement or procedure intended as a skillful or shrewd step toward some objective; stratagem; artifice; scheme — *vi., vt.* **1** to perform or cause to perform a maneuver or maneuvers **2** to manage or plan skillfully or shrewdly; manipulate or scheme **3** *a)* to direct or guide (a vehicle, tool, etc.) with skill and dexterity *b)* to move, lead, get, put, make, compel, etc. (a person or thing) by some stratagem or scheme —*SYN.* TRICK —**ma·neu′ver·a·ble** *adj.* —**ma·neu′ver·a·bil′i·ty** *n.* —**ma·neu′ver·er** *n.*

man-for-man (man′fər man′) *adj.* MAN-TO-MAN (sense 2)

man Friday *see* FRIDAY (sense 2)

man·ful (man′fəl) *adj.* manly; brave, resolute, strong, etc. —**man′ful·ly** *adv.* —**man′ful·ness** *n.*

man·ga (mäŋ′gə, maŋ′-) [*also in italics*] *n.* ⟦Jpn, random pictures⟧ a Japanese genre consisting of comic books and graphic novels, typically black-and-white and featuring stylized characters with large, round eyes —*pl.n.* such comic books and graphic novels

man·ga·bey (maŋ′gə bā′, -bē) *n.* ⟦after *Mangabey,* Madagascar⟧ any of a genus (*Cercocebus*) of large African monkeys having a silky, gray coat, white eyelids, and a long tail

Man·ga·lore (mäŋ′gə lôr′) city in SW India, on Malabar Coast

man·ga·nate (maŋ′gə nāt′) *n.* a salt of manganic acid containing the divalent, negative radical MnO_4

man·ga·nese (maŋ′gə nēs′, -nēz′) *n.* ⟦Fr *manganèse* < It *manganese,* by metathesis < ML *magnesia:* see MAGNESIA⟧ a grayish-white, metallic chemical element, usually hard and brittle, which rusts like iron but is not magnetic: it is used in the manufacture of alloys of iron, aluminum, and copper: symbol, Mn; at. no. 25: see the periodic table of elements in the Reference Supplement

manganese bronze an alloy of copper and zinc containing up to about 3 percent manganese, used in making steamship propellers, toothed wheels, gears, etc.

manganese dioxide a blackish, crystalline or powdery substance, MnO_2, that is a strong oxidizing agent, used in making batteries, matches, etc.

manganese steel a hard, malleable and ductile steel containing 12 to 14 percent of manganese, used in drill bits, crushers, etc.

man·gan·ic (man gan′ik) *adj.* designating or of chemical compounds containing trivalent manganese

manganic acid an acid, H_2MnO_4, known only in the form of its salts

man·ga·nin (maŋ′gə nin) *n.* ⟦MANGAN(ESE) + -IN[1]⟧ an alloy of copper, some manganese, and some nickel, used in rheostats, resistors, etc.

man·ga·nite (-nīt′) *n.* **1** a dark-colored, shiny mineral, MnO(HO), that is an ore of manganese; hydrous manganese oxide **2** any of a series of salts that may be considered as derivatives of manganous acid, the hydroxide of tetravalent manganese

man·ga·nous (maŋ′gə nəs; man gan′əs) *adj.* designating or of chemical compounds containing divalent manganese

mange (mānj) *n.* ⟦ME *manjewe* < OFr *mangeue,* an itch, eating < *mangier* < L *manducare:* see MANGER⟧ any of various skin diseases of mammals caused by parasitic mites and characterized by intense itching, lesions and scabs, and a loss of hair

man·gel-wur·zel (maŋ′gəl wur′zəl, -wurt′-) *n.* ⟦Ger, altered by assoc. with *mangel,* lack < *mangoldwurzel* < *mangold,* beet + *wurzel,* ROOT[1]⟧ a variety of large beet, used as food for cattle, esp. in Europe: also **man′gel**

man·ger (mān′jər) *n.* ⟦ME < OFr *mangeure* < VL **manducatoria,* feeding trough < pp. of L *manducare,* to eat < *mandere,* to chew < IE base **menth-*, to chew > MOUTH⟧ a box or trough to hold fodder for horses or cattle to eat

man·gle[1] (maŋ′gəl) *vt.* **-gled, -gling** ⟦ME *manglen* < Anglo-Fr *mangler,* prob. freq. of OFr *mehaigner,* MAIM⟧ **1** to mutilate or disfigure by repeatedly and roughly cutting, tearing, hacking, or crushing; lacerate and bruise badly **2** to spoil; botch; mar; garble [*a translation that mangles the original text*] —*SYN.* MAIM —**man′gler** *n.*

man·gle[2] (maŋ′gəl) *n.* ⟦Du *mangel* < Ger < MHG, dim. of *mange,* a mangle < L *manganum* < Gr *manganon,* war machine, orig. deceptive device < IE base **meng-*, to embellish deceptively > MIr *meng,* deceit, L *mango,* falsifying dealer⟧ a machine for pressing and smoothing cloth, esp. sheets and other flat pieces, between heated rollers —*vt.* **-gled, -gling** to press in a mangle —**man′gler** *n.*

man·go (maŋ′gō) *n., pl.* **-goes** or **-gos** ⟦Port *manga* < Malay *mangga* < Tamil *mān-kāy* < *mān,* mango tree + *kāy,* fruit⟧ **1** a yellow-red, oblong tropical fruit with thick rind, somewhat acid and juicy pulp, and a hard stone: it is eaten when ripe, or preserved or pickled when unripe **2** the tropical, evergreen, Asian tree (*Mangifera indica*) of the cashew family on which it grows

man·go·nel (maŋ′gə nel′) *n.* ⟦OFr, dim. < L *manganum:* see MANGLE[2]⟧ an obsolete military apparatus for hurling heavy stones and other missiles

man·go·steen (maŋ′gə stēn′) *n.* ⟦Malay *mangustan*⟧ **1** an edible East Indian fruit somewhat like an orange, with a thick, reddish-brown rind and sweet, white, juicy, segmented pulp **2** the tree (*Garcinia mangostana*) of the St. Johnswort family, on which it grows

man·grove (maŋ′grōv′) *n.* ⟦altered (infl. by GROVE) < earlier *mangrowe* < Port *mangue* < Sp *mangle* < the WInd (Taino) name⟧ any of various coastal or aquatic tropical trees or shrubs, esp. of the mangrove family, that form large colonies in swamps or shallow water and provide a habitat for young fish and shrimp —*adj.* designating a family (Rhizophoraceae, order Rhizophorales) of dicotyledonous trees and shrubs that inhabit tidal marshes and river mouths in the tropics

man·gy (mān′jē) *adj.* **-gi·er, -gi·est** **1** having, resembling, or caused by mange **2** shabby and filthy; sordid; squalid **3** mean and low; despicable —**man′gi·ly** *adv.* —**man′gi·ness** *n.*

man·han·dle (man′han′dəl) *vt.* **-dled, -dling** **1** to move or do by human strength only, without mechanical aids **2** to handle (someone) roughly

Man·hat·tan[1] (man hat′'n, mən-) *n.* **1** ⟦see fol.⟧ a member of a North American Indian people, speaking an Algonquian language, that formerly lived on Manhattan Island **2** ⟦after *Manhattan,* New York⟧ [*often* **m-**] a cocktail made of whiskey and sweet vermouth, usually with a dash of bitters and a maraschino cherry

Man·hat·tan[2] (man hat′'n) ⟦< Du prob. < the native name < *manah,* island + *atin,* hill⟧ **1** island in SE N.Y., between the Hudson & East rivers, forming part of New York City: 13 mi (21 km) long: also **Manhattan Island** **2** borough of New York City, consisting of this island, some small nearby islands, & a small bit of the mainland: 22 sq mi (57 sq km) —**Man·hat′tan·ite′** *n.*

Manhattan clam chowder a thick soup made with clams, onions, salt pork, tomatoes, various seasonings, and sometimes potatoes

Man·hat·tan·ize (-īz′) *vt.* **-ized′, -iz′ing** ⟦after MANHATTAN[2] borough⟧ to alter the architectural appearance of (a city) by the construction of skyscrapers and high-rise buildings —**Man·hat′tan·i·za′tion** *n.*

Manhattan Project ⟦code name (1942), after the *Manhattan Engineer District* of the U.S. Army Corps of Engineers, which orig. managed part of the project⟧ the U.S. research project (through 1946) for developing an atomic bomb

man·hole (man′hōl′) *n.* an opening, often with a cover, through which a person can enter a sewer, conduit, ship's tank, etc. for repair work or inspection

man·hood (man′hood′) *n.* ⟦ME *manhod, manhede:* see MAN + -HOOD⟧ **1** the state or time of being a human being or, esp., an adult male human being **2** manly qualities; manliness **3** status or prestige associated with manliness [*public humiliation robbed him of his manhood*] **4** men collectively

man-hour (-our′) *n.* an industrial time unit equal to one hour of work done by one person

☆**man·hunt** (-hunt′) *n.* a hunt for a fugitive or criminal suspect: also written **man hunt**

Ma·ni (mä′nē) A.D. 216?-276?; Persian prophet: see MANICHAEISM

ma·ni·a (mā′nē ə, mān′yə) *n.* ⟦ME < LL < Gr, madness < *mainesthai,* to rage < IE base **men-*, to think, be mentally excited > MIND⟧ **1** wild or violent mental disorder; specif., the manic phase of bipolar affective disorder, characterized generally by abnormal excitability, exaggerated feelings of well-being, flight of ideas, excessive activity, etc. **2** an excessive, persistent enthusiasm, liking, craving, or interest; obsession; craze [*a mania for dancing*]

SYN.—**mania** in its basic sense describes the phase of bipolar affective disorder that is distinguished from *depression;* **delirium** denotes a temporary state of extreme mental disturbance (marked by restlessness, incoherence, and hallucinations) that occurs during fevers, in alcoholic psychosis, etc.; **frenzy,** not used technically in psychiatry, implies extreme emotional agitation in which self-control is lost; **hysteria** has been applied in psychiatry to certain psychogenic disorders characterized by excitability, anxiety, sensory and motor disturbances, and the involuntary simulation of blindness, deafness, etc. In extended use, **mania** suggests a craze for something [*a mania for surfing*], **delirium,** rapturous excitement [*a delirium of joy*], and **hysteria,** an outburst of wild, uncontrolled feeling [*in his hysteria, he alternated between laughing and weeping*]

-ma·ni·a (mā′nē ə, mān′yə) ⟦see prec.⟧ *combining form forming nouns* **1** a (specified) type of mental disorder characterized by an abnormal preoccupation, compulsion, etc. [*pyromania*] **2** a continuing, intense enthusiasm, craving, or liking for (a specified thing) [*bibliomania*]

ma·ni·ac (mā′nē ak′) *adj.* ⟦ML *maniacus*⟧ of, having, or showing mania; maniacal —*n.* **1** a wildly or violently insane person; madman; lunatic **2** [Informal] a person who has an excessive or persistent enthusiasm, liking, or desire for something [*a football maniac*]

-ma·ni·ac (mā′nē ak′) *combining form* 1 *forming nouns* a person affected by a (specified) mania *[kleptomaniac]* 2 *forming adjectives* affected by a (specified) mania

ma·ni·a·cal (mə nī′ə kəl) *adj.* 1 of, having, or showing mania; wildly insane; raving 2 characterized by excessive or persistent enthusiasm —**ma·ni′a·cal·ly** *adv.*

man·ic (man′ik) *adj.* 1 *Psychiatry* having, characterized by, or like mania 2 [Informal] extremely or excessively excited, elated, etc. —**man′ic·al·ly** *adv.*

man·ic-de·pres·sive (-dē pres′iv) *adj.* BIPOLAR (sense 4) —*n.* a person who has BIPOLAR AFFECTIVE DISORDER —**man′ic-de·pres′sion** *n.*

Man·i·chae·ism or **Man·i·che·ism** (man′i kē′iz′əm) *n.* a dualistic religion that combined Zoroastrian, Christian, Gnostic, and other beliefs in a theology of cosmic struggle between Good (light, God, spirit) and Evil (darkness, Satan, matter): it was founded by Mani (L. name *Manichaeus*) in Persia in the 3d cent. A.D.: also **Man′i·chae′an·ism′** —**Man′i·chae′an** *n., adj.* —**Man′i·chee′** *n.*

Man·i·chae·us or **Man·i·che·us** (man′i kē′əs) *var. of* MANI

man·i·cot·ti (man′i kät′ē; *It* mä′nē kôt′tē) *n., pl.* **-ti** or **-tis** ⟦It, lit., muffs, pl. of *manicotto* < *manica,* sleeve < L, sleeve, muff < *manus,* hand: see MANUAL⟧ pasta in the form of long, broad tubes, usually boiled, stuffed with cheese, and baked with a tomato sauce

man·i·cure (man′i kyoor′) *n.* ⟦Fr < L *manus,* a hand + *cura,* care: see CURE⟧ a trimming, cleaning, and sometimes polishing of the fingernails, esp. when done by a manicurist —*vt.* **-cured′**, **-cur′ing** 1 *a)* to trim, polish, etc. (the fingernails) *b)* to give a manicure to (someone) 2 [Informal] to trim, clip, etc. meticulously *[to manicure a lawn]*

man·i·cur·ist (-ist) *n.* a person whose work is giving manicures

man·i·fest (man′ə fest′) *adj.* ⟦ME < OFr *manifeste* < L *manifestus,* earlier *manufestus,* lit., struck by the hand, palpable, evident < *manus,* a hand (see MANUAL) + base akin to *(in)festus:* see INFEST⟧ apparent to the senses, esp. that of sight, or to the mind; evident; obvious; clear; plain —*vt.* ⟦ME *manifesten* < OFr *manifester* < L *manifestare*⟧ 1 to make clear or evident; show plainly; reveal; evince 2 to prove; be evidence of 3 to enter in a ship's manifest —*vi.* to appear to the senses; show itself —*n.* 1 an itemized list of a ship's cargo, to be shown to customs officials 2 a list of the passengers and cargo on an airplane —*SYN.* EVIDENT —**man′i·fest′a·ble** *adj.* —**man′i·fest′ly** *adv.*

man·i·fes·ta·tion (man′ə fes tā′shən, -fəs-) *n.* ⟦LL *manifestatio*⟧ 1 a manifesting or being manifested 2 something that manifests or is manifested *[his smile was a manifestation of joy]* 3 a form in which a being manifests itself or is thought to manifest itself, esp. the material or bodily form of a spirit 4 a public demonstration, as by a government or party for political effect

☆**Manifest Destiny** the 19th-cent. doctrine postulating the continued territorial expansion of the U.S. as its obvious destiny: term current during the annexation of territories in the Southwest and Northwest and of islands in the Pacific and Caribbean

man·i·fes·to (man′ə fes′tō) *n., pl.* **-toes** or **-tos** ⟦It < *manifestare,* MANIFEST⟧ a public declaration of motives and intentions, as by a political party or by an avant-garde movement

man·i·fold (man′ə fōld′) *adj.* ⟦ME < OE *manigfeald:* see MANY & -FOLD⟧ 1 having many and various forms, features, parts, etc. *[manifold wisdom]* 2 of many sorts; many and varied; multifarious: used with a plural noun *[manifold duties]* 3 being such in many and various ways or for many reasons *[a manifold villain]* 4 comprising, consisting of, or operating several units or parts of one kind: said of certain devices —*n.* 1 something that is manifold 2 a pipe with one inlet and several outlets or with one outlet and several inlets, for connecting with other pipes, specif., as in an automobile, for conducting exhausts from each cylinder into a single exhaust pipe —*vt.* 1 to make manifold; multiply 2 to make more than one copy of *[to manifold a letter with carbon paper]* —**man′i·fold′er** *n.* —**man′i·fold′ly** *adv.* —**man′i·fold′ness** *n.*

man·i·kin (man′ə kin) *n.* ⟦Du *manneken* < *man,* MAN + *-ken,* -KIN⟧ 1 [Now Rare] a little man; dwarf 2 an anatomical model of the human body, usually with movable and detachable parts, used in medical schools, art classes, etc. 3 MANNEQUIN

Ma·nil·a[1] (mə nil′ə) *n.* [*often* **m-**] 1 MANILA HEMP 2 MANILA PAPER 3 MANILA ROPE Also sp. **Ma·nil′la**

Ma·nil·a[2] (mə nil′ə) seaport & capital of the Philippines, in SW Luzon, on an inlet (**Manila Bay**) of the South China Sea

Manila hemp [*often* **m- h-**] 1 a Philippine plant (*Musa textilis*) of the banana family 2 a strong, tough fiber from the leafstalks of this plant, used for making high-quality rope, paper, clothing, etc.

Manila paper [*often* **m- p-**] durable, brownish-yellow paper used for envelopes, wrapping paper, etc.: orig. made of Manila hemp, now of various fibers

Manila rope [*often* **m- r-**] strong rope made of Manila hemp

man in the moon, the *personification of* the apparent face, visible from earth, suggested by large craters on the lunar surface

man in the street the average person; ordinary citizen

man·i·oc (man′ē äk′) *n.* ⟦Fr < Tupí *manioca*⟧ CASSAVA

man·i·ple (man′ə pəl) *n.* ⟦L *manipulus,* orig., a handful, bundle < *manus,* a hand (see MANUAL) + base of *plere,* to fill: from use of bundles of hay as standards of the maniples⟧ 1 a subdivision of the ancient Roman legion; one third of a cohort, consisting of either 60 or 120 men 2 ⟦ME *manaple* < MFr < ML(Ec) *manipulus* < L⟧ a small cloth band formerly worn hanging from the left forearm by the celebrant of a Mass

ma·nip·u·lar (mə nip′yoo lər, -yə-) *adj.* ⟦L *manipularis*⟧ 1 of a maniple (in the ancient Roman army) 2 of manipulation —*n.* a soldier of a maniple

ma·nip·u·late (mə nip′yoo lāt′, -yə-) *vt.* **-lat′ed**, **-lat′ing** ⟦back-form. < fol.⟧ 1 to work, operate, or treat with or as with the hand or hands; handle or use, esp. with skill 2 to manage or control artfully or by shrewd use of influence, often in an unfair or fraudulent way *[to manipulate an election by bribing the voters]* 3 *a)* to falsify (figures, accounts, etc.) for one's own purposes or profit; rig *b)* to cause (prices of stock, etc.) to fall or rise by wash sales, matched orders, etc. —*SYN.* HANDLE —**ma·nip′u·la·ble** *adj.*, **ma·nip′u·lat′a·ble** —**ma·nip′u·la′tive** *adj.*, **ma·nip′u·la·to′ry**

ma·nip·u·la·tion (mə nip′yoo lā′shən, -yə-) *n.* ⟦Fr < *manipuler,* to manipulate < *manipule,* pharmacist's term for a handful, orig., a bundle of herbs < L *manipulus:* see MANIPLE⟧ a manipulating or being manipulated; skillful handling or operation, artful management or control, etc.

ma·nip·u·la·tor (mə nip′yoo lāt′ər, -yə-) *n.* a person or thing that manipulates

Man·i·pur (mun′ə poor′) state of NE India, on the border with Myanmar: 8,620 sq mi (22,326 sq km); cap. Imphal

Ma·ni·sa (mä′ni sä′) city in W Turkey: as *Magnesia,* site of a battle (190 B.C.) in which the Romans defeated Antiochus the Great

Man·i·to·ba (man′ə tō′bə) ⟦Cree *manitoowapaaw,* the narrows (of Lake Manitoba), lit., god narrows⟧ 1 province of SC Canada: 213,271 sq mi (552,370 sq km); cap. Winnipeg: abbrev. *MB* or *Man* 2 **Lake** lake in S Manitoba: 1,817 sq mi (4,706 sq km) —**Man′i·to′ban** *adj., n.*

☆**man·i·tou** (man′ə too′) *n.* ⟦Fr, replacing earlier *manito,* etc. < Delaware *manə̂t'u:* cf. Ojibwa *manidoo*⟧ *Folklore* among the Algonquian Indians, any of various spirits or supernatural forces variously conceived of as nature spirits of both good and evil influence: also **man′i·tu′** or **man′i·to′** (-tō′)

Man·i·tou·lin Island (man′ə too′lin) ⟦earlier *Manitoualin* < 18th-c. Ojibwa dial. *manitoowaalink,* lit., at the god's den⟧ Canadian island in N Lake Huron: 1,068 sq mi (2,766 sq km)

Ma·ni·za·les (mä′nē sä′les) city in WC Colombia

man jack *see phr.* EVERY MAN JACK *under* JACK

man·kind (man′kīnd′; *for 1, also* man kīnd′) *n.* ⟦altered (by assoc. with KIND < *mankin* < OE *mancynn* < *man,* MAN, + *cynn,* KIN⟧ 1 all human beings; the human race 2 all human males; the male sex

man·like (man′līk′) *adj.* 1 like or characteristic of a human being 2 like or fit for a man; masculine

man·ly (man′lē) *adj.* **-li·er**, **-li·est** ⟦ME: see MAN & -LY[1]⟧ 1 having the qualities generally regarded as those that a man should have; virile; strong, brave, resolute, honorable, etc. 2 fit for a man; masculine *[manly sports]* —*adv.* [Obs.] in a manly way —*SYN.* MALE —**man′li·ness** *n.*

man-made (-mād′) *adj.* made or caused by human beings; artificial, synthetic, etc. *[a man-made fabric, man-made famine]*

Mann (män; *for 2* man) 1 **(Luis) Hein·rich** (hīn′riH) 1871-1950; Ger. writer: brother of Thomas 2 **Horace** 1796-1859; U.S. educator 3 **Tho·mas** (tō′mäs) 1875-1955; Ger. novelist, in the U.S. 1938-52

man·na (man′ə) *n.* ⟦OE < LL(Ec) < Gr(Ec) < Aram *mannā* < Heb *mān,* orig., prob. *man hu,* lit., what is it?⟧ 1 *Bible* a sweet food miraculously provided for the Israelites in the wilderness: Ex. 16:14-36 2 *a)* divine aid, spiritual sustenance, etc. *b)* anything badly needed that comes unexpectedly 3 *a)* a sweet, gummy juice obtained from a European ash tree (*Fraxinus ornus*), formerly used as a laxative *b)* any of various similar substances exuded by certain plants and insects

Mann Act (man) ⟦after J. R. *Mann* (1856-1922), U.S. Congressman⟧ an act of Congress (June, 1910) prohibiting the interstate transportation of women for immoral purposes, as white slavery

manned (mand) *adj.* having a human operator or crew on board or on site *[a manned spacecraft]*

man·ne·quin (man′ə kin) *n.* ⟦Fr < Du *manneken:* see MANIKIN⟧ 1 a model of the human body, used by tailors, window dressers, artists, etc. 2 a woman whose work is modeling clothes in stores, etc.

man·ner (man′ər) *n.* ⟦ME *manere* < OFr *maniere* < VL **manaria* < L *manuarius,* of the hand < *manus,* a hand: see MANUAL⟧ 1 a way or method in which something is done or happens; mode or fashion of procedure 2 *a)* a way of acting; personal, esp. customary, behavior or bearing *[a sarcastic manner]* *b)* distinguished bearing or behavior 3 [*pl.*] *a)* ways of social life; prevailing social conditions or customs *[a comedy of manners]* *b)* ways of social behavior; deportment, esp. with reference to polite conventions *[good manners, bad manners]* *c)* polite ways of social behavior; deportment conforming with polite conventions *[a child who has no manners]* 4 characteristic style or method in art, music, literature, etc. 5 kind; sort *[what manner of man is he?]* —*SYN.* BEARING —**all manner of** all or various kinds of —**by all manner of means** of course; surely —**by any manner of means** in any way; at all —**by no manner of means** in no way; definitely not —**in a manner of speaking** so to speak; in a certain sense or way —**to the manner born** ⟦in allusion to Shakespeare's *Hamlet* I, iv⟧ 1 accustomed from birth to the way or usage spoken of 2 naturally fitted for a certain thing

man·nered (-ərd) *adj.* 1 having manners, or a manner, of a (specified) sort: used in hyphenated compounds *[ill-mannered]* 2 having or showing a specified manner *[a solemnly mannered ceremony]* 3 artificial, stylized, or affected *[a mannered literary style]*

man·ner·ism (man′ər iz′əm) *n.* 1 excessive use of some distinctive, often affected, manner or style in art, literature, speech, or behavior **2** a peculiarity of manner in behavior, speech, etc. that has become a habit **3** [**M-**] a 16th-cent. style in art characterized by distortion of realistic proportions, contorted figures, an avoidance of classical balance, etc. —**SYN.** POSE[1] —**man′ner·ist** *n., adj.* —**man′ner·is′tic** *adj.*

man·ner·less (-lis) *adj.* lacking good manners; impolite

man·ner·ly (-lē) *adj.* having or showing good manners; well-behaved; polite; courteous —*adv.* politely —**man′ner·li·ness** *n.*

Mann·heim (man′hīm; *Ger* män′-) city in SW Germany, on the Rhine, in the state of Baden-Württemberg

man·ni·kin (man′ə kin) *n. alt. sp. of* MANIKIN

man·nish (man′ish) *adj.* having a quality usually regarded as belonging to or right for a man: used, often disparagingly, in referring to a woman —**SYN.** MALE —**man′nish·ly** *adv.* —**man′nish·ness** *n.*

man·nite (man′īt′) *n.* ⟦MANN(A) + -ITE[2]⟧ *var. of* MANNITOL —**man·nit·ic** (mə nit′ik) *adj.*

man·ni·tol (man′ə tôl′, -tōl′) *n.* ⟦< prec. + -OL[1]⟧ a colorless, crystalline sugar alcohol, $C_6H_8(OH)_6$, occurring in various plants and animals

man·nose (man′ōs′) *n.* ⟦< prec. + -OSE[2]⟧ a monosaccharide found in some plants and produced by the oxidation of mannitol

mano a mano (mä′nō ə mä′nō; *Sp* mä′nô ä mä′nô) ⟦Sp, lit., hand to hand⟧ **1** in or into direct, personal confrontation **2** a duel or other confrontation between two individuals

ma·noeu·vre (mə no͞o′vər, -nyo͞o′-) *n., vi., vt.* **-vred**, **-vring** *chiefly Brit. sp. of* MANEUVER

Man of Galilee *name for* Jesus Christ

man of God **1** a holy man; saint, hermit, etc. **2** a clergyman; minister, priest, rabbi, etc.

man of letters a writer, scholar, editor, etc., esp. one whose work is in the field of literature

Man of Sorrows **1** a person alluded to by Isaiah (Isa. 53:3) and interpreted as being the Messiah **2** *Christianity name for* Jesus Christ

man of the world a man familiar with and tolerant of various sorts of people and their ways; worldly man

man-of-war (man′əv wôr′, -ə wôr′) *n., pl.* **men′-of-war′** an armed naval vessel; warship

man-of-war bird FRIGATE BIRD

ma·nom·e·ter (mə näm′ət ər) *n.* ⟦Fr *manomètre*: coined (1705) by P. Varignon (1654-1722), Fr mathematician < Gr *manos,* rare (taken in sense "thin, sparse") + Fr *-mètre,* -METER⟧ an instrument for measuring the pressure of gases or liquids —**man·o·met·ric** (man′ə met′rik) *adj.*, **man′o·met′ri·cal**

man on horseback a military man with such influence and power over the people as to be, or seem to be, able to seize control and rule as a dictator

man on the street *var. of* MAN IN THE STREET

man·or (man′ər) *n.* ⟦ME *maner* < OFr *manoir* < *manoir,* to stay, dwell < L *manere,* to remain < IE base **men-,* to remain (> Sans *man-,* to delay, stand still), prob. orig. identical with **men-,* to think (> MIND): sense prob. from "stand in thought"⟧ **1** in England *a)* in feudal times, the district over which a lord held authority and which was subject to the jurisdiction of his court *b)* more recently, a landed estate, usually with a main residence, the owner of which still holds some feudal rights over the land **2** in America during colonial times, a district granted as a manor and leased to tenants at a set rental **3** *a)* a mansion *b)* the main residence on an estate or plantation *c)* a lord's mansion with its land —**to the manor born** ⟦by folk etym. < TO THE MANNER BORN (see phr. at MANNER)⟧ accustomed from birth to the ways and privileges associated with nobility or great wealth —**ma·no·ri·al** (mə nôr′ē əl) *adj.*

manor house the main residence of a manor, specif., the hereditary house of the lord of a manor

man·pow·er (man′pou′ər) *n.* **1** power furnished by human physical strength **2** the collective strength or availability for work of the people in any given area, nation, etc. Also written **man power**

man·qué (män kā′) *adj.* ⟦Fr < pp. of *manquer,* to fail, be lacking < It *mancare* < *manco,* deficient < L *mancus,* infirm, defective < base of *manus,* hand: see MANUAL⟧ **1** that falls short of the goal; unsuccessful or defective **2** potential but unrealized; would-be: placed after the noun it modifies [a scholar *manqué*]: also ***man·quée′*** (-kā′) *fem.*

man·rope (man′rōp′) *n. Naut.* a rope serving as a handrail along a gangway, ladder, etc.

man·sard (roof) (man′särd′, -sərd) ⟦Fr *mansarde,* after F. *Mansard* (1598-1666), Fr architect, who revived the use of such roofs⟧ a roof with two slopes on each of the four sides, the lower steeper than the upper

mansard roof

manse (mans) *n.* ⟦LME *manss* < ML *mansus* (or *mansum, mansa*), a dwelling < pp. of L *manere,* to remain, dwell: see MANOR⟧ **1** the residence of a minister, esp. a Presbyterian minister; parsonage **2** [Archaic] a large, imposing house; mansion

man·ser·vant (man′sur′vənt) *n., pl.* **men·ser·vants** (men′sur′vənts) a male servant: also written **man servant**

Mans·field[1] (mans′fēld′), **Katherine** (born *Kathleen Mansfield Beauchamp*) 1888-1923; Brit. short-story writer, born in New Zealand

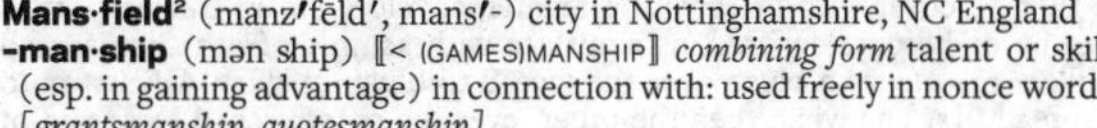

Mans·field[2] (manz′fēld′, mans′-) city in Nottinghamshire, NC England

-man·ship (mən ship) ⟦< (GAMES)MANSHIP⟧ *combining form* talent or skill (esp. in gaining advantage) in connection with: used freely in nonce words [*grantsmanship, quotesmanship*]

man·sion (man′shən) *n.* ⟦ME *mansioun* < OFr *mansion* < L *mansio,* a sojourn, dwelling < pp. of *manere,* to remain, dwell: see MANOR⟧ **1** [Archaic] a manor house **2** a large, imposing house; stately residence **3** [Archaic] *a)* a dwelling place *b)* a separate dwelling place or lodging in a large house or structure: *usually used in pl.* **4** [*pl.*] [Brit.] an apartment house **5** [Obs.] a stay; sojourn **6** *Astrol.* *a)* HOUSE (*n.* 11) *b)* any of the 28 parts of the moon's course occupied on successive days

man-sized (man′sīzd′) *adj.* [Informal] of a size fit for a large or robust man [*man-sized* meal portions]: also **man′-size′**

man·slaugh·ter (-slôt′ər) *n.* the killing of a human being by another; esp., such killing when unlawful but without malice: see also MURDER, HOMICIDE

man·sue·tude (man′swi to͞od′, -tyo͞od′) *n.* ⟦ME < L *mansuetudo* < pp. of *mansuescere,* to tame < *manus,* a hand (see MANUAL) + *suescere,* to accustom < IE base **swedh-,* custom > Gr *ēthos*⟧ gentleness; tameness

Man·sur (man so͝or′) A.D. 712?-775; Arab caliph (754-775): founder of Baghdad: also **al′-Man·sur′**

Man·su·ra (man so͝or′ə) city in N Egypt, on the Nile delta

man·ta (man′tə; *Sp* män′tä) *n.* ⟦Sp < LL *mantum,* a cloak, prob. back-form. < L *mantellum*: see MANTLE⟧ ☆**1** *a)* coarse cotton cloth used for cheap shawls, capes, etc. in Spanish America *b)* a shawl, cape, etc. made of this ☆**2** a horse blanket or horse cloth **3** ⟦AmSp < Sp: from fancied resemblance to a cloak or blanket⟧ any of a family (Mobulidae, order Myliobatiformes) of usually giant rays with winglike pectoral fins, living near the surface of warm seas while feeding on plankton or small fish; devilfish: also **manta ray**

man-tai·lored (man′tā′lərd) *adj.* ⟦from being styled with the simple lines and lack of ornamentation that characterize men's suits, coats, etc.⟧ TAILORED (sense 1)

man·teau (man′tō′; *Fr* män tō′) *n., pl.* **-teaus′** or Fr. ***-teaux′*** (-tō′) ⟦Fr < OFr *mantel*: see MANTLE⟧ **1** a cloak or mantle, esp. for a woman **2** any of various styles of long overcoat, esp. for a woman

Man·te·gna (män te′nyä), **An·dre·a** (än dre′ä) 1431-1506; It. painter & engraver

man·tel (man′təl) *n.* ⟦var. of MANTLE⟧ **1** the facing of stone, marble, etc. about a fireplace, including a projecting shelf or slab above it **2** the shelf or slab

man·tel·et (man′tə lit, mant′lit) *n.* ⟦OFr, dim. of *mantel*: see MANTLE⟧ **1** a short mantle, cape, or cloak **2** a protective shelter or screen; esp., *a)* a movable roof or screen formerly used to protect besiegers from the enemy *b)* any of various bulletproof shields or screens

man·tel·let·ta (man′tə let′ə) *n.* ⟦It, dim. < *mantello* < L *mantellum*: see MANTLE⟧ *R.C.Ch.* a sleeveless vestment worn by cardinals, bishops, etc.

man·tel·piece (man′təl pēs′) *n.* the projecting shelf of a mantel, or this shelf and the side elements framing the fireplace in front

man·tel·tree (-trē′) *n.* **1** a beam, stone, or arch above the opening of a fireplace, supporting the masonry above **2** [Archaic] MANTELPIECE

man·tic (man′tik) *adj.* ⟦Gr *mantikos* < *mantis,* seer, soothsayer: see MANTIS⟧ of, or having powers of, divination; prophetic

-man·tic (man′tik) ⟦< Gr *mantikos*: see prec.⟧ *combining form forming adjectives* of or relating to divination

man·ti·core (man′ti kôr′) *n.* ⟦ME < OFr < L *manticora* < Gr *mantikhōras,* misreading of *martikhoras*⟧ a mythical monster with the body and legs of a lion, the face of a man, and a tail ending in a sting

man·til·la (man til′ə, -tē′ə) *n.* ⟦Sp, dim. of *manta*: see MANTA⟧ **1** a woman's scarf, as of lace, worn over the hair and shoulders, as traditionally in Spain, Mexico, etc. **2** a short mantle, cape, or cloak

man·tis (man′tis) *n., pl.* **-tis·es** or **-tes′** (-tēz′) ⟦ModL < Gr, prophet, seer, kind of insect < IE base **men-,* to think > MIND⟧ any of an order (Mantodea) of slender, elongated insects that feed on other insects and grasp their prey with stout, spiny forelegs: see PRAYING MANTIS, illus.: often called **man′tid** (-tid)

man·tis·sa (man tis′ə) *n.* ⟦L, (useless) addition, makeweight, gain, ? via Etr < Celt: ? so named because it supplements the integral⟧ the decimal part of a logarithm to base 10 as distinguished from the integral part (called the *characteristic*) [.7193 is the *mantissa* of the logarithm 4.7193]

mantis shrimp STOMATOPOD

man·tle (man′təl) *n.* ⟦ME *mantel* < OE *mentel* & OFr *mantel,* both < L *mantellum, mantelum,* a cloth, napkin, cloak, mantle < ? Celt⟧ **1** a loose, sleeveless cloak or cape: often used fig., in allusion to royal robes of state, to connote authority or responsibility **2** anything that cloaks, envelops, covers, or conceals [hidden under the *mantle* of night] **3** a small meshwork hood made of a noncombustible substance, such as a thorium or cerium compound, which when placed over a flame, as in a lantern, gives off a brilliant incandescent light **4** the outer wall and casing of a blast furnace, above the hearth **5** *alt. sp. of* MANTEL **6** *Anat. former term for* the cortex of the cerebrum **7** *Geol.* *a)* the layer of the earth's interior between the crust and the core *b)* *short for* MANTLE ROCK **8** *Zool.* *a)* a major part of a mollusk or similar organism consisting of a sheet of epithelial tissue with muscular, neural, and glandular elements: it covers the viscera and foot under the shell of univalve or bivalve mollusks, secretes the shell, and forms the body of cephalopods *b)* the soft outer body wall of a tunicate or barnacle *c)* the plumage on the back and folded wings of certain birds when it is all the same color —*vt.* **-tled**,

-tling to cover with or as with a mantle; envelop; cloak; conceal —*vi.* **1** to be or become covered, as a surface with scum or froth **2** to spread like a mantle, as a blush over the face **3** to blush or flush **4** *Falconry* to spread first one wing, then the other, over the outstretched legs: said of a perched hawk

Man·tle (mant′'l), **Mick·ey (Charles)** (mik′ē) 1931-95; U.S. baseball player

mantle rock REGOLITH: sometimes written **man′tle·rock′** *n.*

mant·let (mant′lit) *n. var. of* MANTELET (sense 2)

man-to-man (man′tə man′) *adj.* **1** frank, honest, sincere, etc. in a direct, personal way [a *man-to-man* talk] **2** designating or of a type of defense used in various team sports, in which each defensive player guards a specified offensive player

Man·toux test (man to͞o′, man′to͞o′) ⟦after C. *Mantoux* (1877-1947), Fr physician⟧ a test for present or past tuberculosis, in which a small amount of protein from tuberculosis bacteria is injected into the skin

man·tra (man′trə, män′-, mun′-) *n.* ⟦Sans, akin to *mantár-*, thinker: see MANDARIN⟧ **1** *Hinduism* a hymn or portion of text, esp. from the Veda, chanted or intoned as an incantation or prayer **2** a syllable, word, etc. repeated during yogic meditation **3** a word or slogan often repeated, as to provide inspiration [the store manager's *mantra* was "always maximize sales"]

man·tu·a (man′tyo͞o ə, -to͞o ə) *n.* ⟦altered (after fol.) < Fr *manteau* < OFr *mantel,* MANTLE⟧ a mantle or loose gown or cloak formerly worn by women

Man·tu·a (man′cho͞o ə, -to͞o ə) commune in Lombardy, N Italy: birthplace of Virgil: It. name **Man·to·va** (män′tô vä) —**Man′tu·an** *adj., n.*

man·u·al (man′yo͞o əl) *adj.* ⟦ME *manuel* < OFr < L *manualis* < *manus*, a hand < IE **mə-n-és* (akin to **mn̥tos* > Gmc **mund-* > ON & OE *mund*, a hand) < base **mər-, *mən-*, hand⟧ **1** *a)* of or having to do with a hand or the hands *b)* made, done, worked, or used by the hands *c)* involving or doing hard physical work that requires use of the hands **2** without electrical or other power [a *manual* typewriter] **3** *Mech.* designating or of a transmission, specif. an automotive transmission, requiring manual shifting of the gears —*n.* ⟦ME *manuele* < ML *manuale,* manual, service book < LL, case or covering for a book < L *manualis:* see the *adj.*⟧ **1** a handy book of facts, instructions, etc. for use as a guide or reference; handbook **2** any of the separate keyboards of an organ console or harpsichord **3** prescribed drill in the handling of a weapon, esp. a rifle: also **manual of arms** —**man′u·al·ly** *adv.*

manual alphabet a system of communication, esp. one for deaf persons, in which positions of the fingers indicate the letters of the alphabet

ma·nu·bri·um (mə no͞o′brē əm, -nyo͞o′-) *n., pl.* **-bri·a** (-ə) or **-bri·ums** ⟦L, a handle, hilt, haft < *manus,* a hand: see MANUAL⟧ a handlelike structure, process, or part, esp., *a)* the portion of a jellyfish or other cnidarian that bears the mouth at its tip *b)* the uppermost of the three bony segments constituting the breastbone in mammals

Man·uel (man wel′, män-; man′yo͞o əl, man′yo͞o el′) *n.* a masculine name: dim. *Manny*: see EMMANUEL

manuf or **manufac** *abbrev.* **1** manufactured **2** manufacturer

man·u·fac·to·ry (man′yo͞o fak′tər ē, -yə-) *n., pl.* **-ries** ⟦< fol. + FACTORY⟧ FACTORY (sense 1)

man·u·fac·ture (man′yo͞o fak′chər, -yə-) *n.* ⟦Fr < ML *manufactura* < L *manu,* abl. of *manus,* a hand (see MANUAL) + *factura,* a making < *factus,* pp. of *facere,* to make, DO[1]⟧ **1** the making of goods and articles by hand or, esp., by machinery, often on a large scale and with division of labor **2** anything so made; manufactured product **3** the making of something in any way, esp. in a way regarded as merely mechanical —*vt.* **-tured**, **-tur·ing** **1** to make by hand or, esp., by machinery, often on a large scale and with division of labor **2** to work (wool, steel, etc.) into usable form **3** to produce (art, literature, etc.) in a way regarded as mechanical and uninspired **4** to make up (excuses, evidence, etc.); invent; fabricate; concoct —**SYN.** MAKE[1] —**man′u·fac′tu·ra·ble** *adj.*

man·u·fac·tur·er (-chər ər) *n.* a person or company in the business of manufacturing; specif., a factory owner

man·u·mis·sion (man′yo͞o mish′ən) *n.* ⟦OFr < L *manumissio* < pp. of *manumittere:* see fol.⟧ a freeing or being freed from slavery; emancipation

man·u·mit (-mit′) *vt.* **-mit′ted**, **-mit′ting** ⟦ME *manumitten* < OFr *manumitter* < L *manumittere,* lit., to let go from the hand, free < *manu,* abl. of *manus,* a hand (see MANUAL) + *mittere,* to send: see MISSION⟧ to free from slavery; emancipate (a slave, serf, etc.)

ma·nure (mə no͝or′, -nyo͝or′) *vt.* **-nured′**, **-nur′ing** ⟦ME *manouren,* orig., to farm (land) < Anglo-Fr *maynoberer* < OFr *manouvrer,* to cultivate, lit., to work with the hands: see MANEUVER⟧ to put manure on or into (soil) —*n.* ⟦< the *vt.*⟧ organic substances, esp. animal excrement, put on or into the soil to fertilize it —**ma·nur′er** *n.*

ma·nus (mā′nəs) *n., pl.* **ma′nus** ⟦L, hand: see MANUAL⟧ the terminal part of the forelimb of a vertebrate, as the hand of a person or the forefoot of a four-legged animal

man·u·script (man′yo͞o skript′, -yə-) *adj.* ⟦L *manu scriptus,* written by hand < *manu,* abl. of *manus,* hand (see MANUAL) + *scriptus,* pp. of *scribere,* to write: see SCRIBE⟧ **1** written by hand or with a typewriter, not printed **2** designating writing that consists of unconnected letters resembling print; not cursive —*n.* ⟦ML *manuscriptum*⟧ **1** a book or document written by hand, esp. before the invention of printing: see also CODEX **2** a written or typewritten document or paper, esp. the copy of an author's work that is submitted to a publisher or printer **3** writing as distinguished from print

Ma·nu·ti·us (mə no͞o′shē əs, -nyo͞o′-), **Al·dus** (ôl′dəs) (It. name *Aldo Manucci* or *Manuzio*) 1450-1515; It. printer: see also ALDINE

Manx (maŋks) *adj.* ⟦by metathesis < obs. *Maniske* < ON **manskr* < *Man-*, inflectional base of *Mǫn,* Isle of Man < Celt name, as in Welsh *Manau,* OIr *Manu*⟧ of the Isle of Man or its people, language, or culture —*n.* **1** the Celtic language formerly spoken on the Isle of Man and now nearly extinct **2** *pl.* **Manx** any of a breed of domestic cat, originating on the Isle of Man, with a short, dense coat and no tail —**the Manx** the people of the Isle of Man

Manx·man (-mən) *n., pl.* **-men** (-mən) a person born or living on the Isle of Man

Manx·wom·an (-wo͝om′ən) *n., pl.* **-wom′en** (-wim′in) a woman born or living on the Isle of Man

man·y (men′ē) *adj.* **more, most** ⟦ME < OE *manig,* akin to Ger *manch* (OHG *manag*) < IE base **menegh-*, many, richly > Sans *maghā-*, gift, OIr *menicc,* abundant⟧ **1** consisting of some large, indefinite number (of persons or things); numerous **2** relatively numerous (preceded by *as, too,* etc.) —*pl.n.* a large number (*of* persons or things) —*pron.* many persons or things —**a good many** [*with pl. v.*] a relatively large number (of persons or things) —**a great many** [*with pl. v.*] an extremely large number (of persons or things) —**as many** the same number of [to read ten books in *as many* days] —**be (one) too many for someone** [Informal] to be more, stronger, etc. than someone can defeat or successfully deal with —**have one (or a few) too many** [Informal] to become somewhat drunk —**so many** **1** a finite but unspecified number of [works *so many* hours a week] **2** some number of or the same number of [acting like *so many* children] —**the many** **1** the majority of people **2** the masses

USAGE—the idiom **many a (or an, another)** followed by a singular noun or pronoun is equivalent to *many* followed by the corresponding plural (e.g., "*many a* man has tried" means the same thing as "many men have tried")

man·y·fold (men′ē fōld′) *adv.* by many increments [her new book increased her readership *manyfold*]

man·y-sid·ed (men′ē sīd′id) *adj.* **1** having many sides or aspects **2** having many possibilities, qualities, interests, or accomplishments —**man′y-sid′ed·ness** *n.*

man·za·nil·la (man′zə nēl′yə, -nē′ə) *n.* ⟦Sp, dim. of *manzana,* apple: see MANCHINEEL; connection with apples not clear⟧ a dry Spanish sherry

☆**man·za·ni·ta** (man′zə nēt′ə) *n.* ⟦AmSp < Sp, dim. of *manzana,* apple: see MANCHINEEL⟧ any of several shrubs or small trees (genus *Arctostaphylos*) of the heath family, found in the W U.S.

Man·zo·ni (män zō′nē; *It* män dzô′-), **A·les·san·dro (Francesco Tommaso Antonio)** (ä′les sän′drô) 1785-1873; It. poet & novelist

MAO (em′ā′ō′) *n.* ⟦M(ONO)A(MINE) O(XIDASE)⟧ an enzyme that deaminates monoamines: it destroys excessive amounts of many biologically active monoamines, as serotonin, epinephrine, or histamine

Mao·ism (mou′iz′əm) *n.* the communist theories and policies of Mao Tse-tung —**Mao′ist** *adj., n.*

Ma·o·ri (mä′ō rē, mou′rē; mā ôr′ē) *n.* ⟦< Maori: said to mean "native, of the usual kind"⟧ **1** *pl.* **-ris** or **-ri** a member of a Polynesian people native to New Zealand **2** the Austronesian language of this people —*adj.* of the Maoris or their language or culture

mao-tai (mou′tī′) *n.* ⟦after *Mao-t'ai,* town in SW China⟧ a strong, colorless Chinese liquor distilled from grain: also written **mao tai**

Mao Tse-tung (mou′ dzə′do͞oŋ′) 1893-1976; Chin. Communist leader: chairman of the People's Republic of China (1949-59) & of its Communist Party (1949-76): Pinyin *Mao Zedong*

map (map) *n.* ⟦ML *mappa (mundi),* map (of the world) < L *mappa,* napkin, cloth (on which maps were painted): said (by QUINTILIAN) to be of Punic orig.; prob. < TalmudHeb *mappa* < **manpa,* contr. < *menafa,* a fluttering banner⟧ **1** a drawing or other representation, usually on a flat surface, of all or part of the earth's surface, ordinarily showing countries, bodies of water, cities, mountains, etc. **2** a similar representation of part of the sky, showing the relative position of the stars, planets, etc. **3** any maplike representation or delineation **4** [Slang] the face **5** *Genetics* a graphic representation of the relative locations of various genes on a chromosome or plasmid —*vt.* **mapped**, **map′ping** **1** to make a map or maps of; represent or chart on or as on a map **2** to arrange or plan in detail: often with *out* [to *map* out a project] **3** to survey or explore for the purpose of making a map **4** *Genetics* *a)* to locate (a particular gene) on a chromosome or plasmid *b)* to make a genetic map of [to *map* the human genome]: see *n.* 5 above **5** *Math.* to transform, as by a mapping —**put on the map** [Informal] to make well known —☆**wipe off the map** [Informal] to put out of existence —**map′per** *n.*

Map (map), **Walter** 1140?-1209?; Welsh poet & satirist: also, Latin name, **Mapes** (māps, mā′pēz′)

ma·ple (mā′pəl) *n.* ⟦ME < OE *mapel(treo),* akin to ON *mǫpurr*⟧ **1** any of a large genus (*Acer*) of trees of the maple family, grown for wood, sap, or shade **2** the hard, closegrained, light-colored wood of such a tree, used for furniture, flooring, etc. **3** the reddish-yellow or yellowish color of the finished wood **4** the flavor of maple syrup or of the sugar made from this —*adj.* **1** designating a family (Aceraceae, order Sapindales) of dicotyledonous trees and a few shrubs, characterized by opposite, often lobed leaves, small clusters of flowers, and two-winged fruits **2** of or made of maple **3** flavored with maple

maple leaf **1** the national emblem of Canada **2** *pl.* **maple leafs** [*often* **M-L-**] a gold coin of Canada, often bought for investment

☆**maple sugar** sugar made by a further boiling down of maple syrup

☆**maple syrup** syrup made by boiling down the sap of any of various maples, esp. the sugar maple

map·mak·er (map′māk′ər) *n.* a person or firm that makes maps —**map′mak′ing** *n.*

map·ping (map′iŋ) *n. Math.* a transformation taking the points of one space into the points of the same or another space

Ma·pu·to (mə po͞ot′ō) seaport & capital of Mozambique, on the Indian Ocean

ma·quette (ma ket′) *n.* ⟦Fr < It *macchietta,* lit., little spot, dim. of *macchia* < L *macula,* a spot⟧ a small model of a planned sculpture, building, etc.

ma·qui (mä′kē) *n.* ⟦AmSp < Araucanian name⟧ an ornamental Chilean plant (*Aristotelia chilensis,* family Elaeocarpaceae) of the same order (Malvales) as the linden tree: fiber from its bark is used for stringing native musical instruments, and its purple berries are made into a medicinal wine

☆**ma·qui·la·do·ra** (mä kē′lə dôr′ə) *n.* ⟦MexSp < *maquilar,* assemble⟧ a manufacturing facility under foreign ownership in Mexico and typically located near the U.S. border: it is set up to take advantage of low taxes and wages: also **ma·qui·la** (mä kē′lä)

ma·quil·lage (mȧ kē yȧzh′) *n.* ⟦Fr < *maquiller,* to make up, orig., to work, irreg. < OFr *makier,* to do, make < MDu *maken,* akin to MAKE[1]⟧ makeup; cosmetics

ma·quis (mä kē′; *Fr* mȧ kē′) *n.* ⟦Fr < It *macchia,* a thicket, orig. a spot < L *macula,* a spot, stain⟧ **1** a zone of shrubby plants, chiefly evergreens, growing in areas having a Mediterranean climate **2** *pl.* **-quis′** (-kēz′; *Fr,* -kē′) [*often* **M-**] a member of the French underground fighting against the Nazis in WWII

mar[1] (mär) *vt.* **marred**, **mar′ring** ⟦ME *marren* < OE *mierran,* to hinder, spoil, akin to Goth *marzjan,* to offend < IE base **mer-,* to disturb, anger > Sans *mṛ́ṣyate,* (he) forgets, neglects⟧ to injure or damage so as to make imperfect, less attractive, etc.; spoil; impair; disfigure —*n.* [Rare] something that mars; an injury or blemish

mar[2] *abbrev.* **1** marine **2** maritime **3** married

Mar *abbrev.* March

mar·a·bou (mar′ə bo͞o′) *n.* ⟦Fr, *marabout* (see fol.): so named from its contemplative posture⟧ **1** a bare-headed, large-billed African stork (*Leptoptilos crumeniferus*) **2** soft feathers from the wing coverts and tail of the marabou **3** *a)* a delicate, white raw silk thread that can be dyed with the natural gum still in it *b)* a fabric made of this

mar·a·bout (mar′ə bo͞ot′; *for 3, also,* -bo͞o′) *n.* ⟦Fr < Port *marabuto* < Ar *murābit,* hermit⟧ **1** a Muslim hermit or holy man, esp. among the Berbers and Moors **2** the tomb or shrine of such a man **3** *var. of* MARABOU

ma·ra·ca (mə rä′kə) *n.* ⟦Port *maracá* < Tupí⟧ a percussion instrument, played usually in pairs, consisting of a dried gourd or a gourd-shaped rattle with dried seeds or loose pebbles in it, that is shaken

Mar·a·cai·bo (mar′ə kī′bō; *Sp* mä′rä kī′bô) **1** seaport in NW Venezuela **2** **Lake** lake in NW Venezuela, connected by channel with the Gulf of Venezuela: largest lake in South America: *c.* 5,000 sq mi (12,950 sq km)

Mar·a·can·da (mer′ə kan′də) *ancient name for* SAMARKAND

Ma·ra·cay (mä′rä kī′) city in N Venezuela

☆**mar·ag·ing steel** (mär′ā′jiŋ) ⟦MAR(TENSITE) + *aging,* spontaneous hardening of metals during storage⟧ a nickel-iron alloy of extremely high strength, produced from martensite steel by spontaneous hardening at moderate temperatures without quenching

Ma·ra·nhão (mä′rə nyoun′) state of NE Brazil: 128,713 sq mi (333,365 sq km); cap. São Luís

Ma·ra·ñón (mä′rä nyôn′) river that rises in the Andes in WC Peru, flows northwest to N Peru, then east & joins the Ucayali to form the Amazon: *c.* 1,000 mi (1,609 km)

ma·ran·ta (mə rän′tə) *n.* ⟦ModL, after B. *Maranta* (1500-71), It herbalist⟧ any of a genus (*Maranta*) of plants of the arrowroot family, esp. a variety (*M. leuconeura kerchoveana*) with spotted red leaves

ma·ras·ca (mə ras′kə) *n.* ⟦It: see fol.⟧ SOUR CHERRY

mar·a·schi·no (mar′ə shē′nō, -skē′-) *n.* ⟦It < *marasca, amarasca,* kind of cherry < *amaro,* bitter < L *amarus* < IE base **om-,* raw, bitter > OE *ampre,* sorrel⟧ a strong, sweet liqueur or cordial made from the fermented juice of the sour cherry

maraschino cherries cherries in a syrup flavored with maraschino or, now usually, imitation maraschino

ma·ras·mus (mə raz′məs) *n.* ⟦ML < Gr *marasmos,* a wasting away < *marainein,* to quench, cause to waste away: see MARE[3]⟧ a condition of progressive emaciation, esp. in infants, as from malnutrition or an inability to assimilate food —**ma·ras′mic** *adj.*

Ma·rat (mȧ rȧ′), **Jean Paul** (zhän pôl) 1743-93; Fr. Revolutionary leader, born in Switzerland: assassinated by Charlotte Corday

Ma·ra·tha (mə rä′tə) *n.* ⟦Marathi *Marāṭhā* < Sans *Mahārāṣṭra,* lit., great country < *mahā-,* great (see MAGNI-) + *rāṣṭra,* kingdom < *rāj,* to rule: see RAJAH⟧ a member of a people of Maharashtra state in W India

Ma·ra·thi (mə rä′tē) *n.* the Indo-Aryan language of the Marathas

mar·a·thon (mar′ə thän′) *n.* **1** a footrace of 26 miles, 385 yards, run over an open course, esp. as an event of the Olympic games or as an annual event in some cities: after the legend of the Greek runner who ran from Marathon to Athens to tell of the victory over the Persians (490 B.C.) **2** any contest or endeavor that tests endurance

Mar·a·thon (mar′ə thän′) ancient Greek village in E Attica, or a plain nearby, where the Athenians under Miltiades defeated the Persians under Darius I (490 B.C.)

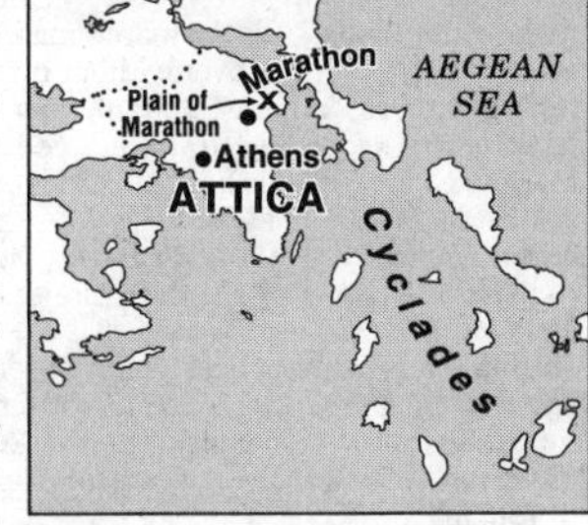

Marathon (5th cent. B.C.)

mar·a·thon·er (-ər) *n.* one who competes in or trains for a marathon —**mar′a·thon′ing** *n.*

ma·raud (mə rôd′) *vi.* ⟦Fr *marauder* < *maraud,* vagabond, prob. special use of dial. Fr *maraud,* tomcat, echoic of cry⟧ to rove in search of plunder; make raids —*vt.* to raid; plunder; pillage —*n.* [Archaic] the act of marauding —**ma·raud′er** *n.*

mar·a·ve·di (mar′ə vā′dē) *n.* ⟦Sp < Ar *Murābiṭīn,* name of a Moorish dynasty at Córdoba (1086-1147) < *murābiṭ:* see MARABOUT⟧ **1** a gold coin used by the Moors in Spain in the 11th & 12th cent. **2** an obsolete Spanish copper coin

mar·ble (mär′bəl) *n.* ⟦ME *marble, marbre* < OFr *marbre* < L *marmor* < Gr *marmaros,* white stone, orig. boulder (meaning infl. by *marmairein,* to shine) < IE base **mer-,* to rub > MARE[3]⟧ **1** a hard, crystalline or granular, metamorphic limestone, white or variously colored and sometimes streaked or mottled, which can take a high polish: it is much used in building and sculpture **2** *a)* a piece or slab of this stone, used as a monument, inscribed record, etc. *b)* a piece of sculpture in marble **3** anything resembling or suggesting marble in hardness, smoothness, coldness, coloration, etc. **4** *a)* a little ball of stone, glass, or clay, used in games *b)* [*pl., with sing. v.*] a children's game in which a marble is propelled by the thumb at other marbles, usually in an attempt to drive them out of a marked circle **5** a marbled pattern; marbling **6** [*pl.*] [Slang] mental soundness; sanity; wits [to lose one's *marbles*] —*adj.* **1** made or consisting of marble **2** like marble in some way; hard, cold, smooth, white, etc., or streaked, mottled, etc. —*vt.* **-bled**, **-bling** to stain or color (book edges) to look mottled or streaked like marble —☆**go for all the marbles** ⟦see *n.* 4⟧ [Slang] to take a great risk in the hope of a great gain —**mar′bly** *adj.*

☆**marble cake** a cake made of light and dark batter mixed to give a streaked appearance like marble

mar·bled (mär′bəld) *adj.* **1** covered in marble or characterized by the use of marble **2** mottled or streaked like marble **3** having fat evenly distributed in narrow streaks: said of meat

☆**mar·ble·ize** (mär′bəl īz′) *vt.* **-ized′**, **-iz′ing** to make, color, grain, or streak in imitation of marble

mar·bling (mär′bliŋ) *n.* **1** the art or process of staining or veining like marble, as the decoration of book edges in marblelike patterns **2** a streaked, veined, or mottled appearance like that of marble [a *marbling* of fat in beef]

marc (märk; *Fr* mȧr) *n.* ⟦Fr < *marcher,* to tread, trample, MARCH[1]⟧ **1** refuse of grapes, seeds, other fruits, etc. after pressing **2** a brandy distilled from it, esp. from grape residue **3** the residue after extraction of a chemical, drug, etc. from a substance

Mar·can (mär′kən) *adj.* of or characteristic of the Evangelist Mark or the book of the New Testament ascribed to him

Marc Antony *see* ANTONY[2], Mark

mar·ca·site (mär′kə sīt′) *n.* ⟦Fr *marcassite* < ML *marcasita* < Ar *marqashītā* < Pers *marqashīshā*⟧ **1** an orthorhombic mineral, FeS_2, that is dimorphic with pyrite; iron sulfide **2** this mineral cut and mounted on silver or other white metal to look like brilliants

mar·ca·to (mär kä′tō) *adj., adv.* ⟦It < pp. of *marcare,* to mark, accent, of Gmc orig.⟧ *Musical Direction* with each note emphasized

Mar·ceau (mȧr sō′), **Mar·cel** (mȧr sel′) (born *Marcel Mangel*) 1923-2007; Fr. mime

mar·cel (mär sel′) *n.* ⟦after *Marcel* Grateau, early 20th-c. Fr hairdresser⟧ a formerly popular hairstyle for women consisting of a series of even waves put with a curling iron in hair cut short: also **marcel wave** —*vt.* **-celled′**, **-cel′ling** to put such waves in (hair)

Mar·cel[1] (mär sel′) *n.* a masculine name: see MARCELLUS[1]

Mar·cel[2] (mȧr sel′), **Ga·bri·el** (gȧ brē el′) 1889-1973; Fr. philosopher

Mar·cel·la (mär sel′ə) *n.* ⟦L⟧ a feminine name: see MARCELLUS[1]

Mar·cel·lus[1] (mär sel′əs) *n.* ⟦L, dim. of *Marcus*⟧ a masculine name: var. *Marcel;* fem. *Marcella*

Mar·cel·lus[2] (mär sel′əs), **(Marcus Claudius)** 268?-208 B.C.; Rom. statesman & general

mar·ces·cent (mär ses′ənt) *adj.* ⟦L *marcescens,* prp. of *marcescere,* to wither, decay < *marcere,* to wither < IE **merk-,* to grow soft, rot < base **mer-,* to rub > MARE[3]⟧ *Bot.* withering but not falling off

march[1] (märch) *vi.* ⟦Fr *marcher,* orig., to tread, trample < OFr, prob. < Frank **markon* < **marka,* MARK[1]: orig. sense prob. "to pace off the boundary"⟧ **1** to walk with regular, steady steps of equal length, usually in a group or military formation **2** to walk in a grave, stately way **3** to advance or progress steadily —*vt.* **1** to cause (troops, etc.) to march **2** to cause or force to go —*n.* **1** the act of marching **2** a regular forward movement; steady advance; progress [the *march* of events] **3** a regular, steady step or pace **4** the distance covered in a period of marching [a day's *march*] **5** a long, tiring walk **6** a piece of music, with a steady, even beat, suitable for marching to **7** an organized walk by a number of people demonstrating on some public issue —**on the march** marching or advancing —**steal a march on** to get an advantage over without being perceived

march² (märch) ***n.*** ⟦OFr < Frank **marka*, MARK¹⟧ a borderland, esp. one in dispute —***vi.*** [Rare] to have a common border (*with*); border —**the Marches 1** borderlands between England & Scotland and between England & Wales **2** *see* MARCHE², Le

March (märch) ***n.*** ⟦ME < OFr *march, marz* < L *Martius (mensis),* (month) of Mars < *Mars,* MARS⟧ the third month of the year, having 31 days: abbrev. *Mar, Mr,* or *M*

Marche¹ (märsh) historical region of central France

Mar·che² (mär′ke), **Le** (le) region of central Italy, on the Adriatic: 3,743 sq mi (9,694 sq km); chief city, Ancona: Eng. name **the March·es** (mär′chiz)

Mär·chen (mer′Hən) ***n.***, *pl.* **-chen** ⟦Ger⟧ a story or tale; esp., a fairy tale or folk tale

march·er¹ (mär′chər) ***n.*** a person who marches

march·er² (mär′chər) ***n.*** **1** a person who lives in a march, or borderland **2** a lord who governed or defended the Marches for England: see THE MARCHES (sense 1) at MARCH²

mar·che·sa (mär kā′zä) ***n.***, *pl.* **-che′se** (-zā) ⟦It, fem. of *marchese:* see fol.⟧ **1** the wife or widow of a marchese **2** an Italian noblewoman ranking just above a countess

mar·che·se (mär kā′zā) ***n.*** ⟦It < OFr *marchis:* see MARQUIS⟧ *pl.* **-che′si** (-zē) an Italian nobleman ranking just above a count; marquis

March hare a hare in breeding time, proverbially regarded as an example of madness

marching orders 1 orders to march, leave, or proceed **2** [Informal] notice of dismissal

mar·chion·ess (mär′shə nis, mär′shə nes′) ***n.*** ⟦ML *marchionissa,* fem. of *marchio,* prefect of the marches < *marcha,* border < Frank **marka,* MARK¹⟧ **1** the wife or widow of a marquess **2** a lady whose rank in her own right equals that of a marquess See also MARQUISE (sense 1)

march·pane (märch′pān′) ***n.*** *var. of* MARZIPAN

Mar·cia (mär′shə) ***n.*** ⟦L, fem. of *Marcius,* name of a Roman gens < *Marcus,* MARCUS⟧ a feminine name: var. *Marsha*

Mar·ci·a·no (mär′sē ä′nō), **Rock·y** (räk′ē) (born *Rocco Francis Marchegiano*) 1923-69; U.S. boxer: world heavyweight champion (1952-56)

Mar·cion·ism (mär′shə niz′əm) ***n.*** ⟦after *Marcion,* Christian Gnostic of the 2d c. A.D.⟧ the doctrines of a rigorous Christian sect of the 2d and 3d cent. that rejected the Old Testament and all but the writings of Paul in the New Testament —**Mar′cion·ite′** (-nīt′) ***n.***

Mar·co·ni (mär kō′nē; *It* mär kô′nē), Marchese **Gu·gliel·mo** (go͞o lyel′mô) 1874-1937; It. physicist: developed wireless telegraphy

☆**Marconi rig** ⟦so named because the structure resembles that used in wireless telegraphy, developed by MARCONI⟧ a popular sailing rig with a tall, triangular mainsail set fore and aft

Marco Polo *see* POLO, Marco

Mar·cus (mär′kəs) ***n.*** ⟦L < *Mars,* MARS⟧ a masculine name: dim. *Marc;* var. *Mark;* fem. *Marcia*

Marcus Aurelius *see* AURELIUS, Marcus

Mar·cy (mär′sē), **Mount** ⟦after W. L. *Marcy,* governor of New York (1833-39)⟧ mountain in N N.Y.: highest peak of the Adirondacks: 5,344 ft (1,629 m)

Mar del Pla·ta (mär′del plät′ə) seaport & resort in E Argentina, south of Buenos Aires

Mar·di Gras (mär′dē grä′) ⟦Fr, lit., fat Tuesday⟧ [*sometimes* **M- g-**] **1** Shrove Tuesday, the last day before Lent: it is a day of merrymaking and carnival, as in New Orleans, often marking the climax of a carnival period **2** CARNIVAL (sense 1)

Mar·duk (mär′dook′) ***n.*** ⟦Bab⟧ *Bab. Myth.* the chief deity, orig. a local sun god

mare¹ (mer) ***n.*** ⟦ME < OE *mere,* fem. of *mearh,* akin to Ger *mähre,* jade, prob. < IE base **marko-,* horse, seen only in Gmc & Celt (Ir *marc,* Welsh *march,* horse)⟧ a fully mature female horse, mule, donkey, burro, etc.; specif., a female horse that has reached the age of five

ma·re² (mä′rā′, -rē′) ***n.***, *pl.* **ma·ri·a** (mä′rē ə, mar′ē ə) ⟦L, sea < IE base **mori* > Goth *marei,* sea, OE *mere,* sea, lake, Welsh *mor,* sea⟧ **1** a sea **2** any of several vast, dark, flat areas visible from the earth on the surface of the moon, Mercury, or Mars

mare³ (mer) ***n.*** ⟦ME < OE, akin to Ger dial. *mahr,* ON *mar* < IE **mora,* incubus < base **mer-,* to rub, seize > Gr *marainein,* to quench, OIr *meirb,* lifeless, OE *mearu,* soft⟧ [Obs.] *Folklore* an evil spirit that causes nightmares

Mare Island (mer) ⟦transl. of Sp *Isla de la Yegua:* said to be for a *mare* that swam to the island and joined a herd of elk⟧ island at the N end of San Francisco Bay, Calif.: site of a U.S. navy yard

ma·re clau·sum (mä′rā klou′səm) ⟦L, closed sea⟧ a portion of the sea under the jurisdiction of a single nation and not open to all others

ma·re li·be·rum (mä′rā lē′bə rəm) ⟦L, free sea⟧ a portion of the sea open to all nations

ma·rem·ma (mə rem′ə) ***n.***, *pl.* **-rem′me** (-ē) ⟦It < L *maritimus:* see MARITIME⟧ fertile, marshy land near the sea, esp. in Italy

Ma·ren·go (mə reŋ′gō) village in the Piedmont, NW Italy: site of a victory (1800) by Napoleon over the Austrians

ma·re nos·trum (mä′rā nôs′trəm) ⟦L, lit., our sea⟧ *Roman name for* the MEDITERRANEAN SEA

mare's-nest (merz′nest′) ***n.*** ⟦proverbial⟧ **1** something supposed to be a wonderful discovery but turning out to be a hoax or a delusion **2** a disorderly or confused condition; mess

mare's-tail (-tāl′) ***n.*** **1** long, narrow formations of cirrus cloud somewhat like a horse's tail in shape, supposed to be a sign of changes in the wind **2** the only species (*Hippuris vulgaris*) of an aquatic family (Hippuridaceae, order Callitrichales) of plants with tiny flowers and narrow, hairlike leaves growing in thick whorls around slender, erect stems **3** HORSEWEED (sense 1)

Mar·fan syndrome (mär′fan) ⟦after Antonin *Marfan* (1858-1942), Fr physician, who first described it (1892)⟧ a hereditary disorder characterized by abnormalities of the blood circulation and the eyes, abnormally long bones in the limbs, and unusually flexible joints: also **Marfan's syndrome**

marg *abbrev.* **1** margin **2** marginal

Mar·ga·ret (mär′gə rit, -grit) ***n.*** ⟦ME < OFr *Margarete* < L *margarita,* a pearl < Gr *margaritēs* < *margaron,* a pearl, ult. < or akin to Sans *mañjaram,* a pearl, orig., bud⟧ a feminine name: dim. *Greta, Madge, Maggie, Marge, Meg, Peg, Peggy;* var. *Margery, Margo, Margot, Marjorie;* equiv. Fr. *Marguerite,* Ger. *Margarete, Gretchen,* Ir. *Megan,* It. *Margherita,* Sp. *Margarita*

Margaret of Anjou 1430-82; queen of Henry VI of England (1445-61; 1470-71)

Margaret of Navarre 1492-1549; queen of Navarre (1544-49): writer & patron of literature: also **Margaret of Angoulême**

Margaret of Valois 1553-1615; queen of Henry IV of France (1589-99): called *Queen Margot*

mar·gar·ic acid (mär gar′ik, -gär′-; mär′gə rik) ⟦Fr *margarique* < Gr *margaron,* a pearl (see MARGARET): from the pearly luster of its crystals⟧ a white, crystalline fatty acid, $C_{17}H_{34}O_2$, obtained from lichens or synthetically

mar·ga·rine (mär′jə rin) ***n.*** ⟦Fr, from the erroneous notion that margaric acid was contained in all fats and oils⟧ a cooking fat or substitute for butter, made of refined vegetable oils (and sometimes rendered animal fat) processed to the consistency of butter, often churned with pasteurized milk or whey: sometimes sp. **mar′ga·rin**

mar·ga·ri·ta (mär′gə rēt′ə) ***n.*** ⟦< Sp *Margarita,* MARGARET⟧ a cocktail made of tequila, lemon or lime juice, and triple sec, typically served in a salt-rimmed glass

Mar·ga·ri·ta (mär′gə rēt′ə) island of Venezuela, just off the N coast: 414 sq mi (1,072 sq km)

mar·ga·rite (mär′gə rīt′) ***n.*** ⟦OFr < L *margarita:* see MARGARET⟧ [Obs.] a pearl

Mar·gate (mär′gāt′, -git) seaport & summer resort in Kent, SE England

mar·gay (mär′gā′) ***n.*** ⟦Fr < Port *maracajá* < Brazilian (Tupí) name⟧ a small ocelot (*Leopardus wiedii*) of Central and South America

marge¹ (märj) ***n.*** ⟦Fr < L *margo,* MARGIN⟧ [Archaic] a border; edge; margin

marge² (märj) ***n.*** [Brit. Informal] *short for* MARGARINE

mar·gent (mär′jənt) ***n.*** ⟦< MARGIN, with unhistoric *-t*⟧ [Archaic] a margin, or edge

Mar·ger·y (mär′jər ē) ***n.*** ⟦ME *Margerie* < OFr < L *margarita:* see MARGARET⟧ a feminine name: dim. *Marge:* see MARGARET

mar·gin (mär′jən) ***n.*** ⟦ME *margine* < L *margo* (gen. *marginis*): see MARK¹⟧ **1** a border, edge, or brink [*the margin of the pond*] **2** the blank space around the printed or written area on a page or sheet **3** a limit to what is desirable or possible **4** *a)* an amount of money, supplies, etc. reserved or allowed beyond what is needed; extra amount for contingencies or emergencies *b)* provision for increase, addition, or advance **5** an amount or degree of difference or inequality [*to win by a wide margin*] **6** *Business, Finance a)* the difference between the cost and the selling price of goods produced, sold, etc. *b)* collateral deposited with a broker by an investor as security against loss, as on an option contract *c)* a customer's equity if his or her account is closed at the prevailing prices *d)* the difference between the face value of a loan and the market value of the collateral put up to secure it **7** *Econ.* the minimum return, below which activities are not profitable enough to be continued **8** *Psychol.* the fringe of consciousness —***vt.*** ⟦L *marginare*⟧ **1** to provide with a margin or border; be a margin to; border **2** to enter, place, or summarize in the margin of a page or sheet **3** *Business, Finance* ☆*a)* to deposit a margin upon *b)* to hold by depositing or adding to a margin upon *c)* to purchase (securities) on margin —**SYN.** BORDER

mar·gin·al (mär′jə nəl) ***adj.*** ⟦ML *marginalis*⟧ **1** written or printed in the margin of a page or sheet **2** of or constituting a margin **3** at, on, or close to the margin or border **4** *a)* close to a margin or limit, esp. a lower limit [*a marginal standard of living*] *b)* minimal; limited *c)* minor; insignificant; not central **5** *a)* on the border between being profitable and being unprofitable [*a marginal business*] *b)* designating land unlikely to produce crops profitably *c)* of or from goods produced and sold at margin [*marginal costs, marginal profits*] —**mar′gin·al′i·ty** (-al′ə tē) ***n.*** —**mar′gin·al·ly** ***adv.***

mar·gi·na·li·a (mär′jə nā′lē ə, -nāl′yə) ***pl.n.*** ⟦ModL < neut. pl. of ML *marginalis*⟧ marginal notes

mar·gin·al·ize (mär′jə nə līz′) ***vt.*** **-ized′**, **-iz′ing** to exclude or ignore, esp. by relegating to the periphery of a group or by diverting the public's attention to something else —**mar′gin·al·i·za′tion** ***n.***

mar·gin·ate (mär′jə nāt′; *for adj. usually,* -nit) ***vt.*** **-at′ed**, **-at′ing** ⟦< L *marginatus,* pp. of *marginare*⟧ to provide with a margin —***adj.*** having a distinct margin: also **mar′gin·at′ed** —**mar′gin·a′tion** ***n.***

Mar·got (mär′gō, -gət) ***n.*** ⟦Fr⟧ a feminine name: var. *Margo:* see MARGARET

mar·gra·vate (mär′grə vāt′, -vit) ***n.*** ⟦see fol. & -ATE²⟧ the territory ruled by a margrave: also **mar·gra·vi·ate** (mär grā′vē āt′, -vē it)

mar·grave (mär′grāv′) ***n.*** ⟦MDu *markgrave* < MHG *marcgrave* < OHG *marcgravo* < *marc* (see MARK¹), a march, border + *graf,* a count, earl⟧ [Historical] 1 a military governor of a march, or border province, in Germany 2 the hereditary title of certain princes of the Holy Roman Empire or Germany —**mar·gra'vi·al** *adj.*

mar·gra·vine (mär'grə vēn') *n.* ⟦Du *markgravin,* fem. of *markgraaf*⟧ the wife of a margrave

mar·gue·rite (mär'gə rēt') *n.* ⟦Fr, a pearl, daisy: see MARGARET⟧ 1 DAISY (sense 1) 2 any of several cultivated chrysanthemums (esp. *Chrysanthemum frutescens*) with a single flower 3 any of various daisylike plants of the composite family

Mar·gue·rite (mär'gə rēt') *n.* ⟦see MARGARET⟧ a feminine name

ma·ri·a (mä'rē ə, mar'ē ə) *n. pl. of* MARE[2]

Ma·ri·a (mə rē'ə, -rī'-) *n.* a feminine name: see MARY[1]

☆**ma·ri·a·chi** (mär'ē ä'chē) *n., pl.* **-chis** ⟦MexSp < Fr *mariage* (see MARRIAGE): from providing music at wedding celebrations⟧ 1 a member of a strolling band of musicians in Mexico, or any similar band elsewhere, typically playing violins, guitars, and trumpets and dressed in traditional CHARRO garb 2 such a band 3 their music —*adj.* of or having to do with these musicians, their music, etc.

ma·ri·age de con·ve·nance (må ryȧzh' də kōnv näns') ⟦Fr⟧ MARRIAGE OF CONVENIENCE

Mar·i·an (mer'ē ən, mar'-) *n.* 1 ⟦var. of MARION[1], but sp. as if < MARY[1] + ANNE[1]⟧ a feminine name: var. *Marianne, Marianna* 2 a devotee of the Virgin Mary 3 a follower or defender of Mary, Queen of Scots —*adj.* 1 of the Virgin Mary 2 of Mary I of England 3 of Mary, Queen of Scots

Ma·ri·an·a Islands (mer'ē an'ə, mar'-) group of islands in the W Pacific Ocean, east of the Philippines: it includes Guam and the U.S. commonwealth of the NORTHERN MARIANA ISLANDS: formerly (except Guam) a Japanese possession and (1947-86) part of the Trust Territory of the Pacific Islands: also **Ma'ri·an'as**

Ma·ria·na·o (mä'ryä nä'ô) city in NW Cuba: suburb of Havana

Marianas Trench deepest known ocean trench in the world, with a maximum depth of *c.* 36,200 ft (*c.* 11,034 m) below sea level, located in the W Pacific near the Mariana Islands: also **Mariana Trench**

Mar·i·anne (mer'ē an', mar'-) *n.* 1 a feminine name: see MARIAN 2 *personification of* the French Republic: depicted as a woman in French Revolutionary costume

Maria Theresa 1717-80; archduchess of Austria: wife of Francis I (1708-65), emperor of the Holy Roman Empire: dowager empress (1765-80): queen of Bohemia & Hungary (1740-80): mother of Marie Antoinette

Ma·ri·bor (mär'i bôr') city in N Slovenia

mar·i·cul·ture (mar'i kul'chər) *n.* ⟦< L *mare,* sea + CULTURE⟧ saltwater aquaculture —**mar'i·cul'tur·ist** *n.*

Ma·rie (mə rē') *n.* a feminine name: see MARY[1]

Marie An·toi·nette (mə rē' an'twə net'; *Fr* må rē än twå net') 1755-93; wife of Louis XVI: queen of France (1774-92): daughter of Maria Theresa: guillotined

Marie Byrd Land region in W Antarctica, on the Amundsen Sea

Marie de France *traditional name for* the author or authors of a group of 12th-cent. Fr. lays

Marie de Médicis *see* MEDICI[2], Maria de'

Marie Louise 1791-1847; 2d wife of Napoleon I & empress of France (1810-15)

Mar·i·et·ta[1] (mer'ē et'ə, mar'-) *n.* a feminine name: see MARY[1]

Mar·i·et·ta[2] (mer'ē et'ə, mar'-) ⟦after MARIE ANTOINETTE⟧ city in SE Ohio, on the Ohio River: 1st permanent settlement (1788) in the Northwest Territory

mar·i·gold (mar'ə gōld') *n.* ⟦ME *marigolde* < *Marie* (prob. the Virgin Mary) + *gold,* GOLD⟧ 1 *a)* any of a genus (*Tagetes*) of annual plants of the composite family, with chiefly red, yellow, or orange flowers *b)* the flower of any of these 2 any of several other plants, usually of the composite family, as the pot marigold

☆**mar·i·jua·na** or **mar·i·hua·na** (mar'ə wä'nə, mär'-; -hwä'-) *n.* ⟦AmSp *marihuana, mariguana* < ? native word blended with personal name *María Juana,* Mary Jane⟧ 1 HEMP (*n.* 1*a*) 2 its dried leaves and flowers, smoked, esp. in the form of cigarettes, for euphoric effects

Mar·i·lyn (mar'ə lin) *n.* a feminine name: see MARY[1]

ma·rim·ba (mə rim'bə) *n.* ⟦Mbundu, a percussive instrument resembling the xylophone, akin to Tshiluba *madimba*⟧ a musical instrument somewhat like a xylophone, consisting of a series of hard wooden bars, usually with resonators beneath, struck with small mallets

marimba

ma·ri·na (mə rē'nə) *n.* ⟦It & Sp, seacoast < L *marinus:* see MARINE⟧ ☆a small harbor or boat basin where dockage, supplies, fuel, etc. are provided for small pleasure craft

mar·i·nade (mar'ə nād') *n.* ⟦Fr < Sp *marinada* < *marinar,* to pickle in brine < *marino* < L *marinus:* see MARINE⟧ a spiced pickling solution, esp. a mixture of oil, wine or vinegar, and spices, in which meat, fish, etc. is steeped, often before cooking —*vt.* **-nad'ed, -nad'ing** MARINATE

ma·ri·na·ra (mä'rə nä'rə, mär'ə ner'ə) *adj.* ⟦< It *alla marinara,* in the style of sailors < *marinaro,* adj., seafaring⟧ 1 designating or of a tomato sauce seasoned with garlic and spices and served with pasta, seafood, etc. 2 served with marinara sauce

mar·i·nate (mar'ə nāt') *vt.* **-nat'ed, -nat'ing** ⟦< It *marinato,* pp. of *marinare,* to pickle in brine < *marino* < L *marinus:* see fol.⟧ to steep (meat, fish, etc.) in a marinade —**mar'i·na'tion** *n.*

ma·rine (mə rēn') *adj.* ⟦ME *maryne* < L *marinus* < *mare,* the sea: see MARE[2]⟧ 1 *a)* of the sea or ocean *b)* inhabiting, found in, or formed by the sea 2 *a)* of navigation on the sea; nautical *b)* of shipping by sea; maritime 3 used, or to be used, at sea [*a marine* engine] 4 *a)* trained for service at sea and on land, as certain troops *b)* of such troops —*n.* 1 *a)* a member of a marine military force ☆*b)* [*often* **M-**] a member of the UNITED STATES MARINE CORPS 2 naval or merchant ships collectively; seagoing ships; fleet [the merchant *marine*] 3 in some countries, the department of government in charge of naval affairs 4 a picture of a ship or a sea scene

☆**Marine Corps** UNITED STATES MARINE CORPS

mar·i·ner (mar'ə nər) *n.* ⟦ME *marinere* < Anglo-Fr *mariner* (OFr *marinier*) < ML *marinarius* < L *marinus,* MARINE⟧ a sailor; seaman

Ma·ri·net·ti (mar'ə net'ē, mär'-), **(Emilio) Fi·lip·po Tom·ma·so** (fē lēp'pô tôm mä'zô) 1876-1944; It. poet

Mar·i·ol·a·try (mer'ē äl'ə trē, mar'-) *n.* ⟦< Gr *Maria,* MARY[1] + -LATRY⟧ veneration of the Virgin Mary, when regarded as carried to an idolatrous extreme

Mar·i·ol·o·gy (-äl'ə jē) *n.* ⟦see prec. & -LOGY⟧ the branch of Christian theology that deals with the Virgin Mary

Mar·i·on[1] (mer'ē ən, mar'-) *n.* ⟦Fr, orig. dim. of *Marie,* MARY[1]⟧ 1 a masculine name 2 a feminine name: see MARY[1]

Mar·i·on[2] (mer'ē ən, mar'-), **Francis** 1732?-95; Am. general in the Revolutionary War: called the *Swamp Fox*

mar·i·o·nette (mar'ē ə net', mer'-) *n.* ⟦Fr, dim. of *Marion:* see MARION[1]⟧ a puppet or little jointed figure made to look like a person or animal and moved by strings or wires from above, often on a miniature stage

☆**Mar·i·po·sa lily** (*or* **tulip**) (mar'ə pō'zə, -sə) ⟦AmSp *mariposa* < Sp, butterfly: from the appearance of the blossoms⟧ 1 any of a genus (*Calochortus*) of plants of the lily family, found in W North America, with tuliplike flowers of white, red, yellow, or violet 2 the flower of any of these plants

mar·ish (mar'ish) [Archaic] *n.* ⟦ME *mareis* < OFr < Frank **marisk,* akin to OE *merisc,* MARSH⟧ a marsh; swamp —*adj.* marshy

Mar·ist (mar'ist, mer'-) *adj.* ⟦Fr *Mariste* < *Marie,* MARY[1]⟧ of or dedicated to the Virgin Mary, esp., of any of several such educational and missionary societies founded in the 19th cent. —*n.* a member of a Marist society

Ma·ri·tain (må rē tan'), **Jacques** (zhäk) 1882-1973; Fr. philosopher

mar·i·tal (mar'ət'l) *adj.* ⟦L *maritalis* < *maritus,* married, a husband < *mas* (gen. *maris*), male⟧ 1 [Obs.] of a husband 2 of marriage; matrimonial; connubial —**mar'i·tal·ly** *adv.*

mar·i·time (mar'ə tīm') *adj.* ⟦L *maritimus* < *mare,* the sea: see MARE[2]⟧ 1 on, near, or living near the sea [*maritime* provinces, a *maritime* people] 2 of or relating to sea navigation, shipping, etc. [*maritime* law] 3 characteristic of sailors; nautical 4 *Meteorol.* of the relatively wet air or climate associated with large bodies of water: see AIR MASS

Maritime Alps S division of the W Alps, along the French-Italian border: highest peak, 10,817 ft (3,297 m)

Maritime Provinces Canadian provinces of Nova Scotia, New Brunswick, & Prince Edward Island: also called **the Mar'i·times'**

Ma·ri·u·pol (mä'rē o͞o'pôl) city in SE Ukraine, on the Sea of Azov: see ZHDANOV

Mar·i·us (mer'ē əs), **Gaius** 157?-86 B.C.; Rom. general & statesman

Ma·ri·vaux (må rē vō'), **Pierre Car·let de Cham·blain de** (pyer kår let shän bland' də) 1688-1763; Fr. playwright & novelist

mar·jo·ram (mär'jə rəm) *n.* ⟦ME *majoran* < OFr *majorane* < ML *maiorana,* prob. altered < L *amaracus* < Gr *amarakos,* marjoram: of Indic orig., akin to Sans *maruva-*⟧ any of a number of perennial plants of the mint family, esp. sweet marjoram

Mar·jo·rie or **Mar·jo·ry** (mär'jə rē) *n.* a feminine name: see MARGARET

mark[1] (märk) *n.* ⟦ME < OE *mearc,* orig., boundary, hence boundary sign, hence sign, akin to Ger *mark,* boundary, boundary mark, *marke,* a token, mark < Gmc **marka* < IE base **mereĝ-,* edge, boundary > L *margo,* MARGIN, OIr *mruig,* borderland⟧ 1 a visible trace or impression on a surface; specif., *a)* a line, dot, or other distinctive feature produced by drawing, coloring, stamping, etc. *b)* a spot, stain, scratch, blemish, mar, bruise, dent, etc. 2 a sign, symbol, or indication; specif., *a)* a printed or written sign or stroke [punctuation *marks*] *b)* a brand, label, seal, tag, etc. put on an article to show the owner, maker, etc. *c)* a sign or indication of some quality, character, etc. [politeness is a *mark* of good upbringing] *d)* a letter or figure used in schools, etc. to show quality of work or behavior; grade (*often used in pl.*) [received good *marks* her sophomore year] *e)* a cross or other sign made on a document as a substitute for a signature by a person unable to write 3 a standard of quality, proficiency, propriety, etc. [failing to come up to the *mark*] 4 importance; distinction; eminence [a man of *mark*] 5 impression; influence [to leave one's *mark* in history] 6 a visible object of known position, serving as a guide or point of reference [a tower as a *mark* for flyers] 7 a line, dot, notch, etc. used to indicate position, as on a graduated scale 8 *a)* an object aimed at; target *b)* an object desired or worked for; end; aim; goal 9 *a)* a person against whom an attack, criticism, ridicule, etc. is directed *b)* [Slang] an intended victim of a swindle 10 a taking notice; heed 11 [Archaic] *a)* a boundary, border, or borderland; march *b)* among Germanic peoples in earlier times, land held or worked in common by a community **12** *Film, Theater* something, as a piece of tape or a chalked line, indicating an actor's predetermined position on a stage or set **13** *Naut.* one of the knots or bits of leather or colored cloth placed at irregular intervals on a lead line to indicate depths in fathoms: cf. DEEP (*n.* 4) **14** *Sports a)* the starting line of a race (often used fig.) [on your *mark!*; a salesman who is quick off the *mark*] *b)* a spare or a strike in bowling —*vt.* **1** to put or make a mark or marks on **2** to identify or designate by or as by a mark or marks [abilities that *mark* one for success] **3** to trace, make, or produce by or as by marks; draw, write, record, etc. **4** to show or indicate by a mark or marks **5** to show plainly; make clear or perceptible [a smile *marking* happiness] **6** to set off as distinctive; distinguish; characterize [scientific discoveries that *marked* the 19th century] **7** to observe; note; take notice of; heed [*mark* my words] **8** to give a grade or grades to; rate [to *mark* examination papers] **9** to put prices on (merchandise) **10** to keep (score, etc.); record **11** to put a subtle mark surreptitiously on the back or edge of (a playing card) for later identification, as in an attempt to cheat **12** *Field Hockey, Soccer, etc.* to stay close to in order to impede the movement of (an opponent) —*vi.* **1** to make a mark or marks **2** to observe; take note **3** *Games* to keep score —**beside the mark** inaccurate, incorrect, irrelevant, etc. —**hit the mark** **1** to achieve one's aim; be successful in one's attempt **2** to be accurate; be right —**make one's mark** to achieve success or fame —**mark down** **1** to make a note of; write down; record ☆**2** *a)* to decrease (a price or prices) *b)* to decrease the price or prices of —**mark off** (or **out**) to mark the limits of; demarcate —**mark out for** to select for or note as selected for —**mark time** **1** to keep time while at a halt by lifting the feet alternately as if marching **2** to suspend progress for a time, as while awaiting developments —**mark up** **1** to cover with marks ☆**2** *a)* to increase (a price or prices) *b)* to increase the price or prices of **3** to add overhead and profit to the cost of in order to arrive at the selling price **4** to put (a legislative bill) into final form —**miss the mark** **1** to fail in achieving one's aim; be unsuccessful in one's attempt **2** to be inaccurate —**wide of the mark** inaccurate, incorrect, irrelevant, etc.

mark[2] (märk) *n.* ⟦ME *marke* < OE *marc* < ON *mǫrk*, a half pound of silver, mark, akin to prec.: orig. prob. in reference to symbol on the balance, later on the silver bar⟧ **1** a former European unit of weight for gold and silver, equal to about eight ounces **2** a unit of value orig. equivalent to about eight ounces of silver; specif., *a)* an obsolete Scottish silver coin *b)* a former money of account of England **3** the former basic monetary unit of Germany, superseded in 1924 by the REICHSMARK: cf. DEUTSCHE MARK **4** DEUTSCHE MARK **5** MARKKA

Mark (märk) *n.* **1** a masculine name: var. *Marc*: see MARCUS **2** *a) Bible* one of the four Evangelists, to whom is ascribed the second Gospel: his day is April 25 (also **Saint Mark**) *b)* the second book of the New Testament, telling the story of Jesus' life (abbrev. *Mk*)

mark·a (mär′kə) *n.* ⟦Serb, akin to Ger *mark*: see MARK[2]⟧ the basic monetary unit of Bosnia and Herzegovina: see the table of monetary units in the Reference Supplement

Mark·an (mär′kən) *adj. Bible alt. sp. of* MARCAN

Mark Antony *see* ANTONY[2], Mark

☆**mark·down** (märk′doun′) *n.* **1** a marking for sale at a reduced price **2** the amount of reduction in price

marked (märkt) *adj.* **1** having a mark or marks (in various senses) **2** singled out to be watched or looked for as an object of suspicion, hostility, etc. [a *marked* man] **3** noticeable; obvious; appreciable; distinct [a *marked* change in behavior] —**mark·ed·ly** (märk′id lē) *adv.* —**mark′ed·ness** *n.*

mark·er (mär′kər) *n.* a person or thing that marks; specif., *a)* a person who keeps score in a game *b)* a device for keeping score *c)* a device for marking lines, as on a tennis court *d)* a bookmark *e)* a gravestone ☆*f)* a milestone or similar sign *g)* GENETIC MARKER *h)* a felt-tip pen, esp. one with a broad tip

mar·ket (mär′kit) *n.* ⟦ME < NormFr < L *mercatus*, trade, marketplace, pp. of *mercari*, to trade < *merx* (gen. *mercis*), wares, merchandise < ? IE base **merk̑-*, to seize⟧ **1** *a)* a gathering of people for buying and selling things, esp. provisions or livestock *b)* the people gathered *c)* the time of such a gathering **2** an open space or a building where goods are shown for sale, usually with stalls or booths for the various dealers **3** a store or shop for the sale of provisions [a meat *market*] **4** a region in which goods can be bought and sold [the Asian *market*] **5** *a)* buying and selling; trade in goods, stocks, etc. [an active *market*] *b)* trade in a specified commodity [the wheat *market*] *c)* a place where such trade is carried on *d)* the group of people associated in such trade **6** *short for* STOCK MARKET **7** opportunity to sell, or demand (for goods or services) [a good *market* for new products] **8** opportunity to buy, or supply (of goods or services) [reduced labor *market*] **9** *a)* MARKET PRICE *b)* MARKET VALUE —*vt.* **1** to send or take to market **2** to offer for sale **3** to sell —*vi.* **1** to deal in a market; buy or sell **2** to buy provisions for the home —**be in the market for** to be seeking to buy or obtain —**be on the market** to be offered for sale —**put on the market** to offer for sale —**mar′ket·eer′** (-kə tir′) *n.* —**mar′ket·er** *n.*

mar·ket·a·ble (-ə bəl) *adj.* **1** *a)* that can be sold; fit for sale *b)* attractive to potential buyers, employers, etc. [a person with highly *marketable* skills] **2** of buying or selling [*marketable* value] —**mar′ket·a·bil′i·ty** *n.*

mar·ket·bas·ket (mär′kit bas′kit) *n.* a selected list of goods and services, usually food and household items regarded as typifying consumer spending over a given time, used to measure the COST OF LIVING: also written **market basket**

market economy an economy in which prices, the supply of goods, etc. are determined by buyers and sellers carrying on business dealings with a relatively high degree of freedom

mar·ket·ing (-iŋ) *n.* **1** the act of buying or selling in a market **2** *a)* all business activity involved in the moving of goods or the providing of services to the consumer *b)* the art or study of selling, advertising, packaging, etc.

market maker a firm which maintains a stable and liquid market for a particular security by buying and selling it as circumstances require

market order an order to buy or sell goods, stock, etc. at the current market price

mar·ket·place (-plās′) *n.* **1** a place, esp. an open place, where goods are offered for sale **2** the world of commerce: often used fig. [the *marketplace* of ideas]

market price the price that a commodity or service brings when sold in a given market; prevailing price

market research the study of the demands or needs of consumers in relation to particular goods or services

market share the percentage of the total sales of some commodity or service accounted for by a given company

market value the price that a commodity or service can be expected to bring when sold in a given market

Mark·ham (mär′kəm) **1** ⟦after Rev. W. *Markham* (1720-1806), Archbishop of York (England)⟧ town in SE Ontario, Canada, northeast of Toronto **2** **Mount** mountain in Antarctica, near the SW edge of the Ross Ice Shelf: 14,270 ft (4,349 m)

mark·ing (mär′kiŋ) *n.* **1** the act of making a mark or marks **2** a mark or marks **3** [*also pl.*] the characteristic arrangement of marks or coloring, as of a plant or animal

mark·ka (mär′kä) *n., pl.* **-kaa** (-kä) ⟦Finn < Swed *mark*: see MARK[2]⟧ the former basic monetary unit of Finland, superseded in 2002 by the EURO

Mar·kov process (mär′kôf) ⟦after A. A. *Markov* (1856-1922), Russ mathematician⟧ a chain of random events in which only the present state influences the next future state, as in a genetic code: also sp. **Mar′koff process**

marks·man (märks′mən) *n., pl.* **-men** (-mən) a person who shoots, esp. one who shoots well —**marks′man·ship′** *n.*

☆**mark·up** (märk′up′) *n.* **1** *a)* a marking for sale at an increased price *b)* the amount of increase in price **2** the amount added to the cost to cover overhead and profit in arriving at the selling price **3** *a)* the putting of a legislative bill into final form *b)* the committee meeting at which this is done **4** *Comput.* a system for tagging text for style, content, and typographical features: in full **markup language**

marl[1] (märl) *n.* ⟦ME < OFr *marle* < ML *margila* (> Ger *mergel*), dim. of L *marga*, marl < Gaul⟧ **1** *Geol.* a soft, crumbly mixture of clay, sand, and limestone in varying proportions, typically containing shell fragments **2** any loose, earthy, crumbly deposit —*vt.* to cover or fertilize with marl —**marl′y** *adj.*

marl[2] (märl) *vt.* ⟦Du *marlen*, prob. freq. < MDu *marren*, to lash, bind, akin to MHG *merren*, to hinder, fasten < IE base **mer-*, to disturb, anger > MAR[1]⟧ to wind marline around (rope), taking a hitch at each turn

Marl·bor·ough (märl′bur′ō, -ə; *Brit* môl′bər ə), 1st Duke of (*John Churchill*) 1650-1722; Eng. general & statesman

Mar·lene (mär lēn′; -lē′nə, -lā′nə) *n.* a feminine name

mar·lin (mär′lin) *n., pl.* **-lin** or **-lins** ⟦< MARLINESPIKE: from the shape⟧ any of several large, slender, deep-sea billfishes, esp. a bluish species (*Makaira nigricans*)

mar·line (mär′lin) *n.* ⟦Du *marlijn*, altered (infl. by *lijn*, LINE[1]) < *marling* < *marlen*: see MARL[2]⟧ a small cord of two loosely twisted strands, used as for winding around ropes or cables to prevent fraying: also **mar′lin** or **mar′ling** (-liŋ)

mar·line·spike or **mar·lin·spike** (-spīk′) *n.* a pointed metal tool for separating the strands of a rope or wire in splicing: also **mar′ling·spike′**

Mar·lowe (mär′lō), **Christopher** 1564-93; Eng. dramatist & poet —**Mar·lo·vi·an** (mär lō′vē ən) *adj.*

mar·ma·lade (mär′mə lād′) *n.* ⟦OFr *marmelade* < Port *marmelada*, orig., confection of quinces < *marmelo*, quince < L *melimelum* < Gr *melimēlon*, sweet apple < *meli*, honey (see MILDEW) + *mēlon*, apple⟧ a jamlike preserve made by boiling the pulp and peel of a citrus fruit with sugar

marmalade tree a tropical American evergreen tree (*Calocarpum sapota*) of the sapodilla family, bearing a plumlike fruit (**marmalade plum**) used for preserving

Mar·ma·ra (mär′mə rə), **Sea of** sea between European & Asiatic Turkey, connected with the Black Sea by the Bosporus & with the Aegean by the Dardanelles: c. 4,300 sq mi (11,137 sq km)

mar·mite (mär′mīt; mär mēt′) *n.* **1** a usually ceramic pot for making soup **2** soup made in, or as if in, such a pot — [**M-**] *trademark for* a brown food spread made from brewer's yeast

Mar·mo·la·da (mär′mô lä′dä) highest peak of the Dolomites, N Italy: 10,965 ft (3,342 m)

mar·mo·re·al (mär môr′ē əl) *adj.* ⟦< L *marmoreus* < *marmor*, MARBLE + -AL⟧ **1** of marble **2** like marble; cold, white, smooth, hard, etc. Also **mar·mo′re·an** —**mar·mo′re·al·ly** *adv.*

mar·mo·set (mär′mə zet′, -set′) *n.* ⟦ME < OFr *marmouset*, grotesque figure < ?: form prob. infl. by *marmouser*, to mumble, grumble, of echoic orig.⟧ any of a family (Callithricidae) of very small New World monkeys of South and Central America, with thick, soft, variously colored fur

mar·mot (mär′mət) *n.* ⟦Fr *marmotte* < earlier *marmottaine,* prob. < L *mus montanus,* mountain mouse⟧ any of a genus (*Marmota*) of thick-bodied, gnawing, burrowing squirrels with coarse fur and a short, bushy tail, as the woodchuck

Marne (märn) river in NE France, flowing northwest & west into the Seine near Paris: scene of two WWI battles in which German offensives were checked

Ma·roc (mȧ rôk′) *Fr. name for* MOROCCO

Mar·o·nite (mar′ə nīt′) *n.* ⟦ML *Maronita,* after *Maro* (lit., master), 5th-c. Syrian monk, founder of the sect⟧ a member of an Eastern Church, originally heterodox but now in communion with the Rom. Catholic Church

ma·roon[1] (mə ro͞on′) *n., adj.* ⟦Fr *marron,* chestnut, chestnut color < It *marrone*⟧ dark brownish-red

ma·roon[2] (mə ro͞on′) *n.* ⟦Fr *marron* < AmSp *cimarrón,* wild, unruly < OSp *cimarra,* thicket⟧ **1** [*sometimes* **M-**] in the West Indies and Suriname, *a)* [Historical] a fugitive black slave *b)* a descendant of such slaves **2** [Rare] a marooned person —*vt.* **1** to put (a person) ashore in some desolate place, as a desert island, and abandon that person there, as pirates or mutineers sometimes did **2** to leave abandoned, isolated, or helpless —*vi.* ☆[Obs.] in the South, to camp out or picnic for several days

mar·plot (mär′plät′) *n.* ⟦ult. < MAR[1] + PLOT⟧ [Rare] a person who mars or spoils some plan by officious interference

Marq *abbrev.* **1** Marquess **2** Marquis

marque[1] (märk) *n.* ⟦ME *mark* < MFr *marque* < Prov *marca,* seizure, reprisal < *marcar,* to seize as a pledge < *marc,* token of pledge < Gmc: see MARK[1]⟧ reprisal: obsolete except in LETTERS OF MARQUE

marque[2] (märk) *n.* ⟦Fr, a sign < *marquer,* to mark < OIt *marcare* < *marca,* a mark < Gmc **marka:* see MARK[1]⟧ **1** a nameplate or emblem, as to identify an automobile **2** a brand of a product, esp. of an automobile

mar·quee (mär kē′) *n.* ⟦false sing. < Fr *marquise* (misunderstood as pl.), an awning, canopy over an officer's tent, lit., marquise: reason for name uncert.⟧ **1** [Chiefly Brit.] a large tent with open sides, esp. one used for some outdoor entertainment ☆**2** a projecting, rooflike structure or sign over the entrance to a theater or other entertainment venue advertising information about current or upcoming attractions —*adj.* [Informal] so well-known or well-publicized as to attract large audiences [*a marquee* event, *marquee* ballplayer]

Mar·que·san (mär kā′sən, -zən) *n.* **1** a member of the indigenous people of the Marquesas Islands **2** the Austronesian language of this people —*adj.* of the Marquesas Islands or their people, language, or culture

Mar·que·sas Islands (mär kā′zəz, -səz) group of islands in French Polynesia, in the E South Pacific: 405 sq mi (1,049 sq km)

mar·quess (mär′kwis) *n.* ⟦var. of MARQUIS⟧ **1** a British nobleman ranking above an earl and below a duke **2** MARQUIS —**mar′quess·ate** (-kwə zit) *n.*

Marquess of Queensberry rules ⟦after John Douglas, 9th *Marquess of Queensberry* (1844-1900), Brit nobleman who supervised their formulation (*c.* 1867)⟧ the basic rules of modern boxing, providing for the use of gloves, the division of a match into rounds, etc.

mar·que·try or **mar·que·terie** (mär′kə trē) *n.* ⟦Fr *marqueterie* < *marqueter,* to spot, inlay < *marque,* a mark < OFr *merc* < ON *merki* < Gmc **marka:* see MARK[1]⟧ decorative inlaid work of wood, ivory, metal, etc., used in furniture and flooring

Mar·quette (mär ket′), **Jacques** (zhäk) 1637-75; Fr. Jesuit missionary & explorer in North America: called *Père Marquette*

mar·quis (mär′kwis; *Fr* mȧr kē′) *n., pl.* **mar′quis·es** or Fr. **mar·quis′** ⟦ME *markis* < OFr *marchis* (later *marquis*) < ML *marchisus,* prefect of a frontier town < *marca,* a borderland < Frank **marka:* see MARK[1]⟧ in some countries of Europe, a nobleman ranking above an earl or count and below a duke: cf. MARQUESS —**mar′quis·ate** (-kwə zit) *n.*

Mar·quis (mär′kwis), **Don(ald Robert Perry)** 1878-1937; U.S. humorist & journalist

mar·quise (mär kēz′) *n.* ⟦Fr, fem. of *marquis*⟧ **1** *a)* the wife or widow of a marquis *b)* a lady whose rank in her own right equals that of a marquis **2** MARQUEE **3** *a)* a ring with jewels set in the shape of a pointed oval *b)* a gem, esp. a diamond, cut in this shape

mar·qui·sette (mär′ki zet′, -kwi-) *n.* ⟦dim. of Fr *marquise,* awning: see MARQUEE⟧ a thin, meshlike fabric used for curtains, dresses, etc.

Marquis of Queensberry rules MARQUESS OF QUEENSBERRY RULES

Mar·ra·kech or **Mar·ra·kesh** (mə rä′kesh, mar′ə kesh′) city in WC Morocco

Mar·ra·no (mə rä′nō) *n., pl.* **-nos** ⟦Sp, lit., swine (expression of contempt) < Ar *muḥarram,* forbidden thing⟧ [*also* **m-**] a Jew living in Spain or Portugal during the Spanish Inquisition who professed Christianity to escape death or persecution, often continuing to observe Judaism secretly: cf. CONVERSO

mar·riage (mar′ij) *n.* ⟦ME *mariage* < OFr < *marier:* see MARRY[1]⟧ **1** the state of being married; relation between spouses; married life; wedlock; matrimony **2** the act of marrying; wedding **3** the rite or form used in marrying **4** any close or intimate union **5** the king and queen of a suit, esp. as a meld in pinochle

mar·riage·a·ble (mar′i jə bəl) *adj.* **1** old enough to get married **2** suitable for marriage [*of a marriageable* age] —**mar′riage·a·bil′i·ty** *n.*

marriage broker a person whose occupation is arranging nuptial matches for others

marriage of convenience ⟦Fr *mariage de convenance*⟧ marriage entered into from calculated self-interest or expediency

marriage portion [Historical] DOWRY (sense 1)

mar·ried (mar′ēd) *adj.* **1** living together as spouses; joined in wedlock **2** having a spouse **3** of marriage or married people; connubial; conjugal **4** closely or intimately joined —*n.* a married person: chiefly in **young marrieds**

mar·ron (mar′ən; *Fr* mȧ rōn′) *n.* ⟦Fr < It *marrone,* chestnut⟧ a large, sweet European chestnut, often used in confectionery

mar·rons gla·cés (mȧ rōn glȧ sā′) ⟦Fr⟧ marrons in syrup or glazed with sugar; candied chestnuts

mar·row (mar′ō) *n.* ⟦ME *merow* < OE *mearg,* akin to Ger *mark,* marrow < IE base **mozgho-,* marrow, brains > Sans *majján-,* marrow⟧ **1** the soft, vascular, fatty tissue that fills the cavities of most bones: also **bone marrow** **2** the innermost, essential, or choicest part; pith **3** vitality **4** [Brit.] VEGETABLE MARROW —**mar′row·y** *adj.*

marrow bean a plump-seeded variety of the common field bean (*Phaseolus vulgaris*), grown for its dry, edible seeds

mar·row·bone (-bōn′) *n.* **1** a bone containing marrow, esp. one used in cooking **2** [*pl.*] [Archaic] the knees: humorous usage

mar·row·fat (-fat′) *n.* a variety of large, rich pea

☆**marrow squash** any variety of oblong squash with a hard, smooth rind

Mar·rue·cos (mär we′kôs) *Sp. name for* MOROCCO

mar·ry[1] (mar′ē) *vt.* **-ried, -ry·ing** ⟦ME *marien* < OFr *marier* < L *maritare* < *maritus,* a husband, married, prob. < IE base **meri,* young wife, akin to **meryo,* young man > Sans *márya-,* man, young man, suitor⟧ **1** *a)* to join as spouses; unite in wedlock *b)* to join (an individual) to another as his or her spouse **2** to take as spouse; take in marriage **3** to join closely or intimately; unite —*vi.* **1** to get married; take a spouse **2** to enter into a close or intimate relationship; unite —**marry off** to give in marriage [*they married off* the last of their children] —**mar′ri·er** *n.*

mar·ry[2] (mar′ē) *interj.* ⟦euphemistic respelling of (the Virgin) MARY[1]⟧ [Archaic] used to express surprise, anger, etc., or, sometimes, merely to provide emphasis

Mars (märz) *n.* ⟦L⟧ **1** *Rom. Myth.* the god of war; identified with the Greek Ares **2** *a personification of* war **3** the seventh largest planet of the solar system and the fourth in distance from the sun: diameter, *c.* 6,790 km (*c.* 4,220 mi); period of revolution, 1.88 earth years; period of rotation, 24.62 hours; two satellites; symbol, ♂

Mar·sa·la (mär sä′lä) *n.* ⟦after *Marsala,* seaport in W Sicily⟧ a dry or sweet, amber-colored fortified wine made in W Sicily

Mar·seil·laise (mär′sə lāz′; *Fr* mȧr se yez′) *n.* ⟦Fr, lit., of Marseille: first sung by Marseille volunteers⟧ the national anthem of France, composed by Rouget de Lisle in 1792 during the French Revolution

Mar·seille (mȧr se′y′; *E* mär sā′) seaport in SE France, on the Gulf of Lions

Mar·seilles[1] (mär sālz′) *n.* [*sometimes* **m-**] a thick, strong, figured or striped cotton cloth with a raised weave, somewhat resembling piqué: originally made in Marseille

Mar·seilles[2] (mär sā′, -sālz′) *Eng. sp. of* MARSEILLE

marsh (märsh) *n.* ⟦ME *mersch* < OE *merisc,* akin to MLowG *mersch, marsch* (> Ger *marsch*) < IE base **mori,* sea > MARE[2]⟧ a tract of low, wet, soft land that is temporarily, or permanently, covered with water, characterized by aquatic, grasslike vegetation; swamp; bog; morass; fen

Marsh (märsh) **1** Dame **Nga·io (Edith)** (nī′ō) 1899-1982; New Zealand writer of detective stories **2 Reginald** 1898-1954; U.S. painter

Mar·sha (mär′shə) *n.* a feminine name: see MARCIA

mar·shal (mär′shəl) *n.* ⟦ME *marescal* < OFr *mareschal* < Frank **marhskalk* or OHG *marahscalh,* lit., horse servant (> ML *marescalcus*) < *marah,* horse (akin to OE *mearh,* horse: see MARE[1]) + *scalh,* servant < IE base **skel-,* to spring⟧ **1** a high official of a royal household or court, as in medieval times, in charge of military affairs, ceremonies, etc. **2** a military commander; specif., *a)* FIELD MARSHAL *b)* in various foreign armies, a general officer of the highest rank *c)* an officer of the highest rank in the British Royal Air Force **3** an official in charge of ceremonies, processions, rank and order, etc. who arranges the order of march ☆**4** an officer of various kinds in the U.S.; specif., *a)* a federal officer appointed to a judicial district to carry out orders and perform functions like those of a sheriff *b)* a minor officer of the law in some cities *c)* the head, or a high-ranking officer, of a police or fire department in some cities —*vt.* **-shaled** or **-shalled, -shal·ing** or **-shal·ling 1** to arrange (troops, things, ideas, etc.) in order; array; dispose [*to marshal* forces for battle] **2** *a)* to direct as a marshal; manage *b)* to lead or guide ceremoniously —**mar′shal·cy** *n.*, **mar′shal·ship′**

Mar·shall[1] (mär′shəl) *n.* a masculine name: var. *Marshal*

Mar·shall[2] (mär′shəl) **1 George C(atlett)** 1880-1959; U.S. general & statesman: U.S. Army chief of staff (1939-45): secretary of state (1947-49) **2 John** 1755-1835; chief justice of the U.S. (1801-35) **3 Thur·good** (thur′ goo͝d) 1908-93; associate justice, U.S. Supreme Court (1967-91)

Marshall Islands ⟦after John *Marshall,* Brit explorer (1788)⟧ country on a group of islands in the W Pacific Ocean, east of the Caroline Islands: formerly a Japanese mandate & formerly (1947-86) part of the Trust Territory of the Pacific Islands: 70 sq mi (181 sq km); cap. Majuro Atoll

Marshall Plan ⟦after Gen. George C. MARSHALL[2], its originator⟧ the U.S.-financed program (1947-51) for the rebuilding of European agriculture and industry after WWII: official name *European Recovery Program*

Mar·shal·sea (mär′shəl sē′) *n.* ⟦ME *marschalcie* < Anglo-Fr *mareschalcie* < ML *marescalcia:* see MARSHAL⟧ **1** a British court of justice, abolished in 1849, under the marshal of the royal household **2** a prison in Southwark, London, for debtors, etc., abolished in 1842

marsh elder ☆any of a genus (*Iva*) of North American plants of the composite family, growing in salt marshes and moist soil

marsh gas a gaseous product, chiefly methane, formed from decomposing vegetable matter, as in marshes
marsh hawk a large, gray American hawk (*Circus cyaneus*) that nests on the ground and preys on mice, frogs, snakes, etc.: the only North American harrier hawk
marsh hen any of several birds, as the rail or coot, living or feeding in marshy areas
marsh·land (märsh′land′) ***n.*** an area or region characterized by marshes or swamps
marsh·mal·low (märsh′mel′ō, -mal′ō) ***n.*** **1** a sweet paste originally made from the root of the marsh mallow, and now made of sugar, starch, corn syrup, and gelatin **2** a soft, spongy confection, in the form of small, rounded pieces coated with powdered sugar, made of this paste
marsh mallow **1** a pink-flowered, perennial, European plant (*Althaea officinalis*) of the mallow family: the root was formerly used for marshmallows and is sometimes used in medicine **2** ROSE MALLOW
marsh marigold a marsh plant (*Caltha palustris*) of the buttercup family, with bright-yellow flowers and shiny, circular leaves, sometimes eaten as greens
marsh·y (mär′shē) ***adj.*** **marsh′i·er, marsh′i·est** **1** of, consisting of, or containing a marsh or marshes **2** like a marsh; soft and wet; boggy; swampy **3** growing in marshes —**marsh′i·ness** ***n.***
Mar·ston (mär′stən), **John** 1576-1634; Eng. dramatist & satirist
Marston Moor moor in Yorkshire, N England: site of a battle (July, 1644) of the English civil war in which Royalist forces were routed by the Parliamentarians
mar·su·pi·al (mär so͞o′pē əl) ***adj.*** **1** of or like a marsupium, or pouch **2** of a superorder (Marsupialia) of mammals that lack a placenta and have an external abdominal pouch (marsupium) containing the teats: the incompletely developed offspring nurses within this pouch for several months after birth to complete its development —***n.*** an animal of this kind, as a kangaroo, opossum, or wombat
mar·su·pi·um (-əm) ***n.***, *pl.* **-pi·a** (-ə) ⟦ModL < L < Gr *marsypion*, dim. of *marsypos*, pouch, bag⟧ **1** a fold of skin on the abdomen of a female marsupial, forming a pouch in which the newborn young are carried **2** a structure like this, in some crustaceans, fishes, etc.
mart (märt) ***n.*** ⟦ME *marte* < MDu, var. of *markt* < VL *marcatus*, for L *mercatus*, MARKET⟧ **1** a market, or trading center **2** [Obs.] *a)* a fair *b)* buying and selling; bargaining *c)* a bargain
Mar·ta·ban (mär′tə bän′), **Gulf of** part of the Andaman Sea, on the S coast of Myanmar
mar·ta·gon (mär′tə gən) ***n.*** ⟦ME < Fr < Turk *martagān*, a turban⟧ a Turk's-cap lily (*Lilium martagon*) having white or purple flowers
Mar·tel (mär tel′), **Charles** A.D. 688?-741; ruler of Austrasia (714-741) & of all the Franks (719-741): checked the Moorish invasion of Europe with a decisive victory near Tours (732): grandfather of Charlemagne
Mar·tel·lo (tower) (mär tel′ō) ⟦It *martello*, a hammer, folk etym. substitution for *mortella*, a tower, after *Mortella*, cape in Corsica, where such a tower was attacked by the English fleet (1794)⟧ [*also* **m- t-**] any of the circular forts of masonry built in the 19th cent. by the British on coasts to protect against invaders
mar·ten (märt′'n) ***n.***, *pl.* **-tens** or **-ten** ⟦ME *martren* < OFr *martrine*, adj. < *martre*, marten < Frank **martar*, akin to Ger *marder*, OE *mearth* < PGmc **marthu-* < IE **martu-*, bride (euphemism for the taboo IE name); akin to **meri*: see MARRY[1]⟧ **1** any of a genus (*Martes*) of small musteline carnivores that live chiefly in trees and have a long, slender body, short legs, and soft, thick, valuable fur **2** the fur
mar·tens·ite (märt′'n zīt′) ***n.*** ⟦after A. *Martens* (1850-1914), Ger metallurgist⟧ a very hard, brittle, solid solution of iron and carbon or the carbide of iron, Fe_3C: the main component of quenched steel —**mar′ten·sit′ic** (-tən zit′ik) ***adj.***
Mar·tha (mär′thə) ***n.*** ⟦LL(Ec) < Gr(Ec) < Aram *Mārthā*, lit., lady, fem. of *mār*, lord⟧ **1** a feminine name: equiv. Fr. *Marthe*, It. & Sp. *Marta* **2** *Bible* sister of Lazarus and Mary, chided by Jesus for being overly concerned with housework while he talked with Mary: Luke 10:40
Martha's Vineyard ⟦after a *Martha* Gosnold and the wild grapes growing there⟧ island off the SE coast of Mass., south of Cape Cod: *c.* 100 sq mi (259 sq km)
Mar·tí (mär tē′), **Jo·sé (Julián)** (hō se′) 1853-95; Cuban poet, essayist, & revolutionary patriot
mar·tial (mär′shəl) ***adj.*** ⟦ME *martialle* < L *martialis*, of Mars⟧ **1** of or suitable for war [*martial songs*] **2** showing a readiness or eagerness to fight; warlike **3** of the army, the navy, or military life; military —**mar′tial·ism′** ***n.*** —**mar′tial·ist** ***n.*** —**mar′tial·ly** ***adv.***

SYN.—**martial** refers to anything connected with or characteristic of war or armies, connoting esp. pomp, discipline, etc. [*martial* music, *martial* law]; **warlike** stresses the bellicose or aggressive nature or temperament that leads to war or results from preparations for war [a *warlike* nation]; **military** applies to anything having to do with armies or soldiers [*military* uniforms, police, etc.] —*ANT.* **pacifist**

Mar·tial (mär′shəl) (*Marcus Valerius Martialis*) A.D. 40?-104?; Rom. epigrammatist & poet, born in Spain
martial art any of various systems of self-defense originating in E Asia, such as karate or kung fu, also engaged in as a sport: *usually used in pl.*
martial law temporary rule by the military authorities over the civilian population, as in an area of military operations in time of war, or when civil authority has broken down: distinguished from MILITARY LAW
Mar·tian (mär′shən) ***adj.*** ⟦L *Martius*, of MARS + -AN⟧ of the planet Mars —***n.*** a being from or living on the planet Mars, as in science fiction
mar·tin (märt′'n) ***n.*** ⟦Fr, ? after ST. MARTIN⟧ any of several swallows (esp. genus *Progne*), as the purple martin and various Old World birds (esp. *Delichon urbica*): see KINGBIRD
Mar·tin[1] (märt′'n) ***n.*** ⟦Fr < L *Martinus* < *Mars* (gen. *Martis*), Mars: hence, lit., warlike⟧ a masculine name: dim. *Marty*
Mar·tin[2] (märt′'n) **1** Saint (A.D. 316?-397?) bishop of Tours: his day is MARTINMAS: also called Saint **Martin of Tours** **2 Homer Dodge** 1836-97; U.S. painter
Mar·ti·neau (märt′'n ō′), **Harriet** 1802-76; Eng. writer & economist
mar·ti·net (märt′'n et′, märt′'n et′) ***n.*** ⟦after Gen. Jean *Martinet*, 17th-c. Fr drillmaster⟧ **1** a very strict military disciplinarian **2** any very strict disciplinarian or stickler for rigid regulations
mar·tin·gale (märt′'n gāl′) ***n.*** ⟦Fr, prob. < Sp *almártaga*, a check, rein < Ar⟧ **1** the strap of a horse's harness passing from the noseband to the girth between the forelegs, to keep the horse from rearing or throwing back its head **2** *a)* a lower stay for the jib boom or flying jib boom of a sailing vessel, to bear the strain of the head stays *b)* DOLPHIN STRIKER **3** a system of betting in which, after a losing wager, the amount bet is doubled or otherwise increased Also **mar′tin·gal′** (-gal′)
☆**mar·ti·ni** (mär tē′nē) ***n.***, *pl.* **-nis** ⟦altered (prob. as assumed sing.) < earlier *Martinez*: said to have originated in *Martinez, Calif.*⟧ a cocktail made of gin (or vodka) and dry vermouth, usually served with a green olive or lemon twist
Mar·ti·nique (mär′tə nēk′) island in the Windward group of the West Indies: overseas department of France: 436 sq mi (1,128 sq km); cap. Fort-de-France
Martin Luther King Day the third Monday in January, a legal holiday in the U.S. commemorating the birthday (Jan. 15) of Martin Luther King, Jr.
Mar·tin·mas (märt′'n məs) ***n.*** ⟦ME *Martinmasse*: see MARTIN[1] & MASS[1]⟧ Saint Martin's day, a church festival held on Nov. 11
mart·let (märt′lit) ***n.*** ⟦Fr *martelet*, prob. < *martinet*, dim. of *martin*⟧ **1** the Old World house martin **2** *Heraldry* a representation of a bird without feet, used as a crest or bearing
mar·tyr (märt′ər) ***n.*** ⟦ME *martir* < OE < LL(Ec) < Gr *martyr*, *martys*, a witness (LGr(Ec), martyr) < IE base **(s)mer-*, to remember, care > L *memor*, mindful, Sans *smárati*, (he) remembers⟧ **1** *a)* any of those persons who choose to suffer or die rather than give up their faith or principles *b)* any person tortured or killed because of his or her beliefs **2** a person who suffers great pain or misery for a long time **3** a person who assumes an attitude of self-sacrifice or suffering in order to arouse feelings of pity, guilt, etc. in others —***vt.*** **1** to put to death or torture for adherence to a belief **2** to torture; make suffer greatly; persecute
mar·tyr·dom (-dəm) ***n.*** ⟦ME *martirdom* < OE *martyrdom*: see prec. & -DOM⟧ **1** the state of being a martyr **2** the death or sufferings of a martyr **3** severe, long-continued suffering; torment
mar·tyr·ize (-īz′) ***vt.*** **-ized′**, **-iz′ing** ⟦ME *martirizen* < LL(Ec) *martyrizare*⟧ to make a martyr of, as by causing to suffer —***vi.*** to be or become a martyr —**mar′tyr·i·za′tion** ***n.***
mar·tyr·ol·o·gy (märt′ər äl′ə jē) ***n.***, *pl.* **-gies** ⟦ML *martyrologium* < LGr *martyrologion*: see MARTYR & -LOGY⟧ **1** a list of martyrs **2** a historical account of religious martyrs, esp. Christian martyrs **3** such accounts collectively **4** the branch of ecclesiastical history dealing with the lives of martyrs —**mar′tyr·ol′o·gist** ***n.***
mar·tyr·y (märt′ər ē) ***n.***, *pl.* **-tyr·ies** ⟦ME *martyrye* < LL(Ec) *martyrium* < LGr(Ec) *martyrion*⟧ a shrine in memory of a martyr
MARV (märv) ***n.*** ⟦*ma(neuverable) r(eentry) v(ehicle)*⟧ a MIRV-like ballistic missile having within each warhead an independent propulsion system that can evade defensive missiles and improve accuracy
mar·vel (mär′vəl) ***n.*** ⟦ME *mervaile* < OFr *merveille*, a wonder < VL *mirabilia*, wonderful things, orig. neut. pl. of L *mirabilis*, wonderful < *mirari*, to wonder at < *mirus*, wonderful: see SMILE⟧ **1** a wonderful or astonishing thing; prodigy or miracle **2** [Archaic] astonishment —***vi.*** **-veled** or **-velled**, **-vel·ing** or **-vel·ling** to be filled with admiring surprise; be amazed; wonder —***vt.*** to wonder at or about: followed by a clause
Mar·vell (mär′vəl), **Andrew** 1621-78; Eng. poet
mar·vel-of-Pe·ru (mär′vəl əv pə ro͞o′) ***n.*** *Bot.* FOUR-O'CLOCK
mar·vel·ous (mär′və ləs) ***adj.*** ⟦ME *merveilous* < OFr *merveillos* < *merveille*: see MARVEL⟧ **1** causing wonder; surprising, astonishing, or extraordinary **2** so extraordinary as to be improbable, incredible, or miraculous **3** very good; fine; splendid Also [Chiefly Brit.] **mar′vel·lous** —**mar′vel·ous·ly** ***adv.***
Mar·vin (mär′vin) ***n.*** ⟦prob. ult. < Gmc **mari*, sea + **winiz*, friend⟧ a masculine name: dim. *Marv*; var. *Mervin*
marv·y (mär′vē) ***adj.*** [Slang] very good; fine; marvelous
Marx (märks) **1 Grouch·o** (grou′chō′) (born *Julius Henry Marx*) 1890-1977; U.S. actor & comedian **2 Karl (Heinrich)** 1818-83; Ger. social philosopher & economist, in London after 1850: founder of modern socialism
Marx·ism (märks′iz′əm) ***n.*** the system of thought developed by Karl Marx, Friedrich Engels, and their followers: see SOCIALISM, COMMUNISM, DIALECTICAL MATERIALISM: also **Marx′i·an·ism′** —**Marx′ist** ***adj., n.***, **Marx′i·an**
Mar·y[1] (mer′ē, mar′ē) ***n.*** ⟦ME *Marie* < OE < LL(Ec) *Maria* < Gr *Maria*, *Mariam* < Heb *Miryām* or Aram *Maryām*, lit., rebellion⟧ **1** a feminine name:

dim. *Mamie, Molly, Polly*; masc. & fem. *Marie, Marion*; var. *Mae, Maria, Marietta, Marilyn, May, Miriam*; equiv. Ir. *Maureen, Moira*, Fr. *Marie, Marion*, Ger., It., & Sp. *Maria*, Pol. *Marya* **2** *Bible a)* mother of Jesus: Matt. 1:18-25: often referred to as the *(Blessed) Virgin Mary, Saint Mary b)* sister of Martha and Lazarus: Luke 10:38-42 *c)* MARY MAGDALENE (see MAGDALENE, sense 2)

Mar·y[2] (mer′ē, mar′ē) **1 Mary I** (*Mary Tudor*) 1516-58; queen of England (1553-58): daughter of Henry VIII & Catherine of Aragon: wife of Philip II of Spain **2 Mary II** 1662-94; queen of England, Scotland, and Ireland (1689-94), ruling jointly with her husband, William III: daughter of James II

Mary Jane ⟦see MARIJUANA⟧ ☆[Slang] MARIJUANA: also **mar′y·jane′** *n.*

Mary Janes ☆⟦< *Mary Jane*, former trademark for such shoes⟧ flat or low-heeled shoes for women or girls, usually with a rounded toe and a single strap that buckles across the instep

Mar·y·land (mer′ə lənd) ⟦after Queen Henrietta *Maria*, wife of CHARLES I of England⟧ state of the E U.S., on the Atlantic: one of the 13 original states: 9,774 sq mi (25,314 sq km); cap. Annapolis: abbrev. *MD* or *Md*

Mar·y·land·er (-lən dər, -lan′-) *n.* a person born or living in Maryland

Mary Magdalene MAGDALENE (sense 2)

Mary, Queen of Scots (*Mary Stuart*) 1542-87; queen of Scotland (1542-67): beheaded

mar·zi·pan (mär′zi pan′, märt′si-; -pän′) *n.* ⟦Ger < It *marzapane*, confection, earlier, the small box containing it, small dry measure, certain weight < ML *matapanus*, Venetian coin with figure of Christ on a throne < Ar *mauthaban*, seated king < *wathaba*, to sit⟧ a confection of ground almonds, sugar, and egg white made into a paste and variously shaped and colored

mas *abbrev.* masculine

-mas (məs) ⟦ME *masse, messe*, MASS[1]⟧ *combining form* a (specified) festival or celebration *[Martinmas]*

Ma·sac·cio (mä sät′chô) (born *Tommaso Guidi*) 1401-28; Florentine painter

Ma·sa·da (mə sä′də, mä sä dä′) ancient Jewish fortress in Israel, near the Dead Sea: site of a prolonged Roman siege (A.D. 72-73) resulting in a mass suicide by the Jews to avoid capture

Ma·sai (mä sī′) *n.* ⟦self-designation in Masai⟧ **1** *pl.* **-sai′** or **-sais′** a member of a people of Kenya and Tanzania **2** the language of this people, belonging to the East Sudanic branch of the Chari-Nile subfamily of the Nilo-Saharan family

ma·sa·la (mə sä′lə) *n.* ⟦Hindi & Urdu, ingredients, spices⟧ **1** in Indian cuisine, any of various blends of ground spices: see also GARAM MASALA **2** a dish flavored with this *[chicken masala]*

Ma·sa·ryk (mȧ′sȧ rik; *E* mas′ə rik) **1 Jan** (yȧn) 1886-1948; Czech statesman: son of Tomáš **2 To·máš Gar·rigue** (tô′mäsh gȧ′rēk) 1850-1937; Czech statesman: 1st president of Czechoslovakia (1918-35)

Mas·ba·te (mäs bä′te) island of the EC Philippines, west of Samar: 1,262 sq mi (3,269 sq km)

masc *abbrev.* masculine

Mas·ca·gni (mäs kän′yē), **Pie·tro** (pye′trô) 1863-1945; It. composer

mas·car·a (mas kar′ə) *n.* ⟦Sp *máscara*, a mask < It *maschera*: see MASK⟧ a cosmetic preparation for coloring or darkening the eyelashes or eyebrows —*vt.* **-car′aed**, **-car′a·ing** to put mascara on

Mas·ca·rene Islands (mas′kə rēn′) group of islands in the W Indian Ocean, east of Madagascar, including Mauritius & Réunion

mas·car·po·ne (cheese) (mas′kär pō′nē) ⟦It < dial. name (in Lombardy)⟧ a very rich, white cream cheese of Italy

☆**mas·con** (mas′kän′) *n.* ⟦*mas(s) con(centration)*⟧ a local concentration of very dense material beneath the surface of the moon

mas·cot (mas′kät′, -kət) *n.* ⟦Fr *mascotte* < Prov *mascot*, dim. of *masco*, sorcerer (< ?): in popular use, after *La Mascotte* (1880), operetta by E. *Audran* (1840-1901), Fr composer⟧ **1** any person, animal, or thing supposed to bring good luck **2** any person, animal, or thing adopted by a group, esp. by a sports team, as a symbol or for good luck *[the team's mascot is a bear]* **3** a distinctive, stylized figure, variously of an animal, character, etc., used to represent a sports team or other organization; often, specif., such a figure portrayed by a costumed person

mas·cu·line (mas′kyo͞o lin, -kyə-) *adj.* ⟦ME *masculyn* < OFr *masculin* < L *masculinus* < *masculus*, male < *mas*, male⟧ **1** male; of men or boys **2** having qualities regarded as characteristic of men and boys, as strength, vigor, boldness, etc.; manly; virile **3** suitable to or characteristic of a man **4** mannish: said of women **5** *Gram.* designating, of, or belonging to the gender of words denoting or referring to males, as well as many other words to which no distinction of sex is attributed **6** *Music* designating or of a cadence ending on an accented note or chord **7** *Prosody a)* ending with a stressed syllable, as a line of verse *b)* designating or of rhyme in which the rhyming elements are stressed final syllables (Ex.: hill/fill, enjoy/destroy) —*n. Gram.* **1** the masculine gender **2** a word or form in this gender —**SYN.** MALE —**mas′cu·line·ly** *adv.* —**mas′cu·lin′i·ty** *n.*

mas·cu·lin·ize (-li nīz′) *vt.* **-ized′**, **-iz′ing** ⟦< prec. + -IZE⟧ to make masculine; esp., to produce male characteristics in (a female) —**mas′cu·lin′i·za′tion** *n.*

Mase·field (mās′fēld′), **John** 1878-1967; Eng. writer: poet laureate (1930-67)

☆**ma·ser** (mā′zər) *n.* ⟦*m(icrowave) a(mplification by) s(timulated) e(mission of) r(adiation)*⟧ a device, operating at microwave frequencies, in which atoms or molecules are raised to a higher energy level and allowed to lose the energy by radiation that is emitted at a very precise frequency: cf. LASER

Ma·se·ru (maz′ə ro͞o′) capital of Lesotho, in the NW part

mash (mash) *n.* ⟦ME *masshe-* < OE *masc-*, in *mascwyrt*, infused malt, akin to Ger *meisch, maisch*, crushed grapes, infused malt < IE base **meiĝh-*, to urinate > L *mingere*: see MICTURITION⟧ **1** crushed or ground malt or meal soaked in hot water for making wort, used in brewing beer **2** a mixture of bran, meal, etc. in warm water, for feeding horses, cattle, etc. **3** any soft mixture or mass **4** [Brit. Informal] mashed potatoes —*vt.* ⟦ME *maschen* < the n.⟧ **1** to mix (crushed malt, etc.) in hot water for making wort **2** to change into a soft or uniform mass by beating, crushing, etc. **3** to crush and injure or damage ☆**4** [Old Slang] to make sexual advances to; flirt with

MASH (mash) *abbrev.* mobile army surgical hospital

mash·er (mash′ər) *n.* one that mashes; specif., *a)* a device for mashing vegetables, fruit, etc. ☆*b)* [Slang] a man who makes unwanted advances to women not acquainted with him, esp. in public places

Mash·had (mə shäd′) city in NE Iran: site of a Shiite shrine

mash·ie (mash′ē) *n.* ⟦Scot, dim. of *mash*, a sledgehammer; ? akin to Fr *massé* (see MASSÉ)⟧ *former term for* number 5 iron: see IRON (*n.* 6)

☆**mash note** ⟦see MASH (*vt.* 4)⟧ [Slang] an effusive note or letter expressing affection or passion for the recipient, usually a stranger or someone known only casually

mash-up (mash′up′) *n.* **1** [Informal] a blend or mixture of incongruous elements, often, specif., one regarded as startling, inept, or inelegant **2** a recorded composition made up of digitally blended sections of other recordings **3** a Web-based application designed to integrate data from two or more sources to produce new content or functionality

Mas·i·nis·sa (mas′ə nis′ə) 238?-148 B.C.; Numidian king who fought as a Roman ally against Hannibal

mas·jid (mus′jid) *n.* ⟦Ar: see MOSQUE⟧ a mosque

mask (mask, mäsk) *n.* ⟦Fr *masque* < It *maschera, mascara*, a mask, prob. < Ar *maskhara*, a clown, buffoonery⟧ **1** a covering for the face or part of the face, to conceal the identity **2** anything that conceals or disguises **3** a person wearing a mask; masker **4** a likeness of a person's face, or face and neck; specif., *a)* a sculptured or molded likeness of the face (cf. DEATH MASK) *b)* a grotesque or comic representation of a face, worn to amuse or frighten, as at Halloween *c)* a sculptured head or face, often grotesque, used as an ornament, as on a building *d)* a figure of a head worn on the stage by an ancient Greek or Roman actor to identify a character and amplify the voice **5** a protective covering for the face or head, as a wire screen *[fencer's mask]* or respirator *[gas mask]* **6** *a)* a covering for the mouth and nose used in administering an anesthetic or oxygen *b)* a piece of paper, etc. worn over the mouth and nose of a surgeon, etc. to prevent infection of a patient, instruments, etc. by exhaled matter **7** a strip of darker color across an animal's face, esp. across the eyes **8** something serving to conceal artillery, military operations, etc. from observation **9** an opaque or translucent material used to modify the exposure of selected areas of a photograph **10** MASQUE (senses 2 & 3) **11** *Zool.* a masklike formation about the head, as the enlarged lower lip of a dragonfly larva —*vt.* **1** to conceal or cover with or as with a mask **2** to conceal or disguise **3** to make (a sound, smell, taste, etc.) less noticeable **4** to protect by covering as with masking tape —*vi.* **1** to put on a mask, as for a masquerade **2** to hide or disguise one's true motives, character, etc.

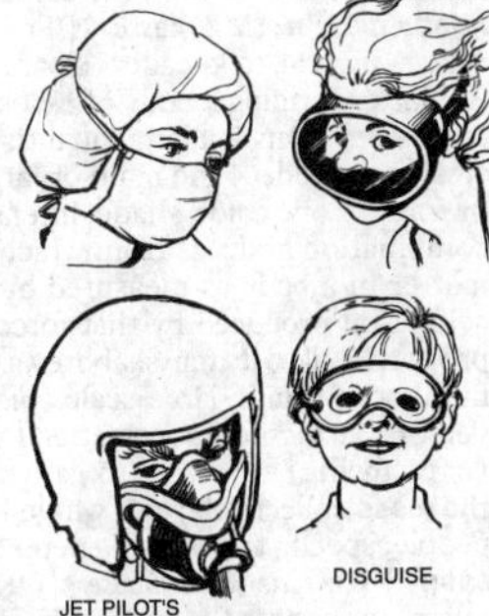

masked (maskt, mäskt) *adj.* **1** wearing a mask **2** concealed, disguised, not apparent, etc. **3** *Bot.* PERSONATE

masked ball a BALL[2] at which masks and fancy costumes are worn

mask·er (mas′kər, mäs′-) *n.* one who wears a mask; specif., a participant in a masque or masquerade

mask·ing tape (-kiŋ) tape for use in covering and protecting surfaces that border on an area to be painted

mas·o·chism (mas′ə kiz′əm, maz′-) *n.* ⟦after Leopold von Sacher-*Masoch* (1835-95), Austrian writer in whose stories it is described⟧ **1** the getting of sexual pleasure from being dominated, mistreated, or hurt physically or otherwise by one's partner **2** the getting of pleasure from suffering physical or psychological pain, inflicted by others or by oneself Cf. SADISM —**mas′o·chist** *n.* —**mas′o·chis′tic** *adj.* —**mas′o·chis′ti·cal·ly** *adv.*

ma·son (mā′sən) *n.* ⟦OFr *maçon* < ML *macio* < Frank **makjo-* < **makon*, akin to OE *macian*, to MAKE[1]⟧ **1** a person whose work is building with stone, brick, concrete, etc. **2** [**M-**] FREEMASON —*vt.* to build of or reinforce with masonry

mason bee a solitary bee (*Osmia cobaltina*) that builds its nest of clay, sand, mud, etc.

Ma·son-Dix·on line (mā′sən dik′sən) ⟦after C. *Mason* & J. *Dixon*, who surveyed it, 1763-67⟧ boundary line between Pa. & Md., regarded, before the Civil War, as separating the free states from the slave states or, now, the North from the South: also **Mason and Dixon's line**

Ma·son·ic (mə sän′ik, mā-) *adj.* [*also* **m-**] of Masons (Freemasons) or Masonry (Freemasonry)

☆**Ma·son·ite** (mā′sən īt′) ⟦after W. H. *Mason* (1877-1947?), U.S. engineer⟧ *trademark for* a kind of hardboard made from pressed wood fibers, used as building material, insulation, etc. —*n.* [*also* **m-**] such hardboard

☆**Mason jar** (mā′sən) ⟦patented (1858) by John L. *Mason* of New York⟧ [*also* **m- j-**] a glass jar having a wide mouth and a screw top, used for preserving foods, esp. in home canning

ma·son·ry (mā′sən rē) *n.* ⟦ME *masonerie* < OFr *maçonnerie* < *maçon,* MASON⟧ **1** the trade or art of a mason **2** work done by or as by a mason, using stone, brick, concrete, etc. **3** [*usually* **M-**] FREEMASONRY

mason wasp any of a genus (*Eumenes,* family Eumenidae) of solitary wasps that build urn-shaped nests of mud

Ma·so·ra or **Ma·so·rah** (mə sō′rə) *n.* ⟦ModHeb *māsōrāh,* tradition < LHeb *māsōreth*⟧ **1** all the accumulated Jewish tradition concerning the correct Hebrew text of the Holy Scriptures **2** the marginal notes on manuscripts of the Holy Scriptures embodying this tradition, compiled from the 2d to the 10th cent. A.D.

Mas·o·rete (mas′ə rēt′) *n.* ⟦< LHeb *māsōreth*⟧ any of the Jewish scribes who compiled the Masora: also **Mas′o·rite′** (-rīt′)

Mas·o·ret·ic (mas′ə ret′ik) *adj.* of the Masora or Masoretes

masque (mask, mäsk) *n.* ⟦see MASK⟧ **1** a masked ball **2** a form of dramatic entertainment popular among the English aristocracy during the 16th and 17th cent., usually based on a mythical or allegorical theme and featuring lavish costumes, scenery, music, dancing, etc.: originally it contained no dialogue **3** a dramatic composition written for such an entertainment, usually in verse —**masqu′er** *n.*

mas·quer·ade (mas′kə rād′) *n.* ⟦altered (by assoc. with prec.) < Fr *mascarade* < It *mascarata,* dial. var. of *mascherata* (< *maschera*): see MASK⟧ **1** a ball or party at which masks and fancy costumes or disguises are worn **2** a costume for such a ball or party **3** *a)* a disguise, false show, or pretense *b)* a living or acting under false pretenses —*vi.* **-ad′ed, -ad′ing 1** to take part in a masquerade **2** to live or act under false pretenses —**mas′quer·ad′er** *n.*

mass (mas) *n.* ⟦ME *masse* < OFr < L *massa,* a lump, mass < Gr *maza,* barley cake < *massein,* to knead < IE base **menk-,* to knead > MINGLE⟧ **1** a quantity of matter forming a body of indefinite shape and size, usually of relatively large size; lump **2** a large quantity or number [*a mass* of bruises] **3** bulk; size; magnitude **4** the main or larger part; majority **5** *Painting* a large area or form of one color, shade, intensity, etc. **6** *Pharmacy* the paste or plastic combination of drugs from which pills are made **7** *Physics* the quantity of matter in a body as measured by its inertia; the ratio of force to the acceleration produced by that force: the gravitational force on an object is proportional to its mass: abbrev. *m*: cf. MATTER (*n.* 2) —*adj.* **1** *a)* of a large number of things; large-scale [*mass* production] *b)* of a large number of persons [*a mass* demonstration] **2** of, characteristic of, or for the masses [*mass* media] — *vt., vi.* to gather or form into a mass —*SYN.* BULK[1] —**in the mass** collectively; as a whole —**the masses** the great mass of common people; specif., the working people, or the lower classes in the social order

Mass[1] (mas) *n.* ⟦ME *masse* < OE *mæsse* < LL(Ec) *missa,* mass, lit., dismissal, orig. pp. of L *mittere,* to dismiss < the words said by the priest *ite, missa est (contio),* go, (the meeting) is dismissed⟧ [*also* **m-**] **1** the Roman Catholic Eucharistic rite consisting of prayers and ceremonies centered on the consecration of bread and wine as a real though mystical reenactment of the sacrifice of Christ on the cross: with differing doctrinal interpretations, the term has sometimes been used of the Eucharistic rite of other denominations **2** a musical setting for certain parts of this rite

Mass[2] *abbrev.* Massachusetts

Mas·sa·chu·sett (mas′ə cho͞o′sit) *n.* ⟦Massachusett name of Great Blue Hill (SW of Boston), lit., at the large hill⟧ **1** *pl.* **-setts** or **-sett** a member of a North American Indian people that lived around Massachusetts Bay **2** the extinct Algonquian language of this people and certain adjacent peoples Also sp. **Mas′sa·chu′set**

Mas·sa·chu·setts (-sits) ⟦after prec.⟧ New England state of the U.S.: one of the 13 original states: 7,840 sq mi (20,306 sq km); cap. Boston: abbrev. *MA* or *Mass*

Massachusetts Bay inlet of the Atlantic, on the E coast of Mass.

mas·sa·cre (mas′ə kər) *n.* ⟦Fr < OFr *maçacre, macecle,* butchery, shambles < ?⟧ **1** *a)* the indiscriminate, merciless killing of a number of human beings *b)* a large-scale slaughter of animals **2** [Informal] an overwhelming defeat, as in sports —*vt.* **-cred** (-kərd), **-cring** (-kər iŋ, -kriŋ) **1** to kill indiscriminately and mercilessly and in large numbers **2** [Informal] to defeat overwhelmingly —*SYN.* SLAUGHTER —**mas′sa·crer** (-kər ər, -krər) *n.*

mas·sage (mə säzh′, -säj′) *n.* ⟦Fr < *masser,* to massage < Ar *massa,* to touch⟧ a rubbing, kneading, etc. of part of the body, usually with the hands, as to stimulate circulation and make muscles or joints supple, to relieve tension, etc. —*vt.* **-saged′, -sag′ing 1** to give a massage to **2** [Informal] to alter or manipulate (data, ideas, etc.) so as to obtain a desired result [the PR department *massaged* the actor's bio] —**mas·sag′er** *n.*

massage parlor a business establishment offering massage, steam baths, etc., often, specif., one that is a front for prostitution and other illicit sexual activity

☆**mas·sa·sau·ga** (mas′ə sô′gə) *n.* ⟦< *Mississauga,* Ojibwa name of river and Indian people in Ontario⟧ a small, gray or brownish rattlesnake (*Sistrurus catenatus*) found in swampy regions in the E and S U.S.

Mas·sa·soit (mas′ə soit′) died 1661; chief of the Wampanoag Indians: signed a treaty with the Pilgrims of Plymouth in 1621

Mass card a printed card indicating to its recipient that the donor has requested a Mass to be offered for a specified person or intention

☆**mass·cult** (mas′kult′) *n.* ⟦MASS + CULT(URE)⟧ [Informal] an artificial, commercialized culture popularized for the masses through the mass media

mass defect *Physics* the difference between the mass of an atom and the sum of the masses of the individual neutrons and protons in its nucleus, expressed in atomic mass units

mas·sé (ma sā′) *n.* ⟦Fr, pp. of *masser,* to make a massé shot < *masse,* billiard cue, lit., mace⟧ a stroke in billiards and pool made by hitting the cue ball off center with the handle of the cue held high, so as to make the ball move in a curve around another ball before hitting the object ball

Mas·sé·na (mȧ sā nȧ′), **An·dré** (än drā′) Duc de Rivoli, Prince d'Essling 1758-1817; Fr. marshal under Napoleon

Mas·se·net (mas′ə nā′; *Fr* mȧs ne′), **Jules (Émile Frédéric)** (zhül) 1842-1912; Fr. composer

mas·se·ter (ma sēt′ər, mə-) *n.* ⟦ModL < Gr *masētēr,* a chewer < *masasthai,* to chew < IE base **menth-* > MOUTH⟧ either of a pair of large muscles in the angle of the lower jaw, which raise the jaw in chewing, etc. —**mas·se·ter·ic** (mas′ə ter′ik) *adj.*

mas·seur (mə sʉr′, -so͞or′, -so͝or′) *n.* ⟦Fr < *masser*: see MASSAGE⟧ a man whose work is giving massages

mas·seuse (mə so͞oz′, -so͞os′) *n.* a woman whose work is giving massages

mas·si·cot (mas′i kät′) *n.* ⟦ME *masticote,* altered (infl. by *mastik,* MASTIC) < MFr < It *marzacotto* < Sp *mezacote* < Ar *shabb qubṭi,* Coptic alum: see COPTIC⟧ a soft, powdery mineral, PbO, used in making rubber, glass, etc.; lead oxide

mas·sif (ma sēf′, mas′if) *n.* ⟦Fr, lit., solid: see MASSIVE⟧ *Geol.* **1** a mountainous mass broken up into separate peaks and forming the backbone of a mountain range **2** a large block of the earth's crust that is isolated by boundary faults and has shifted as a unit

Mas·sine (mȧ sēn′), **Lé·o·nide** (lā ô nēd′) 1896-1979; U.S. ballet dancer & choreographer, born in Russia

Mas·sin·ger (mas′in jər), **Philip** 1583-1640; Eng. dramatist

Mas·si·nis·sa (mas′ə nis′ə) *alt. sp. of* MASINISSA

mas·sive (mas′iv) *adj.* ⟦Fr *massif,* with change of suffix (see -IVE), for OFr *massiz* < VL **massiceus* < L *massa,* MASS⟧ **1** *a)* forming or consisting of a large mass; big and solid; bulky; ponderous *b)* larger or greater than normal [*a massive* dose of medicine] **2** large and imposing or impressive; of considerable magnitude **3** large-scale; extensive [*massive* retaliation] **4** *Geol.* *a)* homogeneous in structure, without stratification, foliation, etc. [*massive* rock formations] *b)* occurring in thick beds, without minor joints and lamination: said of some stratified rocks **5** *Med.* heavy and of wide extent [*massive* hemorrhage] **6** *Mineralogy* irregular in form, though occasionally crystalline in internal structure —*SYN.* HEAVY —**mas′sive·ly** *adv.* —**mas′sive·ness** *n.*

mass·less (mas′lis) *adj.* having no mass: said of some subatomic particles, as a gluon or a photon

mass-mar·ket (mas′mär′kit) *adj.* **1** designating or of goods produced less expensively through large-scale manufacturing and marketed to a broad range of consumers, as through large retailers **2** designating or of a smaller, less expensive paperback book intended for sale at drugstores, supermarkets, newsstands, etc., as well as at bookstores, and typically measuring about four inches wide by seven inches high: cf. TRADE (*adj.* 4) —*vt.* to manufacture a product on a large scale and market it to a broad range of consumers Also written **mass market**

mass media those means of communication that reach and influence large numbers of people, esp. newspapers, popular magazines, radio, and television

☆**mass meeting** a large public meeting to discuss public affairs, demonstrate public approval or disapproval, etc.

☆**mass noun** a noun denoting an abstraction or something that is uncountable, and generally not preceded by *a* or *an* or a numeral: it is typically in a singular construction, but may be singular or plural in form (Ex.: *sympathy, girlhood, butter, news*): cf. COUNT NOUN

mass number *Chem., Physics* the number of neutrons and protons in the nucleus of an atom: the approximate mass of a given nucleus is obtained by multiplying the mass number by the fundamental unit of mass, 1.6605 × 10^{-24} grams ($\frac{1}{12}$ the mass of C^{12} atom)

mas·so·ther·a·py (mas′ō ther′ə pē) *n.* ⟦MASS(AGE) + -O- + THERAPY⟧ physical therapy by means of massage —**mas′so·ther′a·pist** (-pist) *n.*

mass production the production of goods in large quantities, esp. by machinery and division of labor —**mass′-pro·duce′** *vt.* **-duced′, -duc′ing**

mass spectrograph an instrument for analyzing ionized particles by passing them through electric and magnetic fields, typically designed to focus particles of equal mass to a point where they are detected: used esp. to determine the abundance of chemical compounds or isotopes: also **mass spectrometer**

mass transit **1** a large-scale system of public transportation serving a city or metropolitan area **2** such systems collectively

mass·y (mas′ē) *adj.* **mass′i·er, mass′i·est** [Now Rare] massive; weighty, bulky, etc. —**mass′i·ness** *n.*

mast[1] (mast, mäst) *n.* ⟦ME *maste* < OE *mæst,* akin to Ger *mast* < IE **mazdos,* a pole, rod > L *malus,* mast (< **madus* with Sabine *l* for *d*), Ir *maide,* a stick⟧ **1** a tall spar or, now often, a hollow metal structure, sometimes in sections, rising vertically from the keel or deck of a vessel and used to support the sails, yards, radar and radio equipment, etc. **2** a specified section of this [the *topmast*] **3** any vertical pole, as in a crane or derrick **4** a metal post for the support of a radio aerial or television antenna ☆**5** [*also* **M-**] *U.S. Navy* a summary session held by the commanding officer to try minor offenses, hear requests, or give commendations: in full **captain's mast** —*vt.* to put a mast or masts on —**before the mast** ⟦quarters for common sailors were formerly located forward of the foremast⟧ [Archaic] as a common sailor or with the common sailors

mast² (mast, mäst) *n.* ⟦ME *maste* < OE *mæst*, akin to Ger *mast* < IE base **mad-*, moist, dripping (with fat, sap) > MEAT, Gr *mastos*, a breast⟧ beechnuts, acorns, chestnuts, etc., esp. as food for hogs

mast- *combining form* MASTO-: used before a vowel

mas·ta·ba or **mas·ta·bah** (mas′tə bə) *n.* ⟦Ar *maṣṭabah*⟧ an oblong structure with a flat roof and sloping sides, built over the opening of a mummy chamber or burial pit in ancient Egypt and used as a tomb

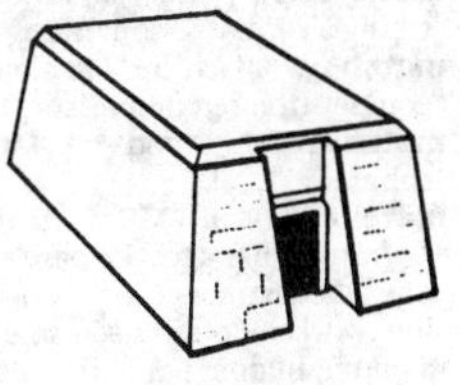
mastaba

mast cell ⟦< Ger *mastzelle* < *mast*, food (see MAST²) + *zelle*, cell < OHG *cella* < L: see CELL⟧ a cell containing large, basophilic granules, found in connective and other bodily tissues

mas·tec·to·my (mas tek′tə mē) *n., pl.* **-mies** ⟦MAST(O)- + -ECTOMY⟧ the surgical removal of all or part of a breast, usually so as to remove cancerous tissue

mas·ter (mas′tər, mäs′-) *n.* ⟦ME *maistre* < OE *mægester*, magister & OFr *maistre*, both < L *magister*, a master, chief, leader, orig., double compar. < base of L *magnus*, great < IE **meĝ(h)-* > MUCH⟧ **1** a person, esp. a man, who rules others or has control, authority, or power over something; specif., *a)* [Old-fashioned] a man who is head of a household or institution *b)* [Archaic] an employer *c)* one who owns a slave or an animal *d)* the captain of a merchant ship *e)* the one that excels in a contest, skill, etc.; victor or superior *f)* [Chiefly Brit.] a male schoolteacher or tutor *g)* a person whose teachings in religion, philosophy, etc. one follows or professes to follow *h)* [**M-**] Jesus Christ (with *our, the,* etc.) **2** someone or something regarded as having control, power, etc. [*master* of the situation] **3** a person very skilled and able in some work, profession, science, etc.; expert; specif., *a)* a highly skilled workman or craftsman qualified to follow his or her trade independently and, usually, to supervise the work of others *b)* an artist regarded as great *c)* *Games, Sports* a person recognized as having achieved the highest degree of skill [chess *master*, golf *master*] **4** [**M-**] a title variously applied to *a)* [Archaic] any man or youth (now superseded by the variant *Mister*, usually written *Mr.* when placed before the name) *b)* a boy regarded as too young to be addressed as *Mr.* (a formal usage) *c)* a man who heads some institution, group, activity, or place *d)* in Scotland, the heir apparent of a viscount or baron **5** *a)* a metal matrix or mold made from the original recording and used to produce phonograph records in quantity *b)* a completed tape recording used to produce discs, cassettes, etc. for sale **6** *Law* any of several court officers appointed to assist the judge by hearing evidence, reporting on certain matters, etc. —*adj.* **1** being a master **2** of a master **3** chief; main; controlling; specif., designating something that controls others or sets a standard or norm [a *master* switch, a *master* sheet of test answers] **4** *a)* designating the largest bedroom in a residence, intended for use by the head of the household *b)* designating any room connected to, or area associated with, such a bedroom [*master* bathroom, *master* suite] —*vt.* **1** to become master of; control, conquer, etc. **2** [Now Rare] to rule or govern as master **3** to become an expert in (an art, science, etc.) **4** to make a MASTER (*n.* 5) of

mas·ter-at-arms (-ət ärmz′) *n., pl.* **mas′ters-at-arms′** *U.S. Navy* a petty officer responsible for keeping order, maintaining discipline, taking charge of prisoners, etc. on a ship or in a shore station

master builder a person skilled in building, as an architect

master chief petty officer *U.S. Navy* an enlisted person of the highest grade, ranking just above a senior chief petty officer

master class a class taught by an accomplished musician who individually instructs advanced students in performance and technique, often before an audience

mas·ter·dom (mas′tər dəm) *n.* [Now Rare] complete control; mastery

mas·ter·ful (mas′tər fəl) *adj.* **1** fond of acting the part of a master; domineering; imperious **2** having or showing the ability of a master; expert; skillful; masterly: usage objected to by some —**mas′ter·ful·ly** *adv.* —**mas′ter·ful·ness** *n.*

SYN.—**masterful** implies such strength of personality as enables one to impose his or her will on others [a *masterful* orchestral conductor]; **domineering** implies the arrogant, tyrannical manner of one who openly tries to dominate another [a *domineering* mother]; **imperious** suggests the arbitrary ruling of an emperor, but connotes less arrogance than **domineering** [the *imperious* old dean of the college]; **magisterial**, while not suggesting an assumption of arbitrary powers, implies an excessive use or display of such inherent powers as a magistrate might have [he dismissed me with a *magisterial* air]

master hand **1** an expert **2** great ability or skill

master key a key that will open every one of a set of locks

mas·ter·ly (mas′tər lē) *adj.* showing the ability or skill of a master; expert [a *masterly* job of repair work] —**mas′ter·li·ness** *n.*

master mason **1** a highly skilled mason **2** [*often* **M- M-**] a Freemason of the third degree

mas·ter·mind (mas′tər mīnd′) *n.* a very intelligent or clever person, esp. one with the ability to plan or direct a group project —*vt.* to be the mastermind of (a project)

Master of Arts (or **Science,** etc.) a degree given by a college or university to a person who has completed a prescribed course of graduate study in the humanities or related studies (or in science, etc.): it ranks above the degree of *Bachelor* and below that of *Doctor*: also **master's (degree)**

master of ceremonies **1** a person who supervises a ceremony ☆**2** a person who presides over an entertainment, as on a radio or television program or in a nightclub, at a banquet, etc., introducing the speakers or performers, filling in the intervals with jokes, etc.

mas·ter·piece (mas′tər pēs′) *n.* ⟦calque of Ger *meisterstück*⟧ **1** a thing made or done with masterly skill; great work of art or craftsmanship **2** the greatest work made or done by a person or group

Mas·ters (mas′tərz), **Edgar Lee** 1869-1950; U.S. poet

☆**master sergeant** *U.S. Mil.* a noncommissioned officer of high rank; in the Army, the rank just above sergeant first class; in the Air Force, the rank just above technical sergeant; in the Marine Corps, the rank just above gunnery sergeant

mas·ter·ship (mas′tər ship′) *n.* **1** the state of being a master; rule; control; dominion **2** the position, duties, or term of office of a master **3** masterly ability; expert skill or knowledge

mas·ter·sing·er (-siŋ′ər) *n.* ⟦calque of Ger *meistersinger*⟧ [Historical] MEISTERSINGER

mas·ter·stroke (-strōk′) *n.* a masterly action, move, or achievement

master tape MASTER (*n.* 5*b*)

mas·ter·work (-wurk′) *n.* MASTERPIECE

mas·ter·y (mas′tər ē, mäs′-) *n., pl.* **-ter·ies** ⟦ME *maistrie* < OFr: see MASTER⟧ **1** mastership; rule; control **2** ascendancy or victory in struggle or competition; the upper hand **3** masterly ability; expert skill or knowledge [his *mastery* of chess] **4** the act of mastering (an art, science, etc.)

mast·head (mast′hed′) *n.* **1** the top part of a ship's mast ☆**2** a box or section printed in each issue of a newspaper or magazine, giving the publishers, owners, and editors, the location of the offices, subscription rates, etc. **3** NAMEPLATE (sense 2) —*vt.* **1** to send (a sailor) to the masthead as a punishment **2** to hoist to or display at the masthead

mas·tic (mas′tik) *n.* ⟦ME *mastik* < OFr *mastic* < LL *mastichum* < L *mastiche* < Gr *mastichē*, akin to *mastichan*: see fol.⟧ **1** a yellowish resin obtained from a small Mediterranean evergreen tree (*Pistacia lentiscus*) of the cashew family, used as an astringent and in making varnish, adhesives, etc. **2** the tree: in full **mastic tree** **3** any of various pasty substances used as adhesives, sealants, etc.

mas·ti·cate (mas′ti kāt′) *vt.* **-cat′ed, -cat′ing** ⟦< LL *masticatus*, pp. of *masticare*, to chew < Gr *mastichan*, to grind the teeth, gnash < *mastax*, a mouth, morsel < IE base **menth-*, to chew, mouth > MOUTH, L *mandere*, to chew⟧ **1** to chew up (food, etc.) **2** to grind, cut, or knead (rubber, etc.) to a pulp —**mas′ti·ca′tion** *n.* —**mas′ti·ca′tor** *n.*

mas·ti·ca·to·ry (-kə tôr′ē) *adj.* of or for mastication; specif., adapted for chewing —*n., pl.* **-ries** any substance to be chewed but not swallowed

mas·tiff (mas′tif) *n.* ⟦ME *mastif* < OFr *mastin* < VL **mansuetinus* < L *mansuetus*, tame; ME form infl. by OFr *mestif*, a mongrel < L *mixtus*, mixed: see MIX⟧ any of a breed of large, powerful dog with hanging lips and drooping ears and having a short, thick, often fawn-colored coat, dark on the muzzle, nose, and ears: formerly used for hunting, now often a watchdog and guard dog: also called **Old English mastiff**

mas·ti·goph·o·ran (mas′ti gäf′ə rən) *n.* ⟦< ModL *Mastigophora* (< Gr *mastix*, gen. *mastigos*, a whip + ModL *-phora*, fem. of *-phorus*: see -PHORE) + -AN⟧ any of a subphylum (Mastigophora) of protozoans, sometimes parasitic, having flagella: certain classes, as dinoflagellates, are also classified as algae by botanists —*adj.* of or relating to the mastigophorans —**mas′ti·goph′o·rous** (-rəs) *adj.*

mas·ti·tis (mas tīt′is) *n.* ⟦< Gr *mastos*, a breast + -ITIS⟧ inflammation of the breast or udder

mas·to- (mas′tō, -tə) ⟦< Gr *mastos*, a breast: see MAST²⟧ *combining form* of or like a breast, or mammary gland [*mastectomy*]

mas·to·don (mas′tə dän′) *n.* ⟦< Fr *mastodonte*, coined (1806) by CUVIER < Gr *mastos* (see prec.) + *odont-*, stem of *odous*, TOOTH: from the nipplelike processes on its molar⟧ any of an extinct family (Mastodontidae) of proboscidean mammals larger than the elephants and having a different structure of the molars: cf. MAMMOTH —**mas′to·don′ic** *adj.*

mas·toid (mas′toid′) *adj.* ⟦Gr *mastoeidēs* < *mastos*, a breast (see MAST²) + *-eidēs*, -OID⟧ **1** shaped like a breast or nipple **2** designating, of, or near a projection of the temporal bone behind the ear —*n.* **1** the mastoid projection **2** [Informal] MASTOIDITIS

mas·toid·ec·to·my (mas′toi dek′tə mē) *n., pl.* **-mies** ⟦see -ECTOMY⟧ the surgical removal of part or all of a mastoid

mas·toid·i·tis (-dīt′is) *n.* inflammation of the mastoid

mas·tur·bate (mas′tər bāt′) *vi., vt.* **-bat′ed, -bat′ing** ⟦< L *masturbatus*, pp. of *masturbari*, altered (by assoc. with *turbare*, to DISTURB) < **manstupro* < *manus*, hand (see MANUAL) + *stuprum*, defilement < IE base **steup-*, to strike, a stick, stump > STEEP¹⟧ to manipulate one's own genitals, or the genitals of (another), for sexual gratification —**mas′tur·ba′tion** *n.* —**mas′tur·ba′tor** *n.* —**mas′tur·ba·to′ry** (-bə tôr′ē) *adj.*

Ma·su·ri·a (mə zoor′ē ə) region with many lakes, in NE Poland: formerly in East Prussia —**Ma·su′ri·an** *adj.*

ma·su·ri·um (mə soor′ē əm, -syoor′-) *n.* ⟦ModL < Ger *Masuren*, prec., where ore thought to contain the element was found + -IUM] *former name for* TECHNETIUM

mat[1] (mat) *n.* [ME *matte* < OE *meatt* < LL *matta* (> Ger *matte*) < Phoen word akin to Heb *mittāh*, a cover] 1 a flat, coarse fabric made of woven or plaited hemp, straw, rope, rushes, etc., often used as a floor covering 2 a piece of this or of corrugated rubber, cocoa fiber, etc., used variously as a DOORMAT, BATHMAT, or removable floor covering for a car 3 *a)* a flat piece of cloth, woven straw, etc., put under a vase, dish, or the like, or used as an ornament, as on a table *b)* a pad, as of rubber or plastic, used to protect the surface of an oven, sink, etc. 4 a thickly padded floor covering, esp. one used in a gymnasium for tumbling, wrestling, etc. 5 anything densely interwoven or felted, or growing in a thick tangle [a *mat* of hair] 6 *Naut.* a thick web of rope yarn, used to protect rigging from wear —*vt.* **mat′ted, mat′ting** 1 to cover with or as with a mat or mats 2 to interweave, felt, or tangle together into a thick mass —*vi.* to be interwoven, felted, or tangled together into a thick mass —**go to the mat** [< *n.* 4 as used in wrestling] [Informal] to engage willingly in a struggle or dispute, as on another's behalf

mat[2] (mat) *adj.* [Fr < OFr *mat*, defeated, exhausted, prob. < L *mattus*, drunk < *madidus*, soaked, drunk < *madere*, to be drenched, drunk < IE base **mad-*, to be wet, drip, juicy, fat > MAST[2], MEAT] MATTE[2] —*n.* [Fr] 1 MATTE[2] 2 a border, as of cardboard or cloth, put around a picture, either as the frame or, usually, between the picture and the frame —*vt.* **mat′ted, mat′ting** 1 to produce a dull finish on (metal, glass, etc.) 2 to apply a mat to (a picture)

mat[3] (mat) *n.* [Informal] a matrix; printing mold

Mat·a·be·le (mat′ə bē′lē) *n., pl.* **-be′le** or **-be′les** [< Zulu name, lit., vanishing (or hidden) people: from "hiding" behind large leather shields in battle] a member of a Zulu people driven out of the Transvaal and into Rhodesia by the Boers in 1837

Ma·ta·di (mä tä′dē) main port of the Democratic Republic of the Congo, on the Congo River

mat·a·dor (mat′ə dôr′) *n.* [Sp, lit., killer < *matar*, to kill < *mate*, checkmate < Ar *māt* < Pers: see CHECKMATE] a bullfighter whose specialty is killing the bull with a sword thrust at the end of a bullfight after performing a series of formalized actions with a cape to anger and tire the animal

Ma·ta Ha·ri (mät′ə hä′rē) (name for *Margaretha Geertruida Zelle*) 1876-1917; Du. dancer: executed by the French as a German spy during WWI

Ma·ta·mo·ros (mä′tä mô′rôs; *E* mat′ə môr′əs) city in NE Mexico, on the Rio Grande, opposite Brownsville, Tex.

Ma·tan·zas (mə tan′zəs; *Sp* mä tän′säs) seaport on the NW coast of Cuba

Ma·ta·pan (mat′ə pan′), **Cape** promontory of the S Peloponnesus, Greece

match[1] (mach) *n.* [ME *macche* < OFr *mesche*, wick of a candle, match < VL **micca*, prob. altered (by assoc. with *muccare*, to snuff a candle, orig., to blow one's nose < L *mucus*, MUCUS) < L *myxa* < Gr, lamp wick, lit., nasal discharge, akin to L *mucus*] 1 [Historical] a wick or cord prepared to burn at a uniform rate, used for firing guns or explosives 2 a slender piece of wood, cardboard, waxed cord, etc. tipped with a composition that catches fire by friction; esp., a SAFETY MATCH

match[2] (mach) *n.* [ME *macche* < OE *(ge)mæcca*, one suited to another, mate < base of *macian*, to MAKE[1]] 1 any person or thing equal or similar to another in some way; specif., *a)* a person, group, or thing able to cope with or oppose another as an equal in power, size, etc. [to meet one's *match*] *b)* a counterpart or facsimile *c)* either of two corresponding things or persons; one of a pair 2 two or more persons or things that go together in appearance, size, or other quality [a purse and shoes that are a good *match*] 3 a contest or game involving two or more contestants; specif., a series of usually three sets in tennis 4 *a)* an agreement to marry or mate *b)* a marriage or mating [to make a good *match*] 5 a person regarded as a suitable or possible mate —*vt.* 1 *a)* [Now Rare] to meet as an antagonist *b)* to compete with successfully 2 to put in opposition (*with*); pit (*against*) 3 to be equal, similar, suitable, or corresponding to in some way [his looks *match* his character] 4 to make, show, produce, or get a competitor, counterpart, or equivalent to [to *match* a piece of cloth] 5 to suit or fit (one thing) to another 6 to fit (things) together; make similar or corresponding 7 to compare ☆8 *a)* to flip or reveal (coins) as a form of gambling or to decide something contested, the winner being determined by the combination of faces thus exposed *b)* to match coins with (another person), usually betting that the same faces will be exposed —*vi.* 1 to be equal, similar, suitable, or corresponding in some way 2 [Obs.] to mate —**match up** 1 MATCH[2] (*vt.* 2) 2 COMPARE (*vi.* 3) —**match′a·ble** *adj.* —**match′er** *n.* —**match′ing** *adj.*

match·board (mach′bôrd′) *n.* any of a number of identical boards with a tongue formed along one edge and a groove cut along the other so that the tongue of one can be fitted into the groove of the next, as in making floors: also **matched board**

match·book (-book′) *n.* ☆a folder of BOOK MATCHES

match·box (-bäks′) *n.* a small box for holding matches

☆**matched order** 1 the pairing of an order to buy stock with an order to sell stock by member brokers on the stock exchange 2 WASH SALE

match·less (mach′lis) *adj.* having no equal; peerless —**match′less·ly** *adv.* —**match′less·ness** *n.*

match·lock (mach′läk′) *n.* [Historical] 1 a type of gunlock in which the charge of powder is ignited by a slow-burning MATCH[1] (sense 1) 2 a musket with such a gunlock

match·mak·ing (-māk′iŋ) *n.* 1 the act or occupation of arranging nuptial matches for others 2 the act or practice of bringing together unmarried people with the hope that they will marry or become romantically involved 3 the arranging of wrestling or boxing matches, etc. —**match′mak′er** *n.*

☆**match·mark** (-märk′) *n.* a mark put on parts, as of a machine, to serve as an aid in assembling them —*vt.* to put such a mark on

match play 1 play in a match, as in tennis 2 *Golf* a form of competitive play in which the score is calculated by counting holes won rather than strokes taken: distinguished from STROKE PLAY

match point *Tennis, etc.* 1 a situation in which the next point scored can decide the winner of the match 2 this point

match·stick (-stik′) *n.* 1 the slender piece of wood, cardboard, etc. constituting a MATCH[1] 2 something thin like this

match·up (mach′up′) *n.* a putting together of two persons or things as for competition or comparison

match·wood (-wood′) *n.* 1 wood for making matches 2 very small pieces; splinters

mate[1] (māt) *n.* [ME < MDu, a companion < *gemate* < Gmc **gamatan* < **ga-*, together (for IE base see COM-) + **mad-*, food, MEAT: hence, orig., one who share meals: cf. COMPANION[1]] 1 *a)* a companion, comrade, or fellow worker (often used in compounds [*classmate*]) *b)* [Brit. Informal] a chum; buddy; pal (often used as a familiar form of address) 2 one of a pair, esp. of a matched pair 3 *a)* a husband or wife; spouse *b)* the male or female of animals paired for propagation 4 [Archaic] an equal; fit associate 5 *Naut.* *a)* an officer of a merchant ship, ranking below the captain; specif., FIRST MATE *b)* an assistant: in the U.S. Navy, *mate* is used in the designators of certain petty officers and ratings, as *machinist's mate, boatswain's mate* —*vt.* **mat′ed, mat′ing** 1 to join as a pair; couple 2 to couple in marriage or sexual union 3 to provide with a mate —*vi.* to become mated

mate[2] (māt) *n., interj., vt.* **mat′ed, mat′ing** [ME *mat* < OFr: see CHECKMATE] CHECKMATE

ma·té (mä′tā′, ma′-) *n.* [AmSp *mate* < Quechua *mati*, calabash: in allusion to the gourd in which it is steeped] 1 a beverage made from the dried leaves of a South American evergreen tree (*Ilex paraguariensis*) of the holly family 2 this tree 3 the dried leaves of this tree Also written **mate**

ma·te·las·sé (mat′lə sā′, mat′ə lə sā′) *adj.* [Fr, pp. of *matelasser*, to stuff, pad < *matelas*, var. of *materas*, MATTRESS] having a surface with a raised design; embossed: said of fabrics —*n.* a fabric with such a surface

mate·lot (mat′lō′, mat′ə lō′) *n.* [Fr: see fol.] [Brit. Informal] SAILOR (sense 1)

mat·e·lote (mat′ə lōt′) *n.* [Fr < *matelot*, sailor < MFr *matenot*, prob. < ON *mǫtunautr*, mate, companion < Gmc **mad-*, food, MEAT + **ganauta* < **ga-* (see MATE[1]) + **nauta*, fellow: for IE base see NEAT[2]] fish stewed in a sauce of wine, oil, onions, mushrooms, etc.

ma·ter (māt′ər, mät′-) *n.* [L, MOTHER[1]] [Informal, Chiefly Brit.] mother: often preceded by *the*

ma·ter·fa·mil·i·as (-fə mil′ē əs) *n.* [L] the mother of a family; woman head of a household

ma·te·ri·al (mə tir′ē əl) *adj.* [LL *materialis* < L *materia*, MATTER] 1 of matter; of substance; relating to or consisting of what occupies space; physical [a *material* object, *material* forces] 2 *a)* of the body or bodily needs, satisfactions, etc.; corporeal, sensual, or sensuous [*material* pleasures] *b)* of or fond of comfort, pleasure, wealth, etc. rather than spiritual or intellectual values; worldly [*material* success] 3 important, essential, or pertinent (*to* the matter under discussion) 4 *Law* important enough to affect the outcome of a case, the validity of a legal instrument, etc. [a *material* witness] 5 *Philos.* of the content or substance of reasoning, as distinguished from the formal element —*n.* 1 what a thing is, or may be, made of; constituent substance; elements, parts, or constituents [raw *material*] 2 ideas, notes, sketches, etc., that may be worked up or elaborated; data 3 cloth or other fabric 4 [*pl.*] implements, articles, etc. needed to make or do something [writing *materials*]

SYN.—**material** is applied to anything that is formed of matter and has substance [*material* objects, possessions, etc.]; **physical** applies either to material things as they are perceivable by the senses or to forces that are scientifically measurable [the *physical* world, the *physical* properties of sound]; **corporeal** applies only to such material objects as have bodily form and are tangible [*corporeal* property] —ANT. **spiritual, mental, psychic**

material cause in Aristotelian philosophy, the constituent element or elements out of which a thing is made

ma·te·ri·al·ism (mə tir′ē əl iz′əm) *n.* [Fr *matérialisme*] 1 *a)* the philosophic doctrine that matter is the only reality and that everything in the world, including thought, will, and feeling, can be explained in terms of matter alone (opposed to IDEALISM) *b)* the doctrine that comfort, pleasure, and wealth are the only or highest goals or values 2 the tendency to be more concerned with material, than with spiritual or intellectual, goals or values

ma·te·ri·al·ist (-ist) *n.* 1 a person who believes in MATERIALISM (sense 1) 2 a person characterized by MATERIALISM (sense 2) —*adj.* of materialism or materialists —**ma·te′ri·al·is′tic** *adj.* —**ma·te′ri·al·is′ti·cal·ly** *adv.*

ma·te·ri·al·i·ty (mə tir′ē al′ə tē) *n.* [ML *materialitas*] 1 the state or quality of being material, or physical 2 matter; substance 3 *pl.* **-ties** something material

ma·te·ri·al·ize (mə tir′ē əl īz′) *vt.* **-ized′, -iz′ing** 1 to give material form or characteristics to; represent in material form 2 to make (a spirit, etc.) appear in bodily form 3 to make materialistic —*vi.* 1 to become fact; develop into something real or tangible; be realized [a plan that never *ma-*

terialized] **2** to take on, or appear in, bodily form: said of spirits, etc. **3** to appear suddenly or unexpectedly —**ma·te′ri·al·i·za′tion** *n.*

ma·te·ri·al·ly (mə tir′ē əl ē) *adv.* **1** with regard to the matter, substance, or content of something, and not to its form **2** with regard to material objects, interests, etc.; physically **3** to a great extent; substantially; considerably

materials science a multidisciplinary science that studies manufacturing materials, esp. high-tech alloys, ceramics, and plastics —**materials scientist**

ma·te·ri·a med·i·ca (mə tir′ē ə med′i kə) ⟦ML < L *materia,* MATTER + *medica,* fem. of *medicus,* MEDICAL⟧ **1** the drugs and other remedial substances used in medicine **2** the branch of medical science that deals with such substances, their uses, etc.

ma·te·ri·el or **ma·té·ri·el** (mə tir′ē el′, -tir′ē əl) *n.* ⟦Fr *matériel:* see MATERIAL⟧ materials and tools necessary to any work, enterprise, etc.; specif., weapons, equipment, supplies, etc. of armed forces: distinguished from PERSONNEL

ma·ter·nal (mə tʉr′nəl) *adj.* ⟦ME < MFr *maternel* < L *maternus* < *mater,* MOTHER[1]⟧ **1** of, like, or characteristic of a mother or motherhood; motherly **2** derived, received, or inherited from a mother **3** related through the mother's side of the family *[maternal* grandparents*]* —**ma·ter′nal·ly** *adv.*

ma·ter·ni·ty (mə tʉr′nə tē) *n., pl.* **-ties** ⟦Fr *maternité* < ML *maternitas* < L *maternus,* prec.⟧ **1** the state of being a mother; motherhood **2** the character or qualities of a mother; motherliness **3** a maternity ward in a hospital —*adj.* **1** for a woman when pregnant or around the time of giving birth *[maternity* dress, *maternity* leave*]* **2** for the care of women giving birth and of newborn babies *[a maternity* ward*]*

mate·y (māt′ē) [Brit. Informal] *adj.* **-i·er, -i·est** ⟦MATE[1] + -Y[3]⟧ friendly; companionable —*n.* a chum; buddy; pal

math[1] (math) *n.* [Informal] *short for* MATHEMATICS —**do the math** [Informal] to consider or analyze a set of facts in order to reach a conclusion

math[2] *abbrev.* **1** mathematical **2** mathematician **3** mathematics

math·e·mat·i·cal (math′ə mat′i kəl) *adj.* ⟦ML *mathematicalis* < L *mathematicus* < Gr *mathēmatikos,* inclined to learn, mathematical < *mathēma,* what is learned < *manthanein,* to learn < IE **mendh-,* to pay attention to, be alert (> Avestan *mazdā,* memory, Ger *munter,* cheerful) < base **men-,* to think > MIND⟧ **1** of, having the nature of, or concerned with mathematics **2** rigorously exact, precise, accurate, etc. Also **math′e·mat′ic** —**math′e·mat′i·cal·ly** *adv.*

mathematical logic SYMBOLIC LOGIC

math·e·ma·ti·cian (math′ə mə tish′ən, math′mə-) *n.* ⟦ME *mathematicion* < MFr *mathematicien*⟧ an expert or specialist in mathematics

math·e·mat·ics (math′ə mat′iks) *n.* ⟦see MATHEMATICAL & -ICS⟧ **1** the group of sciences (including arithmetic, geometry, algebra, calculus, etc.) dealing with quantities, magnitudes, and forms, and their relationships, attributes, etc., by the use of numbers and symbols **2** the act or process of using any of these sciences; computation

Math·er (math′ər) **1 Cot·ton** (kät′'n) 1663-1728; Am. clergyman & writer **2 In·crease** (in′krēs′) 1639-1723; Am. clergyman & writer: father of Cotton

maths (maths) *n.* [Brit. Informal] *short for* MATHEMATICS

Ma·thu·ra (mut′oo rə) city in N India, in Uttar Pradesh, on the Jumna River: sacred Hindu city; reputed birthplace of Krishna

Ma·til·da or **Ma·thil·da** (mə til′də) *n.* ⟦ML *Matilda, Mathildis* < OHG *Mahthilda* < *maht,* might, power + *hiltia,* battle; hence, lit., powerful (in) battle⟧ a feminine name: dim. *Mattie, Matty, Maud, Tilda, Tilly*

mat·in (mat′'n) *n.* ⟦Early ME *matyn* < OFr *matin,* pl. *matines* < ML(Ec) *matutinae (vigiliae),* morning (watches) < L *matutinus,* of the morning, after *Matuta,* goddess of dawn: see MATURE⟧ **1** [*often* **M-**] [*pl., usually with sing. v.*] *a) R.C.Ch.* the first of the seven canonical hours, orig. recited between midnight and dawn, but often at daybreak, usually joined with lauds (matins is now called the *Office of Readings*) *b) Anglican Ch.* MORNING PRAYER **2** [Old Poet.] a morning song, esp. of birds —*adj.* **1** of matins **2** of morning —**mat′in·al** *adj.*

mat·i·nee or **mat·i·née** (mat′'n ā′) *n.* ⟦Fr *matinée* < *matin,* morning: see prec.⟧ a reception or entertainment held in the daytime; esp., a performance, as of a play, held in the afternoon

matinee idol an actor whose looks and manner make him popular with women theatergoers

mat·ing (māt′iŋ) *n.* ⟦prp. of MATE[1]⟧ the act or an instance of joining as a pair, specif. in pair-bonding or sexual union —*adj.* of or having to do with mating *[instinctive mating* rituals of tropical birds*]*

Ma·tisse (mȧ tēs′), **Hen·ri** (än rē′) 1869-1954; Fr. painter

mat·jes herring (mät′yəs) ⟦< Du *maatjesharing,* altered < MDu *medykens hering,* lit., maiden herring (because prepared from herrings that have never spawned)⟧ a reddish herring, filleted and served or packed usually in a spiced wine sauce

Ma·to Gros·so (mät′oo grô′soo) state of WC Brazil: 350,120 sq mi (906,807 sq km); cap. Cuiabá

Ma·to Gros·so do Sul (mät′oo grô′soo dō so͞ol) state of WC Brazil: 138,286 sq mi (358,159 sq km); cap. Campo Grande

mat·rass (ma′trəs) *n.* ⟦Fr *matras,* kind of arrow, blunt borer < Gaul *mataris,* javelin⟧ [Historical] a glass container with a rounded body and a long neck, used by chemists in distilling, etc.

ma·tri- (mā′tri, -trə; ma′-) ⟦< L *mater* (gen. *matris*), MOTHER[1]⟧ *combining form* mother *[matriarch]*: also, before a vowel, **matr-**

ma·tri·arch (mā′trē ärk′) *n.* ⟦prec. + -ARCH⟧ **1** a mother who rules her family or tribe; specif., a woman who is head of a matriarchy **2** a highly respected elderly woman —**ma′tri·ar′chal** (-är′kəl) *adj.*

ma·tri·arch·ate (-är′kit, -kāt′) *n.* **1** a family, tribe, etc. ruled by a matriarch **2** a matriarchal system, as in certain mythical tribes

ma·tri·arch·y (-är′kē) *n., pl.* **-arch′ies** ⟦MATRI- + -ARCHY⟧ **1** a form of social organization in which the mother is recognized as the head of the family or tribe, descent and kinship being traced through the mother **2** government, rule, or domination by women —**ma′tri·ar′chic** *adj.*

ma·tri·ces (mā′trə sēz′, ma′-) *n. alt. pl. of* MATRIX

mat·ri·cide (ma′trə sīd′, mā′-) *n.* ⟦L *matricidium* < *mater,* MOTHER[1] + *caedere,* to kill: see -CIDE⟧ **1** the act of murdering one's mother **2** ⟦L *matricida*⟧ a person who does this —**mat′ri·ci′dal** *adj.*

ma·tric·u·lant (mə trik′yo͞o lənt, -yə-) *n.* a person who has matriculated or is applying for matriculation

ma·tric·u·late (mə trik′yo͞o lāt′, -yə-; *for n.,* -lit, -lāt′) *vt., vi.* **-lat′ed, -lat′ing** ⟦< ML *matriculatus,* pp. of *matriculare,* to register < LL *matricula,* dim. of *matrix:* see MATRIX⟧ to enroll, esp. as a student in a college or university —*n.* a person so enrolled —**ma·tric′u·la′tion** *n.*

mat·ri·fo·cal (ma′trə fō′kəl) *adj.* of a sociological group, as a household, tribe, etc., having a female as its leader

mat·ri·lin·e·al (ma′trə lin′ē əl, mā′trə-) *adj.* ⟦MATRI- + LINEAL⟧ designating or of descent, kinship, or derivation through the mother: also **mat′ri·lin′e·ar** (-lin′ē ər) —**mat′ri·lin′e·al·ly** *adv.*

mat·ri·lo·cal (ma′trə lō′kəl) *adj.* of or relating to a housing pattern or custom in which a married couple lives with or near the wife's parents

mat·ri·mo·ni·al (ma′trə mō′nē əl) *adj.* ⟦Fr < LL *matrimonialis*⟧ of matrimony; marital; nuptial; conjugal —**mat′ri·mo′ni·al·ly** *adv.*

mat·ri·mo·ny (ma′trə mō′nē) *n., pl.* **-nies** ⟦ME *matrimonye* < OFr *matrimoine* < L *matrimonium* < *mater* (gen. *matris*), MOTHER[1]⟧ **1** the act, rite, or sacrament of marriage **2** the state of being husband and wife **3** married life

matrimony vine a shrub (genus *Lycium*) of the nightshade family, with small, pink flowers and reddish berries

ma·trix (mā′triks′) *n., pl.* **ma·tri·ces** (mā′trə sēz′, ma′trə-) or **ma′trix′es** ⟦LL, womb, public register, origin < L, breeding animal < *mater* (gen. *matris*), MOTHER[1]⟧ **1** [Archaic] the womb; uterus **2** that within which, or within and from which, something originates, takes form, or develops; specif., *a)* a die or mold for casting or shaping *b)* an impression from which a large number of phonograph records can be duplicated **3** *Anat. a)* any nonliving, intercellular substance in which living cells are embedded, as in bone, cartilage, etc. *b)* the formative cells from which a nail, tooth, etc. grows **4** *Electronics* a process in which several signals are combined for transmission or recording and then separated for reception or playback **5** *Geol.* the rock or earthy material in which a crystal, pebble, fossil, etc. is enclosed or embedded **6** *Linguis.* a main or independent clause **7** *Math.* a set of numbers or terms arranged in rows and columns between parentheses or double lines **8** *Printing a)* a metal mold for casting the face of type *b)* a papier-mâché, plaster, or similar impression of type, etc., from which a plate can be made, as in stereotypy

ma·tron (mā′trən) *n.* ⟦ME *matrone* < OFr < L *matrona* < *mater,* MOTHER[1]⟧ **1** an older married or widowed woman, esp. one who has a mature appearance and manner **2** a woman superintendent or manager of the domestic arrangements of a hospital, prison, or other institution **3** a woman attendant or guard in charge of women or children, as in an institution —**ma′tron·al** *adj.* —**ma′tron·hood′** *n.*

ma·tron·ize (mā′trən īz′) *vt.* **-ized′, -iz′ing** **1** to make matronly **2** to chaperone

ma·tron·ly (mā′trən lē) *adj.* of, like, characteristic of, or suitable for a matron; specif., *a)* dignified, sedate, etc. *b)* having a full figure, graying hair, etc. —**ma′tron·li·ness** *n.*

☆**matron of honor** a married woman acting as chief attendant to the bride at a wedding: cf. MAID OF HONOR

mat·ro·nym·ic (ma′trə nim′ik) *adj.* ⟦< Gr *mētrōnymikos,* altered by assoc. with L *mater* (gen. *matris*), by analogy with PATRONYMIC⟧ of or derived from the name of the mother or a female ancestor —*n.* a matronymic name

mat·sah (mät′sə) *n. var. of* MATZO

Mat·su (mät′so͞o′, mat′-) island of a small group in Taiwan Strait, administered by Taiwan: 5 sq mi (13 sq km)

Mat·su·do (mät so͞o′dō′) city in SE Honshu, Japan: suburb of Tokyo

Ma·tsu·ya·ma (mä′tsoo yä′mə) seaport on W Shikoku, Japan, on the Inland Sea

Matt *abbrev. Bible* Matthew

matte[1] (mat) *n.* ⟦Fr < dial. *mate,* a lump, prob. ult. < L *matta,* MAT[1]⟧ an impure mixture of sulfides that is produced in smelting the sulfide ores of copper, nickel, lead, etc.

matte[2] (mat) *n.* ⟦var. of MAT[2]⟧ a dull surface or finish, often roughened —*adj.* not shiny or glossy; dull Also sp. **matt**

mat·ted[1] (mat′id) *adj.* **1** closely tangled together in a dense mass *[matted* hair*]* **2** covered with a dense growth **3** covered with or enclosed in matting or mats

mat·ted[2] (mat′id) *adj.* having a matte, or dull finish

mat·ter (mat′ər) *n.* ⟦ME *matiere* < OFr < L *materia,* material, stuff, wood (< base of *mater,* MOTHER[1]), orig., the growing trunk of a tree⟧ **1** what a thing is made of; constituent substance or material **2** what all (material) things are made of; whatever occupies space and is perceptible to the senses in some way: in modern physics, matter and energy are regarded as equivalents, mutually convertible according to Einstein's formula, $E = mc^2$ (i.e., energy equals mass multiplied by the square of the velocity of light); in dualistic thinking, matter is regarded as the opposite of mind, spirit, etc. **3** any specified sort of substance [coloring *matter*] **4** material of thought or expression; what is spoken or written, regarded as distinct from how it is spoken or written; content, as distinguished from manner, style, or form **5** an amount or quantity, usually indefinite [a *matter* of a few days] **6** *a)* something that is the subject of discussion, concern, action, etc.; thing or affair [business *matters*] *b)* cause, occasion, or grounds [no *matter* for jesting] **7** the body of heroic stories and legends, as contained in a folk epic, regarded as central to a culture or literature [the King Arthur stories make up the *matter* of Britain] **8** *a)* a thing of some moment or significance *b)* importance; moment; significance [it's of no *matter*] **9** an unfavorable state of affairs; trouble; difficulty: with *the* [something seems to be the *matter*] **10** documents, letters, etc. sent, or to be sent, by mail [second-class *matter*] **11** a substance discharged by the body; specif., pus **12** *Law* something that is to be proved **13** *Philos.* that which has yet to take on form; undifferentiated substance of reality or experience **14** *Printing a)* written material prepared, or to be prepared, for printing; copy *b)* copy ready to be printed —*vi.* **1** to be of importance or consequence [the things that *matter* to one] **2** to form and discharge pus; suppurate —**as a matter of fact** *see this phrase at* FACT —**for that matter** in regard to that; as far as that is concerned: also **for the matter of that** —**no matter 1** it is of no importance **2** regardless of

Mat·ter·horn (mat′ər hôrn′) mountain of the Pennine Alps, on the Swiss-Italian border: *c.* 14,700 ft (4,481 m)

matter of course a thing to be expected as a natural or logical occurrence in the course of events

mat·ter-of-course (mat′ər əv kôrs′) *adj.* **1** coming as a natural or logical occurrence in the course of events; routine **2** reacting to events in a calm and natural way

mat·ter-of-fact (mat′ər əv fakt′) *adj.* sticking strictly to facts; literal, unimaginative, unemotional, prosaic, etc. —**mat′ter-of-fact′ly** *adv.* —**mat′ter-of-fact′ness** *n.*

Mat·the·an (ma thē′ən) *adj.* of or characteristic of the Evangelist Matthew or the book of the New Testament ascribed to him

Mat·thew (math′yo͞o′) *n.* ⟦ME *Matheu* < OFr < LL(Ec) *Matthaeus* < Gr(Ec) *Matthaios, Matthias*, contr. < *Mattathias* < Heb *mattithyāh*, lit., gift of God⟧ **1** a masculine name: dim. *Matt*; var. *Matthias*; equiv. Fr. *Mathieu*, Ger. & Swed. *Matthaus*, It. *Matteo*, Sp. *Mateo* **2** *Bible a)* one of the twelve Apostles, a customs collector (also called *Levi*) to whom traditionally is ascribed the first Gospel: his day is Sept. 21 (also **Saint Matthew**) *b)* the first book of the New Testament, telling of Jesus' life (abbrev. *Matt* or *Mt*)

Mat·thi·as (mə thī′əs) *n.* ⟦Gr: see prec.⟧ *Bible* one of the Apostles, chosen by lot to replace Judas Iscariot: Acts 1:26: his day is May 14: also **Saint Matthias**

mat·ting[1] (mat′iŋ) *n.* **1** a woven fabric of fiber, as straw or hemp, for mats, floor covering, wrapping, etc. **2** mats collectively **3** the making of mats

mat·ting[2] (mat′iŋ) *n.* ⟦see MATTE[2]⟧ **1** the production of a dull surface or finish on metal, glass, etc. **2** such a surface or finish **3** a mat, or border

mat·tins (mat′'nz) *pl.n. Brit. var. of* matins: see MATIN (*n.* 1)

mat·tock (mat′ək) *n.* ⟦ME *mattok* < OE *mattuc* < VL **mattiuca* < **mattea*, back-form. < L *mateola*, dim. < **matea* < IE base **mat-*, hoe, club > Sans *matyá-*, a harrow⟧ a tool for loosening the soil, digging up and cutting roots, etc.: it is like a pickax but has a flat, adz-shaped blade on one or both sides

mat·tress (ma′trəs) *n.* ⟦ME *materas* < OFr < It *materasso* < Ar *maṭraḥ*, place where something is thrown or laid, cushion⟧ **1** *a)* a casing of strong fabric filled with cotton, hair, foam rubber, etc., usually containing coiled springs, often quilted or tufted at intervals, and used on or as a bed *b)* an inflatable pad used in the same way (in full **air mattress**) *c)* that part of a WATER BED that contains the water, providing cushioned support **2** a mass or mat of interwoven brushwood, poles, etc. used to protect an embankment or dike from erosion, etc.

mat·u·rate (mach′ə rāt′) *vi.* **-rat′ed, -rat′ing** ⟦< L *maturatus*, pp. of *maturare*, to ripen < *maturus*, MATURE⟧ **1** to suppurate; discharge pus **2** to ripen; mature —**ma·tur·a·tive** (mach′ə rāt′iv; mə toor′ə tiv, -tyoor′-) *adj.*

mat·u·ra·tion (mach′ə rā′shən) *n.* ⟦Fr < L *maturatio* < pp. of *maturare*: see prec.⟧ **1** the formation or discharge of pus; suppuration **2** the act or process of maturing, esp. of becoming full-grown or fully developed **3** *Biol.* the final stages in the development of gametes in which, through meiosis, the normal number of chromosomes is reduced by half —**mat′u·ra′tion·al** *adj.*

ma·ture (mə toor′, -choor′, -tyoor′) *adj.* ⟦ME < L *maturus*, seasonable, ripe, mature < IE base **ma-*, good, in good time > L *Matuta*, goddess of dawn⟧ **1** *a)* full-grown (said as of plants or animals) *b)* ripe (said as of fruit) *c)* fully developed (said as of a mind) *d)* adult in age, experience, etc. [a movie for a *mature* audience] *e)* designating, of, or relating to an adult who is of late middle age or older (used as a euphemism) [safety tips for *mature* drivers] **2** fully or highly developed, perfected, worked out, considered, etc. [a *mature* scheme] **3** of a state of full development [*mature* germ cells] **4** due; payable: said of a note, bond, etc. **5** *Geol.* having reached maximum development of topographical form due to erosion, weathering, etc.: said as of a coastline that is relatively stable —*vt.* **-tured′, -tur′ing 1** to bring to full growth or development, or to ripeness **2** to develop or work out fully —*vi.* **1** to become fully grown, developed, or ripe **2** to become due: said of a note, etc. —*SYN.* RIPE —**ma·ture′ly** *adv.* —**ma·ture′ness** *n.*

ma·tu·ri·ty (-ə tē) *n.* ⟦ME *maturite* < L *maturitas*⟧ **1** the state or quality of being mature; specif., *a)* a being full-grown, ripe, or fully developed *b)* a being perfect, complete, or ready **2** *a)* a becoming due *b) pl.* **-ties** the time at which a note, etc. becomes due

ma·tu·ti·nal (mə to͞ot′'n əl, -tyo͞ot′-; *chiefly Brit*, ma′to͞o tī′nəl, -tyo͞o-) *adj.* ⟦L *matutinalis* < *matutinus*, of morning, after *Matuta*, goddess of morning: see MATIN⟧ of or in the morning; early —**ma·tu′ti·nal·ly** *adv.*

mat·zo (mät′sə, -sō) *n.* ⟦Heb *matstsāh*, unleavened⟧ **1** a kind of thin, crisp unleavened bread eaten by Jews during the Passover **2** *pl.* **mat′zos, mat′zot** (-sōt), or **mat′zoth** (-sōt) a piece of this

matzo ball a dumpling made of matzo meal, usually served in chicken broth or soup

matzo meal matzo that has been coarsely ground into meal

maud (môd) *n.* ⟦after ? fol.⟧ a type of Scottish shawl, wrap, or rug made of gray striped plaid

Maud or **Maude** (môd) *n.* a feminine name: see MATILDA

mau·dit (mō dē′) *adj.* ⟦Fr⟧ cursed; damned; wretched

maud·lin (môd′lin) *adj.* ⟦after *Maudlin*, Magdalene < ME *Maudeleyne* < OFr *Madeleine*: Magdalene was often represented with eyes red from weeping⟧ **1** foolishly and tearfully or weakly sentimental **2** tearfully sentimental from too much liquor

Maugham (môm), **W(illiam) Som·er·set** (sum′ər set′) 1874-1965; Eng. novelist & playwright

mau·gre or **mau·ger** (mô′gər) *prep.* ⟦OFr *maugré, malgré*, lit., with displeasure < *mal*, ill + *gré*, pleasure: see MAL- & AGREE⟧ [Archaic] in spite of

Mau·i (mou′ē) ⟦Haw⟧ one of the Hawaiian Islands, southeast of Oahu: 727 sq mi (1,883 sq km)

maul (môl) *n.* ⟦Early ModE phonetic sp. of ME *malle* < OFr *maile* < L *malleus*, a hammer: see MALLEABLE⟧ a very heavy ax or mallet, for driving stakes, wedges, etc. —*vt.* ⟦ME *mallen* < OFr *mailler* < the n.⟧ **1** to injure by beating or tearing; bruise or lacerate **2** to handle roughly or clumsily; manhandle; paw —*SYN.* BEAT —**maul′er** *n.*

maul·stick (môl′stik′) *n. var. of* MAHLSTICK

Mau Mau (mou′ mou′) *pl.* **Mau Mau** or **Mau Maus** a member of a secret society of Kikuyu tribesmen in Kenya, organized *c.* 1951 to fight against white rule: both the movement and its suppression were marked by terrorism and violence

☆**mau-mau** (mou′mou′) *vt.* **-maued′, -mau′ing** ⟦< prec.⟧ [Slang] to coerce or attempt to coerce by the use of threats, intimidation, etc.

maun (män, môn) *vi.* ⟦MScot *mane* < ON *man*, pt. of *munu*, shall, will, lit., intend⟧ [Scot.] must

Mau·na Ke·a (mou′nə kā′ə) ⟦Haw, lit., ? white mountain⟧ nearly extinct volcano on the island of Hawaii: 13,796 ft (4,205 m)

Mauna Lo·a (lō′ə) ⟦Haw, lit., long mountain⟧ active volcano on the island of Hawaii: 13,680 ft (4,170 m)

maund (mônd) *n.* ⟦Hindi & Pers *man* < Sans *manā*, prob. < Sem⟧ a varying unit of weight of certain countries of Asia; esp., a unit of weight of India equal to 40 seers (82.28 lb or 37.35 kg)

maun·der (môn′dər) *vi.* ⟦Early ModE *mander*, to grumble, growl, prob. freq. of obs. *maund*, to beg: sense prob. infl. by MEANDER⟧ **1** to move or act in a dreamy, vague, aimless way **2** to talk in an incoherent, rambling way; drivel —**maun′der·er** *n.*

Maun·dy Thursday (môn′dē) ⟦ME *maunde*, ceremony of washing the feet of the poor < OFr *mandé* < LL(Ec) *mandatum*, commandment of God < L (see MANDATE): from use of *mandatum* at the beginning of the prayer for washing the feet, commemorating Jesus' washing of the disciples' feet: see John 13:5, 34⟧ the Thursday before Easter

Mau·pas·sant (mō pä sän′; *E* mō′pə sänt′), **(Henri René Albert) Guy de** (gē də) 1850-93; Fr. writer of novels & short stories

Mau·reen (mô rēn′) *n.* ⟦Ir *Mairin*, dim. of *Maire*, MARY[1]⟧ a feminine name

Mau·re·ta·ni·a (môr′ə tā′nē ə, -tān′yə) ancient country & Roman province in NW Africa, including areas now in NE Morocco & W Algeria

Mau·ri·ac (mô′rē ak′; *Fr* mô ryȧk′), **Fran·çois** (frän swȧ′) 1885-1970; Fr. novelist & essayist

Mau·rice (môr′is, mär′-; mô rēs′) *n.* ⟦Fr < LL *Mauritius* < *Maurus*, a Moor⟧ a masculine name: var. *Morris*; equiv. Ger. *Moritz*, It. *Maurizio*, Sp. *Mauricio*

Maurice of Nassau Prince of Orange 1567-1625; Du. statesman & military leader

Mau·ri·ta·ni·a (môr′ə tā′nē ə, -tān′yə) country in NW Africa, on the Atlantic: formerly a French protectorate & colony, it became independent in 1960: 397,955 sq mi (1,030,700 sq km); cap. Nouakchott —**Mau′ri·ta′ni·an** *adj., n.*

Mau·ri·ti·us (mô rish′ē əs, -rish′əs) **1** island in the Indian Ocean, east of Madagascar: 720 sq mi (1,865 sq km) **2** country consisting of this island & several nearby islands: discovered by the Portuguese in the 16th cent., it was in turn occupied by the Dutch, the French, & the British; became independent & a member of the Commonwealth in 1968: 788 sq mi (2,040 sq km); cap. Port Louis —**Mau·ri′tian** *adj., n.*

Mau·rois (mô rwä′), **An·dré** (än drā′) (born *Émile Salomon Wilhelm Herzog*) 1885-1967; Fr. writer

Mau·ry (môr′ē), **Matthew Fon·taine** (fän tān′) 1806-73; U.S. naval officer & oceanographer

Mau·so·le·um (mô′sə lē′əm, mä′-; -zə-) *n.*, *pl.* for 2 & 3 **-le′ums** or **-le′a**

(-lē′ə) ⟦L < Gr *Mausōleion*⟧ **1** the tomb of Mausolus, king of Caria, at Halicarnassus: included among the Seven Wonders of the World **2** [**m-**] a large, imposing tomb: humorously applied to any large, somber building or room **3** [**m-**] a building with vaults for the entombment of a number of bodies —**mau′so·le′an** (-ən) ***adj.***

mauve (mōv, môv) ***n.*** ⟦Fr, mallow < L *malva*, MALLOW: from the color of the mallow⟧ **1** a purple dye and pigment that is produced by oxidizing aniline: used on wool, silk, etc. **2** any of several shades of delicate purple —***adj.*** of such a color

☆**ma·ven** (mā′vən) ***n.*** ⟦Yiddish < LHeb *mēvin*⟧ [Informal] an expert or connoisseur, often, specif., a self-proclaimed one: often sp. **ma′vin**

☆**mav·er·ick** (mav′ər ik, mav′rik) ***n.*** ⟦after S. *Maverick* (1803-70), Texas rancher who did not brand his cattle⟧ **1** an unbranded animal, esp. a strayed calf **2** a person who takes an independent stand, as in politics, from his or her party or group

ma·vis (mā′vis) ***n.*** ⟦OFr *mauvis* < ?⟧ SONG THRUSH

ma·vour·neen or **ma·vour·nin** (mə vo͝or′nēn) ***n.*** ⟦Ir *mo muirnīn*⟧ [Irish] my darling

maw[1] (mô) ***n.*** ⟦ME *mawe* < OE *maga*, akin to Ger *magen*, stomach < IE base **mak-*, skin, bag > Welsh *megin*, bellows⟧ **1** *a)* [Archaic] the stomach or its cavity *b)* the stomach of an animal; specif., the fourth stomach of a cud-chewing animal **2** the throat, gullet, jaws, or oral cavity of a voracious animal **3** anything thought of as consuming, devouring, etc. without end

maw[2] (mô) ***n.*** [Dial.] ma; mama; mother

mawk·ish (mô′kish) ***adj.*** ⟦lit., maggoty < ME *mawke*, maggot < ON *mathkr* < IE base **math-*, gnawing vermin > MOTH⟧ **1** having a sweet, weak, sickening taste; insipid or nauseating **2** so weakly or insipidly sentimental as to be sickening —**mawk′ish·ly** ***adv.*** —**mawk′ish·ness** ***n.***

☆**max**[1] (maks) [Slang] ***n., adj.*** MAXIMUM —***vi.*** to reach the maximum, or limit: usually with *out* [classroom capacity *maxes* out at 30] —***vt.*** **1** to cause to reach the maximum or limit [a company that *maxed* out its line of credit] **2** to exhaust or use up (a resource, capacity, etc.) Usually with *out* —**to the max** to the greatest possible degree

max[2] *abbrev.* maximum

Max (maks; *Ger* mäks) ***n.*** a masculine name: fem. *Maxine*: see MAXIMILIAN[1]

☆**max·i** (mak′sē) ***n.***, *pl.* **max′is** ⟦< fol.⟧ [Informal] a very long, usually ankle-length, skirt, dress, coat, etc.

max·i- (mak′sē, -si, -sə) ⟦< MAXI(MUM)⟧ *combining form* **1** maximum, very large, very long [*maxicoat*] **2** of greater scope, extent, etc. than usual or normal: used in nonce compounds, often hyphenated [*maxi*-power]

max·il·la (mak sil′ə) ***n.***, *pl.* **-lae** (-ē) ⟦L, dim., akin to *mala*, a jaw⟧ **1** in vertebrates, the upper jaw, or a major bone or cartilage of the upper jaw **2** in most arthropods, as insects or crabs, one of the first or second pair of accessory jaws or head appendages situated just behind the mandibles

max·il·lar·y (mak′sə ler′ē, mak sil′ə rē) ***adj.*** ⟦L *maxillaris*⟧ designating, of, or near the jaw or jawbone, esp. the upper one; relating to a maxilla or maxillae —***n.***, *pl.* **-lar′ies** a maxillary bone; maxilla

max·il·li·ped (mak sil′i ped′) ***n.*** ⟦< MAXILLA + -PED⟧ any one limb of the three pairs of appendages behind the maxillae in crustaceans, esp. in decapods, modified for aid in feeding

max·il·lo·fa·cial (mak sil′ə fā′shəl) ***adj.*** of or having to do with the jaws and face [a *maxillofacial* surgeon]

max·im (mak′sim) ***n.*** ⟦ME *maxime* < MFr < ML *maxima* < LL *maxima (propositio)*, the greatest (premise), fem. of L *maximus*, greatest, superl. of *magnus*, great: see MAGNI-⟧ a concisely expressed principle or rule of conduct, or a statement of a general truth —***SYN.*** SAYING

Max·im[1] (mak′sim) ***n.*** ⟦after H. S. MAXIM[2]⟧ an early, single-barreled, automatic machine gun: in full **Maxim gun**

Max·im[2] (mak′sim) **1 Hiram Percy** 1869-1936; U.S. inventor: son of Sir Hiram **2** Sir **Hiram Stevens** 1840-1916; Brit. engineer & inventor of weapons & explosives, born in the U.S. **3 Hudson** 1853-1927; U.S. chemist & inventor of explosives: brother of Sir Hiram

max·i·mal (mak′si məl) ***adj.*** highest or greatest possible; of or constituting a maximum —**max′i·mal·ly** ***adv.***

max·i·mal·ist (-məl ist) ***n.*** ⟦prec. + -IST[1]⟧ a person who favors direct or revolutionary action to achieve a goal

Max·i·mil·ian[1] (mak′sə mil′yən) ***n.*** ⟦blend of the L names *Maximus* & *Aemilianus*⟧ a masculine name: dim. *Max*

Max·i·mil·ian[2] (mak′sə mil′yən) **1** (born *Ferdinand Maximilian Joseph*) 1832-67; archduke of Austria: emperor of Mexico (1864-67); executed **2 Maximilian I** 1459-1519; emperor of the Holy Roman Empire (1493-1519) **3 Maximilian II** 1527-76; emperor of the Holy Roman Empire (1564-76)

max·i·mize (mak′sə mīz′) ***vt.*** **-mized′**, **-miz′ing** **1** to increase to the maximum; raise to the highest possible degree; enlarge, intensify, etc. as much as possible **2** to estimate or make appear to be of the greatest possible amount, value, or importance —**max′i·mi·za′tion** (-mə zā′shən, -mī′-) ***n.*** —**max′i·miz′er** ***n.***

max·i·mum (mak′sə məm) ***n.***, *pl.* **-mums** or **-ma** (-mə) ⟦L, neut. of *maximus*, superl. of *magnus*, great: see MAGNI-⟧ **1** the greatest quantity, number, or degree possible or permissible **2** the highest degree or point (of a varying quantity, as temperature) reached or recorded; upper limit of variation **3** *Math.* the largest of a specified set of real numbers —***adj.*** **1** greatest possible, permissible, or reached **2** of, marking, or setting a maximum or maximums

maximum card *Philately* a postcard with an enlarged picture of a commemorative postage stamp, with the stamp itself postmarked on the picture, usually the first day of issue

Max·ine (mak sēn′) ***n.*** a feminine name: see MAX

ma·xi·xe (mə shē′shə) ***n.*** ⟦BrazPort < ?⟧ **1** an old-fashioned Brazilian dance in moderate duple time, similar to the two-step **2** music for this dance

max·well (maks′wel′) ***n.*** ⟦after fol.⟧ the basic unit of magnetic flux in the CGS system, equal to the flux through one square centimeter perpendicular to a magnetic field with an intensity of one gauss: one maxwell equals 10^{-8} weber: abbrev. *Mx*

Max·well (maks′wel′, -wəl), **James Clerk** (klärk) 1831-79; Scot. physicist

may[1] (mā) ***v.aux.***, *pt.* **might** ⟦ME < OE *mæg*, akin to Ger *mag*, OHG & Goth *magan*, lit., to be physically capable of doing < IE base **māgh-*, to be able > MIGHT[2]⟧ **1** used to express ability or power: now generally replaced by CAN[1] **2** used to express possibility or likelihood [it *may* rain] **3** used to express permission [you *may* go] **4** used to express contingency, as in clauses of purpose, result, concession, or condition [they died that we *may* be free] **5** used in exclamations and apostrophes to express a wish, hope, or prayer [*may* he rest in peace] **6** *Law* shall; must As a modal auxiliary, *may* is followed by an infinitive without *to* —***vi.*** **1** used to express possibility or likelihood **2** used to express permission [yes, you *may*]

USAGE—See usage note at CAN[1]

may[2] (mā) ***n.*** ⟦ME < OE *mæg*, kinswoman, woman (? merged with ON *mær*, maiden)⟧ [Archaic] a maiden

May[1] (mā) ***n.*** ⟦OFr *mai* < L (*mensis*) *Maius*, (month) of *Maius*: see MAIA⟧ **1** the fifth month of the year, having 31 days: abbrev. *M* or *My* **2** *a)* springtime *b)* the springtime of life; youth; prime **3** [**m-**] *a)* the English hawthorn (*Crataegus oxyacantha*) with small, lobed leaves and white, pink, or red flowers *b)* its branches or flowers **4** the festivities of May Day

May[2] (mā) ***n.*** ⟦contr. of MARY[1], MARGARET, often assoc. with the name of the month⟧ a feminine name

May[3] (mā), **Cape** ⟦after C. J. *Mey*, 17th-c. Du explorer⟧ peninsula at the southernmost point of N.J.: *c.* 20 mi (32 km) long

Ma·ya[1] (mä′yə, mī′ə) ***n.*** ⟦Sp < native name⟧ **1** *pl.* **-ya** or **-yas** a member of an American Indian people found in Yucatán, Belize, and N Guatemala: the Maya had a highly developed civilization long before the arrival of Europeans early in the 16th cent. **2** the Mayan language of this people —***adj.*** of the Maya or their language or culture; Mayan

Ma·ya[2] (mä′yä′) ***n.*** ⟦Sans *māyā*⟧ **1** *Hinduism* the goddess Devi, or Shakti, consort of Siva **2** [*also* **m-**] in Hinduism and Indian philosophy, the illusory world of the senses

Ma·ya·kov·ski (mä′yä kôf′skē), **Vla·di·mir (Vladimirovich)** (vlä dē′mir) 1893-1930; Russ. poet

Ma·yan (mä′yən, mī′ən) ***adj.*** **1** designating or of an American Indian language family of Central America, consisting of about 25 languages, including Maya, Huastec, and Yucatec **2** MAYA[1] (***adj.***) —***n.*** **1** a member of any of the Indian peoples that speak a Mayan language **2** the Mayan family of languages

☆**May apple** **1** a perennial woodland plant (*Podophyllum peltatum*) of the barberry family, with shield-shaped leaves and a single, large, white, cuplike flower, found in the E U.S. **2** its edible yellow fruit

may·be (mā′bē) ***adv.*** ⟦ME (for *it may be*)⟧ perhaps; possibly

May·day (mā′dā′) ***n.*** ⟦prob. short for Fr (*venez*) *m'aider*, (come) help me⟧ the international radiotelephone signal for help, used by ships and aircraft in distress

May Day May 1: as a traditional spring festival, often celebrated by dancing around a maypole, crowning a May queen, etc.; as a more recent international labor holiday, observed in many countries by parades, demonstrations, etc.

May-De·cem·ber (mā′di sem′bər) ***adj.*** of or designating a marriage or romantic relationship between a young person and a person who is considerably older

May·er (mā′ər), **Louis B(urt)** (born *Eliezer Meir*) 1884-1957; U.S. film producer, born in Russia

may·est (mā′ist, māst) ***v.aux.*** *archaic 2d pers. sing., pres. indic., of* MAY[1]: used with *thou*

May·fair (mā′fer′) exclusive residential district of the West End, London

may·flow·er (mā′flou′ər) ***n.*** **1** any of various plants that flower in May or early spring; esp., ☆*a)* in the U.S., the trailing arbutus, any of several anemones, etc. *b)* in England, the may, cowslip, marsh marigold, etc. **2** [**M-**] the ship on which the Pilgrims came to America (1620)

may·fly (-flī′) ***n.***, *pl.* **-flies′** ⟦so named because thought to be most prevalent in May⟧ any of an order (Ephemeroptera) of delicate, soft-bodied insects with gauzy wings held vertically when at rest: in the adult stage, it lives only hours or a few days, but the aquatic larval stage may last for several years

may·hap (mā hap′, mā′hap′) ***adv.*** ⟦< (*it*) *may hap*(*pen*)⟧ [Archaic] perhaps; maybe: also **may·hap′pen**

may·hem (mā′hem, mā′əm) ***n.*** ⟦see MAIM⟧ **1** [Historical] *Law* the crime of maiming a person, esp. in order to make the person incapable of self-defense **2** destructive or violent disorder

may·ing (mā′iŋ) ***n.*** [*also* **M-**] the celebration of May Day, as by dancing or gathering flowers

May·nard (mā′nərd, -närd′) ***n.*** ⟦ME < Anglo-Fr *Mainard* < OHG *Maganhard* < *magan*, power, strength (see MAY[1]) + *hart*, strong, HARD⟧ a masculine name

may·n't (mā′ənt, mānt) *contraction* may not

may·o (mā′ō) ***n.*** [Informal] *short for* MAYONNAISE

May·o[1] (mā′ō) **1 Charles Horace** 1865-1939; U.S. surgeon **2 William James** 1861-1939; U.S. surgeon; brother of Charles Horace

May·o[2] (mā′ō) county in W Ireland, in Connacht province: 2,084 sq mi (5,398 sq km)

Ma·yon (mä yôn′) active volcano in SE Luzon, Philippines: *c.* 8,000 ft (2,438 m)

may·on·naise (mā′ə nāz′, mā′ə nāz′) ***n.*** ⟦Fr, earlier *mahonnaise,* apparently fem. of *mahonais,* of *Mahón,* Minorca: reason for name unknown⟧ **1** a creamy salad dressing or sauce made by beating together egg yolks, olive oil or other vegetable oil, lemon juice or vinegar, and seasoning **2** a dish of meat or fish made with this **3** any similar creamy dressing used as a condiment

may·or (mā′ər, mer) ***n.*** ⟦ME *mair* < OFr *maire* < L *major,* compar. of *magnus,* great: see MAGNI-⟧ the elected or appointed head of a municipal government, usually the chief administrative official but sometimes a largely ceremonial figure having little executive authority —**may·or·al** (mā′ər əl, mā ôr′əl) ***adj.***

may·or·al·ty (-əl tē) ***n., pl.*** **-ties** ⟦ME *mairalte* < OFr *mairalté*⟧ the office or term of office of a mayor

Ma·yotte (mä yôt′, -yät′) political unit of France, consisting of an island group in the Mozambique Channel of the Indian Ocean: formerly part of the Comoro Islands, it voted to remain affiliated with France while the other islands voted for independence (1974): 144 sq mi (373 sq km)

may·pole (mā′pōl′) ***n.*** [*often* **M-**] a high pole wreathed with flowers, streamers, etc., around which merrymakers dance on May Day

☆**may·pop** (mā′päp′) ***n.*** ⟦altered < *maracock* < AmInd (Algonquian)⟧ **1** the small, yellow, edible fruit of a passionflower (*Passiflora incarnata*) growing in the S U.S. **2** the plant itself

May queen a girl chosen to be queen of the merrymakers on May Day and traditionally crowned with flowers

Mayr (mīr), **Ernst (Walter)** (ernst) 1904-2005; U.S. biologist & naturalist, born in Germany

mayst (māst) ***v.aux., vi.*** *archaic 2d pers. sing., pres. indic., of* MAY[1]: used with *thou*

May·time (mā′tīm′) ***n.*** the month of May: also **May′tide′** (-tīd′)

may tree [Brit.] MAY[1] (sense 3*a*)

may·weed (mā′wēd′) ***n.*** ⟦for *maidweed* < **maythe-weed* < OE *magothe,* mayweed (prob. akin to *mægeth,* maiden) + WEED[2]⟧ DOG FENNEL (sense 1)

May wine ⟦after the month of *May* (see MAY[1]), when the woodruff blossoms⟧ a punch made of white wine flavored with woodruff and garnished with fresh fruit, traditionally strawberries

maz·ard (maz′ərd) ***n.*** ⟦altered (infl. by -ARD) < MAZER⟧ [Obs.] **1** a mazer **2** *a)* the head or skull *b)* the face

Ma·za·rin (má zá ran′; *E* maz′ə rin′), **Jules** (zhül; *E* zho͞ol) Cardinal (born *Giulio Mazarini*) 1602-61; Fr. statesman & prelate, born in Italy

Ma·za·tlán (mä′sät län′) seaport & resort on the Pacific coast of Mexico, in the state of Sinaloa

Maz·da·ism (maz′də iz′əm) ***n.*** ⟦< Avestan *mazda* (see ORMAZD) + -ISM⟧ ZOROASTRIANISM

maze (māz) ***vt.*** **mazed, maz′ing** ⟦ME *masen,* to confuse, puzzle, aphetic for OE *amasian:* see AMAZE⟧ [Now Chiefly Dial.] **1** to stupefy; daze **2** to confuse; bewilder —***n.*** **1** a confusing, intricate network of winding pathways; specif., such a network with one or more pathways that are shut off at their ends, used as in behavioral testing of animals: cf. LABYRINTH (sense 1) **2** any situation characterized by confusing or bewildering complexity

maze

maz·el tov (mä′zəl tôf′, -tōv′) ⟦Heb (often via Yiddish) < *mázal,* luck + *tōv,* good⟧ congratulations; good luck: also written ***maz′el·tov′ interj.***

ma·zer (mā′zər) ***n.*** ⟦ME *maser* < OFr *masere,* maple wood < Gmc, as in OHG *masar,* gnarled growth on oaks, ON *mösurr,* maple, akin to OHG *māsa,* a spot⟧ a large drinking bowl or goblet, orig. of a hard wood, probably maple, later of metal

☆**ma·zu·ma** (mə zo͞o′mə) ***n.*** ⟦Yiddish *mezumon* < Heb *mezūmānim*⟧ [Slang] money

ma·zur·ka or **ma·zour·ka** (mə zur′kə, -zoor′-) ***n.*** ⟦Pol *mazurka,* woman from Mazovia (or Masovia), region of central Poland⟧ **1** a lively Polish folk dance **2** music for this, generally in 3/4 or 3/8 time

ma·zy (mā′zē) ***adj.*** **-zi·er, -zi·est** like a maze; intricately winding; bewildering —**maz′i·ly** ***adv.*** —**maz′i·ness** ***n.***

maz·zard (maz′ərd) ***n.*** ⟦? var. of MAZER⟧ SWEET CHERRY; esp., a wild sweet cherry whose young seedlings are used as a rootstock for cultivated varieties

Maz·zi·ni (mät tsē′nē, mäd dzē′nē), **Giu·sep·pe** (jo͞o zep′pe) 1805-72: It. patriot & revolutionary

mb *abbrev.* **1** megabyte(s) **2** millibar(s)

Mb *abbrev.* megabit(s)

MB *abbrev.* **1** Manitoba **2** megabyte(s)

MBA or **M.B.A.** *abbrev.* Master of Business Administration

Mba·ba·ne (′m bə bä′nē, em-) capital of Swaziland, in the NW part

Mban·da·ka (′m bən dä′kə, em-) city in the W Democratic Republic of the Congo, on the Congo River

mba·qan·ga (′m bə käŋ′gə, em-) ***n.*** ⟦Zulu *umbaqanga,* lit., steamed bread made from cornmeal⟧ a South African urban dance music with a heavy beat

mbd *abbrev.* million barrels per day

MBE *abbrev.* Member of (the Order of) the British Empire

mbi·ra (′m bir′ə, em-) ***n.*** ⟦prob. < name in Shona, a Bantu language of Zimbabwe⟧ a hand-held African musical instrument consisting of a series of metal or wooden strips mounted on a soundboard and, often, having a resonator formed from a gourd: it is played by plucking the strips with the thumbs and forefingers

Mbps *abbrev.* megabits per second

Mbu·ji-Ma·yi (′m bo͝o′jē mī′ē, em-; -mä′yē) city in the SC Democratic Republic of the Congo

Mbun·du (′m bo͞on′do͞o′, em-) ***n.*** **1** *pl.* **-dus′** or **-du′** a member of a group of related peoples of WC Angola **2** the Bantu language of these peoples

mc *abbrev.* **1** MICRO- (sense 4) **2** millicurie(s)

Mc *abbrev.* **1** *Bible* Maccabees **2** megacycle(s)

MC *abbrev.* **1** Master of Ceremonies **2** Medical Corps **3** Member of Congress

Mc-[1] or **M**[c]**-** (mək) *prefix* MAC- [*McDonald*]

☆**Mc-**[2] (mək) ⟦< *Mc(Donald's),* service mark for a chain of fast-food restaurants⟧ [Slang] *prefix* regarded as being inferior, trivial, monotonous, etc., as from being mass-produced or commercialized [*a Mcnewspaper,* a series of *McJobs*]

Mc·Al·len (mə kal′ən) ⟦after J. *McAllen* (1826-1913), local rancher⟧ city in S Tex., in the Rio Grande valley

MCAT *service mark* Medical College Admission Test

☆**Mc·Car·thy·ism** (mə kär′thē iz′əm) ***n.*** ⟦after U.S. Senator Joseph *McCarthy* (served 1946-57), to whom such practices were attributed⟧ the use of indiscriminate, often unfounded, accusations, sensationalism, inquisitorial investigative methods, etc., as in the suppression of political opponents —**Mc·Car′thy·ite′** ***adj., n.***

Mc·Clel·lan (mə klel′ən), **George B(rinton)** 1826-85; Union general in the Civil War

Mc·Clin·tock (mə klin′täk′, -tək), **Barbara** (born *Eleanor McClintock*) 1902-92; U.S. geneticist

Mc·Cor·mack (mə kôr′mək), **John (Francis)** 1884-1945; U.S. tenor, born in Ireland

Mc·Cor·mick (mə kôr′mik), **Cyrus (Hall)** 1809-84; U.S. inventor of the reaping machine

Mc·Coy (mə koi′) ***n.*** ⟦< ?⟧ [Slang] the real person or thing, not a substitute: with *the:* in full **the real McCoy**

Mc·Cul·lers (mə kul′ərz), **Carson** (born *Lula Carson Smith*) 1917-67; U.S. writer

mcf *abbrev.* thousand cubic feet

mcg *abbrev.* microgram(s)

Mc·Guf·fey (mə guf′ē), **William Holmes** 1800-73; U.S. educator: editor of a series of school readers

Mc·Guf·fin (mə guf′in) ***n.*** *alt. sp. of* MACGUFFIN

mCi *abbrev.* millicurie(s)

Mc·In·tosh (mak′in täsh′) ***n.*** ⟦after J. *McIntosh,* who discovered and cultivated it (1796)⟧ a late-maturing variety of red apple: also **McIntosh Red**

Mc·Kin·ley[1] (mə kin′lē), **William** 1843-1901; 25th president of the U.S. (1897-1901): assassinated

Mc·Kin·ley[2] (mə kin′lē), **Mount** ⟦after prec.⟧ *former name for* DENALI

Mc·Kin·ney (mə kin′ē) city in NE Tex., near Dallas

MCL or **M.C.L.** *abbrev.* Master of Civil Law

Mc·Lu·han (mə klo͞o′ən), **(Herbert) Marshall** 1911-80; Cdn. writer & educator

Mc·Mil·lan (mək mil′ən), **Edwin Mat·ti·son** (mat′ə sən) 1907-91; U.S. physicist

Mc·Mur·do Sound (mək mur′dō) arm of the Ross Sea, off the coast of Victoria Land, Antarctica

☆**MCP** *abbrev.* [Slang] male chauvinist pig

Md[1] *abbrev.* Maryland

Md[2] *Chem. symbol for* mendelevium

MD *abbrev.* **1** ⟦L *Medicinae Doctor*⟧ Doctor of Medicine: also **M.D. 2** Maryland **3** Medical Department **4** muscular dystrophy

M-day (em′dā′) ***n.*** the day on which mobilization for war begins

MDiv or **M.Div.** *abbrev.* Master of Divinity

Mdlle *abbrev.* Mademoiselle

MDMA (em′dē′em′ā′) ***n.*** ⟦*m(ethylene)d(ioxy)m(eth)a(mphetamine)*⟧ ECSTASY (sense 4)

Mdme *abbrev.* Madame

MDS or **M.D.S.** *abbrev.* Master of Dental Surgery

mdse *abbrev.* merchandise

MDT *abbrev.* Mountain Daylight Time

MDu *abbrev.* Middle Dutch

me (mē) ***pron.*** ⟦ME < OE, akin to Ger *mich,* acc., *mir,* dat. < IE base **me-* > L *me,* acc., *mi(hi),* dat.⟧ *objective form of* I[2] [help *me;* give *me* the book]

USAGE—*me* is also used as a predicate complement with a linking verb [*it's me*] and in certain comparative constructions [*he runs faster than me,* but he's not as agile as *me*], although both usages are objected to by some

Me *abbrev.* **1** Maine **2** methyl

ME *abbrev.* **1** Maine **2** Master of Education: also **M.E. 3** Mechanical Engineer **4** Medical Examiner **5** Methodist Episcopal **6** Middle English **7** Military Engineer **8** Mining Engineer **9** Most Excellent **10** myalgic encephalomyelitis

me·a cul·pa (mā′ə kul′pə, -ko͝ol′pə) ⟦< L, (by) my fault, I am to blame⟧ [*often in italics*] an apology or an acknowledgment of guilt

mead¹ (mēd) ***n.*** ⟦ME *mede* < OE *meodu*, akin to Ger *met* < IE base **medhu-*, honey > Sans *mādhu*, Gr *methy*, wine, Welsh *medd*, mead⟧ an alcoholic liquor made of fermented honey and water, often with spices, fruit, malt, etc. added

mead² (mēd) ***n.*** ⟦ME *mede* < OE *mæd*, MEADOW⟧ [Old Poet.] *var. of* MEADOW

Mead¹ (mēd), **Margaret** 1901-78; U.S. anthropologist

Mead² (mēd), **Lake** ⟦after E. *Mead* (1858-1936), U.S. engineer⟧ lake in SE Nev. & NW Ariz., formed by Hoover Dam on the Colorado River: *c.* 250 sq mi (647 sq km)

Meade (mēd), **George Gordon** 1815-72; Union general in the Civil War

mead·ow (med′ō) ***n.*** ⟦ME *medow* < OE *mædwe*, oblique case of *mæd* < Gmc **mædwa-* < IE base **mē-*, to MOW¹⟧ **1** a piece of grassland, esp. one used as a pasture or for growing grass for hay **2** low, level grassland near a stream, lake, etc. —**mead′ow·y** ***adj.***

☆**meadow beauty** any of a genus (*Rhexia*) of perennial North American plants of the melastome family, with pink or lavender flowers and large stamens

meadow fescue a tufted perennial grass (*Festuca pratensis*) with narrow, lustrous leaves, used for hay meadows and lawns

mead·ow·land (med′ō land′) ***n.*** land used as a meadow

mead·ow·lark (-lärk′) ***n., pl.*** **-larks′** or **-lark′** any of a genus (*Sturnella*, family Icteridae) of American passerine birds, esp., any of the yellow-breasted North American species (*S. magna* and *S. neglecta*) with a black, V-shaped collar

☆**meadow lily** CANADA LILY

meadow mouse FIELD MOUSE

meadow mushroom a common edible mushroom (*Agaricus campestris*) with pinkish or brown gills, found in open, grassy areas

meadow nematode any of a number of roundworms (genus *Pratylenchus*), parasitic on the roots of various plants

meadow rue any of a genus (*Thalictrum*) of perennial plants of the buttercup family, with leaves like those of rue

meadow saffron COLCHICUM (sense 1)

mead·ow·sweet (med′ō swēt′) ***n.*** **1** any of several spireas, esp., either of two common species (*Spiraea alba* and *S. latifolia*) **2** any of a genus (*Filipendula*) of plants of the rose family, with fragrant, white, pink, or purple flowers in clusters

mea·ger (mē′gər) ***adj.*** ⟦ME *megre* < OFr *megre* (Fr *maigre*) < L *macer*, lean, thin < IE **makro-* < base **māk-*, long and thin > Gr *makros*, long, OE *mæger*, meager⟧ **1** thin; lean; emaciated **2** of poor quality or small amount; not full or rich; inadequate Brit. sp. **mea′gre** —**mea′ger·ly** ***adv.*** —**mea′ger·ness** ***n.***

SYN.—**meager** literally implies an emaciated thinness and, hence, connotes a lack of those qualities which give something richness, vigor, strength, etc. [*meager* cultural resources]; **scanty** implies an inadequacy in amount, number, quantity, etc. of something essential [a *scanty* income]; **scant** is applied to a barely sufficient amount or a stinted quantity [the *scant* attendance at the concert]; **spare** implies less than a sufficient amount but does not necessarily connote great hardship [to live on *spare* rations]; **sparse** applies to a scanty quantity that is thinly distributed over a wide area [his *sparse* hair] —***ANT.*** **ample, abundant, plentiful**

meal¹ (mēl) ***n.*** ⟦ME *mele* < OE *mæl*, a measure, fixed time, meal, akin to Ger *mal*, time, *mahl*, meal < IE base **mē-*, to MEASURE⟧ **1** any of the times, esp. the customary times, for eating, as breakfast, lunch, or dinner **2** the food served or eaten at such a time

meal² (mēl) ***n.*** ⟦ME *mele* < OE *melu*, akin to Ger *mehl* < IE base **mel-*, to grind, soft > MILL¹⟧ **1** any edible grain, or the edible part of any grain, coarsely ground and unbolted [*cornmeal*] **2** any substance similarly ground or powdered

-meal (mēl) ⟦ME *-mele* < OE *-mælum* < *mæl*, measure, time (see MEAL¹) + adv. dat. *-um*⟧ *suffix forming adverbs* by a (specified) amount done or used at one time: obs. except in *inchmeal, piecemeal*

meal·ie (mē′lē) ***n.*** ⟦Afrik *milje* < Port *milho*, millet (in *milho grande*, maize) < L *milium*, MILLET⟧ [South Afr.] **1** CORN¹ (sense 3): *usually used in pl.* **2** an ear of this

Meals on Wheels an agency or service that delivers cooked meals to disabled people and the elderly in their homes: also **meals′-on-wheels′** ***n.***

☆**meal ticket** **1** a ticket entitling the holder to a specified value in meals at a particular restaurant **2** [Slang] a person, job, skill, etc. that one depends on as one's means of support

meal·time (mēl′tīm′) ***n.*** the usual time for serving or eating a meal

meal·worm (-wurm′) ***n.*** the wormlike larva of any of a genus (*Tenebrio*) of darkling beetles, which destroys flour, meal, etc.

meal·y (mēl′ē) ***adj.*** **meal′i·er, meal′i·est** **1** *a)* like meal; powdery, dry, soft, etc. *b)* dry and somewhat crumbly or coarse in texture, with little flavor [a *mealy* apple] **2** of or containing meal **3** sprinkled or covered with meal **4** spotty or flecked: said of color, etc. **5** floury in color; pale **6** MEALY-MOUTHED —**meal′i·ness** ***n.***

meal·y·bug (-bug′) ***n.*** any of a family (Pseudococcidae) of destructive homopteran insects, having a soft body protected by a white, flourlike or cottony wax secretion

meal·y-mouthed (-mouthd′, -moutht′) ***adj.*** not willing to state the facts in simple, direct words; euphemistic and insincere

mean¹ (mēn) ***vt.*** **meant** (ment), **mean′ing** ⟦ME *menen* < OE *mænan*, to mean, tell, complain, akin to Ger *meinen*, to have in mind, have as opinion < IE base **meino-*, opinion, intent > OIr *mian*, wish, desire⟧ **1** to have in mind; intend; purpose [he *means* to go] **2** to intend or design for a certain person or purpose [a gift *meant* for you] **3** to intend to express, signify, or indicate [to say what one *means*] **4** *a)* to be used to convey; denote [the German word "*ja*" *means* "yes"] *b)* to be a sign, indication, or herald of; signify [this *means* war!] —***vi.*** to have a purpose or intention in mind: chiefly in **mean well**, to have good intentions —***SYN.*** INTEND —**mean well by** to have good intentions or friendly, helpful feelings toward

mean² (mēn) ***adj.*** ⟦ME *mene*, common, hence mean < OE *(ge)mæne*, akin to Ger *gemein*, plentiful, COMMON⟧ **1** low in quality, value, or importance; paltry; poor; inferior: now usually in negative constructions [paid no *mean* sum] **2** [Rare] low in social status or rank; of humble origin **3** poor in appearance; shabby [a *mean* dwelling] **4** ignoble; base; small-minded; petty **5** stingy; miserly; penurious ☆**6** bad-tempered; vicious; unmanageable: said of a horse, etc. ☆**7** pettily or contemptibly selfish, bad-tempered, disagreeable, malicious, etc. ☆**8** humiliated or ashamed ☆**9** [Informal] in poor health; not well; ill; indisposed ☆**10** [Slang] *a)* hard to cope with; difficult [to throw a *mean* curve in baseball] *b)* skillful; expert [to play a *mean* game of chess] —***SYN.*** BASE² —**mean′ly** ***adv.*** —**mean′ness** ***n.***

mean³ (mēn) ***adj.*** ⟦ME *mene* < OFr *meien* (Fr *moyen*) < L *medianus*: see MEDIAN⟧ **1** halfway between extremes; in a middle or intermediate position as to place, time, quantity, quality, kind, value, degree, etc. **2** medium; average; middling —***n.*** **1** what is between extremes; intermediate state, quality, course, or procedure **2** avoidance of extremes or excess; moderation **3** *Math.* *a)* a number between the smallest and largest values of a set of quantities, obtained by some prescribed method: unless otherwise qualified, the ARITHMETIC MEAN *b)* the number obtained by multiplying each value of x by the probability (or probability density) of x and then summing (or integrating) over the range of x *c)* the second or third term of a four-term proportion: see also GEOMETRIC MEAN —***SYN.*** AVERAGE

me·an·der (mē an′dər) ***n.*** ⟦L *maeander* < Gr *maiandros* < *Maiandros*, the MAEANDER River (noted for its winding course)⟧ **1** [*pl.*] windings or convolutions, as of a stream **2** an ornamental pattern of winding or crisscrossing lines **3** an aimless wandering; rambling —***vi.*** **1** to take a winding or tortuous course: said of a stream **2** to wander aimlessly or idly; ramble —**me·an′drous** (-drəs) ***adj.***

Me·an·der (mē an′dər) *alt. sp. of* MAEANDER

mean deviation a measure of variability equal to the average of the absolute values of a set of deviations from a specified value, usually the arithmetic mean

mean distance the average of the greatest and least distances in the orbit of a celestial body from its focus

mean·ie or **mean·y** (mē′nē) ***n., pl.*** **mean′ies** [Informal] a person who is mean, selfish, cruel, etc.

mean·ing (mē′niŋ) ***n.*** **1** what is meant; what is intended to be, or in fact is, signified, indicated, referred to, or understood [the *meaning* of a foreign phrase] **2** the practical or essential significance of some concept or quality [a spoiled child who doesn't know the *meaning* of hard work] **3** [Archaic] intention; purpose —***adj.*** **1** that has meaning; significant; expressive **2** intending; having purpose —**mean′ing·ly** ***adv.***

mean·ing·ful (-fəl) ***adj.*** full of meaning; having significance or purpose —**mean′ing·ful·ly** ***adv.*** —**mean′ing·ful·ness** ***n.***

mean·ing·less (-lis) ***adj.*** having no meaning; without significance or purpose; senseless —**mean′ing·less·ly** ***adv.*** —**mean′ing·less·ness** ***n.***

means (mēnz) ***pl.n.*** ⟦< MEAN³, *n.*⟧ **1** [*with sing. or pl. v.*] that by which something is done or obtained; agency [the fastest *means* of travel] **2** *a)* resources or available wealth [to live beyond one's *means*] *b)* great wealth; riches [a person of *means*] —**by all means** **1** without fail **2** of course; certainly —**by any means** in any way possible; at all; somehow —**by means of** by using; with the aid of; through —**by no (manner of) means** not at all; in no way —**means to an end** a method of getting or accomplishing what one wants

mean solar day *see* DAY (*n.* 2)

mean solar time time based on the mean sun: used as the basis for standard time because it has exactly equal divisions: also **mean time**

mean-spir·it·ed (mēn′spir′it id) ***adj.*** characterized by or displaying a propensity to be mean; selfish, malicious, etc. —**mean′-spir′it·ed·ness** ***n.***

means test an investigation of a person's financial resources, made to determine whether that person is eligible for welfare payments, low-cost housing, etc.

means-test (mēnz′test′) ***vt.*** to subject to a means test —**means′-test′ed** ***adj.***

mean sun *Astron.* a hypothetical sun thought of as moving uniformly along the celestial equator at a speed equal to the actual sun's average speed along the ecliptic: hypothesized as a basis for keeping time, because the actual sun does not travel along the ecliptic at a uniform rate: see EQUATION OF TIME

meant (ment) ***vt., vi. pt. & pp. of*** MEAN¹ —***adj.*** destined or seemingly destined [she was *meant* to be a doctor]

mean·time (mēn′tīm′) ***adv.*** MEANWHILE —***n.*** the intervening time

mean·while (mēn′hwīl′, -wīl′) ***adv.*** **1** in or during the intervening time **2** at the same time —***n.*** MEANTIME

Mea·ny (mē′nē), **George** 1894-1980; U.S. labor leader: president of the AFL-CIO (1955-79)

meas *abbrev.* measure

mea·sled (mē′zəld) *adj.* infected with MEASLES (sense 2)

mea·sles (mē′zəlz) *n.* ⟦ME *maseles*, pl. of *masel*, measle, spot (? infl. by *mesel*, leper < OFr < L *misellus*, wretch < *miser*, wretched), akin to OHG *māsa*, a spot, Ger *masern*, measles⟧ **1** *a)* an acute, infectious, communicable disease caused by a paramyxovirus and characterized by small, red spots on the skin, high fever, nasal discharge, etc. and occurring most frequently in childhood; rubeola (often with *the*) *b)* any of various similar but milder diseases; esp., rubella (*German measles*) **2** a disease of cattle and hogs, caused by tapeworm larvae in the flesh *—pl.n.* tapeworm larvae

mea·sly (mēz′lē) *adj.* **-sli·er, -sli·est 1** [Archaic] infected with or caused by MEASLES (sense 1 or 2) **2** [Informal] contemptibly slight, worthless, or skimpy

meas·ur·a·ble (mezh′ər ə bəl, mezh′rə bəl) *adj.* ⟦ME *mesurable* < OFr⟧ that can be measured **—meas′ur·a·bil′i·ty** *n.* **—meas′ur·a·bly** *adv.*

meas·ure (mezh′ər) *n.* ⟦ME *mesure* < OFr < L *mensura* < *mensus*, pp. of *metiri*, to measure < IE base **mē-*, to measure > MEAL[1], Sans *mātrā*, a measure, Gr *metron*⟧ **1** the extent, dimensions, capacity, etc. of anything, esp. as determined by a standard **2** the act or process of determining extent, dimensions, etc.; measurement **3** *a)* a standard for determining extent, dimensions, etc.; unit of measurement, as an inch, yard, or bushel *b)* any standard of valuation, comparison, judgment, etc.; criterion **4** a system of measurement [dry *measure*, board *measure*] **5** an instrument for measuring, or a container of standard capacity [a quart *measure*] **6** a definite quantity measured out or thought of as measured **7** an extent or degree not to be exceeded [remain within *measure*] **8** proportion, quantity, or degree [in large *measure*] **9** a procedure; course of action; step [take *measures* to stop him] **10** a legislative bill, resolution, etc. that is proposed or has been enacted **11** *a)* rhythm in verse; meter *b)* a metrical unit; foot of verse **12** [Archaic] a dance or dance movement, esp. if slow and stately **13** [Old Poet.] a melody or tune **14** [*pl.*] [Rare] *Geol.* related beds or strata, as of coal **15** *Music* the notes or rests, or both, contained between two vertical lines on the staff; bar **16** *Printing* the width of a column or page *—vt.* **-ured, -ur·ing** ⟦ME *mesuren* < OFr *mesurer* < LL *mensurare*, to measure < the L n. *mensura*⟧ **1** to find out or estimate the extent, dimensions, etc. of, esp. by the use of a standard **2** to get, take, set apart, or mark off by measuring: often with *off* or *out* **3** to estimate by comparison; judge; appraise [to *measure* one's foe] **4** to bring into comparison or rivalry: with *against* [to *measure* one's skill against another's] **5** to be a measure of [a clock *measures* time] **6** to adjust or proportion by or as by a standard [to *measure* one's speech by the audience's reactions] **7** to choose or weigh carefully (one's words or actions) **8** [Now Rare] to go over or through; traverse as if measuring *—vi.* **1** to find out or estimate extent, dimensions, etc.; get or take measurements **2** to be of a specified dimension, quantity, etc. when measured [a pole that *measures* ten feet] **3** to allow of measurement **—beyond (or above) measure** so much as not to be measurable; exceedingly; extremely **—for good measure** as a bonus or something extra **—in a measure** to some extent; somewhat **—made to measure** ⟦< the *n.*⟧ made to fit someone's own measurements; custom-made: said of clothes **—measure one's length** to fall, lie, or be thrown down at full length **—measure out** to give out or allot by measuring **—measure swords 1** to duel with swords **2** to fight or contend **—☆measure up** to prove to be competent, qualified, or suitable **—☆measure up to** to come up to; meet (expectations, a standard, etc.) **—take measures** to take action; do things to accomplish a purpose **—take someone's measure** to make an estimate or judgment of someone's ability, character, etc. **—tread a measure** [Archaic] to dance **—meas′ur·er** *n.*

meas·ured (mezh′ərd) *adj.* **1** determined, ascertained, or proportioned by a standard **2** *a)* regular, steady, or uniform *b)* steady, slow, and deliberate [to walk with a *measured* tread] **3** *a)* rhythmic *b)* metrical **4** calculated, restrained, and deliberate; careful and guarded: said of speech, etc. **—meas′ured·ly** *adv.*

meas·ure·less (mezh′ər lis) *adj.* too large to be measurable; vast; immense **—meas′ure·less·ly** *adv.*

meas·ure·ment (-mənt) *n.* **1** a measuring or being measured; mensuration **2** extent, quality, or size as determined by measuring; dimension [a waist *measurement* of 32 inches] **3** a system of measuring or of measures **4** [*pl.*] the bust, waistline, and hip dimensions of a woman

measurement ton TON[1] (sense 5)

measuring cup 1 a standard cup, usually one holding either 8 oz or 16 oz, with marks to show fractional amounts and with a lip for pouring, used to measure ingredients in cooking, esp. liquid ingredients **2** a cup for measuring dry ingredients, usually part of a set in graduated sizes including one CUP (*n.* 4) and ½, ⅓, and ¼ of this

☆**measuring worm** ⟦so called from its way of moving, as if *measuring* the earth: see GEOMETRID⟧ the caterpillar of any geometrid moth: it moves by alternately advancing the front end of its body and bringing the rear end forward to form a loop

meat (mēt) *n.* ⟦ME *mete* < OE < Gmc **mad-*, food, meat < IE base **mad-*, to be moist, trickle > MAST[2], Gr *mastos*, breast⟧ **1** food; esp., solid food, as distinguished from drink: now archaic or dialectal except in the phrase **meat and drink 2** *a)* the flesh of animals used as food, esp. the flesh of mammals or, often, of fowl *b)* [Informal] the FLESH (*n.* 1*a*) of a person [not much *meat* on her bones] **3** the edible, inner part [the *meat* of a nut] **4** the substance, meaning, or gist [the *meat* of a story] **5** one's quarry **6** [Archaic] a meal, esp. dinner **7** [Slang] the external genital organs: a vulgar usage **—☆one's meat** [Slang] something that one especially enjoys or is skillful at

meat and potatoes [Informal] basic elements; essentials; fundamentals

meat-and-po·ta·toes (mēt′'n pə tāt′əz) *adj.* [Informal] **1** basic; fundamental [they talked about the *meat-and-potatoes* issues] **2** ordinary; everyday

meat ax CLEAVER: often used fig. for any method or solution regarded as clumsy, brutal, heavy-handed, etc.

meat·ball (-bôl′) *n.* **1** a small ball of ground meat, seasoned and cooked, often with sauce, gravy, etc. **2** [Slang] a stupid, awkward, or boring person

Meath (mēth) county in E Ireland, in Leinster province: 902 sq mi (2,336 sq km)

☆**meat·head** (mēt′hed′) *n.* [Slang] a stupid person; blockhead

meat hooks ☆[Slang] a person's hands or arms, esp. when regarded as large and clumsy

meat·less (-lis) *adj.* **1** having no meat or food **2** when no meat is to be eaten [a *meatless* Friday] **3** containing no meat or meat substances

meat·loaf (-lōf′) *n.* a baked loaf of ground meat, usually beef or beef and pork, mixed with cracker or bread crumbs, egg, etc.: also written **meat loaf**

meat market ⟦because "flesh" is on display there for selection⟧ [Slang] a bar, nightclub, etc. characterized by its patrons' aggressive pursuit of casual sex

☆**meat·pack·ing** (-pak′iŋ) *n.* the process or industry of slaughtering animals and preparing their meat for market **—meat′pack′er** *n.*

me·a·tus (mē āt′əs) *n., pl.* **-tus·es** or **-tus** ⟦LL, avenue of sensation in the body < L, a passage, pp. of *meare*, to go, pass < IE base **mei-*, to go⟧ a duct-like passage within the body or the external opening of such a passage, as in the ear, nose, or urethra

meat·y (mēt′ē) *adj.* **meat′i·er, meat′i·est 1** of, like, or having the flavor or quality of, meat **2** *a)* full of meat *b)* stout; heavy ☆**3** full of substance; thought-provoking; pithy **—meat′i·ness** *n.*

Mec·ca[1] (mek′ə) *n.* ⟦after fol.: every Muslim is expected to make a pilgrimage to Mecca⟧ [*often* **m-**] **1** any place that draws tourists or visitors of a certain kind [Cooperstown is a *Mecca* for baseball fans] **2** any place that one yearns to go to **3** any goal that one is seeking to achieve **—Mec′can** *adj., n.*

Mec·ca[2] (mek′ə) city in W Saudi Arabia, near the Red Sea: birthplace of Muhammad and hence a holy city & destination for pilgrims in Islam: Ar. name MAKKAH: see also HAJJ **—Mec′can** *adj., n.*

mech *abbrev.* **1** mechanical **2** mechanics **3** mechanism

me·chan·ic (mə kan′ik) *adj.* ⟦L *mechanicus* < Gr *mēchanikos* < *mēchanē*, MACHINE⟧ *archaic var. of* MECHANICAL *—n.* **1** a worker skilled in using tools or in making, operating, and repairing machines, often, specif., one whose occupation is repairing the engines, etc. of motor vehicles **2** [Archaic] a manual laborer

me·chan·i·cal (mə kan′i kəl) *adj.* **1** using or having to do with machinery **2** having skill in the use of machinery or tools **3** produced or operated by machinery or a mechanism **4** of, in accordance with, or using the principles and terminology of, the science of mechanics **5** automatic, as if from force of habit; machinelike; lacking spontaneity, expression, warmth, etc. [to greet someone in a *mechanical* way] **6** [Archaic] of manual labor or manual laborers *—n. Printing* an assemblage of type proofs, pictures, etc. mounted on a sheet of paper, to be photographed for making into a plate **—me·chan′i·cal·ly** *adv.*

mechanical advantage the ratio of the output force of a device that performs useful work to the input force: used in rating the performance of a machine

mechanical drawing 1 technical drawing of the type traditionally done with the use of T squares, scales, compasses, etc. **2** a drawing or diagram of this type

mechanical engineering the branch of engineering having to do with machinery and mechanical power **—mechanical engineer**

mechanical tissue a plant tissue made up of hard, thick-walled cells that add strength to an organ

mech·a·ni·cian (mek′ə nish′ən) *n.* a person skilled in MECHANICS (sense 2); mechanical engineer

me·chan·ics (mə kan′iks) *n.* ⟦see MECHANIC⟧ **1** the branch of physics that deals with the motion of material bodies and the phenomena of the action of forces on bodies: cf. STATICS, DYNAMICS, KINEMATICS **2** theoretical and practical knowledge of the design, construction, operation, and care of machinery *—pl.n.* [*sometimes with sing. v.*] the mechanical aspect; technical part [the *mechanics* of writing]

☆**mechanic's lien** a lien on a building or other property given by statute to those who perform work or furnish materials in the improvement of that property

mech·a·nism (mek′ə niz′əm) *n.* ⟦ModL *mechanismus* < Gr *mēchanē*, MACHINE⟧ **1** the working parts or arrangement of parts of a machine; works [the *mechanism* of a clock] **2** *a)* a system whose parts work together like those of a machine [the *mechanism* of the universe] *b)* any system or means for doing something; esp., a physical or mental process or processes, whether conscious or unconscious, by which some result is produced (cf. DEFENSE MECHANISM) **3** the mechanical aspect; technical part **4** the theory or doctrine that all the phenomena of the universe, particularly life, can ultimately be explained in terms of matter moving in accordance with the laws of nature

mech·a·nist (mek′ə nist) ***n.*** **1** a person who believes in the theory of mechanism **2** *rare var. of* MECHANICIAN

mech·a·nis·tic (mek′ə nis′tik) ***adj.*** **1** of or in accordance with the theory of mechanism **2** of mechanics or mechanical concepts —**mech′a·nis′ti·cal·ly *adv.***

mech·a·nize (mek′ə nīz′) ***vt.*** **-nized′**, **-niz′ing** **1** to make mechanical **2** to do or operate by machinery, not by hand **3** to bring about the use of machinery in (an industry, etc.) **4** to equip (an army, etc.) with motor vehicles, tanks, etc., for greater mobility and striking power —**mech′a·ni·za′tion *n.*** —**mech′a·niz′er *n.***

mech·a·no·re·cep·tor (mek′ə nō ri sep′tər) ***n.*** ⟦< Gr *mēchanē*, MACHINE + RECEPTOR⟧ a type of sensory receptor sensitive to touch, tension, pressure, etc. —**mech′a·no·re·cep′tion *n.*** —**mech′a·no·re·cep′tive *adj.***

mech·an·o·ther·a·py (mek′ə nō′ther′ə pē) ***n.*** ⟦< Gr *mēchanē*, MACHINE + THERAPY⟧ the treatment of disease, injuries, etc. by using mechanical devices, massage, etc. —**mech′an·o′ther′a·pist *n.***

Mech·e·len (mek′ə lən) city in NC Belgium, in Antwerp province

Mech·lin[1] (mek′lin) ***n.*** a fine lace made in Mechelen, with the design clearly outlined by a heavier thread: also **Mechlin lace**

Mech·lin[2] (mek′lin) *Eng. name for* MECHELEN

Meck·len·burg (mek′lən burg′; *Ger*, -boork′) historical region in NE Germany, formerly a German state and now part of the state of Mecklenburg-Western Pomerania

Meck·len·burg-West·ern Pomerania (-wes′tərn) state of NE Germany: 8,946 sq mi (23,170 sq km); cap. Schwerin

mec·li·zine (mek′lə zēn′) ***n.*** ⟦ME(THYL BENZENE) + C(H)L(OROFORM) + -I- + (PIPERA)ZINE⟧ an antihistamine, $C_{25}H_{27}ClN_2$, used for treating nausea and motion sickness

me·co·ni·um (mi kō′nē əm) ***n.*** ⟦ModL < L, meconium, orig. poppy juice < Gr *mēkōnion* < *mēkōn*, poppy < IE **mak(en)-* > OHG *maho* (Ger *mohn*), Russ *mak*⟧ the greenish fecal matter in a fetus, forming the first bowel movement of a newborn infant

me·cop·ter·an (mi käp′tər ən) ***n.*** ⟦< ModL *Mecoptera* < Gr *mēkos*, length (for IE base see MEAGER) + PTER(O)- + -AN⟧ any of an order (Mecoptera) of carnivorous insects, with a head that is greatly elongated into a beak with chewing mouthparts, and, usually, four long, narrow, membranous wings; scorpion fly —**me·cop′ter·ous** (-əs) ***adj.***

med[1] (med) ***adj.*** [Informal] medical [*med* school]

med[2] *abbrev.* **1** medical **2** medicine: see also MEDS **3** medieval **4** medium

Med *abbrev.* Mediterranean

MEd or **M.Ed.** *abbrev.* Master of Education

me·dail·lon or **mé·dail·lon** (mā dī yōn′) ***n.*** ⟦Fr *médaillon*, medal, MEDALLION⟧ *Cooking* MEDALLION (sense 4)

med·al (med′'l) ***n.*** ⟦Fr *médaille* < It *medaglia* < VL **medalia*, a small coin < **medialia* < LL *medialis*, MEDIAL⟧ **1** a small, flat piece of metal with a design or inscription stamped or inscribed on it, made to commemorate some event, or awarded for some distinguished action, merit, etc. **2** a similar piece of metal with a religious figure or design, worn or carried as an aid to piety —***vt.*** **-aled** or **-alled**, **-al·ing** or **-al·ling** [Rare] to honor with a medal —**me·dal·lic** (mə dal′ik) ***adj.***

☆**Medal for Merit** a U.S. military decoration awarded civilians for exceptionally meritorious conduct in the performance of outstanding services

med·al·ist (med′'l ist) ***n.*** **1** a person who designs or makes medals **2** a person who has been awarded a medal **3** *Golf* the low scorer in a qualifying round of medal play preliminary to a match play tournament Also, Brit. sp., **med′al·list**

me·dal·lion (mə dal′yən) ***n.*** ⟦Fr *médaillon* < It *medaglione* < *medaglia*: see MEDAL⟧ **1** a large medal **2** an oval or circular design, portrait, relief carving, etc. resembling a medal in shape and used as a decorative form in architecture, textiles, etc. **3** a metal insignia on a taxicab indicating that the driver or owner has a permit to carry passengers **4** a small round or oval portion of meat or fish, especially of beef or veal

☆**Medal of Freedom** a U.S. decoration awarded to civilians for significant aid in prosecuting a war and, since 1963, to civilians or military persons for any of various achievements

☆**Medal of Honor** the highest U.S. military decoration, awarded by Congress for gallantry at the risk of life above and beyond the call of duty: established 1862

medal play *Golf* STROKE PLAY

Me·dan (mā dän′, mā′dän′) city in N Sumatra, Indonesia, near the Strait of Malacca

Med·a·war (med′ə wər), **Peter (Brian)** 1915-87; Eng. immunologist & writer

med·dle (med′'l) ***vi.*** **-dled**, **-dling** ⟦ME *medlen* < OFr *medler, mesler* (Fr *mêler*), to mix, hence "mix in," meddle < VL **misculare* < L *miscere*, to MIX⟧ **1** to concern oneself with or take part in other people's affairs without being asked, welcomed, or needed; interfere (*in* or *with*) **2** to tamper (*with*) **3** [Obs.] to mingle; combine —***vt.*** [Obs.] to mix; mingle —**med′dler *n.***

med·dle·some (-səm) ***adj.*** meddling or inclined to meddle; interfering —*SYN.* CURIOUS —**med′dle·some·ness *n.***

Mede (mēd) ***n.*** ⟦L *Medus*, pl. *Medi* < Gr *Mēdos*, pl. *Mēdoi*⟧ a person born or living in Media

Me·de·a (mē dē′ə, mə-) ***n.*** ⟦L < Gr *Mēdeia*⟧ *Gr. Myth.* a sorceress who helps Jason get the Golden Fleece and, later, when deserted by him, kills their children

☆**Me Decade** (mē) ⟦coined (1976) by Tom Wolfe, U.S. writer⟧ the decade of the 1970s, thought of as characterized by narcissism, self-indulgence, and a lack of social concern in many, esp. younger, people (the **Me Generation**)

Me·de·llín (mā′dā yēn′) city in NW Colombia

☆**med·e·vac** (med′i vak′) ***n.*** ⟦MED(ICAL) + EVAC(UATION)⟧ **1** emergency evacuation of wounded or ill persons, esp. military personnel, for medical treatment **2** a helicopter or other aircraft used for such evacuation —***adj.*** of or having to do with such an evacuation or the aircraft used —***vt.*** **-vaced′** or **-vacked′**, **-vac′ing** or **-vack′ing** to transport via medevac

med·fly (med′flī′) ***n.***, *pl.* **-flies′** [*also* **M-**] MEDITERRANEAN FRUIT FLY

me·di- (mē′dē, -di, -də) *combining form* MEDIO-: used before a vowel

me·di·a[1] (mē′dē ə) ***n.*** *alt. pl. of* MEDIUM: see MEDIUM (plurals & ***n.*** 3) —**the media** [*usually with sing. v.*] all the means of communication, as newspapers, radio, and TV, that provide the public with news, entertainment, etc., usually along with advertising

me·di·a[2] (mē′dē ə) ***n.***, *pl.* **-di·ae′** (-ē′) ⟦ModL < fem. of L *medius*, middle: see MID[1]⟧ **1** *Anat.* the middle coat of the wall of a blood or lymph vessel **2** ⟦LL, used by PRISCIAN for L *littera media*, intermediate letter: so named as medial between aspirates and tenues⟧ [Historical] *Phonet.* a voiced stop

Me·di·a (mē′dē ə) ancient kingdom in the part of SW Asia that is now NW Iran: cap. Ecbatana

me·di·a·cy (mē′dē ə sē) ***n.*** the state or quality of being mediate

me·di·ad (mē′dē ad′) ***adv.*** ⟦MEDI- + -AD[2]⟧ *Biol.* toward the median plane or axis of a body or part

me·di·ae·val (mē′dē ē′vəl, mid′ē-; mi dē′vəl) ***adj.*** *alt. sp. of* MEDIEVAL —**me′di·ae′val·ism′ *n.*** —**me′di·ae′val·ist *n.***

☆**media event** a public appearance or event deliberately staged to gain publicity from the news media

☆**me·di·a·gen·ic** (mē′dē ə jen′ik) ***adj.*** ⟦MEDIA[1] + -GENIC⟧ attractive and appealing to viewers and readers of the news media

me·di·al (mē′dē əl) ***adj.*** ⟦LL *medialis* < L *medius*, middle: see MID[1]⟧ **1** of or in the middle; neither beginning nor ending; median **2** nearer the median plane or axis of a body or part **3** of an average or mean —***n.*** **1** *Phonet.* CENTRAL (sense 7) **2** *Linguis.* in some alphabets, the form of a letter that is used as neither an initial nor final letter —**me′di·al·ly *adv.***

me·di·an (mē′dē ən) ***adj.*** ⟦L *medianus* < *medius*, middle: see MID[1]⟧ **1** middle; intermediate **2** *a)* designating a line extending from a vertex of a triangle to the middle of the opposite side *b)* designating a line joining the midpoints of the nonparallel sides of a trapezoid **3** *a)* designating the plane that divides a body or part into symmetrical parts *b)* situated in this plane **4** *Statistics* *a)* designating the middle number in a series containing an odd number of items (Ex.: 7 in the series 1, 4, 7, 16, 43) *b)* designating the number midway between the two middle numbers in a series containing an even number of items (Ex.: 10 in the series 3, 4, 8, 12, 46, 72): distinguished from AVERAGE, MEAN[3], MODE —***n.*** **1** a median number, point, or line **2** an artery, vein, nerve, etc. in the middle of the body or along the imaginary plane that bisects the body into the right and left halves ☆**3** the strip of land separating the lanes of opposing traffic of a divided highway: in full **median strip** —**me′di·an·ly *adv.***

Me·di·an (mē′dē ən) ***adj.*** of Media or its people, language, or culture —***n.*** **1** a Mede **2** the language of the ancient Medes

me·di·ant (mē′dē ənt) ***n.*** ⟦It *mediante* < LL *medians*, prp. of *mediare*: see MEDIATE⟧ the third degree of a major or minor scale

me·di·as·ti·num (mē′dē as tī′nəm) ***n.***, *pl.* **-na** (-nə) ⟦ModL < ML *mediastinus*, in the middle (form infl. by L *mediastinus*, servant, medical assistant) < L *medius*, middle: see MID[1]⟧ **1** a membranous partition between two cavities of the body, esp. that separating the lungs or the two pleural sacs **2** the space between the pleural sacs, containing the heart and other chest viscera excluding the lungs —**me′di·as·ti′nal *adj.***

me·di·ate (mē′dē āt′; *for adj.*, -it) ***vi.*** **-at′ed**, **-at′ing** ⟦< LL *mediatus*, pp. of *mediare*, to divide in the middle < L *medius*, middle: see MID[1]⟧ **1** to be in an intermediate position or location **2** to be an intermediary or conciliator between persons or sides —***vt.*** **1** *a)* to settle by mediation [*mediated* the dispute] *b)* to bring about by conciliation [*mediated* a settlement] **2** to be the medium for bringing about (a result), conveying (an object), communicating (information), etc. —***adj.*** **1** [Now Rare] intermediate or intervening **2** dependent on, acting by, or connected through some intervening agency; related indirectly —**me′di·ate·ly *adv.*** —**me′di·a′tor *n.***

me·di·a·tion (mē′dē ā′shən) ***n.*** ⟦ME *mediacioun* < ML *mediatio*⟧ the act or process of mediating; friendly or diplomatic intervention, usually by consent or invitation, for settling differences between persons, nations, etc. —**me′di·a′tive *adj.*** —**me′di·a·to′ry** (-ə tôr′ē) ***adj.***

me·di·a·tize (mē′dē ə tīz′) ***vt.*** **-tized′**, **-tiz′ing** ⟦< Fr or Ger: Fr *médiatiser* (< *médiat* < LL *mediatus*: see MEDIATE), or Ger *mediatisieren* < Fr⟧ to annex (a smaller state) to a larger one, leaving the ruler his or her title and some authority

med·ic[1] (med′ik) ***n.*** ⟦L *medicus*⟧ **1** [Informal] a physician or surgeon ☆**2** a medical student or intern **3** a medical noncommissioned officer who gives first aid in combat; aidman; corpsman **4** *short for* PARAMEDIC[2] (esp. sense 2)

med·ic[2] (med′ik) ***n.*** ⟦ME *medike* < L *medica* < Gr *mēdikē (poa)*, Median (grass), kind of clover from Media < *Mēdikos*, of Media⟧ any of a genus (*Medicago*) of plants, as alfalfa, of the pea family

med·i·ca·ble (med′i kə bəl) ***adj.*** ⟦L *medicabilis*⟧ that can be cured, healed, or relieved by medical treatment

☆**Med·ic·aid** (med′i kād′) ***n.*** ⟦< fol. + AID⟧ [*also* **m-**] a public health program through which certain medical and hospital expenses of those having no income, or a low income, are paid for from state and federal funds

med·i·cal (med′i kəl) ***adj.*** ⟦Fr *médical* < LL *medicalis* < L *medicus*, physician < IE base **med-* (akin to **mē-*: see MEASURE), to measure, consider, wise counselor, doctor > OE *metan*, to measure⟧ of or connected with medicine or the practice or study of medicine —**med′i·cal·ly** ***adv.***

medical examiner **1** a coroner or similar public officer **2** a physician who performs medical examinations, as of applicants for life insurance

med·i·cal·ize (med′i kəl īz′) ***vt.*** **-ized′**, **-iz′ing** to use medical methods or concepts in dealing with (nonmedical problems, conditions, etc.) —**med′i·cal·i·za′tion** ***n.***

medical jurisprudence the application of medical knowledge to questions of law affecting life or property, including ascertaining and certifying the cause of death, proper medical practice, etc.

med·i·ca·ment (med′i kə mənt, mə dik′ə-) ***n.*** ⟦Fr *médicament* < L *medicamentum*⟧ MEDICATION (sense 2)

☆**Med·i·care** (med′i ker′) ***n.*** ⟦MEDI(CAL) + CARE⟧ [*also* **m-**] a national health program through which certain medical and hospital expenses of the aged and the needy are paid for from federal, mostly social security, funds

med·i·cate (med′i kāt′) ***vt.*** **-cat′ed**, **-cat′ing** ⟦< L *medicatus*, pp. of *medicari*, to heal < *medicus*: see MEDICAL⟧ **1** to treat with medicine **2** to add a medicinal substance to; tincture or impregnate with medicine —**med′i·cat′ed** ***adj.*** —**med′i·ca′tive** ***adj.***

med·i·ca·tion (med′i kā′shən) ***n.*** ⟦L *medicatio*⟧ **1** a medicating or being medicated **2** a medicine; substance for curing or healing, or for relieving pain

Me·di·ci[1] (med′ə chē′) ***n.*** name of a family of rich, powerful bankers, merchants, & rulers of Florence & Tuscany in the 14th, 15th, & 16th cent., also noted as patrons of art & literature —**Med′i·ce′an** (-sē′ən, -chē′ən) ***adj.***

Me·di·ci[2] (med′ə chē′) **1 Catherine de′** 1519-89; queen of Henry II of France (1547-59): Fr. name **Cathe·rine de Mé·di·cis** (kȧ trēn′ də mā dē sēs′) **2 Cos·i·mo de′** (kô′zē mô′ de) 1389-1464; head of the Florentine Republic: called *the Elder* **3 Cosimo I de′** 1519-74; grand duke of Tuscany (1569-74): called *the Great* **4 Giu·lio de′** (jo͞o′lyô de) *see* CLEMENT VII **5 Lo·ren·zo de′** (lô ren′tsô de) 1449-92; ruler of Florence (1469-92): called *the Magnificent* **6 Maria de′** 1573-1642; queen of Henry IV of France (1600-10): queen regent (1610-17): Fr. name **Ma·rie de Mé·di·cis** (mȧ rē′ də mā dē sēs′)

me·dic·i·nal (mə dis′ən əl) ***adj.*** ⟦ME *medycinal* < OFr < L *medicinalis*⟧ of, or having the properties of, medicine; curing, healing, or relieving —**me·dic′i·nal·ly** ***adv.***

med·i·cine (med′ə sən; *Brit* med′sən, -sin) ***n.*** ⟦OFr < L *medicina* < *medicus*: see MEDICAL⟧ **1** the science and art of diagnosing, treating, curing, and preventing disease, relieving pain, and improving and preserving health **2** the branch of this science and art that makes use of drugs, diet, etc., as distinguished esp. from surgery and obstetrics **3** *a)* any drug or other substance used in treating disease, healing, or relieving pain *b)* [Obs.] a drug or other substance used for other purposes, as a poison, love potion, etc. ☆**4** among North American Indians, *a)* any object, spell, rite, etc. supposed to have natural or supernatural powers as a remedy, preventive, protection, etc. *b)* magical power —***vt.*** **-cined**, **-cin·ing** to give medicine to; treat medicinally —☆**take one's medicine** to endure just punishment or accept the results of one's action

☆**medicine ball** a large, heavy, leather-covered ball, tossed from one person to another for physical exercise

☆**medicine dance** a ritual dance to drive out disease or make magic, as among North American Indian peoples

Medicine Hat ⟦prob. transl. of Blackfoot *saamis*, headdress of a medicine man⟧ city in SE Alberta, Canada

☆**medicine man** among North American Indians, etc., a man believed to have supernatural powers of curing disease and controlling spirits; shaman

☆**medicine show** [Historical] a show given by entertainers who traveled from town to town, in order to sell cure-alls and nostrums

med·i·co (med′i kō′) ***n.***, *pl.* **-cos′** ⟦It < L *medicus*: see MEDICAL⟧ [Informal] **1** a physician or surgeon; doctor **2** a medical student

med·i·co- (med′i kō′) *combining form* **1** medical **2** medical and [*medicolegal*]

me·di·e·val (mē′dē ē′vəl, mid′ē-; mi dē′vəl) ***adj.*** ⟦< L *medius*, middle (see MID[1]) + *aevum*, AGE + -AL⟧ of, like, characteristic of, or suggestive of the Middle Ages —**me′di·e′val·ly** ***adv.***

Medieval Greek the Greek language as it was used in the Middle Ages, from *c.* A.D. 600 to *c.* 1500

me·di·e·val·ism (-iz′əm) ***n.*** **1** medieval spirit, beliefs, customs, etc. **2** devotion to or acceptance of medieval beliefs, habits, customs, etc. **3** a belief, custom, etc. characteristic of or surviving from the Middle Ages

me·di·e·val·ist (-ist) ***n.*** **1** a student of or specialist in medieval history, literature, art, etc. **2** a person devoted to medieval customs, beliefs, etc.

Medieval Latin the Latin language as it was used throughout Europe in the Middle Ages, from *c.* A.D. 600 to *c.* 1500, with many Latinized borrowings from other languages

☆**med·i·gap** (med′i gap′) ***adj.*** [*also* **M-**] designating or of an insurance policy purchased to supplement the coverage provided by Medicare

me·di·na (mə dē′nə) ***n.*** ⟦native term in N Africa, orig. lit., city < Ar *medinat*, city⟧ the old native quarter of a N African city

Me·di·na (mə dē′nə) city in NW Saudi Arabia: site of Muhammad's tomb & hence a holy city of Islam

me·di·o- (mē′dē ō, -ə) ⟦< L *medius*: see MID[1]⟧ *combining form* MIDDLE

me·di·o·cre (mē′dē ō′kər, mē′dē ō′kər) ***adj.*** ⟦Fr *médiocre* < L *mediocris* < *medius*, middle (see MID[1]) + *ocris*, a peak < IE base **ak-*, sharp > L *acer*⟧ **1** neither very good nor very bad; ordinary; average **2** not good enough; inferior

me·di·oc·ri·ty (mē′dē äk′rə tē) ***n.*** ⟦Fr *médiocrité* < L *mediocritas*⟧ **1** the quality or state of being mediocre **2** mediocre ability or attainment **3** *pl.* **-ties** a person of mediocre abilities or attainments

Medit *abbrev.* Mediterranean

med·i·tate (med′ə tāt′) ***vt.*** **-tat′ed**, **-tat′ing** ⟦< L *meditatus*, pp. of *meditari*, to meditate: for base see MEDICAL⟧ **1** to reflect upon; study, contemplate, etc. **2** to plan or intend —***vi.*** **1** to think deeply and continuously; reflect; muse **2** to engage in or practice MEDITATION (sense 2) —**med′i·ta′tor** ***n.***

med·i·ta·tion (med′ə tā′shən) ***n.*** ⟦ME *meditacioun* < OFr & L: OFr *meditation* < L *meditatio*⟧ **1** act of meditating; deep, continued thought **2** solemn reflection on sacred matters as a devotional act **3** [*often pl.*] oral or written material, as a sermon, based on meditation **4** the practice of quieting the mind by focusing one's attention on one's regular breathing, on a mantra, etc., for the purpose of deepening one's spiritual awareness, reducing stress, etc.

med·i·ta·tive (med′ə tāt′iv) ***adj.*** ⟦LL *meditativus*⟧ **1** meditating or inclined to meditate **2** indicating meditation **3** for or conducive to meditation [*a meditative walk in the garden*] —**SYN.** PENSIVE —**med′i·ta′tive·ly** ***adv.***

Med·i·ter·ra·ne·an[1] (med′ə tə rā′nē ən) ***adj.*** ⟦< L *mediterraneus* < *medius*, middle (see MID[1]) + *terra*, land (see TERRAIN)⟧ **1** [**m-**] [Archaic] *a)* far from the coast; inland (said of land) *b)* surrounded, or almost surrounded, by land; landlocked (said of water) **2** of the Mediterranean Sea or nearby regions **3** designating or of a physical type of the Caucasoid peoples exemplified by the long-headed, short, olive-skinned people living around the Mediterranean Sea: see also ALPINE, NORDIC ☆**4** designating or of a style of furniture made, as through the use of plastic moldings, to simulate the heavy wood, massive lines, and ornate carving of a kind of Renaissance furniture —***n.*** a Mediterranean person

Med·i·ter·ra·ne·an[2] (med′ə tə rā′nē ən) MEDITERRANEAN SEA

Mediterranean climate a climate characterized by warm, dry summers and rainy winters

Mediterranean fever UNDULANT FEVER

Mediterranean flour moth a small, gray moth (*Ephestia kuehniella*) whose larvae are serious pests in flour

Mediterranean fruit fly a small, gall-forming, two-winged fruit fly (*Ceratitis capitata*) whose larvae infest and feed on many kinds of crops, esp. on citrus fruits

Mediterranean Sea large sea surrounded by Europe, Africa, & Asia: *c.* 2,300 mi (3,700 km) long; *c.* 969,100 sq mi (2,509,959 sq km)

me·di·um (mē′dē əm) ***n.***, *pl.* **-di·ums** or **-di·a** (-ə) ⟦L, the middle, neut. of *medius*: see MID[1]⟧ **1** *a)* something intermediate *b)* a middle state or degree; mean **2** an intervening thing through which a force acts or an effect is produced [*copper is a good medium for conducting heat*] **3** *pl. usually* **me′di·a** *a)* any means, agency, or instrumentality *b)* a means of communication that reaches the general public and, often, carries advertising (in this specif. sense, a singular form **media** (*pl.* **medias**) is now often used): see also MEDIA[1] **4** any surrounding or pervading substance in which bodies exist or move **5** environment **6** *Microbiol.* a sterilized nutritive mixture, as enriched agar, for cultivating bacteria, viruses, etc. ☆**7** *pl.* **me′di·ums** a person through whom communications are thought to be sent to the living from spirits of the dead **8** *pl. usually* **me′di·a** any material or technique as used for expression or delineation in art **9** a liquid mixed with pigments to give smoothness —***adj.*** **1** in a middle position; intermediate in quality, amount, degree, size, etc. **2** between rare and well-done: said of cooked meat

medium frequency any radio frequency between 300 kilohertz and 3 megahertz

☆**me·di·um·is·tic** (mē′dē əm is′tik) ***adj.*** of or like a MEDIUM (***n.*** 7)

medium of exchange anything used as a measure of value in exchange for goods and services; currency, checks, etc.

me·di·um-range (mē′dē əm rānj′) ***adj.*** designating or of a gun, missile, etc. that has a range intermediate between short-range and long-range

me·di·um-sized (-sīzd′) ***adj.*** of a medium size; neither large nor small

med·lar (med′lər) ***n.*** ⟦ME *medler* < OFr *medler, meslier* < *mesle*, the fruit < L *mespilum* < Gr *mespilon*⟧ **1** a small tree (*Mespilus germanica*) of the rose family, growing in Europe and Asia **2** its small, brown, applelike fruit, hard and bitter when ripe and eaten or used in preserves when partly decayed

med·ley (med′lē) ***n.***, *pl.* **-leys** ⟦ME *medle* < OFr *medlee*, a mixing < fem. pp. of *medler*: see MEDDLE⟧ **1** a mixture of things not usually placed together; heterogeneous collection; hodgepodge **2** a musical piece made up of tunes or passages from various works **3** MEDLEY RACE **4** [Archaic] MELEE —***adj.*** **1** [Archaic] made up of heterogeneous parts **2** of or having to do with a MEDLEY RACE

medley race *Swimming* a race in which a different stroke must be used for each section: also called **medley relay** when swum as a relay race

Mé·doc (mā dôk′; *E* mā′däk′, mā däk′) ***n.*** a red wine from the Médoc district of the Bordeaux region

meds (medz) ***pl.n.*** [Informal] medications, esp. prescription medications

me·dul·la (mi dul′ə) ***n.***, *pl.* **-las** or **-lae** (-ē) ⟦L, marrow, pith: see SMEAR⟧ **1** *Anat.* *a)* MEDULLA OBLONGATA *b)* the inner substance of an organ, as of the kidney or adrenal gland *c)* bone marrow **2** *Bot.* PITH (sense 1) —**med·ul·lar·y** (med′ə ler′ē, mej′-; mi dul′ər ē) ***adj.***

medulla ob·lon·ga·ta (äb′läŋ gät′ə, -lôŋ-; -gāt′ə) ⟦ModL, oblong medulla⟧ the widening continuation of the spinal cord, forming the lowest part of the brain and containing nerve centers that control breathing, circulation, etc.

medullary ray 1 *Anat.* extensions of the kidney tubules into the cortical substance 2 *Bot.* strands of parenchymal tissue extending from the pith to the bark and separating the vascular bundles in the stems of certain plants (dicotyledons and gymnosperms)

medullary sheath 1 *Anat.* a layer of myelin forming a sheath around certain nerve fibers 2 *Bot.* a ring of primary xylem around the pith of some stems

med·ul·lat·ed (med′əl āt′id, mej′ə lāt′-; mi dul′āt′id) ***adj.*** 1 covered with a medullary substance; having myelin sheaths 2 having a medulla

Me·du·sa (mə do͞o′sə, -dyo͞o′-; -zə) ***n., pl.*** **-sas** or **-sae** (-sē, -zē) ⟦ME *Meduse* < L *Medusa* < Gr *Medousa*, lit., ruler < *medein*, to govern < IE base **med-*: see MEDICAL⟧ 1 *Gr. Myth.* one of the three Gorgons, slain by Perseus: see GORGON 2 ⟦ModL⟧ [**m-**] *Zool.* JELLYFISH

me·du·san (-sən, -zən) ***adj.*** of a medusa, or jellyfish: also **me·du′sal** **—*n.*** a medusa, or jellyfish

me·du·soid (-soid′, -zoid′) ***adj.*** like a medusa, or jellyfish **—*n.*** a medusa-shaped gonophore of a hydrozoan

Med·ved·ev (med vyed′əv), **Dmi·try (Anatolyevich)** (də mē′trē) 1965- ; president of Russia (2008-12); prime minister (2012-)

meed (mēd) ***n.*** ⟦ME *mede* < OE *med*, a recompense, reward, akin to Ger *miete*, pay, rent < IE base **mizdhó-*, reward, pay > Sans *mīḍhá-*, prize⟧ 1 [Archaic] a merited recompense or reward 2 [Obs.] *a)* a bribe *b)* merit; worth

meek (mēk) ***adj.*** ⟦ME *meke* (earlier *meoc*) < ON *miukr*, pliant, gentle < IE base **meug-*, **meuk-*, to slip, slippery, slimy > MUCK, L *mucus*, Gr *myxa*⟧ 1 patient and mild; not inclined to anger or resentment 2 too submissive; easily imposed on; spineless; spiritless 3 [Obs.] gentle or kind **—meek′ly** ***adv.*** **—meek′ness** ***n.***

meer·kat (mir′kat′, mēr′-) ***n.*** ⟦Afrik < Du, name of type of monkey, lit., sea cat⟧ any of various mongooses of SW Africa, esp. a small, grayish one (*Suricata suricatta*) that lives in colonies underground

meer·schaum (mir′shəm, -shôm′) ***n.*** ⟦Ger, lit., sea foam (< *meer*, sea + *schaum*, foam), transl. of ML *spuma maris*, orig. used of coral, calque of Gr *halos hachnē*: name transferred in 18th-c. Ger to a variety of lithomarge⟧ 1 a soft, claylike, orthorhombic mineral, $Mg_4(Si_2O_5)_3(OH)_2 \cdot 6H_2O$, used to make tobacco pipes and other heat-resistant items; hydrous magnesium silicate; sepiolite 2 a pipe with a bowl made of this

Mee·rut (mē′rət) city in W Uttar Pradesh, N India

meet[1] (mēt) ***vt.*** **met**, **meet′ing** ⟦ME *meten* < OE *metan* < base of *mot*, a coming together, meeting: see MOOT⟧ 1 to come upon or encounter; esp., to come up to or face to face with (a person or thing moving from a different direction) 2 to be present at the arrival of [*to meet* a bus] 3 to come into contact, connection, or conjunction with [the ball *met* the bat] 4 *a)* to come into the presence or company of *b)* to be introduced to; get acquainted with *c)* to keep an appointment or engagement with 5 *a)* to encounter in or as in battle; contend with *b)* to deal with; face; match [*to meet* angry words with a laugh] *c)* to refute or deal with effectively [*to meet* an objection] 6 to experience [*to meet* disaster] 7 to come within the perception of (the eye, ear, etc.) 8 *a)* to comply with; satisfy (a demand, etc.) *b)* to pay (a bill, etc.) **—*vi.*** 1 to come together, as from different directions 2 to come into contact, connection, or conjunction 3 to become acquainted; be introduced 4 to be opposed in or as in battle; contend; fight 5 to be united 6 *a)* to come to assemble *b)* to come together for discussion, bargaining, etc. (*with*) **—*n.*** 1 a meeting, gathering, or assembling, as for a sporting event [a track *meet*] 2 the people who so meet or the place of meeting **—meet with** 1 to experience 2 to cause or inspire a (specified) response or reaction [a suggestion that *met with* enthusiasm] 3 to come upon or across; encounter: also [Informal] **meet up with**

meet[2] (mēt) ***adj.*** ⟦ME *mete* < OE *(ge)mæte*, fitting, akin to Ger *gemäss*, commensurable < IE base **med-*: see MEDICAL⟧ [Now Rare] suitable; proper; fit **—meet′ly** ***adv.***

meet-and-greet (mēt′′n grēt′) ***n.*** an informal reception held for the purpose of enabling an author, politician, celebrity, etc. to mingle with a group of people

meet·ing (mēt′iŋ) ***n.*** ⟦see MEET[1]⟧ 1 a coming together of persons or things 2 an assembly; a gathering to discuss or decide matters 3 an assembly or place of assembly for worship, esp. of Friends, or Quakers 4 a series of horse or dog races held during a period of days at a certain track 5 a point of contact; junction

meet·ing·house (-hous′) ***n.*** a building used for public meetings, esp. for worship, as by Friends, or Quakers

meg[1] (meg) ***n.*** [Informal] *short for* MEGABYTE

meg[2] *abbrev.* megohm(s)

meg·a (meg′ə) ***adj.*** [Informal] great in size, quantity, etc., often in relation to others of its kind

meg·a- (meg′ə) ⟦Gr *mega-* < *megas*, great, mighty: see MUCH⟧ *combining form* 1 large, great, powerful [*megacephalic, megaphone*] 2 [Informal] *a)* huge in size, number, etc. [a *mega*-yacht] *b)* to an enormous degree [*mega*-popular] 3 one million; the factor 10^6 [*megahertz, megaton*] Also, before a vowel, **meg-**

meg·a·bit (meg′ə bit′) ***n.*** ⟦prec. + BIT[4]⟧ *Comput.* 1 a unit of storage capacity in a computer system, equal to 1,048,576 (2^{20}) bits 2 loosely, one million bits

☆**meg·a·bucks** (meg′ə buks′) ***pl.n.*** ⟦< MEGA- + BUCK[3]⟧ [Slang] a large, indefinite amount of money

meg·a·byte (-bīt′) ***n.*** ⟦MEGA- + BYTE⟧ 1 a unit of storage capacity in a computer system, equal to 1,048,576 (2^{20}) bytes 2 loosely, one million bytes Abbrev. *MB* or *mb*

meg·a·ce·phal·ic (meg′ə sə fal′ik) ***adj.*** ⟦MEGA- + CEPHALIC⟧ having a large head; esp., having a cranial capacity greater than the average: also **meg′a·ceph′a·lous** (-sef′ə ləs) **—meg′a·ceph′a·ly** (-sef′ə lē) ***n.***

☆**meg·a·church** (meg′ə church′) ***n.*** [Informal] a church, typically Protestant, characterized by a very large congregation and, variously, a large and lavish sanctuary, an array of social programs for members, etc.

meg·a·cy·cle (meg′ə sī′kəl) ***n.*** *former term for* MEGAHERTZ

☆**meg·a·death** (-deth′) ***n.*** ⟦MEGA- + DEATH⟧ one million dead persons: a unit in computing the hypothetical victims of a nuclear explosion

meg·a·dose (-dōs′) ***n.*** an abnormally large dose, esp. of a vitamin

Me·gae·ra (mə jir′ə) ***n.*** ⟦L < Gr *Megaira*, lit., the exalted one (a euphemism) < **megaros*, great < *megas*: see MUCH⟧ *Class. Myth.* one of the three Furies

meg·a·flops (meg′ə fläps′) ***n.*** a unit of processing speed in a computer, equal to one million flops

Meg·a·gae·a (meg′ə jē′ə) ***n.*** ⟦ModL < MEGA- + Gr *gaia*, earth⟧ one of the three primary zoogeographic areas of the earth, including Europe, Africa, Asia, certain islands southeast of Asia, and the polar and temperate areas of North America

meg·a·ga·mete (meg′ə gam′ēt′, -ga mēt′) ***n.*** MACROGAMETE

meg·a·hertz (meg′ə hurts′) ***n., pl.*** **-hertz′** ⟦MEGA- + HERTZ⟧ one million hertz: abbrev. *MHz*

meg·a·hit (meg′ə hit′) ***n.*** ⟦< HIT (*n.* 5)⟧ [Informal] an extremely successful and popular movie, recording, etc.

meg·a·kar·y·o·cyte (meg′ə kar′ē ə sīt′) ***n.*** a large cell found esp. in the bone marrow, that produces blood platelets **—meg′a·kar′y·o·cy′tic** (-sīt′ik) ***adj.***

meg·a·lith (-lith′) ***n.*** ⟦MEGA- + -LITH⟧ a huge stone, esp. one used in Neolithic monuments or in the construction work of ancient peoples: see CROMLECH **—meg′a·lith′ic** ***adj.***

meg·a·lo- (meg′ə lō, -lə) ⟦ModL < Gr < *megas*, large: see MUCH⟧ *combining form* 1 large, great, powerful [*megalomania*] 2 abnormal enlargement [*megalocardia*] Also, before a vowel, **meg′al-**

meg·a·lo·car·di·a (meg′ə lō kär′dē ə) ***n.*** ⟦ModL < prec. + Gr *kardia*, HEART⟧ abnormal enlargement of the heart

meg·a·lo·ce·phal·ic (-sə fal′ik) ***adj.*** MEGACEPHALIC **—meg′a·lo′ceph′a·lous** (-sef′ə ləs) ***adj.*** **—meg′a·lo′ceph′a·ly** (-sef′ə lē) ***n.***

meg·a·lo·ma·ni·a (-mā′nē ə, -mān′yə) ***n.*** ⟦ModL: see MEGALO- & MANIA⟧ 1 *Psychiatry* a mental disorder characterized by delusions of grandeur, power, etc. 2 a passion for obtaining and holding great power, authority, etc. **—meg′a·lo·ma′ni·ac′** ***adj., n.*** **—meg′a·lo·ma·ni′a·cal** (-mə nī′ə kəl) ***adj.*** **—meg′a·lo·man′ic** (-man′ik) ***adj.***

meg·a·lop·o·lis (meg′ə läp′ə lis) ***n.*** ⟦Gr, lit., great city; also used as the name of ancient and modern cities of the Peloponnesus⟧ an extensive, heavily populated, continuously urban area that includes a number of cities **—meg′a·lo·pol′i·tan** (-lō päl′i tən) ***adj., n.***

meg·a·lops (meg′ə läps′) ***n., pl.*** **-lops′** or **-lop′ses** ⟦ModL < MEGAL(O)- + Gr *ōps*, EYE⟧ an advanced larval stage of the true crabs, just preceding the definitive adult stage **—meg′a·lop′ic** ***adj.***

meg·a·lo·saur (meg′ə lō sôr′, -lə-) ***n.*** ⟦< ModL *megalosaurus*: see MEGALO- & -SAURUS⟧ any of a genus (*Megalosaurus*) of huge, flesh-eating theropod dinosaurs of the Jurassic Period: also **meg′a·lo·sau′rus** **—meg′a·lo·sau′ri·an** (-sôr′ē ən) ***adj., n.***

Meg·an (meg′ən, mā′gən) ***n.*** ⟦Ir⟧ a feminine name: see MARGARET

☆**Meg·an's Law** (meg′ənz, mā′gənz) ⟦after *Megan* Kanka, 7-year-old N.J. girl raped and murdered in 1994 by a neighbor previously incarcerated for child molestation⟧ any of various state or local statutes requiring that public notification be given of the whereabouts of persons who have been convicted of certain sexual crimes

☆**meg·a·phone** (meg′ə fōn′) ***n.*** ⟦MEGA- + -PHONE⟧ a large, funnel-shaped device for increasing the volume of the voice and directing it **— *vt., vi.*** **-phoned′**, **-phon′ing** to magnify or direct (the voice) with or as with a megaphone **—meg′a·phon′ic** (-fän′ik) ***adj.***

meg·a·plex (meg′ə pleks′) ***n.*** ⟦MEGA- + -PLEX⟧ a complex of film theaters larger than a MULTIPLEX, typically consisting of 14 or more theaters

meg·a·pod (meg′ə päd′) ***adj.*** ⟦MEGA- + -POD⟧ large-footed **—*n.*** MEGAPODE

meg·a·pode (-pōd′) ***n.*** ⟦see prec.⟧ any of a family (Megapodiidae) of large-footed, ground-dwelling gallinaceous birds of Australia and the East Indies that bury their eggs, often in mounds they have built of earth and vegetation

Meg·a·ra (meg′ə rə) city on the Isthmus of Corinth, central Greece: capital of ancient Megaris

Meg·a·ris (meg′ə ris) ancient district on the E part of the Isthmus of Corinth

meg·a·scop·ic (meg′ə skäp′ik) ***adj.*** ⟦MEGA- + -SCOP(E) + -IC⟧ MACROSCOPIC (sense 1) **—meg′a·scop′i·cal·ly** ***adv.***

meg·a·spo·ran·gi·um (-spō ran′jē əm, -spə-) ***n., pl.*** **-gi·a** (-ə) ⟦ModL: see MEGA- & SPORANGIUM⟧ a sporangium, or spore case, containing only megaspores, as in some ferns

meg·a·spore (meg′ə spôr′) ***n.*** ⟦MEGA- + SPORE⟧ a haploid spore, usually larger than a microspore of the same plant, which gives rise to a female gametophyte: found in all vascular plants that have differentiated sexes in the gametophyte —**meg'a·spor'ic** *adj.*

meg·a·spo·ro·phyll (meg'ə spôr'ə fil') *n.* a sporophyll bearing only megasporangia

me·gass or **me·gasse** (mə gas', -gäs') *n.* BAGASSE

meg·a·star (meg'ə stär') *n.* [Informal] SUPERSTAR

meg·a·the·ri·um (meg'ə thir'ē əm) *n.* ⟦ModL < Gr *megas* (see MEGA-) + *thērion*, beast < *thēr*, wild animal: see FIERCE⟧ any of an extinct genus (*Megatherium*) of very large, plant-eating, ground-dwelling sloths: also **meg'a·there'** (-thir')

meg·a·ton (meg'ə tun') *n.* ⟦MEGA- + TON[2]⟧ the explosive force of one million tons of TNT: a unit for measuring the power of thermonuclear weapons: abbrev. *MT* —**meg'a·ton'nage** *n.*

meg·a·vi·ta·min (meg'ə vīt'ə min) *n.* ⟦MEGA- + VITAMIN⟧ a dosage of a vitamin, mineral, etc. that greatly exceeds the usual recommended levels

meg·a·watt (meg'ə wät') *n.* ⟦MEGA- + WATT⟧ one million watts: abbrev. *MW*

☆**Me Generation** *see* ME DECADE

Me·gid·do (mə gid'ō) ancient town in N Palestine, on the plain of Esdraelon: thought to be the Biblical Armageddon

me·gil·lah (mə gil'ə) *n.* ⟦Yiddish < Heb *megillāh*, scroll, roll; esp. the scroll of the Book of Esther, read aloud on Purim⟧ [Slang] **1** a long or involved explanation, story, etc. **2** a complicated matter

me·gilp (mə gilp') *n.* ⟦< ?⟧ a mixture usually of linseed oil with mastic varnish or turpentine, used in oil paints

☆**MEGO** (mē'gō') *n.* ⟦*m(y) e(yes) g(laze) o(ver)*⟧ **1** a reaction of boredom and indifference **2** something, as a dull news story, that inspires this reaction

meg·ohm (meg'ōm') *n.* one million ohms: symbol, MΩ

me·grim (mē'grim) *n.* ⟦LME *migreime* < OFr *migraine*: see MIGRAINE⟧ **1** *obs. var. of* MIGRAINE **2** [Archaic] a whim, fancy, or fad **3** [*pl.*] [Rare] low spirits; the blues

Mehe·met A·li (me met' ä lē') 1769-1849; viceroy of Egypt (1805-48)

Mei·ji (mā'jē') ⟦Jpn, lit., enlightened government⟧ name adopted by the emperor Mutsuhito of Japan

Meiji Restoration revolution in Japanese life and government that occurred after the accession of Emperor Mutsuhito (1867), characterized by the downfall of feudalism and the shogun and by the creation of a modern state

mein·ie or **mein·y** (mā'nē) *n., pl.* **mein'ies** (-ēz) ⟦ME *menie* < OFr *meisniee*: see MENIAL⟧ **1** [Obs.] feudal retainers or attendants, collectively; retinue or household **2** [Scot.] a crowd; throng; multitude

mei·o·sis (mī ō'sis) *n.* ⟦ModL < Gr *meiōsis* < *meioun*, to make smaller < *meiōn*, less: see MINOR⟧ **1** the process of two consecutive nuclear divisions in the formation of germ cells in animals and of spores in most plants, by which the number of chromosomes ordinarily is reduced from the diploid, or double, number found in somatic cells to the haploid, or halved, number found in gametes and in spores: distinguished from MITOSIS **2** LITOTES —**mei·ot'ic** (-ät'ik) *adj.* —**mei·ot'i·cal·ly** *adv.*

Me·ir (me ir'), **Gol·da** (gōl'də) (born *Goldie Mabovitch*, later *Goldie Myerson*) 1898-1978; Israeli statesman, born in Russia: prime minister of Israel (1969-74)

Meis·sen (mī'sən) city in EC Germany, on the Elbe, in the state of Saxony: noted for its porcelain

Meis·so·nier (me sô nyā'), **Jean Lou·is Er·nest** (zhän lwē er nest') 1815-91; Fr. painter

meis·ter (mīs'tər) *n.* ⟦Ger, master⟧ [Slang] a person involved or skilled in a (specified) thing or activity: usually in compounds [*schlockmeister*]

Meis·ter·sing·er (mīs'tər siŋ'ər, -ziŋ'ər) *n., pl.* **-sing'er** ⟦Ger, lit., master singer⟧ a member of any of several guilds, mainly of workingmen, organized in German cities in the 14th-16th cent. for cultivating music and poetry

Meit·ner (mīt'nər), **Li·se** (lē'zə) 1878-1968; Austrian nuclear physicist, in U.S. & Sweden

meit·ner·i·um (mīt nir'ē əm) *n.* ⟦ModL, after prec. + -IUM⟧ a radioactive chemical element with a very short half-life: a transactinide produced by bombarding bismuth with high-energy nuclear particles: symbol, Mt; at. no. 109: see the periodic table of elements in the Reference Supplement

Mé·ji·co (me'hē kô') *alt. Sp. name for* MEXICO

Mek·nès (mek nes') city in NC Morocco

Me·kong (mā'käŋ', -kôŋ') river in Southeast Asia, flowing from Tibet through SW China & the Indochinese peninsula into the South China Sea: *c.* 2,600 mi (4,184 km)

mel (mel) *n.* ⟦L: see MILDEW⟧ honey, esp. in the pure, clarified form used in pharmacy

me·lam·ed (mə läm'əd) *n., pl.* **-lam'dim** (-dim) ⟦Yiddish < Heb, teacher < *limed*, to teach < root *lmd*, to teach, study⟧ a teacher of children in a heder or other Jewish school

mel·a·mine (mel'ə mēn', -min) *n.* ⟦Ger *melamin* < *melam*, an ammonium thiocyanate distillate < *mel* < ? + *am(monium)*, AMMONIUM + *-in*, -INE[3]⟧ a white, crystalline, cyclic compound, $C_3H_6N_6$, containing three cyanamide molecules in its structure, used in making synthetic resins

☆**melamine resin** any of various thermosetting, synthetic resins made by condensing formaldehyde with melamine and used in making dishes, utensils, adhesives, etc.

mel·an- (mel'ən) *combining form* MELANO-: used before a vowel

mel·an·cho·li·a (mel'ən kō'lē ə) *n.* ⟦ModL < LL: see fol.⟧ **1** [Old-fashioned] DEPRESSION (sense 9) **2** depression of spirits; melancholy —**mel'an·cho'li·ac'** (-kō'lē ak') *adj., n.*

mel·an·chol·y (mel'ən käl'ē) *n., pl.* **-chol'ies** ⟦ME *malencoli* < OFr *melancolie* < LL *melancholia* < Gr < *melas*, black (see MELANO-) + *cholē*, bile, gall: see YELLOW⟧ **1** [Obs.] *a)* black bile: in medieval times considered to be one of the four humors of the body, to come from the spleen or kidneys, and to cause gloominess, irritability, or depression *b)* the condition of having, or the disorder supposed to result from having, too much black bile **2** *a)* sadness and depression of spirits *b)* a tendency to be sad, gloomy, or depressed **3** sad, sober musing; pensiveness —*adj.* **1** sad and depressed; gloomy **2** *a)* causing sadness, gloom, or depression *b)* lamentable; deplorable **3** sadly or soberly musing; pensive **4** [Obs.] having the disorder of melancholy —*SYN.* SAD —**mel'an·chol'ic** *adj.* —**mel'an·chol'i·cal·ly** *adv.*

Me·lanch·thon (mə laŋk'thən), **Philipp** (born *Philipp Schwarzerd*) 1497-1560; Ger. Protestant reformer

Mel·a·ne·sia (mel'ə nē'zhə, -shə) ⟦ModL < Gr *melas*, black (see MELANO-) + *nēsos*, island (see NATANT) + -IA; in reference to the dark skin of the inhabitants⟧ one of the three major divisions of the Pacific islands, south of the equator and including groups from the Bismarck Archipelago to the Fiji Islands

Mel·a·ne·sian (-zhən, -shən) *adj.* of Melanesia or its peoples, languages, or cultures —*n.* **1** a member of any of the indigenous peoples of Melanesia **2** a branch of the Austronesian family of languages, consisting of the languages of Melanesia

mé·lange (mā lônzh', -lônj'; -länzh', -länj') *n.* ⟦Fr < *mêler*, to mix: see MEDDLE⟧ a mixture or medley; hodgepodge

me·lan·ic (mə lan'ik) *adj.* of, characteristic of, or having melanism or melanosis

Mel·a·nie (mel'ə nē) *n.* ⟦< Gr *melaina*, black, dark-skinned, fem. of *melas*: see MELANO-⟧ a feminine name

mel·a·nin (mel'ə nin) *n.* ⟦MELAN(O)- + -IN[1]⟧ a brownish-black pigment found in skin, hair, and other animal or plant tissues

mel·a·nism (-niz'əm) *n.* ⟦MELAN(O)- + -ISM⟧ **1** abnormal development of dark pigmentation in the skin, hair, feathers, etc. **2** darkness of skin, hair, eyes, etc., resulting from a high degree of pigmentation —**mel'a·nis'tic** *adj.*

mel·a·nite (-nīt') *n.* ⟦Ger *melanit*, coined (1799) by A. G. Werner (see WERNERITE) < Gr *melas* (see MELANO-) + Ger *-it*, -ITE[1]⟧ a black variety of andradite garnet

mel·a·nize (-nīz') *vt.* **-nized'**, **-niz'ing** ⟦fol. + -IZE⟧ **1** to darken by the deposition of abnormal amounts of melanin in tissues **2** to make dark

mel·a·no- (mel'ə nō, mə lan'ə) ⟦< Gr *melas* (gen. *melanos*), black < IE base **mel-*, dark, dirty > Sans *mala-*, dirt, MHG *mal*, a spot⟧ *combining form* **1** black, very dark [*melanous*] **2** of melanin [*melanocyte*]

mel·a·no·blast (mel'ə nō blast', mə lan'ə-) *n.* a cell that develops into either a melanocyte or a melanophore

Mel·a·noch·ro·i (mel'ə näk'rō ī') *pl.n.* ⟦ModL < MELAN(O)- + Gr *ōchros*, pale⟧ the darker Caucasoids living around the Mediterranean Sea —**Mel'a·noch'roid'** (-roid') *adj.*

mel·a·no·cyte (mel'ə nō sīt', mə lan'ə-) *n.* ⟦MELANO- + -CYTE⟧ a specialized cell containing melanin

mel·a·noid (mel'ə noid') *adj.* ⟦< Gr *melanoeidēs*, black-looking: see MELANO- & -OID⟧ **1** pigmented black or dark **2** of or like melanosis

mel·a·no·ma (mel'ə nō'mə) *n., pl.* **-mas** or **-ma·ta** (-mə tə) ⟦< ModL: see MELANO- & -OMA⟧ a skin tumor, esp. a malignant one, derived from cells capable of melanin formation

mel·a·no·phore (məl'ə nō fôr', mə lan'ə-) *n.* a chromatophore containing melanin, found esp. in coldblooded animals

mel·a·no·sis (mel'ə nō'sis) *n.* ⟦ModL < Gr *melanōsis*, a becoming black < *melanousthai*, to become black < *melas*: see MELANO-⟧ the abnormal production and deposition of melanin in bodily tissue —**mel'a·not'ic** (-nät'ik) *adj.*

mel·a·no·some (mel'ə nō sōm', mə lan'ə-) *n.* an organelle of a cell containing densely packed melanin pigments along rows of tiny fibers

mel·a·nous (mel'ə nəs) *adj.* ⟦MELAN(O)- + -OUS⟧ having black or dark skin and hair

mel·a·phyre (mel'ə fīr') *n.* ⟦Fr *mélaphyre* < Gr *melas*, black (see MELANO-) + Fr *(por)phyre*, porphyry⟧ [Obs.] any dark-colored porphyritic igneous rock

mel·a·stome (mel'ə stōm') *adj.* ⟦< ModL *Melastoma*, genus name < Gr *melas*, black (see MELANO-) + *stoma*, mouth (see STOMA): so named from the stain caused by the fruit⟧ designating a family (Melastomataceae, order Myrtales) of tropical dicotyledonous plants characterized by showy flowers and leaves with strong longitudinal ribs, including the meadow beauty

mel·a·to·nin (mel'ə tō'nin) *n.* ⟦MELA(NO)- + (SERO)TONIN⟧ a hormone, $C_{13}H_{16}N_2O_2$, produced by the pineal body, that lightens skin pigmentation, inhibits estrus, etc.: its secretion is inhibited by sunlight

Mel·ba (mel'bə), Dame **Nel·lie** (nel'ē) (*Helen Porter Mitchell Armstrong*) 1861-1931; Austral. soprano

Melba toast ⟦after prec., her name altered < MELBOURNE[2]: she was born near the city⟧ [*also* **m- t-**] bread sliced very thin and toasted until brown and crisp

Mel·bourne[1] (mel'bərn), 2d Viscount (*William Lamb*) 1779-1848; Eng. statesman: prime minister (1834; 1835-41)

Mel·bourne[2] (mel'bərn) seaport in SE Australia: capital of Victoria —**Mel·bur'ni·an** *n.*, **Mel·bour'ni·an**

Mel·chi·or (mel′kē ôr′), **Lau·ritz (Lebrecht Hommel)** (lou′rits) 1890-1973; U.S. tenor, born in Denmark

Mel·chiz·e·dek (mel kiz′ə dek′, -kē′zə-) ***n.*** ⟦Heb *malkī-tsedheq*, lit., king of righteousness⟧ *Bible* the priest and king of Salem who blessed Abraham: Gen. 14:18 —***adj.*** ☆*Mormon Ch.* designating or of the higher order of priests: cf. AARONIC

meld¹ (meld) ***vt., vi.*** ⟦Ger *melden*, to announce, akin to OE *meld*, proclamation < IE base **meldh-*, to address a deity > OSlav *moliti*, to ask⟧ *Card Games* to make known, for a score, that one holds (a card or combination of cards), esp. by putting them face up on the table —***n.*** **1** the act of melding **2** a combination of cards melded or to be melded

☆**meld²** (meld) ***vt., vi.*** ⟦merging of MELT + WELD¹⟧ to blend; merge; unite

Mel·e·a·ger (mel′ē ā′jər, -ā′gər) ***n.*** ⟦L < Gr *Meleagros*⟧ *Gr. Myth.* the son of the queen of Calydon and slayer of the Calydonian boar: he is sometimes also listed as one of the Argonauts

me·lee (mā′lā′, mā lā′) ***n.*** ⟦Fr *mêlée* < OFr *meslee*: see MEDLEY⟧ **1** a noisy, confused fight or hand-to-hand struggle among a number of people **2** a confused conflict or mixture Also written **mêlée**

Me·li·an (mē′lē ən) ***adj.*** of or relating to Melos

mel·ic (mel′ik) ***adj.*** ⟦L *melicus* < Gr *melikos* < *melos*, song, musical member, orig., limb < IE base **mel-*, a limb > Cornish *mel*, a knuckle⟧ **1** of song or poetry, esp. early Greek lyric poetry **2** meant to be sung; lyric

mel·i·lot (mel′i lät′) ***n.*** ⟦ME *mellilot* < OFr *melilot* < L *melilotos* < Gr *melilōtos*, kind of clover < *meli*, honey (see MILDEW) + *lōtos*, LOTUS⟧ SWEET CLOVER

Me·lin·da (mə lin′də) ***n.*** a feminine name

mel·i·nite (mel′i nīt′) ***n.*** ⟦Fr *mélinite* < Gr *mēlinos*, quince-yellow < *mēlon*, quince, apple: from its color⟧ a powerful explosive like lyddite, made by combining picric acid with guncotton

mel·io·rate (mēl′yə rāt′) ***vt., vi.*** **-rat′ed, -rat′ing** ⟦< LL *melioratus*, pp. of *meliorare*, to make better < L *melior*, better < IE base **mel-*, strong, big > Gr *mala*, very⟧ to make or become better; improve; ameliorate —**mel′io·ra·ble** (-yə rə bəl) ***adj.*** —**mel′io·ra′tive** (-yə rāt′iv, -yə rə tiv) ***adj.*** —**mel′io·ra′tor** ***n.***

mel·io·ra·tion (mēl′yə rā′shən) ***n.*** **1** a meliorating or being meliorated; improvement **2** *Linguis.* the process by which the meaning or connotation of a word becomes more positive

mel·io·rism (mēl′yə riz′əm) ***n.*** ⟦L *melior*, better (see MELIORATE) + -ISM⟧ **1** the belief that the world naturally tends to get better and, esp., that this tendency can be furthered by human effort **2** the betterment of society by improving people's health, living conditions, etc. —**mel′io·rist** ***n., adj.*** —**mel′io·ris′tic** ***adj.***

me·lis·ma (mə liz′mə) ***n., pl.*** **-ma·ta** (-mə tə) or **-mas** ⟦Gr, song < *melizein*, to sing, modulate < *melos*, song: see MELIC⟧ a succession of different notes sung upon a single syllable, as orig. in plainsong or, now esp., in the ornamental phrases of Near Eastern and Asian music —**mel·is·mat·ic** (mel′iz mat′ik) ***adj.***

Me·lis·sa (mə lis′ə) ***n.*** ⟦Gr, lit., a bee < *meli*, honey: see MILDEW⟧ a feminine name: dim. *Missy*

Me·li·to·pol (mel′ə tō′pəl) city in S Ukraine

Mel·kite (mel′kīt′) ***n.*** ⟦ModL *Melchita* < MGr *melchitēs*, lit., a royalist < Heb *mēlekh*, king⟧ a member of the Eastern Church of the Byzantine rite, as in Egypt, Israel, and Syria: also **Mel′chite**

mell (mel) [Brit. Dial.] ***vi.*** ⟦ME *mellen* < OFr *meller*, var. of *mesler*: see MEDDLE⟧ **1** to mingle; mix **2** to meddle —***vt.*** to mingle; mix

mel·lif·er·ous (me lif′ər əs) ***adj.*** ⟦L *mellifer* < *mel*, honey (see MILDEW) + *-fer* (see -FEROUS) + -OUS⟧ producing honey

mel·lif·lu·ent (mə lif′lo͞o ənt) ***adj.*** ⟦LL *mellifluens*⟧ MELLIFLUOUS —**mel·lif′lu·ence** ***n.***

mel·lif·lu·ous (mə lif′lo͞o əs) ***adj.*** ⟦L *mellifluus* < *mel* (gen. *mellis*), honey (see MILDEW) + *fluere*, to flow: see FLUCTUATE⟧ sounding sweet and smooth; honeyed [*mellifluous* tones] —**mel·lif′lu·ous·ly** ***adv.*** —**mel·lif′lu·ous·ness** ***n.***

Mel·lon (mel′ən), **Andrew William** 1855-1937; U.S. financier: secretary of the treasury (1921-32)

mel·lo·phone (mel′ə fōn′) ***n.*** ⟦MELLO(W) + -PHONE⟧ a valved brass band instrument similar to the French horn: also **mel′lo·pho′ni·um** (-fō′nē əm)

Mel·lo·tron (mel′ə trän′) ⟦prob. < fol. + (ELEC)TRON(IC)⟧ *trademark for* an electronic keyboard instrument that uses tapes of recorded sounds, esp. of orchestral instruments —***n.*** [*also* **m-**] this instrument

mel·low (mel′ō) ***adj.*** ⟦ME *melwe*, ripe, prob. < or akin to OE *melu* (see MEAL²), Fl *meluw*, soft, mellow⟧ **1** soft, sweet, and juicy because ripe: said of fruit **2** full-flavored; matured; not acid or bitter: said of wine, etc. **3** full, rich, soft, and pure; not harsh: said of sound, light, color, weather, etc. **4** moist and rich; loamy: said of soil **5** softened and made gentle, understanding, and sympathetic by age and experience **6** [Informal] genial or convivial, often, specif., from ingesting alcohol or marijuana — ***vt., vi.*** to make or become mellow —***SYN.*** RIPE —**mel′low·ly** ***adv.*** —**mel′low·ness** ***n.***

☆**me·lo·de·on** (mə lō′dē ən) ***n.*** ⟦Ger *melodion*, coined (1806) by J. C. Dietz, Ger inventor, for another instrument < *melodie* < OFr, MELODY⟧ a small keyboard organ in which the tones are produced by drawing air through metal reeds by means of a bellows operated by pedals: it is much like a harmonium

me·lod·ic (mə läd′ik) ***adj.*** ⟦Fr *mélodique* < LL *melodicus*⟧ **1** of, or having the nature of, melody **2** MELODIOUS —**me·lod′i·cal·ly** ***adv.***

me·lod·i·ca (mə läd′i kə, -lō′di-) ***n.*** a modified HARMONICA (sense 1) having a mouthpiece at one end and a small keyboard for sounding the tones

me·lo·di·ous (mə lō′dē əs) ***adj.*** ⟦OFr *melodieus*⟧ **1** containing or producing melody **2** pleasing to hear; sounding sweet; tuneful —**me·lo′di·ous·ly** ***adv.*** —**me·lo′di·ous·ness** ***n.***

mel·o·dist (mel′ə dist) ***n.*** a singer or composer of melodies

mel·o·dize (mel′ə dīz′) ***vt.*** **-dized′, -diz′ing** ⟦ML *melodizare*⟧ **1** to make melodious **2** to set to melody —***vi.*** to make melody or compose melodies —**mel′o·diz′er** ***n.***

mel·o·dra·ma (mel′ō drä′mə, -dram′ə; mel′ə-) ***n.*** ⟦altered (by assoc. with DRAMA) < Fr *mélodrame* < Gr *melos*, a song + Fr *drame* < LL: see DRAMA⟧ **1** [Historical] a sensational or romantic stage play with interspersed songs and an orchestral accompaniment **2** *a)* a drama, as a play or film, characterized by exaggerated conflicts and emotions, stereotyped characters, etc. *b)* such dramas collectively **3** any sensational, extravagantly emotional situation, behavior, etc. —**mel′o·dram′a·tist** (-dram′ə tist) ***n.***

mel·o·dra·mat·ic (mel′ō drə mat′ik, mel′ə-) ***adj.*** of, characteristic of, or like melodrama; sensational and extravagantly emotional —**mel′o·dra·mat′i·cal·ly** ***adv.***

mel·o·dra·mat·ics (-iks) ***pl.n.*** melodramatic behavior

mel·o·dy (mel′ə dē) ***n., pl.*** **-dies** ⟦ME *melodie* < OFr < LL *melodia* < Gr *melōidia* < *melos*, song (see MELIC) + *aeidein*, to sing: see ODE⟧ **1** *a)* pleasing sounds or arrangement of sounds in sequence *b)* musical quality, as in the arrangement of words **2** *Music a)* a sequence of single tones, usually in the same key or mode, to produce a rhythmic whole; often, a tune, air, or song *b)* the element of form having to do with the arrangement of single tones in sequence (distinguished from HARMONY) *c)* the leading part, or voice, in a harmonic composition; the air

SYN.—**melody** refers to the rhythmic arrangement of tones in sequence to express a musical idea; **air**, in strict application, refers to the principal, or leading, melody of a harmonized composition, but it is sometimes used as an equivalent of **tune**, which is the popular term for any easily remembered melody that identifies a song, dance, etc.

mel·oid (mel′oid′) ***n.*** ⟦< ModL *Meloidae* < *meloe*, oil beetle⟧ BLISTER BEETLE —***adj.*** of such beetles

mel·o·lon·thid (mel′ō län′thid′) ***n.*** ⟦< Gr *mēlolonthē*, cockchafer + -ID⟧ any of various scarab beetles whose larvae feed chiefly on roots, including the cockchafers and June bugs —***adj.*** of these beetles

mel·on (mel′ən) ***n.*** ⟦OFr < LL *melo* (gen. *melonis*), for L *melopepo* < Gr *mēlopepōn*, melon < *mēlon*, apple + *pepōn*, ripe⟧ **1** any of several large, juicy, thick-skinned, many-seeded fruits of certain trailing plants of the gourd family, as the watermelon, muskmelon, and cantaloupe **2** any of these plants ☆**3** [Slang] profits, winnings, political spoils, or the like, for distribution among stockholders, etc.: chiefly in **cut a melon**, to distribute such profits, etc.

Me·los (mē′läs′) *var. of* MÍLOS

Mel·pom·e·ne (mel päm′ə nē′) ***n.*** ⟦L < Gr *Melpomenē* < *melpein*, to sing⟧ *Gr. Myth.* the Muse of tragedy

Mel·rose (mel′rōz) village in SE Scotland: site of the ruins of a Cistercian abbey

melt (melt) ***vt., vi.*** ⟦ME *melten* < OE vi. *meltan*, vt. *mieltan* < IE **meld-*, soft < base **mel-*, to grind > MILL¹⟧ **1** to change from a solid to a liquid state, generally by heat **2** to dissolve; disintegrate **3** to disappear or cause to disappear gradually: often with *away* **4** to merge, or appear to merge, gradually; blend [the sea *melting* into the sky at the horizon] **5** to soften; make or become gentle and tender [a story to *melt* our hearts] —***n.*** **1** a melting or being melted **2** something melted **3** the quantity melted at one operation or during one period **4** a dish, esp. a grilled sandwich, containing or covered with a layer of melted cheese [a tuna *melt*] —**melt down** to melt (previously formed metal) so that it can be cast or molded again —**melt in your mouth** **1** to require little or no chewing: said of tender foods **2** to taste especially delicious —**melt′a·ble** ***adj.*** —**melt′er** ***n.*** —**melt′ing·ly** ***adv.***

SYN.—**melt** implies the bringing of a substance from its solid to its liquid state, usually by heat [to *melt* butter]; **dissolve** refers specifically to the reduction of a solid to a liquid by placing it in another liquid so that its particles are evenly distributed among those of the solvent [to *dissolve* sugar in water]; **liquefy** is the general term meaning to change to a liquid state and may be applied to gases as well as solids; **thaw** implies the reducing of a frozen substance to its normal state, usually to a liquid or a semiliquid, by raising its temperature [the ice has *thawed*] —***ANT.*** **solidify, freeze**

melt·age (mel′tij) ***n.*** **1** the act of melting **2** the thing or quantity resulting from melting

melt·down (-doun′) ***n.*** **1** a situation in which a rapid rise in the power level of a nuclear reactor, as from a defect in the cooling system, results in the melting of the fuel rods and the release of dangerous radiation **2** [Informal] a fundamental breakdown in a situation, condition, or system [a *meltdown* of the banking system]

melting point the temperature at which a specified solid becomes liquid

melting pot **1** a container in which metals or other substances are melted; crucible **2** a country, place, or area in which immigrants of various nationalities and races are assimilated

mel·ton (melt′'n) ***n.*** ⟦after *Melton Mowbray*, town in LEICESTERSHIRE⟧ a heavy woolen cloth with a smooth surface and a short nap, used for overcoats

melt·wa·ter (melt′wôt′ər) ***n.*** water produced by the melting of snow or ice

Mel·ville¹ (mel′vil) ***n.*** ⟦< the surname (orig. place name) *Melville*⟧ a masculine name: var. *Melvil*

Mel·ville[2] (mel′vil), **Herman** 1819-91; U.S. novelist & poet
Mel·ville[3] (mel′vil) ⟦after R. Saunders, Viscount *Melville* (1771-1851), First Lord of the Admiralty⟧ **1** island of Canada in the Arctic Ocean, north of Victoria Island: 16,274 sq mi (42,149 sq km) **2** island of Australia, off the N coast: 2,240 sq mi (5,802 sq km)
Melville Peninsula ⟦after Viscount *Melville:* see prec.⟧ peninsula in NE Canada, opposite Baffin Island: *c.* 250 mi (402 km) long
Mel·vin (mel′vin) ***n.*** ⟦< ? *mæl, mæthel,* council + *wine,* friend, protector⟧ a masculine name: dim. *Mel*
mem[1] (mem) ***n.*** ⟦Heb *mēm,* lit., water: see M⟧ the thirteenth letter of the Hebrew alphabet (מ, ם)
mem[2] *abbrev.* **1** member **2** memoir(s) **3** memorandum **4** memorial
mem·ber (mem′bər) ***n.*** ⟦ME *membre* < OE < L *membrum* < IE **mēmsro-,* var. of **mēmso-,* flesh > Sans *māṁsá-,* Goth *mimz,* flesh⟧ **1** a part or organ of a human or animal body; specif., *a)* an arm or leg *b)* the penis **2** a part of a plant considered with regard to structure or position rather than function **3** *a)* a distinct part or element of a whole, as of a mathematical equation, a sentence, a syllogism, a series, a building, a bridge, etc. *b)* a part or division in a system of classification [species are *members* of a genus] **4** a person belonging to some association, society, community, party, etc. **5** [*usually* **M-**] *short for:* ☆*a)* MEMBER OF CONGRESS *b)* MEMBER OF PARLIAMENT —**mem′bered** ***adj.***
☆**Member of Congress** a person who has been elected to the U.S. House of Representatives
Member of Parliament a person who has been elected to the House of Commons
mem·ber·ship (-ship′) ***n.*** **1** the state of being, or status as, a member: with *in* or, in Brit. usage, *of* **2** members collectively, as of an organization **3** the number of members
mem·brane (mem′brān′) ***n.*** ⟦L *membrana,* membrane, fine skin, parchment < *membrum,* MEMBER⟧ **1** a thin, soft, pliable sheet or layer, especially of animal or vegetable tissue, serving as a covering or lining, as for an organ or cell **2** any thin, flexible layer or material designed to separate, filter, etc. —**mem′braned′** ***adj.***
membrane bone a bone developed in a connective tissue membrane rather than in cartilage
mem·bra·nous (mem′brə nəs) ***adj.*** ⟦Fr *membraneux* < L *membraneus*⟧ **1** of, having the nature of, or like membrane **2** characterized by the forming of a membrane: said of some diseases Also **mem′bra·na′ceous** (-nā′shəs)
membranous labyrinth the soft tissue structure conforming to the bony labyrinth of the inner ear
meme (mēm) ***n.*** ⟦short for *mimeme* (< ? MIMESIS + -EME): both words coined by R. Dawkins (b. 1941), Brit biologist, born in Kenya⟧ a concept, belief, or practice conceived as a unit of cultural information that may be passed on from person to person, subject to influences in a way analogous to NATURAL SELECTION
Me·mel (mā′məl; *E* mem′əl) *Ger. name for* KLAIPEDA
me·men·to (mə men′tō) ***n.,*** *pl.* **-tos** or **-toes** ⟦L, imper. of *meminisse,* to remember: for IE base see MIND⟧ **1** [**M-**] *R.C.Ch.* either of two prayers in the canon of the Mass, one for the living and one for the dead, beginning "Memento": term used esp. in ref. to the traditional Latin Mass **2** anything serving as a reminder or warning **3** a souvenir; keepsake
me·men·to mo·ri (mə men′tō mōr′ē, -ī) ⟦L, remember that you must die⟧ any reminder of death
Mem·ling (mem′liŋ), **Hans** 1430?-94; Fl. painter, born in Germany: also **Mem′linc** (-liŋk)
Mem·non (mem′nän′) ***n.*** ⟦L < Gr *Memnōn*⟧ **1** *Gr. Myth.* an Ethiopian king killed by Achilles in the Trojan War and made immortal by Zeus **2** a site at Thebes consisting of two ancient, gigantic statues of an Egyptian pharaoh
mem·o (mem′ō) ***n.,*** *pl.* **-os** *short for* MEMORANDUM
mem·oir (mem′wär′, -wôr′) ***n.*** ⟦Fr *mémoire,* masc., a memorandum, memoir, fem., memory < L *memoria,* MEMORY⟧ **1** a biography, usually one written by someone who knew the subject well **2** [*pl.*] an autobiography, esp. one that is objective and anecdotal in emphasis rather than inward and subjective **3** [*pl.*] a report or record of important events based on the writer's personal knowledge **4** a report or record of a scholarly investigation, scientific study, etc. **5** [*pl.*] the record of the proceedings of a learned society
mem·oir·ist (-ist) ***n.*** a writer of a memoir or memoirs
mem·o·ra·bil·i·a (mem′ə rə bil′ē ə, -bil′yə; -bēl′-) ***pl.n.,*** *sing.* **mem′o·ra′bi·le′** (-ə ra′bi lē′) ⟦L, neut. pl. of *memorabilis,* memorable⟧ things associated with a noteworthy person or event and collected or kept for their historical or sentimental value
mem·o·ra·ble (mem′ə rə bəl) ***adj.*** ⟦L *memorabilis*⟧ worth remembering; notable —**mem′o·ra·bil′i·ty** ***n.*** —**mem′o·ra·bly** ***adv.***
mem·o·ran·dum (mem′ə ran′dəm) ***n.,*** *pl.* **-dums** or **-da** (-də) ⟦ME < L neut. of *memorandus,* to be remembered, ger. of *memorare,* to remember: see MEMORY⟧ **1** *a)* a short note written to help one remember something or remind one to do something *b)* a record of events or observations, esp. one for future use **2** an informal written communication, as from one department to another in an office **3** in diplomacy, a summary or outline of a subject under discussion, reasons for or against some action, etc. **4** *Business* a statement, made by the consignor, of the goods and terms of a consignment sent with the privilege of return **5** *Law* a short written statement of the terms of an agreement, contract, or transaction
me·mo·ri·al (mə môr′ē əl) ***adj.*** ⟦OFr < L *memorialis* < *memoria,* MEMORY⟧ **1** serving to help people remember some person or event; commemorative **2** of memory —***n.*** **1** anything made or done in memory of some person or event, as a monument, trust fund, holiday, charitable donation, etc. **2** an informal diplomatic paper **3** a statement of facts, often with a petition that something be done, sent to a governing body, official, etc. —**me·mo′ri·al·ly** ***adv.***
☆**Memorial Day** a legal holiday in the U.S. (the last Monday in May) in memory of the dead members of the armed forces of all wars; Decoration Day: in some Southern states, **Confederate Memorial Day** is variously observed on April 26, May 10, June 3, etc.
me·mo·ri·al·ist (-ist) ***n.*** **1** a person who draws up, signs, or presents a memorial **2** a writer of a memoir or memoirs
me·mo·ri·al·ize (-īz′) ***vt.*** **-ized′**, **-iz′ing** **1** to commemorate **2** to present a memorial to; petition
me·mo·ri·am (mə môr′ē əm) *see* IN MEMORIAM
mem·o·rize (mem′ə rīz′) ***vt.*** **-rized′**, **-riz′ing** ☆to commit to memory; learn by heart —**mem′o·riz′a·ble** ***adj.*** —**mem′o·ri·za′tion** ***n.*** —**mem′o·riz′er** ***n.***
mem·o·ry (mem′ə rē, mem′rē) ***n.,*** *pl.* **-ries** ⟦ME *memorie* < OFr < L *memoria* < *memor,* mindful, remembering < IE **mimoro-,* redupl. of base **(s)mer-,* to remember, recall > MERIT⟧ **1** the power, act, or process of recalling to mind facts previously learned or past experiences **2** the total of what one remembers **3** a person, thing, happening, or act as recalled to mind **4** the length of time over which remembering extends [a happening within the *memory* of those still living] **5** commemoration or remembrance [in *memory* of his father] **6** the fact of being remembered; posthumous reputation **7** PLASTIC MEMORY **8** *Electronics a)* a device in a computer, guidance system, etc., designed to accept, store, and recall information or instructions; specif., a random-access memory device *b)* storage or storage capacity as of a computer, disk, etc.
memory lane one's memories; esp., one's fond memories: usually in such fig. phrases as **take a trip** (or **walk, stroll,** etc.) **down memory lane**
Mem·phis (mem′fis) **1** capital of ancient Egypt, on the Nile just south of Cairo **2** ⟦after the ancient Egypt city⟧ city in SW Tenn., on the Mississippi —**Mem′phi·an** (-fē ən) ***adj., n.*** —**Mem′phite′** (-fīt′) ***adj., n.***
Mem·phre·ma·gog (mem′fri mā′gäg) ⟦AmInd, lit., beautiful water⟧ lake in N Vt. & S Quebec, Canada: *c.* 27 mi (43 km) long; 2-4 mi (3.2-6.4 km) wide
mem·sa·hib (mem sä′ib, -säb′) ***n.*** ⟦Anglo-Ind < *mem* (< MA'AM) + Hindi *ṣāḥib,* SAHIB⟧ lady; madam: a title used in colonial India by a servant, etc. in speaking to or of a European woman
men (men) ***n. pl.*** *of* MAN
-men (men, mən) *combining form pl. of* -MAN
men·ace (men′əs) ***n.*** ⟦OFr < L *minacia* < *minax* (gen. *minacis*), projecting, threatening < *minari,* to threaten < *minae,* threats, orig. projecting points of walls < IE base **men-,* to project > Cornish *meneth,* mountain⟧ **1** a threat or the act of threatening **2** anything threatening harm or evil **3** [Informal] a person who is a nuisance — ***vt., vi.*** **-aced**, **-ac·ing** to threaten or be a danger (to) —*SYN.* THREATEN —**men′ac·ing** ***adj.*** —**men′ac·ing·ly** ***adv.***
me·nad (mē′nad′) ***n.*** *alt. sp. of* MAENAD
men·a·di·one (men′ə dī′ōn, men′ə dī ōn′) ***n.*** ⟦ME(THYL) + *na*(*phthoquinone*) + DI-[1] + -ONE⟧ a yellow, crystalline powder, $C_{11}H_8O_2$, possessing vitamin K activity and used in medicine
Me·na·do (me nä′dō) seaport in NE Sulawesi, Indonesia
mé·nage or **me·nage** (mā näzh′, mə-) ***n.*** ⟦Fr *ménage* & ME *menage,* both < OFr *manage* < *manoir* (see MANOR), infl. in form and sense by *maisniee,* family < VL **mansionata* < L *mansio:* see MANSION⟧ **1** a household; domestic establishment **2** the management of a household; housekeeping **3** *short for* MÉNAGE À TROIS
mé·nage à trois (mā näzh ȧ trwä′) *pl.* ***mé·nages à trois*** (mā näzh ȧ trwä′) ⟦Fr, household of three⟧ [*often not in italics*] **1** an arrangement by which a married couple and the lover of one or both of them live together **2** any sexual relationship involving three people
me·nag·er·ie (mə naj′ər ē, -nazh′-) ***n.*** ⟦Fr *ménagerie* < *ménage:* see MÉNAGE⟧ **1** a collection of wild or strange animals kept in cages or enclosures for exhibition **2** a place where such animals are kept
Men·ai Strait (men′ī) narrow channel between the NW mainland of Wales & Anglesey Island: 14 mi (22.5 km) long
Me·nam (me näm′) *a former name for* CHAO PHRAYA
Me·nan·der (mə nan′dər) 342?-291? B.C.; Athenian comic dramatist
men·ar·che (mə när′kē) ***n.*** ⟦ModL < Gr *mēn,* month (see MOON) + *archē,* beginning⟧ the first menstrual period of a girl in puberty
Men·ci·us (men′shē əs, -shəs) (L. name of *Meng-tzu*) 372?-289? B.C.; Chin. Confucian philosopher
Menck·en (meŋ′kən), **H(enry) L(ouis)** 1880-1956; U.S. writer, editor, & critic
mend (mend) ***vt.*** ⟦ME *menden,* aphetic < *amenden,* AMEND⟧ **1** to repair (something broken, torn, or worn); restore to good condition; make whole; fix **2** to make better; improve; reform; set right [to *mend* one's manners] **3** to atone for; make amends for: now only in **least said, soonest mended** —***vi.*** **1** to get better; improve, esp. in health **2** to grow together again or heal, as a fracture —***n.*** **1** the act of mending; improvement **2** a mended place, as on a garment —**on the mend** improving, esp. in health —**mend′a·ble** ***adj.*** —**mend′er** ***n.***

SYN.—**mend** is the general word implying a making whole again something that has been broken, torn, etc. [to *mend* a vase, dress, broken bone, etc.]; **repair**, often equivalent to **mend**, is preferred when the object is a relatively complex one that has become damaged or decayed through use, age, exhaustion, etc. [to *repair* an automobile, furnace, etc.]; **patch** and **darn** imply the mending of a hole, tear, etc., the former by inserting or applying a piece of similar material [to *patch* a pair of jeans, a tire, etc.], the latter by sewing a network of stitches across the gap [to *darn* a sock]

men·da·cious (men dā′shəs) ***adj.*** ⟦< L *mendax* (gen. *mendacis*) < IE base **mend-*, a flaw > L *emendare,* EMEND⟧ not truthful; lying or false —**men·da′cious·ly** ***adv.*** —**men·da′cious·ness** ***n.***

men·dac·i·ty (men das′ə tē) ***n., pl.*** **-ties** ⟦LL *mendacitas* < L *mendax*⟧ **1** the quality or state of being mendacious **2** a lie; falsehood

Men·de (men′dā′, men′dē′) ***n., pl.*** **-des′** or **-de′** **1** a member of a people living in Sierra Leone and Liberia **2** the Niger-Congo language of this people

Men·del (men′dəl), **Gre·gor Jo·hann** (grā′gôr yō′hän′) 1822-84; Austrian monk & botanist: founder of genetics

Men·de·le·ev (men′də lā′əf), **Dmi·tri I·va·no·vich** (də mē′trē ē vä′nô vich′) 1834-1907; Russ. chemist

Mendeleev's law ⟦after prec.⟧ *Chem.* PERIODIC LAW

☆**men·de·le·vi·um** (men′də lē′vē əm) ***n.*** ⟦ModL: named in honor of MENDELEEV by its U.S. discoverers⟧ a radioactive, metallic chemical element, one of the actinides, produced by bombarding einsteinium with high-energy alpha particles in a cyclotron: symbol, Md; at. no. 101: see the periodic table of elements in the Reference Supplement

Men·de·li·an (men dē′lē ən, -dēl′yən) ***adj.*** **1** of Gregor Mendel **2** of or according to the principles of heredity formulated by Gregor Mendel

Men·del·ism (men′dəl iz′əm) ***n.*** the theory of heredity as formulated by Gregor Mendel —**Men′del·ist** ***adj., n.***

Mendel's laws the principles of heredity discovered and formulated by Gregor Mendel

Men·dels·sohn (men′dəl sən, -sōn′, -zōn′) **1 Fe·lix** (fā′liks) (full name *Jakob Ludwig Felix Mendelssohn-Bartholdy*) 1809-47; Ger. composer: grandson of Moses **2 Moses** 1729-86; Ger. Jewish philosopher —**Men′dels·sohn′i·an** (-sōn′ē ən) ***adj.***

Men·de·res (men′də res′) **1** river in W Turkey in Asia, flowing west into the Aegean: *c.* 250 mi (402 km): ancient name MAEANDER **2** river in NW Turkey in Asia, flowing west into the Dardanelles: 60 mi (97 km): ancient name SCAMANDER

men·di·cant (men′di kənt) ***adj.*** ⟦L *mendicans* (gen. *mendicantis*), prp. of *mendicare,* to beg < *mendicus,* needy: for base see MENDACIOUS⟧ **1** asking for alms; begging **2** of or characteristic of a beggar **3** designating or of any of various religious orders whose members originally held no personal or community property, living mostly on alms —***n.*** **1** a beggar; person who begs for alms **2** a mendicant friar —**men′di·can·cy** ***n.***, **men·dic·i·ty** (men dis′i tē)

mend·ing (men′diŋ) ***n.*** **1** the act of one who mends **2** things to be repaired by sewing, darning, patching, etc.

Men·do·ci·no (men′də sē′nō), **Cape** ⟦< Sp, prob. < *Mendoza,* surname of a viceroy of New Spain⟧ cape in NW Calif.: westernmost point of the state

Men·do·za (men dō′zə) city in W Argentina

Men·e·la·us (men′ə lā′əs) ***n.*** ⟦L < Gr *Menelaos*⟧ *Gr. Myth.* a king of Sparta: son of Atreus, brother of Agamemnon, and husband of Helen of Troy

Men·e·lik II (men′ə lik) 1844-1913; emperor of Ethiopia (1889-1913)

Me·nén·dez de A·vi·lés (mə nen′dez′ dā ä′vē lās′), **Pe·dro** (pe′drō) 1519-74; Sp. naval officer & explorer: founded St. Augustine, Fla., in 1565

Me·nes (mē′nēz′) fl. *c.* 3100 B.C.; traditionally, 1st king of the 1st dynasty of ancient Egypt

men·folk (men′fōk′) ***pl.n.*** [Informal or Dial.] men: also **men′folks′**

Meng·tzu (muŋ′dzu′) *see* MENCIUS

☆**men·ha·den** (men hād′'n) ***n., pl.*** **-den** or **-dens** ⟦< AmInd (Algonquian) name: orig. sense prob. "fertilizer"⟧ any of a genus (*Brevoortia*) of clupeid fishes of the W Atlantic, used for bait or for making oil and fertilizer

men·hir (men′hir′) ***n.*** ⟦Fr < Bret *men,* stone + *hir,* long⟧ a tall, usually rough, upright megalith, probably erected as a Neolithic monument either alone or as part of a row or circle

me·ni·al (mē′nē əl, mēn′yəl) ***adj.*** ⟦ME *meynal* < Anglo-Fr *meignal* < *meiniee,* a family retainer, servant < OFr *meisniee,* household < L *mansio:* see MANSION⟧ **1** of or fit for servants **2** servile; low; mean —***n.*** **1** a domestic servant **2** a servile, low person —**me′ni·al·ly** ***adv.***

Mé·nière's disease (*or* syndrome) (mān yerz′) ⟦after P. *Ménière* (1799-1862), Fr physician⟧ a malfunctioning of the semicircular canal of the inner ear, characterized by dizziness, nausea, vomiting, a buzzing in the ear, etc.

me·nin·ges (mə nin′jēz′) ***pl.n., sing.*** **me·ninx** (mē′niŋks′) ⟦ModL, pl. of *meninx* < Gr *mēninx* (gen. *mēningos*), a membrane, akin to L *membrum,* MEMBER⟧ the three membranes that envelop the brain and the spinal cord: they are the dura mater, arachnoid, and pia mater —**me·nin′ge·al** (-jē əl) ***adj.***

me·nin·gi·o·ma (mə nin′jē ō′mə) ***n., pl.*** **-mas, -ma·ta** (-mə tə) a usually benign, slow-growing tumor originating in the meninges and sometimes causing brain damage

men·in·gi·tis (men′in jīt′is) ***n.*** ⟦ModL: see MENINGES & -ITIS⟧ inflammation of the meninges, esp. as the result of infection by bacteria or viruses —**men′in·git′ic** (-jit′ik) ***adj.***

me·nin·go·coc·cus (mə niŋ′gō käk′əs) ***n., pl.*** **-coc′ci′** (-käk′sī′) the bacterium (*Neisseria meningitidis*) that is a common cause of meningitis —**me·nin′go·coc′cal** (-käk′əl) ***adj.***, **me·nin′go·coc′cic** (-käk′sik)

Me·nip·pe·an satire (mə nip′ē ən) ⟦after *Menippus* (3d c. B.C.), Gr philosopher⟧ a form of satire that is indirect and nonrealistic in approach and that consists typically of a loosely organized narrative incorporating a series of dialogues between representatives of various points of view

me·nis·cus (mə nis′kəs) ***n., pl.*** **-cus·es** or **-ci′** (-ī′) ⟦ModL < Gr *mēniskos,* dim. of *mēnē,* the MOON⟧ **1** a crescent or crescent-shaped thing **2** a lens that is convex on one side and concave on the other **3** fibrous cartilage within a joint, esp. within the knee **4** *Physics* the curved upper surface of a column of liquid: as a result of capillarity it is concave when the walls of the container strongly attract the liquid (as in the case of water), and it is convex when the liquid is more strongly attracted to itself (as in the case of mercury)

Men·lo Park (men′lō) ⟦after *Menlo Park,* Calif., in turn after *Menlough,* town in GALWAY⟧ village in NE N.J. that was the site of Thomas Edison's workshop (1876-87)

Men·ning·er (men′iŋ ər), **Karl (Augustus)** 1893-1990; U.S. psychiatrist

Men·non·ite (men′ən īt′) ***n.*** ⟦after *Menno* Simons (*c.* 1496-1561), a Du reformer⟧ a member of a Protestant denomination, Anabaptist in origins, founded in the Netherlands in the 16th cent.: Mennonites favor plain dress and oppose military service and the holding of public office: cf. AMISH —***adj.*** of or designating this denomination

me·no (mā′nō) ***adv.*** ⟦It < L *minus*⟧ *Musical Direction* less

me·nol·o·gy (mē näl′ə jē, mə-) ***n., pl.*** **-gies** ⟦ModL *menologium* < LGr *mēnologion* < Gr *mēn,* month, MOON + *logos,* a word, account: see LOGIC⟧ *Eastern Orthodox Ch.* a listing of saints, often with brief biographies and typically arranged in calendar order: also **men·o·log·i·on** (men′ə läg′ē än′, -lō′jē ən) *pl.* **-log′i·a**

☆**Me·nom·i·ni** (mə näm′ə nē′) ***n., pl.*** **-nis′** or **-ni′** ⟦Ojibwa *manoominii,* lit., person of the wild rice⟧ **1** a member of a North American Indian people now living in Wisconsin and formerly living also in the Upper Peninsula of Michigan **2** the Algonquian language of this people Also sp. **Me·nom′i·nee′**

men·o·pause (men′ə pôz′) ***n.*** ⟦< Gr *mēn* (gen. *mēnos*), month, MOON + *pauein,* to bring to an end: see PAUSE⟧ **1** the permanent cessation of menstruation, normally occurring around the age of 50 **2** the period of time preceding this cessation, normally beginning between the ages of 45 and 50; perimenopause —**men′o·paus′al** ***adj.***

me·no·rah (mə nō′rə, -nôr′ə) ***n.*** ⟦Heb *menora,* lamp stand < Aram *nur,* fire; akin to Ar *manārah:* see MINARET⟧ *Judaism* a candelabrum with seven branches, a traditional symbol of Judaism, or with nine branches, used during the festival of Hanukkah

Me·nor·ca (me nôr′kä) *Sp. name for* MINORCA²

men·or·rha·gi·a (men′ə rā′jē ə) ***n.*** ⟦ModL < Gr *mēn* (gen. *mēnos*), month, MOON + -RRHAGIA⟧ excessive menstrual flow —**men′or·rhag′ic** (-raj′ik) ***adj.***

Me·not·ti (mə nät′ē), **Gian Car·lo** (jän kär′lō) 1911-2007; It. operatic composer, in the U.S.

Men·sa (men′sə) ***n.*** ⟦L, lit., table⟧ a S constellation between Dorado and Octans, containing part of the Large Magellanic Cloud

men·sal (men′səl) ***adj.*** ⟦LL *mensalis* < L *mensa,* table, prob. < *mensus:* see MEASURE⟧ **1** [Archaic] of or used at the table **2** having to do with providing food, lodging, etc. for the clergy

mensch (mensh, mench) ***n., pl.*** **mensch′en** (-ən) ⟦Yiddish < Ger, person < OHG *mannisco,* orig., human < *mann,* MAN + *isc-,* -ISH⟧ [Informal] a person, esp. a man, regarded as being honorable and responsible and having strength of character

men·ses (men′sēz′) ***pl.n.*** ⟦L, pl. of *mensis,* month: see MOON⟧ the periodic flow of blood and sloughed-off tissue from the uterus, discharged through the genital tract: it normally occurs about every four weeks in a woman who is not pregnant, from menarche to menopause

Men·she·vik (men′shə vik′) ***n., pl.*** **-viks′** or **-vik′i** (-vē′kē) ⟦Russ *men'ševik* (1903) < *men'še,* smaller, less, compar. of *malyj,* small⟧ a member of the minority faction (*Mensheviki*) of the Russian Social Democratic Workers' Party, which opposed the more radical majority faction (*Bolsheviki*) from 1903 on —***adj.*** of, characteristic of, or like the Mensheviks —**Men′she·vism′** ***n.*** —**Men′she·vist** ***n., adj.***

men's room a restroom or LAVATORY (sense 2a) for men

mens sa·na in cor·po·re sa·no (menz sä′nə in kôr′pə rā′ sä′nō) ⟦L⟧ a sound mind in a sound body

men·stru·al (men′strəl, -stro͞o əl) ***adj.*** ⟦ME *menstruall* < L *menstrualis* < *menstruus,* monthly < *mensis,* month: see MOON⟧ of menstruation

men·stru·ate (men′stro͞o āt′, men′strāt′) ***vi.*** **-at′ed, -at′ing** ⟦< L *menstruatus,* pp. of *menstruare,* to menstruate < *menstruus:* see prec.⟧ to have a menstrual period; undergo menstruation

men·stru·a·tion (men′stro͞o ā′shən, men strā′shən) ***n.*** ⟦ML *menstruatio*⟧ the menses; menstrual flow or a menstrual period

men·stru·ous (men′stro͞o əs, men′strəs) ***adj.*** ⟦ML *menstruosus* < L *menstruus,* monthly < *mensis*⟧ of or having the menses

men·stru·um (men′stro͞o əm) ***n., pl.*** **-stru·ums** or **-stru·a** (-ə) ⟦ML, orig. neut. of L *menstruus* (see prec.): from an alchemistic notion of the power of the menses as a solvent⟧ a liquid that dissolves a solid; a solvent, esp. one used to extract a drug from a plant

men·sur·a·ble (men′shər ə bəl) ***adj.*** ⟦Fr < LL *mensurabilis* < *mensurare:* see MENSURATION⟧ **1** that can be measured; measurable **2** *Music* MENSURAL —**men′sur·a·bil′i·ty** ***n.***

men·su·ral (men′shər əl) ***adj.*** ⟦LL *mensuralis*⟧ **1** of measure **2** *Music* designating or of polyphonic music in which each note is given a strictly determined value

men·su·ra·tion (men′shə rā′shən) ***n.*** ⟦LL *mensuratio* < *mensuratus,* pp. of

mensurare, to measure < L *mensura,* MEASURE⟧ **1** the act, process, or art of measuring **2** the branch of mathematics dealing with the determination of length, area, or volume —**men′su·ra′tive** (-rāt′iv) ***adj.***
mens·wear (menz′wer′) ***n.*** clothing for men: also **men's wear**
-ment (mənt, mint) ⟦OFr < L *-mentum*⟧ *suffix forming nouns* **1** a result or product *[revetment, hutment]* **2** a means, agency, or instrument *[escapement]* **3** the act, art, or process of *[impressment]* **4** the state, condition, fact, or degree of being ____ed *[enchantment]* Final *y* after a consonant becomes *i* before *-ment [embodiment]*
men·tal¹ (ment′'l) ***adj.*** ⟦ME < MFr < LL *mentalis* < L *mens* (gen. *mentis*), MIND⟧ **1** of or for the mind or intellect *[mental* powers, *mental* aids*]* **2** done by, or carried on in, the mind (i.e., without using written symbols) *[mental* arithmetic*]* **3** *a)* of, having, or related to mental illness or any psychiatric disorder *[a mental* patient, *mental* health*]* *b)* [Slang] mentally deranged; insane (often in the phrase **go mental**) **4** for the mentally ill *[a mental* hospital*]* **5** having to do with mind reading, telepathy, etc. —**men′tal·ly** ***adv.***
men·tal² (ment′'l) ***adj.*** ⟦< L *mentum,* the chin < IE base **men-,* to project + -AL⟧ of the chin
mental age an individual's degree of mental development measured in terms of the chronological age of the average individual of corresponding mental ability
mental deficiency *former term for* MENTAL RETARDATION
men·tal·ism (ment′'l iz′əm) ***n.*** the doctrine that all objects exist only when perceived by some mind —**men′tal·is′tic** ***adj.*** —**men′tal·is′ti·cal·ly** ***adv.***
men·tal·ist (-ist) ***n.*** **1** a person who believes in mentalism **2** a person who professes to read minds or tell fortunes
men·tal·i·ty (men tal′i tē) ***n., pl.*** **-ties 1** mental capacity, power, or activity; mind **2** mental attitude or outlook; state of mind
mental retardation a condition, usually present from birth, characterized by intellectual functioning that is below average: until recently, the preferred technical term, with levels defined in terms of IQ and ranging from *borderline* (IQ of 71-84) to *mild* (IQ of 50-55 to approximately 70) to *moderate* (IQ of 35-40 to 50-55) to *severe* (IQ of 20-25 to 35-40) to *profound* (IQ of below 20-25): in technical use, now largely replaced by INTELLECTUAL DISABILITY
men·ta·tion (men tā′shən) ***n.*** ⟦< L *mens* (gen. *mentis*), MIND + -ATION⟧ mental functioning; activity of the mind
men·thene (men′thēn′) ***n.*** ⟦fol. + -ENE⟧ a colorless, oily hydrocarbon, $C_{10}H_{18}$, derived from oil of peppermint or from menthol by dehydration
men·thol (men′thôl′, -thəl) ***n.*** ⟦Ger < L *mentha,* MINT² + *-ol,* -OL¹⟧ a white, waxy, crystalline alcohol, $C_{10}H_{19}OH$, obtained from oil of peppermint and used to add pungency to medicine, cosmetics, cigarettes, etc.
men·tho·lat·ed (men′thə lāt′id) ***adj.*** containing menthol; treated or impregnated with menthol
men·tion (men′shən, -chən) ***n.*** ⟦ME *mencion* < OFr *mention* < L *mentio* < *mens* (gen. *mentis*), MIND⟧ **1** a brief, often incidental, reference or statement **2** a citing for honor —***vt.*** **1** to refer to or speak about briefly or incidentally; specify, as by name **2** to cite for honor —**don't mention it** [Informal] you're welcome; expressions of thanks are not necessary —**make mention of** to mention —**not to mention** with it being hardly necessary even to mention —**men′tion·a·ble** ***adj.***
Men·ton (män tōn′) seaport & resort town on the French Riviera
men·tor (men′tər, -tôr′) ***n.*** ⟦L < Gr *Mentōr,* lit., adviser, akin to Sans *mantár-*: see MANDARIN⟧ **1** [**M-**] *Gr. Myth.* the loyal friend and advisor of Odysseus, and teacher of his son, Telemachus **2** a person, esp. an experienced, older person, who provides personal or professional guidance — ***vt., vi.*** to act as mentor (to) —**men′tor·ship** ***n.***
men·u (men′yo͞o; *occas.* mān′-) ***n., pl.*** **men′us** ⟦Fr, small, detailed < L *minutus:* see MINUTE²⟧ **1** *a)* a detailed list of the foods served at a meal or of the foods available at a restaurant; bill of fare *b)* the foods served **2** a list, displayed as on a computer video screen, of the various operations or options available for selection by the user
Men·u·hin (men′yo͞o in), Sir **Ye·hu·di** (yə ho͞o′dē) 1916-99; U.S. violinist
Men·zies (men′zēz′), Sir **Robert Gordon** 1894-1978; Austral. statesman: prime minister (1939-41; 1949-66)
me·ow or **me·ou** (mē ou′, myou) ***n.*** ⟦echoic⟧ the characteristic vocal sound made by a cat —***vi.*** to make such a sound
mep *abbrev. Mech.* mean effective pressure
me·per·i·dine (mə per′ə dēn′) ***n.*** ⟦ME(THYL) + (PI)PERIDINE⟧ a synthetic, bitter-tasting, crystalline narcotic, $C_{15}H_{21}NO_2$, used as a sedative and analgesic
Meph·is·to·phe·le·an or **Meph·is·to·phe·li·an** (mef′is tə fē′lē ən, mə fis′tə-; mef′ə stäf′ə lē′ən) ***adj.*** **1** of Mephistopheles **2** like Mephistopheles; fiendish, diabolic, crafty, malevolent, sardonic, etc.
Meph·i·stoph·e·les (mef′ə stäf′ə lēz′) ***n.*** ⟦Ger, earlier *Miphostophiles* < ? Heb *mēphītz,* destroyer + *tōphēl,* liar⟧ **1** a devil in medieval legend and later literary and operatic works, to whom Faust, or Faustus, sells his soul for knowledge and power **2** a crafty, powerful, sardonic person Also **Me·phis·to** (mə fis′tō)
me·phit·ic (mə fit′ik) ***adj.*** ⟦LL *mephiticus*⟧ **1** of or caused by mephitis **2** *a)* bad-smelling *b)* poisonous; noxious
me·phi·tis (-fīt′is) ***n.*** ⟦L, earlier *mefitis* < Oscan⟧ **1** a harmful, bad-smelling vapor from the earth, as the exhalation from decomposing organic matter or poisonous gas from a mine **2** a bad smell; stench
☆**me·pro·ba·mate** (mə prō′bə māt′) ***n.*** ⟦*me(thyl) pro(pyl) (dicar)bamate*⟧ a bitter, white, crystalline powder, $C_9H_{18}N_2O_4$, used as a tranquilizer
mEq *abbrev.* milliequivalent
mer *abbrev.* meridian
☆**mer·bro·min** (mər brō′min) ***n.*** ⟦*mer(curic acetate)* + *(di)brom(ofluoresce)in*⟧ MERCUROCHROME
mer·ca·do (mer kä′thô) ***n., pl.*** **-dos** (-thôs) ⟦Sp⟧ a market
Mer·cal·li (intensity) scale (mer kä′lē) ⟦after G. *Mercalli* (1850-1914), It geologist⟧ a numerical scale for measuring the destructive power and major physical effects of an earthquake, ranging from number I (detectable only by seismographs) to number XII (causing extensive landslides, destruction of nearly all buildings, etc.): see the Mercalli scale in the Reference Supplement
mer·can·tile (mʉr′kən tīl′, -til, -tēl′) ***adj.*** ⟦Fr < It < *mercante,* merchant < L *mercans,* prp. of *mercari:* see MERCHANT⟧ **1** of or characteristic of merchants or trade; commercial **2** of mercantilism
mer·can·til·ism (mʉr′kən til iz′əm, -tīl′-, -tēl′-) ***n.*** **1** the doctrine that arose in Europe with the decline of feudalism, that the economic interests of the nation could be strengthened by the government by protection of home industries, as through tariffs, by increased foreign trade, as through monopolies, and by a balance of exports over imports, with a consequent accumulation of bullion **2** COMMERCIALISM —**mer′can·til·ist** ***n., adj.*** —**mer′can·til·is′tic** ***adj.***
mer·cap·tan (mər kap′tan′) ***n.*** ⟦Ger, contr. < ML *mercurium captans,* lit., seizing mercury < L *mercurius,* mercury (see MERCURY, *n.*) + *captans,* prp. of *captare,* to seize, freq. of *capere:* see HAVE⟧ any of a class of thiol compounds analogous to the alcohols, characterized by the substitution of sulfur for oxygen in the OH radical and by strong, unpleasant odors; hydrosulfide
mer·cap·tide (-tīd′) ***n.*** a metallic salt of a mercaptan, characterized by the substitution of a metal for the hydrogen in the SH radical
mer·cap·to (-tō) ***adj.*** ⟦< MERCAPTAN⟧ containing the monovalent radical SH
Mer·ca·tor (mər kāt′ər), **Ge·rar·dus** (jə rär′dəs) ⟦L calque of *(Gerhard) Kremer,* lit., dealer, merchant⟧ 1512-94; Fl. geographer & cartographer
Mercator projection a method of making maps in which the earth's surface is shown with the meridians as parallel straight lines spaced at equal intervals and the parallels of latitude as parallel straight lines intersecting the meridians at right angles but spaced farther apart as their distance from the equator increases: on such maps the area of a country, sea, etc. is more distorted as the distance from the equator increases
mer·ce·nar·y (mʉr′sə ner′ē) ***adj.*** ⟦L *mercenarius* < *merces,* pay, wages, akin to *merx:* see MARKET⟧ **1** working or done for payment only; motivated by a desire for money or other gain; venal; greedy **2** designating a soldier serving for pay in a foreign army —***n., pl.*** **-nar′ies 1** a professional soldier hired to serve in a foreign army **2** a person who gives his or her allegiance to whoever will pay for it —**mer′ce·nar′i·ly** ***adv.*** —**mer′ce·nar′i·ness** ***n.***
mer·cer (mʉr′sər) ***n.*** ⟦OFr *mercier* < *merz,* goods < L *merx,* wares: see MARKET⟧ [Brit.] a dealer in textiles; dry goods merchant
mer·cer·ize (mʉr′sər īz′) ***vt.*** **-ized′, -iz′ing** ⟦after J. *Mercer* (1791-1866), Eng calico dealer⟧ to treat (cotton thread or fabric) under tension with a solution of sodium hydroxide in order to strengthen it, give it a silky luster, and make it more receptive to dyes
mer·cer·y (mʉr′sər ē) ***n., pl.*** **-cer·ies** ⟦ME *mercerie* < OFr⟧ [Brit.] **1** goods sold by a mercer **2** the business or shop of a mercer
mer·chan·dise (mʉr′chən dīz′; *for n., also,* -dīs′) ***n.*** ⟦ME *marchandise* < OFr < *marchant:* see MERCHANT⟧ **1** things bought and sold; goods; commodities; wares **2** [Obs.] buying and selling; trade — ***vt., vi.*** **-dised′, -dis′ing 1** to buy and sell; carry on trade in (some kind of goods) **2** to advertise, promote, and organize the sale of (a particular product) —**mer′chan·dis′er** ***n.***
mer·chan·dis·ing (-dī′ziŋ) ***n.*** that part of marketing involved with promoting sales of merchandise, as by consideration of the most effective means of selecting, pricing, displaying, and advertising items for sale in a retail store
mer·chan·dize (-dīz′) ***vt., vi.*** **-dized′, -diz′ing** *alt. sp. of* MERCHANDISE —**mer′chan·diz′er** ***n.***
mer·chant (mʉr′chənt) ***n.*** ⟦ME *marchant* < OFr *marchant* < VL **mercatans,* prp. of **mercatare,* for L *mercari,* to trade, buy < *merx,* wares: see MARKET⟧ **1** a person whose business is buying and selling goods for profit; trader, esp. one in the wholesale trade who deals with foreign countries **2** a person who sells goods at retail; storekeeper; shopkeeper —***adj.*** **1** of or used in trade; mercantile; commercial **2** of the merchant marine —***vt.*** to carry on trade in; deal in
mer·chant·a·ble (-ə bəl) ***adj.*** MARKETABLE
mer·chant·man (-mən) ***n., pl.*** **-men** (-mən) **1** a ship used in commerce **2** [Archaic] a merchant
merchant marine 1 all the ships of a nation that are used in commerce **2** their personnel
mer·ci (mer sē′) ***interj.*** ⟦Fr⟧ thank you
Mer·cia (mʉr′shə; -shē ə, -sē ə) former Anglo-Saxon kingdom in central & S England
Mer·cian (mʉr′shən; -shē ən, -sē ən) ***adj.*** of Mercia or its people or dialect —***n.*** **1** a person born or living in Mercia **2** the Old English dialect spoken in Mercia
mer·ci·ful (mʉr′si fəl) ***adj.*** full of mercy; having, feeling, or showing mercy; compassionate; lenient, clement, etc. —**mer′ci·ful·ly** ***adv.*** —**mer′ci·ful·ness** ***n.***
mer·ci·less (-lis) ***adj.*** without mercy; having, feeling, or showing no mercy; pitiless, cruel, implacable, etc. —**mer′ci·less·ly** ***adv.*** —**mer′ci·less·ness** ***n.***

mer·cu·rate (mʉr′kyoo rāt′) ***vt.*** **-rat′ed, -rat′ing** to treat or combine with mercury or a compound of mercury —**mer′cu·ra′tion** ***n.***

mer·cu·ri·al (mər kyoor′ē əl) ***adj.*** ⟦ME < L *mercurialis*⟧ **1** [**M-**] of Mercury (the god or planet) **2** of or containing mercury **3** caused by the action or use of mercury **4** having qualities attributed to the god Mercury or supposedly influenced by the planet Mercury; eloquent, clever, shrewd, thievish, etc. **5** having qualities suggestive of mercury; quick, quick-witted, volatile, changeable, fickle, etc. —***n.*** a drug or preparation containing mercury —**mer·cu′ri·al·ly** ***adv.*** —**mer·cu′ri·al·ness** ***n.***

mer·cu·ri·al·ize (-īz′) ***vt.*** **-ized′, -iz′ing 1** to make mercurial **2** to treat with mercury or a compound of mercury —**mer·cu′ri·al·i·za′tion** ***n.***

mer·cu·ric (mər kyoor′ik) ***adj.*** of or containing mercury, esp. divalent mercury

mercuric chloride a very poisonous, white, crystalline compound, $HgCl_2$, used in photography and as an insecticide, antiseptic, etc.

mercuric oxide a poisonous, red powder, HgO, used as an oxidizing agent and a chemical reagent and in the manufacture of pigment, cosmetics, batteries, etc.

☆**mer·cu·ro·chrome** (mər kyoor′ə krōm′) ***n.*** ⟦< *Mercurochrome,* former trademark < *mercury* (see MERCURY, ***n.***) + -CHROME⟧ [*also* **M-**] a green, iridescent compound, $C_{20}H_8Br_2HgNa_2O_6$, that forms a red solution in water; merbromin: used as a mild antiseptic and germicide

mer·cu·rous (mər kyoor′əs, mʉr′kyoo rəs) ***adj.*** of or containing mercury, esp. monovalent mercury

mer·cu·ry (mʉr′kyoor ē, -kyər-) ***n.*** ⟦L *Mercurius,* Mercury, of Etr orig.⟧ **1** [**M-**] *Rom. Myth.* the messenger of the gods, god of commerce, manual skill, eloquence, cleverness, travel, and thievery: identified with the Greek Hermes **2** [**M-**] the smallest of the eight planets in the solar system and the one nearest to the sun: diameter, *c.* 4,880 km (*c.* 3,030 mi); period of revolution, 87.97 earth days; period of rotation, 58.65 earth days; symbol, ☿ **3** ⟦ME < ML *mercurius* < L, *Mercurius,* Mercury: so named by the alchemists because of its fluidity: see QUICKSILVER⟧ *a)* a heavy, silvery-white metallic chemical element, liquid at ordinary temperatures, which sometimes occurs in a free state but usually in combination with sulfur; quicksilver: it is used in thermometers, air pumps, electrical products, etc. and in dental fillings: symbol, Hg; at. no. 80 (see the periodic table of elements in the Reference Supplement) *b)* the mercury column in a thermometer or barometer **4** *pl.* **-ries** [Now Rare] a messenger or guide **5** *Bot. a)* any of a genus (*Mercurialis*) of plants of the spurge family *b)* an edible European plant (*Chenopodium bonus-henricus*) of the goosefoot family

mercury arc an electric discharge passed through ionized mercury vapor, esp. in a mercury-vapor lamp or an electron tube

mercury chloride 1 MERCURIC CHLORIDE **2** CALOMEL

☆**mercury switch** an electric switch consisting of a sealed capsule containing two electrodes at one end and a drop of liquid mercury which can connect the electrodes when tilted to that end

☆**mer·cu·ry-va·por lamp** (-vā′pər) a discharge lamp containing mercury vapor

mer·cy (mʉr′sē) ***n.,*** *pl.* **-cies** ⟦OFr *merci* < L *merces,* hire, payment, reward (in LL, mercy, pity, favor) < *merx,* wares: see MARKET⟧ **1** a refraining from harming or punishing offenders, enemies, persons in one's power, etc.; kindness in excess of what may be expected or demanded by fairness; forbearance and compassion **2** imprisonment rather than the death penalty imposed on those found guilty of capital crimes **3** a disposition to forgive, pity, or be kind **4** the power to forgive or be kind; clemency [*to throw oneself on the mercy of the court*] **5** kind or compassionate treatment; relief of suffering **6** a fortunate thing; thing to be grateful for; blessing [*a mercy he wasn't killed*] —***interj.*** used to express surprise, annoyance, fear, etc. —**at the mercy of** completely in the power of

SYN.—**mercy** implies a kindness or forbearance, as in punishing offenders, in excess of what may be demanded by fairness, or it may connote kindness and sympathy to those in distress; **clemency** refers to a tendency toward mercy in one whose duty it is to punish offenders; **leniency** usually implies mercy or mildness toward offenders where greater strictness might be preferable or expected; **charity,** in this connection, implies a kindly understanding and tolerance in judging others —***ANT.*** **severity, cruelty**

mercy killing EUTHANASIA

mercy seat ⟦transl. (by William TYNDALE, 1530) of Ger *gnadenstuhl,* transl. (by Martin LUTHER[2]) of Gr(Ec) *hilastērion* (< Gr *hilasia,* propitiation: for IE base see SILLY), transl. (in LXX) of Heb *kappōreth*⟧ *Bible* the gold covering on the ark of the covenant regarded as the resting place of God: Ex. 25:17

merde (merd) ***n.*** ⟦Fr⟧ excrement —***interj.*** used to express annoyance, irritation, etc. Somewhat vulgar

mere[1] (mir) ***adj.,*** *superl.* **mer′est** ⟦ME < L *merus,* unmixed, pure < IE base **mer-,* to sparkle > MORNING, OE *amerian,* to purify⟧ **1** nothing more or other than; only (as said to be) [*a mere boy*] **2** [Obs.] unmixed; pure **3** [Obs.] absolute; downright

mere[2] (mir) ***n.*** ⟦ME < OE: see MARE[2]⟧ **1** [Old Poet.] a lake or pond **2** [Brit. Dial.] a marsh **3** [Obs.] *a)* the sea *b)* an arm of the sea

mere[3] (mir) ***n.*** ⟦ME < OE *(ge)mære* < IE base **mei-,* to secure, a post, wooden wall > L *murus,* wall⟧ [Now Dial., Chiefly Brit.] a boundary

-mere (mir) ⟦< Gr *meros,* a part: see MERIT⟧ *combining form* part [*blastomere*]

Mer·e·dith[1] (mer′ə dith) ***n.*** ⟦Welsh, prob. < *mor,* sea + base of *differaf,* I protect; lit., sea protector⟧ a masculine and feminine name

Mer·e·dith[2] (mer′ə dith) **1 George** 1828-1909; Eng. novelist & poet **2 Owen** (pseud. of *Edward Robert Bulwer-Lytton,* 1st Earl of Lytton) 1831-91; Eng. poet & diplomat

mere·ly (mir′lē) ***adv.*** ⟦MERE[1] + -LY[2]⟧ **1** no more than; and nothing else; only **2** [Obs.] absolutely; altogether

☆**mer·en·gue** (mə reŋ′gā) ***n.*** ⟦AmSp < Haitian Creole *méringue,* lit., meringue < Fr *meringue*⟧ **1** a fast ballroom dance in 2/4 rhythm, that originated in the Dominican Republic in the 19th cent.: the dancers keep one leg stiff **2** music for this dance

mer·e·tri·cious (mer′ə trish′əs) ***adj.*** ⟦L *meretricius* < *meretrix* (gen. *meretricis*), a prostitute < *mereri,* to serve for hire, earn: see MERIT⟧ **1** [Obs.] of, like, or characteristic of a prostitute **2** alluring by false, showy charms; attractive in a flashy way; tawdry **3** superficially plausible; specious —**mer′e·tri′cious·ly** ***adv.*** —**mer′e·tri′cious·ness** ***n.***

mer·gan·ser (mər gan′sər) ***n.,*** *pl.* **-sers** or **-ser** ⟦ModL < L *mergus,* diver (waterfowl) < *mergere* (see fol.) + *anser,* GOOSE⟧ any of several fish-eating, diving ducks with a long, slender, serrated bill hooked at the tip and, usually, a crested head, as the large **common merganser** (*Mergus merganser*) and the small **hooded merganser** (*Lophodytes cucullatus*)

merge (mʉrj) ***vi., vt.*** **merged, merg′ing** ⟦L *mergere,* to dip, plunge, sink < IE base **mezg-,* to plunge > Sans *májjati,* (he) sinks under⟧ **1** to lose or cause to lose identity by being absorbed, swallowed up, or combined **2** to join together; unite; combine —**SYN.** MIX —**mer′gence** ***n.***

Mer·gen·thal·er (mʉr′gən thäl′ər, -thôl′-), **Ott·mar** (ät′mär′) 1854-99; U.S. inventor of the Linotype, born in Germany

merg·er (mʉr′jər) ***n.*** a merging; specif., ☆*a)* a combining of two or more companies, corporations, etc. into one, as by issuing stock of the controlling corporation to replace the greater part of that of the other or others *b)* the absorption of one estate, interest, obligation, contract, etc. in another, or of a lesser offense in a greater

Mé·ri·da (me′rē dä′) city in SE Mexico: capital of Yucatán state

me·rid·i·an (mə rid′ē ən) ***adj.*** ⟦OFr *meridien* < L *meridianus,* of noon, southern < *meridies,* noon, the south < older *medidies* < *medius,* MID[1] + *dies,* day: see DEITY⟧ **1** of or at noon **2** of or passing through the highest point in the daily course of any celestial body **3** of or at the highest point of prosperity, splendor, power, etc. **4** of or along a meridian **5** [Rare] southern —***n.*** **1** [Archaic] the highest apparent point reached by a celestial body in its course **2** *a)* the highest point of power, prosperity, splendor, etc.; zenith; apex *b)* the middle period of one's life, regarded as the highest point of health, vigor, etc.; prime **3** [Obs.] noon **4** *Astron.* a GREAT CIRCLE passing through the celestial poles, the observer's zenith and nadir, and the horizon's north and south points: also called **celestial meridian 5** *Geog. a)* a GREAT CIRCLE of the earth passing through the geographical poles and any given point on the earth's surface *b)* either half of such a circle between the poles *c)* any of the lines of longitude running north and south on a globe or map, representing such a half circle **6** [Archaic] distinctive character as of a particular place

me·rid·i·o·nal (mə rid′ē ə nəl) ***adj.*** ⟦OFr < LL *meridionalis* < L *meridianus:* see prec.⟧ **1** southern; southerly **2** of or characteristic of a southern region or people living in the south, esp. in the south of France **3** of or like a meridian —***n.*** [*often* **M-**] a person who lives in a southern region, esp. the south of France

me·rien·da (me ryen′dä) ***n.,*** *pl.* **-das** ⟦Sp⟧ a light meal esp. in the late afternoon

Mé·ri·mée (mā rē mā′), **Pros·per** (prôs per′) 1803-70; Fr. novelist, essayist, & historian

me·ringue (mə raŋ′) ***n.*** ⟦Fr < ?⟧ **1** egg whites mixed with sugar, beaten until stiff, spread over pies, cakes, etc., and often browned in the oven **2** a baked shell made of this mixture, often filled with fruit or ice cream

me·ri·no (mə rē′nō) ***n.,*** *pl.* **-nos** ⟦Sp, prob. after *(Beni) Merin,* name of a Berber tribe of nomads and shepherds⟧ **1** any of a breed of hardy, white-faced sheep with long, fine wool, orig. from Spain **2** the wool **3** a fine, soft yarn made from this wool, often mixed with cotton **4** a soft, thin cloth made of this yarn —***adj.*** designating or of this sheep, wool, yarn, or cloth

Mer·i·on·eth·shire (mer′ē än′ith shir′, -shər) former county of NW Wales, now part of Gwynedd county: also **Merioneth**

mer·i·stem (mer′ə stem′) ***n.*** ⟦< Gr *meristos,* divided < *merizein,* to divide < *meros,* a part (see MERIT) + *-ēm(a),* n. suffix⟧ undifferentiated plant tissue, as the growing tips of roots and stems, the cambium, etc., consisting of actively growing and dividing cells that give rise to various permanent tissues —**mer′i·ste·mat′ic** (-stə mat′ik) ***adj.*** —**mer′i·ste·mat′i·cal·ly** ***adv.***

me·ris·tic (mə ris′tik) ***adj.*** ⟦< Gr *meros,* a part (see fol.) + -ISTIC⟧ *Biol.* **1** having bilateral or longitudinal symmetry of parts [*the meristic higher animals*] **2** having regular, equal segmentation [*meristic worms*]

mer·it (mer′it) ***n.*** ⟦OFr *merite* < L *meritum* < *meritus,* pp. of *merere,* to deserve, earn, akin to *mereri,* to serve for hire < IE base **(s)mer-,* to remember, care (hence provide for, allot a share to) > MOURN, L *memor, mora,* Gr *meros,* a part, *moira,* lot, fate⟧ **1** [*sometimes pl.*] the state, fact, or quality of deserving well or, sometimes, ill; desert **2** worth; value; excellence **3** something deserving reward, praise, or gratitude **4** a reward or honor given for superior qualities or conduct; mark, badge, etc. awarded for excellence **5** [*pl.*] intrinsic rightness or wrongness apart from formalities, emotional considerations, etc. [*to decide a case on its merits*] —***vt.*** to deserve; be worthy of —**mer′it·less** ***adj.***

mer·i·toc·ra·cy (mer′i täk′rə sē) ***n.*** ⟦prec. + -O- + -CRACY; < *The Rise of the Meritocracy,* book (1958) by M. Young (1915-2002), Brit sociologist⟧ **1**

an intellectual elite, based on academic achievement **2** a system in which such an elite achieves special status, as in positions of leadership —**mer′it·o·crat′** *n.* —**mer′it·o·crat′ic** *adj.*

mer·i·to·ri·ous (mer′i tôr′ē əs) *adj.* ⟦ME < L *meritorius,* bringing in money < *meritus:* see MERIT⟧ having merit; deserving reward, praise, etc. —**mer′i·to′ri·ous·ly** *adv.*

☆**merit system** a system of hiring and promoting people to civil service positions on the basis of merit as determined by competitive examinations

merl or **merle** (murl) *n.* ⟦ME *merle* < OFr < LL *merulus* < L *merula,* prob. < IE base *(a)mes- > OE *osle,* Ger *amsel*⟧ [Archaic] the European black thrush (*Turdus merula*)

Mer·leau-Pon·ty (mer lō pōn tē′), **Maurice** 1908-61; Fr. philosopher

mer·lin (mur′lin) *n.* ⟦ME *merlion* < OFr *esmerillon,* dim. of *esmeril,* merlin < OHG *smirl,* merlin⟧ a small, dark falcon (*Falco columbarius*) with a striped, brownish-red breast, of North America and Eurasia

Mer·lin (mur′lin) *n.* ⟦ML *Merlinus* < Welsh *Myrrdin* < Brythonic **Moridūnon* < **mori,* sea + Proto-Celt **dunom,* hill, fortified hill, fort, hence, lit., sea-hill or sea-fortress⟧ *Arthurian Legend* a magician and seer, mentor to King Arthur

mer·lon (mur′lən) *n.* ⟦Fr < It *merlone* < *merlo,* a battlement < ML *merulus* < ?⟧ the solid part of a battlement or parapet, between two crenels

mer·lot (mer lō′) *n.* ⟦Fr⟧ [*also* **M-**] **1** a red grape used in making a number of Bordeaux wines **2** a dark, dry red wine made from this grape, esp. in California

mer·maid (mur′mād′) *n.* ⟦ME *mermayde:* see MERE[2] & MAID⟧ an imaginary sea creature with the head and upper body of a beautiful woman and the tail of a fish

mer·man (mur′man′) *n., pl.* **-men′** (-men′) ⟦ME *mereman:* see MERE[2] + MAN⟧ an imaginary sea creature with the head and upper body of a man and the tail of a fish

mer·o·blas·tic (mer′ō blas′tik) *adj.* ⟦< Gr *meros,* part (see MERIT) + -BLAST + -IC⟧ *Embryology* undergoing only partial cleavage: said of certain ova with much yolk, as birds' eggs: cf. HOLOBLASTIC —**mer′o·blas′ti·cal·ly** *adv.*

mer·o·crine (mer′ō krin, -krīn′, -krēn′) *adj.* ⟦< Gr *meros,* part + *krinein,* to separate: see CRISIS⟧ designating or of any gland producing secretions without obvious damage to its cells

Mer·o·ë (mer′ō ē′) ruined city in N Sudan, on the Nile: capital of ancient Ethiopia

mer·o·mor·phic (mer′ō môr′fik) *adj.* ⟦< Gr *meros,* part (see MERIT) + -MORPHIC⟧ *Math.* designating or of a function of a complex variable that is regular in a given domain except for a finite number of poles

mer·o·plank·ton (mer′ō plaŋk′tən) *n.* ⟦< Gr *meros,* part (see MERIT) + PLANKTON⟧ an organism that is planktonic for only a part of its life cycle, as the barnacle or starfish

-mer·ous (mər əs) ⟦< Gr *meros,* a part (see MERIT) + -OUS⟧ *combining form forming adjectives* having (a specified number or kind of) parts; partite [*trimerous*]

Mer·o·vin·gi·an (mer′ō vin′jē ən, -jən) *adj.* ⟦Fr *Mérovingien* < ML *Merovingi,* descendants of *Merovaeus,* Latinized name of *Merowig,* grandfather of CLOVIS I⟧ designating or of the Frankish line of kings who reigned in Gaul (ancient France) from *c.* A.D. 500 to 751: the line was founded by Clovis I —*n.* a king of this line

mer·o·zo·ite (mer′ō zō′īt) *n.* ⟦< Gr *meros,* part (see MERIT) + ZO(O)- + -ITE[1]⟧ any of various cells produced by multiple fission in the asexual stage of certain protozoans, as the malaria parasite

Mer·ri·mack[1] or **Mer·ri·mac** (mer′ə mak′) *n.* a U.S. frigate armored by the Confederates and engaged by the *Monitor,* a Union ironclad, in the first battle (1862) between ironclads: Confederate name, *Virginia*

Mer·ri·mack[2] (mer′ə mak′) ⟦< AmInd, ? place of swift current⟧ river flowing from S N.H. through NE Mass. into the Atlantic: 110 mi (177 km)

mer·ri·ment (mer′i mənt) *n.* **1** merrymaking; gaiety and fun; mirth; hilarity **2** [Obs.] something that amuses or entertains

mer·ry (mer′ē) *adj.* **-ri·er, -ri·est** ⟦ME *mery* < OE *myrge,* pleasing, agreeable, akin to OHG *murgi,* short < IE base **mreghu-, *mr̥ghu-,* short > Gr *brachys,* L *brevis,* short: basic sense "lasting a short time, seeming brief"⟧ **1** full of fun and laughter; lively and cheerful **2** conducive to fun and laughter; festive [the *merry* month of May] **3** [Archaic] pleasant or amusing —SYN. LIVELY —**make merry** to be festive and full of gaiety; have fun —**mer′ri·ly** *adv.* —**mer′ri·ness** *n.*

mer·ry-an·drew (mer′ē an′dro͞o′) *n.* ⟦prec. + ANDREW: orig. uncert.⟧ [Archaic] a clown or buffoon

mer·ry-go-round (mer′ē gō round′) *n.* **1** a ride, as at an amusement park, consisting of a round, revolving platform with seats often in the form of animals; carousel **2** a whirl or busy round, as of work or pleasure

mer·ry·mak·ing (-māk′iŋ) *n.* fun; conviviality; festivity —*adj.* taking part in merrymaking —**mer′ry·mak′er** *n.*

mer·ry·thought (-thôt′) *n.* ⟦from the belief that the person holding the larger part of the WISHBONE will be granted a wish⟧ [Chiefly Brit.] the wishbone

merry widow [*also* **M- W-**] a woman's undergarment combining a bra, often strapless, a corset ending just below the waist, and garters

MERS (murz) *n.* ⟦*M(iddle) E(ast) r(espiratory) s(yndrome)*: first cases reported from Saudi Arabia⟧ a severe, contagious respiratory illness caused by a coronavirus and characterized by fever, cough, and shortness of breath

Mer·sey (mur′zē) river in NW England, flowing into the Irish Sea through an estuary at Liverpool: 70 mi (113 km)

Mer·sey·side (-sīd′) county in NW England, on the Mersey & the Irish Sea: 253 sq mi (655 sq km)

mer·thi·o·late (mər thī′ə lāt′) *n.* ⟦< *Merthiolate,* former trademark < (*sodium ethyl-*) *mer*(*curi-*) *thio*(*salicy*)*late*⟧ [*also* **M-**] THIMEROSAL

Mer·ton[1] (murt′'n), **Thomas** 1915-68; U.S. Trappist monk & writer

Mer·ton[2] (murt′'n) borough of SW Greater London, England

Mer·vin (mur′vin) *n.* ⟦prob. var. of MARVIN⟧ a masculine name: dim. *Merv;* var. *Mervyn, Merwin, Merwyn:* see MARVIN

mes- (mes, mez) *combining form* MESO-: used before a vowel

☆**me·sa** (mā′sə) *n.* ⟦Sp < L *mensa,* a table: see MENSAL⟧ a small, high plateau or flat tableland with steep sides, esp. in the SW U.S.

Me·sa (mā′sə) ⟦see prec.⟧ city in SC Ariz., on the Salt River, near Phoenix

Me·sa·bi Range (mə sä′bē) ⟦< Ojibwa *missabe wudjiu,* giant mountain⟧ range of hills in NE Minn., containing rich iron ore deposits

mé·sal·li·ance (mā′zə lī′əns, mā zal′ē əns; *Fr* mā zȧ lyäns′) *n.* ⟦Fr < *més-* (< L *mis-*), MIS-[1] + *alliance,* alliance⟧ a marriage with a person of lower social status

mes·arch (mes′ärk′, mez′-) *adj.* ⟦MES- + Gr *archē,* beginning⟧ **1** *Bot.* having the primary xylem maturing from the center toward both the interior and exterior of the stem, as in certain ferns **2** *Ecol.* beginning in a moderately moist habitat

☆**mes·cal** (mes kal′, -käl′) *n.* ⟦Sp *mezcal* < Nahuatl *mexcalli*⟧ **1** a colorless alcoholic liquor of Mexico made from pulque or other fermented agave juice: it is lower in quality and rougher in taste than tequila **2** any plant from which this liquor is made **3** a small, spineless cactus (*Lophophora williamsii*) of N Mexico and the SW U.S., with rounded stems, whose buttonlike tops (**mescal buttons**) are chewed, specif., in religious ceremonies by Mexican Indians, for their hallucinogenic effects

Mes·ca·le·ro (mes′kə ler′ō) *n., pl.* **-ro, -ros** ⟦AmSp, the people of the prec.: so named because they made extensive use of the flesh of the peyote cactus for food, rope fiber, etc.⟧ a member of an Apache people now living mainly in S New Mexico, and formerly living also in Texas and Mexico

mes·ca·line (mes′kə lin, -lēn′) *n.* ⟦MESCAL + -INE[3]⟧ a white, crystalline alkaloid, $C_{11}H_{17}NO_3$, that is a psychedelic drug, obtained from mescal buttons

mes·clun (mes′klən) *n.* ⟦Fr < Prov, mixture⟧ a mixture of salad greens and herbs, as bibb lettuce with dandelion greens, radicchio, and parsley

mes·dames (mā däm′; *Fr* mā dȧm′) *n. pl. of* MADAME, MADAM (sense 1), or MRS.: abbrev. *Mmes*

mes·de·moi·selles (mād mwȧ zel′) *n. Fr. pl. of* MADEMOISELLE (senses 1-2): abbrev. *Mlles*

me·seems (mē sēmz′) *v.impersonal, pt.* **me·seemed′** [Archaic] (it) seems to me: also **me·seem′eth** (-sēm′ith)

mes·em·bry·an·the·mum (mes em′brē an′thə məm, mez-) *n.* ⟦ModL < Gr *mesēmbria,* midday (< *mesos,* MID[1] + *hēmera,* day) + *anthemon,* flower < *anthos,* flower: see ANTHO-⟧ **1** FIG MARIGOLD ☆**2** any of a large group of fleshy, succulent plants of the carpetweed family, sometimes grown for ornament in warm climates, esp., any of several species of a genus (*Carpobrotus*) growing wild in California

mes·en·ceph·a·lon (mes′en sef′ə län′, mez′-) *n., pl.* **-la** (-lə) ⟦ModL: see MESO- & ENCEPHALON⟧ MIDBRAIN —**mes′en·ce·phal′ic** (-sə fal′ik) *adj.*

mes·en·chyme (mes′ən kīm′, mez′-) *n.* ⟦< MES- + ModL *-enchyma,* suffix denoting a type of cell tissue: see PARENCHYMA⟧ *Embryology* that part of the unspecialized mesoderm from which the connective tissues, cartilage, bone, blood, heart, and lymphatic vessels are derived —**mes·en·chy·mal** (mes eŋ′ki məl, mez-) *adj.*

mes·en·ter·on (mes en′tər än′, mez-) *n., pl.* **-ter·a** (-ə) ⟦ModL: see MESO- & ENTERON⟧ MIDGUT —**mes·en′ter·on′ic** *adj.*

mes·en·ter·y (mes′ən ter′ē, mez′-) *n., pl.* **-ter′ies** ⟦ML *mesenterium* < Gr *mesenterion* < *mesos,* MID[1] + *enteron,* intestine: see INTER-⟧ *Anat.* a supporting membrane or membranes enfolding some internal organ and attaching it either to the body wall or to another organ; esp., a double thickness of the peritoneum enfolding most of the small intestine and attaching it to the spinal wall of the abdominal cavity —**mes′en·ter′ic** *adj.*

mesh (mesh) *n.* ⟦earlier *meash,* prob. < MDu *maesche* < ODu *maske* < IE base **mezg-,* to knit, entwine > Lith *mezgù,* to knit together, OE *max,* a net⟧ **1** any of the open spaces of a net, screen, sieve, etc.: a 50-mesh screen is one with 50 such open spaces per linear inch **2** [*pl.*] the threads, cords, etc. forming these openings **3** a net or network **4** a netlike, woven material, as that used for stockings **5** a structure of interlocking metal links **6** anything that entangles, snares, or entraps **7** the engagement of the teeth of gears —*vt.* **1** to entangle ☆**2** to engage: said of gears or gear teeth —*vi.* **1** to become entangled ☆**2** to become engaged: said of gears or gear teeth **3** to fit closely together; interlock **4** to be in harmony, agreement, or accord: often with *with* —**in mesh** in gear; interlocked —**mesh′y** *adj.*

Me·shach (mē′shak′) *n.* ⟦Heb *mēshakh*⟧ *Bible* one of the three captives who came out of the fiery furnace miraculously unharmed: Dan. 3

Me·shed (mə shed′) *var. of* MASHHAD

me·shu·ga (mə sho͝og′ə) *adj.* ⟦Yiddish < Heb *meshuggāh*⟧ [*also in italics*] [Slang] crazy; mad; insane: also **me·shug′ga** or **me·shu′gah**

mesh·u·gas (mish′ə gäs′, mish′ə gäs′) *n.* ⟦Yiddish⟧ [*also in italics*] [Slang] craziness; foolishness; nonsense: also sp. **me′shu·gaas′**

me·shu·ge·neh, me·shug·ge·neh, *or* **me·shu·ga·nah** (mə sho͝og′ə nə) [*also in italics*] [Slang] *adj.* ⟦Yiddish⟧ MESHUGA —*n.* a crazy, eccentric, or foolish person Also **me·shu′ge·ner** or **me·shug′ge·ner** (-nər)

mesh·work (mesh′wurk′) *n.* meshes; network

me·si·al (mē′zē əl, -sē-; mez′ē-, mes′-) *adj.* ⟦< Gr *mesos,* MID[1] + -IAL⟧ **1** of, in, toward, or along the middle; middle; median; esp., designating or of a median plane or line **2** *Dentistry* toward the midline of the face along the curve of the dental arch —**me′si·al·ly** *adv.*

me·sic[1] (mē′zik, -sik; mez′ik, mes′-) *adj.* ⟦MES- + -IC⟧ **1** *Bot.* requiring moderate moisture: said of plants **2** *Ecol.* moderately moist: said of habitats

mes·ic[2] (mes′ik, mez′-; mā′sik, -zik; mē′-) *adj.* ⟦MES(ON) + -IC⟧ *Physics* of a meson

me·sit·y·lene (mi sit′'l ēn′) *n.* ⟦mesityl (< Gr *mesitēs,* mediator < *mesos,* MID[1] + -YL) + -ENE⟧ a colorless, aromatic hydrocarbon, $C_6H_3(CH_3)_3$, found in coal tar or made by distillation of a mixture of sulfuric acid and acetone

mes·mer·ism (mez′mər iz′əm, mes′-) *n.* ⟦Fr *Mesmérisme,* after F. A. *Mesmer* (1734-1815), Ger physician⟧ **1** hypnotism, esp. as practiced by Mesmer in connection with his theory of animal magnetism **2** hypnotic or irresistible attraction; fascination —**mes·mer′ic** (-mer′ik) *adj.* —**mes·mer′i·cal·ly** *adv.* —**mes′mer·ist** *n.*

mes·mer·ize (-iz′) *vt.* **-ized′**, **-iz′ing** **1** [Archaic] HYPNOTIZE (sense 1) **2** to hold the attention of; transfix, captivate, fascinate, etc. —**mes′mer·i·za′tion** *n.* —**mes′mer·iz′er** *n.*

mesne (mēn) *adj.* ⟦Anglo-Fr *meen* < OFr *meien:* see MEAN[3]⟧ *Law* middle; intermediate; intervening: **mesne profits** are profits accruing from the time possession of land has been improperly withheld from its rightful owner until his or her reinstatement in possession of the property —*n.* MESNE LORD

mesne lord a feudal lord holding land from a superior

mes·o- (mes′ō, mez′ō; -ə; mē′sō, -sə) ⟦< Gr *mesos,* middle: see MID[1]⟧ *combining form* in the middle, intermediate [*mesocarp, Mesozoic*]

Mes·o·a·mer·i·ca (mes′ō ə mer′i kə, mez′-) region including parts of modern Mexico and Central America, formerly inhabited by various ancient and pre-Columbian Indian civilizations —**Mes′o·a·mer′i·can** *adj.*

mes·o·ben·thos (mes′ō ben′thäs′, mez′-) *n.* ⟦ModL: see MESO- & BENTHOS⟧ all the animals and plants living on the sea bottom at depths between 200 and 1,000 meters (*c.* 656 to *c.* 3,280 ft)

mes·o·blast (mes′ō blast′, mez′-) *n.* ⟦MESO- + -BLAST⟧ MESODERM —**mes′o·blas′tic** *adj.*

mes·o·carp (-kärp′) *n.* ⟦MESO- + -CARP⟧ the middle layer of the wall of a ripened ovary or fruit —**mes′o·car′pic** *adj.*

mes·o·ce·phal·ic (mes′ō sə fal′ik, mez′-) *adj.* ⟦MESO- + CEPHALIC⟧ having an intermediate head shape with a width of 76 to 80.9 percent of its length from front to back: see also CEPHALIC INDEX: also **mes′o·ceph′a·lous** (-sef′ə ləs) —**mes′o·ceph′a·ly** (-sef′ə lē) *n.*

mes·o·cra·ni·al (mes′ō krā′nē əl, mez′-) *adj.* ⟦MESO- + CRANIAL⟧ MESOCEPHALIC: also **mes′o·cra′nic** (-krā′nik) —**mes′o·cra′ny** (-krā′nē) *n.*

mes·o·crat·ic (mes′ə krat′ik, mez′-) *adj.* ⟦< MESO- + Gr *kratein,* to rule (< *kratos,* strength: see HARD) + -IC⟧ containing 30 to 60 percent of heavy, dark minerals: said esp. of igneous rocks

mes·o·derm (mes′ə durm′, mez′-) *n.* ⟦MESO- + -DERM⟧ the middle layer of cells of an embryo, from which the skeletal, reproductive, muscular, vascular, connective, etc. tissues develop —**mes′o·der′mal** *adj.*, **mes′o·der′mic**

mes·o·gas·tri·um (mes′ō gas′trē əm, mez′-) *n.*, *pl.* **-tri·a** (-ə) ⟦ModL < Gr *mesos* (see MESO-) + *gastēr,* belly (see GASTRO-)⟧ **1** the dorsal mesentery of the stomach of an embryo **2** the region of the abdomen about the navel —**mes′o·gas′tric** *adj.*

mes·o·gle·a or **mes·o·gloe·a** (-glē′ə) *n.* ⟦ModL < Gr *mesos,* MID[1] + LGr *gloia,* glue, akin to Gr *gloios,* sticky oil: see GLUE⟧ a jellylike layer in cnidarians and ctenophores, lying between the ectoderm and the endoderm —**mes′o·gle′al** *adj.*, **mes′o·gloe′al**

mes·o·lim·ni·on (-lim′nē än′, -ən) *n.* ⟦ModL: see MESO- & HYPOLIMNION⟧ an unfrozen lake's thermocline: see EPILIMNION

Mes·o·lith·ic (-lith′ik) *adj.* ⟦MESO- + -LITHIC⟧ [*sometimes* **m-**] designating or of an Old World cultural period (*c.* 10,000-*c.* 8000 B.C.) between the Paleolithic and the Neolithic, characterized by the earliest exploitation of local and relatively permanent food resources and the use of microliths —**the Mesolithic** the Mesolithic period; Middle Stone Age

mes·o·morph (mes′ə môrf′, mez′-) *n.* a person of the mesomorphic physical type —**mes′o·mor′phism′** *n.* —**mes′o·mor′phy** (-fē) *n.*

mes·o·mor·phic (mes′ə môr′fik, mez′-) *adj.* **1** ⟦MESO- + -MORPHIC⟧ of a state intermediate between the liquid and the crystalline; of or like liquid crystal **2** ⟦MESO(DERM) + -MORPHIC⟧ designating or of the muscular physical type, characterized by predominance of the structure developed from the mesoderm: cf. ECTOMORPHIC, ENDOMORPHIC

☆**mes·on** (mes′än′, mez′-; mā′sän′, -zän′; mē′-) *n.* ⟦< MES(OTR)ON⟧ *Particle Physics* any of a group of subatomic particles that are both hadrons and bosons, including the pion and kaon —**me·son·ic** (me sän′ik, -zän′-; mē-) *adj.*

mes·o·neph·ros (mes′ə nef′räs′, mez′-) *n.* ⟦ModL < *meso-,* MESO- + Gr *nephros,* kidney: see NEPHRO-⟧ the excretory organ serving as the adult kidney of fishes and amphibians and as the embryonic kidney of higher vertebrates: the mesonephros and its duct develop into the epididymis and vas deferens in higher vertebrates —**mes′o·neph′ric** *adj.*

mes·o·pause (mes′ə pôz′, mez′-) *n.* ⟦MESO(SPHERE) + PAUSE⟧ an atmospheric transition zone or shell located between the mesosphere and the thermosphere at an altitude of *c.* 80 to 85 km (*c.* 50 to 53 miles) in which temperatures begin to rise with increasing altitude

mes·o·phyll (mes′ə fil′, mez′-) *n.* ⟦< ModL *mesophyllum:* see MESO- & -PHYLL⟧ the soft tissue (*green parenchyma*) inside a leaf, between the lower epidermis and the upper, chiefly concerned in photosynthesis —**mes′o·phyl′lic** *adj.*, **mes′o·phyl′lous**

mes·o·phyte (-fīt′) *n.* ⟦MESO- + -PHYTE⟧ any plant adapted to grow under medium conditions of moisture —**mes′o·phyt′ic** (-fit′ik) *adj.*

Mes·o·po·ta·mi·a (mes′ə pə tā′mē ə) ⟦Gr *mesopotamia (chōra),* lit., (land) between rivers < *mesos,* MID[1] + *potamos,* river, orig., rapids < IE base **pet-*, to fall, rush at > FEATHER⟧ **1** ancient country in SW Asia, between the upper Tigris & Euphrates rivers: a part of modern Iraq **2** loosely, the entire region between these rivers, extending to the Persian Gulf —**Mes′o·po·ta′mi·an** *adj., n.*

Mesopotamia (*c.* 2100 B.C.)

mes·o·sphere (mes′ō sfir′, mez′-) *n.* ⟦MESO- + SPHERE⟧ the atmospheric zone or shell located above the stratopause at an altitude of *c.* 55 to 80 km (*c.* 34 to 50 miles) and characterized by a decrease in temperature with increasing altitude

mes·o·the·li·o·ma (mes′ō thē′lē ō′mə, mez′-) *n.* ⟦< fol. + -OMA⟧ a tumor of the mesothelium, often malignant and thought to be caused most commonly by the inhalation of asbestos particles

mes·o·the·li·um (mes′ō thē′lē əm, mez′-) *n., pl.* **-li·a** (-ə) ⟦ModL < MESO- + *(epi)thelium*⟧ epithelium of mesodermal origin; specif., the thin layer of mesodermal epithelial cells lining the pericardial, pleural, peritoneal, and scrotal cavities

mes·o·tho·rax (-thôr′aks) *n.* the middle one of the three segments of an insect's thorax —**mes′o·tho·rac′ic** (-thô ras′ik) *adj.*

mes·o·tho·ri·um (-thôr′ē əm) *n.* ⟦ModL: see MESO- & THORIUM⟧ **1** a radioactive isotope of radium (**mesothorium 1**), formed from thorium: now usually called *radium-228* **2** a radioactive isotope of actinium (**mesothorium 2**), formed from mesothorium 1: now usually called *actinium-228*

☆**mes·o·tron** (mes′ə trän′, mez′-) *n.* ⟦MESO- + (ELEC)TRON⟧ *former term for* MESON —**mes′o·tron′ic** *adj.*

mes·o·troph·ic (mes′ə träf′ik, mez′-; -trō′fik) *adj.* designating or of a lake, pond, etc. having a moderate amount of plant growth: the mesotrophic stage is intermediate between the oligotrophic and eutrophic stages —**mes′o·troph′y** (-träf′ē) *n.*

mes·o·zo·an (mes′ə zō′ən, mez′-) *n.* ⟦< ModL *Mesozoa* (see MESO- & -ZOA) + -AN: so named from being intermediate in structure between *Protozoa* & *Metazoa*⟧ any of a phylum (Mesozoa) of small, multicellular, wormlike organisms characterized by a very simple, ciliated body with only a mouth, body cavity, and anus: it is a parasite in various marine invertebrates

Mes·o·zo·ic (mes′ə zō′ik, mez′-) *adj.* ⟦MESO- + ZO- + -IC⟧ [*sometimes* **m-**] designating or of the middle geologic era of the Phanerozoic Eon, subdivided into the Triassic, Jurassic, and Cretaceous periods and characterized by the development and extinction of the dinosaurs and the development of the first birds, mammals, and flowering plants —**the Mesozoic** the Mesozoic Era or its rocks: see the geologic time chart in the Reference Supplement

☆**mes·quite** or **mes·quit** (me skēt′, mes′kēt′) *n.* ⟦Sp *mezquite* < Nahuatl *mizquitl*⟧ any of several thorny trees or shrubs (genus *Prosopis*) of the mimosa family, common in the SW U.S. and in Mexico, including the screw bean: the sugary, beanlike, edible pods are used as fodder

Mes·quite (me skēt′) ⟦after the *mesquite* trees found there⟧ city in NE Tex.: suburb of Dallas

mess (mes) *n.* ⟦ME *messe* < OFr *mes* < L *missus,* a course (at a meal), orig. pp. of *mittere,* to send, put: see MISSION⟧ **1** a portion or quantity of food for a meal or dish **2** a portion of soft or semiliquid food, as porridge **3** unappetizing food; disagreeable concoction **4** *a)* a group of people who regularly have their meals together, as in the army *b)* the meal eaten by such a group *c)* the place where this meal is eaten **5** a disorderly or confused collection or mass of things; jumble; hodgepodge **6** *a)* a state of embarrassment, trouble, difficulty, or confusion; muddle *b)* a state of being disorderly, untidy, or dirty ☆*c)* [Informal] a person in either of these states **7** a messy or disorderly place or condition [the house is a *mess!*] —*vt.* **1** to supply meals to **2** to make a mess of; specif., *a)* to make dirty, soiled, or untidy *b)* to bungle; muddle; botch: often with *up* —*vi.* **1** to eat as one of a MESS (sense 4a) **2** to putter (*with*) **3** to meddle (*in* or *with*) —☆**mess around (or about)** **1** to be busy in a desultory way; putter around **2** [Informal] to become involved (*with*) —☆**mess up** [Informal] to make a mess, as by ineptitude; bungle

mes·sage (mes′ij) *n.* ⟦OFr < ML *missaticum* < pp. of L *mittere,* to send: see MISSION⟧ **1** a communication passed or sent by speech, in writing, by signals, etc. **2** a formal, official communication [the President's *message* to Congress] **3** *a)* an inspired communication, as of a prophet or philosopher *b)* the chief idea or theme that a speaker, writer, etc. seeks to communicate [a candidate staying on *message* during an interview] **4** [Archaic] the errand or function of a messenger **5** [Informal] COMMERCIAL — *vt., vi.* **-saged**, **-sag·ing** to send (as) a message —**get the message** [Informal] to understand the implications of an action or, often, specif., of a hint, insinuation, etc. —☆**send a message** [Informal] to convey or communicate one's feelings, desires, etc., often, specif., in a subtle or indirect manner

Mes·sa·li·na (mes′ə lī′nə), **Va·le·ri·a** (və lir′ē ə) A.D. 22?-48; Rom. empress: 3d wife of Claudius I: notorious for her dissolute life: executed

mes·sa·line (mes′ə lēn′, mes′ə lēn′) ***n.*** ⟦Fr⟧ a thin, soft, lustrous twilled silk cloth

mes·sei·gneurs (mes′en yʉrz′; *Fr* mā se nyër′) ***n. pl. of*** MONSEIGNEUR

Mes·se·ne (me sē′nē) town in Messenia: it was the capital of the region in ancient times

mes·sen·ger (mes′ən jər) ***n.*** ⟦ME *messengere* (with unhistoric *-n-*) < OFr *messagier:* see MESSAGE⟧ **1** *a)* a person who carries a message or goes on an errand *b)* a person whose work is delivering telegrams, official dispatches, or the like **2** [Archaic] a harbinger; forerunner **3** *Naut.* a light line tied to a heavier one and used in pulling it as from a ship to a pier

messenger bag a large, durable bag of canvas, nylon, etc. with an adjustable shoulder strap, large flap closure, and, usually, multiple pockets and compartments: so called because originally used by bicycle messengers

messenger RNA a single-stranded form of RNA that carries genetic information for protein synthesis from the DNA in the nucleus to the ribosomes

Mes·se·ni·a (mə sē′nē ə, -sēn′yə) **1** ancient region in the SW Peloponnesus bordering on the Ionian Sea **2** department of modern Greece in the same general area

☆**mess hall** ⟦see MESS, *n.* 4⟧ a room or building where a group, as of soldiers, regularly have their meals

Mes·siaen (mā syan′), **O·li·vier (Eugène Prosper Charles)** (ō lē vyā′) 1908-92; Fr. composer

Mes·si·ah (mə sī′ə) ***n.*** ⟦used by the Geneva translators (1560) for LL(Ec) *Messias* & ME *Messie,* both (ME via OFr < LL) < Gr(Ec) *Messias* < Aram *mĕshīḥā,* Heb *māshīaḥ,* lit., anointed⟧ **1** *Judaism* the promised and expected deliverer of the Jews, who will bring an era of peace and justice **2** *Christianity* Jesus, regarded as the realization of the prophecy that the Messiah would come and, hence, called *the Christ* **3** [**m-**] any expected savior or liberator of a people or country Also, for senses 1 & 2, **Mes·si′as** (-əs) —**Mes·si′ah·ship′** ***n.*** —**Mes·si·an·ic** (mes′ē an′ik) ***adj.***, **mes·si·anic** —**mes·si′a·nism′** ***n.***

Mes·sier (mes′ē ā′; *Fr* me syā′), **Charles** 1730-1817; Fr. astronomer

Messier catalog ⟦after prec.⟧ *Astron.* a listing of 109 galaxies, star clusters, and nebulae: often called **Messier's catalog**

mes·sieurs (mes′ərz; *Fr* mā syö′) ***n. pl. of*** MONSIEUR: abbrev. *MM:* see also MESSRS

Mes·si·na (mə sē′nə) **1** seaport in NE Sicily, on the Strait of Messina **2 Strait of** strait between Sicily & Italy: 2-12 mi (3-19 km) wide; 20 mi (32 km) long

mess jacket ⟦see MESS, *n.* 4⟧ a man's short, closefitting jacket worn for semiformal dress, as by the military, or as part of the uniform of waiters, etc.

mess kit ⟦see MESS, *n.* 4⟧ the compactly arranged metal or plastic plates and eating utensils carried by a soldier or camper for use in the field: also **mess gear**

mess·mate (mes′māt′) ***n.*** ⟦MESS, *n.* 4 + MATE[1]⟧ a person with whom one regularly has meals, as in the army

Messrs (mes′ərz) *abbrev.* messieurs: now used chiefly as the pl. of MR.

mes·suage (mes′wij) ***n.*** ⟦ME < Anglo-Fr *mesuage,* prob. altered < OFr *mesnage:* see MÉNAGE⟧ *Law* a dwelling house with its outbuildings and adjacent land

mess·y (mes′ē) ***adj.*** **mess′i·er**, **mess′i·est** in, like, or characterized by a mess; untidy, disordered, dirty, etc. —**mess′i·ly** ***adv.*** —**mess′i·ness** ***n.***

mes·ti·za (me stē′zə) ***n.*** a woman or girl who is a MESTIZO

mes·ti·zo (me stē′zō) ***n.***, *pl.* **-zos** or **-zoes** ⟦Sp < LL(Ec) *misticius,* of mixed race (transl. of Gr *symmiktos,* commingled) < pp. of L *miscere,* MIX⟧ a person of mixed parentage; esp., in the W U.S. and in Latin American countries, a person having one Spanish or Portuguese parent and one American Indian parent

met[1] (met) ***vt., vi.*** *pt. & pp. of* MEET[1]

met[2] *abbrev.* **1** metaphor **2** metaphysics **3** metropolitan **4** meteorological **5** meteorology

met·a- (met′ə) ⟦< Gr *meta,* along with, after, between, among < IE *meta < base *me-, between > MID[1]⟧ *prefix* **1** change in position or form, alteration, transposition *[metathesis, metasomatism]:* equivalent to TRANS- **2** after *[metapneumonic]:* sometimes, as in medical terms, equivalent to POST- **3** behind, at the back *[metanephros]:* in anatomical terms, equivalent to DORSO- **4** ⟦< supposed analogy to *metaphysics*⟧ going beyond or higher, transcending: used to form terms designating an area of study whose purpose is to examine the nature, assumptions, structure, etc. of a (specified) field *[metalinguistics, metacriticism]* **5** between *[metope]* **6** *Chem.* *a)* a polymer of *[metaldehyde]* *b)* a derivative of *[metaprotein]* *c)* a less hydrated acid or salt *[metaphosphoric acid]* (see ORTHO-, sense 4*a*) *d)* characterized by substitutions in the 1, 3 position in the benzene ring (usually italicized and hyphenated in chemical names) *[meta-aminobenzoic acid]* (see PARA-[1], sense 2*b*, ORTHO-, sense 4*b*) Also (except for sense 6*d*), before a vowel, **met-**

met·a-a·nal·y·sis (met′ə ə nal′ə sis) ***n.***, *pl.* **-ses′** (-sēz′) a research study that combines and analyzes statistics gathered from multiple independent studies

met·a·bol·ic (met′ə bäl′ik) ***adj.*** ⟦Gr *metabolikos*⟧ of, involving, characterized by, or resulting from metabolism —**met′a·bol′ic·al·ly** ***adv.***

me·tab·o·lism (mə tab′ə liz′əm) ***n.*** ⟦< Gr *metabolē,* change < *meta,* beyond (see META-) + *ballein,* to throw (see BALL[2]) + -ISM⟧ the chemical and physical processes continuously going on in living organisms and cells, consisting of anabolism and catabolism

me·tab·o·lite (mə tab′ə līt′) ***n.*** any substance produced by or taking part in metabolism

me·tab·o·lize (-līz′) ***vt., vi.*** **-lized′**, **-liz′ing** to change by or subject to metabolism —**me·tab′o·liz′a·ble** ***adj.***

met·a·car·pal (met′ə kär′pəl) ***adj.*** of the metacarpus —***n.*** any of the bones of the metacarpus

met·a·car·pus (-kär′pəs) ***n.***, *pl.* **-pi′** (-pī′) ⟦ModL, altered < *metacarpium* < Gr *metakarpion* < *meta,* META- + *karpion,* dim. of *karpos:* see CARPUS⟧ **1** the part of the hand consisting of the five bones between the wrist and the fingers **2** the corresponding part of a land vertebrate's forelimb

met·a·cen·ter (met′ə sen′tər) ***n.*** ⟦Fr *métacentre:* see META- & CENTER⟧ that point in a floating body at which a vertical line drawn through its center of buoyancy when it is upright meets the vertical line drawn through its center of buoyancy when it is tipped; center of gravity of the part of a floating body that is not submerged: for stability the metacenter must be above the center of gravity —**met′a·cen′tric** (-trik) ***adj.***

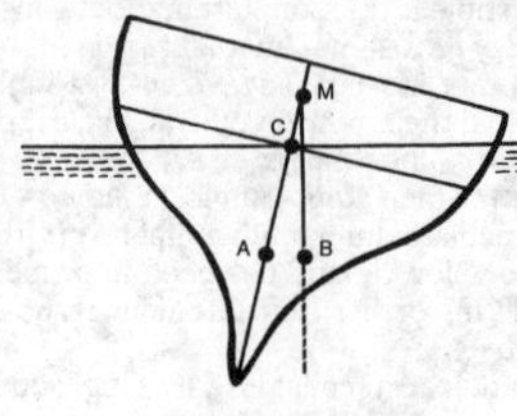

M
C
A
B

metacenter
C, center of gravity; A, center of buoyancy of a floating body; B, center of buoyancy when body is tipped; M, metacenter at point of intersection of verticals MA and MB

met·a·chro·mat·ic (met′ə krō mat′ik) ***adj.*** **1** of metachromatism **2** in microscopy, designating or of a stain that changes color depending on the type of material or tissue being tested, that material's chemical makeup, etc.

met·a·chro·ma·tism (-krō′mə tiz′əm) ***n.*** ⟦< META- + Gr *chroma,* color (see CHROMA) + -ISM⟧ a change of color, esp. as a result of a change in temperature

met·a·da·ta (met′ə dāt′ə, -dat′ə) ***n.*** [*sometimes with pl. v.*] data that describes or underlies other data

met·a·eth·ics (-eth′iks) ***n.*** *Philos.* the branch of ethics dealing with its concepts and methodology

met·a·fic·tion (met′ə fik′shən) ***n.*** **1** fiction in which the mediating function of the author and the technical methods used in writing are self-consciously emphasized and in which the traditional concern with verisimilitude is minimized **2** a work of such fiction —**met′a·fic′tion·al** ***adj.*** —**met′a·fic′tion·ist** ***n.***

met·a·gal·ax·y (-gal′ək sē) ***n.*** *Astron.* the total assemblage of all galaxies, including all intergalactic matter; the measurable material universe —**met′a·ga·lac′tic** (-gə lak′tik) ***adj.***

met·age (mēt′ij) ***n.*** ⟦METE[1] + -AGE⟧ **1** official measurement of contents or weight of coal, grain, etc. **2** the charge for this

met·a·gen·e·sis (met′ə jen′ə sis) ***n.*** ⟦ModL: see META- & -GENESIS⟧ *Biol.* reproduction in which there is alternation of an asexual with a sexual generation, as in many cnidarians —**met′a·ge·net′ic** (-jə net′ik) ***adj.***

me·tag·na·thous (mə tag′nə thəs) ***adj.*** ⟦META- + -GNATHOUS⟧ **1** having the points of the beak crossed, as in the crossbills **2** having larvae that feed by chewing and adults that feed by sucking, as in butterflies and moths —**me·tag′na·thism′** ***n.***

Me·tai·rie (met′ə rē) ⟦< Fr, lit., sharecropping farm, for nearby farms owned by Jesuits⟧ city in SE La.: suburb of New Orleans

met·al (met′'l) ***n.*** ⟦OFr < L *metallum,* metal, mine, quarry < Gr *metallon,* mine, quarry⟧ **1** *a)* any of a class of chemical elements, as iron, gold, or aluminum, generally characterized by ductility, malleability, luster, and conductivity of heat and electricity: these elements act as cations in chemical reactions, form bases with the hydroxyl radical, and can replace the hydrogen of an acid to form a salt *b)* an alloy of such elements, as brass or bronze **2** any substance or thing consisting of metal **3** molten cast iron **4** molten material for making glassware ☆**5** *short for* HEAVY METAL (sense 2) **6** [Chiefly Brit.] ROAD METAL **7** *Heraldry* either of the tinctures gold (*or*) and silver (*argent*) **8** *Printing* *a)* type metal *b)* composed type —***adj.*** made of metal —***vt.*** **-aled** or **-alled**, **-al·ing** or **-al·ling** to cover or supply with metal

met·a·lan·guage (met′ə laŋ′gwij) ***n.*** *Linguis.* a language used to describe or discuss another language

☆**met·a·lin·guis·tics** (met′ə liŋ gwis′tiks) ***n.*** ⟦coined by G. L. Trager (1906-92), U.S. linguist < *metalinguistic,* adj. (< META- + LINGUISTIC) + -ICS⟧ the branch of linguistics dealing with relations between language and other elements of a culture

met·al·ist (met′'l ist) ***n.*** **1** a person who works in metals **2** an advocate of the use of metallic instead of paper money Also sp. **met′al·list**

met·al·ize (-īz′) ***vt.*** **-ized′**, **-iz′ing** **1** to treat, cover, or impregnate with metal or a compound of metal **2** to make metallic Also sp. **met′al·lize′**

metal lath lath made of expanded metal or metal mesh

me·tal·lic (mə tal′ik) ***adj.*** ⟦L *metallicus* < Gr *metallikos*⟧ **1** of, or having the nature of, metal **2** containing, yielding, or producing metal **3** like, characteristic of, or suggestive of metal; specif., *a)* sharp or bitter *[a metallic taste]* *b)* reflectively iridescent *[metallic cloth]* *c)* harsh or rasping *[a metallic sound]* —**me·tal′li·cal·ly** ***adv.***

metallic soap a soaplike substance made by combining the salts of lead, aluminum, and some other metals with fatty acids: it is used in making paint, lubricants, cloth, etc.

☆**met·al·lid·ing** (met′ə lĭd′iŋ) ***n.*** ⟦< METAL + -IDE + -ING⟧ a method of creating alloy coatings on the surface of a wide variety of materials by electrolytically diffusing metals and metalloids into the surface

met·al·lif·er·ous (met′ə lif′ər əs) ***adj.*** ⟦L *metallifer* < *metallum,* METAL + *fere,* to BEAR[1] + -OUS⟧ containing, yielding, or producing metal or ore

met·al·line (met′ə lin, -līn′) ***adj.*** ⟦ME *mettaline* < ML *metallinus*⟧ **1** resembling metal; metallic **2** containing metal or metallic salts

met·al·log·ra·phy (met′ə läg′rə fē) ***n.*** ⟦Fr *métallographie:* see METAL & -GRAPHY⟧ the study of the structure and physical properties of metals and alloys, esp. by the use of the microscope and X-rays —**met·al·lo·graph·ic** (mə tal′ə graf′ik) ***adj.*** —**met·al′lo·graph′i·cal·ly *adv.***

met·al·loid (met′ə loid′) ***n.*** **1** NONMETAL **2** an element having some of, but not all, the properties of metals, as arsenic or silicon —***adj.*** **1** like a metal in appearance **2** of, or having the nature of, a metalloid

met·al·lur·gy (met′ə lur′jē) ***n.*** ⟦ModL *metallurgia* < Gr *metallourgein,* to work in metals or mines < *metallon,* metal, mine + *ergon,* WORK⟧ the science of metals, esp. the science of separating metals from their ores and preparing them for use, by smelting, refining, etc. —**met′al·lur′gi·cal *adj.*, met′al·lur′gic** —**met′al·lur′gi·cal·ly *adv.*** —**met′al·lur′gist *n.***

met·al·smith (met′'l smith′) ***n.*** an artist or craftsman who works with metal, esp. in making sculptures, jewelry, etc.

met·al·ware (met′'l wer′) ***n.*** kitchenware, etc. made of metal

met·al·work (met′'l wurk′) ***n.*** **1** things made of metal **2** METALWORKING

met·al·work·ing (-wur′kiŋ) ***n.*** the act or process of making things of metal —**met′al·work′er *n.***

met·a·math·e·mat·ics (met′ə math′ə mat′iks) ***n.*** the logical study of the nature and validity of mathematical reasoning and proof

met·a·mer (met′ə mər) ***n.*** ⟦< META- + Gr *meros,* a part: see MERIT⟧ *Chem.* a compound exhibiting metamerism with another or others

met·a·mere (met′ə mir′) ***n.*** ⟦META- + -MERE⟧ any of a longitudinal series of similar segments making up the body of a worm, crayfish, etc.

met·a·mer·ic (met′ə mer′ik) ***adj.*** **1** *Chem.* of or exhibiting metamerism **2** *Zool.* of or formed of metameres; segmented —**met′a·mer′i·cal·ly *adv.***

me·tam·er·ism (mə tam′ər iz′əm) ***n.*** **1** ⟦METAMER + -ISM⟧ *Chem.* the type of isomerism in which chemical compounds have identical proportions of the same elements and the same molecular weight, but have radicals differing in type or position, with resulting differences in chemical properties **2** *Zool.* the condition of being made up of metameres

met·a·mor·phic (met′ə môr′fik) ***adj.*** of, characterized by, causing, or formed by metamorphism or metamorphosis

met·a·mor·phism (-môr′fiz′əm) ***n.*** **1** METAMORPHOSIS **2** change in the mineralogical, structural, or textural composition of rocks under pressure, heat, chemical action, etc., which turns limestone into marble, granite into gneiss, etc.

met·a·mor·phose (-fōz′, -fōs′) ***vt., vi.*** **-phosed′, -phos′ing** ⟦Fr *métamorphoser*⟧ to change in form or nature; transform; subject to or undergo metamorphosis or metamorphism —**SYN.** TRANSFORM

met·a·mor·pho·sis (-môr′fə sis, -môr fō′sis) ***n., pl.*** **-ses′** (-sēz′) ⟦L < Gr *metamorphōsis* < *metamorphoun,* to transform, transfigure < *meta,* over (see META-) + *morphē,* form, shape⟧ **1** *a)* change of form, shape, structure, or substance; specif., transformation, as, in myths, by magic or sorcery *b)* the form resulting from such change **2** a marked or complete change of character, appearance, condition, etc. **3** *Biol.* a change in form, structure, or function as a result of development; specif., the physical transformation undergone by various animals during development after the embryonic state, as of the tadpole to the frog or of the larva of an insect to the pupa and the pupa to the adult **4** *Med.* a pathological change of form of some tissues

met·a·neph·ros (met′ə nef′räs′) ***n., pl.*** **-roi′** (-roi′) ⟦ModL < META- + Gr *nephros,* kidney: see NEPHRO-⟧ the excretory organ lying behind the mesonephros in an embryo, which in mammals, reptiles, and birds develops into the permanent, or adult, kidney —**met′a·neph′ric *adj.***

metaph *abbrev.* **1** metaphor **2** metaphysics

met·a·phase (met′ə fāz′) ***n.*** ⟦META- + PHASE[1]⟧ *Biol.* the stage in mitosis and meiosis, after the prophase and before the anaphase, during which the chromosomes are arranged along the equatorial plane of the spindle

met·a·phor (met′ə fôr′) ***n.*** ⟦Fr *métaphore* < L *metaphora* < Gr < *metapherein,* to carry over < *meta,* over (see META-) + *pherein,* to BEAR[1]⟧ a figure of speech containing an implied comparison, in which a word or phrase ordinarily and primarily used of one thing is applied to another (Ex.: the curtain of night, "all the world's a stage"): cf. SIMILE, MIXED METAPHOR —**met′a·phor′ic *adj.*, met′a·phor′i·cal** —**met′a·phor′i·cal·ly *adv.***

met·a·phos·phate (met′ə fäs′fāt′) ***n.*** any salt of metaphosphoric acid

met·a·phos·phor·ic acid (-fäs fôr′ik) glacial phosphoric acid, HPO_3, a deliquescent solid obtained by heating orthophosphoric acid: used as an analytical reagent

met·a·phrase (met′ə frāz′) ***n.*** ⟦ModL *metaphrasis* < Gr < *metaphrazein:* see META- & PHRASE⟧ a translation; esp., a literal, word-for-word translation, as distinguished from a paraphrase —***vt.*** **-phrased′, -phras′ing** **1** to translate, esp. literally **2** to change the wording of —**met′a·phras′tic** (-fras′tik) ***adj.***

met·a·phys·ic (met′ə fiz′ik) ***n.*** METAPHYSICS —***adj.*** [Rare] metaphysical

met·a·phys·i·cal (met′ə fiz′i kəl) ***adj.*** ⟦ML *metaphysicalis*⟧ **1** of, connected with, or having the nature of, metaphysics **2** very abstract, abstruse, or subtle: often a derogatory usage **3** beyond the physical or material; incorporeal, supernatural, or transcendental **4** designating or of the school of early 17th-cent. English poets, including esp. John Donne, George Herbert, Richard Crashaw, and Abraham Cowley, whose verse is characterized by very subtle, highly intellectualized imagery, sometimes deliberately fantastic and far-fetched —**met′a·phys′i·cal·ly *adv.***

met·a·phy·si·cian (-fə zish′ən) ***n.*** ⟦Fr *métaphysicien*⟧ a person who specializes or is versed in metaphysics

met·a·phys·ics (met′ə fiz′iks) ***n.*** ⟦< ML *metaphysica,* neut. pl. < Gr *(ta) meta (ta) physika,* lit., (that) after (the) physics (in reference to the section after the *Physics* in early collections of Aristotle's works)⟧ **1** the branch of philosophy that deals with first principles and seeks to explain the nature of being or reality (*ontology*) and of the origin and structure of the universe (*cosmology*): it is also closely associated with the study of the nature of knowledge (*epistemology*) **2** speculative philosophy in general **3** esoteric, often mystical or theosophical, lore **4** the theory or principles (of some branch of knowledge) **5** popularly, any very subtle or difficult reasoning

met·a·pla·sia (met′ə plā′zhə) ***n.*** ⟦META- + -PLASIA⟧ **1** abnormal change of one type of adult tissue to another **2** conversion of one tissue into another, as of cartilage into bone —**met′a·plas′tic** (-plas′tik) ***adj.***

met·a·plasm (met′ə plaz′əm) ***n.*** **1** ⟦META- + -PLASM⟧ that part of the contents of a cell which consists of lifeless matter, as certain fatty or starch granules **2** ⟦L *metaplasmus,* an irregularity < Gr *metaplasmes,* formation of cases of nouns from a missing nom. < *meta,* over (see META-) + *plassein,* to form (see PLASTIC)⟧ a change in a linguistic form made by the addition, omission, or transposition of a sound or sounds or a syllable or syllables —**met′a·plas′mic *adj.***

met·a·psy·chol·o·gy (-sī käl′ə jē) ***n.*** speculation about the origin, structure, function, etc. of the mind and about the relation between the mental and the physical, regarded as supplemental to psychology —**met′a·psy′cho·log′i·cal** (-kə läj′i kəl) ***adj.***

☆**met·a·se·quoi·a** (-si kwoi′ə) ***n.*** ⟦ModL: see META- & SEQUOIA⟧ DAWN REDWOOD

met·a·so·ma·tism (-sō′mə tiz′əm) ***n.*** ⟦META- + SOMAT(O)- + -ISM⟧ the metamorphic process by which minerals of a rock or ore body are replaced by minerals of a different chemical composition as a result of the action of a fluid, esp. of moving water —**met′a·so·mat′ic** (-sō mat′ik) ***adj.***

met·a·sta·ble (-stā′bəl) ***adj.*** changing readily either to a more stable or less stable condition, as certain electrons; unstable

me·tas·ta·sis (mə tas′tə sis) ***n., pl.*** **-ses′** (-sēz′) ⟦ModL < LL, a passing over, transition < Gr < *methistanai,* to place in another way, change < *meta,* after (see META-) + *histanai,* to place (see STAND)⟧ **1** [Rare] change of form or matter; transformation **2** *Med.* the spread of disease from one part of the body to another unrelated to it, as in the transfer of the cells of a malignant tumor by way of the bloodstream or lymphatics —**met·a·stat·ic** (met′ə stat′ik) ***adj.*** —**met′a·stat′i·cal·ly *adv.***

me·tas·ta·size (-sīz′) ***vi.*** **-sized′, -siz′ing** *Med.* to spread to other parts of the body by metastasis

met·a·tar·sal (met′ə tär′səl) ***adj.*** of the metatarsus —***n.*** any of the bones of the metatarsus

met·a·tar·sus (-tär′səs) ***n., pl.*** **-tar′si′** (-sī′) ⟦ModL: see META- & TARSUS⟧ **1** the part of the human foot consisting of the five bones between the ankle and toes **2** *a)* the corresponding part of a land vertebrate's hind limb *b)* the bone between the tibia and the phalanges in a bird's leg

me·ta·te (mə tät′ā, -tät′ē) ***n.*** ⟦MexSp < Nahuatl *metatl*⟧ a stone with a flat or concave surface on which grain, nuts, etc. can be ground with a smaller stone

me·tath·e·sis (mə tath′ə sis) ***n., pl.*** **-ses′** (-sēz′) ⟦LL < Gr, transposition, a going over < *metatithenai,* to put over, transpose < *meta,* over (see META-) + *tithenai,* to place (see DO[1])⟧ transposition or interchange; specif., *a)* the transposition of sounds in a word or between words (Ex.: "clasp" developed from Middle English "clapse") *b) Chem.* the interchange of elements or radicals between compounds, as when two compounds react with each other to form two new compounds —**met·a·thet·ic** (met′ə thet′ik) ***adj.***, **met′a·thet′i·cal**

met·a·tho·rax (met′ə thôr′aks′) ***n., pl.*** **-tho′rax′es** or **-tho′ra·ces′** (-thôr′ə sēz′) ⟦ModL⟧ the hindmost of the three segments of an insect thorax —**met′a·tho·rac′ic** (-thō ras′ik) ***adj.***

met·a·xy·lem (met′ə zī′ləm) ***n.*** ⟦META- + XYLEM⟧ the outer part of the primary xylem, or woody tissue of a plant, consisting of thick-walled or pitted cells

met·a·zo·an (met′ə zō′ən) ***n.*** ⟦< ModL *Metazoa* (< META- + -ZOA) + -AN⟧ in some systems of classification, any of the very large subkingdom (Metazoa) made up of all animals whose bodies, originating from a single cell, are composed of many differentiated cells arranged into definite organs —***adj.*** of the metazoans

Metch·ni·koff (mech′ni kôf′), **É·lie** (ā lē′) (Russ. *Ilya Ilyich Mechnikov*) 1845-1916; Russ. biologist & bacteriologist, in France

mete[1] (mēt) ***vt.*** **met′ed, met′ing** ⟦ME *meten* < OE *metan,* akin to Ger *messen* < IE **med-* (> L *modus,* Gr *metron*) < base **me-,* to mark off, MEASURE⟧ **1** to allot; distribute; apportion: usually with *out* **2** [Archaic] to measure

mete[2] (mēt) ***n.*** ⟦OFr < L *meta,* boundary, goal < IE **meit-* (var. of **mei-*), post, stake > ON *meithr,* a tree, MIr *methos,* boundary mark⟧ **1** a boundary; limit **2** a boundary mark or line

me·tem·psy·cho·sis (mi tem′sī kō′sis; met′əm sī-) ***n., pl.*** **-ses′** (-sēz′) ⟦LL < Gr *metempsychōsis* < *metempsychoun* < *meta,* over (see META-) + *empsy-*

choun, to put a soul into < *en,* IN[1] + *psychē,* soul, life (see PSYCHE)] in some religious beliefs, the passing of the soul at death into another body, either human or animal; transmigration

met·en·ceph·a·lon (met′en sef′ə län′) *n., pl.* **-la** (-lə) [ModL: see META- & ENCEPHALON] **1** that part of the brain of an embryo from which the pons and cerebellum are derived **2** the part of the hindbrain consisting of the cerebellum and pons —**met′en·ce·phal′ic** (-sə fal′ik) *adj.*

me·te·or[1] (mēt′ē ər, -ē ôr′) *n.* [ME < ML *meteorum* < Gr *meteōron,* pl. *meteōra,* things in the air < *meteōros,* lifted up, in air < *meta,* beyond (see META-) + *eōra,* a hovering in the air (akin to *aeirein,* to lift up)] **1** the luminous phenomenon observed when a meteoroid is heated by its entry into the earth's atmosphere; shooting star; falling star: see FIREBALL **2** loosely, a meteoroid or meteorite **3** *Meteorol.* any atmospheric phenomenon, as precipitation, lightning, or a rainbow

meteor[2] *abbrev.* **1** meteorological **2** meteorology

me·te·or·ic (mēt′ē ôr′ik) *adj.* [ML *meteoricus:* also < METEOR[1] + -IC] **1** atmospheric or meteorological [hail is a *meteoric* phenomenon] **2** of a meteor or meteors **3** like a meteor in swiftness and brilliance [his *meteoric* rise to stardom] —**me′te·or′i·cal·ly** *adv.*

me·te·or·ite (mēt′ē ər īt′) *n.* that part of a relatively large meteoroid that survives passage through the atmosphere and falls to the surface of a planet or moon as a mass of metal or stone —**me′te·or·it′ic** (-it′ik) *adj.*

me·te·or·o·graph (mēt′ē ôr′ə graf′; mēt′ē ər ə-) *n.* [Fr *météorographe:* see METEOR[1] & -GRAPH] an apparatus for automatically recording various weather conditions, as moisture, temperature, etc., at the same time —**me′te·or′o·graph′ic** *adj.*

me·te·or·oid (mēt′ē ər oid′) *n.* any of the many small, solid bodies traveling through outer space, which are seen as meteors when they enter the earth's atmosphere

meteorol *abbrev.* **1** meteorological **2** meteorology

me·te·or·o·log·i·cal (mēt′ē ə rə läj′i kəl, -ôr′ə-) *adj.* **1** of the atmosphere or atmospheric phenomena; of weather or climate **2** of meteorology: also **me′te·or·o·log′ic** —**me′te·or·o·log′i·cal·ly** *adv.*

me·te·or·ol·o·gy (mēt′ē ə räl′ə jē) *n.* [Gr *meteōrologia:* see METEOR[1] & -LOGY] the science of the atmosphere and atmospheric phenomena; study of weather, including weather forecasting —**me′te·or·ol′o·gist** *n.*

meteor shower the appearance of a group of meteors coming from the same area in the sky, usually the result of the earth passing through the trail of a comet: meteor showers are typically named after the constellation closest to the radiant

me·ter[1] (mēt′ər) *n.* [ME *metre* < OFr < L *metrum* < Gr *metron,* measure < IE base **mē-,* to mark off, MEASURE] **1** *a)* rhythm in verse; measured, patterned arrangement of syllables, primarily according to stress or length (see also FOOT, sense 9) *b)* the specific rhythm as determined by the prevailing foot and the number of feet in the line [iambic *meter*] *c)* the specific rhythmic pattern of a stanza as determined by the kind and number of lines **2** the basic pattern of beats in successive measures of a piece of music: it is usually indicated in the time signature **3** [Fr *mètre:* see -METER] the basic unit of linear measure in the metric system, equal to 39.3701 inches: now defined in the SI system as the distance light travels in a vacuum in 1/299,792,458 of a second: abbrev. *m*

me·ter[2] (mēt′ər) *n.* **1** [METE[1] + -ER] a person who measures; esp., an official who measures commodities **2** [< words ending in fol.] *a)* an instrument or apparatus for measuring; esp., an apparatus for measuring and recording the quantity or rate of flow of gas, electricity, or water passing through it ☆*b)* POSTAGE METER ☆*c)* PARKING METER *d)* TAXIMETER —*vt.* **1** to measure or record with a meter or meters **2** to provide in measured quantities ☆**3** to process (mail) with a postage meter

-me·ter (mēt′ər, mi tər) [Fr *-mètre* or ModL *-metrum,* both < Gr *metron,* a measure: see METER[1]] *combining form* **1** a device for measuring (a specified thing) [*thermometer, barometer*] **2** a line of verse having (a specified number of) metrical feet [*heptameter*]

me·ter-kil·o·gram-sec·ond (mēt′ər kil′ə gram′sek′ənd) *adj.* designating or of a system of measurement in which the meter, kilogram, and second are used as the units of length, mass, and time, respectively: abbrev. *MKS:* see the table of weights and measures in the Reference Supplement

☆**meter maid** a woman employed by a police traffic department to monitor parking meters, issue tickets for illegal or overtime parking, etc.

metes and bounds (mēts) [see METE[2]] *Law* the precisely described boundary lines of a parcel of land, as found in a deed

met·es·trus (met es′trəs) *n.* [ModL: see META- & ESTRUS] the quiescent period of the estrous cycle in mammals

☆**meth** (meth) *n.* [Slang] *short for* METHAMPHETAMINE

Meth *abbrev.* Methodist

meth- (meth) *combining form* METHO-: used before a vowel

meth·ac·ry·late (meth ak′rə lāt′) *n.* a salt or ester of methacrylic acid

methacrylate resin any of several plastic substances formed by polymerizing esters of methacrylic acid

meth·a·cryl·ic acid (meth′ə kril′ik) [METH(YL) + ACRYLIC] a colorless liquid, $CH_2{:}C(CH_3)COOH$, prepared by treating acetone cyanohydrin with dilute sulfuric acid: it is readily polymerized and is used in making synthetic resins

meth·a·done (meth′ə dōn′) *n.* [< *(6 di)meth(yl)a(mino-4,4-)d(iphenyl-3-heptan)one*] a synthetic narcotic drug, $C_{21}H_{27}NO$, used in medicine to treat heroin and morphine addicts: it is more potent than morphine, with a longer duration of action and milder withdrawal symptoms

meth·am·phet·a·mine (meth′am fet′ə mēn′, -min) *n.* [METH(O)- + AMPHETAMINE] a white, crystalline derivative of amphetamine, $C_{10}H_{15}N$, used in the form of its hydrochloride as a drug that is more stimulating than amphetamine: a very powerful, potentially habit-forming stimulant often produced and used illicitly

meth·ane (meth′ān′; *Brit* mē′thān′) *n.* [METH(YL) + -ANE] a colorless, odorless, flammable, gaseous alkane, CH_4, present in natural gas and formed by the decomposition of vegetable matter, as in marshes and mines, or produced artificially by heating carbon monoxide and hydrogen: it is the simplest alkane and is used as a fuel, a source of carbon black, etc.

methane series a series consisting of the alkanes, with methane as the first member

me·than·o·gen (mə than′ə jən, -jen′) *n.* an anaerobic microorganism that lives on carbon dioxide and hydrogen and gives off methane, found in swamp sediment, the gut of ruminants, etc. —**me·than′o·gen′ic** (-jen′ik) *adj.*

meth·a·nol (meth′ə nôl′, -nōl′) *n.* [METHAN(E) + -OL[1]] a colorless, volatile, flammable, poisonous liquid, CH_3OH, obtained by the destructive distillation of wood and synthesized chiefly from carbon monoxide and hydrogen: it is used in organic synthesis, as a fuel, solvent, and antifreeze, and in the manufacture of formaldehyde, smokeless powders, paints, etc.; methyl alcohol

meth·an·the·line (meth an′thə lēn′, -lin) *n.* [METH(YL) + *(x)anthe(ne) (carboxy)l(ate)* + -INE[3]] a synthetic drug having an atropinelike action and used in the form of its bromide, $C_{21}H_{26}BrNO_3$, in treating peptic ulcers

meth·aq·ua·lone (meth ak′wə lōn′) *n.* [METH(O)- + *-a-* + *qu(in)a(zo)lone*] a white, crystalline powder, $C_{16}H_{14}N_2O$, used in the form of its hydrochloride salt as a sedative and hypnotic

☆**meth·e·drine** (meth′ə drēn′) *n.* [< *Methedrine,* former trademark] methamphetamine hydrochloride used as a drug

me·theg·lin (mə theg′lin) *n.* [Welsh *meddyglyn* < *medd,* MEAD[1] + *llyn,* juice] an alcoholic liquor made of fermented honey, often containing a spice or medicinal substance: a kind of mead

met·he·mo·glo·bin (met hē′mō glō′bin, -mə-; -hem′ō-, -ə-) *n.* [MET(A)- + HEMOGLOBIN] a brownish, crystalline substance containing ferric iron, formed in the blood by the oxidation of hemoglobin, as by the action of certain drugs or in the decomposition of the blood, and no longer able to combine reversibly with oxygen

☆**me·the·na·mine** (mə thē′nə mēn′, -min) *n.* [< METH(YL) + -EN(E) + AMINE] HEXAMETHYLENETETRAMINE

meth·i·cil·lin (meth′i sil′in) *n.* [METH- + (PEN)ICILLIN] a derivative of penicillin formerly used esp. in treating staphylococcal infections resistant to penicillin

me·thinks (mē thiŋks′) *v.impersonal, pt.* **me·thought′** [ME *me thinketh* < OE *me thyncth* < *me,* me, to me + *thyncth,* it seems < *thyncan,* to seem: see THINK[2]] [Archaic] it seems to me

me·thi·o·nine (mə thī′ə nēn′, -nin) *n.* [ME(THYL) + THION(IC) + -INE[3]] an essential amino acid, $CH_3SCH_2CH_2CH(NH_2)COOH$, that contains sulfur, obtained from various proteins and used as a food supplement and in medicine

meth·o- (meth′ō, -ə) *combining form* methyl [*methamphetamine*]

meth·od (meth′əd) *n.* [Fr *méthode* < L *methodus* < Gr *methodos,* a going after, pursuit, system < *meta,* after (see META-) + *hodos,* a way (see -ODE[1])] **1** a way of doing something; procedure; process; esp., a regular, orderly, definite procedure or way of teaching, investigating, etc. **2** regularity and orderliness in action, thought, or expression; system in doing things or handling ideas **3** regular, orderly arrangement —*adj.* ☆[*often* **M-**] using or suggestive of THE METHOD [a *method* actor] —**the Method** ☆a realistic style of acting in which the actor strives for close personal identification with the role being played

me·thod·i·cal (mə thäd′i kəl) *adj.* [< LL *methodicus* < Gr *methodikos* + -AL] characterized by method; orderly; systematic: also **me·thod′ic** —**me·thod′i·cal·ly** *adv.* —**me·thod′i·cal·ness** *n.*

Meth·od·ism (meth′ə diz′əm) *n.* **1** the beliefs and practices of Methodists, emphasizing personal and social responsibility and John Wesley's ideal of Christian perfection: influenced by Arminianism **2** [**m-**] excessive adherence to systematic procedure

Meth·od·ist (-dist) *n.* **1** a member of any branch of a Protestant Christian denomination that developed from the evangelistic teachings and work of John and Charles Wesley, George Whitefield, and others in the early 18th cent.: so called from the methodical study and worship practiced by the founders in their "Holy Club" at Oxford University (1729) **2** [**m-**] [Rare] one who strictly adheres to method —*adj.* of or characteristic of the Methodists or Methodism: also **Meth′od·is′tic**

meth·od·ize (meth′ə dīz′) *vt.* **-ized′**, **-iz′ing** to make methodical; systematize —**meth′od·iz′er** *n.*

meth·od·ol·o·gy (meth′ə däl′ə jē) *n.* [ModL: see METHOD & -LOGY] **1** the science of method, or orderly arrangement; specif., the branch of logic concerned with the application of the principles of reasoning to scientific and philosophical inquiry **2** *pl.* **-gies** a system of methods, as in any particular science —**meth′od·o·log′i·cal** (-də läj′i kəl) *adj.* —**meth′od·o·log′i·cal·ly** *adv.* —**meth′od·ol′o·gist** *n.*

meth·o·trex·ate (meth′ō treks′āt′) *n.* [< METH(YL) + *-trex-* (< ?) + -ATE[2]] an orange-brown, crystalline powder, $C_{20}H_{22}N_8O_5$, that is a folic acid antagonist: used in medicine, esp. in treating leukemia, various tumors, psoriasis, and rheumatoid arthritis

me·thought (mē thôt′) *v.impersonal pt. of* METHINKS

meth·ox·ide (meth äks′īd′) ***n.*** ⟦METH(YL) + OXIDE⟧ METHYLATE

☆**meth·ox·y·chlor** (meth äks′i klôr′) ***n.*** ⟦METH(YL) + OXY-[1] + *(tri)chlor(omethane)*⟧ a white solid, $Cl_3CCH(C_6H_4OCH_3)_2$, used as an insecticide, esp. against mosquitoes and flies

meths (meths) ***n.*** [Brit. Informal] *short for* METHYLATED SPIRITS

Me·thu·se·lah (mə tho͞o′zə lə, -thyo͞o′-) ***n.*** ⟦Heb *methūshelaḥ,* lit., ? man of the dart, or ? man of Shelah (a Babylonian deity)⟧ **1** *Bible* one of the patriarchs, who lived 969 years: Gen. 5:27 **2** [*usually* **m-**] *Winemaking* a large wine bottle, esp. one for champagne, holding about 6 liters

meth·yl (meth′əl) ***n.*** ⟦Fr *méthyle,* back-form. < *méthylène:* see METHYLENE⟧ the monovalent hydrocarbon radical CH_3, normally existing only in combination, as in methanol —**me·thyl·ic** (me thil′ik) ***adj.***

methyl acetate a colorless, volatile, flammable liquid, $CH_3CO_2CH_3$, used as a solvent, paint remover, etc.

meth·yl·al (meth′ə lal′, meth′ə lal′) ***n.*** ⟦Fr *méthylal* < *méthyle,* methyl + *alcool,* ALCOHOL⟧ a colorless, volatile, flammable liquid, $CH_3OCH_2OCH_3$, that smells like chloroform: it is produced by the incomplete oxidation of methanol and is used as a solvent and in perfumes, organic synthesis, etc.

methyl alcohol METHANOL

meth·yl·a·mine (meth′əl ə mēn′, -əl am′ēn′) ***n.*** ⟦METHYL + AMINE⟧ a colorless, flammable gas, CH_3NH_2, that smells like ammonia and is usually prepared synthetically by heating methanol with ammonia under pressure in the presence of a catalyst: it is used in the manufacture of dyes, pharmaceuticals, insecticides, etc.

meth·yl·ate (meth′ə lāt′) ***n.*** a compound derived from methanol, in which the hydroxyl hydrogen is replaced by a metal —***vt.*** **-at′ed, -at′ing 1** to mix with methanol, often in order to make the resulting mixture undrinkable **2** to introduce a methyl group into (a compound) —**meth′yl·a′tion** ***n.*** —**meth′yl·a′tor** ***n.***

methylated spirits (*or* spirit) ethyl alcohol for general use, made unfit to drink by the addition of methanol

methyl benzene TOLUENE

methyl bromide a colorless, poisonous gas, CH_3Br, with an odor resembling chloroform, used as a refrigerant, fumigant, and in organic synthesis

methyl chloride a colorless, poisonous gas, CH_3Cl, which when compressed becomes a sweet, transparent liquid: it is used as a refrigerant and local anesthetic

meth·yl·ene (meth′ə lēn′) ***n.*** ⟦Fr *méthylène* < Gr *methy,* wine (see MEAD[1]) + *hylē,* wood⟧ the divalent hydrocarbon radical CH_2, normally existing only in combination

methylene blue a bluish-green aniline dye, $C_{16}H_{18}N_3ClS{\cdot}3H_2O$, used as a bacteriologic stain, an antidote in cyanide poisoning, etc.

methyl ethyl ketone a highly flammable liquid, $CH_3COCH_2CH_3$, used as a solvent; butanone

methyl violet GENTIAN VIOLET

met·i·cal (met′i käl′) ***n., pl.*** **met′i·cais′** (-kīsh′) ⟦Port < Ar *mithgal,* former Arab unit of currency once used there⟧ the basic monetary unit of Mozambique: see the table of monetary units in the Reference Supplement

me·tic·u·lous (mə tik′yo͞o ləs, -yə-) ***adj.*** ⟦L *meticulosus,* fearful < *metus,* fear⟧ extremely or excessively careful about details; scrupulous or finicky —*SYN.* CAREFUL —**me·tic′u·lous·ly** ***adv.*** —**me·tic′u·lous·ness** ***n.,*** **me·tic′u·los′i·ty** (-läs′i tē)

mé·tier (mā tyā′) ***n.*** ⟦Fr < OFr *mestier,* ult. < L *ministerium:* see MINISTRY⟧ **1** a trade, profession, or occupation; esp., the work that one is particularly suited for **2** one's area of expertise or strength; forte

mé·tis (mā tēs′, -tē′) ***n., pl.*** **-tis′** ⟦Fr < LL(Ec) *misticius,* of mixed race, born of parents of different nations: present sense in Fr infl. by Sp *mestizo:* see MESTIZO⟧ a person of mixed parentage; esp., in Canada, a person having one French Canadian parent and one American Indian parent

me·tol (mē′tôl′, -tōl′) ***n.*** ⟦< *Metol,* former trademark⟧ a white, soluble powder, $(HOC_6H_4NHCH_3)_2{\cdot}H_2SO_4$, used as a photographic developer

Me·ton·ic cycle (mə tän′ik) ⟦after *Meton,* Athenian astronomer (5th c. B.C.)⟧ a period of about 19 years (almost 235 lunar revolutions), in which the phases of the moon repeat on the same dates as in the previous period: used for determining the date of Easter

met·o·nym (met′ə nim′) ***n.*** ⟦back-form. < fol.⟧ a word or phrase used in metonymy, as a substitute for another

me·ton·y·my (mə tän′ə mē) ***n., pl.*** **-mies** ⟦LL *metonymia* < Gr *metōnymia* < *meta,* other (see META-) + *onoma, onyma,* NAME⟧ a figure of speech in which the name of one thing is used in place of that of another associated with or suggested by it (Ex.: "the White House" for "the President") —**met·o·nym·ic** (met′ə nim′ik) ***adj.,*** **met′o·nym′i·cal**

☆**me-too** (mē′to͞o′) ***adj.*** [Informal] designating or of policies or attitudes, esp. of a politician, adopted from a successful or powerful rival —**me′-too′ism′** ***n.***

met·o·pe (met′ə pē′, met′ōp) ***n.*** ⟦Gr *metopē* < *meta,* between (see META-) + *opē,* an opening, hole in frieze for beam, akin to *ōps,* EYE⟧ any of the square areas, plain or decorated, between triglyphs in a Doric frieze

me·top·ic (mi täp′ik) ***adj.*** ⟦< Gr *metōpon,* forehead (akin to prec.) + -IC⟧ of the forehead; frontal

met·o·pon hydrochloride (met′ə pän′) ⟦< *met(hyldihydr)o(mor)p(hin)on(e)*⟧ a narcotic drug, $C_{18}H_{21}O_3N{\cdot}HCl$, derived from morphine, but slightly more potent: used in medicine to relieve pain

metr- *combining form* METRO-[2]: used before a vowel

me·tral·gi·a (mi tral′jē ə) ***n.*** ⟦ModL < Gr *mētra,* uterus (see METRO-[2]) + -ALGIA⟧ pain in the uterus

☆**met·ra·zol** (me′trə zôl′, -zōl′) ***n.*** ⟦< *Metrazol,* former trademark⟧ PENTYLENETETRAZOL

me·tre (mēt′ər) ***n.*** *Brit. sp. of* METER[1]

met·ric (me′trik) ***adj.*** **1** METRICAL **2** ⟦Fr *métrique*⟧ *a)* of the meter (unit of linear measure) *b)* designating or of the system of measurement based on the meter and the gram: see METRIC SYSTEM —***n.*** a standard for measuring or evaluating something; basis for assessment [a new *metric* for judging success]

met·ri·cal (me′tri kəl) ***adj.*** ⟦L *metricus* < Gr *metrikos* (see METER[1] & -IC) + -AL⟧ **1** of or composed in meter or verse **2** of, involving, or used in measurement; metric —**met′ri·cal·ly** ***adv.***

met·ri·cate (me′tri kāt′) ***vt.*** **-cat′ed, -cat′ing** to change over to the metric system of weights and measures —**met′ri·ca′tion** ***n.***

metric hundredweight a unit of weight equal to 50 kilograms

met·ri·cize (me′tri sīz′) ***vt.*** **-cized′, -ciz′ing** METRICATE

metric mile *Track & Field* a measure of distance equal to 1,500 meters

met·rics (me′triks) ***n.*** the science or art of writing in meter

metric system any of various decimal systems of weights and measures; now, esp., the SI system, in which the centimeter, gram, and second or the meter, kilogram, and second are the basic units: see the table of weights and measures in the Reference Supplement

metric ton a unit of weight, equal to 1,000 kilograms (2,204.623 pounds avoirdupois or 1.1023 short ton or 0.9842 long ton)

met·rist (me′trist, mē′trist) ***n.*** ⟦ML *metrista*⟧ a person skilled in metrics

me·tri·tis (mi trīt′is) ***n.*** ⟦ModL < Gr *mētra,* uterus (see METRO-[2]) + -ITIS⟧ inflammation of the uterus

met·ro[1] (me′trō) ***adj.*** *short for* METROPOLITAN —***n., pl.*** **-ros** [*often* **M-**] a metropolitan government

met·ro[2] (me′trō) ***n., pl.*** **-ros** ⟦Fr *métro,* contr. < *chemin de fer métropolitain:* in England, taken as contr. for *Metropolitan District Railway,* in London⟧ [*often* **M-**] a SUBWAY (sense 2)

met·ro-[1] (me′trō, -trə) ⟦< Gr *metron,* MEASURE⟧ *combining form* measure [*metrology*]

met·ro-[2] (me′trō, -trə) ⟦< Gr *mētra,* uterus < *mētēr,* MOTHER[1]⟧ *combining form* uterus, womb [*metrorrhagia*]

me·trol·o·gy (mi träl′ə jē) ***n.*** ⟦METRO-[1] + -LOGY⟧ **1** the science of weights and measures **2** *pl.* **-gies** a system of weights and measures —**met·ro·log·i·cal** (met′rə läj′i kəl) ***adj.*** —**met′ro·log′i·cal·ly** ***adv.*** —**me·trol′o·gist** ***n.***

met·ro·ni·da·zole (me′trə nī′də zōl′) ***n.*** ⟦ME(THYL) + *-tron-* (< ? NITRO-) + (IM)IDAZOLE⟧ *Med.* a synthetic drug, $C_6H_9N_3O_3$, used to treat bacterial or protozoan infections, esp. amebiasis and trichomoniasis

met·ro·nome (me′trə nōm′) ***n.*** ⟦< METRO-[1] + Gr *nomos,* law: see -NOMY⟧ **1** a clockwork device with an inverted pendulum that beats time at a rate determined by the position of a sliding weight on the pendulum: it is used esp. to help a person maintain regular tempo in practicing on the piano, etc. **2** an electrical device that produces an intermittent sound or flashing light, for similar use —**met′ro·nom′ic** (-näm′ik) ***adj.***

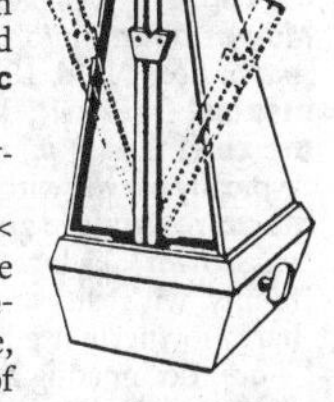
metronome

me·tro·nym·ic (mē′trə nim′ik, me′trə-) ***adj., n.*** MATRONYMIC

me·trop·o·lis (mə träp′ə lis) ***n.*** ⟦LL < Gr *mētropolis* < *mētēr,* MOTHER[1] + *polis,* a state, city: see POLICE⟧ **1** the main city, often the capital, of a country, state, or region **2** any large city or center of population, culture, etc. **3** in ancient Greece, the mother city or state of a colony

met·ro·pol·i·tan (me′trə päl′i tən) ***adj.*** ⟦LL *metropolitanus*⟧ **1** of or constituting a METROPOLIS (senses 1 & 2) **2** designating or of a METROPOLITAN (***n.*** 2) ☆**3** designating or of a population area consisting of a central city and smaller surrounding communities **4** designating or of a mother country as distinguished from a colony, territory, etc. —***n.*** **1** a person who lives in and knows a METROPOLIS (senses 1 & 2) or one who has the characteristic attitudes and manners of such a person **2** ⟦LL(Ec) *Metropolitanus*⟧ *a)* an archbishop having authority over the bishops of a church province *b) Eastern Ch.* a bishop ranking just below a patriarch **3** in ancient Greece, a citizen of a METROPOLIS (sense 3)

met·ro·pol·i·tan·ize (-īz′) ***vt.*** **-ized′, -iz′ing** to cause to be metropolitan or have a metropolitan character —**met′ro·pol′i·tan·ism′** ***n.*** —**met′ro·pol′i·tan·i·za′tion** ***n.***

me·tror·rha·gi·a (mē′trə rā′jē ə, me′trə-) ***n.*** ⟦ModL: see METRO-[2] & -RRHAGIA⟧ nonmenstrual bleeding from the uterus

met·ro·sex·u·al (me′trō sek′sho͞o əl) ***n.*** ⟦METRO[1] + *-sexual,* as in *homosexual, heterosexual,* etc.⟧ [Informal] a fashionable, typically urban, heterosexual man interested in his personal appearance to a degree traditionally associated with women or homosexual men

-me·try (mə trē) ⟦Gr *-metria* < *metron,* MEASURE⟧ *combining form* the process, art, or science of measuring [*bathymetry, psychometry*]

Met·ter·nich (met′ər nik), Prince **(Klemens Wenzel Nepomuk Lothar) von** 1773-1859; Austrian statesman & diplomat

met·tle (met′'l) ***n.*** ⟦var. of METAL, used fig.⟧ quality of character or temperament; esp., high quality of character; spirit; courage; ardor —**on one's mettle** roused or prepared to do one's best

met·tle·some (met′'l səm) ***adj.*** full of mettle; spirited; ardent, brave, etc.: also **met′tled**

Metz (mets) city in NE France, on the Moselle River

meu·nière (mə nyer′) ***adj.*** ⟦Fr *(à la) meunière,* (in the style of) a miller's wife, fem. of *meunier,* a miller⟧ designating fish prepared by being rolled in flour, etc., fried in butter, and sprinkled with lemon juice and chopped parsley

Meur·sault (mər sō′) ***n.*** a dry white wine from the commune of Meursault in Burgundy

Meuse (myo͞oz; *Fr* möz) river flowing from NE France, through Belgium & the Netherlands, into the North Sea: *c.* 575 mi (925 km): Du. name MAAS

MeV or **Mev** *abbrev.* one million (10^6) electron volts

mew¹ (myo͞o) ***n.*** ⟦ME *mewe* < OFr *mue* < *muer,* to change, molt < L *mutare,* to change: see MUTATE⟧ **1** a cage, as for hawks while molting **2** a secret place or den **3** [Obs.] a place of confinement See also MEWS —***vt.*** **1** ⟦< the ***n.***⟧ to confine in or as in a cage; shut up or conceal: often with *up* **2** ⟦ME *mewen* < OFr *muer*⟧ [Archaic] to shed or change (feathers); molt —***vi.*** [Archaic] to molt

mew² (myo͞o) ***n.*** ⟦echoic⟧ the characteristic vocal sound made by a cat —***vi.*** to make this sound

mew³ (myo͞o) ***n.*** ⟦ME *mewe* < OE *mæw,* akin to Ger *möwe* (< LowG): echoic of its cry, as in IE echoic base **mu-* > MOPE⟧ a gull; esp., the common gull (*Larus canus*) of Eurasia and NW North America

mewl (myo͞ol) ***vi.*** ⟦freq. of MEW²⟧ to cry weakly, like a baby; whimper or whine —**mewl′er** ***n.***

mews (myo͞oz) ***pl.n.*** ⟦after *the Mews,* the royal stables in London, built on the site where royal hawks were *mewed:* see MEW¹⟧ [*usually with sing. v.*] [Chiefly Brit.] *a)* stables or carriage houses, now often converted into dwellings, grouped around a court or along an alley *b)* such an alley

Mex *abbrev.* **1** Mexican **2** Mexico

Mex·i·ca·li (mek′si kä′lē) city in NW Mexico, on the U.S. border: capital of Baja California

Mex·i·can (mek′si kən) ***adj.*** of Mexico or its people, language, or culture —***n.*** **1** a person born or living in Mexico **2** [Rare] NAHUATL (sense 2)

☆**Mexican bean beetle** a spotted ladybug beetle (*Epilachna varivestis*) that eats the leaves and pods of bean plants

Mexican hairless any of a breed of small, reddish-gray dog native to Mexico, having no hair except for a tuft on the top of the head

☆**Mexican standoff** a general stalemate, often with the threat of violent confrontation

Mexican War a war between the U.S. and Mexico (1846-48)

Mex·i·co (mek′si kō′) ⟦< Sp *Méjico* < Nahuatl *Mexìtli,* name of the war god⟧ **1** country in North America, south of the U.S.: 761,606 sq mi (1,972,550 sq km); cap. Mexico City **2** state of SC Mexico: 8,286 sq mi (21,461 sq km); cap. Toluca **3 Gulf of** arm of the Atlantic, east of Mexico & south of the U.S.: 582,100 sq mi (1,507,632 sq km) Spanish name MÉJICO, Mexican sp. **Mé·xi·co** (me′hē kô′)

Mexico City capital of Mexico, in the SC part of Mexico

MexSp *abbrev.* Mexican Spanish

Mey·er·beer (mī′ər bir′, -ber′), **Gia·co·mo** (jä′kə mō′) (born *Jakob Liebmann Beer*) 1791-1864; Ger. operatic composer

☆**mez·cal** (mez käl′, -kal′) ***n.*** *var. of* MESCAL

me·ze (me zā′) ***n.,*** *pl.* **-zes′**, **-ze′** ⟦Turk⟧ any of various small appetizers typically served with an aperitif in Greek and Middle Eastern cuisine

me·ze·re·um (mə zir′ē əm) ***n.*** ⟦ModL < LME *mizerion* < ML *mezereon* < Ar *māzariyūn*⟧ **1** a low European shrub (*Daphne mezereum*) of the mezereum family, with clusters of pink or purple flowers in early spring **2** its dried bark, formerly used in liniments and in the treatment of some diseases —***adj.*** designating a family (Thymelaeaceae, order Myrtales) of dicotyledonous plants including daphne Also **me·ze′re·on** (-ən)

me·zu·za (mə zo͞o′zə, -zo͞o′-) ***n.,*** *pl.* **-zot** (-zōt) or **-zas** ⟦Heb *mezuza,* lit., doorpost⟧ *Judaism* a small piece of parchment inscribed with the Shema, from Deuteronomy (6:4-9 & 11:13-21), rolled and put into a case and attached to the doorpost of the home, as commanded in the Biblical passages: also sp. **me·zu′zah**

mez·za·nine (mez′ə nēn′, mez′ə nēn′) ***n.*** ⟦Fr < It *mezzanino* < *mezzano,* middle < L *medianus:* see MEDIAN⟧ **1** a low-ceilinged story between two main stories in a building, usually immediately above the ground floor and in the form of a balcony projecting only partly over the floor below it: also **mezzanine floor** **2** in some theaters, the first few rows of the balcony, separated from the others by an aisle

mez·zo¹ (met′sō, med′zō, mez′ō) *Musical Direction* ***adj.*** ⟦It < L *medius,* middle: see MID¹⟧ medium; moderate; half —***adv.*** moderately; somewhat

mez·zo² (met′sō, med′zō, mez′ō) ***n.,*** *pl.* **-zos** ⟦see prec.⟧ *short for:* **1** MEZZO-SOPRANO **2** MEZZOTINT

mez·zo-re·lie·vo (-ri lē′vō, -ril yev′ō) ***n.,*** *pl.* **-vos′** (-ri lē′vōz′, -ril yev′ōz′) ⟦It *mezzo rilievo:* see MEZZO¹ & RELIEF⟧ sculpture in relief, in which the figures project halfway from the background

mez·zo-so·pra·no (-sə pran′ō, -prä′nō) ***n.,*** *pl.* **-nos** or **-ni** (-prä′nē) ⟦It: see MEZZO¹ & SOPRANO⟧ **1** the range of a female voice between soprano and contralto **2** *a)* a voice or singer with such a range *b)* a part for such a voice —***adj.*** of, for, or having the range of a mezzo-soprano

mez·zo·tint (-tint′) ***n.*** ⟦It *mezzotinto:* see MEZZO¹ & TINT⟧ **1** a method of engraving on a copper or steel plate by scraping or polishing parts of a roughened surface to produce impressions of light and shade **2** an engraving or print so produced —***vt.*** to engrave by this method

mf¹ *abbrev.* **1** machine finish **2** medium frequency: also **MF**

mf² *abbrev.* ⟦It *mezzo forte*⟧ *Musical Direction* moderately loud(ly)

mF *abbrev.* millifarad(s)

MFA or **M.F.A.** *abbrev.* Master of Fine Arts

mfd *abbrev.* manufactured

mfg *abbrev.* manufacturing

MFH *abbrev.* Master of Foxhounds

MFN *abbrev.* MOST FAVORED NATION

mfr *abbrev.* **1** manufacture **2** manufacturer

MFr *abbrev.* Middle French

mg *abbrev.* milligram(s)

Mg *Chem. symbol for* magnesium

MG *abbrev.* **1** machine gun **2** Major General **3** *Football* middle guard: sometimes written **mg**

mgr *abbrev.* manager

Mgr *abbrev.* **1** manager **2** Monseigneur **3** Monsignor

MGr *abbrev.* Medieval (or Middle) Greek

mgt *abbrev.* management: also **mgmt**

mH or **mh** *abbrev.* millihenry; millihenrys

MH *abbrev.* **1** Medal of Honor **2** Most Honorable

MHD *abbrev.* magnetohydrodynamics

MHG *abbrev.* Middle High German

mho (mō) ***n.*** ⟦OHM spelled backward⟧ the former unit of electrical conductance, reciprocal of the ohm

MHR *abbrev.* Member of the House of Representatives

MHz *abbrev.* megahertz

mi¹ (mē) ***n.*** ⟦ML: see GAMUT⟧ *Music* a syllable representing the third tone of the diatonic scale: see SOLFEGGIO

mi² *abbrev.* **1** mile(s) **2** mill(s) **3** minute(s)

Mi *abbrev. Bible* **1** Malachi **2** Micah

MI *abbrev.* **1** Michigan **2** middle initial **3** Military Intelligence

MIA¹ (em′ī′ā′) ***n.,*** *pl.* **MIA's** ⟦see fol.⟧ a person in the armed forces who is lost during combat and who cannot be accounted for as a known casualty

MIA² *abbrev. Mil.* missing in action

Mi·am·i¹ (mī am′ē, -ə) ***n.*** ⟦Fr < Illinois *miamioua*⟧ **1** *pl.* **Mi·am′is** or **Mi·am′i** a member of a North American Indian people formerly of Indiana and nearby areas, that emigrated in the 19th cent. to Oklahoma **2** the Algonquian language of this people

Mi·am·i² (mī am′ē, -ə) ⟦< Sp *Mayaimi,* name for Lake Okeechobee, infl. by name of the Miami Indian people⟧ city on the SE coast of Fla. —**Mi·am′i·an** ***n.***

Miami Beach resort city in SE Fla., on an island opposite Miami

mi·aow or **mi·aou** (mē ou′, myou) ***n., vi.*** *alt. sp. of* MEOW

mi·as·ma (mī az′mə, mē-) ***n.,*** *pl.* **-mas** or **-ma·ta** (-mə tə) ⟦ModL < Gr, pollution < *miainein,* to pollute < IE base **mai-* > OE *mal,* a spot⟧ **1** a vapor rising as from marshes or decomposing animal or vegetable matter: formerly supposed to poison and infect the air, causing malaria, etc. **2** an unwholesome or befogging atmosphere, influence, etc. —**mi·as′mal** ***adj.,*** **mi′as·mat′ic** (-mat′ik), or **mi·as′mic**

mic (mīk) ***n.*** *short for* MICROPHONE

Mic *abbrev. Bible* Micah

mi·ca (mī′kə) ***n.*** ⟦ModL < L, a crumb, grain (< IE **(s)meik-,* var. of base **(s)mei-,* to smear, rub over > OE *smitte,* a smudge): sense infl. by *micare,* to shine, glitter < IE **meik-,* to flicker, blink⟧ any of a group of minerals that are complex silicates that crystallize in thin, somewhat flexible, translucent or colored, easily separated layers, including muscovite, biotite, and lepidolite: mica is resistant to heat and electricity —**mi·ca′ceous** (-kā′shəs) ***adj.***

Mi·cah (mī′kə) ***n.*** ⟦Heb *mīkhā(yah),* lit., who is like (God)?⟧ *Bible* **1** a Hebrew prophet of the 8th cent. B.C. **2** the book of his prophecies: abbrev. *Mic* or *Mi*

mice (mīs) ***n.*** *pl. of* MOUSE

mi·celle (mī sel′, mi-) ***n.*** ⟦ModL *micella,* dim. < L *mica,* a grain, crumb: see MICA⟧ **1** *Biol.* a submicroscopic structural unit composed of a group of molecules, as in living protoplasm, starch grains, etc. **2** *Chem.* a structural unit, as *a)* a colloidal ion composed of an oriented arrangement of molecules *b)* an aggregate of polymerized molecules joined together Also **mi·cel′la** (-sel′ə) *pl.* **-lae** (-ē) —**mi·cel′lar** ***adj.***

Mich *abbrev.* **1** Michaelmas **2** Michigan

Mi·chael (mī′kəl) ***n.*** ⟦LL(Ec) < Gr (LXX & N.T.) *Michaēl* < Heb *mīkhā′ēl,* lit., who is like God?⟧ **1** a masculine name: dim. *Mike, Mickey;* equiv. Fr. *Michel,* It. *Michele,* Sp. *Miguel;* fem. *Michelle, Michele* **2** *Bible* one of the archangels

Mich·ael·mas (mik′əl məs) ***n.*** ⟦ME *Mighelmesse* < OE *Michaeles mæsse:* see prec. & MASS¹⟧ the feast of the archangel Michael, September 29

Michaelmas daisy [Chiefly Brit.] any of various asters, wild or cultivated, that bloom in the fall

miche (mich) ***vi.*** **miched**, **mich′ing** ⟦ME *mychen* < OFr *muchier* < Gaul **mukyare,* to hide, akin to MIr *muchaim,* I conceal < IE base **meug-,* to spy upon⟧ [Brit. Dial.] to skulk

Mi·chel·an·ge·lo (mī′kəl an′jə lō′, mik′əl-) (full name *Michelangelo Buonarroti*) 1475-1564; It. sculptor, painter, architect, & poet

Miche·let (mēsh le′), **Jules** (zhül) 1798-1874; Fr. historian

Mi·chelle or **Mi·chele** (mi shel′, mē-) ***n.*** ⟦Fr *Michèle,* fem. of *Michel,* Michael⟧ a feminine name: see MICHAEL

Mi·chel·son (mī′kəl sən), **Albert Abraham** 1852-1931; U.S. physicist, born in Germany

Mich·i·gan (mish′i gən) ⟦< Fr < Algonquian, lit., great water⟧ **1** Midwestern state of the U.S.: admitted 1837; 56,804 sq mi (147,121 sq km); cap.

Lansing: abbrev. *MI* or *Mich* **2 Lake** one of the Great Lakes, between Mich. & Wis.: 22,300 sq mi (57,757 sq km)

Mich·i·gan·der (-gan′dər) ***n.*** a person born or living in Michigan

Mich·i·ga·ni·an (mish′i gā′nē ən) ***adj.*** of the state of Michigan: usually used in the predicate —***n.*** a person born or living in Michigan Also **Mich′i·gan·ite′**

Mi·cho·a·cán (mē′chō ä kän′) state of WC Mexico: 23,114 sq mi (59,865 sq km); cap. Morelia

mick (mik) ***n.*** ⟦< *Mick,* nickname: see fol.⟧ [Slang] a person of Irish descent: often a derogatory and offensive term

mick·ey (mik′ē) ***n.*** ⟦after *Mickey* (nickname for MICHAEL, taken as typical Irish name), slang for Irishman⟧ [Brit. Slang] spirit; pride; brag: chiefly in the fol. phrases —**take the mickey** to make fun; mock —**take the mickey out of** to deflate (a person)

☆**Mick·ey Finn** ⟦< ?⟧ [*also* **m- f-**] [Slang] a drink, as of liquor, to which something has been added so as to render the unsuspecting drinker stupefied, unconscious, etc.: often shortened to **Mick′ey** or **mick′ey** ***n.,*** *pl.* **-eys**

☆**Mickey Mouse** ⟦< a trademark assoc. with a cartoon character created by Walt DISNEY⟧ [*also* **m- m-**] [Slang] oversimplified, shallow, insignificant, etc. [*a Mickey Mouse* college course]

Mic·kie·wicz (mits kye′vich), **A·dam** (ä′däm) 1798-1855; Pol. poet

mick·le (mik′əl) ***adj., adv., n.*** ⟦ME (Northern) *mikel* < OE *micel,* infl. by ON *mikell:* for IE base see MUCH⟧ [Now Chiefly Scot.] much

Mic·mac (mik′mak′) ***n.*** ⟦Fr < Micmac *miikəmax,* pl. (sing. *miikəmaw*), a self-designation⟧ **1** *pl.* **-macs′** or **-mac′** a member of a North American Indian people of the Maritime Provinces of Canada **2** the Algonquian language of this people

mi·cra (mī′krə) ***n.*** *alt. pl. of* MICRON

mi·cro (mī′krō) ***adj.*** **1** small, very small, or on a small scale [macro and *micro* issues] **2** *short for* MICROECONOMIC —***n.,*** *pl.* **-cros 1** something very small **2** [Informal] *a)* a microwave oven *b)* a microcomputer *c)* a microprocessor

mi·cro- (mī′krō, -krə) ⟦Gr *mikro-* < *mikros,* small < IE *(*s*)*meik-*: see MICA⟧ *combining form* **1** *a)* little, small, minute [*microcosm*] *b)* exceptionally little, abnormally small [*microcephaly*] **2** enlarging or amplifying [*microscope, microphone*] **3** involving microscopes, microscopic [*micrography*] **4** one millionth part of; the factor 10^{-6}: symbol μ: abbrev. *mc* [*microsecond*] Also, before a vowel, **micr-**

mi·cro·a·nal·y·sis (mī′krō ə nal′ə sis) ***n.,*** *pl.* **-ses′** (-sēz′) chemical analysis of very small amounts of matter, typically by means of special equipment, as a microscope —**mi′cro·an′a·lyst** (-an′əl ist) ***n.***

mi·cro·a·nat·o·my (mī′krō ə nat′ə mē) ***n.*** HISTOLOGY —**mi′cro·an′a·tom′i·cal** (-an′ə täm′i kəl) ***adj.***

mi·cro·ar·ray (mī′krō ə rā′) ***n.*** a microscopic array of genetic material placed on a glass slide, a microchip, etc. for analysis, as in genetic research or medicine, or for evaluation, as of the biological effects of a drug

mi·cro·bal·ance (mī′krō bal′əns) ***n.*** an extremely sensitive balance, used to weigh matter that is lighter than one tenth of a gram

mi·cro·bar (mī′krō bär′) ***n.*** ⟦MICRO- + BAR[2]⟧ one millionth of a bar, or one dyne per square centimeter: symbol, μb

mi·cro·bar·o·graph (mī′krō bar′ə graf′) ***n.*** a barograph for recording very small changes in atmospheric pressure

mi·crobe (mī′krōb′) ***n.*** ⟦Fr < Gr *mikro-* (see MICRO-) + *bios,* life (see BIO-)⟧ a microscopic organism; esp., any of the bacteria that cause disease; germ —**mi·cro′bi·al** ***adj.,*** **mi·cro′bic**

mi·cro·bi·ol·o·gy (mī′krō bī äl′ə jē) ***n.*** the branch of biology that deals with microorganisms —**mi′cro·bi′o·log′i·cal** (-ə läj′i kəl) ***adj.,*** **mi′cro·bi′o·log′ic** —**mi′cro·bi·ol′o·gist** ***n.***

☆**mi·cro·brew·er·y** (-bro͞o′ər ē) ***n.,*** *pl.* **-er·ies** a small brewery producing beer or ale of high quality, distinctive flavor, etc., usually for local consumption and distribution

mi·cro·burst (mī′krō burst′) ***n.*** a type of localized downdraft, often associated with thunderstorms, producing very strong, short-lived wind shears

mi·cro·cap·sule (mī′krō kap′səl) ***n.*** a tiny capsule designed to hold a minute amount of a medicine, chemical, etc. that is released when the capsule is melted, dissolved, or broken

mi·cro·ceph·a·ly (mī′krō sef′ə lē) ***n.*** ⟦MICRO- + -CEPHALY⟧ a condition in which the head or cranial capacity is abnormally small: opposed to MACROCEPHALY —**mi′cro·ceph′a·lous** ***adj.,*** **mi′cro·ce·phal′ic** (-sə fal′ik)

mi·cro·chem·is·try (-kem′is trē) ***n.*** the chemistry of microscopic or submicroscopic quantities or objects

☆**mi·cro·chip** (mī′krō chip′) ***n.*** *Electronics* CHIP (***n.*** 8)

mi·cro·cir·cuit (mī′krō sur′kit) ***n.*** ⟦MICRO- + CIRCUIT⟧ a highly miniaturized integrated circuit, used in computers and other electronic devices —**mi′cro·cir′cuit·ry** ***n.***

mi·cro·cli·mate (-klī′mit) ***n.*** ⟦MICRO- + CLIMATE⟧ the climate of a small, distinct area, as a forest, or of a confined space, as a building

mi·cro·cli·ma·tol·o·gy (mī′krō klī′mə täl′ə jē) ***n.*** the study of climate and its characteristics in a small area —**mi′cro·cli′ma·tol′o·gist** ***n.***

mi·cro·cline (mī′krō klīn′) ***n.*** ⟦Ger *mikroklin* (< Gr *mikros,* small + *klinein,* to incline: see LEAN[1]): its cleavage angle differs slightly from 90°⟧ a triclinic feldspar, $KAlSi_3O_8$, that is dimorphic with orthoclase; potassium aluminum silicate

mi·cro·coc·cus (mī′krō käk′əs) ***n.,*** *pl.* **-coc′ci′** (-käk′sī′) ⟦ModL: see MICRO- & -COCCUS⟧ any of a genus (*Micrococcus*) of spherical or egg-shaped bacteria that occur in irregular masses or plates and feed on dead or living matter

mi·cro·code (mī′krō kōd′) ***n.*** permanent basic commands built into a computer that enable its electronic circuits to perform operations

mi·cro·com·put·er (mī′krō kəm pyo͞ot′ər) ***n.*** a PERSONAL COMPUTER; now, esp., a type of early desktop computer equipped with a cathode-ray tube monitor

mi·cro·cop·y (mī′krō käp′ē) ***n.,*** *pl.* **-cop′ies** ⟦MICRO- + COPY⟧ a copy in very greatly reduced size, of printed or graphic matter, produced as by microfilming

mi·cro·cosm (mī′krō kä′zəm) ***n.*** ⟦ME *microcosme* < ML *microcosmus* < LGr *mikros kosmos,* little world: see MICRO- & COSMOS⟧ **1** a little world; miniature universe; specif., *a)* [Historical] the concept that a human being is an epitome of the world *b)* a community regarded as a miniature or epitome of the world *c)* anything regarded as epitomizing, encapsulating, or representing in miniature **2** *Ecol.* a small ecosystem, as a pond —**mi′cro·cos′mic** ***adj.*** —**mi′cro·cos′mi·cal·ly** ***adv.***

microcosmic salt a white, crystalline salt, $Na(NH_4)HPO_4·4H_2O$, used as a reagent in blowpipe analysis because it forms characteristically colored compounds when fused with salts and oxides of metals

mi·cro·crys·tal·line (mī′krō kris′tə lin) ***adj.*** having a crystalline structure that can be seen only with a microscope

mi·cro·cyte (mī′krō sīt′) ***n.*** ⟦MICRO- + -CYTE⟧ an abnormally small red blood corpuscle, occurring esp. in certain types of anemia —**mi′cro·cyt′ic** (-sit′ik) ***adj.***

mi·cro·dont (-dänt′) ***adj.*** ⟦MICR(O)- + -ODONT⟧ having very small teeth: also **mi′cro·dont′ous** —**mi′cro·dont′ism′** ***n.***

mi·cro·dot (-dät′) ***n.*** ⟦MICRO- + DOT[1]⟧ a microcopy of pinhead size, used in espionage, etc.

mi·cro·ec·o·nom·ics (mī′krō ek′ə näm′iks, -ē′kə-) ***n.*** a branch of economics dealing with certain specific factors affecting an economy, as the behavior of individual consumers, the marketing of particular products, etc.: cf. MACROECONOMICS —**mi′cro·ec′o·nom′ic** ***adj.***

mi·cro·e·lec·tron·ics (mī′krō ē′lek trän′iks) ***n.*** ⟦MICRO- + ELECTRONICS⟧ the science dealing with the theory, design, and applications of microcircuits —**mi′cro·e′lec·tron′ic** ***adj.***

☆**mi·cro·en·cap·su·la·tion** (-en kap′sə lā′shən) ***n.*** a process in which tiny particles or droplets of a substance are separately encapsulated for controlled release: used to prolong the action of drugs, solidify liquids, etc. —**mi′cro·en·cap′su·late′** ***vt.*** **-lat′ed, -lat′ing**

mi·cro·en·vi·ron·ment (mī′krō en vī′rən mənt) ***n.*** the environmental conditions of a relatively small, localized area, esp. of a microhabitat

mi·cro·ev·o·lu·tion (-ev′ə lo͞o′shən) ***n.*** ⟦MICRO- + EVOLUTION⟧ small-scale hereditary changes in organisms through mutations and recombinations, resulting in the formation of slightly differing new varieties

mi·cro·far·ad (mī′krō far′ad′, -əd) ***n.*** one millionth of a farad: symbol, μF

mi·cro·fau·na (mī′krō fô′nə) ***n.,*** *pl.* **-nas, -nae** (-nē) **1** minute, esp. microscopic, fauna **2** the animals of a given microhabitat —**mi′cro·fau′nal** ***adj.***

mi·cro·fi·ber (mī′krō fī′bər) ***n.*** **1** a fine polyester fiber of less than one denier **2** a lightweight, waterproof fabric made from this fiber, with the look and feel of silk

mi·cro·fiche (mī′krō fēsh′) ***n.,*** *pl.* **-fich′es** or **-fiche′** ⟦Fr < *micro-,* MICRO- + *fiche,* a small card, mark on a card, orig. a pin, peg < OFr *ficher,* to attach: see FICHU⟧ a small sheet of microfilm on which a number of pages of microcopy can be recorded

mi·cro·film (-film′) ***n.*** **1** film on which documents, printed pages, etc. are photographed in a reduced size for convenience in storage and transportation: enlarged prints can be made from such film, or the film can be viewed by projection **2** reproduction on microfilm — ***vt., vi.*** to photograph on microfilm

mi·cro·fi·nance (mī′krō fī′nans′, -fə nans′) ***n.*** a system that provides financial services and loans to people with very low incomes, as in undeveloped countries

mi·cro·flo·ra (mī′krō flôr′ə) ***n.*** **-ras** or **-rae** (-ē) **1** minute, esp. microscopic, flora **2** the plants of a given microhabitat —**mi′cro·flo′ral** ***adj.***

mi·cro·form (mī′krō fôrm′) ***n.*** any form of photographically reduced document, print, etc., as microfilm or microfiche

mi·cro·fos·sil (mī′krō fäs′əl) ***n.*** a fossilized microorganism or other microscopic fossil

mi·cro·ga·mete (mī′krō gam′ēt′, -ga mēt′) ***n.*** the smaller, usually the male, of a pair of conjugating gametes in heterogamous sexual reproduction

mi·cro·gram (mī′krō gram′) ***n.*** **1** one millionth of a gram: abbrev. *mcg* **2** MICROGRAPH (sense 2)

mi·cro·graph (-graf′) ***n.*** ⟦MICRO- + -GRAPH⟧ **1** an apparatus for doing extremely small writing, drawing, or engraving **2** a photograph or drawing of an object as seen through a microscope **3** an apparatus by which, through the movements of a diaphragm, very slight movements can be recorded in magnified visual form

mi·cro·graph·ics (-graf′iks) ***n.*** the creation, use, and storage of microform systems

mi·crog·ra·phy (mī kräg′rə fē) ***n.*** ⟦MICRO- + -GRAPHY⟧ **1** the description, depiction, or study of microscopic objects **2** the art or practice of writing in tiny characters

mi·cro·grav·i·ty (mī′krō grav′i tē) ***n.*** a nearly weightless condition, as that inside an orbiting spacecraft

☆**mi·cro·groove** (mī′krō gro͞ov′) ***n.*** the very narrow groove in an LP phonograph record

mi·cro·hab·i·tat (mī′krō hab′i tat′) *n.* a small, localized habitat within a larger ecosystem, as a decomposing log in a forest, having conditions that sustain a limited range of animals and plants

mi·cro·in·jec·tion (mī′krō in jek′shən) *n.* an injection made by means of a very thin needle and with the aid of a microscope, as, for example, to insert genetic material into a cell —**mi′cro·in·ject′** *vt.*

mi·cro·in·struc·tion (mī′krō in struk′shən) *n. Comput.* an elementary instruction in microcode

mi·cro·lith (-lith′) *n.* ⟦MICRO- + -LITH⟧ any of various tiny flint tools flaked in two directions and set in bone or wood: characteristic of the Mesolithic period

mi·cro·man·age (mī′krō man′ij) *vt.* **-aged**, **-ag·ing** to manage or regulate very closely, often in a manner regarded as meddlesome or counterproductive —**mi′cro·man′age·ment** *n.*

mi·cro·mere (mī′krō mir′) *n.* ⟦MICRO- + -MERE⟧ any of certain small cells produced by unequal cell division during early embryologic development in many animals, as in mollusks, flatworms, etc.

mi·cro·me·te·or·ite (mī′krō mēt′ē ər īt′) *n.* a very small meteorite, esp. one that drifts through the earth's atmosphere to the ground without becoming incandescent

mi·cro·me·te·or·oid (-mēt′ē ər oid′) *n.* ⟦MICRO- + METEOROID⟧ an extremely small meteoroid

mi·cro·me·te·or·ol·o·gy (-mēt′ē ər äl′ə jē) *n.* ⟦MICRO- + METEOROLOGY⟧ the branch of meteorology that deals with the small-scale processes, physical conditions, and interactions of the lowest part of the atmosphere, esp. in the first few hundred feet above the earth's surface

mi·crom·e·ter[1] (mī kräm′ət ər) *n.* ⟦Fr *micromètre:* see MICRO- & -METER⟧ **1** an instrument for measuring very small distances, angles, diameters, etc., used on a telescope or microscope **2** MICROMETER CALIPER

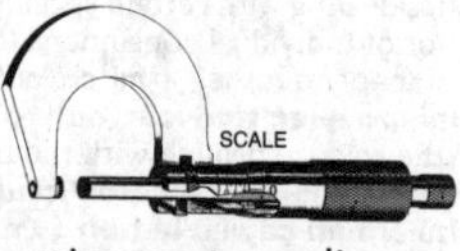

micrometer caliper

mi·cro·me·ter[2] (mī′krō mēt′ər) *n.* ⟦MICRO- (sense 4) + METER[1] (*n.* 3)⟧ MICRON: Brit. sp. **mi′cro·me′tre**

mi·crom·e·ter caliper (*or* **calipers**) (mī kräm′ət ər) calipers with a micrometer screw, for extremely accurate measurement

mi·crom·e·ter screw (mī kräm′ət ər) a finely threaded screw of definite pitch, with a head graduated to show how much the screw has been moved in or out: used in micrometers, etc. to give fine measurements, sometimes to .0001 of an inch

mi·crom·e·try (mī kräm′ə trē) *n.* measurement with micrometers

mi·cro·mi·cro- (mī′krō mī′krō) *combining form* PICO-

mi·cro·mil·li- (-mil′i, -ə) *combining form* NANO-

mi·cro·min·i·a·ture (-min′ē ə chər, -min′i chər) *adj.* of or using extremely small electronic parts, circuits, etc.

mi·cro·min·i·a·tur·ize (-chər īz′) *vt.* **-ized′**, **-iz′ing** to provide with extremely small electronic equipment —**mi′cro·min′i·a·tur·i·za′tion** *n.*

mi·cron (mī′krän′) *n., pl.* **-crons′** or **-cra** (-krə) ⟦ModL < Gr *mikron,* neut. of *mikros,* small, minute: see MICA⟧ a unit of linear measure equal to one millionth of a meter, or one thousandth of a millimeter; micrometer: symbol, µm

Mi·cro·ne·sia (mī′krə nē′zhə, -shə) ⟦ModL < MICRO- + Gr *nēsos,* island (see NATANT) + -IA⟧ country on a group of islands in the W Pacific: 271 sq mi (702 sq km); cap. Palikir

Mi·cro·ne·sian (-zhən, -shən) *adj.* of Micronesia or its peoples, languages, or cultures —*n.* **1** a person born or living in Micronesia **2** the group of Austronesian languages spoken in Micronesia

☆**mi·cron·ize** (mī′krə nīz′) *vt.* **-ized′**, **-iz′ing** ⟦MICRON + -IZE⟧ to reduce to particles of only a few microns in diameter

mi·cro·nu·cle·us (mī′krō no͞o′klē əs, -nyo͞o′-) *n.* the smaller of two types of nuclei present in the cells of ciliated protozoans, associated primarily with reproduction and genetics —**mi′cro·nu′cle·ar** *adj.*

mi·cro·nu·tri·ent (-no͞o′trē ənt, -nyo͞o′-) *n.* ⟦MICRO- + NUTRIENT⟧ any of the chemical elements, as iron, required in minute quantities for growth of an organism —**mi′cro·nu·tri′tion** *n.*

mi·cro·or·gan·ism (-ôr′gə niz′əm) *n.* any microscopic or ultramicroscopic animal, plant, bacterium, virus, etc.

mi·cro·pa·le·on·tol·o·gy (mī′krō pā′lē ən täl′ə jē) *n.* the branch of paleontology that deals with microscopic fossils —**mi′cro·pa′le·on′to·log′i·cal** (-än′tə läj′i kəl) *adj.,* **mi′cro·pa′le·on′to·log′ic** —**mi′cro·pa′le·on·tol′o·gist** *n.*

mi·cro·par·a·site (-par′ə sīt′) *n.* a parasitic microorganism —**mi′cro·par′a·sit′ic** (-sit′ik) *adj.*

mi·cro·phone (mī′krə fōn′) *n.* ⟦MICRO- + -PHONE⟧ an instrument containing a transducer that converts the mechanical energy of sound waves into an electric signal, used in telephony, radio, sound amplification, etc. —**mi·cro·phon·ic** (mī′krə fän′ik) *adj.*

mi·cro·phon·ics (mī′krō fän′iks, -krə-) *n.* ⟦prec. + -ICS⟧ noise in the output of various electronic devices, as a speaker, caused by mechanical vibration of some part

mi·cro·pho·to·graph (-fōt′ə graf′) *n.* **1** a very small photograph requiring enlargement to bring out the details **2** PHOTOMICROGRAPH **3** an enlarged photograph printed from a microfilm —**mi′cro·pho′to·graph′ic** *adj.* —**mi′cro·pho·tog′ra·phy** (-fə täg′rə fē) *n.*

mi·cro·phyte (mī′krō fīt′, -krə-) *n.* ⟦MICRO- + -PHYTE⟧ any microscopically small plant —**mi′cro·phyt′ic** (-fit′ik) *adj.*

mi·cro·print (-print′) *n.* a microphotograph of printed or written matter to be read by means of a magnifying projector or viewer

mi·cro·pro·cess·ing (mī′krō prä′ses′iŋ, -sə siŋ) *n.* the use of microprocessors or a microprocessor

mi·cro·pro·ces·sor (mī′krō prä′ses′ər, -sə sər) *n.* ⟦MICRO- + PROCESSOR⟧ a chip containing the logical elements for performing calculations, carrying out stored instructions, etc.: used as the central processing unit of a microcomputer

mi·cro·pro·gram (mī′krō prō′gram′) *n. Comput.* MICROCODE

mi·cro·pro·gram·ming (mī′krō prō′gram′iŋ, -grəm-) *n. Comput.* the programming of microcode

mi·cro·pub·lish·ing (-pub′lish iŋ) *n.* publication in microform

mi·cro·pyle (mī′krō pīl′) *n.* ⟦Fr < Gr *mikro-* (see MICRO-) + *pylē,* gate⟧ **1** *Bot. a)* a very small opening in the outer coats of an ovule, through which the pollen tube penetrates *b)* the corresponding opening in the developed seed **2** *Zool.* a very small opening in the membrane of an ovum of some animals, through which spermatozoa can enter —**mi′cro·py′lar** (-pī′lər) *adj.*

mi·cro·py·rom·e·ter (mī′krō pī räm′ət ər) *n.* ⟦MICRO- + PYROMETER⟧ an optical instrument for determining temperature, etc. of minute bodies giving off light or heat

mi·cro·ra·di·o·graph (-rā′dē ō graf′) *n.* ⟦MICRO- + RADIOGRAPH⟧ an X-ray photograph showing very small details —**mi′cro·ra′di·o·graph′ic** *adj.* —**mi′cro·ra′di·og′ra·phy** (-rā′dē äg′rə fē) *n.*

mi·cro·scope (mī′krə skōp′) *n.* ⟦ModL *microscopium:* see MICRO- & -SCOPE⟧ an instrument consisting essentially of a lens or combination of lenses, for making very small objects, as microorganisms, look larger so that they can be seen and studied: see also ELECTRON MICROSCOPE

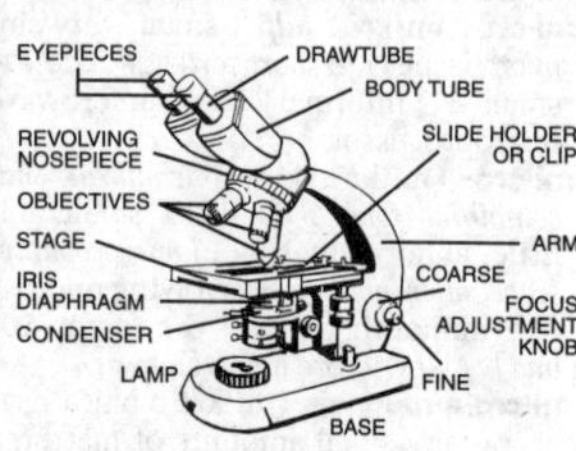

binocular microscope

mi·cro·scop·ic (mī′krə skäp′ik) *adj.* **1** so small as to be invisible or obscure except through a microscope; extremely small; minute **2** of, with, or as if with a microscope **3** like or suggestive of a microscope; searching; minutely observing Also **mi′cro·scop′i·cal** —**mi′cro·scop′i·cal·ly** *adv.*

Mi·cro·sco·pi·um (mī′krə skō′pē əm) *n.* ⟦ModL: see MICROSCOPE⟧ a S constellation between Capricornus and Indus

mi·cros·co·py (mī kräs′kə pē) *n.* the use of a microscope; investigation by means of a microscope —**mi·cros′co·pist** *n.*

mi·cro·sec·ond (mī′krō sek′ənd) *n.* ⟦MICRO- + SECOND[3]⟧ one millionth of a second: symbol, µs

mi·cro·seism (mī′krō sīz′əm) *n.* ⟦< MICRO- + Gr *seismos:* see SEISMIC⟧ a very slight tremor or quivering of the earth's crust that is not related to an earthquake, usually caused by an atmospheric disturbance —**mi′cro·seis′mic** (-sīz′mik, -sīs′mik) *adj.*

mi·cro·some (-sōm′) *n.* ⟦MICRO- + -SOME[3]⟧ any of a number of minute granules in the cytoplasm of an active cell, that are filled with enzymes and thought to be associated with protein synthesis —**mi′cro·so′mal** *adj.*

mi·cro·sphere (mī′krō sfir′) *n.* ⟦MICRO- + -SPHERE⟧ any of various minute globules, as the hollow particles used in making lighter plastics or a cell-like structure resembling a proteinoid

mi·cro·spo·ran·gi·um (mī′krō spō ran′jē əm) *n., pl.* **-gi·a** (-ə) ⟦ModL⟧ a sporangium containing microspores, as the pollen sac of the anther in seed plants

mi·cro·spore (mī′krō spôr′) *n.* a haploid spore, usually smaller than a megaspore of the same plant, which gives rise to a male gametophyte: found in all seed plants, where it is an immature pollen grain, and in many lower vascular plants —**mi′cro·spor′ic** *adj.*

mi·cro·spo·ro·phyll (mī′krō spôr′ə fil′) *n.* a sporophyll bearing only microsporangia

mi·cro·state (mī′krō stāt′) *n.* any very small nation

mi·cro·struc·ture (mī′krō struk′chər) *n.* the structure, as of a metal or alloy, seen under a microscope

mi·cro·sur·ger·y (-sur′jər ē) *n.* surgery performed while viewing through a microscope and using minute instruments or laser beams —**mi′cro·sur′gi·cal** *adj.*

mi·cro·tome (-tōm′) *n.* ⟦MICRO- + -TOME⟧ any of various precision instruments for cutting thin sections, as of organic tissue, for study under the microscope

mi·crot·o·my (mī krät′ə mē) *n.* the skill or work of using a microtome

mi·cro·tone (mī′krō tōn′) *n. Music* an interval smaller than a semitone —**mi′cro·ton′al** *adj.*

mi·cro·tu·bule (mī′krō to͞o′byo͞ol′) *n.* any of a number of small, hollow filaments, composed of long strands of tubulins, that are found in animal or plant cells and are associated esp. with cell structure and movement and with mitosis

mi·cro·vil·lus (mī′krō vil′əs) *n., pl.* **-li′** (-ī′) any of a number of tiny, finger-like structures projecting from the plasma membrane of certain specialized cells

mi·cro·wave (mī′krō wāv′) ***adj.*** **1** designating or of that part of the electromagnetic spectrum associated with the larger infrared waves and the shorter radio waves: used for radar, communications, etc. and generally regarded as from 300,000 to 300 megahertz **2** designating an oven that cooks quickly by causing microwaves to penetrate the food, generating internal heat **3** designed, packaged, etc. for cooking in a microwave oven [*microwave* cookware, *microwave* popcorn] —***vt.*** **-waved′**, **-wav′ing** to cook in a microwave oven —***n.*** **1** any electromagnetic wave of microwave frequency **2** a microwave oven —**mi′cro·wave′a·ble** ***adj.***, **mi′cro·wav′able**

mic·tu·rate (mik′tyoo rāt′, -tə-) ***vi.*** **-rat′ed**, **-rat′ing** ⟦see fol. & -ATE[1]⟧ to discharge urine from the body; urinate

mic·tu·ri·tion (mik′tyoo rish′ən, -tə-) ***n.*** ⟦< L *micturitus,* pp. of *micturire,* to desire to urinate < *mingere,* to urinate < *meiere,* to urinate < IE base **meiĝh-* > MASH⟧ the act of urinating

mid[1] (mid) ***adj.*** ⟦ME < OE *midd-,* akin to Goth *midjis,* ON *mithr* < IE **medhjo-* (> L *medius,* Gr *mesos*) < base **me-,* between⟧ **1** MIDDLE (senses 1 & 2) **2** *Phonet.* articulated with the tongue in a position approximately halfway between high and low: said of certain vowels, as (e) in *set* —***n.*** [Archaic] the middle

mid[2] (mid) ***prep.*** [Old Poet.] *short for* amid: also **'mid**

mid[3] *abbrev.* middle

Mid *abbrev.* Midshipman

mid- (mid) *combining form* middle or middle part of [*midbrain, mid-*June]

mid·af·ter·noon prayer (mid′af tər no͞on′) [*often* **M- P-**] *R.C.Ch.* the fifth of the seven canonical hours; none

mid·air (-er′) ***n.*** any area or point in space not in contact with the ground or some other surface [suspended in *midair*] — ***adj., adv.*** above the ground, in otherwise unoccupied space [two helicopters in a *midair* collision]

Mi·das (mī′dəs) ***n.*** *Gr. Myth.* a king of Phrygia granted the power of turning everything that he touches into gold

Midas touch ⟦after prec.⟧ the seeming ability of certain persons to succeed in every financial undertaking

mid-At·lan·tic (mid′at lan′tik) ***adj.*** characterized by a combination of both British and American elements, influences, etc. [*mid-Atlantic* speech patterns]

mid·brain (mid′brān′) ***n.*** **1** the middle part of the three primary divisions of the brain of a vertebrate embryo **2** the part of the fully developed brain evolved from this; mesencephalon

mid·course (mid′kôrs′) ***adj.*** happening during the middle phase of a flight, journey, or course of action

mid·day (mid′dā′) ***n.*** ⟦ME *middai* < OE *middæg*⟧ the middle of the day; noon —***adj.*** of or at midday

midday prayer [*often* **M- P-**] *R.C.Ch.* the fourth of the seven canonical hours; sext

mid·den (mid′'n) ***n.*** ⟦ME *midding* < Scand, as in Dan *mögdynge* < *mög,* muck + *dynge,* a heap⟧ **1** [Brit.] a dunghill or refuse heap **2** *short for* KITCHEN MIDDEN

mid·dle (mid′'l) ***adj.*** ⟦ME *middel* < OE < *midd-,* MID[1] + *-el,* -LE⟧ **1** halfway between two given points, times, limits, etc.; also, equally distant from all sides or extremities; in the center; mean **2** in between; intermediate; intervening **3** *Gram. a)* denoting the voice or form of a verb whose subject is represented as acting reflexively, or upon itself: in Greek, such verbs are usually passive in grammatical form *b)* in or of the middle voice **4** [**M-**] *Geol.* designating a division of a period or a formation between those called *Upper* and *Lower* **5** [**M-**] designating a stage in language development intermediate between those called *Old* and *Modern* [*Middle* English] —***n.*** **1** a point or part halfway between extremes; middle point, part, time, etc. **2** something intermediate **3** the middle part of the body; waist **4** *Gram.* the middle voice **5** MIDDLE TERM — ***vt., vi.*** **-dled**, **-dling** to put in the middle

SYN.—**middle** refers to the point or part equally distant from either or all sides or extremities and may apply to space, time, etc. [the *middle* of the stage, the day, etc.]; **center** more precisely stresses the point equidistant from the bounding lines or surfaces of any plane or solid figure [the *center* of a circle, globe, etc.] and is sometimes used figuratively [the *center* of town, a trade *center*]; **midst**, usually used in prepositional phrases, denotes a middle part that is surrounded by persons or things or a middle point in some action [in the *midst* of a crowd, one's work, etc.]

middle age the time of life between youth and old age: now typically regarded as including ages from about 40 to about 65

mid·dle-aged (mid′'l ājd′) ***adj.*** in, of, characteristic of, or suitable for middle age

Middle Ages the period of European history between ancient and modern times, A.D. 476-*c.* 1450

Middle America[1] [*also* **m- A-**] ☆the American middle class, regarded as characterized generally by moderate or conservative political attitudes and conventional social values; sometimes, specif., the middle class of Midwestern America —**Middle American**

Middle America[2] the part of America that includes Mexico, Central America, &, sometimes, the West Indies —**Middle American**

Middle Atlantic States New York, New Jersey, Pennsylvania, Delaware, and Maryland

☆**mid·dle·break·er** (mid′'l brāk′ər) ***n.*** LISTER[1]: also ☆**mid′dle·bust′er** (-bus′ tər)

☆**mid·dle·brow** (-brou′) ***n.*** a person regarded as having conventional, middle-class tastes or opinions, and, often, as being pretentious or pseudo-intellectual —***adj.*** of or for a middlebrow

middle C **1** the musical note on the first ledger line below the treble staff and the first above the bass staff **2** the corresponding tone or key

middle class the social class between the aristocracy or very wealthy and the lower working class: people in business and the professions, highly skilled workers, well-to-do farmers, etc. are now generally included in the middle class: see also BOURGEOISIE

middle-class (-klas′) ***adj.*** of, having to do with, or characteristic of the middle class: often used variously to connote conventional, smug, materialistic, etc. attitudes

middle distance **1** the space between the foreground and the background in a picture, view, etc. **2** *Track & Field* a footrace or footrace distance of moderate length, including 800 meters, 1,500 meters, a half mile, or a mile —**mid′dle-dis′tance** ***adj.***

middle ear the part of the ear including the tympanic membrane and the adjacent cavity containing the three small bones (hammer, anvil, and stirrup) that transmit the vibrations of the tympanic membrane to the inner ear

Middle East **1** [Old-fashioned] those regions between the Far East & the Near East: rarely used in this sense since WWII **2** area from Afghanistan to Libya, including Arabia, Cyprus, & Asiatic Turkey —**Middle Eastern** —**Middle Easterner**

Middle English the English language as written and spoken between *c.* 1100 and *c.* 1500, preceded by Old English and followed by Early Modern English: it is characterized by the loss of grammatical gender and most of the inflectional endings of Old English, by the emergence of a syntax based on word order and function words, by the simplification of the pronominal system, and by extensive vocabulary borrowings from French, Latin, and Low German

Middle French the French language as written and spoken between the 14th and 16th centuries

Middle Greek MEDIEVAL GREEK

middle ground **1** MIDDLE DISTANCE (sense 1) **2** an intermediate position between opposing ideas, conflicting viewpoints, etc., by which reconciliation or compromise may be achieved

middle guard *Football* NOSE GUARD

Middle High German the High German language as written and spoken between *c.* 1100 and *c.* 1500

Middle Irish the Irish language as written and spoken from the 10th to the 15th cent.

Middle Kingdom [Historical] *Chinese name for* the CHINESE EMPIRE, considered as the center of the world

middle lamella *Cytology* a thin, sticky membrane between plant cells that cements the cell walls together

Middle Latin MEDIEVAL LATIN

Middle Low German the Low German language as written and spoken between *c.* 1100 and *c.* 1500

mid·dle·man (mid′'l man′) ***n., pl.*** **-men′** (-men′) **1** a trader who buys commodities from the producer and sells them to the retailer or, sometimes, directly to the consumer **2** a go-between; intermediary

☆**middle management** those persons in management at a level below that of upper executives —**middle manager**

mid·dle·most (-mōst′) ***adj.*** MIDMOST (sense 1)

middle name a name, commonly another given name or a maiden name, between the first name and the surname

☆**mid·dle-of-the-road** (-əv *thə* rōd′) ***adj.*** characterized by the avoidance of extremes, as in politics or matters of taste

middle passage [Historical] the passage across the Atlantic from W Africa to the West Indies or America that was the route of the slave trade

Mid·dles·brough (mid′'lz brə) city in NE England, in Cleveland county, on the Tees

middle school a school between elementary school and high school, usually having three or four grades, typically including grades 6 through 8 —**middle schooler** or **mid′dle-school′er** ***n.***

Mid·dle·sex (mid′'l seks′) former county of SE England, now mostly a part of Greater London

mid·dle-sized (-sīzd′) ***adj.*** of medium size

Middle States those eastern states between the New England states and the South; New York, New Jersey, Pennsylvania, Delaware, and Maryland

Middle Stone Age the Mesolithic

Middle Temple *see* INNS OF COURT

middle term the term appearing in both premises of a syllogism but not in the conclusion

Mid·dle·ton (mid′l tən), **Thomas** 1580-1627; Eng. dramatist

mid·dle·weight (mid′'l wāt′) ***n.*** **1** one of average weight **2** a boxer between a junior middleweight and a super middleweight, with a maximum weight of 160 pounds (72.58 kg)

Middle West MIDWEST —**Middle Western**

mid·dling (mid′liŋ) ***adj.*** ⟦MID[1] + -LING[1]⟧ of middle size, quality, grade, etc.; medium; ordinary; mediocre —***adv.*** [Informal] fairly; moderately; somewhat —***n.*** ☆**1** pork or bacon from between the ham and the shoulder **2** [*pl.*] products of medium quality, grade, size, or price **3** [*pl.*] particles of coarsely ground grain, often mixed with bran and used as feed

mid·dy (mid′ē) ***n., pl.*** **-dies** ⟦< slang shortening of MIDSHIPMAN⟧ a loose blouse with a SAILOR COLLAR, worn by women and children: in full **middy blouse**

Mid·east (mid ēst′) MIDDLE EAST —***adj.*** Middle Eastern [*Mideast* peace talks]: also **Mid·east′ern** (-ēs′tərn)

mid·field (mid′fēld′) ***n.*** the area of a playing field midway between the goals, specif., the middle third of the field in soccer and lacrosse

mid·field·er (-ər) ***n.*** *Lacrosse, Soccer* any of the players who play primarily in the midfield area and whose responsibilities are both offensive and defensive

Mid·gard (mid′gärd′) ***n.*** ⟦ON *mithgarthr* < *mithr,* MID[1] + *garthr,* YARD[2]⟧ *Norse Myth.* the earth, regarded as midway between Asgard and the underworld and encircled by a huge serpent: also **Mid′garth′** (-gärth′)

midge (mij) ***n.*** ⟦ME *migge* < OE *mycg,* akin to Ger *mücke* < IE base **mu-,* echoic for fly, gnat > L *musca,* a fly⟧ any of various families (esp. Chironomidae) of small, two-winged, gnatlike dipteran insects, including the gall midges and biting midges

midg·et (mij′it) ***n.*** ⟦dim. of prec.⟧ **1** a person who is much smaller than average, with head, limbs, and trunk proportionate to each other in size: now regarded as somewhat offensive or insulting **2** anything very small of its kind —***adj.*** very small of its kind; miniature —**SYN.** DWARF

Mid Gla·mor·gan (mid′ glə môr′gən) county in SW Wales: 393 sq mi (1,018 sq km)

mid·gut (mid′gut′) ***n.*** **1** the middle part of the alimentary canal in vertebrate embryos **2** the endoderm-lined portion of the digestive tract of arthropods

Mi·di (mē dē′) ⟦Fr, south, lit., midday < *mi-,* half (< L *medius,* MIDDLE) + *di* (< L *dies*), day⟧ the south of France

MIDI (mid′ē) ***n.*** ⟦*m(usical) i(nstrument) d(igital) i(nterface)*⟧ an electronic digital system for musical composition and reproduction, that provides a standard interface connecting electronic musical instruments, such as synthesizers, with computers

mid·i- (mid′ē, -i) ⟦< MID[1], after MINI-⟧ *combining form* of a length to the middle of the calf *[midiskirt]*

Mid·i·an·ite (mid′ē ən īt′) ***n.*** ⟦< Heb *midhyān,* name of a son of Abraham (see Gen. 25:2) + -ITE[1]⟧ *Bible* a member of a nomadic tribe of Arabs that fought the Israelites: Num. 31, Judg. 6-8

mid·i·nette (mid″n et′; *Fr* mē dē net′) ***n.*** ⟦Fr, blend of *midi,* midday + *dinette,* a little lunch < *diner,* to DINE + *-ette,* dim. suffix: in allusion to their customary light lunch⟧ a young Parisian shopgirl, esp. one who works in a dress shop

Mi·di-Pyr·é·nées (mē dē′pir′ə nēz′) metropolitan region of SW France: 15,965 sq mi (41,349 sq km); chief city, Toulouse

mid·i·ron (mid′ī′ərn) ***n.*** ⟦MID- + IRON⟧ *former term for* number 2 iron: see IRON (*n.* 6)

mid·land (mid′lənd) ***n.*** **1** the middle region of a country; interior **2** [**M-**] a Midland dialect —***adj.*** **1** in or of the midland; inland **2** [**M-**] of the Midlands **3** [**M-**] *a)* designating dialects of English spoken or formerly spoken in the Midlands of England and divided into eastern and western groups *b)* designating a dialect of American English spoken in S N.J.; central and S Pa., Ohio, Ind., and Ill.; N Del.; the Shenandoah Valley; the S Appalachians; the upper Piedmont of N.C. and S.C.; Ky.; and N Tenn.

Mid·land (mid′lənd) ⟦from being about midway between Fort Worth and El Paso⟧ city in WC Tex.

Mid·lands (mid′ləndz) highly industrialized region of central England, usually considered to include the present counties of Derbyshire, Leicestershire, Northamptonshire, Nottinghamshire, Staffordshire, Warwickshire, West Midlands, & E Hereford and Worcester: with *the*

mid·leg (mid′leg′, -lāg′) ***n.*** **1** the middle of the leg **2** one of the middle, or second, pair of legs of an insect

mid·life (mid′līf′) ***n.*** MIDDLE AGE: esp. in **midlife crisis**, the sense of uncertainty or anxiety about one's identity, values, relationships, etc. that some people experience in middle age

mid·line (-līn′) ***n.*** a median line

Mid·lo·thi·an (mid lō′*th*ē ən) administrative division of SE Scotland: formerly a county & district

mid·morn·ing prayer (mid′môr′niŋ) [*often* **M- P-**] *R.C.Ch.* the third of the seven canonical hours; terce

mid·most (mid′mōst′) ***adj.*** ⟦ME *mydmest* (with *-most* for *-mest* from 17th c. onward) < OE *midmest* < **middjumo,* in the middle (< IE **medhiemo-,* superl. of **medhjo-,* MID[1]) + superl. suffix *-est,* -EST⟧ **1** exactly in the middle, or nearest the middle; middlemost **2** most secret; inmost —***adv.*** in the middle or midst —***prep.*** in the middle or midst of —***n.*** the middle part

mid·night (-nīt′) ***n.*** **1** twelve o'clock at night; the middle of the night **2** deep darkness —***adj.*** **1** of or at midnight **2** like or suggestive of midnight; very dark *[midnight* blue*]* —**burn the midnight oil** to study or work very late into the night

midnight sun the sun visible at midnight in the arctic or antarctic regions during their summers

mid-o·ce·an·ic ridge (mid ō′shē an′ik) the continuous, double-ridged chain of mountains on the ocean floor, extending through the middle of the Atlantic Ocean and into the Indian and Pacific oceans: also called **mid-o·cean ridge** (mid ō′shən)

mid·point (-point′) ***n.*** a point at or close to the middle or center, or equally distant from the ends

mid·range (mid′rānj′) ***adj.*** intermediate in price, quality, size, etc. —***n.*** **1** the intermediate range of sound frequencies **2** a speaker for reproducing these: cf. TWEETER, WOOFER

mid·rash (mid′räsh) ***n.***, *pl.* **mid·rash·im** (mid rä′shim) or **mid·rash′oth** (-shōt) ⟦Heb *midrash,* explanation⟧ *Judaism* any of the rabbinical commentaries and explanatory notes on the Scriptures, written between the beginning of the Exile and *c.* A.D. 1200 —**the Midrash** these commentaries and notes collectively —**Mid·rash′ic** ***adj.***, **mid·rash′ic**

mid·rib (mid′rib′) ***n.*** the central vein, or rib, of a leaf, usually running from the stem to the apex

mid·riff (-rif) ***n.*** ⟦ME *mydrif* < OE *midhrif* < *midd-* (see MID[1]) + *hrif,* belly (akin to OHG *href,* body) < IE base **krep-,* body > L *corpus*⟧ **1** DIAPHRAGM (sense 1) **2** *a)* the middle part of the torso, between the abdomen and the chest *b)* that part of a woman's garment that covers this part, or that is cut away to expose it —***adj.*** designating or of a garment that bares this part

mid-rise (mid′rīz′) ***adj.*** designating or of a multi-storied building, esp. an apartment house, that is intermediate in height between a low-rise and a high-rise building

mid·sec·tion (-sek′shən) ***n.*** the section in the middle; specif., the midriff region of the body

mid·ship·man (mid′ship′mən, mid ship′-) ***n.***, *pl.* **-men** (-mən) ⟦aphetic for *amidshipmen,* from being *amidships* when on duty⟧ **1** a student in training for the rank of ensign; specif., such a student at the U.S. Naval Academy at Annapolis **2** a junior British naval officer ranking between naval cadet and sublieutenant

mid·ships (mid′ships′) ***adv., adj.*** in or toward the middle of a ship; esp., halfway between bow and stern —***n.*** the middle part of a ship

mid·size or **mid-size** (mid′sīz′) ***adj.*** of or being a size intermediate between large and small *[a midsize* car*]*

mid·sole (mid′sōl′) ***n.*** a layer between the insole and outsole, as of an athletic shoe or a hiking boot

midst (midst, mitst) ***n.*** ⟦ME *middest,* prob. merging of *middes,* gen. of *mid* (with unhistoric *-t*) + *middest,* superl. of *mid,* MID[1]⟧ the middle or central part: now mainly in phrases as below —***prep.*** [Old Poet.] IN THE MIDST OF (see phrase below); amidst; amid —**SYN.** MIDDLE —**in our** (or **your** or **their**) **midst** in among us (or you or them): often used fig. —**in the midst of** **1** in the middle of; surrounded by **2** in the course of; during

mid·stream (mid′strēm′) ***n.*** the middle of a stream

mid·sum·mer (-sum′ər) ***n.*** **1** the middle of summer **2** the time of the summer solstice, about June 21 —***adj.*** of, in, or like midsummer

Midsummer Day June 24, feast of St. John the Baptist

mid·term (-turm′) ☆***adj.*** occurring in the middle of a term —***n.*** **1** the middle of a term ☆**2** a midterm examination, as in a college course

mid·town (mid′toun′) ***adj.*** designating, in, or of the central area of a city or, esp., a metropolis *[midtown* Manhattan, a *midtown* apartment*]* —***n.*** a midtown area

mid-Vic·to·ri·an (mid′vik tôr′ē ən) ***adj.*** **1** of, like, or characteristic of the middle part of Queen Victoria's reign in Great Britain (*c.* 1850-90) or the culture, morals, or art of this period **2** old-fashioned, prudish, morally strict, stuffy, etc. —***n.*** **1** a person who lived during this period **2** a person of mid-Victorian ideas, manners, attitudes, etc.

mid·way (mid′wā′; *also, for adj. & adv.,* -wā′) ***n.*** ⟦ME *midwei* < OE *midweg*⟧ **1** [Obs.] *a)* the middle of the way or distance *b)* a middle way or course ☆**2** ⟦orig. short for *Midway Plaisance,* the amusement area of the Columbian Exposition (1893), in Chicago⟧ that part of a fair or exposition where concessions, sideshows, and other amusements are located — ***adj., adv.*** in the middle of the way or distance; halfway

Midway Islands coral atoll & two islets at the end of the Hawaiian chain: administered by the U.S. Navy: 2 sq mi (5.2 sq km)

mid·week (mid′wēk′) ***n.*** **1** the middle of the week **2** [**M-**] Wednesday: so called by the Friends (Quakers) —***adj.*** in the middle of the week —**mid′week′ly** ***adj., adv.***

Mid·west (mid west′) region of the NC U.S. between the Rocky Mountains & the E border of Ohio, north of the Ohio River & the S borders of Kans. & Mo.

Mid·west·ern (mid wes′tərn) ***adj.*** of, in, or characteristic of the Midwest; Middle Western —**Mid·west′ern·er** ***n.***

mid·wife (mid′wīf′) ***n.***, *pl.* **-wives′** (-wīvz′) ⟦ME *midwyf* < *mid,* with < OE (< Gmc *mithi* < IE **meti-* < base **me-* > MID[1], Ger *mit,* Gr *meta*) + *wif,* woman (see WIFE): basic sense "woman with, woman assisting"⟧ a person (now, esp., a specially trained nurse) whose work is assisting women in childbirth —***vt.*** **-wifed′** or **-wived′**, **-wif′ing** or **-wiv′ing** **1** to assist as a midwife in the birth of (a child) **2** figuratively, to help bring about or bring into being *[to midwife* a resolution to a conflict*]*

mid·wife·ry (mid′wif′rē, -wīf′-; -ər ē) ***n.*** the work of a midwife; esp., the body of knowledge, skills, and practices of a modern midwife

mid·win·ter (mid′win′tər) ***n.*** **1** the middle of winter **2** the time of the winter solstice, about Dec. 22 —***adj.*** of, in, or like midwinter

mid·year (-yir′) ***adj.*** ☆occurring in the middle of the (calendar or academic) year —***n.*** **1** the middle of the year ☆**2** [Informal] a midyear examination, as in a college course

mien (mēn) ***n.*** ⟦aphetic for DEMEAN[2], but altered by assoc. with Fr *mine,* look, air < Bret *min,* muzzle, beak⟧ **1** a way of carrying and conducting oneself; manner **2** a way of looking; appearance —**SYN.** BEARING

Mies van der Ro·he (mēz′ van dər rō′ə), **Lud·wig** (lo͞od′vig) (born *Maria Ludwig Michael Mies*) 1886-1969; U.S. architect, born in Germany

mi·fep·ri·stone (mī fep′ri stōn′, mif′ə pris′tōn′) ***n.*** ⟦ult. < (A)MI(NO)PHE(NOL) + PR(OPYL) + EST(RADIOL) + -ONE⟧ a steroidal drug, $C_{29}H_{35}NO_2$, used orally primarily to terminate pregnancy at the earliest stage by blocking the reception of progesterone

miff (mif) [Informal] ***n.*** ⟦prob. orig. cry of disgust⟧ a trivial quarrel or fit of the sulks; tiff or huff — *vt., vi.* to offend or take offense; put or be put out of humor

MIG (mig) ***n.*** ⟦after Artem *Mi(koyan)* & Mikhail *G(urevich)*, its Soviet designers⟧ any of a series of Russian, orig. Soviet, high-speed, high-altitude jet fighter planes: also written **MiG**

might[1] (mīt) ***v.aux.*** ⟦ME *mihte* < OE, akin to Ger *möchte*⟧ **1** *pt.* of MAY[1] **2** used as a modal auxiliary in verbal phrases with present or future time reference, generally equivalent to MAY[1] in meaning and use, with the following functions: *a)* expressing esp. a shade of doubt or a lesser degree of possibility [it *might* rain] *b)* expressing a lesser degree of permission [*might* I go?] *c)* expressing a lesser degree of obligation [you *might* try to help] —*vi.* used elliptically in the same functions as MIGHT[1] (*v.aux.*)

might[2] (mīt) ***n.*** ⟦ME *mighte* < OE *miht*, akin to Ger *macht* < IE base **māgh-*, to be able > ON *magn*⟧ **1** great or superior strength, power, force, or vigor **2** strength or power of any degree —***SYN.*** STRENGTH

mightn't (mīt′'nt) *contraction* might not

might·y (mīt′ē) ***adj.*** **might′i·er, might′i·est** ⟦ME *myghty* < OE *mihtig*⟧ **1** having might; powerful; strong **2** remarkably large, extensive, etc.; great —***adv.*** [Informal or Dial.] very; extremely —**might′i·ly** ***adv.*** —**might′i·ness** ***n.***

mi·gnon (min′yän′; *Fr* mē nyōn′) ***adj.*** ⟦Fr, for OFr *mignot*, dainty < **min-*, echoic of a caressing cry, as in IE base **mī(n)-*, var. of *mēi-*, gentle, soft > L *mitis*, soft, OIr *min*, gentle⟧ small, delicately formed, and pretty; dainty

mi·gnon·ette (min′yə net′) ***n.*** ⟦Fr *mignonnette*, dim. of *mignon:* see prec.⟧ **1** any of a genus (*Reseda*) of plants of the mignonette family with thick stems and coarse foliage, esp. an annual plant (*R. odorata*) bearing terminal spikes of small greenish, whitish, or reddish flowers **2** any of several similar plants **3** a pale, yellowish green —***adj.*** designating a family (Resedaceae, order Capparales) of dicotyledonous plants and shrubs

mignonette tree HENNA (*n.* 1)

mi·graine (mī′grān′) ***n.*** ⟦Fr < OFr < LL *hemicrania* < Gr *hēmikrania* < *hēmi-*, half + *kranion*, CRANIUM⟧ a type of intense, periodically returning headache, usually limited to one side of the head and often accompanied by nausea, visual disorders, etc. —**mi′grain′ous** ***adj.***

mi·grant (mī′grənt) ***adj.*** ⟦L *migrans*, prp. of *migrare*⟧ migrating; migratory —***n.*** **1** a person, bird, or animal that migrates ☆**2** a farm laborer who moves from place to place to harvest seasonal crops

mi·grate (mī′grāt′) ***vi.*** **-grat′ed, -grat′ing** ⟦< L *migratus*, pp. of *migrare*, to move from one place to another, change < IE **meigw-*, to change location < base **mei-*, to change, exchange, wander⟧ **1** to move from one place to another; esp., to leave one's country and settle in another **2** to move from one region to another with the change in seasons, as many birds and some fishes do **3** to move from place to place to harvest seasonal crops —**mi′gra′tor** ***n.***

SYN.—**migrate** denotes a moving from one region or country to another and may imply, of people, intention to settle in a new land, or, of animals, a periodical movement influenced by climate, food supply, etc.; **emigrate** and **immigrate** are used only of people, **emigrate** specifically denoting the leaving of a country to settle in another, and **immigrate**, the coming into the new country

mi·gra·tion (mī grā′shən) ***n.*** ⟦L *migratio*⟧ **1** the act of migrating **2** a group of people, or of birds, fishes, etc., migrating together **3** *Chem.* *a)* the shifting of one or more atoms from one position in the molecule to another *b)* the movement of ions toward an electrode, under the influence of electromotive force —**mi·gra′tion·al** ***adj.***

mi·gra·to·ry (mī′grə tôr′ē) ***adj.*** **1** migrating; characterized by migration **2** of migration **3** roving; wandering

mih·rab (mē′räb′) ***n.*** ⟦Ar *miḥrāb*⟧ a niche in that wall of a mosque that is closest to Mecca: it indicates the direction toward which Muslims turn to pray

mi·ka·do (mi kä′dō) ***n.***, *pl.* **-dos** ⟦Jpn, lit., exalted gate (i.e., of the Imperial palace) < *mi*, an honorific + *kado*, gate⟧ [*often* **M-**] the emperor of Japan: title no longer used

Mik·a·su·ki (mik′ə so͞o′kē) ***n.*** a Muskogean language spoken by a group of Seminoles in S Florida

mike[1] (mīk) [Informal] ***n.*** a microphone —***vt.*** **miked, mik′ing** **1** to record, amplify, etc. by means of a microphone **2** to attach a microphone to (a person) or set up a microphone in (a room, etc.)

mike[2] (mīk) ***n.*** [Slang] a microgram, as of LSD

mik·vah (mik′və) ***n.*** ⟦TalmudHeb *mikve*, lit., collection of water < root *qwh*, to gather, collect⟧ a bath in which Orthodox Jews immerse themselves for ritual purification, as before the Sabbath or following menstruation: also sp. **mik′veh**

mil[1] (mil) ***n.*** ⟦L *mille*, thousand⟧ **1** a unit of length, equal to one thousandth (0.001) of an inch (0.0254 millimeter), used in measuring the diameter of wire, the thickness of coatings or films, etc. **2** a milliliter, or cubic centimeter **3** a unit of currency in Cyprus, equal to $\frac{1}{1000}$ pound **4** *Mil.* a unit of angle measurement for artillery fire, missile launching, etc., equal to the angle forming an arc that is $\frac{1}{6400}$ of the circumference of a circle

mil[2] (mil) ***n.*** [Slang] *short for* million

mil[3] *abbrev.* **1** mileage **2** military **3** militia

.mil (*often* dät′mil′) *abbrev. Comput.* military: a U.S. domain name

mi·la·dy or **mi·la·di** (mi lā′dē) ***n.***, *pl.* **-dies** ⟦Fr < E *my lady*⟧ **1** an English noblewoman or gentlewoman ☆**2** a woman of fashion: shopkeepers' or advertisers' term

mil·age (mīl′ij) ***n.*** *alt. sp. of* MILEAGE

Mi·lan (mi lan′, -län′) commune in NW Italy, in Lombardy: It. name **Mi·la·no** (mē lä′nô) —**Mil·a·nese** (mil′ə nēz′) ***adj., n.***, *pl.* **-nese′**

milch (milk, milch) ***adj.*** ⟦ME *milche*, milk-giving < OE *-milce*, akin to *meolc*, MILK⟧ [Now Chiefly Dial.] MILK

mild (mīld) ***adj.*** ⟦ME *milde* < OE, akin to Ger *mild* < IE **meldh-* < base **mel-*, to crush, rub fine > MELT, MILL[1]⟧ **1** *a)* gentle or kind in disposition, action, or effect; not severe, harsh, bitter, etc. *b)* not extreme in any way; moderate; temperate [a *mild* winter] **2** having a soft, pleasant taste or flavor; not strong, sour, bitter, biting, or sharp: said of tobacco, cheese, etc. **3** designating steel that is tough but malleable and contains only a small percentage of carbon —***SYN.*** SOFT —**mild′ness** ***n.***

mild·en (mīl′dən) ***vt., vi.*** [Rare] to make or become mild or milder

mil·dew (mil′do͞o′, -dyo͞o′) ***n.*** ⟦ME *mildewe* < OE *meledeaw*, nectar, lit., honeydew, akin to Goth *milith*, honey < IE base **melit-* (> L *mel*, Gr *meli*, honey) + base of OE *deaw*, DEW⟧ **1** a thin, furry, usually whitish coating or discoloration, caused by a fungus, that forms on the surface of various plants, on organic matter, or on damp paper, cloth, bathroom tiles, etc. **2** any fungus that attacks various plants or that produces such a coating or discoloration **3** any plant disease, as powdery mildew, caused by such fungus — ***vt., vi.*** to affect or become affected with mildew —**mil′dew′y** ***adj.***

mild·ly (mīld′lē) ***adv.*** **1** in a mild manner **2** to a mild degree; somewhat —**to put it mildly** to state it with or as if with restraint

Mil·dred (mil′drid) ***n.*** ⟦OE *Myldthryth* < *milde*, mild + *thryth*, power, strength⟧ a feminine name: dim. *Millie, Milly*

mile (mīl) ***n.***, *pl.* **miles**; sometimes, after a number, **mile** ⟦ME < OE *mil*, pl. *mila* < WGmc **milja* < L *milia*, pl. of *mille*, thousand, in *milia passuum*, thousand paces, mile⟧ a unit of length in the FPS system, equal to 5,280 feet or 1,760 yards or 8 furlongs (1.609344 kilometers or 0.869 nautical mile); statute mile: abbrev. *mi* —**a mile a minute** [Informal] very rapidly [to talk *a mile a minute*]

☆**mile·age** (mīl′ij) ***n.*** **1** an allowance for traveling expenses at a specified amount per mile **2** aggregate distance in miles or total number of miles traveled, recorded, etc. **3** rate per mile, as in allowing for travel expenses or in charging for the use of railroad freight cars **4** the number of miles a motor vehicle will go on a gallon of fuel, a tire will run before it wears out, etc. **5** the amount of use, service, or benefit one gets or can get from something

☆**mile·post** (mīl′pōst′) ***n.*** a signpost showing the distance in miles to or from a specified place

mil·er (mīl′ər) ***n.*** one who competes in mile races

Miles (mīlz) ***n.*** ⟦OFr *Miles, Milon* < OHG *Milo*, lit., mild, peaceful⟧ a masculine name

mi·les glo·ri·o·sus (mī′lēz′ glō′rē ō′səs, mē′lās′-) ⟦L < *miles*, soldier + *gloriosus*, boastful: title of a play by PLAUTUS⟧ a braggart, swashbuckling soldier, esp. as a stock character in classical comedy

mile·stone (mīl′stōn′) ***n.*** **1** a stone or pillar set up to show the distance in miles to or from a specified place **2** a significant or important event in history, in the career of a person, etc.

Mi·le·tus (mī lēt′əs) ancient city in Ionia, SW Asia Minor —**Mi·le′sian** (-lē′zhən) ***adj., n.***

MILF (milf) ***n.*** ⟦*m(other) I('d) l(ike to) f(uck)*⟧ [Slang] a middle-aged woman regarded as remarkably attractive sexually, esp. as by younger men: a humorous usage considered vulgar by some: also written **milf**

mil·foil (mil′foil′) ***n.*** ⟦OFr < L *millefolium* < *mille*, thousand + *folium*, leaf (see FOLIATE): from the finely divided leaves⟧ **1** YARROW **2** WATER MILFOIL

Mil·haud (mē yō′), **Da·rius** (dȧ ryüs′) 1892-1974; Fr. composer

mil·ia (mil′ē ə) ***n.*** *pl. of* MILIUM

mil·i·a·ri·a (mil′ē er′ē ə) ***n.*** ⟦ModL < fem. of L *miliarius:* see fol.⟧ an acute skin disease resulting from inflammation of the sweat glands, as from exposure to heat, and characterized by small, white or red eruptions

mil·i·ar·y (mil′ē er′ē, mil′yər ē) ***adj.*** ⟦L *miliarius* < *milium*, MILLET⟧ **1** like a millet seed or seeds **2** *Med.* characterized or accompanied by lesions about the size of millet seeds: said, specif., of a form of tuberculosis which spreads from a primary focus of infection to other parts of the body, forming many minute tubercles

Mil·i·cent (mil′ə sənt) ***n.*** a feminine name: see MILLICENT

mi·lieu (mēl yʉ′, -yo͞o′, -yo͞o′; mil-) ***n.***, *pl.* **-lieus′** ⟦Fr, lit., middle < OFr *mi* (< L *medius:* see MID[1]) + *lieu*, a place < L *locus* (see LOCUS)⟧ an environment; esp., a social or cultural setting: also Fr. **mi·lieu** (mē lyö′), *pl.* **-lieux′** (-lyö′)

mil·i·tan·cy (mil′i tən sē) ***n.*** militant quality, behavior, etc.: often **mil′i·tance**

mil·i·tant (mil′i tənt) ***adj.*** ⟦ME < L *militans*, prp. of *militare*, to serve as a soldier < *miles* (gen. *militis*), soldier⟧ **1** at war; fighting **2** ready and willing to fight; esp., vigorous or aggressive in supporting or promoting a cause —***n.*** a militant person —***SYN.*** AGGRESSIVE —**mil′i·tant·ly** ***adv.***

mil·i·ta·rism (mil′ə tə riz′əm) ***n.*** ⟦Fr *militarisme*⟧ **1** the glorification or prevalence of a military spirit, attitudes, etc. in a nation, or the predominance of the military caste in government **2** the policy of maintaining a strong military organization in aggressive preparedness for war

mil·i·ta·rist (-rist) ***n.*** **1** a person who supports or advocates militarism **2** [Now Rare] an expert or specialist in military affairs —**mil′i·ta·ris′tic** ***adj.*** —**mil′i·ta·ris′ti·cal·ly** ***adv.***

mil·i·ta·rize (mil′i tə rīz′) ***vt.*** **-rized′, -riz′ing** **1** to make military; equip and prepare for war **2** to fill with warlike spirit —**mil′i·ta·ri·za′tion** ***n.***

mil·i·tar·y (mil′ə ter′ē) ***adj.*** ⟦Fr *militaire* < L *militaris* < *miles* (gen. *militis*), soldier⟧ 1 of, characteristic of, for, fit for, or done by soldiers or the armed forces 2 of, for, or fit for war 3 of the army, as distinguished from the navy —*n., pl.* **-tar′ies** 1 the armed forces; military personnel collectively 2 a nation's military establishment —*SYN.* MARTIAL —**mil′i·tar′i·ly** *adv.*

military attaché an officer of the armed forces attached to the staff of an ambassador to another country

☆**mil·i·tar·y-in·dus·tri·al complex** (-in dus′trē əl) ⟦first used by President EISENHOWER in his farewell address (1961)⟧ a nation's military establishment and those industries producing military materiel, viewed as together exerting a powerful influence on foreign and economic policy

military law the code of law concerned with the government and discipline of the armed forces: distinguished from MARTIAL LAW

military police armed forces personnel assigned to police duties; specif., soldiers assigned to police duties in the army

military science the study of military practices and the strategic, tactical, and logistic theories that determine them

military time a system for measuring and recording the time of day, reckoned from midnight to midnight and expressed as a four-digit numeral, the hour followed by minutes (Ex.: 1:30 A.M. = 0130, 1:30 P.M. = 1330, noon = 1200, midnight = 2400)

mil·i·tate (mil′ə tāt′) *vi.* **-tat′ed, -tat′ing** ⟦< L *militatus,* pp. of *militare:* see MILITANT⟧ 1 [Archaic] to serve as a soldier; fight (*against*) 2 to be directed (*against*); operate or work (*against* or, rarely, *for*): said of facts, evidence, actions, etc. [his inexperience *militated* against his candidacy]

mi·li·tia (mə lish′ə) *n.* ⟦L, military service, soldiery < *miles* (gen. *militis*), soldier⟧ 1 *a)* [Archaic] any military force *b)* later, any army composed of citizens rather than professional soldiers, called up in time of emergency ☆2 in the U.S., all able-bodied male citizens between 18 and 45 years old who are not already members of the regular armed forces: members of the National Guard and of the Reserves (of the Army, Air Force, Coast Guard, Navy, and Marine Corps) constitute the **organized militia**; all others, the **unorganized militia** 3 any of various disaffected groups of citizens that are organized as to resemble an army and that oppose the authority of the federal government —**mi·li′tia·man** (-mən) *n., pl.* **-men** (-mən)

mil·i·um (mil′ē əm) *n., pl.* **-i·a** (-ə) ⟦ModL < L: see MILLET⟧ a small, whitish nodule of the skin, somewhat like a millet seed, resulting from retention of the secretion of a sebaceous gland

milk (milk) *n.* ⟦ME < OE *meolc,* akin to ON *mjolk,* Ger *milch* < IE base **melĝ-,* to stroke, press out, wipe off, hence to milk (an animal) > Gr *amelgein,* L *mulgere,* to milk⟧ 1 a white or yellowish emulsion secreted by the mammary glands of female mammals for suckling their young and usually consisting of fats, proteins, sugars, vitamins, and minerals suspended in water 2 cow's milk, or, sometimes, that of goats, camels, etc., drunk by humans as a food or used to make butter, cheese, casein products, etc. 3 any liquid like this, as the juice of various plants or fruits (e.g., coconut milk), or any of various emulsions —*vt.* 1 to draw or squeeze milk from the mammary glands of (a cow, etc.) 2 to extract juice, sap, venom, etc. from 3 to draw out or drain off; extract: often used fig. 4 [Informal] to exploit —*vi.* 1 to give milk 2 to draw milk —*adj.* giving milk; kept for milking [*milk* cows] —**cry over spilt milk** to mourn or regret something that cannot be undone

milk-and-wa·ter (-ən wôt′ər) *adj.* 1 weak; insipid 2 indecisive, ineffectual, etc.

milk chocolate a form of prepared chocolate, used esp. in candies, containing milk and a high proportion of sugar and cocoa butter

milk·er (mil′kər) *n.* 1 a person who milks 2 a machine for milking 3 a cow or other animal that gives milk

milk fever 1 [Now Rare] mild puerperal fever: so called because erroneously attributed to an accumulation of milk in the breasts 2 a disease often occurring in dairy cows shortly after calving, characterized by a drop in blood calcium, paralysis, etc.

milk·fish (-fish′) *n., pl.* **-fish′** a large, silvery food fish (*Chanos chanos*) of an order (Gonorhynchiformes) of toothless bony fishes, found in the tropical Pacific and Indian oceans

milk glass a translucent or nearly opaque whitish glass

milk·i·ness (mil′kē nis) *n.* a milky quality or state

milk leg painful swelling of the leg, caused by inflammation and clotting in the femoral veins, usually as a result of infection during childbirth

milk-liv·ered (milk′liv′ərd) *adj.* ⟦first recorded in KING LEAR, IV, ii: see WHITE-LIVERED⟧ timid; cowardly

milk·maid (milk′mād′) *n.* a girl or woman who milks cows or works in a dairy; dairymaid

milk·man (-man′) *n., pl.* **-men′** (-men′) a man who sells or delivers milk for a dairy

milk of magnesia a milky-white fluid, a suspension of magnesium hydroxide, $Mg(OH)_2$, in water, used as a laxative and antacid

milk run ⟦by analogy with the former delivery of milk to homes on a regular route, or *run*⟧ [Slang] a routine mission, as of a bomber aircraft, that is not expected to be dangerous

☆**milk·shake** (-shāk′) *n.* a drink made of milk, flavoring, and, usually, ice cream, mixed or shaken until frothy

☆**milk·shed** (-shed′) *n.* ⟦MILK + (WATER)SHED⟧ all the dairy farm areas supplying milk for a given city

☆**milk sickness** a rare disease, formerly common in the W U.S., caused by consuming dairy products or flesh from cattle that have eaten any of various poisonous weeds

☆**milk snake** ⟦so named because it was formerly believed to take milk directly from cows⟧ a harmless colubrid snake (*Lampropeltis triangulum*) with brown or reddish bands bordered by black: it feeds on rodents, reptiles, etc.

milk solids the proteins, sugar, minerals, and, sometimes, the fat found in milk

milk·sop (-säp′) *n.* a man seen as timid, ineffectual, effeminate, etc.

milk sugar LACTOSE

milk tooth any of the temporary, first set of teeth of young mammals: normally a child's set consists of 20, including 8 incisors, 4 cuspids, and 8 molars

milk vetch ⟦from the notion that it increases the secretion of milk in goats⟧ any of a genus (*Astragalus*) of plants of the pea family, with deeply cut leaves, flowers in spikes or racemes, and, usually, inflated pods

milk·weed (milk′wēd′) *n.* 1 any of a genus (*Asclepias*) of perennial plants of the milkweed family, with a milky juice, or latex, and pods which when ripe burst to release plumed seeds 2 any of various plants with similar milky juice —*adj.* designating a large family (Asclepiadaceae, order Gentianales) of dicotyledonous plants with a milky juice, including the anglepods and stapelias

milk·wort (-wurt′) *n.* ⟦from the former notion that it increases the secretion of milk in nursing women⟧ any of a genus (*Polygala*) of plants of the milkwort family with showy flowers of various colors —*adj.* designating a family (Polygalaceae, order Polygalales) of dicotyledonous plants, including the gaywings

milk·y (mil′kē) *adj.* **milk′i·er, milk′i·est** 1 like milk; esp., white as milk or having the consistency of milk 2 of, containing, or yielding milk 3 timid, meek, mild, etc.

milky (spore) disease any of several bacterial diseases of the larvae of scarab beetles, as a disease of Japanese beetle grubs, characterized by the milky-white appearance of the infected larvae

Milky Way, the ⟦transl. of L *via lactea,* transl. of Gr *galaxias kyklos:* see GALAXY⟧ the spiral galaxy containing our sun: seen from the earth as a broad, faintly luminous band of stars and interstellar gas arching across the night sky, with the constellation Sagittarius marking the direction to its center

mill[1] (mil) *n.* ⟦ME *melle* < OE *mylen,* akin to OHG *mulin,* ON *mylna,* all < 4th-c. Gmc borrowing < LL *molinae,* pl. of *molina,* mill < LL(Ec) *molina,* of a mill < L *mola,* millstone < IE base **mel-,* to grind, crush > MEAL[2], MILD, Ger *mahlen,* Gr *mylē,* mill, L *mollis,* soft, *molere,* to grind⟧ 1 *a)* a building with machinery for grinding grain into flour or meal *b)* the machine for grinding grain 2 *a)* a machine for grinding or pulverizing any solid material [a countertop coffee *mill*] *b)* a machine for grinding or crushing fruits or vegetables to press out the juice [a cider *mill*] 3 *a)* any of various machines for stamping, shaping, polishing, or dressing metal surfaces, coins, etc., or for making something by some action done again and again ☆*b)* [Informal] an organization, establishment, etc. where things are processed, produced, issued, etc. in a routine, rapid, mechanical way [a diploma *mill,* a divorce *mill*] 4 a building or group of buildings with machinery for manufacturing or processing something; factory [a textile *mill*] 5 a roller of hardened steel with a raised design on it, for making a die or a printing plate by pressure 6 *a)* MILLING CUTTER *b)* MILLING MACHINE 7 a raised edge, ridged surface, etc. made by milling —*vt.* 1 to grind, work, process, form, polish, etc. by, in, or as in a mill 2 to raise and ridge the edge of (a coin), as a safeguard against wear and clipping; knurl 3 [Now Rare] to beat or whip (chocolate, etc.) to a froth —*vi.* ☆to move slowly in a circle, as cattle, or aimlessly, as a confused crowd: often with *around* or *about* —**in the mill** in preparation —**through the mill** [Informal] through a hard, painful, instructive experience, training, test, etc.

☆**mill**[2] (mil) *n.* ⟦for L *millesimus,* thousandth < *mille,* thousand: cf. CENT[1]⟧ one tenth of a cent: $.001: a monetary unit used in calculating but not as a coin

mill[3] (mil) *n.* [Slang] *alt. sp. of* MIL[2]

Mill (mil) 1 **James** 1773-1836; Scot. philosopher, historian, & economist 2 **John Stuart** 1806-73; Eng. philosopher & economist: son of James

☆**mill·age** (mil′ij) *n.* ⟦MILL[2] + -AGE⟧ taxation in mills per dollar of valuation

Mil·lais (mi lā′), Sir **John Everett** 1829-96; Eng. painter

Mil·lay (mi lā′), **Edna St. Vincent** 1892-1950; U.S. poet

mill·cake (mil′kāk′) *n.* the residue left after the oil has been pressed from linseed

mill·dam (-dam′) *n.* 1 a dam built across a stream to raise its level enough to provide water power for turning a mill wheel 2 MILLPOND

milled (mild) *adj.* 1 ground, cut, worked, etc. by or in a mill 2 having the edges raised and ridged or grooved, as a coin; knurled

mille-feuille (mēl fö′y′) *n., pl.* ***mille-feuilles′*** (-fö′y′) ⟦Fr < *mille,* thousand + *feuille,* a leaf⟧ a small pastry consisting of many thin layers of puff pastry, filled with custard, whipped cream, fruit, purée, etc.

mil·le·fi·o·ri or **mil·le·fi·o·re** (mil′ə fē ôr′ē) *n.* ⟦< It *mille fiori,* a thousand flowers⟧ a type of ornamental glasswork created by fusing glass rods (*murrini*) of various colors and diameters, typically in such a way as to form a floral pattern when the bundle is cut and displayed in cross section: see also MURRINE

mille·fleurs or **mille·fleur** (mēl′flur′) *adj.* ⟦< Fr *mille fleurs,* a thousand flowers⟧ having an allover, multicolored pattern of many flowers, as a tapestry or ornamental glassware

mil·le·nar·i·an (mil′ə ner′ē ən) *adj.* ⟦< LL *millenarius,* containing a thousand < L *milleni,* a thousand each < *mille,* thousand + -AN⟧ of 1,000 years; of the millennium —*n.* a person who believes in the coming of THE MILLENNIUM —mil′le·nar′i·an·ism′ *n.*

mil·le·nar·y (mil′ə ner′ē) *adj.* ⟦LL *millenarius:* see prec.⟧ 1 of or consisting of a thousand, esp. a thousand years 2 of THE MILLENNIUM or millenarians —*n., pl.* **-nar′ies** 1 a thousand 2 a thousand years; millennium 3 a thousandth anniversary or its commemoration 4 a millenarian

mil·len·ni·um (mi len′ē əm) *n., pl.* **-ni·ums** or **-ni·a** (-ə) ⟦ModL < L *mille,* thousand + *annus,* year (after L *biennium*): see ANNUAL⟧ 1 any period of 1,000 years [*2000* B.C. *through 1001* B.C. *is the 2d millennium* B.C.] 2 a period of 1,000 years reckoned from a certain time, esp. from the beginning of the Christian Era (A.D. 1) [*the year* A.D. *2001 marks the beginning of the third millennium*] 3 a 1,000th anniversary or its commemoration 4 any period of great happiness, peace, prosperity, etc.; imagined golden age —**the millennium** [*sometimes* **M-**] *Christian Theol.* the period of 1,000 years during which Christ will reign on earth: Rev. 20:1-5 —**mil·len′ni·al** *adj.* —**mil·len′ni·al·ism′** *n.* —**mil·len′ni·al·ist** *n.*

millennium bug the Y2K problem: see Y2K

mil·le·pede (mil′ə pēd′) *n. var. of* MILLIPEDE

mil·le·pore (-pôr′) *n.* ⟦Fr *millépore* < *mille,* thousand + *pore* < L *porus,* PORE[2]⟧ any of an order (Milleporina) of coral-like hydrozoans that form branching or leaflike calcareous masses with small openings on the surface

mill·er (mil′ər) *n.* ⟦ME *mylnere*⟧ 1 a person who owns or operates a mill, esp. a flour mill 2 *a)* MILLING MACHINE *b)* a tool to be used in such a machine 3 any of various moths with wings that look dusty or powdered, suggesting a miller's clothes

Mil·ler (mil′ər) 1 **Arthur (Asher)** 1915-2005; U.S. playwright 2 **Henry (Valentine)** 1891-1980; U.S. writer 3 **Joe** 1684-1738; Eng. stage comedian: *Joe Miller's Jest-book* (1739), a book of jokes attributed to him, was published after his death

mill·er·ite (mil′ər īt′) *n.* ⟦Ger *millerit,* after W. H. *Miller* (1801-80), Brit mineralogist⟧ a soft, yellowish, metallic, rhombohedral mineral, NiS, usually in the form of brittle, fine, hairlike crystals; nickel sulfide

☆**Mill·er·ite** (mil′ər īt′) *n.* [Historical] a follower of William Miller (1782-1849), a U.S. preacher who declared that the end of the world and the second coming of Christ would occur in 1843

mill·er's-thumb (mil′ərz thum′) *n.* SCULPIN (sense 1)

mil·les·i·mal (mi les′ə məl) *adj.* ⟦L *millesimus* < *mille,* thousand + -AL⟧ 1 thousandth 2 of or consisting of thousandths —*n.* a thousandth

mil·let (mil′it) *n.* ⟦ME *milet* < MFr, dim. of *mil* < L *milium,* millet < IE **melēi-,* var. of base **mel-,* to grind > MILL[1], Gr *melinē,* millet⟧ 1 *a)* a cereal grass (*Panicum miliaceum*) whose small grain is used for food in Europe and Asia *b)* the grain 2 any of several other similar grasses or their seed, as foxtail millet and pearl millet

Mil·let (mi lā′; *Fr* mē ye′, -le′), **Jean Fran·çois** (zhän frän swá′) 1814-75; Fr. painter

mil·li- (mil′i, -ə, -ē) ⟦< L *mille,* thousand⟧ *combining form* one thousandth part of; the factor 10^{-3} [*millimeter*]

mil·li·am·pere (mil′ē am′pir) *n.* one thousandth of an ampere: abbrev. *mA*

mil·liard (mil′yərd, -yärd′) *n.* ⟦Fr < *million* (see MILLION) + *-ard* (see -ARD), orig., "large million"⟧ *Brit. var. of* BILLION

mil·li·ar·y (mil′ē er′ē) *adj.* ⟦L *milliarius,* containing a thousand < *mille,* thousand: see MILE⟧ of the ancient Roman mile, or 1,000 paces —*n., pl.* **-ar′ies** an ancient Roman milestone

mil·li·bar (mil′i bär′) *n.* ⟦< MILLI- + Gr *baros,* weight⟧ one thousandth of a bar (1,000 dynes per square centimeter or 100 pascals): 34 millibars equals about one inch of mercury: abbrev. *mb*

Mil·li·cent (mil′i sənt) *n.* ⟦OFr *Melisent* < OHG *Amalaswind* < *amal,* work + **swind-,* strong, akin to Goth *swinths*⟧ a feminine name

mil·li·cu·rie (mil′i kyoor′ē) *n.* one thousandth of a curie: abbrev. *mCi* or *mc*

mil·li·e·quiv·a·lent (mil′i ē kwiv′ə lənt) *n.* ⟦see MILLI-⟧ one thousandth of the equivalent weight of an element or compound: abbrev. *mEq*

mil·li·far·ad (mil′i far′ad, -əd) *n.* one thousandth of a farad: abbrev. *mF*

mil·li·gal (-gal′) *n. Physics* one thousandth of a gal

mil·li·gram (mil′i gram′) *n.* ⟦Fr *milligramme*⟧ one thousandth of a gram (0.0154 grain): abbrev. *mg*

mil·li·hen·ry (-hen′rē) *n., pl.* **-rys** or **-ries** *Elec.* one thousandth of a henry: abbrev. *mH*

Mil·li·kan (mil′i kən), **Robert Andrews** 1868-1953; U.S. physicist

mil·li·li·ter (mil′i lēt′ər) *n.* ⟦Fr *millilitre*⟧ one thousandth of a liter, equal to 1.000027 cubic centimeters (0.0338 fluid ounce or 0.061 cubic inch or 16.234 minims): abbrev. *ml:* Brit. sp. **mil′li·li′tre**

mil·lime (mil′ēm′, -im) *n.* ⟦Fr < *millième,* a thousandth < MFr < *mille,* a thousand < L⟧ a monetary unit of Tunisia, equal to 1/1000 of a dinar

mil·li·me·ter (mil′i mēt′ər) *n.* ⟦Fr *millimètre:* see MILLI- & METER[1]⟧ one thousandth of a meter (0.03937 inch): abbrev. *mm:* Brit. sp. **mil′li·me′tre**

mil·line (mil′līn′) *n.* ⟦MIL(LION) + LINE[1]⟧ 1 a unit of measurement equal to a one-column agate line (of an advertisement) in one million copies of a publication 2 the cost per milline of an advertisement

mil·li·ner (mil′i nər) *n.* ⟦< *Milaner,* inhabitant of MILAN, vendor of bonnets and dress wares from MILAN⟧ a person who designs, makes, trims, or sells women's hats

mil·li·ner·y (mil′i ner′ē) *n.* ⟦< prec. + -ERY⟧ 1 women's hats, headdresses, etc. 2 the work or business of a milliner

mill·ing (mil′iŋ) *vt., vi. prp. of* MILL[1] —*n.* 1 the process or business of grinding grain into flour or meal 2 the grinding, cutting, or processing of metal, cloth, etc. in a mill 3 *a)* the process of ridging the edge of a coin, etc. *b)* the ridging thus produced; milled edge 4 circular or random motion of or as of a herd or crowd

milling cutter any of various rotating toothed cutters used in a milling machine to cut or shape metal parts

milling machine a machine with a table on which material rests as it is fed against a rotating milling cutter

mil·lion (mil′yən) *n.* ⟦ME *milliou*n < OFr *million* < It *milione* < *mille,* thousand < L⟧ 1 a thousand thousands; 1,000,000 2 a million (unspecified but understood) monetary units, as dollars, pounds, francs, etc. 3 an indefinite but very large number: a hyperbolic use —*adj.* amounting to one million in number

mil·lion·aire (mil′yə ner′) *n.* ⟦Fr *millionnaire*⟧ a person whose wealth comes to at least a million dollars, pounds, francs, euros, etc.

mil·lion·air·ess (mil′yə ner′is) *n.* a woman or girl whose wealth comes to at least a million dollars, pounds, francs, euros, etc.: see -ESS

mil·lionth (mil′yənth) *adj.* 1 coming last in a series of a million 2 designating any of the million equal parts of something —*n.* 1 the last in a series of a million 2 any of the million equal parts of something

mil·li·pede (mil′i pēd′) *n.* ⟦< L *millepeda* < *mille,* thousand + *pes* (gen. *pedis*), FOOT⟧ any of a class (Diplopoda) of many-legged arthropods with an elongated body having two pairs of walking legs on each segment

mil·li·rem (-rem′) *n.* one thousandth of a rem

mil·li·sec·ond (-sek′ənd) *n.* one thousandth of a second: abbrev. *ms*

mil·li·sie·vert (-sē′vərt) *n.* one thousandth of a sievert: abbrev. *mSv*

mil·li·volt (-vōlt′) *n.* one thousandth of a volt: abbrev. *mV*

mil·li·watt (-wät′) *n.* one thousandth of a watt: abbrev. *mW*

mill·pond (mil′pänd′) *n.* a pond formed by a milldam, from which water flows for driving a mill wheel

mill·race (-rās′) *n.* 1 the current of water that drives a mill wheel 2 the channel in which it runs

mill·run (-run′) *n.* MILLRACE

mill run ☆1 a quantity of ore whose quality or mineral content is tested by milling 2 the mineral obtained by such testing

mill-run (mil′run′) *adj.* ☆just as it comes out of the mill; ordinary; average; run-of-the-mill

mill·stone (-stōn′) *n.* 1 either of a pair of large, flat, round stones between which grain or other substances are ground 2 stone used for these, usually a hard sandstone or conglomerate 3 a heavy burden 4 something that grinds, pulverizes, or crushes

mill·stream (-strēm′) *n.* the water flowing in a millrace

mill wheel the wheel, usually a water wheel, that drives the machinery in a mill

☆**mill·work** (-wurk′) *n.* 1 doors, window sashes, moldings, etc. made in a planing mill 2 work done in a mill —**mill′work′er** *n.*

mill·wright (-rīt′) *n.* 1 a person who designs or builds mills or installs their machinery 2 a worker who installs, aligns, maintains, and, sometimes, repairs the machinery and heavy equipment in a factory

Milne (miln), **A(lan) A(lexander)** 1882-1956; Eng. playwright, novelist, & writer of children's books

☆**mi·lo** (mī′lō′) *n.* ⟦< Bantu (Sesuto) *maili*⟧ any of a group of grain sorghums with somewhat juicy stalks and compact heads of soft, white or yellow grains

mi·lord (mi lôrd′) *n.* ⟦Fr < E *my lord*⟧ 1 a former continental term of address for an English nobleman or gentleman 2 an Englishman of high social status: often pejorative or mocking [*a haughty young milord*]

Mí·los (mē′läs′) Greek island of the SW Cyclades, in the Aegean Sea: 58 sq mi (150 sq km): It. name **Mi·lo** (mē′lô)

Mi·losz (mē′wôsh, -lôsh), **Czes·law** (ches′wäf, -läf) (born *Czesława Miłosza*) 1911-2004; Pol. poet, born in Russian-held Lithuania: in the U.S. 1960-2004

☆**mil·pa** (mil′pə) *n.* ⟦MexSp (< Nahuatl), cornfield⟧ [Chiefly Dial.] a small tract of arable land cleared from a forest area; specif., in Mexico and Central America, such a tract that is cultivated until the land is exhausted, then abandoned

☆**milque·toast** (milk′tōst′) *n.* ⟦after Caspar *Milquetoast,* character of this sort in a comic strip by H. T. Webster (1885-1952), U.S. cartoonist (< *milk toast,* toast in warm milk)⟧ a person regarded as timid, shrinking, self-abasing, etc.

Mil·stein (mil′stīn′), **Nathan (Mironovich)** 1904-92; U.S. violinist, born in Russia

milt (milt) *n.* ⟦ME *milte,* prob. < Scand (as in Norw *milt, mjelte*), altered (infl. by ON *milti,* spleen) < base of ON *mjolk,* MILK⟧ 1 the reproductive glands of male fishes, esp. when filled with germ cells and the milky fluid containing them 2 such cells and fluid; fish sperm —*adj.* breeding: said of male fishes —*vt.* to fertilize (fish roe) with milt —**milt′er** *n.*

Mil·ti·a·des (mil tī′ə dēz′) died 489? B.C.; Athenian general: defeated the Persians at Marathon in 490

Mil·ton[1] (milt′'n) *n.* ⟦< the surname or place name *Milton* < OE *Middel-tun* (lit., Middletown) & OE *Mylen-tun* (lit., Mill town)⟧ a masculine name: dim. *Milt, Miltie*

Mil·ton[2] (milt′'n), **John** 1608-74; Eng. poet

Mil·ton·ic (mil tän′ik) *adj.* 1 of or relating to John Milton or his writings 2 like Milton's style, esp. in being solemn, elevated, majestic, etc. Also **Mil·to′ni·an** (-tō′nē ən)

Mil·wau·kee (mil wô′kē) ⟦< Fr < Algonquian, lit., good land, council place⟧ city & port in SE Wis., on Lake Michigan

mim (mim) ***adj.*** ⟦echoic of sound made with pursed lips: cf. MUM[5]⟧ [Brit. Dial.] primly quiet or shy; demure

Mi·mas (mī′mas′) ***n.*** ⟦after *Mimas,* in Gr myth., a giant in the war with the gods⟧ a small satellite of Saturn with a gigantic crater

mime (mīm) ***n.*** ⟦L *mimus* < Gr *mimos,* imitator, actor⟧ **1** an ancient Greek or Roman farce, in which people and events were mimicked and burlesqued **2** representation of an action, character, mood, etc. by means of gestures and actions rather than words **3** an actor, often, specif., a street performer, who performs in mime **4** a mimic or pantomimist —***vt.* mimed, mim′ing** to imitate, mimic, or act out as a mime —***vi.*** to act as a mime; play a part with gestures and actions, but without words —**mim′er** ***n.***

☆**mim·e·o·graph** (mim′ē ə graf′) ***n.*** ⟦< former trademark < Gr *mimeomai,* I imitate < *mimos* (see prec.) + -GRAPH⟧ a machine for making copies of written, drawn, or typewritten matter by means of a stencil placed around a drum containing ink —***vt.*** **1** to make copies of on such a machine **2** to make (copies) on such a machine

mi·me·sis (mi mē′sis, mī-) ***n.*** ⟦ModL < Gr *mimēsis,* imitation < *mimos,* imitator⟧ imitation; specif., *a)* *Art, Literature* imitation or representation; often, specif., IMITATION (***n.*** *5b*) *b)* *Biol.* MIMICRY

mi·met·ic (mi met′ik, mī-) ***adj.*** ⟦Gr *mimētikos* < *mimeisthai,* to imitate < *mimos,* actor⟧ **1** of or characterized by imitation; imitative **2** of or characterized by mimicry —**mi·met′i·cal·ly** ***adv.***

mim·ic (mim′ik) ***adj.*** ⟦L *mimicus* < Gr *mimikos* < *mimos,* actor⟧ **1** inclined to copy; imitative **2** of, or having the nature of, mimicry or imitation **3** make-believe; simulated; mock [*mimic* tears] —***n.*** a person or thing that imitates; esp., a performer skilled in mimicry —***vt.* mim′icked, mim′ick·ing** **1** to imitate in speech or action, often so as to ridicule **2** to copy closely; imitate accurately **3** to resemble closely; have or take on the appearance of [an animal's natural coloration that *mimics* the foliage] —**SYN.** IMITATE —**mim′ick·er** ***n.***

mim·ic·ry (mim′ik rē) ***n., pl.*** **-ries** **1** the practice or art, or an instance or way, of mimicking **2** close resemblance, in color, form, or behavior, of one organism to another or to some object in its environment, as of some insects to the leaves or twigs of plants: it serves to disguise or conceal an organism from a predator or prey

Mi·mir (mē′mir′) ***n.*** ⟦ON *Mīmir,* redupl. of Gmc **mer-* < IE base **(s)mer-,* to remember > MOURN⟧ *Norse Myth.* a giant guarding the spring of wisdom at the root of the tree Ygdrasil

mi·mo·sa (mi mō′sə, mī-; -zə) ***n.*** ⟦ModL < L *mimus:* see MIME: from the apparent mimicry of the sensitivity of animal life⟧ **1** any of a large genus (*Mimosa*) of trees, shrubs, and herbs of the mimosa family, growing in warm regions and usually having bipinnate leaves, and heads or spikes of small, white, yellow, or pink flowers **2** any of several similar trees of this family, including the albizia **3** a drink made of champagne and orange juice —***adj.*** designating a family (Mimosaceae, order Fabales) of dicotyledonous, leguminous trees and shrubs, including acacia and mesquite

min *abbrev.* **1** mineralogical **2** mineralogy **3** minim(s) **4** minimum **5** mining **6** minister **7** minor **8** minute(s)

mi·na[1] (mī′nə) ***n., pl.*** **-nae** (-nē) or **-nas** ⟦L < Gr *mna,* of Sem orig., as in Heb *māneh*⟧ a varying unit of weight and money used in ancient Greece, Egypt, etc., generally equal to 1⁄60 talent, 100 drachmas, or 50 shekels

mi·na[2] (mī′nə) ***n.*** *alt. sp. of* MYNA

min·a·ble or **mine·a·ble** (mīn′ə bəl) ***adj.*** that can be mined

mi·na·cious (mi nā′shəs) ***adj.*** ⟦< L *minax* (gen. *minacis*): see MENACE & -OUS⟧ menacing; threatening —**mi·nac′i·ty** (-nas′ə tē) ***n.***

Min·a·ma·ta disease (min′ə mät′ə) ⟦after *Minamata,* Jpn fishing village where first diagnosed⟧ mercury poisoning from industrially contaminated water and fish, often resulting in severe neurological disorders or death

min·a·ret (min′ə ret′, min′ə ret′) ***n.*** ⟦Fr < Turk *menāret* < Ar *manāra(t),* lighthouse, minaret < base of *nār,* fire⟧ a high, slender tower attached to a mosque, with one or more projecting balconies from which a muezzin, or crier, calls the people to prayer

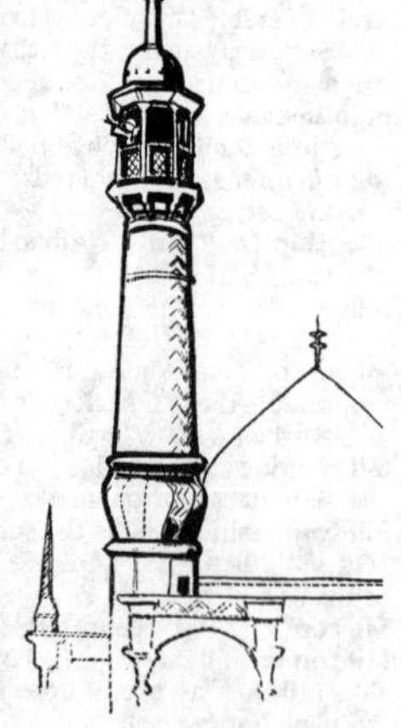
minaret

Mi·nas Basin (mī′nəs) ⟦< Fr *Le Bassin des Mines,* lit., basin of mines, for nearby copper mines⟧ NE arm of the Bay of Fundy, Nova Scotia, Canada: *c.* 60 mi (97 km) long

Mi·nas Ge·rais (mē′nəs zhi rīs′) state of EC Brazil: 227,176 sq mi (588,384 sq km); cap. Belo Horizonte

Mi·na·ti·tlán (mē′nə ti tlän′) city in SE Mexico

min·a·to·ry (min′ə tôr′ē) ***adj.*** ⟦OFr *minatoire* < LL *minatorius* < pp. of L *minari,* to threaten: see MENACE⟧ **1** menacing; threatening **2** conveying or constituting a threat

mi·nau·dière (mē′nō dyer′) ***n.*** ⟦Fr, coquette (obs.) < fem. of adj. *minaudier,* simpering, affected⟧ a woman's small handbag, often lavishly decorated with expensive materials, as precious metals or gems, used for formal wear

mince (mins) ***vt.* minced, minc′ing** ⟦ME *mincen* < OFr *mincier* < VL **minutiare* < L *minutus,* small: see MINUTE[2]⟧ **1** to cut up or chop up (meat, etc.) into very small pieces; hash **2** to lessen the force of; weaken, as by euphemism [let's not *mince* words] —***vi.*** **1** to speak or act with affected elegance or daintiness **2** to walk with short steps or in an affected, dainty manner —***n.*** MINCEMEAT —**not mince matters** to speak frankly —**minc′er** ***n.***

mince·meat (-mēt′) ***n.*** ⟦< *minced meat*⟧ **1** a mixture of chopped apples, spices, suet, raisins, etc., and sometimes meat, used as a pie filling **2** [Obs.] minced meat —**make mincemeat of** **1** to chop into small pieces **2** to defeat or refute completely

mince pie a pie with a filling of mincemeat

minc·ing (min′siŋ) ***adj.*** **1** affectedly elegant or dainty: of a person or a person's speech, manner, etc. **2** characterized by short steps or affected daintiness [a *mincing* walk] —**minc′ing·ly** ***adv.***

mind (mīnd) ***n.*** ⟦ME *mynde* < OE *(ge)mynd,* memory < IE base **men-,* to think > Gr *menos,* spirit, force, L *mens,* mind⟧ **1** memory; recollection or remembrance [her name slips my *mind*] **2** what one thinks; opinion [speak your *mind*] **3** *a)* that which thinks, perceives, feels, wills, etc.; seat or subject of consciousness *b)* the thinking and perceiving part of consciousness; intellect or intelligence *c)* attention; notice *d)* all of an individual's conscious experiences *e)* the conscious and the unconscious together as a unit; psyche **4** the intellect in its normal state; reason; sanity [to lose one's *mind*] **5** a person having intelligence or regarded as an intellect [the great *minds* of today] **6** way, state, or direction of thinking and feeling [the reactionary *mind*] ☆**7** [**M-**] in Christian Science, God: in full **Divine Mind** **8** *Philos.* consciousness and thought as an element in reality: contrasted with MATTER —***vt.*** **1** to direct one's mind to; specif., *a)* [Now Dial.] to perceive; observe *b)* to pay attention to; heed *c)* to obey *d)* to attend to; apply oneself to (a task, etc.) *e)* to tend; take care of; watch over; look after [*mind* the baby] *f)* to be careful about; watch out for [*mind* those rickety stairs] **2** *a)* to care about; feel concern about *b)* to object to; dislike [to *mind* the cold] **3** [Dial.] to remember: sometimes used reflexively **4** [Dial.] to intend; purpose **5** [Now Chiefly Dial.] to remind —***vi.*** **1** to pay attention; give heed **2** to be obedient **3** to be careful; watch out **4** *a)* to care; feel concern *b)* to object —**bear (or keep) in mind** to be mindful of; remember —**be in one's right mind** to be mentally well; be sane —**be of one mind** to have the same opinion or desire —**be of two minds** to be undecided or irresolute —**call to mind** **1** to remember **2** to be a reminder of: also **bring to mind** —**change one's mind** **1** to change one's opinion **2** to change one's intention, purpose, or wish —**give someone a piece of one's mind** to criticize or rebuke someone sharply —**have a good mind to** to feel inclined to —**have half a mind to** to be somewhat inclined to —**have in mind** **1** to remember **2** to think of **3** to intend; purpose —**know one's own mind** to know one's own real thoughts, desires, etc. —**make up one's mind** to form a definite opinion or decision —**meeting of (the) minds** an agreement —**never mind** **1** don't be concerned; it doesn't matter **2** don't be concerned about [*never mind* the cat: she'll be fine here alone] **3** not to mention [it's cold and dark, *never mind* the fact that it's raining] —**on someone's mind** **1** occupying someone's thoughts **2** worrying someone —**out of one's mind** **1** mentally ill; insane **2** frantic (*with* worry, grief, etc.) —**put someone in mind of** to remind someone of —**put (or set) one's mind to** to be determined to —**set one's mind on** to be determined on or determinedly desirous of —**take one's mind off** to stop one from thinking about; turn one's attention from —**to one's mind** in one's opinion —**mind′er** ***n.***

mind-al·ter·ing (mīnd′ôl′tər iŋ) ***adj.*** affecting the mind or state of consciousness; esp., PSYCHEDELIC [a *mind-altering* drug]

Min·da·na·o (min′də nou′, -nä′ō) 2d largest island of the Philippines, at the S end of the group: 36,537 sq mi (94,630 sq km)

mind-bend·ing (mīnd′ben′diŋ) ***adj.*** [Slang] MIND-BLOWING —**mind′-bend′er** ***n.***

mind-blow·ing (mīnd′blō′iŋ) ***adj.*** [Slang] **1** PSYCHEDELIC **2** causing shock, surprise, excitement, etc.; overwhelming **3** difficult to comprehend; confusing —**mind′blow′er** ***n.***

☆**mind-bog·gling** (mīnd′bäg′liŋ) ***adj.*** [Informal] **1** hard to comprehend; confusing **2** surprising, shocking, overwhelming, etc. —**mind′-bog′gler** ***n.***

mind·ed (mīn′did) ***adj.*** **1** having a (specified kind of) mind: used in hyphenated compounds [high-*minded*] **2** having a mind to; inclined; disposed

mind·er (mīn′dər) ***n.*** [Chiefly Brit.] **1** a person who minds, or attends to the needs of, another **2** [Informal] an aide or bodyguard given a degree of control over the actions, whereabouts, etc. of another person

mind-ex·pand·ing (mīnd′ek span′diŋ) ***adj.*** PSYCHEDELIC

mind·ful (mīnd′fəl) ***adj.*** having in mind; aware, heedful, or careful (*of*) [to be *mindful* of the danger] —**mind′ful·ly** ***adv.*** —**mind′ful·ness** ***n.***

mind·less (-lis) ***adj.*** **1** not using one's mind; showing little or no intelligence or intellect; senseless or thoughtless **2** taking no thought; heedless or careless (*of*); unmindful —**mind′less·ly** ***adv.*** —**mind′less·ness** ***n.***

Min·do·ro (min dôr′ō) island of the Philippines, south of Luzon: 3,759 sq mi (9,736 sq km)

mind reader a person who seems or professes to be able to perceive another's thoughts without apparent means of communication —**mind reading**

mind-set (mīnd′set′) ***n.*** a fixed mental attitude formed by experience, education, prejudice, etc.: also written **mind′set′**

mind's eye the imagination

mine[1] (mīn) ***pron.*** ⟦ME *min* < OE, gen. sing of *ic,* I, akin to Ger *mein:* for base see ME⟧ that or those belonging to me: the possessive form of I[2], used without a following noun, often after *of* [that book is *mine; mine* are better; he is a friend of *mine]* —***possessive pronominal adj.*** [Archaic] my: used before a word beginning with a vowel or the letter *h [mine* eyes, *mine* honor]; also used after a noun in direct address *[*daughter *mine]*

mine[2] (mīn) ***n.*** ⟦ME < MFr < VL **mina* < Celt, as in Ir *mein,* Welsh *mwyn,* vein of metal⟧ **1** *a)* a large excavation made in the earth, from which to extract metallic ores, coal, precious stones, salt, or certain other minerals (distinguished from QUARRY[3]) *b)* the surface buildings, shafts, elevators, etc. of such an excavation *c)* a deposit of ore, coal, etc. **2** any great source of supply *[*a *mine* of information*]* **3** a kind of fireworks device that explodes in the air and scatters a number of smaller fireworks **4** *Mil. a)* a tunnel dug under an enemy's trench, fort, etc., esp. one in which an explosive is placed to destroy the enemy or its fortifications *b)* an explosive charge in a container, buried in the ground for destroying enemy troops or vehicles on land, or placed in the sea for destroying enemy ships **5** *Zool.* the burrow of an insect, esp. of a leaf miner —***vi.* mined, min′ing** ⟦ME *minen* < OFr *miner*⟧ to dig a mine; specif., *a)* to dig ores, coal, etc. from the earth *b)* to dig or lay military mines —***vt.* 1** *a)* to dig in (the earth) for ores, coal, etc. *b)* to dig or remove (ores, coal, etc.) from the earth **2** to take from (a source) **3** *a)* to dig a tunnel under (an enemy installation) *b)* to place explosive mines in or under **4** to make hollows under the surface of *[*leaves *mined* by larvae*]* **5** to undermine or ruin slowly by secret methods, plotting, etc.

mine detector an electromagnetic device for locating the position of hidden explosive mines

mine·field (mīn′fēld′) ***n.*** an area on land or in water where explosive mines have been set: often used fig. for any situation fraught with problems or pitfalls

mine·lay·er (mīn′lā′ər) ***n.*** a naval vessel specially designed and equipped to lay explosive mines in the water

min·er (-ər) ***n.*** ⟦ME *minour* < OFr < *miner,* to MINE[2]⟧ **1** a person whose work is digging coal, ore, etc. in a mine **2** [Archaic] a soldier who mines enemy installations, etc.

min·er·al (min′ər əl, min′rəl) ***n.*** ⟦OFr < ML *minerale,* neut. of *mineralis,* mineral < *minera,* ore < VL **mina,* MINE[2]⟧ **1** an inorganic substance occurring naturally in the earth and having a consistent and distinctive set of physical properties (e.g., a crystalline structure, hardness, color, etc.) and a composition that can be expressed by a chemical formula: sometimes applied to substances in the earth of organic origin, such as coal **2** ORE **3** any substance that is neither vegetable nor animal **4** any element or inorganic compound needed by plants and animals for proper growth and functioning, as iron, phosphorus, or nitrate **5** [Brit.] *a)* [*usually pl.*] MINERAL WATER *b)* a flavored, carbonated soft drink —***adj.*** of, like, consisting of, or containing a mineral or minerals

min·er·al·ize (min′ər ə līz′) ***vt.* -ized′, -iz′ing 1** to convert (organic matter) into a mineral; petrify **2** to impregnate (water, etc.) with minerals **3** to convert (a metal) into an ore, as by oxidation —**min′er·al·i·za′tion *n.***

min·er·al·iz·er (-lī′zər) ***n.*** **1** a substance, such as water, acid, or certain gases, which, when dissolved in magma, lowers the melting point and viscosity, promotes crystallization, and influences the formation of minerals **2** an element, as sulfur, arsenic, etc., that combines chemically with a metal to form an ore

☆**mineral jelly** PETROLATUM

min·er·al·o·gy (min′ər äl′ə jē, -al′-) ***n.*** ⟦< MINERAL + -LOGY⟧ **1** the scientific study of minerals **2** *pl.* **-gies** a book about minerals —**min′er·al·og′i·cal** (-ər əl äj′i kəl) ***adj.*, min′er·al·og′ic —min′er·al·og′i·cal·ly *adv.* —min′er·al′o·gist *n.***

mineral oil 1 any oil found in the rock strata of the earth; specif., petroleum **2** any colorless, tasteless oil derived from petroleum and used as a laxative

mineral spring any spring of natural mineral water

mineral tar MALTHA (sense 1)

mineral water water naturally or artificially impregnated with mineral salts or gases

mineral wax OZOCERITE

☆**mineral wool** a fibrous material made from molten rock, slag, or glass and used as insulation in buildings

Mi·ner·va (mi nur′və) ***n.*** ⟦L, prob. < Etr⟧ **1** a feminine name: dim. *Minnie* **2** *Rom. Myth.* the goddess of wisdom, technical skill, and invention: identified with the Greek Athena

mi·ne·stro·ne (min′ə strō′nē) ***n.*** ⟦It < *minestra,* soup < *minestrare,* to serve < L *ministrare:* see MINISTER, *vt.*⟧ a thick vegetable soup containing vermicelli, barley, etc. in a meat broth

mine·sweep·er (mīn′swēp′ər) ***n.*** a naval vessel specially designed and equipped for destroying enemy mines at sea

mine·work·er (mīn′wur′kər) ***n.*** MINER (sense 1)

Ming (miŋ) ***n.*** ⟦Chin, lit., luminous⟧ Chin. dynasty (1368-1644): period noted for scholarly achievements & artistic works, esp. porcelains

min·gle (miŋ′gəl) ***vt.* -gled, -gling** ⟦ME *mengelen,* freq. of *mengen* < OE *mengan,* to mix, akin to Ger *mengen* < IE base **menk-,* to knead > Gr *massein*⟧ **1** to bring or mix together; combine; blend **2** [Now Rare] to make by mixing ingredients; compound —***vi.* 1** to be or become mixed, blended, etc. **2** to join, unite, associate, or take part with others; specif., to interact with others at a party or other social gathering —**SYN.** MIX —**min′gler *n.***

ming tree ⟦after MING⟧ an artificial plant made in imitation of a bonsai

Min·gus (miŋ′gəs), **Charles** (also called *Charlie Mingus*) 1922-79; U.S. jazz bassist & composer

min·gy (min′jē) ***adj.* -gi·er, -gi·est** ⟦prob. altered < MANGY, after STINGY[1]⟧ [Informal] mean and stingy

min·i (min′ē) ***n.*,** *pl.* **minis 1** something that is very small in size or limited in scope, extent, etc., esp. as compared to others of the same kind **2** *short for: a)* MINISKIRT *b)* MINICOMPUTER —***adj.*** very small; specif., much smaller or much more limited than the usual size, scope, extent, etc.

min·i- (min′i, -ə, -ē) ⟦< fol.⟧ *combining form* **1** miniature, very small, very short *[miniskirt]* **2** of lesser scope, extent, etc. than usual: used in nonce compounds, often hyphenated *[mini-*crisis*]*

min·i·a·ture (min′ē ə chər, min′i chər) ***n.*** ⟦It *miniatura,* rubrication, illumination of manuscripts < ML < pp. of L *miniare,* to paint red < *minium,* red lead (see MINIUM): sense infl. by L *minutus,* MINUTE[2]⟧ **1** a small painting or illuminated letter, as in a medieval manuscript **2** *a)* a very small painting, esp. a portrait, done on ivory, vellum, etc. *b)* the art of making such paintings **3** a copy or model on a very small scale **4** a breed of animal or plant much smaller than the ordinary or traditional type —***adj.*** on or done on a very small scale; diminutive; minute —**SYN.** SMALL —**in miniature** on a small scale; greatly reduced

miniature golf a form of golf, played with putters on a small-scale course characterized by a wide variety of ingenious obstacles

min·i·a·tur·ist (min′ē ə chər ist) ***n.*** a painter of miniatures

min·i·a·tur·ize (-īz′) ***vt.* -ized′, -iz′ing** to make in a very small and compact form —**min′i·a·tur′i·za′tion *n.* —min′i·a·tur·iz′er *n.***

min·i·bike (min′ē bīk′) ***n.*** ⟦MINI- + BIKE⟧ a compact type of motorcycle, usually intended for use as an off-road vehicle

☆**min·i·bus** (min′ē bus′) ***n.*,** *pl.* **-bus′es** ⟦MINI- + BUS⟧ a very small bus

min·i·cam (min′ē kam′) ***n.*** ⟦MINI- + CAM(ERA)⟧ a portable television camera operated from the shoulder, for telecasting or videotaping news events, sports, etc.

☆**min·i·camp** (min′ē kamp′) ***n.*** *Sports* a series of small-scale training sessions typically held before a team's regular TRAINING CAMP

min·i·com·put·er (min′ē kəm pyo͞ot′ər) ***n.*** a computer intermediate in size, power, storage capacity, etc. between a mainframe and microcomputer

Min·i·coy (min′i koi′) southernmost island of the Lakshadweep territory, India, off the SW coast of India

Min·ié ball (min′ē, min′ē ā′) ⟦after C. E. *Minié* (1814-79), Fr inventor⟧ a cone-shaped rifle bullet used in the 19th cent.

min·i·fy (min′i fī′) ***vt.* -fied′, -fy′ing** ⟦< L *minor,* less, by assoc. with MAGNIFY⟧ to make or make seem smaller or less important —**min′i·fi·ca′tion *n.* —min′i·fi′er *n.***

min·i·kin (min′i kin) ***n.*** ⟦MDu *minneken,* dim. of *minne,* love: see MINNESINGER & -KIN⟧ **1** [Obs.] a darling **2** [Rare] anything very small and delicate —***adj.*** [Archaic] **1** diminutive **2** affected

min·im (min′im) ***n.*** ⟦ME *mynym* (in sense 3) < L *minimus,* least: see MINIMUM⟧ **1** the smallest unit of liquid measure, equal to 1/60 fluid dram or about half a drop (0.0616 milliliter): the British and Canadian imperial minim equals 1/60 of an imperial fluid dram or 0.0592 milliliter: abbrev. *min* **2** a tiny portion **3** [Chiefly Brit.] HALF NOTE —***adj.*** smallest; tiniest

min·i·ma (min′i mə) ***n.*** *alt. pl. of* MINIMUM

min·i·mal (min′i məl) ***adj.*** **1** smallest or least possible; of or constituting a minimum **2** of or having to do with minimalism or minimal art —**min′i·mal·ly *adv.***

minimal art [*often* **M- A-**] art based on MINIMALISM (sense 2)

min·i·mal·ism (min′i məl iz′əm) ***n.*** **1** action of a minimal or conservative kind **2** a movement in art, dance, music, etc., beginning in the 1960s, in which only the simplest designs, structures, forms, etc. are used, often repetitively, and the artist's individuality is minimized —**min′i·mal·ist *adj.*, *n.***

min·i·mal·ize (min′ə mə līz′) ***vt.* -ized′, -iz′ing** to make minimal; reduce to basic components

min·i·max (min′ē maks′, -i-) ***adj.*** ⟦< MINI(MUM) + MAX(IMUM)⟧ of or having to do with a strategy or technique for minimizing the maximum error or loss —***n.*** such a strategy or technique

min·i·mill (min′ē mil′) ***n.*** a relatively small type of steel mill using, as raw material, scrap melted in an electric furnace rather than iron ore smelted in a blast furnace

min·i·mize (min′i mīz′) ***vt.* -mized′, -miz′ing 1** to reduce to a minimum; decrease to the least possible amount, degree, etc. **2** to estimate or make appear to be of the least possible amount, value, or importance —**SYN.** DISPARAGE —**min′i·mi·za′tion** (-mə zā′shən, -mī′-) ***n.*** —**min′i·miz′er *n.***

min·i·mum (-məm) ***n.*,** *pl.* **-mums** or **-ma** (-mə) ⟦L, neut. of *minimus,* least, superl. < base of *minor,* MINOR⟧ **1** the smallest quantity, number, or degree possible or permissible **2** the lowest degree or point (of a varying quantity, as temperature) reached or recorded; lowest limit of variation **3** *Math.* the smallest of a specified set of real numbers —***adj.* 1** smallest possible, permissible, or reached **2** of, marking, or setting a minimum or minimums

minimum wage 1 a wage set by contract or by law as the lowest that may be paid to employees doing a specified job **2** LIVING WAGE

min·ing (mīn′iŋ) ***n.*** **1** the act, process, or work of removing ores, coal, etc. from a mine, glacial deposit, etc. **2** the act or process of laying explosive mines

min·ion[1] (min′yən) ***n.*** ⟦Fr *mignon,* favorite, darling: see MIGNON⟧ **1** a favorite, esp. one who is a fawning, servile follower: term of contempt **2** a subordinate official, deputy, or the like **3** [Obs.] a mistress or paramour —***adj.*** [Obs.] delicate, dainty, etc.

min·ion[2] (min′yən) ***n.*** *var. of* MINYAN

min·is·cule (min′i skyo͞ol′) *adj. disputed var. of* MINUSCULE (*adj.* 2)
min·i·se·ries or **min·i-se·ries** (min′ē sir′ēz) *n., pl.* **-ries** a TV drama or docudrama broadcast serially in a limited number of episodes
min·ish (min′ish) *vt., vi.* ⟦ME *minusschen* < OFr *menuisier,* to lessen, make small < VL **minutiare* < L *minutus,* MINUTE²⟧ [Archaic] to make or become less; diminish
min·i·skirt (min′ē skurt′) *n.* ⟦MINI- + SKIRT⟧ a very short skirt ending well above the knee —**min′i·skirt′ed** *adj.*
min·i·sode (min′i sōd′) *n.* ⟦MINI- + (EPI)SODE⟧ a very short, abridged version of a television program
min·i·state (min′ē stāt′) *n.* a small country
min·is·ter (min′is tər) *n.* ⟦OFr *ministre* < L *minister,* an attendant, servant, in LL(Ec), Christian preacher < base of L *minor,* MINOR: formed prob. after *magister,* MASTER⟧ **1** a person acting for another as agent and carrying out given orders or designs; specif., *a)* a person appointed by the head of a government to take charge of some department *b)* a diplomatic officer sent to a foreign nation to represent his or her government, usually ranking below an ambassador **2** *a)* anyone authorized to carry out or assist in the spiritual functions of a church *b)* an ordained member of a Protestant church; esp., a pastor **3** the superior of certain Roman Catholic religious orders **4** a person or thing thought of as serving as the agent of some power, force, etc. [*a minister of evil*] —*vt.* ⟦ME *ministren* < OFr *ministrer* < L *ministrare*⟧ [Archaic] **1** to supply; provide **2** to administer —*vi.* **1** to serve as a minister in a church **2** to give help (*to*)
min·is·te·ri·al (min′is tir′ē əl) *adj.* ⟦Fr *ministériel* < LL *ministerialis*⟧ **1** of ministry, a minister, or ministers collectively **2** serving as a minister, or agent; subordinate **3** *a)* having the nature of or characteristic of the administrative functions of government; executive *b)* designating or of an administrative act carried out in a prescribed manner not allowing for personal discretion **4** being a cause; instrumental —**min′is·te′ri·al·ly** *adv.*
minister plenipotentiary *pl.* **ministers plenipotentiary** a diplomatic representative with full authority to negotiate
min·is·trant (min′is trənt) *adj.* ⟦L *ministrans,* prp.: see MINISTER, *vt.*⟧ serving as a minister —*n.* a person who ministers, or serves
min·is·tra·tion (min′is trā′shən) *n.* ⟦ME *ministracion* < L *ministratio* < pp. of *ministrare,* to MINISTER⟧ **1** MINISTRY (sense 2*a*) **2** administration, as of a sacrament **3** the act or an instance of giving help or care; service —**min′is·tra′tive** *adj.*
min·is·try (min′is trē) *n., pl.* **-tries** ⟦ME *mynysterie* < L *ministerium* < *minister,* MINISTER⟧ **1** *a)* the act of ministering, or serving; ministration *b)* that which serves as a means; agency **2** *a)* the office, function, tenure, or service of a religious minister *b)* ministers of religion collectively; clergy **3** *a)* the department under a minister of government *b)* the term of office of such a minister *c)* the building or buildings of such a department *d)* the ministers of a particular government as a group
☆**min·i·track** (min′i trak′) *n.* a system for tracking artificial orbiting satellites by means of signals received from miniature transmitters
min·i·um (min′ē əm) *n.* ⟦L, of Iberian orig., as in Basque *armineá*⟧ **1** the color vermilion **2** RED LEAD
min·i·van (min′ē van′) *n.* ⟦MINI- + VAN³⟧ a motor vehicle for passengers, similar to, but smaller than, a van, usually with windows all around and removable rear seats: also written **mini-van**
min·i·ver (min′ə vər) *n.* ⟦ME *menyuere* < OFr *menu ver,* miniver < *menu,* small (see MENU) < *vair,* VAIR⟧ white fur used for trimming garments, esp. ceremonial robes, as of royalty
mink (miŋk) *n., pl.* **minks** or **mink** ⟦LME *minke* < Scand, as in Swed *menk*⟧ **1** any of several slim, erminelike musteline carnivores with partly webbed feet, esp. a common dark-brown North American species (*Mustela vison*) living in water part of the time **2** its valuable fur, soft, thick, and white to brown in color
min·ke whale (miŋ′kə) ⟦prob. < *Meincke,* surname of a crewman on a 19th-c. Norw whaling ship⟧ a small, swift rorqual whale (*Balaenoptera acutorostrata*) with a dark body and a light belly
Minn *abbrev.* Minnesota
Min·ne·ap·o·lis (min′ē ap′ə lis) ⟦after nearby *Minnehaha* Falls (< Dakota *mní,* water + *xaxa,* waterfall) + Gr *polis,* city⟧ city in E Minn., on the Mississippi, adjacent to St. Paul
min·ne·sing·er (min′i siŋ′ər) *n.* ⟦Ger, altered (< *singer* < *singen,* SING²) < MHG *minnesenger* < *minne,* love < OHG *minna,* orig., loving recollection (for IE base see MIND) + MHG *senger,* a singer < OHG *sangari* < *sang,* SONG + *-ari,* -ER⟧ any of a number of German lyric poets and singers of the 12th to the 14th cent.
Min·ne·so·ta (min′ə sōt′ə) ⟦< Dakota *mnisóta,* Minnesota River, lit., whitish (cloudy or milky) water⟧ Midwestern state of the U.S., adjoining the Canadian border: admitted 1858; 79,610 sq mi (206,189 sq km); cap. St. Paul: abbrev. *MN* or *Minn*
Minnesota Multiphasic Personality Inventory ⟦after the University of prec., where developed⟧ *Psychol.* a true-false test designed to assess personality traits and tendencies
Min·ne·so·tan (min′ə sōt′ən) *adj.* of Minnesota: usually used in the predicate —*n.* a person born or living in Minnesota
Min·ne·wit (min′ə wit), **Peter** *var. of* Peter MINUIT
min·now (min′ō) *n., pl.* **-nows** or **-now** ⟦ME *menow* < or akin to OE *myne,* akin to OHG *muniwa,* prob. < IE base **meni-,* a kind of fish⟧ **1** any of various, usually small, freshwater cyprinoid fishes used commonly as bait **2** any very small fish Also [Informal or Dial.] **min′ny** (-ē), *pl.* **-nies**
Mi·no·an (mi nō′ən, mī-) *adj.* ⟦< MINOS + -AN⟧ designating or of a Bronze Age culture that flourished in Crete *c.* 3000-*c.* 1100 B.C. —*n.* **1** a person living in Minoan Crete **2** the language spoken by the Minoans
mi·nor (mī′nər) *adj.* ⟦ME *menour* < L *minor* < IE **minu-,* small < base **mei-,* to lessen > Gr *meiōn,* less, ON *minni,* smaller⟧ **1** *a)* lesser in size, amount, number, or extent *b)* lesser in importance or rank **2** under full legal age (usually either eighteen or twenty-one years) **3** [Archaic] constituting the minority: said of a party, etc. **4** sad; melancholy; plaintive: from the identification in Occidental music of the minor key with such qualities ☆**5** *Educ.* designating or of a field of study in which students specialize, but less so than in their major **6** *Music a)* designating an imperfect interval smaller than the corresponding major interval by a semitone *b)* characterized by minor intervals, scales, etc. [*the minor key*] *c)* designating a triad having intervals of a minor third between the lower two pitches, and a major third between the upper two pitches *d)* based on the scale pattern of the minor mode (see MINOR SCALE) —*vi.* ☆*Educ.* to make some subject one's minor field of study [*to minor in art*] —*n.* **1** a person under full legal age, who has not yet acquired all civil rights ☆**2** *Educ.* a minor subject or field of study **3** *Music* a minor interval, key, etc. —☆**the minors** the minor leagues, esp. in baseball
minor axis *Geom.* the shorter axis of an ellipse, that passes through the midpoint of, and is perpendicular to, the MAJOR AXIS
Mi·nor·ca¹ (mi nôr′kə) *n.* ⟦after fol.⟧ any of a breed of large chicken with black, white, or buff feathers
Mi·nor·ca² (mi nôr′kə) 2d largest island of the Balearic Islands, east of Majorca: 264 sq mi (684 sq km): Sp. name MENORCA
Mi·nor·ite (mī′nər īt′) *n.* ⟦MINOR, *adj.* + -ITE¹: they regarded themselves as a humbler rank than members of other orders⟧ a Franciscan friar
mi·nor·i·ty (mī nôr′ə tē, mi-; -när′-) *n., pl.* **-ties** ⟦ML *minoritas* < L *minor,* MINOR⟧ **1** the lesser part or smaller number; less than half of a total **2** a group, party, or faction with a smaller number of votes or adherents than the majority **3** *a)* a racial, religious, ethnic, or political group smaller than and differing from the larger population in a community, nation, etc. and often regarded as having particular social or political advantages or disadvantages *b)* a member of such a group (*often used in pl.*) [*scholarship opportunities for minorities*] **4** the period or condition of being under full legal age —*adj.* of or having to do with a group, political party, etc. that constitutes a minority
☆**minor league** any league in a professional sport other than the major leagues —**mi′nor-league′** *adj.*
minor mode *Music* a MODE (*n.* 6*c*) predominantly using the intervals of the minor scale
minor orders *R.C.Ch.* **1** [Historical] four clerical ranks (porter, lector, exorcist, acolyte) conferred before the subdiaconate **2** in the modern Church, the orders of acolyte and lector
minor planet ASTEROID
minor premise in a syllogism, the premise that contains the minor term
Minor Prophets **1** the twelve relatively short books of prophecy in the Bible, from Hosea to Malachi **2** the writers of these books
minor scale *Music* any of the twelve diatonic scales distinguished, from the major scale with the same keynote, by a semitone after the second and seventh tones or after the second, fifth, and seventh tones
minor seminary *R.C.Ch.* a seminary offering typically a high school education and the first two years of college
minor suit *Bridge* diamonds or clubs: so called from their lower value in scoring
minor term in a syllogism, the subject of the conclusion
Mi·nos (mī′näs′) *n.* ⟦Gr *Minōs*⟧ *Gr. Myth.* a king of Crete, son of Zeus by Europa: after he dies he becomes one of the three judges of the dead in the lower world: see also MINOTAUR
Min·o·taur (min′ə tôr′) *n.* ⟦ME *Minotaure* < L *Minotaurus* < Gr *Minōtauros* < *Minōs,* Minos + *tauros,* a bull, akin to L *taurus:* see TAURUS⟧ *Gr. Myth.* a monster with the body of a man and the head of a bull (in some versions, with the body of a bull and the head of a man), confined by Minos in a labyrinth built by Daedalus, and annually fed seven youths and seven maidens from Athens, until killed by Theseus: see also PASIPHAË
min·ox·i·dil (mi näk′sə dil) *n.* ⟦(A)MIN(O)- + OXID(E) + *-il* < ?⟧ a drug, $C_9H_{15}N_5O$, that dilates blood vessels, used internally in treating severe high blood pressure and externally, in a lotion, for treating baldness
Minsk (minsk) capital of Belarus, in the central part
min·ster (min′stər) *n.* ⟦ME *mynstre* < OE *mynster* < LL(Ec) *monasterium,* MONASTERY⟧ any of various large churches or cathedrals: now chiefly in compounds [*Westminster Abbey*]
min·strel (min′strəl) *n.* ⟦ME *menestrel* < OFr, minstrel, servant, orig., official < LL *ministerialis,* imperial officer < L *ministerium,* MINISTRY⟧ **1** any of a medieval class of entertainers who traveled from place to place: known esp. for singing and reciting to musical accompaniment **2** [Old Poet.] a poet, singer, or musician ☆**3** a performer in a minstrel show
☆**minstrel show** ⟦after the Christy *Minstrels,* the first such troupe, organized (*c.* 1842) by Edwin P. Christy in Buffalo, N.Y.⟧ [Historical] a comic variety show presented by a company of performers in blackface
min·strel·sy (-sē) *n., pl.* **-sies** ⟦ME *menestralcie* < OFr *menestralsie*⟧ **1** the art or occupation of a minstrel **2** a group of minstrels **3** a collection of minstrels' ballads or songs
mint¹ (mint) *n.* ⟦ME *mynt* < OE *mynet,* coin, akin to OHG *munizza* < Gmc **munita* < L *moneta,* place for coining money < *Moneta,* epithet of

the goddess Juno, in whose temple in Rome money was coined] 1 *a)* a place where money is coined by authority of the government *b)* [**M-**] a government bureau in charge of this 2 an apparently unlimited supply; large amount [a *mint* of ideas] 3 [Informal] a large amount of money; fortune 4 a source of manufacture or invention —***adj.*** new or in its original condition, as if freshly minted [a postage stamp in *mint* condition] —***vt.*** 1 to coin (money) by stamping metal 2 to invent or create; fabricate —**mint′er** ***n.***

mint[2] (mint) ***n.*** ⟦ME *mynte* < OE *minte,* akin to OHG *minza* < WGmc **minta* < L *menta* < or akin to Gr *mintha*⟧ 1 any of various aromatic plants of the mint family, esp. any of a genus (*Mentha*) whose leaves are used for flavoring and in medicine 2 any of various candies flavored with mint —***adj.*** designating a family (Lamiaceae, order Lamiales) of dicotyledonous plants with fragrant foliage, volatile oil, and square stems, including spearmint, peppermint, basil, and bergamot

mint·age (min′tij) ***n.*** 1 the act or process of minting money 2 the act of inventing or making 3 money produced in a mint 4 the cost of minting money 5 the impression made on a coin

mint jelly (*or* sauce) a jelly (or sauce) flavored with mint leaves, served esp. with lamb

☆**mint julep** a drink consisting of bourbon or brandy, sugar, and mint leaves, typically served in a tall glass packed with crushed ice

mint·y (min′tē) ***adj.*** **mint′i·er, mint′i·est** having the smell or taste of mint

min·u·end (min′yo͞o end′) ***n.*** ⟦L *minuendum,* to be diminished, neut. ger. of *minuere:* see MINUTE[2]⟧ *Arith.* the number or quantity from which another (the *subtrahend*) is to be subtracted

min·u·et (min′yo͞o et′) ***n.*** ⟦Fr *menuet,* orig., minute, tiny < OFr < *menu* (see MENU): from the small steps taken⟧ 1 a slow, stately dance for groups of couples, introduced in France in the 17th cent. 2 the music for this, in 3/4 time: often a movement of certain musical compositions

Min·u·it (min′yo͞o it), **Peter** 1580?-1638; 1st Du. director of New Netherland (1626-31)

mi·nus (mī′nəs) ***prep.*** ⟦LME < L, less, neut. sing. of *minor,* MINOR⟧ 1 reduced by the subtraction of; less [four *minus* two] 2 without; lacking [*minus* a toe] —***adj.*** 1 indicating or involving subtraction [a *minus* sign] 2 somewhat less than the full value of: used after a letter grade [a grade of A *minus*] 3 *Bot.* designating one of two strains of certain fungi and algae which only mate with the opposite (*plus*) strain ☆4 *Elec.* NEGATIVE (*adj.* 4) 5 *Math.* NEGATIVE (*adj.* 6) [a *minus* quantity] —***n.*** 1 a minus sign 2 a negative quantity 3 a negative quality, feature, etc.

mi·nus·cule (min′i skyo͞ol′, mi nus′kyo͞ol′) ***n.*** ⟦Fr < L *minusculus,* rather small, dim. < *minor:* see MINOR⟧ 1 *a)* a small cursive script developed from the uncial and used in medieval manuscripts *b)* a letter in this script 2 any small, or lower-case, letter —***adj.*** 1 of, in, like, or having the nature of minuscules 2 very small; tiny; minute Cf. MAJUSCULE —**mi·nus′cu·lar** ***adj.***

minus sign the sign (−) indicating subtraction or negative quantity

min·ute[1] (min′it) ***n.*** ⟦OFr < ML *minuta* < L (*pars*) *minuta* (*prima*), (first) small (part), term used by Ptolemy for the sixtieth part of a unit in his system of fractions (of the circle, radius, day, later applied also to the hour): see fol.⟧ 1 the sixtieth part of any of certain units; specif., *a)* 1/60 of an hour; sixty seconds *b)* 1/60 of a degree of an arc; sixty seconds (symbol, ′) 2 a very short period of time; moment; instant 3 a specific point in time 4 a measure of the distance usually covered in a minute [five *minutes* from downtown] 5 *a)* a note or memorandum *b)* [*pl.*] an official record of what was said and done at a meeting, convention, etc. —***vt.*** **-ut·ed, -ut·ing** 1 to time to the minute 2 *a)* to make a minute, or memorandum, of; record *b)* to put in the minutes of a meeting, etc. —**the minute (that)** [Informal] just as soon as —**up to the minute** in the latest style, fashion, etc.

mi·nute[2] (mī no͞ot′, -nyo͞ot′; mi-) ***adj.*** ⟦ME < L *minutus,* little, small, pp. of *minuere,* to lessen, diminish < *minor:* see MINOR⟧ 1 very small; tiny 2 of little importance or significance; petty; trifling 3 of, characterized by, or attentive to tiny details; exact; precise —***SYN.*** SMALL —**mi·nute′ness** ***n.***

minute gun a cannon firing at intervals of a minute, as a distress signal or as part of a funeral ceremony

minute hand the longer hand of an analog clock or watch, which indicates the minutes and moves around the dial once every hour

min·ute·ly[1] (min′it lē) ***adj.*** 1 occurring at intervals of a minute 2 occurring very often or continually —***adv.*** 1 every minute 2 often or continually

mi·nute·ly[2] (mī no͞ot′lē, -nyo͞ot′-; mi-) ***adv.*** 1 in a minute manner or in minute detail 2 into tiny pieces

☆**min·ute·man** (min′it man′) ***n., pl.*** **-men′** (-men′) [*also* **M-**] any of the members of the American citizen army at the time of the American Revolution who volunteered to be ready for military service "at a minute's notice"

☆**min·ute steak** (min′it) a small, thin steak that can be cooked quickly

mi·nu·ti·ae (mi no͞o′shə, -nyo͞o′-; -shē ē′, -ī′) ***pl.n., sing.*** **-ti·a** (-shə, -shē ə) ⟦L, pl. of *minutia,* smallness < *minutus,* MINUTE[2]⟧ small or relatively unimportant details

USAGE—*minutiae* is sometimes used as a mass noun, with a singular verb. *Minutia* is often used as a variant of *minutiae,* with plural force and a plural verb. Both variant usages are objected to by some

minx (miŋks) ***n.*** ⟦Early ModE < ? LowG *minsk,* female servant, hussy, person, akin to Ger *mensch:* see MENSCH⟧ a pert, saucy girl or young woman

Min·ya (min′yə), **Al** (al) city in central Egypt, on the Nile

min·yan (min′yən, min yän′) ***n., pl.*** **min′ya·nim′** (-yä nēm′) or **min′yans** ⟦MHeb *minyan* < TalmudHeb, orig., number, quantity < root *mnh,* to number, count⟧ a properly constituted group for a public Jewish prayer service, made up of at least ten Jewish males (in some congregations, males or females) over thirteen years of age

Mi·o·cene (mī′ō sēn′, mī′ə-) ***adj.*** ⟦< Gr *meiōn,* less (see MINOR) + -CENE⟧ [*sometimes* **m-**] designating or of the first geologic epoch of the Neogene, characterized by the joining of what are now Africa, Arabia, and Eurasia and the development of manlike apes —**the Miocene** the Miocene Epoch or its rocks: see the geologic time chart in the Reference Supplement

mi·o·sis (mī ō′sis) ***n., pl.*** **-ses′** (-sēz′) ⟦ModL < Gr *myein,* to close (< IE base **mu-:* see MUTE) + -OSIS⟧ contraction of the pupil of the eye —**mi·ot′ic** (-ät′ik) ***adj., n.***

MIPS (mips) ***n.*** ⟦< *m(illion) i(nstructions) p(er) s(econd)*⟧ a unit of processing speed in a computer, equal to one million instructions per second: often sp. **mips**

Mi·que·lon (mik′ə län′; *Fr* mē klōn′) island in the Atlantic, off the S coast of Newfoundland: part of St-Pierre and Miquelon: 83 sq mi (215 sq km)

mir (mir) ***n.*** ⟦Russ, lit., world⟧ in czarist Russia, a village community of peasant farmers

MIr *abbrev.* Middle Irish

Mi·ra·beau (mir′ə bō′; *Fr* mē rȧ bō′), Comte **(Honoré Gabriel Riqueti) de** 1749-91; Fr. revolutionary, orator, & statesman

mir·a·belle (mir′ə bel′, mir′ə bel′) ***n.*** ⟦Fr, altered < L *myrobalanum,* fruit of a kind of palm tree < Gr *myrobalanan* < *myron,* unguent, perfume + *balanos,* acorn, date⟧ 1 a European variety of plum tree 2 its sweet, small, golden fruit 3 a brandy made from these fruits

mi·ra·bi·le dic·tu (mi rä′bē lā′ dik′to͞o′) ⟦L⟧ wonderful to tell: an interjection

mir·a·cle (mir′ə kəl) ***n.*** ⟦OFr < L *miraculum,* a strange thing, in LL(Ec), miracle < *mirari,* to wonder at < *mirus,* wonderful < IE base **(s)mei-,* to SMILE⟧ 1 an event or action that apparently contradicts known scientific laws and is hence thought to be due to supernatural causes, esp. to an act of God 2 a remarkable event or thing; marvel 3 a wonderful example [a *miracle* of tact] 4 MIRACLE PLAY

miracle drug [Informal] any medicine, esp. a new one, that is, or that is reputed to be, remarkably effective

miracle play any of a class of medieval religious dramas dealing with events in the lives of the saints: cf. MYSTERY PLAY

mi·rac·u·lous (mi rak′yo͞o ləs, -yə-) ***adj.*** ⟦MFr *miraculeux* < ML *miraculosus* < L *miraculum*⟧ 1 having the nature of a miracle; supernatural 2 like a miracle; wonderful; marvelous 3 able to work miracles —**mi·rac′u·lous·ly** ***adv.*** —**mi·rac′u·lous·ness** ***n.***

mir·a·dor (mir′ə dôr′, mir′ə dôr′) ***n.*** ⟦Sp < *mirar,* to observe < L *mirare,* to wonder at, akin to *mirari:* see MIRACLE⟧ a balcony, turret, etc. that affords a fine view

mi·rage (mi räzh′) ***n.*** ⟦Fr < (*se*) *mirer,* to be reflected < VL *mirare,* to look at, for L *mirari:* see MIRACLE⟧ 1 an optical illusion in which the image of a distant object, as a ship or an oasis, is made to appear nearby, floating in air, inverted, etc.: it is caused by the refraction of light rays from the object through layers of air having different densities as the result of unequal temperature distributions 2 something that falsely appears to be real —***SYN.*** DELUSION

Mir·a·mar (mir′ə mär′) city in SE Fla.

Mi·ran·da[1] (mə ran′də) ***n.*** ⟦L, fem. of *mirandus,* strange, wonderful < *mirari:* see MIRACLE⟧ a feminine name: dim. *Mandy*

Mi·ran·da[2] (mə ran′də) ☆***adj.*** ⟦after E. A. *Miranda,* defendant in the 1966 U.S. Supreme Court case establishing these rights⟧ designating or of the legal rights of an arrested person (as that of remaining silent or of being represented by counsel) and the required notification of such a person of those rights

☆**Mi·ran·dize** (mə ran′dīz′) ***vt.*** **-dized′, -diz′ing** ⟦see prec.⟧ to notify (a person under arrest) of the Miranda rights

mire (mīr) ***n.*** ⟦ME < ON *myrr,* akin to *mosi,* MOSS⟧ 1 an area of wet, soggy ground; bog 2 deep mud; wet, soggy earth; slush —***vt.*** **mired, mir′ing** 1 to cause to get stuck in or as in mire 2 to soil or splatter with mud or dirt —***vi.*** to sink or stick in mud

☆**mi·rex** (mī′reks′) ***n.*** ⟦coined from initials of its three developers + *-ex,* arbitrary suffix (suggesting ME *mire,* ant: see PISMIRE & REX)⟧ an insecticide consisting of a chlorinated hydrocarbon, $C_{10}Cl_{12}$, usually mixed with a bait and used esp. against fire ants

Mir·i·am (mir′ē əm) ***n.*** ⟦Heb *miryām*⟧ 1 a feminine name: see MARY[1] 2 *Bible* the sister of Moses and Aaron: Ex. 15:20

mir·i·ness (mīr′ē nis) ***n.*** a miry quality or condition

mirk (murk) ***n.*** *archaic sp. of* MURK —**mirk′y** ***adj.*** **mirk′i·er, mirk′i·est**

mir·li·ton (mir′li tän′) ***n.*** ⟦orig., a small toy flute or kazoo < Fr: echoic; connection with the fruit unknown⟧ CHAYOTE: term used in Cajun cooking

Mi·ró (mē rō′), **Jo·an** (zho͞o än′, hwän) 1893-1983; Sp. painter

mir·ror (mir′ər) ***n.*** ⟦ME *mirour* < OFr *mireor* < VL **miratorium* < *mirare:* see MIRAGE⟧ 1 a smooth surface that reflects the images of objects; esp., a piece of glass coated on the reverse side as with silver or an amalgam 2 anything that gives a true representation or description 3 [Rare] something to be imitated or emulated; model 4 [Archaic] a crystal used by fortune-tellers, sorcerers, etc. —***vt.*** to reflect, as in a mirror; give or show a likeness of

mirror image 1 an image or view of someone or something as seen in a mirror, i.e., with the right side as though it were the left, and vice versa 2 a perfect likeness or exact image: typically a hyperbolic use [a son who is the *mirror image* of his father]

mirth (murth) ***n.*** ⟦ME *myrthe* < OE *myrgth,* pleasure, joy < base of *myrig,* pleasant: see MERRY】 joyfulness, gaiety, or merriment, esp. when characterized by laughter

mirth·ful (murth′fəl) *adj.* full of, expressing, or causing mirth; merry —**mirth′ful·ly** *adv.* —**mirth′ful·ness** *n.*

mirth·less (-lis) *adj.* without mirth; humorless, sad, melancholy, etc. —**mirth′less·ly** *adv.* —**mirth′less·ness** *n.*

☆**MIRV** (murv) *n., pl.* **MIRV's** 【*m(ultiple) i(ndependently targeted) r(eentry) v(ehicle)*】 **1** an intercontinental ballistic missile with several warheads, each of which can be directed to a different target or to the same target at intervals **2** any such warhead —*vt.* **MIRVed, MIRV′ing** to load (a missile) with such warheads —**MIRVed** *adj.*

mir·y (mīr′ē) *adj.* **mir′i·er, mir′i·est 1** full of, or having the nature of, mire; swampy **2** covered with mire; muddy

mir·za (mir′zä′) *n.* 【Pers *mīrza,* contr. < *mīrzādah* < *mir,* prince (< Ar *amīr,* ruler) + *zādah,* son of < *zādan,* to be born < IE base **gen-,* to beget > GENUS】 a Persian title of honor placed after the name of a royal prince or before the name of a high official, scholar, etc.

MIS *abbrev.* management information system

mis-[1] (mis) 【ME < OE & OFr: OE *mis-,* akin to OHG *missa-,* Goth *missa-* (for IE base see MISS[1]); OFr *mes-* < Frank **missi-,* akin to OHG *missa-*】 *prefix* **1** wrong, wrongly, bad, badly *[misdo, misdemeanor]* **2** no, not *[misfire]*

mis-[2] (mis) *combining form* MISO-: used before a vowel

mis·ad·ven·ture (mis′əd ven′chər) *n.* 【ME *mesaventure* < OFr: see MIS-[1] & ADVENTURE】 **1** an unlucky accident; mishap; an instance of bad luck **2** *Eng. Law* death caused accidentally by someone while performing a legal act and with no intent to injure

mis·ad·vise (-əd vīz′) *vt.* **-vised′, -vis′ing** to advise badly —**mis′ad·vice′** (-vīs′) *n.*

mis·a·lign·ment (-ə līn′mənt) *n.* a condition of being badly or improperly aligned —**mis′a·ligned′** *adj.*

mis·al·li·ance (-ə lī′əns) *n.* 【after Fr *mésalliance*】 an improper alliance; esp., an unsuitable marriage

mis·al·ly (-lī′) *vt.* **-lied′, -ly′ing** to ally unsuitably or inappropriately

mis·an·dry (mis′an′drē) *n.* 【MIS(O)- + *-andry* (see POLYANDRY): modeled on MISOGYNY】 hatred of men or the male sex

mis·an·thrope (mis′ən thrōp′, miz′-) *n.* 【Gr *misanthrōpos,* hating mankind < *misein,* to hate + *anthrōpos,* a man: see ANTHROPO-】 a person who hates or distrusts all people: also **mis·an·thro·pist** (mis an′thrə pist, mi zan′-)

mis·an·throp·ic (mis′ən thräp′ik, miz′ən-) *adj.* of or like a misanthrope: also **mis′an·throp′i·cal** —*SYN.* CYNICAL —**mis′an·throp′i·cal·ly** *adv.*

mis·an·thro·py (mi san′thrə pē, mi zan′-) *n.* 【Gr *misanthrōpia*】 hatred or distrust of people in general

mis·ap·ply (mis′ə plī′) *vt.* **-plied′, -ply′ing 1** to use badly, incorrectly, or wastefully *[to misapply one's energies]* **2** to handle dishonestly or illegally *[to misapply an employer's money]* —**mis′ap·pli·ca′tion** (-ap li kā′shən) *n.*

mis·ap·pre·hend (-ap rē hend′) *vt.* to fail to apprehend correctly; misunderstand —**mis′ap·pre·hen′sion** (-hen′shən) *n.*

mis·ap·pro·pri·ate (-ə prō′prē āt′) *vt.* **-at′ed, -at′ing** to appropriate to a bad, incorrect, or dishonest use —**mis′ap·pro′pri·a′tion** *n.*

mis·ar·range (-ə rānj′) *vt.* **-ranged′, -rang′ing** to arrange wrongly or improperly —**mis′ar·range′ment** *n.*

mis·be·come (-bē kum′) *vt.* **-came′, -come′, -com′ing** to be unbecoming to; be unsuitable or unfit for

mis·be·got·ten (-bē gät′'n) *adj.* **1** wrongly or unlawfully begotten; specif., born out of wedlock: also **mis′be·got′ 2** wrongly or badly conceived *[misbegotten rules]*

mis·be·have (-bē hāv′) *vi.* **-haved′, -hav′ing** to behave wrongly *[schoolchildren misbehaving in class]* —*vt.* to conduct (oneself) improperly —**mis′be·hav′er** *n.* —**mis′be·hav′ior** (-yər) *n.*

mis·be·lieve (-bē lēv′) *vi.* **-lieved′, -liev′ing** [Archaic] to hold unorthodox or heretical beliefs or opinions, esp. in religion —**mis′be·lief′** *n.* —**mis′be·liev′er** *n.*

mis·brand (mis brand′) *vt.* to brand or label improperly

misc *abbrev.* **1** miscellaneous **2** miscellany

mis·cal·cu·late (mis kal′kyoo͞ lāt′, -kyə-) *vt., vi.* **-lat′ed, -lat′ing** to calculate incorrectly; miscount or misjudge —**mis′cal·cu·la′tion** *n.*

mis·call (-kôl′) *vt.* to call by a wrong name; misname

mis·car·riage (mis kar′ij; *also, and for 3 usually,* mis′kar′ij) *n.* **1** failure to carry out what was intended *[a miscarriage of justice]* **2** failure of mail, freight, etc. to reach its destination **3** the natural expulsion of an embryo or fetus from the womb before it is sufficiently developed to survive: see also ABORTION

mis·car·ry (mis kar′ē, mis′kar′ē) *vi.* **-ried, -ry·ing 1** *a)* to go wrong; fail: said of a plan, project, etc. *b)* to go astray; fail to arrive: said of mail, freight, etc. **2** to have a MISCARRIAGE (sense 3)

mis·cast (-kast′) *vt.* **-cast′, -cast′ing 1** to cast (an actor) in an unsuitable role **2** to cast (a play or film) with actors unsuited to their roles

☆**mis·ce·ge·na·tion** (mi sej′ə nā′shən, mis′ə jə-) *n.* 【coined (*c.* 1863) < L *miscere,* MIX + *genus,* race (see GENUS) + -ATION】 marriage or sexual relations between a man and woman of different races, esp., in the U.S., between a white and a black: term used esp. in the context of racial segregation

mis·cel·la·ne·a (mis′ə lā′nē ə) *pl.n.* 【L, neut. pl.: see fol.】 *[often with sing. v.]* a miscellaneous collection, esp. of literary works; miscellany

mis·cel·la·ne·ous (mis′ə lā′nē əs) *adj.* 【L *miscellaneus* < *miscellus,* mixed < *miscere,* MIX】 **1** consisting or formed of various kinds; varied; mixed *[a box of miscellaneous candies]* **2** having various qualities, abilities, etc.; many-sided —**mis′cel·la′ne·ous·ly** *adv.* —**mis′cel·la′ne·ous·ness** *n.*

mis·cel·la·ny (mis′ə lā′nē; *Brit* mi sel′ə nē) *n., pl.* **-nies** 【< Fr *miscellanées,* pl. < L *miscellanea,* neut. pl. of *miscellaneus:* see prec.】 **1** a miscellaneous collection, esp. of literary works **2** *[often pl.]* such a collection of writings, as in a book

mis·chance (mis chans′, mis′chans′) *n.* 【ME *mescheance* < OFr *meschance:* see MIS-[1] & CHANCE】 **1** an unlucky accident; misadventure **2** bad luck or an instance of it

mis·chief (mis′chif) *n.* 【ME *meschief* < OFr < *meschever,* to come to grief < *mes-* (see MIS-[1]) + *chever,* come to a head < *chief,* end, head (see CHIEF)】 **1** harm, damage, or injury, esp. that done by a person **2** a cause or source of harm, damage, or annoyance; specif., *a)* action or conduct that causes damage or trouble *b)* a person causing damage or annoyance **3** a tendency or disposition to annoy or vex with playful tricks **4** *a)* a troublesome or annoying act; prank; playful, vexing trick *b)* playful, harmless teasing

mis·chief-mak·er (-māk′ər) *n.* a person who causes mischief; esp., one who creates trouble by gossiping —**mis′chief-mak′ing** *n., adj.*

mis·chie·vi·ous (mis chē′vē əs) *adj. disputed var. of* MISCHIEVOUS
USAGE—a nonstandard form dating back at least to the late 16th cent.

mis·chie·vous (mis′chə vəs) *adj.* 【ME *mischevous* < Anglo-Fr】 **1** causing mischief; specif., *a)* injurious; harmful *b)* prankish; teasing; full of tricks **2** inclined to annoy or vex with playful tricks; naughty: said esp. of a child —**mis′chie·vous·ly** *adv.* —**mis′chie·vous·ness** *n.*
USAGE—see usage note at MISCHIEVIOUS

misch metal (mish) 【Ger *mischmetall* < *mischen,* to mix + *metall,* metal】 an alloy consisting of various rare-earth elements, esp. cerium and lanthanum, used in lighter flints, vacuum tubes, etc.

mis·ci·ble (mis′ə bəl) *adj.* 【ML *miscibilis* < L *miscere,* to MIX】 that can be mixed —**mis′ci·bil′i·ty** *n.*

mis·col·or (mis kul′ər) *vt.* **1** to give a wrong color to **2** to give a false account of; misrepresent

mis·com·mu·ni·ca·tion (mis′kə myo͞o′ni kā′shən) *n.* failure to fully or clearly communicate

mis·con·ceive (mis′kən sēv′) *vt., vi.* **-ceived′, -ceiv′ing** to conceive wrongly; interpret incorrectly; misunderstand —**mis′con·cep′tion** (-sep′shən) *n.*

mis·con·duct (mis′kən dukt′; *for n.* mis kän′dukt) *vt.* **1** to manage badly or dishonestly **2** to conduct (oneself) improperly —*n.* **1** unlawful, bad, or dishonest management, esp. by a governmental or military official; specif., malfeasance **2** willfully improper behavior

mis·con·strue (mis′kən stro͞o′) *vt.* **-strued′, -stru′ing** to construe wrongly; misinterpret or misunderstand —**mis′con·struc′tion** (-struk′shən) *n.*

mis·cop·y (mis käp′ē) *vt., vi.* **-cop′ied, -cop′y·ing** to copy incorrectly

mis·count (mis kount′, mis′kount′; *for n.* mis′kount′) *vt., vi.* to count incorrectly; miscalculate —*n.* an incorrect count, as of votes in an election

mis·cre·ant (mis′krē ənt) *adj.* 【OFr, unbelieving < *mes-* (see MIS-[1]) + *creant,* prp. of *croire,* to believe < L *credere:* see CREED】 **1** villainous; evil **2** [Archaic] unbelieving or heretical —*n.* **1** an evil person; criminal; villain **2** [Archaic] an unbeliever or heretic —**mis′cre·an·cy** *n.*

mis·cre·at·ed (mis′krē āt′id) *adj.* [Archaic] misshapen

mis·cue (mis′kyo͞o′; *for v.* mis kyo͞o′, mis′kyo͞o′) *n.* **1** *Billiards, Pool* a faulty shot in which the tip of the cue slips off the ball **2** a mistake; error —*vi.* **-cued′, -cu′ing 1** to make a miscue **2** *Theater* to miss one's cue or answer the wrong cue

mis·date (mis dāt′, mis′dāt′; *for n.* mis′dāt′) *vt.* **-dat′ed, -dat′ing** to put a wrong date on (a document, letter, etc.) or assign a wrong date to (an event); date incorrectly —*n.* a wrong date

mis·deal (mis dēl′, mis′dēl′; *for n.* mis′dēl′) *vt., vi.* **-dealt′, -deal′ing** to deal (playing cards) incorrectly —*n.* an incorrect deal —**mis′deal′er** *n.*

mis·deed (mis dēd′, mis′dēd′) *n.* a wrong or wicked act; crime, sin, etc.

mis·de·mean·ant (mis′də mēn′ənt) *n. Law* a person guilty or convicted of a misdemeanor

mis·de·mean·or (mis′də mēn′ər) *n.* 【MIS-[1] + DEMEANOR】 **1** the act or an instance of misbehaving; minor transgression **2** *Law* any minor offense, as the breaking of a municipal ordinance, for which statute provides a lesser punishment than for a felony: the penalty is usually a fine or imprisonment for a short time (usually less than one year) in a local jail, workhouse, etc.: Brit. sp. **mis′de·mean′our**

mis·di·ag·nose (mis′dī′əg nōs′, -nōz′) *vt., vi.* **-nosed′, -nos′ing** to make an incorrect diagnosis of (a disease, condition, etc.) —**mis′di′ag·no′sis** (-nō′sis) *n., pl.* **-ses′** (-sēz′)

mis·di·rect (mis′də rekt′) *vt.* to direct wrongly or badly; specif., *a)* to aim (a blow, etc.) badly *b)* to address (a letter) incorrectly *c)* to give incorrect instructions to, esp. as a judge to a jury *d)* to make use of diversions in order to deceive, as a stage magician does —**mis′di·rec′tion** (-rek′shən) *n.*

mis·do (mis do͞o′) *vt.* **-did′, -done′, -do′ing** 【ME *misdoen* < OE *misdon:* see MIS-[1] & DO[1]】 to do wrongly —*vi.* [Obs.] to do evil —**mis·do′er** *n.* —**mis·do′ing** *n.*

mis·doubt (-dout′) [Archaic] *vt.* **1** to have doubt or suspicion about; distrust **2** to fear —*vi.* to have doubts —*n.* suspicion; doubt

mise-en-scène (mē zän sen′) *n.* 【< Fr *mise en scène,* lit., a placing on (the) stage】 **1** *a)* the staging of a play, including the setting, arrangement of the actors, etc. *b)* the direction of a film, emphasizing the image created by setting, props, lighting, actors' movements, etc. **2** general surroundings; environment

mis·em·ploy (mis′əm ploi′) *vt.* to employ, or use, wrongly or badly; misuse —**mis′em·ploy′ment** *n.*

mi·ser (mī′zər) *n.* ⟦< L, wretched, unhappy, ill, worthless⟧ **1** a greedy, stingy person who hoards money for its own sake, even at the expense of personal comfort **2** [Obs.] a miserable person; wretch

mis·er·a·ble (miz′ər ə bəl, miz′rə-) *adj.* ⟦Fr *misérable* < L *miserabilis,* pitiable < *miserari,* to pity < *miser,* wretched⟧ **1** in a condition of misery; wretched, unhappy, suffering, etc. **2** causing misery, discomfort, or suffering [*miserable* weather] **3** bad; inferior; inadequate [a *miserable* performance] **4** pitiable **5** shameful; disgraceful —*n.* [Obs.] a miserable person —**mis′er·a·ble·ness** *n.* —**mis′er·a·bly** *adv.*

Mis·e·re·re (mē′ze rer′ā′) *n.* **1** ⟦ME < LL(Ec), have mercy (imper. of L *misereri,* to feel pity < *miser,* wretched): first word of the psalm in the Vulg.⟧ *Bible* the 51st Psalm, beginning, "Have mercy upon me, O God" **2** a musical setting for this **3** [**m-**] MISERICORD (sense 1)

mis·er·i·cord or **mis·er·i·corde** (mi zer′i kôrd′; *also* miz′ər i-) *n.* ⟦ME *misericorde* < OFr < L *misericordia* < *misericors,* merciful < base of *misereri* (see prec.) + *cor,* HEART⟧ **1** a narrow ledge on the underside of a hinged seat, as in a choir stall, designed to support a person standing at rest against the turned-up seat **2** a dagger used in the Middle Ages for giving the death stroke (*coup de grâce*) to a wounded knight

mi·ser·ly (mī′zər lē) *adj.* like or characteristic of a miser; greedy and stingy —*SYN.* STINGY[1] —**mi′ser·li·ness** *n.*

mis·er·y (miz′ər ē) *n., pl.* **-er·ies** ⟦ME *miserie* < OFr < L *miseria* < *miser,* wretched⟧ **1** a condition of great wretchedness or suffering because of pain, sorrow, poverty, etc.; distress **2** a cause of such suffering; pain, sorrow, poverty, squalor, etc. **3** [Dial.] a pain (*in* some part of the body)

☆**misery index** the sum of the rates of inflation and unemployment at a given time: regarded as being a rough indicator of general economic hardship and public discontent

mis·es·ti·mate (mis es′tə māt′; *for n.,* -mit) *vt.* **-mat′ed, -mat′ing** to estimate incorrectly —*n.* an incorrect estimate —**mis·es′ti·ma′tion** *n.*

mis·fea·sance (mis fē′zəns) *n.* ⟦OFr *mesfaisance* < *mesfaire,* to misdo: see MIS-[1] & FEASANCE⟧ *Law* wrongdoing; specif., the doing of a lawful act in an unlawful or improper manner: distinguished from MALFEASANCE, NONFEASANCE —**mis·fea′sor** (-zər) *n.*

mis·file (mis fīl′, mis′fīl′) *vt.* **-filed′, -fil′ing** to file (papers, etc.) in the wrong place or order

mis·fire (mis fīr′; *for n., usually* mis′fīr′) *vi.* **-fired′, -fir′ing** ⟦MIS-[1] + FIRE, v.⟧ **1** to fail to ignite properly or at the right time: said of an internal-combustion engine **2** to fail to go off, or be discharged: said of a firearm, missile, etc. **3** to fail to achieve a desired effect —*n.* an act or instance of misfiring

mis·fit (mis fit′, mis′fit′; *for n.* mis′fit′) *vt., vi.* **-fit′ted, -fit′ting** to fit badly —*n.* **1** the act or condition of misfitting **2** anything that misfits, as a badly fitting garment **3** a person not suited to a job, associates, etc. **4** a socially maladjusted person

mis·for·tune (mis fôr′chən) *n.* **1** bad luck; ill fortune; trouble; adversity **2** an instance of this; unlucky accident; mishap; mischance —*SYN.* AFFLICTION

mis·give (mis giv′) *vt.* **-gave′, -giv′en, -giv′ing** ⟦MIS-[1] + GIVE⟧ to cause fear, doubt, or suspicion in: said usually of the heart, mind, conscience, etc. [his heart *misgave* him] —*vi.* to feel fear, doubt, suspicion, etc.

mis·giv·ing (-giv′iŋ) *n.* ⟦see prec.⟧ a disturbed feeling of fear, doubt, apprehension, etc.: *usually used in pl.* —*SYN.* QUALM

mis·gov·ern (-guv′ərn) *vt.* to govern, administer, or manage badly —**mis′gov′ern·ment** *n.*

mis·guide (-gīd′) *vt.* **-guid′ed, -guid′ing** to guide wrongly; lead into error or misconduct; mislead —**mis·guid′ance** *n.*

mis·guid·ed (mis gī′dəd, mis′gī′dəd) *adj.* ill-advised, imprudent, wrong-headed, etc. —**mis·guid′ed·ly** *adv.* —**mis·guid′ed·ness** *n.*

mis·han·dle (mis han′dəl) *vt.* **-dled, -dling** to handle badly or roughly; abuse, maltreat, or mismanage —**mis·han′dler** *n.*

mis·hap (mis′hap′) *n.* ⟦ME (see MIS-[1] & HAP[1]), prob. after OFr *mescheance,* mischance⟧ **1** an unlucky or unfortunate accident **2** [Now Rare] bad luck; misfortune

mis·hear (mis hir′) *vt., vi.* **-heard′, -hear′ing** to hear incorrectly or poorly

mi·shi·gas (mi′shi gäs′) *n.* ⟦Yiddish⟧ [*also in italics*] [Slang] *var. of* MESHUGAS: also **mi′she·goss′**

Mi·shi·ma (mish′i mä′), **Yu·ki·o** (yo͞o′kē ō′) 1925-70; Jpn. writer

mish·mash (mish′mash′) *n.* ⟦redupl. of MASH (parallel with Ger *mischmasch,* LowG *miskmask*)⟧ a hodgepodge; jumble: also **mish′mosh′** (-mäsh′)

Mish·na or **Mish·nah** (mish′nä) *n., pl.* **Mish·na·yot** (mish′nä yōt′) ⟦Heb *mishna,* lit., (oral) instruction < root *šnh,* to repeat, (later) learn, teach⟧ **1** the first part of the Talmud, containing traditional oral interpretations of scriptural ordinances (*halakhot*), compiled by the rabbis about A.D. 200 **2** any of these interpretations —**Mish·na′ic** (-nā′ik) *adj.*

mi·shu·ga or **mi·shu·gah** (mi sho͝og′ə, mə-) *adj.* ⟦Yiddish⟧ [*also in italics*] [Slang] *var. of* MESHUGA

mis·im·pres·sion (mis′im presh′ən) *n.* a mistaken impression

mis·in·form (mis′in fôrm′) *vt.* to supply with false or misleading information —**mis′in·form′er** *n.,* **mis′in·form′ant** —**mis′in′for·ma′tion** *n.*

mis·in·ter·pret (-in tur′prit) *vt.* to interpret wrongly; understand or explain incorrectly —**mis′in·ter′pre·ta′tion** *n.* —**mis′in·ter′pret·er** *n.*

mis·join·der (mis join′dər) *n. Law* the improper joining together of parties or of different causes of action in one lawsuit or other legal proceeding

mis·judge (-juj′) *vt., vi.* **-judged′, -judg′ing** to judge wrongly or unfairly —**mis·judg′ment** *n.,* **mis·judge′ment**

mis·know (mis nō′) *vt.* **-knew′, -known′, -know′ing** [Now Rare] to have a misconception of; misunderstand —**mis·knowl′edge** *n.*

Mis·kolc (mish′kôlts′) city in NE Hungary

mis·la·bel (mis lā′bəl) *vt.* **-beled** or **-belled, -bel·ing** or **-bel·ling** to label incorrectly or improperly

mis·lay (-lā′) *vt.* **-laid′, -lay′ing** ⟦see MIS-[1] & LAY[1], v.⟧ to put in a place afterward forgotten or not easily found

mis·lead (-lēd′) *vt.* **-led′, -lead′ing 1** to lead in a wrong direction; lead astray **2** to lead into error (of judgment); deceive or delude **3** to lead into wrongdoing; influence badly —*SYN.* DECEIVE —**mis·lead′er** *n.* —**mis·lead′ing** *adj.* —**mis·lead′ing·ly** *adv.*

mis·like (mik līk′) *vt.* **-liked′, -lik′ing 1** [Archaic] DISPLEASE **2** [Now Rare] to be displeased at; dislike —*n.* [Now Rare] dislike; disapproval

mis·man·age (mis man′ij) *vt., vi.* **-aged, -ag·ing** to manage or administer badly or dishonestly —**mis·man′age·ment** *n.* —**mis·man′a·ger** *n.*

mis·match (mis mach′; *for n.* mis′mach′) *vt.* to match badly or unsuitably —*n.* a bad or unsuitable match

mis·mate (mis māt′) *vt., vi.* **-mat′ed, -mat′ing** to mate badly or unsuitably

mis·name (mis nām′) *vt.* **-named′, -nam′ing** to give or apply an inappropriate name to

mis·no·mer (mis nō′mər) *n.* ⟦ME *misnoumer* < OFr *mesnommer,* inf. used as n. < *mes-,* MIS-[1] + *nommer,* to name < L *nominare:* see NOMINATE⟧ **1** *a)* the act of applying a wrong name or epithet to some person or thing *b)* such a name or epithet **2** an error in naming a person or place in a legal document

mi·so (mē′sō) *n.* ⟦Jpn⟧ a food paste made of soybeans, salt, and, usually, fermented grain, used esp. in Japanese cooking

mis·o- (mis′ō, -ə) ⟦Gr *miso-* < *misein,* to hate⟧ *combining form* hatred of [*misogyny*]

mi·sog·a·my (mi säg′ə mē) *n.* ⟦prec. + -GAMY⟧ hatred of marriage —**mi·sog′a·mist** *n.*

mi·sog·y·ny (mi säj′ə nē) *n.* ⟦Gr *misogynia:* see MISO- & -GYNY⟧ hatred of women or the female sex, esp. by a man —**mi·sog′y·nist** *n.* —**mi·sog′y·nous** *adj.,* **mi·sog′y·nis′tic,** or **mi·sog′y·nic**

mi·sol·o·gy (mi säl′ə jē) *n.* ⟦Gr *misologia:* see MISO- & -LOGY⟧ hatred of argument, debate, or reasoning —**mi·sol′o·gist** *n.*

mis·o·ne·ism (mis′ō nē′iz′əm) *n.* ⟦It *misoneismo* < Gr *miso-,* MISO- + *neos,* NEW + It *-ismo,* -ISM⟧ hatred of innovation or change

mis·per·ceive (mis′pər sēv′) *vt.* **-ceived′, -ceiv′ing** to perceive incorrectly —**mis′per·cep′tion** *n.*

mis·place (mis plās′) *vt.* **-placed′, -plac′ing 1** to put in a wrong place **2** to bestow (one's trust, affection, etc.) on an unsuitable or undeserving object **3** MISLAY —**mis·place′ment** *n.*

mis·play (mis plā′, mis′plā′; *for n.* mis′plā′) *vt., vi.* to play wrongly or badly, as in games or sports —☆*n.* a wrong or bad play or maneuver

mis·plead (mis plēd′, mis′plēd′) *vt., vi.* **-pled′, -plead′ing** to plead incorrectly

mis·plead·ing (-iŋ) *n. Law* an incorrect statement or an omission in pleading, as a misstatement of a cause of action

mis·price (mis prīs′) *vt.* **-priced′, -pric′ing** to price incorrectly

mis·print (mis print′; *for n.* mis′print′) *vt.* to print incorrectly —*n.* an error in printing

mis·pri·sion (mis prizh′ən) *n.* ⟦ME *mesprision* < OFr < pp. of *mesprendre,* to take wrongly < *mes-,* MIS-[1] + *prendre* < L *prehendere,* to take: see PREHENSILE⟧ **1** a mistake, now esp. one due to misreading, either deliberate or unintended, or to misunderstanding **2** scorn; contempt **3** *Law a)* misconduct or neglect of duty, esp. by a public official *b)* act of contempt against a government or court

misprision of felony (or **treason**) *Law* the offense of concealing knowledge of a felony (or treason) by one who has not participated or assisted in it

mis·prize (mis prīz′) *vt.* **-prized′, -priz′ing** ⟦ME *mesprisen* < OFr *mesprisier* < *mes-,* MIS-[1] + *prisier* < LL *pretiare,* to value < L *pretium,* a PRICE⟧ [Rare] to despise or undervalue

mis·pro·nounce (mis′prō nouns′, -prə-) *vt., vi.* **-nounced′, -nounc′ing** to give (a word or words) a pronunciation different from any of the accepted standard pronunciations; pronounce incorrectly —**mis′pro·nun′ci·a′tion** (-nun′sē ā′shən) *n.*

mis·quote (mis kwōt′) *vt., vi.* **-quot′ed, -quot′ing** to quote incorrectly —**mis′quo·ta′tion** *n.*

mis·read (-rēd′) *vt., vi.* **-read′** (-red′), **-read′ing** (-rēd′iŋ) **1** to read wrongly **2** to misinterpret or misunderstand [to *misread* a situation]

mis·reck·on (-rek′ən) *vt.* to reckon or calculate incorrectly

mis·re·mem·ber (mis′rē mem′bər) *vt., vi.* **1** to remember incorrectly **2** [Dial.] to forget

mis·re·port (-rē pôrt′) *vt.* to report incorrectly or falsely —*n.* an incorrect or false report

mis·rep·re·sent (mis′rep rē zent′) *vt.* **1** to represent falsely; give an untrue or misleading idea of **2** to be an improper or bad representative of —**mis′rep·re·sen·ta′tion** *n.*

mis·rule (mis ro͞ol′, mis′ro͞ol′) *vt.* **-ruled′, -rul′ing** to rule badly or unjustly; misgovern —*n.* **1** misgovernment **2** disorder or riot

miss[1] (mis) *vt.* ⟦ME *missen* < OE *missan,* akin to Ger *missen* < IE base **meit(h)-,* to change, exchange > L *mutare,* to change⟧ **1** to fail to hit or land on (something aimed at) **2** to fail to meet, reach, attain, catch, accomplish, see, hear, perceive, understand, etc. **3** to overlook; let (an opportunity, etc.) go by 4 to escape; avoid [he just *missed* being struck] 5 to fail or forget to do, keep, have, be present at, etc. [to *miss* an appointment] 6 to notice the absence or loss of [to suddenly *miss* one's wallet] 7 to feel or regret the absence or loss of [to *miss* one's friends] 8 to be without; lack: now used only in the prp. [this book is *missing* a page] —*vi.* 1 to fail to hit something aimed at; go wide of the mark 2 to fail to be successful 3 to misfire, as an engine 4 [Archaic] to fail to obtain, receive, etc.: with *of* or *in* —*n.* a failure to hit, meet, obtain, see, etc. —**a miss is as good as a mile** missing by a narrow margin has the same practical effect as missing by a wide one —**miss one's guess** to fail to guess or predict accurately —**miss (something) out** [Brit.] to omit or pass over; skip —**miss out on** [Informal] to fail to have, get, take advantage of, etc.

miss[2] (mis) *n., pl.* **miss'es** ⟦contr. of MISTRESS⟧ 1 [**M-**] *a)* a title used in speaking to or of an unmarried woman or a girl and placed before the name [*Miss* Smith, *Miss* Emily Smith, the *Misses* Smith] *b)* [Old-fashioned] a title used in speaking to or of an unmarried woman or a girl and used with just the first name [*Miss* Jane] *c)* a title used in speaking to an unmarried woman or a girl but used without the name ☆*d)* a title given to a young woman winning a (specified) beauty contest or promoting a (specified) product [*Miss* Ohio, *Miss* Cotton] *e)* a title used as before a woman's stage name [*Miss* Judy Garland] 2 a young, unmarried woman or a girl 3 [*pl.*] a series of sizes in clothing for women and girls of average proportions [coats in *misses'* sizes]

Miss *abbrev.* Mississippi

mis·sal (mis'əl) *n.* ⟦ME *missale* < ML(Ec) neut. of *missalis,* of Mass < LL(Ec) *missa,* MASS[1]⟧ 1 [*often* **M-**] a large book containing the prayers, readings, and rubrics authorized by the Roman Catholic Church for the celebration of Mass 2 any small book with such content abridged, for use by people attending Mass

mis·sal·ette (mis'ə let') *n.* a MISSAL (sense 2), esp. one printed periodically or for a special occasion, for distribution at Mass

mis·say (mis sā') *vt., vi.* **-said', -say'ing** [Archaic] 1 to say or speak wrongly 2 to speak evil (of); vilify; abuse; slander

mis·sense mutation (mis'sens') *Genetics* a type of mutation to a specific protein, that results from the substitution, during translation, of one amino acid for another

mis·sent (mis sent') *adj.* designating or of misdirected mail

mis·shape (mis shāp') *vt.* **-shaped', -shap'ing** ⟦ME *mysshapen:* see MIS-[1] & SHAPE⟧ to shape badly; deform

mis·shap·en (mis shāp'ən) *adj.* ⟦ME: see prec.⟧ badly shaped; deformed

mis·sile (mis'əl; *chiefly Brit,* -īl') *adj.* ⟦L *missilis* < *missus:* see MISSION⟧ 1 that can be, or is, thrown or shot, as from a gun 2 [Rare] throwing or shooting missiles —*n.* a weapon or other object, as a spear, bullet, rocket, etc., designed to be thrown, fired, or launched toward a target; often, specif., a guided or ballistic missile

☆**mis·sile·man** (-mən) *n., pl.* **-men** (-mən) one who builds or launches guided or ballistic missiles: also **mis'sil·eer'** (-ir')

mis·sile·ry (mis'əl rē) *n.* ⟦see -RY⟧ 1 the science of building and launching guided or ballistic missiles 2 guided or ballistic missiles collectively

miss·ing (mis'iŋ) *adj.* 1 absent; lost; lacking 2 absent after combat, but not definitely known to be dead or taken prisoner: in full **missing in action**

missing link something necessary for completing a series; specif., a hypothetical fossil of an animal believed to have existed in the evolutionary process intermediate between two known animals, esp. between the anthropoid apes and a human being

mis·sion (mish'ən) *n.* ⟦L *missio,* a sending, sending away < *missus,* pp. of *mittere,* to send < IE base **smeit-,* to throw > Avestan *hamista-,* cast down⟧ 1 a sending out or being sent out with authority to perform a special service; specif., *a)* the sending out of persons by a religious organization to preach, teach, and convert *b)* the sending out of persons to a foreign government to conduct negotiations *c)* the work done by such persons 2 *a)* a group of persons sent by a religious body to spread its religion, esp. in a foreign land *b)* its organization, headquarters, or place of residency *c)* [*pl.*] organized missionary work 3 a group of persons sent to a foreign government to conduct negotiations; diplomatic delegation; embassy 4 a group of technicians, specialists, etc. sent to a foreign country 5 the special duty or function for which someone is sent as a messenger or representative; errand 6 *a)* the special task or purpose for which a person is apparently destined; calling [one's *mission* in life] *b)* a goal or ambition to which a person or group is especially dedicated 7 any charitable, educational, or religious organization for helping persons in need 8 a series of special religious services designed to increase faith or bring about conversion 9 a district without a church of its own, served by a nearby church ☆10 *Mil.* a specific combat operation assigned to an individual or unit; esp., a single combat flight by an airplane or group of airplanes —*adj.* 1 of a mission or missions ☆2 [*often* **M-**] of or in the style of the early Spanish missions in the SW U.S.; specif., designating a type of heavy, dark furniture with simple, square lines —*vt.* 1 to send on a mission 2 to establish a religious mission in (district) or among (a people)

mis·sion·ar·y (-er'ē) *adj.* ⟦ModL (Ec) *missionarius*⟧ of or characteristic of missions or missionaries, esp. religious ones —*n., pl.* **-ar'ies** a person sent on a mission, esp. on a religious MISSION (*n.* 2a): also **mis'sion·er** (-ər)

missionary position ⟦from the notion that Christian foreign missionaries advocated this as the proper sexual position⟧ a position used in sexual intercourse in which the female lies on her back and the male lies on top of her, their faces opposite each other

Missionary Ridge ⟦after the Brainerd *Mission* there⟧ ridge in SE Tenn. & NW Ga.: site of a Union victory (1863) in the Civil War

mission creep [Informal] a gradual broadening of the original objectives of a project or program

mis·sion·ize (-īz') *vi., vt.* **-ized', -iz'ing** to do missionary work (in or among)

mis·sis (mis'iz) *n.* ⟦altered < MISTRESS, MRS.⟧ [Informal or Dial.] 1 one's wife: also used with *the* 2 the mistress of a household: used with *the*

Mis·sis·sau·ga (mis'ə sô'gə) ⟦< Ojibwa < *misi,* large + *sauk,* river mouth⟧ city in SE Ontario, Canada, southwest of Toronto

Mis·sis·sip·pi (mis'ə sip'ē) ⟦< Fr < Illinois *missisipioui,* lit., big river⟧ 1 river in central U.S., flowing from NC Minn. south into the Gulf of Mexico: 2,348 mi (3,779 km): see also MISSOURI[2] (the river) 2 state of the S U.S., on the Gulf of Mexico: admitted 1817; 46,907 sq mi (121,489 sq km); cap. Jackson: abbrev. *MS* or *Miss*

☆**Mis·sis·sip·pi·an** (-ən) *adj.* 1 of the Mississippi River 2 of the state of Mississippi: usually used in the predicate 3 ⟦after the prec. River Valley, site of exposures of such deposits⟧ [*sometimes* **m-**] designating or of the first geologic subdivision or epoch of the Carboniferous Period, characterized by the development of vast limestone deposits, an abundance of ferns, amphibians, and crinoids, and the first winged insects —*n.* a person born or living in Mississippi —**the Mississippian** the Mississippian subdivision or epoch of the Carboniferous Period or its rocks: see the geologic time chart in the Reference Supplement

mis·sive (mis'iv) *n.* ⟦Fr *(lettre) missive* < ML *missivus* < L *missus,* pp. of *mittere,* to send: see MISSION⟧ a letter or written message

Mis·sou·ri[1] (mi zoor'ē) *n.* ⟦Fr, earlier *ouemessourit* < Illinois, lit., person who has a canoe⟧ 1 *pl.* **-ri** a member of a North American Indian people formerly living on the Missouri River in Nebraska and, later, in Oklahoma 2 the Siouan language of this people

Mis·sou·ri[2] (mi zoor'ē, -ə) ⟦< prec.⟧ 1 river in WC U.S., flowing from SW Mont. southeast into the Mississippi: 2,714 mi (4,368 km) 2 Midwestern state of the central U.S.: admitted 1821; 68,886 sq mi (178,414 sq km); cap. Jefferson City: abbrev. *MO* or *Mo*

Mis·sou·ri·an (-ən) *adj.* of the state of Missouri: usually used in the predicate —*n.* a person born or living in Missouri

mis·speak (mis spēk') *vt., vi.* **-spoke', -spok'en, -speak'ing** to speak or say incorrectly

mis·spell (-spel') *vt., vi.* **-spelled'** or **-spelt', -spell'ing** to spell incorrectly —**mis·spell'er** *n.*

mis·spell·ing (-spel'iŋ) *n.* (an) incorrect spelling

mis·spend (-spend') *vt.* **-spent', -spend'ing** to spend improperly or wastefully

mis·state (-stāt') *vt.* **-stat'ed, -stat'ing** to state incorrectly or falsely —**mis·state'ment** *n.*

☆**mis·step** (mis'step', mis step') *n.* 1 a wrong or awkward step 2 a mistake in conduct; faux pas

mis·sus (mis'əz) *n.* [Informal or Dial.] *var. of* MISSIS

miss·y (mis'ē) *n., pl.* **miss'ies** [Informal] miss: diminutive form, used in speaking to or of a young girl

mist (mist) *n.* ⟦ME < OE, darkness, mist, akin to ON *mistr,* dark weather < IE base **meigh-,* to blink, be dim > Sans **mēghá-,* cloud⟧ 1 a large mass of water vapor at or just above the earth's surface resembling a fog, but less dense 2 a thin film of moisture condensed on a surface in droplets 3 *a)* a cloud of dust, smoke, gas, etc. *b)* a fine spray, as of medication or perfume 4 a cloudiness or film before the eyes, dimming or blurring the vision [through a *mist* of tears] 5 anything that dims or obscures the understanding, memory, etc. —*vt.* 1 to make misty; dim or obscure as with a mist 2 to spray the leaves of (a houseplant) with water from a mister —*vi.* to be or become misty

SYN.—**mist** applies to a visible atmospheric vapor of rather fine density, that blurs the vision; **haze** suggests a thin dispersion of smoke, dust, etc. that makes objects indistinct; **fog** suggests a greater density of moisture particles than **mist**, sometimes suggesting a thickness impenetrable by the vision; **smog** is applied to a mixture of fog and smoke of a kind that sometimes appears in industrial centers. The first three terms are also used figuratively [lost in the *mists* of the past, a troublesome *haze* of confusion, in a *fog* of doubt]

mis·take (mi stāk') *vt.* **-took', -tak'en** or [Obs.] **-took', -tak'ing** ⟦ME *mistaken* < ON *mistaka,* to take wrongly: see MIS-[1] & TAKE⟧ 1 to understand or perceive wrongly; interpret or judge incorrectly [*mistake* someone's motives] 2 to take (someone or something) to be another; recognize or identify incorrectly [to *mistake* one twin for the other] —*vi.* [Archaic] to make a mistake —*n.* 1 a fault in understanding, perception, interpretation, etc. 2 an idea, answer, act, etc. that is wrong; error —SYN. ERROR —**and no mistake** [Informal] certainly —**mis·tak'a·ble** *adj.* —**mis·tak'a·bly** *adv.*

mis·tak·en (mi stāk'ən) *adj.* 1 wrong; having an incorrect understanding, perception, etc.: said of persons 2 incorrect; misunderstood; erroneous: said of ideas, etc. —**mis·tak'en·ly** *adv.* —**mis·tak'en·ness** *n.*

Mis·tas·si·ni (mis'tə sē'nē) ⟦< Cree *mista-assini,* lit., the great stone lake⟧ lake in SC Quebec, Canada: 840 sq mi (2,176 sq km)

mis·ter[1] (mis'tər) *n.* ⟦weakened form of MASTER⟧ 1 [**M-**] *a)* a title used in speaking to or of a man and placed before the name or title of office (usually written *Mr.*) ☆*b)* a title before a name of a place, occupation, activity, etc. or before a quality (used to designate a certain man as an example or personification) *[Mr.* Television, *Mr.* Nice Guy*]* ☆**2** *Mil.* the official title of address for *a)* a warrant officer in the army *b)* a cadet in a U.S. service academy *c)* a naval officer below the rank of commander **3** [Informal] sir: in direct address, not followed by a name **4** [Informal or Dial.] one's husband: also used with *the*

mist·er[2] (mis′tər) ***n.*** a bottle with a nozzle for spraying a mist of water, as onto houseplants

mi·ste·ri·o·so (mē ster′ē ō′sō) ***adj., adv.*** ⟦It⟧ [*also in roman type*] *Musical Direction* (in a manner) suggesting mystery

☆**mist·flow·er** (mist′flou′ər) ***n.*** a perennial E American plant (*Eupatorium coelestinum*) of the composite family, with small, purple-flowered heads lacking ray flowers

mis·think (mis thiŋk′) [Archaic] ***vi.*** **-thought′**, **-think′ing** to think mistakenly —***vt.*** to have a bad opinion of

Misti *see* EL MISTI

mis·time (mis tīm′) ***vt.*** **-timed′**, **-tim′ing** **1** to time wrongly; do or say at an inappropriate time **2** to judge incorrectly the time of

mis·tle thrush (mis′əl) a large grayish European thrush (*Turdus viscivorus*) with blackish-brown spots on the breast, that may feed on mistletoe berries

mis·tle·toe (mis′əl tō′) ***n.*** ⟦OE *misteltan* (akin to ON *mistilteinn*) < *mistel,* mistletoe (prob. < Gmc **mista,* dung: from being propagated by seeds in bird dung) + *tan,* a twig⟧ **1** any of various evergreen plants (genera *Phoradendron* and *Viscum*) of the mistletoe family, parasitic on deciduous or evergreen trees, with small, yellowish-green leaves, yellowish flowers, and shiny, white, poisonous berries **2** a sprig of such a plant, hung as a Christmas decoration: by custom, people kiss when standing under it —***adj.*** designating a family (Loranthaceae, order Santalales) of parasitic, dicotyledonous shrubs and small trees

mis·took (mis to͝ok′) ***vt., vi. pt. & obs. pp. of*** MISTAKE

mis·tral (mi sträl′, mis′trəl) ***n.*** ⟦Fr < Prov, lit., master-wind < L *magistralis* < *magister,* MASTER⟧ a cold, dry north wind that blows over the Mediterranean coast of France and nearby regions

Mis·tral (mēs träl′) **1 Fré·dé·ric** (frā dā rēk′) 1830-1914; Fr. Provençal poet **2 Ga·bri·e·la** (gä′brē ä′lä) (born *Lucila Godoy Alcayaga*) 1889-1957; Chilean poet

mis·trans·late (mis′trans lāt′, -tranz-; mis trans′lāt′, -tranz′-) ***vt.*** **-lat′ed**, **-lat′ing** to translate incorrectly —**mis′trans·la′tion** ***n.***

mis·treat (mis trēt′) ***vt.*** to treat wrongly or badly —**mis·treat′er** ***n.*** —**mis·treat′ment** ***n.***

mis·tress (mis′tris) ***n.*** ⟦ME *maistresse* < OFr, fem. of *maistre,* MASTER⟧ **1** a woman who rules others or has control, authority, or power over something; specif., *a)* a woman who is head of a household or institution *b)* [Chiefly Brit.] a female schoolteacher **2** a woman very skilled and able in some work, profession, science, art, etc. **3** [*sometimes* **M-**] something personified as a woman that has control, power, etc. *[*England was *mistress* of the seas*]* **4** *a)* a woman who is in a sexual relationship with, and typically is financially supported by, a man without being married to him *b)* a woman who is in an adulterous relationship with a man married to another woman **5** [Archaic] a sweetheart **6** [**M-**] [Obs.] a title used in speaking to or of a woman and placed before the name: now replaced by *Mrs., Miss,* or *Ms.*

mis·tri·al (mis′trī′əl) ***n.*** *Law* a trial made void because of a prejudicial error in the proceedings, a lack of jurisdiction by the court, or the inability of the jury to agree upon a verdict

mis·trust (mis′trust′, mis trust′) ***n.*** lack of trust or confidence; suspicion; doubt —***vt.*** to have no trust or confidence in (someone or something); doubt —**mis·trust′ful** ***adj.***

mist·y (mis′tē) ***adj.*** **mist′i·er**, **mist′i·est** ⟦ME *misti* < OE *mistig*⟧ **1** of, or having the nature of, mist **2** characterized by or covered with mist **3** *a)* blurred or dimmed, as by mist; indistinct *b)* obscure or vague —**mist′i·ly** ***adv.*** —**mist′i·ness** ***n.***

mist·y-eyed (mis′tē īd′) ***adj.*** **1** having tears in the eyes because of strong feelings **2** emotional, sentimental, dreamy, etc. *[*a *misty-eyed* optimist*]*

mis·un·der·stand (mis′un dər stand′) ***vt.*** **-stood′**, **-stand′ing** to fail to understand correctly; misinterpret

mis·un·der·stand·ing (-stan′diŋ) ***n.*** **1** a failure to understand; mistake of meaning or intention **2** a quarrel or disagreement

mis·un·der·stood (-sto͝od′) ***adj.*** **1** not properly understood **2** not properly appreciated

mis·us·age (mis yo͞o′sij, mis′yo͞o′sij) ***n.*** **1** incorrect usage; misapplication, as of words **2** bad or harsh treatment

mis·use (mis yo͞oz′; *for n.,* mis yo͞os′, mis′yo͞os′) ***vt.*** **-used′**, **-us′ing** **1** to use incorrectly or improperly; misapply **2** to treat badly or harshly; abuse —***n.*** **1** incorrect or improper use **2** [Obs.] bad or harsh treatment

mis·us·er (-yo͞o′zər) ***n.*** **1** a person who misuses something **2** *Law* unlawful use of some privilege, right, benefit, etc.

mis·word (mis wurd′) ***vt.*** to word or phrase incorrectly

mis·write (-rīt′) ***vt.*** **-wrote′**, **-writ′ten**, **-writ′ing** to write incorrectly

Mitch·ell[1] (mich′əl) **1 Maria** 1818-89; U.S. astronomer **2 William** (also called *Billy Mitchell*) 1879-1936; U.S. army officer & aviation pioneer

Mitch·ell[2] (mich′əl), **Mount** ⟦after Elisha Mitchell (1793-1857), U.S. geologist⟧ mountain of the Black Mountains, W N.C.: highest peak of the E U.S.: 6,684 ft (2,037 m)

mite[1] (mīt) ***n.*** ⟦ME < OE, akin to OHG *miza,* a gnat < IE base **mai-,* to cut, cut off > MAD⟧ any of a large subclass (Acari) of tiny, sometimes microscopic, arachnids often parasitic upon animals, insects, or plants, or infesting prepared foods, including many species that transmit diseases

mite[2] (mīt) ***n.*** ⟦ME < MDu, ult. same as prec.⟧ **1** *a)* a very small sum of money or contribution (see WIDOW'S MITE) *b)* [Obs.] a coin of very small value **2** BIT[2] (*n.* 1*b*) **3** a very small creature or object

mi·ter[1] (mīt′ər) ***n.*** ⟦ME *mitre* < OFr < L *mitra* < Gr, a belt, fillet, headband, turban < IE **mitro,* a band < base **mei-,* to bind, tie⟧ **1** a headdress; specif., *a)* a tall, ornamented cap with peaks in front and back, worn by the pope, bishops, and abbots as a mark of office *b)* the official headdress of the ancient Jewish high priest *c)* in ancient Greece, a headband worn by women **2** the office or rank of a bishop; bishopric —***vt.*** to invest with the office of bishop by placing a miter on

miter[1]
(sense 1*a*)

mi·ter[2] (mīt′ər) *Carpentry* ***n.*** ⟦prob. < prec.⟧ **1** a kind of joint formed by fitting together two pieces, beveled to a specified angle (usually 45°) to form a corner (usually a right angle): now usually **miter joint** **2** either of the facing surfaces of such a joint **3** MITER SQUARE —***vt.*** **1** to fit together in a miter joint **2** to bevel the ends or edges of to form a miter joint

miter box a device used to guide the saw in cutting wood at an angle for a miter joint

miter joint

miter square a tool used to mark out angles for miter joints, with two blades set at a 45° angle or adjustable to any angle

☆**mi·ter·wort** (mīt′ər wurt′) ***n.*** *Bot.* BISHOP'S-CAP

Mith·ra·ic (mith rā′ik) ***adj.*** of Mithras or Mithraism

Mith·ra·ism (mith′rā iz′əm, -rə-) ***n.*** the ancient Persian religion based on worship of Mithras —**Mith′ra·ist** ***n., adj.*** —**Mith′ra·is′tic** ***adj.***

Mith·ras (mith′rəs, -ras′) ***n.*** ⟦L < Gr *Mithras* < OPers *Mithra*⟧ the ancient Persian god of light and truth, opponent of darkness and evil: also **Mith′ra** (-rə)

mith·ri·date (mith′rə dāt′) ***n.*** ⟦ML *mithridatum* < LL *mithridatium* < *Mithridatius,* of Mithridates VI, said to have become immune to poisons by taking them in gradually increased doses⟧ [Historical] a substance supposed to be an antidote against all poisons

Mith·ri·da·tes VI (mith′rə dāt′ēz) 132?-63 B.C.; king of Pontus (120-63): called *the Great*

☆**mi·ti·cide** (mīt′i sīd′) ***n.*** ⟦< MITE[1] + -CIDE⟧ any substance used for destroying mites —**mi′ti·ci′dal** ***adj.***

mit·i·gate (mit′ə gāt′) ***vt., vi.*** **-gat′ed**, **-gat′ing** ⟦ME *mitigaten* < L *mitigatus,* pp. of *mitigare,* to make mild, soft, or tender < *mitis,* soft (see MIGNON) + *agere,* to drive: see ACT[1]⟧ **1** to make or become milder, less severe, less rigorous, or less painful; moderate **2** ⟦< confusion with MILITATE⟧ to operate or work (*against*): generally considered a loose or erroneous usage —*SYN.* RELIEVE —**mit′i·ga·ble** (-i gə bəl) ***adj.*** —**mit′i·ga′tion** ***n.*** —**mit′i·ga′tive** ***adj.***, **mit′i·ga·to′ry** (-gə tôr′ē) —**mit′i·ga′tor** ***n.***

Mit·i·lí·ni (mit′′l ē′nē) *alt. sp. of* MYTILENE

mitochondrial DNA DNA contained in mitochondria: it is abundant, highly resistant to damage, and, because it is inherited only through the mother, useful in forensic investigations, in tracing ancestry, and in studying evolutionary change: abbrev. *mtDNA*

mi·to·chon·dri·on (mīt′ō kän′drē ən) ***n., pl.*** **-dri·a** (-ə) ⟦ModL < Gr *mitos,* a thread + *chondrion,* a small cartilage < *chondros:* see CHONDRO-⟧ any of various very small, usually rodlike structures found in the cytoplasm of eukaryotic cells and serving as a center of intracellular enzyme activity: this activity produces the ATP needed to power the cell —**mi′to·chon′dri·al** ***adj.***

mi·to·gen (mīt′ə jən) ***n.*** ⟦< fol. + -GEN⟧ *Genetics* any substance that causes a cell to undergo mitosis —**mi′to·gen′ic** ***adj.***

mi·to·sis (mī tō′sis, mi-) ***n., pl.*** **-ses′** (-sēz′) ⟦ModL < Gr *mitos,* thread + -OSIS⟧ *Biol.* the indirect and more common method of nuclear division of cells, consisting typically of prophase, metaphase, anaphase, and telophase: the nuclear chromatin first appears as long threads which shorten and thicken to form the typical number of chromosomes, each of which splits lengthwise to double in number, with half of each set then moving toward opposite poles of the cell to become reorganized into two new nuclei with the normal number of chromosomes —**mi·tot′ic** (-tät′ik) ***adj.*** —**mi·tot′i·cal·ly** ***adv.***

mi·tral (mī′trəl) ***adj.*** ⟦Fr < ModL *mitralis* < L *mitra,* MITER[1]⟧ of or like a miter or the mitral valve

mitral valve ⟦so named from seeming resemblance in shape to a bishop's miter: see prec.⟧ the valve between the left atrium and left ventricle of the heart, preventing a flow of blood back into the atrium during systole

mi·tre (mīt′ər) ***n., vt.*** **-tred**, **-tring** *Brit. sp. of* MITER[1]

Mi·tro·pou·los (mə trä′pə ləs), **Di·mi·tri** (də mē′trē) 1896-1960; U.S. orchestra conductor, born in Greece

mits·vah (mits′və, mits vä′) ***n., pl.*** **mits′vahs** or **mits·voth′** (-vōt′) *var. of* MITZVAH

mitt (mit) ***n.*** ⟦contr. < MITTEN⟧ **1** a woman's glove, often of lace or net, covering part of the arm, the hand, and sometimes part of the fingers **2** MITTEN **3** a padded glove or mitten for a specified use *[*oven *mitts]* ☆**4** [Slang] a hand ☆5 *a)* *Baseball* a padded glove, with a thumb but typically without distinct fingers, worn for protection by a catcher or first baseman *b)* a boxing glove

Mit·tel·eu·ro·pa (mit′'l yo͞o rō′pə, -oi rō′-) ⟦Ger⟧ central Europe, esp. with reference to its culture, style, or customs: also **Mit′tel-Eu·ro′pa** or **Mit′tel Eu·ro′pa** —**Mit′tel·eu′ro·pe′an** *adj.*, **Mit′tel-Eu′ro·pe′an** (-yoor′ə pē′ən)

mit·ten (mit′'n) *n.* ⟦ME *mytten* < OFr *mitaine* < *mite* (in same sense), prob. orig. metaphorical use of *mite,* cat⟧ **1** a glovelike covering for the hand, with a thumb but no separately divided fingers **2** *former var. of* MITT (sense 1)

Mit·ter·rand (mē te *rän′*; *E* mēt′ər änd′, mit′-), **Fran·çois (Maurice)** (frän swȧ′) 1916-96; Fr. statesman: president of France (1981-95)

mit·ti·mus (mit′i məs) *n.* ⟦L, we send < *mittere:* see MISSION⟧ *Law* a warrant or writ for imprisoning a person convicted of a crime

mitz·vah (mits′və, mits vä′) *n., pl.* **mitz′vahs** or **mitz·voth′** (-vōt′) ⟦Heb *mitsva,* lit., commandment < root *cwh,* to command, order⟧ *Judaism* **1** *a)* a commandment or precept in the Bible or from the rabbis in the Talmud *b)* an act fulfilling such a command **2** a good deed or charitable act

mix (miks) *vt.* ⟦prob. back-form. < *mixt,* mixed, taken as pp. < Fr *mixte* < L *mixtus,* pp. of *miscere,* to mix (> OE *miscian*) < IE base **meik-* > Gr *meignynai,* Welsh *mysgu,* to mix⟧ **1** to put or blend together in a single mass, collection, or compound **2** to make by putting ingredients together [to *mix* a cocktail] **3** to join; combine [to *mix* work and play] **4** to cause to join or associate [to *mix* the fourth- with the fifth-graders at recess] **5** to hybridize **6** to combine or blend electronically (the various sounds of a recording or live performance) on (a tape, record, etc.) —*vi.* **1** to be mixed or capable of being mixed; be blended; mingle **2** to associate or get along [to *mix* with other people] **3** to hybridize —*n.* **1** a mixing or being mixed **2** a muddle; state of confusion ☆**3** *a)* a product of mixing; mixture [cement *mix*] *b)* a commercial mixture of ingredients for preparing a food, usually by adding liquid [cake *mix*] **4** MIXER (sense 3) **5** the blend or combination of sounds in a recording or live performance **6** a mixture of dissimilar components, elements, parts, ideas, etc. —**mix up 1** to mix thoroughly; mingle together **2** to confuse; specif., *a)* to cause confusion in *b)* to mistake for another (with *with*) **3** *a)* to involve or implicate (*in* something regarded as inappropriate, disreputable, etc.) *b)* to involve or associate (*with* someone regarded as inappropriate, disreputable, etc.): usually used in the passive —**mix it up** [Slang] to fight with or as with the fists —**mix′a·ble** *adj.*

SYN.—**mix** implies a combining of things so that the resulting substance is uniform in composition, whether or not the separate elements can be distinguished [to *mix* paints]; **mingle** usually implies that the separate elements can be distinguished [*mingled* feelings of joy and sorrow]; **blend** implies a mixing of different varieties to produce a desired quality [a *blended* tea, whiskey, etc.] or the mingling of different elements to form a harmonious whole [a novel *blending* fact and fiction]; **merge** stresses the loss of distinction of elements by combination or may suggest the total absorption of one thing in another [the companies *merged* to form a large corporation]; **coalesce** implies a union or growing together of things into a single body or mass [the factions *coalesced* into a party of opposition]; **fuse** means to unite by melting together and stresses the indissoluble nature of the union

mix-and-match (miks′ən mach′) *adj.* of or having to do with the combining, as by a consumer, of separate but compatible items to form a set, outfit, etc. [a *mix-and-match* selection of slacks and tops]

mixed (mikst) *adj.* ⟦earlier *mixt:* see MIX⟧ **1** joined or mingled in a single mass or compound; blended **2** made up of different or incongruous parts, groups, elements, classes, races, etc. **3** *a)* consisting of or involving both sexes [a *mixed* doubles match in tennis, a joke unsuitable for *mixed* company] *b)* characterized by or consisting of both positive and negative features, judgments, etc. [critical response to the movie was *mixed*; winning the lottery may be a *mixed* blessing] **4** confused; muddled **5** *Phonet.* central: said of a vowel

☆**mixed bag** an assortment or mixture, esp. of diverse elements, types of people, etc. brought together at random

mixed bud a bud that produces both leaves and flowers: cf. FLOWER BUD, LEAF BUD

mixed drink a drink of alcoholic liquor combined with one or more other ingredients, as wine, water, or another liquor

mixed grill a combination of various meats, as chops, liver or kidneys, and bacon, broiled and served together, often with broiled vegetables

mixed marriage marriage between persons of different religions or races

mixed media 1 *Painting* the use of different media, as watercolors and crayon, in the same composition **2** MULTIMEDIA (senses 1 & 2)

mixed metaphor the use of two or more inconsistent metaphors in a single expression (Ex.: the storm of protest was nipped in the bud)

mixed number a number consisting of a whole number and a fraction, as 3⅔

mixed-up (mikst′up′) *adj.* in a state of befuddlement or turmoil; confused, troubled, etc.

mix·er (mik′sər) *n.* **1** a person or thing that mixes; specif., ☆*a)* a person with reference to his or her ability to get along with others [a good *mixer*] *b)* an electric appliance for mixing or beating foods *c)* a machine for mixing [concrete *mixer*] *d)* a person responsible for combining and balancing visual or sound sources, as for film soundtracks, radio or TV broadcasts, etc. **2** a social gathering, as a dance, for getting people acquainted with one another **3** a beverage, as soda water or ginger ale, for mixing with alcoholic liquor **4** *Electronics* *a)* a device or circuit for combining carriers of differing frequencies to produce a desired carrier *b)* an electrical apparatus in which signals from various audio sources are combined in desired proportions

☆**mix·ol·o·gist** (mik säl′ə jist) *n.* ⟦MIX + *-ologist,* as in *biologist*⟧ [Informal] a person, esp. a bartender, skilled or trained in making and serving mixed drinks

☆**mix·ol·o·gy** (-ə jē) *n.* ⟦back-form. < prec.⟧ [Informal] the work or skill of a mixologist

Mix·tec (mēs′tek′) *n.* **1** *pl.* **-tecs′** or **-tec′** a member of an American Indian people living in the Mexican states of Oaxaca, Guerrero, and Puebla **2** the Mixtecan language of this people

Mix·tec·an (mēs tek′ən) *n.* a branch of a family of American Indian languages spoken in central Mexico

mix·ture (miks′chər) *n.* ⟦LME < L *mixtura* < *mixtus:* see MIX⟧ **1** a mixing or being mixed **2** something made by mixing; esp., *a)* a combination of ingredients, kinds, etc. *b)* a yarn or fabric made of two or more different fibers, often of different colors **3** *Chem.* a substance containing two or more ingredients: distinguished from a chemical compound in that the constituents are not in fixed proportions, do not lose their individual characteristics, and can be separated by physical means

mix-up (miks′up′) *n.* **1** a condition or instance of confusion; tangle **2** [Informal] a fight

Mi·ya·za·ki (mē′yä zä′kē) city in SE Kyushu, Japan

Mi·zar (mī′zär′) *n.* ⟦Ar *mīzār,* lit., waist-cloth, apron⟧ a multiple star, the brighter companion in an optical double star at the middle of the Big Dipper's handle: magnitude, 2.23

mi·zu·na (mi zo͞o′nə) *n.* ⟦Jpn⟧ a Japanese mustard plant whose leaves have a mildly tangy flavor and are used in salads

miz·zen or **miz·en** (miz′ən) *adj.* ⟦LME *meseyn* < or akin to MFr *misaine* < It *mezzana,* fem. of *mezzano,* middle < L *medianus:* see MEDIAN⟧ of the mizzenmast —*n.* **1** a fore-and-aft sail set on the mizzenmast **2** MIZZENMAST

miz·zen·mast (miz′ən mast′; *naut.,* -məst) *n.* ⟦see prec.⟧ **1** the mast third from the bow in a ship with three or more masts **2** the smaller, after mast in a ketch or yawl

miz·zle (miz′əl) [Dial.] *vt., vi.* **-zled, -zling** ⟦LME *misellen,* prob. < LowG, as in Du dial. *miezelen:* for IE base see MIST⟧ to rain in a fine mist; drizzle —*n.* a misty rain; drizzle —**miz′zly** *adj.*

mk *abbrev.* **1** mark (the monetary unit) **2** markka

Mk *abbrev. Bible* Mark

MKS or **mks** *abbrev.* meter-kilogram-second (system): see the table of weights and measures in the Reference Supplement

mkt *abbrev.* market

mktg *abbrev.* marketing

ml *abbrev.* milliliter(s)

ML *abbrev.* Medieval (or Middle) Latin

MLA *abbrev.* Modern Language Association

MLB *abbrev.* **1** *service mark* Major League Baseball **2** *Football* middle linebacker: sometimes written **mlb**

MLD *abbrev.* minimum (or minimal) lethal dose

MLG *abbrev.* Middle Low German

MLK *abbrev.* Martin Luther King, Jr.

Mlle *abbrev.* Mademoiselle

Mlles *abbrev.* Mesdemoiselles

MLowG *abbrev.* Middle Low German

MLS or **M.L.S.** *abbrev.* Master of Library Science

mm[1] (m, um *or other nasalized sound*) *interj.* used to signify *a)* a noncommittal response *b)* an affirmative response *c)* the speaker's hesitation before replying to a question or remark

mm[2] *abbrev.* millimeter(s)

MM *abbrev.* **1** Messieurs **2** Majesties

Mme *abbrev.* Madame

Mmes *abbrev.* Mesdames

mmf *abbrev.* magnetomotive force

MMPI *trademark* Minnesota Multiphasic Personality Inventory

MMR *abbrev.* measles, mumps, and rubella (vaccine or vaccination)

Mn *Chem. symbol for* manganese

MN *abbrev.* Minnesota

mne·mon·ic (nē män′ik) *adj.* ⟦Gr *mnēmonikos* < *mnēmōn,* mindful < *mnasthai,* to remember < IE base **men-,* to think > MIND⟧ **1** helping, or meant to help, the memory [a *mnemonic* device] **2** of mnemonics or memory —*n.* any device or formula used as an aid in memorizing something (Ex.: the phrase "Every Good Boy Does Fine" is a mnemonic for the notes of the strings of a guitar—EGBDF) —**mne·mon′i·cal·ly** *adv.*

mne·mon·ics (-iks) *n.* ⟦see prec.⟧ a technique or system for improving one's ability to memorize something

Mne·mos·y·ne (nē mäs′i nē′, -mäz′-) *n.* ⟦L < Gr *mnēmosynē,* memory < *mnasthai,* to remember: see MNEMONIC⟧ *Gr. Myth.* the goddess of memory, and mother (by Zeus) of the Muses

mo[1] (mō) *n.* [Informal, Chiefly Brit.] *short for* MOMENT (sense 1)

mo[2] *abbrev.* **1** money order **2** month

Mo[1] *abbrev.* **1** Missouri **2** Monday

Mo[2] *Chem. symbol for* molybdenum

MO *abbrev.* **1** Medical Officer **2** Missouri **3** ⟦L *modus operandi*⟧ mode of operation **4** money order

-mo (mō) ⟦< ending of L abl. forms of ordinals, after prep. *in,* as *in duodecimo* (< *duodecimus,* twelfth)⟧ *suffix forming nouns* a book, pamphlet, etc. having (a specified number of) leaves as a result of the folding of a sheet of paper a given number of times [*12mo, duodecimo,* or *twelvemo*]

mo·a (mō′ə) *n.* ⟦< native (Maori) name⟧ any of an extinct order (Dinornithiformes) of ostrichlike flightless birds of New Zealand

Mo·ab[1] (mō′ab′) *n.* ⟦LL(Ec) < Gr(Ec) < Heb *mō′ābh*⟧ *Bible* a son of Lot: Gen. 19:37

Mo·ab[2] (mō′ab′) ancient kingdom east & south of the Dead Sea, now the SW part of Jordan

Mo·ab·ite (mō′ə bīt′) *n.* ⟦ME < LL(Ec) *Moabita* < Gr(Ec) *mōabitis*⟧ **1** a person born or living in Moab **2** the extinct Semitic language spoken by the Moabites —*adj.* of Moab or its people or culture

moan (mōn) *n.* ⟦ME *mone,* prob. < base of OE *mænan,* to complain: see MEAN[1]⟧ **1** [Archaic] a complaint; lamentation **2** a long, low vocal sound as of sorrow or pain or of sexual pleasure **3** any nonvocal sound like this [the *moan* of the wind] —*vi.* **1** to utter a moan or moans **2** to complain, lament, grieve, etc. —*vt.* **1** to say with a moan **2** to complain about; bewail [to *moan* one's fate] —**SYN.** CRY —**moan′er** *n.*

moat (mōt) *n.* ⟦ME *mote* < OFr, orig., mound, embankment, prob. < Gmc **motta,* heap of earth⟧ a deep, broad ditch dug around a fortress or castle, and often filled with water, for protection against invasion —*vt.* to surround with or as with a moat

mob (mäb) *n.* ⟦< L *mobile (vulgus),* movable (crowd)⟧ **1** a disorderly and lawless crowd; rabble **2** any crowd **3** the masses; common people collectively: a contemptuous term **4** [Informal] *a)* a gang of criminals *b)* organized crime, specif. the MAFIA (sense 1) (with *the*) —*vt.* **mobbed, mob′bing 1** to crowd around and attack **2** to crowd around and jostle, annoy, etc., as in curiosity or anger **3** to fill with many people; throng —**SYN.** CROWD[1] —**mob′bish** *adj.*

mob·cap (mäb′kap′) *n.* ⟦< MDu *mop,* woman's cap + CAP[1]⟧ a woman's indoor cap, esp. of the 18th cent., having a high, puffy crown and often tied under the chin

mo·bile (mō′bəl, -bīl′; *for adj. 5-6 & n.,* -bēl′ *or Brit* -bīl′) *adj.* ⟦OFr < L *mobilis,* movable < *movere,* to MOVE⟧ **1** *a)* moving, or capable of moving or being moved, from place to place *b)* movable by means of a motor vehicle or vehicles [a *mobile* X-ray unit] **2** very fluid, as mercury **3** capable of changing rapidly or easily, as in response to different moods, feelings, conditions, needs, or influences; flexible, adaptable, etc. **4** *a)* designating or of a society that allows a relatively free change in social status, and in which social groups mingle freely *b)* designating a person who is experiencing a change in social status [the upwardly *mobile* professional] **5** of or having to do with wireless communications services, devices, etc., esp. cell phones **6** *Art* that is or has to do with a mobile or mobiles —*n.* **1** a piece of abstract sculpture which aims to depict movement, i.e., kinetic rather than static rhythms, as by an arrangement of thin forms, rings, rods, etc. balanced and suspended in midair and set in motion by air currents **2** CELL PHONE

Mo·bile (mō bēl′, mō′bēl′) ⟦< Fr < AmInd < ?⟧ **1** seaport in SW Ala., on Mobile Bay **2** river in SW Ala., formed by the Alabama & Tombigbee rivers & flowing into Mobile Bay: *c.* 45 mi (72 km)

-mo·bile (mō bēl′) ⟦< (AUTO)MOBILE⟧ *combining form* motorized vehicle designed for a (specified) purpose [*bookmobile, snowmobile*]

Mobile Bay arm of the Gulf of Mexico, extending into SW Ala.: *c.* 35 mi (56 km) long

☆**mo·bile home** (mō′bəl) a movable dwelling with no permanent foundation, but able to be connected to utility lines and set more or less permanently at a location: cf. MOTOR HOME

mo·bil·i·ty (mō bil′ə tē) *n.* the quality of being mobile; ability to move, adapt, etc.

mo·bi·lize (mō′bə līz′) *vt.* **-lized′, -liz′ing** ⟦Fr *mobiliser*⟧ **1** *a)* to make mobile, or movable *b)* to put into motion, circulation, or use **2** to bring into readiness for immediate active service in war **3** to organize (people, resources, etc.) for active service or use in any emergency, drive, etc. —*vi.* to become organized and ready, as for war —**mo′bi·liz′a·ble** *adj.* —**mo′bi·li·za′tion** *n.* —**mo′bi·liz′er** *n.*

Mö·bi·us strip (mā′bē əs, mō′-) ⟦after A. F. *Möbius* (1790-1868), Ger mathematician⟧ a one-edged geometric surface with only one continuous side, formed as by giving a 180° twist to a long, narrow rectangle and then connecting the two ends together: also **Möbius band**

mob·oc·ra·cy (mäb äk′rə sē) *n., pl.* **-cies** ⟦MOB + (DEM)OCRACY⟧ **1** rule or domination by a mob **2** the mob as ruler —**mob′o·crat′** *n.* —**mob′o·crat′ic** *adj.*

mob·ster (mäb′stər) *n.* [Informal] a member of a criminal mob; gangster

moc (mäk) *n. short for* MOCCASIN (*n.* 1 & 2)

Mo·çam·bi·que (moo′səm bē′kə) *Port. name for* MOZAMBIQUE

☆**moc·ca·sin** (mäk′ə sən) *n.* ⟦< AmInd (Algonquian), as in Narragansett *mokussin,* Massachusett *mohkisson*⟧ **1** a heelless slipper of soft, flexible leather, worn orig. by North American Indians **2** any slipper more or less like this but with a hard sole and heel **3** WATER MOCCASIN

☆**moccasin flower** CYPRIPEDIUM (sense 1)

mo·cha (mō′kə) *n.* ⟦after *Mocha,* seaport in Yemen⟧ **1** a choice grade of coffee grown orig. in Arabia **2** [Informal] any coffee **3** a flavoring made from an infusion of coffee, or of coffee and chocolate **4** a soft, velvety leather of Egyptian sheepskin, used esp. for gloves **5** chocolate brown —*adj.* **1** flavored with coffee or coffee and chocolate **2** chocolate-brown

mock (mäk) *vt.* ⟦ME *mokken* < OFr *mocquer,* to mock⟧ **1** to hold up to scorn or contempt; ridicule **2** to imitate or mimic, as in fun or derision; burlesque **3** to lead on and disappoint; deceive **4** to defy and make futile; defeat [the impregnable fortress *mocked* the invaders] —*vi.* to show or express scorn, ridicule, or contempt; jeer: often with *at* —*n.* **1** an act of mocking; jibe; sneer **2** a person or thing receiving or deserving ridicule or derision **3** an imitation or counterfeit —*adj.* **1** sham; false; imitation; pretended [a *mock* battle] **2** of or designating a food that imitates another in some way [the filling of *mock* apple pie tastes as if it contains apples] —*adv.* in a false or insincere manner [*mock*-sympathetic words] —**SYN.** IMITATE, RIDICULE —**mock′er** *n.* —**mock′ing·ly** *adv.*

mock·er·y (mäk′ər ē) *n., pl.* **-er·ies** ⟦ME *moquerye* < OFr *moquerie*⟧ **1** a mocking (in various senses) **2** a person or thing receiving or deserving ridicule **3** a false, derisive, or impertinent imitation; travesty; burlesque **4** vain or disappointing effort; futility

mock-he·ro·ic (mäk′hi rō′ik) *adj.* mocking, or burlesquing, any heroic style, action, or character —*n.* a burlesque of something heroic —**mock′-he·ro′i·cal·ly** *adv.*

☆**mock·ing·bird** (mäk′iŋ burd′) *n.* any of various New World passerine birds (family Mimidae), esp. a species (*Mimus polyglottos*) of the U.S. noted for its song and its ability to imitate the calls of many other birds

mock orange ☆any of a genus (*Philadelphus*) of shrubs of the saxifrage family, with fragrant, white flowers resembling those of the orange

mock turtle soup a soup made from calf's head, veal, etc., spiced so as to taste like green turtle soup

mock-up (mäk′up′) *n.* ⟦altered (< MOCK & UP[1]) < Fr *maquette,* a sketch, mock-up < *maquiller,* to pretend, orig. a cant term, to work < dial. *makier,* to make, do < MDu *maken,* akin to MAKE[1]⟧ a scale model, usually a full-sized replica, of a structure or apparatus used for instructional or experimental purposes

mod[1] (mäd) *n.* ⟦< MOD(ERN)⟧ [*also* **M-**] any of the young people in England in the mid-1960s noted for their emphasis on stylish dress, often as a symbol of their alienation from conventional society —*adj.* **1** [*also* **M-**] of or characteristic of the mods or the styles they favored **2** [Informal] of or relating to anything up-to-date, fashionable, stylish, etc., esp. clothes

mod[2] *abbrev.* **1** moderate **2** *Music* moderato **3** modern

mod·a·cryl·ic (mäd′ə kril′ik) *adj.* ⟦*mod(ified) acrylic*⟧ designating or of any of various synthetic fibers that resist combustion, made from long-chain polymers composed primarily of acrylonitrile modified by other polymers: used in making fabrics, carpets, etc.

mod·al (mōd′'l) *adj.* ⟦ML *modalis* < L *modus,* MODE⟧ **1** of or indicating a mode or mood **2** *Gram.* of or expressing mood [a *modal* auxiliary] **3** *a)* *Jazz* of or relating to compositions or improvisations based on an arrangement of modes rather than a series of chord progressions *b)* in popular music, of or characterized by the repetition of one or two chords as a harmonic base **4** *Logic* expressing or characterized by modality **5** *Music* of or composed in any of the medieval church modes **6** *Philos.* of mode, or form, as opposed to substance **7** *Statistics* having to do with a statistical mode —*n. Gram.* MODAL AUXILIARY —**mod′al·ly** *adv.*

modal auxiliary an auxiliary verb that is used with another verb to indicate its mood, as *can, could, may, might, must, shall, should, will,* and *would*: it has no special form in the third person singular and no present or past participle (Ex.: the modal auxiliary *would* indicates the subjunctive mood in "We would go if we could")

mo·dal·i·ty (mō dal′ə tē) *n., pl.* **-ties** ⟦ML *modalitas*⟧ **1** the fact, state, or quality of being modal **2** a special attribute, emphasis, etc. that marks certain individuals, things, groups, etc. **3** *Logic* the qualification in a proposition that indicates that what is affirmed or denied is possible, impossible, necessary, contingent, etc. **4** *Med.* *a)* the employment of, or the method of employment of, a therapeutic agent *b)* a specific sensory channel, as vision or hearing

mode (mōd) *n.* ⟦ME *moede* < L *modus,* measure, manner, mode < IE base **med-,* to measure: see MEDICAL⟧ **1** a manner or way of acting, doing, or being; method or form **2** ⟦Fr < L *modus*⟧ customary usage, or current fashion or style, as in manners or dress **3** *Geol.* the actual mineral composition of an unaltered igneous rock **4** *Gram.* MOOD[2] (sense 1) **5** *Logic* *a)* modality or the form of a proposition with reference to its modality *b)* MOOD[2] (sense 2) **6** *Music* *a)* the selection and arrangement of tones and semitones in a scale, esp. any of such arrangements in medieval church music *b)* a rhythmical system of the 13th cent. *c)* either of the two forms of scale arrangement in later music (MAJOR MODE and MINOR MODE) **7** *Philos.* the form, or way of being, of something, as distinct from its substance **8** *Statistics* the value, number, etc. that occurs most frequently in a given series —**SYN.** FASHION

mod·el (mäd′'l) *n.* ⟦Fr *modèle* < It *modello,* dim. of *modo* < L *modus,* prec.⟧ **1** *a)* a small copy or imitation of an existing object, as a ship, building, etc., made to scale *b)* a preliminary representation of something, serving as the plan from which the final, usually larger, object is to be constructed *c)* ARCHETYPE (sense 1) *d)* a hypothetical or stylized representation, as of an atom *e)* a generalized, hypothetical description, often based on an analogy, used in analyzing or explaining something *f)* a piece of sculpture in wax or clay from which a finished work in bronze, marble, etc. is to be made **2** a person or thing considered as a standard of excellence to be imitated **3** a style or design; specif., any of a series of different styles or designs of a particular product, brand of automobile, etc. *[a heavy-duty model, a 1969 model]* **4** *a)* a person who poses for an artist or photographer *b)* any person or thing serving as a subject for an artist or writer *c)* a person employed to display clothes by wearing them —*adj.* **1** serving as a model, pattern, or standard of excellence *[a model student]* **2** representative of others of the same kind, style, etc. *[a model home]* **3** of or being a small-scale copy of an airplane, ship, etc., esp. one assembled from a KIT[1] (*n. 2d*) as a hobby —*vt.* **-eled** or **-elled, -el·ing** or **-el·ling 1** *a)* to make a model of *b)* to plan, form, or design after a model *c)* to make conform to a standard of excellence *[to model one's behavior on that of one's elders]* **2** to shape or form in or as in clay, wax, etc. **3** to display (a dress, suit, etc.) by wearing **4** in painting, drawing, etc., to create a three-dimensional image of on a flat surface through the use of color, shading, etc. —*vi.* **1** to make a model or models *[to model in clay]* ☆**2** to serve as a MODEL (sense 4) —**mod′el·er** *n.*, **mod′el·ler**

SYN.—**model** refers to a representation made to be copied or, more generally, to any person or thing to be followed or imitated because of excellence, worth, etc.; **example** suggests that which is presented as a sample, or that which sets a precedent for imitation, whether good or bad; a **pattern** is a model, guide, plan, etc. to be strictly followed; **paradigm** is used generally for a conceptual pattern or model and specifically for a concept or principle held within an intellectual or technical field; **archetype** applies to the original pattern serving as the model for all later things of the same kind; **standard** refers to something established for use as a rule or a basis of comparison in judging quality, quantity, etc.

mo·dem (mō′dəm, -dem) *n.* ⟦MO(DULATOR) + DEM(ODULATOR)⟧ a device that converts data to a form that can be transmitted, as over communications lines, to equipment where a similar device reconverts it

Mo·de·na (mōd′′n ə, môd′-; -ä′) commune in N Italy, in Emilia-Romagna

mod·er·ate (mäd′ər it; *for v.*, -āt′) *adj.* ⟦ME *moderat* < L *moderatus*, pp. of *moderare*, to keep within bounds, restrain < *modus:* see MODE⟧ **1** within reasonable limits; avoiding excesses or extremes; temperate or restrained **2** mild; calm; gentle; not violent *[moderate weather]* **3** of average or medium quality, amount, scope, range, etc. *[moderate skills, moderate prices]* —*n.* a person holding moderate views or opinions, as in politics or religion —*vt.* **-at′ed, -at′ing 1** to cause to become moderate; make less extreme, violent, etc.; restrain **2** to preside over (a meeting, etc.) —*vi.* **1** to become moderate **2** to serve as a moderator —**mod′er·ate·ly** *adv.* —**mod′er·ate·ness** *n.*

SYN.—**moderate** and **temperate** are often interchangeable in denoting a staying within reasonable limits, but in strict discrimination, **moderate** implies merely an absence of excesses or extremes, while **temperate** suggests deliberate self-restraint *[moderate demands, a temperate reply]* —*ANT.* **excessive, extreme**

moderate breeze a wind whose speed is 13 to 18 miles per hour: see the Beaufort scale in the Reference Supplement

moderate gale a wind whose speed is 32 to 38 miles per hour: see the Beaufort scale in the Reference Supplement

mod·er·a·tion (mäd′ər ā′shən) *n.* **1** a moderating, or bringing within bounds **2** avoidance of excesses or extremes **3** absence of violence; calmness —**in moderation** to a moderate degree; without excess

mod·e·ra·to (mäd′ə rä′tō, mōd′-) *adj., adv.* ⟦It⟧ [*also in italics*] *Musical Direction* with moderation in tempo

mod·er·a·tor (mäd′ər āt′ər) *n.* ⟦ME *moderatour* < L *moderator*⟧ a person or thing that moderates; specif., *a)* a person who presides at a town meeting, debate, assembly, etc. *b)* the presiding officer of a governing body, as of the Presbyterian Church *c)* a substance, as graphite or heavy water, used to slow down high-energy neutrons in a nuclear reactor

mod·ern (mäd′ərn) *adj.* ⟦Fr *moderne* < LL *modernus* < L *modo*, just now, orig. abl. of *modus:* see MODE⟧ **1** of the present or recent times; specif., *a)* of or having to do with the latest styles, methods, or ideas; up-to-date *b)* designating or of certain contemporary trends and schools of art, music, literature, dance, etc. *c)* [*often* **M-**] designating or of any of various 20th-cent. styles of modernist art, furniture, architecture, etc. **2** of or relating to the period of history after the Middle Ages, from *c.* A.D. 1450 to the present day **3** [*often* **M-**] designating the form of a language in its most recent stage of development —*n.* **1** a person living in modern times **2** a person having modern ideas, beliefs, standards, etc. **3** *Printing* a style of typeface characterized by heavy down strokes contrasting with narrow cross strokes —*SYN.* NEW —**mod′ern·ly** *adv.* —**mod′ern·ness** *n.*

☆**modern dance** a form of dance as a performing art, variously developed in the 20th cent. by Isadora Duncan, Ruth St. Denis, Martha Graham, etc., and characterized by bodily movements and rhythms less formalized than in classical ballet and less firmly bound to predetermined musical form

mod·ern-day (-dā′) *adj.* being of the modern era

Modern English the English language since about the mid-15th cent.: see also EARLY MODERN ENGLISH

Modern Greek the Greek language as spoken and written in Greece since about 1500

Modern Hebrew the Hebrew language as spoken and written in post-biblical times; esp., the language of modern Israel

mod·ern·ism (mäd′ərn iz′əm) *n.* **1** *a)* modern practices, trends, ideas, etc., or sympathy with any of these *b)* an instance of this; a modern idiom, practice, or usage **2** [*often* **M-**] any of several movements variously attempting to redefine Biblical and Christian dogma and traditional teachings in the light of modern science, historical research, etc.: condemned in the Roman Catholic Church in 1907 as a heresy **3** [*often* **M-**] the early 20th-cent. movement or trend in which certain artists and writers, esp. those (as Joyce, T. S. Eliot, and Picasso) of the period between WWI and WWII, broke with established traditions and sought new modes of expression —**mod′ern·ist** *n., adj.*

mod·ern·is·tic (mäd′ərn is′tik) *adj.* **1** of or characteristic of modernism or modernists **2** modern: used esp. to designate certain contemporary trends and schools of art, music, etc., sometimes in a deprecatory sense —*SYN.* NEW —**mod′ern·is′ti·cal·ly** *adv.*

mo·der·ni·ty (mä dur′nə tē, mə-) *n.* **1** the state or quality of being modern **2** *pl.* **-ties** something modern

mod·ern·ize (mäd′ərn īz′) *vt.* **-ized′, -iz′ing** ⟦Fr *moderniser*⟧ to make modern; bring up to date in style, design, methods, etc. —*vi.* to adopt modern ways; become modern —**mod′ern·i·za′tion** *n.* —**mod′ern·iz′er** *n.*

Modern Latin the Latin that has come into use since about 1500, chiefly in scientific literature

mod·est (mäd′ist) *adj.* ⟦Fr *modeste* < L *modestus*, keeping due measure, modest < *modus:* see MODE⟧ **1** having or showing a moderate opinion of one's own value, abilities, achievements, etc.; not vain or boastful; unassuming **2** not forward; shy or reserved *[modest behavior]* **3** behaving, dressing, speaking, etc. in a way that is considered proper or decorous; decent **4** moderate or reasonable; not extreme *[a modest request]* **5** quiet and humble in appearance, style, etc.; not pretentious *[a modest home]* —*SYN.* CHASTE, SHY[1] —**mod′est·ly** *adv.*

Mo·des·to (mə des′tō) ⟦Sp, lit., modest: said to be with ref. to U.S. financier William C. Ralston's modest refusal to have the place named after him⟧ city in central Calif.

mod·es·ty (mäd′is tē) *n.* ⟦Fr *modestie* < L *modestia*⟧ the quality or state of being modest; specif., *a)* unassuming or humble behavior *b)* lack of excesses or pretensions; moderation *c)* decency; decorum

ModGr *abbrev.* Modern Greek

ModHeb *abbrev.* Modern Hebrew

mod·i·cum (mäd′i kəm) *n.* ⟦LME < L, neut. of *modicus*, moderate < *modus:* see MODE⟧ a small amount; bit

mod·i·fi·ca·tion (mäd′ə fi kā′shən) *n.* ⟦MFr < L *modificatio* < pp. of *modificare:* see MODIFY⟧ a modifying or being modified; specif., *a)* a partial or slight change in form or content *b)* a product or result of such a change *c)* *Biol.* a change in an organism caused by its environment and not inheritable *d)* *Linguis.* a change in the form of a morpheme (Ex.: *foot, feet; bath, bathe*) —**mod·i·fi·ca·to·ry** (mäd′ə fik′ə tôr′ē, -fi kə-; -fi kāt′ər ē) *adj.*

mod·i·fi·er (mäd′ə fī′ər) *n.* a person or thing that modifies; esp., a word, phrase, or clause that limits the meaning of another word or phrase *[adjectives and adverbs are modifiers]*

mod·i·fy (mäd′ə fī′) *vt.* **-fied′, -fy′ing** ⟦ME *modifien* < MFr < L *modificare*, to limit, regulate < *modus*, measure (see MODE) + *facere*, to make: see DO[1]⟧ **1** to change or alter; esp., to change slightly or partially in character, form, etc. **2** to limit or reduce slightly; moderate *[to modify a penalty]* **3** *Gram.* to limit the meaning of; qualify *["old" modifies "man" in "old man"]* **4** *Linguis.* to change the form of a morpheme to indicate grammatical relations or derivation —*vi.* to be modified —*SYN.* CHANGE —**mod′i·fi′a·ble** *adj.*

Mo·di·glia·ni (mō′dēl yä′nē), **A·me·de·o** (ä′mā dā′ō) 1884-1920; It. painter, in France

mo·dil·lion (mō dil′yən) *n.* ⟦It *modiglione* < LL **mutilio* < L *mutulus*, modillion, prob. < Etr base **mut-*, a projection⟧ *Archit.* an ornamental block or bracket placed under a projecting cornice, esp. in the Corinthian order

mo·di·o·lus (mō dī′ə ləs) *n., pl.* **-o·li′** (-lī′) ⟦ModL, dim. of L *modius*, measure for grain < *modus*, measure: see MODE⟧ the central bony axis of the cochlea of the ear

mod·ish (mōd′ish) *adj.* in the current mode; in the latest style; fashionable —**mod′ish·ly** *adv.* —**mod′ish·ness** *n.*

mo·diste (mō dēst′, mô-) *n.* ⟦Fr < *mode:* see MODE⟧ [Old-fashioned] a person who makes or deals in fashionable clothes, hats, etc. for women

ModL *abbrev.* Modern Latin

Mo·doc (mō′däk) *n., pl.* **-docs, -doc 1** a member of a North American Indian people living in N California and S Oregon **2** the language of this people, thought to be related to Klamath

Mo·dred (mō′dred′) *n. Arthurian Legend var. of* MORDRED

mod·u·lar (mäj′ə lər) *adj.* ⟦ModL *modularis*⟧ **1** of a module or modulus ☆**2** designating or of units of standardized size, design, construction, etc. that can be arranged or fitted together in a variety of ways

mod·u·late (mäj′ə lāt′) *vt.* **-lat′ed, -lat′ing** ⟦< L *modulatus*, pp. of *modulari*, to regulate, measure off, arrange < *modulus*, dim. of *modus:* see MODE⟧ **1** to regulate, adjust, or adapt to the proper degree **2** to vary the pitch, intensity, etc. of (the voice), often specif. to a lower degree **3** *Radio* to vary the amplitude, frequency, or phase of (an oscillation, as a carrier wave) in accordance with some signal —*vi.* to shift to another key within a musical composition —**mod′u·la′tor** *n.* —**mod′u·la·to′ry** *adj.*

mod·u·la·tion (mäj′ə lā′shən) *n.* ⟦ME *modulacioun* < L *modulatio*⟧ **1** a modulating or being modulated; specif., *a)* *Music* a shifting from one key to another *b)* *Radio* a variation in the amplitude, frequency, or phase of a wave in accordance with some signal **2** a variation in stress or pitch in speaking, as in distinguishing between the merely auxiliary and the lexical uses of a word (Ex.: "*There* is a post office on Main Street," as contrasted with "*There* is the post office")

mod·ule (mäj′o͞ol′) *n.* ⟦Fr *module* < L *modulus*, dim. of *modus:* see MODE⟧ **1**

a standard or unit of measurement; specif., *a)* in classical architecture, the diameter, or one half the diameter, of a column at the base of the shaft, used to determine the proportions or the structure *b)* any of several standardized units of measurement used in architectural planning, in the construction of building materials, etc. [4-inch *module*, 2-foot *module*] ☆2 *a)* any of a set of units, as cabinets, designed to be arranged or joined in a variety of ways *b)* a detachable section, compartment, or unit with a specific purpose or function, as in a spacecraft *c) Electronics* a compact assembly that is a component of a larger unit

mod·u·lus (mäj′ə ləs) ***n.***, *pl.* **-u·li′** (-lī′) ⟦ModL < L: see prec.⟧ **1** *Math.* *a)* the absolute value of a complex number, computed by adding the squares of each part and taking the positive square root of the sum (i.e.: the modulus of $a + bi$ is $\sqrt{a^2 + b^2}$) *b)* a quantity which gives the same remainders when it is the divisor of two quantities *c)* the factor by which a logarithm to one base is multiplied to change it to a logarithm to another base **2** *Physics* a quantity expressing the response of a sample of material to an external stimulus, as mechanical stress: the response is usually expressed as a fractional change in the physical quantity being affected

mo·dus o·pe·ran·di (mō′dəs äp′ə ran′dī, -dē) ⟦L⟧ a way of doing or accomplishing something

modus vi·ven·di (mō′dəs vē ven′dē) ⟦L⟧ **1** a way of living or of getting along **2** a temporary agreement in a dispute pending final settlement; compromise

Moe·bi·us strip (mā′bē əs, mō′-) MÖBIUS STRIP: also **Moebius band**

Moe·si·a (mē′shē ə, -shə) ancient Roman province in SE Europe, between the Danube & the Balkan Mountains

Moe·so-Goth or **Moe·so·goth** (mē′sō gäth′, -gôth′) ***n.*** a member of a Gothic people that lived in Moesia in the 4th and 5th cent. A.D.

Moe·so-Goth·ic or **Moe·so·goth·ic** (mē′sō gäth′ik) ***adj.*** of the Moeso-Goths, their extinct East Germanic language, or their culture

moeurs (mërs) ***pl.n.*** ⟦Fr⟧ the manners, customs, behavior, etc. of a given group

mo·fette or **mof·fette** (mō fet′) ***n.*** ⟦Fr < It *muffare,* to be moldy < Ger *muff,* mold⟧ a vent or fissure in an area of recent volcanic activity, emitting steam, carbon dioxide, and, sometimes, other gases

mog (mäg) ***vi.*** **mogged, mog′ging** ⟦< ?⟧ [Dial.] **1** to plod (*along*) steadily **2** to decamp; move away

Mo·ga·di·shu (mō′gä dē′sho͞o) capital of Somalia: seaport on the Indian Ocean: It. name **Mo′ga·di′scio** (-shō)

Mo·gen David (mō′gən dā′vid, mô′gən dô′vid) *var. of* MAGEN DAVID

mog·gy or **mog·gie** (mäg′ē) ***n.***, *pl.* **-gies** [Brit. Informal] a domestic cat, esp. one of a common or mixed breed

Mo·gi·lev (mō′gə lef′) city in E Belarus, on the Dnieper

mo·gul (mō′gəl) ***n.*** ⟦< fol.: reason for use uncert.⟧ *Skiing* a bump or ridge of closely packed snow, built up on a curve where skiers turn

Mo·gul (mō′gul′, -gəl; mō gul′) ***n.*** ⟦Pers *Mughul* < Mongolian *Mongol,* a Mongol⟧ **1** a Mongol; esp., *a)* any of the Muslims of Mongol descent who conquered India in the 16th cent. *b)* any of their descendants **2** [**m-**] a powerful or important person, esp. one with autocratic power —**Great Mogul** the title of the ruler of the Mongol empire in India

mo·hair (mō′her′) ***n.*** ⟦altered (by assoc. with HAIR) < earlier *mocayare* < OIt *mocajarro* < Ar *mukhayyar,* fine cloth, lit., choice < pp. of *khayyara,* to select⟧ **1** the long, silky hair of the Angora goat **2** yarn, or any of several fabrics for clothing or upholstery, made from this hair, often mixed with other fibers —***adj.*** made of or upholstered with mohair

Mo·ham·med (mō ham′id) **1** *var. of* MUHAMMAD **2 Mohammed II** 1430-81; sultan of Turkey (1451-81): captured Constantinople (1453)

Mohammed Ali *var. of* MEHEMET ALI

Mo·ham·med·an (mō ham′i dən) ***adj.*** of Muhammad or Islam —***n.*** MUSLIM *USAGE*—a term used, esp. formerly, by non-Muslims

Mo·ham·med·an·ism (mō ham′i dən iz′əm) ***n.*** ISLAM: term used, esp. formerly, by non-Muslims

Mohammed Re·za Pah·la·vi (rē zä′ pä′lə vē) 1919-80; shah of Iran (1941-79); deposed

Mo·ha·ve (mō hä′vē) ***n.*** ⟦prob. self-designation < ?⟧ **1** *pl.* **-ves** or **-ve** a member of a North American Indian people living along the Colorado River in Arizona and adjacent areas **2** the Yuman language of this people —***adj.*** of the Mohaves or their language or culture

Mohave Desert *alt. sp. of* MOJAVE DESERT

Mo·hawk[1] (mō′hôk′) ***n.*** ⟦Narragansett *mohowawog,* lit., man-eaters: orig. so named by enemy tribes⟧ **1** *pl.* **-hawks′** or **-hawk′** a member of a North American Indian people formerly living in the Mohawk Valley of New York and now living in Ontario, Quebec, and New York: see FIVE NATIONS **2** the Iroquoian language of this people **3** [*often* **m-**] a haircut characterized by a prominent ridge of longer hair extending along the top of the head from the forehead to the nape of the neck, usually with the sides of the scalp shaven —***adj.*** of the Mohawks or their language or culture

Mo·hawk[2] (mō′hôk′) ⟦after prec.⟧ river in central & E N.Y., flowing into the Hudson: *c.* 140 mi (225 km)

Mo·he·gan (mō hē′gən) ***n.***, *pl.* **-gans** or **-gan** ⟦earlier *Monahegan* < Massachusett, a local place name⟧ a member of a North American Indian people that lived in Connecticut, along the Thames River, and spoke an Algonquian language —***adj.*** of the Mohegans or their culture

mo·hel (mō′əl, moi′əl; *Heb* mô hāl′) ***n.***, *pl.* **mo′hel·im** (-im; *Heb* mô′hā lēm′) ⟦Heb⟧ *Judaism* a person qualified to perform the brith milah, or rite of circumcision

Mo·hen·jo-Da·ro (mō hen′jō dä′rō) an archaeological site in the Indus valley of Pakistan, NE of Karachi, containing ruins of cities from *c.* 3000 to *c.* 1500 B.C.

Mo·hi·can (mō hē′kən) ***n.***, ***adj.*** *var. of* MAHICAN

Mo·ho (mō′hō′) ***n.*** *short for* MOHOROVIČIĆ DISCONTINUITY

Mo·hock (mō′häk′) ***n.*** ⟦var. of MOHAWK[1]⟧ any of a gang of rowdy young men of fashion who attacked and terrorized people in the streets of London in the early 18th cent.

Mo·ho·ro·vi·čić discontinuity (mō′hō rō′və chich′) ⟦after A. *Mohorovičić* (1857-1936), Yugoslav geologist⟧ *Geol.* an irregular dividing line separating the earth's crust from its underlying mantle, situated *c.* 35 km (*c.* 21.7 mi) below the continents and *c.* 5 to 10 km (*c.* 3.1 to 6.2 mi) below the ocean floor

Mohs scale (mōz) ⟦after F. *Mohs* (1773-1839), Ger mineralogist⟧ *Mineralogy* **1** an arbitrary scale used to indicate relative hardness, arranged in 10 ascending degrees: 1, talc; 2, gypsum; 3, calcite; 4, fluorite; 5, apatite; 6, orthoclase; 7, quartz; 8, topaz; 9, corundum; 10, diamond **2** a modification of this scale, retaining its first six minerals and continuing: 7, pure silica glass; 8, quartz; 9, topaz; 10, garnet; 11, fused zircon; 12, corundum; 13, silicon carbide; 14, boron carbide; 15, diamond

mo·hur (mō′hər) ***n.*** ⟦Hindi *muhur, muhr* < Pers *muhr,* a seal, akin to Sans *mudrā,* a seal⟧ a former gold coin of India, equal to 15 rupees

moi·dore (moi′dôr′) ***n.*** ⟦< Port *moeda d'ouro,* coin of gold < *moeda,* coin (< L *moneta,* MONEY) + *ouro,* gold < L *aurum:* see EAST⟧ a former gold coin of Portugal and Brazil

moi·e·ty (moi′ə tē) ***n.***, *pl.* **-ties** ⟦ME *moite* < OFr < L *medietas,* the middle (in LL, half, moiety) < *medius:* see MID[1]⟧ **1** a half; either of two equal, or more or less equal, parts **2** an indefinite share or part **3** *Anthrop.* either of two primary subdivisions in some tribes

moil (moil) ***vi.*** ⟦ME *moillen,* to moisten, make wet < OFr *moillier* < VL **molliare,* to soften < L *mollis,* soft: see MOLLIFY⟧ [Dial.] to toil; drudge —***vt.*** [Archaic] to moisten or soil —***n.*** **1** drudgery; hard work **2** confusion; turmoil —**moil′er** ***n.***

Moi·ra (moi′rə) ***n.***, *pl.* **-rai′** (-rī′) ⟦Gr: see MERIT⟧ *Gr. Myth.* any of the three FATES

moire (mwär, môr) ***n.*** ⟦Fr, watered silk < MOHAIR⟧ a fabric, esp. silk, rayon, or acetate, having a watered, or wavy, pattern

moi·ré (mwä rā′, mô-; môr′ā) ***adj.*** ⟦Fr, pp. of *moirer,* to water < *moire:* see prec.⟧ having a watered, or wavy, pattern, as certain fabrics, stamps, or metal surfaces —***n.*** **1** a watered pattern pressed into cloth, etc. with engraved rollers **2** MOIRE

moist (moist) ***adj.*** ⟦OFr *moiste* < VL **muscidus,* altered (prob. infl. by L *musteus,* of new wine, fresh < *mustum,* MUST[3]) < L *mucidus,* moldy < *mucus,* MUCUS⟧ **1** slightly wet; damp **2** characterized by rain or humidity **3** tearful —*SYN.* WET —**moist′ly** ***adv.*** —**moist′ness** ***n.***

mois·ten (mois′ən) ***vt.***, ***vi.*** to make or become moist —**mois′ten·er** ***n.***

mois·ture (mois′chər) ***n.*** ⟦OFr *moisteur* < *moiste:* see MOIST⟧ water or other liquid causing a slight wetness or dampness —**mois′ture·less** ***adj.***

mois·tur·ize (-īz′) ***vt.***, ***vi.*** **-ized′**, **-iz′ing** to add, provide, or restore moisture to (the skin, air, etc.)

mois·tur·i·zer (-īz′ər) ***n.*** a cosmetic preparation designed to moisturize the skin

Mo·ja·ve (mō hä′vē) ***n.***, ***adj.*** *alt. sp. of* MOHAVE

Mojave Desert desert in SE Calif.: *c.* 15,000 sq mi (38,850 sq km)

☆**mo·ji·to** (mō hē′tō) ***n.***, *pl.* **-tos** ⟦Cuban Sp < *mojo,* sauce + *-ito,* dim. suffix⟧ an iced cocktail made of white rum, soda water, sugar, lime juice, and crushed mint leaves

mo·jo (mō′jō) ***n.*** ⟦prob. of creole orig.; cf. Gullah *moco,* witchcraft⟧ **1** a charm or amulet thought to have magic powers **2** [Slang] power, luck, etc., as of magical or supernatural origin

moke (mōk) ***n.*** ⟦< ?⟧ **1** [Brit. Slang] *a)* a donkey *b)* a stupid fellow **2** [Austral.] an inferior horse; nag

mol[1] (mōl) ***n.*** *alt. sp. of* MOLE[4]

mol[2] *abbrev.* **1** MOLE[4] **2** molecular **3** molecule

mo·la[1] (mō′lə) ***n.***, *pl.* **mo′las** or **mo′la** ⟦ModL < L, a millstone (see MILL[1]): so named from its rough skin and round shape⟧ OCEAN SUNFISH

mo·la[2] (mō′lə, -lä) ***n.*** a fabric made by Panamanian Indians with designs cut through several layers, used for clothing, wall hangings, etc.

mo·lal (mō′ləl) ***adj.*** *Chem.* relating to the mole or gram-molecular weight; specif., designating a solution with a concentration equal to one mole of the solute in 1,000 grams of the solvent

mo·lar[1] (mō′lər) ***adj.*** ⟦L *molaris,* a mill < *mola,* millstone: see MILL[1]⟧ designating or of a tooth or teeth adapted for grinding —***n.*** a molar tooth: in humans there are usually twelve permanent molars, three on each side of each jaw behind the bicuspids

mo·lar[2] (mō′lər) ***adj.*** **1** ⟦MOL(E) + -AR⟧ *Chem.* relating to the mole, or gram-molecular weight; specif., designating a solution containing one mole of solute per liter of solution **2** ⟦< L *moles,* mass (see MOLE[3]) + -AR⟧ *Physics* of a body (of matter) as a whole

mo·lar·i·ty (mō lar′ə tē) ***n.*** ⟦prec. + -ITY⟧ *Chem.* the concentration of a solution expressed as the number of moles of the solute in one liter of solution

mo·las·ses (mə las′iz) ***n.*** ⟦< Port *melaço* < LL *mellaceum,* must < L *mellaceus,* resembling honey < *mel,* honey: see MILDEW⟧ a thick, usually dark-brown syrup produced during the refining of sugar, or from sorghum, etc.

mold[1] (mōld) ***n.*** ⟦ME *moolde* < OFr *molle,* earlier *modle* < L *modulus:* see

MODULE]] 1 a pattern, hollow form, or matrix for giving a certain shape to something in a plastic or molten state 2 a frame, shaped core, etc. on or around which something is modeled 3 a pattern after which something is formed; model 4 something formed or shaped in or on, or as if in or on, a mold; often, specif., a gelatin dessert, aspic, etc. so prepared 5 *a)* the form or shape given by a mold *b)* form or shape in general 6 distinctive character or nature [men of his *mold*] 7 *Archit.* a molding or group of moldings —*vt.* 1 to make or shape in or on, or as if in or on, a mold 2 to work into a certain form or shape; shape 3 to have a strong or important influence on (public opinion, thought, etc.) 4 to fit closely to the outline or contours of 5 to ornament by or with molding 6 to make a mold of or from in order to make a casting —**mold′a·ble** *adj.* —**mold′er** *n.*

mold[2] (mōld) *n.* [[ME *moul, mowlde,* mold, mildew < or akin to ON *mygla* < IE base **meug-, *meuk-*: see MEEK; sp. prob. infl. by fol.]] 1 a downy or furry growth on the surface of organic matter, caused by fungi, esp. in the presence of dampness or decay 2 any fungus producing such a growth 3 any plant disease, as snowmold, caused by such fungus — *vt., vi.* [[< ME *moulen* (with unhistoric *-d-*]] to make or become moldy

mold[3] (mōld) *n.* [[ME *mold* < OE *molde,* dust, ground, earth, akin to Goth *mulda* < IE base **mel-,* to rub away, grind > L *molere,* to grind, MILL[1]]] 1 loose, soft, easily worked soil, esp. when rich with decayed animal or vegetable matter and good for growing plants 2 [Archaic] earth or ground

Mol·dau (môl′dou′) *Ger. name for* VLTAVA

Mol·da·vi·a (mäl dā′vē ə, -dāv′yə) 1 region & former principality in E Europe, east of the Carpathians: merged with Walachia (1861) to form Romania 2 MOLDAVIAN SOVIET SOCIALIST REPUBLIC —**Mol·da′vi·an** *adj., n.*

Moldavian Soviet Socialist Republic a republic of the U.S.S.R.: now MOLDOVA

mold·board (mōld′bôrd′) *n.* [[MOLD[3] & BOARD]] 1 a curved plate of iron attached to a plowshare, for turning over the soil ☆2 a plate like this at the front of a bulldozer or snowplow, angled to push material aside 3 one of the boards used in making a mold for concrete

mold·er (mōl′dər) *vi.* [[freq. of obs. v. *mold,* to molder: see MOLD[3] & -ER]] to crumble into dust; decay; waste away: often with *away* —*vt.* [Now Rare] to cause to molder —**SYN.** DECAY

mold·ing (mōl′diŋ) *n.* 1 the act or process of one that molds 2 something molded 3 *a)* any of various ornamental contours given to cornices, jambs, etc. *b)* a cornice or other projecting or sunk ornamentation, of wood, stone, brick, etc. *c)* a shaped strip of wood, etc., used for finishing or decorating walls (esp. near the ceiling), furniture, etc.

Mol·do·va (môl dō′və) [[Romanian, MOLDAVIA]] country in E Europe: became independent upon the breakup of the U.S.S.R. (1991): 13,067 sq mi (33,843 sq km); cap. Chişinau: formerly, *Moldavian Soviet Socialist Republic* —**Mol·do′van** *adj., n.*

mold·y (mōl′dē) *adj.* **mold′i·er, mold′i·est** [[MOLD[2] + -Y[3]]] 1 covered or overgrown with mold 2 musty or stale, as from age or decay —**mold′i·ness** *n.*

mole[1] (mōl) *n.* [[ME < OE *mal,* akin to Goth *mail* < IE base **mai-,* to spot > Gr *miainein,* to sully]] a small, pigmented spot on the human skin, often slightly raised

mole[2] (mōl) *n.* [[ME *molle,* akin to or < MDu *mol,* < Gmc **mug-* > MOW[2], OHG *mol*: orig. sense, "mound maker"]] 1 any of various small, burrowing insectivores (esp. family Talpidae) with small eyes and ears, shovel-like forefeet, and soft fur: moles live mainly underground 2 a spy who infiltrates and is assimilated into the ranks of an enemy intelligence agency, government staff, etc., usually long before engaging in any spying activities

mole[3] (mōl) *n.* [[Fr *môle* < LGr *mōlos* < L *moles,* a mass, dam, mole < IE **molo-* < base **mo-,* to strive > Gr *mōlos,* effort, Ger *müde,* tired]] 1 a barrier of stone, etc. built in the water as a protection from the force of the waves, as a breakwater 2 a harbor or anchorage so formed or protected

mole[4] (mōl) *n.* [[Ger *mol,* short for *molekulargewicht,* molecular weight]] *Chem.* 1 the quantity of a chemical substance having a weight in grams numerically equal to its molecular weight: one mole of a substance contains 6.022137×10^{23} molecules 2 the amount of a substance containing the same number of units, including molecules, atoms, or ions, as there are atoms in 12 grams of pure carbon-12: a basic unit in the SI system: abbrev. *mol*

mole[5] (mōl) *n.* [[Fr *môle* < L *mola,* false conception, millstone: for IE base see MILL[1]]] 1 a marked growth of grapelike masses of fetal placental tissue 2 any of various fleshy or bloody masses in the uterus

mo·le[6] (mō′lā) *n.* [[MexSp < Nahuatl *molli,* sauce]] any of various spicy Mexican sauces for meat or poultry, typically made with chilies, tomatoes, spices, and ground nuts, esp., such a sauce containing bitter chocolate

Mo·lech (mō′lek′) *n.* [[LL(Ec) *Moloch* < Gr(Ec) (in LXX) < Heb *mōlōkh, mōlekh*]] 1 an ancient Phoenician and Ammonite god, to whom children were sacrificed by burning 2 anything demanding terrible sacrifice

mole cricket any of a family (Gryllotalpidae) of crickets having large front legs specialized for burrowing, and feeding chiefly on roots

mo·lec·u·lar (mə lek′yə lər) *adj.* [[MOLECUL(E) + -AR]] of, consisting of, produced by, or existing between molecules —**mo·lec′u·lar′i·ty** (-lar′ə tē, -lar′ə tē) *n.* —**mo·lec′u·lar·ly** *adv.*

molecular biology a branch of biology that studies the chemical and physical principles associated with the composition, properties, and activities of molecules in living cells

molecular film MONOLAYER

molecular formula a formula which gives the kinds of atoms or radicals and the number of each kind in the molecule of a compound (Ex.: C_6H_6 for benzene)

molecular sieve any of a class of zeolites or similar materials, natural or synthetic, having small, precisely uniform pores in their crystal lattices that can absorb molecules small enough to pass through the pores: used as for separating or drying gases and liquids

molecular weight the relative average weight of a molecule of a substance, expressed by a number equal to the sum of the atomic weights of all atoms in the molecule

mol·e·cule (mäl′ə kyōōl′) *n.* [[Fr *molécule* < ModL *molecula,* dim. of L *moles,* a mass: see MOLE[3]]] 1 the smallest particle of an element or compound that can exist in the free state and still retain the characteristics of the element or compound: the molecules of elements consist of one atom or two or more similar atoms; those of compounds consist of two or more different atoms 2 a small particle

mole fraction *Chem.* the ratio of the number of moles of one constituent of a mixture or solution to the total number of moles of all the constituents

mole·hill (mōl′hil′) *n.* a small ridge or mound of earth, formed by a burrowing mole —**make a mountain out of a molehill** to respond to a trivial problem as if it were a great or important one

mole·skin (-skin′) *n.* 1 the soft, dark-gray skin of the mole, used as fur 2 *a)* a strong, twilled cotton fabric with a soft nap, used for work clothes, etc. *b)* [*pl.*] trousers made of this fabric 3 a soft fabric, often with an adhesive backing, used for foot bandages

mo·lest (mə lest′, mō-) *vt.* [[ME *molesten* < OFr *molester* < L *molestare* < *molestus,* troublesome < *moles,* a burden: see MOLE[3]]] 1 to annoy, interfere with, or meddle with so as to trouble or harm, or with intent to trouble or harm ☆2 to make improper advances to, esp. of a sexual nature 3 to assault or otherwise abuse (esp. a child) sexually —**mo·les·ta·tion** (mō′les tā′shən, mäl′əs-) *n.* —**mo·lest′er** *n.*

Mo·lière (mōl yer′, mō′lē er′; *Fr* mô lyer′) (born *Jean Baptiste Poquelin*) 1622-73; Fr. dramatist

mo·line (mō′lin, mō līn′) *adj.* [[< Anglo-Fr **moliné* < OFr *molin,* a mill < VL **molinum,* for LL *molina,* MILL[1]: from its resemblance to the iron support for the upper millstone]] designating a cross with each arm forked and curved back at the end [a cross *moline*]

Mo·li·se (mō′lē zā′) region of SC Italy: 1,714 sq mi (4,439 sq km)

moll (mäl) *n.* [[< *Moll,* a dim. of MARY[1]]] [Old Slang] 1 GUN MOLL 2 a prostitute

mol·lah (mäl′ə) *n. var. of* MULLAH

mol·li·fy (mäl′ə fī′) *vt.* **-fied′, -fy′ing** [[ME *molifien,* MFr *mollifier* < LL *mollificare,* to soften < L *mollis,* soft (< IE **mḷdu-,* soft < base **mel-,* to crush > MILL[1]) + *facere,* to make, DO[1]]] 1 to soothe the temper of; pacify; appease 2 to make less intense, severe, or violent —**SYN.** PACIFY —**mol′li·fi·ca′tion** *n.* —**mol′li·fi′er** *n.*

mol·lusc (mäl′əsk) *n. alt. sp. of* MOLLUSK —**mol·lus·can** (mə lus′kən) *adj., n.*

mol·lus·coid (mə lus′koid′) *adj.* of or like a mollusk or mollusks

mol·lusk (mäl′əsk) *n.* [[Fr *mollusque* < ModL *Mollusca,* coined by CUVIER < L *mollusca,* a soft-shelled nut < *molluscus,* soft < *mollis*: see MOLLIFY]] any of a large phylum (Mollusca) of invertebrate animals, including the chitons, gastropods, cephalopods, scaphopods, and bivalves characterized by a soft, unsegmented body, typically enclosed wholly or in part in a mantle and a calcareous shell, and usually having gills and a foot —**mol·lus·kan** (mə lus′kən) *adj., n.*

Moll·wei·de projection (môl′vī′də) [[after K. B. *Mollweide* (1774-1825), Ger mathematician]] an equal-area map projection with the whole earth on one map, showing the prime meridian and all parallels of latitude as straight lines and all other meridians as increasing in curvature toward the margins

mol·ly[1] (mäl′ē) *n., pl.* **-lies** [[short for ModL *Mollienisia,* after F. N. *Mollien* (1758-1850), Fr statesman]] any of various brightly colored livebearers (genus *Poecilia*), often kept in aquariums: also sp. **mol′lie**

mol·ly[2] (mäl′ē) *n.* [[< MOLECULAR (infl. by the name MOLLY)]] [also **M-**] [Slang] a powdered form of MDMA

Mol·ly (mäl′ē) *n.* a feminine name: see also MARY[1]

mol·ly·cod·dle (mäl′ē käd′'l) *n.* [[prec. + CODDLE]] a man or boy used to being coddled, or protected, pampered, etc. —*vt.* **-dled, -dling** to pamper; coddle —**mol′ly·cod′dler** *n.*

Molly Ma·guires (mə gwīrz′) 1 a secret society organized in Ireland in 1843 to terrorize landlords' agents in order to prevent evictions ☆2 a secret society of Irish-American miners in E Pennsylvania (*c.* 1865-75), which opposed oppressive industrial and social conditions, sometimes with physical force

Mo·loch (mō′läk′) *n.* 1 *var. of* MOLECH 2 [**m-**] a spiny, brownish, anteating Australian lizard (*Moloch horridus*) similar to a horned toad but of another family (Agamidae)

Mo·lo·kai (mō′lə kī′, mäl′ə-) [[Haw]] one of the Hawaiian Islands, southeast of Oahu: 260 sq mi (673 sq km)

Mo·lo·tov (mäl′ə tôf′, mō′-; -tôv′), **V(yacheslav) M(ikhailovich)** (born *Vyacheslav Mikhailovich Skriabin*) 1890-1986; Russ. statesman: foreign minister of the U.S.S.R. (1939-49; 1953-56)

Molotov cocktail [[after prec.]] a crude grenade consisting of a bottle filled with gasoline, etc. and wrapped in a saturated rag or plugged with a wick: it is ignited and hurled

molt (mōlt) *vi.* [[ME *mouten* (with unhistoric *-l-* after FAULT, in which the letter was orig. silent) < OE *(be)mutian,* to exchange < L *mutare,* to change: see MUTATE]] to cast off or shed the exoskeleton, hair, outer skin, horns, or feathers at certain intervals, prior to replacement of the castoff parts by a new growth: said of reptiles, birds, insects, etc. —*vt.* to replace by molting —*n.* 1 the act or process of molting 2 the parts so shed —**molt′er** *n.*

mol·ten (mōlt′'n) *vt., vi.* ⟦ME⟧ *archaic pp. of* MELT —*adj.* 1 melted or liquefied by heat 2 [Now Rare] made by being melted and cast in a mold

Molt·ke (môlt′kə) 1 Count **Hel·muth (Johannes Ludwig) von** (hel′mo͞ot fôn) 1848-1916; Ger. general 2 Count **Helmuth (Karl Bernhard) von** 1800-91; Ger. field marshal: uncle of Helmuth

mol·to (mōl′tō) *adv.* ⟦It < L *multum,* much⟧ *Musical Direction* very; much

Mo·luc·cas (mō luk′əz, mə-) group of islands of Indonesia, between Sulawesi & New Guinea: 28,767 sq mi (74,506 sq km): also **Molucca Islands** —**Mo·luc′ca** *adj.,* **Mo·luc′can**

mol wt *abbrev.* molecular weight

mo·ly[1] (mō′lē) *n.* ⟦L < Gr *mōly*⟧ 1 *Gr. Myth.* an herb of magic powers given to Odysseus to protect him from Circe's incantation 2 a wild, garliclike European plant (*Allium moly*) of the lily family

mol·y[2] (mäl′ē) *n. short for* MOLYBDENUM

mo·lyb·date (mə lib′dāt) *n.* a salt of molybdic acid

mo·lyb·de·nite (mə lib′də nīt′) *n.* a very soft, lead-gray mineral, MoS_2, the chief ore of molybdenum; molybdenum sulfide

mo·lyb·de·num (mə lib′də nəm) *n.* ⟦ModL: so named (1781) by K. W. Scheele (see SCHEELITE) < *molybdaena,* molybdenite, term used because of resemblance to lead ore < L *molybdaena,* lead, galena < Gr *molybdaina,* piece of lead < *molybdos,* lead⟧ a very hard, lustrous, silver-white metallic chemical element, used in alloys, points for spark plugs, etc.: symbol, Mo; at. no. 42: see the periodic table of elements in the Reference Supplement

mo·lyb·dic (mə lib′dik) *adj. Chem.* designating or of compounds in which molybdenum has a higher valence (usually 3 or 6) than in the corresponding molybdous compounds

mo·lyb·dous (mə lib′dəs) *adj. Chem.* designating or of compounds in which molybdenum has a lower valence than in the corresponding molybdic compounds

mom (mäm) *n.* [Informal] MOTHER[1]

MOMA (mō′mə) *abbrev.* Museum of Modern Art, in New York City: also sp. **MoMA**

☆**mom and pop store (***or* **stand,** *etc.***)** a small, typically family-operated, retail business

Mom·ba·sa (mäm bä′sə, -bas′ə) seaport on the SE coast of Kenya, partly on an offshore island

mome (mōm) *n.* ⟦< ?⟧ [Archaic] a blockhead, fool

mo·ment (mō′mənt) *n.* ⟦ME < L *momentum,* movement, impulse, brief space of time, importance < **movimentum* < *movere,* to MOVE⟧ 1 a brief but indefinite period of time; instant 2 a definite point in time or in a series of events 3 a brief time of being important or outstanding 4 importance; consequence [news of great *moment*] 5 *Mech.* the product, as a torque, of some physical quantity and its distance from the origin of coordinates or an axis 6 *Philos.* any constituent element of a complex entity or process —*SYN.* IMPORTANCE —**the moment** the present or the immediate future

mo·men·tar·i·ly (mō′mən ter′ə lē) *adv.* 1 for a moment or short time 2 in an instant 3 from moment to moment; at any moment

mo·men·tar·y (mō′mən ter′ē) *adj.* ⟦L *momentarius*⟧ 1 lasting for only a moment; passing; transitory 2 recurring every moment; constant 3 likely to occur at any moment —*SYN.* TRANSIENT —**mo′men·tar′i·ness** *n.*

mo·ment·ly (mō′mənt lē) *adv.* [Now Rare] 1 from instant to instant; every moment 2 at any moment 3 for a single moment

mo·men·to (mō men′tō, mə-) *n.* ⟦altered by folk etym. by assoc. with MOMENT⟧ *disputed var. of* MEMENTO

☆**moment of truth** 1 the point in a bullfight when the matador faces the bull for the kill 2 a critical moment or time that tests and reveals one's true self or makes one face the truth

mo·men·tous (mō men′təs, mə-) *adj.* of great moment; very important [a *momentous* decision] —**mo·men′tous·ly** *adv.* —**mo·men′tous·ness** *n.*

mo·men·tum (mō men′təm, mə-) *n., pl.* **-tums** or **-ta** (-tə) ⟦ModL < L: see MOMENT⟧ 1 the impetus of a moving object 2 strength or force that keeps growing or building [a campaign that gained *momentum*] 3 *Mech., Physics* the product of the mass of a particle, body, etc. and its velocity: abbrev. *M*

☆**mom·ism** (mäm′iz′əm) *n.* ⟦coined (1942) by P. Wylie, U.S. writer < MOM & -ISM⟧ excessive, esp. sentimentalized, devotion to mothers or motherhood

mom·ma (mäm′ə) *n.* 1 MAMA 2 [Slang] a woman: sometimes offensive

Momm·sen (mäm′zən, -sən), **The·o·dor** (tā′ə dôr′) 1817-1903; Ger. historian

mom·my (mäm′ē) *n., pl.* **-mies** *child's term for* MOTHER[1]

mom·ser or **mom·zer** (mäm′zər) *n.* ⟦< Yiddish, a bastard < Heb⟧ [Slang] 1 a contemptible person 2 someone thought of as being, variously, mischievous, clever, impudent, deceptive, etc.

Mo·mus (mō′məs) *n.* ⟦L < Gr *Mōmos,* lit., blame, ridicule⟧ *Gr. Myth.* the god of mockery and censure

mon[1] (män) *n. Scot. & North Eng. var. of* MAN

mon[2] *abbrev.* monetary

Mon[1] (mōn) *n.* 1 *pl.* **Mons** or **Mon** a member of a people living in Myanmar east of Yangon 2 the Mon-Khmer language of this people

Mon[2] *abbrev.* Monday

mon- (män) *prefix* MONO-: used before a vowel

Mo·na (mō′nə) *n.* ⟦Ir *Muadhnait,* dim. of *muadh,* noble⟧ a feminine name

mon·a·chal (män′ə kəl) *adj.* ⟦ML(Ec) *monachalis* < LL(Ec) *monachus:* see MONK⟧ MONASTIC —**mon′a·chism′** (-kiz′əm) *n.*

mon·ac·id (män as′id) *adj., n. var. of* MONOACID

Mon·a·co (män′ə kō, mə nä′kō) 1 country in S Europe on the Mediterranean: an independent principality & an enclave in SE France: .75 sq mi (1.95 sq km) 2 its capital, a commune —**Mon′a·can** (-kən) *adj., n.*

mo·nad (mō′nad′, män′ad′) *n.* ⟦LL *monas* (gen. *monadis*) < Gr *monas* (gen. *monados*), a unit, unity < *monos,* alone: see MONO-⟧ 1 a unit; something simple and indivisible 2 *Biol. a)* any simple, single-celled organism, specif., a simple type of flagellated protozoan or protist *b)* any of the four nuclei formed at the completion of meiosis 3 *Chem.* a monovalent atom, element, or radical 4 *Philos.* an entity or elementary being thought of as a microcosm or ultimate unit —*adj.* of a monad or monads —**mo·nad′ic** *adj.,* **mo·nad′i·cal**

mon·a·del·phous (män′ə del′fəs) *adj.* ⟦< MONO- + Gr *adelphos,* brother (< *a-,* copulative + *delphys,* womb: see DOLPHIN) + -OUS⟧ having the stamens united by their filaments into one set or bundle, as some legumes

mo·nad·ism (mō′nad′iz′əm, män′ad-) *n. Philos.* the theory that the universe consists of monads

☆**mo·nad·nock** (mə nad′näk′) *n.* ⟦after Mt. *Monadnock,* N.H.⟧ *Geol.* an isolated rocky hill or mountain rising above a peneplain in an area with a temperate climate: cf. INSELBERG

Mon·a·ghan (män′ə gən) county in Ulster province, in the NE part of the Republic of Ireland: 498 sq mi (1,290 sq km)

Mo·na Li·sa (mō′nə lē′sə, -zə) a famous portrait of a faintly smiling woman, by Leonardo da Vinci: also called *La Gioconda*

mo·nan·drous (mō nan′drəs, mə-) *adj.* ⟦Gr *monandros,* having one husband: see MON- & -ANDROUS⟧ 1 of or characterized by monandry 2 having only one stamen, as some flowers

mo·nan·dry (-drē) *n.* 1 the state or practice of having only one male sex partner over a period of time 2 *Bot.* a monandrous condition

mo·nan·thous (-thəs) *adj.* ⟦MON- + -ANTHOUS⟧ *Bot.* having only one flower, as some plants

mon·arch (män′ərk, -ärk′) *n.* ⟦LME *monarcha* < LL < Gr *monarchēs* < *monos,* alone + *archein,* to rule: see MONO- & -ARCH⟧ 1 [Obs.] the single or sole ruler of a state 2 the hereditary (often constitutional) head of a state; king, queen, etc. 3 a person or thing that surpasses others of the same kind 4 a large, migratory butterfly (*Danaus plexippus*) native to North America, having orange, black-edged wings: the larvae feed on milkweed

mo·nar·chal (mə när′kəl) *adj.* of, like, suitable for, or characteristic of a monarch; royal; regal: also **mo·nar′chi·al** (-kē əl) —**mo·nar′chal·ly** *adv.*

Mo·nar·chi·an·ism (mə när′kē ən iz′əm) *n.* ⟦see MONARCH, -AN, & -ISM⟧ the doctrine of several 2d- and 3d-cent. Christian sects that denied the Trinity altogether or denied the equality of the three persons of the Trinity —**Mo·nar′chi·an** *adj., n.*

mo·nar·chi·cal (mə när′ki kəl) *adj.* 1 of, characteristic of, or like a monarch or monarchy 2 favoring a monarchy Also **mo·nar′chic** —**mo·nar′chi·cal·ly** *adv.*

mon·ar·chism (män′ər kiz′əm, -är-) *n.* ⟦Fr *monarchisme*⟧ monarchical principles or the advocacy of these —**mon′ar·chist** *n., adj.* —**mon′ar·chis′tic** *adj.*

mon·ar·chy (män′ər kē, -är-) *n., pl.* **-ar·chies** ⟦ME *monarchie* < OFr < LL *monarchia* < Gr < *monarchos:* see MONARCH⟧ 1 [Obs.] rule by only one person 2 a government or state headed by a monarch: called *absolute* when there is no limitation on the monarch's power, *constitutional* when there is such limitation

mo·nar·da (mō när′də, mə-) *n.* ⟦ModL, after N. *Monardes,* (1493-1588), Sp botanist⟧ ☆HORSEMINT

mon·as·ter·y (män′ə ster′ē) *n., pl.* **-ter′ies** ⟦ME *monasterie* < LL(Ec) *monasterium* < LGr(Ec) *monastērion* < Gr *monazein,* to be alone < *monos,* alone: see MONO-⟧ 1 a building or residence for monks or others who have withdrawn from the world, as for religious contemplation 2 those living there —*SYN.* CLOISTER —**mon′as·te′ri·al** (-stir′ē əl) *adj.*

mo·nas·tic (mə nas′tik) *adj.* ⟦ME *monastik* < ML(Ec) *monasticus* < LGr(Ec) < Gr *monastikos* < *monazein:* see prec.⟧ 1 of or characteristic of a monastery 2 of or characteristic of monks or nuns or their way of life; ascetic, austere, etc. Also **mo·nas′ti·cal** —*n.* one living a monastic life —**mo·nas′ti·cal·ly** *adv.*

mo·nas·ti·cism (-tə siz′əm) *n.* the monastic system or way of life

Mon·as·tir (mô′nä stir′) *Turk. name for* BITOLA

mon·a·tom·ic (män′ə täm′ik) *adj.* ⟦MON- + ATOMIC⟧ 1 *a)* consisting of one atom (said of a molecule) *b)* having one atom in the molecule 2 containing one replaceable atom or atomic group 3 MONOVALENT (sense 2)

mon·au·ral (män ôr′əl) *adj.* ⟦MON- + AURAL[2]⟧ designating or of sound reproduction in which only one source of sound is used, giving a monophonic effect —**mon·au′ral·ly** *adv.*

mon·ax·i·al (-ak′sē əl) *adj.* having only one axis; uniaxial

mon·a·zite (män′ə zīt′) *n.* ⟦Ger *monazit* < Gr *monazein,* to be alone (see MONASTERY) + Ger *-it,* -ITE[1]: so named because of its isolated crystals⟧ a yellow or brownish-red native phosphate of the rare-earth elements, a major source of thorium, cerium, lanthanum, neodymium, etc.

Mön·chen-Glad·bach (mön′Hən glät′bäkh′) city in WC Germany, in the state of North Rhine-Westphalia

Monck (muŋk), **George** *alt. sp. of* George MONK

Mon·day (mun′dā; *occas.,* -dē) *n.* ⟦ME < OE *monandæg,* moon's day < *monan,* gen. of *mona,* MOON + *dæg,* DAY: transl. of LL *Lunae dies*⟧ the second day of the week: abbrev. *Mon, Mo,* or *M*

☆**Monday morning quarterback** a person who, after the event, offers advice or criticism concerning decisions made by others; one who second-guesses

Mon·days (-dāz′; *occas.*, -dēz′) ***adv.*** during every Monday or most Mondays

monde (mōnd) ***n.*** ⟦Fr < L *mundus*⟧ the world; society

mon Dieu (mōn dyö′) ⟦Fr⟧ my God: an exclamation

mon·do (män′dō) [Slang] ***adj.*** ⟦It, lit., world: n. borrowed for use as modifier < *Mondo cane*, lit., a dog's world, title of It film (1962) documenting episodes of bizarre human behavior⟧ **1** great or huge **2** extremely unconventional or bizarre —***adv.*** very; exceedingly; extremely

Mon·dri·an (män′drē än′), **Piet** (pēt) (born *Pieter Cornelis Mondriaan*) 1872-1944; Du. painter, in France & the U.S.

M-1 (em′wun′) ***n.*** ⟦M(ONEY) + identifying numeral⟧ a measure of a country's money supply, comprising currency in circulation and funds readily convertible into cash, chiefly checking-account deposits: other measures (**M-2, M-3,** etc.) include additional components of money supply, such as time deposits and money market funds

mo·ne·cious (mō nē′shəs, mə-) ***adj.*** *alt. sp. of* MONOECIOUS

Mon·e·gasque (män′ə gask′) ***adj.*** ⟦Fr *monégasque* < Prov *mounegasc* < *Mounegue*, MONACO⟧ of Monaco or its people —***n.*** a person born or living in Monaco

☆**mo·nel·lin** (mō nel′in, mə-) ***n.*** ⟦after *Monell* Chemical Senses Center, Philadelphia, Pa., where first produced⟧ an extremely sweet protein extracted from a W African red berry (*Dioscoreophyllum cumminsii*)

Mo·nel metal (mō nel′) ☆⟦< *Monel*, a trademark for this metal, after A. *Monell* (died 1921), U.S. manufacturer⟧ an alloy mainly of nickel and copper, that is very resistant to corrosion

mo·ner·an (mə nir′ən) ***n.*** ⟦< ModL *Monera* (< Gr *monērēs*, single, solitary) + -AN⟧ any of a kingdom (Monera) of one-celled prokaryotes, including bacteria and blue-green algae, that often form clusters or filaments

Mo·net (mō nā′, mə-; *Fr* mô ne′), **Claude** (klôd; *Fr* klōd) 1840-1926; Fr. impressionist painter

☆**mon·e·tar·ism** (män′ə tər iz′əm) ***n.*** a theory which holds that economic stability and growth result from maintaining a steady rate of growth in the supply of money

mon·e·tar·ist (-ist) ***adj.*** ☆designating, of, or in accordance with monetarism —☆***n.*** an adherent of this theory

mon·e·tar·y (män′ə ter′ē; *occas.* mun′-) ***adj.*** ⟦LL *monetarius*, of a mint < L *moneta*, a MINT[1]⟧ **1** of or having to do with the coinage or currency of a country **2** of or having to do with the supply of money in an economy; specif., designating or of policy that regulates the money supply, as through the periodic adjustment of certain interest rates by a central bank —***SYN.*** FINANCIAL —**mon′e·tar′i·ly** ***adv.***

mon·e·tize (-tīz′) ***vt.*** **-tized′**, **-tiz′ing** ⟦< L *moneta*, a MINT[1] + -IZE⟧ **1** to coin into money **2** to legalize as money —**mon′e·ti·za′tion** ***n.***

mon·ey (mun′ē) ***n.***, *pl.* **-eys** or **-ies** ⟦OFr *moneie* < L *moneta*, a MINT[1]⟧ **1** *a)* standard pieces of gold, silver, copper, nickel, etc., stamped by government authority and used as a medium of exchange and measure of value; coin or coins (also called **hard money**) *b)* any paper note issued by a government or an authorized bank and used in the same way; bank notes; bills (also called **paper money**): see the table of monetary units in the Reference Supplement **2** any substance or article used as money, as bank notes, checks, etc. **3** any definite or indefinite sum of money **4** property; possessions; wealth **5** very wealthy persons or groups **6** any form or denomination of legally current money **7** MONEY OF ACCOUNT **8** money won as a prize **9** [*pl.*] sums of money —**for my money** [Informal] **1** in my opinion **2** as to my preference —**have money to burn** [Informal] to have more money than one needs, so that some can be spent foolishly —**in the money** [Slang] **1** among the winners, as in a contest, race, etc. **2** prosperous; wealthy; successful —**make money** to gain profits; become wealthy —**one's money's worth** full value or benefit —**on the money** [Slang] exact; correct [the prediction was right *on the money*] —**put money into** to invest money in —**put money on** to bet on —**throw good money after bad** to put even more money into a failing investment, in a misguided attempt to save or sustain it —**mon′ey·less** ***adj.***

mon·ey·bag (mun′ē bag′) ***n.*** **1** a bag for holding money **2** [*pl., with sing. v.*] [Informal] a rich person

money belt a belt worn around the waist, with a compartment or pouch for holding or hiding money

mon·ey-chang·er (-chān′jər) ***n.*** **1** a person whose business is money-changing ☆**2** a device designed to hold stacked coins, for making change quickly

mon·ey-chang·ing (-chān′jiŋ) ***n.*** the business or act of exchanging currency, usually of different countries, esp. at a set rate

mon·eyed (mun′ēd) ***adj.*** **1** having much money; rich **2** consisting of, derived from, or representing wealth [*moneyed* interests]

mon·ey·er (mun′ē ər) ***n.*** ⟦ME *moneyour* < OFr *monoier* < L *monetarius*, mint master < *moneta*, MINT[1]⟧ [Archaic] a coiner of money

mon·ey-grub·ber (mun′ē grub′ər) ***n.*** [Informal] a person who is greedily intent on accumulating money —**mon′ey-grub′bing** ***adj., n.***

mon·ey·lend·er (-len′dər) ***n.*** a person whose business is lending money at interest

mon·ey·mak·er (-māk′ər) ***n.*** **1** a person successful at acquiring money **2** something that produces monetary gain, as a lucrative business —**mon′ey·mak′ing** ***adj., n.***

mon·ey·man (-man′) ***n.***, *pl.* **-men′** (-men′) [Informal] **1** a person who provides financial backing for a venture **2** a person involved in managing or regulating financial activities

money market the market for treasury bills, commercial paper, and other securities issued to meet the short-term borrowing requirements of government agencies, banks, large corporations, etc.

money market (mutual) fund a mutual fund that invests chiefly in money-market securities: also written **money-market (mutual) fund**

money of account a monetary denomination used in keeping accounts, esp. one, as the U.S. mill, not issued as a coin or piece of paper money

money order an order for the payment of a specified sum of money, as one issued for a fee at one post office, telegraph office, or bank and payable at another

mon·ey·wort (mun′ē wurt′) ***n.*** ⟦MONEY + WORT[2], after the ModL name *Nummularia* (see NUMMULAR): so called from its coin-shaped leaves⟧ a creeping, perennial European plant (*Lysimachia nummularia*) of the primrose family, with yellow flowers and roundish leaves

Mong *abbrev.* **1** Mongolia **2** Mongolian

mon·ger (muŋ′gər, mäŋ′-) ***n.*** ⟦ME *mongere* < OE *mangere* < L *mango*, dealer in tricked-out wares < ? Gr **mangōn* < *manganon*, device for deceiving: see MANGLE[2]⟧ a dealer or trader —***vt.*** to disseminate, promote, etc., often in a way that is regarded as deceptive or self-serving ➡The ***n.*** and ***prp.***, although still encountered in literal usage, esp. in Brit. English [*fishmonger*], are usually now used fig. and derogatorily in compounds [*hatemonger, scandalmongering*]

mon·go (mäŋ′gō) ***n.***, *pl.* **-gos** ⟦< Khalkha *möngö*⟧ a monetary unit of Mongolia, equal to 1/100 of a tugrik

Mon·gol (mäŋ′gəl, män′-) ***n.*** ⟦< a self-designation; cf. MOGUL⟧ **1** a person born or living in Mongolia **2** KHALKHA —***adj.*** *var. of* MONGOLIAN

Mon·go·li·a (mäŋ gō′lē ə, män-; -gōl′yə) **1** region in EC Asia, consisting of Inner Mongolia & the country of Mongolia **2** country in EC Asia, north of China: 603,909 sq mi (1,564,116 sq km); cap. Ulan Bator

Mon·go·li·an (-ən, -yən) ***n.*** **1** MONGOL (*n.* 1) **2** a family of languages, including Kalmuck and Khalkha, within the Altaic grouping **3** Khalkha, the official language of Mongolia —***adj.*** **1** of Mongolia or its peoples, languages, or cultures **2** designating or affected with Down syndrome: now obsolete as a medical term and regarded as disparaging and offensive

Mongolian hot pot **1** a type of Chinese communal meal consisting of sliced meats and vegetables selected and then simmered in broth in a special cooking pot at the table **2** this cooking pot **3** the food thus cooked

Mongolian idiocy *former term for* DOWN SYNDROME: now considered disparaging and offensive

Mongolian (*or* Mongoloid) idiot [Old-fashioned] a person affected with Down syndrome: now considered disparaging and offensive

Mongolian People's Republic *former name* (1924-92) *for* MONGOLIA (the country)

Mon·gol·ic (mäŋ gäl′ik, män-) ***adj.*** *var. of* MONGOLIAN —***n.*** the Mongolian language; Khalkha

Mon·gol·ism (mäŋ′gəl iz′əm, män′-) ***n.*** [*often* **m-**] *former term for* DOWN SYNDROME: now considered disparaging and offensive

Mon·gol·oid (-oid′) ***adj.*** **1** [Rare] *var. of* MONGOLIAN **2** designating or of one of the major geographical varieties of human beings, including most of the peoples of Asia, the Eskimos, the North American Indians, etc., who are generally characterized by straight black hair, dark eyes with epicanthic folds, and relatively small stature: see RACE[2] **3** [*often* **m-**] of or affected with Down syndrome —***n.*** **1** a member of the Mongoloid population of human beings **2** [*often* **m-**] a person affected with Down syndrome ***USAGE***—both ***adj.*** 3 and ***n.*** 2 are now obsolete as medical terms and are regarded as disparaging and offensive

mon·goose (mäŋ′go͞os′, män′-) ***n.***, *pl.* **-goos′es** ⟦Marathi *mangūs*⟧ any of various civetlike, Old World carnivores (family Viverridae), esp., any of a sometimes domesticated genus (*Herpestes*) noted for their ability to kill poisonous snakes, rodents, etc.

mon·grel (mäŋ′grəl, muŋ′-) ***n.*** ⟦ME *mengrell* < base of OE *mengan*, to mix + dim. suffix *-rel* as in COCKEREL: form infl. by ME *mong*, aphetic < OE *gemong*, mixture: see AMONG⟧ **1** an animal or plant produced by the crossing of different breeds or varieties; esp., a dog of this kind **2** anything produced by indiscriminate mixture —***adj.*** **1** of mixed breed **2** of mixed race, origin, or character: typically a contemptuous or derogatory usage

mon·grel·ize (-īz′) ***vt.*** **-ized′**, **-iz′ing** **1** to mix the type, breed, class, etc. of **2** to intermix in racial or ethnic character: a contemptuous term in the traditional jargon of racism —**mon′grel·i·za′tion** ***n.***

′mongst or **mongst** (muŋst) ***prep.*** [Old Poet.] *short for* AMONGST

Mon·i·ca (män′i kə) ***n.*** ⟦LL < ?⟧ a feminine name; var. *Monique*

mon·ied (mun′ēd) ***adj.*** *alt. sp. of* MONEYED

mon·ies (mun′ēz) ***n.*** *alt. pl. of* MONEY

mon·i·ker (män′i kər) ***n.*** ⟦orig. hobo slang < ?⟧ [Informal] a person's name or nickname: also sp. **mon′ick·er**

mon·i·li·a·sis (män′ə lī′ə sis, mōn′-) ***n.***, *pl.* **-ses′** (-sēz′) ⟦ModL < *Monilia*, genus name for cerain fungi (formerly containing the organism now assigned to *Candida*) < L *monile*, necklace (see fol.): so named from the chains of spores⟧ *former term for* CANDIDIASIS

mo·nil·i·form (mō nil′ə fôrm′, mə-) ***adj.*** ⟦< L *monile* (gen. *monilis*), necklace < IE base **mono-*, neck (> MANE) + -FORM⟧ shaped somewhat like a string of beads; specif., consisting of, or having, a series of alternate swellings and constrictions: said of some plant stems and some insect antennae

mon·ish (män′ish) ***vt.*** [Archaic] ADMONISH

mo·nism (mō′niz′əm, män′iz′əm) ***n.*** ⟦ModL *monismus* < Gr *monos*, single: see MONO-⟧ *Philos.* **1** the doctrine that there is only one ultimate substance or principle, whether mind (*idealism*), matter (*materialism*), or some third thing that is the basis of both **2** the doctrine that reality is an organic whole without independent parts Cf. DUALISM, PLURALISM **—mo′nist** *n.* **—mo·nis′tic** *adj.*, **mo·nis′ti·cal** **—mo·nis′ti·cal·ly** *adv.*

mo·ni·tion (mō nish′ən, mə-) *n.* ⟦ME *monicion* < OFr *monition* < L *monitio* < pp. of *monere,* to warn: see fol.⟧ **1** admonition; warning; caution **2** an official or legal notice; specif., an order issued by a court, as a summons or a command to refrain from doing some act

mon·i·tor (män′i tər) *n.* ⟦L < pp. of *monere,* to warn < IE **moni-* < base **men-,* to think > MIND⟧ **1** a person who advises, warns, or cautions **2** in some schools, a student chosen to help keep order, record attendance, etc. **3** something that reminds or warns **4** any of a family (Varanidae) of usually very large, flesh-eating lizards of Africa, S Asia, and Australia: from the notion that they warn of the presence of crocodiles ☆**5** ⟦after the *Monitor,* first such ship, built in 1862⟧ [Historical] a heavily armored warship with a low, flat deck and heavy guns fitted in one or more revolving turrets ☆**6** a mounting for a nozzle that allows a stream of water to be played in any direction, as in fire fighting **7** a person who monitors a foreign broadcast, etc. **8** any of various devices for checking or regulating the performance of machines, aircraft, guided missiles, etc. **9** an instrument for measuring radioactive contamination by means of the ionizing radiation being emitted **10** any device, typically one of a pair, designed to allow someone to view or listen in on persons or activities in another room or location [a baby *monitor* in a nursery] **11** *Comput.* a video screen for displaying data, graphic images, etc. **12** *Radio, TV* a receiver or speaker, as in the control room of a broadcasting studio, for checking the quality of the transmission **—*vt., vi.*** **1** to watch or check on (a person or thing) as a monitor **2** to observe, check on, or regulate the performance of (a machine, an employee, etc.) **3** to test for radioactive contamination with a monitor **4** to listen in on (a foreign broadcast, telephone conversation, etc.) as for gathering political or military information **5** *Radio, TV* to check the quality of (transmission) with or as with a monitor **—mon′i·tor·ship′** *n.*

mon·i·to·ri·al (män′i tôr′ē əl) *adj.* **1** of a monitor or using a monitor or monitors **2** MONITORY

mon·i·to·ry (män′i tôr′ē) *adj.* ⟦LME *manyterye* < L *monitorius* < *monitor:* see MONITOR⟧ giving or containing monition; admonishing **—*n., pl.*** **-ries** a monitory writing

monk (muŋk) *n.* ⟦ME *munec* < OE *munuc* < LL(Ec) *monachus* < LGr(Ec) *monachos* < Gr, one who lives alone < *monos,* alone: see MONO-⟧ a member of a male religious order living in a monastery or hermitage observing a common rule, under vows of poverty, chastity, and obedience: cf. FRIAR

Monk (muŋk) **1 George** 1st Duke of Albemarle 1608-70; Eng. general & politician **2 The·lo·ni·ous (Sphere)** (thə lō′nē əs) 1920-82; U.S. jazz pianist & composer

monk·er·y (muŋ′kər ē) *n., pl.* **-er·ies** **1** *a)* the way of life, condition, behavior, etc. of monks *b)* [*pl.*] monastic practices or beliefs **2** a monastery A hostile term

mon·key (muŋ′kē) *n., pl.* **-keys** ⟦Early ModE, prob. < or akin to MLowG *Moneke,* name applied in the beast epic *Reynard the Fox* to the son of Martin the Ape < Fr or Sp *mona,* ape < ? Ar *maimūn,* ape, lit., lucky (euphemism: the ape was regarded as the devil) + LowG *-ke,* -KIN⟧ **1** *a)* any of several families of Old and New World primates usually having a flat, hairless face and a long tail *b)* loosely, any of other, similar primates, as a gibbon or chimpanzee **2** the fur of some species of long-haired monkeys **3** a person regarded as somehow like a monkey, as a mischievous or imitative child **4** any of various mechanical devices, as the iron block raised and dropped in a pile driver **—*vi.*** ☆[Informal] to play, fool, trifle, or meddle: often followed by *around, with,* or *around with* —☆**a monkey on one's back** [Slang] **1** addiction to a drug **2** any trying, burdensome obsession, problem, etc. —☆**make a monkey (out) of** to make appear foolish or laughable

☆**monkey bars** an arrangement of horizontal and vertical bars erected as in a playground for children to climb on, swing from, etc.

monkey bread ⟦prob. because the fruit is eaten by monkeys⟧ **1** the fruit of the African baobab tree **2** the baobab tree

☆**monkey business** [Informal] foolish, mischievous, or deceitful tricks or behavior

monkey flower any of a genus (*Mimulus*) of plants of the figwort family, with snapdragonlike flowers having a corolla whose appearance suggests a gape or grimace

monkey jacket [Slang] a man's short, closefitting jacket; often, specif., MESS JACKET

mon·key·pod (-päd′) *n.* **1** a tropical South American tree (*Samanea saman*) of the mimosa family, having clusters of pink flowers and long, edible pods, commonly used as an ornamental **2** the wood of this tree

mon·key·pot (-pät′) *n.* **1** the large, bowl-shaped, woody seed vessel of any of various South American trees (genus *Lecythis*) of the lecythis family **2** any of these trees

monkey puzzle ⟦so named because the tangled branches are difficult to climb⟧ any araucaria tree; esp., a tall tree (*Araucaria araucana*) with stiff pointed leaves, edible nuts, and hard wood, widely grown as an ornamental

☆**mon·key·shine** (-shīn′) *n.* ⟦see SHINE (*n.* 6)⟧ [Informal] a mischievous or playful trick, joke, or prank: *usually used in pl.*

monkey suit [Slang] **1** a uniform **2** a man's dress suit

monkey wrench a wrench with one movable jaw, adjusted by a screw to fit various sizes of a nut, etc. —☆**throw a monkey wrench into** [Informal] to disrupt or prevent the orderly functioning or realization of; sabotage

monk·fish (muŋk′fish′) *n., pl.* **-fish′** or **-fish′es** (see FISH) any of certain species of ANGLER (sense 3), esp. when used as food

Mon-Khmer (mōn′kə mer′) *adj.* designating or of a branch of the Austro-Asiatic family of languages, spoken mainly in Indochina and including Mon and Khmer

monk·hood (muŋk′hood′) *n.* **1** the condition or profession of a monk **2** monks collectively

monk·ish (muŋ′kish) *adj.* of or like monks or monastic life; specif., reclusive, self-denying, etc. **—monk′ish·ly** *adv.*

monk's cloth **1** [Historical] a worsted cloth used for monks' garments **2** a heavy cloth, as of cotton, with a basket weave, used for drapes, etc.

monks·hood (muŋks′hood′) *n.* ⟦so called from its hoodlike flowers⟧ ACONITE

Mon·mouth (män′məth), **Duke of** (*James Scott*) 1649-85; illegitimate son of Charles II & pretender to the Eng. throne: executed for leading an insurrection against James II

Mon·mouth·shire (-shir′, -shər) former county of SE Wales: also **Mon′mouth**

mon·o (män′ō) *adj. short for* MONOPHONIC (sense 2) **—*n.*** ☆[Informal] *short for* INFECTIOUS MONONUCLEOSIS

mon·o- (män′ō, -ə) ⟦Gr *mono-* < *monos,* single, alone < IE base **men-,* small, single > OIr *menb,* small⟧ *prefix* **1** one, alone, single [*monocracy*] **2** containing one atom or one chemical group [*monohydric*] **3** ⟦< *mono*molecular⟧ having a thickness of one molecule [*monolayer*]

mon·o·ac·id (män′ō as′id) *adj. var. of* MONOACIDIC **—*n.*** an acid having only one replaceable hydrogen atom per molecule

mon·o·a·cid·ic (-ə sid′ik) *adj.* **1** designating a base or alcohol one molecular weight of which can react with only one equivalent weight of an acid, or that has one hydroxyl group capable of replacing one acid hydrogen atom **2** having only one acid hydrogen atom per molecule

mon·o·a·mine (-am′ēn′, -ə mēn′) *n.* an amine with one amino group

monoamine oxidase MAO

mon·o·a·tom·ic (-ə täm′ik) *adj. var. of* MONATOMIC

mon·o·bas·ic (-bās′ik) *adj. Chem.* **1** designating an acid the molecule of which contains one hydrogen atom replaceable by a metal or positive radical or capable of reacting with the hydroxyl group **2** designating a compound in which a metal or positive radical replaces one acid hydrogen atom **—mon′o·ba·sic′i·ty** (-bə sis′ə tē) *n.*

mon·o·bloc (män′ō bläk′) *adj.* ⟦Fr⟧ manufactured as a single piece and, often, in a single casting [a plastic *monobloc* chair]

mon·o·car·box·yl·ic (-kär′bäks il′ik) *adj.* having only one carboxylic acid group in the molecule

mon·o·car·pel·lar·y (-kär′pə ler′ē) *adj.* consisting of or having only a single carpel

mon·o·car·pic (-kär′pik) *adj.* ⟦MONO- + -CARPIC⟧ bearing fruit only once, and then dying: said of annuals, biennials, and some long-lived plants, as the bamboos and century plants: also **mon′o·car′pous** (-pəs)

Mo·noc·er·os (mə näs′ər əs) *n.* ⟦L, the unicorn < Gr *monokeras* < *mono-,* MONO- + *keras,* HORN⟧ a S constellation between Orion and Canis Minor

mon·o·cha·si·um (män′ō kā′zē əm, -zhē-; män′ə-) *n., pl.* **-si·a** (-ə) ⟦ModL < MONO- + Gr *chasis,* division, akin to *chainein,* to yawn, GAPE⟧ *Bot.* a cymose or determinate inflorescence having only a single main axis **—mon′o·cha′si·al** *adj.*

mon·o·chla·myd·e·ous (-klə mid′ē əs) *adj.* ⟦< ModL *Monochlamydeae* < MONO- + Gr *chlamyd-,* base of *chlamys,* a mantle + -OUS⟧ having only one series of perianth parts, usually designated as sepals, in the flower

mon·o·chlo·ride (-klôr′īd′) *n.* a chloride containing one chlorine atom per molecule

mon·o·chord (män′ə kôrd′) *n.* ⟦ME *monocorde* < MFr < LL *monochordon* < Gr: see MONO- & CHORD[1]⟧ [Historical] an early acoustic instrument having a single string and a movable bridge set on a graduated scale: later used as a device for determining musical intervals mathematically

mon·o·chro·mat (män′ə krō′mat) *n.* ⟦< L *monochromatos,* one-colored < Gr *monochrōmatos* < *mono-,* MONO- + *chrōma:* see CHROMA⟧ a person who has monochromatism

mon·o·chro·mat·ic (män′ə krō mat′ik) *adj.* ⟦< L *monochromatos* < Gr *monochrōmatos:* see MONOCHROME & -IC⟧ **1** of or having one color **2** of, done in, or having to do with monochrome **3** of or producing electromagnetic radiation of one wavelength or within a very small range of wavelengths **4** of or having monochromatism **—mon′o·chro·mat′i·cal·ly** *adv.*

mon·o·chro·ma·tism (-krō′mə tiz′əm) *n.* ⟦< prec. + -ISM⟧ total colorblindness in which all objects appear as shades of gray

mon·o·chrome (män′ə krōm′) *n.* ⟦ML *monochroma* < Gr *monochrōmos,* of one color: see MONO- & -CHROME⟧ **1** a painting, drawing, design, or photograph in black and white, or in shades of one color often with black or white **2** the art or process of making these **—*adj.*** **1** of or having to do with a single color **2** of or done in monochrome **—mon′o·chro′mic** *adj.* **—mon′o·chro′mist** *n.*

mon·o·cle (män′ə kəl) *n.* ⟦Fr < LL *monoculus,* one-eyed < Gr *monos,* single (see MONO-) + L *oculus,* EYE⟧ an eyeglass for one eye only, typically a lens encircled by a frame with an attached cord **—mon′o·cled** *adj.*

mon·o·cli·nal (män′ō klī′nəl, män′ə-) *adj. Geol.* **1** dipping in one direction: said of strata, or rock layers **2** of strata dipping in the same direction **—*n.*** MONOCLINE

mon·o·cline (män′ō klīn′, män′ə-) *n.* ⟦< MONO- + Gr *klinein,* to incline: see LEAN[1]⟧ a monoclinal rock fold or structure

mon·o·clin·ic (män′ō klin′ik, män′ə-) *adj.* ⟦see prec. & -IC⟧ designating or of a CRYSTAL SYSTEM having three axes of unequal length, only two of which intersect at right angles with each other

mon·o·cli·nous (-klī′nəs) *adj.* ⟦ModL *monoclinus* < MONO- + Gr *klinē*, a bed, couch: see CLINIC⟧ having stamens and pistils in the same flower

mon·o·clon·al (-klōn′əl) *adj.* ⟦MONO- + CLONAL⟧ of cells derived or cloned from one cell

monoclonal antibody *Immunology* an antibody produced by a hybridoma for a specific antigen

mon·o·coque (män′ə käk′, -kōk′) *adj.* ⟦Fr < *mono-*, MONO- + *coque*, a shell < L *coccum*, scarlet berry < Gr *kokkos*, a seed⟧ **1** designating or of a kind of construction, as of a rocket, in which the skin or outer shell bears all or most of the stresses **2** designating or of a kind of construction, as of some racing cars, in which the body and chassis are a unit

mon·o·cot·y·le·don (män′ō kät′ə lēd′'n, män′ə-) *n. Bot.* any of a class (Liliopsida) of angiosperms, including lilies, orchids, and grasses, having an embryo containing only one cotyledon, and characterized by parallel-veined leaves, flower parts in multiples of three, and no secondary growth in stems and roots: often clipped to **mon′o·cot′** —**mon′o·cot′y·le′don·ous** *adj.*

mo·noc·ra·cy (mə näk′rə sē) *n., pl.* **-cies** ⟦MONO- + -CRACY⟧ government by one person —☆**mon·o·crat** (män′ə krat′) *n.* —**mon′o·crat′ic** *adj.*

mo·noc·u·lar (mə näk′yoo lər, -yə-) *adj.* ⟦< LL *monoculus* (see MONOCLE) + -AR⟧ **1** having only one eye **2** of, or for use by, only one eye —*n.* a field glass or telescopic device with a single eyepiece

mon·o·cul·ture (män′ō kul′chər, män′ə-) *n.* ⟦MONO- + CULTURE⟧ **1** the raising of only one crop or product without using the land for other purposes **2** a group, society, etc. characterized by cultural uniformity —**mon′o·cul′tur·al** *adj.*

mon·o·cy·cle (-sī′kəl) *n.* UNICYCLE

mon·o·cy·clic (män′ō sīk′lik) *adj.* **1** of or forming one cycle, circle, whorl, etc. **2** *Chem.* containing one ring of atoms in the molecule

mon·o·cyte (män′ō sīt′, män′ə-) *n.* ⟦MONO- + -CYTE⟧ a large, mononuclear, nongranular white blood cell with a round or kidney-shaped nucleus —**mon′o·cyt′ic** (-sit′ik) *adj.*

Mo·nod (mô nō′), **Jacques Lu·ci·en** (zhäk lü syan′) 1910-76; Fr. biochemist

mon·o·dist (män′ə dist) *n.* a writer or singer of a monody

mon·o·dra·ma (män′ō drä′mə, -dram′ə; män′ə-) *n.* drama acted, or written to be acted, by only one performer —**mon′o·dra·mat′ic** (-drə mat′ik) *adj.*

mon·o·dy (män′ə dē) *n., pl.* **-dies** ⟦LL *monodia* < Gr *monōidia* < *monōidos*, singing alone < *monos*, alone (see MONO-) + *aeidein*, to sing: see ODE⟧ **1** in ancient Greek literature, an ode sung by a single voice, as in a tragedy; lyric solo, generally a lament or dirge **2** a poem in which the poet mourns someone's death **3** a monotonous sound or tone, as of waves **4** *Music a)* an early vocal style having a single voice part with continuo accompaniment, as in Baroque opera *b)* a composition in this style **5** MONOPHONY —**mo·nod·ic** (mə näd′ik) *adj.*, **mo·nod′i·cal** —**mo·nod′i·cal·ly** *adv.*

mo·noe·cious (mō nē′shəs, mə-) *adj.* ⟦< MON(O)- + Gr *oikos*, a house (see ECO-) + -IOUS⟧ **1** *Bot.* having separate male flowers and female flowers on the same plant, as in corn **2** *Zool.* having both male and female reproductive organs in the same individual; hermaphroditic —**mo·noe′cism′** (-siz′əm) *n.*

mon·o·fil·a·ment (män′ō fil′ə mənt, män′ə-) *n.* a single untwisted strand of synthetic material: also **mon′o·fil′**

mo·nog·a·my (mə näg′ə mē) *n.* ⟦Fr *monogamie* < LL(Ec) *monogamia* < Gr: see MONO- & -GAMY⟧ **1** the practice or state of being married to only one person at a time **2** loosely, faithfulness in a relationship between unmarried partners **3** [Rare] the practice of marrying only once during life **4** *Zool.* the practice of having only one mate during a mating season or for life —**mo·nog′a·mist** *n.* —**mo·nog′a·mous** *adj.*, **mon·o·gam·ic** (män′ə gam′ik)

mon·o·gen·e·sis (män′ō jen′ə sis, män′ə-) *n.* ⟦ModL: see MONO- & GENESIS⟧ *Biol.* **1** the hypothetical descent of all living organisms from a single original organism or cell **2** asexual reproduction, as by budding or spore formation

mon·o·ge·net·ic (-jə net′ik) *adj.* **1** of or pertaining to monogenesis **2** designating or of animals without alternating asexual and sexual generations

mon·o·gen·ic (-jen′ik) *adj.* **1** ⟦MONO- + GEN(E) + -IC⟧ *Biol.* designating or of a mode of inheritance in which a character is controlled by one pair of genes **2** ⟦MONO- + -GEN + -IC⟧ *Zool.* producing offspring of one sex only, as females only in some species of aphids —**mo·nog·e·ny** (mə näj′ə nē) *n.*

mo·nog·e·nism (mə näj′ə niz′əm) *n.* ⟦MONO- + -GEN + -ISM⟧ the theory that all human beings are descended from a single pair of ancestors: see POLYGENISM

mon·o·glot (män′ō glät′, män′ə-) *adj.* ⟦Gr *monoglōttos*: see MONO- & (POLY)GLOT⟧ speaking or writing only one language —*n.* a monoglot person

mon·o·gram (män′ə gram′) *n.* ⟦LL *monogramma* < Gr *mono-*, MONO- + *gramma*, letter: see GRAM[1]⟧ a character or figure made up of two or more letters, often initials of a name, combined in a single design: used on writing paper, jewelry, clothing, towels, etc. —*vt.* **-grammed′**, **-gram′ming** to put a monogram on —**mon′o·gram·mat′ic** (-grə mat′ik) *adj.*

mon·o·graph (män′ə graf′) *n.* ⟦MONO- + -GRAPH⟧ **1** [Historical] a treatise on a single genus, species, etc. of plant or animal **2** a book or long article, esp. a scholarly one, on a single subject or a limited aspect of a subject —**mon′o·graph′ic** *adj.*

mo·nog·y·nous (mə näj′ə nəs) *adj.* **1** of or characterized by monogyny **2** *Bot.* having one style or pistil

mo·nog·y·ny (mə näj′ə nē) *n.* ⟦MONO- + -GYNY⟧ the practice or state of being married to only one woman at a time

mon·o·hull (män′ō hul′) *n.* a boat, esp. a sailboat, with a single hull: distinguished from MULTIHULL

mon·o·hy·drate (män′ō hī′drāt′) *n.* a hydrate containing one molecule of water per molecule of combining compound

mon·o·hy·dric (-hī′drik) *adj.* ⟦MONO- + -HYDRIC⟧ MONOHYDROXY

mon·o·hy·drox·y (-hī dräk′sē) *adj.* ⟦MONO- + HYDROXY⟧ having one hydroxyl group in the molecule

mon·o·lay·er (män′ō lā′ər) *n.* a layer or film one molecule thick

mon·o·lin·gual (män′ō liŋ′gwəl, män′ə-) *adj.* ⟦MONO- + LINGUAL⟧ **1** of or in one language **2** using or knowing only one language

mon·o·lith (män′ə lith′) *n.* ⟦Fr *monolithe* < L *monolithus* < Gr *monolithos*, made of one stone < *monos*, single (see MONO-) + *lithos*, stone⟧ **1** a single large block or piece of stone, as in architecture or sculpture **2** something made of a single block of stone, as an obelisk **3** something like a monolith in size, uniformity, etc. —**mon′o·lith′ic** *adj.* —**mon′o·lith′ism′** *n.*

mon·o·logue or **mon·o·log** (män′ə lôg′) *n.* ⟦Fr < Gr *monologos*, speaking alone < *monos*, single (see MONO-) + *legein*, to speak (see LOGIC)⟧ **1** a long speech by one speaker, esp. one monopolizing the conversation **2** a passage or composition, in verse or prose, presenting the words or thoughts of a single character **3** a part of a play in which one character speaks alone; soliloquy **4** a play, skit, or recitation for one actor only **5** the act of a stand-up comedian —**mon′o·log′ic** (-läj′ik) *adj.* —**mon′o·logu′ist** *n.*, **mo·nol·o·gist** (mə näl′ə jist)

mon·o·ma·ni·a (män′ō mā′nē ə) *n.* ⟦ModL: see MONO- & MANIA⟧ **1** an excessive interest in or enthusiasm for some one thing; craze **2** a mental disorder characterized by irrational preoccupation with one subject —**mon′o·ma′ni·ac′** (-mā′nē ak′) *n.* —**mon′o·ma·ni′a·cal** (-mə nī′ə kəl) *adj.*

mon·o·mer (män′ə mər) *n.* ⟦MONO- + Gr *meros*, a part: see MERIT⟧ a simple molecule that can form polymers by combining with identical or similar molecules —**mon′o·mer′ic** (-mer′ik) *adj.*

mo·nom·er·ous (mə näm′ər əs) *adj.* ⟦ModL *monomerus* < Gr *monomerēs*, single (< *mono-*, MONO- + *meros*, a part: see MERIT) + -OUS⟧ having one member, as a fruit of one carpel

mon·o·me·tal·lic (män′ō mə tal′ik, män′ə-) *adj.* **1** of or using one metal **2** of or based on monometallism

mon·o·met·al·lism (-met′'l iz′əm) *n.* **1** use of only one metal, usually gold or silver, as a monetary standard **2** the doctrine or policies supporting this —**mon′o·met′al·list** *n.*

mo·no·mi·al (mō nō′mē əl, mä-) *adj.* ⟦MO(NO)- + (BI)NOMIAL⟧ **1** *Algebra* consisting of only one term **2** *Biol.* consisting of only one word: said of a taxonomic name —*n.* a monomial expression, quantity, or name

mon·o·mo·lec·u·lar (män′ō mə lek′yə lər) *adj.* **1** of a single molecule **2** designating or of a layer one molecule thick

mon·o·mor·phic (män′ō môr′fik) *adj.* ⟦MONO- + -MORPHIC⟧ **1** having only one form **2** having the same or an essentially similar type of structure Also **mon′o·mor′phous** (-fəs)

Mo·non·ga·he·la (mə nän′gə hē′lə, -näŋ′-; -hā′-) ⟦< Algonquian⟧ river in N W.Va. & SW Pa., flowing north to join the Allegheny at Pittsburgh & form the Ohio River: 128 mi (206 km)

mon·o·nu·cle·ar (män′ō noo′klē ər, -nyoo′-) *adj.* **1** *Bot.* having one nucleus in a cell **2** *Chem.* MONOCYCLIC (sense 2)

mon·o·nu·cle·o·sis (män′ō noo′klē ō′sis, -nyoo′-) *n.* ⟦MONO- + NUCLE(US) + -OSIS⟧ **1** INFECTIOUS MONONUCLEOSIS **2** the presence in the blood of an excessive number of cells having a single nucleus

mo·noph·a·gous (mə näf′ə gəs) *adj.* ⟦MONO- + -PHAGOUS⟧ feeding on only one kind of food, as on a certain type of plant

mon·o·pho·bi·a (män′ō fō′bē ə, män′ə-) *n.* ⟦ModL: see MONO- & -PHOBIA⟧ an abnormal fear of being alone —**mon′o·pho′bic** *adj.*

mon·o·phon·ic (män′ō fän′ik, män′ə-) *adj.* **1** of, or having the nature of, monophony **2** designating or of sound reproduction using a single channel to carry and reproduce sounds through one or more loudspeakers

mo·noph·o·ny (mə näf′ə nē) *n.* ⟦MONO- + -PHONY⟧ **1** music having a single melody without accompaniment or harmonizing parts, as in plainsong **2** MONODY

mon·oph·thong (män′əf thôŋ′) *n.* ⟦< Gr *monophthongos*, of or with one sound < *monos*, single (see MONO-) + *phthongos*, a sound, voice⟧ a simple vowel sound during the utterance of which the vocal organs remain in a relatively unchanging position, as (ä), (oo), or (i) —**mon′oph·thong′al** *adj.*

mon·o·phy·let·ic (män′ō fī let′ik, män′ə-) *adj.* ⟦see MONO- & PHYLETIC⟧ *Biol.* **1** of a single stock **2** developed from a single ancestral type —**mon′o·phy′le·tism′** (-fī′lə tiz′əm) *n.*

mon·o·phyl·lous (män′ō fil′əs) *adj.* ⟦Gr *monophyllos* < *monos*, single (see MONO-) + *phyllon*, leaf (see BLOOM[1])⟧ *Bot.* **1** having or consisting of only one leaf **2** having united sepals or petals

Mo·noph·y·site (mə näf′ə sīt′) *n.* ⟦LGr(Ec) *monophysitēs* < Gr *monos*, single (see MONO-) + *physis*, nature (see PHYSIC)⟧ an adherent of an originally 4th- and 5th-cent. theory asserting the existence of only one nature (divine or divine-human) in Christ and opposing the orthodox doctrine of the existence of two distinct natures (one wholly divine, the other wholly human) in the one person of Christ —**Mo·noph′y·sit′ic** (mə näf′ə sit′ik, män′ə fə-) *adj.* —**Mo·noph′y·sit·ism′** *n.*

mon·o·plane (män′ə plān′) *n.* an airplane or glider with only one main supporting surface, or pair of wings

mon·o·ple·gi·a (män′ə plē′jē ə, -plē′jə) *n.* ⟦ModL < MONO- + Gr *plēgē,* a stroke < IE **plēg-,* var. of **plāk-,* to strike > L *plangere:* see FLAW[2]⟧ paralysis of a single limb or part of the body —**mon′o·ple′gic** (-plē′jik, -plej′ik) *adj.*

mon·o·ploid (män′ō ploid′) *adj., n.* ⟦MONO- + -PLOID⟧ *Biol.* HAPLOID

mon·o·pod (män′ə päd′) *n.* a one-legged support, as for a camera

mon·o·pode (män′ə pōd′) *adj.* ⟦LL *monopedius* < Gr **monopodios,* for *monopous* < *monos,* (see MONO-) + *pous* (gen. *podos*), FOOT⟧ having only one foot —*n.* **1** a monopode creature; specif., a member of a fabled race of monopode men **2** MONOPODIUM

mon·o·po·di·um (män′ō pō′dē əm) *n., pl.* **-di·a** (-ə) ⟦ModL: see MONO- & -PODIUM⟧ *Bot.* a single main stem that continues to extend at the apex in its original line of growth, giving off lateral branches or axes, as the trunk of certain pine trees —**mon′o·po′di·al** *adj.*

mon·o·pole (män′ə pōl′) *n.* ⟦MONO- + POLE[2]⟧ a hypothetical elementary particle of great mass, that has only one pole of magnetic charge: in full **magnetic monopole**

mo·nop·o·list (mə näp′ə list) *n.* **1** one who monopolizes or has a monopoly **2** a person who favors monopoly —**mo·nop′o·lis′tic** *adj.* —**mo·nop′o·lis′ti·cal·ly** *adv.*

mo·nop·o·lize (mə näp′ə līz′) *vt.* **-lized′**, **-liz′ing** **1** to get, have, or exploit a monopoly of **2** to take full possession or control of; dominate completely [to *monopolize* a conversation] —**mo·nop′o·li·za′tion** *n.* —**mo·nop′o·liz′er** *n.*

mo·nop·o·ly (mə näp′ə lē) *n., pl.* **-lies** ⟦L *monopolium* < Gr *monopōlion,* right of exclusive sale, *monopōlia,* exclusive sale < *monos,* single (see MONO-) + *pōlein,* to sell < IE base **pel-* > Lith *peĺnas,* wages⟧ **1** exclusive control of a commodity or service in a given market, or control that makes possible the fixing of prices and the virtual elimination of free competition **2** *a)* an exclusive privilege of engaging in a particular business or providing a service, granted by a ruler or by the state *b)* any exclusive possession or control regarded as resembling this [Dad's *monopoly* over the TV remote control] **3** something that is held or controlled as a monopoly **4** a company or combination that has a monopoly —☆[**M-**] *trademark for* a game played on a special board by two or more players: they move according to the throw of dice, engaging in mock real-estate transactions with play money

SYN.—**monopoly** applies to the exclusive control of a commodity, etc., as defined above; a **trust** is a combination of corporations, organized for the purpose of gaining a monopoly, in which stock is turned over to trustees who issue stock certificates to the stockholders: trusts are now illegal in the U.S.; **cartel**, the European term for a trust, now usually implies an international trust; a **syndicate** is now usually a group of bankers, corporations, etc. organized to buy large blocks of securities, afterward selling them in small parcels to the public at a profit; a **corner** is a temporary speculative monopoly of some stock or commodity for the purpose of raising the price

☆**mon·o·pro·pel·lant** (män′ō prə pel′ənt) *n.* ⟦MONO- + PROPELLANT⟧ a liquid or solid rocket propellant combining both fuel and oxidizer in a single substance

mo·nop·so·ny (mō näp′sə nē) *n., pl.* **-nies** ⟦MON(O)- + Gr *opsōnia,* a purchase of fish, catering < *opsōnein,* to buy victuals < *opson,* cooked food, fish < *o-,* with + base of *psōmos,* a morsel⟧ *Econ.* a situation in which there is only one buyer for a particular commodity or service

mon·o·rail (män′ə rāl′) *n.* **1** a single rail serving as a track for cars suspended from it or balanced on it **2** a railway with such a track

mon·o·sac·cha·ride (män′ō sak′ə rīd′) *n.* ⟦MONO- + SACCHARIDE⟧ a carbohydrate, CxH_2xOx, not decomposable by hydrolysis; esp., a hexose sugar, $C_6H_{12}O_6$, as glucose, fructose, or galactose

mon·o·sep·al·ous (-sep′əl əs) *adj. Bot.* GAMOSEPALOUS

mon·o·so·di·um glutamate (män′ə sō′dē əm) a white, crystalline powder, $NaC_5H_8NO_4$, derived from vegetable protein and used in foods as a flavor intensifier

mon·o·some (män′ə sōm′) *n.* ⟦MONO- + -SOME[3]⟧ an unpaired chromosome in an otherwise diploid cell; esp., an unpaired sex chromosome —**mon′o·so′mic** *adj.*

mon·o·sper·mous (män′ō spʉr′məs) *adj.* ⟦MONO- + -SPERMOUS⟧ *Bot.* having only one seed

mon·o·sper·my (män′ō spʉr′mē) *n.* ⟦MONO- + SPERM[1] + -Y[4]⟧ *Zool.* reproduction in which a single sperm cell fertilizes an ovum —**mon′o·sper′mic** *adj.*

mon·o·stele (män′ō stēl′, -stē′lē) *n.* ⟦MONO- + STELE⟧ a stem or root having a single vascular cylinder —**mon′o·ste′lic** *adj.*

mon·o·stich (män′ə stik′) *n.* ⟦LL *monostichum* < Gr *monostichon* < *monos,* single (see MONO-) + *stichos,* a line, verse: see STILE[2]⟧ **1** a poem consisting of one metrical line **2** one line of poetry

mon·o·stome (-stōm′) ⟦MONO- + -STOME⟧ *adj.* having one mouth or sucker, as some larval flatworms: also **mo·nos·to·mous** (mə näs′tə məs)

mon·o·stro·phe (män′ō strō′fē, mə näs′trə fē) *n.* ⟦< Gr *monostrophos:* see MONO- & STROPHE⟧ a poem in which all the stanzas have the same metrical form —**mon·o·stroph·ic** (män′ō sträf′ik) *adj.*

mon·o·sty·lous (män′ō stī′ləs) *adj. Bot.* having only one style

mon·o·syl·lab·ic (män′ō si lab′ik, män′ə-) *adj.* ⟦ML *monosyllabicus*⟧ **1** having only one syllable [a *monosyllabic* word] **2** consisting of monosyllables **3** using, or speaking in, monosyllables, often so as to seem terse or uncommunicative —**mon′o·syl·lab′i·cal·ly** *adv.*

mon·o·syl·la·ble (män′ō sil′ə bəl, män′ə-) *n.* ⟦altered < ML *monosyllaba,* ult. < Gr *monosyllabos:* see MONO- & SYLLABLE⟧ a word of one syllable

mon·o·sym·met·ric (män′ō si met′rik) *adj.* **1** MONOCLINIC **2** ZYGOMORPHIC Also **mon′o·sym·met′ri·cal**

mon·o·the·ism (män′ō thē iz′əm, män′ə-) *n.* ⟦MONO- + THEISM⟧ the belief or doctrine that there is only one God —**mon′o·the′ist** *n., adj.* —**mon′o·the·is′tic** *adj.*, **mon′o·the·is′ti·cal** —**mon′o·the·is′ti·cal·ly** *adv.*

mon·o·tint (män′ō tint′) *n.* MONOCHROME

mo·not·o·cous (mə nät′ə kəs) *adj.* ⟦< Gr *monotokos,* bearing one offspring at a time (< *monos,* MONO- + *tokos,* childbirth: see TOCOLOGY) + -OUS⟧ UNIPAROUS (sense 2)

mon·o·tone (män′ə tōn′) *n.* ⟦< LL *monotonus:* see fol.⟧ **1** *a)* uninterrupted repetition of the same tone *b)* the utterance of words without change of pitch or without expression or feeling **2** monotony or sameness of tone, style, manner, color, etc. **3** a single, unchanging musical tone **4** recitation, chanting, or singing in such a tone **5** a person who can sing only in such a tone —*adj.* MONOTONOUS —**mon′o·ton′ic** (-tän′ik) *adj.*

mo·not·o·nous (mə nät′′n əs) *adj.* ⟦LL *monotonus* < Gr *monotonos:* MONO- & TONE⟧ **1** going on in the same tone without variation **2** having little or no variation or variety **3** tiresome because unvarying —**mo·not′o·nous·ly** *adv.* —**mo·not′o·nous·ness** *n.*

mo·not·o·ny (mə nät′′n ē) *n.* ⟦Fr *monotonie* < Gr *monotonia:* see prec.⟧ **1** sameness of tone or pitch, or continuance of the same tone without variation **2** lack of variation or variety **3** tiresome sameness or uniformity

mon·o·treme (män′ō trēm′, män′ə-) *n.* ⟦< ModL *Monotremata* < Gr *monos,* single (see MONO-) + *trēma,* a hole < IE base **ter-,* to rub, drill > THROW⟧ any of an order (Monotremata) of mammals, consisting of the platypus and the echidnas, which lay eggs and have a single opening for the digestive and urinary tracts and genital organs —**mon′o·trem′a·tous** (-trem′ə təs, -trē′mə-) *adj.*

mo·not·ri·chous (mə nä′tri kəs) *adj.* ⟦MONO- + TRICH(O)- + -OUS⟧ having a single flagellum at one end, as some bacteria

mon·o·type (män′ō tīp′, män′ə-) *n.* ⟦MONO- + -TYPE⟧ **1** *Biol.* the only type of its group, as a single species constituting a genus, a single genus constituting a family, etc. **2** *Art a)* a unique print from a metal or glass plate on which a picture has been made, as with paint or ink *b)* the method of making such prints **3** *Printing* type produced by Monotype —☆[**M-**] *trademark for* a system for mechanically casting and setting metal type, used formerly in printing

mon·o·typ·ic (män′ō tip′ik) *adj.* **1** having only one type, as a genus consisting of only one species **2** having the nature of a monotype

mon·o·un·sat·u·rat·ed (män′ō un sach′ə rāt′id) *adj.* designating or of an organic compound, esp. an oil or fatty acid, having only one double bond: see POLYUNSATURATED, SATURATED (sense 4) —**mon′o·un·sat′u·rate** (-rət) *n.*

mon·o·va·lent (män′ō vā′lənt) *adj.* **1** designating an antibody, or antigen, that combines with only one specific antigen, or antibody **2** *a)* having one valence *b)* having a valence of one (see -VALENT) —**mon′o·va′lence** *n.*, **mon′o·va′len·cy**

mon·ox·ide (mə näk′sīd′) *n.* an oxide with one atom of oxygen in each molecule

mon·o·zy·got·ic (mä′nō zī gät′ik) *adj.* of or from one fertilized egg, as identical twins: also **mon·o·zy·gous** (mä′nə zī′gəs)

Mon·roe (mən rō′) **1 James** 1758-1831; 5th president of the U.S. (1817-25) **2 Marilyn** (born *Norma Jean Mortenson,* later changed to *Norma Jean Baker*) 1926-62; U.S. film actress

Monroe Doctrine the doctrine, essentially stated by President Monroe in a message to Congress (Dec., 1823), that the U.S. would regard as an unfriendly act any attempt by a European nation to interfere in the affairs of the American countries or increase its possessions on the American continents

Mon·ro·vi·a (mən rō′vē ə) seaport & capital of Liberia, on the Atlantic

mons (mänz) *n., pl.* **mon·tes** (män′tēz′) ⟦ModL < L, hill, MOUNT[1]⟧ **1** MONS PUBIS **2** MONS VENERIS

Mons[1] (mōns′) city in SW Belgium: capital of Hainaut province

Mons[2] *abbrev.* Monsieur

Mon·sei·gneur (män′sen yʉr′; *Fr* mōn se nyër′) *n., pl.* **Mes·sei·gneurs** (mes′en yʉrz′; *Fr* mā se nyër′) ⟦Fr, lit., my lord < *mon,* my + *seigneur,* lord < L *senior,* older: see SENIOR⟧ **1** a French title of honor given to persons of high birth or rank or to important church officers **2** [*often* **m-**] a person with this title

mon·sieur (mə syʉr′; *Fr* mə syö′) *n., pl.* **mes·sieurs** (mes′ərz; *Fr* mā syö′) ⟦Fr, lit., my lord (see SIRE): orig. applied to men of high position⟧ **1** a man; gentleman **2** [**M-**] French title, equivalent to *Mr.* or *Sir* Abbrev. *M* or *Mons*

Monsig *abbrev.* **1** Monseigneur **2** Monsignor

Mon·si·gnor (män sēn′yər) *n., pl.* **Mon·si′gnors** or **Mon′si·gno′ri** (-yôr′ē) ⟦It, lit., my lord, MONSEIGNEUR⟧ **1** a title given to certain dignitaries of the Roman Catholic Church **2** [*often* **m-**] a person who has this title

mon·soon (män sōōn′) *n.* ⟦MDu *monssoen* < Port *monção* < Ar *mausim,* a time, a season⟧ **1** a seasonal wind of the Indian Ocean and S Asia, blowing from the southwest from April to October, and from the northeast during the rest of the year **2** the season during which this wind blows from the southwest, characterized by heavy rains **3** any wind that reverses its direction seasonally or blows constantly between land and adjacent water —**mon·soon′al** *adj.*

mons pubis *pl.* **montes pubis** ⟦see MONS & PUBES[1]⟧ the fleshy, rounded area at the lower edge of the human, esp. female, abdomen, that becomes covered with pubic hair at puberty

mon·ster (män′stər) ***n.*** ⟦ME *monstre* < OFr < L *monstrum,* divine portent of misfortune, monster < *monere,* to admonish, warn: see MONITOR⟧ **1** any plant or animal of abnormal shape or structure, as one greatly malformed or lacking some parts; monstrosity **2** any imaginary or fictional creature regarded as unnatural, repulsive, terrifying, etc. **3** something monstrous **4** a person so cruel, wicked, depraved, etc. as to horrify others **5** *a)* any huge animal *b)* [Informal] any huge thing **6** [Archaic] a malformed fetus, esp. one with an excess or deficiency of limbs or parts —***adj.*** [Informal] huge; enormous

mon·ster·a (män′stər ə) ***n.*** any of a genus (*Monstera*) of tropical American plants of the arum family, esp., a tall species (*M. deliciosa*) with huge, deeply lobed leaves and an edible fruit

mon·strance (män′strəns) ***n.*** ⟦ME *munstraunce* < OFr *monstrance* < ML *monstrantia* < L *monstrare,* to show, akin to *monstrum:* see prec.⟧ *R.C.Ch.* a receptacle in which the consecrated Host is exposed for adoration

mon·stre sa·cré (mōn strə sȧ krā′) *pl.* ***mon·stres sa·crés*** (mōn strə sȧ krā′) ⟦Fr, lit., sacred monster⟧ a venerable or popular public figure who is considered above criticism or attack despite eccentricity, controversy, etc.

mon·stros·i·ty (män sträs′ə tē) ***n.*** ⟦LL *monstrositas*⟧ **1** the state or quality of being monstrous **2** *pl.* **-ties** something monstrous

mon·strous (män′strəs) ***adj.*** ⟦LME < OFr *monstreux* < L *monstrosus* < *monstrum:* see MONSTER⟧ **1** abnormally or prodigiously large; huge; enormous **2** very unnatural or abnormal in shape, type, or character **3** having the character or appearance of a monster **4** horrible; hideous; shocking **5** hideously wrong or evil; atrocious —***adv.*** [Chiefly Dial.] very; extremely —**SYN.** OUTRAGEOUS —**mon′strous·ly** ***adv.*** —**mon′strous·ness** ***n.***

mons ven·er·is (ven′ər is) *pl.* **montes veneris** ⟦L, lit., mount of Venus⟧ the mons pubis of the human female

Mont *abbrev.* Montana

mon·tage (män täzh′, mōn-) ***n.*** ⟦Fr, a mounting, setting together < *monter,* MOUNT[2]⟧ **1** *a)* the art or process of making a composite picture by bringing together into a single composition a number of different pictures or parts of pictures and arranging these, as by superimposing one on another, so that they form a blended whole while remaining distinct *b)* a picture so made **2** *Film a)* the process of editing *b)* the art or process of producing a sequence of abruptly alternating scenes or images or a sequence in which superimposed images are shown whirling about, flashing into focus, etc. *c)* such a sequence in a film **3** *a)* any similar technique, as in literature or music, of juxtaposing discrete or contrasting elements *b)* anything that is or is like the result of such a process —***vt.*** **-taged′**, **-tag′ing** to incorporate in a montage

Mon·ta·gnais (män′tən yā′) ***n.*** ⟦Fr, lit., mountaineer⟧ **1** *pl.* **-gnais′** (-yā′, -yāz′) or **-gnaises′** (-yāz′) a member of a North American Indian people of N Quebec **2** the Algonquian language of this people

Mon·ta·gnard (män′tən yärd′, mōn′-) ***n.*** ⟦Fr, lit., mountaineer < *montagne,* MOUNTAIN + *-ard,* -ARD⟧ a member of a people living in the hills of central and S Vietnam

Mon·ta·gu (män′tə gyōō′), Lady **Mary Wort·ley** (wurt′lē) (born *Mary Pierrepont*) 1689-1762; Eng. writer

Mon·ta·gue (män′tə gyōō′) ***n.*** the family name of Romeo in Shakespeare's *Romeo and Juliet*

Mon·taigne (män tān′; *Fr* mōn ten′y′), **Mi·chel (Eyquem) de** (mē shel′ də) 1533-92; Fr. essayist

Mon·ta·le (mōn tä′lā), **Eu·ge·nio** (ā′ōō jā′nyô) 1896-1981; It. poet

Mon·tan·a (män tan′ə) ⟦L *montana,* mountainous regions: see MOUNTAIN⟧ Mountain State of the NW U.S.: admitted 1889; 145,552 sq mi (376,979 sq km); cap. Helena: abbrev. *MT* or *Mont*

Mon·tan·an (-ən) ***adj.*** of Montana: usually used in the predicate —***n.*** a person born or living in Montana

mon·tane (män′tān′, män tān′) ***adj.*** ⟦< L *montanus*: see MOUNTAIN⟧ of or designating a cool, moist ecological zone usually located near the timberline and usually dominated by evergreen trees

mon·tan wax (män′tan) ⟦< L *montanus,* of a mountain (see MOUNTAIN) + WAX[1]⟧ a brown or whitish hydrocarbon wax extracted from lignite and peat, and used in making candles, polishes, etc.

Mon·tauk Point (män′tôk′) ⟦< Algonquian tribal name + POINT⟧ promontory at the easternmost tip of Long Island, N.Y.

Mont Blanc *see* BLANC, Mont

Mont·calm (mänt′käm′; *Fr* mōn kȧlm′), **Lou·is Jo·seph de** (lwē zhō zef′ də) (full name *Louis Joseph de Montcalm-Gozon,* Marquis *de Saint Véran*) 1712-59; Fr. general defeated & killed by Brit. forces under Wolfe at Quebec

Mont Cervin *see* CERVIN, Mont

mont-de-pié·té (mōnd pyā tā′) ***n.***, *pl.* ***monts-de-pié·té*** (mōnd pyā tā′) ⟦Fr < It *monte di pietà,* charitable bank, lit., mount of pity⟧ in France, etc., a government-regulated pawnshop for extending credit to the poor

☆**mon·te** (män′tē) ***n.*** ⟦Sp *monte,* lit., mountain, hence heap of cards (left after players have their shares) < L *mons* (gen. *montis*), MOUNT[1]⟧ **1** a gambling game of Spanish origin played with a special deck of forty cards, in which the players bet against a banker on the suit of cards to be turned up from the deck **2** *see* THREE-CARD MONTE

☆**Mon·te Car·lo**[1] (mänt′ə kär′lō, män′tē-) ⟦after fol.⟧ designating or of a method for obtaining an approximate solution to certain mathematical and physical problems, characteristically involving the replacement of a probability distribution by sample values

Mon·te Car·lo[2] (mänt′ə kär′lō, män′tē-) town in Monaco: gambling resort

mon·teith (män tēth′) ***n.*** ⟦said to be named after a 17th-c. Scot whose coat had a notched hem⟧ a large punch bowl, usually of silver, with a notched brim from which glasses and ladles are hung

Mon·te·ne·gro (mänt′ə nē′grō, -nā′grō; -neg′rō) country in the NW Balkan Peninsula, bordering on the Adriatic: formerly a kingdom and (1946–2003) a constituent republic of Yugoslavia and (2003–06) of Serbia and Montenegro: 5,415 sq mi (14,026 sq km); cap. Podgorica —**Mon′te·ne′grin** (-nē′grin, -nā′grin; -neg′rin) ***adj., n.***, **Mon′te·ne′gran** (-nē′grən, -nā′grən; -neg′rən)

Mon·te·rey (mänt′ə rā′) ⟦< Sp *Puerto de Monterrey,* lit., port of *Monterrey,* after the viceroy of New Spain (1602)⟧ city on the coast of central Calif.: former capital (until 1846) of Calif. region

☆**Monterey Jack** ⟦after *Monterey* County, Calif., where first made + JACK⟧ a mild, light-yellow, semisoft cheese

mon·te·ro (män ter′ō) ***n.***, *pl.* **-ros** ⟦Sp, hunter, lit., mountaineer < *monte,* hill < L *mons,* MOUNT[1]⟧ a round cap with a flap, of a style worn by Spanish huntsmen

Mon·ter·rey (mänt′ə rā′; *Sp* mōn′ter rā′) city in NE Mexico: capital of Nuevo León

mon·tes (män′tēz′) ***n.*** *pl. of* MONS

montes pubis *pl. of* MONS PUBIS

Mon·tes·quieu (män′təs kyōō′; *Fr* mōn tes kyö′), (Baron **de la Brède et de**) (born *Charles Louis de Secondat*) 1689-1755; Fr. jurist & political philosopher

Mon·tes·so·ri[1] (mänt′ə sôr′ē) ***adj.*** designating or of a method of educating young children, devised in 1907 by Maria Montessori, which emphasizes training of the senses and proceeds by guidance and self-direction rather than by rigid control of the child's activities

Mon·tes·so·ri[2] (mänt′ə sôr′ē), **Maria** 1870-1952; It. educator

montes ven·er·is (ven′ər is) *pl. of* MONS VENERIS

Mon·te·ver·di (mänt′ə ver′dē; *It* mōn′te ver′dē), **Clau·dio (Giovanni Antonio)** (klou′dyô) 1567-1643; It. composer

Mon·te·vi·de·o (mänt′ə vi dā′ō) seaport & capital of Uruguay

Mon·te·zu·ma (II) (mänt′ə zōō′mə) 1480?-1520; the last Aztec emperor of Mexico (1502-20)

☆**Montezuma's revenge** ⟦jocular euphemism: after prec.⟧ [Slang] acute infectious diarrhea, esp. when contracted by tourists visiting Mexico

Mont·fort (mänt′fərt) **1 Simon de** 1160?-1218; Fr. soldier: led crusade against Albigenses **2 Simon de** Earl of Leicester 1208?-65; Eng. statesman & soldier: son of Simon (Fr. soldier)

Mont·gom·er·y[1] (munt gum′ər ē, -gum′rē) **1 Bernard Law** (lô) 1st Viscount Montgomery of Alamein 1887-1976; Brit. field marshal in WWII **2 L(ucy) M(aud)** 1874-1942; Cdn. writer, esp. of novels

Mont·gom·er·y[2] (munt gum′ər ē, -gum′rē; mänt-) capital of Ala., in the SC part, on the Alabama River

Mont·gom·er·y·shire (-shir′, -shər) former county of central Wales, now mostly in Powys county: also **Mont·gom′er·y**

month (munth) ***n.*** ⟦ME < OE *monath,* akin to Ger *monat,* ON *manuthr* < Gmc **menōth-* < IE **mēnōt,* month, moon, var. of **mēn:* see MOON⟧ **1** any of the main parts (usually twelve) into which the calendar year is divided: also **calendar month** **2** *a)* the time from any date of one month to the corresponding date of the next *b)* a period of four weeks or 30 days **3** the period of a complete revolution of the moon around the earth with respect to some object; esp., *a)* the period (**synodic month**) marked by two successive lunar conjunctions with the sun, equal on the average to 29.53 days (also called **lunar month**) *b)* the sidereal month **4** one twelfth of the solar year: in full **solar month** —**month after month** every month or for many successive months —**month by month** each month —**month in, month out** every month —**month of Sundays** [Informal] a long time

month·ly (munth′lē) ***adj.*** **1** done, happening, payable, etc. once a month, or every month [*a monthly magazine*] **2** of a month, or of each month —***n.***, *pl.* **-lies** **1** a periodical published once a month **2** [*also pl.*] [Informal] menstruation —***adv.*** once a month; every month

month's mind *R.C.Ch.* a Mass said for the repose of the soul of a person on about the 30th day after the person's death

Mon·ti·cel·lo (män′tə sel′ō, -chel′ō) ⟦It, little mountain⟧ home & burial place of Thomas Jefferson, near Charlottesville, Va.

mon·ti·cule (män′ti kyōōl′) ***n.*** ⟦Fr < LL *monticulus,* dim. of L *mons,* MOUNT[1]⟧ **1** a small mountain or hill **2** a secondary cone of a volcano

Mont·mar·tre (mōn mȧr′tr′) district of Paris, in the N part: noted for its cafes and as an artists' quarter

mont·mo·ril·lon·ite (mänt′mə ril′ə nīt′) ***n.*** ⟦Fr, after *Montmorillon,* France + *-ite,* -ITE[1]⟧ any of a group of very soft, monoclinic clay minerals, $(Na,K,etc.)Al_2Si_4O_{10}(OH)_2 \cdot n\ H_2O$, that expand greatly in water or other liquids

Mont·par·nasse (mōn pȧr nȧs′) section of Paris, on the Left Bank

Mont·pel·ier (mänt pēl′yər) ⟦after fol.⟧ capital of Vt., in the NC part

Mont·pel·lier (mōn pel yā′) city in S France, near the Gulf of Lions

Mont·ra·chet (män′rə shā′, mänt′-; *Fr* mōn rȧ she′) ***n.*** ⟦Fr, after Le *Montrachet,* vineyard where it is produced⟧ **1** a dry white wine of N Burgundy **2** a soft goat cheese of N Burgundy

Mon·tre·al (män′trē ôl′, mun′-) ⟦Fr *Montréal,* after *Mont Royal,* Mount Royal, at its center⟧ **1** city & seaport in SW Quebec, Canada, on an island in the St. Lawrence River **2** this island: 201 sq mi (521 sq km) Fr. name **Mont·ré·al** (mōn rā ȧl′) —**Mon′tre·al′er** ***n.***

Montreal North borough of Montreal: Fr. name **Mont·ré·al-Nord** (mōn rā ȧl nôr′)

Mont·ser·rat (mänt′sə rat′) British island of the Leeward group, in the West Indies: 39.5 sq mi (102 sq km)

Mont-St-Mi·chel (mōn san mē shel′) islet just off the NW coast of France, noted for its fortified abbey

mon·u·ment (män′yə mənt) ***n.*** ⟦OFr < L *monumentum* < *monere,* to remind, warn: see MONITOR⟧ **1** something set up to keep alive the memory of a person or event, as a tablet, statue, pillar, building, etc.; specif., such a marker, statue, or structure placed over a grave or in a cemetery **2** a structure surviving from a former period **3** a writing or the like serving as a memorial **4** *a)* a work, production, etc. of enduring value or significance [*monuments* of learning] *b)* lasting or outstanding evidence or example ☆**5** a stone shaft or other object set in the earth to mark a boundary **6** [Obs.] *a)* a tomb; sepulcher *b)* a statue; effigy See also NATIONAL MONUMENT

mon·u·men·tal (män′yə ment′'l) ***adj.*** ⟦LL *monumentalis*⟧ **1** of, suitable for, or serving as a monument or monuments **2** like a monument; massive, enduring, etc. **3** historically notable, important, or of lasting value **4** very great; colossal [*monumental* ineptitude] **5** *Art* larger than life-size —**mon′u·men·tal′i·ty** (-mən tal′ə tē) ***n.*** —**mon′u·men′tal·ly** ***adv.***

mon·u·men·tal·ize (män′yə ment′'l īz′) ***vt.*** **-ized′**, **-iz′ing** to make a lasting memorial or record of, as with a monument

-mo·ny (mō′nē) ⟦L *-monia, -monium*⟧ *suffix* a resulting condition, state, or thing

Mon·za (môn′tsä) commune in N Italy

mon·zo·nite (män′zə nīt′) ***n.*** ⟦Ger *monzonit,* after Mt. *Monzoni* (in Tyrol), where it occurs⟧ a dark-colored, intrusive igneous rock containing orthoclase and plagioclase in nearly equal quantities, a small amount of quartz, and some biotite

moo (mo͞o) ***n.,*** *pl.* **moos** ⟦echoic⟧ the characteristic vocal sound made by a cow; lowing sound —***vi.*** **mooed**, **moo′ing** to make this sound; low

mooch (mo͞och) [Slang] ***vi.*** ⟦ME *mowchen,* dial. var. of *mychen,* to pilfer: see MICHE⟧ **1** to skulk or sneak **2** to loiter, loaf, or rove about **3** to get food, money, etc. by begging or sponging —***vt.*** **1** to steal; pilfer **2** to get by begging or sponging; cadge —***n.*** a person who sponges off others —**mooch′er** ***n.***

mood[1] (mo͞od) ***n.*** ⟦ME < OE *mod,* mind, soul, courage, akin to Ger *mut,* mental disposition, spirit, courage < IE base **me-*, to strive strongly, be energetic > L *mos,* custom, customary behavior⟧ **1** a particular state of mind or feeling; humor or temper **2** a predominant or pervading feeling, spirit, or tone **3** [*pl.*] fits of morose, sullen, or uncertain temper **4** [Obs.] anger —**in the mood for** having, for the moment, an inclination or fancy for [*in the mood for* ice cream]

SYN.—mood is the broadest of these terms referring to a temporary state of mind and emphasizes the constraining or pervading quality of the feeling [she's in a merry *mood*]; **humor** emphasizes the variability or capriciousness of the mood [he wept and laughed as his *humor* moved him]; **temper**, in this comparison, applies to a mood characterized by a single, strong emotion, esp. that of anger [my, he's in a nasty *temper!*]; **vein** stresses the transient nature of the mood [if I may speak in a serious *vein* for a moment]

mood[2] (mo͞od) ***n.*** ⟦< MODE, altered after prec.⟧ **1** *Gram. a)* a characteristic of verbs that involves the speaker's attitude toward the action expressed, indicating whether this is regarded as a fact (*indicative mood*), as a matter of supposition, desire, possibility, etc. (*subjunctive mood*), or as a command (*imperative mood*); also, an analytic category based on this characteristic (mood is shown by inflection, as in Latin, or analytically with auxiliaries, as English *may, might, should,* or by both) *b)* any of the forms a verb takes to indicate this characteristic **2** *Logic* any of the various forms of valid syllogisms, as determined by the quantity and quality of their constituent propositions

mood-al·ter·ing (mo͞od′ôl′tər iŋ) ***adj.*** capable of causing changes in mood: said esp. of drugs affecting chemical reactions in the brain

mood disorder *Psychol.* a psychiatric disorder, as depression or bipolar affective disorder, characterized by a prolonged period of abnormally altered mood

mood swing an abrupt change in a person's mood, as from elation to sadness, esp. when caused by an underlying physiological or psychiatric condition

mood·y (mo͞o′dē) ***adj.*** **mood′i·er**, **mood′i·est** ⟦ME *modi* < OE *modig*⟧ **1** subject to or characterized by gloomy, sullen moods or changes of mood **2** resulting from or indicating such a mood —**mood′i·ly** ***adv.*** —**mood′i·ness** ***n.***

Mood·y (mo͞o′dē), **Dwight L(yman)** 1837-99; U.S. Christian evangelist

☆**Moog (synthesizer)** (mōg) ⟦< *Moog,* formerly a trademark for this device, after R. A. *Moog* (1934-2005), U.S. engineer who developed it⟧ an early type of music synthesizer

moo goo gai pan (mo͞o′ go͞o gī pan′) ⟦Chin, lit., mushroom chicken slice⟧ a Chinese dish consisting of slices of chicken sautéed with black mushrooms and assorted vegetables

☆**mook** (mo͝ok) ***n.*** ⟦< ? MOKE⟧ [Slang] a person regarded as stupid, inept, negligible, etc.: a dismissive or contemptuous term

☆**moo·la** or **moo·lah** (mo͞o′lä′, -lə) ***n.*** ⟦< ?⟧ [Slang] money

moon (mo͞on) ***n.*** ⟦ME *mone* < OE *mona,* akin to Goth *mēna* < IE **mēn-*, month, moon (> L *mensis,* Gr *mēn,* month, *mēne,* moon) < base **mē-*, to MEASURE⟧ **1** [*often* **M-**] the celestial body that revolves around the earth from west to east in *c.* $27\frac{1}{3}$ days with reference to the stars and once in *c.* $29\frac{1}{2}$ days with reference to the sun, and that accompanies the earth in its yearly revolution about the sun: diameter, *c.* 3,476 km (*c.* 2,160 mi); mean distance from the earth, *c.* 384,404 km (*c.* 238,857 mi); mean density, *c.* $\frac{3}{5}$ that of the earth; mass, *c.* $\frac{1}{81}$; volume, *c.* $\frac{1}{49}$: with *the* **2** this body as it appears during a particular lunar month or period of time, or at a particular time of the month: see NEW MOON, CRESCENT, HALF-MOON, FULL MOON, OLD MOON, FIRST QUARTER, LAST QUARTER **3** a month; esp., a lunar month **4** MOONLIGHT **5** anything shaped like the moon (i.e., an orb or crescent) **6** any natural satellite; esp., a natural satellite of a planet —***vi.*** **1** ⟦from the notion of behaving as if moonstruck⟧ to behave in an idle, dreamy, or abstracted way, as when in love **2** ⟦from an earlier slang use of the n., meaning "buttocks"⟧ [Slang] to engage in the prank of momentarily baring one's buttocks in public —***vt.*** **1** to pass (time) in mooning **2** [Slang] to expose one's buttocks to (someone) as a prank

moon·beam (mo͞on′bēm′) ***n.*** a ray of moonlight

moon-blind (-blīnd′) ***adj.*** having moon blindness

moon blindness **1** night blindness: formerly attributed to the effects of moonlight **2** a disease of horses, of undetermined cause, characterized by recurrent inflammation of the eyes and, eventually, blindness

moon·calf (-kaf′) ***n.*** ⟦from the notion of being influenced by the moon: see LUNATIC⟧ [Archaic] an idiot or fool

☆**moon child** ⟦because the sign is ruled by the moon⟧ *Astrol.* a person born under the sign of Cancer

mooned (mo͞ond) ***adj.*** **1** round or crescent like the moon **2** decorated with moon-shaped marks

moon-eyed (mo͞on′īd′) ***adj.*** **1** MOON-BLIND **2** having the eyes wide open, as from fright or wonder

moon-faced (-fāst′) ***adj.*** having a round face

moon·fish (-fish′) ***n.,*** *pl.* **-fish′** or **-fish′es** (see FISH) **1** either of two species (genus *Selene*) of deep-bodied, sharply compressed jack fishes of the coastal waters of North and South America ☆**2** OPAH

moon·flow·er (-flou′ər) ***n.*** any of a genus (*Calonyction*) of tropical American, perennial twining vines of the morning-glory family, with heart-shaped leaves and large, fragrant white or purple flowers that bloom at night

moon gate a large, circular opening in a wall, through which one can step: originally a feature of Chinese architecture

moon·less (mo͞on′lis) ***adj.*** without moonlight, as during a new moon

moon·let (mo͞on′lit) ***n.*** a small moon or artificial satellite

moon·light (mo͞on′līt′) ***n.*** the light of the moon —***adj.*** **1** of moonlight **2** lighted by the moon **3** done or occurring by moonlight, or at night —***vi.*** ☆to engage in moonlighting —**moon′light′er** ***n.***

☆**moon·light·ing** (-līt′iŋ) ***n.*** ⟦from the usual night hours of such jobs⟧ the practice of holding a second regular job in addition to one's main job

moon·lit (-lit′) ***adj.*** lighted by the moon

☆**moon·port** (mo͞on′pôrt′) ***n.*** ⟦MOON + (AIR)PORT⟧ an installation for launching rockets to the moon

☆**moon·quake** (-kwāk′) ***n.*** a trembling of the surface of the moon, thought to be caused by internal rock slippage or, possibly, meteorite impact

moon·rise (-rīz′) ***n.*** **1** the rising of the upper limb of the moon above the earth's horizon ☆**2** the time of this

moon·scape (-skāp′) ***n.*** ⟦MOON + (LAND)SCAPE⟧ the surface of the moon or a representation of it

moon·seed (mo͞on′sēd′) ***n.*** any of a genus (*Menispermum*) of twining vines of the moonseed family, with small clusters of purple berries and crescent-shaped seeds —***adj.*** designating a family (Menispermaceae, order Ranunculales) of tropical dicotyledonous lianas, shrubs, and trees

moon·set (mo͞on′set′) ***n.*** **1** the passing of the upper limb of the moon below the earth's horizon **2** the time of this

moon·shine (-shīn′) ***n.*** **1** MOONLIGHT **2** foolish or empty talk, notions, plans, etc.; nonsense **3** [Informal] *a)* smuggled whiskey ☆*b)* whiskey unlawfully distilled; often, specif., such whiskey made from corn and not matured in barrels

moon·shin·er (-shīn′ər) ***n.*** ☆[Informal] a person who makes and sells alcoholic liquor unlawfully

moon·shin·y (-shīn′ē) ***adj.*** **1** lighted by the moon **2** like or suggestive of moonlight **3** unreal, visionary, etc.

☆**moon·shot** (mo͞on′shät′) ***n.*** the launching of a spacecraft to the moon

moon·stone (mo͞on′stōn′) ***n.*** a milky-white, translucent feldspar with a pearly luster, used as a gem

moon·struck (mo͞on′struk′) ***adj.*** affected mentally in some way, supposedly by the influence of the moon; specif., *a)* crazed; lunatic; insane *b)* romantically dreamy *c)* dazed or distracted Also **moon′strick′en** (-strik′ən)

☆**moon·walk** (mo͞on′wôk′) ***n.*** a walking about by an astronaut on the surface of the moon

NEW MOON
WAXING CRESCENT
FIRST QUARTER
WAXING GIBBOUS
FULL MOON
WANING GIBBOUS
LAST QUARTER
WANING CRESCENT

phases of the moon

moon·wort (-wʉrt′) *n.* **1** any of a genus (*Botrychium,* family Ophioglossaceae) of ferns bearing a leafy part that is divided into sterile and fertile segments **2** HONESTY (sense 2)
moon·y (mo͞on′ē) *adj.* **moon′i·er, moon′i·est 1** of or characteristic of the moon **2** like the moon, esp. in shape; round or crescent-shaped **3** lighted by the moon **4** like moonlight **5** mooning; listless; dreamy
moor[1] (moor) *n.* ⟦ME *more* < OE *mor,* wasteland, akin to LowG *mor* < IE base **mori-,* sea > MARSH, MERE[2], L *mare,* sea: basic sense "swampy coastland"⟧ [Brit.] **1** [*often pl.*] a tract of open, rolling wasteland, usually covered with heather and often marshy or peaty; heath **2** a tract of land with game preserves
moor[2] (moor) *vt.* ⟦Early ModE < or akin to MDu *maren,* LowG *moren,* to tie⟧ **1** to hold (a ship, etc.) in place by cables or chains attached as to a pier or special buoy (**mooring buoy**), or by two anchors **2** to cause to be held in place; secure —*vi.* **1** to moor a ship, etc. **2** to be secured as by cables
Moor (moor) *n.* ⟦ME *More* < OFr *More, Maure* < L *Maurus,* a Moor, Mauritanian < Gr *Mauros*⟧ **1** a member of a Muslim people of mixed Arab and Berber descent living in NW Africa **2** a member of a group from this people that invaded and occupied Spain in the 8th cent. A.D. —**Moor′ish** *adj.*
moor·age (moor′ij) *n.* **1** a mooring or being moored **2** a place for mooring **3** a charge for the use of such a place
moor·cock (-käk′) *n.* [Brit.] the male moorfowl, or red grouse
Moore (moor) **1 G(eorge) E(dward)** 1873-1958; Eng. philosopher **2 George (Augustus)** 1852-1933; Ir. novelist, playwright, & critic **3 Henry** 1898-1986; Eng. sculptor **4 Marianne (Craig)** 1887-1972; U.S. poet **5 Thomas** 1779-1852; Ir. poet
moor·fowl (moor′foul′) *n.* [Brit.] RED GROUSE
moor·hen (-hen′) *n.* **1** [Brit.] the female moorfowl, or red grouse **2** the nearly worldwide common gallinule (*Gallinula chloropus*)
moor·ing (moor′iŋ) *n.* **1** the act of a person or thing that moors **2** [*often pl.*] the lines, cables, etc. by which a ship, etc. is moored **3** [*pl.*] a place where a ship, etc. is or can be moored **4** [*often pl.*] beliefs, habits, ties, etc. that make one feel secure
moor·land (-lənd) *n.* [Brit.] MOOR[1]
☆**moose** (mo͞os) *n., pl.* **moose** ⟦< Eastern Abenaki *mos*⟧ a deer (*Alces alces*) of N regions, the male of which has huge spatulate antlers and weighs up to 815 kg (*c.* 1,800 lb): it is the largest of the deer family

moose

moose·bird (mo͞os′burd′) *n.* [Cdn.] CANADA JAY
Moose·head Lake (mo͞os′hed′) ⟦transl. of AmInd name⟧ lake in WC Me.: 117 sq mi (303 sq km)
moo shu pork (mo͞o′ sho͞o) a Chinese dish made of shredded pork and vegetables and beaten eggs, sautéed and usually served in a crêpe with hoisin sauce
moot (mo͞ot) *n.* ⟦ME *mote* < OE *mot, gemot,* a meeting & prob. ON *mot* < Gmc base **mot-* > Goth *gamotjan,* to meet⟧ **1** a medieval English assembly of freemen to administer justice, decide community problems, etc. **2** a discussion or argument, esp. of a hypothetical law case, as in a law school —*adj.* **1** subject to or open for discussion or debate; debatable [*a moot* point] **2** not worthy of consideration or discussion because it has been resolved or it no longer needs to be resolved —*vt.* **1** to debate or discuss **2** to propose or bring up for discussion or debate **3** to make so hypothetical as to deprive of significance; make academic or theoretical
moot court a mock court in which hypothetical cases are argued, usually as an academic exercise for students
mop[1] (mäp) *n.* ⟦Early ModE *mappe,* naut. term < ? Walloon *mappe* < L *mappa,* napkin: see MAP⟧ **1** a bundle of loose rags or strands of yarn, a sponge, etc. fastened to the end of a long stick, as for washing or wiping floors **2** anything suggestive of this, as a thick head of hair —*vt.* **mopped, mop′ping** to wash, rub, wipe, or remove with or as with a mop: often with *up* —**mop up 1** [Informal] *a)* to bring to an end; finish *b)* to defeat completely **2** *Mil. a)* to clear (an area) of isolated or scattered remnants of beaten enemy forces *b)* to kill or capture (such remnants) **3** [Informal] to finish a task —**mop (up) the floor with** [Slang] to defeat decisively —**mop′per** *n.*
mop[2] (mäp) *n., vi.* **mopped, mop′ping** ⟦< or akin to MDu *moppen,* MHG *muffen,* to grimace: for base see MOPE⟧ [Archaic] GRIMACE
☆**mop·board** (mäp′bôrd′) *n.* BASEBOARD
mope (mōp) *vi.* **moped, mop′ing** ⟦akin to MDu *mopen,* Swed dial. *mopa* < IE base **mu-,* echoic of sound made with tightly closed lips > MUTTER, L *mutus*⟧ to be gloomy, dull, apathetic, and dispirited —*vt.* **1** to make gloomy, dull, etc.: used reflexively and in the passive **2** to pass in gloom, dullness, etc.: with *away* —*n.* **1** a person who mopes or is inclined to mope **2** [*pl.*] low spirits: with *the* —**mop′er** *n.* —**mop′ey** or **mop′y** *adj.* **mop′i·er, mop′i·est** —**mop′ish** *adj.* —**mop′ish·ly** *adv.*
mo·ped (mō′ped′) *n.* ⟦Ger < *mo(torisiertes) ped(al),* lit., motorized pedal⟧ a bicycle propelled by a small motor
mop·pet (mäp′it) *n.* ⟦dim. of ME *moppe,* rag doll < ?⟧ [Informal] a little child: a term of affection
mop·top (mäp′täp′) *n.* **1** a man's or boy's hairstyle in which the hair is worn in a long bob **2** [Informal] a person with such a hairstyle
mop-up (mäp′up′) *n.* **1** *Mil.* a clearing out or rounding up of scattered remnants of beaten enemy forces in an area **2** [Informal] the final phase of a project or task: often used attributively
mo·quette (mō ket′) *n.* ⟦Fr⟧ a kind of carpet or upholstery fabric with a thick, soft, napped surface
mor (môr) *n.* ⟦Dan, humus < or akin to ON *morth,* a quantity, mass < IE base **mer-,* to rub, grind: see MORDANT⟧ a layer of humus, usually matted or compact, that accumulates on the surface of moist, cool soil
Mor *abbrev.* **1** Morocco **2** Moroccan
MOR *abbrev.* middle-of-the-road: used variously in radio broadcasting to designate styles of popular music that are not extreme
mo·ra (môr′ə, mō′rə) *n., pl.* **mo·rae** (môr′ē, mō′rē) or **mo′ras** ⟦L, delay: see MERIT⟧ **1** *Linguis.* an arbitrary unit of syllabic length **2** *Prosody* the unit of metrical time, equal to the ordinary short syllable, usually indicated by a breve (˘)
Mo·rad·a·bad (mə räd′ə bäd′) city in central Uttar Pradesh, N India
mo·raine (mə rān′, mô-) *n.* ⟦Fr < dial. *morêna* < *morre,* muzzle, akin to Sp *morro,* snout, headland < VL **murru,* echoic word for snout⟧ a mound, ridge, or mass of rocks, gravel, sand, clay, etc. carried and deposited directly by a glacier, along its side (**lateral moraine**), at its lower end (**terminal moraine**), or beneath the ice (**ground moraine**) —**mo·rain′al** *adj.,* **mo·rain′ic**
mor·al (môr′əl, mär′-; *for n. 4,* mə ral′) *adj.* ⟦ME < L *moralis,* of manners or customs < *mos* (gen. *moris*), pl. *mores,* manners, morals (see MOOD[1]): used by CICERO[2] as transl. of Gr *ēthikos*⟧ **1** relating to, dealing with, or capable of making the distinction between right and wrong in conduct **2** relating to, serving to teach, or in accordance with the principles of right and wrong **3** good or right in conduct or character; sometimes, specif., virtuous in sexual conduct **4** designating support, etc. that involves approval and sympathy without action **5** being virtually such because of its effect on thoughts, attitudes, etc., or because of its general results [*a moral* victory] **6** based on strong probability [*a moral* certainty] **7** based on the principle of right conduct rather than legality [*a moral* obligation] **8** *Law* based on general observation of people, on analogy, etc. rather than on what is demonstrable [*moral* evidence] —*n.* **1** *a)* a moral implication or moral lesson taught by a fable, event, etc. *b)* a statement of this lesson, typically the concluding statement of a fable or story **2** [*pl.*] principles, standards, or habits with respect to right or wrong in conduct; ethics; sometimes, specif., standards of sexual behavior —**mor′al·ly** *adv.*

SYN.—**moral** implies conformity with the generally accepted standards of goodness or rightness in conduct or character, sometimes, specif., in sexual conduct [*a moral* person]; **ethical** implies conformity with an elaborated, ideal code of moral principles, sometimes, specif., with the code of a particular profession [*an ethical* lawyer]; **virtuous** implies a morally excellent character, connoting justice, integrity, and often, specif., chastity; **righteous** implies a being morally blameless or justifiable [*righteous* anger] —*ANT.* **immoral**

mo·rale (mə ral′, mô-) *n.* ⟦Fr, fem. of *moral* < L *moralis:* see prec.⟧ moral or mental condition with respect to courage, discipline, confidence, enthusiasm, willingness to endure hardship, etc. within a group, in relation to a group, or within an individual
moral hazard the risk that providing insurance or other indemnification will foster careless, reckless, or dishonest behavior among those receiving such protection
mor·al·ism (môr′ə liz′əm, mär′-) *n.* **1** moral teaching; moralizing **2** a moral maxim **3** belief in or practice of a system of ethics apart from religion
mor·al·ist (môr′ə list, mär′-) *n.* **1** a teacher of or writer on morals; person who moralizes **2** a person who adheres to a system of moralism **3** a person who seeks to impose personal morals on others
mor·al·is·tic (môr′ə lis′tik, mär′-) *adj.* **1** moralizing **2** of moralism or moralists —**mor′al·is′ti·cal·ly** *adv.*
mo·ral·i·ty (mə ral′i tē, mô-) *n., pl.* **-ties** ⟦ME *moralite* < OFr < LL *moralitas* < L *moralis*⟧ **1** moral quality or character; rightness or wrongness, as of an action **2** the character of being in accord with the principles or standards of right conduct; right conduct; sometimes, specif., virtue in sexual conduct **3** principles of right and wrong in conduct; ethics **4** a particular system of such principles **5** moral instruction or a moral lesson **6** a narrative with a moral lesson **7** MORALITY PLAY
morality play any of a class of allegorical dramas of the 15th and 16th cent., the characters of which personify such abstractions as Everyman, Vice, and Virtue
mor·al·ize (môr′ə līz′, mär′-) *vi.* **-ized′, -iz′ing** ⟦Fr *moraliser* < LL *moralizare* < L *moralis*⟧ to think, write, or speak about matters of right and wrong, often in a self-righteous or tedious way —*vt.* **1** *a)* to interpret or explain in terms of right and wrong *b)* to point out the moral in or draw a moral from **2** to improve the morals of —**mor′al·i·za′tion** *n.* —**mor′al·iz′er** *n.*
moral philosophy ETHICS
mo·rass (mə ras′, mô-) *n.* ⟦Du *moeras,* a marsh, fen; earlier *marasch* < OFr *maresc* < Frank **marisk,* a swamp, akin to MARSH⟧ a tract of low, soft, watery ground; bog; marsh; swamp: often used fig. of a difficult, troublesome, or perplexing state of affairs
mor·a·to·ri·um (môr′ə tôr′ē əm) *n., pl.* **-ri·ums** or **-ri·a** (-ə) ⟦ModL < neut. of LL *moratorius,* delaying < L *morari,* to delay < *mora,* a delay: see MERIT⟧ **1**

a legal authorization, usually by a law passed in an emergency, to delay payment of money due, as by a bank or debtor nation **2** the effective period of such an authorization **3** any authorized delay or stopping of some specified activity

mor·a·to·ry (môr′ə tôr′ē) ***adj.*** ⟦LL *moratorius:* see prec.⟧ delaying or postponing; esp., designating or of a law authorizing a moratorium

Mo·ra·va (môr′ə və) **1** *Czech name for* MORAVIA[2] **2** river in Moravia flowing south along the Austrian border, into the Danube: *c.* 230 mi (370 km) **3** river in E Serbia, flowing north into the Danube: 134 mi (216 km)

Mo·ra·vi·a[1] (mô rä′vē ə, -rä′-), **Al·ber·to** (al bur′tō, -ber′tō) (born *Alberto Pincherle*) 1907-90; It. writer

Mo·ra·vi·a[2] (mô rā′vē ə) historical region in the E Czech Republic (formerly in Czechoslovakia)

Mo·ra·vi·an (-ən) ***adj.*** **1** of Moravia or its people or culture **2** of the religious sect of Moravians **—*n.*** **1** a person born or living in Moravia **2** the variety of Czech spoken in Moravia **3** a member of a Protestant sect founded in Saxony (*c.* 1722) by disciples of John Huss from Moravia

☆**mo·ray** (môr′ā′, mô rā′) ***n.*** ⟦Port *moreia* < L *muraena,* kind of fish < Gr *myraina*⟧ any of a family (Muraenidae, order Anguilliformes) of voracious eels of warm seas, characterized by brilliant coloring and found esp. among coral reefs: the Mediterranean moray is valued as a food fish: in full **moray eel**

Mor·ay (mur′ē) administrative division of NE Scotland: formerly a county & district

Moray Firth inlet of the North Sea, on the NE coast of Scotland

mor·bid (môr′bid) ***adj.*** ⟦L *morbidus,* sickly, diseased < *morbus,* disease < IE base **mer-,* to rub, wear away, destroy > MARE[3], L *mortarium,* OIr *meirb,* lifeless⟧ **1** of, having, or caused by disease; unhealthy; diseased **2** resulting from or as from a diseased state of mind; esp., having or showing an unwholesome tendency to dwell on gruesome or gloomy matters **3** gruesome; grisly; horrible *[the morbid* details of a story*]* **4** of diseased parts; pathological *[morbid* anatomy*]* **5** [Obs.] causing disease **—mor′bid·ly *adv.* —mor′bid·ness *n.***

mor·bid·i·ty (môr bid′ə tē) ***n., pl.* -ties** **1** state, quality, or instance of being morbid **2** the rate of disease or proportion of diseased persons in a given locality, nation, etc.

mor·bif·ic (môr bif′ik) ***adj.*** ⟦Fr *morbifique* < LL *morbificare,* to produce disease < L *morbus,* disease (see MORBID) + *facere,* to make, DO[1]⟧ causing or leading to disease

mor·bil·li (môr bil′ī′) ***pl.n.*** ⟦ML, pl. of *morbillus,* dim. of L *morbus,* disease⟧ *former term for* MEASLES

mor·ceau (môr sō′) ***n., pl.* -ceaux′** (-sō′) ⟦Fr: see MORSEL⟧ **1** a morsel; bit; fragment **2** a short composition, passage, or excerpt, as of poetry or music

mor·da·cious (môr dā′shəs) ***adj.*** ⟦< L *mordax* (gen. *mordacis*), biting < base of *mordere,* to bite: see fol. & -OUS⟧ biting, sharp, acrid, or caustic **—mor·da′cious·ly *adv.* —mor·dac′i·ty** (-das′ə tē) ***n.***

mor·dant (môr′dənt) ***adj.*** ⟦ME *mordent* < OFr *mordant,* prp. of *mordre,* to bite < L *mordere* < IE **merd-,* var. of base **mer-:* see MORBID⟧ **1** biting, cutting, caustic, or sarcastic: said of speech, wit, etc. **2** causing corrosion **3** acting as a mordant **—*n.*** **1** a substance used in dyeing to fix the coloring matter, as a metallic compound that combines with the organic dye to form an insoluble colored compound, or lake, in the fiber of the fabric **2** an acid or other corrosive substance used in etching to bite lines, areas, etc. into the surface **—*vt.*** to treat or impregnate with a mordant **—mor′dan·cy *n.* —mor′dant·ly *adv.***

Mor·de·cai (môr′də kī′) ***n.*** ⟦Heb *mordĕkhai*⟧ **1** a masculine name: dim. *Mordy* **2** *Bible* the cousin of Esther (in the Book of Esther), who saved the Jews from the destruction planned by Haman: cf. PURIM

mor·dent (môr′dənt) ***n.*** ⟦Ger < It *mordente,* prp. of *mordere* < L, to bite: see MORDANT⟧ *Music* an ornament made by a single rapid alternation of a principal tone with a subsidiary tone a half step or whole step below: in a **double mordent** there are two alternations: in an **inverted mordent** the subsidiary tone is a half step or whole step above the principal tone

WRITTEN PLAYED
SINGLE
WRITTEN PLAYED
DOUBLE

mordents

mor·di·da (mōr thē′thä) ***n., pl.* -das** ⟦AmSp, lit., a bite⟧ a bribe

Mor·dred (môr′dred′) ***n.*** *Arthurian Legend* treacherous nephew (in some versions, son) of King Arthur: they kill each other in battle

more (môr) ***adj.*** ⟦ME < OE *mara,* greater, used as compar. of *mycel,* big, much (see MUCH): akin to Goth *maiza* < IE base **mē-, *mō-,* big⟧ **1** greater in amount, degree, or number: often used as the comparative of MUCH or MANY *[*we have *more* time than we thought*]* **2** additional; further *[*take *more* tea*]* **—*n.*** **1** a greater amount, quantity, or degree **2** *[with pl. v.] a)* a greater number (of persons or things) *[more* of us are going*] b)* a greater number of persons or things **3** something additional or further *[more* can be said*]* **4** something of greater importance **—*adv.*** ⟦< the above, replacing earlier *mo* (OE *ma*) < IE positive **me-ro-s, *mō-ro-s* < **mē-, *mō-*⟧ **1** in or to a greater degree or extent: used with many adjectives and adverbs (regularly with those of three or more syllables) to form the comparative degree *[more* satisfying, *more* intensely*]* **2** in addition; further; again; longer **—more and more** **1** to an increasing degree; increasingly **2** a constantly increasing amount, quantity, degree, or number (of persons or a specified thing) **—more or less** **1** to some extent **2** approximately **—no more** **1** not more; nothing further *[*let's have *no more* of your insolence*]* **2** no longer in existence *[*the glory that was Rome is *no more]*

More (môr) **1 Hannah** 1745-1833; Eng. writer, esp. of religious tracts **2 Sir Thomas** 1478-1535; Eng. statesman & writer: executed: canonized in 1935: also called **Saint Thomas More**

Mo·re·a (mô rē′ə) *former name for* PELOPONNESUS

mo·reen (mō rēn′, mə-) ***n.*** ⟦prob. < MOIRÉ + *-een,* as in VELVETEEN⟧ a strong fabric, as of wool or cotton, having, esp. formerly, a moiré, or watered, finish

mo·rel (mə rel′, mô-) ***n.*** ⟦Fr *morille* < MDu *morilhe* < OHG *morhila,* dim. of *morha,* carrot, akin to OE *more* < Gmc **morhon* < IE base **mrk-,* edible root > Gr *brakana,* wild herbs⟧ any of a genus (*Morchella*) of edible ascomycetous mushrooms resembling a sponge on a stalk

Mo·re·lia (mô re′lyä) city in central Mexico: capital of Michoacán

mo·rel·lo (mō rel′ō) ***n., pl.* -los** ⟦Fl *marelle,* aphetic < *amarelle* < Ger: see AMARELLE⟧ any of several varieties of sour cherry with dark-red skin and red juice

Mo·re·los (mô re′lôs) state in SC Mexico: 1,908 sq mi (4,942 sq km); cap. Cuernavaca

Mo·re·no Valley (mə rē′nō) city in S Calif.

more·o·ver (môr ō′vər) ***adv.*** in addition to what has been said; besides; further; also: used with conjunctive force

☆**mo·res** (môr′āz′; *also* môr′ēz′) ***pl.n.*** ⟦L, pl. of *mos,* custom: see MOOD[1]⟧ ways of thinking and behaving shared generally by a society or group

more·so (môr′sō′) ***adv.*** *disputed sp. of* more so

Mo·resque (mô resk′) ***adj.*** ⟦Fr < Sp *morisco* < *Moro* < L *Maurus,* MOOR⟧ Moorish in design or decoration, etc. **—*n.*** Moorish design or decoration, characterized by intricate tracery, bright colors, gilt, etc.

Mor·gan[1] (môr′gən) ***n.*** ⟦after Justin *Morgan* (1747-98), New Englander who owned the sire of the breed⟧ ☆any of a breed of strong, light riding horse, usually bay, chestnut, or black in color

Mor·gan[2] (môr′gən) ***n.*** ⟦Welsh, lit., sea dweller (< *mor,* sea: see MARE[2]), akin to Ir *Muirgen*⟧ a masculine and feminine name

Mor·gan[3] (môr′gən) **1 Daniel** 1736-1802; Am. Revolutionary general **2 Sir Henry** 1635?-88; Welsh buccaneer in the Spanish Main **3 John Hunt** 1825-64; Confederate general in the Civil War **4 John Pier·pont** (pir′pänt′) 1867-1943; U.S. financier: son of J. P. Morgan **5 J(ohn) P(ierpont)** 1837-1913; U.S. financier **6 Lewis Henry** 1818-81; U.S. anthropologist **7 Thomas Hunt** 1866-1945; U.S. geneticist

mor·ga·nat·ic (môr′gə nat′ik) ***adj.*** ⟦< ML *(matrimonium ad) morganaticam,* (marriage with) morning gift < *morganaticum,* altered < OHG *morgengeba,* lit., morning gift: gift given to a bride on the day after her marriage (in lieu of any share in the husband's property)⟧ designating or of a form of marriage between a royal or noble person and a person of inferior rank, with the provision that neither the spouse of inferior rank nor any children from the marriage may lay claim to the rank or property of the other spouse **—mor′ga·nat′i·cal·ly *adv.***

☆**mor·gan·ite** (môr′gən īt′) ***n.*** ⟦after J. P. MORGAN[3]⟧ a transparent, rose-colored variety of beryl, used as a gem

Mor·gan le Fay (môr′gən lə fā′) ⟦OFr *Morgain la fée,* lit., Morgan the fairy < Celt, as in OIr *Morrigain,* queen of the incubi, sorceress < **mor-* < IE base **mori-* (see MARE[3]) + OIr *rigain,* queen < IE base **reg-,* to rule: see REGAL⟧ *Arthurian Legend* the evil half sister of King Arthur: in other legends, variously a fairy, water spirit, etc.

mor·gen (môr′gən) ***n., pl.* -gen** or **-gens** ⟦Du & Ger, lit., MORNING: hence area plowed in one morning⟧ **1** a unit of land measure formerly used in the Netherlands and its possessions, and still used in South Africa, equal to about 2 acres **2** a unit of land measure formerly used in Prussia, Denmark, and Norway, equal to about ⅔ acre

Mor·gen·thau (môr′gən thô′), **Henry, Jr.** 1891-1967; U.S. public official: secretary of the treasury (1934-45)

morgue (môrg) ***n.*** ⟦Fr, morgue, earlier, identification room of a prison: orig., "haughty air" < dial. *morre,* snout: see MORAINE⟧ **1** a place where the bodies of unknown dead persons or those dead of unknown causes are kept to be examined, identified, etc. before burial or cremation ☆**2** ⟦so named in ref. to the dead news it contains⟧ the collection of back numbers, photographs, clippings, etc. kept in the office of a newspaper, magazine, etc.

mor·i·bund (môr′i bund′) ***adj.*** ⟦L *moribundus,* dying < *mori,* to die: see MORTAL⟧ **1** dying **2** coming to an end **3** having little or no vital force left **—mor′i·bund′i·ty *n.***

mo·ri·on[1] (môr′ē än′) ***n.*** ⟦OFr < Sp *morrión* < *morra,* crown of the head, snout: see MORAINE⟧ a hatlike, crested helmet without a beaver or visor and with a curved brim coming to a peak in front and in back, worn in the 16th and 17th cent.

mo·ri·on[2] (môr′ē än′) ***n.*** ⟦misreading of L *mormorion* (in early editions of PLINY)⟧ a variety of quartz, dark-brown to black in color

Mo·ris·co (mô ris′kō) ***adj.*** ⟦Sp < *Moro* < L *Maurus,* MOOR⟧ Moorish **—*n., pl.* -cos** or **-coes** a Moor of Spain, specif., one forced to convert to Christianity though often continuing to practice Islam secretly

Mor·i·son (môr′ə sən), **Samuel Eliot** 1887-1976; U.S. historian

Mo·ri·sot (mô rē zō′), **Berthe** (bert) 1841-95; Fr. impressionist painter

☆**Mor·mon** (môr′mən) ***n.*** ⟦explained by Joseph SMITH as *more mon,* more good⟧ a member of the Church of Jesus Christ of Latter-day Saints (commonly called the **Mormon Church**), founded in the U.S. in 1830 by Joseph Smith: among its sacred books is the Book of Mormon, represented by

Smith as his translation of an account of some ancient American peoples by a prophet among them named Mormon *—adj.* of the Mormons or their religion **—Mor′mon·ism′** *n.*

morn (môrn) *n.* ⟦ME *morne* < OE contr. of *morgene,* dat. of *morgen,* MORNING⟧ [Old Poet.] morning

Mor·nay (môr nā′), **Phi·lippe de** (fē lēp′ də) Seigneur du Plessis-Marly 1549-1623; Fr. diplomat & Huguenot leader: also *Duplessis-Mornay*

Mor·nay sauce (môr nā′) ⟦prob. after prec.⟧ a rich white sauce to which grated cheese, usually Swiss or Parmesan, and seasonings have been added

morn·ing (môr′niŋ) *n.* ⟦ME *morweninge* (by analogy with EVENING) < OE *morgen,* morning, akin to Ger < IE base **mer(e)k-,* to glimmer, twilight > obs. Czech *mrkati,* to dawn, grow dark⟧ **1** the first or early part of the day, from midnight, or esp. dawn, to noon **2** the first or early part [the *morning* of life] **3** the dawn; daybreak *—adj.* of, in, or for the morning

morning after [Informal] the morning after a night of excess, when one experiences a hangover, feelings of regret, etc.

morn·ing-af·ter (-af′tər) *adj.* [Informal] **1** of or occurring in the aftermath of some activity, event, etc. of the previous day or night, specif. of an evening of heavy drinking **2** designating or of a pill taken after sexual intercourse to prevent pregnancy

morning dress formal daytime dress for men, including a cutaway (**morning coat**)

☆**morning glory** any of a genus (*Ipomoea*) of plants of the morning-glory family; esp., a twining annual vine (*I. purpurea*), with heart-shaped leaves and trumpet-shaped flowers of lavender, blue, pink, or white

☆**morn·ing-glo·ry** (môr′niŋ glôr′ē) *adj.* designating a family (Convolvulaceae, order Solanales) of twining dicotyledonous vines and some erect shrubs and trees with flowers having five sepals and a funnel-shaped corolla, including some bindweeds and the jalaps and sweet potatoes

morning prayer [*often* **M- P-**] **1** *R.C.Ch.* the second of the canonical hours; lauds **2** *Anglican Ch.* the service assigned to the morning

morn·ings (môr′niŋz) *adv.* during every morning or most mornings

morning sickness a condition of nausea and vomiting, sometimes accompanied by dizziness, headache, etc., affecting many women during the first months of pregnancy and occurring typically in the morning

morning star a planet, esp. Venus, visible in the eastern sky before sunrise; daystar

Mo·ro (môr′ō) *n.* ⟦Sp, lit., Moor < L *Maurus*⟧ **1** *pl.* **-ros** or **-ro** a member of a group of Muslim Malay peoples living in the S Philippines **2** any of the Austronesian languages of these peoples *—adj.* of the Moros

mo·roc·co (mə räk′ō) *n.* **1** a fine, soft leather made, originally in Morocco, from goatskins tanned with sumac **2** any similar leather, as one made from sharkskin Also **morocco leather**

Mo·roc·co (mə räk′ō) kingdom on the NW coast of Africa, bordering on the Atlantic & the Mediterranean; a Muslim kingdom since the 11th cent., from 1912 to 1956 it was divided into a French protectorate (*French Morocco*), a Spanish protectorate (*Spanish Morocco*), & the *international zone of Tangier* (established in 1923): 172,414 sq mi (446,550 sq km); cap. Rabat **—Mo·roc′can** *adj., n.*

☆**mo·ron** (môr′än′) *n.* ⟦arbitrary use (by H. H. Goddard, 1866-1957, U.S. psychologist) of Gr *mōron,* neut. of *mōros,* foolish, akin to Sans *mūrá-,* stupid⟧ **1** a disabled person mentally equal to a child between eight and twelve years old: an obsolescent term: see MENTAL RETARDATION **2** a very foolish or stupid person **—mo·ron′ic** *adj.* **—mo·ron′i·cal·ly** *adv.* **—mo·ron′i·ty** *n.,* **mo′ron·ism′**

Mo·ro·ni (mə rō′nē) capital of Comoros

mo·rose (mə rōs′) *adj.* ⟦L *morosus,* peevish, fretful < *mos* (gen. *moris*), manner: see MOOD[1]⟧ **1** ill-tempered; gloomy, sullen, etc. **2** characterized by gloom **—mo·rose′ly** *adv.* **—mo·rose′ness** *n.*

morph[1] (môrf) *n.* ⟦< Gr *morphē,* form⟧ **1** *Linguis. a)* ALLOMORPH (sense 2) *b)* a representation of an occurrence of a morpheme *c)* a sequence of phonemes isolated from surrounding sequences but not yet assigned to a particular morpheme **2** *Biol.* in a polymorphous species, a group of organisms sharing a particular phenotypic variation

morph[2] (môrf) *vt., vi.* ⟦< (META)MORPH(OSIS)⟧ to transform or be transformed as by MORPHING

morph[3] *abbrev.* morphology

-morph (môrf) ⟦see MORPH[1]⟧ *combining form forming nouns* one having a (specified) form or shape [*pseudomorph*]

☆**mor·phal·lax·is** (môr′fə lak′sis) *n., pl.* **-lax′es′** (-sēz′) ⟦ModL < Gr *morphē,* form + *allaxis,* an exchange < *allassein,* to change, exchange < *allos,* other: see ELSE⟧ *Zool.* the transformation of one part into another during regeneration, as in the growth of an antennule from the stump of an eye in some crustaceans

mor·pheme (môr′fēm′) *n.* ⟦Fr *morphème* < Gr *morphē,* form + Fr *-ème,* as in *phonème,* PHONEME⟧ the smallest meaningful unit or form in a language: it may be an affix (Ex.: *un-* in *undo* or *-er* in *doer*) or a base (Ex.: *do* in *undo* or the single morpheme in *house*) **—mor·phe′mic** *adj.* **—mor·phe′mi·cal·ly** *adv.*

mor·phe·mics (môr fē′miks) *n.* **1** the study of the morphemic systems of languages **2** the description and classification of the morphemes of a specific language

Mor·phe·us (môr′fē əs, môr′fyo͞os′) *n.* ⟦ME < L < Gr *Morpheus,* prob. < *morphē,* form: hence, orig., one who shapes (dreams)⟧ *Gr. Myth.* the god of dreams, son of Hypnos

-mor·phic (môr′fik) ⟦< Gr *morphē,* form + -IC⟧ *combining form forming adjectives* having a (specified) form or shape [*idiomorphic*]

mor·phine (môr′fēn′) *n.* ⟦Ger *morphin* or Fr *morphine* < ModL *morphium,* so named (1811) by F. W. A. Sertürner (1783-1841), Ger pharmacist < L *Morpheus:* see MORPHEUS⟧ a bitter, white or colorless, crystalline narcotic alkaloid, $C_{17}H_{19}NO_3 \cdot H_2O$, derived from opium and used in medicine to relieve pain: also **mor′phi·a** (-fē ə) **—mor·phin′ic** (-fē′nik, -fin′ik) *adj.*

morph·ing (môr′fiŋ) *n.* ⟦< (META)MORPH(OSIS) + *-ing*⟧ a special-effects process used in film or video production in which a series of images created in a digital computer are so smoothly connected that persons or objects seem to change shape, form, etc. in one continuous action

mor·phin·ism (môr′fēn iz′əm, -fin-) *n.* **1** a diseased condition resulting from excessive use of morphine **2** addiction to morphine

mor·pho- (môr′fō, -fə) ⟦MORPH(EME) + *-o-*⟧ *combining form* morpheme [*morphophonemics*]

mor·pho·gen (môr′fə jən) *n.* a chemical substance that regulates morphogenesis

mor·pho·gen·e·sis (môr′fō jen′ə sis) *n.* ⟦ModL: see -MORPH & -GENESIS⟧ *Zool.* the structural changes occurring during the development of an organism, organ, or part **—mor′pho·ge·net′ic** (-jə net′ik) *adj.*

morphol *abbrev.* morphology

mor·phol·o·gy (môr fäl′ə jē) *n.* ⟦Ger *morphologie,* coined (1822) by GOETHE < Gr *morphē,* form + Ger *-logie,* -LOGY⟧ **1** the branch of biology that deals with the form and structure of animals and plants **2** *a)* the branch of linguistics that deals with word structure and with functional changes in the forms of words, such as inflection and compounding *b)* the study of the structure, classification, and relationships of morphemes **3** any scientific study of form and structure, as in physical geography **4** form or structure **—mor′pho·log′i·cal** (-fə läj′i kəl) *adj.,* **mor′pho·log′ic —mor′pho·log′i·cal·ly** *adv.* **—mor·phol′o·gist** *n.*

mor·pho·pho·ne·mics (môr′fō fə nē′miks) *n.* ⟦MORPHO- + PHONEMICS⟧ **1** the study of phonemic variations in morphemes **2** description of such variations in a particular language **—mor′pho·pho·ne′mic** *adj.*

mor·pho·sis (môr fō′sis) *n., pl.* **-ses′** (-sēz′) ⟦ModL < Gr *morphōsis,* form < *morphoun,* to form < *morphē,* form⟧ the mode of developmental formation of an organism or any of its parts

-mor·phous (môr′fəs) ⟦Gr *-morphos* < *morphē,* form⟧ *combining form* -MORPHIC

mor·ris (môr′is, mär′-) *adj.* ⟦< ME *morys,* MOORISH⟧ designating or of an old folk dance formerly common in England, esp. on May Day, in which costumes were worn, often those associated with characters in the Robin Hood legends **—*n.*** this dance

Mor·ris[1] (môr′is, mär′-) *n.* ⟦var. of MAURICE⟧ a masculine name: dim. *Morrie, Morry*

Mor·ris[2] (môr′is, mär′-) **1 Gou·ver·neur** (guv′ər nir′) 1752-1816; Am. statesman & diplomat **2 Robert** 1734-1806; Am. financier & patriot **3 William** 1834-96; Eng. poet, artist, craftsman, & socialist

Morris chair ⟦after William MORRIS[2], who popularized it⟧ an armchair with an adjustable back and removable cushions

Morris Jes·up (jes′əp), **Cape** cape at the N tip of Greenland: northernmost point of land on earth

mor·ro (môr′ō) *n., pl.* **-ros** ⟦Sp: see MORAINE⟧ an isolated hill, ridge, etc., as a bluff or headland

mor·row (mär′ō, môr′-) *n.* ⟦ME *morwe, morwen* < OE *morgen,* MORNING⟧ [Archaic or Literary] **1** morning **2** the next day **3** the time just after some particular event

Mors (môrz, môrs) *n.* ⟦L: see MORTAL⟧ *Rom. Myth.* death personified as a god: identified with the Greek Thanatos

Morse[1] (môrs) *adj.* ⟦after fol.⟧ [*often* **m-**] designating or of a code, or alphabet, consisting of a system of dots and dashes, or short and long sounds or flashes, used to represent letters, numerals, etc. in telegraphy, signaling, and the like: the *international* (or *continental*) *code* was adapted from the original **—*n.*** Morse code

Morse[2] (môrs), **Samuel F(inley) B(reese)** 1791-1872; U.S. artist & inventor of the telegraph

mor·sel (môr′səl) *n.* ⟦OFr, dim. of *mors* < L *morsum,* a bite, piece < pp. of *mordere,* to bite: see MORDANT⟧ **1** a small bite or portion of food **2** a small piece or amount; bit **3** a tasty dish **—*vt.*** to divide into or distribute in small portions

mort[1] (môrt) *n.* ⟦OFr < L *mors,* death: see MORTAL⟧ **1** [Obs.] death **2** a note sounded on a hunting horn when the quarry is killed

mort[2] (môrt) *n.* ⟦? altered (infl. by prec.) < dial. *merth,* excess < ON *mergth,* a multitude; akin to *margr,* much⟧ [Dial.] a great quantity or number

mor·ta·del·la (môr′tə del′ə) *n.* ⟦It < L *murtatum (farcimen),* (sausage) spiced with myrtle, neut. of *myrtatus* < *myrtus,* MYRTLE⟧ a type of Italian bologna

mor·tal (môrt′'l) *adj.* ⟦OFr < L *mortalis* < *mors* (gen. *mortis*), death, akin to *mori,* to die < IE base **mer-,* to die, be worn out > MURDER, Sans *marati,* (he) dies⟧ **1** that must eventually die [all *mortal* beings] **2** of a human being considered as a being who must eventually die **3** of this world **4** of death **5** causing death; deadly; fatal **6** to the death [*mortal* combat] **7** not to be pacified [a *mortal* enemy] **8** very intense; grievous [*mortal* terror] **9** [Informal] *a)* extreme; very great *b)* very long and tedious *c)* conceivable; possible [of no *mortal* good to anyone] **10** *Theol.* causing spiritual death: said of a sin serious in itself, adequately recognized as such, and committed with full consent of one's will: compare VENIAL **—*n.*** a being who must eventually die; esp., a human being; person **—*adv.*** [Dial.] extremely **—SYN.** FATAL **—mor′tal·ly** *adv.*

mor·tal·i·ty (môr tal′ə tē) ***n.*** ⟦ME *mortalite* < OFr < L *mortalitas* < *mortalis,* prec.⟧ **1** the condition of being mortal; esp., the nature of a human being, as having eventually to die **2** death on a large scale, as from disease or war **3** *a)* the proportion of deaths to the population of a region, nation, etc.; death rate *b)* the death rate from a particular disease: in full **mortality rate 4** the number or proportion that fail [the high *mortality* of first-year students] **5** human beings collectively **6** [Obs.] death

mortality table a statistical table, based on a sample group of the population, stating the percentage of people who live to any given age and the life expectancy at any given age

mor·tar (môrt′ər) ***n.*** ⟦ME *mortere* < OE *mortere* & OFr *mortier,* both < L *mortarium,* mixing vessel or trough < IE **mr̥tos,* pulverized < base **mer-,* to rub: see MORBID⟧ **1** a very hard bowl in which softer substances are ground or pounded to a powder with a pestle **2** any machine in which materials are ground or pounded **3** ⟦Fr *mortier*⟧ a short-barreled cannon with a low muzzle velocity, which hurls shells in a high trajectory **4** any of various similar devices, for shooting lifelines, flares, etc. **5** ⟦ME *morter* < MFr *mortier* < L *mortarium,* a mixture of sand and lime: so called from the vessel in which it was made⟧ a mixture of cement or lime with sand and water, used between bricks or stones to bind them together in building, or as plaster —***vt.*** **1** to plaster or bind together with mortar **2** to attack with mortar shells

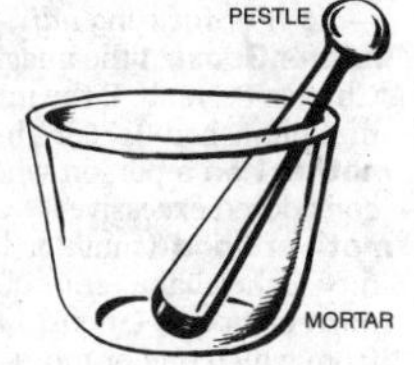

mor·tar·board (-bôrd′) ***n.*** **1** a square board with a handle beneath or with legs, used for holding mortar **2** an academic cap with a square, flat, horizontal top, worn at commencements, etc. in schools and colleges

mort·gage (môr′gij) ***n.*** ⟦OFr *morgage, mort gage,* lit., dead pledge < *mort,* dead (see MORT[1]) + *gage,* GAGE[1]⟧ **1** *a)* the pledging of property to a creditor as security for the payment of a debt *b)* such a debt **2** the deed by which this pledge is made **3** the claim of the mortgagee on the property —***vt.*** **-gaged, -gag·ing 1** *Law* to pledge (property) by a mortgage **2** to put an advance claim or liability on [to *mortgage* one's future]

mort·ga·gee (môr′gi jē′) ***n.*** the lender in a mortgage transaction

mort·ga·gor or **mort·gag·er** (môr′gi jər) ***n.*** the borrower in a mortgage transaction

mor·tice (môrt′is) ***n., vt.*** **-ticed, -tic·ing** *alt. sp. of* MORTISE

☆**mor·ti·cian** (môr tish′ən) ***n.*** ⟦< L *mors,* death (see MORTAL) + -ICIAN⟧ FUNERAL DIRECTOR

mor·ti·fi·ca·tion (môrt′ə fi kā′shən) ***n.*** ⟦ME *mortificacioun* < LL(Ec) *mortificatio* < pp. of *mortificare*⟧ **1** a mortifying or being mortified; specif., *a)* the control of physical desires and passions by self-denial, fasting, etc. *b)* shame, humiliation, etc.; loss of self-respect **2** something causing shame, humiliation, etc. **3** *former term for* GANGRENE

mor·ti·fy (môrt′ə fī′) ***vt.*** **-fied′, -fy′ing** ⟦ME *mortifien* < OFr *mortifier* < LL(Ec) *mortificare,* to kill, destroy < L *mors,* death (see MORTAL) + *facere,* to make, DO[1]⟧ **1** to punish (one's body) or control (one's physical desires and passions) by self-denial, fasting, etc., as a means of religious or ascetic discipline **2** to cause to feel shame, humiliation, chagrin, etc.; injure the pride or self-respect of **3** [Now Rare] to cause (bodily tissue) to decay or become gangrenous **4** to destroy the vitality or vigor of —***vi.*** **1** to practice MORTIFICATION (sense 1*a*) **2** [Now Rare] to decay or become gangrenous —***SYN.*** ASHAMED —**mor′ti·fi′er** ***n.***

Mor·ti·mer (môrt′ə mər) ***n.*** ⟦< Norm surname *Mortimer* < a place name⟧ a masculine name: dim. *Mort, Morty*

mor·tise (môrt′is) ***n.*** ⟦ME *mortays* < MFr *mortaise,* a mortise < Ar *murtazza,* joined, fixed in⟧ a hole or recess cut, as in a piece of wood, to receive a projecting part (*tenon*) shaped to fit into it, or to receive a lock —***vt.*** **-tised, -tis·ing 1** to join or fasten securely, esp. with a mortise and tenon **2** to cut a mortise in

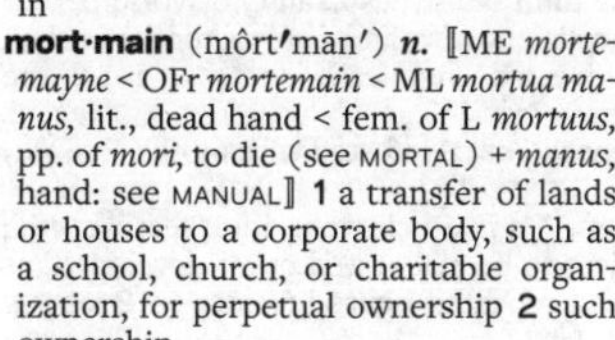

mort·main (môrt′mān′) ***n.*** ⟦ME *mortemayne* < OFr *mortemain* < ML *mortua manus,* lit., dead hand < fem. of L *mortuus,* pp. of *mori,* to die (see MORTAL) + *manus,* hand: see MANUAL⟧ **1** a transfer of lands or houses to a corporate body, such as a school, church, or charitable organization, for perpetual ownership **2** such ownership

Mor·ton[1] (môrt′'n) ***n.*** ⟦orig. surname & place name < OE *Mor-tun* < *mor,* a swamp, MOOR[1] + *tun,* TOWN⟧ a masculine name: dim. *Mort, Morty*

Mor·ton[2] (môrt′'n) **1 Ferdinand Joseph** (born *Ferdinand Joseph Lamothe*) 1890-1941; U.S. jazz pianist & composer: called *Jelly Roll Morton* **2 William Thomas Green** 1819-68; U.S. dentist: introduced the use of ether for anesthesia (1846)

mor·tu·ar·y (môr′cho͞o er′ē) ***n., pl.*** **-ar′ies** ⟦< LL *mortuarius,* of the dead < L *mortuus,* pp. of *mori,* to die: see MORTAL⟧ a place where dead bodies are kept before burial or cremation, as a morgue or funeral home —***adj.*** **1** of or having to do with the burial of the dead **2** of or connected with death

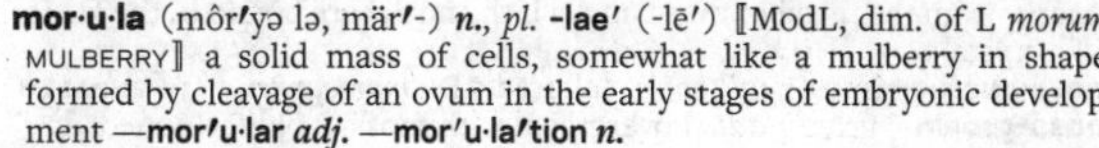

mor·u·la (môr′yə lə, mär′-) ***n., pl.*** **-lae′** (-lē′) ⟦ModL, dim. of L *morum,* MULBERRY⟧ a solid mass of cells, somewhat like a mulberry in shape, formed by cleavage of an ovum in the early stages of embryonic development —**mor′u·lar** ***adj.*** —**mor′u·la′tion** ***n.***

mos *abbrev.* months

mo·sa·ic (mō zā′ik) ***n.*** ⟦LME *musycke* < OFr *musique* < ML *musaicum,* altered < LL *musivum,* mosaic, orig. neut. of L *musivus,* artistic, of a muse < L *musa,* MUSE: sp. altered by assoc. with Fr *mosaïque* < It *mosaico* < same ML source⟧ **1** the process of making pictures or designs by inlaying small bits of colored stone, glass, tile, etc. in mortar **2** inlaid work made by this process **3** a picture or design so made **4** anything resembling this, as a number of aerial photographs pieced together to show a continuous area **5** *Biol.* CHIMERA (*n.* 4) **6** *Bot.* any of the viral diseases that cause wrinkling or mottling of leaves **7** *TV* the photosensitive plate in an iconoscope or other television camera tube —***adj.*** of or resembling mosaic or a mosaic —***vt.*** **-icked, -ick·ing 1** to make by or as by mosaic **2** to decorate with mosaics —**mo·sa′i·cal·ly** ***adv.*** —**mo·sa′i·cist** (-ə sist) ***n.***

Mo·sa·ic (mō zā′ik) ***adj.*** ⟦LL(Ec) *Mosaicus* < Gr(Ec) *Mōsaikos*⟧ of Moses or the writings, principles, etc. attributed to him

mosaic gold 1 a yellow, crystalline powder, stannic sulfide, SnS_2, used as a pigment **2** ORMOLU

mosaic image the collective image produced by the ommatidia of a compound eye

mo·sa·i·cism (mō zā′ə siz′əm) ***n.*** ⟦MOSAIC, *n.* 5 + -ISM⟧ the condition existing when tissues of different genetic makeup occur in the same organism

Mosaic law the ancient law of the Hebrews, ascribed to Moses and contained mainly in the Pentateuch

Mos·cow (mäs′kou′, -kō) capital of Russia, in the W part: Russ. name MOSKVA

Mo·selle[1] (mō zel′; *Fr* mô zel′) ***n.*** **1** a type of white wine produced in the valley of the Moselle River **2** a similar wine made elsewhere

Mo·selle[2] (mō zel′; *Fr* mô zel′) ⟦Fr < L *Mosella*⟧ river in NE France & SW Germany, flowing north into the Rhine at Koblenz: *c.* 320 mi (515 km): Ger. name **Mo·sel** (mō′zəl)

Mo·ses[1] (mō′zəz, -zəs) ***n.*** ⟦LL(Ec) < Gr(Ec) *Mōsēs* < Heb *mōsheh,* prob. < Egypt *mes, mesu,* child, son⟧ **1** a masculine name: dim. *Mo, Mose* **2** *Bible* the leader who brought the Israelites out of slavery in Egypt and led them to the Promised Land, received the Ten Commandments from God, and gave laws to the people

Mo·ses[2] (mō′zəz, -zəs), **Anna Mary Robertson** 1860-1961; U.S. primitive painter: called *Grandma Moses*

☆**mo·sey** (mō′zē) ***vi.*** ⟦prob. < VAMOOSE⟧ [Informal] to move along; now usually, to stroll or amble along

mosh (mäsh) ***vi.*** to engage in a form of dancing to HEAVY METAL music in which dancers freely bump into each other as they jump up and down in an area (**mosh pit**) usually just in front of the bandstand —**mosh′er** ***n.*** —**mosh′ing** ***n.***

mo·shav (mō shäv′) ***n., pl.*** **mo·sha·vim** (mō′shä vēm′) ⟦ModHeb *mōshābh* < Heb, a dwelling⟧ in Israel, a type of settlement consisting of individual leaseholds farmed cooperatively: cf. KIBBUTZ

Mos·kva (môs kvä′) *Russ. name for* MOSCOW

Mos·lem (mäz′ləm, mäs′-) ***n., adj.*** *var. of* MUSLIM

mosque (mäsk) ***n.*** ⟦Early ModE *muskey* < MFr *mosquez* < It *moschea,* ult. < Ar *masjid,* place of adoration, temple < *sajada,* to prostrate oneself, pray⟧ a Muslim temple or place of worship

mos·qui·to (mə skēt′ō) ***n., pl.*** **-toes** or **-tos** ⟦Sp & Port, dim. of *mosca* < L *musca,* a fly: see MIDGE⟧ any of a large family (Culicidae) of two-winged dipteran insects, the females of which have skin-piercing mouthparts used to extract blood from animals, including humans: some varieties are carriers of certain diseases, as malaria and yellow fever —**mos·qui′to·ey** (-ē) ***adj.***

Mosquito Coast region on the Caribbean coast of Honduras & Nicaragua: also **Mos·qui·ti·a** (môs kē′tē ä)

☆**mos·qui·to·fish** (-fish′) ***n., pl.*** **-fish′** a small gambusia fish (*Gambusia affinis*) sometimes introduced into a body of water to control mosquito larvae

☆**mosquito hawk 1** DRAGONFLY **2** NIGHTHAWK (sense 1)

☆**mosquito net (*or* netting)** a very fine cloth mesh or a curtain made of this, for keeping out mosquitoes

moss (môs, mäs) ***n.*** ⟦ME *mos,* a bog, moss < OE, a swamp, akin to ON *mosi,* Ger *moos,* a bog, moss < IE **meus-* (> L *muscus,* moss) < base **meu-,* moist⟧ **1** *a)* any of various classes (esp. Bryopsida) of very small, green bryophytes having stems with leaflike structures and growing in velvety clusters on rocks, trees, moist ground, etc. *b)* a growth of these **2** any of various similar plants, as some lichens and algae —***vt.*** to cover with a growth of moss —**moss′like′** ***adj.***

Mos·sad (mə säd′) ***n.*** ⟦ModHeb, lit., institute, agency⟧ the chief intelligence and secret-service agency of Israel

moss agate a kind of agate containing dark-colored, branchlike markings of manganese or iron oxides

☆**moss·back** (môs′bak′) ***n.*** **1** an old fish, shellfish, turtle, etc. with a greenish growth of algae, etc. over the back **2** [Informal] an old-fashioned or very conservative person

Möss·bau·er (mös′bou′ər), **Ru·dolf Lud·wig** (ro͞o′dôlf′ lo͞ot′viH′) 1929-2011; Ger. physicist

Möss·bau·er effect (môs′bou′ər) ⟦after prec.⟧ the phenomenon in which gamma rays from the nuclei of certain radioactive isotopes do not lose energy from the recoil of those nuclei if the nuclei are bound in the lattice of a crystal

☆**moss·bunk·er** (môs′buŋ′kər) ***n.*** ⟦altered < Du *marsbanker* < ?⟧ MENHADEN

moss-grown (-grōn′) ***adj.*** 1 overgrown with moss 2 old-fashioned; antiquated

☆**moss pink** a hardy, perennial phlox (*Phlox subulata*) forming sprawling mats with bristly, narrow leaves and white, pink, or lavender flowers

moss rose 1 PORTULACA 2 a variety of the cabbage rose with a roughened, mossy flower stalk and calyx

moss·troop·er (-trōōp′ər) ***n.*** ⟦< Scot *moss,* a swamp < ME *mos:* see MOSS⟧ 1 any of the raiders who infested the swampy borderland between England and Scotland in the 17th cent. 2 a marauder

moss·y (môs′ē) ***adj.*** **moss′i·er, moss′i·est** 1 full of or covered with moss or a mosslike growth 2 as if covered with moss 3 like moss —**moss′i·ness *n.***

moss·y·cup oak (môs′ē kup′) ⟦so named from the fringed *cups* of its acorns⟧ BUR OAK

most (mōst) ***adj.*** ⟦ME < OE *mast,* used as superl. of *micel,* big (var. of *mycel:* see MUCH): akin to Goth *maists:* for IE base see MORE⟧ 1 greatest in amount, quantity, or degree: used as the superlative of MUCH 2 greatest in number: used as the superlative of MANY 3 in the greatest number of instances [*most* fame is fleeting] —***n.*** 1 the greatest amount, quantity or degree [to take *most* of the credit] 2 [*with pl. v.*] *a)* the greatest number (*of* persons or things) [*most* of us are going] *b)* the greatest number of persons or things —***adv.*** 1 in or to the greatest degree or extent: used with many adjectives and adverbs (regularly with those of three or more syllables) to form the superlative degree [*most* horrible, *most* quickly] 2 very (often preceded by *a*) [a *most* beautiful morning] 3 ⟦for ALMOST⟧ [Informal] almost; nearly —**at (the) most** at the very limit; not more than —**make the most of** to make the greatest use of; take fullest advantage of —**the most** [Slang] the best or most exciting, attractive, etc.

-most (mōst) ⟦ME, altered (after prec.) < *-mest* < OE < older superl. suffixes, *-ma* + *-est*⟧ *suffix* forming superlatives [*hindmost*]

mos·tac·ci·o·li (mə stä′chē ō′lē) ***n.*** ⟦It⟧ PENNE

most·est (mōs′tist) ***adj., n.*** [Slang] *tautological var. of* MOST ["the hostess with the *mostest*"]

most favored nation the status granted to a nation, as by a trade agreement, that entitles it to receive from the granting nation the most favorable terms of trade that the granter gives to any nation

most·ly (mōst′lē) ***adv.*** 1 for the most part 2 chiefly; principally 3 usually; generally

Mós·to·les (môs′tô les) city in central Spain: suburb of Madrid

Mo·sul (mō sōōl′) city in N Iraq, on the Tigris, opposite the site of ancient Nineveh

mot (mō) ***n.*** ⟦Fr, a word, saying < L *muttum,* a grunt, muttering < IE echoic base **mu-* > MUTTER, MOPE, MEW[3]⟧ *short for* BON MOT

mote[1] (mōt) ***n.*** ⟦ME < OE *mot,* akin to Du, sawdust, grit⟧ a speck of dust or other tiny particle

mote[2] (mōt) ***v.aux.*** ⟦ME *moten* < OE *motan,* akin to Ger *müssen:* basic sense "it is permitted"; *must* (OE *moste*) is the pt. of this v.⟧ [Archaic] may; might

☆**mo·tel** (mō tel′) ***n.*** ⟦MO(TOR) + (HO)TEL: coined (1925) by A. S. Heineman, U.S. architect, for an inn in San Luis Obispo, Calif.⟧ a hotel intended primarily for those traveling by car, usually with easy access from each room to a parking area

mo·tet (mō tet′) ***n.*** ⟦OFr dim. of *mot,* a word: see MOT⟧ *Music* a contrapuntal, polyphonic song, typically of a sacred nature and generally unaccompanied

moth (môth) ***n., pl.*** **moths** (môthz, môths) ⟦ME *motthe* < OE *moththe,* akin to Ger *motte* < IE base **math-,* gnawing vermin⟧ 1 any of various families of chiefly night-flying lepidopteran insects, similar to the butterflies but generally smaller, less brightly colored, and not having the antennae knobbed 2 CLOTHES MOTH

moth·ball (môth′bôl′) ***n.*** a small ball of naphthalene or, sometimes, camphor, the fumes of which repel moths, as from woolens or furs —***vt.*** to store with protective covering or set aside indefinitely for possible future use —***adj.*** in storage or reserve [a *mothball* fleet] —**in (or out of) mothballs** put into (or taken from) a condition of being stored or in reserve

moth-eat·en (-ēt′'n) ***adj.*** 1 gnawed away in patches by moth larvae: said as of cloth 2 decayed or decrepit in appearance; worn-out 3 outdated

moth·er[1] (muth′ər) ***n.*** ⟦ME *moder* < OE *modor,* akin to Ger *mutter* < IE **matér,* mother (> L *mater,* Gr *mētēr,* OIr *māthir*) < **ma-,* echoic of baby talk⟧ 1 a woman who has borne a child; esp., a woman as she is related to her child or children 2 *a)* a stepmother *b)* an adoptive mother *c)* a mother-in-law 3 the female parent of an animal or plant 4 that which gives birth to something, is the origin or source of something, or nurtures in the manner of a mother 5 *a)* a woman having the responsibility and authority of a mother *b)* [*often* **M-**] MOTHER SUPERIOR (used esp. as a title) 6 an elderly woman: used as a title of affectionate respect 7 [Slang] *short for* MOTHERFUCKER: somewhat vulgar —***adj.*** 1 of, like, or like that of a mother 2 derived or learned from or as if from one's mother; native [English is her *mother* tongue] 3 designating a company, institution, etc. from which another or others originated [*mother* church] —***vt.*** 1 to be the mother of; give birth to: often used fig. 2 to look after or care for as a mother does —**the mother of all** something regarded as the biggest, most impressive, or most important of (its kind): often used humorously [*the mother of all* yard sales] —**moth′er·less *adj.***

moth·er[2] (muth′ər) ***n.*** ⟦altered (infl. by prec.) < MDu *moeder,* akin to MLowG *modder:* for IE base see MUD⟧ 1 *short for* MOTHER OF VINEGAR 2 [Obs.] dregs

moth·er·board (-bôrd′) ***n.*** the main interconnecting circuit board in an electronic device, into or on which the various subassemblies, as printed circuit boards, are plugged or wired

Mother Car·ey's chicken (ker′ēz) ⟦< ?⟧ STORM PETREL

mother country MOTHERLAND

mother figure a person who serves as an emotional substitute for one's mother

moth·er·fuck·er (muth′ər fuk′ər) ***n.*** [Vulgar Slang] a person or thing regarded as remarkable, despicable, contemptible, unpleasant, difficult, etc. —**moth′er·fuck′ing *adj.***

Mother Goose 1 the imaginary narrator of a collection of tales (*c.* 1697) by Charles Perrault 2 the imaginary creator of a collection of nursery rhymes first published (1765?) in London

mother hen a person who is protective toward others, often, to a degree considered excessive

moth·er·hood (muth′ər hood′) ***n.*** 1 the state of being a mother; maternity 2 the character or qualities of a mother 3 mothers collectively

moth·er·house (-hous′) ***n.*** *R.C.Ch.* 1 a monastery or other religious house from which one or more additional religious houses have been founded 2 the headquarters of a religious community

Mother Hub·bard (hub′ərd) ⟦after the character in an old nursery rhyme, typically depicted in such a gown⟧ [Historical] a full, loose gown for women

moth·er·ing (muth′ər iŋ) ***n.*** 1 the work or skill of a mother in raising a child or children 2 motherly attention or care, esp. when regarded as fussy or overprotective

moth·er-in-law (-in lô′) ***n., pl.*** **moth′ers-in-law′** the mother of one's husband or wife

moth·er·land (muth′ər land′) ***n.*** 1 one's native land or, sometimes, the land of one's ancestors 2 a country thought of as the origin or source of something

☆**mother lode** 1 the main lode, or vein of ore, in a particular region or district 2 any source regarded as particularly abundant or rich

moth·er·ly (-lē) ***adj.*** 1 of a mother 2 having traits considered typical of mothers; maternally kind, protective, nurturing, etc. —***adv.*** [Archaic] as a mother —**moth′er·li·ness *n.***

moth·er-na·ked (-nā′kid) ***adj.*** as naked as when one was born; completely naked

Mother Nature *personification of* the power or force that seems to regulate the physical world

Mother of God *name for* VIRGIN MARY[2]

moth·er-of-pearl (-əv purl′) ***n.*** ⟦transl. of ML *mater perlarum:* orig. applied to the marine animal, later to the shell⟧ the hard, pearly internal layer of certain marine shells, as of the pearl oyster or abalone, which is used in the arts, in making pearl buttons, etc. —***adj.*** of mother-of-pearl

mother of vinegar ⟦see MOTHER[2]⟧ a stringy, gummy, slimy substance formed by bacteria (genus *Acetobacter*) in vinegar or on the surface of fermenting liquids: used as a starter to make vinegar

☆**Mother's Day** the second Sunday in May, a day set aside (in the U.S.) in honor of mothers

mother ship a ship, spacecraft, etc. from which smaller craft are supported; specif., a large alien spacecraft, as in science fiction

mother superior *pl.* **mother superiors** or **mothers superior** [*often* **M- S-**] a woman who is the head of a religious establishment: often used as a title

mother tongue 1 one's native language 2 a language in its relation to another derived from it

Moth·er·well (muth′ər wel′), **Robert** 1915-91; U.S. painter

Motherwell and Wi·shaw (wish′ô) city in SC Scotland

mother wit native intelligence; common sense

moth·er·wort (-wurt′) ***n.*** ⟦ME *moderwort* (see MOTHER[1] & WORT[2]): from the belief that it was helpful in curing diseases of the uterus⟧ any of a genus (*Leonurus*) of weedy plants of the mint family; esp., an Old World perennial (*L. cardiaca*) with pink or purplish flowers and a spiny, toothed calyx

moth·proof (môth′prōōf′) ***adj.*** treated chemically so as to repel the clothes moth —***vt.*** to make mothproof

moth·y (môth′ē) ***adj.*** **moth′i·er, moth′i·est** 1 infested with moths 2 moth-eaten

mo·tif (mō tēf′) ***n.*** ⟦Fr: see MOTIVE⟧ 1 a main element, idea, feature, etc.; specif., *a)* a main theme or subject to be elaborated on or developed, as in a piece of music or a book *b)* a repeated figure in a design 2 MOTIVE (sense 1)

mo·tile (mōt′'l) ***adj.*** ⟦< L *motus,* pp. of *movere,* to MOVE + -ILE⟧ *Biol.* capable of or exhibiting spontaneous motion —**mo·til·i·ty** (mō til′ə tē) ***n.***

mo·tion (mō′shən) ***n.*** ⟦ME *mocioun* < L *motio* (gen. *motionis*), a moving < *motus,* pp. of *movere,* MOVE⟧ 1 the act or process of moving; passage of a body from one place to another; movement 2 the act of moving the body or any of its parts 3 a meaningful movement of the hand, eyes, etc.; gesture 4 [Rare] the ability to move 5 an impulse; inclination [of one's own *motion*] 6 a proposal; suggestion; esp., a proposal formally made in an assembly or meeting 7 *Law* an application to a court for a ruling, order, etc. 8 *Mech.* a combination of moving parts; mechanism 9 *Music* melodic progression, as a change from one pitch to another in a voice part —***vi.*** to make a meaningful movement of the hand, head, etc.; gesture —***vt.*** to direct or command by a meaningful gesture —**go through the motions** to do something from habit or according to formalities, but without enthusiasm, personal involvement, etc. —**in motion** moving; traveling or in operation —**mo′tion·al** *adj.* —**mo′tion·less** *adj.* —**mo′tion·less·ly** *adv.* —**mo′tion·less·ness** *n.*

motion picture FILM (*n.* 5)

motion sickness sickness caused by the motion of an aircraft, boat, etc. and characterized by nausea, vomiting, and dizziness

motion study *see* TIME STUDY

mo·ti·vate (mōt′ə vāt′) *vt.* **-vat′ed**, **-vat′ing** to provide with, or affect as, a motive or motives; incite, impel, or encourage —**mo′ti·va′tive** *adj.* —**mo′ti·va′tor** *n.*

mo·ti·va·tion (mōt′ə vā′shən) *n.* **1** the act or an instance of motivating **2** anything that motivates **3** desire or enthusiasm to accomplish or achieve something [a talented athlete who lacks *motivation*]

mo·ti·va·tion·al (-shə nəl) *adj.* of or giving motivation; specif., designating or of speeches, recordings, seminars, etc. designed to provide insight, guidance, and encouragement toward achieving self-fulfillment as in one's career or personal life [a *motivational* speaker]

☆**motivational research** the study of factors that influence decision making, esp. those factors that motivate consumers to make particular buying decisions

mo·tive (mōt′iv) *n.* ⟦ME *motif* < OFr *motif* (adj.) < ML *motivus,* moving < L *motus,* pp. of *movere,* to MOVE⟧ **1** some inner drive, impulse, intention, etc. that causes a person to do something or act in a certain way; incentive; goal **2** MOTIF (sense 1) —*adj.* ⟦ML *motivus*⟧ **1** of, causing, or tending to cause motion **2** [Archaic] of, or having the nature of, a motive or motives —*vt.* **-tived**, **-tiv·ing** [Archaic] to supply a motive for; motivate —**SYN.** CAUSE —**mo′tive·less** *adj.*

-mo·tive (mōt′iv) ⟦< prec.⟧ *combining form forming adjectives* moving, of motion [*automotive*]

motive power **1** any power, as steam, electricity, etc., used to impart motion; any source of mechanical energy **2** an impelling force

mo·tiv·ic (mō tiv′ik) *adj.* ⟦< MOTIVE (*n.* 2)⟧ of or having to do with a musical motif

mo·tiv·i·ty (mō tiv′ə tē) *n.* the power of moving or causing motion

mot juste (mō zhōōst′) *pl.* **mots justes** (mō zhōōst′) ⟦Fr⟧ exactly the word or phrase wanted; just the right word or phrase

mot·ley (mät′lē) *adj.* ⟦ME *mottley* < ?⟧ **1** of many colors or patches of color **2** [Historical] wearing many-colored garments [a *motley* fool] **3** having or composed of many different or clashing elements; heterogeneous [a *motley* group] —*n.* **1** cloth of mixed colors **2** [Historical] a garment of various colors, worn by a clown or jester **3** a combination of diverse or clashing elements

Mot·ley (mät′lē), **John Lo·throp** (lō′thrəp) 1814-77; U.S. historian & diplomat

mot·mot (mät′mät′) *n.* ⟦AmSp, echoic of its note⟧ any of a family (Momotidae) of long-tailed, chiefly green, coraciiform birds of tropical and subtropical America, usually nesting in tunnels they make along river banks

mo·to·cross (mō′tō krôs′) *n.* ⟦Fr < *motocyclette,* motorcycle + CROSS-COUNTRY⟧ a race for lightweight motorcycles over a cross-country course with obstacles

mo·to·neu·ron (mō′tə nōōr′än′, -nyōōr′-) *n.* ⟦fol. + NEURON⟧ MOTOR NEURON

mo·tor (mōt′ər) *n.* ⟦L, a mover < *motus,* pp. of *movere,* MOVE⟧ **1** anything that produces or imparts motion **2** an engine; esp., an internal-combustion engine for propelling a vehicle **3** MOTOR VEHICLE **4** *Elec.* a machine for converting electric energy into mechanical energy —*adj.* **1** producing or imparting motion **2** of, having to do with, or powered by a motor or motors [*motor* oil, *motor* parts, a *motor* bicycle] **3** of, by, or for motor vehicles [a *motor* trip] **4** for motorists [a *motor* inn] **5** designating or of a nerve carrying impulses from the central nervous system to a muscle that produces motion **6** of, manifested by, or involving muscular movements [a *motor* reflex, *motor* skills] —*vi.* **1** to ride in a motor vehicle; esp., to travel by automobile **2** [Informal] to walk or otherwise proceed at a swift or steady pace —*vt.* [Chiefly Brit.] to convey by automobile

mo·tor·bike (-bīk′) *n.* [Informal] **1** a bicycle propelled by a motor **2** a light motorcycle

mo·tor·boat (-bōt′) *n.* a boat propelled by an internal-combustion engine or other kind of motor, esp., such a boat that is relatively small

mo·tor·bus (-bus′) *n.* BUS (sense 1): also **motor coach**

☆**mo·tor·cade** (-kād′) *n.* ⟦MOTOR + -CADE⟧ a procession of automobiles or other motor vehicles, specif. as an escort for an important person

mo·tor·car (-kär′) *n.* **1** [Now Chiefly Brit.] AUTOMOBILE ☆**2** a small, open car propelled by a motor and used on a railroad by workers: also written **motor car**

Motor City ⟦from its historical role as center of the U.S. automotive industry⟧ *name for* DETROIT (the city)

mo·tor·cy·cle (-sī′kəl) *n.* ⟦MOTOR + (BI)CYCLE⟧ **1** a two-wheeled (or, if equipped with a sidecar, three-wheeled) vehicle propelled by an internal-combustion engine and resembling a bicycle, but usually larger and heavier, and often having two saddles **2** a similar vehicle having three wheels —*vi.* **-cled**, **-cling** to ride a motorcycle —**mo′tor·cy′clist** (-sīk′list) *n.*

motor drive an electric motor and other parts of a mechanical system for operating a machine or machines

mo·tored (mōt′ərd) *adj.* having a motor or motors: usually used in compounds [*bimotored*]

☆**motor home** a motor vehicle with a van or trucklike chassis, outfitted as a traveling home, usually with self-contained electrical and plumbing facilities: cf. MOBILE HOME

☆**motor hotel** MOTEL: also **motor court**, **motor inn**, or **motor lodge**

mo·tor·ic (mō tôr′ik) *adj. Physiol.* MOTOR (*adj.* 6)

mo·tor·ist (mōt′ər ist) *n.* a person who drives an automobile or travels by automobile

mo·tor·ize (-īz′) *vt.* **-ized′**, **-iz′ing** **1** *a)* to equip with motor-driven vehicles (as in place of horses and horse-drawn vehicles) *b)* to make mobile by designing as part of a motor vehicle or mounting on a motor vehicle **2** to equip (vehicles, machines, etc.) with a motor or motors —**mo′tor·i·za′tion** *n.*

☆**mo·tor·man** (-mən) *n., pl.* **-men** (-mən) **1** a person who drives an electric streetcar or electric locomotive **2** a person who operates a motor

☆**mo·tor·mouth** (-mouth′) *n.* [Slang] a person who talks incessantly: also written **motor-mouth** or **motor mouth**

motor neuron a type of neuron that carries nerve impulses that activate a muscle, gland, etc.: see also SENSORY NEURON

☆**motor pool** a group of motor vehicles kept, as at a military installation, for use as needed by personnel

motor scooter a light motor vehicle resembling a motorcycle, having usually two small wheels with the driver seated over the engine and placing the feet in front resting on a floorboard

motor ship a ship propelled by an internal-combustion engine or engines

☆**motor torpedo boat** a high-speed powerboat equipped with torpedoes and machine guns

motor truck a motor-driven truck for hauling loads

motor vehicle a vehicle on wheels, having its own motor and not running on rails or tracks, for use on streets or highways; esp., an automobile, truck, or bus

mo·tor·way (mōt′ər wā′) *n.* [Chiefly Brit.] FREEWAY

☆**Mo·town** (mō′toun′) *adj.* ⟦< a trademark for phonograph records, etc. < *Mo(tor) Town,* nickname for DETROIT⟧ designating or of a style of rhythm and blues of the 1960s characterized by a strong, even beat and the use of elements derived from black gospel music

Mott (mät), **Lucretia** (born *Lucretia Coffin*) 1793-1880; U.S. abolitionist & women's rights advocate

☆**motte** or **mott** (mät) *n.* ⟦AmSp *mata* < LL *matta,* a cover, MAT[1]⟧ [Southwest] a small grove of trees

mot·tle (mät′'l) *vt.* **-tled**, **-tling** ⟦back-form. < *mottled* < MOTLEY + -ED⟧ to mark with blotches, streaks, and spots of different colors or shades —*n.* **1** such a blotch, streak, or spot **2** a mottled pattern or coloring, as of marble —**mot′tled** *adj.*

mot·to (mät′ō) *n., pl.* **-toes** or **-tos** ⟦It, a word < L *muttum:* see MOT⟧ **1** a word, phrase, or sentence chosen as expressive of the goals or ideals of a nation, group, family, etc. and inscribed on a seal, banner, coin, coat of arms, etc. **2** a maxim adopted as a principle of behavior —**SYN.** SAYING

moue (mōō) *n.* ⟦Fr: see MOW[3]⟧ a pouting grimace; wry face

mouf·lon (mōōf′län′) *n., pl.* **-lons′** or **-lon′** ⟦Fr *mouflon* < It dial. *muffolo,* for *muffione* < LL dial. *mufro,* akin to L *musimo,* wild sheep < a pre-L W Mediterranean native term⟧ **1** *a)* a wild sheep (*Ovis musimon*) native to the mountainous regions of Corsica and Sardinia: the male has large, curving horns *b)* a similar, Asian sheep (*O. orientalis*) **2** the wool of these sheep Also **mouf′flon′**

mouil·lé (mōō yā′) *adj.* ⟦Fr, pp. of *mouiller,* to moisten < VL **molliare* < L *mollis,* soft: see MOLLIFY⟧ *Phonet.* palatalized, as the sound of Spanish *ñ* in *cañon* or French *ll* in *fille*

mou·jik (mōō zhēk′, mōō′zhik′) *n. alt. sp. of* MUZHIK

mou·lage (mōō läzh′) *n.* ⟦Fr < MFr, a molding < *mouler,* to mold < OFr *modle:* see MOLD[1]⟧ **1** the science or practice of making a mold, as in plaster of Paris, of an object, footprint, etc., for use in crime detection **2** such a mold

mould (mōld) *n., vt., vi. chiefly Brit. sp. of* MOLD[1], MOLD[2], MOLD[3] —**mould′y** *adj.* **mould′i·er**, **mould′i·est**

mould·board (-bôrd′) *n. chiefly Brit. sp. of* MOLDBOARD

mould·er (mōl′dər) *vt., vi. chiefly Brit. sp. of* MOLDER

mould·ing (mōl′diŋ) *n. chiefly Brit. sp. of* MOLDING

moule (mōōl) *n.* ⟦Fr⟧ a mussel, esp. an edible variety

mou·lin (mōō lan′) *n.* ⟦Fr, lit., a mill < LL *molinum, molina,* MILL[1]⟧ a nearly vertical hole in a glacier down which flows a stream of water melted from the surface

Mou·lin Rouge (mōō′län rōōzh′) ⟦Fr, red windmill⟧ cabaret near Montmartre in Paris, famed in the late 19th and early 20th cent. for its cancan show

Moul·mein (mool mān′, mōl-) seaport in S Myanmar, on the Gulf of Martaban

moult (mōlt) *n., vt., vi. chiefly Brit. sp. of* MOLT

mound[1] (mound) *n.* ⟦prob. < MDu *mond,* protection, akin to ON *mund,* hand: see MANUAL⟧ **1** a heap or bank of earth, sand, etc. built over a grave, in a fortification, etc. **2** a natural elevation like this; small hill **3** any heap or pile **4** *Baseball* the slightly raised area on which the pitcher stands when pitching —*vt.* **1** [Archaic] to enclose or fortify with a mound **2** to heap up in a mound

mound[2] (mound) *n.* ⟦Fr *monde* < L *mundus,* the world⟧ ORB (*n.* 4)

☆**Mound Builders** a member of any of the early American Indian peoples who built the burial mounds, fortifications, and other earthworks found in the Midwest and the Southwest

mount¹ (mount) ***n.*** ⟦ME < OE *munt* & OFr *mont,* a mount, both < L *mons* (gen. *montis*), hill, mountain < IE base **men-,* to project > Welsh *meneth,* mountain⟧ **1** a mountain or hill: now poetic except before a proper name [*Mount* Shasta] **2** [Obs.] a raised fortification **3** *Palmistry* any fleshy raised part on the palm of the hand

mount² (mount) ***vi.*** ⟦ME *mounten* < OFr *munter* < VL **montare,* lit., to go uphill < L *mons:* see prec.⟧ **1** to climb; ascend: often with *up* **2** to climb up onto something; esp., to get on the back of a horse, on a bicycle, etc. for riding **3** to increase in amount [profits are *mounting*] **—*vt.* 1** to go up; ascend; climb [to *mount* stairs] **2** *a)* to get up on (a horse, bicycle, etc.) for riding *b)* to set (someone) on a horse *c)* to climb or get up on (a platform, stool, etc.) **3** to provide with a horse or horses for riding **4** to climb on (a female) for copulation: said of a male animal **5** to place on something raised: with *on* [*mounting* a statue on a pedestal] **6** to place, fix, or fasten on or in the proper support, backing, etc. for the required purpose; specif., *a)* to fix (a jewel) in a setting *b)* to fix (a specimen) on (a slide) for microscopic study *c)* to arrange (a skeleton, dead animal, etc.) for exhibition *d)* to affix (a picture) to a MAT² or other backing *e)* to affix (a postage stamp) on an album page **7** to furnish the necessary costumes, settings, etc. for producing (a play) **8** *a)* to prepare for and undertake (an expedition, campaign, etc.) *b)* to prepare for and present [to *mount* a major Degas exhibition] **9** *Mil. a)* to raise or adjust (a gun) into proper position for use *b)* to be armed with (a cannon) [a ship that *mounts* six cannons] *c)* to post (a guard) as for sentry duty (see also the phrase MOUNT GUARD at GUARD) **—*n.* 1** the act or manner of mounting (a horse, etc.) **2** a horse, camel, etc. for mounting and riding **3** the opportunity to ride a horse, etc., esp. in a race **4** the support, setting, etc. on or in which something is mounted, as the support for a microscopic slide or the setting for a jewel **—mount′a·ble *adj.* —mount′er *n.***

moun·tain (mount′'n) ***n.*** ⟦ME *montaine* < OFr *montaigne* < VL **montanea,* for L *montana* < *montanus,* mountainous < *mons:* see MOUNT¹⟧ **1** a natural elevation of the earth's surface, typically larger and steeper than a hill **2** [*pl.*] a chain or group of such elevations **3** a large pile, heap, or mound **4** a very large amount **—*adj.* 1** of a mountain or mountains **2** situated, living, or used in the mountains **—the Mountain** ⟦transl. of Fr *la Montagne*⟧ the extreme revolutionary party of Danton and Robespierre, which occupied the highest seats in the French National Assembly in 1793 **—moun′tain·y *adj.***

mountain ash any of a genus (*Sorbus*) of small trees or shrubs of the rose family, with compound leaves and clusters of white flowers and red or orange berries

mountain avens 1 a small evergreen plant (*Dryas octopetala*) of the rose family, found on mountains and in arctic regions **2** a perennial plant (*Geum triflorum*) of the rose family, with reddish flowers and elongated, plumy styles

mountain bike a bicycle having a sturdy frame, handlebars straight across, wide tires with a knobby tread, as many as 21-24 gears, etc., that is suitable for both road and off-road use: sometimes called **mountain bicycle —mountain biker**

mountain cat any of various animals, as the cougar, bobcat, cacomistle, etc.

mountain chain 1 a mountain range **2** two or more relatively adjacent mountain ranges

☆**mountain cranberry** COWBERRY

mountain dew 1 [Obs.] Scotch whiskey **2** [Informal] any whiskey, esp. when illegally distilled, as by Appalachian mountaineers

moun·tain·eer (mount′'n ir′) ***n.* 1** a person who lives in a mountainous region **2** a mountain climber **—*vi.*** to climb mountains, as for sport **—moun′tain·eer′ing *n.***

☆**mountain goat** ROCKY MOUNTAIN GOAT

☆**mountain laurel** an evergreen shrub (*Kalmia latifolia*) of the heath family, with pink and white flowers and poisonous, shiny leaves, native to E North America

☆**mountain lion** COUGAR

☆**mountain mahogany** any of a genus (*Cercocarpus*) of W North American shrubs or small trees of the rose family, with lobed leaves and single dry fruits

moun·tain·ous (mount′'n əs) ***adj.* 1** having or full of mountains **2** like or having the nature of a mountain, specif., very large, tall, steep, etc. **—moun′tain·ous·ly *adv.***

mountain range a series of connected mountains considered as a single system because of geographical proximity or common origin

☆**mountain sheep** any of various wild sheep found in mountain regions; esp., the bighorn

mountain sickness a feeling of weakness, nausea, etc. brought on at high elevations by the rarefied air

moun·tain·side (-sīd′) ***n.*** the side of a mountain

☆**Mountain Standard Time** a standard time used in the zone which includes the Rocky Mountain region of the U.S. corresponding to the mean solar time of the 105th meridian west of Greenwich, England: it is seven hours behind Greenwich time

Mountain State 1 [*also* **M- s-**] any of the eight states of the W U.S. through which the Rocky Mountains pass; Mont., Ida., Wyo., Nev., Utah, Colo., Ariz., or N.Mex. **2** *name for* WEST VIRGINIA

☆**Mountain Time** [*also* **m- t-**] standard time or daylight saving time in the time zone which includes the Rocky Mountain region of the U.S.

moun·tain·top (-täp′) ***n.*** the top of a mountain

Mount·bat·ten (mount bat′'n), **Louis (Francis Albert Victor Nicholas)** ⟦orig. transl. of Ger *Battenberg*⟧ 1st Earl Mountbatten of Burma 1900-79; Brit. admiral

Mount Des·ert (dez′ərt) ⟦< Fr *Isle des Monts Deserts,* lit., island of desert mountains⟧ island off the S coast of Me.: resort: *c.* 100 sq mi (259 sq km)

moun·te·bank (mount′ə baŋk′) ***n.*** ⟦It *montambanco* < *montare,* MOUNT² + *in,* on + *banco,* a bench: see BANK¹⟧ **1** [Historical] a person who mounted a bench, or platform, in a public place and sold quack medicines, usually attracting an audience by tricks, stories, etc. **2** any charlatan, or quack **—*vi.*** to act as a mountebank **—SYN.** QUACK² **—moun′te·bank′er·y *n.***

mount·ed (mount′id) ***adj.* 1** seated on horseback, a bicycle, etc. **2** serving on horseback [*mounted* police] **3** set up and ready for use [*mounted* gun] **4** fixed on or in the proper backing, support, setting, etc. **5** *Mil.* regularly equipped with a means of transportation, as with horses, tanks, armored vehicles, etc.

Mount·ie or **Mount·y** (mount′ē) ***n.,*** *pl.* **-ies** [Informal] a member of the Royal Canadian Mounted Police

mount·ing (mount′iŋ) ***n.* 1** the act of a person or thing that mounts **2** something serving as a backing, support, setting, etc.

Mount Vernon ⟦after Brit Admiral Edward *Vernon* (1684-1757)⟧ home & burial place of George Washington in N Va., on the Potomac, near Washington, D.C.

mourn (môrn) ***vi.*** ⟦ME *mournen* < OE *murnan;* akin to Goth **maúrnan,* to be anxious < IE base **(s)mer-,* to remember: see MERIT⟧ **1** to feel or express sorrow; lament; grieve **2** to grieve for someone who has died; specif., to manifest the conventional signs of such grief, as by wearing black clothing or a mourning band **3** to make the low, continuous sound of a dove **—*vt.* 1** to feel or express sorrow for (something regrettable) **2** to grieve for (someone who has died) **3** to utter in a manner expressing sorrow

mourn·er (môr′nər) ***n.* 1** *a)* a person who is in mourning *b)* any of the persons attending a funeral ☆**2** a person who makes a public profession of penitence at a revival meeting

☆**mourners' bench** a front row of seats at a revival meeting, for those who are to profess penitence

mourn·ful (môrn′fəl) ***adj.* 1** of or characterized by mourning; feeling or expressing grief or sorrow **2** causing sorrow or depression; melancholy **3** having a sound, appearance, etc. that suggests sadness **—mourn′ful·ly *adv.* —mourn′ful·ness *n.***

mourn·ing (môr′niŋ) ***n.* 1** the actions or feelings of one who mourns; specif., the expression of grief at someone's death **2** black clothes, drapery, etc. worn or displayed as a conventional sign of grief for the dead **3** the period during which one mourns the dead **—*adj.*** of or expressing mourning **—mourn′ing·ly *adv.***

mourning band a strip of black crepe or other cloth worn, usually around the arm, to show mourning

mourning cloak a common butterfly (*Nymphalis antiopa*) having purplish-brown wings with a wide yellow border, found throughout Europe and North America

☆**mourning dove** a gray wild dove (*Zenaida macroura*) of the U.S.: so called because its cooing sounds mournful

mouse (mous; *for v., also* mouz) ***n.,*** *pl.* **mice**; for 4, also, **mous′es** ⟦ME *mous* < OE *mus,* akin to Ger *maus* < IE **mūs,* a mouse > Gr *mys,* L *mus,* mouse & *musculus,* MUSCLE⟧ **1** any of a large number of small, widespread rodents belonging to various families and having small ears and a long, thin tail, esp., a species (*Mus musculus*) that commonly infests buildings **2** *a)* [Old-fashioned] a girl or young woman (a term of endearment) *b)* a timid or spiritless person **3** [Slang] a dark, swollen bruise under the eye; black eye ☆**4** ⟦< the shape, motions required for use, and trailing tail-like cord of the earliest devices⟧ *Comput.* a small, hand-held device that is moved about on a flat surface in front of a video screen in such a way as to move or position the cursor or part of the display **—*vi.* moused, mous′ing 1** to hunt for or catch mice **2** to seek about or search for something busily and stealthily **—*vt.* 1** to hunt for **2** [Obs.] to tear or rend as a cat does a mouse

mouse·bird (mous′burd′) ***n.*** COLY

mouse deer CHEVROTAIN

mouse-ear (-ir′) ***n.*** any of various plants, as the hawkweed or chickweed, with short, hairy leaves shaped somewhat like the ear of a mouse

mous·er (mous′ər, mouz′ər) ***n.*** a cat, dog, etc., with reference to its ability to catch mice [some breeds of terrier are excellent *mousers*]

mouse·tail (mous′tāl′) ***n.*** any of a genus (*Myosurus*) of small plants of the buttercup family, with a slender gynoecium resembling the tail of a mouse

mouse·trap (-trap′) ***n.*** a trap for catching mice, specif., a device with a hinged, spring-loaded bar that snaps across the mouse when bait is taken **—*vt.* -trapped′, -trap′ping** ☆to trick or ensnare by means of a feint or stratagem

mous·ey (mous′ē, mouz′ē) ***adj.* mous′i·er, mous′i·est** *alt. sp. of* MOUSY

mous·ing (mous′iŋ, mouz′iŋ) ***n.* 1** the act of hunting or catching mice **2** *Naut.* cord strung across the gap between the point and shank of a hook to keep something attached from slipping off

mous·que·taire (mo͞os kə ter′) ***n.*** ⟦Fr⟧ MUSKETEER

mous·sa·ka (mo͞o sä′kə, mo͞o′sä kä′) ***n.*** ⟦ModGr⟧ a Greek dish consisting typically of sliced eggplant and ground meat arranged in layers, covered with a white sauce and cheese and baked

mousse (mōōs) ***n.*** ⟦Fr, foam, prob. < L *mulsa,* kind of mead < *mulsus,* mixed with honey < *mel,* honey: see MILDEW⟧ **1** any of various light chilled or frozen foods made with egg white, gelatin, whipped cream, etc., combined with fruit or flavoring for desserts, or with fish, meat, etc. **2** an aerosol foam used to help hair stay in place and, sometimes, to add color **—*vt.* moussed, mouss′ing** to shape or style (hair) with mousse

mousse·line (mōōs lēn′) ***n.*** ⟦Fr: see MUSLIN⟧ **1** a sheer fabric somewhat resembling muslin and made of rayon, silk, etc. **2** a fine blown glass with a lacy pattern **3** MOUSSELINE SAUCE

mousseline de laine (də len′) ⟦Fr, muslin of wool⟧ a lightweight woolen cloth, often printed, used for dresses

mousseline de soie (də swå′) ⟦Fr, muslin of silk⟧ a gauzelike silk or rayon cloth with a plain weave

mousseline sauce ⟦so named because of its light, frothy texture⟧ any of various sauces lightened with whipped cream or beaten egg whites; esp., hollandaise sauce containing whipped cream

Moussorgsky, Modest *alt. sp. of* MUSSORGSKY

mous·tache (mus′tash′, mə stash′) ***n.*** *alt. sp. of* MUSTACHE

mous·ta·chi·o (mə stash′ē ō′, -stä′shē ō′; -stash′ō, -stä′shō) ***n., pl.* -os′** *alt. sp. of* MUSTACHIO

Mous·te·ri·an (mōōs tir′ē ən) ***adj.*** ⟦Fr *moustérien:* remains were found at Le *Moustier,* cave in S France⟧ designating or of a Middle Paleolithic culture, associated with the Neanderthal cave people and characterized by the use of flaked hand axes, scrapers, etc.

mous·y (mous′ē, mouz′ē) ***adj.* mous′i·er, mous′i·est 1** of, characteristic of, or like a mouse, in any of various ways; quiet, timid, drab, etc. **2** full of or infested with mice **—mous′i·ness *n.***

mouth (mouth; *for v.* mouth) ***n., pl.* mouths** (mouthz) ⟦ME < OE *muth,* akin to Ger *mund* < IE base **menth-,* to chew > Gr *masasthai,* L *mandere,* to chew⟧ **1** the opening through which an animal takes in food; specif., the cavity, or the entire structure, in the head of any of the higher animals which contains the teeth and tongue and through which sounds are uttered **2** *a)* the mouth regarded as the organ of chewing and tasting *b)* the mouth regarded as the organ of speech **3** a person or animal regarded as a being needing food [six *mouths* to feed] **4** the lips, or the part of the face surrounding the lips **5** a wry expression of the face; grimace: now only in the phrase **make mouths (or a mouth) at 6** any opening regarded as like the mouth; specif., *a)* the part of a river, stream, etc. where the water empties into another body of water *b)* the opening into the earth of a cave, volcano, tunnel, etc. *c)* the opening of a container, through which it is filled or emptied *d)* the front opening in the barrel of a gun *e)* the opening between the jaws of a vise, etc. *f)* the opening between the lips of an organ pipe *g)* the opening in a flute across which the player blows **—*vt.* 1** *a)* to say, esp. in an affected, oratorical, or insincere manner; declaim *b)* to form (a word) with the mouth soundlessly **2** to take or put into the mouth **3** to caress or rub with the mouth or lips **4** to train (a horse) to become accustomed to the bit **—*vi.* 1** to speak in an affected or oratorical manner; declaim **2** [Rare] to make a wry face by twisting the mouth; grimace **—down in (or at) the mouth** ⟦in allusion to the lowered corners of the mouth in a frown or scowl⟧ [Informal] depressed; unhappy; discouraged **—(have) a big mouth** [Informal] (to have) a tendency to talk loudly, excessively, indiscreetly, or impudently **—☆mouth off** [Slang] to talk loudly, excessively, indiscreetly, or impudently **—mouth·er** (mouth′ər) ***n.* —mouth′less *adj.***

mouth-breath·er (mouth′brē′thər) ***n.*** ⟦in allusion to a dazed, open-mouthed expression⟧ [Informal] a slow-witted or socially awkward person **—mouth′-breath′ing *adj.***

mouth·breed·er (mouth′brēd′ər) ***n.*** any of a number of small fishes, as certain cichlids and catfishes, that carry their eggs and young in the mouth

-mouthed (mouthd) *combining form* having a (specified kind of) mouth [loud-*mouthed*]

mouth·feel (mouth′fēl′) ***n.*** the way a particular food or beverage feels in the mouth as it is eaten or drunk [the velvety *mouthfeel* of ice cream]

mouth·ful (mouth′fool′) ***n., pl.* -fuls′ 1** as much as the mouth can hold **2** as much as is usually taken into the mouth at one time **3** a small amount, esp. of food **4** [Informal] a long word or a group of words that is hard to say **5** [Informal] a pertinent, important, or correct remark: chiefly in **say a mouthful**

mouth organ ☆HARMONICA (sense 1)

mouth·part (-pärt′) ***n.*** any of various structures, organs, or appendages around the mouth in arthropods, modified for biting, piercing, sucking, chewing, grasping, etc.: *usually used in pl.*

mouth·piece (-pēs′) ***n.* 1** a part placed at, or forming, a mouth [the *mouthpiece* of a telephone, a pipe, a horse's bit, etc.] **2** the part of a musical instrument held in or to the mouth **3** a person, periodical, etc. used by some other person or persons to express their views, ideas, etc. **4** [Slang] a lawyer who defends criminals

☆**mouth-to-mouth** (mouth′tə mouth′) ***adj.*** designating a method of resuscitation in which the rescuer breathes directly into the mouth and lungs of a person who has stopped breathing

mouth·wash (mouth′wôsh′) ***n.*** a flavored, often antiseptic liquid used for rinsing the mouth or for gargling

mouth·wa·ter·ing (-wôt′ər iŋ) ***adj.*** appetizing enough to make the mouth water

mouth·y (mouth′ē, mouth′ē) ***adj.* mouth′i·er, mouth′i·est** [Informal] overly talkative, esp. in a bombastic or rude way **—mouth′i·ly *adv.* —mouth′i·ness *n.***

mou·ton (mōō′tän′) ***n.*** ⟦Fr, sheep < OFr *moton:* see MUTTON⟧ lambskin or sheepskin, processed and dyed to resemble beaver, seal, etc.

mou·ton·née (mōō′tə nā′) ***adj.*** ⟦Fr, fem. pp. of *moutonner,* make sheeplike < *mouton:* see prec.⟧ rounded like the back of a sheep, as by glacial action: said of rock

mov·a·ble (mōō′və bəl) ***adj.* 1** *a)* that can be moved from one place or position to another; not fixed *b) Law* designating or of personal property as distinguished from real property **2** changing in date from one year to the next [Thanksgiving is a *movable* holiday] **—*n.* 1** something movable **2** *Law* a piece of property that is movable, as furniture; personal property: *usually used in pl.* Also sp. **move′a·ble —mov′a·bil′i·ty *n.* —mov′a·bly *adv.***

move (mōōv) ***vt.* moved, mov′ing** ⟦ME *moven* < Anglo-Fr *mover* < OFr *movoir* < L *movere* < IE base **mew-,* to push away > Sans *mīvati,* (he) shoves⟧ **1** to change the place or position of; push, carry, or pull from one place or position to another **2** to set or keep in motion; actuate, impel, turn, stir, etc. **3** to cause or persuade (*to* act, do, say, speak, etc.); prompt **4** to arouse or stir the emotions, passions, or sympathies of **5** to propose or suggest; esp., to propose formally, as in a meeting **6** to cause (the bowels) to evacuate **7** *Commerce* to dispose of (goods) by selling **—*vi.* 1** to change place or position; go (*to* some place) **2** to change one's place of residence, business, etc. **3** to live or be active in a specified setting or milieu [to *move* in artistic circles] **4** to make progress; advance **5** to take action; begin to act **6** *a)* to be, or be set, in motion *b)* to operate in a certain fixed motion; turn, revolve, etc. (said of machines) **7** to change in price, value, etc. [stocks *moved* lower in heavy trading yesterday] **8** to make a formal appeal or application (*for*) [*move* for a new trial] **9** to evacuate: said of the bowels **10** *Checkers, Chess, etc. a)* to change the position of a piece *b)* to be put in another position (said of a piece) **11** *Commerce* to be disposed of by sale: said of goods **—*n.* 1** the act of moving; a movement **2** one of a series of actions toward some goal **3** a change of residence, business location, etc. **4** *Checkers, Chess, etc.* the act of moving, or a player's turn to move **5** [Slang] an action, device, trick, etc. intended to deceive; esp., in sports, a deceptive maneuver or movement **—SYN.** AFFECT[1] **—☆get a move on** [Slang] **1** to start moving **2** to hurry; go faster **—move in** to take up residence **—☆move in on** [Informal] **1** to draw near, with the intention of capturing **2** to attempt to take over control of (something) from (someone) **—move it!** [Informal] hurry up! get going! **—move on** [Informal] **1** to take one's leave; go away **2** to resume one's normal life, as after a disruptive experience **—move over** to move to another place or position, esp. an adjacent one **—move up** to promote or be promoted **—on the move** [Informal] moving about from place to place **—put the moves (or a move) on** [Slang] to attempt to charm or seduce sexually, as by the use of practiced tricks or remarks

move·ment (mōōv′mənt) ***n.*** ⟦OFr⟧ **1** the act or process of moving; specif., *a)* a motion or action of a person or group *b)* a shift in position *c) short for* BOWEL MOVEMENT *d) Mil.* a change in the location of troops, ships, etc., as part of a maneuver **2** a particular manner of moving **3** *a)* a series of organized activities by people working concertedly toward some goal *b)* the organization consisting of those active in this way **4** a tendency or trend in some particular sphere of activity **5** the pacing, specif. the rapid pacing, of the incidents in a literary work **6** the effect or representation of motion in painting, sculpture, etc. **7** *Mech.* the moving parts of a mechanism; esp., a series of interconnected moving parts [the *movement* of a clock] **8** *Music a)* any of the principal divisions of a symphony, sonata, or other extended composition: each such division typically differs from the others as in structure, tempo, key, etc. *b)* tempo or rhythm *c)* MOTION (*n.* 9) **9** *Prosody* rhythmic flow; cadence

mov·er (mōō′vər) ***n.* 1** a person or thing that moves ☆**2** *a)* a person whose work or business is moving furniture, etc. for those changing residence *b)* [*also pl.*] a business engaged in this work

mover and shaker a person who has power and influence: *usually used in pl.*

☆**mov·ie** (mōō′vē) ***n.*** ⟦contr. < MOVING PICTURE⟧ **1** FILM (*n.* 5) **2** a showing of a film, as in a theater [I'm going to a *movie* tonight] **—the movies 1** the film industry **2** a showing of a film

mov·ie·dom (mōō′vē dəm) ***n.*** FILMDOM

☆**mov·ie·go·er** (-gō′ər) ***n.*** a person who goes to see films, esp. often or regularly **—mov′ie·go′ing *n., adj.***

mov·ie·mak·er (-māk′ər) ***n.*** FILMMAKER **—mov′ie·mak′ing *n.***

mov·ing (mōō′viŋ) ***adj.* 1** that moves; specif., *a)* changing, or causing to change, place or position *b)* causing motion *c)* causing to act; impelling, influencing, etc. *d)* arousing or stirring the emotions or feelings; esp., arousing pathos *e)* of or having to do with a changing of residence [a *moving* date, van, company, etc.] **2** involving a moving motor vehicle [a *moving* violation of a traffic law] **—mov′ing·ly *adv.***

SYN.—moving implies a general arousing or stirring of the emotions or feelings, sometimes, specif., of pathos [a *moving* plea for help]; **poignant** is applied to that which is sharply painful to the feelings [the *poignant* cry of a lost child]; **affecting** applies to that which stirs the emotions, as to tears [the *affecting* scene of their reunion]; **touching** is used of that which arouses such tender feelings as sympathy, gratitude, etc. [her *touching* little gift to me]; **pathetic** applies to that which arouses pity or compassion, sometimes pity mingled with contempt [his *pathetic* attempt at wit]

moving picture [Old-fashioned] FILM (*n.* 5)

moving sidewalk a long, wide conveyor belt designed to move pedestrians short distances, as at an airport

☆**moving staircase** (*or* **stairway**) [Now Chiefly Brit.] ESCALATOR

moving van a large VAN³ (*n.* 1) used for transporting furniture and other belongings, as of a person moving to a new residence

Mov·i·o·la (mo͞o′vē ō′lə) *trademark for* a small motor-driven machine for viewing and editing FILM (*n.* 5) —*n.* [m-] such a machine: also sp. **mov′ie·o′la**

mow¹ (mō) *vt., vi.* **mowed**, **mowed** or **mown**, **mow′ing** ⟦ME *mowen* < OE *mawan,* akin to Ger *mähen* < IE base **mē-, *met-* > L *metere,* to mow⟧ **1** to cut down (standing grass or grain) with a sickle, scythe, lawn mower, etc. **2** to cut grass or grain from (a lawn, field, etc.) —**mow down 1** to cause to fall like grass or grain being cut **2** to kill or destroy as with swift, sudden strokes, gunfire, etc. **3** to overwhelm (an opponent) —**mow′er** *n.*

mow² (mou) *n.* ⟦ME *mowe* < OE *muga,* a heap, pile, akin to ON *mūgi,* a crowd, swath < Gmc **mug-* < IE base **muk-,* heap > Gr *mykōn*⟧ **1** a stack or heap of hay, grain, etc., esp. in a barn **2** the part of a barn where hay or grain is stored; haymow or hayloft

mow³ (mō, mou) *n., vi.* ⟦ME *mowe* < OFr *moue* < Frank **mauwa,* akin to MDu *mouwe*: for IE base see MOPE⟧ [Archaic] GRIMACE

mow·ing (mō′iŋ) *n.* **1** the act of cutting down grass or grain **2** the quantity of grass or grain mowed at one time ☆**3** a field on which grass is grown for hay

☆**mowing machine** a farm machine with a reciprocating blade for mowing standing grain or grass

mown (mōn) *vt., vi. alt. pp. of* MOW¹

mox·a (mäk′sə) *n.* ⟦altered < Jpn *mogusa,* a caustic < *moe kusa,* burning herb⟧ mugwort (*Artemisia vulgaris*) used as a cauterizing agent or counterirritant in moxibustion

mox·i·bus·tion (mäk′sə bus′chən) *n.* ⟦< prec. + (COM)BUSTION⟧ the burning of moxa on the skin in treating various diseases or disorders, as in traditional Chinese and Japanese medicine

☆**mox·ie** (mäk′sē) *n.* ⟦< *Moxie,* trademark for a soft drink⟧ [Slang] courage, pluck, perseverance, etc.; guts

moy·en âge (mwȧ ye näzh′) ⟦Fr⟧ the Middle Ages

Mo·zam·bique (mō′zəm bēk′, -zam-) country in SE Africa, on Mozambique Channel: formerly a Portuguese territory, it became independent in 1975; member of the Commonwealth: 309,496 sq mi (801,590 sq km); cap. Maputo

Mozambique Channel part of the Indian Ocean, between Mozambique & Madagascar: *c.* 1,000 mi (1,609 km) long

Moz·ar·ab (mō zar′əb) *n.* ⟦Sp *mozárabe* < Ar *musta'rib,* would-be Arab⟧ any of the Spanish Christians who were permitted to practice their religion in a modified form during the period of Moorish rule —**Moz·ar′a·bic** *adj.*

Mo·zart (mō′tsärt′), **Wolf·gang A·ma·de·us** (vôlf′gäŋk′ ä′mä dā′o͝os) 1756-91; Austrian composer —**Mo·zar′te·an** *adj.*, **Mo·zar′ti·an** (-tsärt′ē ən)

moz·za·rel·la (mät′sə rel′ə) *n.* ⟦It, dim. of *mozza,* a kind of cheese < *mozzare,* to cut off < *mozzo,* blunt < VL **mutius,* cut off, blunted⟧ a soft, white Italian cheese with a mild flavor, used esp. on pizza, in lasagna, etc.

moz·zet·ta or **mo·zet·ta** (mə zet′ə, mō-) *n.* ⟦It *mozzetta* < *mozzo,* (see prec.), shortened < VL **mutius*⟧ a short cape with a small hood, worn over the rochet by the pope and other high dignitaries of the Roman Catholic Church

mp¹ *abbrev.* melting point

mp² *abbrev.* ⟦It *mezzo piano*⟧ *Musical Direction* moderately soft(ly)

MP *abbrev.* **1** Member of Parliament **2** Military Police **3** Mounted Police **4** Northern Mariana Islands

MPAA *abbrev.* Motion Picture Association of America

mpg *abbrev.* miles per gallon

mph *abbrev.* miles per hour

MP3 (em′pē′thrē′) *n.* ⟦*MP(EG),* abbrev. of *Motion Picture Experts Group* (organization developing standards for digital file formats) + (*audio layer*) *3,* a coding format⟧ **1** a format for processing a digital audio file so as to remove unneeded data and produce a smaller file for transmission on the internet, for use in portable players, etc. **2** an audio file so produced

Mpu·ma·lan·ga (′m po͞o′mə läŋ′gə, em-) province of South Africa, in the N part: 30,259 sq mi (78,371 sq km); cap. Nelspruit

Mr *abbrev.* March

Mr. or **Mr** (mis′tər) *abbrev.* mister: used before the name or title of a man: pl. *Messrs*: see MISTER¹

☆**Mr. Char·lie** (chär′lē) [Slang] a white man or white men collectively: a term used usually derisively by African-Americans

Mr. Clean [Slang] a man who is, or is thought to be, honest and upright; esp., such a man in politics or public life

MRE *abbrev. Mil.* meal (or meals) ready to eat

☆**Mr. Fixit** ⟦see FIX-IT⟧ [Slang] a man who is good at repairing things; specif., a man who is an expert at finding acceptable solutions to difficult problems, situations, etc.

MRI (em′ar′ī′) *n.* ⟦*m(agnetic) r(esonance) i(maging)*⟧ **1** a type of IMAGING that makes use of NUCLEAR MAGNETIC RESONANCE to produce extremely accurate cross-sectional images **2** a noninvasive, diagnostic medical procedure utilizing this type of imaging

mri·dan·gam (mri däŋ′gəm) *n.* ⟦< Sans *mṛdanga,* clayey⟧ *Music* a double-headed, barrel-shaped drum of India: also **mri·dan′ga** (-gə)

mRNA *abbrev.* messenger RNA

Mr. Right [Informal] the man who makes or would make the ideal mate for a particular person: often used hypothetically [she wondered if *Mr. Right* would ever come along]

Mrs. or **Mrs** (mis′iz) *abbrev.* mistress: a title for a woman who is married or has been married, placed before her name [*Mrs.* Smith, *Mrs.* Mary Smith], or, more formally, placed before her husband's name [*Mrs.* Walter Smith]: pl. *Mmes* (see MESDAMES)

MRSA (mur′sə) *n.* ⟦*m(ethicillin-)r(esistant) S(taphylococcus) a(ureus)*⟧ **1** a strain of staphylococcus particularly resistant to antibiotics **2** an infection caused by this strain

ms *abbrev.* **1** manuscript **2** millisecond: also **msec**

MS *abbrev.* **1** manuscript **2** Master of Science **3** Master of Surgery **4** Mississippi **5** motor ship **6** multiple sclerosis **7** ⟦L *memoriae sacrum*⟧ sacred to the memory of Also, for 2 and 7, **M.S.**

☆**Ms.** or **Ms** (miz) *abbrev.* a title free of reference to marital status: used before the name of a woman instead of either *Miss* or *Mrs.*

MSc or **M.Sc.** *abbrev.* Master of Science

MSG *abbrev.* **1** Master Sergeant **2** monosodium glutamate

Msgr *abbrev.* Monsignor

MSgt *abbrev.* Master Sergeant

m'sieur (mə syur′; *Fr* mə syö′) *n.* [Informal] *phonetic sp. of* MONSIEUR

msl *abbrev.* mean sea level

MSM *abbrev.* mainstream media

MSRP *abbrev.* Manufacturer's Suggested Retail Price

MSS *abbrev.* manuscripts: also **mss**

MST *abbrev.* Mountain Standard Time

MSW or **M.S.W.** *abbrev.* Master of Social Work

mt *abbrev.* **1** metric ton **2** mountain

Mt¹ *abbrev.* **1** *Bible* Matthew **2** Mount **3** Mountain

Mt² *Chem. symbol for* meitnerium

MT *abbrev.* **1** Machine Translation **2** Masoretic Text **3** megaton **4** Montana **5** Mountain Time

mtDNA *abbrev.* mitochondrial DNA

mtg *abbrev.* **1** meeting **2** mortgage: also **mtge**

mtn *abbrev.* mountain

Mt Rev *abbrev.* Most Reverend

Mts *abbrev.* Mountains

MTV *service mark* Music Television

mu (mo͞o, myo͞o) *n.* ⟦Gr *my*⟧ the twelfth letter of the Greek alphabet (M, μ)

much (much) *adj.* **more**, **most** ⟦ME *muche* < *muchel,* large, much < OE *mycel,* large in size or quantity < IE base **meĝ(h)-,* large > Gr *megas,* L *magnus*⟧ **1** [Obs.] many in number **2** great in quantity, amount, degree, etc. —*adv.* **more**, **most 1** to a great degree or extent [*much* happier] **2** just about; almost; nearly [*much* the same as yesterday] **3** at frequent intervals; often [do you dine out *much?*] —*n.* **1** a great amount or quantity [*much* to be done] **2** something great, unusual, or outstanding [not *much* to look at] —**a bit much** somewhat excessive —**as much as 1** to the degree that **2** practically; virtually; in effect —**make much of** to treat or consider as of great importance —**much as 1** almost as **2** however; although —**not much of a** not particularly good as a

mu·cha·cha (mo͞o chä′chä) *n., pl.* ***-chas*** (-chäs) ⟦Sp⟧ a girl or young woman

mu·cha·cho (-chô) *n., pl.* ***-chos*** (-chôs) ⟦Sp⟧ a boy or young man

much·ly (much′lē) *adv.* [Informal] very much: used mainly in the humorous phrase **thanks muchly**

much·ness (much′nis) *n.* greatness, as of quantity or degree

much·o (mo͞o′chō) *adj.* ⟦Sp⟧ [*also in italics*] [Slang] much or many; a lot of [in *mucho* trouble]

mu·cic acid (myo͞o′sik) ⟦Fr *mucique* < L *mucus* (see MUCUS) + *-ique,* -IC⟧ a colorless, crystalline acid, $HOOC(CHOH)_4COOH$, formed by oxidizing lactose, gums, etc.

mu·cid (myo͞o′sid) *adj.* ⟦L *mucidus* < *mucere,* to be moldy, akin to *mucus,* MUCUS⟧ [Archaic] moldy; musty

mu·cif·er·ous (myo͞o sif′ər əs) *adj.* ⟦MUC(US) + *-i-* + -FEROUS⟧ producing or secreting mucus

mu·ci·lage (myo͞o′sə lij) *n.* ⟦ME *muscilage* < MFr *mucilage* < LL *mucilago,* musty juice < L *mucere*: see MUCID⟧ **1** any of various thick, sticky substances produced in certain plants ☆**2** any watery solution of gum, glue, etc. used as an adhesive

mu·ci·lag·i·nous (myo͞o′sə laj′ə nəs) *adj.* ⟦MFr *mucilagineux* < ML *mucilaginosus*⟧ **1** of or like mucilage; sticky **2** producing mucilage

mu·cin (myo͞o′sin) *n.* ⟦Fr *mucine*: see MUCUS & -IN¹⟧ any of various glycoproteins in connective tissue, saliva, mucus, etc., that lubricate and protect the body —**mu′cin·ous** *adj.*, **mu′cin·oid′**

mu·cin·o·gen (myo͞o sin′ə jən) *n.* ⟦prec. + *-o-* + -GEN⟧ any of a group of substances from which mucins are derived

muck (muk) *n.* ⟦ME *muk* < or akin to ON *myki,* dung < IE base **meuk-,* slippery, viscous > MEEK, L *mucus*⟧ **1** moist manure **2** black earth containing decaying matter, used as a fertilizer **3** *a)* mire; mud *b)* anything unclean or degrading; dirt; filth —*vt.* **1** to fertilize with muck **2** [Informal] to dirty with or as with muck: often with *up* **3** [Slang] to make a mess of; bungle: often with *up* **4** [Chiefly Brit.] to clean (esp. a stable): usually with *out* —**muck about** (or **around**) [Slang, Chiefly Brit.] to waste time; putter

muck-a-muck or **muck·a·muck** (muk′ə muk′) *n.* [Slang] *var. of* HIGH MUCK-A-MUCK: also **muck′e·ty-muck′**

muck·le (muk′əl) *adj., adv., n.* [Now Chiefly Scot.] *var. of* MICKLE

muck·rake (muk′rāk′) *vi.* **-raked′**, **-rak′ing** ⟦inspired by the allusion by Theodore ROOSEVELT² in a speech (1906) to the man with the *muck rake* in

Bunyan's *Pilgrim's Progress*⟧ ☆to search for and publicize, as in newspapers, any real or alleged corruption or scandal by public figures, esp. politicians —**muck′rak′er** *n.*

muck·worm (muk′wurm′) *n.* **1** a grub, or larva, that lives and develops in manure or mud **2** a miser

muck·y (muk′ē) *adj.* **muck′i·er, muck′i·est** of or like muck; esp., dirty, filthy, etc.

mu·co- (myo͞o′kō, -kə) *combining form* **1** mucus [*mucopolysaccharide*] **2** mucous membrane

mu·coid (myo͞o′koid′) *n.* ⟦MUC(IN) + -OID⟧ any of a group of mucoproteins found in connective tissues, in certain types of cysts, etc. —*adj.* like mucus

mu·co·pol·y·sac·cha·ride (myo͞o′kō päl′i sak′ə rīd′) *n.* ⟦MUCO- + POLYSACCHARIDE⟧ any of a group of complex carbohydrates that provides structural support for connective tissue, lubrication for all body joints, etc.

mu·co·pro·tein (myo͞o′kō prō′tēn′) *n.* any of a group of glycoproteins found in connective tissue, mucous secretions, blood plasma, gastric juice, urine, etc.

mu·co·pu·ru·lent (myo͞o′kō pyoor′ə lənt) *adj.* containing both mucus and pus

mu·co·sa (myo͞o kō′sə) *n., pl.* **-sae** (-sē) or **-sas** ⟦ModL < fem. of L *mucosus,* fol.⟧ MUCOUS MEMBRANE —**mu·co′sal** *adj.*

mu·cous (myo͞o′kəs) *adj.* ⟦L *mucosus,* slimy < *mucus,* MUCUS⟧ **1** of, containing, or secreting mucus **2** like mucus or covered with or as with mucus; slimy —**mu·cos′i·ty** (-käs′ə tē) *n.*

mucous membrane a mucus-secreting membrane lining body cavities and canals connecting with the external air, as the alimentary canal and respiratory tract

mu·cro (myo͞o′krō) *n., pl.* **-cro′nes** (myo͞o krō′nēz) ⟦ModL < L, sharp point < IE base **meuk-,* to scratch > Gr *amychē,* a scratch⟧ *Biol.* a short, sharp point, tip, or process projecting abruptly from certain parts and organs, as at the end of a leaf

mu·cro·nate (myo͞o′krə nit, -nāt′) *adj.* ⟦ModL < L *mucronatus*⟧ ending in a mucro, or sharp point: also **mu′cro·nat′ed** —**mu′cro·na′tion** *n.*

mu·cus (myo͞o′kəs) *n.* ⟦L: see MEEK, MUCK⟧ the thick, slimy secretion of the mucous membranes, that moistens and protects them

mud (mud) *n.* ⟦ME, prob. < a LowG source as in *mudde* < IE **meut* < base **meu-,* wet, musty > MOSS, MOTHER²⟧ **1** wet, soft, sticky earth **2** defamatory remarks; libel or slander —*vt.* **mud′ded, mud′ding** to cover or soil with or as with mud; muddy

mud bath a soaking in, typically, a mixture of mineral waters, volcanic ash, peat, etc.: done as therapy or for relaxation, as at a spa

☆**mud·cat** (mud′kat′) *n.* any of several catfishes living in muddy waters

mud crack a crack formed in mud beds in the course of drying and shrinking, sometimes filled in and preserved when the beds are changed to rock

☆**mud dauber** any of various narrow-waisted wasps (family Sphecidae) that build cells of hard, caked mud for their larvae

☆**mud·der** (mud′ər) *n.* a race horse that performs especially well on a wet, muddy track

mud·dle (mud′'l) *vt.* **-dled, -dling** ⟦< MUD + -LE⟧ **1** to mix up in a confused manner; jumble; bungle **2** to mix or stir (a drink, etc.) **3** to make (water, etc.) turbid **4** to confuse mentally; befuddle, as with alcoholic liquor **5** to confuse (the brain, mind, etc.); befog —*vi.* to act or think in a confused way —*n.* **1** a confused or disordered condition; mess, jumble, etc. **2** mental confusion —**SYN.** CONFUSION —**muddle through** to manage to succeed in spite of apparent blunders or confusion

mud·dle-head·ed (-hed′id) *adj.* stupid; blundering; confused —**mud′dle-head′ed·ness** *n.*

☆**mud·dler** (mud′lər) *n.* a stick for stirring mixed drinks

mud·dy (mud′ē) *adj.* **-di·er, -di·est** **1** full of or spattered with mud **2** *a)* not clear; containing sediment; cloudy [*muddy* coffee] *b)* not light or bright; dull [a *muddy* complexion] **3** confused, obscure, vague, etc. [*muddy* thinking] — *vt., vi.* **-died, -dy·ing** to make or become muddy —**mud′di·ly** *adv.* —**mud′di·ness** *n.*

☆**mud eel** a slime-coated, eel-like siren salamander (*Siren lacertina*) with no hind legs, two short front legs, internal lungs, and external gills: it lives in swamps, ditches, and ponds, in the SE U.S.

mud·fish (-fish′) *n., pl.* **-fish′** or **-fish′es** (see FISH) ☆any of various unrelated fishes that live in mud or muddy water, as the bowfin or killifish

mud·flap (-flap′) *n.* a flap, typically flexible, hung behind a wheel of a motor vehicle to stop water, stones, etc. from being thrown backward

mud flat nearly level muddy land that is flooded at high tide and left uncovered at low tide

mud·flow (mud′flō′) *n.* a massive movement of wet soil, rocks, etc.: see also LAHAR, MUDSLIDE

mud·guard (-gärd′) *n.* **1** *former term for* FENDER (sense *a*) **2** *a)* SPLASH GUARD *b)* a device similar in function, as on a bicycle, which blocks splashing mud or water

mud hen any of various birds that live in marshes, as the coot or gallinule

☆**mud·hole** (-hōl′) *n.* a hole or low place, as in a field or road, full of mud

mud·lark (-lärk′) *n.* [Now Chiefly Literary] a homeless or neglected child

mud·pack (-pak′) *n.* a paste made up of fuller's earth, astringents, etc., used as a facial

☆**mud puppy** any of a genus (*Necturus,* family Proteidae) of gilled, aquatic North American salamanders that hide during the day in mud along the bottom of freshwater streams or lakes

mu·dra (moo drä′) *n.* ⟦Sans, a seal, sign⟧ **1** in ancient India, any identifying symbol or seal **2** a stylized, symbolic gesture used in dances, rituals, etc. of India, specif., an intricate movement or positioning of the hands or fingers

mud·room (mud′ro͞om′) *n.* a room in a house used for the removal and storage of wet or muddy footwear and outerwear

mud·sill (mud′sil′) *n.* the lowest sill of a structure, placed on the foundation or directly on the ground

mud·skip·per (-skip′ər) *n.* any of various goby fishes that are able to leave the water regularly, as when living in mud flats or climbing mangrove roots in search of food

mud·slide (-slīd′) *n.* **1** a slow, viscous mudflow down a gradual slope **2** loosely, any mudflow

mud·sling·ing (-sliŋ′iŋ) *n.* the practice of making unscrupulous, malicious attacks against an opponent, as in a political campaign —**mud′sling′er** *n.*

☆**mud snake** a long, bluish-black colubrid snake (*Farancia abacura*) with a red belly and a nonpoisonous spine at the tip of the tail, found in the SE U.S.

mud·stone (-stōn′) *n.* a fine-grained sedimentary rock that is formed from silt and clay, similar to shale but not distinctly laminated

☆**mud turtle** any of a genus (*Kinosternon*) of musk turtles of North and Central America that live in muddy ponds, streams, etc.

Muen·ster (cheese) (mun′stər, moon′-) ⟦after *Münster,* France, where first made⟧ a mild, light-yellow, semisoft cheese

mues·li (myo͞oz′lē) *n.* ⟦Swiss-Ger dial. *müesli* < Ger *mus,* mush⟧ a breakfast cereal like granola, with rolled oats, shredded apples, raisins, etc.

mu·ez·zin (myo͞o ez′in) *n.* ⟦Ar *mu'adhdhin,* prp. of *adhdhana,* freq. of *adhana,* proclaim < *udhn,* ear⟧ in Muslim countries, a crier, as in a minaret, who calls the people to prayer five times a day

muff (muf) *n.* ⟦Du *mof* < Wal *moufe,* shortened < Fr *moufle,* a mitten < ML *muffla,* glove⟧ **1** a cylindrical covering of fur or other soft material into which the hands are placed from either end to keep them warm **2** a tuft of feathers on the sides of the head, or on the legs, of certain fowl **3** *a) Sports* a failure to hold the ball when attempting to catch it *b)* any bungling action — *vt., vi.* **1** to do (something) badly or awkwardly **2** *Sports* to miss (a catch) or bungle (a play)

muf·fin (muf′ən) *n.* ⟦< dial. *mouffin, moufin,* ? akin to OFr *moufflet,* soft, as in *pain moufflet,* soft bread⟧ a quick bread made with eggs, baked in a small cup-shaped mold: see also ENGLISH MUFFIN

muf·fin·eer (muf′ə nir′) *n.* ⟦so called because orig. used when serving muffins, etc.⟧ a shaker for sprinkling sugar, spices, etc.

muf·fle (muf′əl) *vt.* **-fled, -fling** ⟦ME *muflen,* prob. akin to OFr *enmouflé,* muffled < *moufle,* a mitten: see MUFF⟧ **1** to wrap up in a shawl, blanket, cloak, etc. so as to hide, keep warm, or protect **2** to wrap or cover in order to deaden or prevent sound **3** to deaden (a sound), as by wrapping **4** to prevent the expression of; stifle —*n.* **1** an oven in which pottery, etc. can be fired without being exposed directly to the flame **2** the fleshy bare part of the upper lip and nose of certain mammals, as ruminants or rabbits

muf·fler (muf′lər) *n.* **1** a scarf worn around the throat, as for warmth **2** any of various devices for deadening noises; specif., a device, as on an automobile, for deadening the noise of pressurized exhaust produced by the internal-combustion engine

☆**muf·fu·let·ta** (mo͞o′fə let′ə) *n.* ⟦< It dial. *muffoletta,* the type of round Sicilian loaf used, ? akin to It *muffola,* mitten (< ML *muffla:* see MUFF)⟧ a sandwich of cold meats, cheese, and olive salad on a large, round roll: it originated in New Orleans

muf·ti (muf′tē) *n., pl.* **-tis** ⟦Ar, one who gives a decisive response < *āftā,* to judge⟧ **1** in Muslim countries, an interpreter or expounder of religious law **2** ⟦? in allusion to the dressing gown and tasseled cap worn by an off-duty Brit officer in the early 19th c.⟧ ordinary clothes, esp. when worn by one who normally wears, or has long worn, a military or other uniform

mug¹ (mug) *n.* ⟦prob. < Scand, as in Swed *mugg*⟧ **1** a heavy drinking cup of earthenware or metal, having a handle **2** as much as a mug will hold **3** ⟦because drinking mugs were often ornamented with a human face⟧ [Slang] *a)* the face *b)* the mouth *c)* a grimace *d)* a rough, ugly person; ruffian, thug, etc. *e)* a fool or dupe; sucker ☆*f) short for* MUG SHOT —*vt.* **mugged, mug′ging** **1** to assault usually with intent to rob ☆**2** [Slang] to photograph; esp., to photograph (a person under arrest) for police records —*vi.* **1** to assault a person, usually with intent to rob **2** [Slang] *a)* to make a grimace *b) Theater* to overact by exaggerated facial expressions —**mug's game** [Slang] an undertaking regarded as foolish, pointless, etc.

mug² (mug) *vi.* **mugged, mug′ging** [Brit. Slang] to study hard and hurriedly, as in preparation for an examination; cram: used with *up*

mug·ger¹ (mug′ər) *n.* one who mugs; esp., *a)* one who assaults with intent to rob *b) Theater* one who overacts, esp. by exaggerated facial expressions

mug·ger² (mug′ər) *n.* ⟦Hindi *magar* < Sans *makara,* sea monster⟧ a large, relatively timid crocodile (*Crocodylus palustris*) of India and Malaysia, with a broad, wrinkled snout

mug·gins (mug′inz) *n.* ⟦after pers. name *Muggins,* assoc. with slang *mug,* cardsharp's dupe⟧ [Brit. Slang] a dupe; fool

mug·gy (mug′ē) *adj.* **-gi·er, -gi·est** ⟦< dial. *mug,* mist, drizzle, prob. < or akin to ON *mugga* < IE base **meuk-* > MUCK⟧ hot and damp, with little or no stirring of the air [*muggy* weather] —**mug′gi·ness** *n.*

Mu·ghal (mo͞o′gäl′) *n. var. of* MOGUL (*n.* 1)

mu·gho pine (myo͞o′gō) ⟦prob. via Fr *mugho,* mugho pine < It *mugo*⟧ a Swiss mountain pine (*Pinus mugo*), esp. a shrubby spreading form often used as an ornamental

mug shot any of the photographs taken for police records of the face of a person under arrest

mug·wort (mug′wurt, -wôrt′) *n.* ⟦OE *mycgwyrt* < *mycg,* MIDGE + *wyrt,* WORT[2]⟧ any of various species of artemisia, esp. a tall, Eurasian perennial herb (*Artemisia vulgaris*) having leaves used in folk medicine

☆**mug·wump** (mug′wump′) *n.* ⟦Algonquian *mugquomp,* chief⟧ **1** a Republican who refused to support the party ticket in 1884 **2** any independent, esp. in politics

Mu·ham·mad (moo ham′əd, -häm′-) ⟦Ar, lit., praiseworthy⟧ A.D. 570?-632; Arab prophet: founder of Islam

Mu·ham·mad·an (moo ham′i dən, -häm′-) *adj.* of Muhammad or Islam —*n.* Muslim A term used by non-Muslims

Mu·ham·mad·an·ism (-iz′əm) *n.* Islam: term used by non-Muslims

Muir (myoor), **John** 1838-1914; U.S. naturalist, explorer, & writer, born in Scotland

mu·ja·hi·deen (mo͞o′jä hə dēn′) *pl.n., sing.* **mu′ja·hid′** (-hid′) ⟦Ar *mujāhidīn,* pl. of *mujāhid,* person who fights in a jihad⟧ [*also in italics*] (the members of) a Muslim guerrilla force that claims divine authority for its activities: often sp. **mu′ja·hi·din′, mu′ja·he·din′,** or **mu′ja·he·deen′**

mu·jik (mo͞o zhēk′, mo͞o′zhik′) *n. alt. sp. of* MUZHIK

Muk·den (mook′dən, mook den′) *former name for* SHENYANG

mu·kha·ba·rat (moo kä′bə rät′) *n.* ⟦Ar⟧ [*often* **M-**] the secret police force or intelligence agency in certain Arabic-speaking countries

☆**muk·luk** (muk′luk′) *n.* ⟦Esk *muklok,* a large seal⟧ **1** an Eskimo boot made of sealskin or reindeer skin **2** a boot like this, made of canvas, rubber, etc.

muk·tuk (muk′tuk′) *n.* ⟦Inupiaq *maktak*⟧ blubber and skin of a whale eaten as food

mu·lat·to (mə lät′ō, -lat′ō; myo͞o-) *n., pl.* **-toes** or **-tos** ⟦Sp & Port *mulato,* mulatto, of mixed breed, orig. young mule < *mulo,* mule < L *mulus*⟧ a person with mixed black and Caucasoid ancestry; specif., a person who has one black and one white parent —*adj.* of a mulatto

USAGE—except in technical discourse, now often regarded as disparaging or insulting

mul·ber·ry (mul′ber′ē, -bər ē) *n., pl.* **-ries** ⟦ME *mulberie,* dissimilated var. of *murberie* < OE *morberie* < L *morum,* mulberry, blackberry < IE base **moro-,* blackberry (> Gr *moron,* mulberry, blackberry) + OE *berie,* BERRY⟧ **1** any of a genus (*Morus*) of shrubs and trees of the mulberry family, with milky juice and multiple false fruits which resemble the fruits of the raspberry **2** the edible fruit **3** a dark purplish-red color —*adj.* designating a family (Moraceae, order Urticales) of dicotyledonous plants of wide horticultural and economic importance, including the fig and breadfruit trees

mulch (mulch) *n.* ⟦ME *molsh,* soft, akin to Ger dial. *molsch,* soft: for prob. IE base see MOLD[3]⟧ leaves, straw, peat moss, etc., spread on the ground around plants to prevent evaporation of water from soil, freezing of roots, etc. and for decoration —*vt.* to apply mulch to

mulching mower a lawn mower that shreds blades of grass into very small pieces left on the lawn to decay and return nutrients to the soil

mulct (mulkt) *vt.* ⟦L *mulctare* < *mulcta, multa,* a fine⟧ **1** to punish by a fine or by depriving of something **2** to extract (money, etc.) from (someone), as by fraud or deceit —*n.* a fine or similar penalty

mule[1] (myo͞ol) *n.* ⟦OFr, fem. of *mul* < L *mulus,* mule⟧ **1** the hybrid offspring of a donkey and a horse; esp., the offspring of a jackass and a mare: mules are nearly always sterile: cf. HINNY **2** a small tractor or electric engine used to tow boats along a canal or move mine cars **3** a machine for drawing and spinning cotton fibers into yarn and winding the yarn on spindles **4** a hybrid animal, as the offspring of a canary and some other finch; esp., a sterile hybrid **5** ⟦from the mule's traditional reputation for stubbornness⟧ [Informal] a stubborn person **6** [Slang] a person who smuggles drugs or narcotics into a country

mule[2] (myo͞ol) *n.* ⟦Fr, ult. < L *mulleus,* red or purple shoe < IE base **mel-,* dark-colored > Gr *melas,* black⟧ a shoe that does not cover the heel

☆**mule deer** a long-eared deer (*Odocoileus hemionus*) of the W U.S. & Canada with a black tail

☆**mule skinner** [Informal] a driver of mules: now chiefly historical

mu·le·ta (mo͞o lät′ə, -let′ə) *n.* ⟦Sp, muleta, crutch, orig. dim. of *mula,* a she-mule < L *mulus,* MULE[1]⟧ a red flannel cloth draped over a stick and manipulated by the matador in his series of passes

mu·le·teer (myo͞o′lə tir′) *n.* ⟦OFr *muletier* < *mulet,* dim. of *mule*⟧ a driver of mules

mul·ey (myo͞o′lē, moo′lē) *adj.* ⟦Scot *moiley* < Celt, as in Welsh *moel,* Gael *maol,* hornless, bald < IE base **mai-,* to cut off > MAD⟧ hornless; polled: said of cattle —*n.* **1** a hornless cow **2** any cow

Mul·ha·cén (mool′ä then′) highest mountain in Spain, in the S part, near Granada: 11,420 ft (3,481 m)

Mül·heim (mül′hīm′) city in W Germany, on the Ruhr, in the state of North Rhine-Westphalia: also **Mülheim an der Ruhr** (än der ro͞or′)

Mul·house (mü lo͞oz′) city in E France, near the Rhine

mu·li·eb·ri·ty (myo͞o′lē eb′rə tē) *n.* ⟦LL *muliebritas* < L *muliebris,* womanly, womanish < *mulier,* a woman, prob. < IE **mlyésī,* (the) softer (one), compar. of **ml̥du-* (> L *mollis*) < base **mel-* > MILL[1]⟧ **1** the condition of being a woman; womanhood **2** the qualities characteristic of a woman; womanliness; femininity

mul·ish (myo͞o′lish) *adj.* like or characteristic of a mule; stubborn, obstinate, balky, etc. —**mul′ish·ly** *adv.* —**mul′ish·ness** *n.*

mull[1] (mul) *vt., vi.* ⟦ME *mullen,* to grind < *mul,* dust < OE *myl,* dust: for IE base see MOLD[3]⟧ to cogitate or ponder: usually with *over*

mull[2] (mul) *vt.* ⟦< ?⟧ to heat, sweeten, and flavor with spices (wine, cider, ale, etc.)

mull[3] (mul) *n.* ⟦contr. < *mulmul* < & Pers *malmal*⟧ a thin, soft muslin

Mull (mul) island of the Inner Hebrides, Scotland: 351 sq mi (909 sq km)

mul·lah or **mul·la** (mul′ə, mool′ə) *n.* ⟦Turk, Pers, & Hindi *mulla* < Ar *maulā,* a master, sir⟧ a Muslim teacher or interpreter of the religious law: a general title of respect for a learned man

mul·lein (mul′in) *n.* ⟦ME *moleyne* < OFr *moleine* < *mol,* soft < L *mollis:* see MOLLIFY⟧ any of a genus (*Verbascum*) of tall plants of the figwort family, with spikes of yellow, lavender, or white flowers

mull·er (mul′ər) *n.* ⟦ME *molour,* prob. < *mullen,* to grind: see MULL[1]⟧ any of various mechanical or hand devices for grinding; specif., a flat-bottomed pestle of stone, etc., as for grinding paints or drugs

Mul·ler (mul′ər), **H(ermann) J(oseph)** 1890-1967; U.S. biologist & geneticist

Mül·ler (mul′ər, myo͞ol′-; *Ger* mül′-), **(Friedrich) Max** (maks; *Ger* mäks) 1823-1900; Eng. philologist, mythologist, & Orientalist, born in Germany

mul·let[1] (mul′it) *n., pl.* **-lets** or **-let** ⟦ME *molet* < OFr *mulet,* dim. < L *mullus,* red mullet < Gr *myllos,* kind of fish < ? IE base **mel-*: see MULE[2]⟧ **1** any of a family (Mugilidae) of edible, spiny-finned percoid fishes, both freshwater and marine, having a small mouth and feeble teeth, esp. a striped species (*Mugil cephalus*) **2** any goatfish, esp. a species (*Mullus auratus*) with reddish or golden scales

mul·let[2] (mul′it) *n.* ⟦orig. uncert.⟧ a hairstyle in which the hair is worn short on the top and sides of the head and longer in the back

mul·ley (mool′ē, mo͞o′lē) *adj., n. var. of* MULEY

mul·li·gan (mul′i gən) *n.* ⟦prob. after personal name *Mulligan*⟧ **1** MULLIGAN STEW ☆**2** *Golf* in informal play, a second shot given to a golfer as a substitute for a poorly played shot, for which the golfer is not charged an additional stroke [*to take a mulligan*]

mulligan stew ⟦see prec.⟧ a stew made of odd bits of meat and vegetables

mul·li·ga·taw·ny (mul′i gə tô′nē) *n.* ⟦Tamil *milagutaṇṇir,* lit., pepper water⟧ a spicy soup of S India, made of chicken and vegetables, curry, and, sometimes, rice, coconut, cream, etc.

Mul·li·ken (mul′i kən), **Robert San·der·son** (san′dər sən) 1896-1986; U.S. physicist & chemist

mul·lion (mul′yən) *n.* ⟦prob. altered < OFr *moienel* < *moien,* median < L *medianus,* middle: see MID[1]⟧ a slender, vertical dividing bar between the lights of windows, doors, etc. —*vt.* to furnish with or divide by mullions —**mul′lioned** *adj.*

mull·ite (mul′īt′) *n.* ⟦after *Mull,* island off W coast of Scotland, where the ore is found + -ITE[1]⟧ a very hard, light-colored, orthorhombic mineral, $Al_6Si_2O_{13}$, that is resistant to heat and corrosion: used to make glass, furnace linings, etc.

Mul·tan (mo͞ol tän′) city in NE Pakistan, near the Chenab River

mul·tan·gu·lar (mul taŋ′gyo͞o lər, -gyə-) *adj.* having many angles: said as of certain wrist bones: also **mul′ti·an′gu·lar** (mul′tē aŋ′-)

mul·ti- (mul′ti, -tə, -tē, -tī) ⟦L < *multus,* much, many < IE base **mel-,* strong, big > Gr *mala,* very⟧ *combining form* **1** having, consisting of, or affecting many [*multifold*] **2** more than two, or, sometimes, more than one [*multilateral, multiparous*] **3** many times over [*multimillionaire*] Also, before a vowel, **mult-** The meanings of the following words can be determined by combining the meanings of their component elements:

multibranched
multicelled
multicellular
multichambered
multichannel
multicircuit
multicolor
multicolored
multicomponent
multicylinder
multidenominational
multidimensional
multidirectional
multidwelling
multifamily
multifilament
multifoliate
multifunctional
multihued
multilane
multilayered
multilevel
multilinear
multilobate
multimolecular
multiphase
multipinnate
multipolar
multiracial
multirange
multisegmented
multisite
multiskilled
multispeed
multispiral
multistaminate
multistoried
multistory
multitalented
multitiered
multitrack
multiunit
multiuse
multivalve
multivitamin
multivoiced
multivolume
multiyear

☆**mul·ti·cul·ti** (mul′tē kul′tē) *adj.* [Informal] MULTICULTURAL: often a dismissive or disparaging term

mul·ti·cul·tur·al (mul′tē kul′chər əl) *adj.* **1** of or having to do with various cultures **2** of, having to do with, or advocating multiculturalism

mul·ti·cul·tur·al·ism (mul′tē kul′chər əl iz′əm) *n.* the policy or practice of giving overt recognition to the cultural needs and contributions of all the groups in a society, esp. of those minority groups regarded as having been neglected in the past —**mul′ti·cul′tur·al·ist** *n., adj.*

mul·ti·dis·ci·pli·nar·y (mul′tē dis′ə pli ner′ē) *adj.* of or combining the disciplines of many or several different branches of learning or research

mul·ti·eth·nic (mul′tē eth′nik) ***adj.*** of or having to do with a society, community, etc. made up of people of various ethnic backgrounds

mul·ti·fac·et·ed (mul′tē fas′ət id) ***adj.*** combining a variety of features, parts, or perspectives; complex [*a multifaceted* career]

mul·ti·far·i·ous (mul′tə far′ē əs, -fer′-) ***adj.*** ⟦L *multifarius,* manifold < *multi-,* MULTI- + *-farius,* as in *bifarius:* see BIFARIOUS⟧ having many kinds of parts or elements; of great variety; diverse; manifold —**mul′ti·far′i·ous·ly** ***adv.*** —**mul′ti·far′i·ous·ness** ***n.***

mul·ti·fid (mul′tə fid′) ***adj.*** ⟦L *multifidus:* see MULTI- & -FID⟧ split or branching into many divisions or lobes

mul·ti·flo·ra rose (mul′tə flôr′ə) a rose (*Rosa multiflora*) with thick clusters of small flowers, grown esp. for hedges

mul·ti·fold (mul′tə fōld′) ***adj.*** ⟦MULTI- + -FOLD⟧ **1** doubled or folded many times **2** MANIFOLD

mul·ti·form (-fôrm′) ***adj.*** ⟦< Fr or L: Fr *multiforme* < L *multiformis* < *multi-,* MULTI- + *forma,* FORM⟧ having many forms, shapes, etc. —**mul′ti·for′mi·ty** ***n.***

mul·ti·hull (mul′tē hul′) ***n.*** a boat with two or more hulls joined side by side; esp., a catamaran or trimaran: distinguished from MONOHULL

mul·ti·lat·er·al (mul′ti lat′ər əl) ***adj.*** ⟦MULTI- + LATERAL⟧ **1** many-sided **2** participated in by more than two parties, nations, etc. [*a multilateral* treaty] —**mul′ti·lat′er·al·ism′** ***n.*** —**mul′ti·lat′er·al·ist** ***adj.*** —**mul′ti·lat′er·al·ly** ***adv.***

mul·ti·lev·el marketing (mul′ti lev′əl) any of various, often illegal, marketing schemes in which sellers are rewarded for recruiting new sellers who in turn recruit, resulting in level upon level of sellers

mul·ti·lin·gual (mul′ti liŋ′gwəl) ***adj.*** **1** of or in several languages **2** using or capable of using several languages —**mul′ti·lin′gual·ism′** ***n.*** —**mul′ti·lin′gual·ly** ***adv.*** —**mul′ti·lin′guist** ***n.***

mul·ti·me·di·a (-mē′dē ə) ***n.*** **1** a combination of media, as film, tape recordings, slides, and special lighting effects, used for entertainment or education **2** a combination of communication media, such as television, newspapers, and radio, used in an advertising or publicity campaign **3** MIXED MEDIA (sense 1) **4** a combination of text, data, pictures, sound, video, etc., as on a CD-ROM, for interactive access —***adj.*** for or using multimedia

☆**mul·ti·mil·lion·aire** (-mil′yə ner′) ***n.*** a person whose wealth amounts to many millions of dollars, francs, pounds, etc.

mul·ti·na·tion·al (-nash′ə nəl) ***adj.*** **1** of or involving a number of nations **2** designating a corporation with branches in a number of countries **3** comprising persons of various nationalities —***n.*** a multinational corporation

mul·ti·nu·cle·ate (-no͞o′klē it, -āt′; -nyo͞o′-) ***adj.*** having more than two nuclei: also **mul′ti·nu′cle·at′ed** or **mul′ti·nu′cle·ar**

mul·tip·a·ra (mul tip′ə rə) ***n., pl.*** **-ras** or **-rae′** (-rē′) ⟦ModL < fem. of *multiparus:* see fol.⟧ a woman who is bearing her second child or has borne two or more children

mul·tip·a·rous (mul tip′ə rəs) ***adj.*** ⟦ModL *multiparus:* see MULTI- & -PAROUS⟧ **1** of or being a multipara **2** *Zool.* designating or of a species that normally bears more than one offspring at a birth

mul·ti·par·tite (mul′tə pär′tīt′) ***adj.*** ⟦L *multipartitus* < *multi-,* MULTI- + *pars* (gen. *partis*), PART[2]⟧ **1** divided into many or several parts **2** MULTILATERAL (sense 2)

mul·ti·par·ty (mul′tē pär′tē) ***adj.*** made up of or involving more than one political party

mul·ti·ped (mul′tə ped′) ***adj.*** ⟦L *multipes* (gen. *multipedis*) < *multi-,* MULTI- + *pes* (gen. *pedis*), FOOT⟧ having many feet —***n.*** [Rare] a multiped animal or insect Also **mul′ti·pede′** (-pēd′)

mul·ti·pha·sic (mul′tē fā′zik) ***adj.*** of, characterized by, or involving various phases, aspects, stages, etc. [*multiphasic* testing]

mul·ti·phon·ics (-fän′iks) ***n.*** the technique of producing two or more tones simultaneously, as on a wind instrument or with the voice —**mul′ti·phon′ic** ***adj.***

mul·ti·ple (mul′tə pəl) ***adj.*** ⟦Fr < L *multiplex* < *multi-,* MULTI- + *-plex,* -FOLD: see DUPLEX⟧ **1** having or consisting of many parts, elements, etc.; more than one or once; manifold or complex **2** shared by or involving many **3** many or very many; numerous **4** *Elec.* designating or of a circuit having two or more conductors connected in parallel —***n.*** **1** *Elec.* a group of terminals so arranged that connection with the circuit can be made at any of a number of points **2** *Finance* PRICE-EARNINGS RATIO **3** *Math.* a number which is a product of some specified number and another number [10 is a *multiple* of 5]

☆**mul·ti·ple-choice** (-chois′) ***adj.*** **1** designating a question for which one of several proposed answers is to be selected **2** designating a test made up of such questions

multiple factors *Genetics* a series of two or more pairs of allelic genes, considered to act as a single unit with a cumulative effect in the transmission of certain characters, such as size, pigmentation, etc.

multiple fruit a FALSE FRUIT formed by a fused cluster of the ovaries of several flowers, as a pineapple or mulberry

multiple personality disorder *Psychiatry* a rare dissociative disorder characterized by the seeming existence of two or more independent personalities, each with distinct memories and experiences: also written **mul′ti·ple-per′son·al′i·ty disorder**

multiple sclerosis a chronic disease in which there is scattered demyelination of the central nervous system: it may result in speech defects, loss of muscular coordination, etc.

multiple shop (*or* store) [Brit.] CHAIN STORE

multiple star *Astron.* three or more stars forming one gravitational system that appear to be a single star or a binary star

mul·ti·plet (mul′tə plət) ***n.*** ⟦MULTIPL(E) + -ET⟧ *Physics* **1** a set of quantum mechanical states that are related to each other and whose single energy level can be split into a specific number of distinct energy levels **2** a line in a spectrum composed of a group of related lines

mul·ti·plex (mul′tə pleks′) ***adj.*** ⟦L, MULTIPLE⟧ **1** multiple or manifold **2** designating or of a system for transmitting or receiving simultaneously two or more messages or signals over a common circuit, carrier wave, etc. —***vt.*** to send (messages or signals) by a multiplex system —***n.*** a complex of three or more film theaters in the same building, sharing management, projectionists, etc. —**mul′ti·plex′er** ***n.***, **mul′ti·plex′or**

mul·ti·pli·a·ble (mul′tə plī′ə bəl) ***adj.*** that can be multiplied Also **mul′ti·plic′a·ble** (-plik′ə bəl)

mul·ti·pli·cand (mul′tə pli kand′) ***n.*** ⟦L *multiplicandus,* to be multiplied, ger. of *multiplicare,* MULTIPLY[1]⟧ *Math.* the number that is, or is to be, multiplied by another (the *multiplier*)

mul·ti·pli·cate (mul′tə pli kāt′) ***adj.*** ⟦ME < L *multiplicatus,* pp. of *multiplicare,* to MULTIPLY[1]⟧ [Now Rare] multiple; manifold

mul·ti·pli·ca·tion (mul′tə pli kā′shən) ***n.*** ⟦ME *multiplicacioun* < OFr *multiplication* < L *multiplicatio*⟧ **1** a multiplying or being multiplied **2** *Math.* the process of finding the number or quantity (*product*) obtained by repeated additions of a specified number or quantity (*multiplicand*) a specified number of times (*multiplier*): symbolized in various ways (Ex.: 3 × 4 = 12 or 3 · 4 = 12, which means 3 + 3 + 3 + 3 = 12, to add the number three together four times)

multiplication factor (*or* constant) the ratio of the number of neutrons in a generation to the number of neutrons in the previous generation: when the multiplication factor is equal to or greater than one, a chain reaction is possible

multiplication sign either of two signs (× or ·) used to indicate that the preceding number or quantity is to be multiplied by the following number or quantity (Ex.: 8 × 4 = 32 or $2a \cdot a = 2a^2$)

multiplication table a table showing the results of multiplying each number of a series, usually 1 to 12, by each of the numbers in succession: used as a reference and as a memorization aid

mul·ti·pli·ca·tive (mul′tə pli kāt′iv) ***adj.*** ⟦LL *multiplicativus* < L *multiplicatus,* pp.: see MULTIPLY[1]⟧ tending to multiply or capable of multiplying —**mul′ti·pli·ca′tive·ly** ***adv.***

multiplicative inverse *Math.* RECIPROCAL (***n.*** 2)

mul·ti·plic·i·ty (mul′tə plis′ə tē) ***n.*** ⟦LL *multiplicitas* < L *multiplex,* MULTIPLE⟧ **1** the quality or condition of being manifold or various **2** a great number

mul·ti·pli·er (mul′tə plī′ər) ***n.*** **1** a person or thing that multiplies or increases **2** *Econ.* the ratio between the total increase in income (resulting from the stimulating effect of an initial expenditure) and the initial expenditure itself **3** *Math.* the number by which another number (the *multiplicand*) is, or is to be, multiplied **4** *Physics* any device for multiplying, or intensifying, some effect

mul·ti·ply[1] (mul′tə plī′) ***vt.*** **-plied′**, **-ply′ing** ⟦ME *multiplien* < OFr *multiplier* < L *multiplicare* < *multiplex,* MULTIPLE⟧ **1** to cause to increase in number, amount, extent, or degree **2** *Math.* to find the product of by multiplication —***vi.*** **1** to increase in number, amount, extent, or degree; specif., to increase by procreation **2** *Math.* to perform multiplication —**SYN.** INCREASE

mul·ti·ply[2] (mul′tə plē) ***adv.*** ⟦MULTIPLE + -LY[2]⟧ in multiple ways

mul·ti·pro·cess·ing (mul′ti prä′ses′iŋ, -sə siŋ) ***n.*** the process of using a multiprocessor

mul·ti·pro·ces·sor (-ses′ər, -sə sər) ***n.*** a computer system having two or more central processing units, each sharing main memory and peripherals, in order to simultaneously process programs

mul·ti·pur·pose (mul′ti pʉr′pəs) ***adj.*** having more than one purpose or use [*a multipurpose* community center]

mul·ti·stage (mul′ti stāj′) ***adj.*** having, or operating in, more than one stage; specif., having several propulsion systems that are used and discarded in sequence: said of a rocket or missile

mul·ti·task·ing or **mul·ti-task·ing** (mul′ti task′iŋ) ***n.*** **1** *Comput.* the execution by a single central processing unit of two or more programs at once, either by simultaneous operation or by rapid alternation between the programs **2** the act or an instance of performing various tasks more or less simultaneously —**mul′ti·task′er** ***n.***, **mul′ti-task′er**

mul·ti·tude (mul′tə to͞od′, -tyo͞od′) ***n.*** ⟦OFr < L *multitudo* < *multus,* many: see MULTI-⟧ **1** the quality or state of being numerous, or many **2** [*often pl.*] a large number of persons or things, esp. when gathered together or considered as a unit; host, myriad, etc. **3** the masses: preceded by *the* —**SYN.** CROWD[1]

mul·ti·tu·di·nous (mul′tə to͞od′'n əs, -tyo͞od′-) ***adj.*** ⟦< L *multitudo* (gen. *multitudinis*), multitude + -OUS⟧ **1** very numerous; many **2** consisting of many parts, elements etc.; manifold **3** [Rare] holding a multitude; crowded —**mul′ti·tu′di·nous·ly** ***adv.***

mul·ti·va·lent (mul′ti vā′lənt) ***adj.*** *Chem.* POLYVALENT (sense 2) —**mul′ti·va′lence** ***n.***

mul·ti·var·i·ate (-ver′ē it, -āt′) ***adj.*** *Statistics* involving more than one variable [*multivariate* analysis]

mul·ti·verse (mul′tē vʉrs′, mul′ti-) ***n.*** ⟦MULTI- + (UNI)VERSE⟧ a hypothetical cosmos in which our universe is one of an indefinite number of distinct universes, comprising a range of physical laws

☆**mul·ti·ver·si·ty** (mul′tə vʉr′sə tē) ***n.,*** *pl.* **-ties** ⟦MULTI- + (UNI)VERSITY: coined (1957) by Arthur Bestor (1908-94), U.S. historian⟧ the modern large and complex university with its many colleges, schools, extensions, etc.

mul·ture (mul′chər) ***n.*** ⟦ME *multer* < OFr *molture* < VL **molitura* < pp. of L *molere,* to grind < *mola,* MILL^{1}⟧ [Historical] a fee paid to the owner of a mill for the privilege of having one's grain ground there, usually a percentage of the grain or of the ground flour

mum^{1} (mum) ***n.*** ⟦Ger *mumme:* said to be named after Christian *Mumme,* 15th-c. Ger brewer⟧ a strong beer

mum^{2} (mum) ***vi.*** **mummed, mum′ming** ⟦< OFr *momer* < *momo,* echoic for grimace (as in Sp *momo*)⟧ to wear a mask or costume in fun; specif., to act as a mummer at Christmastime: also sp. **mumm**

☆**mum^{3}** (mum) ***n.*** [Informal] a chrysanthemum

mum^{4} (mum) ***n.*** [Informal, Chiefly Brit.] mother

mum^{5} (mum) ***adj.*** ⟦ME *momme,* echoic of sound made with the lips closed⟧ silent; not speaking —**mum's the word** say nothing

Mum·bai (mo͝om bī′, mum′bī′) seaport in W India, on the Arabian Sea: capital of Maharashtra state: formerly *Bombay*

mum·ble (mum′bəl) ***vt., vi.*** **-bled, -bling** ⟦ME *momelen,* like Ger *mummeln,* Du *mommelen,* of echoic orig.⟧ **1** to speak or say indistinctly and in a low voice, as with the mouth partly closed; mutter **2** [Rare] to chew gently and ineffectively, as with toothless gums —***n.*** a mumbled sound or utterance —***SYN.*** MURMUR —**mum′bler** ***n.*** —**mum′bling·ly** ***adv.***

mum·ble·ty·peg (mum′bəl tē peg′, -dē-) ***n.*** ⟦altered < *mumble-the-peg* < *mumble,* to bite⟧ a children's game in which a jackknife is tossed in various ways to make it land with the blade in the ground, the loser originally having to draw a peg from the ground with his or her teeth

mum·bo-jum·bo (mum′bō jum′bō) ⟦of Afr orig.: meaning, form, & dialect uncert.⟧ **1** [**M- J-**] among certain West African tribes, an idol or god believed to protect the people from evil and terrorize the women into subjection **2** meaningless ritual **3** gibberish

Mum·ford (mum′fərd), **Lewis** 1895-1990; U.S. social philosopher & architectural critic

mum·mer (mum′ər) ***n.*** ⟦MFr *momeur* < OFr *momer:* see MUM^{2}⟧ **1** a person who wears a mask or disguise for fun; specif., in England, any of the masked and costumed persons who travel about, as at Christmastime, acting out traditional pantomimes **2** [Old Slang] an actor in the theater: a derogatory term

mum·mer·y (mum′ər ē) ***n.,*** *pl.* **-mer·ies** ⟦MFr *mommerie* < OFr *momer:* see MUM^{2}⟧ **1** performance by mummers **2** any display or ceremony regarded as pretentious or hypocritical

mum·mi·fy (mum′ə fī′) ***vt.*** **-fied′, -fy′ing** ⟦fol. + -FY⟧ to make into or like a mummy —***vi.*** to shrivel or dry up —**mum′mi·fi·ca′tion** ***n.***

mum·my^{1} (mum′ē) ***n.,*** *pl.* **-mies** ⟦Fr *momie* < ML *mumia* < Ar *mūmiyā,* embalmed body, mummy < Pers *mum,* wax⟧ **1** a dead body preserved by embalming, as by the ancient Egyptians **2** any dead body that has been naturally well preserved **3** any thin, withered person regarded as looking like a mummy

mum·my^{2} (mum′ē) ***n.,*** *pl.* **-mies** [Chiefly Brit.] *child's term for* MOTHER^{1}

mump (mump) ***vt., vi.*** ⟦echoic, or < ? Du *mompelen,* var. of *mommelen,* to mumble⟧ **1** [Dial.] to mumble; mutter **2** ⟦Du *mompen,* to cheat, prob. akin to *mompelen*⟧ [Old Slang] *a)* to beg *b)* to cheat

mumps (mumps) ***n.*** ⟦pl. of obs. *mump,* a grimace: prob. from the patient's appearance⟧ an acute communicable disease, usually of childhood, caused by a paramyxovirus and characterized by swelling of the salivary glands, esp. the parotid, and, in adults, often complicated by inflammation of the testes, ovaries, etc.: often with *the*

mu·mu or **mu-mu** (mo͞o′mo͞o′) ***n.*** *alt. sp. of* MUUMUU

mun *abbrev.* municipal

munch (munch) ***vt., vi.*** ⟦ME *monchen,* prob. echoic alteration of *mangen,* to feast < OFr *manger* < L *manducare:* see MANGER⟧ **1** to chew steadily, often with a crunching sound **2** to snack (on) —**munch′er** ***n.***

Munch (mo͝oŋk), **Ed·vard** (ed′värt′) 1863-1944; Norw. painter

Mun·chau·sen (mun′chou′zən, mo͝on′-; -chô′-), Baron (*Karl Friedrich Hieronymus von Münchhausen*) 1720-97; Ger. soldier & adventurer known for his exaggerated tales of his exploits

Mün·chen (mün′Hən) *Ger. name for* MUNICH

Mün·chen-Glad·bach (-glät′bäkh′) *var. of* MÖNCHEN-GLADBACH

☆**munch·ies** (mun′chēz′) ***pl.n.*** [Informal] **1** food for snacking; snacks **2** a desire for snacks: usually with *the*

☆**munch·kin** (munch′kin) ***n.*** ⟦< *Munchkin,* one of a race of beings having a small human form and an amiable, innocuous nature, in *The Wonderful Wizard of Oz,* novel (1900) by L. Frank BAUM⟧ [Informal] any small person, esp. a small child: often a patronizing or dismissive use

Mun·cie (mun′sē) ⟦after the *Munsee* (Delaware) Indians⟧ city in EC Ind.

Mun·da (mo͝on′də) ***adj.*** designating or of a branch of the Austro-Asiatic family of languages, spoken in areas of NE India

mun·dane (mun dān′, mun′dān′) ***adj.*** ⟦LME *mondeyne* < OFr *mondain* < LL *mundanus* < L *mundus,* world (in LL(Ec), the secular world, as opposed to the church)⟧ **1** of the world; esp., worldly, as distinguished from heavenly, spiritual, etc. **2** commonplace, everyday, ordinary, etc. —***SYN.*** EARTHLY —**mun·dane′ly** ***adv.*** —**mun′dan′i·ty** (-dan′ə tē) ***n.,*** *pl.* **-ties**

mun·dun·gus (mun duŋ′gəs) ***n.*** ⟦orig. facetious use of Sp *mondongo,* tripe⟧ [Archaic] any dark, smelly tobacco

mung bean (muŋ) ⟦*mung,* short for *mungo* < Tamil *mūṅgu* < Hindi *mug* < Sans *mudga*⟧ an annual bean (*Vigna radiata*) of the pea family, grown for green manure and forage and as a source of bean sprouts

mun·go (muŋ′gō) ***n.,*** *pl.* **-gos** ⟦< Yorkshire dial. < ?⟧ the waste of milled wool used to make a cheap cloth

☆**mu·ni** (myo͞o′nē) ***n.,*** *pl.* **mu′nis** MUNICIPAL BOND: *usually used in pl.* —***adj.*** [Informal] MUNICIPAL

Mu·nich (myo͞o′nik) city in SE Germany: capital of the state of Bavaria: Ger. name MÜNCHEN

Munich Pact (*or* **Agreement**) a pact signed in 1938 at Munich by Great Britain and France, ceding the Czech Sudetenland to Nazi Germany: often referred to as an epitome of political appeasement

mu·nic·i·pal (myo͞o nis′ə pəl) ***adj.*** ⟦L *municipalis* < *municeps,* inhabitant of a free town < *munia,* official duties, functions < IE base **mei-,* to exchange (> COMMON, MEAN^{2}) + *capere,* to take (see HAVE)⟧ **1** *a)* of or having to do with a city, town, etc. or its local government *b)* having self-government locally **2** [Rare] of the internal, as distinguished from the international, affairs of a nation —***n.*** ☆*Finance* MUNICIPAL BOND: *usually used in pl.* —**mu·nic′i·pal·ly** ***adv.***

municipal bond a bond issued by a state or local government or by a nonfederal government agency, usually to provide funding for a specified purpose

mu·nic·i·pal·ism (-iz′əm) ***n.*** **1** self-government by a municipality **2** the principle that such government should be fostered —**mu·nic′i·pal·ist** ***n.***

mu·nic·i·pal·i·ty (myo͞o nis′ə pal′ə tē) ***n.,*** *pl.* **-ties** ⟦Fr *municipalité* < *municipal* < L *municipalis,* MUNICIPAL⟧ **1** a city, town, etc. having its own incorporated government for local affairs **2** its governing officials

mu·nic·i·pal·ize (myo͞o nis′ə pəl īz′) ***vt.*** **-ized′, -iz′ing** **1** to bring under the control or ownership of a municipality **2** to make a municipality of —**mu·nic′i·pal·i·za′tion** ***n.***

mu·nif·i·cent (myo͞o nif′ə sənt) ***adj.*** ⟦L *munificens* < *munificus,* bountiful < *munus,* a gift (akin to *munia:* see MUNICIPAL) + *facere,* to make: see DO^{1}⟧ **1** very generous in giving **2** characterized by or indicative of great generosity [*a munificent reward*] —**mu·nif′i·cence** ***n.*** —**mu·nif′i·cent·ly** ***adv.***

mu·ni·ment (myo͞o′nə mənt) ***n.*** ⟦ME < Anglo-Fr < OFr < L *munimentum,* a fortification, defense, protection < *munire,* to furnish with walls, fortify: see MUNITIONS⟧ **1** [Rare] a means of protection or defense **2** ⟦ML *munimentum*⟧ [*pl.*] *Law* a document or documents serving as evidence of inheritances, title to property, etc.

mu·ni·tion (myo͞o nish′ən) ***vt.*** ⟦< fol.⟧ to provide with munitions

mu·ni·tions (-ənz) ***pl.n.*** ⟦< MFr *munition* < L *munitio,* a fortifying, defending < *munire,* to fortify < *moenia,* fortifications < IE base **mei-,* to fortify > MERE^{3}, L *murus,* wall⟧ [*sometimes with sing. v.*] war supplies; esp., weapons and ammunition

Mun·ro (mən rō′), **H(ector) H(ugh)** *see* SAKI

Mun·ster (mun′stər) province of SW Ireland: 9,313 sq mi (24,121 sq km)

Mün·ster (mün′stər) city in WC Germany, in the state of North Rhine-Westphalia

mun·tin (munt′'n) ***n.*** ⟦< obs. *montant* < Fr, prp. of *monter,* to rise < OFr *monter, munter,* MOUNT^{2}⟧ any of the strips of wood or metal used for support between panes of glass, as in a window

munt·jac or **munt·jak** (munt′jak′) ***n.*** ⟦< Jav & Malay *menjangan*⟧ any of a genus (*Muntiacus*) of small jungle deer of Southeast Asia and the East Indies: the males have horns and long, sharp, tusklike canine teeth

mu·on (myo͞o′än′) ***n.*** ⟦MU + (MES)ON⟧ *Particle Physics* an unstable, negatively charged lepton with a mass of 105.7 MeV, *c.* 207 times that of an electron, and a mean lifetime of 2.2×10^{-6} second: it decays into an electron, a neutrino, and an antineutrino —**mu·on′ic** ***adj.***

mu·ral (myo͝or′əl) ***adj.*** ⟦Fr < L *muralis,* of a wall < *murus:* see MUNITIONS⟧ **1** of, on, in, or for a wall **2** like a wall —***n.*** a picture, esp. a large one, painted directly onto a wall or ceiling, or a large photograph, etc. attached directly to a wall

mu·ral·ist (-ist) ***n.*** a painter of murals

Mu·ra·sa·ki Shi·ki·bu (mo͞o′rä sä′kē shē′kē bo͞o′), Lady A.D. 978?-1031?; Jpn. novelist & poet: wrote *The Tale of Genji*

Mu·rat (mü rà′), **Jo·a·chim** (zhô à shan′) 1767-1815; Fr. marshal under Napoleon: king of Naples (1808-15)

Mur·cia (mʉr′shə, -shē ə; *Sp* mo͞or′thyä) **1** region & ancient kingdom of SE Spain: 4,370 sq mi (11,318 sq km) **2** its capital

☆**Mur·cott** (mʉr′kät′) ***n.*** ⟦after *Murcott* Smith, Florida citrus grower, who developed the strain *c.* 1922⟧ *former name for* HONEY TANGERINE

mur·der (mʉr′dər) ***n.*** ⟦ME *murthir, mordre* < OE & OFr: OE *morthor,* akin to ON *morth,* Goth *maurthr;* OFr *mordre* < Frank **morthr:* all ult. < IE **mr̥tóm* < base **mer-* > MORTAL⟧ **1** the unlawful and malicious or premeditated killing of one human being by another; also, any killing done while committing some other felony, as rape or robbery ☆**2** [Informal] something very hard, unsafe, or disagreeable to do or deal with —***vt.*** **1** to kill (a person) unlawfully and with malice **2** to kill inhumanly or barbarously, as in warfare **3** [Informal] to spoil, mar, etc., as in performance [*the song was murdered by the singer*] —***vi.*** to commit murder —***SYN.*** KILL^{1} —☆**get away with murder** [Informal] to escape detection of or punishment for a blameworthy act —**murder will out** ⟦proverbial⟧ **1** a murder or murderer will always be revealed **2** any secret or wrongdoing will be revealed sooner or later —**scream** (**or yell**) **bloody murder** [Informal] to yell or otherwise raise a loud disturbance, as from outrage or fear

mur·der·er (mʉr′dər ər) ***n.*** a person who commits or has committed murder

mur·der·ess (mur′dər is) ***n.*** a woman who commits or has committed murder

mur·der·ous (mur′dər əs) ***adj.*** **1** of, having the nature of, or characteristic of murder; brutal [*a murderous* act] **2** capable or guilty of, or intending, murder ☆**3** [Informal] very difficult, disagreeable, dangerous, trying, etc. —**mur′der·ous·ly** ***adv.*** —**mur′der·ous·ness** ***n.***

Mur·doch (mur′däk′), Dame **(Jean) Iris** 1919-99; Eng. writer, born in Ireland

mure (myoor) ***vt.*** **mured, mur′ing** ⟦ME *muren* < MFr *murer* < LL(Ec) *murare,* to provide with walls < L *murus,* wall: see MUNITIONS⟧ [Archaic] IMMURE

Mu·reş (moo resh′) river flowing west from the Carpathian Mountains into the Tisza in SE Hungary: 470 mi (756 km)

mu·rex (myoor′eks′) ***n., pl.*** **-ri·ces′** (-ə sēz′) or **-rex′es** ⟦ModL < L, the purple fish < IE base **mus* > MOUSE, Gr *myax,* sea mussel⟧ any of a genus (*Murex*) of flesh-eating snails, found in warm salt waters and having a rough, spiny shell: some species yield a purple substance formerly valued as a dye

Mur·frees·bor·o (mur′frēz bur′ō, -ə) ⟦after Col. H. *Murfree* (1752-1809)⟧ city in central Tenn.: site of a Union victory over Confederate forces during the Civil War (1863)

mu·ri·ate (myoor′ē it, -āt′) ***n.*** ⟦Fr < *muriatique:* see fol.⟧ [Now Rare] a salt of hydrochloric acid; chloride, esp. potassium chloride

mu·ri·at·ic acid (myoor′ē at′ik) ⟦Fr *muriatique* < L *muriaticus,* pickled < *muria,* brine < IE **meuro-* < base **meu-,* damp, musty > MOSS, MIRE⟧ hydrochloric acid: now only a commercial term

mu·ri·cate (myoor′i kit, -kāt′) ***adj.*** ⟦< L *muricatus,* pointed, shaped like a purple fish < *murex,* MUREX⟧ rough, with short, sharp points: also **mu′ri·cat′ed**

mu·rid (myoor′id) ***n.*** ⟦< ModL *Muridae* < L *mus* (gen. *muris*), MOUSE⟧ any of a family (Muridae) of rodents, including the Old World rats and mice

Mu·ri·el (myoor′ē əl) ***n.*** ⟦prob. < Celt, as in Ir *Muirgheal* < *muir,* the sea + *geal,* bright⟧ a feminine name

Mu·ri·llo (mōō rē′lyō; *E* myoo ril′ō, mə-), **Bar·to·lo·mé Es·te·ban** (bär′tô lô mā′ es tā′bän′) 1617-82; Sp. painter

mu·rine (myoor′īn, -in) ***adj.*** ⟦L *murinus* < *mus* (gen. *muris*), MOUSE⟧ of the murids, or family of rodents including the Old World rats and mice —***n.*** a murine rodent

murk (murk) ***n.*** ⟦ME *mirke* < ON *myrkr,* dark, akin to OE *mirce,* dark⟧ darkness; gloom —***adj.*** [Archaic] dark or dim

murk·y (mur′kē) ***adj.*** **murk′i·er, murk′i·est** ⟦ME *mirky*⟧ **1** dark or gloomy **2** heavy and obscure with smoke, mist, etc. [the *murky* air of the city] **3** unclear, obscure, cryptic, etc. [the *murky* depths of Transcendentalism] —***SYN.*** DARK —**murk′i·ly** ***adv.*** —**murk′i·ness** ***n.***

Mur·mansk (moor mänsk′) seaport in Russia, on the Barents Sea, on the NW coast of the Kola Peninsula

mur·mur (mur′mər) ***n.*** ⟦ME *murmure* < OFr < L, a murmur, roar, muttering < IE echoic base **mormor-, *murmur-* > Sans *marmara-,* Gr *mormurein*⟧ **1** a low, indistinct, continuous sound, as of a stream or far-off voices **2** a mumbled or muttered complaint **3** an expression of feeling or opinion, regarded as hesitant, restrained, furtive, etc.: *often used in pl.* [*murmurs* of public disapproval] **4** *Med.* any abnormal sound heard by auscultation, esp. of the heart —***vi.*** **1** to make a murmur **2** to mumble or mutter a complaint —***vt.*** to say in a murmur —**mur′mur·a′tion** ***n.*** —**mur′mur·er** ***n.*** —**mur′mur·ing** ***adj., n.***

SYN.—**murmur** implies a continuous flow of words or sounds in a low, indistinct voice and may apply to utterances of satisfaction or dissatisfaction [to *murmur* a prayer]; **mutter** usually suggests angry or discontented words or sounds of this kind [to *mutter* curses]; to **mumble** is to utter almost inaudible or inarticulate sounds in low tones, with the mouth nearly closed [an old woman *mumbling* to herself]

mur·mur·ous (mur′mər əs) ***adj.*** characterized by or making a murmur or murmurs —**mur′mur·ous·ly** ***adv.***

Mur·nau (moor′nou), **F(riedrich) W(ilhelm)** (born *Friedrich Wilhelm Plumpe*) 1888-1931; Ger. film director, in the U.S. after 1926

mur·phy (mur′fē) ***n., pl.*** **-phies** ⟦< Ir surname *Murphy*⟧ [Old Slang] a potato

☆**Mur·phy bed** (mur′fē) ⟦after W. L. *Murphy,* its U.S. inventor (*c.* 1900)⟧ a bed that swings up or folds into a closet or cabinet when not in use

☆**Murphy game** ⟦? after a 19th-c. confidence man of that name⟧ a confidence game in which the victim pays the swindler (**Murphy Man**) for something, as the services of a prostitute, which the swindler promises but the victim never receives

☆**Murphy's Law** ⟦after E. A. *Murphy,* Jr., U.S. engineer who formulated the original version (1949)⟧ a facetiously pessimistic proposition stating that if there is a possibility for something to go wrong, it will go wrong

mur·rain (mur′in) ***n.*** ⟦ME *moreine* < OFr *morine* < VL **morire,* to die < L *mori:* see MORTAL⟧ **1** any of various infectious diseases of cattle **2** [Archaic] a pestilence; plague

Mur·ray[1] (mur′ē, mu′rē) ***n.*** ⟦after the surname *Murray* < ? Celt, as in Welsh *mor,* the sea⟧ a masculine name

Mur·ray[2] (mur′ē, mu′rē) **1 (George) Gilbert (Aimé)** 1866-1957; Eng. classical scholar & statesman, born in Australia **2** Sir **James A(ugustus) H(enry)** 1837-1915; Brit. lexicographer **3 Lind·ley** (lind′lē) 1745-1826; Am. grammarian, in England

Mur·ray[3] (mur′ē) river in SE Australia, flowing from the Australian Alps into the Indian Ocean: 1,596 mi (2,568 km)

murre (mur) ***n., pl.*** **murres** or **murre** ⟦< ?⟧ any of a genus (*Uria*) of swimming and diving alcidine shorebirds

murre·let (mur′lit) ***n.*** ⟦prec. + -LET⟧ any of a number of small auklike birds found chiefly on N Pacific islands

mur·rey (mur′ē) ***n.*** ⟦ME *murry* < OFr *moree,* a dark-red color < ML *moratum* < L *morum,* MULBERRY⟧ a dark purplish-red color; mulberry —***adj.*** of this color

mur·rine (moo rēn′) ***n., pl.*** **-ri′ni** (-rē′nē) or **-rines′** ⟦It < L *murr(h)inus,* adj. form of *murr(h)a,* mineral used for making vases and cups < Iran, as in Pers *mori,* glass ball⟧ a type of multicolored glass made in rods: symmetrical patterns are revealed when the rod is cut and displayed in cross section

Mur·ri·et·a (mur′ē et′ə) ⟦family name of early (19th-c.) settlers⟧ city in SW Calif.

Mur·row (mur′ō), **Edward R(oscoe)** 1908-65; U.S. radio & TV journalist

Mur·rum·bidg·ee (mur′əm bij′ē) river in SE Australia, flowing west into the Murray: *c.* 1,000 mi (1,609 km)

mur·ther (mur′thər) ***n., vt., vi.*** *obs. or dial. var. of* MURDER

mus *abbrev.* **1** museum **2** music **3** musical **4** musician

MusB or **Mus.B.** *abbrev.* ⟦L *Musicae Baccalaureus*⟧ Bachelor of Music: also **MusBac** or **Mus.Bac.**

Mus·ca (mus′kə) ***n.*** ⟦L, a fly: see MIDGE⟧ a S constellation near Crux

Mus·ca·det (mus′kə dā′, moos′-; *Fr* müs kȧ de′) ***n.*** ⟦Fr < Prov, after the variety of grape from which made: akin to MUSCAT⟧ [*also* **m-**] **1** a light, dry white wine from the W Loire valley, France **2** the grape from which it is made

mus·ca·dine (mus′kə din, -dīn′) ***n.*** ⟦altered < *muscadel,* var. of MUSCATEL⟧ an American grape (*Vitis rotundifolia*) grown in the SE U.S., with small leaves, simple tendrils, and small clusters of large, spherical, musky, purple grapes

mus·cae vo·li·tan·tes (mus′ē väl′ə tan′tēz′, mus′kē-) ⟦L, flying flies⟧ specks that appear to float before the eyes, caused by defects or impurities in the vitreous humor; floaters

mus·ca·rine (mus′kə rin, -rēn′) ***n.*** ⟦< ModL (*Amanita*) *muscaria,* fly (agaric) < L *muscarius,* of flies < *musca,* a fly: see MIDGE⟧ an extremely poisonous alkaloid, $C_9H_{21}NO_3$, found in certain mushrooms, rotten fish, etc., that seriously disrupt the neuromuscular system if consumed

mus·cat (mus′kət, -kat′) ***n.*** ⟦Fr < Prov < It *moscato,* musk, wine, lit., having the smell or flavor of musk < LL *muscus,* MUSK⟧ **1** any of several sweet European grapes used in making muscatel and raisins **2** MUSCATEL (sense 1)

Mus·cat (mus kat′) capital of Oman: seaport on the Gulf of Oman

Muscat and Oman *former name for* OMAN (the country)

mus·ca·tel (mus′kə tel′) ***n.*** ⟦ME *muscadelle* < OFr *muscadel* < Prov or < It *moscadello,* orig. dim. of Prov *muscat,* It *moscato,* MUSCAT⟧ **1** a sweet, usually fortified wine made from the muscat **2** MUSCAT (sense 1) Also **mus′ca·del′** (-del′)

mus·cid (mus′id) ***adj.*** ⟦< ModL *Muscidae* < L *musca,* a fly: see MIDGE⟧ of the family (Muscidae) of two-winged dipteran insects that includes the common housefly —***n.*** a muscid insect

mus·cle (mus′əl) ***n.*** ⟦Fr < L *musculus,* a muscle, lit., little mouse (from the fancied resemblance to the movements of a mouse), dim. of *mus,* MOUSE⟧ **1** *a)* any of the bodily organs consisting of bundles of cells or fibers that can be contracted and relaxed to produce bodily movements *b)* the tissue making up such an organ **2** muscular strength; brawn ☆**3** [Informal] power or influence, esp. when based on force or threats of force —***vi.*** **-cled, -cling** ☆[Informal] to make one's way or take control by sheer strength or force, or threats of force: usually with *in* —***vt.*** [Informal] **1** to move (something) by, or as by, muscular exertion **2** to influence, pressure, etc. by force or threat of force

mus·cle-bound (-bound′) ***adj.*** **1** having a muscly physique; often, specif., having muscles so overdeveloped as to result in a stiff, inflexible way of moving **2** not flexible or adaptive; rigid

☆**muscle car** an automobile, esp. in the 1960s, made to look and perform like a racing car, as in being able to accelerate quickly to high speeds, but designed for use on regular roads

mus·cle·head (mus′əl hed′) ***n.*** [Slang] **1** a muscular man, esp. one who is involved in bodybuilding, weight lifting, etc. **2** a dull, stupid person

mus·cle·man (-man′) ***n., pl.*** **-men′** (-men′) **1** [Informal] a man with a well-developed, brawny physique, esp., a bodybuilder **2** [Slang] a bodyguard, esp. one hired to use coercive, physical methods; goon

muscle sense KINESTHESIA

☆**muscle shirt** a casual shirt similar to a T-shirt but without sleeves, ostensibly worn to show off muscular upper arms

mus·cly (mus′lē, -əl ē) ***adj.*** having prominent, well-developed muscles, esp. in the chest and upper arms

mus·co·va·do (mus′kə vā′dō, -vä′-) ***n.*** ⟦Sp *mascabado* (or Port *mascavado*), unrefined, of inferior quality < Sp *mascabar,* to depreciate, contr. < *menoscabar,* to lessen, deteriorate < *menos,* less (< L *minus:* see MINUS) + *acabar,* to achieve < L *ad-,* to + *caput,* HEAD⟧ the dark raw sugar that remains after the molasses has been extracted from the juice of the sugar cane

mus·co·vite (mus′kə vīt′) ***n.*** ⟦formerly called *Muscovy glass:* see -ITE[1]⟧ a very common, light-colored, soft mica, hydrous potassium aluminum silicate, $KAl_2(AlSi_3)O_{10}(OH)_2$, used as an electrical or thermal insulator

Mus·co·vite (mus′kə vīt′) ***n.*** **1** *a)* [Historical] a person born or living in Muscovy *b)* a Russian **2** a person born or living in Moscow —***adj.*** **1** *a)* of Muscovy *b)* Russian **2** of Moscow

Mus·co·vy (mus′kə vē) **1** former grand duchy, surrounding and including Moscow, that expanded into the Russian Empire under Ivan IV (16th cent.) **2** *former name for* RUSSIA

Muscovy duck ⟦altered (by assoc. with prec.) < MUSK DUCK⟧ a large, domesticated, Neotropical duck (*Cairina moschata*) with dark plumage, white wing patches, and a reddish, naked patch on the face

mus·cul- (mus′kyəl) *combining form* MUSCULO-: used before a vowel

mus·cu·lar (mus′kyə lər) *adj.* ⟦< L *musculus* (see MUSCLE) + -AR⟧ **1** of, consisting of, or accomplished by a muscle or muscles **2** having well-developed muscles; strong; brawny **3** suggestive of great physical strength; powerful —**mus′cu·lar′i·ty** (-lar′ə tē) *n.* —**mus′cu·lar·ly** *adv.*

muscular dystrophy a chronic, noncontagious disease characterized by a progressive wasting of the muscles

mus·cu·la·ture (mus′kyə lə chər) *n.* ⟦Fr < L *musculus*⟧ the arrangement of the muscles of a body or of some part of the body; muscular system

mus·cu·lo- (mus′kyə lō, -lə) ⟦< L *musculus,* MUSCLE⟧ *combining form* muscle, muscle and [*musculoskeletal*]

mus·cu·lo·skel·e·tal (mus′kyə lō skel′ə təl, mus′kyə lə-) *adj.* of or relating to musculature and the skeleton together

MusD or **Mus.D.** *abbrev.* ⟦L *Musicae Doctor*⟧ Doctor of Music: also **MusDoc** or **Mus.Doc.**

muse (myo͞oz) *vi.* **mused, mus′ing** ⟦ME *musen* < OFr *muser,* to ponder, loiter, orig., ? to stand with muzzle in the air < ML **musare* < *musum* (> OFr *musel*), snout, MUZZLE⟧ to think deeply and at length; meditate —*vt.* to think or say meditatively —*n.* a musing; deep meditation

Muse (myo͞oz) *n.* ⟦OFr < L *musa* < Gr *mousa,* a Muse, music, eloquence < ? IE base **mendh-*, to pay attention to, be lively > ON *munda,* to strive⟧ **1** *Gr. Myth.* any of the MUSES **2** [**m-**] a person, esp. a woman, who is the object of love or devotion and is regarded as a source of inspiration

mu·se·ol·o·gy (myo͞o′zē äl′ə jē) *n.* ⟦< Gr *mouseion,* MUSEUM + -LOGY⟧ the theory or practice of operating, or managing, a museum —**mu′se·o·log′i·cal** (-ə läj′i kəl) *adj.* —**mu′se·ol′o·gist** (-jist) *n.*

Mus·es (myo͞oz′iz) *pl.n. Gr. Myth.* the nine goddesses who preside over literature and the arts and sciences: Calliope, Clio, Euterpe, Melpomene, Terpsichore, Erato, Polyhymnia (or Polymnia), Urania, and Thalia

mu·sette (myo͞o zet′) *n.* ⟦OFr < *muser,* to play music, MUSE⟧ **1** a small French bagpipe of the 17th and 18th cent. **2** a soft pastoral melody, in imitation of the tunes typically played on this instrument ☆**3** a small bag of canvas or leather for toilet articles, etc., worn suspended from a shoulder strap, as by soldiers or hikers: also **musette bag**

mu·se·um (myo͞o zē′əm) *n.* ⟦L < Gr *mouseion,* place for the Muses or for study < *mousa,* MUSE⟧ an institution, building, or room for preserving and exhibiting artistic, historical, or scientific objects

mush[1] (mush) *n.* ⟦prob. var. of MASH⟧ **1** a thick porridge made by boiling meal, esp. cornmeal, in water or milk **2** any thick, soft, yielding mass **3** [Informal] maudlin sentimentality —*vt.* [Dial., Chiefly Brit.] to make into mush; crush

mush[2] (mush) *interj.* ⟦prob. < *mush on,* altered < Fr *marchons,* let's go < *marcher,* to go, MARCH[1]⟧ used to command sled dogs to start or to go faster —*vi.* to travel on foot over snow with a dog sled —*n.* a journey by mushing

mush·er (mush′ər) *n.* ⟦prec. + -ER⟧ a person who drives a dog sled

mush·room (mush′ro͞om′, -ro͝om′) *n.* ⟦ME *muscheron* < OFr *moisseron* < LL *mussirio* (gen. *mussirionis*)⟧ **1** *a)* any of various rapidly growing, fleshy fungi, typically having a stalk capped with an umbrella-like top; esp., a gill or pore fungus *b)* the fruiting body of such a fungus *c)* an edible fruiting body of such a fungus **2** anything like a mushroom in shape or rapid growth —*vi.* **1** to hunt for and gather wild mushrooms **2** to grow or spread rapidly **3** to flatten out at the end so as to resemble a mushroom

mushroom cloud an enormous, mushroom-shaped cloud of radioactive debris, water vapor, etc., resulting from an aboveground nuclear explosion

mu shu pork (mo͞o′ sho͞o) *alt. sp. of* MOO SHU PORK

mush·y (mush′ē) *adj.* **mush′i·er, mush′i·est 1** *a)* like mush; thick, soft, and yielding *b)* poorly defined; blurry [the old recording had a *mushy* sound] **2** [Informal] affectionate or sentimental in a maudlin fashion —**mush′i·ly** *adv.*

mu·sic (myo͞o′zik) *n.* ⟦ME *musike* < OFr *musique* < L *musica* < Gr *mousikē* (*technē*), musical (art), orig. an art of the Muses < *mousa,* MUSE⟧ **1** the art and science of combining vocal or instrumental sounds or tones in varying melody, harmony, rhythm, and timbre, esp. so as to form structurally complete and emotionally expressive compositions **2** the sounds or tones so arranged, or the arrangement of these **3** any rhythmic sequence of pleasing sounds, as of birds, water, etc. **4** *a)* a particular form, style, etc. of musical composition or a particular class of musical works or pieces [*folk music*] *b)* the body of musical works of a particular style, place, period, or composer **5** the written or printed score of a musical composition **6** ability to respond to or take pleasure in music [*no music* in his soul] —☆**face the music** [Slang] to accept the consequences of one's actions, however unpleasant —**set to music** to compose music for (a poem, etc.)

mu·si·cal (myo͞o′zi kəl) *adj.* ⟦ME < ML *musicalis* < L *musica*⟧ **1** of or for the creation, production, or performance of music **2** having the nature of music; melodious or harmonious **3** fond of, sensitive to, or skilled in music **4** set to music; accompanied by music —*n.* ☆**1** a theatrical or film production, often elaborately costumed and staged, with dialogue developing the story line and an integrated musical score featuring songs and dances in a popular idiom: in full, variously, **musical comedy, musical play,** *or* **musical drama 2** [Archaic] MUSICALE —**mu′si·cal′i·ty** (-kal′ə tē) *n.* —**mu′si·cal·ly** *adv.*

musical chairs a game in which the players march to music around empty chairs (always one fewer than the number of players) and rush to sit down each time the music stops: the player with no seat is eliminated in each round

☆**mu·si·cale** (myo͞o′zi kal′) *n.* ⟦Fr⟧ a party or social affair featuring a musical program

mu·si·cal·ize (myo͞o′zi kəl īz′) *vt.* **-ized′, -iz′ing** to set (a play, novel, film, etc.) to music —**mu′si·cal·i·za′tion** *n.*

musical saw a handsaw held upright between the knees and variously flexed and stroked with a violin bow to produce musical tones

music box an often decorative box containing a mechanism that plays a melody as when the lid is opened

music drama a form of opera, specif. as developed by Richard Wagner, characterized by a continuous flow of orchestral music, with an integrative use of musical themes (*leitmotifs*), and singing that is free from formal division into arias, recitatives, etc.

music hall 1 an auditorium for musical or theatrical productions **2** *a)* [Brit.] a vaudeville theater *b)* VAUDEVILLE (sense 1) in Britain

mu·si·cian (myo͞o zish′ən) *n.* ⟦ME < MFr *musicien*⟧ a person skilled in music; esp., a professional performer, composer, or conductor of music —**mu·si′cian·ly** *adj.* —**mu·si′cian·ship′** *n.*

mu·sick (myo͞o′zik) *vt.* to compose music for (a poem, libretto, etc.) —*vi.* to compose music

music of the spheres ⟦see SPHERE (sense 5)⟧ an ethereal music supposed by Pythagoras and other early mathematicians to be produced by the movements of the heavenly bodies

mu·si·col·o·gy (myo͞o′zi käl′ə jē) *n.* ⟦It *musicologia:* see MUSIC & -LOGY⟧ the systematized study of the science, history, forms, and methods of music —**mu′si·co·log′i·cal** (-kə läj′i kəl) *adj.* —**mu′si·col′o·gist** *n.*

music stand a rack to hold sheets of music for a performer or conductor

music video a recorded performance of music accompanied by synchronized actions, such as a dramatic interpretation of the lyrics or a series of, sometimes surreal, images

Mu·sil (mo͞o′zil), **Robert** 1880-1942; Austrian novelist

mus·ing (myo͞o′ziŋ) *adj.* that muses; meditative —*n.* meditation; reflection: *often used in pl.* —**mus′ing·ly** *adv.*

mu·sique con·crète (mü zēk kōn kret′) ⟦Fr, concrete (as opposed to abstract) music⟧ a type of modern music created by mixing electronically manipulated or distorted instrumental and natural sounds, noises, etc.

mus·jid (mus′jid) *n. alt. sp. of* MASJID

musk (musk) *n.* ⟦OFr *musc* < LL *muscus* < Gr *moschos* < Pers *mušk,* musk < Sans *muṣka,* testicle, dim. of *mus,* MOUSE⟧ **1** a substance with a strong, penetrating odor, obtained from a small sac (**musk bag**) under the skin of the abdomen in the male musk deer: used as the basis of numerous perfumes **2** a similar substance secreted by certain other animals, as the alligator or musk ox **3** the odor of any of these substances, now often created synthetically **4** any of several plants having a musky scent

musk deer a small, hornless deer (*Moschus moschiferus*) of the uplands of central Asia: the male secretes musk and has tusklike upper canines

musk duck 1 an Australian duck (*Biziura lobata*) with an inflatable leathery pouch beneath the lower jaw, spikelike tail feathers, and a musklike odor during the breeding season **2** MUSCOVY DUCK

mus·keg (mus′keg′) *n.* ⟦Cree *maskeek,* swamp⟧ a kind of bog or marsh containing thick layers of decaying vegetable matter, mosses, etc., found esp. in Canada and Alaska and often overgrown with moss

☆**mus·kel·lunge** (mus′kə lunj′) *n., pl.* **-lunge′** ⟦Ojibwa *maaskinoozhe* < *maazh-*, similar to + *ginoozhe,* northern pike⟧ a very large pike (*Esox masquinongy*) of the Great Lakes and upper Mississippi drainages, valued as a game and food fish: also called **mus′kie** (-kē)

mus·ket (mus′kət) *n.* ⟦MFr *mosquet* < It *moschetto,* musket, orig., fledged arrow < *mosca,* a fly < L *musca:* see MIDGE⟧ a smoothbore, long-barreled firearm, used esp. by infantry soldiers before the invention of the rifle

mus·ket·eer (mus′kə tir′) *n.* ⟦Fr *mousquetaire*⟧ **1** a soldier armed with a musket **2** in 17th- and 18th-cent. France, a member of a company of guards attached to the royal household and famed for flamboyant dress

mus·ket·ry (mus′kə trē) *n.* ⟦Fr *mousqueterie*⟧ **1** the skill of firing muskets or other small arms **2** *a)* muskets collectively *b)* musketeers collectively

musk·mel·on (musk′mel′ən) *n.* ⟦MUSK + MELON⟧ **1** any of various round or oblong fruits that grow on different varieties of a trailing vine (*Cucumis melo*) of the gourd family, including cantaloupes and honeydew melons **2** any of these plants, esp. a variety (*Cucumis melo* var. *reticulatus*) having fruit with a musky odor, ribbed netlike skin, and greenish to reddish orange, sweet, juicy flesh

☆**Mus·ko·ge·an** (mus kō′gē ən, -jē-) *adj.* ⟦var. of *Muskhogean,* coined (1891) < MUSKOGEE[2] by J. W. Powell (1834-1902), U.S. ethnologist & geologist⟧ designating or of a North American Indian language family of the SE U.S., consisting of four main branches, including Choctaw-Chickasaw and Creek-Seminole: also sp. **Mus·kho′ge·an**

Mus·ko·gee[1] (mus kō′gē) *n., pl.* **-gees** or **-gee** ⟦Creek *maaskóoki*⟧ CREEK (sense 2)

Mus·ko·gee[2] (mus kō′gē) ⟦< prec.⟧ city in E Okla.

musk ox a hardy goat antelope (*Ovibos moschatus*) of arctic America and Greenland, with a long, coarse, hairy coat, large, curved horns, and a musklike odor

musk plant a perennial North American plant (*Mimulus moschatus*) of the figwort family, with yellow tubular flowers and, sometimes, a musky odor

☆**musk·rat** (musk′rat′) *n., pl.* **-rats′** or **-rat′** **1** any of various American rodents (family Cricetidae) living in water and having glossy brown fur, a long tail, webbed hind feet, and a musklike odor **2** its fur

musk rose a Mediterranean rose (*Rosa moschata*) with fragrant, usually white, flowers

☆**musk turtle** any of a family (Kinosternidae) of small, aquatic turtles having a heavy, musky scent, esp., any of a genus (*Sternotherus*) found in E North America

musk·y (mus′kē) *adj.* **musk′i·er, musk′i·est** of, like, or smelling of musk —**musk′i·ness** *n.*

Mus·lim (muz′ləm, mooz′-, moos′-) *n.* ⟦Ar, devoted believer < *aslama,* to resign oneself (to God)⟧ an adherent of Islam —*adj.* of Islam or the Muslims

mus·lin (muz′lin) *n.* ⟦Fr *mousseline* < It *mussolino* < *mussolo,* muslin, after *Mussolo* (< Ar *Mauṣil*), Mosul, city in Iraq, where it was made⟧ any of various strong, often sheer cotton fabrics of plain weave, esp., a heavy variety used for sheets, pillowcases, etc.

☆**mus·quash** (mus′kwäsh′, -kwôsh′) *n., pl.* **-quash′es** or **-quash′** ⟦< AmInd (Algonquian), akin to Abenaki *muskwessu,* lit., it is red⟧ **1** any of a genus (*Ondatra*) of muskrats of N North America having rudderlike tails that are flat from top to bottom **2** [Chiefly Brit.] the fur of the muskrat

muss (mus) *n.* ⟦prob. var. of MESS⟧ **1** [Informal] a mess; disorder [*done without muss or fuss*] **2** [Dial.] a squabble; row; commotion —*vt.* [Informal] to make messy or disordered; disarrange: often with *up*

mus·sel (mus′əl) *n.* ⟦ME *muscle* < OE, akin to OHG *muscula,* both < VL **muscula,* for L *musculus,* mussel, MUSCLE⟧ any of various bivalve mollusks, specif., *a)* any of a sometimes edible saltwater family (Mytilidae) that anchors to rocks, ships, etc. by byssus threads *b)* any of a freshwater family (Unionidae) that is large-sized and may produce pearls

Mus·set (mü se′), **(Louis Charles) Al·fred de** (ȧl fred′ də) 1810-57; Fr. poet & playwright

Mus·so·li·ni (moo′sə lē′nē), **Be·ni·to** (be nē′tō) 1883-1945; It. dictator: Fascist prime minister of Italy (1922-43): executed: called *Il Duce*

Mus·sorg·sky (mə sôrk′skē, -sôrg′-), **Mo·dest Pe·tro·vich** (mō dest′ pi trō′vich) 1839-81; Russ. composer: also sp. **Musorgsky**

Mus·sul·man (mus′əl mən) *n., pl.* **-mans** ⟦Pers *musulmān,* a Muslim < Ar *muslim*⟧ [Archaic] MUSLIM

muss·y (mus′ē) *adj.* **muss′i·er, muss′i·est** [Informal] messy; disordered, untidy, rumpled, etc.

must[1] (must) *v.aux., pt.* **must** ⟦ME *moste,* pt., had to < OE, pt. of *motan,* may, akin to Goth *(ga)mot,* (I) find room, am permitted, prob. < IE **mōt-,* var. of **med-,* to measure > METE[1]⟧ **1** used to express compulsion, obligation, requirement, or necessity [*I know I must pay her; I knew I must pay her*] **2** used to express probability [*then you must be my cousin; I thought he must be my cousin*] **3** used to express certainty or inevitability [*all men must die; they knew they must die*] ➥As a modal auxiliary, *must* is followed by an infinitive without *to* and is often used in comb., meaning "essential to" or "necessary to" [*a must-see movie, a list of must-do chores*] —*vi.* used elliptically in the same functions as MUST[1] (*v.aux.*) [*shoot if you must*] —*n.* [Informal] something that must be done, had, read, seen, etc. [*this book is a must*] —*adj.* [Informal] that must be done, etc.; necessary; essential [*a book that is must reading*]

must[2] (must) *n.* ⟦Hindi *mast,* intoxicated < Pers *mast* < IE base **mad-,* to be moist > MEAT⟧ a state of frenzy in animals, esp. in the male elephant, usually associated with sexual heat —*adj.* in must

must[3] (must) *n.* ⟦ME < OE < L *mustum,* new wine, neut. of *mustus,* new, fresh < IE base **meu-,* moist > MOSS⟧ the juice pressed from grapes or other fruit before it has fermented; new wine

must[4] (must) *n.* ⟦back-form. < MUSTY⟧ a musty quality or state; mustiness

mus·tache (mus′tash′, mə stash′) *n.* ⟦Fr *moustache* < It *mostacchio,* mustache < MGr *mustaki* < Gr *mystax,* upper lip, mustache < *mastax,* a mouth, jaws < IE base **menth-* > MOUTH⟧ **1** *a)* the hair that a man has let grow out on his upper lip (sometimes used in the plural in reference to the two halves of this growth, esp. when long) *b)* hair growing on the upper lip [*at fourteen he's already getting a mustache*] **2** the hair or bristles growing about the mouth in some animals

mus·ta·chi·o (mə stash′ē ō′, -stä′shē ō′; -stash′ō, -stä′shō) *n., pl.* **-os′** ⟦< Sp *mostacho* or It *mostaccio*⟧ [*also pl.*] a mustache, esp. one that is large, bushy, ornate, etc. —**mus·ta′chi·oed′** *adj.*

Mus·ta·fa Ke·mal (moos′tä fä′ ke mäl′) *see* KEMAL ATATÜRK

☆**mus·tang** (mus′taŋ′) *n.* ⟦AmSp *mestengo* < Sp *mesteño,* belonging to an assoc. of cattlemen, ranging freely < *mesta,* (cattlemen's) group < ML *mixta,* a mixture < fem. of L *mixtus,* a mingling, orig. pp. of *miscere,* MIX⟧ a small wild or half-wild horse of the W Plains of the U.S.

mus·tard (mus′tərd) *n.* ⟦ME *mustarde* < OFr *moustarde* < *moust,* must < L *mustum* (see MUST[3]): the paste was orig. prepared with must as an ingredient⟧ **1** any of several annual herbs (genus *Brassica*) of the crucifer family, with yellow flowers and slender pods containing round seeds **2** the ground or powdered seeds of some species (as *Brassica nigra*) of these plants, often prepared as a paste, used as a pungent seasoning for foods, or as a counterirritant in medicine **3** the dark-yellow color of ground mustard —☆**cut the mustard** [Slang] to come up to expectations or to the required standard; succeed

mustard gas ⟦from its odor, like that of ground mustard⟧ an oily, volatile liquid, $(CH_2ClCH_2)_2S$, used in warfare as a poison gas because of its extremely irritating, blistering, and disabling effects

mustard oil an oil extracted from mustard seed, used in making soap

mustard plaster a paste made with powdered mustard, spread on a cloth and applied to the skin as a counterirritant and rubefacient

mus·tard·y (mus′tər dē) *adj.* of or having the flavor, color, etc. of mustard

mus·tee (mus tē′, mus′tē) *n.* ⟦altered < MESTIZO⟧ **1** OCTOROON **2** any person of mixed ancestry

mus·te·line (mus′tə līn′, -lin) *adj.* ⟦L *mustelinus* < *mustela,* a weasel, akin to *mus,* MOUSE⟧ designating or of a large family (Mustelidae) of fur-bearing carnivores, including the weasel, marten, polecat, and mink

mus·ter (mus′tər) *vt.* ⟦ME *mousteren* < OFr *moustrer,* to exhibit, show < ML *mustrare* < L *monstrare,* to show < *monstrum:* see MONSTER⟧ **1** to assemble or summon (troops, etc.), as for inspection, roll call, or service **2** to put through a roll call **3** to gather together and display; collect; summon: often with *up* [*to muster up strength*] **4** to have in number; amount to —*vi.* to come together or gather; specif., to assemble as for inspection or roll call —*n.* **1** a gathering together or assembling, as of troops for inspection **2** *a)* the persons or things assembled; assemblage *b)* the sum of these **3** the roll, or list, of persons in a military or naval unit: also **muster roll** —*SYN.* GATHER —☆**muster in (or out)** to enlist in (or discharge from) military service —**pass muster** to measure up to the required standards

musth (must) *n., adj. Zool. alt. sp. of* MUST[2]

must·n't (mus′ənt) *contraction* must not

mus·ty (mus′tē) *adj.* **-ti·er, -ti·est** ⟦< ? earlier *moisty* < MOIST⟧ **1** having a stale, moldy smell or taste, as an unused room, food kept in a damp place, etc. **2** stale or trite; worn-out; antiquated [*musty ideas*] **3** dull; apathetic —**mus′ti·ly** *adv.* —**mus′ti·ness** *n.*

mu·ta·ble (myoot′ə bəl) *adj.* ⟦ME < L *mutabilis,* changeable < *mutare,* to change: see MISS[1]⟧ **1** that can be changed **2** tending toward frequent change; inconstant; fickle **3** subject to mutation —**mu′ta·bil′i·ty** *n.,* **mu′ta·ble·ness** —**mu′ta·bly** *adv.*

mu·ta·gen (myoot′ə jən, -jen′) *n.* ⟦MUTA(TION) + -GEN⟧ *Biol.* any agent or substance, as X-rays, mustard gas, etc., capable of noticeably increasing the frequency of mutation —**mu′ta·gen′ic** (-jen′ik) *adj.* —**mu′ta·gen′i·cal·ly** *adv.*

mu·ta·gen·e·sis (myoot′ə jen′ə sis) *n.* ⟦MUTA(TION) + GENESIS⟧ the occurrence or production of mutation

mu·tant (myoot′'nt) *adj.* ⟦< L *mutans,* prp. of *mutare,* to change: see MISS[1]⟧ having to do with or undergoing mutation —*n.* **1** an organism that exhibits MUTATION (sense 3*a*) **2** in science fiction, an organism monstrously altered, as by radiation

mu·tate (myoo′tāt′) *vi., vt.* **-tat′ed, -tat′ing** ⟦< L *mutatus,* pp. of *mutare,* to change: see MISS[1]⟧ to change; specif., to undergo or cause to undergo genetic or linguistic mutation

mu·ta·tion (myoo tā′shən) *n.* ⟦ME *mutacioun* < OFr *mutacion* < L *mutatio* < *mutare,* to change: see MISS[1]⟧ **1** a changing or being changed **2** a change, as in form, nature, qualities, etc. **3** *Biol. a)* a sudden variation in some inheritable characteristic in a germ cell of an individual animal or plant, as distinguished from a variation resulting from generations of gradual change *b)* an individual resulting from such variation; mutant *c)* an abrupt and relatively permanent change in somatic cells that is transmitted only to daughter cells and can be inherited only in plants that reproduce asexually **4** *Linguis. a)* UMLAUT (sense 1*a*) *b)* alternation of consonants under specific conditions, as in variations in the initial consonant of a word in Irish and other Celtic languages —**mu·ta′tion·al** *adj.* —**mu·ta′tion·al·ly** *adv.*

mu·ta·tis mu·tan·dis (moo tät′is moo tän′dis, myoo tät′is myoo-) ⟦L, lit., things being changed that should be changed < *mutatis,* abl. pl. of pp. of *mutare,* to change (see MISS[1]) + *mutandis,* abl. pl. of ger. of this v.⟧ with all due adjustments or modifications having been made

mu·ta·tive (myoot′ə tiv) *adj.* ⟦ML *mutativus*⟧ of, tending toward, or characterized by mutation

mutch·kin (much′kin) *n.* ⟦ME *muchekyn* < obs. Du *mudseken,* a measure of capacity < MDu *mudde,* bushel < ML *modius,* a liquid measure < L, the Roman grain measure < *modus:* see MODE⟧ [Scot.] a unit of liquid measure equal to a little less than a pint

mute (myoot) *adj.* ⟦ME *mewet* < OFr *muet* < *mu* < L *mutus,* silent: for IE base see MOPE⟧ **1** not speaking; voluntarily silent: often used fig. **2** unable to speak **3** not spoken [*a mute appeal*] **4** *Phonet.* SILENT (*adj.* 4*b*) [*the letter e in "mouse" is mute*] —*n.* **1** a person who does not speak; specif., one who, deaf from infancy, has not learned to speak **2** [Historical] a hired mourner at a funeral **3** *Electronics* a setting, control, device, etc., as on a TV receiver or telephone, that may be used to silence the audio temporarily **4** *Music* any of various devices used to soften or muffle the tone of an instrument, as a block placed within the bell of a brass instrument, or a piece set onto the bridge of a violin **5** *Phonet.* a silent letter —*vt.* **mut′ed, mut′ing** **1** to soften or muffle the sound of (a musical instrument, etc.) as with a mute **2** to subdue the intensity of (a color) —**stand mute** *Law* to refuse to plead guilty or not guilty —**mute′ly** *adv.* —**mute′ness** *n.*

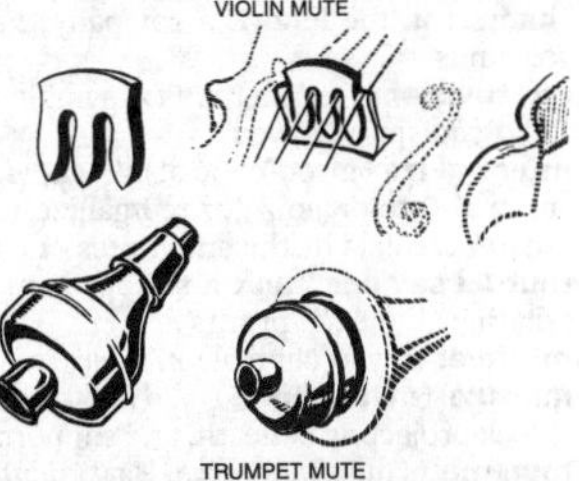
VIOLIN MUTE
TRUMPET MUTE

mute swan a large, white, usually silent swan (*Cygnus olor*) with a black knob at the base of its orange bill: originally of the Old World but now present in NE U.S.

mu·ti·cous (myo͞ot′i kəs) *adj.* ⟦L *muticus*, curtailed, docked, var. of *mutilus*: see fol.⟧ *Bot.* lacking a point or awn; blunt

mu·ti·late (myo͞ot′'l āt′) *vt.* **-lat′ed**, **-lat′ing** ⟦< L *mutilatus*, pp. of *mutilare*, to maim, mutilate < *mutilus*, maimed; akin to Ir *mut*, short⟧ **1** to cut off or damage a limb or other important part of (a person or animal) **2** to damage, injure, or otherwise mar, esp. by removing an essential part or parts [to *mutilate* a novel by censorship] —*SYN.* MAIM —**mu′ti·la′tion** *n.* —**mu′ti·la′tive** *adj.* —**mu′ti·la′tor** *n.*

mu·ti·neer (myo͞ot′'n ir′) *n.* ⟦Fr *mutinier* < OFr *mutin*: see MUTINY⟧ a person who takes part in a mutiny

mu·ti·nous (myo͞ot′'n əs) *adj.* **1** of, engaged in, or inclined to mutiny **2** like or characteristic of mutiny —**mu′ti·nous·ly** *adv.* —**mu′ti·nous·ness** *n.*

mu·ti·ny (myo͞ot′'n ē) *n., pl.* **-nies** ⟦< earlier *mutine*, to rebel < Fr *mutiner* < OFr *mutin*, mutinous < *meute*, a revolt < LL **movita*, movement, ult. < L *movere*, MOVE⟧ revolt against and, often, forcible resistance to constituted authority; esp., rebellion of soldiers or sailors against their officers —*vi.* **-nied**, **-ny·ing** to participate in a mutiny; revolt against constituted authority

mut·ism (myo͞ot′iz′əm) *n.* ⟦Fr *mutisme* < L *mutus*, MUTE⟧ the condition of being mute; esp., a refusal to speak, as a manifestation of a psychotic disorder

mu·ton (myo͞o′tän′) *n.* ⟦MUT(ATION) + -ON⟧ the smallest unit of DNA, possibly one nucleotide, that can produce a mutation

Mu·tsu·hi·to (mo͞ot′sə hēt′ō) 1852-1912; emperor of Japan (1867-1912): see also MEIJI, MEIJI RESTORATION

☆**mutt** (mut) *n.* ⟦prob. contr. < MUTTONHEAD⟧ **1** [Slang] a stupid or incompetent person **2** [Informal] a dog of mixed breed; mongrel

mut·ter (mut′ər) *vi.* ⟦ME *moteren*, akin to Ger *muttern*, ult. < IE echoic base **mu-* (see MOPE) > L *muttire*⟧ **1** to speak in low, indistinct tones without much movement of the lips, as in complaining or in speaking to oneself **2** to complain or grumble **3** to make a low, rumbling, threatening sound, as thunder —*vt.* to say in low, indistinct, often angry or discontented, tones —*n.* **1** the act of muttering **2** something muttered; esp., a complaint or grumble —*SYN.* MURMUR —**mut′ter·er** *n.*

mut·ton (mut′'n) *n.* ⟦ME *moton* < OFr, a ram < ML **multo*, sheep, of Celt orig. as in Welsh *mollt*, Ir *molt*⟧ **1** the flesh of a sheep, esp. a grown sheep, used as food **2** [Rare] a sheep —**mut′ton·y** *adj.*

mutton chop **1** a piece cut from the rib of a sheep for broiling or frying **2** [*pl.*] side whiskers extending along the lower jaw and shaped like mutton chops (i.e., narrow at the top, and broad and rounded at the bottom), with a clean-shaven chin between

mut·ton·head (-hed′) *n.* [Slang] a stupid person

Mut·tra (mut′rə) *former name for* MATHURA

mu·tu·al (myo͞o′cho͞o əl) *adj.* ⟦LME *mutuall* < MFr *mutuel* < L *mutuus*, mutual, reciprocal < *mutare*, to change, exchange: see MISS[1]⟧ **1** *a)* done, felt, etc. by each of two or more for or toward the other or others; reciprocal [*mutual* admiration] *b)* of, or having the same relationship toward, each other or one another [*mutual* enemies] **2** shared in common; joint [our *mutual* friend] **3** designating or of a type of insurance in which the policyholders elect the directors, share in the profits, and agree to indemnify one another against loss —**mu′tu·al′i·ty** (-al′ə tē) *n., pl.* **-ties** —**mu′tu·al·ly** *adv.*

SYN.—**mutual** may be used for an interchange of feeling between two persons [John and Joe are *mutual* enemies] or may imply a sharing jointly with others [the *mutual* efforts of a group]; **reciprocal** implies a return in kind or degree by each of two sides of what is given or demonstrated by the other [a *reciprocal* trade agreement], or it may refer to any inversely corresponding relationship [the *reciprocal* functions of two machine parts]; **common** simply implies a being shared by others or by all the members of a group [our *common* interests]

☆**mutual fund** **1** a fund made up of a number of stocks, bonds, etc. for which shares are issued to investors, with each share representing a fractional interest in the fund **2** a company that manages or markets such a fund or funds

mu·tu·al·ism (-iz′əm) *n.* *Biol.* symbiosis with mutual advantage to both or all organisms involved

mu·tu·al·ize (myo͞o′cho͞o əl īz′) *vt., vi.* **-ized′**, **-iz′ing** **1** to make or become mutual **2** to organize or reorganize (a corporation) so that a majority of shares are held by the employees or customers —**mu′tu·al·i·za′tion** *n.*

☆**mutual savings bank** a savings bank that has no capital, its depositors sharing all the net profits

☆**mu·tu·el** (myo͞o′cho͞o əl) *n.* PARIMUTUEL

mu·tule (myo͞o′cho͞ol′) *n.* ⟦Fr < L *mutulus*: see MODILLION⟧ *Archit.* a flat block projecting beneath, and supporting, the corona of a Doric cornice

☆**muu·muu** (mo͞o′mo͞o′) *n.* ⟦Haw *mu′umu′u*, lit., cut off: so named to distinguish it from styles with yokes and long sleeves⟧ a full, long, loose dress for women, typically in a bright print as originally worn in Hawaii

Muy·bridge (mī′brij′), **Ead·weard** (ed′wərd) (born *Edward James Muggeridge*) 1830-1904; Eng. photographer

Mu·zak (myo͞o′zak′) *trademark for* a system for distributing uninterrupted recorded music via satellite transmission or on compact disc: orig., such music was delivered via radio and telephone lines to restaurants, stores, workplaces, etc. —*n.* **1** the music so distributed, typically intended to be unobtrusive **2** [*often* **m-**] any music regarded as pervasive, bland and monotonous, etc.

mu·zhik (mo͞o zhēk′, mo͞o′zhik′) *n.* ⟦Russ *mužik*, dim. of *muž*, MAN⟧ in czarist Russia, a peasant

muz·zle (muz′əl) *n.* ⟦ME *mosel* < OFr *musel*, snout, muzzle, dim. of *mus* < ML *musum* < ?⟧ **1** the projecting part of the head of a dog, horse, etc., including the mouth, nose, and jaws; snout **2** a device, as of straps, fastened over the mouth of an animal to prevent its biting or eating **3** anything that prevents free speech or discussion **4** the front end of the barrel of a firearm —*vt.* **-zled**, **-zling** **1** to put a muzzle on (an animal) **2** to prevent from talking or expressing an opinion; gag —**muz′zler** *n.*

muz·zle·load·er (-lōd′ər) *n.* any firearm loaded through the muzzle —**muz′zle·load′ing** *adj.*

muzzle velocity the velocity of a projectile as it leaves the muzzle of a firearm: expressed in feet per second

muz·zy (muz′ē) *adj.* **-zi·er**, **-zi·est** ⟦prob. < MU(DDY) + (FU)ZZY⟧ [Informal] **1** confused; befuddled **2** blurred —**muz′zi·ly** *adv.* —**muz′zi·ness** *n.*

mV or **mv** *abbrev.* millivolt(s)

MV *abbrev.* **1** megavolt(s): also **Mv** **2** motor vessel

MVP *abbrev. Sports* most valuable player

mW or **mw** *abbrev.* milliwatt(s)

MW or **Mw** *abbrev.* megawatt(s)

Mwe·ru (′m wā′ro͞o, em-) lake between the Democratic Republic of the Congo & NE Zambia: *c.* 1,700 sq mi (4,403 sq km)

Mx *abbrev.* maxwell

MX missile (em′eks′) ⟦< *m(issile)*, *(e)x(perimental)*⟧ any of a system of U.S. intercontinental ballistic missiles with MIRVed nuclear warheads, designed to be highly mobile and concealable in underground silos

my (mī) ***possessive pronominal adj.*** ⟦ME *mi*, shortened form of *min* used before consonants < OE *min*, of me, my, mine: see MINE[1], ME⟧ of, belonging to, made by, or done by me: also used before some formal titles and polite forms of address [*My* Lord, *my* dear Mr. Brown] —***interj.*** used to express surprise, dismay, disbelief, etc.: often in comb. with other words [oh, *my*! *my* goodness! *my* eye!]

My *abbrev.* May

my- (mī) *combining form* MYO-: used before a vowel

mya *abbrev.* million years ago: sometimes written **MYA**

my·al·gi·a (mī al′jə, -jē ə) *n.* ⟦ModL: see MYO- & -ALGIA⟧ pain in a muscle or muscles —**my·al′gic** *adj.*

myalgic encephalomyelitis CHRONIC FATIGUE SYNDROME

Myan·mar (myän′mär′, mē′ən mär′) country in Southeast Asia, on the Indochinese peninsula: modern state founded in the 18th cent.; under British control from 1885 to 1948: 261,970 sq mi (678,500 sq km); cap. Yangon

my·as·the·ni·a (mī′as thē′nē ə) *n.* ⟦ModL: see MYO- & ASTHENIA⟧ muscular weakness or fatigue —**my′as·then′ic** (-then′ik) *adj.*

myasthenia gra·vis (-grā′vis, -gräv′is) a disease of faulty nerve conduction characterized by myasthenia, esp. of the face and neck

myc- *combining form* MYCO-: used before a vowel

my·ce·li·um (mī sē′lē əm) *n., pl.* **-li·a** (-ə) ⟦ModL < Gr *mykēs*, a mushroom (see MYCO-) + *-lium*, as in EPITHELIUM⟧ the thallus, or vegetative part, of a fungus, made of a mass or network of threadlike tubes —**my·ce′li·al** *adj.*

My·ce·nae (mī sē′nē) ancient city in Argolis, in the NE Peloponnesus

My·ce·nae·an (mī′sə nē′ən) *adj.* **1** of Mycenae **2** designating or of a Bronze Age civilization existing in Greece, Crete, Asia Minor, etc. from *c.* 1700 to *c.* 1100 B.C. Also **My·ce·ne·an** (mī′sə nē′ən, mī′sē′nē ən)

-my·cete (mī′sēt′, mī sēt′) ⟦< fol.⟧ *combining form* a member of a (specified) class, subdivision, or division of fungi or slime molds [*basidiomycete*]

-my·ce·tes (mī sēt′ēz′) ⟦ModL < Gr *mykētes*, pl. of *mykēs*, a mushroom: see MYCO-⟧ *combining form Bot.* the scientific name of a (specified) class of fungi or slime molds [*Discomycetes*]

my·ce·to- (mī sēt′ō, -ə) ⟦< Gr *mykētes*: see prec.⟧ *combining form* fungus [*mycetoma*]: also, before a vowel, **mycet-**

my·ce·to·ma (mī′sə tō′mə) *n.* ⟦prec. + -OMA⟧ a chronic infection of the skin and subcutaneous tissues, esp. of the foot, characterized by a tumorous mass consisting mostly of fungi

my·ce·to·zo·an (mī sēt′ə zō′ən) *n.* ⟦MYCETO- + -ZO(A) + -AN⟧ MYXOMYCETE: term used when the organism is classified as a protozoan (class Eumycetozoa) —*adj.* MYXOMYCETOUS

-my·cin (mī′sin) ⟦< Gr *mykēs*, fungus (see fol.) + -IN[1]⟧ *combining form* a substance, esp. an antibiotic, derived from a fungus [*erythromycin*]

my·co- (mī′kō, -kə) ⟦< Gr *mykēs*, fungus < IE base **meuk-*, slippery > MUCK, L *mucus*⟧ *combining form* fungus [*mycology*]

my·co·bac·te·ri·um (mī′kō bak tir′ē əm) *n., pl.* **-ri·a** (-ə) ⟦ModL: see prec. & BACTERIA⟧ any of a genus (*Mycobacterium*) of rod-shaped, Gram-positive bacteria, as those causing tuberculosis and leprosy

my·col·o·gy (mī käl′ə jē) *n.* ⟦ModL *mycologia*: see MYCO- & -LOGY⟧ **1** the branch of botany dealing with fungi **2** all the fungi of a region —**my·co·log·ic** (mī′kə läj′ik) *adj.*, **my′co·log′i·cal** —**my·col′o·gist** *n.*

my·co·plas·ma (mī′kō plaz′mə) *n.* ⟦ModL: see MYCO- & PLASMA⟧ any of a class (Mollicutes) of bacteria that lack cell walls and may cause disease, esp. of the joints and lungs, in humans and domestic animals, or may be pathogenic for plants

my·cor·rhi·za (mī'kō rī'zə) ***n.***, *pl.* **-zae'** (-zē') or **-zas** ⟦< MYCO- + Gr *rhiza,* ROOT[1]⟧ an intimate symbiotic association of the mycelium of certain fungi with the root cells of some vascular plants, as certain orchids —**my'cor·rhi'zal** ***adj.***

my·co·sis (mī kō'sis) ***n.***, *pl.* **-ses'** (-sēz') ⟦ModL: see MYCO- & -OSIS⟧ **1** the growth of parasitic fungi in any part of the body **2** a disease caused by such fungi —**my·cot'ic** (-kät'ik) ***adj.***

my·co·toxin (mī'kō täks'in, -kə-) ***n.*** a toxin produced by a fungus

my·dri·a·sis (mi drī'ə sis, mī-) ***n.*** ⟦LL < Gr⟧ prolonged or excessive dilatation of the pupil of the eye, as the result of disease or the administration of a drug

myd·ri·at·ic (mid'rē at'ik) ***adj.*** of or causing mydriasis —***n.*** any drug causing mydriasis

my·el- *combining form* MYELO-: used before a vowel

my·e·len·ceph·a·lon (mī'ə len sef'ə län') ***n.***, *pl.* **-la** (-lə) ⟦ModL: see MYELO- & ENCEPHALON⟧ the part of the hindbrain consisting of the medulla oblongata

my·e·lin (mī'ə lin) ***n.*** ⟦Ger < Gr *myelos,* marrow: see MYELO- & -INE[3]⟧ the white, fatty substance forming a sheath about certain nerve fibers —**my'e·lin'ic** ***adj.***

my·e·li·na·tion (mī'ə li nā'shən) ***n.*** the change or maturation of certain nerve cells whereby a layer of myelin forms around the axons, allowing nerve impulses to travel faster: occasionally called **my·e·lin·i·za·tion** (mī'ə lin'ə zā'shən) —**my'e·li·nat'ed** ***adj.***

my·e·li·tis (mī'ə līt'is) ***n.*** ⟦ModL: see fol. & -ITIS⟧ **1** inflammation of the spinal cord **2** inflammation of the bone marrow

my·e·lo- (mī'ə lō) ⟦< Gr *myelos,* marrow, prob. < *myōn,* muscle cluster, muscle < *mys:* see MOUSE⟧ *combining form* **1** bone marrow *[myeloma]* **2** spinal cord *[myelogram]* **3** myelin

my·e·lo·blast (mī'ə lō blast') ***n.*** ⟦prec. + -BLAST⟧ a bone-marrow cell, not normally in the blood, that develops into certain white blood cells (neutrophils, eosinophils, and basophils)

my·e·lo·cyte (mī'ə lō sīt') ***n.*** a type of large cell in the bone marrow, that develops into a granulocyte: it is present in the blood in some forms of leukemia —**my'e·lo·cy'tic** (-sit'ik) ***adj.***

my·e·lo·gen·ic (mī'ə lō jen'ik) ***adj.*** ⟦MYELO- + -GENIC⟧ produced in or by elements of the bone marrow: also **my'e·log'e·nous** (-läj'ə nəs)

my·e·lo·gram (mī'ə lō gram') ***n.*** ⟦MYELO- + -GRAM⟧ an X-ray of the spinal cord, taken after the injection of a substance that will show contrast on a photograph —**my'e·lo·graph'ic** ***adj.*** —**my'e·log'ra·phy** (-läg'rə fē) ***n.***

my·e·loid (mī'ə loid') ***adj.*** ⟦MYEL(O)- + -OID⟧ **1** of, like, or derived from elements of bone marrow **2** of the spinal cord

my·e·lo·ma (mī'ə lō'mə) ***n.***, *pl.* **-mas** or **-ma·ta** (-mə tə) ⟦MYEL(O)- + -OMA⟧ a malignant tumor of the bone marrow, consisting generally of abnormal plasma cells —**my'e·lom'a·tous** (-läm'ə təs, -lō'mə-) ***adj.***

my·i·a·sis (mī ī'ə sis) ***n.*** ⟦< Gr *myia,* fly + -ASIS⟧ infestation of a body area or cavity by fly maggots

☆**My·lar** (mī'lär') *trademark for* a polyester made in thin sheets of great tensile strength, used in insulation, in storage bags, as a fabric, etc. —***n.*** [*occas.* **m-**] this substance

my·na or **my·nah** (mī'nə) ***n.*** ⟦Hindi *mainā*⟧ any of various tropical starlings of Southeast Asia; esp., the HILL MYNA

Myn·heer (mi ner', -nir'; mīn her', -hir') ***n.*** ⟦Du *mijn heer,* my lord: see MILORD⟧ Sir; Mr.: a Dutch title of respect

my·o- (mī'ō, -ə) ⟦< Gr *mys* (gen. *myos*), a muscle, MOUSE⟧ *combining form* muscle, muscle and *[myograph, myoneural]*

MYOB *abbrev.* mind your own business

my·o·blast (mī'ō blast') ***n.*** a small embryonic cell that develops into a muscle cell —**my'o·blast'ic** ***adj.***

myocardial infarction HEART ATTACK

my·o·car·di·o·graph (mī'ō kär'dē ō graf') ***n.*** ⟦MYO- + CARDIOGRAPH⟧ an instrument for recording the movements of the heart muscle

my·o·car·di·tis (-kär dīt'is) ***n.*** ⟦ModL: see -ITIS⟧ inflammation of the myocardium

my·o·car·di·um (-kär'dē əm) ***n.*** ⟦ModL: see MYO- & CARDIO-⟧ the muscular substance of the heart —**my'o·car'di·al** ***adj.***

my·oc·lo·nus (mī äk'lə nəs) ***n.*** ⟦MYO- + CLONUS⟧ involuntary twitching or spasm of a muscle or muscles —**my·o·clon·ic** (mī'ō klän'ik) ***adj.***

my·o·e·lec·tric (mī'ō ē lek'trik) ***adj.*** ⟦MYO- + ELECTRIC⟧ designating or of electricity generated in a muscle or muscles that is then picked up, amplified, and used to operate various attached prosthetic devices: often **my'o·e·lec'tri·cal** —**my'o·e·lec'tri·cal·ly** ***adv.***

my·o·fas·ci·al (mī'ə fā'shē əl, -shəl) ***adj.*** *Anat.* of or having to do with the fascia surrounding, supporting, or connecting muscles

my·o·fi·bril (mī'ə fī'brəl) ***n.*** any of a number of tiny, contractile fibrils composed of actomyosin and bundled together within a muscle cell

my·o·gen·ic (mī'ō jen'ik) ***adj.*** ⟦MYO- + -GENIC⟧ originating in or produced by a muscle

my·o·glo·bin (mī'ō glō'bin, mī'ō glō'-) ***n.*** ⟦MYO- + GLOBIN⟧ an iron-containing protein in muscle, similar to hemoglobin, that receives oxygen from the red blood cells and transports it to the mitochondria of muscle cells, where the oxygen is used in cellular respiration to produce energy

my·o·graph (mī'ō graf') ***n.*** ⟦MYO- + -GRAPH⟧ an instrument for recording muscular contractions —**my'o·gram'** ***n.*** —**my'o·graph'ic** ***adj.*** —**my·og·ra·phy** (mī äg'rə fē) ***n.***

my·ol·o·gy (mī äl'ə jē) ***n.*** ⟦ModL *myologia:* see MYO- & -LOGY⟧ the branch of anatomy dealing with the muscles —**my'o·log'ic** (-ō läj'ik) ***adj.***, **my'o·log'i·cal**

my·o·ma (mī ō'mə) ***n.***, *pl.* **-mas** or **-ma·ta** (-mə tə) ⟦ModL: see MYO- & -OMA⟧ any tumor consisting of muscular tissue —**my·om'a·tous** (-äm'ə təs, -ō'mə-) ***adj.***

my·o·neu·ral (mī'ō noor'əl, -nyoor'-) ***adj.*** ⟦MYO- + NEURAL⟧ pertaining to both muscle and nerve, esp. to the ending of a nerve of a muscle fiber

my·op·a·thy (mī äp'ə thē) ***n.*** ⟦MYO- + -PATHY⟧ any disease of a muscle —**my'o·path'ic** ***adj.***

my·ope (mī'ōp') ***n.*** ⟦Fr < LL *myops* < Gr *myōps,* shortsighted, blinking < *myein,* to close (< ? IE base **mu-,* with closed lips > MOPE, MUTE) + *ōps,* EYE⟧ a person having myopia; nearsighted person

my·o·pi·a (mī ō'pē ə) ***n.*** ⟦ModL < Gr *myōpia* < *myōps:* see prec.⟧ **1** an abnormal eye condition in which light rays from distant objects are focused in front of the retina instead of on it, so that the objects are not seen distinctly; nearsightedness **2** lack of understanding or foresight —**my·op'ic** (-äp'ik) ***adj.*** —**my·op'i·cal·ly** ***adv.***

my·o·sin (mī'ō sin) ⟦< Gr *mys* (gen. *myos*), a muscle, MOUSE + -IN[1]⟧ ***n.*** a protein in muscles: see ACTOMYOSIN

my·o·si·tis (mī'ə sīt'is) ***n.*** ⟦< Gr *myos,* gen. of *mys,* muscle, MOUSE (see MUSCLE) + -ITIS⟧ muscular inflammation, usually resulting in pain, soreness, etc.

my·o·so·tis (mī'ō sōt'is) ***n.*** ⟦ModL < L, mouse ear < Gr *myosōtis* < *mys* (gen. *myos*), MOUSE + *ōtos,* gen. of *ous,* EAR[1]⟧ FORGET-ME-NOT (sense 1)

my·o·tome (mī'ō tōm') ***n.*** ⟦MYO- + -TOME⟧ **1** the body-wall musculature in a single segment of primitive chordates and segmented invertebrates **2** one of the paired mesodermal masses in a vertebrate embryo from which the musculature develops

my·o·to·ni·a (mī'ō tō'nē ə) ***n.*** ⟦MYO- + TON(IC) + -IA⟧ prolonged muscular spasm, often a manifestation of certain diseases of muscles —**my'o·ton'ic** (-tän'ik) ***adj.***

My·ra (mī'rə) ***n.*** ⟦< ? Ir *Moira, Moyra*⟧ a feminine name

Myr·dal (mur'däl, mir'-), **(Karl) Gun·nar** (gun'är) 1898-1987; Swed. economist & sociologist

myr·i·a- (mir'ē ə) ⟦< Gr *myrias:* see fol.⟧ *combining form* **1** many, numerous *[myriapod]* **2** ten thousand; the factor 10^4 *[myrialiter]*

myr·i·ad (mir'ē əd) ***n.*** ⟦< Gr *myrias* (gen. *myriados*), the number ten thousand < *myrios,* countless⟧ **1** [Archaic] ten thousand **2** any indefinitely large number **3** a great number of persons or things —***adj.*** **1** of an indefinitely large number; countless; innumerable **2** of a highly varied nature

myr·i·a·pod (mir'ē ə päd') ***adj.*** ⟦< ModL *Myriapoda:* see MYRIA- & -POD⟧ having many legs: said esp. of millipedes and centipedes —***n.*** a millipede or centipede

my·ris·tic acid (mi ris'tik) ⟦< ModL *Myristica,* name of a genus of trees in the nutmeg family⟧ a white, oily, crystalline fatty acid, $CH_3(CH_2)_{12}COOH$, used in making soaps, cosmetics, and food additives

myr·me·co- (mur'mi kō, -kə) ⟦Gr *myrmēko-* < *myrmēx,* ant < IE base **morwi-* > (PIS)MIRE, OIr *moirb*⟧ *combining form* ant *[myrmecology]*

myr·me·col·o·gy (mur'mi käl'ə jē) ***n.*** ⟦prec. + -LOGY⟧ the branch of entomology dealing with ants —**myr'me·co·log'i·cal** (-kə läj'i kəl) ***adj.*** —**myr'me·col'o·gist** ***n.***

myr·me·coph·a·gous (-käf'ə gəs) ***adj.*** ⟦MYRMECO- + -PHAGOUS⟧ feeding on ants

Myr·mi·don (mur'mə dän', -dən) ***n.***, *pl.* **-dons'** or **Myr·mid·o·nes** (mər mid'ə nēz') ⟦ME *mirmidones* < L *Myrmidones,* pl. < Gr, the Myrmidons⟧ **1** *Gr. Legend* any of the tribe of Thessalian warriors who fight under Achilles, their king, in the Trojan War **2** [**m-**] an unquestioning follower or subordinate

my·rob·a·lan (mī räb'ə lən, mi-) ***n.*** ⟦Fr < L *myrobalanum* < Gr *myrobalanon* < *myron,* plant juice (for base see SMEAR) + *balanos,* a nut, acorn: see GLAND[1]⟧ **1** any of various trees (genus *Terminalia*) of a tropical family (Combretaceare, order Myrtales) of dicotyledonous plants **2** any of their dried prunelike fruits, containing tannin and used for dyeing and tanning **3** CHERRY PLUM

My·ron[1] (mī'rən) ***n.*** ⟦prob. < Gr *Myrōn*⟧ a masculine name

My·ron[2] (mī'rən) Gr. sculptor of the 5th cent. B.C.

myrrh (mur) ***n.*** ⟦ME *mirre* < OE *myrre* & OFr *mirre,* both < L *myrrha* < Gr < Ar *murr,* myrrh, bitter⟧ **1** a fragrant, bitter-tasting gum resin exuded from any of several plants of Arabia and E Africa, used in making incense, perfume, etc. **2** any of these plants; esp., any of several small trees (genus *Commiphora*) of the bursera family

myr·tle (murt''l) ***n.*** ⟦ME *mirtille* < OFr *myrtille* < ML *myrtillus,* dim. < L *myrtus* < Gr *myrtos,* myrtle, prob. < Sem; ? akin to Ar *murr,* myrrh⟧ **1** any of a genus (*Myrtus*) of plants of the myrtle family, with evergreen leaves, white or pinkish flowers, and dark, fragrant berries **2** any of various other plants, as the periwinkle and the California laurel —***adj.*** designating a family (Myrtaceae, order Myrtales) of dicotyledonous, evergreen trees and shrubs, including eucalyptus, guava, clove, and blue gum

Myr·tle (murt''l) ***n.*** ⟦< prec.⟧ a feminine name

my·self (mī self', mə-) ***pron.*** ⟦ME *meself* < OE *me sylf:* see ME & SELF⟧ a form of I[2], used: *a)* as an intensifier [I saw it *myself;* I *myself* saw it] *b)* as a reflexive [I hurt *myself*] *c)* with the meaning "my real, true, or normal self" [I am not *myself* today] (in this construction *my* functions as an adjective and *self* as a noun, and they may be separated) [*my* own sweet *self*] Now sometimes used as a subject or a nonreflexive object in certain contexts [he spoke to John and *myself*]

My·si·a (mish′ē ə) ancient region in NW Asia Minor, on the Propontis —**My′si·an** *adj., n.*

my·sid (mī′sid) *n.* ⟦< ModL *Mysidacea*⟧ any of an order (Mysidacea) of small, shrimplike, malacostracan crustaceans with a carapace over most of the thorax

My·sore (mī sôr′) city in S India

mys·ta·gogue (mis′tə gäg′, -gôg′) *n.* ⟦Fr < L *mystagogus* < Gr *mystagōgos* < *mystēs* (see MYSTERY¹) + *agōgos,* leader < *agein:* see ACT¹⟧ a person who interprets religious mysteries or initiates others into them —**mys′ta·gog′ic** (-gäj′ik) *adj.,* **mys′ta·gog′ic·al** —**mys′ta·go′gy** (-gō′jē) *n.*

mys·te·ri·o·so (mis tir′ē ō′sō) *adj.* **1** MISTERIOSO **2** having a mysterious nature or quality; inexplicable, enigmatic, etc. —*adv.* MISTERIOSO —*n.* someone or something that is mysterioso

mys·te·ri·ous (mis tir′ē əs) *adj.* ⟦< L *mysterium* (see fol.) + -OUS⟧ of, containing, implying, or characterized by mystery —**mys·te′ri·ous·ly** *adv.* —**mys·te′ri·ous·ness** *n.*

SYN.—**mysterious** is applied to that which excites curiosity, wonder, etc. but is impossible or difficult to explain or solve [*a mysterious* murder]; that which is **inscrutable** is completely mysterious and altogether incapable of being searched out, interpreted, or understood [the *inscrutable* ways of God]; **mystical** applies to that which is occult or esoteric in connection with religious rites or spiritual experience

mys·ter·y¹ (mis′tə rē, mis′trē) *n., pl.* **-ter·ies** ⟦ME *mysterye* < L *mysterium* (in N.T., supernatural thing) < Gr *mystērion,* a secret rite (in N.T., divine secret) < *mystēs,* one initiated into the mysteries < *myein,* to initiate into the mysteries, orig., to close: see MYOPE⟧ **1** something unexplained, unknown, or kept secret [the *mystery* of life] **2** *a)* any thing or event that remains so secret or obscure as to excite curiosity [the new employee's past is a bit of a *mystery*] *b)* a novel, story, or play involving such an event, esp. one involving a crime and the gradual discovery of who committed it **3** the quality of being inexplicable; obscurity or secrecy [an air of *mystery* surrounding the affair] **4** [*pl.*] *a)* secret rites or doctrines known only to a small, esoteric group; specif., in ancient Greece, religious ceremonies or doctrines revealed only to the initiated *b)* any of the ancient cults characterized by such ceremonies [the Eleusinian *mysteries*] **5** ⟦? infl. by fol.⟧ MYSTERY PLAY **6** *R.C.Ch. a)* a sacrament; esp. the Eucharist *b)* any of fifteen (or, now often, twenty) events in the lives of Jesus and Mary serving as a subject for meditation during the praying of the rosary **7** *Theol.* any religious truth made known only by divine revelation and accepted through faith

SYN.—**mystery** is applied to something beyond human knowledge or understanding, or it merely refers to any unexplained or seemingly inexplicable matter; **enigma** specifically applies to that whose meaning is hidden by cryptic or ambiguous allusions, and generally, to anything very difficult to explain; a **riddle** is an enigma (usually in the form of a question in guessing games) that involves a paradox; a **puzzle** is a situation, problem, or, often, a contrivance, that requires some ingenuity to solve or explain; **conundrum** is specifically applied to a riddle whose answer is a pun, and generally applied to any puzzling question or problem

mys·ter·y² (mis′tə rē) *n., pl.* **-ter·ies** ⟦altered < ME *misterie,* a trade, craft < ML *misterium,* altered < L *ministerium,* office, occupation (see MINISTER), by confusion with *mysterium* (see prec.)⟧ [Archaic] **1** a craft or trade **2** GUILD (sense 1)

mystery play any of a class of medieval dramatic representations of Biblical events, esp. of the life and death of Jesus: they originated in the church liturgy but were later presented by craft guilds in marketplaces, etc.: cf. MIRACLE PLAY, MORALITY PLAY

mys·tic (mis′tik) *adj.* ⟦ME *mistik* < L *mysticus* < Gr *mystikos,* belonging to secret rites < *mystēs,* one initiated: see MYSTERY¹⟧ **1** of mysteries, or esoteric rites or doctrines **2** MYSTICAL (senses 1, 2, & 4) **3** of obscure or occult character or meaning [*mystic* powers] **4** beyond human comprehension; mysterious or enigmatic **5** filling one with wonder or awe **6** having magic power —*n.* **1** a person initiated into esoteric mysteries **2** a believer in mysticism; specif., one who professes to undergo mystical experiences and so to comprehend intuitively truths beyond human understanding

mys·ti·cal (mis′ti kəl) *adj.* **1** spiritually significant or symbolic; allegorical **2** of mystics or mysticism; esp., relating to or based on intuition, contemplation, or meditation of a spiritual nature **3** MYSTIC (*adj.* 3) **4** mysterious; enigmatic —*SYN.* MYSTERIOUS —**mys′ti·cal·ly** *adv.* —**mys′ti·cal·ness** *n.,* **mys′ti·cal′i·ty** (-kal′ə tē)

mys·ti·cism (mis′tə siz′əm) *n.* **1** the doctrines or beliefs of mystics; specif., the doctrine that it is possible to achieve communion with God through contemplation **2** any doctrine that asserts the possibility of attaining an intuitive knowledge of spiritual truths through meditation **3** vague, obscure, or confused thinking or belief

mys·ti·fy (mis′tə fī′) *vt.* **-fied′**, **-fy′ing** ⟦Fr *mystifier* < *mystère,* mystery (< L *mysterium*) + *-fier,* -FY⟧ **1** *a)* to puzzle or perplex *b)* to bewilder deliberately; play on the credulity of; hoax **2** to involve in mystery or obscurity; make obscure or hard to understand —**mys′ti·fi·ca′tion** *n.* —**mys′ti·fi′er** *n.*

mys·tique (mis tēk′) *n.* ⟦Fr, mystic⟧ an air of glamour, charm, or mystery

myth¹ (mith) *n.* ⟦LL *mythos* < Gr, a word, speech, story, legend⟧ **1** *a)* a traditional story of unknown authorship, ostensibly with a historical basis, but serving usually to explain some phenomenon of nature, the origin of man, or the customs, institutions, religious rites, etc. of a people: myths usually involve the exploits of gods and heroes *b)* such stories collectively; mythology: cf. LEGEND **2** any popular concept or belief regarded as baseless, unscientific, etc. **3** any imaginary person or thing spoken of as though existing

myth² *abbrev.* mythology

myth·ic (mith′ik) *adj.* **1** of, or having the nature of, a myth or myths **2** MYTHICAL (senses 1 & 2)

myth·i·cal (-i kəl) *adj.* **1** existing only in a myth or myths [*a mythical* creature] **2** imaginary, fictitious, or not based on facts or scientific study **3** MYTHIC (sense 1) —*SYN.* FICTITIOUS —**myth′i·cal·ly** *adv.*

myth·i·cize (-ə sīz′) *vt.* **-cized′**, **-ciz′ing** to make into, or explain as, a myth —**myth′i·ciz′er** *n.*

myth·mak·er (mith′māk′ər) *n.* a person who creates myths

myth·mak·ing (mith′māk′iŋ) *n.* the creation of myths

myth·o- (mith′ə, -ō) ⟦< Gr *mythos,* MYTH¹⟧ *combining form* myth [*mythomania*]

my·thog·ra·pher (mi thäg′rə fər) *n.* a person who collects or writes about myths

my·thog·ra·phy (-fē) *n.* **1** a collection of myths **2** the collecting or analysis of myths See MYTH¹ (sense 1)

myth·o·log·i·cal (mith′ə läj′i kəl) *adj.* **1** of mythology **2** mythical; imaginary Also **myth′o·log′ic** —**myth′o·log′i·cal·ly** *adv.*

my·thol·o·gist (mi thäl′ə jist) *n.* **1** an expert in mythology **2** a writer or compiler of myths

my·thol·o·gize (-jīz′) *vi.* **-gized′**, **-giz′ing** ⟦Fr *mythologiser*⟧ **1** to relate or construct a myth or myths **2** to compile, classify, or write about myths —*vt.* MYTHICIZE —**my·thol′o·giz′er** *n.*

my·thol·o·gy (-jē) *n., pl.* **-gies** ⟦ME *methologie* < LL *mythologia* < Gr, a telling of tales or legends < *mythos,* MYTH¹ + *-logia,* -LOGY⟧ **1** the science or study of myths **2** a book of or about myths **3** myths collectively; esp., all the myths of a specific people or about a specific being

myth·o·ma·ni·a (mith′ə mā′nē ə, -mān′yə) *n.* ⟦ModL: see MYTHO- & -MANIA⟧ *Psychiatry* an abnormal tendency to lie or exaggerate —**myth′o·ma′ni·ac′** *adj., n.*

myth·o·poe·ia (mith′ə pē′ə) *n.* ⟦< Gr *mythopoios* < *mythos,* MYTH¹ + *poiein,* to make: see POEM⟧ the making of myths —**myth′o·poe′ic** (-pē′ik) *adj.,* **myth′o·po·et′ic** (-pō et′ik)

myth·os (mith′äs′, -ōs′; mī′thäs′) *n.* ⟦see MYTH¹⟧ **1** MYTH¹ (sense 1) **2** the complex of attitudes, beliefs, etc. most characteristic of a particular group or society

Myt·i·le·ne (mit′'l ē′nē) **1** chief city of Lesbos, on the SE coast **2** LESBOS

myx·e·de·ma (mik′sə dē′mə) *n.* ⟦ModL: see fol. & EDEMA⟧ a disease caused by failure of the thyroid gland and characterized by a drying and thickening of the skin and a slowing down of physical and mental activity —**myx′e·de′ma·tous** (-təs) *adj.*

myx·o- (mik′sō, -sə) ⟦< Gr *myxa,* MUCUS⟧ *combining form* slime or mucus [*myxomycete*]: also, before a vowel, **myx-**

myx·o·ma (mik sō′mə) *n., pl.* **-mas** or **-ma·ta** (-mə tə) ⟦prec. + -OMA⟧ a tumor of connective tissue cells containing a mucuslike material —**myx·o′ma·tous** (-təs) *adj.*

myx·o·ma·to·sis (mik′sə mə tō′sis) *n.* ⟦see prec. & -OSIS⟧ **1** the presence of multiple myxomas **2** an infectious viral disease in rabbits, transmitted by mosquitoes and characterized by tumorous growths resembling myxomas

myx·o·my·cete (mik′sō mī′sēt, -mī sēt′) *n.* ⟦MYXO- + -MYCETE⟧ any of various primitive organisms, usually classified as a thallophyte (division Myxomycota) but also as a mycetozoan, that are found on decaying vegetation, having a vegetative stage in which they move as a protozoan and a dry reproductive stage in which they form spores like a MOLD² (*n.* 2); slime mold —**myx′o·my·ce′tous** (-sē′təs) *adj.*

myx·o·vi·rus (mik′sə vī′rəs) *n.* ⟦MYXO- + VIRUS: from the affinity of such viruses for some mucins⟧ any paramyxovirus or orthomyxovirus: a name for viruses of a former family that is now subdivided into two separate families

N

n[1] or **N** (en) ***n.**, pl.* **n's, N's** **1** the fourteenth letter of the English alphabet: from the Greek *nu*, a borrowing from the Phoenician **2** any of the speech sounds that this letter represents, as, in English, the (n) of *night* **3** a type or impression for *n* or *N* **4** the fourteenth in a sequence or group **5** *Printing* an en (half an em) **6** an object shaped like N —***adj.*** **1** of *n* or *N* **2** fourteenth in a sequence or group **3** shaped like N

n[2] *abbrev.* **1** ⟦L *natus*⟧ born **2** *Chem., Geol., Math.* indefinite number (of) **3** nail **4** name **5** nano- **6** national **7** nephew **8** net **9** neuter **10** *Physics* neutron **11** new **12** nominative **13** noon **14** north **15** northern **16** note (i.e., endnote or footnote) **17** noun **18** number

N[1] *abbrev.* **1** *Chess* knight **2** National **3** Navy **4** neutral (on automotive automatic-shift indicators) **5** newton **6** no **7** Norse **8** North **9** north **10** northern **11** November

N[2] **1** *symbol* Avogadro constant: often written NA **2** *Chem. symbol for* nitrogen

n- *prefix Elec.* negative

'n' or **'n** ('n, ən) ***conj.*** and: an informal spelling [fish *'n'* chips, fun *'n'* games]

Na[1] *abbrev. Bible* Nahum

Na[2] ⟦L *natrium*⟧ *Chem. symbol for* sodium

NA *abbrev.* **1** North America **2** not applicable: also **N/A**

n/a *abbrev. Banking* no account

☆**NAACP** *abbrev.* National Association for the Advancement of Colored People

naan (nän, nan) ***n.*** *alt. sp. of* NAN

nab (nab) ***vt.* nabbed, nab′bing** ⟦< thieves' slang (16th-17th c.) prob. var. of dial. *nap*, to snatch < Scand, as in Dan *nappe*, Swed *nappa*, to snatch⟧ [Informal] **1** to seize suddenly; snatch or steal **2** to arrest or catch (a felon or wrongdoer) —**SYN.** CATCH

NAB *abbrev.* **1** naval air base **2** New American Bible

Nab·a·te·a or **Nab·a·tae·a** (nab′ə tē′ə) ancient kingdom of Arabia, in what is now W Jordan —**Nab′a·te′an** ***adj., n.***, **Nab′a·tae′an**

☆**nabe** (nāb) ***n.*** ⟦altered < NEIGHB(ORHOOD)⟧ [Slang] a neighborhood movie theater

Na·be·rezh·niy·e Chel·ny (nä′bi rizh nē yi chĕl nē′) city in E European Russia, on the Kama River

Nab·lus (nab′ləs, näb′-) city in W Jordan: capital (as *Shechem*) of ancient Samaria

na·bob (nā′bäb′) ***n.*** ⟦Urdu *nawwāb* < Ar *nuwwāb*, pl. of *na'ib*, deputy, viceroy⟧ **1** a native provincial deputy or governor of the old Mogul Empire in India **2** a very rich or important man —**na′bob′ish** ***adj.***

Na·bo·kov (nä bô′kôf, nä′bə kôf′), **Vladimir** 1899-1977; U.S. writer, born in Russia

Na·both (nā′bäth) ***n.*** ⟦Heb *nābhōth*⟧ *Bible* a vineyard owner, killed at Jezebel's behest so that Ahab could seize the vineyard: 1 Kings 21

na·celle (nə sel′) ***n.*** ⟦Fr < LL *navicella*, dim. of L *navis*, a ship: see NAVY⟧ a streamlined enclosure on an aircraft, esp. for an engine

☆**nach·as** or **nach·es** (näkh′əs) ***n.*** ⟦Yiddish *nakhes* < Heb *nachat*, a calmness, repose < *nach*, to rest⟧ [Slang] pleasurable pride, esp. in another's achievements

Nach·lass (näkh′läs′) ***n.*** ⟦Ger⟧ REMAINS (sense 4)

na·chos (nä′chōz′) ***pl.n.***, *sing.* **-cho′** ⟦Sp⟧ tortilla chips topped variously with melted cheese, ground beef, salsa, peppers, beans, etc.

na·cre (nā′kər) ***n.*** ⟦Fr < It *nacchera* < Ar *naqqārah*, small kettledrum⟧ MOTHER-OF-PEARL

na·cre·ous (nā′krē əs) ***adj.*** **1** of or like nacre **2** yielding nacre **3** iridescent; lustrous

na·da (nä′thä; *E* näd′ə) ***n.*** ⟦Sp⟧ nothing

☆**Na-De·ne** (nä′də nā′, -dā-) ***n.*** ⟦< Haida *na*, to dwell, house & Tlingit *na*, people + Athabaskan *dene*, person, people (occurring in various dialect forms): coined (1914) by Edward SAPIR⟧ a proposed grouping of North American Indian language families, including the Athabaskan languages, Tlingit, and Haida

Na·dine (nā dēn′) ***n.*** ⟦Fr < ? Russ *nadyezhda*, hope⟧ a feminine name

na·dir (nā′dər, -dir′) ***n.*** ⟦ME < MFr < ML < Ar *naẓīr*, in *naẓīr as-samt*, lit., opposite to the zenith < *naẓīr*, opposite + *as-samt*, zenith⟧ **1** that point of the celestial sphere directly opposite to the zenith and directly below the observer **2** the lowest point

nae (nā) [Scot.] ***adv.*** no; not —***adj.*** no

naff (naf) ***adj.*** ⟦< ?⟧ [Brit. Informal] **1** inferior in quality or condition **2** tasteless or unfashionable

NAFTA (naf′tə) ***n.*** ⟦*N(orth) A(merican) F(ree) T(rade) A(greement)*⟧ a 1994 FREE TRADE agreement made by the U.S., Canada, and Mexico

Na·fud (nə fo͞od′) desert in the N Arabian Peninsula: *c.* 180 mi (290 km) long; *c.* 140 mi (225 km) wide

nag[1] (nag) ***vt.* nagged, nag′ging** ⟦< Scand (as in Swed *nagga*, obs. Dan *nagge*, to nibble, gnaw, nag) < ON *gnaga*: for IE base see GNAW: for sense development see FRET[1]⟧ **1** to annoy by continual scolding, faultfinding, complaining, urging, etc. **2** to keep troubling, worrying, etc. [*nagged* by a thought] —***vi.*** **1** to urge, scold, find fault, etc. constantly **2** to cause continual discomfort, pain, etc. [a *nagging* toothache] —***n.*** a person, esp. a woman, who nags: also **nag′ger** —**nag′ging·ly** ***adv.*** —**nag′gy** ***adj.*** **-gi·er**, **-gi·est**

nag[2] (nag) ***n.*** ⟦ME *nagge*, akin to obs. Du *negghe* < ?⟧ **1** [Archaic] a small saddle horse; pony **2** [Informal] a horse that is worn-out, old, etc. **3** [Slang] a racehorse, esp. an inferior one

na·ga·na (nə gä′nə) ***n.*** ⟦< Zulu *u(lu)-nakane*⟧ an infectious disease affecting horses and cattle in tropical Africa, caused by a trypanosome (*Trypanosoma brucei*) transmitted by the bite of infected tsetse flies

Na·ga·no (nä gä′nō, nä′gə no) city in WC Honshu, Japan

Na·ga·sa·ki (nä′gə sä′kē) seaport on the W coast of Kyushu, Japan: partly destroyed (Aug. 9, 1945) by a U.S. atomic bomb, the second ever used in warfare: cf. HIROSHIMA

Na·gor·no-Ka·ra·bakh (nä gôr′nō kär′ä bäk′) autonomous region in Azerbaijan, mostly populated by Armenians: 1,700 sq mi (4,403 sq km); cap. Xankändi

Na·go·ya (nä′gô yä′) seaport in S Honshu, Japan, on an inlet of the Pacific

Nag·pur (näg′po͝or′) city in E Maharashtra, W India

nah (nä) ***adv., interj.*** [Informal] no: a negative reply

Nah *abbrev. Bible* Nahum

Na·ha (nä′hä′) seaport on Okinawa, Japan

Na·hua·tl (nä′wät′'l) ***n.*** ⟦Nahuatl *na:waλ*: a self-designation⟧ **1** *pl.* **Na′hua′tls** or **Na′hua′tl** a member of a group of Amerindian peoples of Mexico and Central America, including the Aztecs **2** a Uto-Aztecan language widely spoken in central and W Mexico —**Na′hua′tlan** ***adj., n.***

Na·hum (nā′əm, -həm) ***n.*** ⟦Heb *naḥūm*, lit., comfort⟧ *Bible* **1** a Hebrew prophet of the 7th cent. B.C. **2** the book of his prophecies: abbrev. *Na, Nah,* or *Nh*

NAIA *abbrev.* National Association of Intercollegiate Athletics

nai·ad (nā′ad′, nī′-; -əd) ***n.**, pl.* **-ads′** or **-a·des′** (-ə dēz′) ⟦Fr *naïade* < L *Naias* (gen. *Naiadis*) < Gr *Naias* (pl. *Naïades*) < *naein*, to flow < IE base **(s)na-*, to flow > L *natare*, to swim⟧ **1** [*also* **N-**] *Class. Myth.* any of the nymphs living in and giving life to springs, fountains, rivers, and lakes **2** a girl or woman swimmer **3** *Bot.* any of a family (Najadaceae, order Najadales) of monocotyledonous, submerged freshwater plants, consisting of a single genus (*Najas*) and having linear opposite leaves **4** *Zool.* the aquatic nymph of certain insects, as the dragonfly and mayfly

na·if or **na·ïf** (nä ēf′) ***adj.*** ⟦Fr⟧ *var. of* NAIVE —***n.*** a naive person

nail (nāl) ***n.*** ⟦ME *naile* < OE *nægl*, akin to Ger *nagel* < IE base **onogh*, nail > Sans *ánghri-*, foot, Gr *onyx*, nail, L *unguis*, fingernail⟧ **1** *a)* a thin, horny covering that grows out over the upper tip of a finger or toe *b)* a similar growth on a toe of a bird, reptile, etc.; claw **2** a tapered piece of metal, commonly pointed and having a flattened head, driven with a hammer, and used to hold pieces or parts together, to hang things on, etc. **3** an old cloth measure, equal to 2¼ inches —***vt.*** ⟦ME *nailen* < OE *mæglan*⟧ **1** to attach or fasten together or onto something else with or as with nails **2** to secure, hold, or fasten shut with nails **3** to fix (the eyes, attention, etc.) steadily on an object **4** to discover or expose (a lie, etc.) **5** [Informal] to catch, capture, seize, or intercept **6** [Informal] to hit squarely ☆**7** [Slang] to have sexual intercourse with; esp., to penetrate sexually: mildly vulgar **8** [Slang] to execute or accomplish flawlessly [the gymnast *nailed* her routine] —**hard as nails** callous, unfeeling, remorseless, etc. —**hit the nail on the head** to do or say whatever is exactly right or to the point —**nail down** **1** to fasten tightly with nails **2** [Informal] to settle definitely; clinch —**nail up** **1** to fasten with nails to a wall or at some height **2** to fasten (a door, window, etc.) tightly with nails

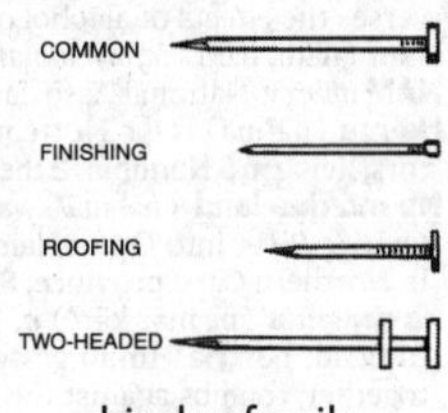

kinds of nails

nail-bit·er (nāl′bīt′ər) ***n.*** ⟦in allusion to the habit of chewing one's fingernails when anxious or nervous⟧ [Informal] a situation or activity, as a suspenseful drama or highly competitive game in sports, with an outcome so uncertain that it creates much tension or anxiety

nail-bit·ing (nāl′bīt′iŋ) *adj.* [Informal] causing tension or anxiety
nail·brush (-brush′) *n.* a small, stiff brush for cleaning the fingernails
☆**nail file** a small, flat file for smoothing and shaping the fingernails and toenails
nail·head (-hed′) *n.* **1** the flattened or, sometimes, rounded head of a nail **2** a decoration resembling the rounded head of a nail
nail polish a kind of lacquer, usually colored, applied to the fingernails or toenails as a cosmetic
nail set a tool used in driving the head of a nail below, or level with, a wood surface
nain·sook (nān′sook′) *n.* ⟦Hindi *nainsukh* < *nain*, the eye + *sukh*, pleasure⟧ a thin, lightweight cotton fabric
nai·ra (nī′rə) *n., pl.* **nai′ra** ⟦altered < NIGERIA⟧ the basic monetary unit of Nigeria: see the table of monetary units in the Reference Supplement
Nairn (nern) former county & former district of NE Scotland: also, for the county, **Nairn′shire** (-shir, -shər)
Nai·ro·bi (nī rō′bē) capital of Kenya, in the SW part
na·ive or **na·ïve** (nä ēv′) *adj.* ⟦Fr, fem. of *naïf* < L *nativus*, natural, NATIVE⟧ **1** unaffectedly or foolishly simple; childlike; artless **2** not suspicious; credulous —**na·ive′ly** *adv.*, **na·ïve′ly**

SYN.—**naive** implies a genuine, innocent simplicity or lack of artificiality but sometimes connotes an almost foolish lack of worldly wisdom [his *naive* belief in the kindness of others]; **ingenuous** implies a frankness or straightforwardness that suggests the simplicity of a child [her *ingenuous* smile at my discomfiture]; **artless** suggests a lack of artificiality or guile that derives from indifference to the effect one has upon others [her *artless* beauty]; **unsophisticated**, like **naive**, implies a lack of worldly wisdom resulting from a life limited in experience [an *unsophisticated* freshman] —*ANT.* **sophisticated**, **artful**

na·ive·té or **na·ïve·té** (nä ēv tā′, -ēv′tā′; nä ē′və tē′, -ev′ə-) *n.* ⟦Fr⟧ **1** the quality or state of being naive; simplicity; artlessness **2** a naive action or remark Also **na·ive′ness** or **na·ïve′ness**, **na·iv·e·ty** or **na·ïv·e·ty** (nä ē′və tē′, -ev′ə-)
na·ked (nā′kid) *adj.* ⟦ME < OE *nacod*, akin to Ger *nackt* < IE base **nogw-*, naked > Sans *nagná-*, L *nudus*⟧ **1** *a)* completely unclothed; bare; nude *b)* uncovered; exposed (said of parts of the body) **2** lacking clothing, means of support, etc.; destitute **3** without protection or defense **4** without conventional or usual covering; specif., *a)* out of its sheath [a *naked* sword] *b)* without grass, vegetation, etc. *c)* without furnishing, decoration, etc. [a *naked* wall] **5** without additions, ornaments, disguises, or embellishments; plain; stark [the *naked* truth] **6** without the aid of a microscope, telescope, etc. [the *naked* eye] **7** *Bot.* without leaves, corolla, ovary, perianth, etc. **8** *Law* lacking a necessary condition; invalid [a *naked* contract] **9** *Zool.* without hair, scales, feathers, shell, etc. —*SYN.* BARE[1] —**na′ked·ly** *adv.* —**na′ked·ness** *n.*
nak·fa (näk′fä) *n.* ⟦Tigrinya, after *Nakfa*, town where a number of battles were fought in the war of independence against Ethiopia⟧ the basic monetary unit of Eritrea: see the table of monetary units in the Reference Supplement
Na·khi·che·van (näkh′yi chē vän′) *Russ. name for* NAXÇIVAN
☆**nal·or·phine** (nal ôr′fēn′) *n.* ⟦< *N-al(lylnorm)orphine*⟧ a white, crystalline derivative of morphine, $C_{19}H_{21}NO_3$, used, usually in the form of its hydrochloride, to counteract the effects of narcotic overdoses and to aid in diagnosing narcotic addiction
☆**nal·ox·one** (nal′ək sōn′) *n.* ⟦< *N-al(lylnor)ox(ymorph)one*⟧ a white, crystalline, nonaddictive, synthetic drug, $C_{19}H_{21}NO_4{\cdot}HCl$, used to counteract the effects of narcotic overdoses: in full **naloxone hydrochloride**
nal·trex·one (nal trek′sōn) *n.* ⟦< *N-al(lyl)* + *-trex-* (< ?) + -ONE⟧ a white, crystalline, nonaddictive synthetic drug, $C_{20}H_{23}NO_4{\cdot}HCl$, that blocks or reverses the effects of alcohol or a narcotic: in full **naltrexone hydrochloride**
Nam (näm, nam) *informal name for* VIETNAM: also written **'Nam**
NAM *abbrev.* National Association of Manufacturers
Na·ma (nä′mä) *n.* ⟦< Hottentot name⟧ **1** the largest group of the Hottentots, living in S Namibia **2** the Khoisan language of this group of Hottentots
Na·ma·qua·land (nə mä′kwə land′) region in SW Africa divided by the Orange River into **Great Namaqualand** in Namibia & **Little Namaqualand** in Northern Cape province, South Africa: also **Na·ma·land** (nä′mə land′)
na·mas·kar (nä məs kär′) *n.* ⟦Hindi < Sans *námas-*, a bow < IE base **nem-*, to bend, bow⟧ a Hindu gesture of salutation made by placing the palms together, thumbs against the chest, and bowing the head slightly —*interj.* [*usually in italics*] used when making this gesture
na·ma·ste (nä′mə stā′) *interj.* ⟦Hindi: see prec.⟧ used when making the namaskar gesture —*n.* [*often not in italics*] NAMASKAR
nam·by-pam·by (nam′bē pam′bē) *adj.* ⟦orig. satirical nickname of *Ambrose Philips*, 18th-c. Eng poet: in ridicule of his sentimental pastorals⟧ **1** weakly sentimental; insipid **2** without vigor **3** wishy-washy —*n.* **1** namby-pamby talk **2** *pl.* **-bies** a namby-pamby person
Nam Co (näm′ tsō′) salt lake in E Tibet: *c.* 700 sq mi (1,813 sq km); 15,200 ft (4,633 m) above sea level
name (nām) *n.* ⟦ME < OE *nama*, akin to Ger *name* < IE base **(o)nomn̥* > L *nomen*, Gr *onoma*, *onyma*⟧ **1** a word or phrase by which an individual person, place, or thing, or a class of things, is known, called, or spoken of **2** a word or words expressing some quality considered characteristic or descriptive of a person or thing, often showing approval or disapproval; epithet **3** the sacred designation of a deity [His ineffable *name*] **4** *a)* fame, reputation, or character [a good *name*] *b)* good reputation **5** a family or clan [the last of his *name*] **6** a distinguished or famous person [the greatest *name* in science] —*adj.* ☆**1** having a good reputation; well-known [a *name* brand] **2** displaying someone's name [*name* tags worn at a convention] —*vt.* **named**, **nam′ing 1** to give a name or title to; entitle; style **2** to designate, mention, or refer to by name **3** to identify by the right name [*name* all the oceans] **4** to nominate or appoint to a post, situation, or office **5** to set or fix; specify (a date, price, etc.) **6** to speak about; mention —**call someone names** to use insulting or abusive names in attacking someone —**in name only** having the title or appearance but not actually; nominally; ostensibly —**in the name of 1** in appeal or reference to **2** by the authority of; as the representative of **3** as belonging to —**know only by name** to be familiar with the name of but not know personally —**name names** to identify specific persons, esp. as doing wrong —**to one's name** belonging to one [but one suit of clothes *to his name*] —**name′a·ble** *adj.*, **nam′a·ble** —**nam′er** *n.*
name brand 1 a well-known brand or trademark **2** a product bearing such a brand or trademark
name-call·ing (-kôl′iŋ) *n.* the use of disparaging or abusive names in attacking another —**name′-call′er** *n.*
name day the feast day of the saint after whom one is named
name-drop·per (-dräp′ər) *n.* a person who seeks to impress others by frequently mentioning famous or important persons he or she knows or pretends to know —**name′-drop′ping** *n.*
name·less (-lis) *adj.* **1** not having or bearing a name **2** left unnamed; anonymous [an embarrassing story about an acquaintance who shall remain *nameless*] **3** not publicly known; obscure **4** lacking a legal name; illegitimate **5** that cannot be described [*nameless* dread] **6** too horrid or painful to specify [*nameless* crimes] —**name′less·ly** *adv.* —**name′less·ness** *n.*
name·ly (-lē) *adv.* ⟦ME: see NAME & -LY[2]⟧ that is to say; specifically
Na·men (nä′mən) *Fl. name for* NAMUR
name of the game the basic or essential quality, situation, goal, etc.: with *the*
name·plate (-plāt′) *n.* **1** a piece of metal, wood, etc. on which a name is inscribed, often, specif., one displayed to identify an office, workstation, etc. **2** a newspaper's name as it appears on the front page
name·sake (-sāk′) *n.* ⟦earlier *name's sake*⟧ a person with the same name as another; specif., *a)* a person in relation to someone he or she is named after *b)* a person in relation to someone named after him or her
Na·mib·i·a (nə mib′ē ə) country in S Africa, on the Atlantic: a former mandate of South Africa, it was administered by South Africa until full independence in 1990; member of the Commonwealth: 318,696 sq mi (825,418 sq km); cap. Windhoek —**Na·mib′i·an** *adj., n.*
Na·mur (nà mür′) **1** province of S Belgium: 1,415 sq mi (3,665 sq km) **2** its capital, on the Meuse River
nan (nän, nan) *n.* ⟦Hindi & Urdu *nān* < Pers⟧ a kind of flat leavened bread of India, made with white flour
na·na (nan′ə, nä′nə) *n. informal term for* GRANDMOTHER
nance (nans) *n.* [Slang] *var. of* NANCY[1] (*n.* 2)
Nan·chang (nän′chäŋ′) city in SE China; capital of Jiangxi province
Nan·cy[1] (nan′sē) *n.* **1** ⟦prob. by faulty division of MINE[2] + *Ancy*, dim. form of ME *Annis*, AGNES[1], confused with ANNE[1]: see ANNA⟧ a feminine name: dim. *Nan* **2** *pl.* **-cies** [*usually* **n-**] [Informal] an effeminate or homosexual man: usually a term of contempt or hostility: also [Chiefly Brit.] **nancy boy**
Nan·cy[2] (nän sē′) city in NE France
Nan·da De·vi (nun′dä dā′vē) mountain of the Himalayas, in N Uttar Pradesh, India: 25,645 ft (7,817 m)
nan·di·na (nan dī′nə, -dē′-) *n.* ⟦ModL < Jpn *nanten*⟧ an ornamental, evergreen shrub (*Nandina domestica*) of the barberry family, having clusters of white flowers and bright red berries
Nan·ga Par·bat (nuŋ′gə pur′bət) mountain of the Himalayas, in W Kashmir: 26,660 ft (8,126 m)
Nan·jing (nän′jiŋ′) ⟦Chin, southern capital (as contrasted with BEIJING)⟧ city in E China, on the Chang; capital of Jiangsu province
nan·keen or **nan·kin** (nan kēn′) *n.* ⟦< fol., whence orig. imported⟧ **1** a buff-colored, durable cotton cloth, originally from China **2** [*pl.*] trousers made of this cloth
Nan·king (nan′kiŋ′, nän′-) *a former transliteration of* NANJING
Nan·nette or **Na·nette** (na net′) *n.* a feminine name: dim. *Nan*: see ANNA
Nan·ning (nän′niŋ′) city in S China; capital of Guangxi autonomous region
nan·no·fos·sil (nan′ō fäs′əl) *n.* ⟦< NANO- + FOSSIL⟧ a microfossil of a planktonic organism
nan·no·plank·ton (nan′ō plaŋk′tən) *n.* ⟦< NANO- + PLANKTON⟧ planktonic organisms smaller than 40 microns in diameter: also sp. **na′no·plank′ton**
nan·ny (nan′ē) *n., pl.* **-nies** ⟦< *Nan*, dim. of ANN(A)⟧ a person whose work is caring for a young child in the child's home
nanny goat ⟦see prec.⟧ a female goat
na·no- (nan′ō, -ə) ⟦< Gr *nanos*, dwarf, akin to *nanna*, aunt: see NUN[1]⟧ *combining form* **1** one billionth part of (a specified unit); the factor 10^{-9} [*nanosecond*] **2** of or having to do with nanotechnology [*nanochip*]
na·no·gram (nan′ə gram′) *n.* one billionth of a gram: abbrev. *ng*
na·no·me·ter (nan′ō mēt′ər) *n.* one billionth of a meter: abbrev. *nm*: Brit. sp. **na′no·me′tre**
na·no·scale (nan′ə skāl′) *adj.* of or measured in nanometers
na·no·sec·ond (nan′ə sek′ənd) *n.* **1** one billionth of a second: abbrev. *ns*, *nsec* **2** a very short period of time; instant

na·no·tech (nan′ō tek′) ***n.*** [Informal] *short for* NANOTECHNOLOGY

na·no·tech·nol·o·gy (nan′ō tek näl′ə jē) ***n.*** a branch of technology dealing with the manipulation of atoms and molecules, as in the production of high-tech materials or microscopic devices —**na′no·tech′no·log′i·cal** (-tek′nə läj′i kəl) ***adj.*** —**na′no·tech·nol′o·gist *n.***

na·no·tube (nan′ə to͞ob′) ***n.*** a nanoscale structure exhibiting extraordinary strength and conductivity and consisting of a cylindrical molecule, typically of carbon

Nan·sen (nän′sən; nan′-), **Fridt·jof** (frit′yäf′) 1861-1930; Norw. arctic explorer, naturalist, & statesman

Nansen bottle ⟦after prec.⟧ an oceanographic instrument used to obtain water samples and temperature readings at various depths in the sea

Nan Shan (nän′shän′) mountain system in NW China, in N Qinghai & S Gansu provinces: highest peak, *c.* 20,000 ft (6,096 m)

Nantes (nänt; *E* nänts, nants) city in W France, on the Loire River

Nan·tuck·et (nan tuk′it) ⟦Massachusett⟧ island of Mass., south of Cape Cod: summer resort: 46 sq mi (119 sq km)

Na·o·mi (nā ō′mē, nī-; nā′ə mē′) ***n.*** ⟦Heb *nōʿomī*, lit., my delight⟧ **1** a feminine name **2** *Bible* the mother-in-law of Ruth: Ruth 1

na·os (nā′äs, nä′-) ***n.***, *pl.* **na′oi** (-oi) ⟦Gr < IE base **nes-*, to unite, be protected > OE *nerian*, Ger *nähren*, to protect, support⟧ **1** an ancient temple **2** the enclosed part of such a temple; cella

nap[1] (nap) ***vi.*** **napped, nap′ping** ⟦ME *nappen* < OE *hnappian*, akin to OHG *hnaffezan*⟧ **1** to doze or sleep lightly for a short time **2** to be careless or unprepared —***n.*** a brief, light sleep; doze

nap[2] (nap) ***n.*** ⟦ME *noppe* < or akin to MDu & MLowG *noppe* (Ger & Dan *hoppe*) < IE **kenebh-* < base **ken-*, to scratch, rub > Ger *nut*, rabbet, Gr *knaptein*, to scratch, tear apart⟧ **1** the downy or hairy surface of cloth formed by short hairs or fibers, esp. when artificially raised by brushing, etc.; pile **2** any such downy surface, as that raised on the flesh side of leather —***vt.*** **napped, nap′ping** to raise a nap on (fabric or leather), as by brushing —**nap′less *adj.***

nap[3] (nap) ***n.*** *short for* NAPOLEON (senses 1 & 2)

-nap (nap) ⟦< KIDNAP⟧ *combining form forming verbs* to seize and carry away; steal: often in nonce combinations *[dognap, petnap]*

Nap·a (nap′ə) ⟦< AmInd < ? *napa*, grizzly bear or *napo*, house⟧ city in W Calif., north of Oakland: center of a winegrowing region (**Napa Valley**)

nap·a (leather) (nap′ə) *alt. sp. of* NAPPA

☆**na·palm** (nā′päm′, -pälm′) ***n.*** ⟦NA(PHTHENE) + PALM(ITATE), constituents used in its manufacture⟧ **1** sodium palmitate or an aluminum soap added to gasoline or oil to form a highly flammable, jellylike substance **2** this substance, used in flame throwers and bombs —***vt.*** to attack or burn with napalm

nape (nāp, nap) ***n.*** ⟦ME < ?⟧ the back of the neck: also **nape of the neck**

Na·per·ville (nā′pər vil′) ⟦after Captain J. *Naper*, its founder⟧ city in NE Ill., west of Chicago

na·per·y (nā′pər ē) ***n.*** ⟦ME *naprye* < MFr *naperie* < OFr *nappe*: see NAPKIN⟧ household linen; esp., table linen

Naph·ta·li (naf′tə lī′) ***n.*** ⟦Heb < *naphtulim*; wrestlings: see Gen. 30:8⟧ *Bible* **1** Jacob's sixth son, whose mother was Bilhah: Gen. 30:7-8 **2** the tribe of Israel descended from him: Num. 1:43

naph·tha (naf′thə, nap′-) ***n.*** ⟦L < Gr *naphtha*, naphtha, bitumen < Pers *neft*, pitch < ? IE base **nebh-*, damp, water > Gr *nephelē*, cloud, fog⟧ **1** a flammable, volatile, oily liquid produced by the fractional distillation of petroleum: it is the fraction that boils between gasoline and kerosene and is used as a fuel, solvent, and illuminant **2** PETROLEUM **3** any of several flammable, volatile liquids produced by the distillation of coal tar, wood, coal, and other carbonaceous materials

naph·tha·lene (-lēn′) ***n.*** ⟦earlier *naphthaline* < prec. + *-l-* + -INE[3]⟧ a white, crystalline, aromatic hydrocarbon, $C_{10}H_8$, produced in the fractional distillation of coal tar: it is used in moth repellents and in the manufacture of certain dyes and other organic compounds: also **naph′tha·lin′** —**naph′tha·le′nic** (-lē′nik, -len′ik) ***adj.***

naph·thene (naf′thēn, nap′-) ***n.*** ⟦NAPHTH(A) + -ENE⟧ CYCLOPARAFFIN —**naph·the′nic** (-thē′nik, -then′ik) ***adj.***

naph·thol (naf′thôl′, -thôl′; nap′-) ***n.*** ⟦NAPHTH(ALENE) + -OL[1]⟧ either of two white, crystalline isomeric compounds, $C_{10}H_7OH$, derived from naphthalene and used as antiseptics and in dyes, pharmaceuticals, etc.

naph·thyl (-thil) ***n.*** ⟦NAPHTH(ALENE) + -YL⟧ a monovalent radical $C_{10}H_7$ derived from naphthalene

Na·pi·er (nāp′yər), **John** 1550-1617; Scot. mathematician: inventor of logarithms

Na·pier·i·an logarithm (nə pir′ē ən) ⟦after prec.⟧ NATURAL LOGARITHM

na·pi·form (nā′pə fôrm′) ***adj.*** ⟦< L *napus*, turnip (see NEEP) + -FORM⟧ large and round at the top, tapering sharply below; turnip-shaped: said of roots

nap·kin (nap′kin) ***n.*** ⟦ME *nappekyn*, dim. < OFr *nappe*, cloth, tablecloth < L *mappa*: see MAP⟧ **1** a small piece of cloth or paper, usually square, used while eating for protecting the clothes and wiping the fingers or lips **2** any small cloth, towel, etc.; esp., *a)* [Brit.] a diaper *b)* [Brit. Dial.] a handkerchief *c)* [Scot.] a kerchief or neckerchief *d)* SANITARY NAPKIN

Na·ples (nā′pəlz) **1** seaport in S Italy, on the Bay of Naples **2** former kingdom occupying the S half of Italy **3 Bay of** inlet of the Tyrrhenian Sea, on the S coast of Italy: *c.* 10 mi (16 km) wide

na·po·le·on (nə pō′lē ən, -pōl′yən) ***n.*** ⟦after fol.⟧ **1** a former gold coin of France, equivalent to 20 francs, with a portrait of Napoleon I (or III) on it **2** *a)* a card game similar to euchre *b)* a bid to take all five tricks in this game **3** a rectangle of puff pastry with a custardlike filling

Na·po·le·on (nə pō′lē ən, -pōl′yən) **1** *see* BONAPARTE[2], Napoleon: in full **Napoleon I** **2 Napoleon II** (born *François Charles Joseph Napoléon Bonaparte*) Duke of Reichstadt 1811-32; titular emperor of France: son of Napoleon I & Marie Louise **3 Napoleon III** *see* LOUIS NAPOLEON

Na·po·le·on·ic (nə pō′lē än′ik) ***adj.*** of, characteristic of, or like Napoleon I, his campaigns, period, etc.

Napoleonic Code *Eng. name for* CODE NAPOLÉON

Na·po·li (nä′pô lē′) *It. name for* NAPLES

nappa (leather) (nap′ə) a soft, supple leather produced, esp. from sheepskin, by tawing

nappe (nap) ***n.*** ⟦Fr, lit., tablecloth < OFr (see NAPKIN): orig. referring to a sheet of water passing over a dam⟧ **1** *Geol.* a mass or sheet of rock that has been moved horizontally by geologic forces **2** *Geom.* either of the two identical portions of a CONE (sense 1*c*) that meet at the vertex: each portion is equivalent to a right circular cone

nap·per[1] (nap′ər) ***n.*** a person who naps or is in the habit of taking naps

nap·per[2] (nap′ər) ***n.*** a person, device, or machine that raises a nap on cloth

nap·py[1] (nap′ē) ***n.***, *pl.* **-pies** ⟦dim. of obs. *nap*, a drinking cup, bowl < ME *nap, hnap* < OE *hnæp*, akin to Ger *napf*⟧ a small, shallow, flat-bottomed dish for serving food

nap·py[2] (nap′ē) ***adj.*** **-pi·er, -pi·est** **1** covered with nap; hairy, downy, shaggy, etc. **2** kinky; frizzy: said esp. of the hair of blacks and sometimes used derogatorily —**nap′pi·ness *n.***

nap·py[3] (nap′ē) [Brit.] ***adj.*** **-pi·er, -pi·est** ⟦prob. < prec.⟧ foaming; heady; strong: said of ale —***n.*** ale

nap·py[4] (nap′ē) ***n.***, *pl.* **-pies** ⟦< NAPKIN + -Y[2]⟧ *Brit. term for* DIAPER (***n.*** 2)

na·prox·en (nə präk′sən) ***n.*** ⟦NA(PHTHYL) + PR(OPIONIC ACID) + OX(Y)- (sense 1) + *-en*, prob. arbitrary suffix⟧ a white, crystalline powder, $C_{14}H_{14}O_3$, used as a nonsteroidal, anti-inflammatory drug to relieve pain and reduce fever, esp. in the treatment of arthritis, migraine, and menstrual cramps

Na·ra (nä′rä) city in S Honshu, Japan, east of Osaka: oldest permanent capital of Japan & chief early Buddhist center (fl. 8th cent. A.D.)

Nar·ba·da (nər bud′ə) river in central India, flowing west into the Arabian Sea: *c.* 800 mi (1,287 km)

☆**narc**[1] (närk) ***n.*** ⟦< NARC(OTIC)⟧ [Slang] a local or federal police agent charged with enforcing the laws restricting the use of narcotics, hallucinogenic drugs, etc.

narc[2] (närk) ***n., vt., vi.*** *alt. sp. of* NARK[1]

nar·ce·ine (när′sē ēn′, -in) ***n.*** ⟦Fr *narcéine* < Gr *narkē*, numbness: see NARCOTIC⟧ a bitter, white, crystalline narcotic alkaloid, $C_{23}H_{27}NO_8$, obtained from opium

nar·cis·sism (när′sə siz′əm; *chiefly Brit*, när sis′iz′əm) ***n.*** ⟦Ger *Narzissismus* (< *Narziss*, fol.) + *-ismus*, -ISM⟧ **1** excessive interest in one's own appearance, comfort, importance, abilities, etc. **2** *Psychoanalysis* arrest at or regression to the first stage of libidinal development, in which the self is an object of erotic pleasure Also **nar′cism′** —**nar′cis·sist *n., adj.*** —**nar′cis·sis′tic *adj.***

Nar·cis·sus (när sis′əs) ***n.*** ⟦L < Gr *Narkissos*⟧ **1** *Gr. Myth.* a beautiful youth who, after Echo's death, is made to pine away for love of his own reflection in a spring and changes into the narcissus **2** *pl.* **-cis′sus, -cis′sus·es,** or **-cis′si** (-ī) ⟦ModL < L < Gr *narkissos*, ? akin to *narkē*, stupor (see NARCOTIC), in reference to the plant's narcotic properties⟧ [**n-**] any of a genus (*Narcissus*) of bulbous plants of the lily family with smooth, linear leaves and six-parted flowers with a cup or tube projecting from the center, including daffodils and jonquils

nar·co (när′kō′) [Slang] ***n.***, *pl.* **-cos** **1** NARC[1] **2** a user of narcotic drugs; addict **3** a person who engages in illegal trade in narcotic drugs —***adj.*** of or having to do with narcotic drugs, their illegal sale, etc.

nar·co- (när′kō, -kə) ⟦< Gr *narkē*: see NARCOTIC⟧ *combining form* **1** narcosis, stupor, or sleep *[narcolepsy]* **2** narcotic drug *[narcosynthesis]* Also, before a vowel, **narc-**

nar·co·a·nal·y·sis (när′kō ə nal′ə sis) ***n.*** ⟦prec. + ANALYSIS⟧ psychotherapy using the method of narcosynthesis but in a slower, gentler manner

nar·co·lep·sy (när′kə lep′sē) ***n.*** ⟦NARCO- + -LEPSY⟧ a chronic neurological disorder characterized by episodes of involuntary sleep and, often, cataplexy, hallucinations, etc. —**nar′co·lep′tic *adj., n.***

nar·co·sis (när kō′sis) ***n.***, *pl.* **-ses** ⟦ModL < Gr *narkōsis* < *narkoun*: see NARCOTIC⟧ a condition of deep stupor which passes into unconsciousness and paralysis, usually caused by a narcotic or certain chemicals

nar·co·syn·the·sis (när′kō sin′thə sis) ***n.*** ⟦NARCO- + SYNTHESIS⟧ a method of treating an acute traumatic neurosis by working with a patient while he or she is under the influence of a hypnotic drug

nar·cot·ic (när kät′ik) ***n.*** ⟦ME *narcotyke* < OFr *narcotique*, orig. adj. < ML *narcoticus* < Gr *narkoun*, to benumb < *narkē*, numbness, stupor < IE **nerk-* < base **(s)ner-*, to twist, entwine > SNARE, NARROW⟧ **1** *a)* a drug, as opium or any of its derivatives (morphine, heroin, codeine, etc.), used to relieve pain and induce sleep: narcotics are often addictive and in excessive doses can cause stupor, coma, or death *b)* loosely, any illicit drug, as LSD or marijuana **2** anything that has a soothing, lulling, or dulling effect —***adj.*** **1** of, like, or capable of producing narcosis **2** of, by, or for narcotic addicts

nar·co·tism (när′kə tiz′əm) ***n.*** **1** NARCOSIS **2** a method producing narcosis **3** addiction to narcotics

nar·co·tize (när′kə tīz′) ***vt.*** **-tized′, -tiz′ing** **1** to subject to a narcotic; stupefy **2** to lull or dull the senses of —**nar′co·ti·za′tion *n.***

nard (närd) ***n.*** ⟦ME *narde* < OFr < L *nardus* < Gr *nardos* < Sem, as in Heb *nērd*, prob. < Sans *nálada-*, nard⟧ *Bot. var. of* SPIKENARD (sense 2)

na·res (ner′ēz′) *pl.n., sing.* **na′ris** (-is) ⟦L: see NOSE⟧ the nasal passages; esp., the nostrils —**nar′i·al** (-ē əl) *adj.*, **nar′ine** (-in, -īn)

Na·rew (nä′ref′) river in NE Poland, flowing west & southwest into the Bug River, near Warsaw: *c.* 270 mi (435 km)

nar·ghi·le (när′gə lē′, -lā′) *n.* ⟦Pers *nārgīleh* < *nargīl*, coconut tree, prob. < Sans *nārikera*, coconut: orig. made of coconut shell⟧ a kind of water pipe for smoking: also sp. **nar′gi·le′** or **nar′gi·leh′**

NARI (när′ē) *service mark* National Association of the Remodeling Industry

nark[1] (närk) [Slang] *n.* ⟦< Romany *nāk*, a nose < Hindi *nāk*, nose: for IE base see NOSE⟧ an informer; stool pigeon — *vt., vi.* **1** to inform on (a person) **2** [Brit.] to make, be, or become annoyed, angry, etc. —**nark it!** [Brit.] stop it! keep quiet! —**nark′y** *adj.*

☆**nark**[2] (närk) *n.* [Slang] *alt. sp. of* NARC[1]

Nar·ra·gan·sett (nar′ə gan′sit) *n.* ⟦earlier (17th c.) *Nanhiggansett, Nanohigganset*, etc. < a Narragansett place name of uncert. meaning⟧ **1** *pl.* **-setts** or **-sett** a member of a North American Indian people living west of Narragansett Bay in Rhode Island **2** the Algonquian language of this people, no longer in use Also sp. **Nar′ra·gan′set** —*adj.* of the Narragansetts or their language or culture

Narragansett Bay ⟦after prec.⟧ inlet of the Atlantic, extending into R.I.: *c.* 30 mi (48 km)

nar·rate (nar′āt′; na rāt′, nə-) *vt., vi.* **-rat′ed, -rat′ing** ⟦< L *narratus*, pp. of *narrare*, to tell, akin to *gnarus*, acquainted with < IE **ĝnoro-* < base **ĝen-*, to KNOW⟧ **1** to tell (a story) in writing or speech **2** to give an account of (happenings, etc.) **3** to read (descriptive or narrative passages), as in a documentary film

nar·ra·tion (na rā′shən, nə-) *n.* ⟦ME *narracion* < OFr < L *narratio*⟧ **1** the act or process of narrating; the telling of a story or of happenings **2** a story or account; narrative **3** writing or speaking that narrates, as history, biography, or fiction —**nar·ra′tion·al** *adj.*

nar·ra·tive (nar′ə tiv) *adj.* ⟦L *narrativus*⟧ **1** of, or having the nature of, narration; in story form **2** occupied or concerned with narration [*a narrative* poet] —*n.* **1** a story; account; tale **2** the art or practice of narrating; narration **3** any official or standard account or explanation, as of a sequence of related events —SYN. STORY[1] —**nar′ra·tive·ly** *adv.*

nar·ra·tol·o·gy (nar′ə täl′ə jē) *n.* the theory and critical study of narrative forms in literature —**nar′ra·to·log′i·cal** *adj.*

nar·ra·tor (nar′āt′ər, -ət-; na rāt′ər, nə-) *n.* ⟦L < *narratus*: see NARRATE⟧ **1** a person who relates a story or account **2** a person who reads descriptive or narrative passages, as in a documentary film

nar·row (nar′ō, ner′ō) *adj.* ⟦ME *narwe* < OE *nearu*, akin to MDu *nare*, OS *naru* < IE base **(s)ner-*, to turn, twist > SNARE, Gr *narkē*, stupor⟧ **1** small in width as compared to length; esp., less wide than is customary, standard, or expected; not wide **2** limited in meaning, size, amount, or extent [*a narrow* majority] **3** limited in outlook; without breadth of view or generosity; not liberal; prejudiced [*a narrow* mind] **4** close; careful; minute; thorough [*a narrow* inspection] **5** with limited margin; with barely enough space, time, etc.; barely successful [*a narrow* escape] **6** limited in means; with hardly enough to live on [*narrow* circumstances] ☆**7** having a relatively high proportion of protein: said of livestock feed **8** [Dial.] stingy; parsimonious **9** *Phonet.* tense: said of certain vowels —*vi.* to decrease in width; contract [the river *narrows* up ahead] —*vt.* **1** to decrease or limit in width [to *narrow* a sidewalk] **2** to decrease or limit the scope, extent, or number of: often with *down* [to *narrow* down one's college options] —*n.* **1** a narrow part or place, esp. in a valley, mountain pass, road, etc. **2** [*usually pl.*] a narrow passage, as between two bodies of water; strait —**nar′row·ly** *adv.* —**nar′row·ness** *n.*

nar·row·cast (-kast′) *vt., vi.* **-cast′, -cast′ing** ⟦prec. + -CAST, as in BROADCAST⟧ to transmit, esp. by cable television, to a specialized or selected audience —*n.* **1** the act of narrowcasting **2** a program that is narrowcast

narrow gauge **1** a width, between the rails of a railroad, less than standard (56.5 in, or 143.5 cm) ☆**2** a narrow-gauge railroad or car —**nar′row-gauge′** *adj.*, **nar′row-gauged′**

nar·row-mind·ed (-mīn′did) *adj.* limited in outlook or lacking in tolerance; not open-minded; bigoted, prejudiced, etc. —**nar′row-mind′ed·ly** *adv.* —**nar′row-mind′ed·ness** *n.*

Nar·rows (nar′ōz, ner′-), **The** strait between Upper & Lower New York Bay, separating Staten Island & Long Island

nar·thex (när′theks′) *n.* ⟦LL(Ec) < LGr(Ec) *narthēx* < Gr, giant fennel: from a fancied resemblance of the porch to the hollow stem⟧ **1** in early Christian churches, a porch or portico at the west end for penitents and others not admitted to the church itself **2** any church vestibule leading to the nave

nar·whal (när′wəl, -hwəl) *n.* ⟦< Scand, as in Norw & Dan *narhval* < ON *nahvalr*, lit., corpse (< IE base **nāu-*, death, corpse) + *hvalr*, WHALE[2] (with reference to the whitish underside)⟧ an arctic toothed whale (*Monodon monoceros*) of the same family (Monodontidae) as the beluga, valued for its oil and ivory: the male has a long, spiral tusk extending from the upper jaw: also **nar′wal** (-wəl) or **nar′whale′** (-hwāl′, -wāl′)

nar·y (ner′ē) *adj.* ⟦altered < *ne'er a*, never a⟧ [Dial. or Literary] not any; no: with *a* or *an* [*nary* a doubt]

☆**NAS** *abbrev.* **1** National Academy of Sciences **2** naval air station

☆**NASA** (nas′ə) *n.* National Aeronautics and Space Administration

na·sal (nā′zəl) *adj.* ⟦ModL *nasalis* < L *nasus*, NOSE⟧ **1** of the nose **2** *Linguis.* *a)* articulated by means of partial or complete closing of the mouth, as at the velum, alveolar ridge, or lips, so that all or part of the breath passes through the nose, as in the consonants (m), (n), and (ŋ) and certain French vowels *b)* characterized by such production of sounds **3** having or characteristic of a vocal tone resulting from reduction in airflow through the nose, as when the nose is pinched or the nasal passages are congested —*n.* **1** *Linguis.* a NASAL (*adj.* 2) sound or a letter or symbol representing such a sound **2** *Anat.* a bone or plate of the nose **3** ⟦ME < OFr *nasal, nasel* < L *nasus*, NOSE⟧ the protective nosepiece of a helmet —**na·sal·i·ty** (nā zal′ə tē) *n.* —**na′sal·ly** *adv.*

na·sal·ize (nā′zəl īz′) *vt.* **-ized′, -iz′ing** to articulate with a nasal sound —*vi.* to speak with nasal sounds See NASAL (*adj.* 2) —**na′sal·i·za′tion** *n.*

Nas·by (naz′bē), **Pe·tro·le·um V.** (pə trō′lē əm) (pseud. of *David Ross Locke*) 1833-88; U.S. humorist

NASCAR (nas′kär′) *service mark* National Association for Stock Car Auto Racing

nas·cent (nas′ənt, nā′sənt) *adj.* ⟦L *nascens*, prp. of *nasci*, to be born: see GENUS⟧ **1** coming into being; being born **2** beginning to form, start, grow, or develop: said of ideas, cultures, etc. **3** *Chem.* designating or of the state of an element just released from a compound and having unusual chemical activity because atoms of the element have not combined to form molecules [*nascent* chlorine] —**nas′cence** *n.*, **nas′cen·cy**

NASDAQ (naz′dak′) *service mark* National Association of Securities Dealers Automated Quotations: an electronic quotation system for over-the-counter trading —*n.* the market in stocks traded in this system: often written **Nasdaq**

nase·ber·ry (nāz′ber′ē) *n., pl.* **-ries** ⟦Sp *níspero*, medlar tree, *néspero*, medlar < L *mespilus*: see MEDLAR⟧ SAPODILLA

Nase·by (nāz′bē) village in Northamptonshire, England: site of a decisive Royalist defeat (1645)

Nash (nash), **Ogden** 1902-71; U.S. writer of humorous verse

Nashe (nash), **Thomas** 1567-1601; Eng. satirist & pamphleteer: also sp. **Nash**

Nash·ville (nash′vil; *locally*, -vəl) ⟦after Gen. Francis *Nash* (1720-77)⟧ capital of Tenn., on the Cumberland River and in Davidson county, with which it constitutes a metropolitan government (**Nash′ville-Da′vid·son**)

na·si·on (nā′zē än′) *n.* ⟦ModL < L *nasus*, NOSE⟧ in craniometry, the point in the skull at which the suture between the two nasal bones meets the suture between these and the frontal bone —**na′si·al** *adj.*

na·so- (nā′zō, -zə) ⟦< L *nasus*, NOSE⟧ *combining form* **1** nose, nasal [*nasoscope*] **2** nose and [*nasofrontal*] Also, before a vowel, **nas-**

na·so·fron·tal (nā′zō frunt′'l) *adj.* of the nose and the frontal bone

na·so·gas·tric (-gas′trik) *adj.* of the nose and stomach: said as of a feeding tube inserted into the stomach via the nose

na·so·phar·ynx (-far′iŋks) *n., pl.* **-pha·ryn′ges′** (-fə rin′jēz′) or **-phar′ynx·es** the part of the pharynx lying directly behind the nasal passages and above the soft palate: see PHARYNX, illus.: cf. LARYNGOPHARYNX, OROPHARYNX —**na′so·pha·ryn′ge·al** (-fə rin′jē əl) *adj.*

Nas·sau[1] (nä′sou′) *n.* name of the princely family of the former German duchy of Nassau, which, as the House of Orange, has ruled the Netherlands since 1815

Nas·sau[2] (nä′sou′; *for 2* na′sô′) **1** region in W Germany: formerly a duchy **2** capital of the Bahamas, on New Providence Island

Nas·ser (nas′ər), **Ga·mal Ab·del** (gä mäl′ äb′dəl) 1918-70; Egypt. statesman: president of Egypt (1956-58): president of the United Arab Republic (1958-70)

Nast (nast), **Thomas** 1840-1902; U.S. political cartoonist & illustrator, born in Germany

nas·tic (nas′tik) *adj.* ⟦< Gr *nastos*, pressed close < *nassein*, to press, squeeze close + -IC⟧ designating, of, or exhibiting movement or change in position of a plant or its parts, as in the opening and closing of flowers, in response to a stimulus but independent of the direction of the stimulus and caused by unequal growth of certain cells, changes in light intensity, etc.

-nas·tic (nas′tik) *combining form* nastic by some (specified) means or in some (specified) direction [*epinastic, hyponastic*]

nas·tur·tium (nə stur′shəm, na-) *n.* ⟦L, kind of cress < **nasitortium*, lit., nose-twist < *nasus*, NOSE + pp. of *torquere*, to turn, twist (see TORT): from the pungent odor of the plant⟧ **1** any of a genus (*Tropaeolum*, family Tropaeolaceae) of dicotyledonous garden plants (order Geraniales) with shield-shaped leaves, and showy, trumpet-shaped, usually red, yellow, or orange spurred flowers **2** the flower

nas·ty (nas′tē) *adj.* **-ti·er, -ti·est** ⟦ME < ? or akin to Du *nestig*, dirty⟧ **1** very dirty, filthy **2** offensive in taste or smell; nauseating **3** morally offensive; indecent **4** very unpleasant; objectionable [*nasty* weather] **5** mean; malicious; ill-humored [*a nasty* temper] **6** very dangerous, troublesome, grievous, etc. [*a nasty* bruise, a *nasty* curveball] —*n., pl.* **-ties** [Informal] an offensive, objectionable, or very unpleasant person or thing —**nas′ti·ly** *adv.* —**nas′ti·ness** *n.*

-nas·ty (nas′tē) ⟦< Gr *nastos* (see NASTIC) + -Y[3]⟧ *combining form forming nouns* a condition of plant growth by a (specified) means or in a (specified) direction [*epinasty*]

nat *abbrev.* **1** national **2** native **3** natural

na·tal (nāt′'l) *adj.* ⟦ME < L *natalis* < *natus*, pp. of *nasci*, to be born: see GENUS⟧ **1** of or connected with one's birth **2** dating from birth **3** native: said of a place

Na·tal (nə tal′; -täl′) **1** former province of E South Africa: now part of KwaZulu-Natal province **2** seaport in NE Brazil: capital of Rio Grande do Norte state

Nat·a·lie (nat′ə lē) ***n.*** ⟦Fr < LL *Natalia* (name given to children born on Christmas Day) < L *natalis (dies)*, natal (day)⟧ a feminine name

na·tal·i·ty (nā tal′ə tē, nə-) ***n.*** ⟦Fr *natalité*⟧ BIRTHRATE

na·tant (nā′tənt) ***adj.*** ⟦L *natans*, prp. of *natare*, to swim < IE **(s)net-* < base **(s)na-*, to flow > Gr *nēchein*, to swim, *nēsos*, island, L *nare*, to swim, OIr *snām*, swimming⟧ swimming or floating; esp., floating on the surface of water

na·ta·tion (nā tā′shən) ***n.*** ⟦L *natatio* < pp. of *natare*: see prec.⟧ the act or art of swimming —**na·ta′tion·al** ***adj.***

na·ta·to·ri·al (nāt′ə tôr′ē əl, nat′-) ***adj.*** ⟦< LL *natatorius* < L *natator*, swimmer (see NATANT) + -AL⟧ of, characterized by, or adapted for swimming: also **na′ta·to′ry**

☆**na·ta·to·ri·um** (-əm) ***n.***, *pl.* **-ri·ums** or **-ri·a** (-ə) ⟦LL < *natatorius*: see prec.⟧ **1** a swimming pool, esp. one indoors **2** a building or facility housing a large swimming pool

☆**natch** (nach) ***adv.*** ⟦altered < NAT(URALLY)⟧ [Slang] naturally; of course

Natch·ez (nach′iz) ***n.*** ⟦Fr < a Natchez place name⟧ **1** *pl.* **Natch′ez** a member of a North American Indian people formerly living in SW Mississippi and later in Oklahoma **2** the extinct language of this people, thought to be related to Muskogean

Natchez Trace early 19th-cent. road following an old Indian trail from Natchez, Miss., to Nashville, Tenn.: often **Natchez Trail**

na·tes (nā′tēz′) ***pl.n.*** ⟦L, pl. of *natis*, akin to Gr *nōton*, the back⟧ the buttocks

Na·than[1] (nā′thən) ***n.*** ⟦Heb *nāthān*, lit., he has given⟧ **1** a masculine name: dim. *Nat, Nate* **2** *Bible* a prophet who rebuked David for the death of Uriah: 2 Sam. 12:1-14

Na·than[2] (nā′thən), **George Jean** 1882-1958; U.S. drama critic & editor

Na·than·ael (nə than′yəl, -ē əl) ***n.*** ⟦LL(Ec) < Gr(Ec) *Nathanaēl* < Heb *nĕthan′ēl*, lit., God has given⟧ **1** a masculine name: dim. *Nat*: now usually sp. **Na·than′iel** **2** *Bible* one of the disciples of Jesus: John 1:45: see also BARTHOLOMEW

nathe·less (nāth′lis, nath′-) ***adv.*** ⟦ME *natheles* < OE < *na*, not, never + *the* (for *thy*, instrumental case of def. art.) + *læs*, less⟧ [Archaic] nevertheless; nonetheless: also **nath′less** (nath′-)

na·tion (nā′shən) ***n.*** ⟦ME *nacion* < OFr < L *natio* < *natus*, born: see NATURE⟧ **1** a stable, historically developed community of people with a territory, economic life, distinctive culture, and language in common **2** the people of a territory united under a single government; country **3** *a)* a people or tribe, specif., a group of North American Indians, sometimes one belonging to a confederation ☆*b)* **[N-]** the territory of a particular Indian people or peoples —**the nations** **1** *Bible* the non-Jewish nations; Gentiles **2** [Old Poet.] all the peoples of the earth —**na′tion·hood′** ***n.***

Na·tion (nā′shən), **Car·ry** (kar′ē) (born *Carry Amelia Moore*) 1846-1911; U.S. temperance leader

na·tion·al (nash′ə nəl) ***adj.*** ⟦Fr⟧ **1** of or having to do with a nation or the nation **2** affecting a (or the) nation as a whole; nationwide in scope, involvement, representation, etc. **3** patriotic or nationalist **4** established, maintained, or owned by the federal government [*a national park*] —***n.*** **1** a person under the protection of a (specified) country: citizen or subject **2** the national headquarters or administration of an organization **3** [*often pl.*] a competition in which participants compete for a nationwide ranking, title, championship, etc. —***SYN.*** CITIZEN —**na′tion·al·ly** ***adv.***

national bank **1** a bank or system of banks owned and operated by a government, as in some foreign countries ☆**2** in the U.S., a bank chartered and regulated by the Department of the Treasury and, since 1913, required to be a member of the Federal Reserve System

national debt the total debt incurred by the central government of a nation

☆**National Guard** in the U.S., the organized militia forces of the individual states, a component of the Army of the U.S. when called into active federal service

☆**National Guard of the United States** those members and units of the National Guard that have been accorded federal recognition as a reserve component of the Army or Air Force of the U.S.

national income the total income earned by a nation's productive factors, including all profits, rents, wages, etc., during a specified period, usually a year; net national product minus indirect business taxes

na·tion·al·ism (nash′ə nəl iz′əm) ***n.*** **1** *a)* devotion to one's nation; patriotism *b)* excessive, narrow, or jingoist patriotism; chauvinism **2** the doctrine that national interest, security, etc. are more important than international considerations **3** the desire for or advocacy of national independence

na·tion·al·ist (-ist) ***n.*** a person who believes in or advocates nationalism —***adj.*** of nationalism or nationalists: also **na′tion·al·is′tic** —**na′tion·al·is′ti·cal·ly** ***adv.***

na·tion·al·i·ty (nash′ə nal′ə tē) ***n.***, *pl.* **-ties** **1** national quality or character **2** the status of belonging to a particular nation by birth or naturalization; identification as to national origin **3** the condition or fact of being a nation **4** a national or ethnic group, esp. of immigrants from some other country: in full **nationality group**

na·tion·al·ize (nash′ə nə līz′) ***vt.*** **-ized′**, **-iz′ing** **1** to make national in character **2** to transfer ownership or control of (land, resources, industries, etc.) to the national government —**na′tion·al·i·za′tion** ***n.*** —**na′tion·al·iz′er** ***n.***

☆**national monument** a natural geographical feature or historic site, as a mountain, canyon, fort, etc., maintained and preserved by the federal government for the public to visit

☆**national park** an area of scenic beauty, historical and scientific interest, etc. maintained and preserved by the federal government for the public to visit

☆**national seashore** any of the coastal areas with beaches, waterfowl, fishing, etc., reserved by the federal government for public use

National Socialism ⟦< Ger *Nationalsozialismus*⟧ the political ideology of Adolf Hitler and the Nazis; Nazism —**National Socialist**

☆**National Weather Service** the division of the Department of Commerce that gathers and compiles data on weather conditions over the U.S., on the basis of which weather forecasts are made

☆**Nation of Islam** an African-American sect of Islam, espousing social and political activism: see also BLACK MUSLIM

na·tion-state (nā′shən stāt′) ***n.*** the modern nation as the representative unit of political organization

na·tion·wide (-wīd′) ***adj.*** by or throughout the whole nation; national —***adv.*** throughout the nation

na·tive (nāt′iv) ***adj.*** ⟦ME *natyf* < MFr *natif* < L *nativus* < *natus*, born: see NATURE⟧ **1** inborn or innate rather than acquired **2** belonging to a locality or country by birth, production, or growth; indigenous [*a native* Bostonian, plants *native* to Florida] **3** related to one as, or in connection with, the place of one's birth or origin [one's *native* land, one's *native* language] **4** simple; natural; free from affectation **5** as found in nature; natural and not refined, adorned, or altered by man **6** occurring in a pure state in nature [*native* gold] **7** of or characteristic of the natives, or indigenous inhabitants, of a place **8** **[N-]** *short for* NATIVE AMERICAN [*Native* land rights] —***n.*** **1** a person born in the place or country indicated **2** *a)* an original or indigenous inhabitant of a region, as distinguished from an invader, explorer, colonist, etc. *b)* an indigenous plant or animal **3** a permanent resident, as distinguished from a temporary resident or visitor —**go native** to adopt the mode of life, often one less complicated, of the native inhabitants —**na′tive·ly** ***adv.*** —**na′tive·ness** ***n.***

SYN.—**native** applies to a person born, or thing originating, in a certain place or country [*a native* Italian, *native* fruits]; **indigenous**, which also suggests natural origin in a particular region, is applied to races or species rather than to individuals [the potato is *indigenous* to South America]; **aboriginal** applies to the earliest known inhabitants (or, rarely, animals or plants) of a region [the Indians are the *aboriginal* Americans]; **endemic**, applied esp. to plants and diseases, implies prevalence in or restriction to a particular region [typhus is *endemic* in various countries] See also **citizen** —*ANT.* **alien, foreign**

Native American AMERICAN INDIAN

na·tive-born (-bôrn′) ***adj.*** of a specified place by birth

☆**native son** a man native to the place in question [the Ohio delegation nominated a *native son*]

☆**na·tiv·ism** (nāt′iv iz′əm) ***n.*** **1** the practice or policy of favoring native-born citizens as against immigrants **2** the revival or preservation of a native culture **3** the theory in philosophy, psychology, and linguistics that certain ideas or capacities are innate and form the basis for moral judgment, the acquiring of knowledge and language, etc. —☆**na′tiv·ist** ***adj., n.*** —☆**na′tiv·is′tic** ***adj.***

na·tiv·i·ty (nə tiv′ə tē, nā-) ***n.***, *pl.* **-ties** ⟦ME *natiuite* < OFr *nativite* < LL *nativitas* < L *nativus*, NATIVE⟧ **1** birth, esp. with reference to place, time, or accompanying conditions **2** **[N-]** a representation of the newborn Jesus, typically as part of a grouping that includes Mary, Joseph, the Magi, etc. **3** *Astrol.* the horoscope for the time of a given person's birth —**the Nativity** **1** the birth of Jesus **2** Christmas Day

natl *abbrev.* national

NATO (nā′tō) ***n.*** North Atlantic Treaty Organization

nat·ro·lite (na′trə līt′, nā′trə-) ***n.*** ⟦Ger *natrolith* < *natron* (< Fr: see fol.) + *-lith*, -LITE⟧ a hard, light-colored, orthorhombic zeolite, $Na_2Al_2Si_3O_{10} \cdot 2H_2O$, characterized by crystals that radiate out, often needlelike, from a central point; hydrous sodium aluminum silicate

na·tron (nā′trän′) ***n.*** ⟦Fr < Sp *natrón* < Ar *naṭrūn* < Gr *nitron*: see NITER⟧ hydrated sodium carbonate, $Na_2CO_3 \cdot 10H_2O$

nat·ter (nat′ər) [Chiefly Brit.] ***vi.*** ⟦var. of dial. *gnatter* < Gmc echoic base > ON *gnata*, to crash noisily & Ger *knattern*, to clatter⟧ **1** to chatter idly; talk on at length **2** to find fault; scold —***n.*** a chat or talk

nat·ty (nat′ē) ***adj.*** **-ti·er**, **-ti·est** ⟦< ? NEAT[1]⟧ trim and smart in appearance or dress [*a natty* suit] —**nat′ti·ly** ***adv.*** —**nat′ti·ness** ***n.***

Na·tu·fi·an (nə to͞o′fē ən) ***adj.*** ⟦after Wady en-*Natuf*, valley in Palestine + -IAN⟧ designating or of a Mesolithic culture of the Near East characterized by microliths, sickles, pestles, etc.: it offers the first evidence of reaping and grinding cereals

nat·u·ral (nach′ər əl, nach′rəl) ***adj.*** ⟦OFr < L *naturalis*, by birth, according to nature⟧ **1** of or arising from nature; in accordance with what is found or expected in nature **2** produced or existing in nature; not artificial or manufactured **3** dealing with nature as an object of study [*a natural* science] **4** in a state provided by nature, without man-made changes; wild; uncultivated **5** of the real or physical world as distinguished from a spiritual, intellectual, or imaginary world **6** *a)* present by virtue of nature; innate; not acquired *b)* having certain qualities, abilities, etc. innately [*a natural* athlete] **7** obviously or seemingly right or proper [he is a *natural* choice to chair the committee] **8** true to nature; lifelike [*a natural* likeness] **9** normal or usual; in the ordinary course of events [*a natural* outcome] **10** free from affectation or artificiality; at ease [*a natural* smile] **11** without a legal relationship; specif., *a)* illegitimate [a *natural* child] *b)* relating biologically rather than by adoption [*natural* parents] **12** with little or no processing, artificial ingredients or preservatives [*natural* food] **13** off-white, light-beige, etc. **14** resulting from age, disease, etc. rather than an accident, violence, etc. [a *natural* death, death from *natural* causes] **15** *Biol.* designating or of a system of classification based on complete structure and characteristics **16** *Music a)* without flats or sharps, as the key of C major *b)* modified in pitch by the sign (♮) *c)* neither sharped nor flatted —*n.* **1** a person without normal intelligence; fool; idiot **2** [Informal] a person who is or seems to be naturally expert ☆**3** [Informal] a thing that is, or promises to be, immediately successful ☆**4** *Craps* a winning roll of 7 or 11 on a first throw **5** *Music a)* a sign (♮) used to remove the effect of a preceding sharp or flat within the measure in which it occurs (in full **natural sign**) *b)* the note so changed *c)* a white key on a piano —**SYN.** NORMAL —**nat′u·ral·ness** *n.*

☆**natural bridge** a natural rock formation suggestive of a bridge

Natural Bridge limestone formation in WC Va., over a tributary of the James River: 215 ft (66 m) high; span *c.* 90 ft (27.4 m)

natural childbirth childbirth involving little or no anesthesia, surgery, etc.

natural gas a mixture of gaseous hydrocarbons, chiefly methane, occurring naturally in the earth, often in association with petroleum deposits, and piped to cities, factories, etc., to be used as a fuel

natural history the study of zoology, botany, mineralogy, geology, and other subjects dealing with the physical world, esp. in a popular way

nat·u·ral·ism (nach′ər əl iz′əm, nach′rə liz′-) *n.* **1** action or thought based on natural desires or instincts **2** *Art, Literature, etc. a)* faithful adherence to nature; realism; specif., the principles and methods of a group of 19th-cent. writers, including Émile Zola, Gustave Flaubert, and Guy de Maupassant, who believed that the writer or artist should apply scientific objectivity and precision in observing and depicting life, without idealizing, imposing value judgments, or avoiding what may be regarded as sordid or repulsive *b)* the quality resulting from the use of such realism **3** *Ethics* the theory that distinctions between good and bad can be reduced to nonnormative or factual terms and statements, according to psychology, biology, etc. **4** *Philos.* the belief that the natural world, as explained by scientific laws, is all that exists and that there is no supernatural or spiritual creation, control, or significance **5** *Theol.* the doctrine that religion does not depend on supernatural experience, divine revelation, etc., and that all religious truth may be derived from the natural world

nat·u·ral·ist (nach′ər əl ist, -rə list) *n.* ⟦Fr *naturaliste*⟧ **1** a person who studies nature, esp. by direct observation of animals and plants **2** a person who believes in or practices naturalism in any form —*adj.* NATURALISTIC

nat·u·ral·is·tic (nach′ər əl is′tik, nach′rə lis′-) *adj.* **1** of natural history or naturalists **2** of or characterized by naturalism in any form **3** in accordance with, or in imitation of, nature; lifelike —**nat′u·ral·is′ti·cal·ly** *adv.*

nat·u·ral·ize (nach′ər əl īz′, nach′rə līz′) *vt.* **-ized′**, **-iz′ing** ⟦Fr *naturaliser*: see NATURAL & -IZE⟧ **1** to confer the rights of citizenship upon (an alien) **2** to adopt and make common (a custom, word, etc.) from another country or place **3** to adapt (a plant or animal) to a new environment; acclimate **4** to explain (occurrences) by natural law, rejecting supernatural influence **5** to make natural or less artificial; free from conventionality —*vi.* **1** to become naturalized, or as if native **2** to study nature —**nat′u·ral·i·za′tion** *n.*

natural law **1** rules of conduct supposedly inherent in the relations between human beings and discoverable by reason; law based upon an assumed innate moral sense **2** a law of nature: see LAW (sense 8*a*) **3** the laws of nature, collectively

natural logarithm a logarithm to the base *e*

nat·u·ral·ly (nach′ər əl ē, nach′rə lē) *adv.* **1** in a natural manner **2** by nature; innately **3** as one might expect; of course

natural number any positive integer, as 1, 2, 3, etc.

natural philosophy *former name for* NATURAL SCIENCE, esp. PHYSICAL SCIENCE

natural resource an actual or potential form of wealth supplied by nature, as coal, oil, water power, timber, arable land, etc.

natural science **1** the systematized knowledge of nature and the physical world, including zoology, botany, chemistry, physics, and geology **2** any of these branches of knowledge

natural selection in evolution, the process by which certain individuals of a species, having characters that help them adapt to their specific environment, tend to leave more progeny and transmit their characters, while other individuals of the same species, less able to adapt, tend to leave fewer progeny or to die out: over the course of generations, the gene pool of the species comes to reflect this adaptation: see also DARWINIAN THEORY

natural theology ⟦L *theologia naturalis*⟧ theology that seeks knowledge of God, the soul, immortality, and natural law through reason and the observation of natural processes

na·ture (nā′chər) *n.* ⟦OFr < L *natura* < *natus*, born, produced: see GENUS⟧ **1** the essential character of a thing; quality or qualities that make something what it is; essence **2** inborn character; innate disposition; inherent tendencies of a person **3** the vital functions, forces, and activities of the organs: often used as a euphemism **4** kind; sort; type [things of that *nature*] **5** any or all of the instincts, desires, appetites, drives, etc. of a person or animal **6** what is regarded as normal or acceptable behavior **7** the sum total of all things in time and space; the entire physical universe **8** [*sometimes* **N-**] the power, force, principle, etc. that seems to regulate the physical universe: often personified, sometimes as MOTHER NATURE **9** the primitive state of man **10** a simple way of life close to or in the outdoors [campers getting back to *nature*] **11** natural scenery, including the plants and animals that are part of it **12** [Archaic] affectionate or kindly feeling **13** *Theol.* the state of humanity viewed hypothetically as unredeemed by grace —**by nature** naturally; inherently —**in a state of nature** **1** completely naked **2** not cultivated or tamed; wild **3** uncivilized —**of (or in) the nature of** having the essential character of; like

-na·tured (nā′chərd) *combining form* having or showing a (specified kind of) nature, disposition, or temperament [good-*natured*]

nature study the study of plant and animal life by direct observation, esp. in an elementary, nontechnical manner

nature worship religious worship of natural forces, phenomena, etc.

na·tur·ism (nā′chər iz′əm) *n.* NUDISM —**na′tur·ist** *n.*

na·tur·o·path (nā′chər ə path′, nach′ər ə-) *n.* a person who practices naturopathy

na·tur·op·a·thy (nā′chər äp′ə thē) *n.* ⟦< NATURE + -O- + -PATHY⟧ a system of treating diseases, largely employing natural agencies, such as air, water, sunshine, etc., and rejecting the use of drugs and medicines —**na′tur·o·path′ic** (nā′chər ə path′ik, nach′ər ə-) *adj.*

Nau·cra·tis (nô′krə tis) ancient Greek city in the Nile delta

☆**Naug·a·hyde** (nôg′ə hīd′) ⟦arbitrary coinage⟧ *trademark for* a kind of imitation leather, used for upholstery, luggage, etc. —*n.* [**n-**] this material

naught (nôt) *pron.* ⟦ME < OE *nawiht* < *na* (see NO[1]) + *wiht* (see WIGHT[1], WHIT)⟧ nothing —*n.* **1** nothing **2** *alt. sp. of* NOUGHT —*adj.* [Obs.] **1** worthless; useless **2** wicked; evil —*adv.* [Archaic] not in the least [it matters *naught*] —**set at naught** [Archaic] to defy; scorn

naugh·ty (nôt′ē) *adj.* **-ti·er**, **-ti·est** ⟦ME *naugti*: see prec.; orig. senses: having *naught*, poor⟧ **1** [Obs.] wicked; bad; evil **2** not behaving properly; mischievous or disobedient: used esp. of children or their behavior **3** showing lack of decorum; improper, indelicate, or obscene —**SYN.** BAD[1] —**naugh′ti·ly** *adv.* —**naugh′ti·ness** *n.*

nau·ma·chi·a (nô mā′kē ə) *n.*, *pl.* **-chi·as** or **-chi·ae′** (-ē′) ⟦L < Gr *naus*, ship (see NAVY) + *machē*, battle⟧ **1** in ancient Rome, a mock or reenacted sea battle presented as a spectacle **2** a place constructed for this

nau·pli·us (nô′plē əs) *n.*, *pl.* **-pli·i′** (-ī′) ⟦L, kind of shellfish < Gr *nauplios*, kind of shellfish said to sail in its shell as in a ship < *naus*, ship (see NAVY) + *pleiein*, to sail⟧ the first larval stage in the development of certain crustaceans, typically unsegmented with only three pairs of appendages, all on the head, and an unpaired median eye

Na·u·ru (nä o͞o′ro͞o) country on an island in the W Pacific, just south of the equator: associated with the Commonwealth & formerly (1947-68) a United Nations trust territory: 8 sq mi (21 sq km)

nau·se·a (nô′zē ə, -sē ə; nô′zhə, -shə) *n.* ⟦L < Gr *nausia*, *nautia*, seasickness < *naus*, a ship, *nautēs*, sailor: see NAVY⟧ **1** a feeling of sickness in the stomach, with an impulse to vomit **2** disgust; loathing —**nau′se·ant** *adj.*, *n.*

nau·se·ate (nô′zē āt′, -sē-, -shē-, -zhē-) *vt.* **-at′ed**, **-at′ing** ⟦< L *nauseatus*, pp. of *nauseare*, to be seasick: see prec.⟧ **1** to cause to feel nausea; make sick **2** [Rare] to feel nausea at; loathe —*vi.* to feel nausea; become sick —**nau′se·at′ing·ly** *adv.* —**nau′se·a′tion** *n.*

nau·seous (nô′shəs, nô′zē əs) *adj.* ⟦L *nauseosus*⟧ **1** causing nausea; specif., *a)* sickening *b)* disgusting **2** feeling nausea; nauseated: usage still objected to by some —**nau′seous·ly** *adv.* —**nau′seous·ness** *n.*

Nau·sic·a·ä (nô sik′ā ə, -ē ə) *n.* in Homer's *Odyssey*, King Alcinoüs's daughter, who discovers and helps the shipwrecked Odysseus

naut *abbrev.* nautical

nautch (nôch) *n.* ⟦Hindi *nāc* < Prakrit *nacca* < Sans *nṛtya*, dancing < *nṛt*, to dance⟧ in India, a performance by professional dancing girls (**nautch girls**)

nau·ti·cal (nôt′i kəl) *adj.* ⟦Fr *nautique* < L *nauticus* < Gr *nautikos* < *nautēs*, sailor, seaman < *naus*, a ship: see NAVY⟧ of or having to do with sailors, ships, or navigation —**nau′ti·cal·ly** *adv.*

nautical mile any of various units of distance for sea and air navigation: in the U.S. since 1959, an international unit of length, equal to one minute of arc of a great circle of the earth or 6,076.12 feet or 1.1508 miles (1,852 meters or 1.852 kilometers): abbrev. *NM*

nau·ti·loid (nôt′'l oid′) *n.* ⟦< ModL *Nautiloidea*: see fol. & -OID⟧ any of a subclass (Nautiloidea) of cephalopods with chambered, coiled, or straight external shells: the nautiluses are the only remaining representatives

nau·ti·lus (nôt′'l əs) *n.*, *pl.* **-lus·es** or **-li′** (-ī′) ⟦ModL < L < Gr *nautilos*, sailor, nautilus < *naus*, a ship: see NAVY⟧ **1** any of two genera (*Nautilus* or *Allonautilus*) of tropical tetrabranchiate cephalopods having a many-chambered, spiral shell with a pearly interior **2** PAPER NAUTILUS —[**N-**] *trademark for* weight-lifting equipment utilizing a mechanical cam that varies the resistance of the weights in proportion to muscular strength

nautilus (sense 1)
(cross section)

nav *abbrev.* **1** naval **2** navigable **3** navigation **4** navigator

NAV *abbrev.* net asset value

Nav·a·jo (nav′ə hō′, nä′və hō′) *n.* ⟦Sp *Navajó*, shortened < *Apaches de Navajó*, lit., Apaches of *Navajó*, area of NW New Mexico < Tewa *navahu′*, arroyo with cultivated fields⟧ **1** *pl.* **-jos′**, **-jo′**, or **-joes′** a member of a North American Indian people living in Arizona, New Mexico, and Utah **2** the Athabaskan language of this people, a member of the Apache grouping Also sp. **Nav′a·ho′**

na·val (nā′vəl) *adj.* ⟦< Fr or L: Fr *naval* < L *navalis* < *navis*, a ship: see NAVY⟧ 1 [Now Rare] of or having to do with ships or shipping 2 of, having, characteristic of, or for a navy, its ships, personnel, etc.

na·va·rin (nȧ vȧ *ran′*) *n.* ⟦Fr⟧ a French stew made with mutton or lamb and onions, turnips, potatoes, and herbs

Na·varre (nə vär′) 1 historical region & former kingdom in NE Spain & SW France 2 region in NE Spain: 4,024 sq mi (10,422 sq km); cap. Pamplona Sp. name **Na·var·ra** (nä vär′rä)

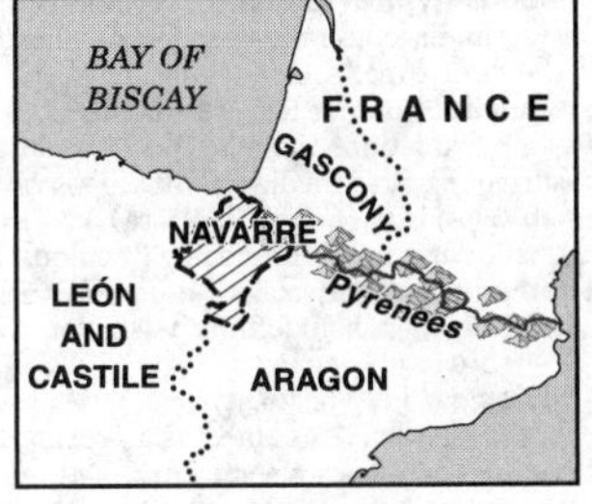

Navarre (sense 1)

nave[1] (nāv) *n.* ⟦ML *navis* < L, ship: see NAVY⟧ that part of some churches between the side aisles, extending from the chancel to the principal entrance, and forming the main part of the building

nave[2] (nāv) *n.* ⟦ME < OE *nafu*, akin to Ger *nabe*: see fol.⟧ the hub of a wheel

na·vel (nā′vəl) *n.* ⟦ME < OE *nafela*, akin to Ger *nabel* < IE base **ombh-*, **nōbh-*, navel > prec., L *umbilicus*, Gr *omphalos*⟧ 1 the small scar, usually a depression in the middle of the abdomen, marking the place where the umbilical cord was attached to the fetus; umbilicus 2 any centrally located point, part, or place

na·vel-gaz·ing (-gāz′iŋ) *n.* ⟦extended from orig. sense, the traditional meditative practice in some Eastern religions of contemplating one's navel as conducive to a trance⟧ [Informal] observation and analysis of oneself in a way regarded variously as pointless, tedious, self-indulgent, obsessive, etc. —**na′vel-gaz′er** *n.*

☆**navel orange** a seedless orange having at its apex a depression like a navel, containing a small, undeveloped secondary fruit

na·vic·u·lar (nə vik′yə lər) *adj.* ⟦LL *navicularis* < L *navicula*, dim. of *navis*, a ship: see NAVY⟧ shaped like a boat: said esp. of certain bones —*n.* any of various boat-shaped bones; esp., *a)* the outer bone of the first row of carpals in the wrist *b)* a bone on the inner side of the human foot, in front of the anklebone

navig *abbrev.* navigation

nav·i·ga·ble (nav′i gə bəl) *adj.* ⟦L *navigabilis* < *navigare*: see fol.⟧ 1 wide or deep enough, or free enough from obstructions, for the passage of ships [a *navigable* river] 2 that can be steered, or directed [a *navigable* balloon] —**nav′i·ga·bil′i·ty** *n.* —**nav′i·ga·bly** *adv.*

nav·i·gate (nav′ə gāt′) *vi.* **-gat′ed**, **-gat′ing** ⟦< L *navigatus*, pp. of *navigare*, to sail < *navis*, a ship (see NAVY) + *agere*, to lead, go (see ACT[1])⟧ 1 to steer, or direct, a ship or aircraft ☆2 to make one's way [to *navigate* through a crowded lobby] 3 [Rare] to travel by ship —*vt.* 1 to travel through or over (water, air, or land) in a ship or aircraft 2 to steer or direct (a ship or aircraft) 3 to plot the course for (a ship or aircraft) 4 to make one's way on or through, esp. in a skillful manner [to *navigate* rush-hour traffic, *navigate* the internet]

nav·i·ga·tion (nav′ə gā′shən) *n.* ⟦L *navigatio*⟧ 1 the act or practice of navigating 2 the science of locating the position and plotting the course of ships and aircraft 3 traffic by ship —**nav′i·ga′tion·al** *adj.* —**nav′i·ga′tion·al·ly** *adv.*

nav·i·ga·tor (nav′ə gāt′ər) *n.* 1 a person who navigates; esp., one skilled or employed in plotting the course for a ship or aircraft 2 an explorer 3 [Brit.] NAVVY

nav·vy (nav′ē) *n., pl.* **-vies** ⟦by shortening of prec. in sense "laborer digging a canal" < NAVIGATION in dial. sense "artificial waterway"⟧ [Brit.] an unskilled laborer, as on canals, roads, etc.

na·vy (nā′vē) *n., pl.* **-vies** ⟦ME *navie* < OFr < VL **navia* < L *navis*, a ship < IE base **nāus*, boat (prob. dugout) > Sans *nāuh*, boat, Gr *naus*, ship, ON *nōr*, ship⟧ 1 [Archaic] a fleet of ships 2 all the warships of a nation 3 [*often* **N-**] the entire military sea force of a nation, including vessels, personnel, stores, shipyards, etc. 4 NAVY BLUE

☆**navy bean** ⟦from common use in the U.S. *Navy*⟧ a small, white variety of kidney bean, dried for use as a food

navy blue ⟦from the color of the uniform of the Brit *navy*⟧ very dark, purplish blue

☆**Navy Cross** a U.S. military decoration awarded to members of the Navy, Marine Corps, or Coast Guard for extraordinary heroism in action

navy yard a shipyard for building and repairing naval ships, storing naval supplies, etc.

naw (nô) *adv., interj. phonetic sp. of* NO[1] (in dial. or informal pronunciation): a negative reply

na·wab (nə wäb′, -wôb′) *n.* ⟦Urdu *nawwāb*: see NABOB⟧ *var. of* NABOB (sense 1)

Nax·çi·van (näkh chē vän′) 1 autonomous republic of Azerbaijan, geographically separated from the rest of the country by Armenia: 2,120 sq mi (5,491 sq km) 2 its capital

Nax·os (naks′äs′; *Gr* näks′ôs′) largest island of the Cyclades, in the SC Aegean: *c.* 170 sq mi (440 sq km)

nay (nā) *adv.* ⟦ME < ON *nei* < *ne*, not + *ei*, ever: see AYE[1]⟧ 1 no: now seldom used except in voting by voice 2 not that only, but also: used to reinforce a statement [I permit, *nay*, encourage it] —*n.* 1 a refusal or denial 2 a negative vote or a person voting in the negative 3 a negative answer —**say someone nay** to refuse or forbid

Na·ya·rit (nä′yä rēt′) state of W Mexico: 10,665 sq mi (27,622 sq km); cap. Tepic

nay·say·er (nā′sā′ər) *n.* ⟦NAY + SAY + -ER⟧ one who opposes, refuses, or denies, esp. habitually

nay·say·ing (nā′sā′iŋ) *n.* the act or an instance of opposing, refusing, or denying —*adj.* that opposes, refuses, etc., esp. habitually

Naz·a·rene (naz′ə rēn′, naz′ə rēn′) *adj.* ⟦ME *Nazaren* < LL(Ec) *Nazarenus* < Gr(Ec) *Nazarēnos*, the Nazarene⟧ of Nazareth or its people or culture —*n.* 1 a person born or living in Nazareth 2 a member of an early sect of Christians of Jewish origin who continued to observe much of the Mosaic law ☆3 a member of the Church of the Nazarene, a Protestant sect 4 [Obs.] a Christian: term formerly used by Muslims, Jews, etc. —**the Nazarene** Jesus

Naz·a·reth (naz′ə rəth) ⟦Heb *natzērath*⟧ town in Galilee, N Israel, where Jesus lived as a child

Naz·a·rite or **Naz·i·rite** (naz′ə rīt′) *n.* ⟦LL(Ec) *Nazaraeus* < Gr(Ec) *Naz-araios*, for Heb *nāzīr* < *nāzar*, to separate, consecrate⟧ among the ancient Hebrews, a person who vowed to abstain from wine, leave the hair uncut, and avoid touching a corpse

Na·zi (nät′sē, nat′-) *adj.* ⟦Ger < *Nati(onalsozialistische Deutsche Arbeiterpartei)*, party name⟧ designating, of, or characteristic of the German fascist political party (*National Socialist German Workers' Party*), founded in 1919 and abolished in 1945: under Hitler it seized control of Germany in 1933, systematically eliminated opposition, and initiated a program of nationalism, rearmament, political aggression, and racism, esp. anti-Semitism —*n.* 1 a member of this party 2 [*often* **n-**] *a)* a supporter of this or any similar party; fascist *b)* loosely, someone regarded as thinking or acting like a Nazi —**Na′zism′** (-siz′əm) *n.*, **Na′zi·ism′** (-sē iz′əm)

Na·zi·fy (-sə fī′) *vt.* **-fied′**, **-fy′ing** [*also* **n-**] to cause to be a Nazi or like the Nazis —**Na′zi·fi·ca′tion** *n.*

Nb[1] *abbrev. Bible* Numbers

Nb[2] *Chem. symbol for* niobium

NB *abbrev.* 1 New Brunswick: also **N.B.** 2 ⟦L *nota bene*⟧ note well: also **n.b.**

NBA *abbrev.* 1 *service mark* National Basketball Association 2 National Book Awards 3 *service mark* National Boxing Association

NBC *service mark* National Broadcasting Company

NbE *abbrev.* north by east

NBS *abbrev.* National Bureau of Standards

NbW *abbrev.* north by west

nc *abbrev.* no charge

NC *abbrev.* 1 New Caledonia 2 North Carolina: also **N.C.**

NCAA *abbrev.* National Collegiate Athletic Association

NCC *abbrev.* National Council of Churches

NCO *abbrev.* noncommissioned officer

☆**NC-17** (en′sē′sev′ən tēn′) *trademark* a film rating meaning "no children under seventeen admitted"

NCTE *abbrev.* National Council of Teachers of English

Nd *Chem. symbol for* neodymium

ND or **N.D.** *abbrev.* North Dakota: also **N Dak**

n.d. *abbrev.* no date

N'Dja·me·na (ən jä′mə nə) capital of Chad, on the Shari river

Ne[1] *abbrev. Bible* Nehemiah

Ne[2] *Chem. symbol for* neon

NE *abbrev.* 1 Naval Engineer 2 Nebraska 3 New England 4 northeast 5 northeastern

né or **ne** (nā) *adj.* ⟦Fr, pp. of *naître*, to be born: see NEE⟧ born: used before the original name of a man who has changed his name, assumed a pseudonym, etc. [George Orwell *né* Eric Blair]

ne- (nē) *combining form* NEO-: used before a vowel

NEA *abbrev.* 1 National Education Association 2 National Endowment for the Arts

Neal (nēl) *n.* ⟦ME *Nel, Neel, Nele*, prob. < Ir *Niul* (Gael *Niall*) < *niadh*, a champion⟧ a masculine name

Ne·an·der·thal (nē an′dər thôl′, -täl′) *adj.* ⟦name of the place in the Rhine Province of Germany where the remains were first found < *Neander*, after Joachim *Neander* (1650-80), Ger hymn writer + Ger *thal, tal*, valley, akin to DALE⟧ 1 designating or of a widespread form of early human being (*Homo sapiens neanderthalensis*) of the Upper Pleistocene: see MOUSTERIAN 2 *a)* crude or primitive *b)* reactionary; regressive —*n.* 1 a Neanderthal human being 2 a person regarded as crude, primitive, reactionary, etc. Often, for *adj.* 1 & *n.* 1, **Ne·an′der·tal′** (-täl′)

neap[1] (nēp) *adj.* ⟦ME *neep* < OE *nep-* in *nepflod*, neap tide⟧ designating a type of tide that occurs after the first and third quarters of the lunar month: at these times the high tides are lower and the low tides are higher than the corresponding tides during SPRING TIDE, because of the gravitational effects of the right-angled alignment of the moon, earth, and sun —*n.* neap tide

neap[2] (nēp) *n.* ⟦prob. < ON, as in Norw dial. *neip*, forked pole⟧ [Dial.] the tongue of a wagon drawn by two animals

Ne·a·pol·i·tan (nē′ə päl′ə tən) *adj.* ⟦L *Neapolitanus* < *Neapolites*, a citizen of Naples < *Neapolis*, Naples < Gr, lit., new town⟧ of Naples or its people —*n.* a person born or living in Naples

☆**Neapolitan ice cream** brick ice cream consisting of several flavors and colors in layers, now typically chocolate, strawberry, and vanilla

near (nir) *adv.* ⟦ME *nere* < ON & OE: ON *nær*, near (orig. compar. of *nā-*):

OE *near*, nearer, compar. of *neah*, NIGH⟧ **1** at or to a relatively short distance in space or time [summer draws *near*] **2** relatively close in degree; almost: now usually *nearly* [*near* right] **3** closely; intimately **4** [Archaic] in a stingy manner —*adj.* **1** close in distance or time; not far **2** close in relationship; akin **3** close in feelings, desires, etc.; close in friendship **4** *a)* close in degree; narrow [a *near* escape] *b)* almost happening [a *near* accident] **5** on the left side, facing forward: said of an animal in double harness, a wagon wheel, etc.: opposed to OFF[1] **6** short or direct [take the *near* way] **7** [Archaic] stingy; niggardly **8** somewhat resembling; approximating [a *near* likeness] —*prep.* at a relatively short distance from in space, time, degree, etc.; close to [towns *near* the border, the hours *near* midnight] — *vt., vi.* to come or draw near (to); approach —**near at hand** very close in time or space —**near′ness** *n.*

☆**near beer** a malt beverage resembling beer but containing no alcohol or no more than a mandated low percentage of alcohol

near·by (nir′bī′) *adj., adv.* near; close at hand

Ne·arc·tic (nē ärk′tik, -är′-) *adj.* ⟦NE(O)- + ARCTIC⟧ designating or of the biogeographic realm that includes the arctic and temperate parts of North America and Greenland

near-death experience (nir′deth′) a set of experiences reportedly felt by many persons who were near death and subsequently resuscitated, typically involving, variously, a feeling of out-of-body awareness, a bright light, a blissful vision of an afterlife, etc.

Near East **1** countries near the E end of the Mediterranean, including those of SW Asia, the Arabian Peninsula, & NE Africa **2** [Historical] the lands occupied by the former Ottoman Empire, including the Balkans —**Near Eastern**

near·er (nir′ər) *adv., adj. compar. of* NEAR —*prep.* less distant from; closer to [a planet *nearer* the sun]

near·est (nir′ist) *adv., adj. superl. of* NEAR —*prep.* least distant from; closest to [the planet *nearest* the sun]

near·ly (nir′lē) *adv.* **1** almost; not quite; all but [*nearly* finished] **2** [Now Rare] closely; intimately [to be *nearly* related] **3** [Archaic] parsimoniously; stingily —**not nearly** not at all; far from

near miss **1** a shell, aerial bomb, etc. that does not score a direct hit on the target but comes close enough to inflict some damage **2** any result that is nearly but not quite successful **3** a narrowly averted collision; a near escape

near·sight·ed (nir′sīt′id) *adj.* having better vision for near objects than for distant ones; myopic —**near′sight′ed·ly** *adv.* —**near′sight′ed·ness** *n.*

near-term (nir′tʉrm′) *adj.* of or for the immediate future

neat[1] (nēt) *adj.* ⟦Fr *net* < L *nitidus*, shining, elegant, smart, trim < *nitere*, to shine < IE base **nei-*, to be active, shine > MIr *nīam*, luster, beauty⟧ **1** unmixed with anything; undiluted; straight: said esp. of liquor drunk without a mixer or chaser **2** [Rare] free of deductions; net **3** *a)* clean and in good order; trim; tidy *b)* characterized by tidiness, skill, and precision [a *neat* worker] *c)* without anything superfluous; simple **4** well-proportioned; shapely **5** cleverly or smartly phrased or done ☆**6** [Slang] nice, pleasing, fine, etc.: a generalized term of approval —**neat′ly** *adv.* —**neat′ness** *n.*

neat[2] (nēt) *n., pl.* **neat** ⟦ME *nete* < OE *neat* (akin to ON *naut*, Du *noot*) < base of *neotan*, to enjoy, possess < IE base **neud-*, to make use of > Lith *naudà*, benefit, possessions⟧ [Now Rare] a bovine animal; ox, cow, etc.

neat·en (nēt′'n) *vt.* ⟦NEAT[1] + -EN⟧ to make neat; cause to be clean, tidy, orderly, or trim: often with *up*

'neath or **neath** (nēth) *prep.* [Old Poet.] *short for* BENEATH

neat·herd (nēt′hʉrd′) *n.* ⟦ME *netherd*: see NEAT[2] & HERD[2]⟧ *rare var. of* COWHERD

neat's-foot oil (nēts′foot′) a light-yellow oil obtained by boiling the feet and shinbones of cattle, used mainly as a dressing for leather: also written **neats′foot′ oil**

neb (neb) *n.* ⟦ME < OE *nebb*, akin to MDu *nebbe*, ON *nef*⟧ [Now Dial., Chiefly Brit.] **1** *a)* the bill of a bird *b)* the snout of an animal **2** the nose or mouth of a person **3** a projecting end or point; nib; tip

Neb *abbrev.* Nebraska

NEB *abbrev.* New English Bible

☆**neb·bish** (neb′ish) *n.* ⟦< Yiddish *nebekh*, pity, pitiably⟧ [Slang] a person regarded as, variously, pitifully inept, ineffective, shy, dull, etc. —**neb′bish·y** *adj.*

NEbE *abbrev.* northeast by east

NEbN *abbrev.* northeast by north

Ne·bo (nē′bō′), **Mount** *Bible* mountain from which Moses saw the Promised Land; summit Pisgah (Deut. 34:1)

Nebr *abbrev.* Nebraska

Ne·bras·ka (nə bras′kə) ⟦< Omaha (a Siouan language) *nibdhathka*, lit., flat river, flat water, name for the PLATTE River⟧ Midwestern state of the NC U.S.: admitted 1867; 76,872 sq mi (199,099 sq km); cap. Lincoln: abbrev. *NE, Neb,* or *Nebr*

Ne·bras·kan (-kən) *adj.* of Nebraska: usually used in the predicate —*n.* a person born or living in Nebraska

neb·u·chad·nez·zar (neb′yə kəd nez′ər, neb′ə-) *n.* ⟦after fol.⟧ [*sometimes* **N-**] *Winemaking* the largest type of wine bottle, esp. one for champagne, holding about 15 liters

Neb·u·chad·nez·zar (neb′yə kəd nez′ər, neb′ə-) ⟦ult. < Akkadian *Nabū-kudur-uṣur*⟧ died 562 B.C.; king of Babylonia (605?-562), who conquered Jerusalem, destroyed the Temple, & deported many Jews into Babylonia (586 B.C.): see 2 Kings 24; Dan. 1-4: also **Neb′u·chad·rez′zar** (-rez′ər)

neb·u·la (neb′yə lə) *n., pl.* **-lae′** (-lē′) or **-las** ⟦ModL < L, vapor, fog, mist < IE base **nebh-*, moist, vapor, cloud > Gr *nephos, nephelē*, cloud, OE *nifol*, mist, darkness⟧ **1** a cloud of interstellar gas or dust: formerly, applied to any hazy, distant celestial object, as a star cluster or an external galaxy **2** *Med. a)* a small, cloudy opacity on the cornea *b)* a liquid preparation used as a spray

neb·u·lar (neb′yə lər) *adj.* of or having to do with a nebula or nebulae

nebular hypothesis any of several hypotheses about the origin of the solar system, based on the theory that the sun and the planets formed at about the same time from a nebula

neb·u·lize (neb′yə līz′) *vt.* **-lized′**, **-liz′ing** ⟦< L *nebula*, mist (see NEBULA) + -IZE⟧ **1** to reduce (a liquid) to a fine spray **2** to spray (a diseased or injured surface) with a medicated liquid —**neb′u·li·za′tion** *n.* —**neb′u·liz′er** *n.*

neb·u·los·i·ty (neb′yə läs′ə tē) *n.* ⟦Fr *nébulosité* < LL *nebulositas*⟧ **1** the quality or condition of being nebulous **2** *pl.* **-ties** NEBULA (*n.* 1)

neb·u·lous (neb′yə ləs) *adj.* ⟦ME *nebulus* < L *nebulosus*⟧ **1** NEBULAR **2** unclear; vague; indefinite Also **neb′u·lose′** (-lōs′) —**neb′u·lous·ly** *adv.* —**neb′u·lous·ness** *n.*

nec·es·sar·i·ly (nes′ə ser′ə lē, nes′ə ser′-) *adv.* **1** because of necessity; by or of necessity **2** as a necessary result; inevitably

nec·es·sar·y (nes′ə ser′ē) *adj.* ⟦ME < L *necessarius* < *necesse*, unavoidable, necessary < *ne-*, not + *cedere*, to give way: see CEDE⟧ **1** that cannot be dispensed with; essential; indispensable [the nutriments *necessary* to life] **2** resulting from necessity; inevitable [a *necessary* result] **3** *a)* that must be done; mandatory; not voluntary *b)* not free to choose; compelled by circumstances [a *necessary* agent] **4** inherent in the situation; undeniable; unavoidable from the premises **5** [Archaic] rendering some essential and intimate service —*n., pl.* **-sar′ies** **1** a necessary thing; thing essential to life, some purpose, etc.: *often used in pl.* **2** [Dial.] a privy or toilet **3** [*pl.*] *Law* those things essential to maintaining a dependent or incompetent in comfort and well-being —***SYN.*** ESSENTIAL

necessary condition **1** *Logic* an antecedent whose denial entails the denial of the consequent **2** something that must exist or occur if something else is to exist or occur Cf. SUFFICIENT CONDITION

necessary evil something undesirable that nevertheless must be tolerated in order to attain a desired end

ne·ces·si·tar·i·an·ism (nə ses′ə ter′ē ən iz′əm) *n.* the theory that every event, including any action of the human will, is the necessary result of a sequence of causes; determinism —**ne·ces′si·tar′i·an** *n., adj.*

ne·ces·si·tate (nə ses′ə tāt′) *vt.* **-tat′ed**, **-tat′ing** ⟦< ML *necessitatus*, pp. of *necessitare* < L *necessitas*, necessity⟧ **1** to make (something) necessary or unavoidable; involve or imply as a necessary condition, outcome, etc. **2** [Now Rare] to compel; require; force [he was *necessitated* to agree] —**ne·ces′si·ta′tion** *n.*

ne·ces·si·tous (-təs) *adj.* ⟦Fr *nécessiteux*: see fol. & -OUS⟧ **1** in great need; destitute; needy **2** that is necessary or essential **3** calling for action; urgent —**ne·ces′si·tous·ly** *adv.* —**ne·ces′si·tous·ness** *n.*

ne·ces·si·ty (-tē) *n., pl.* **-ties** ⟦ME *necessite* < OFr *nécessité* < L *necessitas* < *necesse*: see NECESSARY⟧ **1** the power of natural law that cannot be other than it is; natural causation; physical compulsion placed on man by nature; fate **2** anything that is inevitable, unavoidable, etc. as a result of natural law; that which is necessary in natural sequence **3** *a)* the compulsion or constraint of man-made circumstances, habit, custom, law, etc.; logical or moral conditions making certain actions inevitable or obligatory [faced by the *necessity* to earn a living] *b)* what is required by this social or legal compulsion **4** great or imperative need **5** something that cannot be done without; necessary thing: *often used in pl.* **6** the state or quality of being necessary **7** [Now Rare] want; poverty —***SYN.*** NEED —**of necessity** necessarily; inevitably

Nech·es (nech′iz) ⟦prob. < AmInd tribal name⟧ river in E Tex., flowing southeast into Sabine Lake: 280 mi (451 km): see SABINE[2]

neck (nek) *n.* ⟦ME *nekke* < OE *hnecca*, akin to Ger *nacken* < IE base **ken-*, to bend, squeeze > NOOK, NUT⟧ **1** that part of a human or animal joining the head to the body, including the part of the backbone between the skull and the shoulders **2** a narrow part between the head, or end, and the body, or base, of any object [the *neck* of a violin, the *neck* of a goblet] **3** that part of a garment which covers, encircles, or is nearest the neck **4** the narrowest part of any object, considered to be like a neck; specif., *a)* a narrow strip of land *b)* the narrowest part of an organ [the *neck* of the uterus, the *neck* of a tooth] *c)* the narrowest or tapering part of a bottle, vase, etc. *d)* a strait or channel **5** *Geol.* a vertical column of hardened igneous rock, formerly plugging a volcanic conduit and later exposed by erosion and weathering —☆*vi.* [Slang] to engage in amorous kissing, hugging, and caressing —**break one's neck** [Informal] to try very hard —☆**get it in the neck** [Slang] to be severely reprimanded or punished —**neck and crop** completely; entirely —**neck and neck** ⟦from use in horse racing to describe horses running side by side⟧ even or nearly even during the course of a race or competition [the candidates are *neck and neck* in the polls] —**neck of the woods** ☆[Informal] a region or locality [not from this *neck of the woods*] —**risk one's neck** to put one's life, career, reputation, etc. in danger —**stick one's neck out** [Informal] to expose oneself to possible failure, ridicule, loss, etc. by taking a chance —**win** (or **lose**) **by a neck** **1** *Horse Racing* to win (or lose) by the length of a horse's head and neck **2** to win (or lose) any contest by a narrow margin —**neck′er** *n.*

neck·band (nek′band′) *n.* **1** a band worn around the neck **2** the part of a garment that encircles the neck, esp., the part to which the collar is fastened

neck·cloth (-klôth′, -kläth′) *n.* [Archaic] CRAVAT

Neck·er (nā ker′; *E* nek′ər), **Jacques** (zhäk) 1732-1804; Fr. statesman & financier, born in Switzerland: father of Madame de Stäel

neck·er·chief (nek′ər chif, -chēf′) *n.* ⟦ME *nekkyrchefe*: see NECK & KERCHIEF⟧ a handkerchief or scarf worn around the neck

neck·ing (nek′iŋ) *n.* **1** *Archit.* any small molding around the top of a column below the capital ☆**2** ⟦see NECK, *vi.*⟧ [Slang] the act of kissing and caressing passionately

neck·lace (nek′lis) *n.* ⟦NECK + LACE⟧ **1** a string of beads, jewels, etc. or a chain of gold, silver, etc., worn around the neck as an ornament **2** a gasoline-doused automobile tire draped around a person's neck or shoulders and set ablaze —*vt.* **-laced, -lac·ing** to kill by means of a NECKLACE (*n.* 2)

neck·line (-līn′) *n.* the edge of the neck opening of a garment, specif. with regard to its shape or position at the front of the neck or at the bosom [a blouse with a low *neckline*]

neck·piece (-pēs′) *n.* a decorative scarf, esp. of fur

☆**neck-rein** (-rān′) *vi.* to go to the right if the left rein is lightly pressed against the neck or to the left if the right rein is so pressed: said of a saddle horse —*vt.* to guide (a horse) by such pressure of the reins

neck·tie (-tī′) *n.* **1** a band worn around the neck under a collar and tied in front as a four-in-hand or in a bow **2** a decorative piece of cloth clipped onto the collar to resemble this

☆**necktie party** [Slang] a hanging; esp., a lynching

neck·wear (-wer′) *n.* articles worn about the neck, as neckties or scarves

nec·ro- (nek′rō, -rə) ⟦< Gr *nekros*, dead body < IE base **nek-*, physical death, corpse > L *nex*, death, *nocere*, to injure, *necare*, to kill⟧ *combining form* **1** death [*necrology*] **2** corpse, dead tissue [*necrophagia*] Also, before a vowel, **necr-**

nec·ro·bi·o·sis (nek′rō bī ō′sis) *n.* ⟦ModL < prec. + -BIOSIS⟧ the process of decay and death of tissue cells

ne·crol·a·try (ne kräl′ə trē, nə-) *n.* ⟦NECRO- + -LATRY⟧ worship of, or excessive reverence for, the dead

ne·crol·o·gy (-ə jē) *n., pl.* **-gies** ⟦ModL *necrologium*: see NECRO- & -LOGY⟧ **1** a list of people who have died within a certain period, as that in a newspaper **2** a death notice; obituary —**nec·ro·log·i·cal** (nek′rə läj′i kəl) *adj.* —**nec′ro·log′i·cal·ly** *adv.* —**ne·crol′o·gist** *n.*

nec·ro·man·cy (nek′rə man′sē) *n.* ⟦ME *nigromancie* < OFr *nigromance* < ML *nigromantia* (altered by assoc. with L *niger*, black) < L *necromantia* < Gr *nekromanteia* < *nekros*, corpse (see NECRO-) + *manteia*, divination: see -MANCY⟧ **1** in some occult and religious beliefs, divination by means of communication with the spirits of deceased persons **2** black magic; sorcery —**nec′ro·man′cer** *n.* —**nec′ro·man′tic** *adj.*

nec·ro·pha·gi·a (nek′rə fā′jē ə) *n.* ⟦ModL: see NECRO- & -PHAGY⟧ the eating of dead bodies; esp., the practice of feeding on carrion —**ne·croph·a·gous** (ne kräf′ə gəs) *adj.*

nec·ro·phil·i·a (-fil′ē ə) *n.* ⟦NECRO- + -PHILIA⟧ an abnormal fascination with death and the dead; esp., an erotic attraction to corpses: also **ne·croph·i·lism** (ne kräf′ə liz′əm) —**nec′ro·phile′** (-fīl′) *n.* —**nec′ro·phil′i·ac′** *adj., n.*

nec·ro·pho·bi·a (nek′rə fō′bē ə) *n.* ⟦NECRO- + -PHOBIA⟧ an abnormal fear of death or of dead bodies —**nec′ro·pho′bic** *adj.*

ne·crop·o·lis (ne kräp′ə lis, nə-) *n., pl.* **-lis·es** or **-leis′** (-līs′) ⟦Gr *nekropolis* < *nekros* (see NECRO-) + *polis*, city: see POLICE⟧ a cemetery, esp. one belonging to an ancient city

nec·rop·sy (ne′kräp sē) *n., pl.* **-sies** ⟦see NECRO- & -OPSIS⟧ an examination of a dead body; postmortem: also **ne·cros·co·py** (ne kräs′kə pē)

ne·cro·sis (ne krō′sis, nə-) *n., pl.* **-ses′** (-sēz′) ⟦ModL < LL, a killing < Gr *nekrōsis* < *nekroun*, to make dead, mortify < *nekros*, dead body: see NECRO-⟧ **1** the death or decay of tissue in a particular part of the body, as from loss of blood supply, burning, etc. **2** *Bot.* death of plant tissue, as from disease, frost, etc. —**ne·crose** (ne krōs′, ne′krōs′) *vt., vi.* **-crosed′, -cros′ing** —**ne·crot′ic** (-krät′ik) *adj.*

nec·ro·tiz·ing (nek′rə tīz′iŋ) *adj.* ⟦< *necrotize*, to be affected by necrosis < prec. + -IZE⟧ of or having to do with necrosis

ne·crot·o·my (ne krät′ə mē) *n., pl.* **-mies** ⟦NECRO- + -TOMY⟧ **1** the dissection of corpses **2** the surgical removal of dead bone

nec·tar (nek′tər) *n.* ⟦L < Gr *nektar* < ? base of *necros*, dead body (see NECRO-) + *tar*, who overcomes (akin to Sans *tarati*, he overcomes): hence, death-overcoming: the drink was held to confer immortality⟧ **1** *Class. Myth.* the drink of the gods **2** any very delicious beverage **3** *Bot.* the sweetish liquid in many flowers, used by bees for the making of honey —**nec·tar′e·an** (-ter′ē ən) *adj.*, **nec·tar′e·ous** (-ter′ē əs), or **nec′tar·ous**

nec·tar·ine (nek′tə rēn′, nek′tə rēn′) *n.* ⟦< obs. adj., of, like, as sweet as prec.⟧ a naturally mutated variety (*Prunus persica* var. *nectarina*) of peach, having a smooth skin without down

nec·ta·ry (nek′tər ē) *n., pl.* **-ries** ⟦ModL *nectarium*⟧ an organ or part, esp. of a flower, that secretes nectar —**nec·tar′i·al** (-ter′ē əl) *adj.*

Ned (ned) *n.* ⟦by faulty division of *mine Ed*⟧ a masculine name: see EDGAR[1], EDMUND, EDWARD[1]

NED *abbrev.* New English Dictionary: orig. name of *The Oxford English Dictionary*

Ne·der·land (nā′dər länt′) *Du. name for* the NETHERLANDS

nee or **née** (nā; *now often* nē) *adj.* ⟦Fr, fem. of *né*, pp. of *naître* < L *nasci*, to be born: see GENUS⟧ born: used to indicate the maiden name of a married woman [Mrs. Helen Jones, *nee* Smith]

need (nēd) *n.* ⟦ME *nede* < OE *nied*, akin to Ger *not*, Goth *nauths* < IE **neuti-* < base **neu-*, to collapse with weariness > Welsh *newyn*, starvation⟧ **1** necessity or obligation created by some situation [no *need* to worry] **2** a lack of something useful, required, or desired [to have *need* of a rest] **3** something useful, required, or desired that is lacking; want; requirement [list your daily *needs*] **4** *a)* a condition characterized by hardship or serious deficiency [flood victims in *need* of food and shelter] *b)* a condition of poverty, or extreme want —*vt.* to have need of; want or lack; require: *need* is often used as an auxiliary, either uninflected and followed by an infinitive without *to*, or inflected and followed by an infinitive with *to*, meaning "to be obliged, must" [he *need* not come, he *needs* to be careful] —*vi.* **1** to be necessary; chiefly in impersonal or subjunctive constructions [he *need* not worry] **2** to be in need See also NEEDS —**have need to** to be compelled or required to; must —**if need be** if it is required; if the occasion demands —**need′er** *n.*

SYN.—**need** refers to an urgent requirement of something essential or desirable that is lacking; **necessity**, a more formal word, suggests an imperative need for something indispensable but lacks the emotional connotations of **need** [they are in *need* of food, food is a *necessity* for all living things]; **exigency** refers to a necessity created by some emergency, crisis, or compelling circumstances [the *exigencies* created by the flood]; **requisite** applies to something that is indispensable to a particular end or goal [a sense of rhythm is a *requisite* in a dancer] See also **lack**

need·ful (nēd′fəl) *adj.* **1** necessary; needed; required **2** [Archaic] needy —**need′ful·ly** *adv.* —**need′ful·ness** *n.*

need·i·ness (nēd′ē nis) *n.* the state of being needy

nee·dle (nēd′'l) *n.* ⟦ME *nedle* < OE *nædl*, akin to Ger *nadel* < IE base **(s)nē-*, **(s)nēi-*, to sew, spin > SNOOD, L *nere*, Gr *nein*, to spin⟧ **1** *a)* a small, slender piece of steel with a sharp point at one end and a hole for thread at the other, used for sewing by hand or for surgical sutures *b)* a similar implement with a hole for thread near the pointed end, used esp. on sewing machines **2** *a)* a slender rod of steel, bone, wood, etc. with a hook at one end, used for crocheting *b)* a slender, pointed rod of wood, metal, plastic, etc., used in pairs for knitting **3** STYLUS (*n.* 3b) **4** a pointed instrument used in etching or engraving **5** *a)* the magnetized pointer of a compass *b)* the indicator or pointer of a speedometer or other gauge **6** the thin, short, pointed leaf of such trees as the pine, spruce, etc. **7** NEEDLE VALVE **8** *a)* the sharp, very slender metal tube at the end of a hypodermic syringe, that is introduced into the blood vessel, muscle, etc. ☆*b)* [Informal] a hypodermic injection *c)* any of various other slender, tubelike devices for inserting, as to inflate or inject **9** ELECTRIC NEEDLE **10** any object roughly resembling a needle or its point in shape, as the sharp point of some crystals, a narrow, pointed rock, an obelisk, spire, etc. —*vt.* **-dled, -dling 1** to sew, puncture, etc. with a needle **2** [Informal] *a)* to provoke into doing something; goad; prod *b)* to tease or heckle ☆**3** [Slang] to strengthen by adding alcohol [to *needle* beer] —*vi.* **1** to work with a needle; sew **2** to form needles in crystallization —☆**give someone the needle** [Slang] to goad or heckle —☆**on the needle** [Slang] addicted to narcotics —**nee′dle·like′** *adj.* —**nee′dler** *n.*

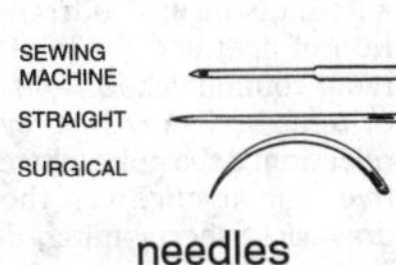

needles

nee·dle·fish (-fish′) *n., pl.* **-fish′** or **-fish′es** (see FISH) any of a family (Belonidae, order Atheriniformes) of elongated, voracious, marine bony fishes with long jaws and sharp, needlelike teeth

nee·dle·point (-point′) *n.* **1** embroidery done with wool thread on canvas, used for upholstery, decorative hangings, pillow covers, etc. **2** a kind of lace made on a paper pattern, with a needle instead of a bobbin: in full **needlepoint lace**

need·less (nēd′lis) *adj.* not needed; unnecessary —**need′less·ly** *adv.* —**need′less·ness** *n.*

needle valve a thin, tapered valve that is usually precisely set to control the flow of fluid through a cone-shaped opening: used esp. in carburetors

nee·dle·wom·an (nēd′'l woom′ən) *n., pl.* **-wom′en** (-wim′in) a woman who does needlework; esp., a seamstress

nee·dle·work (-wurk′) *n.* **1** work done with a needle, as embroidery, crocheting, or sewing **2** the art or practice of such work **3** anything made by such work, as embroidery or cross-stitch —**nee′dle·work′er** *n.*

need·n't (nēd′'nt) *contraction* need not; do not need to or does not need to

needs (nēdz) *adv.* ⟦ME *nedes* < OE *nedes, nydes* < *nied* (see NEED) + *-s*, gen. & adv. suffix⟧ of necessity; necessarily: with *must* [he must *needs* obey]

need·y (nēd′ē) *adj.* **need′i·er, need′i·est 1** in, or characterized by, need, or poverty; not having enough to live on; very poor **2** having or showing a need for affection, emotional support, etc.

neem (nēm) *n.* ⟦Hindi *nīm* < Sans *nimba*⟧ a tall, tropical evergreen tree (*Azadirachta indica*) of the mahogany family, cultivated, esp. in Asia, for its wood and aromatic oil (**neem oil**)

neep (nēp) *n.* ⟦ME *nepe* < OE *næp* < L *napus*, prob. < Gr *napy*, mustard⟧ [Brit. Dial.] a turnip

ne'er (ner) *adv.* [Old Poet.] never

ne'er-do-well (ner′do͞o wel′) *n.* a person who is lazy, idle, irresponsible, etc. —*adj.* lazy, idle, irresponsible, etc.

ne·far·i·ous (nə fer′ē əs) *adj.* ⟦L *nefarius* < *nefas*, crime, sin < *ne-*, not + *fas*, (divine) law, lawful⟧ very wicked; villainous; iniquitous —**ne·far′i·ous·ly** *adv.* —**ne·far′i·ous·ness** *n.*

Nef·er·ti·ti (nef′ər tē′tē) 14th cent. B.C.; queen of Egypt & wife of Ikhnaton: also **Nef′re·te′te** (-rə-)

Ne·fud (nə fo͞od′) *alt. sp. of* NAFUD
neg *abbrev.* **1** negative **2** negatively
ne·gate (ni gāt′) *vt.* **-gat′ed, -gat′ing** ⟦< L *negatus*: see fol.⟧ **1** to deny the existence or truth of **2** to nullify or make ineffective —**ne·ga′tor** *n.*, **ne·gat′er**
ne·ga·tion (ni gā′shən) *n.* ⟦< Fr or L: Fr *négation* < L *negatio* < *negatus*, pp. of *negare*, to deny < *neg(i)-* < *ne-* (see NO[1]) + **-g(h)-* < IE **ĝ(h)i*, intens. particle used after negation⟧ **1** the act or an instance of denying; negative answer; denial **2** the lack or opposite of some positive character or quality [death is the *negation* of life] **3** something negative; nonentity —**ne·ga′tion·al** *adj.*
neg·a·tive (neg′ə tiv) *adj.* ⟦ME *negatife* < OFr or L: OFr *négatif* < L *negativus* < *negatus*: see prec.⟧ **1** containing, expressing, or implying a denial or refusal; that says "no" [a *negative* reply] **2** opposite to something regarded as positive; specif., *a)* lacking in positive character or quality *b)* lacking evidence, affirmation, etc. *c)* having the effect of diminishing, depriving, or denying *d)* faultfinding, antagonistic, destructive, etc. [*negative* criticism, a *negative* political campaign] **3** *Biol.* directed away from the source of a stimulus [*negative* tropism] ☆**4** *Elec. a)* of, generating, or charged with negative electricity *b)* having an excess of electrons **5** *Logic* denying something about a subject ["no reptiles are warmblooded" is a *negative* proposition] **6** *Math.* designating a quantity less than zero, or one to be subtracted; minus quantity **7** *Med.* not having or not demonstrating, showing, or proving the presence or existence of a condition, infection, symptoms, bacteria, etc. [a patient who is *negative* for TB; the X-rays were *negative*] **8** *Optics* forming a VIRTUAL IMAGE by diverging light rays: said of a lens: distinguished from POSITIVE (*adj.* 17) **9** *Photog.* reversing the relation of light and shade of the subject — *adv., interj.* no; not so: used in radio communication —*n.* **1** a word, affix, phrase, etc. that denies, rejects, or refuses (Ex.: *no, not, by no means*) **2** a statement of denial, refusal, or rejection **3** the point of view that denies or attacks the positive or affirmative [the *negative* won the debate] **4** an undesirable element or quality; drawback, shortcoming, defect, etc. **5** an impression of something, as a sculpture, that shows it in reverse **6** [Obs.] the right of veto **7** *Elec.* a terminal, electrode, or plate having an excess of electrons flowing out toward a positive terminal, electrode, or plate, as in a storage battery or dry cell **8** *Math.* a quantity less than zero, or one to be subtracted; minus quantity **9** *Photog.* an exposed and developed photographic film or plate on which light and shadow are the reverse of what they are in the positive printed from this —*vt.* **-tived, -tiv·ing 1** *a)* to refuse; reject ☆*b)* to veto (a candidate, motion, or bill) **2** to deny; contradict **3** to prove false; disprove **4** to counteract; neutralize —*interj.* no! not so! —**in the negative 1** in refusal or denial of a plan, suggestion, etc. **2** with a denial or negative answer —**neg′a·tive·ly** *adv.* —**neg′a·tive·ness** *n.*, **neg′a·tiv′i·ty**
☆**negative electricity** the kind of electricity possessed by an object (as a piece of silk after it has been rubbed with a glass rod) having an excess of electrons: opposed to POSITIVE ELECTRICITY
☆**negative income tax** a proposed system of subsidy payments by the government to those whose annual income is below a certain level
negative sign the sign (-) used to indicate a negative quantity
neg·a·tiv·ism (neg′ə tiv iz′əm) *n.* **1** an attitude or system of thought characterized by doubt and question, rather than approval and acceptance **2** *Psychol.* an attitude characterized by ignoring, resisting, or opposing suggestions or orders coming from other people —**neg′a·tiv·ist** *n., adj.* —**neg′a·tiv·is′tic** *adj.*
neg·a·tron (neg′ə trän′) *n.* ⟦NEGA(TIVE) + (ELEC)TRON⟧ *Particle Physics* the ELECTRON, as distinguished from the positron
Neg·ev (neg′ev′) region in S Israel of partially reclaimed desert: *c.* 4,000 sq mi (10,360 sq km): also **Nég′eb′** (-eb′)
ne·glect (ni glekt′) *vt.* ⟦< L *neglectus*, pp. of *negligere, neglegere*, not to heed, be regardless of < *neg-* (see NEGATION) + *legere*, to gather (see LOGIC)⟧ **1** to ignore or disregard [to *neglect* the advice of others] **2** to fail to care for or attend to sufficiently or properly; slight [to *neglect* one's family] **3** to fail to carry out (an expected or required action) through carelessness or by intention; leave undone —*n.* **1** the action of neglecting **2** lack of sufficient or proper care; negligence; disregard **3** the state of being neglected —**ne·glect′er** *n.*, **ne·glec′tor**

SYN.—**neglect** implies a failure to carry out some expected or required action, either through carelessness or by intention [I *neglected* to wind the clock]; **omit**, in this connection, implies a neglecting through oversight, absorption, etc. [when in New York, one should not *omit* visiting the MOMA]; **overlook** suggests a failure to see or to take action, either inadvertently or indulgently [I'll *overlook* your rudeness this time]; **disregard** implies inattention or neglect, usually intentional [she always *disregards* his wishes]; **ignore** suggests a deliberate disregarding, sometimes through stubborn refusal to face the facts [but you *ignore* the necessity for action]; **slight** implies a disregarding or neglecting in an indifferent or disdainful way [that critic seems to *slight* newer writers]; **forget**, in this connection, implies an intentional disregarding or omitting [after his election, he *forgot* the wishes of the voters]

ne·glect·ful (ni glekt′fəl) *adj.* characterized by neglect; heedless; negligent: often with *of* —*SYN.* REMISS —**ne·glect′ful·ly** *adv.* —**ne·glect′ful·ness** *n.*
neg·li·gee (neg′lə zhā′, neg′lə zhā′) *n.* ⟦Fr *négligée*, fem. of *négligé*, pp. of *négliger*, to neglect < L *negligere*: see NEGLECT⟧ **1** a woman's thin, light, typically loosefitting dressing gown or, now, often, nightgown, usually decorative and of a soft, flowing material **2** any informal, careless, or incomplete attire
neg·li·gence (neg′lə jəns) *n.* ⟦ME *neglygence* < OFr *négligence* < L *negligentia*⟧ **1** the quality or condition of being negligent; specif., *a)* habitual failure to do the required thing *b)* carelessness in manner or appearance; indifference **2** an instance of such failure, carelessness, or indifference **3** *Law* failure to use a reasonable amount of care when such failure results in injury or damage to another
neg·li·gent (neg′lə jənt) *adj.* ⟦ME < OFr *négligent* < L *negligens*, prp. of *negligere*: see NEGLECT⟧ **1** habitually failing to do the required thing; neglectful **2** careless, lax, inattentive, or indifferent —*SYN.* REMISS —**neg′li·gent·ly** *adv.*
neg·li·gi·ble (neg′lə jə bəl) *adj.* ⟦< L *negligere* (see NEGLECT) + -IBLE⟧ that can be neglected or disregarded because small, unimportant, etc.; trifling —**neg′li·gi·bil′i·ty** *n.* —**neg′li·gi·bly** *adv.*
ne·go·tia·ble (ni gō′shə bəl, -shē ə bəl) *adj.* that can be negotiated; specif., *a)* legally transferable to another by endorsement or by proper delivery (said of promissory notes, checks, etc.) *b)* that can be passed, crossed, surmounted, etc. —**ne·go′tia·bil′i·ty** *n.*
ne·go·ti·ate (ni gō′shē āt′, -sē-) *vi.* **-at′ed, -at′ing** ⟦< L *negotiatus*, pp. of *negotiari*, to carry on business < *negotium*, business < *neg-*, not (see NEGATION) + *otium*, ease⟧ to confer, bargain, or discuss with a view to reaching agreement —*vt.* **1** to make arrangements for, settle, or conclude (a business transaction, treaty, etc.) **2** to transfer, assign, or sell (negotiable paper) **3** to succeed in crossing, surmounting, moving through, etc. [to *negotiate* the river rapids] —**ne·go′ti·a′tor** *n.* —**ne·go·ti·a·to·ry** (ni gō′shē ə tôr′ē; *often*, -sē ə tôr′ē) *adj.*
ne·go·ti·a·tion (ni gō′shē ā′shən, -sē-) *n.* ⟦L *negotiatio*⟧ **1** a negotiating **2** [*often pl.*] a conferring, discussing, or bargaining to reach agreement
Ne·gress (nē′gris) *n.* ⟦Fr *négresse*, fem. of *nègre* < Sp or Port *negro*, NEGRO[1]⟧ a black woman or girl
USAGE—now mostly a disparaging term, but still used descriptively within historical contexts: see also -ESS
Ne·gril·lo (nə gril′ō) *n., pl.* **-los** or **-loes** ⟦Sp, dim. of *negro*, NEGRO[1]⟧ a member of any of certain black African peoples of short stature; Pygmy
Ne·gri Sem·bi·lan (ne′grē sem bē′lən) state of Malaysia in W Peninsular Malaysia: 2,565 sq mi (6,643 sq km); cap. Seremban
Ne·gri·to (nə grēt′ō) *n., pl.* **-tos** or **-toes** ⟦Sp, dim. of *negro*, black, NEGRO[1]: in allusion to their small stature & dark skin⟧ a member of any of certain dark-skinned peoples of short stature living in Oceania and Southeast Asia
neg·ri·tude (neg′rə to͞od′, -tyo͞od′; nē′grə-) *n.* ⟦Fr *négritude* < *négre* (< Sp or Port *negro*, black person: see fol.) + *-i-* + *-tude* (see -TUDE): prob. coined (1939) by Aimé Césaire, Martinique poet⟧ [*also* **N-**] the consciousness in black people, esp. Africans, of their cultural heritage, together with an affirmation of the distinctive qualities and values of this heritage
Ne·gro[1] (nē′grō) *n., pl.* **-groes** ⟦Sp & Port *negro*, black, black person < L *niger*, black⟧ **1** a member of any of the indigenous dark-skinned peoples of Africa, living chiefly south of the Sahara **2** a person having some African ancestors; a black person —*adj.* of, relating to, or for Negroes
Ne·gro[2] (nā′grō; *Port* nā′gro͞o; *Sp* nā′grō) **1** river in N Brazil, flowing southeast into the Amazon, near Manaus: *c.* 1,400 mi (2,253 km) **2** river in SC Argentina, flowing east into the Atlantic: *c.* 700 mi (1,127 km)
Ne·groid (nē′groid′) *adj.* ⟦NEGRO[1] + -OID⟧ designating or of one of the major traditional geographic groupings of human beings, including the majority of the peoples of Africa, and peoples of Melanesia, New Guinea, etc. who are generally characterized by a dark skin, black, very curly hair, etc.: loosely called the *black race* See RACE[2] —*n.* a member of the Negroid population
Ne·gro·ni (nə grō′nē) *n.* ⟦It, said to be after C. *Negroni*, count in Florence who invented this combination of ingredients (early 1900s?)⟧ [*often* **n-**] a cocktail of gin, Campari, and sweet vermouth
Ne·gro·phobe (nē′grō fōb′) *n.* ⟦NEGRO[1] + -PHOBE⟧ [*sometimes* **n-**] a person who hates or fears blacks —**Ne′gro·pho′bi·a** (-fō′bē ə) *n.*
Ne·gros (nā′grōs′; *Sp* nā′grōs′) island of the central Philippines, between Cebu & Panay: 4,907 sq mi (12,709 sq km)
ne·gus (nē′gəs) *n.* ⟦after Col. Francis *Negus* (died 1732), who concocted it⟧ a hot beverage made from wine, hot water, and lemon juice, sweetened and spiced
Ne·gus (nē′gəs) *n.* ⟦Amharic *nĕgūš*, king⟧ [Historical] the title of the ruler of Ethiopia
NEH *abbrev.* National Endowment for the Humanities
Ne·he·mi·ah (nē′hi mī′ə, nē′ə-) *n.* ⟦Heb *nehemyāh*, lit., comfort of *Jah* (God)⟧ *Bible* **1** a Hebrew leader of *c.* 5th cent. B.C. **2** the book that tells of his work: abbrev. *Ne* or *Neh*
Neh·ru (nā′ro͞o), **Ja·wa·har·lal** (jə wä′hər läl′) 1889-1964; Indian nationalist leader in India's movement for independence: prime minister (1947-64)
neigh (nā) *vi.* ⟦ME *neyen* < OE *hnægan*, akin to MDu *neyen*, of echoic orig.⟧ to utter the loud, characteristic cry of a horse; whinny —*n.* this cry; a whinny
neigh·bor (nā′bər) *n.* ⟦ME *neighbour* < OE *neahgebur* (akin to Ger *nachbar*) < *neah* (see NIGH) + *gebur*, freeholder, peasant < *ge-*, with + *bur*, farmer < *buan*, to live, cultivate, akin to ON *bua*: see BONDAGE⟧ **1** a person who lives near oneself or another; specif., a person who lives in the same neighborhood as oneself or another **2** a person, country, or thing situated near

another 3 a fellow human being [love thy *neighbor*] 4 any person: used as a term of direct address —*adj.* nearby; adjacent: now rare except in the dial. or informal sense of "being a neighbor [chatting with a *neighbor* lady] —*vt.* 1 to live or be situated near (someone or something) 2 [Rare] to bring near or into close association with —*vi.* 1 to live or be situated nearby 2 to have friendly relations; associate on friendly terms (*with*) Brit. sp. **neighbour**

neigh·bor·hood (nā′bər ho͝od′) *n.* 1 [Archaic] friendly relations, as of neighbors; neighborliness 2 the state or quality of being neighbors 3 a community, district, or area, esp. with regard to some characteristic or point of reference [an old *neighborhood*] 4 the people living near one another [the whole *neighborhood* attended the block party] 5 *Math.* the set of all points which lie within a stated distance of a given point —☆**in the neighborhood of** [Informal] 1 near; close to (a place) 2 about; approximately (the age, amount, etc. specified)

neigh·bor·ing (nā′bər iŋ) *adj.* nearby; adjacent; close together; in the same region —**SYN.** ADJACENT

neigh·bor·ly (nā′bər lē) *adj.* like, characteristic of, or appropriate to neighbors; kind, friendly, sociable, etc. —**neigh′bor·li·ness** *n.*

Neil (nēl) *n.* a masculine name

Nei Mong·gol (nā′ muŋ′go͞o′) *Chin. name for* INNER MONGOLIA

nein (nīn) *adv., interj.* ⟦Ger⟧ no

Neis·se (nī′sə) river in N Europe, flowing from the N Czech Republic into the Oder River on the Polish-German border: *c.* 140 mi (225 km): see ODER

nei·ther (nē′*th*ər, nī′-) *adj., pron.* ⟦ME *naither*, altered (by assoc. with *eyther*, EITHER) < *nauther* < OE *na-hwœther*, lit., not whether (see NO[1], WHETHER), not either of two⟧ not one or the other (of two); not either [*neither* boy went; *neither* of them was invited] —*conj.* 1 not either: the first element of the pair of correlatives *neither ... nor*, indicating negation of both parts of the statement [I could *neither* laugh nor cry]: *neither ... nor* is sometimes used to refer to more than two, although this use is objected to by some [the shop sells *neither* tobacco, beer, nor wine] 2 nor: indicating another, or a further, negative [he does not smoke, and *neither* do I] —*adv.* [Informal or Dial.] any more than the other; also: used after negative expressions [if she won't go, I won't *neither*]

Nejd (nezhd) region in central & E Saudi Arabia: formerly a sultanate

nek·ton (nek′tän′, nek′tən) *n.* ⟦Ger < Gr *nēkton*, neut. of *nēktos*, swimming < *nēchein*, to swim: see NATANT⟧ the larger, aquatic, free-swimming animal life having movements that are largely independent of currents and waves, including squids, fishes, and whales

Nell (nel) *n.* a feminine name: var. *Nellie, Nelly*: see HELEN, ELEANOR

Nel·son[1] (nel′sən) *n.* ⟦< the surname *Nelson* < ME *Nel* (see NEAL) + *son*, SON⟧ a masculine name

Nel·son[2] (nel′sən), **Horatio** Viscount Nelson 1758-1805; Eng. admiral

Nel·son[3] (nel′sən) ⟦so named by Sir T. Button on an expedition into Hudson Bay (1612), after R. *Nelson*, a crew member who died there⟧ river in Manitoba, Canada, flowing from Lake Winnipeg northeast into Hudson Bay: 400 mi (644 km)

Nel·spruit (nel′sproit′) capital of Mpumalanga province, South Africa

ne·lum·bo (nē lum′bō, nə-) *n., pl.* **-bos** ⟦ModL < Sinhalese *nelumbu*⟧ any of a genus (*Nelumbo*, family Nelumbonaceae) of waterlilies with large, dish-shaped leaves and flowers of white to dark red: also **ne·lum′bi·um** (-bē əm)

ne·ma (nē′mə) *n. short for* NEMATODE

Ne·man (nye′mən; *E* nem′ən) river flowing west through Belarus & Lithuania into the Baltic: 597 mi (961 km)

nem·a·thel·minth (nem′ə thel′minth′) *n.* ⟦NEMAT(O)- + HELMINTH⟧ in some former classifications, any of a large phylum (Nemathelminthes) of round, unsegmented worms, many of which are parasitic, as the hookworm, gordian worm, etc.

ne·mat·ic (nē mat′ik, nə-) *adj.* ⟦fol. + -IC⟧ designating a kind of liquid crystal in which the molecules spontaneously align themselves with their axes parallel

nem·a·to- (nem′ə tō′, -tə) ⟦< Gr *nēma* (gen. *nēmatos*), what is spun, thread, akin to *nein*: see NEEDLE⟧ *combining form* thread, threadlike [*nematocyst*]: also, before a vowel, **nemat-**

nem·a·to·cyst (nem′ə tō sist′) *n.* ⟦prec. + -CYST⟧ any of the intracellular stinging structures characteristic of all cnidarians, as the jellyfish: it contains a threadlike sting —**nem′a·to·cys′tic** *adj.*

nem·a·tode (nem′ə tōd′) *n.* ⟦< ModL *Nematoda*: see NEMATO- & -ODE[2]⟧ any of a phylum (Nemata) of worms, often parasites of animals and plants, with long, cylindrical, unsegmented bodies and a heavy cuticle, as the hookworm or pinworm; roundworm

nem·a·tol·o·gy (nem′ə täl′ə jē) *n.* ⟦< prec. + -LOGY⟧ the branch of zoology that deals with nematodes

☆**Nem·bu·tal** (nem′byə tôl′, -tal′) *n.* ⟦former trademark < N(A)[2] + E(THYL) + M(ETHYL) + BU(TYL) + (BARBI)TAL⟧ PENTOBARBITAL SODIUM

nem. con. *abbrev.* ⟦L *nemine contradicente*⟧ (with) no one contradicting; unanimously

nem. diss. *abbrev.* ⟦L *nemine dissentiente*⟧ (with) no one dissenting; unanimously

Ne·me·a (nē′mē ə) valley in Argolis, Greece, in the NE Peloponnesus —**Ne·me·an** (ni mē′ən, nē′mē-) *adj.*

Nemean games a Greek festival held in ancient times every other year at Nemea, consisting chiefly of athletic and musical contests

Nemean lion *Gr. Myth.* a fierce lion killed by Hercules as the first of his twelve labors

ne·mer·te·an (nē mur′tē ən, nə-) *n.* ⟦< ModL *Nemertea* < Gr *Nēmertēs*, name of a sea nymph < *nēmertēs*, unerring⟧ any of a phylum (Nemertea) of usually very elongate, unsegmented marine worms with no body cavity and with a protrusile proboscis, living mostly in coastal mud or sand; ribbon worm —*adj.* of or belonging to these worms: also **nem·er·tine** (nem′ər tin, -tīn′) or **nem′er·tin′e·an** (-tin′ē ən)

nem·e·sis (nem′ə sis) *n., pl.* for 2 & 3 **-ses′** (-sēz′) ⟦L < Gr *nemein*, to distribute, deal out: see -NOMY⟧ 1 [**N-**] *Gr. Myth.* the goddess of retributive justice, or vengeance 2 *a)* just punishment; retribution *b)* one who imposes retribution 3 anyone or anything which seems to be the inevitable cause of someone's downfall or defeat

ne·moph·i·la (nē mäf′ə lə, nə-) *n.* ⟦ModL < Gr *nemos*, a wooded pasture, orig. wooded valley (< IE base *nem-, to bend, form a hollow > NAMASTE) + ModL *-phila*, suffix indicating attraction toward < L, neut. pl. of *-philus*, -PHILOUS⟧ any of a genus (*Nemophila*) of annual W American plants of the waterleaf family, cultivated for garden ornament

ne·ne (nā′nā′) *n.* ⟦Haw *nēnē*⟧ a grayish-brown Hawaiian goose (*Branta sandvicensis*) once nearly extinct

Nen·ets (nen′ets) *n., pl.* **-ets** or **Nen·tsy** (nent′sē) ⟦Russ *n'enyts*, man, person⟧ 1 a member of a group of Samoyed people living in autonomous regions in NE European Russia and NW Siberia 2 the Samoyed language of this people

N Eng *abbrev.* 1 New England 2 North England

ne·o- (nē′ō, -ə) ⟦ModL < Gr *neos*, young, NEW⟧ *combining form* 1 [*often* **N-**] *a)* new, recent, latest [*Neolithic, Neozoic*] *b)* in a new, different, or modified way [*neologism*] *c)* the New World [*Neotropical*] 2 *Chem.* *a)* designating a compound related in some way to an older one [*neoprene*] *b)* indicating a hydrocarbon having at least one carbon atom joined to four other carbon atoms [*neopentane*]

Ne·o·cene (nē′ō sēn′, nē′ə-) *adj.* ⟦prec. + -CENE⟧ *former name for* NEOGENE

ne·o·clas·si·cal (nē′ō klas′i kəl) *adj.* designating or of a revival of classic style and form in art, literature, etc., as in England from *c.* 1660 to *c.* 1740: also **ne′o·clas′sic** —**ne′o·clas′si·cism′** *n.* —**ne′o·clas′si·cist** *n.*

ne·o·co·lo·ni·al·ism (-kə lō′nē əl iz′əm) *n.* the survival or revival of colonialist exploitation by a foreign power of a region that has ostensibly achieved independence —**ne′o·co·lo′ni·al** *adj.* —**ne′o·co·lo′ni·al·ist** *n., adj.*

ne·o·con (nē′ō kän′) *adj., n. short for* NEOCONSERVATIVE

☆**ne·o·con·ser·va·tive** (-kən sur′və tiv) *adj.* designating or of a political movement that evolved in the late 1970s in reaction to liberal and leftist thought, advocating individualism, traditional moral standards, anti-Communist foreign policy, etc. —*n.* a neoconservative person —**ne′o·con·ser′va·tism′** *n.*

ne·o·cor·tex (nē′ō kôr′teks′) *n.* the part of the thin, gray outer layer of the brain's cortex usually associated with human thought and higher intelligence —**ne′o·cor′ti·cal** *adj.*

Ne·o-Dar·win·ism (-där′win iz′əm) *n.* a biological theory which maintains that natural selection is the main factor in the evolution of animals and plants and adjusts this concept to modern genetics

ne·o·dym·i·um (nē′ō dim′ē əm, nē′ə-) *n.* ⟦ModL < *neodymia*, a rare earth (< Gr *neos*, NEW + ModL *(di)dymium*: see DIDYMIUM) + -IUM: so named (1885) by C. A. von Welsbach (see WELSBACH BURNER), from being split from didymium⟧ a silver-colored chemical element, one of the rare-earth elements, used in the coloring of glass and in lasers: symbol, Nd; at. no. 60: see the periodic table of elements in the Reference Supplement

Ne·o·gae·a (nē′ō jē′ə, nē′ə-) *n.* ⟦ModL < NEO- + Gr *gaia*, earth⟧ one of the three primary zoogeographic areas of the earth, coextensive with the Neotropical realm —**Ne′o·gae′an** *adj.*

Ne·o·gene (nē′ə jēn′) *adj.* [*sometimes* **n-**] designating or of the second geologic period of the Cenozoic Era, subdivided into the Miocene and Pliocene epochs: formerly a subdivision of the Tertiary Period —**the Neogene** the Neogene Period or its rocks: see the geologic time chart in the Reference Supplement

ne·o·gen·e·sis (nē′ō jen′ə sis) *n.* ⟦NEO- + -GENESIS⟧ regeneration, esp. of tissue —**ne′o·ge·net′ic** (-jə net′ik) *adj.*

Ne·o-He·bra·ic (nē′ō hē brā′ik, -hi-) *n.* Hebrew as spoken and written since the Diaspora

ne·o·im·pres·sion·ism (-im presh′ən iz′əm) *n.* a late 19th-cent. theory and practice of painting, based on a strict scientific application of impressionist techniques, esp. pointillism —**ne′o·im·pres′sion·ist** *adj., n.*

Ne·o-La·marck·ism (-lə märk′iz′əm) *n.* a theory of inheritance based on a modification and extension of Lamarckism, essentially maintaining the principle that genetic changes can be influenced and directed by environmental factors

Ne·o-Lat·in (-lat′'n) *n.* MODERN LATIN

ne·o·lith (nē′ō lith′, nē′ə-) *n.* ⟦back-form. < fol.⟧ a Neolithic stone tool

Ne·o·lith·ic (nē′ō lith′ik, nē′ə-) *adj.* ⟦NEO- + -LITHIC⟧ [*sometimes* **n-**] designating or of an Old World cultural period (*c.* 8000-*c.* 3500 B.C.) characterized by polished stone tools, pottery, weaving, stock rearing, agriculture, and sometimes megaliths —**the Neolithic** the Neolithic period; New Stone Age

ne·ol·o·gism (nē äl′ə jiz′əm) *n.* ⟦Fr *néologisme*: see NEO-, -LOGY, & -ISM⟧ 1 a new word or a new meaning for an established word 2 the use of, or the practice of creating, new words or new meanings for established words —**ne·ol′o·gist** *n.* —**ne·ol′o·gis′tic** *adj.*, **ne·ol′o·gis′ti·cal**

ne·ol·o·gize (-jīz′) *vi.* **-gized′**, **-giz′ing** ⟦Fr *néologiser*: see fol. & -IZE⟧ to invent, or make a practice of using, neologisms

ne·ol·o·gy (-jē) *n., pl.* **-gies** ⟦Fr *néologie:* see NEO- & -LOGY⟧ NEOLOGISM —**ne·o·log·i·cal** (nē′ō läj′i kəl, nē′ə-) *adj.* —**ne′o·log′i·cal·ly** *adv.*

ne·o·my·cin (nē′ō mī′sin, nē′ə-) *n.* ⟦NEO- + -MYCIN⟧ a broad-spectrum antibiotic obtained from an actinomycete (*Streptomyces fradiae*) and used in the treatment of various infections, esp. of the skin and eye

ne·on (nē′än′) *n.* ⟦ModL: so named (1898) by Sir William RAMSAY, its co-discoverer < Gr *neon,* neut. of *neos,* NEW⟧ a chemical element, one of the noble gases, that is tasteless, odorless, and colorless, found in small quantities in the earth's atmosphere and used in discharge tubes, gas lasers, bright electrical signs, etc.: neon ionizes and glows with light when an electric current is sent through it: symbol, Ne; at. no. 10: see the periodic table of elements in the Reference Supplement —*adj.* **1** containing neon for lighting purposes *[*a *neon* tube*]* **2** *a)* lighted by neon *[*garish *neon* advertising signs*]* *b)* bright, intense, gaudy, etc. *[neon* colors*]*

ne·o·nate (nē′ō nāt′, nē′ə-) *n.* ⟦ModL *neonatus* < *neo-,* NEO- + L *natus,* born: see NATURE⟧ a newly-born individual, esp. an infant during its first month of life —**ne′o·na′tal** *adj.* —**ne′o·na′tal·ly** *adv.*

ne·o·na·tol·o·gy (nē′ō nā täl′ə jē) *n.* the branch of medicine dealing with newborn children up to two months old —**ne′o·na·tol′o·gist** *n.*

ne·o-Na·zi (nē′ō nät′sē) *adj.* of or pertaining to a person or group holding political views associated with or derived from those of Adolf Hitler and Nazism —*n.* a person who holds or advocates neo-Nazi views

neon tetra ⟦descriptive of its bright coloration⟧ a popular tetra (*Hyphessobrycon innesi*) with blue or green back, white belly, and a posterior, red, lateral stripe

ne·o·orth·o·dox·y (nē′ō ôr′thə däk′sē) *n.* a movement in 20th-cent. Protestantism stressing traditional doctrines of the Reformation in reaction to theological liberalism —**ne′o-orth′o·dox** *adj.*

ne·o·pa·gan (nē′ō pā′gən) *n.* a person who practices a form of nature worship in imitation of any of various religions that historically preceded Christianity

ne·o·phyte (nē′ō fīt′, nē′ə-) *n.* ⟦LL(Ec) *neophytus* < Gr *neophytos,* newly planted (in 1 Tim. 3:6, a new convert) < *neos,* NEW + *phytos* < *phyein,* to produce, grow: see BONDAGE⟧ **1** a new convert **2** one just beginning a new kind of life, work, etc.; beginner; novice —**SYN.** AMATEUR

ne·o·pla·sia (nē′ō plā′zhə, -zhē ə) *n.* ⟦NEO- + -PLASIA⟧ the growth of new tissue, esp. the formation of neoplasms

ne·o·plasm (nē′ō plaz′əm) *n.* ⟦NEO- + -PLASM⟧ an abnormal growth of tissue, as a tumor

ne·o·plas·tic (nē′ō plas′tik) *adj.* **1** of or relating to neoplasia or a neoplasm **2** of or relating to neoplasticism

ne·o·plas·ti·cism (nē′ō plas′tə siz′əm) *n.* ⟦NEO- + PLASTIC + -ISM⟧ the principles and methods of the *de Stijl* movement in painting: see DE STIJL

ne·o·plas·ty (nē′ō plas′tē) *n.* ⟦NEO- + -PLASTY⟧ the restoration or repair of a part of the body by plastic surgery

Ne·o·pla·to·nism (nē′ō plāt′′n iz′əm) *n.* a school of philosophy developed by Plotinus, based on a modified Platonism, and postulating a single source from which all forms of existence emanate and with which the soul seeks mystical union —**Ne′o·pla·ton′ic** (-plā tän′ik) *adj.* —**Ne′o·pla′ton·ist** *n.*

☆**ne·o·prene** (nē′ō prēn′) *n.* ⟦NEO- + (CHLORO)PRENE⟧ a synthetic rubber produced by the polymerization of chloroprene: it is highly resistant to oil, heat, light, and oxidation

ne·o·re·al·ism (nē′ō rē′ə liz′əm) *n. Film* a style or movement, esp. in Italy in the 1940s and early 1950s, in which the everyday lives of ordinary, usually poor, people are shown in harshly realistic settings in actual locations —**ne′o·re′al·ist** *adj., n.*

☆**Ne·o·ri·can** (nē′ō rē′kən) *n.* a Puerto Rican who has lived in New York City for some years or has returned to Puerto Rico after living there

Ne·o-Scho·las·ti·cism (nē′ō skə las′tə siz′əm) *n.* a 19th- and 20th-cent. school of philosophy based on scholasticism, esp. Thomism, but also drawing on modern philosophical and scientific concepts

ne·ot·e·ny (nē ät′′n ē) *n.* ⟦ModL *neotenia* < *neo-,* NEO- + Gr *teinein,* to stretch: see TEND[2]⟧ *Zool.* **1** the retention of juvenile characteristics in the adult **2** the development of adult features in the juvenile, as the attainment of sexual maturity in some larvae; paedogenesis —**ne·o·te·nic** (nē′ə tē′nik, -ten′ik) *adj.,* **ne·ot·e·nous** (nē ät′′n əs)

ne·o·ter·ic (nē′ō ter′ik, nē′ə-) *adj.* ⟦LL *neotericus* < Gr *neōterikos* < *neōteros,* compar. of *neos,* NEW⟧ recent; new; newly invented —*n.* a modern person; one accepting new ideas and practices —**ne′o·ter′i·cal·ly** *adv.*

Ne·o·trop·i·cal (-träp′i kəl) *adj.* ⟦NEO- + TROPICAL⟧ designating or of the biogeographic realm that includes South America, the West Indies, Central America, and tropical Mexico: also **Ne′o·trop′ic**

Ne·pal (nə pôl′, -päl′) country in the Himalayas, between India & Tibet: 54,363 sq mi (140,800 sq km); cap. Kathmandu —**Nep·a·lese** (nep′ə lēz′, -lēs′) *adj., n., pl.* **-lese′**

Ne·pal·i (ni pôl′ē, -päl′-; ne-) *n.* **1** a person born or living in Nepal **2** the Indo-Aryan language spoken in Nepal —*adj.* of Nepal or its people, language, or culture

ne·pen·the (nē pen′thē, ni-) *n.* ⟦L *nepenthes* < Gr *nepenthēs,* removing sorrow < *ne-,* not (see NO[1]) + *penthos,* sorrow, grief < IE base **kwenth-,* to suffer, bear > OIr *cessaim,* (I) suffer⟧ a drug supposed by the ancient Greeks to cause forgetfulness of sorrow: also **ne·pen′thes′** (-thēz′) —**ne·pen′the·an** (-thē ən) *adj.*

neph·a·nal·y·sis (nef′ə nal′ə sis) *n., pl.* **-ses′** (-sēz′) ⟦NEPH(O)- + ANALYSIS⟧ the analysis of the data on a map or chart that pertains to clouds and precipitation; also, such a map or chart

neph·e·line (nef′ə lēn′, -lin) *n.* ⟦Fr *néphéline* < Gr *nephelē,* cloud (see NEBULA) + *-ine,* -INE[1]⟧ a hard, light-colored, hexagonal mineral, (Na,K)AlSiO$_4$, used in making glass, china, etc.; sodium potassium aluminum silicate: sometimes called **neph′e·lite′** (-līt′)

neph·e·lin·ite (nef′ə lin īt′) *n.* ⟦< prec. + -ITE[1]⟧ a grayish, fine-grained or porphyritic igneous rock composed mainly of nepheline and pyroxene

neph·e·lo- (nef′ə lō, -lə) ⟦< Gr *nephelē,* a cloud: see NEBULA⟧ *combining form* clouds, cloudy *[nephelometer]*: see NEPHO-: also, before a vowel, **nephel-**

neph·e·lom·e·ter (nef′ə läm′ət ər) *n.* ⟦prec. + -METER⟧ an apparatus for measuring the concentration of a suspension, as of bacteria or other substance, by its scattering of a beam of light

neph·ew (nef′yōō; *chiefly Brit,* nev′-) *n.* ⟦ME *neveu* < OFr < L *nepos* < IE base **nepot-,* grandson, nephew > Sans *napat,* OE *nefa*⟧ **1** *a)* the son of one's brother or sister *b)* the son of one's brother-in-law or sister-in-law **2** an illegitimate son, as of a medieval prelate: a euphemism **3** [Obs.] *a)* grandson *b)* a descendant

neph·o- (nef′ō, -ə) ⟦< Gr *nephos,* cloud: see NEBULA⟧ *combining form* cloud, clouds *[nephology]*: see NEPHELO-: also, before a vowel, **neph-**

ne·phol·o·gy (nē fäl′ə jē, ni-) *n.* ⟦NEPHO- + -LOGY⟧ the branch of meteorology dealing with clouds —**neph·o·log·i·cal** (nef′ō läj′i kəl) *adj.* —**ne·phol′o·gist** *n.*

neph·o·scope (nef′ə skōp′) *n.* ⟦NEPHO- + -SCOPE⟧ an instrument for determining the direction and velocity of the movement of clouds

nephr- *combining form* NEPHRO-: used before a vowel

ne·phral·gi·a (nə fral′jē ə, -fral′jə) *n.* ⟦prec. + -ALGIA⟧ pain in the kidneys

ne·phrec·to·my (nə frek′tə mē) *n., pl.* **-mies** ⟦NEPHR- + -ECTOMY⟧ surgical removal of the kidneys

ne·phrid·i·um (nə frid′ē əm) *n., pl.* **-phrid′i·a** (-ə) ⟦ModL < Gr *nephridion,* dim. of *nephros,* kidney: see NEPHRO-⟧ **1** a waste-discharging tubule with an external excretory pore, found in many invertebrates, as in worms, mollusks, etc. **2** any of the excretory tubules of the pronephros of a vertebrate embryo —**ne·phrid′i·al** *adj.*

neph·rite (nef′rīt′) *n.* ⟦Ger *nephrit* < Gr *nephritēs,* of the kidneys < *nephros,* kidney (see NEPHRO-): formerly worn as a supposed remedy for kidney ailments⟧ a fine-grained, greenish variety of actinolite, that is a less valuable type of jade

ne·phrit·ic (nə frit′ik) *adj.* ⟦LL *nephriticus* < Gr *nephritikos* < *nephros,* kidney: see NEPHRO-⟧ **1** of a kidney or the kidneys; renal **2** of or having nephritis

ne·phri·tis (nə frīt′əs) *n.* ⟦LL < Gr *nephritis:* see fol. & -ITIS⟧ an acute or chronic disease of the kidneys, characterized by inflammation, degeneration, fibrosis, etc.: see BRIGHT'S DISEASE

neph·ro- (nef′rō, -rə) ⟦< Gr *nephros,* kidney < IE base **negwhros,* kidney, testicle > ME *nere,* kidney⟧ *combining form* kidney *[nephrotomy, epinephrine]*

neph·ro·gen·ic (nef′rō jen′ik, -rə-) *adj.* ⟦prec. + -GENIC⟧ **1** arising in the kidneys **2** producing kidney tissue

ne·phrol·o·gy (nə fräl′ə jē) *n.* the branch of medicine dealing with the kidney —**ne·phrol′o·gist** *n.*

neph·ron (nef′rän′, -rən) *n.* ⟦Ger < Gr *nephros:* see NEPHRO-⟧ a single urinary tubule in the vertebrate kidney

ne·phro·sis (nə frō′sis) *n.* ⟦NEPHR- + -OSIS⟧ a degenerative disease of the kidneys, characterized by generalized edema, protein in the urine, and an increase in serum cholesterol —**ne·phrot′ic** (-frät′ik) *adj.*

ne·phrot·o·my (nə frät′ə mē) *n., pl.* **-mies** ⟦NEPHRO- + -TOMY⟧ surgical incision into the kidney, as for removing a stone

ne plus ul·tra (nā plus ul′trə, nē-) ⟦L, lit., no more beyond⟧ the ultimate; esp., the finest, best, most perfect, etc.

nep·o·tism (nep′ə tiz′əm) *n.* ⟦Fr *népotisme* < It *nepotismo* < *nepote,* nephew < L *nepos* (gen. *nepotis*), grandson, NEPHEW: from favoritism shown to "nephews," or illegitimate sons, by medieval prelates⟧ favoritism shown to relatives, esp. in appointment to desirable positions —**nep′o·tist** *n.* —**nep′o·tis′tic** *adj.*

Nep·tune (nep′tōōn′, -tyōōn′) *n.* ⟦ME < L *Neptunus,* prob. < IE **nebhtus* < base **nebh-,* moist > NEBULA⟧ **1** *Rom. Myth.* the god of the sea: identified with the Greek Poseidon **2** the sea personified **3** ⟦ModL⟧ the fourth largest planet of the solar system and normally the eighth in distance from the sun: it has a thin, icy ring system around its equator: diameter, *c.* 49,530 km (*c.* 30,780 mi); period of revolution, 164.79 earth years; period of rotation, 16.11 hours; 13 satellites; symbol, ♆ —**Nep·tu′ni·an** (-ē ən) *adj.*

☆**nep·tu·ni·um** (nep tōō′nē əm, -tyōō′-) *n.* ⟦ModL < L *Neptunus* (see prec.) + -IUM: so named by E. M. MCMILLAN & P. Abelson (1913-2004), U.S. physicists, because its atomic number is next after that of uranium, as the planet Neptune is next beyond Uranus⟧ a silver-colored, radioactive, metallic chemical element, one of the actinides, produced by bombarding uranium atoms with neutrons: symbol, Np; at. no. 93: see the periodic table of elements in the Reference Supplement

neptunium series the radioactive series of nuclides starting with neptunium-237, with a half-life of 2.2 x 10^6 years, and ending with stable bismuth-209: many radionuclides, as plutonium-241 and uranium-237, eventually decay into neptunium-237 and are often considered members of the neptunium series

☆**nerd** (nʉrd) *n.* ⟦< ? arbitrary coinage by Dr. SEUSS for the name of a creature in his children's book *If I Ran the Zoo* (1950)⟧ [Informal] a person regarded as socially dull, unsophisticated, awkward, etc., specif., as from being preoccupied with schoolwork, an intellectual hobby, etc. —**nerd·y** (nʉr′dē) *adj.* **nerd′i·er, nerd′i·est**

Ne·re·id (nir′ē id) *n.* ⟦L *Nereis* (gen. *Nereidis*) < Gr *Nērēis* (gen. *Nērēidos*) < *Nēreus*⟧ *Gr. Myth.* any of the sea nymphs, the fifty daughters of Nereus

ne·re·is (nir′ē is) *n., pl.* **ne·re·i·des** (nē rē′ə dēz′, ni-) ⟦ModL *Nereis* < L: see prec.⟧ any of a genus (*Nereis*) of relatively large carnivorous marine polychaetes (order Phyllodocida, family Nereididae)

Ne·re·us (nir′ē əs, nir′yo͞os′) *n.* ⟦L < Gr *Nereus*, prob. < IE **(s)nāu-* < base **(s)na-*, to flow > NATANT⟧ *Gr. Myth.* a benevolent sea god, father of the fifty Nereids

ne·rit·ic (nē rit′ik, nə-) *adj.* ⟦< Gr *nēritēs*, a sea snail (< *Nereus*, prec.) + -IC⟧ designating or of the ecological zone (**neritic zone**) of the continental shelf extending from low tide to a depth of *c.* 660 ft (*c.* 200 m)

Nernst (nernst), **Wal·ther Her·mann** (väl′tər her′män′) 1864-1941; Ger. physicist & chemist

Ne·ro (nir′ō) (*Nero Claudius Caesar Drusus Germanicus*, born *Lucius Domitius Ahenobarbus*) A.D. 37-68; emperor of Rome (54-68): notoriously cruel & depraved —**Ne·ro′ni·an** (-nē ən) *adj.*, **Ne·ron′ic** (-rän′ik)

ner·o·li (ner′ə lē, nir′-) *n.* ⟦Fr *néroli* < It *neroli, nerolo*, after the Princess of *Nerole* (17th-c.) said to have discovered it⟧ an essential oil distilled from orange flowers and used in perfumery: in full **neroli oil**

Ne·ru·da (ne ro͞o′thä; E nə ro͞o′də), **Pa·blo** (pä′blô) (born *Ricardo Eliezer Neftalí Reyes Basoalto*) 1904-73; Chilean poet

nerv·ate (nʉr′vāt′) *adj. Bot.* having nerves, or veins

ner·va·tion (nər vā′shən) *n.* ⟦< fol. + -ATION⟧ VENATION

nerve (nʉrv) *n.* ⟦ME *nerfe* < OFr *nerf* < L *nervus*, sinew, nerve, string < IE base **(s)nēu-*, to twist, wind > Gr *neuron*, tendon, nerve, OE *sneowan*, to hurry⟧ **1** a sinew or tendon: now only in the phr. **strain every nerve**, to try as hard as possible **2** any of the cordlike fibers or bundles of fibers connecting the bodily organs with the central nervous system (the brain and the spinal cord) and parts of the nervous system with each other, and carrying impulses to and from the brain or a nerve center **3** the pulp of a tooth, including the nerves, blood vessels, etc. **4** emotional control; coolness in danger; courage [*a man of nerve*] **5** strength; energy; vigor **6** [*pl.*] the nervous system regarded as indicating health, emotional stability, endurance, etc. **7** [*pl.*] *a)* nervousness *b)* an attack of this; hysteria **8** [Informal] impudent boldness; audacity; brazenness **9** *Biol.* a rib or vein in a leaf or insect's wing —*vt.* **nerved, nerv′ing** to give strength or courage to —**SYN.** TEMERITY —**get on someone's nerves** [Informal] to make someone irritable or exasperated —**nerve oneself** to collect one's energies or courage for an effort

nerve block a method of local anesthesia in which the passage of impulses through a particular nerve is stopped by the injection of an anesthetic into or near the nerve

nerve cell **1** NEURON **2** a nerve cell body without its processes

nerve center **1** any group of nerve cells that function together in controlling some specific sense or bodily activity, as breathing **2** a control center; headquarters

nerve fiber any of the threadlike elements, either dendrites or axons, making up a nerve

nerve gas any of several poisonous, odorless, colorless, and tasteless liquids that volatilize readily, are rapidly absorbed through the eyes, lungs, or skin, and inactivate the enzyme cholinesterase, causing paralysis of the respiratory and central nervous systems: manufactured as for use in war as a chemical weapon

nerve impulse an electrochemical change that sweeps over a nerve fiber when it is stimulated

nerve·less (nʉrv′lis) *adj.* **1** without strength, vigor, force, or courage; weak; inert; unnerved **2** not nervous; cool; controlled **3** *Biol.* without nerves —**nerve′less·ly** *adv.*

nerve net a network of nerve cells that serves as the simple nervous system of such invertebrates as the hydra and jellyfish

nerve-rack·ing or **nerve-wrack·ing** (-rak′iŋ) *adj.* very trying to one's patience or equanimity; causing irritation or exasperation

Ner·vi (ner′vē), **Pier Lu·i·gi** (pir lo͞o ē′jē) 1891-1979; It. engineer & architect

nerv·ing (nʉr′viŋ) *n. Vet.Med.* removal of part of a nerve trunk, as when it is chronically inflamed

nerv·ous (nʉr′vəs) *adj.* ⟦ME *neruous* < L *nervosus*⟧ **1** [Obs.] strong; sinewy **2** vigorous in expression; animated **3** of the nerves **4** made up of or containing nerves **5** characterized by or having a disordered state of the nerves **6** characterized by or showing emotional tension, restlessness, agitation, etc. **7** fearful; apprehensive —**nerv′ous·ly** *adv.* —**nerv′ous·ness** *n.*, **ner·vos′i·ty** (-väs′ə tē)

☆**nervous breakdown** the sudden onset of a psychotic or neurotic disorder that temporarily impairs a person's ability to function normally, typically precipitated by some crisis or intense, unrelieved stress: a nontechnical term

☆**nervous Nellie** ⟦orig. used of high-strung racehorses: in ref. to *old Nell*, jocular name for a nag⟧ [Slang] a timid person who is easily upset and is hesitant to act

nervous system all the nerve cells and nervous tissues in an organism, including, in the vertebrates, the brain, spinal cord, ganglia, nerves, and nerve centers: it coordinates and controls responses to stimuli and conditions behavior and consciousness

ner·vure (nʉr′vyoor′) *n.* ⟦Fr: see NERVE & -URE⟧ *Biol.* VEIN (*n.* 2 & 3)

nerv·y (nʉr′vē) *adj.* **nerv′i·er, nerv′i·est** **1** [Rare] strong; vigorous; sinewy **2** [Brit.] nervous; excitable; jittery **3** full of courage; bold ☆**4** [Informal] rudely bold; brazen; impudent —**nerv′i·ly** *adv.* —**nerv′i·ness** *n.*

Nes·bit (nez′bit), **E(dith)** 1858-1924; Eng. writer, esp. of children's books

nes·ci·ent (nesh′ənt, -ē ənt) *adj.* ⟦L *nesciens*, prp. of *nescire*, to be ignorant of: see NICE⟧ **1** lacking knowledge; ignorant **2** AGNOSTIC —**nes′ci·ence** *n.*

ness (nes) *n.* ⟦ME *nesse* < OE *næs* & ON *nes*, akin to OE *nosu*, NOSE⟧ a promontory; headland: now chiefly in place names [*Inverness*]

Ness (nes), **Loch** lake in NW Scotland: 23 mi (37 km) long: a large, long-necked, reptilian creature (**Loch Ness monster**) is reputed to live in its deep waters

-ness (nis, nəs) ⟦ME *-nesse* < OE *-nes(s)*, akin to Ger *-niss*, Goth *-nassus* (for *-assus*, with *n-* < end of the preceding component)⟧ *suffix* state, quality, or instance of being [*togetherness, sadness*]

Nes·sel·rode (nes′əl rōd′) *n.* ⟦after Count K. *Nesselrode* (Russ *Nessel'rode*) (1780-1862), Russ statesman of German ancestry⟧ a mixture of preserved fruits, chopped nuts, etc., used in ice cream, puddings, pies, or the like

nest (nest) *n.* ⟦ME < OE, akin to Ger *nest* < IE **nizdos* (< base **ni-*, down + **sed-*, to SIT) > L *nidus*, Welsh *nyth*⟧ **1** the structure made or the place chosen by birds for laying their eggs and sheltering their young **2** *a)* the place used by turtles, hornets, fish, etc. for spawning or breeding *b)* the structure made or the place chosen by any of certain wild animals as its home [*a squirrel's nest*] **3** a cozy or snug place in which to live or rest; retreat **4** *a)* a haunt or den (used esp. in an unfavorable sense) *b)* the people who frequent such a place [*a nest of criminals*] **5** a brood, swarm, or colony of birds, insects, etc. **6** a set or series of similar things, each fitting within the one next larger —*vi.* **1** to build or live in or as in a nest **2** to fit one into another **3** to hunt for birds' nests: usually in the prp. —*vt.* **1** to make a nest for **2** to place or settle in or as in a nest **3** to fit (an object) closely within another **4** *Comput.* to embed (a loop, subroutine, etc.) between the first and last instructions of another —**nest′a·ble** *adj.*

n'est-ce pas? (nes pä′) ⟦Fr, is it not?⟧ isn't that so?

nest egg **1** an artificial or real egg left in a nest to induce a hen to lay more eggs there **2** money, etc. put aside as a reserve or to establish a fund

nest·er (nes′tər) *n.* ⟦NEST (*vi.*) + -ER⟧ [West] a squatter or homesteader who settles on open range land

nes·tle (nes′əl) *vi.* **-tled, -tling** ⟦ME *nestlen* < OE *nestlian*: see NEST & -LE⟧ **1** [Archaic] to build or live in a nest **2** to settle down comfortably and snugly **3** to draw or press close for comfort or in affection **4** to lie sheltered or partly hidden, as a house among trees —*vt.* **1** to rest or press (a baby, one's head, etc.) in a snug, affectionate manner **2** to settle or house as in a nest; shelter —**nes′tler** *n.*

nest·ling (nest′liŋ) *n.* ⟦ME (akin to Ger *nestling*): see NEST & -LING[1]⟧ a young bird not yet ready to leave the nest

Nes·tor (nes′tər, -tôr′) *n.* ⟦L < Gr *Nestōr*, lit., the one who returns, akin to *neomai*, I return < IE base **nes-*, to unite, be concealed > Goth *nasjan*, to save, OE *nesan*, to survive⟧ **1** a masculine name **2** *Gr. Myth.* a wise old counselor to the Greeks at Troy

Nes·to·ri·an·ism (nes tôr′ē ən iz′əm) *n.* the unorthodox doctrine attributed to Nestorius (patriarch of Constantinople, A.D. 428-431) alleging the existence of two persons (one divine, one human) in Jesus Christ: declared heretical in 431 —**Nes·to′ri·an** *n., adj.*

net[1] (net) *n.* ⟦ME < OE *nett*, akin to Ger *netz*, Goth *nati* < IE base **ned-*, to twist together > L *nodus*, a knot⟧ **1** a fabric made from string, cord, etc., loosely knotted or woven in an openwork pattern and used to trap or snare birds, fish, etc. **2** anything that catches or entraps; trap; snare **3** any of various devices made of meshed fabric, used to hold, protect, or mark off something [*a hairnet, tennis net*] **4** a fine, meshed, lacelike cloth, used to make curtains, trim garments, etc. **5** NETWORK (*n.* 2 & 3) **6** *Tennis, Volleyball, etc.* a ball or shuttlecock that hits the net, whether or not it goes over: cf. FAULT (*n.* 8): in full **net ball** **7** [*usually* **N-**] [Informal] *Comput. short for* INTERNET: with *the* —*vt.* **net′ted, net′ting** **1** to make into net or a net **2** to make with net **3** to trap or snare with or as with a net **4** to protect, shelter, or enclose with or as with a net **5** *Tennis, Volleyball, etc.* to hit (the ball or shuttlecock) into the net **6** *Ice Hockey, Soccer, etc.* *a)* to hit (the ball or puck) into the goal, or net, and thereby score a point *b)* to score (a point) by hitting the ball or puck into the goal —*vi.* to make nets or network —**net′like′** *adj.*

net[2] (net) *adj.* ⟦ME, trim, clean < Fr: see NEAT[1]⟧ **1** remaining after certain deductions, as for taxes or expenses, have been made [*net annual income*] **2** designating or of weight excluding the container, packaging, etc. **3** after all considerations; final [*a net result*] —*n.* a net amount, profit, weight, price, result, etc. —*vt.* **net′ted, net′ting** to get or bring in as a net; clear as profit, etc.

.net (*usually* dät′net′) *abbrev. Comput.* network: a widely used domain name

net asset value the value of a mutual fund share, determined by dividing the net assets of the fund by the number of shares issued

net·book (net′bo͝ok′) *n.* ⟦< *netBook*, former trademark for such a computer < (INTER)NET + (NOTE)BOOK⟧ a small, relatively inexpensive notebook computer with limited processing power and data storage, designed primarily for wireless communication and networking, as sending and receiving email, browsing the internet, and using internet-based applications

Neth *abbrev.* Netherlands

neth·er (neth′ər) *adj.* ⟦ME *nethere* < OE *neothera*, akin to Ger *nieder* < IE base **ni-*, down + compar. suffix⟧ **1** lying, or thought of as lying, below the earth's surface [*the nether regions*] **2** lower or under [*the nether tip of a crescent*]

Neth·er·lands (neth′ər ləndz) **1** country in W Europe, on the North Sea:

16,033 sq mi (41,526 sq km); cap. Amsterdam; seat of government, The Hague: usually used with *the* 2 kingdom consisting of the independent states of the Netherlands & now-independent islands of the former Netherlands Antilles Du. name NEDERLAND —**Neth′er·land′er** (-lan′dər, -lən dər) *n.*

Netherlands Antilles former group of islands (dissolved 2010), once a part of the Kingdom of the Netherlands, consisting of some of the Leeward Islands & three islands off the coast of Venezuela: the islands are now variously special municipalities of, or independent nations associated with, the Kingdom of the Netherlands

Netherlands (East) Indies former island possessions of the Netherlands, in the East Indies: now part of Indonesia

Netherlands Guiana *former name for* SURINAME

Netherlands New Guinea *former name for* WEST IRIAN

neth·er·most (neth′ər mōst′) *adj.* ⟦ME *nethermest*: see NETHER & -MOST⟧ lowest; farthest down

neth·er·world (-wurld′) *n.* 1 *Myth., Theol.* the world of the dead or of punishment after death; hell 2 a sphere of human activity or state of existence regarded as corrupt, unwholesome, undesirable, etc. 3 any state of existence regarded as hidden, enigmatic, vague, unclassifiable, etc.

Né·thou (nā to͞o′), **Pic de** (pēk də) *Fr. name for* Pico de ANETO

net national product the total value of a nation's annual output of goods and services minus the value of capital goods used up in the production of this output

net·su·ke (net′skē′, -skā′; -sə kē′, -sə kā′) *n.* ⟦Jpn⟧ an ornamental button or figure of ivory, wood, etc., once used to attach a purse or other article to a kimono sash

Net·tie or **Net·ty** (net′ē) *n.* a feminine name: see ANTOINETTE[1], HENRIETTA, JEANNETTE

net·ting (net′iŋ) *n.* 1 the act or process of making nets 2 the action or right of fishing with nets 3 netted material

net·tle (net′'l) *n.* ⟦ME *netle* < OE *netele*, akin to Ger *nessel* < IE base **ned-*, to twist together > NET[1]: from the use of such plants as a source of spinning fiber⟧ 1 any of a genus (*Urtica*) of annual and perennial weeds of the nettle family with stinging hairs 2 any of various other stinging or spiny plants —*adj.* designating a family (Urticaceae, order Urticales) of chiefly tropical, dicotyledonous plants covered typically with stinging hairs, including the ramie —*vt.* **-tled, -tling** 1 to sting with or as with nettles 2 to irritate; annoy; vex —**SYN.** IRRITATE —**net′tler** *n.*

nettle rash HIVES

net·tle·some (-səm) *adj.* that nettles, or annoys

net ton a unit of weight equal to 2,000 pounds; short ton

net-winged (net′wiŋd′) *adj.* having a network of veins in the wings: said of insects

net·work (net′wurk′) *n.* ⟦NET[1] + WORK⟧ 1 any arrangement or fabric of parallel wires, threads, etc. crossed at regular intervals by others fastened to them so as to leave open spaces; netting; mesh 2 a thing resembling this in some way; specif., *a)* a system of roads, canals, veins, etc. that connect with or cross one another *b)* a group, system, etc. of interconnected or cooperating individuals 3 *Comput. a)* a system, as within a business or university, consisting typically of a server and connected microcomputers, terminals, printers, etc.; specif., a LOCAL AREA NETWORK *b)* a larger system encompassing interconnected computer systems, as from various businesses, universities, etc. 4 *Radio, TV a)* a chain of transmitting stations linked by cable, microwave relay, satellite, etc., usually sharing the same programs *b)* a company that produces programs to be broadcast over such a network 5 the making of nets or netted fabric —*adj.* broadcast over the stations of a network —*vi.* to develop contacts or exchange information with others, as to further a career —*vt.* 1 to organize or integrate into a network 2 *Radio, TV* to present on or broadcast over a network —**net′work′er** *n.*

net·work·ing (-wur′kiŋ) *n.* 1 the developing of contacts or exchanging of information with others in an informal network, as to further a career 2 the interconnection, as over communication lines, of computer systems

Neu·châ·tel (nö shä tel′; *E* no͞o′shə tel′) 1 canton of W Switzerland, on the French border: 310 sq mi (803 sq km) 2 its capital, on the Lake of Neuchâtel 3 **Lake of** lake in W Switzerland: 84 sq mi (218 sq km)

Neu·en·burg (noi′ən boork′) *Ger. name for* NEUCHÂTEL

Neuf·châ·tel (cheese) (no͞o′shä tel′, no͞o′-; *Fr* nö shä tel′) ⟦Fr, after *Neufchâtel*, town in N France⟧ a soft, white cheese prepared from whole milk or skim milk and eaten fresh or cured

neume or **neum** (no͞om, nyo͞om) *n.* ⟦Fr < ML *neuma*, prob. ult. < Syriac *ne'mo*, a sound, tone, song: altered in form and sense by assoc. with Gr *neuma*, a sign, *pneuma*, a breath⟧ 1 any of various notational signs used in medieval church music, originally put above words to be sung so as to show approximate pitch, melody line, etc. 2 in Gregorian chant, a specific musical note, often sustained, or a group of such notes —**neu·mat′ic** *adj.*

neur- (noor, nyoor) *combining form* NEURO-: used before a vowel [*neuralgia*]

neu·ral (noor′əl, nyoor′-) *adj.* ⟦prec. + -AL⟧ of a nerve, nerves, or the nervous system

neural arch a bony or cartilaginous arch resting on the chief part of each vertebra and forming a tunnel through which the nerve cord passes

neural crest *Embryology* a band of cells that lies along the length of the neural tube and developing spinal cord: it is the primordium of many structures, including the spinal ganglia

neu·ral·gi·a (no͞o ral′jə, nyo͞o-; -jē ə) *n.* ⟦ModL: see NEUR- & -ALGIA⟧ severe pain along the course of a nerve or in its area of distribution —**neu·ral′gic** (-jik) *adj.*

neural network a computer system designed to perform tasks or make decisions based on generalized patterns it has derived from data: so called because originally modeled after neuron interconnections and processing methods in the human brain: also **neural net**

neural tube a primitive, tubular, dorsal structure that is formed from ectodermal tissue in the early vertebrate embryo and that develops into the brain and spinal cord

neu·ras·the·ni·a (noor′əs thē′nē ə, nyoor′-) *n.* ⟦ModL: see NEURO- & ASTHENIA⟧ a former category of mental disorder, including such symptoms as irritability, fatigue, weakness, anxiety, and localized pains without apparent physical causes, thought to result from weakness or exhaustion of the nervous system —**neu′ras·then′ic** (-then′ik) *adj., n.*

neu·rec·to·my (no͞o rek′tə mē, nyo͞o-) *n., pl.* **-mies** ⟦NEUR- + -ECTOMY⟧ surgical removal of a nerve or part of a nerve

neu·ri·lem·ma (noor′ə lem′ə, nyoor′-) *n.* ⟦ModL, altered (infl. by Gr *lemma*, skin, peel) < *neurilema* < Gr *neuron*, NERVE + *eilēma*, a covering < *eilyein*, to wind, wrap: see WALK⟧ the thin outer sheath covering a nerve fiber

neu·rine (noor′ēn′, nyoor′-; -in) *n.* ⟦NEUR- + -INE[3]⟧ a ptomaine poison, CH_2:$CHN(CH_3)_3OH$, formed by the dehydration of choline, as during the putrefaction of flesh

neu·ri·tis (no͞o rīt′əs, nyo͞o-) *n.* ⟦ModL: see fol. & -ITIS⟧ inflammation of a nerve or nerves, accompanied by changes in sensory and motor activity in the region of the affected nerve and often associated with a degenerative process —**neu·rit′ic** (-rit′ik) *adj.*

neu·ro- (noor′ō, nyoor′ō; -ə) ⟦< Gr *neuron*, NERVE⟧ *combining form* of a nerve, nerves, or the nervous system [*neuropathology*]

neu·ro·a·nat·o·my (noor′ō ə nat′ə mē, nyoor′-) *n.* a branch of anatomy dealing with the nervous system —**neu′ro·an′a·tom′i·cal** (-an′ə täm′i kəl) *adj.*, **neu′ro·an′a·tom′ic** —**neu′ro·a·nat′o·mist** *n.*

neu·ro·bi·ol·o·gy (-bī äl′ə jē) *n.* a branch of biology that deals with the nervous system and its ability to react, learn, etc. —**neu′ro·bi′o·log′i·cal** *adj.*, **neu′ro·bi′o·log′ic** —**neu′ro·bi·ol′o·gist** *n.*

neu·ro·blast (noor′ō blast′, nyoor′-) *n.* ⟦NEURO- + -BLAST⟧ any of the embryonic cells from which the nerve cells develop

neu·ro·blas·to·ma (noor′ō blas tō′mə, nyoor′-) *n., pl.* **-mas** or **-ma·ta** (-mə tə) a rare type of malignant tumor, found in some young children, that is formed from embryonic nerve cells

neu·ro·chem·is·try (noor′ō kem′is trē, nyoor′-) *n.* the study of the chemistry of the nervous system —**neu′ro·chem′i·cal** *adj., n.* —**neu′ro·chem′ist** *n.*

neu·ro·de·gen·er·a·tive (noor′ō dē jen′ər ə tiv, nyoor′-) *adj.* designating or of a disease or condition, as Alzheimer's disease, characterized by the degeneration of nervous tissue —**neu′ro·de·gen′er·a′tion** (-ā′shən) *n.*

neu·ro·en·do·crine (-en′dō krin′) *adj.* of or having to do with neuroendocrinology

neu·ro·en·do·cri·nol·o·gy (-en′dō kri näl′ə jē) *n.* the science dealing with how hormones and glands interact with the nervous system —**neu′ro·en′do·cri·nol′o·gist** *n.*

neu·ro·fi·bril (-fī′brəl) *n.* a fibril comprising part of a nerve cell —**neu′ro·fi′bril·lar′y** (-fī′brə ler′ē) *adj.*

neu·ro·fi·bro·ma (-fī brō′mə) *n., pl.* **-mas** or **-ma·ta** (-mə tə) a tumor, usually benign, that consists of nerve fibers and connective tissue, caused by an abnormal proliferation of Schwann cells

neu·ro·gen·ic (-jen′ik) *adj.* 1 originating in the nervous system 2 controlled by nerve impulses —**neu′ro·gen′i·cal·ly** *adv.*

neu·rog·li·a (no͞o räg′lē ə, nyo͞o-) *n.* ⟦ModL < NEURO- + MGr *glia*, for Gr *gloios*, GLUE⟧ the connective tissue, consisting of a special type of branched cells, that binds together and supports the nerve tissue of the central nervous system —**neu·rog′li·al** *adj.*

neu·ro·hor·mone (noor′ō hôr′mōn, nyoor′-) *n.* a hormone made by nervous tissue —**neu′ro·hor·mo′nal** (-mō′nəl) *adj.*

neu·ro·hu·mor (-hyo͞o′mər, nyoor′-) *n.* ⟦NEURO- + HUMOR⟧ NEUROTRANSMITTER —**neu′ro·hu′mor·al** *adj.*

neu·ro·hy·poph·y·sis (noor′ō hī päf′ə sis, nyoor′-) *n., pl.* **-ses′** (-sēz′) the posterior lobe and infundibular stalk of the pituitary gland: it secretes various hormones, including oxytocin and vasopressin: cf. ADENOHYPOPHYSIS —**neu′ro·hy′po·phy′se·al** *adj.*, **neu′ro·hy′po·phy′si·al** (-hī′pō fiz′ē əl)

neu·ro·im·ag·ing (noor′ō im′ij iŋ, nyoor′-) *n.* imaging of the structure or activity of the central nervous system

neurol *abbrev.* 1 neurological 2 neurology

neu·ro·lep·tic (noor′ō lep′tik, nyoor′-) *adj.* ⟦Fr *neuroleptique* < Gr *neuron*, NERVE + *lēptos*, seizing < *lambanein*, to seize: see EPILEPSY⟧ tranquilizing —*n.* a tranquilizing drug

neu·rol·o·gy (no͞o räl′ə jē, nyo͞o-) *n.* ⟦ModL *neurologia*: see NEURO- & -LOGY⟧ the branch of medicine dealing with the nervous system, its structure, and its diseases —**neu·ro·log·i·cal** (noor′ə läj′i kəl, nyoor′-) *adj.*, **neu′ro·log′ic** —**neu′ro·log′i·cal·ly** *adv.* —**neu·rol′o·gist** *n.*

neu·rol·y·sis (no͞o räl′ə sis, nyo͞o-) *n.* ⟦ModL: see NEURO- & -LYSIS⟧ 1 destruction or exhaustion of nerve tissue 2 the freeing of a nerve from adhesions —**neu·ro·lyt·ic** (noor′ə lit′ik, nyoor′-) *adj.*

neu·ro·ma (no͞o rō′mə, nyo͞o-) *n., pl.* **-mas** or **-ma·ta** (-mə tə) ⟦ModL: see NEURO- & -OMA⟧ a tumor derived from nervous tissue, or one consisting largely of nerve cells and fibers

neu·ro·mast (no͝or′ō mast′, nyo͝or′-) ***n.*** ⟦NEURO- + Gr *mastos*, breast: see MAST[2]⟧ any of the sense organs found in the lateral line system and the skin of fishes

neu·ro·mus·cu·lar (no͝or′ō mus′kyo͞o lər, nyo͝or′-) ***adj.*** of or involving both nerves and muscles

neu·ron (no͝or′än′, nyo͝or′-) ***n.*** ⟦ModL < Gr *neuron*, NERVE⟧ the structural and functional unit of the nervous system, consisting of the nerve cell body and all its processes, including an axon and one or more dendrites: also **neu′rone′** (-rōn′) —**neu·ro·nal** (no͝or′ə nəl, nyo͝or′-) ***adj.***, **neu·ron·ic** (no͞o rän′ik, nyo͞o-)

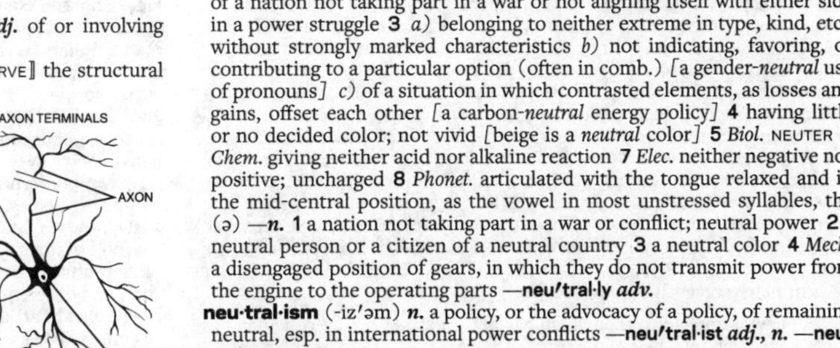

neuron

neu·ro·path (no͝or′ō path′, nyo͝or′-) ***n.*** ⟦< NEUROPATHIC⟧ *former term for* NEUROTIC

neu·ro·pa·thol·o·gy (no͝or′ō pə thäl′ə jē, nyo͝or′-) ***n.*** the branch of pathology dealing with diseases of the nervous system —**neu′ro·pa·thol′o·gist** ***n.***

neu·rop·a·thy (no͝o räp′ə thē, nyo͝o-) ***n.*** ⟦NEURO- + -PATHY⟧ any disease of the nervous system —**neu·ro·path·ic** (no͝or′ō path′ik, nyo͝or′-) ***adj.***

neu·ro·pep·tide (no͝or′ō pep′tīd′, nyo͝or′-) ***n.*** an endorphin or other peptide in neural tissue

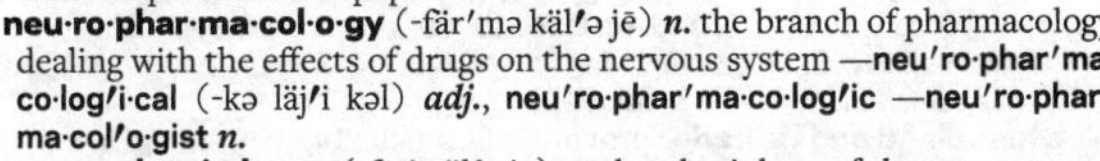

neu·ro·phar·ma·col·o·gy (-fär′mə käl′ə jē) ***n.*** the branch of pharmacology dealing with the effects of drugs on the nervous system —**neu′ro·phar′ma·co·log′i·cal** (-kə läj′i kəl) ***adj.***, **neu′ro·phar′ma·co·log′ic** —**neu′ro·phar′ma·col′o·gist** ***n.***

neu·ro·phys·i·ol·o·gy (-fiz′ē äl′ə jē) ***n.*** the physiology of the nervous system —**neu′ro·phys′i·o·log′i·cal** (-ə läj′i kəl) ***adj.***, **neu′ro·phys′i·o·log′ic** —**neu′ro·phys′i·o·log′i·cal·ly** ***adv.*** —**neu′ro·phys′i·ol′o·gist** ***n.***

neu·ro·psy·chi·a·try (-sī kī′ə trē, -si-) ***n.*** a branch of medicine dealing with psychiatric disorders as they are related to disorders of the nervous system —**neu′ro·psy′chi·at′ric** (-sī′kē a′trik) ***adj.*** —**neu′ro·psy·chi′a·trist** ***n.***

neu·ro·psy·chol·o·gy (-sī käl′ə jē) ***n.*** the science dealing with the effects that the nervous system, esp. the brain, has on behavior —**neu′ro·psy′cho·log′i·cal** (-sī′kə läj′i kəl) ***adj.*** —**neu′ro·psy·chol′o·gist** ***n.***

neu·rop·ter·an (no͝o räp′tər ən, nyo͝o-) ***n.*** ⟦< ModL *Neuroptera* (< NEURO- + PTERO-) + -AN⟧ any of an order (Neuroptera) of carnivorous insects, including the lacewings and ant lions, with four transparent wings and biting mouthparts —**neu·rop′ter·ous** ***adj.***

neu·ro·sci·ence (no͝or′ō sī′əns, nyo͝or′-) ***n.*** any science dealing with the functions, abnormalities, etc. of the nervous system —**neu′ro·sci′en·tist** ***n.***

neu·ro·sis (no͝o rō′sis, nyo͝o-) ***n.***, *pl.* **-ses′** (-sēz′) ⟦ModL: see NEURO- & -OSIS⟧ **1** *Psychiatry* any of various mental disorders in which there is a symptom or group of symptoms that causes psychological pain or discomfort and may be very disabling: common neuroses include anxiety, compulsions, phobias, and depression **2** popularly, any mental state characterized by obsession, chronic anxiety, hypochondria, etc.

neu·ro·sur·ger·y (no͝or′ō sʉr′jər ē, nyo͝or′-) ***n.*** the branch of surgery involving some part of the nervous system, including the brain and the spinal cord —**neu′ro·sur′geon** ***n.*** —**neu′ro·sur′gi·cal** ***adj.***

neu·rot·ic (no͝o rät′ik, nyo͝o-) ***adj.*** of, characteristic of, or having a neurosis —***n.*** a neurotic person —**neu·rot′i·cal·ly** ***adv.*** —**neu·rot′i·cism′** (-ə siz′əm) ***n.***

neu·rot·o·my (no͝o rät′ə mē, nyo͝o-) ***n.***, *pl.* **-mies** ⟦NEURO- + -TOMY⟧ the surgical severing of a nerve, as for relieving pain

neu·ro·tox·in (no͝or′ō täk′sin, nyo͝or′-) ***n.*** a toxin that destroys nerves or nervous tissue —**neu′ro·tox′ic** ***adj.***

neu·ro·trans·mit·ter (no͝or′ō trans′mit′ər, nyo͝or′-; -tranz′-) ***n.*** a biochemical substance, as acetylcholine or norepinephrine, that transmits or inhibits nerve impulses at a synapse

neu·ro·trop·ic (no͝or′ō träp′ik, nyo͝or′-) ***adj.*** ⟦NEURO- + -TROPIC⟧ having an affinity for nervous tissue, as certain viruses and poisons

Neuss (nois) city in W Germany, in the state of North Rhine-Westphalia

neus·ton (no͞os′tän′, nyo͞os′-) ***n.*** ⟦Gr, neut. of *neustos*, swimming (verbal of *nein*, to swim < IE *(s)neu-*, var. of *(s)na-*, > NATANT)⟧ minute organisms, as mosquito larvae, existing in or dependent upon the surface film of a body of water

Neus·tri·a (no͞os′trē ə, nyo͞os′-) W part of the kingdom of the Merovingian Franks in what is now N & NW France —**Neus′tri·an** ***adj., n.***

neut *abbrev.* neuter

neu·ter (no͞ot′ər, nyo͞ot′-) ***adj.*** ⟦ME *neutre* < MFr or L: MFr *neutre* < L *neuter*, neither < *ne-*, not (see NO[1]) + *uter*, either⟧ **1** [Archaic] taking neither side; neutral **2** *Biol. a)* having no sexual organ; asexual *b)* having undeveloped or imperfect sexual organs in the adult, as the worker bee **3** *Gram. a)* designating, of, or belonging to a third gender, existing in many highly inflected languages, consisting of words that have neither masculine nor feminine grammatical gender *b)* neither active nor passive; intransitive (said of verbs) —***n.*** **1** a castrated or spayed animal **2** [Archaic] a neutral person or group **3** *Biol.* a plant or animal lacking, or having undeveloped, sexual organs **4** *Gram. a)* the neuter gender *b)* a word or form in this gender *c)* an intransitive verb —***vt.*** to castrate or spay (an animal)

neu·tral (no͞o′trəl, nyo͞o′-) ***adj.*** ⟦Fr < ML *neutralis* < L, of neuter gender < *neuter*: see prec.⟧ **1** *a)* not taking the side of either of the parties in a dispute or quarrel *b)* not taking part in a war; giving no active aid to any belligerent *c)* not associated with either side in a war, dispute, contest, etc. [*a neutral* corner in a boxing ring] **2** of, belonging to, or characteristic of a nation not taking part in a war or not aligning itself with either side in a power struggle **3** *a)* belonging to neither extreme in type, kind, etc.; without strongly marked characteristics *b)* not indicating, favoring, or contributing to a particular option (often in comb.) [a gender-*neutral* use of pronouns] *c)* of a situation in which contrasted elements, as losses and gains, offset each other [a carbon-*neutral* energy policy] **4** having little or no decided color; not vivid [beige is a *neutral* color] **5** *Biol.* NEUTER **6** *Chem.* giving neither acid nor alkaline reaction **7** *Elec.* neither negative nor positive; uncharged **8** *Phonet.* articulated with the tongue relaxed and in the mid-central position, as the vowel in most unstressed syllables, the (ə) —***n.*** **1** a nation not taking part in a war or conflict; neutral power **2** a neutral person or a citizen of a neutral country **3** a neutral color **4** *Mech.* a disengaged position of gears, in which they do not transmit power from the engine to the operating parts —**neu′tral·ly** ***adv.***

neu·tral·ism (-iz′əm) ***n.*** a policy, or the advocacy of a policy, of remaining neutral, esp. in international power conflicts —**neu′tral·ist** ***adj., n.*** —**neu′tral·is′tic** ***adj.***

neu·tral·i·ty (no͞o tral′ə tē, nyo͞o-) ***n.***, *pl.* **-ties** the quality, state, or character of being neutral; specif., *a)* the status or policy of a nation not participating directly or indirectly in a war between other nations *b)* neutral status, as of a seaport in wartime

neu·tral·ize (no͞o′trə līz′, nyo͞o′-) ***vt.*** **-ized′**, **-iz′ing** ⟦Fr *neutraliser*⟧ **1** to declare (a territory, nation, etc.) neutral in war; declare open to all nations under international law and exempt from attack **2** to make ineffective; destroy or counteract the effectiveness, force, disposition, etc. of **3** *Chem.* to destroy the distinctive or active properties of [an alkali *neutralizes* an acid] **4** *Elec.* to make electrically neutral —**neu′tral·i·za′tion** ***n.*** —**neu′tral·iz′er** ***n.***

neutral spirits [*with sing. or pl. v.*] ethyl alcohol of 190 proof or over, esp. as used for blending with aged whiskeys, or with flavorings to make liqueurs, cordials, etc.

neu·tri·no (no͞o trē′nō, nyo͞o-) ***n.***, *pl.* **-nos** ⟦It, coined by Enrico FERMI < *neutrone* (< fol.) + dim. suffix *-ino*⟧ *Particle Physics* any of three stable leptons having a mass approaching zero and no charge: a neutrino has almost no interaction with matter

neu·tron (no͞o′trän′, nyo͞o′-) ***n.*** ⟦NEUTR(AL) + -ON⟧ *Particle Physics* an uncharged nucleon having a mass of *c.* 1.675×10^{-27} kg (*c.* 939.5729 MeV/c^2, *c.* 1,839 times the mass of an electron): a free neutron, as in nuclear fission, has a half-life of *c.* 14.8 minutes, is readily absorbed by a nucleus, and decays into a proton, an electron, and a neutrino

☆**neutron bomb** a small thermonuclear warhead for battlefield use, releasing large numbers of neutrons intended to disable or kill enemy soldiers without destroying buildings, vehicles, etc.

neutron number the number of neutrons in a given nucleus: it is the difference between the mass number and the atomic number

☆**neutron star** a collapsed star of extremely high density composed almost entirely of neutrons

neu·tro·phil (no͞o′trō fil, nyo͞o′-; -trə-) ***n.*** ⟦< NEUTRAL + -PHIL (var. of -PHILE)⟧ a granular type of phagocytic white blood cell in vertebrate blood, stainable by neutral dyes —***adj.*** easily stained by neutral dyes: often **neu′tro·phil′ic**

Nev *abbrev.* Nevada

Ne·va (nē′və) river in NW Russia, flowing from Lake Ladoga through St. Petersburg into the Gulf of Finland: 46 mi (74 km)

Ne·vad·a (nə vad′ə, -väd′ə) ⟦after SIERRA NEVADA⟧ Mountain State of the W U.S.: admitted 1864; 109,826 sq mi (284,448 sq km); cap. Carson City: abbrev. *NV* or *Nev*

Ne·vad·an (-ən) ***adj.*** of Nevada: usually used in the predicate —***n.*** a person born or living in Nevada

né·vé (nā vā′, nā′vā′) ***n.*** ⟦Fr (Swiss dial.), glacier, ult. < L *nix* (gen. *nivis*), SNOW⟧ **1** FIRN **2** the area above or at the head of a glacier that accumulates firn

Nev·el·son (nev′əl sən), **Louise** 1900-88; U.S. sculptor, born in Russia

nev·er (nev′ər) ***adv.*** ⟦ME *nevere* < OE *næfre* < *ne*, not (see NO[1]) + *æfre*, EVER⟧ **1** not ever; at no time **2** not at all; by no chance; in no case; under no conditions —**never mind** *see the phrase under* MIND

☆**nev·er·mind** (-mīnd′) ***n.*** [Dial.] **1** attention; heed: chiefly in **pay someone (or something) no nevermind** **2** concern; affair

nev·er·more (nev′ər môr′) ***adv.*** never again

nev·er-nev·er (nev′ər nev′ər) ***n.*** [Brit. Slang] the installment plan —***adj.*** imaginary, fantasized, unrealistic, etc.

never-never land ⟦after the imaginary land in *Peter Pan* (1904), play by J. M. BARRIE[1]⟧ an unreal or unrealistic place or situation

nev·er·the·less (nev′ər *thə* les′) ***adv.*** in spite of that; however; nonetheless: often used as a conjunctive adverb: sometimes written **never the less**

Nev·il or **Nev·ille** (nev′əl) ***n.*** ⟦< Norm surname *Nevil*, *Néville*, after *Neuville*, town in Normandy (lit., new city)⟧ a masculine name: dim. *Nev*

Ne·vis (nē′vis, nev′is) island of the country St. Kitts and Nevis: 36 sq mi (93 sq km)

ne·vus (nē′vəs) ***n.***, *pl.* **ne′vi′** (-vī′) ⟦ModL < L *naevus*, birthmark < base of *genus*, GENUS⟧ a birthmark, mole, or other colored spot on the skin —**ne′void′** (-void′) ***adj.***

new (no͞o, nyo͞o) ***adj.*** ⟦ME *newe* < OE *niwe*, akin to Ger *neu* < IE **newos*, new (< base **newo-*) > L *novus*, Gr *neos*, Welsh *newydd*, new⟧ **1** never existing before; appearing, thought of, developed, made, produced, etc. for the first time **2** *a)* existing before, but known or discovered for the first time [*a new* planet] *b)* recently observed, experienced, manifested, etc.; different [a *new* understanding of the problem] *c)* strange; unfamiliar; foreign [languages *new* to him] **3** not yet familiar or accustomed; inexperienced [*new* to the work] **4** *a)* designating the more or most recent of two or more things of the same class, though both may be old [*New* York] *b)* taking the place of the previous one; recently appointed, acquired, etc. [a *new* regime] **5** *a)* recently grown or made; fresh [*new* wine, *new* cars] *b)* harvested early [*new* potatoes] **6** not previously used or worn **7** modern; recent; fashionable; recently current **8** more; additional [two *new* inches of snow] **9** beginning again; starting as a repetition of a cycle, series, etc.; making another start [the *new* moon, the *new* year] **10** having just reached a position, rank, place, etc. [a *new* arrival] **11** refreshed in spirits, health, etc. [a *new* man] **12** [**N-**] MODERN (*adj.* 3) —*n.* something new: with *the* —*adv.* newly; recently —**new′ness** *n.*

SYN.—**new** is applied to that which has never existed before or which has only just come into being, possession, use, etc. [a *new* coat, plan, etc.]; **fresh** implies such newness that the original appearance, quality, vigor, etc. have not been affected by time or use [*fresh* eggs, a *fresh* start]; **novel** implies a newness that is strikingly unusual or strange [a *novel* idea, combination, etc.]; **modern** and **modernistic** apply to that which is of the present time, as distinguished from earlier periods, and connote up-to-dateness, the latter word, sometimes, with derogatory implications; **original** is used of that which is not only new but is also the first of its kind [an *original* plan, melody, etc.] —*ANT.* **old**

New Age [*often* **n- a-**] **1** of or pertaining to a contemporary cultural movement characterized by a concern with spiritual consciousness and variously combining belief in reincarnation and astrology with such practices as meditation, vegetarianism, and holistic medicine **2** designating or of a style of popular instrumental music characterized by simple, repetitive melodies and intended to effect a serene mood

New American Bible an English translation of the Bible for the use of Roman Catholics, made by a group of U.S. scholars and published in 1970

New Amsterdam Dutch colonial town on Manhattan Island: renamed (1664) New York by the British

New·ark (no͞o′ərk, nyo͞o-) ⟦after *Newark*, England⟧ city in NE N.J.

New Bedford ⟦after BEDFORD, England⟧ seaport in SE Mass.

new·bie (no͞o′bē, nyo͞o′-) *n.* [Informal] a person new to a particular occupation, way of life, activity, etc.; novice; beginner

new blood people newly hired, recruited, etc., regarded as a potential source of fresh ideas, renewed vigor, etc.

new·born (no͞o′bôrn′, nyo͞o′-) *adj.* ⟦ME⟧ **1** recently born **2** reborn —*n.* a recently born infant

New Britain largest island of the Bismarck Archipelago, east of New Guinea: 14,100 sq mi (36,519 sq km)

New Brunswick ⟦named to honor George III, who was also elector of *Brunswick*-Lüneburg⟧ province of SE Canada, on the Gulf of St. Lawrence: 27,550 sq mi (71,355 sq km); cap. Fredericton: abbrev. *NB* or *N.B.*

New·burg (no͞o′burg′, nyo͞o′-) *adj.* ⟦< *(lobster) Newburg(h)*, prob. after *Newburgh*, N.Y.⟧ ☆served in a rich, creamy sauce made with butter, egg yolks, and sherry

New Caledonia French island in the SW Pacific, east of Australia: with nearby islands an overseas territory of France: 7,172 sq mi (18,575 sq km); cap. Nouméa

New Castile *see* CASTILE

New·cas·tle (no͞o′kas′əl, nyo͞o′-; -käs′-) **1** seaport in Tyne and Wear, N England, north of Leeds: in full **Newcastle-upon-Tyne** (-tīn′) **2** city in Staffordshire, WC England: in full **Newcastle-under-Lyme** (-līm′) **3** seaport in E New South Wales, Australia, on the Pacific

Newcastle disease ⟦after prec., where it was first recorded⟧ an acute viral disease of poultry and other birds, characterized by pneumonia and encephalomyelitis and caused by a paramyxovirus

New·comb (no͞o′kəm, nyo͞o′-), **Simon** 1835-1909; U.S. astronomer, born in Canada

new·com·er (no͞o′kum′ər, nyo͞o′-) *n.* a recent arrival

New Criticism ⟦< *The New Criticism*, book (1941) by John Crowe RANSOM⟧ ☆a method of literary analysis, in vogue in the mid-20th cent., stressing close examination of the text itself, its tone, imagery, structure, etc.

☆**New Deal** **1** the economic and political principles and policies adopted by President Franklin D. Roosevelt in the 1930s to advance economic recovery and social welfare **2** the Roosevelt administration —**New Dealer**

New Delhi capital of India, in Delhi territory, adjacent to the old city of Delhi

☆**new economics** [*sometimes* **N- E-**] an economic doctrine based on Keynesian theories and stressing the importance of governmental taxing and spending in promoting and maintaining a sound economy

New Egyptian the Egyptian language, *c.* 1600-700 B.C.

new·el (no͞o′əl, nyo͞o′-) *n.* ⟦ME *nowelle* < OFr *nuel*, a nut, fruit pit < LL *nucalis*, like a nut < L *nux* (gen. *nucis*), NUT⟧ **1** the central upright pillar around which the steps of a winding staircase turn **2** the post at the top or bottom of a flight of stairs, supporting the handrail: also **newel post**

New England ⟦so named by Captain John SMITH⟧ ☆the six NE states of the U.S.: Me., Vt., N.H., Mass., R.I., & Conn.: abbrev. **New Eng** —**New Englander**

☆**New England boiled dinner** a dish consisting of meat, often corned beef, and whole potatoes, onions, carrots, cabbage, etc. cooked by boiling

New England clam chowder a thick cream soup made with clams, onions, potatoes, salt pork, milk, and various seasonings

New English ⟦term popularized by Henry SWEET after Ger *neuhochdeutsch*, New High German⟧ the English language since about 1750: cf. EARLY MODERN ENGLISH

New English Bible a British translation of the Bible, from the original languages, published in 1961 (N.T.) & 1970 (O.T.)

Newf *abbrev.* Newfoundland

new·fan·gled (no͞o′faŋ′gəld, nyo͞o′-) *adj.* ⟦ME < *newefangel* < *newe*, NEW + *-fangel* < base of OE *fon*, to take: see FANG⟧ **1** newly done, made, etc.; new; novel: a humorously derogatory term **2** [Now Rare] tending toward or fond of novelty or new things

new-fash·ioned (-fash′ənd) *adj.* **1** recently come into fashion **2** made in a new and different form or style

New Forest partially wooded rural district in SW Hampshire, England: 144 sq mi (373 sq km)

new·found (-found′) *adj.* newly gained or acquired [*newfound* wealth]

New·found·land[1] (no͞o′fənd lənd, -land′; nyo͞o′-; no͞o found′lənd, -land′; nyo͞o-) *n.* ⟦after fol.⟧ any of a breed of large, muscular dog with a long, straight, often black coat, formerly much used in water rescue work and now usually a guard dog or a watchdog

New·found·land[2] (no͞o′fənd lənd, -land′, nyo͞o′-; no͞o found′lənd, -land′, nyo͞o-) ⟦descriptive⟧ **1** island of Canada, off the E coast: 42,031 sq mi (108,860 sq km) **2** *former name for* NEWFOUNDLAND AND LABRADOR: abbrev. *NF, Nfld, Newf,* or *Nfd* —**New′found·land′er** *n.*

Newfoundland and Labrador province of Canada: 143,049 sq mi (370,495 sq km); cap. St. John's: abbrev. *NL, N.L.,* or *Nfld & Lab*

Newfoundland Standard Time a standard time used in Newfoundland and Labrador, Canada: it is three hours and thirty minutes behind Greenwich time

New France French possessions in North America, from the end of the 16th cent. to 1763, including E Canada, the Great Lakes region, & the Mississippi valley

New·gate (no͞o′gāt′, nyo͞o′-) *n.* former prison in London: torn down in 1902

New General Catalog *Astron.* a catalog of star clusters, galaxies, and other non-stellar objects, published in 1888: abbrev. *NGC*

New Georgia **1** group of islands in central Solomon Islands, in the SW Pacific: *c.* 2,170 sq mi (5,620 sq km) **2** largest island of this group: *c.* 1,300 sq mi (3,367 sq km)

New Granada **1** former Spanish possessions, mostly in NW South America, including what is now Colombia, Venezuela, Ecuador, & Panama **2** former country consisting of present-day Colombia & Panama

New Guinea **1** large island in the East Indies, north of Australia: divided between the Indonesian province of Papua and Papua New Guinea: *c.* 330,000 sq mi (854,697 sq km): Indonesian name IRIAN **2** **Trust Territory of** former Australian trust territory including NE New Guinea, the Bismarck Archipelago, Bougainville, & smaller adjacent islands of the Solomons: see PAPUA NEW GUINEA

New·ham (no͞o′əm, nyo͞o′-) borough of E Greater London, England, on the Thames: formed by the merger of the former cities of East Ham & West Ham

New Hamp·shire (hamp′shər, ham′-) ⟦after HAMPSHIRE⟧ New England state of the U.S.: one of the 13 original states: 8,968 sq mi (23,227 sq km); cap. Concord: abbrev. *NH* or *N.H.*

New Hamp·shir·ite (-īt′) **1** of New Hampshire: usually used in the predicate **2** a person born or living in New Hampshire

New Haven city in S Conn., on Long Island Sound

New Hebrides *former name for* VANUATU

New High German *see* GERMAN, HIGH GERMAN

New Ireland island in the Bismarck Archipelago, north of New Britain: 3,340 sq mi (8,651 sq km)

new·ish (no͞o′ish, nyo͞o′-) *adj.* somewhat new

☆**new jack (swing)** a style of rhythm-and-blues music blending rap, disco, funk, soul, etc. and characterized by aggressive, boastful, romantic lyrics

New Jersey (jur′zē) ⟦after JERSEY[2] (the Channel Island)⟧ state of the E U.S., on the Atlantic: one of the 13 original states: 7,417 sq mi (19,211 sq km); cap. Trenton: abbrev. *NJ* or *N.J.*

New Jer·sey·ite (-īt′) **1** of New Jersey: usually used in the predicate **2** a person born or living in New Jersey

New Jerusalem[1] *Bible* the holy city of heaven: Rev. 21:2

New Jerusalem[2], **Church of the** the church of the Swedenborgians: also **New Church**

new journalism [*sometimes* **N- J-**] journalism that incorporates characteristics of and techniques from fiction writing, as by including conversations, a person's thoughts, and other specific details imagined by the writer

☆**New Left** ⟦term coined by C. Wright Mills (1916–62), U.S. sociologist⟧ a political movement that developed in the 1960s in Europe and the U.S. as a loose coalition of organizations, mainly of young people, seeking radical social and economic change

New London city in SE Conn., on Long Island Sound: site of U.S. Coast Guard Academy

new·ly (no͞o′lē, nyo͞o′-) *adv.* **1** recently; lately **2** anew; afresh **3** in a new way or style

new·ly·wed (-wed′) *n.* a recently married person

New·man (no͞o′mən, nyo͞o′-) **1 Alfred** 1901-70; U.S. composer of film scores **2 John Henry** Cardinal Newman 1801-90; Eng. theologian & writer **3 Paul (Leonard)** 1925-2008; U.S. film actor

new·mar·ket (no͞o′mär′kit, nyo͞o′-) ***n.*** ⟦after fol.: orig. worn for riding at the races held there⟧ a long, closefitting coat worn by men and women in the 19th cent.: also **Newmarket coat**

New·mar·ket (no͞o′mär′kit, nyo͞o′-) rural district in Suffolk, E England: scene of many horse-racing events

☆**new math** a system for teaching fundamental concepts of mathematics by the use of SET THEORY

New Mexican 1 of New Mexico: usually used in the predicate **2** a person born or living in New Mexico

New Mexico ⟦transl. of Sp *Nuevo Méjico*⟧ Mountain State of the SW U.S.: admitted 1912; 121,356 sq mi (314,310 sq km); cap. Santa Fe: abbrev. *NM*, *N.M.*, or *N Mex*

new moon 1 the first phase of the moon when it is between the earth and the sun, with its dark side toward the earth: it is followed by the waxing crescent phase **2** the time of the new moon

new-mown (no͞o′mōn′, nyo͞o′-) ***adj.*** freshly mown or cut: said of hay or grass

New Netherland Dutch colony (1613-64) on Manhattan Island & along the Hudson River: taken by England & divided into the colonies of New York & New Jersey

New Or·le·ans (ôr′lē ənz, -lənz; ôr lēnz′) ⟦transl. of Fr *Nouvelle Orléans*, in honor of Philippe II, Duc d'*Orléans* (1674-1723), and after *Orléans*, France⟧ city & port in SE La., on the Mississippi

New·port (no͞o′pôrt′, nyo͞o′-) seaport in Gwent, SE Wales, on the Usk River

Newport News ⟦orig. obscure⟧ seaport in SE Va., on the James River at Hampton Roads

New Providence island of the NC Bahamas: 80 sq mi (207 sq km)

New Revised Standard Version a thorough revision of the Revised Standard Version of the Bible sponsored by the National Council of Churches in the U.S. and published in 1989

news (no͞oz, nyo͞oz) ***n.*** ⟦ME *newes*, novelties (pl. of *newe*, adj.), after OFr *noveles* or ML *nova*, pl. of *novum*, what is new: < L *novus*: see NEW⟧ **1** new information about anything; information previously unknown **2** *a)* reports, collectively, of recent happenings, esp. those broadcast over radio or TV, printed in a newspaper, etc. *b)* any person or thing thought to merit special attention in such reports **3** *short for* NEWSCAST —**make news** to do something that is apt to be reported as news

☆**news agency** an organization that supplies news to newspapers, radio and television stations, etc. that subscribe to its services

news agent *chiefly Brit. var. of* NEWSDEALER

news·boy (no͞oz′boi′, nyo͞oz′-) ***n.*** a boy who sells or delivers newspapers

☆**news·cast** (-kast′, -käst′) ***n.*** ⟦NEWS + -CAST⟧ a program of news broadcast over radio or television —**news′cast′er** ***n.*** —**news′cast′ing** ***n.***

☆**news conference** PRESS CONFERENCE

☆**news·deal·er** (-dēl′ər) ***n.*** a person who sells newspapers, magazines, etc., esp. as a retailer

news·group (no͞oz′gro͞op′) ***n.*** any of a large number of internet discussion sites on a particular topic, set up to display messages and comments from various users in the order of submission

☆**news·hawk** (-hôk′) ***n.*** [Slang] a newspaper reporter

☆**news·hound** (-hound′) ***n.*** [Slang] a broadcast or newspaper reporter

New Siberian Islands group of Russian islands in the Arctic Ocean, between the Laptev & East Siberian seas: *c.* 11,000 sq mi (28,490 sq km)

☆**news·ie** (no͞o′zē, nyo͞o′-) ***n.*** [Slang] **1** NEWSPERSON **2** NEWSDEALER

news·let·ter (no͞oz′let′ər, nyo͞oz′-) ***n.*** a bulletin issued regularly to subscribers, employees, or members of an organization or group, containing news, a calendar of upcoming events, etc.

news·mag·a·zine (-mag′ə zēn) ***n.*** **1** a magazine, often a weekly, concerned with current news, usually divided into departments with analyses and interpretations **2** MAGAZINE (sense 6)

news·mak·er (-māk′ər) ***n.*** a person whose activities or accomplishments are reported as news, esp. one who is a prominent figure in the news

news·man (-man′, -mən) ***n.***, *pl.* **-men′** (-men′, -mən) a newscaster or reporter, esp. a male one

news·mon·ger (-muŋ′gər, -mäŋ′gər) ***n.*** a person who spreads news; esp., a gossip

New South Wales state of SE Australia, on the Pacific: 309,129 sq mi (800,640 sq km); cap. Sydney

New Spain former Spanish viceroyalty (1535-1821) including, at its greatest extent, Mexico, SW U.S., Central America north of Panama, the West Indies, & the Philippines

news·pa·per (no͞oz′pā′pər, nyo͞oz′-; no͞os′-, nyo͞os′-) ***n.*** **1** a publication consisting of folded, unbound sheets of newsprint containing news, editorials, advertisements, etc. and published regularly, typically daily or weekly **2** NEWSPRINT

news·pa·per·ing (-iŋ) ***n.*** news writing; journalism

news·pa·per·man (-man′) ***n.***, *pl.* **-men′** (-men′) **1** a person, esp. a man, who works for a newspaper as a reporter, editor, etc. **2** a person who owns or publishes a newspaper

news·pa·per·wom·an (-wo͝om′ən) ***n.***, *pl.* **-wom′en** (-wim′in) **1** a woman who works for a newspaper as a reporter, editor, etc. **2** a woman who owns or publishes a newspaper

new·speak (no͞o′spēk′, nyo͞o′-) ***n.*** ⟦coined (< NEW + SPEAK) by George ORWELL in his novel *Nineteen Eighty-four* (published 1949)⟧ [*sometimes* **N-**] **1** the deliberate use of ambiguous and deceptive talk, as by government officials, in an attempt to control public opinion **2** such language

news·peo·ple (no͞oz′pē′pəl, nyo͞oz′-) ***pl.n.*** newspersons collectively

news·per·son (-pur′sən) ***n.*** a person involved in the gathering, writing, editing, or reporting of news, often specif. for television or radio

news·print (-print′) ***n.*** a cheap, low-grade paper made mainly from wood pulp and used chiefly for newspapers

news·read·er (-rēd′ər) ***n.*** [Chiefly Brit.] a person who reads the news on a TV or radio broadcast

☆**news·reel** (-rēl′) ***n.*** a short film of recent news events: formerly shown as part of the program in movie theaters

☆**news release** a statement or story prepared for release to the news media, as by a government official or an organization

news·room (-ro͞om′) ***n.*** ☆a room in a newspaper office, or in a radio or television station, where the news is written and edited

news service 1 NEWS AGENCY **2** WIRE SERVICE **3** SYNDICATE (***n.*** 3)

☆**news·stand** (-stand′) ***n.*** a stand at which newspapers, magazines, etc. are sold: also [Brit.] **news stall**

New Stone Age the Neolithic

New Style ⟦opposed to OLD STYLE (sense 1)⟧ the method of reckoning time according to the Gregorian calendar

news·week·ly (no͞oz′wēk′lē, nyo͞oz′-) ***n.***, *pl.* **-lies** a newsmagazine that is published each week

news·wom·an (-wo͝om′ən) ***n.***, *pl.* **-wom′en** (-wim′in) a female newscaster or reporter

☆**news·wor·thy** (-wur′thē) ***adj.*** having the qualities of news; timely and important or interesting —**news′wor′thi·ness** ***n.***

☆**news·y** (no͞o′zē, nyo͞o′-) ***adj.*** **news′i·er**, **news′i·est** [Informal] containing much news —***n.***, *pl.* **news′ies** [Old Informal] a newsboy

newt (no͞ot, nyo͞ot) ***n.*** ⟦ME *neute* < (*a*)*n eute* < OE *efeta*, EFT[1]⟧ any of various small salamanders (family Salamandridae) that can live both on land and in water

New Territories the part of the administrative region of Hong Kong that is on the Chinese mainland

New Testament 1 *Christian Theol.* the promises of God to man that are embodied in the life and teachings of Jesus **2** the part of the Christian Bible that tells of the life and teachings of Jesus and his followers, including the four Gospels, the Acts of the Apostles, the Letters, and the Revelation of Saint John: cf. BIBLE

new·ton (no͞ot′'n, nyo͞ot′'n) ***n.*** ⟦after Sir Isaac NEWTON[2]⟧ the basic unit of force in the SI and MKS systems, equal to the force which imparts to a mass of one kilogram an acceleration of one meter per second per second: abbrev. *N*

New·ton[1] (no͞ot′'n, nyo͞ot′'n) ***n.*** ⟦after surname *Newton* < common Eng place name *Newton* < OE *neowa tun*, new town⟧ a masculine name: dim. *Newt*

New·ton[2] (no͞ot′'n, nyo͞ot′'n), Sir **Isaac** 1642-1727; Eng. mathematician & natural philosopher: formulated the laws of gravity & motion and the elements of differential calculus —**New·to′ni·an** (-tō′nē ən) ***adj., n.***

new town [*often* **N- T-**] any of a number of comprehensively planned, often self-contained, towns and cities built esp. just after WWII in Great Britain, often under government direction

new wave ⟦calque of Fr *nouvelle vague*; see WAVE, ***n.*** 4⟧ any of various new or experimental trends or movements, as in the arts or popular culture

New World[1] designating or of a group of animals or plants native to the Western Hemisphere, esp. the Americas

New World[2] the Western Hemisphere

new year 1 the year just about to begin or just begun: usually with *the* **2** [**N- Y-**] the first day or days of the new year

New Year's (Day) Jan. 1, the first day of a calendar year, usually celebrated as a legal holiday

New Year's Eve the day or, esp., the evening before New Year's Day

New York ⟦after the Duke of *York* and Albany⟧ **1** state of the NE U.S.: one of the 13 original states: 47,214 sq mi (122,283 sq km); cap. Albany: abbrev. *NY* or *N.Y.* **2** city & port in SE N.Y., at the mouth of the Hudson: divided into five boroughs (the Bronx, Brooklyn, Manhattan, Queens, Staten Island): 365 sq mi (946 sq km): often **New York City**

New York Bay inlet of the Atlantic, south of Manhattan, divided by the Narrows into a N section (**Upper New York Bay**) & a S section (**Lower New York Bay**)

New York·er (yôr′kər) **1** *a)* of the state of New York *b)* of the city of New York: usually used in the predicate **2** *a)* a person born or living in the state of New York *b)* a person born or living in the city of New York

New York State Canal System system of waterways connecting Lake Erie & the Hudson River, with branches to lakes Ontario, Champlain, Cayuga, & Seneca: 524 mi (843 km): cf. ERIE CANAL

New Zea·land (zē′lənd) ⟦Du *Nieuw Zeeland*, after ZEELAND⟧ country made up of two large & several small islands in the S Pacific, southeast of Australia: discovered in 1642, became a British colony (1841), & achieved complete independence in 1931; member of the Commonwealth: 103,738 sq mi (268,680 sq km); cap. Wellington —**New Zea′land·er**

next (nekst) ***adj.*** ⟦ME *nexte* < OE *neahst*, *niehst*, superl. of *neah*, NIGH⟧ just before or after in time, space, degree, or rank; nearest; immediately preceding or following —***adv.*** **1** in the time, place, degree, or rank nearest, or immediately preceding or following **2** on the first subsequent occasion [when *next* we meet] —***prep.*** [Archaic] beside; nearest to [sit *next* the tree] —***n.*** **1** the one immediately following **2** one whose turn is next, as in being served —☆**get next to** [Slang] to ingratiate oneself with; become friendly or intimate with —**next door (to)** **1** in, at, or to the next house, building, etc. (adjacent to) **2** almost; nearly —**next to** **1** beside; adjacent to **2** [Informal] following in order of preference [*next to* eating, he likes jogging best]

next-door (nekst′dôr′, neks′-) ***adj.*** in or at the next house, building, etc.

next friend *Law* a person who, though not appointed as a guardian, acts for another legally unable to act for himself or herself

next of kin **1** a person's nearest relative or relatives **2** *Law a)* those persons who may be entitled by statute to share in the estate of one who dies without a will *b)* sometimes, the nearest blood relative as defined by statute

next world, the the afterlife; heaven, hell, etc.

nex·us (nek′səs) ***n., pl.*** **nex′us·es** or **nex′us** ⟦L < pp. of *nectere*, to tie⟧ **1** *a)* a connection, tie, or link between individuals of a group, members of a series, etc. *b)* the group or series so connected **2** a center or focal point

Ney (nā), **Mi·chel** (mē shel′) Duc d'Elchingen, Prince de La Moskova 1769-1815; Fr. military leader under Napoleon I: executed

Nez Percé or **Nez Perce** (nez′ purs′, -pər sā′; *Fr* nā per sā′) ⟦Fr, lit., pierced nose: from early reports of the practice of nose piercing by peoples in the same area⟧ **1** *pl.* **Nez Percé** or **Nez Percés; Nez Perce** or **Nez Perces** (nez′ pur′siz, -pər sāz′; Fr nā per sā′)a member of a North American Indian people living in Idaho, Washington, and Oregon **2** the Sahaptian language of this people

NF *abbrev.* **1** *Pharmacy* National Formulary **2** Newfoundland **3** *Banking* no funds: also **N/F, nf,** or **n/f**

NFC *service mark* National Football Conference

Nfd *abbrev.* Newfoundland

NFL *service mark* National Football League

Nfld *abbrev.* Newfoundland

Nfld & Lab *abbrev.* Newfoundland and Labrador

NFS *abbrev.* not for sale

ng *abbrev.* nanogram(s)

NG *abbrev.* **1** National Guard **2** New Guinea **3** *Football* nose guard: sometimes written **ng**

NGC *abbrev. Astron.* New General Catalog

NGO (en′jē′ō′) ***n., pl.*** **NGOs** ⟦*n(on)g(overnmental) o(rganization)*⟧ a private organization providing humanitarian aid or support as to impoverished or economically underdeveloped nations

NGU *abbrev.* NONGONOCOCCAL URETHRITIS

ngul·trum (əŋ ool′troom; eŋ gool′trəm, ən-) ***n.*** ⟦Bhutanese⟧ the basic monetary unit of Bhutan: see the table of monetary units in the Reference Supplement

Ngu·ni (əŋ gōō′nē) ***n.*** **1** *pl.* **-ni** or **-nis** a member of a group of peoples living in S Africa **2** the group of related Bantu languages of these peoples

ngwee (əŋ gwē′) ***n., pl.*** **ngwee** ⟦Bemba < adj., lit., bright⟧ a monetary unit of Zambia, equal to 1⁄100 of a kwacha

Nh *abbrev. Bible* Nahum

NH or **N.H.** *abbrev.* New Hampshire

NHeb *abbrev.* **1** New Hebrew **2** New Hebrides

NHG *abbrev.* New High German

NHI *abbrev.* [Brit.] National Health Insurance

NHL *service mark* National Hockey League

NHS *abbrev.* National Health Service (Great Britain)

Ni *Chem. symbol for* nickel

NI[1] *abbrev.* Northern Ireland

NI[2] *symbol* ampere-turn(s)

☆**ni·a·cin** (nī′ə sin) ***n.*** ⟦NI(COTINIC) AC(ID) + -IN[1]⟧ NICOTINIC ACID

Ni·ag·a·ra[1] (nī ag′rə, -ag′ə rə) ***n.*** ⟦after NIAGARA FALLS (the waterfall)⟧ a torrent, or flood

Ni·ag·a·ra[2] (nī ag′rə, -ag′ə rə) ⟦< Fr < Iroquoian town name⟧ river between W N.Y. & SE Ontario, Canada, flowing from Lake Erie into Lake Ontario: *c.* 36 mi (58 km)

Niagara Falls **1** large waterfall on the Niagara River: it is divided by an island into two falls, Horseshoe (or Canadian) Falls, *c.* 160 ft (49 m) high, & American Falls, *c.* 167 ft (51 m) high **2** city in W N.Y., near Niagara Falls (the waterfall) **3** city in SE Ontario, Canada, near the waterfall & opposite Niagara Falls, N.Y.

Nia·mey (nyä mā′) capital of Niger, in the SW part, on the Niger River

nib (nib) ***n.*** ⟦var. of NEB⟧ **1** the bill or beak of a bird **2** *a)* [Historical] the split and sharpened end of a quill pen *b)* the point of a pen **3** the projecting end of anything; point See also NIBS —***vt.*** **nibbed, nib′bing** [Obs.] to sharpen and split the end of (a quill) to make a pen

nib·ble (nib′əl) ***vt.*** **-bled, -bling** ⟦LME *nebyllen*, prob. akin to MLowG *nibbelen*: for IE base see NIP[1]⟧ **1** to eat (food) with quick bites, taking only a small amount at a time, as a mouse does **2** to bite at with small, gentle bites —***vi.*** **1** to take small, cautious, or gentle bites: usually with *at* **2** to show little interest in food by taking only small bites intermittently: usually with *at* —***n.*** **1** a small bite, morsel, or quantity **2** the act or an instance of nibbling **3** *a)* a slight tug on a fishing line, as from a fish sampling the bait *b)* [Informal] any display of interest, as from a potential customer or client —**nib′bler** ***n.***

Ni·be·lung (nē′bə looŋ′) ***n., pl.*** **-lungs′** or **-lung′en** (-ən) ⟦Ger⟧ **1** *Gmc. Legend a)* any of a race of dwarfs who owned a magic ring and a hoard of gold, which Siegfried took from them *b)* any of Siegfried's followers **2** in the *Nibelungenlied*, any of the Burgundian kings

Ni·be·lung·en·lied (nē′bə looŋ′ən lēt′) ***n.*** ⟦Ger, lit., song of the Nibelungs: see prec.⟧ a Middle High German epic poem by an unknown author, written in the first decade of the 13th cent. and based on Germanic legends

nib·lick (nib′lik) ***n.*** ⟦Scot, dim. of NIB: so named because of the short "nose" of the original wooden club⟧ *former term for* number 9 iron: see IRON (***n.*** 6)

nibs (nibz) ***n.*** ⟦< ?⟧ [Informal] an important, or esp. self-important, person: preceded by *his* or, occas., *her*

Nica *abbrev.* Nicaragua

NiCad (nī′kad′) ***n.*** ⟦< *Nicad*, a trademark < NI(CKEL) + CAD(MIUM)⟧ *Elec.* a type of rechargeable dry-cell battery with an anode of nickel, a cathode of cadmium, and an alkaline electrolyte: also written **nicad, ni-cad**

Ni·cae·a (nī sē′ə) ancient city in Bithynia, NW Asia Minor: site of two church councils: the Nicene Creed was formulated there in A.D. 325 —**Ni·cae′an** ***adj., n.***

Nicar *abbrev.* Nicaragua

Nic·a·ra·gua (nik′ə rä′gwə) **1** country in Central America, on the Caribbean & the Pacific: declared itself independent from Spain (1821): 49,998 sq mi (129,494 sq km); cap. Managua **2 Lake** lake in S Nicaragua: *c.* 3,100 sq mi (8,029 sq km) —**Nic′a·ra′guan** ***adj., n.***

nic·co·lite (nik′ə līt′) ***n.*** ⟦< ModL *niccolum* (< Swed *nickel*: see NICKEL) + -ITE[1]⟧ a hard, reddish, hexagonal mineral, NiAs, an ore of nickel; nickel arsenide

nice (nīs) ***adj.*** **nic′er, nic′est** ⟦ME, strange, lazy, foolish < OFr *nice, nisce*, stupid, foolish < L *nescius*, ignorant, not knowing < *nescire*, to be ignorant < *ne-*, not (see NO[1]) + *scire*, to know: see SCIENCE⟧ **1** [Obs.] *a)* ignorant; foolish *b)* wanton *c)* coy; shy **2** [Archaic] difficult to please; fastidious; refined; scrupulous **3** *a)* delicate; precise; discriminative; subtle [a *nice* distinction] *b)* calling for great care, accuracy, tact, etc., as in handling or discrimination [a *nice* problem of diplomacy] **4** able to make fine or delicate distinctions **5** *a generalized term of approval meaning variously: a)* agreeable; pleasant; delightful *b)* attractive; pretty *c)* kind and considerate *d)* conforming to approved social standards; respectable *e)* in good taste *f)* good; excellent —***adv.*** **nic′er, nic′est** well, pleasingly, attractively, etc.: variously regarded as nonstandard, dialectal, or informal —***SYN.*** DAINTY —☆**make nice** [Informal] to try to be friendly or cooperative: often with *with* —**nice and** [Informal] altogether, in a pleasing way [likes his tea *nice and* hot] —**nice′ly** ***adv.*** —**nice′ness** ***n.***

Nice (nēs) seaport & resort in SE France

Ni·cene (nī′sēn′, nī sēn′) ***adj.*** of Nicaea

Nicene Council either of two church councils that met in Nicaea in A.D. 325 and A.D. 787; esp., the first of these, that condemned Arianism and adopted the Nicene Creed

Nicene Creed a confession of faith of Christians traditionally attributed to the first Nicene Council and accepted, with some differences in wording, by both the Eastern Church and the Western Church

☆**nice Nelly** [Informal] a prudish or affectedly modest person: also sp. **nice Nellie** —**nice′-Nel′ly** ***adj.***

ni·ce·ty (nī′sə tē) ***n., pl.*** **-ties** ⟦ME *nicete* < OFr, folly < *nice*: see NICE⟧ **1** the quality or state of being nice; specif., *a)* scrupulosity *b)* precision; accuracy; exactness, as of discrimination or perception *c)* fastidiousness; refinement; delicacy of taste **2** the quality of calling for delicacy, accuracy, or precision in handling, discrimination, or adjustment **3** anything involving or calling for delicacy, accuracy, or precision; subtle or minute detail, distinction, etc. **4** something choice, dainty, or elegant —**to a nicety** to a precise degree; exactly

niche (nich; *Brit also* nēsh) ***n.*** ⟦Fr < OFr *nichier*, to nest < VL **nidicare* < L *nidus*, NEST⟧ **1** a recess or hollow in a wall, as for a statue, bust, or vase **2** a place or position particularly suitable to the person or thing in it **3** any small, specialized business market **4** *Ecol. a)* the particular role of an individual species or organism in its community and its environment, including its behavior and its position in the food cycle *b)* the specific space occupied by an organism within its habitat —***vt.*** **niched, nich′ing** to place in or as in a niche

niche

Nich·o·las[1] (nik′ə ləs) ***n.*** ⟦ME < OFr *Nicolas* < L *Nicolaus* < Gr *Nikolaos* < *nikē*, victory + *laos*, the people⟧ a masculine name: dim. *Nick*; equiv. L. *Nicolaus*, Fr. & Sp. *Nicolas*, Ger. *Nikolaus*, It. *Niccolo*, Russ. *Nikolai*

Nich·o·las[2] (nik′ə ləs) **1** Saint (4th cent. A.D.); bishop of Myra: patron saint of Russia, of Greece, & of young people, sailors, etc.: his day is Dec. 6: cf. SANTA CLAUS **2** Saint **Nicholas I** (A.D. 800?-867); pope (858-867): his day is Nov. 13: called *the Great* **3 Nicholas I** 1796-1855; czar of Russia (1825-55) **4 Nicholas II** 1868-1918; last czar of Russia (1894-1917); forced to abdicate; executed

Nicholas of Cu·sa (kyōō′sə, -zə) 1401-64; Ger. cardinal, philosopher, & mathematician

Ni·chrome (nī′krōm′) *trademark for* any of several alloys of nickel, chromium, etc. that have a high electrical resistance, used in the heating coils of appliances, in high temperature furnaces, etc.

nicht wahr? (niHt vär′) ⟦Ger, lit., not true?⟧ isn't that so?

nick (nik) ***n.*** ⟦LME *nyke*, prob. akin to *nocke*, notch⟧ **1** a small notch or slit; esp., a small cut, indentation or chip made accidentally on the edge or surface of wood, metal, china, etc. **2** a notch in the lower side of the shank of a printing type, for identification **3** [Brit. Slang] prison; jail **4** [Brit. Slang] condition; state *[a used car in good nick]* —***vt.*** **1** to make a nick or nicks in **2** [Now Rare] to score or tally by means of notches **3** *a)* to wound superficially *b)* to strike lightly and glancingly **4** to strike or catch at the exact or proper time; hit, guess, grasp, etc. exactly **5** [Slang] to overcharge or cheat **6** [Brit. Slang] *a)* to arrest; nab *b)* to steal —**in the nick of time** exactly when needed; just before it is too late

Nick (nik) ***n.*** a masculine name: see NICHOLAS[1]

nick·el (nik′əl) ***n.*** ⟦Swed: contr. (1754) by A. F. Cronstedt (1722-65), Swed mineralogist < *kopparnickel*, niccolite < Ger *kupfernickel*, false copper (< *kupfer*, COPPER[1] + *nickel*, goblin, devil, pejorative contr. < *Nikolaus*, NICHOLAS[1], prob. infl. by *nix*: see NIX[1]): term used by Ger miners because the ore looks like copper but contains none: see COBALT⟧ **1** a hard, silver-white, malleable metallic chemical element, used extensively in alloys, batteries, and for plating because of its resistance to oxidation: symbol, Ni; at. no. 28: see the periodic table of elements in the Reference Supplement ☆**2** a U.S. or Canadian coin made of an alloy of nickel and copper and equal to 5 cents —***vt.*** **-eled** or **-elled**, **-el·ing** or **-el·ling** to plate with nickel

☆**nick·el-and-dime** (nik′əl ən dīm′) [Informal] ***adj.*** **1** costing or spending little; cheap **2** of little value or importance; minor; petty —***vt.*** **nick′el-** (or **nick′eled-)and-dimed′**, **nick′el-** (or **nick′el·ing-)and-dim′ing** **1** to spend very little on **2** to weaken, erode, destroy, etc. as by the repeated expenditure of small sums or repeated niggling actions —***vi.*** to spend very little —**nickel-and-dime it** (or **one's way**) to succeed or obtain something gradually by the repeated expenditure of small sums or the slow gathering of votes, power, money, etc. in small increments

nick·el·ic (nik′əl ik, nik el′ik) ***adj.*** of or containing nickel, esp. trivalent nickel

nick·el·if·er·ous (nik′əl if′ər əs) ***adj.*** ⟦see NICKEL & -FEROUS⟧ containing nickel *[a nickeliferous ore]*

nick·el-met·al hydride (nik′əl met′'l) a type of long-lasting, rechargeable dry-cell battery commonly used in cell phones, digital cameras, etc.: abbrev. *NiMH*

☆**nick·el·o·de·on** (nik′əl ō′dē ən) ***n.*** **1** ⟦NICKEL + Fr *odéon* < LL *odeum*, ODEUM⟧ an early 20th-cent. theater for exhibiting films, vaudeville, etc., to which the admission was typically five cents **2** ⟦NICKEL + (MEL)ODEON⟧ a player piano or type of jukebox operated by the insertion of a coin, typically a nickel, into a slot

nick·el·ous (nik′əl əs) ***adj.*** containing nickel, esp. divalent nickel

nickel plate a thin layer of nickel placed by electrolysis on objects made of other metal, to improve the finish and prevent rust —**nick′el-plate′** ***vt.*** **-plat′ed**, **-plat′ing**

nickel silver a hard, tough, ductile, malleable, silver-white alloy composed essentially of nickel, copper, and zinc: used in making tableware, electric-resistance wire, etc.

nickel steel a steel alloy made harder, stronger, and more resistant to corrosion than ordinary steel by the addition of up to five percent of nickel

nick·er[1] (nik′ər) ***vi.*** ⟦prob. var. of *nicher, neigher*, freq. of NEIGH⟧ to utter a low whinnying sound: said of a horse —***n.*** this sound

nick·er[2] (nik′ər) ***n.***, *pl.* **-er** ⟦orig. underworld cant < ?⟧ [Brit. Slang] one pound sterling

nick·le (nik′əl) ***n.***, ***vt.*** **-led**, **-ling** *alt. sp. of* NICKEL

nick·nack (nik′nak′) ***n.*** *alt. sp. of* KNICKKNACK

nick·name (nik′nām′) ***n.*** ⟦< *(a)n ekename* < ME *ekename*, surname: see EKE[1] & NAME⟧ **1** an additional or substitute name given to a person, place, or thing: usually descriptive and given in fun, affection, or derision, as "Doc," "Shorty," etc. **2** a familiar, often shorter, form of a proper name, as "Dick" for "Richard" —***vt.*** **-named′**, **-nam′ing** **1** to give a nickname to **2** [Obs.] to misname

Nic·o·bar Islands (nik′ō bär′, nik′ō bär′) group of islands in the Bay of Bengal: 635 sq mi (1,645 sq km): see ANDAMAN ISLANDS

ni·çoise salad (nē swäz′; *Fr* nē swȧz′) [*also* **N- s-**] SALADE NIÇOISE

Nic·o·las (nik′ə ləs) ***n.*** a masculine name: see NICHOLAS[1]

Nic·ole (ni kōl′, nē-) ***n.*** ⟦Fr fem. of *Nicolas:* see NICHOLAS[1]⟧ a feminine name: dim. *Nicky, Nikki*

Nic·ol prism (nik′əl) ⟦after William *Nicol* (1768?-1851), Brit physicist, who invented it (1828)⟧ a prism consisting of two crystals of clear calcite cemented together, used for obtaining polarized light

Ni·cop·o·lis (ni käp′ō lis, nī-) city in ancient Epirus

Nic·o·si·a (nik′ō sē′ə) capital of Cyprus, in the NC part

ni·co·ti·a·na (ni kō′shē ā′nə) ***n.*** ⟦< ModL *nicotiana (herba)*: see NICOTINE⟧ any of a genus (*Nicotiana*) of New World plants of the nightshade family, including tobacco and several species with fragrant flowers, grown as ornamentals

nic·o·tin·a·mide (nik′ə tin′ə mīd′, -tēn′-) ***n.*** a white, crystalline powder, $C_6H_6N_20$, the amide of nicotinic acid: found in the heart, liver, and muscles and used in treating pellagra

nic·o·tine (nik′ə tēn′, nik′ə tēn′) ***n.*** ⟦Fr < *nicotiane*, the tobacco plant < ModL *nicotiana (herba)*, Nicot's (plant), after Jean *Nicot* (1530-1600), Fr ambassador at Lisbon, who first introduced tobacco into France (1560)⟧ a toxic, addictive, water-soluble alkaloid, $C_{10}H_{14}N_2$, found in tobacco leaves —**nic′o·tin′ic** (-tin′ik) ***adj.***

nicotinic acid a white, odorless, crystalline substance, C_6H_5NO, found in protein foods or prepared synthetically: it is a member of the vitamin B complex and is used in the treatment of pellagra

nic·o·tin·ism (nik′ə tēn′iz′əm, -tin′-) ***n.*** a diseased condition caused by the ingestion of nicotine, as from tobacco; nicotine poisoning

nic·tate (nik′tāt′) ***vi.*** **-tat′ed**, **-tat′ing** NICTITATE —**nic·ta′tion** ***n.***

nic·ti·tate (nik′tə tāt′) ***vi.*** **-tat′ed**, **-tat′ing** ⟦< ML *nictitatus*, pp. of *nictitare*, freq. < L *nictare*, to wink: see connive⟧ to wink or blink rapidly, as birds and other animals with a NICTITATING MEMBRANE —**nic′ti·ta′tion** ***n.***

nictitating membrane a transparent third eyelid hinged at the inner side or lower lid of the eye of various animals, serving to keep the eye clean and moist: it is vestigial in humans

nid·der·ing or **nid·er·ing** (nid′ər iŋ) [Archaic] ***n.*** ⟦popularized by Sir Walter SCOTT[2] < error in printed text (1596) by WILLIAM OF MALMESBURY, for ME *nithing* (< ON *nithingr*), mean person, coward⟧ coward; wretch —***adj.*** base; cowardly

nide (nīd) ***n.*** ⟦< L *nidus*, NEST⟧ [Chiefly Brit.] a nest or brood, esp. of pheasants

ni·dic·o·lous (nī dik′ə ləs) ***adj.*** ⟦< L *nidus*, NEST + -COLOUS⟧ **1** remaining in the nest for some time after hatching, as some birds **2** living in the nest of another species

ni·dif·u·gous (nī dif′yo͞o gəs) ***adj.*** ⟦< L *nidus*, NEST + *fugere*, to flee (see FUGITIVE) + -OUS⟧ leaving the nest almost immediately after hatching, as chickens

nid·i·fy (nid′ə fī′) ***vi.*** **-fied′**, **-fy′ing** ⟦L *nidificare* < *nidus*, NEST + *facere*, to make, DO[1]⟧ *Zool.* to build a nest: also **nid′i·fi·cate′** (-fi kāt′), **-cat′ed**, **-cat′ing** —**nid′i·fi·ca′tion** ***n.***

ni·dus (nī′dəs) ***n.***, *pl.* **-di′** (-dī′) or **-dus·es** ⟦L, NEST⟧ **1** a nest, esp. one in which insects or spiders deposit their eggs **2** a breeding place; specif., *a)* a place where spores or seeds germinate *b)* a focus of infection —**ni′dal** ***adj.***

Nid·wal·den (nēd′väl′dən) canton of central Switzerland: 107 sq mi (277 sq km)

Nie·buhr (nē′bo͝or) **1 Bar·thold Ge·org** (bär′tôlt′ gā′ôrk′) 1776-1831; Ger. historian, born in Denmark **2 Rein·hold** (rīn′hōld′) 1892-1971; U.S. clergyman & Protestant theologian

niece (nēs) ***n.*** ⟦ME *nece* < OFr *niece* < LL *neptia* < L *neptis*, granddaughter, niece, akin to *nepos*, NEPHEW⟧ **1** the daughter of one's brother or sister **2** the daughter of one's brother-in-law or sister-in-law **3** an illegitimate daughter, as of a medieval prelate: a euphemism

Nie·der·sach·sen (nē′dər zäkh′zən) *Ger. name for* LOWER SAXONY

ni·el·lo (nē el′ō) ***n.***, *pl.* **-li** (-ē) or **-los** ⟦It < VL **nigellum* < L *nigellus*, somewhat black, dark < *niger*, black⟧ **1** any of a number of alloys of sulfur with silver, lead, copper, etc., characterized by a deep-black color and used to decorate metallic objects by means of inlay **2** the process of decorating with niello **3** something decorated in this way —***vt.*** **-loed**, **-lo·ing** to decorate with niello —**ni·el′list** ***n.***

niels·bohr·i·um (nēlz′bôr′ē əm) ***n.*** ⟦ModL, after *Niels* BOHR⟧ DUBNIUM: symbol, Ns: the name originally proposed by Russian scientists for this element

☆**Niel·sen** (nēl′sən) ***adj.*** ⟦< *Nielsen*, service mark for marketing research provided by U.S. firm ACNielsen, founded by A. C. *Nielsen*, Sr. (1897-1980)⟧ designating or of a RATING[1] (sense 7) used to measure the size of a TV audience

Nie·mey·er (nē′mī′ər), **Oscar** (born *Oscar Niemeyer Soares Filho*) 1907-2012; Brazilian architect

Nie·möl·ler (nē′mö lər), **(Friedrich Gustav Emil) Mar·tin** (mär′tēn) 1892-1984; Ger. Protestant leader

Nier·stein·er (nir′stīn′ər, -shtīn-) ***n.*** ⟦Ger, after *Nierstein*, town on the Rhine, in Germany, where made⟧ a white Rhine wine, made usually from the Riesling grape

Nie·tzsche (nē′chə), **Frie·drich Wil·helm** (frē′driH′ vil′helm′) 1844-1900; Ger. philosopher —**Nie·tzsche·an** (nē′chē ən) ***adj.***, ***n.*** —**Nie′tzsche·an·ism′** ***n.***

nieve (nēv) ***n.*** ⟦ME *neve* < ON *hnefi*⟧ [Archaic or Brit. Dial.] a fist or hand

ni·fed·i·pine (ni fed′ə pēn′) ***n.*** ⟦NI(TRO)- + *-fe-* (< PHENYL) + DI-[1] + *-pine* (< PYRIDINE)⟧ a yellow, crystalline powder, $C_{17}H_{18}N_2O_6$, that dilates blood vessels, used to treat angina pectoris, hypertension, etc.

Ni·fl·heim (niv′əl hām′) ***n.*** ⟦ON *Niflheimr*⟧ *Norse Myth.* the regions of darkness and cold, or realm of the dead

☆**nif·ty** (nif′tē) ***adj.*** **-ti·er**, **-ti·est** ⟦orig. theatrical slang, prob. < MAGNIFICENT⟧ [Informal] attractive, smart, stylish, enjoyable, etc.: a generalized term of approval —***n.***, *pl.* **-ties** [Slang] a nifty person or thing; esp., a clever or witty remark —**nif′ti·ly** ***adv.***

Nig *abbrev.* Nigeria

Ni·ger (nī′jər, nē zher′) **1** river in W Africa, flowing from Guinea through Mali, Niger, & Nigeria into the Gulf of Guinea: *c.* 2,590 mi (4,168 km) **2** country in WC Africa, north of Nigeria: formerly a French territory, it became independent in 1960: 489,191 sq mi (1,267,000 sq km); cap. Niamey

Ni·ger-Con·go (-käŋ′gō) ***adj.*** designating or of a large subfamily of the Niger-Kordofanian language family, covering much of sub-Saharan Africa and including the Bantu, Kwa, and Voltaic branches

Ni·ger·i·a (nī jir′ē ə) country in WC Africa, on the Gulf of Guinea: formerly a British colony & protectorate, it became independent in 1960; a republic since 1963: member of the Commonwealth: 356,669 sq mi (923,768 sq km); cap. Abuja —**Ni·ger′i·an** ***adj.***, ***n.***

Ni·ger-Kor·do·fan·i·an (nī′jər kôr′də fā′nē ən) ***adj.*** designating or of a language family comprising the Niger-Congo subfamily and the Kordofanian subfamily

nig·gard (nig′ərd) ***n.*** ⟦ME *negarde,* prob. < Scand, as in ON *hnøggr,* Norw dial. *nøgg,* afraid, stingy < IE base **kneu-* (var. of **ken-,* to scrape) > OE *hneaw,* sparse, stingy⟧ a stingy person; miser —***adj.*** stingy; miserly

nig·gard·ly (-lē) ***adj.*** **1** like or characteristic of a niggard; stingy; miserly **2** small, few, or scanty, as if given by a niggard *[a niggardly sum]* —***adv.*** in the manner of a niggard; stingily —***SYN.*** STINGY[1] —**nig′gard·li·ness** ***n.***

nig·ger (nig′ər) ***n., adj.*** [Dial. or Slang] Negro

USAGE—originally simply a dialectal variant of *Negro,* the term *nigger* today is used generally by some speakers of black English, but in all other contexts is regarded as virtually taboo because of the legacy of racial hatred that underlies the history of its use among whites, and its continuing use among a minority of speakers as a viciously hostile epithet

nig·gle (nig′əl) ***vi.*** **-gled, -gling** ⟦North Brit dial., prob. akin to Norw dial. *nigla* in same sense⟧ **1** to pay too much attention to petty details; fuss **2** to complain or find fault in a petty or nagging way; carp —**nig′gler** ***n.*** —**nig′gling** ***adj., n.***

nigh (nī) ***adv.*** **nigh′er, nigh′est** ⟦ME *neih* < OE *neah,* akin to Ger *nahe,* Goth *nehw*⟧ **1** [Archaic] near in time, place, etc. **2** [Chiefly Dial.] nearly; almost —***adj.*** **nigh′er, nigh′est** [Chiefly Dial.] **1** near; close **2** on the left: said as of a draft animal —***prep.*** [Archaic] near; near to

night (nīt) ***n.*** ⟦ME *niht* < OE, akin to Ger *nacht* < IE base **nekwt-, *nokwt-* > Gr *nyx* (gen. *nyktos*), L *nox* (gen. *noctis*), night⟧ **1** *a)* the period from sunset to sunrise *b)* the period of actual darkness after sunset and before sunrise; also, a part of this period before bedtime *[a night at the opera]* or the part between bedtime and morning *[a sleepless night]* **2** the evening following a specified day *[Christmas night]* **3** the darkness of night **4** any period or condition of darkness or gloom; specif., *a)* a period of intellectual or moral degeneration *b)* a time of grief *c)* death —***adj.*** **1** of, for, or at night **2** active, working, or in use at night —**make a night of it** to celebrate all or much of the night —**night after night** every night or for many successive nights —**night and day** continuously or continually

night blindness imperfect vision in the dark or in dim light: a symptom of vitamin A deficiency

night-bloom·ing ce·re·us (nīt′blo͞om′iŋ sir′ē əs) any of various cactuses that bloom at night, esp. any of many species (genera *Hylocereus, Selenicereus,* etc.), often grown as houseplants

night·cap (nīt′kap′) ***n.*** **1** a cap worn to bed, esp. formerly, to protect the head from cold **2** [Informal] an alcoholic drink taken just before going to bed or at the end of an evening of partying, a night on the town, etc. ☆**3** [Informal] *Baseball* the second game of a double-header

night·clothes (-klōthz′, -klōz′) ***pl.n.*** clothes to be worn in bed, as pajamas: also written **night clothes**

night·club (-klub′) ***n.*** a place of entertainment open at night for eating, drinking, dancing, etc., and usually having a floor show

night·club·bing (-klub′iŋ) ***n.*** the act or practice of patronizing nightclubs —**night′club′ber** ***n.***

☆**night crawler** (krôl′ər) any large earthworm that comes to the surface at night, commonly used as fish bait

night·dress (-dres′) ***n.*** **1** NIGHTGOWN **2** NIGHTCLOTHES

night·fall (-fôl′) ***n.*** the time in the evening when daylight is last visible; dusk

night·glow (-glō′) ***n.*** airglow occurring during the night

night·gown (-goun′) ***n.*** **1** a loose gown worn in bed by women or girls **2** NIGHTSHIRT **3** [Obs.] a dressing gown

night·hawk (-hôk′) ***n.*** ☆**1** any of various nightjars that feed on flying insects, esp., the common nighthawk (*Chordeiles minor*), which is active during the day or night ☆**2** NIGHT OWL (sense 1)

night heron any of several herons most active at night or twilight

night·ie (nīt′ē) ***n.*** ⟦< NIGHT(GOWN) + -IE⟧ [Informal] NIGHTGOWN (sense 1)

night·in·gale (nīt′'n gāl′) ***n.*** ⟦ME *nigtingale,* for earlier *nihtegale* < OE (akin to Ger *nachtigall*) < *niht,* NIGHT + base of *galan,* to sing, akin to *giellan,* YELL⟧ any of various small European thrushes (genus *Luscinia*) with a russet back and buff to white underparts: the male is known for its varied, melodious singing, esp. at night during the breeding season

Night·in·gale (nīt′'n gāl′), **Florence** 1820-1910; Eng. nurse in the Crimean War: regarded as the founder of modern nursing

night·jar (nīt′jär′) ***n.*** ⟦NIGHT + JAR[1]: from the whirring noise made by the male⟧ any of a family (Caprimulgidae) of goatsuckers; esp., the common European nightjar (*Caprimulgus europaeus*)

night latch a door latch with a bolt opened from the outside by a key, and from the inside by a knob

☆**night letter** a telegram sent at night at a reduced rate, to be delivered the next morning

☆**night·life** (nīt′līf′) ***n.*** **1** attendance at theaters or nightclubs, or similar pleasure-seeking activity, at night **2** theaters, nightclubs, or similar entertainment available at night

night light a small, dim light kept burning all night, as in a hallway, bathroom, or sickroom

night·long (-lôŋ′) ***adj., adv.*** through the entire night; all night

night·ly (nīt′lē) ***adj.*** **1** [Obs.] of, like, or characteristic of the night **2** done or occurring every night —***adv.*** **1** [Obs.] at night **2** night after night; every night

night·mare (nīt′mer′) ***n.*** ⟦ME *nihtmare:* see NIGHT & MARE[3]⟧ **1** [Historical] *Folklore* an evil spirit believed to haunt and suffocate sleeping people **2** a frightening dream, often accompanied by a sensation of oppression and helplessness **3** any experience like a nightmare in its terrifying or distressing aspects —**night′mar′ish** ***adj.***

night owl ☆a person who works at night or otherwise stays up late

night prayer [*often* **N- P-**] *R.C.Ch.* the last of the seven canonical hours; compline

☆**night·rid·er** (nīt′rīd′ər) ***n.*** any of a band of masked, mounted men who perform lawless acts of violence and terror at night to intimidate and terrorize; esp., any of such a band of white men in the S U.S. after the Civil War

nights (nīts) ***adv.*** during every night or most nights

night school a school holding classes in the evening, esp. one for adults unable to attend by day

night·shade (nīt′shād′) ***n.*** ⟦ME *nichtheschode* < OE *nihtscada* (see NIGHT & SHADE): ? with reference to narcotic qualities⟧ **1** any of a large genus (*Solanum*) of chiefly tropical plants of the nightshade family, with five-lobed leaves and flowers of various colors, including the black nightshade **2** BELLADONNA (sense 1) **3** HENBANE —***adj.*** designating a large family (Solanaceae, order Solanales) of poisonous and nonpoisonous dicotyledonous plants chiefly of warm regions, generally having a round stem, rank smell, and watery sap, and including the tobaccos, red peppers, tomatoes, potatoes, petunias, and eggplant

night·shirt (nīt′shurt′) ***n.*** a long, loosefitting, shirtlike garment worn to bed

night·side (-sīd′) ***n.*** the side of a planet, the moon, etc. facing away from the sun

night soil ⟦from being collected at night⟧ excrement removed from a cesspool or privy and used as fertilizer

☆**night·spot** (-spät′) ***n.*** a place of entertainment open at night for drinking and, often, eating and dancing

☆**night·stand** (-stand′) ***n.*** a small table at the bedside

☆**night·stick** (-stik′) ***n.*** a policeman's club; billy club

night table NIGHTSTAND

night·time (-tīm′) ***n.*** the time between dusk and dawn; also, the time between sunset and sunrise

night·walk·er (-wôk′ər) ***n.*** [Obs.] a person, as a thief or prostitute, who goes about at night

night watch **1** a watching or guarding during the night **2** the person or persons doing such guarding **3** the time of their guarding **4** any of the periods into which the night was formerly divided for such guarding: *usually used in pl.*

night watchman a watchman hired for duty at night

night·wear (-wer′) ***n.*** NIGHTCLOTHES

night·y (nīt′ē) ***n., pl.*** **night′ies** [Informal] *alt. sp. of* NIGHTIE

night·y-night (-nīt′) ***interj.*** ⟦redupl.⟧ [Informal] GOOD NIGHT

ni·gres·cent (nī gres′ənt) ***adj.*** ⟦L *nigrescens,* prp. of *nigrescere,* to grow black < *niger,* black⟧ [Rare] **1** becoming or tending to become black **2** blackish —**ni·gres′cence** ***n.***

nig·ri·tude (nig′rə to͞od′, -tyo͞od′) ***n.*** ⟦L *nigritudo* < *niger,* black⟧ [Now Rare] blackness or darkness

ni·gro·sine (nig′rə sēn′, -sin) ***n.*** ⟦< L *niger,* black + -OS(E) + -INE[3]⟧ any of a group of blue-black or black dyes used as pigments

NIH *abbrev.* National Institutes of Health

ni·hil (nī′hil′, nē′-) ***n.*** ⟦L, contr. < *nihilum* < **nehilum* < *ne-,* not (see NO[1]) + *hilum,* little thing, trifle⟧ nothing

ni·hil·ism (nī′ə liz′əm, nē′-; -hi-) ***n.*** ⟦< L *nihil* (see prec.) + -ISM⟧ **1** *Philos. a)* the denial of the existence of any basis for knowledge or truth *b)* the general rejection of customary beliefs in morality, religion, etc. (also **ethical nihilism**) **2** the belief that there is no meaning or purpose in existence **3** *Politics a)* the doctrine that existing social, political, and economic institutions must be completely destroyed in order to make way for new institutions *b)* [**N-**] a movement in Russia (*c.* 1860-1917) which advocated such revolutionary reform and attempted to carry it out through the use of terrorism and assassination *c)* loosely, any violent revolutionary movement involving the use of terrorism —**ni′hil·ist** ***n., adj.*** —**ni′hil·is′tic** ***adj.***

nihil ob·stat (nē′hil ōb′stät) ⟦L, nothing obstructs⟧ **1** *R.C.Ch.* a printed phrase, followed by the name of an officially appointed censor, indicating that the publication carrying the phrase has been examined and judged free of doctrinal or moral error **2** any official indication of nonopposition

Ni·hon (nē′hôn) ⟦short for *Nihon koku* < *Nihon* (< SinoJpn *hi no moto,* lit., where the sun rises: from its location east of mainland Asia) + *koku,* country⟧ *Jpn. name for* JAPAN: in full **Nihon ko·ku** (kō′ko͞o)

Ni·i·ga·ta (nē′ē gä′tä) seaport in N Honshu, Japan, on the Sea of Japan

Ni·i·ha·u (nē′ē hä′o͞o, nē′hou′) ⟦Haw⟧ one of the Hawaiian islands, west of Kauai: 70 sq mi (181 sq km)

Ni·jin·sky (ni zhēn′ski; *E* nə jin′skē), **Vas·lav** (väs läf′) 1890-1950; Russ. ballet dancer

Nij·me·gen (nī′mā′gən; *Du* nī′mā′khən) city in the E Netherlands, on the Waal River

-nik (nik) ⟦< Yiddish or Russ: equiv. to -ER⟧ *suffix* one who is or has to do with (the thing specified) *[beatnik, refusenik]*

Ni·ke (nī′kē) ***n.*** ⟦Gr *Nikē,* prob. < IE base **neik-,* to attack > OE *(ga)næstan,* to fight⟧ *Gr. Myth.* the winged goddess of victory

Nik·kei (nē′kā′) ⟦acronym, after the *Nihon Keizai Shimbun,* Jpn newspaper⟧ *service mark for* an index based upon the current prices of selected companies traded on the Tokyo Stock Exchange: also **Nikkei index**

Nik·ko (nē′kō, nik′ō) town in EC Honshu, Japan: Buddhist religious center

Ni·ko·la·yev (nik′ə lä′yev′) seaport in S Ukraine, on the Bug River

nil (nil) ***n.*** ⟦L, contr. of NIHIL⟧ nothing —***adj.*** zero; so small as not to be measurable [our chances were *nil*]

nil de·spe·ran·dum (nil′ des′pə ran′dəm, -rän′doom) ⟦L⟧ nothing should be despaired of; never despair

Nile (nīl) river in NE Africa, formed at Khartoum, Sudan, by the juncture of the **Blue Nile**, flowing from N Ethiopia, *c.* 1,000 mi (1,610 km) & the **White Nile**, flowing from Lake Victoria, *c.* 1,650 mi (2,655 km), & flowing north through Egypt into the Mediterranean: with the White Nile & a headstream south of Lake Victoria, *c.* 4,160 mi (6,695 km)

Nile green yellowish green —**Nile′-green′** ***adj.***

nil·gai (nil′gī′) ***n., pl.*** **-gais′** or **-gai′** ⟦Pers *nīlgāw*, lit., blue cow < *nīl*, blue + *gāw*, cow: for IE base see COW[1]⟧ a large, gray Indian antelope (*Boselaphus tragocamelus*): the male has short, straight horns and a black mane: also **nil′gau′** (-gô′)

nill (nil) ***vt., vi.*** ⟦ME *nillen* < OE *nyllan* < *ne*, not (see NO[1]) + *willan* (see WILL[1])⟧ [Archaic] not to will (something); refuse [will I, *nill* I]: see also WILLY-NILLY

nil ni·si bo·num (nil′ nē′sē bō′nəm, -noom) ⟦L⟧ *short for* DE MORTUIS NIL NISI BONUM

Ni·lo-Sa·ha·ran (nī′lō sə her′ən) ***n.*** a large family of languages spoken chiefly in N and central Africa and including the Chari-Nile subfamily

Ni·lot·ic (nī lät′ik) ***adj.*** ⟦L *Niloticus* < Gr *Neilōtikos* < *Neilos*, the Nile⟧ **1** of the Nile or the Nile Valley **2** of the peoples living in the valley of the White Nile, including the Dinkas —***n.*** a group of Chari-Nile languages spoken in the upper Nile Valley

nim (nim) ***vt., vi.*** **nam** (näm) or **nimmed, no·men** (nō′mən) or **nome** (nōm), **nim′ming** ⟦ME *nimen* < OE *niman*: see -NOMY⟧ [Archaic] to steal or pilfer

nim·ble (nim′bəl) ***adj.*** **-bler, -blest** ⟦with intrusive *-b-* < ME *nimmel* < OE *numol* < *niman*, to take (see prec.): basic sense "capable of taking"⟧ **1** mentally quick; quick-witted; alert [a *nimble* mind] **2** [Rare] showing mental quickness [a *nimble* reply] **3** moving quickly and lightly —***SYN.*** AGILE —**nim′ble·ness** ***n.*** —**nim′bly** ***adv.***

nim·bo·stra·tus (nim′bō strāt′əs, -strat′əs) ***n.*** ⟦ModL: see fol. & STRATUS⟧ the type of extensive gray cloud that obscures the sun, found at low altitudes and consisting of dense, dark layers of water droplets, rain, or snow: see CLOUD

nim·bus (nim′bəs) ***n., pl.*** **-bi′** (-bī′) or **-bus·es** ⟦L, violent rain, black rain cloud < IE base **nebh-*, moist, cloud > L *nebula*⟧ **1** *Myth.* a bright cloud surrounding gods or goddesses appearing on earth **2** an aura of splendor about any person or thing **3** a halo or bright disk surrounding the head of a divinity, saint, or sovereign in pictures, on medals, etc. **4** any rain-producing cloud

☆**NIMBY** or **Nim·by** (nim′bē) ***n.*** ⟦*n(ot) i(n) m(y) b(ack)y(ard)*⟧ **1** opposition by nearby residents to a proposed building project, esp. a public one, as being hazardous, unsightly, etc. **2** *pl.* **NIMBYs** or **Nim′bys** a person who opposes such a project

Nîmes (nēm) city in S France

NiMH *abbrev.* nickel-metal hydride

NIMH *abbrev.* National Institute of Mental Health

ni·mi·e·ty (ni mī′ə tē) ***n.*** ⟦L *nimietas* < *nimis*, adv., too much (by litotes) < **ne-miis* < *ne-*, not + IE **miis*, compar. of **meio-*, little < base **mei-* > MINOR⟧ excess; redundancy

nim·i·ny-pim·i·ny (nim′ə nē pim′ə nē) ***adj.*** ⟦imitative of mincing speech⟧ fussily dainty or refined; mincing

Nim·itz (nim′its), **Chester William** 1885-1966; U.S. admiral in WWII

Nim·rod (nim′räd′) ***n.*** ⟦Heb *nimrōdh*⟧ **1** *Bible* the son of Cush, referred to as a mighty hunter: Gen. 10:8-9 ☆**2** [**n-**] [Slang] a person regarded as stupid, foolish, awkward, etc.

nin·com·poop (nin′kəm po͞op′) ***n.*** ⟦< ?⟧ a stupid, silly person; fool

nine (nīn) ***adj.*** ⟦ME *nyen* < OE *nigon*, akin to Ger *neun* < IE **enewen* (> Gr *ennea*, L *novem*, nine), prob. extension of base **newo-*, NEW, indicating a new division of the numeral system commencing with 9⟧ totaling one more than eight —***n.*** **1** the cardinal number between eight and ten; 9; IX **2** any group of nine persons or things; esp., a baseball team **3** something numbered nine or having nine units, as a playing card, throw of dice, etc. —**the Nine** the nine Muses —**to the nines** [Informal] **1** to perfection **2** in the most elaborate or showy manner [dressed *to the nines*]

nine ball *Pool* a form of rotation played with the object balls numbered one through nine, in which the winner is the one who pockets the nine ball, either in sequence or by means of a combination shot: also written **9-ball** ***n.*** or **nine′-ball′**

nine days' wonder anything that arouses great excitement and interest, but for only a short time

☆**9/11** (nīn′ē lev′ən, nīn′i-) ⟦numeric representation of the month and the day⟧ September 11, 2001, the day on which four airliners were hijacked by terrorists for use in an attack on the U.S.: two were flown into the towers of the World Trade Center in Manhattan, one into the Pentagon, and the fourth crashed into a Pa. field

nine·fold (nīn′fōld′) ***adj.*** ⟦NINE + -FOLD⟧ **1** having nine parts **2** having nine times as much or as many —***adv.*** nine times as much or as many

☆**9-1-1** or **911** (nīn′wun wun′) ⟦the specific digits in the number⟧ in the U.S., Canada, and some other countries, a three-digit telephone number that may be dialed in an emergency: it connects to a dispatcher who notifies the police, the fire department, or medical personnel as appropriate

nine·pin (-pin′) ***n.*** a pin used in the game of ninepins

nine·pins (-pinz′) ***n.*** a British version of the game of tenpins, in which nine wooden pins are used

nine·teen (-tēn′) ***adj.*** ⟦ME *nynetene* < OE *nigontyne*: see NINE & -TEEN⟧ totaling nine more than ten —***n.*** the cardinal number between eighteen and twenty; 19; XIX

nine·teenth (-tēnth′) ***adj.*** ⟦ME *nyntenthe* < OE *nigonteotha*: see prec. & -TH[2]⟧ **1** preceded by eighteen others in a series; 19th **2** designating any of the nineteen equal parts of something —***n.*** **1** the one following the eighteenth **2** any of the nineteen equal parts of something; 1⁄19 —***adv.*** in the nineteenth place, rank, group, etc.

☆**nineteenth hole** ⟦because it comes after the eighteenth, and last, hole in the round⟧ [Informal] any place, as the bar of a clubhouse, where golfers meet for drinks and conviviality after playing a round of golf

nine·ti·eth (nīn′tē ith) ***adj.*** ⟦ME *nyntithe* < OE *nigenteotha*: see NINETY & -TH[2]⟧ **1** preceded by eighty-nine others in a series; 90th **2** designating any of the ninety equal parts of something —***n.*** **1** the one following the eighty-ninth **2** any of the ninety equal parts of something; 1⁄90 —***adv.*** in the ninetieth place, rank, group, etc.

nine-to-five (nīn′tə fīv′) ***adj.*** ⟦referring to 9:00 A.M. and 5:00 P.M.⟧ of or pertaining to the period of conventional business hours and the work period of the typical office worker: also written **9-to-5**

nine·ty (nīn′tē) ***adj.*** ⟦ME *nigenty* < OE *nigontig*: see NINE & -TY[2]⟧ nine times ten —***n., pl.*** **-ties** the cardinal number between eighty-nine and ninety-one; 90; XC (or LXXXX) —☆**the Gay Nineties** the decade 1890-99 in the U.S. —**the nineties** the numbers or years, as of a century, from ninety through ninety-nine

Nin·e·veh (nin′ə və) capital of ancient Assyria, on the Tigris: ruins opposite modern Mosul in N Iraq

Ning·bo (niŋ′bō′) city in Zhejiang province, E China: also sp. **Ningpo**

Ning·xia-Hui (niŋ′shyä′wē′) autonomous region in NW China, on the border of Inner Mongolia: 65,637 sq mi (169,999 sq km); cap. Yinchuan: former transliteration **Ning′sia′ Hui′** (-shyä′-)

nin·ja (nin′jə) ***n., pl.*** **-ja** or **-jas** ⟦Jpn⟧ any of a class of feudal Japanese warriors highly trained in stealth and employed as spies and assassins

nin·ny (nin′ē) ***n., pl.*** **-nies** ⟦< *(a)n inn(ocent)* + -Y[2]⟧ a fool; dolt

ni·non (nē nän′; *Fr* nē nōn′) ***n.*** ⟦Fr < ?⟧ a thin, sheer fabric like voile, made sometimes of synthetic material, used chiefly for curtains

ninth (nīnth) ***adj.*** ⟦ME *ninthe* < OE *nigonthe*: see NINE & -TH[2]⟧ **1** preceded by eight others in a series; 9th **2** designating any of the nine equal parts of something —***n.*** **1** the one following the eighth **2** any of the nine equal parts of something; 1⁄9 **3** *Music a)* an interval in pitch of an octave and a second *b)* a tone separated from another by such an interval *c)* the combination of two such tones —***adv.*** in the ninth place, rank, group, etc. —**ninth′ly** ***adv.***

ninth chord *Music* a chord consisting of the third, fifth, seventh, and ninth above the root

Ni·nus (nī′nəs) *Latin name for* NINEVEH

Ni·o·be (nī′ō bē′) ***n.*** ⟦L < Gr *Niobē*⟧ *Gr. Myth.* a queen of Thebes, daughter of Tantalus, who, weeping for her slain children, is turned into a stone from which tears continue to flow

ni·o·bi·um (nī ō′bē əm) ***n.*** ⟦ModL: so named (1844) by H. Rose (1795-1864), Ger chemist (for earlier COLUMBIUM) < Gr *Niobē* (because of its close relationship to *tantalum*) + -IUM: see prec. & TANTALUM⟧ a gray or white, metallic chemical element, somewhat ductile and malleable, used in alloy steels, superconducting alloys, in jet engines and rockets, etc.: symbol, Nb; at. no. 41: see the periodic table of elements in the Reference Supplement

Ni·o·brar·a (nī′ə brer′ə) ⟦< Siouan (Omaha), lit., broad, flat river⟧ river flowing from E Wyo. east through N Nebr. into the Missouri: 431 mi (694 km)

Niord (nyôrd) ***n.*** *Norse Myth. var. of* NJORD

nip[1] (nip) ***vt.*** **nipped, nip′ping** ⟦ME *nippen*, prob. < MLowG *nippen* or ON *hnippa* < IE **kneib-* (< base **ken-*, to scrape) > Gr *kniptos*, stingy⟧ **1** to catch or squeeze between two surfaces, points, or edges; pinch or bite **2** to sever (shoots, buds, etc.) by pinching or clipping **3** to check the growth or development of **4** to have a painful or injurious effect on because of cold [frost *nipped* the plants] **5** [Slang] *a)* to snatch *b)* to steal —***vi.*** **1** to give a nip or nips **2** [Brit. Informal] to move quickly or nimbly: with *off, away, along*, etc. —***n.*** **1** the act of nipping; pinch; bite **2** a piece nipped off; small bit **3** a stinging quality, as in cold or frosty air **4** stinging cold; frost **5** a stinging remark **6** a strong flavor; tang —☆**nip and tuck** [Informal] so closely contested as to leave the outcome in doubt; neck and neck

nip[2] (nip) ***n.*** ⟦prob. contr. < *nipperkin* < Du *nippertje*, small measure for liquors < base of *nippen*, to sip, prob. akin to prec.⟧ a small drink of liquor; dram; sip — ***vt., vi.*** **nipped, nip′ping** to drink (liquor) in nips

Nip (nip) ***n.*** ⟦< NIP(PONESE)⟧ [*also* **n-**] [Slang] a Japanese: a term of contempt or hostility

ni·pa (nē′pə, nī′-) ***n.*** ⟦Sp < Malay *nipah*⟧ **1** an Asian palm tree (*Nipa fruticans*) with large bunches of edible fruit and with feathery leaves used in thatching **2** thatch or fruit from the nipa **3** a liquor made from its sap

Nip·i·gon (nip′i gän′), **Lake** ⟦< 18th-c. Fr (*Lac*) *Alimipigon* < Ojibwa (unattested); lit. meaning ? where the water begins⟧ lake in WC Ontario, Canada, north of Lake Superior: 1,870 sq mi (4,843 sq km)

Nip·is·sing (nip′ə siŋ′), **Lake** ⟦< Fr < Ojibwa; lit. meaning prob. "at the lake"⟧ lake in SE Ontario, Canada, between Georgian Bay & the Ottawa River: 350 sq mi (906 sq km)

nip·per (nip′ər) ***n.*** 1 anything that nips, or pinches 2 [*pl.*] any of various tools for grasping or severing wire, etc. as pliers, pincers, or forceps 3 any of certain organs of animals, used in biting, grasping, holding, etc.; specif., *a)* an incisor tooth of a horse *b)* the pincerlike claw of a crab or lobster; chela 4 [Informal, Chiefly Brit.] a small boy; lad 5 [*pl.*] [Old Slang] handcuffs or leg irons

nip·ping (nip′iŋ) ***adj.*** 1 that nips, or pinches 2 sharp; biting; nippy 3 sarcastic —**nip′ping·ly *adv.***

nip·ple (nip′əl) ***n.*** ⟦earlier *neble*, prob. dim. of NEB⟧ 1 the small protuberance on a breast or udder through which, in the female, the milk passes in suckling the young; teat 2 an artificial teatlike part, as of rubber, in the cap of a baby's nursing bottle 3 any projection, part, or thing resembling the nipple of a breast in shape or function; specif., *a)* a short piece of pipe with both ends threaded *b)* a projection with a small opening through which a liquid or grease can be forced

Nip·pon (nip′än′, ni pän′) *var. of* NIHON

Nip·pon·ese (nip′ə nēz′, -nēs′) ***adj., n.,*** *pl.* **-ese′** ⟦< prec.⟧ JAPANESE

Nip·pur (ni po͝or′) ancient city of Sumer, southeast of Babylon on the Euphrates, in what is now SE Iraq

nip·py (nip′ē) ***adj.*** **-pi·er**, **-pi·est** 1 nipping or tending to nip, or pinch 2 cold in a stinging way [*a nippy* autumn morning] 3 [Brit. Informal] quick or nimble —**nip′pi·ness *n.***

nip-up (nip′up′) ***n.*** the acrobatic feat of springing to one's feet from a position flat on one's back

ni·qab (ni käb′) ***n.*** ⟦Ar *niqāb*⟧ an opaque veil, typically having only a slitlike opening for the eyes, worn by some Muslim women to cover the head, neck, and sometimes the chest and shoulders

nir·va·na (nir vä′nə, nər-; -van′ə) ***n.*** ⟦Sans *nirvāṇa* < *nirvā*, to blow out < *nis-*, out + *vā*, to blow: see WIND[1]⟧ [*also* **N-**] 1 *Buddhism* the state of perfect blessedness achieved by the extinction of individual existence and by the absorption of the soul into the supreme spirit, or by the extinction of all desires and passions 2 any place or condition of great peace or bliss

Niš (nēsh) city in E Serbia

Ni·san (nē sän′, nis′ən) ***n.*** ⟦Heb *nīsān*⟧ the seventh month of the Jewish calendar: see the Jewish calendar in the Reference Supplement

☆**ni·sei** (nē′sā′) ***n.,*** *pl.* **ni′sei′** or **ni′seis′** ⟦Jpn, lit., second generation⟧ [*also* **N-**] a native U.S. or Canadian citizen born of immigrant Japanese parents and educated in America: cf. ISSEI, KIBEI, SANSEI

Ni·shi·no·mi·ya (nē′shē nō′mē yä′) city in S Honshu, Japan, west of Osaka

ni·si (nē′sē′, nī′sī′) ***conj.*** ⟦L < *ne-*, not (see NO[1]) + *si*, if (see SO[1])⟧ unless: used in law after *decree, order*, etc. to indicate that it shall take permanent effect at a specified time unless cause is shown why it should not, or unless it is changed by further proceedings

nisi pri·us (prī′əs, prē′-) ⟦L, unless before: used orig. in a writ directing a sheriff to summon a jury to Westminster on a certain date "unless before" that date the trial had been held in his own county⟧ any of various courts in which a cause of action may be originally tried before a jury

Nis·sen hut (nis′ən) ⟦after P. N. *Nissen* (1871-1930), engineer in the Cdn army⟧ a prefabricated shelter of corrugated metal shaped like a cylinder cut vertically in two and resting on its flat surface: first used by the Brit. Army in WWI

nit[1] (nit) ***n.*** ⟦ME *nite* < OE *hnitu*, akin to Ger *niss* < IE base **knid-*, louse, nit, prob. < **ken-*, to scratch⟧ 1 the egg of a louse or similar insect 2 a young louse, etc.

nit[2] (nit) ***n.*** [Informal, Chiefly Brit.] *short for* NITWIT

nite (nīt) ***n., adj.*** *informal sp. of* NIGHT: used as in advertisements, brand names, etc.

ni·ter (nīt′ər) ***n.*** ⟦ME *nitre* < MFr < L *nitrum* < Gr *nitron*, native soda, natron < Heb or Egypt: Heb *netr* < Egypt *ntṛ*⟧ 1 POTASSIUM NITRATE 2 SODIUM NITRATE Also [Chiefly Brit.] **ni′tre**

Ni·te·rói (nē′tə roi′) seaport in SE Brazil, opposite Rio de Janeiro

☆**nit·i·nol** (nit′ə nôl′, -nōl′) ***n.*** ⟦NI(CKEL) + TI(TANIUM) + *N(aval) O(rdnance) L(aboratory)* where discovered⟧ any of several paramagnetic alloys of nickel and titanium that can be heated and shaped: when cooled and deformed, they resume their previous shapes upon being reheated

ni·ton (nī′tän′) ***n.*** ⟦ModL < L *nitere*, to shine + *-on* as in ARGON: so named (1912) by Sir William RAMSAY because it glows in the dark⟧ *former name for* RADON

☆**nit·pick** (nit′pik′) ***vi., vt.*** ⟦back-form. < fol.⟧ [Informal] to find fault with (someone or something) in a manner that is finicky or petty —**nit′-pick′er *n.***

☆**nit-pick·ing** (nit′pik′iŋ) ***adj., n.*** ⟦NIT[1] + PICK[2]⟧ [Informal] (a) paying too much attention to petty details; niggling

nitr- *combining form* NITRO-: used before a vowel

ni·trate (nī′trāt′) ***n.*** ⟦Fr < MFr *nitre*, NITER⟧ 1 *a)* a salt of nitric acid containing the monovalent, negative radical NO_3 *b)* an uncharged ester of this acid 2 potassium nitrate or sodium nitrate, used as a fertilizer —***vt.*** **-trat′ed**, **-trat′ing** to treat or combine with nitric acid or a nitrate; esp., to make into a nitrate

ni·tra·tion (nī trā′shən) ***n.*** the process of nitrating; esp., the introduction of the NO_2 group into an organic compound

ni·tric (nī′trik) ***adj.*** ⟦Fr *nitrique*: see NITER & -IC⟧ 1 of or containing nitrogen 2 designating or of compounds in which nitrogen has a higher valence than in the corresponding nitrous compounds

nitric acid a colorless, fuming acid, HNO_3, that is highly corrosive: prepared by the action of sulfuric acid on nitrates and by the oxidation of ammonia

nitric bacteria soil and water bacteria (genus *Nitrobacter*, etc.) that convert nitrites into nitrates

nitric oxide a colorless gas, NO, prepared by the action of nitric acid on copper or directly from the air by various processes

ni·tride (nī′trīd′) ***n.*** ⟦NITR- + -IDE⟧ a compound of nitrogen with a more electropositive element, as boron

ni·tri·fy (nī′trə fī′) ***vt.*** **-fied′**, **-fy′ing** ⟦Fr *nitrifier*: see NITER & -FY⟧ 1 to combine with nitrogen or nitrogen compounds 2 to impregnate (soil, etc.) with nitrates 3 to cause the oxidation of (ammonium salts, atmospheric nitrogen, etc.) to nitrites and nitrates, as by the action of soil bacteria, etc. —**ni′tri·fi·ca′tion *n.*** —**ni′tri·fi′er *n.***

ni·trile (nī′tril, -trīl′) ***n.*** ⟦NITR- + -ILE⟧ 1 an organic cyanide of the general formula R·C⋮N, yielding the corresponding acid and ammonia on hydrolysis 2 a copolymer of acrylonitrile and butadiene, used in making synthetic latex

ni·trite (nī′trīt′) ***n.*** ⟦NITR- + -ITE[1]⟧ 1 a salt of nitrous acid containing the monovalent, negative radical NO_2 2 an uncharged ester of this acid

ni·tro (nī′trō) ***adj.*** ⟦< fol.⟧ 1 designating certain compounds containing nitrogen and produced by the action of nitric or nitrous acid 2 designating the NO_2 radical or compounds in which one or more NO_2 radicals have replaced atoms of hydrogen —***n.*** ☆[Informal] *short for* NITROGLYCERIN

ni·tro- (nī′trō, nī′trə) ⟦see NITER⟧ *combining form* 1 containing nitrogen compounds made by the action of nitric or nitrous acid and other substances [*nitrocellulose*] 2 containing the NO_2 radical [*nitrobenzene, nitroparaffin*] 3 niter [*nitrobacteria*]

ni·tro·bac·te·ri·a (nī′trō bak tir′ē ə) ***pl.n.,*** *sing.* **-ri·um** (-əm) ⟦ModL: see prec. & BACTERIA⟧ bacteria in the soil that oxidize ammonia compounds into nitrites, or nitrites into nitrates: see NITRIC BACTERIA, NITROUS BACTERIA

ni·tro·ben·zene (-ben′zēn′) ***n.*** a poisonous yellow liquid, $C_6H_5NO_2$, prepared by treating benzene with nitric acid, used in making aniline, as a solvent, etc.

ni·tro·cel·lu·lose (-sel′yo͞o lōs′) ***n.*** any ester of nitric acid and cellulose; esp., a pulplike substance produced by the action of nitric acid upon wood, cotton, etc. in the presence of concentrated sulfuric acid: used in making smokeless explosives, plastics, lacquers, etc. —**ni′tro·cel′lu·los′ic** (-lōs′ ik) ***adj.***

ni·tro·fu·ran (-fyo͝or′an′, -fyo͞o ran′) ***n.*** ⟦NITRO- + FURAN⟧ a furan derivative, $C_4H_3O{\cdot}NO_2$, used to treat bacterial infections

ni·tro·gen (nī′trə jən) ***n.*** ⟦Fr *nitrogène*: so named (1790) by J. A. Chaptal (1756-1832), Fr chemist < Gr *nitron* (see NITER) + Fr *-gène*, -GEN, because niter resulted when it was sparked with oxygen in the presence of caustic potash⟧ a colorless, tasteless, odorless, gaseous chemical element forming nearly four fifths of the atmosphere: it is a component of all proteins and nucleic acids: symbol, N; at. no. 7: see the periodic table of elements in the Reference Supplement

ni·trog·en·ase (nī träj′ə nās′, -nāz′; nī′trə jə-) ***n.*** an enzyme in certain soil bacteria and algae, involved in the capture of nitrogen from the air to form ammonia

nitrogen cycle the cycle of natural processes through which atmospheric nitrogen is converted by nitrogen fixation and nitrification into compounds used by plants and animals in the formation of proteins and is eventually returned by decay and denitrification to its original state

nitrogen dioxide a poisonous, reddish-brown gas, NO_2, used in making nitric acid, as a rocket-fuel oxidizer, etc.: it is also an air pollutant formed from automobile exhausts

nitrogen fixation 1 the conversion of atmospheric nitrogen into nitrogenous compounds by bacteria (**nitrogen fixers**) found in the root nodules of legumes and certain other plants, and in the soil 2 the conversion of free nitrogen into nitrogenous compounds of commercial value by any of various processes —**ni′tro·gen-fix′ing *adj.***

ni·trog·en·ize (nī träj′ə nīz′, nī′trə jə nīz′) ***vt.*** **-ized′**, **-iz′ing** to combine or impregnate with nitrogen or its compounds

nitrogen mustard any of a class of compounds similar to mustard gas, but having an amino nitrogen in place of a sulfur atom: used in the treatment of cancers, etc.

nitrogen narcosis reduction in the ability to think clearly and react quickly, caused by increased air pressure which increases the concentration of nitrogen in bodily tissue and the brain: a special concern of deep-sea divers

ni·trog·e·nous (nī träj′ə nəs) ***adj.*** of or containing nitrogen or nitrogen compounds

nitrogen oxide any of various oxides of nitrogen, esp. one contributing to air pollution, as nitrous oxide, nitric oxide, or nitrogen dioxide

ni·tro·glyc·er·in or **ni·tro·glyc·er·ine** (nī′trō glis′ər in, -trə-) ***n.*** a thick, pale-yellow, flammable, explosive oil, $C_3H_5(ONO_2)_3$, prepared by treating glycerin with a mixture of nitric and sulfuric acids: used in medicine and in making dynamites and propellants

ni·trol·ic acid (nī träl′ik) ⟦NITR- + -OL[1] + -IC⟧ any of a series of acids with the general formula $RC(:NOH)NO_2$, formed by the action of nitrous acid on nitroparaffin

ni·trom·e·ter (nī träm′ət ər) ***n.*** ⟦NITRO- + -METER⟧ an apparatus for measuring the amount of nitrogen, or certain of its gaseous compounds, emitted during a chemical reaction

ni·tro·par·af·fin (nī′trō par′ə fin, -trə-) ***n.*** a nitrogen compound derived from an alkane and containing an NO_2 group in place of one or more of the hydrogen atoms

ni·tros·a·mine (nī′trōs am′ēn′, -in; nī trōs′ə mēn′) ***n.*** ⟦< fol. + AMINE⟧ any of a series of organic compounds derived from amines and containing the N·NO group: they are found in foods, herbicides, and industrial products and are formed in the body from nitrates and nitrites: some are thought to be carcinogenic in humans

ni·tro·so- (nī trō′sō, -sə) ⟦< L *nitrosus,* full of natron < *nitrum:* see NITER⟧ *combining form* of or containing nitrosyl [*nitrosamine*]: also, before a vowel, **nitros-**

ni·tro·syl (nī′trō sil, -sēl; nī trō′sil) ***n.*** ⟦< prec. + -YL⟧ the monovalent radical, or group, NO

ni·trous (nī′trəs) ***adj.*** ⟦L *nitrosus:* see NITROSO-⟧ **1** of, like, or containing niter **2** designating or of compounds in which nitrogen has a lower valence than in the corresponding nitric compounds

nitrous acid an acid, HNO_2, known only in solution or in the form of its salts (*nitrites*)

nitrous bacteria soil and water bacteria (genus *Nitrosomonas,* etc.) that convert ammonia into nitrites

nitrous oxide a colorless, nonflammable gas, N_2O, used as an anesthetic and in aerosols

nit·ty (nit′ē) ***adj.*** **-ti·er, -ti·est** full of nits

☆**nit·ty-grit·ty** (nit′ē grit′ē) ***n.*** ⟦orig. black slang: rhyming euphemism for *shitty*⟧ [Slang] the actual, basic facts, elements, issues, etc.

☆**nit·wit** (nit′wit′) ***n.*** ⟦*nit* (< Ger dial. for *nicht,* not) or ? NIT[1] + WIT[1]⟧ [Informal] a stupid or silly person

Ni·u·e (nē o͞o′ā) island in the SC Pacific, east of Tonga: a self-governing territory in association with New Zealand: 101 sq mi (261 sq km)

NIV *abbrev.* New International Version (of the Bible)

ni·val (nī′vəl) ***adj.*** ⟦L *nivalis* < *nix* (gen. *nivis*), SNOW)⟧ of, or growing in or under, snow

niv·e·ous (niv′ē əs) ***adj.*** ⟦L *niveus,* snowy: see prec.⟧ snowy; snowlike

Ni·ver·nais (nē ver ne′) historical region of central France, southeast of Paris

nix[1] (niks) ***n.*** ⟦Ger *nix,* masc., *nixe,* fem. < OHG *nihhus,* sea beast, *nicchussa,* water sprite, akin to OE *nicor,* ON *nykr,* water sprite < Gmc **nik-, *nikwus-,* water spirit < IE base **neigw-,* to wash > Sans *nénēkti,* (he) washes⟧ *Gmc. Folklore* a water sprite, usually small and of human or partly human form

☆**nix**[2] (niks) ***adv.*** ⟦Ger *nichts*⟧ [Slang] **1** no **2** not at all —***interj.*** [Slang] **1** stop; don't do that **2** I forbid, refuse, disagree, etc. —***n.*** [Slang] nothing —***vt.*** [Informal] to disapprove of or put a stop to

nix·ie[1] (nik′sē) ***n.*** *Gmc. Folklore* a female nix: also **nix·e** (nik′sə)

☆**nix·ie**[2] (nik′sē) ***n.*** ⟦see NIX[2]⟧ a piece of mail with an incorrect, incomplete, or illegible address, usually not deliverable

Nix·on (nik′sən), **Richard M(ilhous)** 1913-94; 37th president of the U.S. (1969-74): resigned under threat of impeachment —**Nix·o′ni·an** (-sō′nē ən) ***adj.***

Ni·zam (ni zäm′, nī zam′) ***n.*** ⟦Hindi & Pers *niẓām* < Ar *niẓām,* to order < *naẓama,* to govern⟧ **1** the title of the native rulers of Hyderabad, India that reigned from 1713 to 1950 **2** *pl.* **ni·zam′** [**n-**] a soldier in the Turkish regular army —**ni·zam′ate *n.***

Nizh·niy Ta·gil (nēzh′nē tä gēl′) city in W Russia, in the EC Urals

Nizh·ny Nov·go·rod (nēzh′nē nôv′gə rət) city in central European Russia, at the Volga & Oka rivers: see GORKI[2]

NJ or **N.J.** *abbrev.* New Jersey

Njord (nyôrd) ***n.*** ⟦ON *Njörthr*⟧ *Norse Myth.* one of the Vanir, father of Frey and Freya

nka *abbrev.* now known as

Nkru·mah (ən kro͞o′mə), **Kwa·me** (kwä′mē) 1909-72; president of Ghana (1960-66)

NL *abbrev.* **1** National League **2** Newfoundland and Labrador: also **N.L.**

n.l. *abbrev.* **1** ⟦L *non liquet*⟧ it is not clear **2** ⟦L *non licet*⟧ it is not lawful **3** *Printing* new line: also **nl**

N Lat *abbrev.* north latitude

NLRB *abbrev.* National Labor Relations Board

nm *abbrev.* nanometer(s)

Nm *abbrev. Bible* Numbers

NM *abbrev.* **1** nautical mile(s) **2** New Mexico: also **N.M., N Mex**

NMI *abbrev.* no middle initial

NMR *abbrev.* nuclear magnetic resonance

NMSQT *trademark* National Merit Scholarships Qualifying Test

NMT *abbrev. Pharmacy* not more than

NNE *abbrev.* north-northeast

NNW *abbrev.* north-northwest

no[1] (nō) ***adv.*** ⟦ME < OE *na* < *ne a,* lit., not ever < IE base **ne, nē,* negative particle > Sans *ná,* Gr *ne-,* L *ne-,* Goth & OHG *ni,* OIr *no*⟧ **1** not [whether or *no*] **2** not in any degree; not at all [*no* worse] **3** nay; not so: the opposite of *yes,* used to deny, refuse, or disagree —***interj.*** **1** it is not so; nay: the opposite of *yes* **2** it cannot be so: used to express surprise, disbelief, dismay, etc. **3** emphatically not: used to give force to a following negative statement or to introduce a fuller or more specific statement —***adj.*** ⟦ME, form of *non, none* (see NONE[1]) used only before a consonant < OE *nan* < *ne an,* lit., not one (see ONE)⟧ not any; not a; not one [*no* errors] —***n.,*** *pl.* **noes** or **nos** **1** an utterance of *no;* refusal or denial **2** a negative vote, or a person voting in the negative; nay —**no can do** [Slang] I (or we) cannot do it

no[2] (nō) ***n.,*** *pl.* **no** [*also* **N-**] *Drama* NOH

no[3] *abbrev.* **1** north **2** northern **3** ⟦L *numero*⟧ number

No *Chem. symbol for* nobelium

NO_x *symbol* nitrogen oxide

NOAA *abbrev.* National Oceanic and Atmospheric Administration (a U.S. agency incorporating the National Weather Service)

☆**no-ac·count** (nō′ə kount′) [Informal] ***adj.*** of no account; worthless; good-for-nothing —***n.*** a shiftless person

No·a·chi·an (nō ā′kē ən) ***adj.*** of Noah or his time: also **No·a·hide** (nō′ə hīd′) or **No′a·chide′** (-kīd′)

No·ah (nō′ə) ***n.*** ⟦Heb *nōah,* lit., rest, comfort⟧ **1** a masculine name **2** *Bible* the patriarch commanded by God to build the ark on which he, his family, and two of every kind of creature survived the Flood: Gen. 5:28-10:32

nob[1] (näb) ***n.*** ⟦later form of KNOB⟧ **1** [Slang] the head **2** *Cribbage* the jack of the same suit as the card cut from the pack: it counts one point for the holder: now called **his nobs**

nob[2] (näb) ***n.*** ⟦< ? prec.⟧ [Slang, Chiefly Brit.] a person of wealth and high social status

nob·ble (näb′əl) ***vt.*** **-bled, -bling** ⟦? freq. of NAB⟧ [Brit. Slang] **1** to disable (a horse), as by drugging to keep it from winning a race **2** to win over by bribery or other underhanded methods **3** to cheat or swindle —**nob′bler *n.***

nob·by (näb′ē) ***adj.*** **-bi·er, -bi·est** ⟦< NOB[2]⟧ [Slang, Chiefly Brit.] of or for nobs; stylish —**nob′bi·ly *adv.***

No·bel (nō bel′), **Al·fred Bern·hard** (ål′fred ber′nård) 1833-96; Swed. industrialist, philanthropist, & inventor of dynamite: established the Nobel prizes

☆**No·bel·ist** (nō bel′ist) ***n.*** a person who has been awarded a Nobel Prize

no·bel·i·um (nō bel′ē əm) ***n.*** ⟦ModL: so named (1957) after *Nobel* Institute in Stockholm, where discovered⟧ a radioactive, metallic chemical element, one of the actinides, produced by the nuclear bombardment of curium: symbol, No; at. no. 102: see the periodic table of elements in the Reference Supplement

Nobel Prize *trademark for* any of the annual international prizes administered by the Nobel Foundation for distinction in physics, chemistry, economics, medicine or physiology, and literature, and for promoting peace

no·bil·i·ty (nō bil′ə tē) ***n.,*** *pl.* **-ties** ⟦ME *nobilite* < OFr *nobilité* < L *nobilitas*⟧ **1** the quality or state of being noble **2** high station or rank in society, esp. when accompanied by a title **3** the class of people of noble rank or having hereditary titles: usually limited in Great Britain to the peerage: usually with *the*

no·ble (nō′bəl) ***adj.*** **-bler, -blest** ⟦OFr < L *nobilis,* lit., well-known < base of *(g)noscere,* to KNOW⟧ **1** [Obs.] famous; illustrious **2** having or showing high moral qualities or ideals, or greatness of character; lofty **3** having excellent qualities; superior **4** grand; stately; splendid; magnificent [*a noble view*] **5** of high hereditary rank or title; aristocratic **6** chemically nonreactive, esp. with acids and air; precious; pure: said of metals, esp. gold, platinum, etc.; also said of any of the six inert, or nearly inert, rare gases in group VIIIA of the periodic table: see the periodic table of elements in the Reference Supplement —***n.*** **1** a person having hereditary rank or title; nobleman; peer **2** a former gold coin of England —**no′ble·ness *n.***

☆**noble fir** a very large fir (*Abies procera*) of the W U.S.

no·ble·man (-mən) ***n.,*** *pl.* **-men** (-mən) a member of the nobility; peer

noble savage [*sometimes* **N- S-**] in Romanticism, primitive man conceived as existing in a virtuous, innocent state uncorrupted by civilization

no·blesse (nō bles′) ***n.*** ⟦ME *noblesce* < OFr < ML *nobilitia*⟧ NOBILITY

no·blesse o·blige (nō bles′ ō blēzh′; *Fr* nô bles ô blēzh′) ⟦Fr, lit., nobility obliges⟧ the assumed obligation of people of high rank or social position to behave nobly or kindly toward others

no·ble·wom·an (nō′bəl wo͝om′ən) ***n.,*** *pl.* **-wom′en** (-wim′in) a woman who is a member of the nobility; peeress

no·bly (nō′blē) ***adv.*** **1** with noble courage or spirit; gallantly **2** *a)* idealistically; loftily *b)* excellently; splendidly **3** with noble heritage

no·bod·y (nō′bäd′ē, -bud′ē, -bə dē) ***pron.*** not any person; not anybody; no one —***n.,*** *pl.* **-bod′ies** a person of no influence, authority, or importance

no-brain·er (nō′brān′ər) ***n.*** [Informal] something so obvious, simple, etc. as to require little thought

no-cal (nō′kal′) ***adj.*** ⟦NO[1] + CAL⟧ having no calories [*no-cal* diet soda]

no·cent (nō′sənt) ***adj.*** ⟦LME < L *nocens,* prp. of *nocere,* to harm: see NECRO-⟧ [Now Rare] **1** causing harm or injury; hurtful **2** guilty or criminal

no·ci·cep·tive (nō′sə sep′tiv) ***adj.*** ⟦< L *nocere* (see prec.) + (RE)CEPTIVE⟧ of, causing, or reacting to pain

nock (näk) ***n.*** ⟦ME *nocke* < Scand, as in Swed dial. *nokke,* notch < IE **kneug-* < base **ken-,* to pinch > NOOK, NUT⟧ **1** a notch for holding the string at either end of a bow **2** a notch in the end of an arrow, for the insertion of the bowstring —***vt.*** **1** to make a notch in (a bow or arrow) **2** to set (an arrow) into the bowstring

noc·tam·bu·lism (näk tam′byo͞o liz′əm) ***n.*** ⟦Fr *noctambulisme* < L *nox* (gen. *noctis*), NIGHT + *ambulare,* to walk (see AMBLE) + *-isme,* -ISM⟧ [Rare] walking in one's sleep; somnambulism —**noc·tam′bu·list *n.***

noc·ti- (näk′ti, -tə) ⟦< L *nox* (gen. *noctis*), NIGHT⟧ *combining form* night [*noctilucent*]: also, before a vowel, **noct-**

noc·ti·lu·ca (näk′tə lo͞o′kə) ***n.*** ⟦ModL < L, something that shines at night < *nox* (gen. *noctis*), NIGHT + *lucere,* to shine < *lux,* LIGHT[1]⟧ any of a genus (*Noctiluca*) of large, spherical, reddish, luminescent dinoflagellates that often occur in vast numbers in the sea, causing the water to glow at night

noc·ti·lu·cent (näk′tə lo͞o′sənt) ***adj.*** ⟦NOCTI- + LUCENT⟧ shining in the night: said esp. of high-altitude clouds (75 to 90 km or 46 to 56 mi above the earth) that reflect twilight to the earth long after sunset or long before sunrise

noc·tu·id (näk′to͞o id, -tyo͞o-) ***n.*** ⟦< ModL *Noctuidae* < L *noctua*, night owl < *nox* (gen. *noctis*), NIGHT⟧ any of a large family (Noctuidae) of mostly dull-colored moths that fly at night and are attracted to lights, including underwing moths and others with very destructive larvae, as cutworms or army worms

noc·tule (näk′to͞ol′, -tyo͞ol′) ***n.*** ⟦Fr < VL **noctula*, owl, bat, dim. < L *noctua*: see prec.⟧ any of a genus (*Nyctalus*) of bats; esp., a large brown species (*N. noctula*) of Europe and the British Isles

noc·turn (näk′tərn) ***n.*** ⟦ME *nocturne* < OFr < ML(Ec) *nocturna* < L *nocturnus*: see fol.⟧ any of the divisions of the office of matins

noc·tur·nal (näk tur′nəl) ***adj.*** ⟦LME < LL *nocturnalis* < L *nocturnus* < *nox* (gen. *noctis*), NIGHT⟧ **1** of, done, or happening in the night **2** functioning or active during the night **3** *Bot.* having blossoms that open at night —**noc·tur′nal·ly** ***adv.***

nocturnal emission an involuntary emission of semen during sleep

noc·turne (näk′turn′) ***n.*** ⟦Fr < L *nocturnus*: see NOCTURNAL⟧ **1** a painting of a night scene **2** a musical composition, esp. for the piano, of a romantic or dreamy character thought appropriate to night

noc·u·ous (näk′yo͞o əs) ***adj.*** ⟦L *nocuus* < *nocere*: see NECRO-⟧ harmful; poisonous; noxious —**noc′u·ous·ly** ***adv.***

nod (näd) ***vi.*** **nod′ded, nod′ding** ⟦ME *nodden*, prob. in basic sense "to shake the head," akin to Ger *notten*, to move about, OHG *hnotōn*, to shake, OE *hnossian*, to knock < IE **kneudh* < base **ken-*, to scratch, scrape > NIP[1]⟧ **1** to bend the head forward slightly and raise it again quickly, as a sign of greeting, command, acknowledgment, invitation, or, specif., of agreement or assent **2** to let the head fall forward involuntarily because of drowsiness; be very sleepy **3** to be inattentive or careless; make a slip **4** to sway back and forth or up and down, or to hang down, as the tops of trees ☆**5** [Slang] to be under the influence of a drug, as heroin —***vt.*** **1** to bend (the head) forward slightly and raise it again quickly **2** to signify (assent, approval, agreement, etc.) by doing this **3** to invite or dismiss by a nod —***n.*** **1** a nodding, as of the head, treetops, etc. **2** a sign of affirmation, assent, favorable decision, etc. [to give or get the *nod*] ➥See also LAND OF NOD —**nod off** to fall asleep, esp. when sitting up —☆**nod out** [Slang] to become unconscious from the effects of a drug —**nod′der** ***n.***

nod·al (nōd′'l) ***adj.*** of or like a node or nodes —**no·dal·i·ty** (nō dal′ə tē) ***n.*** —**nod′al·ly** ***adv.***

nodding acquaintance ⟦see NOD, *vi.* 1⟧ **1** a slight, not intimate, acquaintance with a person or thing **2** a person whom one knows slightly

nod·dle (näd′'l) ***n.*** ⟦ME *nodle* < ?⟧ [Old Informal] the head; pate: a humorous term

nod·dy (näd′ē) ***n.***, *pl.* **-dies** ⟦< ? NOD + -Y[3]⟧ **1** a fool; simpleton **2** any of a genus (*Anous*) of tropical terns with dark body feathers and pale gray crown

node (nōd) ***n.*** ⟦L *nodus*, a knot: see NET[1]⟧ **1** a knot; knob; swelling **2** a point of concentration; central point **3** *Anat.* a knotty, localized swelling; protuberance **4** *Astron.* either of the two points at which the orbit of a celestial body intersects a reference plane, as the ecliptic **5** *Bot.* that part, or joint, of a stem from which a leaf starts to grow **6** *Geom.* the point where a continuous curve crosses or meets itself **7** *Physics* the point, line, or surface of a vibrating object, as a string, that is virtually free of vibration

nodes on a vibrating string

node of Ran·vier (rän vyā′) *pl.* **nodes of Ranvier** ⟦after L. A. *Ranvier* (1835-1922), Fr histologist⟧ any of the constrictions along the myelin sheath that surrounds an axon of a nerve cell: nodes are formed where two Schwann cells meet and are essential to the proper transmission of nerve impulses

nod·i·cal (näd′i kəl, nō′di-) ***adj.*** *Astron.* of the nodes

no·dose (nō′dōs′, nō dōs′) ***adj.*** ⟦L *nodosus*⟧ having nodes; knotty: said of roots, etc. —**no·dos′i·ty** (-däs′ə tē) ***n.***

nod·ule (näj′o͞ol) ***n.*** ⟦L *nodulus*, dim. of *nodus*, a knot: see NET[1]⟧ **1** a small knot or irregular, rounded lump **2** *Anat.* a small node **3** *Bot.* a small knot or joint on a stem or root, esp. one containing nitrogen-fixing bacteria **4** *Geol. a)* a small, hard lump or mass of a mineral or rock that is embedded in a larger rock *b)* a usually small, roundish lump or mass of manganese, cobalt, etc. found on the floor of the sea or a large lake —**nod′u·lar** ***adj.***, **nod′u·lose′**

no·dus (nō′dəs) ***n.***, *pl.* **-di′** (-dī′) ⟦ME < L, a knot, NODE⟧ complication; difficulty; knotty situation, as in a play

no·el or **no·ël** (nō el′) ***n.*** ⟦< Fr *noël* < OFr *nowel, nouel* < L *natalis*, NATAL⟧ **1** a Christmas carol **2** [**N-**] Christmas

No·el (nō′əl; *also, fem.*, nō el′) ***n.*** ⟦OFr *Nouel, Noel*, lit., natal: see prec.: cf. NATALIE⟧ a masculine and feminine name

no·et·ic (nō et′ik) ***adj.*** ⟦Gr *noētikos* < *noēsis* < *noein*, to perceive < *nous*, the mind⟧ of or having to do with the mind or intellect; sometimes, specif., able to be understood only by the intellect

☆**no-fault** (nō′fôlt′) ***adj.*** **1** designating or of a form of insurance which covers certain losses of all persons injured, as in an automobile accident, without regard to fault **2** designating a form of divorce granted without blame being sought or established

no-frills (nō′frilz′) ***adj.*** [Informal] having few or no special services, luxuries, embellishments, etc.

nog[1] (näg) ***n.*** ⟦< ?⟧ a wooden peg or block, esp., a brick-shaped block that is set in a wall to hold nails —***vt.*** **nogged, nog′ging** to fill in (a space in a wall, as between studs) with bricks

nog[2] or **nogg** (näg) ***n.*** ⟦< East Anglian dial. < ?⟧ **1** [Brit.] a kind of strong ale ☆**2** EGGNOG

nog·gin (näg′in) ***n.*** ⟦prob. < prec.⟧ **1** a small cup or mug **2** one fourth of a pint: a measure for ale or liquor ☆**3** [Informal] the head

nog·ging (näg′iŋ) ***n.*** ⟦< NOG[1]⟧ brick masonry built up between wooden uprights, as studs

☆**no-go** (nō′gō′) ***adj.*** ⟦orig. astronauts' jargon⟧ [Informal] **1** not functioning properly or not ready to go **2** designated as an area into which entry is forbidden, restricted, or reputed to be dangerous

no-good (nō′good′) ***adj.*** [Slang] contemptible; despicable

no-growth (nō′grōth′) ***adj.*** of a policy or practice of not welcoming or encouraging new residents, industries, or commercial ventures to a community or area

No·gu·chi (nō go͞o′chē) **1 Hi·de·yo** (hē′de yō′) 1876-1928; U.S. bacteriologist, born in Japan **2 I·sa·mu** (ē′sä mo͞o′) 1904-88; U.S. sculptor

Noh (nō) ***n.***, *pl.* **Noh** ⟦Jpn *nō*⟧ [*also* **n-**] a classic form of Japanese drama with choral music and dancing, using set themes, simple scenery, masked and costumed performers, and stylized acting

☆**no-hit·ter** (nō′hit′ər) ***n.*** a baseball game in which the pitcher allows the opponents no base hits —**no′-hit′** ***adj.***

no·how (nō′hou′) ***adv.*** [Slang or Dial.] in no manner; not at all: usually in negative constructions

noil (noil) ***n.*** ⟦< SW Yorkshire dial. < ?⟧ short or knotted textile fibers combed from the long staple or, sometimes, spun in with longer staple to make yarn

noir (nwär) [*often in italics*] ***n.*** ⟦Fr, black⟧ **1** *short for* FILM NOIR **2** fiction in which mood, plot, etc. are like those of film noir —***adj.*** of or characteristic of noir or film noir —**noir′ish** ***adj.***

noise (noiz) ***n.*** ⟦ME < OFr, noise, quarreling, clamor < L *nausea*: see NAUSEA⟧ **1** *a)* loud or confused shouting; din of voices; clamor *b)* any loud, discordant, or disagreeable sound or sounds **2** a sound of any kind [the *noise* of the rain] **3** [Informal] *a)* gossip; rumor; scandal *b)* a protest or accusation *c)* something that draws public notice *d)* [*often pl.*] [Informal] a hint or indication of someone's opinion, intention, etc. [the White House making *noises* about an upcoming trade agreement] **4** *Electronics* any unwanted electrical signal, esp. within a communication system, that interferes with the sound or image being communicated —***vt.*** **noised, nois′ing** to spread about (a report, rumor, etc.): usually with *about, around*, etc. —***vi.*** [Now Rare] **1** to talk much or loudly **2** to make noise or a noise

SYN.—**noise** is the general word for any loud, unmusical, or disagreeable sound; **din** refers to a loud, prolonged, deafening sound, painful to the ears [the *din* of the jackhammer]; **uproar** applies to a loud, confused sound, as of shouting, laughing, etc., and connotes commotion or disturbance [his remarks threw the audience into an *uproar*]; **clamor** suggests loud, continued, excited shouting, as in protest or demand [the *clamor* of an aroused people]; **hubbub** implies the confused mingling of many voices [the *hubbub* of a subway station]; **racket** refers to a loud, clattering combination of noises regarded as annoyingly excessive [he couldn't work for the *racket* next door] —*ANT.* **quiet**

noise·less (noiz′lis) ***adj.*** with little or no noise; very quiet —**noise′less·ly** ***adv.*** —**noise′less·ness** ***n.***

noise·mak·er (noiz′māk′ər) ***n.*** a person or thing that makes noise; specif., any of various party favors, typically of paper or plastic, for making noise in celebration, as on New Year's Eve

noise pollution loud or excessive noise, as from traffic or industry, regarded as a health or environmental concern

noi·sette (nwä zet′) ***n.*** a small, rounded piece of meat [*noisettes* of veal]

noi·some (noi′səm) ***adj.*** ⟦ME *noyesum* < *noy*, aphetic < *anoy* < OFr *anoi*: see ANNOY & -SOME[1]⟧ **1** injurious to health; harmful **2** having a bad odor; foul-smelling —**noi′some·ly** ***adv.*** —**noi′some·ness** ***n.***

nois·y (noiz′ē) ***adj.*** **nois′i·er, nois′i·est** **1** making, or accompanied by, noise **2** making more sound than is expected or customary **3** full of noise; clamorous [the *noisy* city] —**nois′i·ly** ***adv.*** —**nois′i·ness** ***n.***

☆**no-knock** (nō′näk′) ***adj.*** [Informal] designating or based on laws or provisions which permit police with search warrants to enter a private dwelling by force without announcing or identifying themselves

no·lens vo·lens (nō′lenz vō′lenz) ⟦L⟧ unwilling or willing; whether or not one wishes it; willy-nilly

no·li me tan·ge·re (nō′lī mē tan′jə rē) ⟦L, lit., touch me not⟧ **1** a warning against touching or meddling **2** JEWELWEED

nol·le pros·e·qui (näl′ē präs′i kwī′, -kwē′; nō′-) ⟦L, to be unwilling to prosecute⟧ *Law* **1** formal notice by the prosecutor that prosecution in a criminal case will be ended as to one or more counts, one or more defendants, or altogether **2** similar notice by the plaintiff in a civil suit

no-load (nō′lōd′) ***adj.*** designating or of mutual funds charging no commissions on sales —***n.*** a no-load mutual fund

no·lo con·ten·de·re (nō′lō kən ten′də rē) ⟦L, lit., I do not wish to contest (it)⟧ *Law* a plea by which a defendant in a criminal case does not make a defense but does not admit guilt: it leaves the defendant open to conviction but does not prejudice his or her case in collateral proceedings

no-lose (nō lo͞oz′) ***adj.*** [Informal] designating or of a situation, policy, etc. that is sure to succeed

☆**nol-pros** (näl präs′) ***vt.*** **-prossed′, -pros′sing** ⟦< abbrev. of NOLLE PROSEQUI⟧ *Law* to abandon (all or part of a suit) by entering a nolle prosequi on the court records

nom *abbrev.* nominative

no·ma (nō′mə) *n.* ⟦ModL < Gr *nomē*, a spreading (of sores), lit., a feeding < *nemein*, to distribute: see -NOMY⟧ a severe ulcerous condition of the mouth, occurring esp. in young children as after debilitating disease and usually resulting in gangrene

no·mad (nō′mad′) *n.* ⟦L *nomas* (gen. *nomadis*) < Gr, orig., roaming about for pasture < *nemein*, to pasture, orig., to distribute: see -NOMY⟧ **1** a member of a tribe or people having no permanent home, but moving about constantly in search of food, pasture, etc. **2** any wanderer who has no fixed home —*adj.* nomadic; wandering —**no′mad·ism′** (-mad iz′əm) *n.*

no·mad·ic (nō mad′ik) *adj.* of, characteristic of, or like nomads or their way of life —*SYN.* ITINERANT —**no·mad′i·cal·ly** *adv.*

no man's land **1** a piece of land, usually wasteland, to which no one has a recognized title **2** the unoccupied region separating opposing armies **3** an indefinite area of operation, involvement, jurisdiction, etc. Also written **no′-man's-land′** *n.*

nom·bril (näm′brəl) *n.* ⟦Fr, the navel, for OFr *lombril* < LL **umbiliculus*, dim. < L *umbilicus*, NAVEL⟧ *Heraldry* the point on a shield just below the true center; navel point

nom de guerre (näm′ də ger′; *Fr* nōnd ger′) *pl.* **noms de guerre** (*Fr* nōnd) ⟦Fr, lit., war name⟧ a pseudonym

nom de plume (näm′ də ploom′; *Fr* nōn də plüm′) *pl.* **noms de plume** (*Fr* nōn) ⟦Fr⟧ a pen name; pseudonym —*SYN.* PSEUDONYM

nome (nōm) *n.* ⟦Gr *nomos* < *nemein*, distribute: see -NOMY⟧ a province of ancient Egypt

Nome (nōm) ⟦after nearby Cape *Nome*, prob. < "? *name*," query on an early map, misread as *C. Nome*⟧ city in W Alas., on the S coast of Seward Peninsula

no·men (nō′mən) *n.*, *pl.* **nom·i·na** (näm′i nə) ⟦L, NAME⟧ the second of the three names of an ancient Roman, following the praenomen and preceding the cognomen (Ex.: Marcus *Tullius* Cicero)

no·men·cla·tor (nō′mən klāt′ər) *n.* ⟦L < *nomen*, NAME + *calator*, caller, crier < pp. of *calare*, to call: see CLAMOR⟧ **1** a person, specif. a slave in ancient Rome, who announces the names of guests, etc. **2** a person who invents names for, or assigns them to, things, as in scientific classification

no·men·cla·ture (nō′mən klā′chər; *also, and chiefly Brit*, nō men′klə chər) *n.* ⟦L *nomenclatura*: see prec.⟧ **1** the system or set of names used in a specific branch of learning or activity, as in biology for plants and animals, or for the parts of a particular mechanism **2** the act or a system of naming

no·men·kla·tu·ra (nō′mən klä toor′ə) *n.* ⟦Russ, a listing of positions to be filled < L *nomenclatura*: see NOMENCLATOR⟧ **1** the ruling, bureaucratic elite of the former Soviet Union, made up of members of the Communist Party who were chosen by the party to hold positions of leadership and privilege in government and industry **2** any similar ruling elite

☆**No·mex** (nō′meks′) *trademark for* a lightweight, fire-resistant, nylon fiber made into garments, aircraft upholstery, etc.

-nom·ics (näm′iks) *combining form* economics: used in forming compounds naming a (specified) kind of economic policy or one associated with a (specified) public official [*urbanomics, Reaganomics*]: also **-omics**

nom·i·nal (näm′ə nəl) *adj.* ⟦ME *nominalle* < L *nominalis*, of a name < *nomen*, NAME⟧ **1** of, consisting of, having the nature of, or giving a name or names **2** of or having to do with a noun or nouns **3** in name only, not in fact [the *nominal* leader] **4** very small compared to usual expectations; slight [a *nominal* fee] —*n. Linguis.* a noun or other word or word group, including adjectives, that occurs in grammatical functions typical of nouns; substantive

nom·i·nal·ism (-iz′əm) *n.* ⟦Fr *nominalisme*: see prec. & -ISM⟧ *Philos.* a doctrine of the late Middle Ages that all universal or abstract terms are mere necessities of thought or conveniences of language and therefore exist as names only, with no ideal realities corresponding to them: opposed to REALISM (sense 3a) —**nom′i·nal·ist** *n.*, *adj.* —**nom′i·nal·is′tic** *adj.*

nom·i·nal·ly (-nəl ē) *adv.* **1** in a nominal way **2** in name only **3** by name

nominal value *Econ.* PAR VALUE

nominal wages wages stated in terms of money paid, not in terms of purchasing power

nom·i·nate (näm′ə nāt′) *vt.* **-nat′ed**, **-nat′ing** ⟦< L *nominatus*, pp. of *nominare*, to name < *nomen*, NAME⟧ **1** [Now Rare] to name, call, or designate **2** to name or appoint to an office or position **3** *a)* to name as a candidate for election or appointment; propose for office *b)* to propose as a candidate for an award or honor **4** to enter (a horse) in a horse race —**nom′i·na′tor** *n.*

nom·i·na·tion (näm′ə nā′shən) *n.* ⟦ME, calling by name < OFr < L *nominatio* < pp. of *nominare*: see prec.⟧ the act of nominating or the fact of being nominated

nom·i·na·tive (näm′ə nə tiv; *for adj. 1 & 2, also*, -nāt′iv) *adj.* ⟦ME *nomenatyf* < OFr *nominatif* < L *nominativus*, belonging to a name < pp. of *nominare*: see NOMINATE⟧ **1** appointed or filled by appointment **2** having the name of a person on it, as a stock certificate **3** *Gram.* designating, of, or in the case of the subject of a finite verb —*n.* ⟦L *nominativus (casus)*⟧ **1** the nominative case **2** a word in this case

nom·i·nee (näm′ə nē′, näm′ə nē′) *n.* ⟦NOMIN(ATE) + -EE[1]⟧ a person who is nominated, esp. a candidate for election

no·mo- (nō′mō, -mə; näm′ō, -ə) ⟦< Gr *nomos*, law: see -NOMY⟧ *combining form* law or custom [*nomology*]

nom·o·gram (näm′ə gram′, nō′mə-) *n.* a graphical representation of a set of scales for the variables in a problem, so positioned that a straight line connecting the known values on some scales will provide the unknown values at its intersections with other scales: also **nom′o·graph′**

no·mog·ra·phy (nō mäg′rə fē) *n.* ⟦Gr *nomographia* < *nomos*, law (see -NOMY) + *graphein*, to write: see GRAPHIC⟧ **1** the science of making nomograms **2** the laws for constructing such charts —**nom·o·graph·ic** (näm′ō graf′ik, nō′mə-) *adj.* —**nom′o·graph′i·cal·ly** *adv.*

nom·o·log·i·cal (näm′ə läj′i kəl, nō′mə-) *adj.* conforming to or stating laws of nature or rules of logic

nom·o·thet·ic (näm′ə thet′ik) *adj.* ⟦Gr *nomothetikos* < *nomothetēs* lawgiver < *nomos*, law (see fol.) + *tithenai*, to make, DO[1]⟧ **1** giving or enacting laws **2** based on law **3** of a science of general or universal laws

-no·my (nə mē) ⟦Gr *-nomia* < *nomos*, law < *nemein* to distribute, govern < IE base **nem-*, to assign, take, arrange > L *numerus*, NUMBER, OE *niman*, Ger *nehmen*, to take⟧ *combining form* the systematized knowledge of or the system of laws governing [*astronomy, taxonomy*]

non (nōn) *adv.*, *interj.* ⟦Fr⟧ no

non- (nän, nun) ⟦< L *non*, not < OL *noenum* < *ne-*, negative particle (see NO[1]) + *oinom*, ONE⟧ *prefix* **1** *a)* not *b)* the opposite of [*nonessential*] *c)* excluded (from a specified category) [*nonvoter, nonfiction*] *d)* refusal or failure [*noncooperation*]: used to give a negative or privative force, esp. to nouns, adjectives, and adverbs **2** having the superficial aspect, but not the real value, of: used to give a pejorative force, esp. to nouns [*nonbook, nonevent*] **3** having the value, but not the surface aspect or identity, of: used to indicate potential, but unacknowledged or unrecognized, qualities [*noncandidate, noncampaign*] ➥As used in sense 1, *non-* is less emphatic than IN-[2] and UN-, which often give a word a strong opposite or reverse meaning or force (Ex.: *nonhuman* vs. *inhuman*). A hyphen may be used after *non-* and is generally used when the base word begins with a capital letter. The list at the bottom of this and the following pages includes the more common compounds formed with *non-* that do not have special meanings; they will be understood if "not" is used before the meaning of the base word

no·na- (nō′nə, nän′ə) *combining form* ⟦< L *nonus*, ninth⟧ nine

non·age (nän′ij, nō′nij) *n.* ⟦ME < Anglo-Fr *nounage* < OFr *nonage*: see NON- & AGE⟧ **1** *Law a)* the state of being under the lawful age for doing certain things, as marrying *b)* MINORITY (*n.* 4) **2** the period of immaturity

non·a·ge·nar·i·an (nän′ə jə ner′ē ən, nō′nə-) *adj.* ⟦L *nonagenarius* < *nonageni*, ninety each < *nonaginta*, ninety < base of *noven*, NINE + *-ginta*, -TY[2]⟧ 90 years old, or between the ages of 90 and 100 —*n.* a nonagenarian person

non·ag·gres·sion pact (nän′ə gresh′ən) an agreement between two nations to avoid armed conflict with each other for a specified period

non·a·gon (nän′ə gän′) *n.* ⟦< L *nonus*, ninth (see NOON) + -GON⟧ a plane figure having nine angles and nine sides

non·a·ligned (nän′ə līnd′) *adj.* ☆not aligned politically with a powerful nation or bloc of nations, specif. with either the U.S. or the Soviet Union during the Cold War —**non′a·lign′ment** *n.*

no-name (nō′nām′) *adj.* not famous, distinguished, or recognized [a *no-name* actor, product, etc.] —*n.* a no-name person or thing

non·ap·pear·ance (nän′ə pir′əns) *n.* a failure to appear, esp. in court

non·be·ing (nän′bē′iŋ) *n.* NONEXISTENCE

non·bind·ing (-bīn′diŋ) *adj.* that does not hold one to an obligation, duty, promise, etc. [a *nonbinding* agreement]

☆**non·book** or **non-book** (nän′book′) *n.* a book produced quickly and cheaply, typically a hastily assembled compilation of facts, photographs, etc., often published merely to take advantage of a current fad

nonabrasive
nonabsorbent
nonacademic
nonacceptance
nonacid
nonacidic
nonactinic
nonactive
nonaddictive
nonadjacent
nonadjectival
nonadjustable
nonadministrative
nonadvantageous
nonadverbial
nonaesthetic
nonaffiliated
non-African
nonaggression
nonaggressive
nonagreement
nonagricultural
nonalcoholic
nonalgebraic
nonallergenic
nonallergic
nonalphabetic
nonamendable
non-American
nonanalytic
non-Anglican
nonantagonistic
nonapologetic
nonapostolic
nonappearing
nonapplicable
nonaquatic
non-Arab
non-Arabic
nonaristocratic
nonarithmetical
nonartistic
non-Aryan
non-Asian
nonassertive
nonassessable
nonassignable
nonassimilable
nonassimilation
nonassociative
nonathletic
nonatmospheric
nonattendance
nonattributive
nonauthoritative
nonautomatic
nonautomotive
nonavailability
nonbacterial
nonbasic
nonbeliever
nonbelieving
nonbelligerency
nonbelligerent
non-Biblical
nonbillable
nonblack
nonblooming
nonbreakable
non-British
non-Buddhist
nonbudding
nonbureaucratic
nonburnable
nonbusiness

nonce (näns) *n.* ⟦ME *(for the) nones,* formed by syllabic merging < *(for then) ones,* lit., the once: *then* is the dat. sing. of the def. art.⟧ the present use, occasion, or time; time being: chiefly in **for the nonce**

non·cel·lu·los·ic (nän′sel′yo͞o lōs′ik) *adj.* designating or of synthetic fibers made from materials other than plant derivatives

nonce word a word coined and used for a single or particular occasion

non·cha·lance (nän′shə läns′; nän′shə läns′, -ləns) *n.* the state or quality of being nonchalant —*SYN.* EQUANIMITY

non·cha·lant (nän′shə länt′; nän′shə länt′, -lənt) *adj.* ⟦Fr < *non* (L *non*), not + *chaloir,* to care for < L *calere,* to be warm or ardent: see CALORIE⟧ without warmth or enthusiasm; showing cool lack of concern; casually indifferent —*SYN.* COOL —**non′cha·lant′ly** *adv.*

non·com (nän′käm′) *n.* [Informal] *short for* NONCOMMISSIONED OFFICER

non·com·bat·ant (nän′kəm bat′′nt, nän′käm′bə tənt) *n.* **1** a member of the armed forces whose activities do not include actual combat, as a chaplain or medic **2** any civilian in wartime —*adj.* **1** not involving combat **2** of noncombatants

non·com·mis·sioned officer (nän′kə mish′ənd) an enlisted person of any of various grades in the armed forces, as, in the U.S. Army, from corporal to sergeant major inclusive: see also PETTY OFFICER

☆**non·com·mit·tal** (-kə mit′′l) *adj.* not committing one to any point of view or course of action; not revealing one's position or purpose *[a noncommittal response to a question]* —**non′com·mit′tal·ly** *adv.*

non·com·pete (-kəm pēt′) *adj.* designating or of a contractual agreement according to which an executive, partner, etc. shall not engage in competition with a corporation or firm for a certain period of time after leaving it: also **non′com′pe·ti′tion**

non·com·pli·ance (-kəm plī′əns) *n.* **1** failure to comply; refusal to yield, agree, etc. **2** the state or condition of failing or refusing to comply —**non′com·pli′ant** *adj.*

non com·pos men·tis (nän käm′pōs men′tis) ⟦L⟧ *Law* not of sound mind; mentally incapable of handling one's own affairs: often shortened to **non compos**

non·con·duc·tor (nän′kən duk′tər) *n.* a substance that does not readily transmit certain forms of energy, as sound, heat, and, esp., electricity

non·con·form·ist (-kən fôrm′ist) *n.* **1** a person who does not act in conformity with generally accepted beliefs and practices **2** [**N-**] a British Protestant who does not belong to the Anglican Church; Dissenter —*adj.* not following established customs, beliefs, etc. —**non′con·form′ism′** *n.*

non·con·form·i·ty (-kən fôrm′ə tē) *n.* **1** failure or refusal to act in conformity with generally accepted beliefs and practices **2** [**N-**] refusal to accept the doctrines or follow the practices of the Anglican Church **3** lack of agreement or harmony

non·con·fron·ta·tion·al (nän′kän′frən tā′shə nəl) *adj.* not aggressive, hostile, or threatening

non·co·op·er·a·tion (-kō äp′ər ā′shən) *n.* **1** failure to work together or in unison with a person, group, or organization **2** refusal to cooperate with a government through various acts of civil disobedience, as by nonpayment of taxes: used as a form of protest, as by Mohandas Gandhi against the former British government in India —**non′co·op′er·a·tive** *adj.*

non·cus·to·di·al (nän′kəs tō′dē əl) *adj.* designating or of a parent who, as a result of divorce or separation, does not have custody of a child or children: also written **non′-cus·to′di·al**

non·dair·y (nän′der′ē) *adj.* containing no milk or milk products *[a nondairy cream substitute]*

☆**non·de·nom·i·nat·ed** (nän′di näm′i nāt′id) *adj.* designating or of a postage stamp that has no denomination printed on it

non·de·nom·i·na·tion·al (nän′di näm′i nā′shə nəl) *adj.* not affiliated with any religious denomination

non·de·script (nän′di skript′, nän′di skript′) *adj.* ⟦< L *non,* not + *descriptus,* pp. of *describere,* DESCRIBE⟧ **1** so lacking in recognizable character or qualities as to belong to no definite class or type; hard to classify or describe **2** not interesting; colorless; drab —*n.* a nondescript person or thing

non·dis·junc·tion (nän′dis juŋk′shən) *n. Biol.* the failure of paired chromosomes to pass to separate cells in meiosis

non·du·ra·ble (-do͝or′ə bəl, -dyo͝or′-) *adj.* not durable; specif., designating a power of attorney that does not remain in effect after the person who authorized it becomes incompetent

nondurable goods goods that remain usable for, or must be replaced within, a relatively short period of time, as food, apparel, or fabrics

none¹ (nun) *pron.* ⟦ME < OE *nan* < *ne,* not (see NO¹) + *an,* ONE⟧ **1** not one *[none of the books is interesting]* **2** no one; not anyone *[none of us is ready]* **3** [*with pl. v.*] no persons or things; not any *[many letters were received but none were answered]* **4** not any (of); no part; nothing *[I want none of it, none of the money is left]* —*adv.* in no way; not at all *[none the worse for wear, none the wiser]* —*adj.* [Archaic] not any: used before a vowel *[of none effect]* —**none other than** the actual or very: used to express surprise, interest, etc. at the appearance of a particular person or thing *[standing in the elevator was none other than the mayor]*

none² (nōn) *n.* ⟦OE *non:* see NOON⟧ [*often* **N-**] the fifth of the canonical hours; midafternoon prayer

non·e·go (nän′ē′gō) *n., pl.* **-gos 1** *Philos.* anything or everything that is not the ego **2** the external world

non·en·ti·ty (-en′tə tē) *n., pl.* **-ties 1** the state of not existing **2** something that exists only in the mind or imagination **3** a person or thing of little or no importance

nones (nōnz) *pl.n.* ⟦ME < L *nonae* < *nonus,* ninth: see NOON⟧ [*with sing. or pl. v.*] **1** [*sometimes* **N-**] in the ancient Roman calendar, the ninth day before the ides of a month **2** *var. of* NONE²

non·es·sen·tial (nän′ə sen′shəl) *adj.* **1** not essential; of relatively no importance; unnecessary **2** *Biochem.* designating biological compounds, esp. amino acids, required by living systems, that can be made in adequate amounts from other dietary constituents —*n.* a nonessential person or thing

none·such (nun′such′) *n.* **1** [Archaic] a person or thing unrivaled or unequaled; something or someone unique; nonpareil **2** BLACK MEDIC

---

noncaking
noncalcareous
noncaloric
noncancelable
noncancerous
noncanonical
noncapitalist
noncarbohydrate
noncarbonated
noncarnivorous
noncash
noncategorical
non-Catholic
non-Caucasoid
noncellular
noncensored
noncereal
noncertified
nonchargeable
nonchemical
non-Chinese
non-Christian
nonchurch
noncitizen
noncivilized
nonclassical
nonclassifiable
nonclerical
nonclinical
noncoagulating
noncoercive
noncognitive
noncohesive
noncollaborative
noncollectible
noncollegiate
noncolloid
noncombat
noncombining
noncombustible
noncommercial
noncommissioned
noncommunicable
noncommunicant
noncommunicating
noncommunicative
noncommunist
noncompensating
noncompensatory
noncompetency
noncompetent
noncompeting
noncompetitive
noncompletion
noncomplying
noncompressible
noncompression
noncompulsory
nonconclusive
nonconcurrence
noncondensing
nonconducive
nonconducting
nonconductive
nonconferrable
nonconfidential
nonconflicting
nonconformance
nonconforming
noncongealing
noncongestion
non-Congressional
nonconnective
nonconscious
nonconsecutive
nonconsent
nonconservative
nonconstitutional
nonconstructive
noncontagious
noncontemporary
noncontiguous
noncontinental
noncontinuance
noncontinuous
noncontraband
noncontradiction
noncontradictory
noncontributing
noncontributory
noncontrolled
noncontroversial
nonconventional
nonconvergent
nonconvertible
nonconviction
noncoordinating
noncorporate
noncorrective
noncorroding
noncorrosive
noncredible
noncriminal
noncritical
noncrucial
noncrystalline
nonculpable
noncumulative
noncurrent
noncyclic
noncyclical
non-Czech
non-Darwinian
nondecaying
nondeceptive
nondeciduous
nondeductible
nondefensive
nondeferential
nondeferrable
nondefining
nondelivery
nondemand
nondemocratic
nondepartmental
nondependent
nondepreciating
nonderivative
nondestructive
nondetachable
nondevelopment
nondevotional
nondialectal
nondifferentiated
nondiffractive
nondiffusible
nondiffusing
nondiplomatic
nondirectional
nondirective
nondisciplinary
nondiscrimination
nondiscriminatory
nondisparaging
nondispersion
nondisposal
nondistinctive
nondistributive
nondivergent
nondivisible
nondoctrinaire
nondoctrinal
nondocumentary
nondogmatic
nondomesticated
nondramatic
nondrinker
nondriver
nondrying
nonearning
nonecclesiastical
noneconomic
nonedible
noneditorial
noneducational
noneffective
noneffervescent
nonefficacious
nonefficient
nonelastic
nonelective
nonelectric
nonelectrical
nonelectrolyte
nonelementary
nonemotional
nonempirical
nonendemic
nonenforceable
nonenforcement
non-English
nonepiscopal
nonequal
nonequivalent

no·net (nō net′) ***n.*** ⟦It *nonetto* < *nono,* ninth < L *nonus*⟧ *Music* **1** a composition for nine voices or nine instruments **2** a group of nine performers of such a composition, or any group of nine musicians playing together

none·the·less (nun′*thə* les′) ***adv.*** in spite of that; nevertheless: also written **none the less**

non-Eu·clid·e·an (nän′yoo͞ klid′ē ən) ***adj.*** designating or of a geometry that rejects any of the postulates of Euclidean geometry, esp. the postulate that through a given point only one line can be drawn parallel to another line that does not contain the given point

non·e·vent (nän′ē vent′, nän′i-) ***n.*** [Informal] an event or occurrence that is boring, does not fulfill expectations, or is deliberately staged as for publicity: also written **non-event**

non·ex·ist·ence (nän′eg zis′təns) ***n.*** **1** the condition of not existing **2** something that does not exist —**non′ex·ist′ent** ***adj., n.***

non·fea·sance (nän′fē′zəns) ***n.*** *Law* failure to do what duty requires to be done: distinguished from MALFEASANCE, MISFEASANCE

non·feed·ing (nän′fēd′iŋ) ***adj.*** not feeding: said of an animal, insect, etc. in a dormant stage

non·fer·rous (nän′fer′əs) ***adj.*** **1** not made of or containing iron **2** designating or of metals other than iron

non·fic·tion (nän′fik′shən) ***n.*** **1** prose writing that is not fiction **2** a broad category of books, as in a library, encompassing such writing —**non′fic′tion·al** ***adj.***

non·food (nän′foo͞d′) ***adj.*** **1** designating or of items sold in grocery stores that are not food, such as paper products, magazines, etc. **2** designating or of all commodities other than food, as in calculating statistical economic data

non·gon·o·coc·cal urethritis (nän′gän′ə käk′əl) an inflammation of the urethra that is spread by sexual contact, having symptoms similar to gonorrhea but caused by organisms (esp. *Chlamydia trachomatis*) other than the gonococcus

non-Hodg·kin's lymphoma (nän′häj′kinz) any of various types of lymphoma distinguished from Hodgkin's disease by the lack of a certain kind of malignant cell: also **non′-Hodg′kin lymphoma**

no·nil·lion (nō nil′yən) ***n.*** ⟦Fr < L *nonus,* ninth (see NOON) + Fr *(m)illion*⟧ ☆**1** the number represented by 1 followed by 30 zeros **2** [Brit.] the number represented by 1 followed by 54 zeros —***adj.*** amounting to one nonillion in number

non·in·duc·tive (nän′in duk′tiv) ***adj.*** *Elec.* not inductive [*a noninductive* capacitor]

non·in·ter·ven·tion (-in′tər ven′shən) ***n.*** the state or fact of not intervening; esp., a refraining by one nation from interference in the affairs of another —**non′in′ter·ven′tion·ist** ***adj., n.***

non·in·va·sive (nän′in vā′siv) ***adj.*** *Med.* **1** not entering the skin or a body cavity: said of therapeutic or diagnostic procedures, as ultrasound **2** not spreading to surrounding or to other tissue: said of certain tumors

non·is·sue (nän′ish′oo͞) ***n.*** a point, question, matter, etc. that has been previously resolved or has no relevance to a given situation

non·join·der (nän′join′dər) ***n.*** *Law* failure to include some person in a suit, when such person should have been included either as a plaintiff or defendant

non·judg·men·tal (nän′juj ment′'l) ***adj.*** **1** not making or expressing an opinion regarding a person or thing; impartial **2** avoiding or tending to avoid making value judgments; tolerant

Non·ju·ror (-joor′ər) ***n.*** any of the clergymen of the Church of England who refused to take an oath of allegiance at the accession of William and Mary in 1689 —**non′ju′ring** ***adj.***

non·met·al (-met′'l) ***n.*** any of those elements lacking the characteristics of a metal; specif., any of the electronegative elements (e.g., oxygen, carbon, nitrogen, fluorine, phosphorus, sulfur) whose oxides form acids and stable compounds with hydrogen —**non′me·tal′lic** ***adj.***

non·mor·al (nän′môr′əl) ***adj.*** not connected in any way with morality or ethical concepts; not moral and not immoral

non·nu·cle·ar (nän′noo͞′klē ər) ***adj.*** not nuclear; specif., *a)* not characterized by the use of, or operated by, nuclear energy *b)* not having or involving nuclear weapons

☆**no-no** (nō′nō′) ***n.,*** *pl.* **-nos′** ⟦< *No! No!,* as said in admonishing a young child⟧ [Slang] something that is forbidden or considered unwise to do, say, use, etc.

non·ob·jec·tive (nän′əb jek′tiv) ***adj.*** designating or of art that does not attempt to represent in recognizable form any object or scene in nature; abstract; nonrepresentational —**non′ob·jec′tiv·ism′** ***n.*** —**non′ob·jec′tiv·ist** ***n., adj.***

non ob·stan·te (nän′ äb stan′tē, -ōb stän′tā) ⟦L < *non,* not + *obstans* (gen. *obstantis*), prp. of *obstare*: see OBSTACLE: from use in medieval legal clauses permitting to the king certain actions notwithstanding statutes to the contrary⟧ notwithstanding; despite (a law, ruling, etc.)

no-non·sense (nō′nän′sens) ***adj.*** not indulging in or tolerating nonsense, impracticality, etc.; matter-of-fact; practical and serious

non·ox·y·nol-9 (nän′äk′sə nôl nīn′) ***n.*** ⟦shortened < chemical name, *nonylphenoxypolyethoxyethanol; 9* for the nine units of ethylene oxide in the molecule⟧ a chemical substance used as the spermicide in certain contraceptive preparations: also written **nonoxynol 9**

---

nonethical
non-European
nonevangelical
nonevasion
noneviction
nonevolutionary
nonexchangeable
nonexclusive
nonexecution
nonexecutive
nonexempt
nonexisting
nonexpansive
nonexpendable
nonexperimental
nonexpert
nonexplosive
nonexportable
nonextraditable
nonextraneous
nonfactual
nonfading
non-Fascist
nonfat
nonfatal
nonfattening
nonfederal
nonfederated
nonfiduciary
nonfigurative
nonfinancial
nonfiscal
nonfissile
nonfissionable
nonflammable
nonflowering
nonfluctuating
nonflying
nonfocal
nonforfeiture
nonformal
nonfraudulent
nonfreezing
non-French
nonfricative
nonfulfillment
nonfunctional
nonfunctioning
nonfundamental
nongaseous
nongenerative
nongenetic
non-Gentile
non-German
non-Germanic
nongovernmental
nongranular
non-Greek
nongregarious
nonhabitable
nonharmonious
nonhazardous
non-Hellenic
nonhereditary
nonheritable
nonhistoric
nonhomogeneous
nonhostile
nonhuman
nonhumorous
nonidentical
nonidiomatic
nonimaginary
nonimitative
nonimmune
nonimmunized
nonimperative
nonimportation
nonimpregnated
noninclusive
nonindependent
nonindexed
non-Indian
nonindictable
non-Indo-European
nonindividualistic
nonindustrial
noninfected
noninfectious
noninflammable
noninflammatory
noninflationary
noninflectional
noninformative
noninjurious
noninstructional
noninstrumental
nonintegrated
nonintellectual
nonintelligent
noninterchangeable
nonintercourse
noninterference
noninternational
nonintersecting
nonintoxicating
nonintuitive
noninvolvement
noniodized
nonionized
non-Irish
nonirradiated
nonirrigated
nonirritant
nonirritating
non-Islamic
non-Israeli
non-Israelite
non-Italian
non-Japanese
non-Jew
non-Jewish
nonjudicial
nonjury
non-Latin
nonleafy
nonlegal
nonlethal
nonlicensed
nonlife
nonlimiting
nonlinear
nonliquefying
nonliquid
nonliteral
nonliterary
nonliterate
nonliturgical
nonliving
nonlocal
nonlogical
nonluminous
non-Lutheran
nonmagnetic
nonmailable
nonmaintenance
nonmalignant
nonmalleable
nonmarital
nonmaritime
nonmarket
nonmarketable
nonmartial
nonmaterial
nonmaterialistic
nonmaternal
nonmathematical
nonmechanical
nonmechanistic
nonmedical
nonmedicated
nonmedicinal
nonmelodious
nonmember
nonmembership
nonmenstrual
nonmercantile
nonmetaphysical
nonmetropolitan
nonmigratory
nonmilitant
nonmilitary
nonmineral
nonministerial
nonmobile
non-Mormon
nonmortal
nonmotile
nonmunicipal
nonmusical
non-Muslim
nonmystical
nonmythical
nonnarcotic
nonnational
nonnative
nonnatural
nonnavigable
nonnecessity
nonnegotiable
non-Negro
nonneutral
nonnucleated
nonnumerical
nonnutritive
nonobedience
nonobligatory
nonobservance
nonobservant
nonobstructive
nonoccupational
nonoccurrence
nonodorous
nonofficial
nonoperating
nonoperational
nonoperative
nonopposition
nonoptional
nonoxidizing

non·pa·reil (nän′pə rel′) *adj.* ⟦Fr < *non,* not + *pareil,* equal < VL **pariculus,* dim. of L *par,* equal, PAR[1]⟧ unequaled; unrivaled; peerless —*n.* **1** someone or something unequaled or unrivaled ☆**2** PAINTED BUNTING **3** *a)* any of certain tiny, variously colored pellets of sugar used to decorate cakes, cookies, etc. *b)* a small, rounded wafer of chocolate covered with such pellets

non·par·tic·i·pat·ing (nän′pär tis′ə pāt′iŋ) *adj.* **1** not participating **2** *Insurance* not entitled to participate in the dividends from the profits or surplus of the company —**non′par·tic′i·pa′tion** *n.*

non·par·ti·san (nän′pärt′ə zən) *adj.* **1** not partisan; esp., not controlled or influenced by, or supporting, any single political party **2** designating or having to do with an election in which candidates are not officially identified by party —**non′par′ti·san·ship′** *n.*

non·per·form·ing (nän′pər fôr′miŋ) *adj.* **1** not performing **2** *Banking* in default but still being carried as an asset on the lender's books [a *nonperforming* loan]

non·per·son (nän′pʉr′sən) *n.* a person who is completely ignored, as if he or she does not exist, specif., such a person lacking any legal or social status: cf. UNPERSON

non pla·cet (nän plā′set) ⟦L⟧ it does not please: used in casting a negative vote

non·plus (nän plus′, nän′plus′) *n.* ⟦L *non,* not + *plus,* more: see PLUS⟧ a condition of perplexity in which one is unable to go, speak, or act further —*vt.* **-plussed′** or **-plused′**, **-plus′sing** or **-plus′ing** to put in a nonplus; bewilder —*SYN.* PUZZLE —**non·plussed′** *adj.*, **non·plused′**

non·po·lar (nän′pō′lər) *adj.* not polar or polarized: said esp. of a molecule with a covalent bond

non·pre·scrip·tion (nän′prē skrip′shən, -pri-) *adj.* available without a prescription: said of a drug

non·pro·duc·tive (nän′prə duk′tiv) *adj.* not productive; specif., *a)* not resulting in the production of the goods sought, or in the realization of the effects expected [a *nonproductive* plan] *b)* not directly related to the production of goods, as clerks, salesmen, etc. —**non′pro·duc′tive·ness** *n.*

non·prof·it (nän′präf′it) *adj.* expressly established for or done as public service, charitable work, etc. and not for earning a profit —*n.* a nonprofit organization

non·pro·lif·er·a·tion (nän′prō lif′er ā′shən) *n.* a not proliferating; specif., prevention, as by international agreement, of an increase in the number of nations possessing nuclear weapons

non-pros (nän′präs′) *vt.* **-prossed′**, **-pros′sing** to enter a judgment of non prosequitur against (a plaintiff or the plaintiff's suit)

non pro·se·qui·tur (nän′ prō sek′wi tər) ⟦L, lit., he does not prosecute⟧ *Law* a judgment entered against a plaintiff who fails to appear at the court proceedings or fails to do any other thing procedurally necessary: abbrev. **non pros.**

non·rat·ed (nän′rāt′id) *adj.* **1** not rated **2** *U.S. Navy* designating an enlisted person who is not a petty officer

non rep. *abbrev.* ⟦L *non repetatur,* not to be repeated⟧ *Pharmacy* do not repeat

non·rep·re·sen·ta·tion·al (nän′rep′rē zən tā′shə nəl) *adj.* NONOBJECTIVE: often **non′rep′re·sen·ta′tion·al·ist** —**non′rep′re·sen·ta′tion·al·ism′** *n.*

non·res·i·dent (nän′rez′ə dənt) *adj.* not residing in a specified place; esp., having one's home in some locality other than where one works, attends school, etc. —*n.* **1** one whose permanent home is not where one is staying **2** one who lives away from the locality of one's business, school, etc. —**non·res′i·dence** *n.*, **non·res′i·den·cy** —**non′res·i·den′tial** *adj.*

non·re·sist·ant (nän′ri zis′tənt) *adj.* not resistant; esp., submitting to force or arbitrary authority —*n.* **1** a person who believes that force and violence should not be used to oppose arbitrary authority, however unjust **2** a person who refuses to use force even in self-defense —**non′re·sist′ance** *n.*

non·re·straint (-ri strānt′) *n.* **1** the absence of restraint **2** *Psychiatry* the management of psychotic persons without the use of a straitjacket or other physical restraint

non·re·stric·tive (-ri strik′tiv) *adj.* **1** not restrictive **2** *Gram.* designating a modifier, as a word, phrase, or subordinate clause, that adds information without limiting the reference of the word or phrase it modifies and thus is not essential to the meaning of a sentence: it is set off by punctuation marks ["who is six feet tall" in "John, who is six feet tall, is younger than Bill" is a *nonrestrictive* clause]: cf. RESTRICTIVE

☆**non·sched·uled** (nän′skej′oold) *adj.* designating or of an airline, plane, etc. licensed for commercial flights as warranted by demand rather than on a regular schedule

non·sec·tar·i·an (nän′sek ter′ē ən) *adj.* not sectarian; specif., not confined to or affiliated with any specific religion

non·sense (nän′sens′, nän′səns) *n.* ⟦NON- + SENSE⟧ **1** words or actions that convey an absurd meaning or no meaning at all **2** things of relatively no importance or value; trivialities **3** impudent, foolish, or evasive behavior —*adj.* **1** designating or of syllables or words arranged arbitrarily and without meaning **2** of or designating verse, poetry, or other literary composition consisting of words or syllables that convey an absurd meaning or no meaning at all —*interj.* how foolish; how absurd: an exclamation of impatience, contradiction, contempt, etc.

nonsense mutation *Genetics* a type of mutation that produces an incomplete polypeptide instead of a specific, fully functional protein, caused by the substitution, during translation, of one base pair for another and the premature termination of translation

non·sen·si·cal (nän sen′si kəl) *adj.* unintelligible, foolish, silly, absurd, etc. —**non·sen′si·cal·ly** *adv.* —**non·sen′si·cal·ness** *n.*, **non·sen′si·cal′i·ty** (-kal′ə tē)

non se·qui·tur (nän′ sek′wi tər) ⟦L, lit., it does not follow⟧ **1** *Logic* a conclusion or inference which does not follow from the premises: abbrev. **non seq.** **2** a remark having no bearing on what has just been said

☆**non-sked** (nän′sked′) [Informal] *adj.* NONSCHEDULED —*n.* a nonscheduled airline, plane, etc.

non·skid (nän′skid′) *adj.* having a surface so made as to reduce slipping or skidding: said of a tire, flooring, etc.

non·so·cial (nän′sō′shəl) *adj.* not social —*SYN.* UNSOCIAL

non·stand·ard (-stan′dərd) *adj.* **1** not standard **2** *Linguis.* designating or of dialects or usages, locutions, grammatical constructions, pronunciations, etc. that differ from the standard dialect: cf. SUBSTANDARD

non-start·er (nän′stärt′ər) *n.* [Informal] a course, project, etc. regarded as having no chance of success or acceptance

non·ste·roi·dal (nän′ster oid′′l) *adj.* not containing a steroid or not involving the use of steroids

non·stick (nän′stik′) *adj.* designating or of cookware or kitchen appliances to which foods will not stick

non·stop (nän′stäp′) *adj., adv.* without a stop; continual or continuous

non·stri·at·ed muscle (nän′strī′āt′id) SMOOTH MUSCLE

---

nonpagan
nonpaid
nonparallel
nonparasitic
nonparental
nonparishioner
nonparliamentary
nonparticipant
nonparty
nonpaying
nonpayment
nonperceptual
nonperformance
nonperiodical
nonperishable
nonperishing
nonpermanent
nonpermeable
nonpersistent
nonphilosophical
nonphysical
nonphysiological
nonplastic
nonpoetic
nonpoisonous
nonpolitical
nonporous
nonpossession
nonpredatory
nonpredictable
nonpreferential
nonprejudicial
nonprescriptive
nonpresidential
nonproducer
nonprofessional
nonproficient
nonprofitable
nonprogressive
nonprolific
nonproportional
nonproprietary
nonprotective
nonprotein
non-Protestant
nonproven
nonpsychic
nonpublic
nonpuncturable
nonpunishable
nonpurulent
nonracial
nonradiating
nonradical
nonradioactive
nonratable
nonrational
nonreactive
nonreader
nonrealistic
nonreality
nonreciprocal
nonreciprocating
nonrecognition
nonrecoverable
nonrecurrent
nonrecurring
nonredeemable
nonrefillable
nonreflexive
nonrefundable
nonregimented
nonregistered
nonregulation
nonreigning
nonrelative
nonreligious
nonremission
nonremovable
nonremunerative
nonrenewable
nonrepayable
nonrepentance
nonrepresentative
nonreproductive
nonresidual
nonresonant
nonrestricted
nonretroactive
nonreturnable
nonrevealing
nonreversible
nonrevolving
nonrhetorical
nonrhythmic
nonrigid
nonrival
non-Roman
nonromantic
nonrotating
nonroyal
nonrural
non-Russian
nonsacramental
nonsacred
nonsalable
nonsalaried
nonsaturated
non-Scandinavian
nonscholastic
nonscientific
nonscoring
nonseasonal
nonsecretory
nonsectional
nonsecular
nonsegregated
nonsegregation
nonselective
non-Semitic
nonsensitive
nonsensitized
nonsensory
nonsensuous
nonserious
nonservile
nonsexual
non-Shakespearean
nonshattering
nonsignificant
nonsinkable
non-Slavic
nonsmoker
nonsmoking
nonsocialist
nonsolid
nonsolvent
nonsovereign
non-Spanish
nonspeaking
nonspecialist
nonspecialized
nonspecific
nonspeculative
nonspherical
nonspiritual
nonspottable
nonstaining
nonstandardized
nonstatic
nonstationary
nonstatistical
nonstatutory
nonsticking
nonstrategic
nonstretchable
nonstriker
nonstriking
nonstructural

non·such (nun′such′) ***n.*** *alt. sp. of* NONESUCH

non·suit (nän′so͞ot′) ***n.*** ⟦ME *noun suyt* < Anglo-Fr *nonsute:* see NON- & SUIT⟧ *Law* **1** a judgment against a plaintiff for failing to proceed to trial, to establish a valid case, or to produce adequate evidence **2** the ending of a lawsuit by the voluntary withdrawal of the plaintiff —***vt.*** to bring a nonsuit against (a plaintiff or a plaintiff's case)

non·sup·port (nän′sə pôrt′) ***n.*** failure to provide for a spouse, child, or other legal dependent

non·syl·lab·ic (nän′si lab′ik) ***adj.*** not forming a syllable or the nucleus of a syllable; not syllabic

non trop·po (nôn trôp′pô; *E* nän trō′pō) ⟦It⟧ *Musical Direction* not too much; moderately (Ex.: *adagio ma non troppo,* slowly but not too much so)

non-U (nän′yo͞o′) ***adj.*** ⟦NON- + U[1]⟧ [Informal, Chiefly Brit.] not belonging to or characteristic of the upper class

non·un·ion (nän′yo͞on′yən) ***n.*** failure to mend or unite: said of a broken bone —***adj.*** **1** not belonging to a labor union **2** not made or serviced by union workers or under conditions required by a labor union **3** refusing to recognize, or sign a contract with, a labor union —**non′un′ion·ism′** ***n.*** —**non′un′ion·ist** ***n.***

non·vi·o·lence (-vī′ə ləns) ***n.*** an abstaining from violence or from the use of physical force, as in efforts to obtain civil rights or in opposing government policy: see also CIVIL DISOBEDIENCE, PASSIVE RESISTANCE —**non′vi′o·lent** ***adj.***

non·yl (nän′il) ***n.*** ⟦*non(ane),* a paraffin hydrocarbon from which it is derived + -YL⟧ a monovalent alkyl radical C_9H_{19}, esp., the normal radical $CH_3(CH_2)_7CH_2$

non·ze·ro (nän′zir′ō) ***adj.*** designating a quantity, etc. other than zero: term used in physics, mathematics, etc.

noodge (no͝oj) [Slang] ***vt., vi.*** **noodged, noodg′ing** ⟦< Yiddish *nudyen,* to be tedious, bore < Russ *nudnyi,* tedious: see NUDNIK⟧ to annoy with persistent complaining, asking, urging, etc.; nag —***n.*** a person who noodges

noo·dle[1] (no͞od′'l) ***n.*** ⟦prob. < NODDLE⟧ **1** a simpleton; fool **2** [Slang] the head

☆**noo·dle**[2] (no͞od′'l) ***n.*** ⟦Ger *nudel*⟧ a flat, narrow strip of dry dough, usually made with egg and served in soup, baked in casseroles, etc.

☆**noo·dle**[3] (no͞od′'l) ***vi.*** **-dled, -dling** ⟦prob. echoic var. of DOODLE⟧ [Informal] **1** to play or improvise idly on a musical instrument **2** ⟦prob. < NOODLE[1], sense 2⟧ to explore an idea

☆**noog·ie** (no͝og′ē) ***n.*** ⟦< ?⟧ [*also pl.*] [Slang] a vigorous, playful rubbing or rapping of the knuckles on another's head

nook (no͝ok) ***n.*** ⟦ME (chiefly Northern) *nok,* akin to Norw *nakke,* a hook, ON *hnekkja,* to hem in, drive back, OE *hnecca,* the NECK⟧ **1** a corner of a room, or a part of a room cut off from the main part [a breakfast *nook*] **2** a small recess or secluded spot; retreat

nook·y (no͝ok′ē) ***n.*** [Slang] sexual intercourse: somewhat vulgar: also sp. **nook′ie**

noon (no͞on) ***n.*** ⟦ME < OE *non,* orig., the ninth hour (i.e., 3 P.M. by the Roman method, reckoning from sunrise) < L *nona (hora),* ninth (hour) < *novem,* NINE⟧ **1** *a)* twelve o'clock in the daytime *b)* midday **2** the highest point or culmination —***adj.*** of or occurring at noon or midday

noon·day (no͞on′dā′) ***n., adj.*** noon or midday

no one no person; not anyone; nobody

noon·ing (no͞on′iŋ) ***n.*** [Now Chiefly Dial.] **1** noon or midday ☆**2** a stop at midday for rest or food **3** a meal or refreshment at noon

noon·time (-tīm′) ***n., adj.*** noon or midday: also [Literary] **noon′tide′** (-tīd′)

Noord·bra·bant (nōrt′brä bänt′) *Du. name for* NORTH BRABANT

Noord·hol·land (-hô′länt′) *Du. name for* NORTH HOLLAND

noose (no͞os) ***n.*** ⟦ME *nose,* prob. via Prov *nous* < L *nodus,* knot, NODE⟧ **1** a loop formed in a rope, cord, etc. by means of a slipknot so that the loop tightens as the rope is pulled **2** anything that restricts one's freedom; tie, bond, snare, trap, etc. —***vt.*** **noosed, noos′ing 1** to catch or hold in a noose; trap, ensnare, etc. **2** to form a noose in or of (a rope, cord, etc.) —**the noose** death by hanging

Noot·ka (no͝ot′kə, no͞ot′-) ***n.*** ⟦after *Nootka* Sound, inlet on Vancouver Island⟧ **1** *pl.* **-kas** or **-ka** a member of a North American Indian people living chiefly on Vancouver Island **2** the Wakashan language of this people

no·pal (nō′pəl, nō päl′) ***n.*** ⟦Sp < Nahuatl *no'palli,* prickly pear cactus⟧ any of a genus (*Nopalea*) of cactuses with red flowers, esp. a tropical prickly pear (*N. cochinellifera*)

no-par (nō′pär′) ***adj.*** having no stated par value [a *no-par* stock certificate]

☆**nope** (nōp) ***adv., interj.*** [Slang] no: a negative reply

nor[1] (nôr) ***conj.*** ⟦ME < *ne-,* not, NO[1] + *or:* see OR[1]⟧ and not; or not; and not either Used: *a)* usually as the second in the correlative pair *neither ... nor,* indicating negation of both parts of the statement [I can neither go *nor* stay] *b)* after some other negative, as *not, no, never* [he does not smoke, *nor* does he drink] *c)* poetically, as the first in a pair or series of negative correlatives [*nor* flood *nor* fire] *d)* after an affirmative statement, to introduce a reinforcing negative [he works from dawn to dusk, *nor* does he pause for rest]

nor[2] (nôr) ***conj.*** ⟦Northern ME⟧ [Dial.] than

Nor *abbrev.* **1** Norman **2** North **3** Norway **4** Norwegian

nor' or **nor** (nôr) north: used especially in compounds [*nor'western*]

nor- (nôr) ⟦< NOR(MAL)⟧ *Chem. combining form* **1** normal **2** *a)* a compound lacking a particular radical, often methyl, when compared to another compound [*norepinephrine* vs. epinephrine] *b)* the straight-chain isomer [*norleucine*]

No·ra (nôr′ə) ***n.*** ⟦Ir, contr. of *Honora, Eleanor, Leonora*⟧ a feminine name: see ELEANOR, LEONORA

NORAD (nôr′ad′) ***n.*** North American Air Defense (Command)

nor·a·dren·a·line (nôr′ə dren′ə lin) ***n.*** ⟦see NOR-⟧ NOREPINEPHRINE

Nor·dau (nôr′dou′), **Max Simon** (born *Max Simon Südfeld*) 1849-1923; Ger. writer, physician, & Zionist leader, born in Hungary

Nor·den·skjöld[1] (no͝or′dən shüld′), Baron **Nils A·dolf E·rik** (nils ä′dôlf ā′rik) 1832-1901; Swed. arctic explorer, born in Finland

Nor·den·skjöld[2] (no͝or′dən shüld′) *former name for* LAPTEV SEA

Nor·dic (nôr′dik) ***adj.*** ⟦ModL *Nordicus* < Fr *nordique* < *nord,* north < OE *north,* NORTH⟧ **1** designating or of a physical type of the Caucasoid peoples exemplified by the long-headed, tall, blond people of Scandinavia: see also ALPINE, MEDITERRANEAN[1] **2** of the Germanic peoples of N Europe; specif., of Scandinavia **3** [*sometimes* **n-**] designating or having to do with cross-country skiing or ski jumping: cf. ALPINE

Nord·kyn (nôr′kün′), **Cape** cape in NE Norway: northernmost point of the European mainland

Nord-Pas-de-Ca·lais (nôr pät kä le′) metropolitan region of NE France: 4,793 sq mi (12,414 sq km); chief city, Lille

nor·ep·i·neph·rine (nôr′ep′ə nef′rin, -rēn′) ***n.*** ⟦see NOR-⟧ a hormone or neurotransmitter, $C_8H_{11}NO_3$, related to epinephrine, that is used medically to constrict blood vessels and to stop bleeding: it is secreted by the adrenal medulla or liberated at nerve endings to help transmit nerve impulses

Nor·folk (nôr′fək) **1** ⟦after the county in England⟧ seaport in SE Va., on Hampton Roads & Chesapeake Bay **2** ⟦OE *Northfolc:* see NORTH & FOLK⟧ county in E England, on the North Sea: 2,074 sq mi (5,372 sq km); county seat, Norwich

Norfolk Island Australian island in the SW Pacific, east of New South Wales: 13 sq mi (34 sq km)

Norfolk Island pine an evergreen tree (*Araucaria excelsa*) of the araucaria family, with small needles and branches, commonly grown as a potted plant or outdoors in warm climates

Norfolk jacket (*or* **coat)** a loosefitting, single-breasted, belted jacket with a pocket on each side and box pleats in front and back

Norfolk terrier ⟦after *Norfolk,* England, where developed⟧ any of a breed of short-legged terrier with a dense, wiry coat and ears that droop forward

Nor·ge (nôr′gə) *Norw. name for* NORWAY

no·ri (nō′rē, nôr′ē) ***n.*** ⟦Jpn⟧ laver seaweed that has been dried and pressed into sheets, used esp. for wrapping sushi

no·ri·a (nôr′ē ə) ***n.*** ⟦Sp < Ar *nā'ūra* < Syriac *nā'ōr* < *nĕar,* (he) poured out⟧ a water wheel with buckets at its circumference, used in Spain and the Near East to raise and discharge water

No·ri·cum (nō′rē ko͞om′, nôr′i kəm) ancient Roman province south of the Danube, in the region of modern Austria

norm (nôrm) ***n.*** ⟦L *norma,* carpenter's square, rule, prob. via Etr < Gr *gnōmōn,* carpenter's square, lit., one that knows: see GNOMON⟧ a standard, model, or pattern for a group; esp., *a)* such a standard of achievement as represented by the median or average achievement of a large group *b)* a standard of conduct that should or must be followed *c)* a way of behaving that is typical of a certain group —***vt.*** to adjust (statistical results) so as to compensate for inequalities or differences in performance, as on a standardized test —**SYN.** AVERAGE

Nor·ma (nôr′mə) ***n.*** **1** ⟦< ? L *norma:* see prec.⟧ a feminine name **2** ⟦L: see prec.⟧ a S constellation in the Milky Way between Lupus and Ara

nonsubmissive
nonsubscriber
nonsuccessive
nonsupporting
nonsuppurative
nonsurgical
nonsustaining
nonsymbolic
nonsymmetric
nonsympathizer
nonsymphonic
nonsymptomatic
nonsynchronous
nonsyntactic
nonsynthesized
nonsystematic
nontarnishable
nontaxable
nonteachable
nontechnical
nonterrestrial
nonterritorial
nontheatrical
nontheistic
nontheological
nontherapeutic
nonthinking
nontoxic
nontraditional
nontragic
nontransferable
nontransparent
nontributary
nontropical
nontuberculous
nontypical
nontyrannical
nonulcerous
nonunderstandable
nonuniform
nonuniversal
nonurban
nonusable
nonuse
nonuser
nonutilitarian
nonutilized
nonvascular
nonvegetative
nonvenomous
nonverbal
nonvertical
nonvesicular
nonviable
nonvibratory
nonviolation
nonvirulent
nonviscous
nonvisual
nonvitreous
nonvocal
nonvocational
nonvolatile
nonvolcanic
nonvoluntary
nonvoting
nonwhite
nonworker
nonwoven

nor·mal (nôr′məl) ***adj.*** ⟦L *normalis* < *norma*, a rule: see NORM⟧ **1** conforming with or constituting an accepted standard, model, or pattern; esp., corresponding to the median or average of a large group in type, appearance, achievement, function, development, etc.; natural; usual; standard; regular **2** *Biol.* occurring naturally [*normal* immunity] **3** *Chem.* *a)* designating or of a salt formed by replacing all the replaceable hydrogen of an acid with a metal or metals *b)* designating or of a solution which contains an amount of the dissolved substance chemically equivalent to one gram atom of hydrogen per liter of solution *c)* designating or of a fatty hydrocarbon, the chain of which is continuous rather than branched, in which no carbon atom is united directly to more than two others **4** *Math.* perpendicular; at right angles **5** *Med., Psychol.* *a)* free from disease, disorder, or malformation; specif., average in intelligence or development *b)* mentally sound —***n.*** **1** anything normal **2** the usual state, amount, degree, etc.; esp., the median or average **3** *Math.* a perpendicular; esp., a perpendicular to a line tangent to a curve, at its point of tangency —**nor′mal·cy** (-sē) ***n.***, **nor·mal′i·ty** (-mal′ə tē)

SYN.—**normal** implies conformity with the established norm or standard for its kind [*normal* intelligence]; **regular** implies conformity with the prescribed rule or accepted pattern for its kind [the *regular* working day]; **typical** applies to that which has the representative characteristics of its type or class [a *typical* Southern town]; **natural** implies behavior, operation, etc. that conforms with the nature or innate character of the person or thing [a *natural* comedian]; **usual** applies to that which conforms to the common or ordinary use or occurrence [the *usual* price]; **average**, in this connection, implies conformity with what is regarded as normal or ordinary [the *average* man] —*ANT.* **abnormal, unusual**

normal curve BELL CURVE

normal distribution *Statistics* a symmetrical distribution, represented on a graph by a BELL CURVE, in which the class with the highest frequency is at the center and the classes with the lowest frequencies are at each end

nor·mal·ize (nôr′mə līz′) ***vt.*** **-ized′**, **-iz′ing** to make normal; specif., *a)* to bring to the natural, or usual, state *b)* to bring into conformity with a standard, pattern, model, etc. —***vi.*** to become normal —**nor′mal·i·za′tion** ***n.*** —**nor′mal·iz′er** ***n.***

nor·mal·ly (nôr′mə lē) ***adv.*** **1** in a normal manner **2** under normal circumstances; ordinarily

normal school ⟦based on Fr *école normale*⟧ a school, usually with a two-year program, for training high-school graduates to be elementary schoolteachers

Nor·man[1] (nôr′mən) ***n.*** ⟦OFr *Normant* or ML *Normannus*, both < Frank **nortman* < **nort*, akin to OE *north*, NORTH + **man*, akin to MAN⟧ **1** any of the Scandinavians who occupied Normandy in the 10th cent. A.D. **2** a descendant of the Normans and French who conquered England in 1066 **3** NORMAN FRENCH **4** a person born or living in Normandy —***adj.*** **1** of Normandy or its people, language, or culture **2** designating or of the Romanesque style of architecture as it flourished in Normandy and, after the Norman Conquest, as developed in England: characterized by massive construction, round arches over recessed doors and windows, and carving —**Nor′man·esque′** (-esk′) ***adj.***

Nor·man[2] (nôr′mən) ***n.*** ⟦< OE *Northman*, OHG *Nordemann*, lit., Northman⟧ a masculine name: dim. *Norm*

Nor·man[3] (nôr′mən) ⟦ult. after A. *Norman*, railroad surveyor⟧ city in central Okla., near Oklahoma City

Norman Conquest the conquest of England by the Normans under William the Conqueror in 1066

Nor·man·dy (nôr′mən dē) historical region in NW France, on the English Channel

Norman French **1** the French of the Normans or Normandy, as spoken in England by the Norman conquerors; Anglo-French: it was not imposed on the English as an official language at the Conquest, but gained legal and administrative currency after the accession of Eleanor of Aquitaine as queen (1154) **2** the form of this language used as the legal jargon of England until the late 17th cent. **3** the modern French dialect of Normandy —**Nor′man-French′** ***adj.***

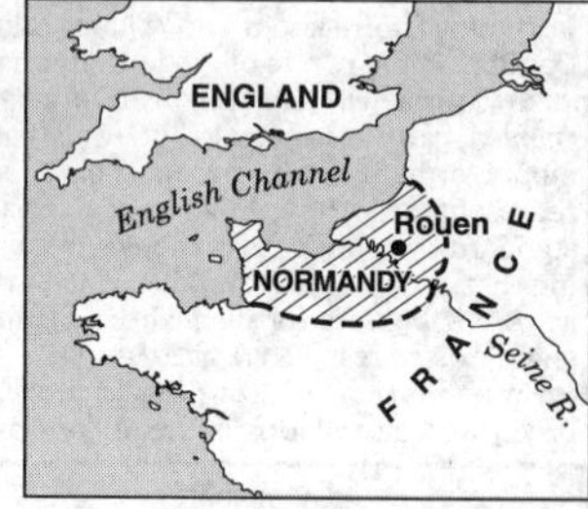

Normandy

Nor·man·ize (nôr′mə nīz′) ***vi.***, ***vt.*** **-ized′**, **-iz′ing** to make or become Norman in style, language, customs, law, etc.

norm·a·tive (nôr′mə tiv) ***adj.*** of or establishing a norm, or standard, now, specif., of behavior —**norm′a·tive·ly** ***adv.***

NormFr *abbrev.* Norman French

Norn (nôrn) ***n.*** ⟦ON *norn* < IE base **(s)ner-*, **(s)nur-*, to SNARL[1], mutter⟧ *Norse Myth.* any of the three goddesses, representing the past, present, and future, who determine the destiny of gods and mortals

Nor·plant (nôr′plant′) ***n.*** ⟦former trademark < *(levo)nor(gestrel) implant* < LEVO- + *norgestrel*, a progestin < NOR- + *(pro)gest(ogen)* (see form at PROGESTIN) + *-rel* (< ?)⟧ a subcutaneous contraceptive implant for women designed to release progesterone or various other steroidal hormones gradually over a period of several years

Nor·ris (nôr′is) **1 Frank** (born *Benjamin Franklin Norris, Jr.*) 1870-1902; U.S. novelist **2 George William** 1861-1944; U.S. senator (1913-43)

Norr·kö·ping (nôr′shö′piŋ) seaport in SE Sweden, on an inlet of the Baltic Sea

Norse (nôrs) ***adj.*** ⟦prob. < Du *Noorsch*, a Norwegian, var. of *Noordsch* < *noord*, NORTH + *-sch*, -ISH⟧ **1** Scandinavian; specif., medieval Scandinavian **2** West Scandinavian (Norwegian, Icelandic, and Faeroese) —***n.*** **1** the Scandinavian group of languages **2** the West Scandinavian group of languages **3** NORWEGIAN See OLD NORSE, ICELANDIC —**the Norse** the people of Scandinavia; specif., *a)* the medieval Scandinavians *b)* the West Scandinavians

Norse·man (nôrs′mən) ***n.***, *pl.* **-men** (-mən) a member of any of the medieval Scandinavian peoples, specif. the Vikings

north (nôrth) ***n.*** ⟦ME < OE, akin to Du *noord*, Ger *nord*, ON *northr* < IE base **ner-*, beneath, below > Gr *nerteros*, lower⟧ **1** the direction to the right of a person facing the sunset; direction of the North Pole from any other point on the earth's surface: the needle of a magnetic compass points to the *magnetic north pole* rather than to the geographic pole **2** the point on a compass at 0° or 360°, directly opposite south **3** a region or district in or toward this direction **4** [*often* **N-**] the northern part of the earth, esp. the arctic regions —***adj.*** **1** in, of, to, toward, or facing the north **2** from the north [a *north* wind] **3** [**N-**] designating the northern part of a continent, country, etc. [*North* Atlantic] —***adv.*** in or toward the north; in a northerly direction —**north of** ⟦fig. use, from the traditionally "higher" position of north on a map or globe⟧ [Informal] more or greater than; above [a salary *north of* $40,000] —**the North** ☆**1** that part of the U.S. which is bounded on the south by Md., the Ohio River, and Mo.; specif., the states opposed to the Confederacy in the Civil War **2** the Northern Hemisphere, esp. as the region comprising the majority of the world's affluent, industrialized nations

North (nôrth), **Frederick** 2d Earl of Guilford 1732-92; Eng. statesman: prime minister of Great Britain (1770-82): called *Lord North*

North America N continent in the Western Hemisphere: *c.* 9,365,000 sq mi (24,256,000 sq km) —**North American**

North·amp·ton (nôrth amp′tən, -hamp′-) **1** NORTHAMPTONSHIRE **2** county seat of Northamptonshire

North·amp·ton·shire (-shir′, -shər) county in central England: 914 sq mi (2,367 sq km); county seat, Northampton

North Borneo *former name for* SABAH

☆**north·bound** (nôrth′bound′) ***adj.*** bound north; going northward

North Brabant province of the S Netherlands, between the Meuse River & the Belgian border: 1,937 sq mi (5,017 sq km); cap. 's Hertogenbosch

north by east the direction, or the point on a mariner's compass, halfway between due north and north-northeast; 11°15′ east of due north

north by west the direction, or the point on a mariner's compass, halfway between due north and north-northwest; 11°15′ west of due north

North Canadian river flowing from NE N.Mex. east & southeast into the Canadian River in E Okla.: 760 mi (1,223 km)

North Carolina ⟦see CAROLINA[1]⟧ state of the SE U.S.: one of the 13 original states; 48,711 sq mi (126,161 sq km); cap. Raleigh: abbrev. *NC* or *N.C.*

North Carolinian **1** of North Carolina: usually used in the predicate **2** a person born or living in North Carolina

North Channel strait between Northern Ireland & SW Scotland: *c.* 80 mi (129 km) long

North Dakota ⟦see DAKOTA[2]⟧ Midwestern state of the NC U.S.: admitted 1889; 68,976 sq mi (178,647 sq km); cap. Bismarck: abbrev. *ND*, *N.D.*, or *N Dak*

North Da·ko·tan (də kōt′ən) **1** of North Dakota: usually used in the predicate **2** a person born or living in North Dakota

North Downs *see* DOWNS

north·east (nôrth′ēst′; *naut.* nôr′-) ***n.*** **1** the direction, or the point on a mariner's compass, halfway between north and east; 45° east of due north **2** a district or region in or toward this direction —***adj.*** **1** in, of, to, toward, or facing the northeast **2** from the northeast [a *northeast* wind] —***adv.*** in or toward the northeast —☆**the Northeast** the NE part of the U.S., sometimes including New York City; esp., New England

northeast by east the direction, or the point on a mariner's compass, halfway between northeast and east-northeast; 11°15′ east of northeast

northeast by north the direction, or the point on a mariner's compass, halfway between northeast and north-northeast; 11°15′ north of northeast

☆**north·east·er** (nôrth′ēs′tər; *naut.* nôr′-) ***n.*** a storm or strong wind from the northeast

north·east·er·ly (-tər lē) ***adj., adv.*** **1** in or toward the northeast **2** from the northeast, as a wind

north·east·ern (-tərn) ***adj.*** **1** in, of, to, toward, or facing the northeast **2** from the northeast [a *northeastern* wind] ☆**3** [**N-**] of or characteristic of the Northeast or New England —**North′east′ern·er** ***n.***

Northeast Passage water route from the Atlantic to the Pacific through the seas north of Europe & Asia

north·east·ward (nôrth′ēst′wərd; *naut.* nôr′-) ***adv., adj.*** toward the northeast —***n.*** a northeastward direction, point, or region

north·east·ward·ly (-wərd lē) ***adv., adj.*** **1** toward the northeast **2** from the northeast [a *northeastwardly* wind]

north·east·wards (-wərdz) ***adv.*** *var. of* NORTHEASTWARD

☆**north·er** (nôr′thər) *n.* a storm or strong wind from the north; esp., a cold wind in the area of or about the Gulf of Mexico or of the Southwestern plains

north·er·ly (-lē) *adj., adv.* **1** in or toward the north **2** from the north, as a wind —*n., pl.* **-lies** a wind from the north

north·ern (nôr′thərn) *adj.* ⟦ME *northerne* < OE *northerna*⟧ **1** in, of, to, toward, or facing the north **2** from the north [*a northern wind*] ☆**3** [**N-**] of or characteristic of the North ☆**4** [**N-**] designating or of a dialect of American English spoken in New England; N.Y.; N N.J. and Pa.; the N counties of Ohio, Ind., Ill., Iowa, and S.Dak.; and Mich., Wis., Minn., and N.Dak.

Northern Cape province of W South Africa: 139,692 sq mi (361,801 sq km); cap. Kimberley

Northern Cross, the the five brightest stars in the constellation Cygnus that seem to form the shape of a cross: often used to mean the entire constellation Cygnus

Northern Crown, the the constellation Corona Borealis

north·ern·er (nôr′thər nər) *n.* **1** a person born or living in the north ☆**2** [*also* **N-**] a person born or living in a U.S. state of THE NORTH (see the phrase at NORTH)

Northern Hemisphere that half of the earth north of the equator

Northern Ireland division of the United Kingdom, in the NE part of the island of Ireland: 5,452 sq mi (14,121 sq km); cap. Belfast

northern lights [*also* **N- L-**] AURORA BOREALIS

Northern Mariana Islands group of islands in the W Pacific Ocean, including all of the Mariana Islands except Guam: a commonwealth in association with the U.S. since 1986, it was formerly part of the Trust Territory of the Pacific Islands (as part of the Mariana Islands): land area 179 sq mi (464 sq km); cap. Saipan: abbrev. *MP*: also **Northern Marianas**

north·ern·most (nôr′thərn mōst′) *adj.* farthest north

northern oriole *see* BALTIMORE ORIOLE

Northern Rhodesia *former name* (1911-64) *for* ZAMBIA

Northern Sporades group of islands in the NW Aegean, west of Thessaly & Euboea

☆**Northern Spy** a yellowish-red winter apple

Northern Territory self-governing territory of N Australia, on the Arafura Sea: 520,902 sq mi (1,349,130 sq km); cap. Darwin

Northern Trans·vaal (trans väl′, tranz-) province of South Africa, in the N part: 47,599 sq mi (123,280 sq km); cap. Pietersburg

North Frigid Zone *see* FRIGID ZONE

North Holland province of the W Netherlands, on the North Sea: 1,567 sq mi (4,059 sq km); cap. Haarlem

north·ing (nôr′thiŋ, -*th*iŋ) *n.* **1** *Naut.* the distance due north covered by a vessel traveling on any northerly course **2** a northerly direction

North Island N island of the two main islands of New Zealand: 44,702 sq mi (115,778 sq km)

North Korea *see* KOREA

north·land (nôrth′land′, -lənd) *n.* [*also* **N-**] **1** the northern region of a country **2** land in the north —**north′land′er** *n.*

North·land (nôrth′land′, -lənd) the Scandinavian Peninsula

North Las Vegas city in SE Nev.: suburb of Las Vegas

North·man (nôrth′mən) *n., pl.* **-men** (-mən) ⟦OE *Northmanna*: see NORTH & MAN⟧ NORSEMAN

north-north·east (nôrth′nôrth′ēst′; *naut.* nôr′nôr′-) *n.* the direction, or the point on a mariner's compass, halfway between due north and northeast; 22°30′ east of due north — *adj., adv.* **1** in or toward this direction **2** from this direction, as a wind

north-north·west (-west′) *n.* the direction, or the point on a mariner's compass, halfway between due north and northwest; 22°30′ west of due north — *adj., adv.* **1** in or toward this direction **2** from this direction, as a wind

North Platte river flowing from N Colo. north into Wyo. & then southeast through W Nebr., joining the South Platte to form the Platte: 618 mi (995 km)

north pole **1** the place where the northern rotational axis intersects the surface of a planet, moon, etc. **2** the zenith of such a place; esp., the zenith (**north celestial pole**) of this place on earth **3** that end of a straight magnet that points to the north when the magnet hangs free **4** [**N- P-**] the place on earth where its northern rotational axis intersects its surface: in full **North Terrestrial Pole**

North Rhine-West·pha·li·a (rīn′ west fā′lē ə, -fāl′yə) state of W Germany: 13,156 sq mi (34,074 sq km); cap. Düsseldorf

North Riding former division of Yorkshire county, England, now part of the county of North Yorkshire

North River lower course of the Hudson River, between New York City & NE N.J.

North Saskatchewan river flowing from SW Alberta east through Saskatchewan, joining the South Saskatchewan to form the Saskatchewan: 760 mi (1,223 km)

North Sea arm of the Atlantic, between Great Britain & the N European mainland: *c.* 164,900 sq mi (427,089 km)

North Star POLARIS

North Temperate Zone *see* TEMPERATE ZONE

North·um·ber·land (nôrth um′bər lənd) northernmost county of England: 1,941 sq mi (5,027 sq km); county seat, Newcastle-upon-Tyne

North·um·bri·a (nôrth um′brē ə) former Anglo-Saxon kingdom in Great Britain, south of the Firth of Forth

North·um·bri·an (-ən) *adj.* **1** of Northumbria or its people or dialect **2** of Northumberland or its people or dialect —*n.* **1** a person born or living in Northumbria **2** the Old English dialect of Northumbria **3** a person born or living in Northumberland **4** the Modern English dialect of Northumberland

north·ward (nôrth′wərd; *naut.* nôr′thərd) *adv., adj.* toward the north —*n.* a northward direction, point, or region

north·ward·ly (-lē) *adv., adj.* **1** toward the north **2** from the north [*a northwardly wind*]

north·wards (-wərdz) *adv. var. of* NORTHWARD

north·west (nôrth′west′; *naut.* nôr′-) *n.* **1** the direction, or the point on a mariner's compass, halfway between north and west; 45° west of due north **2** a district or region in or toward this direction —*adj.* **1** in, of, to, toward, or facing the northwest **2** from the northwest [*a northwest wind*] —*adv.* in or toward the northwest —☆**the Northwest** **1** NORTHWEST TERRITORY **2** the NW part of the U.S., esp. Wash., Oreg., and Ida. **3** the NW part of Canada

northwest by north the direction, or the point on a mariner's compass, halfway between northwest and north-northwest; 11°15′ north of northwest

northwest by west the direction, or the point on a mariner's compass, halfway between northwest and west-northwest; 11°15′ west of northwest

north·west·er (nôrth′wes′tər; *naut.* nôr′-) *n.* a storm or strong wind from the northwest

north·west·er·ly (-tər lē) *adj., adv.* **1** in or toward the northwest **2** from the northwest, as a wind

north·west·ern (-tərn) *adj.* **1** in, of, to, toward, or facing the northwest **2** from the northwest [*a northwestern wind*] ☆**3** [**N-**] of or characteristic of the Northwest —**North′west′ern·er** *n.*

Northwest Passage water route from the Atlantic to the Pacific, through the arctic islands of Canada

Northwest Territories division of N Canada: 440,479 sq mi (1,140,835 sq km); cap. Yellowknife: abbrev. *NT, NWT, N.W.T.*, or *NWTer*

☆**Northwest Territory** region north of the Ohio River, between Pa. & the Mississippi (established 1787): it now forms Ohio, Ind., Ill., Mich., Wis., & part of Minn.

north·west·ward (nôrth′west′wərd; *naut.* nôr′-) *adv., adj.* toward the northwest —*n.* a northwestward direction, point, or region

north·west·ward·ly (-wərd lē) *adv., adj.* **1** toward the northwest **2** from the northwest [*a northwestwardly wind*]

north·west·wards (-wərdz) *adv. var. of* NORTHWESTWARD

North York former city in SE Ontario, Canada, now part of Toronto

North Yorkshire county in N England: 3,208 sq mi (8,309 sq km)

Norw *abbrev.* **1** Norway **2** Norwegian

Nor·walk (nôr′wôk′) ⟦prob. contr. < *North Walk*, a trail from Anaheim Landing⟧ city in SW Calif.: suburb of Los Angeles

Nor·way (nôr′wā′) ⟦OE *Norweg* < ON *Norvegr* < *northr*, NORTH + *vegr*, way: for IE base see WAY⟧ country in N Europe, occupying the W & N parts of the Scandinavian Peninsula: 125,182 sq mi (324,220 sq km); cap. Oslo: Norw. name NORGE

Norway maple a European maple (*Acer platanoides*), commonly grown in the U.S. for shade

Norway pine RED PINE

Norway rat BROWN RAT

Norway spruce a common, evergreen, ornamental spruce (*Picea abies*) with drooping branchlets, large, brown cones, and shiny, dark-green needles

Nor·we·gian (nôr wē′jən) *adj.* ⟦< ML *Norwegia*, Norway < ON *Norvegr* + -AN⟧ of Norway or its people, language, or culture —*n.* **1** a person born or living in Norway **2** either of two official forms of the North Germanic language spoken in Norway, "Book Language" (see BOKMÅL) and "New Norwegian" (see NYNORSK)

Norwegian elkhound any of a breed of medium-sized dog with a short, compact body, a thick, gray coat, and a tail that curls over the back, orig. bred in Norway where it is used in hunting elk and other large game

Norwegian Sea part of the Atlantic between Norway & Iceland

Nor·wich (nôr′ij, -ich) ⟦OE *northwic*: see NORTH & WICK[2]⟧ county seat of Norfolk, E England: known for its cathedral (founded 1096)

Nor·wich terrier (nôr′ij, -ich, -wich) any of a breed of short-legged terrier identical with the Norfolk terrier except that the ears are erect

nos *abbrev.* numbers

nose (nōz) *n.* ⟦ME < OE *nosu*, akin to Ger *nase*, orig. a dual, meaning "the two nostrils" < IE base **nas-*, nostril > Sans *nāsā*, the nose, lit., pair of nostrils, L *nasus*, nose & *naris* (pl. *nares*), nostril⟧ **1** the part of the human face between the mouth and the eyes, having two openings and cavities behind them for breathing and smelling **2** the part that corresponds to this in animals; snout, muzzle, etc. **3** the sense of smell **4** the overall smell of a wine; bouquet **5** the power of tracking or perceiving by or as if by scent [*a nose for news*] **6** anything resembling a nose in shape or position; projecting or foremost part, as a nozzle, spout, prow of a ship, front of an airplane, etc. **7** the nose regarded as a symbol of prying or meddling [*to poke one's nose into another's affairs*] **8** [Slang, Chiefly Brit.] a police spy or informer —*vt.* **nosed**, **nos′ing** **1** to discover or perceive by or as if by the sense of smell **2** to touch or rub with the nose **3** to push with the nose: with *aside, open*, etc. **4** to make or push (a way, etc.) cautiously or slowly with the front forward [*the ship nosed its way into the harbor*] —*vi.* **1** to smell; sniff **2** to pry inquisitively **3** to move cautiously or slowly with the front end forward —☆**by a nose 1** by the length of the animal's nose in horse racing, etc. **2** by a very small margin —**count noses** [Informal] to count the number of people present, voting, etc. —**cut off one's nose to spite one's face** to injure one's own interests, as in a fit of anger or resentment —**follow one's nose** to go straight forward —**have one's nose out of joint** [Informal] to be irritated, annoyed, frustrated, etc. —**lead by the nose** [Informal] to dominate completely —**look down one's nose at** [Informal] to be disdainful of —**nose out 1** to defeat by a very small margin **2** to discover, as by smelling —**nose over** to turn over on its nose: said of an airplane moving along the ground —**on the nose** [Slang] **1** that (a specified horse, etc.) will finish first in a race **2** precisely; exactly —**pay through the nose** [Informal] to pay an unreasonable price —**put someone's nose out of joint** [Informal] to irritate, annoy, frustrate, etc. —**rub someone's nose in** ⟦from the practice, in housebreaking a pet, of rubbing its nose in its urine or feces⟧ [Informal] to keep reminding someone of (something unpleasant, as a mistake he or she made) —**turn up one's nose at** [Informal] to sneer at; scorn —**under one's (very) nose** in plain view

nose bag FEED BAG

nose·band (nōz′band′) ***n.*** that part of a bridle or halter which passes over the animal's nose

nose·bleed (-blēd′) ***n.*** a bleeding from the nose; nasal hemorrhage —***adj.*** ☆⟦in allusion to the possibility of a *nosebleed* at very high altitudes⟧ [Slang] in or of the highest, typically least expensive, seating in a sports stadium, theater, etc.: a humorous usage

nose cone the cone-shaped foremost part of a rocket or missile, usually housing the payload, instruments, etc. and made to withstand intense heat

nose·dive (nōz′dīv′) ***n.*** **1** a swift, steep downward plunge of an airplane, with the nose toward the earth **2** any sudden, sharp drop, as in profits —**nose′-dive′** ***vi.*** **-dived′**, **-div′ing**

nose drops medication administered through the nose with a dropper

☆**no-see-um** (nō sē′əm) ***n.*** ⟦pseudo-AmInd term, altered < *no see (th)em*: in reference to its very small size⟧ BITING MIDGE

nose·gay (nōz′gā′) ***n.*** ⟦NOSE + GAY, in obs. n. sense "gay (bright) object"⟧ a bunch of flowers; small bouquet, esp. for carrying in the hand

☆**nose guard** *Football* the defensive lineman whose position in a three-man or five-man line is directly opposite the offensive center

nose job [Slang] a cosmetic alteration of a person's nose by plastic surgery

nose·piece (-pēs′) ***n.*** **1** that part of a helmet which covers and protects the nose **2** NOSEBAND **3** anything like a nose in form or position, as the lower end of a microscope **4** the bridge of a pair of eyeglasses

nose ring 1 a metal ring passed through the nose of an animal for leading it about **2** a ring of bone or metal worn in the nose as an ornament

☆**nose tackle** *var. of* NOSE GUARD

nos·ey (nō′zē) ***adj.*** **nos′i·er**, **nos′i·est** [Informal] *alt. sp. of* NOSY

nosh (näsh) [Slang] ***vt., vi.*** ⟦< Yiddish < Ger *naschen*, to nibble, taste, akin to *nagen*: see GNAW⟧ to eat (a snack) —***n.*** a snack —**nosh′er** ***n.***

☆**no-show** (nō′shō′) ***n.*** a person who fails to show up when expected, specif., one having a reservation, ticket, appointment, etc. who then fails to use or cancel it

nos·ing (nō′ziŋ) ***n.*** ⟦NOSE + -ING⟧ **1** *a)* the projecting edge of a step; that part of the tread which extends beyond the riser *b)* a strip, as of metal, for protecting this edge from wear **2** any projection like a stair nosing

nos·o- (nōs′ō, nōs′ə) ⟦< Gr *nosos*, disease⟧ *combining form* disease [*nosology*]: also, before a vowel, **nos-**

nos·o·co·mi·al (nōs′ə kō′mē əl) ***adj.*** ⟦< LL *nosocomium*, hospital (< LGr *nosokomeion* < *nosokomos*, one who tends the sick < *nosos* disease + ? *komein*, to take care of) + -AL (sense 1)⟧ of or beginning in a hospital or medical facility; esp., of a hospital-acquired disease or infection

no·sol·o·gy (nō säl′ə jē) ***n.*** ⟦ModL *nosologia*: see NOSO- & -LOGY⟧ **1** classification of diseases **2** the branch of medicine dealing with this —**nos·o·log·i·cal** (näs′ō läj′i kəl) ***adj.***, **nos′o·log′ic** —**nos′o·log′i·cal·ly** ***adv.***

nos·tal·gi·a (nä stal′jə, nô-) ***n.*** ⟦ModL: coined (1688) as a medical term by J. Hofer, Swiss scholar, to transl. Ger *heimweh*, homesickness < Gr *nostos*, a return (akin to *neomai*, I return: see NESTOR) + -ALGIA⟧ **1** a longing to go back to one's home, home town, or homeland; homesickness **2** a longing for something far away or long ago or for former happy circumstances —**nos·tal′gic** (-jik) ***adj.*** —**nos·tal′gi·cal·ly** ***adv.***

nos·tal·gie de la boue (nôs tȧl zhē də lȧ bo͞o′) ⟦Fr, lit., nostalgia or longing for the mud⟧ a desire for or attraction to crudity, vulgarity, depravity, etc.

nos·tal·gist (nä stal′jist) ***n.*** a person who is given to, or indulges in, nostalgic feelings

nos·toc (näs′täk′) ***n.*** ⟦ModL, coined by PARACELSUS⟧ any of a genus (*Nostoc*) of blue-green algae, having twisted, coiled filaments embedded in a gelatinous material and forming spherical colonies

Nos·tra·da·mus (nō′strə dä′məs, nä-; -dā′-) (born *Michel de Notredame*) 1503-66; Fr. astrologer & author of a collection of reputed prophecies

Nos·trat·ic (nä strat′ik) ***adj.*** ⟦< Ger *nostratisch* < L *nostras*, *nostratis*, of our country⟧ designating or of a proposed language superfamily that includes the Indo-European, Afroasiatic, Dravidian, Uralic, Altaic, and Kartvelian families —***n.*** this superfamily of languages

nos·tril (näs′trəl) ***n.*** ⟦ME *nosethirl* < OE *nosthyrl* < *nos*, for *nosu*, the nose + *thyrel*, a hole < *thurh*, through: see NOSE & THROUGH⟧ **1** either of the external openings of the nose **2** the fleshy wall on either side of the nose [*with flaring nostrils*]

nos·trum (näs′trəm) ***n.*** ⟦L, neut. of *noster*, ours (< *nos*, we: see US): ? so called from the seller's calling it "our" remedy⟧ **1** *a)* a medicine prepared by the person selling it *b)* a patent medicine of a kind sold with exaggerated claims; quack medicine **2** a pet scheme for solving some social or political problem; panacea

No sub *abbrev. Pharmacy* dispense brand name as specified instead of the generic equivalent

nos·y (nō′zē) ***adj.*** **nos′i·er**, **nos′i·est** ⟦NOS(E) + -Y[3]⟧ [Informal] given to prying; inquisitive —**nos′i·ly** ***adv.*** —**nos′i·ness** ***n.***

Nosy Par·ker (pär′kər) ⟦prec. + proper name *Parker*: reason for use uncert.⟧ [*also* **n- p-**, **n- P-**] [Informal] a nosy person; busybody

not (nät) ***adv.*** ⟦ME *not*, unstressed form of *noht*, *nought*, *naught*: see NOUGHT⟧ in no manner; to no degree: a particle of negation, or word expressing the idea of *no*, often implying refusal, affirmation of the opposite, etc.: sometimes used elliptically [*whether you like it or not*]

not- (nōt) *combining form* NOTO-: used before a vowel

nota (nōt′ə) ***n.*** *pl. of* NOTUM

no·ta be·ne (nō′tə bā′nā) ⟦L⟧ note well: used to direct attention to something of importance

no·ta·bil·i·a (nōt′ə bil′ē ə) ***pl.n.*** ⟦L, neut. pl. of *notabilis*: see NOTABLE⟧ things worthy of notice

no·ta·bil·i·ty (nōt′ə bil′ə tē) ***n.*** **1** *pl.* **-ties** a person who is notable or prominent **2** the quality of being notable

no·ta·ble (nōt′ə bəl; *for adj. 2, also* nät′-) ***adj.*** ⟦OFr < L *notabilis* < *notare*, to mark, note < *nota*, a mark: see NOTE⟧ **1** worthy of notice; remarkable; outstanding **2** [Archaic] industrious and capable, as in housekeeping —***n.*** **1** a person of distinction; famous or well-known person **2** [**N-**] [Historical] any of the persons of authority, rank, etc. summoned by the king of France as a deliberative assembly in emergencies —**no′ta·bly** ***adv.***

no·tar·i·al (nō ter′ē əl) ***adj.*** **1** of or characteristic of a notary public **2** drawn up or executed by a notary public —**no·tar′i·al·ly** ***adv.***

☆**no·ta·rize** (nōt′ə rīz′) ***vt.*** **-rized′**, **-riz′ing** to certify or attest (a document) as a notary public, esp. with a signature seal —**no′ta·ri·za′tion** ***n.***

no·ta·ry (nōt′ə rē) ***n.***, *pl.* **-ries** ⟦ME *notarye* < OFr *notaire* < L *notarius* < *notare*, to NOTE⟧ *short for* NOTARY PUBLIC

notary public *pl.* **notaries public** or **notary publics** an official authorized to certify or attest documents, take depositions and affidavits, etc.

no·tate (nō′tāt′) ***vt.*** **-tat′ed**, **-tat′ing** ⟦back-form. < fol.⟧ to write or record (esp. music) in notation

no·ta·tion (nō tā′shən) ***n.*** ⟦L *notatio* < *notare*, to NOTE⟧ **1** *a)* the use of a system of signs or symbols to represent words, phrases, numbers, quantities, etc. *b)* any such system, as in mathematics, chemistry, music, etc. **2** a brief note jotted down, as to remind one of something, explain something, etc. **3** the act of noting something in writing —**no·ta′tion·al** ***adj.***

notch (näch) ***n.*** ⟦prob. < ME *(a)n oche* < OFr *oche*, *osche*, a notch < *oschier*, to notch⟧ **1** a concave or V-shaped cut or indentation in an edge or across a surface ☆**2** a narrow pass with steep sides; defile; gap **3** [Informal] a step; grade; degree; peg [*a notch below average*] —***vt.*** **1** to cut a notch or notches in; indent with notches **2** to record or tally, as by means of notches —**notch′er** ***n.***

notched (nächt) ***adj.*** having a notch or indentation: used esp. of a collar in which the seam between the collar and lapel on each side forms a notch

note (nōt) ***n.*** ⟦OFr < L *nota*, a mark, sign, character, letter < *notus*, pp. of *noscere*, to know < *gnoscere*, to KNOW⟧ **1** a mark of some quality, condition, or fact; distinguishing or characteristic feature, mood, tone, etc. [*a note of sadness*] **2** importance, distinction, or eminence [*a person of note*] **3** *a)* a brief statement of a fact, experience, etc. written down for review, as an aid to memory, or to inform someone else; memorandum *b)* [*pl.*] a record of experiences, etc. [*the notes of a journey*] **4** a comment, explanation, or elucidation, as at the foot of a page; annotation **5** notice; heed; observation [*worthy of note*] **6** any of certain types of correspondence; specif., *a)* a short, informal letter *b)* a formal diplomatic or other official communication **7** *a)* a written promise to pay a sum of money or a written acknowledgment of a debt from which a promise of payment can be inferred *b)* a piece of paper currency [*a Federal Reserve note*] **8** a cry or call, as of a bird **9** a signal or intimation [*a note of admonition*] **10** [Archaic] a melody, tune, or song **11** *Music* *a)* a tone of definite pitch, as made by a voice or musical instrument *b)* a symbol for a tone, indicating the duration by its form and the pitch by its position on the staff *c)* a key of a piano or the like —***vt.*** **not′ed**, **not′ing** ⟦ME *noten* < OFr *noter* < L *notare* < *nota*⟧ **1** to pay close attention to; heed; notice; observe **2** to set down in writing; make a note of **3** to mention particularly **4** to denote or indicate **5** to set down in musical notes —**compare notes** to exchange views; confer —**strike the right note** to say, write, or do what is specially apt or pleasing —**take notes** to write down notes, as during a lecture or interview, for later reference

note

note·book (nōt′bo͝ok′) ***n.*** **1** a book of blank or, esp., ruled pages, for writing notes or memorandums **2** a small, lightweight laptop computer: in full **notebook computer**

note·card (-kärd′) ***n.*** 1 a small card, enclosed in an envelope, having a photograph or illustration printed on one side and the other side used for sending short messages 2 an index card or similar card used for recording notes or other information

note·case (-kās′) ***n.*** [Brit.] BILLFOLD

not·ed (nōt′id) ***adj.*** 1 distinguished; well-known; renowned; eminent 2 acknowledged or recorded, esp. officially [*noted* in the council's minutes] —**SYN.** FAMOUS —**not′ed·ly** ***adv.*** —**not′ed·ness** ***n.***

note·less (nōt′lis) ***adj.*** 1 not noted; unnoticed 2 unmusical

note of hand PROMISSORY NOTE

note·pad (-pad′) ***n.*** a small pad of paper, fastened along one edge, on which to jot down notes, reminders, or other information

note·pa·per (-pā′pər) ***n.*** paper for writing notes or letters

note·wor·thy (-wʉr′thē) ***adj.*** worthy of note; deserving notice; outstanding; remarkable; notable —**note′wor′thi·ly** ***adv.*** —**note′wor′thi·ness** ***n.***

not-for-prof·it (nät′fər präf′it) ***adj.*** NONPROFIT

noth·er (nuth′ər) ***adj.*** ⟦altered < ANOTHER as if it were *a nother*⟧ [Slang or Dial.] different; not the same [that's a whole *nother* matter]

noth·ing (nuth′iŋ) ***pron.*** ⟦ME < OE *na thing, nan thing*⟧ 1 *a)* no thing; not anything; naught *b)* no part, element, trace, etc. [*nothing* of kindness in him] 2 *a)* something of little or no value, seriousness, etc.; trifle *b)* a person considered to be of no value or importance —***n.*** 1 nonexistence; nothingness 2 a thing that does not exist 3 *a)* something of little or no value, seriousness, etc.; trifle (see also SWEET NOTHINGS) *b)* a person considered to be of no value or importance 4 a naught; zero; cipher —***adv.*** not at all; in no manner or degree [she looks *nothing* like her parents] —**for nothing** 1 free; at no cost 2 in vain; useless(ly) 3 without reason —☆**in nothing flat** [Informal] in almost no time at all —**make nothing of** 1 to treat as of little importance 2 to fail to understand —**nothing but** only; nothing other than [*nothing but* the truth] —**nothing doing** [Slang] 1 no: used as a refusal of a request 2 no result, accomplishment, etc.: an exclamation of disappointment —**nothing if not** decidedly and unmistakably [he's *nothing if not* prompt] —**nothing less than** no less than; just the same as: also **nothing short of**

noth·ing·ness (-nis) ***n.*** 1 the quality or condition of being nothing or not existing; nonexistence or extinction 2 lack of value, worth, meaning, etc.; uselessness, emptiness, insignificance, etc. 3 unconsciousness or death 4 anything that is nonexistent, worthless, insignificant, useless, etc.

no·tice (nōt′is) ***n.*** ⟦LME < MFr < L *notitia* < *notus*: see NOTE⟧ 1 information, announcement, or warning; esp., formal announcement or warning, as in a newspaper [a legal *notice*] 2 a brief mention or critical review of a work of art, book, play, etc. 3 a written or printed sign giving some public information, warning, or rule 4 *a)* the act of observing; attention; regard; heed; cognizance *b)* courteous attention; civility 5 a formal announcement or warning of intention to end an agreement, relation, or contract at a certain time [to give a tenant *notice*] —***vt.*** **-ticed**, **-tic·ing** 1 *a)* to mention; refer to; comment on *b)* to review briefly 2 *a)* to regard; observe; pay attention to *b)* to be courteous or responsive to —**SYN.** DISCERN —**serve notice** to give formal warning or information, as of intentions; announce —**take notice** to become aware; pay attention; observe

no·tice·a·ble (nōt′is ə bəl) ***adj.*** 1 readily noticed; conspicuous 2 worth noticing; significant —**no′tice·a·bly** ***adv.***

SYN.—noticeable is applied to that which must inevitably be noticed [a *noticeable* coolness in his manner]; **remarkable** applies to that which is noticeable because it is unusual or exceptional [*remarkable* beauty]; **prominent** refers to that which literally or figuratively stands out from its background [a *prominent* nose, a *prominent* author]; an **outstanding** person or thing is remarkable as compared with others of its kind [an *outstanding* sculptor]; **conspicuous** applies to that which is so obvious or manifest as to be immediately perceptible [a *conspicuous* black eye]; **striking** is used of something so out of the ordinary that it leaves a sharp impression on the mind [a *striking* designer gown]

no·ti·fi·a·ble (nōt′ə fī′ə bəl) ***adj.*** that must be reported to health authorities [*notifiable* diseases]

no·ti·fi·ca·tion (nōt′ə fi kā′shən) ***n.*** ⟦ME *notificacioun* < MFr *notification*⟧ 1 a notifying or being notified 2 the notice given or received 3 the letter, form, etc. used to convey such a notice

no·ti·fy (nōt′ə fī′) ***vt.*** **-fied′**, **-fy′ing** ⟦ME *notifien* < MFr *notifier* < L *notificare* < *notus* (see NOTE) + *facere*, to make, DO[1]⟧ 1 to give notice to; inform; announce to 2 [Chiefly Brit.] to give notice of; announce; make known —**no′ti·fi′er** ***n.***

SYN.—notify implies a sending of a formal notice imparting required or pertinent information [*notify* me when you are ready]; **inform** implies a making someone aware of something by sharing knowledge of it [he *informed* me of your decision to join us]; **acquaint** suggests a making familiar with something hitherto unknown to one [she *acquainted* me with her problems]; **apprise** implies a notifying someone of something of particular interest to him or her [I have *apprised* him of your arrival]

no·tion (nō′shən) ***n.*** ⟦Fr < L *notio* < *notus*: see NOTE⟧ 1 *a)* a mental image; general idea *b)* a vague thought 2 a belief; opinion; view 3 a desire; inclination; whim 4 a plan or intention ☆5 a small, useful household article, as a needle, a pin, or thread, sold in a store: *usually used in pl.* —**SYN.** IDEA

no·tion·al (nō′shə nəl) ***adj.*** ⟦ML *notionalis*⟧ 1 of, expressing, or consisting of notions, or concepts 2 imaginary; not actual [to inhabit a *notional* world] ☆3 having visionary ideas; given to whims; fanciful 4 *Gram.* having full lexical, as distinguished from relational, meaning ["have" is *notional* in "we have a problem" and relational in "we have solved a problem"] —**no′tion·al·ly** ***adv.***

no·to- (nōt′ō, nōt′ə) ⟦ModL < Gr *nōton*, the back, akin to L *nates*, buttocks⟧ *combining form* the back, dorsum [*notochord*]

no·to·chord (nōt′ə kôrd′, nōt′ō-) ***n.*** ⟦prec. + CHORD[1]⟧ 1 an elongated, rod-shaped structure composed of cells, forming the primitive supporting axis of the body in the lowest chordates and lying between the digestive tract and the central nervous system 2 a similar structure in the embryonic stages of higher vertebrates, which later is surrounded and replaced by the vertebral column —**no′to·chord′al** ***adj.***

No·to·gae·a (nōt′ə jē′ə) ***n.*** ⟦ModL < Gr *notos*, south, south wind, rain-bringing wind < IE *(*s*)*not-* < base *(*s*)*na-*, to flow > NATANT⟧ one of three primary zoogeographic areas of the earth, including Australia, New Zealand, New Guinea, Sulawesi, and nearby islands: also sp. **No′to·ge′a** —**No′to·gae′an** ***adj.***

no·to·ri·e·ty (nōt′ə rī′ə tē) ***n.*** ⟦Fr *notorieté* < ML *notorietas* < *notorius*: see fol.⟧ 1 the quality or state of being notorious 2 *pl.* **-ties** [Chiefly Brit.] a prominent or well-known person

no·to·ri·ous (nō tôr′ē əs) ***adj.*** ⟦ML *notorius* < LL *notoria*, news, information < *notus*: see NOTE⟧ 1 well-known; publicly discussed 2 widely but unfavorably known or talked about —**SYN.** FAMOUS —**no·to′ri·ous·ly** ***adv.*** —**no·to′ri·ous·ness** ***n.***

no·tor·nis (nō tôr′nis) ***n.*** ⟦ModL < Gr *notos*, the south (see NOTOGAEA) + *ornis*, bird⟧ any of a rare genus (*Notornis*) of nonflying gallinule-like birds of New Zealand

No·tre Dame (nō′trə däm′, -dām′; nōt′ər-; *Fr* nô trə dȧm′) ⟦Fr, lit., Our Lady (Mary, mother of Jesus)⟧ a famous early Gothic cathedral in Paris, built 1163-1257: in full **Notre Dame de Paris**

no-trump (nō′trump′) *Bridge* ***adj.*** designating, of, or having to do with a bid to play with no suit as trump —***n.*** a no-trump bid

Not·ting·ham (nät′iŋ əm) ⟦< OE *Snotingaham* < *Snoting*, people of *Snot* (< *Snot*, personal name < *snotor*, wise + *-inga*, patronymic suffix) + *ham*, HOME⟧ 1 NOTTINGHAMSHIRE 2 county seat of Nottinghamshire, central England

Not·ting·ham·shire (-shir′) ⟦< OE *Snotinghamscir*: see prec. & SHIRE⟧ county in central England: 834 sq mi (2,160 sq km)

no·tum (nōt′əm) ***n.***, *pl.* **-ta** (-ə) ⟦ModL < Gr *nōton*, the back⟧ the back or dorsal portion of an insect segment

not·with·stand·ing (nät′with stan′diŋ, -with-) ***prep.*** in spite of [*notwithstanding* the storm, we flew on]: sometimes in an inverted construction [we flew on, the storm *notwithstanding*] —***adv.*** all the same, nevertheless [he must be told, *notwithstanding*] —***conj.*** in spite of the fact that; although

Nouak·chott (nwäk shät′) capital of Mauritania, in the W part

nou·gat (no͞o′gət) ***n.*** ⟦Fr < Prov *nogat* < *noga*, *nuga*, nut < L *nux*, NUT⟧ a confection of sugar paste with almonds or other nuts, and sometimes fruit

nought (nôt) ***pron.*** ⟦ME < OE *nowiht* < *ne*, not (see NO[1]) + *owiht*, *awiht*, AUGHT⟧ nothing; naught —***n.*** 1 *Arith.* the figure zero (0) 2 *alt. sp. of* NAUGHT —***adj.*** [Obs.] NAUGHT —***adv.*** [Archaic] NAUGHT

Nou·me·a (no͞o′mā ä′) seaport & capital of New Caledonia, on the SE coast

nou·me·non (no͞o′mə nän′, nou′-) ***n.***, *pl.* **-me·na** (-nə) ⟦Ger < Gr *nooumenon*, neut. of *nooumenos*, prp. pass. of *noein*, to perceive < *nous*, *noos*, the mind⟧ in Kantian philosophy, a thing as it is in itself, as such unable to be known through sense perception but postulated as the intelligible ground of a phenomenon: distinguished from PHENOMENON —**nou′me·nal** ***adj.***

noun (noun) ***n.*** ⟦ME *nowne* < OFr *noun*, *nom* < L *nomen*, NAME⟧ *Gram.* any of a class of words naming or denoting a person, thing, place, action, quality, etc. (Ex.: *woman, water, New York, talking, beauty*)

nour·ish (nʉr′ish) ***vt.*** ⟦ME *norischen* < OFr extended stem of *norrir* < L *nutrire*: see NURSE⟧ 1 to feed or sustain (any plant or animal) with substances necessary to life and growth 2 to foster; develop; promote (a feeling, attitude, habit, etc.) —**nour′ish·er** ***n.***

nour·ish·ing (-iŋ) ***adj.*** contributing to health or growth; nutritious —**nour′ish·ing·ly** ***adv.***

nour·ish·ment (nʉr′ish mənt) ***n.*** ⟦ME *norysshement* < OFr *norissement*⟧ 1 a nourishing or being nourished 2 something that nourishes; food; nutriment

nous (no͞os, nous) ***n.*** ⟦Gr *nous*, *noos*⟧ 1 *Philos.* mind, reason, or intellect, specif. as a metaphysical principle 2 [Informal, Chiefly Brit.] shrewdness or understanding; savvy

nou·veau (no͞o vō′, no͞o′vō) ⟦Fr, new⟧ [*often in italics*] ***adj.*** 1 newly appearing, arrived, made, etc.; new [*nouveau* Beaujolais] 2 like or characteristic of a nouveau riche

nou·veau riche (no͞o′vō rēsh′) *pl.* **nou·veaux riches** (no͞o′vō rēsh′) ⟦Fr, newly rich⟧ a person who has only recently become rich: often connoting tasteless ostentation, lack of culture, etc.

nou·velle (no͞o vel′) ⟦Fr, fem. of *nouveau*: see NOUVEAU⟧ [*often in italics*] ***adj.*** 1 new 2 of or characteristic of nouvelle cuisine —***n.*** *short for* NOUVELLE CUISINE

nouvelle cuisine ⟦Fr, new cuisine⟧ a style of French cooking that uses a minimum of fat and starch and emphasizes light sauces and the use of very fresh ingredients, often in unusual combinations prepared simply and served artistically arranged on the plate

Nov *abbrev.* November

no·va (nō′və) ***n.***, *pl.* **-vas** or **-vae** (-vē) ⟦ModL < L *nova* (*stella*), new (star)

< *novus,* NEW⟧ *Astron.* a type of variable star that suddenly increases in brightness by thousands of times, up to 14 magnitudes, and then decreases in brightness over a period of months to years

no·vac·u·lite (nō vak′yoo līt′) ***n.*** ⟦< L *novacula,* razor (< **novare,* to scrape, whet < IE **ksnewā-* < base **kes-,* to scratch, comb > HARDS) + -ITE[1]⟧ a light-colored, hard, extremely fine-grained siliceous sedimentary rock, often used as a whetstone

No·va I·gua·çu (nô′və ē′gwə soo′) city in SE Brazil: suburb of Rio de Janeiro

No·va·ra (nô vä′rä) commune in Piedmont, NW Italy

No·va Sco·tia (nō′və skō′shə) ⟦ModL, New Scotland⟧ province of SE Canada, consisting of a peninsula on the Atlantic, & Cape Breton Island: 20,431 sq mi (52,917 sq km); cap. Halifax: abbrev. *NS* or *N.S.* —**No′va Sco′tian**

no·va·tion (nō vā′shən) ***n.*** ⟦LL *novatio* < L *novare,* to make new < *novus,* NEW⟧ *Law* the substitution of a new obligation or contract for an old one by the mutual agreement of all parties concerned

No·va·ya Zem·lya (nô′vä yä zem lyä′) ⟦Russ *Novaja Zemlja,* lit., new land⟧ archipelago of two large islands & several small ones in NW Russia, between the Barents & Kara seas: *c.* 36,000 sq mi (93,240 sq km)

nov·el (näv′əl) ***adj.*** ⟦ME *novell* < OFr *novel* < L *novellus,* dim. of *novus,* NEW⟧ new and unusual; esp., being the first of its kind —***n.*** ⟦It *novella* < L neut. pl. of *novellus* (see the ***adj.***), hence, orig., new things, news⟧ **1** [Obs.] NOVELLA (sense 1) **2** a relatively long fictional prose narrative with a more or less complex plot or pattern of events, about actions, feelings, motives, etc. of a group of characters **3** the type or form of literature represented by such narratives: with *the* **4** ⟦< LL *novellae (constitutiones)*⟧ *Rom. Law* a new law or decree, specif. one made by Justinian supplementary to the Justinian code: *usually used in pl.* —***SYN.*** NEW —**nov′el·is′tic** ***adj.*** —**nov′el·is′ti·cal·ly** ***adv.***

nov·el·ette (näv′ə let′) ***n.*** SHORT NOVEL, sometimes, specif., one regarded as inferior in quality, banal, overly commercial, etc.

nov·el·et·tish (näv′ə let′ish) ***adj.*** like or characteristic of a novelette; specif., sentimental, contrived, lurid, shallow, etc.

nov·el·ist (näv′ə list) ***n.*** a person who writes novels

nov·el·ize (näv′ə līz′) ***vt.*** **-ized′, -iz′ing** to give the form or characteristics of a novel to; make into or like a novel; specif., to use (a film script) as the basis of a novel —**nov′el·i·za′tion** ***n.***

no·vel·la (nō vel′ə) ***n., pl.*** **-las** or **-le** (-ē) ⟦It: see NOVEL, ***n.***⟧ **1** a short prose narrative, usually with a moral and often satirical, as any of the tales in Boccaccio's *Decameron* **2** SHORT NOVEL

nov·el·ty (näv′əl tē) ***n., pl.*** **-ties** ⟦ME *novelte* < OFr *noveleté* < LL *novellitas*⟧ **1** the quality of being novel; newness; freshness **2** something new, fresh, or unusual; change; innovation **3** a small, often cheap, cleverly made article, usually for play or adornment: *usually used in pl.* —***adj.*** characterized by an innovation or, often, specif., by humorous or faddish gimmickry [a singer with a string of hit *novelty* recordings]

No·vem·ber (nō vem′bər) ***n.*** ⟦ME & OFr *Novembre* < L *November* < *novem,* NINE + *-ber* (< ?): so named as the ninth month of the ancient Roman year, which began with March⟧ the eleventh month of the year, having 30 days: abbrev. *Nov* or *N*

no·ve·na (nō vē′nə) ***n.*** ⟦ML < fem. sing. of L *novenus,* nine each < *novem,* NINE⟧ *R.C.Ch.* the recitation of prayers and the practicing of devotions for nine consecutive days, usually to seek some special favor

Nov·go·rod (näv′gə räd′; *Russ* nôv′gə rət) city in NW Russia: former political & commercial center (11th-15th cent.): since 1999, officially *Velikiy Novgorod*

nov·ice (näv′is) ***n.*** ⟦ME *novis* < OFr *novice* < L *novicius,* new, fresh < *novus,* NEW⟧ **1** a person on probation in a religious group or order before taking vows; neophyte **2** a person new to a particular occupation, activity, etc.; apprentice; beginner; tyro —***SYN.*** AMATEUR

no·vi·lle·ro (nô′vē lye′rô, -vē ye′-) ***n., pl.*** **-ros** (-rôs) ⟦Sp < *novillo,* young bull < L (*bos*) *novellus,* new (bull): see NOVEL⟧ a novice bullfighter

No·vi Sad (nô′vē säd′) city in N Serbia, on the Danube: capital of Vojvodina

no·vi·ti·ate (nō vish′it; *also, and chiefly Brit,* -vish′ē it, -āt′) ***n.*** ⟦Fr *noviciat* < ML *novitiatus*⟧ **1** *a)* the period or state of being a novice *b)* NOVICE **2** the quarters assigned to religious novices Also [Chiefly Brit.] **no·vi′ci·ate**

☆**No·vo·cain** (nō′və kān′) ⟦L *nov(us),* NEW + (C)OCAIN(E)⟧ *trademark for* PROCAINE —***n.*** [*usually* **n-**] any similar local anesthetic, as lidocaine: also sp. **no′vo·caine′**

No·vo·kuz·netsk (nô′vô kooz nyetsk′) city in SC Russia, in the Kuznetsk Basin

No·vo·si·birsk (nô′vô sē birsk′) city in SC Russia, on the Ob River

now (nou) ***adv.*** ⟦ME < OE *nu,* akin to ON Goth, OHG *nu* < IE base **nu-* > Gr *nu,* L *nunc*⟧ **1** *a)* at the present time; at this moment *b)* at once **2** at the time referred to; then; next [*now* the best days of his childhood began] **3** at a time very close to the present; specif., *a)* very recently; not long ago (with *just*) [he left just *now*] *b)* very soon (often with *just*) [they are leaving just *now*] **4** given the situation; with things as they are [*now* we'll never know what happened] —***conj.*** since; seeing that [*now* you've arrived, I can stop worrying] —***n.*** the present time [that's all for *now*] —***adj.*** [Informal] of the present or current time [the *now* generation] —***interj.*** **1** used to signify warning, reproach, etc. [*now,* be careful!] **2** used with no definite meaning, to provide emphasis or to preface or resume one's remarks [*now,* this is where the story really gets interesting] **3** used to express sympathy, concern, consolation, etc. when repeated [*now, now*—it's not so bad after all!] —**from now on** from this time on; after this; in the future —**now and then** sometimes; occasionally: also **now and again**

NOW (nou) ***abbrev.*** **1** National Organization for Women **2** negotiable order of withdrawal

now·a·days (nou′ə dāz′) ***adv.*** ⟦ME *nou adaies* < *now* + *on* + *day* + *-s,* adv. suffix⟧ in these days; at the present time —***n.*** the present time

no·way (nō′wā′) ***adv.*** in no manner; by no means; not at all; nowise: also **no′ways′**: see also phrase NO WAY at WAY

no·where (nō′hwer′, -wer′) ***adv.*** ⟦ME *nowher* < OE *nahwær*⟧ not in, at, or to any place; not anywhere: also [Informal or Dial.] **no′wheres′** —***n.*** **1** a place that is nonexistent, unknown, remote, etc. **2** a place or state of obscurity —**get (or go) nowhere** [Informal] to fail to make progress —**middle of nowhere** [Informal] a very remote or isolated place —**nowhere near** not by a wide margin

no·whith·er (nō′hwith′ər, -with′-) ***adv.*** ⟦ME *nowhider* < OE *nahwider*⟧ [Obs.] in, at, or to no place; nowhere

no-win (nō′win′) ***adj.*** designating or of a situation, policy, etc. that cannot lead to success no matter what measures are taken

no·wise (nō′wīz′) ***adv.*** in no manner; noway

nowt[1] (nout) ***pl.n., sing.*** **nowt** ⟦ME < ON *naut,* cattle, akin to OE *neat:* see NEAT[2]⟧ [Chiefly Scot.] cattle; oxen

nowt[2] (nout) ***pron., n.*** [Dial., Chiefly Brit.] nothing

Nox (näks) ***n.*** ⟦L, NIGHT⟧ *Rom. Myth.* night personified as a goddess: identified with the Greek Nyx

nox·ious (näk′shəs) ***adj.*** ⟦L *noxius* < *noxa,* injury, hurt < *nocere,* to hurt, injure: see NECRO-⟧ **1** harmful to the health; injurious [a *noxious* gas] **2** morally injurious; corrupting; unwholesome —***SYN.*** PERNICIOUS —**nox′ious·ly** ***adv.*** —**nox′ious·ness** ***n.***

noxt *abbrev. Pharmacy* at night

no·yade (nwä yäd′) ***n.*** ⟦Fr < *noyer,* to drown < L *necare,* to kill (in LL, to drown): see NECRO-⟧ a mass execution of persons by drowning, as practiced at Nantes, France, during the Reign of Terror (1794)

noz·zle (näz′əl) ***n.*** ⟦dim. of NOSE⟧ **1** a spout at the end of a hose, pipe, bellows, etc., by which a stream of liquid or gas may be directed and controlled **2** [Slang] the nose

Np *Chem. symbol for* neptunium

NP *abbrev.* Notary Public

n.p. *abbrev.* **1** nisi prius **2** no page or pagination **3** no place (of publication) **4** no publisher

NPR *service mark* National Public Radio

NR *abbrev.* not rated: said of films that have not received a rating

N.R. *abbrev.* ⟦L: see NON REP.⟧ *Pharmacy* do not repeat

NRA *abbrev.* **1** National Recovery Administration **2** *service mark* National Rifle Association

NRC *abbrev.* **1** National Research Council **2** Nuclear Regulatory Commission

NRSV *abbrev.* New Revised Standard Version (of the Bible)

ns *abbrev.* nanosecond(s)

Ns *Chem. symbol for* nielsbohrium

NS *abbrev.* **1** naval station **2** new series **3** New Style **4** Nova Scotia: also N.S. **5** nuclear ship **6** nuclear submarine

n/s *abbrev. Banking* not sufficient funds

NSA *abbrev.* National Security Agency

NSAID (en′sed′, -sād′) ***n., pl.*** **NSAIDs** ⟦*n(on)s(teroidal) a(nti-)i(nflammatory) d(rug)*⟧ *Med.* any of a class of nonsteroidal anti-inflammatory drugs, as aspirin or ibuprofen, used as a pain reliever

NSC *abbrev.* National Security Council

nsec *abbrev.* nanosecond

nsf *abbrev.* not sufficient funds

NSF *abbrev.* National Science Foundation

NSW *abbrev.* New South Wales

NT *abbrev.* **1** New Testament **2** Northern Territory **3** Northwest Territories **4** *Football* nose tackle: sometimes written **nt**

-n't *suffix* not: used with certain verbs in contractions [*aren't*]

NTA *abbrev.* ⟦*n(itrilo)t(ri)a(cetic) acid*⟧ a white, crystalline powder, $N(CH_2COOH)_3$, formerly used in detergents for its biodegradable qualities, but now considered a possible health hazard

nth (enth) ***adj.*** ⟦< (SEVE)NTH, (ELEVE)NTH⟧ **1** expressing the ordinal equivalent to *n* **2** of the indefinitely large or small quantity represented by *n* —**to the nth degree (or power)** **1** to an indefinite degree or power **2** to an extreme

NTP *abbrev.* normal temperature and air pressure: former term for STP

NTSB *abbrev.* National Transportation Safety Board

nt wt *abbrev.* net weight

n-type (en′tīp′) ***adj.*** ⟦< NEGATIVE + TYPE⟧ *Electronics* designating or of negative semiconductor material in which there are more electrons than holes and current is carried through it by the flow of electrons: see HOLE (*n.* 7), P-TYPE

nu[1] (noo, nyoo) ***n.*** ⟦Gr *ny* < Sem, as in Heb *nūn*⟧ the thirteenth letter of the Greek alphabet (Ν, ν)

nu[2] (noo) ***interj.*** ⟦Yiddish < Russ *nu,* WELL[2] (***interj.***)⟧ **1** used to express surprise, agreement, acquiescence, resignation, etc. **2** used to ask a question, with such meanings as "well?", "so?", or "so what?"

Nu *abbrev. Bible* Numbers

NU *abbrev.* Nunavut

nu·ance (no͞o′äns′, nyo͞o′-) *n.* ⟦Fr < *nuer*, to shade < *nue* < VL **nuba*, for L *nubes*, a cloud < IE **sneudh-*, fog (> Welsh *nudd*), prob. < base *(*s*)*na-*, to flow, moisture > NATANT⟧ a slight or delicate variation in tone, color, meaning, etc.; shade of difference

nu·anced (-änst′) *adj.* treated or done so as to show or display small, delicate, or subtle variations, gradations, etc., as in meaning

nub (nub) *n.* ⟦var. of *knub*, for KNOB⟧ **1** *a)* a knob or lump *b)* a small piece ☆**2** [Informal] the point of a story or gist of a matter

nub·bin (nub′in) *n.* ⟦dim. of prec.⟧ ☆**1** a small or imperfect ear of Indian corn **2** anything small or undeveloped [*nubbins* of coal]

nub·ble (nub′əl) *n.* ⟦dim. of NUB⟧ a small knob or lump —**nub′bly** *adj.* **-bli·er, -bli·est**

nub·by (nub′ē) *adj.* **-bi·er, -bi·est** covered with small nubs, or lumps; having a rough, knotted surface; nubbly —**nub′bi·ness** *n.*

Nu·bi·a (no͞o′bē ə, nyo͞o′-) ⟦ML < L *Nubae*, the Nubians < Gr *Noubai*⟧ region & ancient kingdom in NE Africa, west of the Red Sea, in Egypt & Sudan

Nu·bi·an (-ən) *adj.* of Nubia or its people, language, or culture —*n.* **1** a person born or living in Nubia **2** a group of Chari-Nile languages spoken in Nubia

Nubian Desert desert in NE Sudan, between the Nile & the Red Sea

nu·bile (no͞o′bəl, -bīl′; nyo͞o′-) *adj.* ⟦Fr *nubile* < L *nubilis* < *nubere*, to veil oneself, marry < IE base **sneubh-*, to woo, marry > Gr *nymphē*, bride, nymph, Czech *snoubiti*, to woo⟧ **1** marriageable: said of a young woman who seems mature **2** sexually attractive: said of a young woman —**nu·bil′i·ty** *n.*

nu·bi·lous (no͞o′bə ləs, nyo͞o′-) *adj.* ⟦LL *nubilosus*, cloudy, for L *nubilus* < *nubes*, a cloud: see NUANCE⟧ **1** cloudy; misty **2** not clear

nu·buck (leather) (no͞o′buk′, nyo͞o′-) tanned leather similar to suede, but with the nap on the grain side

nu·cel·lus (no͞o sel′əs, nyo͞o-) *n., pl.* **-cel′li′** (-ī′) ⟦ModL < L *nucella*, dim. of *nux* (gen. *nucis*), NUT⟧ *Bot.* the central part of an ovule, containing the embryo sac —**nu·cel′lar** *adj.*

nu·cha (no͞o′kə, nyo͞o′-) *n., pl. Zool.* **-chae** (-kē) ⟦ME < ML < Ar *nukhā*ʿ, spinal marrow⟧ **1** the nape of the neck **2** in insects, the back part of the thorax —**nu′chal** *adj.*

nu·cle·ar (no͞o′klē ər, nyo͞o′-) *adj.* **1** of, like or forming a nucleus **2** of or relating to atomic nuclei [*nuclear* energy] **3** of, characterized by, or operated by the use of nuclear energy [*nuclear* weapons] **4** of, having, or involving nuclear weapons [*nuclear* warfare]

nuclear bomb an atomic bomb or a hydrogen bomb

nuclear emulsion any of various specialized photographic emulsions for recording the characteristic tracks of ionizing particles

nuclear energy the energy released from an atom in nuclear reactions or by radioactive decay; esp., the energy released in nuclear fission or nuclear fusion

☆**nuclear family** a basic social unit consisting of parents and their dependent children living in one household: cf. EXTENDED FAMILY

nuclear fission the splitting of the nuclei of atoms into two fragments of approximately equal mass, accompanied by conversion of part of the mass into energy: the principle of the atomic bomb

nuclear force STRONG INTERACTION

nuclear fusion the fusion of lightweight atomic nuclei, as of tritium or deuterium, into a nucleus of heavier mass, as of helium: the resultant loss in combined mass is converted into energy

nuclear magnetic resonance a phenomenon exhibited by various atomic nuclei when placed in a strong magnetic field, in which they absorb energy from specific, high-frequency radio waves: the measurements of the magnetic moments of these nuclei, esp. of hydrogen, are used in medical diagnostics, chemical research, etc. to study the nature and structure of matter

nuclear medicine the branch of medicine that uses radiation and radioactive materials for diagnosis and therapeutic treatment

nuclear membrane the double-layered membrane of the cell nucleus, separating the nucleoplasm from the cytoplasm and permeable to certain molecules, esp. DNA, RNA, and ATP: now often **nuclear envelope**

nuclear physics the branch of physics dealing with the structure of atomic nuclei, nuclear forces, the interaction between particles and nuclei, the fission process, the study of radioactive decay, etc.

nuclear reactor a device for initiating and maintaining a controlled nuclear chain reaction in a fissile fuel for the production of energy or additional fissile material

nuclear sap KARYOLYMPH

☆**nuclear winter** ⟦term popularized by Carl SAGAN, who attributed its coinage to R. P. Turco (b. 1943), U.S. environmental scientist⟧ a hypothetical condition following nuclear war in which light from the sun is cut off by clouds of smoke and dust, resulting in very low temperatures and consequent devastation of the environment

nu·cle·ase (no͞o′klē ās′, nyo͞o′-) *n.* ⟦NUCLE(O)- + -ASE⟧ any of various enzymes that speed up the hydrolysis of nucleic acids

nu·cle·ate (no͞o′klē it, -āt′; nyo͞o′-; *for v.*, -āt′) *adj.* ⟦L *nucleatus*, having a kernel, pp. of *nucleare*, to become like a kernel < *nucleus*: see NUCLEUS⟧ having a nucleus: also **nu′cle·at′ed** —*vt.* **-at′ed, -at′ing** ⟦< L *nucleatus*⟧ to form into or around a nucleus —*vi.* to form a nucleus —**nu′cle·a′tion** *n.* —**nu′cle·a′tor** *n.*

nu·cle·i (no͞o′klē ī′, nyo͞o′-) *n. alt. pl. of* NUCLEUS

nu·cle·ic acid (no͞o klē′ik, nyo͞o-; -klā′-) ⟦< NUCLE(US) + -IC: because found in the nuclei of cells⟧ any of a group of essential, complex organic acids found in all living cells: the two types, DNA and RNA, consist of long chains of nucleotide units with each unit composed of phosphoric acid, a carbohydrate, and a base derived from purine or pyrimidine

nu·cle·in (no͞o′klē in, nyo͞o′-) *n.* ⟦NUCLE(US) + -IN[1]⟧ any of a group of decomposition substances found in the nuclei of cells that are intermediate to nucleoproteins and nucleic acids

nu·cle·o- (no͞o′klē ō, nyo͞o′-; -ə) *combining form* **1** nucleus [*nucleophile*] **2** nuclear [*nucleoplasm*] **3** nucleic acid [*nuclease, nucleoprotein*] Also, before a vowel, **nu′cle-**

nu·cle·o·cap·sid (no͞o′klē ō kap′sid, nyo͞o′-) *n.* a structural unit of viruses consisting of nucleic acid enclosed by a protein coat, or capsid: see VIRION

nu·cle·oid (no͞o′klē oid′, nyo͞o′-) *n.* ⟦< *nucloid* < NUCL(EUS) + -OID⟧ a region in the cells of prokaryotes that contains nucleic acids but which is not bounded by a membrane: it is analogous in function to the nucleus of eukaryotic cells

nu·cle·o·lus (no͞o klē′ə ləs, nyo͞o-) *n., pl.* **-li′** (-lī′) ⟦ModL < LL, dim. of L *nucleus*⟧ a conspicuous, usually spherical, dense body in the nucleus of most cells, consisting of protein and RNA: ribosomes are produced here: also **nu′cle·ole′** (-klē ōl′) —**nu·cle′o·lar** *adj.*

nu·cle·on (no͞o′klē än′, nyo͞o′-) *n.* ⟦NUCLE(US) + (PROT)ON⟧ *Particle Physics* either of two stable baryons, the proton and the neutron, that make up the nucleus of an atom: see HYPERON —**nu′cle·on′ic** *adj.*

nu·cle·on·ics (no͞o′klē än′iks, nyo͞o′-) *n.* ⟦prec. + -ICS⟧ the branch of physics dealing with nucleons, nuclear phenomena, and the practical applications of nuclear physics

nu·cle·o·phile (no͞o′klē ə fīl′, nyo͞o′-) *n.* ⟦NUCLEO- + -PHILE⟧ an atom or molecule that has an affinity for atomic nuclei or that donates electrons to form a covalent bond —**nu′cle·o·phil′ic** (-fil′ik) *adj.*

nu·cle·o·plasm (-plaz′əm) *n.* ⟦NUCLEO- + -PLASM⟧ the protoplasm that constitutes the nucleus of a cell —**nu′cle·o·plas′mic** *adj.*

nu·cle·o·pro·tein (no͞o′klē ō prō′tēn, nyo͞o′-; -prōt′ē in) *n.* ⟦NUCLEO- + PROTEIN⟧ any of a class of compound proteins consisting of nucleic acid linked to protein, found in the nuclei and surrounding cytoplasm of living cells

nu·cle·o·side (no͞o′klē ō sīd′, nyo͞o′-) *n.* ⟦< NUCLEO- + -OSE[2] + -IDE⟧ any of various compounds consisting of a purine or pyrimidine base linked to a carbohydrate: a major component of a nucleotide

nu·cle·o·some (no͞o′klē ō sōm′, nyo͞o′-) *n.* ⟦NUCLEO- + -SOME[3]⟧ the basic structural unit of chromatin in eukaryotes, composed of eight histone molecules wrapped by a segment of DNA: nucleosomes occur at intervals along a continuous strand of DNA

nu·cle·o·syn·the·sis (no͞o′klē ō sin′thə sis, nyo͞o′-) *n.* ⟦NUCLEO- + SYNTHESIS⟧ the formation of heavier chemical elements from the nuclei of hydrogen or other lighter elements, as in the interior of a star

nu·cle·o·tide (no͞o′klē ō tīd′, nyo͞o′-) *n.* ⟦altered < NUCLEOSIDE⟧ **1** any of several phosphate esters of nucleosides: the basic unit of nucleic acids **2** any of several compounds not found in nucleic acids, which function as coenzymes

nu·cle·us (no͞o′klē əs, nyo͞o′-) *n., pl.* **-cle·i′** (-ī′) or **-cle·us·es** ⟦ModL < L, a nut, kernel, for *nuculeus*, dim. < *nux* (gen. *nucis*), NUT⟧ **1** a thing or part forming the center around which other things or parts are grouped or collected; core **2** anything serving as a center of growth or development [the *nucleus* of a library] **3** *Anat.* a group of nerve cells in the brain or spinal column **4** *Astron.* the bright, central part of the head of a comet **5** *Biol.* the central, usually spherical or oval mass of protoplasm present in most plant and animal cells, containing most of the hereditary material and necessary to such functions as growth, reproduction, etc. **6** *Bot.* the central point in a starch grain **7** *Chem.* in organic chemistry, a fundamental, stable arrangement of atoms, as the benzene ring, that may occur in many compounds by atomic substitution without structural change **8** *Chem., Physics* the central part of an atom, the fundamental particles of which are the proton and (except for hydrogen) neutron: it carries a positive charge and constitutes almost all of the mass of the atom **9** *Phonet.* the most sonorous portion of a syllable, usually a vowel

nu·clide (no͞o′klīd′, nyo͞o′-) *n.* ⟦< prec. + *-ide* < Gr *eidos*, form: see -OID⟧ a specific type of atom as characterized by its nuclear properties, such as the number of neutrons and protons and the energy state of its nucleus —**nu·clid′ic** (no͞o klid′ik, nyo͞o-) *adj.*

nude (no͞od, nyo͞od) *adj.* ⟦L *nudus*, NAKED⟧ **1** completely unclothed or uncovered; naked; bare **2** *Law* without consideration or other legal essential: said esp. of contracts —*n.* **1** a nude person **2** a representation of a nude human figure in painting, sculpture, etc. **3** the condition of being nude; nakedness [in the *nude*] **4** ⟦from approximating the skin color of a white person⟧ any of a range of colors from tan to yellowish or pinkish beige —**SYN.** BARE[1] —**nude′ly** *adv.* —**nude′ness** *n.*

nudge[1] (nuj) *vt.* **nudged, nudg′ing** ⟦prob. akin to Norw dial. *nyggja*, to push, shove, MLowG *nucke*, a sudden push, ult. < IE base **nue-*, to jerk, shove: see INNUENDO⟧ to push or poke gently, esp. with the elbow, in order to get the attention of, hint slyly, etc. —*n.* a gentle push, as with the elbow; jog —**nudg′er** *n.*

nudge[2] (no͝oj) *n., vt., vi.* **nudged, nudg′ing** [Slang] *alt. sp. of* NOODGE

nu·di- (no͞o′di, -də; nyo͞o′-) ⟦< L *nudus*, NAKED⟧ *combining form Biol.* bare, naked [*nudibranch*]

nu·di·branch (-braŋk′) *n.* ⟦< ModL *Nudibranchia*: see prec. & BRANCHIAE⟧ any of an order (Nudibranchia) of marine gastropods without a shell and with external gills —**nu′di·bran′chi·ate** (-braŋ′kē it, -āt′) *adj., n.*

☆**nud·ie** (no͞o′dē, nyo͞o′-) *n.* [Slang] a cheap film exploiting nudity and sex

nud·ism (no͞o′diz′əm, nyo͞o′-) *n.* the practice of going nude, often as a group lifestyle and typically in a private setting, as a person's home or a designated area of a beach or park —**nud′ist** *n., adj.*

nu·di·ty (no͞o′də tē, nyo͞o′-) *n.* ⟦Fr *nudité* < L *nuditas*⟧ **1** the state, quality, or fact of being nude; nakedness **2** *pl.* **-ties** a nude figure, as in art

☆**nud·nik** (nood′nik) *n.* ⟦< Yiddish < Russ *nudnyi*, tedious, tiresome < *nuda*, need, boredom (< IE *neuti- > NEED) + *-nik*, -NIK⟧ [Slang] a dull, tiresome, annoying person

Nu·e·ces (no͞o ā′sās, -səs) ⟦Sp, nuts, for the pecan trees there⟧ river in S Tex., flowing SE into the Gulf of Mexico at Corpus Christi: 315 mi (507 km)

nu·ée ar·dente (no͞o ā′är dänt′) *pl.* **nu·ées ar·dentes** (no͞o ā′zär dänt′) ⟦Fr, lit., burning cloud⟧ a thick, deadly volcanic cloud of steam, dust, ash, etc., that explodes violently, may begin to glow, and rushes down the sides of the volcano

Nu·er (no͞o′ər) *n.* **1** *pl.* **Nu′ers** or **Nu′er** a pastoral people living along the Nile in S Sudan **2** the language of this people

Nue·vo La·re·do (nwā′vô lä rā′dô) city in N Mexico, on the Rio Grande, opposite Laredo, Tex.

Nue·vo Le·ón (nwā′vô lā ôn′) state of NE Mexico: 24,925 sq mi (64,556 sq km); cap. Monterrey

nu·ga·to·ry (no͞o′gə tôr′ē, nyo͞o′-) *adj.* ⟦L *nugatorius* < pp. of *nugari*, to trifle < *nugae*, trifles⟧ **1** trifling; worthless **2** not operative; invalid

nug·get (nug′ət) *n.* ⟦prob. dim. of E dial. *nug*, a lump⟧ **1** a lump; esp., a lump of native gold **2** something small, as an item of information, that is regarded as valuable **3** a small chunk or portion, as of food

nui·sance (no͞o′səns, nyo͞o′-) *n.* ⟦ME *nusance* < OFr < *nuisir, noisir* < L *nocere*, to annoy: see NECRO-⟧ **1** an act, condition, thing, or person causing trouble, annoyance, or inconvenience **2** *Law* a use of one's property that causes danger or annoyance to others or that interferes with others using or enjoying their own property and that is subject to civil action

nuisance tax any excise tax imposed in very small amounts, esp. when considered together with other such small taxes

☆**nuke** (no͞ok, nyo͞ok) [Slang] *n.* ⟦NUC(LEAR)⟧ **1** a nuclear weapon or submarine **2** a nuclear reactor or power plant —*vt.* **nuked, nuk′ing 1** to attack with nuclear weapons **2** to cook (food) in a microwave oven: a jocular usage

Nu·ku·a·lo·fa (no͞o′ko͞o ə lô′fə) capital of Tonga

null (nul) *adj.* ⟦MFr *nul* < L *nullus*, not any, none < OL **n(e) oin(o)los*, not a one < *ne*, not (see NO[1]) + dim. of *oinos* < IE **oinos*: see ONE⟧ **1** without legal force; not binding; invalid: usually in the phrase **null and void 2** amounting to naught; nil **3** of no value, effect, or consequence; insignificant **4** *Math.* designating, of, or being zero, as *a)* having all zero elements [*null* matrix] *b)* having a limit of zero [*null* sequence] *c)* having no members whatsoever [*null* set]

nul·lah (nul′ə) *n.* ⟦Hindi *nālā*, brook, ravine⟧ in India, etc., a watercourse, esp. one that is often dry; gully

nul·li·fi·ca·tion (nul′ə fi kā′shən) *n.* ⟦LL(Ec) *nullificatio*, a despising⟧ **1** a nullifying or being nullified ☆**2** in U.S. history, the refusal of a state to recognize or enforce within its territory any federal law held to be an infringement on its sovereignty

nul·li·fid·i·an (nul′ə fid′ē ən) *n.* ⟦< L *nullus*, none + *fides*, FAITH + -IAN⟧ [Rare] a person having no religious faith

nul·li·fy (nul′ə fī′) *vt.* **-fied′, -fy′ing** ⟦LL(Ec) *nullificare*, to despise < L *nullus*, none (see NULL) + *facere*, to make, DO[1]⟧ **1** to make legally null; make void; annul **2** to make valueless or useless; bring to nothing **3** to cancel out —☆**nul′li·fi′er** *n.*

nul·lip·a·ra (nə lip′ə rə) *n., pl.* **-ras** or **-rae′** (-rē′) ⟦ModL < L *nullus*, none (see NULL) + *parere*, to bring forth, bear: see -PAROUS⟧ a woman who has never given birth —**nul·lip′a·rous** *adj.*

nul·li·pore (nul′ə pôr′) *n.* ⟦< L *nullus*, none (see NULL) + *porus*, PORE[2]⟧ any of several red-spored, coralline red algae that secrete lime

nul·li·ty (nul′ə tē) *n.* ⟦Fr *nullité* < ML *nullitas*⟧ **1** the state or fact of being null **2** *pl.* **-ties** anything that is null, as an act that has no legal force

num *abbrev.* **1** number **2** numeral(s)

Num *abbrev. Bible* Numbers

Nu·man·ti·a (no͞o man′shē ə, nyo͞o-; -shə) ancient city in what is now NC Spain: besieged & captured by Scipio the Younger (133 B.C.)

numb (num) *adj.* ⟦< ME *nome, nomen*, pp. of *nimen*, to take (with unhistoric *-b*): see -NOMY⟧ **1** weakened in or deprived of the power of feeling or moving; benumbed; deadened; insensible [*numb* with cold, *numb* with grief] **2** having the nature of numbness [a *numb* feeling] —*vt.* to make numb —**numb′ly** *adv.* —**numb′ness** *n.*

num·bat (num′bat′) *n.* ⟦< name in a language of Australia⟧ any of a family (Myrmecobiidae) of small, timid Australian marsupials that have no pouch

num·ber (num′bər) *n.* ⟦ME *nombre* < OE < L *numerus*: see -NOMY⟧ **1** *a)* a mathematical unit or value, signifying a quantity, a position in a series, etc., and expressed by a symbol or word or by a group of symbols or words *b)* a figure, letter, word, or a group of these, representing a numerical unit or value: 1, 2, 10, 101 (one, two, ten, one hundred and one) are called *cardinal numbers*; 1st, 2d, 10th, 101st (first, second, tenth, one hundred and first) are called *ordinal numbers* **2** [*pl.*] ARITHMETIC **3** the sum or total of persons or units; aggregate **4** [*with pl. v.*] a collection of persons or things; company; assemblage [a small *number* of people] **5** *a)* [*often pl.*] a large group; many [cut down *numbers* of trees] *b)* [*pl.*] numerical superiority [safety in *numbers*] ☆*c)* [*pl.*] statistics, ratings, etc. [a batter with good *numbers* against left-handers] **6** quantity, as consisting of units [a *number* of errors] **7** one of a series or group that is numbered or thought of as numbered; specif., *a)* a single issue of a periodical [the winter *number* of a quarterly] *b)* a single song, dance, skit, etc. in a program of entertainment ☆*c)* [Old Slang] a pattern of behavior or thought, esp. one regarded as somehow characteristic *d)* a person regarded as merely a unit in some group or process [a caseworker's clients are more than just *numbers*] **8** [Informal] a person or thing singled out [this hat is a cute little *number*]: see also OPPOSITE NUMBER **9** *Gram. a)* a characteristic, as of nouns and verbs, indicating whether a given utterance involves reference to one or more than one entity, or, in some languages, to exactly two; also, an analytic category based on this characteristic *b)* the form a word takes to indicate this characteristic *c)* any of the sets of such forms: see SINGULAR, DUAL NUMBER, PLURAL **10** [*pl.*] [Obs.] *a)* metrical form; meter *b)* metrical lines; verses —*vt.* ⟦ME *nombren* < OFr *nombrer* < L *numerare*, to count < *numerus*⟧ **1** to total the number of persons or things in; count; enumerate **2** to give a number to; designate by number **3** to include as one of a group, class, or category [*numbered* among the missing] **4** to have or comprise; total [a library *numbering* 10,000 volumes] —*vi.* **1** to total; count; enumerate **2** to be numbered; be included —**a number of** an unspecified number of; several or many —**beyond number** too numerous to be counted —☆**by the numbers 1** *Mil.* in prescribed sequence of movements and accompanied by a count **2** in an orderly, methodical, or mechanical way —**someone's (or something's) days are numbered** someone (or something) will not last, survive, or remain in place for much longer [we all knew that *her days* as chairman *were numbered*] —☆**do a number on** [Slang] to abuse or mistreat in some way, as by injuring, disparaging, cheating, or humiliating —☆**get (or have) someone's number** [Slang] to discover (or know) someone's true character or motives —**someone's number is up** [Slang] someone's time to die or suffer punishment has arrived —☆**the numbers** an illegal lottery in which small bets are placed on the order of certain numbers, usually the last three, in some tabulation of sports scores or financial reports published in the daily newspapers: also called **numbers game (or racket)** —**without number** too numerous to be counted —**num′ber·er** *n.*

number crunch·er (krunch′ər) [Informal] **1** a computer used for the rapid execution of many or complex calculations (**number crunching**) **2** a person, as a statistician or accountant, engaged in the processing of large amounts of numerical data

num·ber·less (num′bər lis) *adj.* **1** innumerable; countless **2** without a number or numbers

number line *Math.* a straight line, theoretically extending to infinity in both positive and negative directions from zero, that shows the relative order of the real numbers

number one 1 [Informal] oneself [he's always looking out for *number one*] ☆**2** [Informal] the first or best in quality, standing, importance, etc. **3** ⟦euphemism⟧ [Slang] urine or urination: chiefly a child's term: see also NUMBER TWO (sense 2) —**go (or make) number one** [Slang] to urinate: chiefly a child's term

Num·bers (num′bərz) *n.* ⟦transl. of Gr *Arithmoi* (see ARITHMETIC): so named in allusion to the census⟧ the fourth book of the Pentateuch in the Bible, containing the census of the Hebrews after the Exodus: abbrev. *Nb, Num, Nu*, or *Nm*

number sign a symbol (#) on a keypad or keyboard button; pound sign

number two 1 [Informal] the second in position, ranking, quality, etc. **2** ⟦euphemism⟧ [Slang] feces or defecation: chiefly a child's term: see also NUMBER ONE (sense 3) —**go (or make) number two** [Slang] to defecate: chiefly a child's term

numb·fish (num′fish′) *n., pl.* **-fish′** or **-fish′es** (see FISH) ⟦in ref. to its effect on its victims⟧ an electric ray

numb·ing (num′iŋ) *adj.* causing numbness, esp. in feeling or in mental or emotional response —**numb′ing·ly** *adv.*

num·bles (num′bəlz) *pl.n.* ⟦ME *noumbles* < OFr *nombles*, by dissimilation < L *lumbulus*, dim. of *lumbus*, loin: see LUMBAR⟧ [Obs.] the heart, lungs, etc., as of a deer, used for food: cf. HUMBLE PIE

numb·skull (num′skul′) *n.* [Informal] a stupid person; dolt; dunce

nu·men (no͞o′mən, nyo͞o′-) *n., pl.* **-mi·na** (-mi nə) ⟦L, a deity, akin to *-nuere*, to nod: see INNUENDO⟧ *Rom. Myth.* an indwelling, guiding force or spirit

nu·mer·a·ble (no͞o′mər ə bəl, nyo͞o′-) *adj.* ⟦L *numerabilis*⟧ that can be numbered or counted

nu·mer·al (no͞o′mər əl, nyo͞o′-) *adj.* ⟦LL *numeralis* < L *numerus*, NUMBER⟧ of, expressing, or denoting a number or numbers —*n.* **1** a figure or letter, or a group of figures or letters, expressing a number: see ARABIC NUMERALS, ROMAN NUMERALS **2** [*pl.*] [Chiefly Historical] a cloth representation of the graduation year of one's class, awarded for participation in sports or other activities

nu·mer·ate[1] (no͞o′mər āt′, nyo͞o′-) *vt.* **-at′ed, -at′ing** ⟦< L *numeratus*, pp. of *numerare*: see NUMBER & -ATE[1]⟧ ENUMERATE

nu·mer·ate[2] (no͞o′mər it, nyo͞o′-) *adj.* ⟦< L *numerus*, NUMBER + (LITER)ATE⟧ [Chiefly Brit.] able to understand basic mathematical concepts and perform basic operations —**nu′mer·a·cy** (-ə sē) *n.*

nu·mer·a·tion (no͞o′mər ā′shən, nyo͞o′-) *n.* ⟦ME *numeracioun* < L *numeratio* < *numerare*: see NUMBER⟧ **1** a numbering or counting; calculation **2** a system of numbering

nu·mer·a·tor (no͞o′mər āt′ər, nyo͞o′-) ***n.*** ⟦LL < L *numerare*: see NUMBER⟧ **1** a person or thing that numbers **2** *Math.* the term above or to the left of the line in a fraction [3 is the *numerator* of ¾]

nu·mer·ic (no͞o mer′ik, nyo͞o-) ***adj.*** NUMERICAL

nu·mer·i·cal (no͞o mer′i kəl, nyo͞o-) ***adj.*** **1** of, or having the nature of, number **2** in or by numbers **3** denoting (a) number **4** expressed by numbers, not by letters **5** *Math.* designating or of value regardless of sign [the *numerical* value of −3 is 3] **—nu·mer′i·cal·ly** ***adv.***

numerical taxonomy taxonomic classification into categories or units according to the degree of similarity among individuals and groups, based on numerical analysis of large samples of characteristics that are each given equal value

nu·mer·ol·o·gy (no͞o′mər äl′ə jē, nyo͞o′-) ***n.*** ⟦< L *numerus*, NUMBER + -LOGY⟧ divination by numbers, often, specif., by numbers derived from alphabetic letters, from names, or from words in a text

nu·me·ro u·no (no͞o′mer ō o͞o′nō) ⟦Sp *número uno* & It *numero uno*, number one⟧ [Informal] the very best or the most important one

nu·mer·ous (no͞o′mər əs, nyo͞o′-) ***adj.*** ⟦L *numerosus* < *numerus*, NUMBER⟧ **1** consisting of many persons or things [a *numerous* collection] **2** very many **—nu′mer·ous·ly** ***adv.*** **—nu′mer·ous·ness** ***n.***

Nu·mid·i·a (no͞o mid′ē ə, nyo͞o-) ⟦L < *Numidae*, the Numidians, pl. of *numida*, a nomad < Gr *nomada*, acc. of *nomas*, NOMAD⟧ ancient country in N Africa, mainly in what is now E Algeria

Nu·mid·i·an (-ən) ***n.*** **1** a person born or living in Numidia **2** the language of old Berber inscriptions from this area ***—adj.*** of the Numidians or their language or culture

Numidian crane DEMOISELLE (sense 2)

nu·mi·nous (no͞o′mə nəs, nyo͞o′-) ***adj.*** ⟦< L *numen* (gen. *numinis*), a deity (see NUMEN) + -OUS⟧ **1** of or characteristic of a numen; supernatural; divine **2** having a deeply spiritual or mystical effect

nu·mis·mat·ic (no͞o′miz mat′ik, nyo͞o′-; -mis-) ***adj.*** ⟦Fr *numismatique* < L *numisma* (gen. *numismatis*), a coin < Gr *nomisma*, a coin, lit., what is sanctioned by law < *nomizein*, to sanction < *nomos*, law: see -NOMY⟧ **1** of coins, medals, or tokens **2** of or having to do with currency **3** of numismatics **—nu′mis·mat′i·cal·ly** ***adv.***

nu·mis·mat·ics (-iks) ***n.*** ⟦see prec.⟧ the study or collection of coins, medals, tokens, paper money, etc. **—nu·mis·ma·tist** (no͞o miz′mə tist, nyo͞o-; -mis′-) ***n.***

num·mu·lar (num′yo͞o lər) ***adj.*** ⟦L *nummularius* < *nummulus*, dim. of *nummus*, a coin < Gr *nomimos*, legal < *nomos*: see -NOMY⟧ coin-shaped; circular or oval

num·mu·lite (num′yo͞o līt′) ***n.*** ⟦< L *nummus*, a coin (see prec.) + -LITE⟧ any of a genus (*Nummulites*) of nearly extinct foraminifera with a somewhat disk-shaped shell **—num′mu·lit′ic** (-lit′ik) ***adj.***

num·skull (num′skul′) ***n.*** [Informal] *alt. sp. of* NUMBSKULL

nun¹ (nun) ***n.*** ⟦ME *nunne* < OE < LL(Ec) *nonna*, nun, orig., child's nurse: like Gr *nanna*, aunt, Sans *nanā*, mother, ult. < baby talk⟧ **1** a member of a women's religious order, esp. of one living under a common rule and taking vows of poverty, chastity, and obedience **2** any of various birds; esp., any of a domesticated breed of pigeon

nun² (no͞on, no͝on) ***n.*** ⟦Heb *nūn*, lit., fish⟧ the fourteenth letter of the Hebrew alphabet (נ, ן)

nun·a·tak (nun′ə tak′, no͞o′nə-) ***n.*** ⟦prob. via Dan < Esk⟧ *Geol.* an isolated mountain peak protruding through glacial ice

Nu·na·vut (no͞o′nə vo͞ot′) territory of N Canada: 746,048 sq mi (1,932,255 sq km); cap. Iqaluit: abbrev. *NU* or *Nvt*

Nunc Di·mit·tis (no͝oŋk′ di mit′is) ⟦L, now thou lettest depart: first words of the L version⟧ **1** the song of Simeon, used as a canticle in various liturgies: Luke 2:29-32 **2** [**n- d-**] *a)* departure or farewell, esp. from life *b)* permission to depart; dismissal

nun·cha·ku (nun chä′ko͞o) ***n.***, *pl.* **-kus** or **-ku** ⟦Jpn (Okinawan dialect)⟧ [*also pl.*] a martial-arts weapon consisting of a pair of wooden sticks joined lengthwise by a short cord, chain, etc.: also **nun′chuks′** (-chuks′) ***pl.n.*** or **nun′chucks′** (-chuks′)

nun·ci·a·ture (nun′shē ə chər, -sē-) ***n.*** ⟦It *nunziatura*⟧ the office or term of office of a nuncio

nun·ci·o (nun′shō′, -shē ō′; -sē ō′; no͞on′tsē ō′) ***n.***, *pl.* **-ci·os′** ⟦It *nuncio*, *nunzio* < L *nuntius*, messenger⟧ a prelate officially representing the pope and accredited to a foreign government

nun·cle (nuŋ′kəl) ***n.*** ⟦prob. < *(a)n uncle* or *(mi)n(e) uncle*⟧ *Brit. dial. or obs. var. of* UNCLE

nun·cu·pa·tive (nuŋ′kyo͞o pāt′iv, nun kyo͞o′pə tiv) ***adj.*** ⟦LL *nuncupativus*, so-called, nominal < L *nuncupare*, to name before witnesses as one's heir < *nomen*, NAME + *capere*, to take: see HAVE⟧ *Law* oral, not written: said esp. of wills

nun·na·tion (nu nā′shən) ***n.*** ⟦ModL *nunnatio* < Ar *nūn*, the letter *n*⟧ the addition of final *n* to a word, as in the declension of certain Arabic nouns

nun·ner·y (nun′ər ē) ***n.***, *pl.* **-ner·ies** ⟦ME *nonnerie*: see NUN¹ & -ERY⟧ *former term for* CONVENT **—*SYN.*** CLOISTER

nuoc mam (nwôk mäm′) ⟦Vietnamese⟧ [*also in italics*] a pungent, salty sauce made from fermented fish, used in Vietnamese cooking

nup·tial (nup′shəl, -chəl; *also*, -shə wəl, -chə wəl) ***adj.*** ⟦LME *nupcyalle* < L *nuptialis* < *nuptiae*, marriage < *nuptus*, pp. of *nubere*, to marry: see NUBILE⟧ **1** of marriage or a wedding **2** of or having to do with mating ***—n.*** [*pl.*] a wedding; marriage

Nur·em·berg (no͝or′əm burg′, nyo͝or′-) city in SE Germany, in the state of Bavaria: site of war-crime trials of Nazi officials, held after WWII: Ger. name **Nürn·berg** (nürn′berk′)

Nu·re·yev (no͞o rā′yef), **Rudolf (Hametovich)** 1938-93; ballet dancer, born in the Soviet Union

nurse (nurs) ***n.*** ⟦ME *norse* < OFr *norice* < LL *nutricia* < L *nutricius*, that suckles or nourishes < *nutrix* (gen. *nutricis*), wet nurse < *nutrire*, to nourish < IE **(s)neu-*, var. of base **(s)nā-*, to flow > NATANT, Sans *snāuti*, (she) gives milk, Gr *naein*, to flow⟧ **1** WET NURSE **2** a woman hired to take full care of another's young child or children; nursemaid **3** a person trained to take care of the sick, injured, or aged, to assist surgeons, etc.; specif., a registered nurse or a practical nurse **4** a person or thing that nourishes, fosters, protects, etc. **5** *Zool.* a worker bee or ant that cares for the young ***—vt.*** **nursed**, **nurs′ing** **1** to give milk from the breast to (an infant); suckle **2** to suck milk from the breast of **3** to take care of (a child or children) **4** to bring up; rear **5** to tend (the sick, injured, or aged) **6** to cause to continue, grow, or develop; nourish or foster [to *nurse* a grudge] **7** to treat, or try to cure [to *nurse* a cold] **8** *a)* to use, operate, or handle cautiously or carefully, so as to avoid injury, pain, exhaustion, etc. [to *nurse* an injured leg] *b)* to consume, spend, etc. slowly or carefully so as to conserve [to *nurse* a highball] **9** to clasp; hold carefully; fondle **10** *Billiards* to keep (the balls) close together for a series of caroms ***—vi.*** **1** to be suckled; feed at the breast **2** to suckle a child **3** to tend the sick, injured, etc. as a nurse **—nurs′er** ***n.***

nurse·maid (nurs′mād′) ***n.*** [Old-fashioned] a woman hired to take care of a child or children; nanny: also [Archaic] **nurs′er·y·maid′**

nurse practitioner a registered nurse who has additional training and expertise in certain medical practices, therapies, etc.

nurs·er·y (nur′sə rē, nurs′rē) ***n.***, *pl.* **-er·ies** ⟦ME *norcery*: see NURSE⟧ **1** *a)* an infant's bedroom *b)* a room or apartment in a home, set apart for the children as a playroom, study, dining room, etc. **2** a place where parents may temporarily leave children with trained attendants; specif., *a)* NURSERY SCHOOL *b)* DAY NURSERY **3** a place where young trees or other plants are raised for experimental purposes, for transplanting, or for sale **4** anything that nourishes, protects, develops, or fosters

nurs·er·y·man (-mən) ***n.***, *pl.* **-men** (-mən) a person who owns, operates, or works for a nursery for growing and transplanting trees, shrubs, etc.

nursery rhyme a short, rhymed, usually traditional poem for children

nursery school PRESCHOOL

nurse's aide *pl.* **nurses' aides** or **nurses aides** a nursing assistant, as in a hospital or nursing home, who takes care of the basic needs of patients, including bathing, feeding, taking temperatures, etc.: sometimes sp. **nurse's aid**

nurs·ing (nur′siŋ) ***n.*** **1** the duties or profession of a nurse **2** the medical care given by a nurse

nursing bottle a bottle with a rubber nipple, for feeding liquids to babies

nursing home **1** a residence equipped and staffed to provide care for the infirm, chronically ill, disabled, etc. **2** [Chiefly Brit.] a small private hospital

nurs·ling (nurs′liŋ) ***n.*** **1** a young baby still being breast-fed **2** anything that is being carefully tended or cared for Also **nurse′ling**

nur·ture (nur′chər) ***n.*** ⟦ME < OFr *norreture* < LL *nutritura*, pp. of L *nutrire*, to nourish: see NURSE⟧ **1** anything that nourishes; food; nutriment **2** the act or process of raising or promoting the development of; training, educating, fostering, etc.: also **nur′tur·ance** **3** all the environmental factors, collectively, to which one is subjected from conception onward, as distinguished from one's nature or heredity ***—vt.*** **-tured**, **-tur·ing** **1** to feed or nourish **2** *a)* to promote the development of *b)* to raise by educating, training, etc. **—nur′tur·ant** ***adj.*** **—nur′tur·er** ***n.***

nut (nut) ***n.*** ⟦ME *nutte* < OE *hnutu*, akin to Ger *nuss* < IE **kneu-*, lump, nut (< base **ken-*, to squeeze together) > L *nux*, MIr *cnū*⟧ **1** the dry, one-seeded fruit of any of various trees or shrubs, consisting of a kernel, often edible, in a hard and woody or tough and leathery shell, more or less separable from the seed itself, as the walnut, pecan, chestnut, acorn, etc. **2** the kernel, or meat, of such a fruit **3** loosely, any hard-shell fruit that will keep more or less indefinitely, as a peanut, almond, etc. **4** a small block, usually of metal, with a threaded hole through the center, for screwing onto a bolt, screw, etc. **5** *a)* a ridge of ebony or other hard material at the top of the fingerboard of a stringed instrument, over which the strings pass *b)* the small knob at the end of a violin bow, for tightening or loosening the hairs **6** [Informal] the initial cost of an undertaking, or the amount of money it is necessary to take in before a profit is realized on it **7** [Informal] *a)* a foolish, crazy, or eccentric person *b)* a devotee; fan **8** [Slang] *a)* the head *b)* [*pl.*] the testicles (a somewhat vulgar usage) See also NUTS ***—vi.*** **nut′ted**, **nut′ting** to hunt for or gather nuts **—hard (or tough) nut to crack** a person, problem, or thing difficult to understand or deal with **—off one's nut** [Slang] foolish, silly, or crazy

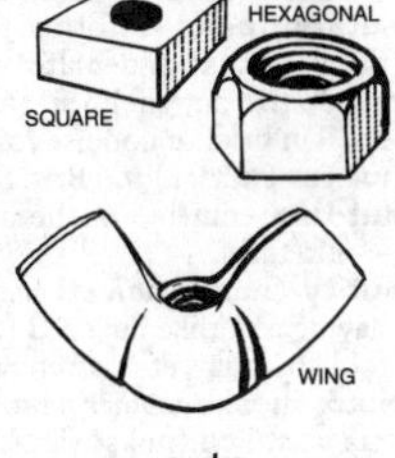

nuts

nu·tant (no͞o′tənt, nyo͞o′-) ***adj.*** ⟦L *nutans*, prp. of *nutare*, to nod, freq. of *nuere*: for IE base see NUDGE¹⟧ with the top bent downward; drooping; nodding: said of plants

nu·ta·tion (no͞o tā′shən, nyo͞o-) ***n.*** ⟦L *nutatio* < *nutare*, to nod: see prec.⟧ **1**

Med. the act or an instance of nodding the head, esp. when involuntary 2 *a)* a periodic variation in the inclination from the vertical of the rotation axis of a spinning body, as a top *b) Astron.* such a small, periodic oscillation of the earth's axis, that slightly varies or nods the earth's precessional motion 3 *Bot.* a slight rotatory movement, as in the stem of a plant, due to the varying rates of growth in its parts —**nu·ta′tion·al** ***adj.***

nut-brown (nut′broun′) ***adj.*** dark-brown, like some ripe nuts

☆**nut case** [Slang] one who is eccentric or crazy: also written **nut′case′** ***n.***

nut·crack·er (nut′krak′ər) ***n.*** 1 an instrument for cracking the shells of nuts, usually consisting of two hinged metal levers, between which the nut is squeezed 2 either of two jaylike corvid birds that feed on nuts; specif., *a)* a white-spotted, dark-brown bird (*Nucifraga caryocatactes*) of Europe *b)* the grayish **Clark's nutcracker** (*N. columbiana*) of W North America

nut·gall (nut′gôl′) ***n.*** a small, nut-shaped gall on the oak and certain other trees

nut·hatch (nut′hach′) ***n.*** ⟦ME *notehach* < *note, nutte,* NUT + **hache* < *hacken,* HACK[1]⟧ any of various small passerine birds (family Sittidae) with a sharp beak and a short tail: they typically search for insects by moving down tree trunks headfirst

nut·house (nut′hous′) ***n.*** [Slang] an institution for hospitalizing the mentally ill

nut·let (nut′lit) ***n.*** 1 a small nut or nutlike fruit 2 the pit, or stone, of a cherry, peach, plum, etc. 3 any of the segments of an ovary which splits into parts, as in plants of the borage and mint families

nut·meat (nut′mēt′) ***n.*** the kernel of a nut, esp. if edible

nut·meg (nut′meg′) ***n.*** ⟦ME *notemygge,* partial transl. of OFr *nois muguete* < Prov *noiz muscade,* lit., musky nut < L *nux,* NUT + LL *muscus,* MUSK⟧ 1 the hard, aromatic seed of an East Indian tree (*Myristica fragrans*) of the nutmeg family: it is grated and used as a spice, and its outer covering yields the spice mace 2 the tree itself —***adj.*** designating a family (Myristicaceae, order Magnoliales) of tropical, dicotyledonous trees

☆**nut·pick** (nut′pik′) ***n.*** a small, sharp instrument for digging out the kernels of cracked nuts

☆**nut pine** any of several pines, esp. a pinyon, with edible seeds

☆**nu·tri·a** (no͞o′trē ə, nyo͞o′-) ***n.*** ⟦Sp < L *lutra,* otter, altered (with *l-* after *lutum,* mire) < IE **udros,* water animal: see OTTER⟧ 1 the only member (*Myocastor coypus*) of a family (Myocastoridae) of South American water-dwelling rodents with webbed feet and a long, almost hairless tail; coypu 2 its short-haired, soft, brown fur, often dyed to look like beaver

nu·tri·ent (no͞o′trē ənt, nyo͞o′-) ***adj.*** ⟦L *nutriens,* prp. of *nutrire,* to nourish: see NURSE⟧ nutritious; nourishing —***n.*** a nutritious substance in a food

nu·tri·ment (no͞o′trə mənt, nyo͞o′-) ***n.*** ⟦L *nutrimentum* < *nutrire,* to nourish: see NURSE⟧ 1 anything that nourishes; food 2 anything that promotes growth, development, or good health

nu·tri·tion (no͞o trish′ən, nyo͞o-) ***n.*** ⟦MFr < L *nutritio, nutricio* < *nutrix,* NURSE⟧ 1 a nourishing or being nourished; esp., the series of processes by which an organism takes in and assimilates food for promoting growth and replacing worn or injured tissues 2 anything that nourishes; nourishment; food 3 the science or study of proper, balanced diet to promote health, esp. in human beings —**nu·tri′tion·al** ***adj.*** —**nu·tri′tion·al·ly** ***adv.***

nu·tri·tion·ist (-ist) ***n.*** a specialist in nutrition

nu·tri·tious (no͞o trish′əs, nyo͞o-) ***adj.*** ⟦L *nutricius:* see NURSE⟧ nourishing; of value as food —**nu·tri′tious·ly** ***adv.*** —**nu·tri′tious·ness** ***n.***

nu·tri·tive (no͞o′trə tiv, nyo͞o′-) ***adj.*** ⟦ME *nutritiff* < OFr *nutritif* < ML *nutritivus*⟧ 1 having to do with nutrition 2 promoting nutrition; nutritious —**nu′tri·tive·ly** ***adv.***

nuts (nuts) [Slang] ***adj.*** ⟦see NUT, *n.* 7 & 8⟧ ☆crazy; foolish —☆***interj.*** used to express disgust, scorn, disappointment, refusal, etc.: often in the phrase **nuts to someone (or something)** —**be nuts about** 1 to be greatly in love with 2 to be very enthusiastic about

nuts and bolts [Informal] the basic elements or practical aspects of something —**nuts′-and-bolts′** ***adj.***

nut·shell (nut′shel′) ***n.*** the shell enclosing the kernel of a nut —**in a nutshell** in brief or concise form; in a few words

nut·ter (nut′ər) ***n.*** [Brit. Slang] NUT (*n.* 7*a*)

nut·ting (nut′iŋ) ***n.*** the act or process of hunting for or gathering nuts —**nut′ter** ***n.***

nut·ty (nut′ē) ***adj.*** **-ti·er, -ti·est** 1 containing or producing many nuts 2 having a nutlike flavor 3 [Slang] *a)* enthusiastic, often to excess *b)* odd, foolish, crazy, etc.: often **nut·sy** (nut′sē) —**nut′ti·ly** ***adv.*** —**nut′ti·ness** ***n.***

Nuuk (no͞ok) *another name for* GODTHÅB

nux vom·i·ca (nuks′ väm′i kə) ⟦ML < L *nux,* NUT + *vomere,* to VOMIT⟧ 1 the poisonous, disklike seed of an Asian tree (*Strychnos nux-vomica*) of the logania family, containing strychnine, brucine, and other alkaloids 2 the tree bearing these seeds 3 a medicine made from the seed, formerly used as a heart stimulant

nuz·zle (nuz′əl) ***vt.*** **-zled, -zling** ⟦ME *noselen* < *nose,* NOSE + freq. *-elen*⟧ 1 to push against or rub with the nose, snout, muzzle, etc. 2 to root up with the nose or snout: said of a pig, etc. —***vi.*** 1 to push or rub with the nose, etc. against or into something 2 to lie close; nestle; snuggle —**nuz′zler** ***n.***

NV *abbrev.* 1 Nevada 2 ⟦Du *Naamloze Vennootschap,* lit., unnamed partnership⟧ public limited liability company or corporation: a legal entity in the Netherlands and certain other countries

Nvt *abbrev.* Nunavut

NW *abbrev.* 1 northwest 2 northwestern

NWbN *abbrev.* northwest by north

NWbW *abbrev.* northwest by west

N-word (en′wurd′), **the** [Informal] the word NIGGER: a euphemism

NWS *abbrev.* National Weather Service

NWT or **NWTer** *abbrev.* Northwest Territories (Canada): also **N.W.T.**

NY or **N.Y.** *abbrev.* New York

nya·la (nyä′lə) ***n.,*** *pl.* **-la** or **-las** ⟦< name in a language of eastern Africa⟧ any of several antelopes (genus *Tragelaphus*) of E Africa, with large, spiral horns

Nya·sa (nyä′sä, nī as′ə), **Lake** *another name for* Lake MALAWI

Nya·sa·land (-land′) *former name for* MALAWI

NYC or **N.Y.C.** *abbrev.* New York City

nyc·ta·lo·pi·a (nik′tə lō′pē ə) ***n.*** ⟦LL < Gr *nyktalōps* < *nyx* (gen. *nyktos*), NIGHT + *alaos,* blind (< *a-,* not + *laein,* to see) + *ōps,* EYE⟧ NIGHT BLINDNESS: cf. HEMERALOPIA —**nyc′ta·lop′ic** (-läp′ik) ***adj.***

nyc·ti- (nik′ti, -tə) ⟦< Gr *nyx* (gen. *nyktos*), NIGHT⟧ *combining form* night [*nyctitropism*]: also, before a vowel, **nyct-**

nyc·ti·tro·pism (nik ti′trə piz′əm) ***n.*** ⟦prec. + -TROPISM⟧ the tendency of the leaves or petals of certain plants to assume a different position at night —**nyc′ti·trop′ic** (-träp′ik) ***adj.***

nyc·to- (nik′tō, -tə) *combining form* NYCTI- [*nyctophobia*]

nyc·to·pho·bi·a (nik′tə fō′bē ə) ***n.*** ⟦prec. + -PHOBIA⟧ an unnatural or excessive fear of darkness or night —**nyc′to·pho′bic** ***adj.***

Nye (nī), **Edgar Wilson** (pseud. *Bill Nye*) 1850-96; U.S. humorist

nyet (nyet) ***adv., interj.*** ⟦Russ *net*⟧ no

nyl·ghai (nil′gī′) ***n.*** *alt. sp. of* NILGAI

☆**ny·lon** (nī′län′) ***n.*** ⟦arbitrary coinage, infl. by (COTT)ON and (RAY)ON⟧ 1 any of a group of synthetic, long-chain polymeric amides with recurring amide groups, made into fiber, yarn, bristles, sheets, molded plastics, etc. that have great strength and elasticity 2 *a)* any of the materials made from nylon *b)* [*pl.*] stockings or pantyhose of nylon fabric

nymph (nimf) ***n.*** ⟦ME *nimphe* < OFr < L *nympha* < Gr *nymphē,* young wife, spring goddess, hence (poetically) water: see NUBILE⟧ 1 *Class. Myth.* any of a group of minor nature goddesses, represented as young and beautiful and living in rivers, mountains, or trees 2 *a)* a lovely young woman *b)* a young woman; maiden: literary or playful usage 3 *Entomology* the young of an insect with incomplete metamorphosis, differing from the adult primarily in size and structural proportions —**nymph′al** ***adj.,*** **nymph′e·an**

nym·pha·lid (nim′fə lid) ***n.*** ⟦< ModL *Nymphalidae* < Gr *nymphē,* nymph: see NUBILE⟧ any of a family (Nymphalidae) of brightly colored butterflies, including the monarch and viceroy, with very short forelegs

nymph·et (nim′fət, nim fet′) ***n.*** ⟦Fr *nymphette,* dim. of *nymphe:* see NYMPH⟧ 1 [Old Poet.] a young or small nymph ☆2 ⟦used in this sense by V. NABOKOV in his novel *Lolita* (1955)⟧ a pubescent girl, esp. one who is sexually precocious —**nym·phet′ic** ***adj.***

nym·pho (nim′fō) ***adj., n.,*** *pl.* **-phos** [Slang] *short for* NYMPHOMANIAC

nym·pho·lep·sy (nim′fō lep′sē, -fə-) ***n.*** ⟦< Gr *nympholēptos,* seized by nymphs (< *nymphē* + *-lēptos,* seized < *lambanein,* to seize, assume: see LEMMA[1]), infl. by EPILEPSY⟧ 1 in ancient times, a state of frenzy that was believed to seize any man who looked at a nymph 2 a violent emotional state arising as from frustrated idealism —**nym′pho·lept′** ***n.***

nym·pho·ma·ni·a (nim′fō mā′nē ə, -fə-; -mān′yə) ***n.*** ⟦ModL < Gr *nymphē,* bride + -MANIA⟧ excessive and uncontrollable desire by a woman for sexual intercourse: cf. SATYRIASIS —**nym′pho·ma′ni·ac′** (-mā′nē ak′) ***adj., n.***

Ny·norsk (nē nôrsk′) ***n.*** ⟦Norw < *ny,* new + *norsk,* Norwegian⟧ the newer of the two standard varieties of Norwegian, created in the mid-1800s and based on dialects of the language as spoken in rural areas: cf. BOKMÅL

NYSE *service mark* New York Stock Exchange

nys·tag·mus (ni stag′məs) ***n.*** ⟦ModL < Gr *nystagmos,* drowsiness < *nystazein,* to be sleepy < IE base **sneud-,* to sleep⟧ involuntary, rapid movement of the eyeball, usually from side to side

nys·ta·tin (nis′tə tin) ***n.*** ⟦*N(ew) Y(ork) Stat(e),* where it was developed + -IN[1]⟧ an antibiotic, $C_{46}H_{77}NO_{19}$, used for treating fungal infections, as candidiasis

Nyx (niks) ***n.*** ⟦Gr, NIGHT⟧ *Gr. Myth.* night personified as a goddess: identified with the Roman Nox

NZ or **N Zeal** *abbrev.* New Zealand

o[1] or **O** (ō) ***n.***, *pl.* **o's, O's 1** the fifteenth letter of the English alphabet: from the Greek *omega* and *omicron,* both borrowed from the Phoenician **2** any of the speech sounds that this letter represents, as, in English, the vowel (ō) of *boat,* (ä) of *hot,* or (ô) of *wrong* **3** a type or impression for *o* or O **4** the fifteenth in a sequence or group **5** an object shaped like O —***adj.* 1** of *o* or O **2** fifteenth in a sequence or group **3** shaped like O; circular or oval in shape

o[2] *abbrev.* **1** octavo **2** old **3** only

O[1] (ō) ***n.***, *pl.* **O's 1** popularly, the figure zero; nought: in printed matter, zero is usually differentiated from the letter O, as in this dictionary: "O" is the character used for the letter, "0" is the character used for the number **2** a blood type: see ABO SYSTEM

O[2] (ō) ***interj.* 1** used in direct address *[O Lord!]* **2** used to express surprise, wonder, fear, pain, etc.: now usually *oh* **3** used at the end of a line in some ballads —***n.***, *pl.* **O's** an instance of this exclamation

USAGE—O and *oh* are now often interchangeable

O[3] *abbrev.* **1** Ocean **2** October **3** Ohio **4** *Physics* ohm(s) **5** *Linguis.* Old [OFr] **6** Ontario **7** *Baseball* out(s) **8** ⟦L *octarius*⟧ *Pharmacy* pint

O[4] *Chem. symbol for* oxygen

o' (ō, ə) ***prep.*** *short for* OF[1] *[will-o'-the-wisp]*

o- *prefix* ORTHO- (sense 4*b*): usually italicized and hyphenated in chemical names

-o (ō) ⟦clipped < words ending in *-o* (e.g. HIPPO, STENO, GRINGO)⟧ *suffix* **1** forming slangy, intensive counterparts of adjectives, nouns, and interjections *[cheapo, freako]* **2** forming slang nouns from adjectives *[weirdo, sicko]*

-o- (ō, ä, ə) *infix* forming compound words: a connective vowel originally used for combining Greek elements only, but now used freely *[sadomasochism, meritocracy]*

O'- (ō) ⟦Ir ō, descendant⟧ *prefix* descendant of: used in Irish surnames *[O'Reilly]*

oaf (ōf) ***n.*** ⟦earlier *auf, ouphe* < ON *alfr,* ELF⟧ **1** [Obs.] CHANGELING (sense 1) **2** a stupid person; specif., a stupid, clumsy fellow; lout —**oaf′ish *adj.*** —**oaf′ish·ly *adv.***

O·a·hu (ō ä′hōō) ⟦Haw⟧ chief island of the Hawaiian Islands: 600 sq mi (1,554 sq km); chief city, Honolulu

oak (ōk) ***n.*** ⟦ME *oke* < OE *ac,* akin to Ger *eiche* < IE base **aig-,* oak > Gr *aigilōps,* a kind of oak⟧ **1** any of a genus (Quercus) of large hardwood trees and bushes of the beech family, bearing acorns **2** the wood of an oak **3** any of various plants with oaklike leaves **4** a wreath of oak leaves **5** woodwork, furniture, etc. made of oak —***adj.*** of oak; oaken

oak apple an applelike gall on oak trees

oak·en (ō′kən) ***adj.*** made of the wood of the oak

Oak·land (ōk′lənd) ⟦after the *oak* groves orig. there⟧ seaport in W Calif., on San Francisco Bay, opposite San Francisco

☆**oak-leaf cluster** (ōk′lēf′) a small, bronze cluster of oak leaves and acorns awarded to the holder of a U.S. Army or Air Force decoration for each new award of that decoration: a silver cluster equals five bronze clusters

Oak·ley (ōk′lē), **Ann·ie** (an′ē) (born *Phoebe Anne Moses*) 1860-1926; U.S. sharpshooter in Buffalo Bill's Wild West Show

Oak Ridge ⟦see OAK LAWN⟧ city in E Tenn., near Knoxville: center for atomic research

oa·kum (ō′kəm) ***n.*** ⟦ME *okom* < OE *acumba,* tow, oakum < *a-,* away, out + *camb,* COMB[1]: lit., what is combed out⟧ loose, stringy hemp fiber gotten by taking apart old ropes and treated as with tar, used as a caulking material

Oak·ville (ōk′vil) ⟦named for an *oak* stave industry there⟧ town in SE Ontario, Canada, on Lake Ontario, near Toronto

☆**oak wilt** a disease of oaks which plugs the vessels of the wood and makes the leaves wilt, caused by an ascomycetous fungus (*Ceratocystis fagacearum*)

oak·y (ō′kē) ***adj.*** tasting of oak sap from the barrel in which it was aged: said of wine, esp. chardonnay

oar (ôr) ***n.*** ⟦ME *ore* < OE *ar,* akin to ON < IE **oyer-,* rudder pole < base **ei-,* **oi-,* pole, rod > Gr *oiēion,* rudder⟧ **1** a long pole with a broad blade at one end, held in place by an oarlock and used in pairs to row a boat: a single oar is sometimes used in steering a boat **2** a person who uses an oar; rower —***vt., vi.*** to row —**put one's oar in** to meddle —**rest on one's oars** to stop to rest or relax, as from satisfaction over past achievements

oared (ôrd) ***adj.*** equipped with oars: often used in hyphenated compounds *[two-oared]*

oar·fish (ôr′fish′) ***n.***, *pl.* **-fish′** or **-fish′es** (see FISH) any of a family (Regalecidae, order Lampriformes) of large, long, narrow, deep-sea bony fishes having a fin along the length of the back and a manelike crest behind the head: some reach a length of 9m (*c.* 29.5 ft) and are responsible for many reports of sea serpents

oar·lock (ôr′läk′) ***n.*** a device, often U-shaped, for holding an oar in place in rowing

oars·man (ôrz′mən) ***n.***, *pl.* **-men** (-mən) a person who rows, esp. one who rows a racing shell —**oars′man·ship′ *n.***

oars·wom·an (ôrz′woom′ən) ***n.***, *pl.* **-wom′en** (-wim′in) a woman or girl oarsman

OAS *abbrev.* Organization of American States

o·a·sis (ō ā′sis) ***n.***, *pl.* **-ses′** (-sēz′) ⟦L < Gr, fertile spot: orig. Coptic⟧ **1** a fertile place in a desert, due to the presence of water **2** any place or thing offering welcome relief as from difficulty or dullness

oast (ōst) ***n.*** ⟦ME *ost* < OE *ast* < Gmc **aist-* < IE base **ai-dh-,* to burn > EDIFY⟧ a kiln for drying hops, malt, or tobacco

oat (ōt) ***n.*** ⟦ME *ote* < OE *ate:* not found in other Gmc languages: prob. < IE base **oid-,* to swell⟧ **1** *[usually pl.]* *a)* a hardy, widely grown cereal grass (*Avena sativa*) *b)* the edible grain of this grass **2** any of various related grasses (genus *Avena*), esp. the wild oats **3** [Obs.] a simple musical pipe made of an oat stalk —☆**feel one's oats** [Slang] **1** to be in high spirits; be frisky **2** to feel and act important

oat·cake (ōt′kāk′) ***n.*** a thin, flat cake made of oatmeal

oat·en (ōt′'n) ***adj.*** of or made of oats, oatmeal, or oat straw

oat·er (ōt′ər) ***n.*** ⟦from *oats* fed to horses⟧ [Slang] WESTERN (*n.* 2)

Oates (ōts), **Titus** 1649-1705; Eng. fabricator of the Popish Plot, a supposed Rom. Catholic plot (1678) to massacre Protestants, burn London, and kill the king

oat grass any of various oatlike grasses; esp., any of several grasses (genera *Arrhenatherum* and *Danthonia*) growing on hillsides and in woods

oath (ōth) ***n.***, *pl.* **oaths** (ōthz, ōths) ⟦ME *oth* < OE *ath,* akin to Ger *eid,* prob. via Celt < IE **oitos* (> OIr *ōeth*) < base **ei-,* to go (basic sense: ? "to advance to take an oath") > YEAR, L *ire,* to go⟧ **1** *a)* a ritualistic declaration, typically based on an appeal to God or a god or to some revered person or object, that one will speak the truth, keep a promise, remain faithful, etc. *b)* the ritual form used in making such a declaration *c)* the thing promised or declared in this way **2** the irreverent or profane use of the name of God or of a sacred thing to express anger or emphasize a statement **3** a swearword; curse —**take oath** to promise or declare by making an oath; swear solemnly —**under** (or **on**) **oath** bound or obligated by having made a formal oath, as in a court of law

oat·meal (ōt′mēl′) ***n.* 1** oats ground or rolled into meal or flakes **2** a porridge made from such oats

OAU *abbrev.* Organization of African Unity: replaced in 2002 by African Union (AU)

Oa·xa·ca (wä hä′kä) **1** state of SE Mexico: 36,820 sq mi (95,363 sq km) **2** its capital: in full **Oaxaca de Juárez**

Ob[1] (ōb; *Russ* ôb′y′) **1** river in W Siberia, flowing from the Altai Mountains northwest & north into the Gulf of Ob: 2,495 mi (4,015 km) **2 Gulf of** arm of the Kara Sea, in NW Siberia: *c.* 600 mi (966 km) long

Ob[2] *abbrev. Bible* Obadiah

OB *abbrev.* **1** obstetrician **2** obstetrics

ob. *abbrev.* **1** ⟦L *obiit*⟧ he (or she) died **2** ⟦L *obiter*⟧ in passing; incidentally

ob- (äb, əb) ⟦< L *ob,* toward, for, about, before < IE base **epi-,* **opi-,* near, at, toward, after > Gr *epi*⟧ *prefix* **1** to, toward, before, in front of *[obtrude]* **2** opposed to, against *[obstinate]* **3** upon, over *[obscure]* **4** completely, totally *[obdurate]* **5** inversely, oppositely *[obovoid]* In words of Latin origin it becomes *oc-* before *c; of-* before *f; o-* before *m;* and *op-* before *p*

Obad *abbrev. Bible* Obadiah

O·ba·di·ah (ō′bə dī′ə) ***n.*** ⟦ult. < Heb *'ōbhadhyāh,* lit., servant of the Lord⟧ **1** a masculine name **2** *a)* *Bible* a Hebrew prophet *b)* the book of his prophecies (abbrev. *Ob* or *Obad*)

O·bam·a (ō bä′mə), **Ba·rack** (bə räk′) (born *Barack Hussein Obama II*) 1961- ; 44th president of the U.S. (2009-)

obb *abbrev.* obbligato

ob·bli·ga·to (äb′li gät′ō) [*also in italics*] *Music* ***adj.*** ⟦It, lit., obliged < L *obligatus,* pp. of *obligare:* see OBLIGE⟧ not to be left out; indispensable: said earlier, generally prior to the 19th cent., of an accompaniment essential to the proper performance of a piece, but now usually of one that can be omitted if necessary: often used as a musical direction —***n.***, *pl.* **-tos** or **-ti** (-ē) **1** an obbligato accompaniment **2** an added melody, usually played by a solo instrument as accompaniment to a vocal performance

ob·con·ic (äb kän′ik) ***adj.*** ⟦OB- + CONIC⟧ *Bot.* conical but attached by the point: also **ob·con′i·cal** (-kän′i kəl)

ob·cor·date (äb kôr′dāt) ***adj.*** ⟦OB- + CORDATE⟧ *Bot.* heart-shaped and joined to the stem at the apex: said of certain leaves

ob·du·rate (äb′door it, -dyoor-) ***adj.*** ⟦ME < L *obduratus,* pp. of *obdurare,* to harden < *ob-,* intens. (see OB-) + *durare,* to harden < *durus,* hard: see DURESS⟧ **1** not easily moved to pity or sympathy; hardhearted **2** hardened and unrepenting; impenitent **3** not giving in readily; stubborn; obstinate; inflexible —*SYN.* INFLEXIBLE —**ob′du·ra·cy** (-ə sē) ***n.*** —**ob′du·rate·ly** ***adv.***

O.B.E. *abbrev.* Officer of (the Order of) the British Empire: sometimes **OBE**

☆**o·be·ah** (ō′bē ə) ***n.*** ⟦of WAfr orig.⟧ [*often* **O-**] a form of religious practice involving magic or witchcraft, that originated in W Africa and is now found in parts of the West Indies, South America, and the S U.S.

o·be·di·ence (ō bē′dē əns) ***n.*** ⟦OFr < L *obedientia* < *obediens:* see fol.⟧ **1** the state, fact, or an instance of obeying, or a willingness to obey; submission **2** *Eccles.* JURISDICTION

o·be·di·ent (ō bē′dē ənt) ***adj.*** ⟦OFr < L *obediens,* prp. of *obedire,* OBEY⟧ obeying or willing to obey; submissive —**o·be′di·ent·ly** ***adv.***

SYN.—**obedient** suggests a giving in to the orders or instructions of one in authority or control [an *obedient* child]; **docile** implies a temperament that submits easily to control or that fails to resist domination [a *docile* servant]; **tractable** implies ease of management or control but does not connote the submissiveness of **docile** and applies to things as well as people [silver is a *tractable,* i.e., malleable, metal]; **compliant** suggests a weakness of character that allows one to yield meekly to another's request or demand [army life had made him *compliant*]; **amenable** suggests such amiability or desire to be agreeable as would lead one to submit readily [she is *amenable* to discipline] —*ANT.* **disobedient, refractory**

o·bei·sance (ō bā′səns, -bē′-) ***n.*** ⟦ME *obeisaunce* < OFr *obeissance* < *obeissant,* prp. of *obeir,* OBEY⟧ **1** a gesture of respect or reverence, such as a bow or curtsy **2** the attitude shown by this; homage; deference —**o·bei′sant** ***adj.***

ob·e·lisk (äb′ə lisk, ō′bə-) ***n.*** ⟦L *obeliscus* < Gr *obeliskos,* a small spit, obelisk, dim. of *obelos:* see OBELUS⟧ **1** a tall, slender, four-sided stone pillar tapering toward its pyramidal top **2** DAGGER (sense 2)

ob·e·lize (äb′ə līz′) ***vt.*** **-lized′**, **-liz′ing** ⟦Gr *obelizein*⟧ to mark with an obelus

ob·e·lus (äb′ə ləs) ***n., pl.*** **-li′** (-lī′) ⟦ME < L, a spit, obelus (in LL, obelisk) < Gr *obelos,* a spit, needle, obelus, obolus⟧ **1** a mark (- or ÷) used in ancient manuscripts to indicate questionable passages or readings **2** DAGGER (sense 2)

obelisk

O·ber·am·mer·gau (ō′bər äm′ər gou′) village in S Germany, in the state of Bavaria: site of a Passion play performed usually every ten years

O·ber·hau·sen (ō′bər hou′zən) city in WC Germany, in the state of North Rhine-Westphalia

O·ber·land (ō′bər länt′) BERNESE ALPS

O·ber·on (ō′bər än′, -ən) ***n.*** ⟦Fr < OFr *Auberon* < Gmc base of ELF, OAF⟧ *Eng. Folklore* the king of fairyland and husband of Titania

o·bese (ō bēs′) ***adj.*** ⟦L *obesus,* pp. of *obedere,* to devour < *ob-* (see OB-) + *edere,* EAT⟧ very fat; stout; corpulent —**o·be′si·ty** ***n.***

o·bey (ō bā′) ***vt.*** ⟦ME *obeien* < OFr *obeir* < L *obedire,* to obey < OL *oboedire* < *ob-* (see OB-) + *audire,* to hear: see AUDIENCE⟧ **1** to carry out the instructions or orders of **2** to carry out (an instruction or order) **3** to be guided by; submit to the control of [to *obey* one's conscience] —***vi.*** to be obedient —**o·bey′er** ***n.***

ob·fus·cate (äb′fəs kāt′) ***vt.*** **-cat′ed**, **-cat′ing** ⟦< L *obfuscatus,* pp. of *obfuscare,* to darken < *ob-* (see OB-) + *fuscare,* to obscure < *fuscus,* dark < IE base **dhus-* > DUSK, DOZE[1], DUST⟧ **1** to cloud over; obscure; make dark or unclear **2** to muddle; confuse; bewilder —**ob′fus·ca′tion** ***n.*** —**ob·fus·ca·to·ry** (äb fus′kə tôr′ē) ***adj.***

OB-GYN or **OB/GYN** (ō′bē′jē′wī′en′) *abbrev.* **1** obstetrical-gynecological **2** obstetrician-gynecologist **3** obstetrics-gynecology Also written **Ob-Gyn** or **Ob/Gyn**

☆**o·bi**[1] (ō′bē) ***n.*** OBEAH

o·bi[2] (ō′bē) ***n.*** ⟦Jpn⟧ a broad sash with a bow in the back, worn with a Japanese kimono

O·bie (ō′bē) ***n.*** ⟦< O(FF-)B(ROADWAY) + -IE⟧ any of the awards given annually in the U.S. for special achievements in off-Broadway productions

o·bit (ō bit′, ō′bit; *also, chiefly Brit* äb′it) ***n.*** ⟦ME *obite* < OFr *obit* < L *obitus,* death < pp. of *obire,* to fall, die < *ob-* (see OB-) + *ire,* to go: see YEAR⟧ OBITUARY

ob·i·ter dic·tum (äb′i tər dik′təm, ō′bi-) ***pl.*** **ob′i·ter dic′ta** (-tə) ⟦L, (something) said incidentally: *obiter,* incidentally (< *ob:* see OB- + *(circ)iter,* near < *circa,* about) + *dictum,* DICTUM⟧ **1** DICTUM (*n.* 2) **2** any incidental remark

o·bit·u·ar·y (ō bich′oo er′ē) ***n., pl.*** **-ar′ies** ⟦ML *obituarius* < L *obitus:* see OBIT⟧ a notice of someone's death, as in a newspaper, usually with a brief biography —***adj.*** of or recording a death or deaths —**o·bit′u·ar′ist** ***n.***

obj *abbrev.* **1** object **2** objection **3** objective

ob·ject (äb′jikt, -jekt; *for v.* əb jekt′, äb-) ***n.*** ⟦ME < ML *objectum,* something thrown in the way < L *objectus,* a casting before, that which appears, orig. pp. of *objicere* < *ob-* (see OB-) + *jacere,* to throw: see JET[1]⟧ **1** a thing that can be seen or touched; material thing that occupies space **2** a person or thing to which action, thought, or feeling is directed **3** what is aimed at; purpose; end; goal **4** a cause for concern: used in negative constructions [money is no *object*] **5** *Gram.* a noun or other substantive that directly or indirectly receives the action of a verb, or one that is governed by a preposition [in "Give me the book," "book" is the direct *object* and "me" is the indirect *object*] **6** *Philos.* anything that can be known or perceived by the mind —***vt.*** **1** [Archaic] *a)* to oppose *b)* to thrust in; interpose *c)* to expose *d)* to bring forward as a reason, instance, etc.; adduce **2** to put forward in opposition; state by way of objection [it was *objected* that the new tax law was unfair] —***vi.*** **1** to put forward an objection or objections; enter a protest; be opposed **2** to feel or express disapproval or dislike —**ob′ject·less** ***adj.*** —**ob·jec′tor** ***n.***

SYN.—**object** implies opposition to something because of strong dislike or disapproval [I *object* to her meddling]; **protest** implies the making of strong, formal, often written objection to something [they *protested* the new tax increases]; **remonstrate** implies protest and argument in demonstrating to another that he or she is wrong or blameworthy [he *remonstrated* against her hostile attitude]; **expostulate** suggests strong, earnest pleading or argument to change another's views or actions [I *expostulated* with him about his self-sacrifice]; **demur** implies the raising of objections or the taking of exception so as to delay action [I *demurred* at her proposal to dine out] See also **intention** —*ANT.* **agree, consent, acquiesce**

object ball *Billiards, Pool* any ball other than the cue ball

object glass OBJECTIVE (*n.* 4)

ob·jec·ti·fy (əb jek′tə fī′, äb-) ***vt.*** **-fied′**, **-fy′ing** ⟦OBJECT + -I- + -FY⟧ **1** to give objective form to; make objective or concrete [to *objectify* warm feelings in a painting] **2** to regard (someone) superficially or treat in a depersonalized way; often, specif., to regard or treat as a SEX OBJECT —**ob·jec′ti·fi·ca′tion** ***n.***

ob·jec·tion (əb jek′shən, äb-) ***n.*** ⟦ME *objeccioun* < LL *objectio* < L *objectus:* see OBJECT⟧ **1** the act of objecting **2** a feeling or expression of opposition, disapproval, or dislike **3** a cause for objecting; reason for opposing, disapproving, or disliking

ob·jec·tion·a·ble (-ə bəl) ***adj.*** **1** open to objection **2** disagreeable; offensive —**ob·jec′tion·a·bly** ***adv.***

ob·jec·tive (əb jek′tiv, äb-) ***adj.*** ⟦ML *objectivus*⟧ **1** of or having to do with a known or perceived object as distinguished from something existing only in the mind of the subject, or person thinking **2** being, or regarded as being, independent of the mind; real; actual **3** determined by and emphasizing the features and characteristics of the object, or thing dealt with, rather than the thoughts and feelings of the artist, writer, or speaker [an *objective* painting or description] **4** without bias or prejudice; detached **5** being the aim or goal [an *objective* point] ☆**6** designating a kind of test, as a multiple-choice or true-false test, that minimizes subjective factors in answering and grading **7** *Gram.* designating or of the case of an object of a transitive verb or preposition **8** *Med.* designating or of a symptom or condition perceptible to others besides the patient —***n.*** **1** anything external to or independent of the mind; something objective; reality **2** something aimed at or striven for **3** *Gram. a)* the objective case *b)* a word in this case **4** *Optics* the lens or lenses nearest to the object observed, as in a microscope or telescope, that serve to focus light to form the image of the object —*SYN.* FAIR[1], INTENTION —**ob·jec′tive·ly** ***adv.*** —**ob·jec′tive·ness** ***n.***

objective complement a word or group of words used in the predicate of a sentence as a modifier or qualifier of the direct object (Ex.: *president* in "We elected him president")

objective correlative ⟦term coined (1919) by T. S. ELIOT[2]⟧ a sequence of events, cluster of images, setting, etc. employed in a literary work to express a certain emotion and evoke it in the reader or viewer

ob·jec·tiv·ism (əb jek′tiv iz′əm, äb-) ***n.*** **1** any of various philosophical doctrines that stress the external, independent existence of what is perceived or known **2** an ethical theory maintaining that the validity of ethical assertions can be determined objectively **3** the use of objective methods in art or literature —**ob·jec′tiv·ist** ***n., adj.*** —**ob·jec′tiv·is′tic** ***adj.***

ob·jec·tiv·i·ty (äb′jek tiv′ə tē) ***n.*** **1** the state or quality of being objective **2** objective reality

ob·jec·tiv·ize (əb jek′tə vīz′, äb-) ***vt.*** **-ized′**, **-iz′ing** OBJECTIFY —**ob·jec′ti·vi·za′tion** ***n.***

object lesson an actual or practical demonstration or exemplification of some principle

ob·jet d'art (äb′zhā där′) ***pl.*** **ob′jets d'art′** (-zhā-) ⟦Fr, lit., object of art⟧ a relatively small object of artistic value, as a figurine, vase, etc.

ob·jet trou·vé (äb′zhā troo vā′) ***pl.*** **ob·jets trou·vés** (äb′zhā troo vā′) ⟦Fr, found object⟧ an ordinary object, as a piece of driftwood, a shell, or a manufactured article, displayed as a work of art

ob·jur·gate (äb′jər gāt′, əb jur′gāt′) ***vt.*** **-gat′ed**, **-gat′ing** ⟦< L *objurgatus,* pp. of *objurgare,* to rebuke, chastise < *ob-* (see OB-) + *jurgare,* to chide, orig., to sue at law < *jus* (gen. *juris:* see JURY[1]) + *agere,* to do, ACT[1]⟧ to chide vehemently; upbraid sharply; rebuke; berate —**ob′jur·ga′tion** ***n.*** —**ob′jur·ga′tor** ***n.*** —**ob·jur′ga·to′ry** (-gə tôr′ē) ***adj.***

obl *abbrev.* **1** oblique **2** oblong

ob·lan·ce·o·late (äb lan′sē ə lit, -lāt′) ***adj.*** ⟦OB- + LANCEOLATE⟧ lance-shaped, with the broad end at the top: said of a leaf

ob·last (äb′last) ***n.*** ⟦Russ *oblast′*⟧ an administrative subdivision, or region, of a republic in the U.S.S.R.

ob·late[1] (äb′lāt′, äb lāt′) ***adj.*** ⟦ModL *oblatus* < OB- + *-latus* as in *prolatus* (see PROLATE): from being thrust forward at the equator⟧ *Geom.* flattened at the poles [an *oblate* spheroid]

ob·late[2] (äb′lāt′) *n.* ⟦ML *oblatus,* offered, thrust forward < pp. of L *offerre:* see OFFER⟧ *R.C.Ch.* a person dedicated to the religious life; esp., a person living in or associated with a religious community but not bound by vows

ob·la·tion (äb lā′shən) *n.* ⟦ME *oblacioun* < OFr *oblation* < L *oblatio,* an offering < *oblatus:* see prec.⟧ **1** an offering of a sacrifice, thanksgiving, etc. to God or a god **2** the thing or things offered; esp., the bread and wine of the Eucharist —**ob·la′tion·al** *adj.*, **ob·la·to·ry** (äb′lə tôr′ē)

ob·li·gate (äb′li gāt′; *for adj.,* -git, -gāt′) *vt.* **-gat′ed, -gat′ing** ⟦< L *obligatus,* pp. of *obligare:* see OBLIGE⟧ to bind by a contract, promise, sense of duty, etc.; put under obligation —*adj.* ⟦ME < L *obligatus*⟧ **1** bound; obliged **2** *Biol.* limited to a certain type of behavior, environment, etc. [an *obligate* parasite]: opposed to FACULTATIVE (sense 4)

ob·li·ga·tion (äb′li gā′shən) *n.* ⟦ME *obligacioun* < OFr *obligation* < L *obligatio*⟧ **1** an obligating or being obligated **2** a binding contract, promise, moral responsibility, etc. **3** a duty imposed legally or socially; thing that one is bound to do by contract, promise, moral responsibility, etc. **4** the binding power of a contract, promise, etc. **5** *a)* the condition or fact of being indebted to another for a favor or service received *b)* a favor or service **6** *Law a)* an agreement or duty by which one person (the *obligor*) is legally bound to make payment or perform services for the benefit of another (the *obligee*) *b)* the bond, contract, or other document setting forth the terms of this agreement —**ob′li·ga′tion·al** *adj.*

ob·lig·a·to·ry (ə blig′ə tôr′ē, äb′lə gə-) *adj.* ⟦LL *obligatorius*⟧ **1** legally, morally, or socially binding; constituting, or having the nature of, an OBLIGATION (sense 3); required **2** *Biol.* OBLIGATE —**ob·lig′a·to′ri·ly** *adv.*

o·blige (ə blīj′, ō-) *vt.* **o·bliged′, o·blig′ing** ⟦ME *obligen* < OFr *obligier* < L *obligare,* to bind, oblige < *ob-* (see OB-) + *ligare,* to bind: see LIGATURE⟧ **1** to compel by moral, legal, or physical force; constrain **2** to make indebted for a favor or kindness done; do a favor for —*vi.* to do a favor or service —**o·blig′er** *n.*

ob·li·gee (äb′li jē′) *n.* ⟦< prec. + -EE[1]⟧ **1** a person obliged to do something for another **2** *Law* a person to whom another is bound by contract

o·blig·ing (ə blī′jiŋ, ō-) *adj.* ready to do favors; helpful; courteous; accommodating —*SYN.* AMIABLE —**o·blig′ing·ly** *adv.*

ob·li·gor (äb′li gôr′, äb′li gôr′) *n.* ⟦< OBLIGE + -OR⟧ *Law* a person who binds himself to another by contract

ob·lique (ō blēk′, ə-; *also, esp. in mil. use,* -blīk′) *adj.* ⟦ME *oblike* < L *obliquus* < *ob-* (see OB-) + *liquis,* awry < IE **leik-,* var. of base **elei-,* to bend > ELL[2]⟧ **1** having a slanting position or direction; neither perpendicular nor horizontal; not level or upright; inclined **2** not straight to the point; not straightforward; indirect **3** evasive, disingenuous, underhanded, etc. **4** indirectly aimed at or attained [*oblique* results] **5** *Anat.* designating or of any of certain muscles obliquely placed and attached **6** *Bot.* having the sides unequal, as some leaves **7** *Geom.* with its axis not perpendicular to its base [an *oblique* cone] **8** *Gram.* designating or of any case except the nominative and the vocative —*n.* an oblique angle, muscle, etc. —*vi.* **ob·liqued′, ob·liqu′ing** to veer from the perpendicular; slant —*adv. Mil.* with a change of direction of approximately 45 degrees —**ob·lique′ly** *adv.* —**ob·lique′ness** *n.*

oblique angle any angle other than a right angle; acute or obtuse angle

ob·liq·ui·ty (ə blik′wə tē) *n., pl.* **-ties** ⟦ME *obliquitee* < L *obliquitas*⟧ **1** the state or quality of being oblique **2** an oblique statement, action, etc. **3** a turning aside from moral conduct or sound thinking **4** *Astron.* the angle between the planes of a planet's equator and its orbit about the sun: for the earth (**obliquity of the ecliptic**) it is currently *c.* 23° 26.5′ and will decrease at the rate of 0.47″ a year for *c.* 1,500 years, at which time it will begin to increase again **5** *Math. a)* deviation of a line or plane from the perpendicular or parallel *b)* the degree of this —**ob·liq′ui·tous** *adj.*

ob·lit·er·ate (ə blit′ər āt′) *vt.* **-at′ed, -at′ing** ⟦< L *obliteratus,* pp. of *obliterare,* to blot out < *ob-* (see OB-) + *littera,* LETTER[1]⟧ **1** to blot out or wear away, leaving no traces; erase; efface **2** to do away with as if by effacing; destroy —*SYN.* ERASE —**ob·lit′er·a′tion** *n.* —**ob·lit′er·a′tive** *adj.* —**ob·lit′er·a′tor** *n.*

ob·liv·i·on (ə bliv′ē ən) *n.* ⟦OFr < L *oblivio* < *oblivisci,* to forget < *ob-* (see OB-) + (prob.) *levis,* smooth < IE base **lei-,* slippery > LIME[1]⟧ **1** a forgetting or having forgotten; forgetfulness **2** the condition or fact of being forgotten **3** official overlooking of offenses; pardon

ob·liv·i·ous (ə bliv′ē əs) *adj.* ⟦ME *obliuyous* < L *obliviosus* < *oblivio;* see prec.⟧ **1** *a)* forgetful (usually with *of*) *b)* unaware or indifferent (usually with *of* or, esp., *to*) **2** causing forgetfulness —**ob·liv′i·ous·ly** *adv.* —**ob·liv′i·ous·ness** *n.*

ob·long (äb′lôŋ′) *adj.* ⟦ME *oblonge* < L *oblongus,* rather long < *ob-* (see OB-) + *longus,* LONG[1]⟧ longer than broad; elongated; specif., *a)* rectangular and longer in one direction than in the other, esp. longer horizontally *b)* elliptical —*n.* an oblong figure

ob·lo·quy (äb′lə kwē) *n., pl.* **-quies** ⟦ME *obliqui* < LL *obloquium* < L *obloqui,* to speak against < *ob-* (see OB-) + *loqui,* to speak⟧ **1** verbal abuse of a person or thing; censure or vituperation, esp. when widespread or general **2** ill repute, disgrace, or infamy resulting from this

ob·nox·ious (əb näk′shəs, äb-) *adj.* ⟦L *obnoxiosus* < *obnoxius,* subject or exposed to danger < *ob-* (see OB-) + *noxa,* harm < base of *nocere,* to hurt: see NECRO-⟧ **1** *a)* exposed or liable to injury, evil, or harm *b)* liable to punishment; censurable **2** very unpleasant; objectionable; offensive —*SYN.* HATEFUL —**ob·nox′ious·ly** *adv.* —**ob·nox′ious·ness** *n.*

ob·nu·bi·late (äb no͞o′bə lāt′, -nyo͞o′-) *vt.* **-lat′ed, -lat′ing** ⟦< L *obnubilatus,* pp. of *obnubilare,* to cover with clouds < *ob-* (see OB-) + *nubilare* < *nubes,* a cloud: see NUANCE⟧ to make unclear, indistinct, vague, etc. [memories *obnubilated* by the passage of time] —**ob·nu′bi·la′tion** *n.*

o·boe (ō′bō) *n.* ⟦It < Fr *hautbois;* see HAUTBOY⟧ **1** a double-reed woodwind instrument having a range of nearly three octaves and a high, penetrating, melancholy tone **2** an organ stop producing an oboelike sound —**o′bo·ist** *n.*

oboe

ob·o·lus (äb′ə ləs) *n., pl.* **-li′** (-lī′) ⟦L < Gr *obolos,* var. of *obelos,* a spit, needle, bar used as money⟧ **1** in ancient Greece *a)* a coin valued at $\frac{1}{6}$ drachma *b)* a weight equal to 11$\frac{1}{4}$ grains **2** any of several small coins formerly current in Europe Also **ob·ol** (äb′əl)

ob·o·vate (äb ō′vāt) *adj.* inversely ovate; having the shape of the longitudinal section of an egg, with the broad end at the top, as some leaves

ob·o·void (äb ō′void) *adj.* ⟦OB- + OVOID⟧ egg-shaped, with the broad end at the top: said of some fruits, etc.

obs *abbrev.* **1** obscure **2** obsolete **3** observation **4** observatory

ob·scene (äb sēn′, əb-) *adj.* ⟦Fr *obscène* < L *obscenus, obscaenus* < *obs-,* var. of *ob-* (see OB-) + *caenum,* filth < IE **k̑weino-* < base **kwei-,* muck, filth > ON *hvein,* swampy land⟧ **1** offensive to one's feelings, or to prevailing notions, of modesty or decency; lewd **2** disgusting; repulsive **3** *Law* designating or of books, films, etc. which when judged by contemporary community standards, are found to appeal to a prurient interest in sex, be patently offensive, and have no serious artistic, scientific, or social value —*SYN.* COARSE —**ob·scene′ly** *adv.*

ob·scen·i·ty (äb sen′ə tē, əb-; *also, chiefly Brit,* -sēn′-) *n.* ⟦Fr *obscénité* < L *obscenitas*⟧ **1** the state or quality of being obscene **2** *pl.* **-ties** an obscene remark, act, event, etc.

ob·scur·ant (äb skyoor′ənt, əb-) *n.* ⟦< L *obscurantem,* acc. of *obscurans,* prp. of *obscurare,* to OBSCURE⟧ a person or thing that obscures, esp. one that opposes or tends to prevent human progress and enlightenment —*adj.* that obscures; of or constituting an obscurant: also **ob·scu·ran·tic** (äb′skyo͞o ran′tik)

ob·scur·ant·ism (äb skyoor′ən tiz′əm, əb-) *n.* **1** opposition to human progress or enlightenment **2** the practice of being deliberately obscure or vague —**ob·scur′ant·ist** *n., adj.*

ob·scu·ra·tion (äb′skyo͞o rā′shən) *n.* ⟦L *obscuratio*⟧ an obscuring or being obscured

ob·scure (əb skyoor′, äb-) *adj.* ⟦OFr *obscur* < L *obscurus,* lit., covered over < *ob-* (see OB-) + IE **skuro-* < base **(s)keu-,* to cover, conceal > HIDE[1], SKY⟧ **1** lacking light; dim; dark; murky [the *obscure* night] **2** not easily perceived; specif., *a)* not clear or distinct; faint or undefined [an *obscure* figure or sound] *b)* not easily understood; vague; cryptic; ambiguous [an *obscure* explanation] *c)* in an inconspicuous position; hidden [an *obscure* village] **3** not well-known; not famous [an *obscure* scientist] **4** *Phonet.* pronounced as (ə) or (i) because it is not stressed; reduced; neutral: said of a vowel —*vt.* **-scured′, -scur′ing** ⟦L *obscurare* < the adj.⟧ **1** to make obscure; specif., *a)* to darken; make dim *b)* to conceal from view; hide *c)* to make less conspicuous; overshadow [a success that *obscured* earlier failures] *d)* to make less intelligible; confuse [testimony that *obscures* the issue] **2** *Phonet.* to make (a vowel) obscure —*n.* [Rare] OBSCURITY —**ob·scure′ly** *adv.* —**ob·scure′ness** *n.*

SYN.—**obscure** applies to that which is perceived with difficulty either because it is concealed or veiled or because of obtuseness in the perceiver [their reasons remain *obscure*]; **vague** implies such a lack of precision or exactness as to be indistinct or unclear [a *vague* idea]; **enigmatic** and **cryptic** are used of that which baffles or perplexes, the latter word implying deliberate intention to puzzle [*enigmatic* behavior, a *cryptic* warning]; **ambiguous** applies to that which puzzles because it allows of more than one interpretation [an *ambiguous* title]; **equivocal** is used of something ambiguous that is deliberately used to mislead or confuse [an *equivocal* answer] —*ANT.* **clear, distinct, obvious**

ob·scu·ri·ty (-skyoor′ə tē) *n.* **1** the quality or condition of being obscure **2** *pl.* **-ties** an obscure person or thing

ob·se·crate (äb′si krāt′) *vt.* **-crat′ed, -crat′ing** ⟦< L *obsecratus,* pp. of *obsecrare,* to beseech (on religious grounds) < *ob-* (see OB-) + *sacrare:* see SACRED⟧ [Rare] to beg for (something) or supplicate (someone); entreat —**ob′se·cra′tion** *n.*

ob·se·quies (äb′si kwēz′) *pl.n.* ⟦< obs. sing. *obsequy* < OFr *obseques* < ML *obsequiae* (pl.) (< L *obsequium,* compliance: see fol.), substituted for L *exsequiae:* see EXEQUIES⟧ funeral rites or ceremonies

ob·se·qui·ous (əb sē′kwē əs, äb-) *adj.* ⟦ME *obsequyouse* < L *obsequiosus* < *obsequium,* compliance < *obsequi,* to comply with < *ob-* (see OB-) + *sequi,* to follow: see SEQUENT⟧ **1** showing too great a willingness to serve or obey; fawning **2** [Archaic] compliant; dutiful —**ob·se′qui·ous·ly** *adv.* —**ob·se′qui·ous·ness** *n.*

ob·serv·a·ble (əb zʉr′və bəl) *adj.* ⟦L *observabilis*⟧ **1** that can be observed; visible; discernible; noticeable **2** deserving of attention; noteworthy **3** that can or must be kept or celebrated [an *observable* holiday] —**ob·serv′a·bly** *adv.*

ob·serv·ance (əb zʉr′vəns) *n.* ⟦ME *observaunce* < OFr *observance* < L *observantia,* attention, regard, in LL(Ec), divine worship⟧ **1** the act or practice of observing, or keeping, a law, duty, custom, rule, etc. **2** a customary act, rite, ceremony, etc. **3** the act of observing, or noting; observation **4** [Archaic] respectful attention; deference **5** *R.C.Ch.* *a)* the rule observed by a religious order *b)* the order observing a specified rule

ob·serv·ant (əb zur′vənt) ***adj.*** ⟦Fr, prp. of *observer,* OBSERVE⟧ **1** strict in observing, or keeping, a law, custom, duty, rule, etc.: often with *of [observant* of the rules of etiquette*]* **2** paying careful attention; keenly watchful **3** perceptive or alert **4** *Judaism* designating or of a person who adheres strictly to traditional religious practices ***—n.*** [**O-**] *former name for* FRIAR MINOR **—ob·serv′ant·ly** ***adv.***

ob·ser·va·tion (äb′zər vā′shən) ***n.*** ⟦ME *observacioun* < L *observatio,* in LL(Ec), reverence, outward display⟧ **1** observance, as of laws, customs, etc. **2** *a)* the act, practice, or power of noticing *b)* something noticed **3** the fact of being seen or noticed *[*seeking to avoid *observation]* **4** *a)* the act or practice of noting and recording facts and events, as for some scientific study *b)* the data so noted and recorded **5** a comment or remark based on something observed **6** *a)* the act of determining the altitude of the sun, a star, etc., in order to find a ship's position at sea *b)* the result obtained ***—adj.*** for observing **—SYN.** REMARK

ob·ser·va·tion·al (-shə nəl) ***adj.*** of or based on observation rather than experimentation

☆**observation car** a railway car with extra-large windows or a transparent dome for facilitating a view of the scenery

observation post an advanced military position from which movements of the enemy can be observed, artillery fire directed, etc.

ob·serv·a·to·ry (əb zur′və tôr′ē) ***n.,*** *pl.* **-ries** ⟦ModL *observatorium* < pp. of L *observare:* see fol.⟧ **1** *a)* a building equipped for scientific observation, esp. such a building with a large telescope for astronomical research *b)* an institution for such research **2** any building or place providing an extensive view of the surrounding terrain

ob·serve (əb zurv′) ***vt.*** **-served′, -serv′ing** ⟦ME *observen* < OFr *observer* < L *observare,* to watch, note < *ob-* (see OB-) + *servare,* to keep or hold < IE base **ser-,* to watch over, guard > Sans *haraiti,* (he) guards⟧ **1** to adhere to, follow, keep, or abide by (a law, custom, duty, rule, etc.) **2** to celebrate or keep (a holiday, etc.) according to custom **3** *a)* to notice or perceive (something) *b)* to pay special attention to **4** to arrive at as a conclusion after study **5** to say or mention casually; remark **6** to examine and study scientifically ***—vi.*** **1** to take notice **2** to comment or remark (*on* or *upon*) **3** to act as an observer **—SYN.** CELEBRATE, DISCERN **—ob·serv′ing·ly** ***adv.***

ob·serv·er (əb zur′vər) ***n.*** **1** a person who observes something; specif., *a)* a soldier manning an observation post *b)* a person who attends an assembly, convention, etc., not as an official delegate but only to observe and report the proceedings *c)* an official, usually a member of a group, sent by a UN committee to collect and report facts on the situation in a special area **2** a member of an aircraft crew, other than a pilot, with certain specialized duties and a special rating (**aircraft observer**)

ob·sess (əb ses′) ***vt.*** ⟦< L *obsessus,* pp. of *obsidere,* to besiege < *ob-* (see OB-) + *sedere,* SIT⟧ to haunt or trouble in mind, esp. to an abnormal degree; preoccupy greatly **—☆*vi.*** to be obsessed or preoccupied: usually with *about, over,* or *on*

ob·ses·sion (əb sesh′ən) ***n.*** ⟦L *obsessio*⟧ **1** the act of an evil spirit in possessing or ruling a person **2** *a)* the fact or state of being obsessed with an idea, desire, emotion, etc. *b)* such a persistent idea, desire, emotion, etc., esp. one that cannot be gotten rid of by reasoning **—ob·ses′sion·al** ***adj.***

ob·ses·sive (əb ses′iv) ***adj.*** of, having the nature of, or causing an obsession or obsessions ***—n.*** a person who has obsessive thoughts **—ob·ses′sive·ly** ***adv.*** **—ob·ses′sive·ness** ***n.***

ob·ses·sive-com·pul·sive (əb ses′iv kəm pul′siv) ***adj.*** designating or of a mental disorder, esp. a neurosis, characterized by compulsive thoughts or actions, irresistible urges, etc., that are unwanted and uncontrollable and interfere with work, social activity, and personal relationships, and often appear as repeated, somewhat ritualistic performances of certain acts ***—n.*** a person who is obsessive-compulsive

ob·sid·i·an (əb sid′ē ən) ***n.*** ⟦ModL *obsidianus* < L *Obsidianus* (*lapis*), a faulty reading in PLINY (altered by assoc. with L *obsidium,* a siege < *obsidere:* see OBSESS) for *Obsianus* (*lapis*), stone of Obsius, finder of a similar stone in Ethiopia⟧ a hard, usually dark-colored or black volcanic glass with conchoidal fracture, often used as a gem

ob·so·lesce (äb′sə les′) ***vi.*** **-lesced′, -lesc′ing** ⟦L *obsolescere:* see OBSOLETE⟧ to be or become obsolescent

ob·so·les·cent (äb′sə les′ənt) ***adj.*** ⟦L *obsolescens*⟧ in the process of becoming obsolete **—ob′so·les′cence** ***n.*** **—ob′so·les′cent·ly** ***adv.***

ob·so·lete (äb′sə lēt′, äb′sə lēt′) ***adj.*** ⟦L *obsoletus,* pp. of *obsolescere,* to go out of use < *ob-* (see OB-) + **-solescere* (< *exolescere,* to grow out of use < *ex-,* EX-[1] + ? *alescere,* to increase: see ADOLESCENT)⟧ **1** no longer in use or practice; discarded **2** no longer in fashion; out-of-date; passé **3** *Biol.* rudimentary or poorly developed as compared with its counterpart in other individuals of a related species, the opposite sex, etc.; vestigial: said of an organ, etc. ***—vt.*** **-let′ed, -let′ing** to make obsolete, as by replacing with something newer **—SYN.** OLD **—ob′so·lete′ly** ***adv.*** **—ob′so·lete′ness** ***n.***

ob·sta·cle (äb′stə kəl) ***n.*** ⟦OFr < L *obstaculum,* obstacle < *obstare,* to withstand < *ob-* (see OB-) + *stare,* to STAND⟧ anything that gets in the way or hinders; impediment; obstruction; hindrance

SYN.—obstacle is used of anything which literally or figuratively stands in the way of one's progress *[*her father's opposition remained their only *obstacle]*; **impediment** applies to anything that delays or retards progress by interfering with the normal action *[*a speech *impediment]*; **obstruction** refers to anything that blocks progress or some activity as if by stopping up a passage *[*your interference is an *obstruction* of justice*]*; **hindrance** applies to anything that thwarts progress by holding back or delaying *[*lack of supplies is the greatest *hindrance* to my experiment*]*; **barrier** applies to any apparently insurmountable obstacle that prevents progress or keeps separate and apart *[*language differences are often a *barrier* to understanding*]*

obstacle course **1** a physical exercise course with barriers, ditches, and other obstacles, used to train military personnel **2** any situation or course of action that presents obstacles or obstructions

ob·stet·ric (əb stet′rik, äb-) ***adj.*** ⟦ModL *obstetricus,* for L *obstetricius,* belonging to a midwife < *obstetrix,* midwife, lit., she who stands before < *ob-* (see OB-) + *stare,* to STAND⟧ of childbirth or obstetrics: also **ob·stet′ri·cal** **—ob·stet′ri·cal·ly** ***adv.***

ob·ste·tri·cian (äb′stə trish′ən) ***n.*** a medical doctor who specializes in obstetrics

ob·stet·rics (əb stet′riks, äb-) ***n.*** ⟦< OBSTETRIC⟧ the branch of medicine concerned with the care and treatment of women during pregnancy, childbirth, and the ensuing period

ob·sti·na·cy (äb′stə nə sē) ***n.*** ⟦ME *obstinacie* < ML *obstinatia,* for L *obstinatio*⟧ **1** the state or quality of being obstinate; specif., *a)* stubbornness *b)* resistance to treatment; persistence, as of a disease **2** *pl.* **-cies** an obstinate act, attitude, etc.

ob·sti·nate (äb′stə nət) ***adj.*** ⟦ME < L *obstinatus,* pp. of *obstinare,* to resolve on < *obstare,* to stand against, oppose < *ob-* (see OB-) + *stare,* to STAND⟧ **1** unreasonably determined to have one's own way; not yielding to reason or plea; stubborn; dogged; mulish **2** resisting remedy or treatment *[*an *obstinate* fever*]* **3** not easily subdued, ended, etc. **—SYN.** STUBBORN **—ob′sti·nate·ly** ***adv.*** **—ob′sti·nate·ness** ***n.***

ob·sti·pa·tion (äb′stə pā′shən) ***n.*** ⟦L *obstipatio* < L *ob-* (see OB-) + *stipare,* to cram, pack: see STIFF⟧ *Med.* severe and persistent constipation

ob·strep·er·ous (əb strep′ər əs, äb-) ***adj.*** ⟦L *obstreperus* < *obstrepere,* to roar at < *ob-* (see OB-) + *strepere,* to roar < IE base *(*s*)*trep-,* to make a loud noise > OE *thræft,* strife⟧ noisy, boisterous, or unruly, esp. in resisting or opposing **—SYN.** VOCIFEROUS **—ob·strep′er·ous·ly** ***adv.*** **—ob·strep′er·ous·ness** ***n.***

ob·struct (əb strukt′) ***vt.*** ⟦< L *obstructus,* pp. of *obstruere,* to block up, build against < *ob-* (see OB-) + *struere,* to pile up: see STREW⟧ **1** to block or stop up (a passage) with obstacles or impediments; dam; clog **2** to hinder (progress, an activity, etc.); impede **3** to cut off from being seen; block (the view) **—SYN.** HINDER[1] **—ob·struct′er** ***n.***, **ob·struc′tor**

ob·struc·tion (əb struk′shən) ***n.*** ⟦L *obstructio*⟧ **1** an obstructing or being obstructed **2** anything that obstructs; hindrance **—SYN.** OBSTACLE

ob·struc·tion·ist (-ist) ***n.*** anyone who obstructs progress; esp., a member of a legislative group who hinders the passage of legislation by various technical maneuvers ***—adj.*** of obstructionists or obstructionism: also **ob·struc′tion·is′tic** **—ob·struc′tion·ism′** ***n.***

ob·struc·tive (əb struk′tiv) ***adj.*** obstructing or tending to obstruct **—ob·struc′tive·ly** ***adv.*** **—ob·struc′tive·ness** ***n.***

ob·stru·ent (äb′stro͞o ənt) ***adj.*** ⟦L *obstruens,* prp. of *obstruere,* to block up: see OBSTRUCT⟧ [Rare] obstructing; esp., blocking a passage of the body ***—n.*** [Rare] something, as a kidney stone, that blocks a passage of the body

ob·tain (əb tān′) ***vt.*** ⟦ME *obteinen* < OFr *obtenir* < L *obtinere,* to obtain, prevail, maintain < *ob-* (see OB-) + *tenere,* to hold: see TENANT⟧ **1** to get possession of, esp. by some effort; procure **2** [Archaic] to arrive at; reach or achieve ***—vi.*** **1** to be in force or in effect; prevail *[*a law that no longer *obtains]* **2** [Archaic] to succeed **—SYN.** GET **—ob·tain′a·ble** ***adj.*** **—ob·tain′er** ***n.*** **—ob·tain′ment** ***n.***

ob·tect (äb tekt′) ***adj.*** ⟦< L *obtectus,* pp. of *obtegere,* to cover over < *ob-* (see OB-) + *tegere,* to cover: see THATCH, ***vt.***⟧ pertaining to an insect pupa in which the appendages and wings are glued down against the body by a secretion: also **ob·tect′ed**

ob·test (äb test′) ***vt.*** ⟦L *obtestari* < *ob-* (see OB-) + *testari,* to witness < *testis,* a witness: see TESTIFY⟧ **1** to beg for; beseech; supplicate **2** to call to witness **—ob′tes·ta′tion** (-tes tā′shən) ***n.***

ob·trude (əb tro͞od′, äb-) ***vt.*** **-trud′ed, -trud′ing** ⟦L *obtrudere* < *ob-* (see OB-) + *trudere,* to thrust: see THREAT⟧ **1** to thrust forward; push out; eject **2** to offer or force (oneself, one's opinions, etc.) upon others unasked or unwanted ***—vi.*** to obtrude oneself (*on* or *upon*) **—SYN.** INTRUDE **—ob·trud′er** ***n.*** **—ob·tru′sion** ***n.***

ob·tru·sive (əb tro͞o′siv, äb-) ***adj.*** ⟦< L *obtrusus,* pp. of *obtrudere* + -IVE⟧ **1** inclined to obtrude **2** obtruding itself; esp., calling attention to itself in a displeasing way **—ob·tru′sive·ly** ***adv.*** **—ob·tru′sive·ness** ***n.***

ob·tund (äb tund′) ***vt.*** ⟦ME *obtunden* < L *obtundere,* to strike at, blunt < *ob-* (see OB-) + *tundere,* to strike < IE *(*s*)*teud-,* to strike > STOCK⟧ to make blunt or dull; make less acute; deaden

ob·tu·rate (äb′to͞o rāt′, -tyo͞o-) ***vt.*** **-rat′ed, -rat′ing** ⟦< L *obturatus,* pp. of *obturare,* to stop up < *ob-* (see OB-) + base akin to *turgere,* to swell: see TURGID⟧ [Rare] to close (an opening); stop up; obstruct **—ob′tu·ra′tion** ***n.*** **—ob′tu·ra′tor** ***n.***

ob·tuse (äb to͞os′, əb-; -tyo͞os′) ***adj.*** ⟦L *obtusus,* blunted, dull, pp. of *obtundere:* see OBTUND⟧ **1** not sharp or pointed; blunt **2** greater than 90 degrees and less than 180 degrees *[*an *obtuse* angle*]* **3** slow to understand or perceive; dull or insensitive **4** not producing a sharp impression; not acute [an *obtuse* pain] —**SYN.** DULL —**ob·tuse′ly** *adv.* —**ob·tuse′ness** *n.*, **ob·tu′si·ty**

ob·verse (äb vurs′, əb-; *also, and for n. always,* äb′vurs′) *adj.* ⟦L *obversus,* pp. of *obvertere,* to turn toward < *ob-* (see OB-) + *vertere,* to turn: see VERSE⟧ **1** turned toward the observer **2** narrower at the base than at the top [an *obverse* leaf] **3** forming a counterpart —*n.* **1** the side, as of a coin or medal, bearing the date and the main image or design: opposed to REVERSE **2** the front or main surface of anything **3** a counterpart **4** *Logic* the negative counterpart of an affirmative proposition, or the affirmative counterpart of a negative ["no one is infallible" is the *obverse* of "everyone is fallible"] —**ob·verse′ly** *adv.*

ob·ver·sion (äb vur′shən, əb-; -zhən) *n.* ⟦LL *obversio* < L *obversus:* see prec.⟧ **1** the act of obverting **2** *Logic* the act of inferring the obverse

ob·vert (äb vurt′, əb-) *vt.* ⟦L *obvertere:* see OBVERSE⟧ **1** to turn so that the main surface or a different surface is shown **2** *Logic* to state the obverse of (a proposition)

ob·vi·ate (äb′vē āt′) *vt.* **-at′ed, -at′ing** ⟦< LL *obviatus,* pp. of *obviare,* to prevent < *obvius:* see fol.⟧ **1** to do away with or prevent by effective measures **2** to make unnecessary: often in the phrase **obviate the need for** [the tall hedge *obviated the need for* a window shade] —**ob′vi·a′tion** *n.*

ob·vi·ous (äb′vē əs) *adj.* ⟦L *obvius,* in the way, lying open: see OB- & VIA⟧ **1** easy to see or understand; plain; evident **2** [Obs.] being in the way —**SYN.** EVIDENT —**ob′vi·ous·ly** *adv.* —**ob′vi·ous·ness** *n.*

ob·vo·lute (äb′və lo͞ot′) *adj.* ⟦L *obvolutus,* pp. of *obvolvere,* to wrap around < *ob-* (see OB-) + *volvere,* to roll: see WALK⟧ having overlapping margins: said of leaves or petals: also **ob′vo·lu′tive** —**ob′vo·lu′tion** *n.*

Ob·wal·den (ôp′väl′dən) canton of central Switzerland: 189 sq mi (490 sq km)

Oc or **oc** *abbrev.* ocean

OC *abbrev.* **1** Officer Commanding **2** Old Catholic

o/c *abbrev.* overcharge

oc- *prefix* OB-: used before *c* [*occur*]

o.c. *abbrev.* ⟦L *opere citato*⟧ in the work cited

oc·a·ri·na (äk′ə rē′nə) *n.* ⟦It, dim. of *oca,* a goose < LL *auca,* a goose (< **avica,* back-form. < L *avicula,* dim. of *avis,* bird): from its fancied resemblance in shape⟧ a small, simple wind instrument shaped like a sweet potato, with finger holes and a mouthpiece: it produces soft, hollow tones

O'Ca·sey (ō kā′sē), **Sean** (shôn) (born *John Casey*) 1880-1964; Ir. playwright

Occam, William of *see* OCKHAM, William of

Oc·cam's razor (äk′əmz) ⟦after William of OCKHAM, who used it often in analyzing problems⟧ a philosophical or scientific principle according to which the best explanation of an event is the one that is the simplest, using the fewest assumptions or hypotheses

occas *abbrev.* **1** occasion **2** occasional **3** occasionally

oc·ca·sion (ə kā′zhən, ō-) *n.* ⟦ME *occasioun* < OFr < L *occasio,* accidental opportunity, fit time < *occasus,* pp. of *occidere,* to fall < *ob-* (see OB-) + *cadere,* to fall: see CASE[1]⟧ **1** a favorable time or juncture; opportunity **2** a fact, event, or state of affairs that makes something else possible [a chance meeting was the *occasion* of the renewal of their friendship] **3** a cause or reason [you have no *occasion* to be angry] **4** *a)* a happening; occurrence *b)* the time at which something happens; particular time [on the *occasion* of our last meeting] **5** a special time or event, suitable for celebration **6** need arising from circumstances **7** [*pl.*] *a)* [Obs.] needs; requirements *b)* [Archaic] affairs; business —*vt.* to be the occasion of; give occasion to; cause —**on occasion** once in a while; sometimes; occasionally —**rise to the occasion** to do whatever suddenly becomes necessary; meet an emergency —**take (the) occasion** to use the opportunity (to do something)

oc·ca·sion·al (ə kā′zhə nəl, ō-) *adj.* **1** occurring on a particular occasion **2** of or for a special occasion [*occasional* verse] **3** acting only on special occasions **4** of irregular occurrence; happening now and then; infrequent **5** designating chairs, tables, etc. intended for occasional or auxiliary use **6** being an OCCASION (*n.* 2)

oc·ca·sion·al·ism (-nəl iz′əm) *n.* in post-Cartesian philosophy, the doctrine that, since mind and matter cannot interact, the intervention of God is required to synchronize corresponding acts of mind and movements of the body

oc·ca·sion·al·ly (ə kā′zhən əl ē, ō-) *adv.* now and then; sometimes; on occasion

oc·ci·dent (äk′sə dənt, -dent′) *n.* ⟦OFr < L *occidens,* direction of the setting sun < prp. of *occidere,* to fall: see OCCASION⟧ [Old Poet.] the west —**the Occident** the part of the world west of Asia, esp. Europe and the Americas

oc·ci·den·tal (äk′sə dent′'l) *adj.* ⟦ME *occidentale*⟧ **1** [Old Poet.] western **2** [**O-**] of the Occident or its people or culture; Western —*n.* [*usually* **O-**] a person born in the Occident or a member of a people of that region

Oc·ci·den·tal·ism (äk′sə dent′'l iz′əm) *n.* the character, culture, customs, etc. of the Occident —**Oc′ci·den′tal·ist** *n.*

Oc·ci·den·tal·ize (-īz′) *vt., vi.* **-ized′, -iz′ing** to make or become Occidental in character, culture, customs, etc.

oc·cip·i·tal (äk sip′it'l) *adj.* ⟦ML *occipitalis*⟧ of the occiput or the occipital bone —*n.* OCCIPITAL BONE —**oc·cip′i·tal·ly** *adv.*

occipital bone the bone that forms the back part of the skull

oc·ci·put (äk′si put′, -pət) *n., pl.* **oc·cip·i·ta** (äk sip′i tə) or **-puts′** ⟦ME < MFr < L < *ob-* (see OB-) + *caput,* HEAD⟧ the back part of the skull or head

oc·clude (ə klo͞od′, ä-) *vt.* **-clud′ed, -clud′ing** ⟦L *occludere* < *ob-* (see OB-) + *claudere,* to CLOSE[2]⟧ **1** to close, shut, or block (a passage) **2** to prevent the passage of; shut in or out **3** to conceal, hide, or obscure **4** *Chem.* to retain or absorb (a gas, liquid, or solid) —*vi. Dentistry* to meet with the cusps fitting close together: said of the upper and lower teeth —**oc·clud′ent** *adj.*

☆**occluded front** *Meteorol.* the front formed when a warm front is overtaken by a cold front and an air mass is forced aloft up the warm-front or cold-front surface

oc·clu·sal (ə klo͞o′zəl, -səl) *adj.* ⟦< L *occlusus* (pp. of *occludere:* see OCCLUDE) + -AL⟧ *Dentistry* **1** of or having to do with OCCLUSION (sense 2) **2** of or having to do with the biting surfaces of the teeth

oc·clu·sion (ə klo͞o′zhən) *n.* **1** an occluding or being occluded **2** *Dentistry* the fitting together of the upper and lower teeth, or the way in which these fit together when the jaws are closed **3** *Meteorol.* OCCLUDED FRONT **4** *Phonet.* the complete closing of the air passages in pronunciation, as of a stop —**oc·clu′sive** *adj.*

oc·cult (ə kult′, ä′kult′) *adj.* ⟦L *occultus,* concealed, pp. of *occulere,* to cover over < *ob-* (see OB-) + *celare,* to hide (see HALL)⟧ **1** hidden; concealed **2** secret; esoteric **3** beyond human understanding; mysterious **4** designating or of certain arts, studies, or practices, as magic, alchemy, or astrology, involving mysterious powers that some people believe can affect the way things happen — *vt., vi.* **1** to hide or become hidden from view **2** *Astron.* to hide by occultation —**the occult** the occult arts or studies —**oc·cult′ly** *adv.*

oc·cul·ta·tion (äk′ul tā′shən) *n.* ⟦ME *occultacioun* < L *occultatio,* a hiding < *occultus:* see prec.⟧ **1** the state of becoming hidden or of disappearing from view **2** *Astron.* the disappearance of a celestial body behind a closer, apparently larger celestial body

occulting light ⟦< prp. of OCCULT (*vi.*)⟧ an intermittent light in a lighthouse, lightship, etc., characterized by a period of light that equals or exceeds the period of darkness

oc·cult·ism (ə kult′iz′əm) *n.* **1** belief in occult forces and powers **2** the practice or study of occult arts —**oc·cult′ist** *n.*

oc·cu·pan·cy (äk′yo͞o pən sē, -yə-) *n., pl.* **-cies** ⟦< fol.⟧ **1** *a)* an occupying; a taking or keeping in possession *b)* the period during which a house, etc. is occupied **2** the condition of being occupied **3** *Law* the taking possession of a previously unowned object, thus establishing ownership

oc·cu·pant (äk′yo͞o pənt, -yə-) *n.* ⟦< L *occupans,* prp. of *occupare,* OCCUPY⟧ **1** a person who occupies a house, post, etc. **2** a person who acquires title to anything by occupancy

oc·cu·pa·tion (äk′yo͞o pā′shən, -yə-) *n.* ⟦OFr < L *occupatio*⟧ **1** an occupying or being occupied; specif., the seizure and control of a country or area by military forces **2** that which chiefly engages one's time; (one's) trade, profession, or business —**oc′cu·pa′tion·al** *adj.* —**oc′cu·pa′tion·al·ly** *adv.*

☆**occupational disease** a disease commonly acquired by people in a particular occupation, as silicosis among miners

☆**occupational therapy** therapy which restores, reinforces, and enhances the abilities of those diseased or injured to care for themselves, return to work, avoid further disability, etc., as by using work and play activity and by teaching techniques for adapting to individual environments

oc·cu·py (äk′yo͞o pī′, -yə-) *vt.* **-pied′, -py′ing** ⟦ME *occupien* < OFr *occuper* < L *occupare,* to take possession of, possess < *ob-* (see OB-) + *capere,* to seize: see HAVE⟧ **1** to take possession of by settlement or seizure **2** to hold possession of by tenure; specif., *a)* to dwell in *b)* to hold (a position or office) **3** to take up or fill up (space, time, etc.) **4** to employ, busy, or engage (oneself, one's attention, mind, etc.) —**oc′cu·pi′er** *n.*

oc·cur (ə kur′) *vi.* **-curred′, -cur′ring** ⟦L *occurrere,* to run, come up to, meet < *ob-* (see OB-) + *currere,* to run: see CURRENT⟧ **1** to be found; exist [fish *occur* in most waters] **2** to present itself; come to mind [an idea *occurred* to him] **3** to take place; happen —**SYN.** HAPPEN

oc·cur·rence (ə kur′əns) *n.* **1** the act or fact of occurring **2** something that occurs; event; incident —**oc·cur′rent** *adj.*

SYN.—**occurrence** is the general word for anything that happens or takes place [an unforeseen *occurrence*]; an **event** is an occurrence of relative significance, especially one growing out of earlier happenings or conditions [the *events* that followed the surrender]; an **incident** is an occurrence of relatively minor significance, often one connected with a more important event [the award was just another *incident* in his career]; an **episode** is a distinct event that is complete in itself but forms part of a larger event or is one of a series of events [an *episode* of his childhood]; a **circumstance** is an event that is either incidental to, or a determining factor of, another event [the *circumstances* surrounding my decision]

OCD *abbrev.* **1** Office of Civil Defense **2** obsessive-compulsive disorder

o·cean (ō′shən) *n.* ⟦ME *occean* < OFr < L *Oceanus* < Gr *Ōkeanos,* the outer sea (in contrast to the Mediterranean), orig. thought of as a great river flowing around the earth⟧ **1** the great body of salt water that covers approximately 71% of the surface of the earth **2** any of its four principal geographical divisions: the Atlantic, Pacific, Indian, or Arctic oceans **3** any great expanse or quantity

☆**o·cean·ar·i·um** (ō′shə ner′ē əm) *n., pl.* **-i·ums** or **-i·a** (-ē ə) ⟦prec. + (AQU)ARIUM⟧ a large salt-water aquarium for ocean fish and animals

☆**o·cean·aut** (ō′shə nôt′) *n.* ⟦< OCEAN + (AQUA)NAUT⟧ AQUANAUT

o·cean·front (ō′shən frunt′) *n.* land, buildings, etc. along an ocean shore —*adj.* of, at, or near the oceanfront [an *oceanfront* hotel]

o·cean·go·ing (ō′shən gō′iŋ) *adj.* of, or made for, travel on the ocean

O·ce·an·i·a (ō′shē an′ē ə) islands in the Pacific, including Melanesia, Micronesia, & Polynesia (incl. New Zealand) &, often, Australia & the Malay Archipelago: now often considered to be a continent when Australia is included as one of its constituent islands: see the table of continents in the Reference Supplement: also **O'ce·an'i·ca** (-i kə) **—O'ce·an'i·an** ***adj., n.***

o·ce·an·ic (ō'shē an'ik) ***adj.*** **1** of, living in, or produced by the ocean **2** like the ocean; vast **3** designating or of the ecological zone (**oceanic zone**) beyond the neritic zone in the ocean **4** [**O-**] of or having to do with Oceania

O·ce·a·nid (ō sē'ə nid') ***n., pl.*** **O'ce·an'i·des'** (-an'i dēz') ⟦Gr *Ōkeanis* (gen. *Ōkeanidos*)⟧ *Gr. Myth.* any of three thousand ocean nymphs, daughters of Oceanus and Tethys

o·ce·an·og·ra·phy (ō'shə näg'rə fē, ō'shē ə-) ***n.*** ⟦< Ger *oceanographie* < Fr *océanographie:* see OCEAN & -GRAPHY⟧ the study of the environment in the oceans, including the waters, depths, beds, animals, plants, etc. **—o'ce·an·og'ra·pher** ***n.*** **—o'ce·an·o'graph'ic** (-nə'graf'ik) ***adj.***, **o'ce·an·o·graph'i·cal**

☆**o·ce·an·ol·o·gy** (-näl'ə jē) ***n.*** ⟦OCEAN + -O- + -LOGY⟧ **1** the study of the sea in all its aspects, including oceanography, geophysical phenomena, undersea exploration, economic and military uses, etc. **2** OCEANOGRAPHY **—o'ce·an·ol'o·gist** ***n.***

O·cean·side (ō'shən sīd') ⟦descriptive⟧ city in SW Calif., near San Diego

ocean sunfish any of a family (Molidae, order Tetraodontiformes) of marine bony fishes with an abruptly truncated body; esp., a large, sluggish fish (*Mola mola*) of tropical and temperate seas

O·ce·a·nus (ō sē'ə nəs) ***n.*** ⟦L < Gr *Ōkeanos:* see OCEAN⟧ *Gr. Myth.* **1** a Titan, father of the Oceanides and ruler of the sea before Poseidon **2** the great outer stream supposedly encircling the earth

oc·el·late (äs'ə lāt'; ō sel'it, -āt') ***adj.*** **1** resembling an ocellus **2** having an ocellus or ocelli **3** spotted Also, for senses 2 & 3, **oc'el·lat'ed**

oc·el·la·tion (äs'ə lā'shən) ***n.*** an eyelike spot

o·cel·lus (ō sel'əs) ***n., pl.*** **-li'** (-ī') ⟦L, dim. of *oculus,* EYE⟧ **1** the simple eyespot of certain invertebrates, as distinguished from the compound eye of an insect or the camera-type eye of vertebrates and cephalopods **2** an eyelike spot, as on a peacock's feathers **—o·cel'lar** ***adj.***

o·ce·lot (äs'ə lət, -lät'; ō'sə-) ***n., pl.*** **-lots** or **-lot** ⟦Fr, use (by BUFFON) of Nahuatl *o:se:lo:λ,* jaguar⟧ any of various wildcats of North and South America with spots that sometimes appear as stripes when several are close together; esp., a large species (*Leopardus pardalis*) with a yellow or gray coat marked with black spots

OCelt *abbrev.* Old Celtic

o·cher (ō'kər) ***n.*** ⟦ME *ocra* < L *ochra* < Gr *ōchra* < *ōchros,* pale, pale-yellow⟧ **1** an earthy clay colored by iron oxide, usually yellow or reddish brown: used as a pigment in paints **2** the color of ocher; esp., dark yellow **—o'cher·ous** ***adj.***

och·loc·ra·cy (äk läk'rə sē) ***n.*** ⟦Fr *ochlocratie* < Gr *ochlokratia* < *ochlos,* a mob, populace + *-kratia,* -CRACY⟧ [Rare] government by the MOB (***n.*** 3); mob rule **—och·lo·crat** (äk'lō krat') ***n.*** **—och'lo·crat'ic** ***adj.***

och·one (ə khōn') ***interj.*** [Scot. or Irish] alas; woe

o·chre (ō'kər) ***n., vt.*** **o'chred**, **o'chring** *alt. sp. of* OCHER **—o'chre·ous** (-kər əs, -krē əs) ***adj.***

o·chroid (ō'kroid') ***adj.*** ⟦Gr *ōchroeidēs:* see OCHER & -OID⟧ resembling ocher; of a dark-yellow color

-ock (ək) ⟦ME *-ok* < OE *-oc, -uc,* dim.⟧ [Archaic] *suffix* little (specified thing) [*hillock*] It has lost its meaning as a diminutive in some words, as *buttock, ruddock*

ock·er (äk'ər) ***n.*** [*also* **O-**] [Austral. Slang] a rough or boorish person

Ock·ham (äk'əm), **William of** 1285?-1349?; Eng. Franciscan nominalist philosopher

Ockham's razor OCCAM'S RAZOR

o'clock (ə kläk', ō-) ***adv.*** **1** of or according to the clock [*nine o'clock* at night] **2** as if on a clock dial, with the number 12 straight ahead or directly overhead: used to indicate direction, esp. of an approaching aircraft

O'Con·nell (ō kän'əl), **Daniel** 1775-1847; Ir. nationalist leader

O'Con·nor (ō kän'ər) **1** **(Mary) Flan·ner·y** (flan'ə rē) 1925-64; U.S. writer **2** **Frank** (born *Michael John O'Donovan*) 1903-66; Ir. writer **3** **Sandra Day** 1930- ; associate justice, U.S. Supreme Court (1981-2006) **4** **Thomas Power** 1848-1929; Ir. journalist & nationalist leader: called *Tay Pay*

☆**o·co·til·lo** (ō'kə tē'yō) ***n., pl.*** **-los** (-yōz) ⟦AmSp, dim. of *ocote,* Mexican pine < Nahuatl *ocoλ,* pine⟧ a spiny, desert candlewood (*Fouquieria splendens*) with scarlet flowers, found in the SW U.S. **—*adj.*** designating a family (Fouquieriaceae, order Violales) of dicotyledonous desert shrubs and trees, including the candlewoods

OCR (ō'sē'är') ***n.*** **1** OPTICAL CHARACTER RECOGNITION **2** OPTICAL CHARACTER READER

oc·re·a (äk'rē ə, ō'krē ə) ***n., pl.*** **-re·ae'** (-rē ē') ⟦ModL < L, a legging, greave < Gr *okris,* a projection, peak, edge < IE **okri-* < base **ak-, *ok-,* sharp > ACID⟧ *Bot.* a tubelike covering around some stems, formed of the united stipules: found esp. in the buckwheat family **—oc're·ate** (-it, -āt') ***adj.***

OCS *abbrev.* Officer Candidate School

OCSO *abbrev.* Order of Cistercians of the Strict Observance (Trappists)

oct *abbrev.* octavo

Oct *abbrev.* October

oct- (äkt) *combining form* **1** OCTA- **2** OCTO- Used before a vowel

oc·ta- (äk'tə) ⟦Gr *okta-* < *oktō,* EIGHT⟧ *combining form* eight [*octagon*]

oc·ta·chord (äk'tə kôrd') ***n.*** ⟦L *octachordus* < Gr *oktachordos,* eight-stringed: see prec. & CHORD[1]⟧ *Music* **1** an octave of the diatonic scale **2** any eight-stringed musical instrument

oc·tad (äk'tad') ***n.*** ⟦Gr *oktas* (gen. *oktados*) < *oktō,* EIGHT⟧ **1** a series or group of eight **2** *Chem.* an element, atom, or radical with a valence of eight

oc·ta·gon (äk'tə gän') ***n.*** ⟦L *octagonum* < Gr *oktagōnos,* eight-cornered: see OCTA- & -GON⟧ a plane figure with eight angles and eight sides **—oc·tag'o·nal** (-tag'ə nəl) ***adj.*** **—oc·tag'o·nal·ly** ***adv.***

oc·ta·he·drite (äk'tə hē'drīt') ***n.*** ⟦< LL *octaedros* (< Gr *oktaedros:* see fol.) + -ITE[1]: orig. thought to crystallize in octahedrons⟧ ANATASE

oc·ta·he·dron (äk'tə hē'drən) ***n., pl.*** **-drons** or **-dra** (-drə) ⟦Gr *oktaedron,* neut. of *oktaedros:* see OCTA- & -HEDRON⟧ a solid figure with eight plane surfaces **—oc'ta·he'dral** ***adj.***

oc·tal (äk'təl) ***adj.*** ⟦OCT(A)- + -AL⟧ **1** of or based on the number eight **2** designating an electronic tube base or its matching socket designed to hold eight equally spaced pins

oc·tam·er·ous (äk tam'ər əs) ***adj.*** ⟦OCTA- + -MEROUS⟧ having eight parts in each whorl: said of flowers: also written **8-merous**

oc·tam·e·ter (äk tam'ət ər) ***n.*** ⟦LL, having eight feet < Gr *oktametros:* see OCTA- & METER[1]⟧ a line of verse containing eight metrical feet or measures

oc·tan (äk'tən) ***adj.*** ⟦< L *octo,* EIGHT + -AN⟧ occurring every eighth day (counting both days of occurrence) **—*n.*** an octan fever, etc.

oc·tane (äk'tān') ***n.*** ⟦OCT(A)- + -ANE⟧ an oily alkane, C_8H_{18}, occurring in petroleum, or any of a group of isomers of this substance

☆**octane number** (*or* **rating**) a number representing the antiknock properties of a gasoline, fuel mixture, etc., determined by the percentage of isooctane that must be mixed with normal heptane to produce the knocking quality of the fuel being tested: the higher the number, the greater the antiknock properties

oc·ta·no·ic acid (äk'tə nō'ik) ⟦< OCTANE + -O- + -IC⟧ CAPRYLIC ACID

oc·ta·nol (äk'tə nôl', -nōl') ***n.*** ⟦OCTAN(E) + -OL[1]⟧ any of four colorless, liquid alcohols, $C_8H_{17}OH$, used in perfumery and as solvents, foam-control agents, etc.

Oc·tans (äk'tanz) ***n.*** ⟦ModL, fol.⟧ a S constellation containing the celestial pole

oc·tant (äk'tənt) ***n.*** ⟦LL *octans,* eighth part < L *octo,* EIGHT⟧ **1** an eighth of a circle; 45° angle or arc **2** an instrument like the sextant, for measuring angles **3** *Astron.* the position of one celestial body when it is 45° distant from another **4** *Math.* any of the eight parts into which a space is divided by three planes intersecting at a single point and at right angles to one another

oc·tave (äk'tiv, -tāv') ***n.*** ⟦OFr < L *octava,* fem. of *octavus,* eighth < *octo,* EIGHT⟧ **1** *a)* the eighth day following a church festival, counting the festival day as the first *b)* the entire period between the festival and this day **2** a group of eight lines of verse; specif., the first eight lines of a Petrarchan sonnet **3** any group of eight **4** *Fencing* a position of thrust or parry in which the hand is rotated with the palm up **5** *Music a)* the eighth tone of an ascending or descending diatonic scale, or a tone seven degrees above or below a given tone in such a scale *b)* the interval of seven diatonic degrees between a tone and either of its octaves *c)* the series of tones contained within this interval, or the keys of an instrument producing such a series *d)* a tone and either of its octaves sounded together *e)* an organ stop producing tones an octave above those ordinarily produced by the keys struck **—*adj.*** **1** consisting of eight, or an octave **2** *Music* producing tones an octave higher [*an octave key*] **—oc·ta·val** (äk tā'vəl, äk'tə vəl) ***adj.***

Oc·ta·vi·a[1] (äk tā'vē ə) ***n.*** ⟦L, fem. of *Octavius*⟧ a feminine name: see OCTAVIUS

Oc·ta·vi·a[2] (äk tā'vē ə) died 11 B.C.; wife of Mark Antony

Oc·ta·vi·an (-ən) *see* AUGUSTUS[2] (the emperor)

Oc·ta·vi·us (-əs) ***n.*** ⟦L < *octavus,* eighth⟧ a masculine name: fem. *Octavia*

oc·ta·vo (äk tā'vō, -tä'-) ***n., pl.*** **-vos** ⟦< L (*in*) *octavo,* (in) eight, abl. of *octavus:* see OCTAVE⟧ **1** the page size of a book made up of printer's sheets folded into eight leaves: the usual size of each leaf is 6 by 9 inches **2** a book consisting of pages of this size Also called *eightvo,* and written **8vo** or **8°** **—*adj.*** consisting of pages of this size

oc·ten·ni·al (äk ten'ē əl) ***adj.*** ⟦< LL *octennium,* period of eight years (< L *octo,* eight + *annus,* year) + -AL⟧ **1** happening every eight years **2** lasting eight years **—oc·ten'ni·al·ly** ***adv.***

oc·tet or **oc·tette** (äk tet') ***n.*** ⟦OCT(A)- + (DU)ET⟧ **1** any group of eight; esp., an OCTAVE (sense 2) **2** *Music a)* a composition for eight voices or eight instruments *b)* a group of eight performers of this, or any group of eight musicians

oc·til·lion (äk til'yən) ***n.*** ⟦Fr < L *octo,* EIGHT + Fr (*m*)*illion*⟧ ☆**1** the number represented by 1 followed by 27 zeros **2** [Brit.] the number represented by 1 followed by 48 zeros **—*adj.*** amounting to one octillion in number

oc·to- (äk'tō, -tə) ⟦Gr *oktō-* < *oktō,* EIGHT⟧ *combining form* eight [*octopus*]

Oc·to·ber (äk tō'bər) ***n.*** ⟦ME < OE < L < *octo,* EIGHT (+ *-ber* < ?): so named as the eighth month of the ancient Roman year, which began with March⟧ **1** the tenth month of the year, having 31 days: abbrev. *Oct* or *O* **2** [Brit.] ale brewed in October

October Revolution *see* RUSSIAN REVOLUTION

oc·to·dec·i·mo (äk'tō des'ə mō') ***n., pl.*** **-mos'** ⟦< L (*in*) *octodecimo,* (in) eighteen, abl. of *octodecimus,* eighteenth⟧ **1** a page size (about 4 by 6 ½ in), 1/18 of a printer's sheet **2** a book with pages of this size Also called *eighteenmo,* and written **18mo** or **18°** **—*adj.*** with pages of this size

oc·to·ge·nar·i·an (äk'tə ji ner'ē ən) ***adj.*** ⟦L *octogenarius,* containing eighty < *octogeni,* eighty each < *octoginta,* eighty: see OCTO- & -TY[2]⟧ 80 years old, or between the ages of 80 and 90 **—*n.*** an octogenarian person

oc·to·nar·y (äk'tə ner'ē) ***adj.*** ⟦L *octonarius* < *octo,* EIGHT⟧ of or consisting of eight or groups of eight **—*n., pl.*** **-nar'ies** **1** a group of eight **2** a stanza of eight lines

oc·to·pod (äk′tə päd′) ***n.*** ⟦< Gr *oktōpous* (gen. *octōpodos*): see fol.⟧ any animal with eight limbs; specif., any of an order (Octopoda) of cephalopod mollusks, including the octopus and the paper nautilus —**oc·top′o·dan** (-täp′ə dən) ***adj., n.*** —**oc·top′o·dous** (-dəs) ***adj.***

oc·to·pus (äk′tə pəs, -poos) ***n., pl.*** **-pus·es, -pi′** (-pī′), or **oc·top·o·des** (äk täp′ə dēz′) ⟦ModL < Gr *oktōpous,* eight-footed < *oktō,* EIGHT + *pous* (gen. *podos*), FOOT⟧ **1** any of various octopods (order Octopoda) having a soft, saclike body, a reduced coelom, an internal vestigial shell, and eight sucker-bearing arms around the mouth **2** anything suggesting an octopus; esp., an organization with branches that reach out in a powerful and influential manner

octopus

☆**oc·to·roon** (äk′tə ro͞on′) ***n.*** ⟦< L *octo,* eight + (QUAD)ROON⟧ [Chiefly Historical] a person who has one black great-grandparent; child of a quadroon and a white

oc·to·syl·lab·ic (äk′tō si lab′ik, -tə-) ***adj.*** **1** containing eight syllables, as a line of verse **2** containing lines of eight syllables

oc·to·syl·la·ble (äk′tō sil′ə bəl, -tə-) ***n.*** a word or a line of verse having eight syllables —***adj.*** OCTOSYLLABIC

oc·troi (äk′troi′; *Fr* ôk trwȧ′) ***n., pl.*** **-trois′** (-troiz′; *Fr,* -trwȧ′) ⟦Fr < *octroyer,* for earlier *ottroyer, otreier,* to grant < VL **auctoricare* < L *auctor:* see AUTHOR⟧ **1** a tax on certain goods entering a town **2** the place where this tax is collected **3** the official or officials collecting this tax

oc·tu·ple (äk′tə pəl, äk to͞o′pəl) ***adj.*** ⟦L *octuplus* < *octo,* EIGHT + *-plus:* see DOUBLE⟧ **1** eightfold **2** consisting of eight parts —***n.*** something eight times as great as something else —***vt.*** **-pled, -pling** to multiply by eight

oc·u·lar (äk′yo͞o lər, -yə-) ***adj.*** ⟦LL *ocularis* < L *oculus,* EYE⟧ **1** of, for, or like the eye **2** by eyesight [an *ocular* demonstration] —***n.*** the lens or lenses constituting the eyepiece of an optical instrument —**oc′u·lar·ly** ***adv.***

oc·u·lar·ist (äk′yo͞o lər ist, -yə-) ***n.*** ⟦prec. + -IST[1]⟧ a person who designs, makes, and fits artificial eyes

oc·u·list (äk′yo͞o list, -yə-) ***n.*** ⟦Fr *oculiste* < L *oculus,* EYE⟧ *former term for:* **1** OPHTHALMOLOGIST **2** OPTOMETRIST

oc·u·lo- (äk′yo͞o lō, -lə; -yə-) ⟦< L *oculus,* EYE⟧ *combining form* eye, eye and [*oculomotor*]

oc·u·lo·mo·tor (äk′yo͞o lō mōt′ər, -yə-) ***adj.*** ⟦prec. + MOTOR⟧ moving the eyeball; specif. designating or of either nerve of the third pair of cranial nerves, arising in the midbrain and supplying four of the six muscles that move each eyeball

od (äd) ***n., pl.*** **od** ⟦Ger, coined by K. v. Reichenbach (1788-1869), Ger scientist⟧ a hypothesized force in nature formerly thought to manifest itself in such phenomena as hypnotism, magnetism, light, etc. —**od′ic** ***adj.***

Od or **'Od** (äd) ***interj.*** ⟦euphemism for *God*⟧ [*often* **o-**] [Archaic] used as a mild oath

OD[1] (ō′dē′) [Slang] ***n., pl.*** **ODs** or **OD's** an overdose, esp. of a narcotic —***vi.*** **OD'd** or **ODed, OD'ing** or **ODing** to take an overdose, esp. a fatal overdose of a narcotic

OD[2] *abbrev.* **1** ⟦L⟧ Doctor of Optometry: also **O.D. 2** Officer of the Day **3** olive drab **4** outside diameter Also, for 3 & 4, **od**

O/D or **o/d** *abbrev.* **1** overdraft **2** overdrawn

o.d. *abbrev.* ⟦L *oculus dexter*⟧ right eye

o·da·lisque or **o·da·lisk** (ō′də lisk′) ***n.*** ⟦Fr *odalisque* < Turk *ōdalik,* chambermaid < *ōdah,* chamber + *-lik,* suffix expressing function⟧ **1** a female slave or concubine in a harem **2** a conventionalized painting of a reclining odalisque as by Ingres or Matisse

ODan *abbrev.* Old Danish

odd (äd) ***adj.*** ⟦ME *odde* < ON *oddi,* point of land, triangle, hence (from the third angle) odd number, akin to OE *ord,* a point < Gmc **uzda-* (> Ger *ort,* place, orig., point) < IE **uds* (< base **ud-,* up > OUT) + **dho-,* var. of **dhē,* to place, put > DO[1]⟧ **1** *a)* being one of a pair of which the other is missing [an *odd* glove] *b)* being the one remaining after the others are paired, grouped, taken, etc. *c)* being one or more of a set, series, or group separated from the others [a few *odd* volumes of Dickens] **2** having a remainder of one when divided by two; not even: said of numbers **3** numbered with an odd number [the *odd* months] **4** *a)* in addition to that mentioned in a round number [ten dollars and some *odd* change] *b)* with a relatively small number over that specified (usually in hyphenated compounds) [twenty-*odd* children] **5** not the usual, regular, habitual, accounted for, etc.; occasional; incidental [*odd* jobs, at *odd* moments] **6** *a)* not usual or ordinary; singular; peculiar; strange *b)* eccentric; unconventional **7** out-of-the-way [in *odd* corners] —***SYN.*** STRANGE —**odd′ly** ***adv.*** —**odd′ness** ***n.***

Odd (äd) ***interj.*** *alt. sp. of* OD

☆**odd·ball** (äd′bôl′) ***n.*** ⟦ODD + BALL[1]⟧ [Slang] an eccentric, unconventional, or nonconforming person —***adj.*** [Slang] strange or unconventional

Odd Fellow a member of the Independent Order of Odd Fellows, a fraternal and benevolent secret society founded in England in the 18th cent.

odd·i·ty (äd′ə tē) ***n.*** **1** the state or quality of being odd; queerness; peculiarity; strangeness **2** *pl.* **-ties** an odd person or thing

☆**odd lot** an amount smaller than the usual unit of trading; specif., a quantity of fewer than 100 shares of stock in a transaction —**odd′-lot′** ***adj.***

odd man out **1** *a)* a method, as in a game, for singling out one person from a group, as by matching coins *b)* the person thus singled out **2** any atypical or unconventional person or thing

odd·ment (äd′mənt) ***n.*** ⟦ODD + -MENT⟧ **1** any of various miscellaneous items **2** a scrap or remnant

odd-pin·nate (äd′pin′āt) ***adj.*** *Bot.* pinnate with an odd, or single, terminal leaflet

odds (ädz) ***pl.n.*** [*sometimes, esp. formerly, with sing. v.*] **1** [Archaic] inequalities **2** [Now Rare] difference or amount of difference **3** difference in favor of one side over the other; advantage **4** an equalizing advantage given or received in betting, based on a given bettor's assumed chance of winning and expressed as a ratio [a winning bettor who got *odds* of 3 to 1 is paid three times as much as he or she bet] —**at odds** in disagreement; quarreling —**by (all) odds** by far; unquestionably —**(the) odds are** the likelihood is

odds and ends scraps; remnants; oddments

odds·mak·er (ädz′māk′ər) ***n.*** a person, usually an expert, who estimates the odds, or advantage, in betting or competing

odds-on (ädz′än′) ***adj.*** having better, often much better, than an even chance of winning [an *odds-on* favorite]

ode (ōd) ***n.*** ⟦Fr < LL *oda* < Gr *ōidē,* song, contr. < *aoidē* < *aeidein,* to sing < IE **aweid-* < base **aw-,* to speak > Sans *vādati,* (he) speaks⟧ **1** a poem written to be sung **2** in modern use, a lyric poem, rhymed or unrhymed, typically addressed to some person or thing and usually characterized by lofty feeling, elaborate form, and dignified style —**od·ic** (ō′dik) ***adj.***

-ode[1] (ōd) ⟦< Gr *hodos,* path, way < IE base **sed-,* to go > L *cedere*⟧ *suffix* way, path [*electrode*]

-ode[2] (ōd) ⟦Gr *-ōdēs, ōdes* < *-ō-,* ending of base or thematic vowel + *-eidēs,* like, -OID⟧ *suffix* something that resembles (a specified thing) [*phyllode, nematode*]

O·den·se (ō′thən sə, -dən-) seaport on N Fyn island, Denmark

O·der (ō′dər) river in central Europe, flowing north through the Czech Republic & Poland into the Baltic: *c.* 560 mi (901 km): it forms, with the Neisse, the boundary (**Oder-Neisse Line**) between Germany & Poland

O·des·sa (ō des′ə) **1** seaport in S Ukraine, on the Black Sea **2** ⟦after the Ukrainian city⟧ city in WC Tex.

O·dets (ō dets′), **Clifford** 1906-63; U.S. playwright

o·de·um (ō dē′əm) ***n., pl.*** **o·de′ums** or **o·de′a** (-ə) ⟦LL < Gr *ōideion* < *ōidē:* see ODE⟧ **1** in ancient Greece and Rome, a roofed building for musical performances **2** a modern concert hall

O·din (ō′din) ***n.*** ⟦Dan < ON *Othinn,* akin to OE *Woden*⟧ *Norse Myth.* the chief deity, god of art, culture, war, and the dead: identified with the Germanic Woden

o·di·ous (ō′dē əs) ***adj.*** ⟦OFr *odieus* < L *odiosus* < *odium,* hatred: see fol.⟧ arousing or deserving hatred or loathing; disgusting; offensive —***SYN.*** HATEFUL —**o′di·ous·ly** ***adv.*** —**o′di·ous·ness** ***n.***

o·di·um (ō′dē əm) ***n.*** ⟦L, hatred, ill will < *odi,* I hate < IE base **od-,* hatred > Gr *odyssasthai,* to be angry, ON *atall,* frightful⟧ **1** *a)* hatred, esp. of a person or thing regarded as loathsome *b)* the state or fact of being hated **2** the disgrace brought on by hateful action; opprobrium

O·do·a·cer (ō′dō ā′sər) A.D. 435?-493; Germanic warrior, 1st barbarian ruler of Italy (476-493)

o·do·graph (ō′də graf′) ***n.*** ⟦< Gr *hodos,* way (see -ODE[1]) + -GRAPH⟧ a device for measuring distance traveled

☆**o·dom·e·ter** (ō däm′ət ər) ***n.*** ⟦Fr *odomètre* < Gr *hodometros* < *hodos,* way (see -ODE[1]) + *metron,* MEASURE⟧ an instrument for measuring the distance traveled by a vehicle

-o·dont (ō dänt′, ə-) ⟦see fol.⟧ *combining form* **1** *forming adjectives* having teeth of a (specified) type [*pleurodont*] **2** *forming nouns* an animal having teeth of a (specified) type

o·dont·o- (ō dän′tō, -tə) ⟦< Gr *odōn, odous* (gen. *odontos*), TOOTH⟧ *combining form* tooth or teeth [*odontoblast, odontology*]: also, before a vowel, **odont-**

o·don·to·blast (ō dänt′ō blast′) ***n.*** ⟦prec. + -BLAST⟧ any of the cells forming the outer surface of the pulp of a tooth and secreting a substance which develops into dentin —**o·don′to·blas′tic** ***adj.***

o·don·to·glos·sum (ō dänt′ō gläs′əm) ***n.*** ⟦ModL < ODONTO- + Gr *glōssa,* a tongue: see GLOSS[2]⟧ any of a genus (*Odontoglossum*) of tropical American, epiphytic orchids with clustered flowers of various colors

o·don·toid (ō dän′toid′) ***adj.*** ⟦Gr *odontoeidēs:* see ODONTO- & -OID⟧ **1** toothlike **2** designating or of a toothlike or peg-shaped process projecting from the second vertebra of the neck, on which the top vertebra moves and rotates

o·don·tol·o·gy (ō′dän täl′ə jē) ***n.*** ⟦Fr *odontologie:* see ODONTO- & -LOGY⟧ the science dealing with the structure, growth, and diseases of the teeth; dentistry —**o·don′to·log′i·cal** (-tō läj′i kəl) ***adj.*** —**o·don′to·log′i·cal·ly** ***adv.*** —**o′don·tol′o·gist** ***n.***

o·don·to·phore (ō dän′tə fôr′) ***n.*** ⟦ODONTO- + -PHORE⟧ a muscular structure of most mollusks, usually protrusile, supporting the radula —**o′don·toph′o·ral** (-täf′ə rəl) ***adj.***

o·dor (ō′dər) ***n.*** ⟦OFr < L < IE base **od-,* to smell, odor > Gr *odmē,* (var. of *osmē*), scent, Swed *os,* smell, suffocating gas⟧ **1** *a)* that characteristic of a substance which makes it perceptible to the sense of smell *b)* a smell, whether pleasant or unpleasant; fragrance, stench, etc. **2** a pervasive atmosphere or quality [an *odor* of intolerance] **3** [Archaic] a perfume or other sweet-smelling substance —***SYN.*** SMELL —**be in bad (or ill) odor** to be in ill repute —**o′dor·less** ***adj.***

o·dor·ant (ō′dər ənt) ***n.*** ⟦prec. + -ANT⟧ any substance or thing that produces a perceptible odor
o·dor·if·er·ous (ō′dər if′ər əs) ***adj.*** ⟦ME < L *odorifer:* see ODOR & -FEROUS⟧ giving off an odor, now often, specif., a strong or offensive one —**o′dor·if′er·ous·ly** ***adv.***
o·dor·ous (ō′dər əs) ***adj.*** having a pronounced odor —**o′dor·ous·ly** ***adv.*** —**o′dor·ous·ness** ***n.***
o·dour (ō′dər) ***n.*** *Brit. sp. of* ODOR
O·do·va·car (ō′dō vā′kər) *var. of* ODOACER
O·dra (ô′drä) *Pol. name for* the ODER
ODu *abbrev.* Old Dutch
-o·dus (ə dəs) ⟦ModL < Gr *-odous* < *odōn,* TOOTH⟧ *combining form* an animal having (a specified kind of) teeth [*ceratodus*]
-o·dyn·i·a (ə din′ē ə, -dīn′-) ⟦ModL < Gr *-odynia* < *odynē,* a pain < IE **od-,* var. of base **ed-,* to EAT⟧ *combining form* pain in (a specified organ or part)
O·dys·se·us (ō dis′ē əs, ō dis′yo͞os′) ***n.*** ⟦Gr⟧ the hero of the *Odyssey,* a king of Ithaca and one of the Greek leaders in the Trojan War: Latin name *Ulysses*
Od·ys·sey (äd′i sē) ***n.*** ⟦L *Odyssea* < Gr *Odysseia*⟧ **1** an ancient Greek epic poem, ascribed to Homer, about the wanderings of Odysseus during the ten years after the fall of Troy **2** *pl.* **-seys** [**o-**] any extended wandering or journey —**Od′ys·se′an** ***adj.***
oe[1] (ō) ***n.*** ⟦< Faeroese *othi* < *othur,* raging < ON *other*⟧ a whirlwind near the Faroe Islands
oe[2] *abbrev.* omissions excepted
Oe *abbrev.* oersted
OE *abbrev.* Old English
oe- a variant spelling for *e-* in many words of Greek and Latin origin [*oecumenical, oestrogen*]
OECD *abbrev.* Organization for Economic Cooperation and Development
oec·u·men·i·cal (ek′yo͞o men′i kəl) ***adj.*** *alt. sp. of* ECUMENICAL
OED *abbrev.* Oxford English Dictionary
oe·de·ma (ē dē′mə) ***n.*** *chiefly Brit. sp. of* EDEMA
Oed·i·pal (ed′i pəl, ē′di-) ***adj.*** [*also* **o-**] of or relating to the Oedipus complex
Oed·i·pus (ed′i pəs, ē′di-) ***n.*** ⟦L < Gr *Oidipous* (< *oidein,* to swell + *pous,* FOOT: lit., swollen foot)⟧ *Gr. Myth.* the son of Laius and Jocasta, king and queen of Thebes, who, raised by the king of Corinth, later returns to Thebes and unwittingly kills his father and marries his mother
Oedipus complex *Psychoanalysis* the unconscious tendency of a child to be attached to the parent of the opposite sex and hostile toward the other parent: its persistence in adult life results in neurotic disorders: orig. restricted to a son's attachment: cf. ELECTRA COMPLEX
oeil-de-boeuf (ëy′ də bëf′) ***n.,*** *pl.* ***oeils-de-boeuf′*** (ëy′-) ⟦Fr, eye of an ox⟧ a round or oval window
oeil·lade (ë yȧd′) ***n.*** ⟦Fr < *oeil,* an eye < L *oculus,* EYE⟧ an amorous or flirting glance; ogle
OEM (ō′ē em′) ***n.*** ⟦*o*(*riginal*) *e*(*quipment*) *m*(*anufacturer*)⟧ **1** a company whose products, such as manufactured parts or computer software, are repackaged and sold by a second company, often as part of a larger system **2** the company that buys the original items and resells them, often under its own name
oe·nol·o·gy (ē näl′ə jē) ***n.*** ⟦< Gr *oinos,* wine (see VINE) + -LOGY⟧ the science or study of wines and winemaking —**oe·no·log·i·cal** (ē′nə läj′i kəl) ***adj.*** —**oe·nol′o·gist** ***n.***
oe·no·mel (ē′nə mel′, en′ə-) ***n.*** ⟦LL *oenomeli* < Gr *oinomeli* < *oinos,* wine (see VINE) + *meli,* honey: see MEL⟧ a beverage of wine and honey, drunk by the ancient Greeks
Oe·no·ne (ē nō′nē) ***n.*** ⟦L < Gr *Oinōnē*⟧ *Gr. Myth.* a nymph deserted by her husband, Paris, for Helen of Troy
oe·no·phile (ē′nə fīl′) ***n.*** ⟦Fr < Gr *oinos,* wine (see VINE) + Fr *-phile,* -PHILE⟧ a person who loves wine; wine connoisseur
o'er (ō′ər, ôr) ***prep., adv.*** [Old Poet.] OVER
oer·sted (ʉr′sted′) ***n.*** ⟦after H. C. *Oersted* (1777-1851), Dan physicist⟧ the basic unit of electromagnetic field strength in the CGS system, equal to a force of one dyne acting upon a unit magnetic pole in a vacuum (79.58 ampere-turns per meter): abbrev. *Oe*
oe·soph·a·gus (ē säf′ə gəs) ***n.*** *chiefly Brit. sp. of* ESOPHAGUS
oes·tro·gen (ēs′trə gən, es′-) ***n.*** *Brit. var. of* ESTROGEN
oes·trous (ē′strəs, es′trəs) ***adj.*** *Brit. var. of* ESTROUS
oes·trus (ē′strəs, es′trəs) ***n.*** *Brit. var. of* ESTRUS
oeu·vre (o͞o′vrə, ʉrv; *Fr* ë′vr′) ***n.,*** *pl.* **oeu·vres** (o͞o′vrəz, ʉrvz; *Fr* ë′vr′) ⟦Fr, lit., work⟧ [*sometimes in italics*] the group consisting of all the works, usually of a lifetime, of a particular writer, artist, or composer
of[1] (uv) ***prep.*** ⟦ME < OE, unstressed var. of *af, æf,* away (from); akin to Ger *ab* < IE base **apo-,* from, away from > L *ab* (see AB-), Gr *apo-*⟧ **1** from; specif., *a)* derived or coming from [men *of* Ohio] *b)* resulting from; caused by; through [to die *of* fever] *c)* proceeding as a product from; by [the poems *of* Poe] *d)* resulting from an operation or process involving [the product *of* 3 and 4] *e)* at a distance from or apart from (a specified reference point) [east *of* the city] *f)* deprived, relieved, or separated from [cured *of* cancer, robbed *of* his money] *g)* from the whole, or total number, constituting [part *of* the time, one *of* her hats] *h)* distinguished as by excellence from among [the greatest *of* our Presidents] *i)* distinguished as the best, most important, etc. from among [the holy *of* holies] *j)* made from; using as its material (a specified substance) [a sheet *of* paper, made *of* tin] **2** is what was done, expressed, etc. by [how wise *of* her!] **3** belonging to [the pages *of* a book, the square root *of* 3, that dog *of* his] **4** *a)* having; possessing [a man *of* property] *b)* containing [a bag *of* nuts] **5** *a)* that is; having the designation of; specified as [the state *of* Utah, a height *of* six feet] *b)* as a way to characterize [a prince *of* a fellow] **6** with (something specified) as object, goal, etc. [a reader *of* books] **7** *a)* having as a distinguishing quality or attribute; characterized by [a man *of* honor, a year *of* plenty] *b)* as characterized with respect to [quick *of* mind, hard *of* heart] **8** concerning; about; with reference to [think well *of* me] **9** set aside for; dedicated to [a day *of* rest] **10** *a)* during [*of* late years] *b)* [Informal] on or at (a specified day, time, etc.) [he came *of* a Friday] **11** before: used in telling time [ten minutes *of* nine] **12** [Archaic] by [rejected *of* men]
NOTE—*of* is also used in various idiomatic expressions (as in *of course*), many of which are entered in this dictionary under the key words
of[2] *abbrev. Baseball* **1** outfield **2** outfielder
OF *abbrev.* Old French
of- (ôf, äf, əf) *prefix* OB-: used before *f* [*offer*]
O'Fao·láin (ō′fə lôn′), **Seán** (shôn) 1900-91; Ir. writer
☆**o·fay** (ō′fā′) ***n.*** [Slang] a white person: a term of contempt
off[1] (ôf, äf) ***adv.*** ⟦LME var. of *of,* OF[1], later generalized for all occurrences of *of* in stressed positions⟧ **1** so as to be or keep away, at a distance, to a side, etc. [to move *off,* to ward *off*] **2** so as to be measured, divided, etc. [to pace *off,* to mark *off*] **3** so as to be no longer on, attached, united, covering, in contact, etc. [take *off* your hat, the paint wore *off*] **4** (a specified distance) away: *a)* in space [a town ten miles *off*] *b)* in time [a date two weeks *off*] **5** *a)* so as to be no longer in operation, function, continuance, etc. [turn the motor *off*] *b)* to the point of completion, extinction, or exhaustion [drink it *off*] **6** so as to be less, smaller, fewer, etc. [to allow 5% *off* for cash] **7** so as to lose consciousness [to doze *off*] **8** away from one's work or usual activity [to take a week *off*] —***prep.*** **1** (so as to be) no longer (or not) on, attached to, united with, covering, in contact with, etc. [it blew *off* the desk; a car went *off* the road] **2** away from but not far from [to live *off* campus, anchored *off* the lee shore] **3** *a)* from the substance of; on [to live *off* an inheritance] *b)* at the expense of **4** coming or branching out from [an alley *off* Main Street] **5** free or relieved from [*off* duty] **6** not up to the usual level, standard, etc. of [*off* one's game] **7** less than; taken from [25% *off* the regular price] **8** [Informal] no longer using, engaging in, supporting, etc.; abstaining from [to be *off* liquor] **9** [Informal] from [I bought it *off* a friend] *Off* as a preposition is often used, chiefly in informal speech, with *of;* however, this idiomatic expression is generally avoided by careful speakers and writers —***adj.*** **1** not on, attached, united, etc. [his hat is *off*] **2** not in operation, function, continuance, etc. [the motor is *off*] **3** gone away; on the way [be *off* to bed] **4** *a)* less, smaller, fewer, etc. [sales are *off*] *b)* lower in value **5** away from work, etc.; absent [the maid is *off* today] **6** not up to what is usual, normal, standard, etc. [an *off* day] **7** more remote; further [on the *off* chance, the *off* side] **8** on the right side, facing forward: said of an animal in double harness, a wagon wheel, etc.: opposed to NEAR **9** in (specified) circumstances [to be well *off*] **10** not correct; in error; wrong [his figures are *off*] **11** [Informal] not quite normal in thinking, behavior, etc.; mildly eccentric **12** *Cricket* designating the side of the field facing the batsman —***n.*** **1** the fact or condition of being off [turn the switch from *off* to on] **2** *Cricket* the off side —***vt.*** [Slang] to kill; murder —***interj.*** go away; stay away —**off and on** now and then; intermittently —**off with!** put off! take off! remove! —**off with you!** go away! depart!
NOTE—*off* is used in various idiomatic expressions, many of which are entered in this dictionary under the key words
off[2] *abbrev.* **1** offered **2** office **3** officer **4** official
-off (ôf, äf) ⟦< OFF[1] ***adv.***: see BAKE-OFF⟧ *combining form* a contest of skill in a (specified) activity or field, esp. one in which finalists compete, as by preparing their own version of a recipe, to determine a champion [a chili cook-*off*]
of·fal (ôf′əl) ***n.*** ⟦ME *ofall,* lit., off-fall⟧ **1** [*with sing. or pl. v.*] waste parts; esp., the entrails, etc. of a butchered animal **2** refuse; garbage
Of·fa·ly (äf′ə lē) county in Leinster province, central Ireland: 771 sq mi (1,997 sq km)
off·beat (ôf′bēt′) ***n.*** *Music* any of the beats of a measure that have weak, or secondary, accents —***adj.*** ☆**1** *Jazz* with a strong, or primary, accent placed on beats that usually receive a weak, or secondary, accent **2** [Informal] not conforming to the usual pattern or trend; unconventional, unusual, strange, etc.
☆**off-Broad·way** (ôf′brôd′wā′) ***adj.*** designating, of, or produced in any theater located in New York City outside the main theatrical district and presenting professional productions that are often unconventional, experimental, low-cost, etc. —***adv.*** in an off-Broadway theater or theaters —***n.*** off-Broadway theaters and their productions collectively Also written **Off Broadway**
off-cen·ter (-sen′tər) ***adj.*** **1** not in the exact center **2** out of balance Also **off′-cen′tered**
off-col·or (ôf′kul′ər) ***adj.*** **1** varying from the usual, standard, or required color ☆**2** not quite proper; now, esp., risqué [an *off-color* joke]
off-du·ty (ôf′do͞ot′ē) ***adj.*** **1** not officially engaged in one's regular duties [an *off-duty* policeman] **2** outside of one's regular job or its work period [*off-duty* employment]
Of·fen·bach[1] (ôf′ən bäk′; *Fr* ôf en bäk′), **Jacques** (zhäk) (born *Jakob Eberscht*) 1819-80; Fr. composer of operettas, born in Germany
Of·fen·bach[2] (ôf′ən bäkh′) city in SW Germany, on the Main River, in the state of Hesse

of·fence (ə fens′) ***n.*** *Brit. sp. of* OFFENSE

of·fend (ə fend′) ***vi.*** ⟦ME *offenden* < OFr *offendre* < L *offendere,* to strike against < *ob-* (see OB-) + *fendere,* to hit, strike: see DEFEND⟧ **1** to break a law, religious commandment, etc.; commit a sin or crime **2** to create resentment, anger, or displeasure; give offense —***vt.*** **1** to hurt the feelings of; cause to feel resentful, angry, or displeased; insult **2** to be displeasing to (the taste, sense, etc.) **3** [Obs.] *a)* to transgress; violate *b)* to cause to sin —**of·fend′er *n.***

SYN.—**offend** implies a causing displeasure or resentment in another, intentionally or unintentionally, by wounding his or her feelings or by a breach of his or her sense of propriety [she will be *offended* if she is not invited]; **affront** implies open and deliberate disrespect or offense [to *affront* someone's modesty]; **insult** implies an affront so insolent or contemptuously rude as to cause deep humiliation and resentment [to *insult* someone by calling him a liar]; **outrage** implies an extreme offense against someone's sense of right, justice, propriety, etc. [he was *outraged* by the offer of a bribe]

of·fense (ə fens′; *also, and for n. 7 always,* ô′fens′) ***n.*** ⟦ME < MFr < L *offensa* < pp. of *offendere:* see prec.⟧ **1** an offending; specif., *a)* the act of breaking a law; sin or crime; transgression *b)* the act of creating resentment, hurt feelings, displeasure, etc. **2** the condition of being offended, esp. of feeling hurt, resentful, or angry; umbrage **3** [Rare] something that causes sinning or wrongdoing **4** something that causes resentment, anger, etc. **5** the act of attacking or assaulting; aggression **6** the person, army, etc. that is attacking ☆**7** *Sports a)* a team when it is attempting to score against an opponent in any contest *b)* the ability to score against an opposing team *c)* the strategy, plays, etc. used in attempting to score against an opposing team —**give offense** to offend; anger, insult, etc. —**on offense** *Sports* engaged in an attempt to score against an opposing team —**take offense** to become offended; feel hurt, angry, etc.

SYN.—**offense** implies displeased or hurt feelings as the result of a slight, insult, etc. [don't take *offense* at my criticism]; **resentment** adds implications of indignation, a brooding over an injury, and ill will toward the offender [a *resentment* cherished for days]; **umbrage** implies offense or resentment at being slighted or having one's pride hurt [he took *umbrage* at the tone of her letter]; **pique** suggests a passing feeling of ruffled pride, usually over a trifle; **displeasure** may describe a feeling varying from dissatisfaction or disapproval to anger and indignation

of·fense·less (ə fens′lis) ***adj.*** **1** not offending **2** lacking or incapable of offense

of·fen·sive (ə fen′siv; *for adj., also* ô′fen′siv) ***adj.*** ⟦ML *offensivus* < L *offensa,* OFFENSE⟧ **1** attacking; aggressive **2** of or for attack ☆**3** designating or of the side that is seeking to score in any contest **4** unpleasant, as to the senses; disgusting; repugnant [an *offensive* odor] **5** causing resentment, anger, etc.; insulting —***n.*** **1** attitude or position of attack: often with *the* **2** an attack or hostile action, esp. by armed forces —**of·fen′sive·ly *adv.*** —**of·fen′sive·ness *n.***

of·fer (ôf′ər, äf′-) ***vt.*** ⟦ME *offren* < OE & OFr: OE *offrian* < LL(Ec) *offerre,* to offer to God, sacrifice; OFr *offrir:* both < L *offerre,* to bring before, present, show < *ob-* (see OB-) + *ferre,* to BEAR[1]⟧ **1** to present to God or a god in an act of worship: often with *up* [to *offer* prayers, *offer* up sacrifices] **2** to present for approval or acceptance; proffer; tender [to *offer* one's services] **3** to present for consideration; suggest; propose [to *offer* a plan] **4** to indicate or express one's willingness or intention (to do something) [to *offer* to go] **5** to show or give signs of [to *offer* resistance] **6** *a)* to present for sale *b)* to bid (a price, etc.) —***vi.*** **1** to make a presentation or sacrifice in worship **2** to occur; present itself [when the opportunity *offers*] **3** [Rare] to make a proposal, as of marriage **4** [Archaic] to make an attempt (*at*) —***n.*** **1** the act of offering **2** something offered; presentation, proposal, suggestion, bid, etc. **3** *Law* a proposal supported by adequate consideration, the full and complete acceptance of which constitutes a contract —**of′fer·er *n.*, of′fer·or**

of·fer·ing (ôf′ər iŋ) ***n.*** **1** the act of making an offer **2** something offered; specif., *a)* a gift or contribution *b)* presentation in worship; oblation ☆*c)* something offered for sale *d)* a theatrical presentation

of·fer·to·ry (ôf′ər tôr′ē) ***n., pl.*** **-ries** ⟦ME *offertorie* < ML(Ec) *offertorium* < LL(Ec), place for offerings < *offerre,* to OFFER⟧ [*often* **O-**] **1** *a)* the part of a Eucharistic service in which the bread and wine, before being consecrated, are offered to God *b)* the prayers said then *c)* a hymn or musical composition used then **2** *a)* the part of a church service during which money offerings are collected from the congregation *b)* the collection itself

off-glide (ôf′glīd′) ***n.*** a glide coming immediately after a speech sound, in which the vocal organs resume their normal inactive position or take the position for articulating a following sound: cf. ON-GLIDE

off-grid (ôf′grid′) ***adj.*** not involving or requiring energy provided by a utility [an *off-grid* solar-heating system]

off·hand (ôf′hand′, -hand′) ***adv.*** without prior preparation or study; at once; extemporaneously —***adj.*** **1** said or done offhand; extemporaneous; unpremeditated **2** casual, curt, informal, brusque, etc. Also **off′hand′ed** —**off′hand′ed·ly *adv.*** —**off′hand′ed·ness *n.***

off-hour (ôf′our′) ***adj.*** not occurring during or pertaining to rush hour, regular business hours, or other busy periods of time [*off-hour* traffic conditions]

of·fice (ôf′is, äf′-) ***n.*** ⟦OFr < L *officium* < *opificium,* doing of work < *opifex,* a worker < *opus,* a work (see OPUS) + *facere,* to DO[1]⟧ **1** something performed or intended to be performed for another; (specified kind of) service [done through someone's good (or ill) *offices*] **2** *a)* a function or duty assigned to someone, esp. as an essential part of his or her work or position *b)* the function or characteristic action of a particular thing **3** a position of authority or trust, esp. in a government, business, institution, etc. [the *office* of president] **4** ☆*a)* any of the branches of the U.S. Government ranking next below the departments [the Printing *Office*] *b)* [Chiefly Brit.] a governmental department [the Foreign *Office*] **5** *a)* the building, room, or series of rooms in which the affairs of a business, professional person, branch of government, etc. are carried on *b)* all the people working in such a place; staff **6** [*pl.*] [Chiefly Brit.] the rooms or buildings of a house or estate in which the servants carry out their duties **7** ⟦ME < ML(Ec) *officium,* divine rite < L, ceremonial observance⟧ [*often* **O-**] a religious service or set of prayers; esp., DIVINE OFFICE —*SYN.* FUNCTION, POSITION —**in** (or **out of**) **office** currently holding (or not holding) power or a particular position of authority

☆**office boy** a boy or man who works in an office, doing odd jobs and errands

of·fice·hold·er (ôf′is hōl′dər) ***n.*** a government official

office hours the hours during which an office is normally open for business or consultation

Office of Readings *R.C.Ch.* the first of the canonical hours; matins

office park a complex of office buildings located on land planted with lawns, trees, bushes, etc.

of·fi·cer (ôf′i sər, äf′-) ***n.*** ⟦ME < Anglo-Fr & OFr *officier* < ML *officiarius* < L *officium,* OFFICE⟧ **1** anyone elected or appointed to an office or position of authority in a government, business, institution, society, etc. **2** a police officer or constable **3** a person appointed to a position of authority in the armed forces; specif., COMMISSIONED OFFICER **4** the captain or any of the mates of a merchant ship **5** in certain honorary societies, a member of any grade above the lowest —***vt.*** **1** to provide with officers **2** to command; direct; manage

officer of the day the military officer in overall charge of the security and guard at a military post for any given day

officer of the deck the officer in charge of a naval ship during a given watch

officer of the guard *Mil.* an officer in immediate command of the interior guard of a garrison

of·fi·cial (ə fish′əl, ō-) ***adj.*** ⟦OFr < LL *officialis*⟧ **1** of or holding an office, or position of authority **2** by, from, or with the proper authority; authorized or authoritative [an *official* request] **3** in a formal or ceremonious manner, often involving persons of authority [an *official* welcome to the city] **4** formally set or prescribed [the *official* date of publication] **5** *Med., Pharmacy* contained in the current pharmacopeia; authorized for use in medicine —***n.*** **1** a person holding office, esp. public office **2** *Sports* one who supervises an athletic contest, as a referee or umpire —**of·fi′cial·ly *adv.***

of·fi·cial·dom (ə fish′əl dəm) ***n.*** **1** officials collectively **2** the domain or position of officials

of·fi·cial·ese (ə fish′əl ēz′) ***n.*** ⟦see -ESE⟧ the pompous, wordy, and involved language typical of official communications and reports

of·fi·cial·ism (ə fish′əl iz′əm) ***n.*** **1** the characteristic practices and behavior of officials; esp., excessive adherence to official routine and regulations; red tape **2** officials collectively; officialdom

of·fi·ci·ant (ə fish′ənt, -ē ənt) ***n.*** ⟦< ML(Ec) *officians* (gen. *officiantis*)⟧ an officiating priest, minister, etc.

of·fi·ci·ar·y (ə fish′ē er′ē) ***n., pl.*** **-ar′ies** ⟦ML *officiarius*⟧ ☆a group of officials —***adj.*** connected with or resulting from the holding of an office

of·fi·ci·ate (ə fish′ē āt′) ***vi.*** **-at′ed, -at′ing** ⟦< ML *officiatus,* pp. of *officiare*⟧ **1** to perform the duties of an office; act as an officer **2** to perform the functions of a priest, minister, rabbi, etc. at a religious ceremony **3** *Sports* to act as referee, umpire, etc. —**of·fi′ci·a′tion *n.*** —**of·fi′ci·a′tor *n.***

of·fic·i·nal (ə fis′i nəl) ***adj.*** ⟦ML *officinalis* < *officina,* storeroom (of a monastery) < L, workshop, contr. of *opificina* < *opifex,* worker: see OFFICE⟧ [Obs.] commonly kept in stock in a pharmacy: said of products or drugs dispensed without prescription —***n.*** [Obs.] an officinal drug or preparation

of·fi·cious (ə fish′əs) ***adj.*** ⟦L *officiosus* < *officium,* OFFICE⟧ **1** [Obs.] ready to serve; obliging **2** offering unnecessary and unwanted advice or services; meddlesome, esp. in a highhanded or overbearing way **3** ⟦after use of Fr *officieux* in this way by diplomats⟧ in diplomacy, unofficial or informal —**of·fi′cious·ly *adv.*** —**of·fi′cious·ness *n.***

off·ing (ôf′iŋ) ***n.*** ⟦< OFF[1]⟧ **1** the distant part of the sea visible from the shore **2** a position at a distance from the shore —**in the offing 1** at some distance but in sight **2** at some indefinite time in the future

off·ish (ôf′ish) ***adj.*** [Informal] STANDOFFISH

off-key (ôf′kē′) ***adj.*** **1** not on the right note; flat or sharp **2** not quite in accord with what is normal, fitting, etc.

off-la·bel (ôf′lā′bəl) ***adj.*** designating or of the legally permitted use of a drug or medical device by a physician to treat a condition for which that drug or device has not been approved officially

off-li·cence (-lī′səns) ***n.*** [Brit.] a shop, counter, etc. at which alcoholic beverages are sold by the bottle for consumption elsewhere

off-lim·its (-lim′its) ***adj.*** **1** designated as a place that cannot be entered, visited, or patronized by a specified group **2** not acceptable or permitted for use, consideration, discussion, etc.

off-line (-līn′) ***adj.*** **1** designating or of equipment not directly connected to and controlled by the central processing unit of a computer **2** not connected to, and therefore not ready to receive data from or transmit data to, a computer or computer network **3** unavailable on, or not done through, the internet or some other computer network —*adv.* independently of the internet or of some other computer network Also written **off′line′**

off·load (-lōd′) *vt., vi.* ⟦OFF[1] + LOAD, prob. orig. transl. of Afrik *aflaai* < Du *afladen*⟧ UNLOAD (*vt.* 1*a*, 2*b*, 4, *vi.*)

☆**off-off-Broad·way** (ôf′ôf′brôd′wā′) *adj.* of or having to do with noncommercial, highly experimental theatrical productions, presented in small halls, cafes, etc. in New York City —*adv.* in such productions or locations —*n.* off-off-Broadway productions collectively Also written **Off-Off-Broadway**

off-peak (ôf′pēk′) *adj.* of or pertaining to periods of time when activity, use, etc. is not at a peak

off-price (ôf′prīs′) *adj.* **1** designating or of retail stores, chains, etc. which sell high-quality merchandise, esp. clothing, at a price lower than the usual retail price **2** of such merchandise or those who manufacture or sell it

off·print (-print′) *n.* a separate reprint of an article, etc. that first appeared in a magazine or other larger publication —*vt.* to reprint (an excerpt, etc.) separately

off-put·ting (-poot′iŋ) *adj.* tending to put one off; distracting, annoying, etc.

off·ramp (-ramp′) *n.* a road leading off a main highway, freeway, etc.

off-road (-rōd′) *adj.* designed for use, occurring, done, etc. off public roads, esp. on a route or course having rough terrain [and *off-road* vehicle, *off-road* racing] —*adv.* on a route or course that is not a public road, esp. one having rough terrain

off·scour·ing (-skour′iŋ) *n.* **1** [*usually pl.*] something scoured off; rubbish; refuse **2** an outcast from society: *usually used in pl.*

off-screen (ôf′skrēn′) *adj., adv.* **1** not in a film, TV show, etc. **2** not in a film FRAME (*n.* 13*b*) or on a TV or computer screen Also, esp. for sense 1, **off′screen′**

off-sea·son (-sē′zən) *n.* a time of the year when the usual activity or business is reduced or not carried on — *adj., adv.* during or for the off-season

off·set (ôf′set′; *for v., usually* ôf set′) *n.* **1** something that is set off, or has sprung or developed, from something else; offshoot; extension; branch; spur **2** anything that balances, counters, or compensates for something else; compensation **3** *rare var. of* OUTSET **4** *Archit.* a ledge or recess formed in a wall by a reduction in its thickness above **5** *Bot.* a side shoot that takes root and starts a new plant **6** *Elec.* a branch off a main power line **7** *Mech.* a curve or bend in a metal bar, pipe, etc. to permit it to pass an obstruction **8** *Printing a)* OFFSET PRINTING *b)* an impression made by this process *c)* an ink smudge transferred from a freshly printed sheet to the one next to it **9** *Surveying* a short distance measured at right angles from the main line to help in computing the area of an irregular plot of ground —*adj.* **1** of, relating to, or being an offset **2** that is offset, off center, or at an angle —*vt.* **-set′**, **-set′ting 1** to balance, complement, counteract, compensate for, etc. **2** to make an offset in **3** *Printing a)* to make (an impression) by offset printing *b)* to smudge with an offset —*vi.* **1** to come out or develop as an offset **2** *Printing* to make an offset

offset printing a printing process in which the inked impression is first made on a rubber-covered roller, then transferred to paper

off·shoot (ôf′shoot′) *n.* anything that branches off, or derives from, a main source; specif., a shoot or stem growing laterally from the main stem of a plant

off·shore (-shôr′) *adj.* **1** moving off or away from the shore [an *offshore* wind] **2** situated or in operation at some distance from shore ☆**3** engaged in outside the U.S. as by U.S. banks or manufacturers [*offshore* investments, *offshore* assembly plants] —*adv.* **1** away or far from the shore; seaward ☆**2** outside the U.S. [to borrow money *offshore*]

off·side (-sīd′) *adj. Sports* not in the proper position for play; specif., *a) Football* over the line of scrimmage or otherwise ahead of the ball before the play has begun, and hence subject to penalty *b) Ice Hockey* moving into the attacking zone ahead of the puck —*adv.* into an offside position [to jump *offside*] —*n.* an offside play Also **off′sides′**

off-site (ôf′sīt′) *adj., adv.* on or at another site, apart from the site of a particular activity or happening [parts assembled *off-site*]

☆**off-speed** (ôf′spēd′) *adj. Baseball* designating or of a pitch, as a change-up, that is slower than a pitcher's fast pitches

off·spring (-spriŋ′) *n., pl.* **-spring′** or **-springs′** ⟦ME *ofspring* < OE: see OFF[1] & SPRING⟧ **1** a child or animal as related to its parent **2** a descendant or descendants collectively; progeny **3** a product, outcome, or result

off·stage (-stāj′) *n.* that part of a stage, as the wings, not visible to the audience —*adj.* in or from the offstage [an *offstage* whisper] —*adv.* **1** in or to the offstage [to go *offstage*] **2** when not actually appearing before the public

off-the-peg (-*th*ə peg′) *adj.* [Chiefly Brit.] ready-made; off-the-shelf; not custom-made

off-the-shelf (-*th*ə shelf′) *adj.* designating commercial products that are ready for use without modification

☆**off-the-wall** (-*th*ə wôl′) *adj.* [Slang] very unusual, eccentric, unconventional, etc.

☆**off-track** (-trak′) *adj.* designating or of legalized betting on horse races, carried on at places away from the racetrack

off-white (-hwīt′, -wīt′) *adj.* of any of various shades of grayish-white or yellowish-white

☆**off year 1** a year in which a major, esp. presidential, election does not take place **2** a year of little production, poor crops, etc. —**off′-year′** *adj.*

O'Fla·her·ty (ō flā′ər tē, -hər tē), **Li·am** (lē′əm) 1897-1984; Ir. writer

OFr *abbrev.* Old French

OFris *abbrev.* Old Frisian

oft (ôft) *adv.* ⟦ME < OE, akin to Ger *oft*, Dan *ofte*, Swed *ofta*, Goth *ufta*⟧ *literary var. of* OFTEN: now chiefly in compounds [an *oft*-heard expression]

of·ten (ôf′ən, äf′-; -tən) *adv.* ⟦ME var. of prec.⟧ many times; repeatedly; frequently —*adj.* [Archaic] frequent

of·ten·times (-tīmz′) *adv.* OFTEN: also [Old Poet.] **oft′times′**

o·fu·ro (ä foor′ō) *n., pl.* **-ros** ⟦Jpn⟧ a traditional Japanese wooden bathtub with steep sides

OG *abbrev.* **1** *Football* offensive guard **2** Officer of the Guard **3** *Philately* original gum Also, for 1 & 3, **og**

Og·bo·mo·sho (äg′bə mō′shō) city in SW Nigeria

Og·den (äg′dən, ôg′-) ⟦after P. S. *Ogden*, a fur trader who explored the region in 1820⟧ city in N Utah

og·do·ad (äg′dō ad′) *n.* ⟦LL(Ec) *ogdoas* (gen. *ogdoadis*) < Gr *ogdoas* < *oktō*, EIGHT⟧ any group of eight

o·gee (ō′jē′, ō jē′) *n.* ⟦ME (pl.) *oggez* < OFr *ogive*, OGIVE⟧ **1** a molding having an S-shaped curve in profile **2** any S-shaped curve or line **3** an ogee arch

ogee arch a pointed arch formed with the curve of an ogee on each side

og·ham (äg′əm, ō′əm) *n.* ⟦Ir < OIr *ogam*⟧ an alphabetic system for writing Old Irish, developed in the 5th and 6th cent. A.D., in which the letters are represented by various combinations of lines or notches as carved along the edge of a memorial stone: also **og′am**

ogee arch

o·give (ō′jīv′, ō jīv′) *n.* ⟦Fr < OFr, < ? Sp *aljibe*, a cistern < Ar *al-ǧubb*, a well⟧ **1** the diagonal rib or groin of a Gothic vault **2** a pointed, or Gothic, arch **3** a similarly shaped nose of a bullet, rocket, or other projectile —**o·gi′val** *adj.*

Og·la·la (äg lä′lə) *n.* ⟦prob. < Siouan, lit., to scatter one's own⟧ **1** *pl.* **-las** or **-la** a member of one member group of the Lakota division of Dakota Indians, living in SW South Dakota **2** the Dakota dialect of the Oglalas

o·gle (ō′gəl, äg′əl) *vi., vt.* **o′gled**, **o′gling** ⟦prob. < LowG *oegeln* (akin to Ger *äugeln*) < *oog*, akin to OE *eage*, EYE⟧ to keep looking (at) boldly and with obvious desire; make eyes (at) —*n.* an ogling look —**o′gler** *n.*

O·gle·thorpe (ō′gəl thôrp′), **James Edward** 1696-1785; Eng. general: founder of the colony of Georgia (1733)

o·gre (ō′gər) *n.* ⟦Fr, prob. < MGr *Ogōr*, a Hungarian, prob. infl. by Fr *orc* < L *Orcus*, Pluto, Hades⟧ **1** in fairy tales and folklore, a man-eating monster or giant **2** a hideous, coarse, or cruel man —**o·gre·ish** (ō′gər ish) *adj.*, **o·grish** (ō′grish)

o·gress (ō′grəs) *n.* a female ogre

oh (ō) *interj.* **1** used to express surprise, wonder, fear, pain, etc. **2** used in direct address, as to attract attention [*oh*, waiter!] **3** used to signify comprehension or acknowledgment of another's statement, explanation, etc. —*n., pl.* **oh's** or **ohs** an instance of this exclamation

OH *abbrev.* Ohio

O'Har·a (ō har′ə), **John** 1905-70; U.S. writer

O. Henry *see* HENRY[2], O.

OHG *abbrev.* Old High German

O'Hig·gins (ō hig′ənz; *Sp* ô ē′gēns), **Ber·nar·do** (ber när′dô) 1778-1842; Chilean revolutionary leader: 1st president of Chile (1817-23)

O·hi·o (ō hī′ō) **1** ⟦< Fr < Iroquoian, lit., fine (or large) river⟧ river formed by the junction of the Monongahela & the Allegheny at Pittsburgh, flowing southwestward into the Mississippi: 981 mi (1,579 km) **2** ⟦after the river⟧ Midwestern state of the NC U.S.: admitted 1803; 40,948 sq mi (106,056 sq km); cap. Columbus: abbrev. *OH* or *O*

O·hi·o·an (ō hī′ō ən) *adj.* of the state of Ohio: usually used in the predicate —*n.* a person born or living in Ohio

ohm (ōm) *n.* ⟦after G. S. *Ohm* (1789-1854), Ger physicist⟧ the basic unit of electric resistance in the SI and MKS systems, equal to the resistance of a circuit in which an electromotive force of one volt maintains a current of one ampere: symbol, Ω —**ohm′ic** *adj.*

ohm·me·ter (ōm′mēt′ər) *n.* ⟦prec. + -METER⟧ an instrument for measuring electrical resistance in ohms or megohms

Ohm's law ⟦see OHM⟧ *Elec.* a law which states that the current in a DC circuit is directly proportional to the applied voltage and inversely proportional to the resistance

o·ho (ō hō′) *interj.* ⟦ME *o ho!*: see O[2] & HO[1]⟧ used to express surprise or triumph, or to taunt a person

oh-oh (ō′ō) *interj. var. of* UH-OH

-o·hol·ic (ə hôl′ik, -häl′-) *combining form* -AHOLIC [*beeroholic*]

oi (oi) *interj. alt. sp. of* OY

-oid (oid) ⟦Gr *-o-eidēs* < -O-, termination of preceding element + *-eidēs*, -oid < *eidos*, a form, shape < IE base **weid-*, to see > IDEA, WISE[1], L *videre*⟧ *suffix* **1** *forming adjectives* like or resembling (something specified) [*crystalloid*] **2** *forming nouns* something resembling (something specified) [*celluloid, android*]

oil (oil) *n.* ⟦ME *oile* < OFr < L *oleum*, oil, olive oil < Gr *elaion*, (olive) oil, akin to *elaia*, OLIVE⟧ **1** any of various kinds of greasy, combustible substances obtained from animal, vegetable, and mineral sources: oils are liquid at ordinary temperatures and soluble in certain organic solvents, as ether, but not in water **2** PETROLEUM **3** any of various substances having the consistency of oil **4** *a)* OIL PAINT *b)* OIL PAINTING **5** [Informal] smooth, hypocritical flattery —*vt.* **1** to smear, lubricate, or supply with oil **2** to bribe: chiefly in **oil the palm (or hand) of** —*adj.* of, from, like, or yielding oil, or having to do with the production or use of oil —**pour oil on troubled waters** to settle quarrels, differences, etc. by calm, soothing methods —☆**strike oil** **1** to discover oil under the ground by drilling a shaft for it **2** to become suddenly wealthy —**oiled** *adj.*

oil beetle any of various small blister beetles (esp. genus *Meloe*) which, when disturbed, produce an oily secretion from the joints of the legs

oil·bird (oil′burd′) *n.* GUACHARO

oil cake a mass of crushed linseed, cottonseed, etc. from which the oil has been extracted, used as livestock feed and as a fertilizer

oil·can (oil′kan′) *n.* a can for holding oil, esp. one with a spout, used for lubricating machinery, etc.

oil·cloth (oil′klôth′) *n.* cloth made waterproof with oil or, now especially, with heavy coats of paint: used to cover tables, shelves, etc.

oil color OIL PAINT

oil·cup (oil′kup′) *n.* a container (in a machine) for releasing oil gradually as lubrication for moving parts

☆**oiled** (oild) *adj.* [Slang] drunk; intoxicated

oil·er (oi′lər) *n.* **1** a person who oils machinery, engines, etc. **2** a device for oiling machinery, etc.; specif., OILCAN **3** a tanker for carrying oil, esp. one used to refuel other ships ☆**4** [Old Informal] an oilskin coat

☆**oil field** an area having valuable deposits of petroleum, often, specif., one with a number of active oil wells

oil·man (-man′, -mən) *n., pl.* **-men′** (-men′, -mən) **1** a person working in an oil field **2** an entrepreneur or executive in the petroleum industry

oil of turpentine TURPENTINE (sense 3)

oil of vitriol ⟦so called because green vitriol was its source⟧ SULFURIC ACID

oil paint an artist's paint made by grinding a pigment in a drying oil, esp. linseed oil

oil painting **1** a picture painted in oil colors **2** the art of painting in oil colors

oil palm a tropical African palm tree (*Elaeis guineensis*) whose seeds yield palm oil

oil pan the lower part of the crankcase of an internal-combustion engine, serving as a lubricating-oil reservoir

oil·pa·per (oil′pā′pər) *n.* paper made transparent and waterproof by treatment with oil

☆**oil patch** [Slang] **1** an area or region where much petroleum is produced **2** the petroleum industry

oil·seed (oil′sēd′) *n.* any seed grown commercially for its oil, as cottonseed or rapeseed

oil shale shale containing hydrocarbons which can be extracted, esp. by distillation

oil·skin (oil′skin′) *n.* **1** cloth made waterproof by treatment with oil **2** [*often pl.*] a garment or outfit made of this, as a coat, or a suit of jacket and trousers

☆**oil slick** a layer of oil, esp. one floating on water and forming a smooth area

oil·stone (oil′stōn′) *n.* a whetstone treated with oil

☆**oil well** a well that supplies petroleum either naturally or by means of a pumping system

oil·y (oi′lē) *adj.* **oil′i·er, oil′i·est** **1** of, like, consisting of, or containing oil **2** covered with oil; fat; greasy **3** too smooth; slippery; unctuous —**oil′i·ly** *adv.* —**oil′i·ness** *n.*

☆**oink** (oiŋk) *n.* ⟦echoic⟧ the grunt of a pig, or a sound in imitation of it —*vi.* to grunt as or like a pig

oint·ment (oint′mənt) *n.* ⟦ME *oignement* < OFr < VL **unguimentum*, for L *unguentum* (see UNGUENT): the *-t-* in Eng from assoc. with obs. v. *oint*, to anoint⟧ a fatty substance applied to the skin for healing or cosmetic purposes; salve; unguent

OIr *abbrev.* Old Irish

Oise (wäz) river flowing from S Belgium southwest through N France into the Seine: 186 mi (299 km)

Oi·strakh (oi′sträkh), **David (Fyodorovich)** 1908-74; Russ. violinist

Oi·ta (oi′tä′; ō ēt′ə) city in NE Kyushu, Japan

oi·ti·ci·ca (oit′i sē′kə) *n.* ⟦Port < native (Tupí) name⟧ a tree (*Licania rigida*) of the rose family, found in NE Brazil and yielding hard, heavy wood and large seeds rich in a drying oil (**oiticica oil**) similar to tung oil

OJ or **oj** (ō′jā) *n.* [Slang] orange juice

☆**O·jib·wa** (ō jib′wā′, -wä′, -wə) *n.* ⟦Ojibwa *ojibwe*, orig. name of an Ojibwa band near Sault Ste. Marie: said to be < a root meaning "puckered up," in allusion to the style of moccasins⟧ **1** *pl.* **-was′** or **-wa′** a member of a North American Indian people living in Michigan, Wisconsin, Minnesota, and Ontario **2** the Algonquian language of this people and certain neighboring groups —*adj.* of the Ojibwas or their language or culture Also **O·jib′way′** (-wā′)

OJT *abbrev.* on-the-job training

☆**OK**[1] or **O.K.** (ō kā′) [Informal] *adj.* ⟦orig. U.S. informal: first known use (March 23, 1839) by C. G. Greene, editor, in the Boston *Morning Post*, as if abbrev. for "oll korrect," facetious misspelling of *all correct;* ? altered < Scot dial. *och aye*, ah yes, oh yes < Gael *och*, ah, oh + AYE[2]⟧ **1** correct; acceptable [*it's OK to wear casual dress to the party*] **2** adequate; satisfactory; good enough [*the entree was OK, but dessert was excellent*] **3** in satisfactory or good condition [*are you feeling OK today?*] **4** comfortable; satisfied [*I'm OK with waiting until tomorrow*] —*adv.* **1** yes; very well: used in reply to a question or to preface or resume one's remarks [*OK, I'll go first*] **2** acceptably; satisfactorily [*am I dressed OK for this restaurant?*] **3** is that acceptable, agreeable, etc. to you?: used, as at the end of a sentence, to ask a question [*we'll have dinner after the movie, OK?*] —*interj.* **1** yes; good, agreed, etc.: used to express satisfaction, agreement, pleasure, etc. [*"Let's leave right away!" "OK!"*] **2** used to express comprehension or acknowledgment of another's statement, explanation, etc. [*"I'll put your umbrella back in the closet." "OK."*] —*n., pl.* **OK's** or **O.K.'s** approval; endorsement —*vt.* **OK'd** or **O.K.'d**, **OK'ing** or **O.K.'ing** to approve or endorse, as by writing "OK" on

OK[2] *abbrev.* Oklahoma

O·ka (ô kä′) river in central European Russia, flowing northeast into the Volga: *c.* 950 mi (1,529 km)

o·ka·pi (ō kä′pē) *n., pl.* **-pis** or **-pi** ⟦native Afr name⟧ an African ruminant (*Okapia johnstoni*) in the same family (Giraffidae) as the giraffe, but having a much shorter neck

O·ka·van·go (ō′kə väŋ′gō) *alt. sp. of* OKOVANGGO

☆**o·kay** (ō kā′) *adj., adv., interj., n., vt.* [Informal] *var. of* OK[1]

O·ka·ya·ma (ô′kä yä′mä) seaport in SW Honshu, Japan, on the Inland Sea

oke[1] (ōk) *n.* ⟦< Turk *ōqah* < Ar *ūqīyah* < Gr *oungia* < L *uncia:* see OUNCE[1]⟧ in Turkey, Egypt, and other countries of the Near East, a unit of weight equal to about 2¾ lb (1.3 kilograms): also **o·ka** (ō′kə)

☆**oke**[2] (ōk) *interj. slang var. of* OK[1]

O·kee·cho·bee (ō′kē chō′bē), **Lake** ⟦< AmInd⟧ lake in SE Fla. at the N edge of the Everglades: 700 sq mi (1,813 sq km): main element of **Okeechobee Waterway**, a system of connected canals, rivers, & lakes across the Fla. peninsula

O'Keeffe (ō kēf′), **Georgia** 1887-1986; U.S. painter

O·ke·fe·no·kee Swamp (ō′kə fə nō′kē) ⟦< AmInd name, lit., trembling earth + SWAMP⟧ swamp in SE Ga. & NE Fla.: *c.* 700 sq mi (1,813 sq km)

O'Kel·ly (ō kel′ē), **Sean T(homas)** (shôn) 1882-1966; Ir. nationalist leader: president of Ireland (1945-59)

☆**o·key-doke** (ō′kē dōk′) *adj., interj.* ⟦redupl. of OK[1]⟧ [Informal] *var. of* OK: also **o′key-do′key** (-dō′kē)

O·khotsk (ō kätsk′; *Russ* ô khôtsk′), **Sea of** arm of the Pacific, off the E coast of Siberia: 537,500 sq mi (1,392,120 sq km)

☆**O·kie** (ō′kē) *n.* ⟦OK(LAHOMA) + -IE⟧ a migratory agricultural worker, esp. one who migrated west from Oklahoma or other areas of the Great Plains because of drought, farm foreclosure, etc., in the late 1930s: often a disparaging term

O·ki·na·wa (ō′kə nä′wə) largest island of the Ryukyus, in the W Pacific northeast of Taiwan: 454 sq mi (1,176 sq km); chief city, Naha —**O′ki·na′wan** *adj., n.*

O·kla·ho·ma (ō′klə hō′mə) ⟦< Choctaw *okla*, people + *homma*, red⟧ state of the SC U.S.: admitted 1907; 68,667 sq mi (177,847 sq km); cap. Oklahoma City: abbrev. *OK* or **Okla**

Oklahoma City capital of Okla., in the central part

O·kla·ho·man (ō′klə hō′mən) *adj.* of Oklahoma: usually used in the predicate —*n.* a person born or living in Oklahoma

O·ko·vang·go (ō′kə väŋ′gō) river in SW Africa, flowing from central Angola southeast into a marshy basin (**Okovanggo Basin**) in N Botswana: *c.* 1,000 mi (1,609 km)

o·kra (ō′krə) *n.* ⟦< WAfr name⟧ **1** a tall annual plant (*Abelmoschus esculentus*) of the mallow family, grown for its slender, ribbed, sticky, green pods **2** the pods, used as a cooked vegetable and in soups, stews, etc. **3** GUMBO (sense 2)

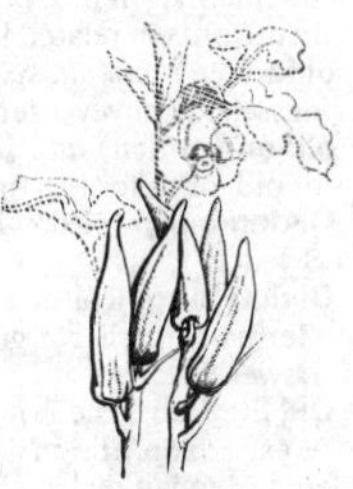
okra

Ok·to·ber·fest (äk tō′bər fest′) *n.* ⟦Ger⟧ **1** a beer-drinking festival held in Munich, Germany, in the fall **2** a similar festival held elsewhere

OL *abbrev.* **1** *Football* offensive lineman: sometimes written **ol** **2** Old Latin

-ol[1] (ôl, ōl) ⟦(ALCOH)OL⟧ *suffix Chem.* an alcohol or phenol [*menthol, thymol*]

-ol[2] (ōl, ôl) *suffix* -OLE

☆**-o·la** (ō′lə) *suffix* **1** forming commercial names **2** forming nouns and adjectives: used as a slangy intensifier [*payola*]

O·laf[1] (ō′ləf, -läf) *n.* ⟦ON *Olafr, Aleifr* < **anulaibar*, lit., descendant of the (original) ancestor < **anu* (< IE **an-*, ancestor > L *anus*, old woman) + *-laibar* (> Leifr, LEIF)⟧ a masculine name: also sp. **O′lav**

O·laf[2] (ō′ləf, -läf) **1 Olaf I** (born *Olaf Tryggvasson*) A.D. 964?-1000; king of Norway (995-1000): subject of many legends **2** Saint **Olaf II** (born *Olaf Haraldsson*) A.D. 995?-1030; king of Norway (1015-28): patron saint of Norway: his day is July 29 **3 Olaf V** 1903-91; king of Norway (1957-91): son of Haakon VII

Ö·land (ö länd′) Swedish island in the Baltic Sea, off the SE coast of Sweden: *c.* 520 sq mi (1,347 sq km)

O·la·the (ō lā′thə) city in NE Kans.: suburb of Kansas City, Mo.

old (ōld) *adj.* **old′er, old′est**: see also ELDER, **eldest** ⟦ME < OE (Anglian) *ald*, WS *eald*, akin to Ger *alt* < IE base **al-*, to grow > L *altus*, old, *alere*, to nourish: basic sense "grown"⟧ **1** having lived or been in existence for a long time; aged **2** of, like, or characteristic of aged people; specif., mature in judgment, wise, etc. 3 of a certain or specified age or duration [a child ten years *old*] 4 made or produced some time ago; not new 5 familiar or known from the past; accustomed [up to his *old* tricks] 6 [*often* **O-**] designating the form of a language in its earliest attested stage [*Old* English] 7 having been in use for a long time; worn out by age or use; shabby 8 that was at one time; former [my *old* teacher] 9 having had long experience or practice [an *old* hand at this work] 10 belonging to the remote past; having existed long ago; ancient [an *old* civilization] 11 dating or continuing from some period long before the present; of long standing [an *old* tradition] 12 designating the earlier or earliest of two or more [the *Old* World] 13 [Informal] dear: a term of affection or cordiality [*old* boy] 14 [Informal] tiresome, annoying, etc., esp. as a result of repetition or monotony [their incessant chatter has gotten *old*] 15 *Geol.* having reached the stage of greatly decreased activity or showing extensive reduction of topographical form: said of streams, mountain ranges, etc. ➡Also used informally as an intensifier, esp. after certain favorable adjectives [a fine *old* time, good *old* Al] —*n.* 1 time long past; yore [days of *old*] 2 a person of a specified age: used in hyphenated compounds [a six-year-*old*] 3 something old: with *the* 4 old people: often with *the* —**old′ness** *n.*

SYN.—**old** implies a having been in existence or use for a relatively long time [*old* shoes, *old* civilizations]; **ancient** specifically implies reference to times long past [*ancient* history]; **antique** is applied to that which dates from ancient times, or, more commonly, from a former period [*antique* furniture]; **antiquated** is used to describe that which has become old-fashioned or outdated [*antiquated* notions of decorum]; **archaic**, in this connection, applies to that which is marked by the characteristics of an earlier period [an *archaic* iron fence surrounded the house]; **obsolete** is applied to that which has fallen into disuse or is out-of-date [*obsolete* weapons] —*ANT.* **new, modern**

old age the advanced years of life, esp. human life, often thought of as being those years after 60 or 65 and characterized by a marked decline in strength and vigor: cf. MIDDLE AGE

Old Bai·ley (bā′lē) historic criminal court in London on Old Bailey Street

old boy 1 [*sometimes* **O- B-**] [Informal, Chiefly Brit.] an alumnus, esp. of a boys' preparatory school 2 a man belonging to a social, professional, etc. group regarded as prestigious or influential, whose members provide one another with assistance or preferential treatment

Old Bulgarian OLD CHURCH SLAVONIC

Old Castile *see* CASTILE

Old·cas·tle (ōld′kas′əl), Sir **John** Lord Cobham 1378?-1417; Eng. Lollard leader: executed as a heretic

Old Catholic a member of any of a number of nationalist churches rejecting various Roman Catholic tenets (esp. papal supremacy and papal infallibility) officially promulgated in relatively recent times: the churches were organized mainly in the late 19th cent.

Old Church Slavonic the South Slavic language used in the 9th-cent. Bible translation by Saint Cyril and his brother, Saint Methodius, and still used as a liturgical language (now called *Church Slavonic*) by Orthodox Slavs but extinct as a vernacular: also called **Old Church Slavic**

☆**old country** the country from which an immigrant came: said esp. of a country in Europe

Old Delhi DELHI (the city)

☆**Old Dominion** *name for* VIRGINIA[2]

Old Dutch the Dutch language in its oldest stage: it is actually recorded on fragmentary relics, but may be reconstructed from a later form and from loanwords in related languages: cf. OLD LOW FRANCONIAN

olde (ōld) *adj. alt. sp. of* OLD: early sp. now used as in the names of businesses to convey a sense of quaint charm

old·en (ōl′dən) *adj.* ⟦ME, inflected form of *old*⟧ [Old Poet.] old; ancient; of old, or of former times

Ol·den·burg[1] (ōl′dən burg′), **Claes** (klas) 1929- ; U.S. sculptor, born in Sweden

Ol·den·burg[2] (ōl′dən burg′; *Ger* ōl′dən boorkh′) 1 former state of NW Germany, earlier a grand duchy 2 city in NW Germany, in the state of Lower Saxony

Old English 1 the Low German language of the Anglo-Saxons, comprising West Saxon, the major literary dialect, and the Kentish, Northumbrian, and Mercian dialects: it was spoken in England from *c.* A.D. 450 to *c.* A.D. 1100 2 BLACK LETTER

Old English sheepdog any of a breed of stocky, muscular, medium-sized dog, originally bred in England as a drover's dog, with a profuse, shaggy coat, usually gray or bluish gray, and, often, no tail

old·er (ōl′dər) *adj.* 1 *alt. compar. of* OLD 2 between middle age and extreme old age: used as an alternative to words which may connote debility, decline, etc.

☆**Old Faithful** noted geyser in Yellowstone National Park, which erupts about every 67 minutes

old·fan·gled (ōld′faŋ′gəld) *adj.* ⟦OLD + (NEW)FANGLED⟧ OLD-FASHIONED

old-fash·ion (ōld′fash′ən) *adj. var. of* OLD-FASHIONED: also written **old fashion** —*n.* ☆*var. of* OLD-FASHIONED: also written **Old Fashion**

old-fash·ioned (ōld′fash′ənd) *adj.* suited to or favoring the styles, methods, manners, or ideas of past times; esp., out-of-date; antiquated; outmoded: also written **old fashioned** —☆*n.* [*usually* **Old-Fashioned**] an iced cocktail containing whiskey, bitters, sweetening, and a small amount of water, and garnished with pieces of fruit: also written **Old Fashioned**

old fogy or **old fogey** *see* FOGY

Old French the French language from *c.* A.D. 800 to *c.* A.D. 1500, esp. French from the 9th to the 14th cent.: cf. MIDDLE FRENCH

Old Frisian a West Germanic language closely related to Old English, preserved in documents from the 13th to the 16th cent.

☆**Old Glory** *name for* the flag of the United States

old gold a soft, yellowish, metallic color

old-growth (ōld′grōth′) *adj.* designating or of a forest characterized by very large, very old trees and great biodiversity

old guard ⟦transl. of Fr *Vieille Garde:* so named in contrast to the Young Guard, formed in 1810⟧ 1 [*also* **O- G-**] the imperial guard, organized by Napoleon I in 1804 2 any group that has long defended a cause 3 the most conservative element of a group, party, etc.

Old·ham (ōl′dəm) city in Greater Manchester, NW England

old hand a person with much skill or experience

Old Harry the Devil; Satan

old hat [Slang] 1 old-fashioned; out-of-date 2 well-known or familiar to the point of being trite or commonplace Used in the predicate

Old Hickory *name for* Andrew JACKSON[1]

Old High German the High German language from its earliest period to the 12th cent.

Old Icelandic the dialect of Old Norse spoken in Iceland from the 9th to the 16th cent.

☆**old·ie** or **old·y** (ōl′dē) *n., pl.* **old′ies** [Informal] an old joke, saying, song, film, etc.

Old Indic 1 the group of Indo-European languages of ancient India including early and classical Sanskrit, as well as Pali and the earliest vernaculars (*Prakrits*) 2 Sanskrit and Vedic

Old Ionic a dialect of ancient Greek: the language of Homer

Old Irish the Gaelic language of Ireland from the earliest period to the 11th cent.

old·ish (ōl′dish) *adj.* somewhat old

old lady [Slang] 1 one's mother 2 one's wife 3 one's girlfriend or mistress, often, specif., when one lives with her

Old Latin the Latin language before *c.* 75 B.C.

old-line (ōld′līn′) *adj.* 1 with an old, well-established history 2 following tradition; conservative

Old Low Franconian the West Germanic language of the Franks of the lower Rhine before *c.* A.D. 1100, the ancestor of Dutch and Flemish: also called **Old Low Frankish**

Old Low German the Low German language from its earliest period to the 12th cent. A.D.

old maid 1 a woman, esp. an older woman, who has never married; spinster: a mild term of contempt 2 a prim, prudish, fussy person 3 a simple card game played with a deck containing one card with no match, the loser being the player left with that card after all the others have been paired —**old′maid′ish** *adj.*

old man [Slang] 1 one's father 2 one's husband 3 [*usually* **O- M-**] any man in authority, as the head of a company, the captain of a vessel, or a military commander: with *the* 4 one's boyfriend or lover, often, specif., when one lives with him 5 old Mr. ____: often used to distinguish the father from the son

☆**Old Man River** *name for* MISSISSIPPI (the river)

old master 1 any of the great European painters before the 18th cent. 2 a painting by any of these

old money [*also* **O- M-**] 1 wealth acquired long ago and passed down through the generations, often regarded as conferring privileged status 2 a person, family, etc. possessing such wealth

old moon the moon in its last quarter; waning crescent

Old Nick ⟦prob. contr. < NICHOLAS[1], but ? *nik- < Gmc *niq-, water sprite, goblin: see NIX[1]⟧ the Devil; Satan

Old Norman French NORMAN FRENCH (sense 1)

Old Norse the North Germanic language spoken in Scandinavia before the 14th cent. and in Iceland to the 16th cent.

Old North French the group of dialects of Old French spoken in N France; esp., the dialects of Picardy and Normandy

Ol·do·wan (ôl′də wän′, -wən; äl′-) *adj.* ⟦after *Olduvai* Gorge, Tanzania, where remains have been found⟧ designating or of the oldest known Lower Paleolithic culture, characterized by pebble tools usually flaked in two directions to form simple cutters, choppers, scrapers, etc.

Old Persian the oldest form of Persian, preserved in stone inscriptions dating from the 7th to the 4th cent. B.C.

Old Pretender *name for* James Francis Edward STUART[2]

Old Prussian a West Baltic language that was once spoken in East Prussia and became extinct in the 17th cent.

old rose a grayish or purplish red —**old-rose** (ōld′rōz′) *adj.*

Old Saxon a West Germanic language, the oldest type of Low German, known chiefly from manuscripts of the 9th and 10th cent. A.D.

old school a group of people who cling to traditional or conservative ideas, methods, etc.

old-school (ōld′sko͞ol′) *adj.* of or faithful to styles, values, etc. regarded as traditional or old-fashioned [an *old-school* cabaret singer]

old school tie 1 a necktie striped in the distinctive colors of any of the exclusive English public schools 2 loyalties, traditions, attitudes, etc. of, or like those of, the graduates of such a school

Old Scratch *see* SCRATCH

Old Slavic OLD CHURCH SLAVONIC

☆**old sledge** SEVEN-UP

☆**Old South** the South before the Civil War

Old Spanish the Spanish language from *c.* 1145 to the 16th cent.

☆**old·squaw** (ōld′skwô′) *n.* a sea duck (*Clangula hyemalis*) of N regions, with mostly black-and-white coloration and a long, pointed tail

old·ster (ōld′stər) *n.* ⟦see -STER⟧ [Informal] a person who is no longer young or middle aged; old or elderly person

Old Stone Age the Paleolithic

Old Style 1 the old method of reckoning time according to the Julian calendar, which was off one day every 128 years 2 [**o- s-**] an old style of type with narrow, light letters having slanted strokes at the top —**old′-style′** *adj.*

Old Testament *Christian designation for* the Holy Scriptures of Judaism, the first of the two general divisions of the Christian Bible: cf. BIBLE

old-time (ōld′tīm′, -tīm′) *adj.* 1 of, like, or characteristic of past times 2 of long standing or experience [*an old-time* journalist]

old-tim·er (ōld′tīm′ər, ōld′tīm′-) *n.* [Informal] 1 a person who has been a resident, employee, member, etc. for a long time ☆2 a person who is old-fashioned ☆3 an old or elderly person; oldster Also written **oldtimer**

old-tim·ey (ōld′tīm′ē) *adj.* [Informal] reminiscent of, or evoking memories of, the manners, ideas, etc. of past times, usually in a positive way

Ol·du·vai Gorge (ōl′də vī′, -do͞o-) gorge in N Tanzania, 30 mi (48 km) long: archaeological site of important hominid fossils

Old Welsh the Welsh language from the earliest period to *c.* 1150

☆**Old West, the** the American West in the second half of the 19th cent., popularly associated with frontier life, cowboys, etc.

old·wife (ōld′wīf′) *n., pl.* **-wives′** (-wīvz′) 1 [Archaic] an old woman ☆2 OLDSQUAW 3 any of various sea fishes

old wives' tale a silly story or superstitious belief

Old World[1] designating or of a group of animals or plants native to the Eastern Hemisphere, esp. Eurasia and Africa

Old World[2] the Eastern Hemisphere; Europe, Asia, and Africa: often used specifically with reference to European culture, customs, etc.

old-world (ōld′wurld′) *adj.* 1 of or from the Old World, esp. Europe 2 having or displaying certain usually good qualities or characteristics associated with European customs, manners, or standards [*old-world* hospitality]

o·lé (ô lā′) *n., interj.* ⟦Sp, prob. < *hola,* hollo, echoic of shout⟧ (an exclamation) used to express approval, triumph, joy, etc., as at a bullfight or in flamenco dancing

-ole (ōl) ⟦< L *oleum,* OIL⟧ *Chem. suffix* 1 any of certain closed-chain compounds with five members [*pyrrole*] 2 any of certain chemical compounds without hydroxyl, esp. any of certain aldehydes and ethers [*anisole*]

o·le·ag·i·nous (ō′lē aj′i nəs) *adj.* ⟦Fr *oléagineux* < L *oleaginus* < *olea,* olive tree (< Gr *elaia,* olive, olive tree)⟧ oily; greasy; unctuous —**o′le·ag′i·nous·ly** *adv.* —**o′le·ag′i·nous·ness** *n.*

o·le·an·der (ō′lē an′dər, ō′lē an′dər) *n.* ⟦ML, earlier also *lorandrum:* altered < ? L *rhododendron*⟧ a poisonous evergreen shrub (*Nerium oleander*) of the dogbane family, with fragrant flowers of white, pink, or red and narrow, leathery leaves

o·le·as·ter (ō′lē as′tər, ō′lē as′tər) *n.* ⟦ME *oliaster* < L < *olea:* see OLEAGINOUS⟧ any of several plants (genus *Elaeagnus*) of the oleaster family, often grown for ornament; esp. the Russian olive —*adj.* designating a family (Elaeagnaceae, order Proteales) of dicotyledonous plants, including buffalo berry

o·le·ate (ō′lē āt′) *n.* a salt or ester of oleic acid

o·lec·ra·non (ō lek′rə nän′, ō′li krā′nän′) *n.* ⟦ModL < Gr *ōlekranon* (for *ōlenokronon*) < *ōlenē,* elbow (see ELL[2]) + *kranion,* the head: see CRANIUM⟧ the part of the ulna projecting behind the elbow joint

OLED (ō′el′ē′dē′) *n.* ⟦*o*(*rganic-*)*l*(*ight-*)*e*(*mitting*) *d*(*iode*)⟧ an LED using an organic semiconductor rather than silicon

o·le·fin (ō′lə fin) *n.* ⟦< Fr (*gaz*) *oléfiant* < L *oleum,* OIL + prp. of Fr *fier,* to make < L *facere:* see DO[1]⟧ ALKENE: also **o′le·fine** (-fin, -fēn′) —**o′le·fin′ic** (-fin′ik) *adj.*

olefin series ETHYLENE SERIES

o·le·ic (ō lē′ik, -lā′-; ō′lē-) *adj.* ⟦< L *oleum,* OIL + -IC⟧ 1 of or obtained from oil 2 of or pertaining to oleic acid

oleic acid an oily, unsaturated fatty acid, $C_{17}H_{33}COOH$, present in the form of the glyceryl ester in most animal and vegetable fats and oils, used in making soap, ointments, etc.

o·le·in (ō′lē in) *n.* ⟦Fr *oléine* < L *oleum,* OIL⟧ 1 a liquid glyceride, $(C_{17}H_{33}CO_2)_3C_3H_5$, present in olive oil and certain other oils and fats 2 the liquid part of any fat, as distinguished from the solid part

☆**o·le·o** (ō′lē ō′) *n. short for* OLEOMARGARINE

o·le·o- (ō′lē ō, -ə) ⟦L < *oleum,* OIL⟧ *combining form* oil, olein, or oleic [*oleograph*]

o·le·o·graph (ō′lē ō graf′, -lē ə-) *n.* ⟦prec. + -GRAPH⟧ a chromolithograph finished so that its surface resembles that of an oil painting on canvas —**o′le·o·graph′ic** *adj.* —**o′le·og′ra·phy** (-äg′rə fē) *n.*

☆**o·le·o·mar·ga·rine** or **o·le·o·mar·ga·rin** (ō′lē ō mär′jə rin) *n.* ⟦Fr *oléomargarine:* see OLEO- & MARGARINE⟧ *former term for* MARGARINE

☆**oleo oil** a butterlike oil obtained from animal fat

o·le·o·res·in (ō′lē ō rez′ən, ō′lē ō rez′-) *n.* 1 a mixture of a resin and an essential oil, as turpentine, occurring naturally in various plants 2 a prepared mixture of an essential oil holding resin in solution

☆**oleo strut** a shock-absorbing strut in the landing gear of some airplanes, consisting of a telescopic cylinder containing oil

O level 1 the first, or ordinary, level of standardized examinations in specific subjects taken by British secondary-school students seeking either a General Certificate of Education and university admission or a Certificate only 2 a pass on any examination at this level See A LEVEL Also written **O′-lev′el** *n.*

ol·fac·tion (äl fak′shən, ōl-) *n.* ⟦< L *olfacere:* see OLFACTORY⟧ 1 the sense of smell 2 the act of smelling

ol·fac·tom·e·ter (äl′fak täm′ət ər, ōl-) *n.* ⟦fol. + -METER⟧ a device for measuring the acuteness of the sense of smell —**ol·fac′to·met′ric** (-tō met′rik) *adj.* —**ol′fac·tom′e·try** *n.*

ol·fac·to·ry (äl fak′tə rē, ōl-) *adj.* ⟦< L *olfactus,* pp. of *olfacere,* to smell < *olere,* to have a smell (akin to *odor,* ODOR) + *facere,* to make: see DO[1]⟧ of the sense of smell: also **ol·fac′tive** (-tiv) —*n., pl.* **-ries** [*usually pl.*] an organ of smell

olfactory bulb the tip of the long, thin lobe (**olfactory lobe**) extending from the bottom of each cerebral hemisphere, from which the olfactory nerve emerges

olfactory nerve either of the first pair of cranial nerves that arise in the mucous membranes within the upper part of the nose and transmit impulses concerned with the sense of smell to the forebrain

ol·fac·tron·ics (äl′fak trän′iks, ōl′-) *n.* ⟦< OLFAC(TORY) + (ELEC)TRONICS⟧ the science that deals with the detection and measurement by instruments of vapors and particles given off by various substances

OLG *abbrev.* Old Low German

Ol·ga (äl′gə, ôl′-, ōl′-) *n.* ⟦Russ < ON *Helga,* holy < *heilagr,* akin to OE *heilag,* HOLY⟧ a feminine name

o·lib·a·num (ō lib′ə nəm) *n.* ⟦ME < ML < Ar *al-luban,* frankincense, akin to Heb *lebōnā* > Gr *libanos*⟧ FRANKINCENSE

ol·i·garch (äl′i gärk′) *n.* ⟦Gr *oligarchēs:* see OLIGO- & -ARCH⟧ any of the rulers of an oligarchy

ol·i·gar·chy (äl′i gär′kē) *n., pl.* **-chies** ⟦Gr *oligarchia:* see fol. & -ARCHY⟧ 1 a form of government in which the ruling power belongs to a few persons 2 a state governed in this way 3 the persons ruling such a state —**ol′i·gar′chic** *adj.*, **ol′i·gar′chi·cal**

ol·i·go- (äl′i gō) ⟦Gr *oligo-* < *oligos,* small, akin to *loigos,* destruction, death < IE base *(*o*)*leig-,* wretched, illness > Lith *ligà,* disease⟧ *combining form* few, scant, small, a deficiency of [*oligochaete*]: also, before a vowel, **olig-**

Ol·i·go·cene (äl′i gō sēn′) *adj.* ⟦prec. + -CENE⟧ [*sometimes* **o-**] designating or of the third and last geologic epoch of the Paleogene, characterized by cold climate, the formation of vast grasslands, and the further development of mammals —**the Oligocene** the Oligocene Epoch or its rocks: see the geologic time chart in the Reference Supplement

ol·i·go·chaete (-kēt′) *n.* ⟦ModL *Oligochaeta:* see OLIGO- & CHAETA⟧ any of a class (Oligochaeta) of annelid worms, as the earthworm, lacking a definite head and having relatively few body bristles: found chiefly in moist soil and fresh water —**ol′i·go·chae′tous** *adj.*

ol·i·go·clase (-klās′) *n.* ⟦Ger *oligoklas* < Gr *oligos* (see OLIGO-) + *klasis,* a fracture (see CLASTIC), in contrast to ORTHOCLASE, because cleavage differs slightly from 90°⟧ a plagioclase feldspar whose composition corresponds to 70 to 90 percent albite

ol·i·go·nu·cle·o·tide (-no͞o′klē ō tīd′, -nyo͞o′-) *n.* a short piece of nucleic acid, usually with less than twenty nucleotides, used in genetic engineering and research

ol·i·goph·a·gous (äl′i gäf′ə gəs) *adj.* ⟦OLIGO- + -PHAGOUS⟧ feeding upon a limited variety of food, as certain caterpillars whose diet is restricted to a few related plants

ol·i·gop·o·ly (äl′i gäp′ə lē) *n., pl.* **-lies** ⟦OLIG(O)- + (MON)OPOLY⟧ control of a commodity or service in a given market by a small number of companies or suppliers —**ol′i·gop′o·list** *n.* —**ol′i·gop′o·lis′tic** *adj.*

ol·i·gop·so·ny (-sə nē) *n., pl.* **-nies** ⟦OLIG(O)- + Gr *opsōnia,* a purchase of food, catering < *opsōnein:* see OPSONIN⟧ control of the purchase of a commodity or service in a given market by a small number of buyers —**ol′i·gop′so·nist** *n.* —**ol′i·gop′so·nis′tic** *adj.*

ol·i·go·sac·cha·ride (äl′i gō sak′ə rīd′) *n.* ⟦OLIGO- + SACCHARIDE⟧ any of a group of carbohydrates consisting of a small number (2 to 10) of simple sugar molecules

ol·i·go·tro·phic (-träf′ik, -trō′fik) *adj.* ⟦OLIGO- + TROPHIC⟧ designating or of a lake, pond, etc. poor in plant nutrient minerals and organisms and usually rich in oxygen at all depths: see also MESOTROPHIC —**ol·i·got·ro·phy** (äl′ə gät′rə fē) *n.*

ol·i·gu·ri·a (äl′i gyoor′ē ə) *n.* ⟦ModL: see OLIGO- & -URIA⟧ a condition characterized by the excretion of an abnormally small amount of urine

o·li·o (ō′lē ō′) *n., pl.* **-os′** ⟦< Sp *olla:* see OLLA⟧ 1 a highly spiced stew of meat and vegetables; olla 2 a collection, or miscellany, as of musical numbers

ol·i·va·ceous (äl′ə vā′shəs) *adj.* ⟦ModL *olivaceus:* see OLIVE & -ACEOUS⟧ of or like the olive; esp., olive-green

ol·i·var·y (äl′ə ver′ē) *adj.* ⟦L *olivarius*⟧ *Anat.* 1 shaped like an olive 2 designating or of either of two oval bodies protruding from the sides of the medulla oblongata

ol·ive (äl′iv) *n.* ⟦OFr < L *oliva* < Gr *elaia*⟧ 1 *a)* an evergreen tree (*Olea europaea*) of the olive family, native to S Europe and the Near East, with leathery leaves, yellow flowers, and an edible fruit *b)* the small, oval fruit of this tree, cured when either green or ripe to be eaten as a relish, or pressed to extract olive oil **2** the wood of this tree **3** any of various plants resembling the olive **4** an olive branch or wreath **5** the dull, yellowish-green color of the unripe olive fruit **6** OLIVE GREEN —***adj.*** **1** of the olive **2** *a)* olive-colored *b)* having a dark complexion tinged with this color **3** designating a family (Oleaceae, order Scrophulariales) of dicotyledonous trees and shrubs with loose clusters of four-parted flowers, including the ashes, lilacs, jasmines, and forsythias

Ol·ive (äl′iv) ***n.*** ⟦< ME *oliva* < L, OLIVE⟧ a feminine name: var. *Olivia*

olive branch **1** the branch of the olive tree, traditionally a symbol of peace **2** any peace offering

olive drab **1** any of various shades of greenish brown, much used as a camouflage color in the armed forces **2** woolen cloth dyed this color and used for uniforms by the U.S. Army **3** [*pl.*] a uniform of this cloth —**ol′ive-drab′** ***adj.***

olive green the color of the unripe olive

o·liv·en·ite (ō liv′ə nīt′, äl′ə və-) ***n.*** ⟦Ger *oliven(erz),* olive (ore) + -ITE[1]⟧ a greenish, soft, orthorhombic mineral, $Cu_2(AsO_4)(OH)$, often found with azurite and malachite; hydrous copper arsenate

olive oil a yellow to greenish oil pressed from ripe olives, used in cooking, salad dressings, liniments, soap, etc.

Ol·i·ver (äl′ə vər) ***n.*** ⟦Fr *Olivier:* form assimilated to OFr *olivier,* olive tree < L *olivarius,* but prob. < MLowG *alfihar,* lit., elf-army < *alf,* elf + *hari,* a host, army⟧ **1** a masculine name **2** one of Charlemagne's twelve peers, a friend of Roland: see ROLAND

Olives, Mount of ridge of hills east of Jerusalem: also **Mount Ol·i·vet** (äl′ə vet′, -vət)

O·liv·i·a (ō liv′ē ə, ə-) ***n.*** a feminine name: see OLIVE

O·liv·i·er (ō liv′ē ā′), **Laurence (Kerr)** Baron Olivier of Brighton 1907-89; Brit. actor

ol·i·vine (äl′ə vēn′) ***n.*** ⟦OLIV(E) + -INE[1]⟧ a hard, greenish mineral, $(Mg,Fe)_2SiO_4$, that is an ore of magnesium, used as a refractory; magnesium iron silicate —**ol′i·vin′ic** (-vin′ik) ***adj.***

ol·la (äl′ə; *Sp* ôl′yä) ***n.*** ⟦Sp < L, a pot: see OVEN⟧ ☆**1** a large-mouthed pot or jar of earthenware **2** a highly spiced stew of meat and vegetables

ol·la-po·dri·da (äl′ə pō drē′də) ***n.*** ⟦Sp, lit., rotten pot < *olla,* pot (< L) + *podrida,* rotten < L *putridus:* see PUTRID⟧ **1** an olla (stew) **2** any assortment, medley, or miscellany; olio

Ol·mec (äl′mek′) ***n., pl.*** **-mecs′** or **-mec′** ⟦< name in Nahuatl, lit., those living in the rubber country⟧ a member of an ancient American Indian people centered in what are now the Mexican states of Tabasco and Veracruz —***adj.*** of the culture of this people, characterized by a highly developed system of agriculture, jade carvings, and sculpture in the form of giant heads

Olm·sted (ōm′sted′, äm′-, -stəd), **Frederick Law** 1822-1903; U.S. landscape architect

ol·o·gy (äl′ə jē) ⟦< fol.⟧ ***n., pl.*** **-gies** a branch of learning; science: a humorous usage

-ol·o·gy (äl′ə jē) ⟦initial medial -O- + -LOGY⟧ *combining form* -LOGY

o·lo·ro·so (ō′lō rō′sō) ***n.*** ⟦Sp < adj., fragrant⟧ a dark, medium-sweet sherry

O·lym·pi·a[1] (ō lim′pē ə, ə-) ***n.*** ⟦L < Gr, fem. of *Olympios,* lit., of Olympus⟧ a feminine name

O·lym·pi·a[2] (ō lim′pē ə, ə-) **1** plain in ancient Elis, W Peloponnesus: site of the ancient Olympic games **2** ⟦after OLYMPIC MOUNTAINS⟧ capital of Wash.: seaport on Puget Sound

O·lym·pi·ad (ō lim′pē ad′, ə-; -əd) ***n.*** ⟦Fr *olympiade* < Gr *Olympias* (gen. *Olympiados*) < *Olympia,* prec. (the plain)⟧ [*often* **o-**] **1** in ancient Greece, any of the four-year periods between Olympic games: used by the Greeks in computing time **2** a celebration of the modern Olympic games

O·lym·pi·an (ō lim′pē ən, ə-) ***n.*** ⟦< LL *Olympianus,* Olympic⟧ **1** *Gr. Myth.* any of the twelve major gods supposed to live on the slopes of Mount Olympus **2** a person born in Olympia **3** any participant in the ancient or modern Olympic games —***adj.*** **1** of Olympia or Mount Olympus **2** like an Olympian god; exalted; celestial; majestic **3** designating or of the Olympic games of ancient Greece

O·lym·pic (ō lim′pik, ə-) ***adj.*** ⟦L *Olympicus* < Gr *Olympikos*⟧ of or having to do with the OLYMPIC GAMES —***n.*** **1** an Olympic game **2** [*pl.*] OLYMPIC GAMES: preceded by *the*

Olympic games **1** an ancient Greek festival consisting of contests in athletics, poetry, and music, held every four years at Olympia to honor Zeus **2** a modern international athletic competition that is generally held every four years in a different location, consisting of summer events, as track and field, swimming, and volleyball, and, in a different city and month, winter events, as skiing, ice skating, and ice hockey: until 1992 all the events were held in the same year but since 1994 the winter events and summer events have been separated by a two-year interval Preceded by *the*

Olympic Mountains one of the Coast Ranges on Olympic Peninsula, NW Wash.: highest peak, Mt. Olympus

Olympic Peninsula peninsula in NW Wash., between Puget Sound & the Pacific

O·lym·pus (ō lim′pəs, ə-), **Mount** ⟦L < Gr *Olympos*⟧ **1** mountain in N Greece, between Thessaly & Macedonia: *c.* 9,580 ft (2,920 m): in Greek mythology, the home of the gods **2** ⟦after the mountain in Greece⟧ highest peak of the Olympic Mountains, NW Wash.: 7,965 ft (2,428 m)

O·lyn·thus (ō lin′thəs) city in ancient Greece, on the Chalcidice Peninsula

om (ōm) ***n.*** ⟦Sans *oṁ*⟧ *Hinduism* a word of affirmation or assent intoned as part of a mantra or as a symbolic mystical utterance during meditation

OM *abbrev.* Order of Merit

-o·ma (ō′mə) ⟦ModL < Gr *-ōma,* group, mass⟧ *suffix* tumor [*lymphoma, sarcoma*]

O·ma·ha (ō′mə hô′, -hä′) ⟦< Fr < name of a Siouan people, lit., ? upstream people⟧ city in E Nebr., on the Missouri River

O·man (ō män′) **1** SE coastal region of Arabia, on the Arabian Sea **2** country in this region: an independent sultanate: 82,031 sq mi (212,460 sq km); cap. Muscat **3 Gulf of** arm of the Arabian Sea, between Iran & Oman in Arabia: *c.* 350 mi (563 km) long —**O·man′i** (-ē) ***adj., n.***

O·mar Khay·yám (ō′mär kī yäm′, -yam′) died 1123; Pers. poet & mathematician: author of *The Rubáiyát*

o·ma·sum (ō mā′səm) ***n., pl.*** **o·ma′sa** (-sə) ⟦ModL < L, bullock's tripe < Gaul⟧ the third division in the stomach of a cud-chewing animal, as the cow

O·may·yad (ō mī′ad) ***n., pl.*** **-yads** or **-ya·des′** (-ə dēz′) ⟦after *Omayya,* great-grandfather of the first caliph in the dynasty⟧ any of a dynasty of caliphs who ruled at Damascus (A.D. 661-750), or of a related branch ruling in Spain (756-1031)

OMB *abbrev.* Office of Management and Budget

om·ber or **om·bre** (äm′bər) ***n.*** ⟦< Fr or Sp: Fr *ombre* < Sp *hombre* < L *homo,* a man: see HOMAGE⟧ a card game played with forty cards by three players, popular in the 17th and 18th cent.

om·bré (äm′brā′, äm brā′) ***adj.*** ⟦Fr, pp. of *ombrer,* to shade < L *umbrare* < *umbra,* shade⟧ shaded or graduated in tone: said of a color

om·buds·man (äm′bədz mən, äm′budz′mən) ***n., pl.*** **-men** (-mən) ⟦Swed < *ombud,* a deputy, representative (< ON *umboth* < *um, umbe,* about < IE **mbhi-,* var. of **ambhi-,* around, on both sides (> AMBI-) + ON *bjotha,* to offer, bid, akin to OE *beodan:* see BID[1]) + *man,* MAN⟧ **1** a public official appointed to investigate citizens' complaints against government agencies or officials that may be infringing on the rights of individuals **2** a person employed by an institution to investigate and attempt to mediate and resolve complaints against it

☆**om·buds·per·son** (äm′bədz pur′sən) ***n.*** OMBUDSMAN: used to avoid the masculine implication of *ombudsman*

om·buds·wom·an (-woom′ən) ***n., pl.*** **-wom′en** (-wim′in) a female serving as an ombudsman

Om·dur·man (äm′door män′) city in WC Sudan, on the Nile, opposite Khartoum

o·me·ga (ō mā′gə, -meg′ə) ***n.*** ⟦Gr ō + *mega,* great (see MEGA-): lit., great (i.e., long) *o,* to distinguish from *o mikron:* see OMICRON⟧ **1** the twenty-fourth and final letter of the Greek alphabet (Ω, ω): in English transliteration, as in the etymologies of this dictionary, it is shown as ō **2** the last (of any series); end

o·me·ga-3 (fatty acid) (-thrē′) ⟦so named because the first double bond in its carbon chain, counting from the last atom (at the end opposite the carboxyl group), is at the third carbon atom; see prec.⟧ a type of polyunsaturated fatty acid in fish oil, shellfish, soybeans, etc., that is associated with lowering cholesterol and LDL levels when consumed in certain amounts

om·e·let or **om·e·lette** (äm′lit; *occas.* äm′ə lit) ***n.*** ⟦Fr *omelette,* earlier *amelette,* by metathesis < *alemette* < *alemelle* < L *lamella,* small plate: see LAMELLA⟧ a dish consisting of beaten eggs, seasonings, etc., cooked or baked in a flat mass and usually served folded over, often with a filling as of jelly, cheese, or mushrooms

o·men (ō′mən) ***n.*** ⟦L < OL *osmen*⟧ a thing or happening believed to foretell a future event, either good or evil; augury —***vt.*** to be an omen of; augur

o·men·tum (ō men′təm) ***n., pl.*** **-ta** (-tə) or **-tums** ⟦L: **o-* (< IE base **eu-,* to put on > L *exuere,* to strip off: see EXUVIAE) + *-mentum,* -MENT⟧ a free fold of the peritoneum connecting the stomach and certain other visceral organs: the **greater omentum** covers the stomach and intestines like an apron over their anterior surfaces, while the **lesser omentum** forms a partial covering of the stomach and common bile duct —**o·men′tal** ***adj.***

o·mer (ō′mər) ***n.*** ⟦Heb *'ōmer*⟧ **1** an ancient Hebrew unit of dry measure equal to one tenth of an ephah **2** [*usually* **O-**] *Judaism* the period of 49 days from the second day of Passover through the day before Shavuot: traditionally a period of partial mourning

o·mer·tà (ô mer tä′) ***n.*** ⟦Sicilian dial. for It *umiltà,* lit., humility (< L *humilitas*), hence submission, acquiescence to group code⟧ in Sicily, a policy or code of keeping silent about crimes and refusing to cooperate with the police

om·i·cron (äm′i krän′, ō′mi-) ***n.*** ⟦Gr *o mikron,* lit., small (i.e., short) *o:* see MICRON, OMEGA⟧ the fifteenth letter of the Greek alphabet (Ο, ο)

om·i·nous (äm′ə nəs) ***adj.*** ⟦L *ominosus*⟧ of or serving as an omen; esp., having the character of an evil omen; threatening; sinister —**om′i·nous·ly** ***adv.*** —**om′i·nous·ness** ***n.***

SYN.—**ominous** implies a threatening character but does not necessarily connote a disastrous outcome [the request was met by an *ominous* silence]; **portentous** literally implies a foreshadowing, especially of evil, but is now more often used of that which arouses awe or amazement because of its prodigious or marvelous character [a *portentous* event]; **fateful** may imply a fatal character or control by fate, but is now usually applied to that which is of momentous or decisive significance [a *fateful* truce conference]; **foreboding** implies a portent or presentiment of something evil or harmful [a *foreboding* anxiety]

o·mis·si·ble (ō mis′ə bəl) ***adj.*** that can be omitted

o·mis·sion (ō mish′ən) *n.* ⟦ME *omissioun* < LL *omissio*⟧ 1 an omitting or being omitted; specif., failure to do as one should 2 anything omitted

o·mis·sive (ō mis′iv) *adj.* ⟦< L *omissus,* pp. of *omittere* + -IVE⟧ failing to do or include; omitting —**o·mis′sive·ly** *adv.*

o·mit (ō mit′) *vt.* **o·mit′ted, o·mit′ting** ⟦ME *omitten* < L *omittere* < *ob-* (see OB-) + *mittere,* to send: see MISSION⟧ 1 to fail to include; leave out 2 to fail to do; neglect 3 [Obs.] *a)* to take no notice of *b)* to let go —**SYN.** NEGLECT —**o·mit′ter** *n.*

om·ma·tid·i·um (äm′ə tid′ē əm) *n., pl.* **-i·a** ⟦ModL, dim. < Gr *omma* (gen. *ommatos*), the eye, akin to *ōps,* EYE⟧ any of the structural elements forming the compound eye of an insect, many crustaceans, etc.: each element is a complete photoreceptor in itself, having a lens, pigment, light-sensitive cells, etc. —**om′ma·tid′i·al** *adj.*

om·mat·o·phore (ə mat′ə fôr′) *n.* ⟦< Gr *ommatos* (see prec.) + -PHORE⟧ EYESTALK

Om·mi·ad (ō mī′ad) *n., pl.* **-ads** or **-a·des′** (-ə dēz′) OMAYYAD

om·ni- (äm′ni, -nē, -nə) ⟦L < *omnis,* all⟧ *combining form* all, everywhere [*omnidirectional*]

om·ni·bus (äm′ni bəs) *n., pl.* **-bus′es** ⟦Fr < *(voiture) omnibus,* lit., (carriage) for all < L, dat. pl. of *omnis,* all⟧ 1 BUS (sense 1) 2 a large volume containing a collection of previously published works, as by a single author or on one theme —*adj.* including many things or having a variety of purposes or uses

om·ni·di·rec·tion·al (äm′ni də rek′shə nəl) *adj.* ⟦OMNI- + DIRECTIONAL⟧ for sending or receiving radio or sound waves in or from any direction

om·ni·far·i·ous (äm′ni fer′ē əs) *adj.* ⟦L *omnifarius,* of all sorts < *omnis,* all + *-farius:* see BIFARIOUS⟧ of all kinds, varieties, or forms

om·nif·ic (äm nif′ik) *adj.* ⟦ML *omnificus* < L *omnis,* all + *facere,* to make, DO[1]⟧ creating all things: also **om·nif′i·cent** (-ə sənt)

om·nip·o·tence (äm nip′ə təns) *n.* ⟦MFr < LL *omnipotentia*⟧ 1 the state or quality of being omnipotent 2 an omnipotent force 3 [**O-**] God

om·nip·o·tent (äm nip′ə tənt) *adj.* ⟦OFr < L *omnipotens* < *omnis,* all + *potens:* see POTENT⟧ having unlimited power or authority; all-powerful —**the Omnipotent** God —**om·nip′o·tent·ly** *adv.*

om·ni·pres·ent (äm′ni prez′ənt) *adj.* ⟦ML *omnipraesens* < L *omnis,* all + *praesens,* PRESENT⟧ present in all places at the same time —**om′ni·pres′ence** *n.*

☆**om·ni·range** (äm′ni rānj′) *n.* ⟦< *omni(directional radio) range*⟧ a navigational system for aircraft in which a network of ground stations send out VHF radio signals that control a display on the instrument panel of an aircraft, showing the pilot the heading of the plane in relation to the source of a specific signal

om·nis·cience (äm nish′əns; *Brit & Cdn,* -nis′ē əns) *n.* ⟦ME < ML *omniscientia*⟧ the state or quality of being omniscient

om·nis·cient (äm nish′ənt; *Brit & Cdn,* -nis′ē ənt) *adj.* ⟦ML *omnisciens* < L *omnis,* all + *sciens,* knowing: see SCIENCE⟧ having infinite knowledge; knowing all things —**the Omniscient** God —**om·nis′cient·ly** *adv.*

om·ni·um-gath·er·um (äm′nē əm gath′ər əm) *n.* ⟦pseudo-L < L *omnium,* gen. pl. of *omnis,* all + GATHER + 'EM⟧ a miscellaneous collection of persons or things

om·ni·vore (äm′ni vôr′) *n.* ⟦< ModL *omnivora* (pl.), old designation for the group containing the pig < L, neut. pl. of *omnivorus:* see fol.⟧ an omnivorous person or animal

om·niv·o·rous (äm niv′ə rəs) *adj.* ⟦L *omnivorus:* see OMNI- & -VOROUS⟧ 1 eating any sort of food, esp. both animal and vegetable food 2 taking in everything indiscriminately, as with the intellect [an *omnivorous* reader] —**om·niv′o·rous·ly** *adv.* —**om·niv′o·rous·ness** *n.*

omn. noct. *abbrev.* ⟦L *omni nocte*⟧ *Pharmacy* every night

o·mo·pha·gi·a (ō′mō fā′jē ə, -fā′jə) *n.* ⟦Gr *ōmophagia* < *ōmos,* raw (< IE base **om-,* raw, bitter > L *amarus,* bitter) + *phagein,* to eat: see -PHAGOUS⟧ the eating of raw flesh —**o·moph·a·gist** (ō mäf′ə jist) *n.* —**o·moph′a·gous** (-gəs) *adj.,* **o′mo·phag′ic** (-faj′ik)

Om·pha·le (äm′fə lē′) *n. Gr. Myth.* a queen of Lydia in whose service Hercules, dressed as a woman, does womanly tasks for three years to appease the gods

om·pha·lo- (äm′fə lō, -lə) ⟦< Gr *omphalos,* NAVEL⟧ *combining form* navel, umbilicus [*omphalocele*]

om·pha·los (äm′fə ləs, -läs′) *n.* ⟦see prec.⟧ 1 NAVEL 2 a central point 3 a rounded stone in Apollo's temple at Delphi, regarded as the center of the world by the ancients

Omsk (ômsk) city in S Asian Russia, on the Irtysh River

on (än, ôn) *prep.* ⟦ME < OE *on, an,* akin to Ger *an,* Goth *ana,* ON *ā* < IE base **an, *anō,* prob. meaning "obliquely toward, slanting toward" > Gr *ana*⟧ 1 in a position above, but in contact with and supported by; upon 2 in contact with (any surface); covering or attached to 3 so as to be supported by [leaning *on* his elbow] 4 in the surface of [a scar *on* the body] 5 *a)* near to; by [a cottage *on* the lake, seated *on* my right] *b)* having as its location [a house *on* Main Street] *c)* assigned to work at or in [*on* the maternity ward, *on* the switchboard] 6 at or during the time of [*on* entering, *on* the first day] 7 having a basis of or having its ground in (something specified) [based *on* her diary, *on* purpose] 8 connected with as a part or member [*on* the faculty] 9 engaged in [*on* a trip] 10 in the state or condition of [*on* parole, *on* fire] 11 in a (specified) manner: chiefly archaic except in phrases with *the* [*on* the sly] 12 as a result of [a profit *on* the sale] 13 in the direction or vicinity of [light shone *on* us] 14 so as to affect [to put a curse *on* someone] 15 regularly following (a regimen), ingesting (medicine), etc., as to promote good health [*on* a diet, *on* penicillin] 16 *a)* through the means or use of [to live *on* bread, running *on* diesel fuel] *b)* through the medium of [*on* the phone, to act *on* TV] *c)* using for transportation [*on* a train] 17 with regard to; concerning [an essay *on* war] 18 coming after: used to indicate repetition [we suffered insult *on* insult] 19 placing obligation or responsibility with [rely *on* me; the onus is *on* him] 20 onto [just throw it *on* the porch] ☆21 chargeable to; at the expense of [have a drink *on* the house; lunch is *on* me] 22 in jazz, popular music, etc., *a)* playing [Jim is *on* guitar] *b)* IN[1] (*prep.* 7a) [he played *on* the Basie band] ☆23 [Informal] habitually using; addicted to [to be *on* drugs] 24 [Informal] carried by [I have no money *on* me] 25 [Informal] constantly nagging at, finding fault with, etc. [the boss has been *on* him all day] 26 *a)* [Dial.] *used variously for* OF[1], AT[1], ABOUT, FOR[1], IN[1] *b)* [Brit.] IN[1] (*prep.* 1, 7a, 11) —*adv.* 1 in or into a situation or position of contacting, being supported by, or covering [put your shoes *on*] 2 in a direction to or toward [he looked *on*] 3 *a)* in advance; forward; ahead [move *on*] *b)* [Brit.] along in time; later; after [thirty years *on,* nothing had changed] 4 lastingly; continuously [she sang *on*] 5 into operation, performance, or action [switch *on* the light] 6 *Baseball* on base 7 *Theater* on stage —*adj.* 1 in action or operation [the TV is *on*] 2 near or nearer 3 arranged or planned for [tomorrow's game is still *on*] 4 [Slang] performing or functioning at a high level of competence [he was really *on* in last night's game] 5 *Cricket* designating that side of the field, or of the wicket, where the batsman stands —*n.* 1 the fact or state of being on 2 *Cricket* the on side —**and so on** and more like the preceding; and so forth —☆**have nothing on** [Informal] 1 to have no unfavorable evidence against 2 to have no advantage over; not as skilled, experienced, successful, etc. in comparison with —☆**have something on** [Informal] to have unfavorable evidence against —**on and off** not continuously; intermittently —**on and on** continuously; at great length —**on to** 1 [Brit.] ONTO (sense 1) ☆2 [Slang] aware of or familiar with; esp., aware of the real nature or meaning of

On (än) *Biblical name for* HELIOPOLIS

ON *abbrev.* 1 Old Norse 2 Ontario

-on (än) *suffix forming nouns* 1 ⟦< *-on* in *argon*⟧ an inert gas [*radon*] 2 ⟦< *-on* in *ion*⟧ a subatomic particle [*neutron*] 3 ⟦< -ONE⟧ *a)* a functional unit [*operon*] *b)* a unit of measure [*photon*]

on·a·ger (än′ə jər) *n., pl.* **-gri′** (-grī′) or **-gers** ⟦ME < L < Gr *onagros,* wild ass < *onos,* ass + *agrios,* wild < *agros,* country, field: see ACRE⟧ 1 a wild ass (*Equus hemionus onager*) of central Asia 2 a catapult for throwing stones, used in ancient and medieval warfare

on-air (än′er′) *adj., adv. Radio, TV* (while) broadcasting or being broadcast

o·nan·ism (ō′nə niz′əm) *n.* ⟦after *Onan,* son of Judah (see Gen. 38:9) + -ISM⟧ 1 COITUS INTERRUPTUS 2 MASTURBATION —**o′nan·ist** *n.* —**o′nan·is′tic** *adj.*

on·board or **on-board** (än′bôrd′) *adv., adj.* ON BOARD (see phrase under BOARD)

once (wuns) *adv.* ⟦ME *ones,* gen. of *on,* ONE⟧ 1 one time; one time only [to eat *once* a day] 2 at any time; at all; ever [she'll succeed if *once* given a chance] 3 at some time in the past; formerly [a *once* famous man] 4 by one degree or grade [a cousin *once* removed] —*conj.* as soon as; if ever; whenever [*once* he has made his point, he will be quiet] —*adj.* former; quondam —*n.* one time [go this *once*] —**all at once** 1 all at the same time 2 suddenly —**at once** 1 immediately 2 at the same time —**for once** for at least one time —**once and again** occasionally —**once (and) for all** finally; decisively; conclusively —**once in a while** now and then; occasionally —**once or twice** not often; a few times —**once upon a time** in the past, esp. a long time ago

☆**once-o·ver** (wuns′ō′vər) *n.* [Informal] 1 a quick, comprehensive look or examination; swiftly appraising glance 2 a quick, cursory or light cleaning or going-over

on·cho·cer·ci·a·sis (äŋ′kō sər kī′ə sis) *n.* ⟦< ModL *Onchocerca* (< Gr *onkos,* barb + *kerkos,* tail) + -IASIS⟧ a fly-transmitted tropical disease in which parasitic filarial worms (genus *Onchocerca*) cause tumors, skin lesions, and blindness; river blindness

on·cid·i·um (än sid′ē əm) *n.* ⟦ModL < Gr *onkos,* barbed hook (for IE base see ANKLE) + ModL *-idium* (< Gr *-idion,* dim. suffix): from form of the labellum⟧ any of a genus (*Oncidium*) of tropical American orchids

on·co- (äŋ′kō, -kə) ⟦< Gr *onkos,* a mass: see ONCOLOGY⟧ *combining form* 1 bulk, mass 2 tumor [*oncogene*]

☆**on·co·gene** (äŋ′kə jēn′) *n.* ⟦< Gr *onkos,* a mass (see fol.) + GENE⟧ any of various genes that, when activated as by radiation or a virus, may cause a normal cell to become cancerous —**on′co·gen′ic** (-jen′ik) *adj.*

on·col·o·gy (än käl′ə jē, äŋ-) *n.* ⟦< Gr *onkos,* a mass (< IE **onk-* < base **enek̂-,* to attain, bear > ENOUGH) + -LOGY⟧ the branch of medicine dealing with neoplasms —**on′co·log′ic** (-kō läj′ik) *adj.* —**on·col′o·gist** *n.*

on·com·ing (än′kum′iŋ) *adj.* 1 coming nearer in position or time; approaching 2 coming forth; emerging —*n.* an approach

on·co·vi·rus (äŋ′kə vī′rəs) *n.* ⟦ONCO- + VIRUS⟧ any of a group of retroviruses variously causing tumors, sarcomas, and leukemias: also **on·cor·na·vi·rus** (äŋ kôr′nə vī′rəs)

one (wun) *adj.* ⟦ME < OE *an,* akin to Ger *ein,* Goth *ains* < IE **oinos* (> Gr *oinē,* L *unus,* OIr *ōen*) < **e-, *ei-,* prefixed pronominal stem meaning "the, this, this one"⟧ 1 being a single thing or unit; not two or more 2 characterized by unity; forming a whole; united; undivided [with *one* accord] 3 designating a person or thing as contrasted with or opposed to another or others [from *one* day to another] **4** being uniquely or strikingly the person or thing specified [the *one* solution to the problem] **5** single in kind; the same [all of *one* mind] **6** designating a single, but not clearly specified, person or thing; a certain [*one* day last week]: also used as an intensive substitute for the indefinite article [she's *one* beautiful girl] —*n.* **1** the number expressing unity or designating a single unit: the lowest cardinal number and the first used in counting a series; 1; I **2** a single person or thing **3** something numbered one or marked with one pip, as the face of a die or domino ☆**4** [Informal] a one-dollar bill —*pron.* **1** some, or a certain, person or thing [*one* of us must go] **2** any person or thing; anybody or anything [when *one* is exhausted, it is wise to rest]: sometimes used affectedly in place of a personal pronoun in the first or second person [what else could *one* do?] **3** the person or thing previously mentioned [they rent a house, but I own *one*] **4** someone by the name of: used preceding the name of someone who is otherwise unknown or who has not previously been mentioned —**all one** making no difference; of no importance —**at one** of the same opinion; in accord —**one and all** everybody —**one after another** each (of a group or series) in succession, esp. rapid succession [to eat an entire bag of peanuts, *one after another*]: also **one after the other** —**one another 1** each one the others [family members who look out for *one another*] **2** each one the other [twins who defend *one another*] See EACH OTHER (at EACH) —**one by one** individually in succession —**one of these days** at some unspecified time in the future —**one of those days** (or **weeks**, etc.) a particularly trying or unfortunate day (or week, etc.) —**one of those things** something that cannot be avoided, helped, changed, etc. —**the one** [Informal] a particular joke or anecdote [have you heard *the one* about the penguin who goes into a bar?]

-one (ōn) ⟦arbitrary use of Gr *-ōnē,* used to signify a female descendant of⟧ *Chem. suffix* **1** ketone [*acetone*] **2** any of certain related compounds containing oxygen [*lactone*]

☆**one-armed bandit** (wun′ärmd′) [Slang] SLOT MACHINE (sense *b*)

☆**one-base hit** (wun′bās′) *Baseball* SINGLE (*n.* 3): also [Slang] **one′-bag′ger** (-bag′ər) *n.*

one-di·men·sion·al (wun′də men′shə nəl) *adj.* having a single dominant aspect, quality, concern, etc. and hence narrow, limited, superficial, etc.

one-eight·y (wun′āt′ē) *n.* [Informal] **1** a turn or revolution of 180° **2** a sharp change in attitude or opinion; about-face Also written **180**

O·ne·ga (ō nē′gə; *Russ* ô nye′gä), **Lake** lake in NW European Russia: *c.* 3,800 sq mi (9,842 sq km)

Onega Bay S arm of the White Sea, extending into NW European Russia: *c.* 100 mi (161 km) long

one-horse (wun′hôrs′) *adj.* **1** drawn by or using a single horse ☆**2** [Informal] having little importance; limited in resources, scope, etc.; petty; inferior

O·nei·da (ō nī′də) *n.* ⟦< Iroquois *Oneiute,* lit., standing rock⟧ **1** *pl.* **-das** or **-da** a member of a North American Indian people living originally near Oneida Lake in New York and now also in Wisconsin and Ontario **2** the Iroquoian language of this people

Oneida Lake ⟦after prec.⟧ lake near Syracuse, N.Y.: part of the New York State Canal System: *c.* 80 sq mi (207 sq km)

O'Neill (ō nēl′), **Eugene (Gladstone)** 1888-1953; U.S. playwright

o·nei·ric (ō nī′rik) *adj.* ⟦< Gr *oneiros,* a dream + -IC⟧ of or having to do with dreams

o·nei·ro·man·cy (ō nī′rō man′sē) *n.* ⟦< Gr *oneiros,* a dream + -MANCY⟧ divination by the interpretation of dreams

☆**one-lin·er** (wun′līn′ər) *n.* a short, witty remark

one-man (wun′man′) *adj.* **1** consisting of, done by, or involving only one person, esp. a man [a *one-man* show] **2** forming an attachment to only one man or to only one man at a time [a *one-man* dog]

one·ness (wun′nis) *n.* **1** singleness; unity **2** unity of mind, feeling, or purpose **3** sameness; identity

☆**one-night stand** (wun′nīt′) **1** a single appearance in one town by a traveling show, lecturer, etc. **2** [Informal] a brief, casual sexual encounter Also [Informal] **one′-night′er** *n.*

one-note (wun′nōt′) *adj.* not changing or varying, as in subject matter or tone; uniform; monotonous

one-off (wun′ôf′, -äf′) [Brit.] *adj.* happening, made, done, etc. only once; not repeated —*n.* something that is one of a kind, not part of a series, etc.

☆**one-on-one** (wun′än wun′) *adj., adv.* **1** *Basketball, Football, etc.* contending individually against a single opposing player **2** in direct, personal confrontation —*n.* a game, sport, etc. in which one individual competes against another individual

101 (wun′ō wun′) *n.* ⟦in allusion to a numeric affix commonly used in naming high-school and college introductory courses⟧ [Informal] the essential facts or principles of a (specified) subject or activity: used in comb. and postpositively [a person who is ignorant of Flirting *101*]

one-piece (wun′pēs′) *adj.* consisting of or fashioned in a single piece [a *one-piece* swimsuit]

on·er·ous (än′ər əs, ōn′-) *adj.* ⟦ME < MFr *onereus* < L *onerosus* < *onus,* a load: see ONUS⟧ **1** burdensome; laborious **2** *Law* involving a legal obligation that equals or exceeds the benefits [*onerous* lease] —**on′er·ous·ly** *adv.* —**on′er·ous·ness** *n.*

SYN.—**onerous** applies to that which is laborious or troublesome, often because of its annoying or tedious character [the *onerous* task of taking inventory]; **burdensome** applies to that which is wearisome or oppressive to the mind or spirit as well as to the body [*burdensome* responsibilities]; **oppressive** stresses the overbearing cruelty of the person or thing that inflicts hardship, or emphasizes the severity of the hardship itself [*oppressive* weather, an *oppressive* king]; **exacting** suggests the making of great demands on the attention, skill, care, etc. [an *exacting* supervisor, *exacting* work]

one·self (wun′self′, wunz′-) *pron.* a person's own self: also **one's self** —**be oneself 1** to function physically and mentally as one normally does **2** to be natural or sincere —**by oneself** alone; unaccompanied —**come to oneself 1** to recover one's senses **2** to recover one's capacity for sound judgment

one-shot (wun′shät′) *adj.* [Slang] **1** happening, appearing, etc. only once **2** being the only one; not part of a series

one-sid·ed (wun′sīd′id) *adj.* **1** on, having, or involving only one side **2** larger or more developed on one side; leaning to one side **3** favoring one side; uneven or unfair; prejudiced **4** uneven or unequal [a *one-sided* race]

one·sie (wun′zē) *n.* ⟦< *Onesies,* a trademark for such garments; prob. < *onesie,* from a traditional children's counting game (*onesie,* twosie, threesie, etc.) < ONE + -SY⟧ ☆a one-piece garment for infants and toddlers that covers the torso, having sleeves, no legs, and snaps at the crotch

one-step (wun′step′) *n.* **1** an early 20th-cent. ballroom dance characterized by quick walking steps in 2/4 time **2** music for this dance —*vi.* **-stepped′**, **-step′ping** to dance the one-step

one-stop (wun′stäp′) *adj.* designating, of, or done at a store, bank, etc. that provides a complete range of goods or services [*one-stop* shopping]

one-time (wun′tīm′) *adj.* **1** at some past time; former **2** done, occurring, etc. only once Also, esp. for sense 1, **one′time′**

one-to-one (wun′tə wun′) *adj.* **1** permitting the pairing of an element of one group with a corresponding element of another group **2** *Math.* designating a correspondence such that each member of a set has just one partner in another set, and no element in either is without a partner

one-track (wun′trak′) *adj.* **1** having a single track ☆**2** [Informal] able or willing to deal with only one thing at a time; limited in scope [a *one-track* mind]

one-trick pony a person with only a single notable skill or feature

one-two (punch) (wun′to͞o′-) **1** *Boxing* a sequence of two quick punches, esp. a jab with the left hand followed at once by a hard blow with the right **2** any sequence of two related actions for a specific result

one-up (wun′up′, wun′-) [Informal] *adj.* having an advantage (over another): also **one up**: often in the phrase **be one-up on** —*vt.* **-upped′**, **-up′ping** to have or seize an advantage over

one-up·man·ship (wun up′mən ship′) *n.* ⟦prec. + (GAMES)MANSHIP⟧ [Informal] the practice of, or skill in, seizing an advantage or gaining superiority over others

one-way (wun′wā′) *adj.* **1** moving, or providing for movement, in one direction only [a *one-way* street, a *one-way* ticket] **2** without any reciprocal action or obligation [a *one-way* contract] **3** TWO-WAY (*adj.* 6)

one-wom·an (wun′wo͝om′ən) *adj.* consisting of, done by, or involving only one woman [a *one-woman* crusade]

on-glide (än′glīd′) *n.* a glide coming before a speech sound, in which the vocal organs take the position for forming that sound, either from their normal inactive position or from their position in articulating a preceding sound: cf. OFF-GLIDE

on·go·ing (än′gō′iŋ) *adj.* that is going on, or actually in process; continuing, progressing, etc.

on·ion (un′yən) *n.* ⟦ME *oynon* < OFr *oignon* < L *unio* (gen. *unionis*), oneness, unity, also a kind of single onion: see UNION⟧ **1** a plant (*Allium cepa*) of the lily family, having an edible bulb with a strong, sharp smell and taste **2** the bulb of this plant, formed of close, concentric layers of leaf bases **3** any of various related plants

onion ring any of the ringlike pieces, served usually as an appetizer, made from sections of sliced onion that are coated with batter and deep-fried

on·ion·skin (un′yən skin′) *n.* **1** the thin, translucent outer coating of an onion ☆**2** a tough, thin, translucent, glossy paper, often used for carbon copies

-o·ni·um (ō′nē əm) ⟦< (AMM)ONIUM⟧ *Chem. suffix forming nouns* **1** any of a group of compounds that are isologues of ammonium [*sulfonium*] **2** a cation [*hydronium*]

on·line (än′līn′) *adj.* **1** designating or of equipment directly controlled by the central processing unit of a computer **2** connected to and ready to receive data from or transmit data to a computer or computer network **3** available on or done through the internet or some other computer network —*adv.* on or by means of the internet or some other computer network Also written **on-line**

on·look·er (än′lo͝ok′ər) *n.* a person who watches without taking part; spectator —**on′look′ing** *adj., n.*

on·ly (ōn′lē) *adj.* ⟦ME < OE *anlic* < *an,* ONE + *-lic,* -LY[1]⟧ **1** alone of its or their kind; by itself or by themselves; sole **2** having no siblings [an *only* child] **3** alone in its or their superiority; best; finest —*adv.* **1** *a)* and no other; and no (or nothing) more; solely; exclusively [drink water *only*] *b)* merely; simply **2** (but) in what follows or in the end [to meet one crisis, *only* to face another] **3** as recently as [elected *only* last fall] —*conj.* [Informal] were it not that; except that; but [I'd have gone, *only* it rained] —**if only** would that; I wish that [*if only* they would leave; *if* they would *only* try harder] —**only too** very; exceedingly

on·o·mas·tic (än′ō mas′tik, än′ə-) *adj.* ⟦Gr *onomastikos* < *onomazein,* to name < *onoma,* NAME⟧ of or having to do with a name or names

on·o·mas·tics (-tiks) ***n.*** ⟦< Fr *onomastique* (n.) < the adj. < Gr *onomastikos*: see prec. & -ICS⟧ **1** the study of the origin, form, meaning, and use of names, esp. proper names **2** a pattern or system serving as a basis for the formation and use of names and terms within a field or category

on·o·mat·o·poe·ia (än′ō mat′ō pē′ə, -mät′-) ***n.*** ⟦LL < Gr *onomatopoiia* < *onoma* (gen. *onomatos*), NAME + *poiein*, to make: see POET[2]⟧ **1** formation of a word by imitating the natural sound associated with the object or action involved; echoism (Ex.: *tinkle, buzz, chickadee*, etc.) **2** the use of words whose sounds reinforce their meaning or tone, as in poetry —**on′o·mat′o·poe′ic** ***adj.***, **on′o·mat′o·po·et′ic** (-pō et′ik) —**on′o·mat′o·poe′i·cal·ly** ***adv.***, **on′o·mat′o·po·et′i·cal·ly**

On·on·da·ga (än′ən dô′gə, -dä′-, -dā′-) ***n.*** ⟦< AmInd (Iroquois) *Ononta′ge′*, lit., on top of the hill (name of the chief Onondaga village)⟧ **1** *pl.* **-gas** or **-ga** a member of a North American Indian people formerly living near Onondaga Lake in New York and now also living in Ontario **2** the Iroquoian language of this people —**On′on·da′gan** ***adj.***

Onondaga Lake ⟦see prec.⟧ salt lake northwest of Syracuse, N.Y.: *c.* 5 sq mi (13 sq km)

on·rush (än′rush′) ***n.*** a headlong dash forward; strong onward rush —**on′rush′ing** ***adj.***

on-screen (än′skrēn′) ***adj., adv.*** **1** in a film, TV show, etc. **2** in a film FRAME (*n.* 13*b*) or on a TV or computer screen Also, esp. for sense 1, **on′screen′**

on·set (än′set′) ***n.*** **1** an attack; assault **2** a beginning; start; appearance [the *onset* of symptoms]

on·shore (än′shôr′) ***adj.*** **1** moving onto or toward the shore [an *onshore* breeze] **2** situated or operating on land [an *onshore* patrol] —***adv.*** toward the shore; landward

on·side (än′sīd′) ***adv.*** *Sports* in the proper position for play; not offside —***adj.*** not offside

☆**onside kick** *Football* a kickoff that is deliberately kicked short in the hope that the kicking team can get possession of the ball

on-site (än′sīt′) ***adj., adv.*** on or at the site of a particular activity or happening [an *on-site* inspection]

on·slaught (än′slôt′) ***n.*** ⟦altered (infl. by SLAUGHTER) < Du *annslag* < *slagen*, to strike: see SLAY⟧ a violent, intense attack

on·stage (än′stāj′) ***adj., adv.*** on a stage, before an audience

on·stream or **on-stream** (än′strēm′) ***adv.*** into operation or production [a new refinery coming *onstream*]

Ont *abbrev.* Ontario

On·tar·i·o (än ter′ē ō) **1** ⟦after Lake *Ontario*⟧ province of SC Canada, between the Great Lakes & Hudson Bay: 350,416 sq mi (907,574 sq km); cap. Toronto: abbrev. *ON* or *Ont* **2** ⟦after the Cdn province⟧ city in S Calif. **3 Lake** ⟦< Fr < Iroquoian, lit., fine lake⟧ smallest & easternmost of the Great Lakes, between N.Y. & Ontario, Canada: 7,540 sq mi (19,529 sq km) —**On·tar′i·an** ***adj., n.***

on·tic (än′tik) ***adj.*** ⟦ONT(O)- + -IC⟧ having the status of real and ultimate existence —**on′ti·cal·ly** ***adv.***

on·to (än′too̅) ***prep.*** **1** to and upon; to a position on ☆**2** [Slang] aware of or familiar with; esp., aware of the real nature or meaning of [they're *onto* our schemes]

on·to- (än′tō, -tə) ⟦< Gr *ōn* (gen. *ontos*), prp. of *einai*, to be < IE base **es-* > IS[1]⟧ *combining form* **1** being, existence [*ontology*] **2** organism [*ontogeny*] Also, before a vowel, **ont-**

on·tog·e·ny (än täj′ə nē) ***n.***, *pl.* **-nies** ⟦prec. + -GENY⟧ the life cycle of a single organism; biological development of the individual: distinguished from PHYLOGENY: also called **on·to·gen·e·sis** (än′tə jen′ə sis) —**on·to·ge·net·ic** (än′tə jə net′ik) ***adj.***, **on′to·gen′ic** (-jen′ik)

ontological argument *Philos.* an a priori argument for the existence of God, asserting that the very conception of a perfect being implies that being's existence outside the human mind

on·tol·o·gy (än täl′ə jē) ***n.*** ⟦ModL *ontologia*: see ONTO- & -LOGY⟧ **1** the branch of metaphysics dealing with the nature of being, reality, or ultimate substance: cf. PHENOMENOLOGY **2** *pl.* **-gies** a particular theory about being or reality —**on·to·log·i·cal** (än′tə läj′i kəl) ***adj.*** —**on′to·log′i·cal·ly** ***adv.*** —**on·tol′o·gist** ***n.***

o·nus (ō′nəs) ***n.*** ⟦L, a load, burden < IE base **enos-* or **onos-* > Sans *ánaḥ*, freight cart⟧ **1** a difficult or unpleasant task, duty, etc.; burden **2** responsibility for a wrong; blame **3** ⟦clip of L *onus probandi*, burden of proving⟧ BURDEN OF PROOF

on·ward (än′wərd) ***adv.*** ⟦ME: see ON & -WARD⟧ toward or at a position or point ahead in space or time; forward: also **on′wards** —***adj.*** moving or directed onward or ahead; advancing [an *onward* trend]

-o·nym (ə nim) ⟦ult. < Gr *onyma* (dial.), *onoma*, NAME⟧ *combining form* name or word [*acronym*]

on·yx (än′iks) ***n.*** ⟦ME *onix* < OFr < L *onyx* < Gr, the NAIL: its color resembles that of the fingernail⟧ **1** a variety of agate with alternate colored layers, used as a semiprecious stone, esp. in making cameos **2** a translucent, finely crystalline calcite, often banded, found in stalagmites: also called **onyx marble**

o·o- (ō′ō, ō′ə) ⟦< Gr *ōion*, EGG[1]⟧ *combining form* egg or ovum [*oogenesis*]

o·o·cyte (ō′ō sīt′, ō′ə-) ***n.*** ⟦prec. + -CYTE⟧ *Embryology* an egg that has not yet undergone maturation

OOD *abbrev.* **1** Officer of the Day **2** Officer of the Deck

oo·dles (o̅o̅d′'lz) ***pl.n.*** ⟦< ?⟧ [Informal] a great amount; very many

o·og·a·mous (ō äg′ə məs) ***adj.*** ⟦OO- + -GAMOUS⟧ characterized by the uniting of a large, nonmotile egg and a small, active sperm for reproduction —**o·og′a·my** (-mē) ***n.***

o·o·gen·e·sis (ō′ō jen′ə sis, ō′ə-) ***n.*** ⟦OO- + -GENESIS⟧ *Biol.* the process by which the ovum is formed in preparation for its development —**o′o·ge·net′ic** (-jə net′ik) ***adj.***

o·o·go·ni·um (-gō′nē əm) ***n.***, *pl.* **-ni·a** (-ə) or **-ni·ums** ⟦ModL < OO- + -GONIUM⟧ **1** the female reproductive organ in certain algae and fungi, consisting of a large cell in which the eggs (*oospheres*) are developed **2** *Embryology* any of the cells from which the oocytes derive

ooh (o̅o̅) ***interj.*** used variously to express surprise, enthusiasm, delight, displeasure, etc. —***vi.*** to utter this exclamation [they *oohed* and aahed over the baby]

o·o·lite (ō′ō līt′, ō′ə-) ***n.*** ⟦Fr *oölithe*: see OO- & -LITE⟧ **1** a tiny, spherical or ellipsoid particle with concentric layers, usually of calcium carbonate, formed in wave-agitated sea waters **2** a rock composed chiefly of oolites Also **o′o·lith** (-lith) —**o′o·lit′ic** (-lit′ik) ***adj.***

o·ol·o·gy (ō äl′ə jē) ***n.*** ⟦OO- + -LOGY⟧ that branch of zoology concerned with the study of eggs, esp. birds' eggs —**o·o·log·i·cal** (ō′ō läj′i kəl, ō′ə-) ***adj.*** —**o·ol′o·gist** ***n.***

oo·long (o̅o̅′lôŋ′) ***n.*** ⟦Chin dial. form of *wulung*, lit., black dragon⟧ a dark tea from China and Taiwan that is partly fermented before being dried

oo·mi·ac or **oo·mi·ak** (o̅o̅′mē ak′) ***n.*** UMIAK

☆**oom·pah** or **oom-pah** (o̅o̅m′pä′) ***n.*** ⟦echoic⟧ the sound of a repeated, rhythmic bass figure played as by a tuba in a polka band, marching band, etc.: also **oom′-pah′-pah′**

☆**oomph** (oomf, o̅o̅mf) ***n.*** ⟦echoic of involuntary expression of approval⟧ **1** [Old Slang] sex appeal **2** [Slang] vigor; energy

o·o·pho·rec·to·my (ō′ō fə rek′tə mē, ō′ə-) ***n.***, *pl.* **-mies** ⟦OOPHOR(O)- + -ECTOMY⟧ the surgical removal of one or both ovaries

o·o·pho·ri·tis (-rīt′is) ***n.*** ⟦ModL: see fol. + -ITIS⟧ inflammation of an ovary or the ovaries

o·o·pho·ro- (ō′ō fə rō′, ō′ə-) ⟦< ModL *oöphoron*, ovary < Gr *ōion*, EGG[1] + *-phoros*, bearing < *pherein*, to BEAR[1]⟧ *combining form* ovary or ovaries [*oophoritis*]: also, before a vowel, **oophor-**

o·o·phyte (ō′ō fīt′, ō′ə-) ***n.*** ⟦OO- + -PHYTE⟧ in plants undergoing alternation of generations, as ferns or mosses, that generation in which the reproductive organs are developed

oops (oops, o̅o̅ps) ***interj.*** used to express sudden or surprised dismay, or, sometimes, implied apology, after one has blundered, tripped, broken something, misspoken, etc.

Oort cloud (ôrt) ⟦after J. *Oort* (1900-92), Du astronomer⟧ a spherical, moving mass of icy cosmic debris thought to exist in the vast region beyond Pluto and to be the source of the long-period comets that orbit the sun

o·o·sperm (ō′ō spurm′, ō′ə-) ***n.*** ⟦OO- + -SPERM⟧ *obs. var. of* ZYGOTE

o·o·sphere (-sfir′) ***n.*** ⟦OO- + -SPHERE⟧ *Bot.* any of the large, spherical, nonmotile, unfertilized eggs that develop in an oogonium

o·o·spore (-spôr′) ***n.*** ⟦OO- + SPORE⟧ *Bot.* a thick-walled, resting spore produced by the fertilization of an oosphere

o·o·the·ca (ō′ō thē′kə, ō′ə-) ***n.***, *pl.* **-cae′** (-sē′) ⟦ModL < OO- + Gr *thēkē*: see THECA⟧ an egg case, as of certain mollusks and insects —**o′o·the′cal** ***adj.***

o·o·tid (ō′ō tid, ō′ə-) ***n.*** ⟦OO- + *-t-* + -ID⟧ a large, haploid cell produced at the second meiotic division, that quickly becomes an egg cell

ooze[1] (o̅o̅z) ***n.*** ⟦ME *wose* < OE *wos*, sap, juice, akin to MLowG *wose*, scum < IE base **wes-*, wet: meaning infl. by OE *wase*, mire: see fol.⟧ **1** an infusion of oak bark, sumac, etc., used in tanning leather **2** ⟦< the v.⟧ *a)* an oozing; gentle flow *b)* something that oozes —***vi.*** **oozed**, **ooz′ing** **1** to flow or leak out slowly, as through very small holes; seep **2** to give forth moisture, as through pores **3** to escape or disappear gradually [hope *oozed* away] —***vt.*** **1** to give forth, or exude (a fluid) **2** to seem to radiate [to *ooze* confidence]

ooze[2] (o̅o̅z) ***n.*** ⟦ME *wose* < OE *wase*, < IE base **weis-*, to flow away > L *virus*⟧ **1** soft mud or slime; esp., the deep layers of sediment at the bottom of a lake, ocean, etc. **2** an area of muddy ground; bog

ooze leather ⟦see OOZE[1] (*n.* 1)⟧ leather of calfskin, sheepskin, or goatskin with a velvety or suede finish on the flesh side

oo·zy[1] (o̅o̅′zē) ***adj.*** **-zi·er**, **-zi·est** ⟦akin to OOZE[1] (*vt.*)⟧ oozing; giving forth moisture —**oo′zi·ly** ***adv.*** —**oo′zi·ness** ***n.***

oo·zy[2] (o̅o̅′zē) ***adj.*** **-zi·er**, **-zi·est** ⟦< OOZE[2]⟧ full of or like ooze; slimy —**oo′zi·ly** ***adv.*** —**oo′zi·ness** ***n.***

op[1] (äp) ***n.*** OP ART

op[2] (äp) ***n.*** [Slang] *short for:* ☆**1** OPERATIVE (*n.* 2) ☆**2** OPPORTUNITY

op[3] *abbrev.* **1** opera **2** operation **3** opposite **4** opus **5** out of print

OP *abbrev.* **1** observation post **2** Order of Preachers (Dominicans) **3** out of print

op- (äp, əp) *prefix* OB-: used before *p* [*oppress*]

o·pac·i·ty (ō pas′ə tē) ***n.*** ⟦Fr *opacité* < L *opacitas* < *opacus*, shady⟧ **1** the state, quality, or degree of being opaque **2** *pl.* **-ties** something opaque, as a spot on the cornea or lens of an eye

o·pah (ō′pə) ***n.*** ⟦WAfr (Ibo) *úbà*⟧ a very large, brightly colored, silvery, marine bony fish (*Lampris guttatus*, order Lampriformes)

o·pal (ō′pəl) ***n.*** ⟦L *opalus* < Gr *opallios* < Sans *úpalaḥ*, (precious) stone⟧ an amorphous, iridescent mineral, $SiO_2 \cdot n\ H_2O$, of various colors, often used as a gem; hydrous silicon oxide

o·pal·es·cent (ō′pə les′ənt) ***adj.*** ⟦prec. + -ESCENT⟧ showing a play of colors like that of the opal; iridescent —**o′pal·esce′** *vi.* **-esced′**, **-esc′ing** —**o′pal·es′cence** *n.* —**o′pal·ine′** (ō′pə lēn′, -līn′, -lin) *adj.*

o·paque (ō pāk′) *adj.* ⟦ME *opake* < L *opacus,* shady⟧ **1** not letting light pass through; not transparent or translucent **2** not reflecting light; not shining or lustrous; dull or dark **3** not allowing electricity, heat, etc. to pass through **4** hard to understand; obscure **5** slow in understanding; obtuse —*n.* **1** anything opaque **2** *Photog.* an opaque liquid used in blocking out parts of a negative —*vt.* **o·paqued′**, **o·paqu′ing 1** to make opaque **2** *Photog.* to apply opaque to (a negative) —**o·paque′ly** *adv.* —**o·paque′ness** *n.*

☆**opaque projector** a projector for throwing images on a screen by reflecting light from opaque objects

☆**op art** (äp) ⟦< OP(TICAL)⟧ a style of abstract painting utilizing geometric patterns or figures to create various optical effects, such as the illusion of movement

op. cit. *abbrev.* ⟦L *opere citato*⟧ in the work cited

ope (ōp) *adj., vt., vi.* **oped**, **op′ing** ⟦ME < *openen*⟧ *old poet. var. of* OPEN

OPEC (ō′pek′) Organization of Petroleum Exporting Countries: an association of major oil-producing nations which seeks to control crude-oil prices by setting production limits for each member nation

☆**Op-Ed** (äp′ed′) *adj.* ⟦*Op(posite) Ed(itorial page)*⟧ [*often* **op-ed**] designating, or appearing on, a page in a newspaper, usually the one opposite the editorial page, that features columns, freelance articles, letters, etc. expressing varied opinions and observations —*n.* an Op-Ed page or an article, column, etc. appearing on an Op-Ed page

o·pen (ō′pən) *adj.* ⟦ME < OE, akin to Ger *offen* < PGmc **upana:* for IE base see UP[1]⟧ **1** *a)* in a state which permits access, entrance, or exit; not closed, covered, clogged, or shut [*open* doors] *b)* closed, but unlocked [the car is *open*] **2** *a)* in a state which permits freedom of view or passage; not enclosed, fenced in, sheltered, screened, etc.; unobstructed; clear [*open* fields] *b)* having few or no trees, houses, etc. [*open* country] **3** unsealed; unwrapped **4** *a)* not covered over; without covering, top, etc. *b)* vulnerable to attack, etc.; unprotected or undefended (see also OPEN CITY) **5** *a)* spread out; unfolded; unclosed; expanded [an *open* umbrella] *b)* describing or of a book, magazine, etc. in which the covers have been spread apart so that the pages can be seen, read, etc. **6** having spaces between; having gaps, holes, interstices, etc. [*open* ranks] **7** free from ice [the lake is *open*] **8** having relatively little snow or frost; mild [an *open* winter] **9** *a)* that may be entered, used, competed in, shared, visited, etc. by all [an *open* meeting] *b)* ready to admit customers, clients, etc. **10** free to be argued or contested; not settled or decided [an *open* question] **11** *a)* free from prejudice or bigotry; not closed to new ideas, etc. [an *open* mind] *b)* liberal; generous **12** ☆*a)* free from legal restrictions [an *open* season on deer] ☆*b)* free from discriminatory restrictions based on race, religion, etc. [*open* housing] ☆*c)* free from effective regulation with respect to drinking, gambling, etc. [the city is wide *open*] *d)* not regulated, organized, or conducted along traditional or conventional lines [*open* marriage, *open* education] **13** characterized by social mobility, political freedom, diversity of opinion, etc. [an *open* society] **14** in force or operation [an *open* account] **15** *a)* not already taken, occupied, or engaged [the job is still *open*] *b)* free to be accepted or rejected *c)* designating or of a date or time when someone, an organization, etc. has no scheduled activity, specif., when a sports team is not scheduled to play a game **16** not closed against access; accessible; available **17** not hidden or secret; generally known; public [an *open* quarrel] **18** frank; candid; direct; honest [an *open* manner] **19** *Math.* of a set of points that is the complement of a closed set of points, as the set of all points outside a circle **20** *Music a)* not stopped by the finger (said of a string) *b)* not closed at the top (said of an organ pipe) *c)* produced by an open string or pipe, or, in wind instruments, brasses, etc., without a slide or key (said of a tone) *d)* not muted **21** *Phonet. a)* articulated with the tongue as low as possible in the mouth; low (said of certain vowels) *b)* articulated with the tongue in the lower of two possible positions [the *open e* and close *e* in Italian] *c)* articulated with the organs of speech not in close contact; fricative (said of certain consonants) *d)* ending in a vowel or diphthong (said of a syllable) **22** *Printing a)* designating or of a style of type the letters of which are cast in outline so that the inside of letters shows white *b)* with wide spacing between words or lines of type; not solid **23** *Sports* designating a stance, as of a golfer or of a batter in baseball, in which the front foot is farther than the rear foot from an imaginary straight line, as one joining tee and green or one joining home plate and second base —*vt.* **1** to make or cause to be open; specif., *a)* to unclose; unfasten [*open* the door] *b)* to remove obstructions from [to *open* a drain] **2** *a)* to make an opening or openings in [to *open* an abscess] *b)* to make or produce (a hole, way, etc.) **3** to make spaces between; spread out; expand [to *open* ranks] **4** *a)* to unclose, unfold, or unroll [to *open* an umbrella] *b)* to spread apart the covers of (a book, magazine, etc.) so that the pages can be seen, read, etc. **5** to make accessible or subject (to an influence or action); expose **6** to make available for use, competition, or participation, without restriction, taxation, fee, etc. **7** to free from prejudice and bigotry; make liberal and generous [to *open* one's mind] **8** to make known, public, etc.; reveal; disclose **9** to begin; enter upon; start; commence [to *open* the bidding, a session, etc.] **10** to cause to start operating, going, etc. [to *open* a new shop] **11** to undo, recall, or set aside (a judgment, settlement, etc.), so as to leave the matter open to further action —*vi.* **1** to become open **2** to spread out; expand; unroll; unfold **3** to become free from prejudice, etc.; become liberal and generous **4** to become revealed, disclosed, etc.; come into view **5** to be or act as an opening; give access: with *to, into, on,* etc. **6** to begin; start **7** to start operating, going, bidding, etc.; specif., in the stock exchange, to show an indicated price level at the beginning of the day [steel *opened* high] **8** to begin a series of performances, games, etc. —*n.* [*usually* **O-**] any of various tournaments, esp. in golf or tennis, open to both professionals and amateurs —*SYN.* FRANK[1] —**open out 1** to make or become extended or larger **2** to develop **3** to disclose to view; reveal —**open to 1** glad or willing to receive, discuss, etc. **2** liable to; subject to **3** available or accessible to or for —**open up 1** to make or become open **2** to spread out; unfold **3** to start; begin **4** [Informal] to begin firing a gun or guns **5** [Informal] to speak freely or with great feeling **6** [Informal] to go or make go faster or as fast as possible —**the open 1** any open, unobstructed space on land or water **2** an unenclosed area; the outdoors **3** public knowledge —**o′pened** *adj.* —**o′pen·ly** *adv.* —**o′pen·ness** *n.*

open admissions the policy or practice of allowing students to enroll in a college or university without regard to their previous academic preparation

open air the outdoors —**o′pen-air′** *adj.*

☆**o·pen-and-shut** (ō′pən ən shut′) *adj.* that can clearly and easily be determined or decided; simple or obvious [an *open-and-shut* case]

open bar a bar as at a banquet, club luncheon, or reception, where guests do not pay for alcoholic drinks

open chain any structural arrangement used in the models and formulas of molecules and consisting of a chain of atoms that does not form a closed geometric figure; specif., a straight or branched chain: see ALIPHATIC, CLOSED CHAIN

open circuit an electrical circuit that does not conduct current because a switch is open, a wire is broken, etc. —**o′pen-cir′cuit** *adj.*

open city a city which is a military objective but is completely demilitarized and left open to enemy occupation in order to gain immunity, under international law, from bombardment and attack

open door 1 unrestricted admission or access **2** equal opportunity for all nations to trade with a given nation, without restrictive terms —**o′pen-door′** *adj.*

o·pen-end (ō′pən end′) *adj.* **1** of or pertaining to an investment company that has no fixed limit to the number of shares issued, so that the shares are issued and redeemed as demand requires **2** allowing the borrowing of additional funds over a period of time on the original security **3** OPEN-ENDED

o·pen-end·ed (-en′did) *adj.* **1** having no set limits as to duration, direction, amount, number, etc.; broad, unlimited, or unrestricted [an *open-ended* discussion] **2** open to change; allowing for modifications as things develop **3** designating or of a question allowing for a freely formulated answer rather than one made by a choice from among predetermined answers —**o′pen-end′ed·ness** *n.*

o·pen·er (ō′pə nər) *n.* **1** a person or thing that opens **2** any of several devices for opening bottles, cans, etc. **3** the first game in a series, the first act in a vaudeville show, etc. ☆**4** [*pl.*] *Poker* cards of sufficient value to allow a player to open the betting —**for openers** [Informal] to begin with

o·pen-eyed (ō′pən īd′) *adj.* **1** having the eyes open or wide open; awake, aware, watchful, amazed, etc. **2** done with the eyes open

o·pen-faced (ō′pən fāst′) *adj.* **1** with the face uncovered **2** having a frank, honest face ☆**3** designating a sandwich without a top slice of bread: also **o′pen-face′**

o·pen·hand·ed (-han′did) *adj.* giving or sharing freely; generous —**o′pen·hand′ed·ly** *adv.* —**o′pen·hand′ed·ness** *n.*

o·pen·heart·ed (-härt′id) *adj.* **1** not reserved; frank; candid **2** kindly; generous —**o′pen·heart′ed·ly** *adv.* —**o′pen·heart′ed·ness** *n.*

o·pen-hearth (ō′pən härth′) *adj.* **1** designating a furnace with a wide, saucer-shaped hearth and a low roof, used in making steel **2** using a furnace of this kind [the *open-hearth* process] **3** of or relating to the use of an open fireplace, esp. for cooking

o·pen-heart surgery (-härt′) surgery involving some type of repair directly to the exposed heart or coronary arteries, etc., during which the blood is diverted, circulated, and oxygenated by mechanical means

open house 1 an informal reception at one's home, with visitors freely coming and going **2** an occasion when a school, institution, etc. is open to visitors for inspection and observation of activities

o·pen·ing (ō′pə niŋ, ōp′niŋ) *n.* ⟦ME *openyng*⟧ **1** a becoming open or causing to be open **2** an open place or part; hole; gap; aperture ☆**3** a clearing in the midst of a wooded area **4** *a)* a beginning; first part; commencement *b)* start of operations; formal beginning *c)* a first performance, as of a play **5** a favorable chance or occasion; opportunity **6** an unfilled position or office for which a person is wanted **7** *Checkers, Chess* the series of moves at the beginning of a game, often a specific, conventional sequence of moves —*adj.* initial or introductory [*opening* remarks]

open letter a letter written as to a specific person, often in attack, criticism, etc., but published in a newspaper or magazine for everyone to read

open market FREE MARKET

o·pen-mind·ed (ō′pən mīn′did) *adj.* having a mind that is open to new ideas; free from prejudice or bias —**o′pen-mind′ed·ly** *adv.* —**o′pen-mind′ed·ness** *n.*

o·pen-mouthed (-mouthd′, -moutht′) *adj.* **1** having the mouth open **2** gaping, as in astonishment **3** clamorous

o·pen-pit mining (ō′pən pit′) a method of mining, usually for metallic ores, in which the waste and ore are completely removed from the sides and bottom of a pit which gradually becomes an enormous canyonlike hole: cf. STRIP MINING

o·pen-pol·li·na·tion (ō′pən päl′ə nā′shən) *n.* the pollination of open flowers by insects, the wind, etc. without human action

☆**open primary** a primary election in which the voter need not declare party affiliation

open punctuation punctuation characterized by the use of relatively few commas or other marks: opposed to CLOSE PUNCTUATION

open sea **1** the expanse of sea away from any coastlines, bays, inlets, etc. **2** HIGH SEAS

open secret something supposed to be secret but known to almost everyone

open ses·a·me (ses′ə mē′) ⟦< "Open sesame!": magic words spoken to open the door of the thieves' den in the story of Ali Baba in *The Arabian Nights*⟧ any unfailing means of gaining admission or achieving some other end

☆**open shop** a factory, business, etc. employing workers without regard to whether or not they are members of a union with which it may have a contract; also, the policy of employing workers in this way

☆**open-source** (-sôrs′) *adj.* designating or of software whose code is made public and which is thus available to any programmer to develop and customize

open stock merchandise, as dishes, available in sets, with individual pieces kept in stock for replacements or additions

o·pen·work (ō′pən wurk′) *n.* ornamental work, as in cloth or metal, with open spaces in the material

op·er·a[1] (äp′ə rə, äp′rə) *n.* ⟦It < L, a work, labor, akin to *opus:* see OPUS⟧ **1** a play having all or most of its text set to music, with arias, recitatives, choruses, duets, trios, etc. sung to orchestral accompaniment, usually characterized by elaborate costuming, scenery, and choreography: see GRAND OPERA, COMIC OPERA **2** the branch of art represented by such plays **3** the score, libretto, or performance of such a play **4** a theater in which operas are given

o·pe·ra[2] (ō′pə rə, äp′ə rə) *n. pl. of* OPUS

op·er·a·ble (äp′ər ə bəl) *adj.* ⟦ML *operabilis:* see OPERATE & -ABLE⟧ **1** practicable or feasible **2** able to function or be operated, as a machine **3** that can be treated by a surgical operation —**op′er·a·bil′i·ty** *n.* —**op′er·a·bly** *adv.*

o·pé·ra bouffe (ô pā rȧ bo͞of′; *E* äp′ə rə bo͞of′) ⟦Fr⟧ comic, esp. farcical, opera

o·pe·ra buf·fa (ô′pe rä bo͞of′fä′) ⟦It⟧ OPÉRA BOUFFE

o·pé·ra co·mique (ô pā rȧ kô mēk′) ⟦Fr, comic opera⟧ French opera with some spoken dialogue: it may or may not be comic

opera glasses small binoculars, often fitted with a handle, for use as at the opera or theater

op·er·a·go·er (äp′ə rə gō′ər, äp′rə-) *n.* a person who attends opera performances, esp. often or regularly

opera hat ⟦so called because worn by a man in formal attire, as for attending the *opera*⟧ a man's tall, collapsible silk hat

opera house a theater chiefly for the performance of operas

op·er·and (äp′ər and′) *n.* ⟦< L *operandum,* neut. ger. of *operari,* to work: see OPERATE⟧ *Math.* that which is operated upon by an operator

op·er·ant (äp′ər ənt) *adj.* ⟦< L *operans,* prp. of *operari:* see OPERATE⟧ **1** operating, or producing an effect or effects **2** *Psychol. a)* designating behavior defined by the resulting stimulus rather than the stimulus which elicits it *b)* designating conditioning in which the desired response, when it occurs, is reinforced by a stimulus —*n.* a person or thing that operates

o·pe·ra se·ri·a (ô′pe rä se′rē ä; *E* äp′ə rə ser′ē ə, -sir′-) ⟦It, serious opera⟧ 18th-cent. opera characterized by the stylized treatment of mythological or classical subjects and the extensive use of arias

op·er·ate (äp′ər āt′) *vi.* **-at′ed, -at′ing** ⟦< L *operatus,* pp. of *operari,* to work < *opus* (gen. *operis*): see OPUS⟧ **1** to be in action so as to produce an effect; act; function; work **2** to bring about a desired or appropriate effect; have a certain influence **3** to carry on strategic military movements **4** to perform a surgical operation —*vt.* **1** [Now Rare] to bring about as an effect **2** *a)* to put or keep in action; work (a machine, etc.) *b)* to conduct or direct the affairs of (a business, etc.); manage

op·er·at·ic (äp′ə rat′ik) *adj.* ⟦< OPERA[1] + *-atic,* as in DRAMATIC⟧ **1** of or like the opera **2** overly dramatic or emotional; histrionic, theatrical, etc. —**op′er·at′i·cal·ly** *adv.*

operating system the software that controls the basic operation of a computer or computer network

op·er·a·tion (äp′ə rā′shən) *n.* ⟦ME *operacion* < OFr < L *operatio*⟧ **1** the act, process, or method of operating **2** the condition of being in action or at work **3** a process or action that is part of a series in some work **4** *a)* any movement or series of movements made in carrying out strategic military plans *b)* [*pl.*] a center where such activities are monitored or supervised, as at an air base *c)* any specific plan, project, venture, etc. (often in nonce compounds) [our neighborhood's *Operation* Cleanup] **5** any surgical procedure performed, usually with the aid of instruments, to remedy a physical ailment or defect **6** *Math.* any process, as addition, division, etc., involving a change or transformation in a quantity —**in operation 1** in the act or process of making, working, etc. **2** having an influence or effect; in force

op·er·a·tion·al (äp′ə rā′shə nəl) *adj.* **1** of, having to do with, or derived from the operation of a device, system, process, etc. **2** *a)* that can be used or operated *b)* in use; operating **3** of or ready for use in a military operation —**op′er·a′tion·al·ly** *adv.*

op·er·a·tion·al·ism (-shə nəl iz′əm) *n. Philos.* the doctrine that no concept or term used in a purportedly factual statement has valid meaning unless it can be defined in terms of repeatable, empirical operations, experimental procedures, etc.: also **op′er·a′tion·ism′** —**op′er·a′tion·al·ist** *n.* —**op′er·a′tion·al·is′tic** *adj.*

op·er·a·tion·al·ize (-shə nəl īz′) *vt.* **-ized′, -iz′ing** to make operational; put into operation —**op′er·a′tion·al·i·za′tion** *n.*

operations research the systematic study of large, complex systems, as in industry, government, or the military, as for the purpose of streamlining operations or in problem solving: also **operations analysis**

op·er·a·tive (äp′ə rə tiv′, -ə rāt′iv) *adj.* ⟦Fr *opératif* < LL(Ec) *operativus*⟧ **1** capable of, characterized by, or in operation **2** *a)* accomplishing what is desired; effective *b)* of primary importance; key; essential [the *operative* word in a sentence] **3** connected with physical work or mechanical action **4** *Surgery* of or resulting from a surgical operation —*n.* **1** a worker, esp. one skilled in industrial work ☆**2** a detective or spy —**op′er·a′tive·ly** *adv.*

op·er·a·tor (äp′ə rāt′ər) *n.* **1** a person who operates; specif., *a)* a person who effects something; agent ☆*b)* a person whose work is operating a machine; specif., a person who operates a telephone switchboard [a telephone *operator*] ☆*c)* a person engaged in financial, commercial, or industrial operations; owner or manager of a mine, railroad, factory, etc. ☆**2** [Slang] a clever, persuasive person who generally manages to achieve his or her ends **3** *Math.* any symbol or term conventionally indicating that a certain process, substitution, etc. is to be carried out

o·per·cu·lar (ō pur′kyo͞o lər, -kyə-) *adj.* of, or having the nature of, an operculum

o·per·cu·late (-lit, -lāt′) *adj.* ⟦L *operculatus*⟧ having an operculum: also **o·per′cu·lat′ed**

o·per·cu·lum (ō pur′kyo͞o ləm, -kyə-) *n., pl.* **-la** (-lə) or **-lums** ⟦ModL < L, lid, dim. < *operire,* to close, shut: for IE bases see OB- & APERTURE⟧ any of various covering flaps or lidlike structures in plants and animals; specif., *a)* the bony covering protecting the gills of fishes *b)* in many gastropods, the horny plate serving to close the shell when the animal is retracted *c)* the lidlike structure of a spore case in mosses *d)* the lidlike structure of a pitcher-shaped leaf

op·er·et·ta (äp′ə ret′ə) *n.* ⟦It, dim. of *opera,* OPERA[1]⟧ a light, comic opera with spoken dialogue

op·er·on (äp′ə rän′) *n.* ⟦< L *operare,* to work (see OPERATE) + -ON⟧ a cluster of genes controlled by a regulatory gene, that functions as a coordinated unit

op·er·ose (äp′ə rōs′) *adj.* ⟦L *operosus* < *opus* (gen. *operis*), work: see OPUS⟧ [Rare] **1** laborious, often, tediously so **2** very busy; industrious

O·phe·lia (ō fēl′yə) *n.* ⟦prob. < Gr *ōphelia,* a help, succor⟧ **1** a feminine name **2** in Shakespeare's *Hamlet,* Polonius's daughter, in love with Hamlet

oph·i·cleide (äf′i klīd′) *n.* ⟦Fr *ophicléide* < Gr *ophis* (see OPHIOLATRY) + *kleis,* a key: for IE base see LOT⟧ an early, brass musical instrument consisting of a long tube doubled back on itself, with keys for fingering

o·phid·i·an (ō fid′ē ən) *n.* ⟦< ModL *Ophidia,* former name of the suborder Serpentes (< Gr *ophis*): see fol. + -AN⟧ a snake or serpent —*adj.* of or like a snake

oph·i·ol·a·try (äf′ē äl′ə trē) *n.* ⟦< Gr *ophis,* a snake (< IE **ogiohi-,* akin to base **eĝhi-,* snake > Arm *iž,* viper) + -LATRY⟧ the worship of serpents

o·phi·o·lite (äf′ē ə līt, ō′fē-) *n.* ⟦< Gr *ophis,* a snake (see prec.) + -LITE⟧ a widespread rock formation containing a mixture of sedimentary, igneous, and metamorphic rocks, thought to be the result of sea-floor rifting or crustal plate collisions

oph·i·ol·o·gy (äf′ē äl′ə jē) *n.* ⟦< Gr *ophis,* a snake (see OPHIOLATRY) + -LOGY⟧ the branch of zoology dealing with snakes —**oph′i·o·log′ic** (-ə läj′ik) *adj.,* **oph′i·o·log′i·cal** —**oph′i·ol′o·gist** *n.*

O·phir (ō′fər) *n.* ⟦Heb *ōphīr*⟧ *Bible* a land rich in gold: 1 Kings 9:28; 10:11; 2 Chron. 8:18

o·phit·ic (ō fit′ik) *adj.* ⟦< L *ophites* < Gr *ophitēs (lithos),* snake (stone) < *ophis,* a snake (see OPHIOLATRY) + -IC⟧ designating a texture of igneous rock, esp. diabase, in which long, flat, narrow crystals of plagioclase feldspar are embedded in augite

Oph·i·u·chus (äf′ē yo͞o′kəs, ō′fē-) *n.* ⟦L, serpent bearer < Gr *ophiouchos,* lit., holding a serpent < *ophis* (see OPHIOLATRY) + base of *echein,* to hold: see SCHEME⟧ a large N and S constellation between Hercules and Scorpius

oph·thal·mi·a (äf thal′mē ə, äp-) *n.* ⟦ME *obtalmia* < LL *ophthalmia* < Gr < *ophthalmos,* the eye: see OPHTHALMO-⟧ a severe inflammation of the eyeball or conjunctiva: also **oph·thal·mi·tis** (äf′thəl mīt′is, äp′-)

oph·thal·mic (äf thal′mik, äp-) *adj.* ⟦LL *ophthalmicus* < Gr *ophthalmikos* < *ophthalmos:* see fol.⟧ of or having to do with the eye

oph·thal·mo- (äf thal′mō, -mə; äp-) ⟦< Gr *ophthalmos,* akin to *ōps,* EYE⟧ *combining form* the eye or eyes [*ophthalmoscope*]: also, before a vowel, **oph·thalm-**

oph·thal·mol·o·gy (äf′thəl mäl′ə jē, -thə-; äp′-) *n.* ⟦prec. + -LOGY⟧ the branch of medicine dealing with the structure, functions, and diseases of the eye —**oph′thal·mo·log′i·cal** (-mə läj′i kəl) *adj.* —**oph′thal·mol′o·gist** *n.*

oph·thal·mo·scope (äf thal′mə skōp′, äp-) *n.* ⟦OPHTHALMO- + -SCOPE⟧ an instrument used to examine the interior of the eye: it consists of a perforated mirror arranged to reflect light from a small bulb into the eye —**oph·thal′mo·scop′ic** (-skäp′ik) *adj.* —**oph·thal·mos·co·py** (äf′thəl mäs′kə pē, äp′-) *n.*

-o·pi·a (ō′pē ə) ⟦Gr *-ōpia* < *ōps,* EYE⟧ *combining form* a (specified) condition or defect of the eye [*hypermetropia*]

o·pi·ate (ō′pē it; *for v.*, -āt′) ***n.*** ⟦ML *opiatum:* see OPIUM⟧ **1** any drug containing opium or any of its derivatives, and acting as a sedative and narcotic **2** anything tending to quiet, soothe, or deaden —***adj.*** **1** containing opium **2** bringing sleep, quiet, or ease; narcotic —***vt.*** **-at′ed, -at′ing 1** [Rare] to treat with an opiate **2** to dull; deaden

o·pine (ō pīn′) ***vt., vi.*** **o·pined′, o·pin′ing** ⟦MFr *opiner* < L *opinari,* to think: see fol.⟧ to express (one's opinion): often used humorously or with mild derision

o·pin·ion (ə pin′yən, ō-) ***n.*** ⟦ME *opinioun* < OFr < L *opinio* < *opinari,* to think, akin to *optare,* to select, desire: see OPTION⟧ **1** a belief not based on absolute certainty or positive knowledge but on what seems true, valid, or probable to one's own mind; judgment **2** an evaluation, impression, or estimation of the quality or worth of a person or thing **3** the formal judgment of an expert on a matter in which advice is sought **4** *Law* the formal statement by a judge, court referee, etc. of the law bearing on a case

SYN.—**opinion** applies to a conclusion or judgment which, while it remains open to dispute, seems true or probable to one's own mind [it's my *opinion* that he'll agree]; **belief** refers to the mental acceptance of an idea or conclusion, often a doctrine or dogma proposed to one for acceptance [religious *beliefs*]; a **view** is an opinion affected by one's personal manner of looking at things [she gave us her *views* on life]; a **conviction** is a strong belief about whose truth one has no doubts [I have a *conviction* of your innocence]; **sentiment** refers to an opinion that is the result of deliberation but is colored with emotion; **persuasion** refers to a strong belief that is unshakable because one wishes to believe in its truth

o·pin·ion·at·ed (-āt′id) ***adj.*** holding unreasonably or obstinately to one's own opinions —**o·pin′ion·at′ed·ly** ***adv.*** —**o·pin′ion·at′ed·ness** ***n.***

o·pin·ion·a·tive (-āt′iv, -ə tiv) ***adj.*** **1** of, or having the nature of, opinion **2** OPINIONATED —**o·pin′ion·a′tive·ly** ***adv.*** —**o·pin′ion·a′tive·ness** ***n.***

o·pi·oid (ō′pē oid′) ***adj.*** designating or of a group of natural or synthetic biochemicals, esp. endorphins, that relieve pain in the same way that opiates do —***n.*** any such biochemical

op·is·thog·na·thous (äp′is thäg′nə thəs) ***adj.*** ⟦< Gr *opisthen,* behind (< IE **opi-*: see OB-) + -GNATHOUS⟧ having receding jaws, as certain insects do

o·pi·um (ō′pē əm) ***n.*** ⟦L < Gr *opion* < *opos,* vegetable juice < IE base **s(w)ekwos-,* plant juice > OProv *sackis*⟧ **1** a yellow to dark brown, addicting, narcotic drug prepared from the juice of the unripe seed capsules of the opium poppy: it contains such alkaloids as morphine, codeine, and papaverine, and is used as an intoxicant and medicinally to relieve pain and produce sleep **2** anything that has a tranquilizing or stupefying effect

o·pi·um·ism (-iz′əm) ***n.*** **1** opium addiction **2** the condition resulting from this

opium poppy an annual poppy (*Papaver somniferum*) with grayish-green leaves and large, white or purple flowers, the source of opium

O·por·to (ō pôr′tō) seaport in N Portugal, on the Douro River: Port. name PÔRTO

☆**o·pos·sum** (ə päs′əm) ***n.,*** *pl.* **-sums** or **-sum** ⟦< AmInd (Algonquian) name, lit., white beast⟧ any of various families (esp. Didelphidae) of marsupials; esp., any of a small, omnivorous, tree-dwelling American species (*Didelphis marsupialis*) with a ratlike, prehensile tail, that is active at night and becomes motionless when endangered

opossum shrimp ⟦by analogy with the pouch of a marsupial⟧ MYSID: the female carries her eggs in a pouch between the legs

opp *abbrev.* **1** opposed **2** opposite **3** opuses

Op·pen·heim·er (äp′ən hī′mər), **J(ulius) Robert** 1904-67; U.S. nuclear physicist

op·po·nen·cy (ə pō′nən sē) ***n.*** opposition; resistance

op·po·nent (ə pō′nənt) ***n.*** ⟦< L *opponens,* prp. of *opponere* < *ob-* (see OB-) + *ponere,* to place: see POSITION⟧ a person who opposes; person against another in a fight, game, debate, argument, etc.; adversary —***adj.*** **1** [Rare] opposite, as in position **2** opposing; adverse; antagonistic **3** *Anat.* bringing parts into opposition: said of a muscle

SYN.—**opponent**, an unemotional word, refers to anyone who is opposed to one, as in a fight, game, debate, etc.; **antagonist** implies more active opposition, especially in a struggle for control or power; **adversary** usually suggests actual hostility in the conflict; **enemy** may imply actual hatred in the opponent and a desire to injure, or it may simply refer to any member of the opposing group, nation, etc., whether or not there is personal animosity or hostility involved; **foe**, now a somewhat literary synonym for **enemy**, connotes more active hostility —***ANT.*** **ally, confederate**

op·por·tune (äp′ər to͞on′, -tyo͞on′) ***adj.*** ⟦ME < MFr < L *opportunus,* lit., at or before the port < *ob-* (see OB-) + *portus,* PORT[1]⟧ **1** right for the purpose; fitting in regard to circumstances: said of time **2** happening or done at the right time; seasonable; well-timed; timely —***SYN.*** TIMELY —**op′por·tune′ly** ***adv.*** —**op′por·tune′ness** ***n.***

op·por·tun·ism (-iz′əm) ***n.*** ⟦Fr *opportunisme*⟧ the practice or policy of adapting one's actions, decisions, etc. to immediate circumstances in order to further one's interests: term often used to suggest unscrupulousness —**op′por·tun′ist** ***n., adj.***

op·por·tun·is·tic (äp′ər to͞o nis′tik, -tyo͞o-) ***adj.*** **1** of or characterized by opportunism ☆**2** designating or of an infection or disease caused by a microorganism (**opportunistic microorganism**) that is normally not virulent but that can cause a serious condition in those with a weakened immune system —**op′por·tun·is′ti·cal·ly** ***adv.***

op·por·tu·ni·ty (äp′ər to͞o′nə tē, -tyo͞o′-) ***n.,*** *pl.* **-ties** ⟦ME *opportunite* < OFr *opportunité* < L *opportunitas* < *opportunus:* see OPPORTUNE⟧ **1** a combination of circumstances favorable for the purpose; fit time **2** a good chance or occasion, as to advance oneself

op·pos·a·ble (ə pō′zə bəl) ***adj.*** **1** that can be opposed, or placed opposite something else **2** *Zool.* *a)* capable of being moved so as to touch the other digits (said of a toe, finger, or, esp., the thumb) *b)* resulting from or characterized by such a digit [an *opposable* grip] —**op·pos′a·bil′i·ty** ***n.***

op·pose (ə pōz′) ***vt.*** **-posed′, -pos′ing** ⟦ME *opposen* < OFr *opposer,* altered (infl. by *poser:* see POSE[1]) < L *opponere:* see OPPONENT⟧ **1** to set against; place opposite, in balance or contrast **2** to contend with in speech or action; resist; withstand —***vi.*** to act in opposition —**op·pos′er** ***n.***

op·po·site (äp′ə zit, -sit) ***adj.*** ⟦OFr < L *oppositus,* pp. of *opponere:* see OPPONENT⟧ **1** set against, facing, or back to back; at the other end or side; in a contrary position or direction: often with *to* **2** characterized by hostility or resistance **3** different in every way; exactly contrary; antithetical **4** being or involving the other of two alternatives [attractive to the *opposite* sex] **5** *Bot.* *a)* growing in pairs, but separated by a stem *b)* having one part on the same radius as another, as a stamen in front of a petal —***n.*** anything opposed or opposite —***adv.*** on opposing sides or in an opposite position —***prep.*** **1** facing; across from **2** *Theater* in a complementary role (of the opposite sex) to [he played *opposite* her] —**op′po·site·ly** ***adv.*** —**op′po·site·ness** ***n.***

SYN.—**opposite** is applied to things that are symmetrically opposed in position, direction, etc. [they sat at *opposite* ends of the table]; **contrary** adds to this connotations of conflict or antagonism [they hold *contrary* views]; **antithetical** implies diametrical opposition so that the contrasted things are as far apart or as different as is possible [our interests are completely *antithetical*]; **reverse** applies to that which moves or faces in the opposite direction [the *reverse* side of a fabric]; **antonymous** is used specifically of words that are so opposed in meaning that each contradicts, reverses, or negates the other [good and bad are *antonymous* terms] —***ANT.*** **same, identical, like**

opposite number a person with reference to another having a comparable position, rank, etc. but in a different place, organization, or situation

op·po·si·tion (äp′ə zish′ən) ***n.*** ⟦ME *opposicioun* < OFr *opposition* < L *oppositio* < *oppositus,* pp. of *opponere:* see OPPONENT⟧ **1** the act of opposing **2** an opposed condition; resistance, contradiction, contrast, hostility, etc. **3** *a)* any person, group, or thing that opposes *b)* [*often* **O-**] a political party opposing, and serving as a check on, the party in power **4** *Astrol., Astron.* the position of two celestial bodies when their celestial longitudes differ by 180°; esp., the position of a superior planet or the full moon when it is in opposition with the sun **5** *Law* the refusal of a creditor to assent to a debtor's release under the bankruptcy law **6** *Logic* the relation of exclusion or inclusion which exists between propositions having the same subject and predicate but differing in quality, quantity, or both —**op′po·si′tion·al** ***adj.*** —**op′po·si′tion·ist** ***n., adj.***

op·press (ə pres′) ***vt.*** ⟦ME *oppressen* < OFr *oppresser* < ML *oppressare* < L *oppressus,* pp. of *opprimere,* to press against < *ob-* (see OB-) + *premere,* PRESS[1]⟧ **1** to weigh heavily on the mind, spirits, or senses of; worry; trouble **2** to keep down by the cruel or unjust use of power or authority; rule harshly; tyrannize over **3** [Obs.] *a)* to crush; trample down *b)* to overpower; subdue —***SYN.*** WRONG —**op·pres′sor** ***n.***

op·pres·sion (ə presh′ən) ***n.*** ⟦OFr < L *oppressio*⟧ **1** an oppressing or being oppressed **2** a thing that oppresses **3** a feeling of being weighed down, as with worries or problems; physical or mental distress

op·pres·sive (ə pres′iv) ***adj.*** ⟦ME *oppressivus* < L *oppressus:* see OPPRESS⟧ **1** hard to put up with; causing great discomfort or fatigue **2** cruelly overbearing; tyrannical **3** weighing heavily on the mind, spirits, or senses; distressing —***SYN.*** ONEROUS —**op·pres′sive·ly** ***adv.*** —**op·pres′sive·ness** ***n.***

op·pro·bri·ous (ə prō′brē əs) ***adj.*** ⟦ME < LL *opprobriosus*⟧ **1** expressing opprobrium; abusive; disrespectful **2** [Now Rare] deserving opprobrium; disgraceful —**op·pro′bri·ous·ly** ***adv.*** —**op·pro′bri·ous·ness** ***n.***

op·pro·bri·um (ə prō′brē əm) ***n.*** ⟦L < *opprobrare,* to reproach < *ob-* (see OB-) + *probrum,* a disgrace < *pro-* (see PRO-[2]) + base of *ferre,* BEAR[1], formed after Gr *propherein,* to bring forward, allege, reproach⟧ **1** the disgrace or infamy attached to conduct viewed as grossly shameful **2** reproachful contempt for something regarded as inferior

op·pugn (ə pyo͞on′) ***vt.*** ⟦ME *oppugnen* < L *oppugnare* < *ob-* (see OB-) + *pugnare* < *pugna,* a fight: see PUGNACIOUS⟧ to oppose with argument; criticize adversely; call in question —**op·pugn′er** ***n.***

op·pug·nant (ə pug′nənt) ***adj.*** ⟦L *oppugnans,* prp.: see prec.⟧ [Rare] hostile; antagonistic —**op·pug′nan·cy** ***n.***

O-prop·o·si·tion (ō′präp′ə zish′ən) ***n.*** *Logic* a particular, negative proposition

Ops (äps) ***n.*** ⟦L, lit., strength, riches: for IE base see OPUS⟧ *Rom. Myth.* the wife of Saturn and goddess of the harvest: identified with the Greek Rhea

op·sin (äp′sin) ***n.*** ⟦prob. back-form. < RHODOPSIN⟧ any of several colorless proteins, found in the rods and cones of the retina, that combine with various forms of retinal to produce light-sensitive pigments such as rhodopsin

-op·sis (äp′sis) ⟦Gr *-opsis* < *opsis,* a sight < *ōps,* EYE⟧ *combining form* sight or view [*stereopsis*]

opsonic index ⟦see OPSONIN⟧ the ratio of the number of bacteria destroyed by phagocytes in an individual's blood serum to the number destroyed in a normal blood serum

op·son·i·fy (äp sän′ə fī′) *vt.* **-fied′**, **-fy′ing** OPSONIZE —**op·son′i·fi·ca′tion** *n.*
op·so·nin (äp′sə nin) *n.* ⟦obs. *opson(ium),* relish (< L < Gr *opsōnion,* food, provisions < *opsōnein,* to buy food < *opson,* meat or any food eaten with bread < *o-,* together with + **psōn,* food, bread, akin to *psōmos,* mouthful) + -IN[1]⟧ a substance in blood serum acting on bacteria and foreign cells to make them more liable to destruction by phagocytes —**op·son′ic** (-sän′ ik) *adj.*
op·so·nize (äp′sə nīz′) *vt.* **-nized′**, **-niz′ing** ⟦see prec.⟧ to make bacteria more liable to destruction by phagocytes —**op′so·ni·za′tion** *n.*
opt[1] (äpt) *vi.* ⟦Fr *opter* < L *optare:* see OPTION⟧ to make a choice: often with *for* —**opt out (of)** to choose not to participate (in)
opt[2] *abbrev.* **1** optical **2** optician **3** optics **4** optional
op·ta·tive (äp′tə tiv) *adj.* ⟦Fr *optatif* < LL *optativus* < pp. of L *optare:* see OPTION⟧ **1** expressing wish or desire **2** designating or of the grammatical mood, as in Greek, which expresses wish or desire —*n.* **1** the optative mood **2** a verb in this mood —**op′ta·tive·ly** *adv.*
op·tic (äp′tik) *adj.* ⟦MFr *optique* < ML *opticus* < Gr *optikos* < *optos,* seen < *ōps,* EYE⟧ of the eye or sense of sight —*n.* **1** an eye: a pretentiously humorous usage, generally in the pl. **2** a lens or an optical instrument
op·ti·cal (äp′ti kəl) *adj.* **1** of or connected with the sense of sight; visual; ocular **2** of the relation between light and vision **3** having to do with optics **4** for aiding vision —**op′ti·cal·ly** *adv.*
optical activity the ability of certain substances to rotate the plane of polarization when transmitting polarized light
optical character reader a device for scanning documents by means of OPTICAL CHARACTER RECOGNITION
optical character recognition electronic identification of alphanumeric characters, esp. those printed on paper, for computer processing or storage
optical disc (*or* disk) any disk on which data, as computer text files, video images, or music, is recorded as microscopic pits to be read by a laser
optical double (star) DOUBLE STAR (sense 2)
optical fiber a wirelike thread of transparent glass or plastic used in fiber optics to carry light signals and images
optical illusion an illusion resulting from any of various visual effects that cause a viewer to misunderstand or misinterpret what he or she actually sees
optical isomerism a type of isomerism in which isomeric compounds differ only in the direction in which they rotate the plane of polarized light
optic axis in anisotropic crystals, a direction along which the velocity of light does not depend on the polarization of the light
optic disk BLIND SPOT (sense 1)
op·ti·cian (äp tish′ən) *n.* ⟦Fr *opticien*⟧ a person who makes or deals in optical instruments, esp. one who prepares and dispenses eyeglasses
optic nerve either of the second pair of cranial nerves, which connect the retina of the eye with the brain
op·tics (äp′tiks) *n.* ⟦< OPTIC⟧ the branch of physics dealing with the nature and properties of light and vision
op·ti·mal (äp′tə məl) *adj.* ⟦OPTIM(UM) + -AL⟧ most favorable or desirable; best; optimum —**op′ti·mal·ly** *adv.*
op·ti·mism (äp′tə miz′əm) *n.* ⟦Fr *optimisme* < L *optimus,* best: see OPTIMUM⟧ **1** *Philos. a)* the doctrine held by Leibniz and others that the existing world is the best possible *b)* the doctrine or belief that good ultimately prevails over evil **2** the tendency to take the most hopeful or cheerful view of matters or to expect the best outcome —**op′ti·mist** (-mist) *n.* —**op′ti·mis′tic** (-mis′tik) *adj.* —**op′ti·mis′ti·cal·ly** *adv.*
op·ti·mize (äp′tə mīz′) *vi.* **-mized′**, **-miz′ing** ⟦< L *optimus,* best (see fol. & -IZE⟧ to be given to optimism —*vt.* to make the most of; develop or realize to the utmost extent; obtain the most efficient or optimum use of —**op′ti·mi·za′tion** (-mə zā′shən, -mī′-) *n.*
op·ti·mum (äp′tə məm) *n., pl.* **-mums** or **-ma** (-mə) ⟦L, neut. of *optimus,* best < *ops,* power, riches: for IE base see OPUS⟧ **1** the best or most favorable degree, condition, amount, etc. **2** *Biol.* the amount of heat, light, moisture, food, etc. most favorable for growth and reproduction —*adj.* most favorable or desirable; best; optimal
op·tion (äp′shən) *n.* ⟦Fr < L *optio* < *optare,* to wish, desire, ult. < IE **op-,* to choose, prefer⟧ **1** the act of choosing; choice **2** the power, right, or liberty of choosing **3** *a)* something that is or can be chosen; choice *b)* an optional item that can be purchased to supplement or enhance another consumer item **4** a contract by which one person, company, etc. gives another, for a consideration, the right to buy, sell, or lease something, sign or renew a contract, etc. at a specified price and within a specified time **5** *Football* an offensive play in which the ball carrier decides whether to hand off, run with, lateral, or pass the football —☆*vt.* **1** *Sports* to transfer (a player) to a minor league with the option of recalling him **2** to grant or acquire by means of an OPTION (*n.* 4); specif., to buy or sell (rights) to (a book, film, etc.) in this way —*SYN.* CHOICE
op·tion·al (äp′shə nəl) *adj.* left to one's option, or choice; not compulsory; elective —**op′tion·al·ly** *adv.*
op·to- (äp′tō, -tə) ⟦< Gr *optos:* see OPTIC⟧ *combining form* pertaining to sight or vision; optical *[optometry, optoelectronics]*
op·to·a·cous·tic (äp′tō ə ko͞os′tik) *adj.* of an effect, technique, etc. in which light, as a laser beam, generates sound waves in a gas or other medium
op·to·e·lec·tron·ics (äp′tō ē′lek trän′iks) *pl.n.* [*with sing. v.*] a branch of electronics involving the use of optical technology —**op′to·e′lec·tron′ic** *adj.*
op·tom·e·ter (äp täm′ət ər) *n.* ⟦OPTO- + -METER⟧ an instrument for determining error in the refractive power of the eye
☆**op·tom·e·trist** (äp täm′ə trist) *n.* a specialist in optometry
op·tom·e·try (äp täm′ə trē) *n.* ⟦OPTO- + -METRY⟧ **1** measurement of the range and power of vision **2** the profession of examining the eyes and measuring errors in refraction and of prescribing glasses to correct these defects —**op·to·met·ric** (äp′tə met′rik) *adj.*, **op′to·met′ri·cal**
op·u·lent (äp′yo͞o lənt, -yə-) *adj.* ⟦L *opulentus* or *opulens* < *ops:* see OPUS⟧ **1** very wealthy or rich **2** characterized by abundance or profusion; luxuriant —*SYN.* RICH —**op′u·lence** *n.*, **op′u·len·cy** —**op′u·lent·ly** *adv.*
o·pun·ti·a (ō pun′shē ə, -shə) *n.* ⟦ModL < L *(herba) Opuntia,* (plant) of Opus, city in LOCRIS⟧ any of a large genus (*Opuntia*) of cactus plants with red, purple, or yellow flowers, pulpy or dry berries, and fleshy, jointed stems, including the prickly pears and chollas
o·pus (ō′pəs) *n., pl.* **o′pus·es** or **o·pe·ra** (ō′pə rə, äp′ə rə) ⟦L, a work < IE **ops* < base **op-,* to work, riches > L *ops,* riches, Sans *ápas-,* work, OE *efnan,* to work, do⟧ **1** a work, esp. a great or pretentious work of art **2** any of the musical works of a composer numbered in order of composition or publication
o·pus·cu·lum (ō pus′kyə lum) *n., pl.* **-la** (-lə) ⟦L, dim. of *opus:* see prec.⟧ [Rare] a minor work, as of literature: also **o·pus′cule′** (-kyo͞ol′)
-o·py (ō′pē) *combining form* -OPIA
or[1] (ôr) *conj.* ⟦ME, in form a contr. of *other, auther,* either, but actually < OE *oththe* (in *āther ... oththe,* either ... or)⟧ a coordinating conjunction introducing an alternative; specif., *a)* introducing the second of two possibilities *[beer or wine] b)* introducing any of the possibilities in a series, but usually used only before the last *[apples or pears or plums; apples, pears, or plums] c)* introducing a synonymous word or phrase *[botany, or the science of plants] d)* introducing the second of two possibilities when the first is introduced by *either* or *whether [either go or stay; decide whether to go or stay] e)* [Old Poet.] substituted for *either* or *whether* as the first correlative *["or in the heart or in the head"]*
or[2] (ôr) *conj., prep.* ⟦ME < OE *ār,* var. of *ær, ere:* see ERE⟧ [Now Chiefly Dial.] before; ere
or[3] (ôr) *n.* ⟦Fr < L *aurum,* gold: for IE base see EAST⟧ *Heraldry* the representation of the metal gold: indicated in engravings by small black dots on a white field
OR *abbrev.* **1** operating room **2** Oregon
-or (ər, ôr) *suffix* **1** ⟦ME *-our* < OFr *-our, -or, -eur* < L *-or, -ator*⟧ a person or thing that (does a specified thing) *[mortgagor, incisor]* **2** ⟦ME *-our* < OFr < L *-or*⟧ quality or condition *[favor, error]*
USAGE—for several words with this suffix, e.g. *ardor, armor, color, endeavor, favor, honor, labor, rumor, savior,* the spelling **-our** is standard usage or a common alternate spelling in most other English-speaking countries (*ardour, armour, colour,* etc.); other words, e.g. *error, liquor, pallor, terror,* are now always spelled with -OR
o·ra (ō′rə, ôr′ə) *n.* ⟦L⟧ *pl. of* OS[3]
or·ach or **or·ache** (ôr′əch, är′-) *n.* ⟦ME *orage* < Anglo-Fr *orache* < OFr *arroche* < VL **atrapica* (for L *atriplex*) < Gr *atraphaxys*⟧ any of a genus (*Atriplex*) of plants of the goosefoot family, widespread in salty or alkaline areas, having usually silvery foliage and small green flowers; esp., **garden orach** (*A. hortensis*), cultivated as a potherb, chiefly in France
or·a·cle (ôr′ə kəl, är′-) *n.* ⟦OFr < L *oraculum,* divine announcement, oracle < *orare,* to speak, pray, beseech < *os* (gen. *oris*), the mouth: see ORAL⟧ **1** among the ancient Greeks and Romans, *a)* the place where, or medium by which, deities were consulted *b)* the revelation or response of a medium or priest **2** *a)* any person or agency believed to be in communication with a deity *b)* any person of great knowledge or wisdom *c)* opinion or statements of any such oracle **3** the holy of holies of the ancient Jewish Temple: 1 Kings 6:16, 19-23
o·rac·u·lar (ô rak′yə lər) *adj.* **1** of, or having the nature of, an oracle **2** like an oracle; wise, prophetic, mysterious, etc. **3** obscure; enigmatic —**o·rac·u·lar·i·ty** (ô rak′yə lar′ə tē) *n.* —**o·rac′u·lar·ly** *adv.*
o·rad (ō′rad′, ôr′ad′) *adv.* ⟦< L *os* (gen. *oris*), the mouth + -AD[2]⟧ toward the mouth or oral region
O·ra·dea (ô räd′yä) city in NW Romania, near the Hungarian border
o·ral (ôr′əl) *adj.* ⟦< L *os* (gen. *oris*), the mouth < IE base **ōus-,* mouth, edge > Sans *ā́-ḥ,* mouth, ON *ōss,* mouth of a stream⟧ **1** uttered by the mouth; spoken **2** of speech; using speech **3** of, involving, or administered through the mouth **4** of or having to do with sexual stimulation of the genitals by a partner's mouth or tongue **5** *Phonet.* having mouth resonance only: distinguished from NASAL **6** *Psychoanalysis a)* designating or of the earliest stage of psychosexual development, in which interest centers around sucking, feeding, and biting *b)* designating or of such traits in the adult as friendliness, generosity, and optimism or aggressiveness and pessimism, regarded as unconscious psychic residues of that stage (cf. ANAL[1], GENITAL) **7** *Zool.* on or of the same side as the mouth —☆*n.* an examination with spoken questions and answers, as at a college: *often used in pl.* —**o′ral·ly** *adv.*

SYN.—**oral** refers to that which is spoken, as distinguished from that which is written or otherwise communicated *[an oral promise, request, etc.]*; **verbal**, though sometimes synonymous with **oral**, in strict discrimination refers to anything using words, either written or oral, to communicate an idea or feeling *[a verbal image, caricature, etc.]*

oral history **1** historical data consisting of personal recollections, usually in the form of a tape-recorded interview **2** the gathering and preservation of such data **3** a historical account based on such data

o·ral·ism (ôr′əl iz′əm) *n.* the theory or practice of teaching deaf people to communicate primarily or exclusively through lip-reading and speaking rather than signing —**o′ral·ist** *adj., n.*

o·ral·i·ty (ô ral′ə tē, ō-) *n.* 1 a reliance on spoken, rather than written, language for communication 2 the fact or quality of being communicated orally

oral surgery a branch of dentistry that uses surgical methods to treat disorders and diseases of the teeth, gums, and jaws —**oral surgeon**

-o·ram·a (ə ram′ə, ə rä′mə) ⟦ult. < Gr *horama*, a view, as in PANORAMA, CYCLORAMA⟧ *combining form* a greater-than-usual number, volume, or variety of a specified thing: used to form commercial names and other words for events and displays [*sportorama*]: also **-o-rama**

O·ran (ō ran′, ō rän′) seaport in N Algeria, on the Mediterranean

o·rang (ō raŋ′) *n. short for* ORANGUTAN

or·ange (ôr′inj, är′-) *n.* ⟦OFr *orenge* < Prov *auranja* (with sp. infl. by L *aurum*, gold, & loss of initial *n* through faulty separation of art. *un*) < Sp *naranja* < Ar *nāranj* < Pers *nārang* < Sans *naranga*, prob. akin to Tamil *naṟu*, fragrant⟧ 1 a reddish-yellow, round, edible citrus fruit, with a sweet, juicy pulp 2 any of various evergreen trees (genus *Citrus*) of the rue family producing this fruit, having white, fragrant blossoms and hard, yellow wood 3 any of several plants or fruits resembling the orange 4 reddish yellow —*adj.* 1 reddish-yellow 2 made with or from an orange or oranges 3 having a flavor like that of oranges

Or·ange[1] (ôr′inj, är′-) *n.* name of the ruling family of the Netherlands: see NASSAU[1] —*adj.* of or having to do with Orangemen

Or·ange[2] (ôr′inj, är′-; *also, for 3 & 4, Fr* ô ränzh′) 1 ⟦prob. named for the *orange* groves there⟧ city in SW Calif.: suburb of Los Angeles 2 river in South Africa, flowing from NE Lesotho west into the Atlantic: *c.* 1,300 mi (2,092 km) 3 former principality of W Europe (12th-17th cent.), now in SE France 4 city in SE France

or·ange·ade (ôr′inj ād′) *n.* ⟦Fr: see ORANGE & -ADE⟧ a drink made of orange juice and water, usually sweetened

Orange Free State province of South Africa, west of Lesotho: formerly a Boer republic (1854-1900) & then a British colony (**Orange River Colony**, 1900-10): 49,992 sq mi (129,480 sq km); cap. Bloemfontein

☆**orange hawkweed** DEVIL'S PAINTBRUSH

Or·ange·man (-mən) *n., pl.* **-men** (-mən) ⟦after the Prince of *Orange*, later WILLIAM III⟧ a member of a secret Protestant society organized in Northern Ireland (1795)

orange pekoe a black tea of Sri Lanka and India: see PEKOE

orange rough·y (ruf′ē) *pl.* **orange rough′y** ⟦*roughy* ? in ref. to the large, *rough*-edged scales on its body⟧ a bright reddish-orange food fish (*Hoplostethus atlanticus*) of an order (Beryciformes, family Trachichthyidae) of deep-sea bony fishes with primitive bony rays

or·ange·ry (ôr′inj rē, är′-) *n., pl.* **-ries** ⟦Fr *orangerie* < *oranger*, orange tree < *orange* (the fruit)⟧ a hothouse or other sheltered place for growing orange trees in cooler climates

☆**orange stick** a small, tapered stick, orig. of orangewood, used in manicuring

or·ange·wood (ôr′inj wood′) *n.* the wood of the orange tree, used as in carving —*adj.* of orangewood

o·rang·u·tan (ə raŋ′ə tan′, -taŋ′) *n.* ⟦Malay *oraṅ utan*, lit., man of the forest < *oraṅ*, man + *utan*, forest, thus, wild man, orig. used of indigenous peoples: first applied to the ape by Europeans⟧ a great ape (*Pongo pygmaeus*) with shaggy, reddish-brown hair, very long arms, small ears, and a hairless face: it is smaller than the gorilla and is found only in the swampy, coastal jungles of Borneo and Sumatra: also **o·rang′ou·tang′** (-taŋ′)

or·ang·y or **or·ang·ey** (ôr′in jē, är′-) *adj.* 1 resembling an orange in taste or smell 2 somewhat orange in color [an *orangy* pink]

o·rate (ō rāt′, ôr′at′) *vi.* **o·rat′ed, o·rat′ing** ⟦back-form. < fol.⟧ to make an oration; speak in a pompous or bombastic manner: a humorously derogatory term

o·ra·tion (ō rā′shən, ô rā′-) *n.* ⟦ME *oracion* < L *oratio* < *orare*, to speak < IE base **ōr-*, to speak, call > Gr *ara*, prayer⟧ a formal public speech, esp. one given at a ceremony —***SYN.*** SPEECH

or·a·tor (ôr′ət ər, är′-) *n.* ⟦ME *oratour* < OFr *orateur* < L *orator*⟧ 1 a person who delivers an oration 2 an eloquent public speaker

Or·a·to·ri·an (ôr′ə tôr′ē ən) *n.* a member of an Oratory

or·a·tor·i·cal (ôr′ə tôr′i kəl, är′-) *adj.* 1 of or characteristic of orators or oratory 2 given to oratory —**or′a·tor′i·cal·ly** *adv.*

or·a·to·ri·o (ôr′ə tôr′ē ō′, är′-) *n., pl.* **-os′** ⟦It, lit., small chapel (< LL(Ec) *oratorium*: see fol.): from the performance of such compositions at the Oratory of Saint Philip Neri in Rome⟧ a long, dramatic musical composition, usually on a religious theme, consisting of arias, recitatives, choruses, etc. sung to orchestral accompaniment but without stage action, scenery, or costumes

or·a·to·ry (ôr′ə tôr′ē, är′-) *n., pl.* **-ries** ⟦ME *oratorie* < L *oratoria*⟧ 1 the art of an orator; skill or eloquence in public speaking 2 ⟦ME *oratorie* < LL(Ec) *oratorium*, place of prayer < L *oratorius*, of an orator (in Eccles. use, of praying) < *orator*⟧ a small chapel, esp. one for private prayer 3 [**O-**] *R.C.Ch.* a religious society of secular priests, esp. that founded by Saint Philip Neri in 1564

orb (ôrb) *n.* ⟦L *orbis*, a circle⟧ 1 a sphere, or globe 2 *a)* any of the celestial bodies, as the sun or moon *b)* [Obs.] the earth *c)* the orbit of a planet 3 [Old Poet.] the eye or eyeball 4 a small globe with a cross on top, as a symbol of royal power 5 [Archaic] *a)* a sphere of activity; province *b)* rank; status 6 [Archaic] a collective body; organized whole 7 [Rare] anything circular in form; circle 8 *Astrol.* the sphere of influence of a planet, star, or house —*vt.* 1 to form into a sphere or circle 2 [Old Poet.] to enclose or encircle —*vi.* 1 [Rare] to move in an orbit 2 [Old Poet.] to take on the shape of an orb —**orbed** *adj.* —**orb′y** *adj.*

or·bic·u·lar (ôr bik′yə lər) *adj.* ⟦ME *orbiculer* < LL *orbicularis* < L *orbiculus*, dim. of *orbis*, a circle⟧ 1 in the form of an orb; spherical or circular 2 *Bot.* round and flat, as some leaves Also **or·bic′u·late** (-lit, -lāt′) or **or·bic′u·lat′ed** (-lāt′id) —**or·bic′u·lar′i·ty** (-lar′ə tē) *n.* —**or·bic′u·lar·ly** *adv.*

or·bit (ôr′bit) *n.* ⟦MFr *orbite* < ML *orbita* < L, path, track < *orbis*, a circle, wheel⟧ 1 the bony cavity containing the eye; eye socket 2 ⟦L *orbita*, path, track⟧ *a)* the actual or imaginary path taken by a celestial body during its periodic revolution around another body *b)* the path taken by an artificial satellite or spacecraft around a celestial body 3 *a)* the range or extent of one's experience or activity *b)* the sphere of influence, as of a nation 4 *Ornithology* the skin around the eye of a bird —*vi.* to move in an orbit or circle —*vt.* 1 to put (a satellite or spacecraft) into an orbit in space 2 to move in an orbit around —**or′bit·al** *adj.*

orbital index the ratio of the greatest height of the orbital cavity to its greatest breadth, times 100

or·bit·er (ôr′bit ər) *n.* 1 one that moves in an orbit ☆2 a spacecraft or artificial satellite designed to orbit a planet or other celestial body

orc (ôrk) *n.* ⟦Fr *orque* < L *orca*, kind of whale, altered (infl. by *orca*, a large tub) < Gr *oruga*, acc. of *oryx*, a large fish⟧ a killer whale or other cetacean identified by early writers as a "sea monster"

ORC *abbrev.* Officers' Reserve Corps

or·ca (ôr′kə) *n.* ⟦L: see ORC⟧ KILLER WHALE

or·ce·in (ôr′sē in) *n.* ⟦ORC(IN) + *-e-* + -IN[1]⟧ a brownish-red, crystalline dye, $C_{28}H_{24}N_2O_7$, the main coloring matter of orchil, obtained from lichens or by treating orcinol with ammonia, and used as a biological stain, reagent, etc.

orch *abbrev.* orchestra

or·chard (ôr′chərd) *n.* ⟦ME < OE *ortgeard* < VL **orto*, for L *hortus*, a garden (see HORTICULTURE) + OE *geard*, YARD[2]⟧ 1 an area of land devoted to the cultivation of fruit trees or nut trees 2 such a stand of trees

or·chard·ist (ôr′chər dist) *n.* a person skilled or engaged in the cultivation of orchards: also **or·chard·man** (ôr′chərd mən), *pl.* **-men** (-mən)

or·ches·tra (ôr′kis trə, ôr′kes′-) *n.* ⟦L < Gr *orchēstra* < *orcheisthai*, to dance < IE base **ergh-*, extension of base **er-*, swift movement, a raising > Sans **ṛghāyati*, (he) rages, Ger *arg*, bad⟧ 1 in ancient Greek theaters, the semicircular space in front of the stage, used by the chorus 2 in modern theaters, the space in front of and lower than the stage, where the musicians sit: in full **orchestra pit** ☆3 *a)* the section of seats on the main floor of a theater, esp. the front section *b)* the main floor of a theater 4 *a)* a usually large group of musicians playing together; often, specif., SYMPHONY ORCHESTRA *b)* the instruments of such a group

or·ches·tral (ôr kes′trəl) *adj.* of, for, by, or like an orchestra —**or·ches′tral·ly** *adv.*

or·ches·trate (ôr′kis trāt′) *vt., vi.* **-trat′ed, -trat′ing** 1 to compose or arrange (music) for an orchestra 2 to furnish (a ballet, etc.) with an orchestral score 3 to coordinate or arrange (something) so as to achieve (a desired result) [to *orchestrate* a compromise] —**or′ches·tra′tion** *n.* —**or′ches·tra′tor** *n.*, **or′ches·trat′er**

or·ches·tri·on (ôr kes′trē ən, -än′) *n.* ⟦ORCHESTR(A) + *-ion*, as in ACCORDION⟧ a mechanical device, somewhat like a barrel organ, that produces music suggestive of that played by of an orchestra or band

or·chi- (ôr′ki) *combining form* ORCHIDO- (sense 1) [*orchiectomy*]

or·chid (ôr′kid) *n.* ⟦< ModL *Orchideae*: so named (1751) by LINNAEUS < **orchid-*, mistaken as stem of L *orchis*: see ORCHIS⟧ 1 a perennial plant of the orchid family, that grows in the ground or as an epiphyte and is characterized by waxy pollen masses, minute seeds, and bilaterally symmetrical flowers with three petals, one of which is lip-shaped with many distinctive forms 2 the flower of such a plant; esp., any of the brightly colored tropical varieties cultivated for wear as a corsage 3 a light bluish-red or pale-purple color —*adj.* 1 of this color 2 designating a worldwide family (Orchidaceae, order Orchidales) of monocotyledonous plants

or·chi·do- (ôr′ki dō, -də) ⟦< **orchidos*, mistaken as gen. of Gr *orchis*, testicle: see ORCHIS⟧ *combining form* 1 testicle [*orchidotomy*] 2 orchid [*orchidology*] Also, before a vowel, **orchid-**

or·chid·ol·o·gy (ôr′ki däl′ə jē) *n.* ⟦prec. + -LOGY⟧ the branch of horticulture dealing with orchids

or·chi·dot·o·my (ôr′ki dät′ə mē) *n., pl.* **-mies** ⟦ORCHIDO- + -TOMY⟧ the surgical incision of a testicle

or·chi·ec·to·my (ôr′kē ek′tə mē) *n., pl.* **-mies** ⟦ORCHI- + -ECTOMY⟧ the surgical removal of one or both testicles; castration

or·chil (ôr′kil, -chil) *n.* 1 any of a number of lichens (genera *Roccella, Dendrographa*, and *Lecanora*) yielding purple dyes 2 any of these, including litmus

or·chis (ôr′kis) *n.* ⟦ModL < L, orchid < Gr, orchid, lit., testicle (< IE base **orĝhi-* > Lith *aržùs*, lustful): from the shape of the roots⟧ an orchid; specif., any of a genus (*Orchis*) with small purplish or white flowers growing in spikes

or·cin·ol (ôr′sə nôl′, -nōl′) *n.* ⟦< It *orcello*, ARCHIL + -IN[1] + -OL[1]⟧ a colorless, crystalline compound, $C_6H_3{\cdot}CH_3(OH)_2$, that becomes red in air, obtained from aloes, lichens, etc. and used as a medicine, in dyes, etc.: also **or′cin** (-sin)

Or·cus (ôr′kəs) ***n.*** *Rom. Myth.* **1** the lower world; Hades **2** Pluto, or Dis

ord *abbrev.* **1** order **2** ordinal **3** ordinance **4** ordinary **5** ordnance

or·dain (ôr dān′) ***vt.*** ⟦ME *ordeinen* < OFr *ordener* < L *ordinare,* to arrange (in LL(Ec), to ordain as a priest) < L *ordo,* ORDER⟧ **1** [Obs.] to put in order; arrange; prepare **2** *a)* to decree; order; establish; enact *b)* to predetermine; predestine **3** to invest with the functions or office of a minister, priest, or rabbi —***vi.*** to command; decree —**or·dain′er** ***n.*** —**or·dain′ment** ***n.***

or·deal (ôr dēl′, ôr′dēl′) ***n.*** ⟦ME *ordal* < OE, akin to Ger *urteil,* judgment < WGmc **uzdailjo-,* what is dealt out < **uzdailjan,* to deal out, allot, adjudge < **uz-,* out + **dailjan* < **dails,* a part, share⟧ **1** an ancient method of trial in which the accused was exposed to physical dangers, from which he or she was supposed to be divinely protected if innocent **2** any difficult, painful, or trying experience; severe trial

architectural orders

or·der (ôr′dər) ***n.*** ⟦OFr *ordre* < L *ordo* (gen. *ordinis*), straight row, regular series, akin to *ordiri,* to lay the warp, hence begin, set in order, prob. < IE base **ar-,* to join, fit > ARM[1], ART[1]⟧ **1** social position; rank in the community **2** a state of peace and serenity; observance of the law; orderly conduct **3** the sequence or arrangement of things or events; series; succession **4** a fixed or definite plan; system; law of arrangement **5** a group or class of persons set off from others by some trait or quality **6** *a)* a group of persons constituting an association formed for some special purpose [the *Order* of Knights Templars] *b)* an association of monks, nuns, etc. following a rule [the Benedictine *order*] **7** *a)* a group of persons distinguished by having received a certain award or citation, as for outstanding service to a state [the *Order* of the Garter] *b)* the insignia of such a group **8** a state or condition in which everything is in its right place and functioning properly; specif., a condition conforming to established rules of orderly procedure, as in a court, legislative body, etc. **9** condition or state in general [not in working *order*] **10** a command, direction, or instruction, usually backed by authority **11** a distinctive group; class; kind; sort [paintings of the highest *order*] **12** an established method or system, as of conduct or action in meetings, worship, court, etc. **13** *a)* a request or commission to make or supply something [an *order* for merchandise or services] *b)* the goods so made or supplied [to deliver a grocery *order*] ☆*c)* a single portion of some food, as served in a restaurant [an *order* of cole slaw] **14** *Archit. a)* any of several classical styles of structure, determined chiefly by the type of column and entablature (see DORIC, IONIC, CORINTHIAN) *b)* a style of building **15** *Biol.* a major category in the classification of animals, plants, etc., ranking above a family and below a class: it can include one family or many similar families: the Latinized order names are capitalized but not italicized (Ex.: Fabales, legumes) **16** *Finance a)* written instructions to pay money or surrender property *b)* a formal demand for payment, as by the endorsement and presentment of a negotiable instrument by its specified payee **17** *Gram.* the arrangement or sequence of elements within a grammatical unit **18** *Law* a direction or command of a court, judge, public body, etc. **19** *Math. a)* a whole number describing the degree or stage of complexity of an algebraic expression *b)* an established sequence of numbers, letters, events, units, etc. *c)* the number of elements in a given group *d)* the number of rows or columns in a determinant or matrix **20** *Theol. a)* any of the nine ranks or grades of angels *b)* any rank or grade in the Christian clergy *c)* [*usually pl.*] the position of ordained minister, priest, etc. *d)* [*usually pl.*] ordination, as of a minister or priest *e)* HOLY ORDERS —***vt.*** **1** to put or keep in order; organize; arrange **2** *a)* to instruct to do something; give an order to; command *b)* to command (someone) to go to or from a specified place [to *order* him out of the house] **3** to request or direct that (something) be supplied, done, carried out, etc. [to *order* merchandise, to *order* a hearing] **4** [Archaic] *Eccles.* to ordain (a priest, etc.) —***vi.*** **1** to give a command **2** to request that something be supplied —***interj.*** used to call for quiet and orderly conduct, as to begin a formal meeting —***SYN.*** COMMAND —**by order of** according to the command of —**call to order** to request to be quiet, as to start (a meeting) —**in order** as a means to; so as to; to: followed by an infinitive [reduce spending *in order* to eliminate debt] —**in (or out of) order** **1** in (or not in) proper sequence or position **2** in (or not in) good or working condition **3** in (or not in) accordance with the rules, as of parliamentary procedure ☆**4** being (or not being) suitable to the occasion —**in order that** so that; to the end that —**in short order** without delay; quickly —**on order** ordered, or requested, but not yet supplied —**on the order of** **1** somewhat resembling; similar to **2** approximately; roughly —**order around** to treat in a domineering manner: also **order about** —☆**tall order** [Informal] a difficult task or requirement —**to order** in accordance with the buyer's specifications —**or′der·er** ***n.***

order arms *Mil.* **1** to bring the rifle to an upright position with its butt on the ground beside the right foot, and remain at attention **2** a command to do this

or·der·ly (ôr′dər lē) ***adj.*** **1** *a)* neat or tidy in arrangement; in good order *b)* arranged in, conforming to, or exhibiting some regular order; systematic **2** well-behaved; law-abiding; peaceful **3** having to do with the recording and transmission of military orders, records, etc. [the *orderly* room] —***adv.*** in regular or proper order; methodically —***n., pl.*** **-lies** **1** *Mil.* an enlisted person assigned to perform personal services for an officer or officers or to carry out a specific task [latrine *orderly*] **2** a male hospital attendant —**or′der·li·ness** ***n.***

order of battle *pl.* **orders of battle** a tabular analysis of the units, commanding officers, weaponry, etc. of a particular army, naval force, etc.; often, specif., such an analysis for a particular battle or campaign

order of magnitude *pl.* **orders of magnitude** **1** *Math.* any of a series of numbers or quantities each of which is the result of adding a unit to its predecessor's exponent while keeping the same base number, as in scientific notation: in base ten, 10 (10^1), 100 (10^2), 1,000 (10^3), etc. represent consecutive orders of magnitude **2** any significant increase or decrease in quantity, value, degree, etc.

Order of the Garter the highest order of British knighthood, instituted *c.* 1344 by Edward III

or·di·nal (ôrd′'n əl) ***adj.*** ⟦ME *ordynal,* conforming to order < LL *ordinalis* < L *ordo,* ORDER⟧ **1** expressing order or succession, specif. of a number in a series: see ORDINAL NUMBER **2** of an order of animals or plants —***n.*** **1** ORDINAL NUMBER **2** [*often* **O-**] *Eccles.* a book of prescribed forms or ceremonies

ordinal number any number used to indicate order (e.g., second, ninth, 25th) in a particular series: distinguished from CARDINAL NUMBER

or·di·nance (ôrd′'n əns) ***n.*** ⟦OFr *ordenance* < *ordener:* see ORDAIN⟧ **1** a direction or command of an authoritative nature **2** that which is held to be a decree of fate or of a deity **3** an established or prescribed practice or usage, esp. a religious rite ☆**4** a governmental, now esp. municipal, statute or regulation —***SYN.*** LAW

or·di·nand (ôrd′'n and′) ***n.*** ⟦LL(Ec) *ordinandus,* ger. of *ordinare,* ORDAIN⟧ a candidate for ordination

or·di·nar·i·ly (ôrd′'n er′ə lē) ***adv.*** **1** usually; as a rule **2** in an ordinary manner or to an ordinary degree

or·di·nar·y (ôrd′'n er′ē) ***n., pl.*** **-nar′ies** ⟦OFr & ML: OFr *ordinarie* < ML(Ec) *ordinarius* < L, an overseer, orig., orderly, regular < *ordo,* ORDER⟧ **1** *a)* an official having jurisdiction within a specified area by right of the office he or she holds; esp., a bishop having such jurisdiction within his or her own diocese ☆*b)* in some states, a judge of probate **2** [Brit.] *a)* a set meal served regularly at the same price *b)* an inn, tavern, etc. where such meals are served **3** an early type of bicycle with one large wheel, and a smaller one behind **4** [*often* **O-**] *Eccles. a)* the form to be followed in a service *b)* the parts of the Mass that are fixed or relatively unvarying; common **5** *Heraldry* any one of the basic heraldic devices; bend, fess, etc. —***adj.*** ⟦ME *ordinarie* < L *ordinarius*⟧ **1** customary; usual; regular; normal **2** *a)* familiar; unexceptional; common; average *b)* relatively poor or inferior; below average **3** *Law* of or having immediate jurisdiction —***SYN.*** COMMON —**out of the ordinary** unusual; extraordinary —**or′di·nar′i·ness** ***n.***

ordinary seaman a merchant seaman of less experience than, and ranking below, an able-bodied seaman

or·di·nate (ôrd′'n it, -āt′) ***n.*** ⟦< ModL *(linea) ordinate (applicata),* (line applied) in (an) ordered manner < L *ordinare,* to arrange: see ORDAIN⟧ *Math.* the vertical Cartesian coordinate on a plane, measured from the x-axis along a line parallel with the y-axis to point P

or·di·na·tion (ôrd′'n ā′shən) ***n.*** ⟦ME *ordinacioun* < L *ordinatio* < *ordinare:* see ORDAIN⟧ **1** the act of ordaining **2** a being ordained, as to the religious ministry

ord·nance (ôrd′nəns) ***n.*** ⟦contr. < ORDINANCE, in restricted meaning⟧ **1** cannons or artillery **2** all military weapons together with ammunition, combat vehicles, etc. and the equipment and supplies used in servicing these **3** a military branch or unit that orders, stores, and supplies ordnance

or·do (ôr′dō) ***n., pl.*** **-dos** or **-di·nes′** (-də nēz′) ⟦L, lit., ORDER⟧ *Eccles.* an annual calendar that gives directions for each day's Mass and Office

or·don·nance (ôrd′'n əns; *Fr* ôr dô näns′) ***n.*** ⟦Fr < OFr *ordenance:* see ORDINANCE⟧ **1** the proper or orderly arrangement of parts, as in a painting or literary work **2** in France, an ordinance, law, or decree

Or·do·vi·cian (ôr′də vish′ən) ***adj.*** ⟦< L *Ordovices,* ancient Celtic tribe in Wales⟧ [*sometimes* **o-**] designating or of the second geologic period of the Paleozoic Era, characterized by the development of abundant marine invertebrates and the first vertebrates —**the Ordovician** the Ordovician Period or its rocks: see the geologic time chart in the Reference Supplement

or·dure (ôr′jər, -dyoor) ***n.*** ⟦OFr < *ord,* filthy < L *horridus,* HORRID⟧ dung; excrement

Or·dzho·ni·kid·ze (ôr′jô ni kēd′ze) *name* (1931-44; 1954-90) *for* VLADIKAVKAZ

ore (ôr) ***n.*** ⟦ME *or* < OE *ar,* brass, copper (< IE base *ayos, metal, copper, bronze, iron > Sans *áyas,* metal, L *aes,* copper) identified with *ora,* unworked metal (akin to ON *aurr,* ferrous sand, gravel)⟧ **1** any natural combination of minerals, esp. one from which a metal or metals can be profitably extracted **2** a natural substance from which a nonmetallic material, such as sulfur, can be extracted

Ore or **Oreg** *abbrev.* Oregon

ö·re (ö′rə) ***n., pl.* ö′re** ⟦Swed < ON *aurar,* a unit of weight, coin < L *aureus,* a gold coin, orig. adj., golden < *aurum,* gold: see EAST⟧ a monetary unit of Sweden, equal to 1/100 of a krona

ø·re (ö′rə) ***n., pl.* ø′re** ⟦Dan & Norw < ON *aurar:* see prec.⟧ a monetary unit equal to 1/100 of a Danish krone or Norwegian krone

o·re·ad (ō′rē ad′) ***n.*** ⟦< L *oreas* (gen. *oreadis*) < Gr *oreias* (gen. *oreiados*) < *oros,* mountain: see ORIENT⟧ *Class. Myth.* a mountain nymph

Ö·re·bro (ö′rə brōō′) city in SC Sweden

o·reg·a·no (ə reg′ə nō; *chiefly Brit* ä′ri gä′nō) ***n.*** ⟦Sp *orégano* < L *origanum* < Gr *origanon*⟧ any of a number of plants (esp. *Origanum vulgare*) of the mint family, the fragrant leaves of which are used for seasoning

Or·e·gon (ôr′i gən, är′-; *also, but not locally,* -gän′) ⟦prob. < AmInd *ouragan* (lit., birch-bark dish), native name of the COLUMBIA[2] (River)⟧ NW coastal state of the U.S.: admitted 1859; 95,997 sq mi (248,631 sq km); cap. Salem: abbrev. *OR, Ore,* or *Oreg*

☆**Oregon fir** DOUGLAS FIR: also **Oregon pine**

☆**Oregon grape** MAHONIA

Or·e·go·ni·an (-gō′nē ən) ***adj.*** of Oregon: usually used in the predicate —***n.*** a person born or living in Oregon

☆**Oregon myrtle** CALIFORNIA LAUREL

Oregon Trail former route extending from the Missouri River in Mo., northwest to the Columbia River in Oreg., much used by westward migrants (*c.* 1840-60): *c.* 2,000 mi (3,219 km)

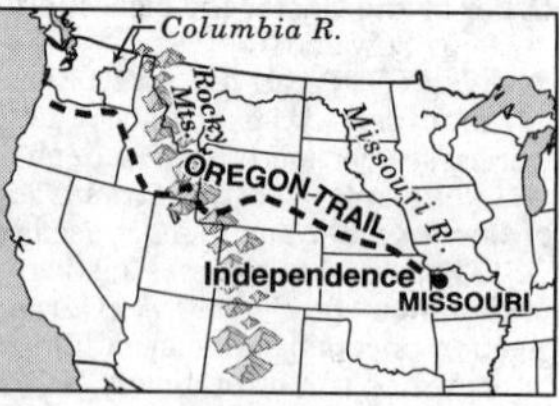

Oregon Trail

O·rel (ô rel′, ôr yôl′) city in W European Russia, on the Oka

O·ren·burg (ôr′ən burg′) city in SE European Russia

☆**Or·e·o** (ôr′ē ō′) ***n., pl.* -os′** ⟦< *Oreo,* trademark for a cookie consisting of a layer of white filling between two chocolate wafers⟧ [*sometimes* **o-**] [Slang] a black person regarded as having adopted the attitudes and behavior of middle-class whites: a term of contempt, esp. as used by other blacks

O·res·tes (ō res′tēz′) ***n.*** ⟦L < Gr *Orestēs* < *oros,* mountain: see ORIENT⟧ *Gr. Myth.* son of Agamemnon and Clytemnestra, who, with the aid of his sister Electra, avenges the murder of his father by killing his mother and her lover Aegisthus

Ö·re·sund (*Swed* ö′rə sund′) strait between Sweden and the Danish island of Zealand: *c.* 80 mi (129 km) long: Dan. name **Ø·re·sund** (*Dan* ö′rə soon′)

Orff (ôrf), **Carl** 1895-1982; Ger. composer

org *abbrev.* **1** organic **2** organization **3** organized

.org (*often* dät′ôrg′) *abbrev. Comput.* organization: a widely used domain name

or·gan (ôr′gən) ***n.*** ⟦ME *organe* < OE *organa* & OFr *organe,* both < L *organum,* tool, implement (in LL(Ec), a church organ) < Gr *organon,* an implement, engine < *ergon,* WORK⟧ **1** *a)* a large wind instrument consisting of various sets of pipes which, as they are opened by corresponding keys on one or more keyboards, allow passage to a column of compressed air that causes sound by vibration *b)* any of several musical instruments producing similar or somewhat similar sounds (cf. ELECTRONIC ORGAN, REED ORGAN, BARREL ORGAN) *c)* [Archaic] any musical instrument; esp., a wind instrument **2** in animals and plants, a part composed of specialized tissues and adapted to the performance of a specific function or functions **3** the penis: a nontechnical use **4** a means or instrument for the performance of some action [an *organ* of local government] **5** a means of communicating ideas or opinions, as a periodical

or·gan·dy or **or·gan·die** (ôr′gən dē) ***n., pl.* -dies** ⟦Fr *organdi* < ?⟧ a very sheer, crisp cotton fabric used for dresses, curtains, etc.

or·gan·elle (ôr′gə nel′) ***n.*** ⟦Ger < ModL *organella* < L *organum* (< Gr *organon:* see ORGAN) + *-ella,* fem. of *-ellus,* dim. suffix⟧ a discrete structure within a cell, as a chloroplast or centriole, characterized by having specialized functions, a usually distinctive chemical composition, and an identifying molecular structure: often found in large numbers in a particular cell

organ grinder a person who plays a barrel organ in the streets

or·gan·ic (ôr gan′ik) ***adj.*** ⟦L *organicus* < Gr *organikos*⟧ **1** of, having the characteristics of, or derived from living organisms **2** of or involving the basic makeup of a thing; inherent; inborn; constitutional **3** made up of systematically interrelated parts; organized ☆**4** *Agric. a)* grown with fertilizers of plant or animal origin, as manure, bone meal, or compost, and without chemical fertilizers or pesticides *b)* characterized by this method [*organic* farming] **5** *Chem. a)* designating or of any chemical compound containing carbon: some of the simple compounds of carbon, as carbon dioxide, are frequently classified as inorganic compounds *b)* designating or of the branch of chemistry dealing with carbon compounds ☆**6** *Law* designating or of the fundamental, or constitutional, law of a state **7** *Med. a)* of or having to do with a bodily organ *b)* producing or involving alteration in the structure of an organ [an *organic* disorder]: cf. FUNCTIONAL (sense 3) —**or·gan′i·cal·ly** ***adv.***

or·gan·i·cism (-ə siz′əm) ***n.*** **1** HOLISM **2** the theory that living processes are a function of the entire, coordinated, autonomous system of an organism, rather than of any of its parts —**or·gan′i·cist** ***n., adj.***

or·gan·ism (ôr′gə niz′əm) ***n.*** **1** any individual animal, plant, bacterium, etc. having various parts or systems that function together as a whole to maintain life and its activities **2** anything resembling a living thing in its complexity of structure or functions —**or′gan·is′mic** ***adj.*, or′gan·is′mal** —**or′gan·is′mi·cal·ly** ***adv.***

or·gan·ist (ôr′gən ist) ***n.*** ⟦< MFr *organiste* or ML *organista*⟧ an organ player

or·gan·i·za·tion (ôr′gə ni zā′shən, -nī-) ***n.*** ⟦ME *organizacion* < ML *organizatio*⟧ **1** an organizing or being organized **2** the manner of being organized; organic structure **3** [Rare] ORGANISM **4** any unified, consolidated group of elements; systematized whole; esp., *a)* a body of persons organized for some specific purpose, as a club, union, or society *b)* the administrative personnel or executive structure of a business *c)* all the functionaries, committees, etc. of a political party —**or′gan·i·za′tion·al** ***adj.*** —**or′gan·i·za′tion·al·ly** ***adv.***

☆**organization man** an employee, esp. an executive, of a large corporation who conforms completely to corporate attitudes and expectations

or·gan·ize (ôr′gə nīz′) ***vt.* -ized′, -iz′ing** ⟦ME *organyzen* < ML *organizare* < L *organum:* see ORGAN⟧ **1** to provide with an organic structure; esp., *a)* to arrange in an orderly way [to *organize* files] *b)* to make into a whole with unified and coherent relationships [to *organize* an essay] *c)* to make plans or arrange for [to *organize* a campaign] **2** to bring into being; establish [to *organize* a corporation] **3** *a)* to enlist in, or cause to form, a labor union ☆*b)* to enlist the employees of (an industry, business, etc.) in a labor union **4** [Informal] to set (oneself) into an orderly state of mind —***vi.*** **1** to become organized ☆**2** to join in some common cause or form some organization, esp. a labor union —**or′gan·iz′a·ble** ***adj.***

organized crime a system or organization of people and groups engaged in criminal activities

or·gan·iz·er (ôr′gə nī′zər) ***n.*** **1** *a)* a person who organizes ☆*b)* a labor-union official whose work is enlisting new members **2** *a)* a device, usually with many compartments, for use in arranging items on a desktop, the contents of a closet, etc. more efficiently *b)* PLANNER (sense 2) **3** *Embryology* any portion of a developing embryo, or any substance produced by it, capable of inducing differentiation in other portions

or·ga·no- (ôr′gə nō, -nə; ôr gan′ō, -ə) ⟦< Gr *organon,* ORGAN⟧ *combining form* **1** organ [*organography*] **2** organic [*organophosphate*]

or·ga·no·chlo·rine (ôr′gə nō klôr′ēn′, ôr gan′ō-) ***n.*** any of a class of organic chemical compounds containing chlorinated hydrocarbons, including dioxins, PCBs, CFCs, and DDT

organ of Cor·ti (kôrt′ē) ⟦after A. *Corti* (1822-76), It anatomist⟧ the spiral structure inside the cochlea of the inner ear, containing the hair cells that are sensitive to sound waves

or·ga·no·gen·e·sis (ôr′gə nō jen′ə sis; ôr gan′ō-) ***n.*** ⟦ModL: see ORGANO- & -GENESIS⟧ *Biol.* the origin and development of organs —**or′ga·no·ge·net′ic** (-jə net′ik) ***adj.***

or·ga·nog·ra·phy (ôr′gə näg′rə fē) ***n.*** ⟦ORGANO- + -GRAPHY⟧ *Biol.* the descriptive study of the organs of animals and plants, esp. the outer parts of plants —**or′ga·no·graph′ic** (-nə graf′ik) ***adj.***

or·ga·no·lep·tic (ôr′gə nō lep′tik; ôr gan′ō-) ***adj.*** ⟦Fr *organoleptique* < Gr *organon,* ORGAN + *lēptikos,* disposed to accept < *lēptos,* verbal of *lambainein,* to seize: see LEMMA[1]⟧ **1** affecting or involving an organ, esp. a sense organ **2** responsive to sensory stimuli

or·ga·no·me·tal·lic (ôr′gə nō mə tal′ik; ôr gan′ō-) ***adj.*** ⟦ORGANO- + METALLIC⟧ *Chem.* designating or of a compound containing carbon and a metal or nonmetal, specif. one in which the metal or nonmetal atom is firmly attached to one or more carbon atoms

or·ga·non (ôr′gə nän′) ***n., pl.* -na** (-nə) or **-nons′** ⟦Gr: see ORGAN⟧ a means of acquiring knowledge; specif., a system of principles for use in philosophical or scientific inquiry

or·ga·no·phos·phate (ôr′gə nō fäs′fāt′, ôr gan′ō-) ***n.*** ⟦ORGANO- + PHOSPHATE⟧ any organic compound containing phosphorus, specif. one used as an insecticide, as malathion

or·ga·no·phos·pho·rus (ôr′gə nō fäs′fə rəs, ôr gan′ō-) ***adj.*** of an organic compound containing phosphorus

or·ga·no·ther·a·py (ôr′gə nō ther′ə pē, ôr gan′ō-) ***n.*** ⟦ORGANO- + THERAPY⟧ the treatment of disease with extracts of animal organs, as of the glands of internal secretion

or·ga·no·trop·ic (ôr′gə nō träp′ik, ôr gan′ə-) ***adj.*** ⟦ORGANO- + -TROPIC⟧ **1** designating or of a substance or virus that travels predominantly to a specific organ **2** having an affinity for a particular bodily organ, organ system, etc.

or·ga·not·ro·pism (ôr′gə nät′rə piz′əm) ***n.*** the affinity for particular organs, organ systems, or somatic tissues exhibited by certain drugs, pathogens, metastatic tumors, etc.

or·ga·num (ôr′gə nəm) ***n., pl.* -nums** or **-na** (-nə) ⟦L: see ORGAN⟧ **1** ORGANON **2** *Music a)* an early type of polyphony based on plainsong, in which the voices are separated by an interval of a fourth, fifth, or octave *b)* a composition in this style

☆**or·gan·za** (ôr gan′zə) ***n.*** ⟦< ? fol.⟧ a thin, stiff fabric of rayon, silk, etc., used for bridal gowns, as underlining for sheer fabrics, etc.

or·gan·zine (ôr′gən zēn′) ***n.*** ⟦Fr *organsin* < It *organzino,* prob. after *Urganğ,* name of a town in Russian TURKESTAN, famous as a silk market in medieval times⟧ **1** a strong raw-silk thread made of twisted strands **2** a fabric made of such threads

or·gasm (ôr′gaz′əm) ***n.*** ⟦Fr *orgasme* < Gr *orgasmos* < *organ,* to swell with moisture, lust < IE base **werg-,* to swell with sap or anger > Sans *ūrjā,* violence, vigor, sap⟧ a frenzy; great excitement; esp., the climax of sexual excitement, as in intercourse, normally accompanied in the male by ejaculation —***vi.*** to have an orgasm —**or·gas′mic** (-gaz′mik) ***adj.,*** **or·gas′tic** (-gas′tik)

or·geat (ôr′zhat′, -jat′) ***n.*** ⟦Fr < Prov *orjat* < *orge,* barley < L *hordeum* < IE base **ĝhrzd,* barley > Ger *gerste*⟧ a syrup or beverage, originally made from barley, flavored with almonds and orange flowers

or·gi·ast (ôr jē ast′) ***n.*** ⟦< Gr *orgiastēs:* see fol.⟧ a person who participates in an orgy

or·gi·as·tic (ôr′jē as′tik) ***adj.*** ⟦Gr *orgiastikos* < *orgiastēs,* one who celebrates orgies < *orgiazein,* to celebrate orgies: see ORGY⟧ having to do with or resembling an orgy

☆**or·gone** (ôr′gōn′) ***n.*** ⟦coined by W. Reich (1897-1957), Austrian psychiatrist in the U.S., prob. < ORG(ASM) + *-one,* as in OZONE⟧ a postulated vital energy permeating the universe: a patient suffering from any of various ills is seated in a special cabinet (**orgone box**) in which this energy is supposed to accumulate

or·gu·lous (ôr′gyə ləs) ***adj.*** ⟦ME < OFr *orguillus* < *orguill,* pride (= Fr *orgueil*) < Frankish⟧ excessively proud; haughty; arrogant

or·gy (ôr′jē) ***n., pl.*** **-gies** ⟦earlier chiefly in pl. < Fr *orgies* < L *orgia,* pl. < Gr, pl., secret rites, akin to *ergon,* WORK⟧ **1** [*usually pl.*] in ancient Greece and Rome, feasting and wild celebration in worship of certain gods, esp. Dionysus **2** any wild merrymaking in a group, esp. with sexual activity **3** unrestrained indulgence in any activity

or·i·bi (ôr′ə bē) ***n.*** ⟦Afrik < Nama *arab*⟧ an African pygmy antelope (*Ourebia ourebia*), having a long tuft of hair growing from each knee and slender, straight horns

o·ri·el (ôr′ē əl) ***n.*** ⟦OFr *oriol* < ML *oriolum,* porch, gallery⟧ a large window built out from a wall and resting on a bracket or a corbel; bay window

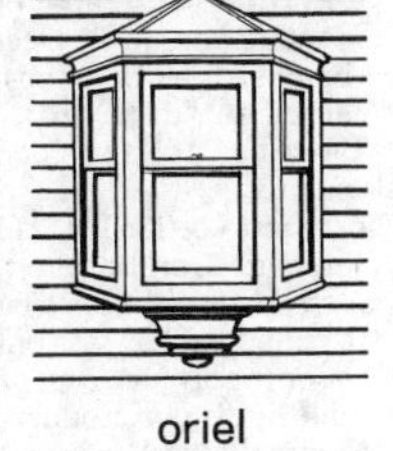
oriel

o·ri·ent (ôr′ē ənt; *also, and for v. usually,* -ent′) ***n.*** ⟦OFr < L *oriens:* see the adj.⟧ **1** [Old Poet.] the east **2** *a)* the quality that determines a pearl's value; luster *b)* a pearl of high quality —***adj.*** ⟦L *oriens,* direction of the rising sun, prp. of *oriri,* to arise < IE base **er-,* to set in motion, elevate > RISE, RUN, Gr *oros,* mountain⟧ **1** brilliant; shining; precious: said originally of pearls, now used more generally **2** [Old Poet.] *a)* eastern; oriental *b)* rising, as the sun —***vt.*** ⟦Fr *orienter* < the adj.⟧ **1** to arrange with reference to the east; esp., to build (a church) with the chief altar at the eastern end **2** to set (a map or chart) in agreement with the points of the compass **3** to adjust with relation to facts or principles; correct **4** *a)* to ascertain for (someone), or make (someone) aware of, his or her location or situation (usually used reflexively) [the lost hikers attempted to *orient* themselves] *b)* to adjust or adapt to a particular situation, market, etc. (often in the pp. and often in comb.) [a youth-*oriented* magazine] —**the Orient 1** [Old-fashioned] the East, including the Near East and the Far East **2** the Far East

o·ri·en·tal (ôr′ē ent′'l) ***adj.*** ⟦ME *orientale* < OFr *oriental* < L *orientalis*⟧ **1** [Old Poet.] eastern **2** being corundum of gemstone quality, but resembling another gem [*oriental* topaz] **3** [*usually* **O-**] *a)* esp. formerly, of the East, including the Near East and the Far East, or its peoples or cultures *b)* of the Far East or its peoples or cultures **4** [**O-**] designating or of the biogeographic realm that includes Southeast Asia, the Philippines, Sumatra, Java, Borneo, and other associated islands —***n.*** [**O-**] **1** [Old-fashioned] a person born in the East, including the Near East and the Far East, or a member of a people of those regions **2** a person born in the Far East or a member of a people of those regions

USAGE—as applied to persons (***adj.*** 3 and the ***n.***), now often regarded as a term of disparagement: cf. ASIAN

O·ri·en·ta·li·a (ôr′ē ən tā′lē ə, -tāl′yə) ***pl.n.*** ⟦ModL < neut. pl. of L *orientalis:* see prec.⟧ art objects, artifacts, documents, books, etc. having their origin in, or written about, the nations and cultures of Asia, specif. the Far East

O·ri·en·tal·ism (ôr′ē ent′'l iz′əm) ***n.*** ⟦ORIENTAL + -ISM⟧ [*also* **o-**] **1** any trait, quality, mannerism, etc. usually associated with people of the East **2** the study of Eastern culture ☆**3** ⟦title of a book (1978) on this subject by E. Said (1935-2003), U.S. academic⟧ a viewpoint, as ascribed to some in the West, in which Asia or specif. the Arabic Middle East is seen variously as exotic, mysterious, irrational, etc.: term used to impute a patronizing attitude —**O′ri·en′tal·ist** ***adj., n.***

O·ri·en·tal·ize (ôr′ē ent′'l īz′) ***vt., vi.*** **-ized′, -iz′ing** to make or become Oriental in character, culture, customs, etc.

Oriental poppy a perennial poppy (*Papaver orientale*), cultivated for its large red, pink, or white flowers

Oriental rug any of various kinds of carpets made in Asia or the Near East, hand-woven in one piece, usually with intricate, colorful designs: also **Oriental carpet**

Oriental shorthair any of a breed of domestic cat, similar to the Siamese but with greenish eyes and often a coat of a solid color

o·ri·en·tate (ôr′ē en tāt′) ***vt.*** **-tat′ed, -tat′ing** ⟦prob. back-form. < fol.⟧ ORIENT —***vi.*** **1** to face east, or in any specified direction **2** to adjust to a situation

o·ri·en·ta·tion (ôr′ē en tā′shən) ***n.*** **1** an orienting or being oriented **2** *a)* position with relation to the points of the compass *b)* the planning of church architecture so that the altar is in the east end **3** familiarization with and adaptation to a situation or environment; specif., *a) Psychol.* awareness of one's environment as to time, space, objects, and persons *b)* a period or process of introduction and adjustment **4** a person's fundamental feelings about or responses to something; specif., a person's sexual identity **5** *Biol.* the position or change of position of an organism or part under a stimulus such as gravity or light **6** *Chem. a)* the position and arrangement of atoms or radicals in a molecule *b)* the ordering of molecules, crystals, etc. so that the axes point in a particular direction

o·ri·en·teer·ing (ôr′ē en tir′iŋ) ***n.*** ⟦< Swed *orientering,* lit., orientation⟧ a timed cross-country competition in which runners follow a course, using compass and map

Orient Express a renowned express passenger train running between Paris &, variously, Vienna, Istanbul (Constantinople), Bucharest, etc.

or·i·fice (ôr′ə fis, är′-) ***n.*** ⟦Fr < LL *orificium* < L *os* (gen. *oris*), a mouth (see ORAL) + *-ficere* < *facere,* to make, DO[1]⟧ a mouth or aperture of a tube, cavity, etc.; opening —**or′i·fi′cial** (-fish′əl) ***adj.***

or·i·flamme (ôr′i flam′) ***n.*** ⟦Fr < OFr *orieflambe* < L *aurea flamma* < *aurum,* gold (see EAST) + *flamma,* FLAME⟧ **1** the ancient royal standard of France, a red silk banner with flame-shaped streamers **2** any battle standard **3** any symbol of courage or devotion

orig *abbrev.* **1** origin **2** original **3** originally

o·ri·ga·mi (ôr′ə gä′mē) ***n.*** ⟦Jpn⟧ **1** a traditional Japanese art of folding paper to form representations of flowers, animals, etc. **2** a paper object so made

Or·i·gen (ôr′i jən, är′-; -jen′) (L. name *Origenes Adamantius*) A.D. 185?-254?; Christian theologian & scholar, born in Alexandria

or·i·gin (ôr′ə jin, är′-) ***n.*** ⟦ME *origyne* < MFr *origine* < L *origo* (gen. *originis*) < *oriri,* to rise: see ORIENT⟧ **1** a coming into existence or use; beginning **2** parentage; birth; lineage **3** [*often pl.*] that in which something has its beginning; source; root; cause **4** *Anat.* the less movable of the two points of attachment of a muscle, usually the end attached to the more rigid part of the skeleton **5** *Math. a)* in a system of Cartesian coordinates, the point at which the axes intersect; base point where the abscissa and ordinate equal zero *b)* any zero reference point from which measurement begins

SYN.—**origin** is applied to that from which a person or thing has its very beginning [the *origin* of a word]; **source** is applied to the point or place from which something arises, comes, or develops [the sun is our *source* of energy]; **beginning** is the basic term for a starting point or place [the *beginning* of a quarrel]; **inception** is specif. applied to the beginning of an undertaking, organization, etc. [Smith headed the business from its *inception*]; **root** suggests an origin so deep and basic as to be the ultimate cause from which something stems [the *root* of the matter]

o·rig·i·nal (ə rij′i nəl) ***adj.*** ⟦OFr < L *originalis*⟧ **1** having to do with an origin; first; earliest **2** never having occurred or existed before; fresh; new; novel **3** capable of or given to inventing or creating something new, or thinking or acting in an independent, individual, fresh way **4** coming from someone as the originator, maker, author, etc. **5** being that from which reproductions, copies, etc. have been made —***n.*** ⟦Fr < the adj.⟧ **1** a pristine form or primary type that has given rise to varieties **2** an original work, as of art or literature, as distinguished from a reproduction, copy, etc. **3** the person or thing represented in a painting or the like **4** *a)* a person with an original and creative mind *b)* an eccentric person **5** [Archaic] an originator —***SYN.*** NEW

o·rig·i·nal·ism (-nəl iz′əm) ***n.*** interpretation of the U.S. Constitution in a way regarded as in accord with the original intent of the Founding Fathers —**o·rig′i·nal·ist** ***adj., n.***

o·rig·i·nal·i·ty (ə rij′i nal′ə tē) ***n.*** ⟦Fr *originalité*⟧ **1** the quality or condition of being original **2** the ability to be inventive or creative

o·rig·i·nal·ly (ə rij′i nəl ē) ***adv.*** **1** with reference to origin, or beginning **2** in the first place; initially **3** in an independent or new way

original sin *Christian Theol.* the sinful state of mankind, originating in THE FALL and inherited from Adam as progenitor of the human race

o·rig·i·nate (ə rij′i nāt′) ***vt.*** **-nat′ed, -nat′ing** ⟦< ML *originatus,* pp. of *originari,* to begin < L *origo:* see ORIGIN⟧ to bring into being; esp., to create (something original); invent —***vi.*** to come into being; begin; start —***SYN.*** RISE —**o·rig′i·na′tion** ***n.*** —**o·rig′i·na′tive** ***adj.*** —**o·rig′i·na′tor** ***n.***

o·ri·na·sal (ôr′ə nā′zəl) ***adj.*** ⟦< L *os* (gen. *oris*), a mouth (see ORAL) + NASAL⟧ *Phonet.* articulated with breath passing through the mouth and the nose at the same time: said as of some French vowels —***n.*** an orinasal sound

O-ring (ō′riŋ′) ***n.*** a ring-shaped seal or washer of rubber, plastic, metal, etc., used to prevent leaks in parts connecting pipes, tubes, rocket sections, etc.

O·ri·no·co (ôr′ə nō′kō) river in Venezuela, flowing from the Brazilian border into the Atlantic: *c.* 1,700 mi (2,736 km)

o·ri·ole (ôr′ē ōl′, -əl) ***n.*** ⟦OFr *oriol* < ML *aureolus* < L, golden, dim. of *aureus* < *aurum,* gold: see EAST⟧ **1** any of an Old World family (Oriolidae) of chiefly yellow-and-black passerine birds, including the **golden oriole**

(*Oriolus oriolus*) **2** any of a genus (*Icterus*, family Icteridae) of American passerine birds, including the Baltimore oriole, that have bright plumage of orange (or yellow) and black, and build hanging nests

O·ri·on (ō rī′ən) *n.* ⟦ME < L < Gr *Ōriōn*⟧ **1** *Class. Myth.* a hunter whom Diana loves but accidentally kills **2** *Astron.* an equatorial constellation between Taurus and Lepus, containing the bright stars Rigel and Betelgeuse

or·i·son (ôr′i zən, -sən) *n.* ⟦ME *oreisun* < OFr *oreison* < LL(Ec) *oratio*, a prayer < L, a speech: see ORATION⟧ [Now Literary] a prayer

O·ri·za·ba (ô′rē sä′bä) **1** volcanic mountain in SE Mexico; highest mountain in Mexico: 18,700 ft (5,700 m) **2** city at the foot of this mountain, in Veracruz state

Ork·ney Islands (ôrk′nē) ⟦< ON *Orkneyjar*, lit., seal islands < *orkn*, a seal + *ey*, ISLAND⟧ group of islands north of Scotland, constituting an administrative division of Scotland: 377 sq mi (976 sq km)

Or·lan·do[1] (ôr lan′dō) *n.* ⟦It⟧ a masculine name: see ROLAND

Or·lan·do[2] (ôr lan′dō; *It* ôr län′dô), **Vit·to·rio E·ma·nue·le** (vēt tô′ryô e′mä nwe′le) 1860-1952; It. statesman: premier of Italy (1917-19)

Or·lan·do[3] (ôr lan′dō) ⟦after *Orlando* Reeves, a soldier killed there in an Indian attack⟧ city in central Fla.

orle (ôrl) *n.* ⟦Fr < OFr *ourle, urle*, dim. < L *ora*, margin, border < *os*, mouth, edge: see ORAL⟧ *Heraldry* the inner border on an escutcheon, following the outline of the edge of the shield

Or·lé·a·nais (ôr lā ȧ ne′) historical region in NC France: chief city, Orléans

Or·le·an·ist (ôr′lē ə nist) *n.* a supporter of the house of Orléans' claim to the French throne through the Duke of Orléans, a younger brother of Louis XIV

Or·lé·ans[1] (ôr lā än′; *E* ôr′lē ən′) *n.* branch of the house of Bourbon, one of whose members (LOUIS PHILIPPE) ruled France, 1830-48

Or·lé·ans[2] (ôr lā än′), **Louis Phi·lippe Jo·seph** Duc **d'** (lwē′ fē lēp′ zhô zef′) 1747-93; Fr. revolutionary: guillotined: father of LOUIS PHILIPPE

Or·lé·ans[3] (ôr lā än′; *E* ôr′lē ən′) city in NC France, on the Loire

☆**Or·lon** (ôr′län′) *n.* ⟦former trademark: arbitrary coinage, after (NYL)ON⟧ [*also* **o-**] **1** a synthetic acrylic fiber somewhat like nylon **2** a fabric made from this fiber

or·lop (ôr′läp) *n.* ⟦ME *ouerlop* < Du *overloop* < *over*, over + *loopen*, to run (see LEAP): so called because it covers the hold⟧ [Now Rare] the lowest deck of a ship with four or more decks

Or·man·dy (ôr′mən dē), **Eugene** (born *Jenő Blau*) 1899-1985; U.S. conductor, born in Hungary

Or·mazd (ôr′məzd) *n.* ⟦Pers < OPers *Auramazda* < Avestan *Ahuro-Mazdao*, wise lord < *ahura*, a god (see OSCAR[2]) + *mazdah-*, name of the highest god < IE **mendh-*, to direct one's mind toward < base **men-*, to think (> MIND) + **dhē-*, to put (< DO[1])⟧ in Zoroastrianism, the supreme deity and creator of the world, or the spirit of good: cf. AHRIMAN: also sp. **Or′muzd**

or·mer (ôr′mər) *n.* ⟦Fr dial. (Channel Islands) < Fr *ormier* < L *auris maris*, ear of the sea (see EAR[1] & MARE[2]): from its shape⟧ [Brit. Dial.] *name for* ABALONE

or·mo·lu (ôr′mə lo͞o′) *n.* ⟦Fr *or moulu*, lit., ground gold < *or* (see OR[3]) + pp. of *moudre* < L *molere*, to grind: see MILL[1]⟧ **1** an imitation gold made of an alloy of copper and tin, used in making ornaments, moldings, cheap jewelry, etc. **2** imitation gold leaf

Or·muz (ôr′muz′, ôr mo͞oz′), **Strait of** *var. of* HORMUZ, Strait of

or·na·ment (ôr′nə mənt; *for v.*, -ment′) *n.* ⟦OFr *ornement* < L *ornamentum* < *ornare*, to adorn (akin to *ordinare*: see ORDAIN)⟧ **1** anything serving to adorn; decoration; embellishment; also, a desirable or needed adjunct **2** something or someone regarded as, or merely as, a decorative accessory **3** an adorning or being adorned; ornamentation **4** mere external display **5** *Music* a tone or tones used to embellish a principal melodic tone —*vt.* to furnish with ornaments or be an ornament to; decorate; beautify —**SYN.** ADORN —**or′na·ment′er** *n.*

or·na·men·tal (ôr′nə ment′'l) *adj.* serving as or pertaining to an ornament; decorative —*n.* something ornamental; specif., a plant or shrub grown for its decorative effect —**or′na·men′tal·ly** *adv.*

or·na·men·ta·tion (ôr′nə men tā′shən) *n.* **1** an ornamenting or being ornamented **2** ornaments collectively; decoration **3** an ornament or embellishment

or·nate (ôr nāt′) *adj.* ⟦ME < L *ornatus*, pp. of *ornare*: see ORNAMENT⟧ **1** heavily ornamented or adorned, often, excessively so **2** showy or flowery [*an ornate writing style*] —**or·nate′ly** *adv.* —**or·nate′ness** *n.*

or·ner·y (ôr′nər ē) *adj.* ⟦altered < ORDINARY⟧ [Informal] **1** having an ugly or mean disposition **2** obstinate —☆**or′ner·i·ness** *n.*

or·nis (ôr′nis) *n.* ⟦Ger < Gr *ornis*, bird: see ORNITHO-⟧ AVIFAUNA

or·nith·ic (ôr nith′ik) *adj.* ⟦Gr *ornithikos* < *ornis*, bird: see ORNITHO-⟧ of or characteristic of birds

or·ni·thine (ôr′nə thēn′, -thin) *n.* ⟦< Gr *ornis*, bird (see ORNITHO-) + -INE[3]⟧ a nonessential amino acid, $NH_2(CH_2)_3CH(NH_2)COOH$, found in animals as a product of urea formation from proteins and in the excrement of birds

or·nith·is·chi·an (ôr′nə this′kē ən, -thish′ē ən) *n.* ⟦< ModL *Ornithischia* < fol. + ISCHIUM⟧ any of an order (Ornithischia) of plant-eating dinosaurs with a birdlike pelvic structure, including the stegosaurus and triceratops —*adj.* of the ornithischians

or·ni·tho- (ôr′nə thō, -thə) ⟦< Gr *ornis* (gen. *ornithos*), bird < IE base **er-*, eagle, large bird > Goth *ara*⟧ *combining form* bird or birds [*ornithology*]: also, before a vowel, **ornith-**

☆**or·ni·thoid** (ôr′nə thoid′) *adj.* ⟦< prec. + -OID⟧ like a bird in appearance or structure

or·ni·thol·o·gy (ôr′nə thäl′ə jē) *n.* ⟦ModL *ornithologia*: see ORNITHO- & -LOGY⟧ the branch of zoology dealing with birds —**or·ni·tho·log·i·cal** (ôr′ni thə läj′i kəl) *adj.* —**or′ni·tho·log′i·cal·ly** *adv.* —**or′ni·thol′o·gist** *n.*

or·ni·tho·pod (ôr′ni thə päd′, ôr nith′ə päd′) *n.* ⟦< ModL *Ornithopoda*: see ORNITHO- & -POD⟧ any of a suborder (Ornithopoda) of ornithischian dinosaurs that walked upright on digitigrade hind feet

or·ni·thop·ter (ôr′nə thäp′tər) *n.* ⟦< ORNITHO- + Gr *pteron*, wing, FEATHER⟧ an experimental type of aircraft designed to be propelled by the flapping of the wings

or·ni·tho·rhyn·chus (ôr′nə thō riŋ′kəs) *n.* ⟦< ORNITHO- + Gr *rhynchos*, bill, snout < IE echoic base **srungh-*, to snort⟧ PLATYPUS

or·ni·tho·sis (ôr′nə thō′sis) *n.* ⟦ModL < ORNITH(O)- + -OSIS⟧ PSITTACOSIS

o·ro- (ō′rō, -rə; ôr′ō, -ə) ⟦< Gr *oros*, mountain: see ORIENT⟧ *combining form* mountain [*orography*]

o·rog·e·ny (ō räj′ə nē) *n.*, *pl.* **-nies** ⟦prec. + -GENY⟧ the formation of mountains through structural disturbance of the earth's crust, esp. by folding and faulting: also called **or·o·gen·e·sis** (ôr′ō jen′ə sis) —**or′o·gen′ic** (-jen′ik) *adj.*, **or′o·ge·net′ic** (-jə net′ik)

o·rog·ra·phy (ō räg′rə fē) *n.* ⟦ORO- + -GRAPHY⟧ the branch of physical geography dealing with mountains: cf. OROLOGY —**or·o·graph·ic** (ôr′ō graf′ik) *adj.*, **or′o·graph′i·cal**

☆**o·ro·ide** (ō′rō īd′, -id; ôr′ō-) *n.* ⟦< Fr *oréide*: see OR[3] & -IDE⟧ an alloy, mainly of copper, tin, and zinc, resembling gold, used in cheap jewelry

o·rol·o·gy (ō räl′ə jē) *n.* ⟦ORO- + -LOGY⟧ the study of mountains, esp. the study of how mountains are formed: cf. OROGRAPHY —**or·o·log·i·cal** (ôr′ō läj′i kəl) *adj.*

O·ro·mo (ō rō′mō) *n.* ⟦self-designation⟧ **1** *pl.* **-mos** or **-mo** a member of a people of S Ethiopia and neighboring regions **2** the Cushitic language of this people

O·ron·tes (ō rän′tēz) river in SW Asia, flowing from Lebanon through Syria & Turkey into the Mediterranean: *c.* 240 mi (386 km)

o·ro·phar·ynx (ō′rō far′iŋks) *n.*, *pl.* **-pha·ryn·ges** (-fə rin′jēz), **-phar′ynx·es** ⟦< L *os* (gen. *oris*), mouth (see ORAL) + PHARYNX⟧ the middle part of the pharynx, located below the nasopharynx and above the laryngopharynx —**o′ro·pha·ryn′ge·al** (-fə rin′jē əl) *adj.*

o·ro·tund (ôr′ə tund′) *adj.* ⟦< L *ore rotundo*, lit., with a round mouth: see ORAL & ROTUND⟧ **1** clear, strong, and deep; resonant: said of the voice **2** bombastic or pompous: said of a style of speaking or writing —**o′ro·tun′di·ty** (-tun′də tē) *n.*

O·roz·co (ô rôs′kô), **Jo·sé Cle·men·te** (hô se′ kle men′te) 1883-1949; Mex. painter

or·phan (ôr′fən) *n.* ⟦LL(Ec) *orphanus* < Gr *orphanos* < IE base **orbho-*, orphan > L *orbus*, bereft, Ger *erbe*, inheritance, *arbeit*, work, Czech *robotnik*, serf⟧ **1** a child whose father and mother are dead: often used fig. **2** [Rare] a child who has lost only one parent by death —*adj.* **1** being an orphan **2** of or for orphans [*an orphan home*] **3** of a product that is medically valuable but is not produced because it lacks a profitable market, as a drug for a rare disease —*vt.* to cause to become an orphan [*orphaned by the war*] —**or′phan·hood′** *n.*

or·phan·age (ôr′fən ij) *n.* **1** the condition of being an orphan **2** an institution that is a home for orphans

Or·phe·us (ôr′fē əs, -fyo͞os′) *n.* ⟦L < Gr⟧ *Gr. Myth.* a poet-musician with magic musical powers who descends to the underworld and tries to lead his wife, Eurydice, back from the dead but fails because he breaks the injunction not to look back at her until they reach the upper world —**Or′phe·an** *adj.*

Or·phic (ôr′fik) *adj.* ⟦L *Orphicus* < Gr *Orphikos*⟧ **1** of or characteristic of Orpheus or the mystic doctrines and rites in worship of Dionysus ascribed to him **2** [*also* **o-**] *a)* like the music attributed to Orpheus; entrancing *b)* mystic; occult; oracular

Or·phism (ôr′fiz′əm) *n.* the rites and religion ascribed to Orpheus as founder

or·phrey (ôr′frē) *n.* ⟦ME *orferay*, taken as sing. of *orfreis*, orphrey < OFr < ML *aurifrigium* < L *aurum*, gold (see EAST) + ML *frisium*, FRIEZE[1]⟧ a richly embroidered decorative band, as on a chasuble

or·pi·ment (ôr′pi mənt) *n.* ⟦OFr < L *auripigmentum*, pigment of gold: see AURIC & PIGMENT⟧ arsenic trisulfide, As_2S_3, having a lemon-yellow color and a resinous luster: it is used as a pigment

or·pine (ôr′pin) *n.* ⟦ME *orpin* < MFr < *orpiment* (see prec.): orig. used of a yellow-flowered plant⟧ any of various plants (esp. genus *Sedum*) of the orpine family, with fleshy leaves and stems, and white, yellow, or purple flowers —*adj.* designating a family (Crassulaceae, order Rosales) of succulent, dicotyledonous plants, including the sempervivums and sedums

Or·ping·ton (ôr′piŋ tən) *n.* ⟦after *Orpington*, village in KENT[2]⟧ any of a breed of large, full-bodied chicken, often brownish yellow in color and with featherless legs, usually raised for its meat

or·rer·y (ôr′ər ē) *n.*, *pl.* **-rer·ies** ⟦after Charles Boyle, Earl of *Orrery* (1676-1731), for whom one was made⟧ a mechanical apparatus consisting of balls of various sizes arranged as on wires, designed to illustrate the relative motions and positions of the sun, earth, moon, and often other planets

or·ris (ôr′is, är′-) *n.* ⟦prob. altered < ME *ireos* < ML *yreos* < Gr *ireos*, made from iris < *iris*, IRIS⟧ any of several European irises, esp. a white-flowered species (*Iris florentina*) whose rootstocks yield orrisroot

or·ris·root (-ro͞ot′) *n.* the rootstock of the orris: pulverized and used in perfumery, tooth powders, etc.

Orsk (ôrsk) city in SE European Russia, on the Ural River

Or·son (ôr′sən) *n.* ⟦< Fr *ourson,* dim. of *ours,* a bear < L *ursus*⟧ a masculine name

ort (ôrt) *n.* ⟦LME *ortus,* pl., prob. < LowG⟧ [Now Chiefly Dial.] a scrap or fragment of food left from a meal: *usually used in pl.*

Or·te·gal (ôr′te gäl′), **Cape** cape in NW Spain, extending into the Bay of Biscay

Or·te·ga y Gas·set (ôr te′gä ē gä set′), **Jo·sé** (hō se′) 1883-1955; Sp. essayist & philosopher

☆**or·thi·con** (ôr′thi kän′) *n.* ⟦fol. + ICON(OSCOPE)⟧ a television camera tube, an improved form of the iconoscope, in which the charges on a photosensitive plate are scanned by a low-velocity electron beam

or·tho- (ôr′thō, -thə) ⟦< Gr *orthos,* straight < IE base **werdh-,* to grow, climb, high > Sans *várdhati,* (he) grows⟧ *combining form* **1** straight, regular, upright *[orthognathous]* **2** at right angles, perpendicular *[orthorhombic]* **3** proper, correct, standard *[orthography]* **4** *Chem. a)* that acid (of a group containing the same nonmetallic element) which has the largest number of OH groups per atom of the nonmetal *[orthophosphoric* acid*]* *b)* characterized by substitutions in the 1, 2 position in the benzene ring: usually italicized and hyphenated in chemical names *[ortho-*aminobenzoic acid*]*: see PARA-[1] (sense 2*b*), META- (sense 6*d*) **5** *Med.* correction of deformities *[orthopedics]* Also (except for sense 4*b*), before a vowel, **orth-**

or·tho·cen·ter (ôr′thə sent′ər) *n. Geom.* the point where the three altitudes of a triangle intersect

or·tho·ce·phal·ic (ôr′thō sə fal′ik) *adj.* ⟦ORTHO- + -CEPHALIC⟧ having a skull whose height is 70.1 to 75 percent of its length, from front to back: see CEPHALIC INDEX: also **or′tho·ceph′a·lous** (-sef′ə ləs) **—or′tho·ceph′a·ly** *n.*

or·tho·chro·mat·ic (-krō mat′ik) *adj.* ⟦ORTHO- + CHROMATIC⟧ designating or of photographic film that is sensitive to all colors except red and deep orange

or·tho·clase (ôr′thō klās′, -klāz′; -thə-) *n.* ⟦Ger *orthoklas* < Gr *orthos* (see ORTHO-) + *klasis,* fracture (< *klan,* to break: see CLASTIC), because of the 90° cleavage⟧ a monoclinic feldspar, $KAlSi_3O_8$, that is dimorphic with microcline; potassium aluminum silicate: see MOHS SCALE

or·tho·don·tics (ôr′thə dän′tiks) *n.* ⟦ModL: see ORTH(O)-, -ODONT, & -ICS⟧ the branch of dentistry concerned with diagnosing, correcting, and preventing irregularities of the teeth and poor occlusion: also **or′tho·don′ti·a** (-dän′shə, -shē ə) **—or′tho·don′tic** *adj.* **—or′tho·don′tist** *n.*

or·tho·dox (ôr′thə däks′) *adj.* ⟦< Fr or LL: Fr *orthodoxe* < LL *orthōdoxus* < LGr(Ec) *orthodoxos,* orthodox (in religion) < Gr *orthos* (see ORTHO-) + *doxa,* opinion < *dokein,* to think: see DECENT⟧ **1** conforming to the usual beliefs or established doctrines, as in religion or politics; approved or conventional *[orthodox* ideas*]*; specif., *a)* conforming to the Christian faith as formulated in the early ecumenical creeds and confessions *b)* [**O-**] strictly conforming to certain rites and traditions of Judaism as formulated by the Torah and Talmud **2** [**O-**] designating or of any of the churches belonging to the Eastern Orthodox Church

Orthodox Eastern Church EASTERN ORTHODOX CHURCH

or·tho·dox·y (ôr′thə däk′sē) *n., pl.* **-dox′ies** ⟦Gr *orthodoxia*⟧ **1** the quality or fact of being orthodox **2** an orthodox belief, doctrine, custom, etc.

or·tho·e·py (ôr thō′ə pē; ôr′thō ə pē, -thō ep′ē) *n.* ⟦ModL *orthoepia* < Gr *orthoepeia* < *orthos,* right + *epos,* a word: see ORTHO- & EPIC⟧ **1** the study of pronunciation; phonology **2** the standard pronunciation of a language **—or·tho·ep·ic** (ôr′thō ep′ik) *adj.,* **or′tho·ep′i·cal —or·tho′e·pist** *n.*

or·tho·gen·e·sis (ôr′thō jen′ə sis) *n.* ⟦ModL: see ORTHO- & -GENESIS⟧ **1** *Biol.* a now discredited theory that states that the progressive evolution of certain organisms in a restricted direction throughout successive generations is independent of outside influences and natural selection **2** *Anthrop.* the theory, no longer accepted, that every culture follows the same fixed course of evolution, uninfluenced by differing environmental factors **—or′tho·ge·net′ic** (-jə net′ik) *adj.*

or·thog·na·thous (ôr thäg′nə thəs) *adj.* ⟦ORTHO- + -GNATHOUS⟧ having the jaws in line, with the lower jaw neither projecting nor receding: also **or′thog·nath′ic** (-nath′ik) **—or·thog′na·thism′** *n.*

or·thog·o·nal (ôr thäg′ə nəl) *adj.* ⟦Fr < *orthogone,* right-angled < L *orthogonius* < Gr *orthogōnios:* see ORTHO- & -GON⟧ having to do with right angles; perpendicular; rectangular **—or·thog′o·nal·ly** *adv.*

or·tho·grade (ôr′thō grād′) *adj.* ⟦ORTHO- + -GRADE⟧ *Zool.* walking with the body upright

or·tho·graph·ic (ôr′thə graf′ik) *adj.* **1** of or characterized by orthography **2** *Geom.* of right angles and perpendicular lines; orthogonal Also **or′tho·graph′i·cal —or′tho·graph′i·cal·ly** *adv.*

orthographic projection a two-dimensional pictorial representation of a three-dimensional object in which the object is shown separately in two or more accurate, scaled-down views, as from the top, front, and side: the views are typically displayed with the top view above and the side view alongside the front view

or·thog·ra·phy (ôr thäg′rə fē) *n., pl.* **-phies** ⟦ME *ortografye* < MFr *ortographie* < L *orthographia* < Gr: see ORTHO- & -GRAPHY⟧ **1** spelling in accord with accepted usage **2** any style or method of spelling **3** spelling as a subject for study **4** ORTHOGRAPHIC PROJECTION **—or·thog′ra·pher** *n.*

☆**or·tho·ker·a·tol·o·gy** (ôr′thō ker′ə täl′ə jē) *n.* ⟦ORTHO- + KERATO- + -LOGY⟧ a branch of optometry that seeks to reduce certain refractive errors in the eye by altering the curvature of the cornea through the application of a series of graduated contact lenses over a period of time

☆**or·tho·mo·lec·u·lar** (ôr′thō mə lek′yə lər) *adj.* ⟦ORTHO- + MOLECULAR⟧ of or involving a regimen in which megavitamins, trace minerals, etc. are taken in an effort to improve the balance of nutrients in the body molecules

or·tho·myx·o·vi·rus (ôr′thō mik′sə vī′rəs) *n.* any of a family (Orthomyxoviridae) of RNA viruses affecting certain vertebrates, primarily causing upper respiratory infections; especially, any of a genus (*Influenzavirus*) causing influenza in human beings

or·tho·pe·dics or **or·tho·pae·dics** (ôr′thə pē′diks) *n.* ⟦< Fr *orthopédique,* orthopedic < *orthopédie* < Gr *orthos,* straight (see ORTHO-) + *paideia,* training of children < *pais* (gen. *paidos*), child: see PEDO-[1]⟧ the branch of medicine dealing with the treatment of deformities, diseases, and injuries of the bones, joints, muscles, etc. **—or′tho·pe′dic** *adj.,* **or′tho·pae′dic —or′tho·pe′dist** *n.,* **or′tho·pae′dist**

or·tho·phos·phate (ôr′thō fäs′fāt′) *n.* ⟦ORTHO- + PHOSPHATE⟧ **1** a salt of orthophosphoric acid containing the trivalent, negative radical PO_4 **2** an uncharged ester of this acid

or·tho·phos·phor·ic acid (-fäs fôr′ik) ⟦ORTHO- + PHOSPHORIC⟧ a clear, colorless, syrupy liquid or a colorless, crystalline solid, H_3PO_4, produced from phosphorus or phosphate rock and used in the manufacture of fertilizers, textiles, etc.

or·tho·psy·chi·a·try (-sī kī′ə trē) *n.* ⟦ORTHO- + PSYCHIATRY⟧ the study and treatment of disorders of behavior and personality, with emphasis on prevention through a clinical approach **—or′tho·psy′chi·at′ric** (-sī′kē a′trik) *adj.* **—or′tho·psy·chi′a·trist** *n.*

or·thop·ter (ôr thäp′tər) *n.* ORNITHOPTER

or·thop·ter·an (ôr thäp′tər ən) *n.* ⟦< ModL *Orthoptera* < ORTHO- + Gr *pteron,* wing, FEATHER⟧ any of a large order (Orthoptera) of mostly plant-eating insects, including crickets, grasshoppers, and katydids, having chewing mouthparts and narrow, hard forewings that cover membranous hind wings in most species, and undergoing gradual metamorphosis **—or·thop′ter·ous** *adj.*

or·thop·tic (ôr thäp′tik) *adj.* ⟦ORTH(O)- + OPTIC⟧ correcting any deviations of the visual axis of the eye, esp. by exercises to strengthen the eye muscles

or·tho·rhom·bic (ôr′thō räm′bik) *adj.* ⟦ORTHO- + RHOMBIC⟧ designating or of a crystal system having three axes of unequal length, each of which intersects at right angles with the others: see CRYSTAL SYSTEM

or·tho·scope (ôr′thə skōp′) *n.* ⟦ORTHO- + -SCOPE⟧ an instrument containing a layer of water which is held in contact with the eye, allowing an examination of the interior of the eye without the distortion due to corneal refraction

or·tho·scop·ic (ôr′thə skäp′ik) *adj.* ⟦< ORTHO- + Gr *skopein,* to view (see SCOPE) + -IC⟧ giving a true flat image without distortion

or·tho·sis (ôr thō′sis) *n., pl.* **-ses′** (-sēz′) ORTHOTIC

or·tho·stat·ic (-stat′ik) *adj.* ⟦ORTHO- + STATIC⟧ of or caused by an upright position *[orthostatic* hypotension*]*

or·thos·ti·chy (ôr thäs′ti kē) *n., pl.* **-chies** ⟦< ORTHO- + Gr *stichos,* a row (see STILE[2]) + -Y[3]⟧ a vertical arrangement of leaves or flowers on a stem **—or·thos′ti·chous** (-kəs) *adj.*

or·thot·ic (ôr thät′ik) *adj.* ⟦< ORTH(O)- + -OTIC⟧ of or having to do with orthotics *[*an *orthotic* shoe*]* **—*n.*** any brace, support, insert, or other orthopedic device used in orthotics

or·thot·ics (ôr thät′iks) *n.* ⟦< prec.⟧ the science of developing and fitting any kind of orthopedic device designed to activate or supplement a weakened or atrophied limb or function **—or·tho·tist** (ôr′thə tist) *n.*

or·tho·trop·ic (ôr′thō träp′ik) *adj.* ⟦ORTHO- + -TROPIC⟧ **1** designating or of a design for bridges in which the structural supporting units also form the deck, or road surface, thus reducing weight and cost of construction **2** *Bot.* designating, of, or showing vertical growth, as most main stems and roots

or·thot·ro·pism (ôr thä′trə piz′əm) *n.* ⟦ORTHO- + -TROPISM⟧ growth, or a tendency to grow, in a vertical direction or position

or·thot·ro·pous (ôr thä′trə pəs) *adj.* ⟦ORTHO- + -TROPOUS⟧ *Bot.* growing straight: said of an ovule with its hilum and micropyle in a straight line

Ort·les (ôrt′lās) **1** range of the E Alps, in N Italy **2** highest peak of this range: 12,792 ft (3,899 m) Ger. name **Ort·ler** (ôrt′lər)

or·to·lan (ôr′tə lən) *n.* ⟦Fr < Prov < It *ortolana,* gardener, ortolan < L *hortulanus,* dim. of *hortus,* a garden (see YARD[2]): from its frequenting gardens⟧ an Old World bunting (*Emberiza hortulana*) prized as a choice food

O·ru·ro (ô roor′ō) city in W Bolivia

Or·ville (ôr′vil) *n.* ⟦Fr; orig. a place name⟧ a masculine name

Or·well (ôr′wel, -wəl), **George** (pseud. of *Eric Arthur Blair*) 1903-50; Eng. writer

Or·well·i·an (ôr wel′ē ən) *adj.* of or like the society portrayed by Orwell in his novel *Nineteen Eighty-four,* characterized by totalitarian government, irrational political concepts, the politicization of everyday language, etc.

-o·ry (ôr′ē, ər ē) *suffix* **1** ⟦ME *-orie* < OFr *-oire* < L *-orius, -oria, -orium*⟧ *forming adjectives* of, having the nature of *[sensory, valedictory]* **2** ⟦ME *-orie* < OFr *-oire, -orie* < L *-orium*⟧ *forming nouns* a place or thing for *[crematory]*

o·ryx (ôr′iks, är′-) *n., pl.* **o′ryx·es** or **o′ryx** ⟦ModL < L, wild goat, gazelle < Gr, lit., pickax (< *oryssein,* to dig: for IE base see RUPTURE): from its pointed horns⟧ any of a genus (*Oryx*) of large African and Asian antelopes with long, straight horns, including the gemsbok

or·zo (ôr′tsō′) *n.* ⟦It, lit., barley⟧ pasta in the shape of grains of rice

os[1] (ōs) *n., pl.* **o·sar** (ō′sär′) ⟦Swed *ås,* ridge, pl. *åsar* < ON *áss* < IE base **omso-,* shoulder > Gr *ōmos,* L *umerus,* shoulder⟧ ESKER

os[2] (äs) *n., pl.* **os′sa** (-ə) ⟦L: see OSSIFY⟧ a bone

os[3] (äs) *n., pl.* **o·ra** (ō′rə, ôr′ə) ⟦L: see ORAL⟧ a mouth; opening

Os *Chem. symbol for* osmium

OS *abbrev.* **1** Old Saxon **2** old series **3** Old Style **4** operating system **5** Ordinary Seaman **6** out of stock Also, for 2 & 6, **os**

o.s. *abbrev.* ⟦L *oculus sinister*⟧ left eye

O·sage[1] (ō sāj′, ō′sāj′) *n.* ⟦< Osage *Wazhazhe*⟧ **1** *pl.* **O·sag′es** or **O·sage′** a member of a North American Indian people that migrated, over time, from the east coast of the U.S. to the Piedmont, then to Missouri, Kansas, and Oklahoma **2** the Siouan language of this people

O·sage[2] (ō sāj′, ō′sāj′) ⟦after prec.⟧ river in central Mo. & E Kans., flowing east into the Missouri: *c.* 500 mi (805 km)

☆**Osage orange** **1** a small thorny tree (*Maclura pomifera*) of the mulberry family, with hard, yellow wood, native to the central U.S. and often used for hedges **2** its greenish-yellow, orange-shaped, inedible fruit

O·sa·ka (ō sä′kə, ō′sä kä′) seaport in S Honshu, Japan

OSB *abbrev.* Order of St. Benedict

Os·born (äz′bərn), **Henry Fair·field** (fer′fēld′) 1857-1935; U.S. paleontologist & biologist

Os·borne (äz′bərn, -bôrn) **1 John (James)** 1929-94; Eng. playwright **2 Thomas Mott** (mät) 1859-1926; U.S. prison reformer

Os·can (äs′kən) *n.* ⟦< L *Oscus,* Oscan + -AN⟧ **1** a member of an ancient people that lived in Campania, in S Italy **2** the Italic language of this people —*adj.* of the Oscans or their language or culture

Os·car[1] (äs′kər) *n.* ⟦OE *Osgar* < *os,* a god, akin to ON *áss* (< IE **ansu-,* a spirit, demon > Avestan *ahura*) + *gar,* a spear⟧ a masculine name

Os·car[2] (äs′kər) ⟦said to be so named from comment ("He reminds me of my Uncle Oscar") made by an Academy official on first seeing the statuette⟧ *trademark for:* **1** ACADEMY AWARD **2** any of the statuettes given to those receiving Academy Awards

Oscar II 1829-1907; king of Norway & Sweden (1872-1905), then of Sweden alone

OSCE *abbrev.* Organization for Security and Cooperation in Europe

Os·ce·o·la (äs′ē ō′lə) 1804?-38; leader of the Seminole Indians

os·cil·late (äs′ə lāt′) *vi.* **-lat′ed, -lat′ing** ⟦< L *oscillatus,* pp. of *oscillare,* to swing < *oscillum,* a swing⟧ **1** to swing or move regularly back and forth **2** to be indecisive in purpose or opinion; vacillate **3** *Physics* to vary regularly between maximum and minimum values, as an electric current —*vt.* to cause to oscillate —*SYN.* SWING —**os′cil·la·to′ry** (-lə tôr′ē) *adj.*

os·cil·la·tion (äs′ə lā′shən) *n.* ⟦L *oscillatio*⟧ **1** the act of oscillating **2** fluctuation; instability; variation **3** *Physics a)* repeated variation in the value of some physical quantity, as position or voltage *b)* a single instance or cycle of such a variation

os·cil·la·tor (äs′ə lāt′ər) *n.* **1** a person or thing that oscillates **2** *Physics* an apparatus, as an electric circuit, for establishing and maintaining oscillations

os·cil·lo·gram (ə sil′ə gram′) *n.* ⟦see -GRAM⟧ a record obtained from an oscillograph

os·cil·lo·graph (-graf′) *n.* ⟦< L *oscillare,* to swing + -GRAPH⟧ an instrument for displaying or recording in the form of a curve the instantaneous values of rapidly varying electrical quantities —**os·cil′lo·graph′ic** *adj.*

os·cil·lo·scope (-skōp′) *n.* ⟦< L *oscillare,* to swing + -SCOPE⟧ a type of oscillograph that visually displays an electrical wave on a fluorescent screen, as of a cathode-ray tube —**os·cil′lo·scop′ic** (-skäp′ik) *adj.*

os·cine (äs′in, -īn′) *adj.* ⟦< ModL *Oscines* < L, pl. of *oscen,* bird whose notes were used in divining < *obs-,* var. of *ob-* (see OB-) + *canere,* to crow, sing (see CHANT, *vi.*)⟧ designating or of the major suborder (Oscines) of passerine birds characterized by a highly developed syrinx, including most common perching birds —*n.* a bird of this suborder

Os·co-Um·bri·an (äs′kō um′brē ən) *n.* a division of the Italic branch of Indo-European, consisting of Oscan and Umbrian

os·cu·lant (äs′kyə lənt) *adj.* ⟦L *osculans,* prp. of *osculari:* see OSCULATE⟧ **1** *Biol.* intermediate; linking; shared: said of a characteristic common to two or more groups, genera, etc. **2** *Zool.* gripping or adhering together

os·cu·lar (äs′kyə lər) *adj.* ⟦L *osculum* (see fol.) + -AR⟧ **1** of the mouth or kissing **2** *Zool.* of an osculum

os·cu·late (äs′kyə lāt′) *vt., vi.* **-lat′ed, -lat′ing** ⟦< L *osculatus,* pp. of *osculari,* to kiss < *osculum,* little mouth: see fol.⟧ to kiss: a pretentious or facetious usage —**os′cu·la′tion** *n.* —**os′cu·la·to′ry** (-lə tôr′ē) *adj.*

os·cu·lum (äs′kyə ləm) *n., pl.* **-la** (-lə) ⟦L, dim. of *os,* a mouth: see ORAL⟧ any of the openings of a sponge though which water passes out

-ose[1] (ōs) ⟦Fr < *(gluc)ose:* see GLUCOSE⟧ *suffix forming nouns* **1** a carbohydrate *[cellulose, sucrose]* **2** the product of a protein hydrolysis *[proteose]*

-ose[2] (ōs) ⟦L *-osus*⟧ *suffix forming adjectives* full of, having the qualities of, like *[filose]*

OSHA (ō′shə) *trademark* Occupational Safety and Health Administration

Osh·a·wa (äsh′ə wə, -wô) city in SE Ontario, Canada, on Lake Ontario

Osh·kosh (äsh′käsh′) ⟦after *Oshkosh* (1795-1858), Menomini chief⟧ city in E Wis., on Lake Winnebago

o·sier (ō′zhər) *n.* ⟦ME *osiere* < OFr < ML *auseria,* willow⟧ **1** any of various willows (esp. *Salix viminalis* and *S. purpurea*) whose lithe branches or stems are used for baskets and furniture **2** a willow branch used for wickerwork ☆**3** any of several North American dogwoods

O·si·ris (ō sī′ris) *n.* ⟦L < Gr < Egypt *Us-år*⟧ *Egypt. Myth.* the god of the lower world and judge of the dead, brother and husband of Isis

-o·sis (ō′sis) ⟦L < Gr *-ōsis* < *-ō-, -o-,* ending of preceding verbal or substantive stem + *-sis*⟧ *suffix forming nouns* **1** state, condition, action *[hypnosis]* **2** an abnormal or diseased condition *[psychosis, mycosis]* **3** increase or formation *[leukocytosis]*

-os·i·ty (äs′ə tē) ⟦< Fr or L: Fr *-osité* < L *-ositas:* see -OSE[2], -ITY⟧ *suffix forming nouns* the quality of being (as specified): corresponds to -OSE[2], -OUS

OSlav *abbrev.* Old (Church) Slavonic

Os·lo (äz′lō, äs′-; *Norw* oos′loo) seaport & capital of Norway, on an inlet of the Skagerrak

Os·man (äz′män′, äz män′) ⟦Turk *Othman* < Ar *'uthmān*⟧ 1259?-1326; Turk. leader & founder of the Ottoman dynasty

Os·man·li (äz män′lē) *n.* ⟦Turk < prec. + *-li,* adj. particle⟧ **1** *pl.* **-lis** an Ottoman Turk **2** TURKISH —*adj.* OTTOMAN

os·mic (äz′mik, äs′-) *adj.* designating or of chemical compounds in which osmium has a higher valence than in the corresponding osmous compounds

os·mics (äs′miks, äz′-) *n.* ⟦< Gr *osmē,* Attic var. of *odmē,* odor (akin to L *odor,* ODOR) + -ICS⟧ the science dealing with smells and the sense of smell

os·mi·rid·i·um (äs′mə rid′ē əm, äz′-) *n.* ⟦fol. + IRIDIUM⟧ IRIDOSMINE

os·mi·um (äz′mē əm, äs′-) *n.* ⟦ModL: so named (1804) by S. Tennant (1761-1815), Eng chemist < Gr *osmē,* ODOR (from the odor of one of its oxides) + -IUM⟧ a very hard, bluish-white, amorphous, metallic chemical element, one of the platinum metals: it occurs in the form of an alloy with platinum and iridium and is used in pen points, electric light filaments, etc., and as a catalyst: symbol, Os; at. no. 76: see the periodic table of elements in the Reference Supplement

os·mom·e·ter (äs mäm′ət ər, äz-) *n.* ⟦< Gr *ōsmos* (see OSMOSIS) + METER[2]⟧ an instrument for measuring osmotic pressure

os·mose (äs′mōs′, äz′-; äs mōs′, äz-) *vt., vi.* **-mosed′, -mos′ing** ⟦backform. < fol.⟧ to subject to, or undergo, osmosis

os·mo·sis (äs mō′sis, äz-) *n.* ⟦ModL, ult. < Gr *ōsmos,* impulse < *ōthein,* to push < IE base **wedh-,* to push, strike > Sans *vádhar-,* deadly weapon⟧ **1** the tendency of a solvent to pass through a semipermeable membrane, as the wall of a living cell, into a solution of higher concentration, so as to equalize concentrations on both sides of the membrane **2** the diffusion of fluids through a membrane or porous partition **3** an apparently effortless absorption of ideas, feelings, attitudes, etc., as if by biological osmosis —**os·mot′ic** (-mät′ik) *adj.* —**os·mot′i·cal·ly** *adv.*

osmotic pressure the pressure exerted by a solvent passing through a semipermeable membrane in osmosis, equal to the pressure that must be applied to the solution in order to prevent passage of the solvent into it

os·mous (äz′məs, äs′-) *adj.* designating or of chemical compounds in which osmium has a lower valence than in the corresponding osmic compounds

os·mun·da (äs mun′də, äz-) *n.* ⟦ModL < OFr *osmonde* < ?⟧ any of a genus (*Osmunda,* family Osmundaceae) of ferns having specialized fronds or portions of fronds bearing dense masses of spore cases

os·mun·dine (äs mun′din, äz-; -dēn′; äs′mən-, äz′-) *n.* ⟦< prec. + -INE[3]⟧ a fibrous mass of dried fern roots, used as a rooting medium for orchids or other air plants

Os·na·brück (ôs′nä brük′; *E* äz′nə brook′) city in NW Germany, in the state of Lower Saxony

os·na·burg (äz′nə burg′) *n.* ⟦altered after prec., where orig. made⟧ a type of coarse, heavy cloth, originally of linen and now of cotton, used in making sacks, work clothes, etc.

OSp *abbrev.* Old Spanish

os·prey (äs′prē, -prā) *n., pl.* **-preys** ⟦LME *ospray,* ult. < L *ossifraga,* osprey, lit., the bone-breaker < *os,* a bone (see OSSIFY) + *frangere,* to BREAK⟧ a large, black-and-white diving bird of prey of a family (Pandionidae) having only one species (*Pandion haliaetus*): it feeds mainly on fish

OSS *abbrev.* Office of Strategic Services

os·sa (äs′ə) *n.* ⟦L⟧ *pl. of* os[2]

Os·sa (äs′ə) mountain in Thessaly, NE Greece: 6,490 ft (1,978 m): see PELION

os·se·in (äs′ē in) *n.* ⟦< L *osseus,* bony < *os,* a bone (see OSSIFY) + -IN[1]⟧ *Biochem.* the organic basis of bone, the part left after the mineral matter is dissolved in dilute acids

os·se·ous (äs′ē əs) *adj.* ⟦L *osseus* < *os,* a bone: see OSSIFY⟧ composed of, containing, or like bone; bony

Os·set (äs′et′) *n.* a member of a people of Ossetia: also **Os′sete′** (-ēt′) —**Os·se·tian** (ä sē′shən) *adj., n.*

Os·se·tia (ä sē′shə, -shē ə) region in the N Caucasus

Os·set·ic (ä set′ik) *adj.* of the Ossets or their language or culture; Ossetian —*n.* the Iranian language spoken by the Ossets

Os·si·an (äsh′ən, äs′ē ən) *n.* ⟦Gael *Oisīn,* dim. of *os,* a fawn⟧ *Gael. Folklore* a bard and hero of the 3d cent.: James MACPHERSON published pieces of poetic prose (1761-65) which he falsely claimed were his translations of Ossian's poetry from old Gaelic manuscripts —**Os·si·an·ic** (äs′ē an′ik, äsh′-) *adj.*

os·si·cle (äs′i kəl) *n.* ⟦< L *ossiculum,* dim. of *os,* a bone: see OSSIFY⟧ a small bone or bonelike structure; esp., any of the three small bones in the tympanic cavity of the ear —**os·sic·u·lar** (ä sik′yə lər) *adj.,* **os·sic′u·late** (-lit, -lāt′)

Os·si·etz·ky (ôs′ē et′skē), **Carl von** (kärl fôn) 1889-1938; Ger. journalist & pacifist

os·sif·er·ous (ä sif′ər əs) *adj.* ⟦< L *os,* a bone (see OSSIFY) + -FEROUS⟧ containing bones, as a geologic deposit

os·si·frage (äs′ə frij) *n.* ⟦L *ossifraga,* OSPREY⟧ [Archaic] **1** LAMMERGEIER **2** OSPREY

os·si·fy (äs′ə fī′) *vt., vi.* **-fied′, -fy′ing** ⟦< L *os* (gen. *ossis*), a bone (< IE base **ost-* > Sans *ásthi,* Gr *osteon,* bone) + -FY⟧ **1** to change or develop into bone **2** to settle or fix rigidly in a practice, custom, attitude, etc. —**os′si·fi·ca′tion** *n.*

os·so bu·co (ôs′sô bo͞o′kô) ⟦It, marrowbone⟧ an Italian dish consisting of veal shanks stewed in white wine with tomatoes, garlic, minced vegetables, etc.

os·su·ar·y (äs′yo͞o er′ē) ***n.***, *pl.* **-ar′ies** ⟦LL *ossuarium* < *ossuarius,* of or for bones < L *os:* see OSSIFY⟧ a container, as an urn or vault, for the bones of the dead

os·te- (äs′tē) *combining form* OSTEO-: used before a vowel

os·te·al (äs′tē əl) ***adj.*** ⟦< Gr *osteon,* a bone (see OSSIFY) + -AL⟧ osseous; bony

os·te·i·tis (äs′tē īt′is) ***n.*** ⟦OSTE(O)- + -ITIS⟧ inflammation of the bone or bony tissue

os·ten·si·ble (ä sten′sə bəl) ***adj.*** ⟦Fr < ML *ostensibilis* < L *ostendere,* to show < *ob(s)-,* against (see OB-) + *tendere,* to stretch: see THIN⟧ **1** apparent; seeming; professed **2** [Rare] clearly evident —**os·ten′si·bly** ***adv.***

os·ten·sive (ä sten′siv) ***adj.*** ⟦Fr *ostensif* < ML *ostensivus*⟧ **1** directly pointing out; clearly demonstrative **2** OSTENSIBLE (sense 1) —**os·ten′sive·ly** ***adv.***

os·ten·ta·tion (äs′tən tā′shən) ***n.*** ⟦ME *ostentacioun* < L *ostentatio* < *ostentare* < *ostendere:* see OSTENSIBLE⟧ showy display, as of wealth or knowledge; pretentiousness —**os′ten·ta′tious** ***adj.*** —**os′ten·ta′tious·ly** ***adv.*** —**os′ten·ta′tious·ness** ***n.***

os·te·o- (äs′tē ō, -ə) ⟦ModL < Gr *osteon,* a bone: see OSSIFY⟧ *combining form* bone or bones *[osteopathy]*

os·te·o·ar·thri·tis (äs′tē ō är thrīt′is) ***n.*** ⟦prec. + ARTHRITIS⟧ a slowly progressive form of arthritis, found chiefly in older people, characterized by cartilage deterioration and bone enlargement

os·te·o·blast (äs′tē ō blast′) ***n.*** ⟦OSTEO- + -BLAST⟧ any cell which develops into bone or secretes substances producing bony tissue —**os′te·o·blas′tic** ***adj.***

os·te·oc·la·sis (äs′tē äk′lə sis) ***n.*** ⟦ModL < OSTEO- + Gr *klasis,* a breaking < *klan,* to break: see CLASTIC⟧ **1** the breaking down and absorption of bony tissue **2** the breaking of a bone to correct a deformity, esp. after a badly healed previous fracture

os·te·o·clast (äs′tē ō klast′) ***n.*** ⟦< OSTEO- + Gr *klastos:* see CLASTIC⟧ **1** any of the large multinucleate cells in bone which absorb or break down bony tissue **2** an instrument used to perform osteoclasis

os·te·o·cyte (äs′tē ō sīt′) ***n.*** any of the branched cells in the tiny cavities of bone, that are involved in the formation of bone

os·te·o·gen·e·sis im·per·fec·ta (äs′tē ō jen′ə sis im′pər fek′tə) ⟦ModL < *osteogenesis,* formation of bone (< OSTEO- + -GENESIS) + L *imperfecta,* fem. of *imperfectus,* IMPERFECT⟧ a rare hereditary disorder of connective tissue, characterized by thin, brittle bones and progressive deafness

os·te·o·gen·ic sarcoma (äs′tē ō jen′ik) OSTEOSARCOMA

os·te·oid (äs′tē oid′) ***adj.*** ⟦OSTE(O)- + -OID⟧ like bone

os·te·ol·o·gy (äs′tē äl′ə jē) ***n.*** ⟦ModL: see OSTEO- & -LOGY⟧ the study of the structure and function of bones —**os′te·o·log′i·cal** (-ō läj′i kəl) ***adj.*** —**os′te·ol′o·gist** ***n.***

os·te·o·ma (äs′tē ō′mə) ***n.***, *pl.* **-mas** or **-ma·ta** (-mə tə) ⟦ModL: see OSTEO- & -OMA⟧ a tumor composed of bony tissue

os·te·o·ma·la·ci·a (äs′tē ō mə lā′shə, -shē ə) ***n.*** ⟦ModL < OSTEO- + *malacia,* a softening of tissue < Gr *malakia,* softness < *malakos,* soft: see MALACO-⟧ a bone disease characterized by a softening of the bones, resulting from deficient bone calcification

os·te·o·my·e·li·tis (-mī′ə līt′is) ***n.*** ⟦ModL: see OSTEO- & MYELITIS⟧ infection of bone marrow or bone structures, usually caused by a bacterium (genus *Staphylococcus*) that produces pus

☆**os·te·o·path** (äs′tē ə path′) ***n.*** a doctor who practices osteopathy

☆**os·te·op·a·thy** (äs′tē äp′ə thē) ***n.*** ⟦ModL: see OSTEO- & -PATHY⟧ a school of medicine and surgery employing various methods of diagnosis and treatment, but placing special emphasis on the interrelationship of the musculo-skeletal system to all other bodily systems —**os′te·o·path′ic** (-ə path′ik) ***adj.*** —**os′te·o·path′i·cal·ly** ***adv.***

os·te·o·phyte (äs′tē ō fīt′) ***n.*** ⟦OSTEO- + -PHYTE⟧ a small bony outgrowth —**os′te·o·phyt′ic** (-fit′ik) ***adj.***

os·te·o·plas·tic (äs′tē ō plas′tik) ***adj.*** ⟦OSTEO- + -PLASTIC⟧ **1** *Anat.* of or pertaining to bone formation **2** *Surgery* of or based on the replacement of bone by restorative operations —**os′te·o·plas′ty** ***n.***

os·te·o·po·ro·sis (-pə rō′sis) ***n.*** ⟦ModL < OSTEO- + *porosis,* a porous condition < L *porus,* a PORE[2] + -OSIS⟧ a bone disorder characterized by a reduction in bone density accompanied by increasing porosity and brittleness, found chiefly in women who have passed menopause

os·te·o·sar·co·ma (äs′tē ō sär kō′mə) ***n.***, *pl.* **-mas** or **-ma·ta** (-mə tə) a common type of sarcoma of the bone characterized by rapid spreading, esp. to the lungs, and pain, swelling, etc. in the large, long bones

os·te·o·sis (äs′tē ō′sis) ***n.*** ⟦ModL: see OSTEO- & -OSIS⟧ the formation of bone

os·te·o·tome (äs′tē ō tōm′) ***n.*** ⟦OSTEO- + -TOME⟧ a surgical instrument for cutting or dividing bone

os·te·ot·o·my (äs′tē ät′ə mē) ***n.***, *pl.* **-mies** ⟦OSTEO- + -TOMY⟧ the surgical operation of dividing a bone or cutting out a piece of bone

Ös·ter·reich (ös′tər rīH′) *Ger. name for* AUSTRIA

Os·ti·a (äs′tē ə) ancient city in Latium, at the mouth of the Tiber, that was the port of Rome

Os·ti·ak (äs′tē ak′) ***n.*** *alt. sp. of* OSTYAK

os·ti·ar·y (äs′tē er′ē) ***n.***, *pl.* **-ar′ies** ⟦L *ostiarius* < *ostium,* door, entrance < *os,* mouth: see ORAL⟧ PORTER[1]

os·ti·na·to (äs′tə nät′ō; *It* ôs′tē nä′tô) ***n.***, *pl.* **-tos′** (-ōz′; *It,* -tôs) or **-ti** (-tē) ⟦It, lit., obstinate⟧ *Music* a short melodic phrase persistently repeated by the same voice or instrument and at the same pitch

os·ti·ole (äs′tē ōl′) ***n.*** ⟦< ModL *ostiolum* < L, dim. of *ostium:* see OSTIARY⟧ a small opening or orifice, as a pore —**os·ti·o·lar** (äs′tē ə lər) ***adj.***

os·ti·um (äs′tē əm) ***n.***, *pl.* **-ti·a** (-ə) ⟦L *ostium:* see OSTIARY⟧ *Anat.* an opening or orifice

os·tler (äs′lər) ***n.*** ⟦ME *osterlere,* var. of *hostelere:* see HOSTLER⟧ *var. of* HOSTLER (sense 1)

os·to·mate (äs′tə māt′) ***n.*** ⟦< fol. + -ATE[2]⟧ a person who has had an ostomy

os·to·my (äs′tə mē) ***n.***, *pl.* **-mies** ⟦prob. back-form. < COLOSTOMY⟧ any surgery connecting a hollow organ to the outside of the body or to another hollow organ, as a colostomy

os·to·sis (äs tō′sis) ***n.*** OSTEOSIS

os·tra·cism (äs′trə siz′əm) ***n.*** ⟦Gr *ostrakismos* < *ostrakizein:* see fol.⟧ **1** in ancient Greece, the temporary banishment of a citizen by popular vote **2** a rejection or exclusion by general consent, as from a group or from acceptance by society

os·tra·cize (äs′trə sīz′) ***vt.*** **-cized′**, **-ciz′ing** ⟦Gr *ostrakizein,* to exile by votes written on tiles or potsherds < *ostrakon,* a shell, potsherd, akin to *osteon,* bone: see OSSIFY⟧ to banish, bar, exclude, etc. by ostracism —***SYN.*** BANISH

os·tra·cod (äs′trə käd′) ***n.*** ⟦< ModL *Ostracoda* < Gr *ostrakon:* see prec.⟧ any of various classes (esp. Ostracoda) of small, freshwater or marine crustaceans, having a bivalve carapace that covers the entire body

os·tra·con (äs′trə kän′) ***n.***, *pl.* **-ca** (-kə) ⟦< Gr *ostrakon,* potsherd⟧ *Archaeol.* a potsherd used in ancient times for writing on, esp., one that preserves ancient writing and survives as an archaeological artifact: *often used in pl.*: also **os′tra·kon′** (-kän′), *pl.* **-ka** (-kə)

Os·tra·va (ôs′trä vä) city in the NE Czech Republic

os·trich (äs′trich, ôs′-) ***n.***, *pl.* **-trich·es** or **-trich** ⟦OFr *ostrusce* < VL *avistruthius* < L *avis,* bird + *struthio,* short for *struthiocamelus,* ostrich < Gr *strouthiokamēlos* < *strouthos,* sparrow + *kamēlos,* CAMEL⟧ **1** a swift-running bird (*Struthio camelus*) of Africa and SW Asia, the only member of its order (Struthioniformes): it is the largest and most powerful of living birds, and has a long neck, very long legs with two toes on each foot, and small, useless wings: the white tail and wing feathers of the male are used in millinery and as trimming **2** ⟦from the erroneous belief that an ostrich buries its head in the sand when in danger⟧ a person who tries to avoid difficult or dangerous situations by refusing to confront them

Os·tro·goth (äs′trə gäth′, -gôth′) ***n.*** ⟦LL *Ostrogothus,* earlier *Austrogoti* (pl.) < Gmc **austra-,* EAST + LL *Gothi:* see GOTH[1]⟧ an East Goth; esp., a member of the group that conquered Italy in the 5th cent. A.D. —**Os′tro·goth′ic** ***adj.***

Ost·wald (ōst′vält), **Fried·rich Wil·helm** (frē′driH vil′helm) 1853-1932; Ger. chemist, born in Latvia

Os·ty·ak (äs′tē ak′) ***n.*** **1** a member of a Finno-Ugric people living in W Siberia **2** the Ugric language of this people

Os·wald (äz′wəld, -wôld′) ***n.*** ⟦OE *Osweald* < *os,* a god + *weald,* power: for IE base see WIELD⟧ a masculine name: dim. *Ozzie*

☆**Os·we·go tea** (äs wē′gō) ⟦after the *Oswego* River, in New York⟧ **1** a North American mint (*Monarda didyma*) with dense terminal heads of brilliant-red flowers **2** the tea brewed from its leaves

Oś·wię·cim (ôsh vyan′tsim) *Pol. name for* AUSCHWITZ

OT *abbrev.* **1** occupational therapy **2** *Football* offensive tackle **3** Old Testament **4** overtime Also, for 2 & 4, **ot**

ot- (ōt) *combining form* OTO-: used before a vowel

o·tal·gi·a (ō tal′jē ə, -jə) ***n.*** ⟦ModL < Gr *ōtalgia:* see OTO- & -ALGIA⟧ an earache; pain in the ear

O·ta·ru (ō tä′ro͞o) seaport on the W coast of Hokkaido, Japan

OTB *abbrev.* off-track betting

OTC *abbrev.* over-the-counter

OTEC *abbrev.* ocean thermal energy conversion: a solar energy conversion system for producing electricity, using warm and cold ocean layers to vaporize and condense a fluid that drives a turbine

O tem·po·ra! O mo·res! (ō tem′pə rə ō môr′āz′) ⟦L⟧ oh, the times! oh, the customs!: a quotation from Cicero

O·thel·lo (ō thel′ō) ***n.*** **1** a tragedy (1604?) by Shakespeare **2** its title character, a noble Moor, who, made madly jealous by the villainous Iago, kills his faithful and loving wife, Desdemona

oth·er (uth′ər) ***adj.*** ⟦ME < OE, akin to Ger *ander,* Goth *anthar* < IE **anteros,* the other of two (< base **an,* there + compar. suffix) > Sans *ántara-*⟧ **1** being the remaining one or ones of two or more *[*Bill and the *other* boys*]* **2** different or distinct from that or those referred to or implied *[*use your *other* foot, not Jane but some *other* girl*]* **3** different in nature or kind *[*it is *other* than you think*]* **4** further or additional *[*to have no *other* coat*]* **5** former *[*the customs of *other* times*]* —***pron.*** **1** the other one *[*each loved the *other]* **2** another or some other person or thing *[*to do as *others* do*]* —***n.*** the opposite *[*hate is the *other* of love*]* —***adv.*** otherwise; differently *[*he can't do *other* than go*]* —**of all others** above all others —**the Other** *[also* **the o-***]* a person, group, or entity perceived as being the opposite of or alien to oneself or one's group —**the other day** (or **night, afternoon,** etc.) on a recent day (or night, afternoon, etc.) —**somehow** (or **somewhere, sometime, something,** etc.) **or other** some unspecified or unknown way (or place, time, thing, etc.) *[somehow or other,* we'll raise the money*]*

☆**oth·er-di·rect·ed** (uth′ər də rek′tid) ***adj.*** guided by or concerned with goals or ideals determined by others rather than by oneself; conformist

oth·er·guess (uth′ər ges′) *adj.* ⟦var. of dial. *othergates,* otherwise⟧ [Obs.] of another kind; different

other half 1 a socioeconomic group other than one's own, esp. a wealthier one: with *the* 2 [Informal, Chiefly Brit.] one's spouse

oth·er·ness (uth′ər nis) *n.* the state or quality of being regarded as different, esp. different in an unfamiliar or unfavorable way, from oneself, one's ethnic group, one's country, etc.

oth·er·where (-hwer′, -wer′) *adv.* [Archaic] in or to another place; elsewhere

oth·er·while (-hwīl′, -wīl′) *adv.* [Now Chiefly Dial.] at some other time or times: also **oth′er·whiles′**

oth·er·wise (uth′ər wīz′) *adv.* ⟦ME *othre wise* < OE *on othre wisan:* see WISE[2]⟧ 1 in another manner; differently [to believe *otherwise*] 2 in all other points or respects [an *otherwise* intelligent person] 3 in other circumstances 4 if not: used as a conjunctive adverb [do it right; *otherwise,* you'll have to do it over] —*adj.* in another condition; different [the answer could not be *otherwise*]

other woman, the [*sometimes* **the O- W-**] the woman in an adulterous relationship with a married man

other world 1 a world believed to exist after or beyond death 2 an ideal or imagined world

oth·er·world·ly (uth′ər wurld′lē) *adj.* being apart from material or earthly interests; spiritual or concerned with life in a future or imaginary world —**oth′er·world′li·ness** *n.*

O·thin (ō′thin) *n. var. of* ODIN

Oth·man (äth′män′, äth män′) *var. of* OSMAN

o·tic (ōt′ik, ät′-) *adj.* ⟦Gr *ōtikos* < *ous* (gen. *ōtos*), EAR[1]⟧ of or connected with the ear

-ot·ic (ät′ik) ⟦Gr *-ōtikos*⟧ *suffix forming adjectives* 1 of or affected with [*neurotic*] 2 producing

o·ti·ose (ō′shē ōs′, ōt′ē-) *adj.* ⟦L *otiosus* < *otium,* leisure⟧ 1 [Rare] idle; indolent 2 ineffective; futile 3 useless; superfluous —***SYN.*** VAIN —**o′ti·ose′ly** *adv.* —**o′ti·os′i·ty** (-äs′ə tē) *n.*

O·tis[1] (ōt′is) *n.* ⟦orig. a surname: popularized as a given name in honor of fol.⟧ a masculine name

O·tis[2] (ōt′is), **James** 1725-83; Am. Revolutionary statesman

o·ti·tis (ō tīt′is) *n.* ⟦ModL: see fol. & -ITIS⟧ inflammation of the ear; esp., inflammation (**otitis media**) of the middle ear

o·to- (ōt′ō, -ə) ⟦< Gr *ous,* (gen. *ōtos*), EAR[1]⟧ *combining form* 1 ear [*otoscope*] 2 ear and [*otolaryngology*]

o·to·cyst (ōt′ō sist′) *n.* ⟦prec. + -CYST⟧ 1 *Embryology* the hollow chamber of ectoderm that develops into the vertebrate inner ear 2 *Zool.* STATOCYST (sense 2) —**o′to·cys′tic** *adj.*

o·to·lar·yn·gol·o·gy (ōt′ō lar′iŋ gäl′ə jē) *n.* ⟦OTO- + LARYNGOLOGY⟧ the branch or practice of medicine dealing with disorders of the ear, nose, and throat —**o′to·lar′yn·gol′o·gist** *n.*

o·to·lith (ōt′ō lith′) *n.* ⟦OTO- + -LITH⟧ 1 a tiny, bonelike particle or stony, platelike structure in the internal ear of lower vertebrates 2 a similar calcareous concretion in the statocyst of many invertebrates —**o′to·lith′ic** *adj.*

☆**o·tol·o·gy** (ō täl′ə jē) *n.* ⟦OTO- + -LOGY⟧ the branch of medicine dealing with the ear and its disorders —**o·to·log·i·cal** (ōt′ō läj′i kəl) *adj.* —**o·tol′o·gist** *n.*

o·to·rhi·no·lar·yn·gol·o·gy (ōt′ō rī′nō lar′iŋ gäl′ə jē) *n.* OTOLARYNGOLOGY

o·to·scle·ro·sis (ōt′ō skli rō′sis) *n.* ⟦OTO- + SCLEROSIS⟧ a growth of spongy bone in the inner ear, causing progressive deafness —**o′to·scle·rot′ic** (-skli rät′ik) *adj.*

o·to·scope (ōt′ə skōp′) *n.* ⟦OTO- + -SCOPE⟧ an instrument for examining the tympanic membrane and external canal of the ear

O·tran·to (ō trän′tō; *It* ô trän′tô), **Strait of** strait between Albania & Italy, connecting the Adriatic & Ionian seas: *c.* 45 mi (72 km) wide

ot·ta·va (ô tä′vä) *adj., adv.* ⟦It⟧ *Musical Direction* ALL'OTTAVA

ot·ta·va ri·ma (ō tä′və rē′mə) ⟦It: see OCTAVE & RHYME⟧ a stanza of eight lines with the rhyme scheme *abababcc:* the Italian form has eleven syllables in a line, the English, usually ten syllables in iambic pentameter

Ot·ta·wa[1] (ät′ə wə, -wä′, -wô′) *n.* ⟦Fr *Outaouois* < Ojibwa *odaawaa*⟧ 1 *pl.* **-was** or **-wa** a member of a North American Indian people of Manitoulin Island and, at various times in the past, other scattered locations south of the upper Great Lakes 2 the Algonquian language of this people, a dialect of Ojibwa, also spoken by some groups known as Ojibwa —*adj.* of the Ottawas or their language or culture

Ot·ta·wa[2] (ät′ə wə, -wä′, -wô′) ⟦after prec.⟧ 1 river in SE Canada, forming the border between Ontario & Quebec, flowing southeast into the St. Lawrence: 696 mi (1,120 km) 2 capital of Canada, in SE Ontario, on the Ottawa River

ot·ter (ät′ər) *n., pl.* **-ters** or **-ter** ⟦ME *oter* < OE, akin to ON *otr* < IE **udros,* a water animal (> Sans *udrá-ḥ*) < base **wed-,* to make wet > WATER⟧ 1 any of various furry carnivores (family Mustelidae) with webbed feet used in swimming and a long, slightly flattened tail; esp., *a)* a North American river species (*Lutra canadensis*) *b)* SEA OTTER 2 the short, thick, lustrous fur of this animal

ot·ter·hound (ät′ər hound′) *n.* any of a breed of large, rough-coated hound with a keen sense of smell, formerly much used in hunting otters: also written **otter hound**

ot·to (ät′ō) *n.* ATTAR

Ot·to (ät′ō) *n.* ⟦OHG *Otho, Odo* < *auda,* rich⟧ a masculine name

Otto I A.D. 912-973; king of Germany (936-973) & emperor of the Holy Roman Empire (962-973): called *the Great*

Ot·to·man (ät′ə mən) *adj.* ⟦Fr < It *Ottomano* < ML *Ottomanus* < Ar *ʿuthmānī,* adj. form of *ʿuthmān,* OSMAN⟧ 1 Turkish 2 of the Ottoman Empire —*n., pl.* **-mans** 1 a Turk belonging to the tribe or family of Osman; Othman 2 ⟦Fr *ottomane* < fem. of adj.⟧ [**o-**] *a)* a low, cushioned seat without a back or arms *b)* a kind of couch or divan, with or without a back *c)* a low, cushioned footstool *d)* a corded fabric of silk, rayon, etc., with wide, flat ribs

Ottoman Empire empire (*c.* 1300-1918) of the Turks, including at its peak much of SE Europe, SW Asia, & NE Africa: cap. (after 1453) Constantinople

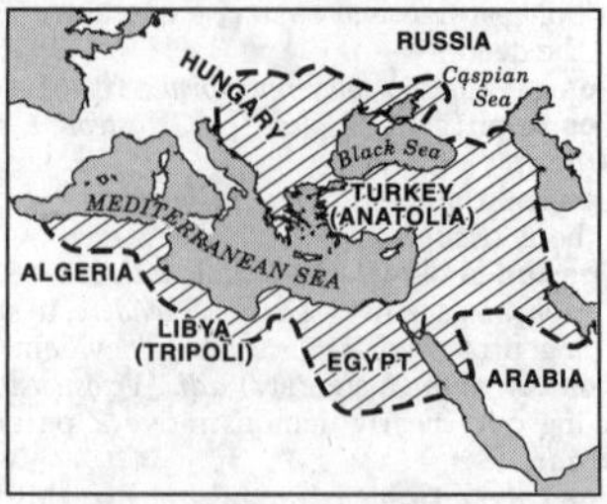

Ottoman Empire (16th cent.)

Ötz·tal Alps (öts′täl) division of the E Alps, along the Austrian-Italian border: highest peak, 12,379 ft (3,773 m)

oua·ba·in (wä bā′in) *n.* ⟦Fr *ouabaine* < *ouabaio,* name of an African tree, source of the substance (< Somali *waabayyo,* arrow poison) + -INE[3]⟧ a poisonous glycoside, $C_{29}H_{44}O_{12}·8H_2O$, made chiefly from the seeds of an African plant (*Strophanthus gratus*) of the dogbane family: it is used in medicine as a substitute for digitalis

Ouach·i·ta (wäsh′i tô, wôsh′-) ⟦< Fr < ?⟧ river flowing from W Ark. southeast & south into the Red River in La.: 605 mi (974 km)

Oua·ga·dou·gou (wä′gə do͞o′go͞o) capital of Burkina Faso, in the central part

oua·na·niche (wä′nä nēsh′) *n., pl.* **-niche′** ⟦CdnFr < Montagnais **wanaʼniš:* cf. *onán,* ouananiche & -ISH, dim. suffix⟧ a small, landlocked salmon of SE Canada

ou·bli·ette (o͞o′blē et′) *n.* ⟦Fr < *oublier,* to forget < VL **oblitare* < pp. of L *oblivisci,* to forget: see OBLIVION⟧ a concealed dungeon having a trap door in the ceiling as its only opening

☆**ouch**[1] (ouch) *interj.* used to express sudden pain

ouch[2] (ouch) *n.* ⟦< ME *(a n)ouche* < OFr *nousche* < Frank **nuskja,* brooch, akin to OHG *nusca,* a clasp < IE base **ned-,* to twist together > NET[1]⟧ 1 a clasp or buckle; specif., an ornament with a clasp, esp. when set with precious stones 2 a setting for a precious stone —*vt.* [Archaic] to ornament as with ouches

oud (o͝od, o͞od) *n.* ⟦Ar *ʿūd,* orig., wood, hence wooden instrument; akin to LUTE[1]⟧ a stringed instrument of the Middle East and N Africa, like a lute

ought[1] (ôt) *v.aux.* used with infinitives and meaning: 1 to be compelled by obligation or duty [he *ought* to pay his debts] 2 to be bound by what is advisable or wise [I *ought* to wear a warmer coat today] 3 to be desirable [you *ought* to meet us for dinner sometime] 4 to be expected or likely [it *ought* to be over soon] Past time is expressed by combining *ought* with the perfect infinitive of the verb being used [I *ought* to have told you] —*n.* ⟦orig., pt. of OWE: ME *aughte* < OE *ahte,* pp. of *agan,* OWE⟧ obligation or duty

ought[2] (ôt) *n.* ⟦var. of AUGHT⟧ anything whatever; aught —*adv.* [Archaic] to any degree; at all; aught

ought[3] (ôt) *n.* ⟦< *(a n)ought*⟧ a nought; the figure zero (0)

ought·n't (ôt′'nt) *contraction* ought not

ou·gui·ya (o͞o gē′ä) *n., pl.* **-ya** ⟦< Ar *ūqīya,* a unit of counting⟧ the basic monetary unit of Mauritania: see the table of monetary units in the Reference Supplement

oui (wē) *adv., interj.* ⟦Fr⟧ yes

☆**Oui·ja** (wē′jə, -jē) ⟦< Fr *oui,* yes + Ger *ja,* yes⟧ *trademark for* a board bearing the alphabet and various symbols, with a planchette that is moved by the fingers to spell out messages, an action believed by some people to be under the direction of spirits

Ouj·da (o͞oj dä′) city in NE Morocco

ounce[1] (ouns) *n.* ⟦OFr *unce* < L *uncia,* a twelfth, twelfth part of a foot or pound, orig., unit, akin to L *unus,* ONE⟧ 1 *a)* a unit of weight, equal to 1/16 pound avoirdupois or 16 drams (28.3495 grams) *b)* a unit of weight, equal to 1/12 pound troy or 20 pennyweights (31.1035 grams) *c)* a unit of weight, equal to 1/12 pound apothecaries' weight or 8 drams (31.1035 grams) *d)* FLUID OUNCE: symbol for all preceding senses, oz 2 any small amount [an *ounce* of prevention]

ounce[2] (ouns) *n.* ⟦ME *once* < OFr < *l'once,* mistaken for *lonce* < VL **luncea* < L *lynx,* LYNX⟧ SNOW LEOPARD

our (our) ***possessive pronominal adj.*** ⟦ME *ure* < OE *ure,* earlier *user,* gen. of *us* (see US), akin to Ger *unser*⟧ of, belonging to, made by, or done by us

ou·ra·ri (o͞o rä′rē) *n.* ⟦var. of CURARE⟧ CURARE

Our Father LORD'S PRAYER

Our Lady Mary, the mother of Jesus; the Virgin Mary

ours (ourz) *pron.* ⟦ME *ures* < *ure,* OUR + gen. *-s,* hence, in form, a double poss.⟧ that or those belonging to us: the possessive form of WE, used without a following noun, often after *of* [this house is *ours; ours* are better; she is a friend of *ours*]

our·self (our self′) *pron.* a form corresponding to OURSELVES, used, as in royal proclamations, by one person who refers to himself or herself as "we": see WE (sense 2)

our·selves (-selvz′) *pron.* ⟦LME *ure selves,* for Midland *ure selven,* replacing *us selven,* lit., us selves] a form of WE, used: *a)* as an intensifier [we *ourselves* saw it] *b)* as a reflexive [we hurt *ourselves*] *c)* with the meaning "our real, true, or normal selves" [we are not *ourselves* when we are upset] (in this construction *our* functions as an adjective and *selves* as a noun, and they may be separated [*our* own sweet *selves*])

USAGE—now sometimes used as a subject or a nonreflexive object in certain contexts [they are younger than *ourselves*]

-ous (əs) [ME < L *-us* & OFr *-ous, -eus,* < L *-osus*] *suffix forming adjectives* **1** having, full of, characterized by [*beauteous, capacious*] **2** *Chem.* having a lower valence than is indicated by the suffix -IC [*mercurous*]

Ouse (o͞oz) **1** river in E England, flowing north into The Wash: 156 mi (251 km): also **Great Ouse** **2** river in N England, joining the Trent to form the Humber: 60 mi (97 km)

ou·sel (o͞o′zəl) ***n.*** *alt. sp. of* OUZEL

oust (oust) ***vt.*** [Anglo-Fr *ouster* < OFr (Fr *ôter*) < L *ostare,* to obstruct < *ob-,* against (see OB-) + *stare,* to STAND] to force or drive out; expel, dispossess, eject, etc. —***SYN.*** EJECT

oust·er (ous′tər) ***n.*** [Anglo-Fr, inf. used as n.: see prec.] **1** a person or thing that ousts **2** *Law* an ousting or being ousted, esp. from real property; legal eviction or unlawful dispossession **3** any expulsion or dismissal

out (out) ***adv.*** [ME < OE *ut,* akin to ON *út,* Ger *aus* < IE base **ud-,* up, up away > Sans *úd-,* L *us(que)*] **1** *a)* away from, forth from, or removed from a place, position, or situation [they live ten miles *out*] *b)* away from home [to go *out* for dinner] *c)* away from shore *d)* on strike **2** into or in the open air [come *out* and play] **3** into or in existence or activity [disease broke *out*] **4** *a)* to a conclusion or result [argue it *out*] *b)* completely, fully, or to the point of exhaustion [tired *out,* dry *out*] *c)* in full bloom, or in leaf **5** into sight or notice [the moon came *out*] **6** *a)* into or in circulation [to put *out* a new style] *b)* into or in society [debutantes who come *out*] **7** *a)* from existence, operation, or activity [fade *out,* burn *out,* die *out*] *b)* away from one's work or usual activity [take time *out* from one's busy day] **8** so as to remove from power or office [vote them *out*] **9** forcefully; aloud [sing *out,* speak *out*] **10** beyond a regular or normal surface, condition, or position [stand *out,* eke *out,* lengthen *out*] **11** away from the interior, center, or midst [spread *out,* reach *out,* branch *out*]: sometimes implying sharing or dividing [deal *out,* sort *out*] **12** from one state, as of composure, harmony, or agreement, into another, as of annoyance, discord, or disagreement [to feel put *out;* friends may fall *out*] **13** into or in disuse, discard, or obsolescence [long skirts went *out*] **14** from a number, group, or stock [pick *out*] **15** [Slang] into or in unconsciousness [to pass *out*] **16** *Baseball* in a manner that results in an out [to fly *out*] —***adj.*** **1** external: usually in comb. [*outpost, outfield*] **2** beyond regular limits **3** outlying; remote **4** going or directed outward [an *out* flight] **5** away from work, school, etc. [*out* because of sickness] **6** bared because of torn clothing, etc. [*out* at the elbow] **7** deviating from what is accurate or right [*out* in one's estimates] **8** *a)* not in effective use, operation, etc. *b)* turned off; extinguished **9** not to be considered; not possible ☆**10** trying or determined: followed by an infinitive [he's *out* to humiliate me] **11** in disagreement; at variance **12** that is not successful or in power **13** deliberating in order to reach a verdict [the jury is still *out*] ☆**14** [Informal] having suffered a financial loss [*out* fifty dollars] **15** [Informal] no longer popular, fashionable, etc.; outmoded **16** [Informal] publicly identified as being homosexual **17** *Baseball* failing or having failed to get on base —***prep.*** **1** out of; through to the outside [he walked *out* the door] **2** along, and away from a central location or some other point of departure [to drive *out* a country road] **3** [Old Poet.] forth from: usually preceded by the preposition *from* used without a distinct meaning or syntactic function [a rousing cry from *out* the trumpet's throat] —***n.*** **1** something that is out **2** a person, group, etc. that is not in power, in office, or in a favored position: *usually used in pl.* ☆**3** [Slang] a way out; means of avoiding something; excuse ☆**4** *Baseball* the failure of a batter or runner to reach base safely ☆**5** *Printing a)* the omission of a word or words *b)* the word or words omitted **6** *Racket Sports* a service or return that lands out of bounds —***vi.*** to come out; esp., to become known [the truth will *out*] —***vt.*** **1** [Now Chiefly Dial.] to put out ☆**2** [Informal] *a)* to identify publicly as a homosexual (a person not previously so identified) *b)* to otherwise publicly reveal information about (someone) that has been kept private or secret [a press story that *outs* an undercover agent] —***interj.*** **1** get out; go away; begone **2** communication completed: term used in radio communication —**go out** *Golf* to play the first nine holes of an 18-hole golf course —**on the outs** [Informal] on unfriendly terms: also, esp. formerly, **at outs** —**out and about** visiting here and there —**out and away** by far; without comparison —**out and out** completely; thoroughly —☆**out for** determined to get or do —**out from under** [Informal] away from difficulty or danger —**out of** **1** from inside of **2** from the number of **3** past the boundaries or scope of; beyond **4** from (material, etc.) [made *out of* stone] **5** because of; for the purpose of [*out of* spite, to make conversation *out of* politeness] **6** given birth by: said of animals **7** not in possession of; having no [*out of* money, *out of* gas] **8** not in a condition [*out of* order, *out of* focus] **9** so as to deprive or be deprived of [cheat *out of* money] —**out of it** [Slang] **1** not sophisticated, fashionable, etc.; not hip, with-it, etc. **2** in a diminished or impaired mental state; specif., confused, intoxicated, unconscious, etc. —**out one's way** [Informal] in, to, or near one's neighborhood —☆**out on one's feet** **1** dazed or stunned, but still standing: said esp. of a boxer **2** completely exhausted —**out there** **1** [Informal] available or in existence [there are lots of good colleges *out there*] **2** [Slang] odd, eccentric, etc. —**out with it!** speak! say what is on your mind!

out- (out) [< prec.] *combining form* **1** situated at or coming from a point away, outside, external [*outbuilding, outpatient*] **2** going away or forth, outward [*outbound*] **3** better, greater, or more than: used to form verbs from verbs, adjectives, or certain nouns naming persons, actors, or agents [*outdo, outsell, outsmart, outgeneral, out-*Herod]: a frequent usage in such self-explanatory terms as the following:

outact	**outleap**
outargue	**outmarch**
outbluff	**outperform**
outboast	**outpitch**
outbox	**outproduce**
outbrag	**outquote**
outclimb	**outrace**
outdance	**outscore**
outdrink	**outshout**
outeat	**outspend**
outfight	**outswim**
outhit	**outwalk**

☆**out·age** (out′ij) ***n.*** [OUT + -AGE] **1** an interruption or suspension **2** a temporary loss of electric power

out-and-out (out′n out′) ***adj.*** complete; thorough

out·back¹ (out′bak′) ***n.*** [after fol.] any remote, sparsely settled region thought of as uncivilized —***adj.*** of such a region

out·back² (out′bak′) [*also* **O-**] the sparsely settled, flat, arid inland region of Australia: usually with *the*

out·bal·ance (out′bal′əns) ***vt.*** **-anced, -anc·ing** to be greater than in weight, value, etc.

out·bid (-bid′) ***vt.*** **-bid′, -bid′ding** to bid or offer more than (someone else)

out·board (out′bôrd′) ***adj., adv.*** **1** outside the hull or bulwarks of, or toward the side of, a ship or boat ☆**2** away from or farther from the hull or fuselage of an aircraft ☆**3** outside the main body of a spacecraft —☆***n.*** **1** OUTBOARD MOTOR **2** a boat with an outboard motor

☆**outboard motor** a portable gasoline engine with a propeller, mounted outboard on the stern of a boat to propel it

out·bound (-bound′) ***adj.*** outward bound

out·brave (out′brāv′) ***vt.*** **-braved′, -brav′ing** **1** to surpass in bravery **2** to face defiantly

out·break (out′brāk′) ***n.*** **1** a breaking out; sudden occurrence, as of disease or war **2** an insurrection or riot

out·breed·ing (-brēd′iŋ) ***n.*** **1** the breeding of stocks or individuals that are not closely related **2** *Anthrop.* a marrying outside one's social group —**out′breed′** ***vt., vi.*** **-bred′, -breed′ing**

out·build·ing (-bil′diŋ) ***n.*** a structure, as a shed or stable, separate from the house or main building

out·burst (out′burst′) ***n.*** a sudden release, as of feeling, energy, noise, etc.

out·cast (out′kast′) ***adj.*** driven out; rejected —***n.*** a person or thing cast out or rejected, as by society

out·caste (out′kast′) ***n.*** in India, a person expelled from his or her caste, or one who belongs to no caste

out·class (out′klas′) ***vt.*** to surpass in excellence by a wide margin

out·come (out′kum′) ***n.*** [ME *utcome*] the way something turns out; result; consequence —***SYN.*** EFFECT

out·crop (out′kräp′; *for v.* out′kräp′) ***n.*** **1** a breaking forth; specif., the emergence of a mineral from the earth so as to be exposed on the surface [an *outcrop* of a vein of coal] **2** any rock formation exposed on the surface or, sometimes, covered by a thin layer of soil, gravel, etc. —***vi.*** **-cropped′, -crop′ping** **1** to emerge from the earth in this way **2** to break forth

out·crop·ping (out′kräp′iŋ) ***n.*** OUTCROP (***n.*** 2)

☆**out·cross** (out′krôs′) ***vt.*** to subject to outcrossing —***n.*** an individual produced by outcrossing

out·cross·ing (-krôs′iŋ) ***n.*** OUTBREEDING (sense 1)

out·cry (-krī′) ***n., pl.*** **-cries′** **1** a crying out **2** a strong objection

☆**out·curve** (-kurv′) ***n.*** *Baseball former term for* CURVE

out·dat·ed (out′dāt′id) ***adj.*** no longer current or popular; behind the times; antiquated

out·dis·tance (out′dis′təns) ***vt.*** **-tanced, -tanc·ing** to leave behind or get ahead of, as in a race

out·do (out′do͞o′) ***vt.*** **-did′, -done′, -do′ing** to exceed or surpass —***SYN.*** EXCEL —**outdo oneself** **1** to do something better than one ever did before or thought one could do **2** to make a supreme effort

out·door (out′dôr′) ***adj.*** **1** being or taking place outdoors **2** of, relating to, or fond of the outdoors

☆**out·doors** (out′dôrz′) ***adv.*** in or into the open; outside a building or shelter —***n.*** **1** any area or place outside a building or shelter **2** countryside, forests, etc. where there are few or no houses: usually with *the*

out·doors·man (out′dôrz′mən) ***n., pl.*** **-men** (-mən) a man who spends much time in the outdoors, as in camping, hunting, or fishing

out·doors·wom·an (out′dôrz′woom′ən) ***n., pl.*** **-wom′en** (-wim′in) a woman who spends much time in the outdoors, as in camping, hunting, or fishing

out·door·sy (out′dôr′zē) ***adj.*** [Informal] of, characteristic of, or fond of the outdoors or outdoor activities

out·er (out′ər) ***adj.*** [ME *outter;* new form < *out* + *-er,* replacing *uttere,* UTTER¹] **1** located farther without; exterior; external **2** relatively far out or far removed [the *outer* regions]

Outer Banks chain of long, narrow, sandy islands, along the coast of N.C.

out·er·coat (out′ər kōt′) ***n.*** a topcoat, overcoat, etc.
outer ear EXTERNAL EAR
Outer Hebrides *see* HEBRIDES, WESTERN ISLES
Outer Mongolia *former name for* MONGOLIA (the country): term used to distinguish from INNER MONGOLIA
out·er·most (out′ər mōst′) ***adj.*** located farthest without
outer planet any of the four planets with an orbit outside the asteroid belt; Jupiter, Saturn, Uranus, or Neptune
outer space **1** space beyond the atmosphere of the earth **2** space outside the solar system
out·er·wear (out′ər wer′) ***n.*** outer garments worn over the usual clothing; specif., topcoats, raincoats, etc.
out·face (out′fās′) ***vt.*** **-faced′**, **-fac′ing** **1** to overcome or subdue with a look or stare **2** to defy or resist
out·fall (out′fôl′) ***n.*** the outlet of a river, sewer, etc.
out·field (out′fēld′) ***n.*** **1** the outlying land of a farm ☆**2** *a)* the playing area of a baseball field beyond the infield *b)* the outfielders collectively
☆**out·field·er** (-fēl′dər) ***n.*** *Baseball* a player whose defensive position is in the outfield; right fielder, center fielder, or left fielder
out·fit (out′fit′) ***n.*** **1** *a)* a set of articles for fitting out, or equipping *b)* the equipment used in any craft or activity; paraphernalia [a mason's *outfit*, camping *outfit*] ☆**2** articles of clothing worn together; ensemble [a fall *outfit*] ☆**3** a group of people associated in some undertaking or activity, as a military unit, business, ranch, etc. **4** a fitting out; equipping —***vt.*** **-fit′ted**, **-fit′ting** to furnish or equip, as with an outfit; fit out —***vi.*** to obtain an outfit —***SYN.*** FURNISH
out·fit·ter (-fit′ər) ***n.*** **1** a person who furnishes, sells, or makes outfits **2** a business that provides equipment and supplies for fishing trips, hunting expeditions, etc.
out·flank (out′flaŋk′) ***vt.*** **1** to go around and beyond the flank of (a body of enemy troops) **2** to thwart; outwit
out·flow (out′flō′) ***n.*** **1** the act of flowing out **2** *a)* that which flows out *b)* the amount flowing out
out·foot (out′foot′) ***vt.*** to run, sail, etc. faster than
☆**out·fox** (-fäks′) ***vt.*** to outwit; outsmart
out·gas (out′gas′) ***vt.*** **-gassed′**, **-gas′sing** to remove or release gases or gaseous elements from
out·gen·er·al (out′jen′ər əl) ***vt.*** **-aled** or **-alled**, **-al·ing** or **-al·ling** to surpass in leadership or management
out·go (out′gō′; *for n.* out′gō′) ***vt.*** **-went′**, **-gone′**, **-go′ing** to surpass, as in achievement; go beyond; outdo —***n.**, pl.* **-goes′** **1** the act of going out **2** that which goes or is paid out; outflow or expenditure
out·go·ing (out′gō′iŋ) ***adj.*** **1** *a)* going out; leaving *b)* retiring from office **2** expansive, friendly, etc. [an *outgoing* personality] —***n.*** **1** the act of going out **2** [*usually pl.*] [Brit.] an outlay; expenses
out-group (out′gro͞op′) ***n.*** all the people not belonging to a specific in-group
out·grow (out′grō′) ***vt.*** **-grew′**, **-grown′**, **-grow′ing** **1** to grow faster or larger than **2** to lose, get rid of, or dispense with in the process of growing or maturing [to *outgrow* one's credulity] **3** to grow too large for [to *outgrow* a suit]
out·growth (out′grōth′) ***n.*** **1** the act of growing out **2** a result; consequence; development **3** that which grows out; offshoot
out·guess (out′ges′) ***vt.*** to outwit in anticipating
out·gun (out′gun′) ***vt.*** **-gunned′**, **-gun′ning** to surpass in weaponry or firepower: often used fig.
out·haul (out′hôl′) ***n.*** *Naut.* a rope used to haul something out into position, specif. the after lower corner of a fore-and-aft sail
out-Her·od (out′her′əd) ***vt.*** to surpass in excess, as in violence or cruelty: usually in the phrase **out-Herod Herod**, Hamlet's reference to the usual characterization of Herod the Great in the old mystery plays
out·house (out′hous′) ***n.*** **1** a building separate from but located near a main building or dwelling ☆**2** a small structure used for defecating or urinating, typically having a seat with a hole over a deep pit
out·ing (out′iŋ) ***n.*** **1** a pleasure trip or holiday outdoors or away from home **2** an outdoor walk, ride, etc. **3** a public performance or appearance, specif. one by a pitcher in a baseball game
☆**outing flannel** a soft, warm cotton fabric in a plain or twill weave with a nap on both sides
out·land (out′land′, -lənd) ***n.*** ⟦ME < OE *utland*⟧ **1** [*usually pl.*] outlying or remote areas; hinterland **2** [Archaic] a foreign land —***adj.*** **1** outlying **2** [Archaic] foreign
out·land·er (out′lan′dər) ***n.*** ⟦prec. + -ER, in part after Du *uitlander,* foreigner: see UITLANDER⟧ a foreigner; alien; stranger
out·land·ish (out′lan′dish) ***adj.*** ⟦ME *utlandisch* < OE *utlendisc* < *utland* + *-isc,* -ISH⟧ **1** [Archaic] foreign; alien **2** very odd, strange, or peculiar; fantastic; bizarre **3** remote; out-of-the-way —***SYN.*** STRANGE —**out′land′ish·ly** ***adv.*** —**out′land′ish·ness** ***n.***
out·last (out last′) ***vt.*** **1** to endure longer than **2** to outlive
out·law (out′lô′) ***n.*** ⟦ME *outlawe* < OE *utlaga* < ON *útlagr,* lit., outlawed: see OUT & LAW⟧ **1** [Historical] a person declared by a court of law to be deprived of legal rights and protection, generally for the commission of some crime: the killing of such a person was not a legal offense **2** a habitual or notorious criminal who is a fugitive from the law **3** a fierce or uncontrollable horse or other animal —***vt.*** **1** [Historical] to declare to be an outlaw **2** in the U.S., to remove the legal force of (contracts, etc.) **3** to declare unlawful or illegal **4** to bar, or ban
out·law·ry (out′lô′rē) ***n.**, pl.* **-ries** **1** an outlawing or being outlawed **2** the state or condition of being an outlaw **3** disregard or defiance of the law
out·lay (out′lā′; *for v.* out lā′, out′lā′) ***n.*** **1** a spending (*of* money, energy, etc.) **2** money, etc. spent —***vt.*** **-laid′**, **-lay′ing** to spend (money)
out·let (out′let′) ***n.*** **1** a passage or vent for letting something out **2** a means of expression [an *outlet* for the emotions] **3** a stream, river, etc. that flows out from a lake **4** *a)* a market for goods *b)* a store, agency, etc. that sells the goods of a specific manufacturer or wholesaler *c)* a retail store that sells defective, damaged, or surplus merchandise at a discount (in full **outlet store**) **5** a mass-media source, as a newspaper or television station ☆**6** any point in an electrical circuit where a plug can be inserted to connect with a power supply **7** an end of a street, alley, etc. that opens onto another street, etc.
out·li·er (out′lī′ər) ***n.*** any person or thing that lies, dwells, exists, etc. away from the main body or expected place; specif., *a)* a person who resides away from his place of work or business *b)* a person who is excluded, or excludes himself, from some group; outsider *c) Geol.* a mass of rock, usually of large size, separated by erosion from the main mass *d) Statistics* an item that is statistically anomalous, compared with others of its group or sample
out·line (out′līn′) ***n.*** **1** a line bounding the limits of an object, showing its shape; contour line **2** a sketch showing only the contours of an object without use of shading **3** [*also pl.*] a general plan without detail **4** a summary of a subject, consisting of a systematic listing of its most important points —***vt.*** **-lined′**, **-lin′ing** **1** to draw a profile of; draw in outline **2** to give or write an outline, or the main points, of —**out′lin′er** ***n.***

SYN.—**outline** is used of the line bounding the limits of an object [the sketch shows only the *outline* of the skyscrapers]; **contour**, specifically applied to the configuration of a land mass, in extension stresses the shape of an object or mass as determined by its outline [the soft *contour* of her waist]; **profile** is used of the outline or contour of the face in a side view or of the outline of any object as it is seen against a background [the *profile* of the trees against the sky]; **silhouette** applies to a profile portrait, esp. of the head and usually in solid black, or it may be used of any dark shape seen against a light background [the *silhouette* of a house against the moonlight] See also **form**

out·live (out′liv′) ***vt.*** **-lived′**, **-liv′ing** **1** to live or endure longer than **2** to live through; outlast
out·look (out′look′) ***n.*** **1** *a)* a place for watching or looking out *b)* the view from such a place **2** the act of looking out **3** mental view or attitude **4** expectation or prospect; probable outcome
out·ly·ing (out′lī′iŋ) ***adj.*** relatively far out from a certain point or center; remote
out·man (out′man′) ***vt.*** **-manned′**, **-man′ning** to surpass in number of men; outnumber
out·ma·neu·ver or **out·ma·noeu·vre** (-mə no͞o′vər) ***vt.*** **-vered** or **-vred**, **-ver·ing** or **-vring** to maneuver with better effect than; outwit
out·match (-mach′) ***vt.*** to be superior to; outdo
out·mi·grant (out′mī′grənt) ***adj.*** leaving one district, region, etc. to take up residence in another in the same country —***n.*** an out-migrant person or animal —**out′-mi′grate′** (-grāt′) ***vi.*** **-grat′ed**, **-grat′ing** —**out′-mi·gra′tion** ***n.***
out·mod·ed (out′mōd′id) ***adj.*** no longer in fashion or accepted; obsolete
out·most (out′mōst′) ***adj.*** ⟦ME, altered (by assoc. with *out*) < *utemest,* UTMOST⟧ most remote; outermost
out·mus·cle (out′mus′əl) ***vt.*** **-cled**, **-cling** [Informal] to overcome or defeat by means of greater power or strength: also written **out-muscle**
out·num·ber (out′num′bər) ***vt.*** to exceed in number
out-of-bod·y (out′əv bäd′ē) ***adj.*** of or characterized by a feeling or mental state in which one perceives one's consciousness as disembodied and able, variously, to observe one's body at a distance, move through physical space, etc. [an *out-of-body* experience]
out-of-date (-dāt′) ***adj.*** no longer in style or use; not current; outmoded; old-fashioned
out-of-door (-dôr′) ***adj.*** OUTDOOR
out-of-doors (-dôrz′) ***adv., n.*** OUTDOORS —***adj.*** OUTDOOR
out-of-pock·et (-päk′it) ***adj.*** **1** designating unbudgeted expenses, or ready cash paid out, as for miscellaneous items ☆**2** designating expenses requiring payment from a person's own financial resources and not covered by insurance, an expense account, etc.
out-of-the-way (-*th*ə wā′) ***adj.*** **1** not near a frequented road or populous place; secluded **2** not common; unusual **3** not conventional or proper
out-of-town·er (-toun′ər) ***n.*** a visitor from another, usually distant, town or city
out·pace (out′pās′) ***vt.*** **-paced′**, **-pac′ing** to surpass; exceed
out·pa·tient (out′pā′shənt) ***n.*** a patient who is treated at a hospital, clinic, etc. but is not lodged there as an inpatient —***adj.*** of or serving outpatients
out·place·ment (out′plās′mənt) ***n.*** assistance in finding a new job, provided, as by an agency hired by the employer, to an employee who has been or is about to be fired
out·play (out′plā′) ***vt.*** to play better than
out·point (-point′) ***vt.*** **1** to score more points than **2** *Naut.* to sail closer to the wind than (another vessel)
out·poll (out′pōl′) ***vt.*** to receive more votes than [the incumbent *outpolled* the challenger by a 2-to-1 margin]

out·port (out′pôrt′) ***n.*** [Cdn.] an isolated fishing village on the Newfoundland coast

out·post (-pōst′) ***n.*** **1** *Mil.* *a)* a small group stationed at a distance from the main force in order to prevent an enemy surprise attack *b)* the place or station occupied by such a group *c)* any military base away from the home country **2** a settlement on a frontier or border **3** any remote place, branch, community, etc.

out·pour (out′pôr′; *for v.* out′pôr′) ***n.*** OUTPOURING —***vt., vi.*** to pour out

out·pour·ing (out′pôr′iŋ) ***n.*** **1** the action of pouring out **2** that which pours out; outflow **3** a release or display of strong feeling

out·put (out′poot′) ***n.*** **1** *a)* the work done or amount produced by a person, machine, production line, manufacturing plant, etc., esp. over a given period *b)* the act of producing **2** *a)* information, resulting from computer processing, that is delivered to a user, as a printout or video display, or transferred to disk or tape *b)* the act or process of delivering or transferring this information **3** *Elec.* *a)* the useful voltage, current, or power delivered by amplifiers, generators, receivers, etc. or by a circuit *b)* the terminal where such energy is delivered —***adj.*** of or relating to computer output —***vt.*** **-put′**, **-put′ting** to deliver or transfer (computer output)

out·rage (out′rāj′) ***n.*** ⟦OFr < *outre,* beyond < L *ultra* (see ULTRA): meaning infl. by assoc. with OUT & RAGE⟧ **1** an extremely vicious or violent act **2** a deep insult or grave offense **3** great anger, indignation, etc. aroused by such an act or offense —***vt.*** **-raged′**, **-rag′ing** **1** to commit an outrage upon or against; specif., *a)* to offend, insult, or wrong grievously *b)* to rape **2** to cause great anger, indignation, etc. in —***SYN.*** OFFEND

out·ra·geous (out rā′jəs) ***adj.*** ⟦OFr *outrageus:* see prec. & -OUS⟧ **1** having the nature of, involving, or doing great injury or wrong **2** exceeding all bounds of decency or reasonableness; very offensive or shocking **3** violent in action or disposition; unrestrained —**out′ra′geous·ly** ***adv.*** —**out′ra′geous·ness** ***n.***

SYN.—**outrageous** applies to that which so exceeds all bounds of right, morality, decency, etc. as to be intolerable [an *outrageous* insult]; **flagrant** implies a glaringly bad or openly evil character in persons or their acts [a *flagrant* sinner, a *flagrant* violation]; **monstrous** and **atrocious** are applied to that which is extremely or shockingly wrong, bad, evil, cruel, etc. [a *monstrous* vice, lie, etc., *atrocious* cruelty, manners, etc.]; **heinous** implies such extreme wickedness as to arouse the strongest hatred and revulsion [a *heinous* crime]

ou·trance (o͞o träns′) ***n.*** ⟦Fr; also, in earlier use, ME < MFr < *outrer,* to pass beyond < *outre:* see OUTRAGE⟧ the extreme limit; utmost extremity

out·range (out′rānj′) ***vt.*** **-ranged′**, **-rang′ing** **1** to have a greater range than **2** to range beyond

☆**out·rank** (-raŋk′) ***vt.*** to exceed in rank

ou·tré (o͞o trā′) ***adj.*** ⟦Fr, pp. of *outrer,* to go too far, overdo < OFr *outre:* see OUTRAGE⟧ **1** exaggerated **2** eccentric; bizarre

out·reach (out′rēch′; *for v., also* out′rēch′) ***vt., vi.*** **1** to reach farther (than); exceed; surpass **2** to reach out; extend —***n.*** **1** the act of reaching out **2** the extent of reach **3** *a)* a program, as by a local church or business, for extending assistance, services, etc. to the community, esp. as an act of charity or goodwill *b)* activities or services undertaken by such a program —***adj.*** designating or of a program designed to provide outreach

out·ride (out′rīd′) ***vt.*** **-rode′**, **-rid′den**, **-rid′ing** **1** to surpass or outstrip in riding **2** to withstand or endure successfully; ride out

out·rid·er (out′rīd′ər) ***n.*** **1** an attendant on horseback who rides out ahead of or beside a carriage, stagecoach, etc. ☆**2** a cowboy who rides over a range, as to prevent cattle from straying **3** a trailblazer; forerunner

out·rig·ger (-rig′ər) ***n.*** **1** any temporary support extending out from a main structure **2** *a)* any of a variety of frameworks extended beyond the rail of a ship for various purposes *b)* a brace holding an oarlock out from the side of a boat, to give the rower more leverage *c)* a timber or other float rigged out from the side of certain canoes to prevent tipping; also, a canoe of this type **3** a sparlike projection, for supporting the lesser airfoils of an airplane or the propellers or engines on an airship

canoe with outrigger

out·right (out′rīt′, out′rīt′) ***adj.*** **1** without reservation; downright **2** straightforward; direct **3** complete; total; whole —***adv.*** **1** entirely; wholly **2** without reservation; openly **3** at once; not by degrees **4** [Obs.] straight ahead

out·run (out′run′) ***vt.*** **-ran′**, **-run′**, **-run′ning** **1** to run faster, farther, or better than **2** to exceed **3** to escape (a pursuer) by or as by running

out·run·ner (out′run′ər) ***n.*** **1** a person or thing that runs out **2** an attendant running beside or before a carriage **3** the leading dog of a team of sled dogs

out·sell (out′sel′) ***vt.*** **-sold′**, **-sell′ing** **1** to sell in greater amounts than **2** to excel in salesmanship **3** [Obs.] to sell for a higher price than

out·set (out′set′) ***n.*** a setting out; beginning; start

out·shine (out′shīn′) ***vt.*** **-shone′** or **-shined′**, **-shin′ing** **1** to shine brighter or longer than (another) **2** to surpass; excel —***vi.*** to shine forth

out·shoot (out′sho͞ot′; *for n.* out′sho͞ot′) ***vt.*** **-shot′**, **-shoot′ing** **1** to shoot more effectively than **2** to shoot out —***vi.*** to shoot out; protrude —***n.*** **1** a shooting or being shot out **2** that which shoots out or protrudes ☆**3** *Baseball former term for* CURVE

out·side (out′sīd′, out′sīd′) ***n.*** **1** the outer side, part, or surface; exterior **2** *a)* outward aspect or appearance; that part of anything that is presented to view *b)* that which is obvious or superficial **3** any place or area not inside —***adj.*** **1** of or on the outside; outer **2** *a)* originating, coming from, or situated beyond given limits; from some other place, person, group, etc. [to accept no *outside* help] *b)* leading to the outside **3** extreme; maximum [an *outside* estimate] **4** mere; slight [an *outside* chance] **5** *Baseball* passing home plate beyond the side of the plate that is farthest from the batter: said of a pitch —***adv.*** **1** on or to the outside **2** beyond certain limits **3** in or into the open air —***prep.*** **1** on or to the outer side of **2** beyond the limits of **3** [Informal] except —**at the outside** at the most; at the absolute limit —**outside of** **1** outside **2** [Informal] other than; except for

out·sid·er (out′sīd′ər, out′sīd′ər) ***n.*** **1** one who is outside or not included; specif., *a)* one not a member of or in sympathy with a given group *b)* one who is socially or emotionally isolated **2** a contender given little chance of winning

out·sit (out′sit′) ***vt.*** **-sat′**, **-sit′ting** **1** to sit longer than (another) **2** to sit beyond the time of

out·size (out′sīz′) ***n.*** **1** a size varying from the usual standard; odd size; esp., an unusually large size **2** a garment or other article of such a size —***adj.*** of nonstandard size; esp., unusually large: also **out′sized′** (-sīzd′)

out·skirts (out′skurts′) ***pl.n.*** **1** districts remote from the center or midst, as of a city; outlying regions: *sometimes, esp. formerly, used in sing.* [much construction throughout the *outskirts* of the city] **2** the outer edge, border, or margin [a shack at the *outskirts* of town]

☆**out·smart** (out′smärt′) ***vt.*** to overcome by cunning or cleverness; outwit —**outsmart oneself** to have one's efforts at cunning or cleverness result in one's own disadvantage

out·soar (out′sôr′) ***vt.*** to soar beyond or higher than

out·sole (out′sōl′) ***n.*** the outermost sole of a shoe, boot, etc.

out·source (out′sôrs′) ***vt.*** **-sourced′**, **-sourc′ing** to transfer (certain manufacturing operations, administrative activities, etc.) to outside contractors, esp. so as to reduce one's operating costs

out·span (out′span′; *for n.* out′span′) [South Afr.] ***vt., vi.*** **-spanned′**, **-span′ning** ⟦Afrik *uitspannen* < Du *uit,* OUT + *spannen,* to harness, akin to OE *spannan,* SPAN[1]⟧ to unyoke or unharness (animals) —***n.*** the act or place of outspanning

out·speak (out′spēk′) ***vt.*** **-spoke′**, **-spo′ken**, **-speak′ing** **1** to speak better or more forcefully than **2** to say boldly or candidly —***vi.*** to speak out boldly or candidly

out·spo·ken (out′spō′kən, out′spō′kən) ***adj.*** **1** unrestrained in speech; frank **2** spoken boldly or candidly —***SYN.*** FRANK[1] —**out′spo′ken·ly** ***adv.*** —**out′spo′ken·ness** ***n.***

out·spread (out′spred′; *also, and for n. always,* out′spred′) ***vt., vi.*** **-spread′**, **-spread′ing** to spread out; extend; expand —***n.*** a spreading out; extension; expansion —***adj.*** spread out; extended; expanded

out·stand (out′stand′) [Archaic] ***vi.*** **-stood′**, **-stand′ing** to stand out plainly; project —***vt.*** to endure

out·stand·ing (out′stan′diŋ) ***adj.*** **1** projecting **2** prominent; distinguished; conspicuous **3** unfulfilled; unsettled **4** unpaid; uncollected **5** that have been issued and sold: said of stocks and bonds **6** unusually fine, admirable, enjoyable, etc.: a general term of approval —***SYN.*** NOTICEABLE —**out′stand′ing·ly** ***adv.***

out·stare (out′ster′) ***vt.*** **-stared′**, **-star′ing** to outdo in staring; stare down; outface

out·sta·tion (out′stā′shən) ***n.*** a post or station in a remote or unsettled area

out·stay (out′stā′) ***vt.*** **1** to stay longer than **2** to stay beyond the time of; overstay

out·stretch (out′strech′) ***vt.*** **1** to stretch out; extend **2** to stretch beyond

out·strip (out′strip′) ***vt.*** **-stripped′**, **-strip′ping** **1** to go at a faster pace than; get ahead of **2** to excel; surpass

out·take (out′tāk′) ***n.*** **1** a scene, or take, photographed or taped for a film or TV program, but not included in the shown version **2** a defective recording of music, etc. not used for commercial release

out·talk (out′tôk′) ***vt.*** to talk more skillfully, loudly, or forcibly than

out·think (out′thiŋk′) ***vt.*** **-thought′**, **-think′ing** **1** to think deeper, faster, or more cunningly than **2** to outwit by such thinking

out·turn (out′turn′) ***n.*** OUTPUT (sense 1*a*)

out·vote (out′vōt′) ***vt.*** **-vot′ed**, **-vot′ing** to defeat in voting

out·ward (out′wərd) ***adj.*** ⟦ME *utward* < OE *utweard:* see OUT & -WARD⟧ **1** having to do with the outside or exterior; outer **2** clearly apparent; observable; visible **3** away from the interior; to or toward the outside **4** having to do with the physical or the body as opposed to the mind or spirit **5** concerning the surface only; superficial —***adv.*** **1** away from the interior or from port; toward the outside **2** visibly; openly; publicly **3** [Obs.] on the outside; externally —***n.*** **1** the outward part; exterior **2** the material or external world **3** outward form or appearance —**out′ward·ness** ***n.***

out·ward·ly (out′wərd lē) ***adv.*** **1** toward or on the outside **2** in regard to external appearance or action

out·wards (out′wərdz) ***adv.*** OUTWARD

☆**out·wash** (out′wôsh′) ***n.*** sand and gravel deposited by meltwater streams in front of glacial ice

out·wear (out′wer′) ***vt.*** **-wore′**, **-worn′**, **-wear′ing** **1** to wear out; use up **2**

to be more lasting than; outlast 3 to outgrow or outlive 4 to exhaust, as in strength

out·weigh (out′wā′) *vt.* 1 to weigh more than 2 to be more important, valuable, etc. than

out·wit (out′wit′) *vt.* **-wit′ted, -wit′ting** 1 to overcome, or get the better of, by cunning or cleverness 2 [Archaic] to be more intelligent than

out·work (out′wurk′; *for v.* out′wurk′) *n. Mil.* a lesser trench or fortification built out beyond the main defenses —*vt.* **-worked′, -work′ing** 1 to work better, faster, or harder than 2 to work out to completion

ou·zel (ōō′zəl) *n.* ⟦ME *osul* < OE *osle,* akin to OHG *amsala,* prob. < IE base **ames-* < **mes-* > L *merula,* Welsh *mwyalch*⟧ 1 RING OUZEL 2 WATER OUZEL

ou·zo (ōō′zō) *n.* ⟦ModGr *ouzon* < ?⟧ a colorless Greek liqueur flavored with aniseed

ov- *combining form* OVI-: used before a vowel

o·va (ō′və) *n. pl. of* OVUM

o·val (ō′vəl) *adj.* ⟦Fr *ovale* < L *ovum,* EGG[1]⟧ 1 shaped like the longitudinal cross section of an egg; elliptical 2 having the form of an egg; ellipsoid —*n.* anything oval —**o′val·ly** *adv.* —**o′val·ness** *n.*

Oval Office ☆the oval-shaped office of the President in the White House: often used fig. to represent the position, authority, or power of the President of the U.S.

o·var·i·ec·to·my (ō ver′ē ek′tə mē) *n., pl.* **-mies** ⟦see -ECTOMY⟧ the surgical removal of one or both ovaries

o·var·i·ot·o·my (-ät′ə mē) *n., pl.* **-mies** 1 a surgical incision into an ovary 2 OVARIECTOMY

o·va·ri·tis (ō′və rīt′is) *n.* ⟦see -ITIS⟧ inflammation of an ovary

o·va·ry (ō′və rē) *n., pl.* **-ries** ⟦ModL *ovarium* < L *ovum,* EGG[1]⟧ 1 *Anat., Zool.* a female reproductive gland producing eggs and, in vertebrates, sex hormones 2 *Bot.* the enlarged, hollow part of the pistil or gynoecium, containing ovules —**o·var·i·an** (ō ver′ē ən) *adj.*

o·vate (ō′vāt′) *adj.* ⟦L *ovatus* < *ovum,* EGG[1]⟧ 1 egg-shaped 2 *Bot.* having the shape of the longitudinal section of an egg, esp. with the broader end at the base

o·va·tion (ō vā′shən) *n.* ⟦L *ovatio* < *ovare,* to celebrate a triumph, akin to Gr *euazein,* to rejoice, *euai,* a cry of Bacchic joy⟧ 1 in ancient Rome, a lesser ceremonial tribute to a hero whose deeds were not great enough to justify a full triumph 2 an enthusiastic outburst of applause or an enthusiastic public welcome

ov·en (uv′ən) *n.* ⟦ME < OE *ofen,* akin to Ger < IE base **auqw-,* cooking vessel > L *aulla, olla*⟧ a compartment or receptacle for baking or roasting food or for heating or drying things

ov·en·bird (uv′ən burd′) *n.* ⟦from the shape of the nest⟧ 1 any of a large family (Furnariidae) of Neotropical passerine birds; esp., any of a genus (*Furnarius*) that builds a two-chambered, dome-shaped nest from clay and dried leaves ☆2 any of various other birds that build a domelike nest on the ground; esp., a North American wood warbler (*Seiurus aurocapillus*)

ov·en·proof (uv′ən prōōf′) *adj.* able to withstand the high temperatures of an oven without breaking, burning, melting, etc. [an *ovenproof* baking pan]: also **ov·en-safe** (uv′ən sāf′, -sāf′)

ov·en·ware (uv′ən wer′) *n.* cookware, as casseroles and pans, designed for use in an oven rather than on a stove

o·ver (ō′vər) *prep.* ⟦ME *ouer* < OE *ofer,* akin to Ger *über, ober* < IE **uper* (orig. a compar. of **upo,* up) > L *super,* Gr *hyper*⟧ 1 *a)* in, at, or to a position up from; higher than; above [a canopy *over* the bed, in water *over* his knees] *b)* on top of [a blanket *over* the bed] *c)* above, in various figurative uses [gloom hung *over* the town; the lecture went *over* our heads] 2 across and down from or down upon [to fall *over* a cliff, to trip *over* a chair] 3 while engaged in; during [we discussed it *over* dinner] 4 upon the surface of [spread the icing *over* the cake] 5 so as to cover or close [shutters *over* the windows] 6 upon: said as of an effect or influence [he cast a spell *over* them] 7 so as to show care, concern, etc. for [watching *over* a flock, hovering *over* the baby] 8 above in authority, position, power, etc. [to rule *over* a nation] 9 authorized or attested by [*over* his signature] 10 in a course leading along or across, or above and to the other side of [fly *over* the lake] 11 on the other side of [a city *over* the border] 12 *a)* here and there in [the tourists dashed *over* the city] *b)* through all parts of [carefully going *over* my notes] 13 during; through [*over* the past ten years] 14 more than, or above, in degree, amount, number, etc. [a moderate increase *over* his current salary, a gift costing *over* five dollars] 15 up to and including; until after [stay *over* Easter] 16 in preference to [chose the red hat *over* the blue one] 17 in spite of; in successful opposition to [we did it *over* his objections] 18 about; concerning [a quarrel *over* politics] 19 through the medium of; on [*over* the telephone or radio] 20 *Arith.* divided by [6 *over* 3 is 2] —*adv.* 1 *a)* above, across, or to the other side *b)* across the brim or edge 2 more; in excess; beyond [three hours or *over*] 3 longer or till a time later [please stay *over*] 4 throughout or covering the entire area [the wound healed *over*] 5 from start to finish; through [think it *over*] 6 *a)* from an upright position [to fall *over*] *b)* upside down; into an inverted position [turn the cup *over*] 7 again; another time; repeated(ly) [do it *over;* many times *over*] 8 at or on the other side, as of an intervening space, or at or to a specified place [*over* in England, come *over* here] 9 from one side, belief, viewpoint, etc. to another [they won him *over*] 10 from one person, etc. to another [hand *over* the money] See also phrases GET OVER, (at GET), PUT OVER, (at PUT) —*adj.* 1 upper, outer, superior, excessive, or extra: often in comb. [*overcoat, overseer, oversupply*] 2 done; finished; past; obsolete [his career is *over*] 3 having reached the other side; having got across 4 [Informal] as a surplus; in excess; extra [to be three hours *over* for the week] —*n.* 1 something in addition; excess; surplus 2 *Cricket a)* the set number of balls bowled during a single turn at one end of the wicket *b)* the period of time during which this takes place 3 *Mil.* a shot that hits or explodes beyond the target —*vt.* to pass above and across —*interj.* 1 turn the page, sheet, etc. over 2 I have finished speaking for the moment — please respond: used in radio communication —**over again** again; another time; anew —**over all** over the whole extent; from end to end —**over and above** in addition to; more than; besides —**over and over (again)** repeatedly; time after time —**over (and done) with** finished; completed; past: said esp. of a difficult or unpleasant task, period, etc. [let's get this job *over with*]

o·ver- (ō′vər) *combining form* 1 *a)* above in position, over, outer, upper [*overhead*] *b)* superior, eminent [*overlord*] 2 *a)* passing across or beyond [*overshoot, overpass, overrun*] *b)* passing over the top or the brim of [*overflow*] 3 denoting movement downward from above [*overwhelm*] 4 across the surface of [*overgrowth, overprint*] 5 more (than), excessive, too much, beyond the normal, extra [*overrate, oversell, oversleep*] 6 overly; excessively [*overeager, overlong*] The list below includes some of the more common compounds formed with *over-* that can be understood if "too much" or "excessively" is added to the meaning of the base word:

overambitious
overanxious
overattentive
overbold
overbusy
overcareful
overcareless
overcautious
overcautiously
overcautiousness
overconscientious
overconservative
overconsumption
overcook
overcritical
overdecorate
overdependent
overeager
overeagerness
overeducate
overemotional
overemphasize
overenthusiastic
overexercise
overexpansion
overfed
overfeed
overfond
overgenerosity
overgenerous
overgenerously
overgreedy
overhasty
overindulge
overinflate
overmedicate
overorganize
overpraise
overprecise
overprivileged
overprize
overrefined
overrefinement
overreligious
overripe
oversensitive
oversentimental
oversolicitous
overspecialize
overstimulate
overstimulation
overstretch
overstrict
oversubtle
oversufficient
oversuspicious
oversweeten
overswing
overtip
overtire
overutilization
overutilize
overzealous
overzealousness

o·ver·a·bun·dance (ō′vər ə bun′dəns) *n.* more than an abundance; superfluity; excess —**o′ver·a·bun′dant** *adj.*

o·ver·a·chieve (-ə chēv′) *vi.* **-chieved′, -chiev′ing** 1 to do better than expected, as in school studies 2 to drive oneself obsessively in trying to reach unreasonable goals —**o′ver·a·chieve′ment** *n.* —**o′ver·a·chiev′er** *n.*

o·ver·act (-akt′) *vt., vi.* to act (a dramatic role) in an exaggerated way

o·ver·ac·tive (-ak′tiv) *adj.* 1 abnormally active [an *overactive* bladder] 2 regarded as excessively active; overly lively, vigorous, etc. [a child with an *overactive* imagination]

o·ver·age[1] (-āj′) *adj.* 1 over the age fixed as a standard 2 so old as to be of no use

o·ver·age[2] (ō′vər ij) *n.* ⟦OVER + -AGE⟧ a surplus or excess, as of goods

o·ver·all (ō′vər ôl′; *for adv.* ō′vər ôl′) *adj.* 1 from end to end 2 including everything; total —*adv.* 1 from end to end 2 in general

☆**o·ver·alls** (ō′vər ôlz′) *pl.n.* 1 loosefitting trousers of some strong cotton cloth, often with a part extending up over the chest, worn, usually over other clothing, to protect against dirt and wear 2 [*sing.*] [Brit.] a smock or other protective outer garment

o·ver·arch (ō′vər ärch′) *vt., vi.* to form an arch over (something)

o·ver·arch·ing (-iŋ) *adj.* 1 forming an arch above or overhead 2 encompassing or linking all that is within its scope, range, etc. [an *overarching* theory, theme, etc.]

o·ver·arm (ō′vər ärm′) *adj.* performed by raising the arm above the shoulder, as a swimming stroke

o·ver·awe (ō′vər ô′) *vt.* **-awed′, -aw′ing** to overcome or subdue by inspiring awe

o·ver·bal·ance (ō′vər bal′əns; *for n.* ō′vər bal′əns) *vt.* **-anced, -anc·ing** 1 OUTWEIGH 2 to throw off balance —*n.* something that outweighs or overbalances

o·ver·bear (ō′vər ber′) *vt.* **-bore′, -borne′, -bear′ing** 1 to press or bear down by weight or physical power 2 to dominate, domineer over, overrule, or subdue —*vi.* to be too fruitful; bear to excess

o·ver·bear·ing (ō′vər ber′iŋ) *adj.* 1 acting in a dictatorial manner; arrogant; domineering 2 of transcending importance; overriding —SYN. PROUD —o′ver·bear′ing·ly adv.

o·ver·bid (ō′vər bid′; *for n.* ō′vər bid′) *vt., vi.* **-bid′**, **-bid′ding** 1 to outbid (another person) 2 to bid more than the worth of (a thing, as one's hand in bridge) —*n.* a higher or excessive bid

o·ver·bill (ō′vər bil′) *vi., vt.* to bill (someone) for charges in excess of the amount to which one is entitled

o·ver·bite (ō′vər bīt′) *n.* a faulty occlusion of the teeth in which the upper incisors and canines project over the lower to an abnormal extent

o·ver·blouse (ō′vər blous′) *n.* a blouse for women, extending below the waist and worn outside the skirt, etc.

o·ver·blow (ō′vər blō′, ō′vər blō′) *vt.* **-blew′**, **-blown′**, **-blow′ing** 1 to blow across, away, or down 2 to cover with something blown, as sand 3 to handle, perform, or promote in an excessive manner; overdo 4 *Music* to blow (a wind instrument) so as to produce overtones

o·ver·blown[1] (ō′vər blōn′) *adj.* past the stage of full bloom

o·ver·blown[2] (ō′vər blōn′) *adj.* 1 stout; obese 2 *a)* overdone; excessive *b)* pompous or bombastic

o·ver·board (ō′vər bôrd′) *adv.* ⟦ME *ouer borde* < OE *ofor bord:* see OVER & BOARD⟧ 1 over a ship's side 2 from a ship into the water —☆**go overboard** [Informal] to go to extremes; esp., to be wildly enthusiastic —**throw overboard** to discard

o·ver·book (ō′vər book′) *vt., vi.* to issue more reservations for (an airline flight, hotel, etc.) than there are accommodations

o·ver·build (ō′vər bild′, ō′vər bild′) *vt., vi.* **-built′**, **-build′ing** 1 to build over or on top of (something) 2 to build too elaborately 3 to erect more buildings than are needed or desirable in (an area)

o·ver·bur·den (ō′vər burd′'n; *for n.* ō′vər burd′'n) *vt.* to burden oppressively; weigh down —*n.* 1 something that overburdens 2 *Geol.* soil, rock, etc. that is covering or overlying a useful deposit, as of ore

o·ver·buy (ō′vər bī′) *vt., vi.* **-bought′**, **-buy′ing** to buy more than is needed or justified by ability to pay

o·ver·call (ō′vər kôl′; *for n.* ō′vər kôl′) *vt., vi.* *Bridge* to make a higher bid than (an opponent or an opponent's bid) when there has been no intervening bid —*n.* such a bid

o·ver·ca·pac·i·ty (ō′vər kə pas′ə tē) *n.* excess capacity for production or service, in relation to the level of demand

o·ver·cap·i·tal·ize (-kap′ət'l īz′) *vt., vi.* **-ized′**, **-iz′ing** 1 to capitalize beyond what is warranted by the state of the business, etc.; furnish too much capital for or overestimate the capital value of (a business) 2 to set the nominal value of the capital of (a corporation) higher than is lawful or justifiable —**o′ver·cap′i·tal·i·za′tion** *n.*

o·ver·cast (ō′vər kast′; *for v., also* ō′vər kast′) *n.* a covering, esp. of clouds —*adj.* 1 cloudy; dark: said of the sky or weather 2 *Sewing* made with overcasting — *vt., vi.* **-cast′**, **-cast′ing** 1 to overcloud; darken 2 *Sewing* to sew over (an edge) with long, loose stitches so as to prevent raveling

o·ver·charge (ō′vər chärj′; *also, and for n. always,* ō′vər chärj′) *vt., vi.* **-charged′**, **-charg′ing** 1 to charge too high a price (to) 2 to overload or fill too full 3 to exaggerate —*n.* 1 an excessive charge 2 a load that is too full or heavy

o·ver·cloud (ō′vər kloud′) *vt., vi.* 1 to darken or cover over with clouds; dim 2 to make or become gloomy, angry, etc. in appearance

☆**o·ver·coat** (ō′vər kōt′) *n.* a coat, esp. a heavy coat, worn over the usual clothing for warmth

o·ver·come (ō′vər kum′) *vt.* **-came′**, **-come′**, **-com′ing** ⟦ME *ouercomen* < OE *ofercuman*⟧ 1 to get the better of in competition, struggle, etc.; conquer 2 to master, prevail over, or surmount [to *overcome* obstacles] 3 to make helpless; overpower or overwhelm [*overcome* by pity] —*vi.* to be victorious; win —SYN. CONQUER

o·ver·com·mit (ō′vər kə mit′) *vt., vi.* **-mit′ted**, **-mit′ting** 1 to commit (oneself or others) to too many obligations, too full a schedule, etc. 2 to promise (something) in a quantity above that which can be provided

o·ver·com·pen·sate (ō′vər käm′pən sāt′) *vt.* **-sat′ed**, **-sat′ing** to give an excessive compensation to —*vi.* 1 *Psychol.* to react to a real or imagined physical or psychological defect with a conscious or unconscious exaggerated drive to compensate for it 2 to make more than the necessary allowance or adjustment —**o′ver·com′pen·sa′tion** *n.* —**o′ver·com·pen′sa·to′ry** (-kəm pen′sə tôr′ē) *adj.*

o·ver·con·fi·dent (ō′vər kän′fə dənt) *adj.* confident without adequate reason; too confident —**o′ver·con′fi·dence** *n.* —**o′ver·con′fi·dent·ly** *adv.*

o·ver·cor·rec·tion (ō′vər kə rek′shən) *n.* ☆HYPERCORRECTION

o·ver·crop (ō′vər kräp′) *vt.* **-cropped′**, **-crop′ping** to deplete the fertility of (land) by overproduction of crops

o·ver·crowd (ō′vər kroud′) *vt.* to crowd with too many people or things

o·ver·de·ter·mine (ō′vər di tur′mən) *vt.* **-mined**, **-min·ing** to bring about through multiple causes or contributory factors

o·ver·de·vel·op (ō′vər di vel′əp) *vt.* 1 to develop too much 2 *Photog.* to develop (a film, plate, etc.) too long or with too strong a developer —**o′ver·de·vel′op·ment** *n.*

o·ver·do (ō′vər doo′) *vt.* **-did′**, **-done′**, **-do′ing** 1 to do too much, or to excess 2 to spoil the effect of by exaggeration [to *overdo* an apology] 3 to cook too long; overcook 4 to overwork; exhaust; tire —*vi.* to do too much; esp., to exhaust oneself by doing too much

o·ver·dose (ō′vər dōs′; *for v.* ō′vər dōs′, ō′vər dōs′) *n.* too large a dose —*vt.* **-dosed′**, **-dos′ing** to dose to excess —*vi.* 1 to take too large an amount of a narcotic, hallucinogen, etc.: often with *on* 2 [Informal] to experience too much of something: often with *on* —**o′ver·dos′age** *n.*

o·ver·draft (ō′vər draft′) *n.* 1 *a)* a withdrawal of money from a bank in excess of the amount credited to the drawer *b)* the amount withdrawn in excess 2 a draft, or current of air, passed over a fire, as in a furnace, or passing down through a kiln

o·ver·draw (ō′vər drô′, ō′vər drô′) *vt.* **-drew′**, **-drawn′**, **-draw′ing** 1 to spoil the effect of by exaggeration; overdo 2 to draw on in excess of the amount credited to the drawer 3 to draw (a bow, etc.) too far

o·ver·dress (ō′vər dres′, ō′vər dres′) *vt., vi.* to dress too warmly, too showily, or too formally for the occasion

o·ver·drive (ō′vər drīv′) *n.* 1 a gear that at a certain speed automatically reduces an engine's power output without reducing its driving speed: used to lessen fuel consumption and engine wear 2 [Informal] a state of intensified activity, productivity, etc.

o·ver·dub (ō′vər dub′) *n.* a recording of sounds, music, etc. that is added to or superimposed on another recording — *vt., vi.* **-dubbed′**, **-dub′bing** to add (sounds, music, etc.) to (an already existing recording)

o·ver·due (ō′vər doo′, -dyoo′) *adj.* 1 past the time for payment 2 delayed in arrival or occurrence beyond the time set or anticipated 3 that should have come about sooner [*overdue* reforms]

o·ver·dye (ō′vər dī′, ō′vər dī′) *vt.* **-dyed′**, **-dye′ing** 1 to subject too long to the dyeing process so as to make too dark 2 to dye over (something previously dyed)

o·ver·eat (ō′vər ēt′) *vi.* **-ate′**, **-eat′en**, **-eat′ing** to eat too much or to the point of surfeit

o·ver-egg (ō′vər eg′) *vt.* [Brit. Informal] to do too much of; elaborate on excessively; overdo: *used mainly in the phrase* **over-egg the** (or **one's**) **pudding**, to mar an undertaking by doing more than is necessary or desirable —**o′ver-egged′** *adj.*

o·ver·es·ti·mate (ō′vər es′tə māt′; *for n.* ō′vər es′tə mit) *vt.* **-mat′ed**, **-mat′ing** to set too high an estimate on or for —*n.* an estimate that is too high —**o′ver·es′ti·ma′tion** *n.*

o·ver·ex·ert (ō′vər eg zurt′) *vt.* to exert too much or too long: often used reflexively —**o′ver·ex·er′tion** *n.*

o·ver·ex·pose (-ek spōz′) *vt.* **-posed′**, **-pos′ing** to expose too much or too long —**o′ver·ex·po′sure** (-spō′zhər) *n.*

o·ver·ex·tend (-ek stend′) *vt.* to extend beyond reasonable limits or beyond one's capacity to meet obligations or commitments —**o′ver·ex·ten′sion** (-ek sten′shən) *n.*

o·ver·fish (ō′vər fish′, ō′vər fish′) *vt., vi.* 1 to fish (a body of water, region, etc.) to excess, depleting the stock of fish or of a certain fish 2 to so deplete (a stock of fish or a certain fish)

o·ver·flow (ō′vər flō′; *also, and for n. always,* ō′vər flō′) *vt.* 1 to flow over or across; flood 2 to flow over the brim or edge of 3 to cause to overflow by filling beyond capacity —*vi.* 1 to flow beyond the limits; run over 2 to be more than full or complete; be superabundant —*n.* 1 an overflowing or being overflowed 2 the amount that overflows; surplus 3 an outlet for overflowing liquids

o·ver·fly (ō′vər flī′, ō′vər flī′) *vt.* **-flew′**, **-flown′**, **-fly′ing** to fly an aircraft over (a specified area) or beyond (a specified place); esp., to fly over (foreign territory) for reconnaissance —**o′ver·flight′** *n.*

o·ver·gar·ment (ō′vər gär′mənt) *n.* an outer garment

☆**o·ver·glaze** (ō′vər glāz′; *for v.* ō′vər glāz′, ō′vər glāz′) *n.* *Ceramics* 1 a second glaze applied over the first 2 a decoration applied over a glaze —*vt.* **-glazed′**, **-glaz′ing** to cover with a glaze or an overglaze

o·ver·graze (ō′vər grāz′) *vt.* **-grazed′**, **-graz′ing** to allow livestock to graze to excess in (pasture, field, etc.) with results detrimental to the land

o·ver·grow (ō′vər grō′, ō′vər grō′) *vt.* **-grew′**, **-grown′**, **-grow′ing** 1 to overspread with growth or foliage so as to cover 2 to grow too large for; outgrow —*vi.* 1 to grow too large or too fast 2 to grow beyond normal size —**o′ver·growth′** *n.*

o·ver·grown (ō′vər grōn′) *adj.* 1 overspread with foliage 2 grown excessively or beyond normal size

o·ver·hand (ō′vər hand′) *adj.* 1 with the hand over the object it grasps 2 performed with the hand raised above the elbow or the arm above the shoulder [an *overhand* pitch] 3 designating or of a style of sewing, or a seam, in which the stitches are passed over two edges to sew them together —*adv.* in an overhand manner —*vt.* ☆to sew overhand —*n.* *Sports* an overhand stroke

overhand knot a kind of knot

o·ver·hang (ō′vər haŋ′; *also, and for n. always,* ō′vər haŋ′) *vt.* **-hung′**, **-hang′ing** 1 to hang or project over or beyond 2 to loom over; threaten —*vi.* to hang over; project or jut out over something —*n.* 1 *a)* the projection of one thing over or beyond another *b)* the amount of such projection *c)* an overhanging or projecting part, as the part of a ship's stern projecting beyond the sternpost 2 *Aeron.* one half the difference in span of the two wings on a biplane or the distance from the last outer strut to the tip of the wing on a monoplane 3 *Archit.* a projection of one part of a structure over another 4 *a)* *Econ.* a surplus, as of a commodity, relative to current demand *b)* an excess of money in circulation, relative to the amount of goods and services available for purchase

o·ver·haul (ō′vər hôl′; *also, and for n. always,* ō′vər hôl′) *vt.* 1 to haul over, as for examination 2 *a)* to check thoroughly for needed repairs *b)* to make the repairs, adjustments, etc. needed to restore (a motor, etc.) to good working order 3 to gain on, catch up with, or overtake —*n.* an overhauling; thorough examination or restoration to good working order

o·ver·head (ō′vər hed′; *for adv.* ō′vər hed′) *adj.* 1 *a)* located or operating above the level of the head ☆*b)* designating a door, as of a garage, that moves into place overhead when opened **2** in the sky **3** on a higher level, with reference to related objects [a machine with an *overhead* drive] **4** having to do with the overhead of a business **5** *Sports* made with a downward motion from above the head [an *overhead* stroke] —*n.* **1** the general, continuing costs involved in running a business, as of rent, maintenance, utilities, etc. **2** *Navy* the ceiling of a compartment **3** *Sports* a type of shot, as in tennis, made with a hard, overhead stroke —*adv.* above the level of the head; aloft

☆**overhead projector** a projector having a flat, transparent top on which a sheetlike transparency is placed, and an overhead mirror that reflects the image on the transparency to a screen

o·ver·hear (ō′vər hir′) *vt.* **-heard′**, **-hear′ing** to hear (something spoken or a speaker) without the speaker's knowledge or intention

o·ver·heat (ō′vər hēt′) *vt., vi.* to make or become too hot

o·ver·heat·ed (-hēt′id) *adj.* **1** subjected to too much heat [*overheated* leftovers] **2** displaying excessive passion or excitement [a romance author's *overheated* prose]

O·ver·ijs·sel (ō′və ri′səl) province of the E Netherlands, bordering on Germany; 1,320 sq mi (3,419 sq km)

o·ver·in·dul·gence (ō′vər in dul′jəns) *n.* excessive indulgence —**o′ver·in·dul′gent** *adj.* —**o′ver·in·dul′gent·ly** *adv.*

o·ver·is·sue (ō′vər ish′o͞o) *n.* an issue, as of bonds or stocks, that exceeds authorization, credit limits, etc.

o·ver·joyed (ō′vər joid′) *adj.* feeling great joy

☆**o·ver·kill** (ō′vər kil′) *n.* **1** the capacity of a nation's nuclear weapon stockpile to kill many times the total population of any given nation **2** much more of something than is necessary, appropriate, etc.; esp., an excess of effort in attempting to achieve some end

o·ver·lad·en (ō′vər lād′'n) *adj.* having too heavy a load

o·ver·land (ō′vər land′, -lənd) *adv., adj.* by, on, or across land

O·ver·land Park (ō′vər lənd) ⟦after the *Overland*, or Santa Fe, Trail which passed through the area⟧ city in NE Kans.: suburb of Kansas City

o·ver·lap (ō′vər lap′; *also, and for n. always,* ō′vər lap′) *vt., vi.* **-lapped′**, **-lap′ping** **1** to lap over; lie upon and extend beyond a part of (something or each other) **2** to extend over part of (a period of time, sphere of activity, etc.); coincide in part (with) —*n.* **1** an overlapping **2** a part that overlaps **3** the amount or extent of overlapping **4** the place of overlapping

o·ver·lay (ō′vər lā′; *also, and for n. always,* ō′vər lā′) *vt.* **-laid′**, **-lay′ing** **1** to lay or spread over **2** to cover or overspread, as with a decorative layer of something **3** *Printing* to place an overlay upon —*n.* **1** anything laid over another thing; covering **2** a decorative layer or the like, applied in overlaying **3** a transparent flap showing additional details, areas of color, etc. placed over a map, art work, etc. ☆**4** in betting, odds which are set higher than expected or warranted **5** *Printing* the paper affixed to the impression surface of a press to help make a uniform impression

o·ver·leaf (ō′vər lēf′) *adj., adv.* on the other side of the page or sheet

o·ver·leap (ō′vər lēp′) *vt.* **-leapt′** (-lept′, -lēpt′) or **-lept′** or **-leaped′**, **-leap′ing** **1** to leap over or across **2** to omit; ignore **3** to overreach (oneself) by leaping too far

o·ver·learn (ō′vər lurn′) *vt.* to learn, as through much repetition, beyond basic proficiency

o·ver·lie (ō′vər lī′) *vt.* **-lay′**, **-lain′**, **-ly′ing** **1** to lie on or over **2** to stifle or smother by lying on

o·ver·load (ō′vər lōd′; *also, and for n. always,* ō′vər lōd′) *vt.* to put too great a load in or on —*n.* too great a load

o·ver·long (ō′vər lôŋ′, ō′vər lôŋ′) *adj., adv.* too long

o·ver·look (ō′vər lo͝ok′; *for n.* ō′vər lo͝ok′) *vt.* **1** to look at from above **2** to give a view of from above **3** to rise above; overtop **4** *a)* to look over or beyond and not see; fail to notice *b)* to ignore; neglect **5** to pass over indulgently; excuse **6** *a)* to oversee; supervise *b)* [Now Rare] to inspect; look over **7** [Archaic] to bewitch by looking at —☆*n.* a height from which to view surroundings —**SYN.** NEGLECT

o·ver·lord (ō′vər lôrd′) *n.* **1** a lord ranking above other lords, esp. in the feudal system **2** any person having great authority or power over others —**o′ver·lord′ship** *n.*

o·ver·ly (ō′vər lē) *adv.* ⟦ME *overliche:* see OVER & -LY[2]⟧ too or too much; excessively

o·ver·man (ō′vər man′, -mən; *for v.* ō′vər man′) *n., pl.* **-men′** (-men′, -mən) a man above others in power or authority —*vt.* **-manned′**, **-man′ning** to supply with more persons than necessary

o·ver·mas·ter (ō′vər mas′tər) *vt.* ⟦ME *overmaistren*⟧ to overcome; conquer; subdue

o·ver·match (ō′vər mach′) *vt.* **1** to be more than a match for **2** to match against a superior opponent

o·ver·much (ō′vər much′) *adj., adv.* too much —*n.* too great a quantity; excessive amount

o·ver·nice (ō′vər nīs′) *adj.* too nice; too fastidious, precise, etc.

o·ver·night (ō′vər nīt′, ō′vər nīt′) *adv.* **1** during or through the night **2** on or during the previous evening **3** suddenly —*adj.* **1** done or going on during or through the night **2** of or for the previous evening **3** staying through the night [an *overnight* guest] ☆**4** of or for a brief trip [an *overnight* bag] —*n.* an overnight stay, usually one away from home —*vi.* to spend the night, usually away from home

o·ver·night·er (ō′vər nīt′ər) *n.* **1** a small piece of luggage for use on a brief trip ☆**2** [Informal] an overnight stay or trip

o·ver·pass (ō′vər pas′; *for v.* ō′vər pas′) ☆*n.* a bridge or other passageway over a road, railway, etc. —*vt.* [Now Rare] **1** to pass over, across, or through **2** to surpass; outdo **3** to overlook; ignore

o·ver·pay (ō′vər pā′, ō′vər pā′) *vt., vi.* **-paid′**, **-pay′ing** **1** to pay too much, or more than (the due amount) **2** to pay too much to (someone) —**o′ver·pay′ment** *n.*

o·ver·per·suade (ō′vər pər swād′) *vt.* **-suad′ed**, **-suad′ing** [Rare] to win over by persuading; esp., to persuade (someone) against one's natural inclinations

o·ver·play (ō′vər plā′, ō′vər plā′) *vt.* **1** to overact, overdo, or overemphasize **2** to overestimate the strength of (one's hand in cards) and be defeated as a result: the phrase **overplay one's hand** is usually used figuratively

o·ver·plus (ō′vər plus′) *n.* ⟦ME *overe-plus,* partial transl. of OFr *surplus,* SURPLUS⟧ **1** an amount left over; surplus ☆**2** too great an amount; excess

o·ver·pop·u·late (ō′vər päp′yo͞o lāt′) *vt.* **-lat′ed**, **-lat′ing** to populate (an area) too heavily for the available sustaining resources —**o′ver·pop′u·la′tion** *n.*

o·ver·pow·er (ō′vər pou′ər) *vt.* **1** to get the better of by superior power; make helpless; subdue **2** to dominate because of superior or excessive strength; overwhelm [a dish *overpowered* by garlic] **3** to supply with more power than is needed —**o′ver·pow′er·ing** *adj.* —**o′ver·pow′er·ing·ly** *adv.*

o·ver·price (ō′vər prīs′) *vt.* **-priced′**, **-pric′ing** to offer for sale at too high a price

o·ver·print (ō′vər print′; *also, and for n. always,* ō′vər print′) *vt.* to print over or on top of (a previously printed surface) —*n.* **1** anything overprinted **2** *a)* anything officially printed over the original design on a stamp *b)* a stamp so overprinted

o·ver·pro·duce (ō′vər prō do͞os′, -dyo͞os′) *vt., vi.* **-duced′**, **-duc′ing** to produce in a quantity that exceeds the need or demand —**o′ver·pro·duc′tion** *n.*

o·ver·proof (ō′vər pro͞of′) *adj.* containing more alcohol than proof spirit does

o·ver·pro·tect (ō′vər prə tekt′) *vt.* to protect more than is necessary or desirable; specif., to exercise excessive, damaging control over (one's child, etc.) in seeking to shield from hurt, conflict, disappointment, etc. —**o′ver·pro·tec′tion** *n.* —**o′ver·pro·tec′tive** *adj.* —**o′ver·pro·tec′tive·ness** *n.*

o·ver·qual·i·fied (ō′vər kwôl′i fīd′, -kwäl′-) *adj.* having more knowledge, education, experience, etc. than needed to qualify for a particular job

o·ver·rate (ō′vər rāt′) *vt.* **-rat′ed**, **-rat′ing** to rate, assess, or estimate too highly

o·ver·reach (ō′vər rēch′, ō′vər rēch′) *vt.* **1** to reach or stretch beyond or above; extend beyond **2** to reach too far for and miss **3** to get the better of by cunning or cheating; outwit —*vi.* **1** to reach too far **2** to strike the forefoot with the hind foot: said of animals —**overreach oneself** **1** to fail because of trying to do more than one can **2** to fail because of being too crafty or eager —**o′ver·reach′er** *n.*

o·ver·re·act (ō′vər rē akt′) *vi.* to react with more energy or force than seems called for, as from strong emotion —**o′ver·re·ac′tion** *n.*

o·ver·rep·re·sent (ō′vər rep′ri zent′) *vt.* to represent in numbers that are greater, or in a proportion that is greater, than is statistically expected or warranted —**o′ver·rep′re·sen·ta′tion** *n.*

o·ver·ride (ō′vər rīd′; *for n.* ō′vər rīd′) *vt.* **-rode′**, **-rid′den**, **-rid′ing** **1** to ride over **2** to trample down **3** to surpass or prevail over **4** to disregard, overrule, or nullify; specif., *a)* to change or cancel (an automatic function) *b)* to overrule (a veto), as by a supermajority vote by the legislature **5** to fatigue (a horse, etc.) by riding too long **6** to pass or extend over ☆**7** to receive a commission on the sales made by (a subagent) **8** *Surgery* to overlap —*n.* **1** the act or an instance of overriding **2** a system or device for changing or canceling an automatic function ☆**3** the commission paid an agent or manager on sales made by his or her representatives

o·ver·rule (ō′vər ro͞ol′) *vt.* **-ruled′**, **-rul′ing** **1** to set aside or decide against by virtue of higher authority; rule against or rule out; annul or reverse **2** to have a dominant influence over; prevail over

o·ver·run (ō′vər run′; *also, and for n. always,* ō′vər run′) *vt.* **-ran′**, **-run′**, **-run′ning** **1** to run or spread out over so as to cover **2** to infest or swarm over, as vermin, or rove over and ravage, as an invading army **3** to invade, defeat, or conquer by a rapid, broad advance **4** to spread swiftly throughout, as ideas, a fad, etc. **5** to run or extend beyond (certain limits) [to *overrun* second base] **6** [Archaic] to outrun **7** *Printing a)* to rearrange (type matter) by shifting from one line to another *b)* to print more copies of (a given work) than ordered —*vi.* **1** to overflow **2** to run over or beyond certain limits —*n.* **1** the act or an instance of overrunning **2** the amount of money by which a product or project exceeds its estimated cost **3** an excess amount produced, as of manufactured goods or copies of printed matter

o·ver·scale (ō′vər skāl′) *adj.* larger than the normal or usual size or large in relation to its surroundings: also **o′ver·scaled′**

o·ver·score (ō′vər skôr′) *vt.* **-scored′**, **-scor′ing** to draw a line over or through (a word, sentence, etc.)

o·ver·seas (ō′vər sēz′) *adv.* abroad; over or beyond the sea —*adj.* **1** of, from, or to countries across the sea; foreign **2** over or across the sea Also [Chiefly Brit.] **o′ver·sea′**

☆**overseas cap** a soft military cap without a visor or brim

o·ver·see (ō′vər sē′) *vt.* **-saw′**, **-seen′**, **-see′ing** ⟦ME *overseen* < OE *oferseon:* see OVER & SEE[1]⟧ **1** to watch over and manage; supervise; superintend 2 to catch sight of (a person or persons in some action) secretly or accidentally 3 to survey; watch 4 [Archaic] to examine; inspect

o·ver·se·er (ō′vər sē′ər) *n.* one who watches over and directs the work of others; supervisor

o·ver·sell (ō′vər sel′) *vt.* **-sold′**, **-sell′ing** 1 to sell more than can be supplied ☆2 to promote, try to persuade, etc. to such an extreme degree as to defeat one's purposes

o·ver·set (ō′vər set′; *also, and for n. always,* ō′vər set′) *vt.* **-set′**, **-set′ting** 1 to overcome or upset 2 to overturn or overthrow 3 to set too great an amount of (type or copy), or too much type for (a given space) —*vi.* to overturn; tip over —*n.* 1 an overturning 2 type matter set and not used

o·ver·sew (ō′vər sō′, ō′vər sō′) *vt.* **-sewed′**, **-sewed′** or **-sewn′**, **-sew′ing** to sew together (two pieces of material) by passing small, close stitches over their coinciding edges; sew overhand

o·ver·sexed (ō′vər sekst′, ō′vər sekst′) *adj.* characterized by an exceptional sexual drive or preoccupation with sexual matters

o·ver·shade (ō′vər shād′) *vt.* **-shad′ed**, **-shad′ing** OVERSHADOW

o·ver·shad·ow (ō′vər shad′ō) *vt.* ⟦ME *ouerschadewen* < OE *ofersceadwian* (see OVER & SHADOW), transl. of LL *obumbrare* in N.T.: see Luke 9:34⟧ 1 *a)* to cast a shadow over *b)* to darken; obscure 2 to be, by comparison, more significant or important than

☆**o·ver·shoe** (ō′vər sho͞o′) *n.* any of various shoes or boots, made of rubber or fabric, designed to be worn over the regular shoe to protect against cold or dampness

o·ver·shoot (ō′vər sho͞ot′, ō′vər sho͞ot′) *vt.* **-shot′**, **-shoot′ing** 1 to shoot or pass over or beyond (a target, mark, etc.); specif., to fly an aircraft beyond (a runway, landing field, etc.) while trying to land 2 to go farther than (an intended or normal limit); exceed —*vi.* to shoot or go too far

o·ver·shot (ō′vər shät′) *adj.* 1 with the upper part or half extending past the lower [an *overshot* jaw] 2 driven by water flowing onto the upper part [an *overshot* water wheel]

o·ver·sight (ō′vər sīt′) *n.* 1 superintendence or supervision, often, specif., as part of governmental regulation 2 an unintentional, careless mistake or omission

o·ver·sim·pli·fy (ō′vər sim′plə fī′) *vt., vi.* **-fied′**, **-fy′ing** to simplify to the point of distortion, as by ignoring essential details —**o′ver·sim′pli·fi·ca′tion** *n.*

o·ver·size (ō′vər sīz′) *adj.* 1 too large 2 larger than the normal or usual; outsize Also **o′ver·sized′** —*n.* a size larger than regular sizes; outsize

☆**o·ver·skirt** (ō′vər skʉrt′) *n.* an outer skirt

o·ver·slaugh (ō′vər slô′) *vt.* ⟦< Du *overslaan,* to pass over, omit < *over* (akin to OVER), + *slaan,* to beat, strike: for IE base see SLAY⟧ ☆1 to pass over (one person) by preferring or promoting another ☆2 to bar or hinder

o·ver·sleep (ō′vər slēp′, ō′vər slēp′) *vi.* **-slept′**, **-sleep′ing** to sleep past the intended time for getting up

☆**o·ver·soul** (ō′vər sōl′) *n.* the universal mind or spirit that animates, motivates, and is the unifying principle of all living things: a concept in the transcendentalist philosophy of Emerson and others

o·ver·spend (ō′vər spend′, ō′vər spend′) *vt.* **-spent′**, **-spend′ing** 1 [Rare] to use till worn out; exhaust 2 to spend more than —*vi.* to spend more than one can afford

☆**o·ver·spin** (ō′vər spin′) *n.* 1 faster or exaggerated spin given to a ball when hitting or throwing it 2 TOPSPIN

o·ver·spread (ō′vər spred′) *vt.* **-spread′**, **-spread′ing** to spread over; cover the surface of

o·ver·state (ō′vər stāt′) *vt.* **-stat′ed**, **-stat′ing** to give an extravagant or magnified account of (facts, truth, etc.); exaggerate —**o′ver·state′ment** *n.*

o·ver·stay (ō′vər stā′) *vt.* to stay beyond the time, duration, or limits of

o·ver·steer (ō′vər stir′) *n.* the tendency of a motor vehicle, esp. a race car, to have its rear tires slide outward on a turn

o·ver·step (ō′vər step′) *vt.* **-stepped′**, **-step′ping** to go beyond the limits of; exceed

o·ver·stock (ō′vər stäk′; *also, and for n. always,* ō′vər stäk′) *vt.* to stock (a store, etc.) with more of (something) than can be readily used —*n.* 1 too large a stock 2 surplus stock, specif. when sold at a reduced price

o·ver·strain (ō′vər strān′) *vt.* to put under very great strain; overwork —*vi.* to exert great effort

o·ver·stride (ō′vər strīd′) *vt.* **-strode′**, **-strid′den**, **-strid′ing** 1 to stride across or over; go beyond 2 to outdo; surpass 3 BESTRIDE

o·ver·strung (ō′vər struŋ′) *adj.* too highly strung; tense

o·ver·stud·y (ō′vər stud′ē) *vt., vi.* **-stud′ied**, **-stud′y·ing** to study too hard or too much —*n.* too much study

o·ver·stuff (ō′vər stuf′, ō′-) *vt.* 1 to stuff with too much of something 2 to upholster (furniture) with deep stuffing —**o′ver·stuffed′** *adj.*

o·ver·sub·scribe (ō′vər səb skrīb′) *vt., vi.* **-scribed′**, **-scrib′ing** to subscribe for more (of) than is available or asked —**o′ver·sub·scrip′tion** (-skrip′shən) *n.*

o·ver·sup·ply (ō′vər sə plī′) *vt.* **-plied′**, **-ply′ing** to supply in excess —*n., pl.* **-plies′** too great a supply

o·vert (ō vʉrt′, ō′vʉrt′) *adj.* ⟦ME *overte* < MFr *overt,* pp. of *ovrir,* to open < VL **operire* < L *aperire,* to open: see APERTURE⟧ 1 not hidden; open; observable; apparent; manifest 2 *Law* done openly and publicly, without attempt at concealment and with evident intent —**o·vert′ly** *adv.*

o·ver·take (ō′vər tāk′) *vt.* **-took′**, **-tak′en**, **-tak′ing** 1 to catch up with and, often, go beyond 2 to come upon unexpectedly or suddenly [a sudden storm *overtook* us] 3 to render outmoded, irrelevant, invalid, etc.: often in the pp. [a once cutting-edge analysis now *overtaken* by recent events]

o·ver·task (ō′vər task′) *vt.* to impose too great or heavy a task or tasks upon

o·ver·tax (ō′vər taks′) *vt.* 1 to tax too heavily 2 to make excessive demands on

o·ver-the-count·er (ō′vər *thə* kount′ər) *adj.* 1 *Finance* designating or of securities sold by traders directly to buyers rather than on the floor of a stock exchange 2 *Pharmacy* sold legally without prescription, as some drugs

o·ver-the-top (ō′vər *thə* täp′) *adj.* [Informal] so unconventional, exaggerated, or excessive as to be considered outrageous, unbelievable, ridiculous, etc.

o·ver·throw (ō′vər thrō′; *also, and for n. always,* ō′vər thrō′) *vt.* **-threw′**, **-thrown′**, **-throw′ing** 1 to throw or turn over; upset 2 to bring down from a position of authority or power; topple 3 to throw a ball or the like beyond (the intended receiver or target) —*n.* 1 an overthrowing or being overthrown 2 destruction; ruin; end —**SYN.** CONQUER

o·ver·time (ō′vər tīm′; *for v., usually* ō′vər tīm′) *n.* 1 time beyond the established limit 2 *a)* working time in addition to standard working hours *b)* pay for work done during this time 3 *Sports* an extra time period added to the game to decide a tie — *adj., adv.* of, for, or during a period of overtime —*vt.* **-timed′**, **-tim′ing** to allow too much time for (a photographic exposure, etc.)

o·ver·tone (ō′vər tōn′) *n.* ⟦transl. of Ger *oberton,* contr. < *oberpartialton,* upper partial tone⟧ 1 *Acoustics, Music* any of the attendant higher tones heard with a fundamental tone produced by the vibration of a given string or column of air, having a frequency of vibration that is an exact multiple of the frequency of the fundamental 2 an implication; nuance: *usually used in pl.* [a reply full of *overtones*]

o·ver·top (ō′vər täp′) *vt.* **-topped′**, **-top′ping** 1 to rise above; exceed in height; tower over 2 to excel; surpass

o·ver·trade (ō′vər trād′, ō′vər trād′) *vi.* **-trad′ed**, **-trad′ing** to trade beyond one's financial means or the market demand

o·ver·train (ō′vər trān′, ō′vər trān′) *vt., vi.* to train too long or too hard

o·ver·trick (ō′vər trik′) *n. Bridge* a trick taken in excess of the number bid

o·ver·trump (ō′vər trump′) *vt., vi. Card Games* to play a trump higher than (a trump already played on a trick)

o·ver·ture (ō′vər chər) *n.* ⟦ME, an opening < OFr < VL **opertura* < L *apertura,* APERTURE⟧ 1 an introductory proposal or offer; indication of willingness to negotiate 2 *a)* a musical introduction to an opera or other large musical work *b)* an independent orchestral composition of varying form 3 in Presbyterian churches, a proposal or question submitted as by the general assembly to the presbyteries 4 any introductory section —*vt.* **-tured**, **-tur·ing** to present as an overture

o·ver·turn (ō′vər tʉrn′; *for n.* ō′vər tʉrn′) *vt.* 1 to turn or throw over; upset 2 to conquer; defeat; ruin —*vi.* to turn or tip over; capsize —*n.* an overturning or being overturned —**SYN.** UPSET

☆**o·ver-un·der** (ō′vər un′dər) *adj.* designating a double-barreled firearm with one barrel over the other

o·ver·use (ō′vər yo͞os′, ō′vər yo͞os′; *for v.* ō′vər yo͞oz′) *n.* too much use —*vt.* **-used′**, **-us′ing** to use too much or too often

o·ver·val·ue (ō′vər val′yo͞o) *vt.* **-val′ued**, **-val′uing** 1 to value too high, or above the actual worth 2 to regard or esteem too highly —**o′ver·val′u·a′tion** *n.*

o·ver·view (ō′vər vyo͞o′) *n.* a general review or survey

o·ver·watch (ō′vər wäch′) *vt.* 1 to watch over 2 [Archaic] to make weary by long watching

o·ver·wea·ry (ō′vər wir′ē) *adj.* weary to the point of exhaustion —*vt.* **-ried**, **-ry·ing** to make overweary; exhaust

o·ver·ween·ing (ō′vər wēn′iŋ) *adj.* ⟦ME *oferweninge,* prp. of *oferwenen* < OE *oferwenan:* see OVER- & WEEN⟧ 1 arrogant; excessively proud 2 exaggerated; excessive —**o′ver·ween′ing·ly** *adv.*

o·ver·weigh (ō′vər wā′) *vt.* 1 OUTWEIGH 2 to burden; oppress; weigh down

o·ver·weight (ō′vər wāt′; *for adj. & v., also,* ō′vər wāt′) *n.* more weight than is needed, desired, or allowed; extra or surplus weight —*adj.* 1 above the normal, desirable, or allowed weight 2 *Finance* holding or containing relatively more of a specified asset, security, etc., as in relation to some benchmark —*vt.* 1 OVERWEIGH 2 *Finance* in investing, to hold a larger amount or proportion of in a portfolio, as in relation to some benchmark [to *overweight* oil stocks]

o·ver·whelm (ō′vər hwelm′, -welm′) *vt.* ⟦ME *oferwhelmen:* see OVER- & WHELM⟧ 1 to pour down upon and cover over or bury beneath 2 to dominate, subdue, obliterate, etc. as because of superior or excessive strength; overpower 3 to overcome emotionally [he was *overwhelmed* by their generosity] 4 [Obs.] to overthrow or overturn —**o′ver·whelm′ing** *adj.* —**o′ver·whelm′ing·ly** *adv.*

o·ver·wind (ō′vər wīnd′, ō′vər wīnd′) *vt.* **-wound′**, **-wind′ing** to wind (a watch spring, etc.) too far or too tightly

o·ver·win·ter (ō′vər wint′ər) *vi.* to pass the winter

o·ver·work (ō′vər wʉrk′, ō′vər wʉrk′) *vt.* 1 to work or use to excess [to *overwork* a horse; to *overwork* an excuse] 2 to decorate the surface of 3 to make very excited or nervous —*vi.* to work too hard or too long —*n.* 1 work that is severe or burdensome 2 work beyond the amount agreed upon; extra work

o·ver·worn (ō′vər wôrn′) *adj.* [Rare] worn-out or exhausted; outworn

o·ver·write (ō′vər rīt′; *also, and for n. always,* ō′vər rīt′) *vt., vi.* **-wrote′**, **-writ′ten**, **-writ′ing** 1 *a)* to write (something) over other writing *b)* to write over (other writing) 2 *Comput.* to record (data) in a file, on a disk, etc. in such a way as to replace data that is already there 3 *a)* to write too much about (some subject) *b)* to write (something) in too flowery or labored a style 4 OVERRIDE (*vt.* 7) —*n.* OVERRIDE

o·ver·wrought (ō′vər rôt′) *adj.* 1 [Archaic] overworked; fatigued 2 very nervous or excited 3 with the surface adorned 4 too elaborate; ornate

o·vi- (ō′vi, -və) ⟦< L *ovum,* EGG[1]⟧ *combining form* egg or ovum *[oviduct, oviform]*: also **o·vo-** (ō′vō)

Ov·id (äv′id) (L. name *Publius Ovidius Naso*) 43 B.C.-A.D. 17?; Rom. poet —**O·vid·i·an** (ä vid′ē ən) *adj.*

o·vi·duct (ō′vi dukt′, äv′i-) *n.* ⟦ModL *oviductus:* see OVI- & DUCT⟧ a duct or tube through which the ova pass from an ovary to the uterus or to the outside

O·vie·do (ô vye′thô) city in NW Spain

o·vif·er·ous (ō vif′ər əs) *adj.* ⟦OVI- & -FEROUS⟧ carrying ova

o·vi·form (ō′vi fôrm′) *adj.* ⟦OVI- & -FORM⟧ egg-shaped

o·vine (ō′vīn′) *adj.* ⟦LL *ovinus* < L *ovis,* sheep: see EWE⟧ of, or having the nature of, sheep

o·vip·a·rous (ō vip′ə rəs) *adj.* ⟦L *oviparus:* see OVI- & -PAROUS⟧ 1 producing eggs that develop and hatch after leaving the body of the female 2 designating or of this type of reproduction See VIVIPAROUS —**o·vi·par·i·ty** (ō′vi par′ə tē) *n.*, **o·vip′a·rous·ness** —**o·vip′a·rous·ly** *adv.*

o·vi·pos·it (ō′vi päz′it, ō′vi päz′it) *vi.* ⟦< OVI- + L *positus,* pp. of *ponere,* to place: see POSITION⟧ to deposit or lay eggs, esp. by means of an ovipositor —**o′vi·po·si′tion** (-pə zish′ən) *n.* —**o′vi·po·si′tion·al** *adj.*

o·vi·pos·i·tor (ō′vi päz′i tər) *n.* ⟦ModL < OVI- + L *positor,* one who places < *ponere:* see prec.⟧ 1 a special organ of many female insects, usually at the end of the abdomen, for depositing eggs, often in a host 2 an extension of the female genital orifice of certain fishes

o·vi·sac (ō′vi sak′) *n.* ⟦OVI- + SAC⟧ 1 OOTHECA 2 *Anat.* an egg receptacle

o·void (ō′void′) *adj.* ⟦OV(I)- + -OID⟧ egg-shaped; ovate: also **o·voi′dal** —*n.* anything of ovoid form

o·vo-lac·to vegetarian (ō′vō lak′tō) ⟦*ovo-* (var. of OVI-) + LACTO-⟧ a vegetarian who eats eggs and dairy products

o·vo·lo (ō′və lō′) *n., pl.* **-li′** (-lē′, -lī′) ⟦obs. It (now *uovolo*), dim. of *ovo* < L *ovum,* EGG[1]⟧ a convex molding, in cross section a quarter of a circle or an ellipse

☆**o·von·ic** (ō vän′ik) *adj.* ⟦after S. R. *Ov(shinsky)* (1922-2012), U.S. inventor + *(electr)onic*⟧ *[also* **O-**] designating, of, or utilizing any of various glassy, amorphous materials that act as semiconductors when subjected to voltage, light, etc.

o·vo·tes·tis (ō′vō tes′tis) *n.* ⟦*ovo-* (var. of OVI-) + TESTIS⟧ a single reproductive organ that produces both sperm and ova, either at different times or concurrently, as in many invertebrates

o·vo·vi·vip·a·rous (ō′vō vī vip′ə rəs) *adj.* ⟦*ovo-* (var. of OVI-) + VIVIPAROUS⟧ designating various animals, as some reptiles, fishes, and snails, which produce eggs with enclosing membranes, that are hatched within the female so that the young are born alive —**o′vo·vi′vi·par′i·ty** (-vī′vi par′ə tē) *n.*, **o′vo·vi·vip′a·rous·ness** —**o′vo·vi·vip′a·rous·ly** *adv.*

ov·u·lar (äv′yoo lər, -yə-; ō′vyoo-, -vyə-) *adj.* ⟦ModL *ovularis* < *ovulum:* see OVULE⟧ of or having to do with an ovule

ov·u·late (äv′yə lāt′, ō′vyə-) *vi.* **-lat′ed, -lat′ing** ⟦back-form. < fol.⟧ to produce and discharge an ovum or ova from an ovary

ov·u·la·tion (äv′yə lā′shən ō′vyə-) *n.* ⟦fol. + -ATION⟧ the process by which a mature ovum escapes from an ovary —**ov′u·la·to′ry** (-lə tôr′ē) *adj.*

ov·ule (äv′yool′, ō′vyool′) *n.* ⟦Fr < ModL *ovulum,* dim. < L *ovum,* EGG[1]⟧ a small egg or seed, esp. one in an early stage of development; specif., *a) Bot.* a structure in seed plants consisting of a nucellus that contains an embryo sac: it develops into a seed after fertilization (see AMPHITROPOUS, ANATROPOUS, CAMPYLOTROPOUS, ORTHOTROPOUS) *b) Zool.* the immature ovum in the graafian follicle

o·vum (ō′vəm) *n., pl.* **o·va** (ō′və) ⟦L, EGG[1]⟧ 1 *Biol.* a mature female germ cell which, generally only after fertilization, develops into a new member of the same species; female gamete; egg 2 *Archit.* an egg-shaped ornament

ow (ou) *interj.* used to express pain or as a cry of pain

owe (ō) *vt.* **owed, ow′ing** ⟦ME *owen* < OE *agan,* to own, possess, have, akin to Goth *aigan,* OHG *eigan* < IE base **ēik-,* to have as one's own, be capable (of) > Sans **īśe,* (he) possesses⟧ 1 to have an obligation to pay; be indebted to the amount of 2 to have or feel the need to do, give, etc., as because of gratitude 3 to have or cherish (a certain feeling) toward another: now only in **owe a grudge** 4 to be indebted *to* someone for the existence of 5 [Obs.] to own; have —*vi.* to be in debt —**owe it to oneself** to be right in doing something, because it is to one's advantage

OWelsh *abbrev.* Old Welsh

Ow·en[1] (ō′ən) *n.* ⟦Welsh < *Owein,* earlier *Ewein,* < Celt **Esuganyos,* akin to Gr *Eugenios:* see EUGENE[1]⟧ a masculine name

Ow·en[2] (ō′ən) 1 Sir **Richard** 1804-92; Brit. anatomist & paleontologist 2 **Robert** 1771-1858; Brit. industrialist & socialist 3 **Wilfred** 1893-1918; Eng. poet

Ow·ens (ō′ənz), **Jesse** (born *James Cleveland Owens*) 1913-80; U.S. track-and-field athlete

Owen Stanley Range mountain range of Papua New Guinea, in SE New Guinea: highest peak, 13,363 ft (4,073 m)

ow·ing (ō′iŋ) *adj.* ⟦ME *owynge*⟧ due; unpaid *[ten dollars owing on a bill]* —**owing to** because of; as a result of

owl (oul) *n.* ⟦ME *owle* < OE *ule,* akin to Ger *eule* < IE echoic base **ul-* > L *ulula,* owl, *ululare,* to howl⟧ any of a worldwide order (Strigiformes) of predatory night birds distinguished by a large, flat face, eyes surrounded by stiff-feathered disks, a short, hooked beak, feathered legs with sharp talons, and soft plumage which permits noiseless flight: applied fig. to a person of nocturnal habits, solemn appearance, etc. —**owl′like′** *adj.*

owl·et (oul′it) *n.* any young or small owl

owl·ish (oul′ish) *adj.* like or characteristic of an owl; specif., *a)* of or having eyes that appear large and round *b)* of or having a solemn or watchful expression —**owl′ish·ly** *adv.* —**owl′ish·ness** *n.*

☆**owl's-clo·ver** (oulz′klō′vər) *n.* any of a genus (*Orthocarpus*) of plants of the figwort family of W North and South America; esp., a California species (*O. purpurascens*) with red or purple upper leaves

own (ōn) *adj.* ⟦ME *owen* < OE *agen,* pp. of *agan,* to possess: see OWE⟧ 1 belonging, relating, or peculiar to oneself or itself: used to strengthen a preceding possessive *[his own book, her own idea]* 2 [Now Rare] related by blood rather than by marriage — *n., pron.* that which belongs to oneself *[the car is his own; I have reasons of my own]* —*vt.* 1 to possess; hold as personal property; have 2 to admit; recognize; acknowledge —*vi.* to confess (*to*) —*SYN.* ACKNOWLEDGE —**come into one's own** to receive what properly belongs to one, esp. acclaim or recognition —**get one's own back** [Informal, Chiefly Brit.] to get or take revenge; get even —**of one's own** belonging strictly to oneself —**on one's own** [Informal] 1 by one's own efforts or on one's own initiative 2 independent of help from others —**own up (to)** to confess (to) —**own′er** *n.* —**own′er·less** *adj.*

own·er·ship (ōn′ər ship′) *n.* 1 the state or fact of being an owner 2 legal right of possession; lawful title (to something); proprietorship —**take ownership (of)** [Informal] to take personal responsibility for (something)

ox (äks) *n., pl.* **ox′en** or [Rare] **ox** ⟦ME < OE *oxa,* akin to Ger *ochse* < IE **ukwsen-,* a bull < base **wegw-, *ūgw-,* wet, sprinkle > HUMOR, HUMID, L *umere,* to be moist⟧ any of several bovid ruminants, as cattle, buffaloes, bison, gaur, and yaks; esp., a castrated, domesticated bull (*Bos taurus*), used as a draft animal

Ox *abbrev.* Oxford

ox- *combining form* 1 OXY-[1] 2 OXA-

ox·a- (äk′sə) ⟦var. < OXY-[1]⟧ *combining form Chem.* oxygen, esp. as replacing carbon in a ring *[oxazine]*

ox·a·cil·lin (äk′sə sil′in) *n.* ⟦OX- + A(ZOLE) + (PENI)CILLIN⟧ a derivative of penicillin used esp. in treating staphylococcal infections resistant to penicillin

ox·a·late (äk′sə lāt′) *n.* ⟦Fr: see fol. & -ATE[2]⟧ 1 a salt of oxalic acid containing the divalent, negative radical $(COO)_2$ 2 an uncharged ester of this acid

ox·al·ic acid (äk sal′ik) ⟦Fr *oxalique* < L *oxalis:* see fol.⟧ a colorless, poisonous, crystalline acid, $(COOH)_2$, found in oxalis and other plants or prepared synthetically and used in dyeing, bleaching, etc.

ox·a·lis (äk′sə lis) *n.* ⟦L, garden sorrel < Gr < *oxys,* acid, sour: see OXY-[2]⟧ WOOD SORREL

ox·a·zine (äk′sə zēn′, -zin) *n.* ⟦OX(A)- + AZINE⟧ any of thirteen compounds having a composition corresponding to the formula C_4H_5NO and composed of molecules which contain four atoms of carbon and one atom each of oxygen and nitrogen united in a ring structure

ox·blood (äks′blud′) *n.* a deep-red color

ox·bow (äks′bō′) *n.* ⟦ME *oxboue:* see OX & BOW[2]⟧ 1 either of the U-shaped parts of an ox yoke: an oxbow passes under and around the neck of a yoked ox ☆2 *a)* something shaped like this, as a bend in a river *b)* the land within such a bend

Ox·bridge (äks′brij) *n.* ⟦OX(FORD) + (CAM)BRIDGE⟧ Oxford and Cambridge universities thought of together, as in terms of their similar organization, traditions, or prestige —*adj.* of or relating to Oxbridge

ox·en (äk′sən) *n. pl. of* OX

ox·eye (äk′sī′) *n.* ⟦ME *oxie:* see OX & EYE⟧ any of several composite plants, as a sunflowerlike perennial plant (*Heliopsis helianthoides*) of E North America

☆**oxeye daisy** DAISY (sense 1)

Oxf *abbrev.* 1 Oxford 2 Oxfordshire

Ox·fam (äks′fam′) *n.* an international organization (in full, *Oxford Committee for Famine Relief*), established in England in 1942 to provide training and financial aid to people in developing countries and disaster areas

ox·ford (äks′fərd) *n.* ⟦after fol.⟧ *[sometimes* **O-**] 1 a type of low shoe laced over the instep: also **oxford shoe** 2 a cotton or rayon fabric with a basketlike weave, used for shirts, etc.: also **oxford cloth**

oxford

Ox·ford (äks′fərd) ⟦OE *Oxenaford* < *oxan,* gen. pl. of *oxa,* OX + *ford,* FORD: originally a place where oxen forded the river⟧ 1 city in SC England; county seat of Oxfordshire & the site of Oxford University 2 OXFORDSHIRE

Oxford gray a very dark gray, approaching black

Oxford movement *[also* **O- M-**] a High-Church, anti-liberal movement within the Church of England, begun at Oxford University in 1833: see TRACTARIANISM

Ox·ford·shire (äks′fərd shir′, -shər) county in SC England: 997 sq mi (2,582 sq km)

ox·heart (äks′härt′) *n.* ⟦so named from its shape⟧ ☆any of various kinds of large cherry

ox·i·dant (äk′si dənt) *n.* an oxidizing agent

ox·i·dase (äk′si dās′, -dāz′) *n.* ⟦OXID(IZE) + -ASE⟧ any oxidoreductase enzyme that acts as a catalyst in oxidation reactions in which oxygen is the electron acceptor

ox·i·da·tion (äk′si dā′shən) ***n.*** ⟦Fr: see OXIDE & -ATION⟧ **1** any process in which oxygen combines with an element or substance, either slowly, as in the rusting of iron, or rapidly, as in the burning of wood **2** the process of increasing the positive valence or of decreasing the negative valence of an element or ion **3** the process by which electrons are removed from atoms or ions Cf. REDUCTION (and REDUCE, ***vt.*** 10) —**ox′i·da′tive** ***adj.***

ox·i·da·tion-re·duc·tion (-rē duk′shən) ***n.*** a chemical reaction in which one of the reactants is reduced (gains one or more electrons) and another reactant is oxidized (loses one or more electrons)

ox·ide (äk′sīd′) ***n.*** ⟦Fr < Gr *oxys,* acid, sour (see OXY-²) + Fr *(ac)ide,* ACID⟧ a binary compound of oxygen with some other element or with a radical

ox·i·dize (äk′si dīz′) ***vt.*** **-dized′**, **-diz′ing** ⟦prec. + -IZE⟧ **1** to unite with oxygen, as in burning or rusting **2** to increase the positive valence or decrease the negative valence of (an element or ion) **3** to remove electrons from (an atom or ion) —***vi.*** to become oxidized —**ox′i·diz′a·ble** ***adj.*** —**ox′i·diz′er** ***n.***

ox·i·do·re·duc·tase (äk′si dō rē duk′tās′, -tāz′) ***n.*** any of a class of enzymes that act as catalysts in chemical reactions involving oxidation-reduction

ox·ime (äk′sēm′, -sim) ***n.*** ⟦< OX(Y)-¹ (sense 1) + IM(IDE)⟧ any of a series of compounds formed by the action of hydroxylamine on an aldehyde or ketone, in which the oxygen atom of the CHO group of the aldehyde, or of the CO group of the ketone, is replaced by the:NOH group

ox·lip (äks′lip′) ***n.*** ⟦OE *oxanslyppe* < *oxan,* gen. of *oxa* (see OX) + *slyppe,* dropping: see SLIP³⟧ a perennial plant (*Primula elatior*) of the primrose family, having yellow flowers in early spring

Ox·nard (äks′närd) ⟦after H. T. *Oxnard,* local businessman⟧ city in SW Calif., near Los Angeles

Oxon *abbrev.* **1** ⟦L *Oxoniensis*⟧ of Oxford **2** ⟦L *Oxonia*⟧ *a)* Oxford *b)* Oxfordshire

Ox·o·ni·an (äk sō′nē ən) ***adj.*** ⟦< ML *Oxonia* < OE *Oxenaford,* OXFORD⟧ of Oxford (England) or Oxford University —***n.*** **1** a student or alumnus of Oxford University **2** a person born or living in Oxford, England

ox·peck·er (äks′pek′ər) ***n.*** any of a genus (*Buphagus*) of African starlings that feed on parasitic ticks found on the hides of large mammals, as cattle

ox·tail (äks′tāl′) ***n.*** the tail of an ox, steer, or cow, esp. when skinned and used in soup, stew, etc.

ox·tongue (äks′tuŋ′) ***n.*** [Obs.] any of a number of plants, as alkanet, with rough, tongue-shaped leaves

Ox·us (äk′səs) *Latin name for* AMU DARYA

ox·y-¹ (äk′si, -sə, -sē) ⟦< OXY(GEN)⟧ *combining form* **1** containing oxygen *[oxyacetylene, oxyhemoglobin]* **2** containing the hydroxyl radical *[oxytetracycline]*: in this sense HYDROXY- is preferred

ox·y-² (äk′si, -sə, -sē) ⟦< Gr *oxys,* sharp, acid < IE **ak̂s-* < base **ak-* > Gr *akmē,* a point, L *acus,* a needle, *acidus,* sour⟧ *combining form* sharp, pointed, acute, or acid *[oxycephaly, oxymoron, oxygen]*

ox·y·a·cet·y·lene (äk′sē ə set′'l ēn′) ***adj.*** ⟦OXY-¹ + ACETYLENE⟧ of or using a mixture of oxygen and acetylene, as for producing an extremely hot flame used in welding or cutting metals *[oxyacetylene* torch*]*

ox·y·ac·id (äk′sē as′id) ***n.*** an acid containing oxygen

ox·y·ceph·a·ly (äk′si sef′ə lē) ***n.*** ⟦< OXY-² + Gr *kephalē,* head: see CEPHALIC⟧ a condition in which the skull has a peaked or somewhat conical shape, specif. as a result of the premature closing of the skull sutures —**ox′y·ce·phal′ic** (-sə fal′ik) ***adj.***, **ox′y·ceph′a·lous** (-sef′ə ləs)

ox·y·gen (äk′si jən) ***n.*** ⟦Fr *oxygène,* altered (1786) < earlier *oxygine,* lit., acid-producing: so named (1777) by LAVOISIER < Gr *oxys* (see OXY-²) + L *gignere,* to beget (see GENUS): from the belief that oxygen is present in all acids⟧ a colorless, odorless, tasteless, gaseous chemical element that occurs free in the atmosphere, forming one fifth of its volume, and in combination in water, sandstone, limestone, etc.: it is very active, combines with nearly all other elements, is the most common element in the earth's crust, and is essential to life processes and to combustion: symbol, O; at. no. 8: see the periodic table of elements in the Reference Supplement —**ox′y·gen′ic** (-jen′ik) ***adj.***, **ox·yg·e·nous** (äk sij′ə nəs)

oxygen acid OXYACID

ox·y·gen·ate (äk′si jə nāt′) ***vt.*** **-at′ed**, **-at′ing** ⟦< Fr *oxygéner* + -ATE¹⟧ to mix, treat, or combine with oxygen —**ox′y·gen·a′tion** ***n.*** —**ox′y·gen·a′tor** ***n.***

ox·y·gen·ize (äk′si jə nīz′) ***vt.*** **-ized′**, **-iz′ing** **1** OXIDIZE **2** OXYGENATE

oxygen tent a transparent enclosure into which oxygen is released, fitted around a bed patient to improve the efficiency of oxygen intake per breath

ox·y·he·mo·glo·bin (äk′si hē′mō glō′bin) ***n.*** ⟦OXY-¹ + HEMOGLOBIN⟧ the bright-red substance that is found in the arterial blood, formed in the lungs by the loose union of hemoglobin with oxygen: it delivers oxygen to the bodily tissues

ox·y·hy·dro·gen (äk′si hī′drə jən) ***adj.*** ⟦OXY-¹ + HYDROGEN⟧ of or using a mixture of oxygen and hydrogen, as for producing a hot flame used in welding or cutting metals *[oxyhydrogen* torch*]*

ox·y·mo·ron (äk′si môr′än′) ***n.***, *pl.* **-rons′** or **-ra** (-rə) ⟦LGr *oxymōron* < neut. of *oxymōros,* acutely silly: see OXY-² & MORON⟧ a figure of speech in which opposite or contradictory ideas or terms are combined (Ex.: thunderous silence, sweet sorrow) —**ox′y·mo·ron′ic** ***adj.***

ox·y·phil (äk′si fil′) ***n.*** ⟦OXY-² + -PHIL⟧ ACIDOPHIL —**ox′y·phil′ic** ***adj.***

ox·y·sul·fide (äk′si sul′fīd′) ***n.*** a compound formed of an element or positive radical with oxygen and sulfur, in which oxygen may be thought of as replacing a part of the sulfur

ox·y·tet·ra·cy·cline (äk′si te′trə sī′klēn′, -klin) ***n.*** ⟦OXY-¹ + TETRA- + CYCL(IC) + -INE³⟧ an antibiotic, $C_{22}H_{24}N_2O_9$, derived from cultures of an actinomycetous bacterium (*Streptomyces rimosus*)

ox·y·to·cic (äk′si tō′sik, -täs′ik) ***adj.*** ⟦< Gr *oxytokion,* medicine for speeding childbirth < *oxys,* sharp, quick (see OXY-²) + *tokos,* birth < *tiktein,* to bear (for IE base see THANE) + -IC⟧ hastening the process of childbirth, as oxytocin does —***n.*** any oxytocic substance

ox·y·to·cin (äk′si tō′sin, -täs′in) ***n.*** ⟦< prec. + -IN¹⟧ a hormone, $C_{43}H_{66}N_{12}O_{12}S_2$, of the posterior pituitary gland, that stimulates contractions in the smooth muscle of the uterus and facilitates the secretion of milk: cf. NEUROHYPOPHYSIS

ox·y·tone (äk′si tōn′) ***adj.*** ⟦Gr *oxytonos* < *oxys,* sharp (see OXY-²) + *tonos,* TONE⟧ having an acute accent on the last syllable —***n.*** an oxytone word

oy (oi) ***interj.*** used to express surprise, pain, grief, worry, etc.

o·yer and ter·mi·ner (ō′yər and tur′mi nər, oi′ər-) ⟦ME, for Anglo-Fr *oyer et terminer,* lit., to hear and determine⟧ **1** a commission issued to English judges authorizing them to hear and determine criminal cases at the assizes **2** formerly in the U.S., the higher criminal courts

o·yez or **o·yes** (ō′yes′) ***interj.*** ⟦ME < Anglo-Fr, hear ye, pl. imper. of *oyer* < L *audire,* to hear: see AUDIENCE⟧ hear ye; attention: traditionally cried out three times by court or public officials to command silence before a proclamation is read —***n.*** a cry of "oyez"

oys·ter (ois′tər) ***n.*** ⟦OFr *oistre* < L *ostrea* < Gr *ostreon,* oyster; akin to *osteon,* a bone: see OSSIFY⟧ **1** any of various bivalve mollusks with an irregularly shaped, unequal shell, living attached to rocks, other shells, etc., and widely used as food **2** the soft, edible part of such a mollusk **3** the oyster-shaped bit of meat contained in a depression on each side of the pelvic bone of a fowl **4** something from which profit or advantage can be extracted *[*the world is my *oyster]* **5** [Informal] a taciturn person —***vi.*** to gather, raise, or dredge oysters

oyster bed a place on the ocean floor naturally suited to, or artificially prepared for, the breeding of oysters

☆**oys·ter·catch·er** (ois′tər kach′ər) ***n.*** any of a family (Haematopodidae) of large, black-and-white shorebirds with a strong, reddish, wedge-shaped beak and stout legs, feeding chiefly on bivalve mollusks; esp., an American species (*Haematopus palliatus*)

oyster crab any of various small, thin-shelled crabs (family Pinnotheridae) that live as commensals in the gill cavities of oysters, clams, etc.

☆**oyster cracker** a small, round, salted soda cracker eaten with oyster stews, soups, etc.

oyster farm a place where oyster beds are maintained

oys·ter·man (ois′tər man′, -mən) ***n.***, *pl.* **-men′** (-men′, -mən) **1** a person who gathers, sells, or raises oysters **2** a vessel used in gathering oysters

oyster mushroom ⟦from resemblance of its cap to an *oyster* shell⟧ any of various fan-shaped mushrooms having gills, esp. an edible one (*Pleurotus ostreatus*) with a short, pale-colored stem, that grows on tree trunks

oyster plant ☆SALSIFY

☆**oyster rake** a rake with a long handle and curved teeth for gathering in oysters from shallow waters

☆**oysters Rockefeller** ⟦after the elder John D. ROCKEFELLER: created (1890s) by a chef at Antoine's, restaurant in New Orleans⟧ oysters on a half shell, topped typically with cooked spinach, cream sauce or butter, bacon, and seasonings, and broiled in a bed of rock salt

☆**oyster stew** a dish consisting of whole oysters in a soup of heated milk or cream, butter, and seasoning

oyster white an off-white color with a creamy cast

oz *symbol* ⟦abbrev. of obs. It *onza* (> It *oncia*)⟧ ounce(s): also, for the plural, **ozs**

☆**Oz·a·lid** (äz′ə lid′) ⟦< DIAZO, by reversal of letters & insertion of *l*⟧ *trademark for* a machine or process for producing positive prints made directly from original drawings or printed material and developed dry in the presence of ammonia vapor —***n.*** **[o-]** such a print

O·zark Mountains (ō′zärk) ⟦< Fr *aux Arcs,* to the (region of the) Arc (Arkansas) Indians⟧ highland region in NW Ark., SW Mo., & NE Okla.: 1,500-2,500 ft (457-762 m) high

O·zarks (ō′zärks) **1** OZARK MOUNTAINS **2 Lake of the** artificial lake in central Mo., formed by a dam on the Osage River: 130 mi (209 km) long

o·zo·ce·rite (ō zō′kə rīt′, -sə-; ō′zō kir′īt′, -sir′-) ***n.*** ⟦Ger *ozokerit* < Gr *ozein* (see fol.) + *kēros,* wax⟧ a brown to black mineral wax sometimes found in sandstone, used to make candles, polishes, etc.: also **o·zo·ke·rite** (ō zō′kə rīt′, ō′zō kir′īt′)

o·zone (ō′zōn′) ***n.*** ⟦Fr < Gr *ozein,* to smell < IE base **od-* > L *odor*⟧ **1** an unstable, pale-blue gas, O_3, with a penetrating odor: it is an allotropic form of oxygen, formed usually by a silent electrical discharge in air, and is used as an oxidizing, deodorizing, and bleaching agent and in the purification of water **2** [Slang] pure, fresh air —**o·zon·ic** (ō zän′ik, -zō′nik) ***adj.***, **o·zo·nous** (ō′zō nəs, -zə-)

ozone layer the atmospheric layer within the stratosphere, extending from a height of *c.* 15 to *c.* 30 km (*c.* 9 to *c.* 18 mi) and having a heavy concentration of ozone: it absorbs harmful ultraviolet radiation from the sun and serves to maintain the temperature of the atmosphere

o·zo·nide (ō′zō nīd′, -zə-) ***n.*** any of a series of compounds formed by the action of ozone on unsaturated organic compounds

o·zo·nize (ō′zō nīz′, -zə-) ***vt.*** **-nized′**, **-niz′ing** **1** to change (oxygen) into ozone **2** to treat or impregnate with ozone —**o′zo′ni·za′tion** ***n.*** —**o′zo·niz′er** ***n.***

o·zo·no·sphere (ō zō′nə sfir′) ***n.*** ⟦< OZONE + -SPHERE⟧ OZONE LAYER

O·zu (ō′zōō), **Ya·su·ji·ro** (yä′sōō jē′rō) 1903-63; Jpn. film director

P

p[1] or **P** (pē) ***n.**, pl.* **p's, P's 1** the sixteenth letter of the English alphabet: from the Greek *pi*, a borrowing from the Phoenician **2** any of the speech sounds that this letter represents, as, in English, the (p) of *peace* **3** a type or impression for *p* or *P* **4** the sixteenth in a sequence or group **5** an object shaped like P ***—adj.*** **1** of *p* or *P* **2** sixteenth in a sequence or group **3** shaped like P **—mind (or watch) one's p's and q's** ⟦prob. orig. a warning to children to distinguish carefully between the similarly formed letters *p* and *q*⟧ to be careful of one's words and actions

p[2] *abbrev.* **1** page **2** part **3** participle **4** past **5** penny; pence **6** per **7** peseta **8** peso **9** petite **10** pico- **11** pint(s) **12** pipe **13** *Baseball* pitcher **14** ⟦L *post meridiem*⟧ PM [7:00 *p*] **15** pole **16** population **17** power **18** pressure **19** pro **20** *Physics* proton

p[3] *abbrev.* ⟦It *piano*: see PIANO[1]⟧ *Musical Direction* soft(ly)

P[1] *abbrev.* **1** *Genetics* parental generation **2** park (on automotive automatic-shift indicators) **3** parking **4** *Chess* pawn **5** peta- **6** *Bible* Peter **7** petite **8** *Baseball* pitcher **9** poise(s) (unit of viscosity) **10** police **11** *Physics* power **12** president **13** *Physics* pressure **14** priest **15** prince **16** *Mil.* prisoner **17** *Rom. History* Publius (the praenomen) **18** *Football* punter: sometimes written **p 19** purl

P[2] *Chem. symbol for* phosphorus

p- *prefix* **1** *Chem.* PARA-[1] (sense 2*b*): usually italicized and hyphenated in chemical names **2** *Elec.* positive

pa (pä, pô) ***n.*** [Informal] FATHER (*n.* 1 & 2)

Pa[1] *abbrev.* **1** pascal(s) (unit of pressure) **2** Pennsylvania

Pa[2] *Chem. symbol for* protactinium

PA[1] (pē′ā′) ***n.*** PUBLIC-ADDRESS SYSTEM

PA[2] *abbrev.* **1** Pennsylvania **2** physician assistant **3** Post Adjutant **4** power of attorney: also **pa 5** press agent **6** purchasing agent

p.a. *abbrev.* per annum

paan (pän) ***n.*** *alt. sp. of* PAN[2]

pa′ang·a (pä äŋ′gə) ***n.**, pl.* **pa′ang′a** ⟦Tongan, a kind of seedpod⟧ the basic monetary unit of Tonga: see the table of monetary units in the Reference Supplement

PABA *abbrev.* para-aminobenzoic acid

☆**Pab·lum** (pab′ləm) ⟦contr. < fol.⟧ *trademark for* a soft, bland cereal food for infants **—*n.*** **[p-]** any oversimplified or bland writing, ideas, etc.

pab·u·lum (pab′yo͞o ləm, -yə-) ***n.*** ⟦L: see FOOD⟧ **1** food or sustenance **2** nourishment for the mind **3** PABLUM

☆**pac** (pak) ***n.*** ⟦shortened < SHOEPAC⟧ **1** [Archaic] a high moccasin; larrigan **2** a high, insulated, waterproof, laced boot, for wear in very cold weather

Pac *abbrev.* Pacific

☆**PAC** (pak) ***n.**, pl.* **PAC's** political action committee

pa·ca (pä′kə, pak′ə) ***n.*** ⟦Port & Sp < Tupí *páca*⟧ any of a genus (*Cuniculus,* family Dasyproctidae) of short-tailed or tailless burrowing, herbivorous rodents of South and Central America, with spotted brown fur and hooflike toes

pace[1] (pās) ***n.*** ⟦ME *pas* < OFr < L *passus,* a step, lit., a stretching out of the leg < pp. of *pandere,* to stretch out < IE base **pet-,* to stretch out > FATHOM⟧ **1** a step in walking, running, etc.; stride **2** a unit of linear measure, equal to the length of a step or stride, variously estimated at from 30 inches to 40 inches: the regulation **military pace** is 30 inches, or 36 inches for double time: the **Roman pace**, measured from the heel of one foot to the heel of the same foot in the next stride, was 5 Roman ft, or 58.1 inches, now known as a **geometric pace**, about 5 ft **3** *a)* the rate of speed in walking, running, etc. *b) Sports* the speed of a ball, shuttlecock, etc. **4** rate of movement, progress, development, etc. **5** a particular way of walking, running, etc. (of a person or animal); gait; walk **6** the gait of a horse in which both legs on the same side are raised together ***—vt.*** **paced, pac′ing 1** to walk or stride back and forth across **2** to measure by paces: often with *off* **3** to train, develop, or guide the pace of (a horse) **4** *a)* to set the pace for (a runner, horse, etc.) *b)* to regulate the rate of progress, development, etc. of, esp. so as to conserve energy or resources **5** to go before and lead **6** to cover (a certain distance) ***—vi.*** **1** to walk with slow or regular steps **2** to raise both legs on the same side at the same time in moving: said of a horse **—change of pace 1** variation in tempo, mood, routine, etc. **2** [Old-fashioned] *Baseball* CHANGE-UP **—go through one's paces** to show one's abilities, skills, etc. **—keep pace (with) 1** to go at the same speed (as) **2** to maintain the same rate of progress, etc. (as) **—off the pace** behind the leader; out of first place **—put through one's paces** to test one's ability, skills, etc. **—set the pace 1** to go at a speed that others try to equal, as in a race **2** to do or be something for others to emulate

pa·ce[2] (pä′chā, pā′sē) ***prep.*** ⟦L, abl. of *pax,* PEACE⟧ with all due respect to: used in expressing polite disagreement

pace car an official starter's car that leads the competing race cars around the track for one lap (**pace lap**) before moving off the track

paced (pāst) ***adj.*** **1** having a (specified) pace: used in hyphenated compounds [fast-*paced*] **2** measured by paces or pacing **3** *Horse Racing* having its pace set by a pacemaker

pace·mak·er (pās′māk′ər) ***n.*** **1** *a)* a runner, horse, automobile, etc. that sets the pace for others, as in a race *b)* a person, group, or thing that leads the way or serves as a model **2** *Anat. a)* a dense network of interwoven, specialized muscle fibers in the right atrium of the heart that controls the rhythm of the electrical impulses that cause the heartbeat *b)* any of several body parts that control the rhythm of a biological activity, as an area in the stomach that controls stomach contractions **3** *Med.* an electronic device implanted within the body and connected to the wall of the heart, designed to provide regular, mild electric shocks that stimulate contraction of the heart muscles and restore normalcy to the heartbeat **—pace′mak′ing *n.***

pac·er (pās′ər) ***n.*** **1** one who paces **2** an animal that paces; esp., a horse bred and trained for pacing in races **3** PACEMAKER (sense 1)

pace·set·ter (pās′set′ər) ***n.*** PACEMAKER (sense 1)

pac·ey (pā′sē) ***adj.*** **pac′i·er, pac′i·est** [Brit.] *alt. sp. of* PACY

pa·cha (pə shä′, pä′shə, pash′ə) ***n.*** PASHA

pa·cha·lic (pə shä′lik) ***n.*** *alt. sp. of* PASHALIK

Pach·el·bel (päkh′əl bel′), **Jo·hann** (yō′hän′) 1653-1706; Ger. composer

pa·chin·ko (pə chiŋ′kō) ***n.*** ⟦Jpn *pachinko,* slingshot, pinball machine, hand gun, etc.: of echoic orig.: use for vertical pinball machine largely after WWII⟧ a Japanese gambling game played on a device like a vertical pinball machine

pa·chi·si (pə chē′zē) ***n.*** ⟦Hindi *pacīsī* < *pacis,* twenty-five (the highest number thrown) < *pãc,* five < Sans *páñca,* FIVE + *-īs* < *bīs,* twenty⟧ in India, a game for four players in which the moves of the pieces around a board are determined by the throwing of cowrie shells

Pa·chu·ca (pä cho͞o′kä) city in EC Mexico: capital of Hidalgo: in full **Pachuca de Sot·o** (di sōt′ō)

☆**pa·chu·co** (pə cho͞o′kō) ***n.**, pl.* **-cos** ⟦MexSp < ?⟧ [Slang] **1** a young Mexican-American man, esp. one belonging to a neighborhood gang or in trouble with the law **2** a Mexican-American: in this use, a contemptuous term

pach·y·derm (pak′ə dʉrm′) ***n.*** ⟦Fr *pachyderme* < Gr *pachydermos,* thick-skinned < *pachys,* thick (< IE base **bheng̑h-,* thick, dense > Sans *bahú-,* dense, much) + *derma,* skin: see DERMA[1]⟧ **1** any of certain large, thick-skinned, hoofed animals, as the elephant, rhinoceros, and hippopotamus, formerly classified together **2** a thick-skinned, insensitive, stolid person **—pach′y·der′mal *adj.*, pach′y·der′mic**

pach·y·der·ma·tous (pak′ə dʉr′mə təs) ***adj.*** **1** of, or having the nature of, a pachyderm **2** thick-skinned; insensitive to criticism, insult, etc.: also **pach′y·der′mous —pach′y·der′ma·tous·ly *adv.***

☆**pach·y·san·dra** (pak′ə san′drə) ***n.*** ⟦ModL < Gr *pachys* (see PACHYDERM) + ModL *-andrus,* -ANDROUS⟧ any of a genus (*Pachysandra*) of low, dense-growing, hardy evergreen plants of the box family, often used for a ground cover in the shade

pa·cif·ic (pə sif′ik) ***adj.*** ⟦Fr *pacifique* < L *pacificus* < *pacificare,* PACIFY⟧ **1** making or tending to make peace; appeasing; conciliatory **2** of a peaceful nature or disposition; not warlike; mild; tranquil; calm Also [Rare] **pa·cif′i·cal —pa·cif′i·cal·ly *adv.***

Pa·cif·ic (pə sif′ik) ***adj.*** of, in, on, or near the Pacific Ocean

pa·cif·i·cate (pə sif′i kāt′) ***vt.*** **-cat′ed, -cat′ing** PACIFY **—pa·cif′i·ca′tor *n.* —pa·cif′i·ca·to′ry** (-kə tôr′ē) ***adj.***

pac·i·fi·ca·tion (pas′ə fi kā′shən) ***n.*** ⟦Fr < L *pacificatio*⟧ a pacifying or being pacified

Pacific Islands, Trust Territory of the former U.S. trust territory in the W Pacific, consisting of the Caroline & Marshall Islands: trusteeship terminated in 1990

Pacific Ocean ⟦< ModL *(mare) Pacificum,* peaceful (sea): so called by Magellan because of its tranquil appearance⟧ largest of the earth's oceans, between Asia and the American continents: *c.* 64,186,300 sq mi (166,241,875 sq km); greatest known depth, 35,809 ft (10,915 m): often **Pacific**

Pacific Rim 1 the coastal regions bordering the Pacific Ocean **2** the countries of these regions, esp. the Asian countries, with respect to their trade relations, political alliances, etc. with each other

☆**Pacific Standard Time** a standard time used in the zone which includes the W states of the continental U.S., corresponding to the mean solar time of the 120th meridian west of Greenwich, England: it is eight hours behind Greenwich time

☆**Pacific Time** [*also* **P- t-**] standard time or daylight saving time in the time zone which includes the W states of the continental U.S.

pac·i·fi·er (pas′ə fī′ər) ***n.*** **1** a person or thing that pacifies ☆**2** a nipple-shaped object of rubber or plastic, for a baby to suck on

pac·i·fism (pas′ə fiz′əm) ***n.*** ⟦Fr *pacifisme:* see PACIFIC & -ISM⟧ opposition to the use of force under any circumstances; specif., refusal for reasons of conscience to participate in war or any military action —**pac′i·fist** ***n., adj.*** —**pac′i·fis′tic** ***adj.*** —**pac′i·fis′ti·cal·ly** ***adv.***

pac·i·fy (pas′ə fī′) ***vt.*** **-fied′**, **-fy′ing** ⟦ME *pacifien* < OFr *pacefier* < L *pacificare* < *pax* (gen. *pacis*), PEACE + *facere,* to make, DO[1]⟧ **1** to make peaceful or calm; appease; tranquilize **2** *a)* to establish or secure peace in (a nation, etc.) ☆*b)* to seek to neutralize or win over (people in occupied areas) —**pac′i·fi′a·ble** ***adj.***

SYN.—**pacify** implies a making quiet and peaceful that which has become noisy or disorderly [to *pacify* a crying child]; **appease** suggests a pacifying by gratifying or giving in to the demands of [to *appease* one's hunger]; **mollify** suggests a soothing of wounded feelings or an allaying of indignation [his compliments failed to *mollify* her]; **placate** implies the changing of a hostile or angry attitude to a friendly or favorable one [to *placate* an offended colleague]; **propitiate** implies an allaying or forestalling of hostile feeling by winning the good will of [to *propitiate* a deity]; **conciliate** implies the use of arbitration, concession, persuasion, etc. in an attempt to win over —ANT. **anger, enrage**

Pa·ci·ni·an corpuscle (pə sin′ē ən) ⟦after Filippo *Pacini* (1812-83), It anatomist⟧ a type of encapsulated sensory nerve ending that is sensitive to touch and vibration, found as in the skin of the hands and feet

pack[1] (pak) ***n.*** ⟦ME *pakke* < MDu *pak* < MFl *pac:* term carried throughout Europe via the Low Countries' wool trade (as in Fr *pacque,* It *pacco,* Ir *pac,* ML *paccus*)⟧ **1** a large bundle of things wrapped or tied up for carrying, as on the back of a person or animal; load **2** a container in which something may be stored compactly [parachute *pack*] **3** a number of similar or related persons or things; specif., *a)* a group or collection [a *pack* of lies] *b)* a package of a standard number [a *pack* of cigarettes] *c)* FILM PACK *d)* a set of playing cards; deck *e)* a set of hunting hounds *f)* a number of wild animals living and hunting together *g)* a united group; gang; set *h)* a unit of Cub Scouts or Brownies under an adult leader **4** ICE PACK **5** *a)* treatment by wrapping a patient in blankets or sheets that are wet or dry and hot or cold *b)* the blankets or sheets used **6** any of various cosmetic pastes applied to the skin and left to dry [*mudpack*] **7** *a)* the amount of food put in cans, etc. in a season or year *b)* a method of packing or canning [cold *pack*] —***vt.*** ⟦ME *pakken*⟧ **1** to make a pack, or bundle, of **2** *a)* to put together compactly in a box, trunk, etc. for carrying or storing *b)* to fill (a box, bag, trunk, etc.) for carrying or storing **3** *a)* to put (food) in (cans, boxes, etc.) for preservation or sale *b)* to package or carry for the purpose of eating away from home [to *pack* a lunch for school] **4** *a)* to fill closely; crowd; cram [a hall *packed* with people] *b)* to crowd or press (people) together **5** to fill in or surround tightly for protection, prevention of leaks, etc. [to *pack* valves] **6** to press together firmly [*packed* earth] **7** to load (an animal) with a pack **8** to carry (goods, equipment, etc.) in or as in a pack: said of an animal **9** to treat with a PACK[1] (***n.*** *5a*) **10** to send (*off*), usually in haste [to *pack* a boy off to school] ☆**11** [Slang] to wear or carry (a gun, etc.), esp. habitually **12** [Slang] *a)* to be able to deliver (a blow, punch, etc.) with force *b)* to provide or contain [a play that *packs* a message] —***vi.*** **1** to make up packs **2** to put one's clothes, belongings, etc. into luggage for a trip [an hour in which to *pack*] **3** to press, crowd, or throng together in a small space **4** to admit of being folded compactly, put in a container, etc. [a suit that *packs* well] ☆**5** to settle into a compact or solid mass **6** to go away in haste: sometimes with *off* —***adj.*** **1** *a)* used in packing *b)* suitable for packing **2** formed in a pack or packs **3** used for carrying packs, loads, etc. [a *pack* animal] —SYN. BUNDLE, GROUP —**pack it in** [Slang] to give up or stop trying, as in discouragement —**send packing** [Informal] to dismiss (a person) abruptly —**pack′a·ble** ***adj.***

pack[2] (pak) ***vt.*** ⟦< ? PACT, but infl. by prec.⟧ to choose or arrange (a jury, court, etc.) in such a way as to get desired decisions, results, etc.

☆**-pack** (pak) *combining form* a package of (a specified number of) cans or bottles, as of beer

pack·age (pak′ij) ***n.*** **1** [Obs.] the act or process of packing **2** a wrapped or boxed thing or group of things; parcel **3** a container, wrapping, etc., esp. one in which a commodity is packed for sale ☆**4** a number of related things regarded as a unit **5** a self-contained component or unit, usually one that is already assembled —☆***vt.*** **-aged**, **-ag·ing** **1** to wrap or box, as for transporting, carrying, etc. **2** *a)* to wrap or seal (a commodity) in a container, wrappings, etc. designed to attract purchasers *b)* to otherwise offer or present in an attractive or enticing way as if for commercial consumption [to *package* a political candidate] **3** to put together or offer as a unit —☆***adj.*** designating or of a plan, offer, etc. by which a number of items are offered as an inseparable unit [*package* deal, *package* tour] —SYN. BUNDLE —**pack′ag·er** ***n.***

☆**package store** a retail store where alcoholic beverages are sold by the bottle for drinking off the premises

pack animal an animal used for carrying packs or loads

pack·er (pak′ər) ***n.*** a person or thing that packs; specif., *a)* a person who packs goods for preservation, transportation, or sale ☆*b)* a person who owns or manages a packing house ☆*c)* a person who transports goods on pack animals

pack·et (pak′it) ***n.*** ⟦MFr *paquet,* dim. of *pacque,* PACK[1]⟧ **1** [Obs.] a parcel of letters **2** a small package or parcel **3** PACKET BOAT **4** [Brit. Informal] a large amount of money **5** *Comput.* in some network architectures, a bundle of data transmitted as a unit —***vt.*** to make up into a packet

packet boat ⟦so called from orig. carrying mail⟧ a boat that travels a regular route, as along a coast or on a river, carrying passengers, freight, etc.

pack·horse (pak′hôrs′) ***n.*** a horse used as a pack animal

pack ice a large, floating expanse of broken ice masses frozen together

pack·ing (pak′iŋ) ***n.*** **1** the act or process of a person or thing that packs; specif., *a)* the large-scale, esp. commercial, processing and packaging of meats, fruits, or vegetables *b) Med.* the filling of a wound or cavity with gauze, etc. to permit drainage and prevent closure **2** any material used to pack, as excelsior, cardboard, etc. used in packages to cushion and brace the contents, a substance put around valves to make them watertight, etc.

packing box (*or* **case**) a large crate or box for storing or shipping goods

packing fraction the ratio of the mass defect of an isotope to its mass number, equal to (M − A) ÷ A, where M is the atomic mass and A is the mass number: usually expressed as parts per 10,000

☆**pack·ing·house** (pak′iŋ hous′) ***n.*** a plant where meats are processed and packed for sale; also, a similar plant for packing fruits and vegetables

pack·man (pak′mən) ***n.***, *pl.* **-men** (-mən) a peddler

☆**pack rat** **1** any of a genus (*Neotoma*) of North American rats that often carry off and hide small articles in their nests **2** [Informal] a person who habitually saves unneeded, miscellaneous items

☆**pack·sack** (pak′sak′) ***n.*** a traveling sack of canvas or leather, usually carried strapped on the shoulders

pack·sad·dle (pak′sad′′l) ***n.*** a saddle with fastenings to secure and balance the load carried by a pack animal

pack·thread (pak′thred′) ***n.*** strong, thick thread or twine for tying bundles, packages, etc.

☆**pack train** a train, or procession, of pack animals

pact (pakt) ***n.*** ⟦OFr < L *pactum,* neut. of *pactus,* pp. of *paciscere,* to agree < base of *pax,* PEACE⟧ an agreement between persons, groups, or nations; compact; covenant

pac·y (pā′sē) ***adj.*** **pac′i·er**, **pac′i·est** [Brit.] maintaining a rapid pace; fast-paced [*pacy* novels, a *pacy* tennis match]

pacz·ki (punch′kē, poonch′-) ***n.***, *pl.* **-ki** or **-kis** ⟦Pol *pączki,* pl. of *pączek,* dim. of *pąk,* bud (for its shape)⟧ a round Polish pastry, similar to a doughnut, usually containing a fruit or cream filling and topped with powdered sugar or a glaze: traditionally eaten in the U.S. on Fat Tuesday

pad[1] (pad) ***n.*** ⟦echoic, but infl. by PAD[3]⟧ the dull sound made by a footstep or staff on the ground

pad[2] (pad) ***n.*** ⟦? var. of POD[1]⟧ **1** a soft, stuffed saddle **2** anything made of or stuffed with soft material to fill out a shape, protect against friction, pressure, jarring, or blows, etc.; cushion [a shoulder *pad,* seat *pad*] **3** a piece of folded gauze, compressed cotton, etc. used as a dressing or protection on a wound, etc. **4** *a)* the foot of certain animals, as the wolf or fox *b)* any of the cushionlike parts on the underside of the foot of some animals ☆**5** the floating leaf of a water plant, as the waterlily **6** a number of sheets of paper for writing or drawing, glued together along one edge; tablet **7** an absorbent cushion soaked with ink for inking a rubber stamp: in full **stamp pad** or **ink pad** **8** LAUNCH PAD **9** [Slang] *a)* a pallet or bed *b)* the apartment, house, etc. where one lives —***vt.*** **pad′ded**, **pad′ding** **1** to stuff, cover, or line with a pad or padding **2** to lengthen (a speech or piece of writing) with unnecessary or irrelevant material ☆**3** to fill (an expense account, bill, etc.) with invented or inflated entries —**on the pad** ☆[Slang] accepting a share of the graft received collectively by members of a police precinct

pad[3] (pad) ***vi.*** **pad′ded**, **pad′ding** ⟦< Du *pad,* PATH[2], akin to LowG *padden*⟧ **1** to travel on foot; walk; tramp **2** to walk or run with a soft, almost soundless, step

Pa·dang (pä däŋ′) seaport on the W coast of Sumatra, Indonesia

pa·dauk (pə douk′) ***n.*** ⟦Burmese⟧ a reddish wood obtained from various leguminous trees (genus *Pterocarpus*) native to Asia and Africa

padded bra a bra with padded cups designed to make the breasts appear fuller

padded cell a cell, or room, for the confinement of violent patients or prisoners, lined with heavy, soft material as a protection against self-inflicted injury

pad·ding (pad′iŋ) ***n.*** **1** the action of a person who pads **2** any soft material, as cotton, felt, etc., used to pad **3** unnecessary or irrelevant material put into a speech or piece of writing, making it longer

Pad·ding·ton (pad′iŋ tən) former borough of London, now part of Westminster

pad·dle[1] (pad′′l) ***n.*** ⟦ME *padell,* small spade < ?⟧ **1** a relatively short pole with a broad blade at one end or sometimes both ends, held in the hands and used to propel and steer a canoe, kayak, etc.: cf. OAR **2** any of various implements shaped like this; specif., *a)* a metal tool for stirring iron in a furnace *b)* a small, flat, wooden instrument for working butter, stirring clay, etc. ☆*c)* a flat stick used for beating clothes in washing them by hand, as in a stream *d)* a flat, wooden stick for administering punishment by beating ☆*e)* a flat, rounded piece of wood with a short handle, used to hit a ball, as in table tennis **3** any of the propelling boards in a water wheel or paddle wheel —*vi.* **-dled, -dling** to propel a canoe, etc. by means of a paddle —*vt.* **1** to propel (a canoe, etc.) by means of a paddle or paddles **2** to punish by beating as with a paddle; spank **3** to stir, work, etc. with a paddle —☆**paddle one's own canoe** to depend entirely on oneself —**pad'dler** *n.*

pad·dle² (pad'l) *vi.* **-dled, -dling** ⟦prob. freq. < PAD³⟧ **1** to move the hands or feet about in the water, as in playing; dabble **2** to walk like a small child; toddle **3** [Archaic] to play idly with the fingers (*on, in,* etc.) —**pad'dler** *n.*

☆**paddle ball** a game similar to handball, but played with a short-handled, perforated paddle

☆**pad·dle·fish** (-fish') *n., pl.* **-fish'** or **-fish'es** (see FISH) any of a family (Polyodontidae, order Acipenseriformes) of large bony fishes of the Mississippi and Chang rivers, with a paddle-shaped snout

☆**paddle tennis** an outdoor game similar to tennis, but using paddles and a modified tennis ball and played on a raised platform

paddle wheel a wheel with paddles set at right angles about its circumference for propelling a steamboat

pad·dle-wheel·er (-hwēl'ər, -wēl'-) *n.* a steamboat propelled by a paddle wheel

paddle wheel

pad·dock¹ (pad'ək) *n.* ⟦ME *paddoke* < *padde* (< OE *pad,* frog, toad) + *-ok,* -OCK⟧ **1** [Scot.] a frog **2** [Archaic] a toad

pad·dock² (pad'ək) *n.* ⟦phonetic alteration of earlier *parrock* < ME *parrok,* enclosed field < OE *pearruc,* enclosure: see PARK⟧ **1** a small field or enclosure near a stable, in which horses are exercised **2** an enclosure at a racetrack, where horses are saddled **3** in Australia, an enclosed piece of land —*vt.* to shut in a paddock

pad·dy (pad'ē) *n., pl.* **-dies** ⟦Malay *padi,* rice in the husk⟧ **1** rice in the husk, growing or gathered **2** rice in general **3** a rice field

Pad·dy (pad'ē) *n., pl.* **-dies** ⟦< nickname for *Pādraig,* Ir form of PATRICK¹⟧ IRISHMAN: a patronizing and formerly derisive term

☆**paddy wagon** ⟦prob. after prec.: see fol.⟧ [Slang] PATROL WAGON

pad·dy·whack (-hwak', -wak') *n.* ⟦orig., an Irishman < PADDY + WHACK: as in "get one's Irish up"⟧ **1** [Brit. Dial.] a rage; temper **2** [Informal] a beating or spanking —*vt.* [Informal] to beat or spank

Pa·der·born (pä'dər bôrn') city in WC Germany, in the state of North Rhine-Westphalia

Pa·de·rew·ski (pad'ə ref'skē; *Pol* pä'de ref'skē), **I·gnace Jan** (ē'nyás' yän') 1860-1941; Pol. pianist, composer, & statesman

pa·di·shah (pä'dē shä') *n.* ⟦Pers *pādshāh* < *pati,* master (< Sans *pāti:* see POTENT) + *shāh,* SHAH¹⟧ a title formerly used for: *a)* a great king; emperor *b)* [*often* **P-**] the shah of Iran *c)* [*often* **P-**] the sultan of Turkey *d)* [*often* **P-**] the British sovereign as emperor of India

pad·lock (pad'läk') *n.* ⟦ME *padlocke* < *pad* (< ?) + *lokke,* LOCK¹⟧ a removable lock with a hinged or pivoting link to be passed through a staple, chain, or eye —*vt.* **1** to fasten with or as with a padlock **2** to close (a building) against entrance

Pa·do·va (pä'dô vä) *It. name for* PADUA

pa·dre (pä'drā, -drē) *n.* ⟦Sp, It < L *pater,* FATHER⟧ **1** father: the title of a priest in Italy, Spain, Portugal, and Latin America **2** [Informal] a priest or chaplain Spanish **pa·dre** (pä'thre), *pl.* **-dres** (-thres); It. **pa·dre** (pä'dre), *pl.* **-dri** (-drē)

pa·dro·ne (pə drō'nē) *n.* ⟦It < L *patronus,* PATRON⟧ **1** patron; master; boss **2** in Italy *a)* a master of a Mediterranean trading ship *b)* an innkeeper ☆**3** [Obs.] a contractor for immigrant Italian laborers in America It. **pa·dro·ne** (pä drô'ne) *pl.* **-ni** (-nē)

pad thai (päd'tī', pad'-) ⟦Thai⟧ [*sometimes* **p-T-**] a Thai dish consisting of stir-fried noodles, bean sprouts, and shrimp or meat, mixed with a sauce and topped with chopped peanuts

Pad·u·a (paj'o͞o ə, pad'yo͞o ə) commune in N Italy, in Veneto: It. name PADOVA

pad·u·a·soy (pad'yo͞o ə soi', paj'o͞o-) *n.* ⟦altered (after prec.) < earlier *poudesoy* < Fr *pou-de-soie*⟧ **1** a rich, corded silk cloth of a kind used in hangings, vestments, etc. **2** a garment made of this

Pa·dus (pā'dəs) *ancient name for* the Po¹

pae·an (pē'ən) *n.* ⟦L < Gr *paian,* hymn < *Paian,* the healing one, epithet of Apollo < *paiein,* to strike, touch < ? IE base **pēu-* > PAVE⟧ **1** in ancient Greece, a hymn of thanksgiving to the gods, esp. to Apollo **2** a song of joy, triumph, praise, etc.

pae·do- (pē'dō, -də) *combining form* PEDO-¹ [*paedogenesis*]: also **paed-**

pae·do·gen·e·sis (pē'dō jen'ə sis) *n.* ⟦prec. + -GENESIS⟧ reproduction by larval or juvenile animal forms —**pae'do·gen'ic** (-jen'ik) *adj.,* **pae'do·ge·net'ic** (-jə net'ik)

pa·el·la (pä yel'ə, pī ā'yä; *Sp* pä e'lyä) *n.* ⟦Catalan, lit., cooking pot < OFr *paelle* < L *patella,* a small pan: see PATELLA⟧ a Spanish dish of rice cooked with chicken, seafood, etc. and seasoned with saffron

pae·on (pē'ən) *n.* ⟦L < Gr (Attic) *paiōn,* PAEAN⟧ *Gr. & Latin Prosody* a foot of three short syllables and one long syllable occurring in any order

pae·sa·no (pī sä'nō, -zä'-) *n., pl.* **pae·sa'ni** (-nē) or Eng. **-nos** ⟦It < LL *pagensis:* see PEASANT⟧ a fellow countryman; esp., a fellow Italian: also **pae·san'**

Paes·tum (pes'təm) ancient Greek city in S Italy

pa·gan (pā'gən) *n.* ⟦ME < LL(Ec) *paganus,* a heathen, pagan (contrasted with Christian or Jew) < L, a peasant, rustic < *pagus,* country < IE base **pak-,* to join, enclose, fasten > FANG, L *pax*⟧ **1** a person who is not a Christian, Muslim, or Jew; heathen: formerly, sometimes applied specif. to a non-Christian by Christians **2** a person who has no religion **3** a person who worships nature or the earth, specif., a NEOPAGAN —*adj.* **1** of pagans or paganism; not Christian, Muslim, or Jewish **2** not religious; heathen ➡The *adj* & *n.* 1-2 are often derogatory or dismissive when not used in historical contexts —**pa'gan·dom** *n.* —**pa'gan·ish** *adj.* —**pa'gan·ism'** *n.*

SYN.—**pagan** and **heathen** are both applied to polytheistic peoples, but **pagan** often refers specifically to ancient peoples, esp. the Greeks and Romans, and **heathen** is applied to any of the peoples regarded as primitive idolaters; **gentile** (often **Gentile**) is applied to one who is not a Jew or, among Mormons, to one who is not a Mormon

Pa·ga·ni·ni (pag'ə nē'nē; *It* pä'gä nē'nē), **Nic·co·lò** (nēk'kô lô') 1782-1840; It. violinist & composer

pa·gan·ize (pā'gə nīz') *vt., vi.* **-ized', -iz'ing** ⟦ML *paganizare*⟧ to make or become pagan —**pa'gan·iz'er** *n.*

page¹ (pāj) *n.* ⟦Fr < L *pagina,* a page < base of *pangere,* to fasten: see PEACE⟧ **1** *a)* one side of a leaf of a book, newspaper, letter, etc. *b)* the printing or writing on such a leaf, often with reference to the particular contents [the sports *pages*] *c)* an entire leaf in a book, etc. **2** [*often pl.*] a record of events [the *pages* of history] **3** an event or series of events that might fill a page [a colorful *page* in his life] **4** *Comput. a)* a unit of memory, consisting of one or more blocks (see BLOCK, *n.* 15) *b) short for* WEB PAGE (see also HOME PAGE) **5** *Printing* the type set for printing a page —*vt.* **paged, pag'ing** PAGINATE —*vi.* to turn pages as in scanning (*through* a book, magazine, etc.) —☆**on the same page** [Informal] in agreement or in a harmonious working relationship —☆**take** (or **borrow**) **a page from** [Informal] to follow the example of; imitate

page² (pāj) *n.* ⟦OFr < ? or akin to It *paggio* < Gr *paidion,* boy, dim. of *pais:* see PEDO-¹⟧ **1** [Historical] a boy training for knighthood, who attended a knight **2** a boy attendant or servant, esp. one serving a person of high rank, as at court **3** a young person, often in uniform, who runs errands, carries messages, etc., as in a legislature or hotel —*vt.* **paged, pag'ing 1** to attend as page ☆**2** to try to find, summon, or notify (a person) by calling out the person's name, as a hotel page does, signaling with an electronic device, as a beeper, etc.

Page (pāj), **Walter Hines** (hīnz) 1855-1918; U.S. journalist, editor, & diplomat

pag·eant (paj'ənt) *n.* ⟦ME *pagent* (with unhistoric *-t*) < earlier *pagyn* < Anglo-L *pagina,* scene displayed on a stage, stage < L, PAGE¹⟧ **1** [Historical] *a)* an individual scene in a medieval mystery play *b)* any of a series of movable outdoor platforms on which a mystery play was performed **2** a spectacular exhibition, elaborate parade, etc., as a procession with floats **3** an elaborate drama, often staged outdoors, celebrating a historical event or presenting the history of a community **4** *short for* beauty pageant: see BEAUTY CONTEST **5** empty pomp or display; mere show

pag·eant·ry (paj'ən trē) *n., pl.* **-ries 1** pageants collectively **2** grand spectacle; gorgeous display **3** empty show or display

page·boy (pāj'boi') *n.* ⟦from its resemblance to the groomed hair of knights' pages⟧ a woman's hairstyle in which the hair is worn straight and close to the head in a long bob, with the ends rolled under

pag·er (pā'jər) *n.* an electronic device that sends or receives a signal and emits a beep, buzz, etc., esp., a small, portable receiver used to contact people for messages

Pag·et (paj'it), Sir **James** 1814-99; Eng. surgeon & pathologist

Paget's disease ⟦both after prec.⟧ **1** a disease that deforms and weakens bones, in which rapid decalcification is followed by excessive calcification **2** a type of cancer usually involving the breast's larger ducts, areola, and nipple

page turner [Informal] any book, esp. a novel, regarded as compellingly interesting, suspenseful, etc.

pag·i·nal (paj'ə nəl) *adj.* ⟦LL *paginalis*⟧ **1** of or consisting of pages **2** page for page

pag·i·nate (paj'ə nāt') *vt.* **-nat'ed, -nat'ing** ⟦back-form. < fol.⟧ to number the pages of (a book, etc.)

pag·i·na·tion (paj'ə nā'shən) *n.* ⟦< L *pagina,* PAGE¹ + -TION⟧ **1** the act of numbering the pages of book, etc. **2** the marks of figures with which pages are numbered in sequence **3** the arrangement and number of pages as noted in a catalog

pa·go·da (pə gō'də) *n.* ⟦Port *pagode,* prob. < Pers *butkadah,* house of idols < *but,* idol + *kadah,* house, dwelling, prob. infl. by Prakrit *bhagodī,* divine, holy < Sans *bhagavatī,* divine, deity⟧ in India and the Far East, a temple in the form of a pyramidal tower of several stories

Japanese pagoda

Pa·go Pa·go (päŋ'ō päŋ'ō, pä'gō pä'gō) seaport on the S coast of Tutuila Island: capital of American Samoa

pa·gu·rid (pə gyoor'id, pag'yo͞o rid) *n.* ⟦< ModL *Paguridae* < L *pagurus,* kind of crab

(< Gr *pagouros* < base of *pagos*, hard object + *oura*, tail) + -ID⟧ any of a family (Paguridae) of marine decapods that have a soft, asymmetrical abdomen and inhabit empty snail shells; hermit crab —*adj.* of or pertaining to the pagurids Also **pa·gu′ri·an** (-ē ən)

pah (pä, pa, pə) *interj.* used to express disgust, contempt, or disbelief

PAH *abbrev.* polycyclic aromatic hydrocarbon

Pa·hang (pä häŋ′) state of Malaysia, in Peninsular Malaysia, on the South China Sea: 13,886 sq mi (35,965 sq km)

pah·la·vi (pä′lə vē) *n., pl.* **-vi** ⟦Pers *pahlawī*, orig., belonging to Riza Khan *Pahlawi* (1877-1944), Shah of Persia⟧ a former gold coin of Iran

Pah·la·vi (pä′lə vē) *n. var. of* PEHLEVI

☆**pa·ho·e·ho·e** (pä hō′ē hō′ē) *n.* ⟦Haw *pāhoehoe*⟧ a type of basaltic rock, usually dark-colored with a smooth, ropy surface, formed in large sheets from fluid, fast-moving lava: cf. AA

paid (pād) *vt., vi. pt. & pp. of* PAY[1] —*adj.* **1** discharged or settled by or as by payment [a *paid* bill] **2** with wages or salary included; with pay [a *paid* vacation]

pail (pāl) *n.* ⟦ME *paile* < OE *pægel*, small measure, wine vessel < LL *pagella* (dim. of L *pagina*, PAGE[1]), a small page, in VL, a measure of area, later a measure of volume: infl. by OFr *paele*, a pan < L *patella*: see PATELLA⟧ **1** a more or less cylindrical container, usually with a curved handle, for holding and carrying liquids, etc.; bucket **2** the amount held by a pail: also **pail′ful′**, *pl.* **-fuls′**

pail·lard (pī yär′; *Fr* pȧ yȧr′) *n.* a slice of meat, esp. veal or chicken, pounded until it is very thin and grilled quickly at high heat

pail·lasse (pal yas′, pal′yas′) *n. alt. sp. of* PALLIASSE

pail·lette (pal yet′; *Fr* pȧ yet′) *n.* ⟦Fr, dim. of *paille*, straw: see PALLET[2]⟧ a small, shiny ornament, as a metal disk, used in decorating women's dresses, etc.; spangle

pain (pān) *n.* ⟦ME *peine* < OFr < L *poena*, penalty, punishment: see PENAL⟧ **1** penalty or punishment: obs. except in **on (or upon or under) pain of**, at the risk of bringing upon oneself (punishment, death, etc.) **2** a sensation of hurting, or strong discomfort, in some part of the body, caused by an injury, disease, or functional disorder, and transmitted through the nervous system **3** the distress or suffering, mental or physical, caused by great anxiety, anguish, grief, disappointment, etc. **4** [*pl.*] the labor of childbirth **5** [*pl.*] great care or effort [to take *pains* with one's work] **6** [Slang] an annoyance: often used in phrases specifying a part of the body (e.g., **pain in the neck**) —*vt.* to cause to suffer; hurt; distress —*vi.* to have or cause pain —*SYN.* EFFORT —**feel no pain** [Slang] to be drunk

Paine (pān) **1 Robert Treat** (trēt) 1731-1814; Am. jurist & statesman **2 Thomas** 1737-1809; Am. Revolutionary patriot, writer, & political theoretician, born in England

pained (pānd) *adj.* **1** hurt or distressed; having the feelings hurt; offended **2** showing pain, irritation, etc. [a *pained* expression]

pain·ful (pān′fəl) *adj.* **1** causing pain; hurting; distressing **2** full of or suffering with pain; aching [a *painful* finger] **3** requiring trouble and care; exacting and difficult **4** annoying or tedious [a long, *painful* lecture] **5** [Archaic] painstaking —**pain′ful·ly** *adv.* —**pain′ful·ness** *n.*

☆**pain·kill·er** (-kil′ər) *n.* a medicine that relieves pain; analgesic —**pain′kill′ing** *adj.*

pain·less (-lis) *adj.* **1** free from or without pain **2** not causing or involving pain —**pain′less·ly** *adv.* —**pain′less·ness** *n.*

pains·tak·ing (pānz′tāk′iŋ, pān′stāk′-) *n.* the act of taking pains; great care or diligence —*adj.* **1** taking pains; very careful; diligent **2** characterized by great care —**pains′tak′ing·ly** *adv.*

paint (pānt) *vt.* ⟦ME *peinten* < OFr *peint*, pp. of *peindre* < L *pingere*, to paint, embroider < IE base **peig-*, to mark by scratching or coloring > Gr *pikros*, sharp, OE *fah*, stained⟧ **1** *a)* to make (a picture, design, etc.) in colors applied to a surface *b)* to depict or portray with paints [to *paint* a landscape] **2** to describe colorfully or vividly; depict in words **3** to cover or decorate with paint; color [to *paint* a wall] **4** to apply cosmetics to; adorn; beautify **5** *a)* to apply (a medicine, etc.) with a brush or swab *b)* to treat (a wound, etc.) in this way —*vi.* **1** to practice the art of painting pictures **2** [Archaic] to use cosmetics —*n.* **1** *a)* a mixture of a pigment with oil, water, etc., in liquid or paste form, applied as with a brush, roller, or spray gun, and used for protective covering or coloring of a surface or for making pictures on canvas, paper, etc. *b)* dry pigment for such use **2** a dried coat of paint **3** *a)* coloring matter, as lipstick, blush, or eye shadow, used as a cosmetic *b)* GREASEPAINT ☆**4** [Chiefly West] PINTO (*n.* 1) ☆**5** ⟦so called from the practice of *painting* the area in a contrasting color⟧ [Informal] *Basketball* FREE THROW LANE: with *the* —**paint out** to cover up with or as with a coat of paint —☆**paint the town (red)** [Slang] to go on a boisterous spree; carouse —**paint′a·ble** *adj.*

☆**paint·ball** (pānt′bôl′) *n.* any of various games in which players, simulating combat, use air guns to shoot pellets filled with colored gel at each other —**paint′ball′er** *n.*

paint·brush (pānt′brush′) *n.* **1** a brush used for applying paint **2** *a)* INDIAN PAINTBRUSH *b)* DEVIL'S PAINTBRUSH

☆**painted bunting** a brightly colored blue, green, red, and brown bunting (*Passerina ciris*) found in the S U.S.

painted cup ☆INDIAN PAINTBRUSH

Painted Desert ⟦so named from the colorful rock strata⟧ desert plateau in NC Ariz., east of the Colorado River

painted turtle a small, brightly colored, freshwater terrapin (*Chrysemys picta*) with webbed feet

paint·er[1] (pānt′ər) *n.* ⟦OFr *peintour*⟧ **1** an artist who paints pictures **2** a person whose work is covering surfaces, as walls, with paint

paint·er[2] (pānt′ər) *n.* ⟦LME *paynter* < OFr *pentour*, ult. < L *pendere*, to hang: see PEND⟧ a rope attached to the bow of a boat for tying it as to a dock or for towing it

☆**paint·er**[3] (pānt′ər) *n.* ⟦altered < PANTHER⟧ *dial. var. of* COUGAR

paint·er·ly (pānt′ər lē) *adj.* **1** of or characteristic of a painter **2** characterized by those qualities related to a painter's techniques in applying colors in masses, esp. with a thick, rough surface texture, as distinguished from linear qualities that emphasize outline and contour —**paint′er·li·ness** *n.*

painter's colic ⟦from the use of lead as an ingredient in paints⟧ LEAD COLIC

paint·ing (pānt′iŋ) *n.* **1** the act or occupation of covering surfaces with paint **2** *a)* the act, art, or occupation of applying paints to canvases, paper, etc. in producing pictures and compositions *b)* a picture or composition so painted

paint·y (pānt′ē) *adj.* **paint′i·er, paint′i·est 1** of, smeared with, or covered with paint **2** having more paint than necessary: said of a picture

pair (per) *n., pl.* **pairs** or **pair** ⟦ME *paire* < OFr < L *paria*, neut. pl. of *par*, equal: see PAR[1]⟧ **1** two similar or corresponding things joined, associated, or used together [a *pair* of gloves] **2** a single thing made up of two corresponding parts that are used together [a *pair* of pants] **3** two persons or animals; specif., *a)* a married, engaged, or courting couple *b)* two mated animals *c)* any two people considered as having something in common [a *pair* of thieves] *d)* a brace; span [a *pair* of oxen] *e)* two legislators on opposing sides of some question who agree to withhold their vote so as to offset each other; also, such an agreement **4** two playing cards of the same denomination **5** [Chiefly Dial.] a set or series [a *pair* of stairs, a *pair* of beads] —*vt.* **1** to make a pair of (two persons or things) by matching, joining, mating, etc. **2** to arrange in pairs **3** to provide with a partner: followed by *with* —*vi.* **1** to form a pair; match **2** to join in marriage; mate —**pair off** to join in, or separate into, pairs

SYN.—**pair** is used of two similar things that are associated together or are necessary in twos for proper use [a *pair* of socks] or of a single thing made up of two corresponding parts [a *pair* of scissors]; **couple** applies to any two similar things that are somehow associated [a *couple* of dollars], or it is used informally to mean several or a few [I must buy a *couple* of things]; a **brace** is a couple, especially of certain birds or animals [a *brace* of pheasants, hounds, etc.]; **yoke** applies to a pair of animals harnessed together for pulling [a *yoke* of oxen]; **span** is used especially of a pair of horses harnessed together

pair bond *Zool.* a monogamous relationship —**pair′-bond′ing** *n.*

pair·ing (per′iŋ) *n.* **1** the act of grouping contestants or teams in a tournament into competing pairs **2** [*pl.*] the list of such pairs

pair-oar (per′ôr′) *n.* a racing shell rowed by two persons who sit one behind the other, each using one oar: also **pair′-oared′ shell**

pair production a process whereby a gamma ray having an energy greater than 1.02 MeV is converted into an electron and positron pair in the strong electric field of a nucleus

pai·sa (pī′sä; *for 2* poi′shä) *n., pl.* **-se** (-se) or **-sas** (-shäz) ⟦Hindi & Beng *paisā* < Sans *pȧd*, one fourth (prob. orig. of a taka)⟧ **1** a monetary unit of India, Nepal, and Pakistan, equal to 1/100 of a rupee **2** a monetary unit of Bangladesh, equal to 1/100 of a taka

pai·san·o[1] (pī sä′nō, -zä′-) *n., pl.* **-os** ⟦Sp < Fr *paysan* < OFr *païsent*: see PEASANT⟧ **1** a fellow countryman **2** [Slang] a comrade; pal

pai·san·o[2] (pī sä′nō, -zä′-) *n., pl.* **-san′i** (-nē) or Eng. **-san′os** ⟦It⟧ *alt. sp. of* PAESANO: also **pai·san** (pī sän′, -zän′)

pais·ley (pāz′lē) *adj.* ⟦after fol., where wool shawls in this pattern were orig. made (*c.* 1800)⟧ [*also* **P-**] **1** designating, of, or having an intricate, multicolored pattern typically of abstract curving figures resembling fat commas, used esp. for textile fabrics: originally derived from designs on cashmere shawls imported into Britain from India **2** made of cloth having such a pattern —*n.* [*also* **P-**] **1** a paisley pattern **2** a paisley cloth, shawl, necktie, etc.

paisley pattern

Pais·ley (pāz′lē) city in SC Scotland, near Glasgow

Pai·ute (pī′yo͞ot′, pī yo͞ot′) *n., pl.* **-utes** or **-ute** ⟦< Shoshonean *pah-ute*, lit., water Ute⟧ **1** a member of a North American Indian people living in Nevada, E California, S Utah, and NW Arizona **2** either of two Uto-Aztecan languages spoken by the Paiutes

pa·ja·mas (pə jä′məz, -jam′əz) *pl.n.* ⟦Hindi *pājāma* < Pers *pāi*, a leg (< IE **ped-*, FOOT) + *jāma*, garment⟧ **1** a pair of loose silk or cotton trousers worn originally in the Near East **2** a loosely fitting sleeping or lounging suit consisting of top and trousers —**pa·ja′ma** *adj.*

Pak *abbrev.* Pakistan

pa·ke·ha (pä′kə hä′, -kē-) *n.* ⟦< Maori⟧ [Chiefly N.Z.] in New Zealand, a person who is not a Maori; esp., a white person

Pa·ki (pak′ē) *n.* ⟦shortened < PAKISTANI⟧ [Brit. Slang] a dark-skinned person of Pakistani or Indian descent: a term of hostility and contempt

Pa·ki·stan (pak′i stan′, pä′ki stän′) country in S Asia, on the Arabian Sea: formed from parts of former British India, it became a dominion (1947-

56) & a republic (1956-72; 1989-99) of the Commonwealth: 310,403 sq mi (803,940 sq km); cap. Islamabad: see also JAMMU AND KASHMIR

Pak·i·stan·i (pak′i stan′ē, pä′ki stä′nē) ***n.*** a person born or living in Pakistan —***adj.*** of Pakistan or its people or culture

pa·ko·ra (pä kôr′ə) ***n.*** ⟦Hindi⟧ in the cuisine of India, a small, spicy fritter containing pieces of vegetables or meat, made usually with a batter of chickpea flour and deep-fried

pal (pal) [Informal] ***n.*** ⟦Romany, brother, mate (for *prāl, phrāl,* in dial. on European continent) < Sans *bhrātar,* BROTHER⟧ an intimate friend; comrade; chum —***vi.*** **palled, pal′ling 1** to associate as pals: with *around* **2** to be a pal (*with* another)

pal·ace (pal′əs) ***n.*** ⟦ME *palais* < OFr < L *palatium,* after *Palatium,* one of the Seven Hills of Rome, where Augustus lived⟧ **1** the official residence of a king, emperor, bishop, etc. **2** any large, magnificent house or building **3** a large, ornate place of entertainment

palace revolution a revolt within the highest ranks of an organization, usually resulting in a change of leadership

pal·a·din (pal′ə din) ***n.*** ⟦Fr < It *paladino* < L *palatinus,* officer of a palace < *palatium:* see PALACE⟧ **1** any of the twelve legendary peers of Charlemagne's court **2** a knight or a heroic champion

pa·lae·o- (pā′lē ō, -ə; *chiefly Brit* pal′ē ō, -ə) *combining form* PALEO-: also **pa′lae-**

pa·laes·tra (pə les′trə) ***n.,*** *pl.* **-trae** (-trē) or **-tras** *alt. sp. of* PALESTRA

pal·an·quin or **pal·an·keen** (pal′ən kēn′) ***n.*** ⟦Port *palanquim* < Indo-Aryan (cf. Hindi *pālkī*) < Sans *palyaṅka, paryaṅka,* bed, couch < *pari-,* around (see PERI-) + *añcati,* (it) bends < IE base **ank-* > ANKLE⟧ [Historical] a covered litter used in S Asia, usually for one person, carried by poles on the shoulders of two or more men

pal·at·a·ble (pal′it ə bəl) ***adj.*** ⟦PALAT(E) + -ABLE⟧ **1** pleasant or acceptable to the taste; fit to be eaten or drunk **2** acceptable to the mind; satisfactory or tolerable —**pal′at·a·bil′i·ty** ***n.,*** **pal′at·a·ble·ness** —**pal′at·a·bly** ***adv.***

pal·a·tal (pal′it′l) ***adj.*** ⟦Fr < L *palatum,* palate⟧ **1** of the palate **2** *Phonet. a)* articulated with the part of the tongue just behind the tip raised against or near the hard palate, as the consonants (y) in *yes* and (H) in German *ich b)* designating a stop, fricative, etc. whose point of articulation is on or near the hard or soft palate, as (ch, j, sh, zh) *c)* front (said of certain vowels) —***n.*** a palatal sound —**pal′a·tal·ly** ***adv.***

pal·a·tal·ize (-īz′) ***vt.*** **-ized′, -iz′ing** *Phonet.* to articulate as a palatal; specif., to change (a nonpalatal sound) into a palatal sound [the original sound represented by *t* in "nature" has been *palatalized* to (ch); Russian contains many *palatalized* sounds] —**pal′a·tal·i·za′tion** ***n.***

pal·ate (pal′it) ***n.*** ⟦ME < L *palatum*⟧ **1** the roof of the mouth, consisting of a hard, bony forward part (the *hard palate*) and a soft, fleshy back part (the *soft palate,* or *velum*) **2** sense of taste: the palate was incorrectly thought to be the organ of taste **3** intellectual taste; liking

pa·la·tial (pə lā′shəl) ***adj.*** ⟦< L *palatium,* PALACE⟧ **1** of, suitable for, or like a palace **2** large and ornate; magnificent; stately —**pa·la′tial·ly** ***adv.***

Pa·lat·i·nate[1] (pə lat′'n āt′, -it) ***n.*** ⟦ML *palatinatus*⟧ **1** [**p-**] the territory ruled by a palatine **2** a person born or living in the Palatinate

Pa·lat·i·nate[2] (pə lat′'n āt′, -it) historical region now part of Germany: in two parts: **Lower Palatinate** or **Rhine Palatinate** (on the Rhine east of Saarland) and the **Upper Palatinate** (in E Bavaria on the Danube): see RHINELAND-PALATINATE

pal·a·tine[1] (pal′ə tīn′, -tin) ***adj.*** ⟦ME < OFr *palatin* < L *palatinus* < *palatium,* PALACE⟧ **1** of a palace **2** having royal privileges [a count *palatine*] **3** of or belonging to a count palatine or earl palatine **4** [**P-**] of the Palatinate —***n.*** **1** an officer of an imperial palace **2** a medieval vassal lord having the rights of royalty in his own territory, or palatinate **3** a fur piece covering the shoulders **4** [**P-**] a person born or living in the Palatinate

pal·a·tine[2] (pal′ə tīn′, -tin) ***adj.*** ⟦Fr *palatin:* see PALATE & -INE[1]⟧ having to do with the palate —***n.*** either of the two bones forming the hard palate

Pal·a·tine (pal′ə tīn′, -tin) *see* SEVEN HILLS OF ROME

Pa·lau (pä lou′) country consisting of a group of islands in the W Pacific Ocean: formerly part of the Trust Territory of the Pacific Islands, the island group became an independent republic in 1994: 177 sq mi (458 sq km); cap. Koror

pa·lav·er (pə lav′ər) ***n.*** ⟦Port *palavra,* a word, speech < LL(Ec) *parabola,* PARABLE⟧ **1** a conference or discussion, as orig. between indigenous Africans and European explorers or traders **2** talk; esp., idle chatter **3** flattery; cajolery —***vi.*** **1** to talk, esp. idly or flatteringly **2** to confer —***vt.*** to flatter or wheedle

Pa·la·wan (pä lä′wän) island in the W Philippines, southwest of Mindoro: 4,550 sq mi (11,784 sq km)

pa·laz·zo (pə lät′sō) ***n.,*** *pl.* **-zos** or It. **-zi** (-sē) ⟦It < L *palatium,* PALACE⟧ **1** a palace **2** any large, stately building

pa·laz·zos (pə lät′sōz) ***pl.n.*** ⟦< prec.⟧ women's pants with wide legs that flare broadly at the ankle: also **palazzo pants**

pale[1] (pāl) ***adj.*** **pal′er, pal′est** ⟦OFr < L *pallidus,* pale: see FALLOW[2]⟧ **1** of a whitish or colorless complexion; pallid; wan **2** lacking intensity or brilliance: said of color, light, etc.; faint; dim **3** feeble; weak [a *pale* imitation] —***vi.*** **paled, pal′ing 1** to become pale **2** to seem weaker or less important —***vt.*** to make pale —**pale′ly** ***adv.*** —**pale′ness** ***n.***

SYN.—**pale**, in this comparison the least connotative of these words, implies merely an unnatural whiteness or colorlessness, often temporary, of the complexion; **pallid** suggests a paleness resulting from exhaustion, faintness, emotional strain, etc.; **wan** suggests the paleness resulting from an emaciating illness; **ashen** implies the grayish paleness of the skin as in death; **livid** refers to a grayish-blue (or now, sometimes, white) complexion, as of one in great rage or fear —*ANT.* **ruddy, rosy**

pale[2] (pāl) ***n.*** ⟦ME < MFr *pal* < L *palus,* a stake < IE base **pak-,* to fasten (as by ramming into the ground) > Gr *passalos,* a peg, stake, L *pax,* peace⟧ **1** a narrow, upright, pointed stake used in fences; picket **2** a fence; enclosure; boundary; restriction: now chiefly fig. [outside the *pale* of the law, beyond the *pale* (of respectability)] **3** a territory or district enclosed within bounds **4** *Bot.* a chaffy bract or scale; esp., a bract at the base of a floret of a composite flower **5** *Heraldry* a vertical band forming the middle third of a shield

pa·le- (pā′lē) *combining form* PALEO-: used before a vowel

pa·le·a (pā′lē ə) ***n.,*** *pl.* **-le·ae′** (-ē′) ⟦ModL < L, chaff < IE base **pel-,* to cover, a skin > FELL[4], FILM⟧ **1** the upper, or inner, thin, membranous bract enclosing the flower in grasses **2** PALE[2] (sense 4)

Pa·le·arc·tic (pā′lē ärk′tik, -är′-) ***adj.*** ⟦PALE(O)- + ARCTIC⟧ designating or of the biogeographic realm that includes Europe, parts of N Africa, and most of Asia: see ORIENTAL (***adj.*** 4)

pale dry light in color and not sweet [*pale dry* sherry]

pa·le·eth·nol·o·gy (pā′lē eth näl′ə jē) ***n.*** ⟦PALE- + ETHNOLOGY⟧ the study of prehistoric races of humans

☆**pale·face** (pāl′fās′) ***n.*** a white person: a term believed by some to have been first used by North American Indians

Pa·lem·bang (pä′lem bäŋ′) seaport in SE Sumatra, Indonesia

Pa·len·que (pä leŋ′kä) village in N Chiapas state, Mexico: site of ancient Mayan ruins

pa·le·o- (pā′lē ō, -ə; *chiefly Brit* pal′ē ō, -ə) ⟦< Gr *palaios,* ancient < IE base **kwel-,* remote > Sans **caramá-,* the last, Gr *tēle,* far, Welsh *pell,* far⟧ *combining form* **1** the Old World [*Paleotropical*] **2** ancient, early, prehistoric, primitive [*Paleozoic, Paleolithic*] **3** involving or dealing with (specified) forms, conditions, phenomena, fossils, etc. of remote, esp. geologic, eras: the following words are examples of this use in compounds:

paleoanthropology
paleobiochemistry
paleobiology
paleobotany
paleoclimatology
paleoecology
paleogeography
paleozoology

Pa·le·o·cene (pā′lē ə sēn′) ***adj.*** ⟦prec. + -CENE⟧ [*sometimes* **p-**] designating or of the first geologic epoch of the Paleogene, characterized by lower sea levels, the development of modern mountain ranges, and the development of flowering plants, birds, and mammals —**the Paleocene** the Paleocene Epoch or its rocks: see the geologic time chart in the Reference Supplement

Pa·le·o·gene (pā′lē ə jēn′) ***adj.*** ⟦< PALEO- + Gr *-genēs,* born: see -GEN⟧ [*sometimes* **p-**] designating or of the first geologic period of the Cenozoic Era, subdivided into the Paleocene, Eocene, and Oligocene epochs: formerly a subdivision of the Tertiary Period —**the Paleogene** the Paleogene Period or its rocks: see the geologic time chart in the Reference Supplement

pa·le·og·ra·phy (pā′lē äg′rə fē) ***n.*** ⟦ModL *palaeographia:* see PALEO- & -GRAPHY⟧ **1** ancient writing or forms of writing, collectively **2** the study of ancient writings —**pa′le·og′ra·pher** ***n.*** —**pa′le·o·graph′ic** (-ō graf′ik) ***adj.,*** **pa′le·o·graph′i·cal**

Pa·le·o-In·di·an (pā′lē ō in′dē ən) ***n.*** a member of the prehistoric people that migrated to America from Asia during the late Pleistocene: they are the ancestors of the American Indians —***adj.*** designating or of the Paleo-Indians or their culture

pa·le·o·lith (pā′lē ə lith′) ***n.*** ⟦PALEO- + -LITH⟧ an unpolished Pleistocene stone tool

Pa·le·o·lith·ic (pā′lē ə lith′ik) ***adj.*** ⟦PALEO- + -LITHIC⟧ [*sometimes* **p-**] designating or of an Old World cultural period (*c.* 2 million-*c.* 10,000 B.C.) before the Mesolithic, characterized by the use of flint, stone, and bone tools, hunting, fishing, and the gathering of plant foods —**the Paleolithic** the Paleolithic period, subdivided into the Lower (to *c.* 150,000 B.C.), Middle (to *c.* 38,000 B.C.), and Upper stages; Old Stone Age

Paleolithic man any of the types of humans of the Paleolithic period, including Java, Neanderthal, and Cro-Magnon man

pa·le·o·mag·net·ism (pā′lē ō mag′nə tiz′əm) ***n.*** **1** the alignment of iron and nickel grains in rock with the earth's magnetic poles, fixed at the time of that rock's formation **2** the study of this alignment, specif. as it relates to the shifting of the earth's magnetic poles over time —**pa′le·o·mag·net′ic** ***adj.*** —**pa′le·o·mag·net′i·cal·ly** ***adv.***

pa·le·on·tog·ra·phy (pā′lē än täg′rə fē) ***n.*** ⟦PALE- + ONTO- + -GRAPHY⟧ the formal description of fossils —**pa′le·on′to·graph′i·cal** (-tō graf′i kəl) ***adj.,*** **pa′le·on′to·graph′ic**

pa·le·on·tol·o·gy (pā′lē ən täl′ə jē, -lē än-) ***n.*** ⟦Fr *paléontologie:* see PALE- & ONTO- & -LOGY⟧ **1** the branch of geology that deals with life forms from the past, esp. prehistoric life forms, through the study of fossils **2** a treatise on this subject —**pa′le·on′to·log′i·cal** (-än′tō läj′i kəl) ***adj.,*** **pa′le·on′to·log′ic** —**pa′le·on·tol′o·gist** ***n.***

pa·le·o·sol (-ə säl′) ***n.*** ⟦< PALEO- + L *solum,* base, soil⟧ a layer of buried, ancient soil

Pa·le·o·zo·ic (pā′lē ə zō′ik) ***adj.*** ⟦PALEO- + ZO- + -IC⟧ [*sometimes* **p-**] designating or of the first geologic era of the Phanerozoic Eon, characterized by the development of the first fishes, amphibians, reptiles, and land plants

—the Paleozoic the Paleozoic Era or its rocks: see the geologic time chart in the Reference Supplement

Pa·ler·mo (pə ler′mō; *It* pä ler′mô) seaport & capital of Sicily, on the N coast

Pal·es·tine (pal′əs tīn′) **1** historical region in SW Asia at the E end of the Mediterranean comprising parts of modern Israel, Jordan, & Egypt: also known as the HOLY LAND **2** British mandated territory in this region, west of the Jordan River, from 1923 to the establishment of the state of Israel (1948) according to the United Nations partition plan (1947) **3** modern region comprising the West Bank & Gaza Strip: usually **Palestinian territories**

Pal·es·tin·i·an (pal′əs tin′ē ən) ***adj.*** **1** of Palestine or its people or culture **2** of the people of Palestine, esp. those Arab peoples that now live in Palestine or whose family or ancestors once lived there **—*n.*** **1** a person, esp. an Arab, born or living in Palestine **2** an Arab whose family or ancestors once lived in Palestine

pa·les·tra (pə les′trə) ***n.***, *pl.* **-trae** (-trē) or **-tras** ⟦L < Gr *palaistra* < *palaiein,* to wrestle⟧ in ancient Greece, a public place for exercise in wrestling and athletics

Pal·es·tri·na (pal′ə strē′nə; *It* pä′les trē′nä), **Gio·van·ni Pier·lu·i·gi da** (jô vän′nē pyer lo͞o ē′jē dä) 1525?-94; It. composer

pal·e·tot (pal′ə tō′) ***n.*** ⟦Fr < OFr *palletoc* < ME *paltok* < ?⟧ [Historical] **1** a man's overcoat **2** a loose jacket worn by women and children

pal·ette (pal′it) ***n.*** ⟦Fr, dim. of *pale,* a shovel < L *pala,* a spade, shovel⟧ **1** a thin board or tablet of wood, plastic, etc., often with a hole for the thumb at one end, on which an artist arranges and mixes paints **2** the colors used by a particular artist or for a particular painting **3** the range of colors available, as in a computer graphics application

palette knife a thin, flexible steel blade with a blunt edge and wooden handle, used by artists to mix colors and clean the palette, and, sometimes, to apply paint

Pa·ley (pā′lē), **William** 1743-1805; Eng. theologian & philosopher

pal·frey (pôl′frē) ***n.***, *pl.* **-freys** ⟦ME < OFr *palefrei* < ML *palafredus,* for LL *paraveredus,* extra post horse < Gr *para,* beside + L *veredus,* post horse < Gaul **voredos* (akin to Welsh *gorwydd,* horse) < **vo-,* down, away (< IE **wo-* < base **au-, *awē*) + **-redos* < IE base **reidh-* > RIDE⟧ [Archaic] a saddle horse, esp. a gentle one for a woman

Pal·grave (pal′grāv′), **Francis Turner** 1824-97; Eng. anthologist

Pa·li (pä′lē) ***n.*** ⟦Sans *pāli,* lit., a row, line, canon, short for *pāli bhāsā,* canon language⟧ the Old Indic Prakrit, or dialect, of the Buddhist scriptures, which has become the religious language of Hinayana Buddhism

Pa·li·kir (pä′lē kir′) capital of Micronesia

☆**pal·i·mo·ny** (pal′ə mō′nē) ***n.*** ⟦PAL + (AL)IMONY⟧ an allowance or a property settlement claimed by or granted to one member of an unmarried couple who separate after having lived together

pal·imp·sest (pal′imp sest′) ***n.*** ⟦L *palimpsestus* < Gr *palimpsēstos,* lit., rubbed again < *palin,* again (see fol.) + *psēn,* to rub smooth < IE base **bhes-,* to rub off, pulverize > L *sabulum,* SAND⟧ a parchment, tablet, etc. that has been written upon or inscribed two or three times, the previous text or texts having been imperfectly erased and remaining, therefore, still partly visible

pal·in·drome (pal′in drōm′) ***n.*** ⟦Gr *palindromos,* running back < *palin,* again (< IE base **kwel-,* to turn > WHEEL) + *dramein,* to run: see DROMEDARY⟧ a word, phrase, or sentence that reads the same backward or forward (Ex.: madam) **—pal′in·drom′ic** (-drō′mik, -drä′-) ***adj.***

pal·ing (pāl′iŋ) ***n.*** **1** the action of making a fence of pales **2** a fence made of pales **3** pales collectively **4** a strip of wood used in making a fence; pale

pal·in·gen·e·sis (pal′in jen′ə sis) ***n.*** ⟦ModL < Gr *palin,* again (see PALINDROME) + *genesis,* birth, GENESIS)⟧ **1** a new birth; regeneration **2** METEMPSYCHOSIS **3** that phase in the development of an individual plant or animal which supposedly repeats the evolutionary history of the taxonomic group to which it belongs; recapitulation: cf. CENOGENESIS **—pal′in·ge·net′ic** (-jə net′ik) ***adj.***

pal·i·node (pal′ə nōd′) ***n.*** ⟦MFr *palinod* < LL *palinodia* < Gr *palinōidia* < *palin,* again (see PALINDROME) + *ōidē,* song: see ODE⟧ **1** an ode or other poem written to retract something said in a previous poem **2** a retraction

pal·i·sade (pal′ə sād′, pal′ə sād′) ***n.*** ⟦Fr *palissade* < Prov *palisada* < *palisa,* a pale < L *palus,* a stake, PALE²⟧ **1** any one of a row of large pointed stakes set in the ground to form a fence used for fortification or defense **2** a fence of such stakes ☆**3** [*pl.*] a line of very steep cliffs, usually along a river **—*vt.*** **-sad′ed, -sad′ing** to fortify or defend with a palisade **—the Palisades** line of steep cliffs in NE N.J. & SE N.Y. on the west shore of the Hudson: *c.* 15 mi (24 km) long

palisade parenchyma a layer of cylindrical cells containing chloroplasts, lying just below the upper epidermis of many leaves with their long axes at right angles to the epidermis

pal·ish (pā′lish) ***adj.*** somewhat pale

pall¹ (pôl) ***vi.*** **palled, pall′ing** ⟦ME *pallen,* aphetic for *appallen,* APPALL⟧ **1** to become cloying, insipid, boring, wearisome, etc. **2** to become satiated or bored **—*vt.*** to satiate, bore, or disgust

pall² (pôl) ***n.*** ⟦ME *pal* < OE *pœll* < L *pallium,* a cover (akin to *palla,* a robe, mantle)⟧ **1** *a)* a cloth covering, typically black, draped over a coffin or catafalque *b)* an overspreading covering, as of dark clouds or black smoke, that cloaks or obscures in a gloomy, depressing way *c)* an overspreading, pervasive atmosphere or spirit of gloom and depression [the sad news cast a *pall* on the proceedings] *d)* [Obs.] a cloak, mantle, or veil **2** a light, square covering, usually of stiffened linen, put on top of the chalice in the Mass **—*vt.*** **palled, pall′ing** to cover with a PALL² (sense 1)

Pal·la·di·an¹ (pə lā′dē ən) ***adj.*** ⟦< L *Palladius* (after PALLAS) + -AN⟧ **1** of Pallas Athena: see PALLAS **2** [*occas.* **p-**] of wisdom or learning

Pal·la·di·an² (pə lā′dē ən) ***adj.*** of or in the classical Roman style of Andrea Palladio

pal·lad·ic (pə lad′ik, -lād′ik) ***adj.*** designating or of chemical compounds containing tetravalent palladium

Pal·la·dio (päl lä′dyô), **An·dre·a** (än dre′ä) (born *Andrea di Pietro*) 1508-80; It. architect

pal·la·di·um (pə lā′dē əm) ***n.*** ⟦ModL: so named (1803) by W. H. Wollaston (see WOLLASTONITE), after the recently discovered asteroid PALLAS + -IUM⟧ a rare, silver-white, ductile, malleable chemical element, one of the platinum metals: it is used as a catalyst, esp. in hydrogenation processes, or in alloys with gold, silver, and other metals: symbol, Pd; at. no. 46: see the periodic table of elements in the Reference Supplement

Pal·la·di·um (pə lā′dē əm) ***n.***, *pl.* **-di·a** (-ə) ⟦L < Gr *palladion,* sacred statue or image, after PALLAS⟧ **1** in ancient Greece and Rome, any statue of the Greek goddess Pallas Athena; specif., the legendary statue in Troy on the preservation of which the safety of the city was supposed to depend **2** [**p-**] anything supposed to ensure the safety of something; safeguard

pal·la·dous (pə lā′dəs, pal′ə dəs) ***adj.*** designating or of chemical compounds containing divalent palladium

Pal·las (pal′əs) ***n.*** ⟦L < Gr⟧ **1** *Gr. Myth.* ATHENA: also **Pallas Athena** **2** ⟦ModL: so named (1802) by H. W. M. Olbers (1758-1840), Ger astronomer, after L *Pallas,* the goddess⟧ the second asteroid discovered (1802), and the second largest (*c.* 610 km or *c.* 380 mi in diameter)

pall·bear·er (pôl′ber′ər) ***n.*** ⟦PALL² + BEARER: formerly, one who held the edges of the pall⟧ one of the persons who attend or bear the coffin at a funeral

pal·let¹ (pal′it) ***n.*** ⟦Fr *palette:* see PALETTE⟧ **1** a wooden tool consisting of a flat blade with a handle; esp., such a tool used by potters for smoothing and rounding **2** PALETTE (sense 1) **3** a low, portable platform, usually double-faced, on which materials are stacked for storage or transportation, as in a warehouse **4** *Bookbinding* a tool used for stamping letters on the binding of a book **5** *Mech.* a part of a machine that changes back-and-forth motion to circular motion, or vice versa, by engaging the teeth of a ratchet wheel; pawl; click; esp., any of the clicks or pawls in a clock or watch escapement, which regulate the speed by releasing one tooth of a ratchet wheel at each swing of the pendulum or turn of the balance wheel

pal·let² (pal′it) ***n.*** ⟦ME *pailet* < MFr *paillet* < OFr *paille,* straw < L *palea,* chaff: see PALEA⟧ a small bed or a pad filled as with straw and used directly on the floor

pal·let³ (pal′it) ***n.*** ⟦ME *palet* < MFr, dim. of *pal,* PALE²⟧ *Heraldry* a vertical stripe half as wide as a pale

pal·let·ize (pal′ə tīz′) ***vt.*** **-ized′, -iz′ing** to store or transport (materials) on pallets

pal·lette (pal′it) ***n.*** ⟦Fr *palette:* see PALETTE⟧ a plate protecting the armpit, in a suit of armor

pal·liasse (pal yas′, pal′yas′) ***n.*** ⟦< Fr *paillasse* < It *pagliaccio* < VL **paleaceum* < L *palea:* see PALEA⟧ a mattress filled with straw, sawdust, etc.

pal·li·ate (pal′ē āt′) ***vt.*** **-at′ed, -at′ing** ⟦< pp. of LL *palliare,* to conceal, cloak, back-form. < L *palliatus,* cloaked < *pallium,* a cloak⟧ **1** to lessen the pain or severity of without actually curing; alleviate; ease **2** to make appear less serious or offensive; excuse; extenuate **—pal′li·a′tion *n.*** **—pal′li·a′tor *n.***

pal·li·a·tive (pal′ē āt′iv, -ə tiv) ***adj.*** serving or tending to palliate; specif., *a)* focusing on relieving the pain or discomfort of an illness, rather than on a cure [*palliative* nursing care] *b)* alleviating *c)* excusing; extenuating **—*n.*** a thing that palliates

pal·lid (pal′id) ***adj.*** ⟦L *pallidus,* PALE¹⟧ faint in color; pale; wan **—*SYN.*** PALE¹ **—pal′lid·ly *adv.*** **—pal′lid·ness *n.***

pal·li·um (pal′ē əm) ***n.***, *pl.* **-li·ums** or **-li·a** (-ə) ⟦L, a cloak, mantle⟧ **1** HIMATION **2** *Anat.* the cerebral cortex with its adjacent white matter **3** *R.C.Ch.* a circular white wool band with pendants, worn over the shoulders by a pope or archbishop **4** *Zool.* the mantle of mollusks and related marine invertebrates

pall-mall (pal′mal′, pel′mel′) ***n.*** ⟦MFr *palemail* < It *pallamaglio* < *palla* (< Langobardic *palla,* akin to OHG *balla,* BALL¹) + *maglio* < L *malleus,* a hammer: see MALLEABLE⟧ **1** an old game in which a boxwood ball was struck by a mallet through an iron ring hung at the end of an alley **2** the alley in which this game was played

pal·lor (pal′ər) ***n.*** ⟦L < base of *pallere,* to be pale, akin to *pallidus,* PALE¹⟧ unnatural paleness, as of the face, associated with poor health, fear, etc.

pal·ly (pal′ē) ***adj.*** [Informal, Chiefly Brit.] of or like a pal; intimate; chummy

palm¹ (päm, pôm; pälm, pôlm) ***n.*** ⟦ME *palme* < OE *palm* < L *palma:* so named because its leaf somewhat resembles the palm of the hand⟧ **1** any of an order (Arecales) of tropical or subtropical monocotyledonous trees and shrubs, having a woody, usually unbranched, trunk and large, evergreen, featherlike or fan-shaped leaves growing in a bunch at the top **2** a leaf of such a tree carried or worn as a symbol of victory, triumph, joy, etc. **3** victory; triumph **4** a representation of a palm leaf or frond given in lieu of a second award of the same military decoration **—*adj.*** designating the only family (Arecaceae) of palms, including the coconut palm, betel palm, and date palm **—bear** (or **carry off**) **the palm** to be the winner; take the prize —**yield the palm to** to acknowledge the superiority of; admit to defeat by —**pal·ma·ceous** (pal māʹshəs, päl-) ***adj.***

palm² (päm, pôm; pälm, pôlm) ***n.*** ⟦altered (infl. by L) < ME *paume* < OFr < L *palma,* palm of the hand < IE base *pele-, broad, flat, spread out > FLOOR, FIELD⟧ **1** the inner part or surface of the hand between the fingers and wrist **2** the part of a glove, mitten, etc. that covers the palm **3** the broad, flat part of an antler, as of a moose **4** a unit of linear measure based either on the width of the hand (3 to 4 inches) or on its length (7 to 9 inches) **5** any broad, flat part at the end of an arm, handle, etc., **6** a piece of leather, often with a metal disc attached, that fits over the palm of the hand, worn for protection in sewing heavy canvas or leather —***vt.*** **1** to hide (something) in the palm or between the fingers, as in a sleight-of-hand trick ☆**2** to momentarily rest (a basketball) in the upturned palm while dribbling: an illegal technique —**have an itching palm** [Informal] to desire money greedily —**palm off** [Informal] to cause, by trickery or deceit, to be accepted as genuine or true

Pal·ma (pälʹmä) seaport on Majorca: capital of Baleares, Spain: in full **Palma de Mal·lor·ca** (*the* mäl yôrʹkä)

pal·mar (palʹmər) ***adj.*** ⟦L *palmaris*⟧ of, in, or corresponding to the palm of the hand

pal·ma·ry (palʹmə rē) ***adj.*** ⟦L *palmarius*⟧ bearing or worthy to bear the palm; preeminent; victorious

pal·mate (palʹmātʹ, päʹ-) ***adj.*** ⟦L *palmatus* < *palma,* PALM²⟧ shaped like a hand with the fingers spread; specif., *a) Bot.* having veins, leaflets, or lobes radiating from a common center (said of some leaves) *b) Zool.* web-footed, as many water birds Also **palʹmat'ed** —**palʹmate'ly *adv.***

pal·mat·i·fid (pal matʹi fid) ***adj.*** ⟦< L *palmatus,* prec. + -FID⟧ having leaves cleft about halfway to the base, but not into separate leaflets

pal·ma·tion (pal māʹshən) ***n.*** **1** the state or quality of being palmate; palmate formation or structure **2** a part or division of a palmate formation

Palm Bay city in EC Fla., near Orlando

Palm Beach ⟦descriptive⟧ town in SE Fla., on the Atlantic; winter resort

palm crab a large tropical land crab (*Birgus latro*) that feeds esp. on coconuts, found on islands in the S Pacific and Indian oceans

Palm·dale (pämʹdālʹ) ⟦transl. of orig. *Palmenthal* < Ger *palme,* palm tree + *thal, tal,* valley (see DELL)⟧ city in SW Calif.: suburb of Los Angeles

palm·er (pämʹər) ***n.*** ⟦ME *palmere* < Anglo-Fr *palmer* < OFr *palmier* < ML *palmarius* < L *palma,* PALM¹⟧ [Historical] a pilgrim carrying a palm leaf to signify the making of a pilgrimage to the Holy Land

Palm·er (pämʹər), **Samuel** 1805-81; Eng. landscape painter & etcher

Pal·mer Peninsula (pämʹər) *former name for* ANTARCTIC PENINSULA

Palm·er·ston (pämʹər stən), 3d Viscount (*Henry John Temple*) 1784-1865; Brit. statesman: prime minister (1855-58; 1859-65)

palm·er·worm (pämʹər wurmʹ) ***n.*** any of various wandering caterpillars feeding on plants

pal·mette (pal metʹ, palʹmetʹ) ***n.*** ⟦Fr < *palme,* palm < L *palma,* PALM¹⟧ *Archit.* a conventional ornament somewhat resembling a palm leaf

pal·met·to (pal metʹō, päl-) ***n., pl.*** **-tos** or **-toes** ⟦Sp *palmito,* dim. < *palma* < L, PALM¹⟧ any of several fan palms; esp., a cabbage palm (*Sabal palmetto*) of the SE U.S.

palm·is·try (pämʹis trē) ***n.*** ⟦altered (by assoc. with PALM²) < ME *paumestrie,* prob. contr. < *paume,* PALM² + *maistrie,* MASTERY⟧ divination of a person's character or fortune by interpreting the lines and marks on that person's palm —**palmʹist *n.***

pal·mi·tate (palʹmi tātʹ) ***n.*** a salt or ester of palmitic acid

pal·mit·ic acid (pal mitʹik) ⟦Fr *palmitique:* see PALM¹ & -ITE¹ & -IC⟧ a colorless, crystalline fatty acid, $CH_3(CH_2)_{14}COOH$, found uncombined in palm oil and as the glyceryl ester in other vegetable and animal fats and oils

pal·mi·tin (palʹmi tin) ***n.*** ⟦Fr *palmitine*⟧ a colorless crystalline compound, $C_{51}H_{98}O_6$, found in palm oil and many other fats: it is the glyceryl ester of palmitic acid

palm leaf the leaf of a palm tree, esp. of one of the palmettos, used to make fans, hats, etc.

palm oil a yellow or reddish, semisolid oil obtained from the fruit of several kinds of palms, esp. the oil palm: used in making soap, candles, etc.

Palm Springs ⟦descriptive⟧ resort city in SW Calif., east of Los Angeles

palm sugar JAGGERY

Palm Sunday the Sunday before Easter, commemorating in Christian churches Jesus' entry into Jerusalem, when palm branches were strewn before him: John 12:12-13: also called *Passion Sunday* or *Second Sunday of the Passion*

palm·top (pämʹtäpʹ) ***n.*** a small, hand-held, battery-operated computer, used to store personal information, send and receive email or faxes, etc.

palm·y (pämʹē) ***adj.*** **palmʹi·er, palmʹi·est** **1** abounding in or shaded by palm trees **2** of or like a palm or palms **3** flourishing; prosperous [*palmy* days]

pal·my·ra (pal mīʹrə) ***n.*** ⟦altered (after fol.) < Port *palmeira* < *palma* < L, PALM¹⟧ a fan palm (*Borassus flabellifer*) grown in India, Sri Lanka, and tropical Africa for its durable wood, its edible fruits, its leaves used for thatching, etc.

Pal·my·ra (pal mīʹrə) ancient city in central Syria, northeast of Damascus: now the site of a village

Pal·o Al·to (palʹō alʹtō) ⟦< MexSp, lit., tall tree (the redwood): see PALOVERDE⟧ city in W Calif., near San Francisco

Pal·o·mar Mountain (palʹə märʹ) ⟦< Sp *palomar,* lit., dovecote⟧ mountain in SW Calif., near San Diego: site of an astronomical observatory: 6,140 ft (1,871 m): formerly, and now popularly, **Mount Palomar**

☆**pal·o·mi·no** (palʹə mēʹnō) ***n., pl.*** **-nos** ⟦AmSp < Sp, dove-colored < L *palumbinus* < *palumbes,* a pigeon, ringdove < IE base *pel-, gray, pale (> PALE¹, FALLOW²): form prob. infl. by L *columba:* see COLUMBARIUM⟧ a golden-tan or cream-colored horse that has a white, silver, or ivory tail and mane and, often, white spots on the face and legs

☆**pa·loo·ka** (pə lo͞oʹkə) ***n.*** ⟦< ?: popularized by Jack Conway (died 1928), U.S. baseball player and sportswriter⟧ [Slang] a clumsy or oafish fellow, esp. an inept athlete

Pa·los (päʹlôs) village & former port in SW Spain, from which Columbus embarked on his 1st voyage

☆**pa·lo·ver·de** (päʹlō verʹdā) ***n.*** ⟦MexSp, lit., green tree < Sp *palo,* a stick, log (< L *palus,* a stake, PALE²) + *verde,* green < L *viridis:* see VERDURE⟧ any of several leguminous trees or shrubs (genera *Parkinsonia* and *Cercidium*) with spiny branches, green bark, and bright-yellow flowers, found in the SW U.S. and Mexico

palp (palp) ***n.*** PALPUS —**palʹpal *adj.***

pal·pa·ble (palʹpə bəl) ***adj.*** ⟦ME < LL *palpabilis* < L *palpare,* to touch, prob. < IE base *pel-, to make move, shake > FEEL⟧ **1** that can be touched, felt, or handled; tangible **2** easily perceived by the senses; audible, recognizable, perceptible, noticeable, etc. **3** clear to the mind; obvious; evident; plain —*SYN.* EVIDENT, PERCEPTIBLE —**palʹpa·bilʹi·ty *n.*** —**palʹpa·bly *adv.***

pal·pate¹ (palʹpātʹ) ***vt.*** **-pat'ed, -pat'ing** ⟦< L *palpatus,* pp. of *palpare,* to touch: see prec.⟧ to examine by touching, as for medical diagnosis —**pal·paʹtion *n.***

pal·pate² (palʹpātʹ, -pit) ***adj.*** ⟦ModL *palpatus:* see PALPUS & -ATE¹⟧ having a palpus or palpi

pal·pe·bral (palʹpə brəl) ***adj.*** ⟦LL *palpebralis* < L *palpebra,* eyelid, akin to *palpare:* see PALPABLE⟧ of or having to do with the eyelids

pal·pi·tate (palʹpə tātʹ) ***vi.*** **-tat'ed, -tat'ing** ⟦< L *palpitatus,* pp. of *palpitare,* freq. of *palpare,* to feel, stroke: see PALPABLE⟧ **1** to beat rapidly or flutter: said esp. of heart action that one is conscious of **2** to throb; tremble —**palʹpi·tant** (-tənt) ***adj.*** —**palʹpi·taʹtion *n.***

pal·pus (palʹpəs) ***n., pl.*** **palʹpiʹ** (-pīʹ) ⟦ModL < L *palpus,* the soft palm of the hand, akin to *palpare:* see PALPABLE⟧ **1** a jointed organ or feeler for touching or tasting, attached to one of the head appendages of insects, lobsters, etc. **2** a fleshy, sensory structure in the oral region of some polychaete worms

pals·grave (pôlzʹgrāvʹ, palzʹ-) ***n.*** ⟦Du *paltsgrave* < *palts* (< L *palatium*), palace + *graaf,* count; akin to Ger *pfalzgraf*⟧ [Historical] in Germany, a count palatine

pal·sy (pôlʹzē) ***n., pl.*** **-sies** ⟦ME *palesie, parlesie* < OFr *paralisie* < L *paralysis,* PARALYSIS⟧ paralysis of any voluntary muscle as a result of some disorder in the nervous system, sometimes accompanied with involuntary tremors —***vt.*** **-sied, -sy·ing** to afflict with or as with palsy; paralyze

pal·sy-wal·sy (palʹzē walʹzē) ***adj.*** ⟦redupl. of *palsy* < *pals,* pl. of PAL + -Y²⟧ [Slang] very friendly; intimate

pal·ter (pôlʹtər) ***vi.*** ⟦freq. formation < dial. *palt,* rag, piece of cloth (< a LowG source): orig. ? with reference to haggling over cloth prices⟧ **1** to talk or act insincerely; prevaricate **2** to deal with facts, decisions, etc. lightly or carelessly; trifle **3** to quibble, as in bargaining —**palʹter·er *n.***

pal·try (pôlʹtrē) ***adj.*** **-tri·er, -tri·est** ⟦prob. < LowG *paltrig,* ragged < *palte,* a rag⟧ **1** practically worthless; trifling; insignificant **2** meager; contemptibly slight —**palʹtri·ness *n.***

pa·lu·dal (pə lo͞odʹ'l, palʹyo͞o dəl) ***adj.*** ⟦ML *paludalis* < L *palus* (gen. *paludis*), marsh < IE base *pel- > FULL¹, Gr *pēlos,* clay, mud, bog⟧ **1** of a marsh or marshes; marshy **2** [Archaic] malarial

pal·y¹ (pāʹlē) ***adj.*** [Archaic] somewhat pale

pal·y² (pāʹlē) ***adj.*** ⟦Late ME < MFr *palé* < *pal,* PALE²⟧ *Heraldry* divided into four or more vertical stripes of equal width, in alternating colors: said of the field of a shield

pal·y·nol·o·gy (palʹi nälʹə jē) ***n.*** ⟦< Gr *palynein,* to strew, sprinkle (< *palē,* fine meal, dust < IE base *pel-, dust, meal > L *pollen*) + -LOGY⟧ the study of living or fossil plant spores and pollen —**palʹy·no·logʹi·cal** (-nə läjʹi kəl) ***adj.*** —**palʹy·nolʹo·gist *n.***

pam *abbrev.* pamphlet

Pam·e·la (pamʹə lə) ***n.*** ⟦apparently coined by Sir Philip SIDNEY² for a character in his *Arcadia* (1590)⟧ a feminine name: dim. *Pam*

Pa·mirs (pä mirzʹ) mountain system mostly in Tajikistan: highest peak, *c.* 25,000 ft (7,620 m): also **Pa·mirʹ**

Pam·li·co Sound (pamʹli kōʹ) ⟦earlier *Pampticough* < Algonquian tribal name⟧ inlet of the Atlantic between the coast of N.C. and narrow offshore islands: *c.* 80 mi (129 km) long

pam·pa (pamʹpə, pämʹ-) ***n.*** ⟦AmSp < Quechua *pámpa,* plain, field⟧ an extensive, treeless plain of South America, esp. of Argentina —**the Pampas** vast plain of S South America, extending from the Atlantic across central Argentina to the Andes

pam·pas grass (pamʹpəs) a giant South American grass (*Cortaderia selloana*) cultivated for use as an ornamental and for its large, plumelike, silvery or pinkish panicles used in bouquets

pam·pe·an (pam pēʹən, pamʹpē-) ***adj.*** of the Pampas or the Indians native to the Pampas —***n.*** a pampean Indian

pam·per (pamʹpər) ***vt.*** ⟦ME *pampren* < LowG source, akin to Fl *pampren* in the same sense⟧ **1** [Obs.] to feed too much; gratify to excess; glut **2** to be overindulgent with; give in easily to the wishes of; coddle [to *pamper* a child] —*SYN.* INDULGE —**pamʹper·er *n.***

pam·pe·ro (päm pāʹrō, -perʹō) ***n., pl.*** **-ros** ⟦AmSp < *pampa:* see PAMPA⟧ a strong, cold wind that blows from the Andes across the South American Pampas

☆**Pam·pers** (pam′pərz) *trademark for* disposable diapers of soft, absorbent paper with an outer covering of thin plastic

pamph *abbrev.* pamphlet

pam·phlet (pam′flit) *n.* ⟦ME *pamfilet* < OFr *Pamphilet,* dim. of ML *Pamphilus,* short for *Pamphilus, seu de Amore,* Pamphilus, or on Love, title of 12th-c. ML amatory poem⟧ **1** a small, thin, unbound book made up of sheets of paper stapled or stitched together and usually having a paper cover **2** something published in this form, usually on some topic of current interest

pam·phlet·eer (pam′flə tir′) *n.* a writer or publisher of pamphlets; esp., one who writes pamphlets dealing polemically with political or social issues —*vi.* to write or publish pamphlets

Pam·phyl·i·a (pam fil′ē ə) ancient region in S Asia Minor, on the Mediterranean

Pam·plo·na (päm plô′nä) city in Navarre, NE Spain: site of an annual festival during which people run with bulls through the streets to the bullring

pan[1] (pan) *n.* ⟦ME *panne* < OE, akin to Ger *pfanne,* early Gmc loanword < VL *panna,* prob. < L *patina,* a pan: see PATELLA⟧ **1** any of many kinds of containers, usually broad, shallow, without a cover, and made of metal, used for domestic purposes: often in comb. *[a frying pan, saucepan, dishpan]* **2** any object or part shaped like a pan; specif., ☆*a)* an open container for washing out gold, tin, etc. from gravel or the like, in mining *b)* either receptacle in a pair of scales *c)* a container for heating, evaporating, etc. **3** the amount a pan will hold **4** any area suggestive of a pan; esp., a hollow, natural or artificial depression in the ground **5** a layer of hard soil, impervious to water; hardpan **6** a small ice floe **7** the part of a flintlock gun that holds the firing powder ☆**8** [Slang] a face —*vt.* **panned, pan′ning 1** to cook in a pan ☆**2** [Informal] to criticize unfavorably, as in reviewing *[to pan a play]* ☆**3** *Mining a)* to wash (gravel, etc.) in a pan, as for separating gold *b)* to separate (gold, etc.) from gravel by washing it in a pan —*vi. Mining* ☆**1** to wash gravel in a pan, searching for gold ☆**2** to yield gold in this process —☆**pan out 1** *Mining* to yield gold, as gravel, a mine, etc. **2** [Informal] to turn out (as specified); transpire; esp., to turn out well; succeed

pan[2] (pän) *n.* ⟦Hindi *pān* < Sans *parṇa,* a leaf, feather: see FERN⟧ **1** a leaf of the betel pepper **2** a mixture of chopped betel nut, lime, and spices, wrapped in this leaf and chewed as a mild stimulant

pan[3] (pan) *Film, TV, etc. vt., vi.* **panned, pan′ning** ⟦< PAN(ORAMA)⟧ to rotate (a camera) horizontally, as to get a panoramic effect or follow a moving object —*n.* **1** the act of panning **2** a shot that is panned

Pan[1] (pan) *n.* ⟦L < Gr⟧ *Gr. Myth.* a god of fields, forests, wild animals, flocks, and shepherds, represented as having the legs (and, often, horns and ears) of a goat: identified with the Roman Faunus

Pan[2] *abbrev.* Panama

PAN *abbrev.* peroxyacetyl nitrate

pan- (pan) ⟦< Gr *pan,* neut. of *pas,* all, every, universal < IE base *$\hat{k}$*eu-,* a swelling, arch > L *cavus,* hollow⟧ *combining form* **1** all *[panchromatic, pantheism]* **2** [**P-**] *a)* of, comprising, embracing, or common to all or every *[Pan-American]* *b)* the cooperation, unity, or union of all members of (a specified nationality, race, church, etc.) *[Pan-Americanism]* **3** *Med.* whole, general; of all or many parts *[panarteritis]* In sense 2, usually followed by a hyphen, as in the following words:

Pan-African	**Pan-European**
Pan-Arabic	**Pan-Islamic**
Pan-Asian	**Pan-Slavic**

pan·a·ce·a (pan′ə sē′ə) *n.* ⟦L < Gr *panakeia* < *panakēs,* healing all < *pan,* all (see prec.) + *akos,* healing, medicine < ? IE base **yĕk-,* to cure > prob. Welsh *iach,* healthy, OIr *hícc,* cure⟧ a supposed remedy or medicine for all diseases or ills; cure-all —**pan′a·ce′an** *adj.*

pa·nache (pə nash′, -näsh′) *n.* ⟦Fr < OFr *pannache* < OIt *pennacchio* < LL(Ec) *pinnaculum,* tuft, plume: see PINNACLE⟧ **1** a plume of feathers, esp. on a helmet **2** dashing elegance of manner; carefree, spirited self-confidence or style; flamboyance

pa·na·da (pə nä′də, -nā′-) *n.* ⟦Sp < *pan* < L *panis,* bread: see FOOD⟧ **1** a dish made of bread boiled to a pulp and flavored **2** a paste made of flour boiled in water or milk, and used as a binding agent, esp. in forcemeats

Pa·na·ji (pə nä′jē) city in SW India: capital of Goa state

Pan·a·ma[1] (pan′ə mä′, -mô′) *n.* ⟦after fol. (the city), once a main distribution center for the hats, which are made in Ecuador⟧ *[also* **p-**] **1** a fine, hand-plaited hat made from select leaves of the jipijapa plant **2** any similar straw hat In full **Panama hat**

Pan·a·ma[2] (pan′ə mä′, -mô′) ⟦< AmSp *Panamá* < native Ind word⟧ **1** country in Central America, on the Isthmus of Panama: formerly a part of Colombia, it became independent in 1903: 30,193 sq mi (78,200 sq km) **2** its capital: seaport on the Gulf of Panama **3 Gulf of** arm of the Pacific, on the S coast of Panama: *c.* 115 mi (185 km) wide **4 Isthmus of** strip of land connecting South America & Central America: 31 mi (50 km) wide at its narrowest point —**Pan′a·ma′ni·an** (-mā′nē ən) *adj., n.*

Panama Canal ship canal across the Isthmus of Panama, connecting the Caribbean Sea (hence, Atlantic Ocean) and the Pacific Ocean: *c.* 50.7 mi (82 km) long: see also CANAL ZONE

Panama Canal Zone CANAL ZONE

Panama City PANAMA[2] (the capital)

Panama hat plant JIPIJAPA (sense 1)

☆**Pan-A·mer·i·can** (pan′ə mer′i kən) *adj.* of North America, South America, and Central America, collectively

☆**Pan-A·mer·i·can·ism** (-iz′əm) *n.* any theory or policy of, or movement toward, political and economic cooperation, mutual social and cultural understanding, international alliance, etc. among the Pan-American nations

Pan·a·mint Range (pan′ə mint) ⟦< name of a division of the Shoshonean Indians⟧ mountain range in SE Calif., forming the W rim of Death Valley: highest peak, 11,045 ft (3,367 m)

☆**pan·a·tel·a** or **pan·a·tel·la** (pan′ə tel′ə) *n.* ⟦AmSp *panatela,* orig., a long, narrow biscuit < It, dim. of *pane,* bread: see PANETTONE⟧ a cigar having a long, slender shape, usually about 5 inches in length and rounded at the mouth end

Pa·nay (pä nī′, pə-) island of the central Philippines, between Mindoro & Negros: 4,446 sq mi (11,515 sq km)

pan·broil (pan′broil′) *vt.* to fry in a pan with little or no fat

pan·cake (pan′kāk′) *n.* **1** a thin, flat cake of batter fried on a griddle or in a pan; griddlecake; flapjack: typically served in a stack **2** an emergency landing in which an airplane levels off higher than for a normal landing, stalls, then drops almost vertically: in full **pancake landing** ☆**3** *short for* PANCAKE MAKEUP —*vi.* **-caked′, -cak′ing 1** to make a pancake landing **2** *a)* to collapse by falling onto stories or levels below (said as of the floors of a multistory building) *b)* to undergo such a collapse (said as of a multistory building) —*vt.* to cause (an airplane) to make a pancake landing

☆**pancake makeup** ⟦after *Pan-Cake Make-Up,* a trademark⟧ a cosmetic or theatrical makeup made of a soluble, matte powder compressed into a thin cake and typically applied with a damp sponge

pan·cet·ta (pän chet′ə, pan-) *n.* ⟦It, dim. of *pancia,* belly < L *pantex:* see PAUNCH⟧ Italian bacon, typically cured with salt and spices rather than by smoking

pan·chax (pan′chaks′, -kaks′) *n.* ⟦ModL⟧ any of various brilliantly colored killifishes (genus *Aplocheilus*) often kept in tropical fish aquariums

pan·chro·mat·ic (pan′krō mat′ik) *adj.* ⟦PAN- + CHROMATIC⟧ sensitive to light of all colors *[panchromatic film]* —**pan·chro·ma·tism** (pan krō′mə tiz′əm) *n.*

pan·cra·ti·um (pan krā′shē əm) *n., pl.* **-ti·a** (-ə) ⟦L < Gr *pankration* < *pan,* all (see PAN-) + *kratos,* strength: see -CRAT⟧ in ancient Greece and Rome, an athletic contest combining boxing and wrestling —**pan·crat′ic** (-krat′ik) *adj.*

pan·cre·as (pan′krē əs, paŋ′-) *n.* ⟦ModL < Gr *pankreas* < *pan,* all (see PAN-) + *kreas,* flesh (see CRUDE)⟧ a large, elongated gland situated behind the stomach and secreting a digestive juice (*pancreatic juice*) into the small intestine: groups of differentiated cells (*islets of Langerhans*) in the gland produce the hormone insulin: the pancreas of animals, used as food, is usually called *sweetbread* —**pan′cre·at′ic** (-at′ik) *adj.*

pan·cre·a·tec·to·my (pan′krē ə tek′tə mē) *n., pl.* **-mies** the surgical removal of all or part of the pancreas

pancreatic juice the clear, alkaline juice secreted by the pancreas into the small intestine, where its constituent enzymes act on food passed down from the stomach

pan·cre·a·tin (pan′krē ə tin, pan krē′-) *n.* **1** any of the pancreatic enzymes or a mixture of these **2** a commercial preparation of pancreas extract taken from cattle or hogs, used as an aid to digestion

pan·cre·a·ti·tis (pan′krē ə tīt′is) *n.* ⟦fol. + -ITIS⟧ inflammation of the pancreas

pan·cre·a·to- (pan′krē ə tō′) ⟦< Gr *pankreat-,* stem of *pankreas,* PANCREAS⟧ *combining form* pancreas *[pancreatitis]*: also, before a vowel, **pancreat-**

pan·da (pan′də) *n.* ⟦Fr < name in Nepal, apparently orig. for the lesser panda⟧ *short for:* **1** GIANT PANDA **2** LESSER PANDA **3** PANDA CAR

panda car ⟦from their distinctive black and white paint, suggestive of the coloration of the GIANT PANDA⟧ [Brit. Slang] a police patrol car

pan·da·nus (pan dā′nəs) *n.* ⟦ModL < Malay *pandan*⟧ SCREW PINE

Pan·da·rus (pan′də rəs) *n.* ⟦L < Gr *Pandaros*⟧ a leader of the Lycians in the Trojan War: in medieval romances and in Boccaccio, Chaucer, and Shakespeare, he acts as the go-between for Troilus and Cressida

Pan·de·an (pan dē′ən) *adj.* of PAN[1]

pan·dect (pan′dekt′) *n.* ⟦Fr *pandecte* < LL *Pandectae,* the Pandects < L, pl. of *pandectes,* an all-inclusive book < Gr *pandektēs,* lit., all-receiving < *pan,* all (see PAN-) + *dechesthai,* to contain, receive < IE **dek̂-:* see DECENT⟧ **1** [*often pl.*] a complete body of laws; legal code **2** [Now Rare] a complete or comprehensive digest —**the Pandects** a digest of Roman civil law in fifty books, compiled for the emperor Justinian in the 6th cent. A.D.; the Digest

pan·dem·ic (pan dem′ik) *adj.* ⟦< LL *pandemus* < Gr *pandēmos* < *pan,* all (see PAN-) + *dēmos,* the people: see DEMOCRACY⟧ prevalent over a whole area, country, etc.; universal; general; specif., epidemic over a large region: said of a disease —*n.* a pandemic disease or outbreak

Pan·de·mo·ni·um (pan′də mō′nē əm) *n.* ⟦ModL < Gr *pan,* all (see PAN-) + *daimōn,* DEMON⟧ **1** the capital of Hell in Milton's *Paradise Lost* **2** HELL **3** [**p-**] *a)* any place or scene of wild disorder, noise, or confusion *b)* wild disorder, noise, or confusion

pan·der (pan′dər) *n.* ⟦< ME *Pandare,* PANDARUS < L *Pandarus*⟧ **1** a go-between in a sexual intrigue; esp., a procurer; pimp **2** a person who provides the means of helping to satisfy the ignoble ambitions or desires, vices, etc. of another Also **pan′der·er** —*vt.* [Archaic] to be a pander for —*vi.* to act as a pander (*to* a person's ignoble ambitions or desires, vices, etc.)

P & H *abbrev.* postage and handling

pan·dit (pun′dit) *n.* ⟦Hindi *paṇḍit:* see PUNDIT⟧ **1** in India, a Brahman who is learned in Sanskrit and in Hindu philosophy, law, and religion **2** [**P-**] a title of respect for such a person: used before the name

P & L *abbrev.* profit and loss

pan·do·ra (pan dôr′ə) ***n.*** ⟦It < LL *pandura:* see BANDORE⟧ BANDORE: also **pan·dore′** (-dôr′)

Pan·do·ra (pan dôr′ə) ***n.*** ⟦L < Gr *Pandōra* < *pan,* all (see PAN-) + *dōron,* a gift: see DATE[1]⟧ *Gr. Myth.* the first mortal woman: out of curiosity she opens a box, letting out all human ills into the world (or, in a later version, letting all human blessings escape and be lost, leaving only hope)

Pandora's box ⟦see prec.⟧ **1** a complex situation fraught with problems and pitfalls **2** something causing or leading to such a situation

pan·dour (pan′door′) ***n.*** ⟦< Fr or < Ger *pandur,* both < Croatian *pàndūr,* constable, prob. < ML *banderius,* one who follows a banner: < WGmc *banda:* see BANNER⟧ **1** a member of a force of 18th-cent. Croatian soldiers in the Austrian army, noted for their brutality **2** any brutal soldier

☆**pan·dow·dy** (pan dou′dē) ***n.,*** *pl.* **-dies** ⟦prob. < obs. Somerset dial. *pandoulde,* custard < PAN[1] + *-doulde* < ?⟧ deep-dish apple pie or pudding, having a top crust only

pan·du·rate (pan′dyoo rit, -doo-; -rāt′) ***adj.*** ⟦< LL *pandura,* PANDORA + -ATE[1]⟧ *Bot.* shaped somewhat like a violin, as some leaves: also **pan·dur·i·form** (pan door′ə fôrm′, -dyoor′ə-)

pan·dy (pan′dē) [Chiefly Scot.] ***n.,*** *pl.* **-dies** ⟦L *pande,* open (your hand), imper. of *pandere,* to extend < IE **pand-,* var. of base **pet-,* to stretch out > FATHOM⟧ a stroke on the palm of the hand with a strap or cane, as a punishment —***vt.*** **-died, -dy·ing** to punish by such a stroke or strokes

pane (pān) ***n.*** ⟦ME *pan* < OFr < L *pannus,* piece of cloth < IE base **pan-,* fabric > Gr *pēnos,* cloth, OE *fana,* banner⟧ **1** a piece or division, esp. if flat and rectangular; specif., *a)* a single division of a window, etc., consisting of a sheet of glass in a frame *b)* such a sheet of glass **2** a panel, as of a door, wall, etc. **3** any of the flat sides, or faces, as of a nut, bolt head, cut diamond, etc. **4** *Philately a)* a separate section of stamps, variously a quarter, half, or full sheet, as cut for sale *b)* a block of stamps sold in a booklet (in full **booklet pane**)

pan·e·gyr·ic (pan′ə jir′ik, -jī′rik) ***n.*** ⟦Fr *panégyrique* < L *panegyricus* < Gr *panēgyris,* public meeting < *pan,* all (see PAN-) + *ageirein,* to bring together⟧ **1** a formal speech or piece of writing praising a person or event **2** high or hyperbolic praise; laudation —**pan′e·gyr′i·cal** ***adj.*** —**pan′e·gyr′i·cal·ly** ***adv.*** —**pan′e·gyr′ist** ***n.*** —**pan′e·gy·rize′** (-jə rīz′) ***vt., vi.*** **-rized′, -riz′ing**

pan·el (pan′əl) ***n.*** ⟦OFr < VL **pannellus,* dim. of L *pannus,* piece of cloth: see PANE⟧ **1** *a)* a piece of cloth placed under a saddle; saddle lining *b)* a soft saddle **2** a section or division of a surface, or one that constitutes a surface; specif., *a)* a section of a fence or railing between two posts *b)* a flat piece, usually rectangular, forming a part of the surface of a wall, door, cabinet, etc., and usually raised, recessed, framed, etc. *c)* a similar piece used for enclosing or covering something or serving as a light diffuser, a built-in heating element in space heating, etc. *d)* a compartment or pane of a window *e)* a section of a tapestry *f)* any of the sections of a comic strip *g)* an insulated board, or flat surface, for instruments or controls, as of an electric circuit, airplane, etc. *h)* any of the sections of the body of an automotive vehicle, typically metal or fiberglass [quarter *panel,* rocker *panel,* etc.] **3** *a)* a thin board for an oil painting *b)* a painting on such a board *c)* any picture very much longer than it is wide **4** ⟦< piece of parchment on which orig. recorded⟧ *a)* a list of persons summoned for jury duty *b)* the persons summoned or the jury itself **5** a group of persons selected for a specific purpose, as judging a contest, discussing an issue publicly, participating on a radio or TV quiz show, etc. **6** a lengthwise strip, as of contrasting material, in a skirt or dress **7** *Aeron. a)* any of the sections of a wing *b)* any of the sections of fabric, etc. used in the envelope of a balloon or airship, or in the canopy of a parachute **8** *Mining* a compartment of a mine —***vt.*** **-eled** or **-elled, -el·ing** or **-el·ling** to cover, provide, fit, or decorate with panels

panel discussion a discussion carried on by a selected group of speakers before an audience

pan·el·ing or **pan·el·ling** (pan′əl iŋ) ***n.*** **1** panels collectively; specif., wood panels covering or for covering an interior wall **2** sections of plastic, wood, or other material from which to cut panels

pan·el·ist (pan′əl ist) ***n.*** a member of a PANEL (*n.* 5)

☆**panel truck** a small, enclosed van or truck, as for carrying cargo

☆**pan·e·tel·a** or **pan·e·tel·la** (pan′ə tel′ə) ***n.*** *alt. sp. of* PANATELA

pan·et·to·ne (pan′i tō′nē; *It* pä′net tô′ne) ***n.*** ⟦It < *panetto,* dim. of *pane,* bread < L *panis:* see FOOD⟧ an Italian sweet yeast bread containing raisins, candied fruits, etc.

☆**pan·fish** (pan′fish′) ***n.*** any small fish that can be fried whole in a pan

pan-fry (pan′frī′) ***vt.*** **-fried′, -fry′ing** to fry in a shallow skillet or frying pan

pan·ful (pan′fool′) ***n.,*** *pl.* **-fuls′** as much as a pan will hold

pang (paŋ) ***n.*** ⟦< ? LME *pronge:* see PRONG⟧ a sudden, sharp, and brief pain, physical or emotional [hunger *pangs*]

pan·ga (päŋ′gə) ***n.*** ⟦< name (in ? Swahili) in E Africa⟧ a long knife with a broad, sometimes hooked, blade, used in Africa as a cutting tool or a weapon

Pan·ge·a (pan jē′ə) ⟦coined (1912) by A. L. Wegener (1880-1930), Ger geologist: < Gr *pan,* all + *gē,* the earth⟧ the large landmass that nearly extended from pole to pole on one side of the earth during the late Paleozoic and early Mesozoic eras: it eventually split, forming Laurasia and Gondwana: often sp. **Pan·gae′a**

pan·gen·e·sis (pan jen′ə sis) ***n.*** ⟦ModL: see PAN- & -GENESIS⟧ a hypothesis of heredity, now discredited, in which each unit or cell of the body throws off minute particles into the blood which are collected in the reproductive cells as the units of hereditary transmission —**pan′ge·net′ic** (-jə net′ik) ***adj.***

Pan·gloss·i·an (pan glôs′ē ən, -gläs′-) ***adj.*** ⟦after Dr. *Pangloss* in Voltaire's *Candide*⟧ foolishly optimistic

pan·go·lin (pan′gō lin, paŋ′-; pan gō′-, paŋ-) ***n.*** ⟦Malay *pĕngulin,* roller < *gulin,* to roll⟧ any of an order (Pholidota) of toothless, scaly mammals of Asia and Africa, feeding on ants and termites and able to roll into a ball when attacked; scaly anteater

Pang·o Pang·o (päŋ′ō päŋ′ō) *var. of* PAGO PAGO

pan·gram (pan′gram′) ***n.*** ⟦PAN- + -GRAM⟧ a sentence containing all the letters of the alphabet; esp., such a sentence in which each letter is used only once

pan·han·dle[1] (pan′han′dəl) ***n.*** **1** the handle of a pan ☆**2** a strip of land projecting like the handle of a pan: often used in place names [the Oklahoma *Panhandle*]

☆**pan·han·dle**[2] (pan′han′dəl) ***vt., vi.*** **-dled, -dling** ⟦prob. back-form. < fol.⟧ [Informal] to beg (from), esp. on the streets

☆**pan·han·dler** (pan′hand′lər) ***n.*** ⟦< PANHANDLE[1] + -ER⟧ [Informal] a beggar, esp. one who begs on the streets

Pan·hel·len·ic (pan′hə len′ik) ***adj.*** **1** of or relating to all the Greek peoples **2** of Panhellenism **3** of all Greek-letter fraternities and sororities

Pan·hel·len·ism (pan hel′ən iz′əm) ***n.*** ⟦see PAN-, HELLENE, & -ISM⟧ [Historical] the theory of, or a movement toward, the political unification of all the Greek peoples

pan·ic[1] (pan′ik) ***n.*** ⟦ME *panyk* < L *panicum,* kind of millet < *panus,* ear of millet, a swelling < IE base **pank-,* to swell > Pol *pąk,* a bud⟧ any of several grasses (genus *Panicum*), as millet, used as fodder: also **panic grass**

pan·ic[2] (pan′ik) ***adj.*** ⟦Fr *panique* < Gr *panikos,* of Pan, after *Pan*⟧ **1** literally, of Pan **2** of sudden fear, as supposedly inspired by Pan **3** having the nature of, or showing or resulting from, panic —***n.*** **1** a sudden, unreasoning, hysterical fear, often spreading quickly **2** a widespread fear of the collapse of the financial system, resulting in unreasoned attempts to turn property into cash, withdraw money, etc. **3** [Slang] a person or thing considered extremely humorous or entertaining —***vt.*** **-icked, -ick·ing** **1** to affect with panic **2** [Slang] to convulse (a listener, audience, etc.) with laughter, delight, etc. —***vi.*** to give way to or show panic —**SYN.** FEAR —☆**push** (or **press** or **hit,** etc.) **the panic button** [Slang] to panic; specif., to react to a crisis with some frantic, often disastrous action —**pan′ic·al·ly** ***adv.*** —**pan′ick·y** ***adj.***

pan·i·cle (pan′i kəl) ***n.*** ⟦L *panicula,* tuft on plants, panicle, dim. of *panus,* a swelling, ear of millet: see PANIC[1]⟧ a loose, irregularly branched, indeterminate flower cluster; compound raceme —**pan′i·cled** ***adj.,*** **pa·nic·u·late** (pa nik′yoo lit, -lāt′), or **pa·nic′u·lat′ed**

pan·ic-strick·en (pan′ik strik′ən) ***adj.*** stricken with panic; badly frightened; hysterical and out of control from fear: also **pan′ic-struck′** (-struk′)

pa·ni·no (pä nē′nō) ***n.,*** *pl.* **-ni** (-nē) ⟦It, dim. of *pane,* bread < L *panis:* see FOOD⟧ [*often in italics*] **1** a small bread roll **2** a grilled sandwich of various combinations of meat, cheese, and vegetables, made with such a roll or with slices of coarse bread and then grilled: also **pa·ni′ni,** *pl.* **-nis**

Pan·ja·bi (pun jä′bē) ***n.*** *alt. sp. of* PUNJABI

pan·jan·drum (pan jan′drəm) ***n.*** ⟦arbitrary formation from a nonsense passage by Samuel Foote (1721-77), Eng actor & playwright⟧ a self-important, pompous official: a satirical title

Pank·hurst (paŋk′hurst′), **Em·me·line** (em′ə līn′, -lēn′) (born *Emmeline Goulden*) 1858-1928; Eng. suffragist

pan·ko (paŋ′kō pän′-) ***n.*** ⟦Jpn < Port *pão,* bread + Jpn *-ko,* flour, crumbs⟧ a type of flaky Jpn. bread crumbs

pan·mix·i·a (pan mik′sē ə) ***n.*** ⟦ModL < PAN- + Gr *mixis,* a mingling, mating (< *meignynai,* to MIX) + -IA⟧ random mating within a breeding population: often **pan·mix′is** (-mik′sis) —**pan·mic′tic** (-mik′tik) ***adj.***

panne (pan) ***n.*** ⟦Fr < OFr *penne,* fur lining, a soft substance < L *penna,* a feather: see PEN[2]⟧ a soft cloth resembling velvet, but having a longer nap and a lustrous finish

pan·nier or **pan·ier** (pan′yər, -ē ər) ***n.*** ⟦ME *panier* < MFr < L *panarium,* breadbasket < *panis,* bread: see FOOD⟧ **1** a large basket; specif., *a)* a wicker basket for carrying loads on the back *b)* either of a pair of baskets hung across the back of a donkey, horse, etc. for carrying loads *c)* a bag, usually one of a pair, for stowing one's gear, hung alongside the wheel of a bicycle or motorcycle **2** *a)* a framework, as of whalebone, wire, etc., used as formerly to puff out a skirt at the hips *b)* a skirt extended or puffed at the hips to give the effect of such a framework

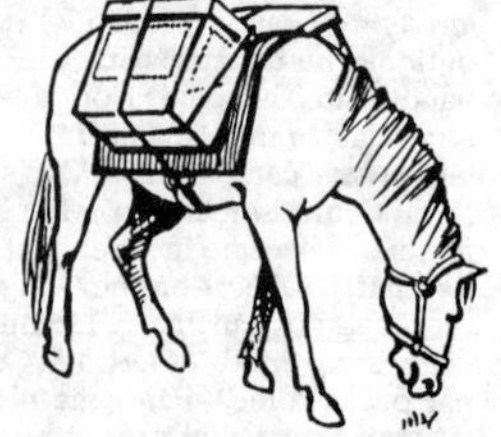
panniers

pan·ni·kin (pan′i kin) ***n.*** ⟦dim. of PAN[1]: see -KIN⟧ [Chiefly Brit.] **1** a small pan **2** a metal cup

Pan·no·ni·a (pə nō′nē ə) ancient Roman province in central Europe, between the Danube & Sava rivers

☆**pa·no·cha** (pə nō′chə, pä nō′chä) ***n.*** ⟦AmSp < Sp *pan,* bread: see PANADA⟧ **1** a coarse sugar made in Mexico **2** *var. of* PENUCHE: also **pa·no′che** (-chē)

pan·o·ply (pan′ə plē) ***n.***, *pl.* **-plies** ⟦Gr *panoplia* < *pan*, all (see PAN-) + *hopla*, arms, pl. of *hoplon*, tool (see HOPLITE)⟧ **1** a complete suit of armor **2** any protective covering **3** any complete or magnificent covering or array —**pan′o·plied** ***adj.***

pan·op·tic (pan äp′tik) ***adj.*** ⟦PAN- + OPTIC⟧ including in one view everything within sight

pan·o·ram·a (pan′ə ram′ə, -rä′mə) ***n.*** ⟦coined (*c.* 1789) by Robert Barker (1739-1806), Scot artist < PAN- + Gr *horama*, a view < *horan*, to see < IE base *wer-, to heed > WARN, GUARD⟧ **1** *a)* a picture or series of pictures of a landscape, historical event, etc., presented on a continuous surface encircling the spectator; cyclorama *b)* a picture unrolled before the spectator in such a way as to give the impression of a continuous view **2** an unlimited view in all directions **3** a comprehensive survey of a subject **4** a continuous series of scenes or events; constantly changing scene —**pan′o·ram′ic** ***adj.*** —**pan′o·ram′i·cal·ly** ***adv.***

pan·pipe (pan′pīp′) ***n.*** ⟦PAN¹ + PIPE⟧ [*also* **P-**] a primitive musical instrument made of a row or rows of reeds or tubes of graduated lengths bound together and played by blowing across the open upper ends: also **pan′pipes** or **Pan's pipes**

pan·sex·u·al (pan sek′sho͞o əl) ***adj.*** displaying or encompassing a broad range of human sexual behavior —**pan′sex·u·al′i·ty** ***n.***

pan·sper·mi·a (pan spur′mē ə) ***n.*** ⟦ModL < Gr < *pan*, all (see PAN-) + *sperma*, seed (see SPERM¹): orig., the ancient Gr doctrine that fundamental elements contain the seeds of all things⟧ the theory that microorganisms distributed throughout the universe are the source of life on earth and elsewhere where conditions favor its survival

panpipe

pan·sy (pan′zē) ***n.***, *pl.* **-sies** ⟦Fr *pensée*, fanciful extension of lit. meaning, a thought < *penser*, to think < L *pensare*: see PENSIVE⟧ **1** any of various violets, esp. a popular garden hybrid (*Viola tricolor hortensis*), with flat, broad, velvety petals in many colors ☆**2** [Slang] an effeminate man; esp., an effeminate male homosexual: a dismissive or contemptuous term

pant¹ (pant) ***vi.*** ⟦ME *panten*, prob. contr. < OFr *pantaisier* < VL **phantasiare*, to suffer from a nightmare < L *phantasia*, idea, notion, nightmare: see FANTASY⟧ **1** to breathe rapidly and heavily; gasp, as from running fast **2** to beat rapidly, as the heart; throb; pulsate **3** to feel strong desire; yearn eagerly: with *for* or *after* **4** to give off steam, smoke, etc. in loud puffs, as an engine —***vt.*** to utter hurriedly and breathlessly; gasp out —***n.*** **1** any of a series of rapid, heavy breaths, as from exertion; gasp **2** a throb, as of the heart **3** a puff, as of an engine

pant² (pant) ***n., adj.*** *see* PANTS

Pan·ta·gru·el (pan′tə gro͞o el′, -gro͞o′əl; pan tag′ro͞o el′; *Fr* pän tȧ grü el′) ***n.*** ⟦< ? name of a minor devil referred to in writings of the late 15th c.⟧ the boisterous, giant son of Gargantua in Rabelais' *Gargantua and Pantagruel*: he is a jovial drunkard characterized by rough, extravagant humor —**Pan·ta·gru·el·i·an** (pan′tə gro͞o el′ē ən) ***adj.*** —**Pan·ta·gru·el·ism** (pan′tə gro͞o′əl iz′əm) ***n.***

pan·ta·lets or **pan·ta·lettes** (pan′tə lets′) ***pl.n.*** ⟦dim. of fol.⟧ **1** long, loose drawers frilled at the ankle and showing beneath the skirt, worn by women during the middle of the 19th cent. **2** detachable ruffles for the legs of drawers

pan·ta·loon (pan′tə lo͞on′) ***n.*** ⟦Fr *Pantalon* < It *Pantalone*, name of a character in 16th-c. Italian comedy, after the Venetian patron saint *Pantalone* or *Pantaleone* (< Gr *pantos*, PANTO- + *leōn*, lion): also used for the garment worn by this character⟧ **1** [**P-**] *a)* a stock character in commedia dell'arte, usually a slender, foolish old man wearing tight trousers extending to the feet *b)* a similar figure in modern pantomime, the butt of the clown's jokes **2** [*pl.*] [Historical] *a)* tight trousers fastened below the calf or strapped under the boots *b)* later, any trousers

pant·dress (pant′dres′) ***n.*** a woman's one-piece garment with the lower part like pants instead of a skirt

pan·tech·ni·con (pan tek′ni kän′) ***n.*** ⟦PAN- + Gr *technikon* (neut. adj.), of the arts < *technē*, art: see TECHNIC⟧ [Brit.] **1** a bazaar where all kinds of things were sold **2** a warehouse **3** a furniture van: also **pantechnicon van**

Pan·tel·le·ri·a (pän tel′le rē′ä) Italian island in the Mediterranean, between Sicily & Tunisia: 32 sq mi (83 sq km)

pan·the·ism (pan′thē iz′əm) ***n.*** ⟦Fr *panthéisme* < *panthéiste* < E *pantheist*, coined (1705) by J. Toland, Ir deist: see PAN-, THEO-, & -ISM⟧ **1** the doctrine that God is not a personality, but that all laws, forces, manifestations, etc. of the universe are God; the belief that God and the universe are one and the same **2** [Historical] the worship, or toleration of worship, of gods of various cults —**pan′the·ist** ***n.*** —**pan′the·is′tic** ***adj.***, **pan′the·is′ti·cal** —**pan′the·is′ti·cal·ly** ***adv.***

pan·the·on (pan′thē än′, -ən; *also, chiefly Brit*, pan thē′ən) ***n.*** ⟦ME *Panteon* < L < Gr *pantheion* < *pan*, all (see PAN-) + *theos*, a god: see THEO-⟧ **1** a temple for all the gods **2** [**P-**] a temple built by Agrippa in Rome in 27 B.C., and rebuilt in the 2d cent. A.D. by Hadrian: used since A.D. 609 as a Christian Church **3** all the gods of a people **4** [*often* **P-**] a building in which famous dead persons of a nation are entombed or commemorated, as the church of Sainte-Geneviève in Paris **5** any group of persons having lasting fame and eminence in a particular field [*the pantheon of British poets*]

pan·ther (pan′thər) ***n.***, *pl.* **-thers** or **-ther** ⟦ME *pantere* < OFr *pantère* < L *panthera* < Gr *panthēr*⟧ **1** a leopard; specif., *a)* a black leopard *b)* a large or fierce leopard **2** COUGAR

☆**pant·ies** (pan′tēz) ***pl.n.*** women's or children's legless underpants: also **pant′ie** (-tē) ***n.***

pant·i·hose (pan′tē hōz′) ***n.*** *alt. sp. of* PANTYHOSE

pan·tile (pan′tīl′) ***n.*** ⟦PAN¹ + TILE⟧ a roofing tile having an S curve, laid with the large curve of one tile overlapping the small curve of the next

pantiles

pan·to (pan′tō) ***n.***, *pl.* **-tos** [Brit.] *short for* PANTOMIME (*n.* 4)

pan·to- (pan′tō, -tə) ⟦< Gr *pantos*, gen. of *pan*: see PAN-⟧ *combining form* all or every [*pantograph*]: also, before a vowel, **pant-**

pan·to·fle or **pan·tof·fle** (pan′tə fəl, pan täf′əl) ***n.*** ⟦LME *pantufle* ? via Prov < It dial. *pantofola*, cork slipper < MGr *pantophellos* whole cork < Gr *pantos* (see prec.) + *phellos*, cork⟧ [Now Literary] SLIPPER

pan·to·graph (pan′tə graf′) ***n.*** ⟦Fr *pantographe*: see PANTO- & -GRAPH⟧ **1** a mechanical device for reproducing a map, drawing, etc. on the same or a different scale, consisting of a framework of jointed rods in a roughly parallelogram form **2** any similar framework, as an extensible arm for a telephone, a trolley on an electric locomotive, etc. —**pan′to·graph′ic** ***adj.***

pan·to·mime (pan′tə mīm′) ***n.*** ⟦L *pantomimus* < Gr *pantomimos* < *pantos* (see PANTO-) + *mimos*, a mimic, actor⟧ **1** in ancient Rome *a)* an actor who played his part by gestures and action without words *b)* a drama played in action and gestures to the accompaniment of music or of words sung by a chorus **2** *a)* any dramatic presentation played without words, using only action and gestures *b)* the art of acting in this way **3** action or gestures without words as a means of expression **4** in England, a type of entertainment presented at Christmastime, ending in a harlequinade —***adj.*** of or like pantomime — ***vt., vi.*** **-mimed′**, **-mim′ing** to express or act in pantomime —**pan′to·mim′ic** (-mim′ik) ***adj.*** —**pan′to·mim′ist** (-mīm′ist) ***n.***

pan·to·then·ate (pan′tō then′āt′, pan täth′ə nāt′) ***n.*** a salt or ester of pantothenic acid

pan·to·then·ic acid (pan′tō then′ik) ⟦Gr *pantothen*, from every side < *pantos* (see PANTO-) + -IC⟧ a yellow, viscous oil, $C_9H_{17}NO_5$, a member of the vitamin B complex, widely distributed in animal and plant tissues and prepared synthetically: thought to be essential for cell growth and used in treating certain anemias

pan·try (pan′trē) ***n.***, *pl.* **-tries** ⟦ME *paneterie* < OFr < ML *panetaria* < L *panis*, bread: see FOOD⟧ **1** a small room or closet off the kitchen, where cooking ingredients and utensils, china, etc. are kept **2** a small room between the kitchen and dining room for storing tableware and for serving **3** a larder or buttery

☆**pants** (pants) ***pl.n.*** ⟦abbrev. of PANTALOONS⟧ **1** an outer garment extending from the waist to the knees or ankles and divided into separate coverings for the legs: more formally called *trousers*: also called **pair of pants** *sing.* **2** drawers or panties As an adjective or in compounds, usually *pant* [*pant legs, pantdress*]

pant·suit (pant′so͞ot′) ***n.*** a woman's suit consisting of a jacket and pants: also **pants suit**

☆**pant·y** (pan′tē) ***n.***, *pl.* **-ies** **1** PANTIES **2** PANTY GIRDLE

panty girdle a girdle with a crotch

pant·y·hose (pan′tē hōz′) ***n.*** a woman's one-piece, closefitting, nylon covering for the hips, legs, and feet: also written **panty hose**

☆**pant·y·waist** (pan′tē wāst′) ***n.*** **1** [Historical] a child's two-piece undergarment that buttoned together at the waist **2** [Slang] a man or youth considered as like a child in lacking strength, courage, etc.; sissy

Panza, Sancho *see* SANCHO PANZA

pan·zer (pan′zər; *Ger* pän′tsər) ***n.*** ⟦Ger, armor < MHG *panzier* < OFr *pancier* < It *pancia*, belly < L *pantex*: see PAUNCH⟧ a German armored vehicle, esp. a tank used in WWII —***adj.*** of or pertaining to a panzer vehicle or division

Pa·o·lo (pä′ô lô) *see* FRANCESCA DA RIMINI

Pao·tou (bou′dō′) *a former transliteration of* BAOTOU

pap¹ (pap) ***n.*** ⟦ME *pappe*, prob. orig. < baby talk⟧ [Archaic] a woman's breast or nipple

pap² (pap) ***n.*** ⟦ME, orig. < baby talk (as in L *papa*)⟧ **1** *a)* any soft or semiliquid food for babies or invalids *b)* any mash, paste, or pulp **2** any oversimplified or bland writing, ideas, etc. ☆**3** money, favors, etc. received because of association with public office

pa·pa (pä′pə, pə pä′) ***n.*** ⟦< baby talk, as also in Fr & L *papa*, Gr *pappas*, father, *pappos*, grandfather⟧ [Informal] FATHER

pa·pa·cy (pā′pə sē) ***n.***, *pl.* **-cies** ⟦ME *papacie* < ML(Ec) *papatia* < LL(Ec) *papa*, bishop, POPE⟧ **1** *a)* the rank of pope; papal office *b)* the term of office of one or more popes *c)* the whole succession of popes **2** [*also* **P-**] the governing of the Roman Catholic Church by the Roman pontiff, its head

pa·pa·dum (pä′pä dəm) ***n.*** ⟦Tamil⟧ a thin, crisp bread or wafer of India, made of lentil flour and usually flavored with pepper and other spices: also sp. **pa′pa·dam** or **pa′pa·dom**

Pa·pa·go (pä′pä gō′) *n., pl.* **-gos′** or **-go′** ⟦< Papago, lit., bean people⟧ **1** a member of a North American Indian people closely related to the Pimas and living mostly near the border between SW Arizona and NW Mexico **2** the Uto-Aztecan language of this people

pa·pa·in (pə pā′in, -pī′in) *n.* ⟦PAPA(YA) + -IN[1]⟧ a protein-splitting enzyme from the juice of unripe papaya, used as a digestive aid, as a meat tenderizer, in pharmacy, etc.

pa·pal (pā′pəl) *adj.* ⟦ME < MFr < ML(Ec) *papalis:* see POPE & -AL⟧ of or relating to a pope or the papacy —**pa′pal·ly** *adv.*

Papal States former territory in central & NC Italy, ruled by the papacy from the 8th cent. until 1870

pa·pa·raz·zi (pä′pə rät′sē) *pl.n., sing.* [*also in italics*] **-zo** (-sō) ⟦after *Paparazzo,* name of a character in F. Fellini's film *La Dolce Vita* (1960)⟧ photographers, often freelance, who take candid shots, often in an intrusive manner, of celebrities for newspapers or magazines

pa·pav·er·ine (pə pav′ər ēn′, -ər in; -pāv′-) *n.* ⟦L *papaver,* poppy + -INE[3]⟧ a white, crystalline alkaloid, $C_{20}H_{21}NO_4$, derived from opium and used in medicine to relax muscles in spasms and as a local anesthetic

pa·paw (pə pô′, pô′pô′) *n.* ⟦< fol.⟧ **1** PAPAYA ☆**2** *a)* a tree (*Asimina triloba*) of the custard-apple family, growing in the central and S U.S. and having an oblong, yellowish, edible fruit with many seeds *b)* its fruit

pa·pa·ya (pə pī′ə, -pä′yə) *n.* ⟦Sp < Carib or Arawak name of the fruit⟧ **1** a tropical American tree (*Carica papaya*) of the papaya family, resembling a palm, having a bunch of large leaves at the top, and bearing a large, oblong, yellowish-orange fruit like a melon **2** its fruit, eaten raw or cooked, and also valued for its juice —*adj.* designating a family (Caricaceae, order Violales) of tropical and subtropical dicotyledonous trees and shrubs

Pa·pe·e·te (pä′pē ā′tā) seaport & chief town on Tahiti: capital of French Polynesia

pa·per (pā′pər) *n.* ⟦ME *papir* < OFr *papier* < L *papyrus* < Gr *papyros,* PAPYRUS⟧ **1** a thin, flexible material made usually in sheets from a pulp prepared from rags, wood, or other fibrous material, and used for writing or printing on, for packaging, as structural material, as a fabric substitute, etc. **2** a single piece or sheet of paper **3** a printed or written sheet; specif., *a)* an official document *b)* an essay, monograph, or dissertation, as read before a learned society, published in a scholarly journal, etc. *c)* a written examination, report, theme, etc. **4** *a)* COMMERCIAL PAPER *b)* PAPER MONEY **5** *short for: a)* NEWSPAPER *b)* WALLPAPER **6** a small wrapper or card of paper, usually including its contents [*a paper* of pins] **7** any material like paper, as papyrus **8** [*pl.*] *a)* documents identifying a person; credentials *b)* a collection of documents, letters, writings, etc., esp. of one person [the Lincoln *papers*] **9** [Slang] *a)* a free pass or passes to a theater, etc. *b)* the people admitted by free passes —*adj.* **1** of paper; made of paper **2** like paper; thin **3** existing only in written or printed form; theoretical; not real [*paper* profits] —*vt.* **1** to cover or line with paper; specif., to cover or decorate with wallpaper **2** to wrap or enclose in paper **3** [Slang] to help to fill (a theater, etc.) by issuing free passes **4** [Archaic] to describe in writing —*vi.* to hang wallpaper —**on paper 1** in written or printed form **2** in theory —**paper over** to conceal or try to cover up (differences, difficulties, unpleasant facts, etc.) —**pa′per·er** *n.*

pa·per·back (pā′pər bak′) *n.* a book bound in paper instead of cloth, leather, etc. —*adj.* designating or of a book bound in paper

☆**paper birch** the North American birch (*Betula papyrifera*), having white or ash-colored, paperlike bark

pa·per·board (pā′pər bôrd′) *n.* ☆a relatively stiff, heavy material, thicker than paper, made from paper pulp

pa·per·bound (pā′pər bound′) *adj.* designating or of a book bound in paper; paperback

pa·per·boy (pā′pər boi′) *n.* a boy who sells or delivers newspapers

☆**paper clip** a flexible clasp, typically of metal wire, for holding loose sheets of paper together by pressure

paper cutter 1 PAPER KNIFE **2** a device or machine for cutting and trimming a number of sheets of paper at a time

paper doll 1 a human figure cut from stiff paper, often printed with the likeness of a popular character or celebrity, used as a plaything **2** [*usually pl.*] a chain of human figures cut from folded paper

pa·per·girl (pā′pər gurl′) *n.* a girl who sells or delivers newspapers

paper gold [Informal] SDR

pa·per·hang·er (pā′pər haŋ′ər) *n.* **1** a person whose work is covering walls with wallpaper ☆**2** [Slang] a person who passes forged checks or counterfeit paper money —**pa′per·hang′ing** *n.*

paper knife a knife for cutting paper, esp. folded paper, as sealed envelopes or the uncut pages of books

pa·per·less (pā′pər ləs) *adj.* functioning or accomplished entirely by electronic means, without paper documents or the use of paper for record keeping [*a paperless* office, *paperless* billing]

pa·per-ma·che (pā′pər mə shā′) *n. var. of* PAPIER-MÂCHÉ

pa·per·mak·ing (pā′pər māk′iŋ) *n.* the making of paper —**pa′per·mak′er** *n.*

☆**paper money** non-interest-bearing notes, as dollar bills, issued by a government or its banks as legal tender

paper mulberry an Asian tree (*Broussonetia papyrifera*) with deeply lobed leaves and red, fleshy, compound fruits: the bark is used to make paper and tapa

paper nautilus 1 any of a genus (*Argonauta*) of small, squidlike octopods: the female secretes a large, frail, paperlike shell to protect her eggs until they hatch; argonaut **2** this shell

☆**paper tiger** a person, nation, etc. that seems to pose a threat but is actually ineffective or powerless

☆**paper trail** a series of records, consisting variously of correspondence, diaries, financial records, etc., that may serve as evidence as of a person's actions

pa·per·weight (pā′pər wāt′) *n.* any small, heavy object, often decorative, set on papers to keep them from being blown away or scattered

☆**pa·per·white** (pā′pər hwīt′) *n.* POLYANTHUS (sense 2)

pa·per·work (pā′pər wurk′) *n.* the keeping of records, filing of reports, etc. incidental to some work or task

pa·per·y (pā′pər ē) *adj.* thin, light, etc., like paper

pap·e·terie (pap′ə trē) *n.* ⟦MFr < *papetier,* paper maker, stationer < *papier,* PAPER⟧ a box of stationery

Pa·phi·an (pā′fē ən) *adj.* ⟦< L *Paphius* + -AN⟧ **1** of Paphos **2** ⟦in reference to the worship of Aphrodite in Paphos⟧ of sexual love; erotic

Paph·la·go·ni·a (paf′lə gō′nē ə) ancient region of N Asia Minor, on the Black Sea

Pa·phos (pā′fäs′) ancient city in SW Cyprus, founded by the Phoenicians

Pa·pia·men·to (pä′pyə men′tō′) *n.* ⟦Sp < Papiamento *papia,* talk, language, prob. (? via Port *papear,* to jabber) of echoic orig. + Sp *-mento,* -MENT⟧ a Spanish-based creole with elements of Dutch and Portuguese, spoken in Curaçao and Aruba: also **Pa′pia·men′tu** (-tōō)

pa·pier col·lé (pȧ pyā kô lā′) *pl.* ***pa·piers col·lés*** (pȧ pyā kô lā′) ⟦Fr, pasted paper: see COLLAGE⟧ a kind of collage in which the pasted objects are grouped for pattern rather than for symbolism

pa·pier-mâ·ché (pā′pər mə shā′) *n.* ⟦Fr *papier,* paper + *mâché,* pp. of *mâcher* (L *masticare*), to chew⟧ a material made of paper pulp mixed with size, glue, etc., that is easily molded when moist and that dries strong and hard —*adj.* made of papier-mâché

pa·pil·i·o·na·ceous (pə pil′ē ō nā′shəs) *adj.* ⟦< L *papilio,* butterfly (< redupl. of IE base **pel-,* to fly, flutter, swim > OE *fifealde,* butterfly) + -ACEOUS⟧ *Bot.* shaped like a butterfly: said of certain flowers, esp. those of some legumes, as the pea

pa·pil·la (pə pil′ə) *n., pl.* **-lae** (-ē) ⟦L, dim. of *papula,* pimple: see PAPULE⟧ **1** *a)* any small nipplelike projection or process of connective tissue, as the small elevations at the root of a developing tooth, hair, feather, etc. or the many and variously shaped elevations on the surface of the tongue *b)* [Rare] the nipple of the breast **2** *Bot.* a tiny, protruding cell —**pap·il·late** (pap′ə lāt′; pə pil′it, -āt′) *adj.,* **pap·il·lose** (pap′ə lōs′)

pap·il·lar·y (pap′ə ler′ē, pə pil′ər ē) *adj.* **1** of, or having the nature of, a papilla **2** provided with, consisting of, or affecting papillae

pap·il·lo·ma (pap′ə lō′mə) *n., pl.* **-ma·ta** (-mə tə) or **-mas** ⟦ModL: see PAPILLA & -OMA⟧ **1** a benign tumor, as a polyp or wart, of the skin or mucous membrane, consisting of a group of thickened, enlarged papillae **2** such a tumor caused by a virus —**pap′il·lom′a·tous** (-läm′ə təs, -lō′mə-) *adj.*

pap·il·lo·ma·vi·rus (pap′ə lō′mə vī′rəs) *n.* ⟦prec. + VIRUS⟧ any of a genus (*Papillomavirus*) of papovaviruses, including the HUMAN PAPILLOMAVIRUS, that cause papillomas

pa·pil·lon (pap′ə län′; *Fr* pȧ pē yōn′) *n.* ⟦Fr, a butterfly (< L *papilio:* see PAPILIONACEOUS): from the shape of the ears⟧ any of a breed of toy spaniel having a long, silky, white coat with colored patches and erect or drooping ears that are fringed

pa·pil·lote (pap′ə lōt′) *n.* ⟦Fr < *papillon,* butterfly: see prec.⟧ a heavy, greased or oiled paper in which food, esp. meat or fish, is wrapped, cooked, and served

pa·pist (pā′pist) *n.* ⟦ModL *papista* < LL(Ec) *papa,* POPE⟧ a Roman Catholic, esp. one who ardently supports the pope —*adj.* of or like a Roman Catholic (esp. one ardently supporting the pope) or the Roman Catholic Church

USAGE—traditionally a pejorative or hostile term

pa·pist·ry (pā′pis trē) *n.* ⟦see prec. & -(E)RY⟧ Roman Catholic beliefs and practices; Roman Catholicism: traditionally a pejorative or hostile term

☆**pa·poose** (pə pōōs′, pa-) *n.* ⟦Narragansett *papoos,* child⟧ a North American Indian baby: now chiefly used in historical contexts

pa·po·va·vi·rus (pə pō′və vī′rəs) *n.* ⟦PAPILLOMA + *po*(*lyoma*) + *va*(*cuolating*) + VIRUS⟧ any of a family (Papovaviridae) of DNA viruses, including the papillomaviruses and polyomaviruses, associated with the growth of tumors in a wide range of animals

pap·pus (pap′əs) *n., pl.* **pap′pi′** (-ī′) ⟦ModL < L < Gr *pappos,* old man, grandfather (see PAPA), hence substance resembling gray hairs⟧ *Bot.* a group or tuft of prongs, bristles, scales, or simple or branched hairs, as on the achenes of the dandelion, forming the modified calyx of the composite and certain other families and serving in the dispersal of the fruit —**pap′pose′** (-ōs′) *adj.,* **pap′pous** (-əs)

pap·py[1] (pap′ē) *n., pl.* **-pies** [Informal or Dial.] FATHER

pap·py[2] (pap′ē) *adj.* **-pi·er, -pi·est** like pap; mushy

pa·pri·ka (pə prē′kə; *chiefly Brit* pap′ri kə) *n.* ⟦Hung < Serb *pàprika* < *pàpar,* pepper < Gr *peperi,* PEPPER⟧ a mild or hot, red, powdered condiment ground from certain capsicums, grown esp. in central Europe and the American tropics

☆**Pap test** (pap) ⟦after G. *Papanicolaou* (1883-1962), U.S. anatomist⟧ the microscopic examination of cells taken as a smear (**Pap smear**) from the cervix of a woman, used as a test for cervical cancer in its early, curable stage

Pap·u·a (pap′yōō ə, -ōō-) **1** PAPUA NEW GUINEA **2 Gulf of** arm of the Coral Sea, on the SE coast of New Guinea: *c.* 225 mi (362 km) wide **3 Territory of** former United Nations trust territory that was administered by Australia, consisting of the SE section of New Guinea and the nearby islands **4** province of Indonesia, occupying the W half of the island of New Guinea: a Dutch territory until 1963: *c.* 141,107 sq mi (365,466 sq km); cap. Jayapura

Pap·u·an (pap′yo͞o ən, -o͞o-) ***adj.*** of Papua or its peoples, languages, or cultures **—*n.*** **1** a person born or living in Papua New Guinea **2** a member of any of the indigenous peoples of New Guinea and nearby islands **3** *a)* any of a group of languages spoken in New Guinea and elsewhere in the SW Pacific *b)* this language group

Papua New Guinea country occupying the E half of the island of New Guinea, & nearby islands, including the former Territory of Papua & the Trust Territory of New Guinea: independent since 1975; member of the Commonwealth: 178,704 sq mi (462,840 sq km); cap. Port Moresby

pap·ule (pap′yo͞ol′) ***n.*** ⟦L *papula* < IE base *pap-, to swell > Sans *pippalah*, berry, *pippali*, peppercorn⟧ a small, usually inflammatory, elevation of the skin; pimple **—pap′u·lar** (-yo͞o lər) ***adj.*** **—pap′u·lose′** (-yo͞o lōs′) ***adj.***

pap·y·ra·ceous (pap′ə rā′shəs) ***adj.*** ⟦L *papyraceus:* see PAPYRUS & -ACEOUS⟧ like paper; papery

pap·y·rol·o·gy (pap′ə räl′ə jē) ***n.*** the study and translation of ancient manuscripts written on papyrus **—pap′y·rol′o·gist *n.***

pa·py·rus (pə pī′rəs) ***n., pl.*** **-ri′** (-rī′) or **-rus·es** ⟦ME *papirus* < L *papyrus* < Gr *papyros*, prob. < Coptic *paparo* < ? Egypt *p′-n-pr-‵*, that of the pharaoh⟧ **1** a tall water plant (*Cyperus papyrus*) of the sedge family, abundant in the Nile region of Egypt and widely cultivated as an ornamental **2** a material for writing on, made from this plant by the ancient Egyptians, Greeks, and Romans, by soaking, pressing, and drying thin slices of its pith laid crosswise **3** any ancient document or manuscript on papyrus

papyrus

par[1] (pär) ***n.*** ⟦L, an equal, orig. adj.: see PART[1]⟧ **1** the established or recognized value of the money of one country in terms of the money of another country, based on a metal accepted as the common standard of value **2** an equal or common status, standing, footing, level, etc.: usually in the phrase **on a par (with) 3** the average or normal state, condition, degree, etc. [*work that is up to par*] **4** *Commerce* the nominal, or face, value of stocks, bonds, etc. **5** *Golf* the number of strokes established as a skillful score for any given hole or for a whole course **—*adj.*** **1** of or at par **2** average; normal **—*vt.*** **parred, par′ring** *Golf* to score par on (a given hole or course) **—par for the course** ⟦in ref. to a golf *course*⟧ that which is normal, usual, or to be expected under the circumstances

par[2] *abbrev.* **1** paragraph **2** parallel **3** parenthesis **4** parish

par- (par) *prefix* PARA-[1] (except sense 2*b*): used before a vowel

pa·ra[1] (pä rä′, pä′rä′) ***n.*** ⟦Turk < Pers *pārah*, a piece, fragment⟧ a monetary unit of Serbia, equal to 1/100 of a dinar

para[2] *abbrev.* **1** paragraph **2** parallel

Para *abbrev.* Paraguay

Pa·rá (pä rä′) **1** river in NE Brazil, the S estuary of the Amazon: *c.* 200 mi (322 km) **2** state of N Brazil, on the Atlantic: 483,849 sq mi (1,253,164 sq km); cap. Belém

par·a-[1] (par′ə) ⟦Gr *para-* < *para*, at the side of, alongside < IE *pera-, var. of *per-, a going beyond > FAR, FORE⟧ *prefix* **1** *a)* by the side of, beside, by, past, to one side, aside from, amiss [*parathyroid, parasite*] *b)* beyond [*paranormal*] *c)* subsidiary to [*paralegal, paramilitary*] **2** *Chem.* *a)* an isomer, modification, polymer, derivative, etc. of (a specified substance) [*paraformaldehyde*] *b)* characterized by substitutions in the 1, 4 position (opposite sides) in the benzene ring (usually italicized and hyphenated in chemical names) [*para-*aminobenzoic acid] (see META-, sense 6*d*, ORTHO-, sense 4*b*) **3** *Med.* *a)* in a secondary or accessory capacity [*parahormone*] *b)* functionally disordered, abnormal [*paramnesia*] *c)* like or resembling [*paratyphoid*] **4** *Nuclear Physics* the form of diatomic molecules in which nuclei have antiparallel spins [*parahydrogen*]

par·a-[2] (par′ə, per′ə) *combining form* **1** ⟦Fr < It *para*, imper. of *parare*, to ward off < L *parare*, PREPARE⟧ protection of or against [*parados*] **2** ⟦< PARA(CHUTE)⟧ using a parachute [*pararescue*]

par·a-a·mi·no·ben·zo·ic acid (par′ə ə mē′nō ben zō′ik, -am′ə nō′-) ⟦PARA-[1] + AMINO- + BENZOIC⟧ a yellowish isomer of aminobenzoic acid, that is a component of folic acid, widely distributed in nature, esp. in yeast, and utilized as a vitamin by organisms that synthesize folic acid: it absorbs ultraviolet light and is used in suntan lotions

par·a·ben (par′ə ben′) ***n.*** ⟦< *para*(*-hydroxy*)*ben*(*zoic acid*)⟧ an ester of para-hydroxybenzoic acid, used as a preservative in cosmetics and pharmaceuticals

par·a·bi·o·sis (-bī ō′sis) ***n.*** ⟦PARA-[1] + -BIOSIS⟧ *Embryology* **1** the union of two animals, naturally or experimentally, as by blood circulatory connections **2** the temporary and reversible suspension of a vital life process **3** the living together of two or more different species, as in mixed flocks of birds or in mixed colonies of ants **—par′a·bi·ot′ic** (-ät′ik) ***adj.***

par·a·blast (par′ə blast′) ***n.*** ⟦PARA-[1] + -BLAST⟧ **1** *Embryology* the nutritive yolk of a meroblastic ovum **2** the portion of a mesoderm that gives rise to vascular and lymphatic tissues **—par′a·blas′tic *adj.***

par·a·ble (par′ə bəl) ***n.*** ⟦ME < MFr *parabole* < LL(Ec) *parabola*, an allegorical relation, parable < L, comparison < Gr *parabolē*, an analogy (< *paraballein*, to throw beside: see PARA-[1] & BALL[2]), in N.T. & LXX, parable: transl. of Heb *mashal*, comparison⟧ a short, simple story, usually of an occurrence of a familiar kind, from which a moral or religious lesson may be drawn

pa·rab·o·la (pə rab′ə lə) ***n.*** ⟦ModL < Gr *parabolē*, lit., application, comparison (see prec.): it is produced by the "application" of a given area to a given straight line⟧ *Geom.* a plane curve which is the path, or locus, of a moving point that remains equally distant from a fixed point (*focus*) and from a fixed straight line (*directrix*); curve formed by the section of a cone cut by a plane parallel to the side of the cone: see ECCENTRICITY (sense 3)

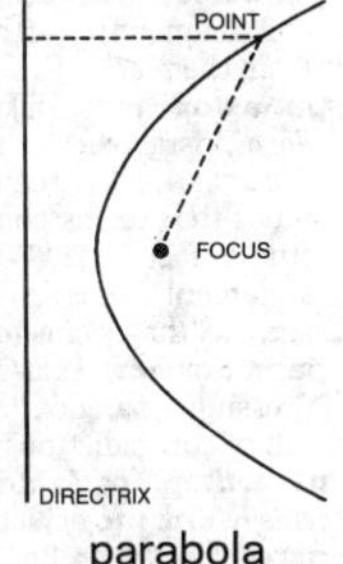

parabola

par·a·bol·ic[1] (par′ə bäl′ik) ***adj.*** ⟦LL *parabolicus* < LGr *parabolikos*⟧ of, in the form of, or expressed by a parable: also **par′a·bol′i·cal —par′a·bol′i·cal·ly *adv.***

par·a·bol·ic[2] (par′ə bäl′ik) ***adj.*** **1** of or like a parabola **2** bowl-shaped, as a reflector, antenna, or microphone, so that sections parallel to the plane of symmetry are parabolas **—par′a·bol′i·cal·ly *adv.***

pa·rab·o·lize (pə rab′ə līz′) ***vt.*** **-lized′, -liz′ing 1** to express in or treat as a parable **2** to make parabolic in shape

pa·rab·o·loid (-loid′) ***n.*** a surface or solid formed so that sections parallel to the plane of symmetry are parabolas and sections perpendicular to it are ellipses (**elliptic paraboloid**), hyperbolas (**hyperbolic paraboloid**), or circles (**paraboloid of revolution**) **—pa·rab′o·loi′dal *adj.***

Par·a·cel·sus (par′ə sel′səs), **(Philippus Aureolus)** (born *Theophrastus Bombastus von Hohenheim*) 1493-1541; Swiss physician & alchemist

par·a·chute (par′ə sho͞ot′) ***n.*** ⟦Fr: see PARA-[2] (sense 1) & CHUTE[1]⟧ **1** a cloth contrivance usually shaped like an umbrella when expanded, and used to retard the falling speed of a person or thing dropping from an airplane, etc.: it is generally carried folded in a pack, from which it is released by a rip cord or other device **2** something shaped like or having the effect of a parachute **3** *Zool.* PATAGIUM (sense 1) **— *vt., vi.* -chut′ed, -chut′ing** to drop or descend by parachute

par·a·chut·ist (-sho͞ot′ist) ***n.*** a person who descends by parachute: also **par′a·chut′er**

par·a·clete (par′ə klēt′) ***n.*** ⟦ME *paraclit* < OFr *paraclet* < LL(Ec) *paracletus* < Gr *paraklētos* (in N.T., the Holy Spirit) < *parakalein*, to call, summon (in N.T., to comfort) < *para-*, PARA-[1] + *kalein*, to call: see CLAMOR⟧ **1** an advocate; intercessor; pleader **2** **[P-]** *Christianity* the Holy Spirit, considered as comforter, intercessor, or advocate

pa·rade (pə rād′) ***n.*** ⟦Fr < Sp *parada*, a parade, place for the exercise of troops < *parar*, to stop (a horse), prepare < L *parare*, PREPARE⟧ **1** ostentatious or pompous display **2** *a)* a military display or assembly; esp., a review of marching troops *b)* a place where troops assemble regularly for parade; parade ground **3** any organized procession or march, as for display **4** *a)* a public walk or promenade *b)* persons promenading or strolling **5** an ostentatious succession of persons or things [*a parade of bestsellers*] **—*vt.*** **-rad′ed, -rad′ing 1** to bring together (troops, etc.) for inspection or display **2** to march or walk through, as for display [*a band parading the streets*] **3** to make a display of; show off [*to parade one's knowledge*] **—*vi.*** **1** to march in a parade or procession **2** to walk about ostentatiously; show off **3** to assemble in military formation for review or display **—on parade** on display **—pa·rad′er *n.***

parade rest *Mil.* **1** a formal position of rest, with the feet 12 inches apart and, when unarmed, hands clasped behind the back; when armed, the left hand is behind the back and the right hand holds the rifle upright with its butt resting on the ground: cf. AT EASE at the entry EASE **2** the command to assume this position

par·a·di·chlo·ro·ben·zene (par′ə dī klôr′ō ben′zēn′, -ben zēn′) ***n.*** ⟦PARA-[1] + DI-[1] + CHLORO- + BENZENE⟧ a white crystalline compound, $C_6H_4Cl_2$, used in protecting clothes from moths, as a deodorant, disinfectant, etc.: see PARA-[1] (sense 2*b*)

par·a·did·dle (par′ə did′'l) ***n.*** ⟦echoic⟧ a pattern of beats on a snare drum executed with alternate strokes of the sticks

par·a·digm (par′ə dīm′, -dim) ***n.*** ⟦Fr *paradigme* < LL *paradigma* < Gr *paradeigma* < *para-*, PARA-[1] + *deigma*, example < *deiknynai*, to show: for IE base see DICTION⟧ **1** *a)* a pattern, example, or model *b)* an overall concept accepted by most people in an intellectual community, as those in one of the natural sciences, because of its effectiveness in explaining a complex process, idea, or set of data **2** *Gram.* an example of a declension or conjugation, giving all the inflectional forms of a word **—*SYN.*** MODEL **—par′a·dig·mat′ic** (-dig mat′ik) ***adj.*** **—par′a·dig·mat′i·cal·ly *adv.***

paradigm shift ⟦term popularized by Thomas S. KUHN⟧ a radical change in, or the superseding of, a prevailing PARADIGM (sense 1*b*)

par·a·di·sa·ic (par′ə di sā′ik) ***adj.*** PARADISIACAL: also **par′a·dis′al** (-dīs′əl) or **par′a·di·sa′i·cal**

par·a·dise (par′ə dīs′, -dīz′) ***n.*** ⟦ME *paradis* < OE & OFr, both < LL(Ec) *paradisus*, heaven, abode of the blessed < L, park, orchard < Gr *paradeisos*, park, garden (in N.T. & LXX, Paradise) < Iran *pardez, akin to Avestan *pairi-daēza*, enclosure < *pairi*, around (see PERI-) + *daēza*, a wall < IE base *dheigh-, to knead clay: see DOUGH⟧ **1** **[P-]** the garden of Eden **2** **[P-]** the abode of the righteous after death; abode of God and the blessed; heaven **3** *a)* any place of great beauty and perfection *b)* any place or condition of great satisfaction, happiness, or delight

Par·a·dise (par′ə dīs′, -dīz′) town in SE Nev., near Las Vegas

par·a·di·si·a·cal (par′ə di sī′ə kəl) ***adj.*** ⟦LL(Ec) *paradisiacus*⟧ of, like, or fit for paradise: also **par′a·dis′i·ac′** (-dis′ē ak′) —**par′a·di·si′a·cal·ly** ***adv.***

par·a·dor (pär′ä thôr′) ***n.***, *pl.* **-dor′es** (-thôr′es) ⟦Sp⟧ esp. in Spain, a government-owned inn or hotel intended for tourists

par·a·dos (par′ə däs′) ***n.*** ⟦Fr < *para-*, PARA-[2] + *dos* < L *dorsum,* back⟧ an embankment of earth along the back of a trench, as to protect against fire from the rear

par·a·dox (par′ə däks′) ***n.*** ⟦L *paradoxum* < Gr *paradoxon,* neut. of *paradoxos,* paradoxical < *para-* (see PARA-[1]) + *doxa,* opinion < *dokein,* to think: see DECENT⟧ **1** [Archaic] a statement contrary to common belief **2** a statement that seems contradictory, unbelievable, or absurd but that may be true in fact (Ex.: "Water, water, everywhere, nor any drop to drink") **3** a statement that is self-contradictory and, hence, false **4** a person, situation, act, etc. that seems to have contradictory or inconsistent qualities

par·a·dox·i·cal (par′ə däk′si kəl) ***adj.*** **1** of, having the nature of, or expressing a paradox or paradoxes **2** fond of using paradoxes **3** seemingly full of contradictions —**par′a·dox′i·cal·ly** ***adv.*** —**par′a·dox′i·cal·ness** ***n.***

par·a·drop (par′ə dräp′) ***n., vt.*** **-dropped′**, **-drop′ping** ⟦PARA-[2] + DROP⟧ *chiefly Brit. var. of* AIRDROP

par·af·fin (par′ə fin) ***n.*** ⟦Ger < L *parum,* too little + *affinis,* akin (see AFFINITY): from its chemical inertness⟧ **1** a white, waxy, odorless, tasteless solid substance consisting of a mixture of straight-chain, saturated hydrocarbons: it is obtained chiefly from the distillation of petroleum and is used for making candles, sealing preserving jars, waterproofing paper, etc. **2** *Chem.* any alkane **3** [Brit.] KEROSENE —***vt.*** to coat or impregnate with paraffin —**par′af·fin′ic** ***adj.***

par·af·fine (-fin, -fēn′) ***n., vt.*** **-fined**, **-fin·ing** *var. of* PARAFFIN

paraffin series METHANE SERIES

paraffin wax PARAFFIN (***n.*** 1)

par·a·gen·e·sis (par′ə jen′ə sis) ***n.*** ⟦ModL: see PARA-[1] & -GENESIS⟧ the order in which closely associated minerals in rocks, veins, etc. have been formed, including their interactions with one another from contact —**par′a·ge·net′ic** (-jə net′ik) ***adj.***

par·a·gon (par′ə gän′, -gən) ***n.*** ⟦MFr (Fr *parangon*) < It *paragone,* a comparison, test, lit., touchstone < *paragonare,* to test, compare < Gr *parakonan,* to whet < *para-*, PARA-[1] + *akonē,* whetstone: for IE base see ACID⟧ **1** a model or pattern of perfection or excellence **2** a perfect diamond weighing a hundred carats or more **3** a large, perfectly round pearl —***vt.*** **1** [Old Poet.] *a)* to put side by side; compare *b)* to be equal to; match **2** [Obs.] to surpass

par·a·graph (par′ə graf′) ***n.*** ⟦MFr *paragraphe* < OFr < ML *paragraphus,* orig., sign marking separation of parts, as of a chapter < Gr *paragraphos* < *para-*, beside (see PARA-[1]) + *graphein,* to write (see GRAPHIC)⟧ **1** a distinct section or subdivision of a chapter, letter, etc., usually dealing with a particular point: it is begun on a new line, often indented **2** a mark (¶) used as by proofreaders to indicate the beginning of a paragraph or as a sign marking material referred to elsewhere **3** a brief article, item, or note in a newspaper or magazine —***vt.*** **1** to mention in a paragraph or paragraphs **2** to separate or arrange in paragraphs —***vi.*** to write paragraphs, esp. for a newspaper —**par′a·graph′er** ***n.***, **par′a·graph′ist** —**par′a·graph′ic** ***adj.***

par·a·graph·i·a (par′ə graf′ē ə) ***n.*** ⟦ModL < Gr *para-*, PARA-[1] + *graphein,* to write: see GRAPHIC⟧ a form of aphasia, usually due to cerebral injury, characterized by the unintentional omission, transposition, or insertion of letters or words in writing

Par·a·guay (par′ə gwā′, -gwī′; *Sp* pä rä gwī′) **1** inland country in SC South America: 157,047 sq mi (406,750 sq km); cap. Asunción **2** river in SC South America, flowing from S Brazil south through Paraguay into the Paraná: *c.* 1,500 mi (2,414 km) —**Par′a·guay′an** ***adj., n.***

Paraguay tea MATÉ

Pa·ra·í·ba (pä rä ē′bä) state of NE Brazil: 21,848 sq mi (56,586 sq km); cap. João Pessoa

par·a·in·flu·en·za (par′ə in′flo͞o en′zə) ***n.*** any of various influenza-like respiratory infections, esp. of children, caused by a paramyxovirus

par·a·keet (par′ə kēt′) ***n.*** ⟦MFr *paroquet,* prob. < *perrot,* PARROT⟧ any of various small, slender parrots with a long, tapering tail

par·a·lan·guage (par′ə laŋ′gwij) ***n.*** nonverbal means of communication, such as tone of voice, laughter, and, sometimes, gestures and facial expressions, that accompany speech and convey further meaning

par·al·de·hyde (pə ral′də hīd′) ***n.*** ⟦PAR(A)- + ALDEHYDE⟧ a colorless liquid, $C_6H_{12}O_3$, produced by the polymerization of acetaldehyde, having a strong, nauseating smell and used in medicine as a hypnotic and sedative

par·a·le·gal (par′ə lē′gəl) ***adj.*** ⟦PARA-[1] + LEGAL⟧ designating or of persons trained to aid lawyers but not licensed to practice law —***n.*** a person doing paralegal work

par·a·leip·sis (par′ə līp′sis) ***n.***, *pl.* **-ses′** (-sēz′) ⟦Gr, omission < *para-*, PARA-[1] + *leipein,* to leave: see LOAN⟧ a rhetorical device in which a point is stressed by suggesting that it is too obvious or well-known to mention, as in the phrase, "not to mention the expense involved": also **par′a·lep′sis** (-lep′-) or **par′a·lip′sis** (-lip′-)

par·a·lin·guis·tics (par′ə liŋ gwis′tiks) ***n.*** the branch of linguistics that deals with paralanguage —**par′a·lin·guis′tic** ***adj.***

Par·a·li·pom·e·non (par′ə li päm′ə nän′) ***n.*** *Douay Bible name for* CHRONICLES

par·al·lax (par′ə laks′) ***n.*** ⟦Fr *parallaxe* < Gr *parallaxis* < *parallassein,* to vary, decline, wander < *para-*, PARA-[1] + *allassein,* to change < *allos,* other: see ELSE⟧ **1** the apparent change in the position of an object resulting from the change in the direction or position from which it is viewed **2** *a)* the amount of angular degree of such change: the parallax of an object may be used in determining its distance from the observer because smaller angles indicate greater distance *b)* *Astron.* the apparent difference in the position of a celestial object with reference to a fixed background when viewed from two distant locations having a triangulated base line equal to the radius of the earth (**diurnal parallax** or **geocentric parallax**) or equal to the radius of the earth's orbit (**annual parallax** or **heliocentric parallax**) **3** the difference between the actual view covered by a camera lens and the apparent view seen through the viewfinder: this may be significant when the object is close to the camera —**par′al·lac′tic** (-lak′tik) ***adj.***

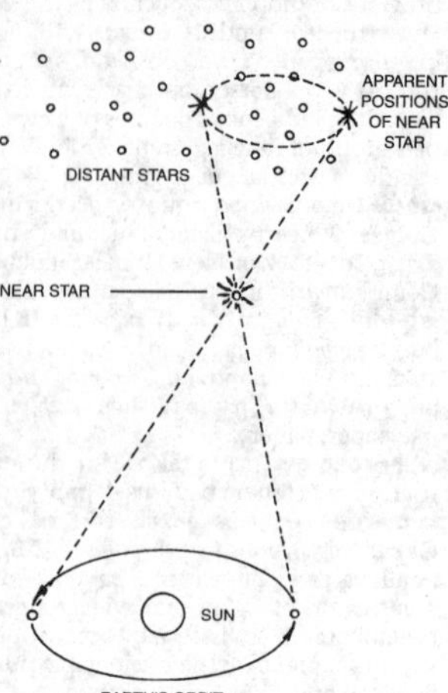

parallax

par·al·lel (par′ə lel′, -ləl) ***adj.*** ⟦Fr *parallèle* < L *parallelus* < Gr *parallēlos* < *para-*, side by side (see PARA-[1]) + *allēlos,* one another < *allos,* other: see ELSE⟧ **1** extending in the same direction and at the same distance apart at every point, so as never to meet, as lines, planes, etc. **2** having parallel parts or movements, as some machines, tools, etc. **3** *a)* closely similar or corresponding, as in purpose, tendency, time, or essential parts *b)* characterized by a balanced or coordinated arrangement of syntactic elements, esp. of phrases or clauses [“I came, I saw, I conquered” is an example of *parallel* structure] **4** *Comput.* *a)* of or for the transmission of data, by means of several channels, a byte or more at a time [a *parallel* port] *b)* having to do with the performing of multiple operations simultaneously [*parallel* processing] (cf. SERIAL, ***adj.*** 5) **5** *Elec.* designating or of a circuit in parallel **6** *Music* having consistently equal intervals in pitch, as two parts of harmony, a series of chords, etc. —***adv.*** in a parallel manner —***n.*** **1** something parallel to something else, as a line or surface **2** any person or thing essentially the same as, or closely corresponding to, another; counterpart **3** the condition of being parallel; conformity in essential points **4** any comparison showing the existence of similarity or likeness **5** *a)* any of the imaginary lines parallel to the equator and representing degrees of latitude on the earth's surface *b)* such a line drawn on a map or globe: in full **parallel of latitude** **6** [*pl.*] a sign (||) used in printing as a reference mark **7** *Elec.* an arrangement of devices in a circuit, in which two or more components have their negative terminals joined to one conductor and their positive to another, so that an identical potential difference is applied to each component: usually in the phrase **in parallel**: cf. SERIES (sense 5) —***vt.*** **-al·leled** or **-al·lelled′**, **-al·lel′ing** or **-al·lel′ling** **1** *a)* to make (one thing) parallel to another *b)* to make parallel to each other **2** to be parallel with; extend parallel to [a road that *parallels* the river] **3** to compare (things, ideas, etc.) in order to show similarity or likeness **4** to be or find a counterpart for; match; equal

parallel bars two parallel wooden bars about 18 inches apart that are set horizontally at the same height on upright posts, used in gymnastics

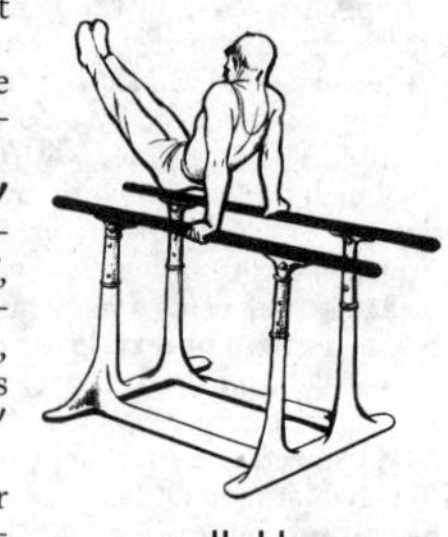
parallel bars

parallel cousin *Anthrop.* a cousin who is the child of one's father's brother or one's mother's sister: see CROSS COUSIN

par·al·lel·e·pi·ped (par′ə lel′ə pī′pəd′, -pip′əd′) ***n.*** ⟦Gr *parallēlepipedon* < *parallēlos,* parallel + *epipedos,* on the ground, plane < *epi,* upon (see EPI-) + *pedon,* the ground < IE **pedom* (> Sans *padám,* footstep) < base **ped-*, FOOT⟧ a solid with six faces, each of which is a parallelogram: also **par′al·lel′e·pip′e·don′** (-pip′ə dän′)

par·al·lel·ism (par′ə lel′iz′əm, -ləl-) ***n.*** ⟦Gr *parallēlismos*⟧ **1** the state of being parallel **2** close resemblance; similarity **3** *a)* the use of parallel structure in writing *b)* an instance of this **4** *Philos.* the doctrine that mind and matter function together synchronously but without any causal interaction

par·al·lel·o·gram (par′ə lel′ə gram′) ***n.*** ⟦Fr *parallélogramme* < L *parallelogrammum* < Gr *parallēlogrammon* < *parallēlos,* PARALLEL + *grammē,* stroke in writing: see GRAM[1]⟧ a plane figure with four sides, having the opposite sides parallel and equal

parallel parking a type of city-street parking in which a vehicle is parked close to and parallel to the curb, typically between two other similarly parked vehicles

pa·ral·o·gism (pə ral′ə jiz′əm) ***n.*** ⟦MFr *paralogisme* < LL *paralogismus* < Gr *paralogismos* < *paralogizesthai,* to reason illogically < *para-*, beyond (see

PARA-[1]) + *logizesthai,* to reason < *logos,* a discourse, reason: see LOGIC⟧ reasoning contrary to the rules of logic; faulty argument —**pa·ral′o·gis′tic** *adj.*

pa·ral·y·sis (pə ral′ə sis) *n., pl.* **-ses′** (-sēz′) ⟦L < Gr *paralysis* < *paralyein,* to loosen, dissolve, or weaken at the side: see PARA-[1] & LYSIS⟧ **1** partial or complete loss, or temporary interruption, of a function, esp. of voluntary motion or of sensation in some part or all of the body **2** any condition of helpless inactivity or of inability to act

paralysis a·gi·tans (aj′i tanz′) PARKINSON'S DISEASE

par·a·lyt·ic (par′ə lit′ik) *adj.* ⟦ME *paraletik* < OFr *paralytique* < L *paralyticus* < Gr *paralytikos*⟧ **1** of, or having the nature of, paralysis **2** having, subject to, or causing paralysis —*n.* a person having paralysis

par·a·lyze (par′ə līz′) *vt.* **-lyzed′**, **-lyz′ing** ⟦Fr *paralyser,* back-form. < *paralysie* < L *paralysis*⟧ **1** to cause paralysis in; make paralytic **2** to bring into a condition of helpless inactivity; make ineffective or powerless —**par′a·ly·za′tion** *n.* —**par′a·lyz′er** *n.*

par·a·mag·net·ic (par′ə mag net′ik) *adj.* designating or of a material, as aluminum or platinum, having a magnetic permeability slightly greater than unity and varying to only a small extent with the magnetizing force —**par′a·mag′net·ism′** (-mag′nə tiz′əm) *n.*

Par·a·mar·i·bo (par′ə mar′i bō′) seaport & capital of Suriname, in the N part

par·a·mat·ta (par′ə mat′ə) *n.* ⟦after *Parramatta,* city in SE Australia⟧ a soft, lightweight dress fabric with a cotton warp and a filling of fine wool

par·a·me·ci·um (par′ə mē′sē əm, -shē əm) *n., pl.* **-ci·a** (-ə) ⟦ModL < Gr *paramēkēs,* oval < *para-,* PARA-[1] + *mēkos,* length, akin to *makros,* long: see MACRO-⟧ any of a genus (*Paramecium*) of one-celled, elongated, slipper-shaped ciliates moving by means of cilia and having a backward-curving oral groove that ends with the mouth

☆**par·a·med·ic**[1] (par′ə med′ik, par′ə med′ik) *n.* ⟦PARA-[2] + MEDIC[1]⟧ a MEDIC[1] (esp. *n.* 3) who parachutes to combat or rescue areas

☆**par·a·med·ic**[2] (par′ə med′ik) *n.* ⟦back-form. < fol.⟧ **1** a person trained to assist a doctor, nurse, etc. **2** a person specially trained to provide emergency medical services, as in or from an ambulance

☆**par·a·med·i·cal** (par′ə med′i kəl) *adj.* ⟦PARA-[1] + MEDICAL⟧ designating or of auxiliary medical personnel, such as midwives, laboratory technicians, nurses' aides, etc.

pa·ram·e·ter (pə ram′ət ər) *n.* ⟦ModL *parametrum* < Gr *para-,* PARA-[1] + *metron,* MEASURE⟧ **1** *Math.* a quantity or constant whose value varies with the circumstances of its application, as the radius line of a group of concentric circles, which varies with the circle under consideration **2** any constant, with variable values, used as a referent for determining other variables **3** *a)* a boundary or limit *b)* a factor or characteristic (*usually used in pl.*): usage objected to by some —**par·a·met·ric** (par′ə met′rik) *adj.*

par·a·mil·i·tar·y (par′ə mil′ə ter′ē) *adj.* ⟦PARA-[1] + MILITARY⟧ designating or of forces working along with, in place of, or in opposition to a regular military organization —*n., pl.* **-tar′ies** a member of a paramilitary force

par·am·ne·sia (par′am nē′zhə) *n.* ⟦PAR(A)- + AMNESIA⟧ *Psychol.* **1** distortion of memory with confusion of fact and fantasy **2** DÉJÀ VU

pa·ra·mo (par′ə mō′) *n., pl.* **-mos′** ⟦AmSp < Sp *páramo* < Celt **paramus,* a plain⟧ any high, barren plain in the South American tropics, esp. in the Andes

par·a·morph (par′ə môrf′) *n.* a mineral that has undergone paramorphism

par·a·mor·phism (par′ə môr′fiz′əm) *n.* ⟦PARA-[1] + -MORPH + -ISM⟧ the process by which the crystal structure of a mineral changes without an alteration in the chemical composition or external form of the mineral —**par′a·mor′phic** *adj.*, **par′a·mor′phous**

par·a·mount (par′ə mount′) *adj.* ⟦Anglo-Fr *paramont* < OFr *par* (L *per*), by + *amont, à mont* (< L *ad montem,* to the hill), uphill⟧ ranking higher than any other, as in power or importance; chief; supreme —*n.* [Rare] supreme ruler; overlord —***SYN.*** DOMINANT —**par′a·mount′cy** (-sē) *n.* —**par′a·mount′ly** *adv.*

par·a·mour (par′ə moor′) *n.* ⟦ME < *par amur* < OFr *par amour,* with love < *par* (L *per*), by + *amour* (L *amor*), love⟧ **1** a lover or mistress; esp., the illicit sexual partner of a married man or woman **2** [Archaic] a sweetheart

par·a·myx·o·vi·rus (par′ə mik′sə vī′rəs) *n.* ⟦PARA-[1] + MYXOVIRUS⟧ any of a family (Paramyxoviridae) of RNA viruses, including those causing mumps, measles, and parainfluenza

Pa·ra·ná (pä′rä nä′) **1** state of S Brazil: 77,108 sq mi (199,709 sq km): cap. Curitiba **2** river port in NE Argentina, on the Paraná River **3** river in S South America, flowing from S Brazil along the SE boundary of Paraguay, through NE Argentina into the Río de la Plata: *c.* 2,000 mi (3,219 km)

pa·rang (pä räŋ′) *n.* ⟦Malay⟧ a heavy knife used as a tool and weapon in Malaysia

par·a·noi·a (par′ə noi′ə) *n.* ⟦ModL < Gr, derangement < *para-,* beside (see PARA-[1]) + *nous,* the mind⟧ *Psychiatry* a mental disorder characterized by systematized delusions, as of grandeur or, esp., persecution, often, except in a schizophrenic state, with an otherwise relatively intact personality

par·a·noid (par′ə noid′) *adj.* **1** of or like paranoia **2** characterized by extreme suspiciousness and anxiety, delusions of persecution, etc.: also **par′a·noi′dal** (-noi′dəl) —*n.* a person afflicted with paranoia Also **par′a·noi′ac′** (-noi′ak′, -ik)

paranoid schizophrenia a chronic form of schizophrenia characterized by hallucinations, grandiose delusions or delusions of persecution, etc.

par·a·nor·mal (par′ə nôr′məl) *adj.* ⟦PARA-[1] + NORMAL⟧ designating or of psychic, occult, supernatural, or other phenomena considered unexplainable by the known forces or laws of nature —**the paranormal** paranormal phenomena, forces, etc.

par·a·nymph (par′ə nimf′) *n.* ⟦LL *paranymphus* < Gr *paranymphos* < *para-,* beside (see PARA-[1]) + *nymphē,* bride: see NUBILE⟧ **1** in ancient Greece, a groomsman who escorted the bridegroom when he went to bring his bride home, or a bridesmaid who escorted the bride to the bridegroom **2** [Literary] a best man or bridesmaid

par·a·pet (par′ə pet′, -pət) *n.* ⟦Fr < It *parapetto* < *parare,* to guard (< L, PREPARE) + *petto,* breast < L *pectus*⟧ **1** a wall or bank used to screen troops from frontal enemy fire, sometimes placed along the top of a rampart **2** a low wall or railing, as along a balcony —**par′a·pet′ed** *adj.*

par·aph (par′əf) *n.* ⟦ME *parafe* < MFr < ML *paraphus,* contr. < *paragraphus,* PARAGRAPH⟧ a flourish made after a signature, originally as a safeguard against forgery

par·a·pher·na·li·a (par′ə fər nāl′yə, -nā′lē ə; -fə-) *pl.n.* ⟦ML, short for *paraphernalia bona,* wife's own goods < LL *parapherna* < Gr, bride's possessions beyond her dower < *para-,* beyond (see PARA-[1]) + *phernē,* a dowry, portion < *pherein,* to BEAR[1]⟧ [*often with sing. v.*] **1** personal belongings **2** articles, usually things used in some activity; equipment; apparatus; specif., the apparatus used in the storage or use of illegal drugs **3** [Obs.] *Law a)* personal property given to a wife by her husband which he may dispose of during his life, but which passes to her at his death *b)* the separate personal property of a wife over which her husband has no control

par·a·phil·i·a (par′ə fil′ē ə, -fil′yə, -fēl′-) *n.* ⟦PARA-[1] + -PHILIA⟧ **1** sexual behavior that is considered deviant or abnormal **2** a sexual act or practice that is considered deviant or abnormal —**par′a·phil′i·ac** *adj., n.*, **par′a·phil′ic**

par·a·phrase (par′ə frāz′) *n.* ⟦Fr < L *paraphrasis* < Gr < *paraphrazein,* to say in other words: see PARA-[1] & PHRASE⟧ **1** *a)* a rewording of something spoken or written, usually for the purpose of making its meaning clearer *b)* the use of this as a literary or teaching device **2** an approximate rendering of a quotation, saying, etc. whose exact words cannot be cited or recalled **3** a free reworking of a musical text or composition —*vt.* **-phrased′**, **-phras′ing** to express in a paraphrase —*vi.* to compose a paraphrase —***SYN.*** TRANSLATION —**par′a·phras′er** *n.*

par·a·phras·tic (par′ə fras′tik) *adj.* ⟦ML *paraphrasticus* < Gr *paraphrastikos*⟧ **1** of, having the nature of, or forming a paraphrase **2** using paraphrase —**par′a·phras′ti·cal·ly** *adv.*

pa·raph·y·sis (pə raf′i sis) *n., pl.* **-ses′** (-sēz′) ⟦ModL < Gr, an offshoot, sucker < *para-* (see PARA-[1]) + *physis,* a growth < *phyein,* to grow: see BE⟧ a sterile, threadlike part found with the spore-bearing organs of some ferns and mosses

par·a·ple·gi·a (par′ə plē′jē ə, -jə) *n.* ⟦ModL < Gr *paraplēgia,* a stroke at one side: see PARA-[1] & -PLEGIA⟧ motor and sensory paralysis of the entire lower half of the body —**par′a·ple′gic** (-plē′jik) *adj., n.*

par·a·prax·is (-prak′sis) *n., pl.* **-es′** (-sēz′) ⟦PARA-[1] + PRAXIS⟧ an action in which one's conscious intention is not fully carried out, as in the mislaying of objects, slips of the tongue and pen, etc.: thought to be generally due to a conflicting unconscious intention: also **par′a·prax′i·a** (-sē ə)

par·a·pro·fes·sion·al (-prō fesh′ə nəl) *n.* ⟦PARA-[1] + PROFESSIONAL⟧ a worker trained to perform certain functions, as in medicine or teaching, but not licensed to practice as a professional

par·a·psy·chol·o·gy (-sī käl′ə jē) *n.* ⟦PARA-[1] + PSYCHOLOGY⟧ the branch of psychology that investigates psychic phenomena, such as telepathy, extrasensory perception, or clairvoyance —**par′a·psy′cho·log′i·cal** (-sī′kə läj′i kəl) *adj.* —**par′a·psy·chol′o·gist** *n.*

par·a·quat (par′ə kwät′) *n.* ⟦PARA-[1] (sense 2) + QUAT(ERNARY)⟧ a highly toxic, soluble yellow solid, $CH_3(C_5H_4N)_2CH_3{\cdot}2CH_3SO_4$, used as a herbicide

☆**par·a·res·cue** (par′ə res′kyoo) *n.* ⟦PARA-[2] + RESCUE⟧ the rescue of a person or persons from a dangerous situation by parachutists

par·a·ros·an·i·line (par′ə rō zan′əl in) *n.* ⟦PARA-[1] + ROSANILINE⟧ a red aniline dye, $C_{19}H_{19}N_3O$, used in coloring fabrics, paper, etc. and as a biological stain

Pará rubber crude rubber obtained from several tropical South American trees (genus *Hevea,* esp. *H. brasiliensis*) of the spurge family

par·a·sail (par′ə sāl′) *n.* ⟦PARA(CHUTE) + SAIL(ING)⟧ a kind of parachute worn for a sport (**par′a·sail′ing**) in which a person is pulled by a motorboat, automotive vehicle, etc. fast enough to glide high above the water or ground —*vi.* to engage in such a sport —**par′a·sail′or** *n.*

par·a·sang (par′ə saŋ′) *n.* ⟦L *parasanga* < Gr *parasangēs* < OPers > Pers *farsang*⟧ an ancient Persian unit of linear measure equal to 30 stadia or 3.455 miles (5.56 kilometers)

par·a·se·le·ne (par′ə sə lē′nē) *n., pl.* **-nae** (-nē) ⟦ModL: see PARA-[1] & SELENE⟧ a moonlike optical illusion caused by moonlight passing through ice crystals in the upper atmosphere —**par′a·se·len′ic** (-len′ik) *adj.*

par·a·sex·u·al (par′ə sek′shoo əl) *adj.* designating or of any reproductive process in which recombination of genes from genetically distinct cells or individuals occurs without meiosis and fertilization, as during bacterial conjugation or by the fusion of nuclei within the multinucleate cells of some fungi

par·a·shah (pär′ə shä′) *n., pl.* **-shoth′** (-shōt′) ⟦Heb *pārāshāh,* lit., an explanation: akin to *perish* > PHARISEE⟧ **1** *a)* any of the sections into which the Pentateuch is divided for reading during a year in the synagogue on the Sabbath *b)* any of various selections from the Pentateuch for reading on the holy days **2** any of the subsections into which such sections are divided

par·a·site (par′ə sīt′) *n.* ⟦L *parasitus* < Gr *parasitos,* one who eats at the table of another, parasite, toady < *para-,* beside (see PARA-[1]) + *sitos,* food, grain⟧ 1 a person, as in ancient Greece, who flattered and amused the host in return for free meals 2 a person who lives at the expense of another or others without making any useful contribution or return; hanger-on 3 *Biol.* a plant or animal that lives on or in an organism of another species from which it derives sustenance or protection without benefit to, and usually with harmful effects on, the host

parasite drag *Aeron.* the drag caused by the parts of an aircraft that do not provide lift, as nacelles, the fuselage, etc.

par·a·sit·ic (par′ə sit′ik) ***adj.*** ⟦L *parasiticus* < Gr *parasitikos*⟧ 1 of or like a parasite; living at the expense of others 2 caused by parasites, as a disease 3 of or designating a subsidiary volcano, crater, etc. that forms on the side of another one Also **par′a·sit′i·cal** —**par′a·sit′i·cal·ly** ***adv.***

par·a·sit·i·cide (par′ə sit′ə sīd′) ***n.*** ⟦< PARASITE + -CIDE⟧ a substance or agent used to destroy parasites —**par′a·sit′i·ci′dal** ***adj.***

par·a·sit·ism (par′ə sit′iz′əm) ***n.*** 1 the state or condition of being a parasite 2 the habits of a parasite 3 in the U.S.S.R., the state of being unemployed 4 *Biol.* a symbiotic association of two kinds of organisms in which the parasite is benefited and the host is usually harmed 5 *Med.* the condition of being infested with parasites

par·a·sit·ize (-sī′tīz′, -si tīz′) ***vt.*** **-ized′, -iz′ing** 1 to live on, in, or with as a parasite 2 to infest with parasites —**par′a·sit′i·za′tion** ***n.***

par·a·sit·oid (-sī′toid′) ***n.*** ⟦PARASIT(E) + -OID⟧ a parasite that ultimately destroys its host, as any of various wasp larvae which feed progressively on the tissues of an immature stage of a host species

par·a·si·tol·o·gy (par′ə sī täl′ə jē, -si-) ***n.*** the science dealing with parasites and parasitism —**par′a·si′to·log′i·cal** (-sīt′ə läj′i kəl) ***adj.*** —**par′a·si·tol′o·gist** ***n.***

par·a·si·to·sis (-sī tō′sis, -si-) ***n.*** ⟦PARASIT(E) + -OSIS⟧ *Med.* any disease caused by parasites

par·a·sol (par′ə sôl′, -säl′) ***n.*** ⟦Fr < It *parasole* < *parare,* to ward off (< L, PREPARE) + *sole* (< L *sol*), SUN[1]⟧ a lightweight umbrella carried as a sunshade

par·a·sym·pa·thet·ic (par′ə sim′pə thet′ik) ***adj.*** ⟦PARA-[1] + SYMPATHETIC⟧ *Physiol.* designating or of that part of the autonomic nervous system whose nerves originate in the midbrain, the hindbrain, and the sacral region of the spinal cord and whose functions include the constriction of the pupils of the eyes, the slowing of the heartbeat, and the stimulation of certain digestive glands: these nerves oppose the sympathetic nerves in the regulation of many body processes

par·a·sym·pa·tho·mi·met·ic (-sim′pə thō′mi met′ik) ***adj.*** ⟦< prec. + MIMETIC⟧ having an effect similar to that produced when the parasympathetic nervous system is stimulated: said of drugs, chemicals, etc.

par·a·syn·ap·sis (-sin ap′sis) ***n.*** ⟦ModL: see PARA-[1] & SYNAPSIS⟧ the union of chromosomes side by side during meiosis

par·a·syn·the·sis (-sin′thə sis) ***n.*** ⟦ModL: see PARA-[1] & SYNTHESIS⟧ *Linguis.* the process of forming words by both compounding and the addition of derivational suffixes (Ex.: *big-hearted* from *big heart* + *-ed,* not *big* + *hearted*) —**par′a·syn·thet′ic** (-sin thet′ik) ***adj.***

par·a·tac·tic (-tak′tik) ***adj.*** 1 *Gram.* of, relating to, or involving parataxis: also **par′a·tac′ti·cal** 2 designating or using a style in which sentences or elements within sentences are set down successively with little or no indication of their relationship —**par′a·tac′ti·cal·ly** ***adj.***

par·a·tax·is (par′ə tak′sis) ***n.*** ⟦ModL < Gr *parataxis,* a placing beside < *para-,* beside (see PARA-[1]) + *tassein,* to place: see TACTICS⟧ *Gram.* the placing of related clauses, phrases, etc. in a series without the use of connecting words (Ex.: "I came, I saw, I conquered"): cf. HYPOTAXIS

☆**par·a·thi·on** (par′ə thī′än′) ***n.*** ⟦PARA-[1] + THION(IC)⟧ a highly poisonous compound, $C_{10}H_{14}O_5NPS$, commercially a colorless to dark-brown liquid, used as an agricultural insecticide

par·a·thor·mone (-thôr′mōn′) ***n.*** ⟦shortened < *parathyroid hormone*⟧ a hormone secreted by the parathyroids, important in the control of the calcium-phosphorus balance of the body: also **parathyroid hormone**

par·a·thy·roid (-thī′roid′) ***adj.*** ⟦PARA-[1] + THYROID⟧ 1 situated alongside or near the thyroid gland 2 designating or of any of usually four small, oval glands on or near the thyroid gland that secrete parathormone —***n.*** a parathyroid gland

par·a·trans·it (par′ə trans′it, -tranz′it) ***n.*** a transportation service, typically involving buses or vans, that provides rides as needed for the disabled or the elderly

par·a·troops (par′ə tro͞ops′) ***pl.n.*** ⟦< PARA(CHUTE) + TROOP⟧ troops trained and equipped to parachute into a combat area —**par′a·troop′** ***adj.*** —**par′a·troop′er** ***n.***

par·a·ty·phoid (par′ə tī′foid′) ***adj.*** ⟦PARA-[1] + TYPHOID⟧ designating, of, or causing an infectious disease closely resembling typhoid fever but usually milder and caused by bacteria (genus *Salmonella*) —***n.*** paratyphoid fever

par·a·vane (par′ə vān′) ***n.*** ⟦PARA-[1] + VANE⟧ either of a pair of torpedo-shaped devices that are towed by cables from the bow of a ship and are used to cut the moorings of submerged mines

par avion (pȧr ȧ vyōn′) ⟦Fr, by airplane⟧ by air mail

☆**par·a·wing** (par′ə wiŋ′) ***n.*** ⟦< PARA(CHUTE) + WING⟧ a winglike, maneuverable parachute that can be steered over short distances to a specific landing site

par·a·zo·an (par′ə zō′ən) ***n.*** ⟦< ModL *Parazoa:* see PARA-[1] & -ZOA⟧ any of the subkingdom (Parazoa) of animals, consisting only of the phylum of sponges, having two tissue layers only and lacking a nervous system and true digestive cavity —***adj.*** of the parazoans

par·boil (pär′boil′) ***vt.*** ⟦ME *parboilen* < OFr *parboullir* < *par* (< L *per*), through, thoroughly + *boullir* (< L *bullire*), to BOIL[1]: meaning infl. in ME & ModE by assoc. of *par* with PART[1]⟧ 1 to boil (meat or vegetables) until partly cooked, as in preparation for roasting 2 to make uncomfortably hot; overheat

par·buck·le (pär′buk′əl) ***n.*** ⟦altered (infl. by BUCKLE[1]) < Early ModE *parbunkel*⟧ 1 a sling for a log, barrel, etc., made by passing a doubled rope around the object and pulling the rope ends through the loop 2 a device for raising or lowering a cylindrical object, consisting of a doubled rope, the middle of which is secured at a given height and the ends passed around the object so that it will move up and down as the ends are hauled in or payed out —***vt.*** **-led, -ling** to raise or lower by using a parbuckle

parbuckles

Par·cae (pär′sē) ***pl.n.*** ⟦L, pl. of *Parca,* one of the Fates, orig., a birth-goddess < *parere,* to give birth: see -PAROUS⟧ FATES

par·cel (pär′səl) ***n.*** ⟦ME < MFr *parcelle* < LL **particella,* for L *particula:* see PARTICLE⟧ 1 a small, wrapped bundle; package 2 a quantity or unit of some commodity put up for sale 3 a group or collection; pack; bunch [*a parcel of fools*] 4 a piece, as of land, usually a specific part of a large acreage or estate 5 a portion or part: now only in **part and parcel**, an inseparable or essential part —***vt.*** **-celed** or **-celled, -cel·ing** or **-cel·ling** 1 to separate into parts and distribute; apportion: with *out* 2 to make up in or as a parcel 3 *Naut.* to wrap in parceling — ***adj., adv.*** [Archaic] part; partly —**SYN.** BUNDLE

par·cel·ing or **par·cel·ling** (pär′səl iŋ) ***n.*** 1 the act of separating into parts and distributing 2 *Naut.* canvas strips, usually covered with tar, wrapped around a rope to protect it

parcel post 1 a mail service and system for carrying and delivering parcels not over a specified weight and size 2 mail handled by this service

par·ce·nar·y (pär′sə ner′ē) ***n.*** ⟦Anglo-Fr *parcenerie* < OFr *parçonerie* < ML *partionaria* < *partionarius:* see fol.⟧ COPARCENARY (***n.*** 1)

par·ce·ner (pär′sə nər) ***n.*** ⟦ME < Anglo-Fr *parcenier* < OFr *parçonnier* < ML *partionarius,* contr. of **partitionarius* < L *partitio:* see PARTITION⟧ COPARCENER

parch (pärch) ***vt.*** ⟦ME *perchen* < ?⟧ 1 to expose (corn, peas, etc.) to great heat so as to dry or roast slightly 2 to dry up with heat; make hot and dry 3 to make very thirsty 4 to dry up and shrivel with cold —***vi.*** to become very dry, hot, thirsty, etc.

Par·chee·si (pär chē′zē) *trademark for* a game like pachisi in which the moves of pieces on a board are determined by the throwing of dice —***n.*** [**p-**] this game or the game of pachisi

parch·ment (pärch′mənt) ***n.*** ⟦ME *parchemin* < OFr < LL *pergamina* < L *(charta) Pergamena,* (paper) of PERGAMUM, where used as a substitute for papyrus: altered in OFr by assoc. with *parche,* parchment < LL *parthica (pellis),* lit., Parthian (leather)⟧ 1 the skin of an animal, usually a sheep or goat, prepared as a surface on which to write or paint 2 paper specially treated to resemble parchment, and used for lampshades, stationery, etc. 3 a document, manuscript, or diploma on parchment

pard[1] (pärd) ***n.*** ⟦ME *parde* < OFr < L *pardus* < Gr *pardos,* prob. < Iran (> Pers *pārs,* panther)⟧ [Archaic] LEOPARD

☆**pard**[2] (pärd) ***n.*** [Slang] *short for* PARDNER

par·die or **par·di** (pär dē′) ***adv., interj.*** ⟦ME *parde* < OFr *par dé* (Fr *pardieu*), by God!⟧ [Archaic] indeed; verily: a mild oath: also sp. **par·dy′**

☆**pard·ner** (pärd′nər) ***n.*** ⟦altered < PARTNER⟧ [Chiefly Dial.] a partner or companion

par·don (pärd′′n) ***vt.*** ⟦ME *pardonen* < OFr *pardoner* < LL *perdonare* < L *per-,* through, quite (see PER-) + *donare,* to give: see DATE[1]⟧ 1 to release (a person) from further punishment for a crime 2 to cancel or not exact penalty for (an offense); forgive 3 *a)* to excuse or forgive (a person) for some minor fault, discourtesy, etc. *b)* to overlook (a discourtesy, etc.) —***n.*** ⟦ME < OFr⟧ 1 a pardoning or being pardoned; forgiveness 2 an official document granting a pardon; specif., a document granting a Church indulgence, esp. as sold by medieval pardoners —***interj.*** 1 pardon me: a mild apology 2 please repeat what you have said: a request for information or clarification, often with the rising intonation of a question —**SYN.** ABSOLVE —**I beg your pardon!** excuse me!: a polite formula of apology, disagreement, etc. —**pardon me** EXCUSE ME (see phrase under EXCUSE) —**par′don·a·ble** ***adj.*** —**par′don·a·bly** ***adv.***

par·don·er (-ər) ***n.*** ⟦ME < Anglo-Fr⟧ 1 a medieval preacher who collected money offerings (as for building a church) to which indulgences were attached 2 a person who pardons

pare (per) ***vt.*** **pared, par′ing** ⟦ME *paren* < MFr *parer,* to prepare, trim, pare < L *parare,* to PREPARE⟧ 1 to cut or trim away (the rind, skin, covering, rough surface, etc.) of (anything); peel 2 to reduce or diminish (costs, etc.) gradually: often with *down* —**par′er** ***n.***

Pa·ré (pȧ rā′), **Am·broise** (än brwäz′) 1517?-90; Fr. surgeon

par·e·gor·ic (par′ə gôr′ik) ***adj.*** ⟦LL *paregoricus* < Gr *parēgorikos* < *parēgoros,* speaking, consoling, soothing < *para-,* on the side of (see PARA-[1]) + *agora,* assembly, AGORA[1]⟧ [Archaic] soothing or lessening pain —***n.*** 1 [Archaic] a medicine that soothes or lessens pain 2 a camphorated tincture of opium, containing benzoic acid, anise oil, etc., used to relieve diarrhea

par·ei·do·li·a (par′ī dō′lē ə) ***n.*** ⟦< PARA-[1] + Gr *eidōlon,* an image, phantom⟧

the imagined perception of a meaningful pattern in something that is random or indefinite

pa·rei·ra (bra·va) (pə rer′ə brä′və) ⟦Port *parreira brava,* wild vine < *parreira,* vine + *brava,* wild⟧ the stem of a South American curare plant

pa·ren (pə ren′, par′ən) ***n.*** *short for* PARENTHESIS (sense 2)

pa·ren·chy·ma (pə reŋ′ki mə, -ren′-) ***n.*** ⟦ModL < Gr, anything poured in beside < *para-,* beside (see PARA-[1]) + *enchyma,* infusion < *enchein,* to pour in < *en-,* in + *cheein,* to pour: see FOUND[3]⟧ **1** *Anat.* the essential or functional tissue of an organ, as distinguished from its connective tissue, blood vessels, etc. **2** *Bot.* a soft tissue made up of thin-walled, undifferentiated living cells with air spaces between them, constituting the chief substance of plant leaves and roots, the pulp of fruits, the central portion of stems, etc. **3** *Zool.* a spongy mass of tissue packing the spaces between the organs of some invertebrates —**pa·ren′chy·mal** ***adj.,*** **par·en·chym·a·tous** (par′en kim′ə təs) —**par′en·chym′a·tous·ly** ***adv.***

par·ent (per′ənt, par′-) ***n.*** ⟦OFr < L *parens,* parent, orig. prp. of *parere,* to beget: see -PAROUS⟧ **1** a mother or father **2** a progenitor or ancestor **3** any animal, organism, or plant in relation to its offspring **4** anything from which other things are derived; source; origin —***adj.*** ☆**1** designating a corporation in relation to a subsidiary that it owns and controls **2** designating anything in relation to something for which it is the source [other books based on this *parent* work] — ***vt., vi.*** to be or act as the parent (of) —**par′ent·hood′** ***n.***

par·ent·age (-ən tij) ***n.*** ⟦LME < MFr⟧ **1** descent or derivation from parents or ancestors; lineage; origin **2** the position or relation of a parent; parenthood

pa·ren·tal (pə rent′'l) ***adj.*** ⟦L *parentalis*⟧ **1** of or characteristic of a parent or parents **2** constituting the source or origin of something **3** *Biol.* designating or of the generation in which fertilization produces hybrids —**pa·ren′tal·ly** ***adv.***

parental leave temporary leave from work, granted to a parent of a newborn

par·en·ter·al (par en′tər əl) ***adj.*** ⟦PAR(A)- + ENTER(O)- + -AL⟧ **1** inside the body but outside the intestine **2** brought into the body through some way other than the digestive tract, as by subcutaneous or intravenous injection —***n.*** a substance for parenteral injection —**par·en′ter·al·ly** ***adv.***

pa·ren·the·sis (pə ren′thə sis) ***n., pl.*** **-ses′** (-sēz′) ⟦LL < Gr < *parentithenai,* to put beside < *para-,* beside (see PARA-[1]) + *entithenai,* to insert < *en-,* in + *tithenai,* to put, place: see DO[1]⟧ **1** an additional word, clause, etc. placed as an explanation or comment within an already complete sentence: in writing or printing it is usually marked off by curved lines, dashes, or commas **2** either or both of the curved lines, ( ), used to mark off parenthetical words, etc. or to enclose mathematical or logical symbols that are to be treated as a single term **3** an episode or incident, often an irrelevant one; interlude

pa·ren·the·size (-sīz′) ***vt.*** **-sized′, -siz′ing 1** *a)* to insert (a word, phrase, etc.) as a parenthesis *b)* to put into parentheses (see PARENTHESIS, sense 2) **2** to place a parenthesis within [to *parenthesize* a talk with jokes]

par·en·thet·i·cal (par′ən thet′i kəl) ***adj.*** ⟦ML *parentheticus*⟧ **1** *a)* of or having the nature of a parenthesis *b)* placed within parentheses (see PARENTHESIS, sense 2) **2** interjected as qualifying information or explanation **3** using or containing parentheses Also **par′en·thet′ic** —**par′en·thet′i·cal·ly** ***adv.***

par·ent·ing (per′ən tiŋ, par′-) ***n.*** the work or skill of a parent in raising a child or children

pa·re·o (pä′rā ōō′) ***n.*** **1** *alt. sp. of* PAREU **2** in the West, the pareu or a similar garment worn by women

par·er·gon (pə rer′gän) ***n., pl.*** **-ga** (-gə) ⟦L, extra ornament < Gr, a lesser work < neut. of *parergos,* adj., beside the main work < *para-* (see PARA-[1]) + *ergon,* WORK⟧ a shorter or less detailed musical or literary composition that is produced at the same time as, derived from, or complementary to a larger work

pa·re·sis (pə rē′sis, par′ə sis) ***n., pl.*** **-ses′** (-sēz′) ⟦ModL < Gr < *parienai,* to relax < *para-* (see PARA-[1]) + *hienai,* to set in motion (see JET[1])⟧ **1** partial or slight paralysis **2** a disease of the brain caused by syphilis of the central nervous system and characterized by inflammation of the meninges, dementia, paralytic attacks, etc.: in full **general paresis** —**pa·ret′ic** (-ret′ik, -rē′tik) ***n., adj.***

par·es·the·si·a (par′es thē′zhə, -zhē ə) ***n.*** ⟦ModL: see PARA-[1] & ESTHESIA⟧ an abnormal sensation, as of burning, prickling, etc. on the skin —**par′es·thet′ic** (-thet′ik) ***adj.***

Pa·re·to (pä re′tô), **Vil·fre·do** (vēl fre′dô) 1848-1923; It. economist & sociologist in Switzerland

pa·re·u (pä′rā ōō′) ***n.*** ⟦Tahitian⟧ a long, colorful wraparound skirt worn by Polynesian men and women: the Tahitian equivalent of the Samoan lava-lava

par·e·ve (pär′ə və, -ve) ***adj.*** ⟦Yiddish *parev*⟧ without either meat or milk products, hence permissible to be eaten with either meat or dairy dishes, in accordance with the laws of kashrut

par ex·cel·lence (pär′ ek′sə läns′; *Fr* pȧ rek se läns′) ⟦Fr, lit., by the way of excellence⟧ in the greatest degree of excellence; beyond comparison; preeminent(ly)

par ex·em·ple (pȧr eg zän′pl') ⟦Fr⟧ for example

par·fait (pär fā′) ***n.*** ⟦Fr, lit., perfect⟧ **1** a dessert made of rich cream, eggs, syrup, etc. frozen together and served in a tall, slender, short-stemmed glass **2** a dessert of layers of ice cream, crushed fruit, etc. in such a glass

par·fleche (pär′flesh′, pär flesh′) ***n.*** ⟦CdnFr *parflèche,* prob. < Fr *parer,* PARRY + *flèche,* arrow: see FLÈCHE⟧ **1** a rawhide with the hair removed by soaking it in water and lye **2** something made of this, as a case or robe

parge (pärj) ***vt.*** **parged, parg′ing** ⟦< fol.⟧ to apply a thin coat of plaster or mortar to (masonry) to seal or smooth the surface —**parg′ing** ***n.***

par·get (pär′jit) ***vt.*** **-get·ed** or **-get·ted, -get·ing** or **-get·ting** ⟦ME *pargeten, pargetten* < MFr *pargeter, parjeter* < *par-* (< L *per:* see PER-), completely + *jeter,* to throw: see JET[1]⟧ to put plaster or mortar on, esp. in a decorative way —***n.*** **1** plaster, mortar, etc. used to coat a masonry surface **2** raised ornamental plasterwork used on walls or ceilings Also, for ***n.,*** **par′get·ing** or **par′get·ting**

par·he·lic (pär hē′lik, -hel′ik) ***adj.*** of or like a parhelion or parhelia: also **par′he·li′a·cal** (-hi lī′ə kəl)

parhelic circle a bright circular halo that appears to intersect the sun in a plane parallel to the horizon: also **parhelic ring**

par·he·li·on (-hē′lē ən, -hēl′yən) ***n., pl.*** **-li·a** (-lē ə, -lē yə) ⟦L *parelion* < Gr *parēlion* < *para-,* beside (see PARA-[1]) + *hēlios,* the sun: see HELIOS⟧ a bright, sunlike optical illusion caused by sunlight passing through ice crystals in the upper atmosphere; sundog

par·i- (par′i) ⟦< L *par* (gen. *paris*): see PAR[1]⟧ *combining form* EQUAL [*paripinnate*]

pa·ri·ah (pə rī′ə; *Brit also* par′ē ə) ***n.*** ⟦Tamil *paṛaiyan,* drummer < *paṛai,* a drum: the pariah was a hereditary drumbeater⟧ **1** a member of one of the lowest social castes in India **2** any person despised or rejected by others; outcast

Par·i·an (per′ē ən, par′-) ***adj.*** **1** of Paros **2** *a)* designating a fine, white marble found in Paros *b)* like this marble **3** designating a fine, white porcelain (**Parian ware**) that resembles Parian marble —***n.*** a person born or living in Paros

Pa·ri·cu·tín (pä rē kōō tēn′) volcanic mountain in WC Mexico, formed by eruptions starting in 1943 & now dormant: *c.* 7,500 ft (2,286 m): also **Pa·rí·cu·tin** (pä rē′kōō tēn′)

pa·ri·es (per′ē ēz′, par′-) ***n., pl.*** **pa·ri·e·tes** (pə rī′ə tēz′) ⟦ModL < L, a wall < IE base *(*s*)*per-*, a bar, spear > SPAR[2], SPEAR⟧ *Biol.* a wall, as of a hollow organ, cavity, or cell: *usually used in pl.*

pa·ri·e·tal (pə rī′ə təl) ***adj.*** ⟦Fr *pariétal* < LL *parietalis* < L *paries:* see prec.⟧ ☆**1** of or having to do with life in a college, esp. with rules (**parietals**) governing visiting in dormitories by members of the opposite sex **2** *Anat.* of, pertaining to, or forming the walls of a cavity or hollow structure; esp., designating either of the two bones between the frontal and occipital bones, forming part of the top and sides of the skull **3** *Bot.* attached to the wall of the ovary, as the placenta in some plants

parietal cell any of the large, oval cells that secrete hydrochloric acid, found in the gastric glands of the mucous membrane that lines the stomach

parietal lobe the part of each hemisphere of the brain between the frontal and the occipital lobes

par·i·mu·tu·el (par′ə myōō′chōō əl) ***n.*** ⟦Fr *pari mutuel* < *pari,* a bet (< *parier,* to bet, orig., to equalize < LL *pariare,* to make equal < L *par:* see PAR[1]) + *mutuel,* MUTUAL⟧ **1** a system of betting on races in which those backing the winners divide, in proportion to their wagers, the total amount bet, minus a percentage for the track operators, taxes, etc. **2** a machine for recording such bets and computing payoffs; totalizator

par·ing (per′iŋ) ***n.*** **1** the act of one who pares something **2** a thin piece or strip pared off, as of the skin of a potato

pa·ri pas·su (pä′rē pä′sōō′, per′ē pas′ōō′) ⟦L⟧ **1** at an equal pace **2** in an equal or like way **3** *Law* without preference or priority

par·i·pin·nate (par′i pin′āt′) ***adj.*** ⟦PARI- + PINNATE⟧ *Bot.* having an equal number of leaflets on either side of the central stalk: said of compound leaves

Par·is[1] (par′is) ***n.*** ⟦L < Gr⟧ *Gr. Legend* a son of Priam, king of Troy: his kidnapping of Helen, wife of Menelaus, causes the Trojan War

Par·is[2] (par′is; *Fr* pȧ rē′) capital of France, in the NC part, on the Seine

Paris green [after prec.] a poisonous, bright-green powder made by reacting sodium arsenite with copper sulfate and acetic acid: now used chiefly as an insecticide

par·ish (par′ish) ***n.*** ⟦ME *parissche* < OFr *parroche* < LL(Ec) *parochia,* for *paroecia* < LGr(Ec) *paroikia,* a diocese < Gr, a sojourning (in a foreign land, or, by early Christians, on earth) < *paroikos,* a stranger < *para-* (see PARA-[1]) + *oikos,* dwelling: see ECO-⟧ **1** a British church district with its own church and clergyman **2** a district of British local civil government, often identical with the original church parish **3** an administrative district of various churches, esp. a part of a diocese, under the charge of a priest or minister **4** *a)* the members of the congregation of any church *b)* the territory in which they live ☆**5** a civil division in Louisiana, corresponding to a county

pa·rish·ion·er (pə rish′ə nər) ***n.*** ⟦ME *parisshoner* < *parishion* (< OFr *paroissien* < *paroiche,* prec.) + -ER⟧ a member of a parish

par·ish-pump (par′ish pump′) ***adj.*** [Brit.] narrow or limited in scope or outlook; of only local interest or significance [*parish-pump* politics]

Pa·ri·sian (pə rē′zhən, pə rizh′ən) ***adj.*** ⟦LME < Fr *parisien*⟧ of or characteristic of Paris, its people or culture, or the variety of French spoken there —***n.*** a person born or living in Paris

Pa·ri·si·enne (pə rē′zhē en′, -zē en′) ***n.*** ⟦Fr, fem. of prec.⟧ a female born or living in Paris

par·i·ty[1] (par′ə tē) ***n., pl.*** **-ties** ⟦Fr *parité* < L *paritas* < *par,* equal: see PAR[1]⟧ **1**

the state or condition of being the same in power, value, rank, etc.; equality **2** resemblance; similarity **3** equivalence in value of one currency expressed in terms of another country's currency **4** equality of value at a given ratio between different kinds of money, commodities, etc. ☆**5** a price for certain farm products, usually maintained by government price supports, designed to keep the purchasing power of the farmer at the level of a designated base period **6** *Math.* the condition existing between two integers that are both odd or both even **7** *Physics* a symmetry property of a wave function: expressed as +1 if no difference can be detected between the wave function and its mirror image, and as −1 if the wave function is changed only in sign

par·i·ty² (par′ə tē) ***n.*** ⟦< L *parere,* to bear (see -PAROUS) + -ITY⟧ *Med.* the state or fact of having borne offspring

park (pärk) ***n.*** ⟦ME *parc* < OFr < ML *parricus* < Iberian **parra* > Sp *parra,* trellis, grape vine⟧ **1** [Historical] *Eng. Law* an enclosed area of land, held by royal grant or prescription, stocked and preserved for hunting **2** an area of land containing pasture, woods, lakes, etc., surrounding a large country house **3** an area of public land; specif., *a)* an area in or near a city, usually laid out with walks, drives, playgrounds, etc., for public recreation *b)* an open square in a city, with benches, trees, etc. *c)* a large area known for its natural scenery and preserved for public recreation by a state or national government **4** BALLPARK ☆**5** [West] a level, open area surrounded by mountains or forest **6** that arrangement of bands, clutches, etc. in an automatic transmission that disengages and locks the drive wheels of a motor vehicle **7** PARKING LOT **8** an area set aside for a particular commercial use; specif., *a)* AMUSEMENT PARK *b)* INDUSTRIAL PARK **9** *Mil.* an area for storing and servicing vehicles and other equipment —***vt.*** **1** to enclose in or as in a park **2** to store (military equipment) in a park ☆**3** to leave (a vehicle) in a place temporarily ☆**4** to maneuver (a vehicle) into a space where it can be left temporarily ☆**5** [Informal] to leave or set in a particular place; deposit **6** *Finance* to transfer (securities) temporarily, as to conceal ownership —***vi.*** to park a vehicle —**park′er *n.***

Park (pärk), **Mun·go** (muŋ′gō) 1771-1806; Scot. explorer in Africa

☆**par·ka** (pär′kə) ***n.*** ⟦Aleut < Russ, skin jacket, fur coat⟧ **1** a hip-length pullover fur garment with a hood, worn in arctic regions **2** a hooded jacket, often with fleece or pile lining

Park Avenue a wealthy residential street in New York City, regarded as a symbol of high society, fashion, etc.

Par·ker (pär′kər) **1 Char·lie** (chär′lē) (born *Charles Christopher Parker, Jr.*) 1920-55; U.S. jazz saxophonist **2 Dorothy** (born *Dorothy Rothschild*) 1893-1967; U.S. writer **3 Theodore** 1810-60; U.S. clergyman, social reformer, & abolitionist

☆**par·ker·house roll** (pär′kər hous′) ⟦after *Parker House,* hotel in Boston where first served⟧ a yeast roll shaped by folding over a flat, round piece of buttered dough

☆**parking lot** an area, often paved, for parking a number of motor vehicles

☆**parking meter** a coin-operated timing device installed near a parking space: drivers pay to park in the space for a certain length of time by inserting coins into the meter

☆**parking orbit** a temporary orbit of an artificial satellite or spacecraft around the earth, moon, etc., prior to carrying out a further maneuver

par·kin·son·ism (pär′kin sən iz′əm) ***n.*** ⟦see fol.⟧ **1** any of various brain disorders characterized by muscle rigidity as in Parkinson's disease, with or without tremor **2** PARKINSON'S DISEASE —**par′kin·son′i·an *adj.***

Par·kin·son's disease (pär′kin sənz) ⟦after James *Parkinson* (1755-1824), Eng physician⟧ a degenerative disease of later life, characterized by a rhythmic tremor and muscular rigidity, caused by degeneration in the basal ganglia of the brain: often **Parkinson's *n.***

Par·kin·son's Law (pär′kin sənz) ⟦propounded by C. Northcote *Parkinson* (1909-93), Brit economist⟧ any of several satirical statements expressed as economic laws, as one to the effect that work expands to fill the time allotted to it

park·land (pärk′land′) ***n.*** wooded land set aside as, or suitable for, a public park

Park·man (pärk′mən), **Francis** 1823-93; U.S. historian

Park Range ⟦descriptive⟧ range of the Rockies, in NC Colo. & S Wyo.: highest peak, 14,284 ft (4,354 m)

Parks (pärks), **Rosa** 1913-2005; U.S. civil rights activist

☆**park·way** (pärk′wā′) ***n.*** **1** a broad roadway bordered and, often, divided with plantings of trees, bushes, and grass **2** *a)* the landscaped center strip or border of a parkway *b)* TREE LAWN

Parl *abbrev.* **1** Parliament **2** Parliamentary

par·lance (pär′ləns) ***n.*** ⟦Anglo-Fr *parlaunce* < OFr < *parler:* see PARLEY⟧ **1** [Archaic] conversation; esp., parley or debate **2** a style or manner of speaking or writing; language; idiom *[*military *parlance]*

par·lan·do (pär län′dō) ***adj., adv.*** ⟦It, speaking < *parlare,* speak⟧ *[also in italics] Musical Direction* to be sung in a style suggesting or approximating speech

☆**par·lay** (pär′lā, -lē; *for v., occas.* pär lā′) ***vt., vi.*** ⟦altered < earlier *paroli* < Fr < It (Neapolitan) dial. < *paro,* an equal, pair < L *par:* see PAR¹⟧ **1** to bet (an original wager plus its winnings) on another race, contest, etc. **2** to exploit (an asset) successfully *[*to *parlay* one's voice into fame*]* —***n.*** a bet or series of bets made by parlaying

par·ley (pär′lē) ***vi.*** ⟦< Fr *parler,* to speak < OFr < LL(Ec) *parabolare,* speak < *parabola,* a speech, PARABLE⟧ to have a conference or discussion, esp. with an enemy; confer —***n.,*** *pl.* **-leys** a talk or conference for the purpose of discussing a specific matter or of settling a dispute, as a military conference with an enemy, under a truce, for discussing terms

par·lia·ment (pär′lə mənt) ***n.*** ⟦ME *parlament* < OFr *parlement* < *parler:* see prec.⟧ **1** an official or formal conference or council, usually concerned with government or public affairs **2** [**P-**] *a)* the national legislative body of Great Britain, composed of the House of Commons and the House of Lords *b)* the body of persons who make up Parliament for the period between elections **3** [**P-**] any of several similar bodies in other countries **4** any of several high courts of justice in France before 1789

par·lia·men·tar·i·an (pär′lə men ter′ē ən) ***n.*** **1** [**P-**] a supporter of the Long Parliament in opposition to Charles I of England; Roundhead **2** a person skilled in parliamentary rules, practice, or debate

par·lia·men·ta·ry (pär′lə ment′ə rē, -men′trē) ***adj.*** **1** of or like a parliament **2** decreed or established by a parliament **3** based on or conforming to the customs and rules of a parliament or other public assembly *[parliamentary* procedure*]* **4** having or governed by a parliament; specif., designating or of a government in which a prime minister or premier holds office only so long as he or she commands a majority in the parliament

par·lor (pär′lər) ***n.*** ⟦ME *parlour* < OFr *parleor* < *parler:* see PARLEY⟧ **1** *a)* [Archaic] a room set aside for the entertainment of guests; formal sitting room *b)* [Old-fashioned] any living room **2** a small, semiprivate sitting room or meeting room apart from the main lounges in a hotel, inn, etc. **3** *a)* [Old-fashioned] a business establishment elegantly furnished to resemble a private sitting room *[*an ice-cream *parlor]* *b)* now, a shop or business establishment of a specified kind, often with some special equipment or furnishings for personal services *[*a beauty *parlor,* tattoo *parlor,* off-track betting *parlor]* Brit. sp. **par′lour**

☆**parlor car** a comfortable railroad passenger car with individual seats

parlor game a game, as charades, typically not requiring special equipment, that is played indoors as by family or friends

par·lor·maid (-mād′) ***n.*** a maid who serves at table, answers the door, etc.

par·lous (pär′ləs) ***adj.*** ⟦ME, contr. of *perilous*⟧ **1** [Literary] perilous; dangerous; risky **2** [Archaic] dangerously clever; cunning, mischievous, shrewd, etc. —***adv.*** [Archaic] extremely; very

Par·ma (pär′mə; *It* pär′mä) commune in N Italy, in Emilia-Romagna

Par·men·i·des (pär men′ə dēz′) 5th cent. B.C.; Gr. Eleatic philosopher

Par·me·san (pär′mə zän′, -zhän′) ***adj.*** ⟦Fr *parmesan* < It *parmigiano,* after *Parma,* city in Italy⟧ of or from Parma, Italy

Parmesan (cheese) a very hard, dry cheese orig. of Italy, made from skimmed cow's milk and usually grated for sprinkling on pasta, soups, etc.

par·mi·gia·na (pär′mə zhä′nə, par′mə zhän′) ***adj.*** ⟦It *Parmigiana,* fem. of *parmigiano,* PARMESAN⟧ prepared with Parmesan cheese: used postpositively *[*eggplant *parmigiana]*: also **par′mi·gia′no** (-zhä′nō)

Par·na·í·ba (pär′nə ē′bə) river in NE Brazil, flowing north into the Atlantic: *c.* 900 mi (1,448 km)

Par·nas·si·an (pär nas′ē ən) ***adj.*** ⟦L *Parnassius*⟧ **1** of Mount Parnassus **2** of the art of poetry **3** of the Parnassians —***n.*** ⟦Fr *parnassien,* after *Le Parnasse contemporain,* title of their first collection (1866)⟧ a member of a school of 19th cent. French poets concerned with form primarily

Par·nas·sus¹ (pär nas′əs) ***n.*** ⟦after fol.⟧ **1** poetry or poets collectively **2** any center of poetic or artistic activity

Par·nas·sus² (pär nas′əs), **Mount** ⟦L < Gr *Parnasos*⟧ mountain in central Greece, near the Gulf of Corinth: 8,061 ft (2,457 m): sacred to Apollo and the Muses in ancient times

Par·nell (pär nəl′), **Charles Stewart** 1846-91; Ir. nationalist leader

pa·ro·chi·al (pə rō′kē əl) ***adj.*** ⟦ME *parochiele* < OFr *parochial* < ML(Ec) *parochialis* < LL(Ec) *parochia:* see PARISH⟧ **1** of or in a parish or parishes **2** restricted to a small area or scope; narrow; limited; provincial *[*a *parochial* outlook*]* —**pa·ro′chi·al·ism′ *n.*** —**pa·ro′chi·al·ist *n.*** —**pa·ro′chi·al·ly *adv.***

parochial school ☆a school supported and run by a church

par·o·dist (par′ə dist) ***n.*** a writer of parodies —**par′o·dis′tic *adj.***

par·o·dy (par′ə dē) ***n.,*** *pl.* **-dies** ⟦Fr *parodie* < L *parodia* < Gr *parōidia,* burlesque song < *para-,* beside (see PARA-¹) + *ōidē,* song (see ODE)⟧ **1** *a)* a literary or musical work imitating the characteristic style of some other work or of a writer or composer in a satirical or humorous way, usually by applying it to an inappropriate subject *b)* the art of writing such works **2** a poor or weak imitation —***vt.*** **-died, -dy·ing** to make a parody of —**SYN.** CARICATURE —**pa·rod·ic** (pə räd′ik) ***adj.,*** **pa·rod′i·cal**

pa·rol (pə rōl′, par′əl) ***n.*** ⟦MFr *parole* < OFr: see fol.⟧ *Law* spoken evidence given in court by a witness: now only in **by parol** —***adj.*** *Law* oral or verbal

pa·role (pə rōl′) ***n.*** ⟦Fr, a word, formal promise < OFr < LL(Ec) *parabola,* a speech, PARABLE⟧ **1** [Now Rare] word of honor; promise; esp., the promise of a prisoner of war to abide by certain conditions, often specif. to take no further part in the fighting, in exchange for full or partial freedom **2** the condition of being on parole ☆**3** *a)* the release of a prisoner whose sentence has not expired, on condition of future good behavior: the sentence is not set aside and the individual remains under the supervision of a parole board *b)* the conditional freedom granted by such release, or the period of it **4** [Obs.] *Mil.* a special password used only by certain authorized persons —***vt.*** **-roled′, -rol′ing** ☆to grant parole to (a prisoner) —**on parole** at liberty under conditions of parole

☆**pa·rol·ee** (pə rō′lē′) ***n.*** ⟦< prec. + -EE¹⟧ a person who has been released from prison on parole

par·o·no·ma·si·a (par′ə nō mā′zhə, -zhē ə) ***n.*** ⟦L < Gr *paronomasia* < *para-,* beside (see PARA-¹) + *onomasia,* naming < *onomazein,* to name < *onoma,* NAME⟧ a pun —**par′o·no·mas′tic** (-mas′tik) ***adj.***

par·o·nym (par′ə nim′) ***n.*** ⟦Gr *parōnymon,* orig. neut. of *parōnymos:* see fol.⟧ a paronymous word

pa·ron·y·mous (pə rän′ə məs) ***adj.*** ⟦Gr *parōnymos* < *para-,* beside (see PARA-[1]) + *onyma,* NAME⟧ derived from the same root; cognate, as the words *differ* and *defer*

Par·os (per′äs′; *Gr* pä′rôs′) island of the Cyclades, in the SC Aegean, west of Naxos: 81 sq mi (210 sq km)

pa·ro·tic (pə rōt′ik, -rät-) ***adj.*** ⟦ModL *paroticus* < Gr *para-,* beside + *ous* (gen. *ōtos*), EAR[1]⟧ situated near the ear

pa·rot·id (pə rät′id) ***adj.*** ⟦ML *parotidus* < L *parotis* (gen. *parotidis*), a tumor near the ear < Gr *parōtis* < *para-,* beside (see PARA-[1]) + *ous* (gen. *ōtos*), EAR[1]⟧ situated near or beside the ear; esp., designating or of either of the salivary glands below and in front of each ear —***n.*** ⟦ML *parotida*⟧ a parotid gland

par·o·ti·tis (par′ə tīt′is) ***n.*** ⟦see -ITIS⟧ inflammation of the parotids; esp., the mumps —**par′o·tit′ic** (-tit′ik) ***adj.***

-par·ous (pər əs) ⟦L *-parus,* < *parere,* to bring forth, bear < IE base **per-,* to give birth to > Gr *portis,* calf⟧ *combining form* bringing forth, producing, bearing [*oviparous, multiparous*]

Par·ou·si·a (pär′o͞o sē′ə, pə ro͞o′zē ə) ***n.*** ⟦Gr(Ec) *parousia* < Gr, lit., presence, arrival < *para-,* PARA-[1] + *ousia,* a being, substance < stem of *ōn,* prp. of *einai,* to be: see ONTO-⟧ SECOND COMING

par·ox·ysm (par′ək siz′əm, pə räk′-) ***n.*** ⟦Fr *paroxysme* < ML *paroxysmus* < Gr *paroxysmos* < *paroxynein,* to excite, sharpen < *para-,* beyond (see PARA-[1]) + *oxynein,* to sharpen < *oxys,* sharp: see OXY-[2]⟧ **1** a sudden attack, or intensification of the symptoms, of a disease, usually recurring periodically **2** a sudden outburst as of laughter, rage, or sneezing; fit; spasm —**par·ox·ys·mal** (par′ək siz′m'l) ***adj.***

par·ox·y·tone (par äk′si tōn′) ***adj.*** ⟦ModL *paroxytonus* < Gr *paroxytonos:* see PARA-[1] & OXYTONE⟧ in Greek grammar, having an acute accent on the next to last syllable —***n.*** a paroxytone word

par·quet (pär kā′) ***n.*** ⟦Fr, a small enclosed section < MFr *parchet,* dim. of *parc,* PARK⟧ ☆**1** the main floor of a theater, esp. that part from the orchestra pit to the parquet circle: usually called *orchestra* **2** a flooring of parquetry —***vt.*** **-queted′** (-kād′), **-quet′ing** (-kā′iŋ) **1** to use parquetry to make (a floor, etc.) **2** to decorate the floor of (a room) with parquetry

☆**parquet circle** the part of a theater beneath the balcony and behind the parquet on the main floor

par·quet·ry (pär′kə trē) ***n.*** ⟦Fr *parqueterie:* see PARQUET⟧ inlaid woodwork in geometric forms, usually of contrasting woods, used esp. in flooring

parr (pär) ***n., pl.*** **parrs** or **parr** ⟦< ?⟧ **1** a young salmon before it enters salt water **2** the young of certain other fishes

Parr (pär), **Catherine** 1512-48; 6th & last wife of Henry VIII of England

par·ra·keet (par′ə kēt′) ***n. alt. sp. of*** PARAKEET

par·ra·mat·ta (par′ə mat′ə) ***n. alt. sp. of*** PARAMATTA

Par·ra·mat·ta (par′ə mat′ə) city in E New South Wales, Australia: suburb of Sydney

par·rel or **par·ral** (par′əl) ***n.*** ⟦ME *perell,* var. of *parail,* aphetic for *aparail,* equipment: see APPAREL⟧ *Naut.* a loop of rope, chain, etc. or metal collar used to join a yard or gaff to a mast in such a way that it can be moved up and down

par·ri·cide (par′ə sīd′) ***n.*** ⟦Fr < L *parricida,* earlier *paricida* < IE base **pāsos,* a relative (> Gr *pēos,* one related by marriage) + L *-cida,* -CIDE⟧ **1** the act of murdering one's parent, someone having a similar relationship, or a close relative **2** ⟦L *parricidium*⟧ a person who does this —**par′ri·ci′dal** ***adj.***

Par·ring·ton (par′iŋ tən), **Vernon Louis** 1871-1929; U.S. literary historian

Par·rish (par′ish), **Max·field** (maks′fēld) 1870-1966; U.S. illustrator & painter

par·rot (par′ət) ***n.*** ⟦Fr dial. *perrot,* prob. after *Perrot,* dim. of *Pierre,* Peter⟧ **1** any of an order (Psittaciformes) of tropical or subtropical birds with a hooked bill, brightly colored feathers, and feet having two toes pointing forward and two backward: some parrots can learn to imitate human speech **2** a person who mechanically repeats the words or acts of others, usually without full understanding —***vt.*** to repeat or imitate, esp. without understanding

parrot fever PSITTACOSIS

par·rot·fish (-fish′) ***n., pl.*** **-fish′** or **-fish′es** (see FISH) any of a family (Scaridae) of brightly colored, tropical, marine percoid fishes with parrotlike jaws

par·ry (par′ē) ***vt.*** **-ried, -ry·ing** ⟦prob. < Fr *parez,* imper. of *parer* < It *parare,* to ward off < L *parare,* to PREPARE⟧ **1** to ward off or deflect (a blow, the thrust of a sword, etc.) **2** to counter or ward off (criticism, a prying question, etc.) by a clever or evasive response —***vi.*** to make a parry or evasion —***n., pl.*** **-ries** **1** a warding off or a turning aside of a blow, thrust, etc., as in fencing **2** an evasion; evasive reply

Par·ry (par′ē), Sir **William Edward** 1790-1855; Eng. naval officer & arctic explorer

parse (pärs) ***vt.*** **parsed, pars′ing** ⟦< L *pars,* a part, in *quae pars orationis?* what part of speech?⟧ **1** to separate (a sentence) into its parts, explaining the grammatical form and function of each of the parts and their interrelation **2** to describe the form, part of speech, and function of (a word in a sentence) **3** to use analytical skills to interpret or comprehend —***vi.*** **1** to parse a sentence, word, etc. **2** to be capable of being parsed

par·sec (pär′sek′) ***n.*** ⟦PAR(ALLAX) + SEC(OND)⟧ a unit of distance, usually used to measure the distance to a star, equal to 206,265 astronomical units (3.0857×10^{13} kilometers or 1.92×10^{13} miles or 3.2616 light years): it is the distance at which an angle of 0° 0′ 1″ (one second of arc) would form a triangle having an opposite side with a length of one astronomical unit: abbrev. *pc*

Par·see or **Par·si** (pär′sē, pär sē′) ***n.*** ⟦Pers *Pārsī,* a Persian < *Pārs,* Persia⟧ a member of a Zoroastrian religious sect in India descended from a group of Persian refugees who fled from the Muslim persecutions of the 7th and 8th cent. —**Par′see·ism′** ***n.***, **Par′si·ism′**

par·si·mo·ni·ous (pär′sə mō′nē əs) ***adj.*** characterized by parsimony; miserly; close —***SYN.*** STINGY[1] —**par′si·mo′ni·ous·ly** ***adv.*** —**par′si·mo′ni·ous·ness** ***n.***

par·si·mo·ny (pär′sə mō′nē) ***n.*** ⟦ME *parcimony* < L *parcimonia* < *parcere,* to spare: akin to *(com)pescere,* to enclose, limit⟧ a tendency to be over-careful in spending; unreasonable economy; stinginess

pars·ley (pärs′lē) ***n.*** ⟦ME *parseli* < OE *petersilie* & OFr *persil,* both < VL **petrosilium* < L *petroselinum* < Gr *petroselinon,* rock parsley < *petros,* stone + *selinon,* celery⟧ a cultivated plant (*Petroselinum hortense*) of the umbel family, with greenish-yellow flowers and aromatic, often curled leaves used to flavor or garnish some foods

pars·leyed (-lēd) ***adj.*** cooked with or sprinkled with parsley [*parsleyed* potatoes]: also sp. **pars′lied**

pars·nip (pärs′nip′) ***n.*** ⟦ME *pasnepe,* altered (infl. by *nepe,* turnip) < OFr *pasnaie* < L *pastinaca* < *pastinare,* to dig up < *pastinum,* two-forked dibble⟧ **1** a biennial plant (*Pastinaca sativa*) of the umbel family, with yellow flowers and a long, thick, sweet, white root used as a vegetable **2** its root

par·son (pär′sən) ***n.*** ⟦ME *persone* < OFr < ML *persona,* a beneficed priest, orig., person < L: see PERSON⟧ **1** an Anglican minister in charge of a parish; rector **2** [Informal] any minister or pastor, esp. a Protestant one

par·son·age (-ij) ***n.*** ⟦ME *personage* < OFr < ML(Ec) *personagium,* ecclesiastical benefice: see prec. & -AGE⟧ the dwelling provided by a church for its minister

Par·sons (pär′sənz), **Tal·cott** (tôl′kät, täl′-; -kət) 1902-79; U.S. sociologist

☆**Par·sons table** (pär′sənz) ⟦after *Parsons* School of Design, in New York⟧ [*also* **p- t-**] a lightweight, square-legged table of geometric design, often made of molded plastic

part[1] (pärt) ***n.*** ⟦ME < OE & OFr, both < L *pars* (gen. *partis*) < IE base **per-,* to sell, hand over in sale, make equal > L *par,* equal, *parare,* to equate⟧ **1** a portion or division of a whole; specif., *a)* any of several equal portions, quantities, numbers, pieces, etc. of which something is composed or into which it can be divided [a cent is a 100th *part* of a dollar] *b)* an essential element or constituent; integral portion which can be separated, replaced, etc. [automobile *parts*] *c)* a portion detached or cut from a whole; fragment; piece *d)* a certain amount but not all [to lose *part* of one's fortune] *e)* a certain amount or section regarded as separate or distinct in some way [a rainy *part* of the country] *f)* a segment or organ of the body of humans and animals *g)* a division of a literary work *h) Math.* an aliquot part **2** a portion assigned or given; share; specif., *a)* something a person must do; share of work or duty [to do one's *part*] *b)* interest or concern [to have some *part* in a matter] *c)* [*usually pl.*] talent; ability [a man of *parts*] *d)* a character or role in a theatrical presentation; also, the words, actions, etc. of a character in a play *e) Music* the score for a particular voice or instrument in a concerted piece; also, any of the voices or instruments in a musical ensemble **3** *a)* a region; area *b)* [*usually pl.*] a portion of a country; district **4** one of the different sides or parties in a transaction, dispute, conflict, etc.: now rare except in the phrase TAKE SOMEONE'S PART (see below) or in legal use [the party of the first *part*] ☆**5** the dividing line formed by combing the hair in different directions —***vt.*** ⟦ME *parten* < OFr *partir* < L *partire,* to divide, separate < the n.⟧ **1** to break or divide into separate parts **2** to comb (the hair) in different directions so as to leave a dividing line **3** to break up (a connection or relationship) by separating those involved **4** to separate (two or more persons or things); break or hold apart **5** to separate (substances) as by a chemical process **6** [Archaic] to distribute; share; apportion **7** *Naut.* to break or undergo the breaking of (a hawser, chain, etc.) —***vi.*** **1** to break or divide into two or more pieces **2** to separate and go different ways, as branches of a river **3** to separate; leave each other; cease associating **4** *a)* to go away; leave; depart (with *from*) *b)* to die —***adj.*** of or having to do with only a part; partial —***adv.*** partly; in part —**for one's part** as far as one is concerned —**for the most part** in the greatest part or to the greatest extent; mostly; generally —**in good part** **1** good-naturedly **2** generally; mostly —**in part** to a certain extent or degree; partly —**on the part of someone** **1** as far as someone is concerned **2** by or coming from someone Also **on someone's part** —**part with** to give up; let go; relinquish —**play a part** **1** to behave unnaturally in an attempt to deceive **2** to participate or share: also **take part** —**take someone's part** to support someone in a struggle or disagreement; side with someone

SYN.—**part** is the general word for any of the components of a whole [a *part* of one's life]; a **portion** is specifically a part allotted to someone [his *portion* of the inheritance]; a **piece** is either a part separated from the whole [a *piece* of pie] or a single standardized unit of a collection [a *piece* of statuary]; a **division** is a part formed by cutting, partitioning, classifying, etc. [the fine-arts *division* of a library]; **section** is equivalent to **division** but usually connotes a smaller part [a *section* of a bookcase]; **segment** implies a part separated along natural lines of division [a *segment* of a tangerine]; a **fraction** is strictly a part contained by the whole an integral number of times, but generally it connotes an insignificant part [he received only a *fraction* of the benefits]; a **fragment** is a relatively small part separated by or as by breaking [a *fragment* of rock] See also **separate** —***ANT.*** **whole**

part[2] *abbrev.* **1** participial **2** participle **3** particular

par·take (pär tāk′) ***vi.*** **-took′, -tak′en, -tak′ing** ⟦back-form. < *partaker,* contr. of *part taker,* transl. of L *particeps* < *pars,* PART[2] + *capere,* to take: see HAVE⟧ **1** to take part (*in* an activity); participate **2** to take a portion or take some; specif., to eat or drink something, esp. in company with others: usually with *of* **3** to have or show a trace (*of*); have some of the qualities (*of*) —*SYN.* SHARE[1] —**par·tak′er** *n.*

part·ed (pärt′id) *adj.* **1** divided; separated **2** [Archaic] dead; departed **3** *Bot.* divided almost to the base, as some leaves

par·terre (pär ter′) *n.* ⟦Fr < *par,* on + *terre,* earth < L *terra:* see TERRACE⟧ **1** an ornamental garden area in which the flower beds and path form a pattern ☆**2** PARQUET CIRCLE

par·the·no·car·py (pär′thə nō kär′pē) *n.* ⟦Ger *parthenokarpie* < Gr *parthenos,* a virgin + *karpos,* fruit: see HARVEST⟧ the development of a ripe fruit without fertilization of the ovules, as in the banana and pineapple —**par′the·no·car′pic** *adj.* —**par′the·no·car′pi·cal·ly** *adv.*

par·the·no·gen·e·sis (pär′thə nō′jen′ə sis) *n.* ⟦ModL < Gr *parthenos,* maiden, virgin + *genesis,* origin: see GENESIS⟧ reproduction by the development of an unfertilized ovum, seed, or spore, as in certain insects or algae: it may be induced artificially by chemical or mechanical means: opposed to ANDROGENESIS —**par′the·no·ge·net′ic** (-jə net′ik) *adj.* —**par′the·no·ge·net′i·cal·ly** *adv.*

Par·the·non (pär′thə nän′, -nən) *n.* ⟦L < Gr *Parthenōn* < *parthenos,* a virgin (i.e., Athena)⟧ the Doric temple of Athena built (5th cent. B.C.) on the Acropolis in Athens: sculpture is attributed to Phidias

Par·then·o·pe (pär then′ə pē′) *n.* ⟦L < Gr *Parthenopē*⟧ *Gr. Myth.* the siren who throws herself into the sea after her songs fail to lure Odysseus into a shipwreck

Par·the·nos (pär′thə näs′) *n.* ⟦< Gr *parthenos*⟧ a virgin: an epithet of several Greek goddesses, esp. of Athena

Par·thi·a (pär′thē ə) ancient country in SW Asia, southeast of the Caspian Sea —**Par′thi·an** *adj., n.*

Parthian shot ⟦in allusion to a trick of *Parthian* archers of shooting at the enemy while in retreat⟧ PARTING SHOT

par·tial (pär′shəl) *adj.* ⟦ME *parcial* < MFr *partial* < LL *partialis* < L *pars,* PART[1]⟧ **1** favoring one person, faction, etc. more than another; biased; prejudiced **2** of, being, or affecting only a part; not complete or total —*n.* **1** PARTIAL TONE **2** a partial artificial denture —**partial to** fond of; having a liking for —**par′tial·ly** *adv.*

par·tial-birth abortion (-burth′) an abortion performed relatively late in pregnancy, in which the living fetus is extracted in stages through the birth canal: a nontechnical term

partial derivative *Math.* the result of differentiating a function of more than one variable with respect to a particular variable, with the other variables kept constant: the notation $\partial f/\partial x$ means the partial derivative of the function f with respect to x

partial fraction any of a set of fractions which add up to a given fraction (Ex.: a/2xy and a/xy are the partial fractions of 3a/2xy)

par·ti·al·i·ty (pär′shē al′ə tē, pär shal′-) *n.* ⟦ME *parcialitee* < MFr *partialité*⟧ **1** the state or quality of being partial; tendency to favor unfairly; bias **2** particular fondness or liking —*SYN.* PREJUDICE

partial tone *Acoustics, Music* any of the pure, or harmonic, tones forming a complex tone; harmonic

par·ti·ble (pär′tə bəl) *adj.* ⟦LL *partibilis* < L *partiri,* to divide < *pars,* PART[1]⟧ that can be divided, separated, or parted; divisible

par·ti·ceps cri·mi·nis (pär′ti seps′ krim′i nis) ⟦L⟧ a partner in crime; accomplice

par·tic·i·pant (pär tis′ə pənt) *adj.* ⟦L *participans,* prp. of *participare:* see fol.⟧ participating —*n.* a person who participates or shares in something

par·tic·i·pate (pär tis′ə pāt′) *vi.* **-pat′ed, -pat′ing** ⟦< L *participatus,* pp. of *participare,* to share, partake < *pars,* PART[1] + *capere,* to take: see HAVE⟧ to have or take a part or share with others (*in* some activity, enterprise, etc.) —*vt.* [Rare] to have or take a part or share in —*SYN.* SHARE[1] —**par·tic′i·pa′tion** *n.,* **par·tic′i·pance** —**par·tic′i·pa′tive** *adj.* —**par·tic′i·pa′tor** *n.*

par·tic·i·pa·to·ry (-pə tôr′ē) *adj.* **1** of or having to do with participation **2** allowing or providing for the participation of all members of a group [*participatory* democracy]

par·ti·cip·i·al (pärt′ə sip′ē əl) *adj.* ⟦L *participialis*⟧ of, based on, or having the nature and use of a participle —**par′ti·cip′i·al·ly** *adv.*

par·ti·ci·ple (pärt′i sip′əl) *n.* ⟦OFr < L *participium* < *particeps,* participating, partaking < *participare,* PARTICIPATE: from participating in the nature of both v. & adj.⟧ *Gram.* a verbal form having some characteristics and functions of both verb and adjective: in English, the present participle ends in *-ing* (*asking*) and the past participle most commonly ends in *-ed* or *-en* (*asked, spoken*): participles are used: *a)* in verb phrases (are *asking,* was *carried*) *b)* as verbs (*seeing* the results, he stopped) *c)* as adjectives (a *laughing* boy, the *beaten* path) *d)* as nouns, i.e., gerunds (*seeing* is *believing*) *e)* as adverbs (*raving* mad) *f)* as connectives (*saving* those present)

par·ti·cle (pärt′i kəl) *n.* ⟦ME *partycle* < MFr *particule* < L *particula,* dim. of *pars,* PART[1]⟧ **1** *a)* an extremely small piece; tiny fragment [a dust *particle*] *b)* the slightest trace; speck [not a *particle* of truth] **2** [Archaic] a clause or article in a document **3** *Gram.* *a)* a short, usually uninflected and invariable part of speech used to express a syntactic or semantic relationship, as an article or any of certain prepositions, conjunctions, or interjections *b)* a prefix or derivational suffix **4** *Physics* ELEMENTARY PARTICLE **5** *R.C.Ch.* a small piece of the consecrated Host or any of the small Hosts given to lay communicants

particle accelerator *Nuclear Physics* ACCELERATOR (sense 3)

particle beam a beam of atomic or subatomic particles which may be accelerated to nearly the speed of light and used experimentally, as in the development of military weapons

☆**par·ti·cle·board** (-bôrd′) *n.* a boardlike building material made by compressing sawdust or wood particles with a resin binder

particle physics the branch of physics employing high-energy particles to study the properties of atomic nuclei and of the elementary particles themselves

par·ti-col·ored (pärt′i kul′ərd) *adj.* ⟦< ME *party,* parti-colored (< Fr *parti,* pp. of *partir:* see PARTY) + COLORED⟧ **1** having different colors in different parts **2** diversified; variegated

par·tic·u·lar (pär tik′yə lər) *adj.* ⟦ME *particuler* < MFr < LL *particularis* < L *particula,* PARTICLE⟧ **1** of or belonging to a single, definite person, part, group, or thing; not general; distinct **2** apart from any other; regarded separately; specific [to rummage for a *particular* earring] **3** out of the ordinary; unusual; noteworthy; special [no *particular* reason for going] **4** dealing with particulars; itemized; detailed **5** not satisfied with anything considered inferior; exacting; extremely careful; fastidious **6** *Logic* designating a proposition that deals with only some members of a class rather than all of them; not universal ["some people have red hair" is a *particular* proposition] —*n.* **1** a separate and distinct individual, fact, item, or instance which may be included under a generalization; single case **2** a detail; item of information; point: *often used in pl.* **3** *Logic* a particular proposition —*SYN.* DAINTY, SPECIAL —**in particular** particularly; especially

par·tic·u·lar·ism (-iz′əm) *n.* **1** undivided adherence or devotion to one particular party, system, interest, theory, etc. **2** the policy of allowing each member or state in a federation to govern independently without regard to the interests of the whole —**par·tic′u·lar·ist** *adj., n.* —**par·tic′u·lar·is′tic** *adj.*

par·tic·u·lar·i·ty (pär tik′yo͞o lar′ə tē) *n., pl.* **-ties** ⟦MFr *particularité* < LL *particularitas*⟧ **1** the state, quality, or fact of being particular; specif., *a)* individuality, as opposed to generality or universality *b)* the quality of being detailed, as a description *c)* attention to detail; painstaking care *d)* the quality of being fastidious or hard to please **2** something particular; specif., *a)* an individual characteristic; peculiarity *b)* a minute detail

par·tic·u·lar·ize (-tik′yə lər īz′) *vt.* **-ized′, -iz′ing** ⟦MFr *particulariser*⟧ to state or name individually or in detail; itemize —*vi.* to give particulars or details —**par·tic′u·lar·i·za′tion** *n.*

par·tic·u·lar·ly (pär tik′yə lər lē, -ler′lē) *adv.* **1** so as to be particular; in detail **2** especially; unusually; extraordinarily **3** specifically

par·tic·u·late (pär tik′yə lit, -lāt′) *adj.* ⟦< L *particula,* PARTICLE + -ATE[1]⟧ of, pertaining to, or consisting of very small, separate particles —*n.* a very minute particle

particulate inheritance *Genetics* inheritance by offspring of distinctive characters from both the father and the mother; Mendelian inheritance

par·ti·er (pärt′ē ər) *n. var. sp. of* PARTYER: see PARTY

part·ing (pärt′iŋ) *adj.* **1** dividing; separating **2** departing **3** given, spoken, done, etc. at parting —*n.* **1** the act of breaking, dividing, or separating **2** a place of division or separation; dividing point or line **3** something that separates or divides **4** a leave-taking or departure **5** death

parting shot any hostile gesture or remark made in leaving

par·ti pris (pȧr tē prē′) ⟦Fr⟧ preconceived opinion

par·ti·san[1] (pärt′ə zən, -sən) *n.* ⟦MFr < It *partigiano* < *parte* < L *pars,* PART[1]⟧ **1** a person who takes the part of or strongly supports one side, party, or person; often, specif., an unreasoning, emotional adherent **2** any of a group of guerrilla fighters; esp., a member of an organized civilian force fighting covertly to drive out occupying enemy troops —*adj.* **1** of, like, or characteristic of a partisan **2** blindly or unreasonably devoted **3** of or having to do with military partisans —*SYN.* FOLLOWER —**par′ti·san·ship′** *n.*

par·ti·san[2] (pärt′ə zən, -sən) *n.* ⟦MFr *partisane* < It *partigiana,* fem. of *partigiano* (see prec.): sense infl. by *pertugiare,* to pierce⟧ a broad-bladed weapon with a long shaft, used esp. in the 16th cent.

par·ti·ta (pär tēt′ə) *n.* ⟦It < fem. pp. of *partire,* to divide < L: see PART[1] (*vt.*)⟧ *Music* **1** [Archaic] a variation **2** an instrumental suite

par·tite (pär′tīt′) *adj.* ⟦L *partitus,* pp. of *partire,* to divide: see PART[1] (*vt.*)⟧ parted; having divisions; divided into parts: often in compounds [*bipartite*]

par·ti·tion (pär tish′ən) *n.* ⟦ME *particioune* < L *partitio*⟧ **1** a parting or being parted; division into parts; separation; apportionment **2** something that separates or divides, as an interior wall dividing one room from another **3** a part or section; portion; compartment **4** *Law* the process of dividing property and giving separate title to those who previously had joint or common title —*vt.* **1** to divide into parts or shares; apportion **2** to set off or divide by a partition —**par·ti′tioned** *adj.* —**par·ti′tion·er** *n.*

par·ti·tive (pärt′ə tiv) *adj.* ⟦ML *partitivus:* see PARTITE & -IVE⟧ **1** used in setting off or separating; making a division **2** *Gram.* *a)* referring to a part of a whole *b)* of or relating to a case expressing reference to a part of a whole —*n.* **1** a partitive word or form **2** the partitive case —**par′ti·tive·ly** *adv.*

par·ti·zan (part′ə zən, -sən) *n., adj. alt. sp. of* PARTISAN[1]

part·let (pärt′lit) *n.* ⟦earlier *patelet* < MFr *patelette,* band of stuff, orig., dim. of *pate,* a paw⟧ a covering for the neck and upper chest, worn chiefly by women in the 16th cent.

part·ly (pärt′lē) *adv.* in some measure or degree; in part; not fully or completely

part·ner (pärt′nər) *n.* ⟦ME *partener,* altered (by assoc. with *part,* PART[1]) < *parcener:* see PARCENER⟧ **1** a person who takes part in some activity in common with another or others; associate; specif., *a)* one of two or more persons engaged in the same business enterprise and sharing its profits and risks: each is an agent for the other or others and is liable, except when limited to his or her own investment, for the debts of the firm *b)* a husband or wife *c)* either of two persons dancing together *d)* either of two players on the same side or team playing or competing against two others, as in bridge or tennis **2** *a)* either of two persons not married to each other but otherwise in an intimate, spouse-like relationship *b)* either of two persons having sex with each other **3** [*usually pl.*] *Naut.* a framework, as of timbers, for supporting a mast, capstan, etc. where it passes through the deck **—*vt.*** **1** to join (others) together as partners **2** to be or provide a partner for

part·ner·ship (-ship′) ***n.*** **1** the state of being a partner; participation **2** the relationship of partners; joint interest; association **3** *a)* an association of two or more partners in a business enterprise *b)* a contract by which such an association is created *c)* the people so associated

part of speech any of the classes of words of a given language to which a word can be assigned: different kinds of grammar have different criteria for classifying words, as form, function or meaning, or combinations of these: in traditional English grammar, patterned after Latin grammar, the parts of speech are noun, verb, adjective, adverb, pronoun, preposition, conjunction, and interjection

par·ton (pär′tän′) ***n.*** ⟦PART(ICLE) + -ON⟧ a particle in nucleons, now identified with quarks

par·took (pär to͝ok′) ***vi. pt. of*** PARTAKE

par·tridge (pär′trij) ***n., pl.*** **-tridg·es** or **-tridge** ⟦ME *partriche* < OFr *perdriz,* earlier *perdiz* < L *perdix* < Gr, prob. akin to *perdesthai,* to break wind (< IE base **perd-* > FART): from whirring sound made by wings on rising to fly⟧ **1** any of a number of medium-sized, short-tailed gallinaceous birds (family Phasianidae), esp., an Old World species (*Perdix perdix*) with an orange-brown head, a grayish neck, and a rust-colored tail, now established in N U.S.: cf. PHEASANT **2** any of various birds resembling the partridge, as the ruffed grouse

Par·tridge (pär′trij), **Eric (Honeywood)** 1894-1979; Brit. lexicographer, born in New Zealand

☆**par·tridge·ber·ry** (pär′trij ber′ē) ***n., pl.*** **-ries** **1** a trailing North American evergreen (*Mitchella repens*) of the madder family with opposite, rounded leaves, pinkish flowers, and red berries **2** its berry

part song a usually homophonic composition for several voices, intended for choral performance without accompaniment: also written **part′-song′** ***n.***

part time as a part-time employee, student, etc. [to work *part time*]

part-time (pärt′tīm′) ***adj.*** designating, of, or engaged in work, study, etc. for specified periods regarded as taking less time than a regular or full schedule

part-tim·er (-tīm′ər) ***n.*** a part-time employee, student, etc.

par·tu·ri·ent (pär to͝or′ē ənt, -tyo͝or′-) ***adj.*** ⟦L *parturiens,* prp. of *parturire,* to be in labor < *parere,* to bring forth: see -PAROUS⟧ **1** giving birth or about to give birth to young **2** of childbirth, or parturition **3** on the point of coming forth with a discovery, idea, etc. **—par·tu′ri·en·cy** ***n.***

par·tu·ri·fa·cient (pär to͝or′i fā′shənt, -tyo͝or′-) ***adj.*** ⟦< L *parturire* (see prec.) + -FACIENT⟧ inducing or easing labor in childbirth **—*n.*** a parturifacient medicine

par·tu·ri·tion (pär′to͞o rish′ən, -tyo͞o-, -cho͞o-) ***n.*** ⟦L *parturitio* < *parturire:* see PARTURIENT⟧ the act of bringing forth young; childbirth

part·way (pärt′wā′) ***adv.*** to some point, degree, or extent less than full, complete, final, etc. [*partway* done]

par·ty (pärt′ē) ***n., pl.*** **-ties** ⟦ME *partie* < OFr < *partir,* to divide < L *partiri* < *pars,* PART[1]⟧ **1** a group of people working together to establish or promote particular theories or principles of government which they hold in common; esp., an organized political group which seeks to elect its candidates to office and thus to direct government policies **2** any group of persons acting together; specif., *a)* a group sent out on a task or mission [a surveying *party*] *b)* a group meeting together socially to accomplish a task [a quilting *party*] *c)* a group assembled for amusement or recreation [a fishing *party*] **3** a gathering for social entertainment, or the entertainment itself, often of a specific nature [a birthday *party,* cocktail *party*] **4** a person who participates or is concerned in an action, proceeding, plan, etc.: often with *to* [to be a *party* to a conspiracy] **5** either of the persons or sides concerned in a legal matter **6** [Informal] a person [the *party* who telephoned] **—*adj.*** **1** of or having to do with a political party [a *party* leader] **2** for a social gathering [*party* clothes] **—*vi.*** **-tied, -ty·ing** ☆**1** to attend or hold social parties **2** [Informal] to take part in social activity, as at a party, in an unrestrained, often boisterous manner, usually while drinking alcoholic beverages, taking drugs, etc. **—par′ty·er** ***n.***

par·ty·go·er (pärt′ē gō′ər) ***n.*** a person who goes to a party or attends many parties

party line **1** a line marking the boundary between adjoining properties ☆**2** a single circuit connecting two or more telephone users with the exchange ☆**3** [*usually pl.*] a political tenet regarded as a line, or boundary, beyond which a political party or its members are not supposed to go **4** the line of policy followed by a political party, esp. a communist party **—par′ty-lin′er** ***n.***

party man a faithful supporter of a political party

party politics political acts and principles directed toward the interests of one political party or its members without reference to the common good

☆**party poop·er** (po͞op′ər) ⟦PARTY + POOP[2] + -ER⟧ [Slang] a spoilsport, esp. one who is too tired or lethargic to participate in the fun of a party: also **party poop**

party wall a wall separating and common to two buildings or properties: each owner has a partial right in its use

pa·rure (pə ro͝or′; *Fr* pȧ rür′) ***n.*** ⟦Fr < OFr < *parer,* to prepare < L *parare,* PREPARE⟧ a matched set of jewelry, as earrings, bracelet, and necklace

par value the value of a stock, bond, etc. fixed at the time of its issue; face value: distinguished from MARKET VALUE

par·ve (pär′və, -ve; *also* pärv) ***adj.*** PAREVE

par·ve·nu (pär′və no͞o′, -nyo͞o′) ***n.*** ⟦Fr, pp. of *parvenir* < L *pervenire,* to arrive < *per,* through (see PER[1]) + *venire,* COME⟧ a person who has suddenly acquired wealth or power, esp. one who is not fully accepted socially by the class associated with the higher position; upstart **—*adj.*** **1** being a parvenu **2** like or characteristic of a parvenu

par·ve·nue (pär′və no͞o′, -nyo͞o′) ***n.*** ⟦Fr⟧ a woman who is a parvenu **—*adj.*** **1** being a parvenue **2** like or characteristic of a parvenue

par·vis (pär′vis) ***n.*** ⟦ME < OFr *parevis* < L *paradisus,* lit., PARADISE: name of the court before St. Peter's in Rome⟧ **1** an enclosed court or yard in front of a building, esp. a church **2** a portico or single line of columns in front of a church

par·vo·line (pär′və lēn′, -lin) ***n.*** ⟦< L *parvus,* small, after (QUIN)OLINE: so named because of its low volatility⟧ any of various isomeric, liquid ptomaines, $C_9H_{13}N$, derived from pyridine and found in decaying fish or meat

par·vo·vi·rus (pär′vō vī′rəs) ***n.*** ⟦< L *parvus,* small + VIRUS⟧ any of a family (Parvoviridae) of very small DNA viruses affecting a wide range of vertebrates and some invertebrates, including viruses which cause acute enteritis in dogs and cats and which can be fatal to puppies and kittens

pas (pä) ***n., pl.*** **pas** (päz; *Fr* pä) ⟦Fr < L *passus,* a step: see PASS[2]⟧ **1** the right to precede; precedence **2** a step or series of steps in dancing

Pas·a·de·na (pas′ə dē′nə) ⟦< Ojibwa *pasadinaa,* valley⟧ **1** city in SW Calif., near Los Angeles **2** ⟦after the city in Calif.⟧ city in SE Tex., near Houston

Pa·sar·ga·dae (pə sär′gə dē′) ancient capital of Persia, built by Cyrus the Great: near modern Shiraz, Iran

Pas·cal[1] (pas kal′) ***n.*** ⟦after fol.⟧ **1** a high-level computer language, written in structured modules: also written **PASCAL** **2** [**p-**] the basic unit of pressure in SI and MKS systems, equal to the pressure of a force of one newton per square meter (0.00001 bar or 0.01 millibar): abbrev. *Pa*

Pas·cal[2] (pas kal′; *Fr* pȧs kȧl′), **Blaise** (blez) 1623-62; Fr. mathematician, physicist, & philosopher

Pas·cal celery (pas′kəl) ⟦< ?⟧ any of several large, dark-green varieties of celery with firm, crisp stalks

Pasch (pask) ***n.*** ⟦ME *pasche* < OFr < LL(Ec) *pascha* < Gr(Ec) (in N.T. & LXX) < Heb *pesach,* usually interpreted "passage", as if < *psḥ,* to pass over, but ? akin to Akkadian *pessû,* lame⟧ **1** PASSOVER **2** EASTER **—pas·chal** (pas′kəl) ***adj.***

paschal lamb[1] **1** among the ancient Hebrews, the lamb slain and eaten at the Passover Seder **2** [*often* **P- L-**] AGNUS DEI (sense 1)

paschal lamb[2] [*often* **P- L-**] *Christianity name for* Jesus Christ

pasch flower (pask) PASQUEFLOWER

Pas·cua (päs′kwä), **Is·la de** (ēs′lä *the*) *Sp. name for* EASTER ISLAND

pas de chat (pä′ də shä′; *Fr* pät shȧ′) ⟦Fr, lit., step of the cat⟧ *Ballet* a cat-like, springing leap

pas de deux (pä′ də do͞o′; *Fr* päd dö′) *pl.* **pas′ de deux′** (-do͞oz′; *Fr* päd dö′) ⟦Fr, step for two⟧ *Ballet* a dance or figure for two performers: a **pas de trois** (pä′də twä′) is for three performers, a **pas de qua·tre** (pä′də kä′trə, -kät′) is for four performers, etc.

pa·se·o (pä se′ô) ***n., pl.*** **-os** ⟦Sp < *pasear,* to walk < *paso,* a step < L *passus:* see PACE[1]⟧ **1** a leisurely walk, esp. in the evening; stroll **2** a street or plaza for strolling **3** the parade of bullfighters into the arena before bullfights

pash[1] (pash) [Now Dial.] ***vt., vi.*** ⟦ME *passchen,* prob. echoic⟧ to hurl or be hurled violently so as to break; smash **—*n.*** a smashing blow

pash[2] (pash) ***n.*** ⟦shortened & altered < PASSION⟧ [Slang] an infatuation

pa·sha (pə shä′, pä′shə, pash′ə) ***n.*** ⟦Turk *paşa*⟧ [Historical] in the Ottoman Empire, *a)* a title of rank or honor placed after the name *b)* a high civil or military official

pa·sha·lik or **pa·sha·lic** (pə shä′lik) ***n.*** ⟦Turk *paşalık* < *paşa* + *-lık,* abstract suffix⟧ the jurisdiction of or area governed by a pasha

pash·mi·na (pəsh mē′nə, pash-) ***n.*** ⟦ult. < Pers *pashm,* wool⟧ **1** a fine, soft fabric made from cashmere **2** a shawl made of this

Pash·to (push′tō, päsh′-) ***n.*** a language of the Iranian branch of the Indo-European language family, spoken in E Afghanistan and N Pakistan: one of the official languages of Afghanistan

Pash·tun (push to͞on′) ***n., pl.*** **-tun** or **-tuns** ⟦Pashto *paštun*⟧ a member of a Pashto-speaking people of E Afghanistan and N Pakistan

Pa·siph·a·ë (pə sif′ā ē′) ***n.*** ⟦L < Gr *Pasiphaē*⟧ *Gr. Myth.* the wife of Minos and mother of the Minotaur by a white bull belonging to Minos

pa·so·do·ble (pä′sô dô′ble) ***n., pl.*** ***pa′so·do′bles*** (-bles) ⟦Sp, double step⟧ **1** spirited music played at bullfights during the entrance (*paseo*) of the bullfighters or during the passes (*faena*) just before the kill **2** a lively dance in duple meter based on this: also written ***pa′so do′ble***

pasque·flow·er (pask′flou′ər) ***n.*** ⟦earlier *passeflower* < MFr *passefleur* < *passer,* PASS[2] + *fleur,* FLOWER, altered by assoc. with Fr *pasque,* PASCH⟧ any of several plants (genus *Anemone*) of the buttercup family; esp., a North American wildflower (*A. patens*) of early spring, having silky, hairy foliage and cup-shaped, bluish, solitary flowers

pas·quin·ade (pas′kwi nād′) ***n.*** ⟦Fr < It *pasquinata,* after *Pasquino,* classical statue in Rome to which it was the custom in the 16th c. to attach satirical verses⟧ a satirical piece of writing that holds its object up to ridicule, formerly one posted in a public place; lampoon: also **pas·quil** (pas′kwil) —***vt.*** **-ad′ed, -ad′ing** to criticize or ridicule with a pasquinade; lampoon

pass[1] (pas, päs) ***n.*** ⟦ME *pas:* see PACE[1]⟧ a narrow passage or opening, esp. between mountains; gap; defile

pass[2] (pas, päs) ***vi.*** ⟦ME *passen* < OFr *passer* < VL **passare* < L *passus,* a step: see PACE[1]⟧ **1** to go or move forward, through, or out **2** to extend; lead *[*a road *passing* around the hill*]* **3** to be handed on or circulated from person to person **4** to go, change, or be conveyed from one place, form, condition, circumstance, possession, etc. to another **5** to be spoken or exchanged between persons, as greetings **6** *a)* to cease; come to an end (often with *away*) *[*the fever *passed]* *b)* to go away; depart **7** to die: a euphemism: usually with *away* or *on* **8** to go by; move by or past **9** to slip by or elapse *[*an hour *passed]* **10** to get or make a way: with *through* or *by* **11** *a)* to go, take place, or be accepted without question, dispute, or challenge *b)* to gain acceptance as a member of a group by assuming an identity with it in denial of one's ancestry, background, etc. **12** to be sanctioned, ratified, or approved by some authority, as a legislative body **13** *a)* to go through a trial, test, examination, or course of study successfully; satisfy given requirements or standards *b)* to be barely acceptable as a substitute **14** to happen; take place; occur **15** *a)* to sit in inquest or judgment *b)* to give a judgment, opinion, or sentence; decide (*on* or *upon* a matter) **16** to be rendered or pronounced *[*the judgment *passed* against us*]* **17** to be expelled, as from the bowels **18** to decline to take one's turn, as in certain card games or board games, or to participate **19** *Craps* to make a winning throw (of the dice) **20** *Sports* to attempt or complete a pass of the ball, puck, etc. —***vt.*** **1** to go by, beyond, past, over, or through; specif., *a)* to leave behind *[*to *pass* others in a race*]* *b)* to undergo; experience (usually with *through*) *c)* to go by without noticing; disregard; ignore (often used fig.) *[*to *pass* one's bus stop; life seems to be *passing* me by*]* *d)* to fail to promote, reward, etc. (usually with *over*) *[*to *pass* over more qualified job applicants*]* ☆*e)* to omit the payment of (a regular dividend) *f)* to go through (a trial, test, examination, course of study, etc.) successfully; satisfy the requirements or standards of *g)* to go beyond or above the powers or limits of; surpass; excel *h)* [Archaic] to cross; traverse **2** to cause or allow to go, move, or proceed; specif., *a)* to send; dispatch *b)* to cause to move in a certain way; direct the movement of *[*to *pass* a comb through one's hair*]* *c)* to guide into position *[*to *pass* a rope around a stake*]* *d)* to cause to go through, or penetrate *e)* to cause to move past *[*to *pass* troops in review*]* *f)* to cause or allow to get by an obstacle, obstruction, etc. *g)* to cause or allow to stand approved; ratify; sanction; enact; approve *h)* to cause or allow to go through an examination, test, etc. successfully *i)* to allow to go by or elapse; spend (often with *away*) *[*to *pass* a pleasant hour*]* *j)* to discharge or expel from the bowels, bladder, etc.; excrete; void ☆*k)* *Baseball* to walk (a batter) **3** to cause to move from place to place or person to person; transport or transmit; specif., *a)* to hand to another *[pass* the salt*]* *b)* to cause to be in circulation *[*to *pass* a bad check*]* *c)* to hand, throw, or hit (a ball, puck, etc.) from one player to another *d)* to hit a tennis ball past (an opponent) so as to score a point **4** [Rare] to pledge **5** *a)* to pronounce or give (an opinion or judgment) *b)* to utter (a remark) **6** to manipulate (cards, etc.) or trick (a person), as by sleight of hand —***n.*** ⟦Fr *passe* < *passer* (see the ***vi.***); partly < the ModE v.⟧ **1** an act of passing; passage **2** *a)* the successful completion of a scholastic course or examination, esp. if without honors *b)* a mark, etc. indicating this **3** an unfortunate or undesirable condition or situation *[*to come to such a sorry *pass]* **4** *a)* a ticket, certificate, etc. giving permission or authorization to come or go freely or without charge *b)* a ticket at a fixed price that permits unlimited rides, as on a bus or train for a specified period *c)* *Mil.* a written leave of absence for a brief period **5** a motion of the hands that is meant to deceive, as in card tricks or magic; sleight of hand **6** a motion or stroke of the hand, as in mesmerism or hypnotism **7** *a)* a motion of the hand as if to strike *b)* a tentative attempt **8** [Informal] a proposal of sexual intimacy, or an attempt to embrace, or kiss, as in seeking sexual intimacy **9** *Aeron.* a flight over a specified point or at a target **10** *Card Games* a declining to bid, play a round, etc. when it is one's turn **11** *Craps* a winning throw (of the dice) **12** *Sports* *a)* in soccer, hockey, etc., an intentional transfer of the ball, puck, etc. to another player during play; also, an attempt to do so, whether or not successful ☆*b)* in football, a throw, esp. a FORWARD PASS, to an offensive teammate *c)* a lunge or thrust made in fencing ☆*d)* a walk in baseball —**SYN.** DIE[1] —**bring to pass** to cause to come about or happen —**come to pass** to come about or happen —**pass for** to be accepted or looked upon as: usually said of an imitation or counterfeit —**pass someone's lips** **1** to be eaten or drunk by someone **2** to be said by someone —**pass off** **1** to come to an end; cease **2** to take place; go through, as a transaction **3** to be accepted or cause to be accepted as genuine, true, etc., esp. through deceit —**pass out** **1** to distribute **2** to become unconscious; faint —**pass over** **1** to disregard; ignore; omit **2** to leave (someone) out of consideration in promotions, appointments, etc. —☆**pass up** to reject, refuse, or let go by *[*to *pass up* an opportunity*]* —**pass′er** ***n.***

pass[3] *abbrev.* **1** passage **2** passenger **3** passive

pass·a·ble (pas′ə bəl) ***adj.*** ⟦ME < MFr < *passer,* PASS[2]⟧ **1** that can be passed, traveled over, or crossed **2** that can be circulated; genuine, as coin **3** satisfactory or barely satisfactory for the purpose; adequate **4** that can be enacted, as a proposed law —**pass′a·ble·ness** ***n.***

pass·a·bly (-ə blē) ***adv.*** **1** well enough; acceptably **2** moderately; somewhat

pass·a·ca·glia (päs′ə käl′yə) ***n.*** ⟦pseudo-It < Sp *pasacalle* < *pasar* (< VL **passare,* PASS[2]) + *calle,* street < L *callis:* so named from often being performed in the streets⟧ **1** a slow, stately Italian, Spanish, or French dance of the 17th c., similar to the chaconne **2** the music for this dance **3** a musical form based on this dance, in 3/4 time and with a continuous ground bass

pas·sade (pə säd′) ***n.*** ⟦Fr < It *passata* < *passare,* PASS[2] < VL: see prec.⟧ *Horsemanship* the movement of a horse backward and forward over the same course

pas·sa·do (pə sä′dō) ***n.,*** *pl.* **-dos** or **-does** ⟦altered < Fr *passade* < It *passata:* see prec.⟧ *Fencing* a thrust or lunge with one foot advanced

pas·sage (pas′ij) ***n.*** ⟦OFr < *passer:* see PASS[2] & -AGE⟧ **1** the act of passing; specif., *a)* movement from one place to another; migration *[*birds of *passage]* *b)* change or progress from one process or condition to another; transition *c)* the enactment of a law by a legislative body **2** permission, right, or a chance to pass **3** a journey, esp. by water; voyage **4** *a)* the accommodations of a passenger, esp. on a ship *b)* the charge for such accommodations **5** a way or means of passing; specif., *a)* a road or path *b)* a channel, duct, etc. *c)* a hall or corridor that is an entrance or exit or onto which several rooms open; passageway **6** that which happens or takes place between persons; interchange, as of blows or words **7** *a)* a short segment of a written work or speech *[*a Bible *passage]* *b)* a section or detail of a painting, drawing, etc. **8** *Med.* a bowel movement **9** *Music* a short section of a composition, especially one displaying technical skill —***vi.*** **-saged, -sag·ing** [Rare] to make a passage, or voyage; journey

pas·sage·way (-wā′) ***n.*** a narrow way for passage, as a hall, corridor, or alley; passage

pas·sage·work (pas′ij wʉrk′) ***n.*** a section of a composition regarded chiefly as a display of the soloist's technical skill: also written **passage work**

Pas·sa·ic (pə sā′ik) ⟦< Delaware *énta pahsá·e·k,* where there is a valley⟧ river in NE N.J.: *c.* 100 mi (161 km)

Pas·sa·ma·quod·dy Bay (pas′ə mə kwäd′ē) ⟦< Micmac *pestəmokati,* lit., place where pollock are plentiful⟧ arm of the Bay of Fundy between Me. & New Brunswick, Canada: *c.* 15 mi (24 km) long

pas·sant (pas′ənt) ***adj.*** ⟦ME (only in sense "excelling, passing") < OFr < prp. of *passer,* PASS[2]⟧ *Heraldry* walking with the head forward and the forepaw farther from the viewer raised *[*a lion *passant]*

pass-band filter (pas′band′) BAND-PASS FILTER

pass·book (pas′book′) ***n.*** BANKBOOK

Pass·chen·daele (pash′ən dāl′) village near Ypres in NW Belgium, obliterated in WWI: site of a bloody, but indecisive, battle (1917)

pas·sé (pa sā′, pä sā′) ***adj.*** ⟦Fr, pp. of *passer,* PASS[2]⟧ **1** out-of-date; old-fashioned **2** [Archaic] not youthful; rather old

☆**passed ball** *Baseball* a misplay by the catcher in which a pitch that could be caught or controlled is missed and a base runner advances to another base as a result: cf. WILD PITCH

passed pawn *Chess* a pawn having no opponent's pawn ahead of it on its file or an adjacent file

pas·sel (pas′əl) ***n.*** ⟦altered < PARCEL⟧ [Informal or Dial.] a group or collection, esp. a fairly large one

passe·men·terie (pas men′trē; *Fr* päs män trē′) ***n.*** ⟦Fr < *passement,* lace < *passer:* see PASS[2] & -MENT⟧ trimming made of gimp, cord, beads, braid, etc.

pas·sen·ger (pas′ən jər) ***n.*** ⟦ME *passager* < MFr < OFr *passage,* PASSAGE: the *n* is unhistoric, as in *messenger*⟧ **1** [Rare] WAYFARER **2** a person traveling in a train, bus, boat, automobile, etc., esp. one not involved in operating the conveyance

☆**passenger pigeon** a variety of North American pigeon (*Ectopistes migratorius*) with a narrow tail longer than its wings: formerly abundant, but extinct since 1914

passe-par·tout (päs′pär to͞o′, pas′-) ***n.*** ⟦Fr, lit., passes everywhere⟧ **1** that which passes or allows passage everywhere **2** a passkey or master key **3** a mat used in mounting pictures **4** a picture mounting in which glass, picture, backing, and often a mat are bound together, as by strips of gummed paper along the edges **5** the gummed paper used for such a mounting

passe·pied (päs pyā′) ***n.*** ⟦Fr < *passer,* PASS[2] + *pied* (< L *pes*), FOOT⟧ **1** a lively, 17th-cent. French dance, similar to the minuet but faster in tempo **2** the music for this

pass·er·by (pas′ər bī′) ***n.,*** *pl.* **pass′ers·by′** a person who passes by: also written **passer-by,** *pl.* **passers-by**

pas·ser·ine (pas′ər in, -īn′) ***adj.*** ⟦L *passerinus* < *passer,* a sparrow⟧ of or pertaining to an order (Passeriformes) of small or medium-sized, chiefly perching songbirds having grasping feet with the first toe directed backward: more than half of all birds are included —***n.*** any such bird

pas seul (pä sël′) ⟦Fr, solo dance⟧ *Ballet* a dance performed by one person

pass-fail (pas′fāl′) ***adj.*** *Educ.* of or designating a grading system in which "pass" or "fail" is recorded instead of a numerical or letter grade *[*a *pass-fail* course*]* —***n.*** such a grading system

pas·si·ble (pas′ə bəl) ***adj.*** ⟦OFr < LL(Ec) < pp. of L *pati,* to suffer: see PASSION⟧ that can feel or suffer: term used chiefly in theology *[*a *passible* divinity*]* —**pas′si·bil′i·ty** ***n.***

pas·sim (pas′im) ***adv.*** ⟦L⟧ here and there; in various parts (of a book, etc.)

pass·ing (pas′iŋ) ***adj.*** ⟦ME⟧ **1** going by, beyond, past, over, or through **2** lasting only a short time; short-lived; fleeting; momentary **3** casual; cursory; incidental [a *passing* remark] **4** satisfying given requirements or standards [a *passing* grade] **5** [Archaic] surpassing; extreme [a woman of *passing* beauty] —***adv.*** [Archaic] exceedingly; unusually; very ['tis *passing* strange] —***n.*** **1** the act of one that passes; specif., death **2** a means or place of passing —**in passing 1** without careful thought; casually **2** incidentally; by the way

passing note (*or* tone) *Music* a note not part of a harmonic scheme but introduced for ornamentation or for smoother transition from one tone or chord to another

passing shot *Tennis* a sharp shot sent past an opposing player who is at the net or moving toward it

pas·sion (pash′ən) ***n.*** ⟦OFr < LL(Ec) *passio,* a suffering, esp. that of Christ (< L *passus,* pp. of *pati,* to endure < IE base **pē-,* to harm > Gr *pēma,* destruction, L *paene,* scarcely): transl. of Gr *pathos*: see PATHOS⟧ **1** *a)* [Archaic] suffering or agony, as of a martyr *b)* [Now Rare] an account of this **2** [**P-**] *a)* the sufferings of Jesus, beginning with his agony in the garden of Gethsemane and continuing to his death on the Cross *b)* any of the Gospel narratives of Jesus' Passion and of accompanying events *c)* an artistic work, as an oratorio or a play, based on these narratives **3** *a)* any one of the emotions, as hate, grief, love, fear, joy, etc. *b)* [*pl.*] all such emotions collectively **4** extreme, compelling emotion; intense emotional drive or excitement; specif., *a)* great anger; rage; fury *b)* enthusiasm or fondness [a *passion* for music] *c)* strong love or affection *d)* sexual drive or desire; lust **5** the object of any strong desire or fondness **6** [Obs.] the condition of being acted upon, esp. by outside influences

SYN.—**passion** usually implies a strong emotion that has an overpowering or compelling effect [his *passions* overcame his reason]; **fervor** and **ardor** both imply emotion of burning intensity, **fervor** suggesting a constant glow of feeling [religious *fervor*], and **ardor**, a restless, flamelike emotion [the *ardors* of youth]; **enthusiasm** implies strongly favorable feelings for an object or cause and usually suggests eagerness in the pursuit of something [her *enthusiasm* for golf]; **zeal** implies intense enthusiasm for an object or cause, usually as displayed in vigorous and untiring activity in its support [a *zeal* for reform] See also **feeling**

pas·sion·al (-shə nəl) ***adj.*** of, characterized by, or due to passion

pas·sion·ate (pash′ə nit) ***adj.*** ⟦ME *passionat* < ML *passionatus*⟧ **1** having or showing strong feelings; full of passion **2** easily angered; hot-tempered **3** resulting from, expressing, or tending to arouse strong feeling; ardent; intense; impassioned [a *passionate* speech] **4** readily aroused to sexual activity; sensual **5** strong; vehement: said of an emotion —**pas′sion·ate·ly *adv.***

SYN.—**passionate** implies strong or violent emotion, often of an impetuous kind [a *passionate* rage]; **impassioned** suggests an expression of emotion that is deeply and sincerely felt [an *impassioned* plea for tolerance]; **ardent** and **fervent** suggest a fiery or glowing feeling of eagerness, enthusiasm, devotion, etc. [an *ardent* pursuit of knowledge, a *fervent* prayer]; **fervid** differs from **fervent** in often suggesting an outburst of intense feeling that is at a fever pitch [a vengeful, *fervid* hatred]

pas·sion·flow·er (pash′ən flou′ər) ***n.*** ⟦from the supposed resemblance of parts of the flowers to Jesus' wounds, crown of thorns, etc.⟧ any of a genus (*Passiflora*) of mostly climbing plants of the passionflower family, with red, yellow, green, white, or purple flowers and usually small, edible, yellow or purple, egg-shaped fruit —***adj.*** designating a family (Passifloraceae, order Violales) of mostly tendril-climbing, tropical, dicotyledonous plants, including the maypop

passion fruit the fruit of a passionflower

Pas·sion·ist (-ist) ***n.*** a member of a Roman Catholic congregation of contemplative religious promoting devotion to the Passion of Jesus: the congregation, founded (1720) in Italy, engages chiefly in missionary work

pas·sion·less (-lis) ***adj.*** free from passion or emotion; impassive; calm —**pas′sion·less·ly *adv.***

Passion play a religious play reenacting the Passion of Jesus

Passion Sunday 1 the fifth Sunday in Lent, two weeks before Easter Sunday: now also called **First Sunday of the Passion 2** *name for* PALM SUNDAY

Pas·sion·tide (-tīd′) ***n.*** the two-week period before Easter

pas·si·vate (pas′ə vāt′) ***vt.*** **-vat′ed, -vat′ing** ⟦fol. + -ATE[1]⟧ *Metallurgy* to treat (a metal) so as to form a protective coating on its surface and reduce its chemical activity —**pas′si·va′tion *n.*** —**pas′si·va′tor *n.***

pas·sive (pas′iv) ***adj.*** ⟦ME *passif* < L *passivus* < *passus*: see PASSION⟧ **1** influenced or acted upon without exerting influence or acting in return; inactive, but acted upon **2** offering no opposition or resistance; submissive; yielding; patient **3** taking no active part; inactive **4** not requiring or using electric power to function [*passive* audio speakers] **5** *a) Chem.* INERT (sense 3) *b)* resistant to corrosion **6** *Finance* of or relating to an investor not involved actively in management, policymaking, etc. [*passive* losses] **7** *Gram. a)* denoting the voice or form of a verb whose subject is the recipient (object) of the action of the verb: opposed to ACTIVE *b)* in or of the passive voice [in "The tree was struck by lightning," *was struck* is a *passive* construction] —***n.*** *Gram.* **1** the passive voice **2** a verb in this voice —**pas′sive·ly *adv.*** —**pas′sive·ness *n.***

pas·sive-ag·gres·sive (-ə gres′iv) ***adj.*** designating or of a kind of seemingly nonassertive behavior characterized by disguised aggression and resistance to the demands of others, esp. as expressed by procrastination or stubbornness

passive immunity 1 immunity (to a disease) acquired by the injection of antibodies from an animal or person who has acquired active immunity **2** temporary immunity acquired by a child from antibodies transferred from the mother, either while the child is in the womb or when the child drinks the mother's milk

passive resistance opposition to a government or occupying power by refusal to comply with orders, or by such nonviolent acts as voluntary fasting or public demonstrations

passive restraint any automatic, built-in system for the protection of automotive vehicle passengers during a crash, as a system using air bags

passive smoking involuntary inhalation of smoke, as by a nonsmoker, from a nearby cigarette, cigar, etc.

pas·siv·ism (pas′iv iz′əm) ***n.*** **1** passive behavior or characteristics **2** the principle of or belief in being passive —**pas′siv·ist** (-ist) ***n.***

pas·siv·i·ty (pa siv′ə tē) ***n.*** ⟦LL *passivitas*⟧ the state or quality of being passive; esp., inaction, inertia, submissiveness, etc.

pass·key (pas′kē′) ***n.*** **1** *a)* MASTER KEY *b)* SKELETON KEY **2** any private key

Pass·o·ver (pas′ō′vər) ***n.*** ⟦PASS[2] + OVER, used to transl. Heb *pesach*: see PASCH⟧ **1** a Jewish holiday (*Pesach*) celebrated for eight (or seven) days beginning on the 15th of Nisan and commemorating the deliverance of the ancient Hebrews from slavery in Egypt: Ex. 12 **2** [**p-**] PASCHAL LAMB[1] (sense 1)

pass·port (pas′pôrt′) ***n.*** ⟦Fr *passeport,* safe-conduct, orig., permission to leave or enter a port < *passer,* PASS[2] + *port,* PORT[1]⟧ **1** a government document issued to a citizen for travel abroad, subject to visa requirements, certifying identity and citizenship: it entitles the bearer to the protection of his or her own country and that of the countries visited **2** SAFE-CONDUCT (senses 1 & 2) **3** anything that enables a person to be accepted, admitted, etc.

☆**pass-through** (pas′thro͞o′) ***n.*** an opening in a wall, as between a kitchen and dining room, often with a shelf, as for passing food

pass·word (pas′wurd′) ***n.*** **1** a secret word or phrase used for identification, as by a soldier wishing to pass a guard **2** a sequence of characters that must be entered in order to gain access to electronically locked or protected computer or security systems, files, etc. **3** any means of gaining entrance, admission, etc.

Pas·sy (pá sē′) **1 Fré·dé·ric** (frā dā rēk′) 1822-1912; Fr. economist **2 Paul É·douard** (pôl ā dwȧr′) 1859-1940; Fr. phonetician: principal originator of the International Phonetic Alphabet: son of Frédéric

past (past, päst) ***vi., vt.*** *rare pp. of* PASS[2] —***adj.*** **1** gone by; ended; over [our *past* troubles] **2** of a former time; bygone **3** immediately preceding; just gone by [the *past* week] **4** having served formerly [a *past* chairman] **5** *Gram.* indicating an action completed or in progress at a former time, or a state or condition in existence at a former time —***n.*** **1** the time that has gone by; days, months, or years gone by **2** what has happened; the history, former life, or experiences of a person, group, or institution: often used to indicate a hidden or questionable past [a woman with a *past*] **3** *Gram. a)* the past tense *b)* a verb form in this tense —***prep.*** **1** beyond in time; later than [five *past* four] **2** beyond in space; farther on than **3** [Obs.] beyond in amount or degree; more than **4** beyond the extent, power, limits, scope, etc. of [*past* belief] —***adv.*** to and beyond a point in time or space; by; so as to pass —**not put it past someone** to judge that someone is not incapable of engaging in some specified action

pas·ta (päs′tə) ***n.*** ⟦It < LL < Gr *pastē*: see fol.⟧ **1** a flour paste or dough made of semolina and dried, as for spaghetti and macaroni, or used fresh, as for ravioli **2** any food or foods made of this

paste (pāst) ***n.*** ⟦ME *past* < OFr *paste* < LL *pasta* < Gr *pastē,* mess of barley porridge < *passein,* to sprinkle⟧ **1** *a)* dough used in making rich pastry *b)* PASTA **2** any of various soft, moist, smooth-textured substances [*toothpaste*] **3** a foodstuff, pounded or ground until fine and made creamy, soft, etc. [almond *paste*] **4** a jellylike candy **5** a mixture of flour or starch, water, and occasionally alum, resin, etc., used as an adhesive for paper or other light materials **6** the moistened clay used in manufacturing pottery and porcelain **7** *a)* a hard, brilliant glass containing oxide of lead, used in making artificial gems; strass *b)* such a gem or gems **8** [Slang] a blow, or punch, as with the fist —***vt.*** **past′ed, past′ing 1** to fasten or make adhere with paste **2** to cover with pasted material [to *paste* a wall with posters] **3** to insert or place (a portion of text, a file, etc. being stored on a computer's clipboard) within another portion of text, a file, etc. **4** [Slang] to hit; punch

paste·board (pāst′bôrd′) ***n.*** **1** a stiff material made of layers of paper pasted together or of pressed and dried paper pulp **2** [Slang] something made of pasteboard, as a playing card or ticket —***adj.*** **1** of or like pasteboard **2** flimsy; sham

pas·tel (pas tel′) ***n.*** ⟦Fr < It *pastello* < VL **pastellum,* dim. of LL *pasta,* PASTE⟧ **1** *a)* ground coloring matter mixed with gum and formed into a crayon *b)* such a crayon **2** a picture drawn with such crayons **3** drawing with pastels as an art form or medium **4** a soft, pale shade of any color —***adj.*** **1** soft and pale: said of colors **2** of pastel **3** drawn with pastels —**pas·tel·ist *n.*, pas·tel·list** (pas tel′ist, pas′tel ist)

past·er (pās′tər) ***n.*** **1** a person or thing that pastes ☆**2** a slip of gummed paper used to paste on or over something; sticker

pas·tern (pas′tərn) ***n.*** ⟦ME *pastron* < MFr *pasturon* < *pasture,* tether for cattle < VL **pastoria,* foot shackle, tether < L *pastorius,* pastoral < *pastor*: see PASTOR⟧ the part of the foot of a horse, sheep, etc. just above the hoof or toes

Pas·ter·nak (pas′tər nak′), **Boris (Leonidovich)** 1890-1960; Russ. poet & novelist

paste-up (pāst′up′) ***n.*** **1** a piece of paper or cardboard on which things are pasted to form a design, working diagram, etc. **2** a collage **3** *Printing* MECHANICAL

Pas·teur (pas tur′; *Fr* pȧs tėr′), **Louis** 1822-95; Fr. chemist & bacteriologist

pas·teur·ism (pas′tər iz′əm) ***n.*** the theories or methods of Louis Pasteur; specif., *a)* PASTEURIZATION *b)* the Pasteur treatment for rabies

pas·teur·i·za·tion (pas′chər i zā′shən, -tər-) ***n.*** ⟦Fr: see fol. & -ATION⟧ a method of destroying disease-producing bacteria and checking the activity of fermentative bacteria, as in milk, beer, or cider, by heating the liquid to a prescribed temperature for a specified period of time

pas·teur·ize (pas′chər īz′, -tər-) ***vt.*** **-ized′**, **-iz′ing** ⟦Fr *pasteuriser,* after Louis PASTEUR + *-iser,* -IZE⟧ to subject (milk, beer, etc.) to pasteurization —**pas′teur·iz′er** ***n.***

Pasteur treatment Pasteur's method of preventing certain diseases, esp. rabies, by increasing the strength of successive inoculations with a specific weakened or attenuated virus

pas·tic·cio (pas tē′chō, päs-) ***n.,*** *pl.* **-tic′ci** (-chē) or **-tic′cios** ⟦It < ML *pasticius* < VL **pasticius,* composed of paste < LL *pasta,* PASTE⟧ PASTICHE

pas·tiche (pas tēsh′, päs-) ***n.*** ⟦Fr < It *pasticcio*⟧ **1** *a)* a literary, artistic, or musical composition made up of bits from various sources; potpourri *b)* a literary, artistic, or musical composition intended to imitate or caricature another artist's style **2** a jumbled mixture; hodgepodge

pas·ti·cheur (pas tē′shər; *Fr* pȧs tē shėr′) ***n.*** ⟦Fr⟧ a writer, artist, musician, etc. who makes pastiches

pas·tie (pas′tē) ***n.*** *alt. sp. of* PASTY[2]

pas·ties[1] (pas′tēz′) ***n.*** *pl. of* PASTY[2]

past·ies[2] (pās′tēz′) ***pl.n.*** a pair of small adhesive coverings for the nipples, worn by stripteasers, exotic dancers, etc.

pas·tille (pas tēl′) ***n.*** ⟦Fr < L *pastillus,* little roll, lozenge < base of *pascere,* to feed: see FOOD⟧ **1** a small tablet or lozenge containing medicine, flavoring, etc. **2** a pellet of aromatic paste, burned for fumigating or deodorizing **3** pastel for crayons **4** a crayon of pastel Also **pas·til** (pas′til)

pas·time (pas′tīm′) ***n.*** ⟦LME *passe tyme,* transl. of Fr *passe-temps*⟧ a way of spending spare time pleasantly; anything done for recreation or diversion, as a hobby

pas·ti·na (päs tē′nə) ***n.*** ⟦It, dim. of *pasta,* PASTA⟧ pasta in very small pieces, usually served in soup

past·i·ness (pās′tē nis) ***n.*** a pasty quality or condition

pas·tis (pas tēs′) ***n.*** ⟦Fr < ?⟧ a French liqueur flavored with licorice and aniseed

past master **1** a person who formerly held the position of master, as in a lodge or club **2** ⟦for *passed master*⟧ a person who has had long experience in some occupation, art, etc.; expert

pas·tor (pas′tər, päs′-) ***n.*** ⟦ME *pastour* < OFr < L *pastor,* shepherd (LL(Ec), minister of a congregation) < *pascere,* to feed: see FOOD⟧ a person, as a priest or minister, in spiritual and jurisdictional charge of a parish, church, congregation, or community —***vt.*** to serve as pastor of

pas·to·ral (-əl) ***adj.*** ⟦ME *pastoralle* < L *pastoralis* < *pastor,* a shepherd: see prec.⟧ **1** of shepherds or their work, way of life, etc. **2** of or portraying rural life or, formerly, a highly conventionalized form of rustic life among shepherds, usually in an idealized way **3** of pastoral literature or a pastoral **4** characteristic of rural life, idealized as peaceful, simple, and natural **5** of or relating to a pastor —***n.*** **1** a piece of literature dealing, usually in an idealized way, with rural life; formerly, specif., a poem, play, etc. treating the rustic lives and loves of shepherds in a conventionalized, artificial manner **2** such writing as a literary form **3** a pastoral picture or scene **4** an official letter or document, as on doctrine or religious observance, issued by a bishop or group of bishops to persons within their jurisdiction **5** *Music* PASTORALE —***SYN.*** RURAL —**pas′to·ral·ism′** ***n.*** —**pas′to·ral·ly** ***adv.***

pas·to·ra·le (pas′tə ral′, -räl′, -rä′lē; *It* päs′tô rä′le) ***n.,*** *pl.* **-ra′les** or It. **-ra′li** (-lē) ⟦It, lit., pastoral⟧ *Music* **1** a composition in simple and idyllic style suggesting rural scenes **2** a forerunner of opera consisting of a dramatic performance on an idyllic subject with incidental music

pas·to·ral·ist (pas′tər əl əst) ***n.*** **1** a person who raises livestock, esp. a nomadic herder **2** a writer whose style or subjects are pastoral

pas·tor·ate (pas′tər it) ***n.*** **1** *a)* the position, rank, or duties of a pastor *b)* a pastor's term of office: also **pas′tor·ship′** **2** the whole body of pastors or a specific group of these

☆**pas·to·ri·um** (pas tôr′ē əm) ***n.*** ⟦< neut. of L *pastorius,* of a shepherd < *pastor:* see PASTOR⟧ [South] a Protestant, esp. Baptist, parsonage

past participle *Gram.* a participle used *a)* with auxiliaries to express, typically, completed action or a time or state gone by (Ex.: *spoken* in "he has spoken") *b)* with auxiliaries to form the passive voice (Ex.: *eaten* in "the snails were all eaten in a moment") *c)* as an adjective (Ex.: *polished* in "polished brass")

past perfect **1** a tense indicating an action as completed or a state as having ended before a specified or implied time in the past; pluperfect **2** a verb form in this tense (Ex.: had gone)

pas·tra·mi (pə strä′mē) ***n.*** ⟦E Yiddish *pastrame* < Pol *bastramy,* dried meat, ult. < Turk *basdyrma*⟧ highly spiced smoked beef, esp. from a shoulder cut

pas·try (pās′trē) ***n.,*** *pl.* **-tries** ⟦see PASTE & -ERY⟧ **1** flour dough or paste made with shortening and used for the crust of pies, tarts, etc. **2** foods made with this, as pies and tarts **3** broadly, all fancy baked goods, including cakes, sweet rolls, etc. **4** a single pie, cake, croissant, etc.

pastry bag an open conical bag with a pierced tip at the narrow end, used for decorating cakes with icing, pressing out dough into various shapes for cookies, etc.

pas·tur·a·ble (pas′chər ə bəl; pas′tyər-) ***adj.*** that can be used for pasture

pas·tur·age (-ij) ***n.*** ⟦OFr: see fol. & -AGE⟧ **1** PASTURE **2** the pasturing of cattle

pas·ture (pas′chər) ***n.*** ⟦OFr < LL *pastura* < L *pascere,* to feed: see FOOD⟧ **1** grass or other growing plants used as food by grazing animals **2** *a)* ground suitable for grazing *b)* a field, plot, etc. set aside for this —***vt.*** **-tured**, **-tur·ing** **1** to put (cattle, etc.) out to graze in a pasture **2** to graze or feed on (grass, etc.) —***vi.*** to feed on growing grass or herbage —**put out to pasture** **1** to put in a pasture to graze **2** to allow or compel to retire from work —**pas′tur·er** ***n.***

pas·ture·land (pas′chər land′) ***n.*** PASTURE (***n.*** 2)

past·y[1] (pās′tē) ***adj.*** **past′i·er**, **past′i·est** of or like paste in color or texture

pas·ty[2] (pas′tē) ***n.,*** *pl.* **pas′ties** ⟦ME *pastee* < OFr *pastée* < *paste,* PASTE⟧ [Brit.] a pie, esp. a meat pie

pat[1] (pat) ***adj.*** ⟦prob. < fol.⟧ **1** apt; timely; opportune **2** exactly suitable **3** so glibly plausible as to seem contrived **4** designating a poker hand to which no cards are drawn because of the unlikelihood of improving it —***adv.*** in a pat manner —**have (down) pat** [Informal] to know or have memorized thoroughly —☆**stand pat** **1** *Poker* to draw no further cards and play the hand as dealt **2** [Informal] to refuse to turn aside from an opinion, course of action, etc. —**pat′ness** ***n.***

pat[2] (pat) ***n.*** ⟦ME *patte,* prob. echoic⟧ **1** a quick, gentle tap, touch, or stroke with the hand or some flat object **2** the sound made by this **3** a small lump or mass, as of butter **4** a mass of animal dung —***vt.*** **pat′ted**, **pat′ting** **1** *a)* to tap, touch, or stroke quickly or gently, esp. with the hand, as in affection, sympathy, or encouragement *b)* to tap or stroke lightly with something flat **2** to flatten, shape, apply, etc. by patting —***vi.*** **1** to pat a surface **2** to move along with a patting sound, as in running —**pat someone down** FRISK (***vt.*** 2) —**pat on the back** **1** a compliment or encouragement **2** to compliment or praise

pat[3] *abbrev.* **1** patent **2** patented

☆**PAT** *abbrev.* ⟦*p(oint) a(fter) t(ouchdown)*⟧ CONVERSION (sense 3)

pa·ta·gi·um (pə tā′jē əm) ***n.,*** *pl.* **-gi·a** (-ə) ⟦ModL < L, gold edging of a tunic, border < Gr *patageion* < *patagein,* to rustle⟧ **1** a fold of skin between the fore and hind limbs of bats, flying squirrels, etc., enabling them to fly or glide through the air **2** a fold of skin between the shoulder and forepart of a bird's wing —**pa·ta′gi·al** ***adj.***

Pat·a·go·ni·a (pat′ə gō′nē ə, -gōn′yə) dry, grassy region in S South America, east of the Andes, including the S parts of Argentina and Chile: often restricted to the portion, *c.* 250,000 sq mi (647,498 sq km), in Argentina —**Pat′a·go′ni·an** (-gō′nē ən, -gōn′yən) ***adj., n.***

pa·ta·phys·ics (pa′tə fiz′iks) ***n.*** ⟦< Fr *pataphysique,* coined by Alfred JARRY, apparently altered < Gr *ta epi ta metaphysika,* the (works) superimposed on the metaphysics: see METAPHYSICS⟧ the study of a realm beyond that of metaphysics: a notion devised by French absurdist writers as a parody of modern science —**pa′ta·phys′i·cal** ***adj.*** —**pa′ta·phy·si′cian** ***n.***

patch[1] (pach) ***n.*** ⟦ME *pacche,* prob. var. of *peche,* a piece < OFr *pieche,* var. of *pece, piece,* PIECE⟧ **1** a piece of material applied to cover or mend a hole or tear or to strengthen a weak spot **2** a dressing applied to a wound or sore **3** a pad or shield worn over an eye, as for protection **4** a surface area differing from its surroundings in nature or appearance *[patches* of snow on the ground*]* **5** a small plot of ground *[*a potato *patch]* **6** *a)* a small piece of any material; scrap; bit; remnant *b)* BEAUTY SPOT (sense 1) **7** the connection of two circuits, pieces of electronic equipment, etc. with a cable (**patch cord**) having plugs or clips on each end, specif. such a connection (*phone patch*) of telephone and radio equipment **8** SHOULDER PATCH **9** [Informal] an indefinite period of time that is relatively short and of a specified character *[*a rough *patch* in their marriage*]* **10** *Comput.* a number of instructions added to a program that has already been translated into machine language, as to correct an error **11** *Pharmacy* an adhesive pad containing a drug or hormone that is to be steadily absorbed through the skin into the bloodstream —***vt.*** **1** to put a patch or patches on **2** to serve as a patch for **3** to form or make by the use of patches *[*to *patch* a quilt*]* **4** to produce or piece together roughly, crudely, or hurriedly: often with *up* or *together* **5** *a)* to connect (electronic circuits, equipment, etc.), as with patch cords *b)* to add (a person) *in* or *into* an electronic communication circuit, as for a conference call or radio transmission —***vi.*** to make electronic connections, as with patch cords —***SYN.*** MEND —**not a patch on** [Informal] not nearly so good as; not of comparable quality as *[*the sequel is *not a patch on* the original movie*]* —**patch up** to bring to an end or settle (differences, a quarrel, etc.) —**patch′er** ***n.***

patch[2] (pach) ***n.*** ⟦prob. < It *paccheo,* dial. var. of *pazzo,* crazy (< ? L *patiens,* sick: see PATIENT): altered by assoc. with prec.⟧ [Archaic] **1** a court jester **2** any clown or fool

patch·ou·li (pach′o͝o lē, pe cho͞o′lē) ***n.*** ⟦Fr, altered < E *patch leaf,* part transl. of Tamil *paccili,* lit., green leaf < *paccu,* green + *ilai,* a leaf⟧ **1** an East Indian mint (*Pogostemon cablin*) that yields a heavy, dark-brown, fragrant oil **2** a perfume made from this oil Often sp. **patch′ou·ly**

patch pocket a pocket made by sewing a patch of shaped material to the outside of a garment

patch reef a relatively small, isolated coral reef

patch test *Med.* a test for determining allergy to a specific substance, made by attaching a sample of it, often a small piece of material saturated with the substance, to the skin and observing the reaction

patch·work (pach′wurk′) *n.* 1 anything formed of irregular, incongruous, odd, or miscellaneous parts; jumble 2 a quilt or other covering made of patches of cloth, etc. sewn together at their edges 3 any design or surface like this

patch·y (pach′ē) *adj.* **patch′i·er, patch′i·est** 1 *a)* made up of or characterized by patches *b)* forming or like patches 2 giving the effect of patches; not consistent or uniform in quality; irregular —**patch′i·ly** *adv.* —**patch′i·ness** *n.*

PATCO (pat′kō) *abbrev.* Professional Air Traffic Controllers' Organization

patd *abbrev.* patented

pat-down (pat′doun′) *n.* the act or an instance of patting down, or frisking, someone

pate (pāt) *n.* ⟦ME < ?⟧ 1 the head, esp. the top of the head 2 the brain or intellect A humorous or derogatory term

pâte (pät) *n.* ⟦Fr⟧ paste; esp., the clay paste used in making pottery or porcelain

pâ·té (pä tā′, pa-) *n.* ⟦Fr⟧ 1 a meat pie 2 a meat paste or spread

-pat·ed (pāt′id) *combining form* having a (specified kind of) pate, or head [*bald-pated*]

pâ·té de foie gras (pä tā′ də fwä′ grä′) ⟦Fr⟧ a paste or spread made of the livers of fattened geese

pa·tel·la (pə tel′ə) *n., pl.* **-las** or **-lae** (-ē) ⟦L, dim. of *patina,* a pan < Gr *patanē* < **petana* < IE base **pet-,* to spread out > FATHOM, L *patere*⟧ 1 a small, shallow pan used in ancient Rome 2 a movable bone at the front of the human knee 3 *Biol.* any panlike formation —**pa·tel′lar** *adj.*

patellar reflex *Med.* a normal reflex kick with extension of the leg at the knee, produced by sharply tapping the tendon below the patella

pa·tel·li·form (pə tel′ə fôrm′) *adj.* ⟦< PATELLA + -FORM⟧ 1 having the form of a flattened cone 2 having the shape of a limpet shell

pat·en (pat′'n) *n.* ⟦ME < OFr *patene* < L *patina:* see PATELLA⟧ a metal disk or plate, esp. one of precious metal for holding the bread in a Eucharistic service

pa·ten·cy (pāt′'n sē, pat′-) *n.* ⟦ML *patentia*⟧ 1 the state or quality of being patent, or obvious 2 *Med.* the state of being open or unobstructed

pat·ent (pat′'nt; *for adj. 2-4 & 8* pāt′'nt, pat′-; *Brit usually* pāt′'nt) *adj.* ⟦ME < MFr & L: MFr *patent* < L *patens,* prp. of *patere,* to be open: see PATELLA⟧ 1 *a)* open to examination by the public (said of a document granting some right or rights, as to land, a franchise, an office, or, now esp., an invention) [*letters patent*] *b)* granted or appointed by letters patent 2 open to all; generally accessible or available 3 obvious; plain; evident [*a patent lie*] 4 open or unobstructed 5 *a)* protected by a patent; patented *b)* of or having to do with patents or the granting of patents [*patent law*] 6 produced or sold as a proprietary product: cf. PATENT MEDICINE 7 new, unusual, individual, etc.: also **patented** 8 *Bot., Zool.* spreading out or open; patulous —*n.* 1 an official document open to public examination and granting a certain right or privilege; letters patent; esp., a document granting the exclusive right to produce, sell, or get profit from an invention, process, etc. for a specific number of years 2 *a)* the right so granted *b)* the thing protected by such a right; patented article or process 3 public land, or title to such land, granted to a person by letters patent 4 any exclusive right, title, or license —*vt.* 1 to grant a patent to or for 2 to secure exclusive right to produce, use, and sell (an invention or process) by a patent; get a patent for —**pat·ent·a·ble** (pat′'nt ə bəl) *adj.*

patent ambiguity (pat′'nt, pāt′-) *Law* uncertainty existing where language employed in an instrument is capable of more than one meaning: see LATENT AMBIGUITY

pat·ent·ee (pat′'n tē′) *n.* a person who has been granted a patent

☆**patent leather** (pat′'nt) leather with a hard, glossy, usually black finish: made by a process formerly patented

pa·tent·ly (pāt′'nt lē, pat′-) *adv.* in a patent manner; clearly; obviously; openly

patent medicine (pat′'nt) a trademarked medical preparation that can be bought without a physician's prescription

patent office (pat′'nt) an office or department for administering patent and trademark laws

pat·en·tor (pat′'n tər) *n.* the grantor of a patent

patent right (pat′'nt) an exclusive right established by patent, esp. the right to an invention

pa·ter (pāt′ər) *n.* ⟦L, FATHER⟧ [Informal, Chiefly Brit.] father: now only a humorous usage

Pa·ter (pāt′ər), **Walter (Horatio)** 1839-94; Eng. essayist & critic

pa·ter·fa·mil·i·as (pāt′ər fə mil′ē əs, pät′-) *n., pl.* **pa′tres′fa·mil′i·as** (pā′ trēz′-) ⟦L⟧ the father of a family; male head of a household

pa·ter·nal (pə tur′nəl) *adj.* ⟦ML *paternalis* < L *paternus* < *pater,* FATHER⟧ 1 of, like, or characteristic of a father or fatherhood; fatherly 2 derived, received, or inherited from a father 3 related through the father's side of the family [*paternal* grandparents] —**pa·ter′nal·ly** *adv.*

pa·ter·nal·ism (-iz′əm) *n.* ⟦prec. + -ISM⟧ a manner, often a patronizing or domineering one, of governing a country, managing employees, etc. that is suggestive of a father's relationship to his children —**pa·ter′nal·ist** *n., adj.* —**pa·ter′nal·is′tic** *adj.* —**pa·ter′nal·is′ti·cal·ly** *adv.*

pa·ter·ni·ty (pə tur′nə tē) *n.* ⟦OFr *paternité* < LL *paternitas* < L *paternus,* paternal < *pater,* FATHER⟧ 1 the state of being a father; fatherhood 2 male parentage; paternal origin 3 origin or authorship in general

paternity leave temporary leave from work granted to the father of a newborn

pa·ter·nos·ter (pät′ər näs′tər, pat′-) *n.* ⟦ME < ML(Ec) < LL(Ec) *Pater noster,* opening words of the Lord's Prayer < L *pater,* FATHER + *noster,* our: see NOSTRUM⟧ 1 the Lord's Prayer, esp. in Latin: often **Pater Noster** 2 *a)* one of the large beads of a rosary on which the Lord's Prayer is said *b)* [Archaic] a rosary

Pat·er·son (pat′ər sən) ⟦after W. *Paterson* (1745-1806), state governor⟧ city in NE N.J., on the Passaic River

path[1] (path, päth) *n.* ⟦ME < OE *pæth,* akin to Ger *pfad,* Du *pad,* prob. early Gmc loanword < Iran (as in Avestan *path-*) < IE base **pent(h)-,* to step, go > FIND, L *pons,* bridge⟧ 1 a track or way worn by footsteps; trail 2 a walk or way for the use of people on foot, as in a park or garden 3 a line of movement; course taken [the *path* of the meteor] 4 a course or manner of conduct, thought, or procedure —**path′less** *adj.*

path[2] *abbrev.* 1 pathological 2 pathology

Pa·than (pə tän′, pət hän′) *n.* ⟦Hindi *paṭhān* < Afghan *pĕstānē,* pl. of *pĕştūn,* an Afghan⟧ PASHTUN

path·break·ing or **path-break·ing** (path′brāk′iŋ) *adj.* pioneering; groundbreaking; innovative

pa·thet·ic (pə thet′ik) *adj.* ⟦LL *patheticus* < Gr *pathētikos,* akin to *pathos,* suffering, PATHOS⟧ 1 expressing, arousing, or intended to arouse pity, sorrow, sympathy, or compassion; pitiful 2 pitifully unsuccessful, ineffective, etc. [a *pathetic* performance] 3 of the emotions: now only in PATHETIC FALLACY Also **pa·thet′i·cal** —*SYN.* MOVING —**pa·thet′i·cal·ly** *adv.*

pathetic fallacy ⟦coined (1856) by John RUSKIN⟧ in literature, the attribution of human feelings and characteristics to inanimate things (Ex.: the angry sea, a stubborn door)

☆**path·find·er** (path′fīn′dər) *n.* one who makes a path or way where none had existed, as in an unknown region, wilderness, etc.

-path·i·a (path′ē ə) ⟦ModL⟧ *combining form* [Obs.] -PATHY (sense 2*a*)

-path·ic (path′ik) ⟦see -PATHY & -IC⟧ *combining form* 1 feeling or suffering in a (specified) way or because of a (specified) condition 2 of or relating to a (specified) approach to disease or treatment

path·o- (path′ō, -ə) ⟦< Gr *pathos:* see PATHOS⟧ *combining form* suffering, disease, feeling [*pathogenesis*]: also, before a vowel, **path-**

path·o·gen (path′ə jən) *n.* ⟦prec. + -GEN⟧ any agent, esp. a microorganism, able to cause disease: also **path′o·gene′** (-jēn′)

path·o·gen·e·sis (path′ə jen′ə sis) *n.* ⟦ModL: see PATHO- & -GENESIS⟧ the production or development of a disease: also **pa·thog·e·ny** (pə thäj′ə nē) —**path′o·ge·net′ic** (-jə net′ik) *adj.*

path·o·gen·ic (-jen′ik) *adj.* producing disease —**path′o·ge·nic′i·ty** (-jə nis′ə tē) *n.* —**path′o·gen′i·cal·ly** *adv.*

pa·thog·no·mon·ic (pə thäg′nō män′ik) *adj.* ⟦Gr *pathognōmonikos* < *pathos,* disease (see PATHOS) + *gnōmonikos,* able to judge < *gnōmōn,* one who knows: see GNOMON⟧ indicating or typical of a particular disease

pathol *abbrev.* 1 pathological 2 pathology

path·o·log·i·cal (path′ə läj′i kəl) *adj.* 1 of pathology; of or concerned with diseases 2 due to or involving disease 3 governed by a compulsion; compulsive [a *pathological* liar] Also **path′o·log′ic** —**path′o·log′i·cal·ly** *adv.*

pa·thol·o·gy (pə thäl′ə jē, pa-) *n., pl.* **-gies** ⟦< Fr *pathologie* or ModL *pathologia* < Gr *pathologia:* see fol. & -LOGY⟧ 1 the branch of medicine that deals with the nature of disease, esp. with the structural and functional changes caused by disease 2 all the conditions, processes, or results of a particular disease 3 any abnormal variation from a sound or proper condition —**pa·thol′o·gist** *n.*

pa·thos (pā′thäs′, -thôs′) *n.* ⟦Gr *pathos,* suffering, disease, feeling, akin to *pathein, paschein,* to suffer, feel < IE base **kwenth-,* to suffer, endure > OIr *cessaim,* I suffer⟧ 1 [Rare] suffering 2 the quality in something experienced or observed which arouses feelings of pity, sorrow, sympathy, or compassion 3 the feeling aroused

SYN.—**pathos** names that quality, in a real situation or in a literary or artistic work, which evokes sympathy and a sense of sorrow or pity; **bathos** applies to a false or overdone pathos that is absurd in its effect; **poignancy** implies an emotional quality that is keenly felt, often to the point of being sharply painful

path·way (path′wā′) *n.* PATH[1]

-pa·thy (pə thē) ⟦ModL < -*pathia* < Gr -*patheia* < *pathos:* see PATHOS⟧ *combining form* 1 feeling, suffering [*telepathy*] 2 *a)* disease [*neuropathy*] *b)* treatment of disease [*osteopathy, homeopathy*]

Pa·ti·a·la (put′ē ä′lə) former state of N India: since 1956, part of Punjab

pa·tience (pā′shəns) *n.* ⟦ME *pacience* < OFr < L *patientia* < *pati,* to suffer: see PASSION⟧ 1 the state, quality, or fact of being patient; specif., *a)* the will or ability to wait or endure without complaint *b)* steadiness, endurance, or perseverance in the performance of a task 2 [Chiefly Brit.] SOLITAIRE (sense 3)

SYN.—**patience** implies the bearing of suffering, provocation, delay, tediousness, etc. with calmness and self-control [her *patience* with children]; **endurance** stresses the capacity to bear suffering or hardship [Job's *endurance* of his afflictions]; **fortitude** suggests the resolute endurance that results from firm, sustained courage [the *fortitude* of the pioneers]; **forbearance** implies restraint under provocation or a refraining from retaliation for a wrong [he acted with *forbearance* toward the hecklers]; **stoicism** suggests such endurance of suffering without flinching as to indicate an almost austere indifference to pain or pleasure —*ANT.* **impatience**

pa·tient (pā′shənt) *adj.* ⟦ME *pacient* < OFr < L *patiens,* patient, prp. of *pati:*

see PASSION⟧ 1 bearing or enduring pain, trouble, etc. without complaining or losing self-control 2 refusing to be provoked or angered, as by an insult; forbearing; tolerant 3 calmly tolerating delay, confusion, inefficiency, etc. 4 able to wait calmly for something desired 5 showing or characterized by patience [*a patient face*] 6 steady; diligent; persevering [*a patient worker*] 7 [Rare] receiving action; passive —*n.* 1 a person receiving care or treatment, esp. from a doctor 2 [Rare] a person who receives an action 3 *Gram.* the word or words designating the person or thing affected by the action of the verb —**patient of** 1 capable of bearing (fatigue, thirst, etc.) 2 admitting of or having (a certain meaning) —**pa′tient·ly** *adv.*

pat·i·na[1] (pat′'n ə) *n., pl.* **-nae′** (-nē′) ⟦L⟧ *var. of* PATEN

pat·i·na[2] (pat′'n ə, pə tē′nə) *n.* ⟦Fr < It, orig., tarnish (on a metal plate), prob. < L, pan: see PATELLA⟧ 1 a fine crust or film on bronze or copper, usually green or greenish-blue, formed by natural oxidation and often valued as being ornamental 2 any thin coating or color change resulting from age, as on old wood or silver

pat·i·nate (pat′'n āt′) *vt.* **-nat′ed, -nat′ing** to produce a patina on —*vi.* to take on a patina Also **pat′i·nize′, -nized′, -niz′ing** —**pat′i·na′tion** *n.*

pat·ine (pat′'n; *for 2* pə tēn′) *n.* 1 PATEN 2 PATINA[2]

pa·ti·o (pat′ē ō′, pät′-) *n., pl.* **-ti·os′** ⟦Sp < VL **patium*, open area, aphetic for L *spatium*, SPACE, infl. by *patere*, to lie open, stretch out: see FATHOM⟧ ☆1 a courtyard or inner area open to the sky, as in Spanish and Spanish-American architecture ☆2 an area, esp. a paved area adjacent to a house, for outdoor lounging, dining, etc.

pa·tis·se·rie (pə tis′ə rē; *Fr* pä tēs rē′) *n.* ⟦Fr *pâtisserie* < MFr < OFr **pastiz*, pastry (< VL *pasticium* < LL *pasta*, dough, PASTE) + *-erie*, -ERY⟧ 1 fancy pastry 2 a shop where such pastry is made and sold

pâ·tis·sier (pä tēs yā′) *n.* ⟦Fr⟧ a chef or baker specializing in cakes, tarts, and other pastry; pastry chef

Pat·mos (pat′məs, pät′-) island of the Dodecanese, in the SE Aegean: traditionally where St. John wrote the Book of Revelation (Rev. 1:9): 13 sq mi (34 sq km)

Pat·na (put′nə, pat′-) city in NE India, on the Ganges: capital of Bihar state

pa·tois (pa′twä′; *Fr* pȧ twȧ′) *n., pl.* **-tois′** (-twäz′; *Fr*, -twȧ′) ⟦Fr < OFr, uncultivated speech, akin to *patoier*, to shake paws, behave crudely < *pate*, paw, akin to Frank **pauta* > PAW[1]⟧ 1 a form of a language differing generally from the accepted standard, as a provincial or local dialect 2 JARGON[1] (sense 4)

Pa·ton (pāt′'n), **Alan (Stewart)** 1903-88; South African novelist

☆**pa·toot·ie** (pə to͞ot′ē) *n.* [Slang] 1 ⟦< *sweet patootie*, ? altered < *sweet potato*⟧ a sweetheart 2 the buttocks: a humorous usage: also **pa·toot′**

pat pend *abbrev.* patent pending

Pa·tras (pä träs′) 1 seaport in W Greece, on the Gulf of Patras 2 **Gulf of** arm of the Ionian Sea, in the NW Peloponnesus: Gr. name **Pá·trai** (pä′trē)

pa·tri- (pā′tri; -trə; pa′-) ⟦L < Gr *patri-* < *patēr*, FATHER⟧ *combining form* father [*patricide*]: also, before a vowel, **patr-**

pa·tri·arch (pā′trē ärk′) *n.* ⟦ME *patriarche* < OFr < LL(Ec) *patriarcha* < Gr(Ec) *patriarchēs* (transl. of Heb *roshe-avot*) < Gr *patria*, family < *patēr*, FATHER + *-archēs* < *archein*, to rule⟧ 1 the father and ruler of a family or tribe, as one of the founders of the ancient Hebrew families: in the Bible, Abraham, Isaac, Jacob, and Jacob's twelve sons were patriarchs 2 a person regarded as the founder or father of a colony, religion, business, etc. 3 a man of great age and dignity 4 the oldest individual of a class or group 5 [*often* **P-**] *a)* a bishop in the early Christian Church, esp. a bishop of Rome, Constantinople, Alexandria, Antioch, or Jerusalem *b) R.C.Ch.* the pope (**Patriarch of the West**), or any of certain bishops ranking immediately after him, as the bishops of Constantinople, Alexandria, Antioch, and Jerusalem *c) Eastern Orthodox Ch.* the highest-ranking bishop at Constantinople, Alexandria, Antioch, Jerusalem, Moscow, Bucharest, etc. *d)* the jurisdictional head of any of certain other churches, as the Coptic, Nestorian, Armenian, etc. *e) Mormon Ch.* a high-ranking member of the Melchizedek priesthood

pa·tri·ar·chal (pā′trē är′kəl) *adj.* of or having to do with a patriarch or patriarchy: now often used with reference to a society, institution, etc. regarded as being under the repressive domination of men [*patriarchal values of the Victorian family*]

pa·tri·arch·ate (pā′trē är′kit, -kāt′) *n.* ⟦ML(Ec) *patriarchatus*⟧ 1 the position, rank, jurisdiction, territory, etc. of a patriarch 2 PATRIARCHY

pa·tri·arch·y (-är′kē) *n., pl.* **-arch′ies** ⟦Gr *patriarchia:* see PATRIARCH⟧ 1 a form of social organization in which the father or the eldest male is recognized as the head of the family or tribe, descent and kinship being traced through the male line 2 government, rule, or domination by men, as in a family or tribe —**pa′tri·ar′chic** *adj.*

pa·tri·ate (pā′trē āt′) *vt.* **-at′ed, -at′ing** ⟦back-form. < REPATRIATE⟧ [Cdn.] to return or turn over full legislative powers, as of amendment, to (a constitution) that were formerly held by the government of another country: a term used in Canada to describe the action of taking over the power to amend the constitution from the British parliament in 1982 —**pa′tri·a′tion** *n.*

Pa·tri·cia (pə trish′ə, -trē′shə) *n.* ⟦L, fem. of *patricius:* see fol.⟧ a feminine name: dim. *Pat, Patsy, Patti, Patty*

pa·tri·cian (pə trish′ən) *n.* ⟦ME *patricion* < MFr *patricien* < L *patricius* < *patres*, senators, lit., fathers, pl. of *pater*, FATHER⟧ 1 in ancient Rome *a)* a member of any of the ancient Roman citizen families *b)* later, a member of the nobility (opposed to PLEBEIAN) *c)* a member of a class of honorary nobility of the later Empire *d)* a chief administrator in the Roman provinces in Africa and Italy 2 a person of high rank in some medieval Italian republics and in certain free cities of the German Empire 3 any person of high social rank; aristocrat —*adj.* ⟦MFr *patricien*⟧ 1 of or characteristic of patricians 2 noble; aristocratic

pa·tri·ci·ate (pə trish′ē it, -āt′; -trish′it) *n.* ⟦ML *patriciatus* < L *patricius*⟧ 1 the rank or position of a patrician 2 the patrician class; aristocracy

pat·ri·cide (pa′trə sīd′, pā′-) *n.* ⟦ML *patricida:* see PATRI- & -CIDE⟧ 1 the act of murdering one's father 2 a person who does this —**pat′ri·ci′dal** *adj.*

Pat·rick[1] (pa′trik) *n.* ⟦L *patricius*, a patrician⟧ a masculine name: dim. *Paddy, Pat, Rick*; fem. *Patricia*

Pat·rick[2] (pa′trik), Saint (A.D. 385?-461?); Brit. missionary in, and a patron saint of, Ireland: his day is March 17

pat·ri·lin·e·al (pa′trə lin′ē əl, pā′trə-) *adj.* ⟦PATRI- + LINEAL⟧ designating or of descent, kinship, or derivation through the father instead of the mother —**pat′ri·lin′e·al·ly** *adv.*

pat·ri·lo·cal (pa′trə lō′kəl) *adj.* of or relating to a housing pattern or custom in which a married couple lives with or near the husband's parents

pat·ri·mo·ny (pa′trə mō′nē) *n., pl.* **-nies** ⟦ME *patrimoigne* < OFr *patrimoine* < L *patrimonium* < *pater*, FATHER + *-monium*, -MONY⟧ 1 property inherited from one's father or ancestors 2 property endowed to an institution, as a church 3 anything inherited, as a characteristic or tendency —**SYN.** HERITAGE —**pat′ri·mo′ni·al** *adj.*

pa·tri·ot (pā′trē ət, -ät′; *chiefly Brit, also* pa′-) *n.* ⟦Fr *patriote* < LL *patriota*, fellow countryman < Gr *patriōtēs* < *patris*, fatherland < *patēr*, FATHER⟧ one who loves and loyally or zealously supports one's own country —**pa′tri·ot′ic** (-ät′ik) *adj.* —**pa′tri·ot′i·cal·ly** *adv.*

pa·tri·ot·ism (pā′trē ə tiz′əm) *n.* ⟦prec. + -ISM⟧ love and loyal or zealous support of one's country

☆**Patriot's Day** the third Monday in April, a legal holiday in Me. and Mass. commemorating the battles of Lexington and Concord (April 19, 1775)

pa·tris·tic (pə tris′tik) *adj.* ⟦Ger *patristisch* < L *patres*, pl. of *pater*, FATHER⟧ of the Fathers of the early Christian Church or their writings and doctrines: also **pa·tris′ti·cal** —**pa·tris′ti·cal·ly** *adv.*

Pa·tro·clus (pə trō′kləs, pa′trō-) *n.* ⟦L < Gr *Patroklos*⟧ *Gr. Myth.* a Greek warrior and friend of Achilles, slain by Hector in the Trojan War

pa·trol (pə trōl′) *vt., vi.* **-trolled′, -trol′ling** ⟦Fr *patrouiller*, altered < OFr *patouiller*, to paddle, puddle, patrol < *pate*, paw: see PATOIS⟧ to make a regular and repeated circuit of (an area, town, camp, etc.) in guarding or inspecting —*n.* ⟦Fr *patrouille* < the *v.*⟧ 1 the act of patrolling 2 a person or persons patrolling 3 *a)* a small group of soldiers sent on a mission, as for reconnaissance *b)* a group of ships, airplanes, etc. used in guarding 4 a subdivision of a troop of Boy Scouts or Girl Scouts —**pa·trol′ler** *n.*

patrol car a police car that is used to patrol an area, usually communicating with headquarters by radio telephone

☆**pa·trol·man** (-mən) *n., pl.* **-men** (-mən) a person who patrols; esp., a police officer assigned to patrol a specific beat

☆**patrol wagon** a small, enclosed truck used by the police in transporting prisoners

pa·tron (pā′trən) *n.* ⟦ME *patroun* < OFr *patrun, patron* < ML & L: ML(Ec) *patronus*, patron saint, patron < L, a protector, defender < *pater*, FATHER⟧ 1 a person empowered with the granting of an English church benefice 2 PATRON SAINT 3 a person corresponding in some respects to a father; protector; benefactor 4 a person, usually a wealthy and influential one, who sponsors and supports some person, activity, institution, etc. [*the patrons of the orchestra*] 5 a customer, esp. a regular customer, of a store, restaurant, etc. 6 in ancient Rome, a person who had freed a slave but still retained a certain paternal control over him or her —**SYN.** SPONSOR

pa·tron·age (pā′trə nij, pa′-) *n.* ⟦OFr: see prec. & -AGE⟧ 1 *a)* the function or status of a patron *b)* support, encouragement, sponsorship, etc. given by a patron 2 [Now Rare] goodwill, favor, courtesy, etc. shown to people considered inferior; condescension 3 *a)* patrons collectively; clientele *b)* business; trade; custom 4 *a)* the power to appoint to office or grant other favors, esp. political ones *b)* the distribution of offices or other favors through this power *c)* the offices, etc. thus distributed

pa·tron·al (pā′trə nəl, pa′-; pə trōn′əl) *adj.* ⟦Fr < LL *patronalis*⟧ of or characteristic of a patron or patron saint; protective

pa·tron·ess (pā′trə nis) *n.* a female patron: see -ESS

pa·tron·ize (pā′trə nīz′, pa′-) *vt.* **-ized′, -iz′ing** 1 to act as a patron toward; sponsor; support 2 to be kind or helpful to, but in a haughty or snobbish way, as if dealing with an inferior 3 to be a regular customer of (a store, merchant, etc.)

patron saint a saint looked upon as the special guardian of a person, place, institution, etc.

pat·ro·nym·ic (pa′trə nim′ik) *adj.* ⟦LL *patronymicus* < Gr *patrōnymikos* < *patēr*, FATHER + *onyma*, NAME⟧ 1 derived from the name of a father or ancestor 2 showing such descent [*a patronymic suffix*] —*n.* 1 a name showing descent from a given person as by the addition of a prefix or suffix (Ex.: *Stevenson*, son of Steven; *O'Brien*, descendant of Brien; *Ivanovna*, daughter of John, used in Russ. after the first name) 2 a family name; surname

pa·troon (pə tro͞on′) *n.* ⟦Du, protector < Fr *patron* < OFr PATRON⟧ ☆a person who held a large estate with manorial rights under a grant from the Dutch government of New Netherland

pat·sy (pat′sē) *n., pl.* **-sies** ⟦prob. altered (after *Patsy*, nickname for PATRICK[1]) < It *pazzo*, crazy⟧ ☆[Slang] a person easily imposed upon or victimized

pat·ten (pat′'n) *n.* ⟦ME *patyn* < MFr *patin* < OFr *pate*, a paw: see PATOIS⟧ any of various thick wooden sandals or clogs formerly worn for walking over wet or muddy ground

pat·ter[1] (pat′ər) *vi.* ⟦freq. of PAT[2]⟧ **1** to make a patter **2** to run or move along so as to make a patter —*n.* a series of quick, light taps *[*the *patter* of rain on leaves*]*

pat·ter[2] (pat′ər) *vt., vi.* ⟦ME *pateren* < *pater*, in *paternoster*, as pronounced in rapid, mechanical recitation⟧ to speak or mumble rapidly or glibly; recite (prayers, etc.) mechanically or thoughtlessly —*n.* **1** language peculiar to a group, class, etc., and not generally understood by outsiders; cant; jargon **2** the glib, rapid speech of salespeople, comedians, magicians, etc. **3** idle, meaningless chatter —**pat′ter·er** *n.*

pat·ter[3] (pat′ər) *n.* a person or thing that pats

pat·tern (pat′ərn) *n.* ⟦ME *patron* < OFr *patrun*, patron, hence something to be imitated, pattern: see PATRON⟧ **1** a person or thing considered worthy of imitation or copying **2** a model or plan used as a guide in making things; set of forms to the shape of which material is cut for assembly into the finished article *[*a dress *pattern]* **3** the full-scale model used in making a sand mold for casting metal **4** something representing a class or type; example; sample **5** an arrangement of form; disposition of parts or elements; design *[*wallpaper *patterns*, the *pattern* of a novel*]* **6** a regular, mainly unvarying way of acting or doing *[*behavior *patterns]* **7** a predictable or prescribed route, movement, etc. *[*traffic *pattern*, landing *pattern]* **8** *a)* grouping or distribution, as of a number of bullets fired at a mark *b)* something, as a diagram, showing such distribution ☆**9** [Now Rare] sufficient material for making a garment —*vt.* **1** to make, do, shape, or plan in imitation of a model or pattern: with *on*, *upon*, or *after* **2** to supply with a pattern or design; mark or decorate with a pattern —*SYN.* MODEL

pat·tern·mak·er (-māk′ər) *n.* a person who makes patterns, as for molds or for various articles to be mass-produced: also **pattern maker**

patter song a musical-comedy song with a simple tune and comic lyrics sung with great rapidity

Pat·ti (pät′tē; *E* pat′ē), **A·de·li·na** (ä′de lē′nä) (born *Adela Juana Maria Patti*) 1843-1919; It. operatic soprano, born in Spain

Pat·ton (pat′'n), **George S(mith)** 1885-1945; U.S. general

pat·ty (pat′ē) *n., pl.* **-ties** ⟦Fr *pâté*: see PÂTÉ⟧ **1** a small pie, esp. a meat pie **2** a small, flat cake of ground meat, fish, etc., usually fried **3** any disk-shaped piece, as of candy

pat·ty-cake (pat′ē kāk′) *n.* ⟦< earlier sp. *pat-a-cake*⟧ **1** the opening words of a nursery rhyme **2** a game played by clapping the hands in rhythm to this rhyme

pat·ty·pan (-pan′) *n.* ⟦orig., a small, round baking pan < PATTY + PAN[1]⟧ a variety of summer squash having a saucer-shaped white fruit, scalloped around the edges

patty shell a small pastry case in which an individual portion of creamed fish, meat, etc. is served

pat·u·lous (pa′tyoo̅ ləs, pach′ə-) *adj.* ⟦L *patulus* < *patere*, to stretch out: see FATHOM⟧ *Bot.* standing open, or spreading —**pat′u·lous·ly** *adv.* —**pat′u·lous·ness** *n.*

patz·er (pat′sər) *n.* ⟦prob. < Ger *patzen*, to bungle, blunder⟧ [Slang] an amateur or inferior chess player

PAU *abbrev.* Pan American Union

pau·ci·ty (pô′sə tē) *n.* ⟦ME *paucyte* < MFr or L: MFr *paucité* < L *paucitas* < *paucus*, FEW⟧ **1** fewness; small number **2** scarcity; dearth; insufficiency

Paul[1] (pôl) *n.* ⟦L *Paulus* (or Gr *Paulos*), Roman surname, prob. < *paulus*, small: akin to *paucus*, FEW⟧ a masculine name: equiv. L. *Paulus*, It. *Paolo*, *Paulo*, Sp. *Pablo*: fem. *Paula*, *Pauline*

Paul[2] (pôl) **1** (original name *Saul*) (died A.D. 67?); a Jew of Tarsus who became the Apostle of Christianity to the Gentiles: author of several Letters in the New Testament: his day is June 29: also **Saint Paul** **2** **Paul I** 1754-1801: czar of Russia (1796-1801): son of Catherine II & Peter III **3** **Paul III** (born *Alessandro Farnese*) 1468-1549; pope (1534-49) **4** **Paul VI** (born *Giovanni Battista Montini*) 1897-1978; pope (1963-78)

Paul·a (pô′lə) *n.* ⟦L, fem. of PAUL[1]⟧ a feminine name: see PAUL[1]

Paul Bun·yan (bun′yən) *American Folklore* a giant lumberjack who, with the help of his blue ox, Babe, performs various superhuman feats

paul·dron (pôl′drən) *n.* ⟦ME *polrond*, aphetic < MFr *espauleron* < *espaule*, the shoulder: see EPAULET⟧ a piece of plate armor to protect the shoulder

Pau·li (pou′lē), **Wolf·gang** (wo͝olf′gaŋ′; *Ger* vôlf′gäŋk′) 1900-58; U.S. physicist, born in Austria

Pauli exclusion principle ⟦after prec.⟧ the principle that no two electrons, protons, etc. in a given system can have the same set of quantum numbers and, thus, that no two can occupy the same space at the same time: see FERMION

Paul·ine[1] (pô′līn′, -lēn′) *adj.* ⟦ModL *Paulinus*⟧ of or characteristic of the Apostle Paul, his writings, or his doctrines

Paul·ine[2] (pô lēn′) *n.* ⟦L *Paulina*, fem. of *Paulinus* < L *Paulus*, PAUL[1]⟧ a feminine name

Paul·ing (pô′liŋ), **Li·nus (Carl)** (lī′nes) 1901-94; U.S. chemist

Paul·ist (pô′list) *n.* ☆a member of a Roman Catholic group, the Society of Missionary Priests of St. Paul the Apostle, founded in New York in 1858

pau·low·ni·a (pô lō′nē ə) *n.* ⟦ModL, after Anna *Pavlovna* (died 1865), daughter of Czar PAUL I⟧ any of a genus (*Paulownia*) of Asian trees of the figwort family, with large, heart-shaped leaves and large, erect clusters of violet flowers; esp., a tree (*P. tomentosa*) having fragrant, violet flowers like those of foxglove

paunch (pônch) *n.* ⟦ME *paunche* < MFr *panche* < L *pantex* (gen. *panticis*), belly < IE base **pank-*, to swell > Russ *puk*, a bundle, bunch⟧ **1** the abdomen, or belly; esp., a large, protruding belly; potbelly **2** RUMEN —**paunch′i·ness** *n.* —**paunch′y** *adj.*

pau·per (pô′pər) *n.* ⟦L, poor person, POOR⟧ **1** [Historical] a person who lives on charity, esp. on tax-supported charity **2** any person who is extremely poor

pau·per·ism (-iz′əm) *n.* the condition of being a pauper

pau·per·ize (pô′pər īz′) *vt.* **-ized′**, **-iz′ing** to make a pauper of; impoverish —**pau′per·i·za′tion** *n.*

pau·piette (pō pyet′) *n.* [*also in italics*] a thin slice of meat or fish rolled around a filling as of meat or vegetables and then braised or fried

pau·ro·me·tab·o·lous (pô′rō mə tab′ə ləs) *adj.* ⟦< Gr *pauros*, small (< IE base **pōu-*: see FEW) + *metabolos*, changeable < *metabolē*, change: see METABOLISM⟧ designating or of a group of insect orders, as orthopterans or hemipterans, in which metamorphosis to the adult state from the juvenile state is gradual and without any sudden, radical change of body form: also **pau′ro·met′a·bol′ic** (-met′ə bäl′ik) *n.* —**pau′ro·me·tab′o·lism′** *n.*

Pau·sa·ni·as (pô sā′nē əs) 2d cent. A.D.; Gr. historian & geographer, probably born in Lydia

pause (pôz) *n.* ⟦ME *pawse* < MFr *pause* < L *pausa* < Gr *pausis*, a stopping < *pauein*, to bring to an end < IE base **paus-*, to let go > OPrus *pausto*, wild⟧ **1** a short period of inaction; temporary stop, break, or rest, as in speaking or reading **2** hesitation; interruption; delay *[*pursuit without *pause]* **3** *a)* a stop or break in speaking or reading, which clarifies meaning *b)* any mark of punctuation indicating this **4** *Music a)* the holding of a tone or rest beyond its written value, at the discretion of the performer *b)* a sign 𝄐 indicating this, written above the note or rest **5** *Prosody* a rhythm break or caesura —*vi.* **paused**, **paus′ing** ⟦Fr *pauser* < L *pausare*, to stop < the n.⟧ **1** to make a pause; be temporarily inactive; stop; hesitate **2** to dwell or linger: with *on* or *upon* —*vt.* to cause to be temporarily inactive; briefly stop the action of (an electronic device, audio or video stream, etc.) —**give someone pause** to make someone hesitant or uncertain —**paus′er** *n.*

pav·ane (pə van′, -vän′) *n.* ⟦Fr < OIt *pavana* < (*danza*) *Pavana*, lit., (dance) of Padua < dial. *Pava*, for *Padua*: assoc. by folk etym. with Fr *pavaner*, to strut, walk like a peacock < L *pavo*, peacock⟧ **1** a slow, stately court dance of Spanish or Italian origin, performed by couples **2** the music for this Also **pav·an** (pav′ən)

Pa·va·rot·ti (pä′və rôt′ē; *It* pä′vä rôt′tē), **Lu·cia·no** (lo͞o chä′nô) 1935-2007; It. operatic tenor

pave (pāv) *vt.* **paved**, **pav′ing** ⟦ME *paven* < OFr *paver* < VL **pavare*, for L *pavire*, to ram, beat < IE base **pēu-*, to strike, chop > Lith *piauti*, L *putare*, to cut⟧ **1** to cover over the surface of (a road, etc.), as with concrete, asphalt, or brick **2** to be the top surface or covering of **3** to cover closely or thickly; overlay —**pave the way (for)** to prepare the way (for); facilitate the introduction (of)

pa·vé (pa vā′) *n.* ⟦Fr, orig. pp. of OFr *paver*, prec.⟧ **1** [Archaic] pavement **2** a setting of jewelry in which the gems are placed close together so that no metal shows

pave·ment (pāv′mənt) *n.* ⟦OFr < L < *pavimentum* < *pavire*, to beat: see PAVE⟧ **1** a paved surface or covering, as of concrete, brick, etc.; specif., *a)* a paved street or road *b)* [Brit.] a sidewalk **2** the material used in paving

pav·er (pā′vər) *n.* **1** a person or thing that paves **2** a brick, stone, etc. used in paving, esp. such a brick specially designed and treated for use in yard or garden walks

Pa·vi·a (pä vē′ä) commune in NW Italy, on the Ticino River

pav·id (pav′id) *adj.* ⟦L *pavidus* < *pavere*, to tremble, orig., be struck down < *pavire*: see PAVE⟧ [Rare] fearful; afraid; timid

pa·vil·ion (pə vil′yən) *n.* ⟦ME *pavilon* < OFr *pavillon* < L *papilio*, butterfly, also tent (from its shape): see PAPILIONACEOUS⟧ **1** a large tent, usually with a peaked top **2** *a)* a building or part of a building, often partly open and highly ornamented, used for entertainment, exhibits, etc., as at a fair or park *b)* a decorative shelter or summerhouse **3** part of a building jutting out from the main part and often ornamented **4** any of the separate or connected parts of a group of related buildings, as of a hospital or sanitarium **5** the part of a brilliant-cut gem between the girdle and the culet —*vt.* to furnish with or shelter in or as in a pavilion

pav·ing (pā′viŋ) *n.* **1** a pavement **2** material for a pavement

pav·ior (pāv′yər) *n.* ⟦altered < ME *pavier* < *paven*, PAVE⟧ **1** a person or thing that paves; paver **2** the material used in paving Also [Chiefly Brit.] **pav′iour**

pav·is (pav′is) *n.* ⟦ME *paveis* < MFr *pavaiz* < It *pavese* after *Pavia*, Italy, where first made⟧ a large shield for protecting the entire body, used in the 14th through 16th cent.: also sp. **pav′ise**

Pav·lov (pav′lôv′; *Russ* pȧ′vlôf′), **I·van Pe·tro·vich** (i vȧn′ pye trô′vich) 1849-1936; Russ. physiologist —**Pav·lov·i·an** (pav lô′vē ən, -lō′-) *adj.*

Pav·lo·va (päv lō′və, pav-; *Russ* pȧv′lô və′), **An·na (Matveyevna)** (än′ä) 1881-1931; Russ. ballet dancer

Pa·vo (pā′vō) *n.* ⟦L, PEACOCK⟧ a S constellation near the celestial pole between Octans and Telescopium

pav·o·nine (pav′ə nīn′, -nin) *adj.* ⟦L *pavoninus* < *pavo*, PEACOCK⟧ **1** of or resembling a peacock **2** iridescent, as a peacock's tail

paw[1] (pô) *n.* ⟦ME *paue* < OFr *poue* < Frank **pauta*, a paw (< pre-Celt **pauta*) > Ger *pfote*⟧ **1** the foot of a four-footed animal having claws **2** [Informal] a hand — *vt., vi.* **1** to touch, dig, hit, strike out (at), etc. with the paws or feet *[*a horse *pawing* the air*]* **2** *a)* to handle (something) clumsily or roughly [she *pawed* angrily through the papers on her desk] *b)* to caress (someone) in a rough or overly familiar way —**paw′er** *n.*

paw² (pô) *n.* [Dial.] pa; papa; father

pawk·y (pô′kē) *adj.* **pawk′i·er, pawk′i·est** [Chiefly Brit.] shrewd and witty; humorously crafty —**pawk′i·ly** *adv.* —**pawk′i·ness** *n.*

pawl (pôl) *n.* ⟦akin ? to Du *pal,* pawl, stake, pole⟧ a mechanical device allowing rotation in only one direction: one type consists of a hinged tongue, the tip of which engages the notches of a ratchet wheel, preventing backward motion

pawn¹ (pôn) *n.* ⟦LME *paun* < MFr *pan,* piece of cloth < L *pannus,* cloth (? used as medium of exchange): see PANE⟧ **1** anything given as security, as for a debt, performance of an action, etc.; pledge; guaranty **2** a hostage **3** the state of being pledged [to put a ring in *pawn*] **4** the act of pawning —*vt.* **1** to give as security; put in pawn **2** to stake, wager, or risk [to *pawn* one's honor] —*SYN.* PLEDGE —**pawn off** PALM OFF (see phrase under PALM²) —**pawn′age** *n.* —**pawn′er** *n.*, **paw′nor**

pawn² (pôn) *n.* ⟦ME *poun* < OFr *peon* < ML *pedo* (gen. *pedonis*), foot soldier < LL, one who has flat feet < L *pes,* FOOT⟧ **1** a chessman of the lowest value: it can be moved only forward and one square at a time (or two squares on its first move), but it captures with a diagonal move **2** a person used to advance another's purposes; tool

pawn·bro·ker (pôn′brōk′ər) *n.* ⟦PAWN¹ + BROKER⟧ a person licensed to lend money at a legally specified rate of interest on articles of personal property left as security —**pawn′bro′king** *n.*

Paw·nee (pô nē′) *n.* ⟦NAmFr *pani* < Illinois < Iowa *panyi*⟧ **1** *pl.* **-nees′** or **-nee′** a member of a group of North American Plains Indian peoples, formerly living in the valley of the Platte River in Nebraska and now living in N Oklahoma **2** the Caddoan language of these peoples —*adj.* of the Pawnees or their language or culture

pawn·shop (pôn′shäp′) *n.* a pawnbroker's shop

pawn ticket a receipt for goods in pawn

paw·paw (pô′pô′) *n. var. of* PAPAW

Paw·tuck·et (pə tuk′it) ⟦< Narragansett, at the falls⟧ city in R.I.

pax (päks, paks) *n.* ⟦ME < ML(Ec) < L, PEACE⟧ **1** [P-] the Roman goddess of peace, identified with the Greek Irene **2** SIGN OF PEACE **3** ⟦in allusion to fol.⟧ [P-] a relatively peaceful political condition resulting from the dominance of a large power: usually in comb. [*Pax* Americana]

Pax Ro·ma·na (päks rō mä′nä, paks rō mā′nə) ⟦L, Roman peace⟧ the comparative peace brought about by Roman rule over the Mediterranean world (27 B.C.-A.D. 180)

pay¹ (pā) *vt.* **paid** or [Obs.] (except in phrase PAY OUT, sense 2) **payed, pay′ing** ⟦ME *paien,* to pay, satisfy < OFr *paiier* < L *pacare,* to pacify < *pax,* PEACE⟧ **1** to give to (a person) what is due, as for goods received, services rendered, etc.; remunerate; recompense **2** to give (what is due or owed) in return, as for goods or services **3** to make a deposit or transfer of (money) [*paid* $50 into the credit union] **4** to discharge or settle (a debt, obligation, expenses, etc.) by giving something in return **5** *a)* to give or offer (a compliment, respects, attention, etc.) *b)* to make (a visit, call, etc.) **6** to yield as a recompense or return [a job that *pays* $90] **7** to be worthwhile or profitable to [it will *pay* him to listen] —*vi.* **1** to give due compensation; make payment **2** to be profitable or worthwhile **3** to yield return or compensation as specified [a stock that *pays* poorly] —*n.* **1** a paying or being paid; payment **2** money paid, esp. for work or services; wages or salary **3** anything, good or bad, given or done in return **4** [Now Rare] a person regarded as a credit risk —*adj.* **1** rich enough in minerals, ore, etc. to make mining profitable [*pay* gravel] **2** operated or made available by depositing coins, submitting credit cards, etc. [a *pay* telephone, *pay* toilet] **3** designating a service, facility, etc. paid for by subscription, fees, etc. [*pay* TV] —**in the pay of** employed and paid by —☆**pay as you go** to pay expenses as they arise —**pay back 1** to repay **2** to retaliate upon —**pay down 1** to pay (a sum of money) as a down payment, with the balance to be paid later **2** to reduce (a debt) over a period of time —**pay for 1** to suffer or undergo punishment because of **2** to atone or make amends for —**pay off 1** to pay all that is owed on (a debt, etc.) or to (a person, as in discharging from employment) **2** to take revenge on (a wrongdoer) or for (a wrong done) **3** to yield full recompense or return, for either good or evil **4** [Informal] to bring about a desired result; succeed **5** *Naut.* to swing or allow to swing away from the wind: said of the bow of a vessel —**pay someone's way** to pay someone's share of the expenses —**pay out 1** to give out (money, etc.); expend **2** to let out (a rope, cable, etc.) gradually —**pay up** to pay in full or on time —**with pay** with wages or salary included [a two-week vacation *with pay*]

SYN.—**pay** is the simple, direct word meaning to give money, etc. due for services rendered, goods received, etc.; **compensate** implies a return, whether monetary or not, thought of as equivalent to the service given, the effort expended, or the loss sustained [one could never be *compensated* for the loss of a child]; **remunerate** stresses the idea of payment for a service rendered, but it often also carries an implication of reward [a bumper crop *remunerated* the farmer for past labors]; to **reimburse** is to pay back what has been expended [the salesman was *reimbursed* for his traveling expenses]; to **indemnify** is to pay for what has been lost or damaged [they were *indemnified* for the war destruction]; **repay** implies a paying back of money given to one or it may refer to a doing or giving of anything in requital [how can I *repay* you for your kindness?]; **recompense** stresses the idea of compensation or requital See also **wage**

pay² (pā) *vt.* **payed, pay′ing** ⟦OFr *peier* < L *picare,* to cover with pitch < *pix,* PITCH¹⟧ to coat as with pitch in order to make waterproof [to *pay* the seams of a wooden ship]

pay·a·ble (pā′ə bəl) *adj.* **1** that can be paid **2** that is to be paid (*on* a specified date); due **3** that is or can be profitable, as a mine or business venture —*n.* [*pl.*] accounts payable

pay·back (pā′bak′) *n.* **1** the act or an instance of paying back **2** return, as on an investment of capital

☆**pay·check** (pā′chek′) *n.* a check in payment of wages or salary

pay·day (pā′dā′) *n.* **1** the day on which salary or wages are paid **2** [Informal] any situation or moment in which a large amount of money is won, awarded, or otherwise acquired

payday lender a business specializing in making payday loans

payday loan a small, short-term loan, typically for two weeks, to be paid back from the borrower's next paycheck on payday: such loans are usually made at a very high rate of interest when annualized

☆**pay dirt** soil, gravel, ore, etc. rich enough in minerals to make mining profitable —**hit** (or **strike**) **pay dirt** [Informal] to discover a source of wealth, success, etc.

pay·ee (pā ē′) *n.* the person to whom a payment is made or owed

pay·er (pā′ər) *n.* the person who pays or is to pay: also sp. **pay′or**

PAYG *abbrev.* pay as you go: a system in which users pay in increments that reflect usage, earnings, etc., rather than in regular, fixed payments

pay·grade (-grād′) *n. Mil.* the grade of a serviceman according to a scale of increasing amounts of base pay

pay·load (pā′lōd′) *n.* **1** a cargo, or the part of a cargo, producing income **2** *a)* a load that consists of anything carried by an aircraft, rocket, etc. that is not essential to its flight operations, including warheads, spacecraft, or passengers *b)* the weight of such a load

pay·mas·ter (pā′mas′tər) *n.* the official in charge of paying wages or salaries to employees

pay·ment (pā′mənt) *n.* **1** a paying or being paid **2** something that is paid **3** penalty or reward

pay·nim (pā′nim) *n.* ⟦ME *painim* < OFr *paienime,* heathendom < LL(Ec) *paganismus,* paganism⟧ [Obs.] **1** a pagan; heathen **2** a non-Christian; esp., a Muslim **3** the pagan world

☆**pay·off** (pā′ôf′) *n.* **1** the act, event, or time of payment **2** a settlement or reckoning **3** that which is paid off; return: recompense **4** [Informal] a bribe **5** [Informal] something coming as a climax or culmination to a series of events, esp. when unexpected or improbable

☆**pay·o·la** (pā ō′lə) *n.* ⟦PAY¹ + *-ola,* as in *Pianola* (former trademark for a player piano) > Tin Pan Alley *pianola,* slang term for the music business⟧ [Informal] **1** the practice of paying bribes or graft for commercial advantage or special favors, as to a disc jockey for unfairly promoting one recording over others **2** this kind of bribe or graft

pay·out (pā′out′) *n.* **1** a paying out; disbursement **2** an amount paid out, as from earnings; dividend

pay-per-view (pā′pər vyoo′) *adj.* TV of or having to do with a system in which a person pays for single showings of films or other programming, as by cable or satellite —*n.* such a system

☆**pay phone** (*or* **station**) a public telephone, usually coin-operated

☆**pay·roll** (pā′rōl′) *n.* **1** a list of employees to be paid, with the amount due to each **2** the total amount needed, or the money on hand, for this for a given period

Pays de la Loire (pā ē′ de lȧ lwȧr′) metropolitan region of NW France: 12,387 sq mi (32,082 sq km); chief city, Nantes

payt or **pay't** *abbrev.* payment

pay·wall (pā′wôl′) *n.* ⟦PAY¹ + (FIRE)WALL⟧ a system designed to prevent visitors to a website, often, specif., to a news website, from viewing certain content without first paying a subscription fee

Paz (päs; *E also* päz), **Oc·ta·vio** (ôk tä′vyô) 1914-98; Mex. poet

☆**pa·zazz** (pə zaz′) *n. var. of* PIZZAZZ

Pb ⟦L *plumbum*⟧ *Chem. symbol for* lead

PB *abbrev.* paperback: also **pb**

PB&J *abbrev.* peanut butter and jelly (sandwich)

PBB (pē′bē′bē′) *n.* ⟦*p(oly)b(rominated) b(iphenyl)*⟧ any of several fat-soluble, cancer-causing substances formerly used as fire retardants

PBGC *abbrev.* Pension Benefit Guaranty Corporation

PBS *service mark* Public Broadcasting Service

PBX (pē′bē′eks′) *n.* ⟦*p(rivate) b(ranch) (e)x(change)*⟧ a telephone system operating within one building, company, etc. and having outside telephone lines

pc *abbrev.* **1** parsec(s) **2** percent **3** petty cash **4** piece **5** postal card **6** postcard **7** price(s) **8** prices current

PC¹ (pē′sē′) *n., pl.* **PCs** or **PC's** PERSONAL COMPUTER

PC² *abbrev.* **1** Past Commander **2** Police Constable ☆**3** politically correct or political correctness **4** Post Commander **5** Privy Council (or Councilor)

P/C or **p/c** *abbrev.* **1** petty cash **2** prices current

p.c. *abbrev.* ⟦L *post cibum*⟧ *Pharmacy* after meals

PCB (pē′sē′bē′) *n.* ⟦*p(oly)c(hlorinated) b(iphenyl)*⟧ any of a group of chlorinated isomers of biphenyl, formerly used in the form of a toxic, colorless, odorless, viscous liquid, esp. as an insulator in electrical equipment

PCP¹ (pē′sē′pē′) *n.* ⟦*p(henyl)c(yclohexyl)p(iperidine)*⟧ a powerful psychedelic drug (*phencyclidine hydrochloride*), $C_{17}H_{25}N \cdot HCl$

PCP² *abbrev.* **1** PNEUMOCYSTIS (PNEUMONIA) **2** primary care physician (or provider)

PCR *abbrev.* polymerase chain reaction
pct *abbrev.* percent
PCV valve (pē′sē′vē′) ⟦*p(ositive) c(rankcase) v(entilation)*⟧ a one-way valve on a motor-vehicle engine for regulating a pollution control system that draws crankcase fumes into the cylinders for burning
pd *abbrev.* **1** paid **2** per diem **3** potential difference
Pd *Chem. symbol for* palladium
PD *abbrev.* **1** per diem **2** Police Department **3** postal district
PDA (pē′dē′ā′) *n.* ⟦*p(ersonal) d(igital) a(ssistant)*⟧ a hand-held, electronic device equipped with a microprocessor, for storing personal information
PDF *abbrev.* Portable Document Format
pdl *abbrev.* poundal(s)
pdq or **PDQ** (pē′dē′kyo͞o′) *adv.* ⟦< *pretty damn* (or *darn*) *quick*⟧ [Slang] right away; immediately
PDT *abbrev.* Pacific Daylight Time
pe (pā) *n.* ⟦Heb, lit., mouth⟧ the seventeenth letter of the Hebrew alphabet (פ, ף): in a text containing points, this letter written with a dot is designated *pe*; without a dot it is *fe*
Pe *abbrev. Bible* Peter
PE *abbrev.* **1** physical education **2** Prince Edward Island **3** Professional Engineer **4** Protestant Episcopal
p/e or **P/E** *abbrev.* price/earnings (ratio)
pea (pē) *n., pl.* **peas** ⟦back-form. < ME *pese, pees,* a pea, taken as pl. < OE *pise* < LL *pisa* < L, pl. of *pisum,* a pea < Gr *pison,* a pea⟧ **1** an annual, tendril-climbing plant (*Pisum sativum*) of the pea family, with white or pinkish flowers and green seedpods **2** its small, round, smooth or wrinkled seed, used as a vegetable **3** *a)* any of various similar plants, as the cowpea *b)* the seed of any of these —*adj.* designating a family (Fabaceae, order Fabales) of leguminous, dicotyledonous plants, including peanuts, clover, vetch, alfalfa, and many beans —**like (two) peas in a pod** exactly alike
pea bean any of various kidney beans; esp., a navy bean
Pea·bod·y (pē′bäd′ē, -bəd ē), **George** 1795-1869; U.S. merchant & philanthropist, in England
☆**Pea·bod·y bird** (pē′bäd′ē, -bəd ē) ⟦echoic of its note⟧ [*also* **p- b-**] WHITE-THROATED SPARROW
peace (pēs) *n.* ⟦ME *pais* < OFr < L *pax* (gen. *pacis*) < IE base **pak-,* to fasten > FANG, L *pacisci,* to confirm an agreement, *pangere,* to fasten⟧ **1** freedom from war or a stopping of war **2** a treaty or agreement to end war or the threat of war **3** freedom from public disturbance or disorder; public security; law and order **4** freedom from disagreement or quarrels; harmony; concord **5** an undisturbed state of mind; absence of mental conflict; serenity: in full **peace of mind** **6** calm; quiet; tranquillity —*vi.* to be or become silent or quiet: obs. except in the imperative —**at peace** **1** free from war **2** quiet; in repose —**hold (or keep) one's peace** to be silent; keep quiet —**keep the peace** to avoid or prevent violation of law and public order —**make one's peace with** to effect a reconciliation with —**make peace** to end hostilities, settle arguments, etc.
Peace (pēs) ⟦after *Peace Point,* where Cree & Beaver Indians made a peace pact⟧ river in W Canada, flowing from N British Columbia east & northeast into the Slave River in NE Alberta: 945 mi (1,521 km)
peace·a·ble (pēs′ə bəl) *adj.* ⟦ME *peisible* < OFr⟧ **1** fond of, inclined toward, or promoting peace; not quarrelsome **2** at peace; peaceful —**peace′a·ble·ness** *n.* —**peace′a·bly** *adv.*
peace conference a conference for the purpose of ending a war or for seeking ways to establish lasting peace
☆**Peace Corps** an agency of the U.S. established in 1961 to provide volunteers skilled in teaching, construction, etc. to assist people of underdeveloped areas abroad
peace·ful (pēs′fəl) *adj.* **1** not quarrelsome; peaceable **2** characterized by peace; free from disturbance or disorder; calm; quiet; tranquil **3** of or characteristic of a time of peace —***SYN.*** CALM —**peace′ful·ly** *adv.* —**peace′ful·ness** *n.*
peace·keep·ing (pēs′kēp′iŋ) *adj.* of or relating to the process of maintaining peace, specif., of the reduction or elimination of armed conflict by the use of neutral troops to enforce a truce or separate hostile groups [UN *peacekeeping* forces]: also written **peace-keeping** —*n.* such a process —**peace′keep′er** *n.*
peace·mak·er (-māk′ər) *n.* a person who makes peace, as by settling the disagreements or quarrels of others —**peace′mak′ing** *n., adj.*
☆**peace·nik** (-nik) *n.* ⟦PEACE + -NIK⟧ [Slang] a person actively opposing, esp. demonstrating against, war or a war: often a disparaging or dismissive term
peace offering ⟦used to transl. Heb *shelem,* lit., thank-offering⟧ **1** an offering or sacrifice in thanksgiving to God: Ezek. 45:15 **2** an offering made to maintain or bring about peace
peace officer an officer entrusted with maintaining law and order, as a sheriff, constable, or policeman
☆**peace pipe** CALUMET
peace sign **1** PEACE SYMBOL **2** a gesture meaning "peace," "love," etc., made by raising and spreading the index and middle fingers, with the palm outwards
peace symbol a symbol for, variously, peace, love, pacifism, etc., consisting of an upside-down, three-pronged Y encircled
peace·time (pēs′tīm′) *n.* a time of freedom from war —*adj.* of or characteristic of such a time
peach[1] (pēch) *n.* ⟦ME *peche* < OFr *pesche* < VL *persica* < pl. of L *persicum* < *Persicum (malum),* Persian (apple)⟧ **1** a small prunus tree (*Prunus persica*) with lance-shaped leaves, pink flowers, and round, juicy, orange-yellow or pinkish-yellow fruit having a fuzzy skin and a single, rough pit **2** its fruit **3** the orange-yellow or pinkish-yellow color of this fruit **4** [Slang] any person or thing that is very good or is well liked
peach[2] (pēch) *vt.* ⟦ME *pechen,* aphetic for *apechen,* via Anglo-Fr < OFr *empechier,* IMPEACH⟧ [Obs.] to name in an indictment; impeach —*vi.* [Slang] to give evidence against another; turn informer
peach·blow (pēch′blō′) *n.* ⟦PEACH[1] + BLOW[3]⟧ **1** a delicate purplish-pink color **2** a porcelain glaze of this color
peach·es-and-cream (pēch′iz ən krēm′) *adj.* clear, fresh, glowing, etc.; often, specif., fair and unblemished with rosy cheeks: said of skin [a *peaches-and-cream* complexion]
peach fuzz **1** the fuzz on a peach **2** [Informal] soft, fine hair; often, specif., an immature or early growth of beard
peach·y (pē′chē) *adj.* **peach′i·er, peach′i·est** **1** peachlike, as in color or texture ☆**2** [Old Slang] fine, excellent, etc. —**peach′i·ness** *n.*
☆**pea coat** ⟦var. of PEA JACKET⟧ a hip-length, double-breasted coat of heavy woolen cloth, worn originally by seamen: also written **pea′coat′** *n.*
pea·cock (pē′käk′) *n., pl.* **-cocks′** or **-cock′** ⟦ME *pacok* < *pa,* peacock (< OE *pea* < early WGmc borrowing < L *pavo,* peacock, ? akin to Gr *taōs,* ? of Asian orig.) + *cok,* COCK[1]⟧ **1** *a)* any male peafowl, esp., one of a species (*Pavo cristatus*) with a crest of plumules and long, brightly colored upper tail coverts that can be spread like a fan and have rainbow-colored, eyelike spots *b)* loosely, any peafowl **2** a vain, strutting person —*vi.* to display vanity in behavior, dress, etc.; strut —**pea′cock′ish** *adj.,* **pea′cock′y**

peacock

Pea·cock (pē′käk′), **Thomas Love** 1785-1866; Eng. novelist & poet
peacock blue a greenish blue
peacock chair ⟦prob. from the shape of its back, suggesting the spread tail of a *peacock*⟧ an armchair, usually of rattan or wicker, with a very high, rounded back
peacock ore ⟦from its iridescent sheen, likened to that of a peacock's plumage⟧ BORNITE
pea·fowl (pē′foul′) *n., pl.* **-fowls′** or **-fowl′** any of various large gallinaceous birds (family Phasianidae) of S Asia, the East Indies, or Africa, as the peacock: now widely domesticated as an ornamental bird
☆**peag** or **peage** (pēg) *n.* ⟦shortened < earlier *wampumpeage:* see WAMPUM⟧ WAMPUM
pea green a light yellowish-green color
pea·hen (pē′hen′) *n.* a female peafowl
☆**pea jacket** (pē′) ⟦altered by folk etym. (infl. by PEA) < Du *pijjekker* < *pij,* coarse, thick cloth + *jekker,* jacket < *jak* < OFr *jaque:* see JACKET⟧ PEA COAT
peak[1] (pēk) *vi.* ⟦< ?⟧ to become sickly; waste away; droop
peak[2] (pēk) *n.* ⟦var. of PIKE[5]⟧ **1** a tapering part that projects; pointed end or top, as of a cap, roof, etc. **2** part of the hairline coming to a point on the forehead; widow's peak **3** [Rare] a promontory **4** *a)* the crest or summit of a hill or mountain ending in a point *b)* a mountain with such a pointed summit **5** the highest or utmost point of anything; height; maximum [the *peak* of production] **6** *Elec.* the maximum value of a varying quantity during a specified period **7** *Naut.* *a)* the top, after corner of a gaff sail *b)* the upper end of the gaff *c)* the narrowed part of the hull, forward or aft **8** *Phonet.* the most sonorous portion of a syllable —*adj.* maximum [*peak* production] —*vt., vi.* **1** to tilt up, as a spar or oar **2** to come or cause to come to a peak; reach or bring to a high, or the highest, point —***SYN.*** SUMMIT
peaked[1] (pēkt, pē′kid) *adj.* ⟦< prec.⟧ having or ending in a peak; pointed
peak·ed[2] (pē′kid) *adj.* ⟦< PEAK[1]⟧ thin and drawn, or weak and wan, as from illness —**peak′ed·ness** *n.*
peak·y (pē′kē) *adj.* ⟦related to PEAK[1] and prec.⟧ having a wan or sickly appearance
peal (pēl) *n.* ⟦ME *pele,* aphetic for *apele,* APPEAL⟧ **1** the loud ringing of a bell or set of bells **2** *a)* a set of tuned bells; chimes; carillon *b)* the ringing of changes on such a set of bells **3** any loud, prolonged sound, as of gunfire, thunder, laughter, etc. —*vi., vt.* to sound in a peal; resound; ring
Peale (pēl) **1** **Charles Will·son** (wil′sən) 1741-1827; Am. portrait painter **2** **James** 1749-1831; Am. painter: brother of Charles **3** **Rembrandt** 1778-1860; Am. painter: son of Charles
pe·an (pē′ən) *n. alt. sp. of* PAEAN
☆**pea·nut** (pē′nut′, -nət) *n.* ⟦PEA + NUT⟧ **1** a spreading, annual vine (*Arachis hypogaea*) of the pea family, with yellow flowers and brittle pods ripening underground and containing one to three edible seeds **2** the pod or any of its seeds **3** [Informal] a small or insignificant person **4** [*pl.*] [Slang] a trifling or relatively small sum of money
☆**peanut butter** a food paste or spread made by grinding roasted peanuts

peanut plant

☆**peanut gallery** [Slang] the topmost balcony section in a theater, where the cheaper seats are located

peanut oil a yellowish oil pressed from peanuts, used in cooking, salad dressings, soaps, medicines, and cosmetics

pear (per) ***n.*** ⟦ME *pere* < OE *peru* < VL **pira* < L pl. of *pirum,* pear, akin to Gr *apion:* of pre-Gr Mediterranean orig.⟧ **1** a tree (*Pyrus communis*) of the rose family, with glossy leaves and greenish, brown, or reddish fruit **2** the soft, juicy fruit, round at the base and narrowing toward the stem

pearl[1] (purl) ***n.*** ⟦ME *perle* < MFr < VL **perla,* **perula,* altered (? after L *sphaerula,* SPHERULE) < L *perna,* a sea mussel, lit., a ham: from the shape of its peduncle⟧ **1** a smooth, hard, usually white or bluish-gray body of varied but usually roundish shape that is an abnormal nacreous growth within the shell of some oysters and certain other bivalve mollusks and forms around a grain of sand, a parasite, or some other foreign object: it is used as a gem **2** MOTHER-OF-PEARL **3** any person or thing regarded as like a pearl in some way, as in size, shape, color, beauty, value, etc. **4** a bluish or pinkish gray —***vt.*** **1** to adorn or cover with pearls or pearl-like drops **2** to make like a pearl in shape —***vi.*** to fish for pearl-bearing mollusks, esp. oysters —***adj.*** **1** of or having pearls **2** like a pearl in shape or color **3** made of mother-of-pearl [*pearl* buttons] —**cast pearls before swine** ⟦see Matt. 7:6⟧ to present something of great interest or value to someone incapable of appreciating it —**pearl′er** ***n.***

pearl[2] (purl) ***vt., vi., n. obs. sp. of*** PURL[2]

Pearl[1] (purl) ***n.*** ⟦< PEARL[1]⟧ a feminine name

Pearl[2] (purl) **1** ⟦named for *pearls* found there⟧ river in central Miss., flowing south into the Gulf of Mexico: 490 mi (789 km) **2** ZHU

pearl ash a refined potash, potassium carbonate

pearl barley barley seed rubbed down into small, round grains: also **pearled barley**

pearl diver (*or* fisher) a person who dives for pearl-bearing mollusks

pearl·es·cent (pər les′ənt) ***adj.*** having the lustrous, bluish-gray or grayish-white color of pearls or mother-of-pearl

pearl gray a pale bluish-gray color

Pearl Harbor ⟦after the *pearl* oysters once there⟧ inlet on the S coast of Oahu, Hawaii, near Honolulu: site of a U.S. naval base bombed by Japan, Dec. 7, 1941

pearl·ite (purl′īt′) ***n.*** ⟦Fr *perlite* < *perle,* PEARL[1] + *-ite,* -ITE[1]⟧ *Metallurgy* a mixture of iron and cementite, which crystallizes during the slow cooling of high-temperature steel and cast iron —**pearl·it′ic** (-it′ik) ***adj.***

pearl·ized (purl′īzd′) ***adj.*** resembling mother-of-pearl

☆**pearl millet** a tall cereal and forage grass (*Pennisetum glaucum*) having pearly white seeds borne in dense spikes

pearl onion a very small, globe-shaped onion, often pickled and served as an appetizer or in cocktails

pearl·y (pur′lē) ***adj.*** **pearl′i·er, pearl′i·est** **1** of or like a pearl, as in color or luster **2** adorned or covered with pearls or mother-of-pearl —**pearl′i·ness** ***n.***

Pearly Gates the gates of heaven: cf. Rev. 21:21

pearly nautilus NAUTILUS (sense 1)

pear·main (per′mān′) ***n.*** ⟦ME *parmayn* < OFr *parmain,* assoc. by folk etym. with *Parma,* Italy, but prob. < OFr *parmaindre,* to remain (< L *permanere:* see PERMANENT), from its long-keeping qualities⟧ a variety of apple

pear-shaped (per′shāpt′) ***adj.*** **1** shaped like a pear; specif., having disproportionately wide hips **2** full, clear, even, and resonant: said of sung tones

Pear·son (pir′sən), **Lester B(owles)** 1897-1972; Cdn. statesman: prime minister (1963-68)

peart (pērt, pyərt) ***adj.*** ⟦var. of PERT[1]⟧ [Dial.] lively, chipper, sprightly, smart, etc. —**peart′ly** ***adv.***

Pear·y (pir′ē), **Robert E(dwin)** 1856-1920; U.S. arctic explorer: his claim that the group he led was the first to reach the North Pole (1909) is disputed

peas·ant (pez′ənt) ***n.*** ⟦LME *paissaunt* < Anglo-Fr *paisant* < MFr *païsent* < OFr < *païs,* country < LL *pagensis,* belonging to the district < *pagus,* district: see PAGAN⟧ **1** any person of the class of small farmers or of farm laborers, as in Europe or Asia **2** a person regarded as coarse, boorish, ignorant, etc.

peas·ant·ry (pez′ən trē) ***n.*** **1** peasants collectively **2** a peasant's rank or condition

Peasants' Revolt the first great popular rebellion in English history (1381), caused by the imposition of an unpopular poll tax: it lasted less than a month and failed as a social revolution

pease (pēz) ***n.*** ⟦see PEA⟧ **1** *pl.* **peas′es** or **peas′en** (-′n) [Obs.] a pea **2** *archaic or Brit. dial. pl. of* PEA

pease·cod or **peas·cod** (pēz′käd′) ***n.*** ⟦ME *pesecod:* see prec. & COD[2]⟧ [Archaic] the pod of the pea plant

pea·shoot·er (pē′sho͞ot′ər) ***n.*** a toy weapon consisting of a tube through which dried peas, etc. are blown

pea soup **1** a heavy soup made from dried split peas or, sometimes, fresh peas **2** a dense, yellowish fog: also [Chiefly Brit.] **pea′soup′er** ***n.***

peat (pēt) ***n.*** ⟦ME *pete* < ML *peta,* piece of turf, prob. < Celt **pett-,* piece > PIECE, Welsh *peth*⟧ **1** partly decayed, moisture-absorbing plant matter found in ancient bogs and swamps, used as a plant covering or fuel **2** a dried block of this used as fuel —**peat′y** ***adj.*** **peat′i·er, peat′i·est**

peat moss **1** any moss which forms peat, esp. sphagnum **2** any peat composed of residues of mosses, used chiefly as mulch **3** [Brit. Dial.] a peat bog

peau de soie (pō′ də swä′) ⟦Fr, lit., skin of silk⟧ a soft, rich silk or rayon cloth with a dull, satiny finish

☆**pea·vey** (pē′vē) ***n., pl.*** **-veys** ⟦prob. after J. *Peavey,* said to be its inventor, *c.* 1872⟧ a heavy wooden lever with a pointed metal tip and hinged hook near the end: used in handling logs: cf. CANT HOOK: also sp. **pea′vy,** *pl.* **-vies**

peb·ble (peb′əl) ***n.*** ⟦ME *pobble* < OE *papol-(stan), popol-(stan),* pebble (stone), prob. of echoic orig.⟧ **1** *a)* a small stone worn smooth and round, as by the action of water *b) Geol.* such a stone, smaller than a cobblestone, with a maximum diameter of 64 mm (*c.* 2.5 in) **2** clear, transparent quartz or a lens made from it **3** a surface grain of pebbly appearance, artificially produced on leather (**pebble leather**), paper, etc. —***vt.*** **-bled, -bling** **1** to cover with pebbles or objects that look like pebbles **2** to stamp (leather, etc.) so as to produce a pebbly appearance

pebble dash ⟦prec. + DASH[1] (prob. ***vt.*** 3)⟧ [Chiefly Brit.] a finish for outer walls in which pieces of crushed rock are set into an outer coat of stucco or cement: also **peb′ble·dash′** ***n.*** —**peb′ble-dash′** ***adj.***, **peb′ble-dashed′**

peb·bly (peb′lē, peb′əl ē) ***adj.*** **-bli·er, -bli·est** **1** having many pebbles **2** having a bumpy, uneven surface or grain resembling pebbles

☆**pe·can** (pē kän′, -kan′; pi-; pē′kän′, -kan′) ***n.*** ⟦18th-c. Mississippi Valley Fr *pacane* < Illinois *pakani*⟧ **1** an olive-shaped, edible nut with a thin, smooth shell **2** the North American tree (*Carya illinoensis*) of the walnut family on which it grows

pec·ca·ble (pek′ə bəl) ***adj.*** ⟦ML *peccabilis* < L *peccare,* to sin⟧ liable to or capable of sin —**pec′ca·bil′i·ty** ***n.***

pec·ca·dil·lo (pek′ə dil′ō) ***n., pl.*** **-loes** or **-los** ⟦Sp *pecadilo,* dim. < *pecado* < L *peccatum,* a sin < *peccare,* to sin⟧ a minor or petty sin or fault

pec·can·cy (pek′ən sē) ***n.*** ⟦LL(Ec) *peccantia* < *peccare,* to sin⟧ **1** sinfulness **2** *pl.* **-cies** a sin

pec·cant (pek′ənt) ***adj.*** ⟦L *peccans,* prp. of *peccare,* to sin⟧ **1** sinful; sinning **2** breaking or disregarding a rule or practice; faulty **3** [Rare] diseased or causing disease —**pec′cant·ly** ***adv.***

pec·ca·ry (pek′ə rē) ***n., pl.*** **-ries** or **-ry** ⟦AmSp *pecari* < Carib *pakira*⟧ any of a family (Tayassuidae) of piglike, artiodactylous mammals of North and South America, with a musk gland, sharp tusks, and porklike flesh

pec·ca·vi (pā kä′vē) ***n., pl.*** **-vis** ⟦L, lit., I have sinned⟧ a confession of sin or guilt

Pe·cho·ra (pe chôr′ə; *Russ* pye chô′rä) river in N European Russia, flowing from the Urals north into the Barents Sea: 1,110 mi (1,786 km)

peck[1] (pek) ***vt.*** ⟦ME *pecken,* var. of *picken,* PICK[3], in specialized senses⟧ **1** to strike with a pointed object, as with a beak **2** to make by doing this [*to peck* a hole] **3** to pick up with the beak; get by pecking —***vi.*** to make strokes as with a pointed object —***n.*** **1** a stroke so made, as with the beak **2** a mark made as by pecking **3** [Informal] a quick, casual kiss [*a peck* on the forehead] —**peck at** **1** to make a pecking motion at **2** [Informal] to eat very little of; eat carefully or sparingly **3** [Informal] to criticize or find fault with constantly

peck[2] (pek) ***n.*** ⟦ME *pek* < OFr, prob. < ML *bika,* liquid measure, ult. < Gr *bikos,* wine jar: see BEAKER⟧ **1** a unit of dry measure, equal to ¼ bushel or 8 dry quarts (8.8096 dry liters or 0.3111 cubic foot): abbrev. *pk* **2** any container with a capacity of one peck **3** [Informal] a large amount, as of trouble

peck·er (pek′ər) ***n.*** **1** a person or thing that pecks **2** [Brit. Informal] courage; spirits: chiefly in the phrase **keep one's pecker up** **3** [Slang] the penis: somewhat vulgar

☆**peck·er·wood** (pek′ər wood′) ***n.*** ⟦orig., dial. term for WOODPECKER⟧ [Dial.] POOR WHITE: a hostile term of contempt or derision

☆**pecking order** ⟦calque of Ger *hackordnung*⟧ **1** a hierarchy among birds, as a flock of hens, based on aggressive pecking in which the most dominant bird pecks all others, the second most dominant bird pecks all others except the most dominant, etc. **2** [Informal] a hierarchy of the members of any group according to relative power, importance, etc. [*the office pecking order*] Also **peck order**

peck·ish (pek′ish) ***adj.*** ⟦PECK[1] + -ISH⟧ [Informal] **1** [Chiefly Brit.] somewhat hungry **2** cross; irritable —**peck′ish·ly** ***adv.*** —**peck′ish·ness** ***n.***

Peck·sniff·i·an (pek snif′ē ən) ***adj.*** ⟦after *Pecksniff,* unctuous hypocrite in Dickens' novel *Martin Chuzzlewit* (1843)⟧ falsely moralistic; hypocritical; insincere

☆**peck·y** (pek′ē) ***adj.*** ⟦PECK[1] (***n.*** 2) + -Y[2]⟧ showing or marked by spots or holes caused by decay [*pecky* cypress]

pe·co·ri·no (cheese) (pek′ə rē′nō) an Italian cheese made of sheep's milk; specif., such a cheese that is dry, sharp, and very hard

Pe·cos (pā′kōs′, -kəs) ⟦< ? AmInd⟧ river in the SW U.S., flowing from N N.Mex. through Tex. into the Rio Grande: 735 mi (1,183 km)

☆**Pecos Bill** *American Folklore* a frontier cowboy who performed such superhuman feats as digging the Rio Grande

pecs (peks) ***pl.n.*** [Slang] pectoral muscles, esp. of a bodybuilder or weight lifter

Pécs (pāch) city in SW Hungary

pec·tase (pek′tās′) ***n.*** an enzyme in fruits that converts pectin into pectic acid

pec·tate (pek′tāt′) ***n.*** a salt or ester of pectic acid

pec·ten (pek′tən) ***n., pl.*** **pec′ti·nes′** (-tə nēz′) ⟦L, a comb < *pectere,* to comb < IE base **pek-,* to pull wool or hair, shorn animal, cattle > FEE⟧ *Zool.* **1** a vascular mass of tissue on the retina of the eye of many birds and reptiles **2** any comblike structure, as a part of the stridulating organ of some spiders

pec·tic (pek′tik) ***adj.*** ⟦Fr *pectique* < Gr *pēktikos,* congealing < *pēktos,* congealed < *pēgnynai,* to fix < IE base **pag̑-,* to fasten: see FANG⟧ of, containing, or derived from pectin

pectic acid a complex, water-insoluble acid, formed by hydrolysis of the methyl ester groups of pectin

pec·tin (pek′tin) ***n.*** ⟦< Gr *pēktos* (see PECTIC) + -IN[1]⟧ a water-soluble carbohydrate, obtained from certain ripe fruits, which yields a gel that is the basis of jellies and jams —**pec′tin·ous** ***adj.***

pec·ti·nate (pek′tə nāt′) ***adj.*** ⟦L *pectinatus,* pp. of *pectinare,* to comb < *pecten:* see PECTEN⟧ having toothlike projections like those on a comb: also **pec′ti·nat′ed** —**pec′ti·na′tion** ***n.***

pec·to·ral (pek′tə rəl) ***adj.*** ⟦< L *pectoralis* < *pectus* (gen. *pectoris*), breast⟧ **1** of or located in or on the chest or breast **2** worn on the chest or breast *[a bishop's pectoral cross]* **3** influenced by or resulting from personal feelings; subjective —***n.*** ⟦ME < MFr < L *pectorale*⟧ **1** something worn on the breast, as an ornamental plate **2** a pectoral fin or muscle

pectoral fin either of a pair of fins, associated with the pectoral girdle, just behind the head of a fish, corresponding to the forelimbs of a higher vertebrate

pectoral girdle *Anat., Zool.* the bony or cartilaginous structures to which the forelimbs (or arms) of a vertebrate are attached

☆**pectoral sandpiper** a large, grayish-brown, American sandpiper (*Calidris melanotos*) with a streaked breast, white belly, and yellow legs

pec·u·late (pek′yoo͞ lāt′, -yə-) ***vt.*** **-lat′ed, -lat′ing** ⟦< L *peculatus,* pp. of *peculari,* to embezzle < *peculium,* private property < *pecus,* cattle: for IE base see FEE⟧ to steal or misuse (money or property entrusted to one's care, esp. public funds); embezzle —**pec′u·la′tion** ***n.*** —**pec′u·la′tor** ***n.***

pe·cu·liar (pi kyo͞ol′yər) ***adj.*** ⟦ME *peculier* < L *peculiaris* < *peculium:* see prec.⟧ **1** of only one person, thing, group, country, etc.; distinctive; exclusive *[a bird peculiar to Australia]* **2** particular; unique; special *[a matter of peculiar interest]* **3** out of the ordinary; queer; odd; strange —***n.*** **1** something belonging to one only, as a privilege **2** [Brit.] a church or parish under a jurisdiction other than that of the diocese in which it is located —***SYN.*** STRANGE —**pe·cu′liar·ly** ***adv.***

pe·cu·li·ar·i·ty (pi kyo͞o′lē er′ə tē) ***n.*** **1** the quality or condition of being peculiar **2** *pl.* **-ties** something that is peculiar, as a trait or habit

pe·cu·ni·ar·y (pi kyo͞o′nē er′ē) ***adj.*** ⟦L *pecuniarius* < *pecunia,* money < *pecus,* cattle: see FEE⟧ **1** of or involving money **2** involving a money penalty, or fine *[a pecuniary offense]* —***SYN.*** FINANCIAL —**pe·cu′ni·ar′i·ly** ***adv.***

ped *abbrev.* **1** pedal **2** pedestrian

PED *abbrev. Sports* performance-enhancing drug

ped- (ped, pēd) *combining form* **1** PEDO-[1] **2** PEDO-[2] **3** PEDI- Used before a vowel

-ped (ped) *combining form* -PEDE

ped·a·gog·ic (ped′ə gäj′ik, -gō′jik) ***adj.*** ⟦Gr *paidagōgikos* < *paidagōgos:* see PEDAGOGUE⟧ of or characteristic of teachers or of teaching: also **ped′a·gog′i·cal** —**ped′a·gog′i·cal·ly** ***adv.***

☆**ped·a·gog·ics** (ped′ə gäj′iks, -gō′jiks) ***n.*** PEDAGOGY

ped·a·gogue or **ped·a·gog** (ped′ə gäg′) ***n.*** ⟦ME *pedagoge* < OFr < L *paedagogus* < Gr *paidagōgos* < *pais,* child (see PEDO-[1]) + *agein,* to lead: see ACT[1]⟧ a teacher; often, specif., a pedantic, dogmatic teacher

ped·a·gog·y (ped′ə gäj′ē, -gō′jē) ***n.*** ⟦Fr *pédagogie* < LL *paedagogia* < Gr *paidagōgia:* see prec.⟧ **1** the profession or function of a teacher; teaching **2** the art or science of teaching; esp., instruction in teaching methods

ped·al (ped′'l; *for adj. 1, also* pēd′-) ***adj.*** ⟦L *pedalis* < *pes* (gen. *pedis*), FOOT⟧ **1** of or having to do with the foot or feet **2** of or operated by a pedal or pedals —***n.*** ⟦MFr *pédale* < It *pedale* < L *pedalis:* see the ***adj.***⟧ **1** a lever operated by the foot, used in transmitting motion, as on a bicycle, or a pad pressed by the foot in activating a mechanism, as on a sewing machine, so as to operate a device **2** such a lever or pad used to change the tone or volume of a musical instrument, as an organ or harp — ***vt., vi.*** **-aled** or **-alled, -al·ing** or **-al·ling** to move or operate by a pedal or pedals; use the pedals (of) —**ped′al·er** ***n.,*** **ped′al·ler**

pe·dal·fer (pi dal′fər) ***n.*** ⟦< Gr *ped(on),* ground (see PEDO-[2]) + L *al(umen),* ALUM[1] + L *fer(rum),* iron⟧ soil containing much alumina and iron oxide and lacking calcium and magnesium carbonates: usually found in forested areas of the tropics characterized by high humidity and temperature —**ped·al·fer·ic** (ped′əl fer′ik) ***adj.***

pedal point *Music* a single continuous tone, usually in the bass, held against the changing figures or harmonies of the other parts

☆**pedal pushers** ⟦used originally for bicycle riding⟧ calf-length pants for women or girls

☆**pedal steel (guitar)** a steel guitar consisting of a rectangular body mounted on legs and having ten or more strings along with pedals for changing pitch: see STEEL GUITAR

ped·ant (ped′'nt) ***n.*** ⟦Fr *pédant,* pedant, schoolmaster < It *pedante,* ult. < Gr *paidagōgos:* see PEDAGOGUE⟧ **1** a person who puts unnecessary stress on minor or trivial points of learning, displaying a scholarship lacking in judgment or sense of proportion **2** a teacher characterized by insistence on exact adherence to a set of arbitrary rules **3** [Obs.] a schoolmaster —**pe·dan′tic** ***adj.*** —**pe·dan′ti·cal·ly** ***adv.***

ped·ant·ry (ped′'n trē) ***n.,*** *pl.* **-ries** ⟦Fr *pédanterie* < It *pedanteria* < *pedante:* see prec.⟧ **1** the qualities, practices, etc. of a pedant; ostentatious display of knowledge, or an instance of this **2** an arbitrary adherence to rules and forms

ped·ate (ped′āt′, -it) ***adj.*** ⟦L *pedatus* < *pes* (gen. *pedis*), FOOT⟧ **1** *Bot.* palmately divided into three main divisions, the two outer divisions forked into smaller ones **2** *Zool. a)* having a foot or feet *b)* like a foot; footlike

ped·dle (ped′'l) ***vi.*** **-dled, -dling** ⟦back-form. < fol.⟧ **1** to go from place to place selling small articles **2** ⟦infl. by PIDDLE⟧ to spend time on trifles; piddle —***vt.*** **1** to carry from place to place and offer for sale **2** to sell or offer for sale: a somewhat dismissive use *[to peddle life insurance]* **3** to deal out or circulate (gossip, ideas, etc.): often used with mild contempt

ped·dler (ped′lər, ped′'l ər) ***n.*** ⟦ME *pedlare, pedlere* < ? *peddare,* peddler < *ped, pedde,* a basket, via dim. *pedle*⟧ a person who peddles

ped·dler·y (ped′lər ē, ped′'l ər ē) ***n.*** **1** the business or trade of a peddler **2** wares sold by a peddler

ped·dling (ped′liŋ, ped′'l iŋ) ***adj.*** ⟦see PEDDLE, ***vi.***⟧ busy with trifles; trifling; petty

-pede (pēd) ⟦< L *pes* (gen. *pedis*), FOOT⟧ *combining form forming nouns* foot or feet *[centipede]*

ped·er·ast (ped′ər ast′) ***n.*** ⟦Fr *pédéraste* < Gr *paiderastēs*⟧ a man who practices pederasty —**ped′er·as′tic** ***adj.*** —**ped′er·as′ti·cal·ly** ***adv.***

ped·er·as·ty (ped′ər as′tē) ***n.*** ⟦ModL *paederastia* < Gr *paiderastia* < *paiderastēs,* lover of boys < *pais* (gen. *paidos*), boy (see PEDO-[1]) + *eran,* to love⟧ sodomy between male persons, esp. as practiced by a man with a boy

pe·des (pē′dēz′, ped′ēz′) ***n.*** *pl. of* PES

ped·es·tal (ped′əs təl) ***n.*** ⟦Fr *piédestal* < It *piedestallo* < *piè* (< L *pes*), FOOT + *di,* of + *stal* (< Gmc **stal,* STALL[1]), a rest, place⟧ **1** the foot or bottom support of a column or pillar **2** a similar base on a lamp, statue, etc. **3** a columnlike stand for displaying a piece of sculpture or other decorative article —***vt.*** **-taled** or **-talled, -tal·ing** or **-tal·ling** to place on or furnish with a pedestal —**put (or set) on a pedestal** to regard with great or excessive admiration; idolize

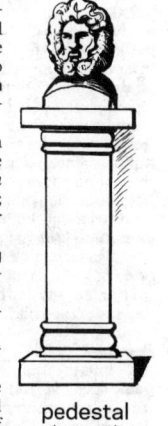

pedestal
(sense 3)

pe·des·tri·an (pi des′trē ən) ***adj.*** ⟦< L *pedester,* on foot < *pes* (gen. *pedis*), FOOT + -IAN⟧ **1** going or done on foot; walking **2** of or for pedestrians *[a pedestrian crossing]* **3** lacking interest or imagination; prosaic; ordinary and dull —***n.*** one who goes on foot; walker —**pe·des′tri·an·ism′** ***n.***

pe·des·tri·an·ize (pə des′trē ən īz′) ***vt.*** **-ized′, -iz′ing** to make (an area, esp. a street) accessible to pedestrians only by closing to use by automobiles, buses, etc.

ped·i- (ped′i, -ə) ⟦< L *pes* (gen. *pedis*), FOOT⟧ *combining form* foot or feet *[pedicab, pedipalp]*

pe·di·a·tri·cian (pē′dē ə trish′ən) ***n.*** a specialist in pediatrics: also **pe·di·at·rist** (pē′dē a′trist, pē dī′ə trist′)

pe·di·at·rics (pē′dē a′triks) ***n.*** ⟦< PED(O)- + -IATRICS⟧ the branch of medicine dealing with the development and care of infants and children, and with the treatment of their diseases, illnesses, etc. —**pe′di·at′ric** ***adj.***

ped·i·cab (ped′i kab′) ***n.*** ⟦PEDI- + CAB[1]⟧ a three-wheeled passenger vehicle, esp. formerly in Southeast Asia, which the driver propels like a bicycle by pedaling

ped·i·cel (ped′i səl) ***n.*** ⟦ModL *pedicellus,* dim. of L *pediculus,* dim. of *pes* (gen. *pedis*), FOOT⟧ **1** *Bot. a)* the stalk of a single flower, fruit, leaf, etc. *b)* the stalk of a grass spikelet **2** *Zool. a)* a small, stalklike structure or support, as the stalk of a sessile organism or the second segment of an insect's antenna *b)* a small, footlike organ or part —**ped′i·cel′late** (-sel′it, -āt′) ***adj.***

ped·i·cle (ped′i kəl) ***n.*** ⟦L *pediculus*⟧ PEDICEL

pe·dic·u·lar (pi dik′yoo͞ lər) ***adj.*** ⟦L *pedicularis* < *pediculus,* dim. of *pedis,* a louse < **pezdis,* akin to *pedere:* see PETARD⟧ **1** of lice **2** infested with lice; lousy

pe·dic·u·late (pi dik′yoo͞ lit, -lāt′) ***adj.*** ⟦< L *pediculus* (see PEDICEL) + -ATE[1]⟧ of an angler fish, characterized by pectoral fins attached to an armlike base and a reduced dorsal fin whose first flexible ray, attached to the head, often serves as a lure —***n.*** any angler fish

pe·dic·u·lo·sis (pi dik′yoo͞ lō′sis) ***n.*** ⟦< L *pediculus* (see PEDICULAR) + -OSIS⟧ infestation with lice —**pe·dic′u·lous** (-yə ləs) ***adj.***

☆**ped·i·cure** (ped′i kyoor′) ***n.*** ⟦Fr *pédicure* < L *pes* (gen. *pedis*), FOOT + *curare,* to care for < *cura:* see CURE⟧ **1** *former term for* PODIATRIST **2** ⟦by analogy with MANICURE⟧ a treatment for the care of the feet; now, esp., a trimming, cleaning, and sometimes polishing of the toenails —**ped′i·cured′** ***adj.*** —**ped′i·cur′ist** ***n.***

ped·i·gree (ped′i grē′) ***n.*** ⟦ME *pedegru, pe de gre* < MFr *pié de grue,* lit., crane's foot < L *pes,* FOOT + *grus,* a crane: from the lines in the genealogical tree⟧ **1** a list of ancestors; record of ancestry; family tree **2** descent; lineage; ancestry **3** a recorded or known line of descent, esp. of a purebred animal **4** the background or origin of a person or thing, esp. as a mark of prestige or distinction *[an Ivy League pedigree]* —**ped′i·greed′** ***adj.***

ped·i·ment (ped′i mənt) ***n.*** ⟦altered (after L *pes,* gen. *pedis,* FOOT) < earlier *periment,* prob. altered < PYRAMID⟧ **1** a low-pitched gable on the front of some buildings in the Grecian style of architecture **2** any similar triangular piece used ornamentally, as over a doorway, fireplace, etc. —**ped′i·men′tal** ***adj.***

ped·i·men·ted (ped′i men′tid) ***adj.*** having a pediment

ped·i·palp (ped′i palp′) ***n.*** ⟦ModL *pedipalpus:* see PEDI- & PALPUS⟧ either of the leglike second pair of appendages of spiders and other arachnids, variously specialized for grasping, sensing, fertilizing, etc.

ped·lar or **ped·ler** (ped′lər, ped′'l ər) ***n.*** *alt. sp. of* PEDDLER —**ped′lar·y** ***n.,*** **ped′ler·y**

pe·do-[1] (pē′dō, -də) ⟦< Gr *pais* (gen. *paidos*), a child < IE base **pou-,* small,

small animal, child > FEW, FOAL⟧ *combining form* child, children, offspring *[pedophilia, pedobaptism]*

ped·o-[2] (ped′ō, -ə) ⟦< Gr *pedon,* the ground < IE base, **ped-,* FOOT⟧ *combining form* ground, soil, earth *[pedocal]*

ped·o·cal (ped′ō kal′) *n.* ⟦< prec. + L *calx* (gen. *calcis*), lime: see CALCIUM⟧ soil containing much lime, commonly formed in prairie regions characterized by low humidity and temperature —**ped′o·cal′ic** *adj.*

☆**pe·do·don·tics** (pē′dō dän′tiks) *n.* ⟦ModL: see PEDO-[1], -ODONT, & -ICS⟧ the branch of dentistry concerned with the care and treatment of children's teeth —**pe′do·don′tic** *adj.* —**pe′do·don′tist** *n.*

ped·o·gen·e·sis (ped′ō jen′ə sis) *n.* ⟦PEDO-[2] + -GENESIS⟧ soil formation —**ped′o·gen′ic** (-jen′ik) *adj.* or **ped′o·ge·net′ic** (-jə net′ik)

☆**pe·dol·o·gy**[1] (pē däl′ə jē) *n.* ⟦PEDO-[1] + -LOGY⟧ the systematic study of the behavior and development of children —**pe·do·log·ic** (pē′dō läj′ik) *adj.*, **pe′do·log′i·cal** —**pe′do·log′i·cal·ly** *adv.* —**pe·dol′o·gist** *n.*

pe·dol·o·gy[2] (pē däl′ə jē) *n.* ⟦PEDO-[2] + -LOGY⟧ the scientific study of soils —**ped·o·log·ic** (ped′ō läj′ik) *adj.* or **ped′o·log′i·cal** —**ped′o·log′i·cal·ly** *adv.* —**pe·dol′o·gist** *n.*

pe·dom·e·ter (pē däm′ət ər, pi-) *n.* ⟦Fr *pédomètre* < L *pes* (gen. *pedis*), FOOT + Gr *metron,* MEASURE⟧ an instrument carried by a walker, which measures approximately the distance covered in walking by recording the number of steps

pe·do·phile (ped′ə fīl′, pē′də-) *n.* an adult who has sexual desire for children

pe·do·phil·i·a (ped′ə fil′ē ə, pē′də-) *n.* ⟦PEDO-[1] + -PHILIA⟧ sexual desire felt by an adult for children —**pe′do·phil′ic** *adj.*

pe·dun·cle (pē duŋ′kəl, pē′duŋ′-) *n.* ⟦ModL *pedunculus,* dim. of L *pes* (gen. *pedis*), FOOT⟧ **1** *Anat.* a stalklike bundle of nerve fibers connecting various parts of the brain **2** *Bot. a)* the stalk of a flower cluster or inflorescence *b)* the stalk of a solitary flower which is regarded as a reduced inflorescence, as in the narcissus **3** *Med.* a narrow, stalklike base of a tumor or polyp **4** *Zool.* a slender, stalklike part, as between the abdomen and middle section of an insect, or the stalk of a goose barnacle; pedicel —**pe·dun·cu·lar** (pē duŋ′kyoo lər) *adj.*

pe·dun·cu·late (pē duŋ′kyoo lit, -lāt′) *adj.* growing on or having a peduncle: also **pe·dun′cu·lat′ed**

pee (pē) [Informal] *vi., vt.* **peed, pee′ing** ⟦orig. euphemistic use of P(ISS)⟧ to urinate —*n.* **1** urine **2** an act of urination

Pee·bles (pē′bəlz) former county of SC Scotland: also **Pee′bles·shire′** (-shir′)

Pee Dee (pē′ dē′) ⟦< AmInd tribal name⟧ river flowing through N.C. & S.C. into the Atlantic: 233 mi (375 km): see YADKIN

peek (pēk) *vi.* ⟦ME *piken* < ?⟧ to glance or look quickly and furtively, esp. through an opening or from behind something —*n.* such a glance

peek·a·boo (pēk′ə boo′) *n.* a game to amuse a young child, in which someone hides his or her face, as behind the hands, and then suddenly reveals it, calling "Peekaboo!" —☆*adj.* made of openwork or sheer fabric: said as of a blouse —*interj.* used as an exclamation in the child's game or to startle or gain attention

peel[1] (pēl) *vt.* ⟦ME *pilien, peolien* < OE **pilian* < L *pilare,* to make bald < *pilus,* hair: see PILE[2]⟧ to cut away or strip off (the rind, skin, covering, surface, etc.) of (anything); pare —*vi.* **1** to shed skin, bark, etc. **2** to come off in layers or flakes, as old paint or sunburned skin **3** [Slang] to undress —*n.* the rind or skin of a fruit or vegetable —*SYN.* SKIN —**keep one's eyes peeled** *see phrase under* EYE —**peel off 1** *Aeron.* to veer away from a flight formation in an abrupt maneuver **2** [Slang] *a)* to depart; leave *b)* to go in another direction —☆**peel out** [Slang] to accelerate an automobile very rapidly, as in a drag race: also **peel rubber (or tires)** —**peel′er** *n.*

peel[2] (pēl) *n.* ⟦ME *pele* < OFr < L *pala,* a spade⟧ a long shovel-like tool used by bakers for moving bread into and out of the ovens

peel[3] (pēl) *n.* ⟦ME *pel* < Anglo-Fr < OFr, a fort, stake < L *palus:* see PALE[2]⟧ a fortified house or tower of a type built during the 16th cent. on the border between Scotland and England

Peel (pēl), Sir **Robert** 1788-1850; Brit. statesman: prime minister (1834-35; 1841-46)

peel·er (pē′lər) *n.* ⟦after prec., who first organized the Irish constabulary⟧ [Old Brit. Slang] a policeman

peel·ing (pē′liŋ) *n.* a peeled-off strip, as of apple skin

peen (pēn) *n.* ⟦prob. < Scand, as in Norw *pænn,* sharpened end of a hammer, Swed *pæna,* to beat out⟧ the part of the head of certain hammers opposite to the flat striking surface: it is often ball-shaped or wedge-shaped —*vt.* to hammer, bend, etc. with a peen

peep[1] (pēp) *vi.* ⟦ME *pepen:* orig. echoic⟧ **1** to make the short, high-pitched cry of a young bird or chick; chirp; cheep **2** to utter a sound or speak in a small, weak voice, as from fear —*n.* **1** a short, high-pitched sound; chirp; cheep **2** the slightest vocal sound *[heard not a peep from him]*

peep[2] (pēp) *vi.* ⟦ME *pepen,* ? akin to *piken,* PEEK⟧ **1** to look through a small opening or from a place of hiding **2** to peer slyly or secretly; take a hasty, furtive look **3** to come into view; show or appear gradually or partially, as though from hiding *[stars peeped through the clouds]* —*vt.* to cause to appear or protrude —*n.* **1** a brief, hasty look or restricted view; secret or furtive glimpse or glance **2** the first appearance; crack, as of dawn

pee-pee[1] (pē′pē′) [Slang] *n.* ⟦redupl. of PEE⟧ urine —**go pee-pee** to urinate *USAGE*—a child's term

pee-pee[2] (pē′pē′) *n.* ⟦shortened < PENIS⟧ [Slang] a penis: a child's term

peep·er[1] (pē′pər) *n.* **1** a person who peeps or pries **2** [Slang] *a)* [*pl.*] the eyes ☆*b)* a private detective

peep·er[2] (pē′pər) *n.* **1** a person or thing that peeps, cheeps, chirps, etc. ☆**2** any of various tree frogs (esp. family Hylidae) that peep in early spring

peep·hole (pēp′hōl′) *n.* a hole to peep through, specif. one cut into a door that allows visitors to be viewed from the inside before the door is opened

Peeping Tom 1 *Eng. Legend* a Coventry tailor who was struck blind after peeping at Lady Godiva **2** [**p- T-**] a person who gets pleasure, esp. sexual pleasure, from watching others, esp. furtively

peep show 1 a pictured scene or group of objects, as in a box, viewed through a small opening, sometimes with a magnifying lens **2** an erotic or pornographic film viewed through a coin-operated device

peep sight a rear sight for a firearm, usually consisting of an adjustable disk with a small opening in the center through which the front sight and target are lined up

pee·pul (pē′pəl) *n.* an Indian fig tree (*Ficus religiosa*): see BO TREE

peer[1] (pir) *n.* ⟦ME *peir* < OFr *per* < L *par,* an equal: see PAR[1]⟧ **1** a person or thing of the same rank, value, quality, ability, etc.; equal; specif., an equal before the law **2** a noble; esp., a British duke, marquess, earl, viscount, or baron **3** a person who is a member of the same group, class, etc. as another *[a professor's academic peers]* —*vt.* [Archaic] to match or equal —**peer of the realm** any of the British peers entitled to a seat in the House of Lords

peer[2] (pir) *vi.* ⟦? aphetic < APPEAR⟧ **1** to look closely and searchingly, or squint, as in trying to see more clearly **2** to come out or show slightly; come partly into sight **3** [Old Poet.] to appear

peer·age (pir′ij) *n.* **1** all the peers of a particular country **2** the rank or dignity of a peer **3** a book or list of peers with their lineage

peer·ess (pir′is) *n.* **1** the wife or widow of a peer **2** a woman having the rank of peer in her own right

peer group all those people of about the same age, status, etc. in a society, regarded as forming a sociological group with a homogeneous system of values

peer·less (pir′lis) *adj.* without equal; unrivaled —**peer′less·ly** *adv.* —**peer′less·ness** *n.*

peer pressure compelling influence to conform to the behavior or expectations of one's PEER GROUP

peer-re·viewed (pir′ri vyood′) *adj.* of or being scientific or scholarly writing or research that has undergone evaluation by other experts in the field (**peer review**) to judge if it merits publication or funding

☆**peet·weet** (pēt′wēt′) *n.* ⟦echoic⟧ SPOTTED SANDPIPER (see SANDPIPER)

☆**peeve** (pēv) [Informal] *vt.* **peeved, peev′ing** ⟦back-form. < PEEVISH⟧ to make peevish or bad-tempered; annoy —*n.* **1** an object of dislike; annoyance **2** a peevish state —*SYN.* IRRITATE

☆**peeved** (pēvd) *adj.* ⟦pp. of prec.⟧ [Informal] irritated; annoyed

pee·vish (pē′vish) *adj.* ⟦ME *pevische* < ?⟧ **1** hard to please; irritable; fretful; cross **2** showing ill humor or impatience, as a glance or remark —**pee′vish·ly** *adv.* —**pee′vish·ness** *n.*

☆**pee·wee** (pē′wē′) *n.* ⟦prob. echoic redupl. of WEE⟧ **1** [Informal] a person or thing that is unusually small **2** *alt. sp. of* PEWEE —*adj.* designating or of an organized sport or sports league for children: also written **pee wee** or **Pee Wee**

pee·wit (pē′wit) *n. var. of* PEWIT

peg (peg) *n.* ⟦ME *pegge,* prob. < LowG source, as in Du *peg,* wooden plug < IE base **bak-,* staff > L *baculum,* stick⟧ **1** a short, usually tapering or pointed piece of wood, metal, etc. used to hold parts together or in place, or to close an opening, as in a barrel **2** a projecting pin or bolt used to hang things on, fasten ropes to, mark degrees of measurement or keep the score in a game, etc. **3** *a)* the distance between pegs *b)* a step or degree *c)* a fixed level, as for a price **4** any of the pins which hold, and are used in regulating the tension of, the strings of a violin or other stringed instrument **5** a point or prong for tearing, hooking, etc. **6** a point of reference, esp. an excuse or reason **7** [Informal] the foot or leg **8** [Informal] an act or instance of throwing; esp., a hard, accurate throw from a baseball fielder **9** [Brit.] CLOTHESPIN **10** [Brit. Informal] a drink, esp. of brandy or whiskey and soda —*vt.* **pegged, peg′ging 1** to put a peg or pegs into so as to fasten, secure, mark, etc. **2** to mark (a boundary, claim, etc.) with pegs: usually with *out* **3** to strike with a peg so as to pierce or hook **4** to fix (a price, etc.) at a particular level **5** to score (points) in cribbage during the play of a hand **6** [Informal] to give support, relevance, or perspective to (an idea, news story, etc.) by relating it to something else **7** [Informal] to identify or categorize *[pegged him as a man of action]* **8** [Informal] to throw; esp., to throw forcefully *[to peg a ball to first base]* —*vi.* **1** to score points in cribbage during the play of a hand **2** to move energetically or quickly: usually with *down, along,* etc. —**off the peg** [Chiefly Brit.] READY-MADE —**peg away (at)** to work steadily and persistently (at) —**round peg in a square hole** a person in a position, situation, etc. for which he or she is unsuited or unqualified: also **square peg in a round hole** —**take down a peg** to lower the pride or conceit of; humble or dispirit

Peg·a·sus (peg′ə səs) *n.* ⟦L < Gr *Pēgasos*⟧ **1** *Gr. Myth.* a winged horse which springs from the body of Medusa at her death **2** a large N constellation between Andromeda and Pisces

peg·board (peg′bôrd′) *n.* ⟦< *Peg-Board,* former trademark⟧ ☆boardlike material, or a piece of this, perforated with rows of holes, for arranging pegs or hooks to hold displays, tools, etc.

Peg·gy (peg′ē) *n.* a feminine name: see MARGARET

peg leg [Informal] **1** an aritifical leg, esp. one made of wood **2** a person with such a leg: now considered an insulting term

peg·ma·tite (peg′mə tīt′) *n.* ⟦< Gr *pēgma* (gen. *pēgmatos*), a framework, something fastened together (< IE base **paĝ-*: see FANG) + -ITE[1]: from its texture⟧ a light-colored, coarsegrained, intrusive igneous rock, usually granitic, containing large crystals of quartz, feldspar, and mica, and sometimes rare minerals: typically found in fissures of other igneous rocks —**peg′ma·tit′ic** (-tit′ik) ***adj.***

peg top 1 a child's spinning top having a metal tip on which it spins 2 [*pl.*] peg-top trousers

peg-top (peg′täp′) ***adj.*** pear-shaped like a peg top; esp., designating trousers that are full at the hips and narrow at the cuffs

peh (pā) ***n.*** *alt. sp. of* PE

Peh·le·vi (pā′lə vē′) ***n.*** ⟦Pers *pahlawī* < *Pahlav,* PARTHIA < OPers *Parthava*⟧ an Iranian language spoken and written in Persia from about the 3d to the 8th cent. A.D.; Middle Persian: the name is often restricted to the literary language of the Zoroastrian books, written *c.* A.D. 224-651

Pei (pā), **I(eoh) M(ing)** 1917- ; U.S. architect, born in China

PEI *abbrev.* Prince Edward Island: also **P.E.I.**

peign·oir (pān wär′, pen-; pān′wär′, pen′-) ***n.*** ⟦Fr < *peigner,* to comb < L *pectinare* < *pecten,* comb: see PECTEN⟧ a woman's full, loose dressing gown like a negligee

pein (pēn) ***n.*** *alt. sp. of* PEEN

Pei·ping (bā′piŋ′) *a former transliteration of* BEIJING

Peip·si (pāp′sē) *Estonian name for* Lake CHUDSKOYE

Pei·pus (pī′po͝os) *Ger. name for* Lake CHUDSKOYE

Pei·rai·évs (pē′re efs′) *Gr. name for* PIRAEUS

Peirce (purs), **Charles San·ders** (san′dərz) 1839-1914; U.S. philosopher & mathematician

pej·o·ra·tion (pej′ə rā′shən, pē′jə-) ***n.*** ⟦ML *pejoratio:* see fol.⟧ *Linguis.* the taking on of a less favorable meaning or connotation

pe·jo·ra·tive (pi jôr′ə tiv, -jär′-; *occas.* pē′jə rāt′iv, pej′ə-) ***adj.*** ⟦< L *pejoratus,* pp. of *pejorare,* to make worse < *pejor,* worse, orig., inclined downward < IE base **ped-,* FOOT⟧ 1 *Linguis.* taking on or giving a meaning or connotation that is less favorable [-ess and -ling are often *pejorative* suffixes] 2 disparaging or derogatory —***n.*** a pejorative word or form —**pe·jo′ra·tive·ly** ***adv.***

pek·an (pek′ən) ***n.*** ⟦CdnFr *pécan, pékan* < extinct Abenaki dialect *pekane*⟧ FISHER (sense 2)

pe·kin (pē′kin′) ***n.*** ⟦Fr *pékin* < *Pékin,* PEKING⟧ a striped silk material, orig. from China

Pe·kin (pē′kin) ***n.*** ⟦see fol.⟧ any of a breed of large, white domestic duck, originating in China, raised esp. for its meat: often **Pe′king** (-kin)

Pe·king (pē′kiŋ′) ⟦< Fr *Pékin,* Jesuit missionaries' sp. of the Chin name: see BEIJING⟧ *a former transliteration of* BEIJING

Peking duck a Chinese dish of roasted duck traditionally served in several courses, including thin pancakes rolled up with pieces of the crisp skin, scallions, and a sauce

Pe·king·ese (pē′kiŋ ēz′; *for n. 3, usually,* -kə nēz′) ***adj.*** of Beijing (Peking) or its people, language, or culture —***n.,*** *pl.* **Pe′king·ese′** (-kə nēz′) 1 a person born or living in Beijing (Peking) 2 the variety of Chinese spoken in Beijing 3 any of a breed of toy dog with a long, straight coat, a heavy mane, prominent eyes, short legs, and a short, wrinkled muzzle, originally bred in China Also **Pe′kin·ese′** (-kə nēz′)

Peking man a type of early human (*Homo erectus pekinensis*) of the Middle Pleistocene, known from fossil remains found near Beijing (Peking), China

pe·koe (pē′kō) ***n.*** ⟦< Amoy Chin dial. *pek-ho,* lit., white down: from being picked while leaves still have the down on them⟧ a fine grade of black tea of Sri Lanka and India, made from the small leaves at the tips of the stem

pel·age (pel′ij) ***n.*** ⟦Fr < OFr *pel,* hair < L *pilus,* hair: see PILE[2]⟧ the coat, or covering, of a mammal, as hair or fur

Pe·la·gi·an (pi lā′jē ən) ***n.*** ⟦ML(Ec) *Pelagianus*⟧ *Christian Theol.* a follower of Pelagius, who affirmed freedom of the will and consequently denied the necessity of divine grace for justification and salvation —***adj.*** of Pelagius, his followers, or those who hold similar doctrines —**Pe·la′gi·an·ism′** ***n.***

pe·lag·ic (pi laj′ik) ***adj.*** ⟦L *pelagicus* < Gr *pelagos,* the sea < IE **plāg-,* to spread out < base **plā-* > PLAIN[1]⟧ of the ocean waters; esp., of the oceanic zone, as distinguished from the benthic regions of the ocean

Pe·la·gi·us (pə lā′jē əs) A.D. 360?-420?; Brit. monk & theologian: see also PELAGIAN

pel·ar·gon·ic acid (pel′är gän′ik, -gō′nik) a monobasic fatty acid, $C_8H_{17}COOH$, obtained from the leaves of a pelargonium or by oxidation of oleic acid: used in lacquers, pharmaceuticals, etc.

pel·ar·go·ni·um (pel′är gō′nē əm) ***n.*** ⟦ModL *Pelargonium* < Gr *pelargos,* stork (after ModL *Geranium:* see GERANIUM), because the carpels resemble a stork's bill⟧ any of a genus (*Pelargonium*) of mostly South African plants of the geranium family, having circular or lobed, often aromatic, leaves and variously colored flowers

Pe·las·gi (pə laz′jī′) ***pl.n.*** the Pelasgians

Pe·las·gi·an (pə laz′jē ən) ***n.*** any of a prehistoric people mentioned by ancient Greek authors and believed to have lived in, variously, Greece, Asia Minor, and the Aegean Islands —***adj.*** of the Pelasgians: also **Pe·las′gic** (-jik)

pel·e·can·i·form (pel′ə kan′ə fôrm′) ***adj.*** of, or having the nature of, an order (Pelecaniformes) of swimming birds having all four toes connected in a webbed foot, including pelicans and cormorants

pe·lec·y·pod (pə les′i päd′) ***n., adj.*** ⟦< Gr *pelekys,* an ax (akin to Sans *paraśú,* battle-ax) + -POD⟧ BIVALVE

Pe·lée (pə lā′), **Mount** volcanic mountain on Martinique, in the West Indies: erupted 1902: 4,429 ft (1,350 m)

pel·er·ine (pel′ər ēn′) ***n.*** ⟦Fr *pèlerine* < *pèlerin,* a pilgrim < L *peregrinus:* see PILGRIM⟧ a woman's cape, often of fur, tapering to long points in the front

Pe·le's hair (pā′lāz′, pē′lēz′) ⟦transl. of Haw *lauoho-o Pele,* after *Pele,* goddess of volcanoes⟧ fine, hairlike filaments of volcanic glass formed naturally from molten lava that hardened while it was subjected to high winds or other turbulence

Pe·le·us (pē′lē əs, pēl′yo͞os′) ***n.*** *Gr. Myth.* a king of the Myrmidons, father of Achilles

pelf (pelf) ***n.*** ⟦ME, akin to (< ?) MFr *pelfre,* booty⟧ 1 [Obs.] ill-gotten gains; booty 2 money or wealth regarded with contempt

Pe·li·as (pē′lē əs, pel′ē-) ***n.*** ⟦L < Gr⟧ *Gr. Myth.* a king of Thessaly and the uncle and guardian of Jason, whom he sends in search of the Golden Fleece

pel·i·can (pel′i kən) ***n.*** ⟦ME < OE *pellicane* < LL(Ec) *pelicanus* < Gr *pelekan* (used in LXX to transl. Heb *ḳā'ath,* bird of prey), akin to *pelekas,* woodpecker, prob. < *pelekys,* an ax (from the shape of the bill)⟧ any of a genus (*Pelecanus,* family Pelecanidae) of pelecaniform birds with a distensible pouch which hangs from the large lower bill and is used to scoop up or store fish

North American white pelican

☆**pelican hook** a hinged hook that can be quickly secured or released by a sliding ring

Pe·li·on (pē′lē ən) mountain in E Thessaly, NE Greece: 5,252 ft (1,601 m): in Greek mythology, the Titans piled Pelion on Ossa & both on Olympus in a futile attempt to reach & attack the gods in heaven

pe·lisse (pə lēs′) ***n.*** ⟦Fr < OFr < VL *pellicia,* for *pellicia (vestis)* < L *pellicius,* made of skins < *pellis,* a skin: for IE base see FELL[4]⟧ a long cloak or outer coat, esp. one made, lined, or trimmed with fur

pel·la·gra (pə lā′grə, -lag′rə) ***n.*** ⟦It < *pelle* (L *pellis*), the skin + *-agra* < Gr *agra,* seizure, akin to *agein:* see ACT[1]⟧ a chronic disease caused by a deficiency of nicotinic acid in the diet and characterized by gastrointestinal disturbances, skin eruptions, and mental disorders: it is endemic in some parts of the world —**pel·la′grous** ***adj.***

pel·la·grin (pə lā′grin) ***n.*** a person who has pellagra

pel·let (pel′it) ***n.*** ⟦ME *pelote* < OFr < VL **pilotta,* dim. of L *pila,* a ball, orig., knot of hair: see PILE[2]⟧ 1 a little ball or rounded mass, as of clay, paper, medicine, compressed food for animals, etc. 2 *a)* a crude projectile of stone, etc., as used in a catapult or early cannon *b)* a bullet or an imitation bullet *c)* any of various pieces of small, usually lead, shot —***vt.*** 1 to make pellets of 2 to shoot or hit with pellets

pel·let·ize (pel′ə tīz′) ***vt.*** **-ized′, -iz′ing** to form (a substance) into pellets; specif., to make pellets of the iron-containing particles recovered from pulverized low-grade iron (ore) —**pel′let·i·za′tion** ***n.***

pel·li·cle (pel′i kəl) ***n.*** ⟦L *pellicula,* dim. of *pellis,* skin: see FELL[4]⟧ 1 a thin skin or film, as on a photographic emulsion or on a liquid 2 *Zool.* a thin nonliving membrane secreted by animal cells, as the envelope covering many protozoans —**pel·lic·u·lar** (pə lik′yo͞o lər) ***adj.,*** **pel·lic′u·late** (-lit, -lāt′)

pel·li·to·ry (pel′i tôr′ē) ***n.,*** *pl.* **-ries** ⟦altered < ME *peritorie* < OFr *paritoire* < L *parietaria* < *parietarius,* of walls < *paries:* see PARIES⟧ 1 any of a genus (*Parietaria*) of plants of the nettle family, often grown as an ornamental: in full **wall pellitory** 2 a Mediterranean plant (*Anacyclus pyrethrum*) of the composite family, whose root was formerly used to relieve toothache: in full **pellitory of Spain**

pell-mell (pel′mel′) ***adv., adj.*** ⟦Fr *pêle-mêle* < OFr *pesle mesle,* redupl. < *mesler,* to mix⟧ 1 in a jumbled, confused mass or manner; without order or method 2 in wild, disorderly haste; headlong —***n.*** a jumble; confusion; disorder Also written **pell′mell′**

pel·lu·cid (pə lo͞o′sid) ***adj.*** ⟦L *pellucidus* < *pellucere,* to shine through < *per,* through (see PER[1]) + *lucere,* to shine < *lux,* LIGHT[1]⟧ 1 transparent or translucent; clear 2 easy to understand; clear and simple in style [*a pellucid* explanation] —**SYN.** CLEAR —**pel·lu·cid·i·ty** (pel′yo͞o sid′ə tē) ***n.,*** **pel·lu′cid·ness** —**pel·lu′cid·ly** ***adv.***

pel·met (pel′mət) ***n.*** ⟦? altered < Fr *palmette,* a palm-leaf ornament on a cornice < *palme,* PALM[1]⟧ a decorative cornice or valance for concealing the fixtures of curtains or drapes

Pe·lop·i·das (pi läp′i dəs) died 364 B.C.; Theban general

Peloponnesian War an intermittent war between Athens and Sparta (431-404 B.C.), ending in victory for Sparta

Pel·o·pon·ne·sus or **Pel·o·pon·ne·sos** (pel′ə pə nē′səs) ⟦< ? *Pelops* (see fol.) + *nesos,* island⟧ peninsula forming the S part of the mainland of Greece —**Pel′o·pon·ne′sian** (-shən, -zhən) ***adj., n.***

Peloponnesus

Pe·lops (pē′läps′) ***n.*** ⟦L < Gr, prob. < *pellos,* dark + *ops,* face: see EYE⟧ *Gr.*

Myth. the son of Tantalus: he is killed and served to the gods as food by his father, but later is restored to life by them

pe·lo·ri·a (pi lō′rē ə, -lôr′ē ə) ***n.*** ⟦ModL < Gr *pelōros,* monstrous < (Aeolic) *pelōr,* monster, var. of *telōr,* for **terōr* < IE **kwerōr* < base **kwer-,* to make, form > OIr *cruth,* shape⟧ an abnormal regularity of form in a flower normally irregular —**pe·lo′ric** ***adj.***

pe·lo·rus (pə lōr′əs, -lôr′-) ***n.*** ⟦? after L *Pelorus,* pilot of Hannibal's ship⟧ *Naut.* a device for taking bearings, consisting of a flat metal ring, equipped with sighting vanes or a small telescope, that fits over a compass card or gyrocompass

pe·lo·ta (pə lōt′ə; *Sp* pe lô′tä) ***n.*** ⟦Sp, lit., a ball < VL **pilotta:* see PELLET⟧ JAI ALAI

pelt[1] (pelt) ***vt.*** ⟦LME *pelten* < ? *pelote,* PELLET⟧ **1** to throw things at; strike with or as with missiles **2** to beat or pound heavily and repeatedly **3** to throw or cast (missiles) —***vi.*** **1** to beat or strike heavily or steadily, as hard rain **2** to rush or hurry —***n.*** **1** [Now Rare] the act of pelting **2** a blow —**(at) full pelt** at full speed —**pelt′er** ***n.***

pelt[2] (pelt) ***n.*** ⟦ME, prob. back-form. < OFr *peleterie:* see PELTRY⟧ **1** the skin of a fur-bearing animal, esp. after it has been stripped from the carcass **2** the human skin: a humorous usage —**SYN.** SKIN

pel·tast (pel′tast′) ***n.*** ⟦L *peltasta* < Gr *peltastēs* < *peltē,* light shield < IE **pelto-,* a cover < base **pel-,* to cover, skin: see FELL[4]⟧ in ancient Greece, a soldier carrying a light shield

pel·tate (pel′tāt′) ***adj.*** ⟦< L *pelta* (< Gr *peltē:* see prec.) + -ATE[1]⟧ *Bot.* shield-shaped; specif., having the stalk attached to the lower surface, at or near the center: said of a leaf —**pel′tate′ly** ***adv.***

pel·ter (pel′tər) ***vt., vi.*** PELT[1]

Pel·tier effect (pel′tyā′, pel tyā′) ⟦after J. *Peltier* (1785-1845), Fr physicist⟧ *Elec.* the liberation or absorption of heat at a junction of two unlike metals through which an electric current is passing

pelt·ing (pel′tiŋ) ***adj.*** ⟦prob. < obs. *pelt,* to haggle, akin ? to PALTRY⟧ [Archaic] mean; miserly; paltry

pelt·ry (pel′trē) ***n., pl.*** **-ries** ⟦ME < OFr *peleterie* < *peletier,* furrier < *pel* (L *pellis*), a skin: see FELL[4]⟧ pelts, or fur-bearing skins, collectively

pel·vic (pel′vik) ***adj.*** of or near the pelvis

pelvic fin either of a pair of fins corresponding to the hind limbs of a higher vertebrate and associated with the pelvic girdle in fishes

pelvic girdle the bony or cartilaginous structures to which the hind limbs or fins of a vertebrate are attached

pelvic inflammatory disease an acute or chronic condition in which inflammation of the cervix, uterus, fallopian tubes, or ovaries, often caused by sexually transmitted microorganisms and characterized by fever, abdominal pain, and discharges of pus, may result in sterility

pel·vis (pel′vis) ***n., pl.*** **-vis·es** or **-ves′** (-vēz′) ⟦ModL < L, basin < IE base **pel-,* container > ON, OE *full,* cup⟧ *Anat., Zool.* any basinlike or funnel-shaped structure; specif., *a)* the basinlike cavity formed by the ring of bones of the pelvic girdle in the posterior part of the trunk in many vertebrates: in humans, it is formed by the ilium, ischium, pubis, coccyx, and sacrum, supporting the spinal column and resting upon the legs *b)* these bones collectively; pelvic girdle *c)* the funnel-shaped part of the kidney leading into the ureter

Pem·ba (pem′bə) island of Tanzania in the Indian Ocean, off the E coast of Africa: 380 sq mi (984 sq km)

Pem·broke[1] (pem′brōk′) ***n.*** the Pembroke Welsh corgi: see WELSH CORGI

Pem·broke[2] (pem′brook′, -brōk′) PEMBROKESHIRE

Pem·broke Pines (pem′brōk′) city in SE Fla.: suburb of Miami

Pem·broke·shire (pem′brook′shir′) former county of SW Wales, now part of Dyfed county

pem·mi·can (pem′i kən) ***n.*** ⟦Cree *pimihkaan* < *pimihkeew,* makes pemmican, makes grease < *pimiy,* grease⟧ **1** dried lean meat, pounded into a paste with fat and preserved in the form of pressed cakes **2** dried beef, suet, dried fruit, etc., prepared as a concentrated high-energy food

pem·phi·gus (pem′fi gəs, pem fi′-) ***n.*** ⟦ModL < Gr *pemphix* (gen. *pemphigos*), bubble < IE echoic base **bamb-, *bhambh-,* to swell⟧ a disease characterized by the formation of watery blisters on the skin, sometimes with itching

pen[1] (pen) ***n.*** ⟦ME < OE *penn,* prob. akin to *pinn,* PIN⟧ **1** a small yard or enclosure for domestic animals **2** the animals so confined **3** any small enclosure —***vt.*** **penned** or **pent, pen′ning** to confine or enclose in or as in a pen

pen[2] (pen) ***n.*** ⟦ME *penne* < OFr, a pen, feather < L *pinna,* var. of *penna,* a feather < **petna* < IE base **pet-,* to fly: see FEATHER⟧ **1** [Historical] a heavy quill or feather trimmed to a split point, used for writing with ink **2** now, any of various devices used in writing or drawing with ink; specif., *a)* a device with a half-tubular metal point split into two nibs, now used esp. by artists and draftsmen *b)* BALLPOINT (PEN) *c)* FOUNTAIN PEN **3** the metal point for a PEN[2] (*n.* 2*a*) **4** *a)* the pen regarded as an instrument of writing *b)* literary style or expression *c)* writing as a profession **5** any of various cartridge-like devices, as one designed to inject a measured dose of medication [insulin *pen*] **6** [Archaic] a feather or quill; esp., a heavy wing feather **7** *Zool.* the quill-shaped internal shell of a squid —***vt.*** **penned, pen′ning** to write with or as with a pen [*penned* verses filled with pain]

☆**pen**[3] (pen) ***n.*** [Slang] a penitentiary

pen[4] (pen) ***n.*** ⟦< ?⟧ a female swan

Pen or **pen** *abbrev.* peninsula

PEN (pen) *abbrev.* International Association of Poets, Playwrights, Editors, Essayists, and Novelists

pe·nal (pē′nəl) ***adj.*** ⟦ME < L *poenalis* < *poena,* punishment (> PAIN) < Gr *poinē,* penalty, fine < IE **kwoina,* punishment < base **kwei-,* to heed, respect, avenge > Sans *cáyatē,* (he) avenges, Lith *káina,* price⟧ **1** of, for, or constituting punishment, esp. legal punishment **2** specifying or prescribing punishment [a *penal* code] **3** making a person liable to punishment [a *penal* offense] —**pe′nal·ly** ***adv.***

penal code a body of law dealing with various crimes or offenses and their legal penalties

pe·nal·ize (pē′nə līz′, pen′ə-) ***vt.*** **-ized′, -iz′ing** **1** to make punishable; set a penalty for (an offense, etc.) **2** to impose a penalty on; specif., to subject to a handicap in a contest as penalty for the infraction of a rule **3** to put at a disadvantage —**pe′nal·i·za′tion** ***n.***

penal servitude imprisonment, usually at hard labor: the legal punishment for conviction of certain crimes

pen·al·ty (pen′əl tē) ***n., pl.*** **-ties** ⟦LME *penalyte* < ML *poenalitas* < L *poenalis:* see PENAL⟧ **1** a punishment fixed by law, as for a crime or breach of contract **2** the disadvantage, suffering, handicap, etc. imposed upon an offender or one who does not fulfill a contract or obligation, as a fine or forfeit; specif., a forfeit paid for withdrawal before maturity of invested funds **3** any unfortunate consequence or result of an act or condition **4** *Sports* any disadvantage, as a loss of yardage or the removal of a player, imposed because of infraction of a rule

penalty box **1** *Ice Hockey* a small, enclosed area just outside the wall surrounding the rink, where a player removed from the game must wait as a penalty **2** *Soccer* the large rectangular area directly in front of each goal where a foul committed by a defensive player may result in a PENALTY KICK: also **penalty area**

penalty kick *Soccer, Rugby, etc.* any kick awarded to a team as a result of a penalty given to an opponent; esp., in soccer, a 12-yard kick from directly in front of the goal, awarded for a foul committed by a defensive player who was inside the goalie's penalty box

pen·ance (pen′əns) ***n.*** ⟦ME < OFr *peneance* < L *paenitentia, poenitentia* < *paenitens:* see PENITENT⟧ **1** *R.C.Ch., Eastern Orthodox Ch.* *a)* a sacrament involving the confession of sin, repentance, and acceptance of the satisfaction imposed, followed by absolution by a priest *b)* the satisfaction imposed, as the recital of certain prayers **2** any act of reparation, self-punishment, etc. done in repentance for a sin or wrongdoing —***vt.*** **-anced, -anc·ing** [Archaic] to impose a penance on —**do penance** to do one or more acts of penance

Pe·nang (pi naŋ′) **1** island off the NW coast of the Malay Peninsula: 110 sq mi (285 sq km) **2** state of Malaysia, in Peninsular Malaysia, including this island & a section of the mainland opposite it: 398 sq mi (1,031 sq km) **3** its capital: seaport on the NE coast of Penang Island

pe·na·tes (pē nā′tēz′) ***pl.n.*** ⟦L, akin to *penus,* inner part of temple of Vesta: see PENETRATE⟧ the household gods of the ancient Romans: see LARES AND PENATES

pence (pens) ***n.*** ⟦ME *pens,* contr. of *penies,* pl. of *peny,* PENNY⟧ *pl. of* PENNY (senses 1*a* & *b*): used also in compounds [*twopence*]

pen·cel (pen′səl) ***n.*** ⟦ME < Anglo-Fr, contr. < OFr *penoncel,* dim. of *penon,* PENNON⟧ [Archaic] a small pennon, or narrow flag

pen·chant (pen′chənt) ***n.*** ⟦Fr < *pencher,* to incline < VL **pendicare* < L *pendere,* to hang: see PENDANT⟧ a strong liking or fondness; inclination; taste

Pen·chi (bun′chē′) *a former transliteration of* BENXI

pen·cil (pen′səl) ***n.*** ⟦ME *pencel* < MFr *pincel* < VL **penicellus* < L *penicillus,* a brush < dim. of *penis,* a tail, PENIS: mod. sense & form infl. by PEN[2]⟧ **1** [Archaic] an artist's small, fine brush **2** the individual style or ability of an artist **3** a slender, rod-shaped instrument of wood, metal, etc. with a center stick of graphite, crayon, etc. that is sharpened to a point for marking, writing, and drawing **4** something shaped or used like a pencil; specif., *a)* a small cosmetic stick as for darkening or redrawing the contours of the eyebrows *b)* a stick of some medicated substance [a styptic *pencil*] **5** a series of lines or rays coming to or spreading out from a point **6** *Math.* a set of lines, planes, etc. passing through a given point or points and satisfying a given equation, as *a)* all the lines passing through a given point *b)* all the planes passing through a given line *c)* all the circles lying in a given plane and passing through two fixed points —***vt.*** **-ciled** or **-cilled, -cil·ing** or **-cil·ling** **1** to mark, write, or draw with or as with a pencil **2** to use a pencil on **3** ⟦metaphoric extension: from being easy to erase⟧ to schedule or assign provisionally: with *in* [she *penciled* him in for dinner next week] —**pen′cil·er** ***n.***, **pen′cil·ler**

☆**pencil pusher** [Informal] a person with a job characterized by monotonous paperwork

pend (pend) ***vi.*** ⟦OFr *pendre* < L *pendere,* to weigh, hang: see fol.⟧ **1** to await judgment or decision **2** [Dial.] to depend

pend·ant (pen′dənt) ***n.*** ⟦ME *pendaunt* < OFr *pendant,* prp. of *pendre* < L *pendere,* to hang < IE base **(s)pen(d)-,* to pull, stretch > SPIN⟧ **1** a hanging ornamental object, as one suspended from an earring or a necklace **2** the stem and ring of a pocket watch **3** either of a pair; match or companion piece **4** anything hanging, as the pull chain on a lamp **5** a decorative piece suspended from a ceiling or roof, as in Gothic architecture —***adj.*** *alt. sp. of* PENDENT —**pend′ant·ly** ***adv.***

Pen·del·i·kón (pen del′ē kôn′) mountain in Attica, Greece, northeast of Athens: known for its fine marble: 3,638 ft (1,109 m)

pend·en·cy (pen′dən sē) ***n.*** the state or condition of being pendent or pending

pend·ent (pen′dənt) ***adj.*** ⟦ME *pendaunt:* see PENDANT⟧ **1** hanging; suspended 2 overhanging 3 undecided; pending —*n. alt. sp. of* PENDANT —**pend′ent·ly** *adv.*

pen·den·tive (pen den′tiv) *n.* ⟦Fr *pendentif* < L *pendens,* prp. of *pendere,* to hang: see PENDANT⟧ *Archit.* any one of the triangular pieces of vaulting springing from the corners of a rectangular area, serving to support a rounded or polygonal dome: usually supported by a single pier

pend·ing (pen′diŋ) *adj.* ⟦prp. of PEND, infl. by Fr *pendant,* L *pendens*⟧ 1 *a)* not decided or determined [*a pending* lawsuit] *b)* being processed but not yet final [patent *pending*] 2 about to happen; impending —*prep.* 1 [Now Rare] throughout the course of; during 2 while awaiting; until [*pending* his arrival]

Pend O·reille (pän′ də rā′) ⟦Fr *pend(re),* to hang + *oreille,* ear: name given by the Fr to local Salishan Indians who wore ear pendants⟧ 1 river in N Ida. & NE Wash., flowing from Pend Oreille Lake into the Columbia River: 100 mi (161 km): see CLARK FORK 2 lake in N Ida.: 148 sq mi (383 sq km)

pen·drag·on (pen drag′ən) *n.* ⟦LME < Welsh < *pen,* head + *dragon,* dragon symbol, war standard, hence leader < L *draco* (gen. *draconis*), cohort's standard⟧ supreme chief or leader: a title used in ancient Britain

pen·du·lous (pen′dyoo ləs, -dyə-, -də-; -jōō-, -jə-) *adj.* ⟦L *pendulus* < *pendere,* to hang: see PENDANT⟧ 1 hanging freely or loosely; suspended so as to swing 2 hanging or bending downward; drooping 3 [Now Rare] vacillating; uncertain —**pen′du·lous·ly** *adv.* —**pen′du·lous·ness** *n.*

pen·du·lum (pen′dyoo ləm, -dyə-, -də-; -jōō-, -jə-) *n.* ⟦ModL < neut. of L *pendulus:* see prec.⟧ a weight hung from a fixed point so as to swing freely to and fro under the combined forces of gravity and momentum: often used in regulating the movement of clocks —**pen′du·lar** *adj.*

Pe·nel·o·pe (pə nel′ə pē) *n.* ⟦L < Gr *Pēnelopē*⟧ 1 a feminine name: dim. *Penny* 2 *Gr. Myth.* Odysseus's wife, who waits faithfully for his return from the Trojan War

☆**pe·ne·plain** or **pe·ne·plane** (pē′nə plān′, pen′ə-) *n.* ⟦L *pene, paene,* almost (see PASSION) + PLAIN[1], PLANE[2]⟧ land worn down by erosion almost to a level plain

pe·nes (pē′nēz′) *n. alt. pl. of* PENIS

pen·e·tra·ble (pen′i trə bəl) *adj.* that can be penetrated —**pen′e·tra·bil′i·ty** *n.* —**pen′e·tra·bly** *adv.*

pen·e·tra·li·a (pen′i trā′lē ə) *pl.n.* ⟦L, neut. pl. of *penetralis,* penetrating, inward⟧ 1 the innermost parts, as of a temple 2 things kept private or secret

pen·e·trance (pen′i trəns) *n.* ⟦< PENETR(ATE) + -ANCE⟧ *Genetics* the degree of regularity with which a gene produces its specific effect in its carriers in a population

pen·e·trant (pen′i trənt) *adj.* ⟦L *penetrans,* prp. of *penetrare*⟧ penetrating; sharp; acute —*n.* a thing that penetrates

pen·e·trate (pen′i trāt′) *vt.* **-trat′ed, -trat′ing** ⟦< L *penetratus,* pp. of *penetrare,* to pierce into, penetrate < base of *penitus,* inward, far within (< *penus,* store of food, storeroom, sanctuary of temple of Vesta < IE base **pen-,* to feed, food) + *(in)trare,* ENTER⟧ 1 *a)* to pass into; find or force a way into or through; enter by or as by piercing *b)* to insert the penis into (the vagina or anus) of 2 to see into, or into the interior of [to *penetrate* the darkness] 3 to have an effect throughout; spread through; permeate 4 to affect or move deeply 5 to grasp mentally; understand —*vi.* 1 to make a way into or through something; pierce 2 to have a marked effect on the mind or emotions

pen·e·trat·ing (pen′i trāt′iŋ) *adj.* 1 that can penetrate [a *penetrating* oil] 2 sharp; piercing [a *penetrating* sound or smell] 3 keen or acute; discerning [a *penetrating* mind] Also **pen′e·tra′tive** (-trāt′iv) —**pen′e·trat′ing·ly** *adv.*, **pen′e·tra′tive·ly**

pen·e·tra·tion (pen′i trā′shən) *n.* ⟦LL *penetratio*⟧ 1 *a)* the act, power, or an instance of penetrating *b)* the act or an instance of inserting the penis into the vagina or anus 2 the depth to which something penetrates, as a military force into enemy territory 3 the extension of the influence of a country over a weaker one by means of commercial investments, loans, diplomatic maneuvers, etc. 4 keenness of mind; discernment; insight

☆**pen·e·trom·e·ter** (pen′i träm′ət ər) *n.* ⟦< PENETR(ATE) + -O- + -METER⟧ 1 an instrument used to measure the hardness of a substance by inserting a needle into the substance in a prescribed manner 2 an instrument that measures the penetrating power of X-rays

Pe·ne·us (pi nē′əs) *ancient name for* PINIÓS

pen·friend (pen′frend′) *n.* [Brit.] PEN PAL

pen·guin (peŋ′gwin, pen′-) *n.* ⟦prob. < Welsh *pen gwyn,* lit., white head (or Bret *pen gouin*): ? in reference to a white headland on a N Atlantic island, near which they were found⟧ 1 *former name for* GREAT AUK 2 any of an order (Sphenisciformes) of flightless birds found in the Southern Hemisphere, having webbed feet and paddlelike flippers for swimming and diving

pen·hold·er (pen′hōl′dər) *n.* 1 the handle or holder into which a pen point fits 2 a container or rack for a pen or pens

pen·i·cil·la·mine (pen′i sil′ə mēn′, -min) *n.* ⟦PENICILL(IN) + AMINE⟧ a white, crystalline chelating drug, $C_5H_{11}NO_2S$, used to treat Wilson's disease, severe cases of rheumatoid arthritis, etc.

pen·i·cil·late (pen′i sil′it, -āt′) *adj.* ⟦< L *penicillus* (see PENCIL) + -ATE[1]⟧ *Biol.* 1 pencil-shaped 2 having a tufted tip of fine hairs Also **pen′i·cil′li·form′** (-i fôrm′) —**pen′i·cil′late·ly** *adv.* —**pen′i·cil·la′tion** *n.*

pen·i·cil·lin (pen′i sil′in) *n.* ⟦< fol. + -IN[1]⟧ any of a group of isomeric, antibiotic compounds with the general formula $C_9H_{11}N_2O_4SR$, obtained from the filtrates of certain molds (esp., *Penicillium notatum* and *P. chrysogenum*) or produced synthetically

pen·i·cil·li·um (pen′i sil′ē əm) *n., pl.* **-li·ums** or **-li·a** (-ə) ⟦ModL < L *penicillus* (see PENCIL): from the tuftlike ends of the conidiophores⟧ any of a genus (*Penicillium*) of imperfect fungi growing as green mold on stale bread, ripening cheese, decaying fruit, etc.: penicillin is derived from some species

pen·in·su·la (pə nin′sə lə) *n.* ⟦L *paeninsula* < *paene,* almost (see PASSION) + *insula,* ISLE⟧ 1 a land area almost entirely surrounded by water and connected with the mainland by an isthmus 2 any land area projecting out into water —**pen·in′su·lar** *adj.*

Peninsular Malaysia territory of Malaysia comprising the former federation of states on the S end of the Malay Peninsula: see MALAYA, Federation of

pe·nis (pē′nis) *n., pl.* **-nis·es** or **-nes′** (-nēz′) ⟦L, tail, penis < IE base **pes-* > Sans *pásas-,* Gr *peos,* OE *fæsl,* penis⟧ the male organ of sexual intercourse: in mammals it is also the organ through which urine is excreted —**pe′nile′** (-nīl′, -nəl) *adj.*

penis envy *Psychoanalysis* the condition of a young girl who envies males in their possession of a penis

pen·i·tence (pen′i təns) *n.* ⟦OFr < L *paenitentia*⟧ the state of being penitent; repentance

SYN.—**penitence** implies sorrow over having sinned or done wrong; **repentance** implies full realization of one's sins or wrongs and a will to change one's ways; **contrition** implies a deep, crushing sorrow for one's sins, with a true purpose of amendment; **compunction** implies a pricking of the conscience and therefore suggests a sharp but passing feeling of uneasiness about wrongdoing; **remorse** implies a deep and torturing sense of guilt; **regret** may refer to sorrow over any unfortunate occurrence as well as over a fault or act of one's own

pen·i·tent (pen′i tənt) *adj.* ⟦OFr < L *paenitens,* prp. of *paenitere,* to repent; prob. akin to *paene,* scarcely: see PASSION⟧ truly sorry for having sinned or done other wrong and willing to atone; contrite; repentant —*n.* 1 a penitent person 2 a person receiving or intending to receive the sacrament of penance —**pen′i·tent·ly** *adv.*

pen·i·ten·tial (pen′i ten′shəl) *adj.* ⟦ML(Ec) *penitentialis*⟧ of, constituting, or expressing penitence or penance —*n.* 1 a penitent 2 a list or book of rules governing religious penance —**pen′i·ten′tial·ly** *adv.*

pen·i·ten·tia·ry (pen′i ten′shə rē) *adj.* ⟦ML *penitentiarius, poenitentiarius* (form and meaning infl. by assoc. with L *poena:* see PENAL) < L *paenitentia* < *paenitens,* PENITENT⟧ 1 of or for penance 2 used in punishing, disciplining, and reforming 3 making one liable to imprisonment in a penitentiary 4 of or in a penitentiary —*n., pl.* **-ries** 1 ⟦ML *penitentiaria* < the adj.⟧ *a)* a prison ☆*b)* a state or federal prison for persons convicted of serious crimes 2 ⟦ML(Ec) *penitentiarius* < the adj.⟧ an office or tribunal headed by a cardinal (**Grand Penitentiary**) and dealing with matters of penance, confession, dispensation, absolution, etc.

pen·knife (pen′nīf′) *n., pl.* **-knives′** (-nīvz′) a small pocketknife; originally, one used in fashioning quill pens

☆**pen·light** or **pen·lite** (pen′līt′) *n.* a flashlight that is about as small and slender as a fountain pen

pen·man (pen′mən) *n., pl.* **-men** (-mən) 1 a person employed to write or copy 2 a person skilled in penmanship 3 an author

pen·man·ship (-ship′) *n.* 1 handwriting considered as an art or skill 2 style or quality of handwriting

Penn[1] (pen), **William** 1644-1718; Eng. Quaker leader: founder of Pennsylvania

Penn[2] or **Penna** *abbrev.* Pennsylvania

pen·na (pen′ə) *n., pl.* **-nae** (-ē) ⟦L: see PEN[2]⟧ a contour feather: see CONTOUR FEATHERS —**pen·na·ceous** (pe nā′shəs) *adj.*

pen name a name used by an author in place of his or her true name; nom de plume —*SYN.* PSEUDONYM

pen·nant (pen′ənt) *n.* ⟦< PENNON, altered by assoc. with PENDANT⟧ 1 any long, narrow, usually triangular flag, as used in naval signal hoists, for a school banner, etc. 2 any such flag symbolizing a championship, esp. in baseball

pen·nate (pen′āt′) *adj.* ⟦L *pennatus,* winged < *penna,* quill, wing: see PEN[2]⟧ *Bot.* PINNATE

pen·ne (pen′ā′) *n.* ⟦It, pl. of *penna,* lit., feather, quill, pen < L *pinna,* feather (see PEN[2]): so named from being cut diagonally like a quill pen⟧ pasta in the form of tubes, cut diagonally on the ends

Pen·nell (pen′əl), **Joseph** 1857-1926; U.S. etcher, book illustrator, & writer

pen·ni (pen′ē) *n., pl.* **-ni·a** (-ə), **-nis,** or **-ni** ⟦Finn, prob. < OFris *penni,* PENNY⟧ a former monetary unit of Finland, equal to $\frac{1}{100}$ of a markka

pen·ni·less (pen′ə lis, -ē-) *adj.* without even a penny; extremely poor —**pen′ni·less·ness** *n.*

Pen·nine Alps (pen′īn′, -in) division of the W Alps, along the Swiss-Italian border, northeast of the Graian Alps: highest peak, *c.* 15,200 ft (4,633 m)

Pennine Chain range of hills in N England, extending from the Cheviot Hills southward to Derbyshire & Staffordshire: highest point, *c.* 3,000 ft (914 m)

pen·non (pen′ən) *n.* ⟦ME *penon* < OFr < *penne,* a feather: see PEN[2]⟧ 1 a long, narrow, triangular or swallow-tailed flag borne on a lance as an ensign, as formerly by knights and lancers 2 any flag or pennant 3 a pinion; wing

pen·non·cel (pen′ən sel′) *n.* [Archaic] *var. of* PENCEL

Penn·syl·va·ni·a (pen′səl vān′yə; *occas.,* -vā′nē ə) ⟦after Admiral William *Penn,* father of the founder, William PENN[1] + L *sylvania,* wooded (land), fem. of *sylvanus* < *sylva, silva,* forest: see SYLVAN⟧ Middle Atlantic State of the NE U.S.: one of the 13 original states: 44,817 sq mi (116,075 sq km); cap. Harrisburg: abbrev. *PA, Pa, Penn,* or *Penna*

Pennsylvania Avenue ⟦after prec.⟧ street in Washington, D.C., location of some of the principal government offices of the U.S., including the White House (1600 Pennsylvania Avenue): often used fig. in ref. to the White House

☆**Pennsylvania Dutch** ⟦*Dutch* < similar-sounding Ger *Deutsch,* German: see DEUTSCHLAND⟧ **1** the descendants of early German immigrants, principally from the Palatinate, who settled mainly in E Pennsylvania **2** the High German dialect of this people: also called **Pennsylvania German** **3** their form of folk art, characterized by carved or painted, stylized decorations of flowers, fruits, birds, etc., as on furniture —**Penn′syl·va′ni·a-Dutch′** *adj.*

☆**Penn·syl·va·ni·an** (pen′səl vān′yən, -vā′nē ən) *adj.* **1** of Pennsylvania: usually used in the predicate **2** ⟦after PENNSYLVANIA, site of exposures of such deposits⟧ [*sometimes* **p-**] designating or of the second and last geologic subdivision or epoch of the Carboniferous Period, characterized by the development of vast deposits of dead, coal-forming plant matter and the first conifers and reptiles —*n.* a person born or living in Pennsylvania —**the Pennsylvanian** the Pennsylvanian subdivision or epoch of the Carboniferous Period or its rocks: see the geologic time chart in the Reference Supplement

pen·ny (pen′ē) *n., pl.* for 1*a* & *b,* **pence;** for 1*c,* 2–4, **pen′nies** ⟦ME *peny* < OE *penig, pening,* akin to Ger *pfennig:* < ? early WGmc borrowing < L *pannus,* cloth: see PAWN[1]⟧ **1** in the United Kingdom and certain other countries, *a)* a monetary unit equal to 1/100 of a pound (in full **new penny:** abbrev. *p*) *b)* before 1971, a monetary unit equal to 1/12 of a shilling (abbrev. *d*) *c)* a coin worth one penny ☆**2** a U.S. or Canadian cent **3** any of several other low-value coins, as a denarius **4** a sum of money: now chiefly in the following phrases —**a pretty penny** [Informal] a large sum of money —**turn an honest penny** to earn money fairly and honestly

-pen·ny (pen′ē, pə nē) *combining form forming adjectives* **1** costing a (specified) number of pennies **2** having a size designated as (a specified number) [*a sixpenny* nail is larger than a *fourpenny* nail, but the numbers in their designations do not specify units of length, weight, etc.]

☆**penny ante** a game of poker in which the ante or limit is a very small amount, as one cent

☆**pen·ny-an·te** (pen′ē an′tē) *adj.* [Informal] having a contemptibly small value

penny arcade a building or hall, as at an amusement park, with various coin-operated game and vending machines, peep shows, photography booths, and the like

penny dreadful [Brit. Informal] a cheap book or magazine containing stories of crime, terror, etc.

☆**penny loafer** a loafer having a narrow band, sewn over the vamp, traditionally with a decorative slot in the center into which a penny may be inserted

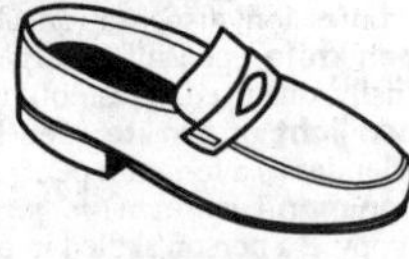
penny loafer

penny pincher a person who is extremely frugal or stingy —**pen′ny-pinch′ing** *n., adj.*

pen·ny·roy·al (pen′ē roi′əl, pen′ē roi′əl) *n.* ⟦altered < earlier *pulyol ryal* < Anglo-Fr *puliol real* < OFr *poliol, pouliol* (< L *puleium:* infl. by assoc. with *pulegium,* fleabane < ?) + *real,* ROYAL⟧ **1** a strongly scented, perennial European mint (*Mentha pulegium*) with bluish-lavender flowers **2** a similar North American mint (*Hedeoma pulegioides*) that yields an aromatic oil

penny stock a highly speculative stock traded over the counter, typically at prices under one dollar per share

pen·ny·weight (pen′ē wāt′) *n., pl.* **-weight′** or sometimes **-weights′** a unit of weight, equal to 1/20 ounce troy or 24 grains (1.5552 grams): abbrev. *pwt*

pen·ny·whis·tle (pen′ē hwis′əl, -wis′-) *n.* ⟦prob. because originally inexpensive⟧ any of various fipple flutes of metal, wood, or plastic with open holes for fingering

pen·ny-wise (pen′ē wīz′) *adj.* careful or thrifty in regard to small matters —**penny-wise and pound-foolish** careful or thrifty in small matters but careless or wasteful in major ones

pen·ny·wort (pen′ē wurt′) *n.* ⟦ME *penywort:* see PENNY & WORT[2]⟧ any of various plants with small round leaves growing in crevices of rocks and walls or in marshy places, as any of a genus (*Hydrocotyle*) of perennial plants of the umbel family and a small North American plant (*Obolaria virginica*) of the gentian family

pen·ny·worth (pen′ē wurth′) *n.* **1** the amount that can be bought for one penny **2** [Now Rare] a bargain **3** a small amount

Pe·nob·scot[1] (pi näb′skät′, -skət) *n.* **1** *pl.* **-scots′** or **-scot′** a member of a North American Indian people living esp. in Maine **2** the Algonquian language of this people, a variety of Abenaki —*adj.* of the Penobscots or their language or culture

Pe·nob·scot[2] (pi näb′skät′, -skət) ⟦< Abenaki *panáwahpskek,* lit., where the rocks widen⟧ river in central Me., flowing south into an arm (**Penobscot Bay**) of the Atlantic: *c.* 350 mi (563 km)

pe·nol·o·gy (pē näl′ə jē) *n.* ⟦< L *poena* or Gr *poinē,* punishment (see PENAL) + -LOGY⟧ the study of the reformation and rehabilitation of criminals and of the management of prisons —**pe·no·log·i·cal** (pē′nə läj′i kəl) *adj.* —**pe·nol′o·gist** *n.*

pen pal a person, esp. a stranger in another country, with whom one arranges a regular exchange of sociable letters

Pen·sa·co·la (pen′sə kō′lə) ⟦Fr < a tribal name; ? equiv. to Choctaw *pąši,* hair + *okla,* people⟧ seaport in NW Fla., on an inlet (**Pensacola Bay**) of the Gulf of Mexico

pen·sée (pän sā′) *n., pl.* **-sées′** (-sā′) ⟦Fr⟧ a thought; reflection

pen·sile (pen′sil, -sīl′) *adj.* ⟦L *pensilis* < pp. of *pendere,* to hang: see PENDANT⟧ **1** hanging **2** having or building a hanging nest

pen·sion (pen′shən; *for n. 3, Fr* pän syōn′) *n.* ⟦ME *pensioun* < MFr < L *pensio,* a paying < pp. of *pendere,* to weigh, pay, hang: see PENDANT⟧ **1** a payment, not wages, made regularly to a person (or to his or her family) who has fulfilled certain conditions of service, reached a certain age, etc. [a soldier's *pension,* an old-age *pension*] **2** a regular payment, not a fee, given to an artist, etc. by a patron; subsidy **3** in France and other continental countries *a)* a boardinghouse *b)* room and board —*vt.* to grant a pension to —**pension off** to dismiss from service, with a pension —**pen′sion·a·ble** *adj.* —**pen′sion·less** *adj.*

pen·sion·ar·y (pen′shə ner′ē) *adj.* ⟦ML *pensionarius*⟧ **1** of or constituting a pension **2** receiving a pension **3** dependent; hireling —*n., pl.* **-ar′ies** **1** a pensioner **2** a hireling

pen·sio·ne (pen syô′ne) *n., pl.* **-ni** (-nē) ⟦It⟧ PENSION (*n.* 3)

pen·sion·er (pen′shə nər) *n.* ⟦ME < MFr *pensionnier* < ML *pensionarius*⟧ **1** a person who receives a pension; pensionary **2** [Obs.] a gentleman-at-arms

pen·sive (pen′siv) *adj.* ⟦ME *pensif* < OFr < *penser,* to think, reflect < L *pensare,* to weigh, consider, freq. of *pendere,* to ponder, weigh, hang: see PENDANT⟧ **1** thinking deeply or seriously, often of sad or melancholy things **2** expressing deep thoughtfulness, often with some sadness —**pen′sive·ly** *adv.* —**pen′sive·ness** *n.*

SYN.—**pensive** suggests a dreamy, often somewhat sad or melancholy concentration of thought [the *pensive* look in her eye]; **contemplative** implies intent concentration of thought as on some abstract matter, often connoting this as a habitual practice [a *contemplative* scholar]; **reflective** suggests an orderly, often analytical turning over in the mind with the aim of reaching some definite understanding [after a *reflective* pause he answered]; **meditative,** on the other hand, implies a quiet and sustained musing, but with no definite intention of understanding or reaching a conclusion [a *meditative* walk in the cloister]

☆**pen·ste·mon** (pen stē′mən, pen′stə-) *n.* ⟦ModL < Gr *penta-,* five + *stēmōn,* warp: see STAMEN⟧ any of a large genus (*Penstemon*) of chiefly North American plants of the figwort family, having five stamens, the fifth of which is bearded and sterile, and bearing tubular, showy, white, pink, red, blue, or purple flowers

pen·stock (pen′stäk′) *n.* ⟦PEN[1] + STOCK⟧ **1** a gate or sluice used in controlling the flow of water ☆**2** a tube or trough for carrying water to a water wheel

pent (pent) *vt. alt. pt. & pp. of* PEN[1] —*adj.* held or kept in; confined; penned: often with *up*

pen·ta- (pen′tə) ⟦Gr *penta-* < *pente,* FIVE⟧ *combining form* five: also, before a vowel, **pent-**

pen·ta·chlo·ro·phe·nol (pen′tə klôr′ə fē′nōl′, -nôl′) *n.* ⟦prec. + CHLORO- + PHENOL⟧ a white powder, C_6Cl_5OH, made by chlorinating phenol: used as a herbicide, fungicide, wood preservative, etc.

pen·ta·cle (pen′tə kəl) *n.* ⟦MFr < ML *pentaculum* < Gr *penta-,* PENTA- + L *-culum,* dim. suffix⟧ a symbol, typically an encircled, five-pointed star, traditionally used in magic

pen·tad (pen′tad′) *n.* ⟦Gr *pentas* (gen. *pentados*) < *pente,* FIVE⟧ **1** the number five **2** a series or group of five **3** a five-year period **4** *Chem.* a pentavalent element or radical

pen·ta·dac·tyl (pen′tə dak′təl) *adj.* ⟦L *pentadactylus* < Gr *pentadaktylos:* see PENTA- & DACTYL⟧ having five fingers or toes on each hand or foot

pen·ta·e·ryth·ri·tol (pen′tə e rith′ri tôl′, -tōl′) *n.* ⟦PENTA- + ERYTHRITOL⟧ a colorless, crystalline compound, $C(CH_2OH)_4$, prepared by reacting acetaldehyde with formaldehyde: used in the manufacture of alkyd resins, explosives, insecticides, etc.

pen·ta·gon (pen′tə gän′) *n.* ⟦L *pentagonum* < Gr *pentagōnon:* see PENTA- & -GON⟧ a plane figure with five angles and five sides —☆**the Pentagon** a five-sided building in Arlington, Va., in which the main offices of the U.S. Department of Defense are located; hence, the U.S. military establishment —**pen·tag·o·nal** (pen tag′ə nəl) *adj.* —**pen·tag′o·nal·ly** *adv.*

pen·ta·gram (pen′tə gram′) *n.* ⟦Gr *pentagrammon,* neut. of *pentagrammos,* having five lines: see PENTA- & -GRAM⟧ **1** a five-pointed star; specif., a PENTACLE **2** any figure of five lines

pen·ta·he·dron (pen′tə hē′drən) *n., pl.* **-drons** or **-dra** (-drə) ⟦ModL: see PENTA- & -HEDRON⟧ a solid figure with five plane surfaces —**pen′ta·he′dral** *adj.*

pen·tam·er·ous (pen tam′ər əs) *adj.* ⟦PENTA- + -MEROUS⟧ *Biol.* made up of five parts or divisions

pen·tam·e·ter (pen tam′ət ər) *n.* ⟦L < Gr *pentametros:* see PENTA- & METER[1]⟧ **1** a line of verse containing five metrical feet or measures; esp., English iambic pentameter (Ex.: "Hĕ jésts | ăt scárs | whŏ név | ĕr félt | ă wóund") **2** verse consisting of pentameters; heroic verse —*adj.* having five metrical feet or measures

pen·tam·i·dine (pen tam′ə dēn′) *n.* ⟦< fol. + AMIDINE⟧ a white, crystalline substance, $C_{23}H_{36}N_4O_{10}S_2$, used as a drug to treat AIDS-related pneumonia or protozoan diseases, esp. trypanosomiasis: in full **pentamidine i·se·thi·o·nate** (ī′sə thī′ə nāt′)

pen·tane (pen′tān′) *n.* ⟦PENT(A)- + -ANE⟧ any of three known isomeric, colorless alkanes, C_5H_{12}, occurring in petroleum, etc.: used as a solvent, in low-temperature thermometers, etc.

pen·tan·gu·lar (pen taŋ′gyo͞o lər, -gyə-) ***adj.*** ⟦PENT(A)- + ANGULAR⟧ having five angles

pen·ta·nol (pen′tə nôl′, -nōl′) ***n.*** ⟦PENTAN(E) + -OL[1]⟧ AMYL ALCOHOL

pen·ta·ploid (pen′tə ploid′) ***adj.*** ⟦PENTA- + -PLOID⟧ *Biol.* having five times the haploid number of chromosomes —***n.*** a pentaploid cell or organism —**pen′ta·ploi′dy** ***n.***

pen·ta·quine (pen′tə kwēn′, -kwin) ***n.*** ⟦PENTA- + QUIN(OLIN)E⟧ a synthetic antimalarial drug, $C_{18}H_{27}N_3O$, used chiefly in the form of its phosphate

pen·tar·chy (pen′tär kē, pen′tär′-) ***n., pl.*** **-chies** ⟦Gr *pentarchia:* see PENTA- & -ARCHY⟧ **1** a federation of five states, each under an individual leader or ruler **2** government by five rulers

pen·ta·stich (pen′tə stik′) ***n.*** ⟦Gr *pentastichos:* see PENTA- & STICH⟧ a poem or stanza of five lines

Pen·ta·teuch (pen′tə to͞ok′, -tyo͞ok′) ***n.*** ⟦LL(Ec) *Pentateuchus* < Gr(Ec) *pentateuchos,* composed of five books < *penta-,* FIVE + *teuchos,* an implement, book < *teuchein,* to make < IE base **dheugh-,* to press > DOUGHTY⟧ the first five books of the Bible —**Pen′ta·teuch′al** ***adj.***

pen·tath·lete (pen tath′lēt′) ***n.*** ⟦blend of fol. & ATHLETE⟧ a participant in a pentathlon

pen·tath·lon (pen tath′län′, -lən) ***n.*** ⟦Gr *pentathlon* < *penta-,* five + *athlon:* see ATHLETE⟧ **1** an athletic contest in which each contestant takes part in five events (long jump, javelin throw, 200-meter dash, discus throw, and 1,500-meter run) **2** in the Olympic games, a contest consisting of cross-country horseback riding, a cross-country run, swimming, foil fencing, and pistol shooting: in full **modern pentathlon**

pen·ta·ton·ic (pen′tə tän′ik) ***adj.*** ⟦see PENTA- & TONIC⟧ designating or of a musical scale having five tones to the octave

pen·ta·va·lent (pen′tə vā′lənt) ***adj.*** **1** having a valence of five **2** having five valences See -VALENT

☆**pen·ta·zo·cine** (pen′tə zō′sēn′, -sin) ***n.*** ⟦PENTA- + (A)Z(O)- + -*ocine,* suffix for an 8-membered ring < L *oc(to),* EIGHT + -INE[3]⟧ a pain-killing, synthetic drug derived from coal tar: used in place of morphine because it is less addictive

Pen·te·cost (pen′tə kôst′, -käst′) ***n.*** ⟦ME < LL(Ec) *pentecoste* < Gr(Ec) *pentēkostē (hēmera),* the fiftieth (day) after Passover < *pentēkonta,* fifty < *pente,* FIVE⟧ **1** SHAVUOT **2** a Christian festival on the seventh Sunday after Easter, celebrating the descent of the Holy Spirit upon the Apostles; Whitsunday

Pen·te·cos·tal (pen′tə kôs′təl, -käs′-) ***adj.*** **1** of or relating to Pentecost ☆**2** designating or of any of various Protestant fundamentalist sects often stressing direct inspiration by the Holy Spirit, as in glossolalia —**Pen′te·cos′tal·ism′** ***n.*** —**Pen′te·cos′tal·ist** ***n.***

Pen·tel·i·cus (pen tel′i kəs) *Latin name for* PENDELIKÓN

Pen·tel·i·kon (pen tel′i kän′) *var. of* PENDELIKÓN

pen·tene (pen′tēn′) ***n.*** AMYLENE

pent·house (pent′hous′) ***n.*** ⟦altered (infl. by HOUSE) < *pentice* < ME *pentis,* penthouse < MFr *apentis* < ML *appenticium* < LL *appendicium,* lit., an appendage < L *appendere:* see APPEND⟧ **1** a small structure, esp. one with a sloping roof, attached to a larger building **2** a sloping roof, or, sometimes, an awning, etc. extending out from a wall or building **3** *a)* an apartment or other houselike structure built upon the roof of a building *b)* a luxury apartment on an upper floor, esp. the top floor, of a building

pen·ti·men·to (pen′tə men′tō) ***n.*** ⟦It, lit., repentance: in allusion to changes in the artist's intentions⟧ **1** *Art* the emergence of lines, images, etc. in a painting that become visible as oil paint grows transparent with age, thus revealing the artist's earlier ideas **2** *pl.* **-ti** (-tē) any such line, image, etc.

Pent·land Firth (pent′lənd) channel between the mainland of Scotland & the Orkney Islands: 6-8 mi (9.7-12.9 km) wide

pent·land·ite (pent′lən dīt′) ***n.*** ⟦Fr, after J. B. *Pentland* (1797-1873), Ir mineralogist⟧ a bronze-colored, brittle mineral, $(Fe,Ni)_9S_8$, that is the chief ore of nickel

pen·to·bar·bi·tal sodium (pen′tō bär′bi tôl′, -täl′) ⟦*pento-* for PENTA- (because of methylbutyl five-carbon group) + BARBITAL⟧ an odorless, white, crystalline powder, $C_{11}H_{17}N_2O_3Na$, soluble in water: used in medicine as a sedative, hypnotic, and analgesic

pen·tode (pen′tōd′) ***n.*** ⟦PENT(A)- + -ODE[1]⟧ an electron tube containing five electrodes, usually a cathode, anode, and three grids: used as a voltage amplifier

pen·to·san (pen′tə san′) ***n.*** ⟦fol. + -AN⟧ any of a group of plant carbohydrates which form pentoses upon undergoing hydrolysis

pen·tose (pen′tōs′) ***n.*** ⟦PENT(A)- + -OSE[1]⟧ any of a group of monosaccharides, $C_5H_{10}O_5$, including ribose and arabinose

pen·to·side (pen′tə sīd′) ***n.*** ⟦prec. + (GLYC)OSIDE⟧ a sugar derivative that yields a pentose on hydrolysis

☆**Pen·to·thal Sodium** (pen′tə thôl′) ⟦*pento-* for PENTA- (because of methylbutyl five-carbon group) + *th(iobarbiturate)* + -AL⟧ THIOPENTAL SODIUM: often shortened to **Pentothal** (a trademark)

pent·ox·ide (pent äk′sīd′) ***n.*** ⟦PENT(A)- + OXIDE⟧ an oxide that contains five oxygen atoms in its molecule

☆**pent·ste·mon** (pent stē′mən, pent′stə-) ***n.*** *var. of* PENSTEMON

pent-up (pent′up′) ***adj.*** held in check; kept inside; not released; unable to be released [*pent-up* emotion]

pen·tyl (pent′'l) ***n.*** ⟦PENT(A)- + -YL⟧ AMYL

pen·tyl·ene·tet·ra·zol (pen′ti lēn′ te′trə zôl′, -zōl′) ***n.*** ⟦< *pent(a-meth)-ylene-tetrazol(e)*⟧ a white, crystalline powder, $C_6H_{10}N_4$, used as a circulatory and respiratory stimulant and formerly in shock therapy

☆**pe·nu·che** or **pe·nu·chi** (pə no͞o′chē) ***n.*** ⟦var. of PANOCHA⟧ a candy resembling fudge, made of brown sugar, milk, butter, and, sometimes, nuts

☆**pe·nuch·le** or **pe·nuck·le** (pē′nuk′əl) ***n.*** *var. of* PINOCHLE

pe·nult (pē′nult′, pi nult′) ***n.*** ⟦L *paenultima* < *paene,* almost (see PASSION) + *ultima,* fem. of *ultimus,* last: see ULTIMATE⟧ the one next to the last; specif., the next-to-the-last syllable in a word: also **pe·nul·ti·ma** (pē nul′ti mə, pi-)

pe·nul·ti·mate (pi nul′tə mət) ***adj.*** ⟦< prec., after ULTIMATE⟧ **1** next to the last **2** of the penult —***n.*** PENULT —**pe·nul′ti·mate·ly** ***adv.***

pe·num·bra (pi num′brə) ***n., pl.*** **-brae′** (-brē′) or **-bras** ⟦ModL < *paene,* almost (see PASSION) + *umbra,* shade⟧ **1** the partly lighted area surrounding the complete shadow (umbra) of a body, as the moon, during an eclipse **2** the less dark region surrounding the dark central area of a sunspot **3** a vague, indefinite, or borderline area —**pe·num′bral** ***adj.***

pe·nu·ri·ous (pe nyoor′ē əs, -noor′-) ***adj.*** ⟦ML *penuriosus* < L *penuria:* see fol.⟧ **1** unwilling to part with money or possessions; mean; miserly; stingy **2** characterized by extreme poverty; impoverished —***SYN.*** STINGY[1] —**pe·nu′ri·ous·ly** ***adv.*** —**pe·nu′ri·ous·ness** ***n.***

pen·u·ry (pen′yo͞o rē, -yə-) ***n.*** ⟦ME *pennury* < L *penuria,* want, scarcity < *paene,* scarcely: see PASSION⟧ lack of money, property, or necessities; extreme poverty; destitution —***SYN.*** POVERTY

☆**Pe·nu·ti·an** (pə no͞ot′ē ən, pə no͞o′shən) ***n.*** ⟦coined (1912) by R. B. Dixon & A. L. Kroeber < *pene* + *uti,* both words for "two" in different languages of this group⟧ a group of remotely related language families, consisting of North American Indian languages of California, British Columbia, and New Mexico

Pen·za (pen′zä) city in central European Russia

Pen·zance (pen zans′) resort city in SW Cornwall, England, on the English Channel

Pen·zi·as (pent′sē əs), **Ar·no Allan** (är′nō) 1933- ; U.S. physicist, born in Germany

pe·on (pē′än′, -ən; *for 3, Brit usually* pyo͞on) ***n.*** ⟦< Sp *peón* or (in sense 2) Port *peão,* both < ML *pedo,* foot soldier: see PAWN[2]⟧ **1** in Spanish America, *a)* a person of the landless laboring class *b)* [Historical] a person forced to work off a debt or to perform penal servitude ☆**2** [Historical] in the SW U.S., a person forced into servitude to work off a debt **3** in India and Southeast Asia, *a)* a foot soldier *b)* a native policeman *c)* an attendant or messenger **4** an unskilled or exploited laborer **5** [Informal] any person of low social status, esp. one employed at menial or tedious work

pe·on·age (pē′ə nij) ***n.*** **1** the condition of a peon **2** the system by which debtors or legal prisoners are held in servitude to labor for their creditors or for persons who lease their services from the state

pe·o·ny (pē′ə nē) ***n., pl.*** **-nies** ⟦ME *pione* < OE *peonie* & OFr *peoine,* both < L *paeonia* < Gr *paiōnia,* after *Paiōn,* epithet of APOLLO, physician of the gods: from its former medicinal use⟧ **1** any of a genus (*Paeonia*) of perennial, often double-flowered, plants of the peony family, with large, showy, pink, white, red, or yellow flowers **2** the flower —***adj.*** designating a family (Paeoniaceae, order Dilleniales) of dicotyledonous plants, including many popular ornamentals with attractive flowers and foliage

peo·ple (pē′pəl) ***n., pl.*** **-ples** ⟦ME *peple* < Anglo-Fr *poeple, people* < OFr *pople* < L *populus,* nation, crowd < ?⟧ **1** *a)* all the persons of a racial, national, religious, or linguistic group; nation, race, etc. [the *peoples* of the world] *b)* a group of persons with common traditional, historical, or cultural ties, as distinct from racial or political unity [the Jewish *people*] **2** [Archaic] a group of creatures [the ant *people*] —***pl.n.*** **1** *pl. of* PERSON (sense 1): see the note **2** the persons belonging to a certain place, community, or class [the *people* of Iowa, *people* of wealth] **3** the members of a group under the leadership, influence, or control of a particular person or body, as members of a group of servants, royal subjects, etc. **4** the members of (someone's) class, occupation, set, race, tribe, etc. [the miner spoke for his *people*] **5** one's relatives or ancestors; family **6** persons without wealth, influence, privilege, or distinction; members of the populace **7** the citizens or electorate of a state **8** persons considered indefinitely [*people* are funny] **9** human beings, as distinct from other animals —***vt.*** **-pled, -pling** ⟦Fr *peupler* < the n.⟧ to fill with or as with people; populate; stock

-peo·ple (pē′pəl) *combining form alt. pl. of* -PERSON: see the note at PERSON (sense 1)

people mover a means of transporting many people over short distances, as a MOVING SIDEWALK or an automated monorail

☆**People's party** *see* POPULIST

People's Republic of China *official name for* CHINA

Pe·or·i·a (pē ôr′ē ə) **1** ⟦Fr *Peouarea,* a tribal name < Illinois *Peouareoua*⟧ city in central Ill., on the Illinois River **2** ⟦after PEORIA, Ill.⟧ city in SC Ariz.: suburb of Phoenix

☆**pep** (pep) [Informal] ***n.*** ⟦< PEPPER⟧ energy; vigor; liveliness; spirit —***vt.*** **pepped, pep′ping** to fill with pep; invigorate: with *up*

pep·er·o·ni (pep′ər ō′nē) ***n.*** *alt. sp. of* PEPPERONI

Pep·in the Short (pep′in) A.D. 714?-768; king of the Franks (751-768): father of Charlemagne

pep·los or **pep·lus** (pep′ləs) ***n.*** ⟦Gr *peplos*⟧ a large shawl or scarf worn draped about the body by women in ancient Greece

pep·lum (pep′ləm) ***n., pl.*** **-lums** or **-la** (-lə) ⟦L < Gr *peplos:* see prec.⟧ **1** PEPLOS **2** a flounce or short, flared flap attached at the waist of a dress, blouse, coat, etc. and extending around the hips

pe·po (pē′pō) *n., pl.* **-pos** ⟦L, species of large melon: see PUMPKIN⟧ any fleshy gourd fruit with a hard rind and many seeds, as the melon or squash
pep·per (pep′ər) *n.* ⟦ME *peper* < OE *pipor* < WGmc borrowing < L *piper* < Gr *peperi,* via Pers < Sans *pippali,* peppercorn⟧ **1** *a)* a pungent condiment obtained from the small, dried fruits of an Indian vine (*Piper nigrum*) of the pepper family (see BLACK PEPPER, WHITE PEPPER) *b)* this smooth, soft-stemmed vine **2** any of various aromatic or pungent plants of several families, as the myrtle or ginger family, used in flavoring foods **3** *a)* CAPSICUM *b)* the fruit of the capsicum; chili pepper, green pepper, red pepper, etc. ☆**4** *Baseball* a warm-up or practice session in which the ball is repeatedly thrown to a batter close by, who bunts it back to be fielded: in full **pepper game** —*adj.* designating a family (Piperaceae, order Piperales) of dicotyledonous plants, including cubeb —*vt.* **1** to sprinkle or flavor with ground pepper **2** to sprinkle freely or thickly **3** to shower or pelt with many small objects [*a roof peppered* with hailstones] **4** to beat or hit with short, quick jabs
pep·per-and-salt (pep′ər ən sôlt′) *adj.* SALT-AND-PEPPER
pep·per·box (pep′ər bäks′) *n.* PEPPER SHAKER
pep·per·corn (pep′ər kôrn′) *n.* ⟦ME *pepercorn* < OE *piporcorn*⟧ **1** the dried berry of any plant of the pepper family, esp. the black pepper **2** something insignificant or trifling
pep·per·grass (pep′ər gras′) *n.* any of a genus (*Lepidium*) of small plants of the crucifer family, with small, whitish flowers and flattened pods, esp. the garden cress
pep·per·idge (pep′ər ij′) *n.* ⟦var. of Brit dial. *pipperidge,* the barberry⟧ ☆BLACK GUM
pepper mill a hand mill used to grind peppercorns
pep·per·mint (pep′ər mint′, -mənt) *n.* **1** an aromatic, perennial plant (*Mentha piperita*) of the mint family, with lance-shaped leaves and whitish or purplish flowers in dense terminal spikes **2** the pungent oil it yields, used for flavoring **3** the flavor of the oil **4** a candy or lozenge flavored with this oil —*adj.* flavored with peppermint
☆**pep·per·o·ni** (pep′ər ō′nē) *n., pl.* **-nis** or **-ni** ⟦< It *peperoni* (sing. *peperone*), cayenne peppers < *pepe,* pepper < L *piper,* PEPPER⟧ a hard, highly spiced Italian sausage
pepper pot **1** PEPPER SHAKER **2** a West Indian stew of vegetables and meat or fish, flavored with cassava juice, red pepper, etc. ☆**3** a hotly seasoned stew of vegetables, dumplings, tripe, etc. **4** a soup of meat and vegetables flavored with hot spices
pepper shaker a container with a perforated top, for sprinkling ground pepper
pepper spray ⟦in ref. to capsicum, a genus of *pepper* plants⟧ an aerosol spray containing capsaicin or other ingredient highly irritating to the eyes, sinuses, etc., used as in defense against an attacker or by the police to subdue unruly or violent persons —**pep′per-spray′** *vt.*
pepper tree a South American ornamental tree (*Schinus molle*) of the cashew family, with panicles of yellowish flowers, pinnately compound leaves, and pinkish-red berries
pep·per·wort (pep′ər wurt′) *n.* **1** PEPPERGRASS **2** any of a genus (*Marsilea,* family Marsileaceae) of water ferns having long-stalked leaves with four leaflets
pep·per·y (pep′ər ē) *adj.* **1** of, like, or highly seasoned with pepper **2** sharp or fiery, as speech or writing **3** hot-tempered; irritable —**pep′per·i·ness** *n.*
☆**pep pill** [Slang] any of various pills or tablets containing a stimulant, esp. amphetamine
☆**pep·py** (pep′ē) *adj.* **-pi·er, -pi·est** [Informal] full of pep, or energy; brisk; vigorous; spirited —**pep′pi·ly** *adv.* —**pep′pi·ness** *n.*
☆**pep rally** a meeting or gathering, as at a school before an athletic event, held to generate enthusiasm
pep·sin (pep′sin) *n.* ⟦Ger: coined (1836) by T. *Schwann* (1810-82), Ger physiologist < Gr *pepsis,* digestion < *peptein,* earlier *pessein,* to cook, digest < IE base **pekw-* > L *coquere,* COOK⟧ **1** a digestive enzyme in the gastric juice of stomach secretions that catalyzes the splitting of proteins into smaller, more absorptive peptides **2** an extract of pepsin from the stomachs of calves, pigs, etc., formerly used as a digestive aid
pep·sin·ate (pep′si nāt′) *vt.* **-at′ed, -at′ing** to treat, mix, or infuse with pepsin
pep·sin·o·gen (pep sin′ə jən) *n.* ⟦< PEPSIN + -O- + -GEN⟧ the inactive precursor of pepsin, synthesized by the gastric glands of the stomach and converted to pepsin by hydrochloric acid
☆**pep talk** [Informal] a talk, as to an athletic team by its coach, designed to instill enthusiasm, determination, etc.
pep·tic (pep′tik) *adj.* ⟦L *pepticus* < Gr *peptikos* < *peptein,* to digest: see PEPSIN⟧ **1** of or aiding digestion **2** of or relating to pepsin **3** related to, or caused by, digestive secretions [*a peptic* ulcer]
pep·ti·dase (pep′ti dās′) *n.* ⟦< fol. + -ASE⟧ any hydrolase enzyme that acts as a catalyst in the splitting of a peptide into amino acids
pep·tide (pep′tīd′) *n.* ⟦PEPT(ONE) + -IDE⟧ any of a group of compounds formed from two or more amino acids by the linkage of amino groups of some of the acids with carboxyl groups of others, or by the hydrolysis of proteins
peptide bond (*or* **linkage**) the bond formed when a carboxyl group of one molecule of an amino acid is condensed with an amino group of a second molecule; the divalent radical CO·NH
pep·tize (pep′tīz′) *vt., vi.* **-tized′, -tiz′ing** ⟦< fol. + -IZE⟧ to change into a colloid, usually through the action of an added chemical; esp., to change (a gel) into a sol
pep·tone (pep′tōn′) *n.* ⟦Ger *pepton* < Gr, neut. of *peptos,* digested < *peptein:* see PEPSIN⟧ any of a group of soluble and diffusible derived proteins formed by the action of enzymes on proteins, as in the process of digestion, or by acid hydrolysis of proteins —**pep·ton′ic** (-tän′ik) *adj.*
pep·to·nize (pep′tə nīz′) *vt.* **-nized′, -niz′ing** **1** to change (proteins) into peptones **2** to subject to the action of pepsin or other protein-converting agents —**pep′to·ni·za′tion** *n.*
Pepys (pēps), **Samuel** 1633-1703; Eng. government official, known for his diary
Pe·quot (pē′kwät′) *n.* ⟦Narragansett, ? lit., people of the shoal⟧ **1** *pl.* **-quots′** or **-quot′** a member of a North American Indian people dominant in E Connecticut until conquered in 1637 **2** the Algonquian language of this people —*adj.* of the Pequots or their language or culture
per[1] (pur) *prep.* ⟦L < IE base **per-,* a going beyond > FAR, FOR[1]⟧ **1** through; by; by means of **2** *a)* for each; for every [fifty cents *per* yard] *b)* during each (used in indicating a rate of motion or activity) [to cover 500 miles *per* day] **3** according to; in accordance with [*per* your instructions]: also **as per** —**as per usual** [Informal] in the usual way; as usual
per[2] *abbrev.* **1** period **2** person
Per *abbrev.* **1** Persia **2** Persian
per- (pur) ⟦L < *per,* through: see PER[1]⟧ *prefix* **1** through, throughout [*perfoliate, peroral*] **2** thoroughly, completely, very [*perfervid*] **3** *Chem. a)* containing a specified element or radical in its maximum, or a relatively high, valence [*perchloric acid*] *b)* containing the maximum amount of the indicated element [*perfluoropropane* (completely fluorinated propane, C_3F_8)] *c)* containing the divalent group O_2 [*peracid*] (sometimes *peroxy-*)
per·ac·id (pur′as′id, pər as′id) *n.* ⟦transl. of Ger *persäure:* see prec. & ACID⟧ **1** an acid containing a larger proportion of oxygen than other acids containing the same elements, as perboric acid or perchloric acid **2** an acid that contains one or more O_2 groups
per·ad·ven·ture (pur′əd ven′chər) [Archaic] *adv.* ⟦ME *perauenture* < OFr *par'aventure* < *par* (L *per*), by + *aventure,* a chance, ADVENTURE⟧ **1** perhaps; possibly **2** by chance —*n.* chance; question; doubt [beyond *peradventure*]
Pe·rae·a (pə rē′ə) a region in ancient Palestine, east of the Jordan, roughly the same as ancient Gilead
Pe·rak (pā′rak′; *Malay* pā′rä) state of Malaysia, in W Peninsular Malaysia, on the strait of Malacca: 8,110 sq mi (21,005 sq km)
per·am·bu·late (pər am′byōō lāt′, -byə-) *vt.* **-lat′ed, -lat′ing** ⟦< L *perambulatus,* pp. of *perambulare* < *per,* through (see PER[1]) + *ambulare,* to walk⟧ **1** to walk through, over, around, etc., esp. in examining or inspecting **2** to walk around so as to officially inspect and maintain the boundary of (a forest, estate, etc.) —*vi.* to walk about; stroll —**per·am′bu·la′tion** *n.* —**per·am′bu·la·to′ry** (-lə tôr′ē) *adj.*
per·am·bu·la·tor (-lāt′ər) *n.* **1** a person who perambulates **2** [Chiefly Brit.] a baby carriage; baby buggy **3** a large wheel with a calibrated mechanism, pushed along on the ground to measure distances, like an odometer
per an·num (pər an′əm) ⟦L⟧ by the year; annually: abbrev. *p.a.,* **per an.**
☆**P-E** (*or* **P/E**) **ratio** PRICE-EARNINGS RATIO
per·bo·rate (pər bôr′āt) *n.* a salt of perboric acid containing the monovalent, negative radical BO_3
per·bor·ic acid (pər bôr′ik) ⟦PER- + BORIC⟧ the hypothetical acid, HBO_3, whose salts, the perborates, are formed by the action of hydrogen peroxide on borates
per·cale (pər kāl′) *n.* ⟦Fr < Pers *pargāla,* fragment, scrap⟧ fine, closely woven cotton cloth, used for bedsheets, etc.
per·ca·line (pur′kə lēn′, pur′kə lēn′) *n.* ⟦Fr < *percale:* see prec.⟧ a fine cotton cloth, usually with a glazed or watered finish, used as for linings or the bindings of books
per cap·i·ta (pər kap′i tə) ⟦ML, lit., by heads, for L *in capita*⟧ for each person
per·ceive (pər sēv′) *vt., vi.* **-ceived′, -ceiv′ing** ⟦ME *perceyven* < OFr *perceivre* < L *percipere,* to take hold of, feel, comprehend < *per,* through + *capere,* to take: see HAVE⟧ **1** to grasp mentally; take note (of); observe **2** to become aware (of) through one of the senses, esp. through sight —*SYN.* DISCERN —**per·ceiv′a·ble** *adj.* —**per·ceiv′a·bly** *adv.* —**per·ceiv′er** *n.*
per·cent (pər sent′) *adv., adj.* ⟦< It *per cento* < L *per centum*⟧ per hundred; in, to, or for every hundred: symbol, % [a 20 *percent* rate means 20 in every 100] —*n.* **1** a hundredth part **2** [Informal] percentage **3** [*pl.*] [Brit.] securities bearing regular interest of a (stated) percentage [the four *percents*] Also written **per cent** or [Now Rare] **per cent.**
per·cent·age (pər sent′ij) *n.* **1** a given part or amount in every hundred **2** any number or amount, as of interest, tax, etc., stated in percent **3** part; portion; share [*a percentage* of the audience] ☆**4** [Informal] *a)* use; advantage; profit [no *percentage* in worrying] *b)* [*usually pl.*] a risk based on favorable odds
per·cen·tile (pər sen′tīl′, -sent′'l) *n.* ⟦PERCENT + -ILE⟧ *Statistics* **1** any of the values in a series dividing the distribution of the individuals in the series into one hundred groups of equal frequency **2** any of these groups —*adj.* of a percentile or division into percentiles
per cen·tum (sen′təm) *now rare var. of* PERCENT (*adv., adj.*)
per·cept (pur′sept′) *n.* ⟦back-form. (after CONCEPT) < PERCEPTION⟧ a recognizable sensation or impression received by the mind through the senses
per·cep·ti·ble (pər sep′tə bəl) *adj.* ⟦LL *perceptibilis* < pp. of L *percipere*⟧ that can be perceived —**per·cep′ti·bil′i·ty** *n.* —**per·cep′ti·bly** *adv.*

SYN.—**perceptible** is applied to anything that can be apprehended by the senses but often connotes that the thing is just barely visible, audible, etc. [a *perceptible* smell of coffee]; **sensible** applies to that which can clearly be perceived [a *sensible* difference in their size]; **palpable** refers to anything that can be perceived by or as by the sense of touch [a *palpable* fog]; **tangible** applies to that which can be grasped, either with the hand or the mind [*tangible* property, ideas, etc.]; **appreciable** is used of that which is sufficiently perceptible to be measured, estimated, etc. or to have significance [an *appreciable* amount] —*ANT.* **imperceptible**

per·cep·tion (pər sep′shən) ***n.*** ⟦L *perceptio* < pp. of *percipere:* see PERCEIVE⟧ **1** *a)* the act of perceiving or the ability to perceive; mental grasp of objects, qualities, etc. by means of the senses; awareness; comprehension *b)* insight or intuition, or the faculty for these **2** *a)* the understanding, knowledge, etc. gotten by perceiving *b)* a specific idea, concept, impression, etc. so formed —**per·cep′tion·al** ***adj.***

per·cep·tive (pər sep′tiv) ***adj.*** ⟦ML *perceptivus*⟧ **1** of or capable of perception **2** able to perceive quickly and easily; having keen insight or intuition; penetrating —**per·cep′tive·ly** ***adv.*** —**per·cep′tive·ness** ***n.***, **per·cep·tiv·i·ty** (pur′sep tiv′ə tē)

per·cep·tu·al (pər sep′cho͞o əl) ***adj.*** of, by means of, or involving perception —**per·cep′tu·al·ly** ***adv.***

perch[1] (purch) ***n.***, *pl.* **perch** or **perch′es** ⟦ME *perche* < OFr < L *perca* < Gr *perkē* < IE base *perk-, speckled, colorful > Ger *farbe,* color, OE *forn,* trout⟧ **1** any of a family (Percidae) of small, spiny-finned, freshwater, percoid food fishes of Europe and America; esp., a yellowish species (*Perca flavescens*) of North America **2** any of various other spiny-finned bony fishes, as the white perch and the surfperches

perch[2] (purch) ***n.*** ⟦ME *perche* < OFr < L *pertica,* a pole, staff⟧ **1** a horizontal rod, pole, etc. provided as a roost for birds **2** anything, as a branch or wire, upon which a bird rests **3** any resting place, position, or vantage point, esp. a high or insecure one **4** *a)* a unit of linear measure equal to 5½ yards (5.029 meters); rod *b)* a unit of land measure equal to 30¼ square yards (25.3 square meters) *c)* a cubic measure for stone, usually equal to 24¾ cubic feet (.70 cubic meters) **5** a pole connecting the front and rear axletrees of a wagon, carriage, etc. —***vi.*** ⟦Fr *percher* < OFr < the n.⟧ to alight or rest on or as on a perch —***vt.*** to place or set on or as on a perch

per·chance (pər chans′) ***adv.*** ⟦ME *par chance* < OFr *par* (L *per*), by + *chance,* CHANCE⟧ [Archaic] **1** by chance; accidentally **2** perhaps; possibly

Perche (persh) historical region in NW France, in Maine & Normandy

perch·er (pur′chər) ***n.*** a person or thing that perches; specif., a bird having feet adapted for perching

Per·che·ron (pur′chə rän′, -shə-) ***n.*** ⟦Fr, after PERCHE, where orig. bred⟧ any of a breed of large draft horse, often black or dark gray in color

per·chlo·rate (pər klôr′āt′) ***n.*** a salt of perchloric acid containing the monovalent, negative radical ClO_4

per·chlo·ric acid (pər klôr′ik) ⟦PER- + CHLORIC⟧ a colorless, liquid acid, $HClO_4$, that is a strong oxidizing agent: its concentrated solutions can form explosive mixtures with reducing agents: used in analytical chemistry, in making solid propellants, etc.

per·chlo·ride (pər klôr′īd′) ***n.*** any chloride in which the amount of chlorine is greater than that present in the ordinary chloride of the same element

per·cip·i·ent (pər sip′ē ənt) ***adj.*** ⟦L *percipiens,* prp. of *percipere:* see PERCEIVE⟧ perceiving, esp. keenly or readily —***n.*** a person who perceives —**per·cip′i·ence** ***n.***, **per·cip′i·en·cy** —**per·cip′i·ent·ly** ***adv.***

Per·ci·val (pur′si vəl) ***n.*** ⟦OFr *Perceval,* prob. < *perce val,* pierce valley: apparently coined by CHRÉTIEN DE TROYES (12th c.)⟧ **1** a masculine name: dim. *Percy;* var. *Perceval* **2** PERCIVALE

Per·ci·vale (pur′si vəl) ***n.*** ⟦see prec.⟧ *Arthurian Legend* a knight who is allowed to see the Holy Grail

per·coid (pur′koid′) ***adj.*** ⟦< L *perca,* PERCH[1] + -OID⟧ of or belonging to a very large order (Perciformes) of bony fishes found in fresh and salt water, including the perches, basses, and sunfishes —***n.*** a fish of this order

per·co·late (pur′kə lāt′; *also, for n.,* -lit) ***vt.*** **-lat′ed, -lat′ing** ⟦< L *percolatus,* pp. of *percolare,* to strain < *per,* through + *colare,* to strain: see COLANDER⟧ **1** to pass (a liquid) gradually through small spaces or a porous substance; filter **2** to drain or ooze through (a porous substance); permeate **3** to brew (coffee) in a percolator —***vi.*** **1** *a)* to pass or ooze through a porous substance *b)* to spread throughout; permeate **2** to become active or lively; start bubbling up, as coffee in a percolator —***n.*** a liquid produced by percolating —**per′co·la′tion** ***n.***

per·co·la·tor (-lāt′ər) ***n.*** **1** a thing that percolates **2** a kind of coffeepot in which the boiling water bubbles up through a tube and filters, through the ground coffee held in a perforated container, back to the bottom of the pot

per con·tra (pər kän′trə) ⟦L⟧ on the contrary

per cu·ri·am (pər kyoor′ē əm′) ⟦L⟧ *Law* by the court: said of a judicial opinion presented as that of the entire court rather than that of any one judge

per·cuss (pər kus′) ***vt.*** ⟦< L *percussus,* pp. of *percutere,* to strike < *per-,* PER- + *quatere,* to shake: see QUASH[2]⟧ to rap gently and firmly, as in medical diagnosis —**per·cus′sor** ***n.***

per·cus·sion (pər kush′ən) ***n.*** ⟦L *percussio* < *percussus:* see prec.⟧ **1** the hitting or impact of one body against another, as the hammer of a firearm against a cap **2** the shock, vibration, etc. resulting from this **3** the percussion instruments of an orchestra, band, etc. or the players of these **4** *Med.* the striking or tapping of the chest, back, etc. with the fingertips so as to determine from the sound produced the condition of internal organs —***adj.*** **1** designating a musical instrument in which the tone or sound is produced when some part of it is struck, as a drum, or shaken, as a tambourine or a maraca **2** of or composed for percussion instruments [a *percussion* quartet]

percussion cap a small container holding a charge that explodes when struck, used as in firing a gun

per·cus·sion·ist (-ist) ***n.*** a musician who plays percussion instruments

percussion lock a gunlock that fires by percussion, as on a firearm

per·cus·sive (pər kus′iv) ***adj.*** of or characterized by percussion —**per·cus′sive′ly** ***adv.*** —**per·cus′sive·ness** ***n.***

per·cu·ta·ne·ous (pur′kyo͞o tā′nē əs) ***adj.*** ⟦PER- + CUTANEOUS⟧ effected or introduced through the skin, as by rubbing, injection, etc. —**per′cu·ta′ne·ous·ly** ***adv.***

Per·cy[1] (pur′sē) ***n.*** ⟦dim. of *Percival;* also after Fr *Perci,* village in Normandy⟧ a masculine name: see PERCIVAL

Per·cy[2] (pur′sē) **1** Sir **Henry** 1364-1403; Eng. soldier & rebel against Henry IV: called *Hotspur* **2 Thomas** 1729-1811; Eng. bishop & collector of early Eng. & Scot. ballads

Per·di·do (per thē′thô), **Mon·te** (môn′te) mountain in the central Pyrenees, NE Spain: 11,007 ft (3,355 m)

per·die (pər dē′) ***adv., interj.*** [Archaic] *var. of* PARDIE

per di·em (pər dē′əm, dī′-) ⟦L⟧ **1** by the day **2** daily **3** paid by the day ☆**4** a daily allowance, as for expenses

per·di·tion (pər dish′ən) ***n.*** ⟦ME *perdicioun* < OFr *perdiciun* < LL(Ec) *perditio* < L *perditus,* pp. of *perdere,* to lose, ruin < *per-,* PER- + *dare,* to give: see DATE[1]⟧ **1** [Archaic] complete and irreparable loss; ruin **2** *Theol. a)* the loss of the soul; damnation *b)* HELL

per·du or **per·due** (pər do͞o′, -dyo͞o′) ***adj.*** ⟦Fr *perdu,* masc., *perdue,* fem., pp. of *perdre,* to lose < L *perdere:* see prec.⟧ out of sight; in hiding; concealed, as in military ambush —***n.*** ⟦< the ***adj.***; also contr. of Fr *sentinelle perdue,* advanced (lit., lost) sentry, or *enfants perdus,* forlorn hope⟧ [Obs.] a soldier on a very dangerous assignment

Per·du (per dü′), **Mont** (mōn) *Fr. name for* Monte PERDIDO

per·dur·a·ble (pər door′ə bəl, -dyoor′-) ***adj.*** ⟦OFr < LL *perdurabilis* < L *perdurare,* to last, endure < *per-,* intens. + *durare:* see PER- & DURABLE⟧ extremely durable or lasting —**per·dur′a·bly** ***adv.***

per·dure (pər door′, -dyoor′) ***vi.*** **-dured′, -dur′ing** ⟦ME *perduren* < L *perdurare,* to continue, endure: see prec.⟧ to remain in existence

père (per) ***n.*** ⟦Fr⟧ **1** father: often used after the surname, like English *Senior* [Alexandre Dumas *père*] **2** [**P-**] the title of certain priests

per·e·gri·nate (per′ə gri nāt′) ***vt.*** **-nat′ed, -nat′ing** ⟦< L *peregrinatus,* pp. of *peregrinari* < *peregrinus:* see PILGRIM⟧ to follow (a route, etc.); travel, esp. walk, along, over, or through —***vi.*** to travel —**per′e·gri·na′tion** ***n.*** —**per′e·gri·na′tor** ***n.***

per·e·grine (per′ə grin, -grīn′, -grēn′) ***adj.*** ⟦L *peregrinus:* see PILGRIM⟧ traveling or migratory —***n.*** PEREGRINE FALCON

peregrine falcon ⟦transl. of L *falco peregrinus*⟧ a swift falcon (*Falco peregrinus*) of nearly worldwide distribution, much used in falconry

Per·el·man (per′əl mən, purl′mən), **S(idney) J(oseph)** 1904-79; U.S. humorist

per·emp·to·ry (pər emp′tə rē) ***adj.*** ⟦LL *peremptorius,* decisive, final < L, destructive, deadly < *peremptus,* pp. of *perimere,* to destroy < *per-,* intens. + *emere,* to take, buy: see REDEEM⟧ **1** *Law a)* barring further action, debate, question, etc.; final; absolute; decisive *b)* not requiring that any cause be shown [a *peremptory* challenge of a prospective juror] **2** that cannot be denied, changed, delayed, opposed, etc., as a command **3** intolerantly positive or assured; imperious [a *peremptory* manner] —**per·emp′to·ri·ly** ***adv.*** —**per·emp′to·ri·ness** ***n.***

per·en·nate (per′ə nāt′, pə ren′āt) ***vi.*** **-nat′ed, -nat′ing** ⟦< L *perennatus,* pp. of *perennare,* to last for many years, endure < *perennis:* see fol.⟧ to survive from year to year for a number of years; be perennial —**per·en·na·tion** (per′ə nā′shən) ***n.***

per·en·ni·al (pə ren′ē əl) ***adj.*** ⟦< L *perennis,* lasting through the year < *per-,* through + *annus,* a year: see PER[1] & ANNUAL⟧ **1** lasting or active throughout the whole year **2** lasting or continuing for a long time [*perennial* youth] **3** returning or becoming active again and again; perpetual **4** having a life cycle of more than two years: said esp. of herbaceous plants that produce flowers and seed from the same root structure year after year —***n.*** **1** a perennial plant **2** a person or thing that is present continuously or reappears regularly —**per·en′ni·al·ly** ***adv.***

pe·re·stroi·ka (per′ə stroi′kə) ***n.*** ⟦Russ *perestrojka,* reconstruction < *perestroit′,* to rebuild, reorganize⟧ the policy of restructuring and reforming the economic, political, and social systems of the U.S.S.R. promoted by Mikhail Gorbachev beginning in the mid 1980s

perf[1] (purf) ***vt.*** *short for* PERFORATE

perf[2] *abbrev.* **1** perfect **2** *Philately* perforated

per·fect (pur′fikt; *for v.* pər fekt′) ***adj.*** ⟦ME *perfit* < OFr *parfit* < L *perfectus,* pp. of *perficere,* to finish < *per-,* through (see PER-) + *facere,* to make, DO[1]: mod. sp. is Latinized⟧ **1** complete in all respects; without defect or omission; sound; flawless **2** in a condition of complete excellence, as in skill or quantity; faultless; most excellent; sometimes used comparatively ["to create a more *perfect* union"] **3** completely correct or accurate; exact; precise [a *perfect* copy] **4** without reserve or qualification; pure; utter; sheer; absolute [a *perfect* fool, *perfect* stranger] **5** designating a binding of books in which pages are glued to cloth or paper at the spine rather than having the signatures sewn together **6** *Bot.* MONOCLINOUS **7** *Gram.* expressing or showing a state reached or an action completed at the time of speaking or at the time indicated: verbs have three perfect tenses: simple (or present) perfect, past perfect (or pluperfect), and future perfect **8** *Music* designating an interval of a unison, fourth, fifth, or octave —*vt.* **1** to bring to completion **2** to make perfect or more nearly perfect according to a given standard, as by training —*n. Gram.* **1** a perfect tense **2** a verb form in a perfect tense —**per·fect′er** *n.* —**per′fect·ness** *n.*

☆**per·fec·ta** (pər fek′tə) *n.* ⟦Sp, perfect⟧ a bet or betting procedure in which one wins if one correctly picks the first and second place finishers in a race

perfect cadence *Music* a cadence, immediately preceded by some form of dominant harmony, and consisting of the tonic triad of the key of the particular section or of the composition in its beginning, with the keynote appearing in both the highest and lowest voice

☆**perfect game** **1** *Baseball* a no-hitter in which no batter on the opposing team reaches base **2** *Bowling* a game in which a bowler rolls twelve successive strikes

per·fect·i·ble (pər fek′tə bəl) *adj.* ⟦ML *perfectibilis*⟧ that can become, or be made, perfect or more nearly perfect —**per·fect′i·bil′i·ty** *n.*

per·fec·tion (pər fek′shən) *n.* ⟦ME *perfeccioun* < OFr < L *perfectio*⟧ **1** the act or process of perfecting **2** the quality or condition of being perfect; extreme degree of excellence according to a given standard **3** a person or thing that is the perfect embodiment of some quality —**to perfection** completely; perfectly

☆**per·fec·tion·ism** (-shə niz′əm) *n.* **1** any doctrine that holds that moral, religious, or social perfection can and should be attained in this life **2** extreme or obsessive striving for perfection, as in one's work —**per·fec′tion·ist** *n., adj.*

per·fec·tive (pər fek′tiv) *adj.* ⟦LL *perfectivus*⟧ **1** [Now Rare] tending to bring to or achieve perfection **2** *Gram.* designating an aspect of verbs, as in Russian, expressing completion of the action or indicating an action that is not repeated —*n.* **1** the perfective aspect **2** a verb in this aspect —**per·fec′tive·ly** *adv.* —**per·fec′tive·ness** *n.*

per·fect·ly (pur′fikt lē) *adv.* **1** so as to be perfect; to a perfect degree **2** completely; fully

perfect number a positive integer which is equal to the sum of all its factors, excluding itself: the first four *perfect numbers* are 6, 28, 496, and 8,128

☆**per·fec·to** (pər fek′tō) *n., pl.* **-tos** ⟦Sp < L *perfectus,* PERFECT⟧ a cigar of a standard shape, thick in the center and tapered at each end

perfect participle PAST PARTICIPLE

perfect pitch *nontechnical term for* ABSOLUTE PITCH

perfect rhyme **1** rhyme in which the stressed vowels and following consonants of the rhyming words correspond, but preceding consonants do not (Ex.: *make, take*) **2** RIME RICHE

perfect square an integer or quantity that is the exact square of another integer or quantity (Ex.: 25 is a perfect square of 5; $x^2 + 2xy + y^2$ is a perfect square of $(x + y)$)

☆**perfect storm** ⟦< *The Perfect Storm,* book (1997) by S. Junger, U.S. writer, and film (2000) about a violent storm in the NE U.S. (1991)⟧ a situation characterized by an extraordinary convergence of conditions or forces that together are favorable or conducive to a given outcome [a *perfect storm* of historical events led to WWI]

per·fer·vid (pər fur′vid) *adj.* ⟦ModL *perfervidus:* see PER- & FERVID⟧ extremely fervid; ardent

per·fid·i·ous (pər fid′ē əs) *adj.* ⟦L *perfidiosus*⟧ characterized by perfidy; treacherous —*SYN.* FAITHLESS —**per·fid′i·ous·ly** *adv.*

per·fi·dy (pur′fə dē) *n., pl.* **-dies** ⟦Fr *perfidie* < L *perfidia* < *perfidus,* faithless < *per fidem (decipi),* (to deceive) through faith < *per* (see PER[1]) + *fides,* FAITH⟧ the deliberate breaking of faith; betrayal of trust; treachery

per·fo·li·ate (pər fō′lē it, -āt′) *adj.* ⟦ModL *perfoliatus* < L *per-* (see PER-) < L *folium,* a leaf: see FOLIATE⟧ having a base surrounding the stem which bears it so that the stem seems to pass through it: said of a leaf —**per·fo′li·a′tion** *n.*

per·fo·rate (pur′fə rāt′; *for adj.,* -rit, -rāt′) *vt., vi.* **-rat′ed, -rat′ing** ⟦< L *perforatus,* pp. of *perforare* < *per,* through + *forare,* to BORE⟧ **1** to make a hole or holes through (something), as by punching or boring; pierce; penetrate **2** to pierce (a sheet of stamps, etc.) with holes in a row —*adj.* PERFORATED —**per′fo·ra·ble** (-fə rə bəl) *adj.* —**per′fo·ra′tor** *n.*

per·fo·rat·ed (pur′fə rāt′əd) *adj.* pierced with holes, esp. a row of holes, as to facilitate tearing

per·fo·ra·tion (pur′fə rā′shən) *n.* **1** a perforating or being perforated **2** a hole made by piercing, ulceration, etc. **3** any of a series of holes punched or drilled, as between postage stamps on a sheet

per·fo·ra·tive (pur′fə rāt′iv) *adj.* ⟦Fr *perforatif* < ML *perforativus*⟧ that perforates readily

per·force (pər fôrs′) *adv.* ⟦ME *par force* < OFr: see PER[1] & FORCE⟧ by or through necessity; necessarily

per·form (pər fôrm′) *vt.* ⟦ME *performen* < Anglo-Fr *parformer,* altered (infl. by *forme,* FORM) < OFr *parfournir,* to perform, consummate < *par* (< L *per-,* intens.) + *fornir,* to accomplish, FURNISH⟧ **1** to act on so as to accomplish or bring to completion; execute; carry out (a task, process, etc.) **2** to carry out; meet the requirements of; fulfill (a promise, command, etc.) **3** to give a performance of; render or enact (a piece of music, a dramatic role, etc.) —*vi.* **1** to carry out or execute an action or process; esp., to take part in a musical program, act in a play, dance, etc. before an audience **2** to admit of being performed as specified [a play that *performs* well] **3** to operate or function: used with regard to a thing's effectiveness [tires that *perform* well on wet pavement] **4** to produce gains or losses as specified [stocks *performed* poorly in the third quarter] —**per·form′a·ble** *adj.* —**per·form′a·bil′i·ty** *n.* —**per·form′er** *n.*

SYN.—**perform**, often a mere formal equivalent for **do**, is usually used of a more or less involved process rather than a single act [to *perform* an experiment]; **execute** implies a putting into effect or completing that which has been planned or ordered [to *execute* a law]; **accomplish** suggests effort and perseverance in carrying out a plan or purpose [to *accomplish* a mission]; **achieve** implies the overcoming of obstacles in accomplishing something of worth or importance [to *achieve* a lasting peace]; **effect** also suggests the conquering of difficulties but emphasizes what has been done to bring about the result [his cure was *effected* by the use of certain drugs]; **fulfill**, in strict discrimination, implies the full realization of what is expected or demanded [to *fulfill* a promise]

per·form·ance (pər fôr′məns) *n.* ⟦LME *parfourmaunce* < MFr⟧ **1** the act of performing; execution, accomplishment, fulfillment, etc. **2** operation or functioning, usually with regard to effectiveness, as of a machine **3** something done or performed; deed or feat **4** *a)* a formal exhibition or presentation before an audience, as a play, musical program, etc.; show *b)* one's part in this

performance art an art form combining elements of other art forms, as painting, film, dance, and drama, in a presentation in which the artist juxtaposes images on various themes and provides a usually non-narrative commentary on them —**performance artist**

per·form·a·tive (pər fôr′mə tiv) *adj.* of or having to do with performance; specif., designating or having to do with a statement that functions as an action and, hence, is neither true nor false ["I apologize" is a *performative* utterance]

performing arts arts, such as drama, dance, and music, that involve performance before an audience

per·fume (pər fyo͞om′; *also, and for n. usually,* pur′fyo͞om′) *vt.* **-fumed′, -fum′ing** ⟦MFr *parfumer* < It *perfumare* < L *per-,* intens. + *fumare,* to smoke < *fumus,* smoke: see FUME⟧ **1** to fill with a fragrant or pleasing odor; scent **2** to put perfume on; dab, spray, etc. with perfume —*n.* ⟦MFr *parfum* < the v.⟧ **1** a pleasing smell or odor; sweet scent, as of flowers; fragrance **2** a substance producing a fragrant or pleasing odor; esp., a volatile oil, as that extracted from flowers, or a substance like this prepared synthetically —*SYN.* SCENT —[Informal] **per·fum′y** *adj.*

per·fum·er (pər fyo͞o′mər) *n.* **1** a person who makes or sells perfumes **2** a person or thing that perfumes

per·fum·er·y (pər fyo͞o′mə rē) *n., pl.* **-er·ies** ⟦PERFUM(E) + -ERY⟧ **1** the trade or art of a perfumer **2** a perfume, or perfumes collectively **3** a place where perfume is made or sold

per·func·to·ry (pər fuŋk′tə rē) *adj.* ⟦LL *perfunctorius* < L *perfunctus,* pp. of *perfungi,* to get rid of, discharge < *per-,* intens. + *fungi,* to perform: see FUNCTION⟧ **1** done without care or interest or merely as a form or routine; superficial [a *perfunctory* examination] **2** without concern or solicitude; indifferent [a *perfunctory* waitress] —**per·func′to·ri·ly** *adv.* —**per·func′to·ri·ness** *n.*

per·fuse (pər fyo͞oz′) *vt.* **-fused′, -fus′ing** ⟦< L *perfusus,* pp. of *perfundere* < *per,* through + *fundere,* to pour: see FOUND[3]⟧ **1** to sprinkle, cover over, or permeate with or as with a liquid; suffuse **2** to pour or spread (a liquid, etc.) through or over something —**per·fu′sion** (-fyo͞o′zhən) *n.* —**per·fu′sive** (-fyo͞o′siv) *adj.*

per·fu·sion·ist (pər fyo͞o′zhə nist) *n.* a medical technician or nurse who monitors and operates equipment that oxygenates the blood, as during open-heart surgery

Per·ga·mum (pur′gə məm) **1** ancient Greek kingdom occupying most of W Asia Minor (fl. 2d cent. B.C.): later a Roman province **2** ancient capital of this kingdom, the present site of Bergama, Turkey

per·go·la (pur′gə lə) *n.* ⟦It, arbor < L *pergula,* arbor, projecting cover < ? **perga,* beams, framework < IE **perg-,* beam, rod > ON *forkr,* pole⟧ an arbor, esp. one with an open roof of cross rafters or latticework supported on posts or columns, usually with climbing vines

Per·go·le·si (per′gō lā′zē, -sē), **Gio·van·ni Bat·tis·ta** (jô vän′nē bät tēs′tä) 1710-36; It. composer

per·haps (pər haps′) *adv.* ⟦PER[1] + *haps,* pl. of HAP[1]⟧ possibly; maybe

pe·ri (pē′rē, pir′ē) *n.* ⟦Pers *parī* < MPers *parīk* < Avestan *pairika,* woman who misleads the faithful by seduction, lit., winged⟧ **1** *Pers. Myth.* a fairy or elf descended from evil angels and barred from paradise until penance has been done **2** any fairylike or elfin being

per·i- (per′ə, -ē) ⟦Gr *peri-* < *peri,* around < IE base **per-,* a going beyond > FAR, FARE, Sans *pari,* Avestan *pairi*⟧ *prefix* **1** around, about, surrounding, enclosing [*periscope, perichondrium*] **2** near [*perinatal*]

per·i·anth (per′ē anth′) *n.* ⟦ModL *perianthium* < Gr *peri-* (see prec.) + *anthos,* a flower: see ANTHO-⟧ the outer envelope of a flower, including the calyx and corolla

per·i·ap·sis (per′ē ap′sis) *n. Astron.* the nearest point to the gravitational center in the orbit of any satellite: see APOAPSIS

per·i·apt (per′ē apt′) *n.* ⟦Fr *périapte* < Gr *periapton* < *periaptein,* to fit about, tie about < *peri-* (see PERI-) + *aptein,* to fasten⟧ AMULET

per·i·blem (per′ə blem′) *n.* ⟦Ger < Gr *periblēma,* robe < *periballein,* to surround < *peri-* (see PERI-) + *ballein,* to throw: see BALL[2]⟧ *Bot.* the meristem that produces the cortex

per·i·car·di·tis (per′ə kär dīt′is) ***n.*** ⟦see -ITIS⟧ inflammation of the pericardium

per·i·car·di·um (per′ə kär′dē əm) ***n., pl.*** **-di·a** (-ə) ⟦ModL < Gr *perikardion,* neut. of *perikardios,* around the heart < *peri-,* around + *kardia,* HEART⟧ in vertebrates, the thin, closed, membranous sac surrounding the heart and the roots of the great blood vessels and containing a clear serous liquid —**per′i·car′di·al** ***adj.***, **per′i·car′di·ac′**

per·i·carp (per′ə kärp′) ***n.*** ⟦ModL *pericarpium* < Gr *perikarpion:* see PERI- & -CARP⟧ *Bot.* the wall of a ripened ovary, sometimes consisting of three distinct layers, the endocarp, mesocarp, and exocarp —**per′i·car′pi·al** ***adj.***

per·i·chon·dri·um (per′ə kän′drē əm) ***n., pl.*** **-dri·a** (-ə) ⟦ModL < PERI- + Gr *chondros,* cartilage, grain: see CHONDRO-⟧ the membrane of white, fibrous connective tissue covering cartilage, except at the joints —**per′i·chon′dri·al** ***adj.***, **per′i·chon′dral** (-drəl)

Per·i·cle·an (per′ə klē′ən) ***adj.*** **1** of Pericles **2** of the period of great commercial, intellectual, and artistic achievement in Athens during the Age of Pericles

Per·i·cles (per′ə klēz′) 495?-429 B.C.; Athenian statesman & general

pe·ric·o·pe (pə rik′ə pē) ***n.*** ⟦LL(Ec) < Gr *perikopē,* orig., a cutting all around < *peri-,* around (see PERI-) + *kopē,* a cutting < base of *koptein,* to cut: see SHAFT⟧ a passage, usually short, from a written work; esp., LECTION (sense 2)

per·i·cra·ni·um (per′ə krā′nē əm) ***n., pl.*** **-ni·a** (-ə) ⟦ModL < Gr *perikranion,* orig. neut. adj., around the skull < *peri-,* around + *kranion,* skull: see CRANIUM⟧ the periosteum of the external surface of the skull —**per′i·cra′ni·al** ***adj.***

per·i·cy·cle (per′ə sī′kəl) ***n.*** ⟦Fr *péricycle* < Gr *perikyklos,* spherical < *peri-,* around + *kyklos,* ring, circle: see WHEEL⟧ the outer layer of the stele in the root and stem of most plants —**per′i·cy′clic** (-sī′klik, -sik′lik) ***adj.***

per·i·cyn·thi·on (per′ə sin′thē ən) ***n.*** ⟦< PERI- + Gr *Kynthion,* neut. of *Kynthios:* see CYNTHIA⟧ the point nearest to the moon in the orbit of a lunar satellite

per·i·derm (per′ə durm′) ***n.*** ⟦ModL *peridermis:* see PERI- & DERMIS⟧ the outer bark and the layer of soft, growing tissue between the bark and the wood in plants —**per′i·der′mal** ***adj.***, **per′i·der′mic**

pe·rid·i·um (pə rid′ē əm) ***n., pl.*** **-i·a** (-ə) ⟦ModL < Gr *pēridion,* dim. of *pēra,* leather sack, wallet⟧ the outer coat of the spore-bearing organ in certain fungi —**pe·rid′i·al** ***adj.***

per·i·dot (per′ə dät′, -dō) ***n.*** ⟦Fr *péridot* < MFr *peritot* < ?⟧ a variety of yellowish-green olivine, used as a gem —**per′i·dot′ic** ***adj.***

per·i·do·tite (per′ə dō′tīt′, pə rid′ə tīt′) ***n.*** ⟦Fr *péridotite* < *péridot,* prec.⟧ any of several coarsegrained, dark igneous rocks consisting mainly of olivine and other ferromagnesian minerals —**per·i·do·tit·ic** (per′i dō tit′ik, pə rid′ō-) ***adj.***

per·i·gee (per′ə jē′) ***n.*** ⟦Fr *périgée* < Late ML *perigaeum* < LGr *perigeion* < Gr *perigeios,* around the earth < *peri-,* near + *gē,* the earth⟧ **1** the point nearest to the earth in the orbit of the moon or of a man-made satellite **2** the lowest or nearest point —**per′i·ge′an** ***adj.***, **per′i·ge′al**

pe·rig·y·nous (pə rij′ə nəs) ***adj.*** ⟦ModL *perigynus:* see PERI- & -GYNOUS⟧ designating sepals, petals, and stamens attached to the rim of a cup or tube which surrounds the ovary but is not attached to it, as in the rose: see EPIGYNOUS, HYPOGYNOUS —**pe·rig′y·ny** (-nē) ***n.***

per·i·he·li·on (per′ə hē′lē ən, -hēl′yən) ***n., pl.*** **-li·ons** or **-li·a** (-ə) ⟦ModL < Gr *peri-,* around + *hēlios,* the SUN[1]⟧ the point nearest the sun in the orbit of a planet, comet, or man-made satellite

per·il (per′əl) ***n.*** ⟦OFr < L *periculum,* danger < base **per-* (as in *experiri,* to try) < IE base **per-,* to try, risk, come over > FEAR, FARE⟧ **1** exposure to harm or injury; danger; jeopardy **2** something that may cause harm or injury —***vt.*** **-iled** or **-illed**, **-il·ing** or **-il·ling** [Archaic] to expose to danger; jeopardize; imperil —***SYN.*** DANGER —**at one's peril** at one's own risk [ignore safety regulations *at your peril*]

per·il·ous (per′ə ləs) ***adj.*** ⟦OFr *perilleus* < L *periculosus*⟧ involving peril or risk; dangerous —**per′il·ous·ly** ***adv.*** —**per′il·ous·ness** ***n.***

per·i·lune (per′ə lo͞on′) ***n.*** ⟦PERI- + LUNE[1]⟧ the orbital point nearest to the moon of an artificial satellite launched from, and in orbit around, the moon

per·i·lymph (per′ə limf′) ***n.*** the fluid that surrounds the membranous labyrinth of the inner ear: cf. ENDOLYMPH

per·i·men·o·pause (per′ə men′ə pôz′) ***n.*** ⟦see PERI-⟧ the period of time preceding menopause, characterized variously by decreased hormone levels, irregular menstrual periods, hot flashes, mood swings, etc.; climacteric; change of life —**per′i·men′o·paus′al** ***adj.***

pe·rim·e·ter (pə rim′ə tər) ***n.*** ⟦L *perimetros* < Gr < *peri-,* around + *metron,* MEASURE⟧ **1** the outer boundary of a figure or area **2** the total length of this **3** an optical instrument for testing the scope of vision and the visual powers of various parts of the retina **4** *Mil.* a boundary strip where defenses are set up —***SYN.*** CIRCUMFERENCE

per·i·met·ric (per′ə me′trik) ***adj.*** **1** of or by a perimeter, or boundary **2** of perimetry Also **per′i·met′ri·cal** —**per′i·met′ri·cal·ly** ***adv.***

pe·rim·e·try (pə rim′ə trē) ***n.*** the testing of the scope of vision by means of a perimeter

per·i·morph (per′ə môrf′) ***n.*** ⟦PERI- + -MORPH⟧ a mineral of one kind enclosing one of another kind

per·i·my·si·um (per′ə miz′ē əm) ***n., pl.*** **-si·a** (-ə) ⟦ModL < *peri-,* PERI- + Gr *mys,* muscle (see MYO-) + -IUM⟧ connective tissue covering and binding together bundles of muscle fibers

per·i·na·tal (per′ə nāt′'l) ***adj.*** ⟦PERI- + NATAL⟧ of, involving, or occurring during the period closely surrounding the time of birth

per·i·neph·ri·um (per′ə nef′rē əm) ***n.*** ⟦ModL < Gr *perinephros,* fat about the kidneys < *peri-,* around + *nephros,* kidney: see NEPHRO-⟧ the envelope of connective and fatty tissue surrounding the kidney

per·i·ne·um (per′ə nē′əm) ***n., pl.*** **-ne′a** (-ə) ⟦ModL < LL *perinaeon* < Gr *perineon* < *peri-,* around + *inein,* to discharge, defecate⟧ the region of the body between the thighs, at the outlet of the pelvis; specif., the small area between the anus and the vulva in the female or between the anus and the scrotum in the male —**per′i·ne′al** ***adj.***

per·i·neu·ri·um (per′ə no͝or′ē əm, -nyo͝or′-) ***n., pl.*** **-ri·a** (-ə) ⟦ModL < PERI- + Gr *neuron,* NERVE⟧ the sheath of dense connective tissue that envelops a bundle of nerve fibers composing a peripheral nerve —**per′i·neu′ri·al** ***adj.***

pe·ri·od (pir′ē əd) ***n.*** ⟦ME *paryode* < MFr *periode* < L *periodus* < Gr *periodos,* a going around, cycle < *peri-,* around + *hodos,* way < IE base **sed-,* to go > Sans *ā-sad-,* go toward⟧ **1** the interval between recurrent astronomical events, as between two full moons **2** the interval between certain happenings [a ten-year *period* of peace] **3** a portion of time, often indefinite, characterized by certain events, processes, conditions, etc.; stage [a *period* of change, the present *period*] **4** any of the portions of time into which an event of fixed duration, as a game or a school day, is divided **5** the full course, or one of the stages, of a disease **6** an occurrence of menstruation; menses: in full **menstrual period** **7** an end, completion, or conclusion, or a point of time marking this [death put a *period* to his plans] **8** *Geol.* a subdivision of an era in geologic time corresponding to the rock strata of a SYSTEM (sense 10): see the geologic time chart in the Reference Supplement **9** *Gram., Rhetoric* *a)* a sentence, esp. a balanced, well-constructed, complex sentence *b)* the natural pause in speaking used to indicate the end of a declarative sentence *c)* the mark of punctuation (.) used to indicate the end of a declarative sentence *d)* the dot (.) following many abbreviations **10** *Math.* the interval from one repetition to the next of a recurrent or self-duplicating function **11** *Music* a group of two or more related phrases ending with a cadence **12** *Physics* the interval of time necessary for a regularly recurring motion to make a complete cycle **13** *Prosody* a rhythm group of two or more cola in the Greek system —***adj.*** of or like that of a particular or appropriate period or age [a Victorian house decorated with *period* furniture, baroque music played on *period* instruments] —***interj.*** [Informal] used to indicate that the preceding statement is the speaker's last, conclusive, word on the subject [be home by midnight or you're grounded, *period!*]

SYN.—**period** is the general term for any portion of time; **epoch** and **era** are often used interchangeably, but in strict discrimination **epoch** applies to the beginning of a new period marked by radical changes, new developments, etc. and **era,** to the entire period [the steam engine marked an *epoch* in transportation, an *era* of revolution]; **age** is applied to a period identified with some dominant personality or distinctive characteristic [the Stone *Age*]; **eon** refers to an indefinitely long period [it all happened *eons* ago]

pe·ri·o·date (pə rī′ə dāt′) ***n.*** a salt of periodic acid containing the monovalent, negative radical IO_4

pe·ri·od·ic (pir′ē äd′ik) ***adj.*** ⟦MFr *periodique* < L *periodicus* < Gr *periodikos*⟧ **1** occurring, appearing, or recurring at regular intervals [a *periodic* fever] **2** occurring from time to time; intermittent **3** of or characterized by periods [the *periodic* motion of a planet] **4** of, characterized by, or expressed in periodic sentences —***SYN.*** INTERMITTENT

per·i·od·ic acid (pur′ī äd′ik) ⟦PER- + IODIC⟧ a white crystalline solid, HIO_4, formed by careful oxidation of iodine or iodic acid: it is a strong oxidizing agent

pe·ri·od·i·cal (pir′ē äd′i kəl) ***adj.*** **1** PERIODIC **2** published at regular intervals, as weekly, monthly, etc. **3** of a periodical —***n.*** a periodical publication

pe·ri·od·i·cal·ly (pir′ē äd′ik lē, -i kə lē) ***adv.*** **1** at regular intervals **2** from time to time; recurrently

pe·ri·o·dic·i·ty (pir′ē ə dis′ə tē) ***n., pl.*** **-ties** ⟦Fr *périodicité* < *période:* see PERIOD⟧ **1** the tendency, quality, or fact of recurring at regular intervals **2** *Chem.* the occurrence of similar properties in elements occupying similar positions in the periodic table

periodic law the principle that the properties of the chemical elements recur periodically when the elements are arranged in increasing order of their atomic numbers

periodic sentence a sentence in which the essential elements, in the main clause, are withheld until the end or separated as by modifiers or subordinate clauses (Ex.: stock prices, as he had warned, had collapsed): cf. LOOSE SENTENCE

periodic system the system governing the classification of the elements: see PERIODIC LAW

periodic table an arrangement of the chemical elements according to their atomic numbers, to exhibit the periodic law: see the periodic table of elements in the Reference Supplement

pe·ri·od·i·za·tion (pir′ē ə di zā′shən) ***n.*** the dividing, as of history or the development of a culture, into distinctive chronological periods

per·i·o·don·tal (per′ē ə dän′təl) ***adj.*** ⟦PERI- + -ODONT + -AL⟧ *Anat.* **1** situated or occurring around a tooth **2** affecting the gums, connective tissues, etc. surrounding the teeth

per·i·o·don·tics (per′ē ə dän′tiks) ***n.*** ⟦see prec. & -ICS⟧ the branch of dentistry concerned with diseases of the bone and tissue supporting the teeth: also **per′i·o·don′ti·a** (-dän′shə, -shē ə) —**per′i·o·don′tic** ***adj.*** —**per′i·o·don′tist** ***n.***

per·i·o·don·ti·tis (-dän tī′tis) ***n.*** any inflammation of the periodontal tissue

per·i·o·don·tol·o·gy (-täl′ə jē) ***n.*** the study of periodontal disease, tissue, etc.

period piece 1 a painting, piece of furniture, novel, etc. considered typical of the period in which it was created; often, specif., one regarded as being of mere historical interest and without lasting artistic merit 2 a novel, film, etc. set in an earlier time period, in which careful attention has been given to the details of its historical setting

per·i·o·nych·i·um (per′ē ə nik′ē əm) ***n.***, *pl.* **-i·a** (-ə) ⟦ModL < Gr *peri-* (see PERI-) + *onych-* < *onyx,* nail + ModL *-ium* (see -IUM)⟧ the epidermis forming the border around a fingernail or toenail

per·i·os·te·um (per′ē äs′tē əm) ***n.***, *pl.* **-te·a** (-ə) ⟦ModL < L *periosteon* < Gr < *peri-,* around + *osteon,* bone: see OSTEO-⟧ the membrane of tough, fibrous connective tissue covering all bones except at the joints —**per′i·os′te·al** (-əl) ***adj.***

per·i·os·ti·tis (per′ē äs tīt′is) ***n.*** ⟦ModL⟧ inflammation of the periosteum —**per′i·os·tit′ic** (-tit′ik) ***adj.***

per·i·os·tra·cum (per′ē äs′trə kəm) ***n.***, *pl.* **-ca** (-kə) ⟦ModL < Gr *peri-,* around (see PERI-) + *ostrakon,* a shell: see OSTRACIZE⟧ a horny covering, secreted as the outermost layer of most mollusk shells, that protects the underlying shell from erosion

per·i·o·tic (per′ē ōt′ik, -ät′ik) ***adj.*** ⟦PERI- + OTIC⟧ surrounding the inner ear; specif., of the bone (**periotic bone**) enclosing the inner ear of mammals

per·i·pa·tet·ic (per′i pə tet′ik) ***adj.*** ⟦Fr *péripatétique* < L *peripateticus* < Gr *peripatētikos* < *peripatein,* to walk about < *peri-,* around + *patein,* to walk < IE base **pent-,* to step, go > FIND⟧ 1 [**P-**] of the philosophy or the followers of Aristotle, who walked about in the Lyceum while he was teaching 2 walking or moving about; not staying in one place; itinerant —***n.*** ⟦ME *parypatetik*⟧ 1 [**P-**] a follower of Aristotle 2 a person who walks from place to place —**SYN.** ITINERANT —**per′i·pa·tet′i·cal·ly** ***adv.***

per·i·pe·tei·a (per′ə pi tē′ə, -tī′-) ***n.*** ⟦Gr, reversal < *peripetēs,* falling in with, changing suddenly < *peri-,* around (see PERI-) + *piptein,* to fall (see FEATHER)⟧ a sudden change of fortune or reversal of circumstances, as in a drama: also **per′i·pe·ti′a** or **pe·rip·e·ty** (pə rip′ə tē)

pe·riph·er·al (pə rif′ə rəl) ***adj.*** 1 of, belonging to, or forming a periphery 2 *a)* lying at the outside or away from the central part; outer; external *b) Anat.* of, at, or near the surface of the body; specif., designating or of that part of a nervous system that branches out from a central nervous system (cf. CENTRAL, sense 6*a*) 3 only slightly connected with what is essential or important; merely incidental —***n.*** a piece of equipment that can be used with a computer to increase its functional range or efficiency, as a printer, scanner, disk, etc. —**pe·riph′er·al·ly** ***adv.***

peripheral vision vision just outside the line of direct sight

pe·riph·er·y (pə rif′ə rē) ***n.***, *pl.* **-er·ies** ⟦MFr *peripherie* < LL *peripheria* < Gr *periphereia* < *peripherēs,* moving around < *peri-,* around + *pherein,* to BEAR[1]⟧ 1 a boundary line, esp. that of a rounded figure; perimeter 2 an outside surface, esp. that of a rounded object or body 3 surrounding space or area; outer parts; environs or outskirts 4 *Anat.* the area surrounding a nerve ending —**SYN.** CIRCUMFERENCE

pe·riph·ra·sis (pə rif′rə sis) ***n.***, *pl.* **-ses′** (-sēz′) ⟦L < Gr < *peri-,* around + *phrazein,* to speak⟧ 1 the use of many words where one or a few would do; roundabout way of speaking or writing; circumlocution 2 an expression that is an instance of this Also **per·i·phrase** (per′i frāz′)

per·i·phras·tic (per′i fras′tik) ***adj.*** ⟦ML *periphrasticus* < Gr *periphrastikos*⟧ 1 of, like, or expressed in periphrasis 2 *Gram.* formed with a particle or an auxiliary verb instead of by inflection (Ex.: the phrase *did sing* used for the inflected form *sang*) —**per′i·phras′ti·cal·ly** ***adv.***

pe·riph·y·ton (pə rif′ə tän′, per′i fīt′ən) ***n.*** ⟦ModL: see PERI- & -PHYTE⟧ the tiny, aquatic plant and animal organisms that attach to objects in the bed of a body of water, as certain algae or insect larvae living on submerged plant stems and leaves

☆**pe·rique** (pə rēk′) ***n.*** ⟦AmFr, supposedly after *Pierre* Chenet, said to have introduced tobacco growing in Louisiana, but prob. < Fr pronun. of E *prick,* vulgar for *penis* (from the shape of the dried, compacted plug)⟧ a strong, rich black tobacco grown only in a small area of Louisiana and used mainly in blending

per·i·sarc (per′ə särk′) ***n.*** ⟦< PERI- + Gr *sarx* (gen. *sarkos*), flesh: see SARCO-⟧ the tough, nonliving, outer skeleton layer of many hydroid colonies

per·i·scope (per′ə skōp′) ***n.*** ⟦PERI- + -SCOPE⟧ 1 a periscopic lens 2 an optical instrument consisting of a tube holding a system of lenses and mirrors or prisms, so arranged that a person looking through the eyepiece at one end can see objects reflected at the other end: used on submerged submarines, etc.

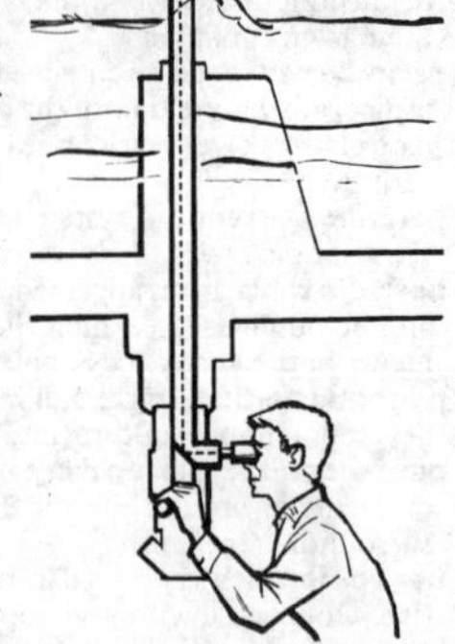
periscope

per·i·scop·ic (per′ə skäp′ik) ***adj.*** 1 providing clear lateral or oblique range of view, as certain lenses 2 of or by a periscope

per·ish (per′ish) ***vi.*** ⟦ME *perischen* < extended stem of OFr *perir* < L *perire,* to go through, perish < *per-,* through (see PER[1]) + *ire,* to go: see YEAR⟧ 1 to be destroyed, ruined, or wiped out 2 to die; esp., to die a violent or untimely death —**SYN.** DIE[1] —**perish the thought!** let's not even consider such a possibility!

per·ish·a·ble (per′ish ə bəl) ***adj.*** that may perish; esp., liable to spoil or deteriorate, as some foods —***n.*** something, esp. a food, liable to spoil or deteriorate —**per′ish·a·bil′i·ty** ***n.***, **per′ish·a·ble·ness**

pe·ris·so·dac·tyl (pə ris′ə dak′təl) ***adj.*** ⟦ModL *perissodactylus* < Gr *perissos,* uneven (< *peri-,* over) + *daktylos,* finger: see DACTYL⟧ having an uneven number of toes on each foot —***n.*** any of an order (Perissodactyla) of hoofed mammals with an uneven number of toes on each foot and a simple stomach, including the horse, tapir, and rhinoceros —**pe·ris′so·dac′ty·lous** (-tə ləs) ***adj.***

per·i·stal·sis (per′ə stal′sis, -stôl′-) ***n.***, *pl.* **-ses′** (-sēz′) ⟦ModL < Gr *peristaltikos* < *peristellein,* to surround, involve < *peri-,* around + *stellein,* to place: for IE base see STALK[1]⟧ the rhythmic, wavelike motion of the walls of the alimentary canal and certain other hollow organs, consisting of alternate contractions and dilations of transverse and longitudinal muscles that move the contents of the canal or organ onward —**per′i·stal′tic** ***adj.*** —**per′i·stal′ti·cal·ly** ***adv.***

per·i·stome (per′ə stōm′) ***n.*** ⟦ModL *peristoma:* see PERI- & STOMA⟧ 1 *Bot.* the fringe of teeth around the opening of the spore case in mosses 2 *Zool.* the area or parts surrounding the mouth or a mouthlike part of various invertebrates —**per′i·sto′mi·al** (-stō′mē əl) ***adj.***

per·i·style (per′ə stīl′) ***n.*** ⟦Fr *péristyle* < L *peristylum* < Gr *peristylon* < *peri-,* around + *stylos,* column: see STYLITE⟧ 1 a row of columns forming an enclosure or supporting a roof 2 any area or enclosure so formed, as a court —**per′i·sty′lar** (-stī′lər) ***adj.***

per·i·the·ci·um (per′ə thē′shē əm, -sē-) ***n.***, *pl.* **-ci·a** (-ə) ⟦ModL < PERI- + Gr *thēkē,* case, box (see THECA) + -IUM⟧ in certain ascomycetous fungi, a flasklike case containing the spore sacs (*asci*) —**per′i·the′ci·al** ***adj.***

per·i·to·ne·um (per′ə tə nē′əm) ***n.***, *pl.* **-ne′a** (-ə) or **-ne′ums** ⟦LL < Gr *peritonaion* < *peri-,* around + *teinein,* to stretch: see THIN⟧ the transparent serous membrane lining the abdominal cavity and reflected inward at various places to cover the visceral organs —**per′i·to·ne′al** ***adj.***

per·i·to·ni·tis (per′ə tə nīt′is) ***n.*** ⟦see -ITIS⟧ inflammation of the peritoneum

pe·rit·ri·chous (pə ri′tri kəs) ***adj.*** ⟦PERI- + TRICH(O)- + -OUS⟧ 1 having flagella evenly distributed over the entire surface of the cell: said of bacteria 2 *Zool.* having a row of cilia around the mouth: said of protozoans —**pe·rit′ri·chous·ly** ***adv.***

pe·ri·tus (pə rēt′əs, pe rē′tʊs) ***n.***, *pl.* **-ri′ti** (-rē′tī′, -rē′tē) ⟦L⟧ an expert; specif., a skilled theologian used as a consultant

per·i·wig (per′ə wig′) ***n.*** ⟦earlier *perwyke,* altered < Fr *perruque:* see PERUKE⟧ 1 [Archaic] any sort of wig 2 a wig of the type worn by men in the 17th and 18th cent., usually powdered: some types are still worn formally, as by certain judges in Great Britain

per·i·win·kle[1] (per′ə wiŋ′kəl) ***n.*** ⟦ME *pervinke* < OE *peruince* < L *pervinca,* periwinkle < *pervincire,* to entwine, bind < *per-* (see PER[1]) + *vincire,* to bind, fetter < IE base **weig-:* see WEAK⟧ any of two genera (*Vinca* or *Catharanthus*) of trailing or erect, evergreen plants of the dogbane family; esp., a creeper (*V. minor*) with blue, white, or pink flowers, grown as a ground cover

per·i·win·kle[2] (per′ə wiŋ′kəl) ***n.*** ⟦< OE *pinewincle* < L *pina,* mussel (< Gr) + OE *-wincle,* akin to Dan dial. *vinkel,* snail shell, OE *winkel,* corner < IE **weng-,* to be curved > WINCH⟧ 1 any of a family (Littorinidae) of small, intertidal saltwater snails having a thick, globular shell: some species are edible 2 the shell of such a snail

per·jure (pʉr′jər) ***vt.*** **-jured, -jur·ing** ⟦ME *parjuren* < OFr *parjurer* < L *perjurare* < *per,* through + *jurare,* to swear: see JURY[1]⟧ to make (oneself) guilty of perjury —**per′jur·er** ***n.***

per·jured (pʉr′jərd) ***adj.*** 1 guilty of perjury [a *perjured* witness] 2 characterized by perjury [*perjured* testimony]: also **per·ju·ri·ous** (pər jʊər′ē əs)

per·ju·ry (pʉr′jə rē) ***n.***, *pl.* **-ries** ⟦ME < OFr *parjurie* < L *perjurium* < *perjurus,* false, breaking oath < *per,* through + *jus* (gen. *juris*), a right, justice: see JURY[1]⟧ 1 the willful telling of a lie while under lawful oath or affirmation to tell the truth in a matter material to the point of inquiry 2 the breaking of any oath or formal promise

perk[1] (pʉrk) ***vt.*** ⟦ME *perken* < ? NormFr *perquer,* var. of OFr *percher,* PERCH[2]⟧ 1 to raise (the head, ears, etc.) briskly or spiritedly 2 to make jaunty or smart in appearance 3 to give or restore freshness, vivacity, etc. to Usually with *up* —***vi.*** 1 to lift one's head, straighten one's posture, etc. jauntily: usually with *up* 2 to become lively or animated; esp., to recover one's spirits: with *up* —***adj.*** [Now Rare] PERKY

perk[2] (pʉrk) ***vt., vi.*** [Informal] *short for* PERCOLATE

perk[3] (pʉrk) ***n.*** [Informal] *short for* PERQUISITE

Per·kins (pʉr′kinz), **Frances** 1882-1965; U.S. social worker: secretary of labor (1933-45)

perk·y (pʉr′kē) ***adj.*** **perk′i·er, perk′i·est** ⟦PERK[1] + -Y[2]⟧ 1 self-confident; aggressive 2 sprightly or lively; saucy; jaunty —**perk′i·ly** ***adv.*** —**perk′i·ness** ***n.***

Per·lis (per′lis) state of Malaysia, in NW Peninsular Malaysia, bordering on Thailand: 307 sq mi (795 sq km)

per·lite (pʉr′līt′) ***n.*** ⟦Fr < *perle,* PEARL[1]⟧ 1 *Geol.* a greenish volcanic glass, similar to obsidian, with a pearly luster and multiple, minute concentric cracks, used as insulation and in making concrete, plaster, etc. 2 PEARLITE —**per·lit·ic** (pər lit′ik) ***adj.***

perm (pʉrm) ***n.*** *short for* PERMANENT —***vt.*** to give a permanent to

Perm (perm) city in E European Russia, on the Kama River

per·ma·frost (pur′mə frôst′) *n.* ⟦PERMA(NENT) + FROST⟧ permanently frozen soil, subsoil, etc.

☆**perm·al·loy** (purm′al′oi, pur′mə loi′) *n.* ⟦PERM(EABILITY) + ALLOY⟧ any of a series of alloys of iron and nickel with high magnetic permeability: used in magnetic cores, for wrapping underwater cables, etc.

per·ma·nence (pur′mə nəns) *n.* ⟦ME < ML *permanentia*⟧ the state or quality of being permanent

per·ma·nen·cy (pur′mə nən sē) *n.* **1** PERMANENCE **2** *pl.* **-cies** something permanent

per·ma·nent (pur′mə nənt) *adj.* ⟦ME < MFr < L *permanens,* prp. of *permanere* < *per,* through + *manere,* to remain: see MANOR⟧ **1** lasting or intended to last indefinitely without change **2** lasting a relatively long time —*n.* a hair wave that is produced as by applying chemical preparations and that remains even after the hair is washed —**per′ma·nent·ly** *adv.*

permanent magnet a magnet, usually of hard steel, which keeps most of its magnetism after it has once been magnetized

permanent press **1** a process in which a fabric is treated with a chemical and heat to make it less likely to wrinkle, thus requiring little or no ironing after washing **2** the condition of a fabric treated by this process —**per′ma·nent-press′** *adj.*

permanent tooth any of the set of 32 adult human teeth that replace the milk teeth, including 4 cuspids, 8 bicuspids, 8 incisors, and 12 molars

permanent wave PERMANENT (*n.*)

per·man·ga·nate (pər maŋ′gə nāt′) *n.* a salt of permanganic acid containing the monovalent, negative radical MnO_4: it is a strong oxidizing agent and is generally dark purple in color

per·man·gan·ic acid (pur′man gan′ik) ⟦PER- + MANGANIC⟧ an unstable acid, $HMnO_4$, that is a strong oxidizing agent in aqueous solution

per·me·a·bil·i·ty (pur′mē ə bil′ə tē) *n.* **1** the state or quality of being permeable **2** *Physics a)* the measure of the ease with which a magnetic field can establish magnetic induction in a particular material *b)* the rate of diffusion of a fluid through a porous body **3** the property of a porous substance, as rock or a membrane, of allowing the flow of a fluid through it

per·me·a·ble (pur′mē ə bəl) *adj.* ⟦ME < L *permeabilis*⟧ that can be permeated; open to passage or penetration, esp. by fluids —**per′me·a·bly** *adv.*

per·me·ance (pur′mē əns) *n.* **1** a permeating or being permeated **2** the reciprocal of magnetic reluctance

per·me·ant (pur′mē ənt) *adj.* that permeates

per·me·ate (pur′mē āt′) *vt.* **-at′ed, -at′ing** ⟦< L *permeatus,* pp. of *permeare* < *per,* through + *meare,* to glide, flow, pass < IE base **mei-,* to go, change, wander > Czech *mijeti,* to pass by⟧ to pass into or through and affect every part of; penetrate and spread through [ink *permeates* blotting paper; a society that is *permeated* with idealism] —*vi.* to spread or diffuse; penetrate: with *through* or *among* —**per′me·a′tion** *n.* —**per′me·a′tive** (-āt′iv) *adj.*

per men·sem (pər men′səm) ⟦L⟧ by the month

Per·mi·an (pur′mē ən) *adj.* ⟦after the city of PERM⟧ [*sometimes* **p-**] designating or of the sixth and last geologic period of the Paleozoic Era, characterized by the formation of Pangea, glaciation in the Southern Hemisphere, development of mountains, esp. in the Appalachians, and an increase in the diversity of land plants and animals —**the Permian** the Permian Period or its rocks: see the geologic time chart in the Reference Supplement

per mill (pər mil′) ⟦< PER[1] + L *mille,* thousand⟧ for every thousand

per·mis·si·ble (pər mis′ə bəl) *adj.* ⟦ME < MFr < ML *permissibilis* < L *permissus,* pp. of *permittere*⟧ that can be permitted; allowable —**per·mis′si·bil′i·ty** *n.* —**per·mis′si·bly** *adv.*

per·mis·sion (pər mish′ən) *n.* ⟦ME < MFr < L *permissio* < pp. of *permittere*⟧ the act of permitting; esp., formal consent; leave; license [*permission* to go]

per·mis·sive (pər mis′iv) *adj.* ⟦ME < MFr *permissif* < ML *permissivus* < pp. of L *permittere*⟧ **1** giving permission; that permits **2** allowing freedom; esp., tolerant of behavior or practices generally disapproved of by others; indulgent; lenient **3** [Archaic] allowable and at one's option —**per·mis′sive·ly** *adv.* —**per·mis′sive·ness** *n.*

per·mit[1] (pər mit′; *for n.* pur′mit′, pər mit′) *vt.* **-mit′ted, -mit′ting** ⟦LME *permitten* < L *permittere* < *per,* through + *mittere,* to send: see MISSION⟧ **1** to allow; consent to; tolerate [smoking is not *permitted* here] **2** to give permission to; authorize [to *permit* the demonstrators to march in the street] **3** to give opportunity for [to *permit* light to enter] —*vi.* to give opportunity or possibility [if the weather *permits*] —*n.* **1** [Now Rare] permission, esp. in writing **2** a document granting permission; license; warrant **3** a printed postal indicia, stamped ticket, etc. [postal *permit,* parking *permit*] —*SYN.* LET[1] —**per·mit′ter** *n.*

☆**per·mit[2]** (pur′mit′, pər mit′) *n.* ⟦altered (infl. by prec.) < Sp *palometa,* orig. dim. of *paloma,* dove: see PALOMINO⟧ an Atlantic pompano fish (*Trachinotus falcatus*) found esp. in the Caribbean

☆**per·mit·tiv·i·ty** (pur′mə tiv′ə tē) *n.* ⟦< PERMIT[1] + -IVE + -ITY⟧ DIELECTRIC CONSTANT

per·mu·ta·tion (pur′myoo tā′shən) *n.* ⟦ME *permutacion* < MFr < L *permutatio* < *permutare:* see fol.⟧ **1** any radical alteration; total transformation **2** *a)* a complete rearrangement, esp. by interchanging *b) Math.* any of the total number of groupings, or subsets, into which a group, or set, of elements can be arranged in a particular order: the permutations of A, B, and C taken two at a time are AB, BA, AC, CA, BC, CB (cf. COMBINATION) —**per′mu·ta′tion·al** *adj.*

per·mute (pər myoot′) *vt.* **-mut′ed, -mut′ing** ⟦ME *permuten* < L *permutare,* to change thoroughly < *per-,* intens. + *mutare,* to change: see MUTATE⟧ **1** [Now Rare] to make different; alter **2** to rearrange the order or sequence of

Per·nam·bu·co (pur′nəm boo′kō, -byoo′-) **1** state of NE Brazil: 38,200 sq mi (98,938 sq km); cap. Recife **2** *former name for* RECIFE

per·ni·cious (pər nish′əs) *adj.* ⟦Fr *pernicieux* < L *perniciosus* < *pernicies,* destruction < *pernecare,* to kill < *per,* thoroughly + *necare,* to kill: see NECRO-⟧ **1** causing great injury, destruction, or ruin; fatal; deadly **2** [Rare] wicked; evil —**per·ni′cious·ly** *adv.* —**per·ni′cious·ness** *n.*

SYN.—**pernicious** applies to that which does great harm by insidiously undermining or weakening [*pernicious* anemia, a *pernicious* dogma]; **baneful** implies a harming by or as by poisoning [a *baneful* superstition]; **noxious** refers to anything that is injurious to physical or mental health [*noxious* fumes]; **deleterious** implies slower, less irreparable injury to the health [the *deleterious* effects of an unbalanced diet]; **detrimental** implies a causing of damage, loss, or disadvantage to something specified [his error was *detrimental* to our cause] —*ANT.* **harmless, innocuous**

pernicious anemia a form of anemia characterized by a gradual reduction in the number of the red blood cells, gastrointestinal and nervous disturbances, etc., due to a deficiency of vitamin B_{12}

per·nick·et·y (pər nik′ə tē) *adj. var. of* PERSNICKETY

Per·nod (per nō′) ⟦Fr⟧ *trademark for* a particular brand of anis —*n.* [*sometimes* **p-**] this liqueur

pe·ro·gi (pi rō′gē) *n., pl.* **-gi** or **-gies** *alt. sp. of* PIEROGI

Pe·rón (pe rōn′, pə-; *Sp* pe rôn′), **Juan (Domingo)** 1895-1974; president of Argentina (1946-55, 1973-74)

per·o·ne·al (per′ə nē′əl) *adj.* ⟦< ModL *peroneus* (< *perone,* fibula < Gr *peronē,* pin, fibula < *perein,* to go through, akin to *peran:* see FARE) + -AL⟧ of or near the fibula

per·o·ral (pər ôr′əl) *adj.* ⟦PER- + ORAL⟧ by, through, or around the mouth

per·o·rate (per′ə rāt′) *vi.* **-rat′ed, -rat′ing** ⟦< L *peroratus:* see fol.⟧ **1** to make a speech, esp. a lengthy oration **2** to sum up or conclude a speech

per·o·ra·tion (per′ə rā′shən) *n.* ⟦L *peroratio* < *peroratus,* pp. of *perorare* < *per,* through + *orare,* to pray, speak: see ORATION⟧ **1** the concluding part of a speech, in which there is a summing up and emphatic recapitulation **2** a high-flown or bombastic speech —**per′o·ra′tion·al** *adj.*

per·ox·i·dase (pər äk′si dās′) *n.* ⟦PER- + OXIDASE⟧ any oxidoreductase enzyme that acts as a catalyst in reactions in which a peroxide is reduced

per·ox·ide (pər äk′sīd′) *n.* ⟦PER- + OXIDE⟧ any oxide containing the O_2 group in which the two atoms of oxygen are linked by a single bond; specif., hydrogen peroxide —*vt.* **-id′ed, -id′ing** to treat with a peroxide; esp. to bleach (hair) with hydrogen peroxide —*adj.* bleached with hydrogen peroxide

☆**per·ox·i·some** (pər äk′si sōm′) *n.* ⟦< prec. + -SOME[3]⟧ any of a group of organelles in some cells of mammals, the leaves of plants, etc., containing enzymes that produce and then decompose hydrogen peroxide and carry out other aspects of cellular metabolism

peroxy- (pər äk′sə) *prefix* PER- (sense 3c)

per·ox·y·a·ce·tyl nitrate (pər äk′sē ə sēt′′l) ⟦PER- + OXY-[1] + ACETYL⟧ an unstable nitrogen compound, found in certain types of smog, that is an irritant, esp. to the eyes and to plants

☆**perp** (purp) *n.* [Slang] the perpetrator of a crime

per·pend[1] (pur′pənd) *n.* ⟦ME *perpoynt* < MFr *parpain* < VL **perpannium*⟧ a large stone extending through a wall from one side to the other, used as a binder: also **per′pent** (-pənt)

per·pend[2] (pər pend′) *vt., vi.* ⟦L *perpendere:* see fol.⟧ [Archaic] to ponder or consider

per·pen·dic·u·lar (pur′pən dik′yoo lər, -yə-) *adj.* ⟦ME *perpendiculer* < OFr < L *perpendicularis* < *perpendiculum,* plumb line < *perpendere,* to weigh carefully < *per-,* intens. + *pendere,* to hang: see PENDANT⟧ **1** at right angles to a given plane or line **2** exactly upright; vertical; straight up or down **3** very steep **4** [**P-**] of or designating the third and latest style of English Gothic architecture of the 14th to the 16th cent., characterized by vertical lines in its tracery —*adv.* in a perpendicular manner —*n.* **1** a device used in finding or marking the vertical line from any point **2** a line at right angles to the plane of the horizon **3** a line or plane at right angles to another line or plane **4** a perpendicular or upright position —**per′pen·dic′u·lar′i·ty** (-lar′ə tē) *n.* —**per′pen·dic′u·lar·ly** *adv.*

per·pe·trate (pur′pə trāt′) *vt.* **-trat′ed, -trat′ing** ⟦< L *perpetratus,* pp. of *perpetrare,* to commit, perpetrate, orig., to bring about, achieve < *per,* thoroughly + *patrare,* to effect, prob. orig. a ritual term < *pater,* FATHER, priest⟧ **1** to do or perform (something evil, criminal, or offensive); be guilty of **2** to commit (a blunder), impose (a hoax), etc. —**per′pe·tra′tion** *n.* —**per′pe·tra′tor** *n.*

per·pet·u·al (pər pech′oo əl) *adj.* ⟦ME *perpetuel* < OFr < L *perpetualis* < *perpetuus,* constant < *perpes* (gen. *perpetis*), continuous < *per-,* through + *petere,* to strive, rush at, fall: see FEATHER⟧ **1** lasting or enduring forever or for an indefinitely long time; eternal; permanent **2** continuing indefinitely without interruption; unceasing; constant [a *perpetual* nuisance] **3** blooming continuously throughout the growing season —*n.* a perpetual plant; esp., a variety of perpetual hybrid rose —*SYN.* CONTINUAL —**per·pet′u·al·ly** *adv.*

perpetual calendar **1** a calendar mathematically arranged so that the correct day of the week can be determined for any given date over a wide range of years **2** a desk calendar adjustable for each of many years

perpetual motion **1** hypothetical ability of some device to move or operate indefinitely by creating its own energy in excess of that used or dissipated 2 the state of such indefinite movement or operation

per·pet·u·ate (pər pech′o͞o āt′) *vt.* **-at′ed, -at′ing** ⟦< L *perpetuatus,* pp. of *perpetuare*⟧ to make perpetual; cause to continue or be remembered; preserve from oblivion —**per·pet′u·a′tion** *n.* —**per·pet′u·a′tor** *n.*

per·pe·tu·i·ty (pur′pə to͞o′ə tē, -tyo͞o′-) *n., pl.* **-ties** ⟦ME *perpetuite* < OFr *perpetuité* < L *perpetuitas*⟧ 1 the state or quality of being perpetual 2 something perpetual, as an annuity or pension to be paid indefinitely or, often specif., for life 3 unlimited time; eternity 4 *Law a)* a limitation upon the transference of an estate: it is valid only for a legally specified period *b)* an estate so limited —**in perpetuity** forever or for an indefinite period

per·pe·tu·um mo·bi·le (pur pech′o͞o um mō′bi lā) ⟦L⟧ PERPETUAL MOTION

Per·pi·gnan (per pē nyän′) city in S France, near the Gulf of Lions & the Spanish border

per·plex (pər pleks′) *vt.* ⟦< ME *perplex,* perplexed < MFr *perplexe* < L *perplexus,* entangled, confused, involved < *per,* through + *plexus,* pp. of *plectere,* to twist, plait: see PLY[1]⟧ 1 to make (a person) uncertain, doubtful, or hesitant; confuse; puzzle 2 to make intricate or complicated; make confusing or hard to understand [to *perplex* an issue] —*n. archaic or rare var. of* PERPLEXITY —*SYN.* PUZZLE —**per·plex′ing** *adj.* —**per·plex′ing·ly** *adv.*

per·plexed (pər plekst′) *adj.* 1 full of doubt or uncertainty; puzzled 2 hard to understand; confusing —**per·plex′ed·ly** (-plek′sid lē) *adv.*

per·plex·i·ty (pər plek′sə tē) *n.* ⟦ME *perplexite* < MFr *perplexité* < LL *perplexitas*⟧ 1 the condition of being perplexed; bewilderment; confusion 2 *pl.* **-ties** something that perplexes 3 something that is perplexed, or complicated

per pro. *abbrev.* ⟦L *per procurationem*⟧ by proxy

per·qui·site (pur′kwə zit) *n.* ⟦ME *perquysite* < ML *perquisitum,* something acquired < neut. pp. of *perquirere,* to obtain, purchase < L, to search diligently for < *per-,* intens. + *quaerere,* to seek: see QUERY⟧ 1 something additional to regular profit or pay, resulting from one's position or employment, esp. something customary or expected 2 a tip or gratuity 3 a privilege or benefit to which a person, institution, etc. is entitled by virtue of status, position, or the like; prerogative; right

Per·rault (pe rō′), **Charles** (shärl) 1628-1703; Fr. writer & compiler of fairy tales

Per·ri·er (per′ē ā′, per′ē ā′) ⟦after *Source Perrier,* spring at Vergèze in S France⟧ *trademark for* an effervescent mineral water from a spring in S France —*n.* this water, or a serving of it

Per·rin (pe *ran*′), **Jean Bap·tiste** (zhän bȧ tēst′) 1870-1942; Fr. physicist

per·ron (per′ən; *Fr* pe rōn′) *n.* ⟦ME *peroun* < OFr *perron* < *pierre,* stone < L *petra* < Gr, rock⟧ 1 an outside staircase, as up the slope of a terrace, leading to a platform at the front entrance of a building 2 such a platform

per·ry (per′ē) *n.* ⟦ME *pereye* < MFr *peré* < VL **piratum,* for LL *piracium* < L *pirum,* PEAR⟧ a fermented drink like cider, made from pear juice, esp. in England

Per·ry[1] (per′ē) *n.* ⟦? orig., a dim. of *Pers* < Fr *Piers* < L *Petrus,* PETER[1]⟧ a masculine name

Per·ry[2] (per′ē) 1 **Matthew C(albraith)** 1794-1858; U.S. naval officer: negotiated U.S.-Japanese trade treaty (1854) 2 **Oliver Haz·ard** (haz′ərd) 1785-1819; U.S. naval officer: defeated the Brit. fleet on Lake Erie (1813): brother of Matthew

pers *abbrev.* 1 person 2 personal

Pers *abbrev.* 1 Persia 2 Persian

per·salt (pur′sôlt′) *n.* a salt of a peracid

perse (purs) *n.* ⟦ME *pers* < OFr < ML *persus* < ? L *Persa,* Persian⟧ a dark grayish-blue color

Perse, St. John *see* SAINT-JOHN PERSE

per se (pər sā′, -sē′) ⟦L⟧ by (or in) itself; intrinsically

per·se·cute (pur′sə kyo͞ot′) *vt.* **-cut′ed, -cut′ing** ⟦LME *persecuten* < MFr *persécuter,* back-form. < *persécuteur* < L *persecutor* < *persequi,* to pursue < *per,* through + *sequi,* to follow: see SEQUENT⟧ 1 to afflict or harass constantly so as to injure or distress; oppress cruelly, esp. for reasons of religion, politics, or race 2 to trouble or annoy constantly [*persecuted* by mosquitoes] —*SYN.* WRONG —**per′se·cu′tive** *adj.,* **per·se·cu·to·ry** (pur′sə kyo͞o tôr′ē, pər sek′yo͞o-) —**per′se·cu′tor** *n.*

per·se·cu·tion (pur′sə kyo͞o′shən) *n.* ⟦ME *persecucion* < OFr < L *persecutio*⟧ a persecuting or being persecuted

Per·se·ids (pur′sē idz) *pl.n.* ⟦< ModL *Perseis* (pl. *Perseïdes*) < Gr *Perseïs,* sprung from Perseus⟧ the heavy meteor showers visible annually about Aug. 12: they appear to radiate from the constellation Perseus

Per·seph·o·ne (pər sef′ə nē) *n.* ⟦L < Gr *Persephonē*⟧ *Gr. Myth.* the daughter of Zeus and Demeter, abducted by Hades (Pluto) to be his wife in the lower world: identified with the Roman Proserpina

Per·sep·o·lis (pər sep′ə lis) capital of the ancient Persian Empire, near the modern city of Shiraz, Iran

Per·se·us (pur′sē əs, -syo͞os′) *n.* ⟦L < Gr⟧ 1 *Gr. Myth.* the son of Zeus and Danae, and slayer of Medusa: he marries Andromeda after rescuing her from a sea monster 2 a N constellation between Andromeda and Auriga, containing the variable star Algol

per·se·ver·ance (pur′sə vir′əns) *n.* ⟦OFr < L *perseverantia* < *perseverans,* prp. of *perseverare:* see fol.⟧ 1 the act of persevering; continued, patient effort 2 the quality of one who perseveres; persistence 3 in Calvinism, the continuance in grace of people elected to eternal salvation —**per′se·ver′ant** *adj.*

per·sev·er·ate (pər sev′ər āt′) *vi.* **-at′ed, -at′ing** ⟦< L *perseveratus,* pp. of *perseverare,* to PERSEVERE⟧ to experience or display perseveration

per·sev·er·a·tion (pər sev′ər ā′shən) *n.* ⟦L *perseveratio* < *perseveratus:* see prec.⟧ 1 the tendency of an idea, impression, experience, etc. to persist or recur, or of an individual to continue a particular mental activity without the ability to shift easily to another at a change in stimulus 2 *Psychiatry* the persistent and pathological repetition of a verbal or motor response, often seen in organic brain disease and schizophrenia —**per·sev′er·a′tive** (-ā′tiv) *adj.*

per·se·vere (pur′sə vir′) *vi.* **-vered′, -ver′ing** ⟦ME *perseveren* < OFr *perseverer* < L *perseverare* < *perseverus,* very severe, strict < *per-,* intens. + *severus,* SEVERE⟧ to continue in some effort, course of action, etc. in spite of difficulty, opposition, etc.; be steadfast in purpose; persist —**per′se·ver′ing·ly** *adv.*

Per·shing (pur′shiŋ, -zhiŋ), **John J(oseph)** 1860-1948; U.S. general: commander in chief of the American Expeditionary Forces in WWI

Per·sia (pur′zhə, -shə) ⟦L < Gr *Persais* < OPers *Pārsa*⟧ 1 *former name for* IRAN[1] 2 PERSIAN EMPIRE

Per·sian (pur′zhən, -shən) *adj.* of Persia, ancient or modern, or its people, language, or culture —*n.* 1 a person born or living in Persia 2 FARSI 3 any of a breed of domestic cat, thought to have originated in Asia Minor, having a stocky build, a long, thick coat, and a broad, round head with a very short muzzle: also **Persian cat**

Persian blinds PERSIENNES

Persian Empire ancient empire in SW Asia, including at its peak (*c.* 500 B.C.) the area from the Indus River to the W borders of Asia Minor & Egypt: it was founded by Cyrus the Great (6th cent. B.C.) & conquered by Alexander the Great (*c.* 328 B.C.)

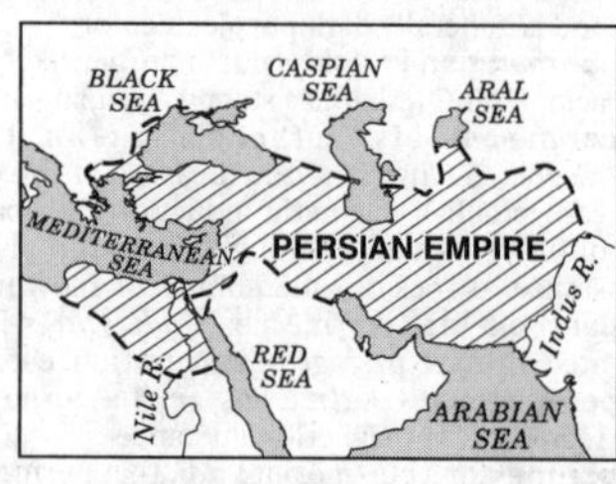

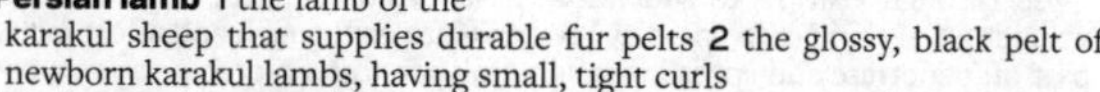
Persian Empire (500 B.C.)

Persian Gulf arm of the Arabian Sea, between SW Iran & Arabia: *c.* 88,800 sq mi (229,991 sq km)

Persian Gulf States group of Arab sheikdoms along the Persian Gulf: Kuwait, Bahrain, Qatar, & United Arab Emirates

Persian Gulf War GULF WAR

Persian lamb 1 the lamb of the karakul sheep that supplies durable fur pelts 2 the glossy, black pelt of newborn karakul lambs, having small, tight curls

Persian rug (*or* carpet) an Oriental rug made in Persia or Iran, having rich, soft colors in any of various intricate, often floral, patterns

per·si·ennes (pur′zē enz′, -sē-; *Fr* per syen′) *pl.n.* ⟦Fr, fem. pl. of *persien,* Persian⟧ outside shutters for windows, having adjustable, horizontal slats like those on Venetian blinds

per·si·flage (pur′sə fläzh′) *n.* ⟦Fr < *persifler,* to banter < *per-* (see PER-) + *siffler,* to whistle, hiss < L *sifilare,* var. of *sibilare:* see SIBILANT⟧ 1 a light, frivolous or flippant style of writing or speaking 2 such talk or writing

☆**per·sim·mon** (pər sim′ən) *n.* ⟦Virginia Algonquian *pessemins,* etc.⟧ 1 any of a genus (*Diospyros*) of trees of the ebony family with white, cup-shaped flowers, hard wood, and yellow or orange-red, plumlike fruit 2 the fruit, sour and astringent when green, but sweet and edible when thoroughly ripe

per·sist (pər sist′, -zist′) *vi.* ⟦MFr *persister* < L *persistere* < *per,* through + *sistere,* to cause to stand, redupl. of base of *stare,* to STAND⟧ 1 to refuse to give up, esp. when faced with opposition or difficulty; continue firmly or steadily 2 to continue insistently, as in repeating a question 3 to continue to exist or prevail; endure; remain —*SYN.* CONTINUE

per·sist·ence (pər sis′təns, -zis′-) *n.* ⟦Fr *persistance*⟧ 1 the act of persisting; stubborn or enduring continuance 2 the quality of being persistent; tenacity: also **per·sist′en·cy** (-tən sē) 3 the continuance of an effect after the removal of its cause [*persistence* of vision causes visual impressions to continue upon the retina for a brief time]

per·sist·ent (pər sis′tənt, -zis′-) *adj.* ⟦L *persistens,* prp. of *persistere:* see PERSIST⟧ 1 refusing to relent; continuing, esp. in the face of opposition, interference, etc.; stubborn; persevering 2 continuing to exist or endure; lasting without change 3 constantly repeated; continued 4 *Bot.* remaining attached permanently or for a longer than normal time, as some leaves, perianths, etc. 5 *Zool. a)* remaining essentially unchanged over a long period of geologic time, as a species *b)* remaining for life (said of such parts retained in the adult that normally disappear or wither at an early stage) —**per·sist′ent·ly** *adv.*

per·snick·e·ty (pər snik′ə tē) *adj.* ⟦< *pernickety* < Scot dial., altered < ? *pertickie,* child's term for PARTICULAR⟧ [Informal] 1 too particular or precise; fastidious; fussy 2 showing or requiring extremely careful treatment

per·son (pur′sən) *n.* ⟦ME *persone* < OFr < L *persona,* lit., actor's face mask, hence a character, person, prob. < Etr *phersu,* mask⟧ 1 *pl.* **-sons** or **peo·ple** (pē′pəl) a human being, esp. as distinguished from a thing or lower animal; individual man, woman, or child: the plural in this sense is now also *people,* which formerly was used only for an indefinite number of persons 2 [Now Rare] an individual regarded slightingly, as one of a lower status 3 *a)* a living human body *b)* bodily form or appearance [to be neat about one's *person]* 4 personality; self; being 5 *Gram.* *a)* a characteristic, as of pronouns and verbs, indicating whether a given utterance refers to the speaker(s), the one(s) spoken to, or the one(s) spoken about; also, an analytic category based on this characteristic *b)* the form a verb takes to indicate this characteristic (see FIRST PERSON, SECOND PERSON, THIRD PERSON) 6 [Archaic] a role in a play; character 7 *Law* any individual or incorporated group having certain legal rights and responsibilities 8 *Christian Theol.* any of the three modes of being (Father, Son, and Holy Spirit) in the Trinity —**in person** while being physically present; bodily; personally —**on someone's person** being carried personally by someone, as in a pocket or purse *[*a cigarette lighter *on her person]*

per·son- (pur′sən) *combining form* person (of either sex): used occas. to avoid the masculine implication of *man-* *[personhood]*

-per·son (pur′sən) *combining form* person of either sex in a (specified) activity, of a (specified) kind, etc.: sometimes used in compounds to avoid the masculine implication of -MAN: pl. form -PEOPLE or -PERSONS: see the note at PERSON (sense 1)

per·so·na (pər sō′nə) ***n.***, *pl.* **-nae** (-nē); for sense 2, usually **-nas** ⟦L: see PERSON⟧ 1 *[pl.]* the characters of a drama, novel, etc. 2 *Psychol.* the outer personality or facade presented to others by an individual

per·son·a·ble (pur′sə nə bəl) ***adj.*** ⟦ME *personabilis*⟧ having a pleasing appearance and personality; attractive —**per′son·a·ble·ness *n.*** —**per′son·a·bly *adv.***

per·son·age (pur′sə nij) ***n.*** ⟦MFr: see PERSON & -AGE⟧ 1 a person of importance or distinction; notable 2 any person 3 a character in history, a play, a novel, etc.

per·so·na gra·ta (pər sən′ə grät′ə) *pl.* **per·so·nae gra·tae** (pər sən′ē grä′ tē) ⟦L⟧ *[often in italics]* a person who is acceptable or welcome; esp., a foreign diplomat acceptable to the government to which he or she is assigned

per·son·al (pur′sə nəl) ***adj.*** ⟦OFr < L *personalis*⟧ 1 of or peculiar to a certain person; private; individual 2 done in person or by oneself without the use of another person or outside agency *[*a *personal* interview*]* 3 involving persons or human beings *[personal* relationships*]* 4 of the person, body, or physical appearance *[personal* hygiene*]* 5 *a)* having to do with the character, personality, intimate affairs, conduct, etc. of a certain person *[*a *personal* remark*]* *b)* tending to make personal, esp. derogatory, remarks *[*to get *personal* in an argument*]* 6 of, like, or having the nature of a person, or rational, self-conscious being 7 *Gram.* indicating grammatical person *[personal* pronouns, *personal* endings of verbs in Greek and other highly inflected languages*]* 8 *Law* of or constituting personal property —***n.*** ☆1 a local news item about a person or persons ☆2 *a)* a short, personal communication placed as in a newspaper *b)* a classified advertisement placed for the purpose of seeking someone to date or have a personal relationship with *c)* *[pl.]* a section of such advertisements, as in a newspaper

personal computer a small, relatively inexpensive computer whose central processing unit is a microprocessor: used in the home, small businesses, etc.

personal effects personal or intimate belongings of an individual, esp. those worn or carried on the person

☆**personal foul** in certain team games, a foul involving bodily contact with an opponent, as unwarranted roughness or hindering

per·son·a·li·a (pur′sə nā′lē ə, -nāl′yə) ***pl.n.*** ⟦< LL, neut. pl. of *personalis,* PERSONAL⟧ personal details concerning, or personal items associated with, an individual's life

per·son·al·ism (pur′sə nə liz′əm) ***n.*** any doctrine or movement which emphasizes the rights and centrality of the individual human being in his or her social, political, intellectual, etc. milieu —**per′son·al·ist *n., adj.*** —**per′son·al·is′tic *adj.***

per·son·al·i·ty (pur′sə nal′ə tē) ***n.***, *pl.* **-ties** ⟦ME *personalite* < LL *personalitas* < *personalis,* personal⟧ 1 [Archaic] the quality or fact of being a person; personhood 2 [Archaic] the quality or fact of being a particular person; personal identity; individuality 3 *a)* qualities of any individual as expressed by attitudes and physical and mental activities; distinctive individual qualities of a person, considered collectively *b)* the complex of qualities and characteristics seen as being distinctive to a group, nation, place, etc. 4 *a)* the sum of such qualities seen as being capable of making, or likely to make, a favorable impression on other people *b)* [Informal] personal attractiveness; engaging manner or qualities 5 a person; specif., *a)* a notable person; personage *b)* a person known for appearances on TV, radio, etc. 6 *[pl.]* remarks, usually of an offensive or disparaging nature, aimed at or referring to a person —**SYN.** DISPOSITION

personality disorder any of a group of psychological disorders characterized by patterns of thought, behavior, and emotional response that differ from cultural norms and that cause distress and interfere with a person's ability to function at work, in relationships, etc.

per·son·al·ize (pur′sə nə līz′) ***vt.*** **-ized′**, **-iz′ing** 1 to apply or understand as applied to a particular person, esp. to oneself 2 PERSONIFY 3 to mark or have marked, as with one's name or initials *[personalized* checks*]*

per·son·al·ly (pur′sə nə lē) ***adv.*** 1 without the help of others; in person *[*to attend to a matter *personally]* 2 as a person *[*I dislike him *personally,* but I admire his art*]* 3 in one's own opinion; speaking for oneself 4 as though directed at oneself *[*to take a remark *personally]*

personal pronoun any of a group of pronouns referring to the speaker(s), the person(s) spoken to, or any other person(s) or thing(s): the English personal pronouns, nominative case form, are: I[2], YOU, HE[1], SHE, IT[1], WE, THEY

personal property any property that is not real property and that is movable or not attached to the land

per·son·al·ty (pur′sə nəl tē) ***n.***, *pl.* **-ties** ⟦Anglo-Fr *personaltie* < LL *personalitas,* PERSONALITY⟧ PERSONAL PROPERTY: opposed to REALTY

per·so·na non gra·ta (pər sän′ə nän grät′ə) *pl.* **per·so·nae non gra·tae** (pər sän′ē nän grä′tē) ⟦L⟧ *[often in italics]* a person who is not acceptable or welcome; esp., a foreign diplomat unacceptable to the government to which he or she is assigned

per·son·ate (pur′sə nāt′; *for adj.,* -nit, -nāt′) ***vt.*** **-at′ed**, **-at′ing** ⟦< L *personatus,* masked < *persona:* see PERSON⟧ 1 to act or play the part of, as in a drama or masquerade; portray 2 to personify 3 *Law* to assume the character or identity of with intent to defraud; impersonate —***adj.*** *Bot.* having two lips and a projection in its throat: said of a tubular corolla, as in the snapdragon —**per′son·a′tion *n.*** —**per′son·a′tor *n.***

per·son·hood (pur′sən hood′) ***n.*** the state or condition of being a person, or individual human being

per·son·i·fi·ca·tion (pər sän′ə fi kā′shən) ***n.*** 1 a personifying or being personified 2 a person or thing thought of as representing some quality, thing, or idea; embodiment; perfect example *[*he is the *personification* of honesty*]* 3 a figure of speech in which a thing, quality, or idea is represented as a person

per·son·i·fy (pər sän′ə fī′) ***vt.*** **-fied′**, **-fy′ing** ⟦Fr *personifier:* see PERSON & -FY⟧ 1 to think or speak of (a thing) as having personality; represent as a person *[*to *personify* a ship by referring to it as "she"*]* 2 to symbolize (an abstract idea) by a human figure, as in art 3 to be a symbol or perfect example of (some quality, thing, or idea); typify; embody —**per·son′i·fi′er *n.***

per·son·nel (pur′sə nel′) ***n.*** ⟦Fr (lit., PERSONAL), prob. infl. by Ger *personal,* earlier *personale* < ML, orig. neut. of L *personalis*⟧ 1 persons employed in any work, enterprise, service, establishment, etc.: distinguished in military usage from MATERIEL 2 a personnel department or office —***adj.*** of or relating to the division within a business or other enterprise whose functions include hiring and training employees, and administering their benefits

person of interest a person who is a subject of a criminal investigation but who has yet to be charged with the crime: term used as by journalists and by some in law enforcement

-per·sons (pur′sənz) *combining form alt. pl. of* -PERSON: see the note at PERSON (sense 1)

per·spec·tive (pər spek′tiv) ***adj.*** ⟦ME < LL *perspectivus* < L *perspicere,* to look through < *per,* through + *specere,* to look: see SPY⟧ 1 of perspective 2 drawn in perspective —***n.*** ⟦ME *perspectif* < ML *(ars) perspectiva,* perspective (art)⟧ 1 the art of picturing objects or a scene in such a way, e.g., by converging lines (**linear perspective**), as to show them as they appear to the eye with reference to relative distance or depth 2 *a)* the appearance of objects or scenes as determined by their relative distance and positions *b)* the effect of relative distance and position 3 the relationship or proportion of the parts of a whole, regarded from a particular standpoint or point in time 4 *a)* a specific point of view in understanding or judging things or events, esp. one that shows them in their true relations to one another *b)* the ability to see things in a true relationship 5 a picture in perspective 6 a distant view; vista —**per·spec′tive·ly *adv.***

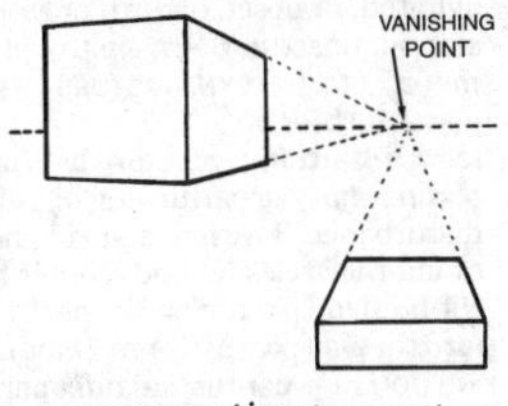

perspective (sense 1)

Per·spex (pur′speks′) *trademark for* a hard, transparent plastic, an acrylic resin similar to Plexiglas —***n.*** [Brit.] **[p-]** this plastic

per·spi·ca·cious (pur′spi kā′shəs) ***adj.*** ⟦< L *perspicax* (gen. *perspicacis*) < *perspicere,* to see through: see PERSPECTIVE⟧ 1 having keen judgment or understanding; acutely perceptive 2 [Archaic] having keen vision —**SYN.** SHREWD —**per′spi·ca′cious·ly *adv.*** —**per′spi·cac′i·ty** (-kas′ə tē) ***n.*,** **per′spi·ca′cious·ness**

per·spic·u·ous (pər spik′yoo əs) ***adj.*** ⟦ME, transparent < L *perspicuus* < *perspicere,* to see through: see PERSPECTIVE⟧ clear in statement or expression; easily understood; lucid —**per·spi·cu·i·ty** (pur′spi kyoo′ə tē) ***n.*,** **per·spic′u·ous·ness** —**per·spic′u·ous·ly *adv.***

per·spi·ra·tion (pur′spə rā′shən) ***n.*** ⟦Fr⟧ 1 the act of perspiring; sweating 2 salty moisture given off in perspiring; sweat

per·spir·a·to·ry (pər spīr′ə tôr′ē) ***adj.*** of, relating to, or causing perspiration

per·spire (pər spīr′) ***vt., vi.*** **-spired′**, **-spir′ing** ⟦Fr *perspirer* < L *perspirare,* to breathe everywhere < *per-,* through + *spirare,* to breathe: see PER- & SPIRIT⟧ to give forth (a characteristic salty moisture) through the pores of the skin; sweat

per stir·pes (pər stur′pēz) ⟦L, by stocks or families < *stirps,* a stalk, stem: see STIRPS⟧ *Law* with the children of any beneficiary who has predeceased the testator receiving the beneficiary's share

per·suade (pər swād′) ***vt.*** **-suad′ed**, **-suad′ing** ⟦MFr *persuader* < L *persuadere* < *per-,* intens. + *suadere,* to urge: see SUASION⟧ 1 to cause to do something by reasoning, urging, or inducement; prevail upon 2 to induce to believe something; convince —**per·suad′a·ble *adj.*** or **per·sua′si·ble** (-swā′sə bəl) —**per·sua′si·bil′i·ty *n.***

per·suad·er (-swā′dər) ***n.*** 1 a person or thing that persuades 2 [Informal] something used to intimidate or deter, as a weapon or punishment

per·sua·sion (pər swā′zhən) ***n.*** ⟦ME < L *persuasio* < pp. of *persuadere*⟧ **1** a persuading or being persuaded **2** power of persuading **3** a strong belief; conviction **4** *a)* a person's particular religion *b)* a particular sect, party, group, etc. **5** [Informal] kind, sort, sex, etc.: used jocularly —***SYN.*** OPINION

per·sua·sive (pər swā′siv) ***adj.*** ⟦Fr *persuasif* < ML *persuasivus* < L *persuasus,* pp. of *persuadere*⟧ having the power, or tending, to persuade —**per·sua′sive·ly** ***adv.*** —**per·sua′sive·ness** ***n.***

per·sul·fate (pər sul′fāt′) ***n.*** ⟦PER- + SULFATE⟧ a salt containing the divalent, negative radical S_2O_8, produced by the electrolysis of a sulfate solution

pert[1] (purt) ***adj.*** ⟦ME, aphetic for *apert* < OFr < L *apertus,* open: see APERTURE⟧ **1** bold or impudent in speech or behavior; saucy; forward **2** chic and jaunty **3** [Dial.] in good spirits or health; lively; brisk **4** [Obs.] clever —**pert′ly** ***adv.*** —**pert′ness** ***n.***

pert[2] *abbrev.* pertaining

per·tain (pər tān′) ***vi.*** ⟦ME *partenen* < OFr *partenir* < L *pertinere,* to stretch out, reach < *per-,* intens. + *tenere,* to hold: see THIN⟧ **1** to belong; be connected or associated; be a part, accessory, etc. *[lands pertaining to an estate]* **2** to be appropriate or suitable *[conduct that pertains to a lady]* **3** to have reference or relevance; be related *[laws pertaining to the case]* —**pertaining to** having to do with; belonging to

Perth (purth) **1** former county of central Scotland: also **Perthshire** (-shir′) **2** city in central Scotland on the Tay **3** capital of Western Australia, in the SW part

per·ti·na·cious (purt′′n ā′shəs) ***adj.*** ⟦< L *pertinax* (gen. *pertinacis*), firm < *per-,* intens. + *tenax,* holding fast < *tenere,* to hold: see THIN⟧ **1** holding firmly to some purpose, belief, or action, often stubbornly or obstinately **2** hard to get rid of; unyielding; persistent —***SYN.*** STUBBORN —**per′ti·na′cious·ly** ***adv.***

per·ti·nac·i·ty (purt′′n as′ə tē) ***n.*** ⟦MFr *pertinacité*⟧ the quality or condition of being pertinacious; stubborn persistence; obstinacy

per·ti·nence (purt′′n əns) ***n.*** the quality of being pertinent or appropriate; relevance: also **per′ti·nen·cy**

per·ti·nent (purt′′n ənt) ***adj.*** ⟦ME < MFr < L *pertinens,* prp. of *pertinere:* see PERTAIN⟧ having some connection with the matter at hand; relevant; to the point —***SYN.*** RELEVANT —**per′ti·nent·ly** ***adv.***

per·turb (pər turb′) ***vt.*** ⟦ME *perturben* < MFr *perturber* < L *perturbare* < *per-,* intens. + *turbare,* to disturb: see TURBID⟧ **1** to cause to be alarmed, agitated, or upset; disturb or trouble greatly **2** to cause disorder or confusion in; unsettle **3** *Astron.* to cause perturbations in (the orbit of a planet, moon, etc.) —***SYN.*** DISTURB —**per·turb′a·ble** ***adj.*** —**per·turb′ed·ly** ***adv.*** —**per·turb′er** ***n.***

per·tur·ba·tion (pur′tər bā′shən) ***n.*** ⟦ME < MFr *perturbacion* < L *perturbatio*⟧ **1** a perturbing or being perturbed **2** something that perturbs; disturbance **3** *Astron.* a small change in an orbit caused by the attraction of another celestial body, other bodies, etc. —**per′tur·ba′tion·al** ***adj.***, **per·tur·ba·tive** (pər tur′bə tiv, pur′tər bāt′iv)

per·tus·sis (pər tus′is) ***n.*** ⟦ModL < L *per-,* intens. + *tussis,* a cough⟧ WHOOPING COUGH —**per·tus′sal** ***adj.***, **per·tus′soid′**

Pe·ru (pə ro͞o′) country in W South America, on the Pacific: 496,226 sq mi (1,285,220 sq km); cap. Lima

Peru current HUMBOLDT CURRENT

Pe·ru·gia (pe ro͞o′jä) commune in Umbria, central Italy

Per·u·gi·no (per′o͞o jē′nō), **Il** (ēl) (born *Pietro di Cristoforo Vannucci*) 1446?-1523; It. painter

pe·ruke (pə ro͞ok′) ***n.*** ⟦Fr *perruque* < It *perruca, parruca*⟧ PERIWIG

pe·rus·al (pə ro͞o′zəl) ***n.*** the act or an instance of perusing

pe·ruse (pə ro͞oz′) ***vt.*** **-rused′, -rus′ing** ⟦LME *perusen,* to use up, prob. < L *per-,* intens. + ME *usen,* to USE⟧ **1** [Obs.] to examine in detail; scrutinize **2** to read carefully or thoroughly; study **3** to read in a casual or leisurely way —**pe·rus′er** ***n.***

Pe·rutz (pə ro͞ots′), **Max Ferdinand** 1914-2002; Brit. molecular biologist, born in Austria

Pe·ru·vi·an (pə ro͞o′vē ən) ***adj.*** of Peru or its people or culture —***n.*** a person born or living in Peru

Peruvian bark CINCHONA (sense 2)

per·vade (pər vād′) ***vt.*** **-vad′ed, -vad′ing** ⟦L *pervadere* < *per,* through + *vadere,* to go: see EVADE⟧ **1** [Now Rare] to pass through; spread or be diffused throughout **2** to be prevalent throughout —**per·va′sion** (-vā′zhən) ***n.***

per·va·sive (pər vā′siv) ***adj.*** tending to pervade or spread throughout —**per·va′sive·ly** ***adv.*** —**per·va′sive·ness** ***n.***

per·verse (pər vurs′) ***adj.*** ⟦ME *pervers* < OFr < L *perversus,* pp. of *pervertere:* see PERVERT⟧ **1** deviating from what is considered right or good; wrong, improper, etc. or corrupt, wicked, etc.; specif., sexually perverted **2** persisting in error or fault; stubbornly contrary **3** obstinately disobedient or difficult; intractable **4** characterized by or resulting from obstinacy or contrariness —***SYN.*** CONTRARY —**per·verse′ly** ***adv.*** —**per·verse′ness** ***n.***

per·ver·sion (pər vur′zhən, -shən) ***n.*** ⟦ME *peruersion* < L *perversio* < pp. of *pervertere*⟧ **1** a perverting or being perverted **2** something perverted; abnormal form **3** any of various sexual acts or practices deviating from what is considered normal; sexual deviation

per·ver·si·ty (pər vur′sə tē) ***n.*** ⟦OFr *perversité* < L *perversitas* < *perversus*⟧ **1** the quality or condition of being perverse **2** *pl.* **-ties** an instance of this

per·ver·sive (pər vur′siv) ***adj.*** ⟦ML *perversivus:* see PERVERSE & -IVE⟧ that perverts or is marked by perversion

per·vert (pər vurt′; *for n.* pur′vurt′) ***vt.*** ⟦ME *perverten* < OFr *pervertir* < L *pervertere,* to overturn, corrupt < *per-,* intens. + *vertere,* to turn: see VERSE⟧ **1** to cause to turn from what is considered right, good, or true; misdirect; lead astray; corrupt **2** to turn to an improper use; misuse **3** to change or misapply the meaning of; misinterpret; distort; twist **4** to bring into a worse condition; debase —***n.*** a perverted person; esp., a person who practices sexual perversion —***SYN.*** DEBASE —**per·vert′er** ***n.*** —**per·vert′i·ble** ***adj.***

per·vert·ed (pər vurt′id) ***adj.*** **1** deviating from what is considered right, good, or true; misdirected, corrupted, etc. **2** of or practicing sexual perversion **3** misinterpreted; distorted —**per·vert′ed·ly** ***adv.*** —**per·vert′ed·ness** ***n.***

per·vi·ous (pur′vē əs) ***adj.*** ⟦L *pervius* < *per,* through + *via,* way: see VIA⟧ **1** allowing passage through; that can be penetrated or permeated **2** having a mind open to influence, argument, or suggestion —**per′vi·ous·ness** ***n.***

pes (pez, pes) ***n.***, *pl.* **pe·des** (pē′dēz′, ped′ēz′) ⟦ModL < L, FOOT⟧ *Zool.* a foot or footlike structure in land vertebrates

Pe·sach (pā′säkh) ***n.*** ⟦Heb *pesaḥ:* see PASCH⟧ PASSOVER

pe·sade (pə säd′, -zäd′, -zäd′) ***n.*** ⟦Fr, altered (prob. infl. by *peser,* to weigh) < *posade* < It *posata,* a halt < *posare,* to halt < L *pausare* < *pausa,* PAUSE⟧ *Horsemanship* a maneuver in which a horse is made to rear

Pes·ca·do·res (pes′kə dôr′ēz, -is) group of islands in Taiwan Strait; a dependency of Taiwan: 49 sq mi (127 sq km)

Pes·ca·ra (pās kä′rä) commune & seaport in central Italy, on the Adriatic

pe·se·ta (pə sāt′ə; *Sp* pe se′tä) ***n.*** ⟦Sp, dim. of *peso,* PESO⟧ the former basic monetary unit of Andorra and Spain, superseded in 2002 by the EURO

pes·e·wa (pes′ə wä′) ***n.***, *pl.* **-was′** or **-wa′** ⟦Akan⟧ a monetary unit of Ghana, equal to $1/100$ of a cedi

Pe·sha·war (pe shä′wər) city in N Pakistan, near the Khyber Pass

Pe·shi·to (pə shē′tō) ***n.*** ⟦Syriac *pshīṭtā,* shortened < *mappaqtā pshīṭtā,* the simple version < *pšaṭ,* to be straightforward⟧ the standard translation of the Old and New Testaments in ancient Syriac: also **Pe·shit·ta** (pə shēt′tä′)

pes·ky (pes′kē) ***adj.*** **-ki·er, -ki·est** ⟦prob. var. of *pesty* < PEST + -Y[2]⟧ [Informal] annoying; disagreeable; troublesome —**pes′ki·ly** ***adv.*** —**pes′ki·ness** ***n.***

pe·so (pā′sō; *Sp* pe′sô) ***n.***, *pl.* **-sos** (-sōz; *Sp,* -sôs) ⟦Sp, lit., a weight < L *pensum,* something weighed < neut. pp. of *pendere:* see PENSION⟧ the basic monetary unit of: *a)* Argentina *b)* Chile *c)* Colombia *d)* Cuba *e)* the Dominican Republic *f)* Mexico *g)* the Philippines *h)* Uruguay: see the table of monetary units in the Reference Supplement

pes·sa·ry (pes′ə rē) ***n.***, *pl.* **-ries** ⟦ME *pessarie* < LL *pessarium* < *pessum* < Gr *pessos,* oval pebble⟧ a device worn in the vagina to support a displaced uterus or to prevent conception

pes·si·mism (pes′ə miz′əm) ***n.*** ⟦Fr *pessimisme* < L *pessimus,* worst, superl. of *pejor,* worse: see PEJORATIVE⟧ **1** *Philos.* *a)* the doctrine or belief that the existing world is the worst possible *b)* the doctrine or belief that the evil in life outweighs the good **2** the tendency to expect misfortune or the worst outcome in any circumstances; practice of looking on the dark side of things —**pes′si·mist** ***n.***

pes·si·mis·tic (pes′ə mis′tik) ***adj.*** of or characterized by pessimism; expecting the worst —***SYN.*** CYNICAL —**pes′si·mis′ti·cal·ly** ***adv.***

Pes·soa (pes′wä), **Fer·nan·do** (fər nan′dō) 1888-1935; Port. poet

pest (pest) ***n.*** ⟦Fr *peste* < L *pestis,* plague⟧ **1** a person or thing that causes trouble, annoyance, discomfort, etc.; nuisance; specif., any destructive or troublesome insect, small animal, weed, etc. **2** [Now Rare] a fatal epidemic disease; esp., bubonic plague

Pes·ta·loz·zi (pes′tə lät′sē), **Jo·hann Hein·rich** (yō′hän′ hīn′riH) 1746-1827; Swiss educational reformer

pes·ter (pes′tər) ***vt.*** ⟦< obs. *impester* < OFr *empestrer,* orig., to hobble a horse at pasture, entangle < VL **impastoriare* < L *in-,* IN-[1] + VL **pastoria,* shackle (see PASTERN): meaning infl. by PEST⟧ **1** to annoy constantly or repeatedly with petty irritations; bother; vex **2** [Obs.] to overcrowd; cram —**pes′ter·er** ***n.***

pest·hole (pest′hōl′) ***n.*** ⟦PEST + HOLE⟧ a place infested or likely to be infested with disease: now usually used fig.

pest·house (pest′hous′) ***n.*** ⟦PEST + HOUSE⟧ [Archaic] a hospital for the isolation of people with contagious or epidemic diseases

pes·ti·cide (pes′tə sīd′) ***n.*** ⟦< PEST + -CIDE⟧ any chemical used for killing insects, weeds, etc. —**pes′ti·ci′dal** ***adj.***

pes·tif·er·ous (pes tif′ər əs) ***adj.*** ⟦ME < L *pestiferus* < *pestis,* plague + *ferre,* to BEAR[1]⟧ **1** *a)* bringing or carrying disease *b)* [Archaic] infected with an epidemic disease **2** dangerous to morals or to the welfare of society; noxious; evil **3** [Informal] annoying; mischievous; bothersome —**pes·tif′er·ous·ly** ***adv.*** —**pes·tif′er·ous·ness** ***n.***

pes·ti·lence (pes′tə ləns) ***n.*** ⟦OFr < L *pestilentia* < *pestilens:* see fol.⟧ **1** any virulent or fatal contagious or infectious disease, esp. one of epidemic proportions, as bubonic plague **2** anything, as a doctrine, regarded as harmful or dangerous

pes·ti·lent (pes′tə lənt) ***adj.*** ⟦ME < L *pestilens* < *pestis,* plague⟧ **1** likely to cause death; deadly **2** [Rare] contagious; pestilential **3** dangerous to the security and welfare of society; pernicious **4** [Archaic] annoying; troublesome —**pes′ti·lent·ly** ***adv.***

pes·ti·len·tial (pes′tə len′shəl) ***adj.*** ⟦ME *pestilencial* < ML *pestilentialis*⟧ **1** of, causing, or likely to cause pestilence or infection **2** like or constituting a pestilence; widespread and deadly **3** pernicious; dangerous; harmful —**pes′ti·len′tial·ly** ***adv.***

pes·tle (pes′əl, -təl) ***n.*** ⟦ME *pestel* < OFr < L *pistillum* < *pinsere,* to pound < IE base **pis-,* to pound, crush > Gr *ptissein,* to stamp⟧ **1** a tool, usually club-shaped, used to pound or grind substances in a mortar **2** any of several tools for pounding, grinding, or stamping — ***vt., vi.*** **-tled, -tling** to pound, grind, crush, etc. with or as with a pestle

☆**pes·to** (pes′tō) ***n.*** ⟦It pp. of *pestare,* to pound, grind < L *pinsere:* see prec.⟧ an Italian sauce that is a purée of fresh basil, garlic, pine nuts, and Parmesan cheese in olive oil, used esp. over pasta

pet[1] (pet) ***n.*** ⟦orig. Scot dial., prob. back-form. < ME *pety,* small: see PETTY⟧ **1** an animal that is tamed or domesticated and kept as a companion or treated with fondness **2** a person who is treated with particular affection or indulgence; favorite —***adj.*** **1** kept or treated as a pet [*a pet duck*] **2** especially liked; favorite **3** greatest; especial; particular [*one's pet peeve*] **4** showing fondness or affection [*a pet name*] —***vt.*** **pet′ted, pet′ting 1** to stroke or pat (now, esp., an animal) affectionately **2** to be indulgent toward; pamper —☆***vi.*** [Informal] to kiss, embrace, fondle, etc., passionately in mutual sexual stimulation —***SYN.*** CARESS —**pet′ter** ***n.***

pet[2] (pet) ***n.*** ⟦< earlier phr. *to take the pet* < ?⟧ a state of sulky peevishness or ill humor —***vi.*** **pet′ted, pet′ting** to be in a pet; sulk

PET[2] *abbrev.* polyethylene terephthalate

Pet *abbrev. Bible* Peter

PET[1] (pet) ***n.*** PET SCAN

PETA (pēt′ə) *abbrev.* People for the Ethical Treatment of Animals

pet·a- (pet′ə) ⟦< ? PENTA-, because the number is 1,000 to the fifth power; perhaps also by analogy with TERA-, as if it were derived from TETRA-⟧ *combining form* one quadrillion; the factor 10^{15}

Pe·tah Tiq·wa (pe tä′ tēk′vä) city in WC Israel

Pé·tain (pā tan′), **Hen·ri Phi·lippe** (än rē fē lēp′) 1856-1951; Fr. general: premier of Fr. government at Vichy (1940-44): convicted of treason (1945)

pet·al (pet′'l) ***n.*** ⟦ModL *petalum* < ML(Ec), a thin metal plate < Gr *petalon,* leaf < *petalos,* outspread < IE base **pet-,* to spread out > FATHOM⟧ any of the component parts, or leaves, of a corolla —**pet′aled** ***adj.,*** **pet′alled**

-pe·tal (pə təl) ⟦< ModL *-petus* (< L *petere,* to rush at, seek: see FEATHER + -AL⟧ *combining form forming adjectives* moving toward, seeking [*basipetal*]

pet·al·o·dy (pet′'l ō′dē) ***n.*** ⟦< PETAL + Gr *-ōdia,* a becoming like < *-ōdes:* see -ODE[2]⟧ *Bot.* the conversion of stamens or other organs into petals

pet·al·oid (-oid′) ***adj.*** ⟦PETAL + -OID⟧ resembling a petal

pet·al·ous (pet′'l əs) ***adj.*** with petals

pé·tanque (pā tänk′) ***n.*** ⟦Fr < Prov *pés tanqués,* feet together (the required stance)⟧ a French game similar to bowls

pe·tard (pi tärd′) ***n.*** ⟦Fr *pétard* < *péter,* to break wind < *pet,* fart < L *peditum* < *peditus,* pp. of *pedere,* to break wind < IE base **pezd-,* of echoic orig.⟧ **1** [Historical] a metal cone or box filled with explosives, fastened in warfare to walls and gates and exploded to force an opening **2** a kind of firecracker —**hoist with** (or **by**) **one's own petard** ⟦in allusion to *Hamlet,* III, iv: see HOISE⟧ destroyed by the very devices with which one meant to destroy others

pet·a·sos or **pet·a·sus** (pet′ə säs′, -səs) ***n.*** ⟦L *petasus* < Gr *petasos* < *petannynai,* to spread out < IE base **pet-* > FATHOM⟧ **1** a flat, wide-brimmed hat worn in ancient Greece **2** the winged hat of Hermes (Mercury)

pet·cock (pet′käk′) ***n.*** ⟦< obs. *pet* (< Fr: see PETARD) + COCK[1]⟧ a small faucet or valve used in draining unwanted or excess water or air from pipes, radiators, boilers, etc.

PETE *abbrev.* polyethylene terephthalate

pe·te·chi·a (pə tē′kē ə) ***n., pl.*** **-chi·ae** (-ē′) ⟦ModL < It *petecchia* < L *pittacium,* label, plaster, patch < Gr *pittakion,* a writing tablet, slip, letter⟧ a small hemorrhagic spot in the skin, mucous membrane, etc. —**pe·te′chi·al** ***adj.***

pe·ter[1] (pēt′ər) ***vi.*** ⟦< ?⟧ ☆[Informal] to become gradually smaller, weaker, etc. and then cease or disappear: with *out*

pe·ter[2] (pēt′ər) ***n.*** ⟦ult. < fol.⟧ [Slang] the penis

Pe·ter[1] (pēt′ər) ***n.*** ⟦ME < LL(Ec) *Petrus* < Gr *Petros* (< *petros,* stone, *petra,* rock) used as transl. of Aram *kēphā,* rock⟧ **1** a masculine name: dim. *Pete:* equiv. L. *Petrus,* Fr. *Pierre,* It. *Pietro,* Sp. *Pedro,* Russ. *Pyotr* **2** *a)* (original name *Simon*) (died A.D. 64?); one of the twelve Apostles, a fisherman, to whom the Letters of Peter are ascribed: considered the first pope: his day is June 29 (also **Simon Peter** or **Saint Peter**) *b)* either of the two Letters of Peter (abbrev. *Pe, Pet*) —**rob Peter to pay Paul** to pay a debt, obligation, etc. by creating or leaving unpaid another

Pe·ter[2] (pēt′ər) **1 Peter I** 1672-1725; czar of Russia (1682-1725): called *the Great* **2 Peter II** 1923-70; king of Yugoslavia (1934-45): son of Alexander I **3 Peter III** 1728-62; czar of Russia (1762): assassinated; succeeded by his wife, Catherine II

Pe·ter·bor·ough (pēt′ər bur′ō, -ə) **1** city in Cambridgeshire, EC England **2** city in SE Ontario, Canada, near Toronto: resort area **3 Soke of** former county of EC England, now part of Cambridgeshire

Peter Pan the title character of J. M. Barrie's play (1904), a young boy who runs away to "Never-Never Land" and never grows up

Peter Pan collar ⟦< traditional costume of prec.⟧ a small, closefitting collar with ends rounded in front, used on women's and children's dresses, blouses, etc.

☆**Peter Principle** ⟦< *The Peter Principle* (1968), book by L. J. Peter (1919-90), U.S. educator, & R. J. Hull (1919-85), Cdn writer⟧ the facetious proposition that each employee in an organization tends to be promoted until reaching his or her level of incompetence

Pe·ters·burg (pēt′ərz burg′) *var. of* ST. PETERSBURG (Russia)

Pe·ter·sham (pēt′ər shəm) ***n.*** ⟦after Lord *Petersham,* who set the fashion (*c.* 1812)⟧ **1** an overcoat made of a rough, heavy woolen cloth **2** this cloth

Pe·ter·son (pē′tər sən), **Roger Tory** 1908-96; U.S. ornithologist, naturalist, & artist

Peter's pence 1 an annual tax, orig. of one penny, paid to the papal see by certain English property owners before the Reformation **2** an annual voluntary donation made by Catholics everywhere to the papal see Also **Peter pence**

pet·i·o·lar (pet′ē ō′lər) ***adj.*** of or attached to the petiole

pet·i·o·late (pet′ē ō lāt′) ***adj.*** ⟦< fol. + -ATE[1]⟧ *Biol.* having a stalk or petiole

pet·i·ole (pet′ē ōl′) ***n.*** ⟦ModL *petiolus* < L, little foot, little leg, stalk, dim. < *pes,* FOOT⟧ **1** *Bot.* LEAFSTALK **2** *Zool.* PEDUNCLE (sense 4)

pet·i·o·lule (pet′ē ō lōōl′, pet′ē ō′-) ***n.*** ⟦ModL *petiolulus* < *petiolus,* prec. + *-ulus,* -ULE⟧ the stalk of a leaflet in a compound leaf

Pe·ti·pa (pə tē pȧ′), **Ma·rius** (mȧ ryüs′) 1818-1910; Fr. dancer & choreographer in Russia

pe·tit (pet′ē) ***adj.*** ⟦OFr: see PETTY⟧ small or of less importance; petty: now used chiefly in law

pe·tit bourgeois (pet′ē, pə tē′) ⟦Fr⟧ a member of the petite bourgeoisie —**pe′tit-bour·geois′** ***adj.***

pe·tite (pə tēt′) ***adj.*** ⟦Fr, fem. of *petit*⟧ small and trim in figure: said of a woman —***SYN.*** SMALL —**pe·tite′ness** ***n.***

petite bourgeoise ⟦Fr⟧ a woman who is a member of the petite bourgeoisie

petite bourgeoisie ⟦Fr⟧ that part of the bourgeoisie of lowest income or status, including small shopkeepers, routine office workers, etc.; the lower middle class

petite si·rah (si rä′, sē-) **1** a dry red wine produced mainly in California **2** the grape from which it is made

pe·tit four (pet′ē fôr′; *Fr* pə tē fōōr′) *pl.* **pe·tits fours** (pet′ē fôrz′; *Fr* pə tē fōōr′) or **pe·tit fours** (pet′ē fôrz′) ⟦Fr, small cake < *petit,* small + *four,* cake, lit., oven < L *furnus:* see FURNACE⟧ a small piece of spongecake, etc. cut in any of various shapes and decorated with icing

pe·ti·tion (pə tish′ən) ***n.*** ⟦OFr < L *petitio* (gen. *petitionis*) < *petere,* to seek, rush at, fall: see FEATHER⟧ **1** a solemn, earnest supplication or request to a superior or deity or to a person or group in authority; prayer or entreaty **2** a formal writing or document embodying such a request, addressed to a specific person or group and often signed by a number of petitioners **3** something that is asked or entreated [*to grant a petition*] **4** *Law* a written formal request or plea in which specific court action is asked for [*a petition for rehearing*] —***vt.*** **1** to address a petition to; ask formally or earnestly **2** to ask for; solicit —***vi.*** to make a petition —***SYN.*** APPEAL —**pe·ti′tion·ar′y** ***adj.*** —**pe·ti′tion·er** ***n.***

pe·ti·ti·o prin·ci·pi·i (pi tish′ē ō′ prin sip′ē ī′) ⟦L, a begging of the question⟧ *Logic* the fallacy of assuming in the premise of an argument the conclusion which is to be proved

pe·tit jury (pet′ē) a group of twelve citizens picked to weigh the evidence in and decide the issues of a trial in court: distinguished from GRAND JURY

pe·tit larceny (pet′ē) *see* LARCENY

pe·tit mal (pə tē′ mäl′, -mal′) ⟦Fr, lit., small ailment⟧ a type of epilepsy in which there are attacks of momentary unconsciousness without convulsions: distinguished from GRAND MAL

pe·tit point (pet′ē) ⟦Fr⟧ **1** a small needlepoint stitch over one vertical and one horizontal canvas thread **2** work done with this stitch, as a picture on canvas

pe·tits pois (pə tē pwȧ′) ⟦Fr, little peas⟧ small green peas

☆**pet·nap·ping** or **pet·nap·ing** (pet′nap′iŋ) ***n.*** ⟦PET[1] + (KID)NAPPING⟧ the stealing of pets, esp. dogs or cats, in order to sell them, as for use in laboratory experiments

Pe·tö·fi (pet′ə fē; *Hung* pe′tö fē), **Sán·dor** (shän′dôr′) 1823-49; Hung. poet & patriot

Pe·tra (pē′trə) ancient Edomite city in SW Jordan

Pe·trarch (pē′trärk′) (It. name *Francesco Petrarca*) 1304-74; It. lyric poet & scholar

Pe·trar·chan sonnet (pi trär′kən) a sonnet composed of a group of eight lines (*octave*) with two rhymes *abba abba,* and a group of six lines (*sestet*) with two or three rhymes variously arranged, typically *cde cde* or *cdc dcd:* the thought or theme is stated and developed in the octave, and expanded, contradicted, etc. in the sestet; Italian sonnet

pet·rel (pe′trəl) ***n.*** ⟦earlier *pitteral* < ?⟧ a member of any of three families (esp. Procellariidae) of small, marine tubenose birds with long wings, including storm petrels and shearwaters

pe·tri dish (pē′trē) ⟦after J. R. *Petri* (1852-1921), Ger bacteriologist⟧ [*also* **P- d-**] a very shallow, cylindrical, transparent glass or plastic dish with an overlapping cover, used for the culture of microorganisms

Pe·trie (pē′trē), Sir **(William Matthew) Flin·ders** (flin′dərz) 1853-1942; Eng. archaeologist & Egyptologist

pet·ri·fac·tion (pe′trə fak′shən) ***n.*** ⟦< fol.⟧ **1** a petrifying or being petrified **2** something petrified Also **pet′ri·fi·ca′tion** (-fi kā′shən) —**pet′ri·fac′tive** ***adj.***

pet·ri·fy (pe′trə fī′) ***vt.*** **-fied′, -fy′ing** ⟦Fr *pétrifier* < L *petra,* stone, rock (< Gr) + *-ficare,* -FY⟧ **1** to replace the normal cells of (organic matter) with silica or other mineral deposits; re-form as a stony substance **2** to make rigid, inflexible, or inert; harden or deaden **3** to paralyze or make numb, as with fear; stupefy; stun —***vi.*** to become petrified —**pet′ri·fied** ***adj.***

Pe·trine (pē′trīn′, -trin) *adj.* ⟦< L *Petrus,* PETER[1] + -INE[1]⟧ of, like, or attributed to the Apostle Peter

petri plate [*also* **P- p-**] *var. of* PETRI DISH

pet·ro- (pe′trō, -trə) ⟦< Gr *petra,* rock, or *petros,* stone⟧ *combining form* **1** rock or stone [*petrography*]: also, before a vowel, **petr- 2** petroleum [*petrochemical*] **3** of or relating to the petroleum business [*petrodollars, petropolitics*]

pet·ro·chem·i·cal (pe′trō kem′i kəl) *n.* ⟦PETRO(LEUM) + CHEMICAL⟧ a chemical derived ultimately from petroleum or natural gas, as an aliphatic or aromatic hydrocarbon —**pet′ro·chem′is·try** (-is trē) *n.*

pet·ro·dol·lars (pe′trō däl′ərz) *pl.n.* ⟦< PETRO- (sense 3) + DOLLAR⟧ the dollar-denominated revenue earned from petroleum exports by oil-producing countries, esp. the members of OPEC —**pet′ro·dol′lar** *adj.*

pet·ro·gen·e·sis (pe′trə jen′ə sis) *n.* ⟦PETRO- (sense 1) + -GENESIS⟧ **1** the branch of petrology that studies the origin and formation of rocks **2** the origin of a rock —**pet′ro·ge·net′ic** (-jə net′ik) *adj.*, **pet′ro·gen′ic** (-jen′ik)

pet·ro·glyph (pe′trō glif′) *n.* ⟦Fr *pétroglyphe* < Gr *petra,* rock + *glyphē,* carving: see GLYPH⟧ a rock carving, esp. a prehistoric one —**pet′ro·glyph′ic** *adj.*

Pet·ro·grad (pe′trə grad′; *Russ* pyet′rô grät′) *name* (1914-24) *for* ST. PETERSBURG (Russia)

pe·trog·ra·phy (pə träg′rə fē) *n.* ⟦ModL *petrographia:* see PETRO- + -GRAPHY⟧ the branch of petrology that deals with the description and classification of rocks, esp. by means of examination under a microscope —**pe·trog′ra·pher** *n.* —**pet·ro·graph·ic** (pe′trō graf′ik) *adj.*, **pet′ro·graph′i·cal** —**pet′ro·graph′i·cal·ly** *adv.*

pet·rol (pe′trəl) *n.* ⟦Fr *pétrole* < ML *petroleum:* see PETROLEUM⟧ *Brit. term for* GASOLINE

☆**pet·ro·la·tum** (pe′trə lāt′əm) *n.* ⟦ModL < fol. + L *-atum,* neut. of *-atus:* see -ATE[2]⟧ a greasy, jellylike substance consisting of a mixture of semisolid hydrocarbons obtained from petroleum: it is used as a base for ointments, in leather dressing, etc.

pe·tro·le·um (pə trō′lē əm) *n.* ⟦ML < L *petra,* rock (< Gr) + *oleum,* OIL⟧ an oily, flammable, liquid solution of hydrocarbons, yellowish-green to black in color, occurring naturally in the rock strata of certain geological formations: when fractionally distilled, it yields paraffin, fuel oil, kerosene, gasoline, etc.

☆**petroleum jelly** PETROLATUM

pe·trol·o·gy (pə träl′ə jē) *n.* ⟦PETRO- + -LOGY⟧ the branch of geology that deals with the classification, location, composition, structure, and origin of rocks —**pet·ro·log·ic** (pe′trō läj′ik) *adj.*, **pet′ro·log′i·cal** —**pet′ro·log′i·cal·ly** *adv.* —**pe·trol′o·gist** *n.*

pet·ro·nel (pe′trə nəl) *n.* ⟦altered (as if < PETRO-) < Fr *petrinal* < OFr *peitrine* (Fr *poitrine*), breast, chest < L *pectus* (gen. *pectoris*), chest: it was rested against the chest in firing⟧ a carbinelike firearm, used in the 15th to 17th cent.

Pe·tro·ni·us (pi trō′nē əs), **(Gaius)** died A.D. 66; Rom. satirist: often called *Petronius Arbiter*

Pet·ro·pav·lovsk (pe′trə päv′ləfsk) city in N Kazakhstan

Pet·ro·pav·lovsk-Kam·chat·skiy (-käm chät′skē) seaport in E Asian Russia, on Kamchatka Peninsula

Pe·tró·po·lis (pə trô′pə lis) city in EC Rio de Janeiro state, Brazil, near Rio de Janeiro

pe·tro·sal (pə trō′səl) *adj.* ⟦< L *petrosus,* rocky: see fol. & -AL⟧ **1** very hard or stony **2** ⟦< ModL *petrosa* < ML *(os) petrosus,* petrosal (bone)⟧ *Anat.* of or located near the petrous part of the temporal bone

pet·rous (pe′trəs, pē′trəs) *adj.* ⟦L *petrosus,* rocky < *petra,* rock < Gr⟧ **1** of or like rock; hard; stony **2** ⟦ML *petrosus*⟧ designating or of that part of the temporal bone which surrounds and protects the internal ear

Pet·ro·za·vodsk (pe′trə zä vôtsk′) city in NW Russia, on Lake Onega

☆**PET scan** (pet) ⟦*p(ositron) e(mission) t(omography)*⟧ a type of tomography that, through the use of radioactive tracers, shows the metabolism, as of glucose, in the body, esp. the brain: used in diagnosing abnormalities —**PET scanner** —**PET scanning**

pet·ti·coat (pet′ē kōt′, pet′i-) *n.* ⟦ME *petycote:* see PETTY & COAT⟧ **1** a skirt, now esp. an underskirt often trimmed at the hemline as with lace or ruffles, worn by women and girls **2** something resembling a petticoat **3** [Old Informal] a woman or girl —*adj.* of or by women; female: a derisive use [*petticoat* government]

pet·ti·fog·ger (pet′i fäg′ər, -fôg′-; pet′ē-) *n.* ⟦PETTY + obs. *fogger* < ?⟧ **1** a lawyer who handles petty cases, esp. one who uses unethical methods in conducting trumped-up cases **2** a trickster; cheater **3** a quibbler; caviler —**pet′ti·fog′** *vi.* **-fogged′**, **-fog′ging** —**pet′ti·fog′ger·y** *n.*

pet·tish (pet′ish) *adj.* ⟦< PET[2] + -ISH⟧ peevish; petulant; cross —**pet′tish·ly** *adv.* —**pet′tish·ness** *n.*

pet·ti·toes (pet′ē tōz′, pet′i-) *pl.n.* ⟦prob. < MFr *petite oye,* goose giblets < fem. of *petit* (see PETTY) + *oye,* goose < LL *auca* (see OCARINA): form and meaning infl. by assoc. with TOE⟧ **1** pigs' feet, as an article of food **2** feet or toes, esp. a child's

PETT scan (pet) ⟦*p(ositron) e(mission) t(ransaxial) t(omography)*⟧ PET SCAN —**PETT scanner** —**PETT scanning**

pet·ty (pet′ē) *adj.* **-ti·er**, **-ti·est** ⟦ME *pety* < OFr *petit* < **pit-*, little < baby talk⟧ **1** relatively worthless or unimportant; trivial; insignificant **2** small-scale; minor **3** *a)* having or showing a tendency to make much of small matters *b)* small-minded; mean, narrow, ungenerous, etc. **4** relatively low in rank; subordinate —**pet′ti·ly** *adv.* —**pet′ti·ness** *n.*

petty bourgeois PETIT BOURGEOIS

petty cash a cash fund for small incidental expenses

petty larceny *see* LARCENY

petty officer *U.S. Navy* an enlisted person of any of the six grades of noncommissioned officers from petty officer third class up to master chief petty officer

pet·u·lant (pech′ə lənt) *adj.* ⟦L *petulans* (gen. *petulantis*), forward, petulant < base of *petere,* to rush at, fall: see FEATHER⟧ **1** [Obs.] forward or insolent **2** impatient or irritable, esp. over petty things; peevish —**pet′u·lance** *n.*, **pet′u·lan·cy** —**pet′u·lant·ly** *adv.*

pe·tu·ni·a (pə to͞on′yə, -tyo͞on′-; -ē ə) *n.* ⟦ModL < Fr *petun* < Tupí, tobacco⟧ any of a genus (*Petunia*) of plants of the nightshade family, with funnel-shaped flowers of various colors and patterns, esp. a common garden annual (*P. hybrida*)

Pevs·ner (*for 1,* pefs′nər *or Fr* pevz ner′; *for 2,* pevz′nər) **1 An·toine** (än twån′) 1886-1962; Fr. sculptor & painter, born in Russia: brother of Naum Gabo **2** Sir **Ni·ko·laus (Barnhard Leon)** (nik′ə ləs) 1902-85; Brit. art historian and author of architectural guidebooks, born in Germany

pew (pyo͞o) *n.* ⟦ME *pewe* < OFr *puie,* balcony, balustrade < L *podia,* pl. of *podium,* balcony: see PODIUM⟧ **1** any of the benches with a back that are fixed in rows in a church **2** any of the boxlike enclosures with seats, in some churches, for the use as of a particular family

☆**pe·wee** (pē′wē′) *n.* ⟦echoic of its call⟧ any of a genus *(Contopus)* of small tyrant flycatchers; esp., the wood pewees

pe·wit (pē′wit, pyo͞o′it) *n.* ⟦echoic of its call⟧ **1** LAPWING ☆**2** PEWEE

pew·ter (pyo͞ot′ər) *n.* ⟦ME *peutre* < OFr *peautre,* akin to It *peltro* < ?⟧ **1** any of various alloys containing mostly tin with varying percentages of antimony, copper, lead, etc. **2** articles made of pewter —*adj.* made of pewter

☆**pe·yo·te** (pā ōt′ē) *n.* ⟦AmSp < Nahuatl *peyotl,* caterpillar, with reference to the down in the center⟧ MESCAL (sense 3): also **pe·yo·tl** (pā ōt′'l)

pf *abbrev.* **1** perfect **2** pfennig **3** preferred

PFC or **Pfc** *abbrev.* Private First Class

pfd *abbrev.* preferred

pfef·fer·nuss (fef′ər no͞os′) *n., pl.* **-nues′se** (-no͞o′sə) ⟦Ger, lit., pepper nut⟧ a small, usually ball-shaped cookie flavored with cinnamon, allspice, anise, etc. and with black pepper, made esp. during the Christmas season

pfen·nig (fen′ig; *Ger* pfen′iH) *n., pl.* **-nigs** or Ger **Pfen·ni·ge** (pfen′i gə) ⟦Ger: see PENNY⟧ a former monetary unit of Germany, equal to 1⁄100 of a deutsche mark

pfft (ft) *interj.* [Informal] used to suggest a sudden ending or fizzling out

Pforz·heim (pfôrts′hīm) city in SW Germany, northwest of Stuttgart, in the state of Baden-Württemberg

pfu·i (fo͞o′ē) *interj.* ⟦Ger, echoic of the sound of spitting⟧ PHOOEY

pg *abbrev.* **1** page **2** paying guest **3** picogram(s)

Pg *abbrev.* **1** Portugal **2** Portuguese

☆**PG[1]** *trademark* a film rating meaning "parental guidance suggested": it indicates that some content of the film may be unsuitable for children under seventeen

PG[2] *abbrev.* **1** paying guest **2** postgraduate

PGA *service mark* Professional Golfers' Association

☆**PG-13** *trademark* a film rating meaning "parents strongly cautioned": it indicates that some content of the film may be unsuitable for children under thirteen

pH (pē′āch′) *n.* ⟦< Fr *p(ouvoir) h(ydrogène)*, lit., hydrogen power⟧ the degree of acidity or alkalinity of a solution; it is the logarithm of the reciprocal of the hydrogen-ion concentration in gram equivalents per liter of solution (Ex: .0000001 gram atom of hydrogen ion per liter yields a numeric reciprocal of ten million, the log of ten million equals 7, therefore 7 is the pH): a pH of 7, the value for pure distilled water, is regarded as neutral; pH values from 7 to 0 indicate increasing acidity and from 7 to 14 indicate increasing alkalinity

ph *abbrev.* **1** phase **2** PHOT[1] **3** *Baseball* pinch hitter: also **PH**

Ph *abbrev. Bible* Philippians

PH *abbrev.* Purple Heart

PHA *abbrev.* Public Housing Administration

Phae·dra (fē′drə, fe′-) *n.* ⟦L < Gr *Phaidra*⟧ *Gr. Myth.* daughter of Minos and wife of Theseus: she kills herself after her stepson, Hippolytus, rejects her advances: see HIPPOLYTUS

Phae·drus (fē′drəs) 1st cent. A.D.; Rom. writer of fables and reputed translator of some of Aesop's fables

Pha·ë·thon (fā′ə thän′) *n.* ⟦L *Phaethon* < Gr *Phaethōn,* lit., shining (< *phaethein,* to shine) < *phaos,* light < IE base **bhā-*, to shine⟧ *Class. Myth.* son of Helios, the sun god: he unsuccessfully tries to drive his father's sun chariot and almost sets the world on fire, but Zeus strikes him down with a thunderbolt

pha·e·ton or **pha·ë·ton** (fā′ə tən, fāt′'n) *n.* ⟦Fr *phaéton* < L *Phaethon:* see prec.⟧ **1** a light, four-wheeled carriage of the 19th cent. drawn by one or two horses, with front and back seats and, usually, a folding top for the front ☆**2** an early type of gasoline automobile somewhat resembling such a carriage; also, later, a touring car

phag- (fag) *combining form* PHAGO-: used before a vowel

phage (fāj) *n. short for* BACTERIOPHAGE

-phage (fāj) ⟦< Gr *phagein:* see -PHAGOUS⟧ *combining form forming nouns* one that eats or destroys (something specified) [*bacteriophage*]

phag·e·de·na or **phag·e·dae·na** (faj′ə dē′nə) *n.* ⟦L *phagedaenos* < Gr *phagedaina* < *phagein,* to eat: see -PHAGOUS⟧ a rapidly spreading ulcer accompanied by sloughing, or the separation of dead tissue —**phag′e·den′ic** (-den′ik) *adj.*

-pha·gi·a (fā′jē ə, -jə) *combining form* -PHAGY
phag·o- (fag′ō, -ə) ⟦< Gr *phagein,* to eat: see -PHAGOUS⟧ *combining form* **1** eating or destroying *[phagocyte]* **2** phagocyte
phag·o·cyte (fag′ə sīt′) *n.* ⟦prec. + -CYTE⟧ any cell, esp. a leukocyte, that ingests and destroys other cells, microorganisms, or other foreign matter in the blood and tissues —**phag′o·cyt′ic** (-sit′ik) *adj.*
phagocytic index the average number of bacteria ingested per leukocyte in an incubated mixture of normal or immune serum, bacteria, and normal leukocytes
phag·o·cy·to·sis (fag′ə sī tō′sis) *n.* ⟦ModL: see PHAGOCYTE & -OSIS⟧ the ingestion and destruction by phagocytes of cells, microorganisms, foreign particles, etc.: see ENDOCYTOSIS —**phag′o·cy·tot′ic** (-tät′ik) *adj.*
-pha·gous (fə gəs) ⟦< Gr *-phagos* < *phagein,* to eat < IE base *bhag-, to allot, receive as share > Sans *bhajati,* (he) allots⟧ *combining form forming adjectives* that eats (something specified) *[entomophagous, ichthyophagous]*
-pha·gy (fə jē) ⟦ModL *-phagia* < Gr *phagein:* see prec.⟧ *combining form forming nouns* the eating of (something specified) *[geophagy]*
phal·ange (fal′anj′, fə lanj′) *n.* ⟦Fr < Gr *phalanges,* pl. of *phalanx*⟧ PHALANX (sense 5)
pha·lan·ge·al (fə lan′jē əl) *adj.* ⟦< ModL *phalangeus* + -AL⟧ of a phalanx or the phalanges: also **pha·lan′gal** (-laŋ′gəl)
pha·lan·ger (fə lan′jər) *n.* ⟦ModL < Gr *phalanx,* bone between two joints of the fingers or toes (see PHALANX): from the structure of the 2d and 3d phalanges of the hind feet⟧ a member of any of various families of small, plant-eating Australian marsupials (order Diprotodontia), living chiefly in trees and often having bushy, prehensile tails, including flying phalangers and cuscuses
pha·lan·ges (fə lan′jēz′) *pl.n. see* PHALANX
phal·an·ster·y (fal′ən ster′ē) *n., pl.* **-ster′ies** ⟦Fr *phalanstère* < *phalange,* phalange + *(mona)stère,* monastery⟧ **1** a socialist community as planned by F. M. C. Fourier **2** any communal association **3** the buildings housing such a community
pha·lanx (fā′laŋks′, fal′aŋks′) *n., pl.* **-lanx′es**; also, and for 5 always, **pha·lan·ges** (fə lan′jēz′) ⟦L < Gr, line of battle, bone between fingers, orig., log < IE base *bhel-, log > BALK⟧ **1** an ancient military formation of infantry in close, deep ranks with shields overlapping and spears extended **2** a massed group of individuals; compact body **3** a group of individuals united for a common purpose **4** the people forming a phalanstery **5** *Anat.* any of the bones forming the fingers or toes
phal·a·rope (fal′ə rōp′) *n.* ⟦Fr < ModL *Phalaropus,* name of the type genus < Gr *phalaris,* coot (akin to *phalos,* white: from its white head) + *pous,* FOOT⟧ any of a family (Phalaropodidae) of small shorebirds: the male rears the young
phal·lic (fal′ik) *adj.* ⟦Gr *phallikos*⟧ **1** of, like, or relating to the phallus **2** of or relating to phallicism **3** GENITAL (sense 2*a*)
phal·li·cism (fal′ə siz′əm) *n.* worship of the phallus as a symbol of the male generative power: also **phal·lism** (fal′iz′əm) —**phal′li·cist** *n.,* **phal′list**
phal·lo·cen·tric (fal′ō sen′trik) *adj.* ⟦< fol. + -CENTRIC⟧ **1** of or characterized by a particularly masculine mode of thought or behavior *[a phallocentric* point of view*]* **2** dominated or controlled unduly by men *[a phallocentric* society*]*
phal·lus (fal′əs) *n., pl.* **-li′** (-ī′) or **-lus·es** ⟦L < Gr *phallos* < IE base *bhel-, to swell > L *follis,* leather sack, *flare,* to blow⟧ **1** a representation or image of the penis as the reproductive organ, worshiped as a symbol of generative power, as in the Dionysiac festivals of ancient Greece **2** *Anat. a)* the penis *b)* the undifferentiated embryonic tissue that develops into the penis or clitoris
-phane (fān) ⟦< Gr *phainein,* to appear: see FANTASY⟧ *combining form* a substance that has a (specified) appearance or resembles (something specified) *[allophane, cymophane]*
phan·er·o·gam (fan′ər ə gam′) *n.* ⟦Fr *phanérogame* < Gr *phaneros,* visible (< *phainein,* to appear: see FANTASY) + *gamos,* marriage (see -GAMY)⟧ *former term for* a seed plant or a flowering plant —**phan′er·o·gam′ic** *adj.,* **phan′er·og′a·mous** (-ər äg′ə məs)
phan·er·o·phyte (-fīt′) *n.* ⟦< Gr *phaneros,* visible (see prec.) + -PHYTE⟧ *Bot.* a perennial plant with its resting buds located well above the ground and exposed to the air
Phan·er·o·zo·ic (fan′ər ə zō′ik) *adj.* ⟦< Gr *phaneros* (see PHANEROGAM) + -ZOIC⟧ *[sometimes* **p-***]* designating or of the geologic eon usually subdivided into the Paleozoic, Mesozoic, and Cenozoic eras —**the Phanerozoic** the Phanerozoic Eon or its rocks: see the geologic time chart in the Reference Supplement
phan·tasm (fan′taz′əm) *n.* ⟦ME *fantasme* < OFr < L *phantasma* < Gr < *phantazein,* to show < stem of *phainein,* to appear: see FANTASY⟧ **1** a perception of something that has no physical reality; figment of the mind; esp., a specter, or ghost: also **phan·tas·ma** (fan taz′mə), *pl.* **-ma·ta** (-mə tə) or **-mas** **2** a deceptive likeness **3** *Philos.* a mental impression of a real person or thing —**phan·tas′mal** (-taz′məl) *adj.,* **phan·tas′mic**
phan·tas·ma·go·ri·a (fan taz′mə gôr′ē ə) *n.* ⟦Fr *fantasmagorie* < Gr *phantasma,* prec. + *agoreuein,* to speak in public < *ageirein,* to assemble (see GREGARIOUS): prob. infl. by Fr *allegorie,* ALLEGORY⟧ **1** an early type of magic-lantern show consisting of various optical illusions in which objects rapidly change size, blend into one another, etc. **2** a rapidly changing series of things seen or imagined, as the figures or events of a dream **3** any rapidly changing scene —**phan·tas′ma·go′ric** *adj.,* **phan·tas′ma·go′ri·cal**
phan·ta·sy (fan′tə sē) *n., pl.* **-sies** *alt. sp. of* FANTASY
phan·tom (fan′təm) *n.* ⟦ME *fantome, fantosme* < OFr *fantosme* < L *phantasma:* see PHANTASM⟧ **1** something that seems to appear to the sight but has no physical existence; apparition; vision; specter **2** something feared or dreaded **3** something that exists only in the mind; illusion **4** a person or thing that is something in appearance but not in fact *[a phantom* of a leader*]* **5** any mental image or representation *[*the *phantoms* of things past*]* —*adj.* of, like, or constituting a phantom; not really existing; illusory
phar *abbrev.* **1** pharmaceutical **2** pharmacist **3** pharmacy
Phar·aoh (far′ō, fer′ō, fā′rō′) *n.* ⟦ME *Pharaon* < OE < LL(Ec) *Pharao* (gen. *Pharaonis*) < LGr *Pharaō* < Heb *paro* < Egypt pr-", great house: cf. Coptic *prro, pouro*⟧ *[sometimes* **p-***]* the title of the kings of ancient Egypt: often used as a proper name in the Bible —**Phar·a·on·ic** (far′ā än′ik, fer′-) *adj.,* **Phar′a·on′i·cal**
pharaoh ant a common, tiny, red ant (*Monomorium pharaonis*) that is a household pest in most of the world
pharaoh hound any of a breed of medium-sized hound, originating in ancient Egypt, having a short coat and large, erect ears
Phar·i·sa·ic (far′ə sā′ik) *adj.* ⟦LL(Ec) *Pharisaicus* < Gr(Ec) *pharisaïkos* < *pharisaios:* see PHARISEE⟧ **1** of the Pharisees **2** ⟦from the notion promulgated in the N.T. that Pharisees were generally so characterized⟧ *[usually* **p-***]* emphasizing or observing the letter but not the spirit of religious law; self-righteous; sanctimonious **3** *[usually* **p-***]* pretending to be highly moral or virtuous without actually being so; hypocritical: also **phar′i·sa′i·cal** —**phar′i·sa′i·cal·ly** *adv.*
Phar·i·sa·ism (far′ə sā′iz′əm) *n.* ⟦ModL *Pharisaïsmus* < Gr(Ec) *pharisaios:* see fol.⟧ **1** the beliefs and practices of the Pharisees **2** ⟦**p-**⟧ pharisaic behavior, character, principles, etc.
Phar·i·see (far′ə sē′) *n.* ⟦ME *pharise* < OE *fariseus* & OFr *pharisé,* both < LL(Ec) *Pharisaeus* < Gr(Ec) *pharasaios* < Aram *perishaiya,* pl. of *perish* < Heb *parush,* orig. adj., separated < root *prš,* cleave, separate⟧ **1** a member of an ancient Jewish group that carefully observed the written law but also accepted the oral, or traditional, law, believed that religious practices should be followed by everyone including high priests, etc.: opposed to SADDUCEE **2** *[often* **p-***]* a pharisaic person —**Phar′i·see′ism′** *n.*
pharm *abbrev.* **1** pharmaceutical **2** pharmacist **3** pharmacology **4** pharmacopeia **5** pharmacy
phar·ma (fär′mə) *n.* the pharmaceutical industry —*adj.* **1** pharmaceutical **2** of or having to do with the pharmaceutical industry
phar·ma·ceu·ti·cal (fär′mə so͞ot′i kəl, -syo͞ot′-) *adj.* ⟦LL *pharmaceuticus* < Gr *pharmakeutikos* < *pharmakeuein,* to practice witchcraft, use medicine < *pharmakon,* a poison, medicine⟧ **1** of pharmacy or pharmacists **2** of or by drugs Also **phar′ma·ceu′tic** —*n.* a pharmaceutical product; drug —**phar′ma·ceu′ti·cal·ly** *adv.*
phar·ma·ceu·tics (-iks) *n.* ⟦< LL⟧ PHARMACY (sense 1)
phar·ma·cist (fär′mə sist) *n.* a person licensed to practice pharmacy; druggist
phar·ma·co- (fär′mə kō) ⟦< Gr *pharmakon,* drug⟧ *combining form* drug or drugs *[pharmacodynamics]*
phar·ma·co·dy·nam·ics (-dī nam′iks) *n.* ⟦prec. + DYNAMICS⟧ the branch of pharmacology that deals with the effect and the reactions of drugs within the body —**phar′ma·co·dy·nam′ic** *adj.*
phar·ma·co·ge·net·ics (-jə net′iks) *n.* ⟦Ger *pharmakogenetik:* see PHARMACO- & GENETICS⟧ the study of genetic variation as revealed by various reactions to a drug
phar·ma·cog·no·sy (fär′mə käg′nə sē) *n.* ⟦< Gr *pharmakon,* drug + *-gnōsia* < *gnōsis,* knowledge: see GNOSIS⟧ the science that deals with medicinal products of plant, animal, or mineral origin in their crude or unprepared state
phar·ma·co·ki·net·ics (fär′mə kō ki net′iks) *n.* ⟦PHARMACO- + KINETICS⟧ the branch of pharmacology that deals with the absorption, distribution, and elimination of drugs by the body —**phar′ma·co·ki·net′ic** *adj.*
phar·ma·col·o·gy (fär′mə käl′ə jē) *n.* ⟦ModL *pharmacologia:* see PHARMACO- & -LOGY⟧ **1** the study of the preparation, qualities, and uses of drugs **2** the science dealing with the effect of drugs on living organisms —**phar′ma·co·log′i·cal** (-kə läj′i kəl) *adj.,* **phar′ma·co·log′ic** —**phar′ma·co·log′i·cal·ly** *adv.* —**phar′ma·col′o·gist** *n.*
phar·ma·co·pe·ia or **phar·ma·co·poe·ia** (fär′mə kō pē′ə) *n.* ⟦ModL < Gr *pharmakopoiia* < *pharmakon,* drug + *poiein,* to make: see POET[1]⟧ **1** an authoritative book containing a list and description of drugs and medicines together with the standards established under law for their production, dispensation, use, etc. **2** [Obs.] a stock of drugs —**phar′ma·co·pe′ial** *adj.,* **phar′ma·co·poe′ial**
phar·ma·co·ther·a·py (fär′mə kō ther′ə pē) *n.* the treatment of disease with drugs
phar·ma·cy (fär′mə sē) *n., pl.* **-cies** ⟦ME *fermacie,* medicine < MFr *farmacie* < LL *pharmacia* < Gr *pharmakeia* < *pharmakon,* drug⟧ **1** the art or profession of preparing and dispensing drugs and medicines **2** a store, office, etc. where drugs and medicines are dispensed
Pha·ros (fer′äs′) small peninsula at Alexandria, Egypt: in ancient times it was an island with a large lighthouse (also called **Pharos**) on it: this lighthouse was one of the Seven Wonders of the World
Phar·sa·li·a (fär sā′lē ə) district in ancient Thessaly, surrounding Pharsalus
Phar·sa·lus (fär sā′ləs) ancient city in S Thessaly, Greece, near which Caesar decisively defeated Pompey (48 B.C.)
pha·ryn·ge·al (fə rin′jē əl, far′ən jē′əl) *adj.* ⟦< ModL *pharyngeus*⟧ of, or in the region of, the pharynx: also **pha·ryn·gal** (fə riŋ′gəl)

phar·yn·gi·tis (far′ən jīt′is) ***n.*** ⟦ModL: see fol. & -ITIS⟧ inflammation of the mucous membrane of the pharynx; sore throat

pha·ryn·go- (fə riŋ′gō) ⟦< Gr *pharynx* (gen. *pharyngos*)⟧ *combining form* pharynx, pharynx and *[pharyngology]*: also, before a vowel, **pharyng-**

phar·yn·gol·o·gy (far′iŋ gäl′ə jē, far′ən-) ***n.*** ⟦prec. + -LOGY⟧ the branch of medicine dealing with the pharynx and its diseases

pha·ryn·go·scope (fə riŋ′gə skōp′) ***n.*** ⟦PHARYNGO- + -SCOPE⟧ an instrument for examining the pharynx —**phar·yn·gos·co·py** (far′iŋ gäs′kə pē, far′ən-) ***n.***

phar·ynx (far′iŋks) ***n.***, *pl.* **pha·ryn·ges** (fə rin′jēz′) or **phar′ynx·es** ⟦ModL < Gr *pharynx* (gen. *pharyngos*), throat < IE **bhorg-*, throat, gullet > L *frumen*⟧ the muscular and membranous cavity of the alimentary canal leading from the mouth and nasal passages to the larynx and esophagus

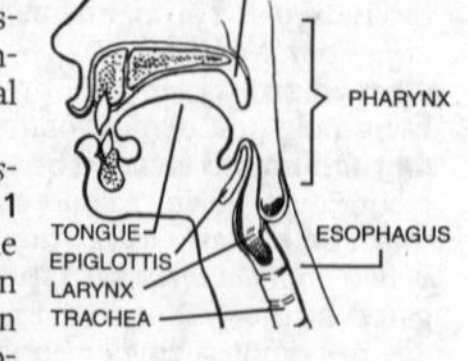

phase[1] (fāz) ***n.*** ⟦ModL *phasis* < Gr < *phainesthai*, to appear, akin to *phainein*: see FANTASY⟧ **1** any of the recurrent stages of variation in the illumination and apparent shape of a moon or a planet **2** any of the stages or forms in any series or cycle of changes, as in development **3** any of the ways in which something may be observed, considered, or presented; aspect; side; part *[a problem with many phases]* **4** *Chem.* a solid, liquid, or gaseous homogeneous form existing as a distinct part in a heterogeneous system *[ice is a phase of* H_2O*]* **5** *Physics* the fractional part of a cycle through which an oscillation, as of light or sound waves, has advanced, measured from an arbitrary starting point **6** *Zool.* any of the characteristic variations in color of the skin, fur, plumage, etc. of an animal, according to season, age, etc. —***vt.*** **phased, phas′ing 1** to plan, introduce, or carry out in phases, or stages: often with *in* or *into* **2** to put in phase —***vi.*** to move by phases —**in (or out of) phase** in (or not in) a state of exactly parallel movements, oscillations, etc.; in (or not in) synchronization —☆**phase out** to bring or come to an end, or withdraw from use, by stages

SYN.—**phase** applies to any of the ways in which something may be observed, considered, or presented, and often refers to a stage in development or in a cycle of changes *[the phases of the moon]*; **aspect** emphasizes the appearance of a thing as seen or considered from a particular point of view *[to consider a problem from all aspects]*; **facet** literally or figuratively applies to any of the faces of a many-sided thing *[the facets of a diamond, a personality, etc.]*; **angle** suggests a specific aspect seen from a point of view sharply limited in scope, or, sometimes, an aspect seen only by a sharply acute observer *[he knows all the angles]*

☆**phase**[2] (fāz) ***vt.*** **phased, phas′ing** *disputed sp. of* FAZE

phase-con·trast microscope (fāz′kän′trast′) a compound microscope that uses special lenses, diaphragms, etc. to alter slightly the paths of light waves from an object, thus producing a diffraction pattern that allows the viewing of transparent parts: also **phase microscope**

phase modulation *Radio* variation in the phase of a carrier wave in accordance with some signal, as speech

☆**phase·out** (fāz′out′) ***n.*** a phasing out; gradual termination or withdrawal

phase rule *Chem.* a generalization in the study of equilibriums between two or more phases of a system, stating that the number of degrees of freedom is equal to the number of components minus the number of phases plus the constant 2, or $F = C - P + 2$

-pha·si·a (fā′zhə, -zhē ə, -zē ə) ⟦ModL < Gr *phanai*, to speak: see PHONO-⟧ *combining form* a (specified) speech disorder *[dysphasia]*: also **-pha·sy**

pha·sic (fā′zik) ***adj.*** of or having to do with a phase or phases

pha·sis (fā′sis, -zis) ***n.***, *pl.* **-ses′** (-sēz′, -zēz′) ⟦ModL⟧ a phase; aspect; way; stage

phas·mid (faz′mid′, fas′-) ***n.*** ⟦< ModL *Phasmida* < Gr *phasma*, an apparition (akin to *phainein*, to show: see FANTASY) + *-ida* < neut. pl. of L *-ides*: see -ID⟧ any of various sticklike or leaflike insects (order Phasmatoptera), including the walking sticks and leaf insects

☆**phat** (fat) ***adj.*** **phat′ter, phat′test** [Slang] **1** fashionable, stylish, etc. **2** very pleasing, excellent, etc.

phat·ic (fat′ik) ***adj.*** ⟦< Gr *phatos*, spoken (< *phanai*, to speak: see PHONO-) + -IC⟧ of, constituting, or given to formulaic talk or meaningless sounds that are used merely to establish social contact rather than to communicate ideas *[phatic expression]* —**phat′i·cal·ly** ***adv.***

PhB or **Ph.B.** *abbrev.* ⟦L *Philosophiae Baccalaureus*⟧ Bachelor of Philosophy

PhC or **Ph.C.** *abbrev.* Pharmaceutical Chemist

PhD or **Ph.D.** *abbrev.* ⟦L *Philosophiae Doctor*⟧ Doctor of Philosophy

pheas·ant (fez′ənt) ***n.***, *pl.* **-ants** or **-ant** ⟦ME *fesant* < Anglo-Fr < OFr *faisan* < L *phasianus* < Gr *phasianos*, after *Phasis*, river of Colchis: the birds are said to have been numerous near its mouth⟧ **1** any of a number of large gallinaceous birds (family Phasianidae), usually with a long, sweeping tail and brilliant feathers: cf. PARTRIDGE ☆**2** any of a number of birds resembling the pheasant, as the ruffed grouse

Phei·di·as (fī′dē əs, fid′ē əs) *var. of* PHIDIAS

Phei·dip·pi·des (fī dip′i dēz′) ⟦prob. altered (by HERODOTUS) after *Philippides*⟧ 5th cent. B.C.; Athenian courier who ran to Sparta to seek aid against the Persians before the battle of Marathon

phel·lem (fel′em′, -əm) ***n.*** ⟦< Gr *phellos*, cork + E *-em*, as in PHLOEM⟧ the layer of dead, corky cells produced externally by the cork cambium in the bark of woody plants; cork

phel·lo·derm (fel′ə durm′) ***n.*** ⟦< Gr *phellos*, cork (akin to *phloos*, bark: see PHLOEM) + -DERM⟧ the layer of soft, living cells developed on the inner side by the phellogen —**phel′lo·der′mal** ***adj.***

phel·lo·gen (fel′ə jen′, -jən) ***n.*** ⟦< Gr *phellos* (see prec.) + -GEN⟧ CORK CAMBIUM —**phel′lo·ge·net′ic** (-jə net′ik) ***adj.***, **phel′lo·gen′ic** (-jen′ik)

phen- (fen) ⟦Fr *phén-* < Gr *phainein*, to show, shine (see FANTASY): term first used to indicate deriv. from coal tar, a byproduct in manufacturing illuminating gas⟧ *combining form* of or derived from benzene *[phenazine]*

phen·a·caine (fen′ə kān′, fē′nə-) ***n.*** ⟦*phen(etidyl)a(cetphenetidine)* + (CO)-CAINE⟧ **1** an organic, crystalline substance, $C_{18}H_{22}N_2O_2$, derived from coal tar **2** its hydrochloride, a local anesthetic, esp. for the eyes

phe·nac·e·tin (fē nas′ə tin) ***n.*** ⟦PHEN- + ACETIN⟧ a white, crystalline powder, $C_2H_5OC_6H_4NHCOCH_3$, used to reduce fever and to relieve headaches and muscular pains; acetophenetidin

phen·a·kite (fen′ə kīt′) ***n.*** ⟦Swed *phenakit* < Gr *phenax* (gen. *phenakos*), cheat + -ITE[1]: from being mistaken for quartz⟧ a very hard, glassy, rhombohedral mineral, Be_2SiO_4, of various colors, sometimes used as a gem; beryllium silicate: often **phen′a·cite′** (-sīt′)

phe·nan·threne (fə nan′thrēn′) ***n.*** ⟦< PHEN- + ANTHR(AC)ENE⟧ a colorless, crystalline hydrocarbon, $C_{14}H_{10}$, an isomer of the anthracene present in coal tar, used in making dyes, explosives, etc.

phe·nate (fē′nāt′, fen′āt′) ***n.*** ⟦PHEN(OL) + -ATE[2]⟧ a salt of carbolic acid (phenol in a dilute aqueous solution) containing the monovalent radical C_6H_5O

phen·a·zine (fen′ə zēn′, -zin) ***n.*** ⟦PHEN- + AZ(O)- + -INE[3]⟧ a tricyclic, yellow, crystalline base, $C_6H_4{:}N_2{:}C_6H_4$, from which many dyes are derived

phen·cy·cli·dine (fen sik′lə din, -sī′klə-; -dēn′) ***n.*** *see* PCP[1]

phe·net·ics (fi net′iks) ***n.*** *Taxonomy* classification based on observable characteristics, without reference to evolutionary relationships —**phe·net′ic** ***adj.*** —**phe·net′i·cist** ***n.***

phe·net·i·dine (fə net′ə dēn′, -din) ***n.*** ⟦< fol. + (AM)ID(O) + -INE[3]⟧ any of three isomeric compounds, $C_2H_5OC_6H_4NH_2$, used in manufacturing phenacetin and dyes

phen·e·tole (fen′ə tōl′) ***n.*** ⟦PHEN(OL) + ET(HYL) + -OLE⟧ a colorless liquid, $C_6H_5OC_2H_5$, the ethyl ether of phenol

Phe·ni·cia (fə nish′ə, -nē′shə) *alt. sp. of* PHOENICIA

phe·no- (fē′nō, -nə; fen′ō, -ə) *combining form* PHEN-

phe·no·bar·bi·tal (fē′nə bär′bi tôl′, -tal′) ***n.*** ⟦prec. + BARBITAL⟧ a white, odorless, crystalline barbiturate, $C_{12}H_{12}N_2O_3$, used as a sedative, sleeping pill, or anticonvulsant

phe·no·cop·y (fē′nō käp′ē) ***n.***, *pl.* **-ies** ⟦PHENO(TYPE) + COPY⟧ *Genetics* an environmentally induced change in an organism that is similar to a mutation but is nonhereditary

phe·no·cryst (fē′nə krist) ***n.*** ⟦Fr *phénocryste* < Gr *phainein*, to show (see FANTASY) + *krystallos*, CRYSTAL⟧ a relatively large and usually conspicuous crystal found in a fine-grained matrix in porphyritic igneous rock

phe·nol (fē′nōl′, -nôl′, -näl′) ***n.*** ⟦PHEN- + -OL[1]⟧ **1** a white crystalline compound, C_6H_5OH, produced from coal tar or by the hydrolysis of chlorobenzene, and used in making explosives, synthetic resins, etc.: it is a strong, corrosive poison with a characteristic odor, and its dilute aqueous solution, commonly called *carbolic acid*, is used as an antiseptic, disinfectant, etc. **2** any of a group of aromatic hydroxyl derivatives of benzene, similar in structure and composition to phenol —**phe·no·lic** (fē nō′lik; -nôl′ik; -näl′-) ***adj.***

phe·no·late (fē′nə lāt′) ***n.*** PHENATE

phenolic resin any of a group of thermosetting resins formed by condensing phenol with various aldehydes, as formaldehyde: used to form molded and cast plastic items

phe·nol·o·gy (fē näl′ə jē, fi-) ***n.*** ⟦contr. < PHENOMENOLOGY⟧ the study of natural phenomena that recur periodically, as migration or blossoming, and of their relation to climate and changes in season —**phe·no·log·i·cal** (fē′nə läj′i kəl) ***adj.*** —**phe′no·log′i·cal·ly** ***adv.*** —**phe·nol′o·gist** ***n.***

phe·nol·phthal·ein (fē′nōl thal′ēn′, -ē in; -fthal′-) ***n.*** ⟦PHENOL + PHTHALEIN⟧ a white to pale-yellow, crystalline powder, $C_{20}H_{14}O_4$, used in making dyes and as an acid-base indicator in chemical analysis: it is red in a solution containing a base and colorless in a solution containing an acid

phenol red a red, crystalline substance, $C_{19}H_{14}O_5S$, used, in dilute solution, as an acid-base indicator and as a test of renal function

phe·nom (fē′näm′) ***n.*** ⟦PHENOM(ENON)⟧ [Slang] one who is extremely talented, able, or skilled; specif., in sports, a young, exceptionally gifted or promising player

phe·nom·e·na (fə näm′ə nə) ***n.*** *pl. of* PHENOMENON

phe·nom·e·nal (fə näm′ə nəl) ***adj.*** **1** of or constituting a phenomenon or phenomena **2** extremely unusual; extraordinary; highly remarkable **3** *Philos.* apparent to or perceptible by the senses —**phe·nom′e·nal·ly** ***adv.***

phe·nom·e·nal·ism (-iz′əm) ***n.*** the philosophic theory that knowledge is limited to phenomena, either because there is no reality beyond phenomena or because such reality is unknowable —**phe·nom′e·nal·ist** ***n.*** —**phe·nom′e·nal·is′tic** ***adj.*** —**phe·nom′e·nal·is′ti·cal·ly** ***adv.***

phe·nom·e·nol·o·gy (fə näm′ə näl′ə jē) ***n.*** ⟦fol. + -LOGY⟧ **1** the philosophical study of phenomena, as distinguished from ontology, the study of being; specif., such a study of perceptual experience in its purely subjective aspect **2** a descriptive or classificatory account of the phenomena of a given body of knowledge, without any further attempt at explanation —**phe·nom′e·no·log′i·cal** (-nō läj′i kəl, -nə-) ***adj.*** —**phe·nom′e·no·log′i·cal·ly** ***adv.*** —**phe·nom′e·nol′o·gist** ***n.***

phe·nom·e·non (fə näm′ə nən, -nän′) ***n.***, *pl.* **-na**; also, esp. for 3 and usually for 4, **-nons′** ⟦LL *phaenomenon* < Gr *phainomenon,* neut. prp. of *phainesthai,* to appear, akin to *phainein:* see FANTASY⟧ **1** any event, circumstance, or experience that is apparent to the senses and that can be scientifically described or appraised, as an eclipse **2** in Kantian philosophy, a thing as it appears in perception as distinguished from the thing as it is in itself independent of sense experience: distinguished from NOUMENON **3** any extremely unusual or extraordinary thing or occurrence **4** [Informal] a person with an extraordinary quality, aptitude, etc.; prodigy

phe·no·thi·a·zine (fē′nō thī′ə zēn′) ***n.*** ⟦PHENO- + THIAZINE⟧ a yellowish, crystalline substance, $C_{12}H_9NS$, used as an insecticide, in the treatment of worm infections in livestock, and in the synthesis of tranquilizers

phe·no·type (fē′nə tīp′) ***n.*** ⟦Ger *phänotypus* < *phänomen* (< LL: see PHENOMENON) + *typus,* TYPE⟧ *Biol.* **1** the manifest characteristics of an organism collectively, including anatomical and behavioral traits, that result from both its heredity and its environment **2** *a)* a group of organisms having a like phenotype *b)* an individual of such a group —**phe′no·typ′ic** (-tip′ik) ***adj.,*** **phe′no·typ′i·cal** —**phe′no·typ′i·cal·ly** ***adv.***

phe·nox·ide (fē näk′sīd′, fi-) ***n.*** PHENATE

phe·nox·y (fē näk′sē, fi-) ***adj.*** ⟦PHEN- + OXY-[1]⟧ containing the monovalent radical C_6H_5O, derived from phenol

phen·yl (fen′əl, fē′nəl) ***n.*** ⟦PHEN- + -YL⟧ the monovalent radical C_6H_5, forming the basis of phenol, benzene, aniline, and various other aromatic compounds

phen·yl·al·a·nine (fen′əl al′ə nēn′, fē′nəl-) ***n.*** ⟦Ger *phenylalanin* < *phenyl,* prec. + *alanin,* ALANINE⟧ an essential amino acid, $C_6H_5CH_2CH(NH_2)COOH$, occurring in proteins: see AMINO ACID

phen·yl·a·mine (-ə mēn′; -am′ēn′, -in) ***n.*** ANILINE

phen·yl·bu·ta·zone (-byo͞ot′ə zōn′) ***n.*** ⟦PHENYL + BUT(YL) + AZ(O)- (sense 1) + -ONE (sense 2)⟧ a white powder, $C_{19}H_{20}N_2O_2$, used as an analgesic, as for the relief of rheumatoid arthritis

phen·yl·ene (fen′ə lēn′, fē′nə-) ***n.*** ⟦PHENYL + -ENE⟧ the divalent radical C_6H_4, derived from benzene by displacement of two hydrogen atoms

phen·yl·ke·to·nu·ri·a (fen′əl kēt′ə no͝or′ē ə, -nyo͝or′-; fē′nəl-) ***n.*** ⟦PHENYL + KETONURIA⟧ a genetic disorder of phenylalanine metabolism, which, if untreated, causes severe mental disability in infants through the accumulation of toxic metabolic products —**phen′yl·ke′to·nu′ric** ***adj.***

phen·yl·pro·pa·nol·a·mine (fen′əl prō′pə näl′ə mēn′, fē′nəl-) ***n.*** ⟦PHENYL + PROPAN(E) + -OL[1] + AMINE⟧ a synthetic, amphetamine-like, crystalline drug, $C_9H_{13}NO{\cdot}HCl$, that constricts the blood vessels, used in nasal decongestants, diet pills, cough medicines, etc.: in full **phenylpropanolamine hydrochloride**

phen·y·to·in (fen′i tō′ən, fə nit′ə win; *also,* fen′i toin′) ***n.*** ⟦*(di)pheny(lhydan)toin*⟧ a crystalline compound, $C_{15}H_{11}N_2O_2$, used as an anticonvulsant

pher·e·sis (fer′ə sis) ***n.*** *var. of* APHERESIS (sense 2)

pher·o·mone (fer′ə mōn′) ***n.*** ⟦< Gr *pherein,* to carry, BEAR[1] + -O- + (HOR)MONE⟧ any of various chemical substances, secreted externally by certain animals, that convey information to, and produce specific responses in, other individuals of the same species —**pher′o·mo′nal** (-mō′nəl) ***adj.***

PHEV *abbrev.* plug-in hybrid electric vehicle

phew (fyo͞o: *conventionalized pronun.*) ***interj.*** a breathy, almost whistling sound used variously to express a sense of relief or to express surprise, disgust, etc.

phi (fī, fē) ***n.*** ⟦MGr *phi* < Gr *phei*⟧ **1** the twenty-first letter of the Greek alphabet (Φ, φ) **2** GOLDEN RATIO (sense 1)

phi·al (fī′əl) ***n.*** ⟦ME *fiole* < OFr < Prov *fiola* < ML < L *phiala* < Gr *phialē,* broad, shallow drinking vessel⟧ a small, cylindrical bottle, usually of glass, for containing liquids; vial

☆**Phi Be·ta Kap·pa** (fī′ bāt′ə kap′ə) ⟦< initial letters of the Gr motto *philosophia biou kybernētēs,* love of learning is the guide of life⟧ **1** an honorary society of U.S. college students in liberal arts and sciences with high scholastic rank: founded 1776 **2** a member of this society

Phid·i·as (fid′ē əs) 5th cent. B.C.; Gr. sculptor: see PARTHENON —**Phid′i·an** (-ən) ***adj.***

Phi·dip·pi·des (fī dip′i dēz′) *alt. sp. of* PHEIDIPPIDES

phil *abbrev.* **1** philology **2** philosophy

Phil *abbrev.* **1** *Bible* Philippians **2** Philippine

phil- (fil) *combining form* PHILO-: used before a vowel

-phil (fil) *combining form* -PHILE [*eosinophil*]

Phil·a·del·phi·a (fil′ə del′fē ə, -fyə) ⟦Gr *philadelphia,* brotherly love < *philos,* loving + *adelphos,* brother: see MONADELPHOUS⟧ **1** ancient city in Lydia, W Asia Minor **2** city & port in SE Pa., on the Delaware River —**Phil′a·del′phi·an** ***adj., n.***

☆**Philadelphia lawyer** ⟦in ref. to Andrew Hamilton of *Philadelphia,* who obtained an acquittal (1735) of J. P. ZENGER from libel charges⟧ [Informal] a clever, shrewd, or tricky lawyer, esp. one skilled in taking advantage of legal technicalities

☆**Philadelphia pepper pot** PEPPER POT (sense 3)

phil·a·del·phus (fil′ə del′fəs) ***n.*** ⟦ModL < Gr *philadelphon,* mock orange < *philadelphos,* loving one's brother < *philein,* to love + *adelphos,* brother: see MONADELPHOUS⟧ MOCK ORANGE

phi·lan·der (fə lan′dər) ***n.*** ⟦< Gr *philandros,* fond of men < *philos,* loving + *anēr,* a man (see ANDRO-): used in fiction as a name for a lover⟧ [Rare] a man who philanders —***vi.*** to regularly enter into casual love affairs: said of a man —**phi·lan′der·er** ***n.***

phil·an·throp·ic (fil′ən thräp′ik) ***adj.*** ⟦Fr *philanthropique*⟧ of, showing, or constituting philanthropy; charitable; benevolent; humane: also **phil′an·throp′i·cal** —**phil′an·throp′i·cal·ly** ***adv.***

SYN.—**philanthropic** implies interest in the general human welfare, esp. as shown in large-scale gifts to charities or the endowment of institutions for human advancement; **humanitarian** implies more direct concern with promoting the welfare of humanity, esp. through reducing pain and suffering; **charitable** implies the giving of money or other help to those in need; **altruistic** implies a putting of the welfare of others before one's own interests and therefore stresses freedom from selfishness

phi·lan·thro·pist (fə lan′thrə pist) ***n.*** a person, esp. a wealthy one, who practices philanthropy

phi·lan·thro·pize (-pīz′) ***vt.*** **-pized′, -piz′ing** to deal with philanthropically —***vi.*** to practice philanthropy

phi·lan·thro·py (fə lan′thrə pē) ***n.*** ⟦LL *philanthropia* < Gr *philanthrōpia* < *philein,* to love + *anthrōpos,* human being: see ANTHROPO-⟧ **1** a desire to help mankind, esp. as shown by gifts to charitable or humanitarian institutions; benevolence **2** *pl.* **-pies** a philanthropic act, gift, institution, etc.

phi·lat·e·ly (fə lat′'l ē) ***n.*** ⟦Fr *philatélie,* coined (1864) < Gr *philos,* loving + *ateleia,* exemption from (further) tax, taken as equivalent of "postage prepaid"⟧ the collection and study of postage stamps, postmarks, stamped envelopes, etc. —**phil·a·tel·ic** (fil′ə tel′ik) ***adj.*** —**phil′a·tel′i·cal·ly** ***adv.*** —**phi·lat′e·list** ***n.***

-phile (fīl, fil) ⟦< Gr *philos,* loving⟧ *combining form forming nouns* one that loves, likes, or is attracted to [*bibliophile, Russophile*]

Philem *abbrev. Bible* Philemon

Phi·le·mon (fi lē′mən, fī-) ***n.*** ⟦L < Gr *Philēmōn,* lit., affectionate < *philein,* to love⟧ **1** *Bible* a book of the New Testament, a letter from the Apostle Paul to his friend Philemon: abbrev. *Philem, Phlm,* or *Phm* **2** *Gr. Myth.* the husband of BAUCIS

Phil·har·mon·ic (fil′här män′ik) ***adj.*** ⟦Fr *philharmonique,* infl. by It *filharmonico* < Gr *philos,* loving + *harmonia,* HARMONY⟧ designating or of a society or other group formed to sponsor a symphony orchestra —***n.*** a symphony orchestra sponsored as by such a society or group: in full **Philharmonic Orchestra**

phil·hel·lene (fil hel′ēn) ***n.*** ⟦see PHILO- & HELLENE⟧ a friend or supporter of the Greeks or Greece —**phil′hel·len′ic** (-hə len′ik) ***adj.*** —**phil·hel′len·ism′** (-ən iz′əm) ***n.***

-phil·i·a (fil′ē ə, fil′yə) ⟦ModL < Gr *philia,* fondness⟧ *combining form forming nouns* **1** tendency toward [*hemophilia*] **2** strong or abnormal attraction to [*Anglophilia, coprophilia*]

-phil·ic (fil′ik) *combining form* -PHILOUS [*lyophilic*]

Phil·ip[1] (fil′ip) ***n.*** ⟦L *Philippus* < Gr *Philippos,* lit., fond of horses < *philos,* loving + *hippos,* horse⟧ **1** a masculine name: dim. *Phil;* var. *Phillip;* equiv. L. *Philippus,* Fr. *Philippe,* Ger. *Philipp,* It. *Filippo,* Sp. *Felipe;* fem. *Philippa* **2** one of the twelve Apostles: his day is May 1: also **Saint Philip**

Phil·ip[2] (fil′ip) **1** (Wampanoag Indian name *Metacomet*) died 1676; chief of the Wampanoag Indians (1662-76): led a war against New England colonists: son of Massasoit: called *King Philip* **2** Prince (born *Philip Battenberg*) 1921- ; Duke of Edinburgh, born in Greece: husband of Elizabeth II of England **3** Saint (1st cent. A.D.); a deacon of the early Christian church: his day is June 6 **4 Philip II** 382-336 B.C.; king of Macedonia (359-336): father of Alexander the Great **5 Philip II** 1165-1223; king of France (1180-1223): also called **Philip Augustus** **6 Philip II** 1527-98; king of Spain (1556-98) & (as **Philip I**) of Portugal (1580-98): sent Armada against England (1588) **7 Philip IV** 1268-1314; king of France (1285-1314): moved the papacy to Avignon (1309): called *the Fair* **8 Philip V** 1683-1746; 1st Bourbon king of Spain (1700-46)

Phi·lip·pa (fi lip′ə) ***n.*** ⟦fem. of PHILIP[1]⟧ a feminine name: see PHILIP[1]

Phi·lip·pi (fi lip′ī′) ancient city in Macedonia, where, in 42 B.C., Mark Antony & Octavius defeated Brutus & Cassius: site of Paul's first preaching of the Gospel in Europe (Acts 16:12) —**Phi·lip′pi·an** ***adj., n.***

Phi·lip·pi·ans (fi lip′ē ənz) ***n.*** a book of the New Testament, a letter from the Apostle Paul to the Christians of Philippi: abbrev. *Ph* or *Phil*

Phi·lip·pic (fi lip′ik) ***n.*** ⟦L *Philippicus* < Gr *Philippikos,* belonging to Philip < *Philippos,* PHILIP[1]⟧ **1** any of the orations of Demosthenes against Philip, king of Macedon **2** [**p-**] any bitter verbal attack

Phil·ip·pine (fil′ə pēn′) ***adj.*** of the Philippine Islands or their peoples

Philippine mahogany **1** any of various Philippine and SE Asian trees (esp. genera *Shorea* and *Dipterocarpus*) of a family (Dipterocarpaceae, order Theales) of dicotyledonous plants **2** the light to dark reddish wood of any of these trees

Phil·ip·pines (fil′ə pēnz′) ⟦ult. after Philip II of Spain: see PHILIP[2]⟧ country occupying a group of *c.* 7,100 islands (**Philippine Islands**) in the SW Pacific off the SE coast of Asia: formerly a Spanish possession (1565-1898) & U.S. possession (1898-1946), it became independent in 1946: 115,831 sq mi (300,000 sq km); cap. Manila

Philippine Sea part of the W Pacific, between the Philippines & the Mariana Islands, south of Japan

Phil·ip·pop·o·lis (fil′ə päp′ə lis) *Gr. name for* PLOVDIV

Philip the Good 1396-1467; duke of Burgundy (1419-67)

Phi·lis·ti·a (fə lis′tē ə) country of the Philistines (fl. 12th-4th cent. B.C.), in ancient SW Palestine

Phil·is·tine (fil′i stēn′, -stīn′; fi lis′tin, -tēn′) ***n.*** ⟦ME < LL(Ec) *Philistinus,* usually pl. *Philistini* < LGr (*Josephus*) *philistinoi* < Heb *pelishtim;* akin to PALESTINE⟧ **1** a member of a non-Semitic people that lived in Philistia and repeatedly warred with the Israelites 2 ⟦adapted < Ger *Philister,* orig. student slang for townspeople⟧ [*usually* **p-**] a person regarded as smugly narrow and conventional in views and tastes, lacking in and indifferent to cultural and aesthetic values —*adj.* 1 of the ancient Philistines or their culture 2 [*often* **p-**] smugly conventional and lacking in culture —**phil′is·tin·ism′** *n.*

Phil·lip (fil′ip) *n.* a masculine name: see PHILIP[1]

Phil·lips[1] (fil′ips) ☆⟦after H. F. *Phillips* (?-1958), its U.S. developer⟧ *trademark for* a screwdriver (**Phillips screwdriver**) with a cross-shaped, pointed tip: used on a screw (**Phillips screw**) that has two slots crossing at the center of the head

Phil·lips[2] (fil′ips), **Wen·dell** (wen′dəl) 1811-84; U.S. abolitionist, reformer, & orator

Phillips curve (fil′ips) ⟦after A. W. H. *Phillips* (1914–75), N.Z. economist, its originator⟧ [*also* **P- C-**] a curve illustrating a theoretical inverse relationship between rates of unemployment and of inflation

Phil·lis (fil′is) *n.* a feminine name: see PHYLLIS

phil·lu·men·y (fi lo͞o′mə nē) *n.* ⟦Gr *philos,* loving + L *lumen,* light + -Y[4]⟧ the study or collection of matchbooks and matchboxes

Phil·ly (fil′ē) *informal name for* PHILADELPHIA (the U.S. city)

Philo (fī′lō) PHILO JUDAEUS

phil·o- (fil′ō, -ə) ⟦< Gr *philos,* loving⟧ *combining form* loving, liking, predisposed to [*philoprogenitive*]

Phil·oc·te·tes (fil′äk tē′tēz′) *n. Gr. Legend* the Greek warrior who kills Paris in the Trojan War with a poisoned arrow given him by Hercules

phil·o·den·dron (fil′ə den′drən) *n.* ⟦ModL < neut. of Gr *philodendros,* loving trees < *philos,* loving + *dendron,* TREE⟧ 1 any of a genus (*Philodendron*) of tropical American vines of the arum family, often with leathery, heart-shaped leaves, used commonly as a houseplant 2 loosely, any similar plant

phi·log·y·ny (fi läj′ə nē) *n.* ⟦Gr *philogynia* < *philein,* to love + *gynē,* woman: see GYNO-⟧ love of or fondness for women —**phi·log′y·nist** *n.* —**phi·log′y·nous** *adj.*

Phi·lo Ju·dae·us (fī′lō jo͞o dē′əs) 20? B.C.-A.D. 50?; Hellenistic Jewish philosopher of Alexandria

philol *abbrev.* philology

phi·lol·o·gy (fi läl′ə jē) *n.* ⟦Fr *philologie* < L *philologia,* love of learning < Gr, love of literature < *philein,* to love + *logos,* word: see LOGIC⟧ 1 [Obs.] the love of learning and literature; study; scholarship 2 *former term for* LINGUISTICS 3 the study of written records, esp. literary texts, in order to determine their authenticity, meaning, etc. —**phil·o·log·i·cal** (fil′ə läj′i kəl) *adj.*, **phil′o·log′ic** —**phil′o·log′i·cal·ly** *adv.* —**phi·lol′o·gist** *n.*

phil·o·mel (fil′ə mel′) *n.* ⟦altered (infl. by L) < ME *Philomene* < ML *Philomena,* for L *Philomela:* see fol.⟧ *old poet. term for* NIGHTINGALE

Phil·o·me·la (fil′ə mē′lə) *n.* ⟦L < Gr < *philein,* to love + *melos,* song⟧ 1 *Gr. Myth.* a princess of Athens raped by Tereus, husband of her sister Procne: the gods change Philomela into a nightingale, Procne into a swallow, and Tereus into a hawk 2 [**p-**] PHILOMEL

phil·o·pro·gen·i·tive (fil′ə prō jen′ə tiv) *adj.* ⟦PHILO- + PROGENITIVE⟧ 1 productive of offspring; prolific 2 *a)* loving offspring, esp. one's own *b)* of such love

philos *abbrev.* philosophy

phi·lo·sophe (fē lô zôf′) *n., pl.* **-sophes′** (-zôf′) ⟦Fr⟧ a French intellectual and writer of the Enlightenment

phi·los·o·pher (fi läs′ə fər) *n.* ⟦ME *philosophre* < OFr *philosophe* < L *philosophus* < Gr *philosophos* < *philos,* loving + *sophos,* wise⟧ 1 a person who studies or is an expert in philosophy 2 a person who lives by or expounds a system of philosophy 3 *a)* a person who meets difficulties with calmness and composure *b)* a person given to philosophizing

philosophers' (*or* **philosopher's) stone** *Alchemy* a substance capable of changing base metals into gold or silver

phil·o·soph·i·cal (fil′ə säf′i kəl) *adj.* ⟦L *philosophicus* < Gr *philosophikos*⟧ 1 of or according to philosophy or philosophers 2 devoted to or learned in philosophy 3 like or suited for a philosopher 4 sensibly composed or calm, as in a difficult situation; rational Also **phil′o·soph′ic** —**phil′o·soph′i·cal·ly** *adv.*

phi·los·o·phize (fi läs′ə fīz′) *vi.* **-phized′**, **-phiz′ing** 1 to deal philosophically with abstract matter; think or reason like a philosopher 2 to express superficial philosophic ideas, truisms, etc.; esp., to moralize —**phi·los′o·phiz′er** *n.*

phi·los·o·phy (fi läs′ə fē) *n., pl.* **-phies** ⟦ME *philosophie* < OFr < L *philosophia* < Gr < *philosophos:* see PHILOSOPHER⟧ 1 [Archaic] love of, or the search for, wisdom or knowledge 2 theory or logical analysis of the principles underlying conduct, thought, knowledge, and the nature of the universe: included in philosophy are ethics, aesthetics, logic, epistemology, metaphysics, etc. 3 the general principles or laws of a field of knowledge, activity, etc. [the *philosophy* of economics] 4 *a)* a particular system of principles for the conduct of life *b)* a treatise covering such a system 5 a study of human morals, character, and behavior 6 mental balance or composure thought of as resulting from the study of philosophy 7 [Obs.] NATURAL PHILOSOPHY

-phi·lous (fi ləs) ⟦< Gr *philos,* loving⟧ *combining form forming adjectives* loving, having an affinity for [*photophilous*]

phil·ter (fil′tər) *n.* ⟦MFr *philtre* < L *philtrum* < Gr *philtron* < *philein,* to love⟧ 1 a potion thought to arouse sexual love, esp. toward a certain person 2 any magic potion —*vt.* to charm or arouse with a philter Also [Chiefly Brit.] **phil′tre** (-tər), **-tred**, **-tring**

phil·trum (fil′trəm) *n., pl.* **-tra** (-trə) ⟦L < Gr *philtron,* love potion, charm, dimple on upper lip: see prec.⟧ the vertical indentation between the upper lip and the nose

phi·mo·sis (fī mō′sis, fi-) *n.* ⟦ModL < Gr *phimōsis,* a muzzling < *phimos,* a muzzle⟧ an abnormal condition, correctable by circumcision, in which the foreskin of the penis is so tight that it cannot be drawn back over the glans —**phi·mot′ic** (-mät′ik) *adj.*

Phin·e·as (fin′ē əs) *n.* ⟦LL *Phinees* < Gr < Heb *pinechas,* prob. < Egypt *penehase*⟧ a masculine name

phish·ing (fish′iŋ) *n.* ⟦< *fishing* (see FISH (*vi.* 2), with sp. infl. by PHREAK⟧ the practice of sending fraudulent email that appears to be from a legitimate business, as a bank or credit card company, in an attempt to deceive an individual into disclosing personal information, as a password or an account number

phiz (fiz) *n.* ⟦contr. < PHYSIOGNOMY⟧ [Old Slang] a face or facial expression

phle·bi·tis (flə bīt′is) *n.* ⟦ModL: see fol. & -ITIS⟧ inflammation of a vein or veins —**phle·bit′ic** (-bit′ik) *adj.*

phleb·o- (fleb′ō, -ə) ⟦< Gr *phleps* (gen. *phlebos*), a vein < IE **bhlegw-,* to swell < base **bhel-,* to blow up, swell > L *flare,* to BLOW[1]⟧ *combining form* vein [*phlebotomy*]: also, before a vowel, **phleb-**

phle·bol·o·gy (flə bäl′ə jē) *n.* the branch of medicine dealing with the study of veins —**phle·bol′o·gist** *n.*

phleb·o·scle·ro·sis (fleb′ō skli rō′sis) *n.* ⟦ModL: see PHLEBO- & SCLEROSIS⟧ hardening of the walls of the veins

phle·bot·o·mize (fli bät′ə mīz′) *vt., vi.* **-mized′**, **-miz′ing** to practice phlebotomy (on); bleed

phle·bot·o·my (fli bät′ə mē) *n.* ⟦ME *flebotomie* < OFr *flebothomie* < LL *phlebotomia* < Gr: see PHLEBO- & -TOMY⟧ 1 the act or practice of bloodletting as a therapeutic measure 2 *Med.* the act or practice of drawing blood from a vein for use in a transfusion, diagnosis, etc. —**phle·bot′o·mist** *n.*

Phleg·e·thon (fleg′i thän, flej′-) *n.* ⟦L < Gr *Phlegethōn,* orig. prp. of *phlegethein,* to blaze: for IE base see FLAGRANT⟧ *Gr. Myth.* a river of fire in Hades

phlegm (flem) *n.* ⟦ME *fleume* < MFr < LL *phlegma,* clammy humor of the body < Gr, inflammation, hence, humors caused by inflammation < *phlegein,* to burn: for IE base see BLACK⟧ 1 the thick, stringy mucus secreted by the mucous glands of the respiratory tract and discharged from the throat, as during a cold 2 [Obs.] that one of the four humors of the body which was believed in medieval times to cause sluggishness or dullness 3 *a)* sluggishness or apathy *b)* calmness or composure —**phlegm′y** *adj.* **-i·er**, **-i·est**

phleg·mat·ic (fleg mat′ik) *adj.* ⟦ME *fleumatike* < OFr < LL *phlegmaticus* < Gr *phlegmatikos* < *phlegma:* see prec.⟧ 1 hard to rouse to action; specif., *a)* sluggish; dull; apathetic *b)* calm; cool; stolid 2 [Obs.] of, like, or producing the humor phlegm Also **phleg·mat′i·cal** —*SYN.* IMPASSIVE —**phleg·mat′i·cal·ly** *adv.*

Phlm *abbrev. Bible* Philemon

phlo·em (flō′em′) *n.* ⟦Ger < Gr *phloos,* bark, akin to *phloiein,* to swell: for IE base see PHLEBO-⟧ the vascular tissue in vascular plants that conducts and distributes sugars and other dissolved foods from the places where the food is produced to the places where it is needed or stored

phloem ray the portion of a vascular ray in a stem which traverses the phloem

phlo·gis·tic (flō jis′tik) *adj.* ⟦< ModL *phlogiston* (see fol.) + -IC⟧ 1 of phlogiston 2 [Obs.] fiery; flaming 3 *Med.* of inflammation; inflammatory

phlo·gis·ton (flō jis′tän, -tən) *n.* ⟦ModL < Gr *phlogistos* < *phlogizein,* to burn, inflame < *phlegein,* to burn: for IE base see BLACK⟧ an imaginary element formerly believed to cause combustion and to be given off by anything burning; matter or principle of fire

phlog·o·pite (fläg′ō pīt′) *n.* ⟦Ger *phlogopit* < Gr *phlogōpos,* fiery (< *phlox,* flame: see PHLOX + *ōps,* face, EYE) + Ger *-it,* -ITE[1]⟧ a brown, monoclinic mica, $K(Mg,Fe)_3AlSiO_{10}(OH,F)_2$, used mainly as an electrical insulator

phlor·i·zin (flôr′i zin, flō rī′zin) *n.* ⟦< Gr *phloos,* bark (see PHLOEM) + *rhiza,* ROOT[1] + -IN[1]⟧ a bitter, white, crystalline glycoside, $C_{21}H_{24}O_{10}$, obtained from the root and bark of certain fruit trees: used experimentally to cause glycosuria because it inhibits cellular absorption of glucose: also **phlo·rid·zin** (flō rid′zin) or **phlo·rhi′zin** (-rī′zin)

phlox (fläks) *n.* ⟦ModL < L, flower, flame < Gr, wallflower, lit., flame < *phlegein,* to burn: for IE base see BLACK⟧ any of a genus (*Phlox*) of chiefly North American plants of the phlox family with opposite leaves and white, pink, red, or bluish flowers —*adj.* designating a family (Polemoniaceae, order Solanales) of dicotyledonous plants, including Jacob's ladder

phlyc·te·na (flik tē′nə) *n., pl.* **-nae** (-nē) ⟦ModL < Gr *phlyktaina,* a blister < *phlyein,* bubble up: for IE base see PHLEBO-⟧ a small blister or pustule —**phlyc·te′nar** *adj.*

phlyc·ten·ule (flik ten′yo͞ol) *n.* ⟦ModL *phlyctenula:* see prec. & -ULE⟧ a small phlyctena —**phlyc·ten′u·lar** *adj.*

Phm *abbrev. Bible* Philemon

Phnom Penh (pə näm′pen′, näm′pen′) capital of Cambodia, at the junction of the Mekong & Tonle Sap rivers

pho (fu, fä, fō) *n.* ⟦Vietnamese < ?⟧ a Vietnamese soup containing rice noodles, thin slices of beef or chicken, and chopped onion

-phobe (fōb) ⟦Fr < L *-phobus* < Gr *-phobos* < *phobos,* fear < IE base **bhegw-,* to flee > Hindi *bhāg-,* Latvian *bēgt,* to flee⟧ *combining form forming nouns* one who fears or hates [*Francophobe*]

pho·bi·a (fō′bē ə, fō′byə) *n.* ⟦ModL < Gr *phobos,* fear: see prec.⟧ an irrational, excessive, and persistent fear of some particular thing or situation

-pho·bi·a (fō′bē ə, fō′byə) ⟦Gr *-phobia* < *phobos,* fear: see -PHOBE⟧ *combining form forming nouns* fear, dread, or hatred of *[photophobia, Russophobia]*

pho·bic (fō′bik) ***adj.*** **1** of or relating to a phobia **2** having a phobia or phobias Often used in comb. *[Francophobic]* —***n.*** a person who has a phobia

Pho·bos (fō′bəs) ***n.*** ⟦Gr *phobos,* lit., fear, personified as an attendant of Ares: see -PHOBE⟧ ☆the larger of the two satellites of Mars: cf. DEIMOS

Pho·cae·a (fō sē′ə) ancient Ionian city in W Asia Minor, on the Aegean

pho·cine (fō′sīn′, -sin) ***adj.*** ⟦< L *phoca,* a seal (< Gr *phōkē*) + -INE[1]⟧ *Zool.* of or relating to the seals

Pho·ci·on (fō′sē än′) 402?-317? B.C.; Athenian statesman & general

Pho·cis (fō′sis) ancient region in central Greece, on the Gulf of Corinth: chief city, Delphi

pho·co·me·li·a (fō′kō mē′lē ə, -mēl′yə) ***n.*** ⟦ModL < Gr *phōkē,* a seal + ModL *-melia,* a condition of limbs < Gr *melos,* limb⟧ the congenital absence or abnormal shortening of arms or legs, often with only short, flipperlike limbs projecting from the body —**pho′co·me′lic** (-mē′lik) ***adj.***

☆**phoe·be** (fē′bē) ***n.*** ⟦echoic, with sp. after fol.⟧ any of a genus (*Sayornis*) of tyrant flycatchers with a grayish or brown back

Phoe·be (fē′bē) ***n.*** ⟦L < Gr *Phoibē,* fem. of *Phoibos:* see fol.⟧ **1** a feminine name **2** *Gr. Myth.* Artemis as goddess of the moon: identified with the Roman Diana **3** [Old Poet.] the moon personified **4** the small outermost satellite of Saturn, having an unusual retrograde orbit

Phoe·bus (fē′bəs) ***n.*** ⟦ME *Phebus* < L *Phoebus* < Gr *Phoibos,* bright one < *phoibos,* bright⟧ **1** *Gr. Myth.* Apollo as god of the sun **2** [Old Poet.] the sun personified

Phoe·ni·cia (fə nish′ə, -nē′shə) ancient region of city-states at the E end of the Mediterranean, in the region of present-day Syria & Lebanon

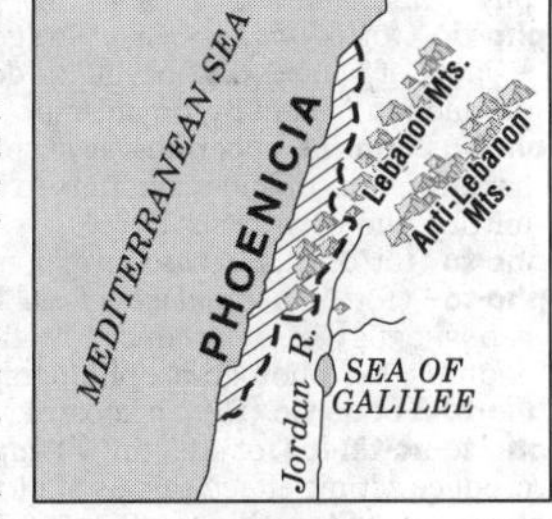

Phoenicia

Phoe·ni·cian (fə nish′ən, -nē′shən) ***adj.*** of Phoenicia or its people, language, or culture —***n.*** **1** a person born or living in ancient Phoenicia **2** the extinct Semitic language of the Phoenicians, closely related to Hebrew

phoe·nix (fē′niks) ***n.*** ⟦altered (infl. by L) < OE & OFr *fenix* < L *phoenix* < Gr *phoinix,* phoenix, dark-red, Phoenician, akin to *phoinos,* blood-red, deadly⟧ **1** *Egypt. Myth.* a beautiful, lone bird which lives in the Arabian desert for 500 or 600 years and then sets itself on fire, rising renewed from the ashes to start another long life: a symbol of immortality **2** [**P-**] a S constellation between Eridanus and Grus

Phoe·nix (fē′niks) ⟦in allusion to the prec.⟧ capital of Ariz., in the SC part, near the Salt River

phon (fän) ***n.*** ⟦< Gr *phōnē,* a sound: see PHONO-⟧ a measure of the apparent loudness level of a sound with respect to a 1,000-cycle-per-second pure tone: based on the subjective judgment of the human ear or on objective comparisons of acoustical measurements

phon- (fōn) *combining form* PHONO-: used before a vowel

pho·nate (fō′nāt′) ***vi.*** ⟦PHON(O)- + -ATE[1]⟧ **-nat′ed, -nat′ing** to produce speech sounds; esp., to utter a voiced sound or sounds —**pho·na′tion** ***n.***

phone[1] (fōn) ***n.*** ⟦Gr *phōnē,* a sound: see PHONO-⟧ *Phonet.* any single speech sound considered as a physical event without reference to its place in the structure of a language

☆**phone[2]** (fōn) ***n., vt., vi.*** **phoned, phon′ing** *short for* TELEPHONE —**phone it in** [Informal] to perform in a perfunctory, mechanical, or uninspired way

-phone (fōn) ⟦< Gr *phōnē,* a sound: see PHONO-⟧ *combining form forming nouns* **1** a device producing or transmitting sound *[saxophone, megaphone]* **2** a telephone *[interphone]*

☆**phone book** [Informal] TELEPHONE BOOK

phone card *see* CALLING CARD (sense 3)

pho·neme (fō′nēm′) ***n.*** ⟦Fr *phonème* < Gr *phōnēma,* a sound < *phōnein,* to sound < *phōnē,* a voice: see PHONO-⟧ *Linguis.* a set of phonetically similar but slightly differing sounds in a language that are heard as the same sound by native speakers and are represented in phonemic transcription by the same symbol *[in English, the phoneme /p/ includes the phonetically differentiated sounds represented by p in "pin," "spin," and "tip"]*: see SEGMENTAL PHONEMES, SUPRASEGMENTAL PHONEMES

pho·ne·mic (fō nē′mik, fə-) ***adj.*** **1** of, characterized by, or based on phonemes **2** of phonemics —**pho·ne′mi·cal·ly** ***adv.*** —**pho·ne′mi·a·za′tion** ***n.*** —**pho·ne′mi·cize′** ***vt.*** **-cized′, -ciz′ing**

pho·ne·mics (fō nē′miks, fə-) ***n.*** ⟦PHONEM(E) + -ICS⟧ **1** the study of the phonemic systems of languages **2** the description and classification of the phonemes of a specific language —**pho·ne′mi·cist** (-mə sist) ***n.***

phone patch *see* PATCH[1] (***n.*** 7)

phone phreak (frēk) ⟦PHONE[2] + respelling of FREAK[1]⟧ [Informal] a person who uses electronic equipment to gain unauthorized access to long-distance telephone services

phone sex **1** the act of engaging in sexually explicit conversation over the telephone for the purpose of sexual gratification **2** such a conversation **3** a commercial service providing the opportunity to engage in such conversation, typically with a woman

phone tag ⟦by analogy with a game of TAG (***n.*** 13)⟧ a series of attempts by two people to speak to each other directly by phone, in which a failed attempt by one person prompts the other person to return the call, also without success: used chiefly of a prolonged sequence of such calls

pho·net·ic (fō net′ik, fə-) ***adj.*** ⟦ModL *phoneticus* < Gr *phōnētikos* < *phōnētos,* to be spoken < *phōnein,* to speak < *phōnē,* a sound: see PHONO-⟧ **1** of speech sounds or the production or transcription of these **2** of phonetics **3** conforming to pronunciation *[phonetic spelling]* **4** of or involving the relatively small differences between related speech sounds, which can be perceived but do not change meaning *[the differences between the sounds represented by p in "tip" and "pit" are phonetic, since substituting one for the other would not change the meanings of the two words]* —**pho·net′i·cal·ly** ***adv.***

phonetic alphabet a set of symbols used in phonetic transcription, having a separate symbol for every speech sound that can be distinguished: see INTERNATIONAL PHONETIC ALPHABET

pho·ne·ti·cian (fō′nə tish′ən) ***n.*** an expert in phonetics

pho·net·ics (fō net′iks, fə-) ***n.*** ⟦see PHONETIC⟧ **1** the study of speech sounds, their production and combination, and their representation by written symbols **2** the description and analysis of the sounds of a particular language *[the phonetics of English]*

pho·ne·tist (fō′nə tist) ***n.*** ⟦< Gr *phōnētos,* to be spoken (see PHONETIC) + -IST[1]⟧ **1** PHONETICIAN **2** a person who uses, or advocates the use of, a system of phonetic spelling

☆**pho·ney** (fō′nē) ***adj., n.*** [Informal] *alt. sp. of* PHONY: the preferred Brit. sp.

-pho·ni·a (fō′nē ə, -nyə) *combining form* -PHONY

phon·ic (fän′ik, fōn′-) ***adj.*** ⟦PHON- + -IC⟧ **1** of, or having the nature of, sound; esp., of speech sounds **2** of or relating to phonics —**phon′i·cal·ly** ***adv.***

phon·ics (fän′iks, fōn′-) ***n.*** ⟦< prec.⟧ **1** the science or study of sound; acoustics **2** a method of teaching beginners to read or enunciate by learning to associate certain letters or groups of letters with the sounds they commonly represent: cf. LOOK-SAY METHOD

pho·no (fō′nō) ***n.*** *short for* PHONOGRAPH

pho·no- (fō′nō, -nə) ⟦< Gr *phōnē,* a sound, voice, akin to *phanai,* to say < IE base **bhā-,* to speak > BAN[1], FAME⟧ *combining form* sound, tone, speech *[phonology]*

pho·no·gram (fō′nə gram′) ***n.*** ⟦prec. + -GRAM⟧ a sign or symbol representing a word, syllable, or sound, as in shorthand —**pho′no·gram′ic** ***adj.,*** **pho′no·gram′mic** —**pho′no·gram′i·cal·ly** ***adv.,*** **pho′no·gram′mi·cal·ly**

pho·no·graph (fō′nə graf′) ***n.*** ⟦PHONO- + -GRAPH⟧ ☆a device for reproducing sound that has been mechanically transcribed in a spiral groove on a circular disc or cylinder: a stylus following the groove in the revolving disc or cylinder transmits vibrations which are converted into sound

pho·no·graph·ic (fō′nə graf′ik) ***adj.*** ☆**1** of a phonograph or the sounds made by one **2** of phonography —**pho′no·graph′i·cal·ly** ***adv.***

pho·nog·ra·phy (fō näg′rə fē, fə-) ***n.*** ⟦PHONO- + -GRAPHY⟧ **1** a written or printed representation of the sounds of speech; phonetic spelling or transcription **2** any system of shorthand based on a phonetic transcription of speech; esp., the system invented by Sir Isaac PITMAN

pho·no·lite (fō′nə līt′) ***n.*** ⟦Fr *phonolithe* < *phono-* (see PHONO-) + *-lithe* (see -LITE): transl. of Ger *klingstein* (see CLINKSTONE)⟧ a fine-grained, extrusive igneous rock consisting chiefly of alkali feldspar and nepheline —**pho′no·lit′ic** (-lit′ik) ***adj.***

pho·nol·o·gy (fō näl′ə jē, fə-) ***n.*** ⟦PHONO- + -LOGY⟧ **1** the study of speech sounds, including phonetics and phonemics **2** an overall description of the sounds of a given language —**pho·no·log·i·cal** (fō′nō läj′i kəl, -nə-) ***adj.,*** **pho′no·log′ic** —**pho′no·log′i·cal·ly** ***adv.*** —**pho·nol′o·gist** ***n.***

pho·nom·e·ter (fō näm′ət ər, fə-) ***n.*** ⟦PHONO- + -METER⟧ an instrument used to measure the intensity and vibration frequency of sound —**pho·nom′e·try** ***n.***

pho·non (fō′nän′) ***n.*** ⟦PHON- + *-on,* as in PHOTON⟧ *Physics* a quantum of vibrational or sound energy in a crystal lattice or solid: often characterized as being heat energy

pho·no·scope (fō′nə skōp′) ***n.*** ⟦PHONO- + -SCOPE⟧ an instrument used to observe or exhibit the properties of a sounding body; esp., such an instrument for testing the quality of strings for musical instruments

pho·no·type (fō′nə tīp′) ***n.*** ⟦PHONO- + -TYPE⟧ a phonetic symbol or character, as used in printing

☆**pho·ny** (fō′nē) [Informal] ***adj.*** **-ni·er, -ni·est** ⟦altered < Brit thieves' argot *fawney,* gilt ring (passed off as gold by swindlers) < Ir *fáinne*⟧ not genuine; false, counterfeit, spurious, pretentious, etc. —***n., pl.*** **-nies** **1** something not genuine; sham; fake **2** a person who is not what he or she pretends to be; one who deceives, dissembles, is insincere, etc.; fraud —**pho′ni·ness** ***n.***

-pho·ny (fə nē, fō′nē) ⟦< Gr *phōnē,* a sound: see PHONO-⟧ *combining form forming nouns* a (specified kind of) sound *[polyphony]*

phoo·ey (fo͞o′ē) ***interj.*** ⟦echoic of the sound of spitting, like (or ? <) Ger *pfui*⟧ used to express contempt, disgust, or mocking disagreement

-phore (fôr, fōr) ⟦ModL *-phorus, -phorum* < Gr *-phoros, -phoron* < *pherein,* to BEAR[1]⟧ *combining form forming nouns* bearer, producer *[carpophore]*

pho·ro·nid (fə rō′nid) ***n.*** ⟦< ModL *Phoronidea,* prob. < L *Phoronis,* Io[1] + *-idea,* neut. pl. suffix⟧ any of a small phylum (Phoronida) of unsegmented, wormlike marine animals, with a U-shaped digestive tract and a lophophore —***adj.*** of or belonging to the phoronids

-phor·ous (fər əs) ⟦ModL *-phorus* < Gr < *pherein,* BEAR[1]⟧ *combining form forming adjectives* bearing, producing *[sporophorous]*

phos·gene (fäs′jēn′) *n.* ⟦so named (1812) by Sir Humphry DAVY < Gr *phōs,* light (see PHOSPHORUS) + *-gene,* -GEN⟧ a colorless, volatile, highly poisonous liquid, $COCl_2$, prepared by the reaction of carbon monoxide with chlorine in the presence of activated charcoal or, orig., in sunlight; carbonyl chloride: used as a poison gas, in organic synthesis, in making dyes, etc.

phosph- *combining form* PHOSPHO-: used before a vowel

phos·pha·tase (fäs′fə tās′) *n.* ⟦< fol. + -ASE⟧ any of various enzymes, found in bodily tissues and fluids, that hydrolyze phosphoric acid esters of organic compounds, liberating phosphate ions

phos·phate (fäs′fāt′) *n.* ⟦Fr < *(acide) phosphorique* < *-ate,* -ATE[2]⟧ **1** *a)* a salt of phosphoric acid containing the trivalent, negative radical PO_4 *b)* an uncharged ester of this acid **2** any substance containing phosphates, used as a fertilizer ☆**3** a soft drink made with soda water, syrup, and, originally, a few drops of phosphoric acid

☆**phosphate rock** any rock, esp. phosphorite, containing large amounts of phosphates, used as a raw material for making fertilizers, phosphorous chemicals, etc.

phos·phat·ic (fäs fat′ik) *adj.* of or containing phosphoric acid or phosphates

phos·pha·tide (fäs′fə tīd′) *n.* ⟦PHOSPHAT(E) + -IDE⟧ a phospholipid having a glycerol component, as lecithin —**phos′pha·tid′ic** (-tid′ik) *adj.*

phos·pha·tize (fäs′fə tīz′) *vt.* **-tized′, -tiz′ing 1** to change into, or treat with, a phosphate or phosphates **2** to treat with phosphoric acid —**phos′pha·ti·za′tion** *n.*

phos·pha·tu·ri·a (fäs′fə to͝or′ē ə, -tyo͝or′-) *n.* ⟦ModL: see PHOSPHATE & -URIA⟧ an excess of phosphates in the urine —**phos′pha·tu′ric** *adj.*

phos·phene (fäs′fēn′) *n.* ⟦< Gr *phōs,* light (see PHOSPHORUS) + *phainein,* to show (see FANTASY)⟧ a sensation of light produced by mechanical or electrical stimulation of the retina, as by pressure on the eyeball through the closed eyelid

phos·phide (fäs′fīd′) *n.* a compound consisting of trivalent phosphorus and another element or a radical

phos·phine (fäs′fēn′, -fin) *n.* ⟦PHOSPH- + -INE[3]⟧ **1** hydrogen phosphide, PH_3, a colorless, poisonous, flammable gas with a garliclike odor **2** a synthetic yellow dye

phos·phite (fäs′fīt′) *n.* ⟦Fr: see fol. & -ITE[1]⟧ **1** a salt of phosphorous acid containing the trivalent, negative radical PO_3 **2** an uncharged ester of this acid

phos·pho- (fäs′fō, -fə) ⟦< PHOSPHORUS⟧ *combining form* phosphorus or phosphoric acid *[phosphoprotein]*

phos·pho·cre·a·tine (fäs′fō krē′ə tēn′, -tin) *n.* ⟦prec. + CREATINE⟧ a compound, $C_4H_{10}N_3O_5P$, in vertebrate muscle, derived from creatine and used as a backup energy source because it reacts with ADP to replenish the ATP and creatine used in muscle contraction

phos·pho·lip·id (fäs′fō lip′id) *n.* ⟦PHOSPHO- + LIPID⟧ any of a group of lipids that contain a phosphate ester as part of the structure and yield on hydrolysis phosphoric acid, an alcohol, fatty acid, and a nitrogenous base: found in all living cells

phos·pho·ni·um (fäs fō′nē əm) *n.* ⟦ModL: see PHOSPHO- & -ONIUM⟧ the monovalent radical PH_4, which is related to PH_3 as the ammonium radical NH_4 is related to NH_3

phos·pho·pro·tein (fäs′fō prō′tēn, -tē in) *n.* any of a group of proteins containing a phosphorous compound, as casein in milk

phos·phor (fäs′fər, -fôr′) *n.* ⟦L *Phosphorus:* see PHOSPHORUS⟧ **1** [**P-**] [Old Poet.] the morning star, esp. Venus **2** PHOSPHORUS: now esp. in **phosphor bronze,** a bronze having a very small amount of phosphorus in it **3** a phosphorescent or fluorescent substance

phos·pho·rate (fäs′fə rāt′) *vt.* **-rat′ed, -rat′ing** ⟦PHOSPHOR(US) + -ATE[1]⟧ to combine or impregnate with phosphorus

phos·pho·resce (fäs′fə res′) *vi.* **-resced′, -resc′ing** ⟦prob. back-form. < fol.⟧ to produce, show, or undergo phosphorescence

phos·pho·res·cence (fäs′fə res′əns) *n.* ⟦Fr: see PHOSPHORUS & -ESCENCE⟧ **1** *a)* the condition or property of a substance of giving off a lingering emission of light after exposure to radiant energy, as light or X-rays *b)* the light thus given off **2** a continuing luminescence without noticeable heat, as from phosphorus when it is slowly oxidized —**phos′pho·res′cent** *adj.*

phos·pho·ret·ed or **phos·pho·ret·ted** (fäs′fə ret′id) *adj.* ⟦< ModL *phosphoretum,* phosphide (< *phosphorus*: see PHOSPHORUS) + -ED⟧ combined or impregnated with phosphorus: also **phos′phu·ret′ed** (-fyo͞o-) or **phos′phu·ret′ted**

phos·phor·ic (fäs fôr′ik) *adj.* ⟦Fr *phosphorique*⟧ of, like, or containing phosphorus, esp. pentavalent phosphorus

phosphoric acid any of several oxygen acids of phosphorus: see ORTHOPHOSPHORIC ACID, METAPHOSPHORIC ACID, and PYROPHOSPHORIC ACID

phos·pho·rism (fäs′fə riz′əm) *n.* chronic phosphorus poisoning

phos·pho·rite (fäs′fə rīt′) *n.* **1** natural calcium phosphate, similar chemically to apatite but without crystal form **2** a sedimentary PHOSPHATE ROCK —**phos′pho·rit′ic** (-rit′ik) *adj.*

phos·pho·ro- (fäs′fə rō, -rə; fäs fôr′ə) *combining form* phosphorus or phosphorescence *[phosphoroscope]*: also, before a vowel, **phosphor-**

phos·phor·o·scope (fäs fôr′ə skōp′) *n.* ⟦prec. + -SCOPE⟧ a device used in observing and measuring the persistence of phosphorescence after the source of light has been removed

phos·pho·rous (fäs′fə rəs, fäs fôr′əs) *adj.* ⟦PHOSPHOR(US) + -OUS⟧ **1** *rare var. of* PHOSPHORESCENT **2** ⟦Fr *phosphoreux*⟧ of, like, or containing phosphorus, esp. trivalent phosphorus

phosphorous acid a white or yellowish, crystalline acid, H_3PO_3, that absorbs oxygen readily: used as a chemical reducing agent and as an analytical reagent

phos·pho·rus (fäs′fə rəs) *n.* ⟦ModL < L *Phosphorus,* morning star < Gr *phōsphoros,* bringer of light < *phōs,* a light, contr. < *phaos* < IE base **bhā-,* to shine > Gr *phainein,* to show (> FANTASY) + -PHOR(O)US⟧ **1** [Archaic] any phosphorescent substance or object **2** a nonmetallic chemical element, normally a white, phosphorescent, waxy solid, becoming yellow when exposed to light: it is poisonous and unites easily with oxygen, so that it ignites spontaneously at room temperature: when heated in sealed tubes it is converted into a red form, which is nonpoisonous and less flammable than the white: when heated under a pressure of 10,000 atmospheres it is converted into a black powder: symbol, P; at. no. 15: a radioactive isotope (**phosphorus-32**) is used in the diagnosis and treatment of certain diseases, as a tracer in chemical and biochemical research, etc.: see the periodic table of elements in the Reference Supplement

phos·pho·ryl·ase (fäs′fə ri lās′) *n.* ⟦PHOSPHOR(O)- + -YL + -ASE⟧ any of a group of enzymes, widely distributed in plant and animal tissues, that help inorganic phosphates break down glycogen and other complex sugars

phos·pho·ryl·ate (fäs′fə ri lāt′) *vt.* **-at′ed, -at′ing** ⟦PHOSPHOR(O)- + -YL + -ATE[1]⟧ to add phosphate to an organic compound —**phos′pho·ryl·a′tion** *n.*

phot[1] (fōt, fät) *n.* ⟦< Gr *phōs* (gen. *phōtos*), a light: see PHOSPHORUS⟧ the basic unit of illumination in the CGS system, equal to one lumen per square centimeter (929.023 foot-candles or 10,000 lux): abbrev. *pt*

phot[2] *abbrev.* **1** photograph **2** photographer **3** photographic **4** photography

pho·tic (fōt′ik) *adj.* ⟦< Gr *phōs* (gen. *phōtos*), a light (see PHOSPHORUS) + -IC⟧ **1** of light **2** *Biol.* having to do with the effect of light upon, or the production of light by, organisms

photic zone the uppermost layer in a body of water, into which daylight penetrates in sufficient amounts to influence living organisms, esp. by permitting photosynthesis

pho·to (fōt′ō) *n., pl.* **-tos** *short for* PHOTOGRAPH

pho·to- (fōt′ō, -ə) *combining form* **1** ⟦< Gr *phōs* (gen. *phōtos*), a light: see PHOSPHORUS⟧ of or produced by light *[photograph, photosynthesis]* **2** ⟦< PHOTOGRAPH⟧ photograph, photography *[photomicrograph]*

pho·to·a·cous·tic (fō′tō ə ko͞os′tik) *adj.* OPTOACOUSTIC

pho·to·ac·tin·ic (fōt′ō ak tin′ik) *adj.* ⟦PHOTO- (sense 1) + ACTINIC⟧ that can produce actinic effect: said as of ultraviolet rays

pho·to·au·to·tro·phic (fōt′ō ôt′ə träf′ik) *adj.* ⟦PHOTO- + AUTOTROPHIC⟧ able to manufacture organic foodstuffs from inorganic materials in the presence of light: said as of green plants and certain bacteria

pho·to·bi·ol·o·gy (fōt′ō bī äl′ə jē) *n.* the branch of biology that deals with the effect of radiant energy, esp. light, on living organisms —**pho′to·bi′o·log′i·cal** (-bī′ə läj′i kəl) *adj.,* **pho′to·bi′o·log′ic** —**pho′to·bi·ol′o·gist** *n.*

pho·to·bi·ot·ic (fōt′ō bī ät′ik) *adj.* ⟦PHOTO- + -BIOTIC⟧ *Biol.* dependent upon light for existence

pho·to·cath·ode (fōt′ō kath′ōd′) *n.* a cathode that emits electrons when activated by radiation, as light

pho·to·cell (fōt′ō sel′) *n.* PHOTOELECTRIC CELL

pho·to·chem·is·try (fōt′ō kem′is trē) *n.* ⟦PHOTO- + CHEMISTRY⟧ the branch of chemistry having to do with the effect of light or other radiant energy in producing chemical action, as in photosynthesis or photography —**pho′to·chem′i·cal** (-i kəl) *adj.*

pho·to·chro·mic (fōt′ō krō′mik) *adj.* ⟦PHOTO- + CHROMIC⟧ designating or of a material, as certain glass or film, which turns dark when exposed to light and returns to its normal transparency with the removal of the light source —**pho′to·chro′mism′** *n.*

pho·to·chron·o·graph (fōt′ō krän′ə graf′) *n.* ⟦PHOTO- + CHRONOGRAPH⟧ **1** *a)* a device formerly used for recording motion in a series of photographs taken at regular, extremely brief, intervals *b)* a photograph so taken **2** an instrument for recording the exact time of an event by exposing a moving photographic plate to the tracing of a thin beam of light synchronized with the event

pho·to·co·ag·u·la·tion (fōt′ō kō ag′yo͞o lā′shən) *n.* ⟦PHOTO- + COAGULATION⟧ a technique using intense light energy, as from a laser, to produce scar tissue: used in treating certain eye disorders, in medical and biological research, etc. —**pho′to·co·ag′u·la′tor** *n.*

pho·to·com·po·si·tion (fōt′ō käm′pə zish′ən) *n.* ⟦< PHOTO- (sense 2)⟧ any of various methods of composing matter for printing, in which light images of type characters or graphics are projected in succession onto a photosensitive surface to produce a negative from which plates can be prepared —**pho′to·com·pose′** (-kəm pōz′) *vt.* **-posed′, -pos′ing**

pho·to·con·duc·tive (fōt′ō kən duk′tiv) *adj.* ⟦< PHOTO- (sense 1)⟧ designating or of a substance, as selenium, which exhibits changed electrical conductivity under varying amounts of radiation —**pho′to·con′duc·tiv′i·ty** (-kän′duk tiv′ə tē) *n.* —**pho′to·con·duc′tor** *n.*

pho·to·cop·y (fōt′ō käp′ē) *n., pl.* **-cop′ies** a copy of printed or other graphic material made by a device (**pho′to·cop′i·er**) which photographically reproduces the original —*vt.* **-cop′ied, -cop′y·ing** to make a photocopy of

pho·to·cur·rent (-kur′ənt) *n.* a stream of electrons released from a photoelectric cell by the action of light

pho·to·de·grad·a·ble (fōt′ō dē grād′ə bəl) *adj.* ⟦PHOTO- + (BIO)DEGRADABLE⟧

that will decompose under exposure to certain kinds of radiant energy, esp. ultraviolet light: said as of certain plastics or insecticides

pho·to·de·tec·tor (fōt′ō dē tek′tər) ***n.*** ⟦PHOTO- + DETECTOR⟧ any electronic device, esp. a photodiode, that responds to or measures the intensity of ultraviolet or infrared radiation or visible light

pho·to·di·ode (fōt′ō dī′ōd′) ***n.*** ⟦PHOTO- + DIODE⟧ *Electronics* a light-sensitive, semiconductor diode, used as a photoelectric cell

pho·to·dis·in·te·gra·tion (fōt′ō dis in′tə grā′shən) ***n.*** ⟦< PHOTO- (sense 1)⟧ *Physics* a nuclear reaction induced by the action of a photon

pho·to·dis·so·ci·a·tion (fōt′ō di sō′shē ā′shən) ***n.*** ⟦< PHOTO- (sense 1)⟧ the breaking up of a substance, esp. a chemical compound, into simpler components by the action of radiant energy

pho·to·dy·nam·ic (fōt′ō dī nam′ik) ***adj.*** of or pertaining to the energy of light; esp., designating a fluorescent substance

pho·to·dy·nam·ics (-dī nam′iks) ***n.*** ⟦PHOTO- + DYNAMICS⟧ **1** the activating effect of light on living organisms, as in causing phototropism in plants **2** the science dealing with this

pho·to·e·las·tic·i·ty (fōt′ō ē′las tis′ə tē) ***n.*** ⟦PHOTO- (sense 1) + ELASTIC + -ITY⟧ the property shown by certain transparent solids, esp. glass and plastics, of producing double refraction when put under tension or compression, thus permitting stress analysis of models of parts —**pho′to·e·las′tic** (-ē las′tik) ***adj.***

pho·to·e·lec·tric (fōt′ō ē lek′trik) ***adj.*** ⟦PHOTO- + ELECTRIC⟧ of or having to do with the electric effects produced by light or other radiation, esp. as in the emission of electrons by certain substances when subjected to light or radiation of suitable wavelength

☆**photoelectric cell** a photodetector that regulates or produces a current or voltage in response to certain types of radiation, esp. visible light: typically incorporated in an electric circuit and used in mechanical devices as to open doors, set off alarms, etc.

pho·to·e·lec·tron (fōt′ō ē lek′trän′) ***n.*** ⟦< PHOTO- (sense 1)⟧ an electron ejected from a system by a photon striking it, or emitted as a result of radiation

pho·to·e·mis·sion (fōt′ō ē mish′ən) ***n.*** ⟦PHOTO- + EMISSION⟧ the ejection of one or more electrons from a substance (**pho′to·e·mit′ter**), usually a metal, when subjected to light or other suitable radiation —**pho′to·e·mis′sive** (-mis′iv) ***adj.***

pho·to·en·grav·ing (fō′tō en grā′viŋ) ***n.*** **1** a photomechanical process by which photographs are reproduced on relief printing plates **2** a printing plate so made **3** a print from such a plate —**pho′to·en·grave′** ***vt.*** **-graved′**, **-grav′ing** —**pho′to·en·grav′er** ***n.***

photo essay a group of photographs arranged, often with accompanying text, to tell a story, evoke a mood, etc.

photo finish **1** a race finish so close that the winner can be determined only from a photograph of the contestants crossing the finish line **2** any close finish of a contest

pho·to·fin·ish·ing (fōt′ō fin′ish iŋ) ***n.*** the process or work of developing exposed photographic film, making prints, etc. —**pho′to·fin′ish·er** ***n.***

pho·to·flash (fōt′ō flash′) ***n.*** FLASH (***n.*** 7)

pho·to·flood (-flud′) ***adj.*** ⟦PHOTO- (sense 2) + FLOOD (***n.*** 4)⟧ *Photog.* designating, of, or using a high-intensity electric lamp or light used for sustained illumination —***n.*** a photoflood bulb, lamp, etc.

pho·to·fluo·rog·ra·phy (fōt′ō flô räg′rə fē, -floo-) ***n.*** the use of photography to record fluoroscopic images on film —**pho′to·fluo′ro·graph′ic** (-flôr′ə graf′ik, -floor′-) ***adj.***

photog *abbrev.* **1** photograph **2** photographer **3** photographic **4** photography

pho·to·gene (fōt′ə jēn′) ***n.*** ⟦see PHOTO- (sense 1) & -GEN⟧ AFTERIMAGE

pho·to·gen·ic (fōt′ə jen′ik) ***adj.*** ⟦PHOTO- + -GENIC⟧ **1** due to or produced by light **2** producing or giving off light; phosphorescent **3** that looks or is likely to look attractive in photographs: said especially of a person —**pho′to·gen′i·cal·ly** ***adv.***

pho·to·ge·ol·o·gy (fōt′ō jē äl′ə jē) ***n.*** the branch of geology that studies geologic features by using photography, esp. photographs taken from an airplane or satellite —**pho′to·ge′o·log′ic** (-jē′ə läj′ik) ***adj.***

pho·to·gram·me·try (fōt′ō gram′ə trē) ***n.*** ⟦*photogram* (var., modeled on -GRAM, of fol.) + -METRY⟧ the art or process of surveying or measuring, as in map making, by taking photographs, esp. aerial photographs —**pho′to·gram·met′ric** (-grə me′trik) ***adj.*** —**pho′to·gram′me·trist** ***n.***

pho·to·graph (fōt′ə graf′) ***n.*** ⟦PHOTO- (sense 1) + -GRAPH⟧ an image or picture made by photography —***vt.*** **1** to take a photograph of **2** to FILM (***vt.*** 2) —***vi.*** **1** to take photographs **2** to appear (as specified) in photographs [to *photograph* well]

pho·tog·ra·pher (fə täg′rə fər) ***n.*** a person who takes photographs, esp. as an occupation

pho·to·graph·ic (fōt′ə graf′ik) ***adj.*** **1** of or like a photograph or photography **2** used in or made by photography **3** retaining or recalling in precise detail [a *photographic* memory] —**pho′to·graph′i·cal·ly** ***adv.***

pho·tog·ra·phy (fə täg′rə fē) ***n.*** ⟦PHOTO- (sense 1) + -GRAPHY⟧ the art or process of capturing images, either on light-sensitive film or electronically in digital form, from which viewable pictures can be produced; activity of someone who uses a camera

pho·to·gra·vure (fōt′ō grə vyoor′) ***n.*** ⟦Fr < *photo* (contr. < *photographe* < PHOTOGRAPH) + *gravure,* engraving < *graver:* see ENGRAVE⟧ **1** a photochemical process by which photographs are reproduced on intaglio printing plates or cylinders **2** a plate or cylinder so made **3** a print from such a plate, usually with a satinlike finish

pho·to·i·on·i·za·tion (fōt′ō ī′ə nə zā′shən) ***n.*** ⟦< PHOTO- (sense 1)⟧ the liberation of one or more electrons from a material as a result of radiation

pho·to·jour·nal·ism (fōt′ō jur′nəl iz′əm) ***n.*** journalism in which news stories or features are presented mainly through photographs —**pho′to·jour′nal·ist** ***n.*** —**pho′to·jour′nal·is′tic** ***adj.***

pho·to·ki·ne·sis (fōt′ō ki nē′sis) ***n.*** ⟦ModL < PHOTO- + *kinesis,* motion < Gr *kinēsis* < *kinein,* to move⟧ *Physiol.* movement in response to light —**pho′to·ki·net′ic** (-net′ik) ***adj.***

pho·to·lith·o·graph (fōt′ō lith′ə graf′) ***n.*** a print made by photolithography —***vt.*** to make a photolithograph of —**pho′to·lith·og′ra·pher** (-li thäg′rə fər) ***n.***

pho·to·li·thog·ra·phy (-li thäg′rə fē) ***n.*** a process of printing from a plate, etc. prepared by methods combining photography and lithography —**pho′to·lith′o·graph′ic** (-lith′ə graf′ik) ***adj.***

pho·to·lu·mi·nes·cence (fōt′ō lo͞o′mə nes′əns) ***n.*** luminescence in response to excitation by light, as in fluorescence and phosphorescence —**pho′to·lu′mi·nes′cent** ***adj.***

pho·tol·y·sis (fō täl′ə sis) ***n.*** ⟦ModL: see PHOTO- & -LYSIS⟧ chemical decomposition due to the action of light —**pho·to·lyt·ic** (fōt′ə lit′ik) ***adj.***

pho·to·map (fōt′ō map′) ***n.*** a map made by imposing a grid on one or more aerial photographs, adding place names, etc. —**pho′to·map′** ***vt., vi.*** **-mapped′**, **-map′ping**

pho·to·me·chan·i·cal (fōt′ō mə kan′i kəl) ***adj.*** ⟦PHOTO- + MECHANICAL⟧ designating or of any process by which printing plates are made by a photographic method —**pho′to·me·chan′i·cal·ly** ***adv.***

pho·tom·e·ter (fō täm′ət ər) ***n.*** ⟦PHOTO- + -METER⟧ an instrument used in measuring the intensity of light, esp. in determining its relative intensity from different sources

pho·tom·e·try (fō täm′ə trē) ***n.*** ⟦ModL *photometria:* see PHOTO- & -METRY⟧ **1** the measurement of the intensity of light **2** the branch of optics dealing with this —**pho·to·met·ric** (fōt′ō me′trik) ***adj.*** —**pho′to·met′ri·cal·ly** ***adv.***

pho·to·mi·cro·graph (fōt′ō mī′krō graf′) ***n.*** ⟦PHOTO- + MICROGRAPH⟧ a photograph taken through a microscope —**pho′to·mi′cro·graph′ic** ***adj.*** —**pho′to·mi·crog′ra·phy** (-mī kräg′rə fē) ***n.***

pho·to·mon·tage (fōt′ō mōn täzh′, -män-) ***n.*** montage done in or with photographs

pho·to·mul·ti·pli·er (fōt′ō mul′tə plī′ər) ***n.*** a photoemissive photoelectric cell which amplifies emitted electrons and converts them into brighter light, an electric signal, etc.

pho·to·mu·ral (fōt′ō myoor′əl) ***n.*** a large photograph used as a mural

☆**pho·ton** (fō′tän′) ***n.*** ⟦PHOT(O)- + (ELECTR)ON⟧ **1** *Particle Physics* a subatomic particle, having energy and momentum but no mass or electric charge, that is the quantum unit of electromagnetic radiation, including light: see also CLASSON **2** a unit of retinal illumination equal to the illumination from a surface having a brightness of one candle per sq meter seen through a pupil area of one sq millimeter —**pho·ton′ic** ***adj.***

pho·to·neg·a·tive (fōt′ō neg′ə tiv) ***adj.*** *Biol.* responding negatively to light, as an earthworm does

pho·to·neu·tron (fōt′ō no͞o′trän′, -nyo͞o′-) ***n.*** ⟦< PHOTO- (sense 1)⟧ a neutron given off in the photodisintegration of an atomic nucleus

pho·ton·ics (fō tän′iks) ***n.*** the branch of physics that deals with photons and their applications in telecommunication, data processing, etc.

pho·to-off·set (fōt′ō ôf′set′) ***n.*** a method of offset printing in which the text or pictures are photographically transferred to a metal plate from which inked impressions are made on the rubber roller

☆**photo opportunity** an opportunity, as at a specially chosen public event, for a politician or other celebrity to be photographed by the press, TV, etc. in a way expected to afford favorable publicity: also [Informal] **photo op** (äp) or **pho′to-op′** ***n.***

☆**pho·to·ox·i·da·tion** (fōt′ō äk′si dā′shən) ***n.*** oxidation induced by light or some other form of radiant energy

pho·to·pe·ri·od (fōt′ō pir′ē əd) ***n.*** the number of daylight hours best suited to the growth and maturation of an organism —**pho′to·pe′ri·od′ic** (-pir′ē äd′ik) ***adj.***

pho·to·pe·ri·od·ism (fōt′ō pir′ē əd iz′əm) ***n.*** *Biol.* the behavioral or physiological reaction of an organism to variations in the duration of light, as, in plants, by flowering or ceasing to flower, or, in certain animals, by changing the daily cycle of activities: also **pho′to·pe′ri·o·dic′i·ty** (-ə dis′ə tē)

pho·toph·i·lous (fō täf′ə ləs) ***adj.*** ⟦PHOTO- + -PHILOUS⟧ *Biol.* thriving in light: also **pho·to·phil·ic** (fōt′ō fil′ik) —**pho·toph′i·ly** (-lē) ***n.***

pho·to·pho·bi·a (fōt′ō fō′bē ə) ***n.*** ⟦ModL: see PHOTO- & -PHOBIA⟧ **1** an abnormal fear of light **2** an abnormal sensitivity to light, esp. of the eyes, as in measles and certain eye conditions —**pho′to·pho′bic** (-fō′bik) ***adj.***

pho·to·phore (fōt′ə fôr′) ***n.*** ⟦PHOTO- + -PHORE⟧ a light organ in bioluminescent animals containing reflective tissue and light-producing cells

pho·to·pi·a (fō tō′pē ə) ***n.*** ⟦< PHOT(O)- + -OPIA⟧ the normal visual perception or vision following light adaptation, as during the day or in bright light: cf. SCOTOPIA —**pho·top′ic** (-täp′ik, -tō′pik) ***adj.***

☆**pho·to·play** (fōt′ō plā′) ***n.*** ⟦PHOTO- (sense 2) + PLAY (***n.*** 8)⟧ *former name for* FILM (***n.*** 5)

pho·to·pos·i·tive (fōt′ō päz′ə tiv) ***adj.*** *Biol.* responding positively to light, as a moth does

pho·to·re·al·ism (fō′tō rē′əl iz′əm) ***n.*** **1** [*also* **P-**] a movement in art, esp. painting, of the 1970s that emphasized realistic accuracy and detail like that of a photograph: also **Photo Realism** **2** such realistic depiction in painting, animation, etc. —**pho′to·re′al·ist** ***adj., n.*** —**pho′to·re′al·is′tic** ***adj.***

pho·to·re·cep·tor (fōt′ō ri sep′tər) *n. Biol.* a sense organ specialized to detect light, as the eye or any of the elements of a compound eye —**pho′to·re·cep′tion** *n.* —**pho′to·re·cep′tive** *adj.*

pho·to·re·con·nais·sance (fōt′ō ri kän′ə səns) *n. Mil.* reconnaissance by means of aerial photographs

pho·to·re·sist (fōt′ō ri zist′) *n.* ⟦PHOTO- (sense 1) + RESIST (*n.*)⟧ a substance that can be made to form a tough film by a photographic process, used to mask electrical circuits before chemical etching

pho·to·re·sis·tive (-zis′tiv) *adj.* PHOTOCONDUCTIVE —**pho·to·re·sis′tor** *n.*

pho·to·sen·si·tive (fōt′ō sen′sə tiv) *adj.* reacting or sensitive to radiant energy, esp. to light —**pho′to·sen′si·tiv′i·ty** *n.*

pho·to·sen·si·tize (-sen′sə tīz′) *vt.* **-tized′**, **-tiz′ing** to make photosensitive —**pho′to·sen′si·ti·za′tion** *n.*

pho·to·set (fōt′ō set′) *vt.* **-set′**, **-set′ting** ⟦< PHOTO- (sense 2)⟧ to set (matter for printing) by photocomposition

Pho·to·shop (fōt′ō shäp′) *trademark for* software for altering digital images —*vt.* **-shopped′**, **-shop′ping** [*usually* **p-**] to alter (a digital image) using such software

pho·to·sphere (fōt′ō sfir′) *n.* ⟦PHOTO- (sense 1) + -SPHERE: orig. sense, "orb of light"⟧ the visible surface of the sun —**pho′to·spher′ic** (-sfer′ik) *adj.*

☆**pho·to·stat** (fōt′ə stat′) *n.* ⟦< *Photostat*, former trademark for the device < PHOTO- (sense 2) + -STAT⟧ **1** [*often* **P-**] a device for making photocopies on special paper **2** a copy so made —*vt.* **-stat′ed** or **-stat′ted**, **-stat′ing** or **-stat′ting** to make a photostat of —**pho′to·stat′ic** *adj.*

pho·to·syn·the·sis (fōt′ō sin′thə sis) *n.* ⟦ModL: see PHOTO- & SYNTHESIS⟧ **1** the biological synthesis of chemical compounds in the presence of light **2** the production of organic substances, chiefly sugars, from carbon dioxide and water occurring in green plant cells supplied with enough light to allow chlorophyll to aid in the transformation of the radiant energy into a chemical form —**pho′to·syn·thet′ic** (-sin thet′ik) *adj.* —**pho′to·syn·thet′i·cal·ly** *adv.*

pho·to·syn·the·size (-sīz′) *vi., vt.* **-sized′**, **-siz′ing** to carry on, or produce by, photosynthesis

pho·to·tax·is (fōt′ō tak′sis) *n.* ⟦ModL: see PHOTO- & -TAXIS⟧ the positive, or negative, response of a freely moving organism toward, or away from, light —**pho′to·tac′tic** (-tik) *adj.*

☆**pho·to·te·leg·ra·phy** (fōt′ō tə leg′rə fē) *n.* **1** ⟦< PHOTO- (sense 1)⟧ communication by means of a heliograph **2** ⟦< PHOTO- (sense 2)⟧ TELEPHOTOGRAPHY (sense 2)

pho·to·ther·a·py (fōt′ō ther′ə pē) *n.* the use of sunlight, lamps, or lasers to treat skin disorders, depression, etc. —**pho′to·ther′a·peu′tic** (-pyo͞ot′ik) *adj.*

pho·to·ther·mic (fōt′ō thur′mik) *adj.* ⟦PHOTO- + THERMIC⟧ of or involving both light and heat

pho·tot·o·nus (fō tät′ə nəs) *n.* ⟦ModL: see PHOTO- & TONE⟧ *Biol.* the state of being responsive to or irritated by exposure to light —**pho·to·ton·ic** (fōt′ō tän′ik) *adj.*

☆**pho·to·tran·sis·tor** (fōt′ō tran zis′tər, -sis′-) *n.* ⟦< PHOTO- (sense 1)⟧ *Electronics* a device combining the function of a photodiode with the amplifying function of a transistor

pho·tot·ro·pism (fō tä′trə piz′əm) *n.* ⟦PHOTO- + TROPISM⟧ any movement of a part of a plant toward or away from light sources: see HELIOTROPISM —**pho·to·trop·ic** (fōt′ō träp′ik) *adj.*

pho·to·tube (fōt′ō to͞ob′, -tyo͞ob′) *n.* ⟦PHOTO(ELECTRIC) + TUBE⟧ a vacuum tube designed to convert light energy into electrical energy by means of a photoemissive cathode

pho·to·type·set·ting (fōt′ō tīp′set′iŋ) *n.* ⟦< PHOTO- (sense 2)⟧ PHOTOCOMPOSITION —**pho′to·type′set′ter** *n.*

pho·to·vol·ta·ic (fōt′ō väl tā′ik) *adj.* ⟦PHOTO- (sense 1) + VOLTAIC⟧ of or having to do with the generation of an electromotive force at the junction of two different materials in response to visible or other radiation

phr *abbrev.* phrase

phrag·mit·es (frag mīt′ēz) *n.* ⟦ModL < Gr *phragmitēs*, growing in hedges < *phragma*, hedge, fence⟧ any of a genus (*Phragmites*) of tall, slender perennial grasses, esp. the common reed (*P. australis*), having plumelike inflorescences, widely distributed in wet or marshy areas

phras·al (frā′zəl) *adj.* of, like, or consisting of a phrase or phrases —**phras′al·ly** *adv.*

phrase (frāz) *n.* ⟦L *phrasis*, diction < Gr < *phrazein*, to speak⟧ **1** a manner or style of speech or expression; phraseology **2** a short, colorful or forceful expression **3** a connected series of movements in a formal dance **4** *Gram.* a sequence of two or more words conveying a single thought or forming a distinct part of a sentence but not containing a subject and predicate: cf. CLAUSE **5** *Linguis.* a group of words that functions as a syntactic unit **6** *Music* a short, distinct part or passage, usually of two, four, or eight measures —*vt., vi.* **phrased**, **phras′ing** **1** to express in a certain way, as by selecting particular words to make a phrase **2** *Music* to mark off or divide (notes) into phrases

phrase·mak·ing (frāz′māk′iŋ) *n.* the coining of memorable or quotable phrases, slogans, etc. —**phrase′mak′er** *n.*

phra·se·o·gram (frā′zē ō gram′) *n.* ⟦PHRASEO(LOGY) + -GRAM⟧ a mark or symbol representing an entire phrase, as in Pitman shorthand

phra·se·ol·o·gist (frā′zē äl′ə jist) *n.* a person skilled at formulating well-turned phrases or one given to using catchy but trite phrases

phra·se·ol·o·gy (frā′zē äl′ə jē) *n., pl.* **-gies** ⟦ModL *phraseologia:* see PHRASE & -LOGY⟧ choice and pattern of words; way of speaking or writing; diction —**phra′se·o·log′i·cal** (-ō läj′i kəl) *adj.*

phras·ing (frāz′iŋ) *n.* **1** the act or manner of formulating phrases; phraseology **2** the manner in which one phrases musical passages

phra·try (frā′trē) *n., pl.* **-tries** ⟦Gr *phratria* < *phratēr*, akin to L *frater*, BROTHER⟧ **1** a subdivision of an ancient Greek phyle **2** any of the similar units, as a group of clans, of a primitive tribe —**phra′tric** *adj.*, **phra′tral**

phreak (frēk) *n.* ⟦< FREAK[1], with sp. infl. by PHONE[2]⟧ [Informal] *short for* PHONE PHREAK

phre·at·ic (frē at′ik) *adj.* ⟦< Fr *phréatique* < Gr *phrear*, a well: see fol.⟧ *Geol.* of, having to do with, or being groundwater

phre·at·o·phyte (frē at′ə fīt′) *n.* ⟦< Gr *phrear* (gen. *phreatos*), a well (< IE **bh(e)reu-*, to boil up see FERVENT) + -PHYTE⟧ a long-rooted plant that absorbs its water from the water table or other permanent ground supply —**phre·at′o·phyt′ic** (-fit′ik) *adj.*

phre·net·ic (fri net′ik) *adj. archaic sp. of* FRENETIC

phren·ic (fren′ik) *adj.* ⟦see fol. & -IC⟧ **1** of the diaphragm **2** of the mind; mental

phren·o- (fren′ō, -ə) ⟦< Gr *phrēn* (gen. *phrenos*), midriff, heart, also mind, mental capacity⟧ *combining form* **1** the diaphragm [*phrenic*] **2** the mind [*phrenology*] Also, before a vowel, **phren-**

☆**phre·nol·o·gy** (fri näl′ə jē) *n.* ⟦prec. + -LOGY⟧ a system, popular esp. in the 19th cent., based on the assumption that an analysis of character can be made by a study of the shape and protuberances of the skull —**phren·o·log·i·cal** (fren′ə läj′i kəl) *adj.* —**phre·nol′o·gist** *n.*

phren·sy (fren′zē) *n., pl.* **-sies** —*vt.* **-sied**, **-sy·ing** *archaic sp. of* FRENZY

Phryg·i·a (frij′ē ə) ancient country in WC Asia Minor

Phryg·i·an (frij′ē ən, frij′ən) *adj.* of Phrygia or its people, language, or culture —*n.* **1** a person born or living in Phrygia **2** the extinct Indo-European language of the ancient Phrygians, preserved only in fragmentary inscriptions

PHS *abbrev.* Public Health Service

phthal·ate (thal′āt′) *n.* ⟦PHTHAL(IC ACID) + -ATE[2] (sense 4*a*)⟧ **1** a salt of phthalic acid containing the divalent, negative radical $C_6H_4(COO)_2$ **2** an uncharged ester of this acid

phthal·ein (thal′ēn′, -ē in; fthal′-) *n.* ⟦< fol. + -IN[1]⟧ any of a group of synthetic dyes manufactured from phenols and phthalic anhydride

phthal·ic acid (thal′ik, fthal′-) ⟦(NA)PHTHAL(ENE) + -IC⟧ any of three isomeric acids, $C_6H_4(COOH)_2$, esp. one (*ortho*-phthalic acid) obtained by oxidation of naphthalene or xylene and used in the manufacture of dyes, medicines, etc.

phthalic anhydride a white, solid substance, $C_6H_4(CO)_2O$, produced by the oxidation of naphthalene and used to make the phthalein dyes, certain synthetic resins, etc.

phthal·in (thal′in, fthal′-) *n.* ⟦PHTHAL(EIN) + -IN[1]⟧ any of a series of compounds produced by the reduction of the phthaleins

phthal·o·cy·a·nine (thal′ə sī′ə nēn′, -nin; fthal′-) *n.* ⟦PHTHAL(IC ACID) + -O- + CYANINE⟧ **1** a blue-green organic compound, $(C_6H_4C_2N)_4N_4$ **2** any of a group of brilliant, green or blue pigments that are metal, esp. copper, derivatives of this compound

phthi·ri·a·sis (thī rī′ə sis, fthi-) *n.* ⟦L < Gr *phtheiriasis* < *phtheir*, a louse + *-iasis*, -IASIS⟧ infestation with lice, esp. the crab louse; pediculosis

phthi·sis (tī′sis, thī′-, fthī′-) *n.* ⟦L < Gr, a decay < *phthiein*, to waste away < IE base **gwhthei-*, to disappear, be destroyed > Sans *kṣáyati*, (he) destroys⟧ any wasting disease, as tuberculosis of the lungs —**phthis·ic** (tiz′ik) *adj.*, *n.* —**phthis′i·cal** *adj.*

phut (ft, fət) *n.* ⟦echoic⟧ a dull, flat, slightly explosive sound, as of an engine dying —**go phut** go out of order; break down

-phy·ce·ae (fī′sē ē′, fis′ē ē′) ⟦ModL < Gr *phykos*, seaweed, orchil, rouge < Sem, as in Heb *puch*, eye shadow⟧ *combining form* seaweed: used in forming the scientific names of classes of algae

-phy·ceous (fish′əs) *combining form forming adjectives* of or belonging to a (specified) class of algae

phy·col·o·gy (fī käl′ə jē) *n.* ⟦< Gr *phykos*, seaweed (see -PHYCEAE) + -LOGY⟧ ALGOLOGY —**phy·col′o·gist** *n.*

Phyfe (fīf), **Duncan** (born *Duncan Fife*) 1768-1854; U.S. cabinetmaker & furniture designer, born in Scotland

phy·la (fī′lə) *n. pl. of* PHYLUM

phy·lac·ter·y (fi lak′tər ē) *n., pl.* **-ter·ies** ⟦ME *filaterie* < ML *phylaterium* < LL(Ec) *phylacteria* (used for Heb *tefilin*, pl. of *tefila*, prayer < root *pll*, to pray, entreat < Gr *phylaktērion*, a safeguard < *phylassein*, to defend, guard > *phylax*, a watchman⟧ **1** TEFILLIN **2** [Rare] something worn as a charm or safeguard

phy·le (fī′lē) *n., pl.* **-lae** (-lē) ⟦ModL < Gr *phylē*, tribe, akin to *phyein:* see BE⟧ the largest political subdivision in the ancient Athenian state

phy·let·ic (fī let′ik) *adj.* ⟦ModL *phyleticus* < Gr *phyletikos* < *phyletēs*, tribesman < *phylē:* see prec.⟧ *Biol.* of or pertaining to a phylum or to an evolutionary line of descent

-phyll (fil) ⟦ModL < Gr *phyllon*, a leaf: see BLOOM[1]⟧ *combining form forming nouns* leaf [*sporophyll*]

Phyl·lis (fil′is) *n.* ⟦L < Gr, lit., leaf: see prec.⟧ a feminine name

phyl·lite (fil′īt′) *n.* ⟦< Gr *phyllon*, a leaf (see BLOOM[1]) + -ITE[1]⟧ a type of metamorphic rock having tiny mica grains that give it a luster: it is intermediate in crystal development between slate and schist

phyl·lo (fē′lō, fī′-) *n.* ⟦< ModGr *phyllon*, thin sheet < Gr: see fol.⟧ dough in very thin sheets which becomes very flaky when baked: used for appetizers, desserts, etc.

phyl·lo- (fil′ō, -ə) ⟦ModL < Gr *phyllon,* a leaf: see BLOOM[1]⟧ *combining form* leaf *[phyllotaxis]*: also, before a vowel, **phyll-**

phyl·lo·clad (fil′ə klad′) *n.* CLADOPHYLL: also **phyl′lo·clade′** (-klād′)

phyl·lode (fil′ōd′) *n.* ⟦ModL *phyllodium* < Gr *phyllōdēs,* leaflike: see PHYLLO- & -ODE[2]⟧ *Bot.* a flat leafstalk that functions as a leaf —**phyl·lo·di·al** (fə lō′dē əl) *adj.*

phyl·loid (fil′oid′) *adj.* ⟦ModL *phylloides:* see PHYLLO- & -OID⟧ like a leaf; leaflike

phyl·lome (fil′ōm′) *n.* ⟦ModL *phylloma* < Gr *phyllōma,* foliage < *phylloun,* to cover with leaves < *phyllon,* a leaf: see BLOOM[1]⟧ *Bot.* a leaf or analogous member —**phyl·lom·ic** (fi läm′ik, -lō′mik) *adj.*

phyl·loph·a·gous (fi läf′ə gəs) *adj.* ⟦PHYLLO- + -PHAGOUS⟧ feeding on leaves

phyl·lo·tax·is (fil′ə tak′sis) *n.* ⟦ModL *phyllotaxis:* see PHYLLO- & -TAXIS⟧ *Bot.* **1** the arrangement of leaves on a stem **2** the study or principles of such arrangement Also **phyl′lo·tax′y** (-tak′sē) —**phyl′lo·tac′tic** (-tak′tik) *adj.*

-phyl·lous (fil′əs) ⟦see PHYLLO- & -OUS⟧ *combining form forming adjectives* having (a specified number or kind of) leaves, leaflets, etc. *[heterophyllous]*

phyl·lox·e·ra (fi läks′ə rə; fil′äk sir′ə) *n., pl.* **-rae′** (-ə rē′; -sir′ē′) or **-ras** ⟦ModL < Gr *phyllon,* a leaf + *xēros,* dry: see BLOOM[1] & SERENE⟧ any of a family (Phylloxeridae) of homopteran insects that attack the leaves and roots of certain plants, including grapevines

phy·lo- (fī′lō, -lə) ⟦< Gr *phylon,* tribe, akin to *phylē,* PHYLE⟧ *combining form* tribe, race, phylum, etc. *[phylogeny]*: also, before a vowel, **phyl-**

phy·log·e·ny (fī läj′ə nē) *n., pl.* **-nies** ⟦Ger *phylogenie,* coined (1866) by E. H. HAECKEL: see prec. & -GENY⟧ **1** the lines of descent or evolutionary development of any plant or animal species **2** the origin and evolution of a division, group, or race of animals or plants: distinguished from ONTOGENY **3** the historical development of a nonliving thing, as a group of languages Also **phy·lo·gen·e·sis** (fī′lō jen′ə sis) —**phy′lo·ge·net′ic** (-jə net′ik) *adj.,* **phy′lo·gen′ic** (-jen′ik) —**phy′lo·ge·net′i·cal·ly** *adv.*

phy·lum (fī′ləm) *n., pl.* **-la** (-lə) ⟦ModL, coined by CUVIER < Gr *phylon,* tribe: see PHYLO-⟧ **1** a major category in the classification of living organisms, esp. animals, ranking above a class and below a kingdom: it can include one class or many similar classes: the Latinized phylum names are capitalized but not italicized (Ex.: Arthropoda, arthropods): cf. DIVISION (*n.* 7) **2** *a)* a language stock *b)* loosely, a language family

-phyre (fir) ⟦Fr < *porphyre:* see PORPHYRY⟧ *combining form* a porphyritic rock

phys *abbrev.* **1** physical **2** physician **3** physics

phys ed (fiz′ ed′) [Informal] PHYSICAL EDUCATION

phys·i·at·rics (fiz′ē a′triks) *n.* ⟦PHYS(IO)- + -IATRICS⟧ the branch of medicine that deals with physical therapy: also **phys′i·at′ry** (-a′trē) —**phys′i·at′rist** (-a′trist) *n.*

phys·ic (fiz′ik) *n.* ⟦ME *fisike* < OFr *fisique* < L *physica,* natural science (in ML, medicine) < Gr *physikē* < *physis,* nature < *phyein,* to produce, become: see BE⟧ **1** *rare var. of* PHYSICS **2** [Archaic] the art or science of healing; medical science **3** a medicine or remedy, esp. a laxative or cathartic —*vt.* **-icked, -ick·ing 1** to dose with medicine, esp. with a cathartic **2** to have a curative effect on; heal

SYN.—physic is the general word for anything taken to relieve constipation or to effect a bowel movement; **laxative** and **aperient** usually refer to milder physics of a kind that are ordinarily taken to promote discharge from the bowels, such as mineral oil, agar, certain fruit juices, etc.: **purgative** and **cathartic** apply to stronger physics, such as castor oil, Epsom salts, calomel, etc., that are more drastic in their action

phys·i·cal (fiz′i kəl) *adj.* ⟦ME *phisical,* having to do with medicine < ML *physicalis* < L *physica:* see prec.⟧ **1** of nature and all matter; natural; material **2** of natural science or natural philosophy **3** of or according to the laws of nature **4** of, or produced by the forces of, physics **5** *a)* of the body as opposed to the mind *[physical exercise]* *b)* preoccupied with bodily or sexual pleasures; carnal *c)* of or marked by aggressive or rough play, activity, etc. —*n.* ☆a general medical examination: in full **physical examination** —*SYN.* BODILY, MATERIAL —**phys′i·cal·ly** *adv.*

physical anthropology a major division of anthropology that deals with the physical characteristics and evolution of humans

physical chemistry the branch of chemistry dealing with the physical changes associated with chemical reactions

☆**physical education** instruction in physical exercise and in the care and hygiene of the human body; esp., a course in gymnastics, athletics, etc., as in a school or college

physical geography the study of the features and nature of the earth's solid surface and oceans, atmosphere and climate, distribution of plant and animal life, etc.

phys·i·cal·ism (fiz′i kəl iz′əm) *n.* the theory that all referential terms in scientific or meaningful statements are reducible to terms connected with physical objects or events, or with their properties —**phys′i·cal·ist** *n.*

phys·i·cal·i·ty (fiz′i kal′ə tē) *n.* **1** the quality or condition of being physical **2** preoccupation with physical, esp. bodily or carnal, matters

physical science any of the sciences that deal with inanimate matter or energy, as physics, chemistry, geology, astronomy, etc.

physical therapy the treatment of disease, inflammation, injury, etc. by such physical means as exercise, massage, infrared or ultraviolet light, electrotherapy, hydrotherapy, or heat

phy·si·cian (fi zish′ən) *n.* ⟦ME & OFr *fisicien* < L *physica:* see PHYSIC⟧ **1** a person licensed to practice medicine; doctor of medicine **2** any medical doctor other than one specializing in surgery **3** any person or thing that heals, relieves, or comforts

physician assistant a person trained and certified to perform various medical procedures under the supervision of a physician: also **physician's assistant**

phys·i·cist (fiz′ə sist) *n.* an expert or specialist in physics

phys·i·co- (fiz′i kō′) ⟦< PHYSICAL⟧ *combining form* physical, physical and *[physicochemical]*

phys·i·co·chem·i·cal (fiz′i kō′kem′i kəl) *adj.* ⟦prec. + CHEMICAL⟧ **1** of or pertaining to both physical and chemical properties, changes, and reactions **2** of or according to physical chemistry —**phys′i·co·chem′i·cal·ly** *adv.*

phys·ics (fiz′iks) *n.* ⟦transl. of L *physica,* physics < Gr *(ta) physika* (lit., natural things), name given to the physical treatises of ARISTOTLE: see PHYSIC⟧ **1** [Obs.] natural philosophy **2** *a)* the science dealing with the properties, changes, interactions, etc. of matter and energy in which energy is considered to be continuous (**classical physics**), including electricity, heat, optics, mechanics, etc., and now also dealing with the atomic scale of nature in which energy is considered to be discrete (**quantum physics**), including such branches as atomic, nuclear, and solid-state physics *b)* a specific system of physics **3** a book or treatise on any of these —*pl.n.* physical properties or processes [the *physics* of flight]

phys·i·o- (fiz′ē ō, -ə) ⟦< Gr *physis,* nature: see PHYSIC⟧ *combining form* **1** nature; natural *[physiography]* **2** physical *[physiology, physiatrics]* Also, before a vowel, **phys·i-**

phys·i·o·crat (fiz′ē ə krat′) *n.* ⟦Fr *physiocrate:* see prec. & -CRAT⟧ a believer in the 18th-cent. French economic theory that land and its products are the only true sources of wealth and hence the only logical basis of revenue, and that freedom of opportunity and trade and security of person and property are essential to prosperity —**phys′i·o·crat′ic** *adj.*

phys·i·og·no·my (fiz′ē äg′nə mē; *chiefly Brit,* -än′ə mē) *n., pl.* **-no·mies** ⟦ME *fisonomie* < MFr *phisonomie* < ML *physonomia* < Gr *physiognōmonia* < *physis,* nature (see PHYSIC) + *gnōmōn,* one who knows: see GNOMON⟧ **1** the practice of trying to judge character and mental qualities by observation of bodily, esp. facial, features **2** the facial features and expression of a person, esp. when regarded as indicative of character **3** apparent characteristics; outward features or appearance —*SYN.* FACE —**phys′i·og·nom′ic** (-äg näm′ik, -ə näm′-) *adj.,* **phys′i·og·nom′i·cal** —**phys′i·og·nom′i·cal·ly** *adv.* —**phys′i·og′no·mist** *n.*

phys·i·og·ra·phy (fiz′ē äg′rə fē) *n.* ⟦PHYSIO- + -GRAPHY⟧ **1** a description of the features and phenomena of nature **2** PHYSICAL GEOGRAPHY **3** GEOMORPHOLOGY —**phys′i·og′ra·pher** *n.* —**phys′i·o·graph′ic** (-ə graf′ik) *adj.,* **phys′i·o·graph′i·cal**

physiol *abbrev.* **1** physiological **2** physiology

phys·i·o·log·i·cal (fiz′ē ə läj′i kəl) *adj.* **1** of physiology **2** characteristic of or promoting normal, or healthy, functioning Also **phys′i·o·log′ic** —**phys′i·o·log′i·cal·ly** *adv.*

physiological saline *Biochem.* a salt solution that has the same osmotic pressure as that found in the blood or tissues

phys·i·ol·o·gy (fiz′ē äl′ə jē) *n.* ⟦Fr *physiologie* < L *physiologia* < Gr: see PHYSIO- & -LOGY⟧ **1** the branch of biology dealing with the functions and vital processes of living organisms or their parts and organs **2** the functions and vital processes, collectively (of an organism, or of an organ or system of organs) —**phys′i·ol′o·gist** *n.*

phys·i·o·ther·a·py (fiz′ē ō′ther′ə pē) *n.* PHYSICAL THERAPY —**phys′i·o·ther′a·pist** *n.*

phy·sique (fi zēk′) *n.* ⟦Fr: see PHYSIC⟧ the structure, constitution, strength, form, or appearance of the body

phy·so·stig·mine (fī′sō stig′mēn′, -min) *n.* ⟦< ModL *Physostigma,* name of the genus including the Calabar bean < Gr *physa,* a bellows (< IE *phus-, var. of *pu-, *phu-, to blow > L *pustula*) + *stigma,* a prick (see STICK) + -INE[3]⟧ a colorless or pinkish crystalline alkaloid, $C_{15}H_{21}N_3O_2$, extracted from the Calabar bean, used in medicine for stimulating intestinal muscles, contracting the pupils of the eyes, etc.

phy·sos·to·mous (fī säs′tə məs) *adj.* ⟦< Gr *physa* (see prec.) + -STOMOUS⟧ *Zool.* having the air bladder connected to the digestive tract by a tube, as certain fishes: also **phy·so·stom·a·tous** (fī′sō stäm′ə təs)

-phyte (fīt) ⟦< Gr *phyton,* a plant, akin to *phyein,* to grow: see BE⟧ *combining form forming nouns* **1** a plant growing in a (specified) way or place *[microphyte, sporophyte, epiphyte]* **2** *Med.* a (specified kind of) growth *[osteophyte]*

phy·tin (fī′tin) *n.* ⟦< Gr *phyton* (see prec.) + -IN[1]⟧ a calcium-magnesium salt derived from various seeds, potatoes, etc., and used as a dietary calcium supplement and in the manufacture of inositol

phy·to- (fīt′ō, -ə) ⟦< Gr *phyton:* see -PHYTE⟧ *combining form* plant, flora, vegetation *[phytogenesis, phytosociology]*: also, before a vowel, **phyt-**

phy·to·a·lex·in (fīt′ō ə lek′sin) *n.* ⟦< prec. + Gr *alexein,* to defend⟧ an antibiotic produced by a plant in response to the intrusion of a disease-producing agent, esp. a fungus

phy·to·chem·i·cal (-kem′i kəl) *n.* any of certain usually brightly colored substances produced by plants, as lycopene, carotene, and lutein (xanthophyll), now thought to assist in boosting the immune system, preventing certain cancers, etc.

phy·to·chem·is·try (-kem′is trē) *n.* the branch of chemistry dealing with the chemical processes associated with plant life and the chemical compounds produced by plants

phy·to·chrome (fīt′ō krōm′) ***n.*** ⟦PHYTO- + -CHROME⟧ a bluish-green plant protein that, in response to variations in red light, regulates the growth of plants

phy·to·flag·el·late (fīt′ō flaj′ə lit, -lāt′) ***n.*** ⟦PHYTO- + FLAGELLATE⟧ a flagellated microorganism with plantlike characteristics, as cell walls and chlorophyll

phy·to·gen·e·sis (fīt′ō jen′ə sis) ***n.*** ⟦PHYTO- + -GENESIS⟧ the science of the origin and development of plants —**phy′to·ge·net′ic** (-jə net′ik) ***adj.***, **phy′to·ge·net′i·cal**

phy·to·gen·ic (fīt′ō jen′ik) ***adj.*** of plant origin, as peat or coal: also **phy·tog·e·nous** (fī täj′ə nəs)

phy·to·ge·og·ra·phy (fīt′ō jē äg′rə fē) ***n.*** the geography of the distribution of plant life

phy·tog·ra·phy (fī täg′rə fē) ***n.*** ⟦ModL *phytographia:* see PHYTO- & -GRAPHY⟧ the branch of botany dealing with the description of plants

phy·to·he·mag·glu·ti·nin (fīt′ō hē′mə glo͞ot′'n in′) ***n.*** ⟦PHYTO- + HEMAGGLUTININ⟧ a lectin, obtained from the red kidney bean, that binds to the membranes of T cells and stimulates metabolic activity, cell division, etc.

phy·to·hor·mone (fīt′ō hôr′mōn′) ***n.*** PLANT HORMONE

phy·to·lith (fīt′ō lith′) ***n.*** ⟦PHYTO- + -LITH⟧ a small opaline rock consisting chiefly of fossil plant remains

phy·tol·o·gy (fī täl′ə jē) ***n.*** ⟦ModL *phytologia:* see PHYTO- & -LOGY⟧ *former term for* BOTANY —**phy′to·log′ic** (-tō läj′ik) ***adj.***, **phy′to·log′i·cal**

phy·to·pa·thol·o·gy (fīt′ō pa thäl′ə jē) ***n.*** ⟦PHYTO- + PATHOLOGY⟧ the study of plant diseases and their control —**phy′to·path′o·log′ic** (-path′ə läj′ik) ***adj.***, **phy′to·path′o·log′i·cal**

phy·toph·a·gous (fī täf′ə gəs) ***adj.*** ⟦PHYTO- + -PHAGOUS⟧ *Zool.* feeding on plants; herbivorous

phy·to·plank·ton (fīt′ō plaŋk′tən) ***n.*** ⟦PHYTO- + PLANKTON⟧ plankton consisting of plants and algae —**phy′to·plank·ton′ic** (-tän′ik) ***adj.***

phy·to·so·ci·ol·o·gy (-sō′sē äl′ə jē, -shē-) ***n.*** ⟦PHYTO- + SOCIOLOGY⟧ a division of ecology concerned particularly with the origin, composition, classification, distribution, etc. of plant communities

phy·tos·ter·ol (fī täs′tər ôl′, -ōl′) ***n.*** ⟦PHYTO- + STEROL⟧ **1** any of several steroidal alcohols found in plants **2** an isomer of cholesterol found in plants

phy·to·tox·ic (fīt′ō täk′sik) ***adj.*** toxic to plants —**phy′to·tox·ic′i·ty** (-täk sis′ə tē) ***n.***

☆**phy·to·tron** (fīt′ō trän′) ***n.*** ⟦PHYTO- + -TRON⟧ any of various chambers, etc. designed to provide a controlled environment for the study of plant growth

pi[1] (pī) ***n.***, *pl.* **pies** ⟦see PIE[2]⟧ **1** a mixed, disordered collection of printing type **2** any jumble or mixture —***vt.*** **pied**, **pie′ing** or **pi′ing** to make jumbled; mix up (type)

pi[2] (pī) ***n.*** ⟦Gr *pi,* earlier *pei* < Sem, as in Heb *pi*⟧ **1** the sixteenth letter of the Greek alphabet (Π, π) **2** *a)* the symbol (π) designating the ratio of the circumference of a circle to its diameter *b)* the ratio itself, equal to 3.14159265+: often approximated as $^{22}/_{7}$

PI *abbrev.* [Slang] private investigator

Pia·cen·za (pyä chen′tsä) commune in N Italy, in Emilia-Romagna, on the Po River

pi·ac·u·lar (pī ak′yo͞o lər, -yə-) ***adj.*** ⟦L *piacularis* < *piaculum,* expiatory sacrifice < *piare,* to appease, expiate; akin to *pius,* PIOUS⟧ **1** making atonement; expiatory **2** calling for expiation or atonement; sinful; wicked

Pi·af (pē′äf′; *Fr* pyȧf), **É·dith** (*Fr* ā dēt′) (born *Édith Giovanna Gassion*) 1915-63; Fr. singer of popular ballads

piaffe (pyaf) ***n.*** ⟦Fr < *piaffer,* to strut, paw the ground, prob. of echoic orig.⟧ a movement in horsemanship in which the animal executes the motions of a slow trot in place —***vt.*** **piaffed**, **piaff′ing** to perform the piaffe

Pia·get (pyä zhā′; *Fr* pyȧ zhe′), **Jean** (zhän) 1896-1980; Swiss psychologist & philosopher

pi·al (pī′əl) ***adj.*** of the pia mater

pi·a ma·ter (pī′ə māt′ər) ⟦ME < ML (lit., gentle mother < fem. of L *pius,* tender, PIOUS + *mater,* MOTHER[1]): used as transl. of Ar *al 'umm al raqīqa*⟧ the vascular membrane immediately enveloping the brain and spinal cord and surrounded by the arachnoid and dura mater

pi·an·ism (pē′ə niz′əm, pē an′iz′əm) ***n.*** the art, technique, or performance of a pianist —**pi′a·nis′tic** ***adj.***

pi·a·nis·si·mo (pē′ə nis′i mō′; *It* pyä nēs′sē mô′) [*also in italics*] *Music* ***adj., adv.*** ⟦It, superl. of *piano:* see PIANO[1], ***adj., adv.***⟧ very soft(ly): often used as a musical direction: opposed to FORTISSIMO —***n.***, *pl.* **-mos′** or It. ***pia·nis′si·mi′*** (-mē′) a pianissimo passage

pi·an·ist (pē′ə nist, pē an′ist) ***n.*** ⟦Fr *pianiste*⟧ a person who plays the piano, esp. a skilled or professional performer

pi·an·o[1] (pē ä′nō, -an′ō) [*also in italics*] *Music* ***adj., adv.*** ⟦It, soft, smooth < L *planus,* smooth, PLANE[2]⟧ soft(ly): often used as a musical direction: opposed to FORTE[2] —***n.***, *pl.* **-an′os** a passage to be performed piano

pi·a·no[2] (pē an′ō) ***n.***, *pl.* **-nos** ⟦It, contr. < *pianoforte*⟧ a large keyboard instrument, each key of which operates a small, felt-covered hammer that strikes and vibrates a corresponding wire or set of wires stretched on a metal frame that is enclosed in a wooden case of various forms: the wires typically produce tones ranging over seven octaves

piano bar a cocktail lounge having a counter and chairs built around a piano at which a musician plays

pi·an·o·for·te (pē an′ō fôrt′, pē an′ō fôr′tā) ***n.*** ⟦It < *piano e forte,* lit., soft and loud: term used (*c.* 1710) by its inventor, *B. Cristofori* (1655-1731), of Padua < *piano* (see PIANO[1]) + *forte,* loud, strong (< L *fortis:* see FORT[1]) from its gradation of tone in contrast with the harpsichord⟧ PIANO[2]

pi·as·sa·va (pē′ə sä′və) ***n.*** ⟦Port *piassaba* < Tupí *piaçába,* a plant name⟧ **1** a stiff, elastic fiber obtained from any of various palms and used in making brushes, brooms, etc. **2** a palm yielding piassava; esp., any of several Brazilian palms (as *Leopoldinia piassaba* and *Attalea funifera*)

pi·as·ter (pē as′tər) ***n.*** ⟦Fr *piastre* < It *piastra,* thin plate of metal, dollar, ult. < L *emplastrum:* see PLASTER⟧ **1** [Obs.] the Spanish dollar **2** a monetary unit equal to $^{1}/_{100}$ of a pound in Egypt, Lebanon, and Syria **3** a former monetary unit of Sudan, equal to $^{1}/_{100}$ of a dinar **4** a former monetary unit of Turkey, equal to $^{1}/_{100}$ of a lira

Piau·í (pyou ē′) state of NE Brazil: 97,444 sq mi (252,379 sq km); cap. Teresina

pi·az·za (pē az′ə, -ä′zə; -at′sə, -ät′sə; *for 1, usually* pē ät′sə *or It* pyät′tsä) ***n.***, *pl.* **-zas** or It. **piaz′ze** (-tse) ⟦It < L *platea:* see PLACE⟧ **1** in Italy, an open public square, esp. one surrounded by buildings **2** a covered gallery or arcade ☆**3** [New England & South] a large, covered porch

☆**pi·bal** (pī′bəl) ***n.*** **1** *short for* PILOT BALLOON **2** observation by means of a pilot balloon

pi·broch (pē′bräk′; *Scot* pē′bräkh′) ***n.*** ⟦Gael *piobaireachd,* pipe music < *piobair,* piper < *piob* (< PIPE) a pipe, bagpipe⟧ a piece of music for the bagpipe, consisting of a theme with variations, usually martial but sometimes dirgelike

pi·ca[1] (pī′kə) ***n.*** ⟦< ? ML(Ec), a directory, church manual (see PIE[4]): ? in reference to type used in printing it⟧ **1** a size of type, 12 point **2** the height of this type, about $^{1}/_{6}$ inch: used as a typographical unit of measure **3** a size of type for typewriters, measuring 10 characters to the linear inch

pi·ca[2] (pī′kə) ***n.*** ⟦ModL < L, magpie: see PIE[3]⟧ an abnormal craving to eat substances not fit for food, as clay or paint

pi·ca·dil·lo (pē′kä dē′ō) ***n.*** ⟦AmSp < *picado,* hash < pp. of Sp *picar,* to pierce, mince⟧ a Latin American, esp. Mexican, dish consisting of spiced ground beef usually served over rice

pic·a·dor (pik′ə dôr′; *Sp* pē′kä thôr′) ***n.***, *pl.* **-dors′** or Sp. **-do′res** (-thô′res) ⟦Sp < *picar,* to prick < VL **piccare* < **piccus,* for L *picus,* woodpecker: see PIE[3]⟧ in bullfighting, any of the horsemen who weaken the neck muscles of the bull by pricking with a lance

pi·can·te (pē kän′tā) ***adj.*** ⟦Sp⟧ **1** hot and spicy; esp., served or prepared with a spicy sauce **2** designating such a sauce Term used in Spanish and Latin American cooking

Pic·ar·dy (pik′ər dē) **1** historical region of N France **2** metropolitan region of modern N France: 7,490 sq mi (19,399 sq km); chief city, Amiens Fr. name **Pi·car·die** (pē kȧr dē′)

pic·a·resque (pik′ə resk′) ***adj.*** ⟦Sp *picaresco* < *pícaro,* rascal, orig. knavish, vile⟧ **1** of, like, or having to do with sharp-witted vagabonds or rogues **2** designating or characteristic of a kind of fiction that originated in Spain and deals episodically with the adventures of a hero who is or resembles such a vagabond or rogue

pi·ca·ro (pē′kä rō′) ***n.***, *pl.* **-ros′** ⟦see prec.⟧ an adventurous rogue or vagabond

pic·a·roon (pik′ə ro͞on′) ***n.*** ⟦Sp *picarón* < *pícaro:* see PICARESQUE⟧ **1** PICARO **2** a pirate or pirate ship

Pi·cas·so (pi kä′sō), **Pa·blo** (pä′blō) (born *Pablo Ruiz y Picasso*) 1881-1973; Sp. painter & sculptor in France

☆**pic·a·yune** (pik′ə yo͞on′, pik′ə yo͞on′) ***n.*** ⟦Fr *picaillon,* small coin, halfpenny < Prov *picaioun* < *picaio,* money, prob. < *pica,* to ring, jingle, strike < VL **piccare:* see PICADOR⟧ **1** a coin of small value, as a former Spanish halfreal of Louisiana **2** anything trivial —***adj.*** trivial or petty; small or small-minded: also **pic′a·yun′ish**

Pic·ca·dil·ly (pik′ə dil′ē) street in London, England: traditional center of fashionable shops, clubs, & hotels

pic·ca·lil·li (pik′ə lil′ē) ***n.*** ⟦prob. < PICKLE: formerly also *piccalillo*⟧ a relish, orig. East Indian, of chopped vegetables, mustard, vinegar, and hot spices

pic·ca·nin·ny (pik′ə nin′ē) ***n.***, *pl.* **-nies** [Dial. or Old Slang] *alt. sp. of* PICKANINNY: now an offensive term of contempt

Pic·card (pi kärd′; *Fr* pē kȧr′), **Au·guste** (ô güst′) 1884-1962; Swiss physicist in Belgium: known for balloon ascents into the stratosphere & descents in a bathyscaph

pic·ca·ta (pi kät′ə, pē-) ***adj.*** designating a dish consisting of a thin, breaded and sautéed slice of veal, chicken, etc. with a sauce of lemon, white wine, and butter [*veal piccata, chicken piccata*]

pic·co·lo (pik′ə lō′) ***n.***, *pl.* **-los′** ⟦It, small⟧ a small instrument of the flute family, pitched an octave above the ordinary flute —***adj.*** small; little; diminutive —**pic′co·lo′ist** ***n.***

pice (pīs) ***n.***, *pl.* **pice** ⟦Hindi *paisā*⟧ **1** a former monetary unit of India, equal to $^{1}/_{64}$ of a rupee **2** PAISA

pic·e·ous (pis′ē əs, pī′sē-) ***adj.*** ⟦L *piceus* < *pix,* PITCH[1]⟧ **1** of or like pitch **2** *Zool.* black as pitch

pich·i·ci·e·go (pich′i sē ā′gō) ***n.***, *pl.* **-gos** ⟦AmSp, prob. < Araucanian *pichi,* small + Sp *ciego* (< L *caecus*), blind⟧ either of two South American armadillos having soft hair on the lower body, esp., the smallest armadillo (*Chlamyphorus truncatus*): also **pich′i·ci·a′go** (-ā′gō, -ä′gō)

pic·i·form (pi′sə fôrm′) ***adj.*** ⟦ModL *piciformis* < L *picus,* woodpecker: see PIE[3]⟧ of, or having the nature of, an order (Piciformes) of birds, including woodpeckers and toucans, having two front and two hind toes for clinging to vertical surfaces

pick[1] (pik) ***vt.*** ⟦ME *pykken,* var. of *picchen,* to PITCH[2]⟧ *Weaving* to throw (a shuttle) —*n.* 1 one passage or throw of the shuttle of a loom 2 one of the weft threads, or filling yarns

pick² (pik) *n.* ⟦ME *pike* < OE *pic,* PIKE⁴⟧ 1 a heavy tool used as in breaking up soil or rock: the metal head is long, narrow, and slightly curved, and pointed at one or both ends, with a wooden handle fitted into its center 2 any of several pointed tools or instruments for picking: usually in comb. [*toothpick*] 3 PLECTRUM 4 *a)* a slender, plastic pin used to hold hair rollers in place ☆*b)* a comb with widely spaced teeth, used for fine, curly hair

pick³ (pik) *vt.* ⟦ME *picken,* akin to MDu *picken, pecken,* ON *pikka;* prob. infl. by OFr *piquer,* to pierce < *pic,* PIKE²⟧ 1 to break up, pierce, or dig up (soil, rock, etc.) with something sharply pointed; use a pick on 2 to make or form (a hole) with something pointed 3 *a)* to dig, probe, or scratch at with the fingers or with something pointed in an attempt to remove *b)* to clear something from (the teeth) in this way 4 to remove by pulling as with the fingers; specif., to pluck or gather (flowers, berries, etc.) 5 to clear (something) in this way; specif., *a)* to prepare (a fowl) by removing the feathers *b)* to remove the fruit from (a tree, orchard, etc.) 6 *a)* to take up (food, etc.) in small pieces, as a bird with its bill; peck *b)* to eat sparingly or daintily 7 to pull (fibers, rags, etc.) apart 8 to choose; select; cull 9 to look for and find excuse or occasion for (a quarrel or fight) 10 to look for purposefully and find [to *pick* flaws] ☆11 *a)* to pluck (the strings on a guitar, banjo, etc.) *b)* to play (a guitar, banjo, etc.) in this way 12 to open (a lock) as with a wire instead of a key, esp. in a stealthy manner 13 to steal from (another's pocket, purse, etc.) —*vi.* 1 to eat sparingly or fussily 2 to thieve or pilfer 3 to use a pick 4 to gather growing berries, flowers, etc. 5 to be picked [grapes *pick* easily] 6 to select or choose, esp. in a careful or fussy manner ☆7 to play the guitar, banjo, etc. —*n.* 1 the act of picking; stroke or blow with something pointed 2 *a)* the act or right of choosing *b)* the person or thing chosen; choice 3 the best or most desirable one or ones 4 the amount of a crop picked at one time ☆5 *Basketball* SCREEN (*n.* 9) —**pick and choose** to choose or select carefully —**pick apart** (or **to pieces**) 1 to separate or tear into many parts 2 to find flaws in by examining critically —**pick at** 1 to eat small portions of, esp. in a dainty or fussy manner 2 [Informal] to nag at; find fault with 3 to toy or meddle with; finger —**pick off** 1 to remove by picking or plucking 2 to hit with a carefully aimed shot ☆3 *Baseball* to throw out (a base runner taking a lead) by means of a throw from the pitcher or catcher before or after a pitch —**pick on** 1 to choose; select 2 [Informal] to single out as for abuse or criticism; annoy; tease —**pick one's way** to progress slowly, choosing each move with care —**pick out** 1 to choose; select 2 to single out from or recognize among a group; distinguish 3 to make out (meaning or sense) 4 to play (a tune) note by note, as on a piano —**pick over** to examine (a number of things) item by item; sort out —**pick up** 1 to grasp and raise or lift; take up 2 to get, gain, find, or learn, esp. by chance or in a casual manner 3 to stop for and take or bring along 4 to take into custody; arrest 5 to accelerate; gain (speed) 6 to regain (health, power, efficiency, etc.); improve 7 to resume (an activity) after a pause 8 *a)* to see, hear, discern, etc. *b)* to receive or be in range to receive (a radio or TV transmission, esp. a distant or weak one) 9 *a)* to find and travel along (a route or trail) *b)* to find and follow [the dog *picked up* the scent] ☆10 to make neat; tidy up 11 to take (a bill) with the intention of paying it 12 [Informal] to become acquainted with casually or informally, often with hope of sexual activity 13 [Informal] to answer or respond to a telephone call —☆**pick up on** [Informal] 1 to become aware of, understand, appreciate, etc. 2 to start to do or use

pick·a·back (pik′ə bak′) *adv., adj., vt.* ⟦var. of *pickapack, pickpack,* redupl. of PACK¹⟧ PIGGYBACK

pick·a·nin·ny (pik′ə nin′ē) *n., pl.* **-nies** ⟦ult. < Sp *pequeño* or Port *pequeno*⟧ [Dial. or Old Slang] a black child: now an offensive term of contempt

pick·ax or **pick·axe** (pik′aks′) *n.* ⟦altered (infl. by AX¹) < ME *pikois* < OFr *picquois,* pickax < *pic,* PIKE²⟧ a pick with a point at one end of the head and a chisel-like edge at the other —*vt., vi.* **-axed′, -ax′ing** to use a pickax (on)

picked¹ (pikt) *adj.* ⟦< PICK³⟧ 1 selected with care [*picked* men] 2 gathered from plants rather than from the ground, as berries

pick·ed² (pik′id, pikt) *adj.* ⟦ME < PICK²⟧ [Now Chiefly Dial.] having a sharp end; pointed

pick·er¹ (pik′ər) *n.* a person or thing that picks; specif., ☆*a)* [Informal] a musician who plays guitar, banjo, etc., esp. in country music *b)* a machine for picking fibers

pick·er² (pik′ər) *n.* ⟦PICK¹ + -ER⟧ *Weaving* a device that throws the shuttle through the warp

pick·er·el (pik′ər əl) *n., pl.* **-el** or **-els** ⟦ME < *pik,* PIKE³ + *-rel,* dim. suffix⟧ 1 any of various small, North American pike fishes (genus *Esox*) 2 WALLEYE (sense 5*b*) 3 [Brit.] a young pike

pick·er·el·weed (pik′ər əl wēd′) *n.* ☆any of a genus (*Pontederia*) of North American aquatic plants of the pickerelweed family, esp. a species (*P. cordata*) with arrow-shaped leaves and spikes of blue-violet flowers, found in shallow waters —*adj.* designating a family (Pontederiaceae, order Liliales) of monocotyledonous, freshwater plants, including the water hyacinth

Pick·er·ing (pik′ər iŋ), **Edward Charles** 1846-1919; U.S. astronomer & physicist

pick·et (pik′it) *n.* ⟦Fr *piquet* < *piquer,* to pierce < *pic,* PIKE²⟧ 1 a stake or slat, usually pointed, used as an upright in a fence, a hitching post for animals, a marker, etc. 2 a group of soldiers or a single soldier stationed, usually at an outpost, to guard a body of troops from surprise attack 3 a ship or airplane that patrols a defense perimeter 4 a person, as a member of a labor union on strike, stationed outside a factory, store, or public building, often carrying a sign, to demonstrate opposition to certain views or practices, keep strikebreakers from entering, or dissuade people from buying —*vt.* 1 to enclose, shut in, or protect with a picket fence or palisade 2 to hitch (an animal) to a picket 3 *a)* to post as a military picket *b)* to guard (a body of troops) with a picket 4 to place pickets, or serve as a picket, at (a factory, etc.) —*vi.* to serve as a PICKET (sense 4) —**pick′et·er** *n.*

☆**picket fence** a fence made of upright pales or stakes

picket line a line or cordon of people serving as pickets

Pick·ett (pik′it), **George Edward** 1825-75; Confederate general

pick·ing (pik′iŋ) *n.* 1 the act of a person who picks 2 [*usually pl.*] something that is or may be picked, or the amount of this; specif., *a)* small scraps or remains that may be gleaned *b)* something gotten by effort, often in a dishonest way; returns or spoils

pick·le (pik′əl) *n.* ⟦ME *pikil* < MDu *pekel* < ? *picken,* to prick, in sense "that which pricks, or is piquant"⟧ 1 any brine, vinegar, or spicy solution used to preserve or marinate food 2 a cucumber preserved in such a solution 3 a chemical bath used to clear metal of scale, preserve wood, etc. 4 [Informal] an awkward or difficult situation; plight —*vt.* **-led, -ling** to treat with or preserve in a pickle solution —*SYN.* PREDICAMENT

pick·led (pik′əld) *adj.* [Slang] intoxicated; drunk

pick·lock (pik′läk′) *n.* 1 a person, esp. a thief, who picks locks 2 an instrument for picking locks

☆**pick-me-up** (pik′mē up′) *n.* [Informal] 1 an alcoholic drink taken to raise one's spirits 2 anything that stimulates, invigorates, refreshes, heartens, etc.

pick·off (pik′ôf′) ☆*n.* ☆*Baseball* a play in which a base runner is picked off: see PICK OFF at PICK³

pick·pock·et (pik′päk′it) *n.* a thief who steals from the pockets of persons, as in crowds

Pick's disease (piks) ⟦after A. *Pick* (1851-1924), Czech physician⟧ a condition characterized by progressive deterioration of the brain with atrophy of the cerebral cortex, esp. the frontal lobes, and evidenced in loss of memory and emotional instability

pick·up (pik′up′) *n.* 1 the act of picking up, as in fielding a rapidly rolling baseball 2 the process or power of increasing in speed; acceleration ☆3 a small, open truck with low sides, for hauling light loads: in full **pickup truck** 4 [Informal] *a)* the act of making the acquaintance of a stranger in a quick and flirtatious way with the hope of a romantic or sexual encounter *b)* a person with whom such an acquaintance is formed ☆5 [Informal] improvement or recovery, as in trade ☆6 [Informal] *a)* a stimulant; bracer *b)* stimulation 7 *a)* in an electric phonograph, a device that produces audio-frequency currents from the vibrations of a needle or stylus moving in a record groove *b)* the pivoted arm holding this device 8 *a)* the reception of sound or light for conversion into electrical energy in the transmitter *b)* the apparatus used for this *c)* any place outside a studio where a broadcast originates *d)* the electrical system connecting this place to the broadcasting station 9 a small microphone attached to a vibrating surface, as in an electric guitar —*adj.* [Informal] 1 assembled informally for a single engagement, contest, etc. [a *pickup* jazz band or baseball team] 2 of a game or job performed or played by those assembled in this way 3 designating a window at a restaurant where prepared food can be bought by customers in cars

Pick·wick (pik′wik), **Mr. (Samuel)** the naive, benevolent president of the Pickwick Club in Dickens' *Pickwick Papers* (1836)

pick·wick·i·an (pik wik′ē ən) *adj.* 1 of or characteristic of Mr. Pickwick or the Pickwick Club 2 special, unusual, or esoteric: said of a meaning of a word or phrase

☆**pick·y** (pik′ē) *adj.* **pick′i·er, pick′i·est** ⟦PICK³ + -Y²⟧ [Informal] overly fastidious or exacting; fussy —**pick′i·ness** *n.*

pic·lo·ram (pik′lə ram′, pī′klə-) *n.* ⟦PIC(OLINE) + (CH)LOR(O)- (sense 2) + AM(INE)⟧ an extremely toxic herbicide and defoliant, $C_6H_3Cl_3N_2O_2$, that persists in the soil and is slow to break down

pic·nic (pik′nik) *n.* ⟦Fr *pique-nique,* prob. < *piquer,* to pick + *nique,* a trifle < OFr *niquier,* to nod⟧ 1 a pleasure outing at which a meal is eaten outdoors ☆2 a shoulder cut of pork, cured like ham: also **picnic ham** or **picnic shoulder** 3 [Slang] *a)* a pleasant experience *b)* an easy task —*vi.* **-nicked, -nick·ing** to hold or attend a picnic —**pic′nick·er** *n.*

pi·co- (pē′kō, pī′-; -kə) ⟦prob. < It *piccolo,* small⟧ *combining form* one trillionth part of; the factor 10^{-12} [*picometer*]

pi·co·cu·rie (pē′kō kyŏŏr′ē, pī′-) *n.* one trillionth of a curie: abbrev. *pCi*

Pi·co del·la Mi·ran·do·la (pē′kō del′ə mə ran′dō lə; *It* pē′kô del′lä mē rän′dô lä′), Count **Gio·van·ni** (jō vän′nē) 1463-94; It. humanist

pi·co·gram (pē′kə gram′, pī′-) *n.* one trillionth of a gram: abbrev. *pg*

pic·o·line (pik′ō lēn′, -lin) *n.* ⟦< L *pix* (gen. *picis*), PITCH¹ + -OL² + -INE³⟧ any of three isomeric, colorless, strong-smelling, liquid bases, $C_5H_4(CH_3)N$, found in the oil produced by the dry distillation of bones and coal: used in insecticides, pharmaceuticals, resins, etc.

pi·co·me·ter (pē′kə mēt′ər, pī′-) *n.* one trillionth of a meter: abbrev. *pm:* Brit. sp. **pi′co·me′tre**

pi·cor·na·vi·rus (pi kôr′nə vī′rəs) *n.* ⟦PICO-, very small (as used here) + RNA + VIRUS⟧ any of a large family (Picornaviridae) of RNA viruses affecting animals, including the enteroviruses and rhinoviruses

pi·co·sec·ond (pē′kə sek′ənd, pī′-) *n.* one trillionth of a second

pi·cot (pē′kō) *n., pl.* **-cots** ⟦Fr < OFr, dim. of *pic,* a point: see PIKE²⟧ any of a number of small, threadlike loops forming an ornamental edging on lace, ribbon, etc. —*vt., vi.* **-coted** (-kōd), **-cot·ing** (-kō iŋ) to edge with such loops

pic·o·tee (pik′ə tē′, pik′ə tē′) *n.* ⟦Fr *picoté,* pp. of *picoter,* to mark with dots or pricks < *picot:* see prec.⟧ a variety of carnation whose light-colored petals are bordered with another, usually darker, color

pic·rate (pik′rāt′) ***n.*** a salt or ester of picric acid, usually highly explosive and sensitive to shock

pic·ric acid (pik′rik) ⟦Fr *picrique:* see PICRO- & -IC⟧ a poisonous, yellow, crystalline, bitter acid, $C_6H_2(NO_2)_3OH$, used in making dyes and explosives and in analytical chemistry

pic·rite (pik′rīt′) ***n.*** ⟦Fr: see fol. & -ITE[1]⟧ a dark, olivine-rich igneous rock —**pic·rit′ic** (-rit′ik) ***adj.***

pic·ro- (pik′rō, -rə) ⟦Fr < Gr *pikros,* bitter < IE base *peig-, *peik-,* colorful, sharp > L *pingere,* to PAINT⟧ *combining form* **1** bitter *[picrotoxin]* **2** picric acid Also, before a vowel, **picr-**

pic·ro·tox·in (pik′rō täk′sin) ***n.*** ⟦prec. + TOXIN⟧ a white, bitter, poisonous, crystalline compound, $C_{30}H_{34}O_{13}$, resembling strychnine in its properties: used as a stimulant in cases of barbiturate poisoning

Pict (pikt) ***n.*** ⟦LME *Pictes,* pl. < LL *Picti* (lit. ? painted people) > OE *Peohtas*⟧ a member of an ancient people of Great Britain that was driven into Scotland by the Britons and the Romans

Pict·ish (pik′tish) ***adj.*** of the Picts or their language or culture —***n.*** the language of the Picts: no clear relationship to any other language has been established

pic·to·gram (pik′tə gram′) ***n.*** a pictograph

pic·to·graph (pik′tə graf′) ***n.*** ⟦< L *pictus* (see PICTURE) + -GRAPH⟧ **1** a picture or picturelike symbol representing an idea, as in primitive writing; hieroglyph **2** PICTOGRAPHY **3** a diagram or graph using pictured objects to convey ideas, information, etc. —**pic′to·graph′ic** ***adj.***

pic·tog·ra·phy (pik täg′rə fē) ***n.*** writing by the use of pictographs; picture writing

Pic·tor (pik′tər) ***n.*** ⟦L, painter: see fol.⟧ a S constellation between Carina and Dorado

pic·to·ri·al (pik tôr′ē əl) ***adj.*** ⟦LL *pictorius* < L *pictor,* painter < pp. of *pingere,* to PAINT⟧ **1** [Rare] of a painter or painting **2** of, containing, or expressed in pictures **3** evoking or suggesting a mental image or picture; vivid; graphic, as a description —☆***n.*** **1** a periodical featuring many pictures **2** a magazine FEATURE (*n.* 5) consisting mainly of pictures —**pic·to′ri·al·ly** ***adv.*** —**pic·to′ri·al·ize′** ***vt.*** **-ized′, -iz′ing** —**pic·to′ri·al·i·za′tion** ***n.***

pic·ture (pik′chər) ***n.*** ⟦ME *pycture* < L *pictura* < *pictus,* pp. of *pingere,* to PAINT⟧ **1** *a)* an image or likeness of an object, person, or scene produced on a flat surface, esp. by painting, drawing, or photography *b)* a printed reproduction of this *c)* an image captured by or with a camera *[tourists taking pictures]* **2** anything closely resembling or strikingly typifying something else; perfect likeness or image *[to be the picture of one's mother, the picture of health]* **3** anything regarded as having the compositional beauty of a painting or drawing **4** a mental image or impression; idea **5** a vivid or detailed description *[a picture of the times]* **6** all the facts or conditions of an event, collectively; situation **7** TABLEAU **8** FILM (*n.* 5) **9** the image or succession of images on a TV or computer screen, as in a telecast or webcast —***vt.*** **-tured, -tur·ing 1** to make a picture of by painting, drawing, photographing, etc. **2** to make visible; show clearly; reflect **3** to describe or explain **4** to form a mental picture or impression of; imagine —**in (or out of) the picture** considered (or not considered) as involved in a situation

picture book a book with pictures or illustrations and little or no text

pic·ture-book (pik′chər bo͝ok′) ***adj.*** so beautiful, neatly maintained, charming, etc. as to be a suitable subject for a book of pictures; picturesque *[a picture-book country inn]*

picture card FACE CARD

picture hat a woman's wide-brimmed hat with plumes, flowers, etc., like those seen in some famous paintings

pic·ture-per·fect (pik′chər pur′fikt) ***adj.*** perfect or flawless

☆**picture show** [Old-fashioned] a film or a theater where films are shown

pic·tur·esque (pik′chər esk′) ***adj.*** ⟦altered (by assoc. with PICTURE) < Fr *pittoresque* < It *pittoresco* < *pittore,* painter < L *pictor,* painter < pp. of *pingere,* to PAINT⟧ **1** like or suggesting a picture; specif., *a)* having a wild or natural beauty, as mountain scenery *b)* pleasantly unfamiliar or strange; quaint **2** suggesting or calling up a mental picture; striking; vivid *[a picturesque description]* —**pic′tur·esque′ly** ***adv.*** —**pic′tur·esque′ness** ***n.***

☆**picture tube** a cathode-ray tube in a TV receiver, monitor, etc., that produces visual images on its screen

picture window a large window, esp. in a living room, that seems to frame the outside view

picture writing 1 writing consisting of pictures or figures representing ideas **2** the pictures or figures so used; pictographs; hieroglyphics

pic·tur·ize (pik′chər īz′) ***vt.*** **-ized′, -iz′ing** to portray in a picture —**pic′tur·i·za′tion** ***n.***

pic·ul (pik′əl) ***n., pl.*** **-ul′** or **-uls′** ⟦< Malay (or Javanese) *pikul,* lit., a man's load < *pikul,* to carry over the shoulders⟧ a unit of weight equal to 100 catties, about 133 pounds (60 kilograms), used in various countries of Southeast Asia

PID (pē′ī′dē′) ***n.*** PELVIC INFLAMMATORY DISEASE

pid·dle (pid′'l) ***vi., vt.*** **-dled, -dling** ⟦prob. euphemistic dim. < base of PISS⟧ **1** to urinate: child's term **2** to dawdle or trifle: sometimes with *away [to piddle the time away]* —**pid′dler** ***n.***

pid·dling (pid′liŋ) ***adj.*** insignificant; trifling; petty

pid·dly (pid′lē, pid′'l ē) ***adj.*** PIDDLING

pid·dock (pid′ək) ***n.*** ⟦< ?⟧ any of a family (Pholadidae) of bivalve mollusks which bore holes in mud, peat, wood, clay, and soft rocks

pidg·in (pij′in) ***n.*** ⟦supposed Chin pronun. of BUSINESS⟧ **1** a mixed language, or jargon, incorporating the vocabulary of one or more languages with a very simplified form of the grammatical system of one of these and not used as the main language of any of its speakers **2** any of various such languages, as pidgin English or bêche-de-mer

pidgin English ⟦see prec.⟧ **1** a simplified form of English used by certain peoples of E Asia and the South Pacific in dealing with foreigners: there are two forms, Chinese pidgin and Melanesian pidgin, the former based on the syntax of Chinese, the latter on the syntax of certain aboriginal languages of Melanesia and N Australia **2** any pidgin based on English

pi-dog (pī′dôg′) ***n.*** ⟦prob. Anglo-Ind contr. of *pariah dog*⟧ a wild Asian dog, often roaming in packs in and around villages

pie[1] (pī) ***n.*** ⟦ME, akin ? to PIE[3]⟧ **1** a baked dish made with fruit, meat, etc., and having either an under crust, an upper crust, or both **2** a layer cake with a filling of custard, cream, jelly, etc. ☆**3** [Slang] *a)* something extremely good or easy *b)* political graft *c)* a total amount to be divided in shares —**(as) easy as pie** [Informal] extremely easy

pie[2] (pī) ***n., vt.*** ⟦< ? prec.⟧ *chiefly Brit. sp. of* PI[1]

pie[3] (pī) ***n.*** ⟦OFr < L *pica,* magpie, akin to *picus,* woodpecker < IE base **(s)piko-,* woodpecker > Ger *specht*⟧ MAGPIE

pie[4] (pī) ***n.*** ⟦transl. of ML(Ec) *pica,* prob. < or akin to prec.⟧ in England, a form or table of rules used before the Reformation in selecting the correct church service or office for the day

PIE *abbrev.* Proto-Indo-European

pie·bald (pī′bôld′) ***adj.*** ⟦PIE[3] + BALD⟧ covered with patches or spots of two colors, esp. with white and black —***n.*** a piebald horse or other animal

piece (pēs) ***n.*** ⟦ME *pece* < OFr < ML **pettia* < Celt **pett-* > Welsh *peth,* part, Bret *pez,* piece⟧ **1** a part or fragment broken or separated from the whole **2** a section, division, or quantity regarded as complete in itself and distinct from the whole of which it is a part **3** any single thing, amount, specimen, example, etc.; specif., *a)* an artistic work or composition, as of music, writing, painting, drama, etc. *b)* an article in a magazine, newspaper, etc. *c)* an action or its result *[a piece of nonsense, business, etc.] d)* a small firearm, as a pistol or rifle *e)* a coin or token *[a fifty-cent piece] f)* one of a set or class, as of silver, china, furniture, etc. *g)* a counter or man, as used in various games; specif., in chess, a chessman other than a pawn **4** the quantity or size, as of cloth or wallpaper, that is manufactured as a unit **5** an amount or unit of work constituting a single job **6** [Now Chiefly Dial.] an indefinite distance or duration; often, specif., a rather short one **7** [Now Chiefly Dial.] a person; individual ☆**8** [Slang] a financial interest; share **9** [Slang] *a)* a woman regarded as a sexual partner *b)* an instance of sexual intercourse: often regarded as vulgar: also [Vulgar Slang] **piece of ass** —***vt.*** **pieced, piec′ing 1** to add a piece or pieces to, as in repairing or enlarging *[to piece a pair of trousers]* **2** to join or unite —***vi.*** [Informal or Dial.] to eat a snack between meals —***SYN.*** PART[1] —**go (or fall) to pieces 1** to break into pieces; fall apart **2** to lose all self-control, morally or emotionally —**of a (or one) piece** of the same sort; alike; consistent (*with*) —**piece together** to join the pieces of, as in mending —☆**speak one's piece** to vent one's views or opinions —**piec′er** ***n.***

pièce de ré·sis·tance (pyes də rā zēs täns′) ⟦Fr⟧ **1** the principal dish of a meal **2** the main item or event in a series

piece-dyed (pēs′dīd′) ***adj.*** dyed after being woven or knitted: said of cloth

piece goods YARD GOODS

piece·meal (pēs′mēl′) ***adv.*** ⟦ME *pecemel* < *pece* (see PIECE) + *-mele:* see -MEAL⟧ **1** piece by piece; in small amounts or degrees **2** into pieces or parts —***adj.*** made or done in pieces or one piece at a time

piece of cake [Informal] a thing easy to do

piece of eight the obsolete Spanish and Spanish-American dollar, equal to eight reals

piece of work a person who is regarded as eccentric, difficult, etc.

piece·work (pēs′wurk′) ***n.*** work paid for at a fixed rate (**piece rate**) per piece of work done —**piece′work′er** ***n.***

pie chart ⟦so called from resemblance of the sectors to wedges into which a *pie* is cut for serving⟧ a graph in the form of a circle divided into sectors in which relative quantities are indicated by the proportionately different sizes of the sectors

pied (pīd) ***adj.*** ⟦ME *pyed,* orig., black and white like a magpie: see PIE[3]⟧ **1** covered with patches or spots of two or more colors; piebald; variegated **2** wearing a garment of this description

pied-à-terre (pyā tä ter′) ***n., pl.*** ***pied-à-terre*** ⟦Fr, lit., foot on the ground⟧ a lodging or dwelling, esp. one used only part time or temporarily

pied-billed grebe (pīd′bild′) a common American grebe (*Podilymbus podiceps*) with a black band around its bill, except in the winter

pied·mont (pēd′mänt′) ***adj.*** ⟦after *Piedmont,* Italy < L *Pedimontium* < *pes* (gen. *pedis*), FOOT + *mons* (gen. *montis*), MOUNT[1]⟧ at the base of a mountain or mountains *[a piedmont stream]* —***n.*** a piedmont area, plain, etc.

Pied·mont (pēd′mänt′) **1** hilly upland region of the E U.S., between the Atlantic coastal plain & the Appalachians, stretching from SE N.Y. to central Ala. **2** region of NW Italy, on the Swiss & French borders: 9,807 sq mi (25,400 sq km); chief city, Turin: It. name **Pie·mon·te** (pye môn′te)

Pied·mon·tese (pēd′män tēz′) ***adj.*** of Piedmont, Italy, or its people or culture —***n., pl.*** **-tese′** a person born or living in Piedmont, Italy

Pied Piper 1 *Gmc. Legend* a musician who rids Hamelin of its rats by leading them with his piping to the river, where they drown: in revenge for not being paid, he pipes the village children to a mountain, where they disappear: in full **Pied Piper of Hamelin 2** [*also* **p- p-**] a leader whom people willingly follow, often, specif., one who leads others into danger or trouble by means of elaborate, false promises

☆**pie-eyed** (pī′īd′) ***adj.*** [Slang] intoxicated; drunk

Pie·gan (pē′gən) ***n., pl.*** **-gans** or **-gan** a member of a subgroup of the Blackfoot Indians

☆**pie in the sky** [Slang] **1** a promise of benefits or a reward in an afterlife or in the remote future **2** an unrealistically Utopian plan or project

☆**pie·plant** (pī′plant′) ***n.*** ⟦PIE[1] + PLANT⟧ the rhubarb: so called from its use in pies

pier (pir) ***n.*** ⟦ME *per* < ML *pera,* ult. < ? or akin to L *petra,* stone < Gr, rock⟧ **1** a heavy structure supporting the spans of a bridge, esp. (as distinguished from an abutment), one supporting the adjacent ends of two center spans of a long bridge **2** a structure built out over the water and supported by pillars or piles: used as a landing place, pleasure pavilion, etc. **3** *Archit. a)* a heavy column, usually square, used to support weight, as at the end of an arch *b)* the part of a wall between windows or other openings *c)* a reinforcing part built out from the surface of a wall

pierce (pirs) ***vt.*** **pierced, pierc′ing** ⟦ME *percen* < OFr *percer* < VL **pertusiare* < L *pertusus,* pp. of *pertundere,* to thrust through < *per,* through + *tundere,* to strike < IE base **(s)teu-,* to push > STOCK⟧ **1** to pass into or through as a pointed instrument does; penetrate; stab **2** to affect sharply the senses or feelings of **3** to make a hole in or through; perforate; bore; specif., to make a hole in an earlobe, lip, nostril, or other part of the body for the purpose of inserting a ring, stud, or other ornament **4** to make (a hole), as by boring or stabbing **5** to force a way into or through; break through **6** to sound sharply through [a shriek *pierced* the air] **7** to penetrate with the sight or mind [to *pierce* a mystery] —***vi.*** to penetrate (*to, into,* or *through* something) —**pierc′er** ***n.*** —**pierc′ing·ly** ***adv.***

Pierce (pirs), **Franklin** 1804-69; 14th president of the U.S. (1853-57)

pierced (pirst) ***adj.*** **1** having a small hole made by piercing; specif., having such a hole in its lobe [*pierced* ears] **2** for wearing in a pierced ear [*pierced* earrings]

pierc·ing (pir′siŋ) ***n.*** **1** a hole pierced in an earlobe, nostril, or other part of the body for the purpose of inserting a ring, stud, or other ornament **2** an ornament worn in such a hole —***adj.*** that can pierce; specif., *a)* penetrating or sharp to the senses [a *piercing* wind, *piercing* cold, a *piercing* cry] *b)* caustic; cutting; sarcastic [*piercing* criticism] *c)* having or showing keen intelligence, perception, or judgment [a *piercing* wit, *piercing* eyes]

pier glass a tall mirror set in the pier, or wall section, between windows

Pi·er·i·a (pī ir′ē ə) ancient region of Macedonia, N Greece

Pi·er·i·an (pī ir′ē ən) ***adj.*** **1** of Pieria, where the Muses were anciently worshiped **2** of the Muses or the arts

pi·er·i·dine (pī er′ə dīn′, -din) ***adj.*** ⟦< ModL *Pieridinae* < Gr *Pieris,* any of the Muses⟧ of a large family (Pieridae) of small or medium-sized butterflies, usually white or yellow with dark markings, including the sulfur and cabbage butterflies

pie·ro·gi (pi rō′gē) ***n., pl.*** **-gies, -gi,** or **-gis** ⟦< Pol⟧ a small casing of dough, usually a triangle or half circle, filled as with a potato-and-cheese or cabbage mixture, boiled, and served with sour cream, melted butter, or sautéed onions: see also PIROGI

Pi·erre[1] (pē er′; *Fr* pyer) ***n.*** ⟦Fr: see PETER[1]⟧ a masculine name: see PETER[1]

Pierre[2] (pir, pē er′) ⟦after *Pierre* Chouteau, early fur trader⟧ capital of S.Dak., on the Missouri River

Pi·er·rot (pē′ər ō′; *Fr* pye rō′) ***n.*** ⟦Fr, dim. of *Pierre,* PETER[1]⟧ a stock comic character in old French pantomime, having a whitened face and wearing loose white pantaloons and a jacket with large buttons

pier table a low table set in the pier, or wall section, between windows, often below a pier glass

Pies·port·er (pēs′pôrt′ər) ***n.*** ⟦after *Piesport,* village in W Germany where produced⟧ a fruity Moselle wine of Germany

Pie·tà (pyā tä′, pē ā′tä) ***n.*** ⟦It, lit., pity < L *pietas,* PIETY⟧ a representation in painting, sculpture, etc. of Mary, the mother, grieving over the body of Jesus after the Crucifixion

Pie·ter·mar·itz·burg (pē′tər mer′its burg′) capital of KwaZulu-Natal province, South Africa

Pie·ters·burg (pē′tərz burg′) capital of Northern Transvaal province, South Africa

pi·e·tism (pī′ə tiz′əm) ***n.*** ⟦Ger *pietismus:* see fol.⟧ **1** [**P-**] the beliefs and practices of the Pietists **2** an exaggerated pious feeling or attitude —**pi′e·tis′tic** (-tis′tik) ***adj.,*** **pi′e·tis′ti·cal** —**pi′e·tis′ti·cal·ly** ***adv.***

Pi·e·tist (pī′ə tist′) ***n.*** ⟦Ger < ModL *(Collegia) pietatis,* lit., (fellowship) of piety⟧ **1** any of a group of Germans who advocated a revival of the devotional ideal in the Lutheran Church in the 17th-18th cent. **2** [**p-**] a pious person

pi·e·ty (pī′ə tē) ***n.*** ⟦OFr *pieté* < LL(Ec) *pietas,* duty to God < L, dutiful conduct, scrupulousness < *pius:* see PIOUS⟧ **1** devotion to religious duties and practices **2** loyalty and devotion to parents, family, etc. **3** *pl.* **-ties** a pious act, statement, belief, etc.

pi·e·zo- (pī ē′zō′, pē ā′-) ⟦< Gr *piezein,* to press < IE **pised-,* to sit on, press < base **epi-,* on + **sed-,* SIT⟧ *combining form* pressure [*piezometer*]

pi·e·zo·chem·is·try (pī ē′zō kem′is trē, pē ā′-) ***n.*** ⟦prec. + CHEMISTRY⟧ the branch of chemistry dealing with the effects of high pressure on chemical reactions

piezoelectric effect *Electronics* the property of certain crystals of generating a voltage when subjected to pressure and, conversely, of undergoing mechanical stress when subjected to an electric field (e.g., alternately expanding and contracting in response to an alternating electric field), as in crystal oscillators, microphones, etc.

pi·e·zo·e·lec·tric·i·ty (pī ē′zō ē′lek tris′ə tē, pē ā′-) ***n.*** ⟦PIEZO- + ELECTRICITY⟧ electricity resulting from the piezoelectric effect —**pi·e′zo·e·lec′tric** ***adj.,*** **pi·e′zo·e·lec′tri·cal** —**pi·e′zo·e·lec′tri·cal·ly** ***adv.***

pi·e·zom·e·ter (pī′ə zäm′ət ər, pē′-) ***n.*** ⟦PIEZO- + -METER⟧ any of various instruments used in measuring pressure or compressibility —**pi·e·zo·met·ric** (pī ē′zō me′trik, pē ā′-) ***adj.*** —**pi′e·zom′e·try** (-ə trē) ***n.***

pif·fle (pif′əl) [Informal] ***n.*** ⟦< Brit dial.⟧ talk, writing, action, etc. regarded as insignificant or nonsensical —***interj.*** nonsense —**pif·fling** (pif′liŋ) ***adj.***

pig (pig) ***n., pl.*** **pigs** or **pig** ⟦ME *pigge,* orig., young pig (replacing OE *swin*) < OE **picga,* as in *picgbread,* mast, pig's food⟧ **1** any swine, esp. the unweaned young of the thick-bodied domesticated species (*Sus scrofa*): see HOG (sense 1) **2** meat from a pig; pork **3** a person regarded as acting or looking like a pig; greedy or filthy person **4** ⟦from the shape or size⟧ *a)* an oblong casting of iron or other metal poured from the smelting furnace *b)* any of the molds in which these are cast *c) short for* PIG IRON **5** [Slang] ☆*a)* a slatternly or sluttish woman *b)* a rude or arrogant person *c)* a police officer (a derogatory term) —***vi.*** **pigged, pig′ging** **1** to bear pigs **2** to live in filth, like a pig: usually with *it* —**buy a pig in a poke** to buy, get, or agree to something without sight or knowledge of it in advance —**pig out** [Slang] to eat too much greedily: often with *on*

pig bed the sand bed into which molten iron is poured in molding pigs

☆**pig·boat** (pig′bōt′) ***n.*** ⟦from resemblance to suckling pigs when several of these are nosed against a tender⟧ [Slang] a submarine

pi·geon[1] (pij′ən) ***n., pl.*** **-geons** or **-geon** ⟦ME *pejon* < MFr *pijon* < LL *pipio* (gen. *pipionis*), chirping bird, squab < L *pipire,* to chirp, of echoic orig.⟧ **1** any of a family (Columbidae, order Columbiformes) of birds with a small head, plump body, long, pointed wings, and short legs: see DOVE ☆**2** CLAY PIGEON **3** a girl or young woman **4** [Slang] a person easily deceived or gulled; dupe

pi·geon[2] (pij′ən) ***n.*** *alt. sp. of* PIDGIN: a spelling not used technically by linguists —**one's pigeon** [Slang, Chiefly Brit.] one's special concern, or business

pigeon breast a deformity of the human chest occurring in rickets, etc., and characterized by a sharply projecting sternum like that of a pigeon —**pi′geon-breast′ed** ***adj.***

pigeon drop ⟦so called because a common form of this swindle begins with the *dropping* of a wallet in front of the victim, or PIGEON[1] (*n.* 4)⟧ a confidence game in which the victim, enticed by a promise to share in the distribution of a large sum of money, hands over personal funds to show good faith

pigeon hawk MERLIN

pi·geon-heart·ed (-härt′id) ***adj.*** cowardly or timid

pi·geon·hole (pij′ən hōl′) ***n.*** **1** a small recess or hole for pigeons to nest in, usually in a compartmented structure **2** a small, open compartment, as in a desk, for filing papers —***vt.*** **-holed′, -hol′ing** **1** to put in the pigeonhole of a desk, etc. **2** to put aside indefinitely, as if intending to ignore or forget; shelve **3** to assign to a category or categories; classify

pi·geon-liv·ered (-liv′ərd) ***adj.*** [Rare] meek or gentle

pigeon pea **1** a tropical plant (*Cajanus cajan*) of the pea family, with yellow flowers, widely grown for its edible seed **2** its seed

pi·geon-toed (-tōd′) ***adj.*** having the feet turned inward

pi·geon·wing (-wiŋ′) ***n.*** ☆**1** a fancy dance step performed by jumping and striking the legs together **2** *Skating* a figure outlining a pigeon wing

☆**pig·fish** (pig′fish′) ***n., pl.*** **-fish′** or **-fish′es** (see FISH) any grunt fish, esp. a species (*Orthopristis chrysoptera*) abundant off the E coast of the U.S. and in the Gulf of Mexico

pig·ger·y (pig′ər ē) ***n., pl.*** **-ger·ies** [Chiefly Brit.] **1** PIGPEN (sense 1) **2** a farm where pigs are raised

pig·gin (pig′in) ***n.*** ⟦< ?⟧ a small wooden pail with one stave extended above the rim to serve as a handle

pig·gish (pig′ish) ***adj.*** of or like a pig; specif., gluttonous or filthy —**pig′gish·ly** ***adv.*** —**pig′gish·ness** ***n.***

pig·gy (pig′ē) ***n., pl.*** **-gies** *child's term for* PIG (*n.* 1) or PIGLET: also sp. **pig′gie** —***adj.*** **-gi·er, -gi·est** PIGGISH

pig·gy·back (pig′ē bak′) ***adv.*** ⟦alt. of PICKABACK⟧ **1** on the shoulders or back [to carry a child *piggyback*] **2** by a piggyback transportation system **3** so as to be fixed to, carried by, connected with, or dependent on something else —***adj.*** **1** on the shoulders or back [to give a child a *piggyback* ride] **2** of a transportation system in which truck trailers are carried on flatcars **3** fixed to, carried by, connected with, or dependent on something else [a local *piggyback* tax on top of the state sales tax] —☆***vt.*** **1** to carry or transport piggyback **2** to place on or upon something in piggyback fashion [*piggyback* a new tax on the current one] —***vi.*** to be placed or held in piggyback fashion

☆**piggy bank** ⟦orig. ? < Scot *pig,* earthenware jar: form & meaning now infl. by PIG⟧ any small savings bank, often one in the form of a pig, with a slot for receiving coins

pig·head·ed (pig′hed′id) ***adj.*** stubborn; obstinate; mulish —**pig′head′ed·ly** ***adv.*** —**pig′head′ed·ness** ***n.***

pig iron ⟦see PIG, *n.* 4⟧ crude iron, as it comes from the blast furnace

pig Latin a playful secret language in which each word is pronounced beginning with its first vowel, and any preceding consonants are moved to the end to form a new syllable with the vowel sound (ā), as "oybay" for *boy:*

a word beginning with a vowel can be handled variously, as in "armay," "armway," or "armhay" for *arm*

pig·let (pig′lit) *n.* a little pig, esp. a suckling

pig·ment (pig′mənt) *n.* ⟦ME < L *pigmentum* < base of *pingere,* to PAINT⟧ **1** coloring matter, usually in the form of an insoluble powder, mixed with oil, water, etc. to make paints **2** any coloring matter in the cells and tissues of plants or animals — *vi., vt.* to take on or cause to take on pigment; color or become colored: also **pig′ment·ize′ -ized′, -iz′ing —pig′men·tar′y** (-mən ter′ē) *adj.*

pig·men·ta·tion (pig′mən tā′shən) *n.* ⟦< LL *pigmentatus,* colored (< L *pigmentum*) + -ION⟧ coloration in plants or animals due to the presence of pigment in the tissue

Pig·my (pig′mē) *adj., n., pl.* **-mies** *alt. sp. of* PYGMY

pi·gno·li·a (pēn yōl′yə, -yōl′ē ə; pig nōl′-) *n.* ⟦altered < It *pignolo* < VL **pineolus,* dim. of L *pineus,* of pine < *pinus,* a pine tree⟧ the edible seed of any of various nut pines: also **pi·gno·li** (pēn yō′lē, pig nō′-)

pig·nut (pig′nut′) *n.* ☆**1** any of several bitter, astringent hickory nuts ☆**2** any of the hickory trees on which these nuts grow

pig·out (pig′out′) *n.* ⟦< PIG OUT (see phr. under PIG)⟧ [Slang] the act or an instance of greedily eating too much: also written **pig-out**

pig·pen (pig′pen′) *n.* **1** a pen where pigs are kept **2** any place that is dirty, messy, untidy, etc.

pigs in blankets ⟦descriptive of their appearance⟧ small frankfurters wrapped in dough and baked, served as an appetizer

pig·skin (pig′skin′) *n.* **1** the skin of a pig **2** leather made from this ☆**3** [Informal] a football

pig·stick·ing (pig′stik′iŋ) *n.* the hunting of wild boars, esp. on horseback and using spears —**pig′stick′er** *n.*

pig·sty (pig′stī′) *n., pl.* **-sties′** PIGPEN

pig·tail (pig′tāl′) *n.* **1** tobacco in a twisted roll **2** *a)* a long braid of hair hanging at the back of the head *b)* any tied or braided lock of hair, esp. either of two such locks worn on each side of the head

pig·weed (pig′wēd′) *n.* ☆**1** any of several coarse weeds (genus *Amaranthus*) of the amaranth family, with dense, bristly clusters of small green flowers **2** any of several goosefoots, esp. lamb's-quarters

pi·ka (pī′kə) *n.* ⟦< Tungusic name⟧ any of a family (Ochotonidae) of small, short-legged lagomorphs with rounded ears, found in rocky areas, usually at high altitudes, in W North America and in Asia

pi·ka·ke (pē′kä kā′) *n.* ⟦Haw pīkake, lit., peacock < E⟧ a jasmine plant (*Jasminum sambac*) commonly found in Hawaii, where its fragrant, white flowers are used in making leis

pike¹ (pīk) *n.* ⟦< TURNPIKE⟧ a highway: now chiefly in the informal phrase **come down the pike,** to happen or appear

pike² (pīk) *n.* ⟦Fr *pique* < *piquer,* to pierce, prick < VL **piccare:* see PICADOR⟧ a weapon, formerly used by foot soldiers, consisting of a metal spearhead on a long wooden shaft —*vt.* **piked, pik′ing** to pierce or kill with a pike

pike³ (pīk) *n., pl.* **pike** or **pikes** ⟦ME *pik,* prob. < *pike* (see fol.), from the pointed head⟧ **1** any of a family (Esocidae, order Salmoniformes) of slender, voracious, freshwater bony fishes with a narrow, pointed head and conspicuous, sharp teeth; esp., a species (*Esox lucius*) of the northern parts of the Northern Hemisphere **2** any of various fishes resembling the true pikes, as the walleye

pike⁴ (pīk) *n.* ⟦ME *pike* < OE *pic,* pickax, prob. akin to OFr, pick, pickax < VL **piccus:* see PICADOR⟧ a spike; point, as the pointed tip of a spear

pike⁵ (pīk) *n.* ⟦ME, prob. < ON *pik* < ? OFr *pique* < L *picus:* see PICADOR⟧ [Brit. Dial.] **1** a peaked summit **2** a mountain or hill with a peaked summit Used esp. in place names

Pike (pīk), **Zeb·u·lon Montgomery** (zeb′yə lən) 1779-1813; U.S. general & explorer

pike·man (pīk′mən) *n., pl.* **-men** (-mən) a soldier armed with a pike

pike·perch (pīk′purch′) *n., pl.* **-perch′** or **-perch′es** a fish of the perch family resembling a pike, as the walleye or the sauger

pik·er (pīk′ər) *n.* ☆⟦orig., prob. one from *Pike* County, Missouri, then applied to Missourians generally: reason for later uses obscure⟧ [Slang] a person who does things in a petty or niggardly way; esp. one who gambles or speculates in an overly cautious way

Pikes Peak (pīks) ⟦after Zebulon PIKE⟧ mountain of the Front Range, central Colo.: 14,110 ft (4,301 m)

pike·staff (pīk′staf′) *n., pl.* **-staves′** (-stāvz′) **1** the shaft of a PIKE² **2** a traveler's staff with a sharp iron or steel point

pi·laf or **pi·laff** (pē′läf′, pi läf′) *n.* ⟦Pers *pilāv*⟧ a dish made of rice or wheat boiled in a seasoned liquid, and often containing meat or fish

pi·las·ter (pi las′tər) *n.* ⟦Fr *pilastre* < It *pilastro* < L *pila,* a pile, column⟧ a rectangular support or pier projecting partially from a wall and treated architecturally as a column, with a base, shaft, and capital

Pi·late (pī′lət), **Pon·tius** (pun′chəs, -shəs; pän′-; pän′tē əs) 1st cent. A.D.; Rom. procurator of Judea, Samaria, & Idumaea (26?-36?) who condemned Jesus to be crucified

Pi·la·tes (pə lät′ēz) *n.* ⟦after J. H. *Pilates* (1880-1967), Ger fitness instructor⟧ an exercise program, usually involving the use of special equipment, designed to strengthen the muscles of the abdomen, lower back, and buttocks and to improve overall flexibility and coordination

pi·lau or **pi·law** (pi lô′) *n. var. of* PILAF

pil·chard (pil′chərd) *n.* ⟦earlier *pilcher* < ?⟧ a member of any of two genera (*Sardina* and *Sardinops*) of small, oily, marine clupeid fishes; esp., the commercial sardine (*Sardina pilchardus*) of W Europe

Pil·co·ma·yo (pēl′kô mä′yô) river flowing from S Bolivia southeast along the Argentine-Paraguayan border into the Paraguay River, near Asunción: *c.* 1,000 mi (1,609 km)

pil·crow (pil′krō′) *n.* ⟦? ult. < OFr *pelagraphe,* PARAGRAPH⟧ a typographical character (¶) used as in marking the beginning of a paragraph: cf. PARAGRAPH (*n.* 2)

pile¹ (pīl) *n.* ⟦ME < MFr < L *pila,* pillar⟧ **1** a mass of things heaped together; heap **2** a heap of wood or other combustible material on which a corpse or sacrifice is burned **3** a large building or group of buildings **4** [Informal] *a)* a large amount or number ☆*b)* a lot of money; fortune **5** *Elec.* a voltaic pile or similar device that produces an electric current; battery ☆**6** *former term for* NUCLEAR REACTOR —*vt.* **piled, pil′ing 1** to put or set in a pile; heap up **2** to cover with a pile; load **3** to accumulate **4** to crash, wreck, etc. Often with *up* —*vi.* **1** to form a pile or heap **2** to move in a mass; crowd: with *in, into, out, on, off,* etc. **3** to crash (*into*) —*SYN.* BUILDING

pile² (pīl) *n.* ⟦ME *pile,* bird's down < L *pilus,* hair < IE base **pilo-* > L *pila,* ball, Gr *pilos,* felt⟧ **1** a soft, velvety, raised surface on a rug, fabric, etc., produced by making yarn loops on the body of the material and, often, shearing them **2** soft, fine hair, as on wool, fur, etc.

pile³ (pīl) *n.* ⟦ME *pil* < OE, akin to Ger *pfeil* < WGmc borrowing < L *pilum,* javelin⟧ **1** a long, heavy timber or beam driven into the ground, sometimes under water, to support a bridge, dock, etc. **2** any similar supporting member, as of concrete **3** *Heraldry* a wedge-shaped bearing with the point usually downward —*vt.* **piled, pil′ing 1** to drive piles into **2** to support or strengthen with piles

pi·le·ate (pī′lē it, pil′ē-; -āt′) *adj.* ⟦L *pileatus* < *pileus*⟧ **1** having a pileus **2** having a crest extending from the bill to the nape, as some birds Also **pi′le·at′ed** (-āt′id)

☆**pileated woodpecker** a large North American woodpecker (*Dryocopus pileatus*) with a black and white body and a red crest

piled (pīld) *adj.* having a PILE² [*a piled carpet*]

pile driver (*or* **engine)** a machine with a drop hammer for driving piles

pi·le·ous (pī′lē əs, pil′ē-) *adj.* ⟦< L *pilus,* hair (see PILE²) + -EOUS⟧ hairy or furry

piles (pīlz) *pl.n.* ⟦ME *pylys* < L *pilae,* pl. of *pila,* a ball, orig. prob. a knot of hair: see PILE²⟧ hemorrhoids

pi·le·um (pī′lē əm, pil′ē-) *n., pl.* **-le·a** (-ə) ⟦ModL < L *pilleum,* felt cap: see PILEUS⟧ *Ornithology* the top of a bird's head from the bill to the nape

pile·up (pīl′up′) *n.* **1** an accumulation as of burdensome tasks **2** [Informal] a collision involving several vehicles

pi·le·us (pī′lē əs, pil′ē-) *n., pl.* **-le·i′** (-ī′) ⟦< L *pilleus* (or *pilleum*), felt cap, akin to *pilus,* hair: see PILE²⟧ **1** a type of brimless cap worn in ancient Rome **2** *Bot.* the cap of a mushroom, or the similar part of the fruiting body of other fungi **3** *Zool.* *a)* the umbrella-shaped disk of a jellyfish *b)* PILEUM

pile·wort (pīl′wurt′) *n.* **1** CELANDINE (sense 2) **2** any of several plants reputed to have medicinal properties

pil·fer (pil′fər) *vt., vi.* ⟦< MFr *pelfrer* < *pelfre,* booty⟧ to steal (esp. small sums or petty objects); filch —**pil′fer·er** *n.*

pil·fer·age (pil′fər ij) *n.* **1** the act or practice of pilfering **2** something pilfered

pil·gar·lic (pil gär′lik) *n.* ⟦altered < *pilled* (peeled) *garlic*⟧ [Now Dial.] **1** a bald head or a baldheaded man **2** a person regarded with mild contempt or feigned pity

pil·grim (pil′grəm) *n.* ⟦ME *pelegrim* < OFr *pelegrin* < LL(Ec) *pelegrinus* < L *peregrinus,* foreigner < *peregre,* from abroad < *per,* through + *ager,* field, country: see ACRE⟧ **1** a person who travels about; wanderer **2** a person who travels to a shrine or holy place as a religious act ☆**3** [**P-**] any member of the band of English Puritans who founded Plymouth Colony in 1620

pil·grim·age (pil′grə mij) *n.* ⟦ME *pilgrymage* < OFr *pelegrinage* < *pelegrin,* prec.⟧ **1** a journey made by a pilgrim, esp. to a shrine or holy place **2** any long journey, as to a place of historical interest

☆**Pilgrim Fathers** the Pilgrims (of Plymouth Colony)

pi·li¹ (pē lē′) *n.* ⟦Tagalog⟧ **1** the edible nut, somewhat like an almond, of a SE Asian tree (*Canarium ovatum*) of the bursera family **2** the tree itself

pi·li² (pī′lī′) *n. pl. of* PILUS

pil·i- (pil′i, -ə; pī′li, -lə) ⟦< L *pilus,* hair: see PILE²⟧ *combining form* hair [*piliform*]

pi·lif·er·ous (pī lif′ər əs) *adj.* ⟦prec. + -FEROUS⟧ having or bearing hair or hairs

pil·i·form (pil′i fôrm′) *adj.* ⟦ModL *piliformis:* see PILI- & -FORM⟧ in the form of a hair; hairlike

pil·ing (pīl′iŋ) *n.* **1** piles collectively **2** a structure of piles

Pil·i·pi·no (pil′i pē′nō) *n.* ⟦Tagalog, altered < obs. Sp *Philippino,* FILIPINO⟧ an official language of the Philippines, based on the variety of Tagalog spoken in and around Manila

pill¹ (pil) *n.* ⟦LME *pylle,* contr. < L *pilula,* dim. of *pila,* a ball: see PILES⟧ **1** a small ball, tablet, capsule, etc. of medicine to be swallowed whole **2** anything unpleasant but unavoidable **3** *a)* something like a pill in shape *b)* [Slang] a baseball, golf ball, etc. **4** [Slang] an unpleasant or boring person —*vt.* **1** to dose with pills **2** to form into pills **3** [Slang] to blackball —*vi.* to form into small balls, as fuzz on a fabric —**the pill (***or* **Pill)** ☆[Informal] any contraceptive drug for women, taken in the form of a pill

pill² (pil) *vt., vi.* ⟦ME *pilien,* to rob, PEEL¹, ult. < ? L *pilare,* to make bald < *pilus,* a hair⟧ **1** [Archaic] to pillage; plunder **2** [Now Brit. Dial.] to peel

pil·lage (pil′ij) *n.* ⟦ME *pilage* < MFr < *piller:* see prec.⟧ **1** the act of plundering **2** that which is plundered; booty; loot —*vt.* **-laged, -lag·ing 1** to deprive of money or property by violence; loot **2** to take as booty or loot —*vi.* to engage in plunder; take loot —**SYN.** RAVAGE, SPOIL —**pil′lag·er** *n.*

pil·lar (pil′ər) *n.* ⟦ME *piler* < OFr < VL **pilare* < L *pila,* column⟧ **1** a long, slender, vertical structure used to support a superstructure; column **2** such a column standing alone as a monument **3** anything like a pillar in form or function, as a formation of ore left standing as a support in a mine **4** a person who is a main support of an institution, movement, etc. —*vt.* to support or brace with or as with pillars —**from pillar to post** from one predicament, place of appeal, etc. to another, usually under harassment

pillar box [Brit.] a pillar-shaped mailbox

Pillars of Hercules two headlands on either side of the Strait of Gibraltar, one at Gibraltar (ancient CALPE) & the other at Ceuta (ancient ABYLA) or Jebel Musa, on the coast of Africa

pill·box (pil′bäks′) *n.* **1** a small, shallow box, often cylindrical, for holding pills **2** a low, enclosed gun emplacement of concrete and steel **3** a woman's cylindrical hat with a low, flat crown

☆**pill bug** any of various isopods capable of rolling up into a ball, as a common species (*Armadillidium vulgare*) found in damp places

pil·lion (pil′yən) *n.* ⟦Gael *pillean* < *peall,* a hide, skin, ult. < L *pellis:* see FELL[4]⟧ **1** a cushion attached behind a saddle for an extra rider, esp. a woman, as in medieval times **2** an extra saddle behind the driver's on a motorcycle

pil·lo·ry (pil′ə rē) *n., pl.* **-ries** ⟦ME *pilory* < OFr *pilori* < ML *pilorium* < L *pila,* column + *-orium,* -ORY⟧ **1** a device consisting of a wooden board with holes for the head and hands, in which petty offenders were formerly locked and exposed to public scorn **2** any exposure to public scorn, etc. —*vt.* **-ried, -ry·ing 1** to punish by placing in a pillory **2** to subject to harsh public criticism or ridicule

pil·low (pil′ō) *n.* ⟦ME *pylwe* < OE *pyle,* akin to Ger *pfühl* < WGmc borrowing of L *pulvinus,* cushion⟧ **1** a cloth case filled with feathers, down, foam rubber, air, etc., used as a support, as for the head in sleeping **2** any object used as a headrest **3** anything like a pillow or cushion, as a pad on which certain laces are made **4** anything that supports like a pillow —*vt.* **1** to rest on or as on a pillow **2** to be a pillow for —*vi.* [Rare] to rest the head on or as on a pillow

pillow block a block that supports the journal of a shaft, spindle, etc.

pil·low·case (pil′ō kās′) *n.* a removable, usually cotton case used to cover a pillow: also **pil′low·slip′** (-slip′)

pillow lace BOBBIN LACE

☆**pillow sham** a decorative cover for a bed pillow

pillow talk intimate, unguarded conversation, as between a husband and wife, while lying in bed

pil·low·y (pil′ō ē) *adj.* like a pillow; soft; yielding

pi·lo·car·pine (pī′lō kär′pēn′, -pin; pil′ō-) *n.* ⟦< ModL *Pilocarpus,* genus name (< Gr *pilos,* felt + *karpos,* fruit: see PILE[2] & CARPO-) + -INE[3]⟧ an alkaloid, $C_{11}H_{16}N_2O_2$, extracted from the leaves of the jaborandi plant and used in medicine to stimulate sweating or to contract the pupil of the eye

pi·lose (pī′lōs′) *adj.* ⟦L *pilosus* < *pilus,* hair: see PILE[2]⟧ covered with hair, esp. fine, soft hair —**pi·los·i·ty** (pī läs′ə tē) *n.*

pi·lot (pī′lət) *n.* ⟦MFr *pilote* < It *pilota, pedoto* < MGr **pēdōtēs* < Gr *pēdon,* oar blade (in pl., rudder), akin to *pous,* FOOT⟧ **1** *a)* [Archaic] HELMSMAN *b)* a person licensed to direct ships into or out of a harbor or through difficult waters **2** a person qualified to operate the controls of an aircraft or spacecraft **3** a guide; leader **4** a device that guides the action of a machine or machine part ☆**5** a metal shield on the front of a locomotive, for deflecting obstructions from the track **6** *a)* PILOT LIGHT (sense 1) *b)* PILOT FILM —*vt.* **1** to act as a pilot of, on, in, or over **2** to guide; conduct; lead —*adj.* **1** that serves as a guide or guiding device **2** that serves as an activating device **3** that serves as a trial unit for experimentation or testing —**pi′lot·less** *adj.*

pi·lot·age (pī′lə tij) *n.* ⟦Fr: see prec. & -AGE⟧ **1** the action or occupation of piloting **2** the fee paid to a pilot **3** aircraft navigation by observation of ground features and the use of charts and maps

pilot balloon a small balloon sent up to determine the direction and velocity of the wind

☆**pilot biscuit** (*or* **bread**) HARDTACK

pilot engine a locomotive sent on ahead of a train, to determine if the track is clear

pilot film (*or* **tape**) a film (or videotape) of a single segment of a projected series of television shows, prepared for showing to prospective commercial sponsors and, sometimes, later broadcast

pilot fish a narrow, spiny-finned jackfish (*Naucrates ductor*) with a widely forked tail, often seen swimming near sharks: often written **pi·lot·fish** (pī′lət fish′) *n., pl.* **-fish′** or **-fish′es** (see FISH)

☆**pi·lot·house** (pī′lət hous′) *n.* an enclosed place as on the bridge of a ship, in which the helmsman stands while steering and from which the ship is usually conned

pi·lot·ing (pī′lət iŋ) *n.* the directing of a ship's movements near land, using landmarks, buoys, soundings, etc.

pilot lamp a tiny electric lamp placed in a circuit to indicate that the current is on

pilot light 1 a small gas burner which is kept burning for use in lighting a main burner when needed: also **pilot burner 2** PILOT LAMP

pilot whale BLACKFISH (sense 1)

pi·lous (pī′ləs) *adj.* PILOSE

Pil·sen (pil′zən) *Ger. name for* PLZEŇ

Pil·sener or **Pil·sner** (pilz′nər, pils′-) *n.* ⟦after prec., where first made⟧ [*often* **p-**] a light lager beer, traditionally served in a tall, conical, footed glass (**Pilsener glass**) —*adj.* of or being this type of beer

Pilt·down man (pilt′doun′) a supposed species of prehistoric human presumed on the basis of skull fragments found in Piltdown (Sussex, England) about 1911 and exposed as a hoax in 1953

pil·u·lar (pil′yoo lər) *adj.* of or like a pill or pills

pil·ule (pil′yool′) *n.* ⟦Fr < L *pilula:* see PILL[1]⟧ a small pill

pi·lus (pī′ləs) *n., pl.* **pi′li′** (-lī′) ⟦L, hair: see PILE[2]⟧ a hair or hairlike structure

☆**Pi·ma** (pē′mə) *n.* ⟦< Sp < Piman word for "no," misunderstood and misapplied by missionaries⟧ **1** *pl.* **-mas** or **-ma** a member of a North American Indian people living in the Gila and Salt river valleys in Arizona **2** the Uto-Aztecan language of this people

☆**Pima cotton** ⟦after *Pima* County, Ariz.⟧ a tough, strong, smooth, long-staple cotton grown in the SW U.S.

☆**Pi·man** (pē′mən) *n.* a branch of the Uto-Aztecan family of languages —*adj.* of the Pimas or their language or culture

pi·men·to (pə men′tō) *n., pl.* **-tos** ⟦Sp *pimiento* < L *pigmentum,* lit., PIGMENT (in VL & ML, plant juice, spiced drink, spice)⟧ **1** a sweet variety of the capsicum pepper, or its red, bell-shaped fruit, used as a relish, as a stuffing for olives, etc. **2** ALLSPICE

pimento cheese a process cheese containing pimentos

pi meson *Particle Physics* PION: also written **pi′-mes′on** *n.*

pi·mien·to (pi myen′tō, -men′-) *n. var. of* PIMENTO

pimp (pimp) *n.* ⟦prob. < or akin to MFr *pimper,* to allure, dress smartly⟧ a man who manages and, often, controls a prostitute or prostitutes and their earnings —*vi.* to act as a pimp —*vt.* [Slang] **1** to promote or exploit: often with *out* **2** to decorate or embellish, specif. in a lavish or garish way: often with *out*

pim·per·nel (pim′pər nel′, -nəl) *n.* ⟦ME *pympernelle* < OFr *piprenelle* < LL *pimpinella,* an herb with medicinal uses, prob. altered < **piperinella,* ult. < L *piper,* PEPPER: its fruit resembles small peppercorns⟧ any of a genus (*Anagallis*) of plants of the primrose family, esp. the **scarlet pimpernel** (*A. arvensis*), with red, white, or blue, starlike flowers which close in bad weather

pimp·ing (pim′piŋ) *adj.* ⟦< dial., prob. akin to Du *pimpel,* weak man, Ger *pimpelig,* womanish⟧ [Archaic] **1** petty; mean **2** sickly; puny

pim·ple (pim′pəl) *n.* ⟦ME *pinplis* (pl.), nasalized < OE *piplian,* to break out in pimples⟧ any small, rounded, usually inflamed swelling of the skin; papule or pustule

pim·ply (pim′plē) *adj.* **-pli·er, -pli·est** having pimples: also **pim′pled** (-pəld)

pin (pin) *n.* ⟦ME *pyn* < OE *pinn,* akin to MHG *pfinne,* a nail, prob. < IE base **bend-,* projecting point > MIr *benn,* peak⟧ **1** a peg of wood, metal, etc., used esp. for fastening or holding things together or as a support on which to hang things **2** a little piece of stiff wire with a pointed end and a flattened or rounded head, used for fastening things together or holding them in place; straight pin **3** something worthless or insignificant; trifle **4** a pointed instrument for holding the hair, a hat, etc. in place **5** *short for* CLOTHESPIN, SAFETY PIN, COTTER PIN, etc. **6** anything like a pin in form, use, etc. **7** an ornament, badge, or emblem having a pin or clasp with which it is fastened to the clothing **8** [Informal] the leg: *usually used in pl.* **9** *Bowling* any of the bottle-shaped pieces of wood, or wood coated with plastic, at which the ball is rolled **10** *Golf* a pole with a flag attached, placed in the hole of a green to mark its location **11** *Med.* a metal rod used to hold a broken bone together **12** *Music* any of the pegs for regulating the tension of the strings of a piano, harp, etc. **13** *Naut. a)* THOLE[1] *b)* any of various pegs or rods used to secure ropes **14** *Wrestling* FALL (*n.* 21*a*) —*vt.* **pinned, pin′ning 1** to fasten with or as with a pin **2** to pierce with a pin **3** to hold firmly in one place or position ☆**4** [Slang] to give one's fraternity pin to, as an informal token of betrothal —**pin down 1** to get (someone) to make a decision, commitment, etc. **2** to determine or confirm (a fact, details, etc.) —☆**pin someone's ears back** [Informal] to beat, defeat, or scold someone soundly —**pin something on someone** [Informal] to lay the blame for something on someone

PIN (pin) *n.* ⟦*p*(*ersonal*) *i*(*dentification*) *n*(*umber*)⟧ an identification number entered on a keypad in order to gain access to a computer, ATM, etc.

pi·na·ceous (pī nā′shəs) *adj.* ⟦PIN(E) + -ACEOUS⟧ of the pine family of trees

pi·ña cloth (pēn′yə) ⟦< Sp *piña,* pineapple, orig., pine cone < L *pinea* < *pineus,* of pine < *pinus,* PINE[1]⟧ a fabric made of the fibers of pineapple leaves

pi·ña co·la·da (pēn′yə kō lä′də) ⟦Sp, lit., pineapple strained⟧ a drink made with pineapple juice, coconut milk, and rum

pin·a·fore (pin′ə fôr′) *n.* ⟦PIN + AFORE⟧ **1** a sleeveless, apronlike garment worn by little girls over a dress **2** a sleeveless housedress worn by women, as over a blouse

Pi·nar del Río (pē när′ del rē′ō) city in W Cuba

pi·nas·ter (pī nas′tər, pi-) *n.* ⟦L, wild pine < *pinus,* PINE[1]⟧ a Mediterranean pine (*Pinus pinaster*) with paired needles and prickly cones

☆**pi·ña·ta** (pin yä′də, pē nyä′tä) *n.* ⟦MexSp < Sp, orig., a pot < It *pignatta,* ult. < L *pinea,* pine cone < *pinus,* pine tree⟧ a decorated figure of clay or papier-mâché, hung up for use in a children's party game: blindfolded players take turns wielding a stick in an effort to break open the figure and release its contents of toys and candy: orig. a part of Mexican Christmas celebrations

☆**pin·ball machine** (pin′bôl′) a device, used for entertainment or gambling, having an inclined board containing a number of pins, springs, holes, etc.

variously marked with scores that are automatically recorded as a ball, released by the player, makes contacts on it

☆**pin boy** *Bowling* a person who set up the pins and returned the ball to the bowler, as in a bowling alley before the time of automatic pinsetters

pince-nez (pans′nā′, pins′nā′; *Fr* pans nā′) ***n.*** ⟦Fr < *pincer,* to pinch + *nez,* nose⟧ *pl.* **pince′-nez′** (-nāz′; *Fr,* -nā′) eyeglasses without temples, kept in place by a spring gripping the bridge of the nose

pin·cer (pin′sər) ***n.*** ⟦< ME *pinsours* < OFr *pincier,* to PINCH⟧ **1** [*pl., with sing. or pl. v.*] a tool with two parts pivoted together to form two handles and two jaws, used in gripping or nipping things **2** [*often pl.*] *Zool.* a grasping claw, as of a crab or lobster; chela —**pin′cer·like′** ***adj.***

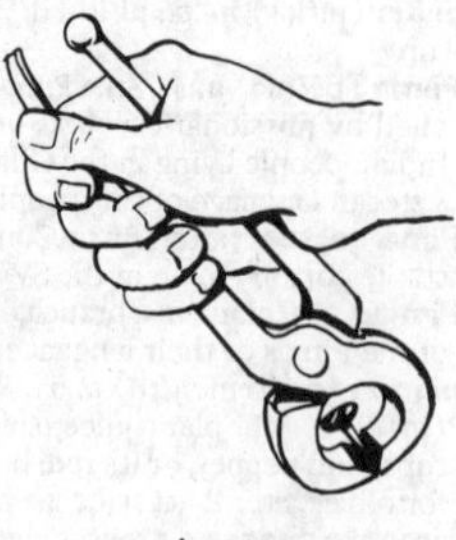

pincers

pincers movement a military maneuver in which simultaneous flank movements are used to converge upon an enemy force or stronghold and cut it off from support and supplies

pinch (pinch) ***vt.*** ⟦ME *pinchen* < NormFr **pincher* < OFr *pincier* < VL **pinctiare* < ? *punctiare,* to prick (see PUNCHEON[1]), infl. by **piccare:* see PICADOR⟧ **1** to squeeze between a finger and the thumb or between two surfaces, edges, etc. **2** to nip off the end of (a plant shoot), as for controlling bud development **3** to press painfully upon (some part of the body) **4** to cause distress or discomfort to **5** to cause to become thin, cramped, etc., as by hunger, pain, cold, etc. **6** to restrict closely; straiten; stint: usually in the passive voice **7** [Slang] *a)* to steal *b)* to arrest **8** *Naut.* to sail (a vessel) too close to the wind when closehauled —***vi.*** **1** to squeeze painfully **2** *a)* to be stingy or niggardly *b)* to be frugal with expenses; economize ☆**3** *Mining* to become narrower; hence, to give (out): said of a vein of ore —***n.*** **1** a pinching; squeeze or nip **2** *a)* the quantity that may be grasped between the finger and thumb *b)* a small amount **3** distress; hardship; difficulty **4** an emergency; urgent situation or time: now usually in the phrase **in a pinch** **5** [Slang] *a)* a theft *b)* an arrest or police raid —***adj.*** ⟦see *n.* 4⟧ *Baseball* of or having to do with a substitute hitter or runner —**pinch pennies** to be very frugal or economical —**pinch′er** ***n.***

pinch bar a kind of crowbar with a pointed, projecting end, used to roll heavy wheels, etc.

pinch·beck (pinch′bek′) ***n.*** ⟦after C. *Pinchbeck,* Eng jeweler who invented it (*c.* 1725)⟧ **1** an alloy of copper and zinc used to imitate gold in cheap jewelry **2** anything cheap or imitation —***adj.*** **1** made of pinchbeck **2** cheap, imitation, sham, etc.

pinch·cock (-käk′) ***n.*** ⟦PINCH + COCK[1]⟧ a clamp used on a flexible tube to control the flow of fluid through it

pinch effect *Physics* the constriction, or compression, of plasma by the action of the magnetic field of a strong electric current flowing through the plasma

pinch·ers (pin′chərz) ***pl.n.*** pincers: see PINCER

☆**pinch-hit** (pinch′hit′) ***vi.*** **-hit′**, **-hit′ting** **1** *Baseball* to bat in place of the batter whose turn it is, esp. when a hit is particularly needed **2** to act as a substitute in an emergency (*for*) —**pinch hitter**

pinch·pen·ny (pinch′pen′ē) ***adj.*** extremely frugal or stingy —***n.*** PENNY PINCHER

Pinck·ney (piŋk′nē), **Charles Cotes·worth** (kōts′wərth) 1746-1825; Am. statesman & diplomat

pin curl a strand of hair formed into a curl and held in place with a bobby pin while it sets

pin·cush·ion (pin′ko͝osh′ən) ***n.*** a small cushion, variously shaped, in which pins and needles are stuck to keep them handy

Pin·dar (pin′dər, -där′) 522?-438? B.C.; Gr. lyric poet

Pin·dar·ic (pin dar′ik) ***adj.*** ⟦L *Pindaricus* < Gr *Pindarikos*⟧ **1** of, characteristic of, or in the style of, Pindar **2** designating an ode having two metrical forms, one for the strophe and antistrophe and another for the epode —***n.*** a Pindaric ode

pin·dling (pind′liŋ, -lin) ***adj.*** ⟦prob. var. of PIDDLING⟧ ☆[Dial.] weak and undersized; puny

Pin·dus (pin′dəs) mountain range in central & NW Greece: highest peak, 8,650 ft (2,637 m)

pine[1] (pīn) ***n.*** ⟦ME < OE *pin* < L *pinus,* pine tree < IE **pitsnus* < base **pi-,* fat > L *pix,* pitch, OE *fæted,* FAT⟧ **1** any of a genus (*Pinus*) of evergreen trees of the pine family, with hard, woody cones and bundles of two to five needle-shaped leaves; many pines are valuable for their wood and their resin, from which turpentine, tar, etc. are obtained **2** the wood of such a tree **3** the odor of pine trees, or a synthetic odor resembling this, often used to scent deodorizers, cleaning solutions, etc. **4** *short for* PINEAPPLE —***adj.*** designating a family (Pinaceae) of conifers having needlelike leaves and, usually, woody cones and valuable wood, including the larches, spruces, firs, and hemlocks

pine[2] (pīn) ***vi.*** **pined**, **pin′ing** ⟦ME *pinen* < OE *pinian,* to torment < *pin,* pain < L *poena:* see PENAL⟧ **1** to waste (*away*) through grief, pain, longing, etc. **2** to have an intense longing or desire; yearn: with *for, after,* or an infinitive —***vt.*** [Archaic] to mourn for

pin·e·al (pin′ē əl) ***adj.*** ⟦Fr *pinéal* < L *pinea,* pine cone < *pinus,* PINE[1]⟧ **1** shaped like a pine cone **2** of the pineal body

pineal body a small, grayish, cone-shaped, glandular outgrowth from the brain of all vertebrates that produces the hormone melatonin: in lower vertebrates, often visible as an external median eye

pine·ap·ple (pīn′ap′əl) ***n.*** ⟦ME *pinappel,* pine cone (see PINE[1] & APPLE): mod. sense from shape of the fruit⟧ **1** a juicy, edible tropical fruit somewhat resembling a pine cone: it consists of the fleshy inflorescence of a collective fruit developed from a spike of flowers **2** the terrestrial plant (*Ananas comosus*) of the pineapple family on which it grows, having a short stem and spiny-edged, recurved leaves **3** [Slang] a hand grenade shaped like a small pineapple —***adj.*** designating a large family (Bromeliaceae, order Bromeliales) of tropical and subtropical, mostly epiphytic, monocotyledonous plants, including the Spanish moss

pineapple

pine cone the cone of a pine tree

☆**pine·drops** (pīn′dräps′) ***n.***, *pl.* **-drops′** a purplish-red, leafless plant (*Pterospora andromedea*) of the heath family, with white flowers: it is parasitic on the roots of pines

pi·nene (pī′nēn′) ***n.*** ⟦PINE[1] + -ENE⟧ either of two isomeric terpenes, $C_{10}H_{16}$, occurring in oil of turpentine and other essential oils: used as a solvent, in synthetic resins, etc.

pine needle the needlelike leaf of a pine tree

pine nut ☆the sweet, edible seed of any of several pines found chiefly in the SW U.S. and in Mexico

Pi·ne·ro (pi nir′ō), Sir **Arthur Wing** 1855-1934; Eng. playwright

pin·er·y (pīn′ər ē) ***n.***, *pl.* **-er·ies** ⟦see PINE[1] + -ERY⟧ ☆**1** a forest of pine trees **2** a pineapple plantation or hothouse

Pines (pīnz), **Isle of** *former name for* Isle of YOUTH

☆**pine·sap** (pīn′sap′) ***n.*** any of various whitish or reddish plants (genus *Monotropa*) of the heath family, including the Indian pipe, that live on dead vegetable material or as parasites on roots

☆**pine siskin** a small, brown finch (*Carduelis pinus*) of North America, with yellow markings on the wings and tail

☆**pine snake** *regional var. of* BULLSNAKE: term used along the E coast of the U.S.

☆**pine straw** pine needles, esp. dried ones

pine tar a viscid, blackish-brown liquid prepared by the destructive distillation of pine wood and used in the preparation of expectorants, disinfectants, tar paints, roofing materials, etc.

pi·ne·tum (pī nē′təm) ***n.***, *pl.* **-ne′ta** (-tə) ⟦L, pine grove < *pinus,* PINE[1]⟧ an arboretum of pine trees, etc.

☆**pine warbler** a small yellow wood warbler (*Dendroica pinus*) with dull-greenish wings, living in the pine forests of the E U.S.

pin·ey (pī′nē) ***adj.*** **pin′i·er**, **pin′i·est** **1** abounding in pines **2** of or like pines; esp., having the odor of pines

pin·feath·er (pin′feth′ər) ***n.*** an undeveloped feather that is just emerging through the skin, usually still encased in a horny sheath

☆**pin·fish** (pin′fish′) ***n.***, *pl.* **-fish′** or **-fish′es** (see FISH) any of several fishes with sharp dorsal spines, esp. a small porgy (*Lagodon rhomboides*) found along the Atlantic coast of the U.S.

pin·fold (pin′fōld′) ***n.*** ⟦ME *pynfold* < OE *pundfald* < *pund,* POUND[3] + *fald,* FOLD[2]⟧ a place where stray cattle, etc. are confined

ping (piŋ) ***n.*** ⟦echoic⟧ **1** the sound made by a bullet striking something sharply **2** any sound somewhat similar to this, as an engine knocking, a sonar echo, etc. — ***vi., vt.*** to make or cause to make such a sound

pin·go (piŋ′gō) ***n.***, *pl.* **-gos** or **-goes** ⟦< Inupiaq *pinguq*⟧ an earth-covered ice hill formed by the upward expansion of underground ice

Ping-Pong (piŋ′pôŋ′) ⟦echoic redupl.⟧ *trademark for* table-tennis equipment —***n.*** [*often* **ping-pong**] TABLE TENNIS — ***vi., vt.*** [**ping-pong**] to move or cause to move back and forth, as between places or between ideas, feelings, etc.

pin·guid (piŋ′gwid) ***adj.*** ⟦L *pinguis,* fat (< **pimos,* fat < IE base **pi-* + L **finguis* < IE base **bhengh-,* thick) + *-id,* as in TORPID⟧ fat; oily; greasy —**pin·guid′i·ty** ***n.***

pin·head (pin′hed′) ***n.*** **1** the head of a pin **2** anything very small or trifling ☆**3** a stupid or silly person

☆**pin·head·ed** (-id) ***adj.*** stupid or silly —**pin′head′ed·ness** ***n.***

pin·hole (pin′hōl′) ***n.*** **1** a tiny hole made by or as by a pin **2** a hole into which a pin or peg goes

pin·ion[1] (pin′yən) ***n.*** ⟦Fr *pignon* < VL **pinnio* < L *pinna,* bucket of a paddle wheel, lit., feather, var. of *penna* (see PEN[2]): assoc. in MFr with *peigner,* to comb: see PEIGNOIR⟧ a small gear, the teeth of which fit into those of a larger gear or those of a rack

pin·ion[2] (pin′yən) ***n.*** ⟦ME *pynyon* < OFr *pignon,* var. of *penon* < L *pinna, penna:* see PEN[2]⟧ **1** *Ornithology* the outermost section of a bird's wing **2** [Old Poet.] a wing **3** [Old Poet.] any wing feather —***vt.*** **1** to cut off or bind the pinions of (a bird) to keep it from flying **2** to bind (the wings) **3** to disable or impede by binding the arms of **4** to confine or shackle

Pi·niós (pēn yôs′) river in Thessaly, E Greece, flowing eastward to the Gulf of Salonika: 125 mi (201 km)

pin·ite (pin′īt′, pī′nīt′) ***n.*** ⟦Ger *pinit,* after *Pini,* mine in Saxony⟧ a grayish, fine-grained, usually amorphous mica that consists chiefly of muscovite, used in making kiln linings, ceramics, etc.

pi·ni·tol (pī′ni tôl′, -tōl′; pin′i-) ***n.*** ⟦< obs. *pinite,* pinitol < Fr < *pin,* pine (< L *pinus*) + *-ite,* -ITE[1] + *-ol,* -OL[2]⟧ INOSITOL

pink[1] (piŋk) ***n.*** ⟦< ?⟧ **1** any of a genus (*Dianthus*) of annual and perennial plants of the pink family with white, pink, or red flowers, often clove-scented **2** the flower **3** its pale-red color **4** ⟦see FLOWER, *n.* 3⟧ the highest or finest example, degree, etc. [the *pink* of perfection] **5** ⟦so named because of tendency toward red (see RED, *n.* 3) views⟧ [Informal] a person whose political or economic views are somewhat leftist: a derogatory term **6** [Brit.] *a)* the scarlet worn by a fox hunter *b)* a fox hunter —***adj.*** **1** designating a family (Caryophyllaceae, order Caryophyllales) of widely distributed, dicotyledonous plants with bright-colored flowers, including the carnation and sweet william **2** pale-red **3** [Informal] somewhat leftist: a derogatory term —**in the pink** [Informal] in good physical condition; healthy; fit —**pink′ish** ***adj.*** —**pink′ness** ***n.***

pink[2] (piŋk) ***vt.*** ⟦ME *pynken* < ? or akin to OE *pyngan,* to prick < L *pungere:* see POINT⟧ **1** to ornament (cloth, paper, etc.) by making perforations in a pattern **2** to cut a saw-toothed edge on (cloth, etc.) to prevent unraveling or for decoration **3** to prick or stab **4** to hurt, as by criticism **5** to adorn; embellish —**pink′er** ***n.***

pink[3] (piŋk) ***n.*** ⟦LME *pynk* < MDu *pinke*⟧ a sailing vessel with a high, narrow stern

pink-col·lar (piŋk′käl′ər) ***adj.*** ⟦from the color's traditional assoc. with women and girls (as opposed to BLUE-COLLAR work traditionally assoc. with men)⟧ designating or of a job or work, as that of a secretary or salesclerk, for which women have been typically hired

pink·en (piŋ′kən) ***vi.*** to become pink

Pink·er·ton (piŋ′kər tən), **Allan** 1819-84; U.S. private detective, born in Scotland

pink·eye (piŋk′ī′) ***n.*** an acute, contagious form of conjunctivitis in which the eyeball and the lining of the eyelid become red and inflamed

pink gin a British cocktail made of gin and bitters

pink·ie[1] (piŋ′kē) ***n.*** ⟦prob. < Du *pinkje,* dim. of *pink,* little finger⟧ **1** the fifth, or smallest, finger: often **pinkie finger** **2** the fifth, or smallest, toe: usually **pinkie toe**

☆**pink·ie**[2] (piŋ′kē) ***n.*** PINK[3]: also sp. **pink′ey** or **pink′y**

pink·ing shears (piŋ′kiŋ) shears with notched blades, used as for pinking the edges of cloth

pink lady ⟦so named from its color, resulting from the use of grenadine⟧ a cocktail made of gin, grenadine, lemon juice, and egg white, shaken with ice and strained

pink·o (piŋ′kō′) [Slang] ***n., pl.*** **-os** PINK[1] (*n.* 5) —***adj.*** PINK[1] (*adj.* 3)

☆**pink·root** (piŋk′ro͞ot′) ***n.*** a plant (*Spigelia marilandica*) of the logania family, with tufted stems and red flowers with yellow throats, native to the SE U.S.

☆**pink salmon** a widespread species (*Oncorhynchus gorbuscha*) of salmon: see HUMPBACK (sense 4)

☆**pink slip** ⟦from the sometime use of *pink* paper for the employee's carbon of the dismissal notice⟧ [Informal] notice to an employee of termination of employment

☆**Pink·ster** (piŋk′stər) ***n.*** ⟦Du < MDu *pinxten* < OS *pinkoston* < Goth *paintēkuste* < Gr(Ec) *pentēkostē:* see PENTECOST⟧ Whitsuntide: name formerly used in New Netherland

☆**pink·ster flower** (piŋk′stər) PINXTER FLOWER

☆**pink tea** [Informal] any frivolous social gathering, esp. one attended largely by women

pink·y[1] (piŋ′kē) ***n., pl.*** **pink′ies** *alt. sp. of* PINKIE[1]

☆**pink·y**[2] (piŋ′kē) ***n., pl.*** **pink′ies** PINK[3]

pin money **1** [Archaic] an allowance of money given to a wife for small personal expenses **2** any small sum of money, as for incidental expenses

pin·na (pin′ə) ***n., pl.*** **-nae** (-ē) or **-nas** ⟦L, a feather: see PEN[2]⟧ **1** *Anat.* the external ear; auricle **2** *Bot.* a primary division of a pinnately compound leaf, esp. of a fern leaf **3** *Zool.* a feather, wing, fin, or similar structure —**pin′nal** ***adj.***

pin·nace (pin′is) ***n.*** ⟦Fr *pinasse* < Sp *pinaza* < VL **pinacea* < L *pinus,* PINE[1]⟧ **1** [Archaic] a small sailing ship, often one used as a tender to a larger ship **2** a ship's boat

pin·na·cle (pin′ə kəl) ***n.*** ⟦ME *pinacle* < MFr < LL(Ec) *pinnaculum,* dim. L *pinna,* pinnacle, feather: see PEN[2]⟧ **1** a small turret or spire on a buttress or a supporting pier **2** a pointed formation, as at the top of a mountain; peak **3** the highest point; culmination; acme —***vt.*** **-cled, -cling** **1** to set on a pinnacle **2** to furnish or adorn with pinnacles **3** to form the pinnacle of —***SYN.*** SUMMIT

pin·nate (pin′āt′, -it) ***adj.*** ⟦ModL *pinnatus* < L < *pinna,* feather, fin: see PEN[2]⟧ **1** resembling a feather **2** *Bot. a)* with leaflets on each side of a common axis in a featherlike arrangement *b)* with a pattern of leaf veins resembling the structure of a feather —**pin′nate′ly** ***adv.*** —**pin·na′tion** ***n.***

pin·nat·i- (pi nat′i, -ə) ⟦< ModL *pinnatus,* prec.⟧ *combining form* pinnately [*pinnatifid*]

pin·nat·i·fid (pi nat′i fid) ***adj.*** ⟦prec. + -FID⟧ having leaves in a featherlike arrangement, with narrow lobes whose clefts extend more than halfway to the axis

pin·nat·i·sect (-sekt′) ***adj.*** ⟦PINNATI- + -SECT⟧ pinnatifid but with the clefts reaching to or almost to the axis

pin·ner (pin′ər) ***n.*** **1** a person or thing that pins **2** a caplike headdress with a long, hanging flap pinned on either side, formerly worn by women

pin·ni·ped (pin′i ped′) ***adj.*** ⟦< ModL *Pinnipedia* < L *pinnapes, pinnipes,* having winged feet < *pinna,* feather, fin (see PEN[2]) + *pes,* FOOT⟧ having finlike feet or flippers —***n.*** a pinniped carnivore, as a seal or walrus Also **pin′ni·pe′di·an** (-pē′dē ən)

pin·nule (pin′yo͞ol′) ***n.*** ⟦ModL *pinnula* < L, dim. of *pinna,* wing, feather: see PEN[2]⟧ **1** any of the smallest divisions of a leaf which is doubly compound, esp. in ferns **2** any of the lateral branches of the arm of a crinoid —**pin′nu·late′** (-yoo lāt′) ***adj.,*** **pin′nu·lat′ed**

pin·ny (pin′ē) ***n., pl.*** **-nies** [Brit. Informal] a pinafore: usually a child's term

pin oak ⟦so named because its dead branches resemble *pins* or pegs stuck into the trunk⟧ **1** either of two tall oaks (*Quercus palustris* and *Q. ellipsoidalis*) of E U.S. used for shade and lumber **2** their wood

Pi·noc·chi·o (pi nō′kē ō′) ***n.*** the title character of a novel (1880) by It. writer C. Collodi (pseud. of Carlo Lorenzini): Pinocchio is a living marionette whose nose lengthens whenever he tells a lie

☆**pi·noch·le** or **pi·noc·le** (pē′nuk′əl, -näk′-) ***n.*** ⟦earlier *binochle* < Ger dial. (Swiss) *binokel* < Fr *binocle,* pince-nez (< ModL *binoculus,* binoculars: see BINOCULAR), taken as synonym for *bésigue,* BEZIQUE, wrongly identified with *besicles,* spectacles (prob. because the game is played with a double deck)⟧ **1** any of a family of card games, usually for three or four persons and typically played with a 48-card deck made up of two of every card above the eight, including the ace **2** the meld of the queen of spades and the jack of diamonds in this game

pi·no·cy·to·sis (pī′nə sī tō′sis, pin′ə-) ***n., pl.*** **-ses′** (-sēz′) ⟦< Gr *pinein,* to drink, after PHAGOCYTOSIS⟧ a type of endocytosis in which the engulfed liquid remains within a separate vacuole —**pi′no·cy′tic** (-sīt′ik) ***adj.,*** **pi′no·cy·tot′ic** (-sī tät′ik)

☆**pi·no·le** (pē nō′lā, -lē; pi-; *Sp* pē nô′le) ***n.*** ⟦AmSp < Nahuatl *pinolli*⟧ [Southwest] flour made of ground corn, mesquite beans, etc.

☆**pi·ñon** (pēn′yän′, pin′-; -yōn′, -yən) ***n.*** *alt. sp. of* PINYON

pi·not (pē′nō, pē nō′) ***n.*** ⟦Fr, lit., little pine (cone): from the shape of the grape cluster⟧ **1** any of several related red or white grapes grown chiefly in Burgundy and Alsace **2** any of the red or white wines made from these grapes

pinot chardonnay [*also* **P- C-**] CHARDONNAY

Pinot Gri·gio (grē′jō, -zhō, -zhē ō) ⟦It, gray pinot, name of the grape: see PINOT⟧ [*also* **p- g-**] a light, dry white wine, originally produced in Italy

pinot noir ⟦Fr, lit., black PINOT⟧ [*also* **P- N-**] **1** the main red-wine grape of the Burgundy region, also used to make champagne **2** a dry red wine made from this grape

pin·point (pin′point′) ***vt.*** **1** to show the location of (a place on a map, etc.) by sticking in a pin **2** to locate, define, or focus on precisely —***n.*** **1** the point of a pin **2** something trifling or insignificant —***adj.*** **1** minute, exact, precise, etc. **2** very fine in texture: said of textiles [*pinpoint* oxford cloth]

pin·prick (pin′prik′) ***n.*** **1** any tiny puncture made by or as by a pin **2** a minor irritation or annoyance

pins and needles a tingling and prickling feeling in some part of the body, esp. in a limb that has been numb —**on pins and needles** in a state of anxious suspense or nervous anticipation

pin·scher (pin′chər, -shər) ***n.*** *see* DOBERMAN PINSCHER

☆**pin·set·ter** (pin′set′ər) ***n.*** **1** PIN BOY **2** a device that automatically sets up bowling pins in their proper place on the alley Also **pin′spot′ter** (-spät′ər)

Pinsk (pēnsk; *E* pinsk) city in SW Belarus

pin·stripe (pin′strīp′) ***n.*** **1** a very narrow stripe **2** *a)* a pattern of such stripes in parallel, as in some fabrics *b)* a fabric having such a pattern *c)* [*pl.*] a suit made of such fabric —**pin′striped′** ***adj.***

pint (pīnt) ***n.*** ⟦ME *pynte* < MFr *pinte* < ML *pinta,* prob. < VL **pincta,* for L *picta,* fem. pp. of *pingere,* to PAINT: orig. prob. a spot marking the level in a measure⟧ **1** *a)* a unit of liquid measure, equal to ½ of a liquid quart or 16 fluid ounces (4 gills or 0.4732 liquid liter): the British and Canadian imperial pint equals 0.5682 liquid liter *b)* a unit of dry measure, equal to ½ of a dry quart or ¹⁄₁₆ peck (0.5506 dry liter or 33.6003 cubic inches) **2** any container with a capacity of one pint **3** [Brit. Informal] a pint of beer Abbrev. *pt*

pin·ta (pin′tə) ***n.*** ⟦AmSp < Sp, a spot < VL **pincta:* see prec.⟧ a contagious skin disease of the tropics, characterized by patches of various colors and caused by a spirochete (*Treponema carateum*)

pin·ta·do (pin tä′dō) ***n., pl.*** **-dos** or **-does** ⟦Port, painted, pp. of *pintar,* to paint < VL **pinctare* < **pinctus,* for L *pictus,* pp. of *pingere,* to PAINT⟧ SPANISH MACKEREL

pin·tail (pin′tāl′) ***n., pl.*** **-tails′** or **-tail′** **1** any of several ducks, esp. a species (*Anas acuta*) with a long neck and long, pointed middle tail feathers ☆**2** any variety of grouse with a long, pointed tail

pin·ta·no (pin tä′nō) ***n., pl.*** **-nos** ⟦AmSp⟧ any of several brightly colored damselfishes (genus *Abudefduf*), as the sergeant major

Pin·ter (pin′tər), **Harold** 1930-2008; Eng. playwright

pin·tle (pin′təl) ***n.*** ⟦ME *pintil,* penis < OE *pintel,* dim. of *pinn:* see PIN⟧ a pin or bolt upon which some other part pivots or turns

☆**pin·to** (pin′tō) ***adj.*** ⟦AmSp, spotted < obs. Sp < VL **pinctus:* see PINTADO⟧ marked with patches of white and another, usually dark, color; piebald or skewbald —***n., pl.*** **-tos** **1** a pinto horse or pony **2** PINTO BEAN

☆**pinto bean** a kind of mottled kidney bean grown in the SW U.S. for food and fodder

Pintsch gas (pinch) ⟦after R. *Pintsch* (1840-1919), Ger inventor of the process⟧ a gas obtained by the destructive distillation of petroleum, formerly used for lighting

pint-size (pīnt′sīz′) ***adj.*** ☆small; tiny: also **pint′-sized′**

pin·up (pin′up′) ***adj.*** **1** that is or can be pinned up on or otherwise fastened to a wall *[a pinup lamp]* ☆**2** [Informal] designating a person whose sexual attractiveness makes her or him a suitable subject for the kind of pictures often pinned up on walls —☆***n.*** [Informal] such a person, picture, etc.

pin·wale (pin′wāl′) ***adj.*** having a fine wale, as some corduroy

☆**pin·weed** (pin′wēd′) ***n.*** any of a genus (*Lechea*) of perennial plants of the rockrose family, with thin stems and leaves, and small purplish or greenish flowers

pin·wheel (pin′hwēl′, -wēl′) ***n.*** **1** a small wheel with variously colored vanes of paper, plastic, etc., pinned to a stick so as to revolve in the wind **2** a fireworks device that revolves and throws off colored lights when set off —***vi.*** to rotate as a pinwheel does; whirl; spin

pin·worm (pin′wurm′) ***n.*** any of various parasitic nematode worms, esp. a species (*Enterobius vermicularis*) often found in the human rectum and large intestine, esp. in children

pinx·it (piŋk′sit) ***v.*** ⟦L⟧ (he or she) painted (it): formerly put after the artist's name on a painting: abbrev. *pinx.*, *pnxt.* or *pxt*

☆**pinx·ter flower** (piŋk′stər) ⟦so named from blossoming at PINKSTER⟧ a variety of azalea (*Rhododendron nudiflorum*) with pink, sweet-smelling flowers, purplish-red at the base

pin·y (pī′nē) ***adj.*** **pin′i·er, pin′i·est** *alt. sp. of* PINEY

Pin·yin (pin′yin′) ***n.*** ⟦Chin *pinyin*, lit., spell sound⟧ [*also* **p-**] system for transliterating Chinese ideograms into the Latin alphabet, adopted by the People's Republic of China in 1979

☆**pin·yon** (pin′yən, pēn′yōn, pēn yōn′) ***n.*** ⟦AmSp *piñón* < Sp, pine nut < *piña*, pine cone < L *pinea* < *pinus*, PINE[1]⟧ **1** any of several small pines (as *Pinus cembroides*, *P. monophylla*, or *P. edulis*) with large, edible seeds, widely distributed in W North America **2** the seed

Pin·zón (pēn thôn′) **1 Mar·tín A·lon·so** (mär tēn′ ä lôn′sô) 1440?-93; Sp. navigator with Columbus; commanded the *Pinta* **2 Vi·cen·te Yá·ñez** (vē *then*′te yä′nyeth) 1460?-1524?; Sp. navigator with Columbus; commanded the *Niña*: brother of Martín

pi·on (pī′än′) ***n.*** ⟦PI[2] + (MES)ON⟧ *Particle Physics* any of three short-lived mesons that may be positive, negative, or neutral: pions have a mass *c.* 270 times that of an electron and play an important role in the binding forces within the nucleus of an atom —**pi·on·ic** (pī än′ik) ***adj.***

pi·o·neer (pī′ə nir′) ***n.*** ⟦Fr *pionnier* < OFr *peonier*, foot soldier < *peon*: see PEON⟧ **1** [Archaic] a member of a military engineer unit trained to construct or demolish bridges, roads, trenches, etc. ☆**2** a person who goes before, preparing the way for others, as an early settler or a scientist doing exploratory work **3** a plant, animal, etc. that starts a new cycle of life in a barren area —***adj.*** **1** being one of the first of its kind **2** of or characteristic of the settlers of a new territory —***vi.*** to be a pioneer —***vt.*** **1** to prepare or open (a way, etc.) ☆**2** to be a pioneer in or of

pi·ous (pī′əs) ***adj.*** ⟦L *pius*, pious, devout, affectionate, good, prob. < IE **pwīyos* < base **peu-*, to clean > L *purus*, PURE⟧ **1** having or showing religious devotion; zealous in the performance of religious obligations **2** springing from actual or pretended religious devotion or moral motives **3** seemingly virtuous; affecting virtue hypocritically **4** sacred, as distinguished from secular or profane **5** [Archaic] having or showing a sense of duty and loyalty to family, friends, etc. —**SYN.** DEVOUT —**pi′ous·ly** ***adv.*** —**pi′ous·ness** ***n.***

pip[1] (pip) ***n.*** ⟦contr. < PIPPIN⟧ **1** a small seed, as of an apple, pear, or orange **2** [Old Slang] a person or thing much admired

pip[2] (pip) ***n.*** ⟦earlier *peep* < ?⟧ **1** any of the suit-indicating figures on playing cards, or any of the dots on dice or dominoes **2** [Informal] a starlike shoulder insignia worn by certain officers in the British army **3** any of the diamond-shaped divisions of the skin of a pineapple **4** a single rootstock or flower of the lily of the valley, peony, etc. **5** BLIP (***n.*** 1)

pip[3] (pip) ***vi.*** **pipped, pip′ping** ⟦var. of PEEP[1]⟧ to peep or chirp, as a young bird —***vt.*** to break through (the shell): said of a hatching bird

pip[4] (pip) ***n.*** ⟦ME *pippe* < MDu < WGmc **pipit* < VL **pipita*, for L *pituita*, phlegm, pip: see PITUITARY⟧ **1** a contagious disease of fowl, characterized by the secretion of mucus in the throat and the formation of a scab on the tongue **2** [Informal] any unspecified human ailment: a jocular usage

pip[5] (pip) ***vt.*** **pipped, pip′ping** [Brit.] to defeat in a competition by a narrow margin

pip·age (pīp′ij) ***n.*** **1** transportation, as of water, gas, oil, etc., by pipes **2** the charge for such transportation **3** a system of such pipes

pi·pal (pē′pəl) ***n.*** ⟦Hindi *pīpal* < Sans *pippala*⟧ PEEPUL

pipe (pīp) ***n.*** ⟦ME < OE < WGmc **pipa* < VL **pipa* < L *pipare*, to cheep, chirp, peep, of echoic orig.⟧ **1** a hollow cylinder or cone, as of reed, straw, wood, or metal, in which air vibrates to produce a musical sound, as in an organ or wind instrument **2** any wind instrument; specif., *a)* [*pl.*] BAGPIPE *b)* a small medieval fipple flute played with the left hand while the right hand beats a tabor **3** a small, shrill whistle, used by a boatswain as in conveying orders to a ship's crew: in full **boatswain's pipe** **4** a high, shrill sound, as of a voice, birdcall, etc. **5** [*often pl.*] the vocal organs, esp. as used in singing **6** a long tube of clay, concrete, metal, plastic, etc., for conveying water, gas, oil, etc. or for use in construction **7** *a)* a tubular organ or canal of the body *b)* [*pl.*] the respiratory organs **8** *a)* a somewhat cylindrical deposit of ore *b)* an opening into a volcano's crater **9** anything tubular in form **10** *a)* a tube with a small bowl at one end, in which tobacco, etc. is smoked *b)* enough tobacco, etc. to fill such a bowl **11** *a)* a large cask for wine, oil, etc., having a capacity of about two hogsheads, or 126 gallons *b)* this volume as a unit of measure ☆**12** [Slang] something regarded as easy to accomplish —***vi.*** **piped, pip′ing** **1** to play on a pipe **2** to utter shrill, reedy sounds or tones **3** *Metallurgy* to develop longitudinal cavities, as steel sometimes does in ingots and castings during solidification **4** *Naut.* to signal a ship's crew by sounding a boatswain's pipe —***vt.*** **1** to play (a tune, etc.) on a pipe **2** to utter in a shrill, reedy voice or tone **3** to affect or bring to some condition or place by or as by playing pipes *[to pipe the clan to battle]* ☆**4** to convey (water, gas, oil, etc.) by means of pipes ☆**5** to provide with pipes **6** to trim (a dress, etc.) with piping **7** to squeeze (icing, dough, or other soft or puréed food) from a pastry bag **8** [Slang] to look at or notice **9** *Naut.* to call together or alert (the crew), make (a specified call), or signal the arrival aboard or the departure of (someone) by sounding a boatswain's pipe —**pipe down** ☆[Slang] to become quiet or quieter; stop shouting, talking, etc. —**pipe in** to convey (esp. transcribed or remote music or speech) by an electric or electronic system —**pipe up** **1** to begin to play or sing (music) **2** to speak up or say, esp. in a piping voice

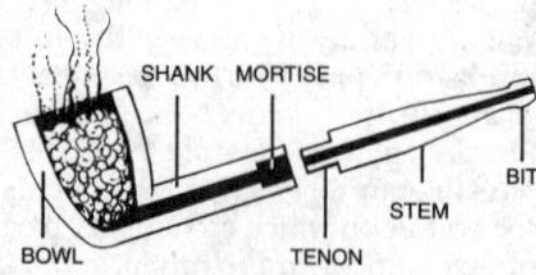

parts of a pipe
(sense 10a)

pipe bomb a crude, handmade bomb with the explosive charge contained in a metal pipe

pipe clay a white, plastic clay used for making clay tobacco pipes or pottery, for whitening leather, etc.

pipe-clay (pīp′klā′) ***vt.*** to whiten with pipe clay

pipe cleaner a short length of thin wires twisted so as to hold tiny tufts of yarn, originally designed to clean the stem of a tobacco pipe but now used variously, as in arts and crafts projects

pipe cutter a tool for cutting metal pipes, with a curved jaw containing one or more disks, the whole tool being rotated around the pipe

☆**pipe dream** ⟦in allusion to hallucinations experienced by opium smokers⟧ [Informal] a fantastic idea, vain hope or plan, etc.

pipe·fish (pīp′fish′) ***n.***, *pl.* **-fish′** or **-fish′es** (see FISH) any of various long, narrow bony fishes (order Gasterosteiformes, family Syngnathidae) with a tubelike snout, of the same family as the sea horses

pipe fitter a skilled worker who installs and maintains pipes, as in a plumbing or refrigeration system

pipe fitting **1** a coupling, elbow, etc. used to connect sections of pipe **2** the work of a pipe fitter

pipe·ful (pīp′fool′) ***n.***, *pl.* **-fuls′** the amount (of tobacco, etc.) put in a pipe at one time

☆**pipe·line** (pīp′līn′) ***n.*** **1** a line of pipes for conveying water, gas, oil, etc. **2** any channel or means whereby something is passed on *[a pipeline of information]* —***vt.*** **-lined′**, **-lin′ing** to convey by, or supply with, a pipeline

☆**pipe of peace** PEACE PIPE

☆**pipe organ** ORGAN (sense 1*a*)

pip·er (pī′pər) ***n.*** ⟦ME *pipere* < OE⟧ a person who plays on a pipe; esp., a bagpiper —**pay the piper** to pay for one's pleasures or bear the consequences of one's actions

pi·per·a·zine (pi per′ə zēn′, pī-; -zin; pip′ər i-) ***n.*** ⟦PIPER(INE) + AZ- + -INE[3]⟧ a crystalline compound, $(C_2H_4NH)_2$, used in treating worm infestations, in insecticides, etc.

pi·per·i·dine (pi per′i dēn′, -din; pip′ər i-) ***n.*** ⟦< fol. + -IDE + -INE[3]⟧ a colorless, liquid hydrocarbon, $(CH_2)_5NH$, found in many alkaloids and obtained by reducing pyridine or by treating piperine with alkali: used in making rubber, oils, fuels, etc.

pip·er·ine (pip′ər ēn′, -in) ***n.*** ⟦L *piper*, PEPPER + -INE[3]⟧ a colorless, crystalline alkaloid, $C_{17}H_{19}NO_3$, found in pepper

pip·er·o·nal (pip′ər ō nal′) ***n.*** ⟦Ger < *piperin*, piperine (see prec.) + *-on*, -ONE + *-al*, -AL⟧ an aldehyde, $C_6H_3(CH_2)OOCHO$, obtained from piperine and having a strong smell like that of heliotrope: used in making perfume

pipe·stem (pīp′stem′) ***n.*** **1** the stem of a tobacco pipe through which the smoke is drawn **2** anything like this in form, as a very thin leg

☆**pipe·stone** (pīp′stōn′) ***n.*** a hard, reddish, claylike stone used by the American Indians to make tobacco pipes

pi·pette or **pi·pet** (pi pet′, pī-) ***n.*** ⟦Fr, dim. of *pipe*, pipe < VL **pipa*: see PIPE⟧ a slender pipe or tube into which small amounts of liquids are taken up by suction, as for measuring —***vt.*** **-pet′ted, -pet′ting** to remove, transfer, or measure (liquid) by means of a pipette

pipe wrench any of several types of wrench, including the Stillson wrench, used to grip and turn pipes and other cylindrical objects

pip·ing (pīp′iŋ) ***n.*** **1** the act of a person who pipes **2** the music made by pipes **3** a shrill voice or sound **4** *a)* a system of pipes *b)* pipes collectively **5** a pipelike fold of material with which edges or seams are trimmed **6** ⟦see PIPE (***vt.*** 7)⟧ *Cooking* ornamental lines made with a PASTRY BAG, as of icing on a frosted cake —***adj.*** **1** playing on a pipe **2** characterized by the music of the "peaceful" pipe rather than of the "warlike" drums, trumpets, etc.; hence, peaceful or tranquil **3** sounding high and shrill —**piping hot** ⟦rough characterization of the hissing sounds made by steaming food⟧ very hot, esp. to an appetizing degree *[piping hot biscuits]*

pip·is·trelle or **pip·is·trel** (pip′i strel′) ***n.*** ⟦Fr *pipistrelle* < It *pipistrello*, altered < OIt *vipistrello* < L *vespertilio*, bat < *vesper*, evening: see VESPER⟧ any of a genus (*Pipistrellus*) of small bats that characteristically fly early in the evening: found in North America and in most of the Eastern Hemisphere

pip·it (pip′it) ***n.*** ⟦echoic of its cry⟧ any of various small, insectivorous birds (esp. genus *Anthus*) of a passerine family (Motacillidae) characterized by a slender bill, streaked breast, and the habit of walking rather than hopping

pip·kin (pip′kin) ***n.*** ⟦? dim. of PIPE, *n.* 11⟧ a small earthenware pot

pip·pin (pip′in) ***n.*** ⟦ME *pipyn* < OFr *pepin*, seed, pip⟧ **1** any of a number of varieties of apple, esp. those cooked in desserts **2** [Brit. Dial.] a small pip, or seed **3** [Slang] a person or thing much admired

☆**pip·sis·se·wa** (pip sis′ə wə) ***n.*** ⟦< ? Abenaki *kpi-pskwáhsawe*, lit., flower of the woods⟧ any of a genus (*Chimaphila*) of North American evergreen plants of the heath family, with pink or white flowers and jagged, leathery leaves formerly used as a diuretic and tonic

pip·squeak (pip′skwēk′) ***n.*** ⟦PIP^3 + SQUEAK⟧ [Informal] anyone or anything regarded as small or insignificant

pip·y (pī′pē) ***adj.*** **pip′i·er, pip′i·est 1** pipelike; tubular **2** sounding like a pipe; shrill —**pip′i·ness *n.***

pi·quant (pē′kənt, -känt, -kwənt) ***adj.*** ⟦Fr, prp. of *piquer*, to prick, sting: see PIKE^2⟧ **1** agreeably pungent or stimulating to the taste; pleasantly sharp or biting **2** exciting agreeable interest or curiosity; stimulating; provocative **3** [Archaic] piercing or stinging; bitter —**pi′quan·cy *n.*, pi′quant·ness** —**pi′quant·ly *adv.***

pique (pēk) ***n.*** ⟦Fr < *piquer*: see prec.⟧ **1** resentment at being slighted or disdained; ruffled pride **2** a fit of displeasure —***vt.* piqued, piqu′ing** ⟦Fr *piquer*⟧ **1** to arouse resentment in, as by slighting; ruffle the pride of **2** to arouse; provoke —***SYN.*** OFFENSE, PROVOKE —**pique oneself on** (or **upon**) to be proud of

pi·qué or **pi·que** (pē kā′) ***n.*** ⟦Fr, pp. of *piquer*, to prick: see PIKE^2⟧ a firmly woven cotton fabric with ribbed, corded, or ridged wales —***adj.*** designating fine seams that have been turned under before sewing, as on women's gloves

pi·quet (pē kā′, -ket′) ***n.*** ⟦Fr < *pic*, term in piquet, orig., prick, sting < *piquer*: see PIKE^2⟧ a card game for two persons, played with 32 cards

pi·ra·cy (pī′rə sē) ***n., pl.* -cies** ⟦ML *piratia* < Gr *peirateia* < *peiratēs*, PIRATE⟧ **1** robbery of ships on the high seas **2** the unauthorized publication, reproduction, or use of a copyrighted or patented work **3** the illegal recording, transmission, or reception of radio or TV broadcasts

Pi·rae·us (pī rē′əs) seaport in SE Greece, on the Saronic Gulf: part of Athens' metropolitan area: Gr. name PEIRAIÉVS

pi·ra·gua (pi rä′gwə, -rag′wə) ***n.*** ⟦Sp: see PIROGUE⟧ **1** a dugout canoe **2** a flat-bottomed, two-masted sailing vessel

Pi·ran·del·lo (pir′ən del′ō; *It* pē′rän del′lô), **Lu·i·gi** (lo͞o ē′jē) 1867-1936; It. playwright & novelist

Pi·ra·ne·si (pir′ə nā′zē; *It* pē′rä ne′zē), **Giam·bat·ti·sta** (jäm′bät tē′stä) 1720-78; It. architect & etcher

pi·ra·nha (pi rä′nə, -ran′ə; pi rän′yə) ***n., pl.* -nhas** or **-nha** ⟦BrazPort < Tupí & Guaraní, toothed fish < *pirá*, fish + *sainha*, tooth⟧ any of various small South American freshwater bony fishes (family Serrasalmidae, order Cypriniformes) having strong jaws and very sharp teeth: they hunt in schools, attacking any animals, including human beings

pi·ra·ru·cu (pē rä′ro͞o ko͞o′) ***n.*** ⟦Port < Tupí *pirá-rucú*, lit., red fish⟧ ARAPAIMA

pi·rate (pī′rət) ***n.*** ⟦ME < L *pirata* < Gr *peiratēs* < *peirān*, to attempt, attack < IE base **per-*, to bring through, penetrate > FARE⟧ **1** a person who practices piracy; esp., a robber of ships on the high seas **2** a ship used by pirates in attacking other vessels **3** one who engages in the illegal recording, transmission, or reception of radio or TV broadcasts —***vt., vi.* -rat·ed, -rat·ing 1** to practice piracy (upon) **2** to take (something) by piracy **3** to publish, reproduce, or make use of without authorization (a literary work, musical recording, film, etc.), esp. in violation of a copyright —**pi·rat·i·cal** (pī rat′i kəl) ***adj.*, pi·rat′ic** —**pi·rat′i·cal·ly *adv.***

pirn (purn, pirn) ***n.*** ⟦ME *pyrne*, by metathesis < ? dial. *prin*, a pin, pointed twig⟧ [Scot.] **1** the bobbin or spool of a weaver's shuttle **2** a fishing reel

pi·ro·gen (pi rō′gən) ***pl.n.*** ⟦Yiddish *pirogn*, sing. *pirog* < Russ: see fol.⟧ small pastry turnovers with a filling

pi·ro·gi (pi rō′gē) ***n., pl.* -gi** or **-gies** ⟦Russ *pirogi*, pl. of *pirog*, pie⟧ a small pastry turnover with a filling, as of meat, cheese, mashed potatoes, etc.: see also PIEROGI

pi·rogue (pi rōg′) ***n.*** ⟦Fr < Sp *piragua* < Carib or Arawak⟧ **1** a dugout canoe **2** any canoe-shaped boat

pi·rosh·ki or **pi·rozh·ki** (pi räsh′kē) ***pl.n.*** ⟦Russ *pyrožki*, sing. *pyrožok*, small pie: see also PIROGI⟧ small pastry turnovers with a filling

pir·ou·ette (pir′o͞o et′) ***n.*** ⟦Fr, spinning top < dial. *piroue*, a top, prob. < VL **piro*, plug, peg < Gr *peiron*, peg⟧ a whirling around on one foot or the point of the toe, esp. in ballet —***vi.* -et′ted, -et′ting** ⟦Fr *pirouetter* < the n.⟧ to do a pirouette

Pi·sa (pē′zə; *It* pē′sä) commune in Tuscany, W Italy, on the Arno River: famous for its Leaning Tower —**Pi′san** (-zən) ***adj., n.***

pis-al·ler (pē zá lā′) ***n.*** ⟦Fr, lit., a getting worse⟧ a last resort

Pi·sa·no (pē sä′nō, -zä′-), **Ni·co·la** (nē kô′lä) 1220?-84?; It. sculptor & architect

pis·ca·ry (pis′kə rē) ***n., pl.* -ries** ⟦ML *piscaria* < L *piscarius*, of fish, of fishing < *piscis*, FISH⟧ **1** *Law* the right of fishing in waters owned by another: now only in **common of piscary 2** a place for fishing

pis·ca·tol·o·gy (pis′kə täl′ə jē) ***n.*** ⟦< L *piscatus*, pp. of *piscari*, to fish (< *piscis*, FISH) + -LOGY⟧ [Rare] the art or science of fishing

Pis·ca·tor (pis kä′tôr), **Erwin** 1893-1966; Ger. theatrical director & producer

pis·ca·to·ri·al (pis′kə tôr′ē əl) ***adj.*** ⟦L *piscatorius* < *piscator*, fisherman < *piscatus*: see PISCATOLOGY⟧ of fishes, fishermen, or fishing: also **pis′ca·to′ry** —**pis′ca·to′ri·al·ly *adv.***

Pis·ces (pī′sēz′; *occas.* pis′ēz′) ***n.*** ⟦ME < L, pl. of *piscis*, FISH⟧ **1** a N constellation between Aries and Aquarius; the Fishes **2** the twelfth sign of the zodiac, entered by the sun about February 21 **3** a person born under the sign of Pisces: also **Pis·ce·an** (pī′sē ən, pis′ē-)

pis·ci- (pis′i, -ə; pī′si, -sə) ⟦< L *piscis*, FISH⟧ *combining form* fish [*piscivorous*]

pis·ci·cul·ture (pis′i kul′chər) ***n.*** ⟦prec. + CULTURE⟧ the breeding and rearing of fish as a science or industry

pis·ci·na (pi sē′nə, -sī′-) ***n.*** ⟦L, tank, cistern, orig., fishpond < *piscis*, FISH⟧ *R.C.Ch.* a basin with a drain, formerly near the altar, now usually in the sacristy, for the disposal of holy water, waste water from washing altar linen, etc.

pis·cine (pī′sēn′, -sīn′, -sin; pis′ēn′, -īn′, -in) ***adj.*** ⟦ModL *piscinus* < L *piscis*, FISH⟧ of or resembling fish

Pis·cis Aus·tri·nus (pis′is ô strī′nəs, pī′sis) ⟦ModL, southern fish < L *piscis*, FISH + *austrinus*, southern < *auster*: see AUSTRAL⟧ a S constellation between Grus and Aquarius, containing the bright star Fomalhaut: also called **Piscis Aus·tra·lis** (ô strā′lis)

pis·civ·o·rous (pi siv′ə rəs, pī-) ***adj.*** ⟦PISCI- + -VOROUS⟧ feeding on fish; fish-eating

pis·co (pēs′kō) ***n.*** ⟦after *Pisco*, town in Peru⟧ a brandy made in Peru

Pis·gah (piz′gə) ***n.*** ⟦Heb *pisga*, lit., peak, summit⟧ *Bible* mountain ridge east of the N end of the Dead Sea: Deut. 3:27: see NEBO, Mount

pish (psh, pish) ***interj., n.*** (an exclamation) used to express disgust or impatience —***vi., vt.*** to utter this exclamation (to)

pish·er (pēsh′ər) ***n.*** ⟦Yiddish < Ger *pisser*, pisser > PISSER, PISS⟧ [*also in roman type*] [Slang] **1** a young, inexperienced, presumptuous person **2** a person or thing of no importance; a nobody or nothing

Pi·sid·i·a (pi sid′ē ə) ancient country in SC Asia Minor, south of Phrygia

pi·si·form (pī′si fôrm′) ***adj.*** ⟦< L *pisum*, PEA + -FORM⟧ resembling a pea in shape and size —***n.*** a small bone on the inner side of the wrist that resembles half a pea

Pi·sis·tra·tus (pi sis′trə təs, pī-) died 527 B.C.; tyrant of Athens (variously from 560 to 527)

pis·mire (pis′mīr′, piz′-) ***n.*** ⟦ME *pissemire* < *pisse*, urine + *mire*, ant (< Scand, as in Dan *myre*, Swed *myra* < IE base **morwi-*, ant > L *formica*): from the odor of formic acid, discharged by ants⟧ [Archaic] an ant

☆**pis·mo clam** (piz′mō) ⟦after *Pismo* Beach, Calif.⟧ a heavy-shelled, edible clam (*Tivela stultorum*) found on sandy beaches along the coast of California and Mexico

pi·so·lite (pī′sə līt′, piz′ə-) ***n.*** ⟦< Gr *pison*, PEA + -LITE⟧ **1** a small, spherical body, commonly composed of calcium carbonate, found in sedimentary rock **2** a sedimentary rock, as limestone, containing many such bodies —**pi′so·lit′ic** (-lit′ik) ***adj.***

piss (pis) [Slang] ***vi.*** ⟦ME *pissen* < OFr *pissier*, prob. of echoic orig.⟧ to urinate —***vt.* 1** to discharge with the urine [*to piss blood*] **2** to make wet by urination [*to piss one's pants*] —***n.*** urine —**piss away** to lose or waste as through carelessness or neglect; squander —**piss off 1** to anger, annoy, irritate, etc. **2** to get away from or out of; leave
USAGE—somewhat vulgar in all uses

piss·ant or **piss-ant** (pis′ant′) ***n.*** ⟦prec. + ANT^1: see PISMIRE⟧ **1** [Dial.] an ant **2** [Slang] a person regarded as insignificant and contemptible —***adj.*** [Slang] insignificant and contemptible The ***adj.*** & ***n.*** 2 considered mildly vulgar by some

Pis·sar·ro (pi sär′ō; *Fr* pē sá rō′), **Camille** 1830-1903; Fr. painter, born in the Virgin Islands

pissed (pist) ***adj.*** **1** ⟦< PISS OFF (see phr. under PISS)⟧ [Slang] angry, irritated, etc. **2** [Slang, Chiefly Brit.] drunk; intoxicated Sometimes considered mildly vulgar

piss-el·e·gant (pis′el′ə gənt) ***adj.*** ⟦from use of PISS, *n.*, as adv., excessively, extremely⟧ [Slang] displaying a contrived, often pretentious, sophistication, opulence, etc.: sometimes considered mildly vulgar —**piss′-el′e·gance *n.***

piss·er (pis′ər) ***n.*** [Slang] a person or thing that is difficult, unpleasant, etc.: sometimes considered mildly vulgar

pis·soir (pē swår′) ***n.*** ⟦Fr < MFr < *pisser*, to urinate < OFr *pissier*: see PISS⟧ a public urinal for men, esp. one located on a street

piss-poor (pis′po͝or′) ***adj.*** ⟦from use of PISS, *n.*, as adv., excessively, extremely⟧ [Slang] **1** characterized by extreme poverty **2** inferior, worthless, etc. Sometimes considered mildly vulgar

pis·tach·i·o (pi stash′ē ō, -stä′shē ō, -stash′ō) ***n., pl.* -chi·os′** ⟦It *pistacchio* < L *pistacium* < Gr *pistakion* < *pistakē*, pistachio tree < OPers *pistah*⟧ **1** a small tree (*Pistacia vera*) of the cashew family **2** its edible, greenish seed: in full **pistachio nut 3** the flavor of this nut **4** a light yellow-green color

☆**pis·ta·reen** (pis′tə rēn′) ***n.*** ⟦prob. orig. < dim. of PESETA⟧ a former Spanish silver coin of the American colonies and the West Indies

piste (pēst) ***n.*** ⟦Fr < It *pista* < *pistare*, to beat: see PISTON⟧ a ski run of hard-packed snow

pis·til (pis′təl) ***n.*** ⟦Fr < L *pistillum*, PESTLE⟧ the seed-bearing organ of a flowering plant consisting of one carpel or of several united carpels

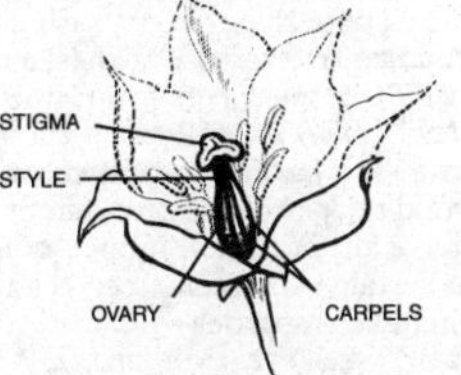

pistil of a tulip

pis·til·late (pis′tə lit, -lāt′) ***adj.*** *Bot.* having a pistil or pistils; specif., having pistils but no stamens

pis·tol (pis′təl) ***n.*** ⟦Fr *pistole* < Ger < Czech *píšťal,* pistol, orig., pipe, prob. < *pisk,* echoic word for a whistling sound⟧ **1** a small firearm made to be held and fired with one hand **2** such a firearm in which the chamber is part of the barrel: cf. REVOLVER **3** *Track & Field* a similar device used to start a race or to signal the beginning of the gun lap: it makes a loud sound but does not fire a projectile ☆**4** [Slang] a remarkable or unusual person, esp. one characterized by eccentric or impetuous behavior —***vt.*** **-toled** or **-tolled, -tol·ing** or **-tol·ling** to shoot with a pistol

pis·tole (pis tōl′) ***n.*** ⟦Fr, earlier *pistolet,* dim. of *pistole* (see prec.): so named in Fr, after debasement of the coin, in punning allusion to a double use of the original name of the coin, *écu,* which also meant "shield"⟧ **1** a former Spanish gold coin **2** any of various similar obsolete gold coins of Europe

pis·to·leer (pis′tə lir′) ***n.*** ⟦Fr *pistolier*⟧ [Obs.] a soldier armed with a pistol

☆**pis·tol-whip** (pis′təl hwip′, -wip′) ***vt.*** **-whipped′, -whip′ping** to beat with a pistol, esp. about the head

pis·ton (pis′tən) ***n.*** ⟦Fr < It *pistone* < *pistare,* to pound, crush < LL, freq. of L *pinsere,* to pound, beat: see PESTLE⟧ **1** the snug-fitting engine part that is forced back and forth within a cylinder by the pressure of combustion, steam, etc. and a reciprocating connecting rod **2** *Music* a sliding valve moved in the cylinder of a brass instrument to change the pitch

piston (sense 1)

Pis·ton (pis′tən), **Walter** 1894-1976; U.S. composer

piston ring a thin split ring fitted into a groove around a piston to seal the cylinder, transfer heat, and control cylinder-wall lubrication

piston rod a connecting rod attached to a piston and the crankshaft

pis·tou (pē sto͞o′) ***n.*** ⟦Fr < Prov⟧ **1** a French sauce like pesto but often without the cheese **2** a soup or other dish flavored with this

☆**pit**[1] (pit) ***n.*** ⟦Du < MDu *pitte,* akin to PITH⟧ the hard stone, as of the plum, peach, or cherry, which contains the seed —***vt.*** **pit′ted, pit′ting** to remove the pit from (a fruit)

pit[2] (pit) ***n.*** ⟦ME < OE *pytt* < early WGmc & NGmc **puttia* (> ON *pyttr,* Ger *pfütze*) < L *puteus,* well, prob. < IE base **pēu-,* to chop, cut > L *pavire,* to beat, strike⟧ **1** a hole or cavity in the ground **2** an abyss **3** hell: used with *the* **4** a covered hole used to trap wild animals; pitfall **5** any concealed danger; trap; snare **6** an enclosed area in which animals are kept or made to fight [*a bear pit*] **7** *a)* the shaft of a coal mine *b)* the coal mine itself **8** a hollow or depression on a part of the human body [*armpit*] **9** a small hollow in a surface; specif., a depressed scar on the skin, as that resulting from smallpox **10** an area below floor level or ground level **11** [Brit.] *a)* the ground floor of a theater, esp. the part at the rear *b)* the spectators in that section **12** the section, often below floor level, in front of the stage, where the orchestra sits ☆**13** the part of the floor of an exchange where a special branch of business is transacted [*corn pit*] ☆**14** *a)* a work area for mechanics, often below floor level, for repairing and servicing automotive vehicles *b)* the area along the side of a track where racing cars make their pit stops ☆**15** in a casino, an area in which gambling tables are set up, specif., the area within a ring of such tables **16** *Bot.* a tiny depression in a plant cell wall —***vt.*** **pit′ted, pit′ting 1** to put, cast, or store in a pit **2** to make pits in **3** to mark with small scars [*pitted* by smallpox] **4** to set (cocks, etc.) in a pit to fight **5** to set in competition (*against*) —***vi.*** **1** to become marked with pits ☆**2** to make a pit stop during an auto race —**the pits 1** [Slang] the worst possible thing, place, condition, etc. ☆**2** PIT[2] (***n.*** *14b*)

pi·ta[1] (pēt′ə) ***n.*** ⟦AmSp < Taino, thread from agave fibers⟧ **1** any of various agave plants yielding a fiber used in paper, etc. **2** the fiber

pi·ta[2] (pēt′ə) ***n.*** ⟦ModHeb *pita* (< SE Judezmo) or ModGr *pitta* (see PIZZA)⟧ **1** a round, hollow, relatively flat bread of the Middle East: also **pita bread 2** a piece of this: it can be split into two layers or cut crosswise to form a pocket for a filling

pit·a·pat (pit′ə pat′) ***adv.*** ⟦redupl. of PAT[2]⟧ with rapid and strong beating; throbbingly —***n.*** a rapid succession of beats or taps —***vi.*** **-pat′ted, -pat′ting** to go pitapat

☆**pit boss** [Informal] a person supervising a casino PIT[2] (***n.*** 15)

pit bull ⟦so named because it was developed for fighting: see PIT[2] (***n.*** 6), BULL TERRIER⟧ a short, heavy, broad-chested dog with large, powerful jaws and a short, smooth coat: also **pit bull terrier**

Pit·cairn (pit′kern) British island in Polynesia, in the South Pacific: settled in 1790 by mutineers from HMS *Bounty*: 1.8 sq mi (4.6 sq km)

pitch[1] (pich) ***n.*** ⟦ME *pich* < OE *pic* < L *pix* (gen. *picis*) < IE base **pi-,* to be fat > FAT⟧ **1** a black, sticky substance formed in the distillation of coal tar, wood tar, petroleum, etc. and used for waterproofing, roofing, pavements, etc. **2** any of certain bitumens, as asphalt, asphaltite, etc. **3** a resin found in certain evergreen trees **4** any of various synthetic substances having pitchlike properties —***vt.*** to cover or smear with or as with pitch

pitch[2] (pich) ***vt.*** ⟦ME *picchen,* ? form of *picken,* to PICK[3]⟧ **1** to set up; erect [*pitch* a tent] **2** to throw; cast, fling, or toss **3** *a)* to toss (coins, quoits, etc.) as at a mark in a contest *b)* to discard by throwing; throw away **4** to set in order for battle: obsolete except in PITCHED BATTLE **5** to fix or set at a particular point, level, degree, etc. **6** [Informal] to try to sell, promote, or convince, using persuasive talk, advertising, etc. ☆**7** *Baseball a)* to throw (the ball) to the batter *b)* to assign (a player) to pitch *c)* to serve as pitcher for (a game, inning, etc.) **8** *Golf* to loft (a ball), esp. in making an approach **9** *Music* to determine or set the key of (a tune, an instrument, or the voice) —***vi.*** **1** to encamp **2** to take up one's position; settle **3** to hurl or toss anything, as hay, a baseball, etc. **4** to fall or plunge headlong **5** to incline downward; dip **6** to plunge or toss with the bow and stern rising and falling abruptly: said of a ship **7** to move in a like manner in the air: said of an aircraft **8** to plunge forward; lurch, as when off balance **9** to act as pitcher in a ballgame **10** to loft a golf ball, as in making an approach —***n.*** **1** act or manner of pitching **2** a throw, fling, toss, etc. **3** *a)* the rising and falling of the bow and stern of a ship in a rough sea *b)* the movement up or down of the nose and tail of an airplane **4** anything pitched **5** the amount pitched **6** a point or degree [*emotion was at a high pitch*] **7** the degree of slope or inclination ☆**8** a card game of the all-fours family in which the suit of the first card led becomes trump ☆**9** [Informal] a line of talk, such as a salesperson uses to persuade customers **10** [Chiefly Brit.] *a)* a playing field [*a cricket pitch*] *b)* a place, often assigned, for pitching a tent or parking a trailer, etc. *c)* a place where a street vendor, street performer, racecourse bookmaker, etc. sets up a stand **11** *Aeron. a)* the adjustable blade angle of the propeller or rotor blade *b)* the distance advanced by a propeller in one revolution **12** *Archit.* the slope of the sides of a roof, expressed by the ratio of its height to its span ☆**13** *Baseball a)* a throw by a pitcher to a batter *b)* a particular type of such a throw [*our ace has three pitches,* a fastball, slider, and curve] *c)* a pitched ball in flight [*the pitch* sailed over the batter's head] **14** *Geol., Mining* the dip of a stratum or vein **15** *Golf* a short, lofted shot, usually to the green **16** *Machinery a)* the distance between corresponding points on two adjacent gear teeth *b)* the distance between corresponding points on two adjacent threads of a screw, measured along the axis **17** *a) Acoustics, Music* that element of a tone or sound determined by the frequency of vibration of the sound waves reaching the ear: the greater the frequency, the higher the pitch *b) Music* a tone used as a standard of pitch for tuning instruments (see CONCERT PITCH) **—*SYN.*** THROW —☆**in there pitching** [Informal] working hard and enthusiastically —☆**make a pitch for** [Informal] to speak in favor or promotion of —**pitch in** [Informal] **1** to set to work energetically **2** to make a contribution —**pitch into** [Informal] **1** to attack physically or verbally **2** to set to work on energetically —**pitch on** (or **upon**) to select; decide on

pitch-black (pich′blak′) ***adj.*** very black or very dark; often, specif., entirely without light

pitch·blende (pich′blend′) ***n.*** ⟦calque of Ger *pechblende* < *pech* (< L *pix*), PITCH[1] + *blende,* BLENDE⟧ a brown to black, radioactive, massive form of uraninite: pitchblende is the chief ore of uranium and radium

pitch circle an imaginary circle that intersects the teeth of a gear at the actual points where the teeth mesh with another gear: the pitch circles of two enmeshed gears are tangent

pitch-dark (pich′därk′) ***adj.*** very dark; often, specif., entirely without light

pitched battle 1 a battle in which placement of troops and the line of combat are relatively fixed before the action **2** a closely fought battle of great intensity

pitch·er[1] (pich′ər) ***n.*** ⟦ME *picher* < OFr *pichier* < VL **piccarium,* var. of *bicarium,* jug, cup: see BEAKER⟧ **1** *a)* a container, usually with a handle and lip, for holding and pouring liquids *b)* as much as a pitcher will hold **2** *Bot.* ASCIDIUM

pitch·er[2] (pich′ər) ***n.*** ⟦PITCH[2] + -ER⟧ a person who pitches; specif., the baseball player who pitches the ball to the opposing batters

pitcher plant any of various plants with slippery, pitcherlike leaves that contain a pool of enzymes that digest trapped insects; esp., any of a family (Sarraceniaceae, order Nepenthales) of dicotyledonous, New World plants that grow in swamps and bogs

pitch·fork (pich′fôrk′) ***n.*** a large, long-handled fork used for lifting and tossing hay, straw, etc. —***vt.*** to lift and toss with or as with a pitchfork

☆**pitch·man** (pich′mən) ***n., pl.*** **-men** (-mən) **1** a person who hawks novelties, jewelry, etc. as from a stand on a city street or at a carnival **2** [Informal] any high-pressure salesperson or advertiser, as on radio

☆**pitch·out** (pich′out′) ***n.*** **1** *Baseball* a ball pitched deliberately away from the plate in anticipation of a play by the catcher to throw out a runner who has moved away from a base **2** *Football* a lateral pass behind the line of scrimmage, usually from the quarterback to another back

☆**pitch pine** any of several resinous pines yielding pitch or turpentine, esp. a pine (*Pinus rigida*) of the E U.S.

pitch pipe a small pipe or set of pipes that produces a tone or tones for establishing the pitch for tuning an instrument or for singing

pitch·stone (pich′stōn′) ***n.*** ⟦calque of Ger *pechstein* < *pech* (< L *pix*), PITCH[1] + *stein,* STONE⟧ a volcanic glass that somewhat resembles pitch and has a higher percentage of water than obsidian or other glassy rocks

pitch·y (pich′ē) ***adj.*** **pitch′i·er, pitch′i·est 1** full of pitch; smeared with pitch **2** thick or sticky like pitch **3** black

pit·e·ous (pit′ē əs) ***adj.*** ⟦ME *piteus* < MFr < OFr *pitous* < LL(Ec) **pietosus* < *pietas:* see PIETY⟧ arousing or deserving pity or compassion **—*SYN.*** PITIFUL —**pit′e·ous·ly** ***adv.*** —**pit′e·ous·ness** ***n.***

pit·fall (pit′fôl′) ***n.*** ⟦ME *pitfalle* < *pit,* PIT[2] + *falle,* a trap < OE *fealle* < *feallan,* to FALL⟧ **1** a lightly covered pit used as a trap for animals **2** an unsuspected difficulty, danger, or error that one may fall into **—*SYN.*** TRAP[1]

pith (pith) *n.* ⟦ME *pithe* < OE *pitha,* akin to MDu *pitte,* pit of a fruit, kernel, pith of a tree⟧ **1** the soft, spongy tissue in the center of certain plant stems **2** the soft core of various other things, as of a bone or feather **3** the spongy, fibrous tissue lining the rind and surrounding the sections of an orange, grapefruit, etc. **4** the essential part; substance; gist **5** importance: now usually in **of great pith and moment** **6** [Archaic] strength; vigor; force —*vt.* **1** to remove the pith from (a plant stem) **2** to pierce or sever the spinal cord of (an animal) in order to kill it or make it insensible for experimental purposes

pith·e·can·thro·pine (pith′i kan′thrə pīn′, -pin) *adj.* ⟦see fol. & -INE[1]⟧ of, belonging to, or resembling a former genus (*Pithecanthropus,* now classified as *Homo erectus*) of extinct early humans, who lived in Java, China, Europe, and Africa: also **pith′e·can′thro·poid′** (-poid′) —*n.* a pithecanthropine human

Pith·e·can·thro·pus e·rec·tus (pith′i kan′thrə pəs ē rek′təs, -kan thrō′pəs) ⟦ModL < Gr *pithēkos,* ape (< IE *bhidh-, dreadful, var. of base *bhōi-, to be afraid > L *foedus,* ugly) + *anthrōpos,* man: see ANTHROPO-; *erectus* < L, upright (see ERECT): so named from having limbs capable of an upright posture and bipedalism⟧ *former name for* JAVA MAN

pith helmet a hat made of pith, cork, or other lightweight material, often with a wide brim, used as a sunshade in hot climates

pith·y (pith′ē) *adj.* **pith′i·er, pith′i·est** **1** of, like, or full of pith **2** terse and full of substance or meaning —*SYN.* CONCISE —**pith′i·ly** *adv.* —**pith′i·ness** *n.*

pit·i·a·ble (pit′ē ə bəl) *adj.* ⟦ME *piteable* < MFr < *pitier:* see PITY⟧ arousing or deserving pity, sometimes mixed with scorn or contempt —*SYN.* PITIFUL —**pit′i·a·ble·ness** *n.* —**pit′i·a·bly** *adv.*

pit·i·er (pit′ē ər) *n.* a person who pities

pit·i·ful (pit′i fəl) *adj.* **1** arousing or deserving pity **2** deserving contempt; despicable **3** [Archaic] full of pity or compassion —**pit′i·ful·ly** *adv.* —**pit′i·ful·ness** *n.*

SYN.—**pitiful** applies to that which arouses or deserves pity because it is sad, pathetic, etc. [the suffering of the starving children was *pitiful*]; **pitiable** is the preferred term when a greater or lesser degree of contempt is mingled with commiseration [the opposition shrank to a *pitiable* minority]; **piteous** stresses the nature of the thing calling for pity rather than its influence on the observer [*piteous* groans]

pit·i·less (pit′ē lis, -i-) *adj.* without pity; unfeeling —*SYN.* CRUEL —**pit′i·less·ly** *adv.* —**pit′i·less·ness** *n.*

pit·man (pit′mən) *n.* **1** *pl.* **-men** (-mən) a person who works in a pit; esp., a coal miner ☆**2** *pl.* **-mans** (-mənz) a type of connecting rod that changes axial motion into linear motion, as in a steering system

Pit·man (pit′mən), Sir **Isaac** 1813-97; Eng. inventor of a system of shorthand

pi·ton (pē′tän′) *n.* ⟦Fr < MFr, a spike, pointed object, akin to OIt *pizza,* a point⟧ a metal spike with an eye to which a rope can be secured: it is driven into rock or ice for support in mountain climbing

Pi·tot-stat·ic tube (pē′tō stat′ik) [*also* **pitot-static tube**] an instrument combining a Pitot tube and a static tube, that measures the difference between the pressures in the two tubes to obtain the relative velocity of a fluid in motion

Pi·tot tube (pē′tō, pē tō′) ⟦after Henri *Pitot* (1695-1771), Fr physicist⟧ **1** [*also* **p- t-**] a small, L-shaped tube which, when inserted vertically into a flowing fluid with its open end facing upstream, measures the total pressure of the fluid and hence, indirectly, the velocity of its flow **2** PITOT-STATIC TUBE

pit saw a large saw used, esp. formerly, to cut timber lengthwise and worked by two people, one standing above the log, the other in a pit below it: also written **pit′saw′** *n.*

pit stop **1** a temporary stop in the pit by a racing car during a race to refuel, change tires, etc. ☆**2** [Slang] *a)* any pause for food, restroom use, etc. during a journey *b)* the place where such a pause is made —☆**make a pit stop** [Slang] to visit a restroom

Pitt (pit) **1 William** 1st Earl of Chatham 1708-78; Eng. statesman: prime minister (1766-68): called *the Great Commoner* **2 William** 1759-1806; Eng. statesman: prime minister (1783-1801; 1804-06): son of William

pit·tance (pit′′ns) *n.* ⟦ME *pitaunce* < OFr *pitance,* portion of food allowed a monk < ML *pietantia* < LL(Ec) *pietas:* see PIETY⟧ **1** a small or barely sufficient allowance of money **2** any small amount or share

pit·ted[1] (pit′id) *adj.* having had the pits removed

pit·ted[2] (pit′id) *adj.* marked with pits or hollows

pit·ter-pat·ter (pit′ər pat′ər) *n.* ⟦ME *pyter-pater:* echoic⟧ a rapid succession of light beating or tapping sounds, as of raindrops —*adv.* with a pitter-patter —*vi.* to fall, move, etc. with a pitter-patter

pit·tos·por·um (pi täs′pər əm) *n.* ⟦ModL < Gr *pitta, pissa,* pitch + *sporos,* seed: so named from the coating of resinous pulp on the seeds⟧ any of a genus (*Pittosporum*) of evergreen trees and shrubs of the pittosporum family from Japan, Australia, etc. —*adj.* designating a family (Pittosporaceae, order Rosales) of decorative, dicotyledonous trees and shrubs

Pitts·burgh (pits′burg′) ⟦after the elder William PITT⟧ city in SW Pa., at the juncture of the Allegheny & Monongahela rivers

pi·tu·i·tar·y (pi to͞o′ə ter′ē, -tyo͞o′-) *adj.* ⟦L *pituitarius* < *pituita,* phlegm, rheum < IE *pitu-, juice, food < base *pei-, *pi-, to be fat > PITCH[1], FAT⟧ **1** [Obs.] of or secreting mucus **2** of the pituitary gland —*n., pl.* **-tar′ies** **1** PITUITARY GLAND **2** any of various preparations made from extracts of the pituitary gland

pituitary gland (*or* body) a small, oval endocrine gland attached by a stalk to the base of the brain and consisting of an anterior and a posterior lobe: it secretes hormones influencing body growth, metabolism, the activity of other endocrine glands, etc.

pit viper any of a subfamily (Crotalinae) of poisonous vipers with a prominent, heat-sensitive pit on each side of the head, as the rattlesnake or copperhead

pit·y (pit′ē) *n., pl.* **pit′ies** ⟦ME *pite* < OFr *pitet* < L *pietas:* see PIETY⟧ **1** sorrow felt for another's suffering or misfortune; compassion; sympathy **2** the ability to feel such compassion **3** a cause for sorrow or regret — *vt., vi.* **pit′ied, pit′y·ing** ⟦< the *n.* or < MFr *pitier* < OFr *piter*⟧ to feel pity (for) —**have (or take) pity on** to show pity or compassion for —**pit′y·ing·ly** *adv.*

SYN.—**pity** implies sorrow felt for another's suffering or misfortune, sometimes connoting slight contempt because the object is regarded as weak or inferior [he felt *pity* for a man so ignorant]; **compassion** implies pity accompanied by an urge to help or spare [moved by *compassion,* I did not press for payment]; **commiseration** implies deeply felt and openly expressed feelings of pity [she wept with her friend in *commiseration*]; **sympathy**, in this connection, implies such kinship of feeling as enables one to really understand or even to share the sorrow, etc. of another [he always turned to his wife for *sympathy*]; **condolence** now usually implies a formal expression of sympathy with another in sorrow [a letter of *condolence*]

pit·y·ri·a·sis (pit′i rī′ə sis) *n.* ⟦ModL < Gr < *pityrion,* bran, scale⟧ **1** any of various skin diseases characterized by the shedding of scaly flakes of epidermis **2** a skin disease of domestic animals, characterized by the formation of dry scales

più (pyo͞o) *adv.* ⟦It < L *plus:* see PLUS⟧ *Musical Direction* more [*più allegro,* more quickly]

Pi·us (pī′əs) **1 Pius II** (born *Enea Silvio de Piccolomini*) 1405-64; pope (1458-64) **2 Pius VII** (born *Luigi Barnaba Chiaramonti*) 1742-1823; pope (1800-23) **3 Pius IX** (born *Giovanni Maria Mastai-Ferretti*) 1792-1878; pope (1846-78) **4** Saint **Pius X** (born *Giuseppe Sarto*) (1835-1914); pope (1903-14): his day is Aug. 21 **5 Pius XI** (born *Achille Ratti*) 1857-1939; pope (1922-39) **6 Pius XII** (born *Eugenio Pacelli*) 1876-1958; pope (1939-58)

Pi·ute (pī′yo͞ot′, pī yo͞ot′) *n. alt. sp. of* PAIUTE

piv·ot (piv′ət) *n.* ⟦Fr, prob. akin to Prov *pua,* tooth of a comb⟧ **1** a point, shaft, pin, etc. on which something turns **2** a person or thing on or around which something turns or depends, etc.; central point **3** a pivoting movement —*adj.* PIVOTAL —*vt.* to provide with, attach by, or mount on a pivot or pivots —*vi.* to turn on or as if on a pivot

piv·ot·al (piv′ət′l) *adj.* **1** of or acting as a pivot **2** on which something turns or depends; central, crucial, critical, etc. —**piv′ot·al·ly** *adv.*

pix[1] (piks) *n. obs. var. of* PYX

☆**pix**[2] (piks) *pl.n.* ⟦var. sp. of pl. of *pic* < PIC(TURE)⟧ [Slang] **1** motion pictures; movies **2** photographs

pix·el (pik′səl) *n.* ⟦prec. + EL(EMENT)⟧ any of the thousands of tiny units or dots that together make up a digital image

pix·ie or **pix·y** (pik′sē) *n., pl.* **pix′ies** ⟦SW Brit dial. *pixey, pisky*⟧ a fairy, elf, or other tiny supernatural being, esp. one that is puckish —**pix′ie·ish** *adj.*, **pix′y·ish**

☆**pix·i·lat·ed** (pik′si lāt′id) *adj.* ⟦altered < *pixy-led,* lost, lit., led astray by pixies, infl. by pp. of verbs in *-late* (as *elated, titillated*)⟧ eccentric, daft, whimsical, puckish, etc.

Pi·zar·ro (pi zär′ō; *Sp* pē thär′rô), **Fran·cis·co** (frän thēs′kô) 1474?-1541; Sp. conqueror of Peru

☆**pi·zazz** or **piz·zazz** (pi zaz′) *n.* ⟦orig. echoic of engine roar⟧ [Informal] **1** energy, vigor, vitality, spirit, etc. **2** smartness, style, flair, etc. — [Slang] **pi·zaz′zy** *adj.*, **piz·zaz′zy**

pizz *abbrev. Musical Direction* pizzicato

☆**piz·za** (pēt′sə) *n.* ⟦It, prob. substitution of *pizza,* point, edge, for ModGr *pitta,* cake⟧ a baked Italian dish consisting of flattened bread dough covered variously with herbs, fresh vegetables, or, typically in the U.S., with tomato sauce, grated cheese, and, often, sausage, mushrooms, pepperoni, etc.

☆**piz·za·ri·a** (pēt′sə rē′ə) *n. disputed sp. of* PIZZERIA

piz·zelle (pit sel′, -zel′; pi-) *n.* an Italian cookie like a thin, crisp waffle, usually flavored with anise

☆**piz·ze·ri·a** (pēt′sə rē′ə) *n.* ⟦It < *pizza,* PIZZA + *-eria,* -ERY⟧ a place where pizzas are prepared and sold

piz·zi·ca·to (pit′si kät′ō; *It* pēt′tsē kä′tô) [*also in italics*] *Music adj.* ⟦It, pp. of *pizzicare,* to pluck, pinch < OIt *pizza,* a point⟧ plucked: a note to performers on stringed instruments to pluck the strings with the finger instead of bowing —*adv.* in a pizzicato manner —*n., pl.* **-ca′ti** (-kät′ē; *It,* -kä′tē) a note or passage played in this way

piz·zle (piz′əl) *n.* ⟦prob. < LowG *pesel* or Fl *pezel,* dim. akin to Du *pees,* a tendon, sinew⟧ the penis of an animal, esp. that of a bull as formerly made into a whip

☆**pj's** (pē′jāz′) *pl.n.* ⟦< P(A)J(AMA)S⟧ *informal var. of* PAJAMAS

pk *abbrev.* **1** pack **2** park **3** peak **4** peck

PK *abbrev. Football* placekicker: sometimes written **pk**

pkg *abbrev.* package(s)

pkt *abbrev.* packet

PKU *abbrev.* phenylketonuria

Pkwy or **Pky** *abbrev.* Parkway

pl *abbrev.* 1 place: also Pl 2 plate 3 plural

pla·ca·ble (plā′kə bəl, plak′ə-) *adj.* ⟦OFr < L *placabilis* < *placare,* to quiet, soothe: see PLEASE⟧ capable of being placated; readily pacified; forgiving —**pla′ca·bil′i·ty** *n.* —**pla′ca·bly** *adv.*

plac·ard (plak′ärd; -ərd; *for v., also* plə kärd′) *n.* ⟦LME *placquart* < MFr *plackart* < MDu *placke,* piece, spot, patch⟧ 1 a notice for display in a public place; poster 2 a small card or plaque —*vt.* 1 to place placards on or in 2 to advertise or give notice of by means of placards 3 to display as a placard —*vi.* to set up placards

pla·cate (plā′kāt′; *occas.* plak′āt′) *vt.* **-cat′ed, -cat′ing** ⟦< L *placatus,* pp. of *placare,* to appease: see PLEASE⟧ to stop from being angry; appease; pacify; mollify —*SYN.* PACIFY —**pla′cat′er** *n.* —**pla·ca′tion** *n.* —**pla′ca′tive** *adj.* —**pla·ca·to·ry** (plā′kə tôr′ē, plak′ə-) *adj.*

place (plās) *n.* ⟦OFr < L *platea,* a broad street (in LL, an open space) < Gr *plateia,* a street < *platys,* broad: see PLATY-⟧ 1 a square or court in a city 2 a short street, often closed at one end 3 space; room 4 a particular area or locality; region 5 *a)* the part of space occupied by a person or thing *b)* situation or state [if I were in his *place*] 6 a city, town, or village 7 a residence; dwelling; house and grounds 8 a building or space devoted to a special purpose [a *place* of amusement] 9 a particular spot on or part of the body or a surface [a sore *place* on the leg] 10 a particular passage or page in a book, magazine, etc., esp. the point where one has temporarily stopped reading [to mark one's *place*] 11 position or standing, esp. one of importance, accorded to one [one's *place* in history] 12 a step or point in a sequence [in the first *place*] 13 the customary, proper, or natural position, time, or character 14 a space used, reserved, or customarily occupied by a person, as a seat in a theater, at a table, etc. 15 an office; employment; position 16 official position 17 the duties of any position 18 the duty, or business (of a person) 19 in racing, the first, second, or third position at the finish, specif. the second position 20 *Arith.* the position of a digit in a number (Ex.: in 12.3 the one is in the ten's *place,* the two in the unit's *place,* and the three in the tenth's *place*) —*vt.* **placed, plac′ing** ⟦Fr *placer*⟧ 1 *a)* to put in a particular place, condition, or relation *b)* to put in an assigned or proper place, as in a sequence or series ☆*c)* to identify by associating with the correct place or circumstances [to *place* somebody's face] 2 to find employment or a position for; appoint to an office 3 to arrange for a desired handling, treatment, or allocation of [to *place* a shipment, to *place* a child for adoption] 4 to assign (a value) 5 to make or give as an estimate 6 to offer (a proposal, problem, etc.) to be considered 7 to repose (confidence, trust, hope, etc.) *in* a person or thing 8 to adjust (the voice) to head or chest register 9 to finish in (a specified position) in a competition [to *place* last] 10 to initiate or effect (a telephone call) —*vi. Sports* to finish among the first three in a contest; specif., to finish second in a horse or dog race —**give place** 1 to make room 2 to yield —☆**go places** [Slang] to achieve success —**in (or out of) place** 1 in (or out of) the customary, proper, or assigned place 2 that is (or is not) fitting, proper, or timely —**in place of** as a substitute for; instead of —**know one's place** to be conscious of one's (inferior) position or rank in life and act accordingly —**put someone in his (or her) place** to humble someone who is overstepping bounds —**run (jog, etc.) in place** to move the legs alternately as in running (jogging, etc.), but remain in the same place, not going forward or backward —**take place** to come into being; happen; occur —**take the place of** to be a substitute for

pla·ce·bo (plə sē′bō) *n., pl.* **-bos** or **-boes** ⟦ME < L, I shall please⟧ 1 *R.C.Ch.* the first antiphon of the vespers for the dead, beginning with the word *placebo* 2 a harmless, unmedicated preparation given as a medicine merely to humor a patient, or used as a control in testing the efficacy of another, medicated substance 3 something said or done to win the favor of another

placebo effect any improvement in a person's medical condition that is ascribed to that person's belief in the effectiveness of the treatment, rather than to the treatment itself

☆**place card** any of the small cards bearing the names of guests and set at the place that each is to occupy at a table

place·kick (plās′kik′) *Football, Rugby, etc. n.* a kick made while the ball is in place, often held in place, on the ground, as in kicking off or in attempting a field goal —*vi.* to kick a ball in this way —**place′kick′er** *n.*

place·man (plās′mən) *n., pl.* **-men** (-mən) [Brit.] a person appointed to a government position as a political reward: usually a derogatory term

place mat a small mat of cloth, paper, etc. serving as an individual table cover for a person at a meal

place·ment (plās′mənt) *n.* 1 a placing or being placed 2 the finding of employment for a person 3 location or arrangement 4 *Football a)* the setting of the ball on the ground in position for a place kick *b)* this position of the ball *c)* PLACEKICK

pla·cen·ta (plə sen′tə) *n., pl.* **-tas** or **-tae** (-tē) ⟦ModL < L, lit., a cake < Gr *plakounta,* acc. of *plakous,* a flat cake < *plax* (gen. *plakos*), a flat object < IE base **plāk-,* flat > L *placere,* to PLEASE⟧ 1 *Anat., Zool. a)* a vascular organ, developed within the uterus of most mammals during gestation from the chorion of the embryo and a part of the maternal uterine wall, that is connected to the embryo by the umbilical cord and that is discharged shortly after birth: it serves as the structure through which nourishment for the fetus is received from, and wastes of the fetus are eliminated into, the circulatory system of the mother *b)* any similar structure in other animals 2 *Bot. a)* that part of the lining of the ovary which bears the ovules *b)* any mass of tissue that bears sporangia or spores —**pla·cen′tal** *adj.*

pla·cen·tate (plə sen′tāt′) *adj.* having a placenta

plac·en·ta·tion (plas′ən tā′shən) *n.* 1 *Anat., Zool. a)* the formation or structure of a placenta *b)* the manner in which the placenta is attached to the uterus 2 *Bot.* the manner in which the placentas are arranged in an ovary

plac·er[1] (plās′ər) *n.* a person who places

☆**plac·er**[2] (plas′ər) *n.* ⟦AmSp (for Sp *placel*) < Catalan, lit., sandbank < *plassa,* a place < L *platea:* see PLACE⟧ a waterborne or glacial deposit of gravel or sand containing heavy ore minerals, as gold or cassiterite, which have been eroded from their original bedrock and concentrated as small particles that can be washed out

☆**plac·er mining** (plas′ər) mining of placer deposits by washing, dredging, or other hydraulic methods

place setting the china, silverware, etc. for setting one place at a table for a meal

place value *Math.* the value assigned to each PLACE (*n.* 20) in a numeral, depending on the BASE[1] (*n.* 16*a*) of the number system

plac·id (plas′id) *adj.* ⟦L *placidus,* akin to *placere,* to PLEASE⟧ undisturbed; tranquil; calm; quiet —*SYN.* CALM —**pla·cid·i·ty** (plə sid′ə tē) *n.,* **plac′id·ness** —**plac′id·ly** *adv.*

Plac·id (plas′id), **Lake** ⟦descriptive⟧ lake in NE N.Y., in the Adirondacks: resort area: *c.* 4 mi (6.4 km) long

plack·et (plak′it) *n.* ⟦prob. altered < PLACARD, in obs. sense "breastplate, top of skirt"⟧ 1 a finished slit with a fastener, as at the waist of a skirt or collar of a shirt, to make it easy to put on and take off 2 [Archaic] *a)* a pocket, esp. in a woman's skirt *b)* a petticoat

plac·oid (plak′oid′) *adj.* ⟦< Gr *plax,* flat plate, tablet (see PLACENTA) + -OID⟧ *Zool.* of or having scales that are periodically shed and replaced, consisting of a dentin base and an enamel-covered surface, as in cartilaginous fishes

pla·fond (plȧ fōn′) *n.* ⟦Fr, ceiling, earlier *platfond* < *plat,* flat (< VL **plattus* < Gr *platys:* see PLATY-) + *fond,* background < L *fundus,* BOTTOM⟧ 1 a decorated ceiling 2 a painted or carved design on a ceiling

pla·gal (plā′gəl) *adj.* ⟦ML *plagalis* < *plaga,* plagal mode < MGr *plagios,* plagal (in Gr, oblique, slanting) < Gr *plagos,* a side, akin to *pelagos,* the sea: see PELAGIC⟧ *Music* 1 designating a mode having a range about a fifth above and a fifth below a control note 2 designating a cadence with the subdominant chord immediately preceding the tonic chord, as in the amen of a religious hymn

plage[1] (plȧzh) *n.* ⟦Fr < It *piaggia* < LL *plagia,* shore < **plagius,* slanting < Gr *plagios,* oblique: see prec.⟧ a sandy beach at a seaside resort area

plage[2] (pläzh) *n.* ⟦< prec.⟧ a bright granular area in the chromosphere of the sun visible on a spectroheliogram that is taken at the wavelengths of the hydrogen or ionized calcium vapor

pla·gi- (plā′jə) *combining form* PLAGIO-

pla·gi·a·rism (plā′jə riz′əm) *n.* ⟦< L *plagiarius,* kidnapper: see PLAGIARY & -ISM⟧ 1 the act of plagiarizing 2 an idea, plot, etc. that has been plagiarized —**pla′gi·a·rist** *n.* —**pla′gi·a·ris′tic** *adj.*

pla·gi·a·rize (plā′jə rīz′) *vt., vi.* **-rized′, -riz′ing** ⟦see fol.⟧ to take (ideas, writings, etc.) from (another) and pass them off as one's own —**pla′gi·a·riz′er** *n.*

pla·gi·a·ry (-rē) *n., pl.* **-ries** ⟦L *plagiarius,* kidnapper, literary thief < *plagium,* kidnapping < *plaga,* hunting net, snare < IE **plāg-,* to spread out: see PELAGIC⟧ 1 *archaic var. of* PLAGIARIST 2 PLAGIARISM

pla·gi·o- (plā′jē ō, -ə) ⟦< Gr *plagios,* oblique < *plagos,* a side: see PLAGAL⟧ *combining form* oblique, slanting [*plagiotropic*]

pla·gi·o·clase (plā′jē ō klās′) *n.* ⟦Ger *plagioklas* < Gr *plagios* (see prec.) + *klasis,* a cleaving, fracture < *klaein,* to break: see CLASTIC⟧ any of a series of triclinic feldspars, ranging in composition from albite to anorthite and found in many rocks

pla·gi·o·trop·ic (plā′jē ə träp′ik) *adj.* ⟦PLAGIO- + -TROPIC⟧ *Bot.* having the longer axes of roots or branches slanting from the vertical line —**pla′gi·o′trop′i·cal·ly** *adv.* —**pla′gi·ot′ro·pism′** (-ä′trə piz′əm) *n.*

plague (plāg) *n.* ⟦ME *plage* < MFr < L *plaga,* a blow, misfortune, in LL(Ec), plague < Gr *plēgē, plaga* < IE **plaga,* a blow < base **plag-,* to strike > FLAW[2]⟧ 1 anything that afflicts or troubles; calamity; scourge 2 any contagious epidemic disease that is deadly; esp., bubonic plague 3 [Informal] a nuisance; annoyance 4 *Bible* any of various calamities sent down as divine punishment: Ex. 9:14, Num. 16:46 —*vt.* **plagued, plagu′ing** 1 to afflict with a plague 2 to vex; harass; trouble; torment —*SYN.* ANNOY —**plagu′er** *n.*

pla·guy or **pla·guey** (plā′gē) *adj.* [Informal or Dial.] annoying; vexatious; disagreeable —*adv.* annoyingly; disagreeably: also **pla′gui·ly**

plaice (plās) *n., pl.* **plaice** or **plaic′es** ⟦ME *plais* < OFr *plaïs* < LL *platessa,* flatfish < Gr *platys,* broad: see PLATY-⟧ any of various American and European flounders (esp. genera *Pleuronectes* and *Hippoglossoides*)

plaid (plad) *n.* ⟦Gael *plaide,* blanket, plaid, contr. < ? *peallaid,* sheepskin⟧ 1 a long piece of twilled woolen cloth with a crossbarred pattern, worn over the shoulder by Scottish Highlanders 2 a fabric with stripes or bars of various colors and widths that cross at right angles 3 any pattern of this kind —*adj.* having a pattern of plaid

plaid·ed (plad′id) *adj.* 1 wearing a plaid 2 made, or having a pattern, of plaid

plain[1] (plān) *adj.* ⟦OFr < L *planus,* flat, level < IE base **plā-,* broad, flat > FLOOR, FIELD⟧ 1 [Obs.] flat; level; plane 2 free from obstructions; open; clear [in *plain* view] 3 clearly understood; evident; obvious [to make one's meaning *plain*] 4 *a)* outspoken; frank; straightforward [*plain* talk] *b)* downright; thoroughgoing [*plain* nonsense] 5 not luxurious or ornate; unembellished [a *plain* coat] 6 not complicated; simple [*plain* sewing] 7 neither good-looking nor ugly [a well-dressed woman with a rather *plain* face] **8** not figured, dyed, or twilled [*plain* cloth] **9** pure; unmixed [*plain* soda] **10** not of high rank or position; such as characterizes the common people; ordinary [a *plain* man] —*n.* [*often pl.*] an extent of relatively level country with few trees; prairie, steppe, etc. —*adv.* clearly or simply [just *plain* tired] —SYN. EVIDENT —**plain′ly** *adv.* —**plain′ness** *n.*

plain[2] (plān) *vi.* ⟦ME *pleynen* < OFr *plaindre* < L *plangere:* see PLAINT⟧ [Now Chiefly Dial.] to complain

plain·chant (plān′chant′) *n.* ⟦Fr⟧ PLAINSONG

plain·clothes (plān′klōthz′, -klōz′) *adj.* dressed in civilian clothes while on duty [a *plainclothes* detective]

plainclothes man a detective or police officer who wears civilian clothes while on duty: also written **plain′clothes′man** (-mən) *n., pl.* **-men** (-mən)

plain dealing straightforward dealing with others

plain Jane a plain, dowdy, unremarkable woman or girl

plain-Jane (plān′jān′) *adj.* ⟦< prec.⟧ [Informal] **1** plain, drab, dull, etc. [*plain-Jane* looks] **2** basic or simple; ordinary; unremarkable

plain-laid (plān′lād′) *adj.* made of three strands laid together with a right-handed twist: said of a rope

Plain People ☆the Mennonites, Dunkers, and Amish people: from their plain dress and simple way of life

Plains (plānz) *adj.* of or having to do with the Great Plains [the *Plains* states]

plain sailing **1** sailing on an unobstructed course **2** a smooth, clear course of action

☆**Plains Indian** a member of any of the North American Indian peoples formerly inhabiting the Great Plains: they were of various linguistic stocks but shared certain cultural traits, such as the nomadic following of bison herds

☆**plains·man** (plānz′mən) *n., pl.* **-men** (-mən) an inhabitant of the plains; esp., a frontiersman on the Great Plains

Plains of Abraham ⟦after *Abraham* Martin (1589-1664), an early settler⟧ a plain near Quebec: site of a battle (1759) of the French and Indian War, in which the British under Wolfe defeated the French under Montcalm

plain·song (plān′sôŋ′) *n.* ⟦transl. of ML *cantus planus*⟧ **1** the monophonic and unmeasured ritual chant of the early Christian church, esp. Gregorian chant **2** any similar religious chant, as in Hindu liturgies

plain-spo·ken (plān′spō′kən) *adj.* speaking or spoken plainly or frankly —**plain′-spo′ken·ness** *n.*

plaint (plānt) *n.* ⟦ME *plainte* < OFr < L *planctus,* lamentation, loud banging < pp. of *plangere,* to beat the breast, lament < IE base **plag-,* to strike > FLAW[2], Gr *plēssein,* to strike⟧ **1** [Old Poet.] lamentation; lament **2** a complaint or grievance

plain·tiff (plān′tif) *n.* ⟦ME *plaintif* < OFr, mournful, making complaint < *plaindre* < *plainte:* see prec.⟧ a person who brings a suit into a court of law; complainant

plain·tive (plān′tiv) *adj.* ⟦ME *pleintif* < OFr *plaintif:* see prec.⟧ expressing sorrow or melancholy; mournful; sad —**plain′tive·ly** *adv.* —**plain′tive·ness** *n.*

plais·ter (plās′tər) *n. obs. var. of* PLASTER

plait (plāt, plat) *n.* ⟦ME *pleit* < OFr < VL **plicta* < pp. of L *plicare,* to fold: see PLY[1]⟧ **1** [Archaic] PLEAT **2** a braid of hair, ribbon, etc. —*vt.* ⟦ME *playten* < the n.⟧ **1** [Archaic] PLEAT **2** to braid or interweave **3** to make by braiding —**plait′er** *n.*

plan (plan) *n.* ⟦Fr, plan, plane, foundation: merging of *plan* (< L *planus:* see PLAIN[1]) with MFr *plant* < It *pianta* < L *planta,* sole of the foot: see PLANT⟧ **1** a drawing or diagram showing the arrangement in horizontal section of a structure, piece of ground, etc. **2** *a)* a scheme or program for making, doing, or arranging something; project, design, schedule, etc. *b)* a method of proceeding **3** any outline or sketch **4** in perspective, any of several planes thought of as perpendicular to the line of sight and between the eye and the object —*vt.* **planned, plan′ning** **1** to make a plan of (a structure, piece of ground, etc.) **2** to devise a scheme for doing, making, or arranging **3** to have in mind as a project or purpose —*vi.* to make plans

SYN.—**plan** refers to any detailed method, formulated beforehand, for doing or making something [vacation *plans*]; **design** stresses the final outcome of a plan and implies the use of skill or craft, sometimes in an unfavorable sense, in executing or arranging this [it was his *design* to separate us]; **project** implies the use of enterprise or imagination in formulating an ambitious or extensive plan [a housing *project*]; **scheme**, a less definite term than the preceding, often connotes either an impractical, visionary plan or an underhanded intrigue [a *scheme* to embezzle the funds]

plan- (plan) *combining form* PLANO- (sense 1): used before a vowel

pla·nar (plā′nər) *adj.* of or pertaining to a point on a surface at which the curvature is zero; of or lying in one plane

pla·nar·i·an (plə ner′ē ən) *n.* ⟦< ModL *Planaria,* name of one genus of these flatworms < LL *planarius,* flat < L *planus,* PLANE[2]⟧ any of a class (Turbellaria) of small, soft-bodied, free-living flatworms moving by means of cilia

pla·na·tion (plā nā′shən) *n.* ⟦PLANE[2] + -ATION⟧ the reduction of a land area by erosion to a nearly flat surface

Plan B ⟦in allusion to the common practice of alphabetically labeling a series of options⟧ [Informal] any alternate or secondary plan or option; fallback

plan·chet (plan′chet, -chit) *n.* ⟦Fr *planchette,* dim. of *planche,* PLANK⟧ a disk of metal to be stamped as a coin

plan·chette (plan shet′) *n.* ⟦Fr: see prec.⟧ a small, heart-shaped or triangular device, often having as one of its supports a pencil, that is supposed to write out a message or, as with a Ouija board, point to letters or words, as it moves with the fingers resting lightly on it

Planck (plänk), **Max (Karl Ernst Ludwig)** (mäks) 1858-1947; Ger. physicist

Planck's constant (plaŋks, pläŋks) ⟦after prec.⟧ *Physics* a universal constant (h) which gives the ratio of a quantum of radiant energy (E) to the frequency (ν) of its source: it is expressed by the equation $E = h\nu$, and its approximate numerical value is 6.626×10^{-34} joule second: often **Planck constant**

plane[1] (plān) *n.* ⟦ME < MFr *plasne* < L *platanus* < Gr *platanos* < *platys,* broad (see PLATY-): from its broad leaves⟧ any of a genus (*Platanus*) of trees of the plane-tree family having maplelike leaves, spherical dry fruits, and bark that sheds in large patches; sycamore

plane[2] (plān) *adj.* ⟦L *planus:* see PLAIN[1]⟧ **1** flat; level; even **2** *Math. a)* lying on a surface that is a plane *b)* of such surfaces —*n.* ⟦L *planum*⟧ **1** a surface that wholly contains every straight line joining any two points lying in it **2** a flat, level, or even surface **3** a level of development, achievement, existence, etc. **4** *short for* AIRPLANE **5** any airfoil; esp., a wing of an airplane —SYN. LEVEL

plane[3] (plān) *n.* ⟦OFr *plaine* < LL *plana* < *planare,* to plane, make level < L *planus:* see PLAIN[1]⟧ a carpenter's tool for shaving a wood surface in order to make it smooth, level, etc. —*vt.* **planed, plan′ing** **1** to make smooth or level with or as with a plane **2** to remove with or as with a plane: with *off* or *away* —*vi.* **1** to work with a plane **2** to do the work of a plane

plane

plane[4] (plān) *vi.* **planed, plan′ing** ⟦Fr *planer* < OFr *plan,* level surface (term used in falconry, in reference to position of bird's wings while soaring) < LL *planare,* to make level: see prec.⟧ **1** to soar or glide **2** to rise partly out of the water while in motion at high speed, as a HYDROPLANE (sense 1) does **3** to travel by airplane

plane angle an angle made by two straight lines that lie in the same plane

plane geometry the branch of geometry dealing with plane figures

plane·load (plān′lōd′) *n.* **1** all the freight or passengers that an airplane can carry or contain **2** the load carried by an airplane

plan·er (plā′nər) *n.* **1** a person or thing that planes ☆**2** a machine that smooths or finishes the surfaces of wood or metal by planing **3** *Printing* a block of wood used with a mallet to level type in a chase

☆**pla·ner tree** (plā′nər) ⟦after J. J. *Planer,* 18th-c. Ger botanist⟧ a small tree (*Planera aquatica*) of the elm family, with ovate leaves and a nutlike fruit, found in the SE U.S.

plan·et (plan′it) *n.* ⟦ME *planete* < OFr < LL *planeta* < Gr *planētēs,* wanderer < *planan,* to lead astray, wander < IE base **plā-,* flat, spread out > PLAIN[1]⟧ **1** [Obs.] any of the celestial objects with apparent motion (as distinguished from the apparently still stars), including the sun, moon, Mercury, Venus, Mars, Jupiter, or Saturn **2** now, a large, opaque, nonluminous mass, usually with its own moons, that revolves about a star; esp., one of the sun's eight major planets: Mercury, Venus, Earth, Mars, Jupiter, Saturn, Uranus, and Neptune: until recently, Pluto had been classified as the ninth major planet: see also ASTEROID, DWARF PLANET **3** *Astrol.* any of the celestial bodies regarded as influencing human lives: traditionally, Mercury, Venus, Mars, Jupiter, Saturn, Uranus, Neptune, Pluto, and the sun and moon

plane table a surveying device for plotting maps in the field: it consists of a drawing board mounted on a tripod with an alidade that can be moved about over the table to establish a reference point

plan·e·tar·i·um (plan′ə ter′ē əm) *n., pl.* **-i·ums** or **-i·a** (-ə) ⟦ModL < LL *planeta,* PLANET + L (*sol*)*arium,* SOLARIUM⟧ **1** ORRERY **2** *a)* a complex revolving projector used to simulate the past, present, or future motions or positions of the sun, moon, planets, and stars on the inside of a large dome *b)* the room or building in which this is contained

plan·e·tar·y (plan′ə ter′ē) *adj.* ⟦Fr *planetaire*⟧ **1** of or having to do with a planet or the planets **2** terrestrial; global **3** wandering; erratic **4** moving in an orbit, like a planet **5** designating or of an epicyclic train of gears, as in an automobile transmission **6** [Rare] *Astrol.* under the influence of a planet

planetary nebula ⟦from its resemblance, when viewed through a telescope, to a PLANET⟧ a glowing, expanding nebula that forms around a collapsing star

plan·e·tes·i·mal (plan′ə tes′i məl, -tez-) *n.* ⟦PLANET + (INFINIT)ESIMAL⟧ in various theories about the origin of the solar system, any of the small, cold masses of rock or ice that merged to form a planet

planetesimal hypothesis any of several theories postulating that the solar system originated with planetesimals

plan·et·oid (plan′ə toid′) *n.* ⟦PLANET + -OID⟧ *former term for* ASTEROID (*n.* 1)

plan·et·ol·o·gy (plan′ə täl′ə jē) *n.* the branch of astronomy that studies and compares the planets and their moons —**plan′et·ol′o·gist** *n.*

plane tree PLANE[1]

plane-tree (plān′trē′) *adj.* designating a family (Platanaceae, order Hamamelidales), of deciduous, dicotyledonous trees, consisting of the plane trees

plan·et-strick·en (plan′it strik′ən) *adj.* [Archaic] **1** believed to be adversely affected mentally or physically by the planets **2** PANIC-STRICKEN Also **plan′et-struck′** (-struk′)

planet wheel a gear that meshes with and revolves around another gear in an epicyclic train

plan·gent (plan′jənt) *adj.* ⟦L *plangens,* prp. of *plangere,* to beat: see PLAINT⟧ **1** beating with a loud or deep sound, as breaking waves, etc. **2** loud or resonant, and, often, mournful-sounding —**plan′gen·cy** (-jən sē) *n.* —**plan′gent·ly** *adv.*

pla·ni- (plā′ni, -nə; plan′i, -ə) ⟦< L *planus,* flat: see PLAIN[1]⟧ *combining form* plane, level, flat *[planisphere]*

pla·nim·e·ter (plə nim′ət ər, plā-) *n.* ⟦Fr *planimètre:* see prec. & -METER⟧ an instrument for measuring the area of a regular or irregular plane figure by tracing the perimeter of the figure —**pla·ni·met·ric** (plā′ni me′trik, plan′i-) *adj.* —**pla·nim′e·try** *n.*

plan·ish (plan′ish) *vt.* ⟦< MFr *planiss-,* extended stem of *planir,* to flatten < *plan,* flat: see PLAN⟧ to toughen, smooth, or polish (metal) by hammering or rolling —**plan′ish·er** *n.*

plan·i·sphere (plan′i sfir′) *n.* ⟦ML *planisphaerium:* see PLANI- & SPHERE⟧ **1** a map or chart that is the projection on a plane of all or part of a sphere **2** a projection on a plane of the celestial sphere, usually with the N or S celestial pole as the center —**plan′i·spher′ic** (-sfer′ik, -sfir′-) *adj.*

plank (plaŋk) *n.* ⟦ME *planke* < NormFr < OFr *planche* < LL *planca,* a board, plank < VL *palanca* < Gr *phalangai* < *phalanx* (gen. *phalangos*): see PHALANX⟧ **1** a long, broad, thick board **2** PLANKING (sense 2) **3** something that supports or sustains ☆**4** any of the articles or principles making up the platform or stated program of a political party —*vt.* **1** to cover, lay, or furnish with planks ☆**2** to broil and serve (steak, fish, etc.) on a board or wooden platter **3** [Informal] *a)* to lay or set (*down*) with force or emphasis ☆*b)* to pay (usually with *down* or *out*) —**walk the plank** to walk to one's death blindfolded and manacled off a plank projecting from the side of a ship, as the victims of pirates were sometimes forced to do

plank·ing (plaŋk′iŋ) *n.* **1** the act of laying planks **2** planks in quantity **3** the planks of a structure

plank·ter (plaŋk′tər) *n.* ⟦Gr *planktēr,* a wanderer < *planktos,* wandering: see fol.⟧ an individual planktonic organism

plank·ton (plaŋk′tən) *n.* ⟦Ger < Gr *planktos,* wandering < *plazesthai,* to wander, akin to *planan:* see PLANET⟧ the usually microscopic animal and plant life found floating or drifting in the ocean or in bodies of fresh water, used as food by nearly all aquatic animals —**plank·ton′ic** (-tän′ik) *adj.*

☆**Planned Parenthood** *service mark for* an organization of community clinics providing information about and assistance with birth control and abortion, sexually transmitted disease, and related issues

plan·ner (plan′ər) *n.* **1** a person who plans, specif., one trained or engaged in planning the development of a city or region **2** a thing that aids in planning, specif. a small calendar, typically in the form of a booklet, with space at each date for listing appointments and activities

Pla·no (plā′nō) ⟦Sp *plano,* plane, flat surface: misunderstood as "plain," for the plains in the area⟧ city in NE Tex.: suburb of Dallas

pla·no- (plā′nō, -nə) ⟦< L *planus,* level, flat: see PLAIN[1]⟧ *combining form* **1** plane, flat *[planography]* **2** having one side plane and (the other as specified) *[plano-concave]*

pla·no-con·cave (plā′nō kän kāv′, -kän′kāv′) *adj.* having one side plane and the other concave

pla·no-con·vex (-kän veks′, -kän′veks′) *adj.* having one side plane and the other convex

pla·nog·ra·phy (plə näg′rə fē, plā-) *n.* ⟦PLANO- + -GRAPHY⟧ any method of printing from a flat surface, as lithography

pla·no·sol (plā′nə säl′, -sôl′) *n.* ⟦< PLANO- + L *solum,* SOIL[1]⟧ *[often* **P-***]* any of an intrazonal group of soils underlain by B-horizons strongly compacted by material leached from surface horizons, developed on nearly flat uplands

plan position indicator a circular radarscope on which signals are shown at radial distances from the center, which represents the location of the transmitter

plant (plant, plänt) *n.* ⟦ME *plante* < OE < L *planta,* sprout, twig, prob. backform. < *plantare,* to smooth the soil for planting < *planta,* sole of the foot < IE **plat-,* var. of base **pla-,* broad, flat > PLAIN[1]⟧ **1** any of a kingdom (Plantae) of eukaryotes generally characterized by the ability to carry on photosynthesis in its cells which contain chloroplasts and have cellulose in the cell wall, including all embryophytes and, formerly, thallophytes **2** a young tree, shrub, or herb, ready to put into other soil for growth to maturity; a slip, cutting, or set **3** an herb, as distinguished from a tree or shrub **4** the tools, machinery, buildings, grounds, etc. of a factory or business **5** the equipment, buildings, etc. of any institution, as a hospital, school, etc. **6** the apparatus or equipment for some particular mechanical operation or process *[the power plant of a ship]* **7** [Slang] a person placed, or thing planned or used, to trick, mislead, or trap —*vt.* ⟦ME *planten* < OE *plantian* & OFr *planter,* both < L *plantare* < the n.⟧ **1** *a)* to put into soil, esp. into the ground, to grow *b)* to set plants in (a piece of ground) **2** to set firmly as into the ground; fix in position **3** to fix in the mind; implant (an idea, etc.) **4** to settle (a colony, colonists, etc.); found; establish **5** to furnish or stock with animals ☆**6** to put a stock of (oysters, young fish, etc.) in a body of water **7** [Slang] to deliver (a punch, blow, etc.) with force **8** [Slang] *a)* to place (a person or thing) in such a way as to trick, trap, etc. *b)* to place (an ostensible news item) in a newspaper, etc. with some ulterior motive, as in order to mold public opinion **9** [Slang] *a)* to hide or conceal *b)* to place (something) surreptitiously where it is certain to be found or discovered —**plant′like′** *adj.*

Plan·tag·e·net (plan taj′ə nit) *n.* name of the ruling family of England (1154-1399)

plan·tain[1] (plan′tin) *n.* ⟦OFr < L *plantago* < *planta,* sole of the foot (see PLANT): from the shape of the leaves⟧ any of a genus (*Plantago*) of plants of the plantain family, usually with rosettes of basal leaves and spikes of tiny, greenish flowers, including many troublesome weeds —*adj.* designating a family (Plantaginaceae, order Plantaginales) of dicotyledonous plants

plan·tain[2] (plan′tin, plan tān′) *n.* ⟦altered (prob. infl. by prec.) < Sp *plátano,* banana tree, lit., plane tree (< L *platanus:* see PLANE[1]), prob. misused for native name (as in Carib *balatana*)⟧ **1** a hybrid banana plant (*Musa × paradisiaca*) that is widely cultivated in the Western Hemisphere **2** the large, firm, curved fruit of this plant: in tropical areas, it is usually cooked while green, before the starch has converted into sugar

plantain lily any of several perennial plants (genus *Hosta*) of the lily family, with broad, strongly ribbed basal leaves and clusters or racemes of trumpet-shaped flowers

plan·tar (plant′ər) *adj.* ⟦L *plantaris* < *planta,* sole of the foot: see PLANT⟧ of or on the sole of the foot

plan·ta·tion (plan tā′shən) *n.* ⟦L *plantatio* < *plantare,* to PLANT⟧ **1** [Archaic] a colony or new settlement ☆**2** an area growing cultivated crops **3** an estate, as in a tropical or semitropical region, cultivated by workers living on it, specif. one located in the S U.S. in the 18th or 19th cent. **4** a large, cultivated planting of trees *[a rubber plantation]*

plant·er (plant′ər) *n.* ☆**1** the owner of a plantation **2** a person or machine that plants **3** a container, usually decorative, for potted or unpotted houseplants **4** [Archaic] a colonist or pioneer

planter's punch ⟦prob. because served by planters (see prec., sense 1)⟧ a chilled drink made of rum, lemon or lime juice, and sugar

plant hormone an organic chemical, as auxin, produced by plant cells and functioning at various sites to regulate growth, turning, metabolic processes, etc.

plan·ti·grade (plan′tə grād′) *adj.* ⟦Fr < L *planta,* sole (see PLANT) + Fr *-grade,* -GRADE⟧ walking on the whole sole, as a human or bear —*n.* a plantigrade animal

plant·ing (plant′iŋ) *n.* **1** the act or an instance of putting seeds or young plants into the soil *[floods delayed spring planting]* **2** something planted, as in a decorative garden or along a border *[plantings of azaleas]*

plant louse APHID

plan·u·la (plan′yoo lə) *n., pl.* **-u·lae′** (-lē′) ⟦ModL < LL, little plane, dim. < L *planus,* flat: see PLAIN[1]⟧ the ciliated larva of a cnidarian —**plan′u·loid′** (-loid′) *adj.*

plaque (plak) *n.* ⟦Fr < MDu *placke,* disk, spot, patch⟧ **1** *a)* any thin, flat piece of metal, wood, etc., with a picture, design in relief, etc., hung as on a wall for ornamentation *b)* a wall tablet inscribed to commemorate an event, identify a building, etc. **2** a platelike brooch worn as a badge or ornament **3** *a)* an abnormal patch on the skin, mucous membrane, etc. *b)* a thin, transparent film on a tooth surface, containing mucin, bacteria, etc.: if not removed it forms tartar and promotes tooth decay *c)* a deposit of fatty or fibrous material in a blood vessel wall

plash[1] (plash) *n.* ⟦ME *plasche* < OE *plæsc,* akin to MDu & MFl *plasch,* pool: prob. echoic⟧ a shallow pool, or puddle

plash[2] (plash) *vt., vi., n.* ⟦echoic⟧ SPLASH

plash[3] (plash) *vt.* ⟦LME *plashen* < OFr *plaissier* < VL **plaxum,* hedge, for L *plexum,* neut. pp. of *plectere,* to weave: see FLAX⟧ to bend and intertwine (branches, stems, etc.) so as to form a hedge

plash·y (plash′ē) *adj.* **plash′i·er, plash′i·est 1** full of puddles; marshy; wet **2** splashing

-pla·si·a (plā′zhə, -zhē ə) ⟦ModL < Gr *plasis,* a molding < *plassein,* to mold: see PLASTIC⟧ *combining form* change, development *[cataplasia]*

plasm (plaz′əm) *n.* PLASMA (senses 2 & 3)

plasm- (plaz′əm) *combining form* PLASMO-: used before a vowel

-plasm (plaz′əm) ⟦< Gr *plasma:* see fol.⟧ *combining form* **1** the formative material of an animal or vegetable cell *[idioplasm]* **2** any of the components of protoplasm *[endoplasm]*

plas·ma (plaz′mə) *n.* ⟦Ger < Gr, something molded < *plassein,* to form: see PLASTIC⟧ **1** a green, somewhat translucent variety of chalcedony **2** the fluid part of blood, lymph, milk, or intramuscular liquid; esp., the fluid part of blood, as distinguished from the corpuscles, used for transfusions **3** PROTOPLASM **4** *a)* any highly ionized gas, as that in a glowing fluorescent lamp *b)* a unique form of matter, as in a star, consisting of highly energized, freely moving ions and electrons **5** a plasma screen display —*adj.* designating or of a flat-screen, high-definition video display consisting of a grid of tiny, gas-filled fluorescent cells that emit colors of varying intensities as the gas is ionized by an electrical signal —**plas·mat′ic** (-mat′ik) *adj.*

plasma cell a type of white blood cell that produces antibodies, formed when a B cell interacts with an antigen: often called **plas·ma·cyte** (plaz′mə sīt′) *n.*

plas·ma·gel (plaz′mə jel′) *n.* ⟦PLASMA + GEL⟧ protoplasm in its more firm and jellylike state

plas·ma·gene (plaz′mə jēn′) *n.* ⟦PLASMA + GENE⟧ any cytoplasmic structure or substance thought to carry inherited characteristics to a subsequent generation but not in a Mendelian manner —**plas′ma·gen′ic** (-jen′ik) *adj.*

plasma membrane a very thin living membrane surrounding the cytoplasm of a plant or animal cell

plas·ma·pher·e·sis (plaz′mə fer′ə sis) *n.* ⟦< PLASM(O)- + Gr *aphairesis:* see APHERESIS⟧ a type of APHERESIS in which blood is taken from a donor

plas·ma·sol (plaz′mə säl′, -sôl′, -sōl′) ***n.*** ⟦PLASMA + SOL³⟧ protoplasm in its more liquid or fluid state

plas·mid (plaz′mid) ***n.*** ⟦PLASM(A) + -ID⟧ a small, DNA-containing, self-reproducing cytoplasmic element that exists outside the chromosome, as in some bacteria: because it can alter a hereditary characteristic when introduced into another bacterium, it is used in recombinant DNA technology

plas·min (plaz′min) ***n.*** ⟦PLASM(A) + -IN¹⟧ a proteolytic enzyme, derived from substances in the blood plasma, that slowly dissolves blood clots

plas·min·o·gen (plaz min′ə jən) ***n.*** ⟦< prec. + -O- + -GEN⟧ a natural, inactive blood protein that is converted to plasmin by urokinase, streptokinase, etc.

plas·mo- (plaz′mō, -mə) *combining form* plasma *[plasmolysis]*

plas·mo·di·um (plaz mō′dē əm) ***n., pl.*** **-di·a** (-ə) ⟦ModL: see PLASMA, -ODE², -IUM⟧ **1** a shapeless mass of protoplasm with many nuclei and no definite size, esp. the vegetative stage of a myxomycete **2** any of a genus (*Plasmodium*) of unicellular sporozoans found in red blood corpuscles, including the parasites that cause malaria

plas·mol·y·sis (plaz mäl′ə sis) ***n.*** ⟦ModL: see PLASMO- & -LYSIS⟧ *Biol.* a shrinking of the protoplasm of a living cell due to loss of water by osmosis

plas·mo·lyze (plaz′mō līz′) ***vt., vi.*** **-lyzed′**, **-lyz′ing** to subject to or undergo plasmolysis

Plas·sey (plä′sē) village in West Bengal, India, north of Calcutta (now called Kolkata): scene of a decisive victory (1757) by which the British established their rule in India

-plast (plast) ⟦< Gr *plastos*, formed < *plassein*, to form: see PLASTIC⟧ *combining form* a unit of protoplasm *[chromoplast]*

plas·ter (plas′tər, pläs′-) ***n.*** ⟦ME < OE *plaster* & OFr *plastre*, both < LL *plastrum*, for L *emplastrum* < Gr *emplastron*, plaster < *emplassein*, to daub over < *en*, on, in + *plassein*, to form: see PLASTIC⟧ **1** a pasty mixture, as of lime or gypsum, sand, and water, which hardens on drying, for coating walls, ceilings, and partitions **2** PLASTER OF PARIS **3** a pasty preparation spread on cloth and applied to the body, used medicinally as a curative or counterirritant —***vt.*** **1** to cover, smear, overlay, etc. with or as with plaster **2** to apply, affix, or display, esp. in a careless or excessive way *[posters plastered all over town]* **3** to make lie smooth and flat **4** to apply PLASTER OF PARIS as a treatment **5** [Informal] to affect or strike with force —**plas′ter·er** ***n.*** —**plas′ter·y** ***adj.***

☆**plas·ter·board** (-bôrd′) ***n.*** thin board consisting of a core of plaster of Paris covered with heavy paper, used in wide sheets as a base or substitute for plaster in walls, partitions, etc.

plaster cast **1** a copy or mold of a statue or other object, cast in plaster of Paris **2** *Surgery* a rigid cast to hold a fractured bone in place and prevent movement, made by wrapping the limb or part with a bandage of gauze soaked in wet plaster of Paris

plas·tered (plas′tərd) ***adj.*** ⟦pp. of PLASTER: orig. mil. slang⟧ [Slang] intoxicated; drunk

plas·ter·ing (plas′tər iŋ) ***n.*** **1** the act or process of applying plaster **2** a coating of plaster as on a wall

plaster of Paris ⟦from use of gypsum from Montmartre in PARIS² in its manufacture⟧ a heavy white powder, calcined gypsum, which, when mixed with water, forms a thick paste that sets quickly: used for casts, moldings, statuary, etc.

plas·ter·work (plas′tər wurk′) ***n.*** a finish or decorative work done by plastering

plas·tic (plas′tik) ***adj.*** ⟦L *plasticus* < Gr *plastikos* < *plassein*, to form, prob. < IE base **plā-*, flat, to smooth out > PLAIN¹⟧ **1** molding or shaping matter; formative **2** *a)* capable of being molded or shaped *b)* made of plastic **3** in a flexible or changing state; impressionable **4** dealing with molding or modeling, as in sculpture ☆**5** *a)* characterized by or exhibiting superficiality or a lack of originality; dehumanized, mass-produced, etc. *[the plastic world of TV advertising]* *b)* hypocritically false or synthetic; phony *[a plastic smile]* ☆**6** [Informal] of or designating a credit card or credit cards, or credit based on their use **7** *Biol.* capable of readily changing or adapting in form, physiology, or behavior **8** *Med.* *a)* of or helpful in the renewal of destroyed or injured tissue *b)* that can be so renewed **9** *Physics* capable of continuous and permanent change of shape in any direction without breaking apart —***n.*** **1** any of various nonmetallic compounds, synthetically produced, usually from organic compounds by polymerization, which can be molded into various forms and hardened, or formed into pliable sheets or films, fibers, flexible or hard foams, etc. for commercial use **2** something made of plastic **3** [Informal] a credit card or credit cards, or credit based on their use —**SYN.** PLIABLE —**plas′ti·cal·ly** ***adv.*** —**plas·tic′i·ty** (-tis′ə tē) ***n.***

-plas·tic (plas′tik) ⟦< Gr *plastikos*: see prec.⟧ *combining form forming adjectives* **1** forming, developing *[homoplastic]* **2** of or relating to (a given noun ending in -PLASM, -PLAST, or -PLASTY) *[rhinoplastic]*

plastic arts **1** arts producing works or effects that are three-dimensional, as sculpture or ceramics **2** arts producing works to be viewed, as sculpture, architecture, painting, and the graphic arts, as distinguished from those involving writing or composing, as music or literature

plastic bomb a bomb made of plastic explosive

plastic explosive a puttylike substance made up in part of explosives, that will adhere to walls, etc. and is detonated by a fuse or electricity

Plas·ti·cine (plas′tə sēn′) ⟦PLASTIC + -INE³⟧ *trademark for* an oil-base modeling paste, used as a substitute for clay or wax —***n.*** [*also* **p-**] this paste

plas·ti·cize (plas′tə sīz′) ***vt., vi.*** **-cized′**, **-ciz′ing** to make or become plastic —**plas′ti·ci·za′tion** ***n.***

plas·ti·ciz·er (-sī′zər) ***n.*** any of various liquid or solid organic substances added to plastics, paints, etc. to modify viscosity, flexibility, or strength

plastic memory the tendency of certain plastics after being deformed to resume their original form when heated

plastic surgery surgery dealing with the repair, restoration, or modification of parts of the body, as by treating an injury or deformity through the use of skin or bone from other parts or from another individual, or as by correcting or enhancing certain features to improve the appearance, as with breast implants or liposuction —**plastic surgeon**

plas·tid (plas′tid) ***n.*** ⟦Ger *plastiden* (pl.) < Gr *plastides*, pl. of *plastis*, fem. of *plastēs*, molder < *plassein*, to form: see PLASTIC⟧ any of several specialized protoplasmic structures occurring in the cytoplasm of some plant cells, in which starch, oil, protein, pigment, etc. are stored

plas·tique (plȧs tēk′) ***n.*** ⟦Fr⟧ [*also in italics*] **1** the technique or action of making very slow movements in dancing or pantomime, like a statue in motion **2** PLASTIC EXPLOSIVE

plas·ti·sol (plas′tə säl′, -sōl′) ***n.*** ⟦PLASTI(C) + SOL³⟧ a liquid dispersion consisting of very small particles of resin in a plasticizer: when heated, the mass first gels and then fuses to become a thermoplastic used as a coating, for molding, etc.

plas·to·gene (plas′tə jēn′) ***n.*** ⟦< Gr *plastos*, formed (see -PLASTY) + E *-gene*, -GEN⟧ a separate genetic particle associated with, and influencing the activity of, the plastids

plas·tron (plas′trən, -trän′) ***n.*** ⟦Fr < It *piastrone* < *piastra*: see PIASTER⟧ **1** a metal breastplate worn under a coat of mail **2** a padded protector worn over the chest by fencers **3** a trimming like a dickey, worn on the front of a woman's dress **4** a starched shirt front **5** the lower, ventral part of the shell of a turtle or tortoise

-plas·ty (plas′tē) ⟦Gr *-plastia* < *plastos*, formed < *plassein*, to form: see PLASTIC⟧ *combining form* plastic surgery involving a (specified) part of the body, source of tissue, or purpose *[rhinoplasty, autoplasty, neoplasty]*

-pla·sy (plā′sē, plas′ē) *combining form* -PLASIA

plat¹ (plat) ***vt.*** **plat′ted**, **plat′ting** ⟦ME *platten*, var. of *playten*: see PLAIT⟧ [Dial.] to plait or braid —***n.*** [Dial.] a plait or braid

plat² (plat) ***n.*** ⟦var. of PLOT, infl. by ME, flat < OFr: see PLATE⟧ **1** a small piece of ground **2** a map or plan, esp. of a piece of land divided into building lots —***vt.*** **plat′ted**, **plat′ting** to make a map or plan of

plat³ *abbrev.* **1** plateau **2** *Mil.* platoon

plat- (plat) *combining form* PLATY-

Pla·ta (plä′tä), **Rí·o de la** (rē′ô de lä) estuary of the Paraná & Uruguay rivers, between Argentina & Uruguay: *c.* 200 mi (322 km)

Pla·tae·a (plə tē′ə) ancient city in Boeotia, EC Greece: site of a battle (479 B.C.) in which the Greeks defeated the Persians: also **Pla·tae′ae** (-ē)

plat·an or **plat·ane** (plat′′n) ***n.*** PLANE¹

plat du jour (plȧ dü zhōōr′) *pl.* ***plats du jour′*** (plȧ) ⟦Fr, dish of the day⟧ the featured dish of the day in a restaurant

plate (plāt) ***n.*** ⟦OFr, flat object < fem. of *plat*, flat < VL **plattus* < Gr *platys*, broad, flat: see PLATY-⟧ **1** a smooth, flat, relatively thin piece of metal or other material **2** a sheet of metal made by beating, rolling, or casting **3** *a)* any of the thin sheets of metal, plastic, etc. used in one kind of armor (**plate armor**) *b)* such armor **4** *a)* a thin, flat piece of metal on which an engraving is, or is to be, cut *b)* an impression taken from the engraved metal **5** a print of a woodcut, lithograph, etc., esp. when used in a book **6** a full-page book illustration of any kind, printed on paper of a stock different from that of the text **7** *a)* dishes, utensils, etc. of silver or gold, collectively *b)* metal dishes, utensils, etc., or any metallic ware, plated with gold or silver **8** a shallow dish, usually circular, from which food is eaten **9** PLATEFUL **10** the food in a dish; a course *[a fruit plate]* **11** food and service for an individual at a meal *[dinner at twenty dollars a plate]* **12** a dish or other container passed in churches, etc. for donations of money **13** *a)* a prize, orig. a gold or silver cup, given to the winner of a race or contest *b)* a contest, esp. a horse race, for such a prize, rather than for stakes (also called **plate race**) **14** PETRI DISH **15** a thin cut of beef from the forequarter, just below the short ribs ☆**16** LICENSE PLATE: *usually used in pl.* **17** *Anat., Zool.* a thin layer, plate, or scale, as of bone or horny tissue; lamina; scute **18** *Archit.* a horizontal wooden girder that supports the trusses or rafters of a roof **19** *Baseball short for* HOME PLATE **20** *Dentistry* *a)* that part of an artificial denture which fits to the mouth and holds the teeth *b)* [*often pl.*] loosely, a full set of false teeth **21** *Elec.* ANODE (senses 1 & 2) **22** *Geol.* any of the slabs making up the earth's crust in PLATE TECTONICS **23** *Philately* the impression surface from which a sheet of postage stamps is printed **24** *Photog.* a sheet of glass, metal, etc., coated with a film sensitive to light, upon which the image is formed **25** *Printing* a cast, to be printed from, made from a mold of set type or from a negative prepared as by photocomposition —***vt.*** **plat′ed**, **plat′ing** **1** to overlay or coat with gold, silver, tin, etc. by a mechanical, chemical, or electrical process **2** to cover, as with metal plates for protection **3** to make a printing plate of **4** to arrange (food) on a plate, esp. in an attractive or appetizing way ☆**5** ⟦< HOME PLATE⟧ *Baseball* to score *[to plate four runs in the top of the first inning]* —**on someone's plate** ⟦in ref. to PLATE, *n.* 8⟧ being, or that is, someone's responsibility *[a promotion will mean a lot more on my plate]* —☆**step up to the plate** **1** *Baseball* to approach, or take one's stance at, home plate: said of a batter **2** [Informal] to take one's turn, willingly accept a challenge, etc.

pla·teau (pla tō′) ***n., pl.*** **-teaus′** or **-teaux′** (-tōz′) ⟦Fr < OFr *platel*, dim. < *plat*: see prec.⟧ **1** an elevated tract of more or less level land; tableland; mesa **2** a period, level, etc. of relative stability, or relatively little change, as can be shown by a flat extent on a graph, etc.; specif., a period in which an individual's learning rate does not improve —*vi.* to become relatively stable or constant, as in position

plate block *Philately* a block of postage stamps with a serial number (**plate number**) in the margin

plat·ed (plāt′id) *adj.* **1** covered or protected with plates, as of armor **2** knitted of two kinds of yarn, one forming the face and the other the back **3** overlaid or coated with a metal, esp. a precious one, by a plating process [silver-*plated*]

plate·ful (plāt′fo͝ol′) *n., pl.* **-fuls′** as much as a plate will hold

plate glass ground and polished, clear glass in thick sheets used for shop windows, mirrors, etc.

plate·let (plāt′lit) *n.* ⟦PLATE + -LET⟧ **1** any of certain round or oval, nonnucleated disks, smaller than a red blood cell and containing no hemoglobin, found in the blood of mammals and associated with the process of blood clotting **2** THROMBOCYTE (sense 1)

plat·en (plat′'n) *n.* ⟦ME *plateyne* < OFr *platine*, flat plate, metal plate < *plat*: see PLATE⟧ **1** a flat metal plate, as that in a printing press which presses the paper against the inked type ☆**2** in a typewriter, the roller against which the keys strike the ribbon and paper

plat·er (plāt′ər) *n.* **1** a person or thing that plates **2** ⟦see PLATE, *n.* 13*b*⟧ an inferior race horse

plate rail a shelflike molding along the upper part of a wall of a room, for holding ornamental plates, etc.

plate tectonics *Geol.* the theory that the earth's surface consists of plates, or large crustal slabs, whose constant motion explains continental drift, mountain building, etc.

plat·form (plat′fôrm′) *n.* ⟦Fr *plate-forme*, lit., flat form: see PLATE & FORM⟧ **1** a raised horizontal surface of wood, stone, or metal; specif., *a)* a raised stage or flooring beside railroad tracks or the like *b)* a raised flooring or stage for performers, speakers, etc. ☆**2** a statement of principles and policies, esp. of a political party **3** a shoe with a platform sole: in full **platform shoe** **4** *Comput. a)* a standard hardware design for use with a compatible operating system, software, etc. *b)* such a compatible system, software, etc. **5** a basic design, process, plan, etc., esp. one that functions as a basis for growth or innovation **6** a means or opportunity for public discussion; forum **7** a means of disseminating information, as through a media outlet, the internet, etc. —*adj.* designating a thick sole of cork, leather, etc. for a shoe

platform bed a bed consisting of a mattress supported by a platform on legs, often with the space below enclosed

☆**platform rocker** a rocking chair that rocks atop an attached, stationary base

☆**platform scale** [*also pl.*] a weighing machine with a platform for holding whatever is to be weighed

☆**platform tennis** a type of PADDLE TENNIS using a rubber ball: the platform is surrounded by a wire screen, off which the ball may be played

Plath (plath), **Sylvia** 1932-63; U.S. poet

plat·ing (plāt′iŋ) *n.* **1** the act or process of a person or thing that plates **2** an external layer of metal plates **3** a thin coating of gold, silver, tin, etc.

pla·tin·ic (plə tin′ik) *adj.* of, like, or containing platinum, esp. tetravalent platinum

plat·i·nize (plat′'n īz′) *vt.* **-nized′**, **-niz′ing** to coat or combine with platinum —**plat′i·ni·za′tion** *n.*

plat·i·no·cy·a·nide (plat′'n ō′sī′ə nīd′) *n.* a double salt of platinous cyanide and another cyanide

plat·i·noid (plat′'n oid′) *adj.* ⟦PLATIN(UM) + -OID⟧ resembling platinum —*n.* **1** an alloy of copper, nickel, zinc, and tungsten, having a strong resistance to electric current: used in resistors, thermocouples, etc. **2** any metal associated with platinum

plat·i·nous (plat′'n əs) *adj.* of, like, or containing platinum, esp. divalent platinum

plat·i·num (plat′'n əm) *n.* ⟦ModL < Sp *platina*, dim. of *plata*, silver < Prov, metal plate, silver bar, silver < VL **plattus*, flat: see PLATE⟧ a silver-colored, malleable, ductile, metallic chemical element that is highly resistant to corrosion and tarnish, used as a chemical catalyst, for acid-proof containers, ignition fuses, jewelry, dental alloys, etc.: symbol, Pt; at. no. 78: see the periodic table of elements in the Reference Supplement —*adj.* ⟦by assoc. with the platinum-plated copy awarded to the performer(s)⟧ ☆designating a record, tape, disc, video, etc. which has registered sales of a specified number, as two million, or value, as $1,000,000: platinum reflects a greater number or value than gold

platinum black a black powder of finely divided metallic platinum, made by reduction of platinum salts: used as a catalyst, as in organic synthesis

☆**platinum blonde** ⟦from the silvery color of the metal⟧ **1** a girl or woman with very light, silvery-blonde hair, natural or bleached **2** such a color

platinum metal any of a group of similar metals, including ruthenium, rhodium, palladium, osmium, iridium, and platinum

plat·i·tude (plat′ə to͞od′, -tyo͞od′) *n.* ⟦Fr < OFr *plat*, flat (see PLATE), infl. by *latitude, rectitude*⟧ **1** a commonplace, flat, or dull quality, as in speech or writing **2** a commonplace or trite remark, esp. one uttered as if it were fresh or original —**plat′i·tu′di·nous** (-to͞od′'n əs) *adj.* —**plat′i·tu′di·nous·ly** *adv.*

SYN.—a **platitude** is a trite remark or idea, esp. one uttered as if it were novel or momentous; a **commonplace** is any obvious or conventional remark or idea; a **truism** is a statement whose truth is widely known and whose utterance, therefore, seems superfluous; a **cliché** is an expression or idea which, though once fresh and forceful, has become hackneyed and weak through much repetition; **bromide** is an informal term for a platitude that is especially dull, tiresome, or annoying

plat·i·tu·di·nize (plat′ə to͞od′'n īz′, -tyo͞od′-) *vi.* **-nized′**, **-niz′ing** to write or speak platitudes

Pla·to (plāt′ō) ⟦Gr *Platōn*⟧ 427?-347? B.C.; Gr. philosopher

Pla·ton·ic (plə tän′ik, plā-) *adj.* ⟦L *Platonicus* < Gr *Platōnikos*⟧ **1** of or characteristic of Plato or his philosophy **2** idealistic, visionary, or impractical **3** [*usually* **p-**] designating or of a relationship, or love, between a man and a woman that is purely spiritual or intellectual and without sexual activity —**pla·ton′i·cal·ly** *adv.*

Platonic year GREAT YEAR

Pla·to·nism (plāt′'n iz′əm) *n.* ⟦ModL *platonismus*⟧ **1** the philosophy of Plato or his school; esp., the doctrine holding that objects of perception are real insofar as they imitate or participate in an independent realm of immutable essences, ideas, or logical forms which constitute the world of essential reality: see IDEALISM **2** the theory or practice of platonic love

Pla·to·nist (plāt′'n ist) *n.* **1** a follower of Plato or his philosophy **2** a person who tends to be abstract, speculative, or idealistic in outlook, rather than empirical or practical: distinguished from ARISTOTELIAN

Pla·to·nize (plāt′'n īz′) *vi.* **-nized′**, **-niz′ing** to follow the philosophy of Plato; philosophize in a Platonic manner —*vt.* to make Platonic

pla·toon (plə to͞on′) *n.* ⟦Fr *peloton*, a ball, group, platoon < OFr *pelote*, a ball: see PELLET⟧ **1** a military unit composed of two or more squads or sections, normally under the command of a lieutenant: it is a subdivision of a company, troop, etc. **2** a group or unit like this [a *platoon* of police] **3** *Sports* any of the specialized squads (as the offensive and defensive squads in professional football) constituting a single team —*vt.* **1** to divide into platoons, or use as or on a platoon ☆**2** *Sports* to alternate (players) at a position [to *platoon* two rookies in right field] —☆*vi. Sports* **1** to be alternated with another player at a position **2** to platoon players at a position

platoon sergeant *U.S. Army* the senior noncommissioned officer in a platoon, equal in grade to a sergeant first class

Platt·deutsch (plät′doich′) *n.* ⟦Ger < Du *platduitsch* < *plat*, plain, clear, lit., flat (< OFr: see PLATE) + *duitsch*, German: see DEUTSCHLAND⟧ the group of West Germanic dialects of N Germany; Low German

Platte (plat) ⟦< Fr *Rivière Platte*, lit., flat river⟧ river formed in central Nebr. by the North Platte & the South Platte rivers, & flowing eastward into the Missouri: 310 mi (499 km)

plat·ter (plat′ər) *n.* ⟦ME *plater* < Anglo-Fr < OFr *plat*: see PLATE⟧ **1** a large plate, usually oval, for serving food, esp. meat or fish **2** the circular, motor-driven surface of a turntable on which phonograph records are played ☆**3** [Old Slang] HOME PLATE ☆**4** [Slang] a phonograph record

Platts·burgh (plats′burg) ⟦after Z. Platt, early settler, *c.* 1784⟧ city in NE N.Y., on Lake Champlain: scene of a British invasion (1814) repulsed by the U.S.

plat·y[1] (plāt′ē) *adj. Geol.* composed of plates, sheets, or slabs, as certain sandstones or limestones

plat·y[2] (plat′ē) *n., pl.* **plat′y**, **plat′ys**, **plat′ies** ⟦clipped < ModL *Platypoecilus*, a genus of fishes < fol. + Gr *poikilos*, many-colored⟧ any of various brightly colored livebearers (genus *Xiphophorus*) native to Central America

plat·y- (plat′ə) ⟦< Gr *platys*, broad, flat < IE **plat-*, var. of base **plā-* > PLAIN[1]⟧ *combining form* broad or flat [*platyhelminth*]

plat·y·hel·minth (plat′ə hel′minth) *n.* ⟦prec. + HELMINTH⟧ any of a phylum (Platyhelminthes) of flat worms with a soft, unsegmented body and a flame cell system, as the planarians, tapeworms, or liver flukes; flatworm —**plat′y·hel·min′thic** *adj.*

plat·y·pus (plat′ə pəs) *n., pl.* **-pus·es** or **-pi′** (-pī′) ⟦ModL < Gr *platypous*, flatfooted < *platys*, flat (see PLATY-) + *pous*, FOOT⟧ a small, aquatic, egg-laying monotreme mammal (*Ornithorhynchus anatinus*) of Australia and Tasmania, with webbed feet, a beaverlike tail, and a ducklike bill; duckbill

platypus

plat·yr·rhine (plat′ə rīn′, -rin) *adj.* ⟦ModL *platyrrhinus* < Gr *platyrrhin*, broad-nosed < *platy* (see PLATY-) + *rhis* (gen. *rhinos*), nose: see RHINO-⟧ having a broad, flat nose with nostrils that open to the side, creating a wide, flat septum —*n.* a platyrrhine animal, esp. the New World monkeys See CATARRHINE

plau·dit (plô′dit) *n.* ⟦< L *plaudite*, pl. imper. of *plaudere*, to applaud⟧ [*usually pl.*] **1** an applauding or round of applause **2** any expression of approval or praise

plau·si·ble (plô′zə bəl) *adj.* ⟦L *plausibilis* < *plaudere*, to applaud⟧ **1** seemingly true, acceptable, etc. **2** seemingly honest, trustworthy, etc.: often implying distrust —**plau′si·bil′i·ty** *n.*, **plau′si·ble·ness** —**plau′si·bly** *adv.*

SYN.—**plausible** applies to that which at first glance appears to be true, reasonable, valid, etc. but which may or may not be so, although there is no connotation of deliberate deception [a *plausible* argument]; **credible** is used of that which is believable because it is supported by evidence, sound logic, etc. [a *credible* account]; **specious** applies to that which is superficially reasonable, valid, etc. but is actually not so, and it connotes intention to deceive [a *specious* excuse] —*ANT.* **genuine, actual**

plau·sive (plô′siv) ***adj.*** **1** [Rare] applauding or showing praise **2** *obs. var. of* PLAUSIBLE

Plau·tus (plôt′əs), **(Titus Maccius)** 254?-184 B.C.; Rom. writer of comic dramas

play (plā) ***vi.*** ⟦ME *plein* < OE *plegan*, to play, be active⟧ **1** to move lightly, rapidly, or erratically; flutter [sunlight *playing* on the waves] **2** to amuse oneself, as by taking part in a game or sport; engage in recreation **3** to take active part in a game or sport [not *playing* because of an injury] **4** to engage in a game for stakes; gamble **5** *a)* to act, deal, or touch carelessly or lightly; trifle (*with* a thing or person) *b)* [Obs.] to engage in sexual activity; dally **6** to perform on a musical instrument **7** to produce or reproduce sounds, esp. musical sounds: said of an instrument, phonograph or tape recorder, etc. **8** to lend itself to performance [a drama that does not *play* well] **9** to act in a specified way; esp., to pretend to be [to *play* dumb] **10** to act in or as in a drama; perform on the stage **11** to be performed or presented in a theater, on radio or TV, etc. [what movie is *playing?*] **12** to move freely within limits, as parts of a machine **13** to be ejected, discharged, or directed repeatedly or continuously, as a fountain, a spotlight, etc.: with *on, over*, or *along* **14** to impose unscrupulously (*on* another's feelings or susceptibilities) **15** [Informal] to achieve acceptance, success, etc. —***vt.*** **1** *a)* to take part in (a game or sport) *b)* to be stationed at (a specified position) in a sport **2** to oppose (a person, team, etc.) in a game or contest **3** to enter or use (a player, etc.) in a game or contest **4** to do (something), as in fun or to deceive [*play* tricks] **5** *a)* to bet ☆*b)* to bet on [*play* the horses] ☆*c)* to act on the basis of [*play* a hunch] ☆**6** to speculate in (the stock market) **7** to cause to move, act, operate, etc.; wield; ply **8** to put (a specified card) into play [to *play* an ace] **9** to cause or effect [to *play* havoc] **10** to perform (music) **11** *a)* to perform on (a musical instrument) *b)* to cause (a phonograph, phonograph record, tape recorder, tape, etc.) to audibly reproduce sounds, images, etc. **12** to accompany or lead (someone) with music: with *in, off*, etc. **13** to perform (a drama or dramatic passage) **14** to act the part of [to *play* Iago, to *play* the fool] **15** to imitate the activities of, as children do for amusement [to *play* teacher, to *play* house] ☆**16** to give performances in [to *play* Boston for a week] **17** to eject or direct (water, light, etc.) repeatedly or continuously (*on, over*, or *along*) **18** to let (a hooked fish) tire itself by tugging at the line ☆**19** to use or exploit (a person) [*played* him for a fool] —***n.*** **1** action, motion, or activity, esp. when free, rapid, or light [the *play* of muscles] **2** freedom or scope for motion or action, esp. of a mechanism **3** activity engaged in for amusement or recreation; sport, games, etc.; often, specif., the natural activities of children **4** fun; joking [to do a thing in *play*] **5** *a)* the playing of a game *b)* the way or technique of playing a game **6** *a)* a maneuver, move, or act in a game; specif., a planned, coordinated action executed by members of a team during a game *b)* a turn at playing **7** the act of gambling **8** a dramatic composition or performance; drama **9** [Informal] publicity or notice, esp. in the news media **10** [Obs.] sexual activity; dalliance —***adj.*** not real; make-believe [a board game using *play* money] —**bring** (or **come**) **into play** to make (or become) implicated, involved, pertinent, etc. —**in** (or **out of**) **play** *Sports* eligible (or not eligible) for continued play, as by being in (or out) of bounds: said of a ball, etc. —**make a play for** [Informal] **1** to employ one's arts and wiles in order to attract, esp. sexually **2** to use all one's skill in order to obtain —**play along** to join in or cooperate, or to pretend to do so —**play around** **1** to engage in trifling activity **2** [Informal] *a)* to engage lightly in passing love affairs *b)* to be sexually unfaithful —**play at** **1** to participate in **2** to pretend to be engaged in **3** to perform or work at halfheartedly —**play back** to audibly reproduce or cause to audibly reproduce (sounds, images, etc.) that have been recorded on (a tape, disc, etc.) —☆**play both ends against the middle** **1** to maneuver alternatives in order to win something, no matter what the outcome **2** to play off opposing factions, etc. against one another to one's own profit —☆**play catch-up ball** *Sports* to adjust one's style of play so as to make up for a lack of points, runs, etc. —**play down** [Informal] to attach little importance, or give little publicity, to; minimize —**play fair** **1** to play according to the rules **2** to behave honorably —☆**play favorites** [Informal] to engage in favoritism —**play for time** to maneuver so as to delay an outcome, gain a respite, etc. —**play into someone's hands** to act in such a way as to give the advantage to someone —**play it** [Informal] to act in a (specified) manner [to *play it* smart] —**play off** **1** to pit (a person or thing) against another ☆**2** in games, to break (a tie) by playing once more **3** to react to or interact with, as in a drama **4** [Archaic] to palm off —**play one's cards well** (or **right**) to use one's resources in the most effective manner —**play out** **1** to play to the finish **2** to develop and eventually conclude **3** PAY OUT (sense 2) (see phrase under PAY[1]) —☆**play up** [Informal] to emphasize or give prominence to —**play through** to pass another foursome or group with their permission, while playing a round of golf —**play up to** [Informal] to try to please by flattery, etc. —**play with oneself** [Informal] to masturbate —**play′a·ble** ***adj.***

☆**pla·ya** (plä′yə) ***n.*** ⟦Sp, lit., beach < Prov < VL *plagia*, coast, side < or akin to Gr, sides < *plagos*, side < IE **plāg-*, flat < base **plā-* > PLAIN[1]⟧ a desert basin that temporarily becomes a shallow lake after heavy rains

play-act (plā′akt′) ***vi.*** **1** to act in a play **2** to pretend; make believe **3** to behave in an affected or dramatic manner —**play′act′ing** ***n.***

☆**play-ac·tion pass** (plā′ak′shən) *Football* a forward pass made by the quarterback after first faking a handoff

play·back (plā′bak′) ***n.*** **1** reproduction of sounds, images, etc. from a recorded disc, tape, etc. **2** the control or device for such reproduction on a player, recorder, etc.

play·bill (plā′bil′) ***n.*** **1** a poster or circular advertising a play **2** a program of a play, listing the cast, staff, etc.

☆**play·book** (plā′book′) ***n.*** **1** a book of plays, or dramas **2** an instruction book put together by a coaching staff, as in football, diagraming the various plays to be used

play·boy (plā′boi′) ***n.*** ☆a man, esp. a man of means, who is given to pleasure-seeking, sexual promiscuity, etc.

☆**play-by-play** (plā′bī plā′) ***adj.*** recounting each play of a game or each incident of a happening as it occurs or occurred —***n.*** such a recounting, as of a sporting event broadcast on TV or radio

played out **1** worn out; exhausted **2** out-of-date Also written **played′-out′** ***adj.***

play·er (plā′ər) ***n.*** **1** a person who plays a game [a football *player*] **2** a performer in a drama; actor **3** a person who plays a musical instrument **4** a gambler **5** a person or group regarded as a chief or legitimate participant in some competitive activity **6** [Slang] a person, esp. a man, who is given to sexual promiscuity, unfaithfulness, etc. ☆**7** *a)* an apparatus attached to a musical instrument, as to a piano, for playing it automatically *b)* a device for playing tapes, records, discs, etc., esp. one that does not also record

☆**player piano** a piano that can play automatically by means of a built-in pneumatic mechanism that depresses the keys in response to signals on a perforated roll

play·fel·low (plā′fel′ō) ***n.*** PLAYMATE

play·ful (plā′fəl) ***adj.*** **1** fond of play or fun; frisky **2** said or done in fun; jocular —**play′ful·ly** ***adv.*** —**play′ful·ness** ***n.***

☆**play·girl** (plā′gurl′) ***n.*** a woman who is given to pleasure-seeking, sexual promiscuity, etc.

play·go·er (plā′gō′ər) ***n.*** a person who goes to the theater frequently or regularly —**play′go′ing** ***n., adj.***

play·ground (plā′ground′) ***n.*** **1** a place, often part of a schoolyard, for outdoor games and recreation **2** a popular resort area

☆**play hook·y** *see* HOOKY

play·house (plā′hous′) ***n.*** ⟦OE *pleghus* < *plega*, a play + *hus*, HOUSE⟧ **1** a theater for live dramatic productions ☆**2** a small house for children to play in **3** a child's toy house or doll house

playing cards cards used in playing various games, arranged in decks of four suits (spades, hearts, diamonds, and clubs): a standard deck has 52 cards

playing field **1** ground for playing games on, esp. as marked out for the playing of a particular game **2** a basis for competition or negotiation: usually characterized according to its relative fairness to both parties: a fig. use [a level *playing field*]

play·let (plā′lit) ***n.*** a short drama

play·list (plā′list′) ***n.*** **1** a limited list of musical recordings or videos that may be played, as on a radio or TV station **2** a select list of digital audio or video files, esp. music files, that have been grouped for playback as on a computer or portable music player

☆**play·mak·er** (plā′māk′ər) ***n.*** a player, as in basketball, who leads the offense by initiating the plays

play·mate (plā′māt′) ***n.*** **1** a companion in games and recreation: term used esp. of children **2** [Informal] a sexual partner in what is regarded as a superficial relationship

play·off (plā′ôf′) ***n.*** **1** a contest or series of contests played to break a tie **2** a contest played to decide a championship, as between the top finishers in the divisions of a league: *usually used in pl.* **3** exhibition of a film

play on words a pun or punning

play·pen (plā′pen′) ***n.*** a small, portable enclosure in which an infant can be left safely to play, crawl, etc.

☆**play·room** (plā′ro͞om′) ***n.*** a recreation room, esp. one for children

play·suit (plā′so͞ot′) ***n.*** a woman's or child's outfit for sports or play, consisting usually of shorts or pants and a shirt

play·thing (plā′thiŋ′) ***n.*** a thing to play with; toy: often used fig.

play·time (plā′tīm′) ***n.*** time for play or recreation

☆**play·wear** (plā′wer′) ***n.*** **1** clothing for casual activity or lounging **2** durable clothing for children, designed for active play

play·wright (plā′rīt′) ***n.*** ⟦see WRIGHT⟧ a person who writes plays; dramatist

play·writ·ing (plā′rīt′iŋ) ***n.*** the art, profession, or work of writing plays

pla·za (plä′zə, plaz′ə) ***n.*** ⟦Sp < L *platea:* see PLACE⟧ **1** *a)* a public square or marketplace in a city or town *b)* an open area, usually paved, between a building and the street or another building, often having statues, shrubs, etc. **2** a complex of shops or buildings, esp. a shopping center **3** a service area along a superhighway, with a restaurant, gas station, etc.

PLC *abbrev.* [Brit.] public limited company

plea (plē) ***n.*** ⟦ME *plai* < OFr *plaid*, suit, plea < L *placitum*, opinion, order, orig. that which is pleasing, orig. neut. pp. of *placere*, to PLEASE⟧ **1** a statement in defense or justification; excuse **2** an earnest and urgent request; appeal; entreaty **3** *Law* *a)* a pleading or allegation, now, esp., in a civil action *b)* the response of a defendant to criminal charges [a *plea* of not guilty]

plea bargain an agreement arrived at by plea bargaining

plea-bar·gain (plē′bär′gən) ***vi.*** to engage in plea bargaining

☆**plea bargaining** pretrial negotiations in which the defendant agrees to plead guilty to a lesser charge in exchange for having a more serious charge dropped

pleach (plēch) ***vt.*** ⟦ME *plechen* < NormFr *plechier*, for OFr *plessier, plaissier*, to weave: see PLASH[3]⟧ to intertwine (the branches of living trees or shrubs) so as to form a hedge, archway, etc.

plead (plēd) ***vi.*** **plead′ed** or **pled** or **plead** (pled), **plead′ing** ⟦ME *pleden* <

OFr *plaidier* < *plaid:* see PLEA⟧ 1 *a)* to present a case in a law court; argue the case of either party *b)* to present a PLEA (sense 3*b*) 2 to make an earnest appeal; supplicate; beg [to *plead* for mercy] —*vt.* 1 to discuss or defend (a law case) by argument 2 to declare oneself to be (guilty or not guilty) in answer to a charge 3 to offer as an excuse or defense [to *plead* ignorance] —*SYN.* APPEAL —**plead′a·ble** *adj.* —**plead′er** *n.* —**plead′ing·ly** *adv.*

plead·ings (plēd′iŋz) *pl.n.* the statements setting forth to the court the claims of the plaintiff and the answer of the defendant

pleas·ance (plez′əns) *n.* ⟦ME *plesaunce* < MFr *plaisance* < *plaisant:* see fol.⟧ 1 [Archaic] pleasure; joy 2 a pleasure ground or garden, usually part of an estate

pleas·ant (plez′ənt) *adj.* ⟦ME *plesaunte* < MFr *plaisant*, prp. of *plaisir*, to PLEASE⟧ 1 agreeable to the mind or senses; pleasing; delightful 2 having an agreeable manner, appearance, etc.; amiable 3 [Obs.] merry; playful —**pleas′ant·ly** *adv.* —**pleas′ant·ness** *n.*

SYN.—**pleasant** and **pleasing** both imply the producing of an agreeable effect upon the mind or senses, but the former word stresses the effect produced [a *pleasant* smile] and the latter, the ability to produce such an effect [her *pleasing* ways]; **agreeable** is used of that which is in accord with one's personal likes, mood, etc. [*agreeable* music]; **enjoyable** implies the ability to give enjoyment or pleasure [an *enjoyable* picnic]; **gratifying** implies the ability to give satisfaction or pleasure by indulging wishes, hopes, etc. [a *gratifying* experience] —*ANT.* **unpleasant, disagreeable**

pleas·ant·ry (plez′ən trē) *n., pl.* **-ries** ⟦Fr *plaisanterie*⟧ 1 the quality or state of being pleasant, or playful, in conversation; jocularity 2 *a)* a humorous remark or action; joke *b)* a polite social remark [to exchange *pleasantries*]

please (plēz) *vt.* **pleased, pleas′ing** ⟦ME *plaisen* < MFr *plaisir* < L *placere*, to please, akin to *placidus*, gentle, mild, *placare*, to calm, soothe < IE **plāk-*, flat, smooth < base **plā-* > PLAIN[1]⟧ 1 to be agreeable to; give pleasure to; satisfy 2 to be the will or wish of [it *pleased* him to remain] —*vi.* 1 to be agreeable; give pleasure; satisfy [to aim to *please*] 2 to have the will or wish; like [to do as one *pleases*]: also used passively [you are *pleased* to scoff] —*adv.* used for politeness in requests or commands to mean "be obliging enough (to)" [*please* sit down] —**if you please** if you wish or like; if you will; if you permit: sometimes used in ironic exclamation —**please God** if it pleases God; if it is God's will —**please oneself** to do as one wishes —**pleas′er** *n.*

pleas·ing (plēz′iŋ) *adj.* giving pleasure; pleasant; agreeable; gratifying —*SYN.* PLEASANT —**pleas′ing·ly** *adv.* —**pleas′ing·ness** *n.*

pleas·ur·a·ble (plezh′ər ə bəl) *adj.* pleasant; enjoyable —**pleas′ur·a·bil′i·ty** (-bil′ə tē) *n.*, **pleas′ur·a·ble·ness** —**pleas′ur·a·bly** *adv.*

pleas·ure (plezh′ər) *n.* ⟦ME, altered < *plesir* < MFr *plaiser*, orig. inf.: see PLEASE⟧ 1 a pleased feeling; enjoyment; delight; satisfaction 2 one's wish, will, or choice [what is your *pleasure*?] 3 a thing that gives delight or satisfaction 4 gratification of the senses; sensual satisfaction 5 amusement; fun —*vt.* **-ured, -ur·ing** 1 to give pleasure to, now specif., sexually 2 to have sexual intercourse with —*vi.* to take pleasure (*in*) —**pleas′ure·ful** *adj.*

SYN.—**pleasure** is the general term for an agreeable feeling of satisfaction, ranging from a quiet sense of gratification to a positive sense of happiness; **delight** implies a high degree of obvious pleasure, openly and enthusiastically expressed [a child's *delight* with a new toy]; **joy** describes a keenly felt, exuberant, often demonstrative happiness [their *joy* at his safe return]; **enjoyment** suggests a somewhat more quiet feeling of satisfaction with that which pleases [our *enjoyment* of the recital] —*ANT.* **displeasure, sorrow, vexation**

pleasure principle *Psychoanalysis* the principle that the governing instinct of the id is to seek pleasure, or gratification, and avoid pain, or unpleasantness: cf. REALITY PRINCIPLE

pleat (plēt) *n.* ⟦ME *pleten*, var. of *playten:* see PLAIT⟧ a flat double fold in cloth or other material, of uniform width and pressed or stitched in place —*vt.* to lay and press (cloth) in a pleat or series of pleats —**pleat′ed** *adj.*

BOX PLEAT

INVERTED PLEAT

COMMON PLEATS

pleat·er (plēt′ər) *n.* a person or thing that pleats; specif., a sewing machine attachment for making pleats

pleb (pleb) *n.* [Informal] PLEBEIAN (*n.* 2)

plebe (plēb) *n.* ⟦Fr *plèbe* < L *plebs*⟧ 1 the plebs in ancient Rome 2 [Obs.] the common people of any nation ☆3 ⟦short for fol.⟧ a member of the freshman class at the U.S. Military Academy or Naval Academy 4 [Slang] PLEBEIAN (*n.* 2)

ple·be·ian (pli bē′ən) *n.* ⟦< L *plebeius* < *plebs*, PLEBS⟧ 1 a member of the ancient Roman lower class: opposed to PATRICIAN 2 one of the common people 3 a vulgar, coarse person —*adj.* 1 of or characteristic of the lower class in ancient Rome or of the common people in any country 2 *a)* vulgar, coarse, or common *b)* commonplace; ordinary —**ple·be′ian·ism′** *n.* —**ple·be′ian·ly** *adv.*

pleb·i·scite (pleb′ə sīt′) *n.* ⟦Fr *plébiscite* < L *plebiscitum* < *plebs*, fol. + *scitum*, decree, neut. pp. of *scire*, to know: see SCIENCE⟧ an expression of the people's will by direct ballot on a political issue, as in choosing between independent nationhood or affiliation with another nation —**ple·bis·ci·tar·y** (plə bis′ə ter′ē) *adj.*

plebs (plebz) *n., pl.* **ple·bes** (plē′bēz′) ⟦L, akin to *plere*, to fill: for IE base see PLENTY⟧ 1 the lower class in ancient Roman society 2 the common people; the masses

plec·tog·nath (plek′täg nath′) *n.* ⟦< ModL *Plectognathi* < Gr *plektos*, twisted (< *plekein*, to braid: for IE base see FLAX) + *gnathos*, jaw: for IE base see CHIN⟧ any of an order (Tetraodontiformes) of bony fishes of warm seas, having a small mouth with powerful jaws and bony or spiny scales, as triggerfishes and trunkfishes —*adj.* of the plectognaths

plec·trum (plek′trəm) *n., pl.* **-trums** or **-tra** (-trə) ⟦L < Gr *plēktron*, device for plucking the lyre < *plēssein*, to strike: see PLAINT⟧ a thin piece of metal, bone, plastic, etc., used for plucking the strings of a guitar, mandolin, etc.: also **plec′tron′** (-trän′, -trən), *pl.* **-tra** (-trə)

pled (pled) *vi., vt. pt. & pp. of* PLEAD

pledge (plej) *n.* ⟦ME *plegge* < OFr *pleige* < ML *plegium* < *plevium*, security, warranty, infl. by Frank **pligi*, liability; akin to OS *plegan*, to warrant⟧ 1 the condition of being given or held as security for a contract, payment, etc. [a thing held in *pledge*] 2 a person or thing given or held as security for the performance of a contract, as a guarantee of faith, etc.; something pawned; hostage 3 a token or earnest 4 a drinking to someone's health to express good will or allegiance; toast 5 a promise or agreement 6 something promised, esp. money to be contributed in regular payments ☆7 a person undergoing a trial period before formal initiation into a fraternity, sorority, etc. —*vt.* **pledged, pledg′ing** 1 to present as security or guarantee, esp. for the repayment of a loan; pawn 2 to drink a toast to 3 to bind by a promise or agreement 4 to promise to give [to *pledge* allegiance, *pledge* money to a fund] ☆5 *a)* to accept tentative membership in (a fraternity, etc.) *b)* to accept as a PLEDGE (*n.* 7) —**take the pledge** [Informal] to make a solemn resolution not to drink alcoholic liquor

SYN.—**pledge** applies to anything given as security for the performance of an act or contract or for the payment of a debt [he gave her a ring as a *pledge*]; **earnest**, in current usage, applies to anything given or done as an indication, promise, or assurance of more to follow [her early triumphs are an *earnest* of her success]; **token** is used of anything serving or given as evidence of authority, genuineness, good faith, etc. [this watch is a *token* of our gratitude]; **pawn** now usually refers to an article left as security for the money lent on it by a pawnbroker; **hostage** is applied to a person handed over as a pledge for the fulfillment of certain terms or one seized and kept to force others to comply with demands

pledg·ee (ple jē′) *n.* a person to whom a pledge is delivered: distinguished from PLEDGOR

pledg·er (plej′ər) *n.* a person who pledges

pledg·et (plej′it) *n.* ⟦< ?⟧ a small compress, sometimes medicated, used as a dressing for a wound or sore

pledg·or (plej′ər, ple jôr′) *n.* *Law* a person who delivers something as security: distinguished from PLEDGEE

-ple·gi·a (plē′jē ə, -jə) ⟦ModL < Gr *-plēgia* < *plēgē*, a stroke, akin to *plēssein*, to strike: see PLAINT⟧ *combining form* paralysis [*paraplegia*]

Plé·iade (plā yàd′) *n.* ⟦Fr: see fol.⟧ 1 a group of seven French poets of the 16th cent. who favored the use of classical forms 2 a small group, usually seven, of brilliant persons: also **ple′iad** or **Ple′iad**

Ple·ia·des (plē′ə dēz′, plī′-), **the**, *sing.* **Ple·iad** (plā′yad′; plē′yad′, -ad′, -əd; plī′-) ⟦ME *Pliades* < L *Pleiades* < Gr⟧ 1 *Gr. Myth.* the seven daughters of Atlas and Pleione, placed by Zeus among the stars 2 [*often with sing. v.*] a cluster of stars in the constellation Taurus, including six bright stars: a seventh bright star (the **Lost Pleiad**) has apparently faded from sight since the original sightings

plein-air (plān′er′; *Fr* ple ner′) *adj.* ⟦Fr, lit., open air⟧ designating, of, or in the manner of certain schools of French impressionist painting of the late 19th cent., engaged mainly in representing observed effects of outdoor light and atmosphere —**plein′-air′ism′** *n.* —**plein′-air′ist** *n.*

plei·o- (plī′ə, -ō) *combining form* PLEO- [*pleiotropy*]

Plei·o·cene (plī′ə sēn′) *adj.* [*sometimes* **p-**] *rare alt. sp. of* PLIOCENE

plei·o·tax·y (plī′ə tak′sē) *n.* ⟦PLEIO- + *-taxy*, an arranging < Gr *-taxia* < *taxis:* see TAXIS⟧ *Bot.* an increase in the number of whorls in a flower

plei·ot·ro·py (plī ä′trə pē) *n.* ⟦PLEIO- + -TROPY⟧ *Genetics* the condition in which a single gene exerts simultaneous effects on more than one character in the offspring: also **plei·ot′ro·pism′** —**plei·o·trop·ic** (plī′ō träp′ik) *adj.* —**plei′o·trop′i·cal·ly** *adv.*

Pleis·to·cene (plīs′tə sēn′) *adj.* ⟦< Gr *pleistos*, most, superl. of *polys*, much (see POLY-[1]) + -CENE⟧ [*sometimes* **p-**] designating or of the first geologic epoch of the Quaternary Period, characterized by a series of advancing and retreating continental glaciers in the Northern Hemisphere and the development of modern humans and toolmaking cultures —**the Pleistocene** the Pleistocene Epoch or its rocks: see the geologic time chart in the Reference Supplement

ple·na·ry (plē′nə rē, plen′ə-) *adj.* ⟦LL *plenarius* < L *plenus*, FULL[1]⟧ 1 full; complete; absolute [*plenary* power] 2 for attendance by all members [a *plenary* session] —*n., pl.* **-ries** a meeting or session for all members or participants —**ple′na·ri·ly** (-rə lē) *adv.*

plenary indulgence *R.C.Ch.* an indulgence remitting in full the temporal punishment incurred by a sinner

plen·i·po·ten·ti·ar·y (plen′i pō ten′shē er′ē, -shə rē) *adj.* ⟦ML *plenipotentiarius* < LL *plenipotens,* possessing full power < L *plenus,* FULL[1] + *potens,* powerful⟧ having or conferring full power or authority [an ambassador *plenipotentiary*] —*n., pl.* **-ar′ies** a person, esp. a diplomatic agent, given full authority to act as representative of a government

plen·ish (plen′ish) *vt.* ⟦ME *plenissen* < MFr *pleniss-,* prp. stem of *plenir,* to fill < L *plenus,* FULL[1]⟧ [Now Scot.] to fill up; stock

plen·i·tude (plen′ə to͞od′, -tyo͞od′) *n.* ⟦OFr < L *plenitudo* < *plenus,* FULL[1]⟧ **1** fullness; completeness **2** abundance; plenty

plen·i·tu·di·nous (plen′ə to͞od′'n əs, -tyo͞od′-) *adj.* **1** marked by plenitude; abundant; full **2** stout; obese

plen·te·ous (plen′tē əs) *adj.* ⟦ME *plentevous* < OFr < *plente,* PLENTY⟧ **1** marked by or being in abundance; plentiful; copious **2** producing abundantly; fruitful; productive —**plen′te·ous·ly** *adv.* —**plen′te·ous·ness** *n.*

plen·ti·ful (plen′ti fəl) *adj.* **1** having or yielding plenty **2** sufficient or more than enough; abundant —**plen′ti·ful·ly** *adv.* —**plen′ti·ful·ness** *n.*

SYN.—**plentiful** implies a large or full supply [a *plentiful* supply of food]; **abundant** implies a very plentiful or very large supply [a forest *abundant* in wild game]; **copious,** now used chiefly with reference to quantity produced, used, etc., implies a rich or flowing abundance [a *copious* harvest, discharge, etc.]; **profuse** implies a giving or pouring forth abundantly or lavishly, often to excess [*profuse* in his thanks]; **ample** applies to that which is large enough to meet all demands [his savings are *ample* to see him through this crisis] —*ANT.* **scarce, scant**

plen·ty (plen′tē) *n., pl.* **-ties** ⟦ME *plente* < MFr *plenté* < L *plenitas* < *plenus,* FULL[1]⟧ **1** prosperity; opulence **2** a plentiful or abundant supply; enough or more than enough **3** a large number; multitude [*plenty* of errors] —*adj.* [Dial.] plentiful; enough; ample [*plenty* time before lunch] —*adv.* [Informal] fully; sufficiently; quite [*plenty* good]

ple·num (plē′nəm, plen′əm) *n., pl.* **-nums** or **-na** (-nə) ⟦ModL < L, neut. of *plenus,* FULL[1]⟧ **1** space filled with matter: opposed to VACUUM **2** fullness **3** a full or general assembly, as of all members of a legislative body **4** *a)* an enclosed volume of gas under greater pressure than that surrounding the container *b)* the state of this

ple·o- (plē′ə, -ō) ⟦< Gr *pleon,* more: see PLEONASM⟧ *combining form* more [*pleomorphism*]

pleochroic halo a dark-colored, microscopic ring around a minute radioactive particle in certain mineral crystals, used in estimating the age of the rocks containing these crystals

ple·och·ro·ism (plē äk′rō iz′əm) *n.* ⟦< PLEO- + Gr *chrōs,* color (see -CHROOUS) + -ISM⟧ the property of some minerals of absorbing selectively various wavelengths of light and of displaying different colors when looked at in the directions of the different crystal axes —**ple·o·chro·ic** (plē′ə krō′ik) *adj.*

ple·o·mor·phism (plē′ə môr′fiz′əm) *n.* ⟦PLEO- + -MORPH(IC) + -ISM⟧ **1** *Biol.* the occurrence of two or more forms in one life cycle **2** POLYMORPHISM (sense 2) —**ple′o·mor′phic** *adj.,* **ple′o·mor′phous** (-fəs)

ple·o·nasm (plē′ə naz′əm) *n.* ⟦LL *pleonasmus* < Gr *pleonasmos* < *pleonazein,* to be in excess < *pleon,* neut. of *pleōn,* more, compar. of *polys,* much: see POLY-[1]⟧ **1** the use of more words than are necessary for the expression of an idea; redundancy (Ex.: "plenty enough") **2** an instance of this **3** a redundant word or expression —**ple′o·nas′tic** *adj.* —**ple′o·nas′ti·cal·ly** *adv.*

ple·o·pod (plē′ə päd′) *n.* ⟦< Gr *pleōn,* prp. of *plein,* to swim (< IE base **pleu-,* to run, FLOW) + -POD⟧ *Zool.* any of the biramous appendages attached to the abdomen of higher crustaceans; swimmeret

ple·si·o·saur (plē′sē ə sôr′) *n.* ⟦< ModL *Plesiosaurus* < Gr *plēsios,* close, near, akin to *pelos,* near (prob. < IE base **pel-,* to push > FELT[1], L *pellere,* to drive) + -SAUR⟧ any of an extinct group (order Sauropterygia) of large water reptiles of the Mesozoic Era, characterized by a small head, long neck, short tail, and four paddlelike limbs: also **ple′si·o·sau′rus**

ples·sor (ples′ər) *n.* PLEXOR

pleth·o·ra (pleth′ə rə) *n.* ⟦ML < Gr *plēthōrē* < *plēthein,* to be FULL[1]⟧ **1** the state of being too full; overabundance; excess **2** an abnormal condition characterized by an excess of blood in the circulatory system or in some part of it

ple·thor·ic (plə thôr′ik) *adj.* **1** of or characterized by plethora [a *plethoric* condition] **2** characterized by excess or profusion; turgid; inflated [a *plethoric* speech] —**ple·thor′i·cal·ly** *adv.*

ple·thys·mo·graph (plə thiz′mə graf′) *n.* ⟦< Gr *plēthysmos,* a multiplying < *plēthymein,* to increase < *plēthys,* a crowd (akin to *plēthein:* see PLETHORA) + GRAPH[1]⟧ any of several instruments for measuring and recording various bodily functions, as the velocity or volume of blood flow, heart rate or breathing rate, changes in the size of organs or limbs, etc. —**ple·thys′mo·graph′ic** *adj.* —**pleth·ys·mog·ra·phy** (pleth′iz mäg′rə fē) *n.*

pleu·ra (plo͝or′ə) *n.* ⟦ML < Gr, rib, side⟧ **1** *pl.* **-rae** (-ē) the thin serous membrane that covers a lung and lines the chest cavity in mammals **2** *pl. of* PLEURON —**pleu′ral** *adj.*

pleu·ri·sy (plo͝or′ə sē) *n.* ⟦ME *pleresye* < MFr *pleurisie* < LL *pleurisis,* for L *pleuritis* < Gr < *pleura,* rib, side⟧ inflammation of the pleura, characterized by difficult, painful breathing and often accompanied by the exudation of liquid into the chest cavity —**pleu·rit·ic** (plo͝o rit′ik) *adj.*

☆**pleurisy root** **1** BUTTERFLY WEED **2** the root of this plant, formerly used as a cure for pleurisy

pleu·ro- (plo͝or′ō, -ə) ⟦< Gr *pleura,* rib, side⟧ *combining form* **1** on or near the side [*pleurodont*] **2** of, involving, or near the pleura [*pleurotomy*] Also, before a vowel, **pleur-**

pleu·ro·dont (plo͝or′ə dänt′) *adj.* ⟦prec. + -ODONT⟧ having teeth growing from the inside of the jawbone instead of from separate sockets, as some lizards —*n.* a pleurodont animal

pleu·ron (plo͝or′än′) *n., pl.* **pleu·ra** (-ə) ⟦ModL < Gr, rib⟧ either of the lateral plates on the thoracic and abdominal segments of an arthropod

pleu·ro·pneu·mo·ni·a (plo͝or′ō no͞o mōn′yə, -nyo͞o-) *n.* ⟦PLEURO- + PNEUMONIA⟧ pneumonia complicated by pleurisy

pleu·rot·o·my (plo͝o rät′ə mē) *n., pl.* **-mies** ⟦PLEURO- + -TOMY⟧ surgical incision of the pleura to permit drainage of exuded liquids

pleus·ton (plo͞os′tän′, -tən) *n.* ⟦< Gr *pleustikos,* fit for sailing < *plein,* to sail, swim (see PLEOPOD) + *-ton,* as in NEUSTON, PLANKTON⟧ small organisms, as algae or gastropods, floating on or near the surface of a body of water —**pleus·ton′ic** *adj.*

Plev·en (plev′ən) city in N Bulgaria: also **Plev′na** (-nä)

plew (plo͞o) *n.* ⟦CdnFr *pelu,* hairy < Fr < L *pilus,* hair: see PILE[2]⟧ [Northwest & Cdn.] a beaver skin

-plex (pleks) ⟦(COM)PLEX (*n.* 2)⟧ *combining form forming nouns* a building, as a condominium or a film theater, consisting of a (specified) number of units or sections [*fourplex, six-plex*]

plex·i·form (plek′si fôrm′) *adj.* ⟦< PLEXUS + -FORM⟧ like, or in the form of, a plexus or network; complex

☆**Plex·i·glas** (plek′si glas′) ⟦< L *plexus,* a twining (see PLEXUS) + GLASS⟧ *trademark for* a lightweight, transparent, thermoplastic synthetic resin, used for aircraft canopies, lenses and windows, etc. —*n.* this material

plex·i·glass (plek′si glas′) *n.* ⟦< prec.⟧ a lightweight material like Plexiglas

plex·or (plek′sər) *n.* ⟦ModL < Gr *plēxis,* a striking, akin to *plēssein,* to strike < IE **plēk-,* a stroke < base **plā-,* flat > PLAIN[1]⟧ *Med.* a small hammer with a soft head, as of rubber, formerly used in percussion

plex·us (plek′səs) *n., pl.* **-us·es** or **-us** ⟦ModL < L, a twining, braid < pp. of *plectere,* to twine, braid; akin to *plicare:* see PLY[1]⟧ **1** a complexly interconnected arrangement of parts; network **2** *Anat.* a network of blood vessels, lymphatic vessels, nerves, etc. [the solar *plexus* (of nerves) in the abdomen]

pli·a·ble (plī′ə bəl) *adj.* ⟦LME *plyable* < MFr < *plier,* to bend, fold < L *plicare,* to fold, bend: see PLY[1]⟧ **1** easily bent or molded; flexible **2** easily influenced or persuaded; tractable **3** adjusting readily; adaptable —**pli′a·bil′i·ty** *n.,* **pli′a·ble·ness** —**pli′a·bly** *adv.*

SYN.—**pliable** and **pliant** both imply capability of being easily bent, suggesting the suppleness of a wooden switch and, figuratively, a yielding nature or adaptability; **plastic** is used of substances, such as plaster or clay, that can be molded into various forms which are retained upon hardening, and figuratively suggests an impressionable quality; **ductile** literally and figuratively suggests that which can be finely drawn or stretched out [copper is a *ductile* metal]; **malleable** literally or figuratively suggests that which can be hammered, beaten, or pressed into various forms [copper is *malleable* as well as ductile] —*ANT.* **inflexible, rigid, brittle**

pli·ant (plī′ənt) *adj.* ⟦ME *plyande* < MFr, prp. of *plier:* see prec.⟧ **1** easily bent; pliable **2** adaptable or compliant —*SYN.* PLIABLE —**pli′an·cy** *n.,* **pli′ant·ness** —**pli′ant·ly** *adv.*

pli·ca (plī′kə) *n., pl.* **-cae** (-sē) ⟦ML, a fold < L *plicare,* to fold: see PLY[1]⟧ *Anat.* a fold or folding, esp. of the skin or mucous membrane

pli·cate (plī′kāt′, -kit) *adj.* ⟦L *plicatus,* pp. of *plicare,* to fold: see PLY[1]⟧ folded or plaited; esp., having parallel folds like a fan [a *plicate* leaf]: also **pli′cat′ed**

pli·ca·tion (plī kā′shən) *n.* ⟦ME *plicacioun* < OFr < L *plicare,* to fold: see PLY[1]⟧ **1** a folding or being folded **2** a fold **3** *Geol.* a fold or crumpling in layered rocks

plic·a·ture (plik′ə chər) *n.* PLICATION (senses 1 & 2)

pli·é (plē ā′) *n.* ⟦Fr < pp. of *plier,* to bend: see PLY[1]⟧ *Ballet* a movement in which the knees are bent outward, with the back held straight

pli·er (plī′ər) *n.* a person or thing that plies

pli·ers (plī′ərz) *pl.n.* ⟦< PLY[1]⟧ small pincers in any of various forms, often with serrated jaws, for gripping small objects, bending wire, etc.: often **pair of pliers**

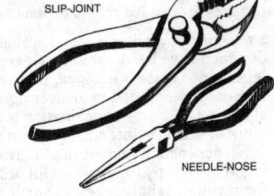

SLIP-JOINT

NEEDLE-NOSE

pliers

plight[1] (plīt) *n.* ⟦ME *plit,* state, condition < Anglo-Fr for OFr *pleit,* a fold, way of folding, condition (see PLAIT): sense infl. by ME *plight* < OE *pliht:* see fol.⟧ a condition or state of affairs; esp., now, an awkward, sad, or dangerous situation —*SYN.* PREDICAMENT

plight[2] (plīt) [Archaic] *vt.* ⟦ME *plihten* < OE *plihtan,* to pledge, expose to danger < *pliht,* a pledge, danger, akin to *pleon,* to risk, Ger *pflicht,* duty⟧ to pledge or promise, or bind by a pledge —*n.* a pledge —**plight one's troth** **1** to pledge one's truth, or one's word **2** to make a promise of marriage

Plim·soll mark (*or* line) (plim′səl, -säl′, -sôl′) ⟦after Samuel *Plimsoll* (1824-98), Eng advocate of legislation against overloading vessels⟧ a line or set of lines on the hull of a merchant ship, showing the depth to which it may legally be loaded

plim·solls (plim′səlz) *pl.n.* ⟦prob. from some fancied resemblance to prec.⟧ [Brit.] lightweight canvas shoes with rubber soles; sneakers: also **plim′soles′** (-sōlz′)

☆**plink** (pliŋk) *n.* ⟦echoic⟧ a light, sharp, ringing or clinking sound —*vt., vi.* **1** to make such sounds on (a piano, banjo, etc.) **2** to shoot at (tin cans or similar targets)

plinth (plinth) *n.* ⟦L *plinthus* < Gr *plinthos*, brick, tile⟧ **1** the square block at the base of a column, pedestal, etc. **2** the base on which a statue is placed **3** a course of brick or stone, often a projecting one, along the base of a wall: also **plinth course 4** a flat block at the base of door trim, an architrave, etc.

Plin·y (plin′ē) **1** (L. name *Gaius Plinius Secundus*) A.D. 23-79; Rom. naturalist & writer: called *the Elder* **2** (L. name *Gaius Plinius Caecilius Secundus*) A.D. 62?-113?; Rom. writer & statesman: nephew of Pliny the Elder: called *the Younger*

pli·o- (plī′ə, -ō) *combining form* PLEO- [*Pliocene*]

Pli·o·cene (plī′ə sēn′) *adj.* ⟦prec. + -CENE⟧ [*sometimes* **p-**] designating or of the second geologic epoch of the Neogene, characterized by the joining of what are now North and South America, the formation of the Arctic ice cap, the extensive migration of mammals between continents, and the development of apelike humans in Africa —**the Pliocene** the Pliocene Epoch or its rocks: see the geologic time chart in the Reference Supplement

☆**Pli·o·film** (plī′ə film′) *n.* ⟦former trademark < PLI(ABLE) + -O- + FILM⟧ [*also* **p-**] a transparent sheeting of chlorinated rubber used for raincoats, as a packaging film, etc.

plique-à-jour (plēk′ä zhoor′; *Fr* plē kà zhoor′) *n.* ⟦Fr, lit., braid letting in daylight⟧ an enameling technique in which the colored enamels are fused into the spaces of a wire framework on a temporary backing; the backing is then removed, producing a translucent effect

plis·sé or **plis·se** (plē sā′, pli-) *n.* ⟦Fr *plissé* < pp. of *plisser*, to pleat < MFr < *pli*, PLY[1], *n.*⟧ **1** a crinkled finish given to cotton, nylon, etc. by treatment with a caustic soda solution **2** a fabric with this finish

PLO *abbrev.* Palestine Liberation Organization

plod (pläd) *vi.* **plod′ded, plod′ding** ⟦of echoic orig.⟧ **1** to walk or move heavily and laboriously; trudge **2** to work steadily and monotonously; drudge —*n.* **1** the act of plodding **2** the sound of a heavy step —**plod′der** *n.* —**plod′ding·ly** *adv.*

Plo·eşti (plô yesht′) city in SC Romania, north of Bucharest: also sp. **Ploieşti**

-ploid (ploid) ⟦< Gr *-ploos*, -fold + -OID⟧ *combining form* of or being a (specified) multiple of the basic (haploid) number of chromosomes characteristic of a group of related organisms [*monoploid*]

ploi·dy (ploi′dē) *n.* ⟦prec. + -Y[3]⟧ the number of chromosome sets in a nucleus

plonk[1] (pläŋk) *vt., vi., n.* ⟦echoic⟧ PLUNK

plonk[2] (pläŋk) *n.* ⟦? altered < Fr *blanc*, white, in *vin blanc*, white wine⟧ [Informal, Chiefly Brit.] cheap, inferior wine

plop (pläp) *vt., vi.* **plopped, plop′ping** ⟦echoic⟧ **1** to drop with a sound like that of something flat falling into water without splashing **2** to drop, or allow to drop, heavily —*n.* a plopping or the sound of this —*adv.* with a plop

plo·sion (plō′zhən) *n.* ⟦< (EX)PLOSION⟧ *Phonet.* **1** the articulation of a plosive sound **2** loosely, the final stage, or sudden release of breath, in the articulation of a plosive

plo·sive (plō′siv) *adj.* ⟦< (EX)PLOSIVE⟧ *Phonet.* produced by the complete stoppage and sudden release of the breath, as the sounds of (p), (b), and (t) —*n.* a plosive sound; stop

plot (plät) *n.* ⟦ME < OE, piece of land: some meanings infl. by COMPLOT⟧ **1** a small area of ground marked off for some special use [*garden plot*, *cemetery plot*] **2** a chart or diagram, as of a building or estate **3** ⟦short for COMPLOT⟧ a secret, usually evil, project or scheme; conspiracy **4** the arrangement of the incidents in a play, novel, narrative poem, etc. —*vt.* **plot′ted, plot′ting 1** *a)* to draw a plan or chart of (a ship's course, etc.) *b)* to mark the position or course of on a map **2** to make secret plans for [*to plot someone's destruction*] **3** to plan the action of (a story, etc.) **4** *Math. a)* to determine or mark the location of (a point) on a graph by means of coordinates *b)* to represent (an equation) by locating points on a graph and joining them to form a curve *c)* to draw (the curve thus determined) —*vi.* to scheme or conspire —**plot′less** *adj.* —**plot′less·ness** *n.*

SYN.—**plot** is used of a secret, usually evil, project or scheme, the details of which have been carefully worked out [*the plot to deprive him of his inheritance failed*]; **intrigue**, implying more intricate scheming, suggests furtive, underhanded maneuvering, often of an illicit nature [*the intrigues at the royal court*]; **machination** stresses deceit and cunning in devising plots or schemes intended to harm someone [*the machinations of the villain*]; **conspiracy** suggests a plot in which a number of people plan and act together secretly for an unlawful or harmful purpose [*a conspiracy to seize the throne*]; **cabal** suggests a small group of political intriguers

Plo·ti·nus (plō tī′nəs) A.D. 205-270; Rom. Neoplatonic philosopher, born in Egypt

plot·line (plät′līn′) *n.* a PLOT (*n.* 4) or subplot

plot·tage (plät′ij) *n.* the area of a plot of land

plot·ter (plät′ər) *n.* **1** a person or thing that plots **2** *Comput.* a peripheral for producing charts, graphs, etc. directly from data

plotz (pläts) *vi.* ⟦< E Yiddish *platsn*, lit., to burst, explode < MHG *platzen*⟧ [Slang] to be overcome with emotion; give way to excitement, anger, delight, etc.

plough (plou) *n., vt., vi. chiefly Brit. sp. of* PLOW

Plov·div (plôv′dif) city in SC Bulgaria

plov·er (pluv′ər, plō′vər) *n., pl.* **-ers** or **-er** ⟦ME < OFr *plovier*, lit., rain bird (reason for name uncert.) < VL **pluviarius* < L *pluvia*, rain (see PLUVIAL)⟧ **1** any of a worldwide family (Charadriidae) of shorebirds, having a short tail, long, pointed wings, a short, stout beak, and, usually, brown or gray feathers **2** any of various similar birds

plow (plou) *n.* ⟦ME *ploh* < Late OE, akin to Ger *pflug*, ON *plógr* < Gmc **plog-* < native Alpine (Rhaetian) base > Langobardic *plovum*⟧ **1** a farm implement used to cut, turn up, and break up the soil ☆**2** any implement like this; specif., *a)* SNOWPLOW (sense 1) *b)* any of various tools for cutting a groove or furrow —*vt.* **1** to cut and turn up (soil) with a plow **2** to make furrows in with or as with a plow **3** to make by or as if by plowing [*to plow one's way through a crowd*] **4** to cut a way through (water) [*a ship plowing the waves*] **5** to clear with a snowplow **6** to invest or spend (as money, capital, etc.): often with *into* [*plowing all extra dollars into an IRA*] **7** [Brit. Slang] to reject (a candidate) in an examination —*vi.* **1** to till the soil with a plow; use a plow **2** to take plowing as specified [*a field that plows easily*] **3** to cut a way (*through* water, snow, etc.) **4** to advance laboriously; plod **5** to begin work vigorously: with *into* **6** to collide forcefully: with *into* **7** [Brit. Slang] to fail in an examination —**plow back** to reinvest (profits) in the same business enterprise —**plow under 1** to bury (crops or vegetation) by plowing, so as to enrich the soil or in seeking to prevent overproduction **2** [Informal] to destroy; obliterate —**plow up 1** to remove with a plow **2** to till (soil) thoroughly —**the Plow** *Astron.* **1** the constellation Ursa Major **2** BIG DIPPER —**plow′a·ble** *adj.* —**plow′er** *n.*

plow·boy (plou′boi′) *n.* **1** [Archaic] a boy who leads a team drawing a plow **2** a country boy

plowed (ploud) *adj.* [Slang] drunk; intoxicated

plow·man (plou′mən) *n., pl.* **-men** (-mən) **1** a man who guides a plow **2** a farm worker; rustic

plow·share (plou′sher′) *n.* the share, or cutting blade, of a moldboard plow

ploy (ploi) *n.* ⟦< ? EMPLOY (*n.* 2)⟧ an action or maneuver intended to outwit or disconcert another person

pluck (pluk) *vt.* ⟦ME *plukken* < OE *pluccian*, akin to Ger *pflücken* < VL **piluccare*, to pull out (> Fr *éplucher*), for L *pilare*, to deprive of hair < *pilus*, hair: see PILE[2]⟧ **1** to pull off or out; pick **2** to drag or snatch; grab **3** to pull feathers or hair from [*to pluck a chicken, pluck eyebrows*] **4** to pull at (the strings of a musical instrument) and release quickly with little jerking movements of the fingers **5** [Slang] to rob or swindle —*vi.* **1** to pull; tug; snatch: often with *at* **2** to pluck a musical instrument —*n.* **1** an act of pulling; tug **2** an animal's heart, liver, lungs, and windpipe, used for food **3** courage to meet danger or difficulty; fortitude —*SYN.* FORTITUDE —**pluck up** to rouse one's (courage) —**pluck′er** *n.*

pluck·y (pluk′ē) *adj.* **pluck′i·er, pluck′i·est** ⟦prec. + -Y[2]⟧ brave; spirited —*SYN.* BRAVE —**pluck′i·ly** *adv.* —**pluck′i·ness** *n.*

plug (plug) *n.* ⟦MDu *plugge*, a bung, plug, block, akin to Ger *pflock*⟧ **1** an object used to stop up a hole, gap, outlet, etc. **2** a natural concretion or formation that stops up a passage, duct, etc. **3** a small wedge or segment cut from something, as from a melon to test its ripeness **4** *a)* a cake of pressed tobacco *b)* a piece of chewing tobacco **5** an electrical connector, as with projecting prongs, designed to be fitted into an outlet, etc., thus making contact or closing a circuit **6** a kind of fishing lure **7** *a)* SPARK PLUG *b)* FIREPLUG ☆*c)* [Old Slang] PLUG HAT **8** [Informal] a defective or shopworn article ☆**9** [Slang] an old, worn-out horse ☆**10** [Informal] a boost, advertisement, etc., esp. one inserted gratuitously in the noncommercial parts of a radio or TV program, magazine article, etc. for someone or something **11** [Informal] a patch of skin containing several hair follicles, for transplanting onto a bald spot **12** *Geol.* igneous rock which has filled in the vent of a dead volcano and hardened: it is often exposed by erosion —*vt.* **plugged, plug′ging 1** to stop up or fill (a hole, gap, etc.) by inserting a plug: often with *up* **2** to insert a plug of (something) *in* a hole or gap ☆**3** to cut a plug from (a melon) to test its ripeness **4** [Informal] *a)* to publicize or boost (a song) by frequent performance ☆*b)* to advertise or publicize, esp. gratuitously in the noncommercial parts of a radio or TV program **5** [Slang] to shoot a bullet into **6** [Slang] to hit with the fist —*vi.* **1** [Informal] to work or study hard and steadily; plod: usually with *away* or *along* **2** to connect with something so as to become attached, to close an electric circuit, etc.: with *into* —**plug in 1** to connect (an electrical device) with an outlet, etc. by inserting a plug in a socket, jack, etc. **2** to be or become connected in this way or in a way regarded as analogous —**pull the plug** [Informal] ☆**1** to disconnect a device being used to maintain a terminal patient's life ☆**2** to put an end to something: often with *on* —**plug′ger** *n.*

plug-and-play (plug′ən plā′) *adj.* of or being a computer component or peripheral designed to work with little or no setting up by the user

plug-com·pat·i·ble (plug′kəm pat′ə bəl) *adj.* designating or of computer equipment that is COMPATIBLE (sense 5) with equipment from another manufacturer

plugged (plugd) *adj.* ☆drilled, with the resulting hole filled with a base metal: said of a coin: often in the phrase **not worth a plugged nickel**

☆**plug hat** [Old Slang] a man's high silk hat

plug-in (plug′in′) *adj.* designed to be plugged in or added on —*n.* something designed to be plugged in or added on; specif., a piece of software designed to enhance the performance of a Web browser or other larger program

☆**plug·o·la** (plə gō′lə) *n.* ⟦PLUG, *n.* 10 + (PAY)OLA⟧ [Slang] **1** covert payment, as to a performer on radio or TV, for favorably mentioning or displaying a particular product or brand name **2** advertising or publicity inserted into the noncommercial parts of a radio or TV program

☆**plug·ug·ly** (plug′ug′lē) ***n.**, pl.* **-lies** ⟦< ?⟧ [Old Slang] a city ruffian or gangster; rowdy

plum (plum) ***n.*** ⟦ME < OE *plume*, akin to Ger *pflaume* < WGmc **pruma* < VL **pruna:* see PRUNE[1]⟧ **1** *a)* any of various small prunus trees bearing a smooth-skinned, edible drupaceous fruit with a flattened stone *b)* the edible fruit **2** any of various trees bearing plumlike fruits **3** ⟦prob. from substitution of raisins for *plums* or prunes in some dishes, which retained their original names⟧ a raisin, when used in pudding or cake [*plum* pudding] **4** the dark bluish-red or reddish-purple color of some plums **5** something choice or desirable; specif., a well-paying job

plum·age (plo͞o′mij) ***n.*** ⟦ME < MFr < *plume*, feather: see PLUME⟧ a bird's feathers, collectively

plu·mate (plo͞o′māt′, -mit) ***adj.*** ⟦ModL *plumatus* < L, pp. of *plumare*, to cover with feathers < *pluma:* see PLUME⟧ *Zool.* resembling a feather, esp. in structure

plumb (plum) ***n.*** ⟦ME *plumbe* < MFr *plomb* < L *plumbum*, LEAD[2] < non-IE source > Gr *molybdos*⟧ a device consisting of a lead weight (**plumb bob**) hung at the end of a line (**plumb line**), used to determine how deep water is or whether a wall, etc. is vertical —***adj.*** perfectly vertical; straight down —***adv.*** **1** in a vertical direction; straight down **2** [Informal] entirely; wholly; absolutely [*plumb* tired out] —***vi.*** ⟦ME *plumben*⟧ [Informal] to work as a plumber —***vt.*** **1** to test or sound with a plumb **2** to discover the facts or contents of; fathom; solve; understand **3** to make vertical **4** to weight or seal with lead **5** to equip with plumbing —**out of plumb** not vertical: also **off plumb**

plumb

plum·ba·go (plum bā′gō) ***n.**, pl.* **-gos** ⟦L *plumbago* < *plumbum*, LEAD[2]⟧ **1** ⟦the substance was orig. known as BLACK LEAD⟧ GRAPHITE **2** *Bot.* LEADWORT —**plum·bag′i·nous** (-baj′i nəs) ***adj.***

plumb bob *see* PLUMB (***n.***)

plum·be·ous (plum′bē əs) ***adj.*** ⟦L *plumbeus* < *plumbum:* see PLUMB⟧ **1** of, like, or containing lead; leaden **2** having a dull-gray color [a *plumbeous* vireo]

plumb·er (plum′ər) ***n.*** ⟦ME < MFr *plummier* < L *plumbarius*, lead worker < *plumbum*, LEAD[2]: see PLUMB⟧ a skilled worker who installs and repairs pipes, fixtures, etc., as of water, drainage, or gas systems in a building

☆**plumber's helper** [Informal] PLUNGER (sense 2): also **plumber's friend**

plum·bic (plum′bik) ***adj.*** ⟦< L *plumbum*, LEAD[2] (see PLUMB) + -IC⟧ of, like, or containing lead, esp. tetravalent lead

plumb·ing (plum′iŋ) ***n.*** **1** the work or trade of a plumber **2** the pipes and fixtures with which a plumber works

plum·bism (plum′biz′əm) ***n.*** ⟦< L *plumbum*, LEAD[2] (see PLUMB) + -ISM⟧ LEAD POISONING

plumb line **1** *see* PLUMB (***n.***) **2** a vertical line

plum·bous (plum′bəs) ***adj.*** ⟦L *plumbosus* < *plumbum*, LEAD[2]: see PLUMB⟧ of, like, or containing lead, esp. divalent lead

plumb rule a narrow board equipped with a plumb line and bob, used by carpenters, masons, etc.

plume (plo͞om) ***n.*** ⟦OFr < L *pluma*, downy part of a feather, small soft feather < IE base **pleus-*, to pluck out, fluff of wool, hair > FLEECE⟧ **1** *a)* a feather, esp. a large, fluffy, or showy one *b)* a cluster of such feathers **2** an ornament made of a large feather or feathers, or of a feathery tuft of hair, esp. when worn on a hat, helmet, etc. as a mark of distinction **3** any token of worth or achievement; prize **4** plumage or down **5** something like a plume in shape or lightness [a *plume* of smoke] **6** *Biol.* a featherlike formation or part **7** *Geol.* a plume-shaped mass of molten rock that rises through the crust from the mantle of the earth and causes volcanic activity —***vt.*** **plumed**, **plum′ing** **1** to provide, cover, or adorn with plumes **2** *a)* to smooth the feathers of (itself) *b)* to preen (its feathers) (said of a bird) **3** to pride (oneself)

plume·let (plo͞om′lit) ***n.*** a small plume or tuft

plu·me·ri·a (plo͞o mir′ē ə) ***n.*** ⟦after C. *Plumier* (1646-1704), Fr botanist⟧ FRANGIPANI (sense 1)

plum·met (plum′it) ***n.*** ⟦ME *plomet* < MFr *plommet*, dim. of *plomb:* see PLUMB⟧ **1** *a)* PLUMB BOB *b)* PLUMB (***n.***) **2** a thing that weighs heavily —***vi.*** **1** to fall or drop straight downward **2** to fall off or decline precipitously [stock prices *plummeted*]

plum·my (plum′ē) ***adj.*** **-mi·er**, **-mi·est** **1** full of or tasting of plums **2** [Brit. Informal] good or desirable: used esp. of a job **3** [Informal] rich, full, and mellow: said of a sound or voice: often (esp. Brit.) used to suggest affectation

plu·mose (plo͞o′mōs′) ***adj.*** ⟦L *plumosus* < *pluma*, feather: see PLUME⟧ **1** having feathers; feathered **2** like a feather —**plu′mose′ly** ***adv.*** —**plu·mos·i·ty** (plo͞o mäs′ə tē) ***n.***

plump[1] (plump) ***adj.*** ⟦LME < MDu *plomp*, unwieldy, bulky, dull: orig. echoic⟧ full and rounded in form; chubby — ***vt., vi.*** to make plump; fill out: sometimes with *up* or *out* —**plump′ish** ***adj.*** —**plump′ly** ***adv.*** —**plump′ness** ***n.***

plump[2] (plump) ***vi.*** ⟦ME *plumpen* < MDu *plompen:* orig. echoic⟧ **1** to fall suddenly or with full impact **2** to come in contact abruptly or heavily (*against* something) **3** [Chiefly Brit.] to vote or opt (*for* someone or something) **4** to offer strong support (*for* someone or something) —***vt.*** to drop, throw, or put down heavily or all at once —***n.*** **1** a falling, plunging, or colliding suddenly or heavily **2** the sound of this —***adv.*** **1** with a plump; suddenly; heavily **2** straight down **3** in plain words; bluntly —***adj.*** blunt; direct

plump[3] (plump) ***n.*** ⟦see prec. & CLUMP⟧ [Now Dial., Chiefly Brit.] a compact group; cluster

plump·er[1] (plum′pər) ***n.*** ⟦< PLUMP[1]⟧ **1** a person or thing that plumps or fattens **2** [Historical] something carried in the mouth to plump out hollow cheeks

plump·er[2] (plum′pər) ***n.*** ⟦< PLUMP[2]⟧ a plumping, or dropping heavily

plum pudding ⟦orig. made with *plums* (fruit of prunus tree)⟧ a rich dessert made of raisins, currants, flour, spices, suet, etc. and boiled or steamed

plum tomato a type of tomato that is pear-shaped or elongated, often used for cooking

plu·mule (plo͞om′yo͞ol, -yəl) ***n.*** ⟦ModL < L *plumula*, dim. of *pluma*, feather: see PLUME⟧ **1** *Bot.* the growing stem tip of the embryo of a seed, above the place of attachment of the cotyledons **2** *Ornithology* a soft down feather of young birds, persisting in some adults

plum·y (plo͞o′mē) ***adj.*** **plum′i·er**, **plum′i·est** **1** covered or adorned with plumes **2** like a plume; feathery

plun·der (plun′dər) ***vt.*** ⟦Ger *plündern* < *plunder*, trash, baggage⟧ **1** to rob or despoil (a person or place) by force, esp. in warfare **2** to take (property) by force or fraud —***vi.*** to engage in plundering —***n.*** **1** the act of plundering; pillage; robbery **2** goods taken by force or fraud; loot; booty ☆**3** [Dial.] personal belongings or household furnishings —***SYN.*** RAVAGE, SPOIL —**plun′der·er** ***n.*** —**plun′der·ous** ***adj.***

plun·der·age (plun′dər ij) ***n.*** **1** robbery; esp., an embezzling of property on shipboard **2** the property embezzled

plunge (plunj) ***vt.*** **plunged**, **plung′ing** ⟦ME *plungen* < OFr *plongier* < VL **plumbicare* < L *plumbum*, LEAD[2]: see PLUMB⟧ to thrust, throw, or force suddenly (*into* a liquid, hole, condition, etc.) [to *plunge* an oar into the water, to *plunge* a country into debt] —***vi.*** **1** to throw oneself, dive, or rush, as into water, a fight, etc. **2** to move violently and rapidly downward or forward **3** to pitch, as a ship **4** to slope steeply, as a road **5** to extend far down in a revealing way [a *plunging* neckline or back] **6** to fall off or decline precipitously **7** [Informal] to spend, gamble, or speculate heavily or rashly —***n.*** **1** *a)* a dive or downward leap *b)* a swim **2** any steep and rapid descent **3** a place for plunging, or swimming **4** [Informal] a heavy, rash investment or speculation —**take the plunge** [Informal] to start on a new and seemingly uncertain enterprise, esp. after some hesitation

plung·er (plun′jər) ***n.*** **1** a person who plunges, or dives **2** a large, rubber suction cup with a long handle, used to free clogged drains **3** any cylindrical device that operates with a plunging motion, as a piston **4** [Informal] a person who acts hastily or recklessly; esp., a rash gambler or speculator

plunk (pluŋk) ***vt.*** ⟦echoic⟧ **1** to pluck or strum (a banjo, guitar, etc.) **2** to throw or put down heavily; plump —***vi.*** **1** to pluck or strum (*on*) **2** to give out a twanging sound, as a banjo **3** to fall or sink heavily —***n.*** **1** the act of plunking or the sound made by this **2** [Informal] a hard blow —***adv.*** with a twang or thud —☆**plunk down** [Informal] to give in payment —**plunk′er** ***n.***

plu·per·fect (plo͞o′pʉr′fikt, plo͞o′pʉr′-) ***adj.*** ⟦LL *plusquamperfectus* < L *plus quam perfectum*, lit., more than perfect⟧ **1** *Gram.* designating or of the past perfect tense in any of certain languages corresponding to the past perfect in English **2** exceptionally perfect: sometimes used as an intensive —***n.*** **1** the past perfect tense **2** a verb form in this tense

plu·ral (ploor′əl) ***adj.*** ⟦ME < L *pluralis* < *plus* (gen. *pluris*), more: see PLUS⟧ **1** of, including, or consisting of more than one; specif., heterogeneous [a *plural* society] **2** designating or of marriage among three or more persons **3** *Gram.* designating or of the category of number that refers to more than one person or thing, or in languages having dual number, more than two —***n.*** *Gram.* **1** the plural number **2** the plural form of a word **3** a word in plural form

plu·ral·ism (ploor′ə liz′əm) ***n.*** **1** the quality or condition of being plural, or of existing in more than one part or form **2** the holding by one person of more than one office or church benefice at the same time **3** *a)* the existence within a nation or society of groups distinctive in ethnic origin, cultural patterns, religion, or the like *b)* a policy of favoring the preservation of such groups within a given nation or society **4** *Philos.* the theory that reality is composed of a multiplicity of ultimate beings, principles, or substances: cf. DUALISM, MONISM —**plu′ral·ist** ***n., adj.*** —**plu′ral·is′tic** ***adj.*** —**plu′ral·is′ti·cal·ly** ***adv.***

plu·ral·i·ty (ploo ral′ə tē) ***n.**, pl.* **-ties** ⟦ME *pluralite* < MFr *pluralité* < LL *pluralitas*⟧ **1** the condition of being plural or numerous **2** a great number; multitude **3** *a)* the holding of two or more church benefices at the same time *b)* any of the benefices so held ☆**4** *a)* the share of votes that the leading candidate, issue, etc. receives in an election, when that share does not exceed one half *b)* the number of such votes that the leading candidate, etc. obtains over the next highest candidate, etc. [if candidate A gets 65 votes, B gets 40, and C gets 35, then A has a *plurality* of 25]: cf. MAJORITY (sense 2) **5** MAJORITY (sense 1)

plu·ral·ize (ploor′ə līz′) ***vt., vi.*** **-ized′**, **-iz′ing** ⟦Fr *pluraliser*⟧ to make or become plural in form or number —**plu′ral·i·za′tion** ***n.*** —**plu′ral·iz′er** ***n.***

plu·ral·ly (ploor′ə lē) ***adv.*** in the plural number or in a plural sense

plu·ri- (ploor′i, -ə) ⟦L < *plus* (gen. *pluris*), several: see PLUS⟧ *combining form* several or many

plu·ri·ax·i·al (ploor′ē ak′sē əl) ***adj.*** ⟦prec. + AXIAL⟧ *Bot.* having several axes; specif., having flowers on secondary shoots

plus (plus) ***prep.*** ⟦L, more < IE **plēyos*, compar. of **pelu-*, much < base **pel-* > FULL[1]⟧ **1** added to *[2 plus 2 equals 4]* **2** increased by; in addition to *[salary plus bonus]* **3** [Informal] with the addition of *[he returned wiser and plus $300]* **—*adj.*** **1** indicating or involving addition *[a plus sign]* **2** positive *[a plus quantity]* **3** somewhat more than the full value of: used after a letter grade *[a grade of B plus]* **4** involving extra gain or advantage *[plus sales, a plus factor]* **5** [Informal] to a great extent or degree; and more; and then some: used postpositively *[she has personality plus]* **6** *Bot.* designating one of two strains of certain fungi and algae which only mate with the opposite (*minus*) strain ☆**7** *Elec.* POSITIVE *[the plus terminal]* **—*adv., conj.*** [Informal] in addition; moreover; and *[we have the time, plus we have the money]* **—*n., pl.*** **plus′es** or **plus′ses** **1** a plus sign **2** an added or favorable quantity or thing **3** a positive quantity

plus ça change, plus c'est la même chose (plü sȧ shänzh′ plü se lȧ mem shōz′) ⟦Fr⟧ the more things change, the more they stay the same: often shortened to ***plus ça change***

plus fours ⟦orig. a tailoring term indicating an added four inches of material for overlap below the knee⟧ baggy knickerbockers worn, esp. formerly, for active sports

plush (plush) ***n.*** ⟦Fr *pluche* < *peluche* < OFr *peluchier*, to pluck < VL **piluccare:* see PLUCK⟧ a fabric with a soft, thick, deep pile **—*adj.*** **1** of or made of plush **2** [Informal] luxurious, as in furnishings

plush·y (plush′ē) ***adj.*** **plush′i·er, plush′i·est** **1** of or like plush ☆**2** [Informal] luxurious; plush **—plush′i·ly** ***adv.*** **—plush′i·ness** ***n.***

plus sign the sign (+) indicating addition or positive quantity

plus size any of a series of sizes in women's garments for full figures

Plu·tarch (ploo′tärk′) A.D. 46?-120?; Gr. biographer & historian

plu·te·us (ploot′ē əs) ***n., pl.*** **-te·i′** (-ī′) ⟦ModL < L, shelf, backrest (< IE **plouto-*, structure of boards > ON *fleythr*, rafter): from being shaped like a painter's easel⟧ *Zool.* the free-swimming, ciliated, larval stage of sea urchins and brittle stars, characterized by elongated, slender arms

Plu·to (ploot′ō) ***n.*** ⟦L < Gr *Ploutōn* < *ploutos*, wealth: see fol.⟧ **1** *Class. Myth.* the god ruling over the lower world: also called *Hades* by the Greeks and *Dis* or *Orcus* by the Romans **2** a large dwarf planet orbiting beyond Neptune: diameter, *c.* 2,270 km (*c.* 1,410 mi); period of revolution, *c.* 248.59 earth years; period of rotation (retrograde), 6.39 earth days; three satellites; symbol, ♇: formerly classified as the ninth major planet

plu·toc·ra·cy (ploo täk′rə sē) ***n., pl.*** **-cies** ⟦Gr *ploutokratia* < *ploutos*, wealth, akin to *plein*, to float, swim (< IE base **pel-* > FULL[1]) + *kratein*, to rule⟧ **1** government by the wealthy **2** a group of wealthy people who control or influence a government

plu·to·crat (ploot′ə krat′) ***n.*** ⟦< Gr *ploutos*, wealth (see prec.) + -CRAT⟧ **1** a member of a wealthy ruling class **2** a person whose wealth is the source of control or great influence **—plu′to·crat′ic** ***adj.*** **—plu′to·crat′i·cal·ly** ***adv.***

plu·ton (ploo′tän′) ***n.*** ⟦Ger, back-form. < *plutonisch*, PLUTONIC⟧ *Geol.* a mass of intrusive igneous rock

Plu·to·ni·an (ploo tō′nē ən) ***adj.*** ⟦L *Plutonius* < Gr *Ploutōnios*⟧ of or like Pluto or the infernal regions

Plu·ton·ic (ploo tän′ik) ***adj.*** ⟦< L *Pluto* (gen. *Plutonis*) + -IC⟧ **1** PLUTONIAN **2** [**p-**] *Geol.* formed at great depth by intense heat and pressure: said of rock, esp. intrusive igneous rock, that is typically coarsegrained and granitelike

☆**plu·to·ni·um** (ploo tō′nē əm) ***n.*** ⟦ModL, after the planet PLUTO + -IUM: so named (1942) by G. T. SEABORG, one of the U.S. physicists who isolated it, because its atomic number is next after that of *neptunium*, as Pluto's orbit is next after Neptune's⟧ a radioactive, metallic chemical element, one of the actinides, found in trace quantities in native uranium ores and produced by bombarding uranium with deuterons: symbol, Pu; at. no. 94: its most important isotope (**plutonium-239**) is used in nuclear weapons and as a reactor fuel: see the periodic table of elements in the Reference Supplement

Plu·tus (ploot′əs) ***n.*** ⟦L < Gr *Ploutos* < *ploutos*, wealth: see PLUTOCRACY⟧ *Gr. Myth.* the blind god of wealth

plu·vi·al (ploo′vē əl) ***adj.*** ⟦L *pluvialis* < *pluvia*, rain < IE **pleu-*, to flow, pour < base **pel-*, to pour, fill > FULL[1], L *pluere*⟧ **1** *a)* of or having to do with rain *b)* having much rain **2** *Geol.* formed by the action of rain

plu·vi·om·e·ter (ploo′vē äm′ət ər) ***n.*** ⟦< L *pluvia*, rain (see prec.) + -METER⟧ RAIN GAUGE **—plu′vi·o·met′ric** (-ə me′trik) ***adj.*** **—plu′vi·om′e·try** ***n.***

plu·vi·ose (ploo′vē ōs′) ***adj.*** ⟦L *pluviosus* < *pluvia:* see PLUVIAL⟧ characterized by much rain; rainy: also **plu′vi·ous** (-əs) **—plu′vi·os′i·ty** (-äs′ə tē) ***n.***

ply[1] (plī) ***vt.*** **plied, ply′ing** ⟦ME *plien* < OFr *plier* < L *plicare*, to fold < IE base **plek-*, to entwine > FLAX⟧ [Now Rare] to bend, twist, fold, or mold **—*vi.*** [Obs.] to bend or submit **—*n., pl.*** **plies** ⟦MFr *pli* < the v.⟧ **1** a single thickness, fold, or layer, as of doubled cloth, plywood, etc. **2** one of the twisted strands in rope, yarn, etc. **3** *a)* the state of being bent or twisted *b)* bias or inclination **—*adj.*** having (a specified number of) layers, thicknesses, or strands: usually in hyphenated compounds *[three-ply]*

ply[2] (plī) ***vt.*** **plied, ply′ing** ⟦ME *plien*, aphetic for *applien*, APPLY⟧ **1** to do work with; wield or use (a tool, faculty, etc.), esp. with energy **2** to work at (a trade) **3** to address (someone) urgently and constantly (*with* questions, etc.) **4** to keep supplying (*with* gifts, food, drink, etc.) in a persistent way **5** to sail regularly back and forth across *[boats ply the channel]* **—*vi.*** **1** to keep busy or work (*at* something or *with* a tool, etc.) **2** to travel regularly (*between* places): said of ships, buses, etc. **3** [Old Poet.] to steer a course **—*SYN.*** HANDLE

Ply·mouth (plim′əth) **1** seaport in Devonshire, SW England, on the English Channel **2** ⟦after the English seaport⟧ town on the SE coast of Mass.: settled by the Pilgrims (1620) as the 1st permanent colonial settlement (**Plymouth Colony**) in New England

☆**Plymouth Rock**[1] ⟦after fol.⟧ any of a breed of domestic chicken with white or gray, barred plumage: formerly raised esp. for its eggs and meat, now usually kept for crossbreeding

Plymouth Rock[2] boulder at Plymouth, Mass., where the Pilgrims who sailed on the *Mayflower* are said to have landed in 1620

ply·wood (plī′wood′) ***n.*** ⟦PLY[1] + WOOD[1]⟧ a construction material made of thin layers of wood glued and pressed together, usually with their grains at right angles to one another

Plzeň (pul′zen yə) city in the W Czech Republic

pm *abbrev.* **1** phase modulation **2** postmortem: also **p.m.** **3** premium

Pm *Chem. symbol for* promethium

PM *abbrev.* **1** ⟦L *post meridiem*⟧ after noon: used to designate the time from noon to midnight: also **P.M.** or **p.m.** or **pm** **2** Past Master **3** Paymaster **4** Police Magistrate **5** Postmaster **6** Prime Minister **7** Provost Marshal

PMG *abbrev.* **1** Paymaster General **2** Postmaster General

pmk *abbrev.* postmark

PMS *abbrev.* PREMENSTRUAL SYNDROME

P/N, PN, p/n, *or* **pn** *abbrev.* promissory note

pneum- (noom, nyoom) *combining form* PNEUMO-: used before a vowel

pneu·ma (noo′mə, nyoo′-) ***n.*** ⟦Gr < *pnein*, to breathe < IE echoic base **pneu-*, to wheeze, breathe > OE *fneosan*, to SNEEZE⟧ the soul or spirit

pneu·mat·ic (noo mat′ik, nyoo-) ***adj.*** ⟦L *pneumaticus* < Gr *pneumatikos* < *pneuma*, breath: see prec.⟧ **1** of or containing wind, air, or gases **2** *a)* filled with compressed air *[pneumatic tire]* *b)* worked by compressed air *[pneumatic drill]* **3** [Informal] having a full, shapely figure; often, specif., having large breasts: said of a woman **4** *Theol.* having to do with the spirit or soul **5** *Zool.* having hollows filled with air, as certain bones in birds **—pneu·mat′i·cal·ly** ***adv.***

pneu·mat·ics (-iks) ***n.*** the branch of physics that deals with the mechanical properties of air and other gases

pneu·ma·to- (noo′mə tō, -tə; nyoo′-; noo mat′ō, -ə; nyoo-) ⟦< Gr *pneuma* (gen. *pneumatos*), air, spirit, breath < *pnein:* see PNEUMA⟧ *combining form* **1** the presence of air or vapor *[pneumatolysis]* **2** breathing *[pneumatometer]* **3** spirit *[pneumatology]*

pneu·ma·tol·o·gy (noo′mə täl′ə jē, nyoo′-) ***n.*** ⟦prec. + -LOGY⟧ *Theol.* **1** the study of spirits or spiritual phenomena **2** any doctrine on the Holy Spirit **—pneu′ma·to·log′ic** (-tə läj′ik) ***adj.***, **pneu′ma·to·log′i·cal**

pneu·ma·tol·y·sis (-täl′ə sis) ***n.*** ⟦ModL: see PNEUMATO- & -LYSIS⟧ the process of rock alteration and mineral formation by the action of gases emitted from solidifying igneous rocks **—pneu′ma·to·lyt′ic** (-tə lit′ik) ***adj.***

pneu·ma·tom·e·ter (noo′mə täm′ət ər, nyoo′-) ***n.*** *Physiol.* an instrument for measuring the capacity or force of the lungs in respiration

pneu·ma·to·phore (noo′mə tō fôr′, -tə-, nyoo′-; noo mat′ō-, -mat′ə-, nyoo-) ***n.*** **1** *Bot.* a porous, woody, specialized branch growing upright into the air from the buried roots of certain swamp trees, as the mangrove, and providing access to the atmosphere **2** *Zool.* a polyp with a gas-filled cavity in siphonophore hydrozoans, serving as a float for the colony

pneu·mec·to·my (noo mek′tə mē, nyoo-) ***n., pl.*** **-mies** the surgical removal of all or part of a lung

pneu·mo- (noo′mō, -mə; nyoo′-) ⟦ModL, contr.: see PNEUMONO-⟧ *combining form* **1** lung *[pneumococcus]* **2** air *[pneumoencephalogram]* **3** respiration *[pneumograph]* **4** pneumonia *[pneumobacillus]*

pneu·mo·ba·cil·lus (noo′mō bə sil′əs, nyoo′-) ***n., pl.*** **-cil′li** (-ī) ⟦ModL: see prec. & BACILLUS⟧ a bacillus (*Klebsiella pneumoniae*) associated with one form of pneumonia

pneu·mo·coc·cus (noo′mō käk′əs, nyoo′-) ***n., pl.*** **-coc′ci′** (-käk′sī′) ⟦ModL: see PNEUMO- & COCCUS⟧ a bacterium (*Streptococcus pneumoniae*) that is a cause of certain diseases, as pneumonia **—pneu′mo·coc′cal** (-käk′əl) ***adj.***, **pneu′mo·coc′cic** (-käk′sik)

pneu·mo·co·ni·o·sis (-kō′nē ō′sis) ***n.*** ⟦ModL < PNEUMO- + Gr *konia* (< *konis*, dust: see INCINERATE) + -OSIS⟧ a disease of the lungs, characterized by fibrosis and caused by the chronic inhalation of mineral dusts, esp. silica and asbestos

pneu·mo·cys·tis (pneumonia) (noo′mō sis′tis, nyoo′-) ⟦ModL: see PNEUMO- & CYST⟧ a form of pneumonia, often associated with AIDS, caused by a fungus (*Pneumocystis jirovecii*)

pneu·mo·en·ceph·a·lo·gram (-en sef′ə lə gram′) ***n.*** ⟦PNEUMO-, air + ENCEPHALOGRAM⟧ an X-ray photograph of the fluid-filled spaces of the brain made after some cerebrospinal fluid has been replaced with air, oxygen, or helium

pneu·mo·gas·tric (-gas′trik) ***adj.*** of the lungs and stomach **—*n.*** *former term for* VAGUS

pneu·mo·graph (noo′mə graf′, nyoo′-) ***n.*** a device for measuring and recording the depth and rate of movement of the chest in respiration

pneu·mo·nec·to·my (noo′mə nek′tə mē, nyoo′-) ***n., pl.*** **-mies** PNEUMECTOMY

pneu·mo·ni·a (noo mōn′yə, nyoo-; *occas.,* -mō′nē ə) ***n.*** ⟦ModL < Gr < *pneumōn*, lung: see PNEUMA⟧ inflammation or infection of the alveoli of the lungs of varying degrees of severity and caused by bacteria, viruses, etc. **—pneu·mon′ic** (-män′ik) ***adj.***

pneu·mo·ni·tis (noo′mə nīt′əs, nyoo′-) ***n., pl.*** **-nit′i·des′** (-nit′ə dēz′) an inflammation of the lung

pneu·mo·no- (no͞o′mə nō, nyo͞o′-) ⟦< Gr *pneumōn*, lung < *pnein*, to breathe: see PNEUMA⟧ *combining form* lung or lungs [*pneumonectomy*]: also, before a vowel, **pneumon-**

pneu·mo·tho·rax (no͞o′mō thôr′aks′, nyo͞o′-) ***n.*** ⟦ModL: see PNEUMO- & THORAX⟧ the presence of air or gas in a pleural cavity, esp. as a result of perforation or rupture of the lung tissue

PNG *abbrev.* Papua New Guinea

pn junction *Electronics* the boundary between two regions in a single crystal of a semiconductor: one region contains an electron acceptor and the other an electron donor

Pnom-Penh (pə näm′pen′, näm′pen′) *alt. sp. of* PHNOM PENH

pnxt. *abbrev.* ⟦L *pinxit*⟧ he (or she) painted it

po *abbrev.* **1** postal order **2** *Baseball* putout(s)

Po[1] (pō) river in N Italy, flowing from the Cottian Alps east into the Adriatic: 405 mi (652 km)

Po[2] *Chem. symbol for* polonium

PO *abbrev.* **1** Petty Officer **2** postal order **3** Post Office **4** post office box **5** purchase order

p.o. *abbrev.* ⟦L *per os*⟧ *Pharmacy* by mouth: sometimes written **po**

POA *abbrev.* power of attorney

poach[1] (pōch) ***vt.*** ⟦ME *pochen* < MFr *pochier*, to pocket < *poche*, pouch, pocket (< Frank **pokka*, pocket: for IE base see POKE[2]): the yolk is "pocketed" in the white⟧ to cook (fish, an egg without its shell, etc.) in water or other liquid near boiling point, or in a small receptacle placed over boiling water

poach[2] (pōch) ***vt.*** ⟦Fr *pocher* < OFr *pochier*, to tread upon, intrude < MHG *bochen, puchen*, to strike upon, plunder, akin to POKE[1]⟧ **1** to soften, tear up, or make holes in (ground) by stamping; trample **2** to mix with water until smooth **3** *a)* to trespass on (private property), esp. for hunting or fishing *b)* to hunt or catch (game or fish) illegally, esp. by trespassing **4** to take (anything) by unfair or illegal methods; steal —***vi.*** **1** to sink into soft or wet earth when walking **2** to become soggy or full of holes when trampled; turn into mud **3** to hunt or fish illegally, esp. by trespassing on **4** *Racket Sports* to return a shot near the net that was intended for one's partner in the back court —**poach′er** ***n.***

POB *abbrev.* Post Office Box

po·bla·no (pō blä′nō) ***n.***, *pl.* **-nos** ⟦< MexSp *chile poblano* < *chile*, chili (pepper) + *poblano*, of PUEBLA⟧ a kind of long, wide, dark-green, moderately hot chili, used esp. in Mexican cooking: also **poblano pepper (or chile)**

po' boy (pō′ boi′) ⟦phonetic sp. imitating New Orleans pronun.⟧ POORBOY: also **po' boy sandwich**

Po·ca·hon·tas (pō′kə hän′təs) 1595?-1617; North American Indian princess: reputed to have saved Captain John Smith from execution: daughter of Powhatan

Po·ca·tel·lo (pō′kə tel′ō) ⟦after an Indian chief who helped railroad builders⟧ city in SE Ida.

po·chard (pō′chərd, -kərd) ***n.***, *pl.* **-chards** or **-chard** ⟦< ? Fr *pocher:* see POACH[2]⟧ any of various European diving ducks (esp. genus *Aythya*), as a species (*A. ferina*) with a blue and black bill

pock (päk) ***n.*** ⟦ME *pocke* < OE *pocc:* for IE base see POKE[2]⟧ **1** a pustule caused by smallpox or some other disease **2** POCKMARK See POX —**pocked** ***adj.***

pock·et (päk′it) ***n.*** ⟦ME *poket* < Anglo-Fr *pokete*, for MFr dial. *poquette*, dim. of *poque, poche:* see POACH[1]⟧ **1** [Archaic] a sack, esp. when used to measure something **2** *a)* a cloth pouch sewn into or on clothing, for carrying money and small articles *b)* any usually small container, compartment, enclosure, etc. **3** a cavity that holds or can hold something **4** a small area or group of a specified type [a *pocket* of poverty] **5** a confining or frustrating situation **6** financial resources; funds; means [a drain on one's *pocket*] **7** a position of being hemmed in by other contestants so as to be held back **8** *Aeron.* AIR POCKET ☆**9** *Baseball* a hollow in a baseball mitt where the ball can be securely caught and held **10** *Bowling* the space between two pins, esp. the head pin and the pin next to it **11** *Football* the protected area behind the offensive line, from which the quarterback passes the ball **12** *Geol. a)* a cavity filled with ore, oil, gas, or water *b)* a small deposit of ore **13** *Pool* any of the pouches at the sides and corners of a billiard or pool table **14** *Zool.* a sac or pouch in an animal's body —***adj.*** **1** *a)* that is or can be carried in a pocket *b)* smaller than standard **2** not widespread; contained; isolated [*pocket* resistance] —***vt.*** **1** to put into a pocket **2** to provide with a pocket or pockets **3** to envelop; enclose **4** to take or receive, often, specif., in a dishonest manner, (money, profits, etc.) for one's own use **5** to put up with (an insult, gibe, etc.) without answering or showing anger **6** to hide, suppress, or set aside [*pocket* one's pride] ☆**7** *Politics* to prevent passage of (a bill) by means of a pocket veto —**in someone's pocket** [Informal] completely under someone's influence —**in pocket** gained or available —**out of pocket 1** *a)* from money at hand ☆*b)* from one's own financial resources [the balance not covered by insurance will have to be paid *out of pocket*] **2** having a financial loss —**pock′et·a·ble** ***adj.*** —**pock′et·less** ***adj.***

pocket battleship [Historical, Chiefly Brit.] a type of German cruiser, originally built within the limits as to tonnage and guns set by the Treaty of Versailles

☆**pocket billiards** POOL[2] (*n.* 2b)

pock·et·book (päk′it bo͝ok′) ***n.*** **1** *a)* a case or folder, as of leather, for carrying money and papers in one's pocket; billfold ☆*b)* a pocket purse formerly used by men ☆**2** a woman's purse or handbag **3** monetary resources

pocket book a book small enough to be carried in one's pocket

pocket borough in Great Britain before 1832, a borough whose representation in Parliament was controlled by one family or person

pock·et·ful (päk′it fo͝ol′) ***n.***, *pl.* **-fuls′** as much as a pocket will hold

☆**pocket gopher** GOPHER[1] (sense 1)

pock·et·knife (päk′it nīf′) ***n.***, *pl.* **-knives′** (-nīvz′) a small FOLDING KNIFE

pocket money cash for small expenses; small change

☆**pocket mouse** any of various small, nocturnal, long-tailed mice (family Heteromyidae) with fur-lined cheek pouches for carrying food to their burrows: found in W and SW North America

pocket park a very small area for public recreation in a city or densely populated neighborhood, with benches, trees, etc.

pock·et-size (päk′it sīz′) ***adj.*** of a relatively small size; esp., of a size to fit in the pocket: also **pock′et-sized′**

☆**pocket veto 1** the indirect veto by the President of the U.S. of a bill presented to him by Congress within ten days of its adjournment, by failing to sign and return the bill before Congress adjourns **2** any similar action

pocket watch a small timepiece, typically attached to a chain, designed to be carried in a pocket

pock·mark (päk′märk′) ***n.*** **1** a scar or pit in the skin left by a pustule, as of smallpox **2** any pit or mark suggestive of this —***vt.*** to pit, cover, or scar with pockmarks —**pock′marked′** ***adj.***

pock·y (päk′ē) ***adj.*** **pock′i·er, pock′i·est 1** of, like, or covered with pocks or pockmarks **2** of or having the pox

po·co (pō′kō) ***adv.*** ⟦It⟧ [*also in italics*] *Musical Direction* somewhat

po·co a po·co (pō′kō ä pō′kō) ⟦It⟧ [*also in italics*] *Musical Direction* little by little

po·co·cu·ran·te (pō′kō ko͞o ran′tē, -kyo͞o-) ***adj.*** ⟦It *poco curante* < *poco* (< L *paucus*, little: see FEW) + *curante*, prp. of *curare*, to care < L *cura*, care: see CURE⟧ caring little; indifferent; apathetic —***n.*** an indifferent or apathetic person —**po′co·cu·ran′te·ism′** (-tē iz′əm) ***n.***, **po′co·cu·ran′tism′** (-tiz′əm)

Po·co·no Mountains (pō′kə nō′) ⟦< ? AmInd⟧ ridge of the Appalachians, in E Pa.: resort area: *c.* 2,000 ft (610 m) high: also **Poconos**

☆**po·co·sin** (pə kō′sən, pō′kō-) ***n.*** ⟦prob. < AmInd⟧ [South] a low, flat, swampy region in savannas of the SE U.S.

pod[1] (päd) ***n.*** ⟦Early ModE < ?⟧ **1** a dry fruit or seed vessel developed from a single carpel enclosing one or more seeds and usually splitting along two sutures at maturity, as a legume **2** a podlike container, as a cocoon of a locust ☆**3** any of various enclosures, as a streamlined housing for a jet engine attached to an aircraft —***vi.*** **pod′ded, pod′ding 1** to bear pods **2** to swell out into a pod —**pod′like′** ***adj.***

☆**pod**[2] (päd) ***n.*** ⟦? special use of prec.⟧ a small group of animals, esp. of seals or whales

pod[3] (päd) ***n.*** ⟦< ?⟧ **1** a sharp groove in certain augers and other tools **2** the socket for the bit in a brace

pod- *combining form* PODO-: used before a vowel

-pod (päd) ⟦< Gr *pous* (gen. *podos*), FOOT⟧ *combining form* **1** *forming nouns a)* foot [*pleopod*] *b)* one having (a specified number or kind of) feet [*arthropod*] **2** *forming adjectives* having (a specified number or kind of) feet Also **-pode** (pōd)

p.o.'d (pē′ōd′) ***adj.*** ⟦< *p(issed) o(ff)* (see the phrase PISS OFF at PISS) + -'D[2]⟧ [Slang] angry, annoyed, irritated, etc.

-po·da (pō də, pə-) ⟦ModL (pl.) < Gr *pous* (gen. *podos*), FOOT⟧ *combining form Zool.* forming the scientific names of certain taxonomic groups: see -POD

po·dag·ra (pə dag′rə, päd′ə grə) ***n.*** ⟦L < Gr < *pous* (gen. *podos*), FOOT + *agra*, seizure⟧ gout, esp. in the big toe —**po·dag′ral** ***adj.*** or **po·dag′ric**

pod·cast (päd′kast′) ***n.*** ⟦< *iPod*, trademark for a portable electronic device + -CAST⟧ a recorded program of talk, music, etc. made available over the internet as a FILE[1] (*n.* 5) that can be downloaded to a computer or portable device for listening or viewing — ***vt., vi.*** to make (a program) available as a podcast

po·des·ta (pō′des tä′, pō′des tä′) ***n.*** ⟦It *podestà* < L *potestas*, power < *potis*, able: see POTENT⟧ **1** a chief magistrate of a medieval Italian town **2** a minor official in an Italian town

Pod·go·ri·ca (päd′gə rēt′sə) capital of Montenegro: see TITOGRAD

podg·y (päj′ē) ***adj.*** **podg′i·er, podg′i·est** [Chiefly Brit.] *var. of* PUDGY

☆**po·di·a·try** (pō dī′ə trē, pə-) ***n.*** ⟦< Gr *pous* (gen. *podos*), FOOT + -IATRY⟧ the profession dealing with the specialized care of the feet and, esp., with the treatment and prevention of foot disorders —**po·di′a·trist** ***n.*** —**po·di·at·ric** (pō′dē a′trik) ***adj.***

pod·ite (päd′īt′) ***n.*** ⟦< -POD + -ITE[1]⟧ *Zool.* **1** an arthropod appendage **2** a clearly defined segment of such an appendage —**po·dit·ic** (pō dit′ik) ***adj.***

po·di·um (pō′dē əm) ***n.***, *pl.* **-di·a** (-ə); also, and for 4 & 5 usually, **-di·ums** ⟦L, balcony, podium, raised place < Gr *(hypo)podion*, footstool < *hypo-*, under + *podion*, dim. of *pous* (gen. *podos*), FOOT⟧ **1** a low wall serving as a pedestal or foundation **2** a low wall separating the seats from the arena in an ancient amphitheater **3** a continuous bench projecting from the walls of a room **4** a low platform, esp. for the conductor of an orchestra; dais **5** LECTERN (sense 2) **6** *Zool.* a hand or foot, or a footlike structure

-po·di·um (pō′dē əm) ⟦ModL < Gr *pous* (gen. *podos*), FOOT⟧ *combining form forming nouns* foot, footlike or supporting part [*monopodium, stylopodium*]

po·do- (pō′dō, -də) ⟦< Gr *pous* (gen. *podos*), FOOT⟧ *combining form* foot or feet

pod·o·carp (pō′də kärp′) ***adj.*** designating a family (Podocarpaceae) of evergreen conifers, including the Huon pine and podocarpus

pod·o·car·pus (pä′də kär′pəs) ***n.*** ⟦ModL < Gr *pous* (gen. *podos*), FOOT +

karpos, fruit: see HARVEST⟧ any of a genus (*Podocarpus*) of tropical evergreen trees and shrubs of the podocarp family with flattened needles, small cones, and fleshy seeds

Po·dolsk (pə dôlsk′) city in W European Russia, south of Moscow

pod·o·phyl·lin (päd′ə fil′in) ***n.*** ⟦< ModL *Podophyllum* < Gr *pous* (gen. *podos*), FOOT + *phyllon,* leaf + -IN[1]⟧ a yellow cathartic resin with a bitter taste, obtained from the rhizome of the May apple

-po·dous (pō dəs, pə-) ⟦see -POD & -OUS⟧ *combining form forming adjectives* having (a specified number or kind of) feet [*gastropodous*]

Po·dunk (pō′duŋk′) ***n.*** ⟦after a village of that name in Mass. or Conn.: prob. of AmInd orig.⟧ [Informal] any hypothetical or actual small town in the U.S., regarded as typically dull, insignificant, etc.

pod·zol (päd′zäl′, -zôl′) ***n.*** ⟦Russ⟧ a type of light-colored, relatively infertile soil, poor in lime and iron, found typically in coniferous forests in cool, humid regions: also **pod′sol′** (-säl′, -sôl′) —**pod·zol′ic** (-zäl′ik) ***adj.***

pod·zol·i·za·tion (päd′zäl i zā′shən, -zôl-) ***n.*** ⟦see prec.⟧ a process of soil formation, esp. in cool, humid regions, in which the upper layers are leached of iron, lime, and alumina, which are then concentrated in underlying layers: also **pod′sol′i·za′tion** (-säl′-, -sôl′-) —**pod′zol·ize′** ***vt.*** **-ized′, -iz′ing**

Poe (pō), **Edgar Allan** 1809-49; U.S. poet, short-story writer, & critic

POE *abbrev.* **1** port of embarkation **2** port of entry

po·em (pō′əm) ***n.*** ⟦MFr *poeme* < L *poema* < Gr *poiēma,* anything made, poem < *poiein,* to make < IE base **kwei-,* to heap up, build, make > Sans *cinōti,* (he) arranges, OSlav *činiti,* to arrange, form⟧ **1** an arrangement of words written or spoken: traditionally a rhythmical composition, sometimes rhymed, expressing experiences, ideas, or emotions in a style more concentrated, imaginative, and powerful than that of ordinary speech or prose: some poems are in meter, some in free verse **2** anything suggesting a poem in its effect

po·e·sy (pō′ə sē′, -zē′) ***n., pl.*** **-sies** ⟦ME *poesie* < OFr < L *poesis* < Gr *poiēsis* < *poiein:* see prec.⟧ **1** *old-fashioned var. of* POETRY **2** [Obs.] *a)* a poem *b)* a motto

po·et[1] (pō′ət) ***n.*** ⟦ME < OFr *poete* < L *poeta* < Gr *poiētēs,* one who makes, poet < *poiein,* to make: see POEM⟧ **1** a person who writes poems or verses **2** a person who displays imaginative power and beauty of thought, language, etc.

poet[2] *abbrev.* **1** poetic **2** poetical **3** poetry

po·et·as·ter (pō′ə tas′tər) ***n.*** ⟦ModL: see POET[1] & -ASTER[2]⟧ a writer of mediocre verse; rhymester; would-be poet

po·ète mau·dit (pô et mō dē′) *pl.* **po·ètes mau·dits** (pô et mō dē′) ⟦Fr, cursed or damned poet⟧ a poet who receives insufficient recognition in his or her own time

po·et·ess (pō′ə tis) ***n.*** a woman or girl who writes poems or verses: see -ESS

po·et·ic (pō et′ik) ***adj.*** ⟦MFr *poétique* < L *poeticus* < Gr *poiētikos*⟧ **1** of, characteristic of, like, or fit for a poet or poetry **2** skilled in or fond of poetry **3** written in verse **4** displaying the beauty, imaginative qualities, etc. found in good poetry —***n.*** POETICS

po·et·i·cal (pō et′i kəl) ***adj.*** POETIC —**po·et′i·cal·ly** ***adv.***

po·et·i·cism (pō et′ə siz′əm) ***n.*** a poetic word or expression, now, usually, one that is old-fashioned or marked by literary affectation

po·et·i·cize (pō et′ə sīz′) ***vt.*** **-cized′, -ciz′ing** **1** to make poetic **2** to express, or deal with, in poetry —***vi.*** to write poetry

poetic justice justice, as in some plays and stories, in which good is rewarded and evil punished, often in an especially fitting way

poetic license **1** deviation from strict fact or from conventional rules of form, style, etc., as by a poet for artistic effect **2** freedom to do this

po·et·ics (pō et′iks) ***n.*** **1** [P-] a famous treatise on poetic drama by Aristotle **2** *a)* the theory or structure of poetry *b)* a treatise on this **3** the poetic theory or practice of a specific poet

po·et·ize (pō′ə tīz′) ***vt., vi.*** **-ized′, -iz′ing** ⟦Fr *poétiser*⟧ POETICIZE

poet laureate *pl.* **poets laureate** or **poet laureates** **1** the court poet of England, appointed for life by the monarch, traditionally to write poems celebrating official occasions, national events, etc. **2** the official or most respected poet of any specific nation, region, etc.

po·et·ry (pō′ə trē) ***n.*** ⟦ME *poetrie* < OFr < ML *poetria* < L *poeta,* POET[2]⟧ **1** the art, theory, or structure of poems **2** poems; poetical works **3** *a)* poetic qualities; the rhythm, feelings, spirit, etc. of poems *b)* the expression or embodiment of such qualities

po-faced (pō′fāst′) ***adj.*** ⟦< ? *po* (= chamber pot) + FACED; by analogy with *poker-faced:* see POKER FACE⟧ [Brit. Informal] **1** expressionless; impassive **2** stern, smug, humorless, etc.

po·go·ni·a (pə gō′nē ə, -gōn′yə) ***n.*** ⟦ModL < Gr *pōgōn,* beard⟧ a small American orchid (*Pogonia ophioglossoides*) with a single white or pinkish flower having a lip tufted with yellow-brown hairs

☆**pog·o·nip** (päg′ə nip′) ***n.*** ⟦< AmInd (Shoshonean)⟧ a heavy winter fog containing ice particles, occurring in the valleys of the Sierra Nevada Mountains and other mountain valleys of the W U.S.

☆**po·go stick** (pō′gō) ⟦arbitrary coinage⟧ a stilt with pedals and a spring at one end, used as a toy to move along in a series of bounds

po·grom (pō′grəm, -gräm′; pō gräm′) ***n.*** ⟦< Russ, earlier, a riot, storm⟧ an organized persecution and massacre, often officially prompted, of a minority group, esp. of Jews (as in czarist Russia) —***SYN.*** SLAUGHTER

☆**po·gy** (pō′gē; *also* päg′ē) ***n., pl.*** **-gies** ⟦shortened < Maine dial. *poghaden,* prob. < Abenaki⟧ **1** MENHADEN **2** a surfperch (*Amphistichus rhodoterus*)

Po Hai (bō′ hī′) *a former transliteration of* BO HAI

☆**poi** (poi, pō′ē) ***n.*** ⟦Haw⟧ a Hawaiian food made of taro root mixed with water, cooked, pounded into a paste, and then fermented slightly

-poi·et·ic (poi et′ik) ⟦< Gr *poiētikos* < *poiētēs:* see POET[2]⟧ *combining form* making, producing, forming

poign·ant (poin′yənt; *Brit, also* poin′ənt) ***adj.*** ⟦ME *poynant* < MFr *poignant,* prp. of *poindre* < L *pungere,* to prick: see POINT⟧ **1** *a)* sharp or pungent to the smell or, formerly, the taste *b)* keenly affecting the other senses [*poignant* beauty] **2** *a)* sharply painful to the feelings; piercing *b)* evoking pity, compassion, etc.; emotionally touching or moving **3** sharp, biting, penetrating, pointed, etc. [*poignant* wit] —***SYN.*** MOVING, PATHOS —**poign′an·cy** ***n.*** —**poign′ant·ly** ***adv.***

poi·ki·lo·ther·mal (poi′ki lō′thʉr′məl) ***adj.*** ⟦< Gr *poikilos,* varying < IE **poiko-,* var. of base **peik-,* colorful (> L *pingere,* to PAINT) + THERMAL⟧ *Zool.* COLDBLOODED (sense 1): also **poi′ki·lo′ther′mic** —**poi′ki·lo′ther′mism′** ***n.***

poi·lu (pwä lōō′, pwä′lōō′; *Fr* pwȧ lü′) ***n.*** ⟦Fr, hairy, virile < *poil,* hair < L *pilus:* see PILE[2]⟧ [Slang] a soldier in the French army: term used esp. in WWI

Poin·ca·ré (pwan kȧ rā′) **1 Jules Hen·ri** (zhül än rē′) 1854-1912; Fr. mathematician **2 Ray·mond** (rā mōn′) 1860-1934; Fr. statesman: prime minister (1912-13; 1922-24; 1926-29); president (1913-20): cousin of Jules

poin·ci·an·a (poin′sē an′ə, -ā′nə, -ä′nə) ***n.*** ⟦ModL, after M. de *Poinci,* early governor of the Fr West Indies⟧ **1** any of a genus (*Caesalpinia*) of small, tropical trees and shrubs of the caesalpinia family, growing in dry, sandy soil and having showy red, orange, or yellow flowers **2** ROYAL POINCIANA

☆**poin·set·ti·a** (poin set′ə, -set′ē ə) ***n.*** ⟦ModL, after Joel R. *Poinsett* (1779-1851), U.S. ambassador to Mexico⟧ a Mexican and Central American plant (*Euphorbia pulcherrima*) of the spurge family, with yellow flowers surrounded by tapering red leaves resembling petals

point (point) ***n.*** ⟦OFr, dot, prick < L *punctum,* dot, neut. of *punctus,* pp. of *pungere,* to prick (< IE base **peuĝ-,* **peuk̂,* to prick, jab > Ger *fichte,* spruce tree, L *pugil,* boxer, *pugnus,* fist); also < OFr *pointe,* sharp end < ML *puncta* < L *punctus*⟧ **1** a minute mark or dot **2** a dot in printing or writing, as a period, decimal point, vowel point, etc. **3** *a)* an element in geometry having definite position, but no size, shape, or extension [a line between two *points*] *b)* a particular or precisely specified position, location, place, or spot [*points* on an itinerary] **4** *a)* any of certain positions where a player is stationed in cricket, lacrosse, and other games *b)* the player at such a position **5** a particular time; exact moment [the *point* of death] **6** a stage, condition, level, or degree reached or indicated [a boiling *point*] **7** a particular detail or element; item [to explain a problem *point* by *point*] **8** *a)* a distinguishing feature; characteristic *b)* a physical characteristic or quality of an animal, used as a standard in judging breeding **9** any of various units used in awarding credit, scoring games, measuring value, etc.; specif., *a)* a penalty unit assessed drivers in a POINT SYSTEM (sense 4) *b) Tennis, etc.* the service and play leading to a scored point [after a let, players must replay the *point*] *c) Anthrop.* a stone, piece of flint, etc. worked manually to a sharp point, as for an arrowhead or spearhead **10** *a)* a sharp or projecting end of something; tip *b)* something with a sharp end **11** needlepoint lace **12** a projecting or tapering piece of land; promontory; cape **13** [*usually pl.*] *a)* the extremities of an animal, esp. a horse, dog, or cat *b)* the coloration of an animal's extremities in contrast to the rest of the coat (said esp. of the face, ears, paws, and tail of a dog or cat) **14** a branch of a deer's antler [a ten-*point* buck] **15** *a)* the exact or essential fact or idea under consideration *b)* the main idea, striking feature, or effective twist of a joke, story, etc. **16** a purpose; aim; object; use [no *point* in complaining] **17** *a)* an impressive or telling argument, fact, or idea [he has a *point* there] ☆*b)* a helpful hint or suggestion **18** the posture of a hunting dog to show the presence and position of game **19** a unit used in rationing commodities, as in time of war **20** a jeweler's unit of weight, equal to 1/100 carat [a 10-*point* diamond] **21** [Historical] a cord with metal tips, used to lace up articles of clothing **22** *Backgammon* any of the 24 triangular spaces on the board **23** *Ballet* the position of being on the tips of the toes **24** *Boxing* one of a number of scoring units awarded to the boxers at the end of each round, used in determining the winner if the fight does not end by knockout or disqualification [to win on *points*] ☆**25** *Craps* the number that the thrower must roll again before rolling a seven in order to win ☆**26** *Educ.* a unit used in grading school or college work and figuring a student's academic average [a grade of A is worth four *points* per credit] **27** *Elec.* *a)* either of the two contacts, tipped with tungsten or platinum, that make or break the circuit in some distributors *b)* [Brit.] an electrical outlet (in full **power point**) **28** *Finance* *a)* a standard unit of value used in quoting changes in the prices of stocks, bonds, etc.; specif., a $1 change in the price of a stock *b)* a unit equal to one percent [a two-*point* rise in interest rates] *c)* an amount equal to one percent; specif., an amount equal to one percent of a loan secured by a mortgage: one or more points may be paid in advance by the borrower **29** *Heraldry* any of certain areas on a shield **30** *Mil.* a small party before an advance guard or behind a rear guard **31** *Navigation* *a)* any of the 32 marks showing direction on the circumference of a compass card *b)* any of the corresponding positions on the horizon *c)* the angle between two successive compass points, equal to 11¼° **32** *Printing* a measuring unit for type bodies and printed matter, equal to about 1/72 of an inch: there are 12 points in a pica **33** [Brit.] *Railroading* SWITCH (*n.* 6a): *usually used in pl.* —***vt.*** **1** *a)* to put punctuation marks or pauses in *b)* to put vowel points on (Hebrew characters) *c)* to mark off (sums or numbers) with points, as esp. a decimal fraction from a whole number (with *off*) **2** to sharpen to a point, as a pencil **3** to give (a story, remark, anecdote, action, etc.) extra force or special emphasis, as by repetition or elaboration: usually with *up* **4** to show or call attention to: usually with *out* [to *point* the way, to *point* out a person's shortcomings] **5** to aim or direct (a gun, finger, etc.) **6** to extend the foot so as to bring (the toe) more nearly in line with the leg **7** to show the presence and location of (game) by standing still and facing toward it: said of hunting dogs **8** *Masonry* to fill or refill and finish the joints of (brickwork or stonework) with mortar: often with *up* [to *point* up a chimney] —*vi.* **1** to direct one's finger or the like (*at* or *to* something) **2** to call attention or allude (*to* something); hint (*at* something) **3** to aim or be directed (*to* or *toward* something); extend in a specified direction [stock futures *point* higher] **4** to point game: said of a hunting dog **5** *Naut.* to sail close to the wind —**at the point of** very close to; on the verge of —**beside the point** not pertinent; irrelevant —**case in point** a pertinent example —**in point of** in the matter of; as concerns [*in point of* fact] —**make a point of 1** to make (something) one's strict rule, habit, or practice **2** to call special attention to —**on (or upon) the point of** almost in the act of; on the verge of —**stretch (or strain) a point** to make an exception or concession —**(up) to a point** within limits; somewhat but not entirely [I trust him ... *to a point*] —**to the point** pertinent; apt —**point′a·ble** *adj.*

point-and-click (point′′n klik′) *adj. Comput.* designating or of an interface designed so that selections and commands can be entered simply, as by clicking a mouse button: see CLICK (*vi.* 3)

point-blank (point′blaŋk′) *adj.* ⟦POINT + BLANK, *n.* 4⟧ **1** *Gunnery a)* aimed horizontally, straight at a mark, at such close range that rise and fall in the projectile's flight need not be considered *b)* of or suitable for such fire [*point-blank* range] **2** straightforward; plain; blunt [a *point-blank* answer] —*adv.* **1** in a direct line; straight **2** without hesitation or quibbling; directly; bluntly [to refuse *point-blank*]

point count *Bridge* **1** a method of evaluating a player's hand in terms of points assigned to it for high cards and extremes of suit distribution **2** the total of such points

point d'ap·pui (pwan dȧ püē′) *pl.* ***points d'ap·pui*** (pwan dȧ püē′) ⟦Fr⟧ point of support, or base, as for a military operation

point-de·vice or **point-de·vise** (point′di vīs′) *adj.* ⟦ME *at point devis*, to an exact point: see DEVICE⟧ [Now Chiefly Literary] completely correct; precise —*adv.* [Archaic] to perfection; meticulously

pointe (pwant) *n., pl.* ***pointes*** (pwant) ⟦Fr, point⟧ *Ballet* (the position of being on) the tip of the toe

point·ed (point′id) *adj.* **1** *a)* having a point, or sharp end *b)* tapering to a point, as a Gothic arch **2** sharp; incisive; to the point, as an epigram **3** clearly aimed at, or referring to, someone [a *pointed* remark] **4** very evident; emphasized; conspicuous **5** ⟦POINT (*n.* 13*b*) + -ED (sense 3)⟧ having coloration of the points in contrast to the rest of the coat: said esp. of the face, ears, paws, and tail of a dog or cat —**point′ed·ly** *adv.* —**point′ed·ness** *n.*

poin·telle (poin tel′) *n.* ⟦prob. < POINT (*n.* 11) + *-elle* < Fr, dim. suffix⟧ a lacy, openwork fabric, often of acrylic, used for blouses, sweaters, etc.

point·er (point′ər) *n.* **1** a person or thing that points **2** a long, tapered rod used by teachers and lecturers for pointing to things on a map, blackboard, etc. **3** an indicator on a clock, meter, scales, etc. **4** any of a breed of large, muscular hunting dog with a short, smooth coat, usually white with liver, black, or yellowish spots, and characterized by its assumption of the classic stance in pointing game: see POINT (*vt.* 7) **5** [Informal] a helpful hint or suggestion —**the Pointers** *Astron.* the two stars in the Big Dipper that are almost in a direct line with the North Star, Polaris

☆**point guard** ⟦< *point*, the position behind the KEY[1] (*n.* 7)⟧ *Basketball* the guard who leads the offense by directing or setting up the plays

poin·til·lism (pwan′tə liz′əm) *n.* ⟦Fr *pointillisme* < *pointiller*, to mark with dots < *pointille*, dot < It *puntiglio*, dim. of *punto* < L *punctus*: see POINT⟧ the method of painting of certain French impressionists, in which a white ground is systematically covered with tiny points of pure color that blend together when seen from a distance, producing a luminous effect —**poin′til·list** *n., adj.* —**poin′til·lis′tic** *adj.*

point lace needlepoint lace

point·less (point′lis) *adj.* **1** without a point **2** without meaning, relevance, or force; senseless; inane —**point′less·ly** *adv.* —**point′less·ness** *n.*

point man 1 the soldier in the front position in a patrol **2** anyone in the forefront of an activity; esp., someone leading an attack on or a movement in support of some proposed program, as in politics

point of honor a matter affecting a person's honor

point of no return 1 the moment on a flight when there is no longer enough fuel to return to the starting point **2** a point in an enterprise, adventure, etc. when participants are too deeply involved or committed to withdraw

point of order a question or challenge as to whether the rules of parliamentary procedure are being observed

point-of-sale (point′əv sāl′) *adj.* of, in, or relating to a place, as in a retail store, where sales are made or purchases checked out [*point-of-sale* advertising]: also **point′-of-pur′chase**

point of view 1 the place from which, or way in which, something is viewed or considered; standpoint **2** a mental attitude or opinion **3** the viewpoint from which a story is narrated [omniscient *point of view*]

point-shav·ing (point′shāv′iŋ) *n.* an illegal scheme in which a player or players on a team purposely act to score fewer points in a game so that the expected SPREAD (*n.* 2*d*) is not achieved

point spread SPREAD (*n.* 2*d*)

point system 1 a system of averaging a student's letter grades by giving them equivalent numerical value in points: the average attained is called the *grade-point average* **2** a system of graduating the sizes of type on a uniform scale of points: see POINT (*n.* 32) **3** any system of writing or printing for the blind, as Braille, in which raised points in certain combinations are used ☆**4** a system in which a certain number of penalty points is added to a driver's record for each violation of the traffic laws, with an accumulation of points leading to possible suspension or revocation of the driver's license

point-to-point (point′tə point′) *n.* [Brit.] a cross-country steeplechase, usually for amateur riders

point·y (point′ē) *adj.* **point′i·er, point′i·est 1** that comes to a sharp point **2** having many points

☆**point·y-head** (point′ē hed′) *n.* [Informal] an intellectual: usually a term of mild derision as used by anti-intellectuals —**point′y-head′ed** *adj.*

poise[1] (poiz) *n.* ⟦ME *pois*, weight < OFr < VL **pesum* < L *pensum*, something weighed < *pendere*, to weigh: see PENDANT⟧ **1** balance; stability **2** ease and dignity of manner; self-assurance; composure **3** the condition of being calm or serene **4** carriage; bearing, as of the body or head **5** [Now Rare] *a)* a suspension of activity in a condition of balance *b)* suspense; irresolution; indecision —*vt.* **poised, pois′ing** ⟦ME *poisen* < OFr *poiser* < *peise*, inflected form of *peser*, to weigh < VL *pesare* < L *pensare*, to weigh out < *pensus*, pp. of *pendere*⟧ **1** to balance; keep steady **2** to suspend: usually passive or reflexive **3** [Rare] to weigh —*vi.* **1** to be suspended or balanced **2** to hover —**SYN.** TACT

poise[2] (poiz) *n.* ⟦Fr, after J. L. M. *Poiseuille* (1799-1869), Fr anatomist⟧ the basic unit of viscosity of a fluid in the CGS system, equal to the force measured in dynes per square centimeter needed to maintain a difference in velocity of one centimeter per second between two parallel planes of a fluid separated by one centimeter (0.1 pascal second): abbrev. P

poised (poizd) *adj.* **1** composed; calm; self-assured **2** balanced **3** suspended, as in motion; readied [an opponent *poised* to strike]

poi·son (poi′zən) *n.* ⟦OFr < L *potio*, POTION⟧ **1** a substance causing illness or death when eaten, drunk, or absorbed even in relatively small quantities **2** anything harmful or destructive to happiness or welfare, such as an idea, emotion, etc. **3** in a nuclear reactor, a substance, as boron, that readily absorbs thermal neutrons from a chain reaction, thereby decreasing the reactivity of a reactor core: it is used for safety or control **4** *Chem.* a substance that inhibits or destroys the activity of a catalyst, enzyme, etc. or that interferes with or checks a reaction —*vt.* **1** to give poison to; harm or destroy by means of poison **2** to put poison on or into **3** to influence wrongfully; corrupt [to *poison* someone's mind] —*adj.* poisonous or poisoned —**poi′son·er** *n.*

☆**poison dogwood** POISON SUMAC

poison gas any toxic chemical agent in the form of a gas or vapor-forming liquid or solid, esp. one used in chemical warfare to kill or harass through inhalation or contact

☆**poison hemlock** HEMLOCK (sense 1)

☆**poison ivy 1** any of several woody vines or shrubs (genus *Rhus*, esp. *R. radicans*), of the cashew family, having leaves of three leaflets, greenish flowers, and ivory-colored berries: it can cause a severe rash on contact **2** a rash or dermatitis so caused

poison ivy

☆**poison oak** poison sumac or any of various poison ivy plants (esp. *Rhus toxicodendron* and *R. diversiloba*)

poi·son·ous (poi′zə nəs) *adj.* capable of injuring or killing by or as by poison; containing, or having the effects of, a poison; toxic; venomous —**poi′son·ous·ly** *adv.* —**poi′son·ous·ness** *n.*

poi·son-pen (poi′zən pen′) *adj.* [Informal] designating or of an abusive letter written out of spite or malice, usually anonymously, to harass the recipient

☆**poison pill** *Business* any defensive measure for preventing the takeover of a corporation by making its acquisition prohibitively expensive for the party attempting to acquire it

☆**poison sumac** a swamp plant (*Rhus vernix*) of the cashew family, with greenish-white flowers, hanging clusters of small grayish fruit, and leaves made up of 7 to 13 leaflets: it can cause a severe rash on contact

Pois·son distribution (pwä sōn′, -sōn′) ⟦after S. D. *Poisson* (1781-1840), Fr mathematician⟧ *Statistics* a frequency distribution that may be regarded as an approximation of the binomial distribution when the number of events becomes large and the probability of success becomes small

Poisson's ratio ⟦see prec.⟧ *Physics* an elastic constant of a material equal to the ratio of contraction sideways to expansion lengthwise when the material is stretched

Poi·tiers (pwȧ tyā′) city in WC France

Poi·tou (pwȧ to͞o′) historical region of WC France

Poi·tou-Cha·rentes (-shə ränt′) metropolitan region of W France: 9,965 sq mi (25,809 sq km); chief city, Poitiers

poke[1] (pōk) *vt.* **poked, pok′ing** ⟦ME *poken* < MDu or LowG⟧ **1** *a)* to push or jab with a stick, finger, etc.; prod *b)* [Slang] to hit with the fist **2** to make by poking [to *poke* a hole in a bag] **3** to stir up (a fire) by jabbing the coals with a poker **4** to thrust (something) forward; intrude [to *poke* one's head out a window] —*vi.* **1** to make jabs with a stick, poker, etc. (*at* something) **2** to intrude; meddle **3** to pry or search: sometimes with *about* or *around* **4** to stick out; protrude **5** to live or move slowly or lazily; loiter; putter; dawdle: often with *along* —*n.* **1** *a)* the act of poking; jab; thrust; nudge *b)* [Slang] a blow with the fist **2** SLOWPOKE **3** a poke bonnet, or its projecting front brim —**poke fun at** to ridicule or deride, esp. satirically or slyly

poke² (pōk) *n.* ⟦OFr *poke, poque* < Frank **pokka* < IE base **beu-*, to blow up, swell > PUCK²⟧ **1** [Dial.] a sack or bag **2** [Archaic] a pocket **3** [Slang] *a)* a wallet or purse *b)* money, esp. all that one has

☆**poke³** (pōk) *n.* ⟦earlier *pocan* < AmInd (Virginian) *puccoon*, weed used for staining⟧ *short for* POKEWEED

☆**poke·ber·ry** (pōk′ber′ē) *n., pl.* **-ries** POKEWEED

poke bonnet a bonnet with a projecting front brim

☆**pok·er¹** (pō′kər) *n.* ⟦< ? Ger *pochspiel*, lit., game of defiance < *pochen*, to defy, orig., to push (< MHG *bochen, puchen*, akin to LowG *poken*, POKE¹) + *spiel*, game⟧ a card game in which the players bet on the value of their hands (of five cards), the bets forming a pool to be taken by the player who remains after all others have dropped out of the betting or who holds the highest hand: there are several varieties: see DRAW POKER, STUD POKER

pok·er² (pō′kər) *n.* **1** a person or thing that pokes **2** a rod, usually of iron, for stirring a fire

☆**poker face** an expressionless face, as of a poker player trying to conceal the nature of his or her hand —**pok′er·faced′** *adj.*

☆**poke·root** (pōk′ro͞ot′) *n.* POKEWEED

☆**poke·weed** (pōk′wēd′) *n.* ⟦see POKE³⟧ a North American plant (*Phytolacca americana*) of the pokeweed family, with clusters of purplish-white flowers, reddish-purple berries, and smooth leaves and stems: the roots and berry seeds are poisonous —*adj.* designating a family (Phytolaccaceae, order Caryophyllales) of dicotyledonous trees, shrubs, and plants

pok·ey (pō′kē) *n., pl.* **pok′eys** or **pok′ies** ⟦< ?⟧ [Slang] a jail: also **pok′y**

pok·y (pō′kē) *adj.* **pok′i·er, pok′i·est** ⟦POKE¹ + -Y²⟧ **1** not lively; slow, dull, dilatory, etc. **2** small and uncomfortable; stuffy [a *poky* room] **3** shabbily dressed; dowdy Also **pok′ey** —**pok′i·ly** *adv.* —**pok′i·ness** *n.*

pol¹ (päl) *n.* [Slang] an experienced politician

pol² *abbrev.* **1** political **2** politics

Pol *abbrev.* **1** Poland **2** Polish

Po·lack (pō′läk′) *n.* ⟦< Pol *Polak*, a Pole⟧ [Slang] a person of Polish descent: a disparaging or derisive term

Po·land (pō′lənd) country in EC Europe, on the Baltic Sea: a kingdom in the Middle Ages, it lost autonomy throughout much of its later history until proclaimed an independent republic in 1918: 120,728 sq mi (312,685 sq km); cap. Warsaw: Pol. name POLSKA

☆**Poland China** any of a breed of large, black hog with white spots on the feet, nose, and tail

po·lar (pō′lər) *adj.* ⟦ML *polaris* < L *polus*: see POLE²⟧ **1** *a)* of, relating to, or near the North or South pole *b)* coming from the region near the North or South pole **2** of a pole or poles **3** having polarity **4** opposite in character, nature, direction, etc. **5** central and guiding, like the earth's pole or the polestar

polar bear a large, white bear (*Thalarctos maritimus*) of coastal arctic regions, usually feeding on fish and seals

polar body a minute cell cast off when a primary oocyte undergoes meiotic division to produce a secondary oocyte and again when the secondary oocyte divides to produce an ovum

polar circle **1** ARCTIC CIRCLE **2** ANTARCTIC CIRCLE

polar continental a type of cold, dry air mass originating at high latitudes over land areas: see AIR MASS

polar coordinates a pair of numbers that locate a point in a plane: one is the distance of the point from a fixed point on a fixed line, and the other is the angle made by the fixed line with the line connecting the two points

polar distance the astronomical coordinate (0° to 180°) measured from the pole of a planet, star, etc. to a point along an hour circle: usually limited in actual use to mean codeclination

polar front *Meteorol.* the boundary or transition region between the cold air of a polar region and the warmer air of the middle or tropical regions

po·lar·im·e·ter (pō′lə rim′ət ər) *n.* ⟦POLARI(ZE) + -METER⟧ **1** an instrument for measuring the degree of polarization of light, or the amount of polarized light in a ray **2** a polariscope made esp. for measuring the optical activity of a substance, esp. a liquid —**po·lar·i·met·ric** (pō lar′i me′trik) *adj.* —**po′lar·im′e·try** (-trē) *n.*

Po·la·ris (pō lar′is) *n.* ⟦ModL < ML *(stella) polaris*, polar (star): see POLE²⟧ a binary Cepheid variable, the brightest star in the constellation Ursa Minor; North Star; Pole Star: magnitude, 1.97: used for navigation, since it is the closest star to the north celestial pole and remains nearly stationary throughout the night

po·lar·i·scope (pō lar′ə skōp′) *n.* ⟦POLARI(ZE) + -SCOPE⟧ **1** an instrument for detecting or demonstrating the polarization of light, or for looking at things in polarized light **2** POLARIMETER (sense 2) —**po·lar′i·scop′ic** (-skäp′ik) *adj.*

po·lar·i·ty (pō lar′ə tē) *n., pl.* **-ties** **1** the tendency of bodies having opposite magnetic poles to arrange themselves so that their two extremities point to the two magnetic poles of the earth **2** any tendency to turn, grow, think, feel, etc. in a certain way or direction, as if because of magnetic attraction or repulsion **3** the fact or condition of being divided into two opposing groups **4** the having or showing of contrary qualities, powers, tendencies, forms, etc.: said as of the roots and stems of a plant or the two electrodes of a battery **5** the condition of being positive or negative with respect to some reference point or object, as electricity

po·lar·i·za·tion (pō′lə ri zā′shən) *n.* ⟦< fol. + -ATION⟧ **1** the producing of polarity in something, or the acquiring of polarity **2** the process or condition of being divided into two opposing groups **3** *Elec.* a condition in which gases produced during electrolysis accumulate on and around the electrodes of an electrical cell and reduce the flow of current by setting up an opposing potential **4** *Optics a)* the condition of electromagnetic or other waves in which the transverse motion or field of the wave is confined to one plane or one direction *b)* the production of this condition

po·lar·ize (pō′lə rīz′) *vt.* **-ized′**, **-iz′ing** ⟦Fr *polariser* < *polaire* < ML *polaris*, POLAR⟧ **1** to give polarity to; produce polarization in **2** to cause to divide into two opposing groups, as through a disagreement over policy —*vi.* to acquire polarity; specif., to separate into diametrically opposed, often antagonistic, groups, viewpoints, etc. —**po′lar·iz′a·ble** *adj.* —**po′lar·iz′er** *n.*

polar lights **1** AURORA BOREALIS **2** AURORA AUSTRALIS

polar maritime a type of cold, wet air mass originating at high latitudes over ocean areas: see AIR MASS

po·lar·og·ra·phy (pō′lər äg′rə fē) *n.* ⟦< POLARIZE + -GRAPHY⟧ an electromechanical technique of analyzing solutions that measures the current flowing between two electrodes in the solution as well as the gradually increasing applied voltage to determine respectively the concentration of a solute and its nature —**po·lar·o·graph·ic** (pō lar′ə graf′ik) *adj.* —**po·lar′o·graph′i·cal·ly** *adv.*

☆**Po·lar·oid** (pō′lə roid′) ⟦POLAR + -OID⟧ *trademark for:* **1** a transparent material containing embedded crystals capable of polarizing light: used in optics, photography, etc. **2** *a)* ⟦short for *Polaroid Land Camera*⟧ a camera that develops the film negative internally and produces a print within seconds after the process is initiated *b)* such a photograph

po·lar·on (pō′lə rän′) *n.* ⟦POLAR(IZATION) + -ON⟧ in solid-state physics, an electron and its surrounding field of polarization as it exists within a crystal lattice

pol·der (pōl′dər) *n.* ⟦Du, prob. akin to POOL¹⟧ an area of low-lying land reclaimed from a sea, lake, or river, as by the building of dikes

pole¹ (pōl) *n.* ⟦ME < OE *pal* < L *palus*, PALE²⟧ **1** a long, slender piece of wood, metal, etc., usually rounded [a tent *pole*, *flagpole*, fishing *pole*] **2** a tapering wooden shaft extending from the front axle of a wagon or carriage and attached by chains or straps to the collars of a span of horses **3** a unit of measure, equal to one rod in linear measure (5.029 m) or one square rod in square measure (25.29 sq m) **4** an assigned starting position at a racetrack, in the front row if there is more than one row and in the innermost lane — *vt., vi.* **poled**, **pol′ing** ☆**1** to push along (a boat or raft) with a pole **2** to manipulate, impel, support, etc. with or as with a pole —**under bare poles** with all sails furled because of high winds

pole² (pōl) *n.* ⟦ME < L *polus*, pole of the heavens, heavens < Gr *polos*, axis of the sphere, firmament < *pelein*, to be in motion < IE base **kwel-*, to turn > WHEEL⟧ **1** either end of any axis, as of the earth, of the celestial sphere, or of a mitotic spindle during cell division **2** the region around the North Pole or that around the South Pole **3** either of two opposed or differentiated forces, parts, or principles, such as the ends of a magnet, the terminals of a battery, motor, or dynamo, or two extremes of opinion **4** *Embryology* either of the two differentiated regions in the early embryo of many animals; specif., the **animal pole** containing little yolk and the **vegetal pole** containing most of the yolk **5** *Math.* a point or points with characteristic properties, as the point of origin of polar coordinates —**poles apart** widely separated; having opposite natures, opinions, etc.; at opposite extremes

Pole¹ (pōl) *n.* a person born or living in Poland

Pole² (pōl), **Reginald** 1500-58; Eng. cardinal: last Rom. Catholic archbishop of Canterbury (1556-58)

pole·ax or **pole·axe** (pōl′aks′) *n., pl.* **-ax′es** ⟦altered (infl. by POLE²) < ME *pollax* < *pol*, POLL + *ax*, AX¹⟧ **1** a long-handled battle-ax **2** any ax with a spike, hook, or hammer opposite the blade —*vt.* **-axed′**, **-ax′ing** to attack or fell with or as with a poleax

☆**pole bean** any of various varieties of the common garden bean, or kidney bean, cultivated to grow as vines twining about poles or other supports: cf. BUSH BEAN

pole·cat (pōl′kat′) *n., pl.* **-cats′** or **-cat′** ⟦ME *polcat*, prob. < OFr *poule* (see POULTRY) + CAT¹⟧ **1** any of several small, Old World weasels, usually having anal glands that eject foul-smelling fluid when the animal is in danger, esp. one (*Mustela putorius*) that is known as a "ferret" when domesticated to kill rats, mice, etc. ☆**2** SKUNK

pole-danc·ing (pōl′dans′iŋ) *n.* a type of erotic performance in which a dancer swings around, and suggestively moves against, a vertically fixed pole —**pole′-danc′er** *n.*

☆**pole horse** a horse harnessed alongside the pole of a wagon or carriage

po·lem·ic (pō lem′ik, pə-) *adj.* ⟦Fr *polémique* < Gr *polemikos* < *polemos*, war < IE **pelem* < base **pel-*, to shake, cause to tremble > L *palpitare*, to tremble⟧ **1** of or involving dispute; controversial **2** argumentative; disputatious Also, esp. for sense 2, **po·lem′i·cal** —*n.* **1** an argument or controversial discussion **2** a person inclined to engage in argument or disputation —**po·lem′i·cal·ly** *adv.*

po·lem·i·cist (pō lem′ə sist, pə-) *n.* a person skilled, or inclined to engage, in polemics: also **pol·e·mist** (päl′ə mist)

po·lem·i·cize (pō lem′ə sīz′, pə-) *vt.* **-cized′**, **-ciz′ing** to engage in polemics; write or speak polemically

po·lem·ics (pō lem′iks, pə-) *n.* ⟦see POLEMIC & -ICS⟧ [*sometimes with pl. v.*] the art or practice of disputation or controversy

po·len·ta (pō len′tə) *n.* ⟦It < L, peeled or pearl barley: for IE base see

POLLEN⟧ cornmeal mush, esp. as used in Italian cuisine as a main or side dish, sometimes containing cheese

pol·er (pōl′ər) *n.* ☆1 POLE HORSE ☆2 a person who poles a boat

pole·star (pōl′stär′) *n.* 1 Polaris, the North Star: usually **Pole Star** 2 a guiding principle 3 a center of attraction

pole vault *Track & Field* 1 an event in which the contestants take turns jumping for height over a horizontal bar set between two upright supports, with the aid of a long, flexible pole: the bar is gradually raised during the contest until a winner is determined 2 a jump in such an event Also [Brit.] **pole jump** —**pole′-vault′** *vi.* —**pole′-vault′er** *n.*

po·lice (pə lēs′) *n.* ⟦Fr < LL *politia*, administration of the commonwealth (in L, the state) < Gr *politeia*, the state, citizenship < *politēs*, citizen < *polis*, city < IE **pel-*, fortress (> Sans *pūr*, town), orig., filled wall, special use of base **pel-*, to flow, fill > FULL[1]⟧ 1 [Archaic] the regulation within a community of morals, safety, sanitation, etc.; public order; law enforcement 2 the governmental department (of a city, state, etc.) organized for keeping order, enforcing the law, and preventing, detecting, and prosecuting crimes 3 *a)* a governmental force, or body of persons, established and maintained for keeping order, etc. *b)* a private organization like this [security *police* at a college] *c)* [*with pl. v.*] the members of any such force *d)* [*with pl. verb*] [Informal] those who act as self-appointed guardians of morality, propriety, style, etc. (usually somewhat disparaging) [the fashion *police*, the language *police*] ☆4 *U.S. Army a)* the work or duty of keeping a camp, post, etc. clean and orderly *b)* [*with pl. v.*] the soldiers charged with such duty [kitchen *police*] —*vt.* **-liced′**, **-lic′ing** 1 to control, protect, or keep orderly with or as police or a similar force [to *police* the streets] ☆2 to make or keep (a military camp, post, etc.) clean and orderly: often with *up*

police action military activity without a declaration of war, undertaken to correct a breach of international law within or by a country

police court in some U.S. states, an inferior court with jurisdiction over minor offenses and misdemeanors, and the power to hold for trial those charged with felonies

police dog 1 a dog, esp. a German shepherd, specially trained to assist police 2 popularly, any German shepherd dog

po·lice·man (-mən) *n., pl.* **-men** (-mən) a member of a police force

police officer a member of a police force

police state a totalitarian state characterized by the use of police, esp. secret police, to suppress dissent and exert repressive control over its citizens

police station the headquarters of a local or district police force

po·lice·wom·an (-wo͝om′ən) *n., pl.* **-wom′en** (-wim′in) a female member of a police force

po·li·cier (pə lēs′ē ā′; *Fr* pô lē syā′) *n.* ⟦< Fr *roman policier*, detective novel⟧ a novel, TV drama, or, esp., film focusing on a realistic depiction of the work of the police in investigating a crime or crimes

pol·i·clin·ic (päl′i klin′ik) *n.* ⟦Ger *poliklinik* < Gr *polis*, city (see POLICE) + Ger *klinik* < Fr *clinique*, CLINIC⟧ the department of a hospital where outpatients are treated: cf. POLYCLINIC

pol·i·cy[1] (päl′ə sē) *n., pl.* **-cies** ⟦ME *policie* < OFr < L *politia* < Gr *politeia*: see POLICE⟧ 1 *a)* [Obs.] government or polity *b)* [Now Rare] political wisdom or cunning 2 wise, expedient, or prudent conduct or management 3 a principle, plan, or course of action, as pursued by a government, organization, individual, etc. [foreign *policy*]

pol·i·cy[2] (päl′ə sē) *n., pl.* **-cies** ⟦altered (infl. by prec.) < MFr *police* < It *polizza* < ML *apodixa* < MGr *apodeixis* < Gr, proof < *apodeiknynai*, to display, make known: see APO- & DICTION⟧ 1 a written contract in which one party guarantees to insure another against a specified loss, damage, injury, etc. in return for payments, usually periodic, called *premiums*: in full **insurance policy** ☆2 *a)* an illegal lottery in which winning numbers are drawn from a revolving drum *b)* THE NUMBERS (see phrase at NUMBER)

pol·i·cy·hold·er (-hōl′dər) *n.* a person to whom an insurance policy is issued

pol·i·cy·mak·ing (-māk′iŋ) *n.* the act or process of setting and directing the course of action to be pursued by a government, business, etc. —**pol′i·cy·mak′er** *n.*

po·li·o (pō′lē ō′) *n. short for* POLIOMYELITIS

po·li·o·my·e·li·tis (pō′lē ō mī′ə lit′is) *n.* ⟦ModL < Gr *polios*, gray + MYELITIS⟧ an acute infectious disease, esp. of children, caused by a viral inflammation of the gray matter of the spinal cord: it is accompanied by paralysis of various muscle groups that sometimes atrophy, often with resulting permanent deformities: also **acute anterior poliomyelitis**

po·li·o·vi·rus (pō′lē ō vī′rəs) *n.* ⟦ModL < prec. + VIRUS⟧ any of three strains of enterovirus causing poliomyelitis

po·lis (pō′lis) *n., pl.* **po′leis′** (-līs′) ⟦Gr *polis*: see POLICE⟧ in ancient Greece, a city-state

pol·i sci (päl′ē sī′) [Informal] *short for* political science

pol·ish (päl′ish) *vt.* ⟦ME *polischen* < inflected stem of OFr *polir* < L *polire*, to polish, prob. < IE base **pel-*, to drive, impel > FELT[1]⟧ 1 *a)* to smooth and brighten, as by rubbing *b)* to coat with polish, wax, etc. and make bright or glossy 2 to improve or refine (someone or someone's manners, appearance, etc.) as by removing crudeness or vulgarity 3 to complete or embellish (a piece of writing, etc.); finish; perfect —*vi.* to take a polish; become glossy, elegant, or refined —*n.* 1 a surface gloss 2 elegance, refinement, cultivation, finish, or the like 3 a substance used for polishing 4 the act of polishing or condition of being polished —**polish off** [Informal] 1 to finish (a meal, job, etc.) completely and quickly 2 to overcome or get rid of (a competitor, enemy, etc.) —**polish up** [Informal] to improve (something) —**pol′ish·er** *n.*

SYN.—**polish** implies a rubbing, as with a cloth or tool and, often, an abrasive, paste, etc., to produce a smooth or glossy surface [to *polish* silver, glass, furniture, etc.]; **burnish** specifically suggests a rubbing of metals to make them bright and lustrous [*burnished* steel]; **buff** implies polishing with a stick or tool covered with specially treated leather (originally buffalo hide) or other material [to *buff* the fingernails]; **shine** implies a making bright and clean by polishing [to *shine* shoes]

Pol·ish (pōl′ish) *adj.* ⟦< POLE[1] + -ISH⟧ of Poland or its people, language, or culture —*n.* the West Slavic language spoken in Poland

Polish Corridor strip of Poland between Germany & East Prussia, giving Poland an outlet to the Baltic Sea (1919-39): *c.* 120 mi (193 km) long; 20-70 mi (32-113 km) wide

pol·ished (päl′isht) *adj.* 1 *a)* made smooth and shiny, as by rubbing *b)* having a naturally smooth and shiny surface 2 elegant; refined 3 without error or flaw; finished [a *polished* performance]

polit *abbrev.* 1 political 2 politics

Po·lit·bu·ro (päl′it byo͝or′ō, pō′lit-) *n.* ⟦Russ *Politbjuro* < *Polit(ičeskoe) Bjuro*, Poliical Bureau⟧ the executive committee of the Communist Party of the Soviet Union and of certain other nations

po·lite (pə līt′) *adj.* ⟦L *politus*, pp. of *polire*, to POLISH⟧ 1 having or showing culture or good taste; polished; cultured; refined [*polite* society, *polite* letters] 2 having or showing good manners; esp., courteous, considerate, tactful, etc. —SYN. CIVIL —**po·lite′ly** *adv.* —**po·lite′ness** *n.*

pol·i·tesse (päl′ə tes′) *n.* ⟦Fr < It *politezza*, cleanliness, courtliness < *pulito*, clean < L *politus*: see prec.⟧ politeness

Po·li·tian (pō lish′ən) (born *Angelo Ambrogini*) 1454-94; It. humanist & poet

pol·i·tic (päl′ə tik′) *adj.* ⟦ME *polytyk* < MFr *politique* < L *politicus* < Gr *politikos*, of a citizen < *politēs*: see POLICE⟧ 1 POLITICAL: archaic except in BODY POLITIC 2 having practical wisdom; prudent; shrewd; diplomatic 3 crafty; unscrupulous 4 prudently or artfully contrived; expedient, as a plan, action, remark, etc. —*vi.* **-ticked′**, **-tick′ing** to engage in political campaigning, vote-getting, etc. —SYN. SUAVE —**pol′i·tic′ly** *adv.*

po·lit·i·cal (pə lit′i kəl) *adj.* ⟦< L *politicus* (see prec.) + -AL⟧ 1 of or concerned with government, the state, or politics 2 having a definite governmental organization 3 engaged in or taking sides in politics [*political* parties] 4 of or characteristic of political parties or politicians [*political* pressure] —**po·lit′i·cal·ly** *adv.*

political action committee an organization representing the interests of a corporation, labor union, trade association, etc. that solicits and collects political campaign contributions from individuals and distributes them to particular candidates

political economy *former term for* ECONOMICS

po·lit·i·cal·ize (-īz′) *vt.* **-ized′**, **-iz′ing** to make political; organize politically —**po·lit′i·cal·i·za′tion** *n.*

political liberty the right to participate in determining the form, choosing the officials, making the laws, and carrying on the functions of one's government

politically correct conforming or adhering to what is regarded as orthodox liberal opinion on matters of sexuality, race, etc.: usually used disparagingly to connote dogmatism, excessive sensitivity to minority causes, etc. —**political correctness**

political science the study of political institutions, or of the principles, organization, and methods of government —**political scientist**

pol·i·ti·cian (päl′ə tish′ən) *n.* ⟦POLITIC + -IAN⟧ 1 a person actively engaged in politics, esp. party politics, professionally or otherwise; often, a person holding or seeking political office: frequently used in a derogatory sense, with implications of seeking personal or partisan gain, scheming, opportunism, etc.: cf. STATESMAN 2 a person skilled or experienced in practical politics or political science

po·lit·i·cize (pə lit′ə sīz′) *vi.* **-cized′**, **-ciz′ing** to talk about, or engage in, politics —*vt.* to make political in tone, character, etc. —**po·lit′i·ci·za′tion** *n.*

pol·i·tick·ing (päl′ə tik′iŋ) *n.* political activity; esp., the process of campaigning for support, votes, etc.

po·lit·i·co (pə lit′ə kō′) *n., pl.* **-cos′** ⟦Sp *político* or It *politico*, both < L *politicus*: see POLITIC⟧ [Informal] POLITICIAN

po·lit·i·co- (pə lit′ə kō′) *combining form* political and [*politico*-economic]

pol·i·tics (päl′ə tiks) *pl.n.* ⟦POLIT(IC) + -ICS⟧ [*with sing. or pl. v.*] 1 the science and art of political government; political science 2 political affairs 3 the conducting of or participation in political affairs, often as a profession 4 political methods, tactics, etc.; sometimes, specif., crafty or unprincipled methods 5 political opinions, principles, or party connections 6 factional scheming for power and status within a group [office *politics*]

pol·i·ty (päl′ə tē) *n., pl.* **-ties** ⟦MFr *politie* < L *politia*: see POLICY[1]⟧ 1 political or governmental organization 2 a society or institution with an organized government; state; body politic 3 a specific form of church government

Polk (pōk), **James K(nox)** 1795-1849; 11th president of the U.S. (1845-49)

pol·ka (pōl′kə) *n.* ⟦Czech, Polish dance, lit., Polish woman < Pol *Polka*, fem. of *Polak*, Pole⟧ 1 a fast dance for couples, developed in Bohemia in the early 19th cent.: the basic step is a hop followed by three small steps 2 music for this dance, in fast duple time —*vi.* to dance the polka

☆**pol·ka dot** (pō′kə, pōl′-) ⟦< prec.: from the popularity of the dance in the late 19th c., term applied to various garments, materials, etc.⟧ 1 one of the small round dots regularly spaced to form a pattern on cloth 2 a pattern or cloth with such dots —**pol′ka-dot′** *adj.*

poll (pōl) *n.* ⟦ME *pol* < or akin to MDu, top of the head, head⟧ 1 the head; esp., the crown, back, or hair of the head 2 an individual person, esp. one among several 3 a counting, listing, or register of persons, esp. of voters 4 a voting or expression of opinion by individuals 5 the amount of voting; number of votes recorded ☆6 [*pl.*] a place where votes are cast and recorded ☆7 *a)* a canvassing of a selected or random group of people to collect information, or to attempt to discover public opinion *b)* a report or record of the results of this 8 the blunt or flat end, as of an ax —*vt.* 1 to cut off or cut short 2 to cut off or trim the wool, hair, horns, or branches of; specif., to pollard (a tree) 3 *a)* to take or register the votes of [*to poll a county*] *b)* to require each member of (a jury, committee, etc.) to declare his or her vote individually 4 to receive (a specified number or proportion of votes) 5 to cast (a vote) 6 to canvass in a POLL (sense 7) —*vi.* to vote in an election —**poll′er** *n.*

pol·lack (päl′ək) *n. alt. sp. of* POLLOCK

Pol·lack (pō′läk′) *n.* [Slang] *alt. sp. of* POLACK: a disparaging or derisive term

pol·lard (päl′ərd) *n.* ⟦POLL + -ARD⟧ 1 a hornless goat, deer, ox, etc. 2 a tree with its top branches cut back to the trunk, so as to cause a dense growth of new shoots —*vt.* to change into a pollard

polled (pōld) *adj.* 1 [Obs.] with the wool, hair, etc. cut off or trimmed 2 lacking horns; hornless

☆**poll·ee** (pō lē′) *n.* a person questioned in a poll

pol·len (päl′ən) *n.* ⟦ModL < L, fine flour, dust < IE base **pel*, dust, meal > L *pulvis*, dust, Gr *palē*, dust⟧ the fine, dustlike mass of grains that are produced in the anthers or microspore sacs of seed plants, containing the male sexual cells (gametophytes) of the plant

pol·len·ate (päl′ə nāt′) *vt.* **-at′ed, -at′ing** *alt. sp. of* POLLINATE

pollen count the number of grains of a specified variety of pollen, usually ragweed, present in a given volume of air, usually a cubic yard, at a specified time and place: used to inform those allergic to pollen of levels that might affect outdoor activity

pol·le·no·sis (päl′ə nō′sis) *n.* ⟦var. of POLLINOSIS: see POLLEN & -OSIS⟧ *alt. sp. of* POLLINOSIS

pollen tube *Bot.* the tubelike growth that emerges from a germinating pollen grain and enters the embryo sac in an ovule: a male gamete passes through it to fertilize the female gamete

pol·lex (päl′eks′) *n., pl.* **pol′li·ces′** (-ə sēz′) ⟦L, thumb, big toe⟧ the innermost digit of a forelimb; esp., the thumb —**pol′li·cal** (-i kəl) *adj.*

pol·li·nate (päl′ə nāt′) *vt.* **-nat′ed, -nat′ing** to transfer pollen from a stamen to the upper tip of the pistil of (the same or a different flower) —**pol′li·na′tion** *n.* —**pol′li·na′tor** *n.*

pol·li·nif·er·ous (päl′ə nif′ər əs) *adj.* ⟦< L *pollen* (gen. *pollinis*) + -FEROUS⟧ 1 bearing or yielding pollen 2 adapted for carrying pollen

pol·lin·i·um (pə lin′ē əm) *n., pl.* **-i·a** (-ə) ⟦ModL < L *pollen:* see POLLEN⟧ *Bot.* a mass of pollen grains stuck together and transferred as a whole in pollination, often by an insect

pol·li·nize (päl′ə nīz′) *vt.* **-nized′, -niz′ing** POLLINATE —**pol′li·niz′er** *n.*

pol·li·no·sis (päl′ə nō′sis) *n.* ⟦ModL < *pollin-*, POLLEN + -OSIS⟧ HAY FEVER

pol·li·wog (päl′ē wäg′, -wôg′) *n.* ⟦ME *polwygle*, prob. < *pol*, POLL + *wigelen*, to WIGGLE⟧ TADPOLE: also **pol′ly·wog′**

pol·lock (päl′ək) *n., pl.* **-lock** or **-locks** any of various marine, gadoid food fishes (genera *Pollachius* and *Theragra*) having tiny scales and a projecting lower jaw

Pol·lock[1] (pō′läk′) *n.* [Slang] *alt. sp. of* POLACK: a disparaging or derisive term

Pol·lock[2] (päl′ək) 1 Sir **Frederick** 3d Baronet 1845-1937; Eng. jurist & writer on law 2 **Jackson** 1912-56; U.S. abstract painter

☆**poll·ster** (pōl′stər) *n.* a person whose work is taking public-opinion polls

poll tax ⟦see POLL⟧ a tax per person, levied on individuals rather than on property: such a tax as a prerequisite for voting is unconstitutional in the U.S.

pol·lu·tant (pə lo͞ot′′nt) *n.* ⟦< fol. + -ANT⟧ something that pollutes; esp., a harmful chemical or waste material discharged into the water or atmosphere

pol·lute (pə lo͞ot′) *vt.* **-lut′ed, -lut′ing** ⟦ME *poluten* < L *pollutus*, pp. of *polluere*, to pollute < **por-*, for *per-*, intens. + *-luere*, to soil < IE base **leu-*, dirt > Gr *lyma*, dirt⟧ 1 to make unclean, impure, or corrupt; defile; dirty 2 to contaminate (water, air, etc.) with harmful chemicals, waste material, etc. —*SYN.* CONTAMINATE —**pol·lut′er** *n.* —**pol·lu′tion** *n.*

pol·lut·ed (pə lo͞ot′id) *adj.* 1 contaminated, specif. with harmful chemicals, waste material, etc. [*polluted streams and rivers*] 2 [Slang] intoxicated; drunk

Pol·lux (päl′əks) *n.* ⟦L, earlier *Polluces* < Gr *Polydeukēs*⟧ 1 *Class. Myth.* the immortal twin of Castor: see DIOSCURI 2 a giant, orange, variable star, actually the brightest star in the constellation Gemini although it is considered the twin of Castor: magnitude, 1.16

Pol·ly (päl′ē) *n.* a feminine name: see MARY[1]

☆**Pol·ly·an·na** (päl′ē an′ə) *n.* ⟦after the young heroine of novels by Eleanor H. Porter (1868-1920), U.S. writer⟧ an excessively or persistently optimistic person —**Pol′ly·an′na·ish** (-an′ə ish) *adj.*, **Pol′ly·an′na-ish**, or **Pol′ly·an′nish** (-an′ish)

po·lo (pō′lō) *n.* ⟦ult. < Tibet dial., var. of *pulu*, properly, the name of the ball⟧ 1 a game played on horseback by two teams of four players each, who attempt to drive a small wooden ball through the opponents' goal with a mallet having a long, flexible handle 2 WATER POLO —**po′lo·ist** *n.*

Po·lo (pō′lō), **Mar·co** (mär′kō) 1254-1324; Venetian traveler in E Asia

polo coat a tailored overcoat of camel's hair or similar fabric

pol·o·naise (päl′ə nāz′, pō′lə-) *n.* ⟦Fr < fem. of *polonais*, Polish⟧ 1 an 18th-cent. dress with the skirt divided in front and worn looped back over an elaborate underskirt, originally in Poland 2 a stately Polish dance in triple time, almost processional in character 3 music for this dance

Po·lo·ni·a (pə lō′nē ə) *n.* ⟦Pol < ML: see fol.⟧ the Polish-American community in a given place outside Poland —**Po·lo′ni·an** *adj., n.*

po·lo·ni·um (pə lō′nē əm) *n.* ⟦ModL: so named (1898) by its co-discoverer Marie CURIE, after her native land, Poland (ML *Polonia*) + -IUM⟧ a radioactive, nonmetallic chemical element formed naturally by the disintegration of radium or synthetically by the neutron irradiation of bismuth followed by beta decay: used as a power source in space satellites, as an aid in inducing electric discharges, etc.: symbol, Po; at. no. 84: see the periodic table of elements in the Reference Supplement

Po·lo·ni·us (pə lō′nē əs) *n.* in Shakespeare's *Hamlet*, a verbose, sententious old courtier, father of Ophelia and Laertes

☆**polo shirt** a knitted pullover sport shirt

Pol Pot (päl′ pät′) (born *Saloth Sar*) 1925-98; Cambodian political leader: de facto ruler (1975-76) & prime minister (1976-79)

Pol·ska (pôl′skä) *Pol. name for* POLAND

Pol·ta·va (pôl tä′vä) city in EC Ukraine: scene of a battle (1709) in which the Russians under Peter the Great defeated Sweden

pol·ter·geist (pōl′tər gīst′) *n.* ⟦Ger < *poltern*, to make noise, rumble (< IE base **bhel-* > BELL[2]) + *geist*, GHOST⟧ a kind of ghost thought by some to be responsible for mysterious noisy disturbances

pol·troon (päl tro͞on′) *n.* ⟦Fr *poltron* < It *poltrone*, coward < *poltro*, colt < VL **pulliter*, prob. < *pullus*, young animal, chick: see POULTRY⟧ a thorough coward; craven —*adj.* cowardly —**pol·troon′er·y** (-ər ē) *n.*

pol·y (päl′ē) *n.* [Informal] *short for* polyester

pol·y-[1] (päl′i, -ə, -ē) ⟦ModL < Gr *poly-* < *polys*, much, many < IE **pelu*, large amount < base **pel-*, to pour, fill > FULL[1]⟧ *combining form* 1 much, many, more than one [*polychromatic*] 2 more than usual, excessive [*polyphagia*] 3 in or of many kinds or parts [*polymorph*]

pol·y-[2] (päl′i, -ə, -ē) *combining form* polymer of; polymerized [*polyvinyl*]

pol·y·a·del·phous (päl′ē ə del′fəs) *adj.* ⟦< Gr *polyadelphos*, with many brothers < *polys*, many (see POLY-[1]) + *adelphos*, brother (see MONADELPHOUS) + -OUS⟧ *Bot.* having stamens joined by their filaments into a number of clusters

pol·y·am·ide (päl′ē am′īd′) *n.* ⟦POLY-[1] + AMIDE⟧ any of various natural or synthetic compounds having two or more amide groups; esp., a polymeric amide, as nylon

☆**pol·y·am·o·ry** (päl′ē am′ə rē) *n.* ⟦< POLY- + L *amor*, love + -Y[4]⟧ the practice of engaging openly in concurrent sexual relationships, in or out of marriage; specif., polygamy —**pol′y·am′o·rous** *adj.*

pol·y·an·drous (päl′ē an′drəs) *adj.* ⟦Gr *polyandros*⟧ 1 practicing polyandry 2 of or characterized by polyandry 3 *Bot.* having many stamens

pol·y·an·dry (päl′ē an′drē, päl′ē an′drē) *n.* ⟦Gr *polyandria* < *poly-*, many + *anēr*, man: see ANDRO-⟧ 1 the state or practice of having two or more husbands at the same time 2 ⟦ModL *polyandria*⟧ *Bot.* the presence of numerous stamens in one flower 3 *Zool.* the mating of one female animal with more than one male —**pol′y·an′dric** *adj.* —**pol′y·an′drist** *n.*

pol·y·an·tha (päl′ē an′thə) *n.* ⟦ModL < Gr *polyanthos:* see fol.⟧ a strain of cultivated roses (*Rosa polyantha*) having numerous small flowers borne in a cluster

pol·y·an·thus (päl′ē an′thəs) *n.* ⟦ModL < Gr *polyanthos:* see POLY-[1] & -ANTHOUS⟧ 1 any of various primroses with many flowers 2 a tender, sweet-scented narcissus (*Narcissus tazetta*) with clusters of small, star-shaped flowers

pol·y·bas·ic (päl′i bās′ik) *adj.* ⟦POLY-[1] + BASIC⟧ 1 designating an acid having more than one hydrogen atom (per molecule) replaceable by basic atoms or radicals 2 designating a salt having more than one atom (per molecule) of a monovalent metal

pol·y·ba·site (päl′i bā′sīt′, pə lib′ə sīt′) *n.* ⟦Ger *polybasit* < Gr *poly-* (see POLY-[1]) + *basis* (see BASE[1]) + Ger *-it*, -ITE[1]⟧ a dark-colored mineral, silver copper antimony sulfide, $(Ag,Cu)_{16}Sb_2S_{11}$, that is an ore of silver

Po·lyb·i·us (pō lib′ē əs) 200?-118? B.C.; Gr. historian

pol·y·car·bon·ate (päl′i kär′bə nit, -nāt′) *n.* any of a class of resins, $(COOC_6H_5C(CH_3)_2C_6H_5O)n$, that are thermoplastic, tough, transparent, and nontoxic and are used in making molded products

Pol·y·carp (päl′i kärp′), Saint (2d cent. A.D.); Gr. bishop of Smyrna: Christian martyr: his day is Feb. 23

pol·y·car·pel·lar·y (päl′i kär′pə ler′ē) *adj. Bot.* having numerous separate or united carpels in the gynoecium

pol·y·car·pic (päl′i kär′pik) *adj.* ⟦POLY-[1] + -CARPIC⟧ *Bot.* 1 capable of flowering and fruiting an indefinite number of times 2 having two or more separate carpels Also **pol′y·car′pous**

pol·y·cen·trism (päl′i sen′triz′əm) *n.* ⟦POLY-[1] + CENT(E)R + -ISM⟧ the existence or advocacy of independent centers of power within a political, esp. communist, system —**pol′y·cen′tric** *adj.* —**pol′y·cen′trist** *adj., n.*

pol·y·chaete (päl′i kēt′) *n.* ⟦< ModL *Polychaeta* < Gr *polychaitēs*, with much hair < *poly-*, POLY-[1] + *chaitē*, hair⟧ any of a class (Polychaeta) of mostly marine, annelid worms, having on most segments a pair of fleshy, leglike appendages bearing numerous bristles —**pol′y·chae′tous** *adj.*

pol·y·chlo·ri·nat·ed bi·phen·yl (päl′i klôr′ə nāt′əd bī′fen′əl, -fē′nəl) PCB

pol·y·chot·o·my (päl′i kät′ə mē) ***n.**, pl.* **-mies** ⟦POLY-[1] + *-chotomy*, as in DICHOTOMY⟧ division or separation into many parts, classes, etc. —**pol′y·chot′o·mous** (-məs) ***adj.***

pol·y·chro·mat·ic (päl′i krō mat′ik) ***adj.*** ⟦POLY-[1] + CHROMATIC⟧ having various or changing colors

pol·y·chrome (päl′i krōm′) ***adj.*** ⟦Fr < Gr *polychrōmos:* see POLY-[1] & -CHROME⟧ **1** POLYCHROMATIC **2** done or decorated in several colors —***n.*** a polychrome work of art

pol·y·chro·my (päl′i krō′mē) ***n.*** ⟦Fr *polychromie:* see prec.⟧ the art of combining many different colors, esp. in painting statues, vases, etc.

pol·y·clin·ic (päl′i klin′ik) ***n.*** ⟦POLY-[1] + CLINIC⟧ a clinic or hospital for the treatment of various kinds of diseases: cf. POLICLINIC

Pol·y·cli·tus or **Pol·y·clei·tus** (päl′i klīt′əs) 5th cent. B.C.; Gr. sculptor: also **Pol′y·cle′tus** (-klēt′-)

pol·y·con·ic projection (päl′i kän′ik) a type of conic map projection in which the parallels are represented as arcs of circles having centers at different points along the straight central meridian and the other meridians are shown as curves

pol·y·cot·y·le·don (päl′i kät′ə lēd′'n) ***n.*** a plant which actually or apparently has more than two cotyledons, as in the gymnosperms —**pol′y·cot′y·le′don·ous** ***adj.***

pol·y·cy·clic (päl′i sīk′lik) ***adj.*** **1** *Biol.* having two or more rings or whorls **2** *Chem.* having two or more rings of atoms in the molecule

polycyclic aromatic hydrocarbon any of a group of common, very stable, aromatic hydrocarbons formed by the incomplete burning of any substance containing carbon, esp. coal, oil, wood, or tobacco: many are known or suspected carcinogens: abbrev. *PAH*

pol·y·cyst·ic (päl′i sis′tik) ***adj.*** made up of or containing many cysts [a *polycystic* kidney]

pol·y·cy·the·mi·a (päl′i sī thē′mē ə) ***n.*** ⟦POLY-[1] + CYT(O)- + -HEMIA⟧ an abnormal increase in the number and concentration of circulating red blood corpuscles

pol·y·dac·tyl (päl′i dak′təl) ***adj.*** ⟦Fr *polydactyle* < Gr *polydaktylos*, many-toed: see POLY-[1] & DACTYL⟧ having more than the normal number of fingers or toes —***n.*** a polydactyl person or animal —**pol′y·dac′tyl·ism′** ***n.***, **pol′y·dac′ty·ly** —**pol′y·dac′ty·lous** ***adj.***

pol·y·e·lec·tro·lyte (päl′ē ē lek′trō līt′) ***n.*** a polymeric electrolyte of high molecular weight that releases either positive or negative ions in solution, used to coagulate and precipitate pollutants and cause them to settle

pol·y·em·bry·o·ny (päl′ē em′brē ə nē) ***n.*** ⟦< POLY-[1] + EMBRYO + -Y[4]⟧ the production of two or more embryos or individuals from a single fertilized ovum

pol·y·ene (päl′ē ēn′) ***n.*** ⟦POLY-[1] + -ENE⟧ an unsaturated compound containing more than two double bonds

pol·y·es·ter (päl′ē es′tər, päl′ē es′tər) ***n.*** ⟦POLY(MER) + ESTER⟧ **1** any of several polymeric synthetic resins formed chiefly by condensing polyhydric alcohols with dibasic acids: used in making plastics, fibers, etc. **2** fabric made of these fibers

☆**pol·y·eth·yl·ene** (päl′ē eth′ə lēn′) ***n.*** ⟦POLY(MER) + ETHYLENE⟧ any of several thermoplastic resins, $(C_2H_4)_n$, made by the polymerization of ethylene: used in making translucent, lightweight, and tough plastics, films, containers, insulation, etc.

polyethylene ter·eph·thal·ate (ter′əf thal′āt′) ⟦< *terephthalate* < TEREPHTHAL(IC ACID) + -ATE[2]⟧ a thermoplastic polyester, $(CH_2CH_2OCOC_6H_4COO)_n$, formed from ethylene glycol, used as a plastic resin to make fabrics, beverage bottles, film, etc.: abbrev. *PETE* or *PET*

po·lyg·a·la (pō lig′ə lə, pə-) ***n.*** ⟦ModL < L, milkwort < Gr *polygalon* < *poly-*, much + *gala*, milk: see GALACTIC⟧ MILKWORT

po·lyg·a·mous (pə lig′ə məs, pō-) ***adj.*** ⟦Gr *polygamos*⟧ **1** of, engaging in, or characterized by polygamy **2** *Bot.* having bisexual flowers and unisexual flowers on the same plant or on different plants —**po·lyg′a·mous·ly** ***adv.***

po·lyg·a·my (pə lig′ə mē, pō-) ***n.*** ⟦Fr *polygamie* < Gr *polygamia:* see POLY-[1] & -GAMY⟧ **1** the state or practice of having two or more spouses at the same time; plural marriage **2** *Zool.* the practice of mating with more than one of the opposite sex —**po·lyg′a·mist** ***n.***

pol·y·genes (päl′ə jēnz′) ***pl.n.*** ⟦< POLY-[1] + GENE⟧ MULTIPLE FACTORS —**pol′y·gen′ic** (-jen′ik) ***adj.***

pol·y·gen·e·sis (päl′ə jen′ə sis) ***n.*** ⟦ModL: see POLY-[1] & GENESIS⟧ **1** derivation from more than one kind of germ cell **2** the theory that different species are descended from different ultimate ancestors —**pol′y·ge·net′ic** (-jə net′ik) ***adj.*** —**pol′y·ge·net′i·cal·ly** ***adv.***

po·lyg·en·ism (pə lij′ə niz′əm) ***n.*** a theory that each race of people is descended from distinct ultimate ancestors: see MONOGENISM

pol·y·glot (päl′i glät′) ***adj.*** ⟦Gr *polyglōttos* < *poly-*, POLY-[1] + *glōtta*, the tongue: see GLOTTIS⟧ **1** speaking or writing several languages **2** containing or written in several languages —***n.*** **1** a polyglot person **2** a polyglot book **3** a mixture or confusion of languages

Pol·yg·no·tus (päl′ig nōt′əs) 5th cent. B.C.; Gr. painter

pol·y·gon (päl′i gän′) ***n.*** ⟦LL *polygonum* < Gr *polygōnon*, neut. of *polygōnos:* see POLY-[1] & -GON⟧ a closed plane figure consisting of straight lines —**po·lyg·o·nal** (pə lig′ə nəl) ***adj.***

po·lyg·o·num (pō lig′ə nəm, pə-) ***n.*** ⟦ModL < L *polygonon* < Gr, kind of plant, knotgrass < *poly-*, many (see POLY-[1]) + *gony*, a joint, KNEE: from the many joints⟧ any of a genus (*Polygonum*) of annual or perennial plants of the buckwheat family, having conspicuous enlarged nodes, ocreae, and small whitish, greenish, or pink flowers in the leaf axils or in terminal clusters

pol·y·graph (päl′i graf′) ***n.*** ⟦Gr *polygraphos*, writing much: see POLY-[1] & -GRAPH⟧ **1** an early device for reproducing writings or drawings **2** an instrument for recording simultaneously changes in blood pressure, respiration, pulse rate, etc., specif. LIE DETECTOR —**pol′y·graph′ic** ***adj.***

po·lyg·y·ny (pə lij′ə nē, pō-) ***n.*** ⟦< ModL *polygynia* < POLY-[1] + Gr *gynē*, woman, wife: see GYNO-⟧ **1** the state or practice of having two or more wives at the same time **2** *Bot.* the fact of having many styles or pistils **3** *Zool.* the mating of a male animal with more than one female —**po·lyg′y·nous** (-nəs) ***adj.***

pol·y·he·dron (päl′i hē′drən) ***n.**, pl.* **-drons** or **-dra** (-drə) ⟦ModL < Gr *polyedron*, neut. of *polyedros:* see POLY-[1] & -HEDRON⟧ a solid figure with usually more than six plane surfaces —**pol′y·he′dral** ***adj.***

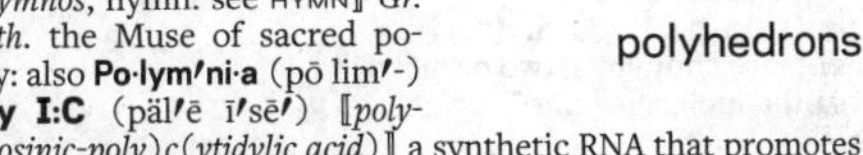

polyhedrons

pol·y·his·tor (päl′ə his′tər) ***n.*** ⟦< Gr *polyistōr*, very learned < *poly-*, POLY-[1] + *histōr*, learned: see HISTORY⟧ POLYMATH —**pol′y·his·tor′ic** (-tôr′ik) ***adj.***

pol·y·hy·dric (päl′i hī′drik′) ***adj.*** ⟦POLY-[1] + HYDR(OXYL) + -IC⟧ containing more than one hydroxyl group (OH) in the molecule: also **pol′y·hy·drox′y** (-hī dräk′sē)

Pol·y·hym·ni·a (päl′i him′nē ə) ***n.*** ⟦L < Gr *Polymnia* < *poly*, POLY-[1] + *hymnos*, hymn: see HYMN⟧ *Gr. Myth.* the Muse of sacred poetry: also **Po·lym′ni·a** (pō lim′-)

pol·y I:C (päl′ē ī′sē′) ⟦*poly-i(nosinic-poly)c(ytidylic acid)*⟧ a synthetic RNA that promotes the production of interferon in the body

pol·y·math (päl′ə math′) ***n.*** ⟦< Gr *polymathēs*, knowing much < *poly-*, POLY-[1] + *manthanein*, to learn: see MATHEMATICAL⟧ a person of great and diversified learning —**pol′y·math′ic** ***adj.***

pol·y·mer (päl′ə mər) ***n.*** ⟦Ger < Gr *polymerēs*, of many parts: see POLY-[1] & -MEROUS⟧ a naturally occurring or synthetic substance consisting of giant molecules formed from polymerization

po·lym·er·ase (pə lim′ər ās′, päl′ə mər ās′) ***n.*** any of various enzymes that promote polymerization, esp. of nucleic acids

polymerase chain reaction a technique in which a DNA sequence is replicated at elevated temperatures by means of a polymerase, eventually producing millions of copies of the sequence: used in genetic analysis, DNA FINGERPRINTING, in detecting minute quantities of cancer cells, etc.

pol·y·mer·ic (päl′ə mer′ik) ***adj.*** ⟦< Ger *polymerisch:* see POLYMER⟧ of or relating to a polymer —**pol′y·mer′i·cal·ly** ***adv.***

po·lym·er·ism (pə lim′ər iz′əm, päl′ə mər-) ***n.*** the condition of being polymeric

po·lym·er·i·za·tion (pə lim′ər ə zā′shən, päl′ə mər-) ***n.*** **1** the process of chaining together many simple molecules to form a more complex molecule with different physical properties **2** the changing of a compound into a polymeric form by this process —**po·lym′er·ize′** (-īz′) ***vt., vi.*** **-ized′**, **-iz′ing**

pol·y·morph (päl′i môrf′) ***n.*** ⟦< Gr *polymorphos:* see POLY-[1] & -MORPH⟧ **1** *Biol.* a polymorphous organism or one of its forms **2** *Chem., Mineralogy* *a)* a substance that can crystallize in different forms *b)* one of these forms

pol·y·mor·phism (päl′i môr′fiz′əm) ***n.*** ⟦POLYMORPH(OUS) + -ISM⟧ **1** *Chem., Mineralogy* the property of certain substances of crystallizing in two or more different forms or systems **2** *Biol.* the condition in which a species has two or more very different morphological forms, as the castes of social insects or the flowers of certain plants **3** *Genetics* the presence of phenotypic variation within a single population

pol·y·mor·pho·nu·cle·ar (päl′i môr′fō no͞o′klē ər, -nyo͞o′-) ***adj.*** having a lobed nucleus, as the neutrophils

pol·y·mor·phous (päl′i môr′fəs) ***adj.*** ⟦Gr *polymorphos:* see POLY-[1] & -MORPH⟧ displaying or taking various forms; specif., of, having, or exhibiting polymorphism: also **pol′y·mor′phic** (-fik) —**pol′y·mor′phous·ly** ***adv.***

pol·y·myx·in (päl′i mik′sin) ***n.*** ⟦< ModL (*Bacillus*) *polymyx(a)* (< *poly-*, POLY-[1] + *-myxa* < Gr *myxa*, MUCUS) + -IN[1]⟧ any of various antibiotics obtained from strains of a soil bacterium (*Bacillus polymyxa*), esp. effective against Gram-negative bacteria

Pol·y·ne·sia (päl′i nē′zhə, -shə) ⟦ModL < Gr *poly-*, POLY-[1] + *nēsos*, island + -IA⟧ a major division of the Pacific islands east of the 180th meridian, including Hawaii, Samoa, Tonga, the Society Islands, the Marquesas Islands, etc.: cf. MELANESIA

Pol·y·ne·sian (päl′i nē′zhən, -shən) ***n.*** **1** a member of any of the indigenous peoples of Polynesia, including the Hawaiians, Tahitians, Samoans, Maoris, Marquesans, Tongans, and other groups **2** a subgroup of the Austronesian language family, consisting of the languages of Polynesia —***adj.*** of the Polynesians or their languages or cultures

pol·y·neu·ri·tis (päl′i no͞o rīt′is, -nyo͞o-) ***n.*** neuritis involving several nerves simultaneously

Pol·y·ni·ces (päl′i nī′sēz′) ***n.*** ⟦Gr *Polyneikēs*, lit., great wrangler < *polys*, much (see POLY-[1]) + *neikos*, quarrel, akin to *Nikē*: see NIKE] *Gr. Legend* a son of Oedipus and Jocasta: see SEVEN AGAINST THEBES

pol·y·no·mi·al (päl′i nō′mē əl) ***n.*** [POLY-[1] + (BI)NOMIAL] an expression or name consisting of more than two terms; specif., *a)* *Algebra* a linear combination of products of integral powers of a given set of variables, with constant coefficients (Ex.: $x^3 + 3x + 2$ or $x^2 - 2xy + y^2$) *b)* *Biol.* a species or subspecies name consisting of more than two terms —***adj.*** consisting of or characterized by polynomials

pol·y·nu·cle·ar (päl′i no͞o′klē ər, -nyo͞o′-) ***adj.*** [POLY-[1] + NUCLEAR] having many nuclei: also **pol′y·nu′cle·ate** (-it)

po·lyn·ya (pä lin′yə, päl′in yä′) ***n.*** [Russ *polyn'ja* < *polyj*, hollow] a usually oblong area of open water surrounded by sea ice

pol·y·o·le·fin (päl′ē ō′lə fin) ***n.*** [POLY-[1] + OLEFIN] any of a group of thermoplastic polymers, as polyethlylene or polypropylene, made from any simple alkene

pol·y·o·ma·vi·rus (päl′ē ō′mə vī′rəs) ***n.*** [POLY-[1] + -OMA + VIRUS] any of a genus (*Polyomavirus*) of papovaviruses that naturally infect wild and laboratory mice, and that cause tumors when injected into newborn mice

pol·yp (päl′ip) ***n.*** [Fr *polype* < L *polypus* < Gr *polypous* < *poly-*, POLY-[1] + *pous*, FOOT] **1** any of various cnidarians, colonial or individual, having a mouth fringed with many small, slender tentacles bearing stinging cells at the top of a tubelike body, as the sea anemone or hydra **2** a smooth projecting growth of hypertrophied mucous membrane in the nasal passages, bladder, rectum, etc.

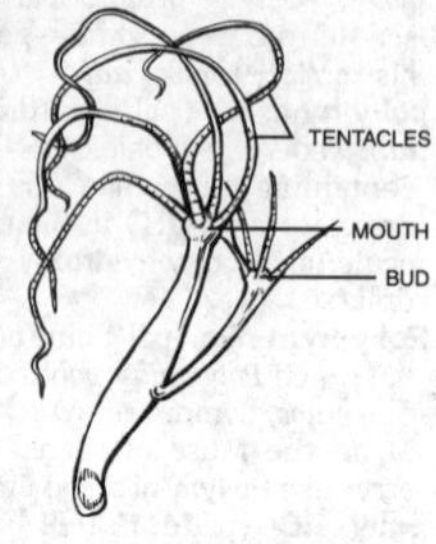

TENTACLES
MOUTH
BUD

polyp (hydra)

pol·y·par·y (päl′i per′ē) ***n.***, *pl.* **-par′ies** [ModL < L *polypus*, prec.] the common base or the connecting tissue to which each member of a colony of polyps is attached: also **pol′y·par′i·um** (-ē əm), *pl.* **-i·a** (-ə)

pol·y·pep·tide (päl′i pep′tīd′) ***n.*** [POLY-[1] + PEPTIDE] a substance containing two or more amino acids in the molecule joined together by peptide bonds

pol·y·pet·al·ous (päl′i pet′'l əs) ***adj.*** [POLY-[1] + PETALOUS] *Bot.* having separate petals

pol·y·pha·gi·a (päl′i fā′jə, -jē ə) ***n.*** [ModL < Gr < *poly-*, POLY-[1] + *phagein*, to eat: see -PHAGOUS] **1** excessive desire for food **2** the eating of or subsistence on many kinds of food —**po·lyph·a·gous** (pə lif′ə gəs) ***adj.***

pol·y·phase (päl′i fāz′) ***adj.*** *Elec.* powered by equal AC voltages or currents that are out of phase

Pol·y·phe·mus (päl′i fē′məs) ***n.*** in Homer's *Odyssey*, a Cyclops who confines Odysseus and his companions in a cave until Odysseus blinds him so that they can escape

☆**pol·y·phe·mus moth** (päl′i fē′məs) a large, brownish American silkworm moth (*Antheraea polyphemus*) with an eyelike spot on each hind wing

pol·y·phe·nol (päl′ē fē′nōl′) ***n.*** [POLY(MER) + PHENOL] a polymeric phenol derived from plants that acts as an antioxidant: it is present especially in red wine, green tea, and certain fruits and is thought to lower the risk and spread of cancer and heart disease

pol·y·phone (päl′i fōn′) ***n.*** *Phonet.* a polyphonic letter or other symbol, or a group of letters or symbols that is polyphonic

pol·y·phon·ic (päl′i fän′ik) ***adj.*** [Gr *polyphōnos*, having many tones: see POLY-[1] & -PHONE] **1** having or making many sounds **2** *Music* *a)* of or characterized by polyphony; contrapuntal *b)* that can produce more than one tone at a time, as a piano **3** *Phonet.* representing more than one sound: said as of the letter *c* as used in *cat* and in *cereal* Also **po·lyph·o·nous** (pə lif′ə nəs) —**pol′y·phon′i·cal·ly** ***adv.***

po·lyph·o·ny (pə lif′ə nē) ***n.*** [Gr *polyphōnia:* see POLY-[1] & -PHONY] **1** multiplicity of sounds, as in an echo **2** *Music* a combining of a number of independent but harmonizing melodies, as in a fugue or canon; counterpoint **3** *Phonet.* the representation of two or more sounds by the same letter, symbol, or group of symbols, as the group *th* as in *then* and in *thin*

pol·y·phy·let·ic (päl′i fī let′ik) ***adj.*** [POLY-[1] + PHYLETIC] *Biol.* derived from more than one ancestral type —**pol′y·phy·let′i·cal·ly** ***adv.***

pol·yp·ide (päl′ip īd′, -id) ***n.*** [POLYP + *-ide* (var. of -ID)] ZOOID (***n.*** 2)

pol·y·ploid (päl′i ploid′) ***adj.*** [POLY-[1] + -PLOID] having the number of chromosomes in the somatic cells three or more times the haploid number —***n.*** a polyploid cell or organism —**pol′y·ploi′dy** ***n.***

pol·y·po·dy (päl′i pō′dē) ***n.***, *pl.* **-dies** [ME *polipodye* < L *polypodium* < Gr *polypodion* < *poly-*, POLY-[1] + *pous* (gen. *podos*), FOOT: from its creeping rootstocks] any of a genus (*Polypodium*, family Polypodiaceae) of ferns with leathery pinnatifid leaves borne on creeping rootstocks

pol·yp·ous (päl′ip əs) ***adj.*** of or like a polyp

pol·y·pro·pyl·ene (päl′i prō′pə lēn′) ***n.*** [POLY(MER) + PROPYLENE] polymerized propylene, a very light, highly resistant, thermoplastic resin used to make coatings, plastic pipe, packaging material, fibers for clothing fabrics, etc.

pol·yp·tych (päl′ip tik′) ***n.*** [Gr *polyptychos*, having many folds < *poly-* (see POLY-[1]) + *ptyx*, a fold] a set of four or more panels with pictures, carvings, etc., often hinged for folding together, used as an altarpiece, etc.

pol·y·rhythm (päl′i rith′əm) ***n.*** [POLY-[1] + RHYTHM] *Music* **1** the use of strongly contrasting rhythms in simultaneous voice parts **2** such a rhythm: *usually used in pl.* —**pol′y·rhyth′mic** ***adj.***

pol·y·ri·bo·some (päl′i rī′bə sōm′) ***n.*** POLYSOME

pol·y·sac·cha·ride (päl′i sak′ə rīd′) ***n.*** [POLY-[1] + SACCHARIDE] any of a group of complex carbohydrates, as starch, that decompose by hydrolysis into a large number of monosaccharide units

pol·y·sa·pro·bic (-sə prō′bik) ***adj.*** [POLY-[1] + SAPROBIC] *Biol.* flourishing in a body of water having a heavy load of decomposed organic matter and almost no free oxygen

poly sci (päl′ē sī′) [Informal] *alt. sp. of* POLI SCI —**pol′y-sci′** ***adj.***

pol·y·se·my (päl′i sē′mē) ***n.*** [ModL *polysemia* < LL *polysemus*, having many meanings < Gr *polysēmos* < *poly-*, POLY-[1] + *sēma*, a sign: see SEMANTIC] the phenomenon of having or being open to several or many meanings —**pol′y·se′mic** (-mik) ***adj.***, **pol′y·se′mous** (-məs)

pol·y·some (päl′i sōm′) ***n.*** [POLY-[1] + -SOME[3]] a collection of ribosomes, probably connected by a single thread of RNA, in which protein synthesis occurs

pol·y·so·mic (päl′i sō′mik) ***adj.*** [< prec. + -IC] *Genetics* having two complete genomes with one or more extra chromosomes that do not form a set

pol·y·sty·rene (päl′i stī′rēn′) ***n.*** a tough, clear, colorless plastic material, a polymer of styrene, used to make chemical apparatus, containers, etc.

pol·y·sul·fide (päl′i sul′fīd′) ***n.*** [POLY-[1] + SULFIDE] a binary compound of sulfur containing more atoms of sulfur than the valence of the combining element requires

pol·y·syl·lab·ic (päl′i si lab′ik) ***adj.*** [ML *polysyllabus* < Gr *polysyllabos* < *poly-*, POLY-[1] + *syllabē*, SYLLABLE + -IC] **1** having several, esp. four or more, syllables **2** characterized by polysyllables Also **pol′y·syl·lab′i·cal** —**pol′y·syl·lab′i·cal·ly** ***adv.***

pol·y·syl·la·ble (päl′i sil′ə bəl) ***n.*** [ML *polysyllaba* < *polysyllabus:* see prec.] a polysyllabic word

pol·y·syn·de·ton (päl′i sin′də tän′, -tən) ***n.*** [ModL < neut. of LGr *polysyndetos*, using many conjunctions < Gr *poly-*, POLY-[1] + *syndetos*, bound together < *syndein*, to bind together: see SYNDETIC] *Rhetoric* the use or repetition of conjunctions in close succession

pol·y·tech·nic (-tek′nik) ***adj.*** [Fr *polytechnique* < Gr *polytechnos*, skilled in many arts < *poly-*, POLY-[1] + *technē:* see TECHNIC] of or providing instruction in many scientific and technical subjects —***n.*** a polytechnic school

pol·y·the·ism (päl′i thē iz′əm, päl′i thē′iz′əm) ***n.*** [Fr *polythéisme* < Gr *polytheos*, of many gods < *poly-*, many (see POLY-[1]) + *theos*, god: see THEO-] belief in or worship of many gods, or more than one god: opposed to MONOTHEISM —**pol′y·the·ist** (-ist) ***adj.***, ***n.*** —**pol′y·the·is′tic** ***adj.***, **pol′y·the·is′ti·cal** —**pol′y·the·is′ti·cal·ly** ***adv.***

pol·y·thene (päl′i thēn′) ***n.*** *chiefly Brit. var. of* POLYETHYLENE

pol·y·to·cous (pə lit′ə kəs) ***adj.*** [< Gr *polytokos*, bearing many offspring (< *poly-*, POLY-[1] + *tokos*, childbirth: see TOCOLOGY) + -OUS] having more than one offspring at a birth

pol·y·to·nal·i·ty (päl′i tō nal′ə tē) ***n.*** [POLY-[1] + TONALITY] *Music* the simultaneous use of two or more keys —**pol′y·ton′al** ***adj.*** —**pol′y·ton′al·ly** ***adv.***

pol·y·troph·ic (päl′i träf′ik, -trōf′-) ***adj.*** [< Gr *polytrophos*, nutritious < *poly-*, many (see POLY-[1]) + *trophos*, feeder < *trephein:* see TROPHIC] obtaining nourishment from more than one kind of organic material: said of many pathogenic bacteria

pol·y·typ·ic (päl′i tip′ik) ***adj.*** [POLY-[1] + -TYP(E) + -IC] **1** *Biol.* having or involving several different types, forms, or variations **2** *Taxonomy* of or pertaining to a category having two or more immediate subdivisions

pol·y·un·sat·u·rat·ed (päl′ē un sach′ə rāt′id) ***adj.*** **1** *Chem.* containing more than one double or triple bond in the molecule **2** designating any of certain vegetable and animal fats and oils with a low cholesterol content —**pol′y·un·sat′u·rate** (-rit) ***n.***

pol·y·u·re·thane (päl′ē yo͝or′ə thān′) ***n.*** any of various synthetic polymers produced by the polymerization of a hydroxyl (OH) radical and an NCO group from two different compounds: used in elastic fibers, cushions, insulation, molded products, coatings, etc.

pol·y·u·ri·a (päl′ē yo͝or′ē ə) ***n.*** [ModL: see POLY-[1] & -URIA] excessive urination, as in some diseases —**pol′y·u′ric** ***adj.***

pol·y·va·lent (päl′i vā′lənt) ***adj.*** **1** *Bacteriology* designating a vaccine effective against many strains of the same species of microorganism **2** *Chem.* *a)* having a valence of more than two *b)* having more than one valence —**pol′y·va′lence** ***n.***

pol·y·vi·nyl (päl′i vī′nəl) ***adj.*** [POLY-[2] + VINYL] designating or of any of a group of polymerized vinyl compounds

polyvinyl chloride PVC

pol·y·vi·nyl·i·dene (-vī nil′ə dēn′) ***adj.*** designating or of any of various polymerized vinylidene compounds

polyvinyl resin VINYL PLASTIC

pol·y·zo·an (päl′i zō′ən) ***n.*** [< POLY-[1] + -ZO(A) + -AN] BRYOZOAN

pol·y·zo·ar·i·um (-zō er′ē əm) ***n.***, *pl.* **-i·a** (-ə) [ModL: see POLY-[1] & -ZO(A) & -ARY] **1** a polyzoan colony **2** its supporting skeleton

Pom (päm) ***n.*** [Austral. & N.Z. Slang] *short for* POMMY: sometimes a derogatory usage

pom·ace (pum′is) ***n.*** [ML *pomacium*, cider < L *pomum*, fruit (in VL, apple)] **1** the crushed pulp of apples or other fruit pressed for juice **2** the crushed matter of anything pressed, as seed for oil

po·ma·ceous (pō mā′shəs) ***adj.*** [ModL *pomaceus* < L *pomum:* see prec.] of or like apples or other pomes

po·made (pä mād′, pō-; pä mäd′, pä′mād′) ***n.*** [Fr *pommade* < It *pomata* < *pomo*, apple < VL **pomum* < L, fruit: orig. perfumed with apple pulp] a perfumed ointment, esp. for grooming the hair: also **po·ma·tum** (pō māt′əm) —***vt.*** **-mad′ed**, **-mad′ing** to apply pomade to

po·man·der (pō′man′dər, pō man′-) ***n.*** ⟦earlier *pomamber* < MFr *pome ambre, pomme d'ambre* < *pome* (see fol.) + *ambre,* amber⟧ **1** *a)* a ball of aromatic substances, as perfumed powder, dried herbs, etc.: originally a supposed safeguard against infection, now placed in drawers, closets, etc. to scent clothing or linens *b)* an ornamental case for carrying or holding this **2** a clove-studded orange, lemon, or apple, serving as an aromatic decoration

pome (pōm) ***n.*** ⟦OFr < VL **poma* < L *pomum,* fruit⟧ *Bot.* a fleshy fruit, as an apple or pear, having united carpels surrounded by a fleshy, usually edible receptacle

pome·gran·ate (päm′gran′it, päm′ə-; pum′-) ***n.*** ⟦ME *pomegarnet* < OFr *pome grenate* < *pome* (see prec.) + *granade* < L *granatum,* pomegranate, lit., having seeds, neut. of *granatus* < *granum,* seed, GRAIN⟧ **1** a round fruit with a red, leathery rind and many seeds covered with red, juicy, edible flesh **2** the bush or small tree (genus *Punica,* esp. *P. granatum*) of the pomegranate family that bears it ***—adj.*** designating a family (Punicaceae, order Myrtales) of dicotyledonous shrubs and small trees

pom·e·lo (päm′ə lō′) ***n., pl.* -los′** ⟦altered (prob. based on POME) < earlier *pomplemous* < Du *pompelmoes,* shaddock⟧ GRAPEFRUIT

Pom·er·a·ni·a (päm′ər ā′nē ə) region in central Europe, on the Baltic, now divided between Poland & Germany

Pom·er·a·ni·an (päm′ər ā′nē ən) ***adj.*** of Pomerania or its people or culture ***—n.*** **1** a person born or living in Pomerania **2** any of a breed of toy dog, developed in Pomerania, with long, coarse hair of a solid color and a bushy tail turned over the back

pom·fret (päm′frət, pum′-) ***n.*** any of a family (Bramidae) of edible, marine percoid fishes

po·mif·er·ous (pō mif′ər əs) ***adj.*** ⟦< L *pomum,* fruit + -FEROUS⟧ bearing fruit, esp. pomes

pom·mel (päm′əl; *for v.* pum′əl) ***n.*** ⟦ME *pomel* < OFr dim. of *pome,* apple: see POME⟧ **1** the knob on the end of the hilt of some swords and daggers **2** the rounded, upward-projecting front part of a saddle ***—vt.* -meled** or **-melled, -mel·ing** or **-mel·ling** PUMMEL

pommel horse *Gym.* **1** a piece of equipment consisting of a HORSE (*n.* 9) with two U-shaped or rounded handles on top, used for acrobatic routines **2** an event in which a male gymnast performs a routine on such a horse

Pom·mern (pôm′ərn) *Ger. name for* POMERANIA

pommes frites (pôm frēt′) ⟦Fr, fried potatoes < pl. of *pomme,* potato (short for *pomme de terre,* lit., apple of the earth) + fem. pl. of *frit,* pp. of *frire,* to fry < OFr < L *frigere:* see FRY[1]⟧ [*also in roman type*] FRENCH FRIES

Pom·my or **Pom·mie** (päm′ē) [Austral. & N.Z. Slang] [*also* **p-**] ***n., pl.* -mies** ⟦< ?⟧ a British person ***—adj.*** British ➥Sometimes a derogatory usage

po·mo (pō′mō′) [Informal] ***adj.*** ⟦PO(ST)MO(DERN)⟧ *short for* POSTMODERN: sometimes **po′-mo′** ***—n.*** *short for* POSTMODERNISM

po·mol·o·gy (pō mäl′ə jē) ***n.*** ⟦ModL *pomologia:* see POME & -LOGY⟧ the science of fruit cultivation **—po′mo·log′i·cal** (-mə läj′i kəl) ***adj.*** **—po·mol′o·gist *n.***

Po·mo·na[1] (pə mō′nə) ***n.*** ⟦L < *pomum,* fruit⟧ *Rom. Myth.* the goddess of fruits and fruit trees

Po·mo·na[2] (pə mō′nə) **1** ⟦after the Roman goddess⟧ city in S Calif., east of Los Angeles **2** MAINLAND (Orkney Islands)

pomp (pämp) ***n.*** ⟦ME < MFr *pompe* < L *pompa* < Gr *pompē,* solemn procession < *pempein,* to send⟧ **1** stately or brilliant display; splendor **2** ostentatious show or display **3** [Obs.] a pageant

pom·pa·dour (päm′pə dôr′) ***n.*** ⟦after fol.⟧ **1** a woman's hairdo in which the hair is swept up high from the forehead, usually over a roll ☆**2** a man's hairdo in which the hair is brushed up high from the forehead

Pom·pa·dour (päm′pə dôr′, -door′; *Fr* pōn pȧ door′), Madame **de** (born *Jeanne Antoinette Poisson*) 1721-64; mistress of Louis XV

☆**pom·pa·no** (päm′pə nō′) ***n., pl.* -no′** or **-nos′** ⟦Sp *pámpano,* a kind of fish, tendril < L *pampinus,* tendril, young shoot⟧ any of various edible, marine North American and West Indian jackfishes (esp. genus *Trachinotus*) with spiny fins and a widely forked tail

Pom·pa·no Beach (päm′pə nō′) ⟦after prec.⟧ city on the SE coast of Fla.

Pom·peii (päm pā′, -pā′ē) ancient city in S Italy, on the Bay of Naples: destroyed by the eruption of Mount Vesuvius (A.D. 79) **—Pom·pei′an** (-pā′ən) ***adj., n.***

Pom·pey (päm′pē, -pā) (L. name *Gnaeus Pompeius Magnus*) 106-48 B.C.; Rom. general & triumvir

pom·pom (päm′päm′) ***n.*** ⟦altered < *pompon*⟧ an ornamental ball or tuft of silk, wool, feathers, etc., as used on clothing or draperies or waved in pairs by cheerleaders

pom-pom (päm′päm′) ***n.*** ⟦echoic⟧ any of several rapid-firing automatic weapons, as an automatic cannon of the Boer War or an antiaircraft cannon of WWII: also **pom′pom′**

pom·pon (päm′pän′) ***n.*** ⟦Fr < MFr *pomper,* to exhibit pomp < *pompe:* see POMP⟧ **1** *var. of* POMPOM **2** *a)* any of various chrysanthemums, dahlias, etc. with small, round flower heads *b)* the flower head

pom·pos·i·ty (päm päs′ə tē) ***n.*** ⟦ME *pomposite* < LL *pompositas:* see fol. & -ITY⟧ **1** the quality of being pompous; ostentation; self-importance **2** *pl.* **-ties** a pompous act, remark, etc.

pom·pous (päm′pəs) ***adj.*** ⟦ME < MFr *pompeus* < LL *pomposus* < L *pompa:* see POMP⟧ **1** [Archaic] full of pomp; stately **2** characterized by exaggerated stateliness; pretentious, as in speech or manner; self-important **—pom′pous·ly *adv.*** **—pom′pous·ness *n.***

☆**Pon·ca** (päŋ′kə) ***n.*** ⟦Ponca *paⁿka,* self-designation⟧ **1** *pl.* **-cas** or **-ca** a member of a North American Indian people living in Nebraska and Oklahoma **2** the Siouan language of this people, a dialect of Omaha ***—adj.*** of the Poncas or their language or culture

ponce (päns) ***n., vi.* ponced, ponc′ing** ⟦Brit slang < ? *pounce on*⟧ [Slang, Chiefly Brit.] PIMP

Pon·ce (pôn′se) ⟦after Juan *Ponce* de León y Loaiza (great-grandson of fol.), who founded it (*c.* 1692)⟧ seaport in S Puerto Rico

Pon·ce de Le·ón (pan′sə dā lē ōn′, -də lē′ən; *Sp* pôn′the *the* le ôn′), **Juan** 1460?-1521; Sp. explorer: discovered Florida while seeking the Fountain of Youth

Pon·chi·el·li (pän′kē el′ē, pôn′-; *It* pôn kyel′lē), **A·mil·ca·re** (ä mēl′kä *re*′) 1834-86; It. operatic composer

pon·cho (pän′chō) ***n., pl.* -chos** ⟦AmSp < Araucanian, woolen cloth⟧ **1** a cloak like a blanket with a hole in the middle for the head, worn in Spanish America **2** any similar garment, esp. a waterproof one worn as a raincoat

pond (pänd) ***n.*** ⟦ME *ponde,* artificially enclosed body of water, form of *pounde,* POUND[3]⟧ a body of water smaller than a lake, often artificially formed **—the pond** the N Atlantic Ocean: a humorous usage

pon·der (pän′dər) ***vt.*** ⟦ME *ponderen* < MFr *ponderer* < L *ponderare,* to weigh < *pondus* (gen. *ponderis*), weight: see POUND[1]⟧ to weigh mentally; think deeply about; consider carefully ***—vi.*** to think deeply; deliberate; meditate **—pon′der·er *n.***

pon·der·a·ble (-ə bəl) ***adj.*** ⟦LL *ponderabilis* < L *ponderare:* see prec.⟧ **1** that can be weighed **2** that can be mentally weighed; appreciable **—pon′der·a·bil′i·ty *n.***

☆**pon·der·o·sa (pine)** (pän′dər ō′sə) ⟦< ModL (*Pinus*) *ponderosa,* lit., heavy (pine) < L *ponderosus:* see fol.⟧ **1** a yellow pine (*Pinus ponderosa*) of W North America, valued for its timber **2** its wood

pon·der·ous (pän′dər əs) ***adj.*** ⟦ME < L *ponderosus* < *pondus,* a weight: see POUND[1]⟧ **1** very heavy **2** unwieldy because of weight **3** that seems heavy; bulky; massive **4** labored and dull [*a ponderous* joke] **—*SYN.*** HEAVY **—pon′der·ous·ly *adv.*** **—pon′der·ous·ness *n.*,** **pon′der·os′i·ty** (-äs′ə tē)

Pon·di·cher·ry (pän′di cher′ē) **1** territory of SE India, chiefly on the Coromandel Coast: before 1954 a part of French India: 190 sq mi (492 sq km) **2** its capital Fr. name **Pon·di·ché·ry** (pōn dē shā *rē*′)

☆**pond lily** WATERLILY

pond scum a mass of filamentous algae forming a green scum on the surface of ponds, etc.

pond·weed (pänd′wēd′) ***n.*** any of a genus (*Potamogeton*) of water plants of the pondweed family, having submerged or floating leaves and spikes of inconspicuous flowers ***—adj.*** designating a family (Potamogetonaceae, order Najadales) of monocotyledonous water plants, including eelgrass

☆**pone**[1] (pōn) ***n.*** ⟦Virginia Algonquian *poan, appoans, apones*⟧ [Chiefly South] **1** bread or cake, esp. corn bread, in the form of small, oval loaves **2** such a loaf or cake

pone[2] (pō′nē) ***n.*** ⟦< L *pone,* imper. of *ponere,* to place: see POSITION⟧ [Now Rare] in various card games, the player to the right of the dealer or, in two-handed games, the player who is not the dealer

pong (pôŋ) ***vi., n.*** ⟦prob. < Romany *pan,* to stink⟧ [Brit. Informal] STINK

pon·gee (pän jē′, pun-; pän′jē) ***n.*** ⟦< Mandarin Chin dial. *pen-chi,* one's own loom⟧ **1** a soft, thin cloth of Chinese or Indian silk, usually left in its natural light-brown color **2** any cloth like this

pon·gid (pän′jid) ***n.*** ⟦< ModL *Pongidae* < Kongo *mpongi* + -IDAE⟧ a great ape

pon·iard (pän′yərd) ***n.*** ⟦Fr *poignard,* altered < MFr *poignal* < VL **pugnalis* < L *pugnus,* fist: see PUGNACIOUS⟧ a dagger ***—vt.*** to stab with a poniard

pons (pänz) ***n., pl.* pon·tes** (pän′tēz′) ⟦ModL < L, bridge < IE base **pent-,* to step, go > FIND⟧ *Anat., Zool.* a piece of connecting tissue; specif., the bridge of white matter at the base of the brain, containing neural connections between the cerebrum, cerebellum, and medulla oblongata

pons as·i·no·rum (pänz′ as′i nō′rəm) ⟦ModL, lit., bridge of asses⟧ **1** *Geom.* the fifth proposition of the first book of Euclid (that the base angles of an isosceles triangle are equal) **2** any problem hard for beginners

pons Va·ro·li·i (və rō′lē ī′) ⟦after Costanzo *Varoli* (1542-75), It anatomist⟧ PONS

Pon·ta Del·ga·da (pôn′tə *the*l gä′*th*ə; *E* pän′tə del gä′də) seaport on São Miguel Island, the Azores

Pont·char·train (pän′chər trān′), **Lake** ⟦after Louis, Comte de *Pontchartrain* (1643-1727), Fr statesman & explorer⟧ shallow saltwater lake in SE La.: 625 sq mi (1,619 sq km)

Pon·ti·ac (pän′tē ak′) 1720?-69; Ottawa Indian chief

Pon·ti·a·nak (pän′tē ä′näk′) seaport in W Kalimantan, Indonesia, on the South China Sea

Pon·tic (pän′tik) ***adj.*** ⟦L *Ponticus* < Gr *Pontikos* < *pontos,* sea (esp. the Black Sea), orig., path: for IE base see PONS⟧ **1** of Pontus **2** of the Black Sea

pon·ti·fex (pänt′i feks′) ***n., pl.* pon·tif·i·ces** (pän tif′i sēz′) ⟦L: see fol.⟧ in ancient Rome, a member of the supreme college of priests (**Pontifical College**)

pon·tiff (pän′tif) ***n.*** ⟦Fr *pontife* < LL(Ec) *pontifex* (gen. *pontificis*), bishop < L, high priest, orig. ? bridge maker, path finder < *pons* (gen. *pontis*), bridge (see PONS) + *facere,* to make, DO[1]⟧ **1** PONTIFEX **2** *a)* a bishop *b)* [**P-**] the pope (in full **Supreme Pontiff**) **3** a high priest

pon·tif·i·cal (pän tif′i kəl) ***adj.*** ⟦ME *pontificall* < L *pontificalis* < *pontifex:* see prec.⟧ **1** having to do with a pontifex or a high priest **2** having to do with or celebrated by a bishop or other high-ranking prelate [*a pontifical* Mass] **3** having to do with the pope; papal **4** having the pomp, dignity, or dogmatism of a pontiff; sometimes, specif., arrogant or haughty —*n.* **1** [*pl.*] a pontiff's vestments and insignia **2** a book of offices for a bishop

pon·tif·i·cate (pän tif′i kit, -kāt′; *for v.,* -kāt′) *n.* ⟦L *pontificatus* < *pontifex:* see PONTIFF⟧ the office, or term of office, of a pontiff —*vi.* **-cat′ed, -cat′ing** ⟦< ML *pontificatus*, pp. of *pontificare*⟧ **1** to officiate as a pontiff **2** to speak or act in a pompous or dogmatic way —**pon·tif′i·ca′tor** *n.*

pon·til (pän′til) *n.* ⟦Fr: see PUNTY⟧ PUNTY

Pon·tine Marshes (pän′tēn′, -tīn′) region in central Italy, southeast of Rome: formerly swampy, now reclaimed

Pontius Pilate *see* PILATE, Pontius

pon·to·nier (pän′tə nir′) *n.* ⟦Fr *pontonnier*⟧ a military engineer or other member of the armed forces who builds, or is in charge of building, a pontoon bridge

pon·toon (pän to͞on′) *n.* ⟦Fr *ponton* < L *ponto* < *pons* (gen. *pontis*), a bridge: see PONS⟧ **1** a flat-bottomed boat **2** any of a number of these, or of some other floating objects, as hollow cylinders, used as supports for a temporary bridge (**pontoon bridge**) **3** either of two floats, as on the landing gear of some airplanes, for landing on water Also ☆**pon′ton** (-tən)

Pon·tor·mo (pôn tôr′mō), **Ja·co·po da** (yä kô′pō dä) (born *Jacopo Carrucci*) 1494-1557?; It. painter

Pon·tus (pän′təs) ⟦L < Gr *Pontos:* see PONTIC⟧ ancient kingdom in NE Asia Minor, on the Pontus Euxinus

Pontus Eux·i·nus (yo͝ok sī′nəs, -sē′nəs) *Latin name for* the BLACK SEA

po·ny (pō′nē) *n., pl.* **-nies** ⟦Scot *powny*, prob. < OFr *poulenet*, dim. of *poulain*, a colt, foal < VL *pullamen*, young animals < L *pullus*, young animal, FOAL⟧ **1** a horse of any of a number of small breeds, usually not over 58 inches high at the withers **2** *a)* something small of its kind ☆*b)* a small liqueur glass or the amount it will hold, typically 1 ounce ☆**3** ⟦? alteration of PONS (ASINORUM)⟧ [Informal] a literal translation of a work in a foreign language, used in doing schoolwork, often dishonestly; crib **4** [Informal] any young horse; foal ☆**5** [Slang] a racehorse **6** [Brit. Slang] the sum of twenty-five pounds —☆*vt., vi.* **-nied, -ny·ing** [Slang] to pay (money), as to settle an account: with *up*

☆**pony express** a system of carrying and delivering mail by riders on swift ponies; specif., such a system in operation from April, 1860, to October, 1861, between St. Joseph, Mo., and Sacramento, Calif.

po·ny·tail (pō′nē tāl′) *n.* a hairstyle in which the hair is gathered and bound at the back of the head and left to hang down: also written **pony tail**

☆**Pon·zi scheme (***or* **game)** (pän′zē) ⟦after C. K. Ponzi (1882-1949), It immigrant to the U.S. who committed investment fraud⟧ a fraudulent investment scheme in which funds paid in by later investors are used to pay artificially high returns to the original investors, thus attracting more new investors and inducing earlier investors to venture even more money

pon·zu (pän′zo͞o′) *n.* ⟦Jpn, alteration (infl. by *-zu*, comb. form of *su*, vinegar) of *ponsu*, mixed drink containing citrus juice < Du *pons*, punch < E PUNCH[3]⟧ a Japanese sauce typically made from rice vinegar, bonito flakes, sweet sake, citrus juice, and often soy sauce

poo (po͞o) *n., vi.* [Slang] *alt. sp. of* POOH[2]

-poo (po͞o) *suffix* forming adjectives and nouns with diminutive force, often disparaging: added to adjectives and nouns, esp. those ending in *-y* or *-ie* [*cutesy-poo, icky-poo*]

☆**pooch**[1] (po͞och) *n.* ⟦< ?⟧ [Informal] a dog

pooch[2] (po͞och) *vt., vi.* [Informal] *used only in the phrase* **pooch out**, to (cause to) protrude, or bulge outward

pood (po͞od) *n.* ⟦Russ *pud* < LowG *pund* < L *pondo*, POUND[1]⟧ a Russian unit of weight, equal to 36.11 pounds (16.38 kilograms)

poo·dle (po͞od′'l) *n.* ⟦Ger *pudel* < LowG *pudel(hund)* < *pudeln*, to splash (akin to PUDDLE) + *hund*, dog: see HOUND[1]⟧ any of a breed of dog with a curly coat in a solid color, usually clipped in one of a variety of patterns: the breed has three varieties differing only in size — *standard*, over 15 in (38 cm) high at the shoulder; *miniature*, 15 in or under but over 10 in (25.4 cm); *toy*, 10 in or under

poof[1] (po͞of, po͝of) *interj.* ⟦echoic of a sudden discharge⟧ **1** used to express suddenness of disappearance. appearance, etc. **2** POOH[1]

poof[2] (po͝of, po͞of) [Brit. Slang] *n.* a male homosexual: a dismissive and offensive term: also **poof′ter** —**poof′y** *adj.*

poo·gle (po͞og′'l) *n.* ⟦< POODLE + BEAGLE⟧ a dog crossbred from a poodle and a beagle

pooh[1] (po͞o) *interj.* ⟦echoic of blowing away⟧ used to express disdain, disbelief, or impatience

pooh[2] (po͞o) *n., vi.* [Slang] *var. of* POOP[3] (*n.* 1 & *vi.*)

pooh-bah (po͞o′bä′) *n.* ⟦after *Pooh-Bah*, a character in Gilbert & Sullivan's *The Mikado* (1885) < POOH[1] + BAH⟧ [Informal] an official or leader who maintains full control as by holding several offices

pooh-pooh (po͞o′po͞o′) *vt.* ⟦redupl. of POOH[1]⟧ to minimize or treat disdainfully; make light of; belittle

pool[1] (po͞ol) *n.* ⟦ME < OE *pol*, akin to Du *poel* & Ger *pfuhl*, prob. ult. < IE base **bhel-*, to shine, glimmer⟧ **1** a small pond, as in a garden **2** a small collection of liquid, as a puddle **3** SWIMMING POOL **4** a deep, still spot in a river ☆**5** a natural, isolated, underground accumulation of oil or gas —*vi.* to form, or accumulate in, a pool

pool[2] (po͞ol) *n.* ⟦Fr *poule*, pool, stakes, orig. hen < LL *pulla*, hen, fem. of L *pullus* (see POULTRY): assoc. in E with prec.⟧ **1** the total amount of the players' stakes played for, as in a single deal of a card game; pot **2** *a)* [Brit.] a game of billiards for such a pool *b)* any of various games related to billiards played typically with object balls numbered from one to fifteen and a cue ball, on a POOL TABLE: the object is to pocket a ball or balls **3** a combination of resources, funds, etc. for some common purpose; specif., ☆*a)* the combined wagers of bettors on a horse race, participants in a lottery, etc., the gains or losses from which are to be divided proportionately *b)* the combined investments of a group of persons or corporations undertaking, and sharing responsibility for, a joint enterprise ☆*c)* a common fund of stockholders, for speculation, manipulation of prices, etc. *d)* the persons or parties forming any such combination ☆**4** a combination of business firms for creating a monopoly in a particular market; trust **5** *a)* a collection of equipment and group of trained personnel, utilized and shared by a group [*a motor pool*] *b)* an informal group of people sharing in some task or responsibility [*a car pool*] —*vt., vi.* ☆to contribute to a pool, or common fund; make a common interest or form a pool (of)

Poole (po͞ol) seaport in Dorsetshire, SE England

☆**pool·room** (po͞ol′ro͞om′) *n.* **1** a room or establishment where pool is played: also **pool hall 2** [Now Rare] a room where bets are placed with a bookmaker

☆**pool·side** (po͞ol′sīd′) *n.* the area adjacent to a swimming pool, often furnished with chaise longues, tables, etc. — *adv., adj.* at or in the poolside [*to dine poolside*]

pool table a table like a billiard table but having a pocket at each corner and at the middle of both sides, for playing pool

poon (po͞on) *n.* ⟦Sinhalese *pūna*⟧ **1** any of several East Indian trees (genus *Calophyllum*) of the St. Johnswort family, whose seeds yield a bitter oil **2** the wood of any of these trees, used esp. in ships, cabinetwork, etc.

Poo·na (po͞o′nə) *alt. sp. of* PUNE

☆**poon·tang** (po͞on′taŋ′) *n.* ⟦prob. altered from Fr *putain*, prostitute⟧ [Vulgar Slang] **1** sexual intercourse with a woman **2** a woman or women collectively regarded only as a sexual partner: a disparaging or dismissive term

poop[1] (po͞op) *n.* ⟦LME *pouppe* < MFr *poupe* < Prov *popa* or It *poppa* < L *puppis*, stern of a ship⟧ **1** the stern section of a ship **2** on sailing ships, a raised deck at the stern: also **poop deck** —*vt.* to break over the poop or stern of: said of following waves

poop[2] (po͞op) [Slang] *vt.* ⟦via dial. < ME *puopen*, to make an abrupt sound, blow, gulp: orig. echoic⟧ to cause to become exhausted, out of breath, etc.; tire: usually in the passive voice —☆**poop out 1** to become exhausted **2** to cease functioning

poop[3] (po͞op) [Informal] *n.* ⟦prob. < vulgar *poop*, to break wind, defecate, feces (< ME *puopen:* see prec.)⟧ **1** excrement; feces ☆**2** the pertinent facts, esp. current inside information —*vi.* to defecate

poop[4] (po͞op) *n.* [Slang] a foolish or contemptible person

☆**poop·er-scoop·er** (po͞o′pər sko͞o′pər) *n.* ⟦redupl. based on POOP[3] + SCOOP (*vt.*)⟧ a scoop for picking up feces dropped by a dog or other pet, as on a city street

Po·o·pó (pô′ô pô′), **Lake** shallow saltwater lake in WC Bolivia: 970 sq mi (2,512 sq km); elevation, *c.* 12,000 ft (3,658 m)

poo-poo (po͞o′po͞o′) *n.* [Slang] excrement: a child's term, now also used in other contexts

☆**poop sheet** ⟦see POOP[3], *n.* 2⟧ a concise compilation of facts or data about a particular subject or subjects

poor (po͝or, pôr) *adj.* ⟦ME *pore* < OFr *povre* < L *pauper*, poor < IE base **pōu-*, small > FEW, FOAL⟧ **1** *a)* lacking material possessions; having little or no means to support oneself; needy; impoverished *b)* indicating or characterized by poverty **2** lacking in some quality or thing; specif., *a)* lacking abundance; scanty; inadequate [*poor crops*] *b)* lacking productivity; barren; sterile [*poor soil*] *c)* lacking nourishment; feeble; emaciated [*a poor body*] *d)* lacking excellence or worth; below average, inferior, bad, etc. or paltry, mean, insignificant, etc. *e)* lacking good moral or mental qualities; mean-spirited; contemptible *f)* lacking pleasure, comfort, or satisfaction [*to have a poor time*] *g)* lacking skill **3** worthy of pity; unfortunate —**the poor** poor, or needy, people collectively —**poor′ness** *n.*

SYN.—**poor** is the simple, direct term for one who lacks the resources for reasonably comfortable living; **impoverished** is applied to one who having once had plenty is now reduced to poverty [*an impoverished aristocrat*]; **destitute** implies such great poverty that the means for mere subsistence, such as food and shelter, are lacking [*left destitute by the war*]; **impecunious** applies to one in a habitual state of poverty and suggests that this results from personal practices [*an impecunious gambler*]; **indigent** implies such relative poverty as results in a lack of luxuries and the endurance of hardships [*books for indigent children*] —*ANT.* **rich, wealthy**

poor box a box, as in a church, for alms for the poor

☆**poor-boy** (po͝or′boi′) *n.* ⟦so named prob. from its large size and low cost⟧ HERO SANDWICH: in full **poor′-boy′ sandwich**

☆**poor farm** [Historical] a farm for paupers, supported by a county or other local government

poor·house (po͝or′hous′) *n.* [Historical] a house or institution for paupers, supported from public funds

poo·ri (po͝or′ē) *n. alt. sp. of* PURI

poor laws *Eng. History* laws that provide for public relief and assistance for the poor

poor·ly (po͝or′lē) *adv.* **1** in a poor manner, as scantily, badly, or defectively **2** with a low opinion; disparagingly [*thought poorly of it*] —*adj.* [Informal] in poor health

poor-mouth (po͝or′mouth′, -mouth′) *vi.* [Informal] to complain about one's lack of money; plead poverty

poor-spir·it·ed (po͝or′spir′it id) ***adj.*** having or showing a poor spirit; cowardly; timorous; abject

☆**poor white** a white person, esp. one born or living in the S U.S., who lives in great poverty and ignorance: often an offensive term

Poot·er·ish (po͞ot′ər ish) ***adj.*** ⟦after Mr. *Pooter,* hero of the humorous Eng novel *The Diary of a Nobody* (1892) by G. & W. Grossmith⟧ [Brit.] of or like a type of middle-class person regarded as unimaginative, conventional, self-important, etc.

poove (po͞ov) ***n.*** [Brit. Slang] *var. of* POOF²: a dismissive and, often, offensive term

pop¹ (päp) ***n.*** ⟦ME *poppe:* echoic⟧ **1** a sudden short, light explosive sound **2** a shot as with a revolver or rifle **3** any carbonated, nonalcoholic beverage: from the sound produced when the cork or cap is removed from the bottle **4** a frozen confection consisting of ice cream or flavored ice on the end of a small stick ☆**5** *Baseball* a ball hit high in the air, usually not beyond the infield —***vi.*** **popped, pop′ping 1** to make, or burst with, a short, light, explosive sound **2** to move, go, come, etc. suddenly and, usually, unexpectedly: often with *up* [to *pop* into a room; new problems kept *popping* up] **3** to open wide suddenly, or protrude, as with amazement: said of the eyes **4** to shoot a firearm ☆**5** *Baseball* to hit the ball high into the air, usually not beyond the infield: often with *out* or *up* **6** [Slang] to offer to pay: with *for* [I'll *pop* for lunch] —***vt.*** ⟦ME *poppen*⟧ ☆**1** to cause to pop: said as of popcorn when it is heated **2** *a)* to fire (a pistol, etc.) *b)* to shoot **3** to put suddenly, quickly, or unexpectedly [to *pop* one's head in at the door] ☆**4** [Slang] to swallow (a pill, capsule, etc.) ☆**5** *Baseball* to hit (the ball) high in the air, usually not beyond the infield —***adv.*** with or like a pop —☆**a pop** [Slang] for each one; per person, per attempt, etc. [we paid $5 *a pop* to get in; a punter averaging 40 yards *a pop*] —**pop off** [Informal] **1** to die suddenly ☆**2** to speak or write thoughtlessly, emotionally, or angrily **3** [Chiefly Brit.] to leave hastily —**pop the question** [Informal] to propose marriage

☆**pop**² (päp) ***n.*** ⟦contr. < *poppa,* var. of PAPA⟧ [Informal] **1** FATHER **2** familiar term of address to any elderly man: also **pops** (päps)

pop³ (päp) ***adj.*** **1** *a)* designating or of music popular with the general public [a *pop* singer, a *pop* album] *b)* POPS¹ **2** intended for the popular taste, esp. as exploited commercially [*pop* culture, *pop* psychology] ☆**3** designating or of a representational art style, esp. in painting and sculpture, using techniques and popular subjects adapted from commercial art, such as comic strips, posters, etc., and the mass media [a *pop* artist] —***n.*** **1** *a)* pop music *b)* a pop song, concert, etc.: see also POPS¹ **2** pop culture ☆**3** pop art

pop⁴ *abbrev.* **1** popular **2** popularly **3** population

POP *abbrev.* point of purchase

☆**pop·corn** (päp′kôrn′) ***n.*** **1** a variety of Indian corn with small ears and hard, pointed grains which pop open into a white, puffy mass when heated **2** the popped grains, usually salted and buttered for eating

☆**popcorn stitch** a crochet stitch made with a number of loose stitches fastened in a common base so that the yarn puffs up, looking much like a piece of popcorn

pope (pōp) ***n.*** ⟦ME < OE *papa* < LL(Ec), a bishop, pope < Gr(Ec) *papas,* bishop < Gr *pappas:* see PAPA⟧ **1** [*often* **P-**] *R.C.Ch.* the bishop of Rome and head of the Church **2** a person regarded as having, or acting as though he has, popelike authority **3** *Eastern Orthodox Ch.* a parish priest —**pope′dom** ***n.***

Pope (pōp) **1 Alexander** 1688-1744; Eng. poet **2 John** 1822-92; Union general in the Civil War

pop·er·y (pōp′ər ē) ***n.*** ⟦POP(E) + -ERY⟧ the doctrines and rituals of the Roman Catholic Church: a hostile term

☆**pop·eyed** (päp′īd′) ***adj.*** having wide, protruding eyes

☆**pop fly** *Baseball* a ball hit high in the air, often, specif., one hit just beyond the infield

pop·gun (päp′gun′) ***n.*** a toy gun that shoots a harmless plug, typically of cork, from the end of the barrel with a popping sound

pop·in·jay (päp′in jā′) ***n.*** ⟦ME *papejai* < MFr *papagai,* altered (infl. by *gai:* see JAY¹) < Ar *babghā′, babbaghā′* < a WAfr language: of echoic orig.⟧ **1** a parrot **2** [Obs.] a target consisting of a wooden parrot on a pole **3** a talkative, conceited person

pop·ish (pōp′ish) ***adj.*** having to do with popery; characteristic of the Roman Catholic Church: a hostile term —**pop′ish·ly** ***adv.*** —**pop′ish·ness** ***n.***

Popish Plot *see* OATES, Titus

pop·lar (päp′lər) ***n.*** ⟦ME *popler* < OFr *poplier* < *peuple* < L *populus*⟧ **1** any of a genus (*Populus*) of trees of the willow family, having soft, fibrous wood, rapid growth, alternate leaves, and flowers borne in catkins **2** the wood of any of these trees **3** *a)* TULIP TREE *b)* TULIPWOOD (sense 1)

Pop·lar (päp′lər) former metropolitan borough of E London, now part of Tower Hamlets

pop·lin (päp′lin) ***n.*** ⟦Fr *papeline,* prob. altered < *(draps de) Poperinghes,* (cloths from) *Poperinge,* city in Flanders, textile center in the Middle Ages⟧ a sturdy fabric of cotton, silk, rayon, etc., in plain weave with fine cross ribbing, used for raincoats, sportswear, etc.

pop·lit·e·al (päp lit′ē əl, päp′li tē′əl) ***adj.*** ⟦< ModL *popliteus* (< L *poples,* gen. *poplitis,* ham of the knee) + -AL⟧ of or near that part of the leg behind the knee

Po·po·ca·té·petl (pô pô′kä te′pet′'l; *E* pō′pə kat′ə pet′'l) volcano in SC Mexico, in W Puebla state: 17,887 ft (5,452 m)

☆**pop·o·ver** (päp′ō′vər) ***n.*** a very light, puffy, hollow muffin that rises over the rim of the baking tin

pop·pa·dom or **pop·pa·dum** (pä′pä dəm) ***n.*** *alt. sp. of* PAPADUM

pop·per (päp′ər) ***n.*** **1** a person or thing that pops ☆**2** a covered wire basket or pan for popping corn ☆**3** [Slang] a capsule containing amyl nitrite or, now more commonly, butyl nitrite, used as a stimulant

Pop·per (päp′ər), Sir **Karl (Raimund)** 1902-94; Brit. philosopher, born in Austria

pop·pet (päp′it) ***n.*** ⟦var. of PUPPET⟧ **1** TAILSTOCK **2** a valve that moves into and from its seat: often cam-driven and spring-loaded for a rapid repeating, popping action as in a gasoline engine: in full **poppet valve 3** any of certain timbers used to support a ship about to be launched **4** *a)* [Obs.] a doll *b)* [Brit. Informal] a term of endearment, as for a child or sweetheart

pop·pied (päp′ēd) ***adj.*** **1** covered with poppies **2** drugging or drugged, as by opium

pop·ping crease (päp′iŋ) *Cricket* a line beyond which the batsman may not go

popping plug a fishing lure that makes a popping sound when pulled along the surface of the water

pop·ple¹ (päp′əl) ***n.*** *dial. var. of* POPLAR (senses 1 & 2)

pop·ple² (päp′əl) ***vi.*** **-pled, -pling** ⟦ME *poplen,* prob. of echoic orig.⟧ to heave, toss, bubble, or ripple, as water in a choppy sea —***n.*** the action of poppling

pop·py (päp′ē) ***n., pl.*** **-pies** ⟦ME *popi* < OE *popæg* < L *papaver*⟧ **1** any of a genus (*Papaver*) of annual and perennial plants of the poppy family, having a milky juice, showy pink, white, red, orange, purple, or yellow flowers, and capsules containing many small seeds, including the opium poppy **2** the flower of any of these plants **3** any of a number of plants of the poppy family resembling the poppy **4** an extract, as opium, made from poppy juice **5** POPPY RED —***adj.*** designating a family (Papaveraceae, order Papaverales) of widely distributed, dicotyledonous plants, including the bloodroot and celandine

☆**pop·py·cock** (päp′ē käk′) ***n.*** ⟦Du *pappekak,* lit., soft dung⟧ [Informal] foolish talk; nonsense —***interj.*** nonsense!

pop·py·head (päp′ē hed′) ***n.*** an ornament often in the form of a small head, fleur-de-lis, or finial, carved at the top of pew ends or stall ends in Gothic churches

poppy red the bright yellowish-red color of some poppies

poppy seed the small, dark seed of the poppy, used, esp. in baking, as a flavoring or topping for bread, rolls, etc.

pop quiz a typically short test given to students without advance warning

pops¹ (päps) ***adj.*** ⟦< POPULAR⟧ designating or of a symphony orchestra that plays semiclassical music or arrangements of popular music —***n.*** a pops orchestra, a pops concert, or a series of pops concerts

☆**pops**² (päps) ***n.*** *see* POP² (***n.*** 2)

☆**Pop·si·cle** (päp′si kəl) ⟦blend of POP¹ & (I)CICLE⟧ *trademark for* a flavored ice frozen around a stick —***n.*** [*also* **p-**] such a confection

pop-top (päp′täp′) ***adj.*** having a tab or ring that is pulled or pushed to make an opening in the top of a container —***n.*** a container with a top like this

pop·u·lace (päp′yə lis) ***n.*** ⟦Fr < It *popolaccio,* mob, rabble < *popolo* < L *populus,* PEOPLE⟧ **1** the common people; the masses **2** POPULATION (sense 1*a*)

pop·u·lar (päp′yə lər) ***adj.*** ⟦L *popularis* < *populus,* PEOPLE⟧ **1** of or carried on by the common people or all the people [*popular* government] **2** appealing to or intended for the general public [*popular* music] **3** within the means of the ordinary person [*popular* prices] **4** accepted among people in general; common; prevalent [a *popular* notion] **5** liked by very many or most people [a *popular* actor] **6** very well liked by one's friends and acquaintances —**SYN.** COMMON —**pop′u·lar·ly** ***adv.***

popular etymology FOLK ETYMOLOGY

popular front [*often* **P- F-**] a coalition of leftist, liberal, and centrist groups and political parties, as in France or Spain to combat fascism in the 1930s

pop·u·lar·i·ty (päp′yə lar′ə tē) ***n.*** ⟦Fr *popularité* < L *popularitas*⟧ the state or quality of being popular

pop·u·lar·ize (päp′yə lə rīz′) ***vt.*** **-ized′, -iz′ing** to make popular; specif., *a)* to cause to be liked by many people *b)* to make understandable to the general public —**pop′u·lar·i·za′tion** ***n.*** —**pop′u·lar·iz′er** ***n.***

pop·u·late (päp′yə lāt′) ***vt.*** **-lat′ed, -lat′ing** ⟦< ML *populatus,* pp. of *populare,* to populate < L *populus,* PEOPLE⟧ **1** to be or become the inhabitants of; inhabit **2** to supply with inhabitants; people

pop·u·la·tion (päp′yə lā′shən) ***n.*** ⟦LL *populatio*⟧ **1** *a)* all the people in a country, region, etc. *b)* the number of these *c)* a (specified) part of the people in a given area [the Japanese *population* of Hawaii] **2** a populating or being populated **3** *Biol.* a group of similar organisms living in the same region, esp. organisms of the same species **4** *Statistics* the total set of items, persons, etc. from which a sample is taken

☆**population explosion** a great and rapid increase in a population, specif., such an increase in the worldwide human population in modern times

☆**Pop·u·list** (päp′yə list) ***n.*** ⟦< L *populus,* PEOPLE + -IST¹⟧ **1** a member of a U.S. political party (**Populist party** or PEOPLE'S PARTY, 1891-1904) advocating free coinage of gold and silver, public ownership of utilities, an income tax, and support of labor and agriculture **2** [**p-**] any person, esp. a politician or political leader, who claims to represent the interests, views, or tastes of the common people, particularly as distinct from those of the rich or powerful: often applied to someone with demagogic tendencies —***adj.*** **1** of the Populist party **2** [**p-**] *a)* of or characteristic of a populist *b)* of or for the common people —**Pop′u·lism′** ***n.***, **pop′u·lism′**

Pop·u·lis·tic (päp′yə lis′tik) ***adj.*** [*also* **p-**] POPULIST

pop·u·lous (päp′yə ləs) ***adj.*** ⟦L *populosus* < *populus*, PEOPLE⟧ full of people; crowded or thickly populated —**pop′u·lous·ly** ***adv.*** —**pop′u·lous·ness** ***n.***

☆**pop-up** (päp′up′) ***n.*** **1** *Baseball* POP[1] (***n.*** 5) **2** *Comput.* a window, containing a message or menu, that appears superimposed over the window in use, often, specif., one containing an advertisement from the Web —***adj.*** of or designating a book designed so that cut-out portions of an illustration lift when the book is opened to its page, producing a three-dimensional effect

por·bea·gle (pôr′bē′gəl) ***n.*** ⟦< Cornish dial. *porgh-bugel*⟧ a large, fierce mackerel shark (*Lamna nasus*) of the N Atlantic, that brings forth living young

por·ce·lain (pôr′sə lin, pôrs′lin) ***n.*** ⟦Fr *porcelaine* < It *porcellana*, orig., a kind of shell < *porcella*, little pig, vulva (< L *porcellus*, dim. of *porcus*, pig, vulva): see FARROW[1]⟧ **1** a hard, white, nonporous, translucent variety of ceramic ware, made of kaolin, feldspar, and quartz or flint **2** porcelain dishes or ornaments, collectively —***adj.*** made of porcelain —**por′ce·la′ne·ous** (-sə lā′nē əs) ***adj.***, **por′cel·la′ne·ous**

porch (pôrch) ***n.*** ⟦ME *porche* < OFr < L *porticus* < *porta*, gate, entrance, passage: see PORT[5]⟧ **1** a covered entrance to a building, usually projecting from the wall and having a separate roof **2** an open or enclosed gallery or room on the outside of a building, as a veranda or sun porch **3** [Obs.] a portico

por·cine (pôr′sīn′, -sin) ***adj.*** ⟦Fr *porcin* < L *porcinus* < *porcus*, hog: see PORK⟧ of or like pigs or hogs

por·ci·no (pôr chē′nō) ***n.***, *pl.* **-ni** (-nē) ⟦It, lit., little pig, dim. of *porco*, pig: reason for name uncert.⟧ a large, fleshy, edible boletus mushroom (*Boletus edulis*) with a brown cap and a thick, white stem; cèpe: *usually used in pl.*: also **por·ci′ni mushroom** (-nē)

por·cu·pine (pôr′kyə pīn′) ***n.***, *pl.* **-pines′** or **-pine′** ⟦ME *porkepyn* < MFr *porc espin*, spinous hog, spine hog < OIt *porcospino* < L *porcus*, pig (see FARROW[1]) + SPINE⟧ any of a terrestrial Old World family (Hystricidae) or an arboreal New World family (Erethizontidae) of rodents, having coarse hair mixed with long, stiff, sharp spines that can be erected

Por·cu·pine (pôr′kyə pīn′) river in N Yukon Territory, Canada, flowing into the Yukon River in NE Alas.: 590 mi (949 km)

por·cu·pine·fish (-fish′) ***n.***, *pl.* **-fish′** or **-fish′es** (see FISH) any of a family (Diodontidae, order Tetraodontiformes) of tropical, marine bony fishes that can erect the long spines on their body by inflating themselves with air or water: also written **porcupine fish**

pore[1] (pôr, pōr) ***vi.*** **pored**, **por′ing** ⟦ME *poren* < ?⟧ **1** [Now Rare] to gaze intently **2** to read or study carefully: with *over* [to *pore* over a book] **3** to think deeply and thoroughly; ponder: with *over*

pore[2] (pôr, pōr) ***n.*** ⟦ME < L *porus* < Gr *poros* < IE **poros*, passage < base **per-*, to bring through > FARE⟧ **1** [Obs.] a passage; channel **2** a tiny opening, usually microscopic, as in plant leaves or skin, through which fluids may be absorbed or discharged **3** a similar opening in rock or other substances

pore fungus a basidiomycete having spores that are produced inside microscopic tubules in the underside of its mushroom

☆**por·gy** (pôr′gē) ***n.***, *pl.* **-gies** or **-gy** ⟦prob. altered < Sp or Port *pargo* < L *pagrus* < Gr *phagros*, sea bream⟧ **1** any of a family (Sparidae) of marine percoid food fishes having spiny fins and a wide body covered with large scales, as the scup, the pinfish, and the sheepshead **2** any of various other fishes, as the menhaden

po·rif·er·an (pō rif′ər ən, pə-) ***n.*** ⟦< L *porus*, PORE[2] + -FER + -AN⟧ SPONGE (sense 1) —***adj.*** of or pertaining to the poriferans

po·rif·er·ous (-əs) ***adj.*** ⟦< L *porus*, PORE[2] + -FEROUS⟧ **1** having pores **2** *Zool.* of the sponges, or poriferans

po·rism (pō′riz′əm, pôr′iz′-) ***n.*** ⟦ME *porysme* < ML *porisma* < Gr, lit., a thing brought < *porizein*, to bring < *poros*, passage: see PORE[2]⟧ *Ancient Math.* a geometrical proposition variously defined, as *a)* a proposition deduced from some other demonstrated proposition; corollary *b)* a proposition that uncovers the possibility of finding such conditions as to make a specific problem capable of innumerable solutions

pork (pôrk) ***n.*** ⟦ME *porc* < OFr < L *porcus*, a pig < IE **porkos*, pig > FARROW[1]⟧ **1** [Obs.] a pig or hog **2** the flesh of a pig or hog, used as food, esp. when used fresh, or uncured ☆**3** [Informal] money, jobs, etc. appropriated, or set aside, as political patronage

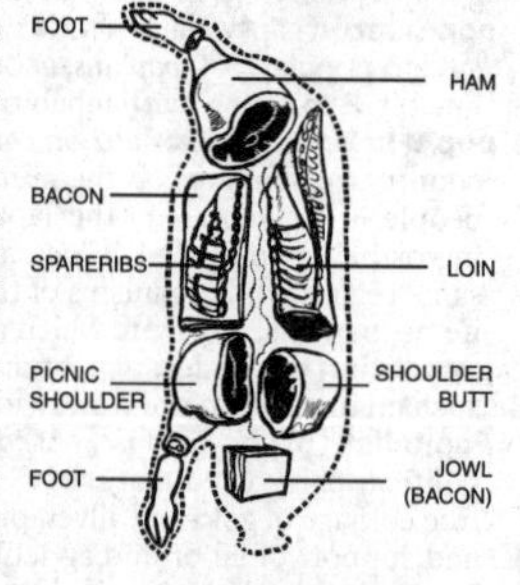

cuts of pork

☆**pork barrel** [Informal] government appropriations for political patronage, as for local improvements to please legislators' constituents: now usually used attributively —**pork′-bar′rel·ing** ***n.***

pork·er (pôr′kər) ***n.*** a hog, esp. a young one, fattened for use as food

pork pie (hat) ⟦so named from its shape⟧ a man's soft hat with a round, flat, low crown and a narrow brim, usually worn slightly flipped up: also written **pork′pie′** ***n.***

pork·y (pôr′kē) ***adj.*** **pork′i·er**, **pork′i·est** **1** of or like pork **2** fat, as though overfed —**pork′i·ness** ***n.***

porn (pôrn) ***n.***, ***adj.*** [Informal] *short for* PORNOGRAPHY, PORNOGRAPHIC: also [Slang] **por·no** (pôr′nō)

por·nog·ra·phy (pôr näg′rə fē) ***n.*** ⟦< Gr *pornographos*, writing about prostitutes < *pornē*, a prostitute, orig. a euphemism, lit., (something) sold, akin to *pernēmi*, to sell (esp. as a slave, or for a bribe) < IE base **per-*, to sell, bring across, come over > FARE + Gr *graphein*, to write: see GRAPHIC⟧ **1** writings, pictures, etc. intended primarily to arouse sexual desire **2** the production of such writings, pictures, etc. —**por·nog′ra·pher** ***n.*** —**por·no·graph·ic** (pôr′nə graf′ik) ***adj.*** —**por′no·graph′i·cal·ly** ***adv.***

☆**por·o·mer·ic** (pôr′ə mer′ik) ***n.*** ⟦arbitrary coinage, prob. < PORO(US) + (POLY)MERIC⟧ a porous, synthetic, leatherlike material, often coated or impregnated with a polymer

po·ros·i·ty (pə räs′ə tē, pō-) ***n.***, *pl.* **-ties** ⟦ME *porositee* < ML *porositas*: see fol. + -ITY⟧ **1** the quality or state of being porous **2** the ratio, usually expressed as a percentage, of the volume of a material's pores, as in rock, to its total volume **3** anything porous **4** PORE[2]

po·rous (pôr′əs) ***adj.*** ⟦ME < ML *porosus* < L *porus*, PORE[2]⟧ full of pores, through which fluids, air, or light may pass —**por′ous·ly** ***adv.*** —**por′ous·ness** ***n.***

por·phy·ra·tin (pôr fir′ə tin) ***n.*** ⟦PORPHYR(IN) + -AT(E) + -IN[1]⟧ any of various complex compounds formed of metals and porphyrins

por·phyr·i·a (pôr fir′ē ə) ***n.*** ⟦ModL < fol. + -IA⟧ an inherited disorder of pigment metabolism with excretion of porphyrins in the urine and dangerous sensitivity to sunlight

por·phy·rin (pôr′fə rin) ***n.*** ⟦< Gr *porphyra*, purple + -IN[1]⟧ any of a group of pyrrole derivatives, found in cytoplasm, that combine with iron and magnesium to form heme and chlorophyll, respectively

por·phy·rit·ic (pôr′fə rit′ik) ***adj.*** ⟦ME *porphiritike* < ML *porphyriticus* < L *porphyrites* < Gr *porphyritēs*⟧ **1** of porphyry **2** like porphyry; having distinct crystals in a fine-grained mass

por·phy·roid (pôr′fə roid′) ***n.*** a metamorphic rock having large crystals embedded in a fine-grained matrix of either igneous or sedimentary origin

por·phy·rop·sin (pôr′fə räp′sin) ***n.*** ⟦< Gr *porphyra*, purple + *opsis*, appearance (< *ōps*, EYE) + -IN[1]⟧ a photosensitive, carotenoid protein pigment found in the rods of the retinas of freshwater vertebrates

por·phy·ry (pôr′fə rē) ***n.***, *pl.* **-ries** ⟦ME *porfirie* < OFr *porfire* < ML *porphyreum*, altered < L *porphyrites* < Gr *porphyritēs* (*lithos*), lit., purple (stone) < *porphyros*, purple⟧ **1** a type of rock quarried in ancient times in Egypt, with large feldspar crystals contained in a purplish groundmass **2** any igneous rock with large, distinct crystals, esp. of alkali feldspar, embedded in a fine-grained matrix

por·poise (pôr′pəs) ***n.***, *pl.* **-pois·es** or **-poise** ⟦ME *porpoys* < OFr *porpeis*, lit., swine fish < L *porcus*, pig (see FARROW[1]) + *piscis*, FISH⟧ **1** any of a family (Phocoenidae) of small, usually gregarious toothed whales found in most seas, with a torpedo-shaped body and a blunt snout **2** a dolphin or any of several small whales

por·ridge (pôr′ij, pär′-) ***n.*** ⟦altered < POTTAGE by confusion with ME *porrey* < OFr *poree* < VL *porrata*, leek broth < L *porrum*, leek, akin to Gr *prason*, leek⟧ **1** [Obs.] pottage **2** a soft food made of cereal or meal boiled in water or milk until thick

por·rin·ger (pôr′in jər) ***n.*** ⟦earlier *pottanger*, *pottager* < Fr *potager*, soup dish: altered by assoc. with prec.⟧ a small, shallow bowl, often of pewter and usually having a flat, horizontal handle

Por·se·na (pôr′si nə), **Lars** (lärz) 6th cent. B.C.; Etruscan king who, according to legend, attacked Rome in an unsuccessful attempt to restore Tarquin to the throne: also **Por·sen·na** (pôr sen′ə)

port[1] (pôrt) ***n.*** ⟦ME < OFr & OE < L *portus*, haven, entrance: see FORD⟧ **1** a harbor **2** a city or town with a harbor where ships can load and unload cargo **3** PORT OF ENTRY

port[2] (pôrt) ***n.*** ⟦after *Oporto*, city in Portugal⟧ a sweet, usually dark-red, fortified wine

port[3] (pôrt) ***vt.*** ⟦MFr *porter* < L *portare*, to carry: see FARE⟧ **1** [Now Rare] to carry **2** to carry, hold, or place (a rifle or sword) in front of one, diagonally upward from right to left, as for inspection —***n.*** ⟦ME *porte* < MFr < the v.⟧ **1** the manner in which one carries oneself; carriage **2** the position of a ported weapon

port[4] (pôrt) ***n.*** ⟦< PORT[1]: so named because it is the side toward the port (dock), since the steering oar (see STARBOARD) prevented docking to the right⟧ the left-hand side of a ship, boat, or airplane as one faces forward: opposed to STARBOARD —***adj.*** **1** of or on this side **2** designating a sailing tack on which the wind passes over the port side — ***vt., vi.*** to move or turn (the helm) to the port side

port[5] (pôrt) ***n.*** ⟦ME < OFr *porte* < L *porta*, door, akin to *portus*: see PORT[1]⟧ **1** [Now Scot.] a portal; gateway, esp. to a town or city **2** *a)* PORTHOLE *b)* a porthole covering **3** an opening, as in a cylinder face or valve face, for the passage of steam, gas, water, etc. **4** *a)* *Electronics* a place at which energy or signals enter or leave a device, circuit, etc. *b)* *Comput.* the circuit, outlet, etc. which serves as a connection between a computer and its peripheral

Port *abbrev.* **1** Portugal **2** Portuguese

port·a- (pôr′tə) *combining form* portable: also sp. **port-a-**

port·a·ble (pôr′tə bəl) ***adj.*** ⟦ME < MFr < LL *portabilis* < *portare*: see FARE⟧ **1** that can be carried **2** *a)* easily carried or moved, esp. by hand [a *portable* TV] *b)* that can be used anywhere because operated by self-contained batteries [a *portable* radio] **3** [Obs.] bearable; endurable —***n.*** something portable —**port′a·bil′i·ty** ***n.*** —**port′a·bly** ***adv.***

por·tage (pôr′tij; *for n. 2 & v., also* pôr täzh′) ***n.*** ⟦ME < MFr < ML *portaticum* < L *portare*, to carry: see FARE⟧ **1** *a)* the act of carrying or transporting *b)* the charge for this ☆**2** *a)* a carrying of boats and supplies overland from one lake or river to another, as during a canoe trip *b)* any route over which this is done — ***vt., vi.* -taged, -tag·ing** ☆to carry (a canoe, supplies, etc.) over a portage

por·tal (pôrt′'l) *n.* ⟦ME < MFr < ML *portale*, orig. neut. of *portalis*, of a door < L *porta:* see PORT[5]⟧ **1** a doorway, gate, or entrance, esp. a large and imposing one **2** any point or place of entry, specif. one where nerves, vessels, etc. enter an organ **3** a website designed to provide access to numerous other sites and, variously, email service, online shopping, etc. —***adj.*** ⟦ML *portalis*⟧ designating, of, or like the vein carrying blood from the intestines, stomach, etc. to the liver

☆**por·tal-to-por·tal pay** (pôrt′'l tə pôrt′'l) wages for workers based on the total time spent from the moment of entering the mine, factory, etc. until the moment of leaving it

por·ta·men·to (pôr′tə men′tō) *n., pl.* **-ti** (-tē) ⟦It < *portare*, to carry < L: see FARE⟧ *Music* a continuous gliding from one note to another, sounding intervening tones; glide

port·ance (pôr′təns) *n.* ⟦Early ModE < MFr < *porter*, to bear: see PORT[3]⟧ [Archaic] one's bearing or demeanor

☆**port-a-pot·ty** (pôr′tə pät′ē) *n.* ⟦< *Porta-Potti*, a trademark for such a structure: see PORTA- & POTTY[1]⟧ a portable, enclosed structure equipped with a toilet, provided for temporary use as at a construction site or large outdoor event

Port Arthur **1** *former name for* LÜSHUN **2** *see* THUNDER BAY

por·ta·tive (pôr′tə tiv) *adj.* ⟦ME < OFr *portatif*, lit., that is carried < L *portatus*, pp. of *portare*, to carry (see FARE) + OFr *-if*, -IVE⟧ **1** of or having the power of carrying **2** portable

Port-au-Prince (pôrt′ō prins′; *Fr* pôr tō prans′) seaport & capital of Haiti, on the Caribbean

port authority a governmental commission in charge of the traffic and regulations of a port

port·cul·lis (pôrt kul′is) *n.* ⟦ME *portcoles* < MFr *porte coleïce* < *porte*, gate + *coleïce*, fem. of *coleis*, sliding < L *colare*, to strain, filter⟧ a heavy iron grating suspended by chains and lowered between grooves to bar the gateway of a castle or fortified town

portcullis

port de bras (pôr′ də brä′) ⟦Fr, carriage of the arms⟧ *Ballet* the positions or movement of the arms

Port du Sa·lut (pôr′ do͞o sa lo͞o′; *Fr* pôr dü sá lü′) ⟦after monastery at *Port du Salut*, France, where orig. made⟧ a creamy, yellowish wholemilk cheese with a brownish crust

Porte (pôrt) *n.* ⟦Fr, short for *la Sublime Porte*, transl. of Turk *Babi Ali*, chief office of the Ottoman Empire, lit., High Gate⟧ the Ottoman Turkish government

porte-co·chere or **porte-co·chère** (pôrt′kō sher′) *n.* ⟦Fr *porte*, a gate (see PORT[5]) + *cochère*, coach, fem. adj. < *coche:* see COACH⟧ **1** a large entrance gateway into a courtyard **2** a kind of porch roof projecting over a driveway at an entrance, as of a house

Port Elizabeth seaport in S South Africa, on the Indian Ocean

porte-mon·naie (pôrt mô ne′; *E* pôrt′mun′ē) *n.* ⟦Fr⟧ a purse or pocketbook

por·tend (pôr tend′) *vt.* ⟦ME *portenden* < L *portendere* < *por-*, akin to *per*, through + *tendere*, to stretch: see THIN⟧ **1** to be an omen or warning of; foreshadow; presage **2** to be an indication of; signify

por·tent (pôr′tent′) *n.* ⟦L *portentum* < *portendere:* see prec.⟧ **1** something that portends an event about to occur, esp. an unfortunate event; omen **2** a portending; significance [a howl of dire *portent*] **3** something amazing; marvel

por·ten·tous (pôr ten′təs) *adj.* ⟦L *portentosus* < *portentum:* see prec.⟧ **1** that portends evil; ominous **2** arousing awe or amazement; marvelous **3** ponderous or pompous; self-important **—SYN.** OMINOUS **—por·ten′tous·ly** ***adv.*** **—por·ten′tous·ness** ***n.***

por·ter[1] (pôr′tər) *n.* ⟦ME < OFr *portier* < LL *portarius* < L *porta*, gate: see PORT[5]⟧ **1** [Chiefly Brit.] a doorkeeper or gatekeeper **2** [Historical] *R.C.Ch.* the lowest of the four minor orders

por·ter[2] (pôr′tər) *n.* ⟦ME *portour* < OFr *porteour* < LL *portator* < L *portare*, to carry: see FARE⟧ **1** a person who carries luggage, etc. for hire or as an attendant at a railroad station, hotel, etc. ☆**2** an employee who sweeps, cleans, does errands, etc. as in a bank, store, or restaurant ☆**3** a railroad employee who waits on passengers in a sleeper or parlor car **4** ⟦< *porter's ale*⟧ a dark-brown beer made from charred or browned malt and produced by rapid fermentation at a relatively high temperature

Por·ter (pôr′tər) **1 Cole** (kōl) 1891-1964; U.S. composer of popular songs **2 David** 1780-1843; U.S. naval officer & diplomat **3 David Dix·on** (dik′sən) 1813-91; Union admiral in the Civil War: son of David **4** Lord **George** 1920-2002; Brit. chemist **5 Katherine Anne** 1890-1980; U.S. short-story writer, essayist, & novelist **6 William Sydney** *see* HENRY[2], O.

por·ter·age (-ij) *n.* **1** a porter's work **2** the charge for this

por·ter·house (pôr′tər hous′) *n.* **1** [Historical] a place where beer and porter (and sometimes steaks and chops) are served ☆**2** ⟦said to be so named from being a specialty at a former New York *porterhouse*⟧ a choice cut of beef from the loin just before the sirloin: in full **porterhouse steak**

port·fo·li·o (pôrt fō′lē ō′) *n., pl.* **-os′** ⟦earlier *porto folio* < It *portafoglio* < *portare* (< L: see FARE), to carry + *foglio* (< L *folium:* see FOLIATE), leaf⟧ **1** a flat, portable case, usually of leather, for carrying loose sheets of paper, manuscripts, and drawings; briefcase **2** such a case for state documents **3** the office of a minister of state or member of a cabinet **4** *a)* all the securities held for investment as by an individual, bank, investment company, etc. *b)* a list of such securities **5** a selection of representative works, as of an artist

port·hole (pôrt′hōl′) *n.* **1** an opening in a ship's side, esp. a round one for admitting light and air, fitted with thick glass and, often, a hinged metal cover **2** an opening to shoot through, in the wall of a fort; embrasure **3** an opening shaped somewhat like this, as in a furnace door

Por·tia (pôr′shə) *n.* ⟦L *Porcia*, fem. of *Porcius*, name of a Roman gens, prob. < *porcus:* see FARROW[1]⟧ a feminine name

por·ti·co (pôr′ti kō′) *n., pl.* **-coes′** or **-cos′** ⟦It < L *porticus:* see PORCH⟧ a porch or covered walk, consisting of a roof supported by columns, often at the entrance or across the front of a building; colonnade

portico

por·tiere or **por·tière** (pôr tyer′, -tē er′, -tir′) *n.* ⟦Fr *portière* < *porte*, door: see PORT[5]⟧ a curtain, usually heavy, hung in a doorway

por·tion (pôr′shən) *n.* ⟦OFr < L *portio* (gen. *portionis*), portion < **partio* < *pars*, PART[1]⟧ **1** a part or limited quantity of anything, esp. that allotted to a person; share **2** the part of an estate received by an heir **3** the part of a man's money or property contributed by his bride; dowry **4** the part of experience supposedly allotted to a person by fate; one's lot; destiny **5** the part of a meal or quantity of food served to a person; serving; helping **—*vt.*** ⟦OFr *portionner*, to divide, separate⟧ to divide into portions; apportion **—SYN.** FATE, PART[1] **—por′tion·er *n.*** **—por′tion·less *adj.***

Port Jackson inlet of the Pacific, in E New South Wales, Australia: harbor of Sydney: 21 sq mi (54 sq km)

Port·land (pôrt′lənd) **1** ⟦after town and island in England⟧ seaport in SW Me., on the Atlantic **2** ⟦after the city in Maine⟧ city & port in NW Oreg., near the confluence of the Columbia & Willamette rivers

port·land cement (pôrt′lənd) ⟦from resemblance of the concrete made from it to stone quarried on the Isle of *Portland*, England⟧ [*sometimes* **P-c-**] a kind of cement that hardens under water, made by burning a mixture of limestone and clay or similar materials

Port Lou·is (lo͞o′is, lo͞o′ē) seaport & capital of Mauritius, on the NW coast

port·ly (pôrt′lē) *adj.* **-li·er, -li·est** ⟦PORT[3] + -LY[1]⟧ **1** large and heavy in a dignified and stately way **2** stout; corpulent **—port′li·ness *n.***

port·man·teau (pôrt man′tō, pôrt′man tō′) *n., pl.* **-teaus** or **-teaux** (-tōz) ⟦Fr *portemanteau* < *porter*, to carry + *manteau*, cloak: see PORT[3] & MANTLE⟧ a traveling case or bag; esp., a stiff leather suitcase that opens like a book into two compartments

portmanteau word ⟦coined by Lewis CARROLL in *Through the Looking-Glass* (1871)⟧ a coined word that is a combination of two other words in form and meaning; blend (Ex.: *smog*, from *smoke* and *fog*)

Port Mores·by (môrz′bē) capital of Papua New Guinea: seaport on the SE coast of New Guinea

Pôr·to (pôr′to͞o) *Port. name for* OPORTO

port·o- (pôr′tə) *combining form var. of* PORTA- [*portophone*]: also sp. **port-o-**

Pôrto A·le·gre (ä le′grə) seaport in S Brazil: capital of Rio Grande do Sul state

por·to·bel·lo (pôr′tə bel′ō) *n., pl.* **-los** a dark mushroom, strong in flavor, having a broad, flat cap that is often grilled and eaten: often **portobello mushroom**

port of call a port that is a regular stopover for ships

port of entry any place where customs officials are stationed to check people and foreign goods entering a country

Port-of-Spain (pôrt′əv spān′) capital of Trinidad and Tobago: seaport on NW Trinidad: also written **Port of Spain**

Por·to No·vo or **Por·to-No·vo** (pôr′tō nō′vō) seaport & constitutional capital of Benin, on the Gulf of Guinea

Por·to Ri·co (pôr′tə rē′kō) *former var. of* PUERTO RICO **—Por′to Ri′can**

Pôr·to Ve·lho (pôr to͞o vā′lyô) city in W Brazil: capital of Rondônia state

Port Phillip Bay inlet of Bass Strait, in S Victoria, Australia: harbor of Melbourne: 762 sq mi (1,974 sq km)

por·trait (pôr′trit, -trāt′) *n.* ⟦MFr, pp. of *portraire:* see PORTRAY⟧ **1** [Obs.] a drawn, painted, or carved picture of something **2** *a)* a painting, drawing, engraving, or sculpture whose subject is an actual person; often, specif., one made from life *b)* a photograph whose posed subject is an actual person **3** a description or dramatic portrayal of a person, society, etc. [a rousing *portrait* of 18th-cent. London]

por·trait·ist (pôr′tri tist) *n.* a person who makes portraits

por·trai·ture (pôr′tri chər) *n.* ⟦ME *purtreiture* < MFr: see fol.⟧ **1** the process, practice, or art of portraying **2** a portrait **3** portraits collectively

por·tray (pôr trā′) *vt.* ⟦ME *purtreien* < MFr *portraire* < L *protrahere*, to draw forth < *pro-*, forth + *trahere*, to DRAW⟧ **1** to make a picture or portrait of; depict; delineate **2** to make a word picture of; describe **3** to play the part of as in a play or film **—por·tray′a·ble *adj.*** **—por·tray′er *n.***

por·tray·al (pôr trā′əl) ***n.*** **1** the act of portraying **2** a portrait; description; representation

por·tress (pôr′tris) ***n.*** ⟦ME: see PORTER[1] & -ESS⟧ a woman doorkeeper, as in a convent

Port Royal town in Jamaica, at the entrance to Kingston harbor: the original town, former capital, was destroyed by an earthquake in 1692

Port Sa·id (sä ēd′, sä′id) seaport in NE Egypt, at the Mediterranean end of the Suez Canal

Port-Sa·lut (pôr′sa lo͞o′; *Fr* pôr sȧ lü′) ***n.*** PORT DU SALUT

Ports·mouth (pôrts′məth) **1** seaport in Hampshire, S England, on the English Channel **2** ⟦after the city in England⟧ seaport in SE Va., on Hampton Roads

Port St. Lu·cie (lo͞o′sē) city in EC Fla.

Por·tu·gal (pôr′chə gəl; *Port* pôr′to͞o gäl′) country in SW Europe, on the Atlantic: formerly a kingdom, it became a republic in 1910: 35,672 sq mi (92,391 sq km); cap. Lisbon

Por·tu·guese (pôr′chə gēz′, -gēs′; pôr′chə gēz′, -gēs′) ***adj.*** of Portugal or its people, language, or culture —***n.*** **1** *pl.* **-guese′** a person born or living in Portugal **2** the Romance language spoken chiefly in Portugal and Brazil

Portuguese East Africa *former alt. name for* MOZAMBIQUE

Portuguese Guinea *former name for* GUINEA-BISSAU

Portuguese India former Portuguese overseas territory consisting of three enclaves in India: see GOA

Portuguese man-of-war any of a genus (*Physalia*) of large, colonial, warm-sea siphonophores having a large, bladderlike sac, with a sail-like structure on top, which enables them to float on the water, and long, dangling tentacles that have powerful stinging cells

Portuguese Timor former (1914-75) Portuguese territory in the Malay Archipelago: now EAST TIMOR

Portuguese water dog any of a breed of medium-sized dog once found along the coast of Portugal, where it was trained to assist fishermen: characterized by a profuse, curly or wavy coat of black, brown, or white

Portuguese West Africa *former alt. name for* ANGOLA

por·tu·lac·a (pôr′chə lak′ə; -lä′kə, -lā′-) ***n.*** ⟦ModL < L, purslane < *portula*, dim. of *porta*, door (see PORT[5]): from the doorlike opening of the seed capsule⟧ a fleshy annual plant (*Portulaca grandiflora*) of the purslane family, usually with yellow, pink, or purple flowers

port-wine stain (pôrt′wīn′) ⟦descriptive⟧ a red or purplish birthmark consisting of dense webs of dilated blood vessels near the surface of the skin: often called **port-wine mark**

pos *abbrev.* **1** position **2** positive

POS *abbrev.* point-of-sale

po·sa·da (pō sä′thä) ***n.***, *pl.* **-das** ⟦Sp < fem. of *posado*, pp. of *posar*, to lodge < L *pausare*, to stop < *pausa*, a PAUSE⟧ in Spanish-speaking countries, an inn —***Las Posadas*** ⟦so named because the procession goes from house to house, reenacting Mary and Joseph's search for lodging in Bethlehem⟧ [*also* **l- p-**] a Mexican Christmas festival marked by candlelight processions from Dec. 16 through Christmas Eve

pose[1] (pōz) ***vt.*** **posed, pos′ing** ⟦ME *posen* < OFr *poser*, to put in position < VL *pausare*, to place, put < L, to stop (see PAUSE): meaning and form altered by assoc. with L *positus*, pp. of *ponere*, to place, put: see POSITION⟧ **1** to put forth; assert (a claim, argument, etc.) **2** to put forward or propose (a question, problem, etc.) **3** to put (a model, photographic subject, etc.) in a certain position or attitude —***vi.*** **1** to assume a certain position or attitude, as in modeling for an artist **2** to strike attitudes for effect; attitudinize **3** to pretend to be what one is not; set oneself up (*as*) [to *pose* as an officer] —***n.*** ⟦Fr < the v.⟧ **1** a bodily attitude, esp. one held for or pictured by an artist, photographer, etc. **2** a way of behaving or speaking that is assumed for effect; pretense —**pose′a·ble** ***adj.***, **pos′a·ble**

SYN.—**pose** refers to an attitude or manner that is assumed for the effect that it will have on others [her generosity is a mere *pose*]; **affectation** is used of a specific instance of artificial behavior intended to impress others [an *affectation* of speech]; a **mannerism** is a peculiarity as in behavior or speech (often originally an affectation) that has become habitual and unconscious [his *mannerism* of raising one eyebrow in surprise]; **airs** (see AIR, ***n.*** 8) is used of an affected pretense of superior manners and graces [she's always putting on *airs*] See also **posture**

pose[2] (pōz) ***vt.*** **posed, pos′ing** ⟦aphetic for APPOSE, OPPOSE⟧ to puzzle or disconcert, as by an almost unanswerable question; baffle

Po·sei·don (pō sī′dən) ***n.*** ⟦L < Gr *Poseidōn*⟧ *Gr. Myth.* god of the sea and of horses: identified with the Roman Neptune

pos·er[1] (pō′zər) ***n.*** ⟦< POSE[1]⟧ a person who poses; esp., a poseur

pos·er[2] (pō′zər) ***n.*** ⟦< POSE[2]⟧ a baffling question or problem

po·seur (pō zʉr′) ***n.*** ⟦Fr⟧ a person who assumes attitudes or manners merely for their effect upon others

posh (päsh) ***adj.*** ⟦prob. < obs. Brit slang *posh*, earlier *push, poosh*, a dandy < ?⟧ [Informal] luxurious and fashionable; elegant —**posh′ly** ***adv.*** —**posh′ness** ***n.***

pos·it (päz′it) ***vt.*** ⟦< L *positus:* see fol.⟧ **1** to set in place or position; situate **2** to set down or assume as fact; postulate **3** to suggest or hypothesize

po·si·tion (pə zish′ən) ***n.*** ⟦MFr < L *positio* < *positus*, pp. of *ponere*, to place < **posinere* < *po-*, away (< IE base **apo-* > L *ab*, from, away) + *sinere*, to put, lay: see SITE⟧ **1** the act of positing, or placing **2** a positing of a proposition; affirmation **3** the manner in which a person or thing is placed or posed, or the manner in which parts are arranged [a dog in a sitting *position*]; specif., any of various customary postures assumed by an individual [the lotus *position*] or a couple [the missionary *position*] **4** one's attitude toward or opinion on a subject; stand [his *position* on foreign aid] **5** the place where a person or thing is, esp. in relation to others; location; situation; site [the ship's *position*] **6** the usual or proper place of a person or thing; station [the players are in *position*] **7** a location or condition in which one has the advantage [to jockey for *position*] **8** a strategic military site **9** a person's relative place, as in society; rank; status **10** a place high in society, business, etc. [a man of *position*] **11** a post of employment; office; job [to apply for a teaching *position*] **12** *Finance* the long or short commitment of a market trader in securities or commodities **13** *Music a)* the arrangement of the notes of a chord with respect to their relative closeness or distance apart [open *position*] *b)* any of the fixed locations on the fingerboard of a violin, etc. that the left hand assumes for fingering a particular series of notes *c)* any of the various points to which a trombone slide may be moved to change the pitch —***vt.*** **1** to put into a particular position; place or station **2** [Rare] to locate —**po·si′tion·al** ***adj.*** —**po·si′tion·er** ***n.***

SYN.—**position** applies to any specific employment for salary or wages, but often connotes white-collar or professional employment; **situation** now usually refers to a position that is open or to one that is desired [*situation* wanted as instructor]; **office** refers to a position of authority or trust, especially in government or a corporation; a **post** is a position or office that carries heavy responsibilities, esp. one to which a person is appointed; **job** is now the common, comprehensive equivalent for any of the preceding terms

position paper a document, esp. a report, explaining a view on a subject, issue, etc., often by outlining a solution or course of action

pos·i·tive (päz′ə tiv) ***adj.*** ⟦ME *positif* < OFr < L *positivus* < *positus:* see POSITION⟧ **1** formally or arbitrarily set; conventional; artificial [a *positive* law] **2** definitely set; explicitly laid down; admitting of no question or modification; express; precise; specific [*positive* instructions] **3** *a)* having the mind set or settled; confident; assured [a *positive* person] *b)* overconfident or dogmatic **4** showing resolution or agreement; affirmative; certain [a *positive* answer] **5** tending in the direction regarded as that of increase, progress, etc. [clockwise motion is *positive*] **6** making a definite contribution; constructive [*positive* criticism] **7** unrelated to anything else; independent of circumstances; absolute; unqualified **8** that has, or is considered as having, real existence in itself, not just in the absence of other attributes [a *positive* good] **9** based, or asserted as based, on reality or facts [*positive* proof] **10** concerned only with real things and experience; empirical; practical **11** [Informal] complete; absolute; out-and-out [a *positive* fool] **12** *Biol.* directed toward the source of a stimulus [*positive* tropism] ☆**13** *Elec. a)* of, generating, or charged with positive electricity *b)* having a deficiency of electrons **14** *Gram. a)* of an adjective or adverb in its simple, uninflected or unmodified form or degree; neither comparative nor superlative *b)* of this degree **15** *Math.* designating a quantity greater than zero, or one to be added; plus **16** *Med.* having or demonstrating, showing, or proving the presence or existence of a condition, an infection, symptoms, bacteria, etc. [a patient who is *positive* for TB, a *positive* TB test] **17** *Optics* forming a REAL[1] (***adj.*** 6) image by converging light rays: said of a lens: distinguished from NEGATIVE (***adj.*** 8) **18** *Photog.* with the light and shade corresponding to those of the subject —***n.*** something positive, as a degree, quality, condition, etc.; specif., *a) Elec.* a terminal, electrode, or plate that attracts a flow of electrons from a negative terminal, electrode, or plate, as in a storage battery or dry cell *b) Gram.* the positive degree; also, a word or form in this degree *c) Math.* a quantity greater than zero, or one to be added; plus quantity *d) Photog.* a photographic print, or a film for use in a projector, on which light and shadow correspond to what they were in the subject —***SYN.*** SURE —**pos′i·tive·ness** ***n.***

☆**positive electricity** the kind of electricity possessed by an object (as a glass rod after it has been rubbed with a piece of silk) having a deficiency of electrons: opposed to NEGATIVE ELECTRICITY

pos·i·tive·ly (-ə təv lē) ***adv.*** in a positive manner: also used in affirmation, equivalent to "I agree" or "quite true" and pronounced (päz′ə tiv′lē)

positive sign the sign (+) used to indicate a positive quantity

pos·i·tiv·ism (päz′ə tiv iz′əm) ***n.*** ⟦Fr *positivisme* < *positif*⟧ **1** the quality or state of being positive; certainty; assurance **2** overconfidence or dogmatism **3** a system of philosophy basing knowledge solely on data of sense experience; esp., a system of philosophy, originated by Auguste COMTE, based solely upon the scientific study of observable phenomena: it rejects speculation about or the search for ultimate origins —**pos′i·tiv·ist** ***n., adj.*** —**pos′i·tiv·is′tic** ***adj.***

pos·i·tiv·i·ty (päz′ə tiv′ə tē) ***n.*** the state or quality of being positive

☆**pos·i·tron** (päz′i trän′) ***n.*** ⟦POSI(TIVE) + (ELEC)TRON⟧ *Particle Physics* a positively charged lepton with the same mass and magnitude of charge as the electron; the antiparticle of an electron

☆**pos·i·tro·ni·um** (päz′i trō′nē əm) ***n.*** ⟦prec. + -IUM⟧ a short-lived atomic system formed of an electron and a positron before they interact to annihilate each other

po·sol·o·gy (pō säl′ə jē) ***n.*** ⟦Fr *posologie* < Gr *posos*, how much (< IE **kwoti* < interrogative base **kwo-* > WHO, WHAT) + Fr *-logie*, -LOGY⟧ *Med.* the scientific study of drug dosages

poss *abbrev.* **1** possession **2** possessive **3** possibly

pos·se (päs′ē) ***n.*** ⟦ML, short for *posse comitatus*, power of the county < L *posse*, to be able (see POTENT) + *comitatus*, county < *comes*, a COUNT[2]⟧ **1** [Historical] a body of men summoned to assist the sheriff in keeping the peace, pursuing felons, etc.: in full **posse co·mi·ta·tus** (käm′ə tāt′əs) ☆2 *a)* in the Old West, a group assembled to hunt for criminal fugitives *b)* a search party 3 [Slang] *a)* a gang, esp. one engaged in selling drugs *b)* any group of people, as of a person's friends and associates, specif. when acting as an entourage

pos·sess (pə zes′) ***vt.*** ⟦LME < MFr *possessier* < L *possessus*, pp. of *possidere*, to possess < *pos-*, contr. < *potis*, able (see POTENT) + *sedere*, to sit⟧ **1** to hold as property or occupy in person; have as something that belongs to one; own **2** to have as an attribute, quality, faculty, etc. [to *possess* wisdom] **3** to have knowledge or mastery of (a language, etc.) **4** to gain strong influence or control over; dominate [*possessed* by an idea] **5** to keep control over or maintain (oneself, one's mind, etc.) **6** to have sexual intercourse with (a woman) **7** to put (someone) in possession of property, facts, etc.; cause to have something specified: usually with *of* **8** [Archaic] to seize or win —**pos·ses′sor *n.***

pos·sessed (pə zest′) ***adj.*** **1** owned **2** controlled by an emotion or as if by an evil spirit; crazed; mad **3** SELF-POSSESSED —**possessed of** in possession of

pos·ses·sion (pə zesh′ən) ***n.*** ⟦OFr < L *possessio*⟧ **1** a possessing or being possessed, as by ownership or occupancy; hold **2** anything possessed **3** [*pl.*] property; wealth **4** territory ruled by an outside country **5** control of oneself: rare except in SELF-POSSESSION **6** *Sports* actual control of the ball or puck in play —**pos·ses′sion·al *adj.***

pos·ses·sive (pə zes′iv) ***adj.*** ⟦L *possessivus*⟧ **1** of possession, or ownership **2** *a)* showing, or characterized by a desire for, possession [a *possessive* child] *b)* having or showing a desire to dominate, control, influence, etc. [a *possessive* mother] **3** *Gram.* designating or of a case, form, or construction expressing possession or some like relationship: in English, this is expressed *a)* by the addition of a final *s* (for nouns and some pronouns) preceded or followed by an apostrophe, or sometimes by the addition of an apostrophe only after a final (s) sound (Ex.: *John's* book, *women's* lives, *boys'* games, *conscience'* sake) *b)* by a change of form in pronouns (Ex.: *I, my, mine; you, your, yours; it, its; who, whose*) *c)* by *of* preceding a form without the possessive ending (Ex.: lives *of men*) or preceding a form in the possessive case (Ex.: a play *of Shakespeare's*, a friend *of mine* — called a **double possessive**): cf. GENITIVE —***n.*** *Gram.* **1** the possessive case **2** a word or phrase in this case —**pos·ses′sive·ly *adv.*** —**pos·ses′sive·ness *n.***

pos·ses·so·ry (pə zes′ə rē) ***adj.*** **1** of, being, or characterizing a possessor **2** of or based upon possession

pos·set (päs′it) ***n.*** ⟦ME < ?⟧ a hot drink made of milk curdled as with ale or wine, usually spiced and sweetened

pos·si·bil·i·ty (päs′ə bil′ə tē) ***n., pl.* -ties** ⟦ME *possibilite* < LL *possibilitas*⟧ **1** the quality or condition of being possible **2** something that is possible **3** [*pl.*] capacity for future success; potential; promise

pos·si·ble (päs′ə bəl) ***adj.*** ⟦OFr < L *possibilis* < *posse*, to be able: see POTENT⟧ **1** that can be; capable of existing **2** that can be in the future; that may or may not happen **3** *a)* that can be done, known, acquired, selected, used, etc., depending on circumstances [a *possible* candidate] *b)* that can happen or be; potential **4** that may be done; permissible **5** that may be a fact or the truth **6** [Informal] that can be put up with; tolerable

***SYN.*—possible** is used of anything that may exist, occur, be done, etc., depending on circumstances [a *possible* solution to a problem]; **practicable** applies to that which can readily be effected under the prevailing conditions or by the means available [a *practicable* plan]; **feasible** is used of that which is likely to be carried through to a successful conclusion and, hence, connotes the desirability of doing so [a *feasible* enterprise]

pos·si·bly (päs′ə blē) ***adv.*** **1** by any possible means; in any case [it can't *possibly* work] **2** by some possibility; perhaps; maybe [it may *possibly* be so]

☆**pos·sum** (päs′əm) [Informal] ***n.*** OPOSSUM —**play possum** to pretend to be asleep, dead, ill, unaware, etc.: an opossum may become motionless when endangered

post[1] (pōst) ***n.*** ⟦ME < OE, akin to Ger *pfosten:* WGmc loanword < L *postis*, post, doorpost < **porstis*, projection < **por-*, akin to FOR[1] + base of *stare*, to STAND⟧ **1** a piece of wood, metal, etc., usually long and square or cylindrical, set upright to support a building, sign, fence, etc. **2** anything like this in shape or purpose **3** any place originally marked by or associated with a post, as the starting or finishing point of a horse race **4** *Basketball* a position of an offensive player near the basket: often with *the* —***vt.*** **1** to put up (a poster, notice, etc.) on (a wall, post, etc.); placard **2** to announce, publicize, or advertise by posting notices, signs, etc. [*post* a reward] ☆**3** to warn persons against trespassing on (grounds, etc.) by posted notices **4** to put (a name) on a posted or published list **5** to denounce by a public notice **6** *Comput.* to make available for viewing on a blog, newsgroup, bulletin board, etc. ☆**7** *Sports* to record (a specified score) —**keep someone posted** to keep someone informed about a developing situation —**post up** *Basketball* to position oneself against (a defender) in the POST[1] (***n.*** 4): said of an offensive player in possession of the ball

post[2] (pōst) ***n.*** ⟦Fr *poste* < It *posto* < VL **postum*, contr. < L *positum*, neut. pp. of *ponere*, to place: see POSITION⟧ **1** the place where a soldier, guard, etc. is stationed **2** *a)* a place where a body of troops is stationed; camp *b)* the troops at such a place; garrison *c)* any place where a person or group is stationed *d)* a position, job, or duty to which a person is assigned or appointed ☆**3** a local unit of a veterans' organization ☆**4** *short for* TRADING POST **5** *Brit. Army* either of two bugle calls (**first post** and **last post**) sounded to indicate the time to retire at night: the last post is also sounded at military funerals and remembrance services —***vt.*** **1** to station at or assign to a post **2** [Brit.] to appoint to a military or naval command ☆**3** to put up or deposit (a bond, etc.) —***SYN.*** POSITION

post[3] (pōst) ***n.*** ⟦Fr *poste* < It *posta*, orig., a station, fem. of *posto:* see prec.⟧ **1** *a)* [Historical] any of a number of riders or runners posted at intervals to carry mail or messages in relays along a route; postrider or courier *b)* a stage of a post route *c)* a station of a post route *d)* a post horse **2** [Chiefly Brit.] *a)* (the) mail *b)* a post office *c)* a mailbox —***vi.*** **1** [Obs.] to travel in posts or stages **2** to travel fast; hasten **3** to rise and sink back in a saddle in rhythm with the horse's trot —***vt.*** **1** *a)* to send by post *b)* to hasten **2** [Chiefly Brit.] to mail ☆**3** to inform, as of events: usually in the passive voice **4** *Bookkeeping a)* to transfer (an item) from a journal to the ledger *b)* to enter in the correct form and place *c)* to enter all necessary items in (a ledger, etc.) —***adv.*** **1** by post **2** speedily

Post (pōst), **Emily** (born *Emily Price*) 1873-1960; U.S. writer on etiquette

post- (pōst) ⟦L < *post*, behind, after < **posti* < IE **pos*, after (prob. < base **apo-*, away > L *ab*) > Gr dial. *pos*, at⟧ *prefix* **1** after in time, later (than), following [*postnatal, post-*obit] **2** after in space, behind [*postcava*] **3** coming after in time, often as a rejection of or in reaction to [*postmodernism*]

post-ac·ti·nide (pōst ak′tə nīd′) ***n.*** TRANSACTINIDE: also called **post-actinide element**

post·age (pōs′tij) ***n.*** ⟦POST[3] + -AGE⟧ the amount charged for mailing a letter or package, esp. as represented by stamps or indicia

☆**postage meter** a machine that prints indicia on mail, indicating that postage has been paid: it records the number of pieces processed and the cost of postage

postage stamp a government stamp to be put on a letter or package as a sign that the postage has been prepaid: it is either a small, printed, adhesive label or a design imprinted on an envelope, postal card, etc.

post·al (pōs′təl) ***adj.*** ⟦Fr < *poste*, POST[3]⟧ having to do with mail or post offices —***n.*** ☆[Informal] a postal card —☆**go postal** ⟦in allusion to widely reported shootings by angry U.S. *postal* workers in the 1990s⟧ [Slang] to become deranged or go berserk, as from stress in the workplace

☆**postal card** a card sold by the post office, with the postage printed on it for mailing without an envelope, used to send short messages

postal code [Cdn.] POSTCODE

postal service POST OFFICE (sense 1)

postal stationery postal items other than stamps issued by a government, as stamped envelopes, postal cards, and aerogrammes

post·ax·i·al (pōst ak′sē əl) ***adj.*** *Anat., Zool.* situated behind the axis of the body or a limb [a *postaxial* muscle]

post-bel·lum (-bel′əm) ***adj.*** ⟦L *post bellum*, lit., after the war⟧ occurring after the war, specif. after the American Civil War

post·box (pōst′bäks′) ***n.*** [Chiefly Brit.] MAILBOX

post·card (-kärd′) ***n.*** **1** a card, usually with a picture on one side, that may be sent through the mail when a stamp is affixed, used to send short messages **2** loosely, a postal card

post·ca·va (pōst kā′və) ***n., pl.* -vae** (-vē) ⟦POST- + (VENA) CAVA⟧ the posterior or inferior vena cava of four-limbed vertebrates —**post′ca′val *adj.***

post chaise a closed, four-wheeled coach or carriage drawn by fast horses, which were changed at each post, used in the 18th and 19th cent. to carry mail and passengers

post-Chris·tian (pōst′kris′chən) ***adj.*** of or designating the modern era, regarded as a time in which the West, esp. Europe, has moved away from its Christian traditions and become fundamentally secular

post·code (pōst′kōd′) ***n.*** [Brit.] a code of numbers and letters used as part of a mailing address: also **post code**

post-con·sum·er (pōst′kən sōōm′ər) ***adj.*** **1** designating or of waste, or refuse, from consumers, often, specif., that which can be recycled **2** designating or of materials made from recycled consumer waste

post·date (pōst dāt′, pōst′dāt′) ***vt.*** **-dat′ed, -dat′ing** **1** to assign a later date to than the actual or current date **2** to write such a date on **3** to be subsequent to

post·di·lu·vi·an (pōst′də lōō′vē ən) ***adj.*** ⟦POST- + DILUVIAN⟧ of the time after the Biblical Flood —***n.*** a postdiluvian person or thing

post·doc (pōst′däk′) ***n.*** **1** a person engaged in postdoctoral research, study, etc. **2** a fellowship or position for postdoctoral work

☆**post·doc·tor·al** (pōst′däk′tər əl) ***adj.*** designating, of, or engaged in study, research, etc. following the doctorate

post·er[1] (pōs′tər) ***n.*** **1** a relatively large printed card or sheet of paper, often illustrated, posted to advertise or publicize something; placard **2** any relatively large piece of commercial art, often a photograph of a celebrity, pinup, etc.

post·er[2] (pōs′tər) ***n.*** **1** a person who traveled by post, or rapidly **2** POST HORSE

poster child ⟦in allusion to the use of children in advertising⟧ a person or thing presented as a symbol or archetype as in advancing some cause: now also **poster boy** (or **girl**, etc.)

poster color an opaque paint with a binder, such as gum or glue, that is water-soluble, used as for posters

poste res·tante (pōst′ re stänt′, -stant′) ⟦Fr, lit., remaining mail⟧ [Brit.] GENERAL DELIVERY

pos·te·ri·or (päs tir′ē ər) ***adj.*** ⟦L, compar. of *posterus*, following < *post*, after: see POST-⟧ **1** later; following after; subsequent **2** coming after in order;

succeeding 3 at or toward the rear; behind; specif., dorsal: opposed to ANTERIOR 4 *Bot.* on the side next to the main stem —*n.* [*formerly also pl.*] the buttocks —**pos·te'ri·or'i·ty** (-ôr'ə tē) *n.* —**pos·te'ri·or·ly** *adv.*

pos·ter·i·ty (päs ter'ə tē) *n.* ⟦ME *posterite* < MFr *postérité* < L *posteritas* < *posterus:* see prec.⟧ 1 all of a person's descendants: opposed to ANCESTRY 2 all succeeding generations

pos·tern (pōs'tərn, päs'-) *n.* ⟦ME < OFr *posterne,* altered < *posterle* < LL *posterula,* a small back door, postern, dim. < *posterus:* see POSTERIOR⟧ a back door or gate; private entrance at the side or rear —*adj.* of or resembling a postern, as in being at the rear, or private

poster paint POSTER COLOR

☆**Post Exchange** *service mark for* a nonprofit general store at an army post or camp

post·ex·il·ic (pōst'ek sil'ik, -eg zil'-) *adj.* of that period of Jewish history following the Babylonian Exile (6th cent. B.C.): also **post'ex·il'i·an** (-ē ən)

post·face (pōst'fās') *n.* ⟦Fr < *post-,* POST- + *-face,* as in *préface,* preface⟧ a concluding statement to a book, explaining or commenting on its purpose, plan, etc.

post·fem·i·nist (pōst'fem'ə nist) *adj.* designating or of the period following the feminist movement of the 1970s, regarded as a time of reevaluation or moderation of feminist principles —*n.* a person holding postfeminist views —**post'fem'i·nism'** *n.*

post·fix (pōst'fiks'; *for v., usually* pōst fiks') *n.* ⟦POST- + (AF)FIX⟧ SUFFIX —*vt.* to suffix

post-free (pōst'frē') *adj.* 1 that can be mailed free of charge 2 [Brit.] POSTPAID

post-game (pōst'gām') *adj.* of or during the period just after an athletic game [a coach's *post-game* press conference]: also written **postgame**

post·gan·gli·on·ic (pōst'gaŋ'glē än'ik) *adj.* lying behind a ganglion; specif., of or pertaining to an axon that leads nerve impulses away from a ganglion to some other part of the body

post·gla·cial (-glā'shəl) *adj.* existing or happening after the disappearance of glaciers from a specific area, esp. after the Pleistocene Epoch

☆**post·grad·u·ate** (pōst'graj'o͞o it) *adj.* 1 of or taking a course of study after graduation, esp. after receipt of the bachelor's degree: see GRADUATE (*adj.* 2) 2 designating or of additional study, training, etc. undertaken after receipt of a doctorate —*n.* a student taking such a course

post·haste (pōst'hāst') *n.* [Archaic] great haste, as of a postrider —*adv.* with great haste

post hoc, er·go prop·ter hoc (pōst' häk' er'gō präp'tər häk') ⟦L⟧ after this, therefore because of this: used in logic to designate the fallacy of thinking that a happening which follows another must be its result: often clipped to **post hoc**

post·hole (pōst'hōl') *n.* a hole dug in the ground to hold the end of an upright post

post horse [Historical] a horse kept at a post house, or inn, for couriers and post chaises or for hire to travelers

post house [Historical] an inn or other place where post horses were kept

post·hu·mous (päs'cho͞o məs, -tyo͞o-) *adj.* ⟦LL *posthumus,* for L *postumus,* after death, orig., last, superl. of *posterus* (see POSTERIOR): altered in LL by assoc. with *humus,* ground or *humare,* to bury (as if meaning "born after the father is buried")⟧ 1 born after the father's death 2 published after the author's death 3 arising, continuing, or coming to pass after one's death [a *posthumous* award] —**post'hu·mous·ly** *adv.*

post·hyp·not·ic (pōst'hip nät'ik) *adj.* of or carried out in the period following a hypnotic trance [*posthypnotic* suggestion]

pos·tiche (pä stēsh') *n.* ⟦Fr, a counterfeit < It *posticcio* < VL *appositicius* < L *appositus:* see APPOSITE⟧ a hairpiece

pos·til·ion or **pos·til·lion** (pōs til'yən, päs-) *n.* ⟦Fr *postillon* < It *postiglione* < *posta,* POST[3]⟧ 1 a person who rides the left-hand horse of the leaders of a four-horse carriage 2 one who rides the left-hand horse of a two-horse carriage when there is no driver

post·im·pres·sion·ism (pōst'im presh'ən iz'əm) *n.* [*often* **P-**] the theory or methods of a group of late 19th-cent. painters, including Cézanne, Van Gogh, and Gauguin, who revolted against the objectivity and naturalism of impressionism and placed emphasis upon the subjective viewpoint of the artist or the formal structure and style of the painting: also written **post-Impressionism** or **Post-Impressionism** —**post'im·pres'sion·ist** *adj., n.* —**post'im·pres'sion·is'tic** *adj.*

post·in·dus·tri·al (-in dus'trē əl) *adj.* designating or of a society in which the economic base has shifted from heavy industry to service industries, technology, etc.

☆**Post-it** (pōst'it') *trademark for* any of the small pieces of colored paper in a pad, each piece backed with a weak adhesive, suitable for temporarily attaching notes to documents or other flat surfaces —*n.* [*often* **p-**] a single piece of such paper

post·li·min·i·um (pōst'li min'ē əm) *n.* ⟦L, a return behind one's threshold < *post,* behind (see POST-) + *limen,* threshold: see LIMEN⟧ in international law, the rule by which persons or things captured in war resume their original status when restored to the jurisdiction of their own country: also **post'lim'i·ny** (-lim'ə nē)

post·lude (pōst'lo͞od') *n.* ⟦POST- + (PRE)LUDE⟧ *Music* 1 a VOLUNTARY played at the end of a church service 2 a musical selection that concludes a performance

post·man (-mən) *n. pl.* **-men** (-mən) MAIL CARRIER

post·mark (pōst'märk') *n.* a post-office mark stamped on a piece of mail, canceling the postage stamp and recording the date and place of sending or receiving —*vt.* to stamp with a postmark

post·mas·ter (pōst'mas'tər) *n.* 1 [Historical] a person in charge of a station for post horses 2 a person in charge of a post office —**post'mas'ter·ship'** *n.*

postmaster general *pl.* **postmasters general** the head of a government's postal system

post·men·o·pause (pōst'men'ə pôz') *n.* the period of time following menopause, when menstruation has ceased permanently —**post'men'o·paus'al** *adj.*

post·me·rid·i·an (pōst'mə rid'ē ən) *adj.* ⟦L *postmeridianus:* see POST- & MERIDIAN⟧ after noon; of or in the afternoon

post me·ri·di·em (pōst'mə rid'ē əm) ⟦L⟧ after noon: abbrev. *P.M., p.m., PM,* or *pm*

post·mil·len·ni·al (pōst'mi len'ē əl) *adj.* existing or happening after the millennium

post·mil·len·ni·al·ism (-iz'əm) *n.* the religious doctrine that the second coming of Christ will occur after, not at, the millennium —**post'mil·len'ni·al·ist** *n.*

post·mis·tress (pōst'mis'tris) *n.* a woman in charge of a post office: term now seldom used

post·mod·ern (pōst'mäd'ərn) *adj.* 1 coming after, and typically in reaction to, modernism in the 20th century, esp. in the arts and literature; specif., of or relating to a diffuse cultural and artistic trend or movement, esp. in art, architecture, and writing, since the 1950s, characterized by eclecticism in style and content, freedom from strict theoretical constraints, indifference to social concerns, etc. 2 designating or of various theories used widely in criticism and interpretation, which question or reject claims of absolute certainty, objective truth, and, as in language or works of art, intrinsic meaning, regarding such claims instead as assertions of privilege, political power, etc. —**post'mod'ern·ism'** *n.* —**post'mod'ern·ist** *adj., n.*

post·mor·tem (pōst'môr'təm) *adj.* ⟦L, lit., after death⟧ 1 happening, done, or made after death 2 having to do with a postmortem examination —*n.* 1 *short for* POSTMORTEM EXAMINATION 2 a detailed examination or evaluation of some event just ended Also written **post-mortem**

postmortem examination AUTOPSY

post·na·sal drip (pōst'nā'zəl) a discharge of mucus from behind the nose onto the surface of the pharynx, as from a cold or allergy

post·na·tal (pōst'nāt''l) *adj.* ⟦POST- + NATAL⟧ after birth; esp., of the period immediately after birth

post·nup·tial (-nup'shəl, -chəl) *adj.* ⟦POST- + NUPTIAL⟧ happening or done after marriage —**post'nup'tial·ly** *adv.*

post-o·bit (-ō'bit) *adj.* ⟦contr. < L *post obitum,* after death < *post,* after + *obitus,* death: see POST- & OBIT⟧ being, or to be, in effect after a specified person's death —*n.* a bond given by a borrower pledging to pay a debt upon the death of a specified person from whom the borrower expects to inherit money: also **post-obit bond**

post office 1 the governmental department in charge of the mails 2 an office or building where mail is sorted for distribution, postage stamps are sold, etc. ☆3 a kissing game for young people played in any of various ways

post-op (pōst'äp') *adj. short for* POSTOPERATIVE —*n.* postoperative care; also, a ward reserved for such care

post·op·er·a·tive (pōst'äp'ər ə tiv, -ər āt'iv) *adj.* of or occurring in the period after a surgical operation —**post'op'er·a·tive·ly** *adv.*

post·or·bit·al (-ôr'bit əl) *adj. Anat., Zool.* situated behind the orbit, or eye socket —*n.* a postorbital bone or scale, as in certain reptiles

post·paid (pōst'pād') *adj.* with the postage prepaid

post·par·tum (pōst'pär'təm) *adj.* ⟦L < *post-,* POST- + *partum,* acc. of *partus,* a bringing forth < *parere,* to bear: see -PAROUS⟧ of the period following childbirth

postpartum depression a condition characterized by persistent and often disabling symptoms of depression, anxiety, etc., experienced by some women in the first weeks or months after childbirth

post·pone (pōst pōn') *vt.* **-poned', -pon'ing** ⟦L *postponere* < *post-,* POST- + *ponere,* to put: see POSITION⟧ 1 to put off until later; defer; delay 2 *Gram.* to put at or near the end of the sentence [the German verb is *postponed*] 3 [Rare] to subordinate —**SYN.** ADJOURN —**post·pon'a·ble** *adj.* —**post·pone'ment** *n.* —**post·pon'er** *n.*

post·po·si·tion (pōst'pə zish'ən) *n.* ⟦< L *postpositus,* pp. of *postponere:* see prec.⟧ 1 a placing after or a being placed after 2 ⟦POST- + (PRE)POSITION⟧ *Gram. a)* the placing of an element after another that is related to it *b)* an element so placed, as an affix that functions as a preposition but follows its object (Ex.: *-ward* in *shoreward*) or an adjective that follows the word it modifies (Ex.: *royal* in *battle royal*)

post·pos·i·tive (pōst'päz'ə tiv) *adj.* ⟦LL *postpositivus* < L *postpositus:* see prec.⟧ *Gram.* placed after or added to a word; suffixed —*n.* a postpositive word —**post'pos'i·tive·ly** *adv.*

post·pran·di·al (-pran'dē əl) *adj.* ⟦POST- + PRANDIAL⟧ after a meal; esp., after-dinner —**post'pran'di·al·ly** *adv.*

post·pro·duc·tion (pōst'prə duk'shən) *n.* the part of film or video production taking place after all the scenes have been shot, during which the final version of the film or tape is edited, the soundtrack is mixed, and music and special effects are added: also written **post-production**

post-ra·cial (pōst'rā'shəl) *adj.* designating or of a society, policies, a politician, etc. regarded as succeeding and transcending a tradition of racial acrimony or, often, specif., a tradition of racism [a *post-racial* generation of voters]

post·rid·er (pōst′rīd′ər) ***n.*** [Historical] a person who carried the post, or mail, on horseback

post road **1** [Historical] a road provided with post houses **2** a road over which the post, or mail, is or formerly was carried

post·script (pōst′skript′) ***n.*** ⟦ModL *postscriptum* < L, neut. pp. of *postscribere* < *post-*, after (see POST-) + *scribere*, to write: see SCRIBE⟧ a note, paragraph, etc. added below the signature in a letter or at the end of a book, speech, etc. as an afterthought or to give supplementary information

post·sea·son (pōst′sē′zən) *Sports* ***n.*** the period just after the regular season, during which playoffs are held —***adj.*** of the postseason

post·sec·ond·ar·y (pōst′sek′ən der′ē) ***adj.*** of or relating to education taking place following graduation from a high school

☆**post time** ⟦see POST[1], ***n.*** 3⟧ the scheduled starting time of a horse race

post-trau·mat·ic stress disorder (pōst′trô mat′ik) a condition characterized by recurring and, often, disabling symptoms of anxiety, depression, etc., that affects some persons well after they experience a traumatic event or situation, as combat

pos·tu·lant (päs′chə lənt, -tyə-) ***n.*** ⟦Fr < L *postulans*, prp. of *postulare:* see fol.⟧ a petitioner or candidate, esp. one for admission into a religious order

pos·tu·late (päs′chə lāt′; *for n., usually*, -lit) ***vt.*** **-lat′ed, -lat′ing** ⟦< L *postulatus*, pp. of *postulare*, to demand < base of *poscere*, to demand < IE **pr̥ḱskā*, question < base **perk-*, to ask > Ger *frage*, question⟧ **1** [Archaic] to claim; demand; require **2** to assume without proof to be true, real, or necessary, esp. as a basis for argument **3** to take as self-evident; assume —***n.*** ⟦ModL *postulatum* < neut. of L *postulatus*⟧ **1** something postulated; assumption or axiom **2** a prerequisite **3** a basic principle —***SYN.*** PRESUME —**pos′tu·la′tion** ***n.***

pos·tu·la·tor (-lāt′ər) ***n.*** **1** one who postulates **2** *R.C.Ch.* an official who pleads for a candidate for beatification or canonization

pos·ture (päs′chər) ***n.*** ⟦MFr < It *postura* < L *positura*, a position < *ponere*, to place: see POSITION⟧ **1** the position or carriage of the body in standing or sitting, often, specif., with respect to the proper alignment of the back, shoulders, and head **2** such a position assumed as in posing for an artist **3** the way things stand; condition with respect to circumstances [the delicate *posture* of foreign affairs] **4** *a)* an attitude of mind; frame of mind *b)* an attitude assumed merely for effect **5** an official stand or position, as that taken by a nation on a major issue —***vt.*** **-tured, -tur·ing** to place in a particular posture; pose —***vi.*** to assume a bodily or mental posture; esp., to assume an attitude merely for effect; pose —**pos′tur·al** ***adj.*** —**pos′tur·er** ***n.***

SYN.—**posture** refers to the habitual or assumed disposition of the parts of the body in standing, sitting, etc. [erect *posture*]; **attitude** refers to a posture assumed either unconsciously, as in manifesting a mood or emotion, or intentionally for carrying out a particular purpose [an *attitude* of watchfulness]; **pose** suggests a posture assumed, usually deliberately, as for artistic effect [to hold a *pose* for a photographer]; **stance** refers to a particular way of standing, esp. with reference to the position of the feet, as in certain sports [the proper *stance* for a golfer]

post·war (pōst′wôr′) ***adj.*** after the (or a) war

po·sy (pō′zē) ***n.***, *pl.* **-sies** ⟦contr. < POESY⟧ **1** [Archaic] a line of poetry or motto inscribed inside a ring, etc. **2** [Old-fashioned] a flower, bouquet, or nosegay

pot[1] (pät) ***n.*** ⟦ME < OE *pott*, akin to Du & Fr *pot* < ML *pottus* < VL *potus*, drinking cup < L, a drink < *potare:* see POTABLE⟧ **1** a round vessel of any size, made as of metal, earthenware, or glass, used for holding liquids, cooking or preserving food, etc. **2** a pot with its contents **3** POTFUL **4** a pot of liquor; drink; potation **5** *short for* FLOWERPOT, LOBSTER POT, CHIMNEY POT, etc. **6** *a)* CHAMBER POT *b)* [Slang] a toilet (with *the*) **7** *a) Poker, etc.* all the money bet at a single time; pool; kitty *b)* [Informal] a large amount, as of money **8** [Informal] a potshot **9** [Slang] POTBELLY —***vt.*** **pot′ted, pot′ting** **1** to put into a pot **2** to preserve in a pot or jar **3** to cook in a pot **4** to shoot (game) for food instead of for sport **5** to hit or secure by or as by a potshot **6** [Informal] to secure, win, or capture; bag —***vi.*** [Informal] to take a potshot; shoot —**go to pot** ⟦from the idea of being chopped into pieces, as meat and vegetables for the stew *pot*⟧ [Informal] to go to ruin; deteriorate

☆**pot**[2] (pät) ***n.*** ⟦contr. < AmSp *potiguaya*⟧ [Informal] MARIJUANA

pot[3] (pät) ***n.*** *short for* POTENTIOMETER

pot[4] *abbrev.* potential

po·ta·ble (pōt′ə bəl) ***adj.*** ⟦Fr < LL *potabilis* < L *potare*, to drink < IE base **pō-*, to drink > Sans *pāti*, (he) drinks, L *bibere*, to drink⟧ fit to drink; drinkable —***n.*** something drinkable; beverage —**po′ta·bil′i·ty** ***n.***

po·tage (pô täzh′) ***n.*** ⟦Fr⟧ soup

pot·ash (pät′ash′) ***n.*** ⟦earlier in pl., *potashes* < Du *potasschen* < *pot*, POT[1] + *asch*, ASH[1]: orig. prepared by evaporating the lixivium of wood ashes in iron pots⟧ **1** *a)* POTASSIUM CARBONATE (esp. when obtained from wood ashes) *b)* POTASSIUM HYDROXIDE **2** any substance containing potassium; esp., salts derived from natural brines, distillery waste, flue dusts of blast furnaces, etc., whose potassium content is expressed in terms of K_2O: used in fertilizers, soaps, etc.

po·tas·si·um (pə tas′ē əm) ***n.*** ⟦ModL: so named < *potassa* < Du *potasch*, POTASH, by Sir Humphry DAVY, who first isolated it from potash⟧ a soft, silver-white, waxlike metallic chemical element, one of the alkali metals, that oxidizes rapidly when exposed to air: it occurs abundantly in nature in the form of its salts, which are used in fertilizers, glass, etc.: symbol, K; at. no. 19: see the periodic table of elements in the Reference Supplement —**po·tas′sic** ***adj.***

po·tas·si·um-ar·gon dating (-är′gän′) an indirect method of dating fossils, esp. those in very ancient volcanic rock, by using potassic minerals in the same strata as a reference: a natural radioactive isotope of potassium, K-40, decays steadily into argon, which accumulates in the minerals and is measured to determine age

potassium bitartrate CREAM OF TARTAR

potassium bromide a white, crystalline compound, KBr, used in photography, medicine, etc.

potassium carbonate a strongly alkaline, white, crystalline compound, K_2CO_3, used in the manufacture of soap and glass, in medicine, etc.

potassium chlorate a colorless, crystalline salt, $KClO_3$, a strong oxidizing agent used in medicine and in the manufacture of explosives, matches, etc.

potassium chloride a colorless, crystalline salt, KCl, used in fertilizers, as a source of potassium salts, etc.

potassium cyanide an extremely poisonous, white, crystalline compound, KCN, used in metallurgy for extracting gold, in electroplating, as an insecticide, etc.

potassium dichromate a yellowish-red, crystalline compound, $K_2Cr_2O_7$, used as an oxidizing agent and in photography, dyeing, etc.

potassium hydrogen tartrate CREAM OF TARTAR

potassium hydroxide a white crystalline salt or deliquescent solid, KOH, used in the manufacture of soap, glass, etc.: it is a very strong alkali and absorbs carbon dioxide from the air

potassium iodide a transparent, crystalline salt, KI, available also as a white, granular powder, used as a feed additive and in medicine, photography, etc.

potassium nitrate a colorless, crystalline compound, KNO_3, used in fertilizers, gunpowder, preservatives, etc., in medicine, and as a reagent and oxidizing agent in chemistry

potassium permanganate a dark-purple, crystalline compound, $KMnO_4$, used as an oxidizing agent, disinfectant, antiseptic, etc.

potassium sulfate a white, crystalline solid, K_2SO_4, used in fertilizers, medicine, etc.

po·ta·tion (pō tā′shən) ***n.*** ⟦ME *potacion* < MFr < L *potatio* < *potare*, to drink: see POTABLE⟧ **1** the act of drinking **2** a drink or draft, esp. of liquor

po·ta·to (pə tāt′ō, -tāt′ə) ***n.***, *pl.* **-toes** ⟦Sp *patata*, var. of *batata*, sweet potato < Taino name⟧ **1** *short for* SWEET POTATO **2** *a)* the starchy, brown-skinned or red-skinned tuber of a widely cultivated plant (*Solanum tuberosum*) of the nightshade family, eaten as a cooked vegetable; the common white potato *b)* this plant

☆**potato beetle** (*or* **bug**) COLORADO BEETLE

☆**potato chip** a very thin slice of potato fried crisp and then usually salted and sometimes flavored: also [Brit.] **potato crisp**

pot-au-feu (pô tō fö′) ***n.*** ⟦Fr, lit., pot on the fire⟧ a French dish made by boiling meat and vegetables, etc.: the broth is customarily strained and served separately

pot·bel·lied (pät′bel′ēd) ***adj.*** **1** having a potbelly **2** having rounded, bulging sides [a *potbellied* stove]

pot·bel·ly (-bel′ē) ***n.***, *pl.* **-lies** a protruding belly

pot·boil·er (-boi′lər) ***n.*** ⟦metaphoric extension: in ref. to the family cooking *pot*⟧ a piece of writing, a painting, etc. done quickly to earn a living and typically of inferior quality

pot-bound (pät′bound′) ***adj.*** *Bot.* having roots so crowded and tangled as to have outgrown its container: said of a potted plant

☆**pot cheese** a type of coarse, dry cottage cheese

po·teen (pō tēn′) ***n.*** ⟦Ir *poitin*, dim. of *poite*, pot⟧ in Ireland, illicitly distilled whiskey

Po·tem·kin (pō tem′kin, pə-), **Gri·go·ri (Aleksandrovich)** (gri gôr′ē) 1739-91; Russ. field marshal & statesman: favorite of Catherine the Great

Potemkin village ⟦after prec., said to have built sham villages to impress Catherine the Great on her tour of the Crimea: story now generally considered apocryphal⟧ a false front or facade

po·ten·cy (pōt′'n sē) ***n.***, *pl.* **-cies** ⟦L *potentia*⟧ **1** the state or quality of being potent, or the degree of this; power; strength **2** capacity for development; potentiality Also, esp. for sense 1, **po′tence** —***SYN.*** STRENGTH

po·tent (pōt′'nt) ***adj.*** ⟦L *potens* (gen. *potentis*), prp. of *posse*, to be able < *potis*, able (< IE base **potis*, master, husband > Sans *pāti*, master) + *esse*, to be: see ESSENCE⟧ **1** having authority or power; mighty; influential [a *potent* monarch] **2** convincing; cogent [a *potent* argument] **3** effective or powerful in action, as a drug or drink **4** able to have an erection and hence to engage in sexual intercourse —**po′tent·ly** ***adv.***

po·ten·tate (pōt′'n tāt′) ***n.*** ⟦ME *potentat* < LL *potentatus* < LL(Ec), power, rule < L *potens:* see prec.⟧ a person having great power; ruler; monarch

po·ten·tial (pō ten′shəl, pə-) ***adj.*** ⟦ME *potenciall* < ML *potentialis* < L *potentia:* see POTENT⟧ **1** that has power; potent **2** that can, but has not yet, come into being; possible; latent; unrealized; undeveloped **3** *Gram.* expressing possibility, capability, power, etc. [the *potential* mood] —***n.*** **1** *a)* something potential; a potentiality *b)* capacity for future success; promise **2** *Elec.* the difference in voltage between two points in an electric circuit or field **3** *Gram.* *a)* the potential mood or aspect *b)* a construction or form in this mood or aspect **4** *Physics* a function whose mathematical derivative is a physical field, as a force or an electric or magnetic field —***SYN.*** LATENT —**po·ten′tial·ly** ***adv.***

potential energy energy that is the result of relative position or structure instead of motion, as in a compressed spring

po·ten·ti·al·i·ty (pō ten′shē al′ə tē, pə-) ***n.*** ⟦ML *potentialitas*⟧ **1** the state or quality of being potential; possibility of becoming, developing, etc.; latency **2** *pl.* **-ties** something potential; a possibility

po·ten·ti·ate (pō ten′shē āt′, pə-) *vt.* **-at′ed, -at′ing** ⟦< L *potentia*, POTENCY + -ATE[1], infl. by Ger *potenziren* < *potenz* < L *potentia*⟧ to increase or multiply (the effect of a drug or toxin) by the preceding or simultaneous administration of another drug or toxin —**po·ten′ti·a′tor** *n.* —**po·ten′ti·a′tion** *n.*

po·ten·til·la (pō′tən til′ə) *n.* ⟦ModL, name of the genus < ML, valerian, dim. of L *potens:* see POTENT⟧ CINQUEFOIL (sense 1)

po·ten·ti·om·e·ter (pō ten′shē äm′ət ər, pə-) *n.* ⟦< POTENTIAL + -METER⟧ *Elec.* any of various devices for measuring, comparing, or controlling electric potentials; specif., a kind of resistor that can be varied, as in a rotary device used to control the volume of a radio, TV, etc.

pot·ful (pät′fo͝ol′) *n., pl.* **-fuls′** as much as a pot will hold

pot·head (pät′hed′) *n.* ⟦POT[2] + -HEAD[2]⟧ ☆[Slang] a habitual user of marijuana

po·theen (pō thēn′) *n. var. of* POTEEN

poth·er (päth′ər) *n.* ⟦< ?⟧ **1** [Archaic] a choking cloud of smoke, dust, etc. **2** an uproar, commotion, fuss, etc. — *vt., vi.* to fuss or bother

pot·herb (pät′hurb′, pät′urb′) *n.* any herb used in cooking or flavoring

pot·hold·er (pät′hōl′dər) *n.* a small pad, or piece of thick cloth, for holding and handling hot pots, etc.

pot·hole (pät′hōl′) *n.* **1** a deep hole or pit; esp., a deep, round hole formed in the rock of a riverbed by gravel whirling in water **2** CHUCKHOLE **3** a deep cave extending downward underground

pot·hook (pät′ho͝ok′) *n.* **1** an S-shaped hook for hanging a pot or kettle over a fire **2** a hooked rod for lifting hot pots, etc. **3** a curved or S-shaped mark in writing

po·thos (pō′thäs, -thōs) *n.* ⟦ModL < name in Sinhalese⟧ any of a genus (*Pothos*) of tropical, Old World vines of the arum family, with thick, waxy, heart-shaped, mottled leaves, including several species that are often used as houseplants: cf. PHILODENDRON (sense 1)

pot·house (pät′hous′) *n.* [Old Informal, Chiefly Brit.] a small alehouse or tavern

pot·hunt·er (pät′hun′tər) *n.* **1** a hunter who kills game indiscriminately, disregarding the rules of sport **2** a person who enters contests merely to win prizes **3** [Informal] an amateur archaeologist

po·tiche (pô tēsh′) *n., pl.* **-tiches′** (-tēsh′) ⟦Fr < *pot*, POT[1]⟧ a tall vase or jar made typically of porcelain, with a rounded or polygonal body narrowing toward the top

po·tion (pō′shən) *n.* ⟦ME *pocion* < OFr < L *potio* < *potare*, to drink: see POTABLE⟧ a drink or liquid dose, as of medicine, poison, or a substance thought to have magic power

☆**pot·latch** (pät′lach′) *n.* ⟦< AmInd (Chinook) *patshatl*, gift⟧ among some American Indians of the N Pacific coast, *a)* [*often* **P-**] a winter festival *b)* a distribution or exchange of gifts during such a festival, often involving the squandering of the host's belongings

pot liquor the liquid left after meat and vegetables have been cooked, often used for broth or gravy: also **pot′lik′ker** *n.*

pot·luck (pät′luk′) *n.* **1** whatever the family meal happens to be [a neighbor invited in to take *potluck*] **2** whatever is available, with little or no choice **3** POTLUCK DINNER

potluck dinner (*or* supper) a dinner to which everyone brings food to share

pot marigold a cultivated calendula (*Calendula officinalis*) with showy yellow or orange flowers

Po·to·mac (pə tō′mək) ⟦< Algonquian; meaning unknown⟧ river in the E U.S., forming a boundary of W.Va., Md., & Va., and flowing into Chesapeake Bay: 285 mi (459 km)

Po·to·sí (pô′tô sē′) **1** city in SW Bolivia, on the slopes of Cerro de Potosí: elevation *c.* 13,340 ft (4,066 m) **2 Cer·ro de** (ser′rô de) mountain of the Andes, in SW Bolivia: 15,843 ft (4,829 m)

☆**pot·pie** (pät′pī′) *n.* a meat pie made in a pot or deep dish, often with only a top crust

pot·pour·ri (pō′po͞o rē′, pō′po͞o rē′) *n.* ⟦Fr < *pot*, POT[1] + *pourri*, pp. of *pourrir*, to rot, transl. of Sp *olla podrida:* see OLLA-PODRIDA⟧ **1** [Obs.] a stew **2** a mixture of dried flower petals with spices, kept as in a jar for its fragrance **3** a medley, miscellany, or anthology

pot roast meat, usually a large cut of beef, cooked in one piece by braising

Pots·dam (päts′dam′; *Ger* pôts däm′) city in E Germany: capital of the state of Brandenburg

pot·sherd (pät′shurd′) *n.* ⟦ME *potschoord:* see POT[1] & SHARD⟧ a piece of broken pottery, esp. one found as an archaeological artifact

pot·shot (pät′shät′) *n.* **1** a pothunter's shot **2** an easy shot, as at close range **3** a random shot **4** a haphazard try **5** a random criticism or attack

pot·stone (pät′stōn′) *n.* a kind of soapstone of which cooking vessels were made in prehistoric times

☆**pot·sy** (pät′sē) *n.* ⟦< ?⟧ [Northeast] HOPSCOTCH

pot·tage (pät′ij) *n.* ⟦ME *potage* < MFr < *pot*, POT[1]⟧ a kind of thick soup or stew made of vegetables, or meat and vegetables

pot·ted (pät′id) *adj.* **1** put into a pot [a *potted* plant] **2** cooked or preserved in a pot or can ☆**3** [Slang] intoxicated; drunk **4** [Chiefly Brit.] condensed or summarized, often to the extent of being superficial, overly terse, etc. [*potted* biographies]

pot·ter[1] (pät′ər) *n.* ⟦ME < Late OE *pottere* < ML *pottarius*⟧ a person who makes earthenware pots, dishes, etc.

pot·ter[2] (pät′ər) *vi., vt.* ⟦freq. formation < obs. *pote* < OE *potian*, to push⟧ *chiefly Brit. var. of* PUTTER[3]

Pot·ter (pät′ər), **(Helen) Be·a·trix** (bē′ə triks′) 1866-1943; Eng. writer & illustrator of children's books

potter's field ⟦so named from a burial place for strangers in Jerusalem, ? orig. a *field* bought from a *potter*: Matt. 27:7⟧ ☆a burial ground for paupers or unknown persons

potter's wheel a rotating horizontal disk, mounted on a vertical shaft and turned by foot or by a motor, upon which clay is molded into bowls, pots, etc.

potter's wheel

☆**potter wasp** MASON WASP

pot·ter·y (pät′ər ē) *n., pl.* **-ter·ies** ⟦LME *poterye* < MFr *poterie* < *potier*, potter < *pot*, POT[1]⟧ **1** a place where earthenware is made; potter's workshop or factory **2** the art or occupation of a potter; ceramics **3** pots, bowls, dishes, etc. made of clay hardened by heat; earthenware

pot·tle (pät′'l) *n.* ⟦ME *potel* < MFr, dim. of *pot*, POT[1]⟧ **1** a former unit of liquid measure, equal to a half gallon **2** a pot or tankard of this capacity, or its contents, as wine, ale, etc.

pot·to (pät′ō) *n., pl.* **-tos** ⟦< name in a Niger-Congo language, as in Wolof *pata*, a kind of tailless monkey⟧ a slow-moving, large-eyed central African prosimian primate (*Perodicticus potto*) of the same family as the lorises and angwantibos

Pott's disease (päts′) ⟦after Percival *Pott* (1714-88), Eng surgeon⟧ tuberculous caries of the vertebrae, resulting in curvature of the spine

pot·ty[1] (pät′ē) *n., pl.* **-ties** ⟦dim. of POT[1]⟧ **1** a small chamber pot for a child **2** a child's chair used for toilet training, consisting of an open seat beneath which a pot is attached: in full **potty chair** **3** a toilet: a child's word

pot·ty[2] (pät′ē) *adj.* **-ti·er, -ti·est** ⟦< POT[1] (sense 4) + -Y[2]⟧ [Brit. Informal] **1** trivial; petty **2** slightly crazy —**pot′ti·ness** *n.*

☆**POTUS** (pōt′əs) *abbrev.* President of the United States

pot-wal·lop·er (pät′wäl′əp ər) *n.* ⟦altered (infl. by *wallop*, to boil) < *potwaller*, lit., a pot boiler < POT[1] + obs. *wall*, to boil < ME *wallen* < OE *weallan* < IE base **wel-*, to turn, roll > WALK⟧ *Eng. History* a man considered a householder by virtue of owning a hearth, and therefore qualified to vote

pouch (pouch) *n.* ⟦ME *pouche* < MFr *poche*, var. of *poque:* see POKE[2]⟧ **1** a small bag or sack for carrying something, as in one's pocket [a leather tobacco *pouch*] ☆**2** a mailbag, specif. one whose opening can be locked, as for sending diplomatic dispatches **3** [Scot.] a pocket (in clothing) **4** [Archaic] a purse **5** *Anat.* any pouchlike cavity or part **6** *Zool. a)* MARSUPIUM (sense 1) *b)* a baglike part, as of a pelican's bill or a gopher's cheeks, used to carry food —*vt.* **1** to put in a pouch **2** to make into a pouch; make pouchy **3** to swallow: said of fish and certain birds —*vi.* to form a pouch or pouchlike cavity

pouched (poucht) *adj.* having a pouch or pouches

pouch·y (pou′chē) *adj.* **pouch′i·er, pouch′i·est** resembling a pouch; baggy —**pouch′i·ness** *n.*

pouf (po͞of) *n.* ⟦Fr, a puff: echoic⟧ **1** an elaborate headdress worn by women, esp. in the 18th cent., and characterized by high rolls or puffs of hair **2** any part of a dress, etc. gathered into a puff, or projection **3** a kind of ottoman or hassock **4** [Brit. Slang] *var. of* POOF[2]: a dismissive and, often, offensive term Also sp. **pouff** or **pouffe**

Pouil·ly Fuis·sé (po͞o yē fwē sā′) ⟦Fr⟧ a dry white Burgundy wine made from the chardonnay grape

Pouil·ly-Fu·mé (po͞o yē fo͞o mā′; *Fr*, -fü mā′) *n.* ⟦Fr⟧ a dry white wine produced in the valley of the Loire from the sauvignon blanc grape: also written **Pouilly Fumé**

pou·lard or **pou·larde** (po͞o lärd′) *n.* ⟦Fr *poularde* < *poule*, hen: see POULTRY⟧ **1** a young hen spayed for fattening **2** any fat young hen

poule (po͞ol) *n.* ⟦Fr, hen: see POULTRY⟧ *Fr. slang for* PROSTITUTE

Pou·lenc (po͞o lank′), **Fran·cis** (frän sēs′) 1899-1963; Fr. composer

poult (pōlt) *n.* ⟦ME *pulte*, contr. of *pulete*, PULLET⟧ any young fowl, as a turkey

poul·ter·er (pōl′tər ər) *n.* ⟦ME *pulter* < MFr *pouletier* < *poulet* (see POULTRY) + -ER⟧ [Brit.] a dealer in poultry and game: also [Archaic] **poul′ter**

poul·tice (pōl′tis) *n.* ⟦earlier *pultes* < ML, thick pap, orig. pl. of L *puls:* see PULSE[2]⟧ a hot, soft, moist mass, as of flour, herbs, mustard, etc., sometimes spread on cloth, applied to a sore or inflamed part of the body —*vt.* **-ticed, -tic·ing** to apply a poultice to

poul·try (pōl′trē) *n.* ⟦ME *pultrie* < MFr *pouleterie* < *poulet*, dim. of *poule*, hen < L *pullus*, chicken, small animal < IE base **pōu-*, **pu-*, small child, small animal > FOAL, FEW, L *puer*, child⟧ domestic fowls raised for meat or eggs; chickens, turkeys, ducks, geese, etc. collectively

poul·try·man (-mən) *n., pl.* **-men** (-mən) **1** a person who raises poultry, esp. commercially **2** a dealer in poultry

pounce[1] (pouns) *n.* ⟦ME *pownce*, talon, prob. altered < MFr *poinçon*, sharp instrument, stiletto: see PUNCHEON[1]⟧ **1** a claw or talon of a bird of prey **2** the act of pouncing; swoop, spring, or leap —*vi.* **pounced, pounc′ing** to swoop down, spring, or leap (*on, upon*, or *at* a person or thing) in, or as in, attacking or seizing: often used fig. —**pounc′er** *n.*

pounce[2] (pouns) *n.* ⟦Fr *ponce* < L *pumex*, PUMICE⟧ **1** a fine powder, as pulverized cuttlefish bone, formerly used to prevent ink from blotting or to prepare the writing surface of parchment **2** a fine powder sprinkled over a stencil to make a design, as on cloth —*vt.* **pounced, pounc′ing** **1** to sprinkle, rub, finish, or prepare with pounce **2** to stencil with pounce

poun·cet box (poun′sit) ⟦prob. < MFr **poncette*, box for prec.⟧ [Archaic] POMANDER (sense 1*b*)

pound[1] (pound) *n.*, *pl.* **pounds**; sometimes, after a number, **pound** ⟦ME < OE *pund*, akin to Ger *pfund:* WGmc loanword < L *pondo*, a pound, orig. abl. of *pondus*, weight (in *libra pondo*, a pound in weight), akin to *pendere:* see PENDANT⟧ **1** *a)* the basic unit of weight in the FPS system, equal to 16 ounces avoirdupois (453.59237 grams) *b)* a unit of weight equal to 12 ounces troy or 12 ounces apothecaries' (373.2418 grams): abbrev. *lb.* (see LIBRA, *n.* 1): symbol, # **2** ⟦orig., the value of a *pound* of Eng silver pennies: see STERLING (*n.* 1)⟧ the basic monetary unit of the United Kingdom, equal to 100 (new) pennies: before 1971 a pound was equal to 20 shillings or 240 pennies: symbol, £ (see LIBRA, *n.* 1): see the table of monetary units in the Reference Supplement: in full **pound sterling** **3** any of the basic monetary units of various countries, as Egypt, Lebanon, and Syria: see the table of monetary units in the Reference Supplement **4** a former Scottish monetary unit (**pound Scots**), originally equal to the British pound **5** *Bible* MINA[1]

pound[2] (pound) *vt.* ⟦altered (with unhistoric *-d*) < ME *pownen* < OE *punian*, akin to Du *puin*, rubbish⟧ **1** to beat to a pulp, powder, etc.; pulverize **2** to strike or drive with repeated, heavy blows **3** to make by pounding **4** to force or impose [*pound* sense into him] —*vi.* **1** to deliver repeated, heavy blows (*at* or *on* a door, etc.) **2** to move with heavy steps or come down heavily while moving **3** to beat heavily; throb —*n.* **1** the act of pounding **2** a hard blow **3** the sound of this; thud; thump —*SYN.* BEAT —**pound out** **1** to flatten, smooth, etc. by pounding **2** *a)* to play, as on a piano, with a very heavy touch *b)* to produce, as on a typewriter, by intense, unremitting effort —☆**pound the pavement** [Slang] to walk the streets, as in looking for work

pound[3] (pound) *n.* ⟦ME *poonde* < OE *pund-* (in comp.), akin to *pyndan*, to shut up⟧ **1** an enclosure, maintained as by a city or county, for confining stray animals until claimed or adopted **2** an enclosure for keeping or sheltering animals **3** an enclosure for trapping animals **4** a place of confinement, as for arrested persons **5** an enclosed area for catching or keeping fish, esp. the inner section of a pound net —*vt.* [Archaic] to confine in a pound

Pound (pound), **Ezra (Loomis)** 1885-1972; U.S. poet, in Italy (1924-45; 1958-72)

pound·age[1] (poun′dij) *n.* **1** a tax, rate, or commission, etc. per pound (sterling or weight) **2** weight in pounds

pound·age[2] (poun′dij) *n.* **1** confinement in or as in a pound, or enclosure **2** the fee required to free animals from a pound

pound·al (poun′dəl) *n.* ⟦POUND[1] + (QUINT)AL⟧ the basic unit of force in the FPS system, equal to the force which imparts an acceleration of one foot per second per second to a mass of one pound (0.1383 newton or 13,825.5 dynes): abbrev. *pdl*

pound·cake (pound′kāk′) *n.* ⟦so named because the traditional recipe calls for a *pound* each of flour, sugar, butter, and eggs⟧ a type of rich, buttery loaf cake

pound·er (poun′dər) *n.* a person or thing that pounds

-pound·er (poun′dər) *combining form* something weighing or worth (a specified number of) pounds: used in hyphenated compounds [*five-pounder*]

pound-fool·ish (pound′fo͞ol′ish) *adj.* not handling large sums of money wisely: see PENNY-WISE

pound·ing (poun′diŋ) *n.* **1** the act of a person or thing that pounds **2** a beating or drubbing **3** a throbbing; pulsation **4** a thorough defeat

☆**pound net** a fish trap consisting of staked nets arranged so as to form an enclosure with a narrow opening

pound of flesh ⟦allusion to Shakespeare's *Merchant of Venice* IV, 1⟧ due measure owed to one, esp. when demanded out of spite or vengeance

pound sign ⟦see POUND[1] (*n.* 1)⟧ a symbol (#) on a button (**pound key**) on a keypad or keyboard

pour (pôr) *vt.* ⟦ME *pouren* < ?⟧ **1** to cause to flow in a continuous stream **2** to emit, discharge, supply, utter, etc. profusely or steadily —*vi.* **1** to flow freely, continuously, or copiously **2** to rain heavily **3** to rush in a crowd; swarm ☆**4** to serve as a hostess at a reception or the like by pouring the tea, coffee, etc. for the guests —*n.* **1** an act of pouring **2** a heavy rain or downpour —☆**pour it on** [Slang] **1** to flatter profusely **2** to increase one's efforts greatly, work very hard, etc. **3** to go very fast —**pour′er** *n.*

pour·boire (po͝or bwär′) *n.*, *pl.* **-boires′** (-bwär′) ⟦Fr < *pour*, for + *boire*, to drink⟧ a tip, or gratuity

pour·par·ler (po͝or′pär lā′; *Fr* po͞or pȧr lā′) *n.* ⟦Fr < *pour*, for + *parler*, to speak⟧ an informal preliminary discussion

pour·point (po͝or′point′) *n.* ⟦ME *purpoynt* < OFr *porpoint*, orig., perforated: altered (based on *pour*, for) < VL * *perpunctus*, pp. of **perpungere* < L *per-*, through (see PER[1]) + *pungere*, to prick: see POINT⟧ a quilted doublet worn in the late Middle Ages

☆**pousse-ca·fé** (po͞os′ka fā′) *n.* ⟦Fr, coffee chaser⟧ **1** a liqueur drunk with after-dinner coffee **2** a drink consisting of several liqueurs poured to form separate layers in a small, slender glass

pous·sette (po͞o set′) *n.* ⟦Fr, dim. of *pousse*, a PUSH⟧ a dance figure in which a couple or couples dance round and round with hands joined —*vi.* **-set′ted**, **-set′ting** to perform a poussette

Pous·sin (po͞o san′), **Ni·co·las** (nē kô lä′) 1594-1665; Fr. painter

pou sto (po͞o′ stō′, pou′) ⟦Gr *pou stō*, where I may stand: from a saying of Archimedes, *dos moi pou stō, kai kinō tēn gēn*, give me (a place) where I may stand, and I will move the earth⟧ **1** a place to stand on **2** a basis of operations

pout[1] (pout) *vi.* ⟦ME *pouten*, ult. < IE base **bu-*, to swell⟧ **1** to thrust out the lips as in sullenness or displeasure **2** to sulk **3** to protrude: said of the lips —*vt.* to thrust out (the lips) —*n.* **1** the act of pouting **2** a fit of sulking: also [Informal] **the pouts**

pout[2] (pout) *n.*, *pl.* **pout** or **pouts** ⟦OE *-pute:* for IE base see prec.⟧ any of several fishes with a stout body, as an eelpout

pout·er (pout′ər) *n.* **1** a person who pouts **2** any of a breed of domestic pigeon with a slender body and long legs, that can distend its crop to produce a large, puffed-up breast

pout·y (pout′ē) *adj.* **pout′i·er**, **pout′i·est** **1** sullen; sulking **2** full and protruding: said of the lips

POV *abbrev.* point of view

pov·er·ty (päv′ər tē) *n.* ⟦ME *poverte* < OFr *povreté* < L *paupertas* < *pauper*, POOR⟧ **1** the condition or quality of being poor; indigence; need **2** deficiency in necessary properties or desirable qualities, or in a specific quality, etc.; inadequacy [*poverty* of the soil, *poverty* of imagination] **3** smallness in amount; scarcity; paucity

SYN.—**poverty**, the broadest of these terms, implies a lack of the resources for reasonably comfortable living; **destitution** and **want** imply such great poverty that the means for mere subsistence, such as food and shelter, are lacking; **indigence**, a somewhat euphemistic term, implies a lack of luxuries which one formerly enjoyed; **penury** suggests such severe poverty as to cause misery, or a loss of self-respect —*ANT.* **wealth, affluence**

poverty line the level of income below which a person or family is considered officially to be in poverty: also **poverty level**

pov·er·ty-strick·en (-strik′ən) *adj.* **1** stricken with poverty; very poor **2** characteristic of, or giving the appearance of, poverty

pow[1] (pō) *n.* [Chiefly Scot.] POLL (sense 1)

pow[2] (pou) *interj.* used to suggest the sound of a shot, explosion, etc. —*n.* such a sound

POW (pē′ō′dub′əl yo͞o′) *n.*, *pl.* **POW's** PRISONER OF WAR

pow·der (pou′dər) *n.* ⟦ME *poudre* < OFr < L *pulvis* (gen. *pulveris*), dust: see POLLEN⟧ **1** any dry substance in the form of very fine, dustlike particles, produced by crushing, grinding, etc. **2** a specific kind of powder [bath *powder*, face *powder*] **3** *a)* a drug in the form of powder *b)* a dose of this **4** *a)* GUNPOWDER *b)* ⟦prob. in reference to swift explosion of powder⟧ [Slang] a sudden or impulsive rush (obs. or Brit. dial. except in the slang phrase ☆**take a powder**, to run away; leave) **5** fine, light, powdery snow, considered best for skiing —*vt.* **1** to sprinkle or cover with or as with powder **2** to apply cosmetic powder to (the body, face, etc.) **3** to make into powder; pulverize —*vi.* **1** to be made into powder **2** to use powder as a cosmetic —**keep one's powder dry** ⟦in ref. to *gunpowder*⟧ to be ready for action —**pow′der·er** *n.*

powder blue pale blue —**pow′der-blue′** *adj.*

powdered sugar granulated sugar ground into a powder

powder horn a container made of an animal's horn, for carrying gunpowder

☆**powder keg** **1** a small barrel used to store gunpowder **2** a potential source of violence, war, disaster, etc.

powder metallurgy the science or process of working metals and alloys by reducing them to powder and shaping this into solids under great heat and pressure

powder monkey **1** [Historical] a boy who carried powder from the magazine to the guns aboard a man-of-war ☆**2** a person who works with explosives, as in oil fields

powder puff a soft pad for applying cosmetic powder

powder room ⟦with ref. to the euphemism *powder one's nose*, to use a lavatory⟧ ☆a lavatory, esp. one for women

pow·der·y (pou′dər ē) *adj.* **1** of, like, or in the form of powder **2** easily crumbled into powder **3** covered with or as with powder

☆**powdery mildew** **1** any of an order (Erysiphales) of ascomycetous fungi that are parasites on the surfaces of higher plants and produce closed fruiting bodies in a powdery mass **2** a plant disease caused by a powdery mildew

Pow·ell (pou′əl; *for 1* pō′əl) **1 Anthony (Dymoke)** 1905-2000; Eng. novelist **2 John Wesley** 1834-1902; U.S. explorer & geologist **3 Lewis Franklin, Jr.** 1907-98; associate justice, U.S. Supreme Court (1972-87)

pow·er (pou′ər) *n.* ⟦ME *pouer* < OFr *poeir*, earlier *poter*, orig. inf. < VL **potere*, to be able, for L *posse*, to be able: see POTENT⟧ **1** ability to do, act, or produce **2** a specific ability or faculty [the *power* of hearing] **3** great ability to do, act, or affect strongly; vigor; force; strength **4** *a)* the ability to control others; authority; sway; influence *b)* [*pl.*] special authority assigned to or exercised by a person or group holding office *c)* legal ability or authority; also, a document giving it **5** a source of physical or mechanical force or energy; force or energy that is at, or can be put to, work [electric *power*, water *power*] **6** the rate at which work is done: abbrev. *P* **7** a person or thing having great influence, force, or authority **8** a nation, esp. one having influence or domination over other nations [a treaty with foreign *powers*] **9** national might or political strength **10** a spirit or divinity **11** [Dial.] a large number or quantity (of something specified) **12** *a)* [Archaic] an armed force; army; navy *b)* military strength [air *power*] **13** *Math.* *a)* the product of the multiplication of a quantity by itself [4 is the second *power* of 2 (2^2)] *b)* EXPONENT (sense 3) **14** *Optics* the degree of magnification of a lens, microscope, telescope, etc., expressed as a ratio of the diameters of image and object —*vt.* to supply with power or with a source of power —*adj.* **1** operated by electricity, a fuel engine, etc. [*power* tools, a *power* mower] **2** served by an auxiliary, engine-powered system that reduces the effort of the operation [*power* steering] 3 producing or carrying electricity [a *power* cell, *power* lines] 4 [Informal] of, for, or signifying persons in business or politics who are regarded as powerful [a *power* lunch, a *power* suit] —**in power** 1 in authority 2 in office —**the powers that be** the persons in control

SYN.—**power** denotes the inherent ability or the admitted right to rule, govern, and determine [the limited *power* of a president]; **authority** refers to the power, because of rank or office, to give commands, enforce obedience, and make decisions [the *authority* of a teacher]; **jurisdiction** refers to the power to rule or decide within certain defined limits [the *jurisdiction* of the courts]; **dominion** implies sovereign or supreme authority [*dominion* over a dependent state]; **sway** stresses the predominance or sweeping scope of power [the Romans held *sway* over the ancient world]; **control**, in this connection, implies authority to regulate, restrain, or curb [under the *control* of a guardian]; **command** implies such authority that enforces obedience to one's orders [in *command* of a regiment] See also **strength**

power alley *Baseball* either of the two areas in the outfield between the outfielders

☆**pow·er·boat** (pou′ər bōt′) *n.* a boat propelled by a motor, esp. such a boat that is relatively large and has an inboard motor

power broker a person who has power and influence, esp. one who operates unofficially or behind the scenes as an intermediary: also written **pow′er·brok′er** *n.*

power dive *Aeron.* a dive speeded up by the use of engine power —**pow′er-dive′** *vi., vt.* **-dived′, -div′ing**

☆**power forward** *Basketball* that one of the two forwards whose function is primarily defensive and who is therefore typically the stronger and larger

pow·er·ful (pou′ər fəl) *adj.* having much power; strong or influential —*adv.* [Dial.] very —**pow′er·ful·ly** *adv.* —**pow′er·ful·ness** *n.*

☆**pow·er·house** (pou′ər hous′) *n.* 1 a building where electric power is generated 2 [Informal] a powerful person, team, etc.

pow·er·less (pou′ər lis) *adj.* without power; weak, feeble, unable, not empowered, etc. —**pow′er·less·ly** *adv.* —**pow′er·less·ness** *n.*

pow·er·lift·ing (pou′ər lift′iŋ) *n.* a type of competitive weight lifting involving the performance of the bench press, dead lift, and squat —**pow′er·lift′er** *n.*

power of appointment the authority granted to a person by deed or will to dispose of the grantor's property

power of attorney a written statement legally authorizing a person to act for another

power pack a unit, as of a radio or TV amplifier, that converts the power-line or battery voltage to required voltages

power plant 1 the entire apparatus serving as the source of power for some particular operation [the *power plant* of an automobile] ☆2 a building where power, esp. electric power, is generated

☆**power play** 1 an offensive play, as in sports, in which force is concentrated in one area; specif., in ice hockey and indoor soccer, one that occurs when the defensive team is shorthanded due to penalties 2 an attempt to attain an end, as in politics or business, through the use of power rather than finesse

power politics 1 political activity, as by an officeholder, characterized by the use of power, influence, etc., usually in ways regarded as somewhat unethical, to effect a desired result 2 international political relations in which each nation attempts to increase its own power and interests by using military or economic coercion

power series *Math.* an infinite series whose terms contain successive, positive, integral powers of a variable

power shovel a large, power-driven excavator having a hinged bucket, controlled by a boom or jointed arm, for scooping

power strip an electrical device consisting of a block of sockets, designed to allow several appliances to be powered from a single outlet

☆**power structure** those persons or groups in a nation, city, organization, etc. who through economic, social, and institutional position constitute the actual ruling power

☆**power takeoff** an accessory unit on a truck, tractor, etc., usually linked to the transmission, allowing engine power to be used for driving other equipment, as a winch

pow·er·train (pou′ər trān′) *n.* DRIVETRAIN

Pow·ha·tan (pou′ə tan′) 1550?-1618; Algonquian Indian chief in E Va.: father of POCAHONTAS

☆**pow·wow** (pou′wou′) *n.* ⟦< Narragansett & Massachusett *powwaw*, priest, orig., prob. "he dreams"⟧ 1 a North American Indian medicine man or priest 2 among North American Indians, a ceremony to conjure the cure of disease, success in war, etc., marked by feasting, dancing, etc. 3 [Chiefly Historical] a conference of or with North American Indians 4 [Informal] any conference or gathering —*vi.* 1 to hold a powwow 2 [Informal] to confer

Pow·ys (pō′is, pou′is) county in central Wales: 1,958 sq mi (5,071 sq km)

pox (päks) *n.* ⟦for *pocks* < ME *pokkes*, pl. of *pokke:* see POCK⟧ 1 any of various diseases characterized by skin eruptions, as smallpox or chickenpox 2 syphilis: usually with *the*

pox·vi·rus (päks′vī′rəs) *n.* ⟦prec. + VIRUS⟧ any of a family (Poxviridae) of very large, complex DNA viruses affecting skin tissue, including those causing smallpox, cowpox, etc.

Po·yang Hu (pô′yäŋ′ ho͞o′) lake in N Jiangxi province, SE China: *c.* 1,000 sq mi (2,590 sq km)

Poz·nań (pôz′nän′y′) city in W Poland, on the Warta River

poz·zuo·la·na (pät′swō lä′nə) *n.* ⟦It < L *puteolana (pulvis)*, (powder of) *Puteoli* (now It *Pozzuoli*), site of the quarries⟧ 1 a volcanic rock, powdered and used in making a hydraulic cement 2 a siliceous or siliceous-and-aluminous material that will, in finely divided form and in the presence of moisture, react with calcium hydroxide to form a cement Also **poz·zo·lan** (pät′sə län′) or **poz′zo·la′na** (-lä′nə) —**poz′zuo·la′nic** *adj.*

pp[1] *abbrev.* 1 pages 2 parcel post 3 past participle 4 postpaid 5 prepaid 6 privately printed

pp[2] *abbrev. Musical Direction* pianissimo

PP *abbrev.* 1 parcel post 2 postpaid 3 prepaid

PPA *abbrev.* phenylpropanolamine

ppb *abbrev.* parts per billion

ppd *abbrev.* 1 postpaid 2 prepaid

PPI *abbrev.* 1 plan position indicator 2 Producer Price Index

ppm *abbrev.* parts per million

PPO (pē′pē′ō′) *n., pl.* **PPO's** ⟦*p(referred) p(rovider) o(rganization)*⟧ a healthcare system in which an organization contracts with particular hospitals, physicians, etc. to provide medical services at a reduced cost, though often allowing prepaid subscribers to be served by providers outside the system with the subscriber sharing a part of the cost

P.P.S., p.p.s., PPS, *or* **pps** *abbrev.* ⟦L *post postscriptum*⟧ an additional postscript

PPV *abbrev.* pay-per-view

PQ *abbrev.* Province of Quebec

pr *abbrev.* 1 pair(s) 2 *Baseball* pinch runner: also **PR** 3 power 4 preferred (stock) 5 present 6 price 7 printed 8 printing 9 pronoun

Pr[1] *abbrev.* 1 Priest 2 Prince 3 Provençal 4 *Bible* Proverbs

Pr[2] *Chem. symbol for* praseodymium

PR or **P.R.** *abbrev.* 1 proportional representation 2 public relations 3 Puerto Rican: a hostile term of contempt 4 Puerto Rico

prac·tic (prak′tik) *adj.* ⟦MFr *practique* < LL *practicus:* see PRACTICE⟧ *obs. var. of* PRACTICAL

prac·ti·ca·ble (prak′ti kə bəl) *adj.* ⟦altered (based on PRACTICE) < Fr *praticable* < *pratiquer*⟧ 1 that can be done or put into practice; feasible [a *practicable* plan] 2 that can be used; usable; useful [a *practicable* tool] —*SYN.* POSSIBLE, PRACTICAL —**prac′ti·ca·bil′i·ty** *n.*, **prac′ti·ca·ble·ness** —**prac′ti·ca·bly** *adv.*

prac·ti·cal (prak′ti kəl) *adj.* ⟦PRACTIC + -AL⟧ 1 of, exhibited in, or obtained through practice or action [*practical* knowledge] 2 *a)* usable; workable; useful and sensible [*practical* proposals] *b)* designed for use; utilitarian 3 concerned with the application of knowledge to useful ends, rather than with theory, speculation, etc. [*practical* science] 4 given to, or experienced from, actual practice [a *practical* farmer] 5 of, concerned with, or dealing realistically and sensibly with everyday activities, work, etc. 6 that is so in practice, whether or not in theory, law, etc.; virtual 7 matter-of-fact; prosaic —**for all practical purposes** so as to amount to; virtually; in effect —**prac′ti·cal·ness** *n.*

SYN.—**practical** stresses effectiveness as tested by actual experience or as measured by a completely realistic approach to life or the particular circumstances involved; **practicable** is used of something that appears to be capable of being put into effect, but has not yet been developed or tried [before the era of electronics, television did not seem *practicable;* today it is but one of the *practical* applications of the science] —*ANT.* **impractical, impracticable**

prac·ti·cal·i·ty (prak′ti kal′ə tē) *n.* 1 the quality or condition of being practical 2 *pl.* **-ties** a practical, rather than theoretical, component or consideration: *often used in pl.* [the *practicalities* of running a small business]

practical joke a trick played on someone, esp. one intended to cause embarrassment or discomfort for the victim —**practical joker**

prac·ti·cal·ly (prak′tik lē, -ti kə lē) *adv.* 1 in a practical manner 2 from a practical viewpoint 3 for all practical purposes; in effect; virtually [*practically* a dictator] 4 [Informal] almost; nearly

☆**practical nurse** a nurse with less training than a registered nurse, often one (**licensed practical nurse**) licensed by the state for certain specified nursing duties

prac·tice (prak′tis) *vt.* **-ticed, -tic·ing** ⟦ME *practisen* < MFr *practiser*, altered < *practiquer* < ML *practicare* < LL *practicus* < Gr *praktikos*, concerning action, practical < *prassein*, to do⟧ 1 to do or engage in frequently or usually; make a habit or custom of [to *practice* thrift] 2 to do repeatedly in order to learn or become proficient; exercise or drill oneself in [to *practice* batting] 3 to put into practice; specif., *a)* to work at (esp. law or medicine) as a profession *b)* to observe, or adhere to (beliefs, ideals, etc.) [to *practice* one's religion] 4 to teach or train through practice; exercise —*vi.* 1 to do something repeatedly in order to learn or acquire proficiency; exercise or drill oneself [to *practice* on the organ] 2 to put knowledge into practice; work at or follow a profession, as medicine, law, etc. 3 [Archaic] to scheme; intrigue —*n.* 1 the act, result, etc. of practicing; specif., *a)* a frequent or usual action; habit; usage [to make a *practice* of being early] *b)* a usual method or custom; convention [the *practice* of leaving a tip for a waitress] 2 *a)* repeated mental or physical action for the purpose of learning or acquiring proficiency *b)* a session of engaging in such action [cheerleading *practice*] *c)* the condition of being proficient or skillful as a result of this [to be out of *practice*] 3 the doing of something as an application of knowledge [the *practice* of a theory] 4 *a)* the exercise of a profession or occupation [the *practice* of law] *b)* a business based on this, often regarded as a legal property [to buy another's law *practice*] 5 [Archaic] intrigue, trickery, a scheme, etc. 6 *Law* the various procedures involved in legal work, in and out of courts —**prac′tic·er** *n.*

SYN.—**practice** implies repeated performance for the purpose of learning or acquiring proficiency [he *practiced* on the violin every day; *practice* makes perfect]; **exercise** implies a putting to or keeping at work [to *exercise* one's rights] or refers to activity, often of a systematic, formal kind, that trains or develops the body or mind [gymnastic *exercises*]; **drill** suggests disciplined group training in which something is taught by constant repetition [to *drill* a squad, an arithmetic *drill*] See also **habit**

prac·ticed (-tist) *adj.* 1 proficient through practice; experienced; skilled 2 learned or perfected by practice

practice teacher STUDENT TEACHER —**practice teaching**

☆**prac·ti·cum** (prak′ti kəm) *n.* ⟦Ger *praktikum* < LL *practicum*, neut. of *practicus*, active: see PRACTICE⟧ a course involving activities emphasizing the practical application of theory, esp. one in which a student gains on-the-job experience in a field of study

prac·tise (prak′tis) *vt., vi.* **-tised, -tis·ing** *chiefly Brit. sp. of* PRACTICE

prac·ti·tion·er (prak tish′ə nər) *n.* ⟦< earlier *practician*, one qualified by practice (< MFr *practicien:* see PRACTICE & -IAN) + -ER⟧ 1 a person who practices a particular profession, art, etc.: often in comb. [general *practitioner*, nurse *practitioner*] ☆2 a Christian Science healer

Pra·do (prä′dō) *n.* Spanish national museum of art in Madrid

prae- (prē) ⟦L: see PRE-⟧ *prefix* PRE-: the preferred form in certain words [*praenomen, praetor*]

prae·di·al (prē′dē əl) *adj.* ⟦ML *praedialis* < L *praedium*, farm, estate < *praes*, surety: see PRESS²⟧ [Historical] 1 of or relating to land or stationary property; landed 2 associated with farming; agrarian 3 owing service as a tenant of land

prae·fect (prē′fekt′) *n. alt. sp. of* PREFECT

prae·mu·ni·re (prē′myōō nī′rē) *n.* ⟦short for ML *praemunire (facias)*, (see to it) that you warn, used for L *praemonere*, to forewarn < *prae-*, before (see PRE-) + *monere*, to warn (see MONITOR)⟧ [Historical] *Eng. Law* 1 any of the writs charging a person with the offense of challenging royal authority, specif. by accepting the authority of the pope over that of the crown 2 the offense itself 3 the penalty for this offense

prae·no·men (prē nō′mən) *n., pl.* **-no′mens** or **-nom′i·na** (-näm′i nə) ⟦L: see PRE- & NAME⟧ the first or personal name of an ancient Roman, preceding the nomen and cognomen (Ex.: *Marcus* Tullius Cicero) —**prae·nom′i·nal** (-näm′i nəl) *adj.*

prae·tor (prē′tər) *n.* ⟦ME (northern) *pretour* < L, for **prae-itor* < *praeire*, to precede < *prae-*, before (see PRE-) + *ire*, to go⟧ a magistrate of ancient Rome, next below a consul in rank —**prae·to·ri·al** (prē tôr′ē əl) *adj.* —**prae′tor·ship′** *n.*

prae·to·ri·an (prē tôr′ē ən) *adj.* 1 of a praetor 2 [*often* **P-**] of or having to do with the bodyguard (**Praetorian Guard**) of a Roman commander or emperor —*n.* 1 a man with the rank of a praetor, or an ex-praetor 2 [*often* **P-**] a member of the Praetorian Guard

prag·mat·ic (prag mat′ik) *adj.* ⟦L *pragmaticus*, skilled in business or law < Gr *pragmatikos* < *pragma*, business, orig. a thing done < *prassein*, to do⟧ 1 [Rare] *a)* busy or active, esp. in a meddlesome way *b)* dogmatic; opinionated 2 having to do with the affairs of a state or community 3 concerned with actual practice, everyday affairs, etc., not with theory or speculation; practical 4 dealing with historical facts, esp. in their causal relationship 5 of or having to do with philosophical pragmatism Also, for senses 1, 3, & 5, **prag·mat′i·cal** —*n.* PRAGMATIC SANCTION —**prag·mat′i·cal·ly** *adv.*

prag·mat·ics (prag mat′iks) *n.* 1 the branch of linguistics concerned with meaning in context, or the meanings of sentences in terms of the speaker's intentions in using them 2 the branch of semiotics dealing with the relationships of signs and symbols to their users

pragmatic sanction [Historical] a royal decree having the force of law

prag·ma·tism (prag′mə tiz′əm) *n.* 1 the quality or condition of being pragmatic ☆2 a method or tendency in philosophy, originating with C. S. Peirce and William James, that determines the meaning and truth of all concepts by their practical consequences —**prag′ma·tist** *n., adj.* —**prag′ma·tis′tic** *adj.*

Prague (präg) capital of the Czech Republic, on the Vltava River: Czech name **Pra·ha** (prä′hä)

Prai·a (prä′yə) capital of Cape Verde

☆**prai·rie** (prer′ē) *n.* ⟦Fr < OFr *praerie* < *pré*, meadow (< L *pratum*, prob. < IE base **prā-*, to bend > MIr *ráith*, fortification, Welsh *bedd-rod*, grave) + *-erie*, -ERY⟧ a large area of level or slightly rolling grasslands, esp. one in the Mississippi Valley

☆**prairie chicken** any of a genus (*Tympanuchus*) of large, brown-and-white grouse with a short, rounded tail, found on the North American prairies and along the coast of the Gulf of Mexico: also **prairie hen**

☆**prairie dog** any of a genus (*Cynomys*, family Sciuridae) of small, burrowing rodents of North America, having a barking cry and living in colonies

☆**prairie oyster** [Informal] 1 a drink made with a raw egg and seasoning, as Worcestershire sauce, taken as a remedy for a hangover 2 [*pl.*] the testicles of a bull calf cooked as food

Prairie Provinces Canadian provinces of Manitoba, Saskatchewan, & Alberta

☆**prairie schooner** a large, box-shaped covered wagon used by pioneers in the 19th cent. to cross the American prairies

☆**prairie soil** [*often* **P- s-**] any of a zonal group of dark, heavy-textured soils, developed under tall grass cover in a temperate, relatively humid climate with moderate rainfall

☆**prairie turnip** BREADROOT

☆**prairie wolf** COYOTE

praise (prāz) *vt.* **praised, prais′ing** ⟦ME *praisen* < OFr *preisier* < LL *pretiare* < L *pretium*, worth, PRICE⟧ 1 [Obs.] to set a price on; appraise 2 to commend the worth of; express approval or admiration of 3 to laud the glory of (God, etc.), as in song; glorify; extol —*n.* 1 a praising or being praised; commendation or glorification 2 [Archaic] a reason or basis for praise —**praise be!** ⟦as in "*Praise be* to God!"⟧ an exclamation of surprise, joy, etc. —**sing someone's praises** to praise someone highly —**prais′er** *n.*

SYN.—**praise** is the simple, basic word implying an expression of approval, esteem, or commendation [to *praise* someone's performance]; **laud** implies great, sometimes extravagant praise [the critics *lauded* the actor to the skies]; **acclaim** suggests an outward show of strong approval, as by loud applause or cheering [he was *acclaimed* the victor]; **extol** implies exalting or lofty praise [the scientist was *extolled* for his work]; **eulogize** suggests formal praise in speech or writing, as on a special occasion [the minister *eulogized* the exemplary life of the deceased]

praise·wor·thy (prāz′wur′thē) *adj.* worthy of praise; laudable; commendable —**praise′wor′thi·ly** *adv.* —**praise′wor′thi·ness** *n.*

Pra·krit (prä′krit) *n.* ⟦< Sans *prākṛta*, natural, simple, vulgar < *pra-* (for IE base see FOR¹), before + *kṛ*, to do, make: cf. SANSKRIT⟧ any of several vernacular, non-Sanskrit Indic languages used in ancient India

☆**pra·line** (prā′lēn′, prä′-) *n.* ⟦Fr, after Marshal Duplessis-*Praslin* (1598-1675), whose cook is said to have invented it⟧ 1 a crisp candy made of nuts, esp. almonds, browned in boiling sugar 2 any of various confections similarly made, esp. a soft or crisp candy patty made of pecans and brown sugar, maple syrup, etc.

prall·tril·ler (präl′tril′ər) *n.* ⟦Ger < *prallen*, to rebound + *triller*, a trill < It *trillo:* see TRILL⟧ *Music* INVERTED MORDENT: see MORDENT

pram¹ (präm, pram) *n.* ⟦Du *praam* < MLowG *prom* < Czech *prám*, ult. < IE base **per-*, to go (see FARE) > FERRY⟧ a small, flat-bottomed boat usually with a square bow; now sometimes, specif., a sailboat made like this

pram² (pram) *n.* ⟦altered < PERAMBULATOR⟧ [Brit.] BABY CARRIAGE

prance (prans) *vi.* **pranced, pranc′ing** ⟦ME *prauncen* < ?⟧ 1 to rise up on the hind legs in a lively way, esp. while moving along: said of a horse 2 to ride on a prancing horse 3 to move about in a way suggestive of a prancing horse; caper 4 to walk or move about in an affected or exaggerated manner —*vt.* to cause (a horse) to prance —*n.* 1 an act or instance of prancing 2 a prancing movement —**pranc′er** *n.* —**pranc′ing·ly** *adv.*

pran·di·al (pran′dē əl) *adj.* ⟦< L *prandium*, late breakfast, luncheon < **pram-*, early (prob. < IE **pṛm-* < base **per*, beyond > FIRST, FROM) + **ed-*, base of *edere*, to EAT + -AL⟧ of a meal, esp. dinner

prang (praŋ) [Slang, Chiefly Brit.] *vt., vi.* ⟦echoic⟧ 1 to cause (an aircraft, vehicle, etc.) to crash 2 to collide with 3 to bomb heavily —*n.* 1 a collision 2 a bombing raid

prank¹ (praŋk) *n.* ⟦Early ModE < ? or akin ? to fol.⟧ a mischievous trick or practical joke —**prank′ster** *n.*

prank² (praŋk) *vt.* ⟦Early ModE, prob. < LowG source, as in Du *pronken*, to make a show⟧ to dress or adorn showily —*vi.* to dress up or make a show

prank·ish (praŋ′kish) *adj.* 1 full of pranks; mischievous or frolicsome 2 like a prank —**prank′ish·ly** *adv.* —**prank′ish·ness** *n.*

prase (prāz) *n.* ⟦Fr < L *prasius* < Gr *prasios*, leek-green < *prason*, leek, akin to L *porrum*, leek⟧ a translucent, greenish variety of chalcedony

pra·se·o·dym·i·um (prā′zē ō dim′ē əm, -sē-) *n.* ⟦ModL < *praseodymia*, a rare earth (< Gr *prasios:* see prec.) + ModL *(di)dymium* (see DIDYMIUM): so named (1885) by C. A. von Welsbach (1858-1929), Austrian chemist, from its spectroscopic line and from being split from didymium⟧ a silvery, malleable chemical element, one of the rare-earth elements, whose salts are generally green in color and are used to color glasses and enamels: symbol, Pr; at. no. 59: see the periodic table of elements in the Reference Supplement

prat (prat) *n.* ⟦< ?⟧ [Slang] the buttocks

prate (prāt) *vi.* **prat′ed, prat′ing** ⟦ME *praten* < MDu, prob. of echoic orig.⟧ to talk much and foolishly; chatter —*vt.* to tell idly; blab —*n.* idle talk; chatter —**prat′er** *n.* —**prat′ing·ly** *adv.*

☆**prat·fall** (prat′fôl′) *n.* a fall on the buttocks, esp. one for comic effect, as in burlesque

prat·in·cole (prat′'n kōl, prat′iŋ-) *n.* ⟦< ModL *pratincola* < L *pratum*, meadow (see PRAIRIE) + *incola*, inhabitant < *in-*, IN-¹ + *colere*, to till: see CULT⟧ any of various small Old World shorebirds (family Glareolidae) with long, pointed wings and a forked tail; esp., the Eurasian pratincole (*Glareola pratincola*)

pra·tique (pra tēk′, prat′ik) *n.* ⟦Fr < *pratiquer* < MFr *practiquer:* see PRACTICE⟧ permission to do business at a port, granted to a ship that has complied with quarantine or health regulations

Pra·to (prä′tô) commune in Tuscany, central Italy, near Florence

prat·tle (prat′'l) *vi., vt.* **-tled, -tling** ⟦MLowG *pratelen*, akin to MDu *praten*, PRATE⟧ 1 PRATE 2 to speak in a childish way; babble —*n.* 1 idle chatter 2 childish babble —**prat′tler** *n.*

pra·u (prä′ōō, prou) *n. var. of* PROA

prawn (prôn) *n.* ⟦ME *prane* < ?⟧ a large shrimp or other similar crustacean —*vi.* to fish for prawns —**prawn′er** *n.*

prax·is (prak′sis) ***n.*** ⟦ML < Gr < *prassein,* to do⟧ **1** practice, as distinguished from theory, of an art, science, etc. **2** established practice; custom **3** [Now Rare] a set of examples or exercises, as in grammar

Prax·it·e·les (prak sit′ə lēz′) ⟦L < Gr *Praxitelēs*⟧ 4th cent. B.C.; Athenian sculptor

pray (prā) ***vt.*** ⟦ME *preien* < OFr *preier* < LL *precare,* for L *precari* < *prex* (gen. *precis*), prayer < IE **prek̑-,* var. of base **perk̑-,* question > Ger *frage,* question⟧ **1** to implore or beseech: now seldom used except as the elliptical form of "I pray you" *[pray* tell me*]* **2** to ask for by prayer or supplication; beg for imploringly **3** to recite (a prayer) silently or aloud **4** [Archaic] to bring about, get, etc. by praying —***vi.*** **1** to ask very earnestly; make supplication, as to a deity **2** to worship God, a god, etc., as by reciting certain set formulas silently or aloud —***SYN.*** APPEAL

prayer[1] (prer) ***n.*** ⟦ME *preiere* < OFr < ML *precaria* < L *precarius,* obtained by begging < *precari,* to entreat: see prec.⟧ **1** the act or practice of praying, as to God or a god **2** an earnest request; entreaty; supplication **3** *a)* a humble and sincere request, as to God or a god *b)* a thought or utterance, as to God or a god, in praise, thanksgiving, confession, etc. *c)* any set formula for praying, as to God or a god **4** [*often pl.*] in some religions, a devotional service consisting chiefly of prayers **5** any spiritual communion, as with God or a god **6** something prayed for or requested ☆**7** [Informal] a chance to succeed *[*the overmatched team doesn't have a *prayer]*

pray·er[2] (prā′ər) ***n.*** a person who prays

prayer beads any string of beads used in praying

prayer book **1** a book of formal religious prayers **2** [**P- B-**] BOOK OF COMMON PRAYER

prayer·ful (prer′fəl) ***adj.*** **1** given to frequent praying; devout **2** like or expressive of prayer —**prayer′ful·ly** ***adv.*** —**prayer′ful·ness** ***n.***

prayer mat PRAYER RUG

prayer meeting any meeting held for the purpose of praying together; specif., such a meeting in some Protestant denominations, usually in the evening and often on Wednesdays, for group prayer, testimonies of faith, singing of hymns, etc.

Prayer of Ma·nas·ses (mə nas′əs) a book of the Old Testament Apocrypha attributed to MANASSEH, King of Judah: abbrev. *Pr of Man*

prayer rug a small rug or carpet used by Muslims to kneel upon while engaged in ritual prayers

prayer shawl TALLIT

prayer wheel a revolving cylinder containing written sacred texts, used by Tibetan Buddhists in praying

praying mantis ⟦so called because the forelegs are often held up and together, suggestive of prayer⟧ MANTIS

PRC *abbrev.* People's Republic of China

pre- (prē, pri) ⟦ME < OFr & L: L *prae-* < *prae,* before, in front of < IE **prai,* var. of base **per,* beyond > FORE, FIRST⟧ *prefix* **1** before in time, earlier (than), prior (to) *[presuppose, prewar]* **2** before in place, in front (of), anterior (to) *[preaxial]* **3** before in rank, superior (to), surpassing *[preeminent]* **4** preliminary to, in preparation for *[preschool]* **5** before the usual or expected time for doing so *[preapprove, preprogrammed]* Cf. PRAE-

praying mantis

preach (prēch) ***vi.*** ⟦ME *prechen* < OFr *precher* < LL(Ec) *praedicare,* to preach the gospel < L, to declare in public, admonish < *prae-,* prec. + *dicare,* to proclaim, akin to *dicere,* to say: see DICTION⟧ **1** to speak in public on religious matters; give a sermon **2** to give moral or religious advice, esp. in a tiresome manner —***vt.*** **1** to expound or proclaim by preaching **2** to advocate by or as by preaching; urge strongly or persistently **3** to deliver (a sermon) —**preach to the choir** to direct arguments to a person or persons who already concur: also **preach to the converted**

preach·er (prē′chər) ***n.*** ⟦ME *prechur*⟧ a person who preaches; esp., a member of the Protestant clergy

preach·i·fy (prē′chə fī′) ***vi.*** **-fied′**, **-fy′ing** [Informal] to preach or moralize in a tiresome manner

preach·ment (prēch′mənt) ***n.*** ⟦ME *prechement* < OFr < LL *praedicamentum:* see PREDICAMENT⟧ a preaching or sermon, esp. a long, tiresome one

preach·y (prē′chē) ***adj.*** **preach′i·er**, **preach′i·est** [Informal] given to or marked by preaching, or moralizing

pre·ad·ap·ta·tion (prē′ad əp tā′shən) ***n.*** the possession of certain characteristics by an organism which make it more adaptable to a future environmental change than similar organisms are —**pre′a·dapt′ive** ***adj.***

pre·am·ble (prē′am′bəl, prē am′-) ***n.*** ⟦ME < MFr *preambule* < ML *praeambulum,* neut. of LL *praeambulus,* going before < L *praeambulare,* to precede < *prae-,* before + *ambulare,* to go: see AMBLE⟧ **1** an introduction, esp. one to a constitution, statute, etc., stating the reasons for it and its purpose **2** an introductory fact, event, etc.; preliminary —***SYN.*** INTRODUCTION

pre·amp (prē′amp′) ***n.*** *short for* PREAMPLIFIER

pre·am·pli·fi·er (prē am′plə fī′ər) ***n.*** in a radio, phonograph, etc., an auxiliary amplifier for boosting the voltage of a weak signal before it reaches the input of the main amplifier

pre·ap·prove (prē′ə pro͞ov′) ***vt.*** **-proved′**, **-prov′ing** **1** to approve in advance **2** to authorize (a person) to obtain (a credit card, loan, etc.) based on CREDIT RATING, not on any formal credit application

pre·ar·range (prē′ə rānj′) ***vt.*** **-ranged′**, **-rang′ing** to arrange beforehand —**pre′ar·range′ment** ***n.***

pre·ax·i·al (prē ak′sē əl) ***adj.*** *Anat.* situated in front of the axis of the body or a limb; esp., of the radial side of the arm or the tibial side of the leg

preb·end (preb′ənd) ***n.*** ⟦ME *prebende* < MFr < ML(Ec) *prebenda* < LL *praebenda,* state support to a private person < neut. pl. ger. of L *praebere,* to grant < *prae-,* before + *habere,* to have⟧ **1** the part of the revenues of a cathedral or collegiate church paid as a clergyman's salary **2** the property or tax that yields such revenue **3** PREBENDARY —**pre·ben·dal** (prē ben′dəl, pri-) ***adj.***

preb·en·dar·y (preb′ən der′ē) ***n.***, *pl.* **-dar′ies** ⟦ME *prebendarie* < ML *praebendarius*⟧ **1** a person receiving a prebend **2** in the Church of England, an honorary canon with only the title of a prebend

pre·bi·o·log·i·cal (prē′bī′ə läj′i kəl) ***adj.*** PREBIOTIC

pre·bi·ot·ic (prē′bī ät′ik) ***adj.*** existing before or making possible the appearance of living organisms *[prebiotic* molecules*]*

prec *abbrev.* preceding

Pre·cam·bri·an (prē kam′brē ən, -kām′-) ***adj.*** [*sometimes* **p-**] designating or of the division of geologic time covering all the time before the Cambrian Period, equivalent to the Archean Eon and the Proterozoic Eon —**the Precambrian** the Precambrian time or its rocks: see the geologic time chart in the Reference Supplement

pre·can·cel (prē kan′səl) ***vt.*** **-celed** or **-celled**, **-cel·ing** or **-cel·ling** to cancel (a postage stamp) before use in mailing: chiefly in the past participle —***n.*** a precanceled stamp —**pre′can′cel·la′tion** ***n.***

pre·can·cer·ous (prē kan′sər əs) ***adj.*** that may become or is likely to become cancerous *[*a *precancerous* mole*]*

pre·car·i·ous (pri ker′ē əs) ***adj.*** ⟦L *precarius:* see PRAYER[1]⟧ **1** dependent upon the will or favor of another person **2** dependent upon circumstances; uncertain; insecure *[*a *precarious* living*]* **3** dependent upon chance; risky *[*a *precarious* foothold*]* **4** dependent upon mere assumption; unwarranted *[*a *precarious* assertion*]* —**pre·car′i·ous·ly** ***adv.*** —**pre·car′i·ous·ness** ***n.***

pre·cast concrete (prē′kast′) concrete in the form of blocks, pillars, bridge sections, etc. that have been cast into form before being put into position

prec·a·to·ry (prek′ə tôr′ē) ***adj.*** ⟦LL *precatorius* < L *precari,* to PRAY⟧ of, having the nature of, or expressing entreaty: also **prec′a·tive** (-tiv)

pre·cau·tion (pri kô′shən) ***n.*** ⟦Fr *précaution* < LL *praecautio* < L *praecautus,* pp. of *praecavere* < *prae-,* before (see PRE-) + *cavere,* to take care: for IE base see HEAR⟧ **1** care taken beforehand; caution used in advance **2** a measure taken beforehand against possible danger, failure, etc. —**pre·cau′tion·ar′y** ***adj.***

pre·ca·va (prē kā′və) ***n.***, *pl.* **-vae** (-vē) ⟦PRE- + (VENA) CAVA⟧ the superior vena cava of four-limbed vertebrates —**pre·ca′val** ***adj.***

pre·cede (prē sēd′, pri-) ***vt.*** **-ced′ed**, **-ced′ing** ⟦ME *preceden* < MFr *précéder* < L *praecedere:* see PRE- & CEDE⟧ **1** to be, come, or go before in time, place, order, rank, or importance **2** to introduce with prefatory remarks, etc. —***vi.*** to be, come, or go before

prec·e·dence (pres′ə dəns; prē sēd′′ns, pri-) ***n.*** ⟦< fol.⟧ **1** the act, right, or fact of preceding in time, order, rank, etc. **2** priority as because of superiority in rank **3** an official or conventional ranking of dignitaries in order of importance Also **prec′e·den·cy**

pre·ced·ent (prē sēd′′nt, pri-; *for n.* pres′ə dənt) ***adj.*** ⟦ME < MFr *précédent* < L *praecedens,* prp. of *praecedere,* to PRECEDE⟧ that precedes; preceding —***n.*** **prec′e·dent** **1** an act, statement, legal decision, case, etc. that may serve as an example, reason, or justification for a later one **2** a practice based upon earlier precedents

prec·e·den·tial (pres′ə den′shəl) ***adj.*** **1** of, having the nature of, or serving as a precedent **2** having precedence; preliminary

pre·ced·ing (prē sēd′iŋ, pri-) ***adj.*** that precedes; going or coming before —***SYN.*** PREVIOUS

pre·cen·sor (prē′sen′sər) ***vt.*** to determine arbitrarily in advance what may or may not be permitted in (books, films, news releases, etc.) —**pre′-cen′sor·ship′** ***n.***

pre·cen·tor (prē sen′tər) ***n.*** ⟦LL *praecentor* < L *praecinere,* to sing or play before: see PRE- & CHANT⟧ a person who directs a church choir or congregation in singing —**pre·cen·to·ri·al** (prē′sen tôr′ē əl) ***adj.*** —**pre·cen′tor·ship′** ***n.***

pre·cept (prē′sept′) ***n.*** ⟦ME < L *praeceptum* < *praecipere,* to admonish, teach < *prae-,* before (see PRE-) + *capere,* to take⟧ **1** a commandment or direction meant as a rule of action or conduct **2** a rule of moral conduct; maxim **3** a rule or direction, as in technical matters **4** *Law* a written order; writ —***SYN.*** DOCTRINE

pre·cep·tive (prē sep′tiv, pri-) ***adj.*** ⟦LL *praeceptivus*⟧ **1** of, having the nature of, or expressing a precept **2** giving precepts; instructive; didactic —**pre·cep′tive·ly** ***adv.***

pre·cep·tor (prē sep′tər, pri-) ***n.*** ⟦L *praeceptor* < *praecipere:* see PRECEPT⟧ **1** a teacher **2** the head of a preceptory —**pre·cep·to·ri·al** (prē′sep tôr′ē əl) ***adj.*** —**pre·cep′tor·ship′** ***n.***

pre·cep·to·ry (prē sep′tə rē, pri-) ***n.***, *pl.* **-ries** ⟦ML *praeceptoria,* estate of a preceptor < L *praeceptor:* see PRECEPT⟧ **1** a provincial community or religious house of the medieval Knights Templars, subordinate to the London Temple **2** its estates

pre·cep·tress (prē sep′tris) ***n.*** a female preceptor

pre·cess (prē ses′, pri-) ***vi.*** ⟦back-form. < fol.⟧ to move by precession

pre·ces·sion (prē sesh′ən, pri-) ***n.*** ⟦ME < LL *praecessio* < L *praecedere,* to PRECEDE⟧ **1** the act of preceding; precedence **2** *Astronomy short for* PRECESSION OF THE EQUINOXES **3** *Mech.* an effect exhibited by a spinning body, as a top, when an applied torque tends to change the direction of its rotational axis, causing this axis generally to describe a cone and to turn at right angles to the direction of the torque —**pre·ces′sion·al** ***adj.***

precession of the equinoxes *Astron.* the occurrence of the equinoxes earlier in each successive sidereal year because of a slow wobble in the earth's axial spin which shifts the equinoctial points slightly westward along the ecliptic: the wobble is caused by the pull of the sun and moon on the earth's equatorial bulges and makes the poles move around a center point (axis of the ecliptic), taking about 25,800 years to return to the same orientation with the stars

pre-Chris·tian (prē′kris′chən) ***adj.*** of, having to do with, or occurring in the time before the Christian era

pre·cinct (prē′siŋkt) ***n.*** ⟦ME *precincte* < ML *praecinctum* < L *praecinctus,* pp. of *praecingere,* to encompass < *prae-,* before (see PRE-) + *cingere,* to surround, gird (see CINCH)⟧ **1** *a)* [*usually pl.*] an enclosure between buildings, walls, etc. *b)* [Chiefly Brit.] the grounds immediately surrounding a religious house or church **2** [*pl.*] environs; a neighborhood ☆**3** *a)* a division of a city, as for police administration *b)* a subdivision of a ward, as for voting purposes **4** [Brit.] an area in a town closed to motor traffic, as for shopping **5** any limited area, as of thought **6** a boundary

pre·ci·os·i·ty (presh′ē äs′ə tē, pres′ē-) ***n.*** ⟦ME *preciousite* < MFr *preciosité* < L *pretiositas* < *pretiosus:* see fol.⟧ great fastidiousness, overrefinement, or affectation, esp. in language

pre·cious (presh′əs) ***adj.*** ⟦ME < OFr *precios* < L *pretiosus* < *pretium,* PRICE⟧ **1** of great price or value; costly **2** of great desirability; held in high esteem [*precious* rights] **3** beloved; dear **4** very fastidious, overrefined, or affected, as in behavior, language, etc. **5** very great [a *precious* liar] —***adv.*** [Informal] very —**pre′cious·ly** ***adv.*** —**pre′cious·ness** ***n.***

precious stone a rare and costly gem: technically, this term is applied to the diamond, emerald, ruby, and sapphire

prec·i·pice (pres′ə pis) ***n.*** ⟦Fr *précipice* < L *praecipitium* < *praeceps,* headlong < *prae-,* before (see PRE-) + *caput,* head (see CHIEF)⟧ **1** a vertical, almost vertical, or overhanging rock face; steep cliff **2** a greatly hazardous situation, verging on disaster

pre·cip·i·tan·cy (prē sip′i tən sē, pri-) ***n.,*** *pl.* **-cies** a being precipitate; great haste; rashness: also **pre·cip′i·tance**

pre·cip·i·tant (prē sip′i tənt, pri-) ***adj.*** ⟦L *praecipitans,* prp. of *praecipitare:* see fol.⟧ PRECIPITATE —***n.*** a substance which, when added to a solution, causes the formation of a precipitate —**pre·cip′i·tant·ly** ***adv.***

pre·cip·i·tate (prē sip′ə tāt′, pri-; *for adj. & n.,* -tit, -tāt′) ***vt.*** **-tat′ed, -tat′ing** ⟦< L *praecipitatus,* pp. of *praecipitare* < *praeceps:* see PRECIPICE⟧ **1** to throw headlong; hurl downward **2** to cause to happen before expected, warranted, needed, or desired; bring on; hasten [to *precipitate* a crisis] **3** *Chem. a)* to cause (a slightly soluble substance) to become insoluble, as by heat or by a chemical reagent, and separate out from a solution *b)* to cause the separation of a suspended liquid or solid from a gas **4** *Meteorol.* to condense (water vapor) and cause to fall to the ground as rain, snow, sleet, etc. —***vi.*** **1** *Chem.* to be precipitated **2** *Meteorol.* to condense and fall to the ground as rain, snow, sleet, etc. —***adj.*** ⟦L *praecipitatus:* see the ***vt.***⟧ **1** falling steeply, rushing headlong, flowing swiftly, etc. **2** acting, happening, or done very hastily or rashly; impetuous; headstrong **3** very sudden, unexpected, or abrupt —***n.*** ⟦ModL *praecipitatum*⟧ a substance that is precipitated out from a solution or gas —***SYN.*** SUDDEN —**pre·cip′i·tate·ly** ***adv.*** —**pre·cip′i·tate·ness** ***n.*** —**pre·cip′i·ta′tive** ***adj.*** —**pre·cip′i·ta′tor** ***n.***

pre·cip·i·ta·tion (prē sip′ə tā′shən, pri-) ***n.*** ⟦MFr *précipitation* < L *praecipitatio*⟧ **1** a precipitating or being precipitated; specif., a headlong fall or rush **2** precipitancy; rash haste; impetuosity **3** a bringing on suddenly; acceleration **4** *Chem. a)* a precipitating or being precipitated from a solution *b)* a precipitate **5** *Meteorol. a)* a depositing of rain, snow, sleet, etc. *b)* rain, snow, sleet, etc. *c)* the amount of this

pre·cip·i·tin (prē sip′ə tin, pri-) ***n.*** ⟦PRECIPIT(ATE) + -IN[1]⟧ an antibody produced in the blood of an animal injected with a soluble antigen: when the antigen is added to blood serum from such an animal, a precipitate forms

pre·cip·i·tin·o·gen (prē sip′ə tin′ə jən, -jen′; pri-) ***n.*** ⟦prec. + -O- + -GEN⟧ the antigen that produces a precipitin —**pre·cip′i·tin′o·gen′ic** (-jen′ik) ***adj.***

pre·cip·i·tous (prē sip′ə təs, pri-) ***adj.*** ⟦MFr *precipiteux* < LL **precipitosus* < L *praeceps:* see PRECIPICE⟧ **1** steep like a precipice; sheer **2** having precipices **3** PRECIPITATE —***SYN.*** STEEP[1] —**pre·cip′i·tous·ly** ***adv.*** —**pre·cip′i·tous·ness** ***n.***

pré·cis (prā sē′, prā′sē′) ***n.,*** *pl.* **pré·cis** (prā sēz′, prā′sēz′) ⟦Fr: see fol.⟧ a concise abridgment; summary; abstract —***vt.*** to make a précis of Also sp. **precis**

pre·cise (prē sīs′, pri-) ***adj.*** ⟦MFr *précis* < L *praecisus,* pp. of *praecidere,* to cut off, be brief < *prae-,* before (see PRE-) + *caedere,* to cut (see -CIDE)⟧ **1** strictly defined; accurately stated; definite **2** speaking definitely or distinctly **3** with no variation; minutely exact [the *precise* amount] **4** *a)* that strictly conforms to usage, rules, etc.; scrupulous; fastidious *b)* too fastidious; finicky —***SYN.*** CORRECT, EXPLICIT —**pre·cise′ness** ***n.***

pre·cise·ly (-lē) ***adv.*** **1** in a precise manner **2** exactly
USAGE—also used as an affirmative reply, equivalent to "I agree"

pre·ci·sian (prē sizh′ən, pri-) ***n.*** a person who is strict and precise in observing rules or customs, esp. of religion; specif., a 16th- or 17th-cent. English Puritan

pre·ci·sion (prē sizh′ən, pri-) ***n.*** ⟦Fr < L *praecisio,* a cutting off⟧ **1** the quality of being precise; exactness, accuracy, etc. **2** the degree of this —***adj.*** **1** characterized by precision, as in measurement, operation, etc. **2** requiring low tolerance, as in manufacturing

pre·ci·sion·ist (prē sizh′ən ist, pri-) ***n.*** a person who attaches great or too great importance to precision

pre·clin·i·cal (prē klin′i kəl) ***adj.*** *Med.* of or in the period of a disease before any of the symptoms appear

pre·clude (prē klo͞od′, pri-) ***vt.*** **-clud′ed, -clud′ing** ⟦L *praecludere,* to shut off < *prae-,* before (see PRE-) + *claudere,* to CLOSE[2]⟧ to make impossible, esp. in advance; shut out; prevent —***SYN.*** PREVENT —**pre·clu′sion** (-klo͞o′zhən) ***n.*** —**pre·clu′sive** (-siv) ***adj.*** —**pre·clu′sive·ly** ***adv.***

pre·co·cial (prē kō′shəl) ***adj.*** ⟦< ModL *praecoces* (< L, pl. of *praecox:* see fol.), precocial birds + -AL⟧ *Ornithology* designating or of birds whose newly hatched young are covered with down and fully active: opposed to ALTRICIAL

pre·co·cious (prē kō′shəs, pri-) ***adj.*** ⟦< L *praecox* < *praecoquere,* to boil beforehand < *prae-,* before (see PRE-) + *coquere,* to mature, COOK⟧ **1** developed or matured to a point beyond that which is normal for the age [a *precocious* child] **2** of or showing premature development —**pre·co′cious·ly** ***adv.*** —**pre·co′cious·ness** ***n.,*** **pre·coc′i·ty** (-käs′ə tē)

pre·cog·ni·tion (prē′käg nish′ən) ***n.*** ⟦LL *praecognitio* < L *praecognitus,* pp. of *praecognoscere,* to foreknow < *prae-,* PRE- + *cognoscere,* to know: see COGNITION⟧ *Parapsychology* the perception of an event, condition, etc. before it occurs, esp. by extrasensory powers —**pre·cog′ni·tive** (-nə tiv) ***adj.***

pre-Co·lum·bi·an (prē′kə lum′bē ən) ***adj.*** of any period in the history of the Western Hemisphere before Columbus arrived in America

pre·con·ceive (prē′kən sēv′) ***vt.*** **-ceived′, -ceiv′ing** **1** [Now Rare] to form a conception or opinion of beforehand **2** to form (an opinion) in advance [a *preconceived* notion]

pre·con·cep·tion (prē′kən sep′shən) ***n.*** ⟦ML *preconceptio*⟧ **1** the act of preconceiving **2** a preconceived idea or opinion **3** bias

pre·con·cert (prē′kən surt′) ***vt.*** ⟦PRE- + CONCERT, v.⟧ to arrange or settle beforehand, as by agreement

pre·con·di·tion (prē′kən dish′ən) ***vt.*** to prepare (someone or something) to behave, react, etc. in a certain way under certain conditions —***n.*** a condition required beforehand if something else is to occur, be done, etc.

pre·co·nize (prē′kə nīz′) ***vt.*** **-nized′, -niz′ing** ⟦ME *preconisen* < ML *praeconizare* < L *praeco* (gen. *praeconis*), public crier (prob. contr. < *praedicator,* proclaimer: see PREACHER) + LL *-izare,* -IZE⟧ **1** to proclaim or extol in public **2** to approve and announce the name of (a new bishop) publicly: said of the pope

pre·con·scious (prē kän′shəs) ***adj.*** *Psychoanalysis* of or pertaining to that part of a person's mental activity which is not immediately conscious, but which can be easily recalled —**the preconscious** preconscious mental activity: see also CONSCIOUS

pre·con·tract (prē kän′trakt′; *for v.* prē′kən trakt′, prē kän′trakt′) [Archaic] ***n.*** a previous contract or pledge, as a betrothal, that bars the making of another —***vt.*** to bind by a previous contract or pledge

pre·cook (prē ko͝ok′) ***vt.*** to cook partially or completely, for final preparation at a later time

pre·cool (prē ko͞ol′) ***vt.*** to cool or refrigerate before packing or shipment

pre·crit·i·cal (prē krit′i kəl) ***adj.*** ⟦PRE- + CRITICAL⟧ coming before a critical period

pre·cur·sor (prē kur′sər, pri-; prē′kur′-) ***n.*** ⟦L *praecursor* < *praecurrere,* to run ahead: see PRE- & CURRENT⟧ **1** a person or thing that goes before; forerunner; harbinger **2** a predecessor, as in office **3** a substance that precedes and is the source of another substance

pre·cur·so·ry (prē kur′sə rē) ***adj.*** ⟦L *praecursorius*⟧ **1** serving as a precursor, or harbinger; indicating something to follow **2** introductory; preliminary

pred *abbrev.* predicate

pre·da·cious or **pre·da·ceous** (prē dā′shəs, pri-) ***adj.*** ⟦< L *praedari,* to prey upon (< *praeda:* see PREY) + -ACEOUS⟧ preying on other animals; predatory —**pre·dac′i·ty** (-das′ə tē) ***n.,*** **pre·da′cious·ness,** or **pre·da′ceous·ness**

pre·date (prē dāt′) ***vt.*** **-dat′ed, -dat′ing** **1** to put a date on (something) that is earlier than the current date **2** to come before in time

pre·da·tion (pri dā′shən) ***n.*** ⟦L *praedatio* < *praedatus,* pp. of *praedari,* to plunder < *praeda,* PREY⟧ **1** the act of plundering or preying **2** the method of existence of predatory animals

pred·a·tor (pred′ə tər) ***n.*** ⟦back-form. < fol.⟧ a predatory person or animal

pred·a·to·ry (pred′ə tôr′ē) ***adj.*** ⟦L *praedatorius* < *praeda,* PREY⟧ **1** of, living by, or characterized by plundering, robbing, or ruthlessly exploiting others **2** living by capturing and feeding upon other animals; predacious —**pred′a·to′ri·ly** ***adv.*** —**pred′a·to′ri·ness** ***n.***

pre·de·cease (prē′dē sēs′, -di-) ***vt., vi.*** **-ceased′, -ceas′ing** to die before (someone else)

pred·e·ces·sor (pred′ə ses′ər, prē′də-; pred′ə ses′ər) ***n.*** ⟦ME *predecessour* < MFr *predecesseur* < LL *praedecessor* < L *prae-,* before (see PRE-) + *decessor,* retiring officer < *decessus,* pp. of *decedere,* to go away, depart < *de-,* from + *cedere,* to go: see CEDE⟧ **1** a person who precedes or preceded another, as in office **2** a thing followed or replaced by another thing, as in use **3** an ancestor; forefather

pre·des·ig·nate (prē dez′ig nāt′) ***vt.*** **-nat′ed, -nat′ing** to designate beforehand —**pre·des′ig·na′tion** ***n.***

pre·des·ti·nar·i·an (prē des′tə ner′ē ən) ***adj.*** ⟦< fol. + -ARIAN⟧ of or believing in predestination —***n.*** a person who believes in predestination —**pre·des′ti·nar′i·an·ism′** ***n.***

pre·des·ti·nate (prē des′tə nit; *for v.,* -nāt′) ***adj.*** ⟦ME *predestynate* < L *praedestinatus*, pp. of *praedestinare*, to PREDESTINE⟧ predestinated or foreordained —*vt.* **-nat′ed, -nat′ing 1** *Theol.* to foreordain by divine decree or intent **2** PREDESTINE —**pre·des′ti·na′tor** *n.*

pre·des·ti·na·tion (prē des′tə nā′shən) *n.* ⟦ME *predestinacioun* < LL(Ec) *praedestinatio*⟧ **1** *Theol.* the doctrine that *a)* God foreordained everything that would happen *b)* God predestines certain souls to salvation and, esp. in Calvinism, others to damnation **2** a predestinating or being predestinated; destiny; fate

pre·des·tine (prē des′tin) *vt.* **-tined, -tin·ing** ⟦ME *predestynen* < L *praedestinare*, to predestine: see PRE- & DESTINE⟧ to destine or decree beforehand; foreordain

pre·de·ter·mine (prē′dē tur′mən) *vt.* **-mined, -min·ing** ⟦LL(Ec) *praedeterminare:* see PRE- & DETERMINE⟧ **1** to determine, decide, or decree beforehand **2** to incline, bias, or impel beforehand; prejudice —**pre′de·ter′mi·nate** (-mə nit) *adj.* —**pre′de·ter′mi·na′tion** *n.*

pre·di·al (prē′dē əl) *adj. alt. sp. of* PRAEDIAL

pred·i·ca·ble (pred′i kə bəl) *adj.* ⟦ML *praedicabilis* < L, praiseworthy < *praedicare:* see PREACH⟧ capable of being predicated —*n.* **1** something predicable **2** *Logic* any of the several sorts of predicate that can be used of a subject, as, in Aristotelian logic, genus, species, difference, property, and accident —**pred′i·ca·bil′i·ty** *n.*, **pred′i·ca·ble·ness** —**pred′i·ca·bly** *adv.*

pre·dic·a·ment (prē dik′ə mənt, pri-) *n.* ⟦ME < LL(Ec) *praedicamentum* < L *praedicare:* see PREACH⟧ **1** a condition or situation, now specif. one that is difficult, unpleasant, embarrassing, or, sometimes, comical **2** [Archaic] CATEGORY (sense 2)

SYN.—**predicament** implies a complicated, perplexing situation from which it is difficult to disentangle oneself; **dilemma** implies a predicament necessitating a choice between equally disagreeable alternatives; **quandary** emphasizes a state of great perplexity and uncertainty; **plight** emphasizes a distressing or unfortunate situation; **fix** and **pickle** are both informal terms loosely interchangeable with any of the preceding, although more precisely **fix** is equivalent to **predicament** and **pickle**, to **plight**

pred·i·cant (pred′i kənt) *adj.* ⟦L *praedicans*, prp. of *praedicare:* see PREACH⟧ preaching —*n.* a preacher; esp., formerly, a Dominican friar

pred·i·cate (pred′i kāt′; *for n. & adj.*, -kit) *vt.* **-cat′ed, -cat′ing** ⟦L *praedicatus*, pp. of *praedicare:* see PREACH⟧ **1** [Obs.] to proclaim; preach; declare; affirm **2** *a)* to affirm as a quality, attribute, or property of a person or thing [to *predicate* the honesty of another's motives] *b)* *Logic* to assert (something) about the subject of a proposition **3** to affirm or base (something) *on* or *upon* given facts, arguments, conditions, etc. **4** to imply or connote —*vi.* to make an affirmation or statement —*n.* ⟦ML *praedicatum*, neut. of *praedicatus:* see the *vt.*⟧ **1** *Gram.* the verb or verbal phrase, including any complements, objects, and modifiers, that is one of the two immediate constituents of a sentence and asserts something about the subject **2** *Logic* something that is affirmed or denied about the subject of a proposition (Ex.: *green* in "grass is green") —*adj. Gram.* being or forming part of the predicate of a sentence [a *predicate* adjective] —**pred′i·ca′tion** *n.* —**pred′i·ca′tive** *adj.* —**pred′i·ca′tive·ly** *adv.*

predicate adjective *Gram.* an adjective that follows a linking verb in a sentence and modifies, or describes, the subject

predicate nominative *Gram.* a noun, pronoun, or phrase that follows a linking verb in a sentence and is identified with the subject

pred·i·ca·to·ry (pred′i kə tôr′ē) *adj.* ⟦LL(Ec) *praedicatorius*, praising, laudatory < *praedicare:* see PREACH⟧ of or having to do with preaching

pre·dict (prē dikt′, pri-) *vt., vi.* ⟦< L *praedictus*, pp. of *praedicere* < *prae-*, before (see PRE-) + *dicere*, to tell: see DICTION⟧ to say in advance (what one believes will happen); foretell (a future event or events) —**pre·dict′a·bil′i·ty** *n.* —**pre·dict′a·ble** *adj.* —**pre·dict′a·bly** *adv.* —**pre·dic′tive** *adj.* —**pre·dic′tive·ly** *adv.* —**pre·dic′tor** *n.*

pre·dic·tion (prē dik′shən, pri-) *n.* ⟦L *praedictio*⟧ **1** a predicting or being predicted **2** the thing predicted or foretold

pre·di·gest (prē′di jest′, -dī-) *vt.* **1** to digest beforehand; specif., to treat (food) as with enzymes for easier digestion when eaten **2** to present (news, information, etc.) in a simplified form: usually used disparagingly —**pre′di·ges′tion** *n.*

pred·i·lec·tion (pred′ə lek′shən, prē′də-) *n.* ⟦Fr *prédilection* < ML *predilectus*, pp. of *prediligere*, to prefer < L *prae-*, before (see PRE-) + *diligere*, to prefer (see DILIGENCE[1])⟧ a preconceived liking; partiality or preference (*for*) —*SYN.* PREJUDICE

pre·dis·pose (prē′di spōz′) *vt.* **-posed′, -pos′ing** to dispose, or make receptive, beforehand; make susceptible [fatigue *predisposes* one to illness]

pre·dis·po·si·tion (prē′dis pə zish′ən, prē dis′-) *n.* the condition of being predisposed; inclination or tendency; predilection

☆**pred·ni·sone** (pred′nə sōn′, -zōn′) *n.* ⟦< *pre(gnane)*, a steroid hydrocarbon (< PREGNANT + -ANE: found in urine during pregnancy) + D(I)- + -(E)N(E) + (CORT)ISONE⟧ a chemical derivative, $C_{21}H_{26}O_5$, of cortisone, but with fewer side effects, used in the treatment of arthritis and certain allergic and inflammatory disorders

pre·dom·i·nant (prē däm′ə nənt, pri-) *adj.* ⟦Fr *prédominant* < ML *predominans*, prp. of *predominari:* see PRE- & DOMINANT⟧ **1** having ascendancy, authority, or dominating influence over others; superior **2** most frequent, noticeable, etc.; prevailing; preponderant —*SYN.* DOMINANT —**pre·dom′i·nance** *n.*, **pre·dom′i·nan·cy**, *pl.* **-cies** —**pre·dom′i·nant·ly** *adv.*

pre·dom·i·nate (prē däm′ə nāt′, pri-; *for adj.*, -nit) *vi.* **-nat′ed, -nat′ing** ⟦< ML *predominatus*, pp. of *predominari:* see PRE- & DOMINATE⟧ **1** to have ascendancy, authority, or dominating influence (*over* others); hold sway **2** to be dominant in amount, number, etc.; prevail; preponderate —*adj.* PREDOMINANT —**pre·dom′i·nate·ly** *adv.* —**pre·dom′i·na′tion** *n.* —**pre·dom′i·na′tor** *n.*

pre·ec·lamp·si·a (prē′i klamp′sē ə) *n.* a disorder that may occur late in pregnancy, characterized by high blood pressure, edema, protein in the urine, etc.: it may develop into eclampsia —**pre′ec·lamp′tic** (-tik) *adj.*

pre·e·lec·tion or **pre-e·lec·tion** (prē′ē lek′shən, prē′ə-) *adj.* occurring before an election —*n.* a choice made in advance

☆**pree·mie** (prē′mē) *n.* ⟦altered < PREM(ATURE) + -IE⟧ [Informal] a prematurely born infant, esp. one weighing less than 2.5 kg (*c.* 5.5 lb)

pre·em·i·nent or **pre-em·i·nent** (prē em′ə nənt) *adj.* ⟦ME < L *praeeminens*, prp. of *praeeminere*, to project forward: see PRE- & EMINENCE⟧ eminent above others; excelling others, esp. in a particular quality; surpassing —*SYN.* DOMINANT —**pre·em′i·nence** *n.*, **pre-em′i·nence** —**pre·em′i·nent·ly** *adv.*, **pre-em′i·nent·ly**

☆**pre·empt** or **pre-empt** (prē empt′) *vt.* ⟦back-form. < fol.⟧ **1** to acquire (public land) by preemption **2** to seize before anyone else can, excluding others; appropriate beforehand **3** to prevent from happening by acting ahead of time; forestall **4** *Radio, TV* to replace (a regularly scheduled program) —*vi. Bridge* to make a preemptive bid —*n. Bridge* a preemptive bid —**pre·emp′tor** *n.*, **pre-emp′tor** —**pre·emp′tor·y** *adj.*, **pre-emp′tor·y**

☆**pre·emp·tion** or **pre-emp·tion** (prē emp′shən) *n.* ⟦< ML *preemptus*, pp. of *preemere*, to buy beforehand < L *prae-*, before (see PRE-) + *emere*, to buy (see REDEEM)⟧ **1** the act or right of buying land, etc. before, or in preference to, others; esp., such a right granted to a settler on public land **2** action taken for the purpose of preventing something else from happening

pre·emp·tive or **pre-emp·tive** (prē emp′tiv) *adj.* **1** of or having to do with preemption **2** of or having to do with an action taken in advance of another possible action to prevent it from happening [a *preemptive* strike in war] **3** *Bridge* designating a high bid intended to shut out or obstruct opposing bids —**pre·emp′tive·ly** *adv.*, **pre-emp′tive·ly**

preen (prēn) *vt.* ⟦ME *preynen*, altered (infl. by *preonen*, to prick with a pin < *preon* < OE, a pin) < *proinen*, to PRUNE[3]⟧ **1** to clean and trim (the feathers) with the beak: said of birds **2** to dress or groom (oneself) in a fussy and self-satisfied way **3** to show satisfaction with or vanity in (oneself) —*vi.* to dress or groom oneself in a fussy and self-satisfied way —**preen′er** *n.*

pre·es·tab·lish or **pre-es·tab·lish** (prē′ə stab′lish) *vt.* to establish in advance

pre·ex·il·ic or **pre-ex·il·ic** (prē′ek sil′ik; -eg zil′-) *adj.* ⟦< PRE- + L *exilium*, exile + -IC⟧ of that period of Jewish history preceding the Babylonian Exile (6th cent. B.C.): also **pre′ex·il′i·an** or **pre′-ex·il′i·an**

pre·ex·ist or **pre-ex·ist** (prē′eg zist′, -ig-) *vt., vi.* ⟦LL *praeexistere*⟧ to exist previously or before (another person or thing) —**pre′ex·ist′ence** *n.*, **pre′-ex·ist′ence** —**pre′ex·ist′ent** *adj.*, **pre′-ex·ist′ent**

pref *abbrev.* **1** preface **2** prefatory **3** preference **4** preferred **5** prefix

pre·fab (prē′fab′) *n.* [Informal] a prefabricated building

pre·fab·ri·cate (prē fab′ri kāt′) *vt.* **-cat′ed, -cat′ing 1** to fabricate beforehand **2** to construct in standardized sections for shipment and quick assembly [a *prefabricated* house] —**pre′fab·ri·ca′tion** *n.*

pref·ace (pref′is) *n.* ⟦ME *prefas* < MFr < ML *prefatia*, for L *praefatio* < *prae-*, before (see PRE-) + *fatus*, pp. of *fari*, to speak: see FAME⟧ **1** [*usually* **P-**] *R.C.Ch.* the introduction to the canon of the Mass, ending with the Sanctus **2** an introductory statement to a book, telling its purpose, plan, etc., esp. a brief one written by the book's author **3** something preliminary or introductory; prelude —*vt.* **-aced, -ac·ing 1** to furnish or introduce with a preface **2** to be or serve as a preface to; begin —*SYN.* INTRODUCTION

pref·a·to·ry (pref′ə tôr′ē) *adj.* ⟦< L *praefatus* (see prec.) + -ORY⟧ of, like, or serving as a preface; introductory —**pref′a·to′ri·ly** *adv.*

pre·fect (prē′fekt′) *n.* ⟦ME *prefecte* < OFr < L *praefectus*, pp. of *praeficere*, to set over: see PRE- & -FY⟧ **1** in ancient Rome, any of various high-ranking officials or chief magistrates in charge of governmental or military departments **2** in modern times, any of various administrative officials; specif., *a)* the head of a department of France *b)* the chief of the Paris police **3** in some private schools, esp. in England, an older student with disciplinary authority

pre·fec·ture (prē′fek′chər) *n.* ⟦L *praefectura*⟧ **1** the office, authority, territory, or residence of a prefect **2** any of the regional districts of Japan administered by a governor —**pre·fec′tur·al** (-chər əl) *adj.*

pre·fer (prē fur′, pri-) *vt.* **-ferred′, -fer′ring** ⟦ME *preferren* < MFr *preferer* < L *praeferre*, to place before < *prae-*, PRE- + *ferre*, BEAR[1]⟧ **1** [Archaic] to put before someone else in rank, office, etc.; promote; advance **2** to put before a magistrate, administrator, court, etc. for consideration, sanction, or redress [to *prefer* charges against an attacker] **3** to put before something or someone else in one's liking, opinion, etc.; like better **4** to give preference or priority to (a creditor, etc.) —**pre·fer′rer** *n.*

pref·er·a·ble (pref′ər ə bəl) *adj.* more desirable; to be preferred —**pref′er·a·bil′i·ty** *n.*, **pref′er·a·ble·ness** —**pref′er·a·bly** *adv.*

pref·er·ence (pref′ər əns) *n.* ⟦MFr *préférence* < ML *praeferentia* < L *praeferens*, prp. of *praeferre*, to PREFER⟧ **1** a preferring or being preferred; greater liking **2** the right, power, or opportunity of prior choice or claim **3** something preferred; one's first choice **4** *a)* a giving of priority or advantage to one person, country, etc. over others, as in payment of debts or granting of credit *b)* such priority or advantage —*SYN.* CHOICE

pref·er·en·tial (pref′ər en′shəl) *adj.* ⟦ML *praeferentia* (see prec.) + -AL⟧ **1** of, having, giving, or receiving preference **2** offering or allowing a preference [a *preferential* ballot] ☆**3** designating a union shop which gives preference, as by contract, to union members in hiring, layoffs, etc. **4** receiving preferences, as in tariffs —**pref′er·en′tial·ism′** ***n.*** —**pref′er·en′tial·ly** ***adv.***

preferential voting a system of voting in which the voter indicates an order of preference for several candidates

pre·fer·ment (prē fur′mənt, pri-) ***n.*** **1** the act of preferring **2** an advancement in rank or office; promotion **3** an office, rank, or honor to which a person is advanced

preferred provider organization PPO

☆**preferred stock** stock on which dividends must be paid before those of common stock: it usually also receives preference in the distribution of assets

pre·fig·u·ra·tion (prē fig′yə rā′shən) ***n.*** **1** the act of prefiguring **2** something in which something else is prefigured; prototype

pre·fig·ure (prē fig′yər, -yoor) ***vt.*** **-ured, -ur·ing** ⟦ME *prefiguren* < LL(Ec) *praefigurare* < L *prae-*, PRE- + *figurare*, to fashion: see FIGURE⟧ **1** to suggest beforehand; be an antecedent figure or type of; foreshadow **2** to picture to oneself, or imagine, beforehand —**pre·fig′ur·a·tive** (-yoor ə tiv, -yər-) ***adj.*** —**pre·fig′ur·a·tive·ly** ***adv.*** —**pre·fig′ur·a·tive·ness** ***n.*** —**pre·fig′ure·ment** ***n.***

pre·fix (prē′fiks′; *for v., also* prē fiks′) ***vt.*** ⟦ME *prefyxen* < MFr *prefixer* < L *praefixus*, pp. of *praefigere* < *prae-*, before (see PRE-) + *figere*, to FIX⟧ **1** to fix to the beginning of a word, etc.; esp., to add as a prefix **2** [Rare] to fix beforehand —***n.*** ⟦ModL *praefixum* < neut. of L *praefixus*: see the *vt.*⟧ **1** a syllable, group of syllables, or word joined to the beginning of another word or a base to alter its meaning or create a new word (Ex.: *pre-* in *precool*, *un-* in *unsure*) **2** a title that is placed before a person's name, as *Dr.* **3** an identifying letter or number placed before another number, etc. —**pre′fix′al** ***adj.*** —**pre′fix′al·ly** ***adv.*** —**pre·fix′ion** ***n.***

pre·flight (prē′flīt′) ***adj.*** coming before a flight or the flying of aircraft [*preflight* instructions]

pre·form (prē fôrm′) ***vt.*** to form in advance

pre·for·ma·tion (prē′fôr mā′shən) ***n.*** **1** previous formation **2** *Biol.* a former theory that every germ cell contains every part of the future organism in miniature, development being merely growth in size

pre·fron·tal (prē frunt′'l) ***adj.*** of, pertaining to, or situated near the front of a structure of the brain or of the head of a vertebrate

pre-game (prē′gām′) ***adj.*** of or during the period just before an athletic game [a *pre-game* warmup]: also written **pregame**

pre·gan·gli·on·ic (prē gaŋ′glē än′ik) ***adj.*** *Zool.* of or pertaining to nerve fibers going from the spinal cord to sympathetic ganglia

preg·gers (preg′ərz) ***adj.*** [Informal, Chiefly Brit.] PREGNANT (sense 1)

preg·na·ble (preg′nə bəl) ***adj.*** ⟦altered (infl. by PREGNANT) < ME *prenable* < MFr < *prendre*, to take < L *prehendere*: see PREHENSILE⟧ **1** that can be captured, as a fortress **2** that can be attacked or injured; assailable or vulnerable —**preg′na·bil′i·ty** ***n.***

preg·nan·cy (preg′nən sē) ***n., pl.*** **-cies** the condition, quality, or period of being pregnant

preg·nant (preg′nənt) ***adj.*** ⟦ME *preignant* < L *pregnans* (gen. *pregnantis*), heavy with young < *prae-*, before (see PRE-) + base of OL *gnasci*, to be born (see GENUS)⟧ **1** having (an) offspring developing in the uterus; that has conceived; with young or with child **2** mentally fertile; prolific of ideas; inventive **3** productive of results; fruitful [a *pregnant* cause] **4** full of meaning, significance, etc. [a *pregnant* silence] **5** filled (*with*); abounding —**preg′nant·ly** ***adv.***

pre·heat (prē hēt′) ***vt.*** to heat beforehand

pre·hen·sile (prē hen′səl; *chiefly Brit*, -sīl′) ***adj.*** ⟦Fr *préhensile* < L *prehensus*, pp. of *prehendere*, to take < *prae-*, PRE- + IE base **ghend-*, **ghed-*, to grasp > GET⟧ adapted for seizing or grasping, esp. by wrapping or folding around something said as of the tail of certain monkeys —**pre·hen·sil·i·ty** (prē′hen sil′ə tē) ***n.***

pre·hen·sion (prē hen′shən) ***n.*** ⟦L *prehensio*⟧ **1** the act of seizing or grasping **2** mental apprehension; comprehension

pre·his·to·ri·an (prē′his tôr′ē ən) ***n.*** an authority on or specialist in prehistory

pre·his·tor·ic (prē′his tôr′ik) ***adj.*** of the period before recorded history: also **pre′his·tor′i·cal** —**pre′his·tor′i·cal·ly** ***adv.***

pre·his·to·ry (prē his′tə rē) ***n.*** **1** history before recorded history, as learned from archaeology, etc. **2** the background of incidents, etc. leading to an event, crisis, etc.

pre·ig·ni·tion (prē′ig nish′ən) ***n.*** in an internal-combustion engine, ignition occurring before the intake valve is closed or before the spark plug fires

pre·in·dus·tri·al (prē′in dus′trē əl) ***adj.*** of or characteristic of a period before industrialization, specif. before the Industrial Revolution

pre·judge (prē juj′) ***vt.*** **-judged′, -judg′ing** ⟦Fr *préjuger* < L *praejudicare*: see PRE- & JUDGE⟧ to judge beforehand, prematurely, or without all the evidence —**pre·judg′er** ***n.*** —**pre·judg′ment** ***n.***, **pre·judge′ment**

prej·u·dice (prej′ə dis) ***n.*** ⟦ME < MFr < L *praejudicium* < *prae-*, before (see PRE-) + *judicium*, judgment < *judex* (gen. *judicis*), JUDGE⟧ **1** a judgment or opinion formed before the facts are known; preconceived idea, favorable or, more usually, unfavorable **2** *a)* a judgment or opinion held in disregard of facts that contradict it; unreasonable bias [a *prejudice* against modern art] *b)* the holding of such judgments or opinions **3** suspicion, intolerance, or irrational hatred of other races, creeds, social classes, etc. **4** injury or harm resulting as from some judgment or action of another or others —***vt.*** **-diced, -dic·ing** **1** to injure or harm, as by some judgment or action **2** to cause to have or show prejudice; bias —**without prejudice** **1** without detriment or injury **2** *Law* without dismissal of or detriment to (a legal right, claim, etc.): often with *to*

SYN.—**prejudice** implies a preconceived and unreasonable judgment or opinion, usually an unfavorable one marked as by suspicion, fear, or hatred [a crime motivated by racial *prejudice*]; **bias** is also preconceived and unreasonable, but often implies a less pernicious or uncompromising quality than **prejudice** [a *bias* against prep schools]; **partiality** implies an inclination to favor a person or thing because of strong fondness or attachment [the conductor's *partiality* for the works of Brahms]; **predilection** implies a preconceived liking, formed as a result of one's background, temperament, etc., that inclines one to a particular preference [he has a *predilection* for murder mysteries]

prej·u·di·cial (prej′ə dish′əl, prej′oo-) ***adj.*** causing prejudice, or harm; injurious; detrimental —**prej′u·di′cial·ly** ***adv.***

pre·kin·der·gar·ten (prē kin′dər gärt′'n) ***n.*** PRESCHOOL: also **pre-k** or **pre-K** (prē′kā′)

prel·a·cy (prel′ə sē) ***n., pl.*** **-cies** ⟦ME *prelacie* < ML(Ec) *praelatia*⟧ **1** *a)* the office or rank of a prelate *b)* prelates collectively: also **prel′a·ture′** (-choor′, -chər) **2** church government by prelates: often a hostile term: also **prel′a·tism′** (-tiz′əm)

pre·lap·sar·i·an (prē′lap ser′ē ən) ***adj.*** of the time before the Fall of Man

prel·ate (prel′it) ***n.*** ⟦ME *prelat* < OFr < LL(Ec) *praelatus*, prelate, orig., ruler < pp. of L *praeferre*, to place before, PREFER⟧ a high-ranking ecclesiastic, as a bishop —**prel′ate·ship′** ***n.*** —**pre·lat·ic** (prē lat′ik, pri-) ***adj.***

pre·lect (prē lekt′) ***vi.*** ⟦< L *praelectus*, pp. of *praelegere*, to read before, lecture: see PRE- & LECTURE⟧ to lecture in public —**pre·lec′tion** ***n.*** —**pre·lec′tor** ***n.***

pre·lim[1] (prē lim′, pri-; prē′lim′) [Slang] ***n.*** *short for* PRELIMINARY

prelim[2] *abbrev.* preliminary

pre·lim·i·nar·y (prē lim′ə ner′ē, pri-) ***adj.*** ⟦< Fr *préliminaire* or ModL *praeliminaris* < L *prae-* (see PRE-) + L *liminaris*, of a threshold < *limen*, threshold (see LIMEN)⟧ coming before or leading up to the main action, discussion, business, etc.; introductory; prefatory; preparatory —***n., pl.*** **-nar′ies** ⟦Fr *préliminaires*, pl.⟧ [*often pl.*] **1** a preliminary step, procedure, etc. **2** *a)* a preliminary examination *b)* a contest or match before the main one —**pre·lim′i·nar′i·ly** ***adv.***

pre·lit·er·ate (prē lit′ər it) ***adj.*** ⟦PRE- + LITERATE⟧ of or belonging to a society not having a writing system for its language

Pre·log (pre′lôg′), **Vladimir** 1906-98; Swiss chemist, born in Bosnia

prel·ude (prel′yood′; prā′lood′, prē′-) ***n.*** ⟦Fr *prélude* < ML *praeludium* < L *praeludere*, to play beforehand < *prae-*, PRE- + *ludere*, to play < *ludus*: see LUDICROUS⟧ **1** anything serving as the introduction to a principal event, action, performance, etc.; preliminary part; preface; opening **2** *Music* *a)* an introductory instrumental composition, such as the first movement of a suite or the overture to an opera *b)* since the 19th cent., any short, romantic composition — ***vt., vi.*** **-ud′ed, -ud′ing** ⟦L *praeludere*⟧ **1** to serve as or be a prelude (to) **2** to introduce by or play (as) a prelude —**pre·lu·di·al** (prē lo͞o′dē əl) ***adj.***

prem *abbrev.* premium

pre·mar·i·tal (prē mar′ət′l) ***adj.*** occurring before marriage

pre·mar·ket (prē′mär′kit) ***adj.*** designating or of trading on the stock market that takes place in the morning, before the start of regular trading hours

pre·ma·ture (prē′mə toor′, -choor′, -tyoor′; *Brit* prem′ə-) ***adj.*** ⟦L *praematurus*: see PRE- & MATURE⟧ happening, done, arriving, or existing before the proper or usual time; too early; specif., born before the full term of gestation —**pre′ma·ture′ly** ***adv.*** —**pre′ma·tu′ri·ty** ***n.***, **pre′ma·ture′ness**

pre·max·il·la (prē′mak sil′ə) ***n., pl.*** **-lae** (-ē) ⟦ModL: PRE- & MAXILLA⟧ either of two bones in the upper jaw of vertebrates, situated between and in front of the maxillae, and fusing with them in the adult human being —**pre·max′il·lar′y** (-maks′i ler′ē) ***adj.***

☆**pre-med** or **pre·med** (prē′med′) ***adj.*** *short for* PREMEDICAL —***n.*** a premedical student or program of studies

pre·med·i·cal (prē med′i kəl) ***adj.*** designating or of the studies preparatory to the study of medicine

pre·med·i·tate (prē med′ə tāt′) ***vt.*** **-tat′ed, -tat′ing** ⟦< L *praemeditatus*, pp. of *praemeditari*: see PRE- & MEDITATE⟧ to think out, plan, or scheme beforehand [a *premeditated* murder] —***vi.*** to think or meditate beforehand —**pre·med′i·tat′ed·ly** ***adv.*** —**pre·med′i·ta′tive** ***adj.*** —**pre·med′i·ta′tor** ***n.***

pre·med·i·ta·tion (prē med′ə tā′shən) ***n.*** **1** the act of premeditating **2** *Law* a degree of planning and forethought sufficient to show intent to commit an act

pre·men·stru·al (prē men′strəl) ***adj.*** occurring before menstruation or a menstrual period

premenstrual syndrome a group of physical and emotional symptoms that may precede a menstrual period, as fluid retention, fatigue, depression, irritability, etc.

pre·mier (pri mir′, -myir′; *Brit* prem′yər) ***adj.*** ⟦ME *primier* < MFr *premier* < L *primarius* < *primus*, first, PRIME⟧ **1** first in importance or rank; chief; foremost **2** first in time; earliest —***n.*** **1** any chief official **2** *the title of* *a)* the prime minister of any of certain countries *b)* the chief executive officer of a Canadian province *c)* the chief minister of an Australian state —**pre·mier′ship** ***n.***

premier danseur ⟦Fr, lit., first dancer⟧ a principal male dancer in a ballet or ballet company

pre·miere (pri mir′, -myer′, -myir′) *n.* ⟦Fr, fem. of *premier:* see PREMIER⟧ **1** a first performance or showing of a play, film, etc. **2** TV the first broadcast of a film, concert, etc. —*adj.* PREMIER —*vt.* **-miered′, -mier′ing** to exhibit (a play, film, etc.) for the first time —*vi.* to be exhibited for the first time Also sp. **première**

première danseuse ⟦Fr, lit., first (female) dancer⟧ a principal female dancer in a ballet or ballet company

pre·mil·len·ni·al (prē′mi len′ē əl) *adj.* of or happening in the period before the millennium —**pre′mil·len′ni·al·ly** *adv.*

pre·mil·len·ni·al·ism (-iz′əm) *n.* the religious doctrine that THE MILLENNIUM will be ushered in by the Second Coming of Christ —**pre′mil·len′ni·al·ist** *n.*

prem·ise (prem′is; *for v., chiefly Brit* pri mīz′) *n.* ⟦ME *premisse* < ML *praemissa* < L *praemissus,* pp. of *praemittere,* to send before < *prae-,* before + *mittere,* to send: see PRE- & MISSION⟧ **1** *a)* a previous statement or assertion that serves as the basis for an argument *b) Logic* either of the two propositions of a syllogism from which the conclusion is drawn (see SYLLOGISM): also sp. [Chiefly Brit.] **prem′iss 2** [*pl.*] *a)* the part of a deed or lease that states the parties involved, the property in conveyance, and other pertinent facts *b)* the property so mentioned **3** [*pl.*] a piece of real estate; house or building and its land [keep off the *premises*] —*vt.* **-ised, -is·ing 1** to state as a premise **2** to introduce or preface (a discourse, etc.) —*vi.* to make a premise —**SYN.** PRESUME

pre·mi·um (prē′mē əm) *n., pl.* **-ums** ⟦L *praemium,* reward, recompense < *prae-,* before + *emere,* to take: see PRE- & REDEEM⟧ **1** a reward or prize, esp. one offered free or at a special low price as an added inducement to buy or do something; bonus **2** an additional amount paid or charged; specif., *a)* an amount paid for a loan in addition to interest *b)* an amount paid, as for stock, above the nominal or par value *c)* additional wages paid as for overtime or dangerous work **3** a payment; specif., *a)* the amount payable or paid, in one sum or periodically, for an insurance policy *b)* [Now Rare] a fee paid for instruction in a trade, etc. *c)* a fee paid by a borrower of stock to the lender, as in short selling **4** very high value [to put a *premium* on punctuality] **5** *Econ.* the amount by which one form of money exceeds another (of the same nominal value) in exchange value, or buying power —*adj.* rated as superior in quality and sold at a higher price —**SYN.** BONUS, REWARD —**at a premium 1** at a value or price higher than normal **2** very valuable, usually because of scarcity

pre-mois·tened (prē mois′ənd) *adj.* moistened ahead of time; specif., infused by the manufacturer with a liquid agent [*pre-moistened* towelettes]

pre·mo·lar (prē mō′lər) *adj.* designating or of any of the bicuspid teeth situated in front of the molars —*n.* a premolar tooth

pre·mon·ish (prē män′ish) *vt., vi.* ⟦PRE- + MONISH⟧ [Rare] to advise or warn in advance

prem·o·ni·tion (prem′ə nish′ən, prē′mə-) *n.* ⟦MFr *premonicion* < LL(Ec) *praemonitio* < L *praemonere* < *prae-,* before + *monere,* to warn: see PRE- & MONITOR⟧ **1** a warning in advance; a forewarning **2** a feeling that something, esp. something bad, will happen; foreboding; presentiment —**pre·mon·i·to·ry** (prē män′i tôr′ē) *adj.*

pre·morse (prē môrs′) *adj.* ⟦L *praemorsus,* pp. of *praemordere,* to bite off, orig. to bite in front or at the end < *prae-,* before + *mordere,* to bite: see PRE- & MORDANT⟧ ending abruptly and unevenly, as if bitten off: said of a leaf or root

pre·mu·ni·tion (prē′myoo͞ nish′ən) *n.* ⟦L *praemunitio,* a strengthening in advance < *praemunire,* to fortify in front < *prae-,* PRE- + *munire,* to fortify: see MUNITIONS⟧ a type of immunity caused by a small number of persistent, latent pathogens in the body

pre·name (prē′nām′) *n.* a given name; forename

pre·na·tal (prē nāt′'l) *adj.* ⟦PRE- + NATAL⟧ before birth or during pregnancy [*prenatal* health care] —**pre·na′tal·ly** *adv.*

Pren·der·gast (pren′dər gast′), **Maurice (Brazil)** 1859-1924; U.S. painter, born in Canada

pre·nom·i·nate (prē näm′ə nāt′; *for adj.,* -nit) [Obs.] *vt.* **-nat′ed, -nat′ing** ⟦PRE- + NOMINATE, based on L *praenominare*⟧ to name, or mention, beforehand —*adj.* previously mentioned

pren·tice or **'pren·tice** (pren′tis) *n.* ⟦ME *prentis,* aphetic for *aprentis,* APPRENTICE⟧ *archaic var. of* APPRENTICE

pre·nup·tial (prē nup′shəl, -chəl) *adj.* ⟦PRE- + NUPTIAL⟧ **1** before a marriage or wedding **2** *Zool.* before mating

prenuptial agreement an agreement made by some couples prior to marriage, for the purpose of settling legal issues, as of ownership and division of property, should the couple later divorce: also [Informal] **pre′nup′**

pre·oc·cu·pan·cy (prē äk′yoo͞ pən sē, -yə-) *n., pl.* **-cies 1** prior occupancy **2** PREOCCUPATION

pre·oc·cu·pa·tion (prē äk′yoo͞ pā′shən, -yə-) *n.* ⟦L *praeoccupatio*⟧ **1** a preoccupying or being preoccupied, esp. mentally **2** something, as an idea, which preoccupies one

pre·oc·cu·pied (prē äk′yoo͞ pīd′, -yə-) *adj.* **1** previously or already occupied **2** *a)* absorbed in one's thoughts *b)* focused on a certain matter [*preoccupied* with losing weight] **3** *Taxonomy* designating or of a name already used and hence no longer available —**SYN.** ABSENT-MINDED

pre·oc·cu·py (prē äk′yoo͞ pī′, -yə-) *vt.* **-pied′, -py′ing** ⟦MFr *preoccuper* < L *praeoccupare:* see PRE- & OCCUPY⟧ **1** to occupy the thoughts of to the virtual exclusion of other matters; engross; absorb **2** to occupy or take possession of before someone else or beforehand

pre-op (prē′äp′) *adj. short for* PREOPERATIVE

pre·op·er·a·tive (prē äp′ər ə tiv, -ər āt′iv) *adj.* of or occurring in the period before a surgical operation —**pre·op′er·a·tive·ly** *adj.*

pre·or·dain (prē′ôr dān′) *vt.* ⟦LL *praeordinare:* see PRE- & ORDAIN⟧ to ordain or decree beforehand; foreordain —**pre′or′di·na′tion** (-ôrd′'n ā′shən) *n.*

pre·or·der or **pre-or·der** (prē ôr′dər) *vt., vi.* to order (an item) prior to the official release or sale date, for later delivery —*n.* **1** the act or an instance of preordering **2** a preordered item

pre-owned (prē ōnd′) *adj.* previously owned; secondhand; used

prep[1] (prep) *adj.* ☆**1** *short for* PREPARATORY [a *prep* school] ☆**2** of or having to do with competitive sports at the high-school level —☆*vi.* **prepped, prep′ping** [Informal] **1** to attend a preparatory school **2** to prepare oneself by study, training, etc. —☆*vt.* to prepare (a person or thing) for something; specif., to prepare (a patient) for surgery, childbirth, etc.

prep[2] *abbrev.* **1** preparation **2** preparatory **3** preposition

☆**pre·pack·age** (prē pak′ij) *vt.* **-aged, -ag·ing** to package (foods or other merchandise) in standard weights or units before selling

pre·paid (prē pād′) *vt. pt. & pp. of* PREPAY

prep·a·ra·tion (prep′ə rā′shən) *n.* ⟦ME *preparacion* < MFr *preparation* < L *praeparatio*⟧ **1** the act or process of preparing **2** the condition of being prepared; readiness **3** something done to prepare; preparatory measure **4** something prepared for a special purpose, as a medicine, cosmetic, condiment, etc. **5** *Music a)* the preparing for a dissonant chord by using the dissonant tone as a consonant tone in the immediately preceding chord *b)* a tone so used —**prep′a·ra′tion·al** *adj.*

pre·par·a·tive (prē par′ə tiv, pri-) *adj.* ⟦ME *preparatif* < MFr < ML *praeparativus*⟧ PREPARATORY —*n.* **1** something preparatory **2** a preparation —**pre·par′a·tive·ly** *adv.*

pre·par·a·to·ry (prē par′ə tôr′ē, pri-; prep′ə rə-) *adj.* ⟦ME < ML *praeparatorius*⟧ **1** that prepares or serves to prepare; preliminary; introductory ☆**2** undergoing preparation, esp. for college entrance [a *preparatory* student] —**preparatory to** in preparation for —**pre·par′a·to′ri·ly** *adv.*

preparatory school a private secondary school for preparing students to enter college

pre·pare (prē par′, pri-) *vt.* **-pared′, -par′ing** ⟦ME *preparen* < MFr *preparer* < L *praeparare* < *prae-,* before (see PRE-) + *parare,* to set in order, get ready, akin to *parere,* to bring forth, bear (see -PAROUS)⟧ **1** to make ready, usually for a specific purpose; make suitable; fit; adapt; train **2** to make receptive; dispose; accustom [to *prepare* someone for bad news] **3** to equip or furnish with necessary provisions, accessories, etc.; fit out [to *prepare* an expedition] **4** to put together or make out of ingredients, parts, etc., or according to a plan or formula; compound [to *prepare* dinner or a medicine] **5** *Music* to use (a dissonant tone) in preparation —*vi.* **1** to make things ready **2** to make oneself ready —**pre·par′ed·ly** (-id lē) *adv.*

pre·pared (-pard′) *adj.* **1** in a ready state; specif., already cooked [*prepared* frozen entrees] ☆**2** *Music* altered for a performance in some way, as with an object placed on one of the strings, in order to modify the timbre [concerto for *prepared* piano]

pre·par·ed·ness (-par′id nis) *n.* the state of being prepared; specif., possession of sufficient armed forces, materiel, etc. for waging war

pre·pay (prē pā′) *vt.* **-paid′, -pay′ing** to pay or pay for in advance —**pre·pay′ment** *n.*

pre·pense (prē pens′) *adj.* ⟦altered < earlier *purpensed* < ME < OFr *purpensé,* pp. of *purpenser,* to meditate < *pur,* pro- + *penser* < L *pensare,* to think: see PENSIVE⟧ planned beforehand; premeditated: see MALICE

pre·plan (prē plan′) *vt.* **-planned′, -plan′ning** to plan in advance

pre·pon·der·ant (prē pän′dər ənt, pri-) *adj.* ⟦L *praeponderans,* prp.⟧ that preponderates; greater in amount, weight, power, influence, importance, etc.; predominant —**SYN.** DOMINANT —**pre·pon′der·ance** *n.,* **pre·pon′der·an·cy** —**pre·pon′der·ant·ly** *adv.*

pre·pon·der·ate (prē pän′dər āt′, pri-) *vi.* **-at′ed, -at′ing** ⟦< L *praeponderatus,* pp. of *praeponderare* < *prae-,* before + *ponderare,* to weigh < *pondus,* weight: see POUND[1]⟧ **1** [Now Rare] to weigh more; be heavier **2** to sink or incline downward, as a scale of a balance **3** to surpass others in amount, number, power, influence, importance, etc.; predominate —**pre·pon′der·a′tion** *n.*

prep·o·si·tion (prep′ə zish′ən) *n.* ⟦ME *preposicioun* < L *praepositio* (< *praepositus,* pp. of *praeponere* < *prae-,* before + *ponere,* to place: see PRE- & POSITION): transl. of Gr *prothesis,* PROTHESIS⟧ **1** in some languages, a relation or function word, as English *in, by, for, with, to,* etc., that connects a lexical word, usually a noun or pronoun, or a syntactic construction, to another element of the sentence, as to a verb (Ex.: he went *to* the store), to a noun (Ex.: the sound *of* loud music), or to an adjective (Ex.: good *for* her) **2** any construction of similar function (Ex.: *in back of,* equivalent to *behind*) —**prep′o·si′tion·al** *adj.* —**prep′o·si′tion·al·ly** *adv.*

prepositional phrase a phrase consisting of a preposition and the noun or noun substitute that is its object

pre·pos·i·tive (prē päz′ə tiv) *adj.* ⟦LL *praepositivus* < L *praeponere:* see PREPOSITION⟧ *Gram.* put before; prefixed —*n.* a prepositive word —**pre·pos′i·tive·ly** *adv.*

pre·pos·i·tor (prē päz′ə tər) *n.* ⟦altered < L *praepositus:* see PROVOST⟧ *Brit. var. of* PREFECT (sense 3)

pre·pos·sess (prē′pə zes′) *vt.* **1** [Obs.] to take or occupy beforehand or before another **2** [Archaic] to prejudice or bias, esp. favorably **3** to impress favorably at once —**pre′pos·ses′sion** *n.*

pre·pos·sess·ing (-iŋ) *adj.* that prepossesses, or impresses favorably; pleasing; attractive —**pre′pos·sess′ing·ly** *adv.*

pre·pos·ter·ous (prē päs′tər əs, pri-) *adj.* ⟦L *praeposterus* < *prae-,* before (see PRE-) + *posterus,* following: see POSTERIOR⟧ **1** [Obs.] with the first last and the last first; inverted **2** so contrary to nature, reason, or common sense as to be laughable; absurd; ridiculous —**SYN.** ABSURD —**pre·pos′ter·ous·ly** *adv.* —**pre·pos′ter·ous·ness** *n.*

pre·po·ten·cy (prē pōt′'n sē) *n., pl.* **-cies** ⟦L *praepotentia:* see PRE- & POTENT⟧ **1** superiority in power, force, or influence **2** *Biol.* the greater capacity of one parent to transmit certain characteristics to offspring: a theory now rejected —**pre·po′tent** *adj.*

prep·py or **prep·pie** (prep′ē) *n., pl.* **-pies** a student at or graduate of a preparatory school —*adj.* **-pi·er, -pi·est** designating, of, or like the fashion, esp. in clothes, associated with preparatory schools

pre·pran·di·al (prē pran′dē əl) *adj.* of, relating to, happening in, or consumed during the time just before dinner: sometimes used humorously [a *preprandial* drink]

pre·preg (prē′preg′) *n.* ⟦< PRE- + *impregnated,* pp. of IMPREGNATE⟧ a strong, flexible composite material, usually a resin impregnated with fibers, formed into lightweight sheets or strips and used in the manufacture of airplane parts, sports equipment, etc.

pre·pro·duc·tion (prē′prə duk′shən) *n.* the process of preparing and planning before actual production begins; specif., the choosing of locations, casting of actors, revision of the script, etc. before the actual shooting of a film —*adj.* of or in the time before actual production begins

pre·pro·gram (prē prō′gram) *vt.* **-grammed** or **-gramed, -gram·ming** or **-gram·ing** to program beforehand: usually in the pp.

prep school PREPARATORY SCHOOL

pre·puce (prē′pyo͞os′) *n.* ⟦ME < MFr < L *praeputium* < *prae-,* PRE- + **putos,* penis < IE base **put-,* a swelling > Lith *pusti,* to swell, Byelorussian *potka,* penis⟧ **1** FORESKIN **2** a fold of skin over the end of the clitoris —**pre·pu′tial** (-pyo͞o′shəl) *adj.*

pre·quel (prē′kwəl) *n.* ⟦PRE- + (SE)QUEL⟧ a novel (or film, etc.) about events that preceded and, often, led up to those of another novel (or film, etc.) that was published (or produced) earlier

Pre-Ra·pha·el·ite (prē ra′fē əl īt′, -raf′ē-) *n.* **1** a member of a society of artists (**Pre-Raphaelite Brotherhood**) led by Dante Gabriel Rossetti, W. Holman Hunt, and J. E. Millais, formed in England in 1848 to encourage painting with the fidelity to nature that they considered characteristic of Italian art before Raphael **2** any Italian painter before Raphael —*adj.* of or characteristic of Pre-Raphaelites

pre·re·cord (prē′ri kôrd′) *vt. Film, Radio, TV* to record (music, a program, etc.) for later use, as for a broadcast

pre·reg·is·ter (prē rej′is tər) *vi.* to register, as for a school or college, before the main registration period —**pre·reg′is·tra′tion** *n.*

pre·req·ui·site (prē rek′wə zit, pri-) *adj.* required beforehand, esp. as a necessary condition for something following —*n.* something prerequisite

pre·rog·a·tive (pri räg′ə tiv, pər äg′-) *n.* ⟦ME *prerogatif* < MFr < L *praerogativa,* called upon to vote first < *praerogare,* to ask before < *prae-,* before + *rogare,* to ask: see ROGATION⟧ **1** a prior or exclusive right or privilege, esp. one peculiar to a rank, class, etc. **2** a distinctively superior advantage **3** [Obs.] priority or precedence —*adj.* of or having a prerogative

pres *abbrev.* **1** present **2** presidency

Pres *abbrev.* **1** Presbyterian **2** President

pre·sa (prā′sə; *It* pre′sä) *n., pl.* **-se** (-sā; *It,* -se) ⟦It, lit., a taking up, seizure < pp. of *prendere,* to take < L *prehendere:* see PREHENSILE⟧ *Music* a sign (:S:, +, or ×) showing where each successive voice enters in a canon

pres·age (pres′ij; *for v.* prē sāj′, pri sāj′, pres′ij) *n.* ⟦ME < MFr < L *praesagium,* a foreboding < *prae-,* before + *sagire,* to perceive: see PRE- & SAGACIOUS⟧ **1** a sign or warning of a future event; omen; portent; augury **2** a foreboding; presentiment **3** [Rare] a prediction **4** foreshadowing quality [of ominous *presage*] —*vt.* **-aged′, -ag′ing** ⟦Fr *présager* < the vt.⟧ **1** to give a presage, or warning, of; portend **2** to have a foreboding or presentiment of **3** to predict —*vi.* **1** [Rare] to have a presentiment **2** to make a prediction —**pre·sag′er** *n.*

pre·sale (prē′sāl′) *adj.* **1** made or done before something goes on sale [*presale* advertising] **2** of or having to do with a presale —*n.* a special sale of merchandise, tickets, etc., held before the regular sale

Presb or **Presby** *abbrev.* Presbyterian

pres·by·cu·sis (prez′bi kyo͞o′sis, pres′-) *n.* ⟦< Gr *presbys,* old + (*a*)*kousis,* hearing < *akouein,* to hear: see ACOUSTIC⟧ the gradual loss of acute hearing with advancing age: also **pres′by·cou′sis** (-ko͞o′sis)

pres·by·o·pi·a (prez′bē ō′pē ə, pres′-) *n.* ⟦ModL < Gr *presbys,* old (see PRIEST) + *ōps,* EYE⟧ a form of farsightedness occurring after middle age, caused by a diminished elasticity of the crystalline lens —**pres′by·ope′** (-ōp′) *n.* —**pres′by·op′ic** (-äp′ik) *adj.*

pres·by·ter (prez′bə tər, pres′-) *n.* ⟦LL(Ec), an elder: see PRIEST⟧ **1** in the early Christian church and in the Presbyterian Church, an elder **2** *Episcopal Ch.* a priest

pres·byt·er·ate (prez bit′ər it, pres-; -ər āt′) *n.* ⟦ML(Ec) *presbyteratus*⟧ **1** the office of a presbyter **2** a body of presbyters

pres·by·te·ri·al (prez′bə tir′ē əl, pres′-) *adj.* of or having to do with a presbyter or presbytery: also **pres·byt′er·al** (-bit′ər əl) —*n.* [**P-**] an organization of women connected with a given presbytery of the Presbyterian Church

pres·by·te·ri·an (-ē ən) *adj.* ⟦< LL(Ec) *presbyterium* (see fol.) + -AN⟧ **1** having to do with church government by presbyters **2** [**P-**] designating or of a church of a traditionally Calvinistic Protestant denomination governed by presbyters, or elders —*n.* [**P-**] a member of a Presbyterian church —**Pres′by·te′ri·an·ism′** *n.*

pres·by·ter·y (prez′bə ter′ē, pres′-) *n., pl.* **-ter′ies** ⟦ME *presbetory* < OFr *presbiterie* < LL(Ec) *presbyterium,* council of elders < Gr(Ec) *presbyterion* < Gr *presbyteros,* elder: see PRIEST⟧ **1** in the Presbyterian Church, *a)* a body of presbyters; specif., an ecclesiastical court and governing body consisting of the minister and representative elders from each church in a district *b)* the district of such a court **2** the part of a church reserved for the officiating clergy **3** [Now Rare] *R.C.Ch.* a priest's house; rectory

pre·school (prē′sko͞ol′) *adj.* designating, of, or for a child between infancy and school age, typically a child three to five years of age —*n.* a school for very young children, usually those three to five years of age —**pre′school′er** *n.*

pres·ci·ence (presh′əns, -ē əns; prē′shəns, -shē əns) *n.* ⟦OFr < LL(Ec) *praescientia* < L *praescire,* to know beforehand: see PRE- & SCIENCE⟧ apparent knowledge of things before they happen or come into being —**pres′ci·ent** *adj.* —**pres′ci·ent·ly** *adv.*

pre·scind (prē sind′, pri-) *vt.* ⟦L *praescindere,* to cut off in front < *prae-,* before (see PRE-) + *scindere,* to cut⟧ to detach, abstract, or isolate mentally or conceptually —*vi.* to detach or isolate oneself; withdraw one's attention (*from*)

Pres·cott (pres′kət), **William H(ickling)** 1796-1859; U.S. historian

pre·scribe (prē skrīb′, pri-) *vt.* **-scribed′, -scrib′ing** ⟦L *praescribere* < *prae-,* before + *scribere,* to write: see PRE- & SCRIBE⟧ **1** to set down as a rule or direction; order; ordain; direct **2** to order or advise as a medicine or treatment: said of physicians, etc. **3** *Law* to invalidate or outlaw by negative prescription —*vi.* **1** to set down or impose rules; dictate **2** to give medical advice or prescriptions **3** *Law a)* to claim a right or title through long use or possession *b)* to become invalidated or outlawed by negative prescription —**pre·scrib′er** *n.*

pre·script (prē skript′; *also, and for n. always,* prē′skript′) *adj.* ⟦L *praescriptus,* pp. of *praescribere:* see prec.⟧ that is prescribed —*n.* ⟦L *praescriptum* < *praescriptus*⟧ something prescribed; direction; rule

pre·scrip·ti·ble (prē skrip′tə bəl, pri-) *adj.* **1** that can be effectively prescribed for [a *prescriptible* illness] **2** acquired or acquirable by PRESCRIPTION (sense 5)

pre·scrip·tion (prē skrip′shən, pri-) *n.* ⟦ME *prescripcion* < L *praescriptio*⟧ **1** the act of prescribing **2** something prescribed; order; direction; prescript **3** *a)* a doctor's written direction for the preparation and use of medicine, the grinding of lenses for eyeglasses, etc. *b)* a medicine so prescribed **4** *a)* a long-established, authoritative custom *b)* a claim based on this **5** *Law a)* the acquirement of the title or right to something through its continued use or possession from time immemorial or over a long period *b)* a right or title so acquired —*adj.* made according to, or purchasable only with, a doctor's prescription [*prescription* lenses; a *prescription* drug]

pre·scrip·tive (prē skrip′tiv, pri-) *adj.* ⟦LL *praescriptivus*⟧ **1** that prescribes **2** based on legal prescription **3** prescribed by custom or long use —**pre·scrip′tive·ly** *adv.*

pre·sea·son (prē′sē′zən) *Sports n.* the period just prior to the regular season, during which teams work out, practice, and play exhibition games —*adj.* of the preseason Often written **pre-season**

pre·se·lect (prē′sə lekt′) *vt.* to select in advance

pre·sell (prē sel′) *vt.* **-sold′, -sell′ing** to sell (something or the rights to something) before the thing exists in finished form [to *presell* condo units in order to finance their construction]

pres·ence (prez′əns) *n.* ⟦OFr < L *praesentia* < *praesens:* see PRESENT, *adj.*⟧ **1** the fact or condition of being present; existence, occurrence, or attendance at some place or in some thing **2** immediate surroundings, or vicinity within close view, of a person [admitted to his *presence*] **3** a person or thing that is present, esp. a person of high station or imposing appearance **4** *a)* a person's bearing, personality, or appearance *b)* impressive bearing, personality, etc. characterized by poise, confidence, etc., often specif. that of a performer before an audience (**stage presence**) **5** an influence or a supernatural or divine spirit felt to be present **6** the quality of sound reproduction with reference to the degree of the apparent reality of the sound **7** [Archaic] people present; an assemblage **8** [Obs.] PRESENCE CHAMBER

presence chamber the room in which a king or other person of rank or distinction formally receives guests

presence of mind ability to think clearly and act quickly and intelligently in an emergency

pres·ent (prez′ənt; *for v.* prē zent′, pri-) *adj.* ⟦OFr < L *praesens,* prp. of *praeesse,* to be present < *prae-,* before (see PRE-) + *esse,* to be (see ESSENCE)⟧ **1** *a)* being at the specified or understood place; at hand; in attendance *b)* existing (*in* a particular thing) [nitrogen is *present* in the air] **2** of or at this time; existing or happening now; in progress **3** now being discussed, considered, written, read, etc. [the *present* writer] **4** [Archaic] readily available, effective, etc. **5** [Obs.] *a)* self-possessed; collected *b)* paying attention **6** *Gram.* indicating action as now taking place (Ex.: she *goes*) or state as now existing (Ex.: the plums *are* ripe), action that is habitual (Ex.: he *speaks* with an accent), or action that is always the same (Ex.: the clock *strikes* twelve at noon): see also HISTORICAL PRESENT —*n.* **1** the present time **2** [Obs.] the present occasion **3** [*pl.*] *a)* the present words or writings *b) Law* this very document [know by these *presents*] **4** *Gram. a)* the present tense *b)* a verb form in this tense **5** ⟦OFr, in phr. *mettre en present à,* to put before (someone), present, offer, hence a gift⟧ something presented, or given; gift —*vt.* **pre·sent′** ⟦ME *pre-*

senten < OFr *presenter* < L *praesentare,* to place before, lit., to make present < *praesens:* see the ***adj.***⟧ **1** to bring (a person) into the presence of, and introduce formally to, another or others **2** *a)* to honor (someone), esp. formally, *with* a gift, award, etc. [the mayor *presented* him with the keys to the city] *b)* to provide or confront (someone) *with* something [this *presents* us with a difficult problem] **3** *a)* to offer for viewing or notice; exhibit; display; show *b)* to offer (a show, exhibit, etc.) to the public **4** to offer for consideration [to *present* a plan, opportunity, etc.] **5** to give (a gift, donation, award, etc.) to a person, organization, etc. **6** to hand over, give, or send (a bill, credentials, etc.) to someone **7** to represent, depict, or interpret in the manner indicated **8** to point or aim (a weapon, etc.) **9** to nominate to an ecclesiastical benefice **10** *Law a)* to put before a legislature, court, etc. for consideration *b)* to bring a charge or indictment against —***vi.* pre·sent′** to come before a physician (*with* a particular symptom, medical history, etc.) —**present arms** *Mil.* **1** to hold a rifle vertically in front of the body, with the muzzle up: a position of salute **2** *a)* this position *b)* the command to assume it

SYN.—**present** and **gift** both refer to something given as an expression of friendship, affection, esteem, etc., but **gift** more often suggests formal bestowal [Christmas *presents*; the painting was a *gift* to the museum]; **donation** applies to a gift of money, etc. for a philanthropic, charitable, or religious purpose, esp. as solicited in a public drive for funds [a *donation* to the orchestra fund]; **gratuity** applies to a gift of money, etc. for services rendered, such as a tip to a waiter See also **give**

pre·sent·a·ble (prē zent′ə bəl, pri-) ***adj.*** ⟦ML *praesentabilis*⟧ **1** capable of being presented; suitable for presentation **2** in proper or suitable attire, order, etc. for being seen, met, etc. by others —**pre·sent′a·bil′i·ty** ***n.,*** **pre·sent′a·ble·ness** —**pre·sent′a·bly** ***adv.***

pres·en·ta·tion (prez′ən tā′shən, prē′zən-) ***n.*** ⟦ME < MFr *presentacion* < LL *praesentatio* < *praesentare:* see PRESENT, ***vt.***⟧ **1** a presenting or being presented **2** something that is presented; specif., *a)* a performance, as of a play *b)* a gift **3** the way in which a food is served; esp., the often artistic arrangement of food on a plate to make it especially appealing **4** *Commerce* PRESENTMENT **5** *Eccles. a)* the naming of a clergyman to a benefice *b)* a request to the bishop to institute the clergyman named **6** *Med.* the position of the fetus in the uterus at the time of delivery, with reference to the part presenting itself at the mouth of the uterus [an arm or breech *presentation*] **7** *Philos., Psychol. a)* anything present in the consciousness at a single moment as an actual sensation or a mental image *b)* anything known by sense perception rather than by description; percept —**pres′en·ta′tion·al** ***adj.***

pre·sen·ta·tion·ism (-iz′əm) ***n.*** *Philos.* the epistemological theory that in perception the mind is directly aware of an external object without any intervening medium: distinguished from REPRESENTATIONALISM

pre·sent·a·tive (prē zent′ə tiv, pri-) ***adj.*** **1** *Eccles.* designating a benefice to or for which a patron has the right of presentation **2** *Philos., Psychol.* known or capable of being known directly, as by sense perception

pres·ent-day (prez′ənt dā′) ***adj.*** of the present time

pres·en·tee (prez′ən tē′) ***n.*** ⟦Anglo-Fr < OFr, pp. of *presenter*⟧ **1** a person presented, as for institution to a benefice **2** a person to whom something is presented

pre·sent·er (prē zent′ər, pri-) ***n.*** **1** a person who presents something or someone **2** [Brit.] HOST[2] (***n.*** 6)

pre·sen·ti·ment (prē zent′ə mənt, pri-) ***n.*** ⟦MFr < *pressentir,* to have a presentiment of < L *praesentire:* see PRE- & SENTIMENT⟧ a feeling that something, esp. of an unfortunate or evil nature, is about to take place; foreboding

pres·ent·ism (prez′ən tiz′əm) ***n.*** the interpretation of past events in the light of present-day attitudes, rather than in the light of their own historical context —**pres′ent·ist** ***adj., n.***

pres·ent·ly (prez′ənt lē) ***adv.*** **1** in a little while; soon **2** at present; now: a usage still objected to by some **3** [Archaic] at once; instantly

pre·sent·ment (prē zent′mənt, pri-) ***n.*** ⟦ME < OFr *presentement* < *presenter:* see PRESENT, ***vt.***⟧ the act of presenting; presentation; specif., *a)* an exhibition; thing presented to view *b)* *Commerce* the producing of a note, bill of exchange, etc. for acceptance or payment at the proper time and place *c)* *Law* the notice taken or report made by a grand jury of an offense on the basis of the jury's own knowledge and observations and without a bill of indictment *d)* *Philos.* PRESENTATION (sense 7)

present participle *Gram.* a participle used *a)* with auxiliaries to show present or continuing action or state of being (Ex.: *growing* in "he is growing") *b)* as an adjective (Ex.: *growing* in "a growing boy")

present perfect **1** a tense indicating an action as completed or a state as having ended at the time of speaking but not at any definite time in the past **2** a verb form in this tense (Ex.: has gone)

pres·er·va·tion (prez′ər vā′shən) ***n.*** ⟦ME < MFr < ML *praeservatio*⟧ a preserving or being preserved

pres·er·va·tion·ist (-ist) ***n.*** a person who advocates taking positive measures to preserve something, as historic buildings, wilderness lands, endangered species, etc.

pre·serv·a·tive (pri zur′və tiv, prē-) ***adj.*** ⟦ME *preseruatyve* < MFr *preservatif* < ML *praeservativus*⟧ having the quality of preserving —***n.*** anything that preserves; esp., a substance added to a food to keep it from spoiling

pre·serve (pri zurv′, prē-) ***vt.*** **-served′**, **-serv′ing** ⟦ME *preserven* < MFr *preserver* < ML *praeservare,* to preserve, protect < LL, to observe beforehand < L *prae-,* PRE- + *servare:* see OBSERVE⟧ **1** to keep from harm, damage, danger, evil, etc.; protect; save **2** to keep from spoiling or rotting **3** to prepare (food), as by canning, pickling, salting, etc., for future use **4** to keep up; carry on; maintain **5** to maintain and protect (game, fish, etc.) in an area, esp. for regulated hunting or fishing —***vi.*** **1** to preserve fruit, etc. **2** to maintain a game preserve —***n.*** **1** [*usually pl.*] fruit preserved whole or in large pieces by cooking with sugar: cf. JAM[2] **2** a place where game, fish, etc. are preserved **3** any place or activity treated as the special domain of some person or group **4** something that preserves or is preserved —**pre·serv′a·ble** ***adj.*** —**pre·serv′er** ***n.***

pre·set (prē′set′; *for v., also* prē set′) ***vt.*** **-set′**, **-set′ting** to set (something, esp. the controls of an automatic apparatus) beforehand —***n.*** something which can be preset; specif., a control, as on a TV, for selecting a previously assigned frequency, command, etc.

pre·shrink (prē shriŋk′) ***vt.*** **-shrank′** or **-shrunk′**, **-shrunk′** or **-shrunk′en**, **-shrink′ing** to shrink by a special process during manufacture so as to minimize further shrinkage in laundering or dry cleaning —**pre·shrunk** (prē shruŋk′, prē′shruŋk′) ***adj.***

pre·side (pri zīd′, prē-) ***vi.*** **-sid′ed**, **-sid′ing** ⟦Fr *présider* < L *praesidere,* to preside over, protect < *prae-,* PRE- + *sedere,* to SIT⟧ **1** to be in the position of authority in an assembly; serve as chairman **2** to have or exercise control or authority: usually with *over* **3** to perform as the featured instrumentalist —**pre·sid′er** ***n.***

pres·i·den·cy (prez′i dən sē) ***n.,*** *pl.* **-cies** ⟦ML *praesidentia* < L *praesidens:* see fol.⟧ **1** the office or function of president **2** the term during which a president is in office ☆**3** [*often* **P-**] the office of President of the U.S. ☆**4** *Mormon Ch. a)* a council of three with local jurisdiction *b)* a council of three that is the highest administrative body (also **First Presidency**) **5** [**P-**] [Historical] any of the three original provinces of British India

pres·i·dent (prez′i dənt, -dent′) ***n.*** ⟦ME < MFr < L *praesidens* < prp. of *praesidere:* see PRESIDE⟧ ☆**1** the highest executive officer of a company, society, university, club, etc. **2** [*often* **P-**] *a)* the chief executive of a republic having no prime minister *b)* in parliamentary governments, the formal head, usually the presiding member of the legislative assembly or council **3** any presiding officer —**pres′i·den′tial** (-den′shəl) ***adj.*** —**pres′i·den′tial·ly** ***adv.***

☆**pres·i·dent-e·lect** (-ē lekt′, -i-) ***n.*** an elected president who has not yet taken office

Presidents' Day in several States, a legal holiday celebrated on the third Monday in February: cf. WASHINGTON'S BIRTHDAY

pres·i·dent·ship (prez′i dənt ship′) ***n.*** [Brit.] the office or term of a president

☆**pre·sid·i·o** (pri sid′ē ō′) ***n.,*** *pl.* **-i·os′** ⟦Sp < L *praesidium,* garrison < *praeses,* guard < *praesidere:* see PRESIDE⟧ a fortified place or military post, esp. in the SW U.S. —**pre·sid′i·al** ***adj.,*** **pre·sid′i·ar′y**

pre·sid·i·um (pri sid′ē əm) ***n.,*** *pl.* **-i·a** (-ə) or **-i·ums** ⟦Russ *prezidium* < L *praesidium:* see prec.⟧ **1** [*often* **P-**] in certain communist countries, a standing committee empowered to act for a larger body, as a legislature **2** [**P-**] the executive committee of the Communist Party of the Soviet Union from 1952 to 1966

pre·sig·ni·fy (prē sig′nə fī′) ***vt.*** **-fied′**, **-fy′ing** to signify or indicate beforehand; foreshadow

Pres·ley (prez′lē), **El·vis (Aron)** (el′vis) 1935-77; U.S. rock-and-roll singer

pre-soak (prē′sōk′) ***vt.*** to soak beforehand; specif., to soak (laundry) in a detergent solution before beginning the regular laundering process

pre-So·crat·ic or **Pre·so·crat·ic** (prē′sə krat′ik) ***adj.*** designating or of the Greek philosophers before Socrates, often, specif., those whose philosophy was cosmological and ontological in emphasis —***n.*** a pre-Socratic philosopher

pre·sort (prē sôrt′, prē′sôrt′) ***vt.*** to sort ahead of time; specif., to sort (large quantities of mail) by ZIP Codes before turning over to the postal service

press[1] (pres) ***vt.*** ⟦ME *pressen* < MFr *presser* < L *pressare,* freq. of *premere,* to press < IE base **per-,* to strike > OSlav *p'rati,* to strike⟧ **1** to act on with steady force or weight; push steadily against; squeeze **2** to depress or touch (a button, key, etc.) as in using an elevator, keyboard, etc. **3** *a)* to extract juice, etc. from by squeezing *b)* to squeeze (juice, etc.) out **4** *a)* to squeeze for the purpose of making smooth, compact, etc.; compress *b)* to iron (clothes, etc.), esp. with a heavy iron or steam machine **5** to embrace closely **6** to force; compel; constrain **7** to urge or request earnestly or persistently; entreat; importune **8** to impose by persistent entreaty; try to force [to *press* a gift on a friend] **9** to lay stress on; be insistent about; emphasize **10** to distress or trouble; harass **11** to urge on; drive quickly **12** to shape (a phonograph record, metal or plastic products, etc.) by use of a form or matrix **13** [Archaic] to crowd; throng **14** [Obs.] OPPRESS —***vi.*** **1** to exert pressure; specif., *a)* to weigh down; bear heavily *b)* to go forward with energetic or determined effort *c)* to force one's way *d)* to crowd; throng *e)* to be urgent or insistent *f)* to try too hard [he strikes out often because he is *pressing*] **2** to react to being pressed, or ironed [this fabric *presses* well] **3** to iron clothes, etc. —***n.*** **1** a pressing or being pressed; pressure, urgency, etc. **2** a crowd; throng **3** an instrument or machine by which something is crushed, squeezed, stamped, smoothed, etc. by pressure **4** a viselike device in which a tennis racket, etc. can be stored to keep it from warping **5** the condition of clothes as to smoothness, creases, etc. after pressing **6** *a)* *short for* PRINTING PRESS *b)* a printing or publishing establishment *c)* the art, business, or practice of printing *d)* newspapers, magazines, news services, etc. in general, or the persons who write for them; journalism or journalists *e)* publicity, criticism, etc. in newspapers, magazines, etc. [*to receive bad press*] 7 a cabinet for storing clothes or other articles; wardrobe, cupboard, etc. ☆8 *Basketball* a defensive tactic in which offensive players are guarded very closely, usually over the full court 9 *Weight Lifting* a lift in which the barbell or weight is pushed away from the body using the arms or legs —SYN. URGE —**go to press** to start to be printed or to begin printing: said as of an edition of a newspaper, book, etc.

press² (pres) *vt.* ⟦altered (infl. by prec.) < obs. *prest*, to enlist for military service by advance pay < OFr *prester* < L *praestare*, to vouch for, warrant < *praes*, surety (< *prae-*, PRE- + *vas*, bail, surety: for IE base see WED) + *stare*, to STAND⟧ 1 to force into military or naval service; impress 2 to force or urge into any kind of service 3 to use in a way different from the ordinary, esp. in an emergency —*n.* 1 an impressment, or forcing into service, esp. naval or military service 2 [Obs.] an order for impressing recruits

☆**press agent** a person whose business is to get publicity in the news media for a person or organization —**press'-a'gent·ry** *n.*

press·board (pres'bôrd') *n.* a smooth, stiff, heavy, often glazed, paper used in presses for finishing paper, etc.

☆**press box** a place reserved for reporters at sports events, etc., as in a stadium

☆**press conference** a collective interview granted to media personnel as by a celebrity or personage

pressed duck 1 the breast and legs of a roast duck served with a sauce made from juices obtained by squeezing the remaining parts in a special press 2 a Chinese dish of steamed duck, boned, pressed, deep-fried, and served with a sauce and toasted almonds

press·er (pres'ər) *n.* one that presses; specif., a person whose work is pressing newly made or freshly cleaned clothes

press gallery a section set apart for newspersons in a chamber where an official body meets

press gang ⟦for *prest gang*: see PRESS²⟧ [Historical] a group of men who round up other men and force them into naval or military service: also **press'gang'** *n.*

press-gang (pres'gaŋ') *vt.* 1 [Historical] to force (someone) into naval or military service by means of a press gang 2 to force (someone) to do something

press·ing (pres'iŋ) *adj.* ⟦prp. of PRESS¹⟧ 1 calling for immediate attention; urgent 2 persistent in request or demand; insistent —*n.* 1 the process or an instance of stamping, squeezing, etc. with a press 2 the result of this, often a series or one of a series of identical articles [*a pressing of phonograph records*] —**press'ing·ly** *adv.*

press kit an assortment of publicity releases, information sheets, etc. for distribution to newspeople

press·man (pres'mən) *n., pl.* **-men** (-mən) 1 an operator of a printing press 2 [Brit.] a newsperson

press·mark (-märk') *n.* [Brit.] CALL NUMBER

press of sail (*or* **canvas**) the maximum amount of sail that a ship can safely carry under given wind conditions

pres·sor (pres'ər) *adj.* ⟦PRESS(URE) + (MOT)OR⟧ designating a nerve which, when stimulated, causes a rise in blood pressure —*n.* a substance capable of raising blood pressure

press release NEWS RELEASE

press·room (pres'ro͞om') *n.* 1 a room containing the printing presses of a newspaper or printing establishment 2 a room for members of the news media, as in the White House

☆**press secretary** a public relations person whose job is to deal with the news media on behalf of a government official or other prominent person

press-up (pres'up') *n.* [Brit.] PUSH-UP

pres·sure (presh'ər) *n.* ⟦OFr < L *pressura*, a pressing (LL(Ec), oppression, affliction) < *pressus*, pp. of *premere*, to PRESS¹⟧ 1 a pressing or being pressed; compression; squeezing 2 a condition of distress; oppression; affliction 3 a sense impression caused by or as by compression of a part of the body 4 a compelling influence; constraining force [*social pressure*] 5 demands requiring immediate attention; urgency 6 *short for: a)* ATMOSPHERIC PRESSURE *b)* BLOOD PRESSURE 7 [Obs.] a mark made by pressing; impression 8 *Physics* force per unit of area: abbrev. *P* —*vt.* **-sured, -sur·ing** ☆1 to exert pressure, or compelling influence, on 2 PRESSURIZE

pressure cabin *Aeron.* a pressurized cabin

☆**pres·sure-cook** (-ko͝ok') *vt.* to cook in a pressure cooker

☆**pressure cooker** 1 an airtight metal container for quick cooking by means of steam under pressure 2 any place or situation characterized by emotional pressure, urgent and persistent demands, etc.

pressure gauge a gauge for measuring the pressure of steam, water, gas, etc.

pressure gradient the rate of decrease in barometric pressure in a given region at a particular time

pressure group any group that exerts pressure upon government officials and the public through lobbies, propaganda, etc. in order to affect legislation or policies

pressure point 1 any of a number of points on the body where an artery passes close to the surface and in front of a bony structure so that pressure applied there will check bleeding from a distal injured part 2 any of various points on the body where pressure is especially effective, as in acupuncture

pressure suit a suit providing an appropriate pressurized environment for an individual who is at high altitudes, in space, etc.

pres·sur·ize (presh'ər īz') *vt.* **-ized', -iz'ing** 1 to keep nearly standard atmospheric pressure inside (an airplane, spacesuit, submarine, etc.) 2 to place under high pressure —**pres'sur·i·za'tion** *n.* —**pres'sur·iz'er** *n.*

press·work (pres'wurk') *n.* 1 the operation or management of a printing press 2 work done by a printing press

prest (prest) [Obs.] *n.* ⟦ME *preste* < OFr < *prester*: see PRESS²⟧ an advance of money, specif. one to men enlisting in the British army or navy —*adj.* ready; prepared

Pres·ter John (pres'tər) a legendary medieval Christian king and priest said to have ruled either in the Far East or in Ethiopia

pre·ster·num (prē stur'nəm) *n.* MANUBRIUM (sense *b*)

pres·ti·dig·i·ta·tion (pres'tə dij'i tā'shən) *n.* ⟦Fr: see fol.⟧ sleight of hand; legerdemain

pres·ti·dig·i·ta·tor (pres'tə dij'ə tāt'ər) *n.* ⟦Fr *prestidigitateur* (based on L *prestigiator*, juggler, deceiver) < *preste*, quick < *presto* (see PRESTO¹) + L *digitus*, finger (see DIGIT)⟧ an expert at prestidigitation

pres·tige (pres tēzh', -tēj') *n.* ⟦Fr, orig., illusion, trick < LL *praestigium* < L *praestigiae*, altered < *praestrigiae*, deceptions < *praestringere*, to bind, orig., to bind fast < *prae-*, PRE- + *stringere*, to bind: see STRAIN¹⟧ 1 the power to impress or influence, as because of success, wealth, etc. 2 reputation based on brilliance of achievement, character, etc.; renown —SYN. INFLUENCE

pres·ti·gious (pres tij'əs, -tē'jəs) *adj.* ⟦L *praestigiosus*, full of deceitful tricks < *praestigium*, delusion: see prec.⟧ 1 [Archaic] of or characterized by legerdemain or deception 2 ⟦re-formed from prec. + -OUS⟧ having or imparting prestige: also **pres·tige'ful**

pres·tis·si·mo (pres tis'i mō'; *It* pres tēs'sē mô') *adj., adv.* ⟦It, superl. of *presto*: see fol.⟧ *Musical Direction* very fast; faster than *presto*: when used other than in musical scores, also in roman type —*n., pl.* **-mos'** *Music* [*also in roman type*] a passage or movement to be performed *prestissimo*

pres·to¹ (pres'tō) *adv., adj.* ⟦It, quick, nimble < L *praestus*, at hand, ready < *praesto*, at hand, available < *prae*, before: see PRE-⟧ *Musical Direction* in fast tempo: when used other than in musical scores, also in roman type —*n., pl.* **-tos** *Music* [*also in roman type*] a passage or movement to be performed *presto*

pres·to² (pres'tō) *interj.* used, as by a magician in a conventional portrayal, to signify, or seemingly command, a sudden change or occurrence —*adv.* suddenly or rapidly

presto chang·o (pres'tō chān'jō) PRESTO² (*interj.*): also sp. **presto change-o**

Pres·ton (pres'tən) city in Lancashire, NW England

☆**pre·stressed concrete** (prē'strest') concrete in which steel cables, wires, etc. are embedded under tension so as to produce compressive stress and lend greater strength

pre·sum·a·ble (prē zo͞om'ə bəl, -zyo͞om'-; pri-) *adj.* that may be presumed, or taken for granted; probable —**pre·sum'a·bly** *adv.*

pre·sume (prē zo͞om', -zyo͞om'; pri-) *vt.* **-sumed', -sum'ing** ⟦ME *presumen* < OFr *presumer* < L *praesumere* < *prae-*, before (see PRE-) + *sumere*, to take: see CONSUME⟧ 1 to take upon oneself without permission or authority; dare (to say or do something); venture 2 to take for granted; accept as true, lacking proof to the contrary; suppose 3 to constitute reasonable evidence for supposing [*a signed invoice presumes receipt of goods*] —*vi.* 1 to act presumptuously; take liberties 2 to rely too much (*on* or *upon*), as in taking liberties [*to presume on another's friendship*] 3 to take something for granted —**pre·sum'ed·ly** (-id lē) *adv.* —**pre·sum'er** *n.*

SYN.—**presume** implies a taking something for granted or accepting it as true, usually on the basis of probable evidence in its favor and the absence of proof to the contrary [*the man is presumed to be of sound mind*]; **presuppose** is the broadest term here, sometimes suggesting a taking something for granted unjustifiably [*this writer presupposes a too extensive vocabulary in children*] and, in another sense, implying that something is required as a preceding condition [*brilliant technique in piano playing presupposes years of practice*]; **assume** implies the supposition of something as the basis for argument or action [*let us assume his motives were good*]; **postulate** implies the assumption of something as an underlying factor, often one that is incapable of proof [*his argument postulates the inherent goodness of man*]; **premise** implies the setting forth of a proposition on which a conclusion can be based See also **assume**

pre·sump·tion (prē zump'shən, pri-) *n.* ⟦ME < OFr *presumpcion* < L *praesumptio*, a taking beforehand < *praesumptus*, pp. of *praesumere*: see prec.⟧ 1 the act of presuming; specif., *a)* an overstepping of proper bounds; forwardness; effrontery *b)* the taking of something for granted 2 the thing presumed; supposition 3 a ground or reason for presuming; evidence that points to the probability of something 4 *Law* the inference that a fact exists, based on the proved existence of other facts

pre·sump·tive (prē zump'tiv, pri-) *adj.* ⟦Fr *présomptif* < LL *praesumptivus* < L *praesumptus*: see prec.⟧ 1 giving reasonable ground for belief [*presumptive evidence*] 2 based on probability; presumed [*an heir presumptive*] —**pre·sump'tive·ly** *adv.*

pre·sump·tu·ous (prē zump'cho͞o əs, pri-) *adj.* ⟦ME < OFr *presunteux* < LL *praesumptuosus* < L *praesumptus*: see PRESUMPTION⟧ too bold or forward; taking too much for granted; showing overconfidence, arrogance, or effrontery —**pre·sump'tu·ous·ly** *adv.* —**pre·sump'tu·ous·ness** *n.*

pre·sup·pose (prē'sə pōz') *vt.* **-posed', -pos'ing** ⟦ME *presupposen* < MFr *presupposer*, altered (based on *poser*, to place) < ML *praesupponere*, pp. *praesuppositus*: see PRE- & SUPPOSE⟧ 1 to suppose or assume beforehand; take for granted 2 to require or imply as a preceding condition [an effect *presupposes* a cause] —*SYN.* PRESUME —**pre′sup·po·si′tion** (-sup ə zish′ən) ***n.***

pret *abbrev.* preterit

prêt-à-por·ter (pre tȧ pôr tā′) ***adj.*** ⟦Fr⟧ READY-TO-WEAR

pre·tax (prē′taks′) ***adj.*** before the payment of taxes

☆**pre·teen** (prē′tēn′) ***n.*** a child who is nearly a teenager

pre·tence (prē tens′, pri-; prē′tens′) ***n.*** *Brit. sp. of* PRETENSE

pre·tend (prē tend′, pri-) ***vt.*** ⟦ME *pretenden,* to intend < MFr *pretendre* < L *praetendere,* to hold forth, allege < *prae-,* before + *tendere,* to stretch: see THIN⟧ 1 to claim; profess; allege [to *pretend* ignorance of the law] 2 to claim or profess falsely; feign; simulate [to *pretend* anger] 3 to make believe, as in children's play [to *pretend* to be astronauts] —***vi.*** 1 to lay claim [to *pretend* to a throne] 2 to make believe in play or in an attempt to deceive; feign —***adj.*** [Informal] make-believe [*pretend* jewelry] —*SYN.* ASSUME

pre·tend·ed (prē ten′did, pri-) ***adj.*** 1 not genuine; feigned 2 reputed or alleged

pre·tend·er (prē ten′dər, pri-) ***n.*** 1 a person who pretends 2 a claimant to a throne 3 an aspirant 4 [P-] in English history, the son or the grandson of James II: see OLD PRETENDER, YOUNG PRETENDER

pre·tense (prē tens′, pri-; prē′tens′) ***n.*** ⟦ME < Anglo-Fr *pretensse* < ML **pretensa* < *praetensus,* alleged < pp. of L *praetendere:* see PRETEND⟧ 1 a claim, esp. an unsupported one, as to some distinction or accomplishment; pretension 2 a false claim or profession 3 a false show of something 4 a pretending, as at play; make-believe 5 a false reason or plea; pretext 6 [Rare] aim; intention 7 pretentiousness; ostentation 8 a pretentious act or remark

pre·ten·sion (prē ten′shən, pri-) ***n.*** ⟦ML *praetensio* < *praetensus:* see prec.⟧ 1 a pretext or allegation 2 a claim, as to a right, title, distinction, etc. 3 assertion of a claim 4 pretentiousness; ostentation

pre·ten·tious (prē ten′shəs, pri-) ***adj.*** ⟦Fr *prétentieux* < *prétention,* pretension + *-eux,* -OUS⟧ 1 making claims, explicit or implicit, to some distinction, importance, dignity, or excellence 2 affectedly grand; ostentatious —**pre·ten′tious·ly** ***adv.*** —**pre·ten′tious·ness** ***n.***

pre·ter- (prēt′ər) ⟦L *praeter-* < *praeter,* beyond, past, compar. of *prae,* before: see PRE-⟧ *prefix* past, beyond, outside the bounds of [*pretermit, preterhuman*]

pre·ter·hu·man (prēt′ər hyo͞o′mən) ***adj.*** beyond that which is human; esp., superhuman

pret·er·it or **pret·er·ite** (pret′ər it) ***adj.*** ⟦ME *preterit* < MFr < L *praeteritus,* gone by, pp. of *praeterire* < *praeter-* (see PRETER-) + *ire,* to go: see YEAR⟧ 1 *Gram.* expressing past action or state 2 [Rare] former —***n.*** 1 the past tense 2 a verb in the past tense

pret·er·i·tion (pret′ər ish′ən) ***n.*** ⟦LL *praeteritio* < L *praeteritus:* see prec.⟧ 1 a passing over; omission 2 *Law* an omitting of one or more legal heirs from a will 3 *Theol.* the passing over by God of those not elect: a doctrine of Calvinism

pre·term (prē′turm′) ***adj.*** ⟦PRE- + TERM[1] (*n.* 3c)⟧ of or having to do with premature birth, or born prematurely —***n.*** a preterm baby

pre·ter·mit (prēt′ər mit′) ***vt.*** **-mit′ted, -mit′ting** ⟦L *praetermittere,* to let go by < *praeter-* (see PRETER-) + *mittere,* to send: see MISSION⟧ 1 to leave out or leave undone; neglect or omit 2 to let pass unnoticed; overlook —**pre′ter·mis′sion** (-mish′ən) ***n.***

pre·ter·nat·u·ral (prēt′ər nach′ər əl) ***adj.*** ⟦ML *praeternaturalis*⟧ 1 differing from or beyond what is normally found in or expected from nature; abnormal [*preternatural* strength] 2 SUPERNATURAL —**pre′ter·nat′u·ral·ism′** ***n.*** —**pre′ter·nat′u·ral·ly** ***adv.***

pre·test (prē′test′; *for v.* prē test′) ***n.*** a preliminary test, as of a product —***vt., vi.*** to test in advance

pre·text (prē′tekst′) ***n.*** ⟦L *praetextum,* neut. of *praetextus,* pp. of *praetexere,* to weave before, pretend: see PRE- & TEXTURE⟧ 1 a false reason or motive put forth to hide the real one; excuse 2 a cover-up; front

pre·tor (prēt′ər) ***n.*** *alt. sp. of* PRAETOR —**pre·to·ri·al** (prē tôr′ē əl) ***adj.*** —**pre·to′ri·an** ***adj., n.***

Pre·to·ri·a (prē tôr′ē ə, pri-) administrative capital of South Africa, in Gauteng province

pre·tri·al (prē′trī′əl) ***adj.*** occurring, presented, or engaged in before a court trial actually begins [a *pretrial* motion] —***n.*** a pretrial proceeding for clearing up points of fact or law

pret·ti·fy (prit′i fī′) ***vt.*** **-fied′, -fy′ing** to make pretty —**pret′ti·fi·ca′tion** ***n.***

pret·ty (prit′ē) ***adj.*** **-ti·er, -ti·est** ⟦ME *prati* < OE *prættig,* crafty < *prætt,* craft, trick⟧ 1 pleasing or attractive in a dainty, delicate, or graceful way rather than through striking beauty, elegance, grandeur, or stateliness 2 *a)* fine; good; nice (often used ironically) [I'm in a *pretty* fix] *b)* adroit; skillful [a *pretty* move] 3 [Archaic] elegant 4 [Now Chiefly Scot.] brave; bold; gallant 5 [Informal] considerable; quite large [a *pretty* price] —***adv.*** 1 *a)* fairly; moderately [*pretty* sure] *b)* [Informal] quite or very [*pretty* angry] 2 **-ti·er, -ti·est** [Informal] prettily [to talk *pretty*] —***n., pl.*** **-ties** a pretty person or thing —***vt.*** **-tied, -ty·ing** to make pretty: usually with *up* —*SYN.* BEAUTIFUL —**pretty nearly** mostly, almost, more or less, etc. [I used up *pretty nearly* all of the flour]: also [Informal] **pretty much** [the spoiled child does *pretty much* what he wants to do] —☆**sitting pretty** [Slang] in a favorable position —**pret′ti·ly** ***adv.*** —**pret′ti·ness** ***n.*** —**pret′ty·ish** ***adj.***

☆**pret·zel** (pret′səl) ***n.*** ⟦Ger *brezel* < OHG *brezitella* < ML **brachiatellum,* dim. of **brachiatum,* biscuit baked in form of crossed arms < L *brachium,* an arm: see BRACE[1]⟧ a usually hard, brittle biscuit made from a slender roll of dough heavily sprinkled with salt and typically baked in the form of a loose knot or as a stick

prev. *abbrev.* 1 previous 2 previously

pre·vail (prē vāl′, pri-) ***vi.*** ⟦ME *prevaylen* < L *praevalere* < *prae-,* before (see PRE-) + *valere,* to be strong: see VALUE⟧ 1 to gain the advantage or mastery; be victorious; triumph: often with *over* or *against* 2 to produce or achieve the desired effect; be effective; succeed 3 to be or become stronger or more widespread; predominate 4 to exist widely; be prevalent —**prevail on** (or **upon**) 1 to persuade or induce; appeal to 2 to make use of for one's own benefit [to *prevail on* a friend's good nature]

pre·vail·ing (-iŋ) ***adj.*** 1 superior in strength, influence, or effect 2 most frequent, noticeable, etc.; predominant 3 widely existing; prevalent —**pre·vail′ing·ly** ***adv.***

SYN.—**prevailing** applies to that which leads all others in acceptance, usage, belief, etc. at a given time and in a given place [a *prevailing* practice]; **current** refers to that which is commonly accepted or in general usage at the time specified or, if unspecified, at the present time [a pronunciation *current* in the 18th century]; **prevalent** implies widespread occurrence or acceptance but does not now connote the predominance of **prevailing** [a *prevalent* belief]; **rife** implies rapidly increasing prevalence and often connotes excitement or alarm [rumors about war were *rife*]

prev·a·lent (prev′ə lənt) ***adj.*** ⟦L *praevalens,* prp. of *praevalere:* see PREVAIL⟧ 1 [Rare] stronger, more effective, etc.; dominant 2 *a)* widely existing *b)* generally practiced, occurring, or accepted —*SYN.* PREVAILING —**prev′a·lence** (-ləns) ***n.*** —**prev′a·lent·ly** ***adv.***

pre·var·i·cate (pri var′i kāt′) ***vi.*** **-cat′ed, -cat′ing** ⟦< L *praevaricatus,* pp. of *praevaricari,* to prevaricate, lit., to walk crookedly < *prae-,* before + *varicare,* to straddle < *varicus,* straddling < *varus,* bent apart < IE base **wa-* > VARY⟧ 1 to turn aside from, or evade, the truth; equivocate 2 to tell an untruth; lie —*SYN.* LIE[2] —**pre·var′i·ca′tion** ***n.*** —**pre·var′i·ca′tor** ***n.***

pre·ven·ient (prē vēn′yənt, pri-) ***adj.*** ⟦L *praeveniens,* prp. of *praevenire:* see fol.⟧ 1 going before; preceding 2 anticipating; expectant 3 *Christian Theol.* antecedent to human action [*prevenient* grace] —**pre·ven′ience** (-yəns) ***n.***

pre·vent (prē vent′, pri-) ***vt.*** ⟦ME *preventen* < L *praeventus,* pp. of *praevenire,* to anticipate < *prae-,* before (see PRE-) + *venire,* to COME⟧ 1 [Obs.] *a)* to act in anticipation of (an event or a fixed time) *b)* to anticipate (a need, objection, etc.) *c)* to precede 2 to stop or keep (*from* doing something) 3 to keep from happening; make impossible by prior action; hinder —***vi.*** to interpose an obstacle —**pre·vent′a·ble** ***adj.***, **pre·vent′i·ble** —**pre·vent′er** ***n.***

SYN.—**prevent** implies a stopping or keeping from happening, as by some prior action or by interposing an obstacle or impediment [to *prevent* disease]; **forestall** suggests advance action to stop something in its course and thereby make it ineffective [try to *forestall* their questions]; **preclude** implies a making impossible by shutting off every possibility of occurrence [locked doors *precluded* his escape]; **obviate** suggests the preventing of some unfavorable outcome by taking necessary anticipatory measures [her frankness *obviated* objections]; **avert** suggests a warding off of imminent danger or misfortune [diplomacy can *avert* war] —*ANT.* **permit, allow**

pre·ven·tion (prē ven′shən, pri-) ***n.*** 1 the act of preventing 2 means of preventing

pre·ven·tive (prē vent′iv, pri-) ***adj.*** preventing or serving to prevent; esp., preventing disease —***n.*** anything that prevents; esp., anything that prevents disease; prophylactic Also **pre·vent′a·tive** (-ə tiv) —**pre·ven′tive·ly** ***adv.*** —**pre·ven′tive·ness** ***n.***

pre·view (prē′vyo͞o′) ***vt.*** to view or show beforehand; receive or give a preview of —***n.*** ☆1 a previous or preliminary view or survey ☆2 *a)* a restricted showing, as of a film, before exhibition to the public generally *b)* a showing of scenes from a film, TV show, etc. in advertising its coming appearance

pre·vi·ous (prē′vē əs) ***adj.*** ⟦L *praevius* < *prae-* (see PRE-) + *via,* way (see VIA)⟧ 1 occurring before in time or order; prior ☆2 [Informal] too soon; premature —**previous to** before —**pre′vi·ous·ly** ***adv.***

SYN.—**previous** generally implies a coming before in time or order [a *previous* encounter]; **prior** adds to this a connotation of greater importance or claim as a result of being first [a *prior* commitment]; **preceding**, esp. when used with the definite article, implies a coming immediately before [the *preceding* night]; **antecedent** adds to the meaning of **previous** a connotation of direct causal relationship with what follows [events *antecedent* to the war]; **foregoing** applies specif. to something previously said or written [the *foregoing* examples]; **former** always connotes comparison, stated or implied, with what follows (termed *latter*) —*ANT.* **following**

previous question the question, put as a motion, whether a matter under consideration by a parliamentary body should be voted on immediately: defeat of the motion permits further consideration

pre·vise (prē vīz′) ***vt.*** **-vised′, -vis′ing** ⟦< L *praevisus,* pp. of *praevidere,* to foresee < *prae-,* PRE- + *videre,* to see: see VISION⟧ [Rare] 1 to foresee or forecast 2 to inform beforehand; warn

pre·vi·sion (prē vizh′ən) ***n.*** ⟦Fr *prévision* < ML *praevisio* < L *praevisus:* see prec.⟧ 1 foresight or foreknowledge 2 a prediction or prophecy —***vt.*** to foresee —**pre·vi′sion·al** ***adj.***, **pre·vi′sion·ar′y**

pre·vo·cal·ic (prē′vō kal′ik) ***adj.*** coming just before a vowel

☆**pre·vo·ca·tion·al** (prē′vō kā′shə nəl) ***adj.*** designating or of counseling, testing, etc. offered to students for career planning and placement in training programs

Pré·vost (d'Ex·iles) (prā vō deg zēl'), **An·toine Fran·çois** (än twán frän swá') 1697-1763; Fr. novelist: called **Abbé Prévost**

☆**pre·vue** (prē'vyo͞o') *n.* PREVIEW (esp. sense 2)

pre·war (prē'wôr') *adj.* before a (or the) war

☆**prex·y** (prek'sē) *n., pl.* **prex'ies** ⟦contr. of PRESIDENT⟧ [Slang] the president, esp. of a college, etc.

prey (prā) *n.* ⟦ME *preye* < OFr *preie* < L *praeda* < base of *prehendere*, to seize: see PREHENSILE⟧ **1** [Archaic] plunder; booty **2** an animal hunted or killed for food by another animal **3** a person or thing that falls victim to someone or something **4** the mode of living by preying on other animals [*a bird of prey*] —*vi.* **1** to plunder; rob **2** to hunt or kill other animals for food **3** to make profit from a victim as by swindling **4** to have a wearing or harmful influence; weigh heavily Generally used with *on* or *upon* —**prey'er** *n.*

preying mantis ⟦by folk etym. < PRAYING MANTIS, because the mantis *preys* on other insects⟧ MANTIS

Prez (prez) *n.* [*also* **p-**] [Slang] the president, as of the United States

PRI *service mark* Public Radio International

Pri·am (prī'əm) *n.* ⟦L *Priamus* < Gr *Priamos*⟧ *Gr. Legend* the last king of Troy, who reigned during the Trojan War: he was the father of Hector and Paris

pri·ap·ic (prī ap'ik) *adj.* ⟦PRIAP(US) + -IC⟧ **1** PHALLIC **2** overly concerned with virility or masculinity

pri·a·pism (prī'ə piz'əm) *n.* ⟦LL *priapismus* < Gr *priapismos* < *priapizein*, to be lewd: see fol.⟧ **1** a pathological condition characterized by persistent erection of the penis, esp. without sexual excitement **2** a lascivious attitude

Pri·a·pus (prī ā'pəs) *n.* ⟦L < Gr *Priapos*⟧ **1** *Class. Myth.* a god, son of Dionysus and Aphrodite, personifying the male procreative power **2** [**p-**] PHALLUS (sense 1)

Prib·i·lof Islands (prib'ə läf') ⟦after G. *Pribylov*, Russ sea captain (*c.* 1786)⟧ group of four Alaskan islands in the Bering Sea, north of the Aleutian Islands: noted as a breeding place of seals

price (prīs) *n.* ⟦ME & OFr *pris* < L *pretium*, price < IE **preti-*, equivalent < base **per-*, to sell, make equal > PAR[1]⟧ **1** the amount of money, etc. asked or paid for something; cost; charge **2** value or worth **3** a reward for the capture or death of a person **4** money or other consideration sufficient to be a bribe or inducement **5** the cost, as in life, labor, sacrifice, etc., of obtaining some benefit or advantage —*vt.* **priced, pric'ing 1** to put a price on; fix the price of **2** [Informal] to ask or find out the price of —**at any price** no matter what the cost —**beyond (or without) price** priceless; invaluable —**price out of the market 1** to force (oneself or one's product) out of competition by charging prices that are too high **2** to exclude in effect (a potential buyer) by charging prices that he or she cannot afford —**pric'er** *n.*

Price (prīs), **(Mary Violet) Le·on·tyne** (lē än'tēn', lē'ən-) 1927- ; U.S. operatic soprano

price control the setting of ceiling prices on basic goods and services by a government, as to fight inflation

☆**price-earn·ings ratio** (prīs'ʉrn'iŋz) the ratio of the current market price of a share of stock to the corporation's annual earnings per share

price fixing the setting or maintenance of prices at a certain level, esp. by competitors in collusion

price gouging ⟦see GOUGE, *vt.* 4⟧ [Informal] the act or an instance of drastically raising the price of something that is temporarily in short supply

price index INDEX (sense 5*b*)

price·less (prīs'lis) *adj.* **1** of inestimable value; beyond price **2** [Informal] very amusing or absurd

☆**price support** support of certain price levels at or above market values, as by government purchase of surpluses

price tag 1 a tag, as on an item of merchandise, indicating the price **2** the price of something: often used fig. [*heavy smoking carries a price tag*]

price war a situation in which competitors selling a certain commodity successively lower prices, as to force one or more out of business

pric·ey (prī'sē) *adj.* **pric'i·er, pric'i·est** [Informal] expensive; dear

prick (prik) *n.* ⟦ME *prike* < OE *prica*, point, dot, akin to Du *prik*, MHG *pfrecken*⟧ **1** a very small puncture or, formerly, dot, made by a sharp point **2** [Archaic] any of various pointed objects, as a thorn, goad, etc. **3** PRICKING **4** a sharp pain caused by or as if by being pricked **5** [Slang] *a)* the penis (considered vulgar by many) *b)* a man regarded as bad-tempered, disagreeable, malicious, etc. (somewhat vulgar) —*vt.* **1** to make (a tiny hole) in (something) with a sharp point **2** to cause to feel sharp pain in [*remorse pricked his conscience*] **3** to mark or trace by dots, points, or punctures **4** to pierce (a horse's foot) to the quick in shoeing, causing lameness **5** to cause to point or stick up: often with *up* **6** [Archaic] to spur or urge on; goad; incite —*vi.* **1** to cause or feel a slight, sharp pain **2** to have a prickly or stinging sensation; tingle **3** to point or stick up: said esp. of ears **4** [Archaic] to spur a horse on; ride fast —*adj.* carried stiffly erect: said of a dog's ears —**prick out (or off)** to transplant (seedlings) as from seed pans to shallow boxes —**prick up one's ears 1** to raise the ears with the points upward: said of an animal **2** to listen closely

prick·er (prik'ər) *n.* **1** a person, animal, or thing that pricks **2** PRICKLE (sense 1)

prick·et (prik'it) *n.* ⟦ME *pryket*, dim.: see PRICK⟧ **1** a small spike on which to stick a candle **2** a candlestick having such a spike **3** a male fallow deer in his second year, with unbranched antlers

prick·ing (-iŋ) *n.* **1** the act or process of one that pricks **2** a prickly feeling

prick·le (prik'əl) *n.* ⟦ME *prykel* < OE *pricel*, earlier *pricels* < base of *prica* (see PRICK) + *-els*, instrumental suffix⟧ **1** any sharp point; specif., a small, sharply pointed spine lacking vascular tissue and growing from the tissue under the outer layer of a plant **2** a prickly sensation; stinging or tingling —*vt.* **-led, -ling 1** to prick, as with a spine or thorn **2** to cause to feel a tingling sensation —*vi.* to tingle

prick·ly (prik'lē) *adj.* **-li·er, -li·est 1** full of prickles **2** stinging; smarting; tingling —**prick'li·ness** *n.*

☆**prickly ash** either of two North American shrubs or trees (genus *Zanthoxylum*) of the rue family, with pinnately compound leaves having paired spines at the base

☆**prickly heat** MILIARIA

☆**prickly pear 1** *a)* any of various cactuses (genus *Opuntia*) having large, flat, oval stem joints and edible fruits: many species have barbed spines *b)* the pear-shaped fruit of such a plant **2** NOPAL

☆**prickly poppy** any of a genus (*Argemone*) of plants of the poppy family, with prickly leaves and yellow juice

pric·y (prī'sē) *adj.* **pric'i·er, pric'i·est** [Informal] *alt. sp. of* PRICEY

pride (prīd) *n.* ⟦ME < OE *pryte* < *prut*, PROUD⟧ **1** *a)* an unduly high opinion of oneself; exaggerated self-esteem; conceit *b)* haughty behavior resulting from this; arrogance **2** proper respect for oneself; sense of one's own dignity or worth; self-respect **3** delight or satisfaction in one's own or another's achievements, in associations, etc. **4** a person or thing in which pride is taken **5** the best of a class, group, society, etc.; pick; flower **6** the best part; prime [*in the pride of manhood*] **7** mettle (in a horse) **8** *a)* a group or family (of lions) *b)* [Informal] any impressive group **9** [Archaic] *a)* magnificence; splendor *b)* ornament **10** [Obs.] sexual desire —*vt.* **prid'ed, prid'ing** [Rare] to make proud —**pride oneself on** to be proud of —**pride'ful** *adj.* —**pride'ful·ly** *adv.* —**pride'ful·ness** *n.*

SYN.—**pride** refers either to a justified or excessive belief in one's own worth, merit, superiority, etc. [*she takes pride in her accuracy*]; **conceit** always implies an exaggerated opinion of oneself, one's achievements, etc. [*blinded by her overweening conceit*]; **vanity** suggests an excessive desire to be admired by others for one's achievements, appearance, etc. [*his vanity is wounded by criticism*]; **vainglory** implies extreme conceit as manifested by boasting, swaggering, arrogance, etc. [*the vainglory of a conquering general*]; **self-esteem** implies a high opinion of oneself, often higher than is held by others —*ANT.* **humility**

Pride (prīd), **Thomas** died 1658; Eng. army officer: in 1648 brought about the expulsion (**Pride's Purge**) of over 100 Royalist & Presbyterian Members of Parliament

☆**pride-of-In·di·a** (prīd'uv in'dē ə) *n.* CHINABERRY (sense 1)

pride of place the first or most important position

prie-dieu (prē dyo͞o', prē'dyo͞o') *n., pl.* **prie-dieux** (prē dyo͞o', prē'dyo͞o') ⟦Fr < *prier*, to pray + *Dieu*, God⟧ a narrow, upright frame with a lower ledge for kneeling on at prayer and an upper ledge, as for a book

pri·er (prī'ər) *n.* a person who pries

priest (prēst) *n.* ⟦ME *prest* < OE *preost* (? with -*o*- by assoc. with *profost*, PROVOST) < LL(Ec) *presbyter*, an elder < Gr *presbyteros*, elder, compar. of *presbys*, old, old man (in LGr(Ec), an elder) < IE **pres-*, ahead < base **per-* (see PER[1], PRE-) + **gwou-*, COW[1], ox (hence, orig., lead-ox)⟧ **1** a person whose function is to make sacrificial offerings and perform other religious rites as an intermediary between deity and worshipers **2** *a)* in the early Christian church, a presbyter, or elder *b)* in hierarchical Christian churches, a clergyman ranking next below a bishop and authorized to administer the sacraments **3** any clergyman —**priest'hood'** *n.*

priest·craft (prēst'kraft') *n.* the craft, methods, etc. of priests: now usually with reference to the unscrupulous use of a priestly office

priest·ess (prēs'tis) *n.* a female priest, esp. of a pagan religion

Priest·ley (prēst'lē) **1 J(ohn) B(oynton)** 1894-1984; Eng. novelist, playwright, & literary critic **2 Joseph** 1733-1804; Eng. scientist & theologian, in the U.S. after 1794: discoverer of oxygen

priest·ly (prēst'lē) *adj.* **-li·er, -li·est** of, like, or suitable for a priest or priests —**priest'li·ness** *n.*

priest-rid·den (prēst'rid''n) *adj.* dominated or tyrannized by priests

prig[1] (prig) *n.* ⟦< 16th-c. cant < ?⟧ **1** a person who is annoyingly smug in his or her moral behavior, attitudes, etc. **2** a person who is annoyingly fastidious about rules, small details, etc. —**prig'ger·y** *n.*, **prig'gism'** —**prig'gish** *adj.* —**prig'gish·ly** *adv.* —**prig'gish·ness** *n.*

prig[2] (prig) *vt.* **prigged, prig'ging** ⟦? akin to prec.⟧ [Brit. Slang] to steal —*vi.* [Scot. or North Eng.] to haggle —*n.* [Brit. Slang] a thief or pickpocket

Pri·go·gine (pri gô'gin, prē'gô zhēn'), **Il·ya** (il yä') 1917-2003; Belgian chemist, born in Russia

prill (pril) *n.* ⟦orig. a mining term in Cornwall < ?⟧ a small, beadlike pellet —*vt.* to make (a substance) into prills

prim[1] (prim) *adj.* **prim'mer, prim'mest** ⟦< ? MFr *prim*, prime, first (also sharp, thin, slender; hence, neat) < L *primus*, first: see PRIME⟧ stiffly formal, precise, moral, etc.; proper; demure — *vt., vi.* **primmed, prim'ming** to assume a prim expression on (one's face or mouth) —**prim'ly** *adv.* —**prim'ness** *n.*

prim[2] *abbrev.* **1** primary **2** primitive

pri·ma ballerina (prē'mə) ⟦It, lit., first ballerina⟧ the principal woman dancer in a ballet company

pri·ma·cy (prī′mə sē) ***n.***, *pl.* **-cies** ⟦ME *primacie* < MFr < ML *primatia* < LL *primas:* see PRIMATE⟧ **1** the state of being first in time, order, rank, etc. **2** the rank, office, or authority of a primate

pri·ma don·na (prē′mə dän′ə, prim′ə-) ⟦It, lit., first lady⟧ **1** the principal woman singer in an opera or concert **2** [Informal] a temperamental, vain, or arrogant person

pri·ma fa·cie (prī′mə fā′shə, -shē) ⟦L⟧ **1** at first sight; on first view, before further examination **2** based on a first impression **3** self-evident

prima facie evidence ⟦see prec.⟧ *Law* evidence adequate to establish a fact or raise a presumption of fact unless refuted

pri·mal (prī′məl) ***adj.*** ⟦ML *primalis* < L *primus,* first: see PRIME⟧ **1** first in time; original; primitive **2** first in importance; primary **3** fundamental; basic [the *primal* urge to procreate]

primal scene *Psychoanalysis* a child's observation of an act of sexual intercourse, esp. between the child's parents

☆**primal therapy** ⟦< *The Primal Scream,* book (1970) by A. Janov, U.S. psychologist⟧ a treatment of mental disorder in which the patient, often in group sessions, is induced to reenact his or her infancy and to express emotions violently in screams, shouts, etc.: also **primal scream (therapy)**

☆**pri·ma·quine** (prī′mə kwēn′) ***n.*** ⟦< L *primus,* first (see PRIME) + QU(IN)INE⟧ a synthetic chemical compound, $C_{15}H_{21}N_3O$, used as a cure for malaria

pri·mar·i·ly (prī mer′ə lē, prī′mer′-) ***adv.*** **1** at first; originally **2** mainly; principally

pri·mar·y (prī′mer′ē, -mə rē) ***adj.*** ⟦ME *prymary* < L *primarius* < *primus,* first: see PRIME⟧ **1** first in time or order of development; primitive; original; earliest **2** from which others are derived; fundamental; elemental; basic **3** designating colors regarded as basic, or as those from which all others may be derived: classification of colors as *primary* varies: see COLOR (***n.*** 2 & 3) **4** of or in the first stage of a sequence; elementary [*primary* school] **5** first in importance; chief; principal; main [a *primary* concern] **6** firsthand; direct [a *primary* source of information] **7** *Chem.* *a)* characterized by or resulting from the replacement of one atom or radical *b)* characterized by groups or radicals that are attached to the end carbon atom of a chain, i.e., to a CH_2 group (Ex.: *primary alcohols,* CH_2OH; *primary amines,* CH_2NH_2) **8** *Elec.* designating or of an inducing current, input circuit, or input coil in a transformer, induction coil, etc. **9** *Geol.* *a)* formed directly by sedimentation, solidification, or precipitation and not subsequently altered (said of rocks) *b)* [Obs.] designating or of the earliest geological periods, up through the Paleozoic Era **10** *Linguis.* having as its fundamental form a base or other element that cannot be broken down: said of derivation **11** *Med.* designating or having to do with the initial medical care given to a patient, before referral to another doctor, a specialist, etc. **12** *Ornithology* designating or of the large, stiff feathers on the last section, or hand, of a bird's wing —***n.***, *pl.* **-ries 1** something first in order, quality, importance, etc. ☆**2** in the U.S., *a)* a local meeting of voters of a given political party to nominate candidates for public office, select delegates to a convention, etc. *b)* DIRECT PRIMARY ELECTION **3** any of the primary colors **4** *Astron.* *a)* a sun, planet, etc. in relation to its satellites *b)* the brighter member of a binary star **5** *Elec.* a primary coil **6** *Ornithology* a primary feather

primary cell a battery cell whose energy is derived from an essentially irreversible electrochemical reaction and which is hence incapable of being efficiently recharged

primary electron in thermionics, any of the electrons falling on a body, distinguished from those emitted by it

primary school 1 ELEMENTARY SCHOOL **2** a separate school usually including the first three elementary grades and, sometimes, kindergarten

primary stress (*or* accent) *Linguis.* **1** the heaviest stress or force given to one syllable in a spoken word or to one word in an utterance; the strongest of the four phonemic degrees of stress **2** a mark (in this dictionary, ′) used to indicate this

primary tooth MILK TOOTH

pri·mate (prī′māt′, -mit; *for 2, usually,* -mit) ***n.*** ⟦ME *primat* < OFr < LL *primas* (gen. *primatis*), of the first, chief < L *primus,* first: see PRIME⟧ **1** [Rare] a person with primacy **2** an archbishop, or the highest-ranking bishop in a province, etc. **3** any of an order (Primates) of mammals characterized esp. by flexible hands and feet, each with five digits, including humans, great apes, monkeys, and lemurs —**pri′mate·ship′** ***n.*** —**pri·ma′tial** (-mā′shəl) ***adj.***

pri·ma·tol·o·gy (prī′mə täl′ə jē) ***n.*** the branch of zoology dealing with primates, esp. the apes, monkeys, and early hominids —**pri′ma·tol′o·gist** ***n.***

pri·ma·ve·ra (prē′mə ver′ə) ***adj.*** ⟦It, lit., spring (the season)⟧ prepared with an assortment of lightly cooked, fresh, usually young vegetables in a light cream sauce [spaghetti *primavera*]

prime (prīm) ***adj.*** ⟦ME < MFr < L *primus,* first < OL *pri,* before < IE base **per-,* beyond > FAR, FIRST⟧ **1** first in time; original; primitive; primary **2** first in rank or authority; chief [the *prime* minister] **3** first in importance or value; principal; main [a *prime* advantage] **4** first in quality; of the highest excellence [*prime* beef] **5** from which others are derived; fundamental; basic **6** *Math.* *a)* of or being a prime number *b)* having no factor in common except 1 [9 and 16 are *prime* to each other] —***n.*** ⟦ME < OE *prim* < L *prima* (*hora*), first (hour): see the ***adj.***⟧ **1** *a)* [*often* **P-**] *R.C.Ch.* a part of the Divine Office orig. assigned to the first hour of daylight (in the Liturgy of the Hours, both Lauds and Prime have been replaced by Morning Prayer) *b)* the first hour of the daylight, conventionally taken to begin about 6 A.M. *c)* the earliest part of something; beginning **2** *a)* springtime *b)* the springtime of life; youth **3** *a)* the best, most vigorous, or most fully mature period or stage of a person or thing [a soprano in her *prime*] *b)* the best part of anything *c)* the best of several or many; pick; cream **4** a symbol (′) used *a)* to distinguish between different values of the same variable *b)* to distinguish a letter, number, or other character from another of the same kind, as A′ *c)* for certain units of measure, as feet or minutes of arc **5** *Math.* PRIME NUMBER **6** *Music* UNISON —***vt.* primed, prim′ing 1** to make ready; prepare [a team *primed* for a game] **2** to prepare (a gun) for firing or (a charge) for exploding by providing with priming or a primer **3** *a)* to get (a pump) into operation by pouring in water until the suction is established *b)* to get (a carburetor, etc.) into operation by adding extra fuel **4** to undercoat, size, etc. (a surface) in preparation as for painting **5** to provide (a person) beforehand with information, answers, etc. —***vi.* 1** to prime a person or thing **2** to let a spray of water mix with the steam forced into the cylinder, as of a steam engine —**prime′ness** ***n.***

prime cost the direct cost of labor and material in producing an article, exclusive of capital, overhead, etc.

prime·ly (prīm′lē) ***adv.*** [Rare] very well; excellently

prime meridian the meridian from which longitude is measured both east and west; 0° longitude: it passes through Greenwich, England

prime minister in parliamentary governments, the chief executive and, usually, head of the cabinet —**prime ministry**

prime mover 1 *a)* the original force in a series of transmissions of force *b)* any initiating or principal force **2** any natural force applied by people to produce power, as muscular energy or flowing water **3** a machine, as a turbine, that converts a natural force into productive power **4** in Aristotelian philosophy, the first cause of all movement, itself unmoved

prime number an integer that can be evenly divided by no other whole number than itself or 1, as 2, 3, 5, or 7: distinguished from COMPOSITE NUMBER

prim·er[1] (prim′ər; *Brit* prī′mər) ***n.*** ⟦ME *prymer* < ML *primarius* < L *primus,* first: see PRIME⟧ **1** a simple book for teaching reading to beginners **2** a textbook giving the first principles of any subject **3** *see* GREAT PRIMER

prim·er[2] (prī′mər) ***n.*** a person or thing that primes; specif., *a)* a small cap, tube, etc. containing an explosive, used to set off a main charge *b)* paint, sizing, etc. used as a preparatory coating on a raw surface

prime rate *Finance* the most favorable interest rate charged by a commercial bank on short-term loans to large corporations: also **prime interest rate** or **prime lending rate**

prime rib a choice cut of beef consisting of the seven ribs immediately before the loin

pri·me·ro (pri mer′ō) ***n.*** ⟦Sp *primera,* fem. of *primero,* first < L *primarius:* see PRIMARY⟧ a card game popular in the 16th and 17th centuries

☆**prime time** *Radio, TV* the hours when the largest audience is regularly available; esp., the evening hours

pri·me·val (prī mē′vəl) ***adj.*** ⟦< L *primaevus* (< *primus,* first: see PRIME + *aevum,* an AGE) + -AL⟧ of the earliest times or ages; primal; primordial [*primeval* forests]

prim·ing (prī′miŋ) ***n.*** **1** the act of a person or thing that primes **2** the explosive used to set off the charge in a gun or in blasting **3** PRIMER[2] (sense *b*)

pri·mip·a·ra (prī mip′ə rə) ***n.***, *pl.* **-a·ras** or **-a·rae′** (-ə rē′) ⟦L < *primus,* first (see PRIME) + *parere,* to bear: see -PAROUS⟧ a woman who is pregnant for the first time or who has borne just one child —**pri·mip′a·rous** ***adj.***

prim·i·tive (prim′i tiv) ***adj.*** ⟦ME *primitif* < MFr < L *primitivus* < *primus,* first: see PRIME⟧ **1** of or existing in the beginning or the earliest times or ages; ancient; original **2** *a)* characteristic or imitative of the earliest ages *b)* crude, simple, rough, uncivilized, etc. **3** not derivative; primary; basic **4** *Anthrop.* of or having to do with a preliterate, generally isolated, culture with a relatively low level of technology **5** *Biol.* *a)* designating or of an organism, organ, etc. at the starting point of its evolutionary development or very little evolved from early ancestral types *b)* PRIMORDIAL (sense 3) —***n.*** **1** a primitive person or thing **2** *a)* an artist or a work of art of an early, esp. preliterate, culture *b)* an artist or a work of art that shows ingenuousness and lack of formal training **3** *Algebra, Geom.* a form from which another is derived **4** *Gram.* the form from which a certain word or other form has been derived; root; base —**prim′i·tive·ly** ***adv.*** —**prim′i·tive·ness** ***n.***

prim·i·tiv·ism (-tiv iz′əm) ***n.*** **1** belief in or practice of primitive ways, living, etc. **2** the qualities, principles, etc. of primitive art or artists —**prim′i·tiv·ist** ***n., adj.***

pri·mo[1] (prē′mō, prī′-) ***adv.*** ⟦L < *primus,* first: see PRIME⟧ to begin with; first of all

pri·mo[2] (prē′mō; *It* prē′mô) ***n.***, *pl.* **pri·mi** (prē′mē) ⟦It, first < L *primus:* see PRIME⟧ *Music* the principal part, as in a duet —***adj.* 1** first ☆**2** [*not in italics*] [Slang] first-rate, first-class, etc.

pri·mo·gen·i·tor (prī′mə jen′i tər, -tôr′) ***n.*** ⟦LL < L *primus,* first (see PRIME) + *genitor,* father < *genitus,* pp. of *gignere:* see GENUS⟧ **1** the earliest ancestor of a family, race, etc. **2** loosely, an ancestor

pri·mo·gen·i·ture (prī′mə jen′i chər) ***n.*** ⟦ML *primogenitura* < L *primus,* first + *genitura,* a begetting < *genitus:* see prec.⟧ **1** the condition or fact of being the firstborn of the same parents **2** *Law* the exclusive right of the eldest son to inherit his father's estate

pri·mor·di·al (prī môr′dē əl) ***adj.*** ⟦ME < LL *primordialis* < L *primordium,* the beginning < *primus,* first (see PRIME) + *ordiri,* to begin (see ORDER)⟧ **1** first in time; existing at or from the beginning; primitive; primeval **2** not derivative; fundamental; original **3** *Biol.* earliest formed in the development of an organism, organ, structure, etc.; primitive —**pri·mor′di·al·ly** ***adv.***

primordial soup the hypothetical, organically rich seas in which the earliest living organisms developed on earth

pri·mor·di·um (prī môr′dē əm) *n., pl.* **-di·a** (-ə) ⟦ModL < L: see PRIMORDIAL⟧ *Embryology* the first recognizable aggregation of cells that will form a distinct organ or part of the embryo

primp (primp) *vt., vi.* ⟦prob. extension of PRIM²⟧ to groom or dress up in a fussy way

prim·rose (prim′rōz′) *n.* ⟦ME *primerose* < MFr, altered (infl. by *rose*, ROSE¹) < OFr *primerole*, primrose < ML *primula*, flower, daisy, primrose < L *primus*, first: see PRIME⟧ **1** any of a genus (*Primula*) of plants of the primrose family, having variously colored, tubelike corollas with five spreading lobes **2** the flower of any of these plants **3** the light yellow of some primroses **4** any of various other plants, as the evening primrose —*adj.* **1** of the primrose **2** light-yellow **3** designating a family (Primulaceae, order Primulales) of dicotyledonous plants principally in the Northern Hemisphere, with flowers in clusters on a leafless stem, including loosestrife and cyclamen

primrose path ⟦popularized after Shakespeare's *Hamlet*, I, iii⟧ **1** the path of pleasure, self-indulgence, etc. **2** a course of action that is deceptively easy, proper, etc. but that can lead to disaster

prim·u·la (prim′yoo lə) *n.* ⟦ML⟧ PRIMROSE (*n.* 1)

pri·mum mo·bi·le (prī′məm mō′bə lē′, prē′məm mō′bi lā′) ⟦ML, first movable thing: see PRIME, *adj.* & MOBILE⟧ *Astron.* in the Ptolemaic system, the tenth and outermost concentric sphere, revolving from east to west around the earth and causing all celestial bodies to revolve with it

pri·mus in·ter pa·res (prī′məs in′tər par′ēz, prē′məs in′tər pär′ās) ⟦L⟧ first among equals

prin *abbrev.* **1** principal **2** principally **3** principle

prince (prins) *n.* ⟦OFr < L *princeps*, first, chief, prince < **primo-caps*, lit., first-taken < *primus* (see PRIME) + *capere*, to take (see HAVE)⟧ **1** [Archaic] any male monarch; esp., a king **2** a ruler whose rank is below that of king; head of a principality **3** a nonreigning male member of a royal family **4** *a)* in Great Britain, a son of the sovereign or of a son of the sovereign *b)* any of various noblemen in other countries ☆**5** *a)* a preeminent person in any class or group [a merchant *prince*] *b)* [Informal] a fine, generous, helpful fellow —**prince′dom** *n.*

Prince Albert ⟦prob. after Albert Edward, Prince of Wales (called *Prince Albert*), later King EDWARD VII⟧ ☆a long, double-breasted frock coat

Prince Charming ⟦partial transl. of Fr *Roi Charmant*, King Charming, hero in *L'Oiseau Bleu* (The Blue Bird), a fairy tale by M. C. d'Aulnoy (1650?-1705)⟧ **1** the romantic hero in various fairy tales, as *Cinderella* **2** a man who embodies or fulfills a woman's fondest romantic hopes

prince consort *pl.* **princes consort** the husband of a queen or empress who is reigning in her own right

Prince Edward Island ⟦after Prince *Edward*, Duke of Kent (1767-1820), father of Queen VICTORIA²⟧ island province of SE Canada, in the S Gulf of St. Lawrence: 2,195 sq mi (5,684 sq km); cap. Charlottetown: abbrev. *PE*, *PEI*, or *P.E.I.*

Prince George ⟦after King GEORGE III⟧ city in EC British Columbia, Canada: resort area

prince·ling (prins′liŋ) *n.* a young, small, or subordinate prince: also **prince′kin** (-kin) or **prince′let** (-lit)

prince·ly (prins′lē) *adj.* **-li·er, -li·est 1** of a prince; royal; regal; noble **2** characteristic of a prince; liberal; generous **3** worthy of a prince; magnificent; lavish —**prince′li·ness** *n.*

Prince of Darkness *name for* SATAN

Prince of Peace *name for* Jesus Christ

Prince of Wales¹ title conferred on the oldest son and heir apparent of a British king or queen

Prince of Wales² **1** ⟦after George, *Prince of Wales*, later King GEORGE IV⟧ island of SE Alas., largest in the Alexander Archipelago: 2,230 sq mi (5,776 sq km) **2 Cape** ⟦after George, *Prince of Wales*, later King GEORGE IV⟧ promontory of the Seward Peninsula, NW Alas., on the Bering Strait: westernmost point of North America **3** ⟦after Albert Edward, *Prince of Wales*, later King EDWARD VII⟧ island of the Arctic Archipelago, Canada: 12,830 sq mi (33,230 sq km)

prince royal the oldest son of a king or queen

prince's-feath·er (prin′siz feth′ər) *n.* a tropical pigweed (*Amaranthus hybridus erythrostachyus*), sometimes grown as a garden flower for its elongated spikes of bristly, red flowers

☆**prince's pine** PIPSISSEWA

prin·cess¹ (prin′sis, -ses′; *Brit* prin ses′, prin′ses′) *n.* ⟦ME *princesse* < MFr: see PRINCE & -ESS⟧ **1** [Archaic] any female monarch; esp., a queen **2** a nonreigning female member of a royal family **3** in Great Britain, *a)* a daughter of the sovereign *b)* a daughter of a son of the sovereign **4** the wife of a prince **5** any woman or girl regarded as like a princess, as in being: *a)* graceful, accomplished, or outstanding in some way *b)* pampered, protected, snobbish, arrogant, etc.

prin·cess² (prin′sis, -ses′; prin ses′) *adj.* ⟦< Fr *princesse*, princess⟧ of or designating a woman's one-piece, closefitting, gored garment, unbroken at the waistline and with a flared skirt: also **prin·cesse′** (-ses′)

princess royal the oldest daughter of a king or queen

Prince·ton (prins′tən) ⟦after the *Prince* of Orange, later WILLIAM III⟧ borough in central N.J., near Trenton: scene of a battle (1777) of the Revolutionary War in which troops led by Washington defeated the British

prin·ci·pal (prin′sə pəl) *adj.* ⟦OFr < L *principalis* < *princeps*: see PRINCE⟧ **1** highest or among the highest in rank, authority, importance, degree, etc. **2** that is or has to do with PRINCIPAL (*n.* 3) —*n.* **1** a principal person or thing; specif., *a)* a chief; head *b)* a governing or presiding officer, specif. of a school *c)* a main actor or performer *d)* either of the combatants in a duel **2** *a)* any of the main end rafters of a roof, supporting the purlins *b)* a roof truss **3** *Finance a)* the amount of a debt, investment, etc. minus the interest, or on which interest is computed *b)* the face value of a stock or bond *c)* the main body of an estate, etc., as distinguished from income **4** *Law a)* a person who employs another to act as his agent *b)* the person primarily responsible for an obligation *c)* a person who commits a crime or is present as an abettor to it (cf. ACCESSORY) **5** *Music a)* any of the principal open stops of an organ *b)* the soloist in a concert *c)* the first player of any section of orchestral instruments except the first violins *d)* the subject of a fugue (opposed to ANSWER) —**SYN.** CHIEF —**prin′ci·pal·ly** *adv.* —**prin′ci·pal·ship′** *n.*

prin·ci·pal·i·ty (prin′sə pal′ə tē) *n., pl.* **-ties** ⟦ME *principalite* < OFr < LL *principalitas*⟧ **1** the rank, dignity, or jurisdiction of a prince **2** the territory ruled by a prince **3** a country with which a prince's title is identified

☆**principal meridian** a meridian line designated as by the government to serve as a reference in land survey

principal parts the principal inflected forms of a verb, from which the other forms may be derived: in English, the principal parts are the infinitive, past tense, and past participle (Ex: *drink, drank, drunk; go, went, gone*): the present participle, derived from the present infinitive with the addition of -ING (sense 1), is sometimes regarded as one of the principal parts

Prín·ci·pe (prin′sə pē′) island in the Gulf of Guinea, off the W coast of Africa: 55 sq mi (142 sq km): see SÃO TOMÉ AND PRÍNCIPE

prin·cip·i·um (prin sip′ē əm) *n., pl.* **-i·a** (-ə) ⟦L, a beginning < *princeps*: see PRINCE⟧ **1** a principle **2** [*pl.*] first principles; fundamentals

prin·ci·ple (prin′sə pəl) *n.* ⟦ME, altered < MFr *principe* < L *principium*: see prec.⟧ **1** the ultimate source, origin, or cause of something **2** a natural or original tendency, faculty, or endowment **3** a fundamental truth, law, doctrine, or motivating force, upon which others are based [moral *principles*] **4** *a)* a rule of conduct, esp. of right conduct *b)* such rules collectively *c)* adherence to them; integrity; uprightness [a man of *principle*] **5** an essential element, constituent, or quality, esp. one that produces a specific effect [the active *principle* of a medicine] **6** *a)* the scientific law that explains a natural action [the *principle* of cell division] *b)* the method of a thing's operation [the *principle* of a gasoline engine is internal combustion] —**in principle** theoretically or in essence —**on principle** because of or according to a principle

prin·ci·pled (-pəld) *adj.* having principles, as of conduct: often in hyphenated compounds [high-*principled*]

prin·cox (prin′käks′) *n.* ⟦earlier also *princocks* < ? PREEN + *cox-*, as in COXCOMB⟧ [Obs.] a coxcomb; fop

prink (priŋk) *vt., vi.* ⟦prob. altered (? infl. by PRIMP) < PRANK²⟧ PRIMP

print (print) *n.* ⟦ME *prente* < OFr *preinte* < *prient*, pp. of *preindre* < L *premere*, to PRESS¹⟧ **1** a mark made in or on a surface by pressing or hitting with an object; impression; imprint [the *print* of a heel] **2** an object for making such a mark, as a stamp, die, seal, mold, etc. **3** an object or mass that has received such a mark [a *print* of butter] **4** a cloth printed with a design, or a dress, blouse, etc. made of this **5** the condition of being printed **6** printed lettering **7** the impression made by inked type [uneven *print*] **8** a picture or design printed from a plate, block, roll, etc., as an etching, woodcut, lithograph, etc. **9** printed matter for reading **10** a photograph, esp. one made from a negative —*vt.* ⟦ME *prenten, printen* < the n.⟧ **1** to mark by pressing or stamping; make a print on or in **2** to press or stamp (a mark, letter, etc.) on or in a surface **3** to draw, trace, carve, or otherwise make (a mark, letter, etc.) on a surface **4** to produce on the surface of (paper, etc.) the impression of inked type, plates, etc. by means of a printing press **5** to perform or cause to be performed all processes connected with the printing of (a book, etc.), as typesetting, presswork, etc. **6** to publish in print [to *print* a story] **7** to write in individual letters resembling standard printed ones, rather than in cursive [*print* your name above your signature] **8** to produce (a photograph, or positive picture) from (a negative) **9** to impress upon the mind, memory, etc. **10** *Comput.* to deliver (information) by means of a printer: often with *out* —*vi.* **1** to practice the art or trade of a printer **2** to produce an impression, print, photograph, etc. [a negative that *prints* well] **3** to write in individual letters resembling standard printed ones, rather than in cursive **4** to produce newspapers, books, etc. by means of a printing press —**in print 1** in printed form; published **2** still being sold by the publisher: said of books, etc. —**out of print** no longer being sold by the publisher: said of books, etc.

print·a·ble (print′ə bəl) *adj.* **1** that can be printed or printed from **2** fit to print —**print′a·bil′i·ty** *n.*

printed circuit an electrical circuit formed by applying conductive material in fine lines or other shapes to an insulating sheet, as by printing with electrically conductive ink or by electroplating

print·er (print′ər) *n.* **1** a person whose work or business is printing **2** a device that prints, esp., *a)* one that makes copies by chemical or photographic means *b)* a device, controlled by a computer, that prints that computer's output on paper

printer's devil ⟦so called ? because apprentices working at early printing presses often became covered with black ink⟧ [Old-fashioned] an apprentice in a print shop

☆**print·er·y** (print′ər ē) *n., pl.* **-er·ies** PRINT SHOP (sense 1)

print·ing (print′iŋ) *n.* 1 the act of a person or thing that prints 2 the production of printed matter 3 the art of a printer 4 something printed; esp., a reprint, revision, or edition, as of a book 5 IMPRESSION (sense 7*c*) 6 written letters made like printed ones

printing press a machine for printing from inked type, plates, or rolls

print·less (print′lis) *adj.* having, making, or leaving no print or mark

print·mak·er (print′māk′ər) *n.* a person who makes prints, etchings, etc. —**print′mak′ing** *n.*

print·out (print′out′) *n.* a paper copy of computer output, as made by a PRINTER (sense 2*b*)

print shop ☆1 a shop where printing is done: also **printing office** 2 a shop where prints, etchings, etc. are sold

pri·on (prē′än′; *also* prī′-) *n.* ⟦*pr*(*oteinaceous*) + *i*(*nfectious*) + -ON: coined by S. B. Prusiner (b. 1942), U.S. neurologist⟧ ☆any of a group of tiny infectious agents composed mainly or entirely of protein: though lacking in demonstrable nucleic acid, prions are capable of self-replication and are thought to be the cause of various degenerative diseases of the nervous systems of vertebrates, as scrapie and kuru

pri·or (prī′ər) *adj.* ⟦L, former, superior, compar. of OL *pri*, before: see PRIME⟧ 1 preceding in time; earlier; previous; former 2 preceding in order or importance; preferred [*a prior* choice] —*n.* ⟦ME < OE & OFr, both < ML(Ec), a prior < L: see the *adj.*⟧ 1 the head of a priory or other religious house 2 in an abbey, the person in charge next below the abbot —*SYN.* PREVIOUS —**prior to** before in time

Pri·or (prī′ər), **Matthew** 1664-1721; Eng. poet

pri·or·ate (prī′ər it) *n.* ⟦ME < ML(Ec) *prioratus* < LL(Ec), preference⟧ 1 the rank, office, or term of a prior: also **pri′or·ship′** 2 PRIORY

pri·or·ess (prī′ər is) *n.* ⟦ME *prioresse* < MFr < ML(Ec) *priorissa:* see PRIOR & -ESS⟧ 1 a woman who heads a priory of nuns 2 in an abbey of nuns, the woman in charge next below the abbess

pri·or·i·tize (prī ôr′ə tīz′) *vt.* **-tized′**, **-tiz′ing** 1 to arrange (items) in order of priority 2 to assign (an item) to a particular level of priority

pri·or·i·ty (prī ôr′ə tē, -är′-) *n., pl.* **-ties** ⟦ME *priorite* < ML *prioritas*⟧ 1 the fact or condition of being prior; precedence in time, order, importance, etc. 2 *a)* a right to precedence over others in obtaining, buying, or doing something *b)* an order granting this, as in an emergency 3 something to be given prior attention

pri·o·ry (prī′ə rē) *n., pl.* **-ries** ⟦ME < Anglo-Fr *priorie* < ML *prioria*⟧ a monastery governed by a prior, or a convent governed by a prioress, sometimes as a subordinate branch of an abbey —*SYN.* CLOISTER

Pri·pet (prē′pet) river in Ukraine & Belarus, flowing through a large, swampy basin (**Pripet Marshes**) into the Dnieper: *c.* 500 mi (805 km): Russ. name **Pri·pyat** (prē′pyät′y′)

Pris·ci·an (prish′ən, -ē ən) (L. name *Priscianus Caesariensis*) fl. A.D. 500: Latin grammarian

Pris·cil·la (pri sil′ə) *n.* ⟦L, dim. of *Prisca*, fem. of *Priscus*, a Roman surname < *priscus*, ancient, primitive, akin to OL *pri:* see PRIME⟧ a feminine name

prise (prīz) *vt.* **prised**, **pris′ing** *Brit. var. of* PRIZE[2] (*vt.*)

prism (priz′əm) *n.* ⟦LL *prisma* < Gr, lit., something sawed < *prizein*, to saw < *priein*, to saw, bite; ? akin to Alb *prish*, (I) destroy, break⟧ 1 *Geom.* a solid figure whose ends are parallel, polygonal, and equal in size and shape, and whose sides are parallelograms 2 a crystalline body whose lateral faces meet at edges that are parallel to each other 3 anything that refracts light, as a drop of water 4 *Optics a)* a transparent body, as of glass, whose ends are equal and parallel triangles, and whose three sides are parallelograms: used for refracting or dispersing light, as into the spectrum *b)* any similar body of three or more sides

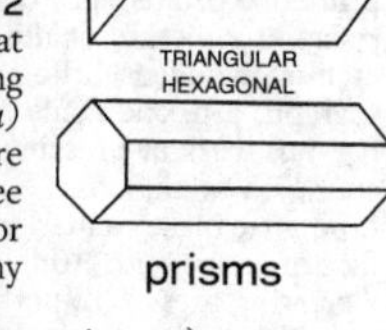

prisms

pris·mat·ic (priz mat′ik) *adj.* ⟦< Gr *prisma* (gen. *prismatos*): see prec. & -IC⟧ 1 of or resembling a prism 2 that refracts light as a prism 3 that forms or resembles prismatic colors 4 many-colored; brilliant; dazzling —**pris·mat′i·cal·ly** *adv.*

prismatic colors the colors of the visible spectrum produced by passing white light through a prism; red, orange, yellow, green, blue, indigo, and violet

pris·ma·toid (priz′mə toid′) *n.* ⟦< Gr *prisma* (gen. *prismatos*), PRISM + -OID, sense 2⟧ a polyhedron with all of its vertices in two parallel planes, as a pyramid or prism

pris·moid (priz′moid′) *n.* ⟦see PRISM & -OID⟧ a prismatoid having polygons with equal numbers of sides as its bases and quadrilaterals as its lateral faces —**pris·moi′dal** *adj.*

pris·on (priz′ən) *n.* ⟦OFr < L < *prensio*, for *prehensio*, a taking < *prehendere*, to take: see PREHENSILE⟧ 1 a place where persons are confined 2 *a)* a building, usually with cells, where convicted criminals, esp. those serving longer sentences, are confined *b)* such a place for holding accused persons who are awaiting, or on, trial (see PENITENTIARY, JAIL, REFORMATORY) 3 the state or condition of being confined, restricted, or limited in any way [in the *prison* of his own desires] —*vt. archaic var. of* IMPRISON

prison camp 1 a camp with minimum security for holding prisoners who are put to work, often outdoors 2 a camp for confining prisoners of war or political prisoners

pris·on·er (priz′nər, priz′ən ər) *n.* ⟦ME < OFr *prisonier*⟧ 1 a person confined in prison, as for some crime 2 a person held in custody 3 a person captured or held captive: often in metaphorical usage [a *prisoner* of love] —**take no prisoners** a command to kill all enemy combatants in a military engagement: phrase often used fig. in describing any ruthless or relentless policy or strategy [a political campaign that *took no prisoners*]

prisoner of war a member of the regular or irregular armed forces of a nation at war held captive by the enemy

prisoner's base a children's game in which each side has a base to which captured opponents are brought

prisoner's dilemma ⟦orig. formulated in terms of hypothetical prisoners⟧ in game theory, a situation in which, if each of the individuals involved chooses the most rational option for gaining his or her own ends, the least desirable outcome for all will necessarily result

☆**priss** (pris) [Informal] *n.* a prissy person —*vi.* to act or move about in a prissy way or manner

☆**pris·sy** (pris′ē) *adj.* **-si·er**, **-si·est** ⟦prob. PR(IM) + (S)ISSY⟧ [Informal] very prim or precise; fussy, prudish, etc. —**pris′si·ly** *adv.* —**pris′si·ness** *n.*

Pris·ti·na (prish′tē nə, pris tē′nə) capital of Kosovo, in the EC part: also sp. **Priština**

pris·tine (pris′tēn′, -tin; pris tēn′; *chiefly Brit* pris′tīn′) *adj.* ⟦L *pristinus*, former < OL *pri*, before: see PRIME⟧ 1 [Archaic] characteristic of the earliest, or an earlier, period or condition; original ☆2 still pure; uncorrupted; unspoiled [*pristine* beauty] 3 having the characteristics of something new and fresh [wearing a *pristine* white pinafore] —**pris′tine′ly** *adv.*

prith·ee (prith′ē) *interj.* ⟦altered < *pray thee*⟧ [Archaic] I pray thee; please

priv. *abbrev.* 1 private 2 *Gram.* privative

pri·va·cy (prī′və sē; *Brit* priv′ə-) *n., pl.* **-cies** ⟦ME *privace:* see PRIVATE & -CY⟧ 1 the quality or condition of being private; withdrawal from company or public view; seclusion 2 secrecy [told in strict *privacy*] 3 one's private life or personal affairs [an invasion of one's *privacy*]

Pri·vat·do·cent (prē vät′dô tsent′) *n., pl.* **-cent′en** (-tsent′'n) ⟦Ger < *privat*, private + *docent, dozent*, teacher: see DOCENT⟧ in German universities, an unsalaried lecturer paid only by students' fees: also sp. **Pri·vat′do·zent′**, *pl.* **-zent′en**

pri·vate (prī′vət) *adj.* ⟦ME *pryvat* < L *privatus*, belonging to oneself, not to the state < *privare*, to separate, deprive < *privus*, separate, peculiar, prob. akin to OL *pri:* see PRIME⟧ 1 of, belonging to, or concerning a particular person or group; not common or general [*private* property, a *private* joke] 2 not open to, intended for, or controlled by the public [a *private* school] 3 for an individual person [a *private* room in a hospital] 4 not holding public office [a *private* citizen] 5 away from public view; secluded [a *private* dining room] 6 not publicly or generally known; confidential [a *private* matter] 7 tending to keep one's personal matters to oneself [a *private* person] 8 carried out on an individual basis [*private* medical practice] 9 engaged in work independent of institutions, organizations, agencies, etc. [*private* detective, *private* tutor] —*n.* 1 [*pl.*] [Informal] the genitals: also **private parts** 2 an enlisted person of either of the two lowest ranks in the U.S. Army or of the lowest rank in the U.S. Marine Corps —**go private** *Finance* to restore private ownership of a corporation by buying back publicly held stock —**in private** privately or secretly; not publicly —**pri′vate·ly** *adv.*

private enterprise FREE ENTERPRISE

private equity equity in a business that is raised from private sources, as opposed to shares that can be traded publicly —**pri′vate-eq′ui·ty** *adj.*

pri·va·teer (prī′və tir′) *n.* ⟦< PRIVAT(E) + -EER⟧ 1 a privately owned and manned armed ship commissioned by a government in a war to attack and capture enemy ships, esp. merchant ships 2 a commander or crew member of a privateer: also ☆**pri′va·teers′man** (-tirz′mən), *pl.* **-men** (-mən) —*vi.* to sail as a privateer

☆**private eye** [Slang] a private detective

☆**private first class** an enlisted person ranking just below a corporal in the U.S. Army and just below a lance corporal in the U.S. Marine Corps: abbrev. *PFC* or *Pfc*

private law that branch of the law dealing with the relationships between individuals: cf. PUBLIC LAW

pri·va·tion (prī vā′shən) *n.* ⟦ME *privacion* < L *privatio* < *privare:* see PRIVATE⟧ 1 a depriving or being deprived; deprivation; specif., the loss or absence of some quality or condition 2 lack of the ordinary necessities of life

pri·va·tism (prī′və tiz′əm) *n.* concern only with one's private life and personal involvements rather than with public affairs, social values, etc. —**pri′va·tist** *adj.*, **pri′va·tis′tic**

priv·a·tive (priv′ə tiv) *adj.* ⟦L *privativus* < pp. of *privare:* see PRIVATE⟧ 1 depriving or tending to deprive 2 characterized by a taking away or loss of some quality 3 *Gram.* indicating negation, absence, or loss —*n. Gram.* a privative term or affix, as A-[2] (sense 3), UN-, NON-, or -LESS —**priv′a·tive·ly** *adv.*

pri·va·tize (prī′və tīz′) *vt.* **-tized′**, **-tiz′ing** to make or hold private; specif., to turn over (a public property, service, etc.) to private interests —**pri′va·ti·za′tion** *n.*

priv·et (priv′it) *n.* ⟦< ?⟧ any of a genus (*Ligustrum*) of shrubs or trees of the olive family, with bluish-black berries and spikes of white flowers, often grown for hedges; esp., the **common privet** (*L. vulgare*)

priv·i·lege (priv′ə lij, priv′lij) *n.* ⟦OFr < L *privilegium*, an exceptional law for or against any individual < *privus*, PRIVATE + *lex* (gen. *legis*), law: see LEGAL⟧ 1 a right, advantage, favor, or immunity specially granted to one; esp., a right held by a certain individual, group, or class, and withheld from certain others or all others **2** a basic civil right, guaranteed by a government **3** an option, as a put or call, to buy or sell a stock —*vt.* **-leged, -leg·ing** **1** to grant a privilege or privileges to **2** to grant special favored status to

priv·i·leged (-lijd) *adj.* **1** having one or more privileges **2** like or having the status of privileged communication; confidential **3** having special favored status **4** *Naut.* designating the vessel that has the right of way: see BURDENED

privileged communication *Law* **1** a communication that one cannot legally be compelled to divulge, as that to a lawyer from a client **2** a communication made under certain circumstances, as in a legislative proceeding, such that it is not actionable as slander or libel

priv·i·ty (priv′i tē) *n., pl.* **-ties** ⟦ME *privete* < OFr < L *privus*, PRIVATE⟧ **1** *a)* private or secret knowledge, as shared between persons *b)* participation in this **2** *Law* a successive relationship to or mutual interest in the same property or rights, established by law or legalized by contract, as between a testator and legatee, lessor and lessee, etc.

priv·y (priv′ē) *adj.* ⟦ME < OFr *prive* < L *privatus*, PRIVATE⟧ **1** [Obs.] private; not public: now only in such phrases as PRIVY COUNCIL **2** [Archaic] hidden, secret, furtive, etc. —*n., pl.* **priv′ies** **1** a toilet; esp., an outhouse **2** *Law* a person who is in privity with another —**privy to** privately informed about —**priv′i·ly** *adv.*

privy council a body of advisors or confidential counselors appointed by or serving a ruler, esp. a monarch —**privy councilor**

privy purse an allowance from the public revenue for the personal expenses of the British sovereign

privy seal in Great Britain, the seal placed on documents which are later to receive the great seal or which are not important enough to receive the great seal

prix fixe (prē fēks′) ⟦Fr, fixed price⟧ **1** a set price for a complete meal **2** such a meal

prize[1] (prīz) *vt.* **prized, priz′ing** ⟦ME *pris:* see PRICE⟧ **1** [Obs.] to set a value upon; price **2** to value highly; esteem —*n.* **1** something offered or given to the winner of a contest **2** something won in a game of chance, lottery, etc. **3** a reward, premium, or the like **4** anything worth striving for; any enviable or highly valued possession **5** [Archaic] a contest or match —*adj.* **1** that has received a prize [*a prize* novel] **2** worthy of a prize; first-rate **3** given as a prize —*SYN.* APPRECIATE, REWARD

prize[2] (prīz) *n.* ⟦ME *prise*, a taking hold < OFr, a taking < fem. pp. of *prendre*, to take < L *prehendere:* see PREHENSILE⟧ **1** [Obs.] the act of capturing **2** something taken by force; esp., a captured enemy ship and its cargo **3** [Dial.] *a)* a tool for prying; lever *b)* leverage —*vt.* **prized, priz′ing** to pry, as with a lever —*SYN.* SPOIL

prize court a court that decides how captured property, esp. that taken at sea in wartime, is to be distributed

prize·fight (prīz′fīt′) *n.* ⟦back-form. < *prizefighter* < PRIZE[1]⟧ a professional boxing match —**prize′fight′er** *n.* —**prize′fight′ing** *n.*

prize money ⟦< PRIZE[2]⟧ money made by taking a prize; specif., profit from the sale of an enemy ship and its cargo captured in war

priz·er (prī′zər) *n.* [Archaic] a person competing for a prize

prize ring **1** a square platform or similar area, enclosed by ropes, for prizefights **2** prizefighting

prize·win·ner (prīz′win′ər) *n.* the winner of a prize

prize·win·ning (prīz′win′iŋ) *adj.* **1** having won, or worthy of, a prize **2** entitling a person to a prize [*a prizewinning* lottery ticket]

p.r.n. *abbrev.* ⟦L *pro re nata*, as the occasion requires⟧ *Pharmacy* as needed; when necessary

pro[1] (prō) *adv.* ⟦L, for < IE base **pro*, forward > Gr *pro*, before, Goth *fra-*, Ger *ver-*⟧ on the affirmative side; favorably —*adj.* favorable —*prep.* favorably disposed toward; for —*n., pl.* **pros** **1** a person who favors the affirmative side of some debatable question **2** an argument in favor of something [the *pros* and cons of a matter] **3** a vote for the affirmative

pro[2] (prō) *adj. short for* PROFESSIONAL (*adj.* 3 & 4) —*n., pl.* **pros** **1** *short for* PROFESSIONAL (*n.* 2*a* & 3) **2** a golfer, tennis player, etc. affiliated with a particular club as a contestant, teacher, etc.

PRO *abbrev.* public relations officer (or office)

pro-[1] (prō) ⟦Gr *pro-* < *pro*, before: see PRO[1]⟧ *prefix* before in place or time [*proclaim, prognosis*]

pro-[2] (prō) ⟦L < *pro*, before, forward, for: see prec.⟧ *prefix* **1** moving forward or ahead of [*proclivity*] **2** forth [*produce*] **3** substituting for, acting for [*procathedral*] **4** defending, supporting [*prolabor*]

pro·a (prō′ə) *n.* ⟦Malay *perahu*, prob. < a Dravidian language⟧ a swift, canoe-like Malayan boat having a lateen sail and one outrigger

pro-a·bor·tion (prō′ə bôr′shən) *adj.* advocating a legal right to obtain an abortion —**pro′-a·bor′tion·ist** *n.*

USAGE—this term is used typically by those opposed to legalized abortion

pro·ac·tive[1] (prō ak′tiv) *adj.* ⟦PRO-[2] + *-active*, as in REACTIVE⟧ assuming an active, rather than passive, role in doing, accomplishing, etc.; taking the initiative [*a proactive* approach to school truancy]

pro·ac·tive[2] (prō ak′tiv) *adj.* ⟦PRO-[1] + *-active*, as in RETROACTIVE⟧ *Psychol.* relating to or caused by previously learned behavior, habits, etc. [*proactive* inhibition]

pro-am (prō′am′) *n.* ⟦PRO[2] + AM(ATEUR)⟧ a sports competition for both amateurs and professionals, usually as a preliminary to a professional tournament

prob *abbrev.* **1** probable **2** probably **3** problem

prob·a·bil·ism (präb′ə bəl iz′əm) *n.* ⟦Fr *probabilisme:* see PROBABLE & -ISM⟧ **1** *Philos.* the doctrine that certainty in knowledge is impossible and that probability is a sufficient basis for action and belief **2** *R.C.Ch.* the principle that in matters concerning which there is more than one probable opinion, it is lawful to follow any one of them —**prob′a·bi·list** *n., adj.*

prob·a·bi·lis·tic (präb′ə bə lis′tik) *adj.* **1** of or based on probabilism **2** of, based on, or involving probability

prob·a·bil·i·ty (präb′ə bil′ə tē) *n., pl.* **-ties** ⟦MFr *probabilité* < L *probabilitas*⟧ **1** the quality or state of being probable; likelihood **2** something probable **3** *Math.* the ratio of the number of times something will probably occur to the total number of possible occurrences —**in all probability** very likely

prob·a·ble (präb′ə bəl) *adj.* ⟦ME < MFr < L *probabilis* < *probare*, to prove: see PROBE⟧ **1** likely to occur or be; that can reasonably but not certainly be expected [the *probable* winner] **2** reasonably so, as on the basis of evidence, but not proved [the *probable* cause of a disease] —**prob·a·bly** (präb′ə blē; *often* präb′lē) *adv.*

probable cause *Law* reasonable grounds for presuming guilt in someone charged with a crime

pro·band (prō′band′) *n.* ⟦< L *probandus*, ger. of *probare*, to test: see PROBE⟧ PROPOSITUS

pro·bang (prō′baŋ′) *n.* ⟦altered (infl. by PROBE) < earlier *provang* < ? obs. *provet*, probe⟧ *Med.* a flexible, slender rod tipped with a sponge, tuft, etc., used for clearing or medicating the esophagus or larynx

pro·bate (prō′bāt′; *for n., Brit,* -bit) *n.* ⟦ME *probat* < L *probatus*, pp. of *probare*, to prove: see PROBE⟧ **1** the act or process of proving before a duly authorized person that a document submitted for official certification and registration, esp. a will, is genuine **2** the judicial certification of a will **3** a certified copy of a probated will ☆**4** all matters coming under the jurisdiction of probate courts —*adj.* having to do with probate or a probate court —*vt.* **-bat′ed, -bat′ing** **1** to establish officially the genuineness or validity of (a will) ☆**2** popularly, to certify in a probate court as mentally unsound

☆**probate court** a court having jurisdiction over the probating of wills, the administration of estates, and, usually, the guardianship of minors and incompetents

pro·ba·tion (prō bā′shən) *n.* ⟦ME *probacion* < OFr < L *probatio* < *probare*, to prove: see PROBE⟧ **1** a testing or trial, as of a person's character, ability to meet requirements, etc. **2** the suspension of sentence of a person convicted but not yet imprisoned, on condition of continued good behavior and regular reporting to a probation officer **3** *a)* the status of a person being tested or on trial [a student on *probation* because of low grades] *b)* the period of testing or trial **4** [Obs.] proof —**pro·ba′tion·ar′y** *adj.*, **pro·ba′tion·al**

pro·ba·tion·er (-ər) *n.* a person on probation

☆**probation officer** an officer appointed by a magistrate to watch over and guide persons placed on probation

pro·ba·tive (prō′bə tiv, präb′ə-) *adj.* ⟦ME *probatiffe* < L *probativus* < *probatus*, pp.: see fol.⟧ **1** serving to test or try **2** providing proof or evidence Also **pro′ba·to′ry** (-tôr′ē)

probe (prōb) *n.* ⟦LL *proba*, proof (in ML, examination) < L *probare*, to test, prove < *probus*, good, proper < IE **probhwos* (> Sans *prabhúḥ*, outstanding) < base **pro*, forward + **bhū*, to grow > BE⟧ **1** a slender, blunt surgical instrument for exploring a wound or the like **2** the act of probing **3** a searching examination; specif., ☆*a)* an investigation, as by a legislative committee, into corruption, etc. *b)* an exploratory advance or patrol ☆**4** an instrumented spacecraft for exploring the upper atmosphere, space, or a celestial body in order to get information about the environment, physical properties, etc. **5** any of various devices, as a Pitot tube or electrode, inserted into an environment for measuring, testing, etc. —*vt.* **probed, prob′ing** **1** to explore (a wound, etc.) with a probe **2** to investigate or examine with great thoroughness —*vi.* to search; investigate —**prob′er** *n.*

pro·ben·e·cid (prō ben′ə sid) *n.* ⟦< PRO(PYL) + BEN(ZOIC A)CID⟧ a white, crystalline drug, $C_{13}H_{19}NO_4S$, that influences the ability of the kidney to separate various compounds from the blood, used to increase the urinary excretion of uric acid in cases of gout and to decrease the urinary excretion of various medicines, esp. penicillin

pro·bi·ot·ic (prō bī ät′ik) *adj.* ⟦PRO-[2] + BIOTIC⟧ designating or of certain microorganisms regarded as being beneficial to health when ingested, as bacteria or yeasts taken to supplement beneficial bacteria that already exist in the digestive tract —*n.* **1** such a microorganism **2** a food, beverage, or dietary supplement containing such microorganisms

pro·bi·ty (prō′bə tē, präb′ə-) *n.* ⟦L *probitas* < *probus*, good, proper: see PROBE⟧ uprightness in one's dealings; integrity

prob·lem (präb′ləm) *n.* ⟦ME *probleme* < MFr < L *problema* < Gr *problēma* < *proballein*, to throw forward < *pro-*, forward + *ballein*, to throw, drive: see PRO-[1] & BALL[2]⟧ **1** a question proposed for solution or consideration **2** a question, matter, situation, or person that is perplexing or difficult **3** *Math.* a proposition requiring solution by mathematical operations, constructions, etc. —*adj.* **1** presenting a problem of human conduct or social relationships [*a problem* novel] **2** very difficult to deal with; esp., very difficult to train or discipline [*a problem* child] —**have a problem with** [Informal] **1** to be unable to understand or do [she *has a problem with* French verbs] **2** to disagree with; disapprove of [I *have a problem with* your plans to paint the kitchen purple] —**no problem!** [Informal] **1** yes!; I will do what you ask!: used in response to a request **2** easily done! **3** you're welcome!

prob·lem·at·ic (präb′lə mat′ik) *adj.* ⟦Fr *problématique* < L *problematicus* < Gr *problematikos* < *problēma* (see prec.) + -AL⟧ **1** having the nature of a problem; hard to solve or deal with **2** not settled; yet to be determined; uncertain Also **prob′lem·at′i·cal** —*n.* an unresolved problem or inherent difficulty, as in a field of study —*SYN.* DOUBTFUL —**prob′lem·at′i·cal·ly** *adv.*

prob·lem·a·tize (prä blem′ə tīz′, präb′ləm-) *vt.* **-tized′**, **-tiz·ing** to demonstrate to be unsettled or uncertain, or more complex than originally assumed or regarded; show to be problematic

pro bo·no (prō bō′nō) ⟦< fol.⟧ designating professional services provided, without compensation, for charitable organizations, poor persons, etc.

pro bo·no pu·bli·co (prō bō′nō pub′li kō′, -po͞ob′li-) ⟦ML⟧ for the public good; for the commonweal

pro·bos·cid·e·an (prō′bə sid′ē ən) *n.* ⟦see fol. & -AN⟧ any of an order (Proboscidea) of large mammals having tusks and a long, flexible, tubelike snout, as the elephant —*adj.* of the proboscideans Also sp. **pro′bos·cid′i·an**

pro·bos·cis (prō bäs′is, -kis) *n., pl.* **-cis·es** or **-ci·des′** (-ə dēz′, -kə dēz′) ⟦L < Gr *proboskis* < *pro-*, before + *boskein*, to feed, graze, prob. akin to *bous*, COW¹⟧ **1** *a)* the trunk of an elephant *b)* a long, flexible snout, as of a tapir **2** any tubular organ for sucking, food-gathering, sensing, etc., as of some insects, worms, and mollusks **3** a person's nose, esp. if large: a jocular usage

proc *abbrev.* **1** proceedings **2** process

pro·caine (prō′kān′) *n.* ⟦PRO-² + (CO)CAINE⟧ a synthetic crystalline compound, $C_{13}H_{20}N_2O_2$·HCl, used as a local anesthetic: in full **procaine hydrochloride**

pro·cam·bi·um (prō kam′bē əm) *n.* ⟦ModL: see PRO-² & CAMBIUM⟧ *Bot.* the meristem or growing layer in the tip of a stem or root, which gives rise to primary phloem, primary xylem, and cambium —**pro·cam′bi·al** *adj.*

pro·carp (prō′kärp′) *n.* ⟦ModL *procarpium:* see PRO-² & -CARP⟧ *Bot.* a female reproductive organ in certain algae

pro·car·y·ote (prō kar′ē ōt′) *n. alt. sp. of* PROKARYOTE

pro·ca·the·dral (prō′kə thē′drəl) *n.* a church used as a temporary substitute for a cathedral

pro·ce·dur·al (prō sē′jər əl, prə-) *adj.* of or having to do with procedure or a procedure —☆*n.* a mystery novel in which much emphasis is placed on the procedures used, esp. by police, in investigating a crime —**pro·ce′dur·al·ly** *adv.*

pro·ce·dure (prō sē′jər, prə-) *n.* ⟦Fr *procédure* < MFr < *proceder:* see fol.⟧ **1** the act, method, or manner of proceeding in some action; esp., the sequence of steps to be followed **2** a particular course of action or way of doing something **3** the established way of carrying on the business of a legislature, law court, etc.

pro·ceed (prō sēd′, prə-) *vi.* ⟦ME *proceden* < MFr *proceder* < L *procedere* < *pro-*, forward + *cedere*, to go: see PRO-² & CEDE⟧ **1** to advance or go on, esp. after stopping **2** to go on speaking, esp. after an interruption **3** to undertake and carry on some action [to *proceed* to eat one's dinner] **4** to move along or be carried on [a project that is *proceeding* well] **5** to take legal action: often with *against* **6** to come forth, issue, or arise (*from*)

pro·ceed·ing (prō sēd′iŋ, prə-) *n.* **1** an advancing or going on with what one has been doing **2** the carrying on of an action or course of action **3** a particular action or course of action **4** [*pl.*] a record of the business transacted by a learned society or other organized group **5** *a)* [*pl.*] legal action *b)* the taking of legal action

pro·ceeds (prō′sēdz′) *pl.n.* the money or profit derived from a sale, business venture, etc.

pro·ce·phal·ic (prō′sə fal′ik) *adj.* ⟦PRO-² + CEPHALIC⟧ of or relating to the front part of the head

pro·cess¹ (prä′ses′, -səs; *chiefly Brit & Cdn*, prō′-) *n., pl.* **pro′cess′es** (-ses′iz, -səs iz; -sə sēz′) ⟦ME < OFr *proces* < L *processus*, pp. of *procedere:* see PROCEED⟧ **1** the course of being done: chiefly in **in process** **2** course (*of* time, etc.) **3** a continuing development involving many changes [the *process* of digestion] **4** a particular method of doing something, generally involving a number of steps or operations ☆**5** a man's hairstyle in which the hair is straightened by applying a chemical preparation and styled **6** *Anat.* a projection or outgrowth from a larger structure, usually a bone [the alveolar *process* of the jaw] **7** *Biol.* an appendage or projecting part of an organism **8** *Law a)* an action or suit *b)* a writ or summons directing a defendant to appear in court or enforcing compliance with a court's orders *c)* the total of such writs in any action or proceeding —*vt.* **1** to prepare by or subject to a special process or method ☆**2** to straighten and style (hair) by the use of a chemical preparation **3** *Law a)* to prosecute *b)* to serve a process on —*adj.* **1** prepared by a special treatment or process **2** of, made by, used in, or using photomechanical or photoengraving methods —**in (the) process of** in or during the course of

pro·cess² (prə ses′, prō-) *vi.* ⟦back-form. < PROCESSION⟧ to go in a procession

processed cheese a cheese made by heating and blending together several natural cheeses with an emulsifying agent: also **process cheese**

pro·ces·sion (prō sesh′ən, prə-) *n.* ⟦OFr < L *processio* < *procedere:* see PROCEED⟧ **1** the act of proceeding, esp. in an orderly manner **2** a number of persons or things moving forward, as in a parade, in an orderly, formal way —*vi.* [Rare] to go in a procession

pro·ces·sion·al (prō sesh′ə nəl, prə-) *adj.* ⟦MFr < ML *processionalis*⟧ of, or used in connection with, a procession —*n.* ⟦ME < ML *processionale*⟧ **1** a book setting forth the ritual to be observed in church processions **2** a hymn sung at the beginning of a church service during the entrance of the clergy **3** any musical composition to be played during a procession

pro·ces·sor or **pro·cess·er** (prä′ses′ər, -səs-) *n.* **1** a person or thing that processes **2** CENTRAL PROCESSING UNIT

process printing a method of reproducing color prints in almost any hue by the use of halftone plates in red, yellow, blue, and usually black

process server *Law* a police officer, sheriff, or deputy who delivers an official order, or process, commanding the person receiving it to be in court at a certain time and place

process shot *Film* a shot in which action takes place in front of a screen on which an image already filmed is projected

pro·ces·su·al (prə sesh′o͞o əl, prō-) *adj.* pertaining to or stressing sociological processes [*processual* archaeology]

pro·cès-ver·bal (prô se ver bȧl′) *n., pl.* **-ver·baux′** (-bō′) ⟦Fr, a verbal process⟧ an official report of proceedings or facts; minutes (of a meeting)

pro-choice (prō′chȯis′) *adj.* advocating a legal right to obtain an abortion —**pro′-choic′er** *n.*

USAGE—the term favored by those supporting legalized abortion

pro·claim (prō klām′, prə-) *vt.* ⟦ME *proclamen* < MFr *proclamer* < L *proclamare* < *pro-*, before + *clamare*, to cry out: see PRO-¹ & CLAMOR⟧ **1** to announce officially; announce to be **2** to show to be [acts that *proclaimed* him a friend] **3** [Rare] to outlaw, ban, or otherwise restrict by a proclamation **4** to extol —*SYN.* DECLARE

proc·la·ma·tion (präk′lə mā′shən) *n.* ⟦ME *proclamacion* < MFr < L *proclamatio*⟧ **1** a proclaiming or being proclaimed **2** something that is proclaimed, or announced officially

pro·clit·ic (prō klit′ik) *adj.* ⟦ModL *procliticus* < Gr *proklinein*, to lean forward < *pro-*, forward (see PRO-¹) + *klinein*, to LEAN¹⟧ *Gram.* dependent on the following word for its stress: said as of a word that forms a phonetic unit with the following, stressed word (Ex.: *for* in "once and for all"), or of certain particles, as in classical Greek —*n.* any such word or particle Cf. ENCLITIC

pro·cliv·i·ty (prō kliv′ə tē) *n., pl.* **-ties** ⟦L *proclivitas* < *proclivus*, downward < *pro-*, before (see PRO-²) + *clivus*, a slope (see DECLIVITY)⟧ a natural or habitual tendency or inclination, esp. toward something discreditable —*SYN.* INCLINATION

Pro·clus (prō′kləs, präk′ləs) A.D. 410?-485; Gr. Neoplatonic philosopher, born in Constantinople

Proc·ne (präk′nē) *n.* ⟦L < Gr *Proknē*⟧ *Gr. Myth.* sister of Philomela and wife of Tereus, transformed into a swallow by the gods: see PHILOMELA

pro·con·sul (prō kän′səl) *n.* ⟦ME < L *pro consule*, (acting) for the consul: see PRO-² & CONSUL⟧ **1** an official of ancient Rome who commanded an army in one or more of the provinces and, often, acted as a provincial governor **2** a governing official in a present-day colony, occupied territory, etc. —**pro·con′sul·ar** (-sə lər) *adj.* —**pro·con′sul·ate** (-sə lit) *n.*, **pro·con′sul·ship′**

Pro·con·sul (prō kän′səl) *n.* ⟦PRO-¹ + *Consul*, name of a famous chimpanzee at the London Zoo (*c.* 1930)⟧ a genus of African ape of the Miocene, a possible ancestor of the chimpanzee and gorilla

Pro·co·pi·us (prə kō′pē əs) 6th cent. A.D.; Byzantine historian

pro·cras·ti·nate (prō kras′tə nāt′, prə-) *vi., vt.* **-nat′ed**, **-nat′ing** ⟦< L *procrastinatus*, pp. of *procrastinare* < *pro-*, forward (see PRO-²) + *crastinus*, belonging to the morrow < *cras*, tomorrow⟧ to put off doing (something unpleasant or burdensome) until a future time; esp., to postpone (such actions) habitually —**pro·cras′ti·na′tion** *n.* —**pro·cras′ti·na′tor** *n.*

pro·cre·ant (prō′krē ənt) *adj.* ⟦L *procreans*, prp. of *procreare:* see fol.⟧ **1** producing young; fruitful **2** of procreation

pro·cre·ate (prō′krē āt′) *vt., vi.* **-at′ed**, **-at′ing** ⟦< L *procreatus*, pp. of *procreare*, to procreate < *pro-*, PRO-² + *creare*, to CREATE⟧ **1** to produce (young); beget (offspring) **2** to produce or bring into existence —**pro′cre·a′tion** *n.* —**pro′cre·a′tive** *adj.* —**pro′cre·a′tor** *n.*

Pro·crus·te·an (prō krus′tē ən) *adj.* **1** of or like Procrustes or his actions **2** designed or acting to secure conformity at any cost; drastic or ruthless

Pro·crus·tes (prō krus′tēz) *n.* ⟦L < Gr *Prokroustēs* < *prokrouein*, to beat out, stretch out < *pro-*, PRO-¹ + *krouein*, to strike: see RUE¹⟧ *Gr. Myth.* a giant of Attica who seizes travelers, ties them to a bedstead, and either stretches them or cuts off their legs to make them fit it

pro·cryp·tic (prō krip′tik) *adj.* ⟦< PRO(TECT) + CRYPTIC⟧ *Zool.* having protective coloration

proc·to- (präk′tō, -tə) ⟦< Gr *prōktos*, anus⟧ *combining form* rectum [*proctology*]

proc·to·dae·um (präk′tō dē′əm) *n., pl.* **-dae′a** (-ə) or **-dae′ums** ⟦ModL < prec. + Gr *hodaios*, on the way < *hodos*, way: see -ODE¹⟧ *Zool.* the end portion of the intestinal tract in many animals, formed in the embryo by a folding in of the body surface at the anus: also **proc′to·de′um** —**proc′to·dae′al** *adj.*

proc·tol·o·gy (präk täl′ə jē) *n.* ⟦PROCTO- + -LOGY⟧ the branch of medicine dealing with the rectum and anus and their diseases —**proc′to·log′ic** (-tə läj′ik) *adj.*, **proc′to·log′i·cal** —**proc·tol′o·gist** *n.*

proc·tor (präk′tər) *n.* ⟦ME *proketour*, contr. < *procuratour:* see PROCURATOR⟧ **1** a person employed to manage the affairs of another; agent; attorney **2** a person who supervises or monitors students, as at an examination —*vt.* to supervise (an academic examination) —**proc·to·ri·al** (präk tôr′ē əl) *adj.* —**proc′tor·ship′** *n.*

proc·to·scope (präk′tə skōp′) *n.* ⟦PROCTO- + -SCOPE⟧ an instrument used for the direct examination of the interior of the rectum —**proc′to·scop′ic** (-skäp′ik) *adj.* —**proc·tos′co·py** (-täs′kə pē) *n., pl.* **-pies**

pro·cum·bent (prō kum′bənt) *adj.* ⟦L *procumbens*, prp. of *procumbere*, to lean forward < *pro-*, forward (see PRO-[2]) + *-cumbere* < *cubare*, to lie down (see CUBE[1])⟧ **1** lying face down **2** *Bot.* trailing along the ground: said of a stem

proc·u·ra·tion (präk′yoo rā′shən, -yə-) ***n.*** ⟦ME *procuracion* < OFr < L *procuratio*⟧ **1** [Obs.] management of another's affairs **2** *a)* POWER OF ATTORNEY *b)* the act of granting power of attorney **3** the act of procuring

proc·u·ra·tor (präk′yə rāt′ər) ***n.*** ⟦ME *procuratour* < OFr < L *procurator* < *procurare:* see fol.⟧ **1** an official of ancient Rome who managed the financial affairs of a province or acted as governor of a lesser province **2** a person employed to manage another's affairs; agent **—proc′u·ra·to′ri·al** (-yə rə tôr′ē əl) ***adj.***

pro·cure (prō kyoor′, prə-) ***vt.*** **-cured′**, **-cur′ing** ⟦ME *procuren* < MFr *procurer*, to procure < L *procurare*, take care of, attend to < *pro-* (see PRO-[2]) + *curare*, attend to < *cura*, care (see CURE)⟧ **1** to get or bring about by some effort; obtain; secure [to *procure* supplies, work, a settlement, etc.] **2** to obtain (persons, esp. women) for the purpose of prostitution **—*vi.*** to obtain persons, esp. women, for the purpose of prostitution **—*SYN.*** GET **—pro·cur′a·ble *adj.*** **—pro·cure′ment *n.***, **pro·cur′ance**, or **pro·cur′al**

pro·cur·er (prō kyoor′ər, prə-) ***n.*** ⟦ME < Anglo-Fr *procurour* < L *procurator:* see PROCURATOR⟧ a person who procures; specif., a man who obtains women for the purpose of prostitution; pimp

pro·cur·ess (prō kyoor′is, prə-; präk′yoo ris) ***n.*** [Rare] a woman who obtains women for the purpose of prostitution

Pro·cy·on (prō′sē än′) ***n.*** ⟦L < Gr *Prokyōn* < *pro-*, before + *kyōn*, dog (see HOUND[1]): it rises before the Dog Star (Sirius)⟧ a binary star, the brightest star in the constellation Canis Minor: magnitude, 0.4

prod[1] (präd) ***vt.*** **prod′ded**, **prod′ding** ⟦< ?⟧ **1** to jab or poke with or as with a pointed stick; goad **2** to urge or stir into action **—*n.*** **1** the act of prodding; jab, poke, thrust, etc. **2** something that prods; specif., a rod or pointed stick used in driving cattle **—prod′der *n.***

prod[2] *abbrev.* **1** produce **2** produced **3** product **4** production

prod·i·gal (präd′i gəl) ***adj.*** ⟦MFr < L *prodigus*, prodigal < *prodigere*, to drive forth or away, waste < *pro-*, forth + *agere*, to drive: see PRO-[2] & ACT[1]⟧ **1** exceedingly or recklessly wasteful **2** extremely generous; lavish [*prodigal* with one's praise] **3** extremely abundant; profuse **—*n.*** **1** a person who wastes his means; spendthrift **2** ⟦after the *prodigal son*, a repentant wastrel who is welcomed back warmly on his homecoming: Luke 15:11-32⟧ a person who returns after a willful absence **—*SYN.*** PROFUSE **—prod′i·gal′i·ty** (-gal′ə tē) ***n.***, *pl.* **-ties** **—prod′i·gal·ly *adv.***

pro·di·gious (prō dij′əs, prə-) ***adj.*** ⟦L *prodigiosus*, marvelous < *prodigium:* see fol.⟧ **1** wonderful; amazing **2** of great size, power, extent, etc.; enormous; huge **3** [Obs.] portentous **—pro·di′gious·ly *adv.*** **—pro·di′gious·ness *n.***

prod·i·gy (präd′ə jē) ***n.***, *pl.* **-gies** ⟦L *prodigium* < *pro-*, before + OL **agiom*, a thing said < *aio*, I say: see ADAGE⟧ **1** [Rare] an extraordinary happening, thought to presage good or evil fortune **2** a person, thing, or act so extraordinary as to inspire wonder; specif., a child of highly unusual talent or genius

pro·drome (prō′drōm′) ***n.*** ⟦Fr < L *prodromus* < Gr *prodromos*, forerunner: see PRO-[1] & -DROME⟧ *Med.* a warning symptom indicating the onset of a disease **—pro·dro·mal** (prō drō′məl) ***adj.***, **pro·drom·ic** (prō dräm′ik)

pro·duce (prə doos′, -dyoos′; prō-; *for n.* prō′doos′, -dyoos′; prä′-) ***vt.*** **-duced′**, **-duc′ing** ⟦L *producere* < *pro-*, forward + *ducere*, to lead, draw: see PRO-[2] & DUCT⟧ **1** to bring to view; offer for inspection [to *produce* identification] **2** to bring forth; bear; yield [a well that *produces* oil] **3** *a)* to make or manufacture [to *produce* steel] *b)* to bring into being; create [to *produce* a work of art] **4** to cause; give rise to [war *produces* devastation] **5** to get (a play, film, TV program, etc.) ready for presentation to the public **6** to supervise (a recording session, musical recording, etc.) and determine the final sound mix of the recording **7** *Econ.* to create (anything having exchange value) **8** *Geom.* to extend (a line or plane) **—*vi.*** to bear, yield, create, manufacture, etc. something **—*n.*** something produced; yield; esp., fresh fruits and vegetables **—pro·duc′i·bil′i·ty *n.*** **—pro·duc′i·ble *adj.***

pro·duc·er (prə doos′ər, -dyoos′-; prō-) ***n.*** **1** a person or thing that produces; specif., one who produces goods and services: opposed to CONSUMER **2** a special type of furnace for making producer gas **3** a person in charge of the financing and coordination of all activities in connection with the production of a play, film, radio or TV program, etc. **4** a person who supervises a recording session and then determines the final sound of the recording mix

producer gas a fuel gas that is a mixture of nitrogen, carbon monoxide, and hydrogen, made by passing air or a mixture of air and steam over incandescent coal or coke

producer goods goods, such as raw materials and machines, that are used in producing other goods: also **producers' goods**

prod·uct (präd′əkt) ***n.*** ⟦ME < ML *productum* < neut. pp. of L *producere:* see PRODUCE⟧ **1** something produced by nature or made by human industry or art **2** [Informal] commercial products collectively, as of a certain kind or from a certain company; merchandise **3** result; outgrowth [a *product* of one's imagination] **4** *Chem.* any substance resulting from a chemical change **5** *Math.* the quantity obtained by multiplying two or more quantities together

pro·duc·tion (prə duk′shən, prō-) ***n.*** ⟦LME < MFr < L *productio*⟧ **1** the act or process of producing **2** the rate of producing or amount produced **3** *a)* something produced; product *b)* a work of art, literature, etc. *c)* a work produced on the stage, as a film, etc. **4** the making of a film or video, specif., the phase involving actual shooting **5** *Econ.* the creation of economic value; producing of goods and services **—*adj.*** designating or of a product, as a motor vehicle or boat, made in quantity for general sale **—☆make a production (out) of** [Informal] to dwell on, fuss over, elaborate, etc. needlessly and annoyingly

☆**production values** the technical elements of a production, as the lighting, decor, or sound in a film, often, specif., such elements that are enhanced to increase audience appeal

pro·duc·tive (prə duk′tiv, prō-) ***adj.*** ⟦ML *productivus* < LL, fit for prolongation < L *productus*, pp. of *producere:* see PRODUCE⟧ **1** producing abundantly; fertile [*productive* soil, a *productive* mind] **2** marked by abundant production or effective results [a *productive* day] **3** bringing as a result (with *of*) [war is *productive* of much misery] **4** *Econ.* of or engaged in the creating of economic value, or the producing of goods and services **5** *Linguis.* designating any affix or method which can be and still is used to make new forms ["non-" is a *productive* prefix] **—pro·duc′tive·ly *adv.*** **—pro·duc·tiv·i·ty** (prō′dək tiv′ə tē, präd′ək-) ***n.***, **pro·duc′tive·ness**

product placement an advertising technique in which a manufacturer pays to have a consumer product appear, as if incidentally, in a film, television show, etc.

pro·em (prō′em) ***n.*** ⟦ME *proheme* < MFr < L *prooemium* < Gr *prooimion* < *pro-*, before + *oimē*, song⟧ [Now Rare] an introduction or preface **—pro·e·mi·al** (prō ē′mē əl) ***adj.***

pro·en·zyme (prō en′zīm′) ***n.*** ⟦PRO-[1] + ENZYME⟧ ZYMOGEN

pro·es·trus (prō es′trəs) ***n.*** ⟦ModL < PRO-[1] + ESTRUS⟧ the time period immediately before estrus, characterized by the development of ovarian follicles and the uterine lining

☆**prof[1]** (präf) ***n.*** [Informal] *short for* PROFESSOR

prof[2] *abbrev.* professional

☆**Prof** *abbrev.* Professor

pro-fam·i·ly (prō′fam′ə lē, -fam′lē) ***adj.*** **1** that favors or benefits families **2** that promotes or protects the well-being of the family, esp. the nuclear family, as a social unit

prof·a·na·tion (präf′ə nā′shən) ***n.*** ⟦Fr < LL(Ec) *profanatio* < L *profanare* < *profanus:* see fol.⟧ a profaning or being profaned; desecration; defilement **—*SYN.*** SACRILEGE **—pro·fan·a·to·ry** (prō fan′ə tôr′ē, prə-) ***adj.***

pro·fane (prō fān′, prə-) ***adj.*** ⟦LME *prophane* < MFr < L *profanus* < *pro-*, before + *fanum*, temple; lit., outside of the temple, hence not sacred, common: see PRO-[1] & FANE⟧ **1** not connected with religion or religious matters; secular [*profane* art] **2** not initiated into the inner mysteries or esoteric knowledge of something **3** not hallowed or consecrated **4** showing disrespect or contempt for sacred things; irreverent **—*vt.*** **-faned′**, **-fan′ing** **1** to treat (sacred things) with irreverence or contempt; desecrate **2** to put to a base or improper use; debase; defile **—pro·fane′ly *adv.*** **—pro·fane′ness *n.*** **—pro·fan′er *n.***

pro·fan·i·ty (prō fan′ə tē, prə-) ***n.*** ⟦LL(Ec) *profanitas*⟧ **1** the state or quality of being profane **2** *pl.* **-ties** something profane; esp., profane language or the use of profane language **—*SYN.*** BLASPHEMY

pro·fess (prō fes′, prə-) ***vt.*** ⟦< L *professus*, pp. of *profiteri*, to avow publicly < *pro-*, before (see PRO-[2]) + *fateri*, to avow, akin to *fari*, to speak: see FABLE⟧ **1** to make an open declaration of; affirm [to *profess* one's love] **2** to claim to have (some feeling, an interest, knowledge, etc.): often connoting insincerity or pretense **3** to practice as one's profession **4** to declare one's belief in [to *profess* Christianity] **5** ⟦ME *professen* < *profes*, professed < L *professus*⟧ to accept into a religious order **—*vi.*** **1** to make profession, or affirmation **2** to make one's PROFESSION (sense 4)

pro·fessed (prō fest′, prə-) ***adj.*** ⟦ME < *profes* (see prec.) + *-ed*, -ED⟧ **1** openly declared; avowed **2** insincerely avowed; pretended **3** having made one's PROFESSION (sense 4) **4** professing to be duly qualified [a *professed* economist] **—pro·fess′ed·ly** (-fes′id lē) ***adv.***

pro·fes·sion (prō fesh′ən, prə-) ***n.*** ⟦OFr < L *professio*⟧ **1** a professing, or declaring; avowal, whether true or pretended [a *profession* of sympathy] **2** *a)* the avowal of belief in a religion *b)* a faith or religion professed **3** *a)* a vocation or occupation requiring advanced education and training, and involving intellectual skills, as medicine, law, theology, engineering, teaching, etc. *b)* the body of persons in any such calling or occupation *c)* loosely, any occupation **4** the act or ceremony of taking vows on formally entering a religious order **—the oldest profession** prostitution: a humorous or euphemistic usage

pro·fes·sion·al (prō fesh′ə nəl, prə-) ***adj.*** **1** of, engaged in, or worthy of the high standards of a profession ☆**2** designating or of a school, esp. a graduate school, offering instruction in a profession **3** earning one's living from an activity, such as a sport, not normally thought of as an occupation **4** engaged in by professional players [*professional* hockey] **5** engaged in a specified occupation for pay or as a means of livelihood [a *professional* writer] **6** *a)* of or having to do with a profession or one's profession [a *professional* journal, an actor's *professional* name] *b)* engaged in a profession **7** being such in the manner of one practicing a profession [a *professional* hatemonger] **—*n.*** **1** a person practicing a profession **2** *a)* a person who engages in some art, sport, etc. for money, esp. as a means of livelihood, rather than as a hobby *b)* PRO[2] (*n.* 2) **3** a person who does something with great skill **—pro·fes′sion·al·ly *adv.***

pro·fes·sion·al·ism (-nəl iz′əm) ***n.*** **1** professional quality, status, etc. **2** the use of professional players in organized sports

pro·fes·sion·al·ize (-nəl īz′) ***vt.*** **-ized′**, **-iz′ing** to cause to have professional qualities, status, etc. **—pro·fes′sion·al·i·za′tion *n.***

pro·fes·sor (prō fes′ər, prə-) *n.* ⟦ME *professoure* < L, teacher < *professus:* see PROFESS⟧ **1** a person who professes something; esp., one who openly declares his or her sentiments, religious beliefs, etc. **2** *a)* a college or university teacher of the highest academic rank; full professor *b)* *short for* ASSISTANT PROFESSOR & ASSOCIATE PROFESSOR *c)* loosely, any college, university, or, occas., secondary-school teacher ☆**3** any person claiming or assumed to be especially skilled or experienced in some art, sport, etc.: a popular or humorous usage —**pro·fes·so·ri·al** (prō′fə sôr′ē əl, prä′-) *adj.* —**pro′fes·so′ri·al·ly** *adv.* —**pro·fes′sor·ship′** *n.*, **pro·fes′sor·ate** (-it)

pro·fes·so·ri·ate (prō′fə sôr′ē it) *n.* ⟦see prec. & -ATE²⟧ **1** academic professors collectively **2** the office or position of a professor; professorship Also **pro′fes·so′ri·at** (-ət)

prof·fer (präf′ər) *vt.* ⟦ME *profren* < Anglo-Fr & OFr *proffrir* < *poroffrir* < *por-*, PRO-² + *offrir* < VL **offerire*, for L *offerre*, to OFFER⟧ to offer (usually something intangible) *[to proffer friendship]* —*n.* ⟦ME & Anglo-Fr *profre* < the v.⟧ an offer or proposal

pro·fi·cient (prō fish′ənt, prə-) *adj.* ⟦L *proficiens*, prp. of *proficere*, to advance < *pro-*, forward + *facere*, to make: see PRO-² & DO¹⟧ highly competent; skilled; adept —*n.* an expert —**pro·fi′cien·cy** (-ən sē) *n.*, *pl.* **-cies** —**pro·fi′cient·ly** *adv.*

pro·file (prō′fīl′) *n.* ⟦It *profilo* < *profilare*, to outline < *pro-* (< L *pro-*), before + *filo* (< L *filum*), thread, line: see PRO¹ & FILE¹⟧ **1** *a)* a side view of the face *b)* a drawing of such a view **2** a view of anything in contour; outline *[the profile of a distant hill]* ☆**3** a short, vivid biographical and character sketch **4** a degree of exposure to or contact with others, esp. the public *[a celebrity who keeps a low profile after a scandal]* **5** *a)* a graph, diagram, piece of writing, etc. presenting or summarizing data relevant to a particular person or thing *b)* a set of characteristics developed for use in identifying a particular person or thing as likely to belong to a certain group, to engage in a certain activity, etc. **6** *Archit.* a side or sectional elevation of a building, etc. —*vt.* **-filed′**, **-fil′ing** **1** to sketch, write, or make a profile of **2** to give or assign a specified profile to **3** to identify or single out by means of a PROFILE (*n.* 5*b*) of —**SYN.** OUTLINE

pro·fil·ing (prō′fīl′iŋ) *n.* use of a PROFILE (*n.* 5*b*) to identify persons, esp., in law enforcement, to identify persons to be investigated, interrogated, etc.

prof·it (präf′it) *n.* ⟦OFr < L *profectus*, pp. of *proficere*, to profit, lit., to advance: see PROFICIENT⟧ **1** advantage; gain; benefit **2** [*often pl.*] *a)* monetary gain from business transactions *b)* the ratio of this to the amount of capital invested *c)* proceeds from property or investments **3** [*often pl.*] the sum remaining after all costs, direct and indirect, are deducted from the income of a business, the selling price, etc. —*vi.* **1** to be of advantage or benefit **2** to reap an advantage, financial or otherwise; benefit —*vt.* to be of profit or advantage to —**prof′it·less** *adj.*

prof·it·a·ble (präf′it ə bəl) *adj.* yielding profit, gain, or benefit —**prof′it·a·bil′i·ty** *n.*, **prof′it·a·ble·ness** —**prof′it·a·bly** *adv.*

profit and loss the gain and loss as from business transactions: applied esp. to an INCOME STATEMENT (**profit and loss statement**)

prof·it·eer (präf′i tir′) *n.* ⟦PROFIT + -EER⟧ a person who makes excessive profits, esp. by taking advantage of a shortage of supply to charge exorbitant prices —*vi.* to be a profiteer

pro·fi·te·role (prə fit′ə rōl′) *n.* ⟦Fr, a small gain, dim. of *profit*, profit: used orig. of any cake or other extra food cooked for and given to the servants⟧ a small cream puff

profit sharing the practice of dividing a share of the profits of a business among employees, in addition to paying their regular wages and salaries —**prof′it-shar′ing** *adj.*

prof·li·gate (präf′li git) *adj.* ⟦L *profligatus*, pp. of *profligare*, to strike to the ground, rout, ruin < *pro-*, forward (see PRO-²) + *fligere*, to drive, dash (see INFLICT)⟧ **1** immoral and shameless **2** extremely wasteful; recklessly extravagant —*n.* a profligate person —**prof′li·ga·cy** (-gə sē) *n.*, **prof′li·gate·ness** —**prof′li·gate·ly** *adv.*

pro for·ma (prō fôr′mə) ⟦L⟧ for (the sake of) form; as a matter of form

pro·found (prō fo͡und′, prə-) *adj.* ⟦ME < OFr *profund* < L *profundus* < *pro-*, forward (see PRO-²) + *fundus*, BOTTOM⟧ **1** very deep or low *[a profound abyss, sleep, etc.]* **2** marked by intellectual depth *[a profound discussion]* **3** intensely felt *[profound grief]* **4** thoroughgoing *[profound changes]* **5** unbroken *[a profound silence]* —*n.* **1** [Archaic] an abyss or deep, as of the ocean **2** something profound —**pro·found′ly** *adv.* —**pro·found′ness** *n.*

pro·fun·di·ty (prō fun′də tē, prə-) *n.*, *pl.* **-ties** ⟦ME *profundite* < MFr < LL *profunditas*⟧ **1** depth, esp. great depth **2** intellectual depth **3** a profound idea, matter, etc.

pro·fuse (prō fyo͞os′, prə-) *adj.* ⟦ME < L *profusus*, pp. of *profundere*, to pour out < *pro-*, forth + *fundere*, to pour: see PRO-² & FOUND³⟧ **1** giving or pouring forth freely; generous, often to excess: usually with *in [profuse in her apologies]* **2** given or poured forth freely and abundantly —**pro·fuse′ly** *adv.* —**pro·fuse′ness** *n.*

SYN.—profuse implies a pouring or giving forth freely, often to the point of excess *[profuse thanks]*; **lavish** implies an unstinted, generous, sometimes unreasonably liberal, giving *[lavish attentions]*; **extravagant** always suggests unreasonably excessive, wasteful spending or giving *[extravagant living]*; **prodigal** implies such reckless extravagance as to suggest eventual impoverishment *[the prodigal heirs to a fortune]*; **luxuriant** suggests production in great and rich abundance *[luxuriant foliage]*; **lush** implies such great luxuriance as to seem excessive *[a lush jungle]* See also **plentiful** —**ANT. limited, scant, spare**

pro·fu·sion (prō fyo͞o′zhən, prə-) *n.* ⟦Fr < L *profusio* < *profusus:* see prec.⟧ **1** a pouring forth with great liberality or wastefulness **2** great liberality or wastefulness **3** rich or lavish supply; abundance

prog[1] (präg) [Dial.] *vi.* **progged**, **prog′ging** ⟦via dial. < ? ME *prokken*, to beg (prob. < LowG)⟧ to prowl about, as in search of food or plunder; forage —*n.* food obtained as by progging

prog[2] *abbrev.* **1** program **2** progressive

pro·gen·i·tive (prō jen′ə tiv, prə-) *adj.* ⟦see fol. & -IVE⟧ capable of begetting offspring; reproductive

pro·gen·i·tor (prō jen′ə tər, prə-; -tôr′) *n.* ⟦ME *progenitour* < MFr *progeniteur* < pp. of *progignere*, to beget < *pro-*, forth + *gignere*, to beget: see PRO-² & GENUS⟧ **1** a forefather; ancestor in direct line **2** a source from which something develops; originator or precursor

prog·e·ny (präj′ə nē) *n.*, *pl.* **-nies** ⟦ME *progenie* < MFr < L *progenies*, descent, lineage, race, family < *progignere:* see prec.⟧ children, descendants, or offspring collectively; issue

pro·ger·i·a (prō jir′ē ə) *n.* ⟦ModL < Gr *progērōs*, prematurely old < *pro*, before + *gēras*, old age + -IA⟧ a rare genetic disorder of childhood, characterized by certain medical and physical conditions associated with old age, including an aged look to the face

pro·ges·ta·tion·al (prō′jes tā′shə nəl) *adj.* ⟦PRO-¹ + GESTATION + -AL⟧ of or involving hormones that, in female mammals, precede, prepare for, or are active in ovulation and pregnancy

pro·ges·ter·one (prō jes′tər ōn′) *n.* ⟦PRO-¹ + GE(STATION) + STER(OL) + -ONE⟧ a steroidal hormone, $C_{21}H_{30}O_2$, secreted by the corpus luteum or prepared synthetically, active in preparing the uterus for the reception and development of the fertilized ovum and the mammary glands for milk secretion

pro·ges·tin (prō jes′tin) *n.* ⟦PRO-¹ + GEST(ATION) + -IN¹⟧ any of various natural or synthetic steroidal hormones, as progesterone, that cause progestational activity, used in birth control pills, in hormone therapy, etc.: often called **pro·ges·to·gen** (prō jes′tə jən)

pro·glot·tid (prō glät′id) *n.* ⟦< ModL *proglottis* (gen. *proglottidis*) < Gr *pro-*, forward + *glōtta*, the tongue: see PRO-¹ & GLOTTIS⟧ any of the segmentlike divisions of a tapeworm's body: each division has both male and female reproductive organs and is essentially an independent organism: also **pro·glot′tis** (-is), *pl.* **-ti·des′** (-i dēz′)

prog·na·thous (präg′nə thəs, präg nā′-) *adj.* ⟦PRO-¹ + -GNATHOUS⟧ having the jaws projecting beyond the upper face: also **prog·nath′ic** (-nath′ik) —**prog′na·thism′** *n.*

prog·no·sis (präg nō′sis) *n.*, *pl.* **-ses′** (-sēz′) ⟦LL < Gr *prognōsis* < *progignōskein* < *pro-*, before (see PRO-¹) + *gignōskein*, to KNOW⟧ a forecast or forecasting; esp., a prediction of the probable course of a disease in an individual and the chances of recovery

prog·nos·tic (präg näs′tik) *n.* ⟦ME *pronostike* < MFr *pronostique* < L *prognosticum* < Gr *prognōstikon* < *progignōskein:* see prec.⟧ **1** a sign or indication of things to come; omen **2** a forecast; prediction —*adj.* ⟦ML *prognosticus* < Gr *prognōstikos*⟧ **1** foretelling; predictive **2** *Med.* of, or serving as a basis for, prognosis

prog·nos·ti·cate (präg näs′ti kāt′) *vt.* **-cat′ed**, **-cat′ing** ⟦< ML *prognosticatus*, pp. of *prognosticare* < *prognosticus:* see prec.⟧ **1** to foretell or predict, esp. from signs or indications **2** to indicate beforehand —**prog·nos′ti·ca′tion** *n.* —**prog·nos′ti·ca′tive** (-kāt′iv) *adj.* —**prog·nos′ti·ca′tor** *n.*

pro·gram (prō′gram′, -grəm) *n.* ⟦< LL & Fr: Fr *programme* < LL *programma* < Gr, edict < *prographein*, to write in public < *pro-*, before + *graphein*, to write: see PRO-¹ & GRAPHIC⟧ **1** [Obs.] *a)* a proclamation *b)* a prospectus or syllabus **2** *a)* the acts, speeches, musical pieces, etc. that make up an entertainment, ceremony, etc. *b)* a printed list of these **3** a scheduled broadcast on radio or television **4** a plan or procedure for dealing with some matter **5** all the activities that can be participated in at a community center, camp, resort, etc. **6** a logical sequence of coded instructions specifying the operations to be performed by a computer in solving a problem or in processing data **7** a series of operations which may be used to control the functions of an electronic device —*vt.* **-grammed′** or **-gramed′**, **-gram′ming** or **-gram′ing** **1** to enter or schedule in a program ☆**2** to prepare the questions and answers for (a textbook or a teaching machine to be used in programmed instruction) **3** *a)* to plan a computer program for (a task, problem, etc.) *b)* to furnish (a computer, chip, etc.) with a program *c)* to incorporate in a computer program **4** to set the program of (an electronic device) **5** to predispose to behave in a certain way, have a certain mindset, etc.; condition *[to program a child for failure]* —*vi.* to plan or prepare a program or programs Also [Chiefly Brit.] **pro′gramme′** —**pro·gram′ma·ble** *adj.*, *n.* —**pro′gram′mer** *n.*, **pro′gram′er**

program director a person in charge of selecting and scheduling programs on radio or TV

pro·gram·mat·ic (prō′grə mat′ik) *adj.* **1** of, or having the nature of, program music **2** of, or having the nature of, a program; often, specif., predictable, mechanical, uninspired, etc.

programmed instruction instruction in which individual students answer questions about a unit of study at their own rate, checking their own answers and advancing only after answering correctly

pro·gram·ming (prō′gram′iŋ, -grə miŋ) *n.* **1** the programs broadcast on radio or TV **2** the schedule, selection, etc. of these programs **3** *a)* the act, process, or work of writing or developing computer programs *b)* the code sequences that make up computer programs

program music instrumental music that is meant to depict or suggest a mood or emotion, or a scene, story, or actual event: cf. ABSOLUTE MUSIC

program trading the use of sophisticated computer programs to execute large orders to buy and sell stocks and futures

prog·ress (präg′res, -rəs; *chiefly Brit & Cdn* prō′gres′; *for v.* prō gres′, prə-) ***n.*** ⟦ME *progresse* < L *progressus*, pp. of *progredi* < *pro-*, before + *gradi*, to step, go: see PRO-[2] & GRADE⟧ **1** a moving forward or onward **2** forward course; development **3** advance toward perfection or to a higher or better state; improvement **4** [Now Rare] an official journey, as of a sovereign —***vi.* pro·gress′ 1** to move forward or onward **2** to move forward toward completion, a goal, etc. **3** to advance toward perfection or to a higher or better state; improve —**in progress** going on; taking place; happening

pro·gres·sion (prō gresh′ən, prə-) ***n.*** ⟦ME < MFr < L *progressio*⟧ **1** a moving forward or onward; progress **2** a sequence or succession, as of acts, happenings, etc. **3** *Math.* a sequence of numbers, each of which is obtained from its predecessor by the same rule: see ARITHMETIC PROGRESSION, GEOMETRIC PROGRESSION **4** *Music a)* the movement forward from one tone or chord to another *b)* a succession of tones or chords —**pro·gres′sion·al** ***adj.***

pro·gres·sive (prō gres′iv, prə-) ***adj.*** ⟦MFr *progressif* < ML *progressivus* < L *progressus:* see PROGRESS⟧ **1** moving forward or onward **2** continuing by successive steps [*a progressive* decline] **3** of, or concerned with, progression **4** designating a tax whose rate increases as the base increases **5** *a)* favoring, working for, or characterized by progress or improvement, as through political or social reform *b)* of or having to do with a person, movement, etc. thought of as being modern or advanced, as in ideas, methods, etc. *c)* LIBERAL (*adj.* 7*b*) ☆**6** of an educational system stressing individuality, self-expression, etc. **7** *Gram.* indicating continuing action or state, or action in progress: used as of certain verb forms (Ex: *am working*, as opposed to the simple form *work*) **8** *Med.* becoming more severe or spreading to other parts: said of a disease **9** [**P-**] *Politics* of a Progressive Party —***n.* 1** a person who is progressive, esp. one who favors political progress or reform **2** [**P-**] a member of a Progressive Party —***SYN.*** LIBERAL —**pro·gres′sive·ly** ***adv.*** —**pro·gres′sive·ness** ***n.***

Progressive Conservative 1 designating or of a former political party of Canada **2** a member of this party

Progressive Party ☆one of three short-lived, minor American political parties, specif., *a)* one organized in 1912 by followers of Theodore Roosevelt *b)* one formed in 1924 under the leadership of Robert M. La Follette *c)* one formed in 1948, originally under the leadership of Henry A. Wallace

pro·gres·siv·ism (prō gres′iv iz′əm, prə-) ***n.*** the doctrines, principles, and practices of progressives —**pro·gres′siv·ist** ***n.***

pro·gres·siv·i·ty (prō′gre siv′ə tē) ***n.*** **1** the quality of being progressive: said of a tax or system of taxation **2** the degree to which a tax or system of taxation is progressive

pro·hib·it (prō hib′it, prə-) ***vt.*** ⟦ME *prohibeten* < L *prohibitus*, pp. of *prohibere*, to prohibit < *pro-*, before (see PRO-[2]) + *habere*, to have (see HABIT)⟧ **1** to refuse to permit; forbid by law or by an order **2** to prevent; hinder —***SYN.*** FORBID —**pro·hib′it·er** ***n.***, **pro·hib′i·tor**

pro·hi·bi·tion (prō′ə bish′ən, -hi-) ***n.*** ⟦ME *prohibicion* < MFr *prohibition* < L *prohibitio*⟧ **1** a prohibiting or being prohibited **2** an order or law that forbids ☆**3** the forbidding by law of the manufacture, transportation, and sale of alcoholic beverages **4** [**P-**] in the U.S., the period (1920-1933) of PROHIBITION (sense 3) by federal law

pro·hi·bi·tion·ist (-ist) ***n.*** ☆**1** one in favor of prohibiting by law the manufacture and sale of alcoholic drinks ☆**2** [**P-**] a member of a U.S. political party (**Prohibition Party**) advocating such prohibition

pro·hib·i·tive (prō hib′ə tiv, prə-) ***adj.*** ⟦Fr *prohibitif* < LL *prohibitivus*⟧ **1** prohibiting or tending to prohibit something **2** such as to prevent purchase, use, etc.: often used in comb. [*cost-prohibitive*] Also **pro·hib′i·to′ry** (-tôr′ē) —**pro·hib′i·tive·ly** ***adv.***

pro·in·su·lin (prō in′sə lin) ***n.*** ⟦PRO-[1] + INSULIN⟧ a polypeptide molecule formed in the islets of Langerhans: hydrolysis of its peptide bonds yields insulin and a biochemically inactive peptide

proj·ect (präj′ekt′, -jikt; *for v.* prō jekt′, prə-) ***n.*** ⟦ME *projecte* < L *projectum*, neut. of *projectus*, pp. of *projicere* < *pro-*, before, forward + *jacere*, to throw: see PRO-[2] & JET[1]⟧ **1** a proposal of something to be done; plan; scheme ☆**2** an organized undertaking; specif., *a)* a special unit of work, research, etc., as in a school, a laboratory, etc. *b)* an extensive public undertaking, as in conservation, construction, etc. ☆**3** [*often pl.*] a complex of inexpensive apartments or houses, esp. one that is publicly owned or financed: in full **housing project** —***vt.* pro·ject′ 1** to propose (an act or plan of action) **2** to throw or hurl forward **3** *a)* to cause (one's voice) to be heard clearly and at a distance *b)* to get (ideas, feelings, one's presence, etc.) across to others effectively **4** to send forth in one's thoughts or imagination [*to project* oneself into the future] **5** to cause to jut out **6** to cause (a shadow, image, etc.) to fall or appear upon a surface **7** EXTRAPOLATE **8** *Geom.* to transform the points of (a geometric figure) into the points of another figure, usually by means of lines of correspondence **9** *Psychol.* to externalize (a thought or feeling) so that it appears to have objective reality —***vi.* 1** to jut out; protrude **2** to be effective in the projection of one's voice, ideas, etc. —***SYN.*** PLAN

pro·jec·tile (prō jek′təl, prə-; *also, chiefly Brit & Cdn*, -tīl′) ***n.*** ⟦Fr < L *projectus:* see prec. & -ILE⟧ **1** an object designed to be hurled or shot forward, as a cannon shell or rocket **2** anything thrown forward —***adj.* 1** designed to be hurled forward, as a javelin **2** hurling forward [*projectile* force] **3** *Zool.* that can be thrust out, as a tentacle

pro·jec·tion (prō jek′shən, prə-) ***n.*** ⟦MFr < L *projectio*⟧ **1** a projecting or being projected **2** something that projects, or juts out **3** something that is projected; specif., *a)* in map making, the representation on a plane of the earth's surface (or the celestial sphere) or of a part thereof *b)* any of various other two-dimensional pictorial representations of a three-dimensional object [axonometric *projection*] **4** a prediction or advance estimate based on known data or observations; extrapolation **5** *Psychiatry* the unconscious act or process of ascribing to others one's own ideas, impulses, or emotions, esp. when they are considered undesirable or cause anxiety **6** *Photog.* the process of projecting an image, as from a transparent slide, upon a screen, etc. —**pro·jec′tion·al** ***adj.***

SYN.—**projection** implies a jutting out abruptly beyond the rest of the surface [the *projection* of the eaves beyond the sides of a house]; **protrusion** suggests a thrusting or pushing out that is of an abnormal or disfiguring nature [*protrusion* of the eyeballs]; **protuberance** suggests a swelling out, usually in rounded form [the tumor on his arm formed a *protuberance*]; **bulge** suggests an outward swelling of a kind that may result from internal pressure [the *bulge* in the can resulted from the fermentation of its contents]

projection booth a small chamber, as in a theater, from which images on film, slides, etc. are projected

☆**pro·jec·tion·ist** (prō jek′shən ist, prə-) ***n.*** the operator of a film or slide projector

projection TV a system made up of lenses, mirrors, and a cathode-ray tube, for projecting video images onto a large screen

pro·jec·tive (prō jek′tiv, prə-) ***adj.*** **1** of or made by projection **2** designating or of a type of psychological test, as the Rorschach test, in which any response the subject makes to the test material will be indicative of personality traits and unconscious motivations

projective geometry the branch of geometry dealing with those properties of a figure (**projective properties**) that do not vary when the figure is projected

pro·jec·tor (prō jek′tər, prə-) ***n.*** a person or thing that projects; specif., a machine for throwing an image on a screen, as from a transparent slide or FILM (*n.* 5*a*)

pro·kar·y·ote (prō kar′ē ōt′) ***n.*** ⟦< Gr *pro-*, before + *karyōtis:* see EUKARYOTE⟧ a single-celled organism lacking a true nucleus: cf. EUKARYOTE —**pro·kar′y·ot′ic** (-ät′ik) ***adj.***

Pro·ko·fi·ev (prō kôf′ē ef′, -kō′fē-), **Ser·gei (Sergeevich)** (ser′gā) 1891-1953; Russ. composer

Pro·ko·pyevsk (prä kô′pyifsk) city in SC Russia, in the Kuznetsk Basin

pro·lac·tin (prō lak′tin) ***n.*** ⟦PRO-[1] + LACT(O)- + -IN[1]⟧ a pituitary hormone stimulating milk secretion in mammals and secretion by the crop gland in certain birds

pro·la·mine (prō′lə mēn′, prō′lə mēn′; prō lam′ēn′, -in) ***n.*** ⟦PROL(INE) + AMINE⟧ any of a class of proteins found esp. in the seeds of cereals, insoluble in water and absolute alcohol, but soluble in 70% alcohol: also **pro·lam·in** (prō lam′in, prō′lə min)

pro·lan (prō′lan′) ***n.*** ⟦Ger < L *proles*, offspring (see PROLIFIC) + Ger *-an*, -AN⟧ *former term for:* **1** FOLLICLE-STIMULATING HORMONE: in full **prolan A 2** LUTEINIZING HORMONE: in full **prolan B**

pro·lapse (prō laps′, prō′laps′) ***n.*** ⟦ModL *prolapsus* < LL, a falling < pp. of L *prolabi*, to fall forward < *pro-*, forward + *labi*, to fall: see PRO-[2] & LAPSE⟧ *Med.* the falling or slipping out of place of an internal organ, as the uterus: also **pro·lap′sus** (-lap′səs) —***vi.* -lapsed′, -laps′ing** *Med.* to fall or slip out of place

pro·late (prō′lāt′) ***adj.*** ⟦L *prolatus*, pp. of *proferre*, to bring forward: see PRO-[1] & BEAR[1]⟧ extended or elongated at the poles [*a prolate* spheroid]

prole (prōl) ***adj., n.*** ⟦popularized by George ORWELL in his novel *Nineteen Eighty-four* (published 1949)⟧ [Informal, Chiefly Brit.] *short for* PROLETARIAN: often a derogatory term

pro·leg (prō′leg′, -lāg′) ***n.*** ⟦PRO-[1] + LEG[1]⟧ any of the stubby limbs attached to the abdomen of certain insect larvae

pro·le·gom·e·non (prō′li gäm′ə nän′, -nən) ***n., pl.*** **-e·na** (-nə) ⟦Gr, neut. pass. prp. of *prolegein*, to say beforehand < *pro-*, before + *legein*, to speak: see PRO-[1] & LOGIC⟧ **1** a preliminary remark **2** [*often pl., with sing. v.*] a preliminary statement or essay; foreword —**pro′le·gom′e·nous** (-nəs) ***adj.***

pro·lep·sis (prō lep′sis) ***n., pl.*** **-ses′** (-sēz′) ⟦L < Gr *prolēpsis*, an anticipating < *prolambanein*, to take before < *pro-*, before + *lambanein*, to take: see LEMMA[1]⟧ an anticipating; specif., *a)* the describing of an event as taking place before it could have done so *b)* the treating of a future event as if it had already happened *c)* the anticipating and answering of an argument before one's opponent has a chance to advance it —**pro·lep′tic** ***adj.***

pro·le·tar·i·an (prō′lə ter′ē ən) ***adj.*** ⟦< L *proletarius*, citizen of the lowest class (see PROLETARY) + -AN⟧ of the proletariat —***n.*** a member of the proletariat; worker

pro·le·tar·i·an·ize (-ə nīz′) ***vt.*** **-ized′, -iz′ing** to make, or treat as, proletarian —**pro′le·tar′i·an·i·za′tion** ***n.***

pro·le·tar·i·at (prō′lə ter′ē ət) ***n.*** ⟦Fr *prolétariat* < L *proletarius:* see fol.⟧ **1** the class of lowest status in ancient Roman society **2** [Rare] the class of lowest status in any society **3** the working class; esp., the industrial working class

pro·le·tar·y (prō′lə ter′ē) ***n., pl.*** **-tar′ies** ⟦L *proletarius*, a propertyless citizen of the lowest class, who served the state only by having children < *proles*, offspring: see PROLIFIC⟧ in ancient Rome, a member of the lowest class of citizens, who had no property

pro-life (prō′līf′) *adj.* opposing a legal right to obtain an abortion —**pro′-lif′er** *n.*
USAGE—this term is used typically by those opposed to legalized abortion

pro·lif·er·ate (prō lif′ə rāt′, prə-) *vt.* **-at′ed, -at′ing** ⟦back-form. < *proliferation* < Fr *prolifération* < *prolifère*, fol. + -ATION⟧ **1** to reproduce (new parts) in quick succession **2** to produce or create in profusion —*vi.* **1** to grow by multiplying new parts, as by budding, in quick succession **2** to multiply rapidly; increase profusely —**pro·lif′er·a′tion** *n.*

pro·lif·er·ous (prō lif′ər əs, prə-) *adj.* ⟦< ML *prolifer* < L *proles* (see fol.) + *ferre*, to BEAR[1] + -OUS⟧ **1** *Bot.* *a)* multiplying freely by means of buds, side branches, etc. *b)* having leafy shoots growing from a flower or fruit **2** *Zool.* reproducing by budding, as coral

pro·lif·ic (prō lif′ik, prə-) *adj.* ⟦Fr *prolifique* < ML *prolificus* < L *proles* (gen. *prolis*), offspring < *pro-*, PRO-[2] + base of *alere*, to nourish (see ALIMENT) + *facere*, to make, DO[1]⟧ **1** producing many young or much fruit **2** turning out many products of the mind [*a prolific* scholar or poet] **3** fruitful; abounding: often with *in* or *of* —*SYN.* FERTILE —**pro·lif′i·ca·cy** (-i kə sē) *n.* —**pro·lif′i·cal·ly** *adv.*

pro·line (prō′lēn′, -lin) *n.* ⟦Ger *prolin*, contr. < *pyrrolidin* < *pyrrol*, PYRROLE + *-id*, -IDE + *-in*, -INE[3]⟧ a nonessential amino acid, C_4H_8NCOOH, formed by the decomposition of proteins: see AMINO ACID

pro·lix (prō liks′, prō′liks′) *adj.* ⟦ME *prolixe* < L *prolixus*, extended, prolix < *pro-*, forth + base of *liquere*, to flow: see LIQUID⟧ **1** so wordy as to be tiresome; verbose **2** using more words than are necessary; long-winded —*SYN.* WORDY —**pro·lix′i·ty** *n.* —**pro·lix′ly** *adv.*

pro·loc·u·tor (prō läk′yoo tər, -yə-) *n.* ⟦L, an advocate < pp. of *proloqui*, to declare < *pro*, for + *loqui*, to speak⟧ **1** a spokesman **2** a chairman

pro·logue (prō′lôg′) *n.* ⟦ME *prologe* < MFr < L *prologus* < Gr *prologos* < *pro-*, before + *logos*, discourse: see PRO-[1] & LOGIC⟧ **1** an introduction to a poem, play, etc.; esp., introductory lines spoken by a member of the cast before a dramatic performance **2** the actor speaking such lines **3** a preliminary act or course of action foreshadowing greater events Also sp. **pro′log′** —*SYN.* INTRODUCTION

pro·logu·ize or **pro·log·ize** (prō′lôg īz′) *vi.* **-ized′, -iz′ing** to compose or deliver a prologue

pro·long (prō lôŋ′, prə-) *vt.* ⟦ME *prolongen* < MFr *prolonguer* < LL *prolongare* < L *pro-*, forth + *longus*, long: see PRO-[2] & LONG[1]⟧ to lengthen or extend in time or space: also **pro·lon′gate′** (-gāt′), **-gat′ed, -gat′ing** —*SYN.* EXTEND —**pro′lon·ga′tion** (-gā′shən) *n.* —**pro·long′er** *n.*

pro·longe (prō länj′) *n.* ⟦Fr < *prolonger:* see prec.⟧ a heavy rope having a hook and toggle, used to drag a gun carriage, etc.

pro·lu·sion (prō loo′zhən) *n.* ⟦L *prolusio*, prelude < *prolusus*, pp. of *proludere*, to play beforehand < *pro-*, before + *ludere*, to play: see PRO-[2] & LUDICROUS⟧ a preliminary part or performance; often, specif., an introductory essay or article —**pro·lu′so·ry** (-sə rē) *adj.*

☆**prom**[1] (präm) *n.* ⟦contr. < PROMENADE⟧ a ball or dance, as of a particular class at a school or college

prom[2] *abbrev.* promontory

PROM (präm) *n.* ⟦*p(rogrammable) r(ead-)o(nly) m(emory)*⟧ a type of ROM chip that can be programmed to a particular user's needs

prom·e·nade (präm′ə nād′, -näd′) *n.* ⟦Fr < *promener*, to take for a walk < LL *prominare*, to drive (animals) onward < L *pro-*, forth (see PRO-[2]) + *minare*, to drive (animals) < *minari*, to threaten (see MENACE)⟧ **1** a leisurely walk taken for pleasure, to display one's finery, etc. **2** a public place for such a walk, as an avenue, the deck of a ship, or the hall of a building **3** ☆*a)* [Old-fashioned] a ball, or formal dance, as at a school; prom *b)* a march of all the guests, beginning a formal ball *c)* a walking or marching figure of a square dance —*vi.* **-nad′ed, -nad′ing** to take a promenade; walk about for pleasure, display, etc. —*vt.* **1** to take a promenade along or through **2** to take or show on or as on a promenade; parade **3** to march (one's partner) as a figure of a square dance —**prom′e·nad′er** *n.*

Pro·me·the·an (prō mē′thē ən, prə-) *adj.* **1** of or like Prometheus **2** life-bringing, creative, or courageously original —*n.* a Promethean person in spirit or deeds

Pro·me·the·us (prō mē′thē əs) *n.* ⟦L < Gr *Promētheus*, lit., forethought < *promēthes*, thinking before < *pro-*, before (see PRO-[1]) + *mathein*, to learn (akin to *manthanein*: see MATHEMATICAL)⟧ *Gr. Myth.* a Titan who steals fire from heaven for the benefit of mankind: in punishment, Zeus chains him to a rock where a vulture (or eagle) comes each day to eat his liver, which grows back each night

☆**pro·me·thi·um** (prō mē′thē əm) *n.* ⟦ModL: so named (1949) for earlier *prometheum*, name proposed by G. M. Coryell, wife of one of the discoverers < Gr *Promētheus* (see prec.) in reference to production by nuclear fission + -IUM⟧ a radioactive chemical element, one of the rare-earth elements, obtained from fission of uranium or neutron bombardment of neodymium and used in phosphorescent paint, as a power source, X-ray source, etc.: symbol, Pm; at. no. 61: see the periodic table of elements in the Reference Supplement

☆**pro·mine** (prō′mēn′, -min) *n.* ⟦< PROM(OTE) + -INE[3]⟧ a substance found in animal cells in minute amounts, that promotes growth and cell division: cf. RETINE

prom·i·nence (präm′ə nəns) *n.* ⟦< MFr < L *prominentia* < *prominens:* see fol.⟧ **1** the state or quality of being prominent **2** something that is prominent or that sticks out, as a hill **3** *Astron.* any of the luminous clouds of solar gas arching from the chromosphere into the much hotter corona: best seen at the edge of the sun, as during an eclipse

prom·i·nent (präm′ə nənt) *adj.* ⟦L *prominens*, prp. of *prominere*, to project < *pro-*, PRO-[2] + *minere*, to project < *minae*, projections, threats: see MENACE⟧ **1** sticking out; projecting [*a prominent* chin] **2** noticeable at once; conspicuous [*prominent* markings] **3** widely known; specif., significant and widely know within a particular field [*a prominent* anthropologist] —*SYN.* NOTICEABLE —**prom′i·nent·ly** *adv.*

prom·is·cu·i·ty (präm′i skyoo′ə tē, prō′mi-) *n., pl.* **-ties** state, quality, or instance of being promiscuous, esp. in sexual relations

pro·mis·cu·ous (prō mis′kyoo əs, prə-) *adj.* ⟦L *promiscuus* < *pro-*, forth (see PRO-[2]) + *miscere*, to MIX⟧ **1** consisting of different elements mixed together or mingled without sorting or discrimination **2** characterized by a lack of discrimination; specif., engaging in sexual intercourse indiscriminately or with many persons **3** without plan or purpose; casual —**pro·mis′cu·ous·ly** *adv.* —**pro·mis′cu·ous·ness** *n.*

prom·ise (präm′is) *n.* ⟦ME *promis* < L *promissum* < *promittere*, to send before or forward < *pro-*, forth + *mittere*, to send: see PRO-[2] & MISSION⟧ **1** an oral or written agreement to do or not to do something **2** indication, as of a successful prospect or future; basis for expectation **3** something promised —*vi.* **-ised, -is·ing 1** to make a promise **2** to give a basis for expectation: often with *well* or *fair* —*vt.* **1** to make a promise of (something) *to* somebody **2** to engage or pledge: followed by an infinitive or a clause [to *promise* to go] **3** to give a basis for expecting **4** [Informal] to declare emphatically; assure **5** [Archaic] to pledge to give in marriage —**prom′is·er** *n.*

Promised Land 1 *Bible* Canaan, promised by God to Abraham and his descendants: Gen. 17:8 **2** [*usually* **p- l-**] any place regarded as the realization of one's hopes

prom·is·ee (präm′i sē′) *n.* *Law* a person to whom a promise is made

prom·is·ing (präm′is iŋ) *adj.* showing promise of success, excellence, etc. —**prom′is·ing·ly** *adv.*

prom·i·sor (präm′i sôr′, präm′i sôr′) *n.* *Law* a person who makes a promise

prom·is·so·ry (präm′i sôr′ē) *adj.* ⟦ML *promissorius* < L *promissor*, one who promises⟧ containing a promise

promissory note a written promise to pay a certain sum of money to a certain person or bearer on demand or on a specified date

pro·mo (prō′mō) [Informal] *adj.* pertaining to or engaged in the promotion or advertisement of a product, entertainment, etc. —*n., pl.* **-mos** a recorded announcement, radio or television commercial, etc. used in a promotional or advertising campaign

prom·on·to·ry (präm′ən tôr′ē) *n., pl.* **-ries** ⟦LL *promontorium* < L *promunturium*, prob. altered (infl. by *mons*, MOUNT[1]) < *prominere:* see PROMINENT⟧ **1** a peak of high land that juts out into a body of water; headland **2** *Anat.* a prominent part

pro·mote (prə mōt′, prō-) *vt.* **-mot′ed, -mot′ing** ⟦ME *promoten* < L *promotus*, pp. of *promovere*, to move forward: see PRO-[2] & MOVE⟧ **1** to raise or advance to a higher position or rank [she was *promoted* to manager] **2** to help bring about or further the growth or establishment of [to *promote* the general welfare] ☆**3** to further the popularity, sales, etc. of, as by publicizing and advertising [to *promote* a product] ☆**4** [Slang] to acquire (something) by devious or cunning means **5** *Chess* to convert (a pawn that has crossed the board and reached the end row) to a more powerful piece: cf. QUEEN (*vt.* 2) ☆**6** *Educ.* to move (a student) forward a grade in school —*SYN.* ADVANCE —**pro·mot′a·ble** *adj.*

pro·mot·er (prə mōt′ər, prō-) *n.* ⟦ME < MFr *promoteur* < ML *promotor*⟧ **1** a person or thing that promotes; specif., a person who begins, secures financing for, and helps to organize an undertaking, as a business or a sports event **2** *Chem.* a substance that will accelerate the effect of a catalyst on a reaction

pro·mo·tion (prə mō′shən, prō-) *n.* ⟦ME < MFr < LL *promotio*⟧ the act or an instance of promoting; specif., *a)* advancement in rank, grade, or position *b)* furtherance of an enterprise, cause, etc.

pro·mo·tion·al (-shən əl) *adj.* of or having to do with the promoting of a product, entertainment, etc. through publicity or marketing; often, specif., offered free of charge or at a discount, as part of such marketing [*a promotional* copy of a new book]

pro·mo·tive (prə mōt′iv, prō-) *adj.* tending to promote

prompt (prämpt) *adj.* ⟦ME *prompte* < MFr < L *promptus*, brought forth, at hand, ready, quick < pp. of *promere*, to bring forth < *pro-*, forth + *emere*, to take: see PRO-[2] & REDEEM⟧ **1** quick to act or to do what is required; ready, punctual, etc. **2** done, spoken, etc. at once or without delay —*n.* **1** *Commerce* *a)* the time limit specified for the payment of an account *b)* the contract in which the due date is specified **2** an act of prompting; reminder **3** *Comput.* a message on a video screen that requests the user to enter information or a command —*vt.* **1** to urge into action; provoke **2** to remind (a person) of something he or she has forgotten; specif., to help (an actor, etc. who has forgotten a line) with a cue **3** to move or inspire by suggestion **4** *Comput.* to request a response from (a user) with a PROMPT (*n.* 3): said of a program, etc. —*SYN.* QUICK —**prompt′ly** *adv.* —**prompt′ness** *n.*

prompt·book (prämpt′book′) *n.* an annotated play script, used by a stage manager or prompter, with detailed directions for action, settings, properties, etc.

prompt·er (prämp′tər) *n.* **1** a person who prompts; specif., one who cues performers when they forget their lines **2** TELEPROMPTER

promp·ti·tude (prämp′tə tood′, -tyood′) *n.* ⟦Fr < LL(Ec) *promptitudo*⟧ the quality of being prompt; promptness

prom·ul·gate (präm′əl gāt′, prō mul′gāt′) *vt.* **-gat′ed, -gat′ing** ⟦< L *promulgatus*, pp. of *promulgare*, to publish < ?⟧ **1** to publish or make known officially (a decree, church dogma, etc.) **2** *a)* to make known the terms of (a new or proposed law or statute) *b)* to put (a law) into effect by publishing its terms **3** to make widespread [to *promulgate* learning and culture] —**prom′ul·ga′tion** *n.* —**prom′ul·ga′tor** *n.*

pro·mulge (prō mulj′) *vt. archaic var. of* PROMULGATE

pro·my·ce·li·um (prō′mī sē′lē əm) *n., pl.* **-li·a** (-ə) ⟦PRO-[1] + MYCELIUM⟧ *Bot.* a short filament bearing small spores, developed in spore germination of rusts and smuts

pron *abbrev.* **1** pronominal **2** pronoun **3** pronounced **4** pronunciation

pro·na·tal·ist (prō nāt′'l ist) *adj.* ⟦PRO-[2] + NATAL + -IST[2]⟧ advocating or supporting a high birthrate

pro·nate (prō′nāt′) *vt., vi.* **-nat′ed, -nat′ing** ⟦< LL *pronatus*, pp. of *pronare*, to bend forward < L *pronus*: see PRONE⟧ **1** to rotate (the hand or forearm) so that the palm faces down or back: see SUPINATE **2** to rotate (the foot) outward and tip it so that the inner side of the sole contacts the ground in walking or running —**pro·na′tion** *n.*

pro·na·tor (prō nāt′ər, prō′nāt′-) *n.* ⟦ModL⟧ a muscle in the forearm by which pronation is effected

prone (prōn) *adj.* ⟦ME < L *pronus* < *pro*, before: see PRO-[1]⟧ **1** lying or leaning face downward **2** lying flat or prostrate; in a horizontal position **3** having a natural bent; disposed or inclined (to) [*prone* to error] **4** groveling; abject **5** [Old Poet.] leaning forward or sloping downward —**prone′ly** *adv.* —**prone′ness** *n.*

SYN.—**prone**, in strict use, implies a position in which the front part of the body lies upon or faces the ground [he fell *prone* upon the ground and drank from the brook]; **supine** implies a position in which one lies on one's back [he snores when he sleeps in a *supine* position]; **prostrate** implies the position of one thrown or lying flat in a prone or supine position, as in great humility or complete submission, or because laid low [the victim lay *prostrate* at the murderer's feet]; **recumbent** suggests a lying down or back in any position one might assume for rest or sleep [she was *recumbent* on the chaise longue] See also **likely** —*ANT.* **erect**

pro·neph·ros (prō nef′räs) *n.* ⟦ModL < *pro-*, PRO-[1] + Gr *nephros*, kidney: see NEPHRO-⟧ *Zool.* a primitive kidney, the most anterior of three pairs of renal organs, functional only during embryonic development in most lower vertebrates, and appearing only transiently in the human embryo —**pro·neph′ric** *adj.*

prong (prôŋ) *n.* ⟦LME *pronge*, akin to MLowG *prangen*, to press, pinch, Ger *pranger*, pillory⟧ **1** any of the pointed ends of a fork; tine **2** any pointed projecting part, as the tip of an antler —*vt.* to pierce, lift, or break up with a prong

pronged (prôŋd) *adj.* having prongs: often used fig. and in comb. to refer to a set of points, means, aspects, etc. [a three-*pronged* strategy]

☆**prong·horn** (prôŋ′hôrn′) *n., pl.* **-horns′** or **-horn′** the only species (*Antilocapra americana*) of a family (Antilocapridae) of ruminants of Mexico and the W U.S., having curved horns, each with one prong, that are shed annually: resembles both the deer and the antelope

pro·no·grade (prō′nə grād′) *adj.* ⟦< L *pronus*, bent forward (see PRONE) + -O- + -GRADE⟧ *Zool.* walking with the body parallel to the ground

pro·nom·i·nal (prō näm′i nəl) *adj.* ⟦LL *pronominalis* < L *pronomen*, fol.⟧ *Gram.* of, or having the function of, a pronoun [the *pronominal* adjective "our"] —**pro·nom′i·nal·ly** *adv.*

pro·noun (prō′noun′) *n.* ⟦altered (infl. by NOUN) < MFr *pronom* < L *pronomen* < *pro*, for + *nomen*, NOUN⟧ *Gram.* any of a small class of relationship or signal words that assume the functions of nouns within clauses or phrases while referring to other locutions within the sentence or in other sentences: *I, you, them, it, ours, who, which, myself, anybody*, etc. are pronouns

pro·nounce (prə nouns′, prō-) *vt.* **-nounced′, -nounc′ing** ⟦ME *pronouncen* < OFr *pronuncier* < L *pronuntiare* < *pro-*, before + *nuntiare*, to announce < *nuntius*, messenger: see PRO-[2] & NUNCIO⟧ **1** to say or declare officially, solemnly, or with ceremony [to *pronounce* a couple husband and wife] **2** to announce or declare (someone or something) to be as specified [to *pronounce* a man guilty] **3** *a)* to articulate (a sound or word); utter the sounds of *b)* to articulate (a word or syllable) in the accepted manner [how do you *pronounce* your family name?] *c)* to indicate the pronunciation of (a word) with symbols —*vi.* **1** to state or pass a judgment; make a pronouncement (*on*) **2** to pronounce words, syllables, etc. —**pro·nounce′a·ble** *adj.* —**pro·nounc′er** *n.*

pro·nounced (prə nounst′, prō-) *adj.* **1** spoken or uttered **2** unmistakable or conspicuous [a *pronounced* limp, *pronounced* chin] —**pro·nounc′ed·ly** (-noun′sid lē) *adv.*

pro·nounce·ment (prə nouns′mənt, prō-) *n.* **1** the act of pronouncing **2** a formal, often authoritative statement of a fact, opinion, or judgment

☆**pron·to** (prän′tō) *adv.* ⟦Sp < L *promptus*: see PROMPT⟧ [Slang] at once; quickly; immediately

pro·nu·cle·us (prō no͞o′klē əs, -nyo͞o′-) *n., pl.* **-cle·i′** (-klē ī′) ⟦ModL: see PRO-[1] & NUCLEUS⟧ *Zool.* the haploid nucleus of either the spermatozoon or the ovum which unite in fertilization to form the fused double (or diploid) nucleus of the fertilized ovum, or zygote —**pro·nu′cle·ar** *adj.*

pro·nun·ci·a·men·to (prə nun′sē ə men′tō, prō-) *n., pl.* **-tos** ⟦Sp *pronunciamiento* < *pronunciar* < L *pronuntiare*: see PRONOUNCE⟧ **1** a public declaration or pronouncement; proclamation **2** MANIFESTO

pro·nun·ci·a·tion (prə nun′sē ā′shən, prō-) *n.* ⟦ME *pronunciacion* < MFr *pronunciation* < L *pronuntiatio*⟧ **1** the act or manner of pronouncing syllables, words, and phrases with regard to the production of sounds and the placing of stress, intonation, etc. **2** *a)* any of the accepted or standard ways of pronouncing a word, etc. *b)* the transcription in symbols of such a way of pronouncing a word, etc. —**pro·nun′ci·a′tion·al** *adj.*

proof (pro͞of) *n.* ⟦ME *profe* < OFr *prueve* < LL *proba* < L *probare*: see PROBE⟧ **1** the act or process of proving; a testing or trying of something **2** anything serving or tending to establish the truth of something, or to convince one of its truth; conclusive evidence **3** the establishment of the truth of something [to work on the *proof* of a theory] **4** a test or trial of the truth, worth, quality, etc. of something [the *proof* of the pudding is in the eating] **5** the quality or condition of having been tested or proved **6** [Obs.] tested or proved strength, as of armor **7** *a)* the relative strength of an alcoholic liquor with reference to the arbitrary standard for proof spirit *b)* this standard, taken as 100 proof: see PROOF SPIRIT **8** *Engraving* a trial impression taken from a plate, block, or stone **9** *Law* all the facts, admissions, and conclusions drawn from evidence which together operate to determine a verdict or judgment **10** *Math.* a process for checking the correctness of a computation, as, in a subtraction problem, by adding the difference to the subtrahend to get the minuend **11** *Numismatics* any of a limited number of coins of a new issue, struck with special care **12** *Photog.* a trial print of a negative **13** *Printing* an impression of composed type taken for checking errors and making changes —*adj.* **1** of tested and proved strength **2** impervious or invulnerable to; able to resist, withstand, etc.: with *against* [*proof* against criticism] **3** used in proving or testing **4** of standard strength: said of alcoholic liquors —*vt.* **1** to make a proof of **2** to make resistant or impervious to something **3** *short for* PROOFREAD

SYN.—**proof**, as compared here, applies to facts, documents, etc. that are so certain or convincing as to demonstrate the validity of a conclusion beyond reasonable doubt; **evidence** applies to something presented before a court, as a witness's statement, an object, etc., which bears on or establishes a fact; **testimony** applies to verbal evidence given by a witness under oath; **exhibit** applies to a document or object produced as evidence in a court

-proof (pro͞of) ⟦< prec.⟧ *combining form* **1** impervious to [*waterproof*] **2** protected from or against [*foolproof, rustproof*] **3** resistant to, unaffected by [*fireproof*]

☆**proof·read** (pro͞of′rēd′) *vt., vi.* **-read′** (-red′), **-read′ing** (-rēd′iŋ) to read and mark corrections on (printers' proofs, etc.) —**proof′read′er** *n.*

proof set a set of coins, one of each denomination, minted annually from highly polished dies, issued for collectors rather than for circulation

proof spirit an alcoholic liquor, or a mixture of alcohol and water, containing by volume 50 percent (in Great Britain and Canada 57.10 percent) ethyl alcohol at 15.6°C (*c.* 60°F)

prop[1] (präp) *n.* ⟦ME *proppe* < MDu, prop, ? akin to Ger *pfropfen*, stopper⟧ **1** a rigid support, as a beam, stake, or pole, placed under or against a structure or part **2** a person or thing that gives support or aid to a person, institution, etc. —*vt.* **propped, prop′ping 1** to support, hold up, or hold in place with or as with a prop: often with *up* **2** to place or lean (something) *against* a support **3** to sustain or bolster

prop[2] (präp) *n. short for* PROPERTY (sense 7)

prop[3] (präp) *n. short for* PROPELLER (as of an aircraft)

prop[4] *abbrev.* **1** proper(ly) **2** property **3** proposition **4** proprietor

pro·pae·deu·tic (prō′pi do͞ot′ik, -dyo͞ot′-) *adj.* ⟦< Gr *propaideuein*, to teach beforehand < *pro-*, before + *paideuein*, to instruct < *pais* (gen. *paidos*), child: see PEDO-[1]⟧ of, or having the nature of, elementary or introductory instruction: also **pro′pae·deu′ti·cal** —*n.* **1** an elementary or introductory subject or study **2** [*pl., with sing. v.*] the basic principles and rules preliminary to the study of some art or science

prop·a·ga·ble (präp′ə gə bəl) *adj.* ⟦< L *propagare* (see PROPAGATE) + -ABLE⟧ capable of being propagated

prop·a·gan·da (präp′ə gan′də) *n.* ⟦ModL, short for *congregatio de propaganda fide*, congregation for propagating the faith: see PROPAGATE⟧ **1** [**P-**] *R.C.Ch.* a committee of cardinals, the Congregation for the Propagation of the Faith, in charge of the foreign missions **2** any systematic, widespread dissemination or promotion of particular ideas, doctrines, practices, etc. to further one's own cause or to damage an opposing one **3** ideas, doctrines, or allegations so spread: now often used disparagingly to connote deception or distortion

prop·a·gan·dism (präp′ə gan′diz′əm; präp′ə gan′-) *n.* the art, system, or use of propaganda —**prop′a·gan′dist** *n., adj.* —**prop′a·gan·dis′tic** (-dis′tik) *adj.* —**prop′a·gan·dis′ti·cal·ly** *adv.*

prop·a·gan·dize (-dīz′) *vt.* **-dized′, -diz′ing 1** to spread (a doctrine or theory) by propaganda **2** to subject to propaganda —*vi.* to organize or spread propaganda

prop·a·gate (präp′ə gāt′) *vt.* **-gat′ed, -gat′ing** ⟦< L *propagatus*, pp. of *propagare*, to peg down, set < *propago*, slip for transplanting < *pro-*, before + *pag-*, base of *pangere*, to fasten: see PEACE⟧ **1** to cause (a plant or animal) to reproduce itself; raise or breed **2** to reproduce (itself); multiply: said of a plant or animal **3** to transmit (hereditary characteristics) by reproduction **4** to spread (ideas, customs, etc.) from one person or place to another **5** to transmit (esp. sound waves or electromagnetic radiation) through a medium —*vi.* to reproduce or multiply, as plants or animals —**prop′a·ga′tive** (-gāt′iv) *adj.* —**prop′a·ga′tor** *n.*

prop·a·ga·tion (präp′ə gā′shən) ***n.*** a propagating or being propagated; specif., *a)* reproduction or multiplication, as of a plant or animal *b)* a spreading, as of ideas, customs, etc.

prop·a·gule (präp′ə gyōōl′) ***n.*** ⟦< ModL *propagulum*, dim. of L *propago*, a shoot, slip: see PROPAGATE⟧ any plant organ or part, as a spore, seed or cutting, used to propagate a new plant

pro·pane (prō′pān′) ***n.*** ⟦PROP(YL) + (METH)ANE⟧ a heavy, colorless, gaseous alkane, C_3H_8, occurring naturally in petroleum and used as a fuel, in aerosols, in refrigerants, etc.

pro·par·ox·y·tone (prō′par äk′sə tōn′) ***adj.*** ⟦Gr *proparoxytonos:* see PRO-[1], PARA-[1], OXYTONE⟧ having an acute accent on the antepenult, as in classical Greek —***n.*** a proparoxytone word

pro pa·tri·a (prō pā′trē ä, -pä′-) ⟦L⟧ for (one's) country

pro·pel (prə pel′, prō-) ***vt.* -pelled′, -pel′ling** ⟦ME *propellen* < L *propellere* < *pro-*, forward + *pellere*, to drive: see FELT[1]⟧ to push, drive, or impel onward, forward, or ahead

pro·pel·lant (prə pel′ənt, prō-) ***n.*** a person or thing that propels; specif., *a)* the explosive charge that propels a projectile from a gun ☆*b)* the fuel and oxidizer used to propel a rocket

pro·pel·lent (prə pel′ənt, prō-) ***adj.*** ⟦L *propellens*, prp.⟧ propelling or tending to propel —***n.*** *alt. sp. of* PROPELLANT

pro·pel·ler (prə pel′ər, prō-) ***n.*** a person or thing that propels; specif., a device (in full **screw propeller**) on a ship or aircraft, consisting typically of two or more blades twisted to describe a helical path as they rotate with the hub in which they are mounted, and serving to propel the craft by the backward thrust of air or water

pro·pend (prō pend′) ***vi.*** ⟦L *propendere*, to hang forward < *pro-*, before + *pendere*, to hang: see PEND⟧ [Obs.] to incline, or be disposed (*to* or *toward* something)

pro·pene (prō′pēn′) ***n.*** ⟦PROP(YL) + -ENE⟧ PROPYLENE

pro·pen·si·ty (prə pen′sə tē) ***n., pl.*** **-ties** ⟦< *propense*, inclined < L *propensus*, pp. of *propendere* (see PROPEND) + -ITY⟧ **1** a natural inclination or tendency; bent **2** [Obs.] favorable inclination; bias (*for*) —***SYN.*** INCLINATION

prop·er (präp′ər) ***adj.*** ⟦ME *propre* < OFr < L *proprius*, one's own⟧ **1** specially adapted or suitable to a specific purpose or specific conditions; appropriate [the *proper* tool for a job] **2** naturally belonging or peculiar (*to*) [weather *proper* to April] **3** conforming to an accepted standard or to good usage; correct [a *proper* spelling] **4** fitting; seemly; right [*proper* modesty] **5** decent; decorous; genteel: often connoting exaggerated respectability ["the *proper* Bostonians"] **6** understood in its most restricted sense; strictly so called: usually following the noun modified [the population of Chicago *proper* (i.e., apart from its suburbs)] **7** [Chiefly Brit.] complete; thorough [a *proper* scoundrel] **8** [Now Chiefly Dial.] *a)* fine; good; excellent *b)* handsome **9** *Eccles.* reserved for a particular day or festival: said of prayers, rites, etc. **10** *Gram. a)* designating a noun that names a specific individual, place, etc., that is not normally used with an article, and that is normally capitalized ["Donald," "Rover," and "Boston" are *proper* nouns, sometimes called *proper* names] (opposed to COMMON) *b)* designating an adjective formed from a proper noun, as *Bostonian* **11** *Heraldry* represented in its natural form or colors —***adv.*** [Dial.] **1** completely; thoroughly **2** properly; correctly —***n.*** [*often* **P-**] *Eccles.* **1** the special office or prayers for a particular day or festival **2** those parts of the Mass which vary according to the particular day or festival —***SYN.*** FIT[1] —**prop′er·ly** ***adv.***

☆**pro·per·din** (prō purd′'n) ***n.*** ⟦< PRO(TEIN) + L *perdere*, to destroy + -IN[1]⟧ a protein present in blood serum and active in the destruction of bacteria and the neutralization of viruses

proper fraction *Math.* a fraction in which the numerator is less, or of lower degree, than the denominator, as ⅖ or x/x^2

proper subset a subset that does not include all the members of the set to which it belongs

prop·er·tied (präp′ər tēd) ***adj.*** owning property

Pro·per·ti·us (prō pur′shəs, -shē əs), **Sextus** 50?-15? B.C.; Rom. poet

prop·er·ty (präp′ər tē) ***n., pl.*** **-ties** ⟦ME *proprete* < OFr *proprieté* < L *proprietas* < *proprius*, one's own⟧ **1** *a)* the right to possess, use, and dispose of something; ownership [*property* in land] *b)* something, as a piece of writing, in which copyright or other rights are held, specif., one acquired for production as a film **2** a thing or things owned; possessions collectively; esp., land or real estate owned **3** a specific piece of land or real estate **4** any trait or attribute proper to a thing or, formerly, to a person; characteristic quality; peculiarity; specif., any of the principal characteristics of a substance, esp. as determined by the senses or by its effect on another substance [the *properties* of a chemical compound] **5** something regarded as being possessed by, or at the disposal of, a person or group of persons [common *property*] **6** *Logic* a quality common to all members of a species or class **7** *Theater, Film, TV* any of the movable articles used as part of the setting or in a piece of stage business, except the costumes, backdrops, etc. —***SYN.*** QUALITY —**prop′er·ty·less** ***adj.***

property man a person in charge of the properties in a theatrical production, film, etc.

property mistress a woman in charge of the properties in a theatrical production, film, etc.

pro·phase (prō′fāz′) ***n.*** ⟦PRO-[1] + PHASE[1]⟧ the first stage in mitosis, during which the chromatin is formed into chromosomes which split into separate paired chromatids

proph·e·cy (präf′ə sē) ***n., pl.*** **-cies** ⟦ME *prophecie* < OFr < LL(Ec) *prophetia* < Gr *prophēteia* (in N.T., gift of speaking under the influence of the Holy Spirit) < *prophētēs:* see PROPHET⟧ **1** prediction of the future under divine or paranormal guidance; act, practice, or ability of a prophet **2** any prediction **3** something prophesied or predicted; specif., the divinely inspired utterance or utterances of a prophet **4** a book of prophecies

proph·e·sy (präf′ə sī′) ***vt.* -sied′, -sy′ing** ⟦ME *prophecien* < MFr *prophecier* < *prophecie:* see prec.⟧ **1** to declare or predict (something) under or as under divine or paranormal guidance **2** to predict (a future event) in any way **3** [Rare] to foreshadow —***vi.*** **1** to speak as a prophet; utter or make prophecies **2** [Rare] to teach religious matters; preach —**proph′e·si′er** ***n.***

proph·et (präf′it) ***n.*** ⟦ME *prophete* < OFr < LL *propheta*, soothsayer, in LL(Ec), prophet < Gr *prophētēs*, interpreter of a god's will (in LXX, a Hebrew prophet; in N.T., an inspired preacher) < *pro-*, before + *phanai*, to speak: see BAN[1]⟧ **1** a person who speaks for God or a god, or as though under divine or paranormal guidance **2** a religious teacher or leader regarded as, or claiming to be, divinely inspired **3** a spokesman for some cause, group, movement, etc. **4** a person who predicts future events in any way —**the Prophet 1** among Muslims, Muhammad ☆**2** among Mormons, Joseph Smith —**the Prophets 1** one of the three major divisions of the Jewish Holy Scriptures, following the Pentateuch and preceding the Hagiographa **2** the authors or subjects of the prophetic books in this division, including Amos, Hosea, Isaiah, Micah, Jeremiah, etc.

proph·et·ess (präf′ə tis) ***n.*** a female prophet: see -ESS

pro·phet·ic (prə fet′ik, prō-) ***adj.*** ⟦MFr *prophetique* < LL(Ec) *propheticus* < Gr *prophētikos*⟧ **1** of, or having the powers of, a prophet **2** of, having the nature of, or containing a prophecy [a *prophetic* utterance] **3** that predicts or foreshadows Also **pro·phet′i·cal** —**pro·phet′i·cal·ly** ***adv.***

pro·phy·lac·tic (prō′fə lak′tik) ***adj.*** ⟦Gr *prophylaktikos* < *prophylassein*, to be on guard < *pro-*, before (see PRO-[1]) + *phylassein*, to guard < *phylax*, guard⟧ preventive or protective; esp., preventing or guarding against disease —***n.*** **1** a prophylactic medicine, device, treatment, etc. ☆**2** a condom

pro·phy·lax·is (prō′fə lak′sis) ***n., pl.*** **-lax′es′** (-sēz′) ⟦ModL < prec., based on Gr *phylaxis*, a watching < *phylax*, guard⟧ **1** the prevention of or protection from disease; prophylactic treatment **2** *Dentistry* a mechanical cleaning of teeth to remove plaque and tartar

pro·pin·qui·ty (prō piŋ′kwə tē, -pin′-) ***n.*** ⟦ME *propinquite* < MFr < L *propinquitas* < *propinquus*, near < *prope*, near⟧ **1** nearness in time or place **2** nearness of relationship; kinship

pro·pi·o·nate (prō′pē ə nāt′) ***n.*** ⟦< fol. + -ATE[2]⟧ a salt or ester of propionic acid

pro·pi·on·ic acid (prō′pē än′ik) ⟦PRO(TO)- + Gr *piōn*, fat (for IE base see FAT) + -IC⟧ a colorless, sharp-smelling, liquid fatty acid, $CH_3CH_2CO_2H$, found in chyme and sweat, and produced from ethanol and carbon monoxide: used in making artificial flavors, perfume esters, preservatives, etc.

pro·pi·ti·ate (prō pish′ē āt′, prə-) ***vt.* -at′ed, -at′ing** ⟦< L *propitiatus*, pp. of *propitiare*, to propitiate < *propitius:* see fol.⟧ to cause to become favorably inclined; win or regain the good will of; appease or conciliate [sacrifices made to *propitiate* the gods] —***SYN.*** PACIFY —**pro·pi′ti·a·ble** (-ē ə bəl) ***adj.*** —**pro·pi′ti·a′tion** ***n.*** —**pro·pi′ti·a′tor** ***n.*** —**pro·pi′ti·a·to′ry** (-ē ə tôr′ē) ***adj.***, **pro·pi′ti·a′tive** (-ē āt′iv, -ē ə tiv)

pro·pi·tious (prō pish′əs, prə-) ***adj.*** ⟦ME *propicius* < OFr < L *propitius*, favorable < *pro-*, before, forward + *petere*, to seek, desire, rush at: see FEATHER⟧ **1** favorably inclined or disposed; gracious [the *propitious* gods] **2** boding well; favorable; auspicious [a *propitious* omen] **3** that favors or furthers; advantageous [*propitious* winds] —***SYN.*** FAVORABLE —**pro·pi′tious·ly** ***adv.*** —**pro·pi′tious·ness** ***n.***

☆**prop·jet** (präp′jet′) ***n.*** TURBOPROP

☆**prop·man** (präp′man′) ***n., pl.*** **-men′** (-men′) *short for* PROPERTY MAN: also written **prop man**

prop·o·lis (präp′ə lis) ***n.*** ⟦L < Gr *propolis*, suburb, also bee glue < *pro-*, before + *polis*, city: see PRO-[1] & POLICE⟧ a brownish, waxy substance collected from the buds of certain trees by bees and used by them to fill crevices in or to seal a honeycomb

pro·pone (prō pōn′) ***vt.* -poned′, -pon′ing** ⟦MScot *proponen* < L *proponere:* see PROPOSE⟧ [Scot.] to bring forward as a plan, excuse, etc.; propose

pro·po·nent (prə pō′nənt, prō-) ***n.*** ⟦< L *proponens*, prp. of *proponere*, to set forth: see PROPOSE⟧ **1** a person who makes a proposal or proposition **2** a person who espouses or supports a cause, etc. **3** *Law* one who propounds something, esp. a will for probate

Pro·pon·tis (prə pän′tis) *ancient name for* Sea of MARMARA

pro·por·tion (prə pôr′shən, prō-) ***n.*** ⟦ME *proporcioun* < MFr *proporcion* < L *proportio* < *pro*, FOR[1] + *portio*, part: see PORTION⟧ **1** the comparative relation between parts, things, or elements with respect to size, amount, degree, etc.; ratio **2** a part, share, or portion, esp. in its relation to the whole; quota **3** relationship between parts or things; esp., harmonious, proper, or desirable relationship; balance or symmetry **4** size, degree, or extent relative to a standard **5** [*pl.*] dimensions [a building of large *proportions*] **6** *Math. a)* an equality between ratios; relationship between four quantities in which the quotient of the first divided by the second is equal to that of the third divided by the fourth (Ex.: 6 is to 2 as 9 is to 3) (also called **geometrical proportion**) *b)* RULE OF THREE —***vt.*** **1** to cause to be in proper relation, harmony, or balance [to *proportion* the punishment to the crime] **2** to arrange the parts of (a whole) so as to be harmonious or properly balanced —***SYN.*** SYMMETRY —**pro·por′tion·ment** ***n.***

pro·por·tion·a·ble (prə pôr′shən ə bəl) ***adj.*** ⟦ME *proporcionable* < LL *proportionabilis*⟧ [Archaic] PROPORTIONAL

pro·por·tion·al (prə pôr′shə nəl, prō-) ***adj.*** ⟦ME *proporcional* < L *proportionalis*] 1 of or determined by proportion; relative 2 having, or being in, proportion [pay *proportional* to work done] 3 *Math.* having the same or a constant ratio —*n.* a quantity in a mathematical proportion —SYN. PROPORTIONATE —**pro·por′tion·al′i·ty** (-shə nal′ə tē) *n.* —**pro·por′tion·al·ly** *adv.*

proportional representation a system of voting that gives minority parties representation in a legislature in proportion to their popular vote

pro·por·tion·ate (prə pôr′shə nit, prō-; *for v.*, -shə nāt′) *adj.* [ME *proporcionate* < LL *proportionatus*] in proper proportion; proportional —*vt.* **-at′ed, -at′ing** to make proportionate; proportion —**pro·por′tion·ate·ly** *adv.*

SYN.—**proportionate** and **proportional** both imply a being in due proportion, the former usually being preferred with reference to two things that have a reciprocal relationship to each other [the output was *proportionate* to the energy expended], and the latter, with reference to a number of similar or related things [*proportional* representation]; **commensurable** applies to things measurable by the same standard or to things properly proportioned; **commensurate**, in addition, implies equality in measure or size of things that are alike or somehow related to each other [a reward *commensurate* with their heroism] —ANT. **disproportionate**

pro·pos·al (prə pōz′əl) *n.* 1 the act of proposing 2 a plan, action, etc. proposed 3 an offer of marriage

SYN.—**proposal** refers to a plan, offer, etc. presented for acceptance or rejection [the *proposal* for a decrease in taxes was approved]; **proposition**, commonly used in place of **proposal** with reference to business dealings and the like, in a strict sense applies to a statement, theorem, etc. set forth for argument, demonstration, proof, etc. [the *proposition* that all men are created equal]

pro·pose (prə pōz′) *vt.* **-posed′, -pos′ing** [LME < OFr *proposer*, altered (infl. by *poser*: see POSE[1]) < L *proponere* (pp. *propositus*), to set forth, display, propose: see PRO-[2] & POSITION] 1 to put forth for consideration or acceptance 2 to purpose, plan, or intend 3 to suggest drinking (a toast) 4 to nominate (someone) for membership, office, etc. —*vi.* 1 to make a proposal; form or declare a purpose or design 2 to offer marriage —SYN. INTEND —**pro·pos′er** *n.*

prop·o·si·tion (präp′ə zish′ən) *n.* [ME *proposicioun* < OFr *proposition* < L *propositio* < *proponere*: see prec.] 1 the act of proposing 2 *a)* something proposed; proposal, plan ☆*b)* an unethical or immoral proposal, specif. one of illicit sexual relations in return for some gain 3 a subject or statement to be discussed or debated ☆4 a proposed deal, as in business ☆5 a person, problem, undertaking, etc. being or to be dealt with 6 [Archaic] a setting forth; offering 7 *Logic* an informative statement whose truth or falsity can be evaluated by means of logic 8 *Math.* a theorem to be demonstrated or a problem to be solved —☆*vt.* to make a proposition, esp. an improper one, to —SYN. PROPOSAL —**prop′o·si′tion·al** *adj.*

propositional function *Logic* an expression containing at least one variable, that becomes a proposition when a constant is substituted for the variable (Ex.: x is a man)

pro·pos·i·tus (prō päz′i təs) *n.*, *pl.* **-ti′** (-tī′) [ModL < L: see PROPOSE] the family member chosen as the starting point in genealogical research, in the investigation of an inheritable disease, etc.

pro·pound (prə pound′, prō-) *vt.* [altered < PROPONE] to put forward for consideration; propose —**pro·pound′er** *n.*

pro·pox·y·phene hydrochloride (prō päk′sə fēn′) [< *prop-* (< PROPIONIC ACID) + OXY-[1] + PHEN-] a white, crystalline, narcotic analgesic, $C_{22}H_{29}NO_2 \cdot HCl$, used for the alleviation of moderate pain

pro·prae·tor or **pro·pre·tor** (prō prēt′ər) *n.* [L *propraetor*, orig. *pro praetore* < *pro*, for + *praetor*, PRAETOR] a magistrate who was sent to govern a Roman province after having served as praetor in Rome

pro·pran·o·lol (prō pran′ə lôl′, -lōl′) [*(iso)pro(pylaminonaphthyloxy-) pr(op)anol* + -OL[2]] *n.* a drug, $C_{16}H_{21}NO_2$, that inhibits the activity of epinephrine and similar substances, used in controlling irregular heartbeats and in treating angina pectoris

pro·pri·e·tar·y (prə prī′ə ter′ē, prō-) *n.*, *pl.* **-tar′ies** [LL *proprietarius* < L *proprietas*: see PROPERTY] 1 a proprietor or owner 2 a group of proprietors 3 proprietorship or ownership ☆4 the grantee or owner of a proprietary colony in colonial America 5 a proprietary medicine —*adj.* 1 belonging to a proprietor 2 holding property 3 of property or proprietorship 4 privately owned and operated [a *proprietary* nursing home] 5 held under patent, trademark, or copyright by a private person or company [a *proprietary* medicine]

☆**proprietary colony** any of certain North American colonies that were granted by the British Crown to an individual or group with full governing rights

pro·pri·e·tor (prə prī′ə tər, prō-) *n.* [irreg. formation < PROPRIET(ARY) + -OR] 1 a person who has a legal title or exclusive right to some property; owner ☆2 the owner of a proprietary colony 3 one who owns and operates a business establishment —**pro·pri′e·tor·ship′** *n.*

pro·pri·e·to·ri·al (prə prī′ə tôr′ē əl, prō-) *adj.* PROPRIETARY (senses 1-3)

pro·pri·e·tress (prə prī′ə tris, prō-) *n.* a female proprietor: see -ESS

pro·pri·e·ty (prə prī′ə tē, prō-) *n.*, *pl.* **-ties** [ME *propriete* < OFr *proprieté*: see PROPERTY] 1 the quality of being proper, fitting, or suitable; fitness 2 conformity with what is proper or fitting 3 conformity with accepted standards of proper manners or behavior 4 [Archaic] *a)* peculiar or proper nature or state *b)* a peculiarity 5 [Obs.] private property —SYN. DECORUM —**the proprieties** accepted standards of behavior in polite society

pro·pri·o·cep·tion (prō′prē ə sep′shən) *n.* *Physiol.* the normal awareness of one's posture, movement, balance, and location based on the sensations received by the proprioceptors

pro·pri·o·cep·tive (prō′prē ə sep′tiv) *adj.* [< L *proprius*, one's own + (RE)CEPTIVE] designating or of stimuli produced in bodily tissues, as the muscles or tendons, and received there by the proprioceptors

pro·pri·o·cep·tor (-tər) *n.* [< L *proprius*, one's own + (RE)CEPTOR] any of the sensory end organs in the muscles, tendons, etc. that are sensitive to the stimuli originated in these organs by the movement of the body or its parts

prop root a root that descends externally from a plant stem into the ground, helping to support the stem, as on a mangrove

☆**props** (präps) *n.* [shortened < *propers* (< *proper respect*)] [Slang] praise, respect, or recognition that is due or deserved

prop·to·sis (präp tō′sis) *n.*, *pl.* **-ses′** (-sēz′) [ModL < LL < Gr *proptōsis* < *propiptein*, to fall forward < *pro-*, before (see PRO-[1]) + *piptein*, to fall: see FEATHER] *Med.* an abnormal protrusion or displacement, as of the eyeball

pro·pul·sion (prə pul′shən) *n.* [< L *propulsus*, pp. of *propellere* (see PROPEL) + -ION] 1 a propelling or being propelled 2 something that propels; propelling or driving force —**pro·pul′sive** *adj.* or **pro·pul′so·ry**

pro·pyl (prō′pil) *n.* [PROP(IONIC ACID) + -YL] the monovalent radical C_3H_7, having two isomeric forms —**pro·pyl′ic** *adj.*

prop·y·lae·um (präp′ə lē′əm) *n.*, *pl.* **-lae′a** (-lē′ə) [L < Gr *propylaion*, orig. neut. of *propylaios*, before the gate < *pro-*, before + *pylē*, gate] in classical architecture, an entrance, vestibule, or portico before a building or group of buildings

propyl alcohol a colorless liquid, $CH_3CH_2CH_2OH$, soluble in water, alcohol, or ether and used in organic synthesis and as a solvent, antiseptic, etc.

pro·pyl·ene (prō′pə lēn′) *n.* [PROPYL + -ENE] an unsaturated, flammable alkene, $CH_3CH{:}CH_2$, a colorless gas obtained in the refining of petroleum, used in making polypropylene, synthetic glycerol, etc.

propylene glycol a colorless, viscous liquid, $C_3H_8O_2$, used as an antifreeze, in the manufacture of polyester resins, etc.

prop·y·lite (präp′ə līt′) *n.* [< Gr *propylon*, gateway (< *pro-*, before + *pylē*, gate) + -ITE[1]] a dark-colored form of andesite altered by the action of hot springs and consisting of such minerals as calcite, chlorite, etc.

pro ra·ta (prō rāt′ə, rät′ə) [L *pro rata (parte)*, according to the calculated (share)] in proportion; proportionate(ly)

☆**pro·rate** (prō rāt′, prō′rāt′) *vt.*, *vi.* **-rat′ed, -rat′ing** [< prec.] to divide, assess, or distribute proportionally —**pro·rat′a·ble** *adj.* —**pro·ra′tion** *n.*

pro·rogue (prō rōg′) *vt.*, *vi.* **-rogued′, -rogu′ing** [ME *prorogen* < MFr *proroguer* < L *prorogare*, to defer, prolong < *pro-*, for + *rogare*, to ask, akin to *regere*, to direct: see RIGHT] 1 [Obs.] to defer; delay; postpone 2 to discontinue or end a session of (a legislative assembly, as the British Parliament) Also **pro′ro·gate′, -gat′ed, -gat′ing** —SYN. ADJOURN —**pro′ro·ga′tion** (-rō gā′shən) *n.*

pros *abbrev.* prosody

pro·sa·ic (prō zā′ik) *adj.* [LL *prosaicus* < L *prosa*, PROSE] 1 of or like prose rather than poetry; often, specif., heavy, flat, unimaginative, etc. 2 commonplace, dull and ordinary [*prosaic* details of everyday life] —**pro·sa′i·cal·ly** *adv.* —**pro·sa′ic·ness** *n.*

pro·sa·ism (prō′zā iz′əm) *n.* [Fr *prosaïsme*] 1 prosaic quality or style 2 a prosaic expression

pro·sce·ni·um (prō sē′nē əm) *n.*, *pl.* **-ni·ums** or **-ni·a** (-ə) [L < Gr *proskēnion* < *pro-*, before + *skēnē*, tent, stage: see SCENE] 1 the stage of an ancient Greek or Roman theater 2 *a)* the apron of a stage *b)* the plane separating the stage proper from the audience and including the arch (**proscenium arch**) and the curtain within it

pro·sciut·to (prə shōō′tō; *It* prô shōōt′tô) *n.* [It < *prosciugare*, to dry out, altered (prob. infl. by *pro-* < L, PRO-[1]) < LL **perexsucare* < *per-* (< L, PER-) + *exsucare*, to extract juice from < L *exsuctus*, pp. of *exsugere*, to suck out: see EX-[1] & SUCK] a spicy Italian ham, cured by drying and served in very thin slices, often with melon

pro·scribe (prō skrīb′) *vt.* **-scribed′, -scrib′ing** [ME *proscriben* < L *proscribere* < *pro-*, PRO-[2] + *scribere*, to write: see SCRIBE] 1 in ancient Rome, to publish the name of (a person) condemned to death, banishment, etc. 2 to deprive of the protection of the law; outlaw 3 to banish; exile 4 to denounce or forbid the practice, use, etc. of; interdict —**pro·scrib′er** *n.*

pro·scrip·tion (prō skrip′shən) *n.* [ME *proscripcioun* < L *proscriptio* < *proscriptus*, pp.] 1 a proscribing or being proscribed 2 prohibition or interdiction —**pro·scrip′tive** *adj.* —**pro·scrip′tive·ly** *adv.*

prose (prōz) *n.* [ME < MFr < L *prosa*, for *prorsa (oratio)*, direct (speech) < *prorsus*, forward, straight on < *proversus*, pp. of *provertere*, to turn forward: see PRO-[2] & VERSE] 1 the ordinary form of written or spoken language, without rhyme or meter; speech or writing, sometimes, specif., nonfictional writing, that is not poetry 2 dull, commonplace talk, expression, quality, etc. —*adj.* 1 of or in prose 2 dull; unimaginative; commonplace; prosaic —*vt.*, *vi.* **prosed, pros′ing** to speak, write, or express (one's thoughts, etc.) in prose or in a prosaic way

pro·sec·tor (prō sek′tər) *n.* [LL(Ec), anatomist < L *prosectus*, pp. of *prosecare*, to cut up < *pro-*, before + *secare*, to cut: see SAW[1]] a person skilled in dissection who prepares subjects for anatomical demonstration

pros·e·cute (präs′ə kyōōt′) *vt.* **-cut′ed, -cut′ing** [ME *prosecuten* < L *prosecutus*, pp. of *prosequi* < *pro-*, PRO-[2] + *sequi*, to follow: see SEQUENT] 1 to follow up or pursue (something) to a conclusion [to *prosecute* a war with vigor] **2** to carry on; engage in **3** *a)* to institute legal proceedings against, or conduct criminal proceedings in court against *b)* to try to get, enforce, etc. by legal process [to *prosecute* a claim] —*vi.* **1** to institute and carry on a legal suit **2** to act as prosecutor —**pros′e·cut′a·ble** *adj.*

☆**prosecuting attorney** a public official, as a district attorney, who conducts criminal prosecutions on behalf of the State or people

pros·e·cu·tion (präs′ə kyo͞o′shən) *n.* ⟦ML *prosecutio* < LL, a following < L *prosecutus:* see PROSECUTE⟧ **1** a prosecuting, or following up **2** *a)* the conducting of criminal proceedings in court against a person *b)* the conducting of any lawsuit **3** the State as the party that institutes and carries on criminal proceedings in court

pros·e·cu·tor (präs′ə kyo͞ot′ər) *n.* ⟦ML < LL, companion, attendant⟧ **1** a person who prosecutes **2** *Law a)* a person who institutes a prosecution in court *b)* PROSECUTING ATTORNEY

pros·e·cu·to·ri·al (präs′ə kyo͞o tôr′ē əl) *adj.* **1** of or having to do with a prosecutor **2** like a prosecutor, as in being relentless, aggressive, etc. in the pursuit of some goal

pros·e·lyte (präs′ə līt′) *n.* ⟦ME *proselite* < LL(Ec) *proselytus* < Gr *prosēlytos,* stranger, sojourner (in N.T., a convert) < 2d aorist stem of *proserchesthai,* to come < *pros,* toward + *erchesthai,* to come, akin to *orcheisthai:* see ORCHESTRA⟧ a person who has been converted from one religion to another, or from one belief, sect, party, etc. to another

pros·e·lyt·ism (präs′ə lə tiz′əm) *n.* **1** the fact of becoming or being a proselyte **2** the act or practice of proselytizing

pros·e·lyt·ize (präs′ə lə tīz′) *vi., vt.* **-ized′**, **-iz′ing** **1** to try to convert (a person), especially to one's religion **2** to persuade to do or join something, especially by offering an inducement —**pros′e·lyt·iz′er** *n.*

☆**pro·sem·i·nar** (prō sem′ə när′) *n.* a seminar open to undergraduate students of advanced standing

pros·en·ceph·a·lon (präs′en sef′ə län′, -lən) *n., pl.* **-la** (-lə) ⟦ModL < Gr *pros,* near + *encephalon:* see ENCEPHALO-⟧ FOREBRAIN —**pros′en′ce·phal′ic** (-en′sə fal′ik) *adj.*

pros·en·chy·ma (präs eŋ′ki mə, -en′-) *n.* ⟦ModL < Gr *pros,* to, toward, near + *enchyma,* infusion: see PARENCHYMA⟧ a tissue of thick-walled, elongated cells without much protoplasm, found in some plants —**pros′en·chym′a·tous** (-kim′ə təs) *adj.*

pros·er (prō′zər) *n.* **1** [Rare] a writer of prose **2** a person who talks or writes in a prosaic or boring manner

Pro·ser·pi·na (prō sur′pi nə) *n.* ⟦L⟧ *Rom. Myth.* the daughter of Ceres and wife of Pluto: identified with the Greek Persephone: also **Pro·ser·pi·ne** (präs′ər pīn′, prō sur′pi nē′)

pro shop a retail shop, as at a golf course or tennis club, specializing in equipment for the sport and, often, managed by a resident PRO² (*n.* 2)

pro·sim·i·an (prō sim′ē ən) *n.* any of a suborder (Strepsirhini) of small, arboreal primates, including lemurs, lorises, and bush babies

pro·sit (prō′zit; *E* prō′sit) *interj.* ⟦Ger < L, 3d pers. sing., subj., of *prodesse,* to do good < *pro,* for + *esse,* to be⟧ to your health: used as a toast

☆**pro·slav·er·y** (prō slāv′ər ē) *adj.* in favor of slavery

☆**pro·so** (prō′sō) *n.* ⟦Russ⟧ MILLET (sense 1*a*)

pro·sod·ic (prō säd′ik) *adj.* of, or according to the principles of, prosody: also **pro·sod′i·cal** —**pro·sod′i·cal·ly** *adv.*

pros·o·dy (präs′ə dē) *n., pl.* **-dies** ⟦ME *prosodye* < L *prosodia* < Gr *prosōidia,* tone, accent, song sung to music < *pros,* to + *ōidē,* song: see ODE⟧ **1** the science or art of versification, including the study of metrical structure, stanza forms, etc. **2** a particular system or style of versification and metrical structure [Dryden's *prosody*]

pro·so·pag·no·si·a (prō′sō pag nō′sē ə, -zē ə) *n.* ⟦ModL < Gr *prosōpon,* person, face (see PROSOPOPOEIA) + *agnōsia,* ignorance: see AGNOSIA⟧ a type of agnosia in which a person cannot recognize familiar faces

pros·o·pog·ra·phy (präs′ə päg′rə fē) *n.* ⟦< ModL < Gr *prosōpon,* person, face (see fol.) + *graphein,* to write: see GRAPHIC⟧ the study of careers, esp. of individuals linked by family, economic, social, or political relationships —**pros·o·po·graph·i·cal** (präs′ə pə graf′i kəl) *adj.*

pro·so·po·poe·ia (prō sō′pō pē′ə) *n.* ⟦L < Gr *prosōpopoiia* < *prosōpon,* person, face, mask (< *pros,* near + *ōps,* EYE) + *poiein,* to make: see POET²⟧ *Rhetoric* **1** a figure in which an absent, dead, or imaginary person is represented as speaking **2** PERSONIFICATION (sense 3)

pros·pect (präs′pekt′) *n.* ⟦ME *prospecte* < L *prospectus,* lookout < *prospicere,* to look forward < *pro-,* forward + *specere,* to look: see SPY⟧ **1** *a)* a broad view; scene *b)* a place affording such a view **2** a mental view or examination; survey **3** the view obtained from any particular point; outlook **4** a looking forward to something; anticipation **5** *a)* something hoped for or expected; anticipated outcome *b)* [*usually pl.*] apparent chance for success **6** a likely or prospective customer, candidate, undertaking, etc. ☆**7** *Mining a)* a place where a mineral deposit is sought or found *b)* a sample of gravel, earth, etc. tested for a particular mineral, or the resulting yield of mineral —*vi.* ☆to explore or search (*for*) [to *prospect* for gold] —*vt.* ☆to explore or search (a place or region) for oil, mineral deposits, etc. —**in prospect** expected

pro·spec·tive (prə spek′tiv, prä-, prō-) *adj.* ⟦LL *prospectivus* < *prospectus:* see prec.⟧ **1** looking toward the future **2** expected; likely; future —**pro·spec′tive·ly** *adv.*

☆**pros·pec·tor** (präs′pek′tər) *n.* ⟦LL, one who looks out⟧ a person who prospects for valuable ores, oil, etc.

pro·spec·tus (prə spek′təs, prä-, prō-) *n.* ⟦L: see PROSPECT⟧ a statement outlining the main features of a new or proposed publication, business enterprise, etc., or the attractions of an established institution such as a college, hotel, etc.; often, specif., a document, made available to investors, containing detailed information about a stock issue, mutual fund, etc.

pros·per (präs′pər) *vi.* ⟦ME *prosperen* < MFr *prosperer* < L *prosperare,* to cause to prosper < *prosperus,* favorable < *prospere,* fortunately < *pro spere* < *pro,* according to (see PRO-²) + stem of *spes,* hope < IE base **spēi-,* to flourish, succeed > SPEED⟧ to succeed, thrive, grow, etc. in a vigorous way —*vt.* [Archaic] to cause to prosper

pros·per·i·ty (präs per′ə tē) *n., pl.* **-ties** ⟦ME *prosperite* < OFr < L *prosperitas* < *prosperus*⟧ prosperous condition; good fortune, wealth, success, etc.

Pros·per·o (präs′pə rō′) *n.* the deposed, magic-working Duke of Milan in Shakespeare's *The Tempest,* exiled on an island with his daughter Miranda

pros·per·ous (präs′pər əs) *adj.* ⟦ME < MFr *prospereus:* see PROSPER & -OUS⟧ **1** having continued success; prospering; flourishing **2** well-to-do; well-off **3** conducive to success; favorable —**pros′per·ous·ly** *adv.*

pross (präs) *n.* [Slang] PROSTITUTE (sense 1*a*): also **pross′ie**

prost (prōst) *interj.* ⟦Ger⟧ PROSIT

pros·ta·cy·clin (präs′tə sī′klin) *n.* ⟦< fol. + CYCL(O)- + -IN¹⟧ a derivative of prostaglandins that forms in the walls of blood vessels, prevents blood clots, and, usually, dilates blood vessels: cf. THROMBOXANE

pros·ta·glan·din (präs′tə glan′din) *n.* ⟦< fol. + GLAND¹ + -IN¹⟧ any of a group of hormonelike fatty acids found throughout the body, esp. in semen, that affect blood pressure, metabolism, body temperature, and other important body processes

pros·tate (präs′tāt′) *adj.* ⟦ML *prostata* < Gr *prostatēs,* one standing before < *proistanai,* to set before < *pro-,* before + *histanai,* to STAND⟧ of or relating to the prostate gland: also **pros·tat′ic** (-tat′ik) —*n.* PROSTATE GLAND

pros·ta·tec·to·my (präs′tə tek′tə mē) *n., pl.* **-mies** ⟦PROSTAT(O)- + -ECTOMY⟧ the surgical removal of all or part of the prostate gland

prostate gland a partly muscular gland surrounding the urethra at the base of the bladder in most male mammals: it secretes an alkaline fluid that is discharged with the sperm

pros·ta·tism (präs′tə tiz′əm) *n.* a chronic disorder of the prostate gland, characterized by enlargement of the gland and resulting in obstruction of the flow of urine

pros·ta·ti·tis (präs′tə tīt′is) *n.* ⟦see -ITIS⟧ inflammation of the prostate gland

pros·ta·to- (präs′tə tō) *combining form* prostate gland: also, before a vowel, **prostat-**

pros·the·sis (präs′thə sis; *for 2, usually* präs thē′-) *n.* ⟦LL < Gr *prosthesis* < *prostithenai* < *pros,* to, at + *tithenai,* to place, DO¹⟧ **1** *var. of* PROTHESIS (sense 1) **2** *pl.* **-the′ses′** (-thē′sēz′) *Med. a)* the replacement of a missing part of the body, as a limb, eye, or tooth, by an artificial substitute *b)* such a substitute

pros·thet·ic (präs thet′ik) *adj.* **1** of a prothesis or prosthetics **2** *Chem.* designating or of any of a number of nonprotein compounds when combined chemically with a protein molecule

pros·thet·ics (präs thet′iks) *n.* ⟦< prec.⟧ the branch of surgery dealing with the replacement of missing parts, esp. limbs, by artificial substitutes —**pros·the·tist** (präs′thə tist) *n.*

☆**pros·tho·don·tics** (präs′thə dän′tiks) *n.* ⟦ModL: see PROSTHETIC, -ODONT, & -ICS⟧ the branch of dentistry dealing with the replacement of missing teeth, as by bridges or artificial dentures: also **pros′tho·don′ti·a** (-dän′shə, -shē ə) —**pros′tho·don′tic** *adj.* —**pros′tho·don′tist** *n.*

pros·tie (präs′tē) *n.* [Slang] PROSTITUTE (sense 1*a*)

pros·ti·tute (präs′tə to͞ot′, -tyo͞ot′) *vt.* **-tut′ed**, **-tut′ing** ⟦< L *prostitutus,* pp. of *prostituere* < *pro-,* before + *statuere,* to cause to stand, akin to *stare,* STAND⟧ **1** to sell the services of (oneself or another) for purposes of sexual intercourse **2** to sell (oneself, one's artistic or moral integrity, etc.) for low or unworthy purposes —*adj.* [Rare] given over to base purposes; debased; corrupt —*n.* **1** *a)* a woman who engages in promiscuous sexual activity for pay; whore; harlot *b)* a man who engages in such activity, esp. homosexual acts, for pay **2** a person, as a writer, artist, etc., who sells his or her services for low or unworthy purposes —**pros′ti·tu′tor** *n.*

pros·ti·tu·tion (präs′tə to͞o′shən, -tyo͞o′-) *n.* ⟦LL(Ec) *prostitutio*⟧ the act or practice of prostituting, or the fact of being prostituted; esp., the trade of a prostitute

pro·sto·mi·um (prō stō′mē əm) *n., pl.* **-mi·a** (-ə) ⟦ModL: see PRO-¹, STOMA, & -IUM⟧ a small, noselike portion of the first body segment in many annelid worms, lying above and overhanging the mouth in earthworms

pros·trate (präs′trāt′) *adj.* ⟦ME *prostrat* < L *prostratus,* pp. of *prosternere,* to lay flat < *pro-,* before + *sternere,* to stretch out < IE base **ster-* > STREW⟧ **1** lying with the face downward in demonstration of great humility or abject submission **2** lying flat, prone, or supine **3** thrown or fallen to the ground **4** *a)* laid low; completely overcome; helpless [*prostrate* with grief] *b)* in a state of physical exhaustion or weakness **5** *Bot.* growing on the ground; trailing —*vt.* **-trat′ed**, **-trat′ing** **1** to throw or put in a prostrate position; lay flat on the ground **2** to lay low; overcome; exhaust or subjugate —**SYN.** PRONE

pros·tra·tion (präs trā′shən) *n.* ⟦LL *prostratio*⟧ **1** a prostrating or being prostrated **2** utter physical or mental exhaustion or helplessness

pro·style (prō′stīl′) *adj.* ⟦L *prostylus* < Gr *prostylos* < *pro-,* before + *stylos,* pillar: see STYLITE⟧ *Archit.* having a portico whose columns, usually four in number, extend in a line across the front only, as in a Greek temple —*n.* **1** such a portico **2** a prostyle building

pros·y (prō′zē) *adj.* **pros′i·er**, **pros′i·est** prosaic; commonplace, dull, uninteresting, etc. —**pros′i·ly** *adv.* —**pros′i·ness** *n.*

Prot *abbrev.* Protestant

prot- *combining form* PROTO-: used before a vowel

pro·tac·tin·i·um (prō′tak tin′ē əm) ***n.*** ⟦ModL: see PROTO- & ACTINIUM⟧ a rare, radioactive, metallic chemical element, one of the actinides, found in pitchblende: symbol, Pa; at. no. 91: see the periodic table of elements in the Reference Supplement

pro·tag·o·nist (prō tag′ə nist) ***n.*** ⟦Gr *prōtagōnistēs* < *prōtos,* first + *agōnistēs,* actor < *agōnizesthai:* see AGONIZE⟧ **1** the main character in a drama, novel, or story, around whom the action centers **2** a person who is a leader, activist, proponent, etc.

Pro·tag·o·ras (prō tag′ə rəs) 481?-411? B.C.; Gr. philosopher: one of the principal Sophists

pro·ta·mine (prōt′ə mēn′, -min) ***n.*** ⟦PROT(O)- + AMINE⟧ any of a class of simple proteins that are soluble in ammonia, do not coagulate by heat, and yield relatively few amino acids upon hydrolysis: used to control hemorrhage

pro·ta·no·pi·a (prō′tə nō′pē ə) ***n.*** ⟦ModL: see PROTO-, AN-[1], & -OPIA⟧ a defect of color vision characterized by the inability to see red

prot·a·sis (prät′ə sis) ***n., pl.*** **-ses′** (-sēz′) ⟦LL < Gr < *proteinein,* to stretch before, present < *pro-,* before + *teinein,* to stretch: see THIN⟧ **1** *Drama* the opening of a play, in which the characters are introduced **2** *Gram.* the clause that expresses the condition in a conditional sentence: opposed to APODOSIS

pro·te·a (prōt′ē ə) ***n.*** ⟦ModL < L *Proteus* (see PROTEUS), with ref. to the wide variety of forms among its species⟧ any of a genus (*Protea*) of mostly tropical, evergreen shrubs and small trees of the protea family, with very large, colorful flowers resembling sunflowers —***adj.*** designating a family (Proteaceae, order Proteales) of ornamental, dicotyledonous trees, shrubs, and plants, including banksia

pro·te·an¹ (prōt′ē ən, prō tē′ən) ***adj.*** **1** [**P-**] of or like Proteus **2** very changeable; readily taking on different shapes and forms **3** showing different abilities or great variety; versatile

pro·te·an² (prōt′ē ən) ***n.*** ⟦PROTE(IN) + -AN⟧ any of a group of insoluble derived proteins that are the first products of the action of water, dilute acids, or enzymes on proteins

pro·te·ase (prōt′ē ās′) ***n.*** ⟦PROTE(IN) + (DIAST)ASE⟧ any hydrolase enzyme, as pepsin or trypsin, that acts as a catalyst in chemical reactions in which a protein is broken down by hydrolysis

protease inhibitor any of a class of synthetic, antiviral drugs that limit or block the production of protease enzymes, which are essential in the reproductive cycle of the AIDS virus

pro·tect (prə tekt′, prō-) ***vt.*** ⟦< L *protectus,* pp. of *protegere,* to protect < *pro-,* before + *tegere,* to cover: see THATCH⟧ **1** to shield from injury, danger, or loss; guard; defend **2** *Commerce* to set aside funds toward the payment of (a note, draft, etc.) at maturity **3** *Econ.* to guard (domestic industry) as by tariffs on imported products —**pro·tect′a·ble** ***adj.***

pro·tec·tant (prə tek′tənt, prō-) ***n.*** a substance applied to some surface in order to protect it from damage or injury

pro·tec·tion (prə tek′shən, prō-) ***n.*** ⟦ME *proteccioun* < MFr *protection* < LL *protectio*⟧ **1** *a)* a protecting or being protected *b)* an instance of this **2** a person or thing that protects **3** a device, as a condom, used to prevent conception or the spread of sexually transmitted diseases **4** a safe-conduct pass or passport ☆**5** [Informal] *a)* money extorted by racketeers threatening violence *b)* bribes paid to officials by racketeers to avoid prosecution **6** *Econ.* the system of protecting domestic products as by taxing imported goods

pro·tec·tion·ism (-iz′əm) ***n.*** *Econ.* the system, theory, or policy of protection —**pro·tec′tion·ist** ***n., adj.***

pro·tec·tive (prə tek′tiv, prō-) ***adj.*** **1** protecting, or serving, intended, or alleged to protect [*a protective* gesture, *protective* custody] **2** *Econ.* serving or intended to protect domestic products, industries, etc. against foreign competition [*a protective* tariff] —**pro·tec′tive·ly** ***adv.*** —**pro·tec′tive·ness** ***n.***

protective coloration (*or* coloring) natural coloration of certain organisms allowing them to blend in with their normal environment and escape detection by enemies

pro·tec·tor (prə tek′tər, prō-) ***n.*** ⟦ME *protectour* < MFr < LL *protector*⟧ **1** a person or thing that protects; guardian; defender **2** *Eng. History a)* a person ruling a kingdom during the minority, absence, or incapacity of the sovereign *b)* [**P-**] the title held by Oliver Cromwell (1653-58) and his son Richard (1658-59), during the British Protectorate (in full **Lord Protector**) —**pro·tec′tor·al** ***adj.*** —**pro·tec′tor·ship′** ***n.***

pro·tec·tor·ate (prə tek′tər it, prō-) ***n.*** **1** government by a protector **2** the office or term of office of a protector **3** *a)* the relation of a strong state to a weaker state under its control and protection *b)* a state or territory so controlled and protected **4** [**P-**] the government of England under Oliver Cromwell and his son Richard (1653-59)

pro·tec·to·ry (-tər ē) ***n., pl.*** **-ries** [Historical] a church-operated institution for the protection of destitute children

pro·tec·tress (-tris) ***n.*** a female protector: see -ESS

pro·té·gé (prōt′ə zhā′, prōt′ə zhā′) ***n.*** ⟦Fr, pp. of *protéger,* to protect < L *protegere:* see PROTECT⟧ a person guided and helped, esp. in the furtherance of his or her career, by another, more influential person

pro·té·gée (prōt′ə zhā′, prōt′ə zhā′) ***n.*** a female protégé

pro·te·id (prō′tē id) ***n.*** *rare var. of* PROTEIN

pro·tein (prō′tēn′, prō′tē in) ***n.*** ⟦Ger < Fr *protéine* < Gr *prōteios,* prime, chief < *prōtos,* first (see PROTO-): from being a chief constituent of plant and animal bodies⟧ any of a large class of complex polymers consisting of long chains of polypeptides often bonded with nucleic acids, lipids, etc.: proteins are found in all cells, are essential to the diet of animals, are the basic components of cartilage, hair, skin, etc., and often function as enzymes, hormones, or antibodies

pro·tein·a·ceous (pro′tē nā′shəs, -tē ə nā′-) ***adj.*** of, having to do with, or resembling protein

pro·tein·ase (prō′tē nās′, -tē ə nās′) ***n.*** PROTEASE

pro·tein·oid (-noid′) ***n.*** any of a group of synthetic, proteinlike polymers formed from amino acids subjected to heat and other conditions such as may have prevailed on earth billions of years ago; primordial protein

pro·tein·u·ri·a (prō′tē nyoor′ē ə, -tē ə nyoor′-) ***n.*** ⟦ModL: see -URIA⟧ the presence of protein in the urine

pro tem·po·re (prō tem′pə rē′) ⟦L⟧ for the time (being); temporary or temporarily: often shortened to **pro tem**

pro·te·o- (prōt′ē ō) *combining form* protein [*proteoclastic*]: also, before a vowel, **pro′te-**

pro·te·o·clas·tic (prōt′ē ō klas′tik) ***adj.*** ⟦< prec. + Gr *klastos,* broken: see CLASTIC⟧ of, related to, or initiating proteolysis

pro·te·ol·y·sis (prōt′ē äl′ə sis) ***n.*** ⟦ModL: see PROTEIN & -LYSIS⟧ *Biochem.* the breaking down of proteins, as by gastric juices, to form simpler substances —**pro′te·o·lyt′ic** (-ō lit′ik) ***adj.***

pro·te·ose (prōt′ē ōs′) ***n.*** ⟦PROTE(IN) + -OSE¹⟧ any of a class of water-soluble products, formed in the hydrolysis of proteins, that can be broken down to peptones

Prot·er·o·zo·ic (prät′ə rə zō′ik, prōt′-) ***adj.*** ⟦< Gr *proteros,* former, compar. of *pro,* forward (see PRO-¹) + ZO- + -IC⟧ [*sometimes* **p-**] designating or of the geologic eon characterized by the development of sedimentary rock, shallow seas, and the first soft-bodied marine invertebrates; Precambrian, esp. late Precambrian —**the Proterozoic** the Proterozoic Eon or its rocks: see the geologic time chart in the Reference Supplement

pro·test (prō test′, prə-; *also, and for n. & adj. always* prō′test′) ***vt.*** ⟦ME *protesten* < MFr *protester* < L *protestari* < *pro-,* PRO-² + *testari,* to affirm < *testis,* witness: see TESTIFY⟧ **1** to state positively; affirm solemnly; assert ☆**2** to make objection to; speak strongly against **3** to make a written declaration of the nonpayment of (a bill of exchange or a promissory note) —***vi.*** **1** to make solemn affirmation **2** to express disapproval; object; dissent —***n.*** **1** the act or an instance of objecting; remonstrance [Eric resigned in *protest*] **2** a document formally objecting to something **3** *Law a)* a written declaration by a notary on behalf of the holder of a bill or note, showing that it has not been honored by the drawer *b)* a written declaration by the master of a ship attesting to the fact that damages or losses were sustained from unavoidable natural causes, and rejecting any liability of the officers and crew *c)* a declaration by a payer, esp. of a tax, disputing the legality or the amount of the payment being made —***adj.*** of or having to do with dissent, esp. political dissent [a *protest* movement, a *protest* vote cast to show dissatisfaction with the party's front-runner] —**SYN.** OBJECT —**under protest** while expressing one's objections; unwillingly —**pro′test′er** ***n.,*** **pro′tes′tor**

Prot·es·tant (prät′əs tənt; *for n. 3 & adj. 2, also* prō tes′tənt, prə-) ***n.*** ⟦Fr < Ger < L *protestans,* prp. of *protestari:* see prec.⟧ **1** any of the German princes and free cities that formally protested to the Diet of Spires (1529) its decision to uphold the edict of the Diet of Worms against the Reformation **2** *a)* any member of the various Christian churches established as a result of the Reformation *b)* loosely, any Christian not belonging to the Roman Catholic or Eastern Orthodox Church **3** [**p-**] a person who protests —***adj.*** **1** of Protestants or Protestant beliefs, practices, etc. **2** [**p-**] protesting —**Prot′es·tant·ism′** ***n.***

☆**Protestant Episcopal Church** the Protestant denomination in the U.S. historically related to the Church of England, and retaining its liturgical and theological forms, but autonomous since 1789: now also called the **Episcopal Church**

Protestant ethic WORK ETHIC: also **Protestant work ethic**

prot·es·ta·tion (prät′es tā′shən, -əs-; prōt′-) ***n.*** ⟦ME *protestacion* < MFr *protestation* < LL *protestatio*⟧ **1** a strong declaration or affirmation **2** the act of protesting **3** a protest; objection

Pro·te·us (prō′tē əs) ***n.*** ⟦ME *Protheus* < L *Proteus* < Gr *Prōteus*⟧ *Gr. Myth.* a minor sea god and servant of Poseidon: he can change his form or appearance at will

pro·tha·la·mi·on (prō′thə lā′mē än′, -ən) ***n., pl.*** **-mi·a** (-ə) ⟦ModL, coined by Edmund SPENSER² (based on EPITHALAMION) < Gr *pro-,* before + *thalamos,* bridal chamber⟧ a song celebrating a marriage: also **pro′tha·la′mi·um** (-əm), *pl.* **-mi·a** (-ə)

pro·thal·li·um (prō thal′ē əm) ***n., pl.*** **-li·a** (-ə) ⟦ModL < Gr *pro-,* before + *thallos,* a shoot (< IE base **dhal-,* to bloom > Alb *dal,* to sprout) + -IUM⟧ *Bot.* a minute, flat, greenish disc of cells bearing sex organs on its lower side, usually attached to the ground by single-celled hairs, and forming the haploid, sexual generation of ferns and similar plants: also **pro·thal·lus** (prō thal′əs), *pl.* **-li′** (-ī′) or **-lus·es** —**pro·thal′li·al** (-ē əl) ***adj.,*** **pro·thal′loid′** (-oid′)

proth·e·sis (präth′ə sis) ***n.*** ⟦LL < Gr, a placing before < *protithenai,* to set before < *pro-,* before + *tithenai,* to place, DO¹⟧ **1** *Gram.* the addition of a syllable or phoneme to the beginning of a word **2** *Eastern Orthodox Ch. a)* the preparation and preliminary oblation of the elements of the Eucharist *b)* the table on which, or the place where, this is done —**pro·thet·ic** (prō thet′ik) ***adj.***

pro·thon·o·tar·y (prō thän′ə ter′ē, prō′thə nōt′ər ē) ***n.***, *pl.* **-tar′ies** ⟦ME < ML *prothonotarius* < LL(Ec) *protonotarius:* see PROTO- & NOTARY⟧ **1** [Now Rare] a chief clerk in some law courts **2** *R.C.Ch.* any of the seven members of the College of Prothonotaries Apostolic, who record important pontifical events: also sometimes held as an honorary title by other ecclesiastics

☆**prothonotary warbler** ⟦said to be so named in reference to the yellow hood worn by certain prothonotaries⟧ a wood warbler (*Protonotaria citrea*) with yellow-orange head and underparts and bluish-gray wings

pro·tho·rax (prō thôr′aks) ***n.***, *pl.* **-rax·es** or **-ra·ces′** (-ə sēz′) ⟦ModL: see PRO-[1] & THORAX⟧ *Zool.* that division of an insect's thorax nearest the head, and bearing the first pair of legs —**pro′tho·rac′ic** (-thō ras′ik) ***adj.***

pro·throm·bin (-thräm′bin) ***n.*** ⟦PRO-[1] + THROMBIN⟧ a factor in the blood plasma that combines with calcium to form thrombin during blood clotting: it is a precursor of thrombin and is synthesized by the liver in the presence of vitamin K

pro·tist (prōt′ist) ***n.*** ⟦< Gr *prōtistos*, first < *prōtos*, first: see PROTO-⟧ *Biol.* in some systems of classification, any of a kingdom (Protista) of one-celled organisms, as algae, yeasts, or protozoans, having characteristics found in both plants and animals —**pro·tis·tan** (prō tis′tən) ***adj., n.***

pro·ti·um (prōt′ē əm, prō′shē-) ***n.*** ⟦ModL: see fol. & -IUM⟧ the most common isotope of hydrogen, hydrogen-1, having a mass number of 1

pro·to- (prōt′ō, -ə) ⟦Gr *prōto-* < *prōtos*, first < IE *p̣ṛto- < base *pro-, early, ahead > L *pro-*, Gr *pro-*⟧ *combining form* **1** first in time, original, primitive *[protoplast]* **2** first in importance, principal, chief *[protonotary]* **3** [**P-**] prehistoric or original: said of a people or language *[Proto-Germanic]* **4** *a) forming nouns* on the way to becoming the (specified) thing or kind of person *[proto-suburbia, a proto-terrorist]* *b) forming adjectives* on the way to having the (specified) quality or relationship *[a proto-Cubist painting]* **5** *Chem.* *a)* being that member of a series of compounds having the lowest proportion of the (specified) element or radical *[protoxide]* *b)* being the parent form of a (specified) substance

pro·to·ac·tin·i·um (prōt′ō ak tin′ē əm) ***n.*** *former name for* PROTACTINIUM

pro·to·col (prōt′ə kôl′, -käl′, -kōl′) ***n.*** ⟦Early ModE *prothocoll* < MFr *prothocole* < ML *protocollum* < LGr *prōtokollon*, first leaf glued to a manuscript (describing the contents) < Gr *prōto-*, PROTO- + *kolla*, glue⟧ **1** an original draft or record of a document, negotiation, etc. **2** ⟦Fr *protocole*⟧ *a)* a diplomatic agreement, esp. one that amends, clarifies, or adds to a treaty *b)* the code of ceremonial forms and courtesies, of precedence, etc. accepted as proper and correct in official dealings, as between heads of state or diplomatic officials **3** in science and medicine, a formal set of rules and procedures to be followed during a particular research experiment, course of treatment, etc. **4** a set of rules governing the communication and the transfer of data between machines, as in a computer system —***vt.*** **-colled′** or **-coled′**, **-col′ling** or **-col′ing** to issue in a protocol —***vi.*** to draw up a protocol

pro·to·gal·ax·y (prōt′ō gal′ək sē) ***n.***, *pl.* **-ies** in some cosmological theories, a huge cloud of dust and hydrogen gas out of which millions of protostars are formed —**pro′to·ga·lac′tic** (-gə lak′tik) ***adj.***

Pro·to-Ger·man·ic (prōt′ō jər man′ik) ***n.*** the hypothetical prehistoric language from which all the Germanic languages, including English, are thought to be descended

pro·to·his·to·ry (prōt′ō his′tə rē) ***n.*** archaeological history in the period immediately preceding recorded history

pro·to·hu·man (-hyo͞o′mən) ***adj.*** of or relating to the humanlike primates that exist or did exist

Pro·to-In·do-Eu·ro·pe·an (prōt′ō in′dō yoor′ə pē′ən) ***n.*** the hypothetical language, reconstructed by modern linguists, from which the INDO-EUROPEAN languages are thought to have descended —***adj.*** of Proto-Indo-European Abbrev. PIE

pro·to·lan·guage (prōt′ō laŋ′gwij) ***n.*** a language that is the documented or the hypothesized and reconstructed parent language of some other language or language group

pro·to·lith·ic (prōt′ə lith′ik) ***adj.*** ⟦PROTO- + -LITHIC⟧ *former name for* EOLITHIC

pro·to·mar·tyr (prōt′ō märt′ər) ***n.*** ⟦ME *prothomartir* < MFr < ML(Ec) *protomartyr* < LGr(Ec) *prōtomartyr:* see PROTO- & MARTYR⟧ the first martyr (in some cause)

pro·ton (prō′tän′) ***n.*** ⟦ModL < Gr *prōton*, neut. of *prōtos*, first: see PROTO-⟧ *Particle Physics* a nucleon carrying a positive charge equal to the negative charge of an electron and having a mass of *c.* 1.673 × 10^{-27} kg (*c.* 938.2796 MeV/c^2, *c.* 1,836 times the mass of an electron): the number of protons in an atom determines the atomic number of a chemical element

pro·to·ne·ma (prōt′ə nē′mə) ***n.***, *pl.* **-ma·ta** (-mə tə) ⟦ModL < Gr *prōto-*, PROTO- + *nēma* (gen. *nēmatos*), thread⟧ *Bot.* a threadlike growth in mosses, arising from a spore and developing small buds that grow into leafy moss plants —**pro′to·ne′mal** ***adj.***

pro·to·ne·phrid·i·um (prōt′ō nē frid′ē əm, -nə-) ***n.*** ⟦PROTO- + NEPHRIDIUM⟧ *Zool.* a tubular, excretory structure in certain invertebrates, as flatworms, rotifers, and some larvae, usually ending internally in flame cells and having an external pore

pro·ton·o·tar·y (prō tän′ə ter′ē, prōt′ə nōt′ər ē) ***n.***, *pl.* **-tar′ies** PROTHONOTARY

☆**proton synchrotron** a synchrotron for accelerating protons and other heavy particles to very high energies

pro·to·nymph (prōt′ə nimf′) ***n.*** ⟦PROTO- + NYMPH⟧ the newly hatched form of various mites —**pro′to·nymph′al** ***adj.***

pro·to·path·ic (prōt′ə path′ik) ***adj.*** ⟦PROTO- + -PATHIC⟧ *Physiol.* designating or of certain sensory nerves having limited sensibility, that respond to heat and pain from a general area

pro·to·plan·et (prōt′ō plan′it) ***n.*** in some cosmological theories, any of the hundreds of swirling clouds of dust and gas that form around a star and eventually evolve into individual planets —**pro′to·plan′e·tar′y** (-i ter′ē) ***adj.***

pro·to·plasm (prōt′ə plaz′əm) ***n.*** ⟦Ger *protoplasma:* see PROTO- & PLASMA⟧ a semifluid, viscous, translucent colloid, the essential living matter of all animal and plant cells: it consists largely of water, proteins, lipids, carbohydrates, and inorganic salts and is differentiated into nucleoplasm and cytoplasm —**pro′to·plas′mic** (-plaz′mik) ***adj.***

pro·to·plast (prōt′ə plast′) ***n.*** ⟦Fr *protoplaste* < LL *protoplastus* < Gr *protoplastos*, formed first < *protos*, first (see PROTO-) + *plastos*, formed < *plassein*, to form: see PLASTIC⟧ **1** a thing or being that is the first of its kind **2** *Biol.* ENERGID **3** *Bot.* a unit of protoplasm, such as makes up a single cell exclusive of the cell wall —**pro′to·plas′tic** ***adj.***

pro·to·star (prōt′ō stär′) ***n.*** in some cosmological theories, any of the millions of swirling clouds of dust and hydrogen gas that form within a protogalaxy and eventually evolve into thermonuclear stars

pro·to·stele (prōt′ə stēl′, -stē′lē) ***n.*** ⟦PROTO- + STELE⟧ a simple, primitive arrangement of conducting tissues in stems and roots of certain lower plants, consisting of a solid cylinder of xylem surrounded by a layer of phloem —**pro′to·ste′lic** ***adj.***

pro·to·troph·ic (prōt′ə träf′ik) ***adj.*** ⟦PROTO- + TROPHIC⟧ able to synthesize its required growth factors: said as of an original organism from which auxotrophic mutants are derived

pro·to·type (prōt′ə tīp′) ***n.*** ⟦Fr < Gr *prōtotypon* < *prōtotypos*, original: see PROTO- & TYPE⟧ **1** the first thing or being of its kind; original; model; pattern; archetype **2** a person or thing that serves as a model for one of a later period **3** a full-scale, operational model, used for demonstration or testing, that incorporates a new design or new features **4** a perfect example of a particular type —**pro′to·typ′al** (-tī′pəl) ***adj.***, **pro′to·typ′ic** (-tip′ik), or **pro′to·typ′i·cal**

pro·tox·ide (prō täk′sīd′) ***n.*** ⟦PROT(O)- + OXIDE⟧ that one of any series of oxides that contains the lowest proportion of oxygen

pro·to·xy·lem (prōt′ō zī′ləm, -lem′) ***n.*** *Bot.* the first formed xylem of a root or stem, produced by the differentiation of the procambium

pro·to·zo·an (prōt′ə zō′ən) ***n.***, *pl.* **-zo′ans** or **-zo′a** (-ə) ⟦< ModL *Protozoa*, name of the subkingdom (see PROTO- & -ZOA) + -AN⟧ any of a subkingdom (Protozoa) of microscopic animals made up of a single cell or a group of more or less identical cells and living in water or as parasites, including ciliates, flagellates, rhizopods, and sporozoans: sometimes **pro′to·zo′on′** (-än′), *pl.* **-zo′ons** or **-zo′a** (-ə) —***adj.*** of the protozoans: often **pro′to·zo′ic** (-ik) or **pro′to·zo′al**

pro·to·zo·ol·o·gy (prōt′ō zō äl′ə jē) ***n.*** ⟦< ModL *Protozoa* (see prec.) + -OLOGY⟧ that branch of zoology dealing with the study of the protozoans

pro·tract (prō trakt′, prə-) ***vt.*** ⟦< L *protractus*, pp. of *protrahere* < *pro-*, forward + *trahere*, to DRAW⟧ **1** to draw out; lengthen in duration; prolong **2** to draw to scale; using a protractor and scale **3** *Zool.* to thrust out; extend: cf. RETRACT (sense 1) —***SYN.*** EXTEND —**pro·tract′ed·ly** ***adv.*** —**pro·tract′ed·ness** ***n.*** —**pro·tract′i·ble** ***adj.*** —**pro·trac′tion** ***n.*** —**pro·trac′tive** ***adj.***

pro·trac·tile (prō trak′təl) ***adj.*** capable of being protracted or thrust out; extensible

pro·trac·tor (prō′trak′tər, prō trak′-) ***n.*** ⟦ML⟧ **1** a person or thing that protracts **2** an instrument in the form of a graduated semicircle, used for plotting and measuring angles **3** *Anat.* a muscle that protracts, or extends, a limb

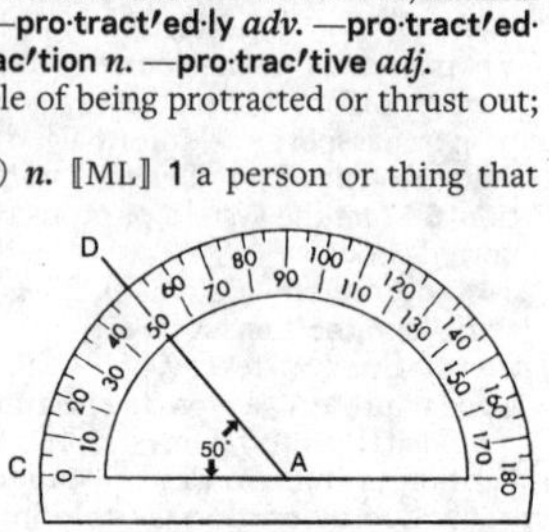

protractor
DAC, angle measured

pro·trep·tic (prō trep′tik) ***adj.*** ⟦< Gr *protreptikos*, instructive < *protrepein*, to urge forward < *pro*, before + *trepein*, to turn: see TROPE⟧ intended as instructional; didactic —***n.*** a book, speech, etc. that is protreptic

pro·trude (prō tro͞od′, prə-) ***vt., vi.*** **-trud′ed**, **-trud′ing** ⟦L *protrudere* < *pro-*, forth + *trudere*, to THRUST⟧ to thrust or jut out; project —**pro·trud′ent** ***adj.***

pro·tru·sile (prō tro͞o′səl, -zəl) ***adj.*** ⟦< L *protrusus*, pp. of *protrudere* (see prec.) + -ILE⟧ that can be protruded, or thrust out, as a tentacle or an elephant's trunk: also **pro·tru′si·ble** (-sə bəl, -zə-)

pro·tru·sion (prō tro͞o′zhən, prə-) ***n.*** ⟦< L *protrusus* (see prec.) + -ION⟧ **1** a protruding or being protruded **2** a protruding part or thing —***SYN.*** PROJECTION

pro·tru·sive (prō tro͞o′siv, prə-) ***adj.*** ⟦< L *protrusus* (see PROTRUSILE) + -IVE⟧ **1** protruding; jutting or bulging out **2** OBTRUSIVE —**pro·tru′sive·ly** ***adv.*** —**pro·tru′sive·ness** ***n.***

pro·tu·ber·ance (prō to͞o′bər əns, -tyo͞o′-; prə-) ***n.*** **1** the condition or fact of being protuberant **2** a part or thing that protrudes; projection; bulge; swelling Also **pro·tu′ber·an·cy** (-ən sē), *pl.* **-cies** —***SYN.*** PROJECTION

pro·tu·ber·ant (prō to͞o′bər ənt, -tyo͞o′-; prə-) ***adj.*** ⟦LL *protuberans*, prp. of *protuberare*, to bulge out < L *pro-*, forth + *tuber*, bump, bulge: see TUBER⟧ bulging or swelling out; protruding; prominent —**pro·tu′ber·ant·ly** ***adv.***

pro·tu·ber·ate (-āt′) ***vi.*** **-at′ed**, **-at′ing** ⟦< LL *protuberatus*, pp. of *protuberare:* see prec.⟧ to bulge or swell out

proud (proud) ***adj.*** ⟦ME < OE *prud* < OFr < LL *prode*, beneficial, back-form. < L *prodesse*, to be useful < *prod-*, var. of *pro-*, PRO-[2] + *esse*, to be: for IE base see IS[1]⟧ **1** having or showing a proper pride in oneself, one's position, one's family, etc. **2** having or showing an overweening opinion of oneself, one's position, etc.; arrogant; haughty **3** feeling or showing great pride or joy, as from being honored **4** that is an occasion or cause of pride; highly gratifying **5** arising from or caused by pride; presumptuous **6** stately; splendid [a *proud* fleet] **7** spirited; of high mettle [a *proud* stallion] **8** [Obs.] valiant —**do oneself proud** [Informal] to do extremely well —**proud of** highly pleased with or exulting in —**proud′ly** ***adv.***

SYN.—**proud** is the broadest term in this comparison, ranging in implication from proper self-esteem or pride to an overweening opinion of one's importance [too *proud* to beg, *proud* as a peacock]; **arrogant** implies an aggressive, unwarranted assertion of superior importance or privileges [the *arrogant* colonel]; **haughty** implies such consciousness of high station, rank, etc. as is displayed in scorn of those one considers beneath one [a *haughty* dowager]; **insolent** implies both haughtiness and great contempt, esp. as manifested in behavior or speech that insults or affronts others [she has an *insolent* disregard for her servant's feelings]; **overbearing** implies extreme, domineering insolence [an *overbearing* supervisor]; **supercilious** stresses an aloof, scornful manner toward others [a *supercilious* intellectual snob]; **disdainful** implies even stronger and more overt feelings of scorn for that which is regarded as beneath one —***ANT.*** **humble**

proud flesh ⟦so called from the notion of swelling up⟧ an abnormal growth of flesh around a healing wound, caused by excessive granulation

Prou·dhon (pro͞o dōn′), **Pierre Jo·seph** (pyer zhō zef′) 1809-65; Fr. socialist & writer

Proust (pro͞ost), **Mar·cel** (mär sel′) 1871-1922; Fr. novelist —**Proust′i·an** ***adj.***

prov *abbrev.* **1** province **2** provincial **3** provisional

Prov *abbrev.* **1** Provençal **2** *Bible* Proverbs **3** Province **4** Provost

prove (pro͞ov) ***vt.*** **proved**, **proved** or **prov′en**, **prov′ing** ⟦ME *proven* < OFr *prover* < L *probare*: see PROBE⟧ **1** to test by experiment, a standard, etc.; subject to a testing process; try out **2** to establish as true; demonstrate to be a fact **3** to establish the validity or authenticity of (esp. a will) **4** to show (oneself) to be capable, dependable, etc. **5** [Archaic] to experience; learn or know by experience **6** *Math.* to test or verify the correctness of (a calculation, etc.) **7** *Printing* to take a proof of (type, etc.) —***vi.*** **1** to be found or shown by experience or trial; turn out to be [a guess that *proved* right] **2** [Archaic] to make trial —**the exception proves the rule** *see* EXCEPTION —☆**prove out** to show or be shown to be satisfactory, accurate, true, etc. —**prov′a·bil′i·ty** ***n.***, **prov′a·ble·ness** —**prov′a·ble** ***adj.*** —**prov′a·bly** ***adv.*** —**prov′er** ***n.***

prov·en (pro͞o′vən) ***vt., vi. pp. of*** PROVE —***adj.*** known to be valid, effective, or genuine [a *proven* method]

prov·e·nance (präv′ə nəns) ***n.*** ⟦Fr < *provenir* < L *provenire*, to come forth < *pro-*, forth + *venire*, to COME⟧ origin; derivation; source

Pro·ven·çal (prō′vən säl′, präv′ən-; *Fr* prô vän sȧl′) ***adj.*** ⟦Fr⟧ of Provence or its people, language, or culture —***n.*** **1** the vernacular of S France, a Romance language comprising several dialects **2** the medieval language of S France, a literary language as cultivated by the troubadours **3** a person born or living in Provence

Pro·vence (prô väns′) ⟦Fr < L *provincia*, PROVINCE⟧ historical region of SE France, on the Mediterranean

Provence-Alpes-Côte d'A·zur (prô väns′ ȧlp′kōt′ dȧ zür′) metropolitan region of SE France: 12,124 sq mi (31,401 sq km); chief city, Marseille

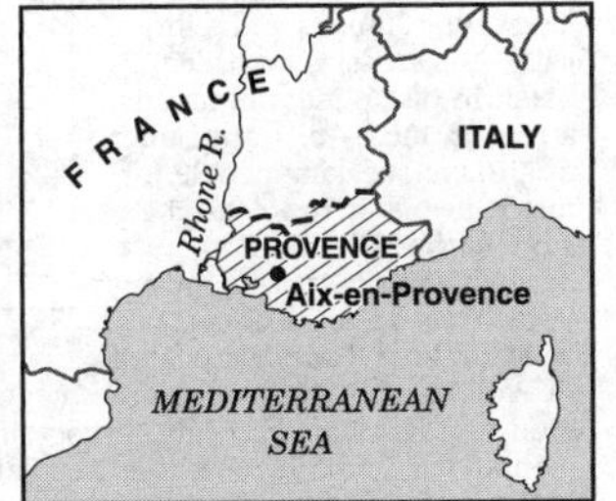

Provence

prov·en·der (präv′ən dər) ***n.*** ⟦ME < MFr *provendre*, var. of *provende* < ML(Ec) *praebenda*: see PREBEND⟧ **1** dry food for livestock, as hay, corn, oats, etc.; fodder **2** [Informal] provisions; food

pro·ve·ni·ence (prō vē′nē əns, -vēn′yəns) ***n.*** ⟦< L *proveniens*, prp. of *provenire*: see PROVENANCE⟧ origin; derivation

pro·ven·tric·u·lus (prō′ven trik′yo͞o ləs, -yə-) ***n., pl.*** **-li′** (-lī′) ⟦ModL: see PRO-[1] & VENTRICULUS⟧ *Zool.* **1** the front part of a bird's stomach, containing digestive glands **2** the thin-walled front part of the stomach of many invertebrates, as earthworms and lobsters

prov·erb (präv′ərb) ***n.*** ⟦OFr *proverbe* < L *proverbium* < *pro-*, PRO-[2] + *verbum*, word: see VERB⟧ **1** a short, traditional saying that expresses some obvious truth or familiar experience; adage; maxim **2** a person or thing that has become commonly recognized as a type of specified characteristics; byword **3** *Bible* an enigmatic saying in which a profound truth is cloaked —***vt.*** ⟦ME *prouerben*⟧ [Archaic] to make a proverb or byword of —***SYN.*** SAYING

pro·ver·bi·al (prə vʉr′bē əl) ***adj.*** ⟦ME < LL *proverbialis*⟧ **1** of, or having the nature of, a proverb **2** expressed in a proverb **3** well-known because commonly referred to [the *proverbial* glamour of Paris] —**pro·ver′bi·al·ly** ***adv.***

Prov·erbs (präv′ərbz) ***n.*** *Bible* a book containing maxims ascribed to Solomon and others: abbrev. *Prov, Prv,* or *Pr*

pro·vide (prə vīd′, prō-) ***vt.*** **-vid′ed**, **-vid′ing** ⟦ME *providen* < L *providere* < *pro-*, PRO-[2] + *videre*, to see: see VISION⟧ **1** [Now Rare] to get ready beforehand **2** to make available; supply **3** to supply (someone) *with* something **4** to state as a condition; stipulate —***vi.*** **1** to prepare (*for* or *against* some probable or possible situation, occurrence, etc.) **2** to make a condition; stipulate **3** to furnish the means of support: usually with *for*

pro·vid·ed (prə vīd′id, prō-) ***conj.*** on the condition or understanding; if; providing: often with *that*

prov·i·dence (präv′ə dəns) ***n.*** ⟦ME < MFr < L *providentia*, foresight < *providens*: see PROVIDENT⟧ **1** a looking to, or preparation for, the future; provision **2** skill or wisdom in management; prudence **3** *a)* the care or benevolent guidance of God or nature *b)* an instance of this **4** [**P-**] God, as the guiding power of the universe

Prov·i·dence (präv′ə dəns) ⟦named by Roger WILLIAMS⟧ capital of R.I., on Narragansett Bay

prov·i·dent (präv′ə dənt) ***adj.*** ⟦ME < L *providens*, prp. of *providere*: see PROVIDE⟧ **1** providing for future needs or events; exercising or characterized by foresight **2** prudent or economical —***SYN.*** THRIFTY —**prov′i·dent·ly** ***adv.***

prov·i·den·tial (präv′ə den′shəl) ***adj.*** ⟦< L *providentia* + -AL⟧ of, by, or as if decreed by divine providence —**prov′i·den′tial·ly** ***adv.***

pro·vid·er (prə vīd′ər, prō-) ***n.*** one that provides; specif., *a)* a working person whose earnings support his or her family [he always has been a good *provider*] *b)* a physician, insurance company, etc. providing services under a healthcare plan *c)* a telecommunications company providing internet service, cell-phone service, cable TV, etc.

pro·vid·ing (prə vīd′iŋ, prō-) ***conj.*** on the condition or understanding; if; provided: often with *that*

prov·ince (präv′ins) ***n.*** ⟦OFr < L *provincia*, province < ? IE **prowo-* (< base **pro-*) > Gr *prōira*, PROW[1], OE *frea*, lord⟧ **1** any of the outside territories controlled and ruled by ancient Rome **2** an administrative division of a country; specif., any of the ten main administrative divisions of Canada **3** *a)* a territorial district; territory *b)* [*pl.*] the parts of a country removed from the capital and the populated, cultural centers **4** proper duties or functions; sphere [enforcing the laws does not fall within the *province* of this commission] **5** an area, division, or branch of learning or activity **6** a division of a country under the jurisdiction of an archbishop or metropolitan **7** a division of the world, smaller than a region, with reference to the plants or animals found there

Prov·ince·town (präv′ins toun′) ⟦after *Province Lands*, title of public land at the end of Cape Cod⟧ resort town in Mass., at the N tip of Cape Cod

pro·vin·cial (prə vin′shəl, prō-) ***adj.*** ⟦ME *prouyncial* < MFr < L *provincialis*⟧ **1** of or belonging to a province **2** having the ways, speech, attitudes, etc. of a certain province **3** of or like that of rural provinces; countrified; rustic **4** designating or of a style, esp. of 18th-cent. European furniture, that was characteristic of the provinces and was a simpler and plainer copy of the style characteristic of the capital and cultural centers: cf. FRENCH PROVINCIAL **5** narrow; limited; unsophisticated [a *provincial* outlook] —***n.*** **1** a native of a province **2** a provincial person; esp., a narrow-minded or unsophisticated person —**pro·vin′cial·ly** ***adv.***

pro·vin·cial·ism (prə vin′shəl iz′əm, prō-) ***n.*** **1** the condition or fact of being provincial **2** narrowness of outlook; exclusive concern with local matters **3** a provincial custom, characteristic, etc. **4** a word, phrase, or pronunciation peculiar to a certain location or dialect Also **pro·vin′ci·al′i·ty** (prə), *pl.* **-ties** —**pro·vin′cial·ist** ***n.***

proving ground a place for testing new equipment, new theories, etc.

pro·vi·rus (prō vī′rəs) ***n.*** ⟦PRO-[1] + VIRUS⟧ the genetic material of a virus, that is merged with the chromosomes of a host cell and can be transmitted to the next generation of cells without causing the destruction of the original host cell —**pro·vi′ral** (-rəl) ***adj.***

pro·vi·sion (prə vizh′ən, prō-) ***n.*** ⟦ME *provysion* < MFr *provision* < L *provisio*, a foreseeing < *provisus*, pp. of *providere*: see PROVIDE⟧ **1** a providing, preparing, or supplying of something **2** *a)* something provided, prepared, or supplied for the future *b)* [*pl.*] a stock of food and other supplies assembled for future needs **3** a preparatory arrangement or measure taken in advance for meeting some future need **4** a clause, as in a legal document, agreement, etc., stipulating or requiring some specific thing; proviso; condition **5** *Eccles.* appointment to an office; esp., advance appointment by the pope to a see or benefice that is not yet vacant —***vt.*** to supply with provisions, esp. with a stock of food —**pro·vi′sion·er** ***n.***

pro·vi·sion·al (prə vizh′ə nəl, prō-) ***adj.*** having the nature of a temporary provision; arranged or established for the time being, pending permanent arrangement or establishment: also **pro·vi′sion·ar′y** (-ner′ē) —***n.*** ☆a postage stamp issued, as by a postmaster, for temporary use pending an official issue —***SYN.*** TEMPORARY —**pro·vi′sion·al·ly** ***adv.***

pro·vi·so (prə vī′zō′, prō-) ***n., pl.*** **-sos′** or **-soes′** ⟦ML *proviso (quod)*, provided (that) < L, abl. of *provisus*, pp. of *providere*: see PROVIDE⟧ **1** a clause, as in a document or statute, making some condition or stipulation **2** a condition or stipulation

pro·vi·so·ry (prə vī′zə rē, prō-) ***adj.*** ⟦ML *provisorius* < L *provisus*: see prec.⟧ **1** containing a proviso; conditional **2** PROVISIONAL —**pro·vi′so·ri·ly** (-zə ri lē) ***adv.***

pro·vi·ta·min (prō vīt′ə min) ***n.*** any ingested substance which can be converted to a vitamin within the organism

Pro·vo[1] (prō′vō) ***n., pl.*** **-vos** ⟦< PROVISIONAL⟧ a member of the Provisional Irish Republican Army, a faction of the Irish Republican Army

Pro·vo² (prō′vō) ⟦renamed (1850) after Étienne *Provot,* early fur trader⟧ city in NC Utah

pro·vo·ca·teur (prə väk′ə tʉr′, prō-) *n.* **1** *short for* AGENT PROVOCATEUR **2** a writer, artist, political activist, etc. whose works, ideas, or activities are regarded as a threat to accepted values or practices

prov·o·ca·tion (präv′ə kā′shən) *n.* ⟦ME *provocacion* < MFr *provocation* < L *provocatio*⟧ **1** an act or instance of provoking **2** something that provokes; esp., a cause of resentment or irritation

pro·voc·a·tive (prə väk′ə tiv, prō-) *adj.* ⟦ME *prouocatyue,* aphrodisiac < LL *provocativus* < L *provocare:* see fol.⟧ provoking or tending to provoke, as to action, thought, feeling, etc.; stimulating, erotic, irritating, etc. —*n.* something that provokes —**pro·voc′a·tive·ly** *adv.* —**pro·voc′a·tive·ness** *n.*

pro·voke (prə vōk′, prō-) *vt.* **-voked′**, **-vok′ing** ⟦ME *provoken* < MFr *provoquer* < L *provocare,* to call forth < *pro-,* PRO-² + *vocare,* to call < *vox,* VOICE⟧ **1** to excite to some action or feeling **2** to anger, irritate, or annoy **3** to stir up (action or feeling) **4** to call forth; evoke [to *provoke* a smile] —**pro·vok′er** *n.*

SYN.—**provoke**, in this connection, implies rather generally an arousing to some action or feeling [thought-*provoking*]; **excite** suggests a more powerful or profound stirring or moving of the thoughts or emotions [it *excites* my imagination]; **stimulate** implies an arousing as if by goading or pricking and, hence, often connotes a bringing out of a state of inactivity or indifference [to *stimulate* one's enthusiasm]; **pique** suggests a stimulating as if by irritating mildly [to *pique* one's curiosity] See also **irritate**

pro·vok·ing (-vōk′iŋ) *adj.* that provokes; esp., annoying or vexing —**pro·vok′ing·ly** *adv.*

pro·vo·lo·ne (prō′və lō′nē, -lōn′) *n.* ⟦It < *provola,* a cheese made from buffalo's milk⟧ a hard, light-colored Italian cheese made from cow's milk, usually smoked and molded in a pear-shaped form

pro·vost (prō′vōst′, präv′əst; *esp. in military use* prō′vō′) *n.* ⟦ME < OE *profost* & OFr *provost,* both < ML *propositus,* for L *praepositus,* chief, prefect, orig. pp. of *praeponere,* to set before, place first < *prae-,* before + *ponere,* to place: see PRE- & POSITION⟧ **1** a superintendent; official in charge **2** the chief magistrate of a Scottish burgh **3** [Obs.] a jailer **4** *Eccles.* the head of a cathedral chapter or principal church **5** *Educ. a)* the head of any of certain colleges in the British Isles ☆*b)* in certain American universities, an administrative official dealing chiefly with faculty, curriculum, etc. —**pro′vost·ship′** *n.*

provost court a military court for trying soldiers or civilians charged with minor offenses in occupied territory

☆**provost guard** a detail of military police under the command of an officer (**provost marshal**)

prow¹ (prou) *adj.* ⟦ME < OFr *prou,* brave, var. of *prud:* see PROUD⟧ [Archaic] valiant; brave

prow² (prou) *n.* ⟦Fr *proue,* earlier *proe* < It dial. (Genoese) *prua* < L *prora* < Gr *prōira,* prow: for IE base see PROVINCE⟧ **1** the forward part of a ship or boat; bow **2** a part like this, as the nose of an airplane

prow·ess (prou′is) *n.* ⟦ME < OFr *prouesse* < *prou:* see prec.⟧ **1** bravery; valor **2** superior ability, skill, etc.

prowl (proul) *vi., vt.* ⟦ME *prollen* < ?⟧ to roam about furtively, as in search of prey or loot —*n.* the act of prowling —**on the prowl** prowling about —**prowl′er** *n.*

☆**prowl car** PATROL CAR

prox. *abbrev.* proximo

prox·e·mics (präk sē′miks) *n.* ⟦PROX(IMITY) + *-emics,* as in PHONEMICS⟧ the study of how people use and structure space or spatial arrangements in work, personal relations, etc. —**prox·e′mic** *adj.*

Prox·i·ma Cen·tau·ri (präk′sə mə sen tô′rē) ⟦ModL, nearest star of CENTAURUS⟧ a red dwarf star near Alpha Centauri: magnitude, 11: at a distance of *c.* 4.22 light-years, it is the closest star to the sun

prox·i·mal (präk′sə məl) *adj.* ⟦< L *proximus* (see fol.) + -AL⟧ **1** proximate; next or nearest **2** *Anat.* situated nearest the center of the body or nearest the point of attachment of a muscle, limb, etc. —**prox′i·mal·ly** *adv.*

prox·i·mate (präk′sə mət) *adj.* ⟦LL *proximatus,* pp. of *proximare,* to come near < L *proximus,* nearest, superl. of *prope,* near⟧ **1** next or nearest in space, order, time, etc. [*proximate* cause] **2** nearly accurate; approximate —**prox′i·mate·ly** *adv.*

prox·im·i·ty (präk sim′ə tē) *n.* ⟦MFr *proximité* < L *proximitas* < *proximus:* see prec.⟧ the state or quality of being near; nearness in space, time, etc.

☆**proximity fuze** an electronic fuze that detonates a bomb, missile, etc. when its sensor detects the target

prox·i·mo (präk′sə mō′) *adv.* ⟦L *proximo* (*mense*), in the next (month), abl. of *proximus:* see PROXIMATE⟧ [Old-fashioned] (in the) next (month) [on the 9th *proximo*]: cf. ULTIMO, INSTANT (*adv.* 2)

prox·y (präk′sē) *n., pl.* **prox′ies** ⟦ME *prokecie,* contr. < *procuracie,* the function of a procurator, ult. < L *procuratio*⟧ **1** the agency or function of a deputy **2** the authority to act for another **3** a document empowering a person to act for another, as in voting at a stockholders' meeting **4** a person empowered to act for another —*SYN.* AGENT

Pro·zac (prō′zak′) *trademark for* FLUOXETINE

prude (pro͞od) *n.* ⟦Fr, back-form. < *prudefemme,* excellent woman < OFr *prud* (see PROUD) + *feme,* woman⟧ a person who is overly modest or proper in behavior, dress, or speech, esp. in a way that annoys others

pru·dence (pro͞od′′ns) *n.* ⟦ME < MFr < L *prudentia* < *prudens:* see PRUDENT⟧ **1** the quality or fact of being prudent **2** careful management; economy

Pru·dence (pro͞od′′ns) *n.* ⟦LL, fem. of *Prudentius* < L *prudentia:* see prec.⟧ a feminine name: dim. *Prue*

pru·dent (pro͞od′′nt) *adj.* ⟦OFr < L *prudens,* for *providens:* see PROVIDENT⟧ **1** capable of exercising sound judgment in practical matters, esp. as concerns one's own interests **2** cautious or discreet in conduct; circumspect; not rash **3** managing carefully and with economy —*SYN.* CAREFUL —**pru′dent·ly** *adv.*

pru·den·tial (pro͞o den′shəl) *adj.* **1** characterized by or resulting from prudence **2** exercising prudence, or sound judgment —**pru·den′tial·ly** *adv.*

prud·er·y (pro͞o′dər ē) *n.* ⟦Fr *pruderie*⟧ the quality or condition of being prudish

Pru·dhoe Bay (pro͞o′dō) inlet of the Beaufort Sea, in N Alas.: site of large oil fields

prud·ish (pro͞o′dish) *adj.* like or characteristic of a prude; too modest or proper —**prud′ish·ly** *adv.* —**prud′ish·ness** *n.*

pru·i·nose (pro͞o′ə nōs′) *adj.* ⟦L *pruinosus,* frosty < *pruina,* hoarfrost, for earlier **pruswina* < IE base **preus-,* to FREEZE⟧ *Bot.* covered with a white, powdery substance or bloom

prune¹ (pro͞on) *n.* ⟦ME < MFr < VL *pruna* < L *prunum* < Gr *proumnon,* plum⟧ **1** a plum dried for eating **2** any of various varieties of plum that can be dried without spoiling ☆**3** [Informal] a sour or disagreeable person

prune² (pro͞on) *vt.* **pruned**, **prun′ing** ⟦ME *prouynen* < OFr *prooignier,* prob. < *provaignier,* to cut < *provain* (< L *propago:* see PROPAGATE), a slip, infl. by *roognier,* to cut off < LL **rotundiare* < L *rotundus,* round: see ROTUND⟧ **1** to remove dead or living parts from (a plant) so as to increase fruit or flower production or improve the form **2** to cut out or get rid of as being unnecessary **3** to reduce or diminish by removing what is unnecessary —*vi.* to cut away or remove unnecessary parts —**prun′er** *n.*

pru·nel·la (pro͞o nel′ə) *n.* ⟦Fr, lit., sloe-colored, dim. < *prune* (see PRUNE¹): prob. because of its orig. color⟧ a strong worsted twill, used, esp. formerly, as for clerical gowns, shoe uppers, etc.

pruning hook a long tool with a hooked blade, or a pair of shears with one hooked blade, for pruning plants

pru·nus (pro͞o′nəs) *n.* ⟦ModL < L, plum tree < Gr *prounos, proumnē*⟧ any of a large genus (*Prunus*) of fruit trees and shrubs of the rose family, including cherry, peach, and plum trees and the blackthorn

pru·ri·ent (proor′ē ənt) *adj.* ⟦L *pruriens* < *prurire,* to itch, long for, be lecherous < IE base **preus-,* to burn, FREEZE > L *pruna,* live coal⟧ **1** having or expressing lustful ideas or desires **2** tending to excite lust; lascivious; lewd **3** [Rare] itching —**pru′ri·ence** *n.*, **pru′ri·en·cy** —**pru′ri·ent·ly** *adv.*

pru·ri·go (pro͞o rī′gō) *n.* ⟦L < *prurire,* to itch: see prec.⟧ a chronic, inflammatory skin disease characterized by pale-red papules and intense itching —**pru·rig′i·nous** (-rij′ə nəs) *adj.*

pru·ri·tus (pro͞o rīt′əs) *n.* ⟦< L, pp. of *prurire,* to itch: see PRURIENT⟧ intense itching of the skin without eruption —**pru·rit′ic** (-rit′ik) *adj.*

Prus *abbrev.* **1** Prussia **2** Prussian

Prus·sia (prush′ə) **1** historical region of N Germany, on the Baltic **2** former kingdom in N Europe (1701-1871) & the dominant state of the German Empire (1871-1919): formally dissolved in 1947

Prus·sian (prush′ən) *adj.* **1** of Prussia or its people, language, or culture **2** like or characteristic of the Junkers and military caste of Prussia, regarded as harsh in discipline, militaristic, arrogant, etc. —*n.* **1** a member of a Baltic-speaking people formerly living in the coastal regions of the SE Baltic **2** a person born or living in Prussia, ancient or modern **3** OLD PRUSSIAN

Prussia (*c.* 1812)

Prussian blue ⟦orig. discovered in PRUSSIA (1704)⟧ **1** any of a group of dark-blue powders, ferrocyanides of iron, used as dyes or pigments; esp., ferric ferrocyanide, $Fe_4[Fe(CN)_6]_3$ **2** a strong, dark blue

Prus·sian·ism (-iz′əm) *n.* the practices and doctrines of the Prussians; specif., the despotic militarism and harsh discipline traditionally associated with the Prussian ruling class

prus·si·ate (prus′ē āt′, -it; prush′-) *n.* ⟦Fr < *prussique* (see fol.) + *-ate,* -ATE²⟧ **1** a salt of hydrocyanic acid **2** *a)* FERROCYANIDE *b)* FERRICYANIDE

prus·sic acid (prus′ik) ⟦Fr *(acide) prussique* < *(bleu de) Prusse,* Prussian (blue): from its chemical relationship to Prussian blue⟧ HYDROCYANIC ACID

Prut (pro͞ot) river in Europe, flowing from SW Ukraine southeastward along the border between Romania & Moldova into the Danube: *c.* 600 mi (966 km)

Prv *abbrev. Bible* Proverbs

pry¹ (prī) *n., pl.* **pries** ⟦back-form. < PRIZE²⟧ **1** a tool for raising or moving something by leverage; lever, crowbar, etc. **2** leverage —*vt.* **pried**, **pry′ing 1** to raise, move, or force with a pry **2** to draw forth or obtain with difficulty [to *pry* money from a miser]

pry² (prī) *vi.* **pried**, **pry′ing** ⟦ME *prien* < ?⟧ to look closely and inquisitively or inquire presumptuously; peer or snoop —*n., pl.* **pries 1** the act of prying **2** a person who is improperly inquisitive

pry·er (prī′ər) ***n.*** *alt. sp. of* PRIER

pry·ing (prī′iŋ) ***adj.*** ⟦prp. of PRY²⟧ improperly curious or inquisitive —***SYN.*** CURIOUS —**pry′ing·ly** ***adv.***

Prze·wal·ski's horse (pshə väl′skēz, shə-) ⟦after N. *Przewalski* (Russ *Prževal'skij*) (1839-88), Russ explorer who discovered it⟧ a small, strong wild horse (*Equus caballus przewalskii*) of Mongolia, characterized by a large head, a short, erect mane, and a light bay color

ps *abbrev.* **1** *Bible* psalm(s) **2** postscript

PS *abbrev.* **1** passenger steamer **2** Privy Seal **3** Public School

P.S., p.s., *or* **PS** *abbrev.* postscript

Psa *abbrev. Bible* Psalms

PSA¹ (pē′es′ā′) ***n.,*** *pl.* **PSAs** ⟦*p*(*rostate-*)*s*(*pecific*) *a*(*ntigen*)⟧ **1** an enzyme secreted by the prostate gland **2** a blood test used to detect prostate cancer by determining if elevated levels of this enzyme are present in the blood

PSA² *abbrev.* public service announcement (on radio or TV)

psalm (säm, sôm; sälm, sôlm) ***n.*** ⟦ME *psalme, saume* < OE *sealm* < LL(Ec) *psalmus* < Gr *psalmos*, a twanging with the fingers (in LXX & N.T., song sung to the harp) < *psallein*, to twitch, pluck⟧ **1** a sacred song or poem; hymn **2** [*usually* **P-**] any of the sacred songs in praise of God constituting the Book of Psalms in the Bible

psalm·book (säm′book′) ***n.*** a collection of psalms for use in religious worship

psalm·ist (säm′ist) ***n.*** a composer of psalms —**the Psalmist** King David, to whom all or certain of the Psalms are variously attributed

psal·mo·dy (säm′ə dē) ***n.*** ⟦ME *psalmodye* < LL(Ec) *psalmodia* < Gr *psalmōdia* < *psalmos* (see PSALM) + *ōidē*, song (see ODE)⟧ **1** the act, practice, or art of singing psalms **2** psalms collectively **3** the arrangement of psalms for singing —**psal′mo·dist** ***n.***

Psalms (sämz, sômz; sälmz, sôlmz) ***n.*** *Bible* a book consisting of 150 psalms: abbrev. *Psa*: also **Book of Psalms**

Psal·ter (säl′tər, sôl′-) ***n.*** ⟦altered (infl. by L) < ME *sauter* < OE *saltere* & OFr *sautier*, both < L *psalterium*, stringed instrument, in LL(Ec), the Psalms < Gr *psaltērion*, harp, in LGr(Ec), the Psalter < *psallein*, to twitch, pluck⟧ **1** the Book of Psalms **2** [*also* **p-**] a version of the Psalms for use in religious services

psal·te·ri·um (säl tir′ē əm, sôl-) ***n.,*** *pl.* **-ri·a** (-ē ə) ⟦ModL < L (see prec.): from the appearance of the many folds it contains⟧ OMASUM

psal·ter·y (säl′tər ē, sôl′-) ***n.,*** *pl.* **-ter·ies** ⟦ME *psauterie* < OFr *sautere, psalterie* < L *psalterium*: see PSALTER⟧ a stringed instrument of the zither family, popular esp. in 12th-15th cent. Europe, having a modified trapezoidal body and a variable number of strings plucked with the fingers of both hands or a pair of quills

psaltery

psam·mite (sam′īt′) ***n.*** ⟦Fr < Gr *psammos*, SAND + *-ite*, -ITE¹⟧ ARENITE —**psam·mit·ic** (sa mit′ik) ***adj.***

psam·mon (sam′än′, -ən) ***n.*** ⟦ModL < Gr *psammos*, SAND⟧ *Ecol.* a group of those microorganisms that live in the water held between sand grains in waterlogged sands

PSAT *trademark* Preliminary Scholastic Aptitude Test

pse·phite (sē′fīt′) ***n.*** ⟦Fr < Gr *psēphos*, pebble (akin to *psammos*, SAND) + *-ite*, -ITE¹⟧ any conglomerate rock —**pse·phit′ic** (-fit′ik) ***adj.***

pse·phol·o·gy (sē fäl′ə jē) ***n.*** ⟦< Gr *psēphos*, pebble (used in voting): see prec. & -LOGY⟧ the statistical evaluation of election returns or of political polls —**pse′pho·log′i·cal** (-fə läj′i kəl) ***adj.*** —**pse·phol′o·gist** ***n.***

pseud¹ (sood, syood) ***n.*** ⟦< *pseudo-intellectual*⟧ [Informal, Chiefly Brit.] a person who affects being an intellectual

pseud² *abbrev.* PSEUDONYM

pseu·de·pig·ra·pha (soo′də pig′rə fə) ***pl.n.,*** *sing.* **-phon′** (-fän′) ⟦ModL < Gr, neut. pl. of *pseudepigraphos*, having a false title < *pseudēs*, false + *epigraphein*, to inscribe < *epi*, upon + *graphein*, to write: see GRAPHIC⟧ [*also* **P-**] a group of early writings not included in the biblical canon or the Apocrypha, some of which were falsely ascribed to biblical characters —**pseu′de·pig′ra·phal** ***adj.,*** **pseu′de·pi·graph′ic** (-pə graf′ik)

pseu·do (soo′dō, syoo′-) ***adj.*** ⟦ME: see fol.⟧ sham; false; spurious; pretended; counterfeit

pseu·do- (soo′dō, -də; syoo′-) ⟦ME < LL < Gr *pseudo-* < *pseudēs*, false < *pseudein*, to deceive⟧ *combining form* **1** fictitious, pretended, or sham [*pseudoscience*] **2** counterfeit or spurious **3** closely or deceptively similar to (a specified thing) [*pseudomorph*] **4** not corresponding to the reality; illusory [*pseudopregnancy*] **5** *Chem.* an isomer or related form of (a specified compound) [*pseudoionone*] Also, before a vowel, **pseud-**

pseu·do·al·um (soo′dō al′əm) ***n.*** ⟦prec. + ALUM¹⟧ any of a class of alums in which the usual monovalent metal of a true alum is replaced by a bivalent metal

pseu·do·carp (soo′də kärp′) ***n.*** ⟦PSEUDO- + -CARP⟧ FALSE FRUIT —**pseu′do·car′pous** ***adj.***

pseu·do·cy·e·sis (soo′dō sī ē′sis) ***n.,*** *pl.* **-ses′** (-sēz′) ⟦ModL < PSEUDO- + Gr *kyēsis*, conception⟧ a physical condition caused by emotional factors or by a tumor, etc., in which a female's body manifests signs of pregnancy, including amenorrhea and enlargement of the abdomen; false pregnancy

Pseu·do-Di·o·ny·si·us (soo′dō dī′ə nish′əs, -nis′ē əs) fl. *c.* A.D. 500; author of Neoplatonic Christian writings that were highly influential in the Middle Ages: *Pseudo-Dionysius* is the traditional name ascribed to this otherwise unknown author, after the Dionysius the Areopagite mentioned in Acts 17:34

pseu·do·e·phed·rine (soo′dō e fe′drin) ***n.*** ⟦PSEUDO- + EPHEDRINE⟧ an isomer of ephedrine, used to relieve nasal congestion

pseu·do·gene (soo′dō jēn′) ***n.*** a genelike section of DNA that has no apparent function

pseu·do·her·maph·ro·dite (soo′dō hər maf′rə dīt) ***n.*** ⟦PSEUDO- + HERMAPHRODITE⟧ a person or animal having gonads of one sex while the external genital organs and secondary sex characters resemble in whole or in part those of the opposite sex —**pseu′do·her·maph′ro·dit′ic** (-rə dit′ik) ***adj.*** —**pseu′do·her·maph′ro·dit′ism′** (-rə dīt′iz′əm) ***n.,*** **pseu′do·her·maph′ro·dism′** (-rə diz′əm)

pseu·dom·o·nas (soo däm′ə nəs) ***n.*** ⟦ModL < PSEUDO- + Gr *monas*: see MONAD⟧ any of a genus (*Pseudomonas*, family Pseudomonadaceae) of aerobic, rod-shaped, Gram-negative bacteria

pseu·do·morph (soo′də môrf′) ***n.*** ⟦< Gr *pseudomorphos*, having a false form: see PSEUDO- & -MORPH⟧ **1** a false or irregular form **2** a mineral possessing the external form characteristic of another —**pseu′do·mor′phism′** (-môr′fiz′əm) ***n.*** —**pseu′do·mor′phous** (-môr′fəs) ***adj.,*** **pseu′do·mor′phic** (-môr′fik)

pseu·do·nym (soo′də nim′) ***n.*** ⟦Fr *pseudonyme* < Gr *pseudōnymos*: see fol.⟧ a fictitious name, esp. one assumed by an author —**pseu′do·nym′i·ty** ***n.***

SYN.—a **pseudonym** is a fictitious name assumed, esp. by a writer, for anonymity, for effect, etc.; **pen name** and **nom de plume** are applied specifically to the pseudonym of a writer; **alias** also refers to an assumed name and, in popular use, is specifically applied to one taken by a criminal to disguise identity; **incognito** is usually applied to a fictitious name temporarily assumed by a famous person, as in traveling, to avoid being recognized

pseu·don·y·mous (soo dän′ə məs) ***adj.*** ⟦Fr *pseudonyme* < Gr *pseudōnymos*, having a false name < *pseudēs*, false + *onyma*, NAME⟧ **1** using a pseudonym **2** written under a pseudonym —**pseu·don′y·mous·ly** ***adv.***

pseu·do·po·di·um (soo′də pō′dē əm) ***n.,*** *pl.* **-di·a** (-ə) ⟦ModL: see PSEUDO- & -PODIUM⟧ a temporary projection of the protoplasm of certain one-celled organisms or of certain cells in multicellular animals, serving as a means of moving about or for taking in food: also **pseu′do·pod′** (-päd′) —**pseu·dop·o·dal** (soo däp′ə dəl) ***adj.,*** **pseu·do·po·di·al** (soo də pō′dē əl)

pseu·do·preg·nan·cy (soo′dō preg′nən sē) ***n.,*** *pl.* **-cies** PSEUDOCYESIS

pseu·do·salt (soo′dō sôlt′) ***n.*** ⟦PSEUDO- + SALT⟧ a compound whose formula is that of a salt, but that does not ionize in solution

pseu·do·sci·ence (soo′dō sī′əns) ***n.*** **1** facts and principles systematized and presented as science, but having no true scientific basis or application **2** any field or theory presuming without warrant to have a scientific basis or application —**pseu′do·sci′en·tif′ic** (-ən tif′ik) ***adj.*** —**pseu′do·sci′en·tist** ***n.***

psf *abbrev.* pounds per square foot

pshaw (shô) ***n., interj.*** (an exclamation) used to express impatience, disgust, contempt, disbelief, etc.

psi¹ (sī, psē) ***n.*** ⟦LGr < Gr *psei*⟧ the twenty-third letter of the Greek alphabet (Ψ, ψ)

psi² (sī) ***adj.*** ⟦prob. < PSYCHIC⟧ of or having to do with psychic or paranormal abilities or phenomena —***n.*** such abilities or phenomena collectively

psi³ *abbrev.* pounds per square inch

PSI *abbrev.* Pollutant Standards Index

psi·lo·cin (sī′lə sin, sil′ə-) ***n.*** ⟦contr. < fol.⟧ a hallucinogenic drug obtained from a fungus (*Psilocybe mexicana*)

psi·lo·cy·bin (sī′lə sī′bin, sil′ə-) ***n.*** ⟦< ModL *Psilocybe* < Gr *psilos*, bare (akin to *psēn*, to rub: see PSORIASIS) + *kybē*, head + -IN¹⟧ a hallucinogenic drug obtained from a fungus (genus *Psilocybe*, esp. *P. mexicana*)

psi·lo·phyte (sī′lə fīt′) ***n.*** ⟦< ModL *Psilophyton*, name used for this grouping of plants < Gr *psilos*, bare (see prec.) + *phyton*, plant: see -PHYTE⟧ any of various extinct, early land plants of the Silurian and Devonian periods, characterized by a simple vascular structure and lacking true roots and leaves

psi particle *Particle Physics* J PARTICLE

psit·ta·cine (sit′ə sīn′, -sin) ***adj.*** ⟦L *psittacinus* < *psittacus*, a parrot (< Gr *psittakos*) + *-inus*, -INE¹⟧ of, resembling, or pertaining to parrots —**psit′ta·cine′ly** ***adv.***

psit·ta·co·sis (sit′ə kō′sis) ***n.*** ⟦ModL < L *psittacus* < Gr *psittakos*, parrot + -OSIS⟧ an acute or chronic disease of birds, esp. birds of the parrot order, caused by a bacterium (*Chlamydia psittaci*): often transmitted to humans, in whom it is characterized by fever and pneumonia

Pskov (pskôf) **1** city near the SE end of Lake Pskov **2 Lake** lake in W European Russia, connected with Lake Chudskoye by a strait: see CHUDSKOYE, Lake

pso·as (sō′əs) ***n.,*** *pl.* **pso′as** ⟦ModL < acc. pl. of Gr *psoa*, muscle of the loins⟧ either of two muscles attached to the lower spinal column, esp. the one that controls certain movements of the thigh —**pso·at·ic** (sō at′ik) ***adj.***

pso·cid (sō′sid, säs′id) ***n.*** ⟦< ModL *Psocidae* (< Gr *psōchos*, dust < *psōchein*, to rub small < IE base **bhes-*, to rub fine > SAND) + *-idae*, -IDAE⟧ any of an order (Psocoptera) of small, winged insects with biting mouthparts, including the book lice

pso·ra·le·a (sō rā′lē ə) ***n.*** ⟦ModL < Gr *psōraleos*, scaly < *psōra*: see

PSORIASIS] any of a large genus (*Psoralea*) of plants of the pea family having scurfy leaves, white to purple flowers, and short pods with single seeds

pso·ra·len (sôr′ə lən) ***n.*** [< ModL *Psoralea*, genus name (see prec.): the substance was first isolated from a species of this genus] any of various derivatives of coumarin used in drugs to treat psoriasis, etc.: when activated by sunlight it causes the skin to darken

pso·ri·a·sis (sə rī′ə sis) ***n.*** [ModL < Gr *psōriasis* < *psōra*, an itch, akin to *psēn*, to rub, scratch, *psammos*, SAND] a chronic skin disease characterized by scaly, reddish patches —**pso·ri·at·ic** (sō′rē at′ik) ***adj.***

PSR *abbrev. Astron.* pulsar

PSRO *abbrev.* Professional Standards Review Organization: a group of doctors and healthcare professionals monitoring the quality of medical care that is paid for by the federal government in a particular geographical area

psst (pst) ***interj.*** [echoic of a hiss] [Informal] used to attract someone's attention, usually in an unobtrusive way

PST *abbrev.* Pacific Standard Time

☆**psych**[1] (sīk) ***vt.*** **psyched, psych′ing** [shortened < PSYCHOANALYZE] [Slang] **1** to cause to be disturbed mentally or excited emotionally: often with *up* **2** to understand the motives or behavior of by intuition or psychological means **3** to intimidate or outwit: often with *out* **4** to prepare (oneself or someone) psychologically: usually with *up*

psych[2] *abbrev.* **1** psychiatric **2** psychiatry **3** psychological **4** psychology

psych- (sīk) *combining form* PSYCHO-: used before a vowel

psy·chas·the·ni·a (sī′kas thē′nē ə, -thēn′yə) ***n.*** [ModL: see PSYCHO- & ASTHENIA] *former term for* a group of neuroses characterized by phobias, obsessions, undue anxiety, etc. —**psy′chas·then′ic** (-then′ik) ***adj.***

psy·che (sī′kē) ***n.*** [Gr *psychē*, the soul, akin to *psychein*, to blow, cool < IE base **bhes-*, to blow > Sans *bábhasti*, (he) blows] **1** the human soul **2** the intellect **3** *Psychiatry* the mind considered as a subjectively perceived, functional entity, based ultimately upon physical processes but with complex processes of its own: it governs the total organism and its interactions with the environment

Psy·che (sī′kē) ***n.*** [L < Gr *psychē*: see prec.] *Rom. Myth.* a maiden who, after undergoing many hardships due to Venus' jealousy of her beauty, is reunited with Cupid and made immortal by Jupiter

☆**psy·che·de·li·a** (sī′kə dē′lē ə, -dēl′yə) ***n.*** [back-form. < fol.] psychedelic drugs or anything associated with their use: a nontechnical term

☆**psy·che·del·ic** (sī′kə del′ik) ***adj.*** [< PSYCHE + Gr *dēloun*, to make manifest: coined (1956), as a n., by H. Osmond (1917-2004), Brit psychiatrist & researcher, in a letter to Aldous HUXLEY] **1** of or causing extreme changes in the conscious mind, as hallucinations, delusions, intensification of awareness and sensory perception, etc. **2** of or associated with psychedelic drugs; specif., simulating the auditory or visual effects of the psychedelic state **3** designating any of various fluorescent colors popularized during the 1960s —***n.*** a psychedelic drug —**psy′che·del′i·cal·ly** ***adv.***

Psyche knot [after PSYCHE] a woman's coiffure in which the hair is coiled in a knot at the back of the head

psy·chi·at·ric (sī′kē a′trik) ***adj.*** **1** of, pertaining to, or associated with psychiatry **2** affecting mental or emotional processes [*psychiatric* side effects] **3** affected by mental illness [*psychiatric* patients] —**psy′chi·at′ri·cal·ly** ***adv.***

psy·chi·a·trist (sī kī′ə trist, si-) ***n.*** a doctor of medicine specializing in psychiatry after postgraduate training

psy·chi·a·try (sī kī′ə trē, si-) ***n.*** [ModL: see PSYCHO- & -IATRY] the branch of medicine concerned with the study, treatment, and prevention of disorders of the mind, including psychoses and neuroses, emotional maladjustments, etc.

psy·chic (sī′kik) ***adj.*** [< Gr *psychikos*, of the soul, spiritual < *psychē*, the soul: see PSYCHE] **1** of or having to do with the psyche, or mind **2** beyond natural or known physical processes **3** apparently sensitive to forces beyond the physical world Also **psy′chi·cal** —***n.*** **1** a person who is supposedly sensitive to forces beyond the physical world **2** a spiritualistic medium —**psy′chi·cal·ly** ***adv.***

psy·cho (sī′kō) ***adj., n., pl.*** **-chos** [Informal] *short for* PSYCHOTIC, PSYCHOPATHIC, PSYCHOPATH, *and, earlier,* PSYCHONEUROTIC

psy·cho- (sī′kō, -kə) [< Gr *psychē*, breath, spirit, soul: see PSYCHE] *combining form* **1** the mind or mental processes [*psychology, psychogenesis*] **2** psychology; psychological methods, practices, etc. [*psychoanalysis, psychohistory*]

psy·cho·a·cous·tics (sī′kō ə ko͞os′tiks) ***n.*** [prec. + ACOUSTICS] the study of how sounds are heard subjectively and of the individual's response to sound stimuli —**psy′cho·a·cous′tic** ***adj.***, **psy′cho·a·cous′ti·cal**

psy·cho·ac·tive (-ak′tiv) ***adj.*** designating or of a drug, chemical, etc. that has a specific effect on the mind

psy·cho·a·nal·y·sis (sī′kō ə nal′ə sis) ***n.*** [ModL: see PSYCHO- & ANALYSIS] **1** a method, developed by Freud and others, of investigating mental processes and of treating neuroses and some other disorders of the mind: it is based on the assumption that such disorders are the result of the rejection by the conscious mind of factors that then persist in the unconscious as repressed instinctual forces, causing conflicts which may be resolved or diminished by discovering and analyzing the repressions and bringing them into consciousness through the use of such techniques as free association, dream analysis, etc. **2** the theory or practice of this —**psy′cho·an′a·lyt′ic** (-an′ə lit′ik) ***adj.***, **psy′cho·an′a·lyt′i·cal** —**psy′cho·an′a·lyt′i·cal·ly** ***adv.***

psy·cho·an·a·lyst (sī′kō an′ə list) ***n.*** a specialist in psychoanalysis

psy·cho·an·a·lyze (sī′kō an′ə līz′) ***vt.*** **-lyzed′, -lyz′ing** to treat or investigate by means of psychoanalysis

☆**psy·cho·bab·ble** (sī′kō bab′əl) ***n.*** [PSYCHO(LOGICAL) + BABBLE: popularized by R. D. Rosen, U.S. author, in his book with this title (1977)] [Informal] talk or writing that employs the language and concepts of psychology and psychiatry in a trite, superficial, or confusing way

☆**psy·cho·bi·og·ra·phy** (sī′kō bī äg′rə fē) ***n.*** a biography dealing with the psychodynamic processes that have affected the development of the subject

psy·cho·bi·ol·o·gy (-bī äl′ə jē) ***n.*** **1** that branch of biology dealing with the interrelationship of the mental processes and the anatomy and physiology of the individual **2** psychology as investigated by biological methods

psy·cho·chem·i·cal (-kem′i kəl) ***n.*** any of various drugs or chemical compounds, as LSD, capable of affecting mental activity —***adj.*** of or pertaining to psychochemicals

☆**psy·cho·dra·ma** (sī′kō drä′mə) ***n.*** *Psychiatry* a form of cathartic therapy in which one or more patients act out by improvisation situations related to a personal problem or a problem common to the group, often before an audience of therapists and fellow patients —**psy′cho·dra·mat′ic** (-drə mat′ik) ***adj.***

psy·cho·dy·nam·ics (sī′kō dī nam′iks) ***n.*** the study of the mental and emotional processes underlying human behavior and its motivation, esp. as developed unconsciously in response to environmental influences —**psy′cho·dy·nam′ic** ***adj.*** —**psy′cho·dy·nam′i·cal·ly** ***adv.***

psy·cho·ed·u·ca·tion·al (sī′kō ej′o͞o kā′shə nəl, -ej′ə-) ***adj.*** designating or of psychological methods, as intelligence tests, used in evaluating learning ability

psy·cho·gen·e·sis (sī′kō jen′ə sis) ***n.*** [ModL: see PSYCHO- & -GENESIS] **1** origination and development within the psyche, or mind; specif., the development of physical disorders as a result of mental conflicts rather than from organic causes **2** the origin and development of the psyche, or mind —**psy′cho·ge·net′ic** (-jə net′ik) ***adj.***

psy·cho·gen·ic (sī′kō jen′ik) ***adj.*** [< prec.] of psychic origin; caused by mental conflicts —**psy′cho·gen′i·cal·ly** ***adv.***

psy·cho·graph (sī′kō graf′) ***n.*** [PSYCHO- + -GRAPH] *Psychol.* a graphic chart outlining the relative strength of personality traits in an individual

psy·cho·graph·ic (sī′kō graf′ik) ***adj.*** **1** of or pertaining to a psychograph **2** of or pertaining to psychographics

psy·cho·graph·ics (sī′kō graf′iks) ***n.*** in marketing and advertising, the study of the values, attitudes, etc. of a consumer population —***pl.n.*** these values, attitudes, etc.

☆**psy·cho·his·to·ry** (sī′kō his′tə rē) ***n.*** **1** the study of historical events by applying psychological theory and methods **2** PSYCHOBIOGRAPHY —**psy′cho·his·tor′i·an** ***n.*** —**psy′cho·his·tor′i·cal** ***adj.***

psy·cho·ki·ne·sis (sī′kō ki nē′sis) ***n.*** [PSYCHO- + Gr *kinēsis*, motion < *kinein*, to move: see CITE] the apparent ability, investigated in parapsychology, to influence physical objects or events by thought processes —**psy′cho·ki·net′ic** (-net′ik) ***adj.***

psychol *abbrev.* **1** psychological **2** psychology

psy·cho·lin·guis·tics (sī′kō liŋ gwis′tiks) ***n.*** [< *psycholinguistic*, adj. (< PSYCHO- + LINGUISTIC) + -ICS] the branch of linguistics that analyzes the psychological factors involved in the perception of and response to linguistic phenomena

psy·cho·log·i·cal (sī′kə läj′i kəl) ***adj.*** **1** of psychology **2** of the mind; mental **3** affecting or intended to affect the mind Also **psy′cho·log′ic** —**psy′cho·log′i·cal·ly** ***adv.***

psychological moment [transl. of Fr *moment psychologique*, a misunderstanding of Ger *psychologischer moment*, psychological momentum or motive] **1** the moment when the mind is most willing to accept a fact, suggestion, etc. **2** the critical moment; most propitious time to act

psychological warfare the use of propaganda or other psychological means to influence or confuse the thinking, undermine the morale, etc. of an enemy or opponent

psy·chol·o·gism (sī käl′ə jiz′əm) ***n.*** any attempt to find psychological bases for historical events, philosophical concepts, etc.: usually a disparaging term

psy·chol·o·gist (sī käl′ə jist) ***n.*** a specialist in psychology

psy·chol·o·gize (sī käl′ə jīz′) ***vi.*** **-gized′, -giz′ing** to reason or theorize psychologically —***vt.*** to analyze psychologically

psy·chol·o·gy (sī käl′ə jē) ***n., pl.*** **-gies** [ModL *psychologia*: see PSYCHO- & -LOGY] **1** *a)* the science dealing with the mind and with mental and emotional processes *b)* the science of human and animal behavior **2** the sum of the actions, traits, attitudes, thoughts, mental states, etc. of a person or group [the *psychology* of the adolescent] **3** a particular system of psychology **4** loosely, techniques intended to manipulate another or others [to use *psychology* on a stubborn child]

psy·cho·met·rics (sī′kō me′triks) ***n.*** [PSYCHO- + METRICS] **1** the theory or practice of measuring mental processes or functions, such as intelligence, as by psychological tests **2** PSYCHOMETRY —**psy′cho·met′ric** ***adj.***, **psy′cho·met′ri·cal** —**psy′cho·met′ri·cal·ly** ***adv.*** —**psy·chom·e·tri·cian** (sī käm′ə trish′ən) ***n.***

psy·chom·e·try (sī käm′ə trē) ***n.*** [PSYCHO- + -METRY] **1** the hypothesized ability to obtain knowledge about an object, or about a person connected with it, through contact with the object **2** PSYCHOMETRICS —**psy·chom′e·trist** ***n.***

psy·cho·mo·tor (sī′kō mōt′ər) ***adj.*** **1** of the motor effects of mental processes **2** designating or of epilepsy with seizures characterized by complex behavioral phenomena

psy·cho·neu·ro·im·mu·nol·o·gy (sī′kō no͞o′rō im′myo͞o näl′ə jē, -nyo͞o′-) ***n.*** the study of how emotional and other psychological responses influence the biochemistry of the brain, hormone production, and the immune response —**psy′cho·neu′ro·im′mu·no·log′i·cal** (-nō läj′i kəl) ***adj.*** —**psy′cho·neu′ro·im′mu·nol′o·gist** ***n.***

psy·cho·neu·ro·sis (sī′kō no͞o rō′sis, -nyo͞o-) ***n.***, *pl.* **-ses′** (-sēz′) ⟦ModL: see PSYCHO- & NEUROSIS⟧ NEUROSIS —**psy′cho·neu·rot′ic** (-rät′ik) ***adj., n.***

psy·cho·path (sī′kō path′, -kə-) ***n.*** ⟦back-form. < PSYCHOPATHY⟧ a person suffering from a mental disorder; specif., PSYCHOPATHIC PERSONALITY

psy·cho·path·ic (sī′kō path′ik, -kə-) ***adj.*** **1** of or characterized by psychopathy **2** suffering from a mental disorder —**psy′cho·path′i·cal·ly** ***adv.***

psychopathic personality **1** a person whose behavior is largely amoral and asocial and who is characterized by irresponsibility, lack of remorse or shame, perverse or impulsive (often criminal) behavior, and other serious personality defects, generally without psychotic attacks or symptoms **2** the personality of such a person

psy·cho·pa·thol·o·gy (sī′kō pə thäl′ə jē) ***n.*** ⟦PSYCHO- + PATHOLOGY⟧ **1** the science dealing with the causes and development of mental disorders **2** psychological malfunctioning, as in a mental disorder —**psy′cho·path′o·log′i·cal** (-path′ə läj′i kəl) ***adj.*** —**psy′cho·pa·thol′o·gist** ***n.***

psy·chop·a·thy (sī käp′ə thē) ***n.*** ⟦PSYCHO- + -PATHY⟧ mental disorder

psy·cho·phar·ma·col·o·gy (sī′kō fär′mə käl′ə jē) ***n.*** the study of the actions of drugs on the mind —**psy′cho·phar′ma·co·log′i·cal** (-kə läj′i kəl) ***adj.***

psy·cho·phys·ics (sī′kō fiz′iks) ***n.*** ⟦PSYCHO- + PHYSICS⟧ the branch of psychology dealing with the functional relations between the mind and physical phenomena —**psy′cho·phys′i·cist** ***n.***

psy·cho·phys·i·ol·o·gy (-fiz′ē äl′ə jē) ***n.*** the study of the interactions between mental and physiological processes —**psy′cho·phys′i·o·log′i·cal** (-fiz′ē ə läj′i kəl) ***adj.***

psy·cho·pomp (sī′kō pämp′) ***n.*** ⟦< Gr *psychopompos*, epithet of Hermes or Charon < *psychē*, soul (see PSYCHE) + *pompos*, escort, guide⟧ *Myth.* an escort of souls to the underworld

psy·cho·sex·u·al (-sek′sho͞o əl) ***adj.*** of or having to do with the psychological aspects of sexuality in contrast to the physical aspects —**psy′cho·sex′u·al′i·ty** (-al′ə tē) ***n.***

psy·cho·sis (sī kō′sis) ***n.***, *pl.* **-ses′** (-sēz′) ⟦ModL: see PSYCHO- & -OSIS⟧ a major mental disorder in which the personality is very seriously disorganized and contact with reality is usually impaired: psychoses are of two sorts, *a)* functional (characterized by lack of apparent organic cause, and principally of the schizophrenic, paranoid, or bipolar type), and *b)* organic (characterized by a pathological organic condition such as brain damage or disease, metabolic disorders, etc.) —**SYN.** INSANITY

psy·cho·so·cial (sī′kō sō′shəl) ***adj.*** of or pertaining to the psychological development of the individual in relation to his or her social environment

psy·cho·so·mat·ic (sī′kō sō mat′ik) ***adj.*** ⟦PSYCHO- + SOMATIC: orig. coined by S. T. COLERIDGE (1830) as *Psycho-somatic*, of the mind and the body together⟧ **1** designating or of a disorder of the body originating in or aggravated by the psychic or emotional processes of the individual **2** designating a system of medicine using a coordinated psychological and physiological approach to the study of the causes and treatment of psychosomatic disorders —***n.*** an individual exhibiting a psychosomatic disorder —**psy′cho·so·mat′i·cal·ly** ***adv.***

psy·cho·sur·ger·y (sī′kō sur′jər ē) ***n.*** brain surgery performed in treating chronic mental disorder

psy·cho·ther·a·peu·tics (sī′kō ther′ə pyo͞ot′iks) ***n.*** PSYCHOTHERAPY —**psy′cho·ther′a·peu′tic** ***adj.***

psy·cho·ther·a·py (sī′kō ther′ə pē) ***n.*** ⟦PSYCHO- + THERAPY⟧ treatment of mental or emotional disorder by any of various means involving communication between a trained person and the patient and including counseling, psychoanalysis, etc. —**psy′cho·ther′a·pist** ***n.***

psy·chot·ic (sī kät′ik) ***adj.*** **1** of, or having the nature of, a psychosis **2** having a psychosis —***n.*** a person who has a psychosis —**psy·chot′i·cal·ly** ***adv.***

psy·chot·o·mi·met·ic (sī kät′ō mī met′ik, -mi-) ***adj.*** ⟦< prec. + -O- + MIMETIC⟧ designating or of certain drugs as LSD and mescaline, that produce hallucinations, symptoms of a psychotic state, and, sometimes, chromosomal breaks —***n.*** a psychotomimetic drug

psy·cho·tox·ic (sī′kō täk′sik) ***adj.*** ⟦PSYCHO- + TOXIC⟧ of or pertaining to certain drugs or chemical compounds, as alcohol, capable of damaging the brain

psy·cho·trop·ic (-träp′ik) ***adj.*** ⟦PSYCHO- + -TROPIC⟧ having an altering effect on the mind, as tranquilizers, hallucinogens, etc. —***n.*** a psychotropic drug

psy·chro- (sī′krō, -krə) ⟦< Gr *psychros*, cold, akin to *psychein*, to cool: see PSYCHE⟧ *combining form* cold *[psychrometer]*

psy·chrom·e·ter (sī kräm′ət ər) ***n.*** ⟦prec. + -METER: orig., thermometer⟧ an instrument with wet- and dry-bulb thermometers, for measuring moisture in the air

psy·chro·phil·ic (sī′krō fil′ik) ***adj.*** ⟦PSYCHRO- + -PHIL(E) + -IC⟧ *Biol.* growing best at low temperatures —**psy′chro·phile′** (-fīl′) ***n.***

psyl·la (sil′ə) ***n.*** ⟦ModL < Gr, flea < IE base **plou-*, var. of **blou-* > L *pulex*, FLEA⟧ any of a family (Psyllidae) of plant-eating, homopterous, jumping lice, often harmful to fruit trees

psyl·li·um (sil′ē əm) ***n.*** ⟦ModL < Gr *psyllion*, fleawort < *psylla*, flea (see prec.): so called because the seeds resemble fleas⟧ the seed of various plantains, used in laxatives and to add fiber to some food products

psy·war (sī′wôr′) ***n.*** *short for* PSYCHOLOGICAL WARFARE

pt *abbrev.* **1** part **2** past tense **3** payment **4** phot(s) **5** pint(s): also, for the plural, **pts** **6** point **7** PORT[4]

Pt[1] *abbrev.* **1** *Bible* Peter **2** Point **3** Port

Pt[2] *Chem. symbol for* platinum

PT *abbrev.* **1** Pacific Time **2** Physical Therapist **3** Physical Therapy

p.t. *abbrev.* pro tempore

pta *abbrev.* peseta

PTA *abbrev.* Parent-Teacher Association

Ptah (p'tä, p'täkh) ***n.*** ⟦Egypt *ptḥ*⟧ *Egypt. Myth.* the chief god of Egyptian Memphis, creator of gods and mortals

ptar·mi·gan (tär′mi gən) ***n.***, *pl.* **-gans** or **-gan** ⟦altered (by assoc. with PTERO-) < earlier *termigan* < Scot *tarmachan*⟧ any of a genus (*Lagopus*) of brownish arctic, subarctic, or alpine grouse with feathered legs and feet, usually having white plumage in the winter

☆**PT boat** (pē′tē′) ⟦*p(atrol) t(orpedo) boat*⟧ MOTOR TORPEDO BOAT

pter·an·o·don (tə ran′ə dän′) ***n.*** ⟦ModL < Gr *pteron*, wing (see FEATHER) + *anodous*, toothless < *an-*, not + *odous* (gen. *odontos*), TOOTH⟧ any of a genus (*Pteranodon*) of large, toothless, Late Cretaceous pterosaurs having a long, bony crest at the back of the head

pter·i·dol·o·gy (ter′i däl′ə jē) ***n.*** ⟦< Gr *pteris* (gen. *pteridos*), fern (akin to *pteron*, FEATHER: from the featherlike shape) + -LOGY⟧ the branch of botany dealing with ferns —**pter′i·do·log′i·cal** (-dō läj′i kəl) ***adj.*** —**pter′i·dol′o·gist** ***n.***

pter·i·do·phyte (ter′i dō fīt′) ***n.*** ⟦< ModL *Pteridophyta* < Gr *pteris* (see prec.) + -PHYTE⟧ in some systems of plant classification, any of a division (Pteridophyta) of plants possessing true vascular roots, stems, and leaves and reproducing by means of spores, including the ferns and lycopods —**pter′i·do′phyt′ic** (-fit′ik) ***adj.***, **pter′i·doph′y·tous** (-däf′i təs)

pter·id·o·sperm (-spurm′) ***n.*** SEED FERN

pter·o- (ter′ō, -ə) ⟦ModL < Gr *pteron*, wing, FEATHER⟧ *combining form* feather, wing *[pterodactyl]*

pter·o·dac·tyl (ter′ə dak′təl) ***n.*** ⟦< ModL *Pterodactylus*: see prec. & DACTYL⟧ **1** PTEROSAUR: now a loose usage **2** any of a suborder (Pterodactyloidea) of pterosaurs of the Jurassic and Cretaceous periods; specif., any of a genus (*Pterodactylus*) of this suborder

pte·ro·ic acid (tə rō′ik) ⟦ult. < Gr *pteron*, FEATHER, wing (because found in pigments in butterfly wings) + -IC⟧ a crystalline acid, $C_{14}H_{12}N_6O_3$, which can react with glutamic acid to form folic acid

pter·o·pod (ter′ə päd′) ***adj.*** ⟦< ModL *Pteropoda*: see PTERO- & -POD⟧ of or relating to certain orders of small, thin-shelled or shell-less gastropod mollusks that swim by means of winglike lobes on the foot —***n.*** any such animal —**pte·rop·o·dan** (tə räp′ə dən) ***adj., n.***

pter·o·saur (ter′ə sôr′) ***n.*** ⟦< ModL *Pterosaurus*: see PTERO- & -SAUR⟧ any of an order (Pterosauria) of flying reptiles of the Mesozoic Era, having wings of skin stretched along the body between the hind limbs and the very long fourth digits of each forelimb

-pter·ous (tər əs) ⟦see PTERO- & -OUS⟧ *combining form forming adjectives* having (a specified number or kind of) wings *[homopterous]*

pte·ryg·i·um (tə rij′ē əm) ***n.***, *pl.* **-i·ums** or **-i·a** (-ə) ⟦ModL < Gr *pterygion*, dim. of *pteryx*, wing, akin to *pteron*, FEATHER⟧ an abnormal, triangular mass of mucous membrane growing over the human cornea from the inner corner of the eye —**pte·ryg′i·al** ***adj.***

pter·y·goid (ter′i goid′) ***adj.*** ⟦< Gr *pteryx*, gen. *pterygos* (see prec.) + -OID⟧ **1** having the form of a wing; winglike **2** designating, of, or near either of two winglike processes in the skull that descend from the sphenoid bone —***n.*** a pterygoid bone or process

pter·y·la (ter′i lə) ***n.***, *pl.* **-lae′** (-lē′) ⟦ModL < PTER(O)- + Gr *hylē*, forest⟧ *Ornithology* any of the special areas on a bird's skin from which feathers grow

ptg *abbrev.* printing

ptis·an (tiz′ən, ti zan′) ***n.*** *var. of* TISANE

PTO *abbrev.* Parent-Teacher Organization

Ptol·e·ma·ic (täl′ə mā′ik) ***adj.*** ⟦Gr *Ptolemaïkos*⟧ **1** of Ptolemy, the astronomer **2** of the Ptolemies who ruled Egypt

Ptolemaic system the theory, systematized by Ptolemy, postulating the earth as the center or fixed point of the universe, around which the celestial bodies move

Ptol·e·ma·ist (täl′ə mā′ist) ***n.*** an adherent or supporter of the Ptolemaic system of astronomy

Ptol·e·my[1] (täl′ə mē) ***n.*** **1** name of a Macedonian dynasty of Egypt founded by Ptolemy I and ruling from 323 to 30 B.C. **2** *pl.* **-mies** a member of this dynasty

Ptol·e·my[2] (täl′ə mē) **1** (L. name *Claudius Ptolomaeus*) 2d cent. A.D.; Alexandrian astronomer, mathematician, & geographer **2** **Ptolemy I** 367?-283 B.C.; general of Alexander the Great: 1st king of the Ptolemaic dynasty (323-285): called *Ptolemy Soter* ("Savior") **3** **Ptolemy II** 309-246 B.C.; king of Egypt (285-246): son of Ptolemy I: called *Ptolemy Philadelphus*

pto·maine (tō′mān′) ***n.*** ⟦It *ptomaina* < Gr *ptōma*, corpse < *piptein*, to fall: see FEATHER⟧ any of a class of alkaloid substances, some of which are poisonous, formed in decaying animal or vegetable matter by bacterial action on proteins

ptomaine poisoning *former term for* FOOD POISONING (erroneously thought to be caused by ptomaines)

pto·sis (tō′sis) ***n.*** ⟦ModL < Gr *ptōsis*, a fall, falling < *piptein*: see FEATHER⟧ a prolapse, or falling of some organ or part; esp., the drooping of the upper eyelid, caused by the paralysis of its muscle —**pto′tic** (-tik) ***adj.***

PTSD *abbrev.* post-traumatic stress disorder
ptu·i (p'to͞o'ē) *interj.* ⟦echoic⟧ used to suggest the sound of spitting: sometimes sp. **ptoo'ey**
PTV *abbrev.* pay television
Pty or **pty** *abbrev.* proprietary
pty·a·lin (tī'ə lin) ***n.*** ⟦< Gr *ptyalon*, spittle < *ptyein*, to spit (of echoic orig.) + -IN[1]⟧ an amylase in the saliva of humans and some other animals that converts starch into various dextrins and maltose
pty·a·lism (tī'ə liz'əm) ***n.*** ⟦Gr *ptyalismos*, a spitting < *ptyalizein*, to spit often < *ptyalon:* see prec.⟧ excessive secretion of saliva
p-type (pē'tīp') ***adj.*** ⟦< POSITIVE + TYPE⟧ *Electronics* designating or of positive semiconductor material in which there are more holes than electrons and current is carried through it by the movement of the holes: see HOLE (*n.* 7), N-TYPE
Pu *Chem. symbol for* plutonium
☆**P.U.** (pē'yo͞o') ***interj.*** [Slang] used to express disgust, revulsion, etc. in response to an offensive odor or to anything felt to be unpleasant or offensive
pub[1] (pub) ***n.*** ⟦contr. < PUBLIC HOUSE⟧ **1** [Chiefly Brit.] a bar or tavern **2** in the U.S., a tavern in traditional English or Irish decor or style
pub[2] *abbrev.* **1** public **2** published (by) **3** publisher **4** publishing
pub-crawl (pub'krôl') [Informal, Chiefly Brit.] ***vi.*** to go from one pub to another as on a drinking spree ***—n.*** the act of, or a period spent in, pub-crawling: also **pub crawl**
pu·ber·ty (pyo͞o'bər tē) ***n.*** ⟦ME *puberte* < L *pubertas* < *puber*, of ripe age, adult, prob. akin to *puer*, boy⟧ the stage of physical development when secondary sex characteristics develop and sexual reproduction first becomes possible: in common law, the age of puberty is generally fixed at fourteen for boys and twelve for girls **—pu'ber·tal** ***adj.***
pu·ber·u·lent (pyo͞o ber'yo͞o lənt) ***adj.*** ⟦< L *puber*, adult, covered with soft down + -ULENT⟧ covered with fine hairs or down
pu·bes[1] (pyo͞o'bēz') ***n.*** ⟦L, pubic hair, groin, akin to prec.⟧ **1** the hair appearing on the body at puberty, esp. the hair at the lower part of the abdomen surrounding the external genitals **2** the region of the abdomen covered by such hair
pu·bes[2] (pyo͞o'bēz') ***n.*** *pl. of* PUBIS
pu·bes·cence (pyo͞o bes'əns) ***n.*** ⟦Fr⟧ **1** the quality or state of being pubescent **2** the soft down that covers the surface of many plants and insects
pu·bes·cent (pyo͞o bes'ənt) ***adj.*** ⟦Fr < L *pubescens*, prp. of *pubescere*, to reach puberty < *pubes*, adult, akin to *puber:* see PUBERTY⟧ **1** reaching or having reached the state of puberty **2** of, having to do with, or characteristic of puberty **3** covered with a soft down, as many plants and insects
pu·bic (pyo͞o'bik) ***adj.*** of or in the region of the pubis or the pubes
pu·bis (pyo͞o'bis) ***n.***, *pl.* **pu'bes'** (-bēz') ⟦ModL < L: see PUBES[1]⟧ that part of either hipbone forming, with the corresponding part of the other, the front arch of the pelvis
publ *abbrev.* **1** published **2** publisher
pub·lic (pub'lik) ***adj.*** ⟦ME < L *publicus:* altered (prob. infl. by *pubes*, adult) < *poplicus*, contr. of *populicus*, public < *populus*, the PEOPLE⟧ **1** of, belonging to, or concerning the people as a whole; of or by the community at large [the *public* welfare, a *public* outcry] **2** for the use or benefit of all; esp., supported by government funds [a *public* park] **3** as regards community, rather than private, affairs **4** acting in an official capacity on behalf of the people as a whole [a *public* prosecutor] **5** known by, or open to the knowledge of, all or most people [to make information *public*, a *public* figure] **6** *Finance* owned by shareholders whose shares can be freely traded, as on an exchange [a *public* company] ***—n.*** **1** the people as a whole; community at large: often preceded by *the* **2** a specific part of the people; those people considered together because of some common interest or purpose [the reading *public*] **—go public 1** to become a publicly owned company by issuing shares for sale to the public **2** to reveal something previously kept private or secret to the public **—in public** openly; not in private or in secrecy
☆**pub·lic-ad·dress system** (pub'lik ə dres') an electronic amplification system, used as in auditoriums or theaters, so that announcements, music, etc. can be easily heard by a large audience
pub·li·can (pub'li kən) ***n.*** ⟦ME < L *publicanus* < *publicus:* see PUBLIC⟧ **1** in ancient Rome, a collector of public revenues, tolls, etc. **2** [Brit.] a saloonkeeper
public assistance financial aid given by the government to persons who are poor, unemployed, etc.
pub·li·ca·tion (pub'li kā'shən) ***n.*** ⟦ME *publicacioun* < L *publicatio* < *publicare:* see PUBLISH⟧ **1** a publishing or being published; public notification **2** the printing and distribution, usually for sale, of books, magazines, newspapers, etc. **3** something published; specif., *a)* a periodical *b)* a work of a particular writer, as an article or book
public debt 1 the total debt of all governmental units, including those of state and local governments **2** NATIONAL DEBT
☆**public defender** an attorney employed at public expense to defend indigent persons accused of crimes
☆**public domain 1** public lands **2** the condition of being free from copyright or patent and, hence, open to use by anyone
public enemy 1 a government with which one's country is at war **2** a hardened criminal or other person who is a menace to society
public house [Brit.] PUB[1] (sense 1)
public housing housing provided by the government, esp. for the poor
public intellectual an intellectual, often a noted specialist in a particular field, who has become well-known to the general public for a willingness to comment on current affairs
pub·li·cist (pub'lə sist) ***n.*** ⟦Fr *publiciste* < (*droit*) *public*, public (law) + *-iste*, -IST[1]⟧ **1** a student of or specialist in public or international law **2** [Rare] a journalist who writes about politics and public affairs **3** ⟦PUBLIC(IZE) + -IST[1]⟧ a person whose business is to publicize persons, organizations, etc.
pub·lic·i·ty (pub lis'ə tē) ***n.*** ⟦Fr *publicité*⟧ **1** the state of being public, or commonly known or observed ☆**2** *a)* any information, promotional material, etc. which brings a person, place, product, or cause to the notice of the public *b)* the work or business of preparing and disseminating such material **3** *a)* notice by the public *b)* any procedure or act that seeks to gain this
pub·li·cize (pub'lə sīz') ***vt.* -cized', -ciz'ing** to give publicity to; draw public attention to
public law 1 a law or statute affecting or applicable to the public generally **2** the branch of law concerned with the relations of individuals to the state and with the state as an entity capable of acting as if a private person
public lending right [Brit.] the right of authors to royalties when their books are borrowed from public libraries
pub·lic·ly (pub'lik lē) ***adv.*** **1** in a public or open manner **2** by, or by consent or agency of, the public
public opinion the opinion of the people generally, esp. as a force in determining social and political action
☆**public relations** relations with the general public as through publicity; specif., those functions of a corporation, organization, etc. concerned with attempting to create favorable public opinion for itself
public school ☆**1** in the U.S., an elementary or secondary school that is part of a system of free schools maintained by public taxes and supervised by local authorities **2** in much of Great Britain, any of a number of endowed, private boarding schools, generally not coeducational, which prepare students for the universities
public servant an elected or appointed government official or a civil-service employee
public service 1 employment by the government, esp. through civil service **2** some service performed for the public with no direct charge, as by a private corporation
☆**pub·lic-serv·ice corporation** (pub'lik sʉr'vis) a private corporation that supplies some essential commodity or service to the public, under governmental regulation
pub·lic-spir·it·ed (pub'lik spir'it id) ***adj.*** having or showing zeal for the public welfare
public utility an organization supplying water, electricity, transportation, etc. to the public, operated, usually as a monopoly, by a private corporation under governmental regulation or by the government directly
public works ☆works constructed by the government for public use or service, as highways or dams
pub·lish (pub'lish) ***vt.*** ⟦ME *publisshen* < extended stem of OFr *publier* < L *publicare*, to make public < *publicus*, PUBLIC⟧ **1** to make publicly known; announce, proclaim, divulge, or promulgate **2** *a)* to issue (a book, newspaper, software, recorded music, digitized information or images, etc.) to the public, as for sale *b)* to issue the written work or works of (a particular author) **3** *Law* to execute (a will) ***—vi.*** **1** to issue books, newspapers, etc. to the public **2** to write books, scholarly papers, etc. that are published **3** to issue a book, newspaper, software, recorded music, etc. in an electronic form, as on a CD-ROM or on the internet: often with *to* **—SYN.** DECLARE **—pub'lish·a·ble** ***adj.***
pub·lish·er (pub'lish ər) ***n.*** a person or firm that publishes, esp. one whose business is the publishing of books, newspapers, magazines, printed music, etc.
pub·lish·ing (pub'lish iŋ) ***n.*** the business or profession of editing, producing, and marketing books, newspapers, magazines, printed music, and, now also, audiobooks, software, etc.
Pub·li·us (po͝ob'lē əs, po͝ob'-) ***n.*** ⟦L⟧ *Rom. History* a masculine praenomen
Puc·ci·ni (po͞o chē'nē), **Gia·co·mo** (jä'kō mō') 1858-1924; It. operatic composer
☆**puc·coon** (pə ko͞on') ***n.*** ⟦see POKE[3]⟧ **1** GROMWELL **2** [Archaic] BLOODROOT **3** [Archaic] a dye from either of these plants
puce (pyo͞os) ***n.*** ⟦Fr, lit., a flea < L *pulex*, flea⟧ brownish purple ***—adj.*** of the color puce
puck[1] (puk) ***n.*** ⟦< dial. *puck*, to strike, akin to POKE[1]⟧ the hard rubber disk used in ice hockey
puck[2] (puk) ***n.*** ⟦ME *puke* < OE *puca*, akin to ON *puki*, devil < IE base **beu-*, to blow up, swell > POUT[1], POKE[2]⟧ *Eng. Folklore* **1** a mischievous sprite or elf **2** [P-] Robin Goodfellow: Puck appears as a character in Shakespeare's *A Midsummer Night's Dream*
puck·a (puk'ə) ***adj.*** *alt. sp. of* PUKKA
puck·er (puk'ər) ***vt., vi.*** ⟦freq. form based on POKE[2]: prob. from the idea of gathering cloth into small baglike folds⟧ to draw up or gather into wrinkles or small folds ***—n.*** a wrinkle or small fold made by puckering **—pucker up** to contract the lips as in preparing to kiss
puck·er·y (-ē) ***adj.*** of, causing, or characterized by puckering
puck·ish (puk'ish) ***adj.*** ⟦< PUCK[2] & -ISH⟧ full of mischief; impish **—puck'ish·ly** ***adv.*** **—puck'ish·ness** ***n.***
pud (po͝od) ***n.*** [Brit. Informal] *short for* PUDDING
PUD *abbrev.* planned unit development
pud·ding (po͝od'iŋ) ***n.*** ⟦ME *puddyng*, altered < ? OFr *boudin*, black pudding

< VL **botellinus* < LL *botellus:* see BOWEL⟧ **1** [Scot. or North Eng.] a sausage made of intestine stuffed with meat, suet, etc. and boiled **2** a soft, mushy or creamy food, usually made with a base of flour, cornstarch, cornmeal, etc., and boiled or baked **3** a sweetened dessert, usually of similar consistency and usually steamed or baked, variously containing eggs, milk, fruit, etc. **4** [Chiefly Brit.] *a)* any dessert *b)* the dessert course of a meal

pud·ding·stone (-stōn′) ***n.*** any conglomerate rock having dark-colored, rounded pebbles that are embedded in a light-colored, fine-grained matrix

pud·dle (pud′'l) ***n.*** ⟦ME *podel,* dim. < OE *pudd,* ditch, akin to LowG *pudel*⟧ **1** a small pool of water, esp. stagnant, spilled, or muddy water **2** a thick mixture of clay, and sometimes sand, with water, that is impervious to water —***vt.*** **-dled, -dling 1** to make muddy **2** to make a thick mixture of (wet clay and sand) **3** to cover with such a mixture to keep water from penetrating **4** to treat (iron) by puddling —***vi.*** to dabble or wallow in dirty or muddy water —**pud′dler** (-lər) ***n.***

pud·dling (pud′liŋ, pud′'l iŋ) ***n.*** ⟦< prec.⟧ **1** the process of working clay, etc. into a puddle **2** the process of making wrought iron from pig iron by heating and stirring it in the presence of oxidizing agents

pud·dly (pud′lē, pud′'l ē) ***adj.*** **-dli·er, -dli·est** having puddles

pu·den·cy (pyo͞od′'n sē) ***n.*** ⟦LL *pudentia* < L *pudens,* prp. of *pudere,* to be ashamed⟧ modesty or prudishness

pu·den·dum (pyo͞o den′dəm) ***n.,*** *pl.* **-den′da** (-də) ⟦ModL < L, neut. of *pudendus,* (something) to be ashamed of < *pudere:* see prec.⟧ **1** the external genitals of the female; vulva **2** [*pl.*] the external genitals of either sex —**pu·den′dal** (-dəl) ***adj.***

pu·deur (pü dėr′) ***n.*** ⟦Fr, modesty⟧ **1** a holding back or concealing from others, as of one's intimate feelings; reserve; restraint **2** modesty or shame, esp. in sexual matters

pudg·y (puj′ē) ***adj.*** **pudg′i·er, pudg′i·est** ⟦< Scot dial., prob. < Scot *pud,* belly, akin to PUCK[2]⟧ short and fat; dumpy —**pudg′i·ness** ***n.***

Pue·bla (pweb′lä) **1** state of SE Mexico: 13,096 sq mi (33,919 sq km) **2** its capital: in full **Puebla de Zaragoza**

☆**pueb·lo** (pweb′lō) ***n.,*** *pl.* **-los** (-lōz); also, for 2, **-lo** ⟦Sp, village, people < L *populus,* PEOPLE⟧ **1** a type of communal village built by certain Amerindian peoples of the SW U.S. and parts of Latin America, consisting of one or more flat-roofed structures of stone or adobe, arranged in terraces and housing a number of families **2** [**P-**] a member of any of the peoples inhabiting pueblos, as a Zuni or Hopi **3** any Indian village in the SW U.S. **4** in Spanish America, a village or town **5** in the Philippines, a municipality; town or township

Pueb·lo (pweb′lō) ⟦see prec.⟧ city in SC Colo., on the Arkansas River

puer·ile (pyoor′əl, -īl′) ***adj.*** ⟦< Fr or L: Fr *puéril* < L *puerilis* < *puer,* boy: see POULTRY⟧ silly or trivial, esp. in a childish way or as a result of immaturity —***SYN.*** YOUNG —**puer′ile·ly** ***adv.***

puer·il·ism (-iz′əm) ***n.*** childishness, esp. as a symptom of emotional disorder in an adult

puer·il·i·ty (pyoor il′ə tē) ***n.*** ⟦Fr *puérilité* < L *puerilitas*⟧ **1** the quality or condition of being puerile; childishness **2** *pl.* **-ties** an instance of this

pu·er·per·al (pyo͞o ur′pər əl) ***adj.*** ⟦< L *puerpera,* woman in labor < *puer,* boy (see POULTRY) + *parere,* to bear (see -PAROUS)⟧ of or connected with childbirth

puerperal fever sepsis occurring, esp. formerly, after childbirth

pu·er·pe·ri·um (pyo͞o′ər pir′ē əm) ***n.*** ⟦L, childbirth: see PUERPERAL⟧ the period or state of confinement during and just after childbirth

Puer·to Ri·co (pwer′tə rē′kō, pôr′-) ⟦Sp, lit., rich port⟧ island in the West Indies which, with small nearby islands, constitutes a commonwealth associated with the U.S.: 3,425 sq mi (8,870 sq km); cap. San Juan: abbrev. *PR* or *P.R.* —**Puer′to Ri′can** (-kən)

puff (puf) ***n.*** ⟦ME *puf* < OE *pyff* < the v.⟧ **1** *a)* a short, sudden burst or gust, as of wind, or an expulsion, as of breath *b)* the sound of this *c)* a small quantity of vapor, smoke, etc. expelled at one time **2** a draw at a cigarette, pipe, etc. **3** a swelling, or a protuberance caused by swelling **4** a shell of soft, light pastry filled with whipped cream, custard, etc. **5** a soft, bulging mass of material, full in the middle and gathered in at the edges **6** a soft roll of hair on the head **7** a soft pad for dabbing powder on the skin or hair **8** a quilted bed covering with cotton, wool, or down filling **9** *a)* [Archaic] vain show; bluff *b)* an advertisement, review, etc., as of a book, containing undue or exaggerated praise —***vi.*** ⟦ME *puffen* < OE *pyffan,* of echoic orig.⟧ **1** to blow in puffs, as the wind **2** *a)* to give forth puffs of smoke, steam, etc. *b)* to breathe rapidly and hard, as from running **3** to move, giving forth puffs: with *away, out, in,* etc. **4** to come in puffs, as smoke **5** *a)* to fill (*out* or *up*), as with air *b)* to become inflated, as with pride (with *out* or *up*) *c)* to swell (*out* or *up*), as skin tissue **6** to take a puff or puffs at a cigarette, pipe, etc. —***vt.*** **1** to blow, drive, give forth, etc. in or with a puff or puffs **2** to swell; distend; inflate **3** to praise unduly **4** to write or print a puff of *[to puff a novel]* **5** to smoke (a cigarette, pipe, etc.) **6** to set (the hair) in soft, round masses or rolls —**puff′ing** ***n.***

puff adder 1 a large, poisonous African viper (*Bitis arietans*) that hisses or puffs loudly when excited ☆**2** HOGNOSE SNAKE

puff·ball (puf′bôl′) ***n.*** any of various round basidiomycetous fungi (esp. order Lycoperdales) that burst at the touch, when mature, and discharge a brown powder

puff·er (puf′ər) ***n.*** **1** a person or thing that puffs ☆**2** either of two families (esp. Tetraodontidae, order Tetraodontiformes) of small, marine bony fishes capable of expanding their body by swallowing water or air

puff·er·y (-ē) ***n.*** exaggerated praise, as in advertising

puf·fin (puf′in) ***n.*** ⟦ME *poffin* < ? assoc. by folk etym. with PUFF, because of the enormous beak or blown-up appearance of the young⟧ any of various northern alcidine shorebirds (esp. genus *Fratercula*) black above and white below, with a short neck, ducklike body, and a large, brightly colored, triangular beak

puffins

puff pastry 1 crisp, flaky pastry in many thin, separate layers, as croissants or napoleons **2** the dough for this pastry, which is interfolded with butter to form the layers

puff·y (puf′ē) ***adj.*** **puff′i·er, puff′i·est 1** blowing or coming in puffs **2** panting; short-winded **3** puffed up; swollen; inflated **4** fat; obese —**puff′i·ly** ***adv.*** —**puff′i·ness** ***n.***

pug[1] (pug) ***n.*** ⟦Early ModE: altered < ? PUCK[2]⟧ **1** any of a breed of small, short-haired dog with a thickset body, square muzzle, deeply wrinkled forehead, and curled tail **2** PUG NOSE

pug[2] (pug) ***vt.*** **pugged, pug′ging** ⟦< dial.: prob. echoic of pounding; orig. sense "to punch, strike"⟧ **1** to temper (clay) for making bricks, earthenware, etc. **2** to fill in with clay, mortar, sand, etc. for soundproofing

pug[3] (pug) ***n.*** [Slang] *short for* PUGILIST

pug[4] (pug) ***n.*** ⟦Hindi *pag*⟧ a footprint or trail (of an animal) —***vt.*** **pugged, pug′ging** to trail by following footprints

Pu·get Sound (pyo͞o′jit) ⟦after Lt. Peter *Puget* of the Vancouver expedition (1792)⟧ inlet of the Pacific in NW Wash.: *c.* 100 mi (161 km) long

pug·gle (pug′əl) ***n.*** ⟦< PUG[1] + BEAGLE⟧ a dog crossbred from a pug and a beagle

pug·ga·ree (pug′ə rē′) ***n.*** ⟦Hindi *pagrī,* turban⟧ **1** in India, a turban **2** a light scarf wrapped around the crown of a sun helmet and hanging behind to protect the back of the neck Also **pug′a·ree′** or **pug·gree** (pug′rē)

pu·gil·ism (pyo͞o′jə liz′əm) ***n.*** ⟦L *pugil,* boxer, pugilist, akin to *pugnare,* to fight (see PUGNACIOUS) + -ISM⟧ BOXING[1] —**pu′gil·ist** ***n.*** —**pu′gil·is′tic** ***adj.***

Pu·glia (po͞o′lyä) *It. name for* APULIA

pug·na·cious (pug nā′shəs) ***adj.*** ⟦< L *pugnax,* combative < *pugnare,* to fight (< IE base **peuĝ-,* to punch > Gr *pygmē,* fist, L *pungere,* to pierce) + -OUS⟧ eager and ready to fight; quarrelsome; combative —***SYN.*** BELLIGERENT —**pug·na′cious·ly** ***adv.*** —**pug·nac′i·ty** (-nas′ə tē) ***n.,*** **pug·na′cious·ness**

pug nose ⟦PUG[1] + NOSE⟧ a nose that is short, thick, and turned-up at the end —**pug′-nosed′** ***adj.***

puis·ne (pyo͞o′nē) [Chiefly Brit.] ***adj.*** ⟦OFr, lit., born later: see PUNY⟧ of lower rank; junior, as in appointment —***n.*** an associate justice as distinguished from chief justice

puis·sant (pwis′ənt; pyo͞o′i sənt, pyo͞o is′ənt) ***adj.*** ⟦OFr, powerful < stem of *poeir,* to be able: see POWER⟧ [Now Chiefly Literary] powerful; strong —**puis′sance** ***n.***

puke (pyo͞ok) ***n., vi., vt.*** **puked, puk′ing** ⟦akin ? to Ger *spucken,* to spit, ult. of echoic orig.⟧ [Informal] VOMIT

puk·ka (puk′ə) ***adj.*** ⟦Hindi *pakka,* ripe, of full weight, cooked < Sans *pakva* < IE base **pekw-,* to COOK⟧ **1** [Anglo-Ind.] good or first-rate of its kind **2** [Brit. Informal] upper-class **3** [Brit.] genuine; authentic

pul (po͞ol) ***n.,*** *pl.* **puls** or **pul** ⟦Pers *pūl* < Turk *pul* < LGr *phollis,* small coin < LL *follis* < L, orig., bellows, hence bag, moneybag: see FOLLICLE⟧ a monetary unit of Afghanistan, equal to 1/100 of an afghani

pu·la (po͞o′lä) ***n.,*** *pl.* **pu′la** ⟦lit., rain, in a Bantu language of Botswana: term used as a greeting or blessing⟧ the basic monetary unit of Botswana: see the table of monetary units in the Reference Supplement

Pu·las·ki (po͞o läs′kē), **Cas·i·mir** (kaz′i mir′) 1748-79; Pol. general in the American Revolutionary army

pul·chri·tude (pul′krə to͞od′, -tyo͞od′) ***n.*** ⟦ME < L *pulchritudo* < *pulcher,* beautiful⟧ physical beauty —☆**pul′chri·tu′di·nous** (-'n əs) ***adj.***

pule (pyo͞ol) ***vi.*** **puled, pul′ing** ⟦echoic⟧ to whimper or whine, as a sick or fretful child does

pu·li (po͞o′lē) ***n.,*** *pl.* **pu′lik** (-lēk) or **pu′lis** ⟦Hung⟧ any of a breed of medium-sized dog with a shaggy coat of a solid color, typically dull black, orig. bred in Hungary for herding sheep

Pul·it·zer (pool′it sər, pyo͞o′lit-), **Joseph** 1847-1911; U.S. newspaper owner & philanthropist, born in Hungary

☆**Pulitzer Prize** any of a number of yearly prizes established by Joseph Pulitzer, given for outstanding work in journalism, literature, and music

pull (pool) ***vt.*** ⟦ME *pullen* < OE *pullian,* to pluck, snatch with the fingers: ? akin to MLowG *pull,* a husk, shell⟧ **1** to exert force or influence on so as to cause to move toward or after the source of the force; drag, tug, draw, attract, etc. **2** *a)* to draw out; pluck out; extract *[to pull a tooth]* *b)* to pick or uproot *[to pull carrots]* **3** to draw apart; rip; tear *[to pull a seam]* **4** to shred (cooked meat) and serve, typically, with a sauce *[a pulled pork sandwich]* ☆**5** to stretch (taffy, etc.) back and forth repeatedly **6** to stretch or strain to the point of injury *[to pull a muscle]* **7** to select, access, or withdraw (a file, form, etc.) *[to pull a patient's medical records]* ☆**8** [Informal] to put into effect; carry out; perform *[to pull a raid]* **9** [Informal] to hold back; restrain *[to pull one's punches]* ☆**10** [Informal] to take (a gun, knife, etc.) from concealment, as to threaten someone: often with *on* *[the robber pulled a gun on the bank teller]* **11** [Dial.] to draw the entrails from (a fowl) **12** *Baseball, Golf* to hit (the ball) and make it go to the left or, if left-handed, to the right **13** *Horse Racing* to rein in or restrain (a horse) so as to keep it from winning **14** *Printing* to take (a proof) on a hand press **15** *Rowing a)* to work (an oar) by drawing it toward one *b)* to propel or transport by rowing —*vi.* **1** to exert force in or for dragging, tugging, or attracting something **2** to take a deep draft of a drink or puff at a cigarette, etc. **3** to be capable of being pulled **4** to move or drive a vehicle *(away, ahead, around, out,* etc.) ☆**5** *Football* to run behind, and parallel to, the line of scrimmage, as to provide blocking for a ballcarrier: said of an offensive lineman —*n.* **1** the act, force, or result of pulling; specif., *a)* a dragging, tugging, attracting, etc. *b)* the act or an instance of rowing *c)* a drink *d)* a puff at a cigarette, etc. *e)* a difficult, continuous effort, as in climbing *f)* the force needed to move a weight, trigger, etc., measured in pounds **2** something to be pulled, as the handle of a drawer, etc. ☆**3** [Informal] *a)* influence or special advantage *b)* drawing power; appeal —**pull a face** *see* MAKE A FACE (at FACE) —**pull apart** to find fault with; criticize —**pull down 1** to tear down, demolish, or overthrow **2** to degrade; humble **3** to reduce **4** [Informal] to get (a specified wage, grade, etc.) —☆**pull for** [Informal] to cheer on, or hope for the success of —**pull in 1** to arrive **2** to draw in or hold back **3** [Informal] to arrest and take to police headquarters —**pull off** [Informal] to bring about, accomplish, or perform —**pull out** ☆**1** to depart ☆**2** to withdraw or retreat ☆**3** to escape from a contract, responsibility, etc. **4** *Aeron.* to level out from a dive or landing approach —**pull over 1** to drive (a vehicle) to or toward the curb or shoulder and come to a stop **2** to induce (someone), as by signaling, to do this —**pull through** [Informal] to get through or over (an illness, difficulty, etc.) —**pull oneself together** to collect one's faculties; regain one's composure, courage, etc. —**pull up 1** to uproot **2** to bring or come to a stop **3** *a)* to drive (a vehicle) to a specified place and come to a stop *b)* to make (an aircraft) nose up sharply **4** to check or rebuke —**pull′er** *n.*

SYN.—**pull** is the broad, general term of this list, as defined in sense 1 of the *vt.* above; **draw** suggests a smoother, more even motion than **pull** [he *drew* his sword from its scabbard]; **drag** implies the slow pulling of something heavy, connoting great resistance in the thing pulled [she *dragged* the desk across the floor]; **tug** suggests strenuous, often intermittent effort in pulling but does not necessarily connote success in moving the object [I *tugged* at the rope to no avail]; **haul** implies sustained effort in transporting something heavy, often mechanically [to *haul* furniture in a truck]; **tow** implies pulling by means of a rope or cable [to *tow* a stalled automobile] —***ANT.*** **push, shove**

pull·back (pool′bak′) *n.* **1** a pulling back; esp., a planned military withdrawal **2** something that retards or hinders **3** a device for pulling something back

pull-down (pool′doun′) *adj. Comput.* designating or of a menu whose options are displayed beneath its title with a click of the mouse

pul·let (pool′it) *n.* ⟦ME *poullet* < OFr *poulet,* dim. of *poule,* hen: see POULTRY⟧ a young hen, usually one not more than a year old

pul·ley (pool′ē) *n., pl.* **-leys** ⟦ME *poley* < OFr *polie* < ML *poleia* < *poledia* < MGr **polidion,* dim. of *polos,* pivot, windlass, axis: see WHEEL⟧ **1** a small fixed wheel, sometimes turning in a block, with a grooved rim in which a rope or chain runs, as to raise a weight attached at one end by pulling on the other end: it changes the direction of effort but provides no mechanical advantage **2** a combination of such wheels, used to increase the mechanical advantage **3** a wheel that turns or is turned by a belt, rope, chain, etc., so as to transmit power

☆**Pull·man** (pool′mən) *n.* **1** ⟦after G. M. *Pullman* (1831-97), U.S. inventor⟧ a railroad passenger car with convertible berths for sleeping: also **Pullman car 2** [*often* **p-**] a suitcase that opens flat and has a hinged divider inside: also **pullman case**

☆**Pullman kitchen** ⟦< prec.⟧ [*also* **p- k-**] a small, compact kitchen, typically built into an alcove, as in some apartments

pull-on (pool′än′) *adj.* designating or of a garment designed to be put on easily, typically one without buttons, zippers, or other fasteners —*n.* a pull-on skirt, shorts, etc.

pul·lo·rum disease (pul lôr′əm) ⟦< ModL *(salmonella) pullorum,* the infecting bacterium < gen. pl. of L *pullus:* see POULTRY⟧ a severe, diarrheal disease of young poultry, caused by a bacterium (*Salmonella pullorum*) and usually transmitted by the infected hen into the egg

pull·out (pool′out′) *n.* **1** the act of pulling out; esp., removal, departure, withdrawal, etc. **2** something meant to be pulled out, as a magazine insert

pull·o·ver (pool′ō′vər) *adj.* that is put on by being pulled over the head —*n.* a pullover sweater, shirt, etc.

pul·lu·late (pul′yə lāt′) *vi.* **-lat′ed, -lat′ing** ⟦< L *pullulatus,* pp. of *pullulare,* to spread out, sprout < *pullulus,* dim. of *pullus:* see POULTRY⟧ **1** to sprout out; germinate; bud **2** to breed quickly **3** to spring up in abundance; teem or swarm —**pul′lu·la′tion** *n.*

pull-up or **pull·up** (pool′up′) *n.* an exercise in which a person chins himself or herself, specif., one in which the bar is gripped with the palms facing away from the exerciser

pul·mo·nar·y (pul′mə ner′ē, pool′-) *adj.* ⟦L *pulmonarius* < *pulmo* (gen. *pulmonis*), lung < IE **pleumon,* lung, orig., floater < base **pleu-,* to swim, float > FLOW: for semantic development see LIGHTS⟧ **1** of, like, or affecting the lungs **2** having lungs or lunglike organs **3** designating the artery conveying blood from the right ventricle of the heart to the lungs or any of the veins conveying oxygenated blood from the lungs to the left atrium of the heart

pul·mo·nate (pul′mə nit, -nāt′) *adj.* ⟦ModL *pulmonatus* < L *pulmo,* lung: see prec.⟧ *Zool.* **1** having lungs or lunglike organs **2** of or belonging to a subclass (Pulmonata) of gastropods having a sort of lung or air sac, as the land snails and slugs, and most freshwater snails —*n.* any member of this subclass

pul·mon·ic (pul män′ik, pool-) *adj.* ⟦Fr *pulmonique*⟧ PULMONARY

☆**pul·mo·tor** (pool′mōt′ər, pul′-) *n.* ⟦< L *pulmo,* lung (see PULMONARY) + MOTOR⟧ an apparatus used in applying artificial respiration by forcing oxygen into the lungs

pulp (pulp) *n.* ⟦Fr *pulpe* < L *pulpa,* flesh, pulp of fruit⟧ **1** a soft, moist, formless mass that sticks together **2** the soft, juicy part of a fruit **3** the pith inside the stem of a plant **4** the soft, sensitive tissue in the center of a tooth, including blood vessels, nerves, etc. **5** a mixture of ground-up, moistened cellulose material, as wood, linen, rags, etc., from which paper is made **6** ore ground to a powder and mixed with water ☆**7** a magazine printed on rough, inferior paper stock made from wood pulp and traditionally characterized by sensational stories of love, crime, etc.: distinguished from SLICK (*n.* 3) —*adj.* ☆of or characteristic of pulp magazines [*pulp* fiction] —*vt.* **1** to reduce to pulp **2** to remove the pulp from —*vi.* to become pulp —**pulp′al** *adj.*

pul·pit (pool′pit, pul′-) *n.* ⟦ME *pulpet* < L *pulpitum,* stage, scaffold (in LL & ML, pulpit) < ?⟧ **1** *a)* a raised platform or high lectern from which a clergyman preaches in a church *b)* preachers collectively *c)* the work of preaching **2** a raised or enclosed area; esp., an elevated control room, as in a steel mill

pulp·wood (pulp′wood′) *n.* **1** soft wood used in making paper **2** wood ground to pulp for paper

pulp·y (pul′pē) *adj.* **pulp′i·er, pulp′i·est** of or like pulp: also **pulp′ous** —**pulp′i·ly** *adv.* —**pulp′i·ness** *n.*

☆**pul·que** (pool′kā; *Sp* pōōl′ke) *n.* ⟦AmSp, prob. of Mex Ind orig.⟧ a cloudy or whitish fermented drink, popular in Mexico, made from the juice of certain agaves, esp. the maguey

pul·sant (pul′sənt) *adj.* pulsating

pul·sar (pul′sär′, -sər) *n.* ⟦PULS(E) + -AR⟧ a rotating neutron star that emits electromagnetic radiation, esp. radio waves, at short and very regular intervals: abbrev. *PSR*

pul·sate (pul′sāt′) *vi.* **-sat′ed, -sat′ing** ⟦< L *pulsatus,* pp. of *pulsare,* to beat < *pulsus:* see PULSE[1]⟧ **1** to beat or throb rhythmically, as the heart **2** to vibrate; quiver

pul·sa·tile (pul′sə təl, -tīl′) *adj.* ⟦ML *pulsatilis*⟧ **1** pulsating **2** played by beating, as a drum

pul·sa·tion (pul sā′shən) *n.* ⟦L *pulsatio*⟧ **1** the act of pulsating; rhythmical beating or throbbing **2** a beat; throb; vibration

pul·sa·tive (pul′sə tiv) *adj.* that pulsates; pulsating

pul·sa·tor (pul′sāt′ər, pul sāt′-) *n.* ⟦L⟧ any of several devices having a throbbing action, as a massage vibrator or a milking machine

pul·sa·to·ry (pul′sə tôr′ē) *adj.* characterized by pulsation

pulse[1] (puls) *n.* ⟦ME *pous* < OFr < L *pulsus (venarum),* beating (of the veins) < *pulsus,* pp. of *pellere,* to beat: see FELT[1]⟧ **1** the regular beating in the arteries, caused by the contractions of the heart **2** any beat, signal, vibration, etc. that is regular or rhythmical **3** the perceptible underlying feelings of the public or of a particular group **4** a variation, characterized by a rise, limited duration, and decline, of a quantity whose value normally is constant; specif., *a) Elec.* a brief surge of voltage or current *b) Radio* a very short burst of electromagnetic waves —*vi.* **pulsed, puls′ing** to pulsate; throb —*vt.* **1** to cause to pulsate **2** to drive (an engine, etc.) by pulses **3** *Elec.* to apply pulses to **4** *Radio* to modify (an electromagnetic wave) by means of pulses —**puls′er** *n.*

pulse[2] (puls) *n.* ⟦ME *pous* < OFr *pouls* < L *puls* (gen. *pultis*), a pottage made of meal or pulse, prob. < Gr *poltos* < IE base **pel-,* dust, meal > L *pollen, pulvis*⟧ **1** the edible seeds of peas, beans, lentils, and similar plants having pods **2** any leguminous plant

pulse height analyzer an instrument that records or counts an electrical pulse if its amplitude falls within specified limits: used in nuclear physics research for the determination of energy spectra of nuclear radiations

pulse·jet (engine) (puls′jet′) a jet engine without a compressor or turbine, in which intermittent combustion provides the thrust

pulse modulation 1 the formation of an intermittent carrier wave by the generation and transmission of a sequence of short, periodic pulses: used in radar **2** the modulation of the amplitude, a characteristic, etc. of a sequence of pulses in order to convey information: often used in codes

pulse radar a radar system using pulse modulation

pul·sim·e·ter (pul sim′ət ər) *n.* a medical instrument for measuring the rate and force of the pulse

pul·som·e·ter (pul säm′ət ər) *n.* ⟦PULS(E) + -O- + -METER⟧ **1** a pump without a piston, that raises water by the sucking effect of condensing steam **2** PULSIMETER

pul·ver·iz·a·ble (pul′vər īz′ə bəl) *adj.* that can be pulverized: also **pul·ver·a·ble** (pul′vər ə bəl)

pul·ver·ize (pul′vər īz′) *vt.* **-ized′, -iz′ing** ⟦MFr *pulveriser* < LL *pulverizare* < L *pulvis,* powder: see POLLEN⟧ **1** to crush, grind, etc. into a powder or dust **2** to break down completely; demolish —*vi.* to be crushed, ground, etc. into powder or dust —**pul′ver·i·za′tion** *n.* —**pul′ver·iz′er** *n.*

pul·ver·u·lent (pul ver′yə lənt, -ə lənt) *adj.* ⟦L *pulverulentus* < *pulvis:* see prec.⟧ **1** consisting of or covered with a powder; powdery **2** crumbling to powder or dust —**pul·ver′u·lence** *n.*

pul·vil·lus (pul vil′əs) *n., pl.* **-li′** (-ī′) ⟦ModL < L, small cushion, contr. <

pulvinulus, dim. of *pulvinus*, cushion⟧ *Zool.* a cushionlike part between the tarsal claws of many insects, as dipterans —**pul·vil′lar** *adj.*

pul·vi·nate (pul′və nāt′, -nit) *adj.* ⟦L *pulvinatus* < *pulvinus*, cushion⟧ **1** cushionlike **2** *Bot.* having a pulvinus —**pul′vi·nate′ly** *adv.*

pul·vi·nus (pul vī′nəs) *n., pl.* **-ni′** (-nī′) ⟦ModL < L, pillow, elevation⟧ *Bot.* an enlarged area at the base of a petiole, at a node, or at the base of a panicled branch, producing movement by growth or swelling

pu·ma (po͞o′mə, pyo͞o′-) *n., pl.* **-mas** or **-ma** ⟦AmSp < Quechua *púma*⟧ COUGAR

pum·ice (pum′is) *n.* ⟦ME *pomis* < OFr < L *pumex* < IE base *(*s*)*poimno-*, FOAM⟧ an extremely porous, glassy, extrusive igneous rock typically light enough to float on water, used as an abrasive and in making soaps, polishes, etc.: also **pumice stone** —*vt.* **-iced**, **-ic·ing** to clean, polish, etc. with pumice —**pu·mi·ceous** (pyo͞o mish′əs) *adj.*

pum·mel (pum′əl) *vt.* **-meled** or **-melled**, **-mel·ing** or **-mel·ling** ⟦< POMMEL⟧ to beat or hit with repeated blows, esp. with the fist —***SYN.*** BEAT

pump[1] (pump) *n.* ⟦ME *pumpe* < MDu *pompe* < Sp *bomba*, prob. of echoic orig.⟧ **1** any of various machines that force a liquid or gas into or through, or draw it out of, something, as by suction or pressure **2** [Informal] the heart —*vt.* **1** to raise or move (fluids) with a pump **2** to remove water, etc. from, as with a pump **3** to drive air into with a pump or bellows **4** to force in, draw out, drive, move up and down, pour forth, etc. by means of a pump or as a pump does **5** to apply force to with a pumping, up-and-down motion **6** [Informal] *a)* to question closely and persistently *b)* to get (information) from a person in this way **7** *Physics* to transfer or inject energy into (particles, the electrons of a laser, etc.) —*vi.* **1** to work a pump **2** to raise or move water, etc. with a pump **3** to move up and down or go by moving up and down like a pump handle or piston **4** to flow in, out, or through by, or as if by, being pumped **5** *Basketball, Football* to fake a shot or a throw —**pump iron** [Slang] to exercise with weights —**pump up 1** to inflate (a tire, ball, etc.) with air **2** [Informal] to fill with confidence, enthusiasm, etc.

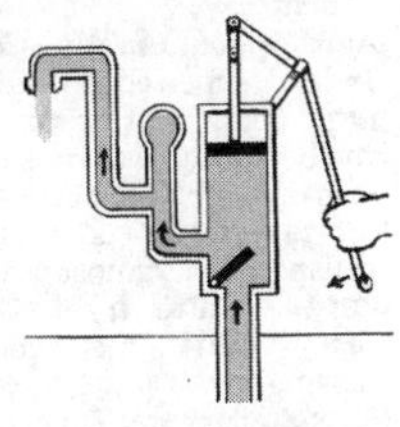
water pump

pump[2] (pump) *n.* ⟦< ? prob. < Fr colloq. *pompe*, boot, shoe, lit. prec.: jocular for a shoe which pumps in the water⟧ a low-cut shoe without straps or ties; esp., such a woman's shoe with a moderate to high heel

pumped (pumpt) *adj.* ☆[Slang] full of confidence, enthusiasm, etc.; pumped up

pump·er (pum′pər) *n.* **1** a person or thing that pumps **2** a fire truck that carries hose and a water tank and can pump water under great pressure

☆**pum·per·nick·el** (pum′pər nik′əl) *n.* ⟦Ger, Westphalian rye bread, earlier a pejorative < *pumpern*, to break wind + *nickel*, a goblin: see NICKEL⟧ a coarse, dark, sour bread made of unsifted rye flour

pump·kin (pump′kin, pum′-; *nonstandard* puŋ′-) *n.* ⟦altered (infl. by -KIN) < *pumpion* < MFr *pompon* < L *pepo* < Gr *pepōn*, lit., cooked by the sun, ripe (hence a gourd not eaten until ripe), akin to *peptein:* see PEPSIN⟧ **1** a large, round, orange-yellow, edible fruit with many seeds **2** the vine (*Cucurbita pepo*) of the gourd family on which it grows **3** [Brit.] any of several varieties of squash (*Cucurbita moschata* and *C. maxima*)

pump·kin·seed (-sēd′) *n.* **1** the seed of the pumpkin ☆**2** a small sunfish (*Lepomis gibbosus*) of North America, greenish-yellow above and orange-yellow below

☆**pump priming** ⟦see PRIME, *vt.* 3⟧ large expenditures by a government, designed to stimulate expenditures by private industry

pun (pun) *n.* ⟦17th-c. clipped form < ? It *puntiglio*, fine point, hence verbal quibble: see PUNCTILIO⟧ the use of a word, or of words which are formed or sounded alike, in such a way as to juxtapose, connect, or bring out two or more of the possible applications of the word or words, usually in a humorous way; a play on words —*vi.* **punned**, **pun′ning** to make a pun or puns

pu·na (po͞o′nä) *n.* ⟦AmSp < Quechua *púna*, high summit⟧ a cold, arid plateau high in the Andes

punch[1] (punch) *n.* ⟦contr. < ME *punchoun:* see PUNCHEON[1]⟧ **1** *a)* a tool driven or pressed against a surface that is to be stamped, pierced, etc. *b)* a tool driven against a nail, bolt, etc. that is to be worked in, or against a pin that is to be worked out **2** a device or machine for making holes, cuts, etc. [a paper *punch*] **3** the hole, cut, etc. made with a punch —*vt.* **1** to pierce, shape, stamp, cut, etc. with a punch **2** to make (a hole, cut, etc.) with or as with a punch

punch[2] (punch) *vt.* ⟦ME *punchen*, orig. var. of *pouncen* (see POUNCE[1]): infl. by prec.⟧ **1** to prod or poke with a stick ☆**2** to herd or drive (cattle) **3** to strike with the fist **4** to depress or push (a push button, a key on a keypad, etc.) —*n.* **1** a thrusting blow with the fist ☆**2** [Informal] effective force; vigor —**beat to the punch** [Informal] to be quicker than (another) in doing something, as in striking a blow —**pull one's punches 1** *Boxing* to deliver blows that are intentionally ineffective **2** [Informal] to attack, criticize, etc. in an intentionally mild or ineffective manner —☆**punch a (time) clock** to insert a timecard into a time clock when coming to or going from work —**punch in** ☆**1** to record the time of one's arrival by means of a time clock **2** to feed (data) as into a computer by pressing buttons or keys —**punch out** ☆**1** to record the time of one's departure by means of a time clock **2** [Slang] to beat up —**punch up 1** [Informal, Chiefly Brit.] to beat up **2** [Informal] to enhance, accentuate, or heighten the effect of [to *punch up* a soup with spices]

punch[3] (punch) *n.* ⟦Hindi *pañca*, five < Sans *páñca* (see FIVE): it orig. consisted of five ingredients⟧ a sweet drink made with fruit juices, carbonated beverages, sherbet, etc., often mixed with wine or liquor, and typically served in cups from a large bowl

Punch (punch) *n.* ⟦contr. after *Punchinello*, earlier *Polichinello*, a character in a Neapolitan puppet play < It *Pulcinella* < VL **pullicinus* < LL *pullicenus*, young chicken, dim. of L *pullus:* see POULTRY⟧ the main character, a hook-nosed and humpbacked figure, of a PUNCH-AND-JUDY SHOW —**pleased as Punch** greatly pleased or gratified

Punch-and-Ju·dy show (punch′ən jo͞o′dē) a traditional puppet show in which the quarrelsome PUNCH constantly fights with his wife, Judy, in a comical way

☆**punch·board** (punch′bôrd′) *n.* a board or card with holes containing concealed slips or disks to be punched out, used in games of chance, raffles, etc.: the slips or disks bear numbers, names, prize designations, or the like

punch bowl a large bowl from which punch is served

☆**punch card** a machine-readable card in which information is encoded as a pattern of punched holes, for interpretation by a data-processing machine

punch-drunk (punch′druŋk′) *adj.* [Informal] **1** having or showing a condition resulting from numerous blows to the head, as from prizefighting, and marked by an unsteady gait, slow muscular movements, hesitant speech, mental confusion, etc. **2** acting dazed or bewildered

pun·cheon[1] (pun′chən) *n.* ⟦ME *punchoun* < MFr *poinçon* < VL **punctio* < *punctiare*, to prick < L *punctus*, pp. of *pungere*, to prick: see POINT⟧ **1** a short, upright wooden post used in a framework ☆**2** a heavy, broad piece of roughly dressed timber with one side hewed flat **3** any of various devices for punching, perforating, or stamping; esp., a figured die used by goldsmiths, etc.

pun·cheon[2] (pun′chən) *n.* ⟦ME *punchion* < OFr *poinçon*, prob. < *poinchon*, var. of *poçon*, pot, small fluid measure, dim. of *pot* < VL *potus:* see POT[1]⟧ **1** a large cask of varying capacity (72-120 gal), for beer, wine, etc. **2** as much as such a cask will hold

punch·er (pun′chər) *n.* a person or thing that punches

pun·chi·nel·lo (pun′chə nel′ō) *n.* ⟦see PUNCH⟧ [*also* **P-**] **1** a prototype of Punch **2** *pl.* **-los** a buffoon; clown

punching bag 1 a stuffed or inflated leather bag hung up so that it can be punched for exercise or practice **2** a person or group repeatedly made the object of blame, derision, anger, etc.

☆**punch·line** (punch′līn′) *n.* the climactic line, typically the last line, of a joke or humorous anecdote

punch press a press in which dies are fitted for cutting, shaping, or stamping metal

punch-up (punch′up′) *n.* [Informal, Chiefly Brit.] **1** a noisy fistfight; brawl **2** a gang fight; rumble

punch·y (pun′chē) *adj.* **punch′i·er**, **punch′i·est** [Informal] ☆**1** forceful; vigorous ☆**2** PUNCH-DRUNK

punc·tate (puŋk′tāt′) *adj.* ⟦ModL *punctatus* < L *punctum*, a POINT⟧ marked with dots or tiny spots, as certain plants and animals: also **punc′tat′ed** —**punc·ta′tion** *n.*

punc·til·i·o (puŋk til′ē ō′) *n., pl.* **-os′** ⟦altered (infl. by L) < Sp *puntillo* or It *puntiglio*, dim. of *punto* < L *punctum*, a POINT⟧ **1** a nice point of conduct, ceremony, etc. **2** observance of petty formalities

punc·til·i·ous (puŋk til′ē əs) *adj.* ⟦Fr *pointilleux* < *pointille* < It *puntiglio:* see prec.⟧ **1** very careful about every detail of behavior, ceremony, etc. [a *punctilious* host] **2** very exact; scrupulous —**punc·til′i·ous·ly** *adv.* —**punc·til′i·ous·ness** *n.*

punc·tu·al (puŋk′cho͞o əl) *adj.* ⟦ME < ML *punctualis* < L *punctus*, a POINT⟧ **1** of, like, or drawn into a single point **2** carefully observant of an appointed time; on time; prompt **3** *archaic var. of* PUNCTILIOUS —**punc′tu·al′i·ty** (-al′ə tē) *n.* —**punc′tu·al·ly** *adv.* —**punc′tu·al·ness** *n.*

punc·tu·ate (puŋk′cho͞o āt′) *vt.* **-at′ed**, **-at′ing** ⟦< ML *punctuatus*, pp. of *punctuare* < L *punctus*, a POINT⟧ **1** to insert a punctuation mark or marks in **2** to break in on here and there; interrupt [a speech *punctuated* with applause] **3** to emphasize; accentuate —*vi.* to use punctuation marks —**punc′tu·a′tor** *n.*

☆**punctuated equilibrium** a theory of evolution holding that characteristics of living organisms remain relatively stable for long periods that are infrequently interrupted, or punctuated, by brief periods of relatively rapid evolutionary change, caused as by climatic or geologic changes: cf. DARWINIAN THEORY

punc·tu·a·tion (puŋk′cho͞o ā′shən) *n.* ⟦ML *punctuatio:* see PUNCTUATE⟧ **1** the act of punctuating; specif., the act or practice of using standardized marks in writing and printing to separate sentences or sentence elements or to make the meaning clearer **2** a system for using such marks **3** such a mark or marks —**punc′tu·a′tive** *adj.*

punctuation mark any of the marks used in punctuation, as a period or comma

punc·tu·late (puŋk′cho͞o lāt′, -lit) *adj.* ⟦< L *punctulum*, dim. of *punctum*, POINT + -ATE[1]⟧ marked with very small dots or holes, as certain plants and animals —**punc′tu·la′tion** *n.*

punc·ture (puŋk′chər) *n.* ⟦ME < L *punctura*, a pricking < L *pungere*, to pierce: see POINT⟧ **1** the act or an instance of perforating or piercing **2** a hole made by a sharp point, as in an automobile tire, the skin, etc. —*vt.* **-tured**, **-tur·ing 1** to perforate or pierce with a sharp point **2** to reduce or put an end to, as if by a puncture [to *puncture* someone's pride] —*vi.* to be punctured —**punc′tur·a·ble** *adj.*

pun·dit (pun′dit) *n.* ⟦Hindi *paṇḍit* < Sans *paṇḍita*, a learned person, orig., learned⟧ **1** *alt. sp. of* PANDIT **2** a person who has or professes to have great learning; actual or self-professed authority —**pun′dit·ry** *n.*

Pune (po͞o′nə) city in W Maharashtra, W India

☆**pung** (puŋ) *n.* ⟦< earlier *tom pung*, altered < an unattested New England Algonquian (e.g. Massachusett) name akin to TOBOGGAN⟧ [Northeast & Cdn.] a boxlike sleigh drawn by one horse

pun·gent (pun′jənt) *adj.* ⟦L *pungens*, prp. of *pungere*, to prick, puncture: see POINT⟧ **1** producing a sharp sensation of taste or smell; acrid **2** sharp and piercing to the mind; poignant; painful **3** sharply penetrating; expressive; biting [*pungent* language] **4** keenly clever; stimulating —**pun′gen·cy** *n.* —**pun′gent·ly** *adv.*

Pu·nic (pyo͞o′nik) *adj.* ⟦L *Punicus*, earlier *Poenicus*, Carthaginian, properly Phoenician < *Poeni*, the Carthaginians < Gr *Phoinix*, Phoenician⟧ **1** of ancient Carthage or its people or culture **2** like or characteristic of the Carthaginians, regarded by the Romans as faithless and treacherous —*n.* the Semitic language spoken in ancient Carthage, a dialect of Phoenician: it survived until *c.* A.D. 500

Punic Wars three wars between Rome and Carthage (264-241 B.C., 218-201 B.C., and 149-146 B.C.), in which Rome was finally victorious

pu·ni·ness (pyo͞o′nē nis) *n.* puny quality or condition

pun·ish (pun′ish) *vt.* ⟦ME *punischen* < extended stem of OFr *punir* < L *punire*, to punish < *poena*, punishment, penalty: see PENAL⟧ **1** to cause to undergo pain, loss, or suffering for a crime or wrongdoing **2** to impose a penalty on a wrongdoer for (an offense) **3** to treat harshly or injuriously [the *punishing* rays of the sun] —*vi.* to deal out punishment —**pun′ish·er** *n.*

SYN.—**punish** implies the infliction of some penalty on a wrongdoer and generally connotes retribution rather than correction [to *punish* a murderer by hanging]; **discipline** suggests punishment that is intended to control or to establish habits of self-control [to *discipline* a naughty child]; **correct** suggests punishment for the purpose of overcoming faults [to *correct* unruly pupils]; **chastise** implies usually corporal punishment and connotes both retribution and correction; **castigate** now implies punishment by severe public criticism or censure [to *castigate* a corrupt official]; **chasten** implies the infliction of tribulation in order to make obedient, meek, etc. and is used especially in a theological sense ["He *chastens* and hastens His will to make known"]

pun·ish·a·ble (pun′ish ə bəl) *adj.* liable to or deserving punishment —**pun′ish·a·bil′i·ty** *n.*

pun·ish·ment (pun′ish mənt) *n.* **1** a punishing or being punished **2** a penalty imposed on an offender for a crime or wrongdoing **3** harsh or injurious treatment

pu·ni·tive (pyo͞o′nə tiv) *adj.* ⟦ML *punitivus* < L *punitus*, pp. of *punire*, to PUNISH⟧ inflicting, concerned with, or directed toward punishment: also **pu′ni·to′ry** —**pu′ni·tive·ly** *adv.* —**pu′ni·tive·ness** *n.*

punitive damages EXEMPLARY DAMAGES

Pun·jab (pun′jäb′, -jab′) ⟦Hindi *Panjāb*, lit., (land of) five rivers < Sans *panj*, five + *ab*, river, water⟧ **1** region in NW India & NE Pakistan, between the upper Indus & Jumna rivers: formerly a province of India, it was divided between India & Pakistan (1947); chief city, Lahore (now in Pakistan) **2** state of India, in this region: 19,445 sq mi (50,362 sq km); cap. Chandigarh

Pun·ja·bi (pun jä′bē) *n.* **1** a person born or living in the Punjab **2** the Indo-Aryan language spoken in the Punjab

pun·ji (pun′jē) *n.* a sharpened, often poisoned, bamboo stake planted in a series as a barricade or planted and concealed in a hole, ditch, etc. as to cut or impale an enemy: usually **punji stick** or **punji stake**

☆**punk**[1] (puŋk) *n.* ⟦prob. var. of SPUNK⟧ any substance, as decayed wood, that smolders when ignited, used as tinder; esp., a chemically treated fungous substance shaped into slender, fragile, light-brown sticks: the glowing tips are used to light fireworks, etc.

punk[2] (puŋk) *n.* ⟦Early ModE slang < ?⟧ **1** [Obs.] a prostitute ☆**2** [Slang] *a)* catamite *b)* a male homosexual *c)* a young hoodlum *d)* any person, esp. a youngster, regarded as inexperienced, insignificant, presumptuous, etc. **3** *a)* PUNK ROCK *b)* a style, originating among fans of punk rock, characterized by motley clothes, oddly clipped hair, etc. —*adj.* ☆**1** [Slang] poor or bad in condition, quality, etc. **2** of or having to do with punk rock or the style called punk —**punk′y** *adj.* **punk′i·er**, **punk′i·est**

pun·kah or **pun·ka** (puŋ′kə) *n.* ⟦Hindi *pankhā* < Sans *pakshaka*, fan < *paksha*, wing⟧ in India, a large fan made from the palmyra leaf, or a large, swinging fan consisting of canvas stretched over a rectangular frame and hung from the ceiling

punk·er (puŋ′kər) *n.* [Informal] **1** a punk-rock musician **2** a person who is a fan of punk rock or who dresses in the punk style

☆**punk·ie** (puŋ′kē) *n.* ⟦dial. Du **punkje* < Delaware *púnkwəs*, dim. of *púnkwəs*, dim. of *púnkw*, ashes, dust: so named from their size⟧ BITING MIDGE

punk rock ⟦see PUNK[2], *n.* 2c⟧ a loud, fast style of rock music that originated in the late 1970s, characterized by deliberately offensive lyrics expressive of alienation and aggression, and, often, parodying mainstream popular music —**punk rocker**

pun·net (pun′ət) *n.* ⟦orig. uncert.⟧ [Chiefly Brit.] a small, shallow basket, as for fruits or vegetables

pun·ster (pun′stər) *n.* ⟦see -STER⟧ a person who habitually makes, or is fond of making, puns: also **pun′ner**

punt[1] (punt) *n.* ⟦< slang of Rugby School, England: ? form of dial. *bunt*, to strike, kick: see BUNT[1]⟧ *Football, etc.* a kick in which the ball is dropped and kicked before it hits the ground, as in relinquishing possession to the other team —*vt. Football, etc.* to kick (a ball) in this way —*vi.* **1** *Football, etc.* to execute a punt **2** [Informal] to avoid taking decisive action —**punt′er** *n.*

punt[2] (punt) *n.* ⟦OE < L *ponto*, punt (in LL, PONTOON)⟧ a flat-bottomed boat with broad, square ends, usually pushed along by a long pole —*vt.* **1** to propel (a boat) by pushing with a pole against the bottom of a shallow river or lake **2** to carry in a punt —*vi.* to go in a punt —**punt′er** *n.*

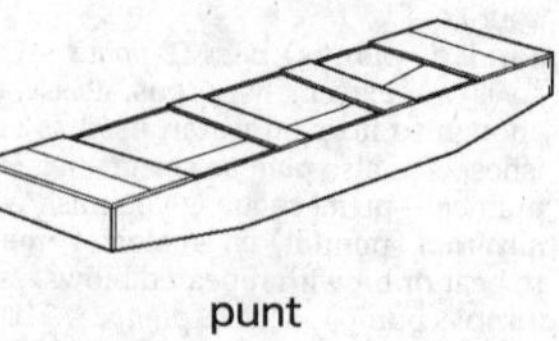
punt

punt[3] (punt) *vi.* ⟦Fr *ponter* < *ponte*, point < Sp *punto* < L *punctum*, a POINT⟧ **1** in certain card games, to bet against the banker **2** [Brit.] to gamble; bet —**punt′er** *n.*

punt[4] (po͝ont) *n.* ⟦Ir (Celt), pound⟧ the former basic monetary unit of Ireland, superseded in 2002 by the EURO

punt[5] (punt) *n.* ⟦< PUNTY, because orig. the place where the metal rod held the bottle and was broken off⟧ *Winemaking* a recess or dimple in the bottom of some wine bottles

Pun·ta A·re·nas (po͞on′tä ä re′näs) seaport in S Chile, on the Strait of Magellan: southernmost city in the world

pun·ty (pun′tē) *n., pl.* **-ties** ⟦Fr *pontil* < It *pontello*, dim. of *punto* < L *punctum*, a POINT⟧ a metal rod on which the molten glass is handled in glassmaking

Punx·su·taw·ney (puŋk′sə tô′nē) ⟦< AmInd name⟧ borough in WC Pa.: site of an annual Groundhog Day celebration

pu·ny (pyo͞o′nē) *adj.* **-ni·er**, **-ni·est** ⟦Fr *puîné*, born later < OFr *puisné* < *puis*, after + *né* < L *natus*, born: see NATURE⟧ of inferior size, strength, or importance; weak; slight

pup (pup) *n.* ⟦contr. < PUPPY⟧ **1** *a)* a young dog; puppy *b)* a young fox, wolf, etc. **2** a young seal, whale, etc. —*vi.* **pupped**, **pup′ping** to give birth to pups

pu·pa (pyo͞o′pə) *n., pl.* **-pae** (-pē) or **-pas** ⟦ModL: so named by LINNAEUS < L, girl, doll, prob. < IE **pup-* < base **pu-*, to swell up, inflate⟧ an insect in the nonfeeding stage of development between the last larval and adult forms, characterized by many anatomical changes and, often, by enclosure in a cell or cocoon —**pu′pal** *adj.*

pu·pate (pyo͞o′pāt′) *vi.* **-pat′ed**, **-pat′ing** to become a pupa; go through the pupal stage —**pu·pa′tion** *n.*

☆**pup·fish** (pup′fish′) *n., pl.* **-fish′** or **-fish′es** (see FISH) any of several small, nearly extinct killifishes (genus *Cyprinodon*) found in desert springs of W North America

pu·pil[1] (pyo͞o′pəl) *n.* ⟦ME *pupille* < MFr < L *pupillus*, *pupilla*, orphan, ward, dim. of *pupus*, boy, *pupa*, girl: see PUPA⟧ **1** a person, esp. a young person, under the supervision of a teacher or tutor, as in school **2** *Civil Law* a minor under the care of a guardian; ward

SYN.—**pupil** is applied either to a child in school or to a person who is under the personal supervision of a teacher [Heifetz was a *pupil* of Leopold Auer]; **student** is applied either to one attending an institution above the elementary level or to one who is making a study of a particular subject [a *student* of social problems]; **scholar**, orig. equivalent to **pupil**, is now usually applied to one who has general erudition or who is highly versed in a particular branch of learning [a linguistics *scholar*]

pu·pil[2] (pyo͞o′pəl) *n.* ⟦Fr *pupille* < L *pupilla*, dim. of *pupa* (see prec. & PUPA): from one's image, like a tiny doll, seen reflected in another's eye⟧ the contractile circular opening, apparently black, in the center of the iris of the eye

pu·pil·age or **pu·pil·lage** (pyo͞o′pə lij) *n.* the state or period of being a pupil

pu·pil·lar·y[1] (pyo͞o′pə ler′ē) *adj.* ⟦Fr *pupillaire* < L *pupillaris* < *pupilla*, PUPIL[1]⟧ of a person who is a pupil

pu·pil·lar·y[2] (pyo͞o′pə ler′ē) *adj.* of the pupil of the eye

pu·pip·a·rous (pyo͞o pip′ə rəs) *adj.* ⟦< PUPA + -PAROUS⟧ designating or of certain dipteran insects, as the sheep tick, bearing young already developed to the stage where they are ready to pupate

pup·pet (pup′ət) *n.* ⟦ME *popet* < OFr *poupette*, dim. of **poupe* < VL **puppa* < L *pupa*, girl, doll: see PUPA⟧ **1** [Obs.] a doll **2** a small, often jointed figure, as of a human being or animal, typically designed to be manipulated, as from within by the fingers of a hand or by strings held from above **3** a person whose actions, ideas, etc. are controlled by another —*adj.* designating or of a state or nation that is ostensibly independent but is actually controlled by another

pup·pet·eer (pup′ə tir′) *n.* a person who operates, designs, or costumes puppets, or produces puppet shows

pup·pet·ry (pup′ə trē) *n.* the art of making or operating puppets or producing puppet shows

puppet show a play or performance with puppets

Pup·pis (pup′is) *n.* ⟦L, poop of a ship⟧ a S constellation between Vela and Columba: see ARGO (sense 2)

pup·py (pup′ē) *n., pl.* **-pies** ⟦ME *popi* < MFr *popee*, doll < **poupe*: see PUPPET⟧ **1** *a)* a young dog *b)* a young fox, seal, etc.; pup **2** [Archaic] an insolent, conceited, or silly young man; whelp ☆**3** [Slang] any person or thing [after the workout, he was one tired *puppy*] —**pup′py·hood′** *n.* —**pup′py·ish** *adj.*

☆**puppy love** immature romantic love between a boy and girl

☆**pup tent** SHELTER TENT

pu·ra·na (poo rä′nə) *n.* ⟦Sans *purāṇāḥ*, lit., ancient, akin to *purāḥ*, before < IE base **per-*: see FORE⟧ [*often* **P-**] any of a group of 18 Hindu epics dealing with creation, the gods, genealogy, etc. in fables, legends, and tales

pur·blind (pur′blīnd′) *adj.* ⟦ME *pur blind:* see PURE & BLIND⟧ **1** [Obs.] completely blind **2** partly blind **3** slow in perceiving or understanding

Pur·cell (pur′səl), **Henry** 1659?-95; Eng. composer

pur·chase (pur′chəs) *vt.* **-chased, -chas·ing** ⟦ME *purchacen* < OFr *pourchacier*, to pursue < *pour*, for (< L *pro:* see PRO[1]) + *chacier*, to CHASE[1]⟧ **1** to obtain for money or by paying a price; buy **2** to obtain at a cost, as of suffering or sacrifice **3** to move or raise by means of a mechanical device **4** *Law* to acquire (land, buildings, etc.) by means other than inheritance or descent —*n.* **1** anything obtained by buying **2** the act of buying **3** [Now Rare] income; return **4** *a)* a firm hold applied to move something mechanically or to keep from slipping *b)* any apparatus for applying such a hold *c) Naut.* TACKLE (*n.* 2) **5** *Law* the acquisition of land, buildings, etc. by means other than inheritance or descent —**pur′chas·a·ble** *adj.* —**pur′chas·er** *n.*

pur·dah (pur′də) *n.* ⟦Urdu & Hindi *pardah*, veil < Pers⟧ **1** the practice among some Hindus and Muslims of secluding women from strangers **2** a curtain or partition used for this **3** the section of a house reserved primarily for women

pure (pyoor) *adj.* **pur′er, pur′est** ⟦ME *pur* < OFr < L *purus*, pure < IE base **peu-*, **pū-*, to purify, cleanse > Sans *punāti*, (he) cleanses, L *putare*, to cleanse, OHG *fowen*, to sift⟧ **1** *a)* free from any adulterant; unmixed [*pure* maple syrup] *b)* free from anything that taints, impairs, infects, etc.; clear [*pure* water or air] **2** simple; mere [*pure* luck] **3** utter; absolute; sheer [*pure* lunacy] **4** free from defects; perfect; faultless **5** free from sin or guilt; blameless **6** virgin or chaste **7** of unmixed stock; purebred **8** restricted to the abstract or theoretical aspects [*pure* physics] **9** *Bible* ceremonially undefiled **10** *Phonet.* articulated without any change in quality and with virtually no movement of the vocal organs; monophthongal [(e) is a *pure* vowel] —*SYN.* CHASTE —**pure′ness** *n.*

pure·bred (pyoor′bred′) *adj.* belonging to a recognized breed with characters maintained through generations of unmixed descent —*n.* a purebred plant or animal

pu·rée or **pu·ree** (pyoo rā′, -rē′; pyoor′ā′) *n.* ⟦Fr *purée* < OFr *purer*, to strain < L *purare*, to purify < *purus*, PURE⟧ **1** a thick, moist, smooth-textured form of cooked vegetables, fruits, etc., usually made by pressing the pulp through a sieve or by whipping it in a blender or food processor **2** a thick, smooth soup made with this —*vt.* **-réed′** or **-reed′**, **-rée′ing** or **-ree′ing** to make a purée of

pure line *Genetics* a breed or strain of animals or plants that maintains a high degree of consistency in certain characters as a result of inbreeding for generations

pure·ly (pyoor′lē) *adv.* **1** in a pure manner; unmixed with anything else **2** merely **3** innocently **4** entirely

pur·fle (pur′fəl) *vt.* **-fled, -fling** ⟦ME *purfilen* < MFr *pourfiler* < *pour*, for (< L *pro:* see PRO[1]) + *fil*, thread: see FILE[1]⟧ **1** to decorate the border of **2** to adorn or edge with metallic thread, beads, lace, etc. —*n.* an ornamental border or trimming, as the inlaid border of a violin: also **pur′fling**

pur·ga·tion (pur gā′shən) *n.* ⟦ME *purgacion* < OFr < L *purgatio*⟧ the act of purging

pur·ga·tive (pur′gə tiv) *adj.* ⟦ME *purgatyf* < MFr *purgatif* < LL *purgativus*⟧ **1** that purges; purging **2** causing bowel movement —*n.* a substance that purges; specif., a cathartic —*SYN.* PHYSIC

pur·ga·to·ri·al (pur′gə tôr′ē əl) *adj.* ⟦< LL *purgatorius* (see fol.) + -AL⟧ **1** serving to atone for sins; expiatory **2** of or like purgatory

pur·ga·to·ry (pur′gə tôr′ē) *n., pl.* **-ries** ⟦ME *purgatorie* < OFr & ML(Ec): OFr *purgatoire* < ML(Ec) *purgatorium* < LL *purgatorius*, cleansing < L *purgare:* see fol.⟧ **1** [*often* **P-**] *Theol.* a state or place in which, in Roman Catholicism and other Christian doctrine, those who have died in the grace of God expiate their sins by suffering **2** any state or place of temporary punishment, expiation, or remorse

purge (purj) *vt.* **purged, purg′ing** ⟦ME *purgen* < OFr *purgier* < L *purgare*, to cleanse < *purus*, clean (see PURE) + *agere*, to do: see ACT[1]⟧ **1** to cleanse or rid of impurities, foreign matter, or undesirable elements **2** to cleanse of guilt, sin, or ceremonial defilement **3** to remove by cleansing; clear (*away, off,* or *out*) **4** *a)* to rid (a nation, political party, etc.) of individuals held to be disloyal or undesirable *b)* to kill or otherwise get rid of (such individuals) **5** *Law* to free from a charge or imputation of guilt **6** *Med. a)* to empty (the bowels) *b)* to cause (a person) to empty the bowels —*vi.* **1** to become clean, clear, or pure **2** to have or effect a thorough bowel movement —*n.* **1** the act of purging **2** that which purges; esp., a purgative, or cathartic **3** the process of ridding a nation, political party, etc. of individuals held to be disloyal or undesirable —**purg′er** *n.*

pu·ri (poor′ē) *n., pl.* **pu′ri** or **pu′ris** ⟦Hindi⟧ a deep-fried wheat bread of India: the flat round of dough puffs out in the hot oil

pu·ri·fi·ca·tion (pyoor′ə fi kā′shən) *n.* the act or an instance of purifying, often, specif., of ritual or religious purifying —**pu·rif′i·ca·to′ry** (pyoo rif′i kə tôr′ē, pyoor′ə fi-) *adj.*

pu·ri·fi·ca·tor (pyoor′ə fi kāt′ər) *n.* ⟦ML⟧ a small linen cloth used in the Eucharist to wipe the chalice and to dry the celebrant's fingers and mouth

pu·ri·fy (pyoor′ə fī′) *vt.* **-fied′, -fy′ing** ⟦ME *purifien* < OFr *purifier* < L *purificare:* see PURE & -FY⟧ **1** to rid of impurities or pollution **2** to free from guilt, sin, or ceremonial uncleanness **3** to free from incorrect or corrupting elements **4** to purge (*of* or *from*) —*vi.* to become purified —**pu′ri·fi′er** *n.*

Pu·rim (poor′im, pōō rēm′) *n.* ⟦Heb *purim*, pl., lit., lots < ? Akkadian *pur*, stone⟧ a Jewish holiday, the Feast of Lots, celebrated on the 14th day of Adar, commemorating the deliverance of the Jews by Esther from a general massacre plotted by Haman: Esth. 9:21

pu·rine (pyoor′ēn′, -in) *n.* ⟦Ger *purin* < L *purus*, pure + ModL *uricum*, uric acid + *-in*, -INE[3]⟧ **1** a colorless, crystalline organic compound, $C_5H_4N_4$, the parent substance of the uric-acid group of compounds **2** any of several basic substances produced by the decomposition of nucleoproteins and having a purine-type molecule, as caffeine, adenine, or guanine

pur·ism (pyoor′iz′əm) *n.* ⟦Fr *purisme* < *pur*, PURE⟧ **1** strict observance of or insistence on precise usage or on application of formal, often pedantic rules, as in language, art, etc. **2** an instance of this —**pur′ist** *n.* —**pu·ris′tic** *adj.*, **pu·ris′ti·cal** —**pu·ris′ti·cal·ly** *adv.*

Pu·ri·tan (pyoor′ə tən) *n.* ⟦< LL *puritas* (see PURITY) + -AN⟧ **1** any member of a Protestant group in England and the American colonies that in the 16th and 17th cent. wanted to make the Church of England simpler in its services and stricter about morals **2** [**p-**] a person regarded as excessively strict in morals and religion —*adj.* **1** of the Puritans or Puritanism **2** [**p-**] PURITANICAL —**Pu′ri·tan·ism′** *n.*, **pu′ri·tan·ism′**

Puritan ethic WORK ETHIC: also **Puritan work ethic**

pu·ri·tan·i·cal (pyoor′ə tan′i kəl) *adj.* **1** [**P-**] of the Puritans or Puritanism **2** extremely or excessively strict in matters of morals and religion Also **pu′ri·tan′ic** —**pu′ri·tan′i·cal·ly** *adv.*

pu·ri·ty (pyoor′ə tē) *n.* ⟦ME *purete* < MFr *pureté* < LL *puritas* < L *purus*, PURE⟧ the quality or condition of being pure; specif., *a)* freedom from adulterating matter *b)* cleanness or clearness *c)* freedom from evil or sin; innocence; chastity *d)* freedom from corrupting elements (said of language, style, etc.) *e)* freedom from mixture with white; color saturation

Pur·kin·je cell (pər kin′jē) ⟦after J. E. *Purkinje* (1787-1869), Bohemian physiologist⟧ any of the large neurons that make up the middle layer of the gray cortex of the cerebellum, characterized by a dense network of dendrites on the outer side and a long, threadlike axon on the inner side

Purkinje fiber ⟦see prec.⟧ any of the specialized cardiac muscle fibers forming a network that carries the electrical impulses controlling contraction of the ventricles

purl[1] (purl) *vi.* ⟦< ? Scand, as in Norw *purla*, to ripple⟧ **1** to move in ripples or with a murmuring sound **2** to move in eddies; swirl —*n.* **1** a purling stream or rill **2** the murmuring sound of purling water

purl[2] (purl) *vt., vi.* ⟦earlier *pirl*, prob. < the n.⟧ **1** PURFLE **2** to edge (lace) with a chain of small loops **3** to form (one or more inverted stitches) in knitting —*n.* ⟦earlier *pyrle* < a Romance source as in It (Venetian) *pirlo*, a joining of warp and woof by twisting together the threads < echoic base **pirl*, to twirl⟧ **1** twisted metal thread, as of gold or silver, used in embroidery **2** a small loop, or a chain of loops, made on the edge of lace **3** an inversion of stitches in knitting to produce a more varied texture: also **purl′ing**

pur·lieu (purl′yōō′, pur′lōō′) *n.* ⟦altered (infl. by Fr *lieu*, place) < Anglo-Fr *puralee* < OFr *puralée* < *puraler*, to go through < *pur-*, *por-* (< L *pro-*, for, but used for *per-*, through) + *aler*, to go: see ALLEY[1]⟧ **1** [Historical] an outlying part of a forest, exempted from forest laws and returned to private owners **2** a place that one visits often or habitually; haunt **3** [*pl.*] *a)* bounds; limits *b)* environs **4** an outlying part, as of a city

pur·lin or **pur·line** (pur′lin) *n.* ⟦ME *purlyn* < ?⟧ a horizontal timber supporting the rafters of a roof

pur·loin (pər loin′, pur′loin′) *vt., vi.* ⟦ME *purlognen* < OFr *purloignier* < *pur-* (L *pro-*), for + *loin*, far < L *longe*, LONG[1]⟧ to steal; filch —**pur·loin′er** *n.*

☆**pu·ro·my·cin** (pyōō′rō mī′sin, pyoor′ō-) *n.* ⟦< PUR(INE) + -O- + -MYCIN⟧ an antibiotic, $C_{22}H_{29}N_7O_5$, produced by a soil actinomycete (*Streptomyces alboniger*), effective against various parasites, bacteria, etc.: it interferes with protein synthesis

pur·ple (pur′pəl) *n.* ⟦ME *purpel* < OE (Northumbrian) *purpl(e)*, dissimilated var. of WS *purpur(e)* < L *purpura*, purple < Gr *porphyra*, shellfish yielding purple dye⟧ **1** a dark color that is a blend of red and blue **2** [Now Rare] *a)* deep crimson *b)* cloth or clothing of such color: an emblem of royalty or high rank —*adj.* **1** of the color purple **2** imperial; royal **3** *a)* ornate or elaborate in literary style (usually used pejoratively) [*purple* prose] *b)* profane or obscene [*purple* language] —*vt., vi.* **-pled, -pling** to make or become purple —**born to (or in) the purple** being of royal or high birth —**the purple** royal or high rank

☆**pur·ple-fringed orchis** (pur′pəl frinjd′) either of two North American orchids (*Habenaria psycodes* and *H. fimbriata*) with purple-fringed flowers

☆**purple gallinule** a gallinule (*Porphyrula martinica*) with purplish wings and legs, usually found in freshwater swamps from the S U.S. to tropical South America

☆**purple grackle** the common grackle

☆**Purple Heart** ⟦descriptive of the original decoration, instituted (1782) by George WASHINGTON[1], a sewn-on *heart*-shaped badge of *purple* cloth; revived as a heart-shaped bronze medal in 1932⟧ a U.S. military decoration awarded to members of the armed forces wounded or killed in action by or against an enemy

☆**purple martin** the largest North American swallow (*Progne subis*), with bluish-black plumage

pur·plish (pur′plish, -pəl ish) ***adj.*** having a purple tinge; somewhat purple: also **pur′ply** (-plē, -pəl ē)

pur·port (pər pôrt′; *also, and for n. always,* pur′pôrt′) ***vt.*** ⟦Anglo-Fr *purporter* < OFr *porporter* < *por-* (< L *pro:* see PRO[1]), forth + *porter,* to bear < L *portare:* see PORT[3]⟧ **1** to profess or claim as its meaning **2** to give the appearance, often falsely, of being, intending, etc. —***n.*** **1** meaning; tenor; sense; drift **2** intention; object —**pur·port′ed** ***adj.*** —**pur·port′ed·ly** ***adv.***

pur·pose (pur′pəs) ***vt., vi.*** **-posed, -pos·ing** ⟦ME *purposen* < OFr *porposer,* var. of *proposer:* see PROPOSE⟧ to intend, resolve, or plan —***n.*** ⟦ME < OFr *porpos*⟧ **1** something one intends to get or do; intention; aim **2** resolution; determination **3** the object for which something exists or is done; end in view —***SYN.*** INTEND, INTENTION —**of set purpose 1** with a specific end in view **2** not accidentally; by design —**on purpose** by design; intentionally —**to good purpose** with a good result or effect; advantageously —**to little (or no) purpose** with little (or no) result or effect; pointlessly —**to the purpose** relevant; pertinent

pur·pose-built (pur′pəs bilt′) ***adj.*** [Brit.] designed and built for a particular purpose or use

pur·pose·ful (pur′pəs fəl) ***adj.*** **1** resolutely aiming at a specific goal **2** directed toward a specific end; not meaningless —**pur′pose·ful·ly** ***adv.*** —**pur′pose·ful·ness** ***n.***

pur·pose·less (pur′pəs ləs) ***adj.*** not purposeful; aimless —**pur′pose·less·ly** ***adv.*** —**pur′pose·less·ness** ***n.***

pur·pose·ly (pur′pəs lē) ***adv.*** with a definite purpose; intentionally; deliberately

pur·pos·ive (pur′pəs iv, pər pō′siv) ***adj.*** **1** serving some purpose **2** having a purpose —**pur′pos·ive·ly** ***adv.***

pur·pu·ra (pur′pyoor ə) ***n.*** ⟦ModL < L: see PURPLE⟧ a condition characterized by purplish patches on the skin or mucous membranes, caused by cutaneous and subcutaneous hemorrhage —**pur·pu·ric** (pər pyoor′ik) ***adj.***

pur·pure (pur′pyoor) ***n.*** ⟦ME < OE(WS): see PURPLE⟧ *Heraldry* the color purple: indicated in engravings by diagonal lines downward from sinister to dexter

pur·pu·rin (pur′pyoor in) ***n.*** ⟦< L *purpura,* PURPLE + -IN[1]⟧ a reddish material, $C_{14}H_5O_2(OH)_3$, isolated from the madder root or produced synthetically: used as a dye, stain, etc.

purr (pur) ***n.*** ⟦echoic⟧ **1** a low, vibratory sound made by a cat when it seems to be pleased **2** any sound like this, as of a quietly running engine —***vi., vt.*** to make, or express with, a purr **2** to speak in a low voice suggestive of contentment, sexual desire, etc.

purse (purs) ***n.*** ⟦ME < OE *purs* < ML *bursa,* bag, purse < LL, hide < Gr *byrsa*⟧ **1** a small bag or pouch for carrying money **2** financial resources; money **3** a sum of money collected as a present or given as a prize ☆**4** a woman's handbag **5** anything like a purse in shape, use, etc. —***vt.*** **pursed, purs′ing 1** [Archaic] to put in a purse **2** *a)* to gather into small folds *b)* to draw (the lips) tightly together, as in disapproval

purse crab PALM CRAB

purse-proud (purs′proud′) ***adj.*** proud of being wealthy

purs·er (pur′sər) ***n.*** ⟦ME, purse-bearer, treasurer⟧ a ship's officer in charge of accounts, tickets, etc., esp. on a passenger vessel

☆**purse seine** a very large net, as for catching tuna, that can be closed like a drawstring purse once it has been set

purse strings ⟦orig., the ends of the drawstring that closes a purse⟧ control over expenditures [*to hold the purse strings in a family*] —**tighten (or loosen) the purse strings** to make funds or the supply of money less (or more) readily available

purs·lane (purs′lin, -lān′) ***n.*** ⟦ME *purcelane* < MFr *porcelaine* < LL *porcilaca,* purslane, altered < L *portulaca:* see PORTULACA⟧ any of various prostrate weeds (genus *Portulaca*) of the purslane family, with pink, fleshy stems and small, yellow, short-lived flowers; esp., an annual (*P. oleracea*) sometimes used as a potherb and in salads —***adj.*** designating a family (Portulacaceae, order Caryophyllales) of dicotyledonous plants, including claytonia and portulaca

pur·su·ance (pər sōō′əns, -syōō′-) ***n.*** ⟦< fol.⟧ a pursuing, or carrying out, as of a project, plan, etc.

pur·su·ant (pər sōō′ənt, -syōō′-) ***adj.*** ⟦ME *poursuiant* < OFr, prp. of *poursuir:* see fol.⟧ [Now Rare] pursuing —**pursuant to 1** following upon **2** in accordance with

pur·sue (pər sōō′, -syōō′) ***vt.*** **-sued′, -su′ing** ⟦ME *pursuen* < OFr *poursuir* < VL *prosequere,* for L *prosequi* < *pro-,* forth + *sequi,* to follow: see SEQUENT⟧ **1** to follow in order to overtake, capture, or kill; chase **2** to proceed along, follow, or continue with (a specified course, action, plan, etc.) **3** to try to find, get, win, etc.; strive for; seek after [*to pursue success*] **4** to have as one's occupation, profession, or study; devote oneself to **5** to continue to annoy or distress; hound [*pursued by bad luck*] —***vi.*** **1** to chase **2** to go on; continue —**pur·su′er** ***n.***

pur·suit (pər sōōt′, -syōōt′) ***n.*** ⟦ME *purseute* < OFr *poursuite*⟧ **1** the act of pursuing **2** an occupation, career, interest, etc. to which one devotes time and energy

pursuit plane *former term for* FIGHTER (sense 3)

pur·sui·vant (pur′si vənt, -swi-) ***n.*** ⟦ME *pursevante* < OFr *poursuivant,* prp. of *poursuivre* < *poursuir:* see PURSUE⟧ **1** in the British Heralds' College, an officer ranking below a herald **2** a follower; attendant

pur·sy[1] (pur′sē) ***adj.*** **-si·er, -si·est** ⟦ME *purcy* < *purcyfe* < Anglo-Fr *pursif,* for OFr *polsif* < *polser,* to push, also breathe, pant < L *pulsare,* to beat < *pulsus:* see PULSE[1]⟧ **1** [Archaic] short-winded, esp. from being obese **2** obese; fat —**pur′si·ness** ***n.***

pur·sy[2] (pur′sē) ***adj.*** **-si·er, -si·est 1** drawn together, like the mouth of a purse with a tightened drawstring; puckered **2** proud of being wealthy

pur·te·nance (purt′'n əns) ***n.*** ⟦ME *portenaunce,* lit., appendage, altered < OFr *partenence* < prp. of *partenir,* to PERTAIN⟧ [Archaic] the viscera of an animal

pu·ru·lent (pyoor′ə lənt, pyoor′yoo-) ***adj.*** ⟦Fr < L *purulentus* < *pus* (gen. *puris*), matter, PUS⟧ of, like, containing, or discharging pus —**pu′ru·lence** ***n.***, **pu′ru·len·cy** —**pu′ru·lent·ly** ***adv.***

Pu·rús (pōō rōōs′) river in South America, flowing from E Peru through NW Brazil into the Amazon: *c.* 2,000 mi (3,219 km)

pur·vey (pər vā′) ***vt.*** ⟦ME *pourveien* < Anglo-Fr *purveier* < OFr *porveir* < L *providere:* see PROVIDE⟧ to furnish or supply (often, specif., food or provisions) —**pur·vey′or** ***n.***

pur·vey·ance (pər vā′əns) ***n.*** ⟦ME *purveance* < OFr⟧ **1** the act of purveying **2** things purveyed; provisions

pur·view (pur′vyōō′) ***n.*** ⟦ME *purveu* < Anglo-Fr (in legal phrases *purveu est,* it is provided, *purveu que,* provided that) < OFr *pourveü,* provided, pp. of *pourveir:* see PURVEY⟧ **1** the body and scope of an act or bill **2** the extent or range of control, activity, or concern; province **3** range of sight or understanding

pus (pus) ***n.*** ⟦L < IE base **pū-, *pu-,* to rot, stink (prob. orig. echoic of cry of disgust) > FOUL, Gr *pyon,* pus, L *putridus,* putrid⟧ the usually yellowish-white liquid matter produced in certain infections, consisting of bacteria, white corpuscles, serum, etc.

Pu·san (pōō′sän′) *a former transliteration of* BUSAN

Pu·sey·ism (pyōō′zē iz′əm) ***n.*** ⟦after E. B. *Pusey* (1800-82), Eng leader of the movement⟧ TRACTARIANISM —**Pu′sey·ite′** (-īt′) ***n.***

push (poosh) ***vt.*** ⟦ME *posshen* < MFr *pousser* < OFr *poulser* < L *pulsare,* to beat < *pulsus:* see PULSE[1]⟧ **1** *a)* to exert pressure or force against, esp. so as to move *b)* to move in this way *c)* to thrust, shove, or drive (*up, down, in, out,* etc.) **2** *a)* to urge on; impel; press *b)* to follow up vigorously; promote (a campaign, claim, etc.) *c)* to extend or expand (business activities, etc.) **3** to bring into a critical state; esp., to make critically in need [*to be pushed for time*] **4** to urge or promote the use, sale, success, etc. of ☆**5** [Informal] to be near or close to [*pushing seventy years of age*] ☆**6** *Baseball, Golf* to hit (the ball) and make it go to the right or, if one is left-handed, to the left —***vi.*** **1** to press against a thing so as to move it **2** to put forth great effort, as in seeking advancement **3** to move forward against opposition **4** to move by being pushed —***n.*** **1** the act of pushing **2** a thing to be pushed so as to work a mechanism **3** a vigorous effort, campaign, etc. **4** an advance against opposition **5** pressure of affairs or of circumstances **6** an emergency **7** [Informal] aggressiveness; enterprise; drive —☆**push comes to shove** [Informal] matters become serious or reach a critical point where some action or decision is required: preceded by *when* or *if* —**push off 1** to move a boat, etc. out into the water by pushing, as with an oar, against the bank or pier **2** [Informal] to set out; depart —**push on** to proceed; continue advancing

push·back (poosh′bak′) ***n.*** a reaction in opposition to a practice, proposal, law, etc.

☆**push·ball** (poosh′bôl′) ***n.*** **1** a game, played by two teams, in which a large ball about six feet in diameter is to be pushed across the opponent's goal **2** such a ball

push broom a wide brush pushed by means of a long handle, used for sweeping large areas

☆**push button** a small knob or button that is pushed to operate something, as by closing an electric circuit

☆**push-but·ton** (poosh′but′'n) ***adj.*** **1** controlled by or carried out by means of a push button **2** highly mechanized, computerized, automatic, etc. [*modern, push-button warfare*]

☆**push·cart** (poosh′kärt′) ***n.*** a cart pushed by hand, esp. one used by street vendors

push·chair (-cher′) ***n.*** [Brit.] STROLLER (sense 3): also **push′-chair′**

push·er (poosh′ər) ***n.*** **1** a person or thing that pushes **2** an airplane with its propeller or propellers mounted behind the engine so that it pushes the aircraft forward: also **pusher airplane** ☆**3** [Slang] a person who sells drugs, esp. narcotics, illegally

push·ing (poosh′iŋ) ***adj.*** **1** aggressive; enterprising; energetic **2** forward; officious —***SYN.*** AGGRESSIVE

Push·kin (poosh′kin), **A·lek·san·dr (Sergeyevich)** (ä′lyik sän′dr′) 1799-1837; Russ. poet, playwright, & short-story writer

☆**push·o·ver** (poosh′ō′vər) ***n.*** [Informal] **1** anything very easy to accomplish **2** a person, group, etc. easily persuaded, defeated, etc.

push·pin (poosh′pin′) ***n.*** a tacklike pin with a large head, used as to affix a notice to a bulletin board

push-pull (poosh′pool′) ***adj.*** *Electronics* designating or of an amplifier circuit in which two tubes or transistors operate 180° out of phase with each other, usually producing a higher output of the desired wave and canceling undesired qualities, as hum

Push·tu (push′tōō) ***n.*** *var. of* PASHTO

push-up or **push·up** (poosh′up′) ***n.*** an exercise in which a person lying face down, with the hands under the shoulders, raises the torso and, often, the knees off the ground by pushing down with the palms: push-ups are usually done in a series by alternately straightening and bending the arms

☆**push·y** (poosh′ē) ***adj.*** **push′i·er, push′i·est** [Informal] annoyingly aggressive and persistent —**push′i·ness** ***n.***

pu·sil·lan·i·mous (pyo͞o′si lan′ə məs) *adj.* ⟦LL(Ec) *pusillanimis* < L *pusillus*, tiny (dim. of *pusus*, little boy, akin to *puer*: see PUERILE) + *animus*, the mind (see ANIMAL) + -OUS⟧ **1** timid, cowardly, or irresolute; fainthearted **2** proceeding from or showing a lack of courage **—SYN.** COWARDLY **—pu′sil·la·nim′i·ty** (-si lə nim′ə tē) *n.* **—pu′sil·lan′i·mous·ly** *adv.*

puss¹ (poos) *n.* ⟦orig. ? echoic of the spitting of a cat: akin to Du *poes*, Swed dial. *pus*, LowG *puus*, cat⟧ [Informal] **1** a domesticated cat: often used in calling a cat **2** [Old-fashioned] a girl or young woman: term of affection

puss² (poos) *n.* ⟦< Irish *pus*, mouth⟧ [Slang] ☆**1** the face ☆**2** the mouth

☆**puss·ley** or **puss·ly** (pus′lē) *n.* PURSLANE

pus·sy¹ (pus′ē) *adj.* **-si·er, -si·est** containing or like pus

puss·y² (poos′ē) *n., pl.* **puss′ies** ⟦dim. of PUSS¹⟧ **1** [Informal] a domesticated cat, esp. a kitten: often used in calling a cat or kitten **2** [Informal] a catkin, as of the pussy willow ☆**3** [Slang] a person, esp. a boy or man, regarded as weak, timid, etc. **4** [Slang] *a)* the female genitals; vulva *b)* a woman regarded merely as a sexual partner (a disparaging or dismissive term) *c)* sexual intercourse with a woman: somewhat vulgar

puss·y·cat (-kat′) *n.* **1** PUSSY² (sense 1) **2** [Informal] a person who is gentle, lenient, meek, etc.

☆**puss·y·foot** (-foot′) *vi.* [Informal] **1** to move with stealth or caution, like a cat **2** to shy away from a definite commitment or from decisive action **—puss′y·foot′er** *n.*

☆**puss·y-whipped** (-hwipt′, -wipt′) *adj.* ⟦see PUSSY², sense 4⟧ [Slang] dominated by one's wife, girlfriend, etc.: somewhat vulgar

☆**pussy willow** any of several willows bearing velvetlike catkins before the leaves; esp., a deciduous shrub or tree (*Salix discolor*) with large, silvery catkins

pus·tu·lant (pus′chə lənt, -tyə-) *adj.* ⟦LL *pustulans*, prp.⟧ causing pustules to form **—*n.*** a pustulant medicine, etc.

pus·tu·lar (pus′chə lər, -tyə-) *adj.* **1** of, or having the nature of, pustules **2** covered with pustules Also **pus′tu·lous**

pus·tu·late (pus′chə lāt′, -tyə-; *for adj.*, -lit, -lāt′) *vt., vi.* **-lat′ed, -lat′ing** ⟦< LL *pustulatus*, pp. of *pustulare*, to blister < *pustula*: see fol.⟧ to form into pustules **—*adj.*** covered with pustules **—pus′tu·la′tion** *n.*

pus·tule (pus′cho͞ol′, -tyo͞ol′) *n.* ⟦L *pustula*, blister, pimple < IE base **pu-*, echoic of blowing out cheeks, puffing > Gr *physa*, breath, bubble⟧ **1** a small elevation of the skin containing pus **2** any small elevation like a blister or pimple

put (poot) *vt.* **put, put′ting** ⟦ME *putten* < or akin to OE *potian*, to push: mod. senses prob. < Scand, as in Dan *putte*, Swed dial. *putta*, to put away, push, akin to OE *pyttan*, to sting, goad⟧ **1** *a)* to drive or send by a blow, shot, or thrust [*to put a bullet in a target*] *b)* to propel with an overhand thrust from the shoulder [*to put the shot*] **2** *a)* to make do something [*to put a dog through its tricks*] *b)* to force [*put an army to flight*] **3** to cause to be in a certain position or place; place; set [*put the box here*] **4** *a)* to cause to be in a specified condition, situation, relation, etc. [*put her at ease*] *b)* to make undergo; subject [*put it to a trial*] **5** to impose [*put a tax on luxuries*] **6** *a)* to bring to bear (*on*); apply (*to*) [*to put one's mind on one's work*] *b)* to bring in or add; introduce; inject [*to put life into a party*] *c)* to bring about; effect [*to put a stop to cheating*] **7** to attribute; assign; ascribe [*to put the blame where it belongs*] **8** to express; state [*put it in plain language*] **9** to translate **10** to present for consideration, decision, etc. [*to put the question*] **11** *a)* to estimate as being (with *at*) [*to put the cost at $50*] *b)* to fix or set (a price, value, etc.) *on* **12** to adapt or fit (words) to music **13** *a)* to bet (money) *on* *b)* to invest (money) *in* or *into* **—*vi.*** to take one's course; move; go (*in, out, back*, etc.) **—*n.*** **1** a cast or thrust; esp., the act of putting the shot **2** an option to sell a given quantity of a stock, commodity, etc. at a specified price and within a specified time: puts are purchased in anticipation of, or to protect against, a decline in the price of the stock, commodity, etc.: cf. CALL (*n.* 17) **—*adj.*** [Informal] immovable; fixed [*stay put*] **—put about 1** to change the course of (a sailing vessel) to another tack **2** to move in another direction **—put across** [Informal] ☆**1** to cause to be understood or accepted **2** to carry out with success **3** to carry out by trickery **—put ahead** to reset the hands of (a clock) to a later time **—put aside** (or **by**) **1** to reserve for later use **2** to give up; discard **—put away 1** PUT ASIDE **2** to consign to a jail, mental hospital, etc. **3** [Informal] to consume (food or drink) **4** PUT DOWN (sense 6) (see phrase below) **—put back 1** to replace **2** to reset the hands of (a clock) to an earlier time ☆**3** to demote (a pupil) **—put down 1** *a)* to crush; repress; squelch *b)* to deprive of authority, power, or position; degrade **2** to write down; record **3** to attribute (to) **4** to consider as; classify **5** to land or make a landing in an aircraft **6** *a)* to kill (an injured or sick animal) as to end its suffering *b)* to kill (a vicious animal, esp. one that is a pet or in captivity) ☆**7** [Informal] to belittle, reject, criticize, or humiliate **—put forth 1** to grow (leaves, shoots, etc.) **2** to bring into action; exert **3** to propose; offer **4** to bring out; publish; circulate **5** to leave a port **—put forward** to advance or present (a plan, etc.) **—put in 1** to enter a port or harbor **2** to enter (a claim, request, etc.) **3** to interpose; insert **4** [Informal] to spend (time) in a specified manner **—put in for** to request or apply for **—put it on** [Slang] to make a pretentious show; pretend or exaggerate **—☆put it over on** [Informal] to deceive; trick **—☆put it there!** [Slang] shake hands with me: an expression of agreement, reconciliation, etc. **—put off 1** to leave until later; postpone; delay **2** to discard **3** to evade; divert **4** to displease or offend **—put on 1** to clothe, adorn, or cover oneself with **2** to take on; add [*to put on a few pounds*] **3** to assume or pretend **4** to apply (a brake, etc.) **5** to stage (a play) **—☆put someone on** to fool someone by playing on that person's credulity; hoax **—☆put someone on to** [Informal] to inform someone about **—put out 1** to expel; dismiss **2** to extinguish (a fire or light) ☆**3** to spend (money) **4** to disconcert; confuse **5** to distress; ruffle; vex **6** to inconvenience **7** *a)* to publish *b)* to produce and distribute *c)* to supply, offer, or display **8** [Slang] to engage in sexual intercourse, often promiscuously: usually said of a woman **9** *Baseball* to cause (a batter or runner) to be out by a fielding play **—put over 1** to postpone; delay ☆**2** [Informal] PUT ACROSS **—☆put something over on** [Informal] to deceive; trick **—put paid to** [Brit.] to put an end to; terminate **—put through** ☆**1** to perform successfully; carry out **2** to cause to do or undergo **3** to connect (someone) by telephone with someone else **—put to it** to place in a difficult situation; press hard **—put up 1** to offer, as for consideration, decision, auction, etc. **2** to offer as a candidate **3** to preserve or can (fruits, vegetables, etc.) **4** to erect; build **5** to lodge, or provide lodgings for ☆**6** *a)* to advance or provide (money) *b)* [Slang] to do or produce what is needed or wanted **7** to arrange (the hair) with curlers, bobby pins, etc. **8** to carry on [*to put up a struggle*] **9** [Informal] to incite (a person) *to* some action **10** to sheathe (one's sword) **—put upon** to impose on; victimize **—put up with** to bear or suffer patiently; tolerate

pu·ta·men (pyo͞o tā′mən) *n., pl.* **-ta′mens** or **-tam′i·na** (-tam′i nə) ⟦ModL < L, that which falls off in pruning, waste < *putare*, to prune, cleanse: see PURE⟧ *Anat.* the outer portion of the corpus striatum: it is associated with movement and with such neurological disorders as Parkinson's disease

pu·ta·tive (pyo͞ot′ə tiv) *adj.* ⟦ME *putative* < L *putativus* < *putare*, to suppose, reckon (orig., to cleanse, set in order, hence compute, consider: see PURE)⟧ generally considered or deemed such; reputed [*a putative ancestor*] **—pu′ta·tive·ly** *adv.*

☆**put-down** (poot′doun′) *n.* [Informal] a belittling remark or crushing retort

Pu·tin (po͞ot′'n), **Vladimir (Vladimirovich)** 1952- ; president (2000-08, 2012-) & prime minister (2008-12) of Russia

put·log (poot′lôg′) *n.* ⟦altered (? infl. by LOG¹) < earlier *putlock* < ? PUT + LOCK¹⟧ in masonry construction, any of the horizontal, wood or metal pieces which support the floor planks of a scaffold and which are themselves supported at one end in holes left temporarily in a wall under construction

Put·nam (put′nəm), **Israel** 1718-90; Am. Revolutionary War general

put-on (poot′än′) *adj.* assumed or feigned [*a put-on smile*] **—*n.*** [Informal] **1** the act of fooling or hoaxing someone by playing on that person's credulity **2** something, as a novel or play, intended as an elaborate hoax or practical joke on the reader or audience

☆**put·out** (poot′out′) *n.* *Baseball* a play in which the batter or runner is retired, or put out

☆**put-put** (put′put′) *n., vi.* **put′-put′ted, put′-put′ting** *alt. sp. of* PUTT-PUTT¹

pu·tre·fac·tion (pyo͞o′trə fak′shən) *n.* ⟦ME *putrefaccion* < LL *putrefactio* < L *putrefacere*: see fol.⟧ the decomposition of organic matter by bacteria, fungi, and oxidation, resulting in the formation of foul-smelling products; a rotting **—pu′tre·fac′tive** *adj.*

pu·tre·fy (pyo͞o′trə fī′) *vt., vi.* **-fied′, -fy′ing** ⟦ME *putrifien* < L *putrefacere*: see PUTRID & -FY⟧ to make or become putrid or rotten; decompose **—SYN.** DECAY **—pu′tre·fi′er** *n.*

pu·tres·cent (pyo͞o tres′ənt) *adj.* ⟦L *putrescens*, prp. of *putrescere*, to become putrid, inchoative of *putrere* < *puter, putris*, rotten: see PUS⟧ **1** becoming putrid; putrefying; rotting **2** of or connected with putrefaction **—pu·tres′cence** *n.*

pu·tres·ci·ble (pyo͞o tres′ə bəl) *adj.* ⟦LL *putrescibilis*⟧ liable to become putrid **—*n.*** a putrescible substance

pu·tres·cine (pyo͞o tres′ēn, -in) *n.* ⟦< L *putrescere* (see PUTRESCENT) + -INE³⟧ a foul-smelling compound, $NH_2(CH_2)_4NH_2$, produced by bacterial fermentation of protein and in the normal metabolism of mammals: it is a precursor of spermine

pu·trid (pyo͞o′trid) *adj.* ⟦Fr *putride* < L *putridus* < *putrere*: see PUTRESCENT⟧ **1** decomposed; rotten and foul-smelling **2** causing, showing, or proceeding from decay **3** morally corrupt; depraved **4** [Informal] very disagreeable or unpleasant **—pu·trid′i·ty** *n.*, **pu′trid·ness —pu′trid·ly** *adv.*

putsch (pooch) *n.* ⟦Ger < Swiss dial., lit., a push, blow⟧ a sudden, planned attempt to overthrow a government **—putsch′ist** *n., adj.*

putt (put) *n.* ⟦< PUT, v.⟧ *Golf* a shot made on the putting green in an attempt to roll the ball into the hole **— *vt., vi.*** to hit (the ball) in making a putt

put·tee (pə tē′, put′ē) *n.* ⟦Hindi *paṭṭī*, bandage < Sans *paṭṭikā* < *paṭṭa*, strip of cloth⟧ a covering for the lower leg, in the form of a cloth or leather gaiter or a cloth strip wound spirally

put·ter¹ (poot′ər) *n.* a person or thing that puts

putt·er² (put′ər) *n.* *Golf* **1** a short, straight-faced club used in putting **2** a person who putts

put·ter³ (put′ər) *vi.* ⟦var. of POTTER²⟧ to busy oneself or proceed in a trifling, ineffective, or aimless way; dawdle: often with *over, along, around*, etc. **—*vt.*** to dawdle or fritter (something) *away*

putt·ing green (put′iŋ) *Golf* the area of smooth, closely mowed turf in which the hole is sunk

put·to (po͞o′tō) *n., pl.* **put′ti** (-tē) ⟦It < L *putus*, var. of *pusus*, boy; akin to *puer*: see POULTRY⟧ a figure of a chubby male child or infant with wings, as in baroque art

☆**putt-putt¹** (put′put′) *n.* ⟦echoic⟧ the chugging sounds made by the engine of a motorboat, motorbike, etc. **—*vi.*** **putt′-putt′ed, putt′-putt′ing** to make, move along, or operate with such sounds

putt-putt[2] (put′put′) ***n.*** ⟦< *Putt-Putt Golf Course*, a service mark, redupl. of PUTT⟧ a game of miniature golf, or the course it is played on

put·ty (put′ē) ***n.*** ⟦Fr *potée*, calcined tin, brass, lit., potful < *pot*, POT[1]⟧ **1** *a)* a soft, plastic mixture of finely powdered chalk and linseed oil, used to secure glass panes, fill small cracks, etc. *b)* any substance like this in consistency, use, etc. **2** PUTTY POWDER **3** a cement of quicklime and water, mixed with plaster of Paris or sand for use as a finishing coat in plastering —***vt.*** **-tied, -ty·ing** to cement, fix, cover, or fill with putty

putty knife a tool having a broad, flexible blade with, often, a squared-off end, for applying and smoothing putty

putty powder powdered oxide of tin, or of tin and lead, used for polishing glass or metals

☆**put·ty·root** (put′ē ro͞ot′) ***n.*** an American orchid (*Aplectrum hyemale*) with clusters of yellowish-brown flowers, one leaf at the base of the stem, and a sticky substance in its bulbs

Pu·tu·ma·yo (po͞o′to͞o mä′yô) river in NW South America, flowing from SW Colombia along the Colombian-Peruvian border into the Amazon in NW Brazil: *c.* 1,000 mi (1,609 km)

put-up (po͝ot′up′) ***adj.*** ⟦< phrase PUT UP⟧ [Informal] **1** planned secretly beforehand **2** contrived, counterfeit, etc. Usually in the phrase **put-up job**

☆**putz** (puts) [Slang] ***n.*** ⟦< Yiddish < Ger, finery, ornament⟧ **1** the penis: mildly vulgar **2** a person regarded as stupid, simple, foolish, etc. —***vi.*** to waste time; putter (*around*)

Pu·vis de Cha·vannes (pü vēd shȧ vȧn′), **Pierre** 1824-98; Fr. painter

puz·zle (puz′əl) ***vt.*** **-zled, -zling** ⟦ME *poselen (inferred < pp. *poselet*), to bewilder, confuse < ?⟧ to perplex; confuse; bewilder; nonplus —***vi.*** **1** to be perplexed, etc. **2** to exercise one's mind, as over the solution of a problem —***n.*** **1** the state of being puzzled; bewilderment **2** a question, problem, etc. that puzzles **3** a toy or problem for testing cleverness, skill, or ingenuity; often, specif., JIGSAW PUZZLE —**puzzle out** to solve by deep thought or study —**puzzle over** to give deep thought to; concentrate on —**puz′zle·ment** ***n.*** —**puz′zler** ***n.***

SYN.—**puzzle** implies such a baffling quality or such intricacy, as of a problem, situation, etc., that one has great difficulty in understanding or solving it; **perplex**, in addition, implies uncertainty or even worry as to what to think, say, or do; **confuse** implies a mixing up mentally to a greater or lesser degree; **confound** implies such confusion as completely frustrates or greatly astonishes one; **bewilder** implies such utter confusion that the mind is staggered beyond the ability to think clearly; to **nonplus** is to cause such perplexity or confusion that one is utterly incapable of speaking, acting, or thinking further; **dumbfound** specifically implies as its effect a nonplused or confounded state in which one is momentarily struck speechless See also **mystery**

PVC (pē′vē′sē′) ***n.*** ⟦*p(oly)v(inyl) c(hloride)*⟧ any of a family of polymers derived from vinyl chloride: they have many uses in various forms, as in rigid plastic pipes and clear, thin food wrapping

Pvt *abbrev. Mil.* Private

PWA[1] (pē′dub′əl yo͞o′ā′) ***n.***, *pl.* **PWA's** ⟦*p(erson) w(ith) A(IDS)*⟧ a person who has an active condition of AIDS

PWA[2] *abbrev.* Public Works Administration

P wave ⟦*p(ressure) wave*⟧ a longitudinal wave that advances by alternate compression and expansion in a solid or fluid medium, like a sound wave

☆**p-whipped** (pē′hwipt′, -wipt′) ***adj.*** [Slang] *var. of* PUSSY-WHIPPED: a euphemism

pwr *abbrev.* power

pwt *abbrev.* pennyweight

PX *service mark* POST EXCHANGE

pxt. *abbrev.* ⟦L *pinxit*⟧ he (or she) painted it

py- (pī) *combining form* PYO-: used before a vowel

pya (pyä) ***n.*** ⟦Burmese⟧ a monetary unit of Myanmar, equal to $1/100$ of a kyat

pyc·nid·i·um (pik nid′ē əm) ***n.***, *pl.* **-i·a** (-ə) ⟦ModL < Gr *pyknos*, thick, tight (< IE base **puk-*, to compress > Alb *puth*, (I) kiss, embrace) + dim. suffix *-idion* (L *-idium*)⟧ a saclike spore case producing asexual spores (*conidia*) on the inside, found in certain ascomycetes and imperfect fungi —**pyc·nid′i·al** ***adj.***

pyc·no- (pik′nō, -nə) ⟦< Gr *pyknos:* see prec.⟧ *combining form* thick, dense [*pycnometer*]

pyc·no·cline (pik′nə klīn′) ***n.*** ⟦prec. + *-cline*, as in ANTICLINE⟧ a layer, zone, or gradient of changing density, esp. a thin layer of ocean water with a density that increases rapidly with depth

pyc·nog·o·nid (pik näg′ə nid) ***n.*** ⟦< ModL *Pycnogonida* < PYCNO- + Gr *gony*, KNEE⟧ any of a class (Pycnogonida) of mostly small saltwater arthropods with very long legs attached to a relatively tiny body

pyc·nom·e·ter (pik näm′ət ər) ***n.*** ⟦PYCNO- + -METER⟧ a vessel of a precise volume used to measure the density of liquids or solids

pyc·no·sis (pik nō′sis) ***n.***, *pl.* **-ses′** (-sēz′) PYKNOSIS —**pyc·not′ic** (-nät′ik) ***adj.***

Pyd·na (pid′nə) ancient city in Macedonia, near the Gulf of Salonika: scene of a battle (168 B.C.) of the final Roman defeat of the Macedonians

pye-dog (pī′dôg′) ***n.*** *alt. sp. of* PI-DOG

py·e·li·tis (pī′ə līt′is) ***n.*** ⟦ModL < Gr *pyelos*, basin (akin to *plynein*, to wash < IE base **pleu-* > FLOW) + -ITIS⟧ inflammation of a kidney pelvis —**py′e·lit′ic** (-lit′ik) ***adj.***

py·e·lo·gram (pī′ə lə gram′) ***n.*** an X-ray picture taken by pyelography

py·e·log·ra·phy (pī′ə läg′rə fē) ***n.*** ⟦< Gr *pyelos*, basin (see PYELITIS) + -GRAPHY⟧ the taking of X-ray pictures of the kidney and ureter after they have been filled with some radiopaque solution

py·e·lo·ne·phri·tis (pī′ə lō′nə frīt′əs) ***n.*** ⟦< Gr *pyelos* (see PYELITIS) + NEPHRITIS⟧ infection of one or both kidneys, usually involving both the pelvis and the functional tissue

py·e·mi·a (pī ē′mē ə) ***n.*** ⟦ModL: see PYO- & -EMIA⟧ a form of blood poisoning caused by the presence in the blood of pus-producing microorganisms that are carried to various parts of the body, producing multiple abscesses, fever, chill, etc. —**py·e′mic** ***adj.***

py·gid·i·um (pī jid′ē əm) ***n.***, *pl.* **-i·a** (-ə) ⟦ModL < Gr *pygidion*, dim. of *pygē*, rump < IE base **pu-*, to swell up > PUPA⟧ *Zool.* the end division of the body of a trilobite or of certain annelids, crustaceans, or insects

pyg·mae·an or **pyg·me·an** (pig mē′ən) ***adj.*** ⟦L *pygmaeus* + -AN⟧ pygmy

Pyg·ma·li·on (pig māl′yən, -mā′lē ən) ***n.*** ⟦L < Gr *Pygmaliōn*⟧ *Gr. Legend* a king of Cyprus and a sculptor: see GALATEA

pyg·moid (pig′moid′) ***adj.*** ⟦fol. + -OID⟧ like the Pygmies, esp. in being of small stature

Pyg·my (pig′mē) ***n.***, *pl.* **-mies** ⟦ME *pigmey* < L *pygmaeus* < Gr *pygmaios*, of the length of the *pygmē*, forearm and fist, also fist: see PUGNACIOUS⟧ **1** a member of any of several groups of African or Asian peoples of small stature described in ancient history and legend **2** a member of any of several modern African (*Negrillo*) and Asian (*Negrito*) peoples of small stature **3** [**p-**] any person, animal, or plant abnormally undersized; dwarf **4** [**p-**] an insignificant person or thing —***adj.*** **1** of the Pygmies **2** [**p-**] *a)* very small *b)* insignificant —**SYN.** DWARF

pygmy chimpanzee BONOBO

pyg·my·ism (-iz′əm) ***n.*** the condition of being a pygmy

py·ja·mas (pə jä′məz, -jam′əz) ***pl.n.*** *Brit. sp. of* PAJAMAS

pyk·nic (pik′nik) ***adj.*** ⟦< Gr *pyknos*, compact, solid (see PYCNIDIUM) + -IC⟧ *former term for* ENDOMORPHIC (sense 3)

pyk·no·sis (pik nō′sis) ***n.***, *pl.* **-ses′** (-sēz′) ⟦< Gr *pyknos*, thick, solid (see PYCNIDIUM) + -OSIS⟧ a process of thickening, esp. in the shrinking nucleus of a degenerating cell —**pyk·not′ic** (-nät′ik) ***adj.***

Pyle (pīl), **Er·nie** (ʉr′nē) (born *Ernest Taylor Pyle*) 1900-45; U.S. journalist

py·lon (pī′län′, -lən) ***n.*** ⟦Gr *pylōn*, gateway, akin to *pylē*, gate⟧ **1** a gateway **2** a truncated pyramid, or two of these, serving as a gateway to an Egyptian temple **3** any slender, towering structure flanking an entranceway, supporting electric lines, marking a course for aircraft, etc. **4** an assembly attached to an airplane, usually under the wing, to hold an engine, fuel tank, weapon, etc. ☆**5** *Football* any of the foam-rubber markers positioned upright at each corner of the end zone

py·lo·rec·to·my (pī′lə rek′tə mē) ***n.***, *pl.* **-mies** ⟦< fol. + -ECTOMY⟧ the surgical removal of the pylorus

py·lo·rus (pī lôr′əs) ***n.***, *pl.* **-ri** (-ī) ⟦LL < Gr *pylōros*, gatekeeper < *pylē*, gate + *ouros*, watchman⟧ the opening, surrounded by muscular tissue, from the stomach into the duodenum, the first part of the small intestine —**py·lor′ic** (-lôr′ik) ***adj.***

Pym (pim), **John** 1583?-1643; Eng. parliamentary leader

py·o- (pī′ō, -ə) ⟦< Gr *pyon*, PUS⟧ *combining form* **1** pus [*pyogenesis*] **2** suppurative [*pyosis*]

py·o·der·ma (pī′ō dʉr′mə) ***n.*** ⟦prec. + DERMA[1]⟧ any bacterial skin infection producing pus —**py′o·der′mic** ***adj.***

py·o·gen·e·sis (-jen′ə sis) ***n.*** ⟦PYO- + -GENESIS⟧ *Med.* the formation of pus; pyosis —**py′o·gen′ic** ***adj.***

py·oid (pī′oid′) ***adj.*** ⟦PY- + -OID⟧ of or like pus

Pyong·yang (pyuŋ′yäŋ′, pyôŋ′yaŋ′) capital of North Korea, in the W part

py·or·rhe·a or **py·or·rhoe·a** (pī′ə rē′ə) ***n.*** ⟦ModL: see PYO- & -RRHEA⟧ **1** a discharge of pus **2** *short for* PYORRHEA ALVEOLARIS —**py′or·rhe′al** ***adj.***, **py′or·rhoe′al**

pyorrhea al·ve·o·la·ris (al vē′ə ler′is) ⟦see ALVEOLUS⟧ a chronic periodontitis of the gums and tooth sockets, characterized by the formation of pus and, usually, by loosening of the teeth

py·o·sis (pī ō′sis) ***n.*** ⟦ModL < Gr *pyōsis:* see PYO- & -OSIS⟧ the formation or discharge of pus; suppuration

pyr- *combining form* PYRO-: used before a vowel

py·ra·can·tha (pī′rə kan′thə, pir′ə-) ***n.*** ⟦ModL: see PYRO- & ACANTHO-⟧ FIRETHORN

pyr·a·lid (pir′ə lid) ***n.*** ⟦< ModL *Pyralidae* < L *pyralis* (gen. *pyralidis*), kind of flying insect < Gr < *pyr*, FIRE: once thought to live in fire⟧ any of a large family (Pyralidae) of small moths with narrow, triangular forewings, broader hind wings, and long legs

pyr·a·mid (pir′ə mid) ***n.*** ⟦L *pyramis* (gen. *pyramidis*) < Gr, pyramid: replaced ME *piramis*, also < L⟧ **1** any huge structure with a square base and four sloping, triangular sides meeting at the top, as those built by the ancient Egyptians for royal tombs **2** an object, formation, structure, or organization shaped like or suggesting a pyramid **3** a crystal form in which as many as 12 sloping faces intersect at a point **4** *Geom.* a solid figure having a polygonal base, the

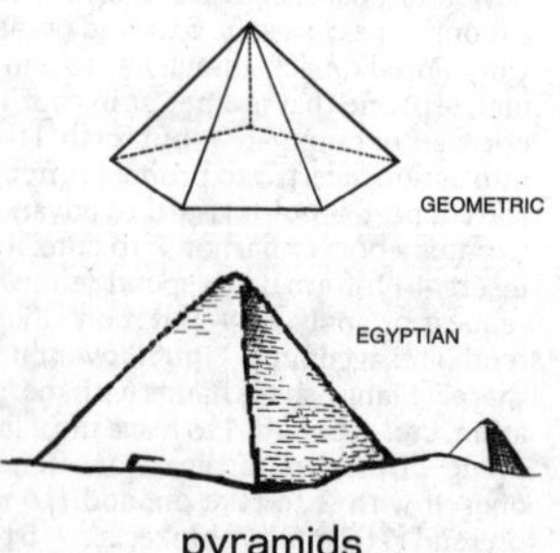

pyramids

sides of which form the bases of triangular surfaces meeting at a common vertex — *vi., vt.* 1 to build up, mass, or heap in the form of a pyramid ☆2 to engage in (a series of buying or selling operations) during an upward or downward trend in the stock market, working on margin with the profits made in the transactions —**the (Great) Pyramids** the three large pyramids at Gîza, Egypt: the largest is the Pyramid of Khufu —**py·ram·i·dal** (pi ram′i dəl, pir′ə mid′'l) *adj.* —**py·ram′i·dal·ly** *adv.* —**pyr′a·mid′ic** *adj.*, **pyr′a·mid′i·cal**

pyramid scheme a moneymaking scheme in which revenues are derived chiefly by recruiting increasingly larger groups of new salespeople or investors, each of whom pays for the right to recruit others in turn

Pyr·a·mus and This·be (pir′ə məs ənd thiz′bē) *Class. Myth.* Babylonian lovers: Pyramus, mistakenly thinking Thisbe has been killed by a lioness, kills himself, and Thisbe, finding his body, kills herself

py·ran (pī′ran′, pī ran′) *n.* ⟦PYR(ONE) + -AN⟧ any of a group of closed-chain compounds containing a ring, C_5H_6O, of one oxygen atom and five carbon atoms

py·rar·gy·rite (pī rär′ji rīt′) *n.* ⟦Ger *pyrargyrit* < Gr *pyr*, FIRE + *argyros*, silver + Ger *-it*, -ITE[1]⟧ a dark-colored, rhombohedral mineral, Ag_3SbS_3, an ore of silver; silver antimony sulfide

pyre (pīr) *n.* ⟦L *pyra* < Gr < *pyr*, FIRE⟧ a pile, esp. of wood, on which a dead body is burned in a funeral rite

py·rene[1] (pī′rēn′) *n.* ⟦ModL *pyrena* < Gr *pyrēn*, stone of a fruit, akin to *pyros*, grain of wheat < IE base **pūro-*, cereal > FURZE⟧ the stone of an apple, pear, or other drupe that contains several seeds

py·rene[2] (pī′rēn′) *n.* ⟦PYR- + -ENE⟧ a colorless hydrocarbon, $C_{16}H_{10}$, obtained from coal tar: its structure consists of the fusion of four benzene rings

Pyr·e·nees (pir′ə nēz′) mountain range along the French-Spanish border: *c.* 300 mi (483 km) long: highest peak, Pico de Aneto —**Pyr′e·ne′an** (-nē′ən) *adj.*

py·re·noid (pī rē′noid) *n.* ⟦< Gr *pyrēn* (gen. *pyrēnos*), PYRENE[1] + -OID⟧ *Bot.* a small structure within a chloroplast, as in some algae, functioning as a center for starch production

py·reth·rin (pī reth′rin, -rē′thrin) *n.* ⟦< fol. + -IN[1]⟧ either of two liquid esters, $C_{21}H_{28}O_3$ or $C_{22}H_{28}O_5$, derived from chrysanthemums: the active ingredient of pyrethrum

py·reth·rum (pī reth′rəm, -rē′thrəm) *n.* ⟦ModL < L < Gr *pyrethron*, feverfew < *pyr*, FIRE⟧ 1 a perennial plant (*Chrysanthemum coccineum*) of the composite family, widely grown for the white, pink, red, or purple flower heads 2 an insecticide made from the dried flower heads of several Old World chrysanthemums, esp. a species (*Chrysanthemum cinerariaefolium*) now grown extensively in the U.S.

py·ret·ic (pī ret′ik) *adj.* ⟦ModL *pyreticus* < Gr *pyretos*, burning heat, fever < *pyr*, FIRE⟧ of, causing, or characterized by fever

☆**Py·rex** (pī′reks′) ⟦arbitrary coinage < PIE[1] + *-r-* + *-ex* (with implication of Gr *pyr*, FIRE + L *rex*, king), arbitrary suffix of manufactured products⟧ *trademark for* a heat-resistant borosilicate glassware used for cooking, lab work, etc. —*n.* [*occas.* **p-**] such glassware

py·rex·i·a (pī rek′sē ə) *n.* ⟦ModL < Gr *pyrexis*, feverishness < *pyressein*, to be feverish < *pyretos*: see PYRETIC⟧ FEVER —**py·rex′i·al** *adj.*, **py·rex′ic**

pyr·he·li·om·e·ter (pīr hē′lē äm′ət ər, pir-) *n.* ⟦PYR- + HELIO- + -METER⟧ an instrument for measuring the amount of energy given off by the sun

pyr·i·dine (pir′ə dēn′, -din) *n.* ⟦PYR- + -ID + -INE[3]⟧ a flammable, colorless or pale-yellow liquid base, C_5H_5N, having a sharp odor: it is produced in the distillation of coal tar or bone oil and is used in the synthesis of vitamins and drugs, as a solvent, etc.

pyr·i·dox·al (pir′ə däk′səl) *n.* ⟦see PYRIDOXINE⟧ an aldehyde, $C_8H_9NO_3$, closely related to vitamin B_6 and exhibiting vitamin activity

pyr·i·dox·a·mine (pir′ə däk′sə mēn′) *n.* ⟦< fol. + AMINE⟧ a crystalline material, $C_8H_{12}N_2O_2$, exhibiting vitamin B_6 activity

pyr·i·dox·ine (pir′ə däk′sēn′, -sin) *n.* ⟦PYRID(INE) + OX(Y)- + -INE[3]⟧ a complex pyridine, $C_8H_{11}NO_3$, one of the vitamins of the B_6 group, found in various foods and prepared synthetically

pyr·i·form (pir′ə fôrm′) *adj.* ⟦ModL *pyriformis* < ML *pyrum*, for L *pirum*, PEAR: see -FORM⟧ pear-shaped: also sp. **pir′i·form′**

py·rim·i·dine (pə rim′ə dēn′, pī-; pir′ə mə dēn′) *n.* ⟦Ger *pyrimidin* < *pyridin*: see PYRIDINE⟧ 1 a colorless, liquid, crystalline organic compound, $C_4H_4N_2$, the fundamental form of a group of bases, some of which are constituents of nucleic acid 2 any of several basic substances produced by the decomposition of nucleoproteins and having a pyrimidine-type molecule, as thymine, cytosine, or uracil

py·rite (pī′rīt′) *n., pl.* **py·ri·tes** (pi rīt′ēz′, pī-; pī′rīts′) ⟦L *pyrites* < Gr *pyritēs*, flint or millstone < *pyritēs* (*lithos*), fire (stone) < *pyr*, FIRE⟧ a hard, brittle, yellow mineral, FeS_2, dimorphic with marcasite and occurring abundantly as a native ore, used to make sulfuric acid; iron sulfide

py·ri·tes (pə rīt′ēz′, pī-; pī′rīts′) *n.* ⟦see prec.⟧ any of various native metallic sulfides, esp. iron pyrites —**py·rit′ic** (-rit′ik) *adj.*, **py·rit′i·cal**

py·ro- (pī′rō, -rə; pir′ō, -ə) ⟦< Gr *pyr* (gen. *pyros*), FIRE⟧ *combining form* 1 fire, heat [*pyromania, pyrometer*] 2 *Chem. a)* a substance derived (from a specified substance) by or as if by the action of heat [*pyrogallic* acid] *b)* an inorganic acid derived from an ortho-acid, as orthophosphoric acid, by the elimination of one molecule of water from two molecules of the acid [*pyrophosphoric* acid] 3 *Geol.* a formation due to the action of heat [*pyroxenite*]

py·ro·cat·e·chol (pī′rō kat′ə chôl′, -chōl′, -kôl′, -kōl′) *n.* ⟦prec. + CATECH(U) + -OL[1]⟧ a white, crystalline phenol, $C_6H_4(OH)_2$, occurring naturally in plants and now usually produced synthetically: used as an antiseptic, as a photographic developer, etc.: also **py′ro·cat′e·chin** (-chin, -kin)

☆**Py·ro·ce·ram** (pī′rō sə ram′) ⟦PYRO- + CERAM(IC)⟧ *trademark for* a heavy, glasslike, ceramic material highly resistant to heat and breakage —*n.* [*also* **p-**] this material

py·ro·chem·i·cal (pī′rō kem′i kəl) *adj.* of chemical action at high temperatures —**py′ro·chem′i·cal·ly** *adv.*

py·ro·clas·tic (pī′rə klas′tik) *adj.* ⟦PYRO- + CLASTIC⟧ of or having to do with rocks formed from material that was explosively ejected from a volcano

py·ro·con·duc·tiv·i·ty (pī′rō kän′duk tiv′ə tē) *n.* *Elec.* conductivity of certain solid insulators that results when they are subjected to high temperatures

py·ro·crys·tal·line (pī′rə kris′tə lin) *adj.* crystallized from molten rock material

py·ro·e·lec·tric (pī′rō ē lek′trik) *adj.* of or showing pyroelectricity —*n.* a pyroelectric substance

py·ro·e·lec·tric·i·ty (pī′rō ē′lek′tris′ə tē) *n.* the development of electric dipoles in certain crystalline materials as a result of temperature changes: often called **pyroelectric effect**

py·ro·gal·late (pī′rə gal′āt′) *n.* a salt or ether of pyrogallol

py·ro·gal·lic acid (pī′rō gal′ik) PYROGALLOL

py·ro·gal·lol (pī′rə gal′ôl′, -ōl′) *n.* ⟦PYRO- + GALL(IC ACID) + -OL[1]⟧ a poisonous, white, crystalline phenol, $C_6H_3(OH)_3$, produced by heating gallic acid: used in medicine, as a developer in photography, etc.

py·ro·gen (pī′rə jən) *n.* ⟦PYRO- + -GEN⟧ *Med.* a substance that produces fever

py·ro·gen·ic (pī′rə jen′ik) *adj.* ⟦PYRO- + -GENIC⟧ 1 producing, or produced by, heat or fever 2 IGNEOUS Also **py·rog·e·nous** (pī räj′ə nəs)

py·rog·ra·phy (pī räg′rə fē) *n.* ⟦PYRO- + -GRAPHY⟧ 1 the art or process of burning designs on wood or leather by the use of heated tools 2 a design so made —**py·rog′ra·pher** *n.* —**py·ro·graph·ic** (pī′rō graf′ik) *adj.*

py·ro·lig·ne·ous (pī′rō lig′nē əs) *adj.* ⟦Fr *pyroligneux* < *pyro-* + L *lignum*, wood: see LIGNEOUS⟧ produced by the destructive distillation of wood

pyroligneous acid a reddish-brown liquid obtained by destructive distillation of wood and containing chiefly acetic acid, methanol, acetone, furfural, and various tars and oils

py·ro·lu·site (pī′rō lo͞o′sīt′, pī räl′yo͞o-) *n.* ⟦Ger *pyrolusit* < Gr *pyr*, FIRE + *lousis*, a washing (< *louein*, to wash < IE base **lou-*, to wash > LATHER) + Ger *-it*, -ITE[1]: used, when heated, to remove color from glass⟧ a very soft, black, tetragonal mineral, MnO_2, an ore of manganese used in making glass, paint, etc.; manganese dioxide

py·rol·y·sis (pī räl′ə sis) *n.* ⟦ModL: see PYRO- & -LYSIS⟧ chemical decomposition of a substance by heat: see CALCINE —**py·ro·lyt·ic** (pī′rō lit′ik) *adj.* —**py′ro·lyt′i·cal·ly** *adv.*

py·ro·mag·net·ic (pī′rō mag net′ik) *adj.* THERMOMAGNETIC

py·ro·man·cy (pī′rə man′sē) *n.* ⟦ME *piromance* < MFr < LL *pyromantia*: see PYRO- & -MANCY⟧ divination by the observation and interpretation of flames

py·ro·ma·ni·a (pī′rə mā′nē ə, -mān′yə) *n.* ⟦ModL: see PYRO- & -MANIA⟧ a persistent compulsion to start destructive fires —**py′ro·ma′ni·ac′** (-mā′nē ak′) *n., adj.* —**py′ro·ma·ni′a·cal** (-mə nī′ə kəl) *adj.*

py·ro·met·al·lur·gy (pī′rə met′ə lur′jē) *n.* metallurgy using high temperatures, as in roasting, smelting, etc., for the extraction of metals from their ores

py·rom·e·ter (pī räm′ət ər) *n.* ⟦PYRO- + -METER⟧ an instrument with which high temperatures, beyond the range of ordinary thermometers, are measured —**py·ro·met·ric** (pī′rō me′trik) *adj.* —**py′ro·met′ri·cal·ly** *adv.* —**py·rom′e·try** (-ə trē) *n.*

py·ro·mor·phite (pī′rə môr′fīt′) *n.* ⟦Ger *pyromorphit*: see PYRO- & -MORPH & -ITE[1]⟧ a semihard, greenish, hexagonal mineral, $Pb_5(PO_4)_3Cl$, an ore of lead; lead phosphate chloride

py·rone (pī′rōn′, pī rōn′) *n.* ⟦Ger *pyron*: see PYRO- & -ONE⟧ 1 either of two isomeric, unsaturated, closed-chain compounds, $C_5H_4O_2$, from which several yellow dyes are derived 2 any of a class of compounds derived from pyrone

py·ro·nine (pī′rə nēn′, -nin) *n.* ⟦Ger *pyronin* < *pyro-*, PYRO- + *-on*, -ONE + *-in*, -INE[3]⟧ any of a small class of dyes, used esp. as histologic stains

py·rope (pī′rōp′) *n.* ⟦ME *pirope* < MFr < L *pyropus*, red bronze < Gr *pyrōpus*, lit., fiery-eyed < *pyr*, FIRE + *ōps*, EYE⟧ a variety of deep-red to black garnet, $Mg_3Al_2(SiO_4)_3$, often used as a gem; magnesium aluminum silicate

py·ro·pho·bi·a (pī′rə fō′bē ə) *n.* ⟦ModL: see PYRO- & -PHOBIA⟧ an excessive or irrational fear of fire

py·ro·phor·ic (pī′rə fôr′ik) *adj.* ⟦< ModL *pyrophorus* (< Gr *pyrophoros* < *pyr*, FIRE + *pherein*, to BEAR[1]) + -IC⟧ capable of igniting spontaneously when exposed to air, as certain finely divided metals

py·ro·phos·phate (pī′rə fäs′fāt′) *n.* a salt or ester of pyrophosphoric acid

py·ro·phos·phor·ic acid (pī′rə fäs fôr′ik) ⟦PYRO- + PHOSPHORIC⟧ a viscous liquid acid, $H_4P_2O_7$, which crystallizes when left standing at ordinary temperatures and is easily converted to orthophosphoric acid upon dilution with water

py·ro·pho·tom·e·ter (pī′rə fō täm′ət ər) *n.* ⟦PYRO- + PHOTOMETER⟧ an optical instrument for measuring extremely high temperatures

py·ro·phyl·lite (pī′rə fil′īt′) *n.* ⟦Ger *pyrophyllit*: see PYRO- & PHYLL(O)- & -ITE[1]⟧ a very soft, greasy, monoclinic mineral, $AlSi_2O_5(OH)$, that is similar to talc in structure, used as a lubricant and in making rubber, soap, etc.; hydrous aluminum silicate

py·ro·sis (pī rō′sis) ***n.*** ⟦ModL < Gr *pyrōsis*, a burning < *pyroun*, to burn < *pyr*, FIRE⟧ HEARTBURN

py·ro·stat (pī′rə stat′) ***n.*** ⟦PYRO- + -STAT⟧ a thermostat, esp. one for high temperatures

py·ro·sul·fate (pī′rə sul′fāt′) ***n.*** a salt of pyrosulfuric acid

py·ro·sul·fu·ric acid (pī′rə sul fyoor′ik) ⟦PYRO- + SULFURIC⟧ a strong, crystalline acid, $H_2S_2O_7$, prepared commercially as a heavy, oily, fuming liquid: used in making explosives and dyes, as a sulfating agent, etc.

py·ro·tech·nic (pī′rə tek′nik) ***adj.*** ⟦Fr *pyrotechnique* < Gr *pyr*, FIRE + *technē*, art: see TECHNIC⟧ **1** of fireworks **2** designating or of devices or materials that activate propellants, safety systems, signals, etc. in spacecraft, by igniting or exploding on command **3** brilliant; dazzling *[pyrotechnic wit]* Also **py′ro·tech′ni·cal** —**py′ro·tech′ni·cal·ly** ***adv.***

py·ro·tech·nics (pī′rə tek′niks) ***n.*** ⟦see prec.⟧ the art of making and using fireworks: also **py′ro·tech′ny** (-nē) —***pl.n.*** **1** *a)* a display of fireworks *b)* fireworks; esp., rockets, flares, smoke bombs, etc., as for signaling *c)* pyrotechnic devices in spacecraft **2** a dazzling display, as of eloquence, wit, virtuosity, etc. —**py′ro·tech·ni′cian** (-tek nish′ən) ***n.***, **py′ro·tech′nist**

py·rox·ene (pī räk′sēn′) ***n.*** ⟦Fr *pyroxène* < Gr *pyr*, FIRE + *xenos*, stranger: from its being foreign to igneous rocks⟧ any of a group of monoclinic or orthorhombic silicate minerals usually containing iron or magnesium but not the hydroxyl radical, and commonly found in igneous rocks —**py′rox·en′ic** (-sen′ik) ***adj.***

py·rox·e·nite (pī räk′sə nīt′) ***n.*** a dark-colored, coarsegrained, intrusive igneous rock composed mainly of pyroxene

py·rox·y·lin or **py·rox·y·line** (pī räk′sə lin) ***n.*** ⟦Fr *pyroxyline* < Gr *pyr*, FIRE + *xylon*, wood⟧ nitrocellulose, esp. in less highly nitrated and explosive forms than guncotton

pyr·rhic[1] (pir′ik) ***n.*** ⟦L *pyrrhicha* < Gr *pyrrhichē*, war dance⟧ a war dance of the ancient Greeks

pyr·rhic[2] (pir′ik) ***n.*** ⟦L *pyrrhichius* < Gr *pyrrhichios (pous)*, pyrrhic (foot)⟧ a metrical foot of two short or unaccented syllables —***adj.*** of or made up of pyrrhics

Pyr·rhic victory (pir′ik) ⟦Gr *Pyrrhikos*⟧ a too-costly victory: in reference to either of two victories of Pyrrhus, king of Epirus, over the Romans in 280 and 279 B.C., with very heavy losses

Pyr·rho·nism (pir′ə niz′əm) ***n.*** **1** the doctrine taught by Pyrrho (*c.* 360-*c.* 270 B.C.), a Gr. Skeptic, that all knowledge, including the testimony of the senses, is uncertain **2** extreme skepticism —**Pyr′rho·nist** ***n.***

pyr·rho·tite (pir′ə tīt′) ***n.*** ⟦< Gr *pyrrhotēs*, redness (< *pyrrhos*, flame-colored < *pyr*, FIRE) + -ITE[1]⟧ a bronze-colored, typically magnetic, hexagonal mineral, $Fe_{x-1}Sx$, usually found with pentlandite; iron sulfide

☆**pyr·rhu·lox·i·a** (pir′oo läk′sē ə, pir′ə-) ***n.*** ⟦ModL < *Pyrrhula* (< Gr *pyrrhoulas*, a red-colored bird < *pyrrhos*, flame-colored < *pyr*, FIRE) + *Loxia*, the crossbill genus < Gr *loxos*, crosswise + -IA⟧ a brownish-gray and red cardinal (*Cardinalis sinuatus*) having a crest and large, parrotlike bill, found in the SW U.S. and N Mexico

Pyr·rhus[1] (pir′əs) ***n.*** *Gr. Myth.* Achilles' son

Pyr·rhus[2] (pir′əs) 318?-272 B.C.; king of Epirus (305?-272 B.C.)

pyr·role (pir′ōl, pi rōl′) ⟦Ger *pyrrol* < Gr *pyrrhos*, fiery (< *pyr*, FIRE) + *-ol*, -OLE⟧ ***n.*** a colorless, pungent, slightly basic liquid, C_4H_5N, found in bile pigments, chlorophyll, and hematin, and obtained from coal tar, bone oil, etc.

py·ru·vic acid (pī rōō′vik, pi-) ⟦< PYR- + L *uva*, grape + -IC⟧ a colorless, liquid or crystalline organic acid, $CH_3COCOOH$, produced by the oxidation of lactic acid: it is a key intermediate in protein, fat, and carbohydrate metabolism in the cell and in the production of ATP

Py·thag·o·ras (pi thag′ə rəs) 6th cent. B.C.; Gr. philosopher & mathematician, born on Samos —**Py·thag′o·re′an** (-ə rē′ən) ***adj.***, ***n.***

Py·thag·o·re·an·ism (pi thag′ə rē′ən iz′əm) ***n.*** the philosophy of Pythagoras, the main tenets of which are the transmigration of the soul and the belief in numbers as the ultimate elements of the universe

Pythagorean theorem *Geom.* the theorem that in a right triangle the hypotenuse squared is equal to the sum of the squares of the other sides (i.e., $c^2 = a^2 + b^2$)

Pyth·i·a (pith′ē ə) ***n.*** the title of the high priestess of the oracle of Apollo at Delphi in ancient Greece

Pyth·i·ad (pith′ē ad′, -əd) ***n.*** ⟦< Gr *Pythios:* see fol.⟧ the period of four years from one celebration of the Pythian games to the next

Pyth·i·an (pith′ē ən) ***adj.*** ⟦< L *Pythius* < Gr *Pythios*, of *Pythō*, older name for DELPHI and its environs⟧ **1** of Apollo as patron of Delphi and the oracle located there **2** designating or of the games held at Delphi every four years by the ancient Greeks in honor of Apollo

Pyth·i·as (pith′ē əs) ***n.*** *see* DAMON AND PYTHIAS

py·thon (pī′thän′, -thən) ***n.*** ⟦L < Gr *Pythōn* < *Pythō:* see PYTHIAN⟧ **1** [**P-**] *Gr. Myth.* an enormous serpent that lurks in the cave of Mount Parnassus and is slain by Apollo **2** any of a genus (*Python*, family Boidae) of very large, nonvenomous snakes of Asia, Africa, and Australia, that squeeze their prey to death **3** popularly, any large snake that squeezes its prey to death

py·tho·ness (pī′thə nis) ***n.*** ⟦ME *phitonesse* < MFr *phitonise* < ML *phytonissa* < LL(Ec) *pythonissa* < Gr *Pythōn* < *Pythō:* see PYTHIAN⟧ **1** a priestess of Apollo at Delphi **2** any woman soothsayer; prophetess

py·thon·ic[1] (pī thän′ik, pi-) ***adj.*** ⟦LL(Ec) *pythonicus*, prophetic; ult. < Gr *Pythōn:* see PYTHON⟧ of or like an oracle; prophetic

py·thon·ic[2] (pī thän′ik, pi-) ***adj.*** of or like a python

py·u·ri·a (pī yoor′ē ə) ***n.*** ⟦ModL: see PY- & -URIA⟧ the presence of pus in the urine

pyx (piks) ***n.*** ⟦ME *pixe* < L *pyxis* < Gr, box < *pyxos*, the box tree⟧ **1** *a)* the container in which the consecrated wafer of the Eucharist is kept *b)* a small container for carrying the Eucharist to the sick **2** a box in a mint, in which specimen coins are placed until the test for purity and weight

pyx·id·i·um (pik sid′ē əm) ***n.***, *pl.* **-i·a** (-ə) ⟦ModL < Gr *pyxidion*, dim. of *pyxis:* see prec.⟧ PYXIS (sense 3)

☆**pyx·ie** (pik′sē) ***n.*** ⟦contr. < the genus name⟧ a creeping, dicotyledonous evergreen plant (*Pyxidanthera barbulata*) with small, leathery leaves and white, star-shaped flowers, native to the E U.S.

pyx·is (pik′sis) ***n.***, *pl.* **pyx′i·des′** (-si dēz′) ⟦ME < L: see PYX⟧ **1** a vase with a cover, used by the ancient Greeks and Romans **2** a small box or case **3** *Bot.* a dehiscent, dry fruit whose upper portion splits off as a lid, as the fruit of a pimpernel

Pyx·is (pik′sis) ***n.*** ⟦ModL, short for *Pyxis nautica*, mariner's compass < L *pyxis:* see PYX⟧ a S constellation between Puppis and Antlia: see ARGO (sense 2)

q[1] or **Q** (kyo͞o) ***n., pl.*** **q's, Q's** **1** the seventeenth letter of the English alphabet: via Latin from the early Greek *koppa*, a borrowing from the Phoenician **2** any of the speech sounds that this letter represents, as, in English words, where it is typically followed by *u* (except in words borrowed from Arabic), the (kw) of *queen* or (k) of *conquer* **3** a type or impression for *q* or Q **4** the seventeenth in a sequence or group **5** an object shaped like Q —***adj.*** **1** of *q* or Q **2** seventeenth in a sequence or group **3** shaped like Q

q[2] *abbrev.* **1** *Pharmacy* every **2** quart **3** quarter **4** quarterly **5** quarto **6** query **7** question **8** quintal **9** quire

Q[1] (kyo͞o) ***n.*** ⟦*q(uality factor)*⟧ *Electronics* the ratio of energy stored to energy lost in a component or substance: often called **Q factor**

Q[2] *abbrev.* **1** ⟦L *quadrans*⟧ farthing **2** Quebec **3** Queen **4** *Chess* queen **5** quetzal **6** *Rom. History* Quintus (the praenomen)

Q[3] *symbol Physics* electric charge

Qad·da·fi (kə dä′fē), **Mu·am·mar al-** (mo͞o′ə mär′ al′-) 1942-2011; Libyan political leader (1969-2011): also **Qa·dha′fi**

qAM *abbrev.* ⟦prob. < L *quaque*, every + AM[2] (sense 2)⟧ *Pharmacy* every morning

qa·nat (kä nät′) ***n.*** ⟦Pers < Ar *ḳanāt*, reed, pipe, channel⟧ an ancient system of deep underground tunnels and wells built in the Middle East to channel water from a mountain to a dry lower region

Q and A or **Q & A** *abbrev.* question and answer

qat (kät) ***n.*** *alt. sp. of* KHAT

Qa·tar (kä tär′, kä′tär′; kut′ər, gut′-) country occupying a peninsula of E Arabia, on the Persian Gulf: entered into treaty relations with Great Britain in 1878 & became an independent emirate in 1971: 4,416 sq mi (11,437 sq km); cap. Doha —**Qa·tar·i** (kə tär′ē, gə-) ***adj., n.***

QB *abbrev.* **1** *Football* quarterback: sometimes written **qb** **2** Queen's Bench **3** *Chess* queen's bishop

QC *abbrev.* **1** Quebec **2** Queen's Counsel

q.d. *abbrev.* ⟦L *quaque die*⟧ *Pharmacy* every day

q.e. *abbrev.* ⟦L *quod est*⟧ which is

Q.E.D. *abbrev.* ⟦L *quod erat demonstrandum*⟧ which was to be demonstrated or proved

Q.E.F. or **q.e.f.** *abbrev.* ⟦L *quod erat faciendum*⟧ which was to be done

Qeshm (kesh′əm) island of Iran, in the Strait of Hormuz: 460 sq mi (1,191 sq km)

QF *abbrev.* quick-firing

Q fever ⟦< Q(UERY): so named because of many unanswered questions about the disease when first identified⟧ a mild illness characterized by fever, headache, muscular pains, and pneumonia, transmitted by contact or ticks, and caused by a rickettsia (*Coxiella burnetii*)

qh *abbrev.* ⟦L *quaque hora*⟧ *Pharmacy* every hour

qhs *abbrev.* ⟦prob. < L *quaque*, every + *hora somni*, lit., hour of sleep⟧ *Pharmacy* at bedtime

qi (chē) ***n.*** *alt. sp. of* CHI[2]: also written **Qi**

Qi·a·na (kē än′ə) ***n.*** ⟦former trademark: arbitrary coinage⟧ a synthetic fabric resistant to stains, wrinkles, etc. and textured like silk, satin, jersey, etc.

q.i.d. *abbrev.* ⟦L *quater in die*⟧ *Pharmacy* four times a day

Qing·dao (chiŋ′dou′) seaport in Shandong province, NE China, on the Yellow Sea

Qing·hai (chiŋ′hī′) **1** province of NW China, northeast of Tibet: 278,379 sq mi (720,999 sq km); cap. Xining **2** salt lake in the NE part of this province: *c.* 2,200 sq mi (5,698 sq km)

Qin·huang·dao (chin′hwäŋ′dou′) seaport in NE Hebei province, NE China

Qin·ling Shan (chin′liŋ′ shän′) mountain range in NC China, extending across Gansu, Shaanxi, & Henan provinces: highest peak, *c.* 13,500 ft (4,115 m)

qin·tar (kin tär′) ***n.*** ⟦Alb, ult. < L *centenarius*, relating to a hundred: see CENTENARY⟧ a monetary unit of Albania, equal to $\frac{1}{100}$ of a lek

Qi·qi·har (chē′chē′här′) city in Heilongjiang province, NE China

Qishm (kish′əm) *var. of* QESHM

☆**qi·vi·ut** (kē′vē o͞ot′, -vē ət) ***n.*** ⟦Esk⟧ **1** the fine, soft, light-brown inner layer of hair of the musk ox **2** yarn spun from this hair

QKt *abbrev. Chess* queen's knight

ql *abbrev.* quintal

QM *abbrev.* Quartermaster

Qo *abbrev.* ⟦for Heb *qōhēleth*, alt. transliteration of *kohelet*: see ECCLESIASTES⟧ *Bible* Ecclesiastes

Qom (ko͝om) city in NC Iran

qoph (kôf) ***n.*** *alt. sp. of* KOPH

q.p. or **q.pl.** *abbrev.* ⟦L *quantum placet*⟧ as much as you please

qq or **Qq** *abbrev.* quartos

qq.v. *abbrev.* ⟦L *quae vide*⟧ which: used in referring to words, passages, etc. as in a book

qr *abbrev.* ⟦L *quadrans*⟧ **1** farthing **2** quarter **3** quire

QR *abbrev. Chess* queen's rook

Q rating ⟦*q(uotient) rating*⟧ a figure, based on opinion polls, intended to reflect how relatively popular and recognizable a given TV performer is with audiences

QR Code (kyo͞o′är′) ⟦< *q(uick) r(esponse)*⟧ *trademark for* a data-encoding system involving a small, digitally encoded pattern of squares and dots designed to be read as by a smartphone scanner and having a wide range of commercial applications —[**QR c-**] such an encoded pattern

qs *abbrev.* quarter section (of land)

q.s. *abbrev.* ⟦L *quantum sufficit*⟧ *Pharmacy* as much as will suffice; enough

qt *abbrev.* **1** quantity **2** quart(s): also, for the plural, **qts**

q.t. (kyo͞o′tē′) ***n.*** ⟦< *q(uie)t*⟧ [Informal] quiet: chiefly in the phrase **on the q.t.**, secretly: also **Q.T.**

Q-tip (kyo͞o′tip′) ***n.*** ⟦< *Q-Tips*, a trademark for such swabs⟧ a swab consisting of a short stick of wood, paper, or plastic with wads of cotton at one or both ends

qto *abbrev.* quarto

qtr *abbrev.* quarter: also **Qtr** or **QTR**

qty *abbrev.* quantity

qu *abbrev.* **1** quart **2** quarter **3** quarterly **4** queen **5** query **6** question

qua (kwā, kwä) ***prep.*** ⟦L, abl. sing. fem. of *qui*, WHO⟧ in the function, character, or capacity of; as [the President *qua* Commander in Chief]

quaa·lude (kwā′lo͞od′) ***n.*** ⟦< *Quaalude*, a former trademark⟧ [*also* **Q-**] METHAQUALONE

quack[1] (kwak) ***vi.*** ⟦echoic⟧ to utter the characteristic sound or cry of a duck, or a sound like it —***n.*** the sound made by a duck, or any sound like it

quack[2] (kwak) ***n.*** ⟦short for QUACKSALVER⟧ **1** an untrained person who practices medicine fraudulently **2** any person who pretends to have knowledge or skill in a particular field; charlatan —***adj.*** **1** characterized by pretentious claims with little or no foundation **2** dishonestly claiming to effect a cure —***vi.*** to engage in quackery

SYN.—**quack** and **charlatan** both apply to a person who unscrupulously pretends to knowledge or skill he or she does not possess, but **quack** almost always is used of a fraudulent or incompetent practitioner of medicine; **mountebank**, in modern use, applies to a person who resorts to cheap and degrading methods in his or her work, etc.; **impostor** applies especially to a person who fraudulently impersonates another and, more generally, to anyone who is a hypocrite; **faker** applies to a person who practices deception or misrepresentation

quack·er·y (kwak′ər ē) ***n.*** the claims or methods of a quack

☆**quack grass** ⟦var. of QUICK GRASS⟧ COUCH GRASS

quack·ish (kwak′ish) ***adj.*** **1** like or characteristic of a quack **2** boastfully pretentious —**quack′ish·ly** ***adv.***

quack·sal·ver (kwak′sal′vər) ***n.*** ⟦MDu (> Du *kwaksalver*) < *quacken*, to quack, brag, boast + *zalf*, salve, akin to Ger *salbe*, SALVE[1]⟧ [Now Rare] a quack; charlatan

quad[1] (kwäd) ***n.*** *short for:* **1** QUADRANGLE (of a college) **2** QUADRICEPS **3** QUADRUPLET —***adj.*** *short for* QUADRAPHONIC

quad[2] (kwäd) *Printing* ***n.*** ⟦< QUAD(RAT)⟧ a piece of type metal lower than the face of the type, used for spacing, to fill blank lines, etc. —***vt.*** **quad′ded**, **quad′ding** to fill out (a line) by means of quads

quad[3] (kwäd) ***n.*** *alt. sp. of* QUOD

☆**quad**[4] (kwäd) ***n.*** a unit of energy equal to one quadrillion Btu

quad[5] *abbrev.* **1** quadrangle **2** quadrant **3** quadruplicate

quadr- *combining form* QUADRI-: used before a vowel

Quad·ra·ges·i·ma (kwä′drə jā′zi mə, -jes′i-) ***n.*** ⟦LL(Ec) < fem. of L *quadragesimus*, fortieth < *quadraginta*, forty < base of *quattuor*, FOUR⟧ *old name for:* **1** [Obs.] the forty days of Lent **2** the first Sunday in Lent: also **Quadragesima Sunday**

quad·ra·ges·i·mal (kwä′drə jā′zi məl, -jes′i-) ***adj.*** ⟦ML *quadragesimalis*: see prec.⟧ **1** lasting forty days: said of Lent **2** [**Q-**] Lenten; of or suitable for Lent

quad·ran·gle (kwä′draŋ′gəl) ***n.*** ⟦ME < MFr < LL *quadrangulum* < L *quadr-* < *quattuor*, FOUR + *angulus*, ANGLE[1]⟧ **1** *Geom.* a plane figure with four angles and four sides **2** *a)* an area, as of a college campus, surrounded on its four sides by buildings *b)* the buildings surrounding a quadrangle ☆**3** the area of land charted on each of the atlas sheets published by the U.S. Geological Survey —**quad·ran′gu·lar** (-draŋ′gyo͞o lər, -gyə-) *adj.*

quad·rant (kwä′drənt) *n.* ⟦ME < L *quadrans,* fourth part < *quadrare:* see QUADRATE⟧ **1** a fourth part of the circumference of a circle; an arc of 90° **2** a quarter section of a circle **3** any piece or part shaped like a quarter section of a circle **4** an instrument similar to the sextant in design and function, and superseded by it **5** *Geom.* any of the four parts formed by rectangular coordinate axes on a plane surface —**quad·ran′tal** (-drant′əl) *adj.*

☆**quad·ra·phon·ic** (kwä′drə fän′ik) *adj.* ⟦< L *quadra-* (< *quattuor,* FOUR) + PHONIC⟧ designating or of sound reproduction, as on records or tapes or in broadcasting, using four channels to carry and reproduce through separate speakers a blend of sounds from separate sources: also **quad′ra·son′ic** (-sän′ik)

quad·rat (kwä′drət) *n.* ⟦ME, var. of fol.⟧ **1** QUAD[2] **2** *Ecol.* a sampling plot, usually one square meter, used to study and analyze plant or animal life

quad·rate (kwä′drit, -drāt′; *for v.,* -drāt′) *adj.* ⟦ME < L *quadratus,* pp. of *quadrare,* to make square < *quadrus,* a square < *quattuor,* FOUR⟧ **1** square or nearly square; rectangular **2** *Zool.* designating a bone or cartilage of the skull in birds, bony fishes, amphibians, and reptiles, to which the lower jaw is joined —*n.* ⟦ME < L *quadratum* < *quadratus*⟧ **1** a square or rectangle **2** a square or rectangular space, thing, etc. **3** *Zool.* the quadrate bone —*vi.* **-rat′ed, -rat′ing** to square; agree (*with*) —*vt.* to make square; make (something) conform

quad·rat·ic (kwä drat′ik) *adj.* ⟦prec. + -IC⟧ **1** [Rare] square **2** *Algebra* involving a quantity or quantities that are squared but not raised to a higher power —*n.* *Algebra* a quadratic term, expression, or equation —**quad·rat′i·cal·ly** *adv.*

quadratic equation *Algebra* an equation in which the second power, or square, is the highest to which the unknown quantity is raised

quad·rat·ics (kwä drat′iks) *n.* the branch of algebra dealing with quadratic equations

quad·ra·ture (kwä′drə chər) *n.* ⟦LL *quadratura* < L *quadratus:* see QUADRATE⟧ **1** the act of squaring **2** the construction of a square equal in area to a given surface [*the quadrature* of a circle] **3** *Astron.* a configuration of a superior planet or the moon in which the angle between it and the sun, as seen from the earth, is 90°

quad·ren·ni·al (kwä dren′ē əl) *adj.* ⟦< L *quadriennium* (see fol.) + -AL⟧ **1** happening every four years **2** lasting four years —*n.* **1** QUADRENNIUM **2** a quadrennial event or occurrence —**quad·ren′ni·al·ly** *adv.*

quad·ren·ni·um (kwä dren′ē əm) *n., pl.* **-ni·ums** or **-ni·a** (-ə) ⟦L *quadriennium* < *quadri-* (see fol.) + *annus,* year (see ANNUAL)⟧ a period of four years

quad·ri- (kwäd′ri) ⟦L < *quattuor,* FOUR⟧ *combining form* four, four times, fourfold [*quadrilingual*]

quad·ric (kwä′drik′) *adj.* ⟦< L *quadra,* a square (akin to *quattuor,* FOUR) + -IC⟧ *Math.* of the second degree: used of a function with more than two variables —*n.* a quantic of the second degree

quad·ri·cen·ten·ni·al (kwä′dri sen ten′ē əl) *n.* ⟦QUADRI- + CENTENNIAL⟧ a 400th anniversary or its commemoration

quad·ri·ceps (kwä′dri seps′) *n., pl.* **-ceps′** ⟦ModL < QUADRI- + L *-ceps* < *caput,* the HEAD⟧ a muscle with four heads, or points of origin; esp., the large muscle at the front of the thigh, which extends the leg —**quad′ri·cip′i·tal** (-sip′i təl) *adj.*

quad·ri·fid (kwä′dri fid′) *adj.* ⟦L *quadrifidus:* see QUADRI- & -FID⟧ divided into four parts, as a leaf or petal

quad·ri·ga (kwä drī′gə) *n., pl.* **-gae** (-gē, -jē) ⟦L, sing. of *quadrigae,* team of four < *quadri-* (see QUADRI-) + *jugum,* YOKE⟧ in ancient Rome and Greece, a two-wheeled chariot drawn by four horses abreast

quad·ri·lat·er·al (kwä′dri lat′ər əl) *adj.* ⟦< L *quadrilaterus* (see QUADRI- & LATERAL) + -AL⟧ four-sided —*n.* **1** *Geom.* a plane figure having four sides and four angles **2** a four-sided area —**quad′ri·lat′er·al·ly** *adv.*

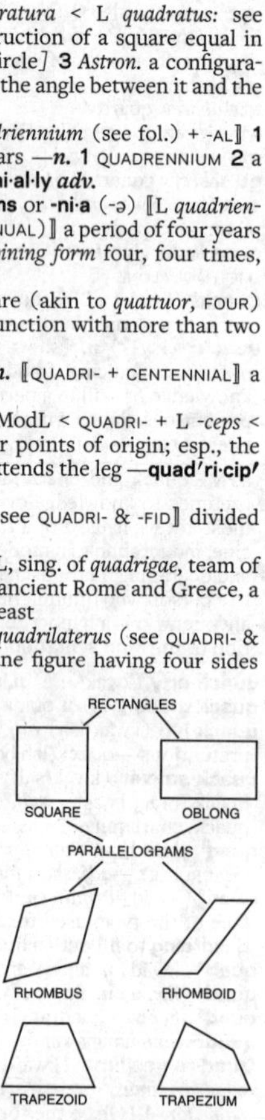

quad·ri·lin·gual (kwä′dri liŋ′gwəl) *adj.* ⟦QUADRI- + LINGUAL⟧ **1** of or in four languages **2** using or capable of using four languages

quadrilaterals

qua·drille[1] (kwə dril′, kwä-) *n.* ⟦Fr, orig., one of four groups of horsemen participating in certain exercises < Sp *cuadrilla,* dim. < *cuadro,* four-sided battle square < L *quadra,* a square: see QUADRIC⟧ **1** a dance of French origin, similar to the cotillion but performed by sets of four couples **2** a kind of square dance evolved from this, in which four couples arranged in a square perform at least five figures **3** music for either of these dances

qua·drille[2] (kwə dril′, kwä-) *n.* ⟦Fr, altered by assoc. with prec. < Sp *cuartillo,* dim. < *cuarto,* fourth < L *quartus:* see QUART[1]⟧ a card game, popular in the 18th cent., played by four persons

qua·drille[3] (kwə dril′, kwä-) *adj.* ⟦Fr *quadrillé* < *quadrille,* a square < Sp *cuadrillo,* a small square: see QUADRILLE[1]⟧ marked with intersecting lines to form squares or rectangles: also **qua·drilled′** (-drild′)

quad·ril·lion (kwä dril′yən) *n.* ⟦Fr < *quadri-* (see QUADRI-) + (MIL)LION⟧ **1** the number represented by 1 followed by 15 zeros **2** [Brit.] the number represented by 1 followed by 24 zeros —*adj.* amounting to one quadrillion in number —**quad·ril′lionth** *adj., n.*

quad·ri·par·tite (kwä′dri pär′tīt′) *adj.* ⟦ME < L *quadripartitus,* pp. of *quadripartire,* to divide into four parts: see QUADRI- & PART[2]⟧ **1** made up of or divided into four parts **2** shared in or formulated by four persons, nations, etc. [*a quadripartite* pact]

quad·ri·ple·gi·a (kwä′dri plē′jē ə, -jə) *n.* ⟦ModL: see QUADRI- (because it affects all four limbs) & -PLEGIA⟧ total paralysis of the body from the neck down —**quad′ri·ple′gic** (-plē′jik) *adj., n.*

quad·ri·sect (kwä′dri sekt′) *vt.* ⟦< QUADRI- + L *sectus,* pp. of *secare:* see SAW[2]⟧ to divide into four equal parts

quad·ri·va·lent (kwä′dri vā′lənt; kwä′dri vä′-) *adj.* TETRAVALENT: see -VALENT —**quad′ri·va′lence** *n.,* **quad′ri·va′len·cy**

quad·riv·i·al (kwä driv′ē əl) *adj.* ⟦ML *quadrivialis* < L *quadrivium,* meeting of four roads < *quadri-* (see QUADRI-) + *via,* road (see VIA)⟧ **1** having or being four roads meeting in a point **2** of the quadrivium

quad·riv·i·um (kwä driv′ē əm) *n.* ⟦ML < L: see prec.⟧ in the Middle Ages, the higher division of the seven liberal arts, consisting of arithmetic, geometry, astronomy, and music: cf. TRIVIUM

quad·roon (kwä dro͞on′) *n.* ⟦Sp *cuarterón* < *cuarto,* a fourth < L *quartus:* see QUART[1]⟧ [Chiefly Historical] a person who has one black grandparent; child of a mulatto and a white

quad·ru·ma·nous (kwä dro͞o′mə nəs) *adj.* ⟦formed (based on QUADRUPED) < L *quadru-* (see QUADRUPED) + *manus,* hand (see MANUAL)⟧ *Zool.* **1** having all four feet adapted to function as hands **2** of a group of primates, including monkeys and great apes, having such adaptation —**quad·ru·mane** (kwä′dro͞o mān′, -drə-) *n.*

quad·rum·vi·rate (kwä drum′və rit, -rāt′) *n.* ⟦QUADR- + (TRI)UMVIRATE⟧ **1** government by four persons **2** any group of four persons associated in office or authority

quad·ru·ped (kwä′dro͞o ped′, -dro͞o-, -drə-) *n.* ⟦L *quadrupes* (gen. *quadrupedis*) < *quadru-* (used for *quadri-,* QUADRI-, esp. before *p*), four + *pes,* FOOT⟧ an animal, esp. a mammal, with four feet —*adj.* having four feet —**quad·ru·pe·dal** (kwä dro͞o′pə dəl; kwä′dro͞o pēd′'l, -ped′'l) *adj.*

quad·ru·ple (kwä dro͞o′pəl, kwə-; kwä′drə pəl) *adj.* ⟦MFr < L *quadruplus* < *quadru-* (see prec.) + *-plus,* as in *duplus:* see DOUBLE⟧ **1** consisting of or including four **2** four times as much or as many; fourfold **3** *Music* containing four beats to the measure [*quadruple* time] —*n.* an amount four times as much or as many — *vt., vi.* **-pled, -pling** to make or become four times as much or as many; multiply by four

quad·ru·plet (kwä dro͞o′plit, -drup′lit; kwə-; kwä′drə plit) *n.* ⟦dim. of prec.⟧ **1** any of four offspring from the same pregnancy **2** a collection or group of four, usually of one kind

quad·ru·plex (kwä′drə pleks′, -dro͞o-) *adj.* ⟦L < *quadru-* (see QUADRUPED) + *-plex,* -fold: see DUPLEX⟧ **1** fourfold ☆**2** designating or of a former system of telegraphy in which four messages could be sent simultaneously over one wire, two in either direction

quad·ru·pli·cate (kwä dro͞o′pli kāt′; *for adj. & n.,* -kit, -kāt′) *vt.* **-cat′ed, -cat′ing** ⟦< L *quadruplicatus,* pp. of *quadruplicare,* to quadruple < *quadruplex:* see prec.⟧ to quadruple; make four identical copies of —*adj.* **1** fourfold **2** designating the fourth of identical copies **3** *Math.* raised to the fourth power —*n.* any of four identical copies or things —**in quadruplicate** in four identical copies —**quad·ru′pli·ca′tion** *n.*

quae·re (kwē′rē, kwir′ē) [Archaic] *v. imper.* ⟦L, imper. of *quaerere,* to ask⟧ inquire: used as a note suggesting further investigation of a point —*n.* a query or question

quaes·tor (kwes′tər, kwēs′-) *n.* ⟦L, contr. < *quaesitor* < *quaesitus,* pp. of *quaerere,* to inquire⟧ an official of ancient Rome, with various, chiefly financial, duties —**quaes′tor·ship′** *n.*

quaff (kwäf, kwaf) *vt., vi.* ⟦Early ModE, prob. (by misreading of *-ss-* as *-ff-*) < LowG *quassen,* to overindulge (in food and drink)⟧ to drink deeply in a hearty or thirsty way —*n.* **1** the act of quaffing **2** a drink that is quaffed —**quaff′er** *n.*

quag (kwag, kwäg) *n.* ⟦< ?⟧ [Rare] a bog or marsh

quag·ga (kwag′ə) *n., pl.* **-ga** or **-gas** ⟦obs. Afrik < the native (? Hottentot) name⟧ an extinct zebra (*Equus quagga*) of South Africa

quag·gy (kwag′ē, kwäg′ē) *adj.* **-gi·er, -gi·est** **1** like a quagmire; boggy; soft and miry **2** soft; flabby

quag·mire (kwag′mīr′, kwäg′-) *n.* ⟦QUAG + MIRE⟧ **1** wet, boggy ground, yielding under the foot **2** a difficult or inextricable position [*a quagmire* of debts]

☆**qua·hog** or **qua·haug** (kō′häg′, -hôg′ *in quahog-gathering localities; also* kwō′-, kwô′-, kwä′-) *n.* ⟦Narragansett *poquaûhock*⟧ an edible clam (*Mercenaria mercenaria*) of the E coast of North America, having a large, thick, hard shell

quaich or **quaigh** (kwākh) *n.* ⟦Gael *cuach,* cup < LL *caucus,* cup < or akin to Gr *kaukos*⟧ [Scot.] a small, shallow drinking cup, usually with two handles

Quai d'Or·say (kā dôr sā′; *Fr* kā dôr se′) **1** a street along the bank of the Seine in Paris, on which are located the offices of the French Ministry of Foreign Affairs **2** the French Ministry of Foreign Affairs

quail[1] (kwāl) *vi.* ⟦ME *quailen,* prob. < OFr *coaillier* < L *coagulare,* to COAGULATE⟧ to draw back in fear; lose heart or courage; cower

quail[2] (kwāl) *n., pl.* **quails** or **quail** ⟦ME *quaille* < OFr < ML *cuacula,* of echoic orig.⟧ any of a number of small, short-tailed gallinaceous birds (family Phasianidae), including the bobwhite: cf. PARTRIDGE

quaint (kwānt) *adj.* ⟦ME *cointe* < OFr < L *cognitus,* known: see COGNITION⟧ **1** [Obs.] clever or skilled **2** [Now Rare] wrought with skill; ingenious **3** unusual or old-fashioned in a pleasing way **4** singular; unusual; curious **5** fanciful; whimsical —*SYN.* STRANGE —**quaint′ly** *adv.* —**quaint′ness** *n.*

quake (kwāk) *vi.* **quaked, quak′ing** ⟦ME *quaken* < OE *cwacian*⟧ **1** to tremble or shake, as the ground does in an earthquake **2** to shudder or shiver, as from fear or cold —*n.* **1** a shaking or tremor **2** an earthquake, moonquake, etc.

Quak·er (kwā′kər) *n.* ⟦orig. derisive: said to be so called from an admonition of George Fox[2] to "quake" at the word of the Lord⟧ a member of the SOCIETY OF FRIENDS; Friend —**Quak′er·ish** *adj.* —**Quak′er·ism′** *n.* —**Quak′er·ly** *adj., adv.*

☆**Quaker gun** a dummy gun or cannon, as of wood: so called from the Quakers' opposition to war and militarism

☆**Quak·er-la·dies** (kwā′kər lā′dēz) *pl.n.* bluets

Quaker meeting a religious meeting of Quakers, characterized by long periods of silent meditation and prayer

☆**quaking aspen** a North American poplar (*Populus tremuloides*) with small, flat-stemmed leaves that tremble in the lightest breeze

quaking grass any of a genus (*Briza*) of annual or perennial grasses having delicate spikelets on very thin stalks that tremble in the lightest breeze

quak·y (kwā′kē) *adj.* **quak′i·er, quak′i·est** inclined to quake; shaky —**quak′i·ly** *adv.* —**quak′i·ness** *n.*

qua·le (kwā′lē, kwä′-) *n., pl.* **qua′li·a** (-lē ə) ⟦L, neut. sing. of *qualis,* of what kind < base of *qui,* who: see WHAT⟧ *Philos.* a quality, as whiteness, loudness, etc., abstracted as an independent, universal essence from a thing

qual·i·fi·ca·tion (kwôl′ə fi kā′shən, kwäl′-) *n.* ⟦ML *qualificatio*⟧ **1** a qualifying or being qualified **2** a modification or restriction; limiting condition **3** any quality, skill, knowledge, experience, etc. that fits a person for a position, office, profession, etc.; requisite **4** a condition that must be met in order to exercise certain rights

qual·i·fied (kwôl′ə fīd′, kwäl′-) *adj.* **1** having met conditions or requirements set **2** having the necessary or desirable qualities; fit; competent **3** limited; modified [to give *qualified* approval] —*SYN.* ABLE —**qual′i·fi′ed·ly** (-fī′id lē, -fīd′-) *adv.*

qual·i·fi·er (kwôl′ə fī′ər, kwäl′-) *n.* **1** a person or thing that qualifies; specif., *a)* a person who meets set requirements *b)* a word, as an adjective or adverb, or a group of words, that modifies or limits the meaning of another word or group of words **2** *Sports* a preliminary round or tournament for determining the contestants who qualify to play in the final round or in another tournament

qual·i·fy (kwôl′ə fī′, kwäl′-) *vt.* **-fied′, -fy′ing** ⟦Fr *qualifier* < ML *qualificare* < L *qualis,* of what kind (see QUALE) + *facere,* to make, DO[1]⟧ **1** to describe by giving the qualities or characteristics of **2** to make fit for an office, occupation, exercise of a right, etc. **3** to make legally capable; give a specific right to; license **4** to modify; restrict; limit; make less positive [to *qualify* one's approval] **5** to moderate; soften [to *qualify* a punishment] **6** to change the strength or flavor of (a liquid, etc.) **7** *Gram.* to limit or modify the meaning of (a word or group of words) —*vi.* to be or become qualified, as by meeting requirements —**qual′i·fi′a·ble** *adj.* —**qual′i·fy′ing·ly** *adv.*

qual·i·ta·tive (kwôl′ə tāt′iv, kwäl′-) *adj.* ⟦LL *qualitativus*⟧ having to do with quality or qualities —**qual′i·ta′tive·ly** *adv.*

qualitative analysis the branch of chemistry dealing with the determination of the elements or ingredients of which a compound or mixture is composed

qual·i·ty (kwôl′ə tē, kwäl′-) *n., pl.* **-ties** ⟦ME *qualite* < OFr < L *qualitas* < *qualis,* of what kind: see QUALE⟧ **1** any of the features that make something what it is; characteristic element; attribute **2** basic nature; character; kind **3** the degree of excellence which a thing possesses **4** excellence; superiority **5** [Now Rare] position, capacity, or role **6** *a)* [Now Rare] high social position *b)* [Now Chiefly Dial.] people of high social position **7** *Acoustics* the property of a tone determined by its overtones; timbre **8** *Logic* that characteristic of a proposition according to which it is classified as affirmative or negative **9** *Phonet.* the distinctive character of a vowel sound as determined by the resonance of the vocal cords and the shape of the air passage above the larynx when the sound is produced —*adj.* of high quality [*quality* goods]

SYN.—**quality,** the broadest in scope of these terms, refers to a characteristic (physical or nonphysical, individual or typical) that constitutes the basic nature of a thing or is one of its distinguishing features [the *quality* of mercy]; **property** applies to any quality that belongs to a thing by reason of the essential nature of the thing [elasticity is a *property* of rubber]; **character** is the scientific or formal term for a distinctive or peculiar quality of an individual or of a class, species, etc. [a hereditary *character*]; an **attribute** is a quality assigned to a thing, esp. one that may reasonably be deduced as appropriate to it [omnipotence is an *attribute* of God]; **trait** specif. applies to a distinguishing quality of a personality [enthusiasm is one of his outstanding *traits*]

quality circle any of the small groups of workers that, as a management technique, meet regularly to suggest and discuss ways to improve production

☆**quality control** a system for maintaining desired standards in a product or process, esp. by inspecting samples of the product

quality of life the relative degree to which an individual's basic human needs are met, in regard to health, self-fulfillment, social interaction, etc. —**qual′i·ty-of-life′** *adj.*

quality time a period of time spent, typically with one's child or family, engaging in activities intended to promote closeness

qualm (kwäm, kwôm, kwôlm) *n.* ⟦ME *qualme* < OE *cwealm,* death, disaster (akin to Ger *qual,* pain, Swed *kvalm,* nausea) < base of *cwellan,* to kill (see QUELL): all extant senses show melioration of the orig. meaning⟧ **1** a sudden, brief feeling of sickness, faintness, or nausea **2** a sudden feeling of uneasiness or doubt; misgiving: *usually used in pl.* **3** a twinge of conscience; scruple: *usually used in pl.*

SYN.—**qualm** implies a painful feeling of uneasiness arising from a consciousness that one is or may be acting wrongly [he had *qualms* about having cheated on the test]; **scruple** implies doubt or hesitation arising from difficulty in deciding what is right, proper, just, etc. [to break a promise without *scruple*]; **compunction** implies a twinge of conscience for wrongdoing, now often for a slight offense [to have no *compunctions* about telling a white lie]; **misgiving** implies a disturbed state of mind resulting from a loss of confidence as to whether one is doing what is right [*misgivings* of conscience]

qualm·ish (-ish) *adj.* **1** having or producing qualms **2** having the nature of a qualm —**qualm′ish·ly** *adv.*

☆**quam·ash** (kwäm′ash′, kwə mash′) *n.* CAMASS

quan·da·ry (kwän′də rē, -drē) *n., pl.* **-ries** ⟦earlier *quandare,* prob. orig. jocular pseudo-L < L *quande,* var. of *quam,* how much (see QUANTITY) + *-are,* inf. suffix⟧ a state of uncertainty; perplexing situation or position; dilemma —*SYN.* PREDICAMENT

quan·dong or **quan·dang** (kwän′däŋ′) *n.* ⟦native name⟧ **1** a small Australian tree (*Eucarya acuminata*) of the sandalwood family, whose edible fruit has a single stone containing an edible kernel **2** this fruit or stone Also **quan′tong′** (-täŋ′)

quang·o (kwaŋ′gō) *n.* ⟦*qu(asi-)a(utonomous) n(on)g(overnmental) o(rganization)*⟧ [Chiefly Brit.] a public advisory and administrative organization, as a board, composed of private citizens appointed by the government which provides funds for operation

quan·ta (kwän′tə) *n. pl. of* QUANTUM

quan·tal (kwän′təl) *adj.* ⟦QUANT(UM) + -AL⟧ of or having to do with quanta or quantum mechanics

quan·ta·some (kwän′tə sōm′) *n.* ⟦< L *quanta,* pl. of *quantum,* how much (see QUANTUM) + -SOME[3]⟧ in the membrane of a chloroplast, any of the highly ordered structures containing many molecules of chlorophyll: quantasomes are thought to be the essential unit of photosynthesis

quan·tic (kwän′tik) *n.* ⟦< L *quantus,* how much (see QUANTUM) + -IC⟧ *Math.* a rational, homogeneous integral function of two or more variables

quan·ti·fi·er (kwänt′ə fī′ər) *n. Logic* a word, term, prefix, symbol, etc. that quantifies

quan·ti·fy (kwänt′ə fī′) *vt.* **-fied′, -fy′ing** ⟦ML *quantificare* < L *quantus,* how much (see QUANTITY) + *facere,* to make, DO[1]⟧ **1** to determine or express the quantity of; indicate the extent of; measure **2** to express in quantitative terms, or as a numerical equivalent **3** *Logic* to make the quantity or extension of (a term or symbol) clear and explicit by the use of a quantifier, as *all, none,* or *some* —**quan′ti·fi′a·ble** *adj.* —**quan′ti·fi·ca′tion** *n.*

quan·tile (kwän′tīl′, -til) *n.* ⟦< QUANT(ITY) + -ILE⟧ *Statistics* any of the values of a random variable dividing the distribution of the individuals into a given number of groups of equal frequency

quan·ti·tate (kwänt′ə tāt′) *vt.* **-tat′ed, -tat′ing** ⟦back-form. < fol.⟧ to measure or determine the quantity of —**quan′ti·ta′tion** *n.*

quan·ti·ta·tive (kwänt′ə tāt′iv) *adj.* ⟦ML *quantitativus*⟧ **1** having to do with quantity **2** capable of being measured **3** having to do with the quantity of a speech sound **4** having to do with a system, as in classical prosody, in which syllables are classified as long and short —**quan′ti·ta′tive·ly** *adv.* —**quan′ti·ta′tive·ness** *n.*

quantitative analysis the branch of chemistry dealing with the accurate measurement of the amounts or percentages of the various components of a compound or mixture

quantitative inheritance *Genetics* the inheritance in offspring of distinctive characters, as stature in man, that are influenced by the combined activity of multiple factors and that are subject to modification by environment

quan·ti·ty (kwänt′ə tē) *n., pl.* **-ties** ⟦ME *quantite* < OFr < L *quantitas* < *quantus,* how great < *quam,* how, how much < IE interrogative base **kwo-* > WHO, WHAT⟧ **1** an amount; portion **2** any indeterminate bulk, weight, or number **3** the exact amount of a particular thing **4** [*also pl.*] a great amount or number [to buy a commodity in *quantity*] **5** that property of anything which can be determined by measurement **6** *Logic* that characteristic of a proposition according to which it is classified as universal or particular **7** *Math. a)* a thing that has the property of being measurable in dimensions, amounts, etc. or in extensions of these which can be expressed in numbers or symbols *b)* a number or symbol expressing a mathematical quantity **8** *Phonet., Prosody* the relative length, or duration, of a vowel, continuant consonant, or syllable

quan·tize (kwän′tīz′) *vt.* **-tized′, -tiz′ing** ⟦< fol. + -IZE⟧ **1** *Math.* to express in multiples of a basic unit **2** *a) Physics* to limit (an observable quantity) to multiples of some small, indivisible unit, as a quantum *b)* to express in terms of the quantum theory —**quan′ti·za′tion** *n.*

quan·tum (kwän′təm) *n., pl.* **-ta** (-tə) ⟦L, neut. sing. of *quantus,* how much: see QUANTITY⟧ **1** quantity, or amount **2** a specified quantity; portion **3** in the quantum theory, a (or the) fixed, elemental unit, as of energy, angular momentum, etc.

quantum chromodynamics [*with sing. v.*] a theory that describes the forces and interactions of quarks and gluons in hadrons: see also COLOR (*n.* 19), CHROMODYNAMICS

quantum electrodynamics [*with sing. v.*] *Physics* a theory that applies the principles of the quantum theory to electrodynamics: it describes how photons interact electromagnetically with electrons, protons, etc.

quantum jump (*or* **leap)** **1** a sudden alteration in the energy level of an atom or molecule **2** any sudden and extensive change or advance, as in a program or policy

quantum mechanics [*with sing. v.*] a physical theory that describes the motion of objects by the principles of quantum theory

quantum number a number expressing the magnitude of a physical quantity in units appropriate to a given quantum mechanical system

quantum physics *see* PHYSICS (sense 2*a*)

quantum theory the theory that energy is not absorbed or radiated continuously but discontinuously, and only in multiples of definite, indivisible units (*quanta*)

qua·qua·ver·sal (kwā′kwə vur′səl) *adj.* ⟦< LL *quaquaversus* (< L *quaqua*, in all directions, redupl. of *qua*, in what direction + *versus*, pp. of *vertere*, to turn: see VERSE) + -AL⟧ *Geol.* directed outward from a common center toward all points of the compass; dipping uniformly in all directions

quar *abbrev.* **1** quarter **2** quarterly

quar·an·tine (kwôr′ən tēn, kwär′-) *n.* ⟦It *quarantina*, lit., space of forty days < *quaranta*, forty < L *quadraginta* < base of *quattuor*, FOUR⟧ **1** *a)* the period, orig. 40 days, during which an arriving vessel suspected of carrying contagious disease is detained in port in strict isolation *b)* the place where such a vessel is stationed **2** any isolation or restriction on travel or passage imposed to keep contagious diseases, etc. from spreading **3** the state of being quarantined **4** a place where persons, animals, or plants having contagious diseases, etc. are kept in isolation, or beyond which they may not travel **5** any period of seclusion, social ostracism, etc. —*vt.* **-tined′**, **-tin′ing** **1** to place under quarantine **2** to isolate politically, commercially, socially, etc. —**quar′an·tin′a·ble** *adj.*

quark (kwôrk, kwärk) *n.* ⟦arbitrary use (by M. GELL-MANN) of a word used by James JOYCE[2] in *Finnegans Wake* (1939), prob. < archaic *quark*, to croak, of echoic orig.⟧ ☆*Particle Physics* any of a set of elementary particles that bind together in various combinations to form hadrons: see also FLAVOR (*n.* 5), COLOR (*n.* 19), FERMION

Quarles (kwôrlz), **Francis** 1592-1644; Eng. poet

quar·rel[1] (kwôr′əl, kwär′-) *n.* ⟦ME *quarel* < OFr < ML *querellus* < VL **quadrellum*, dim. of L *quadrus*, a square⟧ **1** a bolt or arrow with a quadrangular head, shot from a crossbow **2** a small, diamond-shaped or square pane of glass, as in a latticed window

quar·rel[2] (kwôr′əl, kwär′-) *n.* ⟦ME *quarel* < OFr *querele* < L *querela*, complaint < *queri*, to complain, lament < IE base **kwes-*, to pant, snort > WHEEZE⟧ **1** a cause for dispute **2** a dispute or disagreement, esp. one marked by anger and deep resentment **3** a falling out; breaking up of friendly relations —*vi.* **-reled** or **-relled**, **-rel·ing** or **-rel·ling** **1** to find fault; disagree [I don't *quarrel* with your beliefs] **2** to have a heated dispute or disagreement, often, specif., with a resultant breach in friendship —**quar′rel·er** *n.*, **quar′rel·ler**

SYN.—**quarrel** implies heated verbal strife marked by anger and resentment and often suggests continued hostility as a result; **wrangle** suggests a noisy dispute in which each person is vehemently insistent on his or her views; **altercation** implies verbal contention which may or may not be accompanied by blows; **squabble** implies undignified, childish wrangling over a small matter; **spat** is the informal term for a petty quarrel and suggests a brief outburst that does not have a significant effect on a relationship —*ANT.* **agreement, harmony**

quar·rel·some (kwôr′əl səm, kwär′-) *adj.* inclined or ready to quarrel —*SYN.* BELLIGERENT —**quar′rel·some·ly** *adv.* —**quar′rel·some·ness** *n.*

quar·ri·er (kwôr′ē ər, kwär′-) *n.* a person who works in a stone quarry: also **quar′ry·man** (-mən) *pl.* **-men** (-mən)

quar·ry[1] (kwôr′ē, kwär′ē) *n.*, *pl.* **-ries** ⟦var. of QUARREL[1]⟧ a square or diamond-shaped piece of glass, tile, etc.

quar·ry[2] (kwôr′ē, kwär′ē) *n.*, *pl.* **-ries** ⟦ME *querre*, orig., parts of the prey put on the hide and fed to dogs < OFr *cuiree*, altered (infl. by *cuir*, a hide) < ML **corata*, viscera < L *cor*, heart⟧ **1** an animal that is being hunted down, esp. with dogs or hawks; prey **2** anything being hunted or pursued

quar·ry[3] (kwôr′ē, kwär′ē) *n.*, *pl.* **-ries** ⟦ME *quarey* < ML *quarreia*, contr. of *quarreria*, *quadraria*, lit., place where stones are squared < L *quadrare*, to square: see QUADRATE⟧ a place where building stone, marble, or slate is excavated, as by cutting or blasting —*vt.* **-ried**, **-ry·ing** **1** to excavate from a quarry **2** to make a quarry in (land)

quart[1] (kwôrt) *n.* ⟦ME < MFr *quarte* < fem. of OFr *quart*, a fourth < L *quartus*, fourth < base of *quattuor*, FOUR⟧ **1** *a)* a unit of liquid measure, equal to ¼ of a liquid gallon or 2 liquid pints or 32 fluid ounces (0.94635 liquid liters): the British and Canadian imperial quart equals 1.1365 liquid liters *b)* a unit of dry measure, equal to ¼ dry gallon or ⅛ peck or 2 dry pints (1.1012 dry liters or 67.2006 cubic inches) **2** any container with a capacity of one quart Abbrev. *qt*

quart[2] (kärt) *n.* ⟦Fr *quarte*: see prec.⟧ *alt. sp. of* QUARTE

quart[3] *abbrev.* **1** quarter **2** quarterly

quar·tan (kwôrt′'n) *adj.* ⟦ME *quartaine* < MFr *(fièvre) quartaine* < L *(febris) quartana*, (fever) occurring every fourth day, fem. of *quartanus* < *quartus*, fourth: see QUART[1]⟧ occurring every fourth day, counting both days of occurrence: said of a fever —*n.* a type of malaria in which the paroxysms occur every fourth day

quarte (kärt; *Fr* kȧrt) *n.* ⟦Fr, fem. of *quart*, fourth⟧ *Fencing* the fourth position (of thrust or parry) in which the hand is turned nails up, and the point of the weapon is about eye level

quar·ter (kwôrt′ər) *n.* ⟦ME *quartre* < OFr *quartier* < L *quartarius*, fourth part < *quartus*, fourth: see QUART[1]⟧ **1** any of the four equal parts of something; fourth **2** one fourth of a hundredweight: 25 pounds in the U.S., 28 pounds in Great Britain **3** one fourth of a yard, or 9 inches; span **4** one fourth of a pound ☆**5** one fourth of a mile; two furlongs **6** *a)* one fourth of a year; three months *b)* any of the three terms, of about eleven weeks each, which make up an academic year in some schools and colleges **7** *a)* one fourth of an hour; 15 minutes *b)* the moment marking the end of each fourth of an hour ☆**8** *a)* one fourth of a dollar; 25 cents *b)* a U.S. or Canadian coin equal to 25 cents: the U.S. quarter is made of copper and nickel **9** any leg of a four-legged animal, with the adjoining parts **10** *a)* any of four main points of the compass *b)* any of the four divisions of the horizon as marked off by these points *c)* any of the regions of the earth thought of as under these divisions **11** a particular district or section in a city [the Latin *quarter*] **12** [*pl.*] lodgings; place of abode **13** mercy granted to a surrendering foe **14** a particular person, group, place, etc., esp. one serving as a source or origin [news from the highest *quarters*] **15** the part forming the side of a shoe from the heel to the vamp **16** *Astron.* *a)* the period of time in which the moon makes about one fourth of its revolution around the earth *b)* the first or last quarter phase of the moon, when it appears half lighted ☆**17** *Basketball, Football, etc.* any of the four periods into which a game is divided **18** *Heraldry* *a)* any of the four equal divisions of a shield *b)* the bearing occupying such a division **19** *Naut.* *a)* the after part of a ship's side, between the beam and the stern *b)* a direction at a 45° angle aft of either beam *c)* [*pl.*] an assembly of crew members as for muster or at assigned stations for a specific drill or emergency —*vt.* **1** to divide into four equal parts **2** loosely, to separate into any number of parts **3** to defile (the body of a person put to death) by dismembering it or cutting it into quarters **4** to provide lodgings for; specif., to assign (soldiers) to lodgings **5** to cover (an area) by passing back and forth over it in many directions like hounds in hunting; search intensively **6** *Heraldry* *a)* to place or bear (different coats of arms) on the quarters of a shield *b)* to add (a coat of arms) to a shield **7** *Mech.* to set (a crank, etc.) at right angles to the connecting part —*vi.* **1** to be lodged or stationed (*at* or *with*) **2** to range over an area like hounds in hunting **3** to swim, sail, etc. at an angle because of the wind, current, etc. —*adj.* constituting a quarter; equal to a quarter —**at close quarters** at close range; close together —**cry quarter** to beg for mercy

quar·ter·age (kwôrt′ər ij) *n.* ⟦ME < OFr: see prec. & -AGE⟧ **1** a quarterly assessment, payment, allowance, etc. **2** [Rare] *a)* quarters for troops *b)* the provision of quarters or cost of this

☆**quar·ter·back** (kwôrt′ər bak′) *n.* *Football* an offensive back who calls the play, takes the ball from the center, and then passes, hands off, etc. —*vt.*, *vi.* **1** to act as quarterback for (a team) **2** to direct or lead; manage

quarter crack SANDCRACK

quarter day any of the four days regarded as beginning a new quarter of the year, when quarterly payments on rents, etc. are due

quar·ter·deck (kwôrt′ər dek′) *n.* ⟦so called because orig. half the length of the half deck⟧ **1** the after part of the upper deck of a ship, usually reserved for officers **2** *U.S. Navy* the part of the upper deck of a ship reserved for official ceremonies and as the station of the officer of the deck in port

quar·tered (kwôrt′ərd) *adj.* **1** divided into quarters **2** provided with quarters or lodgings **3** quartersawed

quar·ter·fi·nal (kwôrt′ər fin′əl) *adj.* *Sports* designating or of the round of matches immediately preceding the semifinals in a tournament —*n.* a quarterfinal match —**quar′ter·fi′nal·ist** *n.*

quarter grain the grain of quartersawed lumber

☆**quarter horse** ⟦after its great sprinting speed at a *quarter* of a mile⟧ any of a breed of light, muscular horse of a solid, usually dark color: because of its quick reactions it is much used in Western range work and in rodeos

quar·ter-hour (kwôrt′ər our′) *n.* **1** fifteen minutes **2** the point marking the first quarter or third quarter of an hour

quar·ter·ing (kwôrt′ər iŋ) *adj.* **1** moving toward a ship so as to strike either quarter [a *quartering* sea or wind] **2** lying at right angles —*n.* **1** the act of dividing into quarters **2** the act of passing back and forth over an area like hounds in hunting **3** the providing of quarters for soldiers, etc. **4** *Heraldry* *a)* the division of a shield into quarters *b)* any of these, or the coat of arms on it

quar·ter·ly (kwôrt′ər lē) *adj.* **1** occurring or appearing at regular intervals four times a year **2** consisting of a quarter —*adv.* **1** once every quarter of the year **2** *Heraldry* in or by quarters, as a shield —*n.*, *pl.* **-lies** a publication issued every three months

quar·ter·mas·ter (kwôrt′ər mas′tər) *n.* **1** *Mil.* an officer whose duty it is to provide troops with quarters, clothing, equipment, etc. **2** *Naut.* a petty officer or mate trained to steer a ship, perform navigational duties, etc.

Quartermaster Corps the branch of the U.S. Army that supplies food, water, fuel, clothing, etc. to soldiers

quar·tern (kwôrt′ərn) *n.* ⟦ME *quarteroun* < OFr *quarteron* < *quart:* see QUART[1]⟧ **1** [Obs.] a fourth part; quarter **2** [Brit.] one fourth of a pint, a peck, or of various other weights and measures

quarter note *Music* a note having one fourth the duration of a whole note

quarter panel any of the four main sections of body paneling on an automotive vehicle; esp., either of the main sections of body paneling between the doors and the trunk

quar·ter-phase (kwôrt′ər fāz′) *adj. Elec.* TWO-PHASE

quarter round a convex decorative molding, in cross section a quarter of a circle

☆**quar·ter·saw** (kwôrt′ər sô′) *vt.* **-sawed′**, **-sawed′** or [Chiefly Brit.] **-sawn′**, **-saw′ing** to saw (a log) into quarters lengthwise and then into boards, in order to show the grain of the wood to advantage; also, to produce (boards) in this way

☆**quarter section** a unit of land area, equal to one quarter of a square mile or 160 acres (64.752 hectares)

quarter sessions [Historical] a local court, as in England or the U.S., that sits quarterly; specif., an English local court having civil and criminal jurisdiction, except in cases involving the most serious crimes

quar·ter·staff (kwôrt′ər staf′) *n., pl.* **-staves′** (-stāvz′) ⟦? from being held a *quarter* of the length from its end⟧ **1** a stout, iron-tipped, wooden staff, six to eight feet long, formerly used in England as a weapon **2** the use of the quarterstaff in fighting, often as a sport

quarter tone (*or* **step**) *Music* an interval of one half of a semitone

quar·tet (kwôr tet′) *n.* ⟦Fr *quartette* < It *quartetto,* dim. of *quarto* < L *quartus,* fourth: see QUART[1]⟧ **1** any group of four persons or things **2** *Music a)* a composition for four voices or four instruments *b)* a group of four performers of such a composition, or any group of four musicians playing together Also [Archaic] **quar·tette**

quar·tic (kwôrt′ik) *adj.* ⟦< L *quartus,* fourth (see QUART[1]) + -IC⟧ *Math.* of the fourth degree —*n.* a quantic of the fourth degree

quar·tile (kwôr′tīl, kwôrt′'l) *n.* ⟦ML *quartilis* < L *quartus,* fourth: see QUART[1]⟧ *Statistics* **1** any of the values in a series dividing the distribution of the individuals in the series into four groups of equal frequency **2** any of these groups

quar·to (kwôrt′ō) *n., pl.* **-tos** ⟦< L *(in) quarto* < *in,* in + *quarto,* abl. of *quartus,* fourth: see QUART[1]⟧ **1** the page size of a book made up of sheets each of which is folded twice to form four leaves, or eight pages, about nine by twelve inches in size **2** a book made of pages folded in this way —*adj.* having four (quarto) leaves to the sheet

quartz (kwôrts) *n.* ⟦Ger *quarz* < ?⟧ any of various crystallized forms of silica that are transparent, translucent, or colored, used in many ways, esp. as a gem or in making glass, lenses, or quartz crystals: see MOHS SCALE —**quartz′ose′** (-ōs′) *adj.*

quartz crystal *Electronics* a thin, natural or synthetic, piezoelectric crystal of silicon dioxide cut and ground to a precise thickness so as to vibrate at a particular frequency when supplied with energy

quartz glass FUSED QUARTZ

quartz·if·er·ous (kwôrt sif′ər əs) *adj.* ⟦QUARTZ + -I- + -FEROUS⟧ consisting of or yielding quartz

quartz·ite (kwôrt′sīt′) *n.* ⟦QUARTZ + -ITE[1]⟧ **1** a very hard, metamorphic sandstone so firmly cemented that breakage occurs through grains rather than between them **2** any sandstone tightly cemented with quartz

☆**quartz lamp** a high-intensity mercury-vapor lamp with a housing of fused quartz that remains cooler and more transparent than glass

☆**qua·sar** (kwā′zär′, -sär′) *n.* ⟦< *quas(i-stell)ar (radio source)*: so named (1964) by H.-Y. Chiu, Chin-Am physicist⟧ any of a number of starlike celestial objects that emit immense amounts of light and, often, radio waves, characterized by having spectral lines with very large redshifts: quasars are thought to be the most distant and oldest observable objects in the universe

quash[1] (kwäsh, kwôsh) *vt.* ⟦altered (infl. by fol.) < ME *quassen* < MFr *quasser* < LL *cassare,* to annihilate, destroy < L *cassus,* empty < *castus,* pp. of *carere,* to lack: see CASTE⟧ *Law* to annul or set aside (an indictment)

quash[2] (kwäsh, kwôsh) *vt.* ⟦ME *quashen* < MFr *quasser* < L *quassare,* to shake, shatter, shiver, intens. < *quassus,* pp. of *quatere,* to shake, break < IE base **kwēt-*, **kut-*, to shake, akin to **skut-* > SHUDDER⟧ to quell or suppress (an uprising) —**quash′er** *n.*

qua·si (kwā′zī′, -sī′; kwä′zē, -sē) *adv.* ⟦L, as if, as it were, just as < *quamsi* < *quam,* as, how + *si,* if, whether: see QUANTITY & SO[1]⟧ as if; in a sense or manner; seemingly; in part —*adj.* seeming [a *quasi* scholar] Often hyphenated as a prefix to a noun, adjective, or adverb [*quasi*-judicial]

quasi contract *Law* an obligation, equivalent to a contractual obligation, created by law in the absence of a contract, to prevent unfair gain by one party at the expense of another

qua·si·crys·tal (-kris′təl) *n. Physics* any of a class of solid materials characterized by an irregular, repetitive structural arrangement of atoms that is intermediate between the orderly structure of a crystal and the amorphous structure of a glass —**qua′si·crys′tal·line** (-kris′tə lin) *adj.*

qua·si-ju·di·cial (-jo͞o dish′əl) *adj.* having to do with powers that are to some extent judicial, as those of certain federal or state boards and commissions

qua·si·par·ti·cle (-pärt′i kəl) *n. Physics* a phonon, exciton, or other similar entity that has particlelike properties, as mass or energy

qua·si-stel·lar radio source (-stel′ər) QUASAR: also called **quasi-stellar object**

quass (kə väs′) *n. alt. sp. of* KVASS

quas·si·a (kwäsh′ə, -ē ə; kwäs′ē ə) *n.* ⟦ModL, after Graman *Quassi,* black slave of Suriname who prescribed it for fever, *c.* 1730⟧ **1** any of a genus (*Quassia*) of shrubs and trees of the quassia family **2** the wood of either of two tropical trees (*Picrasma excela* or *Quassia amara*) of the quassia family, used in making furniture **3** a bitter drug extracted from this wood, used in insecticides and, formerly, in medicine —*adj.* designating a family (Simaroubaceae, order Sapindales) of tropical American dicotyledonous shrubs and trees having alternate pinnate leaves, including ailanthus

qua·ter·nar·y (kwät′ər ner′ē, kwə tʉr′nə rē) *adj.* ⟦L *quaternarius* < *quaterni,* four together, four each < *quater,* four times < base of *quattuor,* FOUR⟧ **1** consisting of four; in sets of four **2** [*usually* **Q-**] designating or of the third geologic period of the Cenozoic Era, characterized by a series of ice ages, the first toolmaking cultures, and the rise of modern human culture **3** *Chem. a)* designating a compound or alloy containing four different components or elements [*quaternary* silver] *b)* being, of, or containing an atom linked to four carbon atoms [a *quaternary* nitrogen atom] —*n., pl.* **-nar′ies** (-nar′ies) **1** the number four **2** a set of four —**the Quaternary** the Quaternary Period or its rocks: see the geologic time chart in the Reference Supplement

quaternary ammonium compound any of a class of compounds in which the four hydrogen atoms of the ammonium radical are replaced by other groups, generally organic radicals: used as solvents, disinfectants, etc.

qua·ter·ni·on (kwə tʉr′nē ən, kwä-) *n.* ⟦ME < LL *quaternio* < L *quaterni:* see QUATERNARY⟧ **1** a set of four **2** *Math.* an expression that is the sum of four terms, one of which is real and three of which contain imaginary units, and that can be written as the sum of a scalar and a three-dimensional vector

quat·rain (kwä′trān′, kwä trān′) *n.* ⟦Fr < *quatre* < L *quattuor,* FOUR⟧ a stanza or poem of four lines, often rhyming *abab, abba,* or *abcb*

quat·re·foil (kat′ər foil′, ka′trə-) *n.* ⟦ME *quaterfoyle* < MFr *quatrefeuille* < *quatre* (< L *quattuor,* FOUR) + *feuille* (< L *folium,* leaf: see FOIL[2])⟧ **1** a flower with four petals or a leaf with four leaflets **2** *Archit.* a circular design made up of four converging arcs

quat·tro·cen·tist (kwät′trō chen′tist) *n.* an Italian artist or writer of the quattrocento

quat·tro·cen·to (kwät′trō chen′tō) *n.* ⟦It, four hundred: short for *mille quattrocento,* one thousand four hundred⟧ the 15th cent. as a period in Italian art and literature

qua·ver (kwā′vər) *vi.* ⟦ME *quaveren,* freq. of Early ME *cwafien,* to shake, tremble < OE **cwafian,* prob. < IE base **gwēbh-*, wobbly, flabby, tadpole > Ger *quappe* & Du *kwabbe,* tadpole⟧ **1** to shake or tremble **2** to be tremulous: said of the voice **3** *Music* to make a trill or trills in singing or playing —*vt.* **1** to utter in a tremulous voice **2** *Music* to sing or play with a trill or trills —*n.* **1** a tremulous quality in a voice or tone **2** [Chiefly Brit.] EIGHTH NOTE —**qua′ver·er** *n.* —**qua′ver·ing·ly** *adv.* —**qua′ver·y** *adj.*

quay (kē, kā, kwā) *n.* ⟦ME *kei* < MFr *cai* < Celt (as in Welsh *cae* & Bret *kai,* enclosure) < IE base **kagh-*, to enclose > HEDGE: E sp. infl. by Fr *quai* (OFr *cai*), of same orig.⟧ a wharf, usually of concrete or stone, for use in loading and unloading ships

quay·age (kē′ij, kā′-, kwā′-) *n.* ⟦Fr⟧ **1** the charge made for using a quay **2** quays collectively

Que *abbrev.* Quebec

quean (kwēn) *n.* ⟦ME *queyne* < OE *cwene,* akin to *cwen,* QUEEN & Goth *qino,* woman < IE base **gwenā,* woman > QUEEN, Sans *ganā,* goddess, Gr *Gynē,* woman⟧ **1** [Archaic] *a)* a bold, brazen woman; hussy *b)* a prostitute **2** [Scot.] a girl or unmarried woman **3** *alt. sp. of* QUEEN (sense 7)

quea·sy (kwē′zē) *adj.* **-si·er**, **-si·est** ⟦Late ME *qwesye* < Gmc echoic base, as in LowG dial. *quesen,* to grumble, grouse⟧ **1** causing nausea **2** affected with nausea **3** squeamish; qualmish; easily nauseated or disgusted **4** causing or feeling discomfort; uneasy **5** [Archaic] difficult to please; fastidious **6** [Archaic] troublous; hazardous —**quea′si·ly** *adv.* —**quea′si·ness** *n.*

Que·bec (kwi bek′) ⟦Fr *Québec,* earlier *Quebecq, Kébec,* prob. < Algonquian name of region where the city was built⟧ **1** province of E Canada, between Hudson Bay & the Gulf of St. Lawrence: 523,696 sq mi (1,356,367 sq km): abbrev. QC or *Que* **2** capital of this province: seaport on the St. Lawrence River: also **Quebec City** Fr. name **Québec** (kā bek′) —**Que·bec′er** *n.*, **Que·beck′er**

Que·be·cois (kā be kwä′) *n., pl.* **-cois′** ⟦CdnFr *Québécois*⟧ a French-speaking person born or living in the province of Quebec

que·bra·cho (kā brä′chō) *n., pl.* **-chos** ⟦AmSp, contr. < *quiebrahacha,* lit., ax breaker (because of the hardness of the wood) < *quebrar,* to break + *hacha,* ax⟧ **1** a tropical American tree (*Schinopsis lorentzii*) of the cashew family, whose hard wood yields an extract used in tanning **2** a South American tree (*Aspidosperma quebracho-blanco*) of the dogbane family, whose bark yields alkaloids formerly used in medicine **3** the wood or bark of either of these trees

Quech·ua (kech′wä, -wə) *n.* ⟦Sp < Quechua *qheswa, qhechwa,* temperate valleys⟧ **1** *pl.* **-uas** or **-ua** a member of a group of South American Indian peoples dominant in the former Inca Empire **2** the language of these peoples, now spoken widely in Peru, Bolivia, Ecuador, Colombia, Argentina, and Chile —**Quech′uan** (-wän, -wən) *adj., n.*

Quech·u·ma·ran (kech′o͞o mə rän′) *n.* ⟦coined < prec. + (AY)MARA + *-n*⟧ a proposed language stock comprising Quechua and Aymara

queen (kwēn) *n.* ⟦ME *quen* < OE *cwen:* see QUEAN⟧ **1** the wife of a king **2** a woman who rules over a monarchy in her own right; female sovereign **3** a woman foremost or judged to be foremost among others in certain attributes or accomplishments, as beauty, etc. **4** a place or thing regarded as the best or most beautiful of its kind **5** the fully developed, reproductive female in a colony of bees, ants, or termites **6** a playing card with a conventionalized picture of a queen on it **7** [Slang] a male homosexual, specif. one with pronounced feminine characteristics: term of contempt or derision **8** *Chess* the most powerful piece, permitted to move any number of unoccupied squares in a horizontal, vertical, or diagonal direction —*vt.* **1** to make (a girl or woman) a queen **2** *Chess* to make a queen of (a pawn that has reached the opponent's end of the board): cf. PROMOTE (*vt.* 5) —*vi.* to reign as queen —**queen it** to act like a queen; domineer —**queen′dom** *n.* —**queen′hood′** *n.* —**queen′like′** *adj.*

☆**Queen Anne's lace** ⟦after ANNE[2]: see fol.⟧ WILD CARROT

Queen Anne style ⟦after ANNE[2] (1665-1714), queen of Great Britain and Ireland (1702-14)⟧ **1** a style of English architecture of the early 18th cent., characterized by construction in red brick, forms modified from classical architecture, and simple, elegant, and stately ornamentation **2** a style of furniture of the same period, characterized by simple, curved lines and the use of upholstery and veneering

Queen Charlotte Islands ⟦after an explorer's ship, the *Queen Charlotte*⟧ group of islands in British Columbia, Canada, off the W coast: 3,705 sq mi (9,596 sq km)

queen consort the wife of a reigning king

queen dowager the widow of a king

queen·ly (kwēn′lē) *adj.* **-li·er, -li·est** of, like, or fit for a queen or queens; royal; regal —**queen′li·ness** *n.*

Queen Mab (mab) *Eng. Folklore* a fairy queen who controls people's dreams

Queen Maud Land region in Antarctica, south of Africa: it is claimed by Norway

Queen Maud Range mountain range in Antarctica, south of the Ross Ice Shelf: peaks over 13,000 ft (3,962 m)

queen mother a queen dowager who is mother of a reigning sovereign

☆**queen of the prairie** a perennial North American meadowsweet (*Filipendula rubra*), having small, peach-colored flowers

queen olive a large olive with a long, slender pit

queen post *Carpentry* either of a pair of vertical posts set between the rafters and the base, or tie beam, of a truss, at equal distances from the apex: cf. KING POST

queen posts

queen regent **1** a queen reigning in behalf of another person **2** *rare var. of* QUEEN REGNANT

queen regnant a queen reigning in her own right

Queens (kwēnz) ⟦after *Queen* Catherine, wife of CHARLES II of England⟧ borough of New York City, on W Long Island, east of Brooklyn

Queen's Bench, Queen's Counsel, Queen's English, *etc. see* KING'S BENCH, KING'S COUNSEL, KING'S ENGLISH, etc.

Queens·ber·ry rules (kwēnz′ber′ē, -bər ē) *see* MARQUESS OF QUEENSBERRY RULES

☆**queen-size** (kwēn′sīz′) *adj.* larger than usual, but smaller than king-size [*a queen-size* bed is 60 by 80 in]

Queens·land (kwēnz′land′, -lənd) state of NE Australia: 668,208 sq mi (1,730,650 sq km); cap. Brisbane

queen's metal *former term for* any of several alloys containing antimony and tin and resembling britannia metal

queen truss *Carpentry* a truss with queen posts

queer (kwir) *adj.* ⟦N Eng & Scot dial: via beggars' cant < ? Ger *quer,* crosswise, in the orig. sense (MHG *twer*), "crooked"⟧ **1** differing from what is usual or ordinary; odd; singular; strange **2** slightly ill; qualmish or giddy **3** [Informal] doubtful; suspicious **4** [Informal] having mental quirks; eccentric **5** [Slang] counterfeit; not genuine ☆**6** [Slang] homosexual: in general usage, still chiefly a slang term of contempt or derision, but lately used as by some academics and homosexual activists as a descriptive term without negative connotations —*vt.* [Slang] **1** to spoil the smooth operation or success of **2** to put (oneself) into an unfavorable position —*n.* [Slang] **1** counterfeit money **2** a strange or eccentric person ☆**3** [Slang] a homosexual: see note at *adj.* 6 —*SYN.* STRANGE —☆**be queer for** [Slang] to have a strong liking for; be obsessed with —**queer′ish** *adj.* —**queer′ly** *adv.* —**queer′ness** *n.*

quell (kwel) *vt.* ⟦ME *quellen* < OE *cwellan,* to kill, akin to *qwalu,* death, Ger *quälen,* torment, afflict < IE base **gwel-,* to stab, pain, death > OIr *at-baill,* (he) dies⟧ **1** to crush; subdue; put an end to **2** to quiet; allay —*n.* [Obs.] a killing; murder —**quell′er** *n.*

quel·que chose (kel kə shōz′) ⟦Fr, something⟧ a trifle

Que·moy (kē moi′) island of a small group in Taiwan Strait; part of the political unit of Taiwan

quench (kwench) *vt.* ⟦ME *quenchen* < OE *cwencan,* to extinguish, caus. of *cwincan,* to go out, akin to Fris *kwinka,* MHG *verquinen,* to pass away < IE base **gwey-,* to complain, weep⟧ **1** to extinguish; put out [*to quench* fire with water] **2** to overcome; subdue; suppress **3** to satisfy; slake [*to quench* one's thirst] **4** to cool (hot steel, etc.) suddenly by plunging into water, oil, or the like —**quench′a·ble** *adj.* —**quench′er** *n.* —**quench′less** *adj.*

que·nelle (kə nel′) *n.* ⟦Fr < Ger *knödel,* dumpling < MHG *knode,* a knot, akin to KNOT[1]⟧ a seasoned dumpling of minced meat or fish poached in water

Quen·tin (kwent′'n) *n.* ⟦Fr < L *Quintinus* < *Quintus,* Roman praenomen < *quintus,* the fifth: see QUINTET⟧ a masculine name: var. *Quintin*

que pa·sa (kā pä′sə) ⟦Sp⟧ what is happening?: often used as an informal greeting

quer·ce·tin (kwur′sə tin) *n.* ⟦< L *quercetum,* oak forest < *quercus,* oak (< IE base **perkwus,* oak > FIR[2]) + -IN[1]⟧ the yellow, crystalline dyestuff, $C_{15}H_{10}O_7$, extracted from the inner bark of the black oak and also produced synthetically —**quer·cet·ic** (kwər set′ik, -sēt′-) *adj.*

quer·cine (kwur′sin, -sīn′) *adj.* ⟦LL *quercinus* < L *quercus,* oak: see prec.⟧ of the oak

quer·cit·ron (kwur′si trən, kwər sit′rən) *n.* ⟦< ModL *quercus* < L, oak (see QUERCETIN) + CITRON⟧ **1** the inner part of the bark of a North American black oak (*Quercus velutina*), containing tannin and used in tanning and dyeing **2** a yellow dye made from this bark

Que·ré·ta·ro (kə rāt′ə rō′; *Sp* ke re′tä rô′) **1** state of central Mexico: 4,544 sq mi (11,769 sq km) **2** its capital

que·rist (kwir′ist) *n.* one who queries, or questions

quern (kwurn) *n.* ⟦ME *querne* < OE *cweorn,* akin to ON *kvern* < IE base **gwer-,* heavy > L *gravis,* Gr *barys*⟧ a primitive hand mill, esp. for grinding grain

quer·u·lous (kwer′ə ləs, -yə-) *adj.* ⟦L *querulus* < *queri,* to complain: see QUARREL[2]⟧ **1** inclined to find fault; complaining **2** full of complaint; peevish —**quer′u·lous·ly** *adv.* —**quer′u·lous·ness** *n.*

que·ry (kwir′ē, kwer′ē) *n., pl.* **-ries** ⟦< L *quaere,* 2d pers. sing., imper., of *quaerere,* to ask, inquire⟧ **1** a question; inquiry **2** a doubt **3** a question mark (?) placed after a question or used to question the accuracy of written or printed matter —*vt.* **-ried, -ry·ing** **1** to call in question; ask about **2** to question (a person) **3** to mark with a QUERY (sense 3) —*vi.* to ask questions or express doubt —*SYN.* ASK

ques *abbrev.* question

ques·a·dil·la (kās′ə dē′yə) *n.* ⟦MexSp < Sp *queso,* cheese < L *caseus*: see CHEESE[1]⟧ **1** a Mexican dish consisting of a flour tortilla filled with cheese, squash blossoms, or a spicy mixture, then folded and deep-fried **2** a grilled dish like this, consisting of two flour tortillas with a layer of cheese and, variously, chicken, peppers, vegetables, etc. between them

Ques·nay (kā ne′), **Fran·çois** (frän swå′) 1694-1774; Fr. economist & physician

quest (kwest) *n.* ⟦ME < OFr *queste* < ML *questa* < VL **quaesita,* thing sought for < L *quaesitus,* pp. of *quaerere,* to seek, ask, inquire⟧ **1** a seeking; hunt; pursuit **2** in medieval romance, a chivalric journey undertaken by a knight in order to procure or achieve a particular object or end **3** any journey or undertaking in pursuit of a typically lofty or noble goal **4** [Archaic] a jury of inquest —*vi.* **1** to follow the track of game, or to bay in pursuit of game, as hounds do **2** to go in search —*vt.* to search for; seek —**quest′er** *n.*

ques·tion (kwes′chən, -tyən) *n.* ⟦ME < Anglo-Fr *questiun* < OFr *question* < L *quaestio* < pp. of *quaerere,* to ask, inquire⟧ **1** an asking; inquiry **2** something that is asked; interrogative sentence, as in seeking to learn or in testing another's knowledge; query **3** doubt; uncertainty [no *question* of his veracity] **4** something in controversy before a court **5** a problem; matter open to discussion or inquiry **6** a matter or case of difficulty [not a *question* of money] **7** *a)* a point being debated or a resolution brought up for approval or rejection before an assembly *b)* the procedure of putting such a matter to a vote —*vt.* ⟦LME *questyonen* < MFr *questionner* < the n.⟧ **1** to ask a question or questions of; interrogate; put queries to **2** to express uncertainty about; doubt **3** to dispute; challenge —*vi.* to ask a question or questions —*SYN.* ASK —**beside the question** not related to the subject under discussion —**beyond (all) question** beyond dispute; without any doubt; certainly: also **without question** —**in question** being considered, debated, etc. —**out of the question** impossible; not to be considered —**ques′tion·er** *n.*

ques·tion·a·ble (kwes′chən ə bəl, -tyən-) *adj.* **1** that can or should be questioned or doubted; open to doubt [*a questionable* story] **2** suspected with good reason of being immoral, dishonest, unsound, etc. **3** not definitely as specified; uncertain [of *questionable* excellence] —*SYN.* DOUBTFUL —**ques′tion·a·ble·ness** *n.* —**ques′tion·a·bly** *adv.*

ques·tion·less (kwes′chən lis, -tyən-) *adj.* **1** unquestionable; indubitable **2** asking no questions; unquestioning —*adv.* [Now Rare] beyond question; unquestionably

question mark **1** a mark of punctuation (?) put after a sentence, word, etc. to indicate a direct question, and also used to express doubt, uncertainty, etc.; interrogation mark ☆**2** an unknown factor

ques·tion·naire (kwes′chə ner′, -tyə-) *n.* ⟦Fr: see QUESTION, *vt.*⟧ a written or printed form used in gathering information on some subject or subjects, consisting of a set of questions to be submitted to one or more persons

ques·tor (kwes′tər) *n. alt. sp. of* QUAESTOR

Quet·ta (kwet′ə) capital of Baluchistan province, Pakistan

quet·zal (ket säl′) *n.* ⟦AmSp < Nahuatl *quetzaltototl* < *quetzalli,* tail feather + *tototls,* bird⟧ **1** a crested trogon bird (*Pharomachrus mocinno*) of Central America, usually brilliant green above and red below, with long, streaming tail feathers in the male **2** *pl.* **-zal′es** (-sä′les) the basic monetary unit of Guatemala: see the table of monetary units in the Reference Supplement

Quet·zal·co·atl (ket säl′kō ät′'l) *n.* a principal god of the Aztecs, symbolized by a feathered serpent

queue (kyo͞o) *n.* ⟦Fr < OFr *coue* < L *coda,* var. of *cauda,* tail⟧ **1** a plait of hair worn hanging from the back of the head; pigtail **2** [Chiefly Brit.] a line or file of persons, vehicles, etc. waiting as to be served **3** a stored arrangement of computer data or programs, waiting to be processed —*vi.* **queued,**

queu′ing [Chiefly Brit.] to form in or be part of a line or file while waiting to be served, etc.: often with *up*

que·zal (ke säl′) *n. var. of* QUETZAL

Que·zon (kā′sän′), **Ma·nuel Lu·is** (män wel′ lo͞o ēs′) 1878-1944; Philippine statesman: 1st president of the Philippines (1935-44): in full **Manuel Luis Quezon y Mo·li·na** (ē mō lē′nə)

Que·zon City (kā′sän′) former capital of the Philippines: absorbed into Manila in 1975

quib·ble (kwib′əl) *n.* ⟦dim. < obs. *quib* < L *quibus,* abl. pl. of *qui,* which, WHO: *quibus* was common in legal documents⟧ **1** [Obs.] a play on words; pun **2** an evasion of the main point as by emphasizing some petty detail; cavil **3** a petty objection or criticism —*vi.* **-bled, -bling** to evade the truth of a point under discussion by caviling; resort to a quibble —**quib′bler** *n.*

quiche (kēsh) *n.* ⟦Fr < Ger dial. (Lorraine) *küche,* dim. of Ger *kuchen,* CAKE⟧ a dish consisting of unsweetened custard baked in a pastry shell with various ingredients, as bacon, cheese, or spinach, and served hot

quiche Lor·raine (kēsh lô ren′) ⟦Fr, lit., Lorraine pastry: see prec.⟧ a quiche made with cheese and crisp bits of bacon

quick (kwik) *adj.* ⟦ME *quik,* lively, alive < OE *cwicu,* living: see BIO-⟧ **1** [Archaic] living; alive **2** *a)* rapid; swift [a *quick* walk] *b)* done with promptness; prompt [a *quick* reply] *c)* acting swiftly [a *quick* worker] **3** lasting only a moment [a *quick* look] **4** *a)* prompt to understand or learn [a *quick* mind] *b)* designating a reference source designed to provide basic or essential information in a format that is easy to use **5** sensitive; acutely perceptive [a *quick* sense of smell] **6** easily stirred; fiery [a *quick* temper] **7** sharply curved [a *quick* turn] **8** [Archaic] pregnant —*adv.* quickly; rapidly —*n.* **1** the sensitive flesh under a toenail or fingernail **2** the deepest feelings or sensibilities [cut to the *quick* by the insult] —*vt.* [Archaic] to animate; invigorate —**the quick** those who are alive; the living: archaic except in the phrase **the quick and the dead** —**quick′ly** *adv.* —**quick′ness** *n.*

SYN.—**quick** implies ability to respond rapidly as an innate rather than a developed faculty [a *quick* mind]; **prompt** stresses immediate response to a demand as resulting from discipline, practice, etc. or from willingness [*prompt* to obey, a *prompt* acceptance]; **ready** also implies preparation or willingness and, in another sense, connotes fluency, expertness, etc. [a *ready* sympathy, jest, etc.]; **apt**, in this connection, implies superior intelligence or a special talent as the reason for quickness of response [an *apt* pupil] See also **agile, fast** —*ANT.* **slow**

quick assets *Finance* cash on hand, current accounts receivable, and all other highly liquid assets excluding merchandise or inventory

☆**quick bread** any bread, as muffins or corn bread, leavened with baking powder, soda, etc. so that it may be baked as soon as the batter or dough is mixed

quick clay a water-saturated clay that changes rapidly to a fluid state when jarred or crushed, as by an earthquake or pile driver

quick·en (kwik′ən) *vt.* ⟦ME *quickenen* < ON *kvikna,* akin to OE *cwician* < *cwicu,* living: see QUICK⟧ **1** to animate; enliven; revive **2** to arouse; stimulate; stir **3** to cause to move more rapidly; hasten —*vi.* **1** to become enlivened; revive **2** *a)* to begin to show signs of life, as a fetus in the womb *b)* to enter the stage of pregnancy in which the movement of the fetus can be felt **3** to become more rapid; speed up [the pulse *quickens* with fear] —*SYN.* ANIMATE —**quick′en·er** *n.*

quick-fire (kwik′fīr′) *adj.* RAPID-FIRE: also **quick′-fir′ing**

☆**quick fix** an easy and expedient solution or remedy, esp. one producing results that are temporary, illusory, or counterproductive

☆**quick-freeze** (kwik′frēz′) *vt.* **-froze′, -fro′zen, -freez′ing** to subject (raw or freshly cooked food) to sudden freezing so that the flavor and natural juices are retained and the food can be stored at low temperatures for a long time

quick grass ⟦see QUITCH, QUICK⟧ COUCH GRASS

☆**quick·ie** (kwik′ē) [Informal] *n.* anything done or made quickly; specif., *a)* a movie made quickly and cheaply *b)* a hurriedly consumed drink of alcoholic liquor *c)* a hasty act of sexual intercourse —*adj.* done, completed, attained, etc. in less time than is usual or desirable

quick·lime (kwik′līm′) *n.* ⟦ME *quykke lyme,* based on L *calx viva*⟧ a product consisting chiefly of calcium oxide, obtained by roasting limestone, marble, shells, etc.; unslaked lime

quick·sand (kwik′sand′) *n.* ⟦ME *quykkesand:* see QUICK & SAND⟧ a deep, semifluid deposit or bed of sand in which an animal, heavy object, etc. may be trapped or engulfed

quick·set (kwik′set′) *n.* [Chiefly Brit.] **1** a live slip or cutting, as of hawthorn, planted with others to grow into a hedge **2** a hedge, as of hawthorn

quick·sil·ver (kwik′sil′vər) *n.* ⟦ME < OE *cwicseolfor* < *cwicu,* living (see QUICK) + *seolfor,* SILVER: transl. of L *argentum vivum,* lit., living silver: from its liquid form⟧ mercury: see MERCURY (*n. 3a*) —*vt.* to cover with mercury —*adj.* **1** of or like mercury **2** suggestive of mercury; specif., quick, lively, brilliant, etc.

quick·step (kwik′step′) *n.* **1** the step for marching in quick time **2** *Music* a march in the rhythm of quick time **3** a spirited dance step or a combination of such steps, as in ballroom dancing

quick-tem·pered (kwik′tem′pərd) *adj.* easily angered

quick time the normal rate of marching: in the U.S. Army, 120 (30-inch) paces a minute

quick-wit·ted (kwik′wit′id) *adj.* nimble of mind; alert —**quick′-wit′ted·ly** *adv.* —**quick′-wit′ted·ness** *n.*

quid[1] (kwid) *n.* ⟦< OE *cwidu,* var. of *cudu,* CUD⟧ a piece, as of tobacco, to be chewed

quid[2] (kwid) *n., pl.* **quid** ⟦? orig. slang use of L *quid,* something, esp. in QUID PRO QUO⟧ [Brit. Informal] a sovereign, or one pound sterling

quid·di·ty (kwid′ə tē) *n., pl.* **-ties** ⟦ML *quidditas* < L *quid,* what, neut. of *quis,* WHO⟧ **1** the essential quality of a thing **2** a trifling distinction; quibble

quid·nunc (kwid′nuŋk′) *n.* ⟦L, lit., what now?⟧ an inquisitive, gossipy person; busybody

quid pro quo (kwid′ prō kwō′) ⟦L, something for something⟧ **1** one thing in return for another **2** something equivalent; substitute

qui·es·cent (kwī es′ənt, kwē-) *adj.* ⟦L *quiescens,* prp. of *quiescere,* to become quiet: see fol.⟧ quiet; still; inactive —*SYN.* LATENT —**qui·es′cence** *n.* —**qui·es′cent·ly** *adv.*

qui·et (kwī′ət) *adj.* ⟦ME *quiete* < OFr < L *quietus,* pp. of *quiescere,* to become quiet < *quies* (gen. *quietis*), rest < IE base **kweye-,* to rest > WHILE⟧ **1** still; calm; motionless **2** *a)* not noisy; hushed [a *quiet* motor] *b)* not speaking; silent **3** not agitated, as in motion; gentle [a *quiet* sea] **4** not easily excited or disturbed [a *quiet* disposition] **5** not ostentatious or pretentious [*quiet* furnishings] **6** not forward; unobtrusive [a *quiet* manner] **7** secluded [a *quiet* den] **8** secret; private; concealed [let's keep this matter *quiet*] **9** peaceful and relaxing [a *quiet* evening at home] **10** *Commerce* not busy [a *quiet* day on the stock exchange] —*n.* **1** a quiet state or condition; calmness, stillness, inactivity, freedom from noise, etc. **2** a quiet or peaceful quality; freedom from turmoil or agitation —*vt.* **1** to make quiet; calm or pacify, bring to rest, etc. **2** to allay (fear, doubt, etc.) **3** *Law* to make (a title) unassailable by freeing the fact of ownership from interference, disturbance, or question —*vi.* to become quiet: usually with *down* —*adv.* in a quiet manner —**qui′et·er** *n.* —**qui′et·ly** *adv.* —**qui′et·ness** *n.*

qui·et·en (kwī′ət′n) *vt., vi.* ⟦prec. + -EN⟧ [Brit.] to make or become quiet

qui·et·ism (kwī′ə tiz′əm) *n.* ⟦It *quietismo* < L *quietus:* see QUIET & -ISM⟧ **1** a mysticism based on spiritual passivity; specif., a mysticism so minimizing or so completely rejecting human volition and effort as, often, to produce indifference to one's lot in an afterlife and to engender a sense of being incapable of any personal merit or guilt **2** lack of concern about what may happen; apathy —**qui′et·ist** *n., adj.* —**qui′et·is′tic** *adj.*

qui·e·tude (kwī′ə to͞od′, -tyo͞od′) *n.* ⟦Fr *quiétude* < LL *quietudo*⟧ a state of being quiet; rest; calmness

qui·e·tus (kwī ēt′əs) *n.* ⟦< ME *quietus (est)* < ML, (he is) quit < L, QUIET⟧ **1** discharge or release from debt, obligation, or office **2** discharge or release from life; death **3** anything that kills **4** anything that serves to quiet, curb, or end an activity

quiff[1] (kwif) *n.* ⟦< ?⟧ [Chiefly Brit.] a lock or tuft of hair; esp., a forelock

quiff[2] (kwif) *n.* ⟦< Brit navy slang *quiff* (v.), have sexual intercourse < ?⟧ ☆[Slang] a sexually promiscuous woman: mildly vulgar

quill (kwil) *n.* ⟦ME *quil,* hollow stalk, weaver's quill, prob. < MLowG or MDu, as in LowG *quiele,* quill of a feather < ? IE base **gwel-,* to stick, stab⟧ **1** any of the large, stiff wing or tail feathers of a bird **2** the hollow, horny stem of a feather; calamus **3** any of the spines of a porcupine or hedgehog **4** any of various things made from the quill of a feather, specif., a pen for writing **5** a musical pipe made of a hollow stem, reed, or cane **6** a weaver's spindle or bobbin **7** a hollow shaft in certain mechanical devices **8** *Pharmacy* a small roll of dried bark, as of cinchona, cinnamon, etc. —*vt.* **1** to form with or into quillings **2** to wind (thread or yarn) on a QUILL (sense 6) **3** to cover or pierce with quills, as of a porcupine

quil·lai·a (ki lī′ə, kwi lā′yə) *n.* ⟦Sp < the Araucanian native name⟧ SOAPBARK (sense 1): also **quil·lai** (ki lī′) or **quil·la·ja** (kwi lā′yə, -lā′jə)

☆**quill·back** (kwil′bak′) *n., pl.* **-back′** or **-backs′** a North American freshwater fish (*Carpiodes cyprinus*) of the sucker family, with the front margin of the dorsal fin quill-like and elongate

Quil·ler-Couch (kwil′ər ko͞och′), Sir **Arthur Thomas** (pseud. Q) 1863-1944; Eng. writer & editor

quill·ing (kwil′iŋ) *n.* a band of material fluted into small ruffles so as to resemble a row of quills

quill·wort (kwil′wərt′) *n.* any of an order (Isoetales) of lycopods with short, fleshy stems and tufts of long, hollow, quill-like leaves whose bases contain spore cases

Quil·mes (kēl′mes) city in E Argentina, on the Río de la Plata: suburb of Buenos Aires

quilt (kwilt) *n.* ⟦ME *quilte* < OFr < L *culcita,* bed, mattress < IE base **kwelek-* > Sans *kūrcaḥ,* bundle, roll⟧ **1** a bedcover made of two layers of cloth filled with down, cotton, wool, etc. and stitched together in lines or patterns to keep the filling in place **2** anything used as a quilt **3** anything quilted or like a quilt —*vt.* **1** to make or stitch as or like a quilt [to *quilt* a potholder] **2** to sew up or fasten between two pieces of material **3** to line or pad with a quiltlike material —☆*vi.* to make a quilt or quilts —**quilt′er** *n.*

quilt·ing (kwil′tiŋ) *n.* **1** the act or process of making quilts **2** *a)* material for making quilts *b)* quilted work ☆**3** QUILTING BEE

☆**quilting bee (***or* **party)** a social gathering of women at which they work together sewing quilts

quin (kwin) *n.* [Brit.] *short for* QUINTUPLET (sense 1)

quin·a·crine hydrochloride (kwin′ə krēn′) ⟦QUIN(INE) + ACR(ID)INE⟧ ATABRINE

qui·na·ry (kwī′nə rē) *adj.* ⟦L *quinarius* < *quini,* five each < *quinque,* FIVE⟧ consisting of five; in sets of five —*n., pl.* **-ries** a set of five

quince (kwins) *n.* ⟦ME *qwince,* orig. pl. of *quyn* < OFr *cooin* < VL **cotoneum,* for L *cydonium* < Gr *kydōnion (mēlon),* Cydonian (apple) < *Kydōnia,* Cydonia, town on N coast of Crete⟧ 1 a golden or greenish-yellow, hard, apple-shaped fruit of a small tree (*Cydonia oblonga*) of the rose family, used in preserves 2 the tree

quin·cen·te·nary (kwin sen′tə ner ē, kwin′sen ten′ər ē) *adj.* of a 500th anniversary —*n., pl.* **-nar·ies** a 500th anniversary or its commemoration Also **quin·cen·ten·ni·al** (kwin′sen ten′ē əl)

quin·cunx (kwin′kuŋks′) *n.* ⟦L, lit., five twelfths < *quinque,* FIVE + *uncia,* a twelfth: see OUNCE[1]⟧ 1 an arrangement of five objects in a square, with one at each corner and one in the middle 2 *Bot.* an arrangement of five-petaled flowers in which two petals are inferior, two are exterior, and one is partly interior and partly exterior —**quin·cun′cial** (-kun′shəl) *adj.*, **quin·cunx′i·al** (-kuŋk′shəl, -sē əl) —**quin·cun′cial·ly** *adv.*

quin·dec·a·gon (kwin dek′ə gän′) *n.* ⟦< L *quindecim,* fifteen < *quinque,* FIVE + *decem,* TEN + *-agon,* for -GON⟧ *Geom.* a plane figure with fifteen angles and fifteen sides

quin·de·cen·ni·al (kwin′di sen′ē əl) *adj.* ⟦< L *quindecim* (see prec.) + *-ennial,* as in BIENNIAL⟧ 1 happening every fifteen years 2 lasting fifteen years —*n.* a fifteenth anniversary or its commemoration

Quine (kwīn), **Willard van Or·man** (ôr′mən) 1908-2000; U.S. logician & philosopher

qui·nel·la (kwi nel′ə, kē-) *n.* ⟦AmSp *quiniela,* orig. a ball game with five players (later a wager or combination of wagers on the scores of the players; hence any wager against the house) < *quina,* five (on dice) < L *quini,* five each < *quinque,* FIVE⟧ a form of betting, esp. in horse racing, in which the bettor, to win, must pick the first two finishers, in whichever order they finish: also **qui·nie·la** (kē nye′lə)

quin·ic acid (kwin′ik) ⟦< *quina* (see QUININE) + -IC⟧ a colorless, crystalline acid, $C_6H_7(OH)_4{\cdot}COOH$, prepared from cinchona bark, coffee beans, etc.

quin·i·dine (kwin′ə dēn′, -din) *n.* ⟦< *quina* (see fol.) + -ID + -INE[3]⟧ a colorless, crystalline alkaloid, $C_{20}H_{24}N_2O_2$, isomeric with and resembling quinine, extracted from cinchona bark

qui·nine (kwī′nīn′; *chiefly Brit* kwi nēn′) *n.* ⟦< *quina,* cinchona bark (< Sp < Quechua *quinina,* medicinal plant) + -INE[3]⟧ 1 a bitter, crystalline alkaloid, $C_{20}H_{24}N_2O_2$, extracted from cinchona bark 2 any compound of this, as quinine sulfate, used in medicine for various purposes, esp. for treating malaria

quinine water TONIC (*n.* 2*a*)

☆**quin·nat salmon** (kwin′at′) ⟦< ? AmInd⟧ CHINOOK SALMON

qui·no·a (ki nō′ə; *also, and for 2 usually,* kēn′wä′) *n.* ⟦Sp *quínua* < Quechua *kínwa*⟧ 1 an Andean goosefoot (*Chenopodium quinoa*), raised by the Indians for its edible seeds 2 its seeds, used as a food

quin·oid (kwin′oid′) *n.* ⟦QUIN(ONE) + -OID⟧ a substance resembling quinone in structure, properties, etc.

qui·noi·dine (kwi noi′dēn, -din) *n.* ⟦prec. + -INE[3]⟧ a brownish substance containing a mixture of alkaloids formed in the process of extracting quinine from cinchona, formerly used as a substitute for quinine

quin·o·line (kwin′ə lēn′, -lin) *n.* ⟦QUIN(INE) + -OL[1] + -INE[3]⟧ 1 a colorless, liquid compound, C_9H_7N, obtained by the destructive distillation of bones, coal tar, and various alkaloids, or by synthesis: it is used in making antiseptics, dyes, etc. and as a solvent 2 any of various derivatives of quinoline

qui·none (kwi nōn′, kwin′ōn′) *n.* ⟦QUIN(IC ACID) + -ONE⟧ 1 either of two isomeric compounds, $C_6H_4O_2$, especially the yellow, crystalline isomer used in making dyes 2 any of a series of compounds of this type

qui·non·i·mine (kwi nōn′ə mēn′, -min) *n.* ⟦< prec. + IMINE⟧ a crystalline compound, C_6H_5NO, derived from a quinone by the replacement of an oxygen atom by an imino group

quin·o·noid (kwin′ə noid′, kwi nō′noid) *adj.* ⟦QUINON(E) + -OID⟧ like quinone in structure, properties, etc.

quin·qua·ge·nar·i·an (kwin′kwə jə ner′ē ən, kwiŋ′-) *adj.* ⟦< L *quinquagenarius* < *quinquageni,* fifty each < *quinquaginta,* fifty < *quinque,* FIVE + *-ginta* < IE **-k̂omt-* < base **dek̂m̥,* TEN⟧ 50 years old, or between the ages of 50 and 60 —*n.* a person of this age

Quin·qua·ges·i·ma (kwin′kwə jā′zi mə, -jes′i-; kwiŋ′-) *n.* ⟦LL *quinquagesima (dies),* fiftieth (day), i.e., before Easter, fem. of L *quinquagesimus,* fiftieth: cf. prec.⟧ *former term for* the Sunday before Lent: also **Quinquagesima Sunday**

quin·que- (kwin′kwə, kwiŋ′-) ⟦< L *quinque,* FIVE⟧ *combining form* five or a multiple of five [*quinquefoliolate*]: also, before a vowel, **quinqu-**

quin·que·fo·li·o·late (kwin′kwə fō′lē ə lit, -lāt′; kwiŋ′-) *adj.* ⟦prec. + FOLIOLATE⟧ *Bot.* having five leaflets

quin·quen·ni·al (kwin kwen′ē əl, kwiŋ-) *adj.* ⟦< L *quinquennis,* of five years < *quinque,* FIVE + *annus,* year + -AL⟧ 1 happening every five years 2 lasting five years —**quin·quen′ni·al·ly** *adv.*

quin·quen·ni·um (kwin kwen′ē əm, kwiŋ-) *n., pl.* **-ni·ums** or **-ni·a** (-ə) ⟦L < *quinquennis:* see prec.⟧ a period of five years: also **quin·quen′ni·ad′** (-ē ad′)

quin·que·va·lent (kwin′kwə vā′lənt, kwiŋ′-) *adj.* ⟦L *quinque,* FIVE + -VALENT⟧ PENTAVALENT: see also -VALENT —**quin′que·va′lence** *n.*, **quin′que·va′len·cy**

quin·sy (kwin′zē) *n.* ⟦ME *quinaci* < ML *quinancia* < LL *cynanche* < Gr *kynanchē,* inflammation of the throat, lit., dog-choking < *kyōn,* dog (see HOUND[1]) + *anchein,* to choke (see ANGER)⟧ *former term for* TONSILLITIS

quint (kwint) *n.* [Informal] *short for* QUINTUPLET (sense 1)

quin·tain (kwin′tin) *n.* ⟦ME *qwaintan* < OFr *quintaine* < ML *quintana* < L *quintana (via),* street in a Roman camp separating the fifth maniple from the sixth (later, marketplace) < *quintanus,* of the fifth < *quintus,* fifth: see QUINTET⟧ an object supported by a crosspiece on a post, used by knights as a target in tilting

quin·tal (kwin′təl) *n.* ⟦ME < MFr < ML *quintale* < Ar *qinṭār,* ult. < L *centenarius:* see CENTENARY⟧ 1 HUNDREDWEIGHT (sense 1) 2 a unit of weight in the metric system, equal to 100 kilograms (220.4623 pounds avoirdupois): abbrev. *q* or *ql*

quin·tan (kwin′tən) *adj.* ⟦L *quintanus* < *quintus,* fifth: see QUINTET⟧ occurring every fifth day (counting both days of occurrence) —*n.* a quintan fever

Quin·ta·na Ro·o (kin tän′ə rō′ō; *Sp* kēn tä′nä rô′ô) state of SE Mexico, on E Yucatán Peninsula: 19,440 sq mi (50,349 sq km); cap. Chetumal

quinte (kant) *n.* ⟦Fr, fem. of *quint,* fifth: see QUINTET⟧ *Fencing* the fifth position (of defense or parry), similar to the fourth but with the hand lower and the point farther to the left

Quintero, Joaquín Álvarez *see* ÁLVAREZ QUINTERO, Joaquín

quin·tes·sence (kwin tes′əns) *n.* ⟦ME *quyntencense* < MFr *quinte essence* < ML *quinta essentia*⟧ 1 in ancient and medieval philosophy, the fifth essence, or ultimate substance, of which the heavenly bodies were thought to be composed: distinguished from the four elements (air, fire, water, and earth) 2 the pure, concentrated essence of anything 3 the most nearly perfect or most typical manifestation of a quality or thing —**quin′tes·sen′tial** (-te sen′shəl) *adj.*

quin·tet or **quin·tette** (kwin tet′) *n.* ⟦< Fr or It: Fr *quintette* < It *quintetto,* dim. of *quinto,* a fifth < L *quintus* < base of *quinque,* FIVE⟧ 1 any group or set of five persons or things 2 *Music a)* a composition for five voices or five instruments, as for string quartet and piano *b)* a group of five performers of such a composition, or any group of five musicians playing together

quin·tile (kwin′til, -tīl′) *n.* ⟦< L *quintus,* a fifth (see prec.) + -ILE⟧ 1 *Astrol.* the aspect of two celestial bodies 72°, or one fifth of a circle, apart 2 *Statistics a)* any of the values in a series dividing the distribution of the individuals in the series into five groups of equal frequency *b)* any of these groups

Quin·til·ian (kwin til′yən) (L. name *Marcus Fabius Quintilianus*) A.D. 35?-96?; Rom. rhetorician, born in Spain

quin·til·lion (kwin til′yən) *n.* ⟦Fr < L *quintus,* a fifth (see QUINTET) + Fr, (M)ILLION⟧ 1 the number represented by 1 followed by 18 zeros 2 [Brit.] the number represented by 1 followed by 30 zeros —*adj.* amounting to one quintillion in number —**quin·til′lionth** *adj., n.*

Quin·tin (kwint′'n) *n.* a masculine name: dim. *Quint:* see QUENTIN

quin·tu·ple (kwin to͞o′pəl, -tyo͞o′-; kwin′tə pəl) *adj.* ⟦MFr < ML *quintuplus* < L *quintus,* a fifth (see QUINTET) + *-plus:* see DOUBLE⟧ 1 consisting of or including five 2 five times as much or as many; fivefold —*n.* an amount five times as much or as many — *vt., vi.* **-pled**, **-pling** to make or become five times as much or as many; multiply by five

quin·tu·plet (kwin tup′lit; kwin to͞o′plit, -tyo͞o′-; kwin′tə plət) *n.* ⟦dim. of prec.⟧ 1 any of five offspring from the same pregnancy 2 a collection or group of five, usually of one kind

quin·tu·pli·cate (kwin to͞o′pli kāt′, -tyo͞o′-; *for adj. & n.,* -kit, -kāt′) *vt.* **-cat′ed**, **-cat′ing** ⟦LL *quintuplicatus,* pp. of *quintuplicare,* to quintuple < *quintuplex:* see QUINTUPLE⟧ to quintuple; make five identical copies of —*adj.* 1 fivefold 2 designating the fifth of identical copies —*n.* any of five identical copies or things —**in quintuplicate** in five identical copies —**quin·tu′pli·ca′tion** *n.*

Quin·tus (kwin′təs) *n.* ⟦L⟧ *Rom. History* a masculine praenomen

quip (kwip) *n.* ⟦contr. < earlier *quippy* < L *quippe,* indeed, forsooth < *quid,* WHAT + *-pe,* emphatic enclitic⟧ 1 a witty or, esp. formerly, sarcastic remark or reply; jest or gibe 2 a quibble; cavil 3 something curious or odd —*vt.* **quipped**, **quip′ping** [Now Rare] to direct quips, or gibes, at —*vi.* to utter quips or a quip —**quip′ster** *n.*

qui·pu (kē′po͞o, kwip′o͞o) *n.* ⟦AmSp *quipo* < Quechua *khípu* (also sp. *quipu*), knot⟧ a device consisting of an arrangement of cords variously colored and knotted, used by the ancient Peruvians to keep accounts, record events, etc.

quire[1] (kwīr) *n., vt., vi.* **quired**, **quir′ing** *archaic sp. of* CHOIR

quire[2] (kwīr) *n.* ⟦ME *quair* < OFr *quaer,* book of loose pages < VL *quaternum,* paper packed in lots of four pages < L *quaterni,* four each: see QUATERNARY⟧ a set of 24 or 25 sheets of paper of the same size and stock, the twentieth part of a ream

Quir·i·nal[1] (kwir′ə nəl, kwi rī′nəl) *n.* ⟦see fol.⟧ the Italian government —*adj.* 1 of or situated on the Quirinal 2 of Quirinus

Quir·i·nal[2] (kwir′ə nəl, kwi rī′nəl) ⟦L *Quirinalis,* after *Quirinus:* see fol.⟧ one of the SEVEN HILLS OF ROME: site of a palace used (1870-1946) as a royal residence, later as the presidential residence

Qui·ri·nus (kwi rī′nəs) *n.* ⟦L, akin to fol.⟧ *Rom. Myth.* an early god of war: later identified with Romulus

Qui·ri·tes (kwi rīt′ēz) *pl.n.* ⟦L, pl. of *Quiris,* orig., inhabitant of *Cures* (a Sabine town); later, Roman citizen⟧ in ancient Rome, the people as civilians

quirk (kwʉrk) *n.* ⟦< ?⟧ 1 *a)* a sudden twist, turn, or stroke [*a quirk of fortune*] *b)* a flourish in writing 2 an evasion, subterfuge, or quibble 3 a peculiarity, peculiar trait, or mannerism 4 [Now Rare] a clever turn of speech; sally; quip 5 *Archit.* a groove running lengthwise in a molding —*vt.* *Archit.* to form with quirks —**quirk′i·ly** *adv.* —**quirk′i·ness** *n.* —**quirk′y** *adj.* **quirk′i·er**, **quirk′i·est**

☆**quirt** (kwʉrt) *n.* ⟦AmSp *cuarta,* quirt, long whip < Sp *cuerda,* rope < L *chorda:* see CORD⟧ a riding whip with a braided leather lash and a short handle —*vt.* to strike with a quirt

quis·ling (kwiz′liŋ) ***n.*** ⟦after V. *Quisling* (1887-1945), Norw politician who betrayed his country to the Nazis and became its puppet ruler⟧ a traitor

quit (kwit) ***vt.*** **quit** or [Now Chiefly Brit.] **quit′ted, quit′ting** ⟦ME *quiten* < OFr *quiter* < ML *quittus, quietus,* free: see QUIET⟧ **1** to free (oneself) *of* **2** to discharge (a debt or obligation); repay **3** to stop having, using, or doing (something); give up **4** to leave; depart from **5** to stop, discontinue, or resign from **6** [Archaic] to conduct (oneself) —***vi.*** **1** *a)* to stop or discontinue doing something *b)* to give up or stop trying, as in discouragement **2** to give up one's position of employment; resign —***adj.*** ⟦ME *quite* < OFr < ML *quietus*⟧ clear, free, or rid, as of an obligation —***SYN.*** ABANDON, STOP

quitch (kwich) ***n.*** ⟦OE *cwice* < base of *cwicu,* alive (see QUICK): prob. after the great vitality of the plant⟧ COUCH GRASS

quit·claim (kwit′klām′) ***n.*** ⟦ME *quitclayme* < Anglo-Fr *quiteclame* < the v.⟧ **1** the release or relinquishment of a claim, action, right, or title **2** a deed or other legal paper in which a person relinquishes to another a claim or title to some property or right without guaranteeing or warranting such title: in full **quitclaim deed** —***vt.*** ⟦ME *quite clamen* < Anglo-Fr & OFr *quiteclamer:* see QUIT & CLAIM⟧ to give up a claim or title to, esp. by a quitclaim deed

quite (kwīt) ***adv.*** ⟦ME *quite:* see QUIT, ***adj.***⟧ **1** completely; entirely [are you *quite* convinced yet?] **2** really; truly; positively [*quite* the best view available] **3** to some, or a considerable, degree or extent; very or fairly [*quite* warm outside] —**not quite** just short of [it's *not quite* noon] —☆**quite a few (**or **bit,** etc.**)** [Informal] more than a few (or bit, etc.) —**quite (so)!** certainly! I agree!

Qui·to (kē′tō) capital of Ecuador, in the NC part

quit·rent (kwit′rent′) ***n.*** a rent paid in lieu of required feudal services: also written **quit-rent**

quits (kwits) ***adj.*** ⟦ME, prob. contr. < ML *quittus,* var. of *quietus*: see QUIETUS⟧ on even terms, as by discharge of a debt, retaliation in vengeance, etc. —☆**call it quits** [Informal] **1** to stop working, playing, etc. **2** to stop being friendly or intimate; end an association —**cry quits** [Chiefly Brit.] to declare oneself even with another; agree to stop competing

quit·tance (kwit′'ns) ***n.*** ⟦ME *quitance* < OFr < *quiter:* see QUIT⟧ **1** *a)* discharge from a debt or obligation *b)* a document certifying this; receipt **2** recompense; repayment; reprisal

quit·ter (kwit′ər) ***n.*** ☆[Informal] a person who quits or gives up easily, without trying hard

quit·tor (kwit′ər) ***n.*** ⟦ME *quiture* < OFr *cuiture,* cooking < L *coctura* < pp. of *coquere,* to COOK⟧ a foot disease of horses characterized by a pus-forming fistula on the coronet

quiv·er[1] (kwiv′ər) ***vi.*** ⟦ME *quiveren* < OE *cwifer-,* eager, akin to MDu *quiveren* < IE base **gwei-,* to live, lively: see BIO-⟧ to shake with a tremulous motion; tremble —***n.*** the act or condition of quivering; tremor; tremble —**quiv′er·y** ***adj.***

quiv·er[2] (kwiv′ər) ***n.*** ⟦ME *quyuere* < OFr *coivre* < Gmc **kukur* (> OE *cocer,* quiver, sheath, Ger *köcher,* quiver), prob. a loanword from the Huns⟧ **1** a case for holding arrows **2** the arrows in it

qui vive? (kē vēv′) ⟦Fr, (long) live who? (i.e., which monarch or ruler do you support?, whose side are you on?), 3d pers. sing., pres. subj., of *vivre,* to live (< L *vivere*) + *qui,* who (< L)⟧ who goes there?: a sentry's challenge —**on the qui vive** on the lookout; on the alert

Quixote, Don *see* DON QUIXOTE

quix·ot·ic (kwik sät′ik) ***adj.*** **1** [*often* **Q-**] of or like Don Quixote **2** extravagantly chivalrous or foolishly idealistic; visionary; impractical or impracticable: also **quix·ot′i·cal** —**quix·ot′i·cal·ly** ***adv.***

quix·ot·ism (kwik′sə tiz′əm) ***n.*** **1** quixotic character or practice **2** a quixotic act or idea Also **quix′ot·ry** (-trē)

quiz (kwiz) ***n., pl.*** **quiz′zes** ⟦prob. arbitrary use of L *quis,* what (i.e., what sort of person or thing?)⟧ **1** [Obs.] *a)* an odd or eccentric person *b)* a practical joke; hoax ☆**2** a questioning; esp., a short oral or written examination to test knowledge —***vt.*** **quizzed, quiz′zing** **1** [Obs.] to make fun of **2** [Now Rare] to look at, often specif., inquisitively, teasingly, etc. ☆**3** *a)* to ask questions of [to *quiz* the suspect] *b)* to test the knowledge of [to *quiz* the class] —***SYN.*** ASK —**quiz′zer** ***n.***

☆**quiz·mas·ter** (kwiz′mas′tər) ***n.*** the master of ceremonies on a quiz program

☆**quiz program (**or **show)** a radio or television program in which a group of people compete in answering questions

quiz·zi·cal (kwiz′i kəl) ***adj.*** ⟦< QUIZ + -IC + -AL⟧ **1** odd; comical **2** teasing; bantering **3** perplexed; questioning —**quiz′zi·cal′i·ty** (-kal′ə tē) ***n.*** —**quiz′zi·cal·ly** ***adv.***

Qum (koom) *alt. sp. of* QOM

Qum·ran (koom rän′) region in NW Jordan, near the Dead Sea: site of the caves in which the Dead Sea Scrolls were found

quod (kwäd) ***n.*** ⟦prob. var. of *quad,* contr. < QUADRANGLE (of a prison)⟧ [Slang, Chiefly Brit.] prison; jail

quod·li·bet (kwäd′lə bet′) ***n.*** ⟦LME < ML *quodlibeta,* disputation < L *quod libet,* as you will < *quod,* neut. of *qui,*WHO + *libet,* 3d pers. sing., pres. of *libere,* to please⟧ **1** an academic debate or exercise in argument, esp. on a theological question **2** a humorously incongruous musical parody, esp. of well-known melodies or texts

quo·hog (kō′hăg′, -hôg′ *in quohog-gathering localities; also,* kwō′-, kwô′-, kwä′-) ***n.*** *var. of* QUAHOG

quoin (koin, kwoin) ***n.*** ⟦var. of COIN⟧ **1** the external corner of a building; esp., any of the large, squared stones by which the corner of a building is marked **2** a wedgelike piece of stone, etc., such as the keystone or one of the pieces of an arch **3** a wedge-shaped wooden or metal block used to lock up type in a galley or form, to keep casks from rolling, etc. —***vt.*** **1** to secure with a quoin **2** to furnish with quoins, or corners

quoins
(sense 1)

quoit (kwoit; *chiefly Brit* koit) ***n.*** ⟦ME *coyte* (Anglo-Fr *jeu de coytes*), prob. < OFr *coite,* cushion (< L *culcita:* see QUILT): ? orig., a cushion target⟧ **1** a ring of rope or flattened metal, used in the game of quoits **2** [*pl., with sing. v.*] a game somewhat like horseshoes, in which players throw such rings at a peg (*hob* or *tee*) in an effort to encircle it —***vt.*** to throw like a quoit

quo ju·re? (kwō joor′ē, -joor′ā) ⟦L⟧ by what right?

quok·ka (kwä′kə) ***n.*** ⟦< name in a language of Australia⟧ a small wallaby (*Setonix brachyurus*) with a short tail

quo mo·do (kwō mō′dō) ⟦L⟧ **1** in what manner? **2** in the manner that

quon·dam (kwän′dəm, -dam) ***adj.*** ⟦L⟧ that was at one time; former [a *quondam* companion]

☆**Quon·set hut** (kwän′sit) ⟦< *Quonset,* a trademark, after *Quonset* Point, R.I., where first manufactured⟧ a prefabricated shelter made of corrugated metal, shaped like a longitudinal half of a cylinder resting on its flat surface

quo·rum (kwôr′əm) ***n.*** ⟦L, gen. pl. of *qui,* WHO: from use in court commissions⟧ **1** [Historical] the number of justices of the peace required to be present at sessions of English courts **2** the minimum number of members required to be present at an assembly or meeting before it can validly proceed to transact business **3** a select group or company

quot *abbrev.* quotation

quo·ta (kwōt′ə) ***n.*** ⟦ML, short for L *quota pars,* how large a part: fem. of *quotus:* see QUOTE⟧ **1** a share or proportion which each of a number is called upon to contribute, or which is assigned to each; proportional share ☆**2** the number or proportion that is allowed or admitted [immigration *quotas*]

quot·a·ble (kwōt′ə bəl) ***adj.*** worthwhile quoting or suitable for quotation —**quot′a·bil′i·ty** ***n.*** —**quot′a·bly** ***adv.***

quo·ta·tion (kwō tā′shən) ***n.*** ⟦ML *quotatio*⟧ **1** the act or practice of quoting **2** the words or passage quoted **3** *Commerce a)* the current quoted price of a stock, bond, commodity, etc. *b)* a document containing such a price or prices, usually an offer to sell that which is quoted

quotation mark **1** either of a pair of punctuation marks (" ... ") used to enclose a direct quotation, a word or phrase being used in a special way, or the title of a short written work, as a story, poem, or song **2** either of a pair of single marks (' ... ') for enclosing a quotation within a quotation (Ex.: She said, "Remember this, 'Always think before you speak.'") In British English, the function of these pairs of marks is reversed

quote (kwōt) ***vt.*** **quot′ed, quot′ing** ⟦altered (infl. by L) < ME *coten* < ML *quotare,* to mark the number of, divide into chapters < L *quotus,* of what number < IE **kwoti-,* how many < interrogative base **kwo-* > WHO⟧ **1** to reproduce or repeat a passage from or statement of [to *quote* Chaucer] **2** to reproduce or repeat (a passage from a book, a statement, etc.) **3** to refer to as authority or an example; cite **4** *Commerce* to state (a price) or state the price of (something) **5** *Printing* to enclose in quotation marks —***vi.*** to make a quotation, as from a book or author —***n.*** [Informal] **1** QUOTATION **2** QUOTATION MARK —***interj.*** I shall quote: used in speech to signal the beginning of a quotation —**quot′er** ***n.***

quote-un·quote (kwōt′un kwōt′) ***interj.*** used as before a word or phrase to indicate a direct quotation: often used to mean "purportedly" or "so-called" [the *quote-unquote* "free offer" cost me five dollars in postage]

quoth (kwōth) ***vt.*** ⟦ME *quath* < OE *cwæth,* pret. of *cwethan,* to speak, say, akin to Goth *quithan,* to say⟧ [Archaic] said: the past tense, followed by a subject in the first or third person, and taking as its object the words being repeated

quoth·a (kwō′thə) ***interj.*** ⟦altered < *quoth he,* used ironically⟧ [Archaic] indeed: used, following the repetition of another's words, to express sarcasm or contempt

quo·tid·i·an (kwō tid′ē ən) ***adj.*** ⟦ME *cotidian* < OFr < L *quotidianus* < *quotidie,* daily < *quot,* as many as (for IE base see QUOTE) + *dies,* day⟧ **1** daily; recurring every day **2** everyday; usual or ordinary —***n.*** anything, esp. a fever, that recurs daily

quo·tient (kwō′shənt) ***n.*** ⟦ME *quocient* < L *quoties, quotiens,* how often, how many times < *quot,* how many⟧ **1** *Math. a)* the result obtained when one number is divided by another *b)* the whole-number part of this result *c)* the fraction indicating this division **2** *Math.* the result obtained when one algebraic expression is divided by another **3** the degree to which some characteristic, element, etc. is present [a rise in our population's anxiety *quotient*]

quo war·ran·to (kwō′ wə ran′tō, -rän′-) ***pl.*** **-tos** ⟦ML, by what warrant < L *quo,* abl. of *qui,* who, which + ML *warrantus,* warrant⟧ **1** [Historical] a writ ordering a person to show by what right he exercises an office, franchise, or privilege **2** a legal proceeding undertaken to recover an office, franchise, or privilege from the person in possession, initiated as upon an information

Qu·ran (koo rän′, -ran′) ***n.*** *var. of* KORAN: now the preferred form in many contexts: also sp. **Qur'an** or **Qur'aan** —**Qu·ran′ic** ***adj.***

q.v. *abbrev.* ⟦L *quod vide*⟧ which see: used in referring to a passage, etc. as in a book

qwer·ty keyboard (kwurt′ē) ⟦< the *q, w, e, r, t,* and *y* keys at the upper left of a typewriter⟧ a keyboard having the arrangement of alphabetical and numerical keys found on the traditional typewriter

qy *abbrev.* query

R

r[1] or **R** (är) *n., pl.* **r's, R's** **1** the eighteenth letter of the English alphabet: from the Greek *rho,* a borrowing from the Phoenician **2** any of the speech sounds that this letter represents, as, in English, the (r) of *rude* **3** a type or impression for *r* or *R* **4** the eighteenth in a sequence or group **5** an object shaped like R —*adj.* **1** of *r* or *R* **2** eighteenth in a sequence or group **3** shaped like R —**the three R's** *see* THREE R'S

r[2] *abbrev.* **1** radius **2** range **3** rare **4** received **5** *Printing* recto **6** retired **7** right **8** rod(s) **9** roentgen(s) **10** *Card Games* rubber **11** *Baseball* run(s)

☆**R**[1] (är) *trademark for* a film rating meaning "restricted": it indicates that persons under seventeen may be admitted to the film only when accompanied by a parent or adult guardian

R[2] *abbrev.* **1** ⟦L *Rex*⟧ king **2** ⟦L *Regina*⟧ queen **3** Rabbi **4** *Chem.* radical, esp. organic radical **5** Rankine **6** *Math.* ratio **7** Reaumur **8** registered (trademark): symbol, ® **9** regular (clothing size) **10** Republican **11** *Elec.* resistance **12** right **13** River **14** Road **15** roentgen(s) **16** *Chess* rook **17** Route **18** ruble **19** *Baseball* run(s) **20** rupee **21** ⟦L *recipe*⟧ *Pharmacy* take: also ℞ **22** Thursday

R[3] *symbol Physics, Chem.* molar gas constant

Ra[1] (rä) *n.* ⟦Egypt *r',* sun, day⟧ *Egypt. Myth.* the sun god and principal deity: usually depicted as having the head of a hawk and wearing the solar disk as a crown

Ra[2] *Chem. symbol for* radium

RA *abbrev.* **1** Rear Admiral **2** *Astron.* right ascension **3** Royal Academician **4** Royal Academy

ra·bat (rab′ē, rə bat′) *n.* ⟦MFr, rabat, orig. (collar) turned down < OFr *rabattre:* see REBATE[1]⟧ a plain, black dickey worn with a clerical collar by some clergymen

Ra·bat (rə bät′) capital of Morocco, in the NW part, on the Atlantic

ra·ba·to (rə bāt′ō, -bät′-) *n., pl.* **-tos** ⟦altered < MFr, a turning down < *rabattre:* see REBATE[1]⟧ a large linen or lace collar of the 16th and 17th cent., worn up at the back or turned down so as to fall over the shoulders

Rab·bah (rab′ə) *n. Bible* chief city of the Ammonites: site now occupied by Amman, Jordan: also **Rab′bath** (-əth)

rab·bet (rab′it) *n.* ⟦ME *rabet* < OFr *rabat, rabbat,* a beating down < *rabattre:* see REBATE[1]⟧ a groove or recess cut in the edge of a board, plank, etc. in such a way that another piece may be fitted into it to form a joint (**rabbet joint**) —*vt.* **1** to cut a rabbet in **2** to join by means of a rabbet —*vi.* to be joined by a rabbet

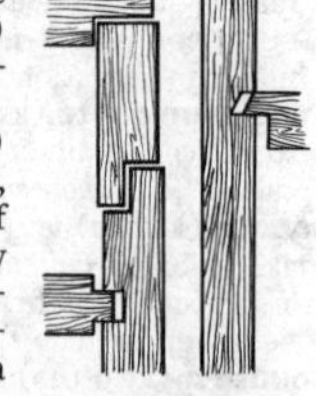

rabbets

rab·bi (rab′ī) *n., pl.* **-bis** ⟦ME < OE < LL(Ec) < Gr(Ec) *rhabbi* < Heb *rabi,* my master, my lord < *rav,* teacher, master + *-i,* my⟧ **1** *Judaism* a scholar and teacher of the Jewish law; now, specif., an ordained Jew, usually the spiritual head of a congregation, qualified to decide questions of law and ritual and to perform marriages, supervise religious education, etc. **2** [Slang] a sponsor; influential friend

rab·bin (-in) *n.* ⟦Fr < ML *rabbinus*⟧ *archaic var. of* RABBI

rab·bin·ate (rab′i nit, -nāt′) *n.* **1** the position or office of rabbi **2** rabbis collectively

Rab·bin·ic (rə bin′ik) *adj.* **1** designating the Hebrew language as used in the writings of rabbis of the Middle Ages **2** [r-] RABBINICAL

rab·bin·i·cal (-i kəl) *adj.* ⟦< ML *rabbinus* + -ICAL⟧ **1** of the rabbis, their doctrines, learning, language, etc., esp. in the early Middle Ages **2** of or for the rabbinate —**rab·bin′i·cal·ly** *adv.*

rab·bin·ism (rab′i niz′əm) *n.* rabbinical teachings and traditions

rab·bit (rab′it) *n., pl.* **-bits** or **-bit** ⟦ME *rabette,* young of the cony, prob. < MFr dial. *rabotte* < MDu *robbe,* Fl *robbe*⟧ **1** any of various swift, burrowing mammals (order Lagomorpha), smaller than most hares and characterized by soft fur, long ears, a stubby tail, and the bearing of naked young: see HARE **2** the fur of a rabbit **3** loosely, any hare **4** *short for* WELSH RABBIT **5** *Track & Field* a runner who, early in the race, sets a fast pace, as to spur on teammates or exhaust a strong competitor —*vi.* **1** to hunt rabbits **2** [Brit. Informal] to talk continuously about unimportant matters; ramble: often with *on* —**rab·bi·ty** (rab′i tē) *adj.*

☆**rabbit ears** [*with pl. v.*] **1** [Informal] an indoor television antenna, consisting of two adjustable rods that swivel apart at a V-shaped angle **2** [Slang] excessive sensitivity to criticism, taunting, etc.: said as of a ballplayer

☆**rabbit fever** TULAREMIA

rabbit punch *Boxing* a short, sharp blow to the back of the neck

rab·bit·ry (rab′i trē) *n., pl.* **-ries** a place where domesticated rabbits are kept; rabbit hutch

rabbit's (*or* **rabbit) foot** ☆a talisman or good-luck charm made from, or made to resemble, the hind foot of a rabbit

rab·ble[1] (rab′əl) *n.* ⟦ME *rabel* < ? or akin to ML *rabulus,* brawling, noisy < L *rabula,* a brawling advocate < *rabere:* see RABID⟧ a noisy, disorderly crowd; mob —*vt.* **-bled, -bling** to attack as or by a rabble; mob —**the rabble** the common people; the masses: a term of contempt

rab·ble[2] (rab′əl) *n.* ⟦Fr *râble* < OFr *roable* < ML *rotabulum,* poker < L *rutabulum,* stirrer < *ruere,* to rake up < IE base **reu-,* to dig up > RID[1], RUBBLE⟧ an iron bar used to stir and skim molten iron in puddling —*vt.* **-bled, -bling** to stir or skim with such a bar

rab·ble·ment (-mənt) *n.* [Now Rare] **1** a noisy disturbance, as by a rabble, or mob **2** a rabble; mob

rab·ble-rous·er (-rouz′ər) *n.* a person who tries to arouse people to anger, hatred, or violent action by appeals to emotions, prejudices, etc.; demagogue —**rab′ble-rous′ing** *adj., n.*

Ra·be·lais (rab′ə lā′; *Fr* rȧ ble′), **Fran·çois** (frän swȧ′) 1494?-1553; Fr. satirist & humorist

Ra·be·lai·si·an (rab′ə lā′zhən, -zē ən) *adj.* of or like Rabelais or his works; broadly and coarsely humorous, satirical, etc.

rab·id (rab′id; *for 3, occas.* rā′bid) *adj.* ⟦L *rabidus* < *rabere,* to rage, prob. < IE base **rabh-,* to be violent, raging > Sans *rábhas-,* violence, force, L *rabies,* madness⟧ **1** violent; raging **2** fanatic or unreasonably zealous in beliefs, opinions, or pursuits **3** of or having rabies —**ra·bid·i·ty** (rə bid′ə tē) *n.,* **rab′id·ness** —**rab′id·ly** *adv.*

ra·bies (rā′bēz) *n.* ⟦L, madness < *rabere:* see prec.⟧ an acute, infectious viral disease of mammals, that attacks the central nervous system: it can be transmitted to people through the bite of an infected animal and is characterized by choking, convulsions, inability to swallow, etc.

☆**rac·coon** (ra ko͞on′) *n., pl.* **-coons′** or **-coon′** ⟦< Virginia Algonquian *aroughcun*⟧ **1** any of a genus (*Procyon,* family Procyonidae) of small, tree-climbing, American carnivores, active largely at night and characterized by long, yellowish-gray fur, black, masklike markings across the eyes, and a long, black-ringed tail **2** its fur

☆**raccoon dog** a small, tree-climbing and burrowing dog (*Nyctereutes procyonoides*) of Asia, resembling the raccoon in appearance and having long, loose fur and a short, thick tail

race[1] (rās) *n.* ⟦ME (North) *ras(e)* < ON *rās,* a running, rush, akin to OE *ræs,* swift movement, attack < IE **eras-,* to flow, move rapidly < base **er-, *or-,* to set in motion > RUN, ORIENT⟧ **1** a competition of speed in running, skating, riding, etc. **2** [*pl.*] a series of such competitions for horses, cars, etc. on a regular course **3** any contest or competition likened to a race [*the race for mayor, a race for power*] **4** a steady onward movement or course **5** the span of life **6** *a)* a swift current of water *b)* the channel for a current of water, esp. one built to use the water industrially [*a millrace*] **7** a channel or groove for the moving parts of a machine, as the groove for the balls in a ball bearing **8** *Aeron.* SLIPSTREAM —*vi.* **raced, rac′ing** **1** to take part in a competition of speed; run a race **2** to go or move swiftly **3** to move or revolve so swiftly as to be out of control, because of less resistance or a lighter load: said of machinery —*vt.* **1** to compete with in a competition of speed **2** to enter or run (a horse, etc.) in a race **3** *a)* to cause to go swiftly *b)* to cause (an engine) to run at high speed with the drive gears disengaged

race[2] (rās) *n.* ⟦Fr < It *razza* < ?⟧ **1** any of the different varieties or populations of human beings distinguished by *a)* physical traits such as hair color and texture, eye color, skin color, or body shape: traditionally, the three primary divisions are Caucasoid, Negroid, and Mongoloid, although many subdivisions of these are also called *races b)* blood types *c)* genetic code patterns *d)* all their inherited characteristics which are unique to their isolated breeding population **2** *a)* the state of belonging to such a population *b)* the qualities, traits, etc. belonging, or supposedly belonging, to such a population **3** loosely, *a)* any geographical population *b)* any population sharing the same activities, habits, ideas, etc. **4** any group of people having the same ancestry; family; clan; lineage **5** *Biol.* *a)* a subspecies, or variety *b)* BREED (*n.* 1) **6** [Rare] distinctive flavor, taste, etc., as of wine —*adj.* ☆[Historical] designating or of music, films, etc. featuring black performers and intended mainly for a black audience [*an early record company specializing in race music*] —**the (human) race** all people collectively

race·course (rās′kôrs′) *n.* an open course, usually unprepared, used in cross-country racing, as through a forest, field, etc.

race·horse (-hôrs′) ***n.*** a horse bred and trained for racing

ra·ce·mate (rā sē′māt, rə-; ras′ə māt′) ***n.*** **1** a salt or ester of racemic acid **2** a racemic salt

ra·ceme (rā sēm′, rə-) ***n.*** ⟦L *racemus,* cluster of grapes⟧ an unbranched flower cluster, consisting of a single central stem or rachis, along which individual flowers grow on small stalks at intervals, blooming from the base toward the apex, as in the lily of the valley

ra·ce·mic (-sē′mik) ***adj.*** ⟦< prec. + -IC: for sense see fol.⟧ *Chem.* **1** consisting of an optically inactive, equimolecular mixture of the dextrorotatory and levorotatory forms of certain substances **2** designating or of a compound formed of such a mixture

racemic acid ⟦< RACEME: orig. found in grapes⟧ a transparent, colorless, crystalline compound occurring in nature with *d*-tartaric acid: it is an optically inactive isomer of tartaric acid

rac·e·mism (ras′ə miz′əm, rā sē′miz′əm) ***n.*** **1** the quality or condition of being racemic **2** RACEMIZATION

rac·e·mi·za·tion (ras′ə mi zā′shən) ***n.*** the conversion of an optically active substance into a racemic form

rac·e·mose (ras′ə mōs′) ***adj.*** ⟦L *racemosus*⟧ arranged in, or bearing, a raceme or racemes

rac·er (rās′ər) ***n.*** **1** any person, animal, vehicle, etc. that takes part in races ☆**2** any of several slim, swift, harmless colubrid snakes (genus *Coluber*), as the American blacksnake

☆**race riot** violence and fighting in a community, brought on by racial conflicts and hatreds

race·run·ner (rās′run′ər) ***n.*** ☆any of a genus (*Cnemidophorus,* family Teiidae) of very active, long-tailed lizards, found chiefly in warm regions of North and South America

race·track (rās′trak′) ***n.*** a course prepared for racing, esp. an oval track for horse races or dog races

race·walk·ing (rās′wôk′iŋ) ***n.*** the competitive sport of walking at high speed while maintaining foot contact with the ground at all times —**race′walk′er *n.***

☆**race·way** (rās′wā′) ***n.*** **1** a narrow channel for water **2** any conduit for carrying and protecting electric wires **3** RACE[1] (sense 7) **4** a racetrack for harness racing **5** a racetrack for drag racing, stock cars, etc.

Ra·chel[1] (rā′chəl) ***n.*** ⟦LL(Ec) < Gr(Ec) *Rhachēl* < Heb *rachel,* lit., ewe⟧ **1** a feminine name: dim. *Rae* **2** *Bible* the younger of the two wives of Jacob, and mother of Joseph and Benjamin: Gen. 29-35

Ra·chel[2] (rà shel′) (born *Élisa Félix*) 1820?-58; Fr. actress, born in Switzerland

ra·chil·la (rə kil′ə) ***n., pl.*** **-lae** (-ē) ⟦ModL, dim. of *rachis:* see fol.⟧ the central stalk of a grass spikelet, to which the glumes and florets are attached

ra·chis (rā′kis) ***n., pl.*** **ra′chis·es** or **ra·chi·des** (rak′ə dēz′, rā′kə-) ⟦ModL < Gr *rhachis,* backbone < IE base **wrāĝh-,* thorn, point > Lith *rãžas,* stubble⟧ **1** SPINAL COLUMN **2** *Bot.* the principal axis of an inflorescence or of a compound leaf **3** *Zool.* the shaft of a feather, esp. that part bearing the barbs

ra·chi·tis (rə kīt′əs, ra-) ***n.*** ⟦ModL < Gr *rhachitis,* inflammation of the spine: see prec. & -ITIS⟧ RICKETS —**ra·chit′ic** (-kit′ik) ***adj.***

Rach·ma·ni·noff (räk män′i nôf′), **Ser·gei V(assilievich)** (ser′gā) 1873-1943; Russ. composer, conductor, & pianist: also sp. **Rach·man′i·nov′** (-nôf′)

ra·cial (rā′shəl) ***adj.*** **1** of or characteristic of a RACE[2] **2** having to do with a difference in RACE[2]; between races [*racial* tensions] —**ra′cial·ly *adv.***

ra·cial·ism (-iz′əm) ***n.*** RACISM —**ra′cial·ist *n., adj.***

rac·i·ly (rā′sə lē) ***adv.*** in a racy manner

Ra·cine[1] (ra sēn′; *Fr* rà sēn′), **Jean Bap·tiste** (zhän bà tēst′) 1639-99; Fr. poet & dramatist

Ra·cine[2] (rə sēn′) ⟦Fr, root, after Fr name of the nearby Root River < ?⟧ city in SE Wis., on Lake Michigan

rac·i·ness (rā′sē nis) ***n.*** the quality of being racy

racing form a chart, booklet, etc. containing information, such as past performance, post position, odds, etc., about a program of horse races at a track or number of tracks

racing homer a kind of homing pigeon used for racing

rac·ism (rā′siz′əm) ***n.*** **1** belief in or doctrine asserting racial differences in character, intelligence, etc. and the superiority of one race over another or others: racist doctrine also, typically, seeks to maintain the supposed purity of a race or the races **2** any program or practice of racial discrimination, segregation, etc., specif., such a program or practice that upholds the political or economic domination of one race over another or others **3** feelings or actions of hatred and bigotry toward a person or persons because of their race —**rac′ist *n., adj.***

rack[1] (rak) ***n.*** ⟦ME *racke* < LowG *rack* < IE **rek-,* to project, bar > ROCK[2]⟧ **1** a framework, grating, case, stand, etc. for holding or displaying various things [clothes *rack,* dish *rack,* pipe *rack,* bomb *rack*]: often used in combination: see HATRACK, HAYRACK, etc. **2** *a)* a triangular form for arranging billiard balls at the beginning of a game of pool *b)* the billiard balls as set up before the break **3** a lift used for automotive vehicles **4** a frame for holding cases of type **5** a toothed bar into which a pinion, worm gear, etc. meshes for receiving or transmitting motion, as in automotive steering systems **6** a pair of antlers **7** an instrument of torture having a frame on which the victim's body is bound and stretched until the limbs are pulled out of place **8** any great mental or physical torment, or its cause **9** a wrenching or upheaval, as by a storm —***vt.*** ⟦prob. < MDu *recken*⟧ **1** to arrange in or on a rack **2** to torture on a rack **3** to trouble, torment, or afflict [a body *racked* with pain] **4** *a)* to oppress by unfair demands, esp. by exacting exorbitant rents *b)* to raise (rents) to an exorbitant degree —**off the rack** ready-made: said of clothing —**on the rack** in a very difficult or painful situation —**rack one's brains** (or **brain**) to try very hard to remember or think of something —**rack up** [Slang] **1** to gain, score, or achieve [to *rack up* a victory] **2** to be the victor over or beat decisively **3** to knock down, as with a punch **4** to injure, wreck, or destroy, as in an accident [*racked up* the car]

rack[2] (rak) ***n., vi.*** ⟦< ?⟧ SINGLE-FOOT

rack[3] (rak) ***n.*** ⟦var. of WRACK[1]⟧ destruction; wreckage: now only in **go to rack and ruin,** to become ruined

rack[4] (rak) ***n.*** ⟦ME *rac,* prob. < Scand, as in ON *reka,* to drive, Norw, Swed dial. *rak,* a wreck: for IE base see WREAK⟧ a broken mass of clouds blown by the wind —***vi.*** to be blown by the wind: said of clouds

rack[5] (rak) ***vt.*** ⟦LME *rakken* < Prov *arracar* < *raca,* husks and stems of grapes, thick dregs⟧ to draw off (cider, wine, etc.) from the dregs

rack[6] (rak) ***n.*** ⟦< ? RACK[1]⟧ **1** the neck or forepart of the spine, especially of mutton or pork **2** the rib section of lamb, usually including eight or nine pairs of ribs, used for a roast or for rib chops: in full **rack of lamb**

rack-and-pin·ion (rak′ən pin′yən) ***adj.*** designating or of an automotive steering system having a RACK[1] (***n.*** 5) and a pinion

rack·et[1] (rak′it) ***n.*** ⟦prob. echoic⟧ **1** a noisy confusion; loud and confused talk or activity; uproar **2** [Archaic] a period of lively, exciting social life or revelry ☆**3** *a)* a scheme for or the practice of obtaining money illegally, esp. one involving fraud or extortion *b)* [Informal] any dishonest scheme or practice ☆**4** [Slang] *a)* an easy, profitable source of livelihood *b)* any business, profession, or occupation —***vi.*** **1** to make a racket; take part in a noisy activity **2** [Now Rare] to lead a boisterous social life; revel **3** to ramble or travel in a casual, reckless way, as in search of excitement: often with *around* —**SYN.** NOISE

rack·et[2] (rak′it) ***n.*** ⟦MFr *raquette,* earlier *rachette,* palm of the hand < ML *rasceta (manus),* palm (of the hand) < Ar *rāḥa(t),* palm of the hand⟧ **1** a light bat for tennis, badminton, etc., with a network of catgut, silk, nylon, etc., in an oval or round frame attached to a handle **2** a snowshoe **3** loosely, the paddle used in table tennis **4** [*pl., with sing. v.*] the game of racquets

☆**rack·et·eer** (rak′ə tir′) ***n.*** ⟦RACKET[1], ***n.*** 3 + -EER⟧ a person who obtains money illegally, as by bootlegging, fraud, or, esp., extortion —***vi.*** to obtain money in any of these ways —**rack′et·eer′ing *n.***

rack·et·y (rak′ə tē) ***adj.*** **1** making a racket; very noisy **2** characterized by revelry or boisterousness

rack railway COG RAILWAY

rack-rent (rak′rent′) ***n.*** ⟦RACK[1], ***vt.*** 4 + RENT[1]⟧ an excessively high rent; esp., a rent whose annual amount is equal, or almost equal, to the value of the property —***vt.*** to exact rack-rent from

rack-rent·er (-ər) ***n.*** one who pays or exacts rack-rent

ra·clette (ra klet′) ***n.*** ⟦Fr < *racler,* to scrape < VL **rasclare* (for **rasiculare*) < L *rasus,* a scraping, orig., pp. of *radere:* see RAT⟧ a Swiss dish of cheese melted before an open fire, scraped onto a plate, and served with boiled potatoes and small sour pickles

☆**ra·con** (rā′kän′) ***n.*** ⟦RA(DAR BEA)CON⟧ RADAR BEACON

rac·on·teur (rak′än tʉr′, -ən-) ***n.*** ⟦Fr < *raconter,* to RECOUNT[1]⟧ a person skilled at telling stories or anecdotes, esp. in an urbane or sophisticated manner

☆**ra·coon** (ra ko͞on′) ***n., pl.*** **-coons′** or **-coon′** *alt. sp. of* RACCOON

rac·quet (rak′it) ***n.*** **1** *alt. sp. of* RACKET[2] **2** [*pl., with sing. v.*] a game like court tennis, played in an enclosure with four walls

☆**rac·quet·ball** (-bôl′) ***n.*** a game similar to handball, but played with a short-handled racket

rac·y (rā′sē) ***adj.*** **rac′i·er, rac′i·est** ⟦RACE[2] + -Y[2]⟧ **1** having the characteristic taste, flavor, or quality associated with the original or genuine type [*racy* fruit] **2** lively; spirited; vigorous **3** piquant; pungent ☆**4** somewhat indecent; suggestive; risqué [a *racy* novel]

rad[1] (rad) ***n.*** ⟦< RAD(IATION)⟧ a basic unit of an absorbed dose of radiation, equal to the absorption of 100 ergs of energy per gram of material or 0.01 joule per kilogram of material (0.01 gray or 1.1 roentgen)

rad[2] *abbrev.* **1** radian(s) **2** radical **3** radius **4** radix

☆**ra·dar** (rā′där′) ***n.*** ⟦*ra(dio) d(etecting) a(nd) r(anging)*⟧ **1** any of various systems or devices using reflected radio waves to locate fixed objects and track moving ones: a radar system typically consists of a transmitter, receiver, and display screen, and is used in navigation, air traffic control, meteorology, mapping, etc. **2** a special ability to perceive, recognize, or find a particular kind of thing, behavior, etc. [a teacher's *radar* for plagiarism] —**on** (or **off**) **the** (or **someone's**) **radar screen** noticed (or unnoticed) by someone —**under** (or **below**) **the** (or **someone's**) **radar** **1** beyond someone's ability to notice or perceive **2** not attracting someone's attention; not making an impression on someone

☆**radar beacon** a beacon with its transmitter and other components that emits radar waves for reception and display, indicating its range or bearing, or both, from a receiving set: it is usually a transponder that returns coded signals only when triggered by a specific radar pulse

☆**ra·dar·scope** (-skōp′) ***n.*** ⟦RADAR + -SCOPE⟧ an oscilloscope that visually displays the reflected radio beams picked up by a radar receiver

Rad·cliffe (rad′klif′), **Ann** (born *Ann Ward*) 1764-1823; Brit. novelist

rad·dle[1] (rad′'l) ***vt.*** **-dled, -dling** ⟦< dial. *raddle,* a slender rod interwoven

in a fence < Anglo-Fr *reidele,* cart rail, stout pole < OFr *ridelle* < MHG *reidel,* cudgel⟧ INTERWEAVE (sense 1)
rad·dle² (rad′'l) ***n., vt.*** **-dled, -dling** *var. of* RUDDLE
rad·dled (rad′'ld) ***adj.*** ⟦< prec.: in ref. as to the heavily rouged or made-up face of an old woman⟧ [Chiefly Brit.] showing signs of wear or old age; run-down, worn-out, etc.
ra·di·al (rā′dē əl) ***adj.*** ⟦< ML *radialis:* see RADIUS⟧ **1** *a)* of or like a ray or rays; branching out in all directions from a common center *b)* having or characterized by parts that branch out in this way **2** of or situated like a radius **3** *Anat.* of or near the radius or forearm —***n.*** **1** a radial part or structure **2** RADIAL (PLY) TIRE —**ra′di·al·ly** ***adv.***
radial (arm) saw a circular saw suspended from a pivoted horizontal arm along which it can be moved
radial engine an internal combustion engine with cylinders arranged radially like wheel spokes
radial keratotomy a surgical operation for correcting nearsightedness in which a series of minute, shallow incisions in a radial pattern are made in the cornea
radial (ply) tire a motor vehicle tire having a foundation of plies of rubberized cords running at right angles to the center line of the tread: it provides better handling, etc. than a bias ply tire
ra·di·an (rā′dē ən) ***n.*** ⟦< RADIUS⟧ the basic unit of plane angle in the SI system, equal to 57° 17′ 44.8″ (57.29578°, the angle formed at the center of a circle by two radii cutting off an arc whose length is equal to the radius of the circle): one degree equals 0.017454 radian and 360 degrees equals 2π radians: abbrev. *rad*
ra·di·ance (rā′dē əns) ***n.*** the quality or state of being radiant; brightness: also **ra′di·an·cy** (-ən sē)
ra·di·ant (-ənt) ***adj.*** ⟦L *radians,* prp. of *radiare:* see RADIATE⟧ **1** sending out rays of light; shining brightly **2** filled with light; bright [*a radiant* morning] **3** showing pleasure, love, well-being, vitality, etc.; beaming [*a radiant* smile] **4** issuing (from a source) in or as in rays; radiated [*radiant* energy] —***n.*** **1** the point or object from which heat or light emanates **2** *Astron.* the point on the celestial sphere from which a shower of meteors appears to come —***SYN.*** BRIGHT —**ra′di·ant·ly** ***adv.***
radiant energy energy traveling in waves; esp., electromagnetic radiation, as heat, light, or X-rays
radiant flux the flow of radiant energy; the rate at which radiant energy passes through a given area
radiant heating a method of heating a space by means of radiation, as from electric coils, hot-water or steam pipes, etc. installed in the floor or walls
ra·di·ate (rā′dē āt′; *for adj.,* -it, -āt′) ***vi.*** **-at′ed, -at′ing** ⟦< L *radiatus,* pp. of *radiare,* to radiate < *radius,* ray: see RADIUS⟧ **1** to send out rays of heat, light, etc.; be radiant **2** to come forth or spread out in rays [heat *radiating* from a stove] **3** to branch out in lines from a center [highways *radiating* from a city] —***vt.*** **1** to send out (heat, light, etc.) in rays **2** to give forth or spread (happiness, love, etc.) as if from a center —***adj.*** **1** having rays or raylike parts; radial **2** *Bot.* having ray flowers or florets **3** *Zool.* having radial symmetry, as a jellyfish
ra·di·a·tion (rā′dē ā′shən) ***n.*** ⟦L *radiatio*⟧ **1** the act or process of radiating; specif., the process in which energy in the form of rays of light, heat, etc. is sent out through space from atoms and molecules as they undergo internal change **2** the rays sent out; radiant energy **3** radial arrangement of parts **4** *Biol.* ADAPTIVE RADIATION **5** *Nuclear Physics* energy emitted as electromagnetic waves, as gamma or X-rays, or as energetic nuclear particles, as neutrons, alpha and beta particles, etc. —**ra′di·a′tion·al** ***adj.*** —**ra′di·a′tive** ***adj.***
radiation sickness sickness produced by overexposure to radiation, as from X-rays or atomic explosions, and characterized by nausea, diarrhea, bleeding, loss of hair, and increased susceptibility to infection
ra·di·a·tor (rā′dē āt′ər) ***n.*** anything that radiates; specif., ☆*a)* a series of pipes or coils through which hot water or steam circulates so as to radiate heat into a room, etc. ☆*b)* a cooling device of tubes and fins, as in an automobile, through which circulating coolant passes *c)* any radioactive material or body *d) Radio* a portion of any transmitting antenna capable of producing radio-frequency energy
rad·i·cal (rad′i kəl) ***adj.*** ⟦ME < LL *radicalis* < L *radix* (gen. *radicis*), ROOT¹⟧ **1** *a)* of or from the root or roots; going to the foundation or source of something; fundamental; basic [*a radical* principle] *b)* extreme; thorough [*a radical* change in one's life] **2** *a)* favoring fundamental or extreme change; specif., favoring basic change in the social or economic structure *b)* [**R-**] designating or of any of various modern political parties, esp. in Europe, ranging from moderate to conservative in program **3** *Bot.* of or coming from the root **4** *Math.* having to do with the root or roots of a number or quantity —***n.*** **1** *a)* a basic or root part of something *b)* a fundamental **2** *a)* a person holding radical views, esp. one favoring fundamental social or economic change *b)* [**R-**] a member or adherent of a Radical party **3** *Chem.* a group of two or more atoms that acts as a single atom and goes through a reaction unchanged, or is replaced by a single atom: it is normally incapable of separate existence **4** *Math. a)* the indicated root of a quantity or quantities, shown by an expression written under the radical sign *b)* RADICAL SIGN —***SYN.*** LIBERAL —**rad′i·cal·ness** ***n.***
rad·i·cal·ism (-iz′əm) ***n.*** **1** the quality or state of being radical, esp. in politics **2** radical principles, ideals, methods, or practices
rad·i·cal·ize (-īz′) ***vt., vi.*** **-ized′, -iz′ing** to make or become politically radical —**rad′i·cal·i·za′tion** ***n.***
rad·i·cal·ly (rad′i kəl ē, rad′ik lē) ***adv.*** **1** *a)* as regards root or origin *b)* fundamentally; basically; completely **2** in a manner characterized by radicalism
radical sign the sign ($\sqrt{}$ or $\sqrt{}$) used before a quantity to indicate that the square root (or a specified root indicated by an imposed index number) is to be extracted: derived from the *r* in Latin *radix,* root
rad·i·cand (rad′i kand′) ***n.*** ⟦< L *radicandum,* neut. ger. of *radicare,* to take root < *radix,* ROOT¹⟧ the quantity under a radical sign
ra·dic·chio (rə dē′kyō, rä-) ***n., pl.*** **-chios** ⟦It⟧ a variety of chicory, with purplish-red, slightly bitter leaves that form an oval head, used in salads
rad·i·ces (rad′ə sēz′, rā′də-) ***n.*** *alt. pl. of* RADIX
rad·i·cle (rad′i kəl) ***n.*** ⟦L *radicula,* dim. of *radix,* ROOT¹⟧ **1** *Anat.* the rootlike beginning of a nerve, vein, etc. **2** *Bot. a)* the lower part of the axis of an embryo seedling; strictly, the root part; often, the hypocotyl, sometimes together with the root *b)* a rudimentary root
ra·di·i (rā′dē ī′) ***n.*** *alt. pl. of* RADIUS
☆**ra·di·o** (rā′dē ō′) ***n.*** ⟦contr. < RADIOTELEGRAPHY⟧ **1** the practice or science of communicating over a distance by converting sounds or signals into electromagnetic waves and transmitting these directly through space, without connecting wires, to a receiving set, which changes them back into sounds, signals, etc. **2** *pl.* **-os′** such a receiving set, esp. one adapted for receiving the waves of the assigned frequencies of certain transmitters or broadcasting stations **3** *a)* broadcasting by radio as an industry, entertainment, art, etc. *b)* all the facilities and related activities of such broadcasting —***adj.*** **1** of, using, used in, sent by, or operated by radio **2** having to do with electromagnetic wave frequencies between *c.* 10 kilohertz and *c.* 300,000 megahertz — ***vt., vi.*** **-oed′, -o′ing** to send (a message, etc.) or communicate with (a person) by radio
ra·di·o- (rā′dē ō, -ə) ⟦Fr < L *radius,* ray: see RADIUS⟧ *combining form* **1** ray, raylike **2** by radio [*radiotelegraph*] **3** by means of radiant energy [*radiothermy*] **4** radioactive [*radiotherapy*]
ra·di·o·ac·tive (rā′dē ō ak′tiv) ***adj.*** ⟦prec. + ACTIVE⟧ giving off, or capable of giving off, radiant energy in the form of particles or rays, as alpha, beta, and gamma rays, by the spontaneous disintegration of atomic nuclei: said of certain elements, as plutonium, radium, thorium, and uranium, and their products —**ra′di·o·ac′tive·ly** ***adv.*** —**ra′di·o·ac·tiv′i·ty** (-ak tiv′ə tē) ***n.***
☆**radioactive dating** the determination of the age of an artifact, bone, rock, etc. based on the known rates of decay of radioactive isotopes of various elements
radioactive series a series of unstable radioactive elements and isotopes, in which a given element or isotope beginning the series decays into and is succeeded by the next in the series, and so on until a stable nucleus is arrived at
radio astronomy the branch of astronomy that deals with radio-frequency radiation from space in order to obtain data and information about particular regions in the universe —**radio astronomer**
☆**ra·di·o·au·to·graph** (-ôt′ə graf′) ***n.*** AUTORADIOGRAPH —**ra′di·o·au′to·graph′ic** ***adj.*** —**ra′di·o·au·tog′ra·phy** (-ô täg′rə fē) ***n.***
☆**radio beacon** a radio transmitter that gives off special signals continuously to help ships or aircraft determine their positions or come in safely, as at night or in a fog
radio beam *see* BEAM (***n.*** II, 3)
ra·di·o·bi·ol·o·gy (rā′dē ō bī äl′ə jē) ***n.*** ⟦RADIO- + BIOLOGY⟧ the branch of biology dealing with the effects of radiation on living organisms and with biological studies using radioactive tracers —**ra′di·o·bi′o·log′i·cal** (-bī′ə läj′i kəl) ***adj.*** —**ra′di·o·bi·ol′o·gist** ***n.***
☆**ra·di·o·broad·cast** (rā′dē ō brôd′kast′) ***n.*** a broadcast by radio — ***vt., vi.*** **-cast′** or **-cast′ed, -cast′ing** to broadcast by radio —**ra′di·o·broad′cast′er** ***n.***
☆**ra·di·o·car·bon** (-kär′bən) ***n.*** carbon-14: see CARBON
radiocarbon dating CARBON DATING
ra·di·o·chem·is·try (-kem′is trē) ***n.*** the branch of chemistry dealing with radioactive phenomena —**ra′di·o·chem′i·cal** (-i kəl) ***adj.***
radio compass a direction finder, used chiefly in navigation
radio control control as of pilotless aircraft, garage doors, etc. by means of radio signals
ra·di·o·el·e·ment (-el′ə mənt) ***n.*** a radioactive element that has no stable isotopes
radio frequency any frequency between normally audible sound waves and the infrared light portion of the spectrum, lying between *c.* 10 kilohertz and *c.* 1,000,000 megahertz
radio galaxy a galaxy emitting stronger radio waves than a normal galaxy
ra·di·o·gen·ic (-jen′ik) ***adj.*** ⟦RADIO- + -GENIC⟧ produced by ionizing radiation
ra·di·o·gram (rā′dē ō gram′) ***n.*** **1** a message sent by radio **2** RADIOGRAPH **3** ⟦< *radiogram(ophone)*⟧ [Brit.] RADIO-PHONOGRAPH
ra·di·o·graph (-graf′, -gräf′) ***n.*** ⟦RADIO- + -GRAPH⟧ a picture produced on a sensitized film or plate by X-rays —**ra′di·og′ra·pher** (-äg′rə fər) ***n.*** —**ra′di·o·graph′ic** ***adj.*** —**ra′di·o·graph′i·cal·ly** ***adv.*** —**ra′di·og′ra·phy** ***n.***
☆**ra·di·o·im·mu·no·as·say** (-im′yə nō as′ā) ***n.*** the technique of immunoassay in which radioactive tracers are introduced into the substance to be analyzed
ra·di·o·i·so·tope (rā′dē ō ī′sə tōp′) ***n.*** a naturally occurring or artificially created radioactive isotope of a chemical element: used in medical therapy, biological research, etc.
ra·di·o·la·bel (rā′dē ō lā′bəl) ***vt.*** **-beled** or **-belled, -bel·ing** or **-bel·ling** to label with a radioactive tracer —***n.*** TRACER (***n.*** 4)
ra·di·o·lar·i·an (-ler′ē ən) ***n.*** ⟦< ModL *Radiolaria* < *radiolus,* dim. of L *ra-*

dius, ray (see RADIUS): from the radiating pseudopodia⟧ any of several classes of one-celled deep-sea protozoans with long, slender pseudopodia and a spiny, or solid but perforated, skeleton of silica

ra·di·o·lo·ca·tion (-lō kā′shən) ***n.*** the use of radar in finding the location and direction of objects

ra·di·ol·o·gy (rā′dē äl′ə jē) ***n.*** ⟦RADIO- + -LOGY⟧ the science dealing with X-rays, ultrasound, tomography, etc., esp. as used in medicine for diagnosing and treating disease and injury —**ra′di·o·log′ic** (-ə läj′ik) ***adj.***, **ra′di·o·log′i·cal** (-ə läj′i kəl) —**ra′di·o·log′i·cal·ly** ***adv.*** —**ra′di·ol′o·gist** ***n.***

ra·di·o·lu·cent (rā′dē ō lo͞o′sənt) ***adj.*** ⟦RADIO- + LUCENT⟧ offering little or no resistance to the passage of X-rays or other forms of radiant energy —**ra′di·o·lu′cen·cy** ***n.***

ra·di·ol·y·sis (rā′dē äl′ə sis) ***n.*** ⟦RADIO- + -LYSIS⟧ chemical decomposition brought about by radiation —**ra′di·o·lyt′ic** (-ə lit′ik) ***adj.***

☆**ra·di·o·me·te·or·o·graph** (rā′dē ō mēt′ē ər ə graf′) ***n.*** a device for the automatic transmission by radio of the data from a set of meteorological instruments

ra·di·om·e·ter (rā′dē äm′ə tər) ***n.*** ⟦RADIO- + -METER⟧ **1** a device containing a set of vanes that are blackened on one side and suspended on an axis in a vacuum: the vanes rotate on exposure to sunlight **2** an instrument for measuring radiant energy in any part of the electromagnetic spectrum —**ra·di·o·met·ric** (rā′dē ō me′trik) ***adj.*** —**ra′di·om′e·try** ***n.***

ra·di·o·mi·met·ic (rā′dē ō mi met′ik) ***adj.*** producing action and effects similar to those produced by radiation

☆**ra·di·on·ics** (rā′dē än′iks) ***n.*** ⟦RADIO + (ELECTRO)NICS⟧ *former term for* ELECTRONICS

ra·di·o·nu·clide (rā′dē ō no͞o′klīd′, -nyo͞o′-) ***n.*** ⟦RADIO- + NUCLIDE⟧ a radioactive nuclide

ra·di·o·paque (rā′dē ō pāk′) ***adj.*** ⟦RADIO- + (O)PAQUE⟧ not allowing the passage of X-rays, gamma rays, or other forms of radiant energy —**ra′di·o·pac′i·ty** (-ō pas′ə tē) ***n.***

ra·di·o·phar·ma·ceu·ti·cal (rā′dē ō fär′mə so͞ot′i kəl, -syo͞ot′-) ***n.*** a radioactive drug, compound, etc. used in physiological study or in the diagnosis and treatment of disease

☆**ra·di·o·phone** (rā′dē ō fōn′) ***n.*** RADIOTELEPHONE

☆**ra·di·o·pho·no·graph** (rā′dē ō fō′nə graf′) ***n.*** a radio and phonograph combined in one unit and sharing some components, as the amplifier and speaker(s)

ra·di·o·pho·to (-fōt′ō) ***n.***, *pl.* **-tos** a photograph or picture transmitted by radio: also **ra′di·o·pho′to·graph′** (-fōt′ə graf′)

ra·di·os·co·py (rā′dē äs′kə pē) ***n.*** ⟦RADIO- + -SCOPY⟧ *former term for* FLUOROSCOPY —**ra′di·o·scop′ic** (-ə skäp′ik) ***adj.***

ra·di·o·sen·si·tive (rā′dē ō sen′sə tiv) ***adj.*** sensitive to, or susceptible to destruction by, X-rays or other forms of radiant energy —**ra′di·o·sen′si·tiv′i·ty** ***n.***

☆**ra·di·o·sonde** (rā′dē ō sänd′) ***n.*** ⟦Fr < *radio* (see RADIO) + *sonde,* a sounding line < *sonder,* to SOUND[4]⟧ a compact package of meteorological instruments and a radio transmitter, carried aloft as by a small balloon to measure and transmit to ground observers temperature, pressure, and humidity data from the upper atmosphere

radio source any celestial source of radio-frequency radiation, esp. a supernova, an external galaxy, or a quasar

radio spectrum the complete range of frequencies of electromagnetic radiation useful in radio communication, commonly ranging between 10 kilohertz and 300,000 megahertz

ra·di·o·stron·ti·um (rā′dē ō strän′shē əm, -tē əm) ***n.*** radioactive strontium, esp. strontium-90

ra·di·o·tel·e·graph (-tel′ə graf′) ***n.*** WIRELESS TELEGRAPHY: also **ra′di·o·te·leg′ra·phy** (-tə leg′rə fē) —**ra′di·o·tel′e·graph′ic** ***adj.***

ra·di·o·tel·e·phone (-tel′ə fōn′) ***n.*** the equipment needed at one station to carry on two-way voice communication by radio waves only —**ra′di·o·te·leph′o·ny** (-tə lef′ə nē) ***n.***

radio telescope *Astron.* a radio antenna or an array of antennas with the component parts, designed to receive, collect, and measure radio waves from celestial sources or spacecraft

ra·di·o·ther·a·py (-ther′ə pē) ***n.*** ⟦RADIO- + THERAPY⟧ the treatment of disease by the use of X-rays or rays from a radioactive substance

ra·di·o·ther·my (rā′dē ō thur′mē) ***n.*** ⟦RADIO- + (DIA)THERMY⟧ **1** the treatment of disease or alleviation of pain by radiant heat **2** shortwave diathermy

ra·di·o·tho·ri·um (rā′dē ō thôr′ē əm) ***n.*** ⟦ModL⟧ a radioactive isotope of thorium, of mass number 228, formed from mesothorium 2

ra·di·o·trac·er (-trā′sər) ***n.*** *Biol.* a radioactive tracer

radio wave any electromagnetic wave at a radio frequency

rad·ish (rad′ish) ***n.*** ⟦ME < earlier *radiche* < OE *rædic* < L *radix* (gen. *radicis*), lit., ROOT[1]: form infl. by Fr *radis,* of same orig.⟧ **1** an annual plant (*Raphanus sativus*) of the crucifer family, with an edible root **2** the pungent root, eaten raw as a relish or in a salad

ra·di·um (rā′dē əm) ***n.*** ⟦ModL < L *radius,* ray (see RADIUS) + -IUM: so named (1898), because it emits rays, by Pierre & Marie CURIE & G. Bémont (1857-1932), Fr chemist⟧ a radioactive, metallic chemical element, one of the alkaline-earth metals, found in very small amounts in pitchblende and other minerals containing uranium: it undergoes spontaneous atomic disintegration through several stages, emitting alpha, beta, and gamma rays and finally forming an isotope of lead: radium is used in neutron sources and in the treatment of cancer and other diseases: symbol, Ra; at. no. 88: see the periodic table of elements in the Reference Supplement

radium therapy the treatment of cancer or other diseases by the use of radium

ra·di·us (rā′dē əs) ***n.***, *pl.* **-di·i′** (-ī′) or **-us·es** ⟦L, rod, spoke (of a wheel), hence radius, ray (of light), ? akin to *radix,* ROOT[1]⟧ **1** a raylike or radial part, as a spoke of a wheel **2** *a)* any straight line extending from the center to the periphery of a circle or sphere *b)* the length of such a line **3** *a)* the circular area or distance limited by the sweep of such a line [no house within a *radius* of five miles] *b)* the distance a ship or airplane can travel and still return to its point of origin without refueling **4** an extent, scope, range, etc. of a limited or specified kind [within the *radius* of one's experience] **5** *a)* the shorter and thicker of the two bones of the forearm, on the same side as the thumb *b)* a corresponding bone of the forelimb of a four-legged animal **6** *Zool. a)* any of the planes of division of the body of a radially symmetrical animal *b)* any of various longitudinal veins in the wing of an insect

radius vector *pl.* **radii vec·to·res** (vek tôr′ēz) or **radius vectors** **1** a straight line joining the origin of a vector, located at the intersection of two coordinates, to a given point lying in the same plane **2** a vector whose point of origin is fixed and whose terminal point ranges over a given curve or surface, as a straight line connecting the sun with the earth at any point of the earth's orbit

ra·dix (rā′diks) ***n.***, *pl.* **rad·i·ces** (rad′ə sēz′, rā′də-) or **ra′dix·es** ⟦L, ROOT[1]⟧ **1** the root of a plant **2** RADICLE **3** *Linguis.* a root, or base **4** *Math.* a number made the base of a system of numbers

RAdm *abbrev.* Rear Admiral

Rad·nor·shire (rad′nər shir′) former county of EC Wales, now part of Powys county: also called **Rad′nor**

Ra·dom (rä′dôm′) city in EC Poland

ra·dome (rā′dōm′) ***n.*** ⟦RA(DAR) + DOME⟧ a dome-shaped housing for protecting a radar antenna, esp. on aircraft, without modifying its electromagnetic radiation

ra·don (rā′dän′) ***n.*** ⟦RAD(IUM) + -ON⟧ a radioactive, gaseous chemical element, one of the noble gases, formed, together with alpha rays, as a first product in the atomic disintegration of radium: symbol, Rn; at. no. 86: see the periodic table of elements in the Reference Supplement

rad·u·la (raj′o͝o lə) ***n.***, *pl.* **-lae′** (-lē′) ⟦ModL < L, scraper < *radere,* to scrape: see RAT⟧ in most mollusks, a ribbonlike structure found in the mouth, bearing numerous rows of teeth, usually used to tear up food and take it into the mouth —**rad′u·lar** ***adj.***

☆**rad·waste** (rad′wāst′) ***n.*** ⟦< *rad(ioactive) waste*⟧ radioactive waste material

Rae (rā) ***n.*** a feminine name: see RACHEL[1]

Rae·burn (rā′bərn), Sir **Henry** 1756-1823; Scot. painter

Rae·ti·a (rē′shə, -shē ə) *alt. sp. of* RHAETIA

RAF *abbrev.* Royal Air Force

raff (raf) ***n.*** ⟦ME *raf:* see RIFFRAFF⟧ **1** RIFFRAFF **2** [Brit. Dial.] rubbish; trash

raf·fi·a (raf′ē ə) ***n.*** ⟦< Malagasy *rofia*⟧ **1** a palm tree (*Raphia ruffia*) of Madagascar, with large, pinnate leaves **2** fiber from its leaves, used as string or woven into baskets, hats, etc.

raf·fi·né (rà fē nā′) ***adj.*** ⟦Fr⟧ refined; cultivated

raf·fi·nose (raf′ə nōs′) ***n.*** ⟦< Fr *raffiner,* to refine < *re-,* RE- + *affiner,* to refine < *a-* (< L *ad,* to) + *fin,* FINE[1] + *-ose,* -OSE[1]⟧ a sweetish, crystalline trisaccharide, $C_{18}H_{32}O_{16}\cdot 5H_2O$, derived from sugar beets, cottonseed, etc.

raff·ish (raf′ish) ***adj.*** ⟦RAFF + -ISH⟧ **1** having a carelessly unconventional style or manner **2** tawdry; vulgar; low —**raff′ish·ly** ***adv.*** —**raff′ish·ness** ***n.***

raf·fle[1] (raf′əl) ***n.*** ⟦ME *rafle* < MFr, dice game, lit., a raking in < OHG *raffel,* a rake, scraper, akin to OE *hreppan,* to touch, grasp < IE base **(s)ker-,* to cut > HARVEST⟧ a lottery in which each participant buys a chance or chances to win a prize —***vt.*** **-fled, -fling** to offer as a prize in a raffle: often with *off* —***vi.*** [Now Rare] to take part in a raffle: with *for* —**raf′fler** ***n.***

raf·fle[2] (raf′əl) ***n.*** ⟦prob. < Fr, a sweeping together, raking in: see prec.⟧ a jumble or tangle, esp. of ropes, canvas, etc. on a ship

raf·fle·si·a (ra flē′zhə, -zhē ə, -zē ə) ***n.*** ⟦ModL, after Sir T. S. *Raffles* (1781-1826), Brit governor in Sumatra⟧ any of a genus (*Rafflesia*) of foul-smelling, dicotyledonous, Malaysian plants of a parasitic family (Rafflesiaceae, order Rafflesiales) characterized by gigantic, stemless flowers and no leaves

raft[1] (raft) ***n.*** ⟦ME *rafte,* beam, rafter < ON *raptr,* log: see RAFTER[1]⟧ **1** a flat, buoyant structure of logs, boards, barrels, etc. fastened together; specif., one used like a boat as in an emergency or in shallow water **2** a similar structure anchored in a river or lake and used by divers, swimmers, etc. **3** a flat-bottomed, inflatable device, as of rubber, for floating on water —***vt.*** **1** to transport on a raft **2** to make into a raft —***vi.*** to travel, work, etc. on a raft

raft[2] (raft) ***n.*** ⟦< RAFF, sense 2 (with unhistoric *-t*)⟧ [Informal] a large number, collection, or quantity; lot

raf·ter[1] (raf′tər) ***n.*** ⟦ME < OE *ræfter;* akin to ON *raptr,* log < IE base **rep-,* post, beam⟧ any of the boards or planks that slope from the ridge of a roof to the eaves and serve to support the roof

raft·er[2] (raf′tər) ***n.*** a person who rafts

rafts·man (rafts′mən) ***n.***, *pl.* **-men** (-mən) a man who operates, or works on, a raft

rag[1] (rag) ***n.*** ⟦ME *ragge* < OE *ragg-* (in *raggig,* ragged) < ON *rögg,* tuft of hair < IE base **reu-,* to tear up > RUG, L *ruere,* to tumble down, rake up, *rudis,* rough⟧ **1** a waste piece of cloth, esp. one that is old or torn **2** a small piece of cloth for dusting, cleaning, washing, etc. **3** anything considered to resemble a rag in appearance or in lack of value 4 [*pl.*] *a)* old, worn clothes *b)* any clothes (used humorously) (see GLAD RAGS) ☆5 the axis and white, tough membrane of citrus fruits 6 cotton and other cloth fibers used in making high-quality papers for documents, stationery, etc. 7 [Slang] a newspaper, esp. one viewed with contempt —*adj.* 1 made of rags [*a rag mop*] 2 [Informal] of or involved in the manufacture and sale of clothing, esp. women's clothing [*the rag trade*] —**chew the rag** [Slang] to chat

rag² (rag) *vt.* **ragged, rag′ging** ⟦< 19th-c. Brit university slang < ?⟧ [Slang] 1 to tease, scold, criticize, or nag: often with *on* 2 [Brit.] to play a practical joke or jokes on —*n.* [Brit.] 1 an act or instance of ragging 2 (one of) a series of activities by university students to raise money for charity

rag³ (rag) *n.* ⟦< ?⟧ a roofing slate with one rough side

rag⁴ (rag) *n.* ⟦RAG(TIME)⟧ ☆a composition in ragtime —☆*vt.* **ragged, rag′ging** to play in ragtime

ra·ga (rä′gə) *n.* ⟦Sans *rāga,* lit., color, akin to *rajayati,* (he) dyes < IE base **reg-,* to color > Gr *rhegma,* dyed material⟧ any of a large number of traditional melody patterns with characteristic intervals, rhythms, and embellishments, used by Hindu musicians as source material for improvisation

rag·a·muf·fin (rag′ə muf′in) *n.* ⟦ME *Ragamoffyn,* name of a demon in *Piers Plowman:* sense prob. infl. by RAG¹⟧ a dirty, ragged person; esp., a poor, ragged child

rag·bag (rag′bag′) *n.* 1 a bag for rags or cloth scraps 2 a collection of odds and ends; miscellaneous assortment

rag doll a traditional type of child's doll made from cloth and stuffed as with cloth scraps

rage (rāj) *n.* ⟦OFr < LL *rabia,* rage, madness; akin to *rabere,* to rage: see RABID⟧ 1 [Obs.] insanity 2 a furious, uncontrolled anger; esp., a brief spell of raving fury 3 a great force, violence, or intensity, as of the wind 4 strong emotion, enthusiasm, or desire —*vi.* **raged, rag′ing** 1 to show violent anger in action or speech 2 to be forceful, violent, uncontrolled, etc. [*a raging sea, a raging fever*] 3 to spread unchecked, as a disease —*SYN.* ANGER, FASHION —**(all) the rage** anything arousing widespread enthusiasm or interest; craze; fad —**rag′ing·ly** *adv.*

ragg (rag) *adj.* made of or designating a sturdy yarn made up of multiple light and dark, esp. cream and gray, strands producing a flecked pattern [*a ragg sweater*]

rag·ged (rag′id) *adj.* ⟦< RAG¹ + -ED⟧ 1 shabby or torn from wear; tattered [*a ragged shirt*] 2 dressed in shabby or torn clothes 3 uneven; rough; jagged [*a ragged edge*] 4 shaggy; unkempt [*ragged hair*] 5 not finished; imperfect; uneven [*a ragged style*] 6 harsh; strident [*a ragged voice*] —☆**run ragged** to cause to be exhausted, as by constant pressure or harassment —**rag′ged·ly** *adv.* —**rag′ged·ness** *n.*

☆**ragged edge** the extreme edge, like that of a precipice; verge [*the ragged edge of poverty*] —**on the ragged edge** precariously close to loss of self-control, mental stability, etc.

ragged robin a perennial plant (*Lychnis flos-cuculi*) of the pink family, with loose clusters of pink or red flowers

rag·ged·y (rag′i dē) *adj.* somewhat ragged, or tattered

rag·gle-tag·gle (rag′əl tag′əl) *adj.* ⟦extended < RAGTAG⟧ of an odd or heterogeneous mixture; motley

rag·i or **rag·gee** (rag′ē) *n.* ⟦Hindi *rāgī* < Sans *rāgin,* red, akin to *rāga:* see RAGA⟧ a cereal grass (*Eleusine corocana*) of Africa and India whose grain is a staple food

rag·lan (rag′lən) *n.* ⟦after Lord *Raglan* (1788-1855), Brit commander in chief in the Crimean War⟧ a loose overcoat or topcoat with sleeves that continue in one piece to the collar, so that there are no seams at the shoulder —*adj.* designating or of such a sleeve, or having such sleeves

raglan sleeves

rag·man (rag′man′) *n., pl.* **-men′** (-men′) a man who collects, buys, and sells rags, old paper, etc.

Rag·na·rok (rag′nə räk′) *n.* ⟦ON *ragna rǫk,* judgment of the gods < *ragna,* gen. pl. of *regin,* gods, lit., the counselors (< IE base **rek-,* to order) + *rǫk,* tale, fate (< *rekja,* to declare < IE base **reĝ-,* to put in order > RIGHT); confused with *ragnarøkkr,* twilight of the gods⟧ *Norse Myth.* the destruction of the world in the last great conflict between the gods and the forces of evil

ra·gout (ra go͞o′) *n.* ⟦Fr *ragoût* < *ragoûter,* to revive the appetite of < *re-,* RE- + *à* (< L *ad*), to + *goût* (< L *gustus*), taste: see GUSTO⟧ a highly seasoned stew of meat and vegetables —*vt.* **-gouted′** (-go͞od′), **-gout′ing** (-go͞o′iŋ) to make into a ragout

rag·pick·er (rag′pik′ər) *n.* a person who makes a living by picking up and selling rags and junk

☆**rag rug** a rug made of rag strips woven or sewn together

rag·tag (rag′tag′) *n.* ⟦RAG¹ + TAG⟧ the lowest classes; rabble: usually **ragtag and bobtail** —*adj.* 1 raggedy, unkempt, disorderly, etc. 2 made up of mixed or ill-sorted elements

☆**rag·time** (rag′tīm′) *n.* ⟦prob. < *ragged time,* in reference to syncopation⟧ 1 a type of American music, mostly composed but sometimes improvised, popular from about 1890 to 1920 and characterized by strong syncopation in even time: it was influential in the development of jazz 2 its syncopated rhythm

☆**rag·top** (rag′täp′) *n.* [Slang] CONVERTIBLE (*n.* 2)

Ra·gu·sa (rə go͞o′zə) *It. name for* DUBROVNIK

rag·weed (rag′wēd′) *n.* ⟦from the tattered appearance of the leaves⟧ ☆any of a genus (*Ambrosia*) of chiefly North American plants of the composite family, having tassel-like, greenish flowers which yield large amounts of wind-borne pollen, a major cause of hay fever

rag·wort (-wurt′) *n.* ⟦see prec.⟧ GROUNDSEL

☆**rah** (rä) *interj.* hurrah: used in cheering for a team

☆**rah-rah** (rä′rä′) *adj.* ⟦< prec.⟧ [Informal] uncritically enthusiastic

raid (rād) *n.* ⟦North Eng var. of ROAD, preserving etym. sense, "a riding": used orig. of an incursion along the border⟧ 1 *a)* a sudden, hostile attack, esp. by troops, military aircraft, etc., or by armed, usually mounted, bandits intent on looting *b)* any act or instance of entering to remove or capture something [*a midnight raid on a refrigerator*] 2 any sudden invasion of a place, as by police, for discovering and dealing with violations of the law ☆3 an attempt, as by a business concern, to lure employees from a competitor 4 a deliberate attempt by one or more speculators to cause a quick, unexpected fall in stock market prices — *vt., vi.* to make a raid or raids (on) —**raid′er** *n.*

rail¹ (rāl) *n.* ⟦ME *raile* < OFr *reille* < L *regula,* RULE⟧ 1 a bar of wood, metal, etc. placed horizontally between upright posts to serve as a barrier or support 2 a fence or railing; specif., the fence surrounding the infield of a racetrack 3 any of a series of parallel metal bars laid upon crossties or in the ground to make a track for railroad cars, streetcars, etc. 4 a railroad or railway as a means of transportation [*to travel by rail*] 5 a horizontal piece of wood separating the panels in doors or wainscoting 6 the rim of a billiard table 7 *Naut.* a narrow, wooden or metal piece forming the top of a ship's bulwarks —*vt.* to supply with rails or a railing; fence —*adj.* of or pertaining to a railway or railroad —**(go) off the rails** 1 (to go) off the proper course 2 (to become) insane —☆**ride on a rail** to place on a rail and carry out of the community: extralegal punishment in which the victim was usually tarred and feathered beforehand

rail² (rāl) *vi.* ⟦ME *raylen* < MFr *railler* < Prov *ralhar* < VL **ragulare,* to bray < LL *ragere,* to bellow⟧ to speak bitterly or reproachfully; complain violently: with *against, at,* or *about* —**rail′er** *n.*

rail³ (rāl) *n., pl.* **rails** or **rail** ⟦ME *rayle* < MFr *raale* < *raaler,* to screech, rattle < VL **rasclare,* to grate: orig. echoic⟧ any of a number of gruiform marsh birds (family Rallidae), characterized by short wings and tail, long toes, and a harsh cry

rail·bird (rāl′burd′) *n.* ⟦< the notion of standing close to the action at the *rail* surrounding the infield of a racetrack⟧ [Slang] an avid or frequent spectator at horse races or, sometimes, other games or sports, as at a poker or football game

rail·head (rāl′hed′) *n.* 1 the farthest point to which rails have been laid in a railroad 2 *Mil.* the point on a railroad at which supplies are unloaded and distributed

rail·ing (rā′liŋ) *n.* 1 materials for rails 2 rails collectively 3 a fence or balustrade made of rails and posts

rail·ler·y (rā′lər ē) *n., pl.* **-ler·ies** ⟦Fr *raillerie:* see RAIL² & -ERY⟧ 1 light, good-natured ridicule or satire; banter 2 a teasing act or remark

rail·road (rāl′rōd′) *n.* 1 a road laid with parallel steel rails along which cars carrying passengers or freight are drawn by locomotives 2 a complete system of such roads, including land, rolling stock, stations, etc. 3 the persons or corporation owning and managing such a system —*vt.* ☆1 to transport by railroad ☆2 [Informal] to rush through quickly, esp. so quickly as to prevent careful consideration [*to railroad a bill through Congress*] ☆3 [Slang] to cause to go to prison on a trumped-up charge or with too hasty a trial —*vi.* ☆to work on a railroad —**rail′road′er** *n.*

☆**railroad flat** ⟦so called by analogy with a line of boxcars standing end to end on a track⟧ an apartment of rooms in a line, entered one from another, with no hallway

rail·road·ing (-iŋ) *n.* 1 the building or operation of railroads 2 the act or process of one that railroads

☆**rail-split·ter** (-split′ər) *n.* a person who splits logs into rails, as for fences —**the Rail-Splitter** name for Abraham LINCOLN²

rail·way (rāl′wā′) *n.* 1 any track with rails for guiding wheels; specif., a road laid with parallel steel rails along which run passenger cars that are lighter than railroad cars 2 RAILROAD

rai·ment (rā′mənt) *n.* ⟦ME *rayment,* aphetic for *arayment:* see ARRAY & -MENT⟧ [Archaic] clothing; wearing apparel; attire

rain (rān) *n.* ⟦ME *rein* < OE *regn,* akin to Ger *regen* < IE base **rek̂-,* var. of **reĝ-,* moist, wet > L *rigare,* to wet, moisten: see IRRIGATE⟧ 1 water falling to earth in drops larger than 0.5 mm (0.02 in) that have been condensed from the moisture in the atmosphere 2 the falling of such drops; shower or rainstorm 3 *a)* rainy weather *b)* [*pl.*] seasonal rainfalls; the rainy season (preceded by *the*) 4 a rapid falling or propulsion of many small particles or objects [*a rain of ashes*] —*vi.* 1 to fall: said of rain, and usually in an impersonal construction [*it is raining*] 2 to fall like rain [*bullets rained about him*] 3 to cause rain to fall: said of the heavens, clouds, etc. —*vt.* 1 to pour down (rain or something likened to rain) 2 to give in large quantities [*to rain praises on someone*] —**rain cats and dogs** [Informal] to rain heavily —☆**rain out** to cause (an event) to be postponed or canceled because of rain —**rain′less** *adj.*

rain·bow (rān′bō′) *n.* ⟦ME *reinbowe* < OE *regnboga:* see prec. & BOW²⟧ 1 an arc or ring containing the colors of the spectrum in consecutive bands, formed in the sky by the refraction, reflection, and dispersion of light in rain or fog 2 a multicolored array or assortment 3 a wide range or selection —*adj.* 1 of many colors 2 *a)* of or involving the collaboration of members of diverse groups, esp. racial or minority groups *[a rainbow* commission to study housing*]* *b)* designating a political coalition of diverse racial or minority groups

Rainbow Bridge ⟦descriptive of its shape⟧ natural sandstone bridge in S Utah: 278 ft (85 m) long; 290 ft (88 m) high

rainbow fish 1 GUPPY 2 any of a number of brightly colored ocean fishes, as the wrasses

☆**rainbow trout** a widespread, chiefly freshwater game trout (*Salmo gairdneri*), native to the mountain streams and rivers of the Pacific Coast of North America

☆**rain check** 1 the stub of a ticket to a ballgame or other outdoor event, entitling the holder to be admitted at a future date if the original event is rained out 2 an offer to renew or defer an unaccepted invitation or offer 3 a coupon, issued by a store to a customer, which guarantees that an item that is on sale at a reduced price but has been sold out may be purchased by that customer in the future at the lower price

☆**rain·coat** (rān′kōt′) *n.* a waterproof or water-repellent coat for giving protection from rain

rain dance a ceremonial dance performed as by some American Indian peoples to end a drought

rain·drop (-dräp′) *n.* a single drop of rain

rain·fall (-fôl′) *n.* 1 a falling of rain; shower 2 the amount of precipitation falling over a given area in a given period of time: it is stated in terms of the depth of water that has fallen into a rain gauge

rain·for·est (-fôr′ist, -fär′-) a dense, evergreen forest, often, specif., one in a tropical region, having abundant rainfall throughout the year: also written **rain forest**

rain gauge an instrument for measuring rainfall

Rai·nier (rā nir′, rə-), **Mount** ⟦after an 18th-c. Brit Adm. *Rainier*⟧ mountain of the Cascade Range, in WC Wash.: 14,410 ft (4,392 m)

☆**rain·mak·er** (rān′māk′ər) *n.* 1 a person who tries to make rain fall; specif., *a)* a North American Indian medicine man using rituals to influence the rain gods *b)* [Informal] a meteorologist or aircraft pilot involved in seeding clouds or the like ☆2 [Slang] *a)* an influential person who can bring success or new vigor to an enterprise *b)* a person, esp. an attorney, who attracts new clients or business to a firm, practice, etc. —**rain′mak′ing** *n.*

☆**rain·out** (rān′out′) *n.* an event that has been postponed or canceled because of rain

rain·proof (-pro͞of′) *adj.* not letting rain through; shedding rain —*vt.* to make rainproof

rain·spout (rān′spout′) *n.* DOWNSPOUT

rain·squall (rān′skwôl′) *n.* a brief, violent windstorm with rain

rain·storm (-stôrm′) *n.* a storm with a heavy rain

rain·wa·ter (-wôt′ər, -wät′-) *n.* water that is falling or has fallen as rain, and is soft, containing relatively little soluble mineral matter

rain·wear (-wer′) *n.* rainproof clothing

rain·y (rā′nē) *adj.* **rain′i·er, rain′i·est** 1 characterized by rain, esp. much rain *[the rainy* season*]* 2 wet with rain 3 bringing rain *[rainy* winds*]* —**rain′i·ness** *n.*

rainy day a possible future time of difficulty or need

Rai·pur (rī′po͝or′) city in EC India

raise (rāz) *vt.* **raised, rais′ing** ⟦ME *raisen* < ON *reisa,* caus. of *risa,* to RISE⟧ 1 *a)* to cause to rise; move to a higher level; lift; elevate *b)* to bring to or place in an upright position 2 to construct or erect (a building, etc.) 3 *a)* to wake from sleep *b)* to stir up; arouse; incite *[to raise* a revolt*]* 4 to increase in size, value, amount, etc. *[to raise* prices*]* 5 to increase in degree, intensity, strength, etc. *[to raise* one's voice*]* 6 to improve the position, rank, or situation of *[to raise* oneself from poverty*]* 7 to cause to arise, appear, come, etc.; esp., to bring back as from death; reanimate *[to raise* the dead*]* 8 to cause to come about; provoke; inspire *[the joke raised* a laugh*]* 9 to bring forward for consideration *[to raise* a question*]* 10 to collect, gather, or procure (an army, money, etc.) 11 to utter (a cry, shout, etc.) 12 to bring to an end; remove *[to raise* a siege*]* 13 to cause to become light; leaven (bread, etc.) 14 *a)* to cause to grow or to breed *[to raise* corn or cattle*]* *b)* to bring up or rear (children) 15 to establish radio communication with 16 to cause (a blister) to form 17 to make (a nap on cloth) with teasels, etc. ☆18 *Commerce* to increase by fraud the face value of (a check, etc.) 19 *Naut.* to cause (land, another ship, etc.) to seem to rise over the horizon by approaching it; come within sight of ☆20 *Bridge* to increase (one's partner's bid in a suit or in no-trump) 21 *Phonet.* to change the sound of (a vowel) by putting the tongue in a higher position ☆22 *Poker* to bet more than (the highest preceding bet or bettor) —*vi.* 1 [Dial.] to rise or arise ☆2 *Poker* to increase the bet —*n.* 1 an act of raising 2 *a)* an increase in amount ☆*b)* an increase in salary or wages, or in a bet —*SYN.* LIFT —**raise Cain** (or **the devil** or **hell** or **a rumpus** or **the roof,** etc.) [Slang] to create a disturbance; cause trouble

raised (rāzd) *adj.* 1 made in low relief; embossed 2 having a napped surface, or having the pile cut with a design in relief: said of fabric 3 leavened with yeast rather than baking powder or soda

rai·sin (rā′zən) *n.* ⟦OFr *reisin* < VL **racimus* < L *racemus,* cluster of grapes⟧ any of various kinds of sweet grapes, usually seedless, dried for eating

rai·son d'é·tat (re zōn dā tȧ′) ⟦Fr, reason of state⟧ a diplomatic or political reason

rai·son d'être (rā′zōn det′, det′rə; *Fr* re zōn de′tr′) ⟦Fr⟧ reason for being; justification for existence

rai·son·neur (re zō̂ nër′) *n.* ⟦Fr, one who argues or reasons⟧ a character in a play, novel, etc. who serves as spokesman for the author's views

raj (räj) *n.* ⟦Hindi < *rājya,* kingdom: see fol.⟧ in India, rule; government —**the Raj** the British government in, or its dominion over, the states of India

ra·jah or **ra·ja** (rä′jə, -jä) *n.* ⟦Hindi *rājā* < Sans *rājan* < *rāj,* to rule < IE base **reĝ-,* to put in order > RIGHT, L *rex,* king⟧ 1 a prince or chief in India 2 a Malay or Javanese chief

Ra·jah·mun·dry (rä′jä mun′drē) city in NE Andhra Pradesh, SE India

Ra·jas·than (rä′jäs tän′) state of NW India, on the Pakistani border: 132,139 sq mi (342,239 sq km); cap. Jaipur

Raj·kot (räj′kōt′) city in Gujarat state, W India

Raj·put (räj′po͞ot′) *n.* ⟦Hindi *rājpūt,* prince < Sans *rājaputra* < *rājan,* king (see RAJAH) + *putra,* son < IE base **pu-,* small, child > POULTRY⟧ a member of a Hindu people, a former ruling caste of N India: also sp. **Raj′poot′**

rake[1] (rāk) *n.* ⟦ME < OE *raca;* akin to ON *reka,* spade, Ger *rechen,* a rake < IE base **reĝ-,* to direct, put in order > RIGHT⟧ 1 any of various long-handled tools with teeth or prongs at one end, used for gathering loose grass, hay, leaves, etc., or for smoothing broken ground 2 any of various similar toothed devices *[oyster rake]* ☆3 [Informal] *short for* RAKE-OFF —*vt.* **raked, rak′ing** ⟦ME *raken* < the n.; also in part < ON *raka,* to scrape, shave⟧ 1 *a)* to gather or scrape together with or as with a rake *b)* to make (a lawn, etc.) tidy with a rake 2 to gather with great care 3 to scratch or smooth with a rake, as in leveling broken ground 4 to cover (a fire) with ashes 5 to scratch or scrape 6 to search through minutely; scour 7 to direct gunfire along (a line of troops, the deck of a ship, etc.): often fig. 8 to look over rapidly and searchingly —*vi.* 1 to use a rake 2 to search as if with a rake 3 to scrape or sweep: with *over, across,* etc. —**rake in** to gather an abundant amount of rapidly —**rake up** to uncover facts or gossip about (the past, a scandal, etc.)

rake[2] (rāk) *n.* ⟦contr. of RAKEHELL⟧ a dissolute, debauched man of fashion

rake[3] (rāk) *vi.* **raked, rak′ing** ⟦< ? or akin to Swed *raka,* to project, akin to OE *hrægan,* to project < IE base **krek-,* **krok-,* to project⟧ to be slightly inclined; slant, as a ship's masts, etc. —*vt.* to cause to slant or incline —*n.* 1 a slanting or inclination *a)* away from the perpendicular *[the rake* of a mast*]* *b)* away from the horizontal *[the rake* of a stage*]* 2 the angle made by the edge of a cutting tool and a plane perpendicular to the surface that is being worked on

rake[4] (rāk) *vi.* **raked, rak′ing** ⟦ME *raken* < OE *racian,* to speed forward: for IE base see RAKE[1]⟧ 1 to fly after game: said of a hawk 2 to run after game with the nose to the track instead of in the wind: said of a hunting dog

rake·hell (rāk′hel′) [Archaic or Literary] *n.* ⟦prob. altered (< RAKE[1] & HELL) < ME *rakel,* rash, wild⟧ a dissolute, debauched man; rake —*adj.* immoral; dissolute

☆**rake-off** (-ôf′) *n.* ⟦RAKE[1] + OFF[1]: orig. gambler's term for part of stakes raked off by the croupier as profit for the house⟧ [Informal] a commission, rebate, or share, esp. when received in an illegitimate transaction

ra·ki or **ra·kee** (rä kē′, rak′ē) *n.* ⟦Turk *rakı* < Ar *ʿaraq:* see ARRACK⟧ an alcoholic liquor made from grape juice, grain, etc. in the Middle East and S Europe

rak·ish[1] (rāk′ish) *adj.* ⟦< RAKE[3] + -ISH⟧ 1 having a trim, neat appearance suggesting speed: said of a ship 2 having a smartly trim, casual look; dashing; jaunty —**rak′ish·ly** *adv.* —**rak′ish·ness** *n.*

rak·ish[2] (rāk′ish) *adj.* like a RAKE[2]; dissolute —**rak′ish·ly** *adv.* —**rak′ish·ness** *n.*

ra·ku (rä′ko͞o) *n.* ⟦Jpn⟧ a kind of earthenware, originally developed for the Japanese tea ceremony in the 16th cent., that has been fired and glazed and then quickly fired again, leaving a blackened, distinctively variegated pattern

rale (räl) *n.* ⟦Fr < *râler,* to rattle < MFr *raaler:* see RAIL[3]⟧ *Med.* an abnormal sound, as rattling or bubbling, accompanying the normal sound of breathing, and usually indicating a diseased condition of the lungs or bronchi

Ra·legh or **Ra·leigh** (rô′lē, rä′lē), Sir **Walter** 1552?-1618; Eng. statesman, explorer, & poet; beheaded

Ra·leigh (rô′lē, rä′lē) ⟦after prec.⟧ capital of N.C., in the central part

ral·len·tan·do (räl′ən tän′dō) *adj., adv.* ⟦It, prp. of *rallentare,* to slow down < *re-* (< L *re-*), again + *allentare,* to slacken < L *ad-,* to + *lentus,* slow⟧ *Musical Direction* gradually slowing: abbrev. **rall**

ral·ly[1] (ral′ē) *vt.* **-lied, -ly·ing** ⟦Fr *rallier* < OFr *re-,* again + *alier,* to join: see ALLY⟧ 1 to gather together (retreating troops) so as to bring back into a state of order 2 to summon or bring (persons) together for a common purpose 3 to bring back to action; revive *[to rally* one's spirits*]* —*vi.* 1 to come back to a state of order: said esp. of retreating troops 2 to come together for a common purpose, esp. to assist or support a cause, person, etc. 3 to come in order to help *[to rally* to the side of a friend*]* 4 to come back to action, normal strength, etc.; revive *[to rally* from a fever*]* 5 *Racket Sports* to take part in a rally 6 *Finance* to rise in price after having fallen: said of stocks, etc. 7 *Sports* to come from behind in scoring —*n., pl.* **-lies** 1 a rallying or being rallied; specif., a gathering of people, as a PEP RALLY, for a common purpose 2 an organized automobile run, esp. of sports cars on public roads, designed to test driving skills: also sp. **ral′lye** 3 *Racket Sports* an exchange of several strokes before the point is won —*SYN.* STIR[1] —**ral′li·er** *n.*

ral·ly[2] (ral′ē) *vt., vi.* **-lied, -ly·ing** ⟦Fr *rallier,* to RAIL[2]⟧ to tease or mock playfully; ridicule; banter

ral·ly·ist (-ist) *n.* a driver who competes in an automobile rally
Ralph (ralf; *Brit usually* rāf) *n.* ⟦ON *Rathulfr* (akin to OE *Rædwulf*) < *rath,* counsel (for IE base see READ[1]) + *ulfr,* WOLF⟧ a masculine name: equiv. Fr. *Raoul*
ram (ram) *n.* ⟦ME *ramme* < OE *ramm,* akin to MDu & OHG *ram* < Gmc **ramma,* prob. < **rama-,* strong, sharp, bitter > ON *rammr*⟧ **1** a male sheep **2** BATTERING RAM **3** [Historical] a metal projection on the bow of a warship below the waterline, used to pierce enemy vessels **4** HYDRAULIC RAM **5** the weight, or striking part, of a pile driver **6** the plunger of a force pump —*vt.* **rammed, ram′ming 1** to strike against with great force; drive into **2** to force into place; press or drive down *[to ram* a charge into a gun*]* **3** to force (an idea, legislative bill, etc.) to be accepted: often with *across* or *through* **4** to stuff or cram (*with* something) —*vi.* **1** to strike with force; crash **2** to move rapidly —**the Ram** Aries, the constellation and first sign of the zodiac —**ram′mer** *n.*
☆**RAM**[1] (ram) *n.* **1** random-access memory **2** *pl.* **RAMs** a random-access memory chip See RANDOM-ACCESS
RAM[2] *abbrev.* Royal Academy of Music
Ra·ma (rä′mə) *n.* ⟦Sans *Rāma*⟧ any of three of the incarnations of the Hindu god Vishnu, esp. the seventh: see RAMACHANDRA
-ram·a (ram′ə, rä′mə) *combining form* -ORAMA *[autorama, gospelrama, Kinderama]*
Ra·ma·chan·dra (rä′mə chun′drə) *n.* ⟦Sans *Rāmacandra*⟧ Rama, the seventh incarnation of the Hindu god Vishnu: the hero of the Ramayana
☆**ra·ma·da** (rə mä′də) *n.* ⟦AmSp⟧ a covered porch for shade, sometimes thatched
Ram·a·dan (ram′ə dän′, räm′-) *n.* ⟦Ar *ramaḍān,* lit., the hot month < *ramaḍ,* state of being parched⟧ **1** the ninth month of the Muslim year, a period of daily fasting from sunrise to sunset **2** the fasting in this period
ram·a·pith·e·cine (räm′ə pith′ə sīn′, -sēn′, -sin) *adj.* ⟦ModL < *Ramapithecus* (< *Rāma,* name of an Indian prince + *-pithecus,* ape: see PITHECANTHROPUS ERECTUS): see -INE[1]⟧ of or relating to a genus (*Ramapithecus*) of extinct hominoids from Asia, Africa, and Europe that were considered by some authorities to be ancestral to humans —*n.* a ramapithecine hominoid
Ra·mat Gan (rä′mət gän′, rə mät′ gän′) city in W Israel, northeast of Tel Aviv
Ra·ma·ya·na (rä mä′yə nə) *n.* ⟦Sans *Rāmāyaṇa*⟧ one of the two great epics of India, written in Sanskrit some time after the Mahabharata and telling of Rama
Ram·a·zan (ram′ə zän′, räm′-) *n. var. of* RAMADAN
ram·ble (ram′bəl) *vi.* **-bled, -bling** ⟦var. of ME *romblen,* freq. of *romen,* to ROAM⟧ **1** to roam about; esp., to walk or stroll about idly, without any special goal **2** to talk or write aimlessly, without connection of ideas **3** to grow or spread in all directions, as a vine —*vt.* to roam through —*n.* a rambling; esp., an aimless stroll
ram·bler (ram′blər) *n.* **1** a person or thing that rambles **2** any of certain climbing roses, with clusters of relatively small flowers ☆**3** RANCH HOUSE (sense 2)
Ram·bouil·let (ram′bə lā′; *Fr* rän bo͞o ye′) *n.* ⟦after *Rambouillet,* town in N France⟧ any of a breed of large sheep originally bred in France from merino sheep imported from Spain: it yields long, fine wool and good-quality mutton
☆**ram·bunc·tious** (ram buŋk′shəs) *adj.* ⟦earlier *rambustious,* altered (prob. by assoc. with RAM) < ROBUSTIOUS⟧ wild, disorderly, boisterous, unruly, etc. —**ram·bunc′tious·ly** *adv.* —**ram·bunc′tious·ness** *n.*
ram·bu·tan (ram bo͞ot′'n) *n.* ⟦Malay, name of the fruit, lit., hairy < *rambut,* hair⟧ **1** the red or yellow, spiny, egg-shaped, edible fruit of a Malayan tree (*Nephelium lappaceum*) of the soapberry family **2** the tree
Ra·meau (ra mō′), **Jean Phi·lippe** (zhän fē lēp′) 1683-1764; Fr. composer & organist
ram·e·kin or **ram·e·quin** (ram′ə kin) *n.* ⟦Fr *ramequin* < MDu *rammeken,* cheese dish < dial. var. of *rom,* cream, akin to OE *ream,* Ger *rahm*⟧ **1** a food mixture, specif. one made of bread crumbs, cheese, and eggs, baked in individual baking dishes **2** such a baking dish
ra·men (rä′mən) *pl.n.* ⟦Jpn⟧ *[sometimes with sing. v.]* Japanese noodles of wheat flour, usually served in broth with pieces of vegetables and meat
ra·men·tum (rə men′təm) *n., pl.* **-ta** (-tə) ⟦ModL < L, scrapings, shavings < *radere,* to scrape (see RAT) + *-mentum,* -MENT⟧ *Bot.* any of the thin, brown scales found on fern leaves and stems
Ram·e·ses (ram′ə sēz′) *n. var. of* RAMSES[1]
ra·met (rā′met′) *n.* ⟦< L *ramus,* branch (see ROOT[1]) + -ET⟧ *Biol.* any of the members of a clone
ra·mi (rā′mī′) *n. pl. of* RAMUS
ram·ie (ram′ē, rā′mē) *n.* ⟦Malay *rami*⟧ **1** a perennial plant (*Boehmeria nivea*) of the nettle family, grown in warm climates for the strong bast fiber of the stems **2** this fiber, used for making cloth
ram·i·fi·ca·tion (ram′ə fi kā′shən) *n.* ⟦MFr < pp. of ML *ramificare*⟧ **1** a ramifying or being ramified; specif., the arrangement of branches or offshoots, as on a plant **2** the result of ramifying; specif., *a)* a branch or offshoot *b)* a derived effect, consequence, or result *[the ramifications* of an act*]*
ram·i·form (ram′ə fôrm′) *adj.* ⟦< L *ramus,* branch (see ROOT[1]) + -FORM⟧ branched or branchlike
ram·i·fy (-fī′) *vt., vi.* **-fied′, -fy′ing** ⟦Fr *ramifier* < ML *ramificare* < L *ramus,* branch (see ROOT[1]) + *facere,* to make, DO[1]⟧ to divide or spread out into branches or branchlike divisions
ram·jet (engine) (ram′jet′) a jet engine, without moving parts, in which the air for oxidizing the fuel is continuously compressed by being rammed into the inlet by the high velocity of the aircraft
ram·mer (-ər) *n.* a person or thing that rams
ram·mish (-ish) *adj.* of or like a ram, or male sheep; specif., *a)* having a rank smell *b)* lustful
Ra·mo·na (rə mō′nə) *n.* ⟦Sp, fem. of *Ramón,* RAYMOND⟧ a feminine name: see RAYMOND
ra·mose (rā′mōs′, rə mōs′) *adj.* ⟦L *ramosus* < *ramus,* branch: see ROOT[1]⟧ **1** bearing many branches **2** branching
ra·mous (rā′məs) *adj.* **1** *var. of* RAMOSE **2** branchlike
ramp[1] (ramp) *n.* ⟦Fr *rampe* < OFr *ramper:* see fol.⟧ **1** a sloping, sometimes curved, surface, walk, road, etc. joining different levels ☆**2** a means for boarding or leaving a plane, as a staircase on wheels rolled up to the door **3** a concave bend or curve where a handrail or coping changes its direction, as at a staircase landing **4** a sloping runway for launching boats, as from trailers —*vt.* to provide with a ramp: usually in the pp. —**ramp up** [Informal] to increase or augment *[to ramp up* factory production*]*
ramp[2] (ramp) *vi.* ⟦ME *rampen* < OFr *ramper,* to climb, clamber < Frank **rampon,* to cramp together < Gmc **rampa,* claw, akin to MDu *ramp,* cramp < IE **(s)kremb-,* var. of base **(s)kerb(h)-,* to twist, curve > SHRIMP, HARP⟧ **1** *a)* to stand upright on the hind legs *b) Heraldry* to be depicted rampant **2** to assume a threatening posture **3** to move or rush threateningly, violently, or with fury; rampage —*n.* the act of ramping
ramp[3] (ramp) *n.* ⟦taken as sing. of *ramps,* var. of dial. *rams,* wild garlic < ME < OE *hramsa,* wild garlic < IE base **krem-* > Gr *kremyon,* MIr *crem,* Lith *kermùšė*⟧ a wild leek (*Allium tricoccum*) having a pair of broad basal leaves in spring, followed by a naked flower stalk: its strongly flavored bulbs are edible
ram·page (ram′pāj′; *for v., also* ram pāj′) *vi.* **-paged′, -pag′ing** ⟦orig. Scot & North Eng dial., prob. < RAMP[2]⟧ to rush violently or wildly about; rage —*n.* an outbreak of violent, raging behavior: chiefly in **on the** (or **a**) **rampage** —**ram·pa′geous** *adj.* —**ram·pa′geous·ly** *adv.* —**ram·pa′geous·ness** *n.* —**ram′pag′er** *n.*
ramp·ant (ram′pənt) *adj.* ⟦ME < OFr, prp. of *ramper:* see RAMP[2]⟧ **1** growing luxuriantly; flourishing *[rampant* plants*]* **2** spreading unchecked; widespread; rife **3** violent and uncontrollable in action, manner, speech, etc. **4** *Archit.* having one abutment higher than the other: said of an arch **5** *a)* rearing up on the hind legs *b) Heraldry* depicted thus in profile, with one forepaw raised above the other *[a lion rampant]* —**ramp′an·cy** *n.* —**ramp′ant·ly** *adv.*
ram·part (ram′pärt′, -pərt) *n.* ⟦Fr *rempart* < *remparer,* to fortify a place < *re-,* again + *emparer* < Prov *amparer,* to fortify < L *ante,* before + *parare,* to PREPARE⟧ **1** an embankment of earth, usually surmounted by a parapet, encircling a castle, fort, etc., for defense against attack **2** any defense or bulwark —*vt.* to protect as with a rampart
ram·pike (ram′pīk′) *n.* ⟦< ?⟧ [Cdn.] an upright dead tree, esp. one that is blackened and without branches as a result of fire
ram·pi·on (ram′pē ən) *n.* ⟦altered < ? Fr *raiponce,* It *raponzolo* < ML *rapunculus,* dim. < L *rapum,* turnip: see RAPE[2]⟧ a European bellflower (*Campanula rapunculus*) with thick, fleshy, white roots that are used with the leaves in salads or cooked, esp. formerly, as a vegetable
ramps (ramps) *n. var. of* RAMP[3]
ram·rod (ram′räd′) *n.* **1** a rod used for ramming down the charge in a gun that is loaded through the muzzle ☆**2** a person in charge, esp. one who is rigid or unyielding —*vt.* **-rod′ded, -rod′ding** ☆to push, direct, or manage in a rigid or unyielding way *[to ramrod* a bill through Congress*]*
Ram·say (ram′zē) **1 Allan** 1686-1758; Scot. poet & bookseller **2 George** *see* DALHOUSIE, Earl of **3** Sir **William** 1852-1916; Brit. chemist, born in Scotland
Ram·ses[1] (ram′sēz′, -zēz′) *n.* name of 11 kings who ruled Egypt (1315?-1090? B.C.)
Ram·ses[2] (ram′sēz′, -zēz′) **1 Ramses I** died 1314? B.C.; founder of the Ramses dynasty **2 Ramses II** died 1225 B.C.; king of Egypt (1292-25): often identified as the Pharaoh of Exodus **3 Ramses III** died 1167 B.C.; king of Egypt (1198?-67)
Rams·gate (ramz′gāt′) seaport & resort in Kent, SE England, on the English Channel
ram·shack·le (ram′shak′əl) *adj.* ⟦back-form. < *ramshackled,* for earlier *ransackled,* pp. of *ransackle,* freq. of RANSACK⟧ loose and rickety; likely to fall to pieces; shaky *[a ramshackle* old building*]*
ram·til (ram′til) *n.* ⟦Hindi *rāmtil* < Sans *rāma,* RAMA + *tila,* sesame⟧ a weedy annual plant (*Guizotia abyssinica*) of the composite family, whose seeds yield an oil used in India for cooking, and for soaps and illumination
ram·u·lose (ram′yə lōs′) *adj.* ⟦L *ramulosus* < *ramulus,* dim. of *ramus:* see fol.⟧ having many small branches
ra·mus (rā′məs) *n., pl.* **-mi′** (-mī′) ⟦ModL < L, branch: see ROOT[1]⟧ *Biol.* a branch or branchlike projecting part
ran (ran) *vi., vt. pt. of* RUN
☆**ranch** (ranch) *n.* ⟦< RANCHO⟧ **1** a large farm, esp. in the W U.S., with its buildings, lands, etc., for the raising of cattle, horses, or sheep in great numbers **2** any large farm devoted to the raising of a particular crop or livestock *[a fruit ranch]* **3** all the people living and working on a ranch **4** *short for* RANCH HOUSE —*vi.* to work on or manage a ranch —*vt.* to raise on a ranch
☆**ranch dressing** a creamy salad dressing containing buttermilk
☆**ranch·er** (ran′chər) *n.* **1** a person who owns or manages a ranch **2** a cowboy **3** RANCH HOUSE

☆**ran·che·ro** (ran cher′ō; *Sp* rän che′rô) ***n.***, *pl.* **-ros** (-ōz; *Sp*, -rôs) ⟦AmSp⟧ in the SW U.S. and Mexico, a person who owns or works on a ranch

☆**ranch house** **1** the owner's residence on a ranch **2** a style of house in which all the rooms are on one floor, usually with a garage attached

Ran·chi (rän′chē) city in S Bihar, NE India

☆**ranch·man** (ranch′mən) ***n.***, *pl.* **-men** (-mən) a person who owns or works on a ranch

☆**ran·cho** (ran′chō, rän′-) ***n.***, *pl.* **-chos** ⟦AmSp, small farm < Sp, small farm, group who eat together, mess < *ranchear,* to build huts < Fr *(se) ranger,* to make room < *ranger:* see RANGE⟧ **1** a hut or group of huts for ranch workers **2** RANCH

Ran·cho Cu·ca·mon·ga (ran′chō ko͞o′kə mäŋ′gə) ⟦< prec. + Shoshonean *kukamonga,* sandy place⟧ city in S Calif., near San Bernardino

ran·cid (ran′sid) ***adj.*** ⟦L *rancidus* < *rancere,* to be rank⟧ **1** having the bad smell or taste of stale fats or oils; spoiled **2** repugnant —**ran·cid′i·ty** (-sid′ə tē) ***n.***, **ran′cid·ness** —**ran′cid·ly** ***adv.***

ran·cor (raŋ′kər) ***n.*** ⟦ME *rancour* < OFr *rancor* < LL, rankness, in LL(Ec), rancor < L *rancere,* to be rank⟧ a continuing and bitter hate or ill will; deep spite or malice: Brit. sp. **ran′cour** —**ran′cor·ous** ***adj.*** —**ran′cor·ous·ly** ***adv.***

rand[1] (rand) ***n.*** ⟦ME *rande,* border, strip < OE *rand, rond,* brink, shield, akin to ON *rönd,* shield rim, OHG *rant,* shield boss < IE base **rem-,* to support > RIM⟧ a leather strip attached to the back of a shoe sole to level it before the heel is put on

rand[2] (rand, ränd) ***n.***, *pl.* **rand** ⟦Afrik, orig., shield < Du, akin to OE *rand:* see prec.⟧ the basic monetary unit of South Africa: see the table of monetary units in the Reference Supplement

Rand[1] (rand), **Ayn** (īn) (born *Alisa Rosenbaum*) 1905-82; U.S. writer & philosopher, born in Russia

Rand[2] (rand), **the** WITWATERSRAND

Ran·dal or **Ran·dall** (ran′dəl) ***n.*** ⟦< OE *Randwulf* (or ON *Ranthulfr*) < *rand,* shield (see RAND[1]) + *wulf,* WOLF⟧ a masculine name: dim. *Randy*

R & B or **r & b** *abbrev.* rhythm and blues

R & D *abbrev.* research and development

Ran·dolph[1] (ran′dôlf′) ***n.*** ⟦ML *Randulfus* < OE *Randwulf:* see RANDAL⟧ a masculine name: dim. *Randy*

Ran·dolph[2] (ran′dôlf′), **John** 1773-1833; U.S. statesman & orator

ran·dom (ran′dəm) ***n.*** ⟦ME *randoun* < OFr *randon,* violence, speed (in *a randon,* violently) < *randir,* to run violently < Frank **rant,* a running, akin to OHG *rinnan,* to RUN⟧ impetuous and haphazard movement: now only in **at random**, without careful choice, aim, plan, etc.; haphazardly —***adj.*** **1** lacking aim or method; purposeless; haphazard **2** not uniform; esp., of different sizes: said of stones, etc. in certain types of masonry **3** *Statistics* of statistical sample selection in which all possible samples have equal probability of selection —**ran′dom·ly** ***adv.*** —**ran′dom·ness** ***n.***

SYN.—**random** applies to that which occurs or is done without careful choice, aim, plan, etc. [a *random* remark]; **haphazard** applies to that which is done, made, or said without regard for its consequences, relevance, etc. and therefore stresses the implication of accident or chance [a *haphazard* selection of books]; **casual** implies a happening or seeming to happen by chance without intention or purpose and often connotes nonchalance, indifference, etc. [a *casual* acquaintance]; **desultory** suggests a lack of method or system, as in jumping from one thing to another [his *desultory* reading in the textbook]; **chance** emphasizes accidental occurrence without prearrangement or planning [a *chance* encounter] —**ANT. deliberate**

☆**ran·dom-ac·cess** (ran′dəm ak′ses) ***adj.*** *Comput.* designating or of a volatile memory that allows data to be accessed directly and does not require following a sequence of storage locations

ran·dom·ize (-īz′) ***vt.*** **-ized′**, **-iz′ing** to select or choose (items of a group) in a random order to obtain an unbiased result, often by using a table of random numbers —**ran′dom·i·za′tion** (-də mi zā′shən, -mī′-) ***n.*** —**ran′dom·iz′er** ***n.***

random variable *Statistics* a variable whose values are determined independently according to a probability distribution

random walk *Math.* a sequence of movements in which the direction of each successive move is determined entirely at random

R & R *abbrev.* **1** *Mil.* rest and recuperation (leave): also **R and R** **2** rest and relaxation (or recreation) **3** rock-and-roll: also **r & r**

ran·dy (ran′dē) ***adj.*** **-di·er**, **-di·est** ⟦prob. < *rand,* dial. var. of RANT + -Y[2]⟧ **1** [Chiefly Scot.] coarse; crude; vulgar **2** sexually aroused; amorous; lustful —***n.***, *pl.* **-dies** [Scot.] a vulgar, quarrelsome woman; shrew

rang (raŋ) ***vi.***, ***vt.*** *pt. of* RING[1]

range (rānj) ***vt.*** **ranged**, **rang′ing** ⟦ME *rangen* < OFr *ranger,* var. of *rengier,* to arrange in a circle, row (> ME *rengen*) < *renc* < Frank **hring,* akin to OE, OHG *hring,* RING[2]⟧ **1** to arrange in a certain order; esp., to set in a row or rows **2** to put into the proper class or classes; systematize **3** to place with others in a cause, party, etc. [to *range* oneself with the rebels] **4** to put (a gun, telescope, etc.) in a line with the target or object, at a proper angle of elevation; train **5** [Now Rare] to make level or even **6** to travel over or through; roam about [to *range* the woods] **7** to travel or move along [to *range* the coastline] ☆**8** to put out (cattle, etc.) to graze on a range **9** to arrange (the anchor cable) in even rows on deck —***vi.*** **1** to extend, reach, or lie in a given direction or in a row [hills *ranging* toward the south] **2** to wander about; roam **3** to move about an area, as in hunting [dogs *ranging* through the woods] **4** to have a specified range [a gun that *ranges* five miles] **5** to vary between stated limits [children *ranging* in age from 5 to 12] **6** *Biol.* to be native to a specified region —***n.*** ⟦ME *reng* < OFr *renc*⟧ **1** a row, line, or series; rank **2** a class, kind, or order **3** a series of connected mountains or hills considered as a single system **4** *a)* the maximum effective horizontal distance that a weapon can fire its projectile *b)* the horizontal distance from a weapon to its target *c)* the path of flight for a missile or rocket *d)* the distance to or from any target, goal, or object of interest [to view a wild animal at close *range*] **5** the maximum distance a plane, etc. can travel without fueling **6** *a)* a place for shooting practice *b)* a place for testing rockets in flight **7** the full extent over which something moves or is heard, seen, understood, effective, etc.; scope [the *range* of one's studies] **8** full extent of pitch, from highest to lowest tones, of a voice, instrument, composition, etc. **9** a wandering or roaming ☆**10** a large, open area of land over which livestock can wander and graze **11** the limits of possible variations of amount, degree, etc. [a wide *range* of prices] **12** a unit for cooking, typically including an oven and surface heating units and usually operated by gas or electricity ☆**13** in U.S. public surveying, a strip of land between two meridian lines six miles apart, constituting a row of townships **14** *Biol.* the region to which a plant or animal is native **15** *Math.* the set of all distinct values that may be taken on by a given function **16** *Statistics* the difference between the largest and smallest values in a sample —☆***adj.*** of a range, or open grazing place

SYN.—**range** refers to the full extent over which something is perceivable, effective, etc. [the *range* of his knowledge]; **reach** refers to the furthest limit of effectiveness, influence, etc. [beyond the *reach* of my understanding]; **scope** implies considerable room and freedom of range, but within prescribed limits [does it fall within the *scope* of this dictionary?]; **compass** also suggests completeness within limits regarded as a circumference [he did all within the *compass* of his power]; **gamut**, in this connection, refers to the full range of shades, tones, etc. between the limits of something [the full *gamut* of emotions]

range finder any of various instruments for determining the distance of a target or object from an observer, or from a gun, camera, etc.: also **range′find′er** ***n.***

range·land (rānj′land′) ***n.*** RANGE (***n.*** 10)

Range·ley Lakes (rānj′lē) ⟦after a family of early landowners in this region⟧ chain of lakes in W Me. & NE N.H.

rang·er (rān′jər) ***n.*** ⟦ME *raunger,* a forest officer: see RANGE⟧ **1** one who ranges; a wanderer **2** *a)* any of a group of mounted troops for patrolling a region ☆*b)* [*often* **R-**] any of a group of soldiers, trained for raiding and close combat **3** *a)* in England, the chief official of a royal park or forest ☆*b)* in the U.S., a warden who patrols government parks and forests

Ran·goon (ran go͞on′, raŋ-) *former name for* YANGON

rang·y (rān′jē) ***adj.*** **rang′i·er**, **rang′i·est** **1** able or inclined to range about ☆**2** long-limbed and slender [*rangy* cattle] ☆**3** having an open range; spacious —**rang′i·ness** ***n.***

ra·ni (rä′nē) ***n.*** ⟦Hindi *rānī* < Sans *rājñī,* fem. of *rājan:* see RAJAH⟧ in India, the wife of a rajah or a woman who is a queen or princess in her own right: also sp. **ra′nee**

ra·nid (rā′nid, ran′id) ***n.*** ⟦< ModL *Ranidae* < L *rana,* a frog⟧ any of a large family (Ranidae) of frogs having teeth in the upper jaw

rank[1] (raŋk) ***n.*** ⟦MFr *renc* < OFr *ranc, renc:* see RANGE⟧ **1** a row, line, or series **2** an orderly arrangement **3** a social division or class; stratum of society [people from all *ranks* of life] **4** a high position in society; high degree; eminence [a person of *rank*] **5** an official grade or position [the *rank* of captain] **6** a relative position, usually in a scale classifying persons or things; grade; degree [a poet of the first *rank*] **7** any of the rows of squares on a chessboard extending from side to side, perpendicular to the files **8** *Mil.* *a)* a row of soldiers, vehicles, etc. placed side by side, or abreast of one another (cf. FILE[1] ***n.*** 3) *b)* [*pl.*] the body of soldiers of an army, as distinguished from the officers [to rise from the *ranks*] (often used metaphorically to refer to the ordinary members of any group, as opposed to its leaders) **9** *Music* STOP (***n.*** *9a*) —***vt.*** **1** to place in a rank or ranks **2** to assign a certain rank, or position, to ☆**3** to have a higher rank than; outrank —***vi.*** **1** to hold a certain rank, or position [to *rank* third on a list] **2** [Archaic] to form a rank or move in ranks —**close ranks** to bring troops, etc. into close formation, as for defensive purposes: often used fig. —☆**pull (one's) rank on** [Slang] to take advantage of one's military rank in enforcing commands or one's high position or seniority in making demands on (a subordinate)

rank[2] (raŋk) ***adj.*** ⟦ME *ranke* < OE *ranc,* strong, proud, akin to MLowG *rank,* slender, erect, long and thin < IE base **reĝ-,* put in order, stretch out > RIGHT⟧ **1** growing vigorously and coarsely; overly luxuriant [*rank* grass] **2** producing or covered with a luxuriant crop; extremely fertile **3** strong and offensive in smell or taste; rancid **4** in bad taste; coarse **5** complete; utter [*rank* deceit] **6** [Obs.] in sexual heat —**rank′ly** ***adv.*** —**rank′ness** ***n.***

rank and file **1** the body of soldiers of an army, as distinguished from the officers **2** the common people, as distinguished from leaders or officials; specif., the ordinary members of a labor union, political party, etc., as opposed to its leaders

Ran·ke (räŋ′kə), **Le·o·pold von** (lā′ō pôlt′ fôn) 1795-1886; Ger. historian

rank·er (raŋ′kər) ***n.*** [Brit.] **1** a soldier in the ranks **2** a commissioned officer promoted from the ranks

Ran·kine (raŋ′kin) ***adj.*** ⟦after William J. M. *Rankine* (1820-72), Scot physicist⟧ designating or of an absolute-temperature scale in which a measurement interval equals a Fahrenheit degree and in which 0° is equal to −459.69°F, so that the freezing point of water is 491.69°R

Ran·kine-cy·cle engine (-sī′kəl) ⟦see prec.⟧ a type of steam engine involving a continuous cycle of vaporization of liquid and condensation back to liquid in a sealed system: developed experimentally for use in automobiles to reduce polluting emissions, utilize cheaper fuels, etc.

rank·ing (raŋ′kiŋ) *adj.* ☆1 of the highest rank *[the ranking officer]* ☆2 prominent or outstanding *[a ranking composer]* —*n.* 1 the act or an instance of listing persons or things in order of importance, achievement, quality, etc. 2 such a listing 3 a position within such a listing

ran·kle (raŋ′kəl) *vi., vt.* **-kled, -kling** ⟦ME *ranclen* < OFr *rancler* < *raoncle, draoncle,* a fester, ulcer < ML *dracunculus* < L, dim. of *draco,* DRAGON⟧ 1 [Obs.] to fester; become or make inflamed 2 to cause or cause to have long-lasting anger, rancor, resentment, etc.

ran·sack (ran′sak′) *vt.* ⟦ME *ransaken* < ON *rannsaka* < *rann,* house (akin to OE *ærn,* Goth *razn* < IE base *(*e*)*re-,* to REST[1]) + *-saka* < *sœkja,* to SEEK⟧ 1 to search thoroughly; examine every part of in searching 2 to search through for plunder; pillage; rob —**ran′sack′er** *n.*

ran·som (ran′səm) *n.* ⟦ME *raunson* < OFr *raençon* < L *redemptio,* REDEMPTION⟧ 1 the redeeming or release of a captive or of seized property by paying money or complying with other demands 2 the price thus paid or demanded 3 deliverance from sin; redemption —*vt.* 1 to obtain the release of (a captive or property) by paying the demanded price 2 [Now Rare] to release after such payment 3 to deliver from sin; redeem —*SYN.* RESCUE —**ran′som·er** *n.*

Ran·som (ran′səm), **John Crowe** (krō) 1888-1974; U.S. poet & critic

rant (rant) *vi., vt.* ⟦< obs. Du *ranten,* to rave, akin to Ger *ranzen,* to be noisy, *anranzen,* to affront⟧ to talk or say in a loud, wild, extravagant way; declaim violently; rave —*n.* ranting speech —**rant′er** *n.* —**rant′ing·ly** *adv.*

ran·u·la (ran′yə lə) *n., pl.* **-las, -lae** (-lē) ⟦L, little frog, cyst on a cow's tongue, dim. of *rana,* frog: so called ? from fancied resemblance⟧ a cyst under the tongue, as caused by the obstruction of a salivary gland duct

ra·nun·cu·lus (rə nuŋ′kyo͞o ləs) *n., pl.* **-lus·es** or **-li′** (-lī′) ⟦ModL < L, tadpole, medicinal plant, dim. of *rana,* frog⟧ BUTTERCUP

rap[1] (rap) *vt.* **rapped, rap′ping** ⟦ME *rappen,* prob. of echoic orig.⟧ 1 to strike quickly and sharply; tap ☆2 [Slang] to criticize sharply —*vi.* 1 to knock quickly and sharply ☆2 to perform rap or a rap ☆3 [Slang] to talk; chat ☆4 [Slang] to talk seriously and frankly with another or others, often in an informal setting —*n.* 1 a quick, sharp knock; tap ☆2 [Slang] blame or punishment, as a prison sentence: usually in **beat (or take) the rap**, escape (or receive) the blame or punishment, or **bum rap**, unfair blame or punishment ☆3 [Slang] a talking; chat ☆4 [Slang] a serious, frank talk ☆5 *a)* a kind of popular music in which rhymed verses are chanted or declaimed to the accompaniment of forceful and repetitive rhythms, played usually on drums or synthesizers (also **rap music**) *b)* a rap song or recording —**rap on the knuckles** a mild reprimand or light sentence —**rap out** to say or utter sharply *[to rap out an order]*

rap[2] (rap) *n.* ⟦< ?⟧ 1 in the early 18th cent., a counterfeit halfpenny in circulation in Ireland 2 [Informal] the least bit: now usually in **not care (or give) a rap**, not care anything at all

rap[3] (rap) *vt.* **rapped** or **rapt, rap′ping** ⟦back-form. < RAPT⟧ [Now Rare] 1 to seize 2 to transport with rapture: now only in the pp.

ra·pa·cious (rə pā′shəs) *adj.* ⟦< L *rapax* (gen. *rapacis*) < *rapere,* to seize (see RAPE[1]) + -OUS⟧ 1 taking by force; plundering 2 greedy or grasping; voracious 3 living on captured prey; predatory —**ra·pa′cious·ly** *adv.* —**ra·pac·i·ty** (rə pas′ə tē) *n.,* **ra·pa′cious·ness**

Ra·pa Nu·i (rä′pä no͞o′ē) *local name for* EASTER ISLAND

rape[1] (rāp) *n.* ⟦ME, prob. < the v.⟧ 1 *a)* the crime of engaging in sexual acts, esp. involving penetration of the vagina or anus, usually forcibly, with a person who has not consented; specif., this crime committed by a man upon a woman or girl *b)* STATUTORY RAPE 2 [Archaic] the act of seizing and carrying away by force 3 the plundering or violent destruction (*of* a city, etc.), as in warfare 4 any outrageous assault or flagrant violation —*vt.* **raped, rap′ing** ⟦ME *rapen* < L *rapere,* to seize < IE base **rep-,* to seize > ON *refsa,* to punish, OE *repsan,* to reprove⟧ 1 [Archaic] to seize and carry away by force 2 to commit rape on; violate 3 to plunder or destroy —*vi.* to commit rape

rape[2] (rāp) *n.* ⟦ME < L *rapa, rapum,* turnip < IE base **rap-* > Ger *rübe,* beet, Gr *rhapys, rhaphys*⟧ an annual Old World plant (*Brassica napus*) of the crucifer family, whose seeds yield an oil and whose leaves are used for fodder

rape[3] (rāp) *n.* ⟦Fr *râpe* < ML *raspa,* ult. < or akin to OHG *raspon,* to scrape together: see RASP⟧ the crushed pulp of grapes after the juice has been extracted

☆**rape kit** a set of materials, variously including swabs, microscope slides, storage bags, labels, etc., designed for the gathering of forensic evidence from a victim of sexual assault

rape oil a thick oil extracted from rapeseed, used as a lubricant, illuminant, etc.: also **rapeseed oil**

rape·seed (rāp′sēd′) *n.* the seed of the rape plant

Raph·a·el[1] (raf′ē əl, rā′fā el′) *n.* ⟦LL(Ec) < Gr(Ec) *Rhaphaēl* < Heb *refael,* lit., God hath healed⟧ 1 a masculine name 2 an archangel mentioned in the Apocrypha

Ra·pha·el[2] (rä′fā el′, -fī-) (born *Raffaello Santi* or *Sanzio*) 1483-1520; It. painter & architect

ra·phe (rā′fē) *n.* ⟦ModL < Gr *rhaphē,* seam < *rhaptein,* to stitch together < IE **werp-, *wrep-,* to turn, twist > RHAPSODY⟧ 1 *Anat.* a seamlike joining of the two lateral halves of an organ, as of the tongue 2 *Bot. a)* a ridge of tissue along the side of an ovule, indicating the position of the vascular bundle which supplies the developing seed *b)* the line of union of the two carpels in the fruit of members of the umbel family *c)* a longitudinal fissure along the center of certain diatom shells

ra·phi·a (rā′fē ə, raf′ē ə) *n. var. of* RAFFIA

ra·phide (rā′fid, raf′id) *n., pl.* **raph·i·des** (raf′ə dēz′, rā′fidz) ⟦ModL < Gr *rhaphis* (gen. *rhaphidos*), needle: for IE base see RAPHE⟧ *Bot.* a needle-shaped crystal, usually of calcium oxalate, developed singly, or more often in bundles, in a plant cell

rap·id (rap′id) *adj.* ⟦L *rapidus* < *rapere,* to seize, rush: see RAPE[1]⟧ moving, progressing, or occurring with speed; swift; fast; quick —☆*n.* 1 [*usually pl.*] a part of a river where the current is relatively swift, as because of a narrowing of the riverbed 2 a rapid transit car, train, or system —*SYN.* FAST[1] —**ra·pid·i·ty** (rə pid′ə tē) *n.,* **rap′id·ness** —**rap′id·ly** *adv.*

Rap·i·dan (rap′i dan′) ⟦< ?⟧ river in NC Va., flowing eastward from the Blue Ridge Mountains into the Rappahannock: *c.* 90 mi (145 km)

Rapid City ⟦from its location on *Rapid* Creek⟧ city in W S.Dak., in the Black Hills

rapid eye movement REM

rap·id-fire (rap′id fīr′) *adj.* 1 firing or capable of firing shots in rapid succession: said of guns 2 done, delivered, proceeding, or carried on swiftly and sharply *[rapid-fire talk]*

☆**rapid transit** a system of public transportation in an urban area, using electric trains running along an unimpeded right of way

ra·pi·er (rā′pē ər, rāp′yər) *n.* ⟦Fr *rapière,* orig. adj., in OFr *espee* (sword) *rapiere* < ? *râper,* to rasp, ult. < OHG *raspon,* to scrape together: see RASP⟧ a slender, two-edged sword used chiefly for thrusting

rap·ine (rap′in, -īn′) *n.* ⟦OFr < L *rapina* < *rapere,* to snatch, seize: see RAPE[1]⟧ the act of seizing and carrying off by force others' property; plunder; pillage

ra·pi·ni (rä pē′nē) *n.* ⟦It, pl. of *rapino,* dim. of *rapo,* akin to *rapa,* turnip < L *rapa, rapum:* see RAPE[2]⟧ BROCCOLI RAAB

☆**rap·ist** (rāp′ist) *n.* a person who has committed rape

Rap·pa·han·nock (rap′ə han′ək) ⟦< Virginia Algonquian, prob. lit., the river that flows back again⟧ river in NE Va., flowing southeastward into Chesapeake Bay: *c.* 185 mi (298 km)

rap·pa·ree (rap′ə rē′) *n.* ⟦Ir *rapaire,* orig., pikeman < *rapaire,* short pike⟧ 1 [Historical] an Irish freebooting soldier 2 a plunderer or robber

rap·pee (ra pē′) *n.* ⟦Fr (*tabac*) *râpé,* grated (tobacco), pp. of *râper,* to rasp, ult. < OHG *raspon,* to scrape together: see RASP⟧ a strong snuff made from coarse, dark tobacco leaves

rap·pel (ra pel′, rə-) *n.* ⟦Fr, lit., a recall < *rappeler,* to call back < OFr *rapeler* (see REPEAL): from the idea of bringing back the rope⟧ a descent by a mountain climber, as down a sheer face of a cliff, by means of a double rope anchored above and arranged around the climber's body so as to control the slide downward —*vi.* **-pelled′, -pel′ling** to make such a descent

rap·pen (räp′ən) *n., pl.* **-pen** ⟦Ger < *rappe,* RAVEN[1]: in pejorative allusion to the eagle on an earlier Alsatian coin⟧ *Ger. name for* the Swiss centime

rap·per (rap′ər) *n.* a person or thing that raps; specif., *a)* a door knocker ☆*b)* a person who performs rap music

rap·port (ra pôr′, rə-) *n.* ⟦Fr < OFr *raport,* agreement, accord, lit., a bringing back < *raporter,* to bring back < *re-* (< L *re-*), again + *aporter,* to bring < L *apportare* < *ad-,* to + *portare,* to carry: see PORT[3]⟧ relationship; esp., a close or sympathetic relationship; agreement; harmony

rap·por·teur (rap′ôr tʉr′) *n.* ⟦Fr < *rapporter* (see prec.) + *-eur,* -OR⟧ a person appointed to prepare reports, studies, etc. as for a committee or conference

rap·proche·ment (ra′prōsh män′; *Fr* rȧ prôsh män′) *n.* ⟦Fr < *rapprocher,* to bring together: see RE-, APPROACH, & -MENT⟧ an establishing, or esp. a restoring, of harmony and friendly relations

rap·scal·lion (rap skal′yən) *n.* ⟦< earlier *rascallion,* extension of RASCAL⟧ a rascal; rogue

☆**rap sheet** ⟦see RAP[1] (*n.* 2)⟧ [Informal] a person's police record of arrests and convictions

rapt (rapt) *adj.* ⟦L *raptus,* pp. of *rapere,* to snatch, seize: see RAPE[1]⟧ 1 [Now Rare] carried away in body or spirit (*to* heaven, etc.) 2 carried away with joy, love, etc.; enraptured 3 completely absorbed or engrossed (*in* meditation, study, etc.) 4 resulting from or showing rapture *[a rapt look]*

rap·tor (rap′tər, -tôr′) *n.* ⟦L, plunderer < pp. of *rapere,* to snatch (see RAPE[1])⟧ 1 BIRD OF PREY 2 [Informal] *short for* VELOCIRAPTOR

rap·to·ri·al (rap tôr′ē əl) *adj.* 1 predatory: said esp. of a bird of prey 2 adapted for seizing prey *[raptorial claws]*

rap·ture (rap′chər) *n.* ⟦ML *raptura:* see RAPT & -URE⟧ 1 the state of being carried away with joy, love, etc.; ecstasy 2 an expression of great joy, pleasure, etc. 3 a carrying away or being carried away in body or spirit: now rare except in theological usage —*vt.* **-tured, -tur·ing** [Now Rare] to enrapture; fill with ecstasy —*SYN.* ECSTASY —**the rapture** [*often* **the R-**] in some Christian theologies, the bodily ascent into heaven just before Armageddon of those who are saved (see SAVE[1], *vt.* 8) —**rap′tur·ous** *adj.* —**rap′tur·ous·ly** *adv.*

☆**rapture of the deep** NITROGEN NARCOSIS: so called from its initial intoxicating effect

Ra·pun·zel (rə pun′zəl) *n.* ⟦< Ger *rapunzel,* CORN SALAD: in the tale, Rapunzel's parents steal this herb from the witch's garden⟧ in a folk tale, a girl who is imprisoned in a tower by a witch and rescued by a prince who climbs to her by means of her extraordinarily long hair

ra·ra a·vis (rer′ə ā′vis) *pl.* **ra·rae a·ves** (rer′ē ā′vēz) ⟦L, lit., strange bird⟧ an unusual or extraordinary person or thing; rarity

rare[1] (rer) ***adj.*** **rar′er, rar′est** ⟦ME < MFr < L *rarus,* loose, thin, scarce, prob. < IE base *(*e*)*re-,* loose > Gr *erēmos,* solitary⟧ **1** not frequently encountered; scarce; unusual **2** unusually good; excellent *[a rare* scholar*]* **3** not dense; thin; tenuous *[rare* atmosphere*]* **4** [Obs.] not close together; scattered —**rare′ness** ***n.***

rare[2] (rer) ***adj.*** **rar′er, rar′est** ⟦earlier *rear* < ME *rere* < OE *hrere,* lightly boiled (basic sense prob. "disturbed, moved") < base of *hreran,* to move⟧ not completely cooked; underdone; partly raw: said esp. of meat —**rare′ness** ***n.***

rare[3] (rer) ***vi.*** **rared, rar′ing 1** [Dial.] REAR[2] (esp. ***vi.*** 1 & 2) ☆**2** [Informal] to be eager, enthusiastic, etc.: used in prp. *[raring* to go*]*

rare·bit (rer′bit) ***n.*** ⟦altered < (WELSH) RABBIT⟧ WELSH RABBIT

rare earth 1 any of certain basic oxides much alike in physical and chemical properties; specif., any of the oxides of the rare-earth elements **2** any of the rare-earth elements

rare-earth element any of the series of metallic chemical elements, with consecutive atomic numbers of 57 (lanthanum) through 71 (lutetium) inclusive: see LANTHANIDE: often called **rare-earth metal**

rar·ee show (rer′ē) ⟦< pronun. (by Savoyard showmen) of *rare show*⟧ **1** a portable PEEP SHOW (sense 1) **2** any street show

rar·e·fy (rer′ə fī′) ***vt., vi.*** **-fied′, -fy′ing** ⟦ME *rarefien* < MFr *rarefier* < L *rarefacere* < *rarus,* RARE[1] + *facere,* to make, DO[1]⟧ **1** to make or become thin, or less dense *[*the *rarefied* mountain air*]* **2** to make or become more refined, subtle, or lofty: usually in the pp. *[a rarefied* sense of humor*]* —**rar′e·fac′tion** (-fak′shən) ***n.*** —**rar′e·fac′tive** ***adj.***

rare·ly (rer′lē) ***adv.*** **1** infrequently; seldom **2** beautifully, skillfully, excellently, etc. **3** uncommonly; exceptionally

rare·ripe (rer′rīp′) ***adj.*** ⟦*rare,* dial. var. of RATHE + RIPE⟧ ripening early —***n.*** a fruit or vegetable that ripens early

rar·i·fy (rer′ə fī′) ***vt., vi.*** **-fied′, -fy′ing** *alt. sp. of* RAREFY

rar·i·ty (rer′ə tē) ***n.*** ⟦L *raritas*⟧ **1** the quality or condition of being rare; specif., *a)* uncommonness; scarcity *b)* excellence *c)* lack of density; thinness **2** *pl.* **-ties** something remarkable or valuable because rare

Ra·ro·ton·ga (rä′rō tôŋ′gə) largest of the Cook Islands, in the South Pacific: 26 sq mi (67 sq km)

ras·bo·ra (raz bôr′ə) ***n.*** ⟦ModL < ? name in a language of the East Indies⟧ any of a large genus (*Rasbora*) of small, freshwater, tropical cyprinoid fishes of Southeast Asia, often kept in aquariums

ras·cal (ras′kəl) ***n.*** ⟦ME *rascaile* < OFr *rascaille,* scrapings, dregs, rabble < **rasquer,* to scrape < VL **rasicare* < L *rasus:* see RAZE⟧ **1** a scoundrel; rogue; scamp: now usually used jokingly or affectionately, as of a mischievous child **2** [Archaic] one of the rabble —***adj.*** [Rare] low; dishonest; base

ras·cal·i·ty (ras kal′ə tē) ***n.*** **1** the character or behavior of a rascal **2** *pl.* **-ties** a low, mean, or dishonest act

ras·cal·ly (ras′kə lē) ***adj.*** of or like a rascal; base; dishonest; mean —***adv.*** in a rascally manner

rase (rāz) ***vt.*** **rased, ras′ing** *Brit. sp. of* RAZE

rash[1] (rash) ***adj.*** ⟦ME *rasch,* prob. < OE **ræsc,* akin to ON *röskr,* Ger *rasch*⟧ **1** too hasty or incautious in acting or speaking; reckless **2** characterized by too great haste or recklessness *[a rash* act*]* **3** [Obs.] bringing quick results —**rash′ly** ***adv.*** —**rash′ness** ***n.***

rash[2] (rash) ***n.*** ⟦MFr *rasche* < VL **rasica,* a scraping: see RASCAL⟧ **1** an eruption of spots on the skin, usually temporary **2** a sudden appearance of a large or excessive number of instances *[a rash* of complaints*]*

rash·er (rash′ər) ***n.*** ⟦< ? obs. *rash,* to cut < OFr *raser:* see RAZE⟧ **1** a thin slice of bacon or, rarely, ham, for frying or broiling ☆**2** a serving of several such slices

Rasht (räsht, rasht) city in NW Iran

Rask (räsk), **Ras·mus Kris·tian** (räs′moos krēs′tyän) 1787-1832; Dan. philologist

Ras·mus·sen (räs′moo sən), **Knud (Johan Victor)** (kə no͞oth′) 1879-1933; Dan. arctic explorer

ra·so·ri·al (rə sôr′ē əl) ***adj.*** ⟦< ModL *Rasores,* lit., scratchers < L *rasus* (see RAZE) + -IAL⟧ characteristically scratching the ground for food, as a chicken

rasp (rasp, räsp) ***vt.*** ⟦ME *raspen* < OFr *rasper* < OHG *raspon,* to scrape together, akin to OE *hrespan,* to strip, spoil⟧ **1** to scrape or rub with or as with a file **2** to utter in a rough, grating tone **3** to grate upon; irritate *[*giggling that *rasped* his nerves*]* —***vi.*** **1** to scrape roughly; grate **2** to make a rough, grating sound —***n.*** **1** a type of rough file with raised points instead of ridges, used esp. on wood **2** a rough, grating sound **3** an act of rasping —**rasp′er** ***n.*** —**rasp′ing·ly** ***adv.***

rasp·ber·ry (raz′ber′ē, -bər ē) ***n., pl.*** **-ries** ⟦earlier *raspis berry* < *rasp, raspis,* raspberry (prob. same word as ME *raspis,* kind of wine) + BERRY⟧ **1** the small, juicy, edible, aggregate fruit of various brambles (genus *Rubus*) of the rose family, consisting of a cluster of red, purple, or black drupelets **2** any plant bearing this fruit **3** ⟦< rhyming slang *raspberry tart,* fart⟧ [Slang] a sound of derision, contempt, etc. made by expelling air forcibly so as to vibrate the tongue between the lips

Ras·pu·tin (ras pyo͞ot′'n), **(Grigori Yefimovich)** (orig. surname *Vilkin*) 1871?-1916; Russ. mystic & faith healer: connected to the court of Czar Nicholas II

rasp·y (ras′pē, räs′-) ***adj.*** **rasp′i·er, rasp′i·est 1** rasping; grating **2** easily irritated —**rasp′i·ness** ***n.***

ras·sle (ras′əl) ***n., vi., vt.*** **-sled, -sling** *dial. or informal var. of* WRESTLE

Ras·ta·far·i·an (ras′tə far′ē ən, räs′tə fär′-) ***n.*** ⟦< *Ras Tafari,* earlier name of HAILE SELASSIE⟧ a member of a Jamaican religious sect which holds that Haile Selassie was divine and a savior, that Ethiopia is Eden, and that blacks will eventually be repatriated to Africa: also called **Ras·ta** (räs′tə) —**Ras′ta·far′i·an·ism′** ***n.***

ras·ter (ras′tər) ***n.*** ⟦Ger, screen < ML *rastrum,* rake < L, hoe, mattock < *rasus:* see RAZE⟧ the pattern of illuminated horizontal scanning lines formed on a picture tube when no signal is being received

rat (rat) ***n.*** ⟦ME *ratte* < OE *ræt,* akin to Ger *ratz, ratte* < PGmc **ratto* < ? IE base **red-,* **rōd-,* to scratch, gnaw > L *radere,* to scrape, *rodere,* to gnaw⟧ **1** any of numerous long-tailed rodents of various families (esp. Muridae and Cricetidae) resembling, but larger than, the mouse: rats are very destructive pests and carriers of highly contagious diseases, as bubonic plague and typhus ☆**2** a small pad formerly used in certain styles of women's coiffures to make the hair look thicker **3** [Slang] a sneaky, contemptible person; specif., *a)* an informer; stool pigeon *b)* a worker who is a scab *c)* a person who deserts or betrays a cause **4** [Slang] a person who spends a great deal of time at, in, or on a (specified) place *[a* gym *rat,* a mall *rat]* —***vi.*** **rat′ted, rat′ting 1** to hunt for rats, esp. with dogs **2** [Slang] *a)* to desert or betray a cause, movement, etc. as rats are reputed to desert a sinking ship *b)* to act as a stool pigeon; inform (*on*) —***vt.*** ☆**1** to tease (the hair) **2** [Slang] to inform on or betray (someone): with *out [*his comrades will not *rat* him out*]* —**smell a rat** to suspect a trick, plot, etc.

rat·a·ble (rāt′ə bəl) ***adj.*** **1** that can be rated, or estimated, etc. **2** figured at a certain rate; proportional **3** [Brit.] liable to the payment of taxes (rates) —**rat′a·bly** ***adv.***

rat·a·fi·a (rat′ə fē′ə) ***n.*** ⟦Fr, prob. of Creole orig.⟧ **1** a cordial or liqueur made from fruit or fruit kernels, esp. by maceration in brandy, and often flavored with almonds **2** [Brit.] a small almond macaroon: in full **ratafia biscuit**

rat·a·plan (rat′ə plan′) ***n.*** ⟦Fr: echoic of drumming⟧ the beating of a drum, or a sound like this — ***vi., vt.*** **-planned′, -plan′ning** to make such a sound (on)

rat-a-tat (rat′ə tat′) ***n.*** ⟦echoic⟧ a series of sharp, quick rapping sounds: also **rat′-a-tat′-tat′**

ra·ta·touille (rat′ə twē′, -to͞o′ē; rät′ə-) ***n.*** ⟦Fr < *ra-,* intensifier + *ta-,* redupl. syllable + *touiller,* to mix < L *tudiculare,* to stir about < *tudicula,* device for crushing olives, dim. of *tudes,* hammer < root of *tundere,* to strike: see STUDY⟧ a vegetable stew of eggplant, zucchini, tomatoes, onions, and peppers, flavored with garlic and basil or other herbs and served hot or cold

rat·bite fever (rat′bīt′) an infectious disease that is transmitted by the bite of an infected rat or other animal, characterized by a bluish-red rash, attacks of fever, and muscular pain, and caused by either a spirochete (*Spirillum minus*) or by a bacillus (*Streptobacillus moniliformis*)

ratch·et (rach′it) ***n.*** ⟦earlier *rochet* < Fr, lance head, distaff < It *rocchetto,* bobbin, spindle, dim. of *rocca,* distaff < Goth **rukka,* akin to OHG *roccho,* spindle, distaff < IE base **ruk*(*k*)*-,* spun yarn⟧ **1** a toothed wheel (in full **ratchet wheel**) or bar whose teeth slope in one direction so as to catch and hold a pawl, which thus prevents backward movement **2** such a pawl **3** such a wheel (or bar) and pawl as a unit: used in some wrenches, screwdrivers, etc. to allow motion in only one direction — ***vt., vi.*** to (cause to) change in increments: usually with *up* or *down [*to *ratchet* up interest rates*]*

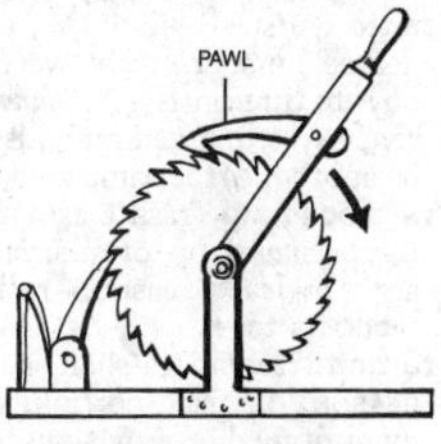

PAWL

ratchet wheel

rate[1] (rāt) ***n.*** ⟦OFr < L *rata* (*pars*), reckoned (part), fem. of *ratus,* pp. of *reri,* to reckon < IE **rē-,* var. of base **ar-,* to fit, join > ART[1], ORDER⟧ **1** the amount, degree, etc. of anything in relation to units of something else *[*the *rate* of pay per month, *rate* of speed per hour*]* **2** a fixed ratio; proportion **3** a price or value; specif., the cost per unit of some commodity, service, etc. *[*insurance *rate]* **4** speed of movement or action *[*to read at a moderate *rate]* **5** the amount of time gained or lost by a timepiece within a specified period **6** [Now Rare] a class or rank *[*of the first *rate]* **7** [Brit.] a local property tax: *usually used in pl.* **8** [Obs.] amount; quantity **9** *U.S. Navy* the grade of a petty officer within a rating *[*the sailor's *rate* is Quartermaster first class*]* —***vt.*** **rat′ed, rat′ing 1** to estimate the value, worth, strength, capacity, etc. of; appraise **2** *a)* to put into a particular class or rank *b) U.S. Navy* to assign a rate to **3** to consider; esteem *[*they are *rated* among the best*]* **4** to fix or determine the rates for **5** [Informal] to deserve *[*to *rate* an increase*]* —***vi.*** **1** to be classed or ranked **2** to have value, status, or rating —***SYN.*** ESTIMATE —**at any rate 1** in any event; whatever happens **2** at least; anyway

rate[2] (rāt) ***vt., vi.*** **rat′ed, rat′ing** ⟦ME *raten* < ? OFr *reter,* to blame, accuse < L *reputare,* to count: see REPUTE⟧ to scold severely; chide

rate·a·ble (rāt′ə bəl) ***adj.*** *alt. sp. of* RATABLE

ra·tel (rāt′'l, rät′-) ***n.*** ⟦Afrik, short for *rateldas* < Du *raat,* honeycomb + *das,* badger; akin to Ger *dachs*⟧ a fierce badger (*Mellivora capensis*) of India and tropical Africa

rate of exchange EXCHANGE RATE

rate·pay·er (rāt′pā′ər) ***n.*** **1** [Brit.] a person who pays rates, or local taxes **2** a customer of a public utility

-rat·er (rāt′ər) *combining form* one of a (specified) rate, or class: used in hyphenated compounds *[*second-*rater]*

☆**rat fink** [Slang] 1 a person who is obnoxious or contemptible 2 an informer or traitor

☆**rat·fish** (rat′fish′) *n., pl.* **-fish′** or **-fish′es** (see FISH) CHIMAERA (sense 2)

rathe (rāth) *adj.* ⟦ME < OE *hræth,* var. of *hræd,* quick, speedy < IE base **kret-,* to shake > MIr *crothaim,* (I) shake⟧ [Archaic] 1 quick; prompt; eager 2 coming or happening early in the day, year, etc.; esp., blooming or ripening early in the season Also **rath** (rath, räth)

Ra·the·nau (rä′tə nou′), **Wal·ther** (väl′tər) 1867-1922; Ger. industrialist & statesman: assassinated

rath·er (rath′ər, räth′-; *for interj.* ra′thur′, rä′-) *adv.* ⟦ME < OE *hrathor,* compar. of *hrathe, hræthe,* quickly: see RATHE⟧ 1 [Obs.] more quickly; sooner 2 more willingly; preferably [would you *rather* have tea?] 3 with more justice, logic, reason, etc. [one might *rather* say] 4 more accurately; more precisely [his sister, or *rather,* stepsister] 5 on the contrary; quite conversely [not a help, *rather* a hindrance] 6 somewhat; to some degree [*rather* hungry] —*interj.* [Chiefly Brit.] yes; certainly —**had rather** [Brit.] would rather —**rather than** instead of; in place of —**would rather** 1 would choose to 2 would prefer that

rat·hole (rat′hōl′) *n.* 1 a hole made or used by a rat 2 [Informal] any place characterized by squalor ☆3 [Informal] anything thought of as a thorough waste of money or resources: often in such phrases as **throw down a rathole,** to spend (money) on such a thing

☆**raths·kel·ler** (rath′skel′ər, rät′-) *n.* ⟦Ger < *rath* (now *rat*) (akin to READ[1]), council, town hall + *keller,* cellar: because frequently located in the cellar of the city hall⟧ a restaurant, usually below the street level, where beer is served

rat·i·fy (rat′ə fī′) *vt.* **-fied′, -fy′ing** ⟦ME *ratifien* < MFr *ratifier* < ML *ratificare* < L *ratus* (see RATE[1]) + *facere,* to make, DO[1]⟧ to approve or confirm; esp., to give official sanction to —*SYN.* APPROVE —**rat′i·fi·ca′tion** (-fi kā′shən) *n.* —**rat′i·fi′er** *n.*

ra·ti·né (rat′′n ā′) *n.* ⟦Fr, frizzed, tufted (of the nap) < pp. of OFr **raster,* to scrape, ult. < L *rasus:* see RAZE⟧ a coarse, loosely woven fabric of cotton, wool, rayon, etc., with a nubby or knotty surface: also **ra·tine** (ra tēn′)

rat·ing[1] (rāt′iŋ) *n.* ⟦see RATE[1]⟧ 1 *a)* a rank, class, or grade; specif., a classification of military or naval personnel according to specialized skills and training [Quartermaster is a Navy *rating*] *b)* [Brit.] an enlisted person in the Navy 2 a placement in a certain rank or class 3 an expression in horsepower, British thermal units, etc. of the effectiveness or operational limit of an engine, furnace, etc. 4 an evaluation of the credit or financial standing of a businessman, firm, etc. 5 an amount determined as a rate 6 *Film* a classification, based on content, restricting the age of those who may attend ☆7 *Radio, TV* a figure, measured by statistical sampling, reflecting the relative size of an audience for a program, time period, etc.

rat·ing[2] (rāt′iŋ) *n.* ⟦see RATE[2]⟧ a scolding; sharp reprimand

ra·tio (rā′shō, -shē ō′) *n., pl.* **-tios** ⟦L: see REASON⟧ 1 a fixed relation in degree, number, etc. between two similar things; proportion [a *ratio* of two boys to three girls] 2 *Finance* the relative value of gold and silver in a currency system based on both 3 *Math.* the quotient of one quantity divided by another of the same kind, usually expressed as a fraction

ra·ti·oc·i·nate (rash′ē äs′ə nāt′, rat′-; -ō′sə nāt′) *vi.* **-nat′ed, -nat′ing** ⟦< L *ratiocinatus,* pp. of *ratiocinari,* to reckon < *ratio:* see REASON⟧ to think or argue logically; reason —**ra′ti·oc′i·na′tion** *n.* —**ra′ti·oc′i·na′tive** *adj.* —**ra′ti·oc′i·na′tor** *n.*

ra·tion (rash′ən, rā′shən) *n.* ⟦MFr < ML *ratio,* ration < L, a reckoning: see REASON⟧ 1 a fixed portion; share; allowance 2 a fixed allowance or allotment of food or provisions, esp. a fixed daily allowance, as for a soldier 3 [*pl.*] food or food supply, as for soldiers, explorers, etc. —*vt.* 1 to supply with a ration or rations 2 to distribute (food, clothing, etc.) in rations, as in times of scarcity —*SYN.* FOOD

ra·tion·al (rash′ən əl) *adj.* ⟦ME *racional* < L *rationalis* < *ratio:* see REASON⟧ 1 of, based on, or derived from reasoning [*rational* powers] 2 able to reason; reasoning; in possession of one's reason or sanity 3 showing reason; not foolish or silly; sensible [a *rational* argument] 4 *Math. a)* designating or of a real number or quantity expressible as the ratio of two integers, with the second integer not being equal to zero: all integers and fractions are rational numbers (cf. IRRATIONAL, sense 3) *b)* designating a function expressible as the quotient of two polynomials —**ra′tion·al·ly** *adv.* —**ra′tion·al·ness** *n.*

SYN.—**rational** implies the ability to reason logically, as by drawing conclusions from inferences, and often connotes the absence of emotionalism [man is a *rational* creature]; **reasonable** is a less technical term and suggests the use of practical reason in making decisions, choices, etc. [a *reasonable* solution to a problem]; **sensible,** also a nontechnical term, implies the use of common sense or sound judgment [you made a *sensible* decision] —*ANT.* **irrational, absurd**

ra·tion·ale (rash′ə nal′) *n.* ⟦ML < L, neut. of *rationalis,* prec.⟧ 1 the fundamental reasons, or rational basis, for something 2 a statement, exposition, or explanation of reasons or principles

ra·tion·al·ism (rash′ən əl iz′əm) *n.* ⟦RATIONAL + -ISM⟧ 1 the principle or practice of accepting reason as the only authority in determining one's opinions or course of action 2 *Philos.* the doctrine that knowledge comes from the intellect in itself without aid from the senses; intellectualism —**ra′tion·al·ist** *n., adj.* —**ra′tion·al·is′tic** *adj.* —**ra′tion·al·is′ti·cal·ly** *adv.*

ra·tion·al·i·ty (rash′ə nal′ə tē) *n.* ⟦LL(Ec) *rationalitas*⟧ 1 the quality or condition of being rational; reasonableness or the possession or use of reason 2 *pl.* **-ties** a rational act, belief, etc.

ra·tion·al·ize (rash′ən ə līz′) *vt.* **-ized′, -iz′ing** 1 to make rational; make conform to reason 2 to explain or interpret on rational grounds 3 [Chiefly Brit.] to apply modern methods of efficiency to (an industry, agriculture, etc.) 4 *Math.* to remove the radical signs from (an expression) without changing the value 5 *Psychol.* to devise superficially rational, or plausible, explanations or excuses for (one's acts, beliefs, desires, etc.), usually without being aware that these are not the real motives —*vi.* 1 to think in a rational or rationalistic manner 2 to rationalize one's acts, beliefs, etc. —**ra′tion·al·i·za′tion** *n.* —**ra′tion·al·iz′er** *n.*

rat·ite (rat′īt) *adj.* ⟦< L *ratitus,* marked with the figure of a raft < *ratis,* raft, prob. < IE base **rēt-, *rōt-,* beam > ROOD⟧ designating a former group (Ratitae) of large, flightless birds of various orders having a flat breastbone without the keel-like ridge of flying birds —*n.* any bird with such a breastbone, as the cassowary, ostrich, or kiwi

rat kangaroo any of various ratlike kangaroos (esp. genera *Bettongia* and *Potorous*) about the size of a rabbit

rat·line (rat′lin) *n.* ⟦altered by folk etym. < LME *ratling, radeling* < ?⟧ any of the small, relatively thin pieces of tarred rope which join the shrouds of a ship and serve as the steps of a ladder for climbing the rigging: also sp. **rat′lin**

rat mite a widespread tropical mite (*Ornithonyssus bacoti*) of the same order (Parasitiformes) as ticks: it is carried by rats and can cause skin inflammations or transmit typhus to human beings by its bite

ra·toon (ra to͞on′) *n.* ⟦Sp *retoño* < *retoñar,* to sprout again < *re-* (< L *re-*), again + *otoñar,* to grow in autumn < L *autumnare* < *autumnus,* AUTUMN⟧ a shoot growing from the root of a plant (esp. the sugar cane) that has been cut down —*vi.* to grow ratoons, or grow as a ratoon

☆**rat race** [Informal] a mad scramble or intense competitive struggle, as in the business world

☆**rats** (rats) *interj.* [Slang] used to signify disgust, disappointment, etc.

rats·bane (rats′bān′) *n.* rat poison; esp., trioxide of arsenic

☆**rat snake** any of several large, harmless, rodent-eating colubrid snakes (genus *Elaphe*) of E and SW North America

rat·tail (rat′tāl′) *adj.* shaped like a rat's tail; slim and tapering: also **rat′tailed′** —*n.* GRENADIER (sense 3)

rattail cactus a small, often cultivated cactus (*Aporocactus flagelliformis*) with weak, cylindrical, creeping or drooping stems, native to Mexico and Central America

rat·tan (ra tan′, rə-) *n.* ⟦Malay *rotan* < ? *rautan,* a thing that has been cleaned by stripping off the outside⟧ 1 a tall palm tree (genera *Calamus* and *Daemonorops*) with long, slender, tough stems 2 a stem of any of these trees, used in making furniture, etc. 3 a cane or switch made from this

rat·teen (ra tēn′) *n.* ⟦Fr *ratine:* see RATINÉ⟧ a coarse, heavy, twilled woolen cloth, popular in 18th-cent. Britain

rat·ter (rat′ər) *n.* 1 a dog or cat skilled at catching rats 2 [Slang] a betrayer or informer

rat·tish (rat′ish) *adj.* like or characteristic of a rat

rat·tle[1] (rat′′l) *vi.* **-tled, -tling** ⟦ME *ratelen,* prob. of WGmc echoic orig., akin to Ger *rasseln*⟧ 1 to make a series of sharp, short sounds in quick succession 2 to go or move with such sounds [a wagon *rattling* over the stones] 3 to talk rapidly and incessantly; chatter: often with *on* —*vt.* 1 to cause to rattle [to *rattle* the handle of a door] 2 to utter or perform rapidly ☆3 to confuse or upset; disconcert [to *rattle* a speaker with catcalls] —*n.* 1 a quick succession of sharp, short sounds 2 a rattling noise made by air passing through the mucus of a partly closed throat: cf. DEATH RATTLE 3 a noisy uproar; loud chatter ☆4 *a)* a series of horny rings at the end of a rattlesnake's tail, used to produce a rattling sound *b)* any of these 5 a device, as a baby's toy or a percussion instrument, made to rattle when shaken —*SYN.* EMBARRASS —**rattle around in** to live or work in (a house, office, etc.) that is too big for one's needs

rat·tle[2] (rat′′l) *vt.* **-tled, -tling** ⟦back-form. < *ratling* (taken as prp.), var. of RATLINE⟧ to provide with ratlines: usually with *down*

rat·tle·box (-bäks′) *n.* ☆any of a genus (*Crotalaria*) of plants of the pea family, having small seeds that rattle in the inflated pods when ripe

rat·tle·brain (-brān′) *n.* a frivolous, talkative person: also **rat′tle·pate′** (-pāt′) —**rat′tle·brained′** *adj.*

rat·tler (rat′lər) *n.* 1 a person or thing that rattles ☆2 a rattlesnake ☆3 [Slang] a freight train

☆**rat·tle·snake** (rat′′l snāk′) *n.* any of various poisonous American pit vipers (genera *Crotalus* and *Sistrurus*), having an interlocking series of horny rings at the end of the tail that produce a rattling or buzzing sound when shaken

diamondback rattlesnake

☆**rattlesnake plantain** any of a genus (*Goodyera*) of small terrestrial orchids with spotted leaves and yellowish-white flower spikes

☆**rattlesnake root** 1 any of a number of perennial plants (genus *Prenanthes*) of the composite family, with small, cylindrical, drooping heads and intensely bitter roots, formerly considered a cure for snakebite 2 any of various other plants formerly considered such a cure

☆**rattlesnake weed** an American hawkweed (*Hieracium venosum*) having purple-veined basal leaves and a naked flowering stem

rat·tle·trap (rat′'l trap′) ***n.*** anything worn out, rickety, or rattling; esp., a dilapidated old automobile

rat·tling (rat′liŋ) ***adj.*** **1** that rattles **2** [Informal] very fast, good, lively, etc. —***adv.*** [Informal] very [*a rattling* good time]

rat·tly (rat′lē, -'l ē) ***adj.*** that rattles or tends to rattle; noisy

rat·toon (ra to͞on′) ***n., vi. alt. sp. of*** RATOON

rat·trap (rat′trap′) ***n.*** **1** a trap for catching rats **2** a hopeless situation; desperate predicament **3** [Informal] a dirty, run-down building

rat·ty (rat′ē) ***adj.*** **-ti·er, -ti·est 1** of or like a rat **2** full of rats **3** [Slang] shabby or run-down

rau·cous (rô′kəs, rä′-) ***adj.*** ⟦L *raucus* < IE echoic base **reu-*, to give hoarse cries, mutter > L *rumor,* OE *reon,* to lament⟧ **1** hoarse; rough-sounding [*a raucous* shout] **2** loud and rowdy [*a raucous* party] —**rau′cous·ly *adv.*** —**rau′cous·ness *n.***

☆**raunch** (rônch, ränch) ***n.*** ⟦< fol.⟧ [Slang] **1** a raunchy quality **2** raunchy things

☆**raun·chy** (rôn′chē, rän′-) ***adj.*** **-chi·er, -chi·est** ⟦< ?⟧ [Informal] **1** of poor quality, appearance, etc.; dirty, cheap, sloppy, etc. **2** frankly and crudely sexual in content or tone; earthy, risqué, etc. —**raun′chi·ness *n.***

Rau·schen·berg (rou′shən bərg), **Robert** 1925-2008; U.S. artist whose work combines elements of painting & sculpture

rau·wol·fi·a (rô wo͝ol′fē ə, rou-) ***n.*** ⟦ModL, after L. *Rauwolf,* 16th-c. Ger botanist⟧ **1** any of a genus (*Rauwolfia*) of tropical, mostly poisonous, trees and shrubs of the dogbane family, some of which contain medicinal substances **2** the powdered whole root of a plant (*Rauwolfia serpentina*) yielding various alkaloids, esp. reserpine

rav·age (rav′ij) ***n.*** ⟦Fr < OFr *ravir:* see RAVISH⟧ **1** the act or practice of violently destroying; destruction **2** [*usually pl.*] ruin; devastating damage [the *ravages* of time] —***vt.*** **-aged, -ag·ing** ⟦Fr *ravager* < the ***n.***⟧ to destroy violently; ruin —***vi.*** to commit ravages —**rav′ag·er *n.***

SYN.—**ravage** implies violent destruction, usually in a series of depredations or over an extended period of time, as by an army or a plague; **devastate** stresses the total ruin and desolation resulting from a ravaging; **plunder** refers to the forcible taking of loot by an invading or conquering army; **sack** and **pillage** both specifically suggest violent destruction and plunder by an invading or conquering army, **sack** implying the total stripping of all valuables in a city or town; **despoil** is equivalent to **sack** but is usually used with reference to buildings, institutions, etc.

rave (rāv) ***vi.*** **raved, rav′ing** ⟦ME *raven,* prob. < OFr *raver,* var. of *rever, resver,* to roam (> Fr *rêver,* to dream) < ? *re-*, RE- + **esver,* to roam, wander < VL **exvagare,* for L *evagari,* to roam about (< *e-*, for *ex-*, out + *vagari*): see VAGARY⟧ **1** to talk incoherently or wildly, as in a delirious or demented state **2** to talk with great or excessive enthusiasm (*about*) **3** to rage or roar, as a storm —***vt.*** to utter incoherently —***n.*** **1** an act or instance of raving **2** a raving action or speech **3** a kind of loosely organized dance party, lasting through the night, that originated in Britain in the 1980s: a rave features TECHNO music and typically includes the use of psychedelic drugs ☆**4** [Informal] an extremely or excessively enthusiastic commendation: often used attributively

rav·el (rav′əl) ***vt.*** **-eled** or **-elled, -el·ing** or **-el·ling** ⟦MDu *ravelen* (Du *rafelen*), akin to LowG *rabbeln,* Dan dial. *vrøvle:* for IE base see RHAPSODY⟧ **1** [Now Rare] to make complicated or tangled [parts of his argument were all *raveled* up] **2** to separate the parts, esp. threads, of; untwist; unweave; unravel **3** to make clear; disentangle —***vi.*** **1** to become separated into its parts, esp. threads; become unwoven; fray (*out*) **2** [Archaic] to become complicated or tangled —***n.*** **1** a raveled part in a fabric; raveling **2** a tangled mass or complication —**rav′el·er *n.*, rav′el·ler**

Ra·vel (rə vel′), **Mau·rice (Joseph)** (mō rēs′) 1875-1937; Fr. composer

rav·el·ing or **rav·el·ling** (rav′ə liŋ, rav′liŋ) ***n.*** **1** the act of something that ravels or is raveled **2** anything raveled; esp., a thread raveled from knitted or woven material

rav·el·ment (rav′əl mənt) ***n.*** a raveling or becoming raveled; esp., entanglement or complication

ra·ven[1] (rā′vən) ***n.*** ⟦ME < OE *hræfn,* akin to ON *hrafn,* Ger *rabe* < IE echoic base **ker-*, **kor-*, imitative of harsh sounds > Gr *korax,* L *corvus,* raven: so named from its cry⟧ any of various large crows; esp., the largest crow (*Corvus corax*), with a straight, sharp beak, found in Europe, Asia, and North America —***adj.*** black and lustrous

rav·en[2] (rav′ən) ***vt.*** ⟦OFr *raviner* < *ravine* < L *rapina,* RAPINE⟧ **1** to devour greedily **2** [Obs.] to seize forcibly —***vi.*** **1** to prowl hungrily; search for prey or plunder **2** to devour food or prey greedily **3** to have a voracious appetite —***n. alt. sp. of*** RAVIN

rav·en·ing (rav′ə niŋ) ***adj.*** ⟦prp. of prec.⟧ greedily searching for prey —***n.*** RAVIN

Ra·ven·na (rə ven′ə) commune in NC Italy, in Emilia-Romagna

rav·e·nous (rav′ə nəs) ***adj.*** ⟦ME *ravynous* < OFr *ravinos* < *ravine:* see RAVEN[2]⟧ **1** greedily or wildly hungry; voracious or famished **2** very eager for gratification [*ravenous* for praise] **3** very rapacious —**rav′e·nous·ly *adv.*** —**rav′e·nous·ness *n.***

rav·er (rā′vər) ***n.*** **1** a person or thing that raves **2** a person who attends a rave, esp. a person who attends raves regularly

rave-up (rāv′up′) ***n.*** [Slang] **1** [Brit.] a wild party **2** an exciting, energetic musical performance, esp. in popular music

rav·in (rav′ən) ***n.*** ⟦ME *ravine* < OFr: see RAVEN[2]⟧ **1** a violent preying or plundering; rapine **2** anything captured; prey or plunder — ***vt., vi. alt. sp. of*** RAVEN[2]

ra·vine (rə vēn′) ***n.*** ⟦Fr, violent rush, flood: see RAVEN[2]⟧ a long, deep hollow in the earth's surface, esp. one worn by the action of a stream; large gully or small gorge

rav·ing (rā′viŋ) ***adj.*** **1** raging; delirious; frenzied ☆**2** [Informal] exciting great admiration or praise; notable [*a raving* beauty] —***adv.*** so as to cause raving [*raving* mad] —***n.*** delirious, incoherent speech

ra·vi·o·li (rav′ē ō′lē) ***n.*** ⟦It dial., pl. of *raviolo,* dim. of *rava,* for It *rapa,* turnip < L *rapum,* turnip, beet: see RAPE[2]⟧ **1** pasta in the form of small casings of dough, often square, filled with seasoned ground meat, cheese, etc., boiled, and served in broth or with a sauce **2** *pl.* **-li** or **-lis** one of these filled casings

rav·ish (rav′ish) ***vt.*** ⟦ME *ravishen* < inflectional stem of OFr *ravir,* to carry away < VL **rapire,* for L *rapere,* to seize: see RAPE[1]⟧ **1** to seize and carry away forcibly **2** to rape (a woman) **3** to transport with joy or delight; enrapture —**rav′ish·er *n.*** —**rav′ish·ment *n.***

rav·ish·ing (-iŋ) ***adj.*** causing great joy or delight; entrancing —**rav′ish·ing·ly *adv.***

raw (rô) ***adj.*** ⟦ME *rawe* < OE *hreaw,* akin to Ger *roh* < IE base **kreu-*, clotted blood, bloody flesh > L *crusta,* lit., congealed blood: see CRUDE, CRUEL⟧ **1** not cooked **2** in its natural condition; not changed by art, dilution, manufacture, aging, etc. [*raw* wool, *raw* whiskey] **3** not processed, edited, interpreted, etc. [*raw* data] **4** not yet processed, cleaned, etc. as by chemical treatment; untreated [*raw* sewage] **5** inexperienced; not yet developed or trained [*a raw* recruit] **6** with the skin rubbed or torn off; sore and inflamed [*a raw* cut] **7** uncomfortably cold and damp; bleak [*a raw* wind] ☆**8** *a)* brutal or coarse in frankness *b)* indecent; bawdy **9** [Informal] harsh or unfair [*a raw* deal] —***n.*** [Rare] a raw or inflamed spot on the body —**in the raw 1** in the natural state; without cultivation, refinement, etc. ☆**2** naked; nude —**raw′ly *adv.*** —**raw′ness *n.***

Ra·wal·pin·di (rä′wəl pin′dē) city in NE Pakistan

raw bar a restaurant or counter at which uncooked shellfish are served

raw·boned (rô′bōnd′) ***adj.*** lean; gaunt

raw·hide (-hīd′) ***n.*** **1** an untanned or only partially tanned cattle hide ☆**2** a whip, cord, etc. made of this —☆***vt.*** **-hid′ed, -hid′ing** to beat or drive with such a whip

☆**ra·win** (rā′win) ***n.*** ⟦< *ra(dio) win(d)*⟧ **1** a method of observing upper-air currents, using signals from a specially designed balloon equipped with radar or a radio-direction finder **2** the winds so observed

☆**ra·win·sonde** (-sänd′) ***n.*** ⟦prec. + (RADIO)SONDE⟧ a method of observing the upper-air conditions, including wind direction and speed, temperature, pressure, and relative humidity, using signals from a radiosonde that is being tracked with radar or a radio-direction finder

raw material 1 material still in its natural or original state, before processing or manufacture **2** anything that is capable of being processed, converted, changed, etc. to produce something else [her personal experiences could provide the *raw material* for a really good novel]

raw silk 1 silk reeled from the cocoon, with the sericin still in it **2** a silk fabric of a slub weave, used for suits, etc.

ray[1] (rā) ***n.*** ⟦OFr *rai* < L *radius:* see RADIUS⟧ **1** *a)* any of the thin lines, or beams, of light that appear to come from a bright source *b)* a graphic representation of one of these, as in heraldry **2** *a)* any of several lines radiating from a center; radius *b)* any straight line that extends from a point **3** a disclosure of mental or spiritual enlightenment [*a ray* of intelligence] **4** a tiny amount; slight trace [*a ray* of hope] **5** *Bot. a)* RAY FLOWER *b)* any of the pedicels, or flower stalks, of an umbel *c)* a medullary ray **6** *Physics a)* a stream of particles given off by a radioactive substance *b)* any of the particles in such a stream *c)* a straight line along which any part of a wave of radiant energy is regarded as traveling from its source to any given point *d)* a beam of radiant energy of very small diameter **7** *Zool. a)* any of the bony spines supporting the fin membrane of a fish *b)* any of the sectors of a radially symmetrical animal, as a starfish —***vi.*** **1** to shine forth in rays **2** to radiate —***vt.*** **1** to send out in rays; emit **2** to supply with rays or radiating lines —**ray′less *adj.*** —**ray′like′ *adj.***

ray[2] (rā) ***n.*** ⟦ME < MFr *raie* < L *raia*⟧ any of several orders (esp. Rajiformes) of cartilaginous fishes with a horizontally flat body, both eyes on the upper surface, widely expanded fins at each side, and a slender or whiplike tail, as the eagle rays, electric rays, and skates

Ray[1] (rā) ***n.*** a masculine name: see RAYMOND

Ray[2] (rā; *for 2* rī, rā) **1 Man** (born *Emmanuel Radnitsky*) 1890-1976; U.S. painter & photographer **2 Sat·ya·jit** (sät yä′jēt, -jit) 1921-92; Indian film writer & director

ray flower any of the flowers around the margin of the flower head of certain composite plants, as the daisy or aster: also **ray floret**

Ray·leigh (rā′lē), 3d Baron (*John William Strutt*) 1842-1919; Eng. physicist

Rayleigh scattering ⟦after prec.⟧ a type of scattering that occurs when light waves pass through particles that are smaller than the wavelength: this type of scattering in the atmosphere makes the sky appear blue

Rayleigh wave ⟦after Baron RAYLEIGH, who first described them⟧ any of the undulating surface waves present in a solid having uniform properties; esp., any such wave on the earth's surface, caused by an earthquake

Ray·mond (rā′mənd) ***n.*** ⟦NormFr *Raimund* < Frank *Raginmund,* lit., wise protection < Gmc **ragina-*, counsel (as in Goth *ragin,* judgment) + **mund-*, hand, protection (as in OHG *munt*)⟧ a masculine name: dim. *Ray;* fem. *Ramona*

Ray·naud's phenomenon (rā nōz′) ⟦after M. *Raynaud* (1834-81), Fr physician⟧ a secondary circulatory disorder, often associated with a primary vascular disease, characterized by changes of blood flow resulting in white, bluish, or red hands and feet: as a primary disorder caused by cold or emotion it is known as **Raynaud's disease**

☆**ray·on** (rā′än′) *n.* ⟦arbitrary coinage suggested by RAY[1] as descriptive of its sheen + *-on* as in COTTON⟧ **1** any of various textile fibers synthetically produced by pressing cellulose acetate or some other cellulose solution through very small holes and solidifying it in the form of filaments **2** any of various woven or knitted fabrics made of such fibers

raze (rāz) *vt.* **razed, raz′ing** ⟦ME *rasen* < OFr *raser* < VL **rasare,* to shave, scrape, freq. < L *rasus,* pp. of *radere,* to scrape: see RAT⟧ **1** [Archaic] to scrape or graze; wound slightly **2** [Now Rare] to scrape or shave off; erase **3** to tear down completely; level to the ground; demolish —*SYN.* DESTROY

ra·zee (rā zē′) *n.* ⟦Fr *rasé* (as in *vaisseau rasé,* leveled vessel), pp. of *raser,* to level, scrape: see prec.⟧ a wooden warship made lower by the removal of the upper deck —*vt.* **-zeed′, -zee′ing** to remove the upper deck of (a warship)

ra·zor (rā′zər) *n.* ⟦ME *rasour* < OFr < *raser:* see RAZE⟧ **1** a sharp-edged cutting instrument for shaving off or cutting hair: cf. STRAIGHT RAZOR, SAFETY RAZOR **2** SHAVER (sense 2)

ra·zor·back (-bak′) *n.* **1** a wild hog, originating from domestic stock, of the S U.S., with a slender body, a ridged back, and long legs **2** a rorqual whale **3** a sharp, narrow ridge

ra·zor·bill (-bil′) *n.* an auk (*Alca torda*) of the N Atlantic coasts, with sooty black head and neck, white breast and belly, and a black, compressed bill encircled by a white band: its wings are black as seen from above and white as seen from below

☆**razor clam** any of several rapidly burrowing clams (esp. family Solenidae) of sandy beaches, having elongated, narrow shells somewhat resembling a straight razor

razor wire wire with sharp cutting edges or fitted with sharp spurs, typically extended in coils for use as a barrier

☆**razz** (raz) [Slang] *vt.* ⟦contr. < RASPBERRY⟧ to tease, ridicule, deride, heckle, etc. —*n.* RASPBERRY (sense 3)

☆**raz·zle-daz·zle** (raz′əl daz′əl) *n.* ⟦redupl. of DAZZLE⟧ [Slang] a flashy display intended to confuse, bewilder, or deceive

☆**razz·ma·tazz** (raz′mə taz′) *n.* ⟦prob. altered < prec.⟧ [Slang] **1** lively spirit; excitement **2** flashy quality or display; showiness

Rb *Chem. symbol for* rubidium

RB *abbrev. Football* running back: sometimes written **rb**

RBC *abbrev.* **1** red blood cell **2** red blood (cell) count

☆**RBI** or **rbi** (är′bē′ī′, *sometimes* rib′ē) *n., pl.* **RBIs** or **RBI, rbi's** or **rbi** ⟦*r(un) b(atted) i(n)*⟧ a run driven in by a batter: an official statistic

RC *abbrev.* **1** Red Cross **2** remote control **3** Roman Catholic

RCAF *abbrev.* Royal Canadian Air Force

RC Ch *abbrev.* Roman Catholic Church

rcd *abbrev.* received

RCMP *abbrev.* Royal Canadian Mounted Police

r-col·or (är′kul′ər) *n. Phonet.* an *r*-like acoustic quality given to a vowel, produced by retroflex articulation

RCP *abbrev.* Royal College of Physicians

rcpt *abbrev.* receipt

RCS *abbrev.* Royal College of Surgeons

Rct *abbrev. U.S. Army* Recruit

rd *abbrev.* **1** rod **2** round **3** rutherford(s)

Rd *abbrev.* Road

RD *abbrev.* **1** *Banking* refer to drawer: also **R/D** **2** registered dietitian: also R.D. **3** Rural Delivery

RDA *abbrev.* Recommended Daily (*or* Dietary) Allowance: the amount of protein, vitamins, etc. suggested for various age groups by the National Food and Nutrition Board

re[1] (rā) *n.* ⟦It < L *re(sonare):* see GAMUT⟧ *Music* a syllable representing the second tone of the diatonic scale: see SOLFEGGIO

re[2] (rē, rā) *prep.* ⟦L, abl. of *res,* thing: see REAL[1]⟧ in the matter of; as regards: short for IN RE

Re[1] *abbrev.* rupee

Re[2] *Chem. symbol for* rhenium

RE *abbrev.* **1** Reformed Episcopal **2** Right Excellent

re- (rē, ri, rə) ⟦< Fr or L: Fr *re-, ré-* < L *re-, red-,* back, backward⟧ *prefix* **1** back, returning to a previous state [*return, relapse, recall*] **2** again, anew, over again [*refurbish, recount, regelation*] It is used with a hyphen: 1) to distinguish between a word in which the prefix means simply "again" or "anew" and a word of similar form having a special meaning or meanings [*re-collect, recollect*] 2) to avoid ambiguity in the formation of nonce words [*re-urge*] 3) esp. previously, before elements beginning with *e* [*re-examine,* now usually *reexamine*] The list at the bottom of this and the following pages contains some of the more common words in which *re-* means simply *again* or *anew* Words with special meanings are entered in their proper alphabetical places in the vocabulary

-'re *suffix* are: used in contractions, sometimes very informally [*they're* not here; *what're* you doing?]

reach (rēch) *vt.* ⟦ME *rechen* < OE *ræcan,* akin to Ger *reichen* < IE **rēiĝ-,* to stretch out, extend the hand, akin to base **reĝ-,* straight, stretch, direct > RIGHT⟧ **1** to thrust out or extend (the hand, etc.) **2** to extend to, or touch, by thrusting out, throwing something, etc. **3** to obtain and hand over [*reach* me the salt] **4** to go as far as; attain [to *reach* town by night] **5** to carry as far as; penetrate to [the news *reached* him late] **6** to add up to; come to [to *reach* thousands of dollars] **7** to have influence on; affect; impress **8** to get in touch with, as by telephone —*vi.* **1** to thrust out the hand, foot, etc. **2** to stretch, or be extended, in amount, influence, space, time, etc. [power that *reaches* into other lands] **3** to be added; amount (with *to* or *into*) **4** to carry; penetrate, as sight, sound, etc. **5** to try to obtain something; make an attempt **6** to try too hard to make a point, joke, etc. **7** *Naut.* to sail on a reach —*n.* **1** the act of stretching or thrusting out **2** the power of stretching, obtaining, etc. **3** the distance or extent covered in stretching, obtaining, influencing, etc. **4** a continuous, uninterrupted extent or stretch [a vast *reach* of still water] ☆**5** a pole joining the rear axle to the forward part of a wagon **6** any of the levels of importance or distinction in a group or organization; echelon: *usually used in pl.* [the upper *reaches* of society] **7** [Informal] a belief, action, etc. that is unreasonable or questionable [it's a *reach* to think of such a fool as president] **8** *Naut.* a tack sailed with the wind coming more or less from abeam: it may be a **close reach,** with the wind forward of the beam; a **beam reach,** with the wind abeam; or a **broad reach,** with the wind abaft the beam —**reach′a·ble** *adj.* —**reach′er** *n.*

SYN.—**reach,** the broadest of these terms, implies an arriving at some goal, destination, point in development, etc. [he's *reached* the age of 60]; **gain** suggests the exertion of considerable effort to reach some goal [they've *gained* the top of the hill]; **achieve** suggests the use of skill in reaching something [we've *achieved* a great victory]; **attain** suggests a being goaded on by great ambition to gain an end regarded as beyond the reach of most persons [she has *attained* great fame in her profession]; **accomplish** implies success in completing an assigned task [to *accomplish* an end] See also **range**

reach-me-down (-mē doun′) [Informal, Chiefly Brit.] *adj.* **1** ready-made **2** not original; hackneyed —*n.* [*pl.*] second-hand or ready-made clothing

re·act (rē akt′) *vi.* ⟦< LL *reactus,* pp. of *reagere* < L *re-,* again + *agere,* to ACT[1]⟧ **1** to act in return or reciprocally **2** to act in opposition **3** to act in a reverse way; go back to a former condition, stage, etc. **4** to respond to a stimulus; be affected by some influence, event, etc. **5** *Chem.* to act with another substance in producing a chemical change —*vt.* to cause to react; specif., to produce a chemical change in

re-act (rē′akt′) *vt.* to act or do again

re·act·ance (rē ak′təns) *n.* ⟦REACT + -ANCE⟧ *Elec.* opposition to the flow of alternating current in a circuit or circuit element, caused by inductance or capacitance and measured in ohms: symbol, X

re·act·ant (-tənt) *n.* any of the substances participating in a chemical reaction

re·ac·tion (rē ak′shən) *n.* **1** a return or opposing action, force, influence, etc. **2** a response, as to a stimulus or influence **3** a movement back to a former or less advanced condition, stage, etc.; esp., such a movement or tendency in economics or politics; extreme conservatism **4** *Chem. a)* the mutual action of substances undergoing chemical change *b)* a process that involves changes within the nucleus of an atom *c)* the state resulting from such changes **5** *Med. a)* an action induced by resistance to another action *b)* the effect produced by an allergen *c)* a depression or exhaustion of energy following nervous tension, overstimulation, etc. *d)* an increased activity following depression **6** *Physiol., Psychol.* an organic response to a stimulus —**re·ac′tion·al** *adj.*

re·ac·tion·ar·y (-shə ner′ē) *adj.* of, characterized by, or advocating reaction, esp. in politics —*n., pl.* **-ar′ies** a reactionary person; advocate of reaction, esp. in politics Also [Now Rare] **re·ac′tion·ist**

reaction engine an engine, as a jet or rocket engine, that generates thrust by the reaction to an ejected stream of hot exhaust gases, ions, etc.

reaction formation *Psychoanalysis* an unconscious reaction in which a feeling or trait finds expression as the exact opposite of a repressed feeling or impulse

reaction time *Psychol.* the lapse of time between stimulation and the beginning of the response

re·ac·ti·vate (rē ak′tə vāt′) *vt.* **-vat′ed, -vat′ing** **1** to make active again ☆**2** to place (an inactivated military unit, ship, etc.) back on an active status —*vi.* to be reactivated —**re·ac′ti·va′tion** *n.*

re·ac·tive (-tiv) *adj.* **1** tending to react **2** of, caused by, or showing reaction or reactance —**re·ac′tive·ly** *adv.* —**re·ac′tive·ness** *n.* —**re′ac·tiv′i·ty** *n.*

re·ac·tor (-tər) *n.* **1** a person or thing that reacts or undergoes a reaction **2** *a)* NUCLEAR REACTOR *b)* a container used for the production of chemical reactions **3** *Elec.* a device, as a coil or capacitor, inserted in a circuit to introduce reactance **4** *Med.* a person or animal having a positive reaction to a particular foreign substance

read[1] (rēd) *vt.* **read** (red), **read·ing** (rēd′iŋ) ⟦ME *reden,* to explain, hence to read < OE *rædan,* to counsel, interpret; akin to Ger *raten,* to counsel,

reabsorb
reabsorption
reaccept
reaccommodate
reaccompany
reaccredit
reaccuse
reaccustom
reacquaint
reacquaintance
reacquire
reacquisition

advise < IE **rē-dh, *rə-dh* < base **ar-, *(a)rē-*, to join, fit > ART[1], ARM[1], L *reri*, to think, *ratio*, a reckoning⟧ **1** *a)* to get the meaning of (something written, printed, embossed, etc.) by using the eyes, or for Braille, the finger tips, to interpret its characters or signs *b)* *short for* PROOFREAD **2** to utter aloud (printed or written matter) **3** to interpret movements of (the lips of a person speaking) **4** to know (a language) well enough to interpret its written form **5** *a)* to understand the nature, significance, or thinking of as if by reading [to *read* a person's character in her face, to *read* someone's mind] *b)* to ascribe (an underlying meaning or significance) to (with *into*) [don't *read* anything into his straightforward reply] **6** *a)* to interpret (signals, etc.) *b)* to interpret (dreams, omens, tea leaves, lines in the palm of a hand, etc.) **7** to foretell (the future) **8** to interpret or understand (a printed passage) as having a particular meaning **9** to interpret (a musical composition) in a particular way, as in conducting **10** to have or give as a reading in a certain passage [this edition *reads* "show," not "shew"] **11** [Brit.] to study, as at a university; esp., to major in [to *read* law] **12** to record and show; register [the thermometer *reads* 80°] **13** to put into a (specified) state by reading [to *read* a child to sleep] **14** [Slang] to hear and understand [I *read* you loud and clear] **15** *Comput.* to access (data or a file) from (a disk, tape, etc.) —*vi.* **1** to read something written, printed, etc., as words, music, books, etc. **2** to utter or repeat aloud the words of written or printed matter **3** to learn by reading: with *about* or *of* **4** to study **5** to have or give a particular meaning when read [a poem that *reads* several ways] **6** to contain, or be drawn up in, certain words [the sentence *reads* as follows] **7** to admit of being read as specified [a story that *reads* well] —*n.* **1** an act of reading [a quick *read* of the headlines] **2** something for reading [a novel that's a good *read*] **3** [Chiefly Brit.] a period of time spent reading —**read out** to display or record with a readout device —**read out of** to expel from (a political party, society, etc.) by public reading of dismissal —**read someone a lecture (**or **lesson)** to scold or reprimand someone —**read up (on)** to become well informed (about) by reading

read[2] (red) *vt., vi. pt. & pp. of* READ[1] —*adj.* having knowledge gotten from reading [she is widely *read* in American history]

Read (rēd), Sir **Herbert (Edward)** 1893-1968; Eng. art & literary critic

read·a·ble (rēd′ə bəl) *adj.* **1** interesting or easy to read **2** LEGIBLE —**read′a·bil′i·ty** *n.*, **read′a·ble·ness** —**read′a·bly** *adv.*

re·ad·dress (rē′ə dres′) *vt.* **1** to address or occupy (oneself) anew **2** to change the address on (a letter, etc.) **3** to address or speak to once more

read·er (rēd′ər) *n.* **1** a person who reads **2** a person appointed or elected to read lessons, prayers, etc. aloud in church: cf. LECTOR **3** a person who reads and evaluates manuscripts for a publication **4** *short for* PROOFREADER **5** a person who records the readings of meters, etc., as for a public utilities company: in full **meter reader** **6** *a)* a schoolbook containing stories, poems, etc. for use in teaching how to read *b)* an anthology or omnibus **7** [Brit.] a university teacher ranking below a professor: approximately equivalent to an associate professor in the U.S. **8** an assistant who reads and marks examinations, themes, etc. for a professor ☆**9** a magnifying device for viewing microfilm or a microfiche **10** one who reads, or interprets, lines in the palm of a hand, tea-leaf patterns, horoscopes, etc., as to predict the future

read·er·ship (-ship′) *n.* **1** the people who read a particular publication, author, etc. or the estimated number of these **2** the state or position of being a reader

read·i·ly (red′ə lē) *adv.* ⟦ME *redili:* see READY & -LY[2]⟧ **1** without hesitation; willingly **2** without delay; quickly **3** without difficulty; easily

read·i·ness (-ē nis) *n.* the quality or state of being ready

read·ing (rēd′iŋ) *adj.* **1** inclined to read or study **2** made or used for reading —*n.* **1** the act or practice of a person who reads; perusal, as of books **2** a public entertainment at which literary material is read aloud **3** the extent to which a person has read **4** material read or meant to be read **5** the amount measured as by a barometer or thermometer **6** the form of a specified word, sentence, or passage in a particular edition of a literary work **7** a particular interpretation or performance, as of something written or composed

Read·ing (red′iŋ) city in SC England; county seat of Berkshire

reading desk LECTERN

reading room **1** a room, as in a club or library, for reading and writing ☆**2** [R- R-] a place for religious study maintained by Christian Scientists

re·ad·just (rē′ə just′) *vt.* to adjust again; rearrange

re·ad·just·ment (-mənt) *n.* **1** a readjusting or being readjusted **2** *Finance* rearrangement of the financial structure of a corporation: cf. REORGANIZATION

read-on·ly (rēd′ōn′lē) *adj. Comput.* designating or of a file whose contents can be read or viewed, but not altered: see also ROM

read-only memory ROM

read·out (rēd′out′) *n.* **1** the act of retrieving information from storage in a digital computer **2** *a)* information taken from a computer or scientific instrument and displayed visually or recorded, typically for immediate use *b)* an electronic device for displaying such information —*adj.* of or pertaining to any device that presents data output, as in numbers, letters, etc., for immediate use

read·y (red′ē) *adj.* **read′i·er**, **read′i·est** ⟦ME *redie* < OE *ræde*, ready, prepared (for riding), akin to *ridan*, to ride, Ger *bereit*, ready, ON *greithr*, prepared, Goth *garaiths*, arranged: for IE base see RIDE⟧ **1** prepared or equipped to act or be used immediately [*ready* to go, *ready* for occupancy] **2** unhesitant; willing [a *ready* worker] **3** *a)* likely or liable immediately [*ready* to cry] *b)* apt; inclined [always *ready* to blame others] **4** clever and skillful mentally or physically; dexterous [a *ready* wit] **5** done or made without delay; prompt [a *ready* reply] **6** convenient or handy to use; available immediately [*ready* cash] **7** [Obs.] at hand; present: a response to a roll call —*vt.* **read′ied**, **read′y·ing** to get or make ready; prepare: often used reflexively —*n.* [Brit. Informal] ready money; cash at hand: usually with *the* —*SYN.* QUICK —**at the ready** in a position or state of being prepared for immediate use [to hold a gun *at the ready*] —**make ready** **1** to prepare; get in order **2** to dress

read·y-made (red′ē mād′) *adj.* **1** made so as to be ready for use or sale at once; not made-to-order [*ready-made* suits] **2** commonplace; stock [*ready-made* opinions] **3** conveniently available and suitable [no *ready-made* solutions to difficult social problems] —*n.* **1** something that is ready-made **2** ⟦orig. *Readymades*, pl.n., as used in a passage in French (1915) by Marcel DUCHAMP⟧ *Art* an ordinary, usually mass-produced object displayed as a work of art; also, a composition consisting of more than one such object

read·y-mix (-miks′) *adj.* ready to be used just as it is or after the addition of liquid [*ready-mix* concrete]

☆**ready room** a room where aircraft crews gather for briefing before flights

read·y-to-wear (-tə wer′) *n.* ready-made clothing —*adj.* of, designating, or dealing in such clothing [*ready-to-wear* fashions]

read·y-wit·ted (-wit′id) *adj.* QUICK-WITTED

Rea·gan (rā′gən), **Ronald (Wilson)** 1911-2004; 40th president of the U.S. (1981-89)

re·a·gent (rē ā′jənt) *n.* ⟦RE- + AGENT⟧ *Chem.* a substance used to detect or measure another substance or to convert one substance into another by means of the reaction which it causes

re·a·gin (rē ā′jin) *n.* ⟦< prec. + -IN[1]⟧ a type of antibody in the blood associated with some allergic diseases

re·ais (rā ish′) *n. pl. of* REAL[3] (sense 2)

re·al[1] (rē′əl, rēl) *adj.* ⟦OFr < ML *realis* < L *res*, thing < IE base **rei-*, property, thing > Sans *rai*, wealth, property⟧ **1** existing or happening as or in fact; actual, true, etc.; not merely seeming, pretended, imagined, fictitious, nominal, or ostensible **2** *a)* authentic; genuine *b)* not pretended; sincere **3** designating wages or income as measured by purchasing power **4** *Law* of or relating to permanent, immovable things [*real* property] **5** *Math.* designating or of the part of a complex number that is not imaginary: all irrational and rational numbers are real numbers **6** *Optics* of or relating to an image made by the actual meeting of light rays at a point **7** *Philos.* existing objectively; specif., *a)* actual; not merely possible or ideal *b)* essential, absolute, ultimate; not relative, derivative, etc. —*n.* anything that actually exists, or reality in general: with *the* —*adv.* [Informal] very —*SYN.* TRUE —**for real** [Slang] real or really

re·al[2] (rē′əl; *Sp* re äl′) *n., pl.* **re′als** or Sp. **re·a·les** (re ä′les) ⟦Sp & Port, lit., royal < L *regalis:* see REGAL⟧ a former monetary unit and silver coin of Spain and its possessions

re·al[3] (re äl′) *n.* **1** *sing. of* REIS **2** *pl.* **re·ais′** ⟦Port: see prec.⟧ the basic monetary unit of Brazil: see the table of monetary units in the Reference Supplement

real estate **1** land, including buildings or improvements on it and its natural assets, as water **2** the profession or work of an agent in the purchase and sale of real estate **3** the buying and selling of real estate for investment or speculation

re·al·gar (rē al′gər) *n.* ⟦ME < ML, ult. < Ar *rahj al-ghār*, lit., dust of the cave < *rahj*, dust + *al*, the + *ghār*, cave, mine: orig. obtained by mining⟧ a bright orange-red, monoclinic mineral, AsS, used in fireworks, paints, etc.; arsenic sulfide

re·a·li·a (rē ā′lē ə, rē al′ē ə) *n.* ⟦LL, neut. pl. of *realis*, real⟧ objects from everyday life, used as in teaching a foreign language

re·a·lign (rē′ə līn′) *vt., vi.* to align again; specif., to readjust alliances or working arrangements between or within (countries, political parties, etc.) —☆**re′a·lign′ment** *n.*

re·al·ism (rē′ə liz′əm) *n.* ⟦< Ger *realismus* < ModL < ML *realis*, REAL[1] + *-ismus*, -ISM⟧ **1** a tendency to face facts and be practical rather than imaginative or visionary **2** the picturing in art and literature of people and things as they really appear to be, without idealizing: see also NATURALISM (sense 2) **3** *Philos.* *a)* the doctrine that universal or abstract terms are objectively actual (opposed to NOMINALISM) *b)* the doctrine that material objects exist in themselves, apart from the mind's consciousness of them (cf. IDEALISM, sense 4*a*)

re·al·ist (-list) *n.* **1** a person concerned with real things and practical matters rather than those that are imaginary or visionary **2** a believer in or advocate of realism **3** an artist or writer whose work is characterized by realism

re·al·is·tic (rē′ə lis′tik) *adj.* **1** of, having to do with, or in the style of, realism or realists **2** tending to face facts; practical rather than visionary —**re′al·is′ti·cal·ly** *adv.*

re·al·i·ty (rē al′ə tē) *n., pl.* **-ties** ⟦ML *realitas*⟧ **1** the quality or fact of being real **2** something that is real; fact **3** the quality of being true to

readmission	readmittance	readoption	reaffiliate	reaffirmation
readmit	readopt	readorn	reaffirm	

life 4 *Philos.* that which is real —*adj.* TV designating or of programming, a show, etc. that features people, who are not actors, engaged in unscripted activity, often in contrived situations —**in reality** in fact; actually

reality check an instance of confronting or acknowledging the facts about something and thus dispelling unrealistic notions

reality principle *Psychoanalysis* the principle that the governing purpose of the ego is to satisfy the impulses of the id in realistic and socially appropriate ways: cf. PLEASURE PRINCIPLE

re·al·i·za·tion (rē′ə li zā′shən) ***n.*** 1 a realizing or being realized 2 something realized

re·al·ize (rē′ə līz′) ***vt.*** **-ized′, -iz′ing** ⟦REAL[1] (*adj.*) + -IZE, after Fr *réaliser*⟧ 1 to make real; bring into being; achieve 2 to make appear real 3 to understand fully; apprehend 4 to convert (assets, rights, etc.) into money 5 to gain; obtain [to *realize* a profit] 6 to be sold for, or bring as profit (a specified sum) —**re′al·iz′a·ble** ***adj.*** —**re′al·iz′er** ***n.***

re·al-life (rē′əl līf′) ***adj.*** actual; not imaginary

re·al·ly (rē′ə lē, rē′lē) ***adv.*** ⟦ME *rialliche:* see REAL[1] & -LY[2]⟧ 1 in reality; in fact; actually 2 truly or genuinely [a *really* hot day] —***interj.*** indeed: used to express surprise, irritation, doubt, etc.

realm (relm) ***n.*** ⟦ME *reame,* later *realme* < OFr, altered (by assoc. with *reiel* > ROYAL) < *reaume* < L *regimen,* rule: see REGIMEN⟧ 1 a kingdom 2 a region; sphere; area [the *realm* of thought] 3 *Ecol.* any of the primary biogeographic regions of the earth

real number *Math.* any rational or irrational number not having an imaginary part

re·al·po·li·tik (rā äl′pô′lə tēk′) ***n.*** ⟦Ger⟧ [*also* **R-**] foreign policy determined by expediency rather than ethics or world opinion; power politics

☆**real time** time in which the occurrence of an event and the reporting or recording of it are almost simultaneous

☆**real-time** (rēl′tīm′) ***adj.*** 1 of or pertaining to a mode of computer operation in which the computer collects data, computes with it, and uses the results to control a process as it happens 2 ⟦see prec.⟧ involving no perceptible or significant time lag, as between the transmission and reception of data [a *real-time* system for videoconferencing]

☆**Re·al·tor** (rē′əl tər, -tôr′) ⟦< fol. + -OR⟧ *service mark for* a real estate broker or appraiser who is a member of the National Association of Realtors —***n.*** [**r-**] a real estate agent

re·al·ty (rē′əl tē) ***n.*** ⟦REAL[1] + -TY[1]⟧ 1 REAL ESTATE 2 [Obs.] fidelity; honesty

real-world (rēl′wurld′) ***adj.*** in, from, or having to do with actual experience or practice, rather than being theoretical, idealistic, or impractical

ream[1] (rēm) ***n.*** ⟦ME *rem* < MFr *raime* < It *risma* < Ar *rizma,* bale, packet < *razama,* to pack together⟧ 1 a unit of measure for a quantity of paper: the quantity varies from 480 sheets (20 quires) to 516 sheets, depending on the manufacturer 2 [*pl.*] [Informal] a great amount

ream[2] (rēm) ***vt.*** ⟦ME dial. *remen* < OE *reman,* akin to *ryman,* lit., to make roomy < base of *rum:* see ROOM⟧ 1 *a)* to enlarge (a hole) as with a reamer *b)* to enlarge the bore of (a gun) 2 to countersink or taper (a hole) 3 to remove (a defect) with a reamer ☆4 to extract the juice from (a lemon, orange, etc.) 5 to use a reamer on (a pipe bowl) ☆6 [Slang] *a)* to cheat or deceive *b)* to scold; berate (often with *out*)

ream·er (-ər) ***n.*** a person or thing that reams; specif., *a)* a sharp-edged tool for enlarging or tapering holes *b)* JUICER *c)* an implement for scraping out the caked lining of a pipe bowl

re·an·i·mate (rē an′ə māt′) ***vt.*** **-mat′ed, -mat′ing** to give new life, power, vigor, courage, etc. to —**re·an′i·ma′tion** ***n.***

reap (rēp) ***vt.*** ⟦ME *repen* < OE *ripan,* akin to RIPE < IE **reib-* < base **rei-,* to tear, pull out, rend > ROW[1], RIVE⟧ 1 to cut (grain) with a scythe, sickle, or reaping machine 2 to gather (a crop, harvest, etc.) by cutting 3 to cut or harvest grain from (a field) 4 to gain or obtain as the reward of action, conduct, work, etc. —***vi.*** to reap a harvest, reward, etc.

reap·er (rēp′ər) ***n.*** ⟦ME *reper* < OE *ripere*⟧ 1 a person who reaps 2 a machine for reaping grain —**the (Grim) Reaper** death: often personified as a shrouded skeleton bearing a scythe

re·ap·por·tion (rē′ə pôr′shən) ***vt.*** to apportion again; specif., to change the geographical distribution of (a legislature) so that each legislator represents approximately the same number of constituents —**re′ap·por′tion·ment** ***n.***

re·ap·praise (rē′ə prāz′) ***vt.*** **-praised′, -prais′ing** to make a fresh appraisal of; reconsider —**re′ap·prais′al** ***n.***

rear[1] (rir) ***n.*** ⟦prob. back-form. < REARWARD[1], REAR GUARD⟧ 1 the back or hind part of something 2 the place or position behind or at the back [at the *rear* of the house] 3 the part of a military or naval force farthest from the enemy ☆4 [Slang] the buttocks —***adj.*** of, at, or in the rear [a *rear* entrance] —**bring up the rear** to come at the end, as of a procession; be last in order

rear[2] (rir) ***vt.*** ⟦ME *reren* < OE *rǣran,* caus. of *risan,* to RISE⟧ 1 to put upright; elevate 2 to build; erect 3 to grow or breed (animals or plants) 4 to bring up by educating, nurturing, training, etc.; raise [to *rear* a child] —***vi.*** 1 to rise or stand on the hind legs: said as of a horse 2 to rise (*up*), as in anger 3 to rise high, as a mountain peak —***SYN.*** LIFT

rear admiral *U.S. Navy* an officer ranking above a commodore and below a vice admiral

rear end 1 the back part of something 2 [Slang] the buttocks

rear-end (rir′end′) ***vt.*** to crash into, or cause one's vehicle to crash into, the back end of (another vehicle)

rear·guard (rir′gärd′) ***adj.*** of or relating to resistance against something, as prevailing opinion or the action of a dominant political force, regarded as unlikely to be overcome or avoided

rear guard ⟦ME *rier garde* < Anglo-Fr *reregard* < OFr < *riere,* backward (< L *retro:* see RETRO-) + *gard,* GUARD⟧ a military detachment to protect the rear of a main force or body

re·arm (rē ärm′) ***vt., vi.*** 1 to arm again 2 to arm with new or more effective weapons —**re·ar′ma·ment** ***n.***

rear·most (rir′mōst′) ***adj.*** farthest in the rear; last

re·ar·range (rē′ə rānj′) ***vt.*** **-ranged′, -rang′ing** 1 to arrange again 2 to arrange in a different manner

re·ar·range·ment (-mənt) ***n.*** 1 a rearranging or being rearranged 2 a new arrangement 3 *Chem.* a redistribution of atoms or atomic groups within a molecule, forming the molecule of a different substance

rear·view mirror (rir′vyo͞o′) a mirror in or on a vehicle that allows the driver to view the area behind the vehicle

rear·ward[1] (rir′wôrd′) ***n.*** ⟦ME *rerewarde* < Anglo-Fr: see REAR GUARD & WARD⟧ *archaic var. of* REAR[1]

rear·ward[2] (-wərd) ***adj.*** ⟦REAR[1] + -WARD⟧ at, in, or toward the rear —***adv.*** backward; toward the rear: also **rear′wards** (-wərdz)

rear-wheel drive (rir′hwēl′, -wēl′) an automotive power delivery system that provides driving power only to the rear wheels

rea·son (rē′zən) ***n.*** ⟦ME *reisun* < OFr < L *ratio,* a reckoning, reason: see READ[1]⟧ 1 an explanation or justification of an act, idea, etc. 2 a cause or motive 3 the ability to think, form judgments, draw conclusions, etc. 4 sound thought or judgment; good sense 5 normal mental powers; a sound mind; sanity —***vi.*** 1 to think coherently and logically; draw inferences or conclusions from facts known or assumed 2 to argue or talk in a logical way —***vt.*** 1 to think logically about; think out systematically; analyze 2 to argue, conclude, or infer: now usually with a clause introduced by *that* as the object 3 to support, justify, etc. with reasons 4 to persuade or bring by reasoning (*into* or *out of*) —***SYN.*** CAUSE, THINK[1] —**by reason of** because of —**in** (or **within**) **reason** in accord with what is reasonable —**out of all reason** unreasonable —**with reason** justifiably; rightly

rea·son·a·ble (-ə bəl) ***adj.*** ⟦ME *raisonable* < OFr < L *rationabilis*⟧ 1 able to reason 2 amenable to reason; just 3 using or showing reason, or sound judgment; sensible 4 *a)* not extreme, immoderate, or excessive *b)* not expensive —***SYN.*** RATIONAL —**rea′son·a·ble·ness** ***n.*** —**rea′son·a·bly** ***adv.***

rea·son·ing (-iŋ) ***n.*** 1 the drawing of inferences or conclusions from known or assumed facts; use of reason 2 the proofs or reasons resulting from this

rea·son·less (-lis) ***adj.*** 1 not having the ability to reason 2 not reasonable; illogical or senseless —**rea′son·less·ly** ***adv.***

re·as·sure (rē′ə sho͝or′) ***vt.*** **-sured′, -sur′ing** 1 to assure again; repeat a confident declaration or promise 2 to restore the confidence of 3 [Brit.] REINSURE —**re′as·sur′ance** (-əns) ***n.*** —**re′as·sur′ing·ly** ***adv.***

re·a·ta (rē ät′ə) ***n.*** *alt. sp. of* RIATA

Re·au·mur or **Ré·au·mur** (rā′ə myo͝or′; *Fr* rā ō mür′) ***adj.*** ⟦after R. A. F. de *Réaumur* (1683-1757), Fr physicist & naturalist⟧ designating or of a temperature scale which registers the boiling point of water at 80° and the freezing point at 0°

reave[1] (rēv) ***vt.*** **reaved** or **reft, reav′ing** ⟦ME *reven* < OE *reafian,* akin to Ger *rauben,* to ROB⟧ [Archaic] to take away by violence; seize; rob

reave[2] (rēv) ***vt.*** **reaved** or **reft, reav′ing** ⟦ME *reven,* altered (by assoc. with *reven:* see prec.) < ON *rifa,* to tear < IE **reip-,* var. of base **rei-* > L *rima,* a crack⟧ [Archaic] to break, split, tear, or the like

☆**reb** (reb) ***n.*** [*often* **R-**] *short for* REBEL (*n.* 3)

Reb (reb) ***n.*** ⟦Yiddish *reb* < *rebe* < Heb *rabi:* see RABBI⟧ a Jewish title of respect equivalent to *Mister:* used with the given name

re·bap·tize (rē bap′tīz′) ***vt.*** **-tized′, -tiz′ing** ⟦LL(Ec) *rebaptizare*⟧ 1 to baptize again 2 to give a new name to —**re·bap′tism′** ***n.***

re·bar (rē′bär′) ***n.*** ⟦< *re(inforcing) bar*⟧ 1 framework of ribbed bars of steel, designed to reinforce a block or slab of concrete from within 2 one such bar

---

realliance
reallocation
reallot
re-ally
reanalyze
reannex
reanoint
reappear
reappearance
reapplication
reapply
reappoint
reappointment
reargue
rearouse
rearrest
reascend
reassemble
reassembly
reassert
reassertion
reassess
reassign
reassimilate
reassociate
reassume
reassumption
reattach
reattack
reattain
reattempt
reauthenticate
reauthorize
reavail
reawaken

re·bar·ba·tive (ri bär′bə tiv) *adj.* ⟦Fr *rébarbatif* < MFr < *(se) rebarber,* to resist, earlier to face (the enemy), lit., to face beard-to-beard < *barbe,* beard < L *barba*⟧ repellent, unattractive, forbidding, grim, etc.

re·bate¹ (rē′bāt′; *also, for v.,* ri bāt′) *vt.* **-bat′ed, -bat′ing** ⟦ME *rebaten* < OFr *rabattre* < *re-,* RE- + *abattre:* see ABATE⟧ **1** *a)* to give back (part of an amount paid) *b)* to make a deduction from (a bill) *c)* to give a rebate to **2** [Rare] to reduce; lessen **3** [Archaic] to make dull; blunt —*vi.* to give rebates —*n.* ⟦Fr *rabat* < the v.⟧ a return of part of an amount paid, as for goods or services, serving as a reduction or discount

re·bate² (rē′bāt′, rab′it) *n., vt.* **-bat′ed, -bat′ing** *var. of* RABBET

re·ba·to (rə bät′ō) *n. var. of* RABATO

reb·be (reb′e) *n.* ⟦Yiddish < Heb *rabi,* RABBI⟧ **1** a highly venerated spiritual leader or teacher, esp. of a Hasidic sect **2** a teacher in a Jewish school, as a yeshiva

reb·bet·zin (reb′i tsin) *n.* ⟦Yiddish, fem. of prec.⟧ the wife of a rabbi

re·bec or **re·beck** (rē′bek′) *n.* ⟦Fr, altered < OFr *rebebe* < Ar *rabāb*⟧ a three-stringed, pear-shaped musical instrument played with a bow: a precursor of the violin, used during the Middle Ages

Re·bec·ca (ri bek′ə) *n.* ⟦LL(Ec) < Gr(Ec) *Rhebekka* < Heb *rivka,* lit., noose, connection⟧ **1** a feminine name: dim. *Becky, Reba* **2** *Bible* the wife of Isaac and mother of Jacob and Esau: Gen 25:20: usually sp. **Re·bek′ah**

reb·el (reb′əl; *for v.,* ri bel′) *n.* ⟦ME < OFr *rebelle* < L *rebellis,* rebel, rebellious < *rebellare:* see the *vi.*⟧ **1** one who engages in armed resistance against the established government of one's country **2** a person who resists authority or convention ☆**3** [*often* **R-**] *name for* a Confederate soldier in the Civil War: term used chiefly by Northerners —*adj.* **1** rebellious **2** of rebels —*vi.* **re·bel′, -belled′, -bel′ling** ⟦ME *rebellen* < OFr *rebeller* < L *rebellare* < *re-,* again + *bellare,* to wage war < *bellum,* war: see DUEL⟧ **1** to be a rebel against the established government of one's country **2** to resist authority or convention [to *rebel* against one's parents] **3** to feel or show strong aversion; be repelled [his mind *rebels* at the thought]

reb·el·dom (reb′əl dəm) *n.* **1** any area held by rebels ☆**2** [*often* **R-**] the Confederate States during the Civil War

re·bel·lion (ri bel′yən) *n.* ⟦ME < MFr < L *rebellio:* see REBEL⟧ **1** an act or state of armed resistance to one's government **2** a defiance of or opposition to any kind of authority or control

re·bel·lious (ri bel′yəs) *adj.* ⟦ME *rebellous*⟧ **1** resisting authority; engaged in rebellion **2** of or like rebels or rebellion **3** opposing any kind of control; defiant **4** difficult to treat or handle [a *rebellious* cowlick] —**re·bel′lious·ly** *adv.* —**re·bel′lious·ness** *n.*

re·birth (rē burth′, rē′burth′) *n.* **1** a new or second birth, as through reincarnation or spiritual regeneration **2** a reawakening; renaissance; revival

reb·o·ant (reb′ō ənt) *adj.* ⟦L *reboans,* prp. of *reboare,* to resound < *re-,* back + *boare,* to bellow, roar < Gr *boan* < IE echoic base **bu-*⟧ [Old Poet.] loudly reverberating

re·boot (rē bo͞ot′) *vi., vt.* **1** *Comput.* to boot again, as to restore the computer to operation after a program failure **2** [Informal] to do over or remake (something) —*n.* [Informal] the act or an instance of rebooting

re·born (rē bôrn′) *adj.* born again; having new life, spirit, etc.; regenerated

re·bound (rē′bound′; *for v., also* ri bound′) *vi.* ⟦ME *rebounden* < OFr *rebondir*⟧ **1** to bound back; spring back upon impact with something **2** to reecho or reverberate **3** to leap or spring, as in recovery [his spirits *rebounded*] ☆**4** *Basketball* to seize a REBOUND (*n.* 2a) —*vt.* **1** to make bound or spring back **2** to return (a sound) —*n.* **1** the act or an instance of rebounding; recoil **2** *Sports* ☆*a)* a basketball that bounces off the backboard or basket rim, or a hockey puck that bounds back after an attempted goal *b)* a play made by recovering such a rebound —**on the rebound 1** after it bounces off the ground, a wall, etc. **2** immediately after and while reacting strongly to a rejection, as in love

☆**re·bo·zo** (ri bō′zō; *Sp* re bô′thô, -sô) *n., pl.* **-zos** (-zōz; *Sp,* -thôs, -sôs) ⟦Sp, a shawl < *rebozar,* to muffle < *re-* (< L, RE-) + *bozo,* mouth, akin to *boca,* mouth, ult. < L *bucca:* see BUCCAL⟧ in Spain and some Spanish American countries, a long scarf worn by women around the head and shoulders

re·broad·cast (rē brôd′kast′, -käst′) *vt., vi.* **re·broad′cast′** or, in radio, occas. **re·broad′cast′ed, re·broad′cast′ing 1** to broadcast again **2** to broadcast (a program, etc. received in a relay system from another station) —*n.* **1** the act of rebroadcasting **2** a program, etc. that is being or has been rebroadcast

re·buff (ri buf′) *n.* ⟦MFr *rebuffe* < It *rabbuffo* < *rabbuffare,* to disarrange, altered by metathesis (prob. infl. by *buffare,* to blow) < *baruffare,* to scuffle < Langobardic **biraufan,* akin to OHG *biroufan,* to tussle, pluck out⟧ **1** an abrupt, blunt refusal of offered advice, help, etc. **2** any check or repulse —*vt.* **1** to refuse bluntly; snub **2** to check or repulse

re·build (rē bild′) *vt.* **-built′, -build′ing 1** to build anew **2** to restore to a previous condition **3** to repair or remodel extensively, as by taking apart and reconstructing, often with new parts —*vi.* to build again

re·buke (ri byo͞ok′) *vt.* **-buked′, -buk′ing** ⟦ME *rebuken* < Anglo-Fr *rebuker* < OFr *rebuchier* < *re-,* back + *buchier,* to beat < *buche,* stick, billet < Gmc **buska*⟧ **1** to blame or scold in a sharp way; reprimand **2** [Obs.] to force back —*n.* a sharp reprimand —**re·buk′er** *n.*

re·bus (rē′bəs) *n.* ⟦Fr *rébus* < L, abl. pl. of *res,* thing (see REAL¹), lit., (meaning indicated) by things⟧ a kind of puzzle consisting of pictures of objects, signs, letters, etc., the combination of whose names suggests words or phrases [a picture of an eye followed by an L followed by an ampersand is a *rebus* for "island"]

re·but (ri but′) *vt.* **-but′ted, -but′ting** ⟦ME *rebuten* < Anglo-Fr *reboter* < OFr *rebuter* < *re-,* back + *buter,* to thrust, push: see BUTT²⟧ **1** to contradict, refute, or oppose, esp. in a formal manner by argument, proof, etc., as in a debate **2** [Obs.] to force back; repel —*vi.* to provide opposing arguments —*SYN.* DISPROVE —**re·but′ta·ble** *adj.*

re·but·tal (-but′'l) *n.* a rebutting, esp. in law

re·but·ter (-but′ər) *n.* **1** a person or thing that rebuts **2** ⟦n. use of Anglo-Fr *reboter:* see REBUT⟧ *Law* a defendant's reply to a plaintiff's surrejoinder

☆**rec¹** (rek) *n. short for* RECREATION: used in compounds, as **rec room, rec hall**

rec² *abbrev.* **1** receipt **2** recipe **3** record(ed) **4** recording

re·cal·ci·trant (ri kal′si trənt) *adj.* ⟦L *recalcitrans,* prp. of *recalcitrare,* to kick back (in LL, to disobey) < *re-,* back + *calcitrare,* to kick < *calx,* heel: see CALCAR⟧ **1** refusing to obey authority, custom, regulation, etc.; stubbornly defiant **2** hard to handle or deal with —*n.* a recalcitrant person —**re·cal′ci·trance** *n.,* **re·cal′ci·tran·cy** —**re·cal′ci·trant·ly** *adv.*

re·cal·ci·trate (-trāt′) *vt.* **-trat′ed, -trat′ing** ⟦L *recalcitrare:* see prec.⟧ [Rare] to refuse to obey; be stubborn in opposition —**re·cal′ci·tra′tion** *n.*

re·cal·cu·late (rē kal′kyə lāt′) *vt.* **-lat′ed, -lat′ing** to calculate again, esp. in order to detect and correct an error —**re·cal′cu·la′tion** *n.*

re·ca·les·cence (rē′kə les′əns) *n.* ⟦< L *recalescens,* prp. of *recalescere,* to grow hot again < *re-,* again + *calescere,* to grow hot < *calere,* to be warm: see CALORIE⟧ a sudden and temporary increase in glow and temperature of hot iron or steel when it reaches one or more particular temperatures in the cooling process —**re′ca·les′cent** *adj.*

re·call (ri kôl′; *also, & for n. & vt. 4 usually,* rē′kôl′) *vt.* **1** to call back; ask or order to return; specif., to ask purchasers to return (an imperfect or dangerous product), often so that a manufacturing defect can be corrected **2** to bring back to mind; remember **3** to take back; cancel; annul; revoke; withdraw ☆**4** to remove from office by the process of recall **5** to bring (the mind, attention, etc.) back, as to the immediate situation **6** [Old Poet.] to revive —*n.* **1** the act of recalling **2** the ability to remember; memory **3** *Mil.* a signal, as on a bugle or drum, calling soldiers back to camp or ranks ☆**4** the process of removing, or right to remove, an official from office by popular vote, usually after using petitions to call for such a vote —**re·call′a·ble** *adj.*

ré·ca·mier (rā kȧ myā′) *n.* ⟦after fol.⟧ [*occas.* **R-**] a type of couch, usually backless, with gracefully scrolled ends

Ré·ca·mier (rā kȧ myā′), Madame (born *Jeanne Françoise Julie Adelaïde Bernard*) 1777-1849; Fr. social leader in intellectual & literary circles

re·cant (ri kant′) *vt., vi.* ⟦L *recantare* < *re-,* back, again + *cantare,* freq. of *canere,* to sing: see CHANT⟧ to withdraw or renounce (beliefs or statements formerly held), esp. in a formal or public manner —**re·can·ta·tion** (rē′kan tā′shən) *n.* —**re·cant′er** *n.*

re·cap¹ (rē kap′; *also, and for n. always,* rē′kap′) *vt.* **-capped′, -cap′ping** ⟦RE- + CAP¹⟧ ☆to put a new tread on (a worn pneumatic tire) by cementing a strip of crude rubber to the old casing and vulcanizing in a mold; retread —☆*n.* a recapped tire; retread —**re·cap′pa·ble** *adj.*

re·cap² (rē′kap′) *n.* ⟦< RECAPITULATION⟧ a summary or brief restatement — *vt., vi.* **-capped′, -cap′ping** ⟦< RECAPITULATE⟧ to repeat briefly, as in an outline; summarize Informal except in broadcast journalism

re·cap·i·tal·ize (rē′kap′ət 'l īz′) *vt.* **-ized′, -iz′ing** to capitalize again; specif., to change the capital structure of (a corporation) —**re·cap′i·tal·i·za′tion** *n.*

re·ca·pit·u·late (rē′kə pich′ə lāt′) *vi., vt.* **-lat′ed, -lat′ing** ⟦< pp. of LL *recapitulare:* see RE- & CAPITULATE⟧ to repeat briefly, as in an outline; summarize —*SYN.* REPEAT

re·ca·pit·u·la·tion (-pich′ə lā′shən) *n.* ⟦ME *recapitulacion* < MFr or LL: MFr *recapitulation* < LL *recapitulatio*⟧ **1** the act of recapitulating **2** a summary, or brief restatement **3** PALINGENESIS (sense 3) **4** *Music* the section of a composition which restates themes presented earlier; esp., the final division of the sonata form —**re′ca·pit′u·la′tive** *adj.,* **re′ca·pit′u·la·to′ry** (-lə tôr′ē)

re·cap·ture (rē kap′chər) *vt.* **-tured, -tur·ing 1** to capture again; retake; get back by capture; reacquire ☆**2** to get by RECAPTURE (*n.* 2) **3** to bring back by remembering [to *recapture* a feeling] —*n.* **1** a recapturing or being recaptured ☆**2** the placing in reserve or the taking by the government under law of a fixed portion of all business earnings exceeding a specified percentage of property value ☆**3** that which is recaptured **4** POSTLIMINIUM

re·cast (rē kast′, -käst′; *for n.* rē′kast′, -käst′) *vt.* **-cast′, -cast′ing 1** to cast again or anew **2** to improve the form of by redoing; reconstruct [to *recast* a sentence] **3** to calculate or count again **4** *a)* to provide a new cast for (a play) *b)* to put (an actor) in a different role —*n.* **1** the act of recasting **2** a new form produced by recasting

rec·ce (rek′ē) [Brit. Slang] *n.* RECONNAISSANCE — *vt., vi.* **-ced, -ce·ing** RECONNOITER

recd or **rec'd** *abbrev.* received

re·cede¹ (ri sēd′) *vi.* **-ced′ed, -ced′ing** ⟦L *recedere:* see RE- & CEDE⟧ **1** *a)* to go or move back from a former position [flood waters *receded*] *b)* to draw

rebeautify
rebid
rebiddable
rebill
rebind
reboil
reburial
rebury
rebutton
recalibrate
recarbonize
recarry
recatalog

back, resulting in less of something behind (said as of a boundary) [*a receding* hairline, *receding* coastline] **2** to withdraw (*from*) [to *recede* from a promise] **3** to slope backward **4** to become more distant, and hence indistinct [early memories *recede*] **5** to become less; diminish [*receding* prices]

☆**re·cede**[2] (rē′sēd′) ***vt.* -ced′ed, -ced′ing** to cede back

re·ceipt (ri sēt′) ***n.*** ⟦altered (infl. by L) < ME *receite* < Anglo-Fr, for OFr *recete* < ML *recepta* < L, fem. of *receptus,* pp. of *recipere:* see RECEIVE⟧ **1** *old-fashioned var. of* RECIPE **2** a receiving or being received **3** a written acknowledgment that something, as goods, money, etc., has been received **4** [*pl.*] the thing or amount received, as money taken in by a business —***vt.*** **1** to mark (a bill) paid ☆**2** to write a receipt for (goods, etc.) —☆***vi.*** to write a receipt

☆**re·ceipt·or** (-ər) ***n.*** **1** a person who receipts **2** *Law* a person who receipts as bailee for attached property

re·ceiv·a·ble (ri sē′və bəl) ***adj.*** ⟦ME *resceyuable* < Anglo-Fr *receivable,* for OFr *recevable:* also < fol. + -ABLE⟧ **1** that can be received **2** due; requiring payment [accounts *receivable*] **3** suitable for acceptance —***n.*** [*pl.*] accounts or bills receivable

re·ceive (ri sēv′) ***vt.* -ceived′, -ceiv′ing** ⟦ME *receiven* < Anglo-Fr *receivre* < OFr < L *recipere* < *re-,* back + *capere,* to take: see HAVE⟧ **1** to take or get (something given, offered, sent, etc.); acquire or accept **2** to encounter; experience [to *receive* acclaim] **3** to have inflicted on one; undergo; suffer [to *receive* a blow] **4** to take the effect or force of; bear [all four wheels *receive* the weight equally] **5** to react to as specified [a performance that was well *received*] **6** to apprehend mentally; get knowledge of or information about; learn [to *receive* news] **7** to accept mentally as authentic, valid, etc. **8** *a)* to let enter; admit *b)* to have room for; hold; contain [a cistern *receives* rainwater] **9** to grant admittance to or greet (visitors or guests) **10** *Radio, TV* to detect (a radio or TV transmission) and convert it into sounds or images **11** *Sports* to catch (a pass, throw, etc.) —***vi.*** **1** to get, accept, take, or acquire something; be a recipient **2** to admit or greet guests or visitors **3** *Radio, TV* to convert incoming electromagnetic waves into sound or light, thus reproducing the sounds or images being transmitted **4** *Sports a)* to be the team set to return the ball on a kickoff *b)* to be the player or team that returns or attempts to return a serve —**be on the receiving end** [Informal] **1** to be the recipient of a gift, or favor **2** to be the target or victim of an attack **3** *Sports* to act as the receiver

SYN.—**receive** means to get by having something given, told, or imposed, and may or may not imply the consent of the recipient [to *receive* a gift, a blow, etc.]; **accept** means to receive willingly or favorably, but it sometimes connotes acquiescence rather than explicit approval [he was *accepted* as a member, to *accept* the inevitable]; **admit** stresses permission or concession on the part of the one that receives [I will not *admit* him in my home]; **take,** in this connection, means to accept something offered or presented [we can't *take* money from you] —*ANT.* **give**

re·ceived (ri sēvd′) ***adj.*** accepted; considered as standard

Received Pronunciation the pronunciation, commonly used in Brit. broadcasting, of RECEIVED STANDARD

Received Standard the form of British English spoken by the upper socioeconomic classes, esp. by graduates of the public schools and of Oxford and Cambridge

re·ceiv·er (ri sē′vər) ***n.*** **1** a person who receives; specif., *a)* one who officially receives money for others; collector or treasurer *b)* one who knowingly receives stolen goods for gain or concealment; fence *c) Football* an offensive player designated to receive a forward pass; esp., a player, other than a running back, who is ordinarily eligible to receive a forward pass, as a wide receiver or tight end *d) Law* one appointed by a court to administer or hold in trust property in bankruptcy or in a lawsuit *e) Tennis, etc.* the player receiving the service **2** a thing that receives; specif., *a)* a receptacle; esp., a chemical receptacle connected with a retort, tube, etc., into which a distilled product passes *b)* an apparatus or device that converts incoming electromagnetic waves or electrical signals into audible or visual signals, as a radio or television receiving set, or that part of a telephone which is held to the ear

re·ceiv·er·ship (-ship′) ***n.*** **1** *Law* the duties or office of a receiver **2** the state of being administered or held by a receiver

☆**receiving blanket** a small, lightweight blanket, usually of cotton, for wrapping around a baby

receiving line at formal gatherings, the host, hostess, guests of honor, and others, who stand in a row to greet guests

receiving set an apparatus for receiving radio or television signals; receiver

re·cen·sion (ri sen′shən) ***n.*** ⟦L *recensio* < *recensere,* to revise < *re-,* again + *censere,* to value: see CENSURE⟧ **1** a revising of a text on the basis of a critical examination of sources **2** a revised text so produced

re·cent (rē′sənt) ***adj.*** ⟦MFr < L *recens* < *re-,* again + IE base **ken-,* emerge freshly, new > Gr *kainos,* new⟧ **1** done, made, etc. just before the present time; modern; new **2** of a time just before the present **3** [**R-**] designating or of the Holocene Epoch of geologic time —**the Recent** the Holocene Epoch or its rocks —**re′cent·ly *adv.*** —**re′cent·ness *n.*, re′cen·cy**

re·cep·ta·cle (ri sep′tə kəl) ***n.*** ⟦ME < L *receptaculum* < *receptare,* freq. of *recipere:* see RECEIVE⟧ **1** anything used to contain or hold something else; container; vessel **2** an electrical wall outlet designed for use with a plug **3** ⟦ModL *receptaculum*⟧ *Bot. a)* the enlarged upper end of the stalk of a flowering plant, on which the flower parts grow *b)* any of a number of cuplike or disklike structures supporting spores, sex organs, etc.

re·cep·tion (ri sep′shən) ***n.*** ⟦ME *recepcion* < OFr *reception* < L *receptio* < pp. of *recipere:* see RECEIVE⟧ **1** *a)* a receiving or being received *b)* the manner of this [a friendly *reception*] **2** a social function, often formal, for the receiving of guests **3** response or reaction, as to something presented **4** *Radio, TV* the manner of receiving, with reference to the relative quality of reproduction [good or poor *reception*]

re·cep·tion·ist (-ist) ***n.*** a person employed in an office to receive callers, give information, etc.

reception room a room as in a house, office, etc. for receiving visitors, clients, etc. as they arrive

re·cep·tive (ri sep′tiv) ***adj.*** ⟦ML *receptivus* < L *receptus:* see RECEIPT⟧ **1** receiving or tending to receive, take in, admit, or contain **2** inclined to the favorable reception of a request, suggestion, etc. **3** able or ready to receive new ideas **4** of reception or receptors —**re·cep′tive·ly *adv.*** —**re·cep′tive·ness *n.*, re·cep′tiv′i·ty**

re·cep·tor (-tər) ***n.*** ⟦ME *receptour* < OFr < L *receptor* < *receptus:* see RECEIPT⟧ **1** a receiver (in various senses) **2** *Biochem.* any of a group of substances, mainly proteins, found esp. on the surface of a cell, that combine with specific molecules, hormones, antibodies, drugs, viruses, etc. **3** *Physiol.* a nerve ending or group of nerve endings specialized for the reception of stimuli; sense organ

re·cess (rē′ses; *also, & for v. usually,* ri ses′) ***n.*** ⟦L *recessus* < pp. of *recedere:* see RECEDE[1]⟧ **1** a receding or hollow place, as in a surface, wall, etc.; niche **2** a secluded, withdrawn, or inner place [subterranean *recesses,* the *recesses* of the subconscious] **3** *a)* a temporary withdrawal from or halting as of work, business, or study *b)* in elementary school, a scheduled period of relaxation or play, esp. outdoors **4** *Anat.* a small cavity, hollow, indentation, etc. in an organ or part —***vt.*** **1** to place or set in a recess **2** to form a recess in ☆**3** to halt temporarily [to *recess* a hearing] —☆***vi.*** to take a recess

re·ces·sion[1] (ri sesh′ən) ***n.*** ⟦L *recessio* < pp. of *recedere:* see RECEDE[1]⟧ **1** a going back or receding; withdrawal **2** a procession leaving a place of assembly **3** a receding part, as of a wall **4** *Econ.* a temporary falling off of business activity during a period when such activity has been generally increasing —**re·ces′sion·ar′y *adj.***

re·ces·sion[2] (rē sesh′ən) ***n.*** ⟦RE- + CESSION⟧ a ceding back, as to a former owner

re·ces·sion·al (ri sesh′ən əl) ***adj.*** of a recession —***n.*** a piece of music for a RECESSION[1] (sense 2)

re·ces·sive (ri ses′iv) ***adj.*** ⟦< L *recessus* (see RECESS) + -IVE⟧ **1** receding or tending to recede **2** *Genetics* designating or relating to that one of any pair of allelic hereditary factors which, when both are present in the germ plasm, remains latent: opposed to DOMINANT —***n.*** *Genetics* a recessive character or characters —**re·ces′sive·ly *adv.*** —**re·ces′sive·ness *n.***

re·charge (rē chärj′; *also, & for n. always,* rē′chärj′) ***vt., vi.* -charged′, -charg′ing** to charge again (in various senses) —***n.*** the act of recharging —**re·charge′a·ble *adj.*** —**re·charg′er *n.***

ré·chauf·fé (rā shō fā′) ***n.,*** *pl.* **-fés′** (-fā′) ⟦Fr, pp. of *réchauffer,* to warm over < *ré-,* again + *échauffer,* to heat < LL **excalefare,* for L *excalefacere* < *ex-,* intens. + *calefacere,* to heat: see CHAFE⟧ **1** a dish of leftover food reheated **2** any used or old material worked up in a new form; rehash

re·cher·ché (rə sher′shā, -sher′shā′) ***adj.*** ⟦Fr, pp. of *rechercher:* see RESEARCH⟧ **1** sought out with care; rare; choice; uncommon **2** having refinement or studied elegance **3** too refined; too studied

re·cid·i·vism (ri sid′ə viz′əm) ***n.*** ⟦< L *recidivus* < *recidere,* to fall back < *re-,* back + *cadere,* to fall (see CASE[1]) + -ISM⟧ habitual or chronic relapse, or tendency to relapse, esp. into crime or antisocial behavior —**re·cid′i·vist *n., adj.*** —**re·cid′i·vis′tic *adj.*, re·cid′i·vous**

Re·ci·fe (rə sē′fə) seaport in NE Brazil, on the Atlantic: capital of Pernambuco state

rec·i·pe (res′ə pē′) ***n.*** ⟦L, imper. of *recipere:* see RECEIVE⟧ **1** *former term for* PRESCRIPTION (sense 3): see Rx[2] **2** a list of materials and directions for preparing a dish or drink **3** any procedure for accomplishing something

re·cip·i·ent (ri sip′ē ənt) ***n.*** ⟦< L *recipiens,* prp. of *recipere:* see RECEIVE⟧ a person or thing that receives —***adj.*** receiving, or ready or able to receive —**re·cip′i·ence *n.*, re·cip′i·en·cy**

re·cip·ro·cal (ri sip′rə kəl) ***adj.*** ⟦< L *reciprocus,* returning, reciprocal < **reco-prokos,* backwards and forwards < **recos* (< *re-,* back + **cos* < ?) + IE **proko-,* ahead (> Gr *proka,* forthwith) < base **pro-,* forward, ahead + -AL⟧ **1** done, felt, given, etc. in return [hoping for a *reciprocal* favor] **2** present or existing on both sides; each to the other; mutual [to feel a *reciprocal* affection] **3** corresponding but reversed or inverted **4** equivalent or interchangeable; corresponding or complementary **5** *Gram.* expressing mutual action or relation ["each other" is traditionally called a *reciprocal* pronoun] **6** *Math.* of the reciprocals of quantities, or their relations —***n.*** **1** anything that has a reciprocal action on or relation to another; complement, counterpart, equivalent, etc. **2** *Math.* the quantity resulting from the division of 1 by the given quantity; quantity which multiplied by the given quantity equals 1 (Ex.: the *reciprocal* of 7 is $\frac{1}{7}$, of $\frac{1}{7}$ is 7) —*SYN.* MUTUAL —**re·cip′ro·cal′i·ty** (-kal′ə tē) ***n.*** —**re·cip′ro·cal·ly *adv.***

re·cip·ro·cate (-kāt′) ***vt.* -cat′ed, -cat′ing** ⟦< L *reciprocatus,* pp. of *recipro-*

recelebrate
recelebration
recertify
rechannel
rechart
recharter
recheck
rechew

care < *reciprocus:* see prec.] 1 *a)* to give and get, do, feel, etc. reciprocally; interchange *b)* to give, do, feel, etc. in return; return in kind or degree 2 to cause to move alternately back and forth —*vi.* 1 to make some sort of return for something done, given, etc. 2 to move alternately back and forth; interchange position 3 [Archaic] to be correspondent or equivalent —**re·cip'ro·ca'tion** *n.* —**re·cip'ro·ca'tive** *adj.*, **re·cip'ro·ca·to'ry** (-kə tôr'ē) —**re·cip'ro·ca'tor** *n.*

reciprocating engine any engine in which the movement of the pistons back and forth causes the rotary motion of the crankshaft

rec·i·proc·i·ty (res'ə präs'ə tē) *n., pl.* **-ties** ⟦Fr *réciprocité*⟧ 1 reciprocal state or relationship; mutual action, dependence, etc. 2 mutual exchange; esp., exchange of special privileges between two countries, to the advantage of both, as mutual reduction of tariffs

re·ci·sion (ri sizh'ən) *n.* ⟦L *recisio* < *recidere,* to cut back: see RE- + -CIDE⟧ a rescinding or annulling

ré·cit (rā sē') *n., pl.* **-cits'** (-sē') ⟦Fr, account, narrative, story⟧ *Literature* a narrative, or story, esp. that part in which the events are recounted as distinguished from the parts containing commentary, description, dialogue, etc.

re·cit·al (ri sīt''l) *n.* ⟦RECIT(E) + -AL⟧ 1 *a)* a reciting; specif., a telling of facts, events, etc. in detail *b)* what is so told; account, story, or description 2 a detailed statement 3 a musical or dance program given by a soloist, soloists, or small ensemble —**re·cit'al·ist** *n.*

rec·i·ta·tion (res'ə tā'shən) *n.* ⟦L *recitatio*⟧ 1 a reciting, as of facts, events, etc.; recital 2 *a)* a saying aloud in public of something memorized *b)* a piece of prose or verse memorized for this ☆3 *a)* a reciting by pupils of answers to questions on a prepared lesson *b)* a class meeting or period in which this occurs

rec·i·ta·tive (res'ə tə tēv') *n.* ⟦It *recitativo* < L *recitare,* fol.⟧ *Music* 1 a type of declamatory singing, with the rhythm and tempo of speech, but uttered in musical tones, used in the prose parts and dialogue of operas and oratorios 2 a work or passage in this style 3 music for such passages —*adj.* having the nature, or in the style or manner, of recitative

re·cite (ri sīt') *vt.* **-cit'ed, -cit'ing** ⟦ME *reciten* < OFr *reciter* < L *recitare:* see RE- & CITE⟧ 1 to repeat or say aloud from or as from memory, esp. in a formal way; give a recitation on (a lesson) in class or of (a poem, speech, etc.) before an audience 2 to tell in detail; give an account of; narrate; relate 3 to enumerate —*vi.* 1 to repeat or say aloud something memorized ☆2 to recite a lesson or part of a lesson in a class —**re·cit'er** *n.*

reck (rek) *vi., vt.* ⟦ME *recken* < OE *reccan;* akin to OHG *ruohhen*⟧ [Archaic] 1 to have care or concern (*for*) or take heed (*of*) [*he recks* not of the peril] 2 to concern or be of concern; matter (*to*) [*it recks* him not]

reck·less (rek'lis) *adj.* ⟦ME *reckeles* < OE *recceleas:* see prec. & -LESS⟧ 1 careless; heedless 2 not regarding consequences; headlong and irresponsible; rash —**reck'less·ly** *adv.* —**reck'less·ness** *n.*

Reck·ling·hau·sen (rek'liŋ hou'zən) city in W Germany, in the state of North Rhine-Westphalia

reck·on (rek'ən) *vt.* ⟦ME *rekkenen* < OE *-recenian,* akin to Ger *rechnen,* to count < IE base **reĝ-,* to put in order, straight > RIGHT, L *regere,* to rule⟧ 1 to count; figure up; compute 2 *a)* to consider as; regard as being [*reckon* them friends] *b)* to judge; consider; estimate 3 [Informal or Dial.] to think; suppose —*vi.* 1 to count up; figure 2 [Informal] to depend or rely (*on*) [*reckoning* on good weather] 3 [Informal] to think; suppose —*SYN.* CALCULATE, RELY —**reckon with** 1 to balance or settle accounts with 2 to take into consideration —**reck'on·er** *n.*

reck·on·ing (-iŋ) *n.* 1 the act of one who reckons; count or computation 2 a measuring of possibilities for the future; calculated guess 3 *a)* a bill; account *b)* the settlement of an account *c)* the settlement of rewards or penalties for any action [day of *reckoning*] 4 [Rare] *Naut. short for* DEAD RECKONING

re·claim (ri klām') *vt.* ⟦ME *reclaimen* < OFr *réclamer* < L *reclamare,* to cry out against: see RE- & CLAIM⟧ 1 to rescue or bring back (a person or people) from error, vice, etc. to ways of living or thinking regarded as right; reform 2 to make (wasteland, desert, etc.) capable of being cultivated or lived on, as by filling, ditching, or irrigating 3 to recover (useful materials) from waste products 4 to retrieve (something lost, taken away, deposited temporarily, etc.); get back into one's possession 5 [Obs.] to tame or subdue (a hawk) —*n.* reclamation [beyond *reclaim*] —*SYN.* RECOVER —**re·claim'a·ble** *adj.* —**re·claim'ant** *n.*, **re·claim'er**

rec·la·ma·tion (rek'lə mā'shən) *n.* ⟦Fr *réclamation* < L *reclamatio*⟧ 1 a reclaiming or being reclaimed; esp., the recovery of wasteland, desert, etc. by ditching, filling, or irrigating 2 the process or industry of obtaining useful materials from waste products

ré·clame (rā klàm') *n.* ⟦Fr < *réclamer:* see RECLAIM⟧ 1 publicity or notoriety 2 a seeking for, or skill in getting, publicity

rec·li·nate (rek'lə nāt') *adj.* ⟦< L *reclinatus,* pp. of *reclinare:* see fol.⟧ *Bot.* bending downward, as a leaf or stem

re·cline (ri klīn') *vt.* **-clined', -clin'ing** ⟦ME *reclynen* < L *reclinare* < *re-,* back + *clinare,* to lean: see INCLINE⟧ to cause to lean or lie back or down; lay back —*vi.* to lie or lean back or down; specif., to rest or repose lying down —**rec·li·na·tion** (rek'lə nā'shən) *n.*

re·clin·er (-klī'nər) *n.* 1 one that reclines 2 an upholstered armchair with a movable back and seat that can be adjusted for reclining: also **reclining chair**

rec·luse (rek'lo͞os, ri klo͞os') *adj.* ⟦ME < OFr *reclus* < LL(Ec) *reclusus* < L, pp. of *recludere,* to shut off < *re-,* back + *claudere:* see CLOSE²⟧ [Now Rare] RECLUSIVE —*n.* a person who lives a secluded, solitary life

re·clu·sion (ri klo͞o'zhən) *n.* ⟦ME *reclucioun*⟧ the condition or fact of becoming or being a recluse

re·clu·sive (-klo͞o'siv) *adj.* shut away from the world; secluded; solitary

rec·og·ni·tion (rek'əg nish'ən) *n.* ⟦L *recognitio* < *recognitus,* pp. of *recognoscere:* see RECOGNIZANCE⟧ 1 *a)* a recognizing or being recognized; acknowledgment; admission, as of a fact *b)* acknowledgment and approval, gratitude, etc. [in *recognition* of her services] 2 formal acknowledgment by a government of the independence and sovereignty of a state newly created, as by secession, or of a government newly set up, as by revolution 3 identification of some person or thing as having been known before or as being of a certain kind 4 notice, as in passing; greeting; salutation —**re·cog·ni·to·ry** (ri käg'nə tôr'ē) *adj.*, **re·cog'ni·tive** (-tiv)

rec·og·niz·a·ble (rek'əg nī'zə bəl) *adj.* that can be recognized —**rec'og·niz'a·bil'i·ty** *n.* —**rec'og·niz'a·bly** *adv.*

re·cog·ni·zance (ri käg'ni zəns, -kän'i-) *n.* ⟦ME *reconissance* < OFr *reconaissance* < *reconnoisant,* prp. of *reconoistre* < L *recognoscere,* to recall to mind < *re-,* again + *cognoscere,* to know: see COGNITION⟧ 1 *Law a)* an obligation of record entered into before a court or magistrate, binding a person to do or not do something, be in court at a certain time, etc. *b)* a sum of money pledged and subject to forfeit if this obligation is not fulfilled 2 *archaic var. of* RECOGNITION 3 [Obs.] a symbol, token, or badge

rec·og·nize (rek'əg nīz') *vt.* **-nized', -niz'ing** ⟦altered (infl. by prec.) < extended stem of OFr *reconoistre:* see prec.⟧ 1 to be aware of as something or someone known before, or as the same as that known [to *recognize* an old friend after many years] 2 to know by some detail, as of appearance; identify [to *recognize* a butterfly by its coloring] 3 to be aware of the significance of [to *recognize* symptoms] 4 to acknowledge the existence, validity, authority, or genuineness of [to *recognize* a claim] 5 to accept as a fact; admit; accept [to *recognize* defeat] 6 to acknowledge as worthy of appreciation or approval [to *recognize* devotion] 7 to acknowledge the legal standing of (a government, state, etc.) by some formal action, as by entering into diplomatic relations 8 to show acquaintance with (a person) by greeting ☆9 to acknowledge as having the right to speak, as in a meeting —**rec'og·niz'er** *n.*

re·cog·ni·zee (ri käg'ni zē', -kän'i-) *n.* *Law* a person in whose favor a recognizance is entered

re·cog·ni·zor (-zôr') *n.* *Law* a person who enters into a recognizance

re·coil (ri koil'; *also for n., esp. of weapons,* rē'koil') *vi.* ⟦ME *recoilen* < OFr *reculer* < *re-,* back + *cul* < L *culus,* the anus, buttocks: see CULET⟧ 1 *a)* to draw back, fall back, or stagger back; retreat *b)* to start or shrink back, as in fear, surprise, or disgust 2 to fly back when released, as a spring, or kick back when fired, as a gun 3 to return to or as to the starting point or source; react (*on* or *upon*) —*n.* 1 the act of recoiling 2 the state of having recoiled; reaction 3 the distance through which a gun, spring, etc. recoils

re-coil (rē koil') *vt., vi.* to coil anew or again

re·coil·less (ri koil'lis) *adj.* designating or of a firearm designed to minimize recoil, as by means of vents for the escape of gases

re·coin (rē koin') *vt.* to coin anew or again —**re·coin'age** (-ij) *n.*

rec·ol·lect (rek'ə lekt') *vt.* ⟦< L *recollectus:* see fol.⟧ 1 to call back to mind; recall; remember, esp. with some effort 2 to recall to (oneself) something temporarily forgotten —*vi.* to have a recollection; remember

re-col·lect (rē'kə lekt') *vt.* ⟦orig. < L *recollectus,* pp. of *recolligere* (see RE- & COLLECT¹); later felt as < RE- + COLLECT¹⟧ 1 to gather together again (what has been scattered) 2 to collect or rally (one's thoughts, strength, courage, etc.) 3 to recover or compose (oneself): in this sense sometimes written **re'col·lect'**

rec·ol·lec·tion (rek'ə lek'shən) *n.* ⟦Fr *récollection* < ML *recollectio*⟧ 1 the act or power of recollecting, or calling back to mind; remembrance 2 what is recollected [*recollections* of youth] 3 [Archaic] *a)* calmness of mind *b)* religious meditation —**rec'ol·lec'tive** *adj.*

re·com·bi·nant (rē käm'bə nənt) *n.* *Genetics* an organism in which recombination has occurred

recombinant DNA any recombined DNA, esp. that formed in the laboratory by splicing together pieces of DNA from different species, as to create new life forms, modify existing ones, or produce useful biological chemicals, as insulin

re·com·bi·na·tion (rē käm'bə nā'shən) *n.* 1 a combining again 2 *Genetics* the appearance in offspring of new combinations of allelic genes not present in either parent, produced from the mixing of genetic material, as by crossing-over

rec·om·mend (rek'ə mend') *vt.* ⟦ME *recomenden* < ML *recommendare:* see RE- & COMMEND⟧ 1 to give in charge; commit; entrust [*recommended* to our care] 2 to suggest favorably as suited for some use, function, position, etc. [to *recommend* a book, a doctor, etc.] 3 to make acceptable or pleasing [much on the island to *recommend* it] 4 to advise; counsel; suggest [to *recommend* that something be done] —**rec'om·mend'a·ble** *adj.* —**rec'om·mend'a·to'ry** *adj.* —**rec'om·mend'er** *n.*

rec·om·men·da·tion (-mən dā'shən) *n.* ⟦ME *recomendacion* < ML

recircle
recirculate
reclassification
reclassify
reclean
reclosable
reclothe
recode
recodify
recolonize
recolor
recombine
recommence

recommendatio⟧ 1 the act of recommending, or calling attention to, a person or thing as suited to some purpose 2 anything that recommends or makes a favorable or pleasing impression; specif., a letter recommending a person or thing 3 advice; counsel

re·com·mit (rē′kə mit′) *vt.* **-mit′ted, -mit′ting** 1 to commit again 2 to refer (a question, bill, etc.) back to a committee —**re′com·mit′ment** *n.*, **re′com·mit′tal**

rec·om·pense (rek′əm pens′) *vt.* **-pensed′, -pens′ing** ⟦ME *recompensen* < MFr *recompenser* < LL *recompensare:* see RE- & COMPENSATE⟧ 1 to repay (a person, etc.); reward; compensate 2 to make repayment or requital for; compensate (a loss, injury, etc.) —*n.* 1 something given or done in return for something else; repayment, remuneration, requital, or reward 2 something given or done to make up for a loss, injury, etc.; compensation —*SYN.* PAY[1]

re·com·pose (rē′kəm pōz′) *vt.* **-posed′, -pos′ing** 1 to compose again; rearrange, recombine, or reconstitute 2 to restore to composure —**re·com·po·si·tion** (rē′käm′pə zish′ən) *n.*

re·con[1] (rē′kän′, ri kän′) *n. short for* RECONNAISSANCE

re·con[2] (rē′kän′) *n.* ⟦REC(OMBINATION) + -ON⟧ the smallest section of DNA that can be recombined

rec·on·cil·a·ble (rek′ən sīl′ə bəl) *adj.* that can be reconciled —**rec′on·cil′a·bil′i·ty** *n.* —**rec′on·cil′a·bly** *adv.*

rec·on·cile (rek′ən sīl′) *vt.* **-ciled′, -cil′ing** ⟦ME *reconsilen* < OFr *reconcilier* < L *reconciliare:* see RE- & CONCILIATE⟧ 1 to make friendly again or win over to a friendly attitude 2 to settle (a quarrel, difference, etc.) 3 to make (arguments, ideas, texts, accounts, etc.) consistent, compatible, etc.; bring into harmony 4 to make content, submissive, or acquiescent (*to*) [to become *reconciled* to one's lot]

rec·on·cil·i·a·tion (rek′ən sil′ē ā′shən) *n.* ⟦ME *reconsiliacion* < MFr *reconciliation* < L *reconciliatio*⟧ a reconciling or being reconciled: also **rec′on·cile′ment** (-sīl′mənt) —**rec′on·cil′i·a·to′ry** *adj.*

rec·on·dite (rek′ən dīt′; *occas.* ri kän′dīt′) *adj.* ⟦L *reconditus,* pp. of *recondere,* to put back, hide < *re-*, back + *condere,* to put together, store up, hide < *con-*, together + *-dere* < IE base **dhē-*, to put > DO[1]⟧ 1 beyond the grasp of the ordinary mind or understanding; profound; abstruse 2 dealing with abstruse or difficult subjects 3 obscure or concealed —**rec′on·dite′ly** *adv.* —**rec′on·dite′ness** *n.*

re·con·di·tion (rē′kən dish′ən) *vt.* to put back in good condition, as by cleaning, patching, or repairing

re·con·nais·sance (ri kän′ə səns, -zəns) *n.* ⟦Fr, earlier *reconnoissance:* see RECOGNIZANCE⟧ an exploratory survey or examination, as in seeking out information about enemy positions or installations, or as in making a preliminary geologic or engineering survey

rec·on·noi·ter (rek′ə noit′ər, rē′kə-) *vt., vi.* ⟦Fr *reconnoître,* old form of *reconnaître* < OFr *reconoistre:* see RECOGNIZANCE⟧ to make a reconnaissance (of): also [Chiefly Brit.] **rec′on·noi′tre, -tred, -tring** —**re′con·noi′ter·er** *n.*, **re′con·noi′trer** (-noi′trər)

re·con·sid·er (rē′kən sid′ər) *vt.* 1 to consider again; think or argue over again, esp. with a view to changing a decision 2 to take up again in a meeting (a matter discussed and voted on before) —*vi.* to reconsider a matter —**re′con·sid′er·a′tion** *n.*

re·con·sign·ment (rē′kən sīn′mənt) *n.* 1 a consigning again or anew 2 *Commerce* a change (made in transit) in the route, destination, or consignee as indicated in the original bill of lading

re·con·sti·tute (rē kän′stə to͞ot′, -tyo͞ot′) *vt.* **-tut′ed, -tut′ing** to constitute again or anew; reconstruct, reorganize, or recompose; specif., to restore (a dehydrated or condensed substance) to its full liquid form by adding water —**re·con′sti·tu′tion** *n.*

re·con·struct (rē′kən strukt′) *vt.* 1 to construct again; rebuild; make over 2 to build up, from remaining parts or other evidence, a concept or reproduction of (something in its original or complete form) —**re′con·struc′tive** *adj.*

re·con·struc·tion (-struk′shən) *n.* 1 *a)* the act of reconstructing *b)* something reconstructed 2 [R-] the process, after the Civil War, of reorganizing the Southern states which had seceded and reestablishing them in the Union 3 [R-] the period of this (1867-77)

☆**Re·con·struc·tion·ism** (-iz′əm) *n.* a 20th-cent. movement in Judaism that stresses a dynamic creativity in adjusting to modern times, as by the adaptation and reinterpretation of traditional observances

re·con·vert (rē′kən vurt′) *vt., vi.* to change back, as to a former status, form, religion, or opinion —**re′con·ver′sion** *n.*

re·con·vey (rē′kən vā′) *vt.* to convey again or back, as to a former owner or place —**re′con·vey′ance** *n.*

re·cord (ri kôrd′; *for n. & adj.* rek′ərd) *vt.* ⟦ME *recorden,* to report, repeat (also, to sing, practice a tune, warble) < OFr *recorder,* to recount, recite, repeat < L *recordari,* to call to mind, remember < *re-*, again + *cor* (gen. *cordis*), mind, HEART⟧ 1 *a)* to put in writing, print, etc. for future use; draw up an account of [to *record* the day's events] *b)* to make a permanent or official note of [to *record* a vote] 2 *a)* to indicate automatically and permanently, as on a graph or chart [a seismograph *records* earthquakes] *b)* to show, as on a dial [a thermometer *records* temperatures] 3 to remain as evidence of [metal tools *record* a superior civilization] 4 *a)* to register (sound or visual images) in some permanent form by mechanical or digital means for later reproduction, as on a playback device *b)* to register the performance of (a musician, actor, composition, etc.) on discs, tapes, etc. in this way —*vi.* 1 to record something 2 to admit of being recorded —*n.* **rec′ord** ⟦ME < OFr < the v.⟧ 1 the condition of being recorded 2 *a)* anything that is written down and preserved as evidence; account of events *b)* anything that serves as evidence of an event, etc. *c)* an official written report of public proceedings, as in a legislature or court of law, preserved for future reference 3 anything that written evidence is put on or in, as a register or monument ☆4 *a)* the known or recorded facts about anyone or anything, as about one's career *b)* the recorded offenses or crimes of a person who has been arrested one or more times ☆5 something on which sound or visual images have been recorded; esp., a thin, flat, grooved disc for playing on a phonograph 6 the best performance, highest speed, greatest amount, highest rate, etc. achieved, esp. when officially recorded 7 *Comput.* a group of logically related fields, dealt with as a unit: cf. FILE[1] (*n.* 5), FIELD (*n.* 12) ☆8 *Sports* the number of games, matches, etc. won and lost by a team or person —*adj.* **rec′ord** establishing a record as the best, largest, etc. [a *record* crop] —☆**go on record** to state one's opinions publicly or officially —**like a broken record** ⟦in ref. to an imperfection on a phonograph record that causes the tonearm to keep tracking the same section⟧ repeating the same words or message over in a mechanical or tiresome way —☆**off the record** not for publication or public release; confidential(ly) —**on (the) record** recorded; publicly or officially declared or known

☆**record changer** a phonograph device that automatically sets records in succession on the turntable, as from a stack of records on the turntable spindle

re·cord·er (ri kôr′dər) *n.* ⟦ME < Anglo-Fr *recordour*⟧ 1 a person who records; esp., an officer appointed or elected to keep records of deeds or other official papers 2 in some cities, a judge who has the same criminal jurisdiction as a police judge 3 a machine or device that records; esp., TAPE RECORDER 4 ⟦ME < *recorden,* to sing, warble: see RECORD⟧ any of a group of wind instruments, with eight finger holes and a fipple in a straight tube with the mouthpiece at one end

recorder

re·cord·ing (ri kôr′diŋ) *adj.* that records —*n.* 1 the act of one that records 2 *a)* what is recorded, as on a disc or tape *b)* the quality of this; esp., its acoustic or visual fidelity to the original *c)* the record itself

re·cord·ist (ri kôr′dist) *n.* one who makes sound recordings, as for films

record player any of various devices on which phonograph records may be played

re·count[1] (ri kount′) *vt.* ⟦ME *recounten* < Anglo-Fr *reconter:* see RE- & COUNT[1]⟧ 1 to tell in detail; give an account of; narrate 2 to tell in order or one by one

re·count[2] (rē′kount′; *for n.* rē′kount′) *vt.* ⟦RE- + COUNT[1]⟧ to count again —*n.* a second or additional count, as of votes

re·count·al (ri kount′'l) *n.* a recounting; narration

re·coup (ri ko͞op′) *vt.* ⟦Fr *recouper* < *re-*, again + *couper,* to cut, strike: see COUP⟧ 1 *a)* to get back an equivalent for; make up for [to *recoup* a loss] *b)* to regain [to *recoup* one's health] 2 to pay back; reimburse 3 *Law* to deduct or hold back (a part of what is due), having some reasonable claim to do so —*n.* an act of recouping —*SYN.* RECOVER —**re·coup′a·ble** *adj.* —**re·coup′ment** *n.*

re·course (rē′kôrs′, ri kôrs′) *n.* ⟦ME *recours* < OFr < L *recursus,* a running back: see RE- & COURSE⟧ 1 a turning or seeking for aid, safety, etc. [to have *recourse* to the law] 2 that to which one turns or may turn in seeking aid, safety, etc. [one's last *recourse*] 3 *Commerce, Law* the right to demand payment from the maker or endorser of a negotiable instrument, as a bill of exchange: usually in **without recourse**, without obligation to pay (added by the endorser to a bill of exchange to escape possible liability)

re·cov·er (ri kuv′ər) *vt.* ⟦ME *recoveren* < OFr *recovrer* < L *recuperare:* see RECUPERATE⟧ 1 *a)* to get back (something lost or stolen) *b)* to regain (health, consciousness, etc.) 2 to compensate for; make up for [to *recover* losses] 3 *a)* to get (oneself) back to a state of control, balance, or composure *b)* to catch or save (oneself) from a slip, stumble, betrayal of feeling, etc. 4 to reclaim (land from the sea, useful substances from waste, etc.) 5 *Law* to get or get back by final judgment in a court [to *recover* damages] 6 *Sports* to gain or regain control or possession of (a fumbled, muffed, wild, or free ball, puck, etc.) —*vi.* 1 to regain health, balance, or control 2 to catch or save oneself from a slip, stumble, self-betrayal, etc. 3 *Law* to succeed in a claim; receive judgment in one's favor 4 *Sports* to recover a ball, puck, etc. —**re·cov′er·a·ble** *adj.*

SYN.—**recover** implies a finding or getting back something that one has lost in any manner [to *recover* stolen property, one's self-possession, etc.];

---

recommission
recompress
recompute
reconception
reconceptualize
recondense
reconduct
reconfiguration
reconfigure
reconfine
reconfirm
reconquer
reconquest
reconsecrate
reconsign
reconsole
reconsolidate
reconsult
recontaminate
reconvene
recook
recopy

regain more strongly stresses a winning back of something that has been taken from one [to *regain* a military objective]; **retrieve** suggests diligent effort in regaining something [he was determined to *retrieve* his honor]; **recoup** implies recovery of an equivalent in compensation [I tried to *recoup* my losses]; **reclaim** implies recovery or restoration to a better or useful state [to *reclaim* wasteland]

re·cov·er (rē kuv′ər) *vt.* to cover again or anew

re·cov·er·ing (ri kuv′ər iŋ) *adj.* abstaining from the use of an addictive substance [a *recovering* alcoholic]

re·cov·er·y (ri kuv′ər ē, -kuv′rē) *n., pl.* **-er·ies** ⟦ME *recoverie* < Anglo-Fr⟧ **1** the act or an instance of recovering; specif., *a)* a regaining of something lost or stolen *b)* a return to health, consciousness, etc. *c)* a regaining of balance, control, composure, etc. *d)* a retrieval of a capsule, nose cone, etc. after a spaceflight or launch *e)* the removal of valuable substances from waste material, byproducts, etc. **2** *Sports* a return to a position of guard, readiness, etc., as after a lunge in fencing or a stroke in rowing **3** a process of attempting to change dysfunctional behavior, as by abstaining from an addictive substance [an alcoholic in *recovery*]

☆**recovery room** a hospital room where postoperative patients are kept for close observation and care

rec·re·ant (rek′rē ənt) [Archaic or Literary] *adj.* ⟦ME < OFr prp. of *recreire,* to surrender allegiance < ML *recredere,* to give in or up < L *re-*, back, again + *credere,* to believe: see CREED⟧ **1** cowardly; craven **2** failing to keep faith; disloyal; traitorous —*n.* **1** a coward; craven **2** a disloyal person; traitor —**rec′re·an·cy** *n.*, **rec′re·ance** —**rec′re·ant·ly** *adv.*

rec·re·ate (rek′rē āt′) *vt.* **-at′ed, -at′ing** ⟦< L *recreatus,* pp. of *recreare,* to restore, refresh, create anew: see RE- & CREATE⟧ to put fresh life into; refresh or restore in body or mind, esp. after work, by play, amusement, or relaxation —*vi.* to take recreation —**rec′re·a′tive** *adj.*

re-cre·ate (rē′krē āt′) *vt.* **-at′ed, -at′ing** to create again or in a new form —**re′-cre·a′tion** *n.* —**re′-cre·a′tive** *adj.*

rec·re·a·tion (rek′rē ā′shən) *n.* ⟦ME *recreacioun* < MFr *recreation* < L *recreatio:* see RECREATE⟧ **1** refreshment in body or mind, as after work, by some form of play, amusement, or relaxation **2** any form of play, amusement, or relaxation used for this purpose, as games, sports, or hobbies —**rec′re·a′tion·al** *adj.*

☆**recreational vehicle** *see* RV[1]

rec·re·a·tion·ist (rek′rē ā′shən ist) *n.* a person who engages in recreation, esp. outdoor recreation such as camping, boating, hunting, etc.

☆**recreation room (**or **hall)** a room, as in a home (or a public hall), equipped for amusement and relaxation or for social activities

rec·re·ment (rek′rə mənt) *n.* ⟦< Fr or L: Fr *récrément* < L *recrementum* < *re-*, back + *cernere,* to separate: see HARVEST⟧ [Now Rare] the worthless part of anything; waste; dross —**rec′re·men′tal** *adj.*

re·crim·i·nate (ri krim′ə nāt′) *vi.* **-nat′ed, -nat′ing** ⟦< ML *recriminatus:* see RE- & CRIMINATE⟧ to answer an accuser by accusing that person in return; reply with a countercharge —**re·crim′i·na′tion** *n.* —**re·crim′i·na·to′ry** (-ə nə tôr′ē) *adj.*, **re·crim′i·na′tive**

☆**rec room (**or **hall)** (rek) *short for* RECREATION ROOM (*or* HALL)

re·cru·desce (rē′kroo̅ des′) *vi.* **-desced′, -desc′ing** ⟦L *recrudescere* < *re-*, again + *crudescere,* to become harsh or raw < *crudus,* raw, CRUDE⟧ to break out again after a period of latency or relative inactivity; become active again, as a disease —**re′cru·des′cence** *n.* —**re′cru·des′cent** *adj.*

re·cruit (ri kroo̅t′) *vt.* ⟦Fr *recruter* < *recrute,* a recruit, lit., new growth < *recrû,* pp. of *recroître,* to grow again < L *re-*, again + *crescere,* to grow, increase: see CRESCENT⟧ **1** to raise or strengthen (an army, navy, etc.) by enlisting personnel **2** to enlist (personnel) into an army or navy **3** *a)* to enlist (new members), as for a party or organization *b)* to hire or engage the services of **4** [Rare] *a)* to increase or maintain by supplying anew; replenish *b)* to revive or restore (health, strength, etc.) **5** to seek to enroll (students) in a college, university, etc., as for the purpose of playing a varsity sport —*vi.* **1** to enlist new personnel, esp. for a military force **2** [Rare] *a)* to get new supplies of something, as in replacement *b)* to regain health, strength, etc. **3** to seek to enroll students, as athletes to play a varsity sport, in college, university, etc. —*n.* **1** a newly enlisted or drafted soldier, sailor, etc. **2** a new member of any group, body, or organization —**re·cruit′er** *n.* —**re·cruit′ment** *n.*

rect *abbrev.* **1** receipt **2** rectangle **3** rectangular

rec·tal (rek′təl) *adj.* of, for, or near the rectum —**rec′tal·ly** *adv.*

rec·tan·gle (rek′taŋ′gəl) *n.* ⟦Fr < ML *rectangulum* < L *rectus* (see RECTI-) + *angulus,* ANGLE[1]⟧ **1** any four-sided plane figure with four right angles **2** any such figure or shape that is not a square; oblong

rec·tan·gu·lar (rek taŋ′gyə lər) *adj.* **1** shaped like a rectangle; having four sides and four right angles **2** having right-angled corners, or a base in the form of a rectangle, as a building **3** right-angled —**rec·tan′gu·lar′i·ty** (-lar′ə tē) *n.* —**rec·tan′gu·lar·ly** *adv.*

rectangular coordinates CARTESIAN COORDINATES

rec·ti- (rek′tə, -ti) ⟦LL < L *rectus,* straight, right < pp. of *regere,* to lead straight, direct, guide, rule: see RIGHT⟧ *combining form* straight, right [*rectilinear*]: also, before a vowel, **rect-**

rec·ti·fi·er (rek′tə fī′ər) *n.* **1** a person or thing that rectifies, as by correction or adjustment **2** *Elec.* a device, esp. a diode, that converts alternating current into direct current

rec·ti·fy (rek′tə fī′) *vt.* **-fied′, -fy′ing** ⟦ME *rectifien* < MFr *rectifier* < LL *rectificare:* see RECTI- & -FY⟧ **1** to put or set right; correct; amend **2** to adjust, as in movement or balance; adjust by calculation **3** *Chem.* to refine or purify (a liquid) by distillation, esp. by fractional or repeated distillations **4** *Elec.* to convert (alternating current) to direct current **5** *Math.* to find the length of (a curve) —**rec′ti·fi′a·ble** *adj.* —**rec′ti·fi·ca′tion** *n.*

rec·ti·lin·e·ar (rek′tə lin′ē ər) *adj.* ⟦< LL *rectilineus* < *recti-* (see RECTI-) + *linea,* LINE[1] + -AR⟧ **1** moving in a straight line **2** forming a straight line **3** bounded or formed by straight lines **4** characterized by straight lines **5** *Optics* corrected so as not to distort straight lines: said of a type of lens Also **rec′ti·lin′e·al** —**rec′ti·lin′e·ar·ly** *adv.*

rec·ti·tude (rek′tə too̅d′, -tyoo̅d′) *n.* ⟦ME < MFr < LL *rectitudo* < L *rectus,* right: see RECTI-⟧ **1** conduct according to moral principles; strict honesty; uprightness of character **2** correctness of judgment or method **3** [Rare] straightness

rec·to (rek′tō) *n., pl.* **-tos** ⟦< ModL (*folio*) *recto,* on the right side of (a leaf) < L, abl. of *rectus:* see RECTI-⟧ *Printing* **1** any right-hand page of a book **2** the front side of a leaf Opposed to VERSO

rec·to- (rek′tō, -tə) ⟦< L *rectum:* see RECTUM⟧ *combining form* rectum, rectum and [*rectocele*]: also, before a vowel, **rect-**

rec·to·cele (rek′tə sēl′) *n.* ⟦prec. + -CELE⟧ a hernial protrusion of the rectum into the vagina

rec·tor (rek′tər) *n.* ⟦ME < L < pp. of *regere,* to rule: see RIGHT⟧ **1** [Obs.] a ruler, governor, or leader **2** an Episcopal minister in charge of a parish **3** in the Church of England, *a)* a member of the clergy who holds the rights and tithes of a parish *b)* the priest leading a team ministry **4** *R.C.Ch.* *a)* a priest heading a seminary, college, etc. *b)* sometimes, a pastor or other head priest **5** in certain schools, colleges, and universities, the head or headmaster —**rec′tor·ate** (-it) *n.* —**rec·to′ri·al** (-tôr′ē əl) *adj.*

rec·to·ry (rek′tər ē) *n., pl.* **-ries** ⟦ML *rectoria*⟧ **1** the house in which an Episcopal minister lives **2** in the Church of England, *a)* a benefice held by a rector *b)* the house in which a rector lives **3** *R.C.Ch.* the house in which a parish priest lives

rec·trix (rek′triks) *n., pl.* **rec·tri·ces** (rek′trə sēz′, rek trī′sēz) ⟦ModL < L, fem. of *rector,* director: see RECTOR⟧ *Ornithology* any of the large tail feathers of a bird, that are important for controlling the direction of flight

rec·tum (rek′təm) *n., pl.* **-tums** or **-ta** (-tə) ⟦ModL < L *rectum* (*intestinum*), lit., straight (intestine) < *rectus:* see RECTI-⟧ the lowest, or last, segment of the large intestine, extending, in humans, from the sigmoid flexure to the anus

rec·tus (rek′təs) *n., pl.* **-ti′** (-tī′) ⟦ModL < L *rectus* (*musculus*), lit., straight (muscle): see RECTI-⟧ any of various straight muscles, as of the eye, neck, or thigh

re·cum·bent (ri kum′bənt) *adj.* ⟦L *recumbens,* prp. of *recumbere* < *re-*, back + *-cumbere;* akin to *cubare,* to lie down: see CUBE[1]⟧ **1** *a)* lying down; reclining; leaning *b)* resting; idle **2** *Biol.* designating a part that leans or lies upon some other part or surface —*SYN.* PRONE —**re·cum′ben·cy** *n.* —**re·cum′bent·ly** *adv.*

re·cu·per·ate (ri koo̅′pə rāt′, -kyoo̅′-) *vt.* **-at′ed, -at′ing** ⟦< L *recuperatus,* pp. of *recuperare,* to recover: akin to *recipere,* to bring back, recover: see RECEIVE⟧ to get back, or recover (losses, health, etc.) —*vi.* **1** to be restored to health, strength, etc.; get well again; recover **2** to recover losses, etc. —**re·cu′per·a′tion** *n.* —**re·cu′per·a′tive** (-pə rāt′iv, -pə rə tiv) *adj.*, **re·cu′per·a·to′ry** —**re·cu′per·a′tor** *n.*

re·cur (ri kʉr′) *vi.* **-curred′, -cur′ring** ⟦L *recurrere,* lit., to run back, return < *re-*, back + *currere,* to run: see COURSE⟧ **1** to have recourse (*to*) **2** to return, as in thought, talk, or memory [*recurring* to an earlier question] **3** to occur again, as in talk or memory; come up again for consideration **4** to happen or occur again, esp. after some lapse of time; appear at intervals

re·cur·rence (ri kʉr′əns) *n.* ⟦< fol.⟧ the act or an instance of recurring; reoccurrence, return, repetition, etc.

re·cur·rent (-ənt) *adj.* ⟦L *recurrens,* prp.⟧ **1** appearing or occurring again or periodically **2** *Anat.* turning back in the opposite direction: said of certain arteries and nerves —*SYN.* INTERMITTENT —**re·cur′rent·ly** *adv.*

recurring decimal REPEATING DECIMAL

re·cur·sion (ri kʉr′zhən) *n.* ⟦LL *recursio,* a running back, return < *recurrere:* see RECUR⟧ a generating of the next number or result in a series by reapplying the algorithm on which the series is based to the number or result in the series that preceded it

re·cur·sive (ri kʉr′siv) *adj.* ⟦L *recurs-* (stem of *recurrere,* to run back: see RECUR) + -IVE⟧ **1** reapplying the same formula or algorithm to a number or result in order to generate the next number or result in a series **2** returning again and again to a point or points already made [a *recursive* style of writing]

re·cur·vate (rē kʉr′vit, -vāt′) *adj.* ⟦L *recurvatus,* pp.⟧ recurved; bent back

re·curve (rē kʉrv′) *vt., vi.* **-curved′, -curv′ing** ⟦L *recurvare* < *re-*, back + *curvare* < *curvus:* see CURVE⟧ to curve or bend back or backward

rec·u·sant (rek′yoo zənt, ri kyoo̅′zənt) *n.* ⟦L *recusans,* prp. of *recusare,* to reject < *re-*, against + *causari,* to dispute, pretend < *causa,* reason, CAUSE⟧ **1** a person who refuses to obey an established authority; specif., in England in the 16th to 18th cent., a Roman Catholic who refused to attend the services of the Church of England or to recognize its authority **2** any dissenter or nonconformist —*adj.* of or like a recusant —**rec′u·san·cy** *n.*

recross **recrown** **recrystallize** **recultivate**

re·cuse (ri kyo͞oz′) *vt., vi.* **-cused′, -cus′ing** ⟦ME *recusen* < MFr *recuser* < L *recusare:* see prec.⟧ to disqualify or withdraw from a position of judging, as because of prejudice or personal interest —**re·cus′al** *n.*

re·cy·cle (rē sī′kəl) *vt.* **-cled, -cling** **1** to pass through a cycle or part of a cycle again, as for checking, treating, etc. **2** to use again and again, as a single supply of water in cooling, washing, diluting, etc. **3** *a)* to treat or process in order to use again *b)* to gather up and turn in (empty bottles and cans, old newspapers, etc.) to be so treated or processed **4** to alter or adapt to a new use or function [*recycle* an old tenement into condominiums] **5** to use again; bring back; reuse [*recycle* a speech from a previous campaign] —*vi.* **1** to pass through a cycle, system, etc. and return to the starting point again or repeatedly [the electronic flash *recycles* in 5 seconds; the water *recycles* through the cooling system] **2** to engage in recycling empty bottles, old newspapers, etc. —**re·cy′cla·ble** (-klə bəl) *adj.* —**re·cy′cler** (-klər, -kəl ər) *n.* —**re·cy′cling** *n.*

red (red) *n.* ⟦ME < OE *read,* akin to Ger *rot,* ON *rauthr* < IE base **reudh-,* red > Gr *erythros,* L *ruber, rufus,* red, *rubere,* to be red, OIr *rūad,* Lith *raũdas,* red⟧ **1** a primary color, or any of a spread of colors at the lower end of the visible spectrum, varying in hue from that of blood to pale rose or pink: see COLOR **2** a pigment producing this color **3** ⟦from the red flag symbolizing revolutionary socialism⟧ [*often* **R-**] [Informal] a political radical or revolutionary; esp., a communist **4** anything colored red, as a red space on a roulette wheel, a red checker piece, or red clothing **5** *short for* RED WINE **6** [Slang] a red capsule of secobarbital, a barbiturate: *usually used in pl.* —*adj.* **red′der, red′dest** **1** having or being of the color red or any of its hues **2** having red hair **3** *a)* having a reddish or coppery skin *b)* florid, flushed, or blushing *c)* bloodshot *d)* sore; inflamed **4** *a)* [*often* **R-**] politically radical or revolutionary; esp., communist *b)* [**R-**] of the Soviet Union **5** ⟦see BLUE STATE⟧ [Informal] Republican —☆**in the red** ⟦see RED INK⟧ in debt or losing money —☆**into the red** ⟦see RED INK⟧ into debt or an unprofitable financial condition —**see red** [Informal] to be or become angry —**red′ly** *adv.*

re·dact (ri dakt′) *vt.* ⟦ME *redacten* < L *redactus,* pp. of *redigere,* to bring into a certain condition, reduce to order (see RE- & ACT[1]): in sense 2, prob. back-form. < fol.⟧ **1** to write out or draw up (a proclamation, edict, etc.); frame **2** to arrange in proper form for publication; edit **3** to delete (private or sensitive information) from a document, in preparation for publication —**re·dac′tor** *n.*

re·dac·tion (ri dak′shən) *n.* ⟦Fr *rédaction* < LL *redactio:* see prec.⟧ **1** the preparation of written work for publication; editing, reediting, or revision **2** an edited work; esp., a reissue or new edition **3** deletion of private or sensitive information from a document, in preparation for publication

red admiral ⟦see ADMIRAL⟧ a purplish-black European and North American butterfly (*Vanessa atalanta*) with white spots near the tips of the forewings and bright-orange bands across the forewings and bordering the hind wings

red alert **1** a warning of imminent danger **2** a state or condition with such a warning in effect

red algae any of a division (Rhodophycota) of photosynthetic thallophytes, including reddish, brownish-red, pink, or purple algae that form shrublike masses in the depths of the oceans

Red Angus a variety of Angus beef cattle, with a reddish coat

red ant any reddish ant, esp. the pharaoh ant

red·bait (red′bāt′) *vi., vt.* ⟦< RED, *adj.* 4 + BAIT, *vt.* 2⟧ [*often* **R-**] to denounce (a person or group) as being communist, esp. with little or no evidence —**red′bait′er** *n.*

☆**red·bel·ly dace** (-bel′ē) either of two E North American, brightly colored, freshwater dace fishes (genus *Phoxinus*)

red·bird (-burd′) *n.* any of several predominantly red-colored birds, as the cardinal or scarlet tanager

red blood cell ERYTHROCYTE: also called **red blood corpuscle**

red-blood·ed (red′blud′id) *adj.* high-spirited and strong-willed; vigorous, lusty, etc.

red·breast (-brest′) *n.* ⟦ME *redbrest,* robin⟧ **1** any of several birds with a reddish breast; esp., the American robin, the European robin, or the knot ☆**2** a sunfish (*Lepomis auritus*) with an orange-red belly, found in the E U.S.

red·brick or **red-brick** (-brik′) *adj.* ⟦from the typical building material (in contrast to the stone of Oxford and Cambridge)⟧ designating or of a British university or college other than Oxford or Cambridge; esp., any of the newer ones in the provinces: often connoting social inferiority —*n.* a redbrick university or college

Red·bridge (red′brij′) borough of NE Greater London, England

☆**red·bud** (-bud′) *n.* CERCIS

☆**red·bug** (-bug′) *n.* any of various red insects, as a cotton stainer or chigger

red·cap (-kap′) *n.* ⟦first used (1892) when John Williams, a porter in Grand Central Station, New York City, encircled his cap with a red flannel strip to gain attention⟧ ☆**1** a baggage porter, as in a railroad station **2** [Brit. Informal] a military policeman

red carpet **1** a long red carpet or runner, laid out at a reception or other special event for guests to walk on ☆**2** a very grand or impressive welcome and entertainment: with *the* —**roll out the red carpet (for)** to welcome and entertain in a grand and impressive style —**red′-car′pet** *adj.*

☆**red cedar** **1** any of a number of juniper trees or shrubs with bluish, berrylike fruit and red wood; esp., *a)* the **eastern red cedar** (*Juniperus virginiana*) of E North America, with fragrant wood often used to line closets and chests *b)* the **Rocky Mountain red cedar** (*J. scopulorum*), valued for lumber **2** the wood of any of these

red cell ERYTHROCYTE

☆**red cent** [Informal] a cent; penny; trifling amount: esp. in **not worth a red cent, not give a red cent,** etc.

red clay *Geol.* **1** clayey material colored red by iron oxide **2** a soft, reddish clay deposit, restricted to the deepest parts of the ocean bottom and containing volcanic, meteoritic, and other insoluble material

Red Cloud 1822-1909; Dakota Indian chief

red clover a kind of clover (*Trifolium pratense*) with flowers in reddish, ball-shaped heads, grown for fodder and forage

red·coat (red′kōt′) *n.* a British soldier in a uniform with a red coat, as during the American Revolution

red coral any of various gorgonian corals of warm seas; esp., a species (*Corallium nobile*) often taken from the Mediterranean region, whose smooth, hard, blood-red skeleton is used for jewelry

red corpuscle ERYTHROCYTE

Red Crescent ⟦after fol.: see CRESCENT (*n.* 4)⟧ a Muslim organization equivalent to the Red Cross: its symbol is a red crescent

Red Cross **1** a red Greek cross on a white ground (*Geneva cross*), emblem of neutrality in war, adapted from the Swiss flag, with colors reversed, and used since 1864 to mark hospitals, ambulances, etc., esp. in time of war **2** an international society (in full **International Red Cross**) for the relief of suffering in time of war or disaster: its emblem is the Geneva cross **3** any national branch of the International Red Cross

redd[1] (red) *vt., vi.* **redd** or **redd′ed, redd′ing** ⟦ME (North Eng & Scot) *redden* < OE *hreddan,* to free, take away: sense infl. by assoc. with OE *gerǣdan,* to put in order < *rǣde,* prepared: see READY⟧ [Informal or Dial.] to put in order; make (a place) tidy: usually with *up*

redd[2] (red) *n.* ⟦< ?⟧ the spawning area of trout or salmon

red deer **1** a deer (*Cervus elaphus*) native to Europe and Asia ☆**2** the white-tailed deer in its reddish summer coat

red·den (red′'n) *vt.* to make red —*vi.* to become red; esp., to blush or flush

red·dish (red′ish) *adj.* somewhat red —**red′dish·ness** *n.*

red·dle (red′'l) *n., vt.* **-dled, -dling** *var. of* RUDDLE

☆**red-dog** (red′dôg′) *n., vt., vi.* **-dogged′, -dog′ging** ⟦< RED (the traditional color of shirt worn by the defense in scrimmages) + DOG (*vt.* 1)⟧ *Football* BLITZ (*n.* 3, *vt.* 2, *vi.*)

☆**red drum** a large, edible drum fish (*Sciaenops ocellatus*) of the Atlantic coast of the U.S.

red dwarf *pl.* **red dwarfs** or occas. **red dwarves** a star that is cooler on its surface, smaller, and of fainter luminosity than the sun

red dye any of several artificial red pigments added to cosmetics or food

rede (rēd) [Archaic] *n.* ⟦ME < OE *rǣd* (akin to Ger *rat*) < base of *rǣdan,* to interpret (see READ[1]: the *vt.* is the same word, with retained ME sp.)⟧ **1** counsel; advice **2** a plan; scheme **3** a story; tale **4** an interpretation —*vt.* **red′ed, red′ing** **1** to advise; counsel **2** to interpret (dreams, omens, etc.) **3** to narrate; tell

☆**red·ear** (red′ir′) *n.* a sunfish (*Lepomis microlophus*) of the central and SE U.S., with bright red gill covers

re·dec·o·rate (rē dek′ə rāt′) *vt., vi.* **-rat′ed, -rat′ing** to renovate or change the colors, furnishings, decorations, etc. of (a house, room, office, etc.) —**re·dec′o·ra′tion** *n.*

re·deem (ri dēm′) *vt.* ⟦LME *redemen* < MFr *redimer* < L *redimere* < *re(d)-,* back + *emere,* to get, buy < IE base **em-,* to take > Lith *imù,* OSlav *imǫ,* to take⟧ **1** to buy back **2** to get back; recover, as by paying a fee **3** to pay off (a mortgage or note) ☆**4** *a)* to convert (paper money) into gold or silver coin or bullion *b)* to convert (stocks, bonds, etc.) into cash *c)* to turn in (trading stamps or coupons) for a prize, premium, discount, etc. **5** *a)* to set free by paying a ransom *b)* to deliver from sin and its penalties, as by a sacrifice made for the sinner **6** to fulfill (a promise or pledge) **7** *a)* to make amends or atone for [to *redeem* a blunder] *b)* to restore (oneself) to favor by making amends *c)* to make worthwhile; justify —**SYN.** RESCUE —**re·deem′a·ble** *adj.,* **re·demp′ti·ble** (-demp′tə b'l)

re·deem·er (-ər) *n.* **1** a person who redeems **2** [**R-**] Jesus Christ: often with *the*

re·de·mand (rē′di mand′, -mänd′) *vt.* **1** to demand again **2** to demand back; demand the return of

re·demp·tion (ri demp′shən) *n.* ⟦ME *redempcion* < OFr < L *redemptio,* a buying back, in LL(Ec), release from sin < *redemptus,* pp. of *redimere:* see REDEEM⟧ **1** a redeeming or being redeemed (in various senses) **2** something that redeems —**the Redemption** *Christian Theol.* the redeeming of humanity and its reconciliation with God through the suffering and death of Jesus Christ —**re·demp′tion·al** *adj.*

☆**re·demp·tion·er** (-ər) *n.* ⟦prec. + -ER⟧ [Historical] a person who paid for passage to America by a period of service as an indentured servant

re·demp·tive (ri demp′tiv) *adj.* ⟦ML *redemptivus*⟧ **1** serving to redeem **2** of redemption Also **re·demp′to·ry**

Re·demp·tor·ist (ri demp′tər ist) *n.* ⟦Fr *rédemptoriste* < LL(Ec) *redemptor,* redeemer < L, a contractor, one who releases a debtor by paying his creditor < *redemptus:* see REDEMPTION⟧ a member of the Congregation of the Most Holy Redeemer, a Roman Catholic congregation of men doing missionary work, esp. among the poor

---

redamage
redecide
rededicate
rededication
redefine
redefinition
redeliver
redemonstrate

re·de·ploy (rē′di ploi′) *vt., vi.* to move (troops, etc.) from one front or area to another —**re′de·ploy′ment** *n.*

re·de·vel·op (rē′di vel′əp) *vt.* **1** to develop again **2** to rebuild, restore, or improve (an area, as of run-down houses) —**re′de·vel′op·ment** *n.*

red·eye (red′ī′) *n.* ☆**1** any of various fishes having red eyes, as the rock bass **2** RED-EYED VIREO ☆**3** [Slang] strong, cheap whiskey

☆**red-eye** (red′ī′) *adj.* ⟦from the bloodshot eyes of someone who has not slept⟧ [Slang] designating a late-night or all-night commercial airline flight —*n.* [Slang] such a flight

☆**red-eyed vireo** (red′īd′) a North American vireo (*Vireo olivaceus*) with gray and olive-green coloring

red-eye gravy gravy made by adding water and, usually, a little black coffee to the juices left in the pan in which ham has been fried

red-faced (red′fāst′) *adj.* **1** having a red or ruddy face **2** showing, as by blushing, a feeling of embarrassment; ashamed

red feed any of several red, surface-living, saltwater copepods (esp. *Calanus finmarchicus*), used as food by fishes

☆**red·fin** (red′fin′) *n.* any of various fishes having reddish fins, as a pickerel (*Esox americanus*) of E North America

red fir **1** any of various firs with reddish wood, as the **California red fir** (*Abies magnifica*) **2** the wood of any of these trees ☆**3** DOUGLAS FIR

red·fish (-fish′) *n., pl.* **-fish′** or **-fish′es** (see FISH) any of various fishes with a reddish coloration, as the red drum

red flag **1** a warning flag **2** [Informal] something serving as a warning of trouble or danger ahead **3** [Informal] something that arouses anger, irritation, revolt, etc.

red-flag (red′flag′) *vt.* **-flagged′**, **-flag′ging** to mark, designate, or otherwise call attention to as being risky, unsuitable, etc.

☆**red-flan·nel hash** (red′flan′əl) [Dial.] hash made of ground corned beef, potatoes, and beets

☆**red fox** **1** a common fox (*Vulpes vulpes*) of Europe and North America: cf. SILVER FOX **2** the reddish fur of this fox

red giant a star of low surface temperature but with great luminosity resulting from its great size

red grouse a reddish-brown ptarmigan (*Lagopus lagopus scotica*) of the British Isles that does not turn white in winter

Red Guard a member of the militant activist groups in China in the late 1960s

red gum **1** *a)* any of several Australian eucalyptus trees *b)* the wood of any of these trees ☆**2** SWEET GUM (senses 1 & 2)

red-hand·ed (red′han′did) *adv.* ⟦from the image of the hands covered with a victim's blood⟧ **1** while committing a crime or doing some wrong **2** in an undeniably incriminating or compromising situation

red hat a flat, wide-brimmed red hat presented to a new cardinal by the pope as a symbol of the cardinal's rank

red·head (red′hed′) *n.* **1** a person with red hair ☆**2** a North American diving duck (*Aythya americana*): the male is similar to the canvasback in having a red head, black breast, and grayish body

red·head·ed (-hed′id) *adj.* having red hair, as a person, or a red head, as a bird

☆**redheaded woodpecker** a North American woodpecker (*Melanerpes erythrocephalus*), with a bright-red head and neck, black back, and white underparts

red heat **1** the temperature at which a substance is red-hot **2** the state of being at this temperature

red herring **1** a smoked herring **2** something used to divert attention from the basic issue: from the practice of drawing a herring across the trace in hunting, to distract the hounds **3** *Finance* [Informal] a preliminary prospectus, subject to amendment, for an issue of securities: from the notice printed on the front in red ink

red hind a red-spotted grouper (*Epinephelus guttatus*) ranging from the West Indies to Brazil; cabrilla

red-hot (red′hät′) *adj.* **1** hot enough to glow; very hot **2** very excited, angry, ardent, etc. **3** very new; current [*red-hot* news] —☆*n.* [Informal] a frankfurter; hot dog

re·di·a (rē′dē ə) *n., pl.* **re′di·ae′** (-dē ē′) ⟦ModL, after F. *Redi,* 17th-c. It naturalist⟧ a larval stage of many trematodes, usually parasitic in a host snail, produced by a sporocyst and producing daughter rediae or cercariae

re·di·al (rē dī′əl; *for n.* rē′dī′əl) *vt., vi.* to dial (a telephone number) again —*n.* an electronic telephone device that stores a number so that it can be dialed again automatically, as by pushing a single button

Red Indian ⟦in allusion to the typical skin color, perceived as reddish brown: as distinguished from the *Indian* of India⟧ [Chiefly Brit.] an American Indian: now considered offensive by some

red·in·gote (red′iŋ gōt′) *n.* ⟦Fr, altered < E *riding coat*⟧ **1** [Historical] a man's long, full-skirted overcoat **2** a long, unlined, lightweight coat, open down the front, worn by women

red ink ⟦from the use of *red ink* to enter debits in account books⟧ **1** a deficit or loss shown in the accounts of a bank, company, etc. **2** the condition of showing such a loss or deficit

red·in·te·grate (ri din′tə grāt′) *vt.* **-grat′ed**, **-grat′ing** ⟦ME *redintegraten* < L *redintegratus,* pp. of *redintegrare:* see RE- & INTEGRATE⟧ to make whole or perfect again; reunite; reestablish

red·in·te·gra·tion (ri din′tə grā′shən) *n.* ⟦ME *redyntegracyon* < L *redintegratio*⟧ **1** a redintegrating or being redintegrated **2** *Psychol.* the tendency to respond to a later stimulus in the same way as to an earlier complex stimulus of which the later one was a part

re·di·rect (rē′də rekt′, -dī-) *vt.* to direct again or to a different place —☆*adj. Law* designating the examination of one's own witness again, after cross-examination by the opposing lawyer —**re′di·rec′tion** *n.*

re·dis·count (rē dis′kount) *vt.* to discount (esp. commercial paper) for a second time —*n.* **1** the act or process of rediscounting **2** rediscounted commercial paper —**re′dis·count′a·ble** *adj.*

rediscount rate ☆the rate of interest charged by a district Federal Reserve Bank for rediscounting top-grade commercial paper offered by its member banks

re·dis·trib·ute (rē′dis trib′yo͞ot) *vt.* **-ut·ed**, **-ut·ing** to distribute again or in a different way —**re′dis·tri·bu′tion** *n.* —**re′dis·trib′u·tive** *adj.*

☆**re·dis·trict** (rē dis′trikt) *vt.* to divide anew into districts, esp. so as to reapportion electoral representatives

red·i·vi·vus (red′i vī′vəs) *adj.* ⟦LL < L, renewed, renovated < *red-,* RE- + *vivus,* living < *vivere:* see QUICK⟧ restored to life; reborn; reincarnated: usually used metaphorically [a Napoleon *redivivus*]

red lead red oxide of lead, Pb_3O_4, derived from massicot, used in making paint, in glassmaking, etc.

red-let·ter (red′let′ər) *adj.* designating a memorable or joyous day or event: from the custom of marking holidays on the calendar in red ink

red light **1** any danger or warning signal; specif., a red lamp, flare, etc. **2** a red signal on a traffic light, indicating that a vehicle should come to a full stop

☆**red-light district** (red′līt′) a district (in a town or city) containing many brothels: such brothels formerly displayed red lights

red·line (red′līn′) *n.* the maximum safe speed, power, etc. of an engine, usually indicated by a red line or mark on a gauge, as a tachometer —*vi.* **-lined′**, **-lin′ing** to attain the maximum safe speed, power, etc. [a car that *redlines* at 7,500 rpm] —*vt.* to refuse to provide loans or insurance in (a neighborhood) by redlining —**red′lin′er** *n.*

red line the red line, parallel to the goal lines, that divides an ice hockey rink in half: cf. BLUE LINE

☆**red·lin·ing** (red′līn′iŋ) *n.* ⟦from the practice of outlining such areas in red on a map⟧ the systematic refusal by some lending institutions or insurance companies to issue mortgage loans or insurance on property in certain neighborhoods regarded by them as deteriorating

red man ⟦see REDSKIN (*n.* 2)⟧ ☆[Old-fashioned] a North American Indian: now an offensive term

red maple a tall E North American maple (*Acer rubrum*) that has reddish twigs, leaves that turn scarlet in the fall, and wood used for furniture

red meat meat that is red before cooking; esp., beef or mutton as distinguished from pork, veal, poultry, etc.

☆**red·neck** or **red-neck** (red′nek′) *n.* ⟦from the reddened, sunburned necks characteristic of agricultural workers⟧ [Slang] a poor, white, rural Southerner, often, specif., one regarded as ignorant, bigoted, violent, etc.: often a derogatory term

red·ness (-nis) *n.* the state or quality of being red

re·do (rē do͞o′) *vt.* **-did′**, **-done′**, **-do′ing** **1** to do again or do over **2** to redecorate (a room, etc.) —*n.* the act or an instance of redoing

☆**red oak** **1** any of several oaks having leaves with sharp-tipped lobes, dark bark, and acorns which require two years to mature **2** the reddish, hard wood of such a tree

red ocher a red, earthy hematite, used as a pigment

red·o·lence (red′'l əns) *n.* the quality or state of being redolent: also **red′o·len·cy** —*SYN.* SCENT

red·o·lent (-ənt) *adj.* ⟦OFr < L *redolens,* prp. of *redolere,* to emit a scent < *re(d)-,* intens. + *olere,* to smell (akin to *odor,* ODOR)⟧ **1** sweet-smelling; fragrant **2** smelling (*of*) [*redolent* of the ocean] **3** suggestive or evocative (*of*) —**red′o·lent·ly** *adv.*

Re·don (rə dōn′), **O·di·lon** (ô dē lōn′) 1840-1916; Fr. painter & lithographer

☆**red osier** **1** a shrubby dogwood (*Cornus stolonifera*) with dark-red branches and white or bluish fruit **2** any of several willows with reddish or purple stems

re·dou·ble (rē dub′əl) *vt.* **-bled**, **-bling** ⟦LME *redoublen* < MFr *redoubler:* see RE- & DOUBLE⟧ **1** *a)* to make twice as much or twice as great *b)* to make much greater; intensify [*redouble* your efforts] **2** to make echo or reecho **3** to refold; double back **4** [Archaic] to repeat —*vi.* **1** to become twice as great or twice as much **2** to reecho **3** to turn backward, as on one's tracks **4** *Bridge* to further increase the point value or penalty of a bid which an opponent has doubled —*n. Bridge* a redoubling

re·doubt (ri dout′) *n.* ⟦Fr *redoute* < It *ridotta* < ML *reductus,* refuge, orig. pp. of L *reducere:* see REDUCE⟧ **1** *a)* a breastwork outside a fortification, to defend approaches, etc. *b)* a breastwork within a fortification **2** any stronghold

re·doubt·a·ble (-ə bəl) *adj.* ⟦ME *redowtable* < MFr *redoutable* < *redouter,* to fear, dread < L *re-,* intens. + *dubitare,* to DOUBT⟧ **1** formidable; fearsome [a *redoubtable* foe] **2** commanding respect [a *redoubtable* logician] —**re·doubt′a·bly** *adv.*

---

redeposit	**redesign**	**rediscover**	**redissolve**
redescend	**redetermine**	**rediscovery**	**redistill**
redescribe	**redifferentiate**	**redispose**	**redivide**

re·dound (ri dound′) *vi.* ⟦ME *redounden* < MFr *redonder* < L *redundare,* to overflow < *re(d)-,* intens. + *undare,* to surge, swell < *unda,* a wave: see WATER⟧ **1** to have a result or effect (*to* the credit or discredit, etc. of someone or something) **2** to come back; react; recoil (*upon*): said of honor or disgrace **3** [Obs.] to surge up or overflow

red·out (red′out′) *n.* ⟦RED + (BLACK)OUT⟧ a blurring of vision, as if by a red mist, caused by the forcing of blood into the head during feet-first acceleration, as in flying

re·dox (rē′däks′) *n.* ⟦< *red(uction-)ox(idation)*⟧ *Chem.* OXIDATION-REDUCTION

red panda LESSER PANDA

red-pen·cil (red′pen′səl) *vt.* **-ciled** or **-cilled, -cil·ing** or **-cil·ling** to edit or revise with or as if with a pencil having red lead

red pepper 1 any of various capsicums having a many-seeded green fruit that turns red when it is ripe: see CAPSICUM **2** the fruit

red pine a large pine (*Pinus resinosa*), with long, brittle needles in groups of two and reddish brown bark

Red Planet, the *name for* the planet Mars

red·poll (red′pōl′) *n.* ⟦RED + POLL⟧ any of a number of finches (genus *Acanthis*) with a red patch on the head and a black chin

Red Poll (pōl) any of a breed of medium-sized, reddish beef and dairy cattle with no horns, originating in Norfolk and Suffolk counties, England

re·draft (rē′draft′, -dräft′; *for v.* rē draft′, -dräft′) *n.* **1** a second or later draft or framing, as of a legislative bill **2** a new draft on the original drawer or endorser of a protested bill of exchange, for the amount of the bill plus charges and costs —*vt.* to draft again or anew

re·dress (ri dres′; *for n., usually* rē′dres′) *vt.* ⟦ME *redressen* < OFr *redrecier:* see RE- & DRESS⟧ **1** to set right; rectify or remedy, often by making compensation for (a wrong, grievance, etc.) **2** [Now Rare] to make amends to —*n.* **1** a compensation or satisfaction, as for a wrong done **2** the act of redressing —*SYN.* REPARATION —**redress the balance (**or **scales)** to make a fair adjustment; see that justice is done —**re·dress′a·ble** *adj.* —**re·dress′er** *n.*

re-dress (rē dres′) *vt.* to dress again

Red River 1 river flowing southeast along the Texas-Oklahoma border, through SW Ark. & central La. into the Mississippi: 1,018 mi (1,638 km) **2** river flowing north along the North Dakota-Minnesota border into Lake Winnipeg in Manitoba, Canada: *c.* 310 mi (499 km): in full **Red River of the North 3** river in Southeast Asia, flowing from Yunnan province, China, southeast across Vietnam, into the Gulf of Tonkin: *c.* 500 mi (805 km): Annamese name HONG; Chin. name YUAN

☆**red·root** (red′ro͞ot′, -ro͝ot′) *n.* any of various plants with red roots, as *a)* a small shrub (genus *Ceanothus*) of the buckthorn family *b)* a marsh plant (*Lachnanthes tinctoria*) of the bloodwort family, with sword-shaped leaves and flat clusters of small, woolly, yellow flowers, found along the Atlantic coast of the U.S. *c)* PIGWEED (sense 1) *d)* BLOODROOT

red salmon SOCKEYE SALMON

Red Sea sea between NE Africa & W Arabia, connected with the Mediterranean Sea by the Suez Canal & with the Indian Ocean by the Gulf of Aden: *c.* 1,400 mi (2,253 km) long: *c.* 174,900 sq mi (452,989 sq km)

red·shank (red′shaŋk′) *n.* either of two European sandpipers with reddish legs, esp. the more common species (*Tringa totanus*)

red·shift (red′shift′) *n. Astron.* the shift of spectral lines toward the longer wavelengths and lower frequencies at the red end of the spectrum in a luminous celestial body, indicating that the light source is moving rapidly away from the observer: thought to be a Doppler effect explaining an expanding universe, or the result of a strong gravitational field: cf. BLUESHIFT: also written **red shift** —**red′shift′ed** *adj.*

☆**red·shirt** (red′shurt′) [Informal] *vt.* ⟦from the traditional red shirts worn by the scrimmage team, with whom such players may continue to practice⟧ to withdraw (a player) from a varsity team for a year so that the player will be eligible for athletics an extra year later —*n.* such a player

red-shoul·dered hawk (red′shōl′dərd) a dark-colored, North American hawk (*Buteo lineatus*) having a reddish patch on each shoulder and thick bands of white on the tail feathers

red siskin a South American finch (*Çarduelis cucullata*) with a black head and red body, sometimes kept as a cage bird

red·skin (red′skin′) *n.* **1** ⟦descriptive⟧ a kind of white potato that has a reddish skin: in full **redskin potato 2** ⟦in allusion to the typical skin color, perceived as reddish brown⟧ an American Indian: now considered by many to be an offensive term

☆**red snapper 1** a reddish, edible, deep-water snapper fish (*Lutjanus campechanus*) of the Gulf of Mexico and W Atlantic **2** any of several other reddish fishes, as a rockfish (*Sebastes ruberrimus*) of the E Pacific

red spider any of a number of small spider mites that can defoliate plants

red squill 1 a variety of sea onion having red bulbs which yield a powder used chiefly in rat poison **2** this powder

☆**red squirrel** a common North American tree squirrel (genus *Tamiasciurus*) with reddish fur

red·start (-stärt′) *n.* ⟦RED + obs. *start* < ME *stert,* tail < OE *steort:* see STARK-NAKED⟧ **1** any of a genus (*Phoenicurus*) of small European thrushes with a reddish tail, esp. a common species (*P. phoenicurus*) ☆**2** any of various wood warblers; esp. the **American redstart** (*Setophaga ruticilla*), the male of which is black and orange above and white below

red state ⟦see BLUE STATE⟧ a state whose voters chose predominantly the Republican candidate in the most recent presidential election: cf. BLUE STATE —**red stat′er**

red-tailed hawk (red′tāld′) a large, North American hawk (*Buteo jamaicensis*) having a reddish tail and wing feathers that are dark brown on the upper side but light-colored on the underside

red tape ⟦from the tape commonly used to tie official papers⟧ **1** official forms and routines **2** too great attention to regulations and routine, resulting in delay in getting business done

☆**red tide** a reddish discoloration of sea waters, caused by large numbers of red dinoflagellates (esp. genera *Gymnodinium* and *Gonyaulax*) that kill fish and other organisms by releasing poisonous products

red·top (-täp′) *n.* ⟦from the reddish panicle of some forms⟧ ☆a grass (*Agrostis gigantea*) grown in the cooler parts of North America for hay, pasturage, and lawns

re·duce (ri do͞os′, -dyo͞os′) *vt.* **-duced′, -duc′ing** ⟦ME *reducen* < L *reducere,* to lead back < *re-,* back + *ducere,* to lead: see DUCT⟧ **1** *a)* to lessen in any way, as in size, weight, amount, value, price, etc.; diminish *b)* to put into a simpler or more concentrated form **2** to bring into a certain order; systematize **3** to break up into constituent elements by analysis **4** *a)* to put into a different form [to *reduce* a talk to writing] *b)* to change to a different physical form, as by melting, crushing, grinding, etc. **5** to lower, as in rank or position; demote; downgrade **6** *a)* to bring to order, attention, obedience, etc., as by persuasion or force *b)* to subdue or conquer (a city or fort) by siege or attack **7** *a)* to bring into difficult or wretched circumstances [a people *reduced* to poverty] *b)* to compel by need to do something [*reduced* to stealing] **8** *a)* to weaken in bodily strength; make thin [*reduced* to skin and bones] *b)* to thin (paint, lacquer, etc.), as with turpentine **9** *Arith.* to change in denomination or form without changing in value [to *reduce* fractions to their lowest terms] **10** *Chem. a)* to decrease the positive valence of (an element or ion) *b)* to increase the number of electrons of (an atom, element, or ion) *c)* to remove the oxygen from; deoxidize *d)* to combine with hydrogen *e)* to bring into the metallic state by removing nonmetallic elements **11** *Cooking* to boil (a liquid) in order to decrease the volume and concentrate the flavors **12** *Phonet.* to articulate (a vowel) in a central position, giving it a neutral quality, as in an unstressed syllable **13** *Photog.* to weaken or lower the density of (a negative or print) by removing metallic silver **14** *Surgery* to restore (a broken bone, displaced organ, etc.) to normal position or condition —*vi.* **1** to become reduced **2** to lose weight, as by dieting —*SYN.* DECREASE —**re·duc′i·bil′i·ty** *n.* —**re·duc′i·ble** *adj.* —**re·duc′i·bly** *adv.*

re·duc·er (-ər) *n.* **1** a person or thing that reduces **2** *Mech.* a fitting for connecting two pipes of different size **3** *Photog.* a solution that dissolves silver, used to decrease the density of a negative or positive image

reducing agent any substance that reduces another substance, or brings about reduction, and is itself oxidized in the process

reducing glass a biconcave lens used for reducing the visual size of something viewed through it

re·duc·tase (ri duk′tās′, -tāz′) *n.* ⟦REDUCT(ION) + -ASE⟧ any of a class of enzymes that catalyze biochemical reductions

re·duc·ti·o ad ab·sur·dum (ri duk′tē ō′ ad ab sur′dəm, -äd äb-; -shē ō′-) ⟦L, reduction to absurdity⟧ *Logic* the proof of a proposition by showing its opposite to be an obvious falsity or self-contradiction, or the disproof of a proposition by showing its consequences to be impossible or absurd: often shortened to ***reductio***

re·duc·tion (ri duk′shən) *n.* ⟦LME *reduccion* < MFr *reduction* < L *reductio* < *reductus,* pp. of *reducere*⟧ **1** a reducing or being reduced **2** anything made or brought about by reducing, as a smaller copy, lowered price, sauce of concentrated liquid, etc. **3** the amount by which anything is reduced —**re·duc′tion·al** *adj.*

reduction division MEIOSIS (sense 1)

re·duc·tion·ism (-iz′əm) *n.* any method or theory of reducing data, processes, or statements to seeming equivalents that are less complex or developed: usually a disparaging term —**re·duc′tion·ist** *n., adj.* —**re·duc′tion·is′tic** *adj.*

re·duc·tive (ri duk′tiv) *adj.* ⟦ML *reductivus*⟧ **1** of or characterized by reduction or reductionism **2** reducing or tending to reduce —**re·duc′tive·ly** *adv.*

re·duc·tor (-tər) *n. Chem.* any apparatus for carrying out the reduction of metallic ions in solution for purposes of analysis; specif., a long tube filled with granular zinc for reducing a ferric solution to its ferrous salt

re·dun·dan·cy (ri dun′dən sē) *n., pl.* **-cies** ⟦L *redundantia*⟧ **1** the state or quality of being redundant; superfluity **2** a redundant quantity; overabundance **3** the use of redundant words **4** the part of a redundant statement that is superfluous **5** [Brit.] discharge from a job or employment because of not being needed; dismissal Also **re·dun′dance**

re·dun·dant (-dənt) *adj.* ⟦L *redundans,* prp. of *redundare:* see REDOUND⟧ **1** more than enough; overabundant; excess; superfluous **2** using more words than are needed; wordy **3** unnecessary to the meaning: said of words and affixes **4** [Brit.] laid off from work as no longer needed; discharged; dismissed —*SYN.* WORDY —**re·dun′dant·ly** *adv.*

re·du·pli·cate (ri do͞o′plə kāt′, -dyo͞o′-; *for adj. & n., usually,* -kit) *vt.* **-cat′ed, -cat′ing** ⟦< LL *reduplicatus,* pp. of *reduplicare:* see RE- & DUPLICATE⟧ **1** to redouble, double, or repeat **2** *a)* to double (a root syllable or other element) so as to form an inflected or derived form of a word (as *tom-*

redraw redrill redrive redry

tom), sometimes with certain changes, as of the vowel (as in *chitchat*) *b)* to form (words) by such doubling —*vi.* to be or become reduplicated —*adj.* **1** reduplicated; doubled **2** VALVATE (sense 2*a*) —*n.* something reduplicated

re·du·pli·ca·tion (ri do͞o′plə kā′shən, -dyo͞o′-) *n.* ⟦LL *reduplicatio*⟧ **1** a reduplicating or being reduplicated **2** something produced by reduplicating, as a word containing a reduplicated element **3** the element added in a reduplicated word form —**re·du′pli·ca′tive** *adj.*

re·du·vi·id (ri do͞o′vē id, -dyo͞o′-) *n.* ⟦< ModL *Reduviidae* < L *reduvia,* hangnail, remnant < OL *redivia* < **reduere,* to strip away < *red-,* RE- + *-uere* < IE base **eu-,* to put on⟧ ASSASSIN BUG

re·dux (rē′duks′) *adj.* ⟦L < *reducere:* see REDUCE⟧ that has been brought back, revived, restored, etc.: used postpositively and, often, fig.

☆**red velvet cake** a rich cake, flavored with cocoa and colored red, often layered with a cream cheese frosting

red·ware (red′wer′) *n.* ⟦RED + *ware,* seaweed < ME *war* < OE < IE **woiso-,* twig, wand, rod < base **wei-,* to twist, bend > WIRE⟧ any of several large, brown, leathery, edible kelps (genus *Laminaria*)

red water TEXAS FEVER

red wine any wine made from dark, purplish grapes when the grape skins are left with the juice after pressing to allow the absorption of reddish coloring agents during fermentation

red·wing (-wiŋ′) *n.* **1** a small European thrush (*Turdus iliacus*) with an orange-red patch on the underside of the wings ☆**2** RED-WINGED BLACKBIRD

☆**red-winged blackbird** (red′wiŋd′) a North American blackbird (*Agelaius phoeniceus*) with a bright-red patch on each wing near the shoulder in the male: also **redwing blackbird**

red wolf a small, reddish wolf (*Canis rufus*) of the SE U.S.

red·wood (-wood′) *n.* ☆**1** a giant evergreen (*Sequoia sempervirens*) of the baldcypress family, having fire-resistant bark, enduring, soft wood, and needlelike leaves: found in coastal regions of California and S Oregon ☆**2** BIG TREE **3** any of a number of trees with reddish wood or yielding a red dye **4** the wood of any of these trees

red worm BLOODWORM

☆**red zone** *Football* that portion of the playing field within 20 yards of the defender's goal line: term used when an offensive play or series begins here —**red′-zone′** *adj.*

re·ech·o or **re-ech·o** (rē ek′ō) *vt., vi.* **-ech′oed, -ech′o·ing** to echo back or again; resound —*n., pl.* **-ech′oes** the echo of an echo Also **re·ëch′o**

reed (rēd) *n.* ⟦ME *rede* < OE *hreod,* akin to OHG *hriot* < IE base **kreut-,* to shake, tremble⟧ **1** *a)* any of various tall, slender grasses (esp. genus *Phragmites*), with plumelike inflorescences, growing in wet or marshy land *b)* the stem of any of these grasses *c)* such plants or stems collectively, specif. as material for thatching, basketwork, etc. **2** a rustic musical instrument made from a hollow stem or stalk and played by blowing through it **3** an ancient Hebrew unit of linear measure equal to 6 cubits: Ezek. 40:3 **4** a device on a loom, by means of which threads are drawn between the separated threads of the warp **5** [Old Poet.] an arrow **6** *Archit.* a small, rounded molding; reeding **7** *Music a)* a thin strip of some flexible substance, as cane, placed at the opening of the mouthpiece of certain wind instruments, as the clarinet: when vibrated by the breath, it produces a musical tone *b)* an instrument with a reed or reeds *c)* in some organs, a similar device that vibrates in a current of air *d)* [*pl.*] the reed instruments (esp., in jazz, the saxophones and clarinets) of an orchestra, band, etc., or the players of these instruments: see also DOUBLE-REED —*adj.* **1** designating an instrument whose sound is produced by a vibrating reed or reeds, specif., the oboe, clarinet, saxophone, English horn, or bassoon **2** of or for such an instrument or instruments [*a reed* section] —*vt.* to thatch or decorate with reeds

OBOE REED (SIDE VIEW)

OBOE REED (TOP VIEW)

CLARINET MOUTHPIECE WITH REED (SIDE VIEW)

reeds

Reed (rēd) **1 John (Silas)** 1887-1920; U.S. journalist & radical **2 Walter** 1851-1902; U.S. army surgeon & bacteriologist

☆**reed·bird** (rēd′burd′) *n. dial. name for* BOBOLINK

reed·buck (-buk′) *n., pl.* **-buck′** or **-bucks′** ⟦transl. of Du *rietbok*⟧ any of a genus (*Redunca*) of small African antelopes with widely spread hooves and, in the males, backward-sloping, ringed horns turned inward and forward near the tips

reed·ing (-iŋ) *n.* **1** a small, rounded, decorative molding **2** a set of such moldings, as on a column **3** knurling along the edge of a coin

reed mace *Brit. name for* CATTAIL

reed·man (rēd′man′) *n., pl.* **-men′** (-men′) *Jazz* a person, esp. a man, who plays a reed instrument or, often, several such instruments, usually various saxophones

reed organ an organ with a set of free metal reeds instead of pipes to produce the tones: cf. REED PIPE

reed pipe an organ pipe in which the tone is produced by a current of air striking a vibrating reed in an opening in the pipe: cf. FLUE PIPE

reed stop **1** a set of reed pipes (in an organ) operated by one knob **2** the knob

re·ed·u·cate or **re-ed·u·cate** (rē ej′ə kāt′) *vt.* **-cat′ed, -cat′ing** to educate again or anew, esp. so as to rehabilitate or adapt to new situations —**re·ed′u·ca′tion** *n.*, **re-ed′u·ca′tion** —**re·ed′u·ca′tive** *adj.*, **re-ed′u·ca′tive**

reed·y (rēd′ē) *adj.* **reed′i·er, reed′i·est** **1** full of reeds **2** made of reed or reeds **3** like a reed; slender, fragile, etc. **4** having the timbre of a reed instrument; specif., having a thin, piping sound like certain reed instruments within the higher range —**reed′i·ly** *adv.* —**reed′i·ness** *n.*

reef[1] (rēf) *n.* ⟦prob. via Du or MLowG *rif* < ON, lit., RIB⟧ **1** a line or ridge of rock, coral, or sand lying at or near the surface of the water **2** *Mining* a bed or vein of ore; lode —**SYN.** SHOAL[2]

reef[2] (rēf) *n.* ⟦ME *riff* < or akin to ON *rif* (< IE **reip-,* a strip < base **rei-,* to tear, cut > RIVE): orig. used of cords for reefing⟧ *Naut.* a part of a sail which can be folded or rolled up and made fast to reduce the area exposed to the wind, as during a storm —*vt.* **1** to reduce the size of (a sail) by taking in part of it **2** to lower (a spar or mast) or reduce the projection of (a bowsprit)

reef·er[1] (rē′fər) *n.* **1** a person who reefs **2** a short, thick, double-breasted coat in the style of a seaman's jacket ☆**3** ⟦by analogy with the rolled *reef* of a sail⟧ [Slang] a marijuana cigarette

☆**reef·er**[2] (rē′fər) *n.* ⟦altered contr. of REFRIGERATOR⟧ [Slang] a refrigerated freight car, truck, ship, etc.

reef knot a square knot used for reefing sails

reek (rēk) *n.* ⟦ME < OE *rec,* akin to ON *reykr,* Ger *rauch* < ? IE base **reug-,* cloud, smoke⟧ **1** vapor; fume **2** a strong, unpleasant smell; stench **3** [Scot. or North Eng.] smoke —*vi.* ⟦ME *reken* < OE *reocan*⟧ **1** to give off steam or smoke **2** to have a strong, offensive smell **3** to be permeated with anything very unpleasant —*vt.* **1** to expose to the action of smoke or fumes **2** to emit or exude (vapor, fumes, etc.) —**reek′y** *adj.*

reel[1] (rēl) *vi.* ⟦ME *relen* < the n.: from the sensation of whirling⟧ **1** to give way or fall back; sway, waver, or stagger as from being struck **2** to lurch or stagger about, as from drunkenness or dizziness **3** to go around and around; whirl **4** to feel dizzy; have a sensation of spinning or whirling —*vt.* to cause to reel —*n.* ⟦ME *rele* < OE *hreol:* see REEL[3]⟧ a reeling motion; whirl, stagger, etc.

reel[2] (rēl) *n.* ⟦prob. < prec., n.⟧ **1** *a)* a lively Scottish dance *b) short for* VIRGINIA REEL **2** music for either of these

reel[3] (rēl) *n.* ⟦ME < OE *hreol* < Gmc **hrehulaz* < IE base **krek-,* to strike, make a weaving motion > Gr *krekein,* to weave, Latvian *krekls,* shirt⟧ **1** a frame or spool on which thread, wire, tape, film, a net, etc. is wound **2** such a frame set on the handle of a fishing rod, to wind up or let out the line **3** the quantity of wire, thread, film, tape, etc. usually wound on one reel **4** in some lawn mowers, a set of spiral steel blades rotating on a horizontal bar set between wheels — *vt., vi.* to wind on a reel —**reel in** **1** to wind on a reel **2** to pull in (a fish) by winding a line on a reel —**reel off** to tell, write, produce, etc. easily and quickly —**reel out** to unwind from a reel —☆**(right) off the reel** without hesitation or pause

reel-to-reel (-to͞o rēl′) *adj.* designating or of a tape recorder using two separate reels, on which the tape must be threaded

re-embroidered (rē′im broi′dərd) *adj.* embellished with beads, tiny pearls, ribbon, etc. sewn on, usually by hand: said as of lace for bridal gowns

re·en·act (rē′ən akt′) *vt.* **1** to enact again **2** to portray or act out (a past incident or historical event) [eyewitnesses being asked to *reenact* the events of a crime, a Civil War battle *reenacted* by people in period costume] —**re′en·act′ment** *n.* —**re′en·ac′tor** *n.*

re·en·force or **re-en·force** (rē′in fôrs′) *vt.* **-forced′, -forc′ing** REINFORCE

re·en·ter or **re-en·ter** (rē en′tər) *vt., vi.* **1** to enter again (in various senses) **2** to return or return to [a spacecraft designed to *reenter* the earth's atmosphere]

re·en·trant or **re-en·trant** (-trənt) *adj.* that reenters; specif., pointed inward, as an angle —*n.* a reentrant angle or part —**re·en′trance** *n.*, **re-en′trance**

reentrant angle in a polygon, an interior angle greater than 180°, with its point turning back into the figure rather than out from it

re·en·try or **re-en·try** (rē en′trē) *n., pl.* **-tries** **1** a reentering; specif., a coming back, as of a space vehicle, into the earth's atmosphere **2** a second or repeated entry **3** *Card Games* a card that can win a trick and thus regain the lead **4** *Law* a coming into possession again under a right reserved in a prior transfer of property

reeve[1] (rēv) *n.* ⟦ME *reve,* earlier *irefe* < OE *gerefa* < *ge-* + base of **rof,* row, number⟧ **1** *Eng. History a)* the chief officer, under the king, of a town or district *b)* the overseer and chief peasant of a manor **2** the elected head of a village or town council in certain Canadian provinces

reeve[2] (rēv) *vt.* **rove** or **reeved, rove** or **rov′en, reev′ing** ⟦prob. < Du *reven,* to reef, in sense "use a rope in or as in reefing"⟧ *Naut.* **1** to pass (the end of a line) through a block, ring, etc. **2** to fasten by passing through or around something **3** to pass a line through (a block, ring, etc.)

redye	**reembody**	**reemphasize**	**reenlistment**	**reevaluation**
reedit	**reembrace**	**reemploy**	**reequip**	
reelect	**reemerge**	**reendow**	**reestablish**	
reelection	**reemergence**	**reengage**	**reestablishment**	
reembark	**reemphasis**	**reenlist**	**reevaluate**	

reeve[3] (rēv) ***n.*** ⟦< ?⟧ a female RUFF[1] (sense 3)

re·ex·am·i·na·tion or **re-ex·am·i·na·tion** (rē′ig zam′ə nā′shən) ***n.*** **1** a second or repeated examination **2** *Law* the questioning of one's own witness after, and about matters taken up in, the cross-examination

re·ex·am·ine or **re-ex·am·ine** (rē′ig zam′in) ***vt.*** **-ined**, **-in·ing** **1** to examine again **2** *Law* to subject to reexamination

ref[1] (ref) [Informal] ***n.*** *short for* REFEREE (sense 2) — ***vt., vi.*** **reffed**, **ref′fing** *short for* REFEREE

ref[2] *abbrev.* **1** referee **2** reference **3** reformed **4** refund

re·face (rē fās′) ***vt.*** **-faced′**, **-fac′ing** to put a new face, facing, or surface on

Ref Ch *abbrev.* Reformed Church

re·fect (ri fekt′) ***vt.*** ⟦LME *refecken* < pp. of L *reficere:* in later use, back-form. < fol.⟧ [Archaic] to refresh with food or drink

re·fec·tion (ri fek′shən) ***n.*** ⟦OFr < L *refectio* < pp. of *reficere,* to remake, restore < *re-,* again + *facere,* to make, DO[1]⟧ **1** food or drink taken after a period of hunger or fatigue; refreshment **2** a light meal; lunch

re·fec·to·ry (-tər ē) ***n., pl.*** **-ries** ⟦LME < LL *refectorium* < pp. of L *reficere:* see prec.⟧ a dining hall in a monastery, college, etc.

refectory table a long, narrow, rectangular table, as that used in a refectory

re·fer (ri fur′) ***vt.*** **-ferred′**, **-fer′ring** ⟦ME *referren* < MFr *referer* < L *referre* < *re-,* back + *ferre,* to BEAR[1]⟧ **1** to assign or attribute (*to*) as cause or origin **2** to assign, or regard or name as belonging (*to* a kind, class, date, etc.) **3** to submit (a quarrel, question, etc.) for determination or settlement **4** to send or direct (someone) *to* someone or something for aid, information, etc. —***vi.*** **1** to relate or apply (*to*); be concerned or deal **2** to direct attention, or make reference or allusion (*to*) [*to refer* to an earlier event] **3** to turn for information, aid, or authority (*to*) [*to refer* to a map] **4** *Gram.* to apply *to* an antecedent: said of a pronoun [in "the man who spoke", "who" *refers* to the antecedent "man"] —**ref·er·a·ble** (ref′ər ə bəl, ri fur′-) ***adj.***, **re·fer′ra·ble**, or **re·fer′ri·ble** —**re·fer′rer** ***n.***

SYN.—**refer** implies deliberate, direct, and open mention of something [he *referred* in detail to their corrupt practices]; **allude** implies indirect, often casual mention, as by a hint or a figure of speech [although she used different names, she was *alluding* to her family]

ref·er·ee (ref′ə rē′) ***n.*** **1** a person to whom something is referred for decision **2** an official who enforces the rules in certain sports contests; specif., the chief official in a football game **3** *Law* a person appointed by a court to study, take testimony in, judge, and report on, a matter **4** an academic authority who examines and evaluates an article, book, etc. with regard to its fitness for publication **5** [Brit.] a person, esp. one with good credentials, given as a reference in seeking employment —***vi.*** **-eed′**, **-ee′ing** to act as referee —***vt.*** to act as referee for (a game, sport, etc.) or regarding (a legal matter, scholarly article, etc.) —**SYN.** JUDGE

ref·er·ence (ref′ər əns, ref′rəns) ***n.*** **1** a referring or being referred; esp., submission of a problem, dispute, etc. to a person, committee, or authority for settlement **2** *a)* the directing of attention to a person or thing *b)* a mention or allusion **3** *a)* an indication, as in a book or article, of some other work or passage to be consulted *b)* the work or passage so indicated *c)* the mark or sign, as a number, letter, or symbol, directing the reader to a footnote, etc. (in full **reference mark**) **4** *a)* the giving of the name of another person who can offer information or recommendation *b)* the person so indicated *c)* a written statement of character, qualification, or ability, as of someone seeking a position; testimonial **5** *a)* use or consultation to get information, as an aid in research, etc. *b)* a book, etc. used for reference **6** something by which other things are indicated or positioned, against which other things are measured or compared, etc.: often used attributively [let that tree be our *reference* point as we plan the rest of the landscaping] —***adj.*** designating or of books and other materials for use in research, as in a library —***vt.*** **-enced**, **-enc·ing** to provide with references —**in** (or **with**) **reference to** concerning; regarding —**make reference to** to refer to; mention

reference library (*or* **department**) a library, or a department of a large library, whose collection is open for use on the premises only

ref·er·en·dum (ref′ə ren′dəm) ***n., pl.*** **-dums** or **-da** (-də) ⟦ModL < L, a carrying back, ger. or neut. ger. of *referre:* see REFER⟧ ☆**1** *a)* the submission of a law, proposed or already in effect, to a direct vote of the people, as in superseding or overruling the legislature *b)* the vote itself **2** a note sent by a diplomatic agent to the agent's own government, asking for specific instructions

ref·er·ent (ref′ər ənt) ***n.*** ⟦< L *referens,* prp.⟧ **1** something referred to **2** *Linguis.* the object, concept, event, etc. referred to by a term or expression

ref·er·en·tial (ref′ə ren′shəl) ***adj.*** ⟦< REFERENCE (as if < L **referentia*) + -AL⟧ **1** containing a reference **2** used for reference —**ref′er·en′tial·ly** ***adv.***

re·fer·ral (ri fur′əl) ***n.*** **1** a referring or being referred, as for professional service, etc. **2** a person who is referred or directed to another person, an agency, etc.

referred pain pain, felt in a particular area of the body, that originates elsewhere in the body

re·fill (rē fil′; *for n.* rē′fil′) ***vt., vi.*** to fill again —***n.*** a new filling; esp., *a)* a unit to replace the contents of a container that is not itself discarded after use [*a refill for a ball point pen*] *b)* any additional filling of a prescription for medicine —**re·fill′a·ble** ***adj.***

re·fi·nance (rē′fə nans′, rē fī′nans′) ***vt.*** **-nanced′**, **-nanc′ing** to finance again; specif., to provide or obtain a new loan or more capital for

re·fine (ri fīn′) ***vt.*** **-fined′**, **-fin′ing** ⟦RE- + FINE[1], v., based on Fr *raffiner,* to purify⟧ **1** to make fine or pure; free from impurities, dross, alloy, sediment, etc.; purify; clarify **2** to free from imperfection, coarseness, crudeness, etc.; make more elegant or cultivated; impart polish to **3** to make more subtle or precise —***vi.*** **1** to become fine or pure; become free from impurities, etc. **2** to make something more polished or elegant —**refine on** (or **upon**) to improve, as by adding refinements —**re·fin′er** ***n.***

re·fined (ri fīnd′) ***adj.*** ⟦pp. of prec.⟧ **1** made free from other matter, or from impurities; purified **2** free from crudeness or coarseness; cultivated; elegant **3** characterized by great subtlety, precision, etc.

re·fine·ment (ri fīn′mənt) ***n.*** **1** *a)* a refining or being refined *b)* the result of this **2** delicacy or elegance of language, speech, manners, etc.; polish; cultivation **3** a development; improvement; elaboration **4** a fine distinction; subtlety

re·fin·er·y (ri fīn′ər ē) ***n., pl.*** **-er·ies** ⟦< REFINE + -ERY, based on Fr *raffinerie*⟧ an establishment or plant for refining, or purifying, such raw materials as oil, metal, or sugar

re·fin·ish (rē fin′ish) ***vt.*** to change or restore the finish of (furniture, woodwork, etc.) —**re·fin′ish·er** ***n.***

re·fit (rē fit′; *also, and for n. usually,* rē′fit′) ***vt., vi.*** **-fit′ted**, **-fit′ting** to make or be made ready or fit for use again, as by repairing, reequipping, or resupplying —***n.*** an act or instance of refitting

refl *abbrev.* **1** reflection **2** reflective **3** reflex **4** reflexive

re·flag (rē flag′) ***vt.*** **-flagged′**, **-flag′ging** to register and sail (a ship) under a foreign nation's flag, as in order to extend to it military protection against a belligerent

re·flate (rē flāt′) ***vt., vi.*** **-flat′ed**, **-flat′ing** to bring about reflation in (an economy)

☆**re·fla·tion** (rē flā′shən) ***n.*** ⟦RE- + (IN)FLATION⟧ the use of fiscal and monetary policies that increase the money supply, so as to counteract a decline in the general level of prices —**re·fla′tion·ar′y** ***adj.***

re·flect (ri flekt′) ***vt.*** ⟦ME *reflecten* < MFr *reflecter* < L *reflectere* < *re-,* back + *flectere,* to bend⟧ **1** to bend or throw back (light, heat, or sound) **2** to give back an image of; mirror or reproduce **3** to cast or bring back as a consequence: with *on* [deeds that *reflect* honor on him] **4** to express or show [skills that *reflect* years of training] **5** to recollect or realize after thought (*that*) **6** to fold or turn back: usually used in pp. —***vi.*** **1** to be bent or thrown back [light *reflecting* from the water] **2** to bend or throw back light, heat, sound, etc. [a *reflecting* surface] **3** *a)* to give back an image or likeness *b)* to be mirrored **4** to think seriously; contemplate (*on* or *upon*) **5** to cast blame or discredit (*on* or *upon*) —**SYN.** CONSIDER, THINK[1]

re·flec·tance (ri flek′təns) ***n.*** *Physics* the ratio of the amount of electromagnetic radiation, usually light, reflected from a surface to the amount originally striking the surface

reflecting telescope any of several telescopes having as the objective a paraboloid mirror mounted at the lower end of the tube and using various systems of mirrors for viewing the image by reflecting the incident light to an eyepiece; reflector

re·flec·tion (ri flek′shən) ***n.*** ⟦ME *reflexion* < MFr < LL *reflexio*⟧ **1** a reflecting or being reflected **2** the throwing back by a surface of sound, light, heat, etc. **3** anything reflected; specif., an image; likeness **4** *a)* the fixing of the mind on some subject; serious thought; contemplation *b)* the result of such thought; idea or conclusion, esp. if expressed in words **5** *a)* blame; discredit *b)* a remark or statement imputing discredit or blame *c)* an action bringing discredit **6** *Anat.* a turning or bending back on itself —**re·flec′tion·al** ***adj.***

re·flec·tive (ri flek′tiv) ***adj.*** **1** reflecting **2** of or produced by reflection **3** meditative; thoughtful —**SYN.** PENSIVE —**re·flec′tive·ly** ***adv.*** —**re·flec′tive·ness** ***n.***, **re′flec·tiv′i·ty**

re·flec·tor (ri flek′tər) ***n.*** **1** a person or thing that reflects; esp., a surface, object, etc. that reflects light, sound, heat, or the like, as a piece of glass or metal, highly polished and usually concave, which reflects and directs radiant energy, as beams of light, sound waves, etc., in a desired direction **2** REFLECTING TELESCOPE **3** a layer of material that reflects escaping neutrons back into the core of a nuclear reactor or bomb

☆**re·flec·tor·ize** (-īz′) ***vt.*** **-ized′**, **-iz′ing** **1** to treat or process (something) so that it reflects light **2** to furnish with reflectors

re·flet (rə fle′) ***n.*** ⟦Fr, reflection, earlier *reflés* < It *riflesso* < L *reflexus* (see fol.); sp. altered by assoc. with L *reflectere*⟧ luster or iridescence, as a metallic glaze on pottery

re·flex (rē′fleks′; *for v., also* ri fleks′) ***n.*** ⟦< L *reflexus,* reflected, pp. of *reflectere:* see REFLECT⟧ **1** *a)* reflection, as of light *b)* light or color resulting from reflection **2** a reflected image, likeness, or reproduction **3** *a)* *Physiol.* a reflex action *b)* any quick, automatic or habitual response *c)* [*pl.*] ability to react quickly and effectively [a boxer with good *reflexes*] —***adj.*** **1** turned, bent, or reflected back **2** *a)* coming in reaction or reflection [a *reflex* effect] *b)* *Physiol.* designating or of an involuntary action, as a sneeze, resulting from a stimulus that is carried by an afferent nerve to a

reexchange
reexhibit
reexperience
reexplain
reexport
refabricate
refashion
refasten
refigure
refile
refilm
refilter
refind
refire
refix

nerve center and the response that is reflected along an efferent nerve to some muscle or gland **3** *Electronics* designating or of a device, circuit, etc. that has two different functions **4** *Geom.* designating an angle greater than a straight angle (180°) **—*vt.*** **1** to bend, turn, or fold back **2** to cause to undergo a reflex process **—re′flex·ly *adv.***

reflex arc *Physiol.* the entire nerve path involved in a reflex action

reflex camera a camera in which the image formed by the lens is reflected by a mirror onto a ground-glass plate to help in focusing

re·flex·ion (ri flek′shən) ***n.*** *Brit. sp. of* REFLECTION

re·flex·ive (-siv) ***adj.*** ⟦ML *reflexivus*⟧ **1** having to do with the act or process of reflecting **2** automatic, habitual, unthinking, etc. [a smile that seemed merely *reflexive,* not heartfelt] **3** of or having to do with a marked thematic concern in a work of fiction with the creative process employed in the composition of that work **4** *Gram. a)* designating or expressing a grammatical relation in which a verb's subject and an object in the sentence refer to the same person or thing, serving to indicate that the action of the verb is directed back to the subject (Ex.: "Gary hurt himself," "Jane threw a party for herself") *b)* designating a verb, pronoun, etc. in such a relation **—*n.*** a reflexive verb or pronoun **—re·flex′ive·ly *adv.*** **—re·flex′ive·ness *n.*, re·flex·iv·i·ty** (rē′flek siv′ə tē)

re·flex·ol·o·gy (rē′fleks äl′ə jē) ***n.*** a practice involving the use of acupressure or massage of the hands or, esp., the feet to relieve pain in other parts of the body, reduce tension, etc. **—re′flex·ol′o·gist *n.***

ref·lu·ent (ref′lo͞o ənt) ***adj.*** ⟦L *refluens,* prp. of *refluere,* to flow back: see RE- & FLUCTUATE⟧ flowing back; ebbing, as the tide to the sea **—ref′lu·ence *n.***

re·flux (rē′fluks′) ***n.*** ⟦ME < ML *refluxus* < pp. of L *refluere:* see prec.⟧ a flowing back; ebb; specif., regurgitation of food or gastric acid from the stomach to the esophagus

re·for·est (rē fôr′ist, -fär′-) ***vt., vi.*** to plant new trees on (land once forested) **—re′for·est·a′tion *n.***

re·form (ri fôrm′) ***vt.*** ⟦ME *reformen* < OFr *reformer* < L *reformare:* see RE- & FORM⟧ **1** to make better by removing faults and defects; correct [to *reform* a calendar] **2** *a)* to make better by putting a stop to abuses or malpractices or by introducing better procedures, etc. *b)* to put a stop to (abuses, etc.) **3** to cause or persuade (a person) to give up misconduct and behave better **4** *Chem.* to heat (petroleum products) under pressure, with or without catalysts, to produce cracking and a greater yield of gasoline or an improved octane number **—*vi.*** to become better in behavior **—*n.*** **1** a correction of faults or evils, as in government or society; social or political improvement **2** an improvement in character and conduct; reformation **3** a movement aimed at removing political or social abuses **—*adj.*** ☆[**R-**] designating or of a movement in Judaism that attempts to make rational thought compatible with historical Judaism, stressing its ethical aspects and not requiring strict observance of traditional Orthodox ritual **—re·form′a·ble *adj.*** **—re·form′a·tive *adj.***

re-form (rē fôrm′) ***vt., vi.*** to form again

ref·or·ma·tion (ref′ər mā′shən) ***n.*** ⟦ME *reformacion* < L *reformatio*⟧ a reforming or being reformed **—the Reformation** the 16th-cent. religious movement that aimed at reforming the Roman Catholic Church and resulted in establishing the Protestant churches **—ref′or·ma′tion·al *adj.***

☆**re·form·a·to·ry** (ri fôr′mə tôr′ē) ***adj.*** reforming or aiming at reform **—*n.*, *pl.* -ries** **1** an institution to which young offenders convicted of lesser crimes are sent for training and discipline intended to reform rather than punish them **2** a penitentiary for women

re·formed (ri fôrmd′) ***adj.*** **1** improved or corrected, as in behavior or morals, or made better by the removal of errors, abuses, etc. **2** [**R-**] designating or of a Protestant church or churches, esp. Calvinist or Zwinglian as distinguished from Lutheran

reformed spelling any of various proposed systems for simplifying the spelling of English words, esp. by establishing a consistent application of phonetic values and dropping unpronounced letters

re·form·er (ri fôr′mər) ***n.*** **1** a person who seeks to bring about reform, esp. political or social reform **2** [**R-**] any of the leaders of the Reformation

re·form·ism (-miz′əm) ***n.*** the practice or advocacy of reform, esp. political or social reform **—re·form′ist *n.*, *adj.***

☆**reform school** REFORMATORY (sense 1)

re·fract (ri frakt′) ***vt.*** ⟦< L *refractus,* pp. of *refringere,* to turn aside < *re-,* back + *frangere,* to BREAK⟧ **1** to cause (a ray or wave of light, heat, or sound) to undergo refraction **2** *Optics* to measure the degree of refraction of (an eye or lens) **—re·frac′tive *adj.*** **—re·frac′tive·ly *adv.*** **—re·frac·tiv·i·ty** (rē′frak tiv′ə tē) ***n.*, re·frac′tive·ness**

refracting telescope **1** a telescope in which a large biconvex lens causes light rays to converge to a focus, forming an image magnified by a biconvex eyepiece **2** a similar telescope in which the converging rays are intercepted by a biconcave eyepiece

re·frac·tion (ri frak′shən) ***n.*** ⟦LL *refractio*⟧ **1** the bending of a ray or wave of light, heat, or sound as it passes obliquely from one medium to another of different density, in which its speed is different, or through layers of different density in the same medium **2** *Astron.* the bending of the rays of light from a star or planet, greatest when the star or planet is lowest in the sky, so that it seems higher than it really is **3** *Optics a)* the ability of the eye to refract light entering it, so as to form an image on the retina *b)* the measuring of the degree of refraction of an eye

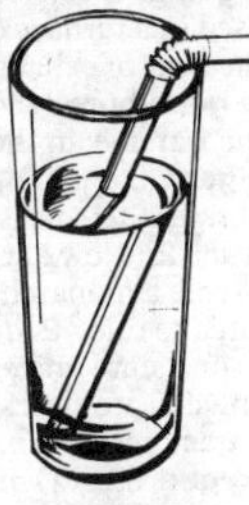

illusion caused by refraction

refractive index INDEX OF REFRACTION

re·frac·tom·e·ter (rē′frak täm′ət ər) ***n.*** an instrument for measuring refraction, as of the eye

re·frac·tor (ri frak′tər) ***n.*** **1** something that refracts **2** REFRACTING TELESCOPE

re·frac·to·ry (ri frak′tər ē) ***adj.*** ⟦altered < obs. *refractary* < L *refractarius* < *refractus:* see REFRACT⟧ **1** hard to manage; stubborn; obstinate: said of a person or animal **2** resistant to heat; hard to melt or work: said of ores or metals **3** *a)* not yielding to treatment, as a disease *b)* able to resist disease **—*n.*, *pl.* -ries** something refractory; specif., a heat-resistant material used in lining furnaces, etc. **—re·frac′to·ri·ly *adv.*** **—re·frac′to·ri·ness *n.***

re·frain[1] (ri frān′) ***vi.*** ⟦ME *refreinen* < OFr *refrener* < L *refrenare* < *re-,* back + *frenare,* to curb < *frenum,* rein⟧ to hold back; keep oneself (*from* doing something); forbear **—*vt.*** [Archaic] to hold back; curb

SYN.—**refrain** usually suggests the curbing of a passing impulse in keeping oneself from saying or doing something [although provoked, she *refrained* from answering]; **abstain** implies voluntary self-denial or the deliberate giving up of something [to *abstain* from liquor]; **forbear** suggests self-restraint manifesting a patient endurance under provocation [to *forbear* venting one's wrath]

re·frain[2] (ri frān′) ***n.*** ⟦ME *refreine* < MFr *refrain* < OFr *refraindre,* to break, repress, modulate < VL **refrangere,* for L *refringere,* to break off: see REFRACT⟧ **1** a phrase, verse, or verses repeated at intervals in a song or poem, as after each stanza **2** music for this

re·fran·gi·ble (ri fran′jə bəl) ***adj.*** ⟦< VL **refrangere* (see prec.)⟧ that can be refracted, as light rays **—re·fran′gi·bil′i·ty *n.*, re·fran′gi·ble·ness**

re·fresh (ri fresh′) ***vt.*** ⟦ME *refreschen* < OFr *refrescher:* see RE- & FRESH[1]⟧ **1** to make fresh by cooling, wetting, etc. [rains *refreshing* parched plants] **2** to make (another or oneself) feel cooler, stronger, more energetic, etc. than before, as by food, drink, or sleep **3** to replenish, as by new supplies; renew **4** to revive or stimulate (the memory, etc.) **5** *Comput.* to generate a fresh display of or on [to *refresh* a Web page, *refresh* a PC screen] **—*vi.*** **1** [Archaic] to take refreshment, as food or drink **2** to reinvigorate someone: said as of food, drink, or sleep **3** *Comput.* to be regenerated or have a regenerated display [a PC screen that automatically *refreshes* 60 times per second] **—*SYN.*** RENEW **—re·fresh′er *n.***

refresher course a course for reviewing material previously studied or for updating information or skills

re·fresh·ing (-iŋ) ***adj.*** **1** that refreshes **2** pleasingly new or different **—re·fresh′ing·ly *adv.***

re·fresh·ment (-mənt) ***n.*** ⟦ME *refreshement* < MFr *refreschement*⟧ **1** a refreshing or being refreshed **2** something that refreshes, as food, drink, or rest **3** [*pl.*] food or drink or both, esp. as a light meal

☆**refried beans** (rē′frīd′) ⟦transl. of MexSp *frijoles refritos*⟧ a Mexican dish consisting of beans, esp. pinto beans, that have been simmered till tender, then seasoned, mashed, and fried

re·frig·er·ant (ri frij′ər ənt) ***adj.*** ⟦L *refrigerans,* prp.⟧ **1** that refrigerates; that cools or freezes something **2** reducing heat or fever **—*n.*** **1** a medicine used to reduce fever **2** a substance used in refrigeration; specif., any of various liquids that vaporize at a low temperature, used in mechanical refrigeration

re·frig·er·ate (-ə rāt′) ***vt.*** **-at′ed, -at′ing** ⟦< L *refrigeratus,* pp. of *refrigerare,* to make cool or cold < *re-,* intens. + *frigerare,* to cool < *frigus,* cold: see FRIGID⟧ **1** to make or keep cool or cold; chill **2** to preserve (food, biologicals, etc.) by keeping cold or freezing **—re·frig′er·a′tion *n.*** **—re·frig′er·a′tive *adj.*, re·frig′er·a·to′ry** (-ə rə tôr′ē)

re·frig·er·a·tor (-rāt′ər) ***n.*** something that refrigerates; esp., a box, cabinet, or room in which food, drink, etc. are kept cool, as by ice or mechanical refrigeration

☆**refrigerator car** a railroad car equipped to keep perishable freight, as food, refrigerated in transit

re·frin·gent (ri frin′jənt) ***adj.*** ⟦L *refringens,* prp. of *refringere:* see REFRACT⟧ refracting; refractive

reft (reft) ***vt.*** *alt. pt. & pp. of* REAVE[1] and REAVE[2] **—*adj.*** robbed or bereft (*of* something)

re·fu·el (rē fyo͞o′əl, -fyo͞ol′) ***vt.*** **-fu′eled** or **-fu′elled, -fu′el·ing** or **-fu′el·ling** to supply again with fuel **—*vi.*** to take on a fresh supply of fuel

ref·uge (ref′yo͞oj′) ***n.*** ⟦OFr < L *refugium* < *refugere,* to retreat < *re-,* back + *fugere,* to flee: see FUGITIVE⟧ **1** shelter or protection from danger, difficulty, etc. **2** a person or thing that gives shelter, help, or comfort **3** a place of safety; shelter; safe retreat **4** an expediency or shift; action taken to escape trouble or difficulty **—*vt.*** **-uged′, -ug′ing** [Archaic] to give refuge to **—*vi.*** [Archaic] to take refuge **—*SYN.*** SHELTER

ref·u·gee (ref′yo͞o jē′, ref′yo͞o jē′) ***n.*** ⟦Fr *réfugié,* pp. of *réfugier* < L *refugere:* see prec.⟧ a person who flees from home or country to seek refuge elsewhere, as in a time of war or of political or religious persecution

refloat	**refocus**	**reformulate**	**reframe**
reflourish	**refold**	**refortify**	**refreeze**
reflower	**reforge**	**refracture**	**refry**

re·fu·gi·um (ri fyo͞o′jē əm) *n., pl.* **-gi·a** (-jē ə) ⟦L: see REFUGE⟧ a small, isolated area that has escaped the extreme changes undergone by the surrounding area, as during a period of glaciation, allowing the survival of plants and animals from an earlier period

re·ful·gent (ri ful′jənt) *adj.* ⟦L *refulgens,* prp. of *refulgere,* to reflect light: see RE- & FULGENT⟧ shining; radiant; glowing; resplendent —**re·ful′gence** *n.,* **re·ful′gen·cy**

re·fund[1] (ri fund′; *also, and for n. always,* rē′fund′) *vt.* ⟦ME *refunden* < MFr or L: MFr *refonder* < L *refundere* < *re-,* back + *fundere,* to pour: see FOUND[3]⟧ to give back or pay back (money, etc.); repay —*vi.* to make repayment —*n.* the act of refunding or the amount refunded; repayment —**re·fund′a·ble** *adj.*

re·fund[2] (rē fund′) *vt.* ⟦RE- + FUND⟧ 1 to fund again or anew 2 *Finance a)* to use borrowed money, esp. the proceeds from the sale of a bond issue, to pay back (a loan) before or at maturity *b)* to replace (an old bond issue) with a new bond issue, often at a lower rate of interest

re·fur·bish (ri fur′bish) *vt.* ⟦RE- + FURBISH⟧ to brighten, freshen, or polish up again; renovate —**re·fur′bish·ment** *n.*

re·fus·al (ri fyo͞o′zəl) *n.* 1 the act of refusing 2 the right or chance to accept or refuse something before it is offered to another; option

re·fuse[1] (ri fyo͞oz′) *vt.* **-fused′, -fus′ing** ⟦ME *refusen* < OFr *refuser* < LL **refusare* < L *refusus,* pp. of *refundere:* see REFUND[1]⟧ 1 to decline to accept; reject 2 *a)* to decline to do, give, or grant *b)* to decline (with an infinitive object) [*to refuse to go*] 3 *a)* to decline to accept or submit to (a command, etc.); decline to undergo *b)* to decline to grant the request of (a person) 4 to stop short at (a fence, etc.), without jumping it: said of a horse 5 [Obs.] to renounce —*vi.* to decline to accept, agree to, or do something —*SYN.* DECLINE —**re·fus′er** *n.*

ref·use[2] (ref′yo͞os′, -yo͞oz′) *n.* ⟦ME < OFr *refus,* pp. of *refuser:* see prec.⟧ anything thrown away or rejected as worthless or useless; waste; trash; rubbish —*adj.* thrown away or rejected as worthless or useless

re·fuse·nik (ri fyo͞oz′nik) *n.* ⟦calque of Russ *otkaznik* < *otkaz,* refusal⟧ a Soviet citizen, esp. a Jew, refused permission to emigrate: also sp. **re·fus′nik**

ref·u·ta·tion (ref′yə tā′shən) *n.* ⟦L *refutatio* < *refutatus,* pp.⟧ 1 the act of refuting, or proving false or wrong; disproof 2 something that refutes, as an argument Also **re·fut·al** (ri fyo͞ot′'l)

re·fute (ri fyo͞ot′) *vt.* **-fut′ed, -fut′ing** ⟦L *refutare,* to repel, check: see RE- & CONFUTE⟧ 1 to prove (a person) to be wrong; confute 2 to prove (an argument or statement) to be false or wrong, by argument or evidence 3 to deny the truth or validity of: usage objected to by some —*SYN.* DISPROVE —**re·fut·a·ble** (ri fyo͞ot′ə bəl, ref′yə tə bəl) *adj.* —**re·fut′a·bly** *adv.* —**re·fut′er** *n.*

reg[1] (reg) *n.* ⟦Ar⟧ *Geol.* a large desert area covered with coarse gravel and small stones

reg[2] (reg) *n.* [Slang] *short for* REGULATION [*government regs*]

reg[3] *abbrev.* 1 regiment 2 region 3 registered 4 registrar 5 regular 6 regulation

re·gain (ri gān′) *vt.* ⟦MFr *regaigner:* see RE- & GAIN[1]⟧ 1 to get back into one's possession; recover 2 to succeed in reaching again; get back to —*SYN.* RECOVER

re·gal (rē′gəl) *adj.* ⟦ME < MFr or L: MFr *regal* < L *regalis* < *rex* (gen. *regis*), a king, akin to *regere,* to rule: see RIGHT⟧ 1 of a monarch; royal 2 characteristic of, like, or fit for a monarch; splendid, stately, magnificent, etc. —**re′gal·ly** *adv.*

re·gale (ri gāl′) *vt.* **-galed′, -gal′ing** ⟦Fr *régaler* < the n.⟧ 1 to entertain by providing a splendid feast 2 to delight with something pleasing or amusing —*vi.* to feast —*n.* ⟦Fr *régal,* earlier *régale* < *ré-* (see RE-) + OFr *gale,* joy, pleasure (see GALLANT)⟧ [Archaic] 1 a feast 2 a choice food; delicacy 3 refreshment —**re·gale′ment** *n.* —**re·gal′er** *n.*

re·ga·li·a (ri gāl′yə, -gā′lē ə) *pl.n.* ⟦L, neut. pl. of *regalis:* see REGAL⟧ 1 [Obs.] rights or privileges belonging to a king; prerogatives of sovereignty 2 the emblems and insignia of royalty, as a crown or scepter 3 the insignia or decorations of any rank or position, or of an order or society 4 splendid clothes; finery

re·gal·i·ty (ri gal′ə tē) *n., pl.* **-ties** ⟦ME *regalite* < ML *regalitas:* see REGAL & -ITY⟧ 1 kingship; royalty; sovereignty 2 a right or privilege belonging to a monarch

☆**regal moth** any of various saturniid moths; esp., a large moth (*Citheronia regalis*), also called hickory horned devil, with a heavy, red, hairy body and dull green wings with red veins and yellow spots

Re·gan (rē′gən) *n.* in Shakespeare's *King Lear,* the younger of Lear's two cruel and disloyal daughters

re·gard (ri gärd′) *n.* ⟦ME < OFr < *regarder:* see RE- & GUARD⟧ 1 a firm, fixed look; gaze 2 consideration; attention; concern [*to have some regard for one's safety*] 3 respect and affection; esteem [*to have high regard for one's teachers*] 4 [*pl.*] good wishes; respects; affection [*give my regards to your father*] 5 [Obs.] aspect; appearance —*vt.* ⟦ME *regarden* < OFr *regarder*⟧ 1 to observe or look at with a firm, steady gaze; look at attentively 2 to take into account; consider 3 [Archaic] to give attentive heed to or show concern for 4 to hold in affection and respect [*to regard one's friends highly*] 5 to think of in a certain light; consider [*to regard taxes as a burden*] 6 to have relation to; concern; have reference to [*that which regards our welfare*] —*vi.* 1 to look; gaze 2 to pay heed or attention —**as regards** concerning —**in** (or **with**) **regard to** concerning; with respect to —**in this** (or **that**) **regard** concerning the point just mentioned —**without regard to** without considering

SYN.—**regard** is the most neutral of the terms here, in itself usually implying evaluation of worth rather than recognition of it [*the book is highly regarded by authorities*]; **respect** implies high valuation of worth, as shown in deference or honor [*a jurist respected by lawyers*]; **esteem,** in addition, suggests that the person or object is highly prized or cherished [*a friend esteemed for her loyalty*]; **admire** suggests a feeling of enthusiastic delight in the appreciation of that which is superior [*one must admire such courage*]

re·gard·ant (ri gär′dənt) *adj.* ⟦ME: see prec.⟧ *Heraldry* looking backward, with the head in profile [*a lion regardant*]

re·gard·ful (ri gärd′fəl) *adj.* 1 observant; heedful; mindful: often with *of* 2 showing regard; respectful or considerate —**re·gard′ful·ly** *adv.*

re·gard·ing (ri gär′diŋ) *prep.* with regard to; concerning; about

re·gard·less (ri gärd′lis) *adj.* without regard; heedless; unmindful; careless —☆*adv.* [Informal] without regard for, or in spite of, objections, difficulties, etc.; anyway —**regardless of** in spite of; notwithstanding [*regardless of the cost*] —**re·gard′less·ly** *adv.*

re·gat·ta (ri gät′ə, ri gat′ə) *n.* ⟦It (Venetian) *regata,* gondola race, lit., a striving for mastery < *rigattare,* to compete, wrangle < *ri-* (< L *re-,* RE-) + *grattare,* to scratch < Gmc **kratton* > Ger *kratzen*⟧ 1 a boat race 2 a series of such races

re·ge·la·tion (rē′jə lā′shən) *n.* ⟦see RE- & GELATION[1]⟧ a refreezing together of pieces of ice after a pressure, which has caused melting at a temperature below the normal melting point, has been removed —**re′ge·late′** (-lāt′), *vi.* **-lat′ed, -lat′ing**

re·gen·cy (rē′jən sē) *n., pl.* **-cies** ⟦ME *regencie* < ML *regentia*⟧ 1 the position, function, or authority of a regent or group of regents 2 a group serving as regents 3 a country or territory governed by a regent or group of regents 4 the time during which a regent or regency governs —*adj.* [**R-**] designating or of a style of furniture of the French or British regencies, the French style characterized by scrollwork combined with natural forms, many curves, and strict balance and proportion, the English style by less massive forms and featuring metal or ebony inlay on mahogany and rosewood —**the Regency** 1 in England, the period (1811-20) during which George, Prince of Wales, acted as regent 2 in France, the period (1715-23) during which Philip, Duke of Orléans, acted as regent

re·gen·er·ate (ri jen′ə rit; *for v.,* -rāt′) *adj.* ⟦LME *regenerat* < L *regeneratus,* pp. of *regenerare,* to reproduce, in LL(Ec), to regenerate: see RE- & GENERATE⟧ 1 spiritually reborn 2 renewed or restored, esp. after a decline to a low or abject condition —*vt.* **-at′ed, -at′ing** 1 to cause to be spiritually reborn 2 to cause to be completely reformed or improved 3 to form or bring into existence again; reestablish on a new basis 4 *Biol.* to grow anew (a part to replace one hurt or lost) 5 *Chem.* to produce (a compound, product, etc.) again chemically, as from a derivative or by modification to a physically changed, but not chemically changed, form 6 *Electronics a)* to cause oscillation or to increase the amplification of (a signal) by feeding energy back from an amplifier output to its input *b)* to receive (imperfectly formed electrical signals) for retransmission in substantially perfect form 7 *Mech.* to use (heat, energy, pressure, etc. which would otherwise be wasted) by employing special arrangements or devices 8 *Physics* to restore (a battery, catalyst, etc.) to its original state or properties —*vi.* 1 to form again, or be made anew 2 to be regenerated, or spiritually reborn 3 to have a regenerative effect —**re·gen′er·a·cy** (-ə sē) *n.,* **re·gen′er·ate·ness** —**re·gen′er·ate·ly** *adv.*

re·gen·er·a·tion (ri jen′ə rā′shən) *n.* ⟦ME *regeneracioun* < LL(Ec) *regeneratio*⟧ a regenerating or being regenerated; specif., *a)* a being renewed, reformed, or reconstituted *b)* a spiritual rebirth *c) Biol.* the renewal or replacement of any hurt or lost part, as the claw of a lobster *d) Electronics* the act or process of regenerating signals

re·gen·er·a·tive (ri jen′ər ə tiv, -ā′tiv) *adj.* ⟦ME < MFr < ML *regenerativus*⟧ 1 regenerating or tending to regenerate 2 of or characterized by regeneration —**re·gen′er·a′tive·ly** *adv.*

re·gen·er·a·tor (-rāt′ər) *n.* 1 a person or thing that regenerates 2 a device used in a furnace or engine to preheat incoming air or gas by exposing it to the heat of exhaust gases

Re·gens·burg (rā′gənz burg′; *Ger* rā′gəns bo͝orkh′) city in SE Germany, on the Danube, in the state of Bavaria

re·gent (rē′jənt) *adj.* ⟦ME < MFr or ML: MFr *regent* < ML *regens* < L, prp. of *regere,* to rule: see RIGHT⟧ 1 acting in place of a king or ruler [*a prince regent*] 2 [Now Rare] acting as ruler; ruling —*n.* ⟦ME⟧ 1 a person appointed to rule a monarchy when the sovereign is absent or too young or incapacitated to rule ☆2 *a)* a member of the governing board of certain institutions, as of a state university or a state system of schools *b)* any of certain other university officers 3 [Now Rare] a ruler; governor —**re′gent·ship′** *n.*

re·ges (rē′jēz′) *n. pl. of* REX (*n.* 2)

reg·gae (reg′ā) *n.* ⟦< ? *ragga,* ? short for *ragamuffin*⟧ a form of popular music of Jamaican origin, characterized by a strong, syncopated rhythm and influenced by rhythm and blues and calypso

Reg·gio di Ca·la·bri·a (re′jō dē kə lä′brē ə) seaport in Calabria, S Italy, on the Strait of Messina: also **Reggio Calabria**

Reg·gio nel·l'E·mi·lia (re′jō nel′ā mēl′yə) commune in NC Italy, in Emilia-Romagna: also **Reggio Emilia**

reg·i·cide (rej′ə sīd′) ***n.*** ⟦ML *regicida* < L *rex* (gen. *regis*), a king (see RIGHT) + *-cida* (see -CIDE)⟧ **1** one who kills, or is responsible for the killing of, a monarch, esp. of one's own country **2** ⟦ML *regicidum*⟧ the killing of a monarch —**reg′i·ci′dal** ***adj.***

re·gift (rē′gift′) ***vt., vi.*** to present (a thing that one has received as a gift) to (someone) as if it were a new gift —**re·gift′ing** ***n.***

re·gime or **ré·gime** (rə zhēm′, rā-) ***n.*** ⟦Fr *régime* < L *regimen:* see fol.⟧ **1** *a)* a form of government or rule; political system *b)* a particular administration or government **2** a social system or order **3** the period of time that a person or system is in power **4** REGIMEN (sense 2)

reg·i·men (rej′ə mən) ***n.*** ⟦ME < L, rule, government < *regere,* to rule: see RIGHT⟧ **1** [Rare] *a)* the act of governing; government; rule *b)* a particular system of government; regime **2** a regulated system of diet, exercise, medication, etc. for therapy or the maintenance or improvement of health

reg·i·ment (rej′ə mənt; *for v.,* -ment′) ***n.*** ⟦ME < MFr < LL *regimentum* < L *regere,* to rule: see RIGHT⟧ **1** a military unit consisting of two or more battalions and forming a basic element of a division: since 1963 no longer a tactical unit in the U.S. Army **2** a large number (of persons, etc.) **3** [Obs.] rule; government —***vt.*** **1** to form into a regiment or regiments **2** to assign to a regiment or group **3** to form into an organized or uniform group or groups; organize systematically **4** to organize in a rigid system under strict discipline and control —**reg′i·men′tal** ***adj.*** —**reg′i·men′tal·ly** ***adv.*** —**reg′i·men·ta′tion** ***n.***

reg·i·men·tals (rej′ə ment′′lz) ***pl.n.*** **1** the uniform and insignia worn by a particular regiment **2** military uniform

Re·gi·na[1] (ri jē′nə; *also, and for 2 usually,* -jī′-) ***n.*** ⟦L, a queen, fem. of *rex:* see RIGHT⟧ **1** a feminine name: dim. *Gina* **2** *pl.* **-nae** (-nē) [*also* **r-**] queen: the official title of a reigning queen [Victoria *Regina*]

Re·gi·na[2] (ri jī′nə) ⟦after Queen Victoria, called Victoria *Regina*⟧ capital of Saskatchewan, Canada, in the S part

re·gi·nal (ri jī′nəl) ***adj.*** ⟦ML *reginalis* < L *regina:* see REGINA[1]⟧ of, like, fit for, or characteristic of a queen; queenly; royal

Reg·i·nald (rej′ə nəld) ***n.*** ⟦ML *Reginaldus* < OHG *Raganald, Raginold* < Gmc **ragina-,* **ragna-,* judgment, counsel + **waldan,* to rule: see WIELD⟧ a masculine name: dim. *Reggie;* var. *Reynold;* equiv. Fr. *Regnault, Renaud,* Ger. *Reinhold,* It. *Rinaldo,* Sp. *Reynaldos*

re·gion (rē′jən) ***n.*** ⟦ME *regioun* < Anglo-Fr *regiun* < OFr *region* < L *regio* < *regere,* to rule: see RIGHT⟧ **1** a large and indefinite part of the surface of the earth; district **2** a division of the world characterized by a specific kind of plant or animal life **3** an area; place; space **4** a particular part of the world or universe **5** an administrative division of a country, as in Italy **6** a sphere or realm, as of art or science **7** a division or part of an organism, often called after its main part or organ [the abdominal *region*] **8** any of the levels used to describe the atmosphere or ocean

re·gion·al (rē′jə nəl) ***adj.*** **1** of a whole region, not just a locality **2** of some particular region, district, etc.; local; sectional —***n.*** something extending over or representing a region or regions [a statewide basketball tournament consisting of several *regionals*] —**re′gion·al·ly** ***adv.***

re·gion·al·ism (-iz′əm) ***n.*** **1** the division of a country into small administrative regions **2** regional quality or character **3** devotion to one's own geographical region **4** a word, custom, etc. peculiar to a specific region **5** *Literature* the usually realistic depiction in stories, plays, etc. of a particular region of a country, esp. a rural region, and of the influence of its history, customs, etc. on the lives of the characters —**re′gion·al·ist** ***n., adj.*** —**re′gion·al·is′tic** ***adj.***

re·gion·al·ize (rē′jə nə līz′) ***vt.*** **-ized′**, **-iz′ing** to divide or organize into, administrate as, etc. a region or regions —**re′gion·al·i·za′tion** ***n.***

ré·gis·seur (rā zhē sër′) ***n.*** ⟦Fr, manager, steward < *régir,* to govern, manage⟧ a stage director

reg·is·ter (rej′is tər) ***n.*** ⟦ME *registre* < MFr < ML *registrum,* altered form of *regestum* < LL *regesta,* records, neut. pl. of L *regestus,* pp. of *regerere,* to record, lit., to bring back < *re-,* back + *gerere,* to bear⟧ **1** *a)* a record or list of names, events, items, etc., often kept by an official appointed to do so *b)* a book in which this is kept *c)* an entry in such a book or record **2** ⟦prob. altered < ME *registrer*⟧ a person who keeps such a record, esp. one legally appointed; registrar **3** registration; registry; enrollment **4** a device, as a meter or counter, for recording fares paid, money deposited, etc. [a cash *register*] **5** *a)* a device in a stove or furnace for controlling the draft, etc. ☆*b)* an opening into a room by which the amount of warm or cold air passing, as through a duct leading from a furnace or ventilator, can be controlled **6** *Comput.* a storage location in the central processing unit, as for holding data to be processed **7** *Linguis.* that aspect of usage having to do with vocabulary, pronunciation, punctuation, level of formality, etc., chosen by a user in a particular social context **8** *Music a)* a division of the compass of the human voice or of an instrument all the tones of which are of similar quality *b)* a set of organ pipes controlled by a given stop or the tone quality produced by such a set **9** *Photog.* the exact alignment of images, materials, etc., as two negatives **10** *Printing a)* exact matching in position of pages, lines, etc. on opposite sides of a single sheet *b)* exact imposition of successive colors as they are printed over each other —***vt.*** ☆**1** *a)* to enter in or as in a record or list; enroll or record officially *b)* to transcribe permanently, as if in a register **2** to indicate on or as on a scale [a thermometer *registers* temperature] **3** to show, as by facial expression [to *register* surprise] **4** to commit (valuable mail) to a special postal service for safeguard by payment of a special fee: see REGISTERED MAIL **5** *Printing* to cause to be in register —***vi.*** ☆**1** to enter one's name in a register, as of a hotel **2** to have one's name placed on the list of those eligible to vote in an election, by making application in the prescribed way **3** to enroll in a school, college, etc. **4** to make an impression **5** *Music* to select and combine organ or harpsichord registers **6** *Printing* to be in register —**SYN.** LIST[1] —**reg′is·tra·ble** (-trə bəl) ***adj.***

reg·is·tered (-tərd) ***adj.*** officially recorded or enrolled; specif., *a)* designating bonds, etc. having the owner's name listed in a register *b)* designating a dog, horse, cow or bull, etc. having its ancestry recorded and authenticated by a breeders' association established to promote the breed *c)* legally certified or authenticated

registered mail **1** a postal service for sending mail of high monetary value: a record of sending the mail is provided, it is signed for by each postal employee handling it, signed for by the addressee, and may be insured **2** mail sent by this service

☆**registered nurse** a nurse who, after completing extensive training and passing a state examination, is qualified to perform complete nursing services

register ton *see* TON[1] (sense 4)

reg·is·trant (rej′is trənt) ***n.*** ⟦Fr < ML *registrans,* prp.⟧ a person who registers

reg·is·trar (rej′i strär′) ***n.*** ⟦ME *registrer* < ML *registrarius*⟧ **1** *a)* a person charged with keeping a register ☆*b)* a college or university official responsible for registering students, maintaining their records, etc. **2** a bank or trust company charged with keeping a record of the shares of a corporation and making certain that the number of shares issued does not exceed the number authorized

reg·is·tra·tion (rej′i strā′shən) ***n.*** ⟦ML *registratio*⟧ **1** a registering or being registered **2** an entry in a register **3** the number of persons registered **4** *Music a)* the act or technique of registering *b)* the combination of organ or harpsichord registers chosen for playing a given piece of music

reg·is·try (rej′is trē) ***n., pl.*** **-tries** **1** REGISTRATION **2** an office where registers are kept **3** an official record or list; register **4** a certificate showing the nationality of a merchant ship as recorded in an official register

Re·gi·us professor (rē′jəs, -jē əs) ⟦ModL < L *regius,* royal < *rex* (gen. *regis*), a king: see RIGHT⟧ [*often* **R- P-**; *sometimes* **r- p-**] any of the professors at certain British universities who hold chairs founded by the Crown

reg·let (reg′lit) ***n.*** ⟦Fr *réglet* < *règle,* a rule < L *regula:* see RULE⟧ **1** *Archit.* a flat, narrow molding, used to separate panels, etc. **2** *Printing a)* a flat strip of wood, lower than the typeface, used to separate lines of type *b)* reglets collectively

reg·nal (reg′nəl) ***adj.*** ⟦ML *regnalis* < L *regnum,* REIGN⟧ of a sovereign, sovereignty, or reign

reg·nant (-nənt) ***adj.*** ⟦L *regnans,* prp. of *regnare:* see REIGN⟧ **1** reigning; ruling [a queen *regnant*] **2** of greatest power; predominant **3** prevalent; widespread —**reg′nan·cy** ***n.***

reg·o·lith (reg′ə lith′) ***n.*** ⟦< Gr *rhēgos,* blanket, orig. colored rug (akin to *rhezein,* to dye) + -LITH⟧ the loose, unconsolidated material, residual or transported, that rests on the bedrock; mantle rock

re·gorge (ri gôrj′) ***vt.*** **-gorged′**, **-gorg′ing** ⟦Fr *regorger:* see RE- & GORGE⟧ to throw up or back; disgorge —***vi.*** to flow or gush back, as water

reg·o·sol (reg′ə sôl′, -säl′) ***n.*** ⟦< REGO(LITH) + L *solum,* SOIL[1]⟧ [*often* **R-**] a soil made up of unconsolidated material without stones and without distinct horizons

re·gress (rē′gres; *for v.* ri gres′) ***n.*** ⟦ME *regresse* < L *regressus,* pp. of *regredi,* to go back, return < *re-,* back + *gradi,* to go: see GRADE⟧ **1** a going or coming back **2** the right or privilege of this **3** backward movement; retrogression —***vi.*** **1** to go back; return; move backward **2** to undergo regression —**re·gres′sor** ***n.***

re·gres·sion (ri gresh′ən) ***n.*** ⟦L *regressio*⟧ **1** a regressing, or going back; return; movement backward **2** RETROGRESSION **3** *Astron.* the slow westward shifting of the nodes of an orbit, caused by a perturbation: the complete cycle of the regression of the nodes of the moon's orbit around the earth takes about 18.6 years **4** *Biol.* reversion to an earlier or simpler form, or to a general or common type **5** *Med.* a gradual subsiding of a disease or its symptoms **6** *Psychoanalysis* reversion to earlier or more infantile behavior patterns **7** *Statistics* an estimation technique in which functions or coefficients within functions are designed to estimate values of a dependent variable

re·gres·sive (ri gres′iv) ***adj.*** **1** regressing or tending to regress **2** of, like, or characteristic of regression **3** designating a tax that becomes proportionately lower as the tax base increases —**re·gres′sive·ly** ***adv.***

re·gret (ri gret′) ***vt.*** **-gret′ted**, **-gret′ting** ⟦ME *regretten* < OFr *regreter,* to bewail the dead < *re-* + Gmc base as in OE *gretan,* ON *grata,* Goth *gretan,* to weep⟧ **1** to feel sorry about or mourn for (a person or thing gone, lost, etc.) **2** to feel troubled or remorseful over (something that has happened, one's own acts, etc.) Also used conventionally, as in politely declining an invitation [the mayor *regrets* that he will be unable to attend your reception] —***n.*** **1** a troubled feeling or remorse over something that has happened, esp. over something that one has done or left undone **2** sorrow over a person or thing gone, lost, etc. **3** [*pl.*] a response declining an invi-

regild
regive
reglaze
reglorify
reglue
regrade
regraft
regrant

tation [he sent his *regrets* before the deadline] —*SYN.* PENITENCE —**re·gret′ful** *adj.* —**re·gret′ful·ly** *adv.* —**re·gret′ful·ness** *n.* —**re·gret′ter** *n.*

re·gret·ta·ble (-ə bəl) *adj.* to be regretted; unfortunate —**re·gret′ta·bly** *adv.*

re·group (rē gro͞op′) *vt.* to group again; reassemble or reorganize —*vi.* **1** to reassemble or reorganize, as troops after a battle **2** to collect oneself, as after a loss or setback

Regt *abbrev.* **1** Regent **2** Regiment

reg·u·la·ble (reg′yə lə bəl) *adj.* that can be regulated

reg·u·lar (reg′yə lər) *adj.* ⟦ME *reguler* < MFr < L *regularis,* of a bar (in LL, regular) < *regula:* see RULE⟧ **1** conforming in form, build, or arrangement to a rule, principle, type, standard, etc.; orderly; symmetrical [*regular* features] **2** characterized by conformity to a fixed principle or procedure **3** *a)* usual; customary [his *regular* seat] ☆*b)* not a substitute; established [the *regular* quarterback] ☆*c) Philately* for general, unrestricted use [a *regular* issue of stamps] **4** consistent or habitual in action [a *regular* customer] **5** *a)* recurring at set times or functioning in a normal way [a *regular* pulse] *b)* defecating at more or less fixed intervals **6** conforming to a standard or to a generally accepted rule or mode of conduct; proper **7** properly qualified [a *regular* doctor] **8** CUBIC (sense 3) **9** [Informal] thorough; absolute; complete [a *regular* nuisance] ☆**10** [Informal] pleasant, friendly, reliable, etc. [a *regular* fellow] **11** *Bot.* having all similar parts of the same shape and size; symmetrical: said of flowers **12** *Eccles.* of or belonging to a religious order whose members are bound by vows, specif. solemn vows: often postpositive [a canon *regular*] **13** *Gram.* conforming to the usual pattern in inflection, formation, etc.; specif., WEAK (*adj.* 15) **14** *Math. a)* having all angles and sides equal, as a polygon *b)* having identical regular polygons for all its faces arranged in the same way around all vertices (said of a polyhedron) *c)* uniform with respect to a certain characteristic **15** *Mil. a)* designating or of the permanently constituted, or standing, army of a country *b)* designating soldiers recognized in international law as legitimate combatants in warfare ☆**16** *Politics* designating, of, or loyal to the recognized party leadership, candidates, etc. —*n.* **1** *Eccles.* a member of a regular religious order **2** a member of a regular army ☆**3** a regular member of an athletic team, not a substitute **4** a clothing size for persons, esp. for men, of average height and build **5** [Informal] one who is regular, as in attendance ☆**6** *Politics* a person who is loyal to the recognized party leadership, candidates, etc. —*SYN.* NORMAL, STEADY —**reg′u·lar′i·ty** (-lar′ə tē) *n., pl.* **-ties** —**reg′u·lar·ly** *adv.*

Regular Army the permanent, or standing, army of the United States; the United States Army: cf. ARMY OF THE UNITED STATES

reg·u·lar·ize (reg′yə lə rīz′) *vt.* **-ized′**, **-iz′ing** to make regular —**reg′u·lar·i·za′tion** *n.*

reg·u·late (reg′yə lāt′) *vt.* **-lat′ed**, **-lat′ing** ⟦< LL *regulatus,* pp. of *regulare,* to rule, regulate < L *regula,* a RULE⟧ **1** to control, direct, or govern according to a rule, principle, or system; specif., to impose a body of regulations on a particular industry, type of business, etc. **2** to adjust to a particular standard, rate, degree, amount, etc. [*regulate* the heat] **3** to adjust (a clock, etc.) so as to make operate accurately **4** to make uniform, methodical, orderly, etc. —**reg′u·la′tive** (-lāt′iv, -lə tiv) *adj.* —**reg′u·la·to′ry** (-lə tôr′ē) *adj.*

reg·u·la·tion (reg′yə lā′shən) *n.* ⟦ME *regulatio*⟧ **1** a regulating or being regulated **2** a rule, ordinance, or law by which conduct, etc. is regulated; specif., one of a body of rules or laws governing an industry, institution, or type of business **3** *Embryology* the process by which a structure, damaged or partially changed in an early stage of an animal embryo, adjusts to the disturbance and develops normally —*adj.* **1** ordered or required by regulation; prescribed [a *regulation* uniform] **2** usual; normal; ordinary; regular —*SYN.* LAW

reg·u·la·tor (reg′yə lāt′ər) *n.* ⟦ML⟧ a person or thing that regulates; specif., *a)* a mechanism for controlling or governing the movement of machinery, the flow of liquids, gases, electricity, steam, etc.; governor *b)* the part of the works of a watch or clock by which its speed is adjusted *c)* an accurate timepiece serving as a standard by which others are regulated

Reg·u·lus[1] (reg′yə ləs) *n.* ⟦ModL < L, dim. of *rex,* a king: see RIGHT⟧ **1** a multiple star, the brightest star in the constellation Leo: magnitude, 1.36 **2** *pl.* **-lus·es** or **-li′** (-lī′) [**r-**] *Chem., Metallurgy a)* ⟦because of its ready combination with gold, the "king of metals"⟧ metallic antimony (in full **regulus of antimony**) *b)* impure metal produced by the smelting or reduction of various ores *c)* partly purified metal that sinks to the bottom of a crucible or furnace in smelting

Reg·u·lus[2] (reg′yə ləs), **(Marcus Atilius)** died 250? B.C.; Rom. consul & general in the 1st Punic War

re·gur·gi·tate (ri gur′jə tāt′) *vi.* **-tat′ed**, **-tat′ing** ⟦< ML *regurgitatus,* pp. of *regurgitare,* to regurgitate < *re-,* back + LL *gurgitare,* to flood < *gurges* (gen. *gurgitis*): see GORGE⟧ to rush, surge, or flow back —*vt.* **1** to cause to surge or flow back; specif., to bring (partly digested food) from the stomach back to the mouth **2** [Informal] to repeat (information, an idea, etc.) without modification, interpretation, etc. [students that merely *regurgitate* facts during an exam] —**re·gur′gi·tant** *adj.*

re·gur·gi·ta·tion (ri gur′jə tā′shən) *n.* ⟦ML *regurgitatio*⟧ a regurgitating; specif., *a)* the return of partly digested food from the stomach to the mouth, as in a ruminant animal *b)* a backward flow of blood due to the imperfect closure of a heart valve

re·hab (rē′hab′) [Informal] *n. short for* REHABILITATION —☆*vt.* **-habbed′**, **-hab′bing** *short for* REHABILITATE [to *rehab* an old house] —☆*vi.* to undergo rehabilitation —**re′hab′ber** *n.*

re·ha·bil·i·tate (rē′hə bil′ə tāt′, rē′ə-) *vt.* **-tat′ed**, **-tat′ing** ⟦< ML *rehabilitatus,* pp. of *rehabilitare,* to restore: see RE- & HABILITATE⟧ **1** to restore to rank, privileges, or property which one has lost **2** to restore the good name or reputation of; reinstate in good repute **3** to put back in good condition; reestablish on a firm, sound basis **4** *a)* to bring or restore to a normal or optimal state of health, constructive activity, etc. by medical treatment and physical or psychological therapy *b)* to prepare (a disabled person, an inmate, etc.) for useful employment or successful integration into society by counseling, training, etc. —**re′ha·bil′i·ta′tion** *n.* —**re′ha·bil′i·ta′tive** *adj.*

re·hash (rē′hash′, -hash′; *for v., also* rē hash′) *vt.* ⟦RE- + HASH[1]⟧ to work up again or go over again [to *rehash* the same old arguments] —*n.* the act or result of rehashing [a *rehash* of an earlier book]

re·hear (rē hir′) *vt.* **-heard′** (-hurd′), **-hear′ing** *Law* to hear (a case) a second time —**re·hear′ing** *n.*

re·hears·al (ri hur′səl) *n.* ⟦ME *rehersaille:* see fol. & -AL⟧ **1** the act of rehearsing, reciting, or recounting [a *rehearsal* of her troubles] **2** a drilling or repeating for practice before future performance **3** *a)* a practice performance of a play, concert, etc., or of part of it, in preparation for a public or formal performance *b)* any practice, exercise, or drill; trial —**in rehearsal** being rehearsed, as a play

re·hearse (ri hurs′) *vt.* **-hearsed′**, **-hears′ing** ⟦ME *rehercen* < OFr *rehercer,* lit., to harrow again < *re-,* again + *hercer,* to harrow < *herce,* a harrow: see HEARSE⟧ **1** to repeat aloud as heard or read; recite **2** to tell in detail; narrate or describe in sequence and at length **3** *a)* to perform (a play, concert, etc.) for practice, in preparation for a public or formal performance *b)* to repeat or practice as if rehearsing [to *rehearse* an alibi] **4** to drill or train (a person) by rehearsal —*vi.* to rehearse a play, concert, etc.

re·heat (rē hēt′) *vt.* to heat again; specif., to add heat to (a fluid), as in an afterburner —**re·heat′er** *n.*

Rehn·quist (ren′kwist′), **William H(ubbs)** 1924-2005; associate justice, U.S. Supreme Court (1972-86): chief justice of the U.S. (1986-2005)

Re·ho·bo·am (rē′hə bō′əm) *n.* ⟦Heb *rechavam,* lit., prob., enlarger of the people⟧ **1** *Bible* the first king of Judah: 2 Chron. 9:31-12:16 **2** [*usually* **r-**] *Winemaking* a wine bottle, esp. one for champagne, holding about 4.5 liters, about three times as much as a magnum: see JEROBOAM (sense 2)

re·hy·drate (rē hī′drāt′) *vt.* **-drat′ed**, **-drat′ing** to restore water or other liquid to (something that has been dehydrated) —**re′hy·dra′tion** *n.*

Reich (rīk; *Ger* rīH) *n.* ⟦Ger < OHG *rihhi,* akin to OE *rice,* Goth *reiki* < IE base **reĝ-,* to put in order, straight > RIGHT⟧ **1** the Holy Roman Empire, regarded as the first German empire (**First Reich**) **2** Germany or the German government; specif., *a)* the German Empire from 1871 to 1919 (**Second Reich**) *b)* the German republic from 1919 to 1933 (*Weimar Republic*) *c)* the German fascist state under the Nazis from 1933 to 1945 (**Third Reich**)

reichs·mark (rīks′märk′; *Ger* rīHs′märk′) *n., pl.* **-marks′** or **-mark′** ⟦Ger: see prec. & MARK[2]⟧ the basic monetary unit of Germany from 1924 to 1948

Reichs·tag (rīks′täg′; *Ger* rīHs′täk) *n.* ⟦Ger < *Reich* (see REICH) + *tag,* session, meeting, lit., DAY: see DIET[2]⟧ the former legislative assembly of Germany

re·i·fy (rē′ə fī′) *vt.* **-fied′**, **-fy′ing** ⟦< L *res,* thing (see REAL[1]) + -FY⟧ to treat (an abstraction) as substantially existing, or as a concrete material object —**re′i·fi·ca′tion** *n.*

reign (rān) *n.* ⟦ME *regne* < OFr < L *regnum* < *regere,* to rule: see RIGHT⟧ **1** royal power, authority, or rule; sovereignty **2** dominance, prevalence, or sway [the *reign* of good will] **3** the period of rule, dominance, sway, etc. —*vi.* ⟦ME *regnen* < OFr *regner* < L *regnare,* to rule < *regnum*⟧ **1** *a)* to rule as a sovereign *b)* to hold the title of sovereign, as in a constitutional monarchy **2** to hold sway; prevail or predominate [when peace *reigns*]

Reign of Terror **1** the period of the French Revolution from 1793 to 1794, during which many persons were executed as counterrevolutionaries **2** [**r- of t-**] any period of time during which those in control coerce or subdue others, as by causing fear or threatening violence

rei·ki (rā′kē) *n.* ⟦Jpn, universal life energy < *rei,* soul, spirit + *ki,* vital energy, analogous to CHI[2]: so named by its creator, Mikao Usui (1865-1926), Jpn scholar⟧ an alternative healing technique thought by some to reduce stress, pain, etc. through the transfer of a certain kind of energy from the hands of a practitioner to parts of the body of a person suffering from such symptoms

re·im·burse (rē′im burs′) *vt.* **-bursed′**, **-burs′ing** ⟦RE- + archaic *imburse,* to pay, after Fr *rembourser* < *re-,* again + *embourser,* to pay < *en-,* in + *bourse,* PURSE⟧ **1** to pay back (money spent) **2** to repay or compensate (a person) for expenses, damages, losses, etc. —*SYN.* PAY[1] —**re′im·burs′a·ble** *adj.* —**re′im·burse′ment** *n.*

re·im·pres·sion (rē′im presh′ən) *n.* a second impression; specif., a reprint, as of a book, from the original plates

Reims (rēmz; *Fr* rans) city in NE France: scene of Germany's surrender to the Allies (1945)

rein (rān) *n.* ⟦ME *rene* < OFr *resne* < VL **retina* < L *retinere:* see RETAIN⟧ **1**

---

regrind	**rehandle**	**rehire**	**reignite**	**reimpregnate**
regrow	**rehang**	**rehospitalize**	**reimplant**	**reimprison**
regrowth	**reharden**	**rehouse**	**reimpose**	**reimprisonment**

a narrow strap of leather attached to each end of the bit in the mouth of a horse, and held by the rider or driver to control the animal: *usually used in pl.* **2** [*pl.*] a means of guiding, controlling, checking, or restraining [the *reins* of government] —*vt.* to guide, control, check, or restrain with or as with reins —*vi.* **1** to stop or slow down a horse, etc. with or as with reins: with *in* or *up* **2** [Archaic] to submit to or be controlled by reins: said of a horse —**draw rein 1** to tighten the reins **2** to slow down or stop Also **draw in the reins** —**give (free) rein to** to allow to act without restraint —**keep a rein on** to check, control, or restrain

re·in·car·nate (rē'in kär'nāt') *vt.* **-nat'ed, -nat'ing** to incarnate again; cause to undergo reincarnation

re·in·car·na·tion (rē'in kär nā'shən) *n.* ⟦see prec.⟧ **1** rebirth of the soul in another body, as in Hindu religious belief **2** a new incarnation or embodiment **3** the doctrine or belief that the soul reappears after death in another and different bodily form

rein·deer (rān'dir') *n., pl.* **-deer'** or occas. **-deers'** ⟦ME *reindere* < ON *hreindýri* < *hreinn,* reindeer (< IE **kerei-,* horned animal < base **ker-,* top of the head, horn > HORN, L *cerebrum*) + *dýr,* animal, DEER⟧ any of a genus (*Rangifer*) of large deer, including the caribou, with branching antlers in both sexes, found in northern regions: it is domesticated as a beast of burden and as a source of milk, meat, and leather

Reindeer Lake ⟦? transl. of AmInd name⟧ lake in NE Saskatchewan & NW Manitoba, Canada: 2,467 sq mi (6,390 sq km)

reindeer moss any of various intricately branched, spongy lichens (genus *Cladonia*), esp. a gray lichen (*C. rangiferina*) eaten by grazing animals in the Arctic and, sometimes, by people

Rein·er (rīn'ər), **Fritz** (frits) (*Frederick Martin Reiner,* born *Frigyes Reiner*) 1888-1963; U.S. conductor, born in Hungary

re·in·force (rē'in fôrs') *vt.* **-forced', -forc'ing** ⟦RE- + *inforce,* var. of ENFORCE⟧ **1** to strengthen (a military, naval, or air force) with additional troops, ships, planes, etc. **2** to increase the number or amount of **3** to strengthen or make stronger, as by patching, propping, adding new material, etc. **4** to make stronger or more compelling [to *reinforce* one's arguments] **5** *Psychol.* to increase the probability of (a response to a stimulus) by giving a reward or ending a painful stimulus —**re'in·forc'er** *n.*

reinforced concrete concrete masonry containing steel bars or mesh to increase its tensile strength

re·in·force·ment (-mənt) *n.* **1** a reinforcing or being reinforced **2** anything that reinforces **3** [*pl.*] additional troops, ships, etc. **4** *Physiol., Psychol.* any action or event that reinforces a response

Rein·hardt (rīn'härt') **1 Ad(olph)** 1913-67: U.S. painter **2 Djan·go** (jaŋ'gō) (born *Jean Baptiste*) 1910-53; Belgian jazz guitarist **3 Max** (born *Max Goldmann*) 1873-1943; Austrian theatrical director & producer in Germany and later in the U.S.

reins (rānz) *pl.n.* ⟦ME *reines* < OFr *reins* < L *renes,* pl. of *ren,* kidney⟧ [Archaic] **1** the kidneys, or the region of the kidneys **2** the loins, thought of as the seat of the emotions and affections **3** the emotions and affections

re·in·state (rē'in stāt') *vt.* **-stat'ed, -stat'ing** to instate again; restore to a former condition, position, etc. —**re'in·state'ment** *n.*

re·in·sure (rē'in shoor') *vt.* **-sured', -sur'ing** to insure again, esp. under a contract by which one insurer transfers all or part of the risk to another insurer —**re'in·sur'ance** *n.* —**re'in·sur'er** *n.*

re·in·ter·pret (rē'in tur'prət) *vt.* to interpret again; specif., to give a new explanation or exposition of —**re'in·ter'pre·ta'tion** *n.*

re·in·vent (rē'in vent') *vt.* to invent again or anew [a new kind of western that *reinvents* the genre] —**reinvent the wheel** to go through the pointless effort of creating or devising something already in existence —**re'in·ven'tion** *n.*

reis (rās) *pl.n., sing.* **re·al** (re äl') ⟦Port, pl. of *real,* REAL[3]⟧ a former Portuguese and Brazilian money of account

re·is·sue (rē ish'ōō) *vt.* **-sued, -su·ing** to issue again —*vi.* to come forth again —*n.* a second or later issue, as of a book or recording

REIT (rēt) *n.* ⟦*r*(*eal*) *e*(*state*) *i*(*nvestment*) *t*(*rust*)⟧ a corporation that invests the shareholders' money in real estate and loans for real-estate development

re·it·er·ate (rē it'ər āt') *vt.* **-at'ed, -at'ing** ⟦< L *reiteratus,* pp. of *reiterare,* to repeat: see RE- & ITERATE⟧ to repeat (something done or said); say or do again or repeatedly —*SYN.* REPEAT —**re·it'er·a'tion** *n.* —**re·it'er·a'tive** (-ər āt'iv, -ər ə tiv) *adj.* —**re·it'er·a'tive·ly** *adv.*

reive (rēv) *vt.* REAVE[1] —**reiv'er** *n.*

re·ject (ri jekt'; *for n.* rē'jekt') *vt.* ⟦LME *rejecten* < L *rejectus,* pp. of *reicere, rejicere,* to throw or fling back < *re-,* back + *jacere,* to throw: see JET[1]⟧ **1** to refuse to take, agree to, accede to, use, believe, etc. **2** to discard or throw out as worthless, useless, or substandard; cast off or out **3** to pass over or skip from (a record set by a record changer) without playing **4** to throw up (food); vomit **5** to rebuff; esp., to deny acceptance, care, love, etc. to (someone) [a *rejected* child] **6** *Physiol.* to fail to accept immunologically (a part or organ grafted or transplanted into the body) —*n.* a rejected thing or person —*SYN.* DECLINE —**re·ject·ee** (ri jek'tē') *n.* —**re·ject'er** *n.,* **re·jec'tor** —**re·jec'tion** *n.* —**re·jec'tive** *adj.*

rejection slip a form or note from a publisher, rejecting a work submitted for possible publication

re·jig·ger (rē jig'ər) *vt.* to adjust or alter the arrangement, structure, terms, etc. of: also [Brit.] **re·jig', -jigged', -jig'ging**

re·joice (ri jois') *vi.* **-joiced', -joic'ing** ⟦ME *rejoissen* < inflectional stem of OFr *rejoïr* < *re-,* again + *joïr,* to be glad < VL **gaudire,* for L *gaudere,* to rejoice: see JOY⟧ to be glad, happy, or delighted; be full of joy: often with *at* or *in* —*vt.* [Archaic] to make glad; delight —**re·joic'ing·ly** *adv.*

re·joic·ing (ri jois'iŋ) *n.* **1** the action or feeling of one who rejoices **2** [*often pl.*] an occasion for joy

re·join[1] (rē join') *vt.* ⟦< MFr *rejoindre:* see fol.⟧ **1** to come into the company of again **2** to join together again; reunite **3** to become a member of again after a lapse in membership —*vi.* to become joined together again

re·join[2] (ri join') *vt.* ⟦LME *rejoynen* < Anglo-Fr *rejoyner,* to reply to a charge < MFr *rejoindre,* to join again: see RE- & JOIN⟧ to say in answer —*vi.* **1** to answer **2** *Law* to answer the plaintiff's replication —*SYN.* ANSWER

re·join·der (ri join'dər) *n.* ⟦LME *rejoyner* < Anglo-Fr substantive use of inf. *rejoindre:* see prec.⟧ **1** *a)* an answer to a reply *b)* a reply; answer **2** *Law* the defendant's answer to a plaintiff's replication

re·ju·ve·nate (ri jōō'və nāt') *vt.* **-nat'ed, -nat'ing** ⟦< RE- + L *juvenis,* YOUNG + -ATE[1]⟧ **1** *a)* to make feel or seem young again; bring back to youthful strength, appearance, etc. *b)* to make seem new or fresh again **2** *Geol.* *a)* to increase the grade and speed of flow of (a stream), usually by uplift of the surrounding land *b)* to give youthful land forms to (a region), as steep slopes —*vi.* to restore or reacquire a youthful or new appearance —*SYN.* RENEW —**re·ju've·na'tion** *n.* —**re·ju've·na'tor** *n.*

re·ju·ve·nes·cence (ri jōō'və nes'əns) *n.* ⟦< L *re-,* again < *juvenescens,* prp. of *juvenescere,* to become young < *juvenis,* YOUNG⟧ renewal of youthfulness —**re·ju've·nes'cent** *adj.*

rel *abbrev.* **1** relating **2** relative(ly) **3** religion

re·laid (rē lād') *vt. pt. & pp. of* RE-LAY

re·lapse (ri laps'; *also, and for n. usually,* rē'laps') *vi.* **-lapsed', -laps'ing** ⟦< L *relapsus,* pp. of *relabi,* to slip or slide back: see RE- & LAPSE⟧ to slip or fall back into a former condition, esp. after improvement or seeming improvement; specif., *a)* to fall back into illness *b)* to fall back into bad habits, wrongdoing, etc.; backslide —*n.* **1** the act or an instance of relapsing **2** the recurrence of a disease after apparent improvement —**re·laps'er** *n.*

relapsing fever any of various acute infectious diseases caused by certain spirochetes (genus *Borrelia*) transmitted by ticks or lice, and characterized by recurrent attacks of fever and chills

re·late (ri lāt') *vt.* **-lat'ed, -lat'ing** ⟦< L *relatus,* pp. of *referre,* to bring back: see REFER⟧ **1** to tell the story of or give an account of; narrate; recount **2** to connect or associate, as in thought or meaning; show as having to do with; show a relation between [to *relate* theory and practice] —*vi.* **1** *a)* to have some connection or relation (*to*) *b)* to show sympathetic understanding and awareness in one's personal relationships *c)* to understand and sympathize or agree with someone or something: with *to* [I can't *relate* to what you're saying] **2** to have reference (*to*) —**re·lat'a·ble** *adj.* —**re·lat'er** *n.*

re·lat·ed (ri lāt'id) *adj.* **1** narrated; recounted; told **2** connected or associated, as by origin or kind; specif., connected by kinship, marriage, etc.; of the same family **3** *Music* closely connected melodically or harmonically: said of tones, chords, etc. —**re·lat'ed·ness** *n.*

SYN.—**related,** applied to persons, implies close connection through consanguinity or, less often, through marriage [we are *related* through our mothers], applied to things, close connection through common origin, interdependence, etc. [*related* subjects]; **kindred** basically suggests blood relationship but in extension connotes close connection as because of similar nature, tastes, goals, etc. [we are *kindred* souls]; **cognate** now usually applies to things and suggests connection because of a common source [*cognate* languages]; **allied,** applied to persons, suggests connection through voluntary association; applied to things, connection through inclusion in the same category [*allied* sciences]; **affiliate** usually suggests alliance of a smaller or weaker party with a larger or stronger one as a branch or dependent [several companies are *affiliated* with this corporation]

re·la·tion (ri lā'shən) *n.* ⟦ME *relacion* < MFr or L: MFr *relation* < L *relatio:* see RELATE⟧ **1** a narrating, recounting, or telling **2** what is narrated or told; account; recital **3** connection or manner of being connected or related, as in thought, meaning, etc. **4** connection of persons by blood, marriage, etc.; kinship **5** a person connected with another or others by blood, marriage, etc.; member of the same family; relative **6** [*pl.*] *a)* the connections or dealings between or among persons in business or private affairs *b)* sexual intercourse *c)* the connections or dealings between or among groups, peoples, nations, states, etc. [foreign and trade *relations*] **7** *Law* *a)* the statement of a relator at whose complaint an action is begun *b)* the referring of an act or proceeding to a time before its completion or enactment,

reinaugurate
reincite
reincorporate
reincur
reinduce
reinfect
reinflate
reinform
reinfuse
reinhabit
reinoculate
reinscribe
reinsert
reinspect
reinspire
reinstall
reinstitute
reinstruct
reinter
reinterment
reinterrogate
reintrench
reintroduce
reintroduction
reinvest
reinvestigate
reinvestment
reinvigorate
reinvite
reinvolve
rejudge
rekindle
reknit
relabel
relace

as the time of its taking effect —**in (or with) relation to** concerning; regarding; in reference to

re·la·tion·al (ri lā′shə nəl) *adj.* **1** of relation or relations **2** showing or specifying relation **3** *Gram.* showing relations of syntax: said of conjunctions, prepositions, relative pronouns, etc.

re·la·tion·ship (ri lā′shən ship′) *n.* **1** the quality or state of being related; connection **2** connection by blood, marriage, etc.; kinship **3** a particular instance of being related **4** a continuing attachment or association between persons, firms, etc., specif., one between lovers

rel·a·tive (rel′ə tiv) *adj.* ⟦< MFr or L: MFr *relatif* < L *relativus* < L *relatus:* see RELATE⟧ **1** related each to the other; dependent upon or referring to each other [to stay in the same *relative* positions] **2** pertinent; relevant [documents *relative* to a legal case] **3** regarded in relation to something else; comparative [living in *relative* comfort] **4** meaningful only in relationship; not absolute ["cold" is a *relative* term] **5** *Gram.* *a)* designating a word that introduces a dependent clause and refers to an antecedent ["which" is a *relative* pronoun in "the hat which you bought"] *b)* introduced by such a word [a *relative* clause] —*n.* **1** a relative word, term, or thing **2** a person connected with another by blood, marriage, etc.; kinsman or kinswoman **3** a plant or animal in the same taxonomic division as another —**relative to 1** relevant to; concerning; about **2** corresponding to; in proportion to —**rel′a·tive·ness** *n.*

relative humidity the amount of moisture in the air as compared with the maximum amount that the air could contain at the same temperature, expressed as a percentage: cf. ABSOLUTE HUMIDITY

rel·a·tive·ly (-lē) *adv.* in a relative manner; in relation to or compared with something else; not absolutely [a *relatively* minor matter]

relative major *Music* the major key which has the same key signature as a given minor key [G major is the *relative major* of E minor, both having a key signature of one sharp, i.e., F♯]

relative minor *Music* the minor key which has the same key signature as a given major key [E minor is the *relative minor* of G major, both having a key signature of one sharp, i.e., F♯]

rel·a·tiv·ism (-iz′əm) *n. Philos.* any theory of ethics or knowledge based on the idea that all values or judgments are relative, differing according to circumstances, persons, cultures, etc. —**rel′a·tiv·ist** *n.* —**rel′a·tiv·is′tic** *adj.*

rel·a·tiv·i·ty (rel′ə tiv′ə tē) *n.* **1** the condition, fact, or quality of being relative **2** the close dependence of one occurrence, value, quality, etc. on another **3** *Philos.* *a)* RELATIVISM *b)* RELATIVITY OF KNOWLEDGE **4** *Physics* the fact, principle, or theory of the relative, rather than absolute, character of motion, velocity, mass, etc., and the interdependence of matter, time, and space: as developed and mathematically formulated by Albert Einstein and H. A. Lorentz in the **special (or restricted) theory of relativity** and by Einstein in the **general theory of relativity** (an extension covering the phenomena of gravitation), the theory of relativity includes the statements that: 1) there is no observable absolute motion, only relative motion 2) the velocity of light is constant and not dependent on the motion of the source 3) no energy can be transmitted at a velocity greater than that of light 4) the mass of a body in motion is a function of the energy content and varies with the velocity 5) matter and energy are equivalent 6) time is relative 7) space and time are interdependent and form a four-dimensional continuum 8) the presence of matter results in a "warping" of the space-time continuum, so that a body in motion passing nearby will describe a curve, this being the effect known as gravitation, as evidenced by the deflection of light rays passing through a gravitational field

relativity of knowledge *Philos.* the theory that all knowledge is relative to the mind, or that things can be known only through their effects on the mind, and that consequently there can be no knowledge of reality as it is in itself

rel·a·tiv·ize (rel′ə tiv īz′) *vt.* **-ized′**, **-iz′ing** to think of or treat as relative —**rel′a·tiv·i·za′tion** *n.*

re·la·tor (ri lāt′ər) *n.* ⟦L⟧ **1** a person who relates, or tells; relater **2** *Law* a private person at whose prompting or complaint a public action is begun to bring in question the exercise of an office, franchise, etc.

re·lax (ri laks′) *vt.* ⟦ME *relaxen,* to loosen < L *relaxare* < *re-*, back + *laxare,* to loosen, widen < *laxus,* loose: see LAX⟧ **1** to make looser, or less firm or tense [to *relax* one's grip] **2** to make less strict or severe; soften [to *relax* discipline] **3** to abate; reduce; slacken [to *relax* one's efforts] **4** to release from intense concentration, hard work, worry, etc.; give rest to [to *relax* the mind] **5** to treat (tightly curled hair) with a chemical solution so as to loosen the curls —*vi.* **1** to become looser or less firm, as the muscles **2** to become less tense or stern, as one's features **3** to become less strict, or milder, as discipline **4** to become easier, or less stiff, in manner **5** to rest from effort, worry, or work, as by lying down, engaging in recreation, etc.

re·lax·ant (ri lak′sənt) *adj.* of, pertaining to, or causing relaxation, esp. reduction of muscular tension —*n.* a relaxant drug or agent

re·lax·a·tion (rē′lak sā′shən) *n.* ⟦L *relaxatio* < pp. of *relaxare*⟧ **1** a relaxing or being relaxed; loosening, lessening of severity, etc. **2** *a)* a lessening of or rest from work, worry, or effort *b)* recreation or other activity for bringing this about

re·lax·ed·ly (ri lak′sid lē) *adv.* in a relaxed manner

re·lax·er (ri lak′sər) *n.* **1** one that relaxes **2** a chemical solution that loosens the curls of tightly curled hair

☆**re·lax·in** (ri lak′sin) *n.* ⟦RELAX + -IN[1]⟧ a polypeptide hormone associated with pregnancy, used experimentally to relax the pelvic ligaments, as in childbirth

re·lay (rē′lā′; *for v., also* ri lā′) *n.* ⟦ME *relai* < MFr *relais,* pl., orig., hounds kept as reserves at points along the course of a hunt < *relaier,* to leave behind < *re-* (see RE-) + *laier,* to leave, let: see DELAY⟧ **1** a fresh supply of dogs, horses, etc. kept in readiness to relieve others in a hunt, on a journey, etc. **2** a crew of workers relieving others at work; shift **3** *a)* RELAY RACE *b)* any of the legs, or laps, of a relay race **4** an act or instance of conveying or transmitting by or as by relays **5** SERVOMOTOR **6** *Electronics* an electromagnetic or electronic switching device activated by a signal and usually used to control a large current or to activate another device or circuit —*vt.* **-layed′**, **-lay′ing 1** to convey by relays **2** to convey as if by relays; receive and pass on (a message, news, etc.) **3** to supply or replace with a relay or relays **4** *Elec.* to control, operate, or send on by a relay

re-lay (rē lā′) *vt.* **-laid′**, **-lay′ing** to lay again or anew: also **re′lay′**

relay race a race between two or more teams, each runner going in turn only a part of the total distance

re·lease (ri lēs′) *vt.* **-leased′**, **-leas′ing** ⟦ME *relesen* < OFr *relaisser* < L *relaxare:* see RELAX⟧ **1** to set free, as from confinement, duty, work, etc. **2** to let go or let loose [to *release* an arrow] **3** to grant freedom from a tax, penalty, obligation, etc. **4** to set free from pain, cares, etc.; relieve ☆**5** to permit to be issued, shown, published, broadcast, etc.; put into circulation **6** *Law* to give up or surrender to someone else (a claim, right, etc.) —*n.* **1** a setting free or being set free; deliverance; liberation **2** a freeing or being freed from a tax, obligation, etc. **3** *a)* a relief from pain, cares, etc. *b)* relief from emotional tension through a spontaneous, uninhibited expression of an emotion **4** a document authorizing release, as from an obligation, from prison, etc. **5** the act of letting loose something caught, held in position, etc. **6** a device to release a catch, etc., as for starting or stopping a machine ☆**7** *a)* the act of releasing a book, film, news story, etc. to the public *b)* the book, film, news story, etc. released **8** *Music* *a)* the act or method of ending a tone ☆*b)* the third group of eight measures in a common form of 32-bar chorus, as in a popular tune, which supplies a bridge between repetitions of the melody **9** *Law* *a)* a giving up or surrender to someone else, as of a claim or right *b)* the document by which this is done; quitclaim —*SYN.* FREE

re-lease (rē lēs′) *vt.* **-leased′**, **-leas′ing** to lease again

☆**released time** a period or periods when a person is freed from regular duties, esp. teaching, to allow time for other tasks or activities: also **release time**

rel·e·gate (rel′ə gāt′) *vt.* **-gat′ed**, **-gat′ing** ⟦< L *relegatus,* pp. of *relegare,* to send away < *re-*, away, back + *legare,* to send: see LEGATE⟧ **1** to exile or banish (someone) *to* a specified place **2** to consign or assign to an inferior position: usually with *to* **3** to assign to a class, sphere, realm, etc.; classify as belonging to a certain order of things **4** to refer, commit, or hand over for decision, action, etc. —*SYN.* COMMIT —**rel′e·ga′tion** *n.*

re·lent (ri lent′) *vi.* ⟦ME *relenten,* to melt, ult. < L < *re-*, again + *lentus,* flexible, pliant, slow: see LITHE⟧ **1** to soften in temper, resolution, etc.; become less severe, stern, or stubborn **2** [Obs.] to melt —*SYN.* YIELD

re·lent·less (-lis) *adj.* **1** not relenting; harsh; pitiless **2** persistent; unremitting —**re·lent′less·ly** *adv.* —**re·lent′less·ness** *n.*

rel·e·vant (rel′ə vənt) *adj.* ⟦ML *relevans,* prp. of *relevare,* to bear upon < L, to lift up: see RELIEVE⟧ bearing upon or relating to the matter in hand; pertinent; to the point —**rel′e·vance** *n.*, **rel′e·van·cy** —**rel′e·vant·ly** *adv.*

SYN.—**relevant** implies close logical relationship with, and importance to, the matter under consideration [*relevant* testimony]; **germane** implies such close natural connection as to be highly appropriate or fit [your reminiscences are not truly *germane* to this discussion]; **pertinent** implies an immediate and direct bearing on the matter in hand [a *pertinent* suggestion]; **apposite** applies to that which is both relevant and happily suitable or appropriate [an *apposite* analogy]; **applicable** refers to that which can be brought to bear upon a particular matter or problem [your description is *applicable* to several people]; **apropos** is used of that which is opportune as well as relevant [an *apropos* remark] —*ANT.* **inappropriate, extraneous**

re·le·vé (rə lə vā′) *n.* ⟦Fr < adj., raised < pp. of *relever,* to raise or lift (again)⟧ *Ballet* a raising onto the toe or toes or the tip of the toe

re·li·a·ble (ri lī′ə bəl) *adj.* that can be relied on; dependable; trustworthy —**re·li′a·bil′i·ty** *n.*, **re·li′a·ble·ness** —**re·li′a·bly** *adv.*

SYN.—**reliable** is applied to a person or thing that can be counted upon to do what is expected or required [a *reliable* assistant]; **dependable** refers to a person or thing that can be depended on as in an emergency and often connotes levelheadedness or steadiness [a *dependable* friend]; **trustworthy** applies to a person, or sometimes a thing, whose truthfulness, integrity, discretion, etc. can be relied on [a *trustworthy* source of information]; **trusty** applies to a person or thing which continued experience has shown to be completely trustworthy or dependable [my *trusty* steed]

re·li·ance (-əns) *n.* **1** the act of relying **2** trust, dependence, or confidence **3** a thing relied on

re·li·ant (-ənt) *adj.* having or showing trust, dependence, or confidence; dependent (*on*) —**re·li′ant·ly** *adv.*

rel·ic (rel′ik) *n.* ⟦ME *relike* < OFr *relique* < L *reliquiae,* pl., remains < *relinquere:* see RELINQUISH⟧ **1** *a)* an object, custom, etc. that has survived,

relaunch relaunder relearn relet

wholly or partially, from the past *b)* something that has historic interest because of its age and associations with the past, or that serves as a keepsake, or souvenir **2** [*pl.*] remaining fragments; surviving parts; ruins **3** RELICT (*n.* 2) **4** *Eccles.* the body or a body part of, or some object associated with, a saint, martyr, etc., kept and reverenced as a memorial, as in the Roman Catholic and Eastern Orthodox churches

re·lict (ri likt′; *for n.* rel′ikt) ***adj.*** ⟦L *relictus,* pp. of *relinquere:* see RELINQUISH⟧ [Archaic] surviving the death of another; esp., widowed —***n.*** **1** ⟦LL *relicta* < L *relictus*⟧ [Archaic] a widow **2** ⟦< the adj.⟧ *a) Ecol.* a plant or animal species living on in isolation in a small local area as a survival from an earlier period or as a remnant of an almost extinct group *b) Geol.* a physical feature, mineral, structure, etc. remaining after other components have wasted away or been altered

re·lief (ri lēf′) ***n.*** ⟦ME *releef* < OFr *relief* < *relever:* see RELIEVE⟧ **1** *a)* an easing, as of pain, discomfort, or anxiety *b)* a lightening of a burden, as of taxation, oppression, etc. **2** anything that lessens tension or strain, or offers a pleasing change, as to the mind or eye **3** aid in the form of goods or money given, as by a government agency, to persons unable to support themselves **4** any aid given in times of need, danger, or disaster, as supplies sent into a flooded area **5** *a)* release from work or duty *b)* the person or persons bringing such release by taking over a post **6** a payment made by the heir of a feudal vassal to the overlord on taking over an estate **7** ⟦Fr < It *relievo* < *rilevare,* to raise: see RELIEVE⟧ *Archit., Sculpture a)* the projection of figures and forms from a flat surface, so that they stand wholly or partly free *b)* a work of art so made **8** *Law* the assistance or redress sought by a complainant in a court, esp. a court of equity **9** *Literature, Drama a)* sharp contrast, as of ideas, actions, or events *b)* comic scenes in a serious drama or film (in full **comic relief**) **10** *a) Painting* the apparent solidity or projection of objects, obtained by modeling and gradation in color, etc. *b)* distinctness of outline; contrast **11** *Geol. a)* the differences in height, collectively, of land forms in any particular area *b)* these differences as shown by lines, colors, raised areas, etc. on a map **12** *Printing* a method of printing in which the image is carried on raised surfaces; letterpress —☆***adj.*** *Baseball* designating a pitcher who replaces another during a game, esp. one who is regularly used in this way —**in relief** carved or molded so as to project from a surface —**on relief** receiving government aid because of poverty, unemployment, etc.

relief map a map showing by color, raised areas, etc., the different heights of landforms, as hills and valleys

relief valve SAFETY VALVE

re·lieve (ri lēv′) ***vt.*** **-lieved′**, **-liev′ing** ⟦ME *releven* < OFr *relever* < L *relevare,* to lift up again < *re-,* again + *levare,* to raise: see LEVER⟧ **1** *a)* to ease, lighten, or reduce (pain, anxiety, etc.) *b)* to free (a person) from pain, discomfort, anxiety, etc. *c)* to restore (a part of the body, the mind, etc.) to well-being **2** *a)* to lighten the pressure, stress, weight, etc. on (something) *b)* to lighten (pressure, stress, etc.) **3** *a)* to give aid or assistance to [to *relieve* the poor] *b)* to bring or send help to [to *relieve* a besieged city] **4** *a)* to set free from a burden, obligation, grievance, etc. *b)* to remove (a burden, etc.) **5** *a)* to set free from duty or work by replacing with oneself or another [to *relieve* a nurse] ☆*b) Baseball* to serve as a relief pitcher for (another pitcher) **6** to make less tedious, monotonous, etc. by being or providing a pleasing change **7** to set off by contrast; make distinct or prominent —☆***vi.*** *Baseball* to serve as a relief pitcher —**relieve oneself** to urinate or defecate —**re·liev′a·ble** ***adj.*** —**re·liev′er** ***n.***

SYN.—**relieve** implies the reduction of misery, discomfort, or tediousness sufficiently to make it bearable [they played a game to *relieve* the monotony of the trip]; **alleviate** implies temporary relief, suggesting that the source of the misery remains unaffected [drugs to *alleviate* the pain]; **lighten** implies a cheering or gladdening as by reducing the weight of oppression or depression [nothing can *lighten* the burden of our grief]; **assuage** suggests a softening or pacifying influence in lessening pain, calming passion, etc. [her kind words *assuaged* his resentment]; **mitigate** implies a moderating or making milder of that which is likely to cause pain [to *mitigate* a punishment]; **allay** suggests an effective, although temporary or incomplete, calming or quieting [we've *allayed* their suspicions] See also **comfort**

re·lie·vo (ri lē′vō, ril yev′ō) ***n.***, *pl.* **-vos** RELIEF (sense 7)

relig *abbrev.* **1** religion **2** religious

re·li·gi·o- (rə lij′ē ō′) *combining form* religion, religious, religion and [*religio*-political]

re·li·gion (ri lij′ən) ***n.*** ⟦ME *religioun* < OFr or L: OFr *religion* < L *religio,* reverence for the gods, holiness, in LL(Ec), a system of religious belief < ? *religare,* to bind back < *re-,* back + *ligare,* to bind, bind together; or < ? *re-* + IE base **leĝ-,* to collect > LOGIC, Gr *legein,* L *legere*⟧ **1** *a)* belief in a divine or superhuman power or powers to be obeyed and worshiped as the creator(s) and ruler(s) of the universe *b)* expression of such a belief in conduct and ritual **2** *a)* any specific system of belief and worship, often involving a code of ethics and a philosophy [the Christian *religion,* the Buddhist *religion,* etc.] *b)* any system of beliefs, practices, ethical values, etc. resembling, suggestive of, or likened to such a system [humanism as a *religion*] **3** the state or way of life of a person in a monastery, convent, etc. **4** any object of conscientious regard and pursuit —☆**get religion** [Informal] **1** to become religious **2** to become very conscientious or earnest about something

re·li·gion·ism (-iz′əm) ***n.*** religious zeal, esp. when excessive or affected —**re·li′gion·ist** ***n.***

re·li·gi·os·i·ty (ri lij′ē äs′ə tē) ***n.*** ⟦ME *religiosite* < LL(Ec) *religiositas*⟧ the quality of being religious, esp. of being excessively, ostentatiously, or mawkishly religious —**re·li′gi·ose′** (-ōs′) ***adj.***

re·li·gious (ri lij′əs) ***adj.*** ⟦OFr < L *religiosus*⟧ **1** characterized by adherence to religion or a religion; devout; pious; godly **2** of, concerned with, appropriate to, or teaching religion [*religious* books] **3** belonging to a community of monks, nuns, etc. **4** conscientiously exact; careful; scrupulous —***n.***, *pl.* **-gious** a member of a community of monks, nuns, etc. —*SYN.* DEVOUT —**re·li′gious·ly** ***adv.*** —**re·li′gious·ness** ***n.***

Religious Society of Friends the full *name for* SOCIETY OF FRIENDS

re·line (rē līn′) ***vt.*** **-lined′**, **-lin′ing** **1** to mark with new lines **2** to provide with a new lining

re·lin·quish (ri liŋ′kwish) ***vt.*** ⟦LME *relinquissen* < extended stem of OFr *relinquir* < L *relinquere* < *re-,* from + *linquere,* to leave: see LOAN⟧ **1** to give up; abandon (a plan, policy, etc.) **2** to renounce or surrender (something owned, a right, etc.) **3** to let go (a grasp, hold, etc.) —**re·lin′quish·ment** ***n.***

SYN.—**relinquish** implies a giving up of something desirable and connotes compulsion or the force of necessity [we will not *relinquish* our advantage]; **abandon**, in this connection, implies a complete and final relinquishment, as because of weariness, discouragement, etc. [do not *abandon* hope]; **waive** suggests a voluntary relinquishing by refusing to insist on one's right or claim to something [to *waive* a jury trial]; **forgo** implies the denial to oneself of something, as for reasons of expediency or altruism [I must *forgo* the pleasure of your company this evening] —*ANT.* **keep, retain**

rel·i·quar·y (rel′ə kwer′ē) ***n.***, *pl.* **-quar′ies** ⟦Fr *reliquaire* < L *reliquiae:* see RELIC⟧ *Eccles.* a case or other container in which relics are kept and displayed for veneration

rel·ique (rel′ik, rə lēk′) ***n.*** *archaic var. of* RELIC

re·liq·ui·ae (ri lik′wē ē′) ***pl.n.*** ⟦L: see RELIC⟧ remains, as of fossil organisms

rel·ish (rel′ish) ***n.*** ⟦ME *reles* < OFr *relais,* something remaining < *relaisser:* see RELEASE⟧ **1** distinctive or characteristic flavor [a *relish* of garlic in the stew] **2** a trace or touch (*of* some quality); hint or suggestion [a *relish* of malice in his action] **3** an appetizing flavor; pleasing taste **4** *a)* pleasure; enjoyment; zest [to listen with *relish*] *b)* liking or craving [showing little *relish* for the task] **5** anything that gives pleasure, zest, or enjoyment; attractive quality **6** *a)* any of a variety of foods, as pickles, olives, piccalilli, or raw vegetables, served with a meal to add flavor or as an appetizer *b)* a pickled condiment, as for use on hot dogs or hamburgers, usually consisting of finely chopped pickled cucumbers with spices, sugar, vinegar, etc. —***vt.*** **1** [Now Rare] to give flavor **2** to enjoy; like —***vi.*** **1** to taste or have the flavor (*of* something) **2** to have a pleasing taste

re·live (rē liv′) ***vt.*** **-lived′**, **-liv′ing** to experience again (a past event) as in the imagination

re·lle·no (re yā′nō) ***n.*** *short for* CHILE RELLENO

☆**re·lo·cate** (rē lō′kāt′) ***vt., vi.*** **-cat′ed**, **-cat′ing** **1** to locate again **2** to move to a new location —**re′lo·ca′tion** ***n.***

re·lu·cent (ri lo͞o′sənt) ***adj.*** ⟦L *relucens,* prp. of *relucere:* see RE- & LUCENT⟧ reflecting light; bright

re·luct (ri lukt′) ***vi.*** ⟦L *reluctari* (see RELUCTANT): in later use prob. back-form. < fol. or RELUCTANT⟧ [Rare] **1** to struggle (*against*); revolt (*at*) **2** to offer opposition; show reluctance

re·luc·tance (ri luk′təns) ***n.*** **1** the fact or state of being reluctant; unwillingness **2** [Rare] opposition; revolt **3** *Elec.* the resistance offered to magnetic flux by a magnetic circuit, equal to the magnetomotive force divided by the magnetic flux: similar to the resistance in an electric circuit Also [Rare] **re·luc′tan·cy**

re·luc·tant (-tənt) ***adj.*** ⟦L *reluctans,* prp. of *reluctari,* to resist < *re-,* against + *luctari,* to struggle: see LOCK[1]⟧ **1** opposed in mind (*to* do something); unwilling; disinclined **2** marked by unwillingness [a *reluctant* answer] **3** [Rare] struggling against; resisting; opposing —**re·luc′tant·ly** ***adv.***

SYN.—**reluctant** implies an unwillingness to do something, as because of distaste, irresolution, etc. [I was *reluctant* to join]; **disinclined** suggests a lack of desire for something, as because it fails to suit one's taste or because one disapproves of it [I feel *disinclined* to argue]; **hesitant** implies a refraining from action, as because of fear, indecision, etc. [don't be *hesitant* about asking this favor]; **loath** suggests strong disinclination or a decided unwillingness [I am *loath* to depart]; **averse** suggests a sustained, although not extreme, disinclination [not *averse* to borrowing money] —*ANT.* **inclined, disposed, eager**

rel·uc·tiv·i·ty (rel′ək tiv′ə tē) ***n.*** the ability of a substance to conduct magnetic flux, measured by the ratio of the intensity of the magnetic field to the magnetic induction of the substance: it is the reciprocal of magnetic permeability

re·lume (rē lo͞om′) ***vt.*** **-lumed′**, **-lum′ing** ⟦RE- + (IL)LUME⟧ [Archaic] **1** to light again; rekindle **2** to light up again; illuminate or shine on again Also **re·lu′mine** (-lo͞o′mən) ***vt.*** **-mined**, **-min·ing**

re·ly (ri lī′) ***vi.*** **-lied′**, **-ly′ing** ⟦ME *relien,* to rally < OFr *relier* < L *religare:* see RELIGION⟧ **1** to have confidence; trust [you can *rely* on their willingness to help] **2** to look to for support or aid; depend Used with *on* or *upon*

SYN.—to **rely** (*on* or *upon*) a person or thing is to have confidence, usually on the basis of past experience, that what is expected will be done [*she can be relied on to keep the secret*]; to **trust** is to have complete faith or assurance that one will not be let down by another [*to trust in God*]; to **depend** (*on* or *upon*) a person or thing is to be assured of support or aid from that person or thing [*he can depend on his wife for sympathy*]; to **count** (*on*) or, informally, to **reckon** (*on*) something is to consider it in one's calculations as certain [*they counted, or reckoned, on my going*]; to **bank** (*on*), an informal term, is to have confidence like that of one who is willing to risk money on something [*don't bank on their help*]

rem (rem) *n., pl.* **rem** ⟦*r(oentgen) e(quivalent), m(an)*⟧ a basic unit used to measure the amount of biological damage caused by various types of ionizing radiation, equal to the dose that produces the same amount of damage in human tissue as one roentgen of X-rays or gamma rays (0.01 sievert)

REM (rem) *n., pl.* **REMs** ⟦*r(apid) e(ye) m(ovement)*⟧ *Psychol.* the periodic, rapid, jerky movement of the eyeballs under closed lids during stages of sleep associated with intense dreaming

re·main (ri mān′) *vi.* ⟦ME *remainen* < OFr *remaindre* < L *remanere* < *re-*, back, behind + *manere,* to stay: see MANOR⟧ **1** to be left or left over when the rest has been taken away, destroyed, or disposed of in some way **2** *a)* to stay while others go *b)* to stay in the same place [*remain in the house*] **3** to continue; go on being [*to remain a cynic*] **4** to continue to exist; endure; persist; last [*a remaining memory*] **5** to be left to be dealt with, done, said, etc. —*SYN.* STAY[3]

re·main·der (-dər) *n.* ⟦ME *remaindre* < Anglo-Fr substantive use of OFr inf.: see prec.⟧ **1** those remaining **2** what is left when a part is taken away; the rest **3** a copy or number of copies of a book still held by a publisher when the sale has fallen off, usually disposed of at a greatly reduced price **4** *Law* an estate of expectancy but not in possession, as when land is conveyed by the same deed to one person while alive and at death to another and that person's heirs **5** *Math. a)* what is left when a smaller number is subtracted from a larger *b)* what is left undivided when one number is divided by another that is not one of its factors —*adj.* [Rare] remaining; leftover —*vt.* to sell (books, etc.) as remainders

SYN.—**remainder** is the general word applied to what is left when a part is taken away [*the remainder of a meal, one's life, etc.*]; **residue** and **residuum** apply to what remains at the end of a process, as after the evaporation or combustion of matter or after the settlement of claims, etc. in a testator's estate; **remnant** is applied to a fragment, trace, or any small part left after the greater part has been removed [*remnants of cloth from the ends of bolts*]; **balance** may be used in place of **remainder**, but in strict use it implies the amount remaining on the credit or debit side

re·mains (ri mānz′) *pl.n.* **1** what is left after part has been used, destroyed, etc.; remainder; remnant **2** vestiges or traces of the past **3** a corpse; specif., the parts or fragments of a dead body remaining after decomposition **4** writings left unpublished by an author at the time of death: in full **literary remains** —*SYN.* BODY

re·make (rē māk′; *for n.* rē′māk′) *vt.* **-made′**, **-mak′ing** to make again or anew —*n.* **1** the act of remaking **2** something remade, as a film

re·man (rē man′) *vt.* **-manned′**, **-man′ning 1** to man (a boat, etc.) again **2** to give new manliness or courage to

re·mand (ri mand′; *for n., also* rē′mand′) *vt.* ⟦ME *remaunden* < OFr *remander* < LL *remandare,* to notify in return < L *re-*, back + *mandare,* to order: see MANDATE⟧ **1** to send back; order to go back **2** *Law a)* to send (a prisoner or accused person) back into custody, as to await trial or further investigation *b)* to send (a case) back to a lower court for additional proceedings —*n.* a remanding or being remanded

rem·a·nence (rem′ə nəns) *n.* [see fol.] *Elec.* the magnetic flux remaining in a substance after the magnetizing force has been withdrawn

rem·a·nent (-nənt) *adj.* ⟦ME < L *remanens,* prp.⟧ [Now Rare] remaining; leftover

re·mark (ri märk′) *vt.* ⟦Fr *remarquer* < *re-* + *marquer,* to mark < It *marcare* < *marca,* a mark < Gmc **marka:* see MARK[1]⟧ **1** *a)* to notice; observe; perceive *b)* to give consideration or be responsive to **2** to say or write as an observation or comment **3** [Obs.] to mark; distinguish; indicate —*vi.* to make an observation or comment: with *on* or *upon* —*n.* **1** the act of noticing, perceiving, or observing [*a man worthy of remark*] **2** something said briefly; comment; casual observation **3** REMARQUE

SYN.—**remark** applies to a brief, more or less casual statement of opinion, etc., as in momentarily directing one's attention to something [*a remark about clothes*]; an **observation** is an expression of opinion on something to which one has given some degree of special attention and thought [*the warden's observations on prison reform*]; a **comment** is a remark or observation made in explaining, criticizing, or interpreting something [*comments on a novel*]; **commentary** is usually applied as a collective noun to a series of explanatory notes or annotations [*a commentary on Aristotle's Politics*]

re·mark·a·ble (ri mär′kə bəl) *adj.* **1** worthy of remark or notice **2** unusual; extraordinary —*SYN.* NOTICEABLE —**re·mark′a·ble·ness** *n.* —**re·mark′a·bly** *adv.*

re·marque (ri märk′) *n.* ⟦Fr: see REMARK⟧ **1** a mark, esp. a small design or sketch, made on the margin of an engraved plate and appearing only on proofs, to identify a particular stage of the plate **2** a plate, print, or proof bearing such a mark

Re·marque (ri märk′), **E·rich Ma·ri·a** (er′ik mə rē′ə) (born *Erich Paul Remark*) 1898-1970; Ger. novelist; later a U.S. citizen

re·mas·ter (rē mas′tər) *vt.* to MASTER (*vt.* 4) again, esp. so as to improve sound or images by using newer technology

Rem·brandt (rem′brant′, -bränt′) (born *Rembrandt Harmensz van Rijn*) 1606-69; Du. painter & etcher

re·me·di·a·ble (ri mē′dē ə bəl) *adj.* ⟦ME < MFr < L *remediabilis*⟧ that can be remedied —**re·me′di·a·ble·ness** *n.* —**re·me′di·a·bly** *adv.*

re·me·di·al (ri mē′dē əl) *adj.* ⟦LL *remedialis*⟧ **1** providing, or intended to provide, a remedy ☆**2** *Educ.* designating or of any special course of study for helping students overcome deficiencies in specific skills, abilities, or knowledge [*remedial reading*] —**re·me′di·al·ly** *adv.*

re·me·di·ate (ri mē′dē āt′) *vt.* **-at′ed**, **-at′ing** ⟦back-form. < fol.⟧ to provide a remedy for

re·me·di·a·tion (ri mē′dē ā′shən) *n.* ⟦< fol. + -ATION⟧ **1** the act or process of remedying ☆**2** *Educ.* the act or process of remedying or overcoming learning disabilities or problems —**re·me′di·a′tion·al** *adj.*

rem·e·dy (rem′ə dē) *n., pl.* **-dies** ⟦ME *remedie* < Anglo-Fr < OFr *remede* < L *remedium* < *re-*, again + *mederi,* to heal, akin to *medicus:* see MEDICAL⟧ **1** any medicine or treatment that cures, heals, or relieves a disease or bodily disorder or tends to restore health **2** something that corrects, counteracts, or removes an evil or wrong; relief; redress **3** *Law* a means, as court action, by which violation of a right is prevented or compensated for; legal redress —*vt.* **-died**, **-dy·ing 1** to cure or heal, as with medicine **2** to put back in proper condition; put right **3** to correct or remove (an evil, etc.) —*SYN.* CURE —**rem′e·di·less** *adj.*

re·mem·ber (ri mem′bər) *vt.* ⟦ME *remembren* < OFr *remembrer* < LL *rememorare* < L *re-*, back, again + *memorare,* to bring to remembrance < *memor,* mindful: see MEMORY⟧ **1** to have (an event, thing, person, etc.) come to mind again; think of again [*suddenly remembering an appointment*] **2** to bring back to mind by an effort; recollect; recall [*to try to remember a name*] **3** to bear in mind; keep in the memory; be careful not to forget **4** to keep (a person) in mind with some feeling, as of pleasure, gratitude, etc. **5** *a)* to keep (a person) in mind for a present, legacy, etc. *b)* to give a present or tip to **6** to mention (a person) to another as sending regards or greetings [*remember me to your mother*] **7** [Archaic] to remind —*vi.* **1** to bear something in mind or call something back to mind **2** to have memory or the use of one's memory —**re·mem′ber·er** *n.*

re·mem·brance (ri mem′brəns) *n.* ⟦ME < OFr: see prec. & -ANCE⟧ **1** a remembering or being remembered **2** the power to remember **3** something remembered; memory **4** the extent of time over which one can remember **5** an object that serves to bring to mind or keep in mind some person, event, etc.; souvenir, gift, keepsake, memento, etc. **6** commemoration [*in remembrance of the deceased*] **7** [*pl.*] greetings

Remembrance Day in Canada, a day (Nov. 11) honoring veterans of WWI and WWII

re·mem·branc·er (-brən sər) *n.* ⟦ME < Anglo-Fr: see REMEMBRANCE & -ER⟧ **1** a person who reminds another of something, esp. one engaged or appointed to do so **2** [*usually* **R-**] in England, any of certain officials, specif., one responsible for collecting debts owed to the sovereign **3** a reminder; memento

Remembrance Sunday a British holiday, observed on the Sunday closest to Armistice Day (Nov. 11), honoring veterans of WWI and WWII

rem·i·ges (rem′ə jēz′) *pl.n., sing.* **re·mex** (rē′meks) ⟦ModL, pl. of *remex* < L, rower < *remus,* oar (see ROW[2]) + *agere,* to move (see ACT[1])⟧ the large quill feathers of a bird's wing; the primary and secondary contour feathers —**re·mig·i·al** (ri mij′ē əl) *adj.*

re·mind (ri mīnd′) *vt., vi.* ⟦RE- + MIND, v.⟧ to put (a person) in mind (*of* something); cause (a person) to remember

re·mind·er (ri mīn′dər) *n.* a person or thing that reminds; thing to help one remember something else

re·mind·ful (ri mīnd′fəl) *adj.* **1** mindful; remembering **2** reviving memory; reminding; reminiscent

Rem·ing·ton (rem′iŋ tən), **Frederic** 1861-1909; U.S. painter, sculptor, & illustrator

rem·i·nisce (rem′ə nis′) *vi.* **-nisced′**, **-nisc′ing** ⟦back-form. < fol.⟧ to think, talk, or write about remembered events or experiences

rem·i·nis·cence (rem′ə nis′əns) *n.* ⟦Fr *réminiscence* < LL *reminiscentia:* see fol.⟧ **1** the act of remembering or recollecting past experiences **2** a memory or recollection **3** [*pl.*] an account, written or spoken, of remembered experiences **4** something that suggests or recalls something else; reminder

rem·i·nis·cent (-ənt) *adj.* ⟦L *reminiscens,* prp. of *reminisci* < *re-*, again + *memini,* to remember: for IE base see MIND⟧ **1** having the nature of or characterized by reminiscence **2** given to reminiscing, or recalling past experiences **3** bringing to mind something else; suggestive (*of*) —**rem′i·nis′cent·ly** *adv.*

re·mise (ri mīz′) *vt.* **-mised′**, **-mis′ing** ⟦LME *remisen* < MFr *remis,* pp. of *remettre,* to send back < L *remittere:* see REMIT⟧ *Law* to give up a claim to; release by deed

remanufacture	**remarriage**	**rematch**	**remelt**	**remigrate**
remap	**remarry**	**remeasure**	**remerge**	**remilitarize**

re·miss (ri mis′) *adj.* ⟦L *remissus,* pp. of *remittere:* see REMIT⟧ **1** careless in, or negligent about, attending to a task; lax in the performance of duty **2** characterized by carelessness or negligence **3** [Now Rare] not energetic; languid —**re·miss′ly** *adv.* —**re·miss′ness** *n.*

SYN.—**remiss** implies the culpable omission or the careless or indifferent performance of a task or duty [*remiss* in one's obligations]; **negligent** and **neglectful** both imply failure to attend to something sufficiently or properly, but **negligent** often stresses this as a habit or trait [*negligent* in dress], and **neglectful** carries an implication of intentional and culpable disregard [a mayor *neglectful* of pledges made to the voters]; **derelict** implies flagrant neglect of a duty or obligation; **lax** implies looseness in satisfying or enforcing requirements, observing standards or rules, etc. [*lax* discipline]; **slack**, in this connection, implies lack of necessary diligence, efficiency, etc., as because of laziness or indifference [*slack* service in a restaurant]

re·mis·si·ble (-ə bəl) *adj.* ⟦Fr *rémissible* < LL *remissibilis* < pp. of L *remittere*⟧ that can be remitted or forgiven, as sin —**re·mis′si·bil′i·ty** *n.*

re·mis·sion (ri mish′ən) *n.* ⟦OFr < L *remissio,* a sending back, in LL(Ec), forgiveness of sin < pp. of *remittere:* see fol.⟧ the act or an instance of remitting; specif., *a)* forgiveness or pardon, as of sins or crimes *b)* cancellation of or release from a debt, tax, penalty, etc. *c)* a lessening or abating, as of heat or cold, pain, etc. *d)* a relatively prolonged lessening or disappearance of the symptoms of a disease —**re·mis′sive** *adj.*

re·mit (ri mit′; *for n., also* rē′mit′) *vt.* **-mit′ted, -mit′ting** ⟦ME *remytten* < L *remittere* (pp. *remissus*), to send back, in LL(Ec), to forgive sin < *re-,* back + *mittere,* to send: see MISSION⟧ **1** to forgive or pardon (sins, offenses, etc.) **2** *a)* to refrain from exacting (a payment, tax, etc.) *b)* to refrain from inflicting (a punishment) or enforcing (a sentence or fine); cancel **3** to let slacken; decrease [without *remitting* one's efforts] **4** *a)* to submit or refer (a matter) for consideration, judgment, etc. *b) Law* REMAND (*vt.* 2) **5** to put back, as into a state or position **6** to put off; postpone **7** to send (money) in payment [please *remit* the full amount by the date shown] **8** [Obs.] to give up; surrender —*vi.* **1** *a)* to become more moderate in force or intensity *b)* to have its symptoms lessen or disappear (said of a disease) **2** to send money, as in payment; pay —*n.* **1** the act or an instance of remitting **2** [Brit.] the area of responsibility, expertise, etc. of a person, agency, etc. —**re·mit′ment** *n.* —**re·mit′ta·ble** *adj.* —**re·mit′ter** *n.*

re·mit·tal (ri mit′'l) *n.* REMISSION

re·mit·tance (ri mit′'ns) *n.* ⟦< REMIT + -ANCE⟧ **1** *a)* the sending of money, as by mail *b)* the money sent **2** [*pl.*] money sent home, as to relatives, by persons working abroad

remittance man a man who lives abroad supported by remittances from home; esp., formerly, one who lived in one of the British colonies or dominions

re·mit·tent (ri mit′'nt) *adj.* ⟦L *remittens,* prp.⟧ remitting; abating for a while or at intervals, and then returning, as a fever —*n.* a remittent fever —**re·mit′tent·ly** *adv.*

re·mix (rē miks′; *for n.* rē′miks′) *vt.* **-mixed′, -mix′ing** to mix again; specif., to MIX (*vt.* 6) (sounds) on (a tape, disc, etc.) in a different way —*n.* a mixing or being mixed again; specif., a new MIX (*n.* 5) of sounds in a recording —**re′mix′er** *n.*

rem·nant (rem′nənt) *n.* ⟦ME, contr. < *remenant* < OFr, orig. prp. of *remaindre:* see REMAIN⟧ **1** what is left over; remainder; residue **2** [*often pl.*] a small remaining part, quantity, or number of persons or things **3** a trace; last remaining indication of what has been [a *remnant* of his former pride] **4** a piece of cloth, ribbon, etc. left over or unsold, as at the end of a bolt —*adj.* remaining —*SYN.* REMAINDER

re·mod·el (rē mäd′'l) *vt.* **-eled** or **-elled, -el·ing** or **-el·ling** **1** to model again **2** to make over; rebuild

re·mo·lade (rā′mə läd′) *n. var. of* RÉMOULADE

☆**re·mon·e·tize** (rē män′ə tīz′) *vt.* **-tized′, -tiz′ing** to reinstate as legal tender [to *remonetize* silver] —**re·mon′e·ti·za′tion** *n.*

re·mon·strance (ri män′strəns) *n.* ⟦LME < MFr < ML *remonstrantia*⟧ **1** the act or an instance of remonstrating; protest, complaint, or expostulation **2** a document setting forth certain points or listing complaints, grievances, etc.

re·mon·strant (-strənt) *adj.* ⟦ML *remonstrans,* prp.⟧ remonstrating or objecting; expostulatory —*n.* **1** a person who remonstrates **2** [**R-**] one of the Arminians in Holland who presented a remonstrance in 1610 setting forth their differences from strict Calvinism —**re·mon′strant·ly** *adv.*

re·mon·strate (ri män′strāt′; *also, chiefly Brit* rem′ən-) *vt.* **-strat′ed, -strat′ing** ⟦< ML *remonstratus,* pp. of *remonstrare,* to demonstrate < L *re-,* again + *monstrare,* to show: see MONSTRANCE⟧ **1** to say or plead in protest, objection, complaint, etc. **2** [Obs.] to point out; show; demonstrate —*vi.* to present and urge reasons in opposition or complaint; protest; object; expostulate —*SYN.* OBJECT —**re·mon·stra·tion** (rē′män strā′shən; *also, chiefly Brit* rem′ən-) *n.* —**re·mon′stra·tive** (-strə tiv) *adj.* —**re·mon′stra·tive·ly** *adv.* —**re·mon′stra′tor** *n.*

rem·o·ra (rem′ər ə, rə môr′ə) *n.* ⟦L, lit., hindrance < *re-,* back + *mora,* a delay: for IE base see MOURN⟧ **1** any of a family (Echeneidae) of small, marine percoid fishes with an oval sucking disc on top of the head, by which they cling to sharks and other larger fishes, turtles, passing ships, etc. **2** anything that hinders or impedes

re·morse (ri môrs′) *n.* ⟦ME *remors* < OFr < LL *remorsus* < L, pp. of *remordere* < *re-,* again + *mordere,* to bite: see MORDANT⟧ **1** a deep sense of guilt or self-reproach over a wrong or blunder **2** pity; compassion: now only in **without remorse**, pitilessly —*SYN.* PENITENCE

re·morse·ful (-fəl) *adj.* full of remorse; feeling, expressing, or caused by remorse —**re·morse′ful·ly** *adv.* —**re·morse′ful·ness** *n.*

re·morse·less (-lis) *adj.* without remorse; pitiless; merciless; ruthless; cruel —**re·morse′less·ly** *adv.* —**re·morse′less·ness** *n.*

re·mote (ri mōt′) *adj.* **-mot′er, -mot′est** ⟦ME < L *remotus,* pp. of *removere,* to REMOVE⟧ **1** distant in space; far off; far away **2** far off and hidden away; secluded **3** far off in (past or future) time [a *remote* ancestor] **4** distant in connection, relation, bearing, or the like [a question *remote* from the subject] **5** distantly related by blood or marriage [a *remote* cousin] **6** distant in human relations; aloof [*remote* and cold in his manner] **7** slight; faint [a *remote* chance] **8** not immediate or primary; far removed in influence [the *remote* causes] **9** *Comput.* occurring or located off-site: opposed to LOCAL (*adj.* 6) —*n.* **1** *Radio, TV* a usually live broadcast originating outside a studio **2** REMOTE CONTROL (sense 2) —*SYN.* FAR —**re·mote′ly** *adv.* —**re·mote′ness** *n.*

remote control **1** control of aircraft, missiles, etc. from a distance, as by radio waves **2** a hand-held device used to control the operation of a television set, garage door, etc. from a distance

remote sensing the use of satellites to gather data, images, etc., as to study the earth or other bodies of the solar system

re·mo·tion (ri mō′shən) *n.* ⟦ME *remocion* < L *remotio* < *remotus:* see REMOVE⟧ **1** the act of removing; removal **2** [Obs.] the act of departing; departure

ré·mou·lade (rā′mə läd′) *n.* ⟦Fr < dial. *remolat,* horseradish, ult. < L *armoracia*⟧ a cold sauce made with a mayonnaise base in which are mixed spices, herbs, capers, etc.: served with seafood, such as shrimp, or as a salad dressing

re·mount (rē mount′; *also, and for n. usually,* rē′mount′) *vt., vi.* ⟦ME *remounten* < OFr *remonter*⟧ to mount again —*n.* a fresh horse, or a supply of fresh horses, to replace another or others

re·mov·a·ble (ri mo͞ov′ə bəl) *adj.* ⟦ML *removibilis*⟧ that can be removed —**re·mov′a·bil′i·ty** *n.* —**re·mov′a·bly** *adv.*

re·mov·al (ri mo͞ov′əl) *n.* **1** a removing or being removed; esp., *a)* a taking away or being taken away *b)* dismissal from an office or position *c)* a change of place, residence, etc. **2** *Law* the transfer of a case from one court to another, esp. from a state court to a federal court

re·move (ri mo͞ov′) *vt.* **-moved′, -mov′ing** ⟦ME *remouen* < OFr *remouvoir* < L *removere:* see RE- & MOVE⟧ **1** to move (something) from where it is; lift, push, transfer, or carry away, or from one place to another **2** to take off [to *remove* one's coat] **3** to do away with; specif., *a)* to kill or assassinate *b)* to dismiss, as from an office or position *c)* to get rid of; eliminate [to *remove* the causes of war] **4** to take, extract, separate, or withdraw (someone or something *from*) —*vi.* **1** [Old Poet.] to go away **2** to move away, as to another residence or place of business; move **3** to be removable [paint that *removes* easily] —*n.* **1** the act of removing **2** the distance between one thing and another [living at a far *remove* from here] **3** any step, interval, or degree [but one short *remove* from victory] **4** [Brit.] a move to another residence or place of business: a formal usage

re·moved (ri mo͞ovd′) *adj.* **1** *a)* distant in relationship *b)* of a younger or older generation [one's first cousin once *removed* is the child of one's first cousin] **2** remote; distant; disconnected: with *from* —*SYN.* FAR

re·mov·er (ri mo͞ov′ər) *n.* a person or thing that removes something [a paint *remover*]

Rem·scheid (rem′shīt′) city in W Germany, in the Ruhr Basin, in the state of North Rhine-Westphalia

☆**re·mu·da** (rə mo͞o′də) *n.* ⟦AmSp < Sp *remuda (de caballos),* relay (of horses) < *remudar,* to exchange < *re-* (< L, RE-) + *mudar,* to change < L *mutare:* see MUTATE⟧ in the Southwest, a group of extra saddle horses kept as a supply of remounts

re·mu·ner·ate (ri myo͞o′nə rāt′) *vt.* **-at′ed, -at′ing** ⟦< L *remuneratus,* pp. of *remunerari,* to reward, remunerate < *re-,* again + *munus* (gen. *muneris*), gift < IE **moini-:* see COMMON⟧ to pay or compensate (a person) for (work or service done, loss incurred, etc.); reward; recompense —*SYN.* PAY[1] —**re·mu′ner·a·ble** *adj.* —**re·mu′ner·a′tor** *n.*

re·mu·ner·a·tion (ri myo͞o′nə rā′shən) *n.* ⟦L *remuneratio*⟧ **1** the act of remunerating **2** that which remunerates; reward; pay; recompense; compensation

re·mu·ner·a·tive (ri myo͞o′nə rāt′iv, -rə tiv) *adj.* **1** remunerating **2** affording remuneration; profitable —**re·mu′ner·a′tive·ly** *adv.* —**re·mu′ner·a′tive·ness** *n.*

Re·mus (rē′məs) *n.* ⟦L⟧ *Rom. Myth.* the twin brother of ROMULUS

ren·ais·sance (ren′ə säns′, -zäns′; ren′ə säns′, -zäns′; *chiefly Brit* ri nā′səns) *n.* ⟦Fr < *renaître,* to be born anew < OFr *renestre* < *re-* + VL **nascere,* for L *nasci,* to be born: see GENUS⟧ **1** a new birth; rebirth; renascence **2** *a)* [**R-**] the style and forms of art, literature, architecture, etc. of the Renaissance *b)* [*often* **R-**] any revival of art, literature, or learning similar to the Renaissance —*adj.* [**R-**] **1** of, characteristic of, or in the style of the Renaissance **2** designating or of a style of architecture developed in Italy and W Europe between 1400 and 1600, characterized by the revival and

remixture **remodification** **remold** **remultiply**
remobilize **remodify** **remortgage**

adaptation of classical orders and design —**the Renaissance 1** the great revival of art, literature, and learning in Europe in the 14th, 15th, and 16th cent., based on classical sources: it began in Italy and spread gradually to other countries and marked the transition from the medieval world to the modern **2** the period of this revival

Renaissance man (or **woman)** ⟦from embodying the qualities of an idealized person of the Renaissance⟧ a highly cultivated man (or woman) who is skilled and well-versed in many fields of knowledge, work, etc., as in the arts and sciences

re·nal (rē′nəl) ***adj.*** ⟦< Fr or LL: Fr *rénal* < LL *renalis* < L *renes,* kidneys⟧ of or near the kidneys

renal corpuscle MALPIGHIAN BODY (sense 2)

Re·nan (rə nän′), **(Joseph) Er·nest** (er nest′) 1823-92; Fr. historian & essayist

re·nas·cence (ri nas′əns, -nās′-) ***n.*** ⟦< fol.⟧ [*also* **R-**] RENAISSANCE

re·nas·cent (-ənt) ***adj.*** ⟦L *renascens,* prp. of *renasci,* to be born again: see RE- & GENUS⟧ acquiring or showing new life, strength, or vigor

ren·con·tre (ren känt′ər; *Fr* rän kōn′tr′) ***n.*** RENCOUNTER

ren·coun·ter (ren kount′ər) ***vt., vi.*** ⟦Fr *rencontrer:* see RE- & ENCOUNTER⟧ [Rare] **1** to meet in or as in battle **2** to meet casually —***n.*** **1** a hostile meeting; conflict or contest, as a battle or debate **2** a casual meeting, as with a friend

rend (rend) ***vt.*** **rent, rend′ing** ⟦ME *renden* < OE *rendan,* akin to OFris *renda* < IE base **rendh-,* to tear apart > RIND, Sans *randhram,* fissure, split⟧ **1** to tear, pull, or rip with violence: with *from, off, away,* etc. **2** to tear, pull apart, rip up, or split with violence [a tree *rent* by lightning]: often used fig. [a roar *rends* the air] **3** to tear (one's clothing) to show grief, anguish, etc. —***vi.*** to tear; burst; split apart —**SYN.** TEAR[1]

ren·der (ren′dər) ***vt.*** ⟦ME *rendren* < OFr *rendre* < VL **rendere,* for L *reddere,* to restore < *re(d)-,* back + *dare,* to give: see DATE[1]⟧ **1** to give, hand over, deliver, present, or submit, as for approval, consideration, payment, etc. [to *render* an account of one's actions, *render* a bill] **2** to give (*up*); surrender [to *render* up a city to the enemy] **3** to give in return or requital [to *render* good for evil] **4** to give (*back*); restore [to *render* back another's gift] **5** to give or pay (something due or owed) [to *render* thanks, *render* obedience] **6** to cause to be or become; make [to *render* someone helpless] **7** *a)* to give or provide (aid) *b)* to do (a service) **8** to represent; depict; specif., to make a drawing of in perspective **9** to perform or interpret by performance; recite (a poem), play (music), treat (a subject, as in painting), act out (a role) **10** to express in other words; esp., to translate: often with *into* **11** *a)* to obtain by melting [to *render* lard] *b)* to melt down (fat) **12** to pronounce or declare (a judgment, verdict, etc.), as in a court **13** *Masonry* to apply a coat of plaster directly to (brickwork, stonework, etc.) —***n.*** a payment, usually in goods or services, as for rent in feudal times —**ren′der·a·ble** ***adj.*** —**ren′der·er** ***n.***

ren·der·ing (-iŋ) ***n.*** the act of one who renders; specif., *a)* an interpretation or rendition *b)* a translation *c)* a perspective drawing depicting an architect's conception of a finished building, bridge, etc. *d) Masonry* a coat of plaster applied directly to brickwork, etc. (also **rendering coat**)

ren·dez·vous (rän′dā vo͞o′, -dē-, -də-) ***n., pl.*** **-vous′** (-vo͞oz′) ⟦Fr: substantive use of *rendez-vous,* betake or present yourself (or yourselves)⟧ **1** a place designated for a meeting or assembling, as of troops, ships, airplanes, space vehicles, etc. **2** a place where people are in the habit of meeting or gathering **3** *a)* an agreement or appointment between two or more persons, esp. between lovers, to meet at a certain time or place *b)* the meeting itself —***vi.*** **-voused′** (-vo͞od′), **-vous′ing** (-vo͞o′iŋ) to meet or assemble at a certain time or place —***vt.*** to assemble (troops, etc.) at a certain time or place

ren·di·tion (ren dish′ən) ***n.*** ⟦MFr, altered (infl. by *rendre,* to RENDER) < L *redditio* (< pp. of *reddere*): see RENDER⟧ a rendering or result of rendering; specif., ☆*a)* a performance or interpretation (*of* a piece of music, a role, etc.) *b)* a translation or version *c)* the giving over, as according to federal law, of a fugitive to the state or region having jurisdiction [*rendition* of fugitive slaves by Northern states]

Re·nee (rə nā′) ***n.*** a feminine name

ren·e·gade (ren′ə gād′) ***n.*** ⟦Sp *renegado,* pp. of *renegar,* to deny < ML *renegare* < L *re-,* again + *negare,* to deny (see NEGATION); the word replaces ME *renagat* < ML *renegatus,* pp. of *renegare*⟧ **1** a person who abandons one religion for another; apostate **2** a person who abandons a party, movement, etc. and goes over to the other side; traitor; turncoat **3** a fugitive from the law; outlaw —***adj.*** of or like a renegade; disloyal

ren·e·ga·do (ren′ə gā′dō, -gä′-) ***n., pl.*** **-does** ⟦Sp, see prec.⟧ *archaic var. of* RENEGADE

re·nege (ri nig′, -neg′) ***vi.*** **-neged′, -neg′ing** ⟦ML *renegare:* see RENEGADE⟧ **1** to back out of an agreement; go back on a promise **2** *Card Games* to fail to follow suit when required and able to do so; revoke —***vt.*** [Archaic] to deny; renounce —***n.*** *Card Games* the act or an instance of reneging; revoke —**re·neg′er** ***n.***

re·ne·go·ti·ate (rē′nə gō′shē āt′) ***vi., vt.*** **-at′ed, -at′ing** to negotiate again; specif., to review (a contract) with a view to obtaining more equitable or favorable terms —**re′ne·go′ti·a·ble** ***adj.*** —**re′ne·go′ti·a′tion** ***n.***

re·new (ri no͞o′, -nyo͞o′) ***vt.*** ⟦ME *renewen* < *re-* + *newe* (see NEW), after L *renovare:* see RENOVATE⟧ **1** to make new or as if new again; make young, fresh, or strong again; bring back into good condition **2** to give new spiritual strength to **3** to cause to exist again; reestablish; revive **4** to begin again; take up again; resume [to *renew* negotiations] **5** to go over again; say again; repeat [to *renew* one's objections] **6** *a)* to replace as by a fresh supply of [to *renew* provisions] *b)* to refill with a fresh supply **7** to give or get an extension of [to *renew* a lease] —***vi.*** **1** to become new or as new again; be renewed **2** to begin again; start over —**re·new′ed·ly** ***adv.*** —**re·new′er** ***n.***

SYN.—renew is the most direct but also the broadest term here, implying a making new again by replacing what is old, worn, exhausted, etc. [to *renew* a stock of goods]; to **renovate** is to clean up, replace or repair worn parts, etc. so as to bring back to good condition; to **restore** is to bring back to an original or unimpaired condition after exhaustion, illness, dilapidation, etc. [to *restore* an old castle]; **refresh** implies a restoring of depleted strength, vigor, etc. by furnishing something needed [a *refreshing* sleep]; **rejuvenate** implies a restoring of youthful appearance, vigor, etc. [she felt *rejuvenated* after the heart surgery]

re·new·a·ble (ri no͞o′ə bəl, -nyo͞o′-) ***adj.*** **1** that can be renewed [a *renewable* lease] **2** *Ecol.* that can be replenished by normal ecological cycles, as solar, wind, or water power [*renewable* energy] —**re·new′a·bil′i·ty** ***n.***

re·new·al (ri no͞o′əl, -nyo͞o′-) ***n.*** **1** a renewing or being renewed **2** an instance of renewing, or something renewed

Ren·frew (ren′fro͞o′) former county & former district of SW Scotland

Ren·frew·shire (-shir′, -shər) **1** *another name for* RENFREW (the county) **2** administrative division of SW Scotland

ren·i- (ren′ə, rē′nə) ⟦< L *renes,* kidneys⟧ *combining form* kidney, kidneys [*reniform*]: also **ren·o-**; before a vowel, **ren-**

ren·i·form (ren′ə fôrm′, rē′nə-) ***adj.*** ⟦ModL *reniformis:* see prec. & -FORM⟧ shaped like a kidney

re·nin (rē′nin) ***n.*** ⟦< L *renes,* kidneys + -IN[1]⟧ a proteolytic enzyme, formed in the kidneys, that helps produce angiotensin, which is a powerful pressor responsible for hypertension

re·ni·tent (ri nīt′'nt, ren′ə tənt) ***adj.*** ⟦< Fr or L: Fr *rénitent* < L *renitens,* prp. of *reniti,* to resist < *re-,* back + *niti,* to struggle⟧ **1** resisting pressure; resistant **2** opposing stubbornly; recalcitrant —**re·ni′ten·cy** ***n.***

ren·min·bi (ren′min bē′) ***n., pl.*** **-bi′** ⟦< Mandarin *jen min pi,* lit., people's currency⟧ in the People's Republic of China, money or currency: see YUAN

Rennes (ren) city in NW France

ren·net (ren′it) ***n.*** ⟦ME *rennen,* to cause to coagulate < OE *gerennan* < *ge-,* together (see CO-) + Gmc **rannjan,* to cause to run < base of **rinnan* (> RUN) + **-jan,* caus. suffix⟧ **1** *a)* the membrane lining the stomach of an unweaned animal, esp. the fourth stomach of a calf *b)* the contents of such a stomach **2** *a)* an extract of this membrane or of the stomach contents, containing rennin and used to curdle milk, as in making cheese or junket *b)* any substance used to curdle milk **3** RENNIN

ren·nin (ren′in) ***n.*** ⟦< prec. + -IN[1]⟧ a coagulating enzyme that can curdle milk, found in rennet

Re·no (rē′nō) ⟦after U.S. Gen. J. L. *Reno* (1823-62)⟧ city in W Nev.

Re·noir (rən wär′, ren′wär′; *Fr* rə nwȧr′) **1 Jean** 1894-1979; Fr. film director: son of Pierre Auguste **2 Pierre Au·guste** (pyer ō güst′) 1841-1919; Fr. painter

re·nounce (ri nouns′) ***vt.*** **-nounced′, -nounc′ing** ⟦ME *renouncen* < OFr *renoncer* < L *renuntiare* < *re-,* back + *nuntiare,* to tell < *nuntius,* messenger: see NUNCIO⟧ **1** to give up (a claim, right, belief, etc.), usually by a formal public statement **2** to give up (a pursuit, practice, way of living or feeling, etc.) **3** to cast off or disown; refuse further association with; repudiate [to *renounce* a son] —***vi.*** *Law* to give up a right, trust, etc. —**re·nounce′ment** ***n.*** —**re·nounc′er** ***n.***

ren·o·vate (ren′ə vāt′) ***vt.*** **-vat′ed, -vat′ing** ⟦< L *renovatus,* pp. of *renovare,* to renew < *re-,* again + *novare,* to make new < *novus,* NEW⟧ **1** to make fresh or sound again, as though new; clean up, replace worn and broken parts in, repair, etc. **2** to refresh; revive —**SYN.** RENEW —**ren′o·va′tion** ***n.*** —**ren′o·va′tive** ***adj.*** —**ren′o·va′tor** ***n.***

re·nown (ri noun′) ***n.*** ⟦ME *renoun* < Anglo-Fr < OFr *renom* < *renommer,* to name again or often, make famous < *re-,* again + *nom(m)er,* to name < L *nominare* < *nomen,* NAME⟧ **1** great fame or reputation; celebrity **2** [Obs.] report or rumor —***vt.*** [Obs.] to make famous

re·nowned (ri nound′) ***adj.*** having renown; famous —**SYN.** FAMOUS

☆**rens·se·laer·ite** (ren′sə lə rīt′, ren′sə lir′īt) ***n.*** ⟦after Stephen Van *Rensselaer* (1764-1839), Am general and statesman + -ITE[1]⟧ a fibrous variety of talc, used for ornamental articles

rent[1] (rent) ***n.*** ⟦ME < OFr *rente* < LL **rendita* (pp. of **rendere:* see RENDER), for L *reddita (pecunia),* paid (money)⟧ **1** a stated return or payment for the temporary possession or use of a house, land, or other property, made, usually at fixed intervals, by the tenant or user to the owner **2** [Obs.] *a)* real estate or other property yielding an income *b)* income; revenue **3** *Econ. a)* income from the use of land *b)* an additional amount paid or accruing to the owner of an economic resource, as a tract of land, that is the result of some special or unique attribute, as a desirable location —***vt.*** **1** *a)* to get temporary possession and use of (a house, land, etc.) by paying rent *b)* to get the temporary use of (a car, tool, furniture, etc.) by paying a fee **2** to give temporary possession and use of in return for the payment of rent or a fee; lease or let: often with *out* —***vi.*** ☆**1** to be leased or let for rent or a fee **2** to lease or let a place or thing —**SYN.** HIRE —☆**for rent** available to be rented —**rent′a·ble** ***adj.***

rent² (rent) *vt., vi. pt. & pp. of* REND

rent³ (rent) *n.* ⟦n. use of obs. or dial. *rent,* var. of REND⟧ **1** a hole or gap made by rending or tearing, as a torn place in cloth, a fissure in the earth, etc. **2** a breach of relations, as between persons or in an organized group; schism

rent·al (rent′'l) *n.* ⟦ME < Anglo-Fr < ML *rentale*⟧ **1** an amount paid or received as rent **2** an income from rents received **3** a house, apartment, car, etc. offered for rent **4** the act of renting —*adj.* of, in, or for rent

rent boy [Brit. Slang] a young male prostitute

rente (ränt) *n., pl.* **rentes** (ränt) ⟦Fr: see RENT¹⟧ **1** in France, annual income or revenue **2** [*usually pl.*] *a)* the bonds, stocks, etc. representing the consolidated debt of the French government *b)* interest paid on this

rent·er (rent′ər) *n.* **1** a person who pays rent for the use of property **2** an owner who rents out property

rent-free (rent′frē′) *adj., adv.* without payment of rent

ren·tier (rän tyā′) *n., pl.* **-tiers′** (-tyā′) ⟦Fr < *rente:* see RENTE⟧ a person who has a fixed income from land, bonds, etc.

re·nun·ci·a·tion (ri nun′sē ā′shən) *n.* ⟦ME < L *renuntiatio* < *renuntiatus,* pp. of *renuntiare:* see RENOUNCE⟧ **1** the act or an instance of renouncing; a giving up formally or voluntarily, often at a sacrifice, of a right, claim, title, etc. **2** a written statement or declaration of this —**re·nun′ci·a·tive** (-ə tiv) *adj.,* **re·nun′ci·a·to′ry** (-ə tôr′ē)

re·o·pen (rē ō′pən) *vt., vi.* **1** to open again **2** to begin again; resume [to *reopen* a debate]

re·or·der (rē ôr′dər) *n.* a second or similar order for certain goods from the same dealer —*vt.* **1** to give a reorder for; order again **2** to put in order again —*vi.* to order goods again

re·or·gan·i·za·tion (rē ôr′gə ni zā′shən) *n.* **1** a reorganizing or being reorganized **2** *Finance* a thorough reconstruction of a business corporation, comprising a considerable change in capital structure, as effected after, or in anticipation of, a failure and receivership: cf. READJUSTMENT

re·or·gan·ize (rē ôr′gə nīz′) *vt., vi.* **-ized′, -iz′ing** to organize again or anew; effect a reorganization (of) —**re·or′gan·iz′er** *n.*

re·o·vi·rus (rē′ō vī′rəs) *n.* ⟦*r(espiratory) e(nteric) o(rphan) virus:* for *orphan,* see ECHOVIRUS⟧ any of a family (Reoviridae) of RNA viruses, including the rotaviruses, that infect various plants and animals

rep¹ (rep) *n.* ⟦Fr *reps* < E *ribs:* see RIB⟧ a fabric of silk, wool, cotton, rayon, etc., with a ribbed or corded surface

rep² (rep) *n.* [Informal] *short for:* **1** REPERTORY THEATER **2** REPRESENTATIVE (sense 2) **3** REPUTATION **4** REPETITION

rep³ (rep) *n., pl.* **rep** ⟦*r(oentgen) e(quivalent) p(hysical)*⟧ a dosage of any ionizing radiation that will produce upon absorption in living tissues a rise in energy equal to that produced by one roentgen of X-ray or gamma-ray radiation

rep⁴ *abbrev.* **1** ⟦L *repetatur*⟧ *Pharmacy* let it be repeated **2** repeat **3** report(ed) **4** reporter

Rep *abbrev.* **1** Representative **2** Republic **3** Republican

re·pack·age (rē pak′ij) *vt.* **-aged, -ag·ing** to package again, esp. in or as in a better or more attractive package

re·paid (ri pād′) *vt., vi. pt. & pp. of* REPAY

re·pair¹ (ri per′) *vt.* ⟦ME *repairen* < OFr *reparer* < L *reparare* < *re-,* again + *parare,* to get ready, PREPARE⟧ **1** to put back in good condition after damage, decay, etc.; mend; fix **2** to renew; restore; revive [to *repair* one's health] **3** to amend; set right; remedy [to *repair* a mistake] **4** to make amends for; make up or compensate for (a wrong, injury, etc.) —*n.* **1** the act, process, or work of repairing **2** [*usually pl.*] an instance of repairing or work done in repairing **3** the state of being repaired, or fit for use [a car kept in *repair*] **4** state with respect to being repaired [a house in bad *repair*] —**SYN.** MEND —**re·pair′a·ble** *adj.* —**re·pair′er** *n.*

re·pair² (ri per′) *vi.* ⟦ME *repairen* < OFr *repairer* < LL *repatriare* < L *re-,* back + *patria,* native country < *(terra) patria,* (land) of one's father, fem. of *patrius* < *pater,* FATHER⟧ **1** to go or betake oneself (*to* a place) **2** to go often, customarily, or in numbers **3** [Obs.] to return —*n.* [Archaic] a place to which one repairs; resort; haunt

re·pair·man (-mən, -man′) *n., pl.* **-men** (-mən, -men′) a person whose work is repairing things

re·pand (ri pand′) *adj.* ⟦L *repandus,* bent backward < *re-,* back + *pandus,* bent < IE base **pandos* > ON *fattr,* bent over, supple⟧ *Bot.* having a wavy margin, as some leaves

rep·a·ra·ble (rep′ə rə bəl) *adj.* ⟦Fr *réparable* < L *reparabilis*⟧ that can be repaired, mended, remedied, etc. —**rep′a·ra·bly** *adv.*

rep·a·ra·tion (rep′ə rā′shən) *n.* ⟦ME *reparacion* < MFr < LL *reparatio* < pp. of L *reparare:* see REPAIR¹⟧ **1** a repairing or being repaired; restoration to good condition **2** a making of amends; making up for a wrong or injury **3** *a)* anything paid or done to make up for something else; compensation *b)* [*usually pl.*] compensation by a nation defeated in a war for economic losses suffered by the victor or for crimes committed against individuals, payable in money, labor, goods, etc.

SYN.—reparation refers to the making of amends, specif. the paying of compensation, for some wrong or injury [war *reparations*]; **restitution** implies return to the rightful owner of something that has been taken away, or of an equivalent [he made *restitution* for the libel]; **redress** suggests retaliation or resort to the courts to right a wrong [to seek *redress* for an injury]; **indemnification** refers to reimbursement, as by an insurance company, for loss, damage, etc.

re·par·a·tive (ri par′ə tiv) *adj.* **1** repairing or tending to repair; mending, etc. **2** of or involving reparation

rep·ar·tee (rep′är tē′, -tā′) *n.* ⟦Fr *repartie,* fem. pp. of *repartir,* to return quickly a thrust or a blow, reply < *re-,* back + *partir* (L *partire*), to PART²⟧ **1** a quick, witty reply **2** a series of such rejoinders **3** skill in making witty replies —**SYN.** WIT¹

re·par·ti·tion (rē′pär tish′ən) *n.* **1** the act of partitioning; distribution **2** the act of partitioning again; redistribution —*vt.* to effect a repartition of

re·pass (rē pas′, -päs′) *vi., vt.* ⟦Fr *repasser*⟧ to pass back or again —**re·pas′sage** *n.*

re·past (ri past′, -päst′) *n.* ⟦ME < OFr < *re-,* RE- + *past,* food < L *pastus* < pp. of *pascere,* to feed: see FOOD⟧ **1** *a)* food and drink for a meal *b)* a meal **2** [Archaic] *a)* the eating of food, as at a meal *b)* mealtime **3** [Obs.] food —*vi.* [Now Rare] to eat or feast

re·pa·tri·ate (rē pā′trē āt′; *for n., usually,* -it) *vt., vi.* **-at′ed, -at′ing** ⟦< LL *repatriatus,* pp. of *repatriare:* see REPAIR²⟧ to send back or return to the country of birth, citizenship, or allegiance [to *repatriate* prisoners of war] —*n.* a person who has been repatriated —**re·pa′tri·a′tion** *n.*

re·pay (ri pā′) *vt.* **-paid′, -pay′ing** ⟦OFr *repaier*⟧ **1** to pay (money borrowed in the past) to (a person, bank, etc. that loaned it) [please *repay* the loan fully next week; I *repaid* her last week] **2** to make some return for; compensate [*repay* a kindness] **3** to give or make some return or recompense to (a person), as for some service **4** to do or give (an equivalent) in return [to *repay* a visit] —*vi.* **1** to make a repayment or return **2** to reward or punish —**SYN.** PAY¹ —**re·pay′a·ble** *adj.* —**re·pay′ment** *n.*

re·peal (ri pēl′) *vt.* ⟦ME *repelen* < OFr *rapeler:* see RE- & APPEAL⟧ **1** to withdraw officially or formally; revoke; cancel; annul [*repeal* a law] **2** [Obs.] to call back, as from exile —*n.* the act of repealing; revocation; abrogation —**SYN.** ABOLISH —**re·peal′a·ble** *adj.* —**re·peal′er** *n.*

re·peat (ri pēt′; *for n., also* rē′pēt′) *vt.* ⟦ME *repeten* < OFr *repeter* < L *repetere* < *re-,* again + *petere,* to demand, rush at, fall: see FEATHER⟧ **1** to say or utter again; reiterate [to *repeat* a remark] **2** to say over or through; recite (a poem, etc.) **3** to say (something) as said by someone else **4** to tell to someone else [to *repeat* a secret] **5** *a)* to do or make again; do over again [to *repeat* a test] *b)* to make happen again or undergo again [to *repeat* an adventure] **6** to say again what has been said before by (oneself) **7** to present (itself or themselves) again —*vi.* **1** to say or do again what has been said or done before **2** to recur [experiences *repeat*] **3** to continue to be tasted, as because of belching: often with *on* [foods that *repeat* on one] ☆**4** to vote (illegally) more than once in the same election —*n.* **1** the act of doing or saying again; repetition **2** *a)* anything said, done, or occurring again *b)* a rebroadcast of a radio or television program **3** *Music a)* a passage repeated in playing *b)* either of two signs used to mark the end (:‖) and, when appropriate, the beginning (‖:) of such a passage —**re·peat′a·bil′i·ty** *n.* —**re·peat′a·ble** *adj.*

SYN.—repeat is the common, general word meaning to say, do, make, present, etc. over again [will you *repeat* that question, please?]; **iterate** and **reiterate** both suggest a repeating, either once or several times, but **reiterate** strongly implies insistent repetition over and over again [he keeps *reiterating* his innocence]; **recapitulate** suggests a repeating briefly of the main points in a discourse in summarizing [she will *recapitulate* her account of the ball game at 8:00 o'clock]

re·peat·ed (-id) *adj.* said, made, done, or happening again, or again and again —**re·peat′ed·ly** *adv.*

re·peat·er (-ər) *n.* **1** a person or thing that repeats **2** a watch or clock which, upon activation of a spring, will strike the time, sometimes to the nearest minute ☆**3** REPEATING FIREARM ☆**4** a person who has been convicted a number of times for violating the law ☆**5** a person who fraudulently votes more than once in the same election ☆**6** a device, broadcasting station, etc. that receives electrical signals and then amplifies and retransmits them ☆**7** *Educ.* a student who fails a course or grade, and then repeats it **8** *Math.* REPEATING DECIMAL

repeating decimal a decimal number in which, beyond a certain point, some digit or group of digits is repeated indefinitely (Ex.: 0.47382382382...)

☆**repeating firearm** a firearm that can fire a number of shots (from a magazine or clip) without being reloaded

re·pel (ri pel′) *vt.* **-pelled′, -pel′ling** ⟦ME *repellen* < L *repellere,* to drive back < *re-,* back + *pellere,* to drive: see PULSE¹⟧ **1** to drive or force back; hold or ward off [to *repel* an attack] **2** to refuse to accept, agree to, or submit to; reject [to *repel* advances] **3** to refuse to accept (a person); spurn [to *repel* a suitor] **4** *a)* to cause distaste or dislike in; disgust [the odor *repelled* him] *b)* to cause (insects, etc.) to react by staying away **5** *a)* to be resistant to, or present an opposing force to [a coating that *repels* moisture] *b)* to fail to mix with or adhere to [water *repels* oil] —*vi.* **1** to drive off, or offer

renumber
reobserve
reobtain
reoccupy
reoccur
reoccurrence
reoppose
reorchestrate
reordain
reordination
reorient
reoutfit
repacify
repack
repaint
repanel
repaper
repark
repave
re-pay

an opposing force to, something **2** to cause distaste, dislike, or aversion —**re·pel′ler** *n.*

re·pel·lent (-ənt) *adj.* ⟦L *repellens*⟧ **1** that repels; pushing away or driving back **2** *a)* causing distaste, dislike, or aversion; repulsive *b)* causing insects, etc. to react by staying away **3** able to resist the absorption of liquid, esp. water, to a limited extent [a water-*repellent* raincoat] —*n.* something that repels; specif., *a)* a solution applied to fabric to make it water-repellent *b)* any substance used to repel insects Also **re·pel′lant** —**re·pel′lence** *n.*, **re·pel′len·cy** —**re·pel′lent·ly** *adv.*

re·pent[1] (ri pent′) *vi.* ⟦ME *repenten* < OFr *repentir* < VL *repoenitere* < L *re-*, again + *poenitere*, for *paenitere:* see PENITENT⟧ **1** to feel sorry or self-reproachful for what one has done or failed to do; be conscience-stricken or contrite: often with *of* **2** to feel such regret or dissatisfaction over some past action, intention, etc. as to change one's mind about: often with *of* [to *repent* of one's generosity] **3** to feel so contrite over one's sins as to change, or decide to change, one's ways; be penitent —*vt.* **1** to feel sorry, contrite, or self-reproachful over (an error, sin, etc.) **2** to feel such regret or dissatisfaction over as to change one's mind about [to *repent* one's kindness] —**re·pent′er** *n.*

re·pent[2] (rē′pənt) *adj.* ⟦L *repens*, prp. of *repere*, to creep: see REPTILE⟧ *Biol.* creeping or crawling

re·pent·ance (ri pen′təns) *n.* a repenting or being penitent; feeling of sorrow, etc., esp. for wrongdoing; compunction; contrition; remorse —*SYN.* PENITENCE

re·pent·ant (-tənt) *adj.* ⟦ME < OFr, prp.⟧ **1** repenting; penitent **2** characterized by or indicative of repentance —**re·pent′ant·ly** *adv.*

re·peo·ple (rē pē′pəl) *vt.* **-pled**, **-pling** ⟦ME *repeoplen* < OFr *repeupler*⟧ **1** to people anew; provide with new inhabitants **2** to restock with animals

re·per·cus·sion (rē′pər kush′ən, rep′ər-) *n.* ⟦L *repercussio* < pp. of *repercutere*, to rebound, strike back: see RE- & PERCUSSION⟧ **1** [Archaic] a driving back or being driven back by something resistant; rebound; recoil **2** reflection, as of light or sound; reverberation **3** a far-reaching, often indirect effect of or reaction to some event or action: *usually used in pl.* —**re′per·cus′sive** *adj.*

rep·er·toire (rep′ər twär′, rep′ə-) *n.* ⟦Fr *répertoire* < LL *repertorium:* see fol.⟧ **1** the stock of plays, operas, roles, songs, etc. that a company, actor, singer, etc. is familiar with and ready to perform **2** all the musical or theatrical works of a particular category, or of a particular writer, composer, etc., available for performance ☆**3** the stock of special skills, devices, techniques, etc. of a particular person or particular field of endeavor

rep·er·to·ry (rep′ər tôr′ē, rep′ə-) *n.*, *pl.* **-ries** ⟦LL *repertorium*, an inventory < L *repertus*, pp. of *reperire*, to find out, discover < *re-*, again + *parere*, to produce, invent, bear: see -PAROUS⟧ **1** *a)* a repository for useful things; storehouse *b)* the things stored; stock; collection **2** REPERTOIRE **3** the system of producing and presenting plays, operas, etc. engaged in by repertory theaters

repertory theater a theater in which a permanent company presents several plays, operas, etc. for a season, usually alternating them in limited runs

rep·e·tend (rep′ə tend′, rep′ə tend′) *n.* ⟦L *repetendus*, to be repeated, ger. of *repetere*, to REPEAT⟧ **1** a repeated sound, word, or phrase; refrain **2** *Math.* the digit or digits repeated indefinitely in a repeating decimal

ré·pé·ti·teur (rā pā tē tër′) *n.* ⟦Fr⟧ [*often not in italics*] a person who acts as a coach for and directs rehearsals of singers, dancers, etc., as in opera or ballet

rep·e·ti·tion (rep′ə tish′ən) *n.* ⟦MFr *repeticion* < L *repetitio*⟧ **1** the act of repeating; a doing or saying again, or again and again **2** *a)* something repeated *b)* something made by repeating, as a copy or imitation

rep·e·ti·tious (-əs) *adj.* full of or characterized by repetition, esp. tiresome or boring repetition —**rep′e·ti′tious·ly** *adv.* —**rep′e·ti′tious·ness** *n.*

re·pet·i·tive (ri pet′ə tiv) *adj.* of or characterized by repetition —**re·pet′i·tive·ly** *adv.*

repetitive strain (or **stress**) **injury** **1** an injury causing a condition characterized by sharp pains in the hand, wrist, back, etc. due usually to muscle strain caused by repetitive actions performed as during work or while exercising **2** such a condition: also **repetitive stress syndrome**

re·phrase (rē frāz′) *vt.* **-phrased′**, **-phras′ing** to phrase again, esp. in a different way

re·pine (ri pīn′) *vi.* **-pined′**, **-pin′ing** ⟦RE- + PINE[2]⟧ to feel or express unhappiness or discontent; complain; fret —**re·pin′er** *n.* —**re·pin′ing·ly** *adv.*

re·place (ri plās′) *vt.* **-placed′**, **-plac′ing** **1** to place again; put back in a former or the proper place or position **2** to take the place of; supplant [workers *replaced* by automated equipment] **3** to provide a substitute or equivalent for [to *replace* a worn tire] **4** to put back or pay back; restore; return [to *replace* embezzled funds] —**re·place′a·ble** *adj.* —**re·plac′er** *n.*

SYN.—**replace** implies a taking the place of someone or something that is now lost, gone, destroyed, worn out, etc. [we *replace* defective tubes]; **displace** suggests the ousting or dislodgment of a person or thing by another that replaces it [he had been *displaced* in her affections by another man]; **supersede** implies a replacing with something superior, more up-to-date, etc. [the steamship *superseded* the sailing ship]; **supplant** suggests a displacing that involves force, fraud, or innovation [the prince had been *supplanted* by an impostor]

re·place·ment (-mənt) *n.* **1** a replacing or being replaced **2** a person or thing that takes the place of another, esp. of one that has worn out, broken down, etc. **3** a member of the armed forces available for assignment to fill a vacancy or complete a quota; reinforcement **4** in crystallography, the replacing of an angle or edge by one face or more **5** *Geol.* the process of very gradual solution and simultaneous deposition by which one kind of mineral is substituted for another

re·play (rē plā′; *also, and for n. always*, rē′plā′) *vi.*, *vt.* to be played or play again —*n.* something replayed; esp., an instant replay

re·plead·er (rē plēd′ər) *n.* ⟦obs. *replead*, to plead again + -ER, sense 3⟧ *Law* **1** a second pleading **2** the right or privilege of pleading again **3** a court order requiring the parties to plead again

re·plen·ish (ri plen′ish) *vt.* ⟦ME *replenissen* < prp. stem of OFr *replenir:* see RE- & PLENISH⟧ **1** to make full or complete again, as by furnishing a new supply [to *replenish* a stock of goods] **2** to supply again with fuel or the like **3** [Archaic] REPEOPLE (sense 1) —**re·plen′ish·er** *n.* —**re·plen′ish·ment** *n.*

re·plete (ri plēt′) *adj.* ⟦ME < OFr *replet* < L *repletus*, pp. of *replere* < *re-*, again + *plere*, to fill: see FULL[1]⟧ **1** well-filled or plentifully supplied **2** stuffed with food and drink; gorged —*n.* HONEY POT (sense 1)

re·ple·tion (ri plē′shən) *n.* **1** the state of being replete, or plentifully supplied **2** the state of having eaten and drunk to surfeit

re·plev·in (ri plev′in) *n.* ⟦ME < Anglo-Fr *replevine* < OFr *replevir*, to warrant, pledge < *re-*, again + *plevir*, to pledge < ML *plevium*, warranty, PLEDGE⟧ *Law* **1** the recovery of goods by the person claiming to own them, on a promise to test the matter in court and give the goods up again if defeated **2** the writ by which one takes over the goods —*vt.* REPLEVY

re·plev·y (ri plev′ē) *vt.* **-plev′ied**, **-plev′y·ing** ⟦OFr *replevir:* see prec.⟧ *Law* **1** to seize or take back (goods) under a writ of replevin **2** [Rare] to release (a person) on bail —*n.* REPLEVIN —**re·plev′i·a·ble** (-ē ə bəl) *adj.*, **re·plev′i·sa·ble** (-i sə bəl)

rep·li·ca (rep′li kə) *n.* ⟦It, a repetition, orig., reply < ML, an answer < L *replicare:* see REPLY⟧ **1** a reproduction or copy of a work of art, esp. a copy by the maker of the original **2** any very close reproduction or copy; facsimile —*SYN.* COPY

rep·li·cate (rep′li kit; *for v.*, -kāt′) *adj.* ⟦L *replicatus*, pp. of *replicare:* see REPLY⟧ *Bot.* folded back on itself, as a leaf —*n. Statistics* any of the individual experiments in a replication —*vt.* **-cat′ed**, **-cat′ing** **1** to fold; bend back **2** to repeat, duplicate, copy, reproduce, etc. **3** [Rare] to reply —*vi.* to be replicated or to undergo replication —**rep′li·ca·ble** *adj.*

rep·li·ca·tion (rep′li kā′shən) *n.* ⟦ME *replicacioun* < MFr *replication* < L *replicatio* < pp. of *replicare:* see REPLY⟧ **1** a folding back; fold **2** a reply, or answer; esp., a reply to an answer **3** repetition of a sound; echo **4** the act of repeating, duplicating, copying, reproducing, etc. **5** a copy; reproduction **6** *Law* REPLY (*n.* 3) **7** *Statistics* the exact duplication of an experiment for verification, criticism, or extension of previous results

rep·li·con (rep′li kän′) *n.* ⟦< prec. + -ON⟧ a specific sequence of nucleic acid that replicates as a unit when activated

re·ply (ri plī′) *vi.* **-plied′**, **-ply′ing** ⟦ME *replyen* < OFr *replier* < L *replicare*, to fold back, make a reply < *re-*, back + *plicare*, to fold: see PLY[1]⟧ **1** to answer, or respond, in speech or writing **2** to respond by some action [to *reply* to the enemy's fire with a barrage] **3** to echo **4** *Law* to answer a defendant's plea —*vt.* to say in answer [she *replied* that she disapproved] —*n.*, *pl.* **-plies′** **1** an answer, or response, in speech or writing **2** a response by some action **3** *Law* the plaintiff's answer to the defendant's plea; specif., the answer to a counterclaim —*SYN.* ANSWER —**re·pli′er** *n.*

☆**re·po** (rē′pō) *n.*, *pl.* **-pos** **1** [Slang] something repossessed **2** *informal var. of* REPURCHASE AGREEMENT

repo man ⟦< REPOSSESS⟧ [Slang] a person whose job is repossessing merchandise from buyers who have failed to make payments when due

re·port (ri pôrt′) *vt.* ⟦ME *reporten* < OFr *reporter*, to carry back < L *reportare* < *re-*, back + *portare*, to carry: see PORT[3]⟧ **1** to give an account of, often at regular intervals; give information about (something seen, done, etc.); recount **2** to carry and repeat (a message, etc.) **3** to write an account of for presentation to others or for publication, as in a newspaper **4** to make known the presence, approach, etc. of [to *report* strange aircraft overhead] **5** to give a formal statement or official account of; announce formally (the results of an investigation, etc.) **6** to present or return (something referred for study, action, etc.) with the conclusions reached or recommendations made: often with *out* [the committee *reported* the bill out] **7** to make a charge about (something) or against (someone) to a person in authority [to *report* a rudeness, to *report* a thief] —*vi.* **1** to make a report **2** to work as a reporter **3** to present oneself or make one's presence known [to *report* for duty] **4** to be responsible or subordinate (*to* a superior) —*n.* ⟦ME < OFr < the v.⟧ **1** rumor; gossip; common talk [*report* has it that you will resign] **2** reputation [a person of good *report*] **3** a statement or account brought in and presented, often for publication [a *report* of a battle] **4** a formal or official presentation of facts or of the record of some proceedings, an investigation, etc. **5** a loud, resounding

re-petition
rephotograph
repigment
replan
replant
replantation
replaster
replate
replead
repledge
replunge
repolish
repopularize
repopulate

noise, esp. one made by an explosion **6** *Law a)* a formal account or record of a court case, decision, etc. *b)* [*pl.*] the official records, published periodically, of court cases, decisions, etc. —**re·port′a·ble** *adj.*

re·port·age (ri pôrt′ij, rep′ər täzh′) ***n.*** **1** the act or process of reporting news events **2** written reports, articles, etc. that deal with current events in a journalistic manner

☆**report card** a periodic report, in writing, on a pupil's progress, sent to the pupil or to the parents or guardian: often used fig. of any critical report or evaluation

re·port·ed·ly (ri pôrt′id lē) ***adv.*** according to report or reports

re·port·er (ri pôrt′ər) ***n.*** ⟦ME *reportour* < OFr *reporteur*⟧ a person who reports; specif., *a)* a person authorized to report legal or legislative proceedings [a court *reporter*] *b)* a person who gathers information and writes reports for publication in a newspaper, magazine, etc. *c)* a person who reports news on radio or television —☆**rep·or·to·ri·al** (rep′ər tôr′ē əl) *adj.* —☆**rep′or·to′ri·al·ly** *adv.*

re·pos·al (ri pō′zəl) ***n.*** [Obs.] the act of reposing

re·pose[1] (ri pōz′) ***vt.*** **-posed′**, **-pos′ing** ⟦LME *reposen* < OFr *reposer* < LL *repausare* < L *re-*, again + LL *pausare:* see POSE[1]⟧ to lay or place for rest: often reflexive [to *repose* oneself on a bed] —***vi.*** **1** to lie at rest **2** to rest from work, travel, exercise, etc. **3** to rest in death or a grave **4** to lie quiet and calm **5** to lie, rest, or be supported [shale *reposing* on a bed of limestone] **6** [Archaic] to have trust (*in*); rely (*on* or *upon*) —***n.*** **1** a reposing, or resting **2** *a)* rest *b)* sleep **3** peace of mind; freedom from worry or troubles **4** calm or ease of manner; composure **5** calm; tranquillity; peace **6** harmony of form or color, giving an effect of tranquillity, as in painting

re·pose[2] (ri pōz′) ***vt.*** **-posed′**, **-pos′ing** ⟦ME *reposen* < L *repositus:* see REPOSITORY⟧ **1** [Rare] to place; put **2** to place (trust, confidence, etc.) *in* someone **3** to place (power, management, etc.) *in* the control of some person or group

re·pose·ful (-fəl) ***adj.*** full of repose; tranquil —**re·pose′ful·ly** *adv.*

re·pos·it (ri päz′it) ***vt.*** ⟦< L *repositus:* see REPOSITORY⟧ **1** to deposit or store, as for safekeeping **2** [Rare] to replace

rep·o·si·tion[1] (rep′ə zish′ən, rē′pə-) ***n.*** ⟦LL *repositio*⟧ a repositing or being reposited; specif., replacement, as of a part of the body by a surgical operation

re·po·si·tion[2] (rē′pə zish′ən) ***vt.*** ⟦RE- + POSITION⟧ to put into a new or different position

re·pos·i·to·ry (ri päz′ə tôr′ē) ***n.***, *pl.* **-ries** ⟦LME *repositorie* < L *repositorium* < *repositus,* pp. of *reponere,* to put back < *re-*, back + *ponere,* to place: see POSITION⟧ **1** a box, chest, closet, or room in which things may be placed for safekeeping **2** [Now Rare] a building for exhibiting objects; museum **3** a burial vault; sepulcher **4** any thing or person thought of as a center of accumulation or storage [a *repository* of information] **5** a person to whom something is entrusted or confided; confidant —***adj.*** acting gradually over a period of time: said of a drug

re·pos·sess (rē′pə zes′) ***vt.*** **1** to get possession of again; specif., to take back from a buyer who has failed to make payments when due **2** [Now Rare] to put in possession again —**re′pos·ses′sion** (-zesh′ən) ***n.***

re·pous·sé (rə po͞o sā′) ***adj.*** ⟦Fr, pp. of *repousser,* to push back < *re-*, back + *pousser,* PUSH⟧ **1** formed in relief, as a pattern on thin metal beaten up from the underside **2** decorated with such patterns —***n.*** **1** a pattern or surface made in this way **2** the art or process of hammering metal in this way

repp (rep) ***n.*** *alt. sp. of* REP[1]

repr *abbrev.* **1** represented **2** representing **3** reprint(ed)

rep·re·hend (rep′ri hend′) ***vt.*** ⟦ME *reprehenden* < L *reprehendere* < *re-*, back + *prehendere:* see PREHENSILE⟧ **1** to reprimand or rebuke (a person) **2** to find fault with (something done); censure —**SYN.** CRITICIZE

rep·re·hen·si·ble (-hen′sə bəl) ***adj.*** ⟦ME *reprehensyble* < LL(Ec) *reprehensibilis*⟧ deserving to be reprehended —**rep′re·hen′si·bil′i·ty** ***n.*** —**rep′re·hen′si·bly** *adv.*

rep·re·hen·sion (-hen′shən) ***n.*** ⟦ME *reprehencion* < L *reprehensio*⟧ the act of reprehending; reproof or censure —**rep′re·hen′sive** (-siv) ***adj.*** —**rep′re·hen′sive·ly** *adv.*

rep·re·sent (rep′ri zent′) ***vt.*** ⟦ME *representen* < OFr *representer* < L *repraesentare* < *re-*, again + *praesentare:* see RE- & PRESENT, ***vt.***⟧ **1** to present or picture to the mind **2** *a)* to present a likeness or image of; portray; depict *b)* to be a likeness or image of, as a picture or statue may be **3** to present in words; describe, state, or set forth; specif., *a)* to describe as having a specified character *b)* to set forth forcibly or earnestly, so as to influence action, persuade hearers, make effective protest, etc. **4** *a)* to be a sign or symbol for; stand for; symbolize [x *represents* the unknown] *b)* to denote by symbols, characters, etc. [to *represent* quantities by letters] **5** to be the equivalent of; correspond to, as in a different place or time [a cave *represented* home to them] **6** *a)* to present, produce, or perform (a play, etc.) *b)* to act the part of (a character), as in a play **7** to act or stand in place of; be an agent, proxy, or substitute for **8** to speak and act for by duly conferred authority, as an ambassador for a country or a legislator for constituents **9** to serve as a specimen, example, type, or instance of; exemplify or typify —**rep′re·sent′a·ble** ***adj.***

rep·re·sen·ta·tion (rep′ri zen tā′shən) ***n.*** ⟦ME < MFr < L *repraesentatio*⟧ **1** a representing or being represented (in various senses); specif., the fact of representing or being represented in a legislative assembly **2** legislative representatives, collectively **3** a likeness, image, picture, etc. **4** [*often pl.*] a description, account, or statement of facts, allegations, or arguments, esp. one intended to influence action, persuade hearers, make protest, etc. **5** the production or performance of a play, etc. **6** *Law* a statement or implication of fact, oral or written, as made by one party to induce another to enter into a contract

rep·re·sen·ta·tion·al (-shə nəl) ***adj.*** **1** of or characterized by representation **2** designating or of art that represents in recognizable form objects in nature —**rep′re·sen·ta′tion·al·ly** *adv.*

rep·re·sen·ta·tion·al·ism (-shə nəl iz′əm) ***n.*** **1** the theory or practice of representational art **2** *Philos.* the theory that the mind apprehends external objects only through the medium of percepts or ideas: distinguished from PRESENTATIONISM —**rep′re·sen·ta′tion·al·ist** ***n.***

rep·re·sent·a·tive (rep′rə zen′tə tiv) ***adj.*** ⟦ME < MFr or ML: MFr *représentatif* < ML *repraesentativus*⟧ **1** representing or serving to represent; specif., *a)* picturing; portraying; reproducing *b)* acting or speaking, esp. by due authority, in the place or on behalf of another or others; esp., serving as a delegate in a legislative assembly **2** composed of persons duly authorized, as by election, to act and speak for others [a *representative* assembly] **3** of, characterized by, or based on representation of the people by elected delegates [*representative* government] **4** being an example or type of a certain class or kind of thing; typical [a building *representative* of modern architecture] —***n.*** **1** a person or thing enough like the others in its class or kind to serve as an example or type **2** a person duly authorized to act or speak for another or others; specif., *a)* a member of a legislative assembly *b)* a salesperson or agent for a business firm ☆**3** [**R-**] a member of the lower house of Congress (*House of Representatives*) or of a state legislature —**rep′re·sent′a·tive·ly** *adv.* —**rep′re·sent′a·tive·ness** ***n.***

re·press (ri pres′) ***vt.*** ⟦ME *repressen* < L *repressus,* pp. of *reprimere:* see RE- & PRESS[1]⟧ **1** to keep down or hold back; restrain [to *repress* a sigh] **2** to put down; subdue **3** to control so strictly or severely as to prevent the natural development or expression of [to *repress* a child] **4** *Psychiatry a)* to force (ideas, impulses, etc. painful to the conscious mind) into the unconscious *b)* to prevent (unconscious ideas, impulses, etc.) from reaching the level of consciousness (cf. SUPPRESS) —**re·press′i·ble** ***adj.*** —**re·pres′sive** ***adj.*** —**re·pres′sive·ly** *adv.* —**re·pres′sive·ness** ***n.***

re-press (rē pres′) ***vt.*** ☆to press again; esp., to make new copies of (a recording) from the original master

re·pressed (ri prest′) ***adj.*** affected by, showing, or resulting from repression

re·pres·sion (ri presh′ən) ***n.*** ⟦ME *repressioun* < ML *repressio*⟧ **1** a repressing or being repressed **2** *Psychiatry a)* the mechanism by which ideas, impulses, etc. are repressed *b)* something repressed in this way

re·pres·sor (ri pres′ər) ***n.*** something that represses; esp., a protein produced in a cell that prevents the synthesis of a specific enzyme: also sp. **re·press′er**

re·prieve (ri prēv′) ***vt.*** **-prieved′**, **-priev′ing** ⟦earlier *repry* < Anglo-Fr *repris* < MFr, pp. of *reprendre,* to take back, prob. altered by assoc. with ME *repreven,* REPROVE⟧ **1** to postpone the punishment of; esp., to postpone the execution of (a person condemned to death) **2** to give temporary relief to, as from trouble or pain —***n.*** a reprieving or being reprieved; specif., *a)* postponement of a penalty, esp. that of death; also, a warrant ordering this *b)* a temporary relief or escape, as from trouble or pain

rep·ri·mand (rep′rə mand′, -mänd′; *also, for v.,* rep′rə mand′, -mänd′) ***n.*** ⟦Fr *réprimande* < L *reprimenda,* fem. of *reprimendus,* that is to be repressed < *reprimere,* to repress: see RE- & PRESS[1]⟧ a severe or formal rebuke, esp. by a person in authority —***vt.*** to rebuke severely or formally

re·print (rē print′; *also, and for n. always,* rē′print′) ***vt.*** to print again; print an additional impression of, usually without change —***n.*** **1** something reprinted; specif., *a)* an additional impression, usually without change, of something previously printed, as a book or pamphlet *b)* OFFPRINT *c) Philately* a stamp, not to be used for postage, printed from the original plate, often with different paper and ink, after the issue of the stamp has ceased **2** the act or an instance of reprinting —**re·print′er** ***n.***

re·pris·al (ri prī′zəl) ***n.*** ⟦ME *reprisail* < MFr *reprisaille* < It *rappresaglia* < *riprendere,* to take back < L *reprehendere:* see REPREHEND⟧ **1** [Historical] the forcible seizure of property or subjects in retaliation for an injury inflicted by another country **2** the act or practice of using force, short of war, against another nation to obtain redress of grievances **3** injury done, or the doing of injury, in return for injury received; retaliation or an act of retaliation, specif. in war, as the killing of prisoners

re·prise (ri prīz′; *for n. 2 & vt., usually* rə prēz′) ***n.*** ⟦ME < OFr, fem. of *repris,* pp. of *reprendre,* to take back < L *reprehendere:* see REPREHEND⟧ **1** *Eng. Law* a deduction and payment, as for an annuity, out of income from lands: *usually used in pl.* **2** *Music a)* RECAPITULATION *b)* any repetition or copying of a song, part of a song, role, etc. performed earlier **3** an instance of performing, presenting, or stating again [a movie *reprise* of her stage role] —***vt.*** **-prised′**, **-pris′ing** **1** to present a reprise of (a song) **2** to perform, present, or state again [a novel that *reprises* its author's favorite themes]

re·pro (rē′prō′) ***n.***, *pl.* **-pros′** *short for:* **1** [Informal] REPRODUCTION (sense 2) **2** REPRODUCTION PROOF: also **repro proof**

re·proach (ri prōch′) ***vt.*** ⟦LME *reprochen* < OFr *reprochier* < VL **repropiare* < L *re-*, back + *prope,* near⟧ **1** to accuse of and blame for a fault so as to make feel ashamed; rebuke; reprove **2** [Rare] to bring shame and disgrace

re-pose | repot | repour | re-present | re-price

upon; be a cause of discredit to —*n.* **1** shame, disgrace, discredit, or blame, or a source, cause, or occasion of this **2** a blaming or reproving; rebuke **3** an expression of blame or reproof **4** [Obs.] an object of blame, censure, scorn, etc. —**re·proach′a·ble** *adj.* —**re·proach′er** *n.* —**re·proach′ing·ly** *adv.*

re·proach·ful (-fəl) *adj.* full of or expressing reproach, or blame, censure, etc. —**re·proach′ful·ly** *adv.* —**re·proach′ful·ness** *n.*

rep·ro·bate (rep′rə bāt′; *for adj. & n., often,* -bit) *vt.* **-bat′ed, -bat′ing** ⟦ME *reprobaten* < LL(Ec) *reprobatus,* pp. of *reprobare:* see REPROVE⟧ **1** to disapprove of strongly; condemn **2** to reject **3** *Theol.* to damn —*adj.* **1** *a)* unprincipled *b)* totally bad; corrupt; depraved **2** *Theol.* damned —*n.* **1** an unprincipled or totally bad person **2** *Theol.* a person damned; lost soul

rep·ro·ba·tion (rep′rə bā′shən) *n.* ⟦ME *reprobacioun* < LL(Ec) *reprobatio*⟧ **1** the act of reprobating **2** disapproval; censure **3** rejection **4** *Theol.* the state of being damned —**rep′ro·ba′tive** *adj.*

re·pro·cess (rē prä′ses) *vt.* **1** to process again so as to reuse **2** to reclaim plutonium, uranium, etc. from (the spent fuel rods of a nuclear reactor) for reuse

reprocessed wool wool cloth respun and rewoven from the raveled fibers of unused cloth, such as the waste or clippings from a garment factory

re·pro·duce (rē′prə do͞os′, -dyo͞os′) *vt.* **-duced′, -duc′ing** to produce again; make, form, or bring into existence again or anew in some way; specif., *a)* to produce by generation or propagation; bring forth one or more other individuals of (the kind or species) by sexual or asexual processes *b)* to make (a lost part or organ) grow again *c)* to bring about or promote the reproduction of (plants or animals) *d)* to make a copy, close imitation, duplication, etc. of (a picture, sound, writing, etc.) *e)* to bring (a past scene, etc.) before the mind again; re-create mentally by imagination or memory *f)* to repeat —*vi.* **1** to produce offspring; bring forth others of its kind **2** to undergo reproduction, or copying, duplication, etc. —**re′pro·duc′er** *n.* —**re′pro·duc′i·ble** *adj.*

re·pro·duc·tion (rē′prə duk′shən) *n.* **1** a reproducing or being reproduced **2** something made by reproducing; copy, close imitation, duplication, etc. **3** the process, sexual or asexual, by which animals and plants produce new individuals —*SYN.* COPY

reproduction proof an especially fine proof of type, engraving, etc., usually on glossy paper, to be photographed for making a printing plate

re·pro·duc·tive (rē′prə duk′tiv) *adj.* **1** reproducing or tending to reproduce **2** of, for, or relating to reproduction —**re′pro·duc′tive·ly** *adv.* —**re′pro·duc′tive·ness** *n.*

re·prog·ra·phy (ri präg′rə fē) *n.* ⟦REPRO(DUCTION) + -GRAPHY⟧ reproduction of written or printed materials, documents, drawings, etc. by mechanical or, esp., xerographic processes: also **re′pro·graph′ics** —**re·prog′ra·pher** *n.* —**re′pro·graph′ic** *adj.*

re·proof (ri pro͞of′) *n.* ⟦ME *reprove* < OFr *reprouve* < *reprouver*⟧ the act of reproving or something said in reproving; rebuke; censure: also **re·prov′al** (-pro͞o′vəl)

re·prove (ri pro͞ov′) *vt.* **-proved′, -prov′ing** ⟦ME *reproven* < OFr *reprouver* < LL(Ec) *reprobare:* see RE- & PROVE⟧ **1** to speak to in disapproval; rebuke **2** to express disapproval of (something done or said); censure **3** [Obs.] to refute; disprove **4** [Obs.] to convince or convict —**re·prov′a·ble** *adj.* —**re·prov′er** *n.* —**re·prov′ing·ly** *adv.*

rept *abbrev.* report

rep·tant (rep′tənt) *adj.* ⟦L *reptans,* prp. of *reptare,* to crawl, creep: see fol.⟧ *Biol.* creeping or crawling

rep·tile (rep′tīl′, -təl) *n.* ⟦LL(Ec) < neut. of L *reptilis,* crawling < *reptus,* pp. of *repere,* to creep < IE base **rēp-,* to creep, crawl > Lith *réplioti,* to creep, OHG *rebo,* tendril⟧ **1** any of a class (Reptilia) of typically coldblooded vertebrates having lungs, an entirely bony skeleton, a body covered with scales or horny plates, and a heart with two atria and, usually, a single ventricle, including the snakes, lizards, turtles, crocodiles, and dinosaurs **2** a mean, sneaky, groveling person —*adj.* ⟦L *reptilis*⟧ of, like, or characteristic of a reptile; reptilian

rep·til·i·an (rep til′ē ən, -til′yən) *adj.* **1** of the reptiles **2** like or characteristic of a reptile **3** sneaky, mean, groveling, etc. —*n.* REPTILE

Repub *abbrev.* **1** Republic **2** Republican

re·pub·lic (ri pub′lik) *n.* ⟦MFr *république* < L *respublica* < *res,* thing, affair, interest (see REAL[1]) + *publica,* fem. of *publicus,* PUBLIC⟧ **1** *a)* a state or nation in which the supreme power rests in all the citizens entitled to vote (the *electorate*) and is exercised by representatives elected, directly or indirectly, by them and responsible to them *b)* the form of government of such a state or nation *c)* a specified republican regime of a nation [the Fifth *Republic* of France] **2** any group whose members are regarded as having a certain equality or common aims, pursuits, etc. [the *republic* of letters] **3** a state or nation with a president as its titular head **4** any of the constituent territorial and political units of the U.S.S.R., Yugoslavia, etc.

re·pub·li·can (ri pub′li kən) *adj.* **1** of, characteristic of, or having the nature of, a republic **2** favoring, or in accord with the nature of, a republic ☆**3** [**R-**] of, belonging to, or characteristic of the Republican Party —*n.* **1** a person who favors a republican form of government ☆**2** [**R-**] a member of the Republican Party —**re·pub′li·can·ize′** (-īz′) *vt.* **-ized′, -iz′ing**

re·pub·li·can·ism (-iz′əm) *n.* **1** republican form of government **2** *a)* republican principles, doctrines, etc. *b)* adherence to these ☆**3** [**R-**] the principles, policies, etc. of the Republican Party

☆**Republican Party** **1** one of the two major political parties in the U.S., organized in 1854 to oppose the extension of slavery **2** a former political party in the U.S., organized by Thomas Jefferson: see DEMOCRATIC PARTY

Republican River ⟦after the "*Republican* Pawnees," so called from their form of government⟧ river flowing from E Colo. east & southeast through Nebr. & Kans., joining the Smoky Hill River to form the Kansas River: 445 mi (716 km)

re·pub·li·ca·tion (rē′pub li kā′shən) *n.* **1** publication anew **2** a book, pamphlet, etc. published again

Republic of the Congo *see* CONGO

re·pub·lish (rē pub′lish) *vt.* **1** to publish again **2** *Law* to execute (a will once revoked) a second time

re·pu·di·ate (ri pyo͞o′dē āt′) *vt.* **-at′ed, -at′ing** ⟦< L *repudiatus,* pp. of *repudiare,* to put away, divorce < *repudium,* separation, a divorce < *re-,* away, back + base of *pudere,* to feel shame⟧ **1** to refuse to have anything to do with; disown or cast off publicly **2** *a)* to refuse to accept or support; deny the validity or authority of (a belief, a treaty, etc.) *b)* to deny the truth of (a charge, etc.) **3** to refuse to acknowledge or pay (a debt or obligation): said esp. of a government —*SYN.* DECLINE —**re·pu′di·a′tion** *n.* —**re·pu′di·a′tor** *n.*

re·pugn (ri pyo͞on′) *vt., vi.* ⟦ME *repugnen* < MFr *repugner* < L *repugnare* < *re-,* back + *pugnare,* to fight: see PUGNACIOUS⟧ [Now Rare] to oppose or resist

re·pug·nance (ri pug′nəns) *n.* ⟦ME < MFr < L *repugnantia* < *repugnans,* prp. of *repugnare:* see prec.⟧ **1** inconsistency or contradiction **2** extreme dislike or distaste; aversion; antipathy Also **re·pug′nan·cy** —*SYN.* AVERSION

re·pug·nant (-nənt) *adj.* ⟦ME < MFr < L *repugnans:* see prec.⟧ **1** contradictory; inconsistent [actions *repugnant* to his words] **2** offering resistance; opposed; antagonistic [*repugnant* forces] **3** causing repugnance; distasteful; offensive; disagreeable [a *repugnant* odor] —*SYN.* HATEFUL —**re·pug′nant·ly** *adv.*

re·pulse (ri puls′) *vt.* **-pulsed′, -puls′ing** ⟦< L *repulsus,* pp. of *repellere,* REPEL⟧ **1** to drive back; repel, as an attack **2** to repel with discourtesy, coldness, indifference, etc.; refuse, reject, or rebuff **3** to be repulsive, or disgusting, to —*n.* ⟦L *repulsa* < *repulsus*⟧ **1** a repelling or being repelled **2** a refusal, rejection, or rebuff

re·pul·sion (ri pul′shən) *n.* ⟦LL *repulsio*⟧ **1** a repelling or being repelled **2** strong dislike, distaste, or aversion; repugnance **3** *Physics* the mutual action by which bodies or particles of matter tend to repel each other: opposed to ATTRACTION

re·pul·sive (ri pul′siv) *adj.* ⟦ML *repulsivus*⟧ **1** tending to repel **2** causing strong dislike or aversion; disgusting; offensive **3** characterized by, or having the nature of, repulsion —**re·pul′sive·ly** *adv.* —**re·pul′sive·ness** *n.*

re·pur·chase agreement (rē pur′chəs) an agreement to sell certain securities and then purchase them again on a specified date, usually within a few days, thereby serving the function of a secured loan that meets the short-term financing needs of both buyer and seller

re·pur·pose (rē pur′pəs) *vt., vi.* **-posed, -pos·ing** to use or reuse (something that already exists) for another purpose or in another form

rep·u·ta·ble (rep′yə tə bəl) *adj.* **1** in good repute; having a good reputation; well-thought-of; respectable **2** regarded as proper usage; standard [a *reputable* word] —**rep′u·ta·bil′i·ty** *n.* —**rep′u·ta·bly** *adv.*

rep·u·ta·tion (rep′yo͞o tā′shən, -yə-) *n.* ⟦ME *reputacioun* < L *reputatio* < *reputatus,* pp. of *reputare:* see fol.⟧ **1** estimation in which a person or thing is commonly held, whether favorable or not; character in the view of the public, the community, etc.; repute **2** such estimation when favorable; good repute; good name [to lose one's *reputation*] **3** fame; distinction **4** the general character of being thought of as specified; name [to have the *reputation* of being a cheat] —**rep′u·ta′tion·al** *adj.*

re·pute (ri pyo͞ot′) *vt.* **-put′ed, -put′ing** ⟦ME *reputen* < MFr *reputer* < L *reputare* < *re-,* again + *putare,* to think: see PUTATIVE⟧ to consider or account (a person or thing) to be as specified; generally suppose or regard: usually in the passive [your neighbor is *reputed* to be rich] —*n.* REPUTATION (senses 1 & 3)

re·put·ed (-id) *adj.* generally accounted or supposed to be such [the *reputed* owner] —**re·put′ed·ly** *adv.*

req *abbrev.* **1** request **2** require(d) **3** requisition

re·quest (ri kwest′) *n.* ⟦ME < OFr *requeste* < ML *requesta* < fem. pp. of VL **requaerere:* see REQUIRE⟧ **1** the act of asking, or expressing a desire, for something; solicitation or petition **2** something asked for [to grant a *request*] **3** the state of being asked for or wanted; demand [a song much in *request*] —*vt.* **1** to express a wish or desire for; ask for, esp. in a polite or formal way: often followed by an infinitive or by a clause beginning with *that* **2** to ask (a person) to do something —**by request** in response to a request —**re·quest′er** *n.,* **re·quest′or**

Re·qui·em (rek′wē əm; rā′kwē-, rē′-) *n.* ⟦ME < L, acc. of *requies,* rest (see RE- & QUIET): first word of the Introit in the Latin Mass for the Dead⟧ [*also* **r-**] **1** *R.C.Ch.* a Mass for one or more deceased persons **2** a musical setting for this; also, any musical service, hymn, or dirge for the dead **3** any dirgelike song, chant, or poem

requiem shark ⟦Fr *requiem,* altered by folk etym. (? in allusion to the danger of its attack) < *requien, requin,* shark, swindler < ?⟧ any of a large family (Carcharhinidae, order Carcharhiniformes) of voracious, chiefly tropical, sharks

---

reprobe
reprogram
reprosecute
re-prove
repurchase
repurify
repursue
requalify

re·qui·es·cat (in pa·ce) (rā′kwē es′kät′ in pä′chā′, rek′wē-) ⟦L, subjunc. of *requiescere* (see RE- & QUIESCENT); *pace,* abl. of *pax,* PEACE⟧ may he or she rest (in peace): a prayer for a dead person: the phrase ***re′qui·es′cant′ (in pace)*** (-känt′) means "may they rest (in peace)"

re·quire (ri kwīr′) ***vt.* -quired′, -quir′ing** ⟦ME *requiren* < base of OFr *requerre* < VL **requaerere,* for L *requirere* < *re-,* again + *quaerere,* to ask⟧ **1** to ask or insist upon, as by right or authority; demand [to *require* obedience] **2** to order; command [to *require* someone to be present] **3** to be in need of; need [to *require* help] **4** to call for as necessary or appropriate [work that *requires* a steady hand] **5** to demand by virtue of a law, regulation, etc. [what is *required* by law] **6** [Archaic] to ask for; request —***vi.*** [Now Rare] to make a demand —***SYN.*** DEMAND, LACK

re·quire·ment (-mənt) ***n.*** **1** the act or an instance of requiring **2** something required; something obligatory or demanded, as a condition [the *requirements* for college entrance] **3** something needed; necessity; need

req·ui·site (rek′wə zit) ***adj.*** ⟦L *requisitus,* pp. of *requirere:* see REQUIRE⟧ required, as by circumstances; necessary for some purpose; indispensable [the *requisite* supplies for a journey] —***n.*** something requisite —***SYN.*** ESSENTIAL, NEED

req·ui·si·tion (rek′wə zish′ən) ***n.*** ⟦L *requisitio* < *requisitus,* pp. of *requirere:* see REQUIRE⟧ **1** a requiring, as by right or authority; formal demand **2** a formal written order, request, or application, as for equipment or tools **3** the fact or condition of being demanded for service or use **4** [Rare] a requirement; indispensable condition **5** *Law* a demand by one government upon another for the surrender of a fugitive criminal —***vt.*** **1** to demand or take, as by authority [to *requisition* food for troops] **2** [Now Rare] to demand from; make demands on [to *requisition* a town for food] **3** to submit a written order or request for (equipment, etc.)

re·quit·al (ri kwīt′'l) ***n.*** **1** a requiting or being requited **2** something given or done in return; repayment, reward, retaliation, or compensation

re·quite (ri kwīt′) ***vt.* -quit′ed, -quit′ing** ⟦RE- + *quite,* obs. var. of QUIT⟧ **1** to make return or repayment for (a benefit, service, etc., or an injury, wrong, etc.) **2** to make return or repayment to for a benefit, injury, etc.; reward or retaliate against **3** [Now Rare] to give or do in return —**re·quit′er *n.***

re·ra·di·a·tion (rē′rā′dē ā′shən) ***n.*** *Physics* radiation resulting from the emission of previously absorbed radiation

rere·dos (rir′däs′) ***n.*** ⟦ME *rerdos,* aphetic < Anglo-Fr *areredos* < OFr *arere* (see ARREARS) + *dos,* back (see DOSSER[1])⟧ an ornamental screen or partition wall behind an altar in a church

re·re·lease or **re-re·lease** (rē′ri lēs′) ***vt.* -leased′, -leas′ing** to release (a film, recording, etc.) again —***n.*** something rereleased

re·route (rē rout′, -ro͞ot′) ***vt.* -rout′ed, -rout′ing** to send by a new or different route

re·run (rē run′; *for n.* rē′run′) ***vt.* -ran′, -run′, -run′ning** to run again —***n.*** **1** the act of rerunning ☆**2** *a)* a rebroadcast of a TV program, series, etc. *b)* a showing of a film after the first run ☆**3** such a program, film, etc.

res[1] (rās, rēz, rez, res) ***n., pl.* res** ⟦L *res,* a thing: see REAL[1]⟧ *Law* **1** a thing; object **2** matter; case; point; action

res[2] *abbrev.* **1** research **2** reservation **3** reserve **4** residence **5** resident **6** resides **7** resigned **8** resolution

res ad·ju·di·ca·ta (ə jo͞o di kät′ə) ⟦L⟧ [Now Rare] *var. of* RES JUDICATA

re·sal·a·ble (rē sāl′ə bəl) ***adj.*** that can be sold again

re·sale (rē′sāl′) ***n.*** the act or an instance of reselling something —***adj.*** of or having to do with reselling [a car's *resale* value]

re·sched·ule (rē skej′o͞ol, -əl) ***vt.* -uled, -ul·ing** **1** to schedule again or anew **2** to adjust the terms of (a loan), as by extending the period over which the borrower may make payments

re·scind (ri sind′) ***vt.*** ⟦L *rescindere* (pp. *rescissus*), to cut off < *re-,* back + *scindere,* to cut: see SCISSION⟧ to revoke, repeal, or cancel (a law, order, etc.) —***SYN.*** ABOLISH —**re·scind′a·ble *adj.*** —**re·scind′er *n.***

re·scis·sion (ri sizh′ən) ***n.*** ⟦LL *rescissio*⟧ the act of rescinding —**re·scis·so·ry** (ri sis′ə rē, -siz′-) ***adj.***

re·script (rē′skript′) ***n.*** ⟦L *rescriptum* < *rescriptus,* pp. of *rescribere* < *re-,* back + *scribere,* to write: see SCRIBE⟧ **1** an order or decree issued by a Roman emperor or by the pope in answer to some presented difficulty or point of law **2** any official decree or order **3** *a)* the act of rewriting *b)* something rewritten; copy

res·cue (res′kyo͞o) ***vt.* -cued, -cu·ing** ⟦ME *rescuen* < OFr *rescourre* < *re-,* again + *escorre,* to shake, move < L *excutere,* to shake off, drive away < *ex-,* off + *quatere,* to shake: see QUASH[2]⟧ **1** to free or save from danger, imprisonment, evil, etc. **2** *Law* to take (a person or thing) out of legal custody by force —***n.*** the act or an instance of rescuing; deliverance —***adj.*** designating or of an animal, esp. a dog or cat, that has been adopted as a pet from a pound, animal shelter, etc. —**res′cu·a·ble *adj.*** —**res′cu·er *n.***

SYN.—**rescue** implies prompt action in freeing someone or something from imminent danger or destruction or in releasing someone from captivity [the lifeguard *rescued* the drowning child]; **deliver** implies a setting free from confinement or from some restricting situation [*deliver* me from those interminable sermons]; **redeem** suggests a freeing from bondage or from the consequences of sin, or a reclaiming, as from pawn, deterioration, etc. [how can I *redeem* my good name?]; **ransom** specifically implies the payment of what is demanded in order to free one held captive; **save,** in this connection, is a general, comprehensive synonym for any of the preceding terms

re·search (rē′surch′, ri surch′) ***n.*** ⟦MFr *recerche* < *recercher,* to travel through, survey: see RE- & SEARCH⟧ [*sometimes pl.*] careful, systematic, patient study and investigation in some field of knowledge, undertaken to discover or establish facts or principles —***vi.*** to do research; make researches —***vt.*** to do research on or in; investigate thoroughly —**re·search′a·ble *adj.*** —**re′search′er *n.*,** **re′search′ist**

re·seat (rē sēt′) ***vt.*** **1** to seat again or in another seat **2** to supply with a new seat or seats **3** to reposition on its SEAT (***n.*** *5b*)

re·seau or **ré·seau** (rā zō′) ***n., pl.* -seaux′** (-zōz′, -zō′) ⟦Fr < OFr *resel,* dim. of *roiz* < VL *retis,* for L *rete,* net: see RETINA⟧ **1** a network; specif., *a)* a grid of fine lines forming little squares of a standard size: used with celestial photographs and plates for reference or measurement *b)* a network of meteorological stations throughout the world **2** a netted ground or meshed foundation in lace

re·sect (ri sekt′) ***vt.*** ⟦< L *resectus,* pp. of *resecare,* to cut off < *re-,* RE- + *secare,* to cut: see SAW[1]⟧ *Surgery* to perform a resection of (some part)

re·sec·tion (ri sek′shən) ***n.*** ⟦L *resectio* < *resectus:* see prec.⟧ **1** *Surgery* the removal of part of an organ, bone, etc. **2** *Surveying* a method of determining the location of a point by taking observations from it to points of known location

re·sec·to·scope (ri sek′tə skōp′) ***n.*** a thin, hollow, flexible surgical instrument inserted through the urethra or vagina for use in the biopsy of tissue or the removal of lesions from the prostate gland, bladder, or uterus —**re·sec′to·scop′ic** (-skäp′ik) ***adj.***

re·se·da (ri sē′də) ***n.*** ⟦ModL < L, a plant < ?, but said (by Pliny) to be orig. imper. of *resedare,* to allay, used in a charm accompanying its medicinal use⟧ MIGNONETTE (sense 3)

re·sell (rē sel′) ***vt.* -sold′** (-sōld′), **-sell′ing** to sell (something one has bought or otherwise acquired); specif., to sell (goods) retail at marked-up prices —***vi.*** to be resold [merchandise that *resells* quickly]

re·sem·blance (ri zem′bləns) ***n.*** ⟦ME < Anglo-Fr⟧ **1** the state, fact, or quality of resembling; similarity of appearance, or, sometimes, of character; likeness **2** a point, degree, or sort of likeness **3** something that resembles; likeness or semblance (*of* someone or something) **4** [Obs.] characteristic appearance **5** [Obs.] likelihood; probability —***SYN.*** LIKENESS

re·sem·ble (ri zem′bəl) ***vt.* -bled, -bling** ⟦ME *resemblen* < OFr *resembler* < *re-,* again + *sembler* < L *simulare:* see SIMULATE⟧ **1** to be like or similar to in appearance or nature **2** [Archaic] to liken or compare

re·send (rē send′) ***vt.* -sent′, -send′ing** to send again or send back

re·sent (ri zent′) ***vt.*** ⟦Fr *ressentir* < OFr *resentir* < *re-,* again + *sentir,* to feel < L *sentire:* see SEND⟧ to feel or show displeasure and hurt or indignation over (some act, remark, etc.) or toward (a person), from a sense of being injured or offended

re·sent·ful (-fəl) ***adj.*** feeling or showing resentment —**re·sent′ful·ly *adv.*** —**re·sent′ful·ness *n.***

re·sent·ment (-mənt) ***n.*** ⟦Fr *ressentiment:* see RESENT⟧ a feeling of displeasure and indignation, from a sense of being injured or offended —***SYN.*** OFFENSE

re·ser·pine (ri sur′pin, -pēn′; res′ər pēn′) ***n.*** ⟦Ger *reserpin,* prob. arbitrary contr. < ModL *Rauwolfia serpentina* + Ger *-in,* -INE[3]⟧ a crystalline alkaloid, $C_{33}H_{40}N_2O_9$, extracted from the root of various rauwolfias (esp. *Rauwolfia serpentina*), used in the treatment of hypertension and some forms of mental illness

res·er·va·tion (rez′ər vā′shən) ***n.*** ⟦ME < ML *reservatio*⟧ **1** the act of reserving or that which is reserved; specif., *a)* a withholding of a right, interest, etc. *b)* that part of a deed or contract which provides for this ☆*c)* public land set aside for some special use [an Indian *reservation,* military *reservation*] ☆*d)* an arrangement by which a hotel room, theater or airline ticket, etc. is set aside and held until called for ☆*e)* anything so reserved in advance ☆*f)* the promise of or a request for such an arrangement **2** *a)* a limiting condition or qualification, tacit or expressed, as in an agreement [an evaluation made without *reservation*] *b)* a doubt or misgiving (*often used in pl.*) [to make a promise with mental *reservations*]

re·serve (ri zurv′) ***vt.* -served′, -serv′ing** ⟦ME *reserven* < OFr *reserver* < L *reservare* < *re-,* back + *servare:* see OBSERVE⟧ **1** to keep back, store up, or set apart for later use or for some special purpose **2** to hold over to a later time **3** to set aside or have set aside for a special person, etc. [to *reserve* a theater seat] **4** to keep back or retain for oneself [to *reserve* the right to refuse] —***n.*** **1** something kept back or stored up, as for later use or for a special purpose **2** a limitation or reservation: now rare except in **without reserve** (see phrase below) **3** the practice of keeping one's thoughts, feelings, etc. to oneself; self-restraint or aloofness in speech and manner **4** reticence; silence **5** restraint and control in artistic expression; freedom from exaggeration or extravagance **6** [*pl.*] *a)* available participants kept out of action for use in an emergency or for replacing active groups or units, as in sports or warfare *b)* personnel or units in the armed forces not on active

reradiate
reread
rerecord
reroll
resaddle
resail
resalute
rescore
rescreen
reseal
reseed
resegregate
reseize
reseizure
resentence
re-serve

duty but subject to call; militia (with *the*) **7** cash, or assets readily turned into cash, held out of use by a bank, insurance company, or business to meet expected or unexpected demands: see also LEGAL RESERVE ☆**8** land set apart for a special purpose [a forest *reserve*] —*adj.* being, or having the nature of, a reserve or reserves [a *reserve* supply] —**in reserve** reserved for later use or for some person —**without reserve** **1** subject to no limitation **2** without any minimum or asking price: said of goods offered at auction

☆**reserve bank** a bank in which the reserves of other banks are deposited; specif., FEDERAL RESERVE BANK

☆**reserve clause** a condition in the contracts of professional baseball players, allowing team owners to extend contracts for one additional year

re·served (ri zurvd′) *adj.* **1** kept in reserve; set apart for some purpose, person, etc. **2** self-restrained in speech and manner; reticent —**re·serv′ed·ly** (-zur′vid lē) *adv.* —**re·serv′ed·ness** *n.*

re·serv·ist (ri zur′vist) *n.* a member of a country's military reserves

res·er·voir (rez′ər vwär′, rez′ə-; -vwôr, -vôr′) *n.* [Fr *réservoir* < *réserver:* see RESERVE] **1** a place where anything is collected and stored, generally in large quantity; esp., a natural or artificial lake or pond in which water is collected and stored for use **2** a receptacle or part (in an apparatus) for holding a fluid, as oil or ink **3** a large supply; esp., an extra or reserve supply **4** *Biol.* *a)* a part, sac, or cavity in some animals or plants in which fluid collects or into which products are secreted *b)* a species of organism that serves as an immune host for a parasite that can cause disease in another species (in full **reservoir host**)

re·set (rē set′; *for n.* rē′set′) *vt.* **-set′**, **-set′ting** to set again (a broken bone, type, a gem, bowling pins, an electrical contact switch, etc.) —*n.* **1** the act of resetting **2** something reset **3** a plant that is planted again **4** a device for resetting something

res ges·tae (jes′tē, -tā, -tī′) [L, lit., things done, deeds] *Law* facts that are so closely connected with the occurrence in question as to be considered a part of it, and are thus admissible as evidence

resh (rāsh) *n.* [Heb *rēsh,* lit., the head] the twentieth letter of the Hebrew alphabet (ר)

re·shape (rē shāp′) *vt.* **-shaped′**, **-shap′ing** to shape again or give new shape or form to

re·ship (rē ship′) *vt.* **-shipped′**, **-ship′ping** **1** to ship again **2** to transfer to another ship —*vi.* **1** to go on a ship again; embark again **2** to sign as a member of a ship's crew for another voyage —**re·ship′ment** *n.* —**re·ship′per** *n.*

Resht (resht) *var. of* RASHT

re·shuf·fle (rē shuf′əl) *vt.* **-fled**, **-fling** **1** to shuffle again **2** to rearrange or reorganize —*n.* a reshuffling or being reshuffled, or the result of this

re·side (ri zīd′) *vi.* **-sid′ed**, **-sid′ing** [ME *resyden* < MFr *resider* < L *residere* < *re-,* back + *sedere,* to SIT] **1** to dwell for a long time; have one's residence; live (*in* or *at*) **2** to be present or inherent; exist (*in*): said of qualities, etc. **3** to be vested (*in*): said of rights, powers, etc.

res·i·dence (rez′i dəns, -dens′) *n.* [ME < MFr < ML *residentia*] **1** the act or fact of residing **2** the fact or status of living or staying in a place while working, going to school, carrying out official duties, etc., esp. long enough to qualify for certain rights, privileges, etc. **3** the place in which a person or thing resides; dwelling place; abode; esp., a house **4** a large or imposing house; mansion **5** the time during which a person resides in a place

res·i·den·cy (-dən sē) *n., pl.* **-cies** **1** RESIDENCE (esp. senses 1, 2, & 5) ☆**2** *a)* a period of advanced, specialized medical or surgical training at a hospital *b)* the position or tenure of a doctor during this period

res·i·dent (-dənt, -dent′) *adj.* [ME < L *residens,* prp.] **1** living in a place for some continuous period; having a residence (*in* or *at*); residing **2** living or staying in a place while working, carrying on official duties, etc.; being in residence **3** present, inherent, or intrinsic in something **4** not migratory: said of birds, etc. —*n.* **1** a person who lives in a place, as distinguished from a visitor or transient ☆**2** a doctor who is serving a residency **3** a bird or animal that is not migratory

☆**resident commissioner** in the House of Representatives, a nonvoting representative of a U.S. dependency

res·i·den·tial (rez′ə den′shəl) *adj.* **1** of or connected with residence **2** of, characterized by, or suitable for residences, or homes [a *residential* neighborhood] ☆**3** chiefly for residents rather than transients [a *residential* hotel] —**res′i·den′tial·ly** *adv.*

res·i·den·ti·ar·y (rez′ə den′shē er′ē, -shə rē) *adj.* [ML *residentiarius*] **1** living in a place; resident **2** of, requiring, or bound to an official residence —*n., pl.* **-ar′ies** **1** a resident **2** *Eccles.* a clergyman bound to an official residence

re·sid·u·al (ri zij′o͞o əl) *adj.* [see RESIDUE & -AL] of, or having the nature of, a residue or residuum; left over after part or most is taken away; remaining —*n.* **1** what is left at the end of a process; something remaining ☆**2** the fee paid to a performer for each rerun of filmed or taped material, as on television: *often used in pl.* **3** *Geol.* MONADNOCK **4** *Math.* the difference between an actual value of some variable and a mean or other estimated value —**re·sid′u·al·ly** *adv.*

re·sid·u·ar·y (-o͞o er′ē) *adj.* **1** of, or having the nature of, a residue or residuum; remaining; leftover **2** *Law* *a)* receiving the residue of an estate after specific bequests [a *residuary* legatee] *b)* giving the disposition of the residue of an estate after specific bequests [the *residuary* clause in a will]

res·i·due (rez′ə do͞o′, -dyo͞o′) *n.* [ME < MFr *residu* < L *residuum,* neut. of *residuus,* remaining < *residere:* see RESIDE] **1** that which is left over after part is taken away; remainder; rest **2** *Chem.* the matter remaining at the end of a process, as after evaporation, combustion, or filtration; residual product **3** *Law* that part of a testator's estate which is left after all claims, charges, and bequests have been satisfied —*SYN.* REMAINDER

re·sid·u·um (ri zij′o͞o əm) *n., pl.* **-sid′u·a** (-ə) [L] RESIDUE —*SYN.* REMAINDER

re·sign (ri zīn′) *vt.* [ME *resignen* < MFr *resigner* < L *resignare* < *re-,* back + *signare,* to SIGN] **1** to give up possession of; relinquish (a claim, etc.) **2** to give up (an office, position, etc.) —*vi.* to give up an office, position of employment, etc., esp. by formal notice: often with *from* —**resign oneself (to)** to submit or become reconciled (to); accept (something) passively

res·ig·na·tion (rez′ig nā′shən) *n.* [ME < MFr *resignation* < ML *resignatio*] **1** *a)* the act of resigning *b)* formal notice of this, esp. in writing **2** patient submission; passive acceptance; acquiescence

re·signed (ri zīnd′) *adj.* feeling or showing resignation; submissive; yielding and uncomplaining —**re·sign′ed·ly** (-zīn′id lē) *adv.* —**re·sign′ed·ness** *n.*

re·sile (ri zīl′) *vi.* **-siled′**, **-sil′ing** [MFr *resiler* < L *resilire* < *re-,* back + *salire,* to JUMP: see SALIENT] **1** to bounce or spring back; rebound; specif., to come back into shape or position after being pressed or stretched: said of elastic bodies **2** to withdraw or recoil: often with *from* [they *resiled* from their arrangement; we *resile* from personal attacks]

re·sil·ience (ri zil′yəns, -ē əns) *n.* the quality of being resilient; esp., *a)* the ability to bounce or spring back into shape, position, etc. *b)* the ability to recover strength, spirits, good humor, etc. quickly; buoyancy Also **re·sil′ien·cy**

re·sil·ient (-yənt, -ē ənt) *adj.* [L *resiliens,* prp. of *resilire:* see RESILE] **1** bouncing or springing back into shape, position, etc. after being stretched, bent, or, esp., compressed **2** recovering strength, spirits, good humor, etc. quickly; buoyant —*SYN.* ELASTIC —**re·sil′ient·ly** *adv.*

res·in (rez′ən) *n.* [ME < MFr *resine* < L *resina* < or akin to Gr *rhētinē*] **1** any of various solid or semisolid organic substances, typically clear or translucent with a yellowish or brownish color, exuded from various plants and trees: natural resins are soluble in ether, alcohol, etc., and are used in varnishes and lacquers, as modifiers in synthetic plastics, etc. **2** *a)* SYNTHETIC RESIN *b)* ROSIN —*vt.* to treat or rub with resin

res·in·ate (rez′ə nāt′) *vt.* **-at′ed**, **-at′ing** to impregnate or treat with resin

resin canal *Bot.* a tubular, intercellular opening containing resin, often found in the wood and needles of gymnosperms

res·in·if·er·ous (rez′ə nif′ər əs) *adj.* yielding resin: said of trees, etc.

res·in·oid (rez′ə noid′) *adj.* like resin —*n.* **1** a resinoid substance **2** GUM RESIN

res·in·ous (-nəs) *adj.* [L *resinosus*] **1** of or like resin **2** obtained from resin **3** containing resin Also **res′in·y**

res ip·sa lo·qui·tur (ip′sə läk′wə tər) [L] the thing speaks for itself

re·sist (ri zist′) *vt.* [ME *resisten* < MFr *resister* < L *resistere* < *re-,* back + *sistere,* to set, caus. of *stare,* to STAND] **1** to withstand; oppose; fend off; stand firm against; withstand the action of **2** *a)* to oppose actively; fight, argue, or work against *b)* to refuse to cooperate with, submit to, etc. [to *resist* conscription] **3** to keep from yielding to, being affected by, or enjoying [to *resist* temptation] —*vi.* to oppose or withstand something; offer resistance —*n.* a substance that resists, esp. something applied as a protective coating —**re·sist′er** *n.*

re·sist·ance (ri zis′təns) *n.* [ME < MFr *resistence* < LL *resistentia*] **1** the act of resisting, opposing, withstanding, etc. **2** power or capacity to resist; specif., the ability of an organism to ward off disease **3** opposition of some force, thing, etc. to another or others **4** a force that retards, hinders, or opposes motion **5** [*often* **R-**] the organized underground movement in a country fighting against a foreign occupying power, a dictatorship, etc., as in France during the Nazi occupation **6** *Elec.* *a)* the property of a component by which it resists the flow of electricity, usually measured in ohms and equal to the ratio of the voltage to the current: it is the reciprocal of conductance (abbrev. *R*) (see IMPEDANCE) *b)* RESISTOR **7** *Psychoanalysis* the active psychological opposition to the bringing of unconscious, usually repressed, material to consciousness

resistance plasmid any of a group of bacterial plasmids carrying genetic information that provide resistance to antibiotic drugs: some resistance plasmids are able to transfer themselves, and hence resistance, during conjugation

re·sist·ant (-tənt) *adj.* [L *resistens,* prp.] offering resistance; resisting: often used in comb. [heat-*resistant* glass] —*n.* a person or thing that resists

Re·sis·ten·cia (rā′sē sten′syä) city in N Argentina, on the Paraná River

re·sist·i·ble (ri zis′tə bəl) *adj.* that can be resisted —**re·sist′i·bil′i·ty** *n.*

re·sis·tive (ri zis′tiv) *adj.* resisting, tending to resist, or capable of resistance —**re·sis′tive·ly** *adv.*

re·sis·tiv·i·ty (rē′zis tiv′ə tē, ri zis′-) *n.* **1** property of, capacity for, or tendency toward resistance **2** *Elec.* resistance per unit of area or volume, measured in ohms per meter: the reciprocal of conductivity

re·sist·less (ri zist′lis) *adj.* **1** that cannot be resisted; irresistible **2** without power to resist; unresisting —**re·sist′less·ly** *adv.* —**re·sist′less·ness** *n.*

---

resettle
resew
resharpen
reshine
reshow
re-sign
resilver

re·sist·o·jet (ri zis′tə jet′) *n.* ⟦< fol. + JET[1]⟧ a jet engine that obtains its thrust from a propellant heated by a resistance device using electrical power

re·sis·tor (ri zis′tər) *n. Elec.* a component with a specific resistance, used to control the current in a circuit

res ju·di·ca·ta (jo͞o′di kät′ə) ⟦L, thing decided⟧ *Law* a matter already decided by judicial authority

re·sole (rē sōl′; *for n.*, rē′sōl′) *vt.* **-soled′**, **-sol′ing** to put a new sole on (a shoe, etc.) —*n.* a new sole for a shoe, etc.

re·sol·u·ble (ri zäl′yə bəl, rez′əl yə bəl) *adj.* ⟦LL *resolubilis* < L *resolvere*⟧ that can be resolved —**re·sol′u·bil′i·ty** *n.*, **re·sol′u·ble·ness**

res·o·lute (rez′ə lo͞ot′) *adj.* ⟦L *resolutus*, pp. of *resolvere:* see RE- & SOLVE⟧ having or showing a fixed, firm purpose; determined; resolved; unwavering —*SYN.* FAITHFUL —**res′o·lute′ly** *adv.* —**res′o·lute′ness** *n.*

res·o·lu·tion (rez′ə lo͞o′shən) *n.* ⟦ME *resolucioun*, dissolution < MFr *resolution* < L *resolutio* < *resolutus:* see prec.⟧ **1** *a)* the act or process of resolving something or breaking it up into its constituent parts or elements *b)* the result of this **2** *a)* a resolving, or determining; deciding *b)* the thing determined upon; decision as to future action; resolve **3** a resolute quality of mind **4** a formal statement of opinion or determination adopted by an assembly or other formal group **5** a solving, as of a puzzle, or answering, as of a question; solution **6** that part of a play, novel, etc., typically after the climax, in which the plotlines are concluded or clarified **7** *Med.* the subsidence or disappearance of swelling, fever, or other manifestation of disease **8** *Music a)* the passing of a dissonant chord (or tone in a chord) to a consonant chord (or tone) *b)* a chord or tone to which such passing occurs **9** *a) Physics* the capability of an optical system, or other imaging system, of making clear and distinguishable the separate parts or components of an object *b)* the clarity and sharpness of an image or of a video or computer screen, camera, etc. that displays or captures an image as measured in dots (or pixels) per inch [a picture made with high *resolution*]

re·solv·a·ble (ri zäl′və bəl, -zôl′-) *adj.* that can be resolved —**re·solv′a·bil′i·ty** *n.*

re·solve (ri zälv′, -zôlv′) *vt.* **-solved′**, **-solv′ing** ⟦ME *resolven* < L *resolvere:* see RE- & SOLVE⟧ **1** to break up into separate, constituent elements or parts; analyze **2** to change or transform: used reflexively [a discussion that *resolved* itself into an argument] **3** to cause (a person) to decide [the flood that *resolved* him to sell] **4** to reach as a decision or intention; determine [to *resolve* to go] **5** *a)* to find the solution or an answer to (a problem); solve *b)* to make a decision about [to *resolve* the points at issue] *c)* to explain or make clear; show the resolution of (a problem, a fictional plot, etc.) *d)* to remove or dispel (doubt, etc.) **6** to decide by vote; make a formal decision about; express by resolution, as an assembly does **7** [Obs.] to cause to dissolve or melt **8** *Chem.* to separate (an optically inactive compound or mixture) into its optically active components **9** *Med.* to cause (a swelling, fever, etc.) to subside or disappear **10** *Music* to cause (a chord or tone) to undergo resolution **11** *Physics* to make distinguishable the individual parts of (an image, radar echo, etc.) —*vi.* **1** to be resolved, as by analysis **2** to come to a decision; make a resolution; determine **3** *Music* to undergo resolution —*n.* **1** fixed purpose or intention; firm determination **2** a formal resolution, as of an assembly —*SYN.* DECIDE —**re·solv′er** *n.*

re·solved (ri zälvd′, -zôlvd′) *adj.* firm and fixed in purpose; determined; resolute —**re·solv′ed·ly** (-zäl′vid lē, -zôl′-) *adv.*

re·sol·vent (ri zäl′vənt, -zôl′-) *adj.* that resolves; causing solution or resolution —*n.* **1** something that resolves; specif., a medicine that reduces swelling **2** something that resolves problems, equations, etc.

resolving power **1** a measure of the smallest distance between two points in the image of an optical system when the two points can be distinguished as separate **2** the ability of a photographic emulsion to produce a picture containing fine detail

res·o·nance (rez′ə nəns) *n.* ⟦LME *resonnaunce* < MFr *resonance* < L *resonantia*, an echo⟧ **1** the quality or state of being resonant **2** reinforcement and prolongation of a sound or musical tone by reflection or by sympathetic vibration of other bodies **3** *a)* the quality of having an intensity of emotion or richness of expression that evokes or reinforces a sympathetic response *b)* an underlying or pervasive quality of a particular type, esp. in a work of art or literature [an apocalyptic *resonance*] **4** *Chem.* the property of certain molecules of having two or more structures in which only the positions of electrons differ: these structures are approximations of the true structure, which cannot be described graphically, but is best represented by a mathematical expression **5** *Elec.* a condition arising in an electric circuit in which *a)* the current or voltage flow is at maximum amplitude, produced when the frequency of the electrical source is varied, or *b)* the current or voltage is in phase respectively with the applied current or voltage, or *c)* the natural frequency of the circuit is the same as that of the incoming signal **6** *Med.* the sound produced in the percussion of some part of the body, esp. of the chest **7** *Physics a)* the effect produced when the amplitude of oscillation of a body is greatly increased by a periodic force at the same or nearly the same frequency *b)* a vibration caused by this phenomenon **8** *Phonet.* the intensification of, and particular quality given to, a speech sound, resulting from its vibrating in a resonating cavity, as the pharynx, the mouth, or the nose, or a combination of these

res·o·nant (-nənt) *adj.* ⟦L *resonans*, prp. of *resonare*, to resound: see RE- & SOUND[1], *vi.*⟧ **1** resounding or reechoing [a *resonant* sound] **2** producing resonance; increasing the intensity of sounds by sympathetic vibration [*resonant* walls] **3** full of, characterized by, or intensified by, resonance [a *resonant* voice, a *resonant* passage in a novel] **4** of or in resonance —**res′o·nant·ly** *adv.*

res·o·nate (-nāt′) *vi.* **-nat′ed**, **-nat′ing** ⟦< L *resonatus*, pp. of *resonare:* see prec.⟧ **1** to be resonant **2** to produce resonance —*vt.* to make resonant

res·o·na·tor (-nāt′ər) *n.* **1** a device for producing resonance or increasing sound by resonance **2** an acoustic guitar with a circular metal device of this kind, rather than the traditional wooden soundboard: in full **resonator guitar** **3** *Electronics* an apparatus or system, as a piezoelectric crystal or a circuit, capable of being put into oscillation by oscillations in another system

re·sorb (ri sôrb′, -zôrb′) *vt.* ⟦L *resorbere* < *re-*, again + *sorbere*, to suck up: see SLURP⟧ to absorb again —**re·sorp′tion** (-sôrp′shən) *n.* —**re·sorp′tive** *adj.*

res·or·cin·ol (ri zôr′si nôl′, -nōl′) *n.* ⟦RES(IN) + ORCINOL⟧ a colorless, crystalline compound, $C_6H_4(OH)_2$, prepared synthetically or by fusing certain resins with caustic alkalies and used in making dyes, celluloid, pharmaceuticals, etc.: also **res·or′cin** (-sin)

re·sort (ri zôrt′) *vi.* ⟦ME *resorten* < OFr *resortir* < *re-*, again + *sortir*, to go out: see SORTIE⟧ **1** to go; esp., to go often, customarily, or generally **2** to have recourse; go or turn (*to*) for use, help, support, etc. [to *resort* to harsh measures] —*n.* ⟦ME < OFr < the v.⟧ **1** a place to which people go often or generally, esp. one for rest or recreation, as on a vacation **2** a frequent, customary, or general going, gathering together, or visiting [a place of general *resort*] **3** a person or thing that one goes or turns to for help, support, etc. **4** a going or turning for help, support, etc.; recourse [to have *resort* to relatives] —*SYN.* RESOURCE —**as a last resort** as the last available means —**re·sort′er** *n.*

re·sound (ri zound′) *vi.* ⟦altered (infl. by SOUND[1]) < ME *resounen* < OFr *resoner* < L *resonare* < *re-* + *sonare:* for IE base see SOUND[1]⟧ **1** to echo or be filled with sound; reverberate **2** to make a loud, echoing, or prolonged sound **3** to be echoed; be repeated or prolonged: said of sounds **4** to be celebrated; be extolled [an act that *resounded* through the ages] —*vt.* **1** to give back (sound); echo **2** to give forth, utter, or repeat loudly **3** to proclaim (praises, etc.)

re·sound·ing (ri zoun′diŋ) *adj.* **1** reverberating; ringing sonorously **2** thoroughgoing; complete [a *resounding* victory] **3** high-sounding —**re·sound′ing·ly** *adv.*

re·source (rē′sôrs′, -zôrs′; ri sôrs′, -zôrs′) *n.* ⟦Fr *ressource* < OFr < *resourdre*, to arise anew < *re-*, again + *sourdre*, to spring up < L *surgere:* see SURGE⟧ **1** something that lies ready for use or that can be drawn upon for aid or to take care of a need **2** [*pl.*] available money or property; wealth; assets **3** [*pl.*] something that a country, state, etc. has and can use to its advantage [natural *resources*, including coal and oil] **4** a means of accomplishing something; measure or action that can be resorted to, as in an emergency; expedient **5** [*pl.*] a source of strength or ability within oneself: in full **inner resources** **6** ability to deal promptly and effectively with problems, difficulties, etc.; resourcefulness

SYN.—**resource** applies to any thing, person, action, etc. to which one turns for aid in time of need or emergency [what *resource* is left us?]; **resort** is usually used of a final resource, qualified as by *last* [we'll take the train as a last *resort*]; **expedient** refers to something used to effect a desired end, specifically to something used as a substitute for the usual means [the daybed was an excellent *expedient* for accommodating unexpected guests]; **makeshift** applies to a quick expedient and, as a somewhat derogatory term, connotes an inferior substitute, carelessness, etc. [she served sandwiches as a *makeshift* for dinner]; **stopgap** refers to a temporary expedient, to be replaced when the usual means is again available [he's just a *stopgap* until a new manager is appointed]

re·source·ful (ri sôrs′fəl, -zôrs′-) *adj.* able to deal creatively and effectively with problems, difficulties, etc. —**re·source′ful·ly** *adv.* —**re·source′ful·ness** *n.*

resp *abbrev.* **1** respective(ly) **2** respiration **3** respondent

re·spect (ri spekt′) *vt.* ⟦< L *respectus*, pp. of *respicere*, to look at, look back on, respect < *re-*, back + *specere*, to look at: see SPY⟧ **1** *a)* to feel or show honor or esteem for; hold in high regard *b)* to consider or treat with deference or dutiful regard **2** to show consideration for; avoid intruding upon or interfering with [to *respect* others' privacy] **3** to concern; relate to —*n.* ⟦ME *respecte* < L *respectus*, a looking at, respect, regard: pp. used as n.⟧ **1** a feeling of high regard, honor, or esteem [to have *respect* for a great artist] **2** the state or condition of being held in honor or esteem [to have the *respect* of one's sons] **3** deference or dutiful regard [*respect* for the law] **4** consideration; courteous regard [to have *respect* for the feelings of others] **5** [*pl.*] courteous expressions of regard: now chiefly in **pay one's respects**, to show polite regard by visiting or presenting oneself **6** a particular point or detail [right in every *respect*] **7** reference; relation [with *respect* to the problem] —*SYN.* REGARD —**in respect of** with reference to; as regards

resituate	**resolder**	**re-solve**	**resow**	**respeak**
resketch	**resolidification**	**re-sort**	**respace**	**respecify**
resmooth	**resolidify**	**re-sound**	**respade**	

re·spect·a·bil·i·ty (ri spek′tə bil′ə tē) ***n.**, pl.* **-ties** **1** the quality or state of being respectable **2** respectable character, reputation, or social status **3** respectable people as a group **4** [*pl.*] patterns of living or behaving regarded as respectable

re·spect·a·ble (ri spek′tə bəl) ***adj.*** ⟦ML *respectabilis*⟧ **1** worthy of respect or esteem; estimable **2** conforming to socially acceptable behavior, attitudes, taste, etc.; proper; correct **3** fairly good in quality; of moderate excellence [a *respectable* meal] **4** fairly large in size, number, or amount [a stock earning a *respectable* dividend] **5** good enough to be seen, used, etc.; presentable [a *respectable* pair of shoes] —**re·spect′a·bly** ***adv.***

re·spect·er (ri spek′tər) ***n.*** a person who respects —**respecter of persons** one whose behavior toward people is influenced by their social status, prestige, etc.: Acts (KJV) 10:34: usually used in the negative [fairly judged by one who is no *respecter of persons*]

re·spect·ful (ri spekt′fəl) ***adj.*** full of or characterized by respect; showing deference or dutiful regard —**re·spect′ful·ly** ***adv.*** —**re·spect′ful·ness** ***n.***

re·spect·ing (ri spek′tiŋ) ***prep.*** concerning; about

re·spec·tive (ri spek′tiv) ***adj.*** ⟦ML *respectivus* < L *respectus:* see RESPECT⟧ **1** as relates individually to each of two or more persons or things; several [they went their *respective* ways] **2** [Obs.] worthy of respect **3** [Obs.] heedful; attentive

re·spec·tive·ly (-lē) ***adv.*** in regard to each of two or more, in the order named [the first and second prizes went to Mary and George, *respectively*]

re·spell (rē spel′) ***vt.*** to spell again; specif., to spell (a word) in a different, usually phonetic, system so as to indicate the pronunciation

Re·spi·ghi (re spē′gē), **Ot·to·ri·no** (ôt′tô rē′nô) 1879-1936; It. composer

res·pi·ra·ble (res′pər ə bəl, ri spīr′ə bəl) ***adj.*** ⟦Fr < LL *respirabilis*⟧ **1** that is fit to be breathed **2** that can respire; capable of breathing —**res′pi·ra·bil′i·ty** ***n.***

res·pi·ra·tion (res′pə rā′shən) ***n.*** ⟦ME *respiracioun* < L *respiratio* < *respiratus,* pp.⟧ **1** act or process of respiring; breathing; inhaling and exhaling air **2** the processes by which a living organism or cell takes in oxygen from the air or water, distributes and utilizes it in oxidation, and gives off products of oxidation, esp. carbon dioxide **3** an analogous process in anaerobic organisms involving some substance other than free oxygen —**res′pi·ra′tion·al** ***adj.***

res·pi·ra·tor (res′pə rāt′ər) ***n.*** **1** any device, as of gauze, worn over the mouth and nose to prevent the inhaling of harmful substances, to warm the air breathed, etc. **2** VENTILATOR (sense 2)

res·pi·ra·to·ry (res′pər ə tôr′ē, ri spīr′ə-) ***adj.*** ⟦ML *respiratorius*⟧ of, for, or involving respiration or the respiratory system

respiratory pigment any of several colored protein substances, as hemoglobin and hemocyanin, in the circulatory system of animals and some plants, that combine reversibly with oxygen that is carried to the tissues

respiratory quotient the ratio between the volume of carbon dioxide eliminated and the volume of oxygen consumed by an animal, organism, etc. during a given period of time

respiratory system the system of organs involved in the exchange of carbon dioxide and oxygen between an organism and its environment

re·spire (ri spīr′) ***vi.*** **-spired′, -spir′ing** ⟦ME *respiren* < OFr *respirer* < L *respirare* < *re-,* back + *spirare,* to breathe: see SPIRIT⟧ **1** to breathe or carry on respiration; inhale and exhale air **2** [Old Poet.] to breathe freely or easily again, as after exertion or anxiety —***vt.*** to breathe

res·pite (res′pit) ***n.*** ⟦ME < OFr *respit* < L *respectus:* see RESPECT⟧ **1** a delay or postponement; esp., postponement of the carrying out of a death sentence; reprieve **2** an interval of temporary relief or rest, as from pain, work, or duty; lull —***vt.*** **-pit·ed, -pit·ing** to give a respite to

re·splend·ent (ri splen′dənt) ***adj.*** ⟦ME < L *resplendens,* prp. of *resplendere:* see RE- & SPLENDENT⟧ **1** shining brightly; full of splendor; dazzling **2** brilliantly showy; magnificent or sumptuous; splendid [the peacock is *resplendent* in iridescent plumage] —**re·splend′ence** ***n.***, **re·splend′en·cy** —**re·splend′ent·ly** ***adv.***

re·spond (ri spänd′) ***vi.*** ⟦ME *responden* < OFr *respondre* < L *respondere* < *re-,* back + *spondere,* to pledge: see SPONSOR⟧ **1** to answer; reply **2** to act in return, as if in answer **3** to have a positive or favorable reaction [an infection that *responded* to treatment] ☆**4** *Law* to be answerable or liable —***vt.*** to say in answer; reply —***n.*** **1** *Archit.* an engaged column, pilaster, etc. supporting an arch **2** *Eccles. former term for* RESPONSE —**SYN.** ANSWER

re·spond·ent (ri spän′dənt) ***adj.*** ⟦L *respondens,* prp.⟧ responding; answering —***n.*** **1** a person who responds **2** *Law* the party who responds to a petition, as in equity, divorce, or appellate proceedings; the defendant in such proceedings —**re·spond′ence** ***n.***, **re·spond′en·cy**

re·spond·er (-dər) ***n.*** **1** a person or thing that responds **2** *Electronics* a device that indicates reception of a signal; specif., TRANSPONDER

re·sponse (ri späns′) ***n.*** ⟦ME *respounse* < ML *respons* < L *responsum,* neut. of *responsus,* pp. of *respondere:* see RESPOND⟧ **1** something said or done in answer; reply or reaction **2** *Eccles.* *a)* a word or words used in replying to or affirming a prayer, reading, or exhortation *b)* RESPONSORY **3** *Electronics* the ratio of the output to the input, as for a given frequency, of a device or system operating under specified conditions **4** *Physiol., Psychol.* any biological reaction or behavior resulting from the application of a stimulus

re·spon·si·bil·i·ty (ri spän′sə bil′ə tē) ***n.**, pl.* **-ties** **1** condition, quality, fact, or instance of being responsible; obligation, accountability, dependability, etc. **2** a thing or person that one is responsible for

re·spon·si·ble (ri spän′sə bəl) ***adj.*** ⟦MFr < L *responsus:* see RESPONSE⟧ **1** expected or obliged to account (*for* something, *to* someone); answerable; accountable **2** involving accountability, obligation, or duties [a *responsible* position] **3** that can be charged with being the cause, agent, or source of something [the moisture that is *responsible* for the rust] **4** able to distinguish between right and wrong and to think and act rationally, and hence accountable for one's behavior **5** *a)* readily assuming obligations, duties, etc.; dependable; reliable *b)* able to pay debts or meet business obligations —**re·spon′si·ble·ness** ***n.*** —**re·spon′si·bly** ***adv.***

SYN.—**responsible** applies to one who has been delegated some duty or responsibility by one in authority and who is subject to penalty in case of default [she is *responsible* for making out the reports]; **answerable** implies a legal or moral obligation for which one must answer to someone sitting in judgment [he is not *answerable* for the crimes of his parents]; **accountable** implies liability for which one may be called to account [you will be held *accountable* for anything you may say]

re·spon·sion (ri spän′shən) ***n.*** ⟦MFr < L *responsio*⟧ **1** [Rare] a responding **2** [*pl.*] prior to 1960, the first of three examinations for the BA degree at Oxford University, England

re·spon·sive (ri spän′siv) ***adj.*** ⟦< Fr or LL: Fr *responsif* < LL *responsivus*⟧ **1** that gives or serves as an answer or response **2** *a)* reacting easily or readily to suggestion or appeal [a *responsive* audience] *b)* sensitive to, and readily reacting to, stimuli, changes, control mechanisms, etc. [a *responsive* stock market, sailboat, etc.] **3** containing or consisting of responses [*responsive* reading in church] —**re·spon′sive·ly** ***adv.*** —**re·spon′sive·ness** ***n.***

re·spon·so·ry (ri spän′sə rē) ***n.**, pl.* **-ries** ⟦ME *responsorye* < ML(Ec) *responsorium,* response (in worship)⟧ *Eccles.* a responsive verse or set of verses, esp. from the Psalms, used as in the Divine Office

res pu·bli·ca (po͞o′bli kə, pub′li-) ⟦L, lit., public thing: see REPUBLIC⟧ the state; commonwealth; republic

res·sen·ti·ment (rə sän tē män′) ***n.*** ⟦Fr, lit., resentment⟧ a feeling of bitter anger or resentment together with a sense of frustration at being powerless to express this hostility overtly

rest[1] (rest) ***n.*** ⟦ME < OE, akin to Ger *rast* < IE base **ere-,* **rē-,* rest > Gr *erōē,* rest (from battle), OE *row,* Ger *ruhe,* rest, quiet, Goth *razn,* house⟧ **1** *a)* peace, ease, and refreshment as produced by sleep *b)* sleep or repose, or a period of this **2** refreshing ease or inactivity after work or exertion **3** a period or occasion of inactivity, as during work or on a journey **4** *a)* relief from anything distressing, annoying, tiring, etc. *b)* peace of mind; mental and emotional calm; tranquillity **5** the repose of death **6** absence of motion; state of being still; immobility **7** a resting or stopping place; shelter or lodging place, as for travelers, sailors, etc. **8** a thing or device for supporting something; support: often used in comb. [a *footrest*] **9** *Music* *a)* a measured interval of silence between tones *b)* any of various symbols indicating the length of such an interval **10** *Prosody* a short pause in a line of verse; caesura —***vi.*** ⟦ME *restan* < OE *ræstan* < the n.; infl. in some senses (esp. 5) by L *restare,* to stop, remain, & the deriv. Fr *rester*⟧ **1** *a)* to get peace, ease, and refreshment by sleeping, lying down, etc. *b)* to sleep **2** to get ease and refreshment by ceasing from work or exertion **3** to be at ease or at peace; be tranquil **4** to be dead **5** to be or become quiet, still, or inactive for a while **6** to remain without change or further action [to let a matter *rest*] **7** to be, or seem to be, supported; specif., *a)* to lie, sit, or lean *b)* to be placed, based, or founded (*in, on, upon,* etc.) **8** to be placed or imposed as a burden or responsibility **9** to be or lie [the fault *rests* with him] **10** to be directed or fixed [my eyes *rested* on the picture] **11** to rely; depend **12** *Agric.* to remain unplowed or uncropped; lie fallow ☆**13** *Law* to end voluntarily the introduction of evidence in a case —***vt.*** **1** to give rest to; refresh by rest **2** to place, put, or lay for ease, support, etc. [to *rest* one's head on a pillow] **3** to base; ground [to *rest* an argument on trivialities] **4** to direct or fix (the eyes, etc.) **5** to bring to rest; stop ☆**6** *Law* to end voluntarily the introduction of evidence in (a case) —**at rest** in a state of rest; specif., *a)* asleep *b)* immobile *c)* free from distress, care, etc. *d)* dead —**lay to rest** to bury (a dead person) —**rest′er** ***n.***

musical rests

rest[2] (rest) ***n.*** ⟦ME < MFr *reste* < OFr *rester,* to rest, remain < L *restare,* to stop, stand, rest, remain < *re-,* back + *stare,* to STAND⟧ **1** what is left after part is taken away; remainder **2** [*with pl. v.*] the others Used with *the* —***vi.*** ⟦ME *resten* < OFr *rester*⟧ to go on being; continue to be; remain (as specified) [*rest* assured that we will go] —***vt.*** [Obs.] to cause to remain; keep ["God *rest* ye merry, gentlemen"]

rest[3] (rest) ***n.*** ⟦ME aphetic, var. of *arest,* an ARREST⟧ a support for the butt of a lance, projecting from the side of the breastplate in medieval armor

rest area a basic service area, esp. on an expressway, providing restrooms, parking space for resting in one's car, and, often, vending machines

re·state (rē stāt′) ***vt.*** **-stat′ed, -stat′ing** to state again, esp. in a different way —**re·state′ment** ***n.***

☆**res·tau·rant** (res′tə ränt′, -rənt; res′tränt′) ***n.*** ⟦Fr, substantive use of prp. of *restaurer:* see RESTORE⟧ a place where meals can be bought and eaten

resplice
resplit
respread
restabilize
restaff
restage
restamp
restart

res·tau·ra·teur (res′tə rə tʉr′, -to͝or′) ***n.*** ⟦Fr < MFr, that which restores < ML *restaurator,* one who restores⟧ a person who owns or operates a restaurant: also **res·tau·ran·teur** (res′tə rän tʉr′, -to͝or′)

rest cure a treatment, as for nervous disorders, consisting of complete rest, often with special diet, etc.

rest·ful (rest′fəl) ***adj.*** **1** full of or giving rest **2** at rest; quiet; peaceful **3** having a soothing or peaceful effect [*restful* colors] —***SYN.*** COMFORTABLE —**rest′ful·ly** ***adv.*** —**rest′ful·ness** ***n.***

rest·har·row (rest′har′ō) ***n.*** ⟦ME *rest,* contr. < *arest* (see ARREST) + HARROW[1]: the tough roots obstruct the harrow⟧ any of a genus (*Ononis*) of leguminous, Old World plants with clusters of white, pink, or yellow flowers

rest home a residence equipped and staffed to provide general care, as for aged persons or convalescents

res·ti·form (res′tə fôrm′) ***adj.*** ⟦ModL *restiformis* < L *restis,* rope (for IE base see RUSH[2]) + *-formis,* -FORM⟧ ropelike or cordlike; specif., designating either of two cordlike bundles of nerve fibers (**restiform bodies**) connecting the medulla oblongata with each hemisphere of the cerebellum

rest·ing (res′tiŋ) ***adj.*** **1** being in a state of rest; quiescent **2** *Biol.* remaining dormant for a period of time, as certain spores or eggs **3** *Cytology* not actively dividing: said of a cell, cell nucleus, etc.

res·ti·tu·tion (res′tə to͞o′shən, -tyo͞o′-) ***n.*** ⟦ME < MFr < L *restitutio* < *restitutus,* pp. of *restituere,* to set up again, restore < *re-,* again + *statuere,* to set up: see STATUE⟧ **1** a giving back to the rightful owner of something that has been lost or taken away; restoration **2** a making good for loss or damage; reimbursement **3** a return to a former condition or situation **4** *Physics* the recovery of its shape by an elastic body after pressure or strain is released —***SYN.*** REPARATION —**res′ti·tu′tive** ***adj.***

res·tive (res′tiv) ***adj.*** ⟦ME *restyfe* < OFr *restif* < *rester:* see REST[2]⟧ **1** refusing to go forward; balky, as a horse **2** hard to control; unruly; refractory **3** nervous or impatient under pressure or restraint; restless; unsettled —***SYN.*** CONTRARY —**res′tive·ly** ***adv.*** —**res′tive·ness** ***n.***

rest·less (rest′lis) ***adj.*** **1** characterized by inability to rest or relax; uneasy; unquiet **2** having or giving no rest or relaxation; disturbed or disturbing [*restless* sleep] **3** never or almost never quiet or still; always active or inclined to action **4** seeking change; discontented —**rest′less·ly** ***adv.*** —**rest′less·ness** ***n.***

rest mass *Physics* the mass of a body when its velocity is zero: according to one view of the special theory of relativity, an object's mass increases as its speed increases

Rest of Esther a book of the Old Testament Apocrypha consisting of verses in the Septuagint text of the book of Esther that are not in the Hebrew text

res·to·ra·tion (res′tə rā′shən) ***n.*** ⟦ME *restauration* < MFr < LL *restauratio*⟧ **1** a restoring or being restored; specif., *a)* reinstatement in a former position, rank, etc. *b)* restitution for loss, damage, etc. *c)* a putting or bringing back into a former, normal, or unimpaired state or condition **2** a representation or reconstruction of the original form or structure, as of a building, fossil animal, etc. **3** something restored —**the Restoration 1** the reestablishment of the monarchy in England in 1660 under Charles II **2** the period of the reign of Charles II (1660-85): sometimes taken as including the reign of James II (1685-88)

re·stor·a·tive (ri stôr′ə tiv) ***adj.*** ⟦ME *restoratif* < MFr < ML *restaurativus*⟧ **1** of restoration **2** tending to restore or capable of restoring; esp., capable of restoring health, strength, consciousness, etc. —***n.*** something that restores; esp., something that restores to consciousness, as smelling salts

re·store (ri stôr′) ***vt.*** **-stored′**, **-stor′ing** ⟦ME *restoren* < OFr *restorer* < L *restaurare* < *re-,* again + *-staurare,* to place, erect: see STORE⟧ **1** to give back (something taken away, lost, etc.); make restitution of **2** to bring back to a former or normal condition, as by repairing, rebuilding, altering, etc. [to *restore* a building, painting, etc.] **3** to put (a person) back in a place, position, rank, etc. [to *restore* a king to his throne] **4** to bring back to health, strength, etc. **5** to bring back into being, use, etc.; reestablish [to *restore* order, a system of government, etc.] —***SYN.*** RENEW —**re·stor′a·ble** ***adj.*** —**re·stor′er** ***n.***

restr *abbrev.* restaurant

re·strain (ri strān′) ***vt.*** ⟦ME *restreinen* < OFr *restreindre* < L *restringere* < *re-,* back + *stringere,* to draw tight: see STRICT⟧ **1** to hold back from action; check; suppress; curb **2** to keep under control **3** to deprive of physical liberty, as by shackling, arresting, etc. **4** to limit; restrict —**re·strain′a·ble** ***adj.*** —**re·strain′ed·ly** ***adv.***

SYN.—**restrain**, the term of broadest application in this list, suggests the use of strong force or authority either in preventing, or in suppressing and controlling, some action [try to *restrain* your zeal]; **curb**, **check**, and **bridle** derive their current implications from the various uses of a horse's harness, **curb** implying a sudden, sharp action to bring something under control [to *curb* one's tongue], **check** implying a slowing up of action or progress [to *check* inflationary trends], and **bridle** suggesting a holding in of emotion, feelings, etc. [to *bridle* one's envy]; **inhibit**, as used in psychology, implies a suppressing or repressing of some action, thought, or emotion [her natural verve had become *inhibited*] —***ANT.*** **free**

re·strained (ri strānd′) ***adj.*** characterized by restraint; exercising, or showing the results of, self-discipline or rational control; controlled

re·strain·er (ri strā′nər) ***n.*** **1** a person or thing that restrains **2** *Photog.* a chemical, such as potassium bromide, added to a developer to retard its action

restraining circle 1 any of three circles on the floor of a basketball court used for jump balls: other players must remain outside the circle during a jump ball **2** any of five circles similarly used for face-offs in ice hockey

restraining order a court order demanding cessation of a specified activity; specif., such an order demanding that a person stop bothering or harassing another

re·straint (ri strānt′) ***n.*** ⟦ME *restreinte* < OFr *restrainte* < *restreindre,* to RESTRAIN⟧ **1** a restraining or being restrained **2** a restraining influence or action **3** a means or instrument of restraining **4** a loss or limitation of liberty **5** control of emotions, impulses, etc.; reserve; constraint

restraint of trade interruption of the free movement of goods in commerce; restriction or prevention of business competition, as by monopoly, price fixing, etc.

re·strict (ri strikt′) ***vt.*** ⟦< L *restrictus,* pp. of *restringere:* see RESTRAIN⟧ to keep within certain limits; put certain limitations on; confine —***SYN.*** LIMIT

re·strict·ed (ri strik′tid) ***adj.*** limited; confined; specif., ☆*a)* limited to authorized personnel (said of documents, data, etc.) ☆*b)* excluding a certain group or groups; esp., limited to white gentiles —**re·strict′ed·ly** ***adv.***

re·stric·tion (ri strik′shən) ***n.*** ⟦ME *restriccion* < MFr *restriction* < L *restrictio*⟧ **1** a restricting or being restricted **2** something that restricts; limitation

restriction enzyme any of various enzymes that chemically break DNA into strands at specific locations

re·stric·tion·ism (-īz′əm) ***n.*** the policy of favoring restriction, as of trade, immigration, etc. —**re·stric′tion·ist** ***n., adj.***

re·stric·tive (ri strik′tiv) ***adj.*** ⟦ME < MFr *restrictif*⟧ **1** restricting or tending to restrict; limiting [*restrictive* regulations] **2** *Gram.* designating a modifier, as a word, phrase, or subordinate clause, that limits the reference of the word or phrase it modifies and thus is essential to the meaning of a sentence: it is not set off by punctuation ["who laughed" in "the person who laughed is my friend" is a *restrictive* relative clause]: cf. NONRESTRICTIVE —**re·stric′tive·ly** ***adv.*** —**re·stric′tive·ness** ***n.***

☆**restrictive covenant** a provision that restricts the action of a party to an agreement, as any covenant (unenforceable by law) seeking to prevent the sale of real estate to a member of a specified minority group

☆**rest·room** (rest′ro͞om′) ***n.*** a room or rooms, as in an office building, sports arena, or restaurant, equipped with toilets, washbowls, etc.: also **rest room**

re·struc·ture (rē struk′chər) ***vt.*** **-tured**, **-tur·ing** **1** to provide a new structure or organization for; specif., to change the structure of (a corporation), as by consolidating operations, shutting down unprofitable divisions, etc. **2** to alter the terms of (a contract or agreement) after it has gone into effect [to *restructure* a loan by lengthening the payment period]

rest stop 1 SERVICE PLAZA **2** REST AREA

re·sult (ri zult′) ***vi.*** ⟦ME *resulten* < ML *resultare* < L, to spring back, rebound, freq. of *resilire,* to leap back: see RESILE⟧ **1** to happen or issue as a consequence or effect: often with *from* [floods *resulting* from heavy rains] **2** to end as a consequence (*in* something) [heavy rains *resulting* in floods] —***n.*** **1** *a)* anything that comes about as a consequence or outcome of some action, process, etc. *b)* [*pl.*] the consequence or consequences desired **2** the number, quantity, etc. obtained by mathematical calculation; answer to a problem —***SYN.*** EFFECT, FOLLOW

re·sult·ant (ri zult′'nt) ***adj.*** ⟦L *resultans,* prp.⟧ **1** that results; following as a consequence **2** resulting from two or more forces or agents acting together —***n.*** **1** something that results; result **2** *Physics* a force, velocity, etc. with an effect equal to that of two or more such forces, etc. acting together —**re·sult′ant·ly** ***adv.***

re·sume (ri zo͞om′, -zyo͞om′) ***vt.*** **-sumed′**, **-sum′ing** ⟦ME *resumen,* to assume < MFr *resumer* < L *resumere* < *re-,* again + *sumere,* to take: see CONSUME⟧ **1** *a)* to take, get, or occupy again [to *resume* one's seat] *b)* to take back or take on again [to *resume* a former name] **2** to begin again or go on with again after interruption [to *resume* a conversation] **3** to summarize or make a résumé of —***vi.*** to begin again or go on again after interruption —**re·sum′a·ble** ***adj.***

ré·su·mé (rez′ə mā′; *for 1, also* rā′zo͞o mā′, -zyo͞o-) ***n.*** ⟦Fr, pp. of *résumer:* see prec.⟧ **1** a summing up; summary ☆**2** a statement of a job applicant's previous employment experience, education, etc.: also written **resume** or **resumé**

re·sump·tion (ri zump′shən) ***n.*** ⟦ME *resumpcioun* < L *resumptio* < *resumptus,* pp. of *resumere*⟧ the act of resuming

re·su·pi·nate (ri so͞o′pə nāt′, -syo͞o′-) ***adj.*** ⟦L *resupinatus,* pp. of *resupinare,* to bend back < *re-,* back + *supinus,* SUPINE⟧ *Bot.* having an upside-down appearance, as the flower of an orchid; inverted —**re·su′pi·na′tion** ***n.***

re·su·pine (rē′so͞o pīn′, -syo͞o-) ***adj.*** ⟦L *resupinus,* back-form. < *resupinare:* see prec.⟧ SUPINE (sense 1)

☆**re·sur·face** (rē sʉr′fis) ***vt.*** **-faced**, **-fac·ing** to put a new surface on —***vi.*** **1** to come to the surface again **2** to reappear or become known again after a

resterilize	**restraighten**	**restretch**	**restuff**	**resubmit**
restimulate	**re-strain**	**restrike**	**restyle**	**resubscribe**
restitch	**restratify**	**restring**	**resubject**	**resummon**
restock	**restrengthen**	**restudy**	**resubmerge**	**resupply**

period of absence or obscurity [after years in retirement, he *resurfaced* in TV commercials]

re·surge (ri surj′) *vi.* **-surged′, -surg′ing 1** ⟦L *resurgere,* to rise again, in LL(Ec), to rise from the grave: see RE- & SURGE⟧ to rise again; be resurrected **2** ⟦RE- + SURGE⟧ to surge back again

re·sur·gent (-sur′jənt) *adj.* ⟦L *resurgens,* prp.⟧ rising or tending to rise again; resurging —**re·sur′gence** *n.*

res·ur·rect (rez′ə rekt′) *vt.* ⟦back-form. < fol.⟧ **1** to raise from the dead or the grave; bring back to life **2** to bring back into notice, practice, use, etc. —*vi.* to rise from the dead

res·ur·rec·tion (rez′ə rek′shən) *n.* ⟦ME *resurreccion* < OFr *resurrection* < LL(Ec) *resurrectio* < L *resurrectus,* pp. of *resurgere:* see RESURGE⟧ **1** *a)* a rising from the dead, or coming back to life *b)* the state of having risen from the dead **2** a coming back into notice, practice, use, etc.; revival, as of old customs —**the Resurrection** *Theol.* **1** the rising of Jesus from the dead after his death and burial **2** the rising of all the dead at the Last Judgment —**res′ur·rec′tion·al** *adj.*

res·ur·rec·tion·ism (-ĭz′əm) *n.* the stealing of bodies from graves, esp. for dissection

res·ur·rec·tion·ist (-ist) *n.* **1** [Historical] BODY SNATCHER **2** a person who brings something back into use or notice again

☆**resurrection plant 1** any of various small plants which curl up when dry and spread their branches or become green again when watered, including several lycopods (genus *Selaginella*) **2** ROSE OF JERICHO

re·sus·ci·tate (ri sus′ə tāt′) *vt.* **-tat′ed, -tat′ing** ⟦< L *resuscitatus,* pp. of *resuscitare,* to revive < *re-,* again + *suscitare,* to raise up, revive < *sus-,* for *sub-,* SUB- + *citare,* to arouse: see CITE⟧ to revive or revitalize; bring back to life; esp., to revive (someone in a faint, apparently dead, etc.), as by artificial respiration —*vi.* to revive, esp. to come back to life or consciousness again —**re·sus′ci·ta′tion** *n.* —**re·sus′ci·ta′tive** *adj.*

re·sus·ci·ta·tor (-tāt′ər) *n.* a person or thing that resuscitates; esp., an apparatus for giving artificial respiration by forcing air or oxygen into the lungs

res·ver·a·trol (rez vir′ə trôl′) *n.* ⟦< RES(INOUS) + VERATR(UM) + -OL[1]⟧ an antimicrobial substance, $C_{14}H_{12}O_3$, that occurs naturally in some plants, fruits, and seeds and acts as an antioxidant

ret[1] (ret) *vt.* **ret′ted, ret′ting** ⟦ME *retten, reten* < MDu *reten, reeten* < IE **reud-:* see ROTTEN⟧ to dampen or soak (flax, hemp, timber, etc.) in water in order to separate the fibers from the woody tissue

ret[2] *abbrev.* **1** retail **2** retain **3** retired **4** return(ed)

re·ta·ble (ri tā′bəl) *n.* ⟦Fr < Sp *retablo* < *re-,* behind (< L *re-,* back) + *tabla,* shelf < L *tabula:* see TABLE⟧ GRADINE (sense 2)

re·tail (rē′tāl′; *for vt. 2, usually* ri tāl′) *n.* ⟦ME *retaile* < OFr *retaille,* lit., a cutting < *retailler,* to cut up < *re-,* again + *tailler,* to cut: see TAILOR⟧ the sale of goods or articles individually or in small quantities directly to the consumer: cf. WHOLESALE —*adj.* **1** of, connected with, or engaged in the sale of goods at retail **2** designating or of a banking or financial institution providing services to, or primarily to, consumers, rather than to corporations or to other banks [a *retail* broker, *retail* lending] —*adv.* in relatively small quantities or at a retail price —*vt.* ⟦ME *retaylen*⟧ **1** to sell individually or in small quantities; sell directly to the consumer **2** to repeat or pass on (gossip, secrets, etc.) to others —*vi.* to be sold at retail [books that *retail* at a dollar] —**at retail** directly to the consumer at retail prices —**re′tail′er** *n.*

re·tain (ri tān′) *vt.* ⟦ME *reteynen* < OFr *retenir* < LL **retenere,* for L *retinere* < *re-,* back + *tenere,* to hold: see THIN⟧ **1** to hold or keep in possession **2** to keep in a fixed state or condition **3** to continue to have or hold in [to *retain* heat] **4** to continue to practice, use, etc. **5** to keep in mind **6** to hire, or arrange in advance for the services of, by paying a retainer ☆**7** *Educ.* to require (a student who has failed) to repeat a grade in school —**re·tain′a·ble** *adj.* —**re·tain′ment** *n.*

retained object *Gram.* an object in a passive construction that is the same as the direct or indirect object in the corresponding active construction (Ex.: "money" in "He was given the money by me")

re·tain·er[1] (ri tān′ər) *n.* **1** a person or thing that retains **2** a person serving another, esp. someone of rank; servant, attendant, adherent, etc. **3** any of several devices used to retain; specif., *a)* a groove, frame, etc. within which roller bearings are held *b)* a device designed to hold teeth in position after they have been adjusted by orthodontics

re·tain·er[2] (ri tān′ər) *n.* ⟦ME *reteyner:* see RETAIN & -ER, sense 3⟧ *Law* **1** the act of engaging the services of a lawyer, consultant, etc. **2** a fee paid in advance to make such services available when needed —**on retainer** hired, engaged, etc. by a RETAINER[2] (sense 2): said as of a lawyer

retaining wall a wall built to keep a bank of earth from sliding, or from being eroded as by an adjacent stream

re·take (rē tāk′; *for n.* rē′tāk′) *vt.* **-took′, -tak′en, -tak′ing 1** to take again, take back, or recapture ☆**2** to photograph again —*n.* **1** a retaking ☆**2** a film or video scene rephotographed or to be rephotographed

re·tal·i·ate (ri tal′ē āt′) *vi.* **-at′ed, -at′ing** ⟦< LL *retaliatus,* pp. of *retaliare,* to require, retaliate < L *re-,* back + *talio,* punishment in kind (see TALION), akin to Welsh *tāl,* compensation⟧ to return like for like; esp., to return evil for evil; pay back injury for injury —*vt.* to return an injury, wrong, etc. for (an injury, wrong, etc. given); requite in kind —**re·tal′i·a′tion** *n.* —**re·tal′i·a′tive** *adj.*, **re·tal′i·a·to′ry** (-tal′yə tôr′ē, -tal′ē ə-)

re·tard (ri tärd′; *for n. 2* rē′tärd′) *vt.* ⟦LME *retarden* < OFr *retarder* < L *retardare* < *re-,* back + *tardare,* to make slow < *tardus,* slow: see TARDY⟧ to hinder, delay, or slow the advance or progress of —*vi.* to be delayed or undergo retardation —*n.* **1** a retarding; delay **2** [Slang] *a)* a retarded person (an offensive term of contempt) *b)* a stupid or foolish person (considered somewhat offensive by many)

re·tard·ant (ri tärd′′nt) *n.* something that retards; esp., a substance that delays a chemical reaction —*adj.* that retards or tends to retard

☆**re·tard·ate** (ri tär′dāt′) *n.* ⟦< L *retardatus,* pp. of *retardare,* to RETARD⟧ a mentally retarded person: term now sometimes considered offensive

re·tar·da·tion (rē′tär dā′shən) *n.* ⟦ME < L *retardatio*⟧ **1** a retarding or being retarded **2** something that retards; hindrance **3** *short for* MENTAL RETARDATION **4** a decrease in velocity **5** the degree to which something is retarded —**re·tard·a·tive** (ri tär′də tiv) *adj.*, **re·tard′a·to′ry** (-tôr′ē)

re·tard·ed (-tär′did) *adj.* **1** slowed or delayed in development or progress **2** having or characteristic of MENTAL RETARDATION: term now sometimes considered offensive **3** [Slang] inept, ineffectual, pathetic, etc.: a general term of contempt or derision considered offensive by many because of the word's traditional medical use

re·tard·er (ri tär′dər) *n.* something that retards, as a substance used to delay a chemical reaction

retch (rech) *vi.* ⟦ME **rechen* < OE *hrǣcan,* to clear the throat, hawk < *hraca,* clearing of the throat, spittle < IE echoic base **ker-* > RING[1], RAVEN[1]⟧ to undergo the straining action of vomiting, esp. without bringing anything up

retd *abbrev.* **1** retained **2** retired **3** returned

re·te (rēt′ē) *n., pl.* **re·ti·a** (rēt′ē ə; rē′shə, -shē ə) ⟦ME *riet* < L *rete,* net: see RETINA⟧ *Anat.* a network or plexus, as of blood vessels or nerve fibers

re·tem (rē′tem) *n.* ⟦Ar *ratam,* collective of *ratana*⟧ a leguminous desert shrub (*Retama raetam*) with small, white flowers: the juniper of the Bible

re·tene (rē′tēn, ret′ēn) *n.* ⟦< Gr *rhētinē,* RESIN⟧ a hydrocarbon, $C_{18}H_{18}$, obtained from resinous woods and fossil resins

re·ten·tion (ri ten′shən) *n.* ⟦ME *retencioun* < MFr *retention* < L *retentio*⟧ **1** a retaining or being retained **2** power of or capacity for retaining **3** *a)* a remembering; memory *b)* ability to remember **4** *Med.* the retaining within the body of matter normally excreted

re·ten·tive (-tiv) *adj.* ⟦ME *retentif* < MFr < LL *retentivus*⟧ **1** retaining or tending to retain **2** having the power of or capacity for retaining **3** *a)* tenacious [a *retentive* memory] *b)* having a good memory —**re·ten′tive·ly** *adv.* —**re·ten′tive·ness** *n.*

re·ten·tiv·i·ty (rē′ten tiv′ə tē) *n.* **1** the power of or capacity for retaining **2** the power of remaining magnetized after the force of magnetization has stopped

re·think (rē thiŋk′) *vt.* **-thought′, -think′ing** to think over again, with a view to changing; reconsider

re·ti·a·ri·us (rē′shē er′ē əs) *n., pl.* **-ri·i′** (-ī′) ⟦L < *rete,* net: see RETINA⟧ in ancient Rome, a gladiator armed with a piece of netting and a trident

re·ti·ar·y (rē′shē er′ē) *adj.* ⟦< L *rete,* net (see RETINA) + -ARY⟧ **1** of or like nets or net-making **2** building nets, as certain spiders **3** armed with a net

ret·i·cence (ret′ə səns) *n.* ⟦< Fr or L: Fr *réticence* < L *reticentia*⟧ the quality or state, or an instance, of being reticent; reserve: also **ret′i·cen·cy**

ret·i·cent (-sənt) *adj.* ⟦L *reticens,* prp. of *reticere,* to be silent < *re-,* again + *tacere,* to be silent: see TACIT⟧ **1** silent or uncommunicative; disinclined to speak readily, often, specif., habitually so **2** having a restrained, quiet, or understated quality —**ret′i·cent·ly** *adv.*

ret·i·cle (ret′ə kəl) *n.* ⟦L *reticulum:* see RETICULE⟧ *Optics* a network of very fine lines, wires, etc. in the focus of the eyepiece of an optical instrument

re·tic·u·lar (ri tik′yə lər) *adj.* ⟦ModL *reticularis* < L *reticulum:* see RETICULE⟧ **1** of or like a net; netlike **2** intricate; entangled —**re·tic′u·lar·ly** *adv.*

re·tic·u·late (-lit; *also, and for v. always,* -lāt′) *adj.* ⟦L *reticulatus* < *reticulum:* see RETICULE⟧ **1** like a net or network; netlike **2** *Bot.* having the veins arranged like the threads of a net: said of leaves Also **re·tic′u·lat′ed** —*vt.* **-lat′ed, -lat′ing** to divide or mark so as to look like network —*vi.* to be divided or marked like network —**re·tic′u·late·ly** *adv.*

re·tic·u·la·tion (ri tik′yə lā′shən) *n.* ⟦ML *reticulatio*⟧ a reticulate arrangement, formation, or pattern; network

ret·i·cule (ret′ə kyo͞ol′) *n.* ⟦Fr *réticule* < L *reticulum,* dim. of *rete,* net: see RETINA⟧ **1** a woman's small handbag, originally made of netting and usually having a drawstring **2** RETICLE

re·tic·u·lo·cyte (ri tik′yə lō sīt′) *n.* ⟦ModL < L *reticulum* (see prec.) + -CYTE⟧ a young circulating erythrocyte showing a network of fibers in the cell when stained —**re·tic′u·lo·cyt′ic** (-sit′ik) *adj.*

re·tic·u·lo·en·do·the·li·al (-en′də thē′lē əl) *adj.* ⟦< ModL *reticulum* (see RETICULE) + ENDOTHELIAL⟧ designating or of the system of macrophages found in the bone marrow, liver, spleen, etc., including all the phagocytic cells except the granular leukocytes: they can take up certain dyes, bacteria, etc.

re·tic·u·lum (ri tik′yə ləm) *n., pl.* for 1, 3, & 4, **-la** (-lə) ⟦L: see RETICULE⟧ **1** a netlike pattern or structure; network **2** [**R-**] a S constellation between Dorado and Horologium **3** *Biol.* any network or netlike structure, as the weblike structure found in the protoplasm of many cells **4** *Zool.* the second chamber of the stomach of cud-chewing animals, as cows

---

resurvey	**retabulate**	**retax**	**retelevise**	**retest**
reswallow	**retack**	**reteach**	**retell**	**retestify**
resynthesize	**retape**	**retear**	**retemper**	**rethread**

re·ti·form (rēt′ə fôrm′, ret′-) ***adj.*** ⟦ModL *retiformis* < L *rete,* net (see fol.) + *-formis,* -FORM⟧ having crisscrossed lines; netlike in form; reticulate

ret·i·na (ret′'n ə) ***n.,*** *pl.* **-nas** or **-nae′** (-ē′) ⟦ML, prob. < L *rete* (gen. *retis*), net < IE base **ere-,* loose, separate > Gr *erēmos,* solitary, Lith *rẽtis,* sieve, & (prob.) L *rarus,* rare⟧ the innermost coat lining the interior of the eyeball, containing various layers of photoreceptive cells that are directly connected to the brain by means of the optic nerve

Ret·in-A (ret′'n ā′) *trademark for* a substance containing tretinoin, used especially in the treatment of acne

ret·i·nac·u·lum (ret′'n ak′yə ləm) ***n.,*** *pl.* **-la** (-lə) ⟦ModL < L, that which holds back, tether < *retinere,* to RETAIN + dim. suffix⟧ *Biol.* an often hooked or sticky structure, band, etc. serving to hold parts, seeds, eggs, etc. together or in place —**ret′i·nac′u·lar** (-lər) ***adj.***

ret·i·nal (ret′'n əl) ***adj.*** ⟦RETIN(A) + -AL (sense 1)⟧ of or related to a retina —***n.*** ⟦RETIN(A) + -AL (sense 3*a*)⟧ *Biochem.* **1** a yellowish carotenoid, $C_{20}H_{28}O$, liberated when rhodopsin or iodopsin is transformed by the action of light **2** a similar carotenoid, $C_{20}H_{26}O$, formed by the action of light on porphyropsin

ret·ine (ret′ēn) ***n.*** ⟦RET(ARD) + -INE[3]⟧ a substance found in animal cells in minute amounts, that retards growth and cell division: cf. PROMINE

ret·i·nene (ret′'n ēn′) ***n.*** ⟦RETIN(A) + -ENE⟧ *Biochem.* RETINAL

ret·i·ni·tis (ret′'n īt′is) ***n.*** ⟦ModL: see RETINA & -ITIS⟧ inflammation of the retina

retinitis pig·men·to·sa (pig men tō′sə) ⟦ModL < *pigmentosa,* fem. of *pigmentosus,* pigmentary < *pigmentum,* paint, PIGMENT; see prec.⟧ an inherited, incurable eye disease that gradually destroys the retina and optic nerve, slowly reducing the field of vision until total blindness occurs

ret·i·no·blas·to·ma (ret′'n ō blas tō′mə) ***n.,*** *pl.* **-mas** or **-ma·ta** (-mə tə) a rare, often inherited, malignant tumor that forms in the retina, usually of a young child

ret·i·no·ic acid (ret′'n ō′ik) ⟦so named as a chemical derivative of RETINOL⟧ a vitamin A derivative, $C_{20}H_{28}O_2$, used in the treatment of acne, skin wrinkles, etc.

ret·i·noid (ret′'n oid′) ***n.*** ⟦fol. + -OID (sense 2)⟧ any of a large class of natural or synthetic, photosensitive chemical compounds that are similar to vitamin A, including retinoic acid and retinal

ret·i·nol (ret′'n ôl′, -äl′, -ōl′) ***n.*** ⟦RETIN(A) + -OL[1]: it is necessary for adequate night vision⟧ VITAMIN A

ret·i·nop·a·thy (ret′'n äp′ə thē) ***n.,*** *pl.* **-thies** any disease, inflammation, etc. of the retina

ret·i·nos·co·py (ret′'n äs′kə pē) ***n.*** ⟦< RETINA + -SCOPY⟧ a method for checking the proper refraction of the eye, in which the retina is illuminated with a retinoscope and observations of the reflected light rays are made —**ret′i·no·scop′ic** (-ə skäp′ik) ***adj.*** —**ret′in·o·scope′** (ret′'n ə skōp′) ***n.***

ret·i·nue (ret′'n o͞o′, -yo͞o′) ***n.*** ⟦ME *retenue* < OFr, fem. of *retenu,* pp. of *retenir:* see RETAIN⟧ a body of assistants, followers, or servants attending a person of rank or importance; train of attendants or retainers

re·tire (ri tīr′) ***vi.*** **-tired′, -tir′ing** ⟦Fr *retirer* < *re-,* back + *tirer,* to draw < VL **tirare*⟧ **1** to go away, retreat, or withdraw to a private, sheltered, or secluded place **2** to go to bed **3** to give ground, as in battle; retreat; withdraw **4** to give up one's work, business, career, etc., esp. because of advanced age **5** to move back or away, or seem to do so —***vt.*** **1** to withdraw or move in retreat [*to retire* troops from an action] **2** *a)* to take (money) out of circulation *b)* to take up or pay off (stocks, bonds, bills, etc.) **3** to cause to retire from a position, job, or office **4** to withdraw from use [*to retire* outdated machinery] ☆**5** *Baseball* to end the batting turn of (a batter, side, etc.) by putting the batter, side, etc. out

re·tired (ri tīrd′) ***adj.*** **1** withdrawn or apart from the world; in seclusion; secluded **2** *a)* having given up one's work, business, career, etc., esp. because of advanced age *b)* of or for such retired persons

☆**re·tir·ee** (ri tīr′ē′) ***n.*** a person who has retired from work, business, etc.: also **re·tir′ant** (-ənt)

re·tire·ment (ri tīr′mənt) ***n.*** **1** a retiring or being retired; specif., withdrawal from work, business, etc. because of age **2** *a)* privacy; seclusion *b)* a place of privacy or seclusion —***adj.*** of, having to do with, or for retirement or retired persons [*a retirement* community]

re·tir·ing (ri tīr′iŋ) ***adj.*** **1** that retires **2** drawing back from contact with others, from publicity, etc.; reserved; shy —**re·tir′ing·ly** ***adv.***

re·took (rē to͝ok′) ***vt.*** *pt. of* RETAKE

☆**re·tool** (rē to͞ol′) ***vt., vi.*** **1** to adapt the machinery of (a factory) to the manufacture of a different product by changing the tools and dies **2** to reorganize to meet new or different needs or conditions

re·tor·sion (ri tôr′shən) ***n.*** ⟦var. of RETORTION⟧ *Law* a retaliation; reprisal; esp., in international law, mistreatment by one country of the citizens or subjects of another in retaliation for similar mistreatment received

re·tort[1] (ri tôrt′) ***vt.*** ⟦< L *retortus,* pp. of *retorquere,* to twist back < *re-,* back + *torquere,* to twist: see TORT⟧ **1** to turn (an insult, epithet, deed, etc.) back upon the person from whom it came **2** to answer (an argument, etc.) in kind **3** to say in reply or response —***vi.*** to reply, esp. in a sharp, quick, or witty way, or in kind —***n.*** **1** a quick, sharp, or witty reply, esp. one that turns the words of the previous speaker back upon that speaker **2** the act or practice of making such a reply —***SYN.*** ANSWER

re·tort[2] (ri tôrt′) ***n.*** ⟦Fr *retorte* < ML *retorta* < L, fem. of *retortus* (see prec.): so called because its long neck is bent downward⟧ **1** a container, generally of glass and with a long tube, in which substances are distilled, as in a laboratory **2** a vessel in which ore is heated to extract a metal, coal is heated to produce gas, etc.

re·tor·tion (ri tôr′shən) ***n.*** ⟦ML *retortio* < L *retortus:* see RETORT[1]⟧ **1** a turning, bending, or twisting back or being turned, bent, or twisted back **2** RETORSION

re·touch (rē tuch′; *for n., also* rē′tuch′) ***vt.*** ⟦Fr *retoucher:* see RE- & TOUCH⟧ **1** to touch up or change details in (a painting, essay, etc.) in order to improve it **2** *Photog.* to change (a negative or print) by adding details or removing blemishes, etc. —***n.*** **1** the act or process of retouching **2** a detail that is changed in retouching **3** something, as a photograph, that has been retouched —**re·touch′er** ***n.***

re·trace (ri trās′) ***vt.*** **-traced′, -trac′ing** ⟦Fr *retracer:* see RE- & TRACE[1]⟧ **1** to go back over again, esp. in the reverse direction [*to retrace* one's steps] **2** to trace again the story of, from the beginning **3** to go over again visually or in memory —**re·trace′a·ble** ***adj.***

re-trace (rē trās′) ***vt.*** **-traced′, -trac′ing** to trace (a drawing, engraving, etc.) over again

re·tract (ri trakt′) ***vt., vi.*** ⟦ME *retracten:* in sense 1 < L *retractus,* pp. of *retrahere,* to draw back < *re-,* back + *trahere,* to DRAW; in sense 2 < MFr *retracter* < L *retractare,* to draw back, withdraw < *re-,* back + *tractare,* to pull, draw, freq. of *trahere*⟧ **1** to draw back or in [*to retract* claws]: cf. PROTRACT (sense 3) **2** to withdraw or disavow (a statement, promise, offer, charge, etc.); recant —**re·tract′a·bil′i·ty** ***n.*** —**re·tract′a·ble** ***adj.*** —**re·trac′tive** ***adj.***

re·trac·tile (ri trak′təl, -tīl′) ***adj.*** ⟦Fr *rétractile*⟧ **1** that can be retracted, or drawn back or in: said as of the claws of a cat **2** of retraction [*retractile* power] —**re·trac·til·i·ty** (rē′trak til′ə tē) ***n.***

re·trac·tion (ri trak′shən) ***n.*** ⟦ME *retraccion* < LL *retractio*⟧ **1** a retracting or being retracted; specif., *a)* withdrawal, as of a statement, promise, charge, etc. *b)* a drawing or being drawn back or in **2** power of retracting

re·trac·tor (-tər) ***n.*** a person or thing that retracts; esp., *a)* a muscle that retracts an organ, protruded part, etc. *b)* a surgical instrument or device for drawing back a part or organ, as the flesh at the edge of an incision

re·tral (rē′trəl) ***adj.*** ⟦< L *retro,* backward + -AL⟧ at, near, or toward the back; posterior —**re′tral·ly** ***adv.***

re·tread (rē tred′; *for n.* rē′tred′) ***vt.*** RECAP[1] —***n.*** **1** RECAP[1] ☆**2** [Slang] a person who is called back or returns to service, esp. military service

re-tread (rē tred′) ***vt.*** **-trod′, -trod′den** or **-trod′, -tread′ing** to tread again

re·treat (ri trēt′) ***n.*** ⟦ME *retret* < OFr *retraite* < pp. of *retraire,* to draw back < L *retrahere:* see RETRACT⟧ **1** a going back or backward; withdrawal in the face of opposition or from a dangerous or unpleasant situation **2** withdrawal to a safe or private place **3** a safe, quiet, or secluded place **4** *a)* a period of retirement or seclusion, for an individual or a group, for prayer, study, spiritual renewal, etc. *b)* an organized group withdrawal from regular activities for a given purpose, as by colleagues meeting away from the office and engaging in exercises for promoting teamwork, creativity, etc. **5** a residential institution for the care of the aged, mentally ill, etc. **6** *Mil.* *a)* the withdrawal of troops, ships, etc. from a position, esp. when forced by enemy attack *b)* a signal for such a withdrawal *c)* a signal given by bugle or drum at sunset for lowering the national flag *d)* the ceremony at which this is done —***vi.*** ⟦ME *retreten*⟧ **1** to withdraw; make a retreat **2** to slope backward —***vt.*** **1** to lead or draw back **2** *Chess* to withdraw (a piece), as from a dangerous position —***SYN.*** SHELTER —**beat a retreat** **1** *Mil.* to signal for retreat by beating a drum **2** to retreat in a hurry —**re·treat′ant** ***n.***

re·trench (rē trench′) ***vt.*** ⟦MFr *retrencher:* see RE- & TRENCH⟧ **1** to cut down or reduce (esp. expenses); curtail **2** to cut off or out; omit or delete —***vi.*** **1** to reduce expenses; economize **2** to consolidate one's strength, as for further efforts

re·trench·ment (-mənt) ***n.*** ⟦MFr⟧ **1** a retrenching; esp., a reduction of expenses **2** a rampart or breastwork within the main fortification **3** the act of consolidating one's strength, as for further efforts

ret·ri·bu·tion (re′trə byo͞o′shən) ***n.*** ⟦ME *retribucioun* < OFr *retribution* < LL(Ec) *retributio* < L *retributus,* pp. of *retribuere,* to repay < *re-,* back + *tribuere,* to pay: see TRIBUTE⟧ **1** [Archaic] suitable repayment for one's actions; requital **2** punishment for evil done —**re·trib·u·tive** (ri trib′yoo tiv) ***adj.,*** **re·trib′u·to′ry** (-tôr′ē) —**re·trib′u·tive·ly** ***adv.***

re·triev·al (ri trē′vəl) ***n.*** **1** the act or process of retrieving **2** possibility of recovery or restoration

re·trieve (ri trēv′) ***vt.*** **-trieved′, -triev′ing** ⟦ME *retreven* < inflected stem of OFr *retrouver* < *re-,* again + *trouver,* to find: see TROVER⟧ **1** to get back; recover **2** to restore; revive [*to retrieve* one's spirits] **3** to rescue or save **4** to set right or repair (a loss, error, etc.); make good **5** to recall to mind ☆**6** *Comput.* to gain access to (data) that is on a floppy disk, hard drive, etc. **7** *Hunting* to find and bring back (killed or wounded small game): said of dogs **8** *Racket Sports* to return (a ball that is hard to reach) —***vi.*** *Hunting* to retrieve game —***n.*** **1** any retrieval ☆**2** a retrieving of the ball in tennis, etc. —***SYN.*** RECOVER —**re·triev′a·ble** ***adj.***

re·triev·er (-ər) ***n.*** **1** a person or thing that retrieves **2** a dog trained to retrieve birds and some other small game, esp., any of several breeds of dog developed for this purpose

retie
retitle
retold
retrain
retransfer
retranslate
retransmission
retransmit
re-treat
re-treatment
retrial
retrim

ret·ro[1] (re′trō) *n., pl.* **-ros** *short for* RETROROCKET

ret·ro[2] (re′trō) *adj.* designating, of, or suggesting a style of an earlier time that has been revived: said of clothing, hairstyles, etc.

ret·ro- (re′trō, -trə) ⟦L < *retro,* backward < *re-,* back + *-tro,* as in INTRO-⟧ *combining form* backward, back, behind [*retroact, retroflex*]

ret·ro·act (re′trō akt′) *vi.* ⟦< L *retroactus,* pp. of *retroagere,* to drive back, reverse < prec. + *agere,* to drive: see ACT[1]⟧ **1** to act in opposition; react **2** to have reference to or influence on things done in the past

ret·ro·ac·tion (-ak′shən) *n.* ⟦RETRO- + ACTION⟧ **1** opposed, reverse, or reciprocal action; reaction **2** ⟦prec. + -ION⟧ effect, as of a law, on things done prior to its enactment or effectuation

ret·ro·ac·tive (-ak′tiv) *adj.* ⟦Fr *rétroactif:* see RETROACT & -IVE⟧ **1** having application to or effect on things done prior to its enactment [*a retroactive* law] **2** going into effect as of a specified date in the past [*a retroactive* increase] —**ret′ro·ac′tive·ly** *adv.* —**ret′ro·ac·tiv′i·ty** *n.*

ret·ro·cede[1] (re′trə sēd′) *vi.* **-ced′ed, -ced′ing** ⟦L *retrocedere,* to recede: see RETRO- & CEDE⟧ to go back; recede —**ret′ro·ces′sion** (-sesh′ən) *n.*

ret·ro·cede[2] (re′trə sēd′) *vt.* **-ced′ed, -ced′ing** ⟦Fr *rétrocéder* < ML *retrocedere* < L: see prec.⟧ to cede or give back (territory) *to* —**ret′ro·ces′sion** (-sesh′ən) *n.*

ret·ro·choir (re′trə kwīr′) *n.* ⟦RETRO- + CHOIR < ML *retrochorus*⟧ a church area behind the choir space or behind the main altar

ret·ro·dic·tion (re′trə dik′shən) *n.* ⟦RETRO- + *-diction,* as in PREDICTION⟧ the explaining or interpreting of a past event, action, etc. by inference based on information currently available —**ret′ro·dict′** *vt.* —**ret′ro·dic′tive** *adj.*

☆**ret·ro·fire** (re′trə fīr′) *vt.* **-fired′, -fir′ing** to ignite (a retrorocket) —*vi.* to become ignited: said of a retrorocket —*n.* the igniting of a retrorocket

☆**ret·ro·fit** (re′trə fit′) *n.* ⟦RETRO- & FIT[1]⟧ a change in design, construction, or equipment, as of an aircraft or machine tool already in operation, in order to incorporate later improvements — *vt., vi.* **-fit′ted, -fit′ting** to modify with a retrofit

ret·ro·flex (re′trə fleks′) *adj.* ⟦L *retroflexus,* pp. of *retroflectere:* see RETRO- & FLEX[1]⟧ **1** bent or turned backward **2** *Phonet.* articulated with the tip of the tongue raised and bent slightly backward toward the hard palate Also **ret′ro·flexed′** —*n. Phonet.* a retroflex sound

ret·ro·flex·ion or **ret·ro·flec·tion** (re′trə flek′shən) *n.* **1** *a)* the condition of being retroflex *b) Med.* the bending backward of an organ, esp. of the body of the uterus, upon itself **2** *Phonet. a)* retroflex articulation *b)* the acoustic quality produced by this

ret·ro·grade (re′trə grād′) *adj.* ⟦ME < L *retrogradus* < *retrogradi,* to go backward: see RETRO- & GRADE⟧ **1** moving or directed backward; retiring or retreating **2** inverse or reverse: said of order **3** going back or tending to go back to an earlier, esp. worse, condition; retrogressive **4** [Obs.] opposed; contrary **5** *a) Astron.* moving in an orbit opposite to the usual orbital direction of similar celestial bodies, as opposite to the direction of the earth in its journey around the sun *b) Astrol.* designating motion, real or apparent, on the celestial sphere in a direction from east to west **6** *Music* designating motion backward in a melody, specif. so as to begin with the last note and end with the first —*vi.* **-grad′ed, -grad′ing** ⟦L *retrogradi*⟧ **1** [Archaic] to go, or seem to go, backward **2** to become worse; decline; deteriorate; degenerate **3** *Astron.* to have a retrograde motion —**ret′ro·gra·da′tion** (-grā dā′shən, -grə dā′-) *n.* —**ret′ro·grade′ly** *adv.*

retrograde amnesia amnesia for events that happened just before the injury, shock, etc. which caused it

ret·ro·gress (re′trə gres′, re′trə gres′) *vi.* ⟦L *retrogressus,* pp. of *retrogradi:* see RETROGRADE⟧ to move backward, esp. into an earlier, less complex, or worse condition; decline; degenerate —**ret′ro·gres′sive** *adj.* —**ret′ro·gres′sive·ly** *adv.*

ret·ro·gres·sion (re′trə gresh′ən) *n.* **1** any retrogressing **2** *Biol.* a return to a lower, less complex stage or state; degeneration

ret·ro·len·tal (re′trə len′təl) *adj.* ⟦< RETRO- + L *lens,* gen. *lentis* (see LENS) + -AL⟧ situated behind the lens of the eye

☆**ret·ro·rock·et** or **ret·ro-rock·et** (re′trō räk′it) *n.* ⟦RETRO- + ROCKET[1]⟧ a small rocket on a larger rocket or spacecraft, that produces thrust in a direction opposite to the direction of flight in order to reduce speed, as for maneuvering

re·trorse (ri trôrs′) *adj.* ⟦L *retrorsus,* contr. of *retroversus,* bent backward < *retro,* back + *versus,* pp. of *vertere,* to turn: see VERSE⟧ *Biol.* bent or turned backward or downward —**re·trorse′ly** *adv.*

ret·ro·spect (re′trə spekt′) *n.* ⟦< L *retrospectus,* pp. of *retrospicere,* to look back < *retro-,* back + *specere,* to look: see SPY⟧ a looking back on or thinking about things past; contemplation or survey of the past —*vi.* [Rare] to look back in thought or refer back (*to*) —*vt.* [Rare] to look or think back on —**in retrospect** in reviewing the past

ret·ro·spec·tion (re′trə spek′shən) *n.* ⟦prec. + -ION⟧ **1** act, instance, or faculty of looking back on or reviewing past events, experiences, etc. **2** reference to a past event **3** a survey of past life or experiences

ret·ro·spec·tive (re′trə spek′tiv) *adj.* ⟦RETROSPECT + -IVE⟧ **1** looking back on or directed to the past, past events, etc. **2** looking or directed backward [*a retrospective* view of the river] **3** applying to the past; retroactive —*n.* a representative exhibition of the lifetime work of an artist —**ret′ro·spec′tive·ly** *adv.*

re·trous·sé (re′trōō sā′) *adj.* ⟦Fr, pp. of *retrousser,* to turn up: see RE- & TRUSS⟧ turned up at the tip [*a retroussé* nose]

ret·ro·ver·sion (re′trə vʉr′zhən, -shən) *n.* ⟦< L *retroversus* (see RETRORSE) + -ION⟧ **1** a turning back **2** a turning or tilting backward (*of* an organ or part), esp. of the uterus

Ret·ro·vir (re′trə vir′) *trademark for* ZIDOVUDINE

ret·ro·vi·rus (re′trō vī′rəs) *n.* any of a family (Retroviridae) of RNA viruses which have a virion that makes REVERSE TRANSCRIPTASE, including the viruses that cause leukemia and AIDS —**ret′ro·vi′ral** *adj.*

ret·si·na (ret sē′nə, ret′si nə) *n.* ⟦ModGr, prob. < It *resina* (< L), RESIN⟧ a Greek wine flavored with pine resin

re·turn (ri tʉrn′) *vi.* ⟦ME *retournen* < OFr *retourner:* see RE- & TURN⟧ **1** to go or come back, as to a former place, condition, practice, opinion, etc. **2** to go back in thought or speech [*to return* to the subject] **3** to revert to a former owner **4** to answer; reply; retort —*vt.* **1** to bring, send, carry, or put back; restore or replace **2** to give, send, or do (something equivalent to what has been given, sent, or done); give, send, or do in requital or reciprocation [*to return* a visit, compliment, etc.] **3** to produce (a profit, revenue, etc.); yield **4** *a)* to report or announce officially or formally *b)* to turn in (a writ, account, or statement) to a judge or other official **5** to elect or reelect, as to a legislature **6** to replace (a weapon) in its holder **7** to turn back or in the opposite direction **8** to reflect (sound, light, etc.) **9** *Archit.* to turn away from, or cause to continue on at an angle to, the previous line of direction **10** *Card Games* to respond to (one's partner's lead) with a lead of the same suit **11** *Law* to render (a verdict) **12** *Sports* to hit, throw, or run back (a ball) —*n.* ⟦ME *retorn* < the v.⟧ **1** a coming or going back, as to a former place, condition, etc. **2** a bringing, sending, carrying, or putting back; restoration or replacement **3** *a)* something returned *b)* [*pl.*] unsold merchandise returned to the distributor by a retailer or merchandise returned to a retailer by a purchaser **4** a coming back again; reappearance; recurrence [many happy *returns* of the day] **5** something done or given as an equivalent for that received; repayment; requital; reciprocation **6** *a)* profit made on an exchange of goods *b)* [*often pl.*] yield, profit, or revenue, as from labor, investments, etc. *c)* yield per unit as compared to cost per unit; rate of yield **7** an answer; reply; retort **8** a report; esp., *a)* an official or formal report, as of the financial condition of a company *b)* [*usually pl.*] a report on a count of votes at polling places [election *returns*] *c)* a form on which taxable income is reported and tax is computed (in full **(income) tax return**) **9** *Archit. a)* the continuation, as of a molding or colonnade, in a different direction, often at a right angle *b)* a bend or turn, as in a line or wall *c)* the section between two such bends **10** *Card Games* a lead in response to one's partner's lead **11** *Law a)* the bringing or sending back of a writ, subpoena, summons, etc. to the proper court or official *b)* a certified report by an election official, assessor, etc. *c)* a court officer's endorsement on any such document **12** *Sports a)* a hitting or throwing back of a ball *b)* a ball so returned *c)* a running back of a football received on a kick or by an interception —*adj.* **1** of or for a return or returning [*return* postage] **2** given, sent, done, etc. in return [*a return* match] **3** occurring again [*a return* performance] **4** returning or returned **5** changing or reversing direction or formed by a change or reversal in direction, as a bend in a road —**in return** as a return; as an equivalent, response, etc. —**re·turn′er** *n.*

re·turn·a·ble (ri tʉr′nə bəl) *adj.* **1** that can or may be returned **2** that must be returned, as a court writ —*n.* a container, esp. a glass bottle as for beer or a soft drink, on which a refundable deposit is paid and which can be returned for reuse

☆**re·turn·ee** (ri tʉr′nē′) *n.* a person who returns, as home from military service or to school after dropping out

returning officer [Brit.] an official in charge of an election in a district

return ticket **1** a ticket for the trip back to the original starting point **2** [Brit.] a round-trip ticket

re·tuse (ri tōōs′, -tyōōs′) *adj.* ⟦L *retusus,* dull, pp. of *retundere,* to beat back < *re-,* back + *tundere,* to strike: see OBTUND⟧ *Bot.* having a blunt or rounded apex with a small notch, as some leaves

Reu·ben[1] (rōō′bən) *n.* ⟦via LL(Ec) < Gr(Ec) < Heb *reuven,* lit., behold, a son < *reu,* imper. of *raa,* to see + *ben,* son⟧ **1** a masculine name: dim. *Rube, Ruby* **2** *Bible a)* the eldest son of Jacob and Leah: Gen. 29:32 *b)* the tribe of Israel descended from him: Num. 1:20-21

☆**Reu·ben**[2] (rōō′bən) *n.* ⟦prob. after *Reuben* Kay, Omaha grocer (*c.* 1930)⟧ a sandwich made with rye bread, filled usually with corned beef, sauerkraut, Swiss cheese, and a dressing and served hot: in full **Reuben sandwich**

re·u·ni·fy (rē yōō′nə fī′) *vt., vi.* **-fied′, -fy′ing** to unify again after being divided —**re·u′ni·fi·ca′tion** *n.*

re·un·ion (rē yōōn′yən) *n.* ⟦Fr *réunion* < ML *reunio:* see RE- & UNION⟧ **1** the act of reuniting **2** a gathering of persons after separation [*a family reunion*]

Ré·u·nion (rā ü nyōn′; *E* rē yōōn′yən) island in the Indian Ocean, east of Madagascar: overseas department of France: 968 sq mi (2,507 sq km); cap. St-Denis

re·u·nite (rē′yōō nīt′) *vt., vi.* **-nit′ed, -nit′ing** ⟦< ML *reunitus,* pp. of *reunire:* see RE- & UNITE[1]⟧ to unite again; bring or come together again —**re′u·nit′er** *n.*

☆**re-up** (rē up′) *vi.* **-upped′, -up′ping** ⟦RE- + (SIGN) UP (see phr. under SIGN)⟧ [Informal] to reenlist, as in a branch of the armed forces

Reu·ther (rōō′thər), **Walter (Philip)** 1907-70; U.S. labor leader

---

retry
retune
retwist
retype
reupholster
reusable
reuse
reutilize
reutter

rev[1] (rev) [Informal] ***n.*** a revolution, as of the crankshaft of an engine —***vt.*** **revved, rev′ving 1** to increase the revolutions per minute of (an engine, motor, etc.) **2** to accelerate, intensify, etc. Usually with *up* —***vi.*** to undergo revving

rev[2] *abbrev.* **1** revenue **2** reverse **3** review(ed) **4** revise(d) **5** revision **6** revolution **7** revolving

Rev *abbrev.* **1** *Bible* Revelation **2** Reverend

re·val·u·ate (rē val′yo͞o āt′) ***vt.*** **-at′ed, -at′ing** to make a new valuation or appraisal of —**re·val′u·a′tion** ***n.***

☆**re·vamp** (rē vamp′) ***vt.*** to vamp again or anew; specif., to renovate or revise; make over —***n.*** the act or result of revamping

re·vanche (rə vänsh′) ***n.*** ⟦Fr⟧ revenge; specif., REVANCHISM

re·vanch·ism (rə vanch′iz′əm) ***n.*** ⟦< Fr *revanche* < MFr *revancher* < *re-*, RE- + *vencher*, var. of *vengier:* see REVENGE & -ISM⟧ a spirit of revenge moving a defeated nation to aggressively seek restoration of lost territory, authority, etc. —**re·vanch′ist** ***adj., n.***

re·veal[1] (ri vēl′) ***vt.*** ⟦ME *revelen* < OFr *reveler* < L *revelare*, lit., to draw back the veil < *re-*, back + *velum*, VEIL⟧ **1** to make known (something hidden or kept secret); disclose; divulge **2** to expose to view; show; exhibit; display **3** *Theol.* to make known by supernatural or divine means —***n.*** ⟦term used by stage magicians⟧ [Slang] the act or an instance of revealing something, esp. as part of a dramatic climax —**re·veal′a·ble** ***adj.*** —**re·veal′ment** ***n.***

SYN.—**reveal** implies a making known of something hidden or secret, as if by drawing back a veil [to *reveal* one's identity]; **disclose** suggests a laying open, as to inspection, of what has previously been concealed [she refuses to *disclose* her intentions]; **divulge** suggests that what has been disclosed should properly have been kept secret or private [do not *divulge* the contents of this letter]; **tell** may also imply a breach of confidence [kiss and *tell*] but more commonly suggests the making known of necessary or requested information [*tell* me what to do]; **betray** implies either faithlessness in divulging something [*betrayed* by an informer] or inadvertence in revealing something [his blush *betrayed* embarrassment] —*ANT.* **conceal, hide**

re·veal[2] (ri vēl′) ***n.*** ⟦< ME *revalen*, to bring down < MFr *revaler* < *re-*, back + *avaler*, to lower < *aval*, downward < *à* (L *ad*, to) + *val*, VALE[1]⟧ **1** that part of the side of an opening for a window or door which is between the outer edge of the opening and the frame of the window or door **2** the entire side of such an opening; jamb

revealed religion religion in general, or a specific religion, viewed as founded, made known, and developed by divine intervention and communication

re·veal·ing (ri vē′liŋ) ***adj.*** **1** providing insight or information that was formerly unknown or kept hidden [a *revealing* interview with a persistent reporter] **2** exposing more of the body to view than usual; low-cut, brief, etc. [a *revealing* evening gown] —**re·veal′ing·ly** ***adv.***

re·veg·e·tate (rē vej′ə tāt′) ***vt.*** **-tat′ed, -tat′ing** to plant or replant (barren or, esp., denuded land) with vegetation —**re·veg′e·ta′tion** ***n.***

rev·eil·le (rev′ə lē; *Brit & Cdn* ri val′ē, -vel′-) ***n.*** ⟦< Fr *réveillez(-vous)*, imper. of *(se) réveiller*, to wake up < *ré-* (< L *re-*) + *veiller* (< L *vigilare*, to watch: see VIGILANT)⟧ *Mil.* **1** a signal on a bugle, drum, etc. at some fixed time early in the morning to waken soldiers or sailors or call them to first assembly **2** the first assembly of the day

rev·el (rev′əl) ***vi.*** **-eled** or **-elled, -el·ing** or **-el·ling** ⟦ME *revelen* < MFr *reveler*, to revel, lit., to rebel < L *rebellare:* see REBEL⟧ **1** to make merry; be noisily festive **2** to take much pleasure; delight (*in*) [to *revel* in one's freedom] —***n.*** ⟦ME < MFr < the v.⟧ **1** boisterous festivity; merrymaking; revelry **2** [*often pl.*] an occasion of merrymaking or boisterous festivity; celebration —**rev′el·er** ***n.***, **rev′el·ler**

rev·e·la·tion (rev′ə lā′shən) ***n.*** ⟦ME *reuelacioun* < OFr *revelation* < LL(Ec) *revelatio* < pp. of L *revelare*⟧ **1** a revealing, or disclosing, of something **2** something disclosed; disclosure; esp., a striking disclosure, as of something not previously known or realized **3** *Theol. a)* communication, by a divinity or by divine agency, of divine truth or knowledge; specif., God's manifestation of the divinity or of the divine will to humanity *b)* an instance of this *c)* that which is so communicated, disclosed, or manifested *d)* something, as a writing or event, containing or showing such a communication, disclosure, or manifestation **4** [**R-**] the last book of the New Testament, ascribed to John (in full **The Revelation of Saint John the Divine**); Apocalypse: abbrev. *Rev* or *Rv:* also **Revelations** —**rev′e·la′tor** ***n.*** —**rev′e·la·to′ry** (-lə tôr′ē) ***adj.***

rev·el·ry (rev′əl rē) ***n., pl.*** **-ries** ⟦ME *revelrie*⟧ reveling; noisy merrymaking; boisterous festivity

rev·e·nant (rev′ə nənt) ***n.*** ⟦Fr < prp. of *revenir*, to come back: see REVENUE⟧ **1** a person who returns, as after a long absence **2** GHOST (sense 2)

re·venge (ri venj′) ***vt.*** **-venged′, -veng′ing** ⟦ME *revengen* < OFr *revenger* < *re-*, again + *venger*, to take vengeance < L *vindicare:* see VINDICATE⟧ **1** to inflict damage, injury, or punishment in return for (an injury, insult, etc.); retaliate for **2** to take vengeance in behalf of (a person, oneself, etc.); avenge —***vi.*** [Obs.] to take vengeance —***n.*** **1** the act of revenging; vengeance **2** what is done in revenging **3** desire to take vengeance; vindictive spirit **4** a chance to retaliate or get satisfaction, as by a return match after a defeat —*SYN.* AVENGE —**be revenged** to get revenge —**re·veng′er** ***n.*** —**re·veng′ing·ly** ***adv.***

re·venge·ful (-fəl) ***adj.*** VENGEFUL —*SYN.* VINDICTIVE —**re·venge′ful·ly** ***adv.*** —**re·venge′ful·ness** ***n.***

rev·e·nue (rev′ə no͞o′, -nyo͞o′) ***n.*** ⟦ME < MFr < fem. pp. of *revenir*, to return, come back < *re-*, back + *venir* < L *venire*, to COME⟧ **1** the return from property or investment; income **2** *a)* an item or source of income *b)* [*pl.*] items or amounts of income collectively, as of a nation **3** the income from taxes, licenses, etc., as of a city, state, or nation **4** the governmental service that collects certain taxes

☆**rev·e·nu·er** (rev′ə no͞o′ər, -nyo͞o′-) ***n.*** [Informal] a Treasury Department revenue agent, esp. one concerned with halting illegal alcohol distilling and bootlegging

revenue stamp a stamp, as on a bottle of liquor, that shows a tax has been paid

☆**re·verb** (ri vʉrb′; *for n., also* rē′vʉrb′) ***n.*** **1** an electronic or mechanical device for simulating the effect of sound reverberation, used with electronically amplified musical instruments or for recordings **2** such an effect —***vt., vi.*** REVERBERATE

re·ver·ber·ant (ri vʉr′bə rənt) ***adj.*** ⟦L *reverberans*, prp.⟧ reverberating; reechoing; resonant

re·ver·ber·ate (-bə rāt′; *for adj.*, -bə rit) ***vt.*** **-at′ed, -at′ing** ⟦< L *reverberatus*, pp. of *reverberare*, to beat back, repel < *re-*, again + *verberare*, to beat < *verber*, a lash, whip, akin to VERBENA⟧ **1** to cause (a sound) to reecho **2** *a)* to reflect (light, etc.) *b)* to deflect (heat, flame, etc.), as in a reverberatory furnace **3** to subject to treatment in a reverberatory furnace or the like —***vi.*** **1** to reecho or resound **2** *a)* to be reflected, as light or sound waves *b)* to be deflected, as heat or flame in a reverberatory furnace **3** to recoil; rebound **4** to have repercussions: said as of an event or action [a governmental decision *reverberating* throughout the entire economy] —***adj.*** [Rare] reverberated

re·ver·ber·a·tion (ri vʉr′bə rā′shən) ***n.*** ⟦ME < ML *reverberatio*⟧ **1** a reverberating or being reverberated; a reechoing or being reechoed; reflection of light or sound waves, deflection of heat or flame, etc. **2** something reverberated; reechoed sound, reflected light, etc. **3** a far-reaching effect of some event or action **4** *Physics* multiple reflection of sound waves in a confined area so that the sound persists after the source is cut off

re·ver·ber·a·tive (ri vʉr′bə rāt′iv, -rə tiv) ***adj.*** **1** reverberating or tending to reverberate **2** having the nature of reverberation —**re·ver′ber·a′tive·ly** ***adv.***

re·ver·ber·a·tor (-bə rāt′ər) ***n.*** something that produces reverberation, as a reverberatory furnace

re·ver·ber·a·to·ry (-bə rə tôr′ē) ***adj.*** **1** operating or produced by reverberation **2** deflected: said as of flame or heat **3** designating or of a furnace or kiln in which ore, metal, etc. is heated by a flame deflected downward from the roof —***n.*** such a furnace or kiln

re·vere[1] (ri vir′) ***vt.*** **-vered′, -ver′ing** ⟦< Fr or L: Fr *révérer* < L *revereri* < *re-*, again + *vereri*, to fear, feel awe < IE base **wer-*, to heed > WARN⟧ to regard with deep respect, love, and awe; venerate

SYN.—**revere** implies a regarding with great respect, affection, honor, or deference [a poet *revered* by all]; **reverence**, more or less equivalent to **revere**, is usually applied to a thing or abstract idea rather than to a person [they *reverence* the memory of their parents]; **venerate** implies a regarding as sacred or holy [to *venerate* saints or relics]; **worship**, in strict usage, implies the use of ritual or verbal formula in paying homage to a divine being, but broadly suggests intense love or admiration of any kind [he *worshiped* his wife]; **adore**, in strict usage, implies a personal or individual worshiping of a deity, but in broad usage, it suggests a great love for someone and, informally, a great liking for something [I *adore* your hat]

re·vere[2] (ri vir′) ***n.*** *var. of* REVERS

Re·vere (ri vir′), **Paul** 1735-1818; Am. silversmith & patriot: rode from Boston to Lexington (April 18, 1775) to warn the colonists that British troops were coming

rev·er·ence (rev′ə rəns, rev′rəns) ***n.*** ⟦OFr < L *reverentia* < *reverens:* see REVERENT⟧ **1** a feeling or attitude of deep respect, love, and awe, as for something sacred; veneration **2** a manifestation of this; specif., a bow, curtsy, or similar gesture of respect; obeisance **3** the state of being revered **4** [**R-**] a title used in speaking to or of a member of the clergy: preceded by *Your* or by *His* or *Her* —***vt.*** **-enced, -enc·ing** to treat or regard with reverence; venerate —*SYN.* AWE, HONOR, REVERE[1]

rev·er·end (rev′ə rənd, rev′rənd) ***adj.*** ⟦ME < MFr < L *reverendus*, ger. of *revereri:* see REVERE[1]⟧ **1** worthy of reverence; deserving to be revered: used with *the* as an honorific epithet for a member of the clergy, prefixed to the first name or initials and last name, and, in very formal use, preceding another title [the *Reverend* A. B. Smith, the *Reverend* Dr. Ann B. Smith, the *Reverend* Mr. Jones] **2** of or characteristic of the clergy —***n.*** [Informal] a member of the clergy

rev·er·ent (rev′ə rənt, rev′rənt) ***adj.*** ⟦LME < L *reverens*, prp. of *revereri:* see REVERE[1]⟧ feeling, showing, or characterized by reverence —**rev′er·ent·ly** ***adv.***

rev·er·en·tial (rev′ə ren′shəl) ***adj.*** ⟦ML *reverentialis*⟧ showing or caused by reverence —**rev′er·en′tial·ly** ***adv.***

rev·er·ie (rev′ə rē) ***n.*** ⟦Fr *rêverie* < MFr, delirium < *rever*, roam: see RAVE⟧ **1** dreamy thinking or imagining, esp. of agreeable things; fanciful musing; daydreaming **2** a dreamy, fanciful, or visionary notion or daydream

revaccinate
revalorization
revalue
revarnish

re·vers (ri vir′, -ver′) ***n.***, *pl.* **-vers′** (-virz′, -verz′) ⟦Fr < L *reversus:* see REVERSE⟧ **1** a part (of a garment) turned back to show the reverse side or facing, as a lapel **2** a piece of trimming made to look like this

re·ver·sal (ri vur′səl) ***n.*** ⟦LME *reversall:* see fol. & -AL⟧ **1** a reversing or being reversed; esp., a change to the opposite as in one's fortune **2** *Law* annulment, change, or revocation, as of a lower court's decision

re·verse (ri vurs′) ***adj.*** ⟦ME *revers* < OFr < L *reversus,* pp. of *revertere:* see REVERT⟧ **1** *a)* turned backward; opposite or contrary, as in position, direction, order, etc. *b)* with the back showing or in view **2** reversing the usual effect so as to show white letters, etc. on a black background **3** acting or moving in a way or direction opposite or contrary to the usual **4** causing movement backward or in the opposite direction *[reverse* gear*]* **—*n.*** **1** the opposite or contrary of something **2** the back or rear of something; specif., the side, as of a coin or medal, not bearing the main image or design: opposed to OBVERSE **3** the act or an instance of reversing; change to the opposite **4** a change from good fortune to bad; defeat, check, or misfortune **5** a mechanism, etc. for reversing, as a gear arrangement in a transmission that causes a machine, motor vehicle, etc. to run backward or in the opposite direction **6** a reversing movement ☆**7** *Football* a type of play in which a ball carrier running toward a sideline gives the ball to a teammate going the opposite way **—*vt.*** **-versed′**, **-vers′ing** **1** to turn backward, in an opposite position or direction, upside down, or inside out **2** to change to the opposite; alter completely **3** to cause to go or move backward or in an opposite direction **4** to exchange or transpose **5** to transfer (the charges for a telephone call) to the party being called **6** *Law* to revoke or annul (a decision, judgment, etc.) **—*vi.*** **1** to move, go, or turn backward or in the opposite direction **2** to put a motor, engine, etc. in reverse; reverse the action of a mechanism **—*SYN.*** OPPOSITE **—re·verse′ly *adv.*** **—re·vers′er *n.***

☆**reverse discrimination** discrimination against certain groups, esp. white males, regarded as having benefited from former policies of discrimination in hiring, college admissions, etc. directed against certain other groups, as minorities, women, etc.

reverse engineering the process of making or designing a product by first examining a competitor's product and then applying the information thus obtained **—re·verse′-en′gi·neer′ *vt.***

reverse mortgage a loan typically given to an older person who owns a house, usually disbursed in monthly installments, and charged against the homeowner's equity

reverse osmosis a method of extracting essentially pure, fresh water from polluted or salt water by forcing the water under pressure against a semipermeable membrane, which passes the pure water molecules and filters out salts and and other dissolved impurities

reverse psychology a manipulative technique whereby one seemingly advocates the opposite of what one actually wants another to do: not a technical term

reverse transcriptase an enzyme that makes DNA from RNA, found in retroviruses and widely used in recombinant DNA technology: cf. TRANSCRIPTASE

re·vers·i·ble (ri vur′sə bəl) ***adj.*** **1** that can be reversed; specif., made so that either side can be used as the outer side; finished on both sides: said of cloth, coats, etc. **2** that can reverse; specif., that can change and then go back to the original condition by a reversal of the change: said of a chemical reaction, etc. **—*n.*** a reversible coat, jacket, etc. **—re·vers′i·bil′i·ty *n.*** **—re·vers′i·bly *adv.***

re·ver·sion (ri vur′zhən, -shən) ***n.*** ⟦ME < MFr < L *reversio* < *reversus:* see REVERSE⟧ **1** a turning or being turned the opposite way; reversal **2** a reverting, or returning, as to a former state, custom, or belief **3** *Biol. a)* a return to a former or primitive type; atavism *b)* the return, or reappearance, of characteristics present in early ancestral generations but not in those that have intervened *c)* an individual or organism with such characteristics **4** *Law a)* the right of succession, future possession, or enjoyment *b)* the return of an estate to the grantor or the grantor's heirs by operation of law after the period of a grant is over *c)* an estate so returning **—re·ver′sion·ar′y *adj.***, **re·ver′sion·al**

re·ver·sion·er (-ər) ***n.*** *Law* a person who has a reversion or a right to receive an estate in reversion

re·vert (ri vurt′) ***vi.*** ⟦ME *reverten* < OFr *revertir* < VL **revertire,* for L *revertere* < *re-,* back + *vertere,* to turn: see VERSE⟧ **1** to go back in action, thought, speech, etc.; return, as to a former practice, opinion, state, or subject **2** *Biol.* to return to a former or primitive type; show ancestral characteristics normally no longer present in the species **3** *Law* to go back to a former owner or the heirs of such owner **—*n.*** a person or thing that reverts; esp., one who returns to a previous faith **—re·vert′i·ble *adj.***

rev·er·y (rev′ər ē) ***n.***, *pl.* **-er·ies** REVERIE

re·vest (rē vest′) ***vt.*** ⟦ME *revesten* < OFr *revestir* < LL *revestire,* to reclothe < L *re-,* again + *vestire,* to clothe: see VEST, *vt.*⟧ **1** to vest (someone) again with possession, power, or office; reinvest; reinstate **2** to vest (office, powers, etc.) again **—*vi.*** to become vested again (*in*); revert to a former owner or holder

re·vet (ri vet′) ***vt.*** **-vet′ted**, **-vet′ting** ⟦Fr *revêtir* < OFr *revestir:* see prec.⟧ to provide or protect with a revetment

re·vet·ment (-mənt) ***n.*** ⟦see prec. & -MENT⟧ **1** a facing of stone, cement, sandbags, etc., as to protect a wall or a bank of earth **2** RETAINING WALL **3** an embankment or wall as of sandbags or earth, constructed to protect against strafing, shell fragments, etc.

re·view (ri vyōō′; *for vt. 1,* rē′-) ***n.*** ⟦MFr *reveue* < *revu,* pp. of *revoir* < L *revidere* < *re-,* again + *videre,* to see: see VISION⟧ **1** a looking at or looking over again **2** a general survey, report, or account **3** a looking back on; retrospective view or survey, as of past events or experiences **4** reexamination; specif., judicial reexamination, as by a higher court of the decision of a lower court **5** a critical report and evaluation, as in a newspaper or magazine, of a recent book, play, etc., or of a performance, concert, etc. **6** a magazine containing articles of criticism and appraisal, often in a specific field *[*a law *review]* **7** the act or process of going over a lesson or subject again, as in study or recitation **8** REVUE **9** an examination or inspection; specif., a formal inspection, as of troops on parade or of ships, by a high-ranking officer, or as a ceremony honoring some dignitary **—*vt.*** ⟦RE- + VIEW; also < the *n.*⟧ **1** [Now Rare] to view, or look at, again **2** to look back on; view in retrospect **3** to survey in thought, speech, or writing; make or give a survey of **4** to examine or inspect; specif., to inspect (troops, etc.) formally **5** to give or write a critical report and evaluation of (a recent book, play, performance, etc.) **6** to reexamine; specif., to reexamine judicially (a lower court's decision) **7** to go over (lessons, a subject, etc.) again, as in study or recitation **—*vi.*** to review books, plays, etc., as for a newspaper

re·view·al (-əl) ***n.*** the act of reviewing; review

re·view·er (-ər) ***n.*** a person who reviews; esp., one who reviews books, plays, etc. as for a newspaper

re·vile (ri vīl′) ***vt.*** **-viled′**, **-vil′ing** ⟦ME *revilen* < OFr *reviler,* to regard or treat as vile < *re-,* RE- + *viler,* to humiliate < *vil,* VILE⟧ to use abusive or contemptuous language in speaking to or about; call bad names **—*vi.*** to use abusive language **—*SYN.*** SCOLD **—re·vile′ment *n.*** **—re·vil′er *n.***

re·vise (ri vīz′) ***vt.*** **-vised′**, **-vis′ing** ⟦Fr *reviser* < L *revisere* < *re-,* back + *visere,* to survey, freq. of *videre,* to see: see VISION⟧ **1** to read over carefully and correct, improve, or update where necessary *[*to *revise* a manuscript, a *revised* edition of a book*]* **2** to change or amend *[*to *revise* tax rates*]* **—*n.*** **1** a revising or a revised form of something; revision **2** *Printing* a proof taken after corrections have been made, for looking over or correcting again **—re·vis′al *n.*** **—re·vis′er *n.***, **re·vi′sor**

Revised Standard Version a revision of the American Standard Version of the Bible, made by a group of U.S. scholars and published in 1946 (N.T.) & 1952 (O.T.)

Revised Version a revision, or recension, of the Authorized, or King James, Version of the Bible, made by a committee of U.S. and British scholars and published in 1881 (N.T.) & 1885 (O.T.)

re·vi·sion (ri vizh′ən) ***n.*** ⟦LL *revisio*⟧ **1** act, process, or work of revising **2** the result of this; revised form or version, as of a book, manuscript, etc. **—re·vi′sion·ar′y *adj.***, **re·vi′sion·al**

re·vi·sion·ist (-ist) ***n.*** **1** a Marxist advocating socialism by means of gradual reforms rather than through revolution **2** a person who advocates a radically different theory or interpretation, as of particular historical events, from that which is generally accepted **—*adj.*** of revisionists or their policy or practice **—re·vi′sion·ism′ *n.***

re·vis·it (rē viz′it) ***vt.*** **1** to visit again **2** to reconsider or reevaluate: often used postpositively in the pp., as in essay or book titles *[*"Mark Twain *Revisited*"*]*

re·vi·so·ry (ri vī′zə rē) ***adj.*** of, or having the nature or power of, revision *[*a *revisory* committee*]*

re·vi·tal·ize (rē vīt′'l īz′) ***vt.*** **-ized′**, **-iz′ing** to bring vitality, vigor, etc. back to after a decline **—re·vi′tal·i·za′tion *n.***

re·viv·al (ri vī′vəl) ***n.*** a reviving or being revived; specif., *a)* a bringing or coming back into use, attention, or being, after a decline *b)* a new or return presentation of a play, film, etc. some time after it has first been presented *c)* restoration to vigor or activity *d)* a returning to life or consciousness *e)* a stirring up of religious faith by fervid evangelistic preaching at public meetings ☆*f)* such a meeting or a series of such meetings with public confession of sins and professions of renewed faith *g) Law* renewal of validity, as of a judgment or contract

re·viv·al·ism (-iz′əm) ***n.*** **1** the fervid spirit or methods characteristic of religious revivals **2** a desire to revive former ways

re·viv·al·ist (-ist) ***n.*** **1** a person who promotes or conducts religious revivals **2** a person who revives former ways, institutions, etc. **—re·viv′al·is′tic *adj.***

Revival of Learning (*or* **Letters** *or* **Literature**) the Renaissance as related to learning and literature

re·vive (ri vīv′) ***vi., vt.*** **-vived′**, **-viv′ing** ⟦ME *reviven* < OFr *revivre* < L *revivere* < *re-,* again + *vivere,* to live: see BIO-⟧ **1** to come or bring back to life or consciousness; resuscitate **2** to come or bring back to a healthy, vigorous, or flourishing condition after a decline **3** to come or bring back into use or attention **4** to become or make valid, effective, or operative again **5** to come or bring to mind again **6** to produce (a play) or exhibit (an old film) again after an interval **—re·viv′a·bil′i·ty *n.*** **—re·viv′a·ble *adj.*** **—re·viv′er *n.***

re·viv·i·fy (ri viv′ə fī′) ***vt.*** **-fied′**, **-fy′ing** ⟦Fr *revivifier* < LL(Ec) *revivificare:* see RE- & VIVIFY⟧ to put new life or vigor into; cause to revive **—*vi.*** to revive **—re·viv′i·fi·ca′tion *n.*** **—re·viv′i·fi′er *n.***

rev·i·vis·cent (rev′ə vis′ənt) ***adj.*** ⟦L *reviviscens,* prp. of *reviviscere* < *re-,*

reverification
reverify
revibrate
revictual
revindicate
revisualize

back + *vivescere,* inchoative of *vivere,* to live: see BIO-⟧ coming or bringing back to life or vigor; reviving —**rev′i·vis′cence** *n.*

rev·o·ca·ble (rev′ə kə bəl, ri vō′kə-) *adj.* ⟦ME < MFr < L *revocabilis*⟧ that can be revoked —**rev′o·ca·bil′i·ty** *n.* —**rev′o·ca·bly** *adv.*

rev·o·ca·tion (rev′ə kā′shən) *n.* ⟦ME < MFr < L *revocatio* < pp. of *revocare*⟧ a revoking or being revoked; cancellation; repeal; annulment

rev·o·ca·to·ry (rev′ə kə tôr′ē) *adj.* ⟦ME < LL *revocatorius*⟧ revoking or tending to revoke; containing or expressing a revocation

re·voice (rē vois′) *vt.* **-voiced′**, **-voic′ing** **1** to voice again, or in answer; echo **2** to restore the proper tone to (an organ pipe, etc.)

re·vok·a·ble (ri vō′kə bəl) *adj. var. of* REVOCABLE

re·voke (ri vōk′) *vt.* **-voked′**, **-vok′ing** ⟦ME *revoken* < MFr *revoquer* < L *revocare* < *re-,* back + *vocare,* to call < *vox,* VOICE⟧ **1** to withdraw, repeal, rescind, cancel, or annul (a law, permit, etc.) **2** [Now Rare] to recall —*vi. Card Games* to fail to follow suit when required and able to do so; renege —*n. Card Games* the act or an instance of revoking —**SYN.** ABOLISH

re·volt (ri vōlt′) *n.* ⟦Fr *révolte* < *révolter,* to revolt < It *rivoltare* < VL **revolutare,* for L *revolvere:* see REVOLVE⟧ **1** a rising up against the government; rebellion; insurrection **2** any refusal to submit to or accept authority, custom, etc. **3** the state of a person or persons revolting —*vi.* ⟦Fr *révolter*⟧ **1** to rise up against the government **2** to refuse to submit to authority, custom, etc.; rebel; mutiny **3** to turn away (*from*) in revulsion **4** to be disgusted or shocked; feel repugnance: with *at* or *against* —*vt.* to fill with revulsion; disgust —**re·volt′er** *n.*

re·volt·ing (-vōl′tiŋ) *adj.* **1** engaged in revolt; rebellious **2** causing revulsion; disgusting; repulsive; offensive; loathsome —**re·volt′ing·ly** *adv.*

rev·o·lute (rev′ə lo͞ot′) *adj.* ⟦L *revolutus,* pp. of *revolvere:* see REVOLVE⟧ rolled backward or downward at the tips or margins, as some leaves

rev·o·lu·tion (rev′ə lo͞o′shən) *n.* ⟦ME *revolucion* < OFr < LL *revolutio* < L *revolutus,* pp. of *revolvere:* see REVOLVE⟧ **1** *a)* the movement of an orbiting celestial object, as a star or planet, completely around another object (cf. ROTATION, sense 2) *b)* apparent movement of the sun and stars around the earth *c)* the time taken for a body to go around an orbit and return to its original position **2** *a)* a turning or spinning motion of a body, shaft, etc. around a center or axis; rotation *b)* one complete turn of such a rotating body, shaft, etc. **3** a complete cycle of events [the *revolution* of the seasons] **4** a complete or radical change of any kind [a *revolution* in modern physics] **5** overthrow of a government, form of government, or social system by those governed and usually by forceful means, with another government or system taking its place [the American *Revolution* (1775), the French *Revolution* (1789), the Chinese *Revolution* (1911), the Russian *Revolution* (1917)]

rev·o·lu·tion·ar·y (-shə ner′ē) *adj.* **1** of, characterized by, favoring, or causing a revolution in a government or social system **2** bringing about or constituting a great or radical change [a *revolutionary* design] ☆**3** [**R-**] of or having to do with the American Revolution **4** revolving or rotating —*n., pl.* **-ar′ies** a person who favors or takes part in a revolution

Revolutionary calendar FRENCH REVOLUTIONARY CALENDAR

☆**Revolutionary War** *see* AMERICAN REVOLUTION (sense 2)

rev·o·lu·tion·ist (-shə nist) *n.* REVOLUTIONARY

rev·o·lu·tion·ize (-shə nīz′) *vt.* **-ized′**, **-iz′ing** **1** to make a complete and basic change in; alter drastically or radically [automation has *revolutionized* industry] **2** [Rare] to bring about a political revolution in

re·volve (ri välv′, -vôlv′) *vt.* **-volved′**, **-volv′ing** ⟦ME *revolven* < L *revolvere* < *re-,* back + *volvere,* to roll: see WALK⟧ **1** to turn over in the mind; reflect on **2** to cause to travel in a circle or orbit **3** to cause to rotate, or spin around an axis —*vi.* **1** to move in a circle or orbit around a point **2** to spin or turn around a center or axis; rotate **3** to be oriented (*around* or *about* something regarded as a center) **4** to recur at intervals; occur periodically **5** to be pondered or reflected on —**re·volv′a·ble** *adj.*

re·volv·er (ri väl′vər, -vôl′-) *n.* ☆**1** a handgun equipped with a revolving cylinder containing several cartridges so that it can be fired repeatedly without being reloaded **2** a person or thing that revolves

re·volv·ing (-viŋ) *adj.* **1** that revolves: said of an airport beacon, etc. ☆**2** *Finance a)* designating a fund kept for making loans, payments, etc. and regularly replenished, as from repayments *b)* designating credit, as for a charge account, that is renewed for a stated amount as regular proportional payments are made

☆**revolving door** **1** a door consisting of two to five upright panels hung on a central axle, and turned around automatically or by pushing on one of the panels: used to keep out drafts of air **2** anything like a revolving door, as *a)* something that leads back to a previous place or condition [for some criminals, the justice system is a *revolving door* back to the streets] *b)* a place or situation through which a stream of persons passes, as a job with a high turnover rate

re·volv·ing-door (ri väl′viŋ dôr′, -vôl′-) *adj.* [Informal] **1** designating or of the practice in which a former employee of a government department goes to work for a private company regulated by that department **2** having a high turnover of personnel, members, etc.: said of a company, organization, etc.

re·vue (ri vyo͞o′) *n.* ⟦Fr, REVIEW⟧ a type of musical show consisting of loosely connected skits, songs, and dances, often parodying topical matters

re·vul·sion (ri vul′shən) *n.* ⟦< Fr or L; Fr *révulsion* < L *revulsio* < *revulsus,* pp. of *revellere,* to pluck away < *re-,* back + *vellere,* to pull < IE base **wel-,* to snatch, seize, injure > OE *wol,* pestilence, ON *valr,* the slain on the battlefield⟧ **1** [Rare] a withdrawal **2** [Archaic] a sudden, complete, and violent change of feeling; abrupt, strong reaction in sentiment **3** extreme disgust, shock, or repugnance; feeling of great loathing —**SYN.** AVERSION —**re·vul′sive** *adj.*

re·ward (ri wôrd′) *n.* ⟦ME < NormFr, for OFr *regarde*⟧ **1** something given in return for good or, sometimes, evil, or for service or merit **2** money offered, as for the capture of a criminal, the return of something lost, etc. **3** compensation; profit **4** *Psychol.* a return for correct response to a stimulus —*vt.* ⟦ME *rewarden* < NormFr *rewarder,* for OFr *regarder:* see REGARD⟧ **1** to give a reward to **2** to give a reward for **3** to serve as a reward to or for —**re·ward′a·ble** *adj.* —**re·ward′er** *n.*

SYN.—reward usually refers to something given in recompense for a good deed or for merit [he received a *reward* for saving the child]; **prize** applies to something won in competition or, often, in a lottery or game of chance [she won first *prize* in the golf tournament]; **award** implies a decision by judges but does not connote overt competition [we received an *award* for the best news story of the year]; **premium,** in this connection, applies to a reward offered as an inducement to greater effort or production [to pay a *premium* for advance delivery]

re·ward·ing (ri wôr′diŋ) *adj.* giving a sense of reward, or return [a *rewarding* experience] —**re·ward′ing·ly** *adv.*

re·wind (rē wīnd′; *for n.* rē′wīnd′) *vt.* **-wound′**, **-wind′ing** to wind again; specif., to wind (film or tape) back onto the original reel —*n.* **1** something rewound **2** the act of rewinding

re·wire (rē wīr′) *vt., vi.* **-wired′**, **-wir′ing** to wire again or anew; specif., *a)* to put new wires or wiring in or on (a house, motor, etc.) *b)* to telegraph again

re·word (rē wurd′) *vt.* **1** to state or express again in other words; change the wording of **2** [Rare] to repeat in the same words

re·work (rē wurk′) *vt.* to work again; specif., *a)* to rewrite or revise *b)* to process (something used) for use again

re·writ·a·ble (rē rīt′ə bəl) *adj.* designed to allow digital information to be recorded on it and overwritten repeatedly [a *rewritable* compact disc]: sometimes sp. **re·write′a·ble**

re·write (rē rīt′; *for n.* rē′rīt′) *vt., vi.* **-wrote′**, **-writ′ten**, **-writ′ing** **1** to write again **2** to write over in different words or a different form; revise ☆**3** to write (news turned in by a reporter) in a form suitable for publication —☆*n.* an article so written —**re·writ′er** *n.*

Rex (reks) *n.* ⟦L, a king: see RIGHT⟧ **1** a masculine name **2** *pl.* **re·ges** (rē′jēz) [*also* **r-**] king: the official title of a reigning king [George *Rex*] **3** [*also* **r-**] any of a breed of domestic cat with a short, curly coat and a long, slender tail

rex·ine (rek′sēn′, -sīn′) *n.* ⟦< *Rexine,* a trademark⟧ [Brit.] a kind of imitation leather used for book covers, upholstery, etc.

Reye's syndrome (rīz) ⟦after R. D. *Reye,* Austral pathologist who first described it (1963)⟧ a rare, acute, often fatal disease, usually of children, characterized by neurological disorders, swelling of the brain, and enlargement of the liver: it is associated with the use of aspirin for certain viral illnesses

Rey·kja·vík (rā′kyə vēk′, -vik′) seaport & capital of Iceland, on the SW coast

Rey·nard (ren′ərd, rā′nərd, rā′närd′) *n.* ⟦OFr *Renard, Renart* < OHG *Reginhart* < Gmc **ragina,* counsel, judgment (< IE base **reĝ-,* to put in order > RIGHT) + *hard,* bold, brave: see HARD⟧ **1** the fox in the medieval cycle of fables *Reynard the Fox* **2** [*often* **r-**] a name for any fox in fable and folklore

Reyn·old (ren′əld) *n.* a masculine name: see REGINALD

Reyn·olds (ren′əldz), Sir **Joshua** 1723-92; Eng. portrait painter

Reynolds number ⟦after O. *Reynolds* (1842-1912), Eng physicist⟧ a dimensionless parameter used to determine the nature of fluid flow along surfaces and around objects, as in a wind tunnel

Rey·no·sa (rā nō′sä) city in N Mexico, on the Rio Grande, opposite McAllen, Tex.

rf *abbrev.* **1** radio frequency **2** *Baseball a)* right field *b)* right fielder Also **RF**

Rf *Chem. symbol for* rutherfordium

R factor RESISTANCE PLASMID

RFD *abbrev.* Rural Free Delivery

RFID (är′ef ī dē′) *n.* ⟦*r*(*adio*) *f*(*requency*) *id*(*entification*)⟧ a system consisting of a tag with an embedded electronic chip that emits a radio signal, and a scanning device for reading that signal: used for identification, tracking merchandise, assessing fees, etc.

RFP *abbrev.* request for proposal

Rg *Chem. symbol for* roentgenium

rh or **RH** *abbrev.* right hand

Rh[1] *see* RH FACTOR

Rh[2] *Chem. symbol for* rhodium

rhab·do·coele (rab′də sēl′) *n.* ⟦< ModL *Rhabdocoela* < Gr *rhabdos,* rod (< IE **werb-* < base **wer-,* to turn, bend) + *koilia,* body cavity: see -COELE⟧ any of various small turbellarian flatworms, characterized by having an unbranched, saclike digestive cavity

rhab·do·man·cy (rab′də man′sē) *n.* ⟦LL *rhabdomantia* < Gr *rhabdomanteia*

revote
rewaken
rewarm
rewash
reweave
reweigh
reweld
rewin
rezone

< *rhabdos,* rod (see prec.) + *manteia,* divination (see -MANCY)⟧ divination by means of a rod or wand; esp., the art of seeking underground water or minerals by means of a divining rod; dowsing —**rhab′do·man′cer** *n.*

rhab·do·my·o·ma (rab′dō mī ō′mə) *n.* ⟦ModL < Gr *rhabdos,* rod (see RHABDOCOELE) + MYOMA⟧ *Med.* a tumor composed of striated muscular fibers

rhab·do·vi·rus (rab′dō vī′rəs) *n.* ⟦< Gr *rhabdos,* rod (see RHABDOCOELE) + VIRUS⟧ any of a large family (Rhabdoviridae) of RNA viruses with a wide range of animal hosts and vectors, including the virus that causes rabies

rha·chis (rā′kis) *n.* RACHIS

Rhad·a·man·thus (rad′ə man′thəs) *n.* ⟦L < Gr *Rhadamanthos*⟧ *Gr. Myth.* a son of Zeus and Europa, rewarded for his exemplary justice by being made, after his death, a judge of the dead in the lower world: also **Rhad′a·man′thys** (-this) —**Rhad′a·man′thine** (-thin) *adj.*

Rhae·ti·a (rē′shə, -shē ə) ancient Roman province in the region of modern Bavaria, E Switzerland, & the Tirol —**Rhae′ti·an** (-shən, -shē ən) *adj., n.*

Rhaetian Alps division of the central Alps, mostly in E Switzerland: highest peak, *c.* 13,300 ft (4,054 m)

Rhae·to-Romance (rē′tō rō′mans, -rō mans′) *n.* the group of closely related Romance dialects, including Romansch and Ladin, spoken in SE Switzerland, the Tirol, and N Italy —*adj.* of Rhaeto-Romance Also **Rhae′to-Ro·man′ic** (-man′ik)

-rha·gi·a (rā′jē ə, -jə) *combining form* -RRHAGIA

rham·nose (ram′nōs′) *n.* ⟦< ModL *Rhamnus,* genus of shrubs (< Gr *rhamnos,* buckthorn < IE *werb-: see RHABDOCOELE) + -OSE[1]⟧ a methyl pentose, $C_6H_{12}O_5$, occurring in many plants as a glycoside

rhap·sode (rap′sōd′) *n.* ⟦Gr *rhapsodos*⟧ in ancient Greece, a person who recited rhapsodies, esp. one who recited epic poems as a profession

rhap·sod·ic (rap säd′ik) *adj.* ⟦Gr *rhapsōidikos*⟧ of, characteristic of, or having the nature of, rhapsody; extravagantly enthusiastic; ecstatic: also **rhap·sod′i·cal** —**rhap·sod′i·cal·ly** *adv.*

rhap·so·dist (rap′sə dist) *n.* **1** RHAPSODE **2** a person who rhapsodizes

rhap·so·dize (-dīz′) *vi.* **-dized′**, **-diz′ing** **1** to speak or write in an extravagantly enthusiastic manner **2** to recite or write rhapsodies —*vt.* to recite or utter as a rhapsody

rhap·so·dy (rap′sə dē) *n., pl.* **-dies** ⟦Fr *r(h)apsodie* < L *rhapsodia* < Gr *rhapsōidia* < *rhapsōidos,* one who strings songs together, reciter of epic poetry < *rhaptein,* to stitch together (< IE **werp-,* **wrep-,* extension of base **wer-,* to turn, bend > WORM, WRAP, RAVEL) + *ōidē,* song: see ODE⟧ **1** in ancient Greece, a part of an epic poem suitable for a single recitation **2** any ecstatic or extravagantly enthusiastic utterance in speech or writing **3** great delight; ecstasy **4** [Obs.] a miscellany **5** *Music* an instrumental composition of free, irregular form, suggesting improvisation

rhat·a·ny (rat′'n ē) *n., pl.* **-nies** ⟦Sp *ratania, rataña* < Quechua *ratánia,* astringent⟧ **1** the strongly astringent root of any of several South American dicotyledonous plants (genus *Krameria,* family Krameriaceae, order Polygalales) **2** any of these plants

Rhe·a (rē′ə) *n.* ⟦L < Gr⟧ **1** *Gr. Myth.* daughter of Uranus and Gaea, wife of Cronus, and mother of Zeus, Poseidon, Hades, Demeter, Hera, and Hestia: identified with the Roman Ops and the Phrygian Cybele **2** a large satellite of Saturn **3** [**r-**] any of an order (Rheiformes) of large, flightless birds of South America, smaller than an ostrich and having three toes and a feathered head and neck

-rhe·a (rē′ə) *combining form* -RRHEA

rhe·bok (rē′bäk′) *n.* ⟦Afrik *reebok* < MDu *reeboc,* male roe < *ree,* roe (see ROE[2]) + *boc,* BUCK[1]⟧ a rare South African antelope (*Pelea capreolus*) with woolly, brownish-gray hair, found on rocky mountainsides

Rheims (rēmz; *Fr* rans) *former sp. of* REIMS

Rhein (rīn) *Ger. name for* the RHINE

Rhein·gold (rīn′gōld′; *Ger* rīn gôlt′) *n.* ⟦Ger, Rhine gold⟧ *Gmc. Legend* the hoard of gold guarded by the Rhine maidens and afterward owned by the Nibelungs and Siegfried: see RING OF THE NIBELUNG

Rhein·land-Pfalz (rīn′länt′pfälts′) *Ger. name for* RHINELAND-PALATINATE

Rhen·ish (ren′ish) *adj.* ⟦< L *Rhenus,* Rhine + -ISH: replacing ME *Rinische* < MHG *rinisch* < *rin,* Rhine⟧ of the Rhine or the regions around it —*n.* [Now Rare] RHINE WINE

rhe·ni·um (rē′nē əm) *n.* ⟦ModL < L *Rhenus,* Rhine + -IUM: so named (1925) by its discoverers W. Noddack (1893-1960), I. Tacke, & O. Berg, Ger chemists⟧ a rare, metallic chemical element that is a silver-white solid or a gray-to-black powder, used in thermocouples, electrodes, etc.: symbol, Re; at. no. 75: see the periodic table of elements in the Reference Supplement

rhe·o- (rē′ə, -ō) ⟦< Gr *rheos,* current < *rheein,* to flow: see STREAM⟧ *combining form* a flow, current [*rheology, rheostat*]

rhe·o·base (rē′ə bās′) *n.* ⟦prec. + BASE[1]⟧ *Physiol.* the minimum electric current of unlimited duration needed to excite a nerve or muscle tissue: cf. CHRONAXIE —**rhe′o·bas′ic** (-bā′sik) *adj.*

rhe·ol·o·gy (rē äl′ə jē) *n.* ⟦RHEO- + -LOGY⟧ the branch of physics dealing with the flow and deformation of matter, embracing elasticity, viscosity, and plasticity —**rhe′o·log′i·cal** (-ə läj′i kəl) *adj.* —**rhe·ol′o·gist** *n.*

rhe·om·e·ter (rē äm′ət ər) *n.* ⟦RHEO- + -METER⟧ an instrument for measuring velocity of fluid flow, as of the blood in circulation —**rhe′o·met′ric** (-ə me′trik) *adj.*

rhe·o·phile (rē′ə fīl′) *n.* ⟦RHEO- + -PHILE⟧ an animal or plant best adapted for living in flowing water

rhe·o·stat (-stat′) *n.* ⟦RHEO- + -STAT⟧ a variable resistor for changing the resistance of an electrical circuit without interrupting the circuit, used as for regulating the brightness of electric lights —**rhe′o·stat′ic** *adj.*

rhe·o·tax·is (rē′ə tak′sis) *n.* ⟦ModL: see RHEO- & TAXIS⟧ a positive, or negative, response of a freely moving organism to flow with, or against, a current of water, air, etc. —**rhe′o·tac′tic** (-tak′tik) *adj.*

rhe·ot·ro·pism (rē ät′rə piz′əm) *n.* ⟦RHEO- + -TROPISM⟧ the tendency of an organism, esp. a plant, to respond to the stimulus of a current of water, air, etc. by some change in the direction of growth —**rhe′o·trop′ic** (-ə träp′ik) *adj.*

rhe·sus (rē′səs) *n.* ⟦ModL, arbitrary use of L *Rhesus* (Gr *Rhēsos*), proper name⟧ a brownish-yellow macaque (*Macaca mulatta*) of India, often kept in zoos and used extensively in biological and medical research: in full **rhesus monkey**

rhet *abbrev.* **1** rhetoric **2** rhetorical

rhe·tor (rēt′ər) *n.* ⟦ME *rethor* < L *rhetor* < Gr *rhētōr* < *eirein,* to speak: see WORD⟧ **1** in ancient Greece and Rome, a master or teacher of rhetoric **2** an orator

rhet·o·ric (ret′ər ik) *n.* ⟦ME *rethorike* < OFr or L: OFr *rethorique* < L *rhetorica* < Gr *rhētorikē (technē),* rhetorical (art) < *rhētōr,* orator: see prec.⟧ **1** *a)* the art of using words effectively or persuasively in speaking or writing; esp., now, the art of prose composition *b)* skill in this *c)* a treatise or book on this **2** artificial eloquence; language that is showy and elaborate but largely empty of clear ideas or sincere emotion

rhe·tor·i·cal (ri tôr′i kəl) *adj.* **1** of, having the nature of, or according to rhetoric **2** using or characterized by mere rhetoric, or artificial eloquence; showy and elaborate in style —**rhe·tor′i·cal·ly** *adv.*

rhetorical question a question asked only for effect, as to emphasize a point, no answer being expected

rhet·o·ri·cian (ret′ə rish′ən) *n.* ⟦ME *rethoricien* < OFr⟧ **1** a person skilled in rhetoric **2** a teacher of rhetoric **3** a person who writes or speaks in a rhetorical, or showy, elaborate manner

rheum (ro͞om) *n.* ⟦ME *reume* < OFr < L *rheuma* < Gr, a flow, moist discharge, akin to *rheein,* to flow: see STREAM⟧ **1** any watery discharge from the mucous membranes, as of the mouth, eyes, or nose **2** a cold; rhinitis —**rheum′y** *adj.* **rheum′i·er**, **rheum′i·est**

rheu·mat·ic (ro͞o mat′ik) *adj.* ⟦ME *reumatike* < OFr *reumatique* < L *rheumaticus* < Gr *rheumatikos:* see prec.⟧ of, caused by, characteristic of, or having rheumatism —*n.* a person who has rheumatism —**the rheumatics** [Dial.] rheumatic pains —**rheu·mat′i·cal·ly** *adv.*

rheumatic disease any of a group of diseases of the connective tissue, of uncertain causes, including rheumatoid arthritis, gout, and rheumatic fever

rheumatic fever an acute or chronic inflammatory disease usually induced by a preceding infection with certain hemolytic streptococci, characterized variously by fever, pain and swelling of the joints, inflammation of the heart, etc., and typically occurring in children and young adults

rheu·ma·tism (ro͞o′mə tiz′əm) *n.* ⟦L *rheumatismus,* rheum < Gr *rheumatismos* < *rheumatizein,* to suffer from a flux < *rheuma:* see RHEUM⟧ *nontechnical term for* any of various painful conditions of the joints and muscles, characterized by inflammation, stiffness, etc., including rheumatoid arthritis, bursitis, and neuritis

rheu·ma·toid (ro͞o′mə toid′) *adj.* of or like rheumatism

rheumatoid arthritis a chronic disease whose cause is unknown, characterized by inflammation, pain, and swelling of the joints accompanied by spasms in adjacent muscles and often leading to deformity of the joints

rheumatoid factor an antibody usually found in the blood serum of people with rheumatoid arthritis

rheu·ma·tol·o·gy (ro͞o′mə täl′ə jē) *n.* ⟦RHEUMAT(ISM) + -OLOGY⟧ the branch of medicine dealing with the study and treatment of rheumatic diseases —**rheu′ma·tol′o·gist** *n.*

☆**Rh factor** (är′āch′) ⟦< RH(ESUS): from having been discovered first in the blood of rhesus monkeys⟧ a group of antigens, determined by heredity and usually present in human red blood cells, which may cause hemolytic reactions during pregnancy or after transfusion of blood containing this factor into someone lacking it: see RH POSITIVE, RH NEGATIVE

☆**rhig·o·lene** (rig′ə lēn′) *n.* ⟦< Gr *rhigos,* frost (see FRIGID) + -OL[2] + -ENE⟧ a colorless, volatile liquid distilled from petroleum and consisting primarily of pentane and butane, formerly used as a local anesthetic

Rhin (ran) *Fr. name for* the RHINE

rhin- (rīn) *combining form* RHINO-: used before a vowel

rhi·nal (rī′nəl) *adj.* ⟦RHIN(O)- + -AL⟧ of the nose; nasal

Rhine (rīn) ⟦Ger *Rhein* < Celt *Rēnos* < IE **erei-* < base **er-,* set in motion > RUN⟧ river in W Europe, flowing from E Switzerland north through Germany, then west through the Netherlands into the North Sea: *c.* 820 mi (1,320 km): Ger. name RHEIN, Fr. name RHIN, Du. name RIJN

Rhine·land (rīn′land′, -lənd) **1** that part of Germany west of the Rhine **2** RHINE PROVINCE

Rhine·land-Pa·lat·i·nate (rīn′lənd′ pə lat′'n āt′) state of SW Germany: 7,663 sq mi (19,847 sq km); cap. Mainz

rhi·nen·ceph·a·lon (rī′nen sef′ə län′) *n., pl.* **-la** (-lə) ⟦ModL: see RHINO- & ENCEPHALON⟧ the part of the brain that receives sensory information from the olfactory nerves —**rhi′nen·ce·phal′ic** (-sə fal′ik) *adj.*

Rhine Province former province of Prussia, now divided between North Rhine-Westphalia & Rhineland-Palatinate

rhine·stone (rīn′stōn′) *n.* ⟦transl. of Fr *caillou du Rhin:* so named because orig. made from pieces of quartz found in the RHINE⟧ a colorless artificial gem made of hard glass that is cut so as to look somewhat like a cut diamond

Rhine wine 1 any of various wines produced in the Rhine Valley, esp. any such light white wine 2 a wine of this type produced elsewhere

rhi·ni·tis (rī nīt′is) ***n.*** ⟦ModL: see RHINO- & -ITIS⟧ inflammation of the nasal mucous membrane

rhi·no¹ (rī′nō) ***n.***, *pl.* **-nos** or **-no** *short for* RHINOCEROS

rhi·no² (rī′nō) ***n.*** ⟦< ?⟧ [Brit. Slang] money; cash

rhi·no- (rī′nō, -nə) ⟦< Gr *rhis* (gen. *rhinos*), the nose⟧ *combining form* nose [*rhinology*]

rhi·noc·er·os (rī näs′ər əs) ***n.***, *pl.* **-os·es** or **-os** ⟦ME *rinoceros* < L *rhinoceros* < Gr *rhinokerōs*, lit., nose-horned < *rhis* (see prec.) + *keras*, HORN⟧ any of a family (Rhinocerotidae) of large, heavy, thick-skinned, plant-eating, perissodactylous mammals of tropical Africa and Asia, with one or two upright horns on the snout —**rhi·noc′er·ot′ic** (-ät′ik) ***adj.***

rhinoceros beetle any of several medium to very large, dark-colored, tropical scarab beetles: so called because of a hornlike projection on the head of the male

rhi·no·lar·yn·gol·o·gy (rī′nō lar′in gäl′ə jē) ***n.*** ⟦RHINO- + LARYNGOLOGY⟧ the branch of medicine dealing with diseases of the nose and larynx —**rhi′no·lar′yn·gol′o·gist *n.***

rhi·nol·o·gy (rī näl′ə jē) ***n.*** ⟦RHINO- + -LOGY⟧ the branch of medicine dealing with the nose and its diseases —**rhi·nol′o·gist *n.***

rhi·no·phar·yn·gi·tis (rī′nō far′in jīt′is) ***n.*** ⟦RHINO- + PHARYNGITIS⟧ inflammation of the mucous membrane of the nose and pharynx, as in the common cold

rhi·no·plas·ty (rī′nō plas′tē) ***n.*** ⟦RHINO- + -PLASTY⟧ plastic surgery of the nose —**rhi′no·plas′tic *adj.***

rhi·nor·rhe·a (rī′nə rē′ə) ***n.*** ⟦RHINO- + -RRHEA⟧ a mucous discharge from the nose

rhi·no·scope (rī′nə skōp′) ***n.*** ⟦RHINO- + -SCOPE⟧ an instrument for examining the internal passages of the nose —**rhi·nos·co·py** (rī näs′kə pē) ***n.***

rhi·no·vi·rus (rī′nō vī′rəs) ***n.*** ⟦RHINO- + VIRUS⟧ any of a large genus (*Rhinovirus*) of picornaviruses that are the chief infectious agents causing the common cold

rhi·zo- (rī′zō, -zə) ⟦< Gr *rhiza*, ROOT¹⟧ *combining form* root [*rhizopod*]: also, before a vowel, **rhiz-**

rhi·zo·bi·um (rī zō′bē əm) ***n.***, *pl.* **-bi·a** (-ə) ⟦ModL < prec. + Gr *bios*, life: see BIO-⟧ any of a genus (*Rhizobium*) of rod-shaped, nitrogen-fixing bacteria found in nodules on the roots of certain leguminous plants, as the bean and clover

rhi·zo·car·pous (rī′zō kär′pəs) ***adj.*** ⟦RHIZO- + -CARPOUS⟧ having perennial roots but annual stems and leaves: said of perennial plants

rhi·zo·ceph·a·lan (-sef′ə lən) ***n.*** ⟦RHIZO- + CEPHAL(OUS) + -AN⟧ any of an order (Rhizocephala) of cirriped crustaceans that live as internal parasites on crabs —**rhi′zo·ceph′a·lous *adj.***

rhi·zoc·to·ni·a (rī′zäk tō′nē ə) ***n.*** ⟦ModL < Gr *rhiza*, ROOT¹ + *ktonos*, murder < *kteinein*, to kill, akin to Sans *kṣaṇómi*, (I) injure⟧ any of various imperfect fungi (genus *Rhizoctonia*), some of which cause various diseases of many garden vegetables and ornamental plants

rhi·zo·gen·ic (rī′zō jen′ik) ***adj.*** ⟦RHIZO- + -GENIC⟧ *Bot.* producing roots: also **rhi·zog′e·nous** (-zäj′ə nəs) or **rhi′zo·ge·net′ic** (-jə net′ik)

rhi·zoid (rī′zoid′) ***adj.*** ⟦RHIZ(O)- + -OID⟧ rootlike —***n.*** any of the rootlike filaments in a moss, fern, etc. that attach the plant to the substratum —**rhi·zoi′dal *adj.***

rhi·zome (rī′zōm′) ***n.*** ⟦ModL *rhizoma* < Gr *rhizōma* < *rhizousthai*, to take root < *rhiza*, ROOT¹⟧ a creeping stem lying, usually horizontally, at or under the surface of the soil and differing from a root in having scale leaves, bearing leaves or aerial shoots near its tips, and producing roots from its undersurface —**rhi·zom′a·tous** (-zäm′ət əs, -zō′mət-) ***adj.***

rhizome of grass

rhi·zo·mor·phous (rī′zō môr′fəs) ***adj.*** ⟦RHIZO- + -MORPHOUS⟧ *Bot.* formed like a root; root-shaped

rhi·zo·pod (rī′zə päd′) ***n.*** ⟦RHIZO- + -POD⟧ any of a superclass (Rhizopoda) of one-celled protozoans with pseudopodia, including the amoebas, foraminifera, and myxomycetes —**rhi·zop′o·dan** (-zäp′ə dən) ***adj., n.*** —**rhi·zop′o·dal** (-dəl) ***adj.***, **rhi·zop′o·dous** (-dəs)

rhi·zo·pus (-pəs) ***n.*** ⟦ModL < RHIZO- + Gr *pous*, FOOT⟧ any of a genus (*Rhizopus*) of fungi, including the common bread mold and other species that cause various rots

rhi·zo·sphere (-sfir′) ***n.*** ⟦Ger *rhizosphäre*: see RHIZO- & SPHERE⟧ *Ecol.* the part of the soil enclosing and influenced by the roots of a plant

rhi·zot·o·my (rī zät′ə mē) ***n.***, *pl.* **-mies** ⟦RHIZO- + -TOMY⟧ a surgical cutting of the spinal nerve roots, esp. of the posterior nerves, as for relieving pain

☆**Rh negative** (är′āch′) not having Rh factor: said of blood or of persons

rho (rō) ***n.*** ⟦Gr *rhō* < Sem: cf. Heb *rosh* (see ROSH HASHANA), *rēsh* (see RESH)⟧ the seventeenth letter of the Greek alphabet (Ρ, ρ)

Rho·da (rō′də) ***n.*** ⟦L *Rhode* < Gr *Rhodē* < *rhodon*, rose < OPers *wṛda* > Ar *ward*⟧ a feminine name

rho·da·mine (rō′də mēn′, -min) ***n.*** ⟦RHOD(O)- + AMINE⟧ any of a group of synthetic dyes ranging in color from red to pink, obtained by condensation of phthalic anhydride with an amino derivative of phenol

Rhode Island (rōd) ⟦officially, *State of Rhode Island and Providence Plantations*: Aquidneck, largest island in Narragansett Bay, was renamed *Rhode Island* (reason uncert.); mainland towns were the *Providence Plantations*⟧ New England state of the U.S.: one of the 13 original states: 1,045 sq mi (2,706 sq km); cap. Providence: abbrev. *RI* or *R.I.*

Rhode Islander a person born or living in Rhode Island

☆**Rhode Island Red** any of a breed of domestic chicken with reddish-brown feathers and a black tail, bred in the U.S. from a red Malay game fowl, raised esp. for its meat

Rhodes¹ (rōdz), **Cecil (John)** 1853-1902; Brit. financier & colonial administrator in South Africa

Rhodes² (rōdz) ⟦Gr *Rhodos*⟧ 1 largest island of the Dodecanese, in the Aegean: 545 sq mi (1,412 sq km) 2 seaport on this island

Rhodes grass ⟦after C. RHODES¹⟧ a tender, perennial, creeping grass (*Chloris gayana*) of Africa, cultivated for forage in the S U.S.

Rho·de·si·a (rō dē′zhə, -zhē ə) former region in S Africa, including NORTHERN RHODESIA (now ZAMBIA) & SOUTHERN RHODESIA (now ZIMBABWE) —**Rho·de′sian *adj., n.***

Rhodesian man ⟦after NORTHERN RHODESIA, where the first skeletal remains were found in 1921⟧ an early African human (*Homo sapiens rhodesiensis*) of the Upper Pleistocene, distinguished by long, sturdy limb bones, massive brow ridges, and a large face

Rhodesian Ridge·back (rij′bak′) any of a breed of strong, short-haired hunting dog developed in S Africa, with a light tan or light reddish-tan coat and a ridge along the spine formed by the hair growing forward

Rhodes scholarship any of a number of scholarships for two or three years of study at Oxford University, England, established by the will of C. J. Rhodes for selected students (**Rhodes scholars**) from the British Commonwealth and the U.S.

Rho·di·an (rō′dē ən) ***adj.*** of Rhodes or its people or culture —***n.*** a person born or living on Rhodes

rho·dic (rō′dik) ***adj.*** of or containing rhodium, esp. tetravalent rhodium

rho·di·um (rō′dē əm) ***n.*** ⟦ModL: so named (1804) by its discoverer, W. H. Wollaston (see WOLLASTONITE) < Gr *rhodon*, rose (see RHODA), after the color of a dilute solution of its salts + -IUM⟧ a hard, gray-white metallic chemical element, one of the platinum metals, used in alloys with platinum and gold in thermocouples and as an electrical contact material, and in unalloyed form to electroplate optical instruments, silverware, jewelry, etc.: symbol, Rh; at. no. 45: see the periodic table of elements in the Reference Supplement

rho·do- (rō′dō, -də) ⟦< Gr *rhodon*, rose: see RHODA⟧ *combining form* rose, rose-red [*rhodolite*]: also, before a vowel, **rhod-**

rho·do·chro·site (rō′də krō′sīt′) ***n.*** ⟦Ger *rhodochrosit* < Gr *rhodochrōs*, rose-colored (< *rhodon*, rose: see RHODA) + *chrōsis*, a coloring < *chrōs*, color, akin to *chrōma*: see CHROME + Ger *-it*, -ITE¹⟧ a glassy pinkish-to-gray mineral, $MnCO_3$, an ore of manganese

rho·do·den·dron (-den′drən) ***n.*** ⟦ModL < Gr *rhododendron* < *rhodon*, rose (see RHODA) + *dendron*, TREE⟧ any of a genus (*Rhododendron*) of trees and shrubs of the heath family, mainly evergreen, with showy flowers of pink, white, or purple

rho·do·lite (rō′də līt′) ***n.*** ⟦RHODO- + -LITE⟧ a pink or rose-red variety of garnet, often used as a gem

rho·do·mon·tade (räd′ə mən tād′, rō′də-; -täd′) ***n., adj., vi.*** *archaic sp. of* RODOMONTADE

rho·do·nite (rōd′'n īt′) ***n.*** ⟦Ger *rhodonit* < Gr *rhodon*, rose (see RHODA) + Ger *-it*, -ITE¹⟧ a glassy, pink-to-brown, triclinic mineral, $MnSiO_3$, used as an ornamental stone; manganese silicate

Rhod·o·pe (räd′ə pē) mountain system in S Bulgaria extending into NE Greece: highest peak, 9,595 ft (2,925 m)

rho·do·plast (rō′də plast′) ***n.*** ⟦RHODO- + -PLAST⟧ a plastid found in red algae, containing red pigment as well as chlorophyll

rho·dop·sin (rō däp′sin) ***n.*** ⟦< Gr *rhodon*, a rose (see RHODA) + *opsis*, sight (see -OPSIS) + -IN¹⟧ a purplish, photosensitive protein pigment that is essential for vision in dim light, found in the rods of the retina: also called *visual purple*: see OPSIN

rho·do·ra (rō dôr′ə) ***n.*** ⟦ModL, earlier name of the genus < L, kind of plant: said to be of Gallic orig.⟧ a deciduous rhododendron (*Rhododendron canadense*) native to NE North America, that bears pink flowers in the spring

rhomb (rämb, räm) ***n.*** ⟦Fr *rhombe* < L *rhombus*⟧ *var. of* RHOMBUS

rhom·ben·ceph·a·lon (räm′ben sef′ə län′) ***n.*** ⟦ModL: see RHOMBUS & ENCEPHALON⟧ the hindbrain, including the cerebellum, pons, and medulla oblongata

rhom·bic (räm′bik) ***adj.*** 1 of, or having the form of, a rhombus 2 having a rhombus as the base or cross section: said of solid figures 3 bounded by rhombuses 4 ORTHORHOMBIC

rhom·bo·he·dral (räm′bə hē′drəl) ***adj.*** 1 of or having to do with a rhombohedron 2 designating or of a crystal system having three axes of equal length, none of which intersects at right angles with another: see CRYSTAL SYSTEM

rhom·bo·he·dron (räm′bə hē′drən) ***n.***, *pl.* **-drons** or **-dra** (-drə) ⟦ModL: see RHOMBUS & -HEDRON⟧ a six-sided prism each face of which is a rhombus

rhom·boid (räm′boid′) ***n.*** ⟦Fr *rhomboïde* < L *rhomboides* < Gr *rhomboeidēs*, rhomboid-shaped: see RHOMBUS & -OID⟧ a parallelogram without right angles and only the opposite sides equal —***adj.*** 1 shaped like a rhomboid 2 shaped somewhat like a rhombus —**rhom·boi′dal *adj.***

rhom·boi·de·us (räm boi′dē əs) ***n.***, *pl.* **-de·i′** (-ī′) ⟦ModL *(musculus) rhomboideus*, rhomblike (muscle) < L *rhomboides*, prec. + *-eus*, -OUS⟧ either of two muscles arising from the upper thoracic vertebrae and inserting into the scapula

rhom·bus (räm′bəs) ***n., pl.*** **-bus·es** or **-bi′** (-bī′) ⟦L < Gr *rhombos,* object that can be turned, akin to *rhembein,* to turn, whirl < IE **wremb-* < base **wer-,* to turn, bend > WORM, WARP⟧ an equilateral parallelogram, esp. one without right angles

rhon·chus (räŋ′kəs) ***n., pl.*** **-chi′** (-kī′) ⟦L, a snoring < Gr *rhonchos,* var. of *renchos* < IE base **srenk-,* to snore > OIr *srennim,* (I) snore⟧ a rattling sound, somewhat like snoring heard on auscultation of the chest when there is a partial bronchial obstruction; dry rale —**rhon′chal** (-kəl) ***adj.,*** **rhon′chi·al** (-kē əl)

Rhone or **Rhône** (rōn) ⟦Fr *Rhône,* prob. < Celt *Rodanos,* stream name, lit., the flowing one < IE **ered-,* to flow < base **er-* > RUN⟧ river flowing from SW Switzerland south through France into the Gulf of Lions: 505 mi (813 km)

Rhône-Alpes (rōn alp′, -älp′; *Fr* rōn ȧlp′) metropolitan region of SE France: 16,872 sq mi (43,698 sq km); chief city, Lyon

rho·ta·cism (rōt′ə siz′əm) ***n.*** ⟦ModL *rhotacismus* < MGr *rhōtakizein,* to make wrong use of the letter *rhō* + L *-ismus,* -ISM⟧ the change of a sound, esp. (s) or (z), to the sound (r)

☆**Rh positive** (är′āch′) having Rh factor: said of blood or of persons

rhu·barb (ro͞o′bärb′) ***n.*** ⟦ME *rubarbe* < OFr *rheubarbe* < ML *rheubarbarum,* altered < LL *rha barbarum* < Gr *rhēon barbaron,* foreign rhubarb < *rhēon,* rhubarb (< Pers *rēwend*) + *barbaron,* foreign, BARBAROUS⟧ **1** any of a genus (*Rheum*) of perennial, large-leaved plants of the buckwheat family; esp., the domestic pieplant (*R. rhaponticum*), having large, cordate leaf blades borne on long, thick stalks: the stalks are cooked into a sauce or baked in pies, but the blades are poisonous **2** the roots and rhizomes of various Asian rhubarbs, used as a cathartic ☆**3** ⟦? from the practice in early radio broadcasts of repeating "rhubarb" in simulating crowd noises⟧ [Slang] a heated discussion or argument

rhumb (rum, rumb) ***n.*** ⟦< Port & Sp *rumbo,* prob. < L *rhombus:* see RHOMBUS⟧ **1** RHUMB LINE **2** any of the 32 points of a mariner's compass

☆**rhum·ba** (rum′bə, ro͝om′bə) ***n. alt. sp. of*** RUMBA

rhumb line the course of a ship that keeps a constant compass direction, represented on a map, chart, or globe by a line that cuts across all meridians at the same angle

rhyme (rīm) ***n.*** ⟦ME *rime* < OFr < *rimer,* to rhyme, prob. < Frank **rim,* row, series, akin to OE, OHG *rim,* series, number < IE **rei-* (> OIr *rim,* number) < base **are-,* to join, fit (> ART[1], RATIO, RITE): form infl. by assoc. with L *rhythmus,* RHYTHM⟧ **1** a piece of verse, or poem, in which there is a regular recurrence of corresponding sounds, esp. at the ends of lines **2** such verse or poetry in general **3** correspondence of sound between stressed syllables at the ends of words or lines of verse; specif., PERFECT RHYME (sense 1) **4** a word that corresponds with another in sound, esp. end sound —***vi.*** **rhymed, rhym′ing 1** to make verse, esp. rhyming verse **2** to form a rhyme ["more" *rhymes* with "door"] **3** to be composed in metrical form with rhymes **4** to be in accord or agreement [the eyewitness accounts *rhyme* on the essential points] —***vt.*** **1** to put into rhyme **2** to compose in metrical form with rhymes **3** to use as a rhyme or rhymes —**rhyme or reason** order or sense: preceded by *without, no,* etc.

rhym·er (rīm′ər) ***n.*** a maker of rhymes, or poems; esp., a rhymester

rhyme royal a stanza of seven lines in iambic pentameter rhyming *ababbcc,* first used in English by Chaucer

rhyme scheme the pattern of rhymes, esp. end rhymes, used in a piece of verse, usually indicated by letters [ababbcc is the *rhyme scheme* of rhyme royal]

rhyme·ster (rīm′stər) ***n.*** ⟦see -STER⟧ a maker of trivial or inferior rhyme or verse; poetaster

rhyming slang a form of language play, esp. as used by cockneys, in which a phrase is substituted for a single word with which the last word of the phrase rhymes (Ex.: *trouble and strife* used for *wife, apples and pears* for *stairs*)

rhyn·cho·ce·pha·li·an (riŋ′kō sə fā′lē ən) ***adj.*** ⟦< Gr *rhynchos,* snout + *kephalē,* head (see CEPHALIC) + -IAN⟧ designating or of a nearly extinct order (Rhynchocephalia) of lizardlike, beaked reptiles: the only two existing species are tuataras —***n.*** any member of this order

rhyn·coph·o·ran (riŋ käf′ə rən) ***n.*** ⟦< ModL *Rhyncophora* < Gr *rhynchos,* snout + *-phoros,* bearer (see -PHORE) + -AN⟧ any of various beetles, including the weevils, having the head extended to form a snout

rhy·o·lite (rī′ə līt′) ***n.*** ⟦Ger *rhyolit* < Gr *rhyax,* stream (of lava) + *lithos,* stone⟧ a light-colored igneous rock with a fine-grained, granitelike texture

rhythm (rith′əm) ***n.*** ⟦< Fr or L: Fr *rythme* < L *rhythmus* < Gr *rhythmos,* measure, measured motion < base of *rheein,* to flow: see STREAM⟧ **1** *a)* flow, movement, procedure, etc. characterized by basically regular recurrence of elements or features, as beat, or accent, in alternation with opposite or different elements or features [the *rhythm* of speech, dancing, the heartbeat, etc.] *b)* such recurrence; pattern of flow or movement **2** an effect of ordered movement in a work of art, literature, drama, etc. attained through patterns in the timing, spacing, repetition, accenting, etc. of the elements **3** *Biol.* a periodic occurrence in living organisms of specific physiological changes, as the menstrual cycle, or a seasonal or daily variation in some activity, as sleep or feeding, in response to geophysical factors **4** *Music a)* basically regular recurrence of grouped strong and weak beats, or heavily and lightly accented tones, in alternation; arrangement of successive tones, usually in measures, according to their relative accentuation and duration *b)* the form or pattern of this [waltz *rhythm*] *c)* instruments on which the rhythm can be played; specif., RHYTHM SECTION: cf. TIME, TEMPO, METER[1] **5** *Prosody a)* basically regular recurrence of grouped stressed and unstressed, long and short, or high-pitched and low-pitched syllables in alternation; arrangement of successive syllables, as in metrical units (*feet*) or cadences, according to their relative stress, quantity, or pitch *b)* the form or pattern of this [iambic *rhythm*] —**rhyth·mic** (rith′mik) ***adj.,*** **rhyth′mi·cal** —**rhyth′mi·cal·ly** ***adv.***

☆**rhythm and blues** a form of American popular music, influenced by the blues and characterized by a strong beat: rock-and-roll derives from it

rhythm band a band that plays percussion instruments, specif. one composed of children who do so in order to learn about musical rhythm

rhythm guitar the guitar part, as in pop music, providing rhythmic chordal accompaniment to a vocalist or lead instrument

rhyth·mic·i·ty (rith mis′ə tē) ***n.*** regularity in tempo, cyclic occurrence, etc.; rhythmic quality

rhyth·mics (rith′miks) ***n.*** science or system of rhythm and rhythmical forms

rhyth·mist (rith′mist) ***n.*** a person using or skilled in rhythm or one having a good sense of rhythm

rhythm method ⟦see RHYTHM (*n.* 3)⟧ a method of birth control in which a couple refrains from sexual intercourse on those days during a woman's menstrual cycle when she is likely to conceive

rhythm section those instruments in a band that mainly supply rhythm: in jazz, usually the piano, double bass, drums, and sometimes guitar; in popular music, usually the guitar, electric bass, drums, and often keyboard

rhyt·i·dec·to·my (rit′i dek′tə mē) ***n., pl.*** **-mies** ⟦< Gr *rhytis* (stem *rhytid-*), wrinkle + -ECTOMY⟧ plastic surgery of the face to remove wrinkles, skin folds, etc.; face-lifting

rhy·ton (rī′tän′) ***n.*** ⟦Gr, neut. of *rhytos,* flowing, akin to *rheein,* to flow: see STREAM⟧ an ancient Greek cup shaped like a drinking horn and typically made in the form of an animal's head

R.I. ***abbrev.*** **1** ⟦L *Rex et Imperator*⟧ King and Emperor **2** ⟦L *Regina et Imperatrix*⟧ Queen and Empress **3** Rhode Island: also **RI**

ri·a (rē′ə, rē′ä) ***n.*** ⟦Ger < Sp *ría,* estuary < *río,* river < VL *rius,* for L *rivus,* brook, stream < IE **reiwos* < base **er-,* to set in motion > RUN⟧ a long, narrow, wedge-shaped inlet, uniformly widening and deepening toward the sea

ri·al (rē äl′, rē ôl′) ***n.*** ⟦Pers < Ar *riyāl* < Sp *real,* REAL[2]⟧ the basic monetary unit of: *a)* Iran *b)* Oman *c)* Yemen: see the table of monetary units in the Reference Supplement

ri·al·to (rē al′tō) ***n., pl.*** **-tos** ⟦after *Rialto,* island in Venice, Italy, formerly a center of business & trade⟧ **1** a theater district **2** a trading area or marketplace

ri·ant (rī′ənt) ***adj.*** ⟦Fr, prp. of *rire* < L *ridere,* to laugh: see RIDICULE⟧ laughing; smiling; merry; cheerful

☆**ri·a·ta** (rē ät′ə) ***n.*** ⟦AmSp *reata:* see LARIAT⟧ [West] LARIAT

rib (rib) ***n.*** ⟦ME *ribbe* < OE *rib,* akin to ON *rif,* Ger *rippe* < IE base **rebh-,* to arch over, roof over > Gr *ereptein,* to crown, OSlav *rebro,* rib⟧ **1** any of the arched bones attached posteriorly to the vertebral column and enclosing the chest cavity: in humans there are twelve pairs of such bones: see TRUE RIBS, FALSE RIBS, FLOATING RIBS **2** *a)* a cut of meat having one or more ribs *b)* [*pl.*] *short for* SPARERIBS **3** a wife: in humorous reference to the Biblical creation of Eve from Adam's rib (Gen. 2:21-22) **4** a raised ridge in cloth, esp. in knitted material **5** any of the curved crosspieces extending from the keel to the top of the hull in a ship, forming its framework **6** the structural crosspieces attached to a spar for shaping and strengthening an airplane wing **7** any narrow riblike piece used to form, strengthen, or shape something [a *rib* of an umbrella] **8** *Archit. a)* a long curved piece in an arch *b)* any of the transverse and intersecting arches of a vault **9** *Bot.* any of the main veins in a leaf —***vt.*** **ribbed, rib′bing 1** to provide, form, or strengthen with a rib or ribs **2** to put ribs in; mark with ribs **3** ⟦prob. < RIB-TICKLER⟧ [Slang] to tease or make fun of; kid

rib·ald (rib′əld) ***adj.*** ⟦ME *ribaude* < OFr *ribaud,* debauchee < *riber,* to be wanton < OHG *riban,* to copulate, lit., to rub < IE **wreip-,* to twist > Gr *rhipē,* a throw, rush, storm⟧ characterized by coarse or vulgar joking or mocking; esp., dealing with sex in a humorously earthy or direct way —***n.*** a ribald person —**SYN.** COARSE

rib·ald·ry (-rē) ***n.*** ⟦ME *ribawdrye* < OFr *ribauderie:* see prec. & -ERY⟧ **1** ribald language or humor **2** *pl.* **-ries** an example of ribald language or humor

rib·and (rib′ənd, -ən) ***n. archaic var. of*** RIBBON

ri·ba·vi·rin (rī′bə vī′rin) ***n.*** ⟦prob. < RIB(ONUCLEIC) A(CID) + VIR(US) + -IN[1]⟧ a synthetic, broad-spectrum antiviral drug, $C_8H_{12}N_4O_5$

rib·band (rib′band′, -ənd, -ən) ***n.*** ⟦RIB + BAND[1]⟧ a long, flexible piece of wood or metal fastened across the ribs of a ship to hold them in place while the outside planking or plating is being put on

rib·bing (rib′iŋ) ***n.*** **1** an arrangement or series of ribs, as in knitted fabric or a ship's framework **2** [Informal] the act or an instance of teasing or ridiculing playfully

rib·bit (rib′it) ***interj., n.*** ⟦echoic⟧ (used to suggest) the croaking of a frog

rib·bon (rib′ən) ***n.*** ⟦ME *riban* < MFr *riban, ruban* < ? MDu *ringband,* collar < *ring,* RING[2] + *band,* akin to BAND[1]⟧ **1** *a)* a narrow strip of silk, rayon, velvet, etc. finished at the edges and of various widths, used for decoration, tying things, etc. *b)* material in such strips **2** anything suggesting such a strip [a *ribbon* of blue sky] **3** [*pl.*] torn strips or shreds; tatters [a garment torn to *ribbons*] ☆**4** a narrow strip of inked cloth or plastic against which type characters strike for printing, as in a typewriter **5** *a)* a small strip of colored cloth worn as a badge or awarded as a prize, symbol of honor or achievement, etc. *b)* *Mil.* a strip of cloth, often of many colors, worn on the left breast of the uniform to indicate an award of a decoration or medal **6** [*pl.*] [Informal] reins used in driving —***vt.*** **1** to decorate, trim, or mark with or as with a ribbon or ribbons **2** to split or tear into ribbonlike strips or shreds —***vi.*** to extend or form in a ribbonlike strip or strips —**rib′bon·like′** ***adj.***

rib·bon-cut·ting (rib′ən kut′iŋ) ***n.*** a ceremony marking the official opening of a site, the commencement of its construction, etc., typically involving the cutting of a ribbon suspended as across an entrance

rib·bon·fish (-fish′) ***n.***, *pl.* **-fish′** or **-fish′es** (see FISH) any of a family (Trachipteridae, order Lampriformes) of elongated, marine bony fishes having a compressed, ribbonlike body

ribbon worm NEMERTEAN

rib cage the cagelike anatomical structure formed by the ribs and sternum

Ri·bei·rão Prê·to (rē′bā roun′ prā′to͞o) city in SE Brazil, in São Paulo state

Ri·be·ra (ri ber′ə; *Sp* rē be′rä), **Jo·sé** (hô se′) 1588?-1652?; Sp. painter in Naples: called *Lo Spagnoletto*

rib-eye (steak) (rib′ī′) a beefsteak cut from the rib section, with the bone removed: also written **ribeye (steak)**

rib·grass (rib′gras′) ***n.*** a weedy plantain (*Plantago lanceolata*) with ribbed leaves

rib·ier (grape) (rib′yər) a large, black variety of European or Californian table grape (*Vitis vinifera*)

ri·bo·fla·vin (rī′bə flā′vin) ***n.*** ⟦RIBO(SE) + FLAVIN⟧ a yellow crystalline B vitamin, $C_{17}H_{20}N_4O_6$, found in milk, eggs, liver, kidney, fruits, leafy vegetables, yeast, etc.; vitamin B_2: its deficiency in the diet causes stunted growth, loss of hair, etc.: also sp. **ri′bo·fla′vine**

ri·bo·nu·cle·ase (rī′bō no͞o′klē ās′, -nyo͞o′-) ***n.*** ⟦RIBO(SE) + NUCLEASE⟧ any of a group of enzymes that split RNA

ri·bo·nu·cle·ic acid (rī′bō no͞o klē′ik, -nyo͞o-) ⟦RIBO(SE) + NUCLEIC ACID⟧ RNA

ri·bo·nu·cle·o·side (rī′bō no͞o′klē ə sīd′, -nyo͞o′-) ***n.*** any of various nucleosides in which the purine or pyrimidine base is combined with the carbohydrate ribose

ri·bo·nu·cle·o·tide (rī′bō no͞o′klē ə tīd′, -nyo͞o′-) ***n.*** any of various nucleotides in which the carbohydrate component is ribose: a structural unit of RNA

ri·bose (rī′bōs′) ***n.*** ⟦< Ger *rib(onsäure)*, a tetra-hydroxy acid (< arbitrarily altered elements of *arabinose*, ARABINOSE + *säure*, acid) + -OSE[1]⟧ a pentose sugar, $C_5H_{10}O_5$, that is a basic component of RNA, riboflavin, etc.

ribosomal RNA a form of RNA that is one of the constituent elements of ribosomes and is associated with messenger RNA and transfer RNA in the synthesis of proteins

ri·bo·some (rī′bə sōm′) ***n.*** ⟦< RIBOSE + -SOME[3]⟧ a minute, spherical particle composed of RNA and proteins and present in great numbers in the cytoplasm of cells: proteins are manufactured at the ribosomal surface following genetic instructions carried there by messenger RNA —**ri′bo·so′mal** (-sō′məl) ***adj.***

ri·bo·zyme (rī′bə zīm′) ***n.*** ⟦RIBO(NUCLEIC ACID) + (EN)ZYME⟧ a molecule of RNA that acts as an enzyme, used in genetic research and gene therapy

rib·tick·ler (rib′tik′lər) ***n.*** [Slang] an esp. funny joke, remark, or story —**rib′-tick′ling** ***adj.***

rib·wort (rib′wurt′) ***n.*** RIBGRASS

-ric (rik) ⟦ME *-riche, -ricke,* realm, power < OE *rice*, reign, dominion: see REICH⟧ *combining form* jurisdiction, realm

Ri·car·do (ri kär′dō), **David** 1772-1823; Eng. economist

rice (rīs) ***n.*** ⟦ME *rys* < OFr *ris* < It *riso* < L *oryza* < Gr *oryza, oryzon:* of Asian orig.; akin to Pashto *vrižē*, Sans *vrīhiḥ*, rice⟧ **1** an aquatic cereal grass (esp. *Oryza sativa*) grown widely in warm climates, esp. in East Asia **2** the starchy seeds or grains of this grass, used as food —***vt.*** **riced, ric′ing** to put (soft foods, as cooked potatoes) through a ricer

Rice (rīs), **Elmer** (born *Elmer Reizenstein*) 1892-1967; U.S. playwright

rice·bird (rīs′burd′) ***n.*** **1** JAVA SPARROW ☆**2** [Chiefly South] BOBOLINK

rice paper **1** a thin paper made from the straw of the rice grass **2** a fine, delicate paper made by cutting and pressing the pith of the rice-paper plant

rice-pa·per plant (rīs′pā′pər) a shrubby plant (*Tetrapanax papyriferus*) of the ginseng family: see RICE PAPER

☆**ric·er** (rīs′ər) ***n.*** a utensil with small holes through which soft food, as cooked potato, is forced to produce short strands resembling grains of rice in size and shape

ri·cer·car (rē′chər kär′) ⟦It < *ricercare*, seek, search⟧ ***n.*** any of various polyphonic instrumental compositions of the 16th and 17th cent.: also **ri·cer·ca·re** (rē′chər kär′ə; *It* rē′cher kä′re), *pl.* **-ca′ri** (-kär′ē; *It,* -kä′rē)

rich (rich) ***adj.*** ⟦ME *riche* < OE & OFr: OE *rice*, noble, powerful: see RIGHT⟧ **1** having more than enough of material possessions; owning much money or property; wealthy **2** having abundant natural resources [*a rich country*] **3** well-supplied (*with*); abounding (*in*) [*rich in minerals*] **4** worth much; valuable [*a rich prize*] **5** of valuable materials or fine, elaborate workmanship; costly and elegant [*rich gifts*] **6** elaborate; luxurious; sumptuous [*a rich banquet*] **7** having an abundance of good constituents or qualities; specif., *a)* full of nutritious or choice ingredients, esp. fats and sugar, and spices, etc. [*rich pastries*] *b)* full of strength and flavor; full-bodied [*rich coffee*] **8** *a)* full, deep, and mellow (said of sounds, the voice, etc.) *b)* deep; intense; vivid (said of colors) *c)* very fragrant (said of odors) **9** having a high proportion of fuel to air [*a rich fuel mixture*] **10** abundant; plentiful; ample [*a rich fund of stories*] **11** yielding or producing in abundance [*rich soil, a rich silver mine*] **12** [Informal] *a)* abounding in humor; very amusing *b)* absurd; preposterous —**the rich** wealthy people collectively —**rich′ness** ***n.***

SYN.—**rich** is the general word for one who has more money or income-producing property than is necessary to satisfy normal needs; **wealthy** adds to this connotations of grand living, influence in the community, a tradition of richness, etc. [*a wealthy banker*]; **affluent** suggests a continuing increase of riches and lavish spending resulting from it [*to live in affluent circumstances*]; **opulent** suggests the possession of great wealth as displayed in luxurious or ostentatious living [*an opulent mansion*]; **well-to-do** implies sufficient prosperity for easy living —*ANT.* **poor**

Rich·ard[1] (rich′ərd) ***n.*** ⟦ME *Rycharde* < OFr *Richard* < OHG *Richart* < Gmc **rik-*, king (akin to L *rex:* see RIGHT) + **harthuz*, strong: for IE base see HARD⟧ a masculine name: dim. *Dick, Rich, Rick*; equiv. It. *Riccardo*, Sp. *Ricardo*

Rich·ard[2] (rich′ərd) **1 Richard I** 1157-99; king of England (1189-99): son of Henry II: called **Richard Coeur de Li·on** (kurd′ lē ōn′, kur′ də lē′ən) or **Richard the Lion-Hearted** **2 Richard II** 1367-1400; king of England (1377-99): last Plantagenet king; deposed: son of Edward, the Black Prince **3 Richard III** 1452-85; king of England (1483-85): last king of the house of York

Richard Roe (rō) ⟦see DOE⟧ a name used in law courts, legal papers, etc. to refer to a person whose actual name is unknown, esp. to the second person of two when both names are unknown (the first person being referred to as *John Doe*)

Rich·ards (rich′ərdz), **I(vor) A(rmstrong)** 1893-1979; Eng. literary critic in the U.S.

Rich·ard·son[1] (rich′ərd sən) **1 Henry Handel** (pseud. of *Ethel Florence Lindesay Richardson Robertson*) 1870-1946; Austral. novelist **2 Henry Hobson** 1838-86; U.S. architect **3 Sir Ralph (David)** 1902-83; Brit. actor **4 Samuel** 1689-1761; Eng. novelist

Rich·ard·son[2] (rich′ərd sən) ⟦after A. S. *Richardson*, 19th-c. railroad official⟧ city in NE Tex.: suburb of Dallas

Ri·che·lieu (rish′lo͞o′, -ə lo͞o′; *Fr* rē shə lyö′), Duc **de** (born *Armand Jean du Plessis*) 1585-1642; Fr. cardinal & statesman: chief minister of Louis XIII (1624-42)

rich·en (rich′ən) ***vt.*** to make rich or richer

rich·es (rich′iz) ***pl.n.*** ⟦ME sing. n. *richess* < OFr *richesse* < *riche:* see RICH⟧ valuable possessions; much money, property, etc.; wealth

rich·ly (rich′lē) ***adv.*** **1** in a rich manner **2** abundantly; amply; fully

Rich·mond (rich′mənd) ⟦Richmond, N.Y., named after Duke of *Richmond*, son of Charles II; other U.S. cities, & Cdn city, after the London borough⟧ **1** *former name for* STATEN ISLAND (the borough) **2** capital of Va.; seaport on the James River **3** seaport in W Calif., on San Francisco Bay **4** city in SW British Columbia, Canada, on several islands at the mouth of the Fraser River **5** borough of SW Greater London, England: in full **Rich′mond-on-Thames′** (-än temz′)

Richmond Hill town in SE Ontario, Canada, near Toronto

rich rhyme RIME RICHE

☆**Rich·ter scale** (rik′tər) ⟦devised by C. *Richter* (1900-85), U.S. seismologist⟧ a logarithmic scale for indicating the magnitude of earthquakes using data from a seismograph: each step represents a magnitude that is about 10 times greater than the preceding step, with 1 indicating a disturbance detectable only by instruments and 7 one that can cause major damage to buildings: see the Richter scale in the Reference Supplement

ri·cin (rī′sin, ris′in) ***n.*** ⟦< L *ricinus*, castor-oil plant⟧ an extremely toxic protein found in the castor bean and isolated as a white powder: it agglutinates red blood corpuscles

ric·in·o·le·ic acid (rī si nō lē′ik, ris′-; -nō′lē ik) ⟦prec. + OLEIC⟧ an unsaturated fatty acid, $C_{18}H_{34}O_3$, found as an ester of glycerin in castor oil and used in soaps, textile finishing, etc.

ric·in·o·le·in (rī′si nō′lē ən) ***n.*** the glycerol ester, $C_{57}H_{104}O_9$, of ricinoleic acid: it is the main constituent of castor oil

rick[1] (rik) ***n.*** ⟦ME *rec, reek* < OE *hreac*, akin to Du *rook*, ON *hruga*, a heap < IE **(s)kreuk-* > RIDGE⟧ **1** a stack of hay, straw, etc. in a field, esp. one covered or thatched for protection from rain ☆**2** a pile of firewood like a cord, but of less width ☆**3** a set of shelves for storing barrels or boxes —***vt.*** to pile (hay, etc.) into ricks

rick[2] (rik) ***vt., n.*** ⟦prob. < ME *wricken:* see WRICK⟧ [Brit.] sprain or wrench

Rick·en·back·er (rik′ən bak′ər), **Ed·die** (ed′ē) (born *Edward Vernon Rickenbacker*) 1890-1973; U.S. aviator & aviation executive

rick·ets (rik′its) ***n.*** ⟦altered < ? Gr *rhachitis*, RACHITIS⟧ a disease of the skeletal system, chiefly of children, resulting from vitamin D deficiency and characterized by a softening and, often, bending of the bones

☆**rick·ett·si·a** (ri ket′sē ə) ***n.***, *pl.* **-si·ae′** (-ē′) or **-si·as** ⟦ModL, after H. T. *Ricketts* (1871-1910), U.S. pathologist + -IA⟧ any of several families (esp. Rickettsiaceae) of Gram-negative bacteria that are the causative agents of certain diseases, as typhus or Rocky Mountain spotted fever: they are transmitted to animals and humans by the bite of certain lice, ticks, etc. in whose bodies they live as parasites —**rick·ett′si·al** ***adj.***

rick·et·y (rik′it ē) ***adj.*** **1** of or having rickets **2** weak in the joints; tottering **3** liable to collapse or break down because weak or unsteady —**rick′et·i·ness** ***n.***

☆**rick·ey** (rik′ē) ***n.*** ⟦said to be after a Col. *Rickey*⟧ a drink made of carbonated water, lime juice, and, usually, an alcoholic liquor, esp. gin (**gin rickey**)

☆**rick·rack** (rik′rak′) ***n.*** ⟦redupl. of RACK[1]⟧ flat, zigzag braid for trimming dresses, etc.

rick·shaw (rik′shô′) ***n.*** ⟦shortened & altered < JINRIKISHA⟧ **1** a small, two-wheeled, covered carriage pulled by one or more persons, esp. formerly in East Asia **2** any of various similar three-wheeled vehicles, as a PEDICAB (in full **cycle rickshaw**) or a small motorized vehicle with a single seat in front for the driver (in full **auto rickshaw**) Also sp. **rick′sha′**

rick·y-tick (rik′ē tik′) ***adj.*** ⟦echoic⟧ [Slang] **1** designating, producing, or of popular music, as of the 1920s, with a mechanical, regular beat and fast tempo **2** old-fashioned; corny Also **rick′y-tick′y** (-tik′ē)

RICO (rē′kō) *abbrev.* Racketeer Influenced and Corrupt Organizations (Act)

ric·o·chet (rik′ə shā′; *Brit, esp. formerly,* -shet′) ***n.*** ⟦Fr; used first in *fable du ricochet* (story in which the narrator constantly evades the hearers' questions) < ?⟧ **1** the oblique rebound or skipping of a bullet, stone, etc. after striking a surface at an angle **2** a bullet, etc. that ricochets —***vi.*** **-cheted′** (-shād′) or [Brit.] **-chet′ted** (-shet′id), **-chet′ing** (-shā′iŋ) or [Brit.] **-chet′ting** (-shet′iŋ) ⟦Fr *ricocher* < the n.⟧ to make a ricochet motion —***SYN.*** SKIP[1]

ri·cot·ta (ri kät′ə) ***n.*** ⟦It < L *recocta,* recooked, fem. pp. of *recoquere,* to boil again: see RE- & COOK⟧ **1** a soft, dry or moist Italian cheese made from whey obtained in the production of other cheeses **2** a cheese like this made in the U.S. from whole milk or from whey and whole milk

ric·tus (rik′təs) ***n.*** ⟦ModL < L, open mouth < pp. of *ringi,* to gape⟧ **1** a sustained gaping, as of a bird's beak or an animal's mouth **2** the opening so produced **3** a fixed, gaping grin —**ric′tal** ***adj.***

rid[1] (rid) ***vt.*** **rid** or **rid′ded, rid′ding** ⟦ME *ridden,* earlier *ruden* < ON *rythja,* to clear (land), akin to OE *ryddan,* OHG *riuten* < IE **reudh-* < base **reu-,* to tear up, dig out > RIP[1], RUG⟧ **1** to free, clear, relieve, or disencumber, as of something undesirable: usually with *of* [to *rid* oneself of superstitions] **2** [Obs.] to save or deliver, as from danger, difficulty, etc.; rescue (*from, out of,* etc.) —**be rid of** to be freed from or relieved of (something undesirable) —**get rid of 1** to get free from or relieved of (something undesirable) **2** to do away with; destroy; kill

rid[2] (rid) ***vi., vt.*** *archaic pt. & pp. of* RIDE

rid·a·ble or **ride·a·ble** (rīd′ə bəl) ***adj.*** **1** that can be ridden [a *ridable* horse] **2** that can be ridden over, through, etc. [a *ridable* path]

rid·dance (rid′'ns) ***n.*** a ridding or being rid; clearance or removal, as of something undesirable, or deliverance, as from something oppressive —**good riddance** welcome relief or deliverance: often used as an exclamation of satisfaction at getting rid of someone or something

rid·den (rid′'n) ***vi., vt.*** *pp. of* RIDE —***adj.*** dominated or obsessed (by the thing specified): used in compounds [fear-*ridden*]

rid·dle[1] (rid′'l) ***n.*** ⟦ME *ridil* < OE *rædels,* akin to *rædan,* to guess, READ[1]⟧ **1** a problem or puzzle in the form of a question, statement, etc. so formulated that some ingenuity is required to solve or answer it **2** any puzzling, perplexing, or apparently inexplicable person or thing, as a difficult problem or enigmatic saying; enigma —***vt.*** **-dled, -dling** to solve or explain (a riddle) —***vi.*** to propound riddles; speak enigmatically —***SYN.*** MYSTERY[1]

rid·dle[2] (rid′'l) ***n.*** ⟦ME *ridil* < OE *hriddel,* earlier *hridder* < base of *hridrian,* to sift, winnow, akin to Ger *reiter* < IE base **(s)ker-,* to cut, separate > HARVEST⟧ a coarse sieve for grading gravel, separating chaff from grain, etc. —***vt.*** **-dled, -dling 1** to sift through such a sieve **2** to make many holes in; puncture throughout [a body *riddled* with bullets] **3** to affect every part of [a book *riddled* with errors]

ride (rīd) ***vi.*** **rode, rid′den, rid′ing** ⟦ME *riden* < OE *ridan,* akin to Ger *reiten* < IE base **reidh-,* to go, be in motion > L *reda,* four-wheel carriage⟧ **1** *a)* to sit on and be carried along by a horse or other animal, esp. one controlled by the rider *b)* to be carried along (*in* a vehicle, *on* a bicycle, etc.) *c)* to move along as if so carried *d)* to move along or be carried or supported in motion (*on* or *upon*) [tanks *ride* on treads] **2** to be fit for riding or admit of being ridden [a car that *rides* smoothly] **3** *a)* to move or float on the water *b)* [Now Rare] to lie at anchor [the ships *riding* close to shore] **4** to seem to be floating in space **5** to overlap, as bones in a joint **6** to be dependent (*on*) [the change *rides* on his approval] **7** to be placed as a bet (*on*) ☆**8** [Informal] to continue undisturbed, with no action taken [let the matter *ride*] —***vt.*** **1** to sit on or in and control so as to move along [to *ride* a horse, a bicycle, etc.] **2** *a)* to move along on or be mounted, carried, or supported on [to *ride* the waves, to *ride* a merry-go-round] *b)* to rest on, as by overlapping *c)* to operate partially by keeping the foot on the pedal [to *ride* the brake] **3** to move over, along, or through (a road, fence, area, etc.) by horse, car, etc. **4** to cover (a specified distance) by riding **5** to engage in or do by riding [to *ride* a race] **6** to cause to ride; carry; convey **7** to mount (a female) as for copulation **8** to control, dominate, tyrannize over, or oppress: often in the past participle [*ridden* by doubts] **9** [Informal] to torment, harass, or tease by making the butt of ridicule, criticism, etc. —***n.*** **1** *a)* a riding; esp., a journey by horse, car, bicycle, etc. *b)* a means or opportunity to ride, as by automobile [do you have a *ride* home?] *c)* the way a car, etc. rides **2** a road, track, etc. for riding, esp. on horseback **3** a roller coaster, Ferris wheel, or other thing to ride, as at an amusement park —***SYN.*** BAIT —**ride down 1** to hit and knock down by riding against **2** to overtake by riding **3** to overcome **4** to exhaust (a horse, etc.) by riding too long or too hard —**ride out 1** to stay afloat or aloft during (a storm, etc.) without too much damage **2** to withstand or endure successfully —**ride up** to move upward out of place: said of an article of clothing —☆**take for a ride** [Slang] **1** to take somewhere, as in a car, and kill **2** to cheat or swindle

Ride (rīd), **Sally K(risten)** 1951-2012; U.S. astronaut: 1st U.S. woman in space (1983)

☆**ride cymbal** *Jazz* a medium-sized cymbal suspended over a set of drums, used for maintaining rhythm patterns since the advent of bop

rid·er (rīd′ər) ***n.*** **1** a person who rides **2** *a)* an addition or amendment to a document such as a contract *b)* a clause, usually dealing with some unrelated matter, added to a legislative bill when it is being considered for passage **3** any of various devices or pieces moving along or mounted on something else —**rid′er·less** ***adj.***

rid·er·ship (-ship′) ***n.*** the passengers using a particular system of public transportation over a given period of time, or the estimated number of these

ridge (rij) ***n.*** ⟦ME *rigge* < OE *hrycg,* akin to ON *hrygr,* backbone, Ger *rücken,* back < IE **(s)kreuk-,* a hump, mound < base **(s)ker-,* to bend > L *curvus,* bent, *circus,* a ring⟧ **1** [Obs.] an animal's spine or back **2** the long, narrow top or crest of something, as of an animal's back, a wave, a mountain, etc. **3** a long, narrow elevation of land or a similar range of hills or mountains **4** any raised line or raised narrow strip, as in corded fabric, plowed land, etc. **5** the horizontal line formed by the meeting of two sloping surfaces [the *ridge* of a roof] **6** a long, narrow high-pressure area on a weather map — ***vt., vi.*** **ridged, ridg′ing 1** to mark or be marked with a ridge or ridges **2** to form into or furnish with a ridge or ridges

Ridge·back (rij′bak′) ***n.*** *see* RHODESIAN RIDGEBACK

ridge·line (rij′līn′) ***n.*** the line or surface along the top of a ridge

ridge·ling or **ridg·ling** (-liŋ) ***n.*** ⟦prob. < RIDGE + -LING[1]: ? in reference to assumed location of the testes⟧ a horse or domestic animal in which one or both testes have failed to pass down into the scrotal sac

ridge·pole (rij′pōl′) ***n.*** the horizontal timber or beam at the ridge of a roof, to which the upper ends of the rafters are attached: also **ridge′piece′** (-pēs′)

ridg·y (rij′ē) ***adj.*** **ridg′i·er, ridg′i·est** having, or rising in, a ridge or ridges

ri·dic (ri dik′, rē-) ***adj.*** [Slang] *short for* RIDICULOUS

rid·i·cule (rid′i kyo͞ol′) ***n.*** ⟦Fr < L *ridiculum,* a jest, laughable (thing), neut. of *ridiculus,* laughable, comical < *ridere,* to laugh < IE **wrizd-,* to avert the face (> Sans *vrīda,* embarrassment) < base **wer-,* to turn⟧ **1** *a)* the act of making someone or something the object of scornful laughter by joking, mocking, etc.; derision *b)* words or actions intended to produce such laughter **2** [Archaic] *a)* an absurdity *b)* foolishness —***vt.*** **-culed′, -cul′ing** to make the object of scornful laughter; make fun of; deride

SYN.—**ridicule** implies a making fun of someone or something and often connotes a dismissive contempt [he *ridiculed* her new hairdo]; **deride** suggests scornful or malicious censure in ridiculing [to *deride* another's beliefs]; **mock** implies a ridiculing that is intended to humiliate someone, esp. by caricaturing that person's peculiarities [it is cruel to *mock* his lisp]; **taunt** implies insulting ridicule, esp. by jeering and repeatedly calling attention to some humiliating fact [they *taunted* him about his failure]

ri·dic·u·lous (ri dik′yə ləs) ***adj.*** ⟦L *ridiculosus* (< *ridiculum:* see prec.) or *ridiculus*⟧ deserving ridicule —***SYN.*** ABSURD —**ri·dic′u·lous·ly** ***adv.*** —**ri·dic′u·lous·ness** ***n.***

rid·ing[1] (rīd′iŋ) ***adj.*** **1** that rides **2** used in or for riding or traveling [a *riding* costume, *riding* horses] ☆**3** designed to be operated by a rider [a *riding* mower] —***n.*** the act of a person or thing that rides

ri·ding[2] (rīd′iŋ) ***n.*** ⟦ME *(t)riding* < OE *-thrithing,* a third part (only in L contexts) < ON *thrithjungr* < *thrithi,* THIRD: initial *t* was lost to the preceding sound in compounds formed with *North-, East-,* and *West-*⟧ **1** any of the three former administrative divisions (*North Riding, East Riding,* and *West Riding*) of Yorkshire, England **2** any similar division in the Commonwealth; specif., a Canadian electoral district

riding master a person who teaches horseback riding

riding school a school where horseback riding is taught

☆**rid·ley** (rid′lē) ***n.*** ⟦< ? surname *Ridley*⟧ any of a genus (*Lepidochelys,* family Cheloniidae) of gray or olive marine turtles of tropical waters with a broad, heart-shaped shell

Rid·ley (rid′lē), **Nicholas** 1500?-55; Eng. bishop & Protestant reformer: burned at the stake for heresy

ri·dot·to (ri dät′ō) ***n.,*** *pl.* **-tos** ⟦It, festival, REDOUBT⟧ a social gathering, often in masquerade, with music and dancing, popular in 18th-cent. England

Rief·en·stahl (rē′fən stôl′, -shtôl′), **Len·i** (len′ē) (born *Bertha Helene Amalie Riefenstahl*) 1902-2003; Ger. filmmaker & photographer

ri·el (rē el′) ***n.*** ⟦? altered < Ar *riyāl* or Sp *real:* see RIAL, REAL[2]⟧ the basic monetary unit of Cambodia: see the table of monetary units in the Reference Supplement

Rie·mann·i·an geometry (rē män′ē ən) ⟦after G. F. B. *Riemann* (1826-66), Ger mathematician⟧ a form of non-Euclidean geometry in which there are no parallel lines, since its figures can be conceived as constructed on a curved surface where all straight lines intersect, and in which the sum of the angles of a triangle exceeds 180°

Ri·en·zi (rē en′zē), **Co·la di** (kō′lä dē) 1313?-54; Rom. patriot & political reformer: also **Ri·en′zo** (-zō)

Ries·ling (rēz′liŋ, rēs′-) ***n.*** ⟦Ger < earlier *rüssling* < ?⟧ [*also* **r-**] **1** a dry to sweet white Rhine wine **2** the white grape from which it is made

☆**rif** (rif) [Slang] ***n.*** ⟦*r(eduction) i(n) f(orce)*⟧ the act of dismissing an employee, esp. from a government job, as by eliminating the position —***vt.*** **riffed, rif′fing** to dismiss from employment

Rif (rif) mountain range along the NE coast of Morocco, extending from the Strait of Gibraltar to the Algerian border: highest peak, *c.* 8,000 ft (2,438 m): also *Er Rif*

RIF *abbrev.* reduction in force

ri·fam·pin (rī fam′pin) *n.* ⟦< *rifamycin* (< *rifa-* < ? + -MYCIN), an antibiotic derived from a fungus⟧ a derivative, $C_{43}H_{58}N_4O_{12}$, of an antibiotic prepared from a culture of soil bacteria (*Streptomyces mediterranei*), used in treating tuberculosis, spinal meningitis, etc. by inhibiting the RNA synthesis of the bacteria: also **ri·fam′pi·cin** (-pə sin)

rife (rīf) *adj.* ⟦ME *rif* < OE *ryfe,* akin to MDu *riif,* abundant, ON *rifr,* desired < IE **reip-* < base **rei-*: see REAP⟧ **1** frequently or commonly occurring; widespread [malicious gossip was *rife*] **2** *a)* abundant *b)* abounding [an interpretation *rife* with error] —**SYN.** PREVAILING —**rife′ness** *n.*

☆**riff** (rif) *n.* ⟦orig. a term in jazz: prob. altered < REFRAIN[2]⟧ **1** a constantly repeated musical phrase used esp. as background for a soloist or as the basic theme of a final chorus **2** [Informal] a short, incisive comment, passage, or scene, often one of several functioning as variations on a theme, in a speech, novel, film, etc. —*vi.* **1** to play a riff **2** [Informal] to make use of a riff or riffs

Riff[1] (rif) *n., pl.* **Riffs** or **Riff′i** (-ē) a member of a Berber people living in the Rif and nearby regions —**Riff′i·an** *adj., n.*

Riff[2] (rif) *alt. sp. of* RIF

rif·fle (rif′əl) *n.* ⟦< ? or akin to Ger *riffel,* groove, furrow < EFris, akin to OE *rifelung,* wrinkle < IE base **rei-,* to tear > REAP⟧ ☆**1** *a)* a shoal, reef, or shallow in a stream, producing a stretch of ruffled or choppy water *b)* a stretch of such water *c)* a ripple or the ripples of such water **2** *a)* a contrivance, as of bars or slats, put across the bottom of a sluice to form grooves or open spaces for catching and holding particles of gold in mining *b)* any of the bars, slats, etc. *c)* any of the grooves or spaces **3** the act or a manner of riffling cards —*vt., vi.* **-fled, -fling** ⟦< ? Ger *riffeln,* to form riffles, groove: see the *n.*⟧ **1** to form, become, or flow over or through, a riffle **2** to leaf rapidly through (a book, etc.), as by letting the edges or corners of the pages slip lightly across the thumb **3** to shuffle (playing cards) by holding part of the deck in each hand, raising the corners or edges slightly, and causing the cards to fall alternately together

riff·raff (rif′raf′) *n.* ⟦earlier *rif and raf,* every scrap < OFr *rif et raf, rifle et rafle:* see RIFLE[2] & RAFFLE[2]⟧ **1** [*often with pl. v.*] those people regarded as worthless, disreputable, etc.; rabble **2** [Dial.] worthless stuff

ri·fle[1] (rī′fəl) *vt.* **-fled, -fling** ⟦Fr *rifler,* to scrape, scratch < OFr < MHG *riffeln,* to scratch, heckle (flax) < OHG *riffilon,* akin to RIPPLE[2]⟧ **1** to cut spiral grooves on the inside of (a gun barrel, etc.) ☆**2** ⟦< the *n.*⟧ to hurl or throw with great speed —*n.* ⟦short for *rifled gun*⟧ **1** ☆*a)* a gun, fired from the shoulder, with spiral grooves cut into the inner surface of the barrel (see RIFLING) *b)* a rifled artillery piece **2** [*pl.*] troops armed with rifles

ri·fle[2] (rī′fəl) *vt.* **-fled, -fling** ⟦ME *riflen* < OFr *rifler,* to plunder, orig., to scratch: see prec.⟧ **1** *a)* to ransack and rob (a place); pillage; plunder *b)* [Now Rare] to search and rob (a person) **2** to take as plunder; steal —*vi.* to search hurriedly, sometimes with dishonest intent [to *rifle* through a stranger's purse] —**ri′fler** *n.*

☆**ri·fle·man** (-mən) *n., pl.* **-men** (-mən) one who uses, or is skilled in using, a rifle; specif., an infantryman armed with a rifle

rifle range a place for target practice with a rifle

☆**ri·fle·ry** (rī′fəl rē) *n.* the skill or practice of shooting at targets with a rifle

ri·fling (rī′fliŋ) *n.* **1** the cutting of spiral grooves on the inside of a gun barrel to make the projectile spin when fired, thus giving the shot greater accuracy and distance **2** a series or system of such grooves

rift[1] (rift) *n.* ⟦ME < Dan, fissure < *rive,* to tear < ON *rifa:* see RIVE⟧ **1** an opening caused by or as if by splitting; cleft; fissure **2** an open break in a previously friendly relationship **3** *Geol.* a large fault along which tectonic movement was mainly lateral — *vt., vi.* to burst open; split

☆**rift**[2] (rift) *n.* ⟦? var. of obs. *riff,* altered < REEF[1]⟧ a shallow, often rocky place in a stream, forming rapids

rift valley *Geol.* a stretch of lowland lying along a portion of a rift

Rift Valley GREAT RIFT VALLEY

rig (rig) *vt.* **rigged, rig′ging** ⟦LME *riggen* < Scand, as in Norw *rigga,* to bind, splice⟧ **1** *a)* to fit (a ship, mast, etc.) with sails, shrouds, etc. *b)* to fit (sails, shrouds, etc.) to a ship's masts, yards, etc. **2** to assemble and adjust the wings, fuselage, etc. of (an aircraft) **3** to fit (*out*); equip **4** to put together, prepare for use, or arrange, esp. in a makeshift or hurried fashion: often with *up* **5** to arrange in a dishonest way for selfish advantage; manipulate fraudulently; fix [to *rig* an election] **6** [Informal] to dress; clothe; attire: usually with *out* —*n.* **1** the distinctive arrangement of sails, masts, and rigging on a vessel ☆**2** any apparatus for a special purpose; equipment; gear [a ham radio operator's *rig*] ☆**3** equipment for drilling an oil well ☆**4** *a)* a carriage, cart, etc. with its horse or horses *b)* a tractor-trailer or, sometimes, the tractor alone *c)* [Informal] any vehicle **5** [Old Informal] dress or costume, esp. if odd or showy

Ri·ga (rē′gə) **1** seaport & capital of Latvia, on the Gulf of Riga **2 Gulf of** inlet of the Baltic Sea, between NW Latvia & SW Estonia: *c.* 100 mi (161 km) long; *c.* 60 mi (97 km) wide

rig·a·doon (rig′ə do͞on′) *n.* ⟦Fr *rigodon, rigaudon:* said to be after *Rigaud,* dancing master who invented the dance⟧ **1** a once popular lively dance for couples, with a jumping step **2** music for this

rig·a·ma·role (rig′ə mə rōl′) *n. var. of* RIGMAROLE

ri·ga·to·ni (rig′ə tō′nē) *n.* ⟦It, pl. < *rigato,* pp. of *rigare,* to mark with lines < *riga,* line⟧ pasta in the form of short, wide tubes with lengthwise ridges

Ri·gel (rī′jəl, -gəl) *n.* ⟦Ar *rijl,* foot: so called because it marks the left foot of Orion in ancient diagrams of the constellation⟧ a supergiant, binary, variable star, the brightest star in the constellation Orion: magnitude, 0.18: see BETELGEUSE

rig·ger (rig′ər) *n.* a person who rigs; specif., *a)* a person who works with hoisting tackle and the like *b)* a person whose work is assembling the fuselage, wings, etc. of aircraft *c)* a person who packs parachute assemblies *d)* a person who works with an oil rig

rig·ging (-iŋ) *n.* **1** the ropes, chains, and other gear used to support, position, and control the masts, sails, yards, etc. of a vessel ☆**2** equipment; gear

right (rīt) *adj.* ⟦ME < OE *riht,* straight, direct, right, akin to Ger *recht* < IE base **reĝ-,* straight, stretch out, put in order > RICH, RECKON, L *regere,* to rule, *rex,* king, *regula,* a rule⟧ **1** [Obs.] not curved; straight: now only in mathematics [a *right* line] **2** *a)* formed by, or with reference to, a straight line or plane perpendicular to a base [a *right* angle] *b)* having the axis perpendicular to the base [a *right* cylinder] **3** in accordance with justice, law, morality, etc.; upright; virtuous [*right* conduct] **4** *a)* in accordance with fact, reason, some set standard, etc.; correct; true [the *right* answer] *b)* correct in thought, statement, or action [to be *right* in one's answer] **5** *a)* fitting; appropriate; suitable *b)* most convenient or favorable *c)* reputable, approved, fashionable, etc. [she always associates with the *right* people] *d)* [Brit. Informal] genuine; absolute [he made a *right* fool of himself] **6** designating the side, surface, etc. meant to be seen; designating the finished, principal, or upper side or surface [the *right* side of cloth] **7** *a)* sound; normal [in one's *right* mind] *b)* mentally sound or normal; sane [not quite *right*] **8** having sound health or good spirits **9** in a satisfactory condition, or in good order [to make things *right* again] **10** *a)* designating or of that side of one's body which is toward the east when one faces north, the side of the more-used hand in most people *b)* designating or of the corresponding side of anything *c)* closer to the right side of a person directly before and facing the thing mentioned or understood [the top *right* drawer of a desk] **11** of the side or bank of a river on the right of a person facing downstream **12** of the political right; conservative or reactionary —*n.* **1** what is right, or just, lawful, morally good, proper, correct, etc. **2** *a)* that which a person has a just claim to; power, privilege, etc. that belongs to a person by law, nature, or tradition [the *right* of free speech] *b)* [*often pl.*] an interest in property, real or intangible (cf. COPYRIGHT) **3** *a)* all or part of the right side *b)* what is on the right side *c)* a direction or location on the right side (often with *the*) *d)* a turn toward the right side [take a *right* at the fork] ☆**4** *Baseball short for* RIGHT FIELD **5** *Boxing a)* the right hand *b)* a blow delivered with the right hand **6** *Finance a)* the privilege given to a company's stockholders of buying shares in a new issue of stock, usually at a price below the current market price *b)* the negotiable certificate indicating this privilege **7** ⟦from the arrangement of seats of the various parties in some European legislatures⟧ [*often* **R-**] *Politics* a conservative or reactionary position, esp. one varying from moderate capitalism to fascism, or a party or group advocating this: often with *the* —*adv.* ⟦ME < OE *rihte*⟧ **1** in a straight line; straight; directly [go *right* home] **2** *a)* properly; fittingly *b)* favorably, conveniently, or well **3** completely; thoroughly [soaked *right* through his coat] **4** exactly; precisely [*right* here, *right* now] ☆**5** without pause or delay; immediately [come *right* down] **6** according to law, justice, etc.; in an upright way; rightly [to do *right* by someone] **7** correctly or accurately **8** on or toward the right hand or side **9** very; extremely [to know something *right* well]: informal except in certain titles [the *right* honorable, the *right* reverend] —*interj.* agreed; OK; I understand —*vt.* **1** to put in or restore to an upright or proper position [to *right* a capsized boat] **2** to correct; make conform with fact, etc. **3** to put in order; set right [to *right* a room] **4** to do justice to (a person); make amends to **5** to make amends for (a wrong, etc.); redress or avenge —*vi.* to get into or resume an upright or proper position —**by right (or rights)** in justice; properly —**in one's own right** through one's own authority, ability, etc.; without dependence on another or others —**in the right** on the side supported by truth, justice, etc. —**right away (or off)** without delay or pause; at once —☆**right on!** [Slang] precisely! exactly! that's right!: an exclamation of approval or encouragement —**to rights** [Informal] in or into good or proper condition or order

right·a·bout (rīt′ə bout′) *n.* **1** RIGHTABOUT-FACE **2** the direction opposite, as faced after turning completely about — *adv., adj.* with, in, or by a right-about-face

right·a·bout-face (-fās′) *n.* **1** a turning directly about so as to face in the opposite direction **2** a complete reversal of belief, conduct, etc. —*interj.* used as a military command to perform a rightabout-face

right angle an angle of 90 degrees; angle made by the meeting of two straight lines perpendicular to each other

right-an·gled (rīt′aŋ′gəld) *adj.* having or forming one or more right angles; rectangular: also **right′-an′gle**

right ascension *Astron.* the angular distance of the hour circle of a celestial body from the vernal equinox, measured eastward along the celestial equator and expressed in degrees (from 0 to 360) or, more commonly, in hours (from 0 to 24), minutes, and seconds: it is used with DECLINATION (sense 6) to find an exact position in the sky: abbrev. *RA*

right brain the right cerebral hemisphere of the human brain, which includes areas associated with abstraction, artistic ability, and emotional response: popularly regarded as the center of creativity and imagination —**right′-brain′** *adj.* —**right′-brained′** *adj.*

right circular cylinder *see* CYLINDER (sense 1*a*)

right·eous (rī′chəs) *adj.* ⟦altered, by analogy with adjs. in -EOUS < ME *rihtwis* < OE: see RIGHT & -WISE] 1 acting in a just, upright manner; doing what is right; virtuous [a *righteous* man] 2 morally right; fair and just [a *righteous* act] 3 morally justifiable [full of *righteous* anger] ☆4 [Slang] good, excellent, satisfying, pleasant, authentic, etc. —*SYN.* MORAL —**right′eous·ly** *adv.* —**right′eous·ness** *n.*

☆**right field** *Baseball* 1 the area in the outfield behind the first and second basemen 2 the defensive position of the outfielder (**right fielder**) who plays there

right·ful (rīt′fəl) *adj.* 1 fair and just; right 2 having a just, lawful claim, or right [the *rightful* owner] 3 belonging or owned by just or lawful claim, or by right [a *rightful* rank] 4 proper or fitting —**right′ful·ly** *adv.* —**right′ful·ness** *n.*

right-hand (rīt′hand′) *adj.* 1 being on or directed toward the right 2 of, for, or with the right hand 3 most helpful or reliable [the president's *right-hand* man] 4 plain-laid

right-hand·ed (-han′did) *adj.* 1 using the right hand more skillfully than, and in preference to, the left 2 done with the right hand 3 made for use with the right hand 4 designating one who swings a bat, club, etc. leftward 5 turning left to right; worked by clockwise motion 6 DEXTRAL (sense 3) 7 having an asymmetrical molecular or crystal structure that is conventionally viewed as having certain components on the right side: said of an isomer that is the mirror image of a one that is left-handed —*adv.* 1 with the right hand [to throw *right-handed*] 2 in such a way that the bat, club, etc. swings leftward [to bat *right-handed*] —**right′-hand′ed·ly** *adv.* —**right′-hand′ed·ness** *n.* —**right′-hand′er** *n.*

right heart the half of the heart, containing the right ventricle and right atrium, which supplies dark-red, oxygen-deficient venous blood to the lungs for oxygenation

right·ist (rīt′ist) *n.* a person whose political position is of the RIGHT (*n.* 7), esp., a conservative or reactionary —*adj.* conservative or reactionary —**right′ism′** *n.*

right·ly (rīt′lē) *adv.* [see RIGHT & -LY[2]] 1 with justice; fairly 2 properly; suitably; fitly 3 correctly

right-mind·ed (rīt′mīn′did) *adj.* thinking or believing what is right; having correct views or sound principles —**right′-mind′ed·ly** *adv.* —**right′-mind′ed·ness** *n.*

right·ness (rīt′nis) *n.* 1 soundness of moral principles; integrity 2 agreement with truth or fact; correctness 3 appropriateness; suitability

right·o (rī tō′, rīt′ō) *interj.* [Informal, Chiefly Brit.] yes; certainly

right of search the right of a nation at war to stop the merchant ships of neutral nations on the high seas and search them for contraband or the like, the finding of which makes the ship liable to seizure

right of way 1 the right, established by common or statutory law, of one ship, automobile, etc. to cross in front of another; precedence in moving, as at intersections 2 right of passage, as over another's property 3 a route that it is lawful to use ☆4 *a)* a strip of land used by a railroad for its tracks *b)* land over which a public road, an electric power line, etc. passes Also written **right-of-way** *n.*

☆**right-on** (rīt′än′) *adj.* [Slang] sophisticated, informed, current, etc.

right stuff, the [Informal] superior ability combined with fortitude, self-discipline, etc.

right-to-life (rīt′tə līf′) *adj.* designating or of any movement, political party, etc. opposed to abortion, esp. legalized abortion —**right′-to-lif′er** *n.*

☆**right-to-work** (rīt′tə wurk′) *adj.* designating or of a law, state, etc. that prohibits compulsory union membership as a condition of employment

right triangle a triangle with a right angle

right·ward (rīt′wərd) *adv., adj.* on or toward the right: also **right′wards** *adv.*

☆**right whale** [reason for name uncert.] any of a family (Balaenidae) of large-headed baleen whales lacking a dorsal fin and longitudinal wrinkles on the throat and chest

right wing [see RIGHT, *n.* 7] the more conservative or reactionary section of a political party or group —**right′-wing′** *adj.* —**right′-wing′er** *n.*

right·y (rīt′ē) *n., pl.* **right′ies** [Slang] ☆1 a right-handed person 2 a person with right-wing political views or affiliations

rig·id (rij′id) *adj.* [L *rigidus* < *rigere*, to be stiff, numb < IE base *(*s*)*rig*-, cold > FRIGID] 1 not bending or flexible; stiff and hard [a *rigid* metal girder] 2 not moving; set 3 severe; strict; exacting [a *rigid* taskmaster] 4 *a)* not deviating; rigorous [*rigid* regulations] *b)* precise; exact [*rigid* specifications] 5 *Aeron.* having a rigid framework that encloses containers for the gas: said of an airship —**ri·gid·i·ty** (ri jid′ə tē) *n.*, **rig′id·ness** —**rig′id·ly** *adv.*

ri·gid·i·fy (ri jid′ə fī′) *vt., vi.* **-fied′**, **-fy′ing** to make or become rigid —**ri·gid′i·fi·ca′tion** *n.*

rig·ma·role (rig′mə rōl′) *n.* [altered < *ragman roll* < ME *rageman rolle*, a long list or document] 1 foolish or incoherent rambling talk; nonsense 2 a foolishly involved, fussy, or time-wasting procedure

rig·or (rig′ər; *for 4 & 5, occas.* rī′gôr) *n.* [ME < MFr *rigueur* < L *rigor* < *rigere*: see RIGID] 1 harshness or severity; specif., *a)* strictness or inflexibility [the *rigor* of martial law] *b)* extreme hardship or difficulty [the *rigors* of life] *c)* inclemency, as of weather 2 exactness in precision or accuracy; exactitude 3 a severe, harsh, or oppressive act, etc. 4 stiffness; rigidity; specif., a condition of rigidity in bodily tissues or organs, in which there is no response to stimuli 5 a shivering or trembling, as in the chill preceding a fever Brit. sp. **rig′our** —*SYN.* DIFFICULTY

rig·or·ism (rig′ər iz′əm) *n.* [Fr *rigorisme*] strictness or severity, as in religion, moral code, artistic style, etc. —**rig′or·ist** *n.*

rig·or mor·tis (rig′ər môr′tis; *occas.* rī′gôr) [ModL, stiffness of death] the progressive stiffening of the muscles that occurs several hours after death as a result of the coagulation of the muscle protein

rig·or·ous (rig′ər əs) *adj.* [OFr < ML *rigorosus*] 1 very strict or harsh [a *rigorous* rule, master, etc.] 2 very severe or sharp [a *rigorous* climate] 3 rigidly precise; thoroughly accurate or exact [*rigorous* scholarship] —**rig′or·ous·ly** *adv.* —**rig′or·ous·ness** *n.*

Rig Veda (rig) [Sans *Ṛigveda* < *ṛic*, praise, hymn + *veda*, knowledge: see WISE[1]] the oldest, longest book of the Hindu Vedas, containing over 1,000 hymns

Riis (rēs), **Jacob August** 1849-1914; U.S. journalist & social reformer, born in Denmark

Ri·je·ka (rē yek′ə) seaport in W Croatia, on the Adriatic

Rijn (rān) *Du. name for the* RHINE

rijst·ta·fel or **rijs·ta·fel** (rīs′tä′fəl) *n.* [Du < *rijst*, rice (< MDu *rijs* < OFr *ris*, RICE) + *tafel*, table < MDu *tafele* < VL **tavola* < L *tabula*, TABLE] an Indonesian meal in which rice is served with a wide variety of foods and sauces in side dishes

Riks·mål (rēks′môl, riks′-) *n.* [Norw < *rike*, realm + *mål*, language] *former name for* BOKMÅL

rile (rīl) *vt.* **riled**, **ril′ing** [var. of ROIL] [Informal or Dial.] 1 ROIL 2 to anger; irritate

Ri·ley (rī′lē), **James Whit·comb** (hwit′kəm) 1849-1916; U.S. poet

ri·lie·vo (rē lye′vô) *n., pl.* **-vi** (-vē) [It: see RELIEF] *Archit., Sculpture* RELIEF (sense 7)

Ril·ke (ril′kə), **Rai·ner Ma·ri·a** (rī′nər mä rē′ä) (born *René Karl Wilhelm Johann Maria Rilke*) 1875-1926; Austrian lyric poet, born in Prague

rill (ril) *n.* [< Du *ril* or LowG *rille* < **ridula*, dim. of Gmc base seen in OE *rith*, small stream] a little brook; rivulet —*vi.* to flow in or like a rill

rille or **rill** (ril) *n.* [Ger *rille*, a furrow; akin to prec.] *Astron.* any of several long, narrow trenches or valleys on the moon's surface

rill·et (ril′it) *n.* [dim. of RILL] a tiny rill; brooklet

ril·lettes (ri lets′; *Fr* rē yet′) *pl.n.* [*with sing. or pl. v.*] bits of meat, fish, or fowl, esp. pork, cooked in seasoned fat, mashed into a paste, and preserved in the fat for use as a spread for bread

rim (rim) *n.* [ME *rime* < OE *rima*, edge, border, akin to ON *rimi*, ridge < IE base **rem*-, to support, rest upon, rest > Sans *rámatē*, (he) stands still, rests] 1 an edge, border, or margin, esp. of something circular; often, a raised or projecting edge or border 2 *a)* the outer, circular part of a wheel *b)* the metal flange surrounding the wheel of an automotive vehicle, on which the tire is mounted 3 [*pl.*] FRAME (*n.* 3e) 4 *Basketball* the metal hoop to which the net is attached —*vt.* **rimmed**, **rim′ming** 1 to put or form a rim on or around 2 to put around or along a rim [to *rim* a margarita glass with salt] 3 to roll around the rim of [the golf ball *rimmed* the hole] —*SYN.* BORDER —**rim′less** *adj.*

Rim·baud (ram bō′; *Fr* ran bō′), **(Jean Nicolas) Ar·thur** (år tür′) 1854-91; Fr. poet

rime[1] (rīm) *n., vi., vt.* **rimed**, **rim′ing** [see RHYME] *alt. sp. of* RHYME —**rim′er** *n.*

rime[2] (rīm) *n.* [ME < OE *hrim*, akin to ON < IE base **krei*-, to touch lightly > OE *hrinan*, to touch] FROST (sense 3) —*vt.* **rimed**, **rim′ing** to coat with rime

rime riche (rēm rēsh′) *pl.* **rimes riches** (rēm rēsh′) [Fr, lit., rich rhyme] rhyming of words or syllables pronounced and sometimes spelled alike but differing in meaning, as *dear* and *deer*

☆**rim·fire** (rim′fīr′) *adj.* designating a cartridge with the primer set in the rim of the base: cf. CENTERFIRE

Ri·mi·ni (rim′ə nē, rē′mə-) seaport in NC Italy, on the Adriatic

rim·ple (rim′pəl) *n., vt., vi.* **-pled**, **-pling** [ME *rimpyl*, prob. < OE *hrympel*; akin to MDu, MLowG *rimpe*: see RUMPLE] [Now Rare] wrinkle; rumple; crease

☆**rim·rock** (rim′räk′) *n.* rock forming the rim or upper part of a steep slope or precipice

☆**rim·shot** (rim′shät′) *n.* a sharp sound produced by striking a drumstick either against the rim and head of a snare drum simultaneously or against another drumstick held so that it rests on the rim and head: also written **rim shot**

Rim·sky-Kor·sa·kov (rim′skē kôr′sə kôf′), **Ni·ko·lai An·dre·ye·vich** (nē kô lī′ än dryā′ye vich) 1844-1908; Russ. composer: also sp. **Rimski-Korsakoff**

rim·y (rī′mē) *adj.* **rim′i·er**, **rim′i·est** covered with rime; frosty

rind (rīnd) *n.* [ME *rinde* < OE *rind*, *rinde* < base of *rendan*, to REND] 1 a thick, hard or tough natural outer covering, as of a watermelon, grapefruit, or orange 2 any outer layer or skin suggestive of this, as of bacon or certain cheeses —*SYN.* SKIN

rin·der·pest (rin′dər pest′) *n.* [Ger *rinder*, pl. of *rind*, horned beast (< IE base **ker*-, head, HORN) + *pest*, plague] an acute, infectious disease of cattle, sheep, and goats caused by a paramyxovirus and characterized by fever and by hemorrhagic inflammation and ulceration of the mucous membrane of the alimentary canal

ring[1] (riŋ) *vi.* **rang** or [Now Chiefly Dial.] **rung**, **rung**, **ring′ing** [ME *ringen* < OE *hringan* < IE echoic base **ker*- > RAVEN[1], CREAK, L *corvus*, crow] 1 to give forth a clear, resonant sound when struck or otherwise caused to vibrate, as a bell 2 to produce, as by sounding, a specified impression on the hearer [promises that *ring* false] 3 to cause a bell or bells to sound, esp. as a summons [to *ring* for a maid] 4 to sound loudly or be full of sound; be resonant; resound [the room *rang* with laughter] 5 to have a sensation as of ringing, humming, etc.: said of the ears or head —*vt.* **1** to cause (a bell, etc.) to ring **2** to sound (a peal, knell, etc.) by or as by ringing a bell or bells **3** to signal, proclaim, announce, summon, etc. by or as by ringing [*chimes rang* the hours] **4** to test (coins, etc.) by the sound produced in striking on something hard **5** [Chiefly Brit.] to call by telephone: often with *up* **6** [Slang] to substitute (originally a racehorse) fraudulently: often with *in* —*n.* **1** the sound of a bell **2** *a)* any similar sound [the *ring* of laughter] *b)* any loud sound, esp. when repeated, continued, or reverberated, as the intermittent sound an incoming call triggers on a telephone **3** the characteristic sound or impression (*of* some feeling) [the *ring* of sincerity] **4** a set of bells **5** the act of ringing a bell, etc. **6** [Informal] a telephone call: chiefly in **give someone a ring**, to telephone someone —**ring a bell** ☆to stir up a memory; sound familiar —**ring down the curtain 1** to signal for a theater curtain to be lowered **2** to end something —**ring in** (or **out**) **1** to punch in (or out): see PUNCH² **2** to usher in (or out) —**ring off** [Chiefly Brit.] to end a telephone call; hang up —☆**ring the bell** [Informal] to achieve a success: originally in allusion to hitting the bull's-eye and so causing a bell to ring in target shooting —**ring up** ☆to record or enter (a specified amount) on a cash register —**ring up the curtain 1** to signal for a theater curtain to be raised **2** to begin something

ring² (riŋ) *n.* ⟦ME < OE *hring,* akin to OHG, ON *hringr,* Du *ring,* Goth **hrings* < IE *(*s*)*krengh-* < base *(*s*)*ker-,* to turn, bend > Gr *kirkos,* ring, L *cortina,* round vessel⟧ **1** a circular band, usually of precious metal and often set with gems, worn on the finger as an ornament or a symbol of betrothal, marriage, etc. **2** a circular band of metal, plastic, etc., used to connect, hang, seal, decorate, etc. a thing or things [a key *ring,* a napkin *ring*] **3** *a)* a circular line, mark, or figure *b)* a line, mark, stain, etc. along the edge or periphery of something [a *ring* of dirt around the inside of a bathtub] **4** the outer edge or border of something circular; rim, as of a wheel **5** a circular cut made, or a circle of bark cut from, around the trunk or a branch of a tree **6** ANNUAL RING **7** any of the turns in a helix or spiral **8** a circular course, as in dancing **9** a number of people or things grouped in a circle ☆**10** a group of people working together to advance their own interests, esp. by questionable or illegal manipulation and control, as in business, politics, etc. **11** an enclosed area, often circular, for contests, exhibitions, etc. [a circus *ring*] **12** *a)* an enclosure, now usually a square, canvas-covered area set off by stakes and ropes, in which boxing and wrestling matches are held *b)* the sport or profession of boxing; prizefighting (with *the*) *c)* [*pl.*] *Gym.* two wooden rings suspended from a ceiling, used for acrobatic feats and routines (usually with *the*) *d)* [*pl.*] *Gym.* a competitive event in which the rings are used (usually with *the*) **13** a contest or competition, esp. a political one, as in *throw one's hat into the ring*: see phrase at HAT **14** *Astron.* a thin, flat, reflective band of orbiting particles, probably ice crystals and dust, encircling a planet, as Saturn or Uranus, along its equatorial plane at altitudes below the Roche limit **15** *Chem.* CLOSED CHAIN **16** *Geom.* the space between two concentric circles **17** *Math.* a set of elements that has two operations, addition and multiplication, and the properties of being a commutative group under addition, of being closed and associative under multiplication and addition, and in which multiplication is distributive over addition —*vt.* **ringed**, **ring′ing 1** to surround or encircle with or as with a ring **2** to form into a ring or rings **3** to furnish with a ring or rings **4** to put a ring through the nose of (an animal), as to prevent rooting or fighting **5** to circle about and so hem in (animals) **6** in some games, to toss a ring, horseshoe, quoit, etc. so that it encircles (a peg) **7** to girdle (a tree) —*vi.* **1** to form in a ring or rings **2** to move in a circular or curving course; run, fly, etc. in circles or spirals

☆**ring-a-le·vi·o** (riŋ′ə lē′vē ō′) *n.* ⟦< prec. + RELIEVE⟧ a children's game in which members of one group try to find and capture hiding members of another group: a captured player is kept in a circle drawn on the ground and is set free when tagged by a teammate

ring bearer an attendant, typically a young boy, who formally carries the rings at a wedding

ring·bolt (riŋ′bōlt′) *n.* a bolt with a ring at the head

ring·bone (-bōn′) *n.* any pathological bony growth on the pastern bones of a horse, often causing lameness

ring·dove (-duv′) *n.* any of various Eurasian pigeons with markings around the neck; esp., a small dove (*Streptopelia risoria*)

ringed (riŋd) *adj.* **1** wearing or having a ring or rings **2** decorated or marked with a ring or rings **3** encircled by a ring or rings **4** formed like a ring or of rings

rin·gent (rin′jənt) *adj.* ⟦L *ringens,* prp. of *ringi,* to gape⟧ **1** having the mouth wide open; gaping **2** *Bot.* having its petals separated by a distinct gap: said of certain flowers

ring·er² (riŋ′ər) *n.* **1** a horseshoe or quoit thrown so that it encircles the peg **2** such a throw

ring·er¹ (riŋ′ər) *n.* **1** a person or thing that rings a bell, chime, etc. ☆**2** [Slang] *a)* a horse, player, etc. fraudulently entered, or substituted for another, in a competition *b)* any substitute *c)* a person or thing very closely resembling another (now usually **dead ringer**)

Ring·er's solution (*or* **fluid**) (riŋ′ərz) ⟦after S. *Ringer* (1835-1910), Eng physiologist⟧ *Biochem., Med.* a solution of the chlorides of sodium, potassium, and calcium in purified water that has the same osmotic pressure as that found in blood or tissues, used in physiological research, to correct dehydration, etc.

ring finger the finger next to the little finger, esp. of the left hand: the wedding ring is usually worn on this finger

ring·git (riŋ′git) *n., pl.* **-git** ⟦Malay, lit., jagged: from the serrated edge of the original coins⟧ the basic monetary unit of Malaysia: see the table of monetary units in the Reference Supplement

ring·hals (riŋ′hals) *n., pl.* **-hals** or **-hals·es** ⟦Afrik, obs. sp. of *rinkals* < Du *ring* (see RING²) + *hals,* neck: see COLLAR⟧ a small, rough-skinned spitting cobra (*Hemachatus hemachatus*) of S Africa that usually sprays jets of venom at the eyes of an aggressor

ring·lead·er (riŋ′lēd′ər) *n.* ⟦RING² + LEADER⟧ a person who leads others, esp. in unlawful acts, opposition to authority, etc.

ring·let (-lit) *n.* ⟦dim. of RING²⟧ **1** a little ring or circle **2** a curl of hair, esp. a long one —**ring′let·ed** *adj.*

ring·mas·ter (riŋ′mas′tər, -mäs′-) *n.* a person who directs performances, as in a circus ring

☆**ring·neck** (riŋ′nek′) *n.* a ring-necked bird, snake, etc.

ring-necked (riŋ′nekt′) *adj. Zool.* having a distinctive colored stripe or stripes around the neck

☆**ring-necked duck** a North American duck (*Aythya collaris*), the male of which has a black breast, neck, and back with a faint coppery ring around the neck

ring-necked pheasant an Asian game fowl (*Phasianus colchicus*) with a whitish collar around the neck in the male, now widely introduced and bred in North America, Europe, etc.

☆**ringneck snake** any of a genus (*Diadophis*) of small colubrid snakes with a yellow or orange ring around the neck, common throughout North America: also **ring-necked snake**

Ring of Fire beltlike region, roughly surrounding the Pacific Ocean, characterized by frequent volcanic and seismic activity caused by the colliding of moving crustal plates

Ring of the Nibelung *Gmc. Legend* the ring made from the Rheingold by Alberich, leader of the Nibelungs, a race of dwarfs

ring ouzel a European thrush (*Turdus torquatus*) with a white crescent across the breast

ring·side (riŋ′sīd′) *n.* **1** the space or place just outside the ring, as at a boxing match or circus **2** any place that provides a close view of something —*adj., adv.* at, in, or from this place

ring-streaked (-strēkt′) *adj.* having streaks of color around the body

ring·tail (riŋ′tāl′) *n.* a ring-tailed animal, as a cacomistle or raccoon

ring-tailed (-tāld′) *adj.* having colored bands or stripes around the tail

ring·tone (-tōn′) *n.* a brief digital recording of music or other sound that plays whenever a call is received on a cell phone

☆**ring·toss** (-tôs′) *n.* a game in which rings made of rope, etc. are tossed so as to encircle a peg

ring·worm (-wurm′) *n.* any of various contagious skin diseases caused by related varieties of fungus and characterized by itching and the formation of ring-shaped, discolored patches covered with scales or vesicles

rink (riŋk) *n.* ⟦ME(Scot), earlier *renk* < OFr *renc,* RANK¹⟧ **1** *a)* a smooth expanse of ice marked off for the game of curling *b)* a part of a bowling green of a suitable size for a match *c)* the players on one side in a game of curling, bowls, or quoits **2** *a)* a smooth expanse of ice, often enclosed and artificially prepared, for ice-skating or hockey *b)* a smooth floor, usually of wood and enclosed, for roller-skating *c)* a building enclosing either of such rinks

☆**rink·y-dink** (riŋ′kē diŋk′) *adj.* ⟦? altered < RICKY-TICK⟧ [Slang] shoddy, cheap, worn-out, or corny

rinse (rins) *vt.* **rinsed**, **rins′ing** ⟦ME *rincen* < OFr *rincer,* earlier *reïncier* < VL **recentiare,* to renew, rinse, purify < L *recens,* fresh, RECENT⟧ **1** to wash lightly, esp. by dipping into water or by letting water run over, into, or through **2** *a)* to remove soap, dirt, or impurities from in this way, esp. as a final part of washing *b)* to remove (soap, dirt, etc.) in this way **3** to flush (the mouth or teeth), as with clear water **4** *a)* to dip (fabrics, garments, etc.) into a dye solution *b)* to use a rinse on (the hair) —*n.* **1** the act of rinsing **2** the water or solution used in rinsing **3** a substance mixed with water and used to rinse or tint hair —**rins′er** *n.*

rins·ing (rin′siŋ) *n.* [*usually pl.*] **1** *a)* the liquid in or with which anything has been rinsed *b)* DREGS **2** the act of one that rinses; rinse

Ri·o (rē′ō) *informal name for* RIO DE JANEIRO (the city)

Ri·o Bran·co (rē′o͞o brun′ko͞o) city in W Brazil: capital of Acre state

Rí·o Bra·vo (rē′ō brä′vō) *Mex. name for* the RIO GRANDE (river flowing into the Gulf of Mexico): also **Río Bravo del Nor·te** (del nôr′te)

Ri·o de Ja·nei·ro (rē′ō dā′ zhə ner′ō, -dē′-; *Port* rē′o͞o də zhə nā′ro͞o) **1** state of SE Brazil: 16,954 sq mi (43,911 sq km); cap. Rio de Janeiro **2** its capital, a seaport in the SE coast

Río de la Plata *see* PLATA, Río de la

Rí·o de O·ro (rē′ō dā ôr′ō) *former name for* SPANISH SAHARA

Ri·o Gran·de (*for 1,* rē′ō grand′; -gran′dē, -grän′dā; *for 2 & 3, Port* rē′o͞o grun′də) ⟦Sp, lit., great river⟧ **1** river flowing from S Colo. south through N.Mex., then southeast as the boundary between Texas and Mexico into the Gulf of Mexico: 1,885 mi (3,034 km) **2** river in SE Brazil, in the states of Minas Gerais & São Paulo; headstream of the Paraná: *c.* 650 mi (1,046 km) **3** seaport in SE Brazil, on the Atlantic

Ri·o Gran·de do Nor·te (rē′o͞o grun′də do͞o nôr′tə) state of NE Brazil: 20,582 sq mi (53,307 sq km); cap. Natal

Ri·o Gran·de do Sul (rē′o͞o grun′də do͞o so͞ol′) southernmost state of Brazil: 108,905 sq mi (282,063 sq km); cap. Pôrto Alegre

Ri·o·ja (rē ō′hä; *Sp* rē ô′hä) *n.* [*sometimes* **r-**] any of various wines, esp. dry red wines, produced in La Rioja, a region of N Spain

Rí·o Mu·ni (rē′ō mo͞o′nē) mainland portion of Equatorial Guinea, on the Gulf of Guinea: 10,042 sq mi (26,009 sq km)

ri·ot (rī′ət) ***n.*** ⟦ME < OFr *riote* < *rihoter,* to make a disturbance⟧ **1** wild or violent disorder, confusion, or disturbance; tumult; uproar **2** a violent public disturbance of the peace, by a number of persons (specified, in law, usually as three or more) assembled together **3** an unrestrained outburst, as of laughter **4** a brilliant, vivid display *[a riot of color]* **5** [Now Rare] *a)* wild, loose living; debauchery *b)* unrestrained revelry *c)* a wild, noisy feast or revel ☆**6** [Informal] an extremely amusing person, thing, or event **—*vi.*** ⟦ME *rioten* < OFr *rihoter*⟧ **1** to take part in a tumult or disturbance of the peace **2** [Now Rare] *a)* to live in a wild, loose manner *b)* to engage in unrestrained revelry *c)* to indulge without restraint; revel (*in* something) **—*vt.*** [Now Rare] to waste (money, time, etc.) in disorderly or profligate living **—run riot** ⟦orig. of dogs barking on the wrong scent⟧ **1** to run wild; act without restraint, control, or discipline **2** to grow in luxuriance or profusion **—ri′ot·er *n.***

Riot Act an English law, passed in 1715, providing that if twelve or more persons are unlawfully assembled and disturbing the public peace they must disperse on proclamation (*reading the Riot Act*) or be held guilty of felony **—read someone the riot act** [Informal] to upbraid or forcefully warn someone

☆**riot gun** a small firearm, esp. a short-barreled shotgun, used to disperse rioters

ri·ot·ous (rī′ət əs) ***adj.*** ⟦ME < OFr *rioteus*⟧ **1** *a)* having the nature of a riot *b)* engaging in rioting or inciting to riot **2** without restraint; disorderly; boisterous **3** dissolute; profligate *[riotous living]* **4** luxuriant or profuse **—ri′ot·ous·ly *adv.* —ri′ot·ous·ness *n.***

rip[1] (rip) ***vt.* ripped, rip′ping** ⟦LME *rippen,* prob. < or akin to MFl, to tear < IE *reub-: see RUB⟧ **1** *a)* to cut or tear apart roughly or vigorously *b)* to remove by or as by so cutting or tearing (with *off, out, away,* etc.) *c)* to make (a hole) in this way *d)* to slash with a sharp instrument *e)* to cut, tear, etc. (stitches) so as to open (a seam, hem, etc.) **2** to saw (wood) along the grain **—*vi.*** **1** to become torn or split apart **2** [Informal] to move with speed or violence **—*n.*** **1** a torn place or burst seam; tear; split **2** the act of ripping **—*SYN.*** TEAR[1] **—☆let her (or ’er) rip** [Slang] to go ahead; continue without restraint **—rip into** [Informal] to attack violently or sharply, often with words **—rip off** [Slang] ☆**1** to steal or rob ☆**2** to cheat, exploit, or take advantage of **—☆rip on** [Slang] to criticize harshly

☆**rip**[2] (rip) ***n.*** ⟦< ? prec.⟧ an extent of rough, broken water caused as by the meeting of cross currents or tides or the interaction of currents and wind

rip[3] (rip) ***n.*** ⟦var. of *rep,* prob. abbrev. of REPROBATE⟧ **1** [Old Informal] a dissolute, dissipated person **2** [Slang] a worthless thing: now chiefly in the phrase **(not) give a rip,** to (not) care even a little

R.I.P. or **RIP** *abbrev.* REQUIESCAT (IN PACE)

ri·par·i·an (ri per′ē ən, rī-) ***adj.*** ⟦< L *riparius* < *ripa,* river bank < IE **reipā,* steep edge < base **rei-,* to slit, cut > RIVE, REAP⟧ **1** of, adjacent to, or living on the bank of a river or, sometimes, of a lake, pond, etc. **2** designating any right enjoyed by the owner of riparian land

rip cord **1** a cord fastened to the gas bag of a balloon or dirigible in such a way that pulling it opens the bag, releasing gas and causing a rapid descent **2** a cord, etc. pulled to open a parachute during descent

ripe (rīp) ***adj.* rip′er, rip′est** ⟦OE, akin to REAP⟧ **1** fully grown or developed; specif., ready to be harvested and used for food, as grain or fruit **2** like ripe fruit, as in being ruddy and full *[ripe lips]* **3** sufficiently advanced, as by being kept in storage or subjected to treatment, to be ready for use *[ripe wine, ripe cheese]* **4** fully or highly developed by study, experience, etc.; mature as in judgment, knowledge, etc. *[ripe wisdom]* **5** *a)* characterized by full physical or mental development *[a person of ripe years]* *b)* advanced in years *[the ripe age of ninety]* **6** ready to do, receive, or undergo something; fully prepared *[ripe for marriage]* **7** ready for some operation, treatment, or process *[a boil ripe for lancing]* **8** sufficiently advanced; far enough along (*for* some purpose): said of time **9** having a strong, unpleasant smell **—ripe′ly *adv.* —ripe′ness *n.***

SYN.—**ripe,** in its basic application, implies readiness to be harvested, eaten, used, etc. *[ripe apples, cheese, etc.]* and, in extended use, full readiness for action, etc. *[ripe for change]*; **mature** implies full growth or development, as of living organisms, the mind, etc. *[a mature tree, mature judgment]*; **mellow** suggests the qualities typical of ripe fruit, such as softness, sweetness, etc. and therefore stresses the absence of sharpness, harshness, etc. *[a mellow flavor, mood, etc.]*; **adult** is applied to a person who has reached complete physical or mental maturity, or legal majority, and to ideas, etc. that show mature thinking **—*ANT.* unripe, immature**

rip·en (rī′pən) ***vi., vt.*** to become or make ripe; mature, age, cure, etc. **—rip′en·er *n.***

☆**rip-off** (rip′ôf′) ***n.*** [Slang] **1** the act or an instance of stealing, cheating, exploiting, misrepresenting, etc. **2** a product that is overpriced, esp. one that is inferior or an imitation

ri·poste or **ri·post** (ri päst′, -pōst′) ***n.*** ⟦Fr *riposte* < It *risposta* < *rispondere* < L *respondere:* see RESPOND⟧ **1** *Fencing* a sharp, swift thrust made after parrying an opponent's lunge **2** a sharp, swift response or retort **—*vi.* -post′ed, -post′ing** to make a riposte

ripped (ript) ***adj.*** [Slang] ☆**1** under the influence of a drug; high ☆**2** intoxicated; drunk ☆**3** trim and muscular *[a set of ripped abs]*

rip·per (rip′ər) ***n.*** **1** a person who rips **2** a thing that rips; device or tool for ripping

rip·ping (rip′iŋ) ***adj.*** **1** that rips or tears **2** [Old Slang, Chiefly Brit.] excellent; fine; splendid **—rip′ping·ly *adv.***

rip·ple[1] (rip′əl) ***vi.* -pled, -pling** ⟦prob. < RIP[1] + -LE, sense 3⟧ **1** *a)* to form or have little waves or undulating movements on the surface, as water or grass stirred by a breeze *b)* to flow with such waves or movements on the surface *c)* to be formed or set in small folds or waves, as cloth or hair **2** to give the effect of rippling water, as by alternately rising and falling *[laughter rippling through the hall]* **—*vt.*** **1** to cause to ripple **2** to give a wavy form or appearance to **3** to make (a sound, tone, etc.) that ripples **—*n.*** **1** a small wave or undulation, as on the surface of water **2** a movement, appearance, or formation suggesting this **3** a sound like that of rippling water **4** a small rapid in a stream **—*SYN.*** WAVE **—rip′pler *n.***

rip·ple[2] (rip′əl) ***vt.* -pled, -pling** ⟦ME *rypelen* < or akin to MLowG or MDu *repelen,* akin to OHG *riffilon,* to scrape, *riffila,* a saw < IE **reib-* > REAP⟧ to remove the seeds from (flax, hemp, etc.) with a toothed implement resembling a comb **—*n.*** such an implement **—rip′pler *n.***

Rip·ple (rip′əl) ***n.*** ⟦former trademark⟧ any cheap wine

ripple effect the spreading effects experienced as the result of a single event

ripple mark any of the ripply lines on the surface of sand, mud, etc. caused by waves, wind, or both

rip·plet (rip′lit) ***n.*** a little ripple

rip·ply (-lē) ***adj.* -pli·er, -pli·est** characterized by ripples

rip·rap (rip′rap′) ***n.*** ⟦echoic redupl. of RAP[1]⟧ ☆**1** a foundation or wall made of large chunks of stone thrown together irregularly or loosely, as in water or on a soft bottom ☆**2** chunks of stone used for this **—☆*vt.* -rapped′, -rap′ping** **1** to make a riprap in or on **2** to strengthen with riprap

☆**rip-roar·ing** (-rôr′iŋ) ***adj.*** [Slang] boisterous; uproarious

rip·saw (-sô′) ***n.*** ⟦RIP[1] + SAW[1]⟧ a saw with coarse teeth, for cutting wood along the grain

☆**rip·snort·er** (-snôrt′ər) ***n.*** [Slang] a person or thing that is strikingly active, forceful, exciting, wild, rambunctious, etc. **—rip′snort′ing *adj.***

rip·stop (rip′stäp′) ***adj.*** designating or of a fabric, esp. nylon, woven with extra threads in a pattern to make runs or tears less likely and used for parachutes, garments, etc.

rip·tide (-tīd′) ***n.*** ⟦RIP[2] + TIDE[1]⟧ a current opposing other currents, producing violently disturbed water; esp., the strong, narrow flow of seawater that rushes seaward after incoming waves pile up on the shore: also written **rip tide**

Rip·u·ar·i·an (rip′yo͞o wer′ē ən) ***adj.*** ⟦< ML *Ripuarius* (prob. < L *riparius,* RIPARIAN) + -AN⟧ of a group of Franks that settled along the Rhine near Cologne in the 4th cent. A.D. **—*n.*** a Ripuarian Frank

Rip van Win·kle (rip′ van wiŋ′kəl) the title character of a story (1819) by Washington Irving: Rip awakens after a twenty-year sleep to find everything changed

rise (rīz) ***vi.* rose, ris·en** (riz′ən), **ris′ing** ⟦ME *risen* < OE *risan,* akin to OHG *rīsan,* ON *rísa* < IE **ereis-,* extension of base **er-,* to set in motion, raise > RUN, L *oriri,* to rise, Gr *ornynai,* to arouse⟧ **I.** *to get up* **1** to stand or assume a vertical or more nearly vertical position, after sitting, kneeling, or lying **2** to get up after sleeping or resting **3** to rebel; revolt **4** to end an official assembly or meeting; adjourn **5** *Theol.* to return to life; become resurrected **II.** *to go up* **1** to go to a higher place or position; ascend **2** to appear above the horizon *[the moon rose just after 8:00]* **3** to attain greater height or a higher level *[the river rose rapidly]* **4** to advance in social status, rank, importance, etc.; become rich, famous, successful, etc. **5** to become erect or rigid **6** to form an elevation; extend upward *[the tower rising above the trees]* **7** to have an upward incline or slant *[hills rising steeply]* **8** to move upward to the surface of the water, as a fish seeking to take a fly, bait, etc. **III.** *to increase in some way* **1** to increase in amount, degree, quantity, price, etc. **2** to increase in volume of sound; become louder, shriller, etc. **3** to become stronger, more vivid, more buoyant, etc. *[his spirits rose]* **4** to become larger and puffier: used esp. of dough containing yeast **IV.** *to appear by or as by rising* **1** to originate, begin, or spring up **2** to have its source: said of a stream **3** to happen; occur **4** to become apparent to the senses or the mind *[land rising ahead of the ship]* **5** to be stirred up; become aroused *[to make someone's temper rise]* **6** to be built *[a house rising on the hill]* **—*vt.*** to cause to rise, as birds from cover or a fish to the surface of the water **—*n.*** **1** the actual or refracted appearance of the sun, moon, etc. above the horizon **2** upward movement; ascent **3** an advance in social status, rank, importance, etc. **4** the appearance of a fish at the water's surface **5** a piece of high or rising ground; hill **6** a slope upward **7** the vertical height of something, as of a flight of stairs or a single step **8** an increase in *a)* height, as of water level *b)* volume or pitch of a sound *c)* degree, amount, price, value, etc. **9** a beginning, origin, springing up, etc. **10** the distance from the top of the inseam to the waistband, as in pants or underwear **11** [Brit.] a raise (in wages, etc.) **—get a rise out of** [Slang] to draw a desired response from by teasing or provoking **—give rise to** to cause to appear or come into existence **—rise to** to prove oneself capable of coping with *[to rise to the challenge]*

SYN.—**rise** and **arise** both imply a coming into being, action, notice, etc., but **rise** carries an added implication of ascent *[empires rise and fall]* and **arise** is often used to indicate a causal relationship *[accidents arise from carelessness]*; **spring** implies sudden emergence *[weeds sprang up in the garden]*; **originate** is used in indicating a definite source, beginning, or prime cause *[psychoanalysis originated with Freud]*; **derive** implies a proceeding or developing from something else that is the source [this word *derives* from the Latin]; **flow** suggests a streaming from a source like water ["Praise God, from whom all blessings *flow*"]; **issue** suggests emergence through an outlet [not a word *issued* from his lips]; **emanate** implies the flowing forth from a source of something that is nonmaterial or intangible [rays of light *emanating* from the sun]; **stem** implies outgrowth as from a root or a main stalk [modern detective fiction *stems* from Poe]

ris·er (rī′zər) ***n.*** 1 a person or thing that rises; specif., a person who gets up after sleep in a specified way [an early *riser*] 2 any of the vertical pieces between the steps in a stairway 3 a vertical pipe as for the flow of a liquid or gas

ris·i·bil·i·ty (riz′ə bil′ə tē) ***n.,*** *pl.* **-ties** 1 the quality or state of being risible; ability or inclination to laugh ☆2 [*usually pl.*] a sense of the ridiculous or amusing; appreciation of what is laughable

ris·i·ble (riz′ə bəl) ***adj.*** ⟦Fr < LL *risibilis* < L *risus,* pp. of *ridere,* to laugh: see RIDICULE⟧ 1 able or inclined to laugh 2 of or connected with laughter 3 causing laughter; laughable; funny; amusing

ris·ing (rī′ziŋ) ***adj.*** 1 that rises; going up, ascending, mounting, advancing, sloping upward, etc. 2 advancing to adult years; growing; maturing [the *rising* generation] 3 *Astrol.* ASCENDANT (sense 3) ☆4 [Informal or Dial.] *a)* fully as much as; somewhat more than *b)* approaching; nearing (in these meanings sometimes construed as a preposition) [a man *rising* fifty] **—*n.*** 1 the act or process of a person or thing that rises; esp., an uprising; revolt; insurrection 2 something that rises; specif., *a)* a projection or prominence *b)* [Dial.] a boil, abscess, etc.

risk (risk) ***n.*** ⟦Fr *risque* < It *risco, risico* < *risicare,* to risk < VL **risicare*⟧ 1 the chance of injury, damage, or loss; dangerous chance; hazard 2 *Insurance a)* the chance of loss *b)* the degree of probability of loss *c)* the amount of possible loss to the insuring company *d)* a person or thing with reference to the risk involved in providing insurance *e)* the type of loss that a policy covers, as fire, storm, etc. **—*vt.*** ⟦Fr *risquer*⟧ 1 to expose to the chance of injury, damage, or loss; hazard [to *risk* one's life] 2 to incur the risk of [to *risk* a fight] **—*SYN.*** DANGER **—at risk** in danger of damage, injury, loss, etc. **—risk′er *n.***

risk capital VENTURE CAPITAL

risk·y (ris′kē) ***adj.*** **risk′i·er, risk′i·est** involving risk; hazardous; dangerous **—risk′i·ly *adv.*** **—risk′i·ness *n.***

Ri·sor·gi·men·to (ri sôr′jə men′tō) ***n.*** ⟦It, resurrection⟧ 1 the 19th-cent. movement for the liberation and unification of Italy 2 the period of this

ri·sot·to (ri zō′tō, -sō′tō; -zät′ō, -sät′ō) ***n.*** ⟦It < *riso,* rice⟧ an Italian dish with a creamy texture, typically made from a short-grained rice that is sauteed and then simmered in broth: the rice may then be flavored as with cheese, butter, vegetables, etc.

ris·qué (ris kā′) ***adj.*** ⟦Fr, pp. of *risquer,* to RISK⟧ very close to being improper or indecent; suggestive, esp. sexually so [a *risqué* anecdote]

ris·sole (ris′ōl′; *Fr* rē sôl′) ***n.*** ⟦Fr, ult. < LL *russeolus,* reddish < L *russus*: see RUSSET⟧ a small ball or roll of minced meat or fish often mixed with bread crumbs, etc., enclosed in a pastry and fried

ris·so·lé (rē′sō lā′) ***adj.*** ⟦Fr < pp. of *rissoler,* to brown, fry⟧ fried in deep fat until brown: said esp. of potatoes

ri·stra (rē′strä) ***n.,*** *pl.* **-stras** ⟦Sp, a string, as of garlic bulbs braided together⟧ [*also in roman type*] a string of dried chilies or a length of braided dried garlic bulbs, hung for storage or decoration

rit *abbrev.* ritardando

Ri·ta (rēt′ə) ***n.*** ⟦shortened < Sp *Margarita* or It *Margherita*: see MARGARET⟧ a feminine name

Rit·a·lin (rit′'l in) ⟦< ?⟧ *trademark for* a stimulant, $C_{14}H_{19}NO_2 \cdot HCl$, used to treat depression, hyperactivity in children, etc.

ri·tar·dan·do (rē′tär dän′dō′) ***adj., adv.*** ⟦It, prp. of *ritardare,* to delay, slow down < L *retardare,* RETARD⟧ *Musical Direction* becoming gradually slower: when used other than in a musical score, also in roman type **—*n.,*** *pl.* ***-dos′*** [*also in roman type*] *Music* a passage to be performed *ritardando* Also ***ri·tard*** (ri tärd′)

rite (rīt) ***n.*** ⟦ME < L *ritus* < IE **rēi-,* var. of base **ar-,* to join, fit > ART[1], READ[1], RATE[1], ARITHMETIC⟧ 1 a ceremonial or formal, solemn act, observance, or procedure in accordance with prescribed rule or custom, as in religious use [marriage *rites*] 2 any formal, customary observance, practice, or procedure [the *rites* of courtship] 3 *a)* a prescribed form or particular system of ceremonial procedure, religious or otherwise; ritual [the Scottish *rite* of Freemasonry] *b)* [*often* **R-**] liturgy; esp., any of the historical forms of the Eucharistic service [the Byzantine *rite*] 4 [*also* **R-**] any of the Christian Churches, either historical or contemporary [the Eastern *Rite,* the Roman *Rite*] **—*SYN.*** CEREMONY

rite of passage 1 a ceremony, often religious, marking a significant transition in a person's life, as birth, puberty, marriage, or death 2 an event, achievement, etc. in a person's life regarded as having great significance Also [Fr.] ***rite de pas·sage*** (rēt də pä säzh′)

ri·tor·nel·lo (rit′ər nel′ō; *It* rē′tôr nel′lô) ***n.,*** *pl.* **-los** or **-li** (-lē) ⟦It, dim. of *ritorno,* a return < *ritornare,* to return < *ri-* (< L *re-*), RE- + *tornare* (< L), to TURN⟧ *Music* 1 an instrumental interlude before or after an aria, scene, etc. in early, esp. 17th-cent., operas 2 a tutti section recurring in a concerto grosso or rondo

rit·u·al (rich′ōō əl) ***adj.*** ⟦L *ritualis*⟧ of, having the nature of, or done as a rite or rites [*ritual* dances] **—*n.*** 1 a set form or system of rites, religious or otherwise 2 the observance of set forms or rites, as in public worship 3 a book containing rites or ceremonial forms 4 any practice, action, or procedure performed or observed regularly, consistently, etc. 5 ritual acts or procedures collectively **—*SYN.*** CEREMONY **—rit′u·al·ly *adv.***

rit·u·al·ism (-iz′əm) ***n.*** 1 observance, use, or study of ritual 2 excessive devotion to ritual **—rit′u·al·ist *n., adj.*** **—rit′u·al·is′tic *adj.*** **—rit′u·al·is′ti·cal·ly *adv.***

rit·u·al·ize (-īz′) ***vi.*** **-ized′, -iz′ing** to engage in or promote ritualism **—*vt.*** 1 to make a ritual of 2 to give the character of ritual to **—rit′u·al·i·za′tion *n.***

☆**ritz·y** (rit′sē) ***adj.*** **ritz′i·er, ritz′i·est** ⟦after the *Ritz* hotels, known for their opulence, founded by César Ritz (1850-1918), Swiss-born hotelier⟧ [Slang] luxurious, fashionable, elegant, etc. **—ritz′i·ness *n.***

riv *abbrev.* river

ri·val (rī′vəl) ***n.*** ⟦Fr < L *rivalis,* orig., one living near or using the same stream as another < *rivus,* brook < IE **reie-,* to flow < base **er-*: see RISE⟧ 1 a person who tries to get or do the same thing as another, or to equal or surpass another; competitor 2 a person or thing that can equal or surpass another in some way; person or thing that can bear comparison [plastics and other *rivals* of many metals] 3 [Obs.] an associate or companion in some duty **—*adj.*** acting as a rival; competing **—*vt.*** **-valed** or **-valled, -val·ing** or **-val·ling** 1 [Archaic] to try to equal or surpass; compete with 2 to equal in some way; be a match for **—*vi.*** [Archaic] to be a rival; compete (*with*)

ri·val·rous (rī′vəl rəs) ***adj.*** 1 being a rival or rivals 2 of or involving rivalry

ri·val·ry (-rē) ***n.,*** *pl.* **-ries** the act of rivaling or the fact or condition of being a rival or rivals; competition **—*SYN.*** COMPETITION

rive (rīv) ***vt.*** **rived, rived** or **riv′en, riv′ing** ⟦ME *riven* < ON *rifa* < IE base **rei-,* to tear, slit > RIFT[1], REAP, ROW[1]⟧ 1 to tear apart; rend 2 to split; cleave 3 to break or dismay (the heart, spirit, etc.) **—*vi.*** to be or become rived

riv·en (riv′ən) ***vt., vi. alt. pp. of*** RIVE **—*adj.*** torn apart or split

riv·er[1] (riv′ər) ***n.*** ⟦ME *rivere* < OFr *riviere* < VL *riparia* < L *riparius*: see RIPARIAN⟧ 1 a natural stream of water larger than a creek and emptying into an ocean, a lake, or another river 2 any similar or plentiful stream or flow [a *river* of lava] **—☆sell down the river** ⟦from the former practice of selling and sending slaves to plantations on the lower Mississippi River, where conditions were esp. harsh⟧ [Informal] to betray, deceive, abuse, etc. **—☆up the river** ⟦from the practice of sending convicts *up* the Hudson, from New York City to Sing Sing⟧ [Slang] to or confined in a penitentiary **—riv′er·like′ *adj.***

riv·er[2] (rī′vər) ***n.*** a person or thing that rives

Ri·ve·ra (ri ver′ə), **Di·e·go** (dē ā′gō) 1886-1957; Mex. painter

riv·er·bank (riv′ər baŋk′) ***n.*** a stretch of land, usually rising, at the edge of a river

river basin the area drained by a river and its tributaries

riv·er·bed (riv′ər bed′) ***n.*** the channel in which a river flows or has flowed

river blindness ONCHOCERCIASIS

riv·er·boat (riv′ər bōt′) ***n.*** a large boat with a flat bottom or shallow draft for use in carrying passengers and cargo on rivers

riv·er·front (riv′ər frunt′) ***n.*** land along the shore of a river **—*adj.*** near, at, or of the riverfront [a *riverfront* park]

riv·er·head (riv′ər hed′) ***n.*** the source of a river

riv·er·ine (riv′ər īn′, -ēn′, -in) ***adj.*** 1 on or near the banks of a river; riparian 2 of, like, or produced by a river or rivers

Riv·ers (riv′ərz), **Larry** (born *Yitzroch Loiza Grossberg*) 1923-2005; U.S. painter

riv·er·side (riv′ər sīd′) ***n.*** the bank of a river **—*adj.*** on or near the bank of a river

Riv·er·side (riv′ər sīd′) ⟦after the Santa Ana *River,* near which it is located⟧ city in S Calif.

riv·er·walk (riv′ər wôk′) ***n.*** a scenic walkway along the side of a river

riv·er·weed (riv′ər wēd′) ***n.*** ☆any of a genus (*Podostemon,* family Podostemaceae) of small, many-branched, aquatic dicotyledonous plants (order Podostemales) adhering to stones by means of suckerlike roots

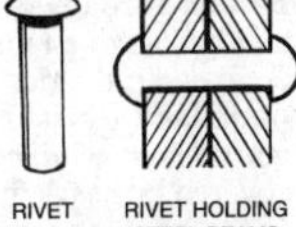

RIVET — RIVET HOLDING STEEL BEAMS TOGETHER

riv·et (riv′it) ***n.*** ⟦ME *ryvette* < MFr *rivet* < *river,* to clinch < ?⟧ 1 a metal bolt or pin with a head on one end, used to fasten plates or beams together by passing it through holes in them and then hammering down the plain end into a head so as to lock it in place 2 a similar device used to fasten or strengthen seams, as on work clothes **—*vt.*** 1 to fasten with a rivet or rivets 2 to hammer or spread the end of (a bolt, etc.) into a head, for fastening something 3 to fasten or secure firmly 4 to fix or hold (the eyes, attention, etc.) firmly **—riv′et·er *n.***

Riv·i·er·a (riv′ē er′ə) coastal strip along the Mediterranean from La Spezia, Italy, to west of Cannes, France: a famous resort area

riv·u·let (riv′yə lit) ***n.*** ⟦earlier *rivolet* < It *rivoletto,* dim. of *rivolo,* dim. of *rivo,* stream < L *rivus,* brook, stream: see RIVAL⟧ a little stream; brook

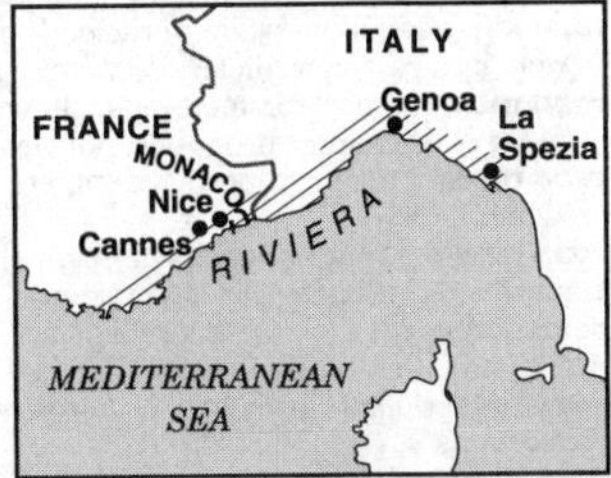

Riviera

riv·u·lose (riv′yə lōs′) ***adj.*** ⟦< L *rivulus,* rivulet (dim. of *rivus,* brook, stream: see RIVAL) + -OSE²⟧ having thin, winding lines

rix-dol·lar (riks′däl′ər) ***n.*** ⟦< obs. Du *rijcksdaler,* lit., dollar of the realm < *rijck,* realm (akin to Ger *reich*) + *daler:* see DOLLAR⟧ any of several old silver coins of Germany, the Netherlands, or Scandinavia

Ri·yadh (rē yäd′) capital of Saudi Arabia, in the central part

ri·yal (rē yäl′, -yôl′) ***n., pl.*** **-yals′** ⟦Ar *riyāl* < Sp *real:* see REAL²⟧ the basic monetary unit of: *a)* Qatar *b)* Saudi Arabia: see the table of monetary units in the Reference Supplement

Ri·zal (rē säl′), **Jo·sé** (hô se′) 1861-96; Philippine writer & patriot

Riz·zi·o (rit′sē ō′), **David** 1533?-66; It. musician: secretary to & favorite of Mary, Queen of Scots: murdered

rm *abbrev.* **1** ream **2** room

Rm *abbrev. Bible* Romans

RMA *abbrev.* Royal Military Academy

RMC *abbrev.* Royal Military College

rms *abbrev.* root mean square

RMS *abbrev.* **1** Royal Mail Service **2** Royal Mail Ship

Rn *Chem. symbol for* radon

RN¹ (är′en′) ***n., pl.*** **RNs** REGISTERED NURSE

RN² *abbrev.* Royal Navy

RNA (är′en′ā′) ***n.*** ⟦R(IBO)N(UCLEIC) A(CID)⟧ a nucleic acid that is an essential component of all cells, composed of a long, usually single-stranded chain of nucleotide units that contain the sugar ribose; ribonucleic acid: see MESSENGER RNA, TRANSFER RNA, RIBOSOMAL RNA

RNA polymerase any of various polymerases that help form RNA by using DNA or RNA as a template

RNA virus any virus having RNA as its genetic material: see VIRUS (sense 2*a*)

rnd *abbrev.* round

RNR *abbrev.* Royal Naval Reserve

ro *abbrev.* **1** recto **2** rood

Ro *abbrev. Bible* Romans

RO *abbrev.* Royal Observatory

☆**roach¹** (rōch) ***n.*** **1** *short for* COCKROACH **2** [Slang] the butt of a marijuana cigarette

roach² (rōch) ***n., pl.*** **roach** or **roach′es** ⟦ME *roche* < OFr < Gmc, as in MLowG *roche,* OE *ruhha,* roach, akin to OE *ruh,* ROUGH: prob. because of the rough skin⟧ **1** either of two N European freshwater cyprinoid fishes (genus *Rutilus*) **2** any of various similar American fishes, as the California minnow (*Hesperoleucus symmetricus*)

roach³ (rōch) ***vt.*** ⟦< ?⟧ ☆**1** to brush (a person's hair) so that it arches over into a roll ☆**2** to cut (a horse's mane) so that it stands up —***n.*** ☆**1** hair or a mane brushed or cut by roaching **2** the curved edge of a sail

roach back an arched back, esp. of a horse

road (rōd) ***n.*** ⟦ME *rode,* a riding < OE *rad,* a ride, traveling on horseback, way; akin to *ridan,* to RIDE⟧ **1** a way made for traveling between places, esp. distant places, by automobile, horseback, etc.; highway **2** a way; path; course [the *road* to fortune] ☆**3** *short for* RAILROAD **4** [*often pl.*] ROADSTEAD —***adj.*** *Sports* designating or having to do with a game or games played on another team's field, court, etc. —☆**down the road** [Informal] at a later time; in the future —**on the road 1** traveling, esp. as a salesman **2** on tour: said as of a troupe of actors **3** playing on the home field, court, etc. of another team or other teams —**one for the road** [Informal] a last alcoholic drink before leaving —**take to the road** to start traveling; set out —**the end of the road** the place or time at which something, esp. something long-standing, comes to an end —**the road** all the cities and towns visited by touring theatrical companies, musicians, etc.

☆**road agent** a highwayman, esp. on Old West stagecoach routes

☆**road·bed** (rōd′bed′) ***n.*** **1** *a)* the foundation laid to support the ties, rails, and ballast of a railroad *b)* a layer of crushed rock, cinders, etc. immediately under the ties **2** the foundation or surface of a road or highway

road·block (-bläk′) ***n.*** **1** an obstruction in a road; specif., *a) Mil.* a blockade of logs, wire, cement, etc., for holding up enemy vehicles at a point covered by heavy fire *b)* a blockade, often of patrol cars, set up by police, as for stopping a fugitive, inspecting vehicles, etc. **2** any hindrance or obstacle in the way of an objective —***vt.*** to obstruct with a roadblock

☆**road hog** [Slang] a person who drives a vehicle in the middle of the road, making it hard or impossible for others to pass

road·house (-hous′) ***n.*** a tavern, inn, or, esp., nightclub on a country road

road·ie (rōd′ē) ***n.*** ⟦ROAD + -IE⟧ [Slang] a person hired to travel with musicians on tour, for the purpose of handling equipment, running errands, etc.

road·kill (rōd′kil′) ***n.*** [Slang] the body of an animal that has been killed on a road by a passing vehicle: also written **road kill**

road map 1 a map for motorists, showing the roads of a given region **2** any set of directions, proposals, policies, etc. for achieving some objective

road metal broken stones, cinders, etc. used in making roads, ballasting roadbeds, etc.

road movie a film in which the main characters travel, often, specif., by motor vehicle, having various encounters and adventures along the way

road racing any type of racing done on a course of public roads or on one designed to resemble such roads

☆**road rage** violent anger in a motorist, as in reaction to stressful driving conditions

☆**road·run·ner** (rōd′run′ər) ***n.*** a long-tailed, crested, desert cuckoo (*Geococcyx californianus*) of the SW U.S. and N Mexico, that can run swiftly: also written **road runner**

☆**road·show** (rōd′shō′) ***n.*** **1** a show presented by a theatrical troupe on tour **2** the showing of a film at selected theaters with reserved seats and an admission price higher than the usual ticket price

road·side (-sīd′) ***n.*** the side of a road —***adj.*** on or at the side of a road [a *roadside* park]

road·stead (-sted′) ***n.*** ⟦ROAD + STEAD⟧ a protected place near shore, not as enclosed as a harbor, where ships can anchor

road·ster (-stər) ***n.*** ☆**1** an earlier type of open automobile with a single seat for two or three persons, a fabric top, and a luggage compartment or rumble seat **2** a horse for riding or driving on the road

road test a test of a vehicle, tires, etc. under actual operating conditions —**road′-test′** ***vt.***

road trip 1 a trip to another city or region by a sports team to play games ON THE ROAD **2** a trip, esp. an extended one, in a motor vehicle

road warrior ⟦< *The Road Warrior,* title of a science-fiction film (1981)⟧ a person who travels extensively, as on business trips

road·way (-wā′) ***n.*** a road; specif., that part of a road traveled on by vehicles

road·work (-wurk′) ***n.*** **1** work done in repairing or building roads **2** distance running or jogging as part of an exercise program, esp. of a boxer's training program

roam (rōm) ***vi.*** ⟦ME *romen* < or akin to OE *aræman,* to rise < IE **erei-* < base **er-,* to set in motion > RISE, RUN⟧ to travel from place to place, esp. with no special plan or purpose; go aimlessly; wander —***vt.*** to wander over or through [to *roam* the streets] —***n.*** the act of roaming; ramble —**roam′er** ***n.***

roam·ing (rōm′iŋ) ***n.*** a customer's use of a cellular phone outside the region served by his or her carrier

roan¹ (rōn) ***adj.*** ⟦OFr < OSp *roano* < L *ravidus,* grayish < *ravus,* grayish-yellow, tawny⟧ of a solid color, as reddish brown, brown, or black, with a thick sprinkling of white hairs: said chiefly of horses —***n.*** **1** a roan color **2** a roan horse or other animal

roan² (rōn) ***n.*** ⟦MScot, after ? ROUEN⟧ a soft, flexible sheepskin used in bookbinding, often treated to look like morocco

Ro·a·noke (rō′ə nōk′) ⟦< Carolina Algonquian: meaning unknown⟧ **1** river flowing from SW Va. southeast through NE N.C. into Albemarle Sound: *c.* 380 mi (612 km) **2** city in SW Va., on this river **3** island off the coast of N.C.: site of abortive English colony (1585-87)

roar (rôr) ***vi.*** ⟦ME *raren* < OE *rarian,* akin to Ger *rehren* < IE echoic base **rei-,* to cry out > Sans *rāyati,* (he) bellows, ON *rāmr,* hoarse⟧ **1** to make a loud, deep, rumbling cry, as a lion does **2** to breathe with a loud, rasping noise as a result of exertion or disease: said of a horse **3** to talk or laugh loudly and boisterously **4** to make a loud noise in moving, operating, etc.: said of an engine, cannon, etc. **5** to resound with a noisy din —***vt.*** **1** to utter in or express with a loud, deep sound **2** to make, put, force, etc. by roaring [to *roar* oneself hoarse] —***n.*** **1** a loud, deep, rumbling sound, as of a lion or bull, a person in pain, a cheering crowd, etc. **2** a loud burst of laughter **3** a loud noise, as that made by crashing waves, a storm, a motor, etc.; din —**roar′er** ***n.***

roar·ing (rôr′iŋ) ***n.*** **1** the act of an animal, person, etc. that roars **2** the loud, deep sound made by an animal, etc. that roars **3** a disease of horses, characterized by loud, hoarse, rasping breathing —***adj.*** **1** *a)* that roars; loud; noisy *b)* boisterous, brawling, etc. **2** [Informal] very active or successful; brisk [a *roaring* business] —***adv.*** to the point of being noisy, boisterous, etc. [*roaring* drunk]

roaring forties the stormy oceanic areas between 40° and 50° south latitude

roast (rōst) ***vt.*** ⟦ME *rosten* < OFr *rostir* < Frank **raustjan,* akin to OHG *rosten* < *rost,* gridiron, roast⟧ **1** to cook (something) with little or no moisture, as in an oven, over an open fire, or in hot embers [to *roast* a chicken, an ox, an ear of corn, etc.] **2** to dry, parch, or brown (coffee beans, nuts, etc.) by exposure to heat **3** to expose to great heat **4** to heat (an ore) in a furnace in the presence of oxygen or air so as to form oxides **5** to warm (oneself), as at a fireplace **6** [Informal] to criticize severely or ridicule without mercy —***vi.*** **1** to roast meat, etc. **2** to be cooked by being roasted **3** to be or become very hot —***n.*** **1** something roasted; esp., roasted meat or a piece of roasted meat **2** a cut of meat for roasting **3** a particular type of roasted coffee [a dark *roast*] **4** a roasting or being roasted ☆**5** a picnic at which food is roasted and eaten [a steer *roast*] **6** [Informal] *a)* severe criticism or ridicule ☆*b)* an entertainment, typically a banquet, at which the guest of honor is the object of good-natured ridicule —***adj.*** roasted [*roast* pork] —**roast′ing** ***adj.***

roast·er (rōs′tər) ***n.*** **1** a person or thing that roasts **2** a special pan, oven, or apparatus for roasting meat, etc. **3** a young pig, chicken, etc. suitable for roasting **4** *Astron.* a hot, gassy, giant, extrasolar planet located very close to its sun

rob (räb) ***vt.*** **robbed, rob′bing** ⟦ME *robben* < OFr *rober* < Gmc **raubon,* akin to OHG *roubon,* OE *reafian* < IE **reup-:* see RUB⟧ **1** *a) Law* to take personal property from unlawfully by using or threatening force and violence; commit robbery upon *b)* popularly, to steal something from in any way, as by embezzlement or burglary *c)* to plunder or rifle *d)* [Now Rare] to take by stealing or plundering **2** to deprive (someone) *of* something belonging or due, or take or withhold something from unjustly or injuriously [the accident *robbed* him of health] —***vi.*** to commit robbery —**rob′ber** ***n.***

rob·a·lo (rä′bə lō′, rō′bə-) ***n., pl.*** **-los′** or **-lo′** ⟦Sp *róbalo* or Port *robalo* < Catalan *llobarro;* ult. < L *lupus,* wolf, also a kind of fish: see WOLF⟧ SNOOK¹

rob·and (rä′bənd) ***n.*** ⟦earlier *raband* & *robbin* < MDu *rabant* < *ra,* sailyard (see ROCK²) + *bant,* BAND¹] a piece of cord or spun yarn, used to fasten the head of a square sail to a yard, spar, etc.

robber baron 1 a nobleman of feudal times who robbed people traveling through his domain ☆2 any of a number of U.S. capitalists of the late 19th cent. who acquired vast wealth by exploitation and ruthlessness

robber fly any of a large family (Asilidae) of hairy dipterous flies of varying size that prey on other insects

rob·ber·y (räb′ər ē) ***n., pl.*** **-ber·ies** [ME *roberie* < OFr: see ROB & -ERY] 1 act or practice of robbing 2 *Law* the felonious taking of personal property in the possession or immediate presence of another by the use of violence or intimidation —**SYN.** THEFT

Robbia, Luca Della *see* DELLA ROBBIA, Luca

Rob·bins (räb′ənz), **Jerome** (born *Jerome Rabinowitz*) 1918-98; U.S. dancer & choreographer

robe (rōb) ***n.*** [ME < OFr, robe, orig. booty, spoils < Gmc **rauba,* plunder: see ROB] 1 a long, loose or flowing outer garment; specif., *a)* such a garment worn on formal occasions, to show rank or office, etc., as by a judge or bishop *b)* a bathrobe or dressing gown 2 [*pl.*] [Archaic] clothes; costume; dress ☆3 *short for* LAP ROBE — ***vt., vi.*** **robed, rob′ing** to dress in or cover with a robe or robes

robe de cham·bre (rôb′də shän′br′) *pl.* ***robes de cham·bre*** (rôb) [Fr, lit., robe of (the) chamber] a dressing gown

Rob·ert¹ (räb′ərt) ***n.*** [OFr < OHG *Hruodperht* < *hruod-,* fame, praise < IE base **kar-,* to praise, boast + *perht,* BRIGHT] a masculine name: dim. *Bob, Bobby, Rob, Robbie, Robby*; var. *Robin, Rupert*; fem. *Roberta, Robin*

Rob·ert² (räb′ərt) **1 Robert I** died 1035; duke of Normandy (1028?-35): father of William the Conqueror **2 Robert I** *see* BRUCE²

Ro·ber·ta (rə bur′tə, rō-) ***n.*** a feminine name: see ROBERT¹

Rob·erts (räb′ərts), **John G(lover), Jr.** 1955- ; chief justice of the U.S. (2005-)

Robe·son (rōb′sən), **Paul** 1898-1976; U.S. singer, actor, & political activist

Ro·bes·pierre (rōbz′pē er′, -pyer′; *Fr* rô bes pyer′), **Max·i·mi·lien (François Marie Isidore de)** (mȧk sē mē lyan′) 1758-94; Fr. revolutionist & Jacobin leader: guillotined

rob·in (räb′ən) ***n.*** [< ME *Robin* < OFr, dim. of *Robert*] ☆1 a North American thrush (*Turdus migratorius*) with a dull-red breast and belly 2 a small European thrush (*Erithacus rubecula*) with an orangish-red breast and face

Rob·in (räb′ən) ***n.*** [masc. name altered < ROBERT¹; fem. name may be < prec.] a feminine and masculine name: see ROBERT¹

Robin Good·fel·low (good′fel′ō) *Eng. Folklore* a mischievous sprite or fairy: identified with Puck

Robin Hood *Eng. Legend* a 12th-cent. outlaw who lived with his followers in Sherwood Forest and robbed the rich to help the poor

☆**rob·in's-egg blue** (räb′ənz eg′, -āg′) [in ref. to the color of the *egg* of the American *robin*] a light greenish blue

Rob·in·son (räb′ən sən) **1 Edwin Arlington** 1869-1935; U.S. poet **2 Jack·ie** (jak′ē) (born *Jack Roosevelt Robinson*) 1919-72; U.S. baseball player

Robinson Cru·soe (kro͞o′sō′) the title hero of Daniel Defoe's novel (1719), a sailor who, shipwrecked on a tropical island, survives by various ingenious contrivances until rescued years later

☆**ro·ble** (rō′blā′) ***n.*** [AmSp < Sp, oak < L *robur,* hard variety of oak: see ROBUST] any of several oak trees of the SW U.S.; esp., a tall, white oak (*Quercus lobata*) of California

ro·bo·call (rō′bō kôl′) ***n.*** [< *robo-* < fol. + CALL] 1 a telephone call made, as on behalf of a political campaign, by means of automated dialing and intended typically to reach a wide public 2 a prerecorded message conveyed in this way

ro·bot (rō′bät′, -bət) ***n.*** [coined by K. ČAPEK in his play *R.U.R.* (transl. as *Rossum's Universal Robots*) (1920) < Czech *robota,* forced labor < OSlav *rabota,* menial labor < *rabu,* servant < IE base **orbho-*: see ORPHAN] 1 *a)* an anthropomorphic mechanical being, as in science fiction *b)* any mechanical device operated automatically, esp. by remote control, to perform repetitive or complex tasks, as in manufacturing 2 any person who acts or works in a way regarded as mechanical and without originality —**ro·bot·ic** (rō bät′ik) ***adj.***

robot bomb a jet-propelled winged missile with an automatic pilot and a warhead: see CRUISE MISSILE

☆**ro·bot·ics** (rō bät′iks) ***n.*** [ROBOT + -ICS: coinage attributed to I. ASIMOV] the science or technology of robots, including their design, manufacture, use, etc.

ro·bot·ize (rō′bə tīz′) ***vt.*** **-ized′, -iz′ing** 1 to make automatic 2 to cause (a person) to become or act like a robot —**ro′bot·i·za′tion** ***n.***

Rob Roy [< *Rob Roy,* nickname of Robert MacGregor (1671?-1734), Scot outlaw] [*often* **r- r-**] a cocktail made of Scotch whisky, sweet vermouth, and bitters

Rob·son (räb′sən), **Mount** [prob. after C. *Robertson* (1793-1842), an officer of the Hudson's Bay Company in the region] mountain in E British Columbia; highest peak of the Canadian Rockies: 12,972 ft (3,954 m)

ro·bust (rō bust′, rō′bust′) ***adj.*** [L *robustus,* oaken, hard, strong < *robur,* hard variety of oak, hardness, strength, earlier *robus,* prob. akin to *ruber,* RED] 1 *a)* strong and healthy; full of vigor; hardy *b)* strongly built or based; muscular or sturdy 2 suited to or requiring physical strength or stamina [*robust* work] 3 rough; coarse; boisterous 4 full and rich, as in flavor [a *robust* port wine] —**ro·bust′ly** ***adv.*** —**ro·bust′ness** ***n.***

ro·bus·ta (rō bus′tə, -bo͞os′-) ***adj.*** [ModL, former species name < L, fem of *robustus,* prec.] designating or of one of the two main types of coffee (*Coffea canephora*) produced commercially, which grows at lower altitudes, mainly in Africa, and is less aromatic than ARABICA —***n.*** this coffee

ro·bus·tious (rō bus′chəs) ***adj.*** [ROBUST + -IOUS] strong and sturdy; also, rough, coarse, boisterous, etc.: now archaic except in facetious usage —**ro·bus′tious·ly** ***adv.***

roc (räk) ***n.*** [Ar *rukhkh* < Pers *rukh*] *Arabian & Pers. Legend* a bird of prey, so huge and strong that it can carry off large animals

ROC *abbrev.* Republic of China (Taiwan)

Ro·ca (rō′kə), **Cape** cape in SW Portugal, near Lisbon: westernmost point of continental Europe: Port. name **Ca·bo da Ro·ca** (kä′bo͞o də rô′kə)

roc·am·bole (räk′əm bōl′) ***n.*** [Fr < Ger *rockenbolle* < *rocken, roggen,* RYE¹ + *bolle,* bulb] a European onion (*Allium scorodoprasum*) bearing a cluster of small bulbs used like garlic cloves for flavoring

Ro·cham·beau (rō′sham bō′; *Fr* rô shän bō′), Comte **de** (*Jean Baptiste Donatien de Vimeur*) 1725-1807; Fr. general: commanded Fr. forces against the British in the Am. Revolutionary War

Roch·dale (räch′dāl′) borough of Greater Manchester in NW England: one of the earliest English cooperative societies was founded there (1844)

Roche limit (rōsh) [after E. *Roche* (1820-83), Fr astronomer] the lowest possible altitude at which a natural satellite can form and orbit, withstanding the fragmenting force of the gravitational pull of a planet or other primary celestial body: see also RING² (***n.*** 14)

Ro·chelle salt (rō shel′) [after La *Rochelle,* France, where discovered] a colorless crystalline compound, potassium sodium tartrate, $KNaC_4H_4O_6 \cdot 4H_2O$, used as a laxative, in baking powders, and, in electronics, as a piezoelectric material

roche mou·ton·née (rōsh′ mo͞o tä nā′) *pl.* **-nées′** (-nā′, -nāz′) [Fr, sheep-shaped rock] *Geol.* a bare hummock of rock, usually smoothed on the upstream side and grooved on the other by glacial action

Roch·es·ter¹ (räch′əs tər, rä′ches′tər), **2d Earl of** (*John Wilmot*) 1647-80; Eng. poet

Roch·es·ter² (räch′əs tər, rä′ches′tər) 1 [after N. *Rochester* (1752-1831), Revolutionary officer] city & port in W N.Y., on Lake Ontario 2 [after the city in N.Y.] city in SE Minn. 3 city in Kent, SE England

roch·et (räch′it) ***n.*** [ME < OFr < *roc,* cloak < MHG < OHG *hroc, roch*] a knee-length, narrow-sleeved, light outer garment of linen and lace, worn by prelates in some ceremonies

rock¹ (räk) ***n.*** [ME *rokke* < OFr *roche* < ML *rocca*] 1 a large mass of stone forming a peak or cliff 2 *a)* a large stone detached from the mass; boulder *b)* broken pieces of any size of such stone *c)* any stone, large or small 3 *a)* mineral matter variously composed, formed in masses or large quantities in the earth's crust by the action of heat, water, etc. *b)* a particular kind or mass of this 4 anything or anyone like or suggesting a rock, as in strength, stability, dependability, etc. ☆5 ROCKFISH 6 *a)* [Chiefly Brit.] a hard candy made in sticks *b)* *short for* ROCK CANDY 7 [Slang] a diamond or other gem ☆8 [Slang] crack cocaine or a single piece of it —☆**between a rock and a hard place** in a predicament; specif., faced with equally unpleasant alternatives —**get one's rocks off** [< slang term *rocks,* testicles] 1 to experience orgasm; ejaculate: a vulgar use 2 to feel any great or satisfying pleasure or excitement: somewhat vulgar —**on the rocks** [Informal] 1 *a)* in or into a condition of ruin or catastrophe *b)* in trouble or approaching ruin [a marriage that is *on the rocks*] 2 without money; bankrupt ☆3 served over ice cubes: said of liquor, wine, etc.

rock² (räk) ***vt.*** [ME *rocken* < OE *roccian,* prob. akin to Ger *rücken,* to pull, push < IE **rek-,* to project, totter (> ON, MDu *rā,* sailyard) < base **reg-,* to put in order, stretch out > RIGHT] 1 to move or sway back and forth or from side to side (a cradle, a child in the arms, etc.), esp. in a gentle, quieting manner 2 to bring into a specified condition by moving or swaying in this way [to *rock* a baby to sleep] 3 *a)* to move or sway strongly; shake; cause to tremble or vibrate [the explosion *rocked* the house] *b)* to upset emotionally 4 *Engraving* to prepare the surface of (a plate) for a mezzotint by roughening with a ROCKER (sense 5) 5 *Mining* to wash (sand or gravel) in a ROCKER (sense 4) —***vi.*** 1 to move or sway back and forth or from side to side, as a cradle 2 to move or sway strongly; shake; vibrate 3 to be rocked, as ore 4 [Slang] *a)* to be thrilling, boisterous, etc. [the party didn't really start to *rock* until midnight] *b)* to take part in social activity, as at a party or nightclub, in an unrestrained, often boisterous, manner [they showed up ready to *rock*] *c)* to be excellent, highly satisfying, etc. (used to express enthusiastic approval) [the new video game *rocks!*] —***n.*** 1 the act of rocking 2 a rocking motion ☆3 *a)* ROCK-AND-ROLL *b)* popular music evolved from rock-and-roll, variously containing elements of folk music, country music, etc. and now often emphasizing loudness, distortion, the use of electronic synthesizers, etc.

☆**rock·a·bil·ly** (räk′ə bil′ē) ***n.*** [prec. + *-a-* + (HILL)BILLY] an early form of rock-and-roll with a strong country music influence

☆**rock-and-roll** (räk′′n rōl′) ***n.*** [prob. first so used (1951) by Alan Freed, Cleveland disc jockey: use of *rock, roll, rock and roll,* etc., with ref. to sexual intercourse, is traditional in blues] a form of popular music that evolved in the 1950s from rhythm and blues, characterized by the use of electric guitars, a strong rhythm with an accent on the offbeat, and youth-oriented lyrics

☆**rock and rye** rye whiskey bottled with pieces of rock candy and slices of fruit

☆**rock·a·way** (räk′ə wā′) ***n.*** [after *Rockaway,* N.J., where formerly made] a light horse-drawn carriage with four wheels, open sides, and a standing top

☆**rock bass** a freshwater game sunfish (*Ambloplites rupestris*) of E North America

☆**rock bottom** the lowest level or point; very bottom —**rock-bot·tom** (räk′ bät′əm) ***adj.***

rock·bound (-bound′) ***adj.*** surrounded or covered by rocks [a *rockbound* inlet or coast]

rock brake any of a genus (*Cryptogramma*, family *Polypodiaceae*) of ferns that grow in rocky ground

rock candy large, hard, clear crystals of sugar formed on a string dipped in a solution of boiled sugar

rock climbing the sport or pastime of scaling natural or artificial cliff faces —**rock climber**

☆**rock cod** any of various marine fishes found around rocks, as various rockfishes

Rock Cornish (hen) CORNISH (sense 2*b*)

rock crystal a transparent, esp. colorless, quartz

rock dove the European wild pigeon (*Columba livia*) from which most domestic varieties are derived: now widespread in most cities of the Northern Hemisphere

Rock·e·fel·ler (räk′ə fel′ər) **1 John D(avison)** 1839-1937; U.S. industrialist & philanthropist **2 John D(avison), Jr.** 1874-1960; U.S. industrialist & philanthropist: son of John Davison **3 Nelson A(ldrich)** 1908-79; vice president of the U.S. (1974-77): son of John Davison, Jr.

rock·er (räk′ər) ***n.*** **1** a person who rocks a cradle, etc. **2** either of the curved pieces on the bottom of a cradle, rocking chair, etc. ☆**3** ROCKING CHAIR **4** a cradle for washing sand or gravel in gold mining **5** a small steel plate with a toothed and curved edge, for roughening and thus preparing the surface of a mezzotint plate **6** one of the curved stripes below the chevron of a noncommissioned officer above sergeant ☆**7** [Informal] *a)* a performer, fan, etc. of rock music *b)* a rock song performed with a heavily accented rhythm at a fast tempo —**off one's rocker** [Slang] crazy; insane

rocker arm an armlike piece attached to a rockshaft, as in automotive engines

rocker panel any of the sections of body paneling below the doors of an automotive vehicle

rock·er·y (räk′ər ē) ***n.***, *pl.* **-er·ies** [Chiefly Brit.] ROCK GARDEN

rock·et[1] (räk′it) ***n.*** ⟦It *rocchetta*, spool or bobbin, rocket, orig. dim. of *rocca*, distaff < OHG *roccho*, distaff: from the resemblance in shape⟧ **1** any of various devices, typically cylindrical, containing liquid or solid propellants which when ignited produce hot gases or ions that escape through a rear vent and drive the container forward by the principle of reaction: simple rockets are used mainly as fireworks, signals, and projectile weapons, while more complex rockets are used to propel guided missiles, ballistic missiles, and spacecraft: see also ROCKET ENGINE, ROCKET MOTOR **2** a spacecraft, missile, probe, etc. propelled by a rocket —***vi.*** **1** to go like a rocket; dart ahead swiftly **2** to travel in a rocket **3** to soar; rise rapidly [prices *rocketed*] —***vt.*** **1** to convey in a rocket **2** to attack by firing a rocket at **3** to propel with or as with sudden force [a hit song *rocketing* a singer to stardom]

rock·et[2] (räk′it) ***n.*** ⟦Fr *roquette* < It *rochetta*, var. of *ruchetta*, dim. < *ruca*, rocket < L *eruca*, kind of colewort⟧ **1** any of various plants of the crucifer family, with white, yellow, pink, or purple flowers; esp., **sea rocket** (genus *Cakile*) found along seashores in Europe and North America **2** ARUGULA: also **rocket salad** **3** DAME'S VIOLET

rock·et·eer (räk′ə tir′) ***n.*** an expert in rocketry

rocket engine a reaction engine carrying its liquid fuel and liquid oxidizing agent in separate tanks: the fuel and oxidizer are brought together and ignited in a combustion chamber to create hot, explosive gas that escapes through a nozzle, providing a powerful thrust: cf. ROCKET MOTOR

rocket launcher any of various devices that launch rockets; specif., *a)* a rocket-launching device on a truck or tanklike vehicle, or the vehicle itself *b)* a rocket-launching device on a ship, airplane, etc. *c)* a portable rocket-launching weapon, as a bazooka

rocket motor a rocket engine, specif. one having a solid propellant formed into a long, hollow cylinder: the cylinder serves as the combustion chamber when the propellant is ignited

rock·et·ry (räk′ə trē) ***n.*** **1** the science of designing, building, and launching rockets **2** rockets collectively

rocket scientist [Informal] a scientist specializing in rocketry: now chiefly a fig. or ironic usage in negative constructions [it doesn't take a *rocket scientist* to figure this out]

rocket ship a rocket-propelled spaceship

☆**rock·et·sonde** (räk′it sänd′) ***n.*** ⟦ROCKET[1] + SONDE⟧ *Meteorol.* a rocket designed for weather observations in the area beyond the range of balloons, esp. between altitudes of 100,000 and 250,000 ft

rock·fall (räk′fôl′) ***n.*** **1** a landslide involving the fall of rocks **2** the pile of rocks formed by such a landslide Sometimes written **rock fall**

rock·fish (räk′fish′) ***n.***, *pl.* **-fish′** or **-fish′es** (see FISH) any of various fishes of rocky coastal areas, as the striped bass, various groupers, and various scorpaenids (genus *Sebastes*)

Rock·ford (räk′fərd) ⟦in allusion to the *rocky*-bottomed *ford* there⟧ city in N Ill.

rock garden a garden with flowers and plants growing on rocky ground or among rocks variously arranged

rock hind a spotted, edible sea bass (*Epinephelus adscensionis*) of tropical Atlantic and Caribbean waters

☆**rock·hound** (räk′hound′) ***n.*** ⟦ROCK[1] + HOUND[1] (***n.*** 3)⟧ [Informal] a person whose hobby is hunting for and collecting rocks, esp. semiprecious stones

Rock·ies (räk′ēz) ROCKY MOUNTAINS

rock·i·ness (räk′ē nis) ***n.*** a rocky quality or state

☆**rocking chair** a chair mounted on rockers or springs, so as to allow a rocking movement when a person is seated

rocking horse a toy horse mounted on rockers or springs and big enough for a child to ride

rocking chair

rock lobster SPINY LOBSTER

☆**rock maple** SUGAR MAPLE

Rock·ne (räk′nē), **Knute (Kenneth)** (no͞ot) 1888-1931; U.S. football coach, born in Norway

☆**rock 'n' roll** (räk′'n rōl′) *var. of* ROCK-AND-ROLL

rock oil *chiefly Brit. term for* PETROLEUM

☆**rock·oon** (rä ko͞on′, räk′o͞on) ***n.*** ⟦ROCK(ET) + (BAL-LOON⟧ a high-altitude sounding system in which a rocket is launched upward from a balloon that has reached its maximum altitude

rock pigeon ROCK DOVE

☆**rock rabbit** **1** HYRAX **2** PIKA

rock-ribbed (räk′ribd′) ***adj.*** **1** having rocky ridges or elevations [*rock-ribbed* coasts] **2** firm; rigid; unyielding [a *rock-ribbed* policy]

rock·rose (-rōz′) ***n.*** CISTUS —***adj.*** designating a family (Cistaceae, order Violales) of bushy dicotyledonous plants, including pinweed and cistus

rock salt common salt, natural sodium chloride, occurring in solid form, esp. in rocklike masses; halite

rock·shaft (-shaft′, -shäft′) ***n.*** a machine shaft designed to rock back and forth on its journals rather than to revolve

☆**rock squirrel** a ground squirrel (*Citellus variegatus*) with a gray body and black head, living mostly in rocky areas in the W U.S. and in Mexico

rock tripe any of a genus (*Umbilicaria*) of large lichens, green on top and black beneath, attached to a rock surface

rock·weed (räk′wēd′) ***n.*** any of a number of seaweeds, as fucus, that grow on rocks

Rock·well (räk′wel′), **Norman (Percevel)** 1894-1978; U.S. illustrator

rock wool a fibrous material that looks like spun glass, made from molten rock or slag by passing a blast of steam through the fluid; mineral wool: it is used for insulation, esp. in buildings

rock·y[1] (räk′ē) ***adj.*** **rock′i·er, rock′i·est** **1** full of or containing rocks **2** consisting of rock **3** like a rock; firm, hard, unfeeling, etc. **4** full of obstacles or difficulties [the *rocky* road to success]

rock·y[2] (räk′ē) ***adj.*** **rock′i·er, rock′i·est** **1** *a)* [Now Rare] inclined to rock, or sway; unsteady; wobbly *b)* uncertain; shaky **2** [Slang] weak or dizzy, as from illness; unwell

☆**Rocky Mountain goat** a white goat antelope (*Oreamnos americanus*) of the mountains of NW North America, with a thick, shaggy coat and small, slender, black horns that curve backward

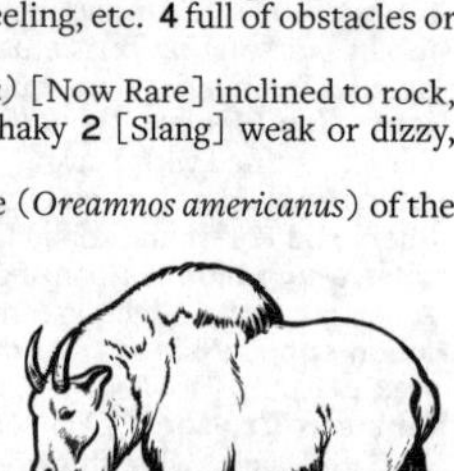
Rocky Mountain goat

Rocky Mountains ⟦transl. < Fr *Montaignes Rocheuses*⟧ mountain system in W North America, extending from central N.Mex. to N Alas.: over 3,000 mi (4,828 km) long; highest peak, Mt. Elbert

Rocky Mountain sheep the bighorn sheep of the Rocky Mountains

☆**Rocky Mountain spotted fever** ⟦from being first discovered in the ROCKY MOUNTAINS⟧ an acute infectious disease caused by a rickettsia (*Rickettsia rickettsii*), transmitted to human beings by certain ticks (esp. genus *Dermacentor*), and characterized by fever, muscular pains, and skin eruptions

ro·co·co (rə kō′kō; *occas.* rō′kə kō′) ***n.*** ⟦Fr < *rocaille*, rock work, shell work < *roc* < OFr *roche*, ROCK[1]⟧ **1** [*occas.* **R-**] a style of architecture, decorative art, music, etc. of the early 18th cent. developed from and in reaction to the Baroque and characterized by profuse and delicate ornamentation, reduced scale, lightness, grace, etc. **2** a style of architecture, music, etc. regarded, often disparagingly, as like this —***adj.*** **1** of or in rococo **2** too profuse and elaborate in ornamentation; florid and tasteless

rod (räd) ***n.*** ⟦ME *rodde* < OE *rodd*, akin to ON *rudda*, club, prob. < IE base **rēt-*, **rōt-*, bar, beam > L *retae*, trees on a river bank⟧ **1** a straight, slender shoot or stem cut from, or still part of, a bush or tree **2** *Bible* an offshoot or branch of a family or tribe; stock or race **3** any straight, or almost straight, stick, shaft, bar, staff, etc., of wood, metal, or other material [curtain *rods*, a lightning *rod*] **4** *a)* a stick or switch, or a bundle of sticks or switches, for beating as punishment *b)* punishment; chastisement (usually with *the*) **5** *a)* a staff, scepter, etc., carried as a symbol of office, rank, or power *b)* power; authority; often, tyrannical rule **6** FISHING ROD **7** a stick used to measure something **8** *a)* a unit of length in the FPS system, equal to 16.5 feet or 5.5 yards (5.0292 meters) (abbrev. *rd*) *b)* a square rod, equal to 30.25 square yards (25.2929 square meters) ☆**9** [Slang] a pistol or revolver ☆**10** [Slang] *short for* HOT ROD **11** *Anat.* any of the rod-shaped cells in the retina of the vertebrate eye that are sensitive to dim light **12** *Bacteriology* any microorganism shaped like a bacillus —☆**ride (**or **hit) the rods** [Slang] to steal a ride on a freight train —**rod′like′** ***adj.***

rode[1] (rōd) ***vi., vt.*** *pt. & archaic pp. of* RIDE

rode[2] (rōd) ***n.*** ⟦< ?⟧ the line attached to the anchor of a small boat

ro·dent (rōd′'nt) ***adj.*** ⟦L *rodens*, prp. of *rodere*, to gnaw: see RAT⟧ **1** gnawing **2** of or like a rodent or rodents —***n.*** any of a very large order (Rodentia) of gnawing mammals, including rats, mice, squirrels, and beavers, characterized by constantly growing incisors adapted for gnawing or nibbling; esp., in popular usage, a rat or mouse

☆**ro·dent·i·cide** (rō den′tə sīd′) ***n.*** ⟦prec. + -I- + -CIDE⟧ a poison used for killing rodents, esp. rats and mice

☆**ro·de·o** (rō′dē ō′; *also* rō dā′ō) ***n.***, *pl.* **-os′** ⟦Sp, a going around, cattle ring < *rodear,* to surround < L *rotare:* see ROTATE⟧ **1** [Now Rare] a roundup of cattle **2** a public exhibition of the skills of cowboys, typically involving competition in broncobusting, lassoing, etc. —***vi.*** **ro′de·oed′, ro′de·o′ing** to take part in a rodeo

Rod·er·ick (räd′ər ik, räd′rik) ***n.*** ⟦ML *Rodericus* < OHG *Hrodrich* < *hruod-,* fame (see ROBERT[1]) + Gmc **rik-,* a king (akin to L *rex:* see RIGHT)⟧ a masculine name: dim. *Rod;* equiv. Sp. *Roderigo*

Rod·gers (rä′jərz), **Richard** 1902-79; U.S. composer of musicals

Ro·din (rō dan′), **(François) Au·guste (René)** (ō güst′) 1840-1917; Fr. sculptor

rod·man (räd′mən) ***n.***, *pl.* **-men** (-mən) ☆a person who carries the leveling rod in surveying

Rod·ney (räd′nē) ***n.*** ⟦< surname *Rodney,* after *Rodney Stoke,* England⟧ a masculine name: dim. *Rod*

rod·o·mon·tade (räd′ə mən tād′, rō′də-; -täd′) ***n.*** ⟦Fr < *rodomont,* braggadocio, after It *Rodomonte,* boastful Saracen leader in Ariosto's *Orlando Furioso*⟧ arrogant boasting or blustering, ranting talk —***adj.*** arrogantly boastful —***vi.*** **-tad′ed, -tad′ing** to boast; brag

roe[1] (rō) ***n.*** ⟦ME *rowe, rowne,* akin to (or < ?) ON *hrogn,* akin to OHG *rogo* < IE base **krek-* > Latvian *kur̃kulis,* frog's eggs⟧ **1** fish eggs, esp. when still massed in the ovarian membrane **2** the swollen ovaries or expelled eggs of certain crustaceans, as the coral of a lobster

roe[2] (rō) ***n.***, *pl.* **roe** or **roes** ⟦ME *ro* < OE *ra,* akin to OHG *reho,* MDu *ree* < IE **roiko-* < base **rei-,* **roi-,* striped, spotted > Latvian *raibs,* colorful, striped, Sans *riśya,* male antelope⟧ a small, agile, graceful European and Asian deer (*Capreolus capreolus*): also called **roe deer**

Roe·bling (rō′bliŋ), **John A(ugustus)** 1806-69; U.S. civil engineer & bridge designer, born in Germany

roe·buck (rō′buk′) ***n.***, *pl.* **-bucks′** or **-buck′** the male of the roe deer

roent·gen (rent′gən, ren′chən) ***n.*** ⟦after fol.⟧ a basic unit of exposure to X-rays, gamma rays, or other ionizing radiation, equal to the amount of radiation that will produce an electric charge of 0.000258 coulomb per kilogram of dry air: abbrev. *R*

Roent·gen (rent′gən; *Ger* rënt′gən), **Wil·helm Con·rad** (vil′helm′ kôn′ rät′) 1845-1923; Ger. physicist: discoverer of X-rays

roent·gen·i·um (rent gen′ē əm) ***n.*** ⟦after prec.⟧ a radioactive chemical element with a very short half-life: a transactinide produced by bombarding bismuth with nickel atoms: symbol, Rg; at. no. 111: see the periodic table of elements in the Reference Supplement

roent·gen·o- (rent′gə nə, ren′chə nə) *combining form* Roentgen rays, X-rays [*roentgenology*]

roent·gen·o·gram (-gram′) ***n.*** ⟦prec. + -GRAM⟧ a photograph taken with X-rays

roent·gen·og·ra·phy (rent′gə nä′grə fē, ren′chə nä′-) ***n.*** ⟦see prec.⟧ photography by the use of X-rays —**roent′gen·o·graph′ic** (-nə graf′ik) ***adj.*** —**roent′gen·o·graph′i·cal·ly** ***adv.***

roent·gen·ol·o·gy (-näl′ə jē) ***n.*** ⟦ROENTGENO- + -LOGY⟧ the study and use of X-rays, esp. in connection with the diagnosis and treatment of disease —**roent′gen·o·log′ic** (-nə läj′ik) ***adj.*** —**roent′gen·ol′o·gist** ***n.***

Roentgen ray [*also* **r- r-**] [Old-fashioned] X-RAY

Roeth·ke (ret′kē), **Theodore** 1908-63; U.S. poet

ro·ga·tion (rō gā′shən) ***n.*** ⟦ME *rogacioun* < L *rogatio,* question, in LL(Ec), prayer, entreaty < *rogare,* to ask, orig., to stretch out the hand; akin to *regere:* see RIGHT⟧ **1** *Eccles.* solemn ceremonial petitioning, specif. on the Rogation Days: *usually used in pl.* **2** in ancient Rome, *a)* a consul's or tribune's proposal of a law to be passed or rejected by the people *b)* such a proposed law

Rogation Days the three days before Ascension Day, formerly a time widely observed as a period of solemn ceremonial petitioning

Rog·er[1] (rä′jər) ***interj.*** ⟦< conventional name of international signal flag for *R*⟧ [*also* **r-**] **1** received: term used in radio communication to indicate reception of a message **2** [Informal] right; OK

Rog·er[2] (rä′jər) ***n.*** ⟦OFr < OHG *Ruodiger, Hrodger* (akin to OE *Hrothgar*) < *hruod-, ruod-,* fame (see ROBERT[1]) + **ger,* spear⟧ a masculine name

Rog·ers (rä′jərz) **1 Bruce** 1870-1957; U.S. typographer & book designer **2 Robert** 1731-95; Am. frontier soldier **3 Will** (born *William Penn Adair Rogers*) 1879-1935; U.S. humorist & actor

Ro·get (rō zhā′), **Peter Mark** 1779-1869; Eng. writer & physician: compiler of a thesaurus

rogue (rōg) ***n.*** ⟦< 16th-c. thieves' slang < ? L *rogare,* to ask: see ROGATION⟧ **1** [Obs.] a wandering beggar or tramp; vagabond **2** a rascal; scoundrel **3** a fun-loving, mischievous person **4** an elephant or other animal that wanders apart from the herd and is fierce and wild **5** *Biol.* an individual varying markedly from the standard, esp. an inferior one —***vt.*** **rogued, ro′guing 1** to cheat **2** to destroy (plants, etc.) as biological rogues **3** to remove such plants, etc. from (land, etc.) —***vi.*** to live or act like a rogue —***adj.*** **1** acting in defiance of established laws, customs, etc. [*a rogue* nation] **2** lacking required authorization, supervision, etc. [a *rogue* intelligence operation]

ro·guer·y (rō′gər ē) ***n.***, *pl.* **-guer·ies** the behavior or an act of a rogue; specif., *a)* trickery; cheating; fraud *b)* playful mischief

☆**rogues' gallery** a collection of the photographs of criminals, as used by police in identification

rogue wave a huge and powerful wave that occurs on the open ocean without warning, thought to be caused by the merging of a series of smaller waves or by the crossing of waves with strong currents running in different directions

ro·guish (rō′gish) ***adj.*** of, like, or characteristic of a rogue; specif., *a)* dishonest; unscrupulous *b)* playfully mischievous —**ro′guish·ly** ***adv.*** —**ro′guish·ness** ***n.***

Ro·hyp·nol (rō hip′nôl′) *trademark for* a powerful, synthetic benzodiazepine drug, $C_{16}H_{12}FN_3O_3$, used as a sedative and hypnotic: it is illegal in the U.S. and often cited as a drug used in date rape

ROI *abbrev.* return on investment

roil (roil) ***vt.*** ⟦Fr *rouiller* < OFr *rouil, roille,* rust, mud, ult. < L *robigo,* rust, akin to *ruber,* RED⟧ **1** to make (a liquid) cloudy, muddy, or unsettled by stirring up the sediment **2** to stir up; agitate **3** to make angry or irritable; rile —***vi.*** to be agitated

roil·y (roi′lē) ***adj.*** **roil′i·er, roil′i·est 1** turbid; muddy **2** agitated

roist·er (rois′tər) ***vi.*** ⟦< earlier *roister* (n.), loud bully < OFr *ruistre* < L *rusticus:* see RUSTIC⟧ **1** to boast or swagger **2** to be lively and noisy; revel boisterously —**roist′er·er** ***n.*** —**roist′er·ous** ***adj.***

ROK *abbrev.* Republic of (South) Korea

☆**ro·la·mite** (rō′lə mīt′) ***n.*** ⟦arbitrary coinage based on ROLL⟧ an almost frictionless bearing consisting of two or more rollers on a flexible metal band, that serves as a suspension system in various devices, as switches, valves, pumps, etc.

Ro·land (rō′lənd, rä′-) ***n.*** ⟦OFr < OHG *Hruodland* < *hruod-,* fame (see ROBERT[1]) + *land,* LAND⟧ **1** a masculine name: var. *Rowland;* equiv. It. *Orlando* **2** a legendary hero famous for his strength, courage, and chivalrous spirit who appears in the *Chanson de Roland* and other stories of the Charlemagne cycle

role (rōl) ***n.*** ⟦Fr *rôle,* lit., a roll: from roll containing actor's part⟧ **1** a part, or character, that an actor plays in a performance **2** the part assumed by a participant in role-playing or in a role-playing game **3** a function or office assumed by someone [an advisory *role*] Often written **rôle**

role model a person, esp. one who is unusually effective or inspiring, who serves as a model for others in some social role, an occupation, etc.

role-play·er (rōl′plā′ər) ***n.*** **1** a participant in ROLE-PLAYING **2** a participant in a ROLE-PLAYING GAME

role-play·ing (rōl′plā′iŋ) ***n.*** **1** a technique in training or psychotherapy in which participants assume and act out roles so as to resolve conflicts, practice appropriate behavior for various situations, etc. **2** a kind of sexual activity in which the participants assume and act out roles —**role′-play′** ***vt., vi.***

role-playing game any of various kinds of games in which participants assume the roles of fictional characters in a highly imaginative setting, usually under the supervision of someone who predetermines the storyline and enforces the rules

Rolf·ing (rôl′fiŋ, räl′-) ⟦after Ida *Rolf* (1896-1979), U.S. biochemist⟧ *service mark for* a form of intensive massage for relaxing and repositioning muscle and connective tissue, realigning body posture, and relieving emotional tensions

roll (rōl) ***vi.*** ⟦ME *rollen* < OFr *roller* < VL **rotulare* < L *rotula:* see the ***n.***⟧ **1** *a)* to move by turning on an axis or over and over *b)* to rotate about its axis lengthwise, as a spacecraft in flight **2** a throw of dice **3** *a)* to move or be moved on wheels *b)* to travel in a wheeled vehicle *c)* [Informal] to travel in a manner regarded as carefree, confident, etc. [the band *rolled* into town for a two-night gig] **4** to travel about; wander **5** to pass; elapse [the years *rolled* by] **6** *a)* to flow, as water, in a full swelling or sweeping motion [the waves *rolling* against the boat] *b)* to be carried in a flow **7** to extend in gentle swells or undulations **8** to make a loud, continuous rising and falling sound [thunder *rolls*] **9** to rise and fall in a full, mellow cadence: said of sound, speech, etc. **10** to trill or warble **11** to form a ball or cylinder when turned over and over on itself: said as of cloth or yarn **12** to turn in a circular motion or move back and forth [with eyes *rolling*] **13** to rock from side to side [the ship pitched and *rolled*] **14** to walk by swaying **15** to become flattened or spread under a roller **16** to make progress; advance [start *rolling*] **17** to start operating [the presses *rolled*] **18** to take part in a bowling game **19** [Informal] to have plenty; abound (*in*) [*rolling* in wealth] ☆**20** *Football* to move laterally: said of the passer: in full **roll out** —***vt.*** **1** to move by turning on an axis or over and over [to *roll* a hoop] **2** to move or send on wheels or rollers **3** to cause to start operating **4** to move or send in a full, sweeping motion **5** to beat (a drum) with blows in rapid, light succession **6** to utter with full, flowing sound [to *roll* one's words] **7** to pronounce or say with a trill [to *roll* one's r's] **8** to give a swaying motion to [waves *rolling* the ship along] **9** to move gently around and around or from side to side [the baby *rolled* her head] **10** to make into a ball or cylinder by winding over and over itself or something else [to *roll* a cigarette] **11** to wrap or enfold, as in a covering [to *roll* a child in a blanket] **12** to make flat, smooth, or spread out as by using a roller, rolling pin, etc. ☆**13** *a)* to throw (dice) as in the game of craps *b)* to make (a specified throw) with dice [she *rolled* a four] ☆**14** [Slang] to rob (a drunken or sleeping person) **15** *Bowling a)* to throw (a ball) *b)* to make (a certain play or score) [to *roll* a strike] *c)* to take part in (a game or games) [to *roll* three games] **16** *Printing* to spread ink on (type, a form, etc.) with a roller —***n.*** ⟦ME *rolle* < OFr < L *rotula, rotulus,* dim. of *rota,* wheel < IE **roto-,* var. of base **ret(h)-,* to run, roll > OIr *rethim,* (I) run, OHG *rad,* wheel⟧ **1** the act or an instance of rolling **2** *a)* a paper, parchment, etc. that is rolled up; scroll *b)* something that is, or looks as if, rolled up **3** a register; catalog **4** a list of names for checking attendance; muster roll **5** a measure of something rolled into a cylinder [*a roll of wallpaper*] **6** a cylindrical mass of something [*a sausage roll*] **7** any of various foods that are rolled during preparation, as *a)* any small portion of bread, variously shaped *b)* thin cake covered with fruit, nuts, etc. and rolled [*a pecan roll*] *c)* beef, veal, etc. rolled and cooked **8** a roller (in various senses) **9** a swaying or rolling motion **10** a rapid succession of light blows on a drum **11** a loud, reverberating sound; peal, as of thunder **12** a full, cadenced flow of words **13** a trill or warble **14** a slight swell or rise on the surface of something, as land ☆**15** [Slang] money; esp., a wad of paper money **16** *Aeron.* a maneuver in which an airplane in flight performs one complete rotation around its longitudinal axis **17** *Bookbinding* a revolving tool used in making an impression or pattern —*SYN.* LIST[1] —**a roll in the hay** [Slang] sexual intercourse —**be on a roll** [Informal] to have a series of successes; go from success to success —**roll around** to recur, as in a cycle [*winter rolled around again*] —**roll back 1** to move back ☆**2** to reduce (prices) to a previous or standard level by government action and control —**roll in** to assemble, arrive, or appear, usually in large numbers or amounts —**roll one's eyes** ⟦see *vi.* 12⟧ to move the eyes upward or from side to side as a gesture of impatience, exasperation, contempt, etc. —**roll out 1** to flatten into a sheet by rolling **2** to spread out by unrolling **3** [Slang] to get out of bed **4** *Business* to introduce (a new product) **5** *Football see vi.* 20 —**roll over** ☆**1** to refinance (a maturing note, etc.) ☆**2** to reinvest (funds) so as to defer the payment of taxes **3** [Informal] to submit; give in or give up **4** [Informal] to defeat overwhelmingly —**roll up 1** to make or put into the form of a roll **2** to wrap up by turning over and over **3** to acquire or increase by accumulation **4** [Informal] to arrive in a vehicle —**roll with the punches** ⟦in ref. to a boxer's ability to move in the same direction as a thrown punch so as to lessen its force⟧ [Informal] to cope with adverse circumstances by adapting oneself to them —**strike off (***or* **from) the rolls** to expel from membership

Rol·land (rô län′), **Ro·main** (rô man′) 1866-1944; Fr. writer

☆**roll·a·way** (rōl′ə wā′) *adj.* having rollers for easy moving and storing when not in use [*a rollaway bed*]

☆**roll·back** (-bak′) *n.* a rolling back; specif., a reduction of prices to a previous level by government control

☆**roll bar** a strong steel bar that passes over and across the width of the interior compartment in some automotive vehicles so as to reduce injury to the driver and passengers if the vehicle rolls over: used esp. in racing

roll call 1 the reading aloud of a roll, or list of names, as to check attendance in a classroom, military formation, etc. **2** the fixed time, or a signal (as on a bugle), for such a reading

☆**rolled oats** hulled oats flattened between rollers to make oatmeal

roll·er (rōl′ər) *n.* **1** a person or thing that rolls (in various senses) **2** any of various rolling cylinders or wheels; specif., *a)* a cylinder of metal, wood, etc. over which something is rolled for easier movement *b)* a cylinder on which something is rolled up or wound [*the roller of a shade, a hair roller*] *c)* a heavy cylinder of metal, stone, etc. used to crush or smooth something *d)* a cylinder covered with a napped fabric, fixed on a tool with a handle and used for applying paint *e) Printing* a cylinder, usually of hard rubber, for spreading ink on the form just before the paper is impressed **3** a long bandage in a roll **4** a heavy, swelling wave that breaks on the shoreline **5** any of various birds that roll (in various senses); specif., *a)* any of a family (Coraciidae) of Old World, tropical coraciiform birds that roll and tumble in flight, as the **Eurasian roller** (*Coracias garrulus*) *b)* a canary that rolls, or trills, its notes —*adj.* of or having to do with roller skating [*roller rink*] —*SYN.* WAVE

☆**roller bearing** a bearing in which the shaft turns with rollers, generally of steel, arranged in a ringlike track: used to reduce friction

☆**Roll·er·blade** (rōl′ər blād′) *trademark for* a kind of IN-LINE SKATE —*n.* [**r-**] any IN-LINE SKATE —**roll′er·blad′ing** *n.*

☆**roller coaster 1** an amusement ride in which small, open cars move on tracks that dip and curve sharply **2** something, as a situation, relationship, or series of events, characterized by frequent abrupt and unpredictable change

roller derby ⟦< *Roller Derby*, a service mark⟧ a team game, characterized by rough play, in which roller skaters race around a banked, oval track trying to score points by lapping opponents

☆**roller skate** SKATE[1] (sense 2) —**roll′er-skate′** *vi.* **-skat′ed, -skat′ing** —**roller skater**

roller towel a long continuous towel suspended on a roller, or a very long towel fed through a device that rolls up the used part on a roller

roll film a strip of photographic film rolled on a spool for a series of consecutive exposures

rol·lick (räl′ik) *vi.* ⟦< ? FROLIC⟧ to play or behave in a lively, carefree way; romp —**rol′lick·ing** *adj.*, **rol′lick·some**

roll·ing (rōl′iŋ) *adj.* **1** that rolls (in various senses); specif., rotating or revolving, recurring, swaying, surging, resounding, trilling, etc. **2** having or forming curves or waves [*rolling hills*] —*n.* the action, motion, or sound of something that rolls or is rolled

rolling hitch a knot in which one or more turns are made between two hitches

rolling mill 1 a factory in which metal bars, sheets, etc. are rolled out **2** a machine used for such rolling

rolling pin a smooth, heavy cylinder of wood, glass, etc., usually with a handle at each end, used to roll out dough

rolling stock all the locomotives, cars, etc. of a railroad, or the trucks, trailers, etc. of a trucking company

roll·mops (rōl′mäps′) *n.* ⟦Ger *rollmops*, orig. Berlin dial. < *rollen*, to ROLL + *mops*, pug dog⟧ a fillet of fresh herring rolled up on a pickle or onion and marinated

Rol·lo (räl′ō) A.D. 860?-931?; Norse conqueror of Normandy: 1st duke of Normandy (911-927)

roll-on (rōl′än′) *adj.* designating any of various commercial products, as a deodorant lotion, that are applied to the skin by means of a rotating ball within the top of the dispenser —*n.* such a product

☆**roll·out** (rōl′out′) *n.* **1** *Business* the introduction of a new product **2** *Football* a play in which the quarterback moves laterally in preparing to throw a pass

roll·o·ver (-ō′vər) *n.* ⟦< ROLL OVER (see phr. under ROLL)⟧ ☆**1** the refinancing of a maturing note, etc. ☆**2** the reinvesting of funds in such a way as to defer the payment of taxes **3** a traffic accident in which a vehicle tips or rolls over

Rolls Royce (rōlz′rois′) ⟦< *Rolls-Royce*, a trademark for a luxury automobile⟧ [Informal] something that is the most luxurious or the highest quality of its kind

☆**roll-top** (rōl′täp′) *adj.* made with a flexible top of parallel slats that slides back [*a roll-top desk*]

roll-up (rōl′up′) *n.* a food shaped into a cylinder, typically consisting of a flat ingredient rolled around a filling, as of a meat or vegetable: also written **roll′up′**

☆**roll·way** (-wā′) *n.* a chute down which logs can be rolled or slid, as into a river for transportation

☆**Ro·lo·dex** (rō′lə deks′) ⟦arbitrary coinage < ROLL + arbitrary suffix⟧ *trademark for* a desktop file in the form of a rotating device or a shallow tray, in which cards containing names, addresses, etc. are held securely in place for ready reference

Röl·vaag (rōl′väg), **O·le Ed·vart** (ō′lē ed′värt) 1876-1931; U.S. novelist, born in Norway and writing in Norwegian

ro·ly-po·ly (rō′lē pō′lē) *adj.* ⟦redupl. of ROLL⟧ short and plump; pudgy —*n., pl.* **-lies 1** a roly-poly thing or person, esp. a child **2** [Chiefly Brit.] a pudding made of suet pastry spread with jam, rolled up, and boiled, steamed, etc. **3** [Austral.] a tumbleweed

rom *abbrev.* roman (type)

Rom[1] (räm) *n., pl.* **Rom** or **Ro·ma** (rō′mə) ⟦see ROMANY⟧ **1** a Gypsy man or boy **2** any member of the Gypsy people

Rom[2] *abbrev.* **1** Roman **2** Romance (language) **3** Romania **4** Romanian **5** *Bible* Romans

ROM (räm) *n.* ⟦*r(ead-)o(nly) m(emory)*⟧ **1** computer memory whose contents can be read but not altered **2** a memory chip that can be read but not altered

Ro·ma[1] (rō′mə) *n. pl. of* ROM[1]

Ro·ma[2] (rô′mä) *It. name for* ROME[2]

Ro·ma·ic (rō mā′ik) *adj.* ⟦ModGr *Rhōmaikos* < Gr *Rhōmaïkos*, Roman (of the Eastern empire) < *Rhōmē*, Rome < L *Roma*⟧ of modern Greece or its language —*n.* the modern Greek vernacular

ro·maine (rō mān′, rō′mān′) *n.* ⟦Fr < *(laitue) romaine*, lit., Roman (lettuce): said to be so called because brought to the papal court at Avignon by the chamberlain to Charles V and Charles VI: see ROMAN⟧ a major group of lettuce varieties having long, coarse leaves and a long, slender head: also **romaine lettuce**

Ro·mains (rô man′), **Jules** (zhül) (born *Louis Farigoule*) 1885-1972; Fr. novelist, poet, & playwright

ro·man (rô män′) *n., pl.* **-mans′** (-män′) ⟦Fr < OFr *romanz*: see ROMANCE⟧ **1** a type of metrical narrative developed in France in the Middle Ages **2** a novel

Ro·man (rō′mən) *adj.* ⟦< ME & L: ME *Romain* < OFr < L *Romanus* < *Roma*, Rome⟧ **1** *a)* of, characteristic of, or derived from the city, esp. the ancient city, of Rome or its people or culture *b)* of, characteristic of, or derived from the ancient empire of Rome or its people or culture **2** LATIN (*adj.* 1 & 5) **3** of the Roman Catholic Church **4** [*usually* **r-**] designating or of the upright style of printing types most common in modern use; not italic —*n.* **1** *a)* a person born or living in Rome *b)* a citizen of ancient Rome **2** [Rare] the Italian spoken in Rome **3** [*usually* **r-**] roman type or characters **4** [Informal] a Roman Catholic: a mildly offensive term

ro·man à clef (rō′män nä klā′) *pl.* **romans à clef** (rō′män-) ⟦Fr, novel with a key⟧ [*often in italics*] a novel in which real persons appear under fictitious names

Roman alphabet LATIN ALPHABET

Roman arch a semicircular arch

Roman architecture the style of architecture used by the ancient Romans, characterized by the rounded arch, vault, and dome, thick, massive walls, and the use of much brick and concrete

Roman calendar the calendar used by the ancient Romans before the Julian calendar: it consisted first of ten months, later twelve

Roman candle a kind of fireworks device consisting of a long tube that sends out balls of fire, sparks, etc.

Roman Catholic 1 of the Roman Catholic Church **2** a member of the Roman Catholic Church —**Roman Catholicism**

Roman Catholic Church the Christian church headed by the pope (Bishop of Rome)

ro·mance (rō mans′, rō′mans′) *n.* ⟦ME < OFr *romanz* < *romanz (escrire)*, (to write) in Roman (i.e., the vernacular, not Latin) < VL *Romanice (scribere)* < L *Romanicus,* Roman⟧ 1 a long medieval narrative in verse or prose, orig. written in one of the Romance dialects, about the adventures of knights and other chivalric heroes 2 a fictitious tale of wonderful and extraordinary events, characterized by a nonrealistic and idealizing use of the imagination 3 a type of novel in which the emphasis is on love, adventure, etc. 4 the type of literature comprising such stories 5 excitement, love, and adventure of the kind found in such literature; romantic quality or spirit 6 the tendency to derive great pleasure from romantic adventures; romantic sentiment 7 an exaggeration or fabrication that has no real substance 8 a love affair 9 *Music* a short, lyrical, usually sentimental piece, suggesting a love song —*vi.* **-manced′, -manc′ing** 1 to make up false or exaggerated stories 2 to think or talk about romantic things 3 [Informal] to make love; court; woo —*vt.* [Informal] 1 to make love to; woo 2 to seek to gain the favor of, as by flattery; court —**ro·manc′er** *n.*

Ro·mance (rō mans′, rō′mans′) *adj.* ⟦< obs. Fr *(langue) romance,* Romance language < OFr *romanz:* see prec.⟧ designating, of, or constituting any of the languages derived from Vulgar Latin, as Italian, Spanish, French, Portuguese, or Romanian —*n.* these languages as a group

Roman Empire empire established (27 B.C.) by Augustus, succeeding the Roman Republic: at its peak it included W & S Europe, Britain, Asia Minor, N Africa, & the lands of the E Mediterranean: divided (A.D. 395) into the EASTERN ROMAN EMPIRE and the WESTERN ROMAN EMPIRE

Ro·man·esque (rō′mə nesk′) *adj.* ⟦Fr < It *romanesco, romanzesco* < *romanzo* < OFr *romanz:* see ROMANCE & -ESQUE⟧ 1 designating or of a style of European architecture of the 11th and 12th cent., based on the Roman and characterized by the use of the round arch and vault, thick, massive walls, interior bays, etc. 2 designating or of a style of painting, sculpture, etc. corresponding to this —*n.* the Romanesque style of architecture, painting, etc.

Roman Empire (A.D. 100)

ro·man-fleuve (rô män flëv′) *n., pl.* **ro·mans-fleuves** (rô män flëv′) ⟦Fr, river novel⟧ a long novel, often in a number of volumes, dealing with a cross section of society, several generations of a family, etc.

Roman holiday ⟦after the ancient Roman gladiatorial contests⟧ entertainment acquired at the expense of others' suffering, or a spectacle yielding such entertainment

Rom·a·ni (räm′ə nē, rō′mə-) *n.* ⟦Romani *romani,* fem. & pl. of *romano,* Gypsy < *rom,* a man, husband, Gypsy < Sans *ḍombaḥ,* low-caste musician⟧ 1 *pl.* **-ni** or **-nies** GYPSY (*n.* 1) 2 the Indo-Aryan language of the Gypsies, which occurs with dialectal variations in each of the countries where they live —*adj.* of the Gypsies or their language or culture

USAGE—for *n.* 1 and *adj.*, this term is now often preferred over *Gypsy*

Ro·ma·ni·a (rō mā′nē ə, -mān′yə; ro͞o-) country in the NE Balkan Peninsula, on the Black Sea: 91,699 sq mi (237,500 sq km); cap. Bucharest

Ro·ma·ni·an (-mān′yən, -mā′nē ən) *adj.* of Romania or its people, language, or culture —*n.* 1 a person born or living in Romania 2 the Romance language spoken in Romania

Ro·man·ic (-man′ik) *adj., n.* ⟦L *Romanicus*⟧ ROMANCE

Ro·man·ism (rō′mən iz′əm) *n.* 1 Roman Catholicism: hostile usage 2 the spirit and influence of ancient Rome

Ro·man·ist (-ist) *n.* ⟦ModL *Romanista*⟧ a person who studies or is expert in Roman law, antiquities, etc.

Ro·man·ize (-īz′) *vt.* **-ized′, -iz′ing** 1 to make Roman in character, spirit, etc. 2 to make Roman Catholic 3 to respell in the ROMAN ALPHABET —*vi.* 1 to follow or be influenced by Roman customs, law, etc. 2 to conform to Roman Catholicism —**Ro′man·i·za′tion** *n.*

Roman law the code of laws of ancient Rome: the basis for the modern legal system in many countries

Roman nose a nose with a high, prominent bridge

Roman numerals the Roman letters used as numerals until the 10th cent. A.D.: in Roman numerals I = 1, V = 5, X = 10, L = 50, C = 100, D = 500, and M = 1,000 ➥Other numbers are formed from these by adding or subtracting: the value of a symbol following another of the same or greater value is added (e.g., III = 3, XV = 15); the value of a symbol preceding one of greater value is subtracted (e.g., IX = 9); and the value of a symbol standing between two of greater value is subtracted from that of the second, the remainder being added to that of the first (e.g., XIX = 19). Roman numerals are commonly written in capitals, though they may be written in lowercase letters, as in numbering subdivisions (e.g., Act IV, scene iii). A bar over a letter indicates multiplication by 1,000 (e.g., $\bar{V}$ = 5,000)

Ro·ma·no (rō mä′nō) *n.* ⟦It, ROMAN⟧ a dry, sharp, very hard cheese orig. of Italy, made from sheep's, cow's, or goat's milk, usually grated for sprinkling on pasta, soups, etc.

Ro·ma·nov[1] (rō′mə nôf′, rō mä′nôf) *n.* name of the ruling family of Russia (1613-1917): also sp. **Romanoff**

Ro·ma·nov[2] (rō′mə nôf′, rō mä′nôf), **Mi·kha·il Feo·do·ro·vich** (mē khä ēl′ fyô′dô rô vich) 1598-1645; 1st Romanov czar & founder of the dynasty

Ro·mans (rō′mənz) *n.* a book of the New Testament, a message from the Apostle Paul to the Christians of Rome: abbrev. *Rm, Ro,* or *Rom*

Ro·mansch or **Ro·mansh** (rō mänsh′, -mansh′) *n.* ⟦Romansch *rumansch, rumonsch* < VL *romanice:* see ROMANCE⟧ the Rhaeto-Romance dialect spoken in the Swiss canton of the Grisons, or Graubünden: sometimes used interchangeably as a name for Ladin or for all the Rhaeto-Romance dialects

ro·man·tic (rō man′tik) *adj.* ⟦Fr *romantique* < obs. *romant* (see ROMAUNT) + *-ique,* -IC⟧ 1 of, having the nature of, characteristic of, or characterized by romance 2 without a basis in fact; fanciful, fictitious, or fabulous 3 not practical; visionary or quixotic [a *romantic* scheme] 4 full of or dominated by thoughts, feelings, and attitudes characteristic of or suitable for romance; passionate, adventurous, idealistic, etc. [a *romantic* youth] 5 *a)* of, characteristic of, or preoccupied with ardent, idealized lovemaking or courtship *b)* suited for romance or lovemaking [a *romantic* night] 6 [*also* **R-**] of or characteristic of Romanticism and the Romantic Movement: contrasted with CLASSIC, CLASSICAL, REALISTIC, etc. —*n.* 1 a romantic person 2 [*often* **R-**] an adherent of Romanticism, as in literature or music —**ro·man′ti·cal·ly** *adv.*

ro·man·ti·cism (rō man′tə siz′əm) *n.* 1 romantic spirit, outlook, tendency, etc. 2 [*usually* **R-**] ROMANTIC MOVEMENT 3 [*also* **R-**] the spirit, attitudes, style, etc. of, or adherence to, the Romantic Movement or a similar movement: contrasted with CLASSICISM, REALISM, etc.

ro·man·ti·cist (-sist) *n.* an adherent of Romanticism in literature, painting, music, etc.

ro·man·ti·cize (-sīz′) *vt.* **-cized′, -ciz′ing** to treat or regard romantically; give a romantic character to or interpretation of —*vi.* to have or uphold romantic ideas, attitudes, etc. —**ro·man′ti·ci·za′tion** *n.*

Romantic Movement the revolt in the late 18th and early 19th cent. against the artistic, political, and philosophical principles that had become associated with neoclassicism: characterized in literature, music, painting, etc. by freedom of form, emphasis on feeling, originality, and the creative imagination and on the artist's own personality, and by sympathetic interest in nature, medievalism, the common man, etc.

Rom·a·ny (räm′ə nē, rō′mə-) *adj., n., pl.* **-ny** or **-nies** *alt. sp. of.* ROMANI

ro·maunt (rō mänt′, -mônt′) *n.* ⟦OFr *romant,* var. of *romanz:* see ROMANCE⟧ [Archaic] ROMANCE (*n.* 1 & 2)

Rom·berg (räm′bərg), **Sigmund** 1887-1951: U.S. composer, born in Hungary

Rom Cath *abbrev.* Roman Catholic

☆**Rome**[1] (rōm) *n.* ⟦after *Rome* Township, S Ohio, where first grown⟧ a somewhat tart, red winter apple: in full **Rome Beauty**

Rome[2] (rōm) ⟦L *Roma,* of Etr orig.⟧ capital of Italy, on the Tiber River: formerly, the capital of the Roman Republic, the Roman Empire, & the Papal States: It. name ROMA[2]

Ro·me·o (rō′mē ō′) *n., pl.* for 2 & 3, **-os′** ⟦It < *Romolo* < L *Romulus*⟧ 1 the hero of Shakespeare's tragedy *Romeo and Juliet* (c. 1595), son of Montague and lover of Juliet, daughter of Capulet: at the death of the lovers their feuding families become reconciled 2 *a)* a man who is an ardent lover *b)* a philanderer ☆3 [**r-**] a man's house slipper with elastic in the sides

Rom·ford (rum′fərd, räm′-) former municipal borough in Essex, SE England: now part of Havering, near London

Rom·ish (rō′mish) *adj.* Roman Catholic: a derogatory term

Rom·mel (räm′əl), **Erwin (Johannes Eugen)** 1891-1944; Ger. field marshal in WWII

Rom·ney (rum′nē, räm′-), **George** 1734-1802; Eng. painter

romp (rämp) *n.* ⟦< earlier *ramp,* vulgar woman, hussy, prob. < ME *rampen* < OFr *ramper:* see RAMP[2]⟧ 1 a person who romps, esp. a girl 2 ⟦< the *vi.*⟧ boisterous, lively play or frolic 3 *a)* an easy, winning gait in a race [to win in a *romp*] *b)* an easy victory —*vi.* 1 to play or frolic in a boisterous, lively way 2 to win with ease in a race, contest, etc.

romp·er (räm′pər) *n.* 1 a person who romps 2 [*pl.*] a type of loosefitting, one-piece garment, esp. for very young children

Rom·u·lus (räm′yoo ləs) *n.* ⟦L⟧ *Rom. Myth.* a son of Mars and founder and first king of Rome, deified as Quirinus: he and his twin brother, Remus, left as infants to die in the Tiber, are suckled by a she-wolf

Ron·ald (rän′əld) *n.* ⟦Scot < ON *Rögnvaldr,* akin to OHG *Raganald:* see REGINALD⟧ a masculine name: dim. *Ron*

ron·deau (rän′dō) *n., pl.* **-deaux** (-dōz) ⟦Fr, earlier *rondel* < *rond,* ROUND[1]⟧ 1 a short, lyrical poem of usually fifteen lines (three stanzas), with only two rhymes and with an unrhymed refrain at the end of the second and third stanzas 2 *a)* RONDO *b)* a medieval French monophonic or polyphonic song with many repetitions of two themes or phrases

ron·del (rän′dəl, rän del′) *n.* ⟦ME < OFr: see prec.⟧ 1 a kind of rondeau, usually with fourteen lines, two rhymes, and the first two lines used as a refrain in the middle and at the end (the second line occasionally being omitted at the end) 2 a circular object; esp., a small round or disk-shaped bead used as a spacer, as in a necklace: also **ron·delle** (rän del′)

ron·do (rän′dō) *n., pl.* **-dos** ⟦It < Fr *rondeau:* see RONDEAU⟧ *Music* a composition or movement, often the last movement of a sonata, having its principal theme stated three or more times in the same key, interposed with subordinate themes

Ron·dô·nia (rôn dô′nyä) state in W Brazil, on the Bolivian border: 92,090 sq mi (238,512 sq km); cap. Pôrto Velho

ron·dure (rän′jər, -dyoor) *n.* ⟦Fr *rondeur* < *rond,* ROUND[1]⟧ [Rare] a circle or sphere; roundness

ro·nin (rō′nin) *n., pl.* **-nin** ⟦Jpn⟧ in feudal Japan, a samurai who lost his lord and was forced to wander, often living as a bandit

Ron·sard (rōn sȧr′), **Pierre de** (pyer də) 1524-85; Fr. poet

Rönt·gen (rent′gən; *Ger* rënt′gən), **Wilhelm Conrad** *alt. sp. of* ROENTGEN

rood (ro͞od) *n.* ⟦ME *rode* < OE *rod,* a cross, measure; akin to *rodd:* see ROD⟧ **1** [Archaic] a cross as used in crucifixion; specif., the cross on which Jesus was crucified **2** any cross representing this; crucifix, esp. a large one at the entrance to the chancel or choir of a medieval church, often supported on a rood beam or rood screen **3** [Brit.] *a)* an old unit of linear measure varying locally from 5½ to 8 yards; sometimes, 1 rod *b)* an old unit of land measure usually equal to ¼ acre (40 square rods)

rood screen an ornamental screen, usually with a rood above it supported by a beam (**rood beam**), serving as a partition between the nave and the chancel of a church

roof (ro͞of, roof) *n., pl.* **roofs** ⟦ME *rof* < OE *hrof,* akin to ON, roof, shed < IE base **krapo-* > OSlav *stropŭ,* roof⟧ **1** the outside top covering of a building **2** figuratively, a house or home **3** the top or peak of anything *[the roof of the world]* **4** anything like a roof in position or use *[the roof of the mouth]* —*vt.* to provide or cover with or as with a roof —**hit the roof** ⟦fig., as if one were propelled upward by the explosion of anger⟧ [Informal] to become suddenly or violently angry —**raise the roof** [Slang] **1** to be very noisy, as in applause, anger, celebration, etc. **2** to complain loudly —**through the roof** [Informal] at or to an extremely high point or level *[a TV show with ratings through the roof]* —**roof′less** *adj.*

roof·er (-ər) *n.* a person who builds or repairs roofs

☆**roof garden** **1** a garden on the flat roof of a building **2** the roof or top floor of a high building, decorated as a garden and used as for a restaurant

roof·ie (ro͞of′ē) *n.* [Slang] a dose of Rohypnol in tablet form

roof·ing (-iŋ) *n.* **1** the act of covering with a roof **2** material for a roof or roofs **3** a roof

roof·line (ro͞of′līn′, roof′-) *n.* the outline or contour of the roof of a building, automobile, etc.

roof·top (-täp′) *n.* the roof of a building

roof·tree (-trē′) *n.* **1** the ridgepole of a roof **2** a roof

rook[1] (rook) *n.* ⟦ME *roc* < OE *hroc,* akin to Ger *ruch* < IE echoic base **ker-* > CROW[1], RAVEN[1]⟧ **1** a gregarious European crow (*Corvus frugilegus*) with a bare spot by its bill **2** a swindler; cheat — *vt., vi.* ⟦prob. from the bird's thievishness⟧ to swindle, cheat, defraud, etc.

rook[2] (rook) *n.* ⟦ME *rok* < OFr *roc* < Ar *rukhkh* < Pers *rukh*⟧ *Chess* either of the two corner pieces shaped like a castle tower: it can move in a vertical or horizontal direction only over any number of consecutive, unoccupied squares; castle

rook·er·y (rook′ər ē) *n., pl.* **-er·ies** **1** a breeding place or colony of rooks **2** a breeding place or colony of other gregarious birds or animals, as penguins or seals **3** [Now Rare] a crowded tenement house or tenement district; esp., a slum

rook·ie (rook′ē) *n.* ⟦altered < ? RECRUIT⟧ **1** [Slang] an inexperienced recruit in the army or on a police force ☆**2** *Sports* a first-year or first-time player in a particular league, event, etc. **3** [Informal] any beginner or novice

rook·y (rook′ē) *adj.* full of or inhabited by rooks

room (ro͞om, room) *n.* ⟦ME *roum* < OE *rum,* akin to ON, OHG < IE base **rewe-,* to open, room > L *rus,* land⟧ **1** space, esp. enough space, to contain something or in which to do something *[room for one more, room to move around in]* **2** suitable scope or opportunity *[room for doubt]* **3** a space within a building enclosed by walls or separated from other similar spaces by walls or partitions **4** [*pl.*] living quarters; lodgings; apartment **5** the people gathered together in a room **6** [Obs.] a position or office —☆*vi.* to occupy living quarters; have lodgings; lodge —*vt.* to provide with a room or lodgings

room and board sleeping accommodations and meals offered together, as in some rooming houses

room clerk a clerk at a hotel or motel who registers guests, assigns them rooms, etc.

☆**room·er** (ro͞om′ər) *n.* a person who rents a room or rooms to live in; lodger

☆**room·ette** (ro͞o met′) *n.* a small room for one person in a railroad sleeping car

room·ful (ro͞om′fool′) *n., pl.* **-fuls′** **1** as much or as many as will fill a room **2** the people or objects in a room, collectively

☆**room·ie** (ro͞om′ē) *n.* [Informal] ROOMMATE

☆**rooming house** a house with furnished rooms for rent

☆**room·mate** (ro͞om′māt′) *n.* a person with whom one shares a room or rooms

room service specialized service, as in some hotels, providing food and beverages to guests in their rooms

room temperature a comfortable indoor temperature, generally between 20 and 25°C (68 to 77°F): term used esp. for this range considered as suitable for serving certain foods or at which certain chemical or physical processes can take place *[a wine best served at room temperature]*

room·y (ro͞om′ē) *adj.* **room′i·er, room′i·est** having plenty of room; spacious —**room′i·ly** *adv.* —**room′i·ness** *n.*

☆**roor·back** or **roor·bach** (roor′bak′) *n.* ⟦after Baron von *Roorback,* imaginary author of a nonexistent book, *Roorback's Tour . . .,* said to contain spurious charges against presidential candidate James K. POLK (1844)⟧ a false or slanderous story devised for political effect, esp. against a candidate for office

roose (ro͞oz; *Scot* röz) *vt.* **roosed, roos′ing** ⟦ME n. *ros,* v. *rosen* < ON n. *hros,* v. *horsa*⟧ [Scot. or North Eng.] praise

Roo·se·velt[1] (rō′zə velt′, ro͞o′zə-) *n.* a masculine name

Roo·se·velt[2] (rō′zə vəlt, -velt′; ro͞o′zə velt′) **1 (Anna) Eleanor** 1884-1962; U.S. writer & delegate to the United Nations: wife of Franklin **2 Franklin Del·a·no** (del′ə nō′) 1882-1945; 32d president of the U.S. (1933-45) **3 Theodore** 1858-1919; 26th president of the U.S. (1901-09)

roost (ro͞ost) *n.* ⟦ME < OE *hrost,* akin to MDu *roest* < IE base **kred-,* timberwork > OSlav *krada,* woodpile, Goth *hrōt,* roof⟧ **1** a perch on which birds, esp. domestic fowls, can rest or sleep **2** a place with perches for birds **3** a place for resting, sleeping, etc. —*vi.* **1** to rest, sit, sleep, etc. on a perch **2** to stay or settle down, as for the night —**come home to roost** to have repercussions, esp. disagreeable ones; boomerang —**rule the roost** to be master

roost·er (ro͞os′tər) *n.* ⟦prec. + -ER⟧ the adult male of the chicken and other, similar birds

roost·er·tail (ro͞os′tər tāl′) *n.* ⟦descriptive: suggestive of the shape of a *rooster's tail*⟧ a full spray or cloud, as of water in the wake of a speeding boat or dust from a speeding car: also written **rooster tail**

root[1] (ro͞ot, root) *n.* ⟦ME *rote* < Late OE < ON *rot,* akin to OE *wyrt,* Ger *wurzel* < IE base **wrād-,* twig, root > Gr *rhiza,* L *radix,* root, *ramus,* branch⟧ **1** [*often pl.*] the part of a plant, usually below the ground, that lacks nodes, shoots, and leaves, holds the plant in position, draws water and nourishment from the soil, and stores food **2** [*often pl.*] loosely, any underground part of a plant, as a rhizome **3** the attached or embedded part of a bodily structure, as of the teeth, hair, nails, or tongue **4** the source, origin, or cause of an action, quality, condition, etc. **5** a person or family that has many descendants; ancestor **6** [*pl.*] the close ties one has with some place or people as through birth, upbringing, long and sympathetic association, etc. **7** a lower or supporting part; base **8** an essential or basic part; core *[the root of the matter]* **9** *Math. a)* a quantity that, multiplied by itself a specified number of times, produces a given quantity *[4 is the square root (4 × 4) of 16 and the cube root (4 × 4 × 4) of 64] b)* a number that, when substituted for the unknown quantity in an equation, will satisfy the equation **10** *Music* the basic tone of a chord, on which the chord is constructed; often, the fundamental **11** *Linguis.* the fundamental element of a word or form, exclusive of all affixes and inflectional phonetic changes —*vi.* **1** to begin to grow by putting out roots **2** to become fixed, settled, etc. —*vt.* **1** to fix the roots of in the ground **2** to establish; settle **3** to cause (a cutting from a plant) to develop roots, as by placing in water or in sand, soil, etc. —*SYN.* ORIGIN —**by the roots** completely, including the root *[to pull up a weed by the roots]* —**root up** (or **out** or **away**) to pull out by the roots; remove or destroy completely —**take root** **1** to begin growing by putting out roots **2** to become settled or established

root[2] (ro͞ot; *for vt. & vi. 1-3, also,* root) *vt.* ⟦formerly also *wrote, rout* < ME *wroten* < OE *wrotan,* to root up < *wrot,* snout < IE base **wer-,* to tear up > L *rostrum,* beak⟧ to dig or turn (*up* or *out*) with or as with the snout —*vi.* **1** to dig in the ground, as with the snout **2** to search about; rummage *[to root through the litter]* **3** [Informal] to work hard; drudge *[to root for a living]* ☆**4** *a)* to encourage a contestant or team by applauding and cheering *b)* to lend moral support to someone seeking success, recovery, etc.: usually with *for* —**root′er** *n.*

Root (ro͞ot), **Elihu** 1845-1937; U.S. statesman: secretary of state (1905-09)

root·age (ro͞ot′ij, root′-) *n.* **1** a taking root or being firmly fixed by means of roots **2** the roots of a plant, collectively

☆**root beer** a carbonated drink made of or flavored with extracts from the roots and bark of certain plants

root borer any insect or insect larva that bores into the roots of plants

root canal **1** a small, tubular channel, normally filled with pulp, in the root of a tooth **2** a treatment or procedure involving the opening, cleaning, filling, etc. of a root canal

root cap the loose cells at the tip of a growing root, rubbed off by the motion of the root tip through the soil and constantly renewed from within

root cellar an underground storage room for vegetables, esp. root crops

root climber *Bot.* a climber that adheres to its support by means of roots

root crop a crop, as turnips or beets, grown for the edible roots

root hair *Bot.* any of the thin-walled, hairlike tubular outgrowths from a growing root, which serve to absorb water and minerals from the soil

roo·tle (ro͞ot′'l) *vi.* **roo′tled, roo′tling** [Brit.] ROOT[2] (*vi.* 1 & 2)

root·less (-lis) *adj.* having no roots or no stabilizing ties, as to society —**root′less·ly** *adv.* —**root′less·ness** *n.*

root·let (-lit) *n.* a little root or small branch of a root

root mean square *Statistics* the value of a quantity or the effective value of a periodic quantity, as a current, equal to the square root of the average (arithmetic mean) of the squares of a set of values

roots music **1** traditional music of a particular geographic region or cultural group **2** music influenced by or composed in the style of such music

root·stock (ro͞ot′stäk′, root′-) *n.* **1** *Bot. a)* RHIZOME *b)* a plant onto which another is grafted as a new top **2** *Zool.* the rootlike, attached portion of a hydroid colony

root·y (ro͞ot′ē, root′ē) *adj.* **root′i·er, root′i·est** **1** having many roots **2** like a root or roots —**root′i·ness** *n.*

rope (rōp) *n.* ⟦ME *rop* < OE *rap,* akin to Ger *reif* (Goth *raip*) < IE **reip-,* rag, piece of cloth < base **rei-,* to tear > REAP, REEF[2]⟧ **1** a thick, strong cord made of intertwisted strands of fiber, thin wires, leather strips, etc. **2** [*pl.*] such cords strung between posts to enclose a boxing ring **3** *a)* such a cord, or a noose made of it, for hanging a person *b)* death by hanging (with *the*) **4** LASSO **5** *a)* a length, esp. a thick, flexible length, of something [*a rope* of taffy, a *rope* of hair] *b)* a ropelike string of things put together by or as by twisting, twining, braiding, or threading [*a rope* of pearls] **6** a ropelike, sticky formation in a liquid, as in wine —*vt.* **roped, rop′ing 1** to fasten, tie, or confine with or as with a rope **2** to connect or tie together (esp. mountain climbers) by a rope **3** to separate, mark off, or enclose with a rope: usually with *in, off,* or *out* ☆**4** to catch or throw with a lasso —*vi.* to become ropelike and sticky [to cook candy until it *ropes*] —**give someone (enough) rope** to allow someone freedom of action in the expectation that that person will overreach himself or herself —**on the ropes 1** *Boxing* knocked against the ropes **2** [Slang] near collapse or ruin —☆**rope in** [Slang] to entice or trick into doing something —**the end of one's rope** the end of one's endurance, resources, etc. —**the ropes** [Informal] the details or procedures of something [a new employee learning *the ropes*] —**rop′er** *n.*

rop·er·y (rōp′pər ē) *n., pl.* **-er·ies 1** [Now Rare] a place for the manufacture of ropes **2** [Archaic] ROGUERY

rope·walk (rōp′wôk′) *n.* a long, low, narrow building, shed, etc. in which ropes are made

rope·walk·er (-wôk′ər) *n.* a performer who walks or does tricks on a tightrope: also **rope′danc′er** (-dan′sər, -dän′-) —**rope′walk′ing** *n.*

rop·y (rō′pē) *adj.* **rop′i·er, rop′i·est 1** forming sticky, stringy threads, as some liquids do; glutinous **2** like a rope or ropes **3** [Brit. Informal] *a)* bad, poor, inferior, etc. *b)* somewhat unwell: also **rop′ey** —**rop′i·ness** *n.*

☆**roque** (rōk) *n.* ⟦< CROQUET⟧ a formalized variety of croquet played with short-handled mallets on a hard court with a raised border

Roque·fort (rōk′fərt) ⟦after *Roquefort,* town in S France where made⟧ *trademark for* a strong cheese made from ewe's milk and veined with bluish streaks produced by BLUE MOLD

roq·ue·laure (räk′ə lôr′, rō′kə-) *n.* ⟦Fr, after the Duc de *Roquelaure* (1656-1738)⟧ a heavy cloak, usually knee-length, often fur-trimmed and silk-lined, worn by men in the 18th cent.

ro·quet (rō kā′) *vt., vi.* **-queted′** (-kād), **-quet′ing** (-kā′iŋ) ⟦< CROQUET⟧ *Croquet, etc.* to cause one's ball to hit (another player's ball) —*n.* the act of roqueting

ro·quette (rō ket′) *n.* ⟦Fr: see ROCKET[2]⟧ ARUGULA

ror·qual (rôr′kwəl) *n.* ⟦Fr < Norw *röyrkval* < ON *reytharhvalr* < *reythr,* rorqual (prob. akin to *rautha* < IE base **reudh-,* RED) + *hvalr,* WHALE[1]: hence lit., red whale, from the reddish streaks in the skin⟧ any of a family (Balaenopteridae) of baleen whales with a well-developed dorsal fin and longitudinal furrows on its belly and throat; esp., any of a genus (*Balaenoptera*) that includes the sei whale and blue whale

Ror·schach test (rôr′shäk′) ⟦after H. *Rorschach* (1884-1922), Swiss psychiatrist⟧ *Psychol.* a test for the analysis of personality, in which the person being tested tells what is suggested to him or her by a standard series of inkblot designs: his or her responses are then analyzed and interpreted

Ro·sa (rō′zə; *It* rô′zä), **Mon·te** (mänt′ē; *It* môn′te) mountain in the Pennine Alps, on the Swiss-Italian border: 15,217 ft (4,638 m)

ro·sa·ceous (rō zā′shəs) *adj.* ⟦ModL *rosaceus* < L, made of roses⟧ **1** of the rose family of plants **2** like a rose **3** rose-colored; rosy

Ros·a·lie (rō′zə lē′, räz′ə-) *n.* ⟦Fr, prob. < L *rosalia,* annual ceremony of hanging garlands of roses on tombs < *rosa,* ROSE[1]⟧ a feminine name

Ros·a·lind (räz′ə lind) *n.* ⟦Sp *Rosalinda,* as if from *rosa linda,* pretty rose, but prob. ult. < OHG *Roslindis* < Gmc **hros,* HORSE + *lindi,* LITHE⟧ a feminine name

Ros·a·lyn (räz′ə lin, rōz′-) *n.* a feminine name: var. *Rosalynn*

Ros·a·mond or **Ros·a·mund** (räz′ə mənd, rō′zə-) *n.* ⟦ME *Rosamunda* < OFr *Rosamonde* or Sp *Rosamunda* < ML *Rosamunda,* as if < L *rosa munda,* clean rose, but ult. < OHG *Hrosmund* < Gmc *hros,* HORSE + **mund-,* hand, protection: see MANUAL⟧ a feminine name: dim. *Roz*

ros·an·i·line (rō zan′ə lin, -lēn′, -līn′) *n.* ⟦ROS(E) + ANILINE⟧ a crystalline base, $C_{20}H_{21}N_3O$, made by heating aniline and toluidine with nitrobenzene: many aniline dyes are derivatives of it

ro·sar·i·an (rō zer′ē ən) *n.* ⟦< L *rosarium,* a rose garden (see ROSARY) + -AN⟧ a person who cultivates roses

Ro·sa·ri·o (rō zär′ē ō′; *Sp* rô sä′ryô) city & port in EC Argentina, on the Paraná River

ro·sa·ry (rō′zər ē) *n., pl.* **-ries** ⟦ME *rosarie* < L *rosarium,* rose garden (in ML, rosary, garland of roses) < neut. of *rosarius,* of roses < *rosa,* ROSE[1]⟧ **1** *R.C.Ch.* *a)* a string of beads, consisting typically of one short set followed by a loop of five (sometimes fifteen) full sets of beads (there are one large bead and ten small beads in each full set), used to keep count as one prays: the Apostle's Creed is said at the beginning; at each large bead an Our Father; at each small one, a Hail Mary; at the end of each set, the lesser doxology *b)* this group of prayers **2** any string of beads used in praying

☆**ros·coe** (räs′kō) *n.* [Old Slang] a gun, esp. a handgun

Ros·coe (räs′kō) *n.* ⟦< ?⟧ a masculine name

Ros·com·mon (räs käm′ən) county in Connacht province, WC Ireland: 951 sq mi (2,463 sq km)

rose[1] (rōz) *n.* ⟦ME < OE < L *rosa* < Gr *rhodon:* see RHODA⟧ **1** any of a genus (*Rosa*) of shrubs of the rose family, characterized by prickly stems, pinnate leaves, and fragrant flowers with five petals that are usually white, yellow, or, often specif., red or pink **2** the flower of any of these plants **3** any of several similar or related plants **4** pinkish red or purplish red **5** ROSETTE **6** a round, perforated nozzle for a hose, sprinkling can, etc. **7** *a)* a form in which gems, esp. diamonds, are cut, with a flat, round base and a multifaceted upper surface *b)* a gem cut in this way **8** a compass card or a representation of this, as on maps —*adj.* **1** of or having to do with a rose or roses **2** rose-colored **3** rose-scented **4** designating a large and widely distributed family (Rosaceae, order Rosales) of wild and cultivated dicotyledonous shrubs and trees, including cinquefoils, meadowsweets, hawthorns, strawberries, apples, peaches, and almonds —*vt.* **rosed, ros′ing** to make rose-colored; specif., to flush (the cheeks, etc.) —**come up roses** [Informal] to turn out very well —**under the rose** SUB ROSA —**rose′like′** *adj.*

rose[2] (rōz) *vi., vt. pt. of* RISE

Rose (rōz) *n.* ⟦see ROSE[1]⟧ a feminine name: dim. *Rosie;* var. *Rosita;* equiv. It. & Sp. *Rosa*

ro·sé (rō zā′) *n.* ⟦Fr, lit., pink⟧ a pink wine made from certain red-wine grapes, with the skins left in the juice during early fermentation just long enough to tinge it with color

☆**rose acacia** a shrubby plant (*Robinia hispida*) of the pea family, with bristly stems and large, rose-colored flowers, native to the SE U.S. and often cultivated

ro·se·ate (rō′zē it, -āt′) *adj.* ⟦< L *roseus,* rosy < *rosa,* ROSE[1] + -ATE[1]⟧ **1** rose-colored; rosy **2** bright, cheerful, or optimistic —**ro′se·ate·ly** *adv.*

Ro·seau (rō zō′) seaport & capital of Dominica, on the SW coast

rose·bay (rōz′bā′) *n.* **1** RHODODENDRON **2** OLEANDER

☆**rose-breast·ed grosbeak** (-bres′tid) a North American passerine bird (*Pheucticus ludovicianus,* family Emberizidae), the male of which is black and white, with a rose-colored triangular patch on the breast, and pink wing lining

rose·bud (-bud′) *n.* the bud of a rose

rose·bush (-boosh′) *n.* a shrub that bears roses

rose campion MULLEIN PINK

rose chafer ☆a small North American scarab beetle (*Macrodactylus subspinosus*) that, as a larva, feeds on plant roots, and, as an adult, on leaves and flowers: also called **rose bug**

rose-col·ored (-kul′ərd) *adj.* **1** pinkish-red or purplish-red **2** bright, cheerful, or optimistic —**through rose-colored glasses** with optimism, esp. undue optimism

Rose·crans (rōz′kranz′), **William Starke** (stärk) 1819-98; Union general in the Civil War

☆**rose fever** a kind of hay fever believed to be caused by the pollen of roses: also **rose cold**

☆**rose·fish** (rōz′fish′) *n., pl.* **-fish′** or **-fish′es** (see FISH) any of several reddish food fishes, as two scorpionfishes (*Sebastes marinus* and *Helicolenus dactylopterus*) of the Atlantic

rose geranium any of several pelargoniums grown for their pleasant aroma

rose mallow any of several plants (genus *Hibiscus*) of the mallow family, with showy flowers; esp., a marsh species (*H. palustris*) having large pink, red, or white flowers

rose·mar·y (rōz′mer′ē) *n.* ⟦altered (after ROSE[1] & MARY[1]) < earlier *rosmarine* < L *ros marinus* (also *ros maris*), lit., dew of the sea < *ros,* dew (< IE **rosā* < **eres,* to flow: see RACE[1]) + *marinus,* MARINE⟧ an evergreen herb (*Rosmarinus officinalis*) of the mint family, native to the Mediterranean region, with clusters of small, light-blue flowers and leaves that yield a fragrant essential oil, used in perfumes, in cooking, etc.

Rose·mar·y (rōz′mer′ē, -mə rē) *n.* ⟦see prec.⟧ a feminine name: var. **Rose·ma·rie** (rōz′mə rē′)

☆**rose moss** PORTULACA

rose of Jericho an Asian plant (*Anastatica hierochuntica*) of the crucifer family, with oval leaves and spikes of small, white flowers: it curls up tightly when dry and expands again when moistened

rose of Sharon ⟦after Heb *Shārōn:* see SHARON[2]⟧ ☆**1** a hardy plant (*Hibiscus syriacus*) of the mallow family, with white, red, pink, or purplish flowers **2** a plant mentioned in the Bible, variously identified as a tulip, crocus, etc.: S. of Sol. 2:1 **3** [Chiefly Brit.] a shrubby species (*Hypericum calycinum*) of St. Johnswort, with large yellow flowers

rose oil attar of roses: see ATTAR

ro·se·o·la (rō′zē ō′lə, rō zē′ə lə) *n.* ⟦ModL, dim. < L *roseus,* rosy⟧ **1** any rose-colored rash **2** a condition or disease causing such a rash; specif., RUBELLA

rose quartz a variety of quartz, pink to deep rose in color, often used for gems, esp. when translucent

☆**rose·slug** (rōz′slug′) *n.* the sluglike larva of certain sawflies (esp. *Endelomyia aethiops*) that eats the leaves of roses

Ro·set·ta stone (rō zet′ə) a tablet of gray granite found in 1799 at Rosetta, a town in Egypt: because it bore parallel inscriptions in Greek and in ancient Egyptian demotic and hieroglyphic characters, it provided a key to the deciphering of ancient Egyptian writing

ro·sette (rō zet′) *n.* ⟦Fr < OFr, dim. of *rose,* a rose < L *rosa,* ROSE[1]⟧ **1** an ornament made of ribbons, threads, etc. gathered or tufted in the shape of a rose **2** any formation, arrangement, etc. resembling or suggesting a rose **3** *Archit.* a painted or sculptured ornament, usually circular, having petals and leaves radiating symmetrically from the center **4** *Bot.* a circular cluster of leaves, petals, or other organs, esp. such a cluster produced at the base of a plant as a means of overwintering

rosette

Rose·ville (rōz′vil′) city in central Calif.: suburb of Sacramento

rose water a preparation consisting of water and attar of roses, used as a perfume

rose window a decorative circular window with a roselike symmetrical pattern of tracery divided by mullions arranged like the spokes of a wheel

rose window

rose·wood (rōz′wood′) ***n.*** ⟦from its odor⟧ **1** any of a number of valuable hard, reddish, black-streaked woods, sometimes with a roselike odor, obtained from certain tropical trees (esp. genus *Dalbergia* of the pea family) and used in making furniture, pianos, etc. **2** a tree yielding such wood

Rosh Ha·sha·na (rōsh′ hə shō′nə, -shä′-; *Heb* rōsh′ hä shä nä′) ⟦Heb *rosh-hashana,* lit., head (or first) of the year⟧ the Jewish New Year, celebrated on the 1st and 2d days of Tishri: also sp. **Rosh Hashona** or **Rosh Hashanah**

Ro·si·cru·cian (rō′zə kroo͞′shən, räz′ə-) ***n.*** ⟦*Rosicruc-* (< L *rosa,* a rose + *crux,* gen. *crucis,* a cross), Latinized form of the Ger name of the reputed founder, Christian *Rosenkreuz* + -IAN⟧ **1** any of a number of persons in the 17th and 18th cent. who professed to be members of a secret society said to have various sorts of occult lore and power **2** a member of any of several later groups with doctrines and practices said to be based on those of these persons; esp., the Rosicrucian Order, or the Ancient Mystic Order Rosae Crucis (AMORC) —***adj.*** of or characteristic of the Rosicrucians —**Ro′si·cru′cian·ism′** ***n.***

ros·i·ly (rō′zə lē) ***adv.*** **1** in a rosy manner; brightly; cheerfully; optimistically **2** with a rosy color

ros·in (räz′ən) ***n.*** ⟦ME, altered < MFr, *resine,* RESIN⟧ the hard, brittle resin, light-yellow to almost black in color, remaining after oil of turpentine has been distilled from crude turpentine or obtained from chemically treated pine stumps: it is used in making varnish, inks, soaps, insulation, etc., and is rubbed on violin bows to prevent slipping on the strings, or on the hands to prevent slipping on gymnastic equipment, etc. —***vt.*** to rub with rosin —**ros′in·ous** ***adj.***, **ros′in·y**

ros·i·ness (rō′zē nis) ***n.*** a rosy quality or state

rosin oil a viscous, odorless oil, obtained by the fractional distillation of rosin and used as a lubricant, etc.

☆**ros·in·weed** (räz′ən wēd′) ***n.*** **1** any of a genus (*Silphium*) of North American plants of the composite family that have resinous juice, sticky foliage, and strong odors, including the compass plant **2** any of several similar resinous plants

Ro·si·ta (rō zēt′ə) ***n.*** a feminine name: see ROSE

Ross[1] (rôs) ***n.*** ⟦< Gael *ros,* headland: surname and region in Scotland⟧ masculine name

Ross[2] (rôs) **1 Betsy** (Mrs. *Elizabeth Griscom Ross*) 1752-1836; Am. woman reputed to have made the first Am. flag with stars and stripes **2 Harold W(allace)** 1892-1951; U.S. magazine editor **3** Sir **James Clark** 1800-62; Brit. polar explorer **4** Sir **John** 1777-1856; Brit. arctic explorer, born in Scotland: uncle of Sir James **5** Sir **Ronald** 1857-1932; Eng. pathologist, born in India

Ross and Crom·ar·ty (rôs′ and kräm′ər tē) former county & former district of N Scotland

Ross Dependency ⟦see ROSS SEA⟧ region in Antarctica, south of New Zealand and south of 60° latitude: administered by New Zealand: *c.* 160,000 sq mi (414,398 sq km)

Ros·set·ti (rə zet′ē, -set′ē) **1 Christina (Georgina)** 1830-94; Eng. poet **2 Dante Gabriel** 1828-82; Eng. Pre-Raphaelite painter & poet: brother of Christina

Ross Ice Shelf frozen S section of the Ross Sea, between Victoria Land & Marie Byrd Land: also called **Ross Shelf Ice**

Ros·si·ni (rôs sē′nē; *E* rô sē′nē, rō-), **Gio·ac·chi·no (Antonio)** (jô′äk kē′nô) 1792-1868; It. composer

Ross Sea ⟦after Sir James Clark Ross[2], who discovered it⟧ arm of the Pacific, along the coast of Antarctica, east of Victoria Land

Ros·tand (rôs tän′), **Ed·mond** (ed mōn′) 1868-1918; Fr. dramatist & poet

ros·tel·late (räs′tə lāt′, -lit) ***adj.*** ⟦ModL *rostellatus* < *rostellum:* see fol.⟧ having a rostellum

ros·tel·lum (räs tel′əm) ***n.***, *pl.* **-la** (-ə) ⟦Modl < L, dim. of *rostrum:* see ROSTRUM⟧ **1** *Bot.* a sterile, flaplike modified stigma that separates the anthers from the stigmas in some orchids **2** *Zool. a)* a small, rounded projection bearing hooks on the head of certain tapeworms *b)* a beak-shaped, sucking mouthpart in certain insects —**ros·tel′lar** (-ər) ***adj.***

ros·ter (räs′tər) ***n.*** ⟦Du *rooster,* orig., gridiron (< *roosten,* to roast), hence a grating, list (from the ruled paper used in making lists)⟧ **1** a list of military or naval personnel or groups, specif. one showing their regular assignments and periods of duty **2** any similar list, as the list of active players on a sports team

Ros·tock (räs′täk′; *Ger* rôs′tôk′) seaport in NE Germany, on the Baltic, in the state of Mecklenburg-Western Pomerania

Ros·tov (rä′stäv′, -stôf′; *Russ* rô stôf′) city in SW Russia, at the mouth of the Don: also called **Ros′tov′-on-Don′** (-än dän′)

ros·tral (räs′trəl) ***adj.*** ⟦LL *rostralis*⟧ **1** of, in, or on a rostrum **2** decorated with rostrums, or beaks of ships [*rostral* pillars]

ros·trate (-trāt′) ***adj.*** ⟦L *rostratus*⟧ having a rostrum

ros·trum (räs′trəm) ***n.***, *pl.* **-trums** or **-tra** (-trə) ⟦L, beak, in pl., speakers' platform (see 1*b*) < *rosus,* pp. of *rodere,* to gnaw, peck: see RAT⟧ **1** in ancient Rome, *a)* a curved, beaklike projection at the prow of a ship; esp., such a projection on a war galley, used for ramming enemy vessels; beak *b)* the speakers' platform in the Forum, decorated with such beaks taken from captured ships **2** *a)* any platform, stage, etc. for public speaking *b)* public speaking, or public speakers collectively **3** *Biol.* a beak or beaklike part

Ros·well (räz′wel′) ⟦after *Roswell* Smith, whose son, Van C. Smith, settled there in 1871⟧ city in SE N.Mex.: near the reputed site of a crash (1947) of an aircraft thought by some to have been a UFO

ros·y (rō′zē) ***adj.*** **ros′i·er, ros′i·est** ⟦ME⟧ **1** like a rose, esp. in color; rose-red or pink; often, blushing or flushed with a healthy, blooming red [*rosy* cheeks] **2** [Archaic] made or consisting of, or adorned with, roses **3** bright, promising, cheerful, etc. [a *rosy* future]

rosy finch ☆any of a genus (*Leucosticte*) of finches of W North America and E Asia, with grayish to black plumage tinted bright pink on the wings, rump, tail, etc.

rot (rät) ***vi.*** **rot′ted, rot′ting** ⟦ME *roten* < OE *rotian,* akin to Du *rotten:* for IE base see ROTTEN⟧ **1** to decompose gradually by the action of bacteria, fungi, etc.; decay; spoil **2** to fall or pass (*off, away,* etc.) by decaying **3** to become unhealthy, sickly, etc. [to *rot* in prison] **4** to become morally corrupt; degenerate —***vt.*** **1** to cause to rot, or decompose **2** RET[1] —***n.*** ⟦ME < ON, akin to OE *rotian*⟧ **1** a rotting or being rotten; decay, decomposition, or putrefaction **2** a rotting or rotten thing or part **3** any of various diseases; esp., a necrotic inflammatory disease of specific organs or tissues of domestic animals, as foot rot **4** any of various plant diseases caused by fungi or bacteria and characterized by decay **5** [Slang] nonsense; rubbish; twaddle; bosh —***interj.*** nonsense: an exclamation of disgust, contempt, annoyance, etc. —**SYN.** DECAY

ro·ta (rōt′ə) ***n.*** ⟦L, wheel: see ROLL⟧ **1** [Chiefly Brit.] a roster, esp. one listing the rotation of duties **2** [**R-**] *R.C.Ch.* an ecclesiastical court of appeal in Rome, as for matrimonial cases

ro·tam·e·ter (rō tam′ət ər, rōt′ə mēt′ər) ***n.*** ⟦prec. + -METER⟧ an instrument for measuring the rate of flow of a fluid by means of a movable float inserted in a vertical tube

☆**Ro·tar·i·an** (rō ter′ē ən) ***n.*** a member of a Rotary Club —***adj.*** of Rotarians or Rotary Clubs —**Ro·tar′i·an·ism′** ***n.***

ro·ta·ry (rōt′ə rē) ***adj.*** ⟦ML *rotarius* < L *rota,* wheel: see ROLL⟧ **1** turning around a central point or axis, as a wheel; rotating **2** *a)* having a rotating part or parts *b)* having blades that rotate on a hub rather than a reel [a *rotary* lawn mower] **3** occurring around an axis [*rotary* motion] —***n.***, *pl.* **-ta·ries** **1** a rotary machine or engine **2** [**R-**] ROTARY CLUB ☆**3** TRAFFIC CIRCLE

☆**Rotary Club** any local organization of an international service club (**Rotary International**) of business and professional people, founded in Chicago in 1905

rotary engine **1** an engine in which rotary motion is produced directly, without reciprocating parts, as a steam turbine or Wankel engine **2** an early type of radial engine with the cylinders rotating around a stationary crankshaft

rotary press a printing press with curved plates mounted on cylinders that rotate against and print on paper fed either in individual sheets or from a continuous roll or web

ro·ta·ry-wing aircraft (-wiŋ′) an aircraft, as the helicopter, which is partly or wholly sustained in the air by lifting surfaces (*rotors*) revolving around a vertical axis

ro·tate (rō′tāt′, rō tāt′) ***vi., vt.*** **-tat′ed, -tat′ing** ⟦< L *rotatus,* pp. of *rotare,* to turn < *rota,* wheel: see ROLL⟧ **1** to turn around or cause to turn around a center point or axis; revolve **2** to go or cause to go in a regular and recurring succession of changes; take, or cause to take, turns [to *rotate* crops] —***adj.*** ⟦< L *rota,* wheel + -ATE[1]⟧ shaped like a wheel, with radiating parts, as the corolla of some flowers —**ro·tat·a·ble** (rō′tāt′ə bəl, rō tāt′-) ***adj.***

ro·ta·tion (rō tā′shən) ***n.*** ⟦L *rotatio*⟧ **1** a rotating or being rotated **2** the spinning motion around the axis of a celestial body: cf. REVOLUTION (sense 1*a*) **3** regular and recurring succession of changes [a *rotation* of duties] ☆**4** *Pool* a game in which the balls must be pocketed in the order of their numbers —**ro·ta′tion·al** ***adj.***

rotation of crops CROP ROTATION

ro·ta·tive (rō′tāt′iv, rō tāt′iv, rōt′ə tiv) ***adj.*** **1** rotating or occurring in rotation **2** of, causing, or caused by rotation —**ro′ta·tive·ly** ***adv.***

ro·ta·tor (rō′tāt′ər) ***n.*** **1** a person or thing that rotates **2** *pl.* **ro·ta·tor·es** (rō′tə tôr′ēz′) *Anat.* a muscle that serves to rotate a part of the body

rotator cuff a group of muscles, under the deltoid muscle, covering the shoulder joint and connecting the humerus to the scapula: it controls shoulder rotation

ro·ta·to·ry (rōt′ə tôr′ē) ***adj.*** **1** of, or having the nature of, rotation **2** that rotates; rotary **3** going or following in rotation **4** causing rotation

ro·ta·vi·rus (rōt′ə vī′rəs) ***n.*** ⟦ModL < L *rota,* a wheel (see ROLL, ***n.***) + VIRUS⟧ any of a genus (*Rotavirus*) of wheel-shaped reoviruses that cause gastroenteritis, esp. in infants

ROTC *abbrev.* Reserve Officers' Training Corps

rotche or **rotch** (räch) ***n.*** ⟦for earlier *rotge* < Du *rotje,* brant goose, prob. via Fl *rotgoes* < Norw *ròtgås* < ON *hrotgás* < **hrot-,* echoic of its cry + *gás,* akin to OE *gos,* GOOSE⟧ DOVEKIE

rote[1] (rōt) ***n.*** ⟦ME < ?⟧ a fixed, mechanical way of doing something; routine —***adj.*** of or having to do with learning through memorization —**by rote** by means of memorization; specif., by means of the mechanical repetition of facts as a method of memorizing them [to learn the multiplication table *by rote*]

rote[2] (rōt) ***n.*** ⟦prob. via ME dial. < Scand, as in ON *rauta,* to roar, akin to OHG *rōz,* a weeping, wailing: for IE base see RAUCOUS⟧ the sound of the surf beating on the shore

rote[3] (rōt) ***n.*** ⟦ME < OFr < Frank **hrōta* (akin to OHG *hrotta*) < Celt *chrotta* > Welsh *crwth,* CROWD[2]⟧ a medieval stringed instrument, variously supposed to have been a kind of lyre, lute, or harp

ro·te·none (rōt′'n ōn′) ***n.*** ⟦Jpn *roten,* derris + -ONE⟧ a white, odorless, crystalline substance, $C_{23}H_{22}O_6$, obtained from the roots of certain plants, as derris and cube, and used in insecticides

rot·gut (rät′gut′) ***n.*** ⟦ROT + GUT⟧ ☆[Slang] raw, low-grade whiskey or other liquor

Roth·er·ham (räth′ər əm) city in South Yorkshire, NC England

Roth IRA (rôth, räth) ⟦after Senator W. V. *Roth* (1921-2003), Senate Finance Committee chairman who sponsored legislation creating this kind of account⟧ *see* IRA[1]

Roth·ko (räth′kō′), **Mark** (born *Marcus Rothkovich*) 1903-70; U.S. painter, born in Russia

Roth·schild[1] (rôth′chīld′, rôths′-, räth′-, räths′-; *Ger* rōt′shilt′) ***n.*** name of a family of European bankers

Roth·schild[2] (rôth′chīld′, rôths′-, räth′-, räths′-; *Ger* rōt′shilt′) **1 Mey·er An·selm** (mī′ər än′zelm) 1743-1812; Ger. founder of the banking house of Rothschild: also **Meyer Am·schel** (äm′shəl) **2 Nathan Meyer** 1777-1836; Eng. banker, born in Germany: son of Meyer Anselm

ro·ti (rō′tē) ***n.*** ⟦Hindi⟧ a soft, round flat bread of India, often served wrapped around a filling as of curried meat

rô·ti (rō tē′) ***n.*** ⟦Fr < pp. of *rôtir,* to roast < MFr *rostir* < OFr: see ROAST⟧ ROAST (***n.*** 1)

ro·ti·fer (rōt′ə fər) ***n.*** ⟦ModL < L *rota,* wheel + -FER⟧ any of a phylum (Rotifera) of microscopic invertebrate animals found mostly in fresh waters, having one or more rings of cilia at the front end of the body that, when vibrated, resemble rotating wheels —**ro·tif·er·al** (rō tif′ər əl) ***adj.***, **ro·tif′er·ous** (-əs) —**ro·tif′er·an** ***adj., n.***

ro·ti·form (-fôrm′) ***adj.*** ⟦ModL *rotiformis* < L *rota,* wheel + *-formis,* -FORM⟧ shaped like a wheel

☆**ro·tis·ser·ie** (rō tis′ər ē) ***n.*** ⟦Fr < MFr *rostisserie* < *rostisseur,* one who roasts meats for sale < *rostir,* to ROAST⟧ **1** a shop where meats are roasted and sold **2** a grill with an electrically turned spit —***adj.*** ⟦< *Rotisserie League Baseball,* a trademark for such a game⟧ designating or of a sports fantasy league, game, etc.

rot·l (rät′'l) ***n., pl.* rot′ls** or **ar·tal** (är′täl′) ⟦Ar *raṭl*⟧ a unit of weight used in Muslim regions, varying locally from about one to about five pounds

☆**ro·to** (rōt′ō) ***n., pl.* -tos** *short for* ROTOGRAVURE

☆**ro·to·gra·vure** (rōt′ə grə vyoor′) ***n.*** ⟦< L *rota,* wheel + GRAVURE⟧ **1** a printing process using photogravure cylinders on a rotary press **2** a print or newspaper pictorial section printed by this process

ro·tor (rōt′ər) ***n.*** ⟦contr. of ROTATOR⟧ **1** any of various rotating mechanical parts; specif., *a)* the rotating part of a motor, dynamo, etc. (cf. STATOR) *b)* in the distributor of a gasoline engine, the part that momentarily connects each spark plug wire to the high voltage from the coil *c)* in disc brakes, the part to which the wheel is usually mounted **2** a system of airfoils, together with their hub, that rotates around a vertical axis, as on a helicopter

ro·tor·craft (-kraft′, -kräft′) ***n.*** ROTARY-WING AIRCRAFT: also **rotor plane**

☆**ro·to·till·er** (rōt′ə til′ər) ***n.*** ⟦E *roto-* (< L *rota,* a wheel: see ROLL, ***n.***) + TILLER[2]⟧ a motorized cultivator that loosens the soil by means of rotary blades —**ro′to·till′ *vt.***

rot·ten (rät′'n) ***adj.*** ⟦ME *roten* < ON *rotinn* < IE **reud-* < base **reu-,* to tear, rip open (> RUDE): prob. used orig. of flax left to soak and rot⟧ **1** in a decayed or decomposed state; spoiled, putrefied, tainted, etc. **2** having a bad odor because of decomposition or decay; putrid; foul-smelling **3** morally corrupt or offensive; dishonest, open to bribery, etc. **4** unsound or weak, as if decayed within **5** soft or easily broken as because of decomposition; friable: said of rocks, ice, etc. **6** [Slang] very bad, unsatisfactory, nasty, etc. —**rot′ten·ly** ***adv.*** —**rot′ten·ness** ***n.***

rotten borough **1** in England (before the Reform Act of 1832), a borough with only a few voters but with the right to send a representative to Parliament **2** any electoral district or political unit with greater representation than its population warrants

rot·ten·stone (rät′'n stōn′) ***n.*** a siliceous limestone decomposed to a friable state, used for polishing metals

rot·ter (rät′ər) ***n.*** ⟦< ROT⟧ [Slang, Chiefly Brit.] a despicable fellow; cad, bounder, etc.

Rot·ter·dam (rät′ər dam′; *Du* rô′tər däm′) seaport in SW Netherlands, in the Rhine delta

Rott·weil·er (rät′wī′lər, rôt′vī′lər) ⟦after *Rottweil,* town in S Germany where orig. used for herding⟧ ***n.*** any of a breed of large, strong dog with a short tail and short, black hair with tan markings

ro·tund (rō tund′) ***adj.*** ⟦L *rotundus,* akin to *rota,* wheel: see ROLL⟧ **1** round or rounded out; plump or stout **2** full-toned; sonorous [a *rotund* voice] —**ro·tun′di·ty** ***n.***, **ro·tund′ness** —**ro·tund′ly** ***adv.***

ro·tun·da (rō tun′də) ***n.*** ⟦It *rotonda* < L *rotunda,* fem. of *rotundus:* see prec.⟧ a round building, hall, or room, esp. one with a dome

Rou·ault (rōō ō′), **Georges** (zhôrzh) 1871-1958; Fr. painter

rou·ble (rōō′bəl) ***n.*** *alt. sp. of* RUBLE

rou·é (rōō ā′, rōō′ā′) ***n.*** ⟦Fr, pp. of *rouer,* to break on the wheel < L *rota,* wheel (see ROLL): said orig. to be used (*c.* 1720) of the dissolute companions of the Duc d'Orléans⟧ a dissipated man; debauchee; rake

Rou·en (rōō än′; *Fr* rwän) city & port in NW France, on the Seine

rouge[1] (rōōzh) ***n.*** ⟦Fr < the adj., red < L *rubeus,* reddish: see see RUBY⟧ **1** any of various reddish cosmetics in powder, paste, or liquid form, esp. a red or reddish cream, for adding color to the cheeks or lips: a cosmetic used esp. formerly: cf. BLUSH (***n.*** 3) **2** a reddish powder, mainly ferric oxide, for polishing jewelry, metal, etc. —***vt.* rouged, roug′ing** to color with rouge —***vi.*** to use cosmetic rouge

rouge[2] (rōōzh) ***n.*** ⟦orig. slang term at Eton, a scrimmage < ?⟧ in Canadian football, the scoring of a point by the team that is punting when the receiving team takes the ball behind the goal line and does not run it back into the field of play — ***vi., vt.* rouged, roug′ing** to carry out or cause to carry out a rouge

rouge et noir (rōōzh′ ā nwär′) ⟦Fr, red and black⟧ a gambling game in which the betting is on two groups of cards, designated red and black, that are dealt face up

Rou·get de Lisle (rōō zhed lēl′), **Claude Jo·seph** (klōd zhō zef′) 1760-1836; Fr. army officer & composer: wrote the *Marseillaise:* also **Rouget de L'Isle**

rough (ruf) ***adj.*** ⟦ME *ruh, rugh* < OE *ruh,* akin to Ger *rauh* < IE **reuk* < base **reu-,* to tear, tear out (> RUG, ROTTEN): prob. basic sense "hairy, woolly"⟧ **1** *a)* not smooth or level; having bumps, projections, etc.; uneven [a *rough* surface] *b)* not easily traveled over or through because rocky, overgrown, wild, etc. [*rough* country] **2** shaggy or bristly [an animal with a *rough* coat] **3** characterized by violent action, motion, agitation, disturbance, or irregularity; specif., *a)* stormy; tempestuous [*rough* weather] *b)* boisterous or disorderly [*rough* play] **4** harsh, rude, brutal, etc.; not gentle or mild [a *rough* temper] **5** sounding harsh; discordant; jarring **6** tasting harsh or astringent [*rough* wine] **7** coarse, as texture, cloth, food, etc. **8** *a)* coarse in manner, tastes, etc.; lacking refinement or culture [*rough* men, *rough* language] *b)* regarded as being risky, dangerous, offensive, etc., often as a result of lacking in conventional social controls [a *rough* crowd, neighborhood, etc.] **9** lacking refinements, comforts, and conveniences [the *rough* life of a pioneer] **10** not refined, polished, or prepared; natural, crude, etc. [a *rough* diamond] **11** not finished, elaborated, perfected, etc. [a *rough* sketch] **12** not worked out in detail; without claim to be exact or complete; approximate [a *rough* estimate] **13** requiring muscular energy rather than skill or intelligence [*rough* labor] **14** [Informal] difficult, severe, or disagreeable [a *rough* time] **15** *Phonet.* articulated with an aspirate; having the sound (h) —***n.*** **1** rough ground **2** rough material or condition **3** the rough part, aspect, etc. of something ☆**4** a rough sketch or draft **5** [Chiefly Brit.] a rough person; rowdy; tough **6** *Golf* any part of the course where grass, weeds, etc. are allowed to grow, uncut, forming a hazard or obstacle —***adv.*** **1** in a rough manner; roughly **2** [Brit.] without shelter; outdoors [to sleep *rough*] —***vt.*** **1** to make rough; roughen: often with *up* **2** *a)* to handle or treat roughly or brutally (usually with *up*) *b) Football, etc.* to subject (an opponent) to intentional and unnecessary roughness **3** to make, fashion, sketch, shape, or cut roughly: usually with *in* or *out* [to *rough* out a scheme] **4** to apply some preparatory or preliminary process or treatment to —***vi.*** **1** [Rare] to become rough **2** to behave roughly [a penalty for *roughing*] —**in the rough** in a rough or crude state —**rough it** to live without customary comforts and conveniences, as in camping —**rough′ish** ***adj.*** —**rough′ly** ***adv.*** —**rough′ness** ***n.***

☆**rough·age** (ruf′ij) ***n.*** rough material; coarse substance; specif., coarse food or fodder, as bran, straw, vegetable peel, etc., containing a relatively high proportion of cellulose and other indigestible constituents and serving in the diet as a stimulus to peristalsis

rough-and-read·y (ruf′ən red′ē) ***adj.*** **1** rough, or crude, rude, unpolished, etc., but effective enough [*rough-and-ready* methods] **2** characterized by rough vigor and prompt action rather than refinement, formality, or nicety [a *rough-and-ready* fellow]

rough-and-tum·ble (-tum′bəl) ***adj.*** violent and disorderly, with no concern for rules [a *rough-and-tumble* fight] —***n.*** a fight or struggle of this kind

rough bluegrass a cultivated bluegrass (*Poa trivialis*) often grown in shady or moist spots as a lawn grass

rough breathing ⟦transl. of L *spiritus asper*⟧ **1** in written Greek, the mark (ʽ) placed over an initial vowel or ρ (rho) to show that in ancient Greek it was pronounced with a preceding (h) sound, or aspirate **2** the sound thus indicated

rough·cast (ruf′kast′, -käst′) ***n.*** **1** a coarse stucco for covering outside surfaces, as walls **2** a rough pattern or form, or crudely made model —***vt.* -cast′, -cast′ing** **1** to cover (walls, etc.) with roughcast **2** to make or shape in a rough form

rough-dry (-drī′) ***vt.* -dried′, -dry′ing** to dry (washed laundry) without ironing: also written **roughdry** —***adj.*** washed and dried but not ironed

rough·en (ruf′ən) ***vt., vi.*** to make or become rough

rough fish any fish that is not a game fish and that has no commercial value

rough-hew (-hyōō′) ***vt.* -hewed′, -hewed′** or **-hewn′, -hew′ing** **1** to hew (timber, stone, etc.) roughly, or without finishing or smoothing **2** to form roughly; give crude shape to Also written **roughhew**

☆**rough·house** (ruf′hous′) ***n.*** [Old Slang] rough, boisterous, or rowdy play, fighting, etc., esp. indoors —***vt.* -housed′, -hous′ing** [Old Slang] to treat (a person) roughly or boisterously —***vi.*** [Informal] to take part, esp. indoors, in rough, boisterous, or rowdy play, fighting, etc. —**rough′hous′ing** ***n.***

☆**rough-leg·ged hawk** (-leg′id, -legd′; -lā′gid, -lāgd′) a large hawk (*Buteo lagopus*) having legs covered with feathers to the base of the toes

☆**rough·neck** (-nek′) *n.* **1** [Informal] a rough, crude person, esp. one who is quarrelsome and disorderly; rowdy **2** a worker on an oil drilling rig, esp. a member of the crew which feeds pipe into the well —*vi.* to work as a roughneck —**rough·neck′ing** *n.*

rough·rid·er (-rīd′ər) *n.* **1** a person who breaks horses so that they can be ridden **2** a person who does much hard, rough riding ☆**3** [**R-**] a member of a volunteer cavalry regiment organized by Theodore Roosevelt and Leonard Wood for service in the Spanish American War (1898): also written **Rough Rider**

rough·shod (-shäd′) *adj.* shod with horseshoes that have calks, or metal points, to prevent slipping —**ride roughshod over** to treat in a harsh, arrogant, inconsiderate manner; domineer over

rough trade [Slang] tough, brutal, or sadistic homosexual men, esp. when available for casual sexual activity

rouille (ro͞o ē′) *n.* ⟦Fr, lit., rust: so named from its color⟧ a creamy sauce of garlic and hot red pepper

rou·lade (ro͞o läd′) *n.* ⟦Fr < *rouler,* to ROLL⟧ **1** a musical ornament consisting of a rapid succession of tones sung to one syllable **2** a slice of meat rolled, usually with a filling of minced meat, and cooked

rou·leau (ro͞o lō′) *n., pl.* **-leaux′** (-lōz′) or **-leaus′** ⟦Fr, dim. of *rôle,* a ROLL⟧ **1** a small roll of something; esp., a roll of coins, generally of the same denomination, stacked in a paper wrapper **2** a roll or fold, as of ribbon for trimming hats, etc.

rou·lette (ro͞o let′) *n.* ⟦Fr < OFr *roelette,* dim. of *roele,* small wheel < LL *rotella,* dim. < L *rota,* wheel: see ROLL⟧ **1** a gambling game played by rolling a small ball around a shallow bowl with an inner disk (**roulette wheel**) revolving in the opposite direction: the ball finally comes to rest in one of the red or black, numbered compartments into which this disk is divided, thus determining the winning bets **2** a small toothed wheel attached to a handle, for making rows of marks or dots, as in engraving, or incisions, as between postage stamps **3** a series of small, consecutive incisions made in the paper between the stamps in a sheet of stamps, to facilitate their separation —*vt.* **-let′ted, -let′ting** to make marks, dots, or incisions in or on with a roulette

roulette wheel

Rou·ma·ni·a (ro͞o mā′nē ə, -mān′yə) *var. of* ROMANIA —**Rou·ma′ni·an** *adj., n.*

Rou·me·li·a (ro͞o mē′lē ə, -mēl′yə) *alt. sp. of* RUMELIA

round[1] (round) *adj.* ⟦ME < OFr *roont* < L *rotundus:* see ROTUND⟧ **1** shaped like a ball; spherical; globular **2** *a)* shaped like a circle, ring, or disk; circular *b)* shaped like a cylinder (in having a circular cross section); cylindrical **3** curved in shape like part of a sphere or circle **4** not angular; plump or stout **5** involving, or done in or with, a circular motion [*a round* dance] **6** *a)* not lacking part; full; complete [*a round* dozen] *b)* completed; perfected **7** completed by progressing through a course which, as if circular, returns to the starting point [*a round* trip] **8** constituting, or expressed by, a whole number, or integer; not fractional **9** expressed in units divisible by ten, one hundred, etc., rather than exactly [500 is a *round* number for 498, 503, etc.] **10** large in amount, size, etc.; considerable [*a round* sum] **11** mellow and full in tone; sonorous [rich *round* tones] **12** brisk; vigorous and rapid [*a round* pace] **13** outspoken; plain and blunt; straightforward **14** *Phonet.* articulated with the lips forming a circular or oval opening; rounded [*a round* vowel] —*n.* **1** something round or rounded; thing or part that is spherical, globular, circular, curved, annular, or cylindrical **2** *a)* a rung of a ladder *b)* a crossbar connecting the legs of a chair **3** the rounded part of the thigh of a beef animal, between the rump and the leg **4** movement in a circular course or about an axis **5** ROUND DANCE **6** a series or succession of actions, events, etc. that is completed at, or as if at, the point where it began [*a round* of parties] **7** the complete extent; whole range [the *round* of human beliefs] **8** [*often pl.*] a regular, customary course or circuit, as by a watchman of a station, a doctor of hospital patients, a drinker of a number of bars, etc. **9** a single serving, as of drinks, to each of a group **10** *a)* a single shot from each of a number of rifles, artillery pieces, etc. fired together, or a shot from a single gun (cf. SALVO[1]) *b)* ammunition for a single shot; cartridge, shell, etc. **11** a single outburst, as of applause, cheering, etc.; salvo **12** a circular slice, as of bread **13** *Archery* a specified number of arrows shot at a target from a specified distance according to the rules **14** *Games, Sports* a single period or division of action, usually one of a series [*a round* of poker]; specif., *a) Boxing* any of the timed periods of a fight; a round is now generally limited to three minutes, and the interval between rounds to one minute *b) Golf* a number of holes as a unit of competition, esp. eighteen **15** *Music a)* a short song for two or more voices, in which the second starts when the first reaches the second phrase, etc. and upon concluding each voice begins again, as in a canon *b)* [*pl.*] the ringing in sequence of a set of bells from the smallest to the largest, in change ringing —*vt.* **1** to make round: often with *off* **2** to deprive of angularity or make plump: usually with *out* **3** to express as or convert to a round number: usually with *off* or *up* or *down* [to *round* 9.5 up to 10 or down to 9]: see *adj.* 9 **4** to complete; finish; perfect: usually with *out* or *off* **5** to make a circuit of; pass around [we *rounded* the island] **6** to make a turn about [to *round* a corner] **7** to cause to move in a circular course **8** [Now Rare] to encircle; surround **9** *Phonet.* to articulate with the lips forming a circular or oval opening —*vi.* **1** to make a complete or partial circuit; move in a curved or circular course **2** *a)* to turn; reverse direction *b)* to attack or oppose suddenly or unexpectedly; turn (*on*) **3** to become round or plump: often with *out* **4** to develop (*into*) [the talk *rounded* into a plan] —*adv.* **1** AROUND (*adv.* 1 & 3) **2** for each of several; to include all in a group [not enough to go *round*] **3** by a circuitous course; in a roundabout way **4** with a rotating or revolving movement —*prep.* AROUND In the U.S., *round* (*adv. & prep.*) is generally superseded by *around;* in Great Britain, *round* is preferred for most senses See also phrases under BRING, COME, etc. —**go the round (or rounds) 1** to be circulated among a number of people: said of a story, rumor, etc. **2** to walk one's regular course or circuit, as a watchman does: also **make one's rounds** —**in the round 1** with the audience or congregation seated all around a central stage, altar, etc.: cf. ARENA THEATER **2** in full and completely rounded form, not in relief: said of sculpture **3** in full and realistic detail —**out of round** not having perfect roundness —**round about 1** in or to the opposite direction **2** in every direction around —**round in** *Naut.* to haul in on (a line) —**round to** *Naut.* to turn the bow of a vessel into the wind —**round up** ☆**1** to drive (cattle, horses, etc.) together; collect in a herd, group, etc. ☆**2** [Informal] to gather, collect, or assemble —**round′ness** *n.*

SYN.—**round**, the most inclusive of these words, applies to anything shaped like a circle, sphere, or cylinder, or like a part of any of these; **spherical** applies to a round body or mass having the surface equally distant from the center at all points; **globular** is used of things that are ball-shaped but not necessarily perfect spheres; **circular** is applied to round lines, or round flat surfaces, in the shape of a ring or disk, and it may or may not imply correspondence in form with a perfect circle; **annular** applies to ringlike forms or structures, as the markings in a cross section of a tree

round[2] (round) *vt., vi.* ⟦ME *rounen* (+ unhistoric *-d*) < OE *runian,* to whisper: see RUNE⟧ [Obs.] to whisper (to)

round·a·bout (roun′də bout′) *adj.* **1** not straight or straightforward; indirect; circuitous [*roundabout* answers] **2** encircling; enclosing; surrounding —*n.* **1** something that is indirect or circuitous ☆**2** a short, tight jacket or coat formerly worn by men and boys **3** [Brit.] *a)* TRAFFIC CIRCLE *b)* MERRY-GO-ROUND

round angle an angle of 360°

☆**round clam** QUAHOG

round dance 1 a dance with the dancers arranged or moving in a circle **2** any of several dances, as the waltz, polka, fox trot, etc., performed by couples and characterized by revolving or circular movements

round·ed (roun′did) *adj.* **1** made round **2** developed or diversified, in regard to tastes, abilities, etc.: often in hyphenated compounds [*a well-rounded* person] **3** *Phonet.* articulated with the lips forming a circular or oval opening; labialized —**round′ed·ness** *n.*

roun·del (roun′dəl) *n.* ⟦ME < OFr *rondel,* orig. dim. of *roont,* ROUND[1]⟧ **1** [Archaic or Rare] something round, or circular **2** a round ornamental panel, plate, niche, etc. **3** a small, round window or pane **4** *a)* [Archaic] a rondeau *b)* an English variation of the rondeau, with eleven lines (three stanzas), the fourth and eleventh being the refrain **5** ROUNDELAY (sense 2)

roun·de·lay (roun′də lā′) *n.* ⟦MFr *rondelet,* dim. of *rondel:* see prec.⟧ **1** *a)* a simple song in which some phrase, line, etc. is continually repeated *b)* music for such a song **2** a dance in a circle; roundel

round·er (roun′dər) *n.* **1** [Obs.] a person who makes a round or rounds, as a watchman **2** a person or thing that rounds; specif., a tool for rounding corners or edges **3** [*pl., with sing. v.*] a British game somewhat like baseball ☆**4** ⟦from the idea of making the rounds of bars, etc.⟧ [Old Informal] a dissolute person or drunkard

round hand careful handwriting in which the letters are rounded, distinct, full, and almost vertical

Round·head (round′hed′) *n.* a member or supporter of the Parliamentary, or Puritan, party in England during the English civil war (1642-52): originally a derisive term, with reference to the Puritans' close-cropped hair in contrast to the Cavaliers' long hair

round·heels (round′hēlz′) *n.* ⟦from the notion that wearing shoes with rounded heels makes it difficult to remain standing: orig. used of an easily beaten prizefighter⟧ [Old Slang] a woman who consents readily to sexual intercourse: also **round′heel′**

round·house (round′hous′) *n.* ⟦orig., a lockup, after Du *rondhuis,* guardhouse⟧ ☆**1** a circular building, with a turntable in the center, used for storing and repairing locomotives **2** a cabin on the after part of the quarterdeck on old sailing ships ☆**3** *Baseball a)* a pitch with a wide curve *b) Boxing* a wide swing or hook, as to the head ☆**4** *Card Games* in pinochle, a meld consisting of a king and queen of each of the four suits

round·ish (roun′dish) *adj.* somewhat round

round·let (round′lit) *n.* ⟦ME *roundelet* < MFr *rondelet:* see ROUNDELAY⟧ a small circle or circular thing

☆**round lot** the unit, or a multiple thereof, in which securities, commodities, etc. are typically traded; specif., 100 shares of stock in a transaction: cf. ODD LOT

round·ly (round′lē) *adv.* **1** in a round form; circularly, spherically, etc. **2** in a round manner; specif., *a)* vigorously, bluntly, severely, etc. [he was *roundly* rebuked] *b)* fully; completely and thoroughly

round of beef ROUND[1] (*n.* 3)

round robin ⟦ROUND[1] + pers. name *Robin*⟧ **1** a document, as a petition, protest, etc., with the signatures written in a circle to conceal the order of signing **2** a contest or tournament, as in tennis, chess, etc., in which every entrant is matched with every other one **3** a letter circulated among the members of a group, which is signed and forwarded by each in turn, often with additional comments, etc.

Round Rock city in central Tex., near Austin

round-shoul·dered (round′shōl′dərd) ***adj.*** stooped because the shoulders are bent forward

rounds·man (roundz′mən) ***n., pl.*** **-men** (-mən) a person who makes rounds, esp. of inspection

round steak a steak cut from a round of beef

round·ta·ble (round′tā′bəl) ***n.*** ⟦< fol.⟧ **1** a group gathered together for an informal discussion or conference **2** such a discussion or conference —***adj.*** of or pertaining to a roundtable

Round Table *Arthurian Legend* **1** the large table around which King Arthur and his knights sit: it is circular to avoid disputes about precedence **2** King Arthur and his knights, collectively

round-the-clock (round′thə kläk′) ***adj., adv.*** throughout the day and night; without interruption

☆**round trip 1** a trip to a place and back again **2** ROUNDHOUSE (sense 4) —**round′-trip′** ***adj.***

round-trip·per (round′trip′ər) ***n.*** ☆[Slang] *Baseball* a home run

round turn one complete turn, as of a rope, around something

round·up (round′up′) ***n.*** ☆**1** *a)* the act of driving cattle, etc. together on the range and collecting them in a herd, as for branding, inspection, or shipping *b)* the herd of cattle, etc. thus collected *c)* the cowboys, horses, etc. that do this work ☆**2** any similar driving together, collecting, or gathering *[a roundup* of suspected persons*]* ☆**3** a summary, as of information, news, etc.

round·worm (round′wurm′) ***n.*** NEMATODE

roup (ro͞op) ***n.*** ⟦prob. akin to or < MFr *roupie,* snivel < ?⟧ an infectious disease of poultry, characterized by mucous discharge from the eyes and nasal passages —**roup′y** ***adj.*** **roup′i·er, roup′i·est**

rouse[1] (rouz) ***vt.*** **roused, rous′ing** ⟦LME *rowsen:* orig. technical term in hawking & hunting, hence prob. < Anglo-Fr or OFr⟧ **1** to cause (game) to rise from cover, come out of a lair, etc.; stir up to flight or attack **2** to stir up, as to anger or action; excite **3** to cause to come out of a state of sleep, repose, unconsciousness, etc.; wake **4** *Naut.* to pull with force, esp. by hand; haul —***vi.*** **1** to rise from cover, etc.: said of game **2** to come out of a state of sleep, repose, etc.; wake **3** to become active —***n.*** **1** the act of rousing **2** a violent stir —***SYN.*** STIR[1] —**rous′er** ***n.***

rouse[2] (rouz) ***n.*** ⟦aphetic for CAROUSE (from mistaking *drink carouse* as *drink a rouse*)⟧ [Archaic] **1** a drink of liquor **2** a carousal

rous·ing (rou′ziŋ) ***adj.*** **1** that rouses; stirring *[a rousing* speech*]* **2** very active or lively; vigorous; brisk *[a rousing* business*]* **3** extraordinary; remarkable —**rous′ing·ly** ***adv.***

Rous·seau (ro͞o sō′) **1 Hen·ri** (än rē′) 1844-1910; Fr. primitive painter: called *Le Douanier* (The Customs Officer) **2 Jean Jacques** (zhän zhäk) 1712-78; Fr. political philosopher & writer, born in Switzerland **3 (Pierre Étienne) Thé·o·dore** (tā ô dôr′) 1812-67; Fr. landscape painter

Rous·sil·lon (ro͞o sē yōn′) historical region of S France bordering on the Pyrenees & the Gulf of Lions

roust (roust) ***vt.*** ⟦dial. form of ROUSE[1] with unhistoric *-t*⟧ **1** to rouse or stir (*up*) **2** to rout or drive (*out*)

roust·a·bout (rous′tə bout′) ***n.*** ⟦prec. + ABOUT⟧ ☆**1** a deckhand or waterfront laborer ☆**2** a laborer in a circus who helps set up the tents, etc. ☆**3** an unskilled or transient laborer, as on a ranch or in an oil field

rout[1] (rout) ***n.*** ⟦ME *route* < OFr, troop, band, lit., part broken off < L *rupta:* see ROUTE⟧ **1** a disorderly crowd; noisy mob; rabble **2** a disorderly flight or retreat, as of defeated troops *[to be put to rout]* **3** an overwhelming defeat **4** [Archaic] *a)* a group of people; company; band *b)* a band of followers; retinue **5** [Archaic] a large, fashionable social gathering in the evening —***vt.*** **1** to put to disorderly flight **2** to defeat overwhelmingly —***SYN.*** CONQUER

rout[2] (rout) ***vi.*** ⟦var. of ROOT[2]⟧ **1** to dig for food with the snout, as a pig; root **2** to poke or rummage about —***vt.*** **1** to dig up or turn over with the snout **2** to force out —**rout out 1** to expose to view **2** to scoop, gouge, or hollow out (metal, wood, etc.) **3** to make (a person) get out —**rout up 1** to find or get by turning up or poking about ☆**2** to make (a person) get up

route (ro͞ot, rout) ***n.*** ⟦ME < OFr *route, rote* < L *rupta (via),* (path) broken through < fem. of *ruptus,* pp. of *rumpere,* to break: see RUPTURE⟧ **1** a road, way, or course for traveling; esp., a highway **2** a course taken to achieve some end *[an unorthodox career route]* ☆**3** *a)* a regular course traveled as in delivering mail, milk, newspapers, etc. *b)* a set of customers whom one regularly visits to make deliveries, solicit sales, etc. **4** [Archaic] an order for troops to march —***vt.*** **rout′ed, rout′ing** ☆**1** to direct, send, forward, or transport by a specified route *[to route* goods through Omaha*]* ☆**2** to fix the order of procedure of (a series of operations, etc.) *[to route* orders through the sales department*]* —☆**go the route** [Informal] *Baseball* to pitch an entire game

rout·er[1] (rout′ər) ***n.*** ⟦see ROUT[2]⟧ a person or thing that routs out or a tool for routing out; specif., *a)* a plane for gouging out recesses and smoothing the bottoms of grooves (in full **router plane**) *b)* a machine for routing out areas on a wood or metal surface

rout·er[2] (rout′ər) ***n.*** ⟦< ROUTE⟧ a person or thing that routes; specif., a device that coordinates the transmission of data packets within and between computer networks: see PACKET (***n.*** 5)

rou·tine (ro͞o tēn′) ***n.*** ⟦Fr < *route:* see ROUTE⟧ **1** a regular, more or less unvarying procedure, customary, prescribed, or habitual, as of business or daily life **2** such procedure in general *[to dislike routine]* **3** a theatrical skit or act ☆**4** a series of steps, bodily movements, etc. in a dance performance, in gymnastics, etc. **5** a set of computer instructions for performing a specific operation —***adj.*** having the nature of, using, or by routine —**rou·tine′ly** ***adv.***

rou·ti·nier (ro͞o tē nyā′) ***n.*** ⟦Fr⟧ a person who adheres to a routine; esp., a competent but uninspired orchestra conductor

rou·tin·ism (ro͞o tēn′iz′əm) ***n.*** adherence to or prevalence of routine —**rou·tin′ist** ***n.***

☆**rou·tin·ize** (ro͞ot′'n īz′, ro͞o tē′nīz′) ***vt.*** **-ized′, -iz′ing** to make routine; reduce to a routine —**rou′tin·i·za′tion** ***n.***

roux (ro͞o) ***n.*** ⟦Fr *roux (beurre),* reddish-brown (butter) < L *russus:* see RUSSET⟧ a cooked mixture of melted butter (or other fat) and flour, used for thickening sauces, soups, gravies, etc.

ROV (är′ō′vē′) ***n., pl.*** **ROVs** ⟦*r(emotely) o(perated) v(ehicle)*⟧ any of various unmanned robotic devices operated remotely and used in underwater research and maintenance

rove[1] (rōv) ***vi.*** **roved, rov′ing** ⟦ME *roven,* orig. an archery term as vt. < ?⟧ **1** to wander about; go from place to place, esp. over an extensive area, with no particular course or destination; roam **2** to look around: often used fig., as to suggest sexual unfaithfulness *[a husband with a roving* eye*]* —***vt.*** to wander over; roam through *[to rove* the woods*]* —***n.*** the act of roving; a ramble

rove[2] (rōv) ***vt.*** **roved, rov′ing** ⟦< ?⟧ to twist (fibers) together and draw out into roving before spinning —***n.*** *Brit. var. of* ROVING

rove[3] (rōv) ***vt.*** *alt. pt. & pp. of* REEVE[2]

rove beetle any of a large family (Staphylinidae) of swiftly moving beetles with a long, slender body and very short elytra: they feed chiefly on decomposing organic matter

rov·en (rō′vən) ***vt.*** *alt. pp. of* REEVE[2]

rov·er[1] (rō′vər) ***n.*** ⟦ROVE[1] + -ER⟧ **1** a person, animal, or thing that roves, or wanders **2** *Archery* *a)* a mark, or target, chosen at random *b)* any of several set marks for distance shooting *c)* an archer who shoots for distance **3** [**R-**] a traditional name for a pet dog: sometimes used informally to refer to the typical pet dog **4** *a)* LUNAR ROVER *b)* an unmanned robotic vehicle equipped with cameras, etc. and designed for use as in exploring the surface of an extraterrestrial planet or the ocean floor

rov·er[2] (rō′vər) ***n.*** ⟦ME < MDu, robber < *roven,* to rob (for IE base see RUPTURE): prob. merged with prec.⟧ [Archaic] a pirate or pirate ship

rov·er[3] (rō′vər) ***n.*** **1** a person who operates a machine for roving fibers **2** such a machine

rov·ing (-viŋ) ***n.*** ⟦< ROVE[2]⟧ **1** the strand of twisted and drawn-out fibers of cotton, wool, silk, etc. from which yarns are made **2** the process of preparing such a strand

Rov·no (räv′nō′, -nə; rôv′-) city in W Ukraine

row[1] (rō) ***n.*** ⟦ME *rowe* < OE *ræw,* akin to Ger *reihe* < IE base **rei-,* to tear, split > RIVE, REAP⟧ **1** a number of people or things arranged so as to form a line, esp. a straight line **2** any of a series of such horizontal lines in parallel, as of seats in a theater or airplane, corn in a field, etc. **3** in a TABLE (***n.*** 4b), any of the parallel series of cells running across **4** a street with a line of buildings on either side, specif. one with occupants or establishments of a specified kind *[fraternity row]* —***vt.*** to arrange or put in a row or rows —☆**hard (or long) row to hoe** anything difficult or wearisome to do —**in a row** in succession; consecutively

row[2] (rō) ***vt.*** ⟦ME *rowen* < OE *rowan,* akin to ON *roa* < IE base **erē-,* to row, oar > RUDDER, L *remus,* oar, Gr *eretēs,* rower⟧ **1** to propel (a boat, etc.) on water by or as by using oars **2** to convey in or on a boat, etc. propelled in this way **3** to employ (a specified number of oars): said of a boat **4** to use (oarsmen, a stroke, etc. as specified) in rowing, esp. in a race **5** to engage in (a race) by rowing **6** to row against in a race —***vi.*** **1** to use oars in propelling a boat **2** to be propelled by means of oars: said of a boat **3** to engage in the sport of ROWING (sense 2) —***n.*** **1** an act or period of rowing **2** a trip made by rowboat —**row′er** ***n.***

row[3] (rou) ***n.*** ⟦back-form. < ? ROUSE[1], with loss of *-se,* as in PEA or CHERRY⟧ a noisy quarrel, dispute, or disturbance; squabble, brawl, or commotion —***vi.*** to make, or take part in, a noisy quarrel or disturbance

row·an (rō′ən, rou′-) ***n.*** ⟦< Scand, as in Norw *rogn, raun,* ON *reynir,* akin to ON *rauthr,* RED: from the color of the fruit⟧ **1** the European mountain ash (*Sorbus aucuparia*), a tree with pinnately compound leaves, white flowers, and red berries **2** either of two similar American mountain ashes **3** the orange or red berry of a rowan: also **row′an·ber′ry** (-ber′ē), *pl.* **-ries**

row·boat (rō′bōt′) ***n.*** a small boat made to be rowed

☆**row·dy** (rou′dē) ***n., pl.*** **-dies** ⟦< ? ROW[3]⟧ a person whose behavior is rough, quarrelsome, and disorderly; hoodlum —***adj.*** **-di·er, -di·est** having the nature of or characteristic of a rowdy; rough, quarrelsome, etc. —**row′di·ly** ***adv.*** —**row′di·ness** ***n.*** —**row′dy·ish** ***adj.*** —**row′dy·ism′** ***n.***

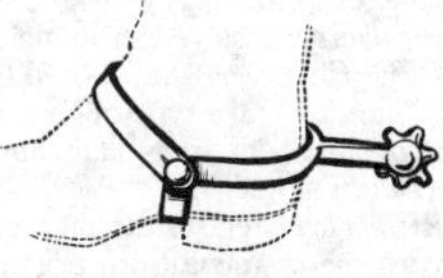
rowel

row·el (rou′əl) ***n.*** ⟦ME *rowelle* < OFr *roele:* see ROULETTE⟧ a small, revolving wheel with sharp projecting points, forming the end of a spur —*vt.* **-eled** or **-elled**, **-el·ing** or **-el·ling** to spur or prick (a horse, etc.) with or as with a rowel

row·en (rou′ən) ***n.*** ⟦ME *rewayn* < NormFr **rewain,* for OFr *regain* < *regainer:* see RE- & GAIN¹⟧ the second crop of grass or hay in one season; aftermath

Ro·we·na (rō ē′nə) ***n.*** ⟦< ? OE **Hrothwina* < *hroth,* fame, akin to OHG *hruod-* (see ROBERT¹) + *wina,* a friend, fem. of *wine:* see EDWIN⟧ a feminine name

☆**row house** (rō) any of a line of identical houses joined along the sides by common walls

row·ing (rō′iŋ) ***n.*** **1** the act of a person who rows a boat **2** the sport of racing long, narrow boats, as shells or sculls, in which the oarsmen sit in a line, each pulling on a single oar

rowing machine a type of exercise equipment that simulates the activity of rowing

Row·land (rō′lənd) ***n.*** a masculine name: see ROLAND

Row·land·son (rō′lənd sən), **Thomas** 1756-1827; Eng. caricaturist & painter

row·lock (räl′ək, rul′-; rō′läk′) ***n.*** ⟦altered (infl. by ROW²) < earlier OARLOCK⟧ *chiefly Brit. term for* OARLOCK

☆**Rox·anne** (räk san′) ***n.*** a feminine name: dim. *Roxie*; var. *Roxanna*

Rox·burgh (räks′bər ə) former county & former district of S Scotland: also, for the county, **Rox′burgh·shire′** (-shir′, -shər)

Roy (roi) ***n.*** ⟦as if < OFr *roy* (Fr *roi*), a king, but prob. < Gael *rhu,* red⟧ a masculine name

roy·al (roi′əl) ***adj.*** ⟦ME *roial* < OFr < L *regalis,* REGAL⟧ **1** of, from, by, or to a king, queen, or other sovereign [the *royal* family, a *royal* edict, the *royal* allowance] **2** having the rank of a sovereign **3** of a kingdom, its government, etc. [the *royal* fleet] **4** *a)* founded, chartered, or helped by, or under the patronage of, a sovereign [the *Royal* Society] *b)* in the service of a sovereign or of the Crown **5** *a)* suitable for a sovereign; magnificent, splendid, etc. [*royal* robes] *b)* like or characteristic of a sovereign; majestic, stately, etc. [a *royal* bearing] **6** unusually large, great, fine, etc. —***n.*** **1** a large size of paper, 20 by 25 inches (for printing) or 19 by 24 inches (for writing) **2** a small sail set next above a topgallant sail, on a royal mast **3** [*sometimes* **R-**] [Informal] a member of a royal family —**roy′al·ly** ***adv.***

royal blue a deep, vivid reddish or purplish blue

royal fern a tall, often aquatic, bushy fern (*Osmunda regalis*) of a family (Osmundaceae) of ferns characterized by special fronds that contain sporangia

☆**royal flush** *Poker* the highest straight flush, consisting of the ace, king, queen, jack, and ten of any one suit

roy·al·ism (roi′əl iz′əm) ***n.*** **1** the principles of royal government; monarchism **2** adherence to monarchism

roy·al·ist (-ist) ***n.*** **1** an adherent of royalism; person who supports a monarch or a monarchy, esp. in times of revolution, civil war, etc. **2** [**R-**] *a)* a supporter of Charles I of England; Cavalier ☆*b)* a supporter of the British in the American Revolution; Tory *c)* a supporter of the Bourbons in France —***adj.*** of royalists or royalism

royal jelly a highly nutritious mixture secreted by the maxillary glands in young honeybee workers, fed to all larvae for the first few days and then fed to only those larvae chosen to be queens

royal mast a small mast next above a topgallant mast

☆**royal palm** any of several tall, feather palm trees (genus *Roystonea*) native to Florida and the West Indies, extensively planted because of their rapid growth and adaptability

royal poinciana a tropical tree (*Delonix regia*) of the caesalpinia family, with a flat crown of twice pinnately compound leaves and masses of intense scarlet flowers

royal purple **1** [Archaic] deep crimson: cf. PURPLE (sense 2) **2** a dark, bluish purple

royal road an easy way of reaching an objective

roy·al·ty (roi′əl tē) ***n.,*** *pl.* **-ties** ⟦ME *roialte* < OFr < ML *regalitas* < L *regalis,* REGAL⟧ **1** the rank, status, or power of a king or queen; royal position, dignity, etc.; sovereignty **2** a royal person or, collectively, royal persons **3** [Archaic] a royal domain or realm; kingdom **4** royal quality or character; nobility, magnanimity, etc. **5** [*usually pl.*] [Archaic] a right, privilege, or prerogative of a monarch **6** [Rare] *a)* a royal right, as over some natural resource, granted by a monarch to a person, corporation, etc. *b)* payment for such a right **7** *a)* a share of the proceeds or product paid to the owner of a right, as a patent, for permission to use it or operate under it *b)* such a share paid to one from whom lands rich in oil or minerals are leased *c)* a share of proceeds, usually a specified percentage, paid for the work of an author, composer, etc. by the publisher

Royce (rois), **Josiah** 1855-1916; U.S. philosopher

roz·zer (räz′ər) ***n.*** ⟦< ? Romany *roozlo,* strong⟧ [Brit. Slang] a policeman

RP *abbrev.* Received Pronunciation

RPG (är′pē′jē′) ***n.,*** *pl.* **RPGs** ⟦prob. < *r*(*ocket-*)*p*(*ropelled*) *g*(*renade*) (*launcher*)⟧ **1** a type of grenade equipped with a simple rocket-propulsion system **2** a grenade launcher designed to shoot this type of grenade: see LAUNCHER (sense 2)

RPh *abbrev.* registered pharmacist

rpm *abbrev.* revolutions per minute

rps *abbrev.* revolutions per second

rpt *abbrev.* **1** repeat **2** report

RPV *abbrev.* remotely piloted vehicle (an unmanned aircraft operated by remote control)

RQ *abbrev.* respiratory quotient

RR *abbrev.* **1** railroad **2** Right Reverend **3** Rural Route: also **R.R.**

-rrha·gi·a (rā′jē ə, -jə) ⟦ModL < Gr < *rhēgnynai,* to burst < IE base **wrēg-,* to break > Lith *režti,* to cut, tear⟧ *combining form* abnormal discharge, excessive flow [*menorrhagia*]: also **-rrhage** (rij) or **-rrhag·y** (rā′jē)

-rrhe·a (rē′ə) ⟦ModL < Gr *-rrhoia* < *rheein,* to flow: see STREAM⟧ *combining form* flow, discharge [*seborrhea*]: also **-rrhoe′a**

RR Ly·rae variable (är′är′ lī′rē) ⟦RR, astronomical code designation of tenth variable + *Lyrae,* gen. of L *Lyra,* LYRA⟧ any of the very regular, short-period, pulsating variable stars having periods between 1.5 and 29 hours

rRNA *abbrev.* ribosomal RNA

Rs *abbrev.* rupees

RSFSR *abbrev.* Russian Soviet Federated Socialist Republic

RSI *abbrev.* REPETITIVE STRAIN (*or* STRESS) INJURY

RSV *abbrev.* Revised Standard Version (of the Bible)

RSVP¹ (är′es vē pē′) ***n.,*** *pl.* **RSVP's** or **RSVPs** ⟦< fol.⟧ a reply to an invitation —***vi.*** **RSVP'd** or **RSVPd**, **RSVP'ing** or **RSVPing** to reply to an invitation

RSVP² *abbrev.* ⟦Fr abbrev. of *répondez s'il vous plaît*⟧ please reply: also **R.S.V.P.**

rt *abbrev.* right

Rt *abbrev. Bible* Ruth

rte *abbrev.* route

Rt Hon *abbrev.* Right Honorable

Rt Rev *abbrev.* Right Reverend

Ru¹ *abbrev. Bible* Ruth

Ru² *Chem. symbol for* ruthenium

ru·a·na (ro͞o ä′nə) ***n.*** ⟦AmSp⟧ a kind of poncho worn originally in Colombia and Peru

Ru·an·da (ro͞o än′də) ***n.*** RWANDA¹

Ru·an·da-U·run·di (ro͞o än′də o͝o ro͝on′dē) former Belgian-administered United Nations trust territory in EC Africa: divided (1962) into the independent countries of RWANDA² & BURUNDI

rub (rub) ***vt.*** **rubbed**, **rub′bing** ⟦ME *rubben,* akin to Dan *rubbe,* EFris *rubben* < IE **reup-,* to tear out < base **reu-,* to dig, tear out > ROB, RIP¹, RUG, RUBBLE, L *rumpere,* to break⟧ **1** to move one's hand, a cloth, etc. over (a surface or object) with pressure and friction, in a circular or back-and-forth motion **2** to move (one's hand, a cloth, etc.) over, or spread or apply (polish, etc.) on or over, a surface or object in this way **3** to move (a thing) against something else, or move (things) over each other with pressure and friction: often followed by *together,* etc. **4** to apply pressure and friction to, for cleaning, polishing, smoothing, etc. **5** to put into a specified condition by applying pressure and friction [to *rub* oneself dry] **6** to make sore or chafed by rubbing **7** to force, cause to go, etc. (*in, into,* etc.) by rubbing **8** to remove by rubbing (*out, off, away,* etc.) —***vi.*** **1** to move with pressure and friction (*on, against,* etc.) [the tire *rubbing* against the fender] **2** to rub something; exert pressure and friction on something **3** to admit of being rubbed or removed by rubbing: often with *off, out,* etc. **4** to arouse anger or irritation **5** figuratively, to be imparted, as through contact or influence: said of a quality, skill, behavior, etc. [let's see if her teacher's manners will *rub off*] —***n.*** **1** the act or an instance of rubbing; specif., a massage **2** an obstacle, hindrance, or difficulty **3** a place or spot that has been rubbed until rough or sore **4** something that irritates, annoys, offends, etc., as a jeer or rebuke **5** a mixture of herbs and spices, a liquid ingredient such as oil, etc. applied by spreading on meat or fish prior to grilling, barbecuing, etc. —**rub along** (or **on** or **through**) [Chiefly Brit.] to manage or keep going in spite of difficulties —**rub down** **1** to massage **2** to smooth, polish, wear down, etc. by rubbing —**rub elbows with** [Informal] to associate or mingle with (famous or prominent people, etc.): also **rub shoulders with** —**rub it in** [Slang] to keep on mentioning to someone his or her failure or mistake, often with some malice —☆**rub off on** to be left on (something or someone) as a mark, as by rubbing or, figuratively, by personal contact or influence —**rub out** **1** to erase or be erased by rubbing ☆**2** [Slang] to kill or murder —**rub the wrong way** [Informal] to be annoying, irritating, etc. to

Ru·bái·yát (ro͞o′bī yät′, ro͞o′bī yät′; -bē-) ***n.*** ⟦Ar, lit., the quatrains < *rubā'īyāt,* pl. of *rubā'īyā,* quatrain, fem. of *rubā'ī,* composed of four < *arba'a,* four⟧ a long poem in quatrains (rhyming *aaba*), written by OMAR KHAYYÁM and well known in a free translation by Edward FitzGerald

Rub' al Kha·li (ro͝ob′ äl kä′lē) large desert of S Arabia: *c.* 250,000 sq mi (647,498 sq km)

ru·basse (ro͞o bas′, -bäs′) ***n.*** ⟦< Fr *rubace* < *rubis:* see RUBY⟧ a variety of crystalline quartz containing bits of hematite that produce a ruby-red color

ru·ba·to (ro͞o bät′ō) [*also in italics*] *Music* ***adj., adv.*** ⟦It < (*tempo*) *rubato,* stolen (time)⟧ with some notes arbitrarily lengthened (or shortened) in performance and, often, others correspondingly changed in length; (in a manner) intentionally and temporarily deviating from a strict tempo: also used as a musical direction —***n.*** **1** rubato modification or execution **2** *pl.* **-tos** a rubato passage, phrase, etc.

rub·ba·boo or **rub·a·boo** (rub′ə bo͞o′) ***n.*** ⟦CdnFr *rababou* < ? Algonquian: cf. Cree *-aapoy,* Ojibwa *-aabo,* soup, broth, liquid⟧ a soup made from pemmican boiled in water, sometimes thickened with flour

rub·ber¹ (rub′ər) ***n.*** **1** a person or thing that rubs, as in polishing, scraping, massaging, etc. **2** ⟦from orig. use as an eraser⟧ an elastic substance produced by coagulating and drying the milky sap (*latex*) of various tropical plants, esp. a tree (*Hevea brasiliensis*) of the spurge family: now most often produced synthetically or by chemically altering latex to obtain desired characteristics for use in making automobile tires, electrical insulation, molded objects and parts, etc.: in pure form rubber is a white, unsaturated hydrocarbon, having the formula $(C_5H_8)_n$ **3** something made of this substance; specif., *a)* [Chiefly Brit.] an eraser ☆*b)* a low-cut overshoe of rubber *c)* [Slang] a condom ☆**4** *Baseball* an oblong rubber slab set in the pitcher's mound: the pitcher's foot must touch the rubber as each pitch is thrown —*adj.* made of rubber —*vi.* ☆[Old Slang] *short for* RUBBERNECK —**rub'ber·like'** *adj.*

rub·ber[2] (rub'ər) *n.* ⟦< ?⟧ *Bridge* a series of three games, two of which must be won to win the series: see also RUBBER GAME

rubber band a narrow, continuous band of rubber as for holding small objects together

rubber cement an adhesive made of unvulcanized rubber in a solvent that quickly evaporates when exposed to air

☆**rubber check** ⟦from the notion that it "bounces": see BOUNCE (*vi.* 4)⟧ [Slang] a check that is worthless because of insufficient funds in the drawer's account

rubber game any game played to break a tie resulting when each side has won the same number of games: also **rubber match**

rub·ber·ize (rub'ər īz') *vt.* **-ized'**, **-iz'ing** to coat or impregnate with rubber or some rubber solution

☆**rub·ber·neck** (rub'ər nek') [Informal] *n.* a person who stretches his or her neck or turns the head to gaze about in curiosity, as a motorist who slows to look at a traffic accident: also **rub'ber·neck'er** —*vi.* to look at things or gaze about in this way

rubber plant **1** any plant yielding a milky sap (*latex*) from which crude rubber is formed **2** an Asian tree (*Ficus elastica*) of the mulberry family, with large, glossy, leathery leaves: often used as an ornamental houseplant

rubber stamp **1** a STAMP (*n.* 3*a*) made of rubber, pressed on an inking pad and used for printing signatures, dates, emblems, etc. ☆**2** [Informal] *a)* a person, bureau, legislature, etc. that approves or endorses something in a routine manner, without thought *b)* any routine approval

rub·ber-stamp (rub'ər stamp') *vt.* **1** to put the impression of a rubber stamp on ☆**2** [Informal] to approve or endorse in a routine manner, without thought —☆*adj.* routinely approved or approving

rub·ber·y (rub'ər ē) *adj.* like rubber in appearance, elasticity, toughness, etc. —**rub'ber·i·ness** *n.*

rub·bing (rub'iŋ) *n.* an impression of a design, picture, etc. incised or in relief on a surface (as of a gravestone), taken by placing a piece of paper on it and rubbing over the paper with graphite, wax, etc.

rubbing alcohol any of various liquid mixtures consisting mainly of either denatured ethyl alcohol or isopropyl alcohol, used to cleanse, cool, or soothe the skin

rub·bish (rub'ish) *n.* ⟦ME *robous, robys:* ult. < base of RUB⟧ **1** any material rejected or thrown away as worthless; trash; refuse **2** worthless, foolish ideas, statements, etc.; nonsense —*vt.* [Brit. Informal] TRASH[1] (*vt.* 3*a*) —**rub'bish·y** *adj.*

rub·ble (rub'əl) *n.* ⟦ME *robel;* akin to prec., RUB⟧ **1** rough, irregular, loose fragments of rock, broken from larger bodies either by natural processes or artificially, as by blasting **2** masonry made of rubble; rubblework **3** debris from buildings, etc., resulting from earthquake, bombing, etc. —**rub·bly** (rub'lē) *adj.* **-bli·er**, **-bli·est**

rub·ble·work (-wurk') *n.* masonry made of rubble or roughly dressed, irregular stones

rub·down (rub'doun') *n.* a brisk rubbing of the body, as in massage

☆**rube** (ro͞ob) *n.* ⟦< *Rube,* nickname of REUBEN[1]⟧ [Slang] a person from a rural region who lacks polish and sophistication; rustic

ru·be·fa·cient (ro͞o'bə fā'shənt) *adj.* ⟦L *rubefaciens,* prp. of *rubefacere,* to redden < *rubeus,* red (see RUBY) + *facere,* to make, DO[1]⟧ causing redness, as of the skin —*n. Med.* any external application, as a salve or plaster, causing redness of the skin

ru·be·fac·tion (ro͞o'bə fak'shən) *n.* **1** the act or process of making red, as with a rubefacient **2** redness of the skin, esp. as caused by a rubefacient

☆**Rube Gold·berg** (ro͞ob' gōld'bərg) ⟦after *Rube* (Reuben Lucius) *Goldberg* (1883-1970), U.S. cartoonist, known for his drawings of comically intricate contrivances⟧ designating any very complicated invention, machine, scheme, etc. laboriously contrived to perform a seemingly simple operation

ru·bel·la (ro͞o bel'ə) *n.* ⟦ModL, neut. pl. of L *rubellus,* reddish < *ruber,* RED⟧ a mild, infectious, communicable viral disease, characterized by swollen glands, esp. of the back of the head and neck, and small red spots on the skin; German measles

ru·bel·lite (ro͞o bel'īt', ro͞o'bə līt') *n.* ⟦< L *rubellus* (see prec.) + -ITE[1]⟧ a red variety of tourmaline, used as a gem

Ru·ben·esque (ro͞o'bə nesk') *adj.* **1** of, characteristic of, or like the art of Rubens; colorful, sensual, opulent, etc. **2** full and shapely; voluptuous: said of a woman's figure

Ru·bens (ro͞o'bənz), **Peter Paul** 1577-1640; Fl. painter

ru·be·o·la (ro͞o'bē ō'lə, ro͞o bē'ə lə) *n.* ⟦ModL, neut. pl. dim. of L *rubeus,* red: see RUBY⟧ MEASLES (sense 1*a*)

ru·bes·cent (ro͞o bes'ənt) *adj.* ⟦L *rubescens,* prp. of *rubescere,* to grow red < *rubere,* to redden < *ruber,* RED⟧ becoming red; specif., blushing or flushing —**ru·bes'cence** *n.*

Ru·bi·con (ro͞o'bi kän') [L *Rubico* (gen. *Rubiconis*)] small river in N Italy that formed the boundary between Cisalpine Gaul & the Roman Republic: when Caesar crossed it (49 B.C.) at the head of his army to march on Rome, he began the civil war with Pompey —**cross the Rubicon** to commit oneself to a definite act or decision; take a final, irrevocable step

ru·bi·cund (ro͞o'bi kənd) *adj.* ⟦Fr *rubicond* < L *rubicundus* < *ruber,* RED⟧ reddish; ruddy —**ru'bi·cun'di·ty** (-kun'də tē) *n.*

ru·bid·i·um (ro͞o bid'ē əm) *n.* ⟦ModL: so named (1861) by R. W. BUNSEN & G. R. KIRCHHOFF < L *rubidus,* red < *ruber,* RED (from the red lines in its spectrum) + -IUM⟧ a soft, silvery-white, metallic chemical element, one of the alkali metals, that ignites spontaneously in air and reacts violently in water: used in photocells and in filaments of vacuum tubes: symbol, Rb; at. no. 37: see the periodic table of elements in the Reference Supplement

ru·bied (ro͞o'bēd') *adj.* colored like a ruby; deep-red

ru·big·i·nous (ro͞o bij'ə nəs) *adj.* ⟦LL *rubiginosus* < L *rubigo,* rust, akin to *rubeus,* red: see RUBY⟧ rust-colored; reddish-brown: also **ru·big'i·nose'** (-nōs')

Ru·bin·stein (ro͞o'bin stīn') **1 An·ton (Grigorevich)** (än tôn') 1829-94; Russ. pianist & composer **2 Arthur** or **Ar·tur** (är'to͝or') 1887-1982; U.S. pianist, born in Poland

ru·bi·ous (ro͞o'bē əs) *adj.* [Old Poet.] ruby-colored; red

ru·ble (ro͞o'bəl) *n.* ⟦Russ *rubl'*⟧ the basic monetary unit of Belarus, Russia, and Tajikistan: see the table of monetary units in the Reference Supplement

ru·bric (ro͞o'brik) *n.* ⟦ME *rubryke* < MFr *rubriche* < L *rubrica,* red ocher, hence title (esp. of a law) written in red, rubric < *ruber,* RED⟧ **1** in early books and manuscripts, a chapter heading, initial letter, specific sentence, etc. printed or written in red, decorative lettering, etc. **2** any heading, title, etc., as of a chapter or section **3** a direction, as in a prayer book, for conducting religious services **4** an explanatory comment, or gloss **5** the title or a heading of a law **6** an established custom or rule of procedure —*adj.* **1** inscribed in red **2** [Archaic] red or reddish

ru·bri·cal (-brə kəl) *adj.* of, prescribed by, or according to rubrics, esp. liturgical rubrics —**ru'bri·cal·ly** *adv.*

ru·bri·cate (ro͞o'brə kāt') *vt.* **-cat'ed**, **-cat'ing** ⟦< L *rubricatus,* pp. of *rubricare,* to redden < *rubrica:* see RUBRIC⟧ **1** to mark, color, or illuminate (a book, etc.) with red; write or print in red letters **2** to provide with or regulate by rubrics —**ru'bri·ca'tion** *n.* —**ru'bri·ca'tor** (-kāt'ər) *n.*

ru·bri·cian (ro͞o brish'ən) *n.* a specialist in rubrics

ru·by (ro͞o'bē) *n., pl.* **-bies** ⟦ME < OFr *rubi,* ult. < L *rubeus,* reddish; akin to *ruber,* RED⟧ **1** a clear, deep-red variety of corundum, valued as a precious stone **2** something having made of this stone, as a watch bearing **3** *a)* deep red *b)* something having this color —*adj.* deep-red

Ru·by (ro͞o'bē) *n.* ⟦see prec.⟧ a feminine name

☆**ru·by-throat·ed hummingbird** (-thrōt'id) a common North American hummingbird (*Archilochus colubris*), the male of which has a metallic green back and a red throat

ruche (ro͞osh) *n.* ⟦Fr, lit., beehive < OFr *rusche* < Celt, as in Gaul *rusca,* bark (used for making beehives)⟧ a fluting or pleating of lace, ribbon, muslin, net, etc. for trimming dresses, esp. at the wrist and neck

ruched (ro͞osht) *adj.* **1** pleated or gathered into ruches [*ruched* silk] **2** having ruches [a *ruched* collar, neckline, or dress]

ruch·ing (ro͞o'shiŋ) *n.* **1** ruches collectively; trimming made of ruches **2** material used to make ruches

ruck[1] (ruk) *n.* ⟦ME *ruke,* a heap < ON *hroki,* a heap, pile; akin to *hruga:* see RICK[1]⟧ **1** [Archaic] a heap or stack, as of fuel **2** a large quantity, mass, or crowd **3** the horses left behind by the leaders in a race **4** the multitude or mass of undistinguished, ordinary people or things; common run

ruck[2] (ruk) *n., vt., vi.* ⟦prob. via dial. < ON *hrukka*⟧ crease, fold, wrinkle, or pucker

ruck·le (ruk'əl) *vt., vi.* **ruck'led**, **ruck'ling** *Brit. var. of* RUCK[2]

ruck·sack (ruk'sak', ro͝ok'-) *n.* ⟦Ger < dial. form of *rücken,* the back (see RIDGE) + *sack* < OHG *sac* (see SACK[1])⟧ a kind of knapsack strapped over the shoulders

☆**ruck·us** (ruk'əs) *n.* ⟦prob. a merging of fol. & RUMPUS⟧ [Informal] noisy confusion; uproar; row; disturbance

ruc·tion (ruk'shən) *n.* ⟦altered < INSURRECTION, orig. with reference to the Irish Insurrection (1798)⟧ [Informal] a riotous outbreak or uproar; noisy disturbance or quarrel

☆**rud·beck·i·a** (rud bek'ē ə) *n.* ⟦ModL, after O. *Rudbeck* (1630-1702), Swed botanist⟧ any of a genus (*Rudbeckia*) of perennial North American plants of the composite family, with conical disks and showy yellow, orange, or maroon ray flowers, including the black-eyed Susan

rudd (rud) *n.* ⟦akin to ME *rude* < OE *rudu,* red; akin to *read,* RED⟧ a European freshwater minnow (*Scardinius erythrophthalmus*) with yellow-orange eyes and red fins, now introduced in the U.S.

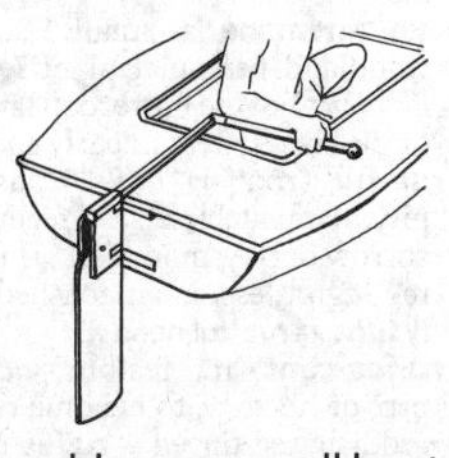
rudder on a small boat

rud·der (rud'ər) *n.* ⟦ME *rother* < OE; akin to Ger *ruder:* see ROW[2]⟧ **1** a broad, flat, movable piece of wood or metal hinged vertically at the stern of a boat or ship, used for steering **2** a movable piece attached to the vertical stabilizer of an aircraft, etc., used for controlling direction to the left or right **3** something serving to guide, direct, or control —**rud'der·less** *adj.*

rud·der·post (-pōst') *n.* **1** the sternpost,

or in some ships an added vertical member, to which the rudder is fastened 2 RUDDERSTOCK

rud·der·stock (-stäk′) ***n.*** the part of a vessel's rudder by which it is pivoted to the sternpost or rudderpost

rud·dle (rud′'l) ***n.*** ⟦< dial. *rud,* red ocher < ME *rude:* see RUDD⟧ RED OCHER —***vt.*** **-dled, -dling 1** to color or mark with red ocher, esp. to mark sheep thus **2** to cause to flush; redden

rud·dle·man (-mən) ***n., pl.*** **-men** (-mən) a person who sells ruddle

rud·dock (rud′ək) ***n.*** ⟦ME *ruddok* < OE *rudduc* < *rudu,* red (see RUDD) + *-uc,* -OCK⟧ [Brit. Dial.] ROBIN (sense 2)

rud·dy (rud′ē) ***adj.*** **-di·er, -di·est** ⟦ME *rudi* < OE *rudig* < *rudu,* red: see RUDD⟧ **1** having a healthy red color *[a ruddy complexion]* **2** red or reddish **3** ⟦euphemism for BLOODY⟧ [Brit. Informal] confounded: an intensive: also used adverbially —**rud′di·ness** ***n.***

☆**ruddy duck** a small, North American duck (*Oxyura jamaicensis*), the breeding male of which has a brownish-red neck and upper body, black crown, white cheeks, and blue bill

rude (ro͞od) ***adj.*** **rud′er, rud′est** ⟦OFr < L *rudis,* akin to *rudus,* debris, rubble < IE **reud-,* to tear apart < base **reu-,* to tear out, dig up > RUG, ROTTEN⟧ **1** crude or rough in form or workmanship *[a rude hut]* **2** barbarous or ignorant *[rude savages]* **3** *a)* lacking refinement, culture, or elegance; uncouth, boorish, coarse, vulgar, etc. *b)* [Brit.] indecent; obscene *[a rude joke]* **4** discourteous; unmannerly *[a rude reply]* **5** rough, violent, or harsh *[a rude awakening]* **6** harsh in sound; discordant; not musical *[rude tones]* **7** having or showing little skill or development; primitive *[rude drawings]* **8** not carefully worked out or finished; not precise *[a rude appraisal]* **9** sturdy; robust; rugged *[rude health]* —**rude′ly** ***adv.*** —**rude′ness** ***n.***

SYN.—**rude,** in this comparison, implies a deliberate lack of consideration for others' feelings and connotes, especially, insolence, impudence, etc. *[it was rude of you to ignore your uncle]*; **ill-mannered** connotes ignorance of the amenities of social behavior rather than deliberate rudeness *[a well-meaning but ill-mannered fellow]*; **boorish** is applied to one who is rude or ill-mannered in a coarse, loud, or overbearing way; **impolite** impiies merely a failure to observe the forms of polite society *[it would be impolite to leave so early]*; **discourteous** suggests a lack of dignified consideration for others *[a discourteous reply]*; **uncivil** implies a disregarding of even the most elementary of good manners *[her uncivil treatment of the waiter]* —**ANT. polite, civil**

ru·der·al (ro͞o′dər əl) ***n.*** ⟦< ModL *ruderalis,* growing in rubble < L *rudus* (gen. *ruderis*), rubbish (see prec.) + *-alis,* -AL⟧ any weedy plant growing in waste places or in rubbish, along the wayside, etc. —***adj.*** weedy

rud·er·y (ro͞od′ər ē) ***n.*** **1** the quality of being rude (in various senses); rudeness **2** *pl.* **-er·ies** a rude act or expression

ru·di·ment (ro͞o′də mənt) ***n.*** ⟦L *rudimentum* < *rudis:* see RUDE⟧ **1** a first principle, element, or fundamental, as of a subject to be learned: *usually used in pl. [the rudiments of physics]* **2** a first slight beginning or appearance, or undeveloped form or stage, of something: *usually used in pl.* **3** *Biol.* an incompletely developed organ or part; specif., a vestigial organ or part with no functional activity; vestige

ru·di·men·ta·ry (ro͞o′də men′tər ē, -men′trē) ***adj.*** of, or having the nature of, a rudiment or rudiments; specif., *a)* elementary *b)* incompletely or imperfectly developed *c)* vestigial: sometimes **ru′di·men′tal** —**ru·di·men·tar·i·ly** (ro͞o′də men ter′ə lē, -men′tər ə lē) ***adv.*** —**ru′di·men′ta·ri·ness** ***n.***

Ru·dolf (ro͞o′dôlf′, -dälf′), **Lake** *another name for* Lake TURKANA

Ru·dolf I (ro͞o′dôlf′, -dälf′) 1218-91; Ger. king & emperor of the Holy Roman Empire (1273-91): founder of the Habsburg dynasty: also called **Rudolf I of Habsburg**

Ru·dolph (ro͞o′dôlf′, -dälf′) ***n.*** ⟦Ger *Rudolf* < OHG *Rudolf, Hrodulf* < *hruod-,* fame (see ROBERT[1]) + *wolf,* WOLF⟧ a masculine name: dim. *Rudy;* var. *Rodolph, Rolf, Rollo;* equiv. Fr. *Rodolphe,* Ger. *Rudolf,* It. & Sp. *Rodolfo*

rue[1] (ro͞o) ***vt.*** **rued, ru′ing** ⟦ME *reowen* < OE *hreowan,* akin to Ger *reuen,* to regret, ON *hryggr,* sorrowful, prob. < IE base **kreu-,* to strike, beat > Gr *krouein*⟧ **1** to feel remorse or repentance for (a sin, fault, etc.) **2** to wish (an act, promise, etc.) undone or unmade; regret —***vi.*** to be sorrowful or regretful —***n.*** [Archaic] sorrow, repentance, or regret

rue[2] (ro͞o) ***n.*** ⟦OFr < L *ruta* < Gr *rhytē*⟧ any of a genus (*Ruta*) of strong-scented shrubs of the rue family, esp. an herb (*R. graveolens*) with yellow flowers and bitter-tasting leaves formerly used in medicine —***adj.*** designating a family (Rutaceae, order Sapindales) of woody dicotyledonous plants, including the gas plant and the citrus plants

☆**rue anemone** a small, North American, woodland perennial plant (*Anemonella thalictroides*) of the buttercup family, with white or pinkish flowers in early spring

rue·ful (ro͞o′fəl) ***adj.*** **1** causing sorrow or pity; lamentable **2** *a)* feeling or showing sorrow or pity; mournful *b)* feeling or showing regret, esp. in an abashed way —**rue′ful·ly** ***adv.*** —**rue′ful·ness** ***n.***

ru·fes·cent (ro͞o fes′ənt) ***adj.*** ⟦L *rufescens,* prp. of *rufescere,* to become red < *rufus,* RED⟧ reddish; red-tinged —**ru·fes′cence** ***n.***

ruff

ruff[1] (ruf) ***n.*** ⟦contr. of RUFFLE[1], ***n.***⟧ **1** a high, frilled or pleated collar of starched muslin, lace, etc., worn by men and women in the 16th and 17th cent. **2** a band of distinctively colored or protruding feathers or fur around the neck of an animal or bird **3** a Eurasian sandpiper (*Philomachus pugnax*), the male of which grows a large ruff during the breeding season: the female is called a *reeve* —**ruffed** ***adj.***

ruff[2] (ruf) *Card Games* ***vt., vi.*** ⟦OFr *roffle,* earlier *ronfle,* altered < ? *triomphe:* see TRUMP[1]⟧ TRUMP[1] —***n.*** ⟦< the v.⟧ the act of trumping

ruff[3] (ruf) ***n.*** ⟦ME *ruffe* < ? *rugh,* ROUGH⟧ **1** a small, spotted, European freshwater perch (*Acerina cernua*): also sp. **ruffe 2** any of various Atlantic butterfishes (genus *Centrolophus*)

☆**ruffed grouse** a North American game bird (*Bonasa umbellus*) with neck feathers that can be extended into a ruff: also called *partridge* in the N U.S. and *pheasant* in the S U.S.

ruf·fi·an (ruf′ē ən, ruf′yən) ***n.*** ⟦Fr *rufian* < It *ruffiano,* a pander < dial. *roffia,* filth < Gmc **hruf-,* scurf (akin to OHG *ruf,* OE *hreof*) < IE base **kreup-* > Lith *kraupus,* rough: E sense infl. by ROUGH⟧ a brutal, violent, lawless person; tough or hoodlum —***adj.*** brutal, violent, and lawless: also **ruf′fi·an·ly** —**ruf′fi·an·ism′** ***n.***

ruf·fle[1] (ruf′əl) ***vt.*** **-fled, -fling** ⟦ME *ruffelen* < ON or MLowG, as in LowG, ON *hrufla,* to scratch⟧ **1** to take away the smoothness of; wrinkle; ripple *[wind ruffling the water]* **2** to gather into ruffles **3** to put ruffles on as trimming **4** to make (feathers, etc.) stand up in or as in a ruff, as a bird when frightened **5** to disturb, irritate, or annoy **6** to turn over (the pages of a book, etc.) rapidly —***vi.*** **1** to become uneven, wrinkled, etc. **2** to become disturbed, irritated, etc. —***n.*** **1** a strip of cloth, lace, etc., gathered in pleats and puckers and used for trimming **2** something like this, as a bird's ruff **3** a disturbance —**ruffle (someone's) feathers** [Informal] to disturb, irritate, or annoy (someone) —**ruf′fly** ***adj.*** **-fli·er, -fli·est**

ruf·fle[2] (ruf′əl) ***n.*** ⟦also earlier *ruff,* prob. echoic⟧ a low, continuous beating of a drum, not so loud as a roll — ***vi., vt.*** **-fled, -fling** to beat (a drum, etc.) with a ruffle

ru·fi·yaa (ro͞o′fē yä′) ***n., pl.*** **-yaa′** ⟦< name in Maldivian (a language related to Sinhalese) < Hindi *rūpiyah,* RUPEE⟧ the basic monetary unit of the Maldives: see the table of monetary units in the Reference Supplement

RU-486 (är′yo͞o′fôr′āt′ē siks′) ***n.*** ⟦< *R(oussel) U(claf),* name of its Fr manufacturer⟧ MIFEPRISTONE: also written **RU486** or **RU 486**

ru·fous (ro͞o′fəs) ***adj.*** ⟦L *rufus,* reddish, RED⟧ brownish-red

Ru·fus (ro͞o′fəs) ***n.*** ⟦L, red-haired, RED⟧ a masculine name

rug (rug) ***n.*** ⟦< Scand, as in Norw dial. *rugga,* coarse coverlet, Swed *rugg,* shaggy hair, ON *rǫgg,* long hair < IE base **reu-,* to tear out: see RUDE⟧ **1** a piece of thick, often napped fabric, woven strips of rag, an animal skin, etc. used as a floor covering: usually distinguished from CARPET in being a single piece of definite shape, not intended to cover the entire floor **2** *chiefly Brit. term for* LAP ROBE ☆**3** [Slang] a toupee

ru·ga (ro͞o′gə) ***n., pl.*** **-gae** (-jē) ⟦ModL < L, a wrinkle < IE **rug-* < **werg-,* to turn < base **wer-*⟧ *Anat., etc.* a wrinkle, fold, or ridge, as in the lining of the stomach, vagina, or palate: *usually used in pl.* —**ru′gate** (-gāt, -git) ***adj.***

Rug·by[1] (rug′bē) ***n.*** **1** famous school for boys located in Rugby, England: founded 1567 **2** *[usually* **r-***]* a kind of football popular in England, played by two opposing teams of usually 15 players: action is continuous and the oval ball may be passed laterally or backward, kicked forward, or carried: a forerunner of American tackle football, first played at Rugby school: in full **Rugby football**

Rug·by[2] (rug′bē) city in Warwickshire, central England

rugby shirt a jersey, usually of brightly colored striped fabric with a white collar and placket, worn for playing rugby or as casual attire

rug·e·lach (rug′ə lukh′) ***n., pl.*** **-lach′** a small pastry consisting of a square of dough with two opposite corners folded over a centered filling of nuts or jam

rug·ged (rug′id) ***adj.*** ⟦ME, rough, shaggy, prob. < Scand, as in Swed *rugga,* to roughen: for IE base see RUG⟧ **1** having irregular projections and depressions; uneven in surface or contour; rough; wrinkled *[rugged ground, a rugged coast]* **2** strong, irregular, and wrinkled: said of the face or facial features **3** stormy; tempestuous *[rugged weather]* **4** sounding harsh *[rugged tones]* **5** severe; harsh; hard; stern *[a rugged life]* **6** not polished, cultivated, refined, or elegant; rude *[rugged manners]* ☆**7** strong; robust; sturdy; vigorous **8** [Informal] requiring great skill, strength, endurance, etc. *[a rugged test]* —**rug′ged·ly** ***adv.*** —**rug′ged·ness** ***n.***

rug·ger (rug′ər) ***n.*** [Brit. Informal] *var. of* RUGBY[1]

ru·go·la (ro͞o′gə lə) ***n.*** ⟦prob. akin to It *ruca,* ROCKET[2]⟧ ARUGULA

☆**ru·go·sa rose** (ro͞o gō′sə) ⟦< ModL *Rosa rugosa,* lit., wrinkled rose < L *rosa,* ROSE[1] + *rugosus,* wrinkled < *ruga,* a wrinkle: see RUGA⟧ an upright, hardy species (*Rosa rugosa*) of rose having rough leaves with furrowed veins, often planted for hedges

ru·gose (ro͞o′gōs′, ro͞o gōs′) ***adj.*** ⟦L *rugosus:* see prec.⟧ *Biol.* having or full of wrinkles; corrugated; ridged *[a rugose leaf]*: also **ru′gous** (-gəs) —**ru·gos·i·ty** (ro͞o gäs′ə tē) ***n., pl.*** **-ties**

Ruhr (ro͝or; *Ger* ro͞o′ər) **1** river in WC Germany, flowing west into the Rhine: 145 mi (233 km) **2** major coal-mining & industrial region centered in the valley of this river: also called **Ruhr Basin**

ru·in (ro͞o′ən) ***n.*** ⟦ME *ruine* < OFr < L *ruina* < *ruere,* to fall, hurl to the ground < IE **ereu-* < base **er-,* to set in motion, erect > RUN, RISE⟧ **1** [Archaic] a falling down, as of a building, wall, etc. **2** *[pl.]* the remains of a fallen building, city, etc., or of something devastated, decayed, etc. **3** *a)* a destroyed or dilapidated building, town, etc. *b)* a person regarded as being physically, mentally, or morally a wreck of what he or she was **4** the state of being destroyed, decayed, dilapidated, etc. **5** downfall, destruction, devastation, etc.; specif., *a)* complete loss of means, solvency, position, etc. *b)* moral downfall **6** any cause of a person's downfall, destruction, etc. [gambling was his *ruin*] —*vt.* to bring or reduce to ruin; specif., *a)* to destroy, spoil, or damage irreparably *b)* to impoverish or make bankrupt *c)* to deflower or seduce (a woman) and, often, specif., thereby render her unmarriageable, disgraced, etc. —*vi.* [Archaic] to go or come to ruin —**ru′in·er** *n.*

SYN.—**ruin** implies a state of decay, disintegration, etc. especially through such natural processes as age and weather [the barn is in a state of *ruin*]; **destruction** implies annihilation or demolition, as by fire, explosion, flood, etc. [the *destruction* of the village in an air raid]; **havoc** suggests total destruction or devastation, as following an earthquake or hurricane; **dilapidation** implies a state of ruin or shabbiness resulting from neglect [the *dilapidation* of a deserted house]

ru·in·ate (ro͞o′ə nāt′) *vt., vi.* **-at′ed, -at′ing** ⟦< ML *ruinatus,* pp. of *ruinare,* to ruin < L *ruina:* see prec.⟧ [Archaic] to ruin

ru·in·a·tion (ro͞o′ə nā′shən) *n.* ⟦< prec. + -ION⟧ **1** a ruining or being ruined **2** anything that ruins or causes ruin

ru·in·ous (ro͞o′ə nəs) *adj.* ⟦ME *ruinouse* < L *ruinosus*⟧ **1** falling or fallen into ruin; dilapidated; decayed **2** bringing or tending to bring ruin; very destructive or harmful; disastrous [*ruinous* floods] —**ru′in·ous·ly** *adv.* —**ru′in·ous·ness** *n.*

Ruis·dael (rois′däl′, rīs′-; *Du* rēs′däl′), **Ja·cob van** (yä′kôp vän′) 1628?-82; Du. landscape painter

rule (ro͞ol) *n.* ⟦ME *reule* < OFr *rieule* < L *regula,* ruler, straightedge < *regere,* to lead straight, rule: see RIGHT⟧ **1** *a)* an authoritative regulation for action, conduct, method, procedure, arrangement, etc. [the *rules* of the school] *b)* an established practice that serves as a guide to usage [the *rules* of grammar] **2** a complete set or code of regulations in a religious order [the Benedictine *rule*] **3** a fixed principle that determines conduct; habit; custom [to make it a *rule* never to hurry] **4** something that usually or normally happens or obtains; customary course of events [famine is the *rule* following war] **5** *a)* government; reign; control *b)* the period of reigning of a particular ruler or government **6** a ruler or straightedge **7** [Obs.] way of acting; behavior **8** *Law a)* a regulation or guide established by a court governing court practice and procedure *b)* a declaration, order, etc. made by a judge or court in deciding a specific question or point of law *c)* a legal principle or maxim **9** *Math.* a method or procedure prescribed for computing or solving a problem **10** *Printing a)* a thin strip of metal, the height of type, used to print straight or decorative lines, borders, etc. *b)* a line so printed —*vt.* **ruled, rul′ing 1** to have an influence over; guide [to be *ruled* by one's friends] **2** to lessen; restrain [reason *ruled* his fear] **3** to have authority over; govern; direct [to *rule* a country] **4** to be the most important element of; dominate [action *rules* the plot] **5** to settle officially or by decree; determine [a law *ruled* unconstitutional by a federal court] **6** *a)* to mark lines on with or as with a ruler *b)* to mark (a line) thus **7** *Astrol.* to be the chief influence or guide: said of a PLANET (sense 3) [the zodiac sign Aries is *ruled* by the planet Mars] —*vi.* **1** to have supreme authority; govern **2** to be at a specified rate or level; prevail: said of prices, commodities, etc. **3** to issue a formal decree about a question —SYN. GOVERN, LAW —**as a rule** usually; ordinarily —**rule out 1** to exclude, as by decision **2** to prevent; make impossible

ruled surface *Geom.* a surface that is the locus of all points on a moving straight line, as a plane, cone, etc.

rule of three *Math.* the method of finding the fourth term of a proportion when three terms are given: the product of the first and last terms is equal to the product of the second and third

rule of thumb ⟦from the method of measuring by the thumb⟧ **1** a rule based on experience or practice rather than on scientific knowledge **2** any method of estimating that is practical though not precise

rul·er (ro͞o′lər) *n.* **1** a person or thing that rules or governs **2** a thin strip of wood, metal, etc. with a straight edge and markings in whole and fractional units of length, as inches or centimeters, used in drawing straight lines, measuring length, etc. **3** a person or device that rules lines on paper, etc. —**rul′er·ship′** *n.*

rul·ing (ro͞o′liŋ) *adj.* that rules; specif., *a)* governing *b)* predominating *c)* prevalent —*n.* **1** the act of governing **2** an official decision, esp. one made by a court or judge **3** *a)* the making of ruled lines *b)* the lines so made

rum[1] (rum) *n.* ⟦short for *rumbullion,* orig. Devonshire dial., uproar, tumult < ?⟧ **1** an alcoholic liquor distilled from fermented sugar cane, molasses, etc. ☆**2** alcoholic liquor in general

rum[2] (rum) *adj.* ⟦< obs. *rum,* good, great < ? *Rom,* a Gypsy: see ROMANI⟧ [Informal, Chiefly Brit.] **1** odd; strange; queer **2** bad, poor, etc. [a *rum* joke]

ru·ma·ki (rə mä′kē) *n., pl.* **-ki** ⟦orig. uncert.; perhaps < Jpn⟧ an appetizer of E Asian origin consisting of a piece of marinated chicken liver wrapped, together with a slice of water chestnut, in a strip of bacon and broiled

Ru·ma·ni·a (ro͞o mā′nē ə, -mān′yə) *var. of* ROMANIA —**Ru·ma′ni·an** *adj., n.*

rum·ba (rum′bə, ro͝om′bə) *n.* ⟦AmSp, prob. of Afr orig.⟧ **1** a dance of Cuban origin and complex rhythm **2** a modern ballroom adaptation of this, with strong rhythmic movements of the lower part of the body **3** music for, or in the rhythm of, this dance —*vi.* to dance the rumba

rum·ble (rum′bəl) *vi.* **-bled, -bling** ⟦ME *romblen,* prob. < MDu *rommelen* < IE base **reu-* > RUNE, RUMOR⟧ **1** to make a deep, heavy, continuous, rolling sound, as thunder **2** to move or go with such a sound **3** [Slang] to participate in a RUMBLE (*n.* 5) —*vt.* **1** to cause to make, or move with, such a sound **2** to utter or say with such a sound **3** to polish, mix, etc. in a rumble, or tumbling box —*n.* **1** a deep, heavy, continuous, rolling sound **2** a widespread expression of discontent or restiveness **3** a space for luggage or a small extra seat, as for servants, in the rear of a carriage **4** TUMBLING BOX ☆**5** [Slang] a fight between gangs, esp. of teenagers —**rum′bler** *n.* —**rum′bling·ly** *adv.* —**rum′bly** *adj.*

☆**rumble seat** in some earlier automobiles, an open seat in the rear, behind the roofed seat, which could be folded shut when not in use

rumble strip a ridged section of pavement alongside a highway or on a roadway preceding a hazard, as a dangerous curve or construction zone, that, when driven over by a passing motor vehicle, causes loud rumbling and vibration: *usually used in pl.*

rum·bus·tious (rum bus′chəs) *adj.* ⟦altered (? after RUM[1]) < ROBUSTIOUS⟧ [Chiefly Brit.] rambunctious, boisterous, unruly, etc.

Ru·me·li·a (ro͞o mē′lē ə, -mēl′yə) former Turkish possessions in the Balkan Peninsula, including Macedonia, Thrace, & an autonomous province (**Eastern Rumelia**) that was annexed to Bulgaria in 1885

ru·men (ro͞o′mən) *n., pl.* **-mi·na** (-mə nə) ⟦ModL < L, throat, gullet < IE **reusmen,* rumination, throat > Sans *rōmantha*⟧ the first stomach of a ruminant

Rum·ford (rum′fərd), Count *see* THOMPSON, Benjamin

Ru·mi (ro͞o′mē) (full name *Jalāl al-Dīn Muhammad Rūmī*) 1207-73; Persian theologian, mystic, & poet

ru·mi·nant (ro͞o′mə nənt) *adj.* ⟦L *ruminans,* prp. of L *ruminare,* to ruminate < *rumen,* RUMEN⟧ **1** chewing the cud **2** of the cud-chewing animals **3** meditative; thoughtful —*n.* any of the suborders (Ruminantia and Tylopoda) of four-footed, cud-chewing artiodactylous mammals: cattle, buffalo, goat, deer, antelope, and giraffe have a stomach with four chambers (the *rumen, reticulum, omasum,* and *abomasum*) and the camel, llama, and chevrotain have a stomach with three chambers —**ru′mi·nant·ly** *adv.*

ru·mi·nate (-nāt′) *vt., vi.* **-nat′ed, -nat′ing** ⟦< L *ruminatus,* pp. of *ruminare:* see prec.⟧ **1** to chew (the cud), as a cow does **2** to turn (something) over in the mind; meditate (on) —**ru′mi·na′tion** *n.* —**ru′mi·na′tive** *adj.* —**ru′mi·na′tive·ly** *adv.* —**ru′mi·na′tor** *n.*

rum·mage (rum′ij) *n.* ⟦aphetic < MFr *arrumage* < *arrumer,* to stow cargo in the hold < *aruner,* to arrange < *run, rum,* ship's hold < Frank **rum,* akin to OE *rum,* ROOM⟧ **1** miscellaneous articles; odds and ends **2** a rummaging, or thorough search —*vt.* **-maged, -mag·ing 1** to search through (a place, receptacle, etc.) thoroughly, esp. by moving the contents about, turning them over, etc.; ransack **2** to get, find, or turn up by or as by searching thoroughly: with *up* or *out* —*vi.* to search diligently, now sometimes haphazardly, as through the contents of a receptacle —**rum′mag·er** *n.*

rummage sale a sale of contributed miscellaneous articles, used or new, to raise money as for charitable purposes

rum·mer (rum′ər) *n.* ⟦Du *roemer* < *roemen,* to praise (akin to OHG *hruom,* praise, *hruod-,* fame: see ROBERT[1]) hence, orig., a glass used for drinking toasts⟧ a large drinking glass or cup

rum·my[1] (rum′ē) *adj.* **-mi·er, -mi·est** ⟦RUM[2] + -Y[2]⟧ [Informal, Chiefly Brit.] odd; strange; queer —☆*n.* ⟦< ? the *adj.*⟧ a card game, played in many variations, in which the object is to match cards into sets of the same denomination or sequences of the same suit

rum·my[2] (rum′ē) *adj.* **-mi·er, -mi·est** ⟦RUM[1] + -Y[2]⟧ of or like rum —*n., pl.* **-mies** ☆[Slang] a drunkard

ru·mor (ro͞o′mər) *n.* ⟦ME *rumour* < OFr < L *rumor,* noise < IE echoic base **reu-,* to roar, grumble > RUNE, OE *reotan,* to complain⟧ **1** general talk not based on definite knowledge; mere gossip; hearsay **2** an unconfirmed report, story, or statement in general circulation **3** [Archaic] fame **4** [Obs.] loud protest, clamor, etc. —*vt.* to tell, report, or spread by rumor or as a rumor Brit. sp. **ru′mour**

ru·mor·mon·ger (-muŋ′gər, -mäŋ′-) *n.* a person who spreads rumors

rump (rump) *n.* ⟦ME *rumpe* < ON *rumpr,* akin to Ger *rumpf,* trunk (of the body) < IE base **remb-, *romb-,* to chop, notch > Czech *roubiti,* to chop⟧ **1** the hind part of the body of an animal, where the legs and back join, or the sacral part of a bird **2** a cut of meat, usually beef, from this part, behind the loin and above the round: see BEEF, illus. **3** the buttocks **4** the last, unimportant or inferior part; mere remnant **5** a legislature or other body having only a remnant of its former membership, as because of expulsions, and hence regarded as unrepresentative and without authority

Rum·pel·stilts·kin (rum′pəl stilt′skin) *n. Gmc. Folklore* a dwarf who saves the life of a maiden by spinning flax into gold in exchange for her first child: he agrees to free her from the bargain if she can guess his name

rum·ple (rum′pəl) *n.* ⟦MDu *rompel* < *rompe,* a wrinkle, akin to OE *hrympel,* a wrinkle < IE **(s)kremb-,* to twist: see SHRIMP⟧ an uneven fold or crease —*vt., vi.* **-pled, -pling 1** to make rumples (in) **2** to make or become disheveled or tousled —**rum′ply** *adv.*

Rump Parliament 1 the part of the Long Parliament remaining after the purge of 1648 until disbanded by Cromwell in 1653 **2** the same body recalled in 1659 and disbanded in 1660

rum·pus (rum′pəs) *n.* ⟦< ?⟧ [Informal] an uproar or commotion

☆**rumpus room** *former term for* RECREATION ROOM (*or* HALL)

☆**rum·run·ner** (rum′run′ər) *n.* a person, ship, etc. engaged in smuggling alcoholic liquor —**rum′run′ning** *n.*

run (run) *vi.* **ran** or [Dial.] **run, run, run′ning** ⟦altered (with vowel prob. infl. by pp.) < ME *rinnen, rennen* < ON & OE: ON *rinna,* to flow, run, *renna,* to cause to run (< Gmc **rannjan*); OE *rinnan, iornan:* both < Gmc **renwo* <

IE base *er-, to set in motion, excite > RAISE, L *origo*, ORIGIN⟧ **1** to go by moving the legs rapidly, faster than in walking, and (in a two-legged animal) in such a way that for an instant both feet are off the ground **2** *a)* to go rapidly; move swiftly *b)* to resort (*to*) for aid [always *running* to the police] **3** to associate or consort (*with*) **4** to go, move, grow, etc. easily and freely, without hindrance or restraint **5** to go away rapidly; flee **6** to make a quick trip (*up to, down to, over to*, etc. a specified place) for a brief stay **7** *a)* to take part in a contest or race ☆*b)* to be a candidate in an election **8** to finish a contest or race in the specified position [to *run* last] **9** to swim in migration, as upstream or inshore for spawning, etc.: said of fish **10** to go, as on a schedule; ply between two points [a bus that *runs* between Chicago and Detroit] **11** to go or pass lightly and rapidly [his eyes *ran* over the page] **12** to be current; circulate [a rumor *running* through the town] **13** to climb or creep: said of plants [a vine *running* over the wall] **14** to move continuously or incessantly: often used fig. [his tongue *ran* on and on] **15** to ravel lengthwise in a knitted fabric **16** to function or operate with or as with parts that revolve, slide, etc. [a machine that is *running*] **17** to recur or return to the mind **18** to flow [a *running* stream] **19** to melt and flow [the wax *ran*] **20** *a)* to spread when put on a surface, as a liquid *b)* to spread over or be diffused through cloth, etc. when moistened, as colors *c)* to be subject to such spreading of color, as fabric **21** to be wet or covered with a flow [eyes *running* with tears] **22** to give passage to a fluid; specif., *a)* to discharge pus, mucus, etc. *b)* to leak, as a faucet **23** to elapse [the days *ran* into weeks] **24** *a)* to appear in print [the newspaper *ran* with a misspelled headline; her editorial *ran* in the Sunday edition] *b)* to appear or be presented continuously or in a continuing series [a play that *ran* for a year] **25** *a)* to continue in effect or force [a law *running* for twenty years] *b)* to continue to occur; recur [talent *runs* in the family] **26** to be characterized by having, producing, using, etc.: with *to* [their taste *runs* to exotic foods] **27** *a)* to extend in or as in a continuous line [a fence *running* through the woods] *b)* to include so as to show variety (with *from* and *to*) [a repertoire *running* from tragedy to comedy] **28** to pass into a specified condition, situation, etc. [to *run* into trouble] **29** to sail or float (aground, etc.): said of a ship **30** to be written, expressed, played, etc. in a specified way [the adage *runs* like this] **31** to be or continue at a specified size, price, amount, etc. [apples *running* four to the pound] **32** *Naut.* to sail with the wind coming from astern —*vt.* **1** to run along or follow (a specified course or route) **2** to travel over; cover by running, driving, etc. [horses *ran* the range] **3** to do or perform by or as by running [to *run* a race] **4** to subject oneself to (a risk); incur ☆**5** *a)* to get past or escape by going through [to *run* a blockade] *b)* to go past or through without making a required stop [to *run* a stop sign or a red light] **6** to pursue or hunt (game, etc.) **7** to compete with in or as in a race; vie with **8** *a)* to enter (a horse, etc.) in a race ☆*b)* to put up or support as a candidate for election **9** *a)* to make run, move, operate, etc. *b)* to cause to go between points, as on a schedule *c)* to cause (a motor or engine) to idle for a while *d)* to make (a stocking) run **10** to bring, lead, or force into a specified condition, situation, etc. by or as by running [to *run* oneself into debt] **11** *a)* to carry or convey, as in a ship or vehicle; transport *b)* to carry (taxable or outlawed goods) in or out illegally; smuggle **12** to drive, force, or thrust (an object) into, through, or against something **13** to make go, move, pass, flow, etc., esp. rapidly, in a specified way, direction, place, etc. [to *run* water into a glass] **14** ☆*a)* to be in charge of; manage [to *run* a household] ☆*b)* to keep, feed, or graze (livestock) *c)* to perform the steps of (an experiment, test, etc.) *d)* to cause to undergo a test, procedure, process, etc. **15** to cost (an amount) [boots that *run* $20] **16** to mark, draw, or trace (lines, as on a map) **17** to extend, pass, or trace in a specified way or direction [to *run* a story back to its source] **18** to undergo or be affected by (a fever, etc.) **19** to flow with, discharge, or pour forth [gutters *running* blood] **20** to melt, fuse, or smelt (ore) **21** to cast or mold, as from molten metal; found ☆**22** to print; esp., to publish (an advertisement, story, etc.) in a newspaper or magazine **23** *Billiards* to complete successfully (a specified number of strokes, shots, etc.) in uninterrupted sequence **24** *Bridge* to lead the cards of (a suit, often, specif., an established suit), thereby taking a series of tricks **25** *Comput.* to cause (a program, software, etc.) to operate or start operating **26** *Golf* to cause (a ball) to roll, esp. on a green —*n.* **1** an act or period of running or moving rapidly **2** *a)* a race for runners *b)* a running pace; rapid gait *c)* capacity for running **3** the distance covered or time spent in running **4** a trip; journey; esp., *a)* a single, customary, or regular trip, as of a train, ship, or plane *b)* a quick trip, esp. for a brief stay *c)* ROUTE (sense 3) **5** *a)* movement onward, progression, or trend [the *run* of events] *b)* a continuous course or period of a specified condition, action, etc. [a *run* of good luck] **6** direction or course, as of the grain of wood, a vein of ore, etc. **7** a continuous course of performances, showings, etc. [a play that had a *run* of a year] **8** a series of continued, sudden, or urgent requests or demands, as by customers for certain goods, or by bank depositors for their funds **9** a period of being in public demand or favor **10** three or more playing cards in unbroken order in the same suit; sequence **11** a continuous extent of something **12** a flow or rush of water, etc., as of the tide **13** a small, swift stream, as a brook or rivulet **14** *a)* a period during which some fluid flows readily *b)* the amount of flow **15** *a)* a period of operation of a machine *b)* the output during this period **16** *a)* a kind, sort, or class, as of goods *b)* the ordinary, usual, or average kind or type **17** something in, on, or along which something else runs; specif., *a)* an inclined pathway or course [a ski *run*] *b)* a track, channel, trough, pipe, etc. *c)* an enclosed area in which domestic animals or fowl can move about freely or feed [a chicken *run*] *d)* in Australia, a large grazing area or ranch *e)* a well-defined trail or path made and used by animals [a buffalo *run*] **18** freedom to use all the facilities or move freely in any part (*of* a place) [to have the *run* of an estate] **19** *a)* a number of animals in motion together *b)* a large number of fish migrating together, as upstream or inshore for spawning *c)* such migration of fish ☆**20** a ravel lengthwise in something knitted, as in hosiery ☆**21** *Baseball* a point scored whenever a base runner successfully touches all four bases in the proper order without being out **22** *Billiards* an uninterrupted sequence of successful strokes, shots, etc. **23** *Cricket* a scoring point, made by a successful running of both batsmen from one wicket to the other **24** *Mil.* the approach to the target made by an airplane in bombing, strafing, etc. **25** *Comput.* one execution of a program **26** *Music* a rapid succession of tones, as a roulade **27** *Naut.* the after part of a ship's bottom, from where it starts to curve up and in toward the stern —*adj.* **1** melted; made liquid **2** poured or molded while in a melted state [*run* metal] **3** drained or extracted, as honey **4** having migrated and spawned: said of fish —**a run for one's money** **1** powerful competition **2** some satisfaction for what one has expended, as in betting on a near winner in a race —**in the long run** in the final outcome; ultimately —**in the short run** in the beginning; at first; initially —**on the run** **1** running **2** hurrying from place to place or task to task **3** running away; in retreat —☆**run across** to encounter by chance —**run after** **1** to pursue or follow **2** [Informal] to seek the company or companionship of —**run along** to leave or depart —**run around** [Informal] to be sexually unfaithful; cheat —☆**run (off) at the mouth** or **run one's mouth** [Informal] to talk loudly, excessively, or imprudently —**run away** **1** to flee **2** to desert one's home or family **3** to escape and run loose, as a horse —**run away with** **1** to depart and take with one; esp., to steal **2** to carry out of control [his enthusiasm *ran away with* him] **3** *a)* to outdo greatly all other contestants or performers in *b)* to get (a prize, honors, etc.) in this way —**run back** to carry (a football) toward the opponent's goal, as after receiving a kickoff —**run down** **1** to cease to run, or stop operating, as a mechanical device, through lack of power **2** to run, ride, or drive against so as to knock down **3** to pursue and capture or kill **4** to search out the source of **5** to speak of slightingly or injuriously; disparage **6** to lessen or lower in worth, quality, etc.; make or become run-down **7** to read through rapidly ☆**8** *Baseball* to catch and tag (a base runner trapped between two bases) —**run for it** to run in order to escape or avoid something —**run in** **1** to include or insert, as something additional **2** [Informal] to make a brief stop or visit at a place ☆**3** [Slang] to take into legal custody; arrest **4** *Printing* to make continuous without a break or paragraph —**run into** **1** to encounter by chance **2** to run, ride, or drive against so as to hit; collide with **3** to add up to (a large sum of money): also **run to** —**run off** ☆**1** to print, typewrite, make copies of, etc. **2** to cause to be run, performed, played, etc. **3** to decide the winner of (a race, etc.) by a runoff **4** to drive (animals, trespassers, etc.) off or away **5** to flow off; drain **6** RUN AWAY —**run on** **1** *a)* to continue or be continued *b)* *Printing* to continue without a break or new paragraph **2** to add (something) at the end **3** to talk continuously —**run out** **1** to come to an end; expire or become used up, exhausted, etc. **2** to force to leave; drive out —**run out of** to use up a supply of (something) —**run out on** [Informal] to abandon or desert —☆**run out the clock** *Basketball, Football* to maintain control of the ball in the closing minutes of a game —**run over** **1** to ride or drive over as with an automobile **2** to overflow **3** to go beyond a limit **4** to examine, rehearse, etc. rapidly or casually —**run rings (**or **circles) around** [Informal] **1** to run much faster than **2** to do much better than; surpass or outdo —**run scared** [Slang] to base one's actions upon the possibility or likelihood of failure —**run through** **1** to use up, spend, etc. quickly or recklessly **2** to pierce **3** RUN OVER (sense 4) —**run up** **1** to raise, rise, make, or build rapidly **2** to let (bills, debts, etc.) accumulate **3** to sew with a rapid succession of stitches —**run with** [Informal] **1** to associate or socialize with **2** to adopt or publicize (an account, explanation, etc.) readily or eagerly, often, specif., before it has been verified [local media *ran with* the story of his past arrest] —**the runs** [Slang] a case of diarrhea

run·a·bout (run′ə bout′) ***n.*** **1** a person who runs about from place to place **2** a light, one-seated, open carriage ☆**3** a light, one-seated, open automobile; roadster ☆**4** a light motorboat

run·a·gate (-ə gāt′) ***n.*** ⟦altered (< RUN + obs. *agate*, on the way) < ME *renegat*, apostate, villain < OFr < ML *renegatus:* see RENEGADE⟧ [Archaic] **1** a runaway; fugitive or deserter **2** a person who drifts or wanders about; vagabond

run·a·round (-ə round′) ***n.*** ☆**1** [Informal] a series of evasive excuses, deceptions, delays, etc.: usually in **get (**or **give) the runaround** **2** *Printing* an arrangement of type in shorter lines than the rest of the text, as around an illustration

run·a·way (-ə wā′) ***n.*** **1** a person, animal, etc. that is running away or has run away; specif., *a)* a fugitive or deserter *b)* a horse, team of horses, etc. that has broken loose from control of the rider or driver *c)* a minor who has fled his or her home or family **2** the act of running away **3** a runaway race or victory —***adj.*** **1** running away or having run away; escaping, eloping, or breaking loose from control [*runaway* lovers, a *runaway* horse] **2** of or done by runaways or running away [a *runaway* marriage] **3** easily won, as a race, or decisive, as a victory **4** *a)* rising rapidly, as prices *b)* characterized by an uncontrolled rise of prices [*runaway* inflation] ☆**5** relocated in order to evade agreements with a local union, local taxes, etc. [a *runaway* shop]

☆**run·back** (-bak′) ***n.*** *Football* the act of running back with the ball, as after receiving the kickoff or intercepting a forward pass

run·ci·ble spoon (run′sə bəl) ⟦name of a table utensil of indefinite form referred to by Edward LEAR[2] in his humorous poem "The Owl and the Pussycat" (1871) < ? obs. *rounceval,* huge (< ?) + -IBLE⟧ any of various utensils with broad tines and a spoonlike shape

run·ci·nate (run′sə nit, -nāt′) ***adj.*** ⟦L *runcinatus,* pp. of *runcinare,* to plane off < *runcina,* a plane (formerly understood as "saw")⟧ *Bot.* irregularly saw-toothed, with the teeth or lobes curved backward, as some leaves

Run·di (ro͞on′dē) ***n.*** **1** *pl.* **-dis** or **-di** a member of a people living in Burundi **2** the Bantu language of this people

run·dle (run′dəl) ***n.*** ⟦ME *rundel:* see ROUNDEL⟧ **1** [Archaic] a rung, or round, as of a ladder **2** any of the bars in a lantern pinion **3** something that rotates, as a wheel or the drum of a capstan

rund·let (rund′lit) ***n.*** ⟦ME *roundelet* < MFr *rondelet,* dim. of *rondelle,* little tun or barrel, round shield, dim. of *rond,* ROUND[1]⟧ [Archaic] **1** a small barrel or cask for liquor **2** the capacity of such a cask, usually taken as equal to about 18 wine gallons

run·down (run′doun′) ***n.*** **1** a concise summary or outline ☆**2** *Baseball* the act of running down a base runner

run-down (run′doun′) ***adj.*** **1** not wound and therefore not running, as a spring-operated clock **2** in poor physical condition, as from overwork; debilitated **3** fallen into disrepair; dilapidated

rune (ro͞on) ***n.*** ⟦ME *roun* < OE *run,* secret, mystery, runic character; re-adopted in the 17th c. in form of ON *rūn:* both < IE echoic base **reu-,* hoarse sound, roar, grumble > Welsh *rhin,* secret, L *raucus,* hoarse; in sense 3a < Finn *runo,* poem, canto < ON *rūn*⟧ **1** any of the characters of an alphabet (*futhark*) probably derived from a Greek script and used by the Scandinavians and other early Germanic peoples from about A.D. 300 **2** [*often pl.*] something inscribed or written in such characters **3** *a)* a Finnish or Old Norse poem or canto *b)* [Old Poet.] any poem, verse, or song, esp. one that is mystical or obscure

rung[1] (ruŋ) ***n.*** ⟦ME *rong* < OE *hrung,* staff, rod, pole, akin to Ger *runge;* for prob. IE base see RING[2]⟧ **1** any sturdy stick, bar, or rod, esp. a rounded one, used as a crossbar, support, etc.; specif., *a)* any of the crosspieces constituting the steps of a ladder *b)* a supporting crosspiece, as between the legs of a chair **2** a stage or degree in a scale, as of social acceptance **3** [Scot.] a cudgel

rung[2] (ruŋ) ***vi., vt. pp. & now chiefly dial. pt. of*** RING[1]

ru·nic (ro͞o′nik) ***adj.*** ⟦ModL *runicus* < ON *rūn,* a RUNE⟧ **1** of, pertaining to, or set down in runes **2** like runes in decorative interlaced effect, as knots and other figures on monuments, etc. of ancient peoples of N Europe **3** mystical; obscure

run-in (run′in′) ***adj.*** *Printing* that is run in or inserted: see the phrase RUN IN (sense 4) at the entry RUN —***n.*** **1** run-in matter ☆**2** [Informal] a quarrel, fight, etc.

run·let[1] (run′lit) ***n.*** ⟦RUN (*n.* 13) + -LET⟧ a runnel, or rivulet

run·let[2] (run′lit) ***n.*** RUNDLET

run·nel (run′əl) ***n.*** ⟦ME *rinel, runel* < OE *rynel* < base of *rinnan,* to RUN⟧ **1** a small stream; rivulet **2** a small channel or watercourse

run·ner (run′ər) ***n.*** ⟦ME *renner*⟧ **1** a person, animal, or thing that runs; specif., *a)* a racer ☆*b) Baseball* BASE RUNNER ☆*c) Football* a player running with the ball **2** a person who runs errands, carries messages, etc., as for a bank or brokerage house **3** a smuggler **4** a person who operates or manages something, as a machine **5** *a)* a long, narrow, decorative cloth for the top of a table, chest of drawers, etc. *b)* a long, narrow rug, as for a hall or corridor **6** a long ravel, as in hose; run **7** *a)* a long, slender, horizontal trailing stem that puts out roots along or just below the ground at its tip or its nodes, thus producing new plants; stolon *b)* any plant that spreads in this way, as the strawberry **8** any of various twining plants [the scarlet *runner*] **9** something on or in which something else moves, as a sliding part in machinery or the support along which a sliding door moves ☆**10** either of the long, narrow pieces of metal or wood on which a sled or sleigh slides ☆**11** the blade of a skate **12** a ring, loop, etc. that can slide along a strap, rod, etc., often one to which another part or parts can be attached **13** *Metallurgy* a channel through which molten metal is poured into a mold; gate **14** *Zool.* any of various edible jack fishes of warm seas, as a bluish species (*Caranx crysos*) and a striped bluish species (*Elagatis bipinnulata*)

runner bean *chiefly Brit. name for* POLE BEAN

run·ner-up (run′ər up′) ***n.,*** *pl.* **-ners-up′** **1** a person or team that finishes second in a race, contest, tournament, etc. **2** any of those finishing behind the winner but in positions of contention

run·ning (run′iŋ) ***n.*** **1** the act of a person or thing that runs (in various senses); racing, managing, proceeding, etc. **2** the condition of a track with reference to its use in a race **3** *a)* that which runs, or flows *b)* the amount or quantity that runs —***adj.*** **1** moving, passing, or advancing rapidly **2** *a)* run at a rapid gait [a *running* race] *b)* trained to race at this gait (said of a horse) **3** flowing [*running* water] **4** cursive: said of handwriting **5** melting; becoming liquid or fluid **6** discharging liquid; esp., discharging pus, etc. [a *running* sore] **7** creeping or climbing: said of plants **8** going, or in operation, as machinery **9** in a straight line; linear: said of measurement [a *running* foot] **10** going on, extending, etc. without interruption; continuous [a *running* commentary, a *running* pattern] **11** prevalent [*running* costs] **12** in progress; current [a *running* account] **13** concurrent; simultaneous [a *running* translation] **14** moving or going easily or smoothly **15** moving when pulled, as a rope **16** done in a run with a running start [a *running* jump] **17** of the normal run (of a train, bus, etc.) [*running* time] **18** of or appropriate for running for exercise or sport [a *running* shoe] —***adv.*** in succession; consecutively [for five days *running*] —**in (or out of) the running** in (or out of) the competition; having a (or no) chance to win

☆**running back** *Football* an offensive back, usually one of a pair, responsible primarily for rushing the ball; halfback or fullback

☆**running board** esp. formerly, a footboard, or step, along the lower part of the side of an automobile, etc.

running bowline a slipknot incorporating a bowline knot

running fire **1** a rapid succession of shots, as from soldiers in ranks **2** a rapid succession, as of remarks, questions, etc.

☆**running gear** **1** the wheels, axles, frame, etc. of a cart or carriage **2** the parts of a motor vehicle not producing or controlling power, including the frame, suspension, steering, and brakes

running hand handwriting in which the letters are slanted and close together, formed without often lifting the pen or pencil from the paper

running head (*or* title) a descriptive head or title printed at the top of every page or, sometimes, every other page, of a book, periodical, report, etc.

running knot SLIPKNOT

running lights the lights that a vehicle, as a ship or aircraft, traveling at night is required to display

☆**running mate** **1** a horse used in a race to set the pace for another horse from the same stable **2** a candidate for the lesser of two closely associated offices, as for the vice-presidency, in his or her relationship to the candidate for the greater office

running rigging the movable parts of a vessel's rigging, as halyards and sheets, used to position and control sails, booms, etc.: cf. STANDING RIGGING

running stitch a basic sewing stitch, in which the needle and thread run over and under small portions of fabric at regular intervals to form a straight or curving broken line: used in gathering, basting, darning, quilting, embroidery, etc.

run·ny (run′ē) ***adj.*** **-ni·er, -ni·est** **1** that flows, esp. too freely **2** that keeps on discharging mucus [a *runny* nose] —**run′ni·ness *n.***

Run·ny·mede (run′ē mēd′) meadow on the S bank of the Thames, southwest of London: see MAGNA CARTA

run·off (run′ôf′) ***n.*** ☆**1** something that runs off, as rain in excess of the amount absorbed by the ground **2** a deciding, final race, election, etc. as in case of a tie

run-of-the-mill (run′əv *th*ə mil′) ***adj.*** not special; ordinary; average

☆**run-of-the-mine** (-mīn′) ***adj.*** ⟦see RUN, *n.* 16*b*⟧ **1** not graded according to size or quality: said of coal **2** RUN-OF-THE-MILL Also **run′-of-mine′**

run-on (run′än′) ***adj.*** **1** *Printing* that is run on: see the phrase RUN ON (sense 1*b*) at the entry RUN **2** *Prosody* designating or of a line of verse that has little or no natural syntactic pause between it and the next line: cf. END-STOPPED, ENJAMBMENT —***n.*** run-on matter

run-on sentence a syntactic structure consisting of two or more complete sentences faultily run together as one

runt (runt) ***n.*** ⟦< ?⟧ **1** a stunted, undersized, or dwarfish animal **2** the smallest animal of a litter **3** [Slang] an insignificant person —**runt′i·ness *n.*** —**runt′y *adj.* runt′i·er, runt′i·est**

run-through (run′thro͞o′) ***n.*** a rehearsal, as of a dramatic or musical work or section, straight through from beginning to end

run-up (run′up′) ***n.*** **1** [Chiefly Brit.] a preparatory period preceding an important event ☆**2** a substantial, often rapid, increase in cost, price, value, etc.

☆**run·way** (run′wā′) ***n.*** a way, as a channel, track, chute, groove, trough, etc., in, on, or along which something runs, or moves; specif., *a)* the channel or bed of a stream *b)* a strip of leveled, usually paved ground, for use by airplanes in taking off and landing *c)* a track or ramp for wheeled vehicles *d)* a beaten path made by deer, etc. *e)* a narrow platform extending from a stage out into the audience

Run·yon (run′yən), **(Alfred) Da·mon** (dā′mən) 1884-1946; U.S. journalist & short-story writer: famous for humorous, slangy accounts of colorful urban characters —**Run′yon·esque′ *adj.***

ru·pee (ro͞o′pē, ro͞o pē′) ***n.*** ⟦Hindi *rūpiyah* < Sans *rūpyaḥ,* wrought silver⟧ the basic monetary unit of: *a)* India *b)* Mauritius *c)* Nepal *d)* Pakistan *e)* the Seychelles *f)* Sri Lanka: see the table of monetary units in the Reference Supplement

Ru·pert (ro͞o′pərt) ***n.*** ⟦Ger *Ruprecht, Rupprecht:* see ROBERT[1]⟧ a masculine name

ru·pes·trine (ro͞o pes′trin) ***adj.*** ⟦< L *rupes,* rock (after LACUSTRINE) < base of *rumpere,* to break: see RUPTURE⟧ *Biol.* growing on or living among rocks: also **ru·pic′o·lous** (-pik′ə ləs)

ru·pi·ah (ro͞o pē′ə) ***n.*** ⟦< Hindi *rūpiyah,* RUPEE⟧ the basic monetary unit of Indonesia: see the table of monetary units in the Reference Supplement

rup·ture (rup′chər) ***n.*** ⟦LME *ruptur* < MFr *rupture* < L *ruptura* < *ruptus,* pp. of *rumpere,* to break < IE **reup-* < base **reu-,* to tear out, tear apart, break > ROB, RUB⟧ **1** the act of breaking apart or bursting, or the state of being broken apart or burst; breach **2** a breaking off of friendly or peaceful relations, as between countries or individuals **3** *Med.* a hernia; esp., *a)* an abdominal or inguinal hernia *b)* a forcible tearing or bursting of an organ or part, as of a blood vessel, the bladder, etc. — ***vt., vi.*** **-tured, -tur·ing** **1** to break apart or burst **2** to affect with, undergo, or suffer a rupture

ru·ral (roor′əl) ***adj.*** ⟦ME < MFr < LL *ruralis* < L *rus* (gen. *ruris*), the country < IE **rewos,* space < base **rewe-,* to open, ROOM⟧ **1** of or characteristic of the country, country life, or country people; rustic **2** living in the country **3** having to do with farming; agricultural —**ru′ral·ly *adv.***

SYN.—**rural** is the comprehensive, nonspecific word referring to life on the farm or in the country as distinguished from life in the city [*rural* schools]; **rustic** stresses the contrast between the supposed crudeness and unsophistication of the country and the polish and refinement of the city [*rustic* humor]; **pastoral** suggests the highly idealized primitive simplicity of rural life, originally among shepherds; **bucolic**, in contrast, suggests a down-to-earth rustic simplicity or artlessness [her *bucolic* suitor] —*ANT.* **urban**

☆**rural delivery** delivery of mail by carriers on routes in rural areas: formerly **rural free delivery**

ru·ral·ism (-iz'əm) ***n.*** **1** rural quality or character **2** rural life **3** a rural idiom, characteristic, feature, etc. Also **ru·ral·i·ty** (roo ral'ə tē), *pl.* **-ties**

ru·ral·ist (-ist) ***n.*** one who leads or advocates a rural life

ru·ral·ize (roor'ə līz') ***vt.*** **-ized'**, **-iz'ing** to make rural —***vi.*** to live for a time in the country —**ru'ral·i·za'tion** ***n.***

Ru·rik (ro͞o'rik) died A.D. 879; Scand. chief regarded as the founder of the 1st Russian dynasty (862?-1598)

Ru·ri·ta·ni·an (roor'ə tā'nē ən) ***adj.*** ⟦after *Ruritania,* imaginary kingdom in novels by Anthony Hope⟧ of, like, or characteristic of some quaint, romantic, unreal place

Rus *abbrev.* **1** Russia **2** Russian

ruse (ro͞oz, ro͞os) ***n.*** ⟦Fr < MFr < OFr *reuser,* to deceive < L *recusare,* to be reluctant, refuse: see RECUSANT⟧ a stratagem, trick, or artifice —*SYN.* TRICK

Ru·se (ro͞o'sē) city in N Bulgaria, on the Danube

rush[1] (rush) ***vi.*** ⟦ME *ruschen* < Anglo-Fr *russher* < MFr *ruser,* to repel, avert, orig., to mislead < OFr *reuser:* see RUSE⟧ **1** *a)* to move or go swiftly or impetuously; dash *b)* to dash recklessly or rashly **2** to make a swift, sudden attack or assault (*on* or *upon*); charge **3** to pass, come, go, come into view, act, etc. swiftly, suddenly, or hastily [a thought *rushing* into the mind] ☆**4** *Football* to run with the ball after a direct snap from the center or after a handoff or pitchout —***vt.*** **1** to move, send, push, drive, etc. swiftly, violently, or hastily [we *rushed* him to the hospital] **2** to do, make, or cause to move, go, or act, with unusual or excessive speed or haste; hurry [to *rush* an order, a person at work, etc.] **3** *a)* to make a swift, sudden attack or assault on; charge *b)* to overcome or capture by such an attack or assault ☆**4** [Informal] *a)* to lavish attentions on, as in courting *b)* to entertain with parties or the like prior to inviting to join a fraternity or sorority ☆**5** *Football a)* to run with (the ball) after a direct snap from the center or after a handoff or pitchout *b)* BLITZ —***n.*** **1** the act or an instance of rushing; specif., an eager movement of many people, as to do something or to get to a place [a *rush* to buy concert tickets, the California *gold* rush] **2** intense activity; busyness; haste; hurry [the *rush* of modern life] **3** a sudden, swift attack or assault; onslaught ☆**4** the period during which fraternity or sorority recruitment takes place **5** a press, as of business or traffic, necessitating unusual haste or effort [the morning *rush*] **6** [Slang] *a)* the first, sudden euphoric effect of taking a narcotic, amphetamine, etc. *b)* a sudden thrill of pleasure ☆**7** *Football* a play in which an offensive back rushes with the ball **8** [*usually pl.*] *Film* a first print made shortly after the filming of a scene or scenes, for inspection as by the director —***adj.*** **1** necessitating haste [*rush* orders] **2** characterized by a RUSH[1] (*n.* 5) [*rush* hours] —**with a rush** suddenly and forcefully —**rush'er** ***n.***

rush[2] (rush) ***n.*** ⟦ME *rusche* < OE *risc,* akin to MDu *risch,* Norw *rusk* < IE base **rezg-,* to plait, twist > Sans *rájju,* L *restis,* cord⟧ **1** any of a genus (*Juncus*) of plants of the rush family, having small, greenish flowers: rushes usually grow in wet places and the round stems and pliant leaves of some species are used in making baskets, mats, ropes, etc. **2** any of various similar plants, as the bulrushes or horsetails —***adj.*** designating a family (Juncaceae, order Juncales) of grasslike monocotyledonous plants with a 6-parted perianth, tufted leaves, and the fruit in capsules

Rush (rush), **Benjamin** 1745-1813; Am. physician: signer of the Declaration of Independence

rush candle a candle made with the pith of a rush as the wick: also **rush'light'** ***n.*** or **rush light**

☆**rush·ee** (rush ē') ***n.*** a college student who is being rushed by a fraternity or sorority

☆**rush hour** a time of the day when business, traffic, etc. are especially heavy —**rush'-hour'** ***adj.***

Rush·more (rush'môr'), **Mount** ⟦after C. E. *Rushmore,* N.Y. mining attorney⟧ mountain in the Black Hills, W S.Dak., on which are carved huge heads (60 ft, 18 m, high) of U.S. presidents Washington, Jefferson, Lincoln, & Theodore Roosevelt: 6,200 ft (1,890 m)

rush·y (rush'ē) ***adj.*** **rush'i·er**, **rush'i·est** **1** made of, full of, or covered with rushes (plants) **2** like a rush

rusk (rusk) ***n.*** ⟦Sp *rosca,* twisted roll of bread, lit., a spiral < VL **rosicare,* to gnaw⟧ **1** sweet, raised bread or cake toasted in an oven, or baked a second time, after slicing, until browned and crisp **2** a piece of this

Rus·kin (rus'kin), **John** 1819-1900; Eng. writer, art critic, & social reformer

Russ *abbrev.* **1** Russia **2** Russian

Rus·sell[1] (rus'əl) ***n.*** ⟦< surname *Russell,* orig. dim. of Fr *roux,* reddish < OFr *rous:* see RUSSET⟧ a masculine name: dim. *Russ;* var. *Russel*

Rus·sell[2] (rus'əl) **1 Bertrand (Arthur William)** 3d Earl Russell 1872-1970; Brit. philosopher, mathematician, & writer **2 Charles M(arion)** 1864-1926; U.S. painter **3 George William** (pseud. Æ or A.E.) 1867-1935; Ir. poet & essayist **4** Lord **John** 1st Earl Russell of Kingston Russell 1792-1878; Eng. statesman: prime minister (1846-52; 1865-66): grandfather of Bertrand **5 Lillian** (born *Helen Louise Leonard*) 1861-1922; U.S. singer & actress

Russell's viper ⟦after P. *Russell,* 18th-c. Brit physician⟧ a very poisonous viper (*Vipera russeli*) of SE and SC Asia, with a pale-brown body and ringlike black spots edged with white or yellow

rus·set (rus'it) ***n.*** ⟦ME < OFr *rousset,* dim. of *rous* < L *russus,* reddish < IE **rudhso-* < base **reudh-,* RED⟧ **1** yellowish brown or reddish brown **2** a coarse homespun cloth, reddish-brown or brownish, formerly used for clothing by country people **3** a winter apple with a rough, mottled skin —***adj.*** **1** yellowish-brown or reddish-brown **2** made of russet (cloth) **3** [Archaic] rustic, simple, etc.

Rus·sia (rush'ə) ⟦< Russ *Rus'*⟧ **1** former empire (1547-1917) in E Europe & N Asia, ruled by the czars: cap. St. Petersburg: in full **Russian Empire** **2** loosely, the UNION OF SOVIET SOCIALIST REPUBLICS **3** RUSSIAN SOVIET FEDERATED SOCIALIST REPUBLIC, esp. the European part **4** country in E Europe and N Asia, stretching from the Baltic Sea to the Pacific & from the Arctic Ocean to the Chinese border: formerly the Russian Soviet Federated Socialist Republic, established as a country in 1991 upon the breakup of the U.S.S.R.: 6,592,772 sq mi (17,075,200 sq km); cap. Moscow: official name **Russian Federation**

Russia leather a fine, smooth leather, usually dyed dark red, orig. made in Russia of hides treated with oil from birch bark: used in bookbinding, etc.

Rus·sian (rush'ən) ***adj.*** of Russia or its people, language, or culture —***n.*** **1** *a)* a person born or living in Russia *b)* loosely, any citizen of the U.S.S.R. **2** a member of the chief Slavic people of Russia **3** the East Slavic language of the Russians

Russian blue any of a breed of domestic cat, thought to have originated in Arkhangelsk, with a soft, dense, grayish blue or silvery-blue coat and green eyes

☆**Russian dressing** mayonnaise mixed with chili sauce, chopped pickles, pimentos, etc.: used as a salad dressing

Rus·sian·ize (-īz') ***vt.*** **-ized'**, **-iz'ing** to make Russian in character —**Rus'sian·i·za'tion** ***n.***

Russian olive a small, hardy tree (*Elaeagnus angustifolia*) of the oleaster family, with silvery leaves and fragrant yellow flowers, often grown for windbreaks or ornament

Russian (Orthodox) Church an autonomous branch of the Eastern Orthodox Church

Russian Revolution **1** the revolution of 1917 in which the government of the czar was overthrown: it consisted of two distinct revolutions, the first (*February Revolution*) being the uprising of March (February, Old Style), in which a parliamentarian government headed by Kerensky came to power, the second (*October Revolution*) being the uprising of November (October, Old Style), in which this government was replaced by the Soviet government led by the Bolsheviks (Communists) under Lenin **2** sometimes, the October Revolution alone

☆**Russian roulette** **1** a deadly game of chance in which a person spins the cylinder of a revolver holding only one bullet, aims the gun at his or her head, and pulls the trigger **2** any activity potentially destructive to its participants

Russian Soviet Federated Socialist Republic a republic of the U.S.S.R.: see RUSSIA (the country)

☆**Russian thistle** a spiny weed (*Salsola kali*) of the goosefoot family: it matures into a spherical tumbleweed

Russian Turkestan the part of Turkestan formerly under Soviet control comprising the Kirghiz, Tadzhik, Turkmen & Uzbek republics and sometimes Kazakhstan: also called *Western Turkestan*

Russian wolfhound *former name for* BORZOI

Rus·si·fy (rus'ə fī') ***vt.*** **-fied'**, **-fy'ing** RUSSIANIZE —**Rus'si·fi·ca'tion** ***n.***

Rus·ski (rus'kē, ro͞os'-) [Slang] ***n.***, *pl.* **-skies** or **-skis** ⟦< Russ *russkij,* Russian, or < RUSSIAN + *-ski, -sky,* suffix in Slavic surnames, used jocularly⟧ **1** RUSSIAN (*n.* 1) **2** [*pl.*] the government or leaders of the U.S.S.R. —***adj.*** RUSSIAN Also sp. **Rus'skie** or **Rus'sky**, *pl.* **-skies** or **-skis**

NOTE—mild term of contempt, esp. formerly

Rus·so- (rus'ō, -ə) *combining form* Russian, Russian and [*Russophile*]

Rus·so·phile (rus'ə fīl') ***n.*** ⟦prec. + -PHILE⟧ a person who strongly admires Russia or its people, culture, customs, influence, etc.

rust (rust) ***n.*** ⟦ME < OE, akin to Ger *rost* < IE base **reudh-,* RED⟧ **1** the reddish-brown or reddish-yellow coating formed on iron or steel by oxidation, as during exposure to air and moisture: it consists mainly of ferric oxide, Fe_2O_3, and ferric hydroxide, $Fe(OH)_3$ **2** any coating or film formed on any other metal by oxidation or corrosion **3** any stain or formation resembling iron rust **4** any habit, influence, growth, etc. injurious to usefulness, to the mind or character, etc. **5** disuse of mental or moral powers; inactivity; idleness **6** the color of iron rust; reddish brown or reddish yellow **7** *Bot. a)* any of various plant diseases characterized by a spotted reddish or brownish discoloration of stems and leaves *b)* any of an order (Uredinales) of basidiomycetous fungi causing rust (in full **rust fungus**) —***vi., vt.*** **1** to affect or be affected by a rust fungus **2** to become or cause to be coated with rust, as iron **3** to deteriorate or spoil, as through disuse [a mind that has *rusted*] **4** to become or make rust-colored

☆**Rust Belt** [*also* **r- b-**] that part of the U.S. comprising many of the states of the Midwest and the Northeast, characterized as an area marked by diminishing urban populations, aging factories, decreasing production as of steel and automobiles, etc.

rust-col·ored (rust'kul'ərd) ***adj.*** having the color of iron rust; reddish-brown or reddish-yellow

rus·tic (rus'tik) ***adj.*** ⟦LME *rustyk* < MFr *rustique* < L *rusticus* < *rus,* the country: see RURAL⟧ 1 of or living in the country, as distinguished from cities or towns; rural 2 lacking refinement, elegance, polish, or sophistication; specif., *a)* simple, plain, or artless *b)* rough, awkward, uncouth, or boorish 3 made of rough, bark-covered branches or roots [*rustic* furniture] 4 *Masonry* having a rough surface or irregular, deeply sunk, deliberately conspicuous joints; rusticated —*n.* a country person, esp. one regarded as unsophisticated, simple, awkward, uncouth, etc. —**SYN.** RURAL —**rus′ti·cal·ly** *adv.* —**rus·tic′i·ty** (-tis′ə tē) *n.*

rus·ti·cal (-ti kəl) *adj., n. archaic var. of* RUSTIC

rus·ti·cate (rus′tə kāt′) *vi.* **-cat′ed, -cat′ing** ⟦< L *rusticatus,* pp. of L *rusticari,* to rusticate < *rusticus:* see RUSTIC⟧ 1 to go to the country 2 to live or stay in the country; lead a rural life —*vt.* 1 to send to, or cause to live or stay in, the country 2 [Brit.] to suspend (a student) temporarily from a university 3 to make (a person, etc.) rustic 4 to make or finish (masonry) in the rustic style —**rus′ti·ca′tion** *n.* —**rus′ti·ca′tor** *n.*

Rus·tin (rus′tin), **Bay·ard** (bī′ərd) 1910-87; U.S. civil rights leader

rus·tle[1] (rus′əl) *vi., vt.* **-tled, -tling** ⟦ME *rustelen,* freq. formation < ME *rouslen,* akin to earlier Fl *ruysselen* < WGmc echoic base⟧ to make or cause to make an irregular succession of soft sounds, as of leaves being moved by a gentle breeze or of papers being shuffled —*n.* such a succession of sounds —**rus′tling·ly** *adv.*

rus·tle[2] (rus′əl) *vi., vt.* **-tled, -tling** ⟦< ? RUSH[1] + HUSTLE⟧ 1 [Informal] to work or proceed with, or move, bring, or get by, energetic or vigorous action ☆2 *a)* [Archaic] in the W U.S., to round up (cattle, horses, etc.) *b)* [Informal] to steal (cattle, horses, etc.) —☆**rustle up** [Informal] to collect or get together, as by foraging —**rus′tler** *n.*

rust·proof (rust′pro͞of′) *adj.* resistant to rust —*vt.* to make rustproof

rust·y (rus′tē) *adj.* **rust′i·er, rust′i·est** ⟦ME < OE *rustig*⟧ 1 coated with rust, as a metal, or affected with the disease of rust, as a plant 2 consisting of or caused by rust 3 not working freely, easily, or quietly because of, or as if because of, rust; stiff or rasping in operation 4 *a)* impaired by disuse, neglect, etc. [to find one's golf game *rusty*] *b)* having lost facility through lack of practice [to be a little *rusty* in chess] 5 having the color of rust 6 faded, old-looking, or shabby —**rust′i·ly** *adv.* —**rust′i·ness** *n.*

rut[1] (rut) *n.* ⟦< ? MFr *route,* ROUTE⟧ 1 a groove, furrow, or track, esp. one made in the ground by the passage of wheeled vehicles 2 a fixed, routine course of action, thought, etc., esp. one regarded as monotonous —*vt.* **rut′ted, rut′ting** to make a rut or ruts in

rut[2] (rut) *n.* ⟦ME *rutte* < OFr *ruit* < L *rugitus,* a roaring (as of deer in rut) < *rugire,* to roar < IE **reuk-* < echoic base **reu-,* to roar, cry hoarsely > OE *ryn,* OSlav *rykati,* to roar⟧ 1 the periodic sexual excitement, or heat, of certain mammals: applied esp. to males, often specif. to those male ruminants in which it occurs once a year: cf. ESTRUS 2 the period during which this occurs —*vi.* **rut′ted, rut′ting** to be in rut

ru·ta·ba·ga (ro͞ot′ə bā′gə, ro͞ot′ə bä′gə) *n.* ⟦Swed dial. *rotabagge* < *rot* (< ON *rot,* ROOT[1]) + *bagge,* ram, thick object < ON *baggi* > BAG⟧ 1 a turniplike plant (*Brassica napobrassica*) of the crucifer family, with a large, yellow root 2 this edible root

ruth (ro͞oth) *n.* ⟦ME *reuthe* < *reowen:* see RUE[1]⟧ [Now Rare] 1 pity; compassion 2 sorrow; grief; remorse

Ruth[1] (ro͞oth) *n.* ⟦LL(Ec) < Heb *rut,* prob. contr. < *re'ut,* companion⟧ 1 a feminine name 2 *Bible a)* a Moabite widow deeply devoted to her mother-in-law, Naomi, for whom she left her own people to later become the wife of Boaz of Bethlehem *b)* the book that tells her story (abbrev. *Rt* or *Ru*)

Ruth[2] (ro͞oth), **Babe** (born *George Herman Ruth*) 1895-1948; U.S. baseball player

Ru·the·ni·a (ro͞o thē′nē ə, -thēn′yə) ⟦ML, Russia⟧ region in W Ukraine, a former province of Czechoslovakia

Ru·the·ni·an (-thē′nē ən, -thēn′yən) *n.* 1 a member of a group of Ukrainians living in Ruthenia and E Slovakia 2 the variety of Ukrainian spoken by the Ruthenians —*adj.* of Ruthenia or its people, language, or culture

ru·then·ic (ro͞o then′ik, -thē′nik) *adj.* designating or of chemical compounds containing ruthenium with a higher valence than in the corresponding ruthenious compounds

ru·the·ni·ous (-thē′nē əs) *adj.* designating or of chemical compounds containing ruthenium with a lower valence than in the corresponding ruthenic compounds

ru·the·ni·um (-thē′nē əm) *n.* ⟦ModL: so named (1828) by G. W. Osann, Estonian-Russian chemist who produced it in impure form < ML *Ruthenia,* Russia (source of the ore) + -IUM⟧ a rare, very hard and brittle, silver-gray chemical element, one of the platinum metals, used as a hardener in alloys of platinum and palladium and as a catalyst: symbol, Ru; at. no. 44: see the periodic table of elements in the Reference Supplement

ruth·er·ford (ruth′ər fərd, ruth′-) *n.* ⟦after Ernest RUTHERFORD⟧ a unit for measuring radioactive decay, equal to the mass (of a given substance) required to give off one million disintegrations per second; one million becquerels: symbol, rd

Ruth·er·ford (ruth′ər fərd, ruth′-) 1 **Ernest** Baron Rutherford of Nelson 1871-1937; Brit. physicist, born in New Zealand 2 **Joseph Franklin** 1869-1942; U.S. leader of Jehovah's Witnesses

Rutherford atom ⟦after Ernest RUTHERFORD⟧ the atom postulated as analogous to the solar system, with electrons revolving around a small, central, positive nucleus that constitutes practically the entire mass of the atom

ruth·er·for·di·um (ruth′ər fôr′dē əm, ruth′-) *n.* ⟦ModL, after Ernest RUTHERFORD + -IUM⟧ a radioactive chemical element with a very short half-life: a transactinide produced by bombarding californium or plutonium with high-energy nuclear particles: symbol, Rf; at. no. 104: see the periodic table of elements in the Reference Supplement

ruth·ful (ro͞oth′fəl) *adj.* ⟦ME *reuthful*⟧ [Now Rare] full of ruth; feeling, showing, or arousing pity or sorrow —**ruth′ful·ly** *adv.* —**ruth′ful·ness** *n.*

ruth·less (-lis) *adj.* ⟦ME *reutheles*⟧ having or showing no pity; merciless; relentless [a *ruthless* competitor] —**SYN.** CRUEL —**ruth′less·ly** *adv.* —**ruth′less·ness** *n.*

ru·ti·lant (ro͞ot′'l ənt) *adj.* ⟦L *rutilans,* prp. of *rutilare,* to have a reddish glow < *rutilus:* see fol.⟧ [Rare] glowing, gleaming, etc.

ru·tile (ro͞o′tēl′, -tīl′) *n.* ⟦< Fr or Ger: Fr < Ger *rutil* < L *rutilus,* red; akin to *rufus, rubeus,* RED⟧ a hard, reddish, tetragonal form of titanium dioxide, an ore of titanium

ru·tin (ro͞ot′'n) *n.* ⟦Ger < ModL *Ruta,* genus name for RUE[2], a source of this substance⟧ a yellowish, powdery bioflavonoid, $C_{27}H_{30}O_{16}$, found in many plants, esp. buckwheat and tobacco

Rut·land (rut′lənd) former county of EC England, now part of Leicestershire: also **Rut′land·shire′** (-shir′, -shər)

Rut·ledge (rut′lij) 1 **Ann** 1813?-35; alleged fiancée of young Abraham Lincoln 2 **Edward** 1749-1800; Am. statesman: signer of the Declaration of Independence 3 **John** 1739-1800; Am. statesman: brother of Edward

rut·tish (rut′ish) *adj.* in or inclined to rut (sexual heat); lustful —**rut′tish·ly** *adv.* —**rut′tish·ness** *n.*

rut·ty (rut′ē) *adj.* **-ti·er, -ti·est** having or full of ruts [a *rutty* road]

Ru·wen·zo·ri (ro͞o′wen zôr′ē) group of mountains in EC Africa, on the border of Uganda & the Democratic Republic of the Congo: identified with the "Mountains of the Moon" referred to by ancient writers: highest peak, Mt. Stanley

Ruys·dael (rois′däl′, rīs′-; *Du* rēs′däl′), **Jacob van** *alt. sp. of* Jacob van RUISDAEL

Ruy·ter (roi′tər, rī′-), **Mi·chiel A·dri·aans·zoon de** (mē khēl′ ä′drē än′sən də) 1607-76; Du. admiral

Rv *abbrev. Bible* Revelation

☆**RV**[1] (är′vē′) *n., pl.* **RVs** ⟦*R(ecreational) V(ehicle)*⟧ any of various vehicles, as campers, trailers, and motor homes, outfitted as a place to live, as when camping out

RV[2] *abbrev.* Revised Version (of the Bible)

R-val·ue (är′val′yo͞o) *n.* a measurement indicating the resistance of a given thickness of material, esp. insulating material, to the flow of heat: the higher the R-value, the greater the insulation

RW *abbrev.* 1 Right Worshipful 2 Right Worthy

Rwan·da[1] (ro͞o än′də) 1 a member of a Bantu people living in Rwanda and the Democratic Republic of the Congo 2 the Bantu language of this people

Rwan·da[2] (ro͞o än′də) country in EC Africa, east of the Democratic Republic of the Congo: formerly part of Ruanda-Urundi: member of the Commonwealth: 10,169 sq mi (26,338 sq km); cap. Kigali —**Rwan′dan** *adj., n.*

Rwy or **Ry** *abbrev.* Railway

Rx[1] (är′eks′) *n.* ⟦< fol.⟧ a remedy, cure, or the like suggested for any disorder or problem

Rx[2] ⟦altered < ℞, conventional symbol for L *recipe:* see RECIPE⟧ *symbol* PRESCRIPTION (sense 3)

-ry (rē) *suffix* -ERY [*foundry, Englishry, papistry*]

Ry·an (rī′ən) *n.* a masculine name

ry·a rug (rē′ə) ⟦Swed *rya (matta)* < ON *ry,* coarse woolen cover, akin to OE *ryhe:* for IE base see ROUGH⟧ a decorative hand-woven area rug or tapestry of Scandinavian origin, with a thick pile and, usually, an abstract design

Ry·a·zan (rē′ə zän′, -zän′y′) city in W European Russia, near the Oka River

Ry·binsk (ri′binsk′) 1 city in W European Russia, on Rybinsk Reservoir: see ANDROPOV 2 artificial lake on the upper Volga: *c.* 1,800 sq mi (4,662 sq km): in full **Rybinsk Reservoir**

Ry·der (rī′dər), **Albert Pink·ham** (piŋk′əm) 1847-1917; U.S. painter

rye (rī) *n.* ⟦ME < OE *ryge,* akin to Ger *roggen* < IE base **wrughyo-,* rye > Lith *rugỹs,* rye grain⟧ 1 a hardy cereal grass (*Secale cereale*) widely grown for its grain and straw 2 the grain or seeds of this plant, used for making flour and whiskey, and as feed for livestock ☆3 whiskey distilled wholly or chiefly from this grain 4 *short for* RYE BREAD

rye bread a bread made altogether or partly of rye flour, often with caraway seeds added

rye·grass (rī′gras′) *n.* any of a genus (*Lolium*) of annual or short-lived perennial grasses, often grown for lawns or as forage

Ryle (rīl) 1 **Gilbert** 1900-76; Brit. philosopher 2 Sir **Martin** 1918-84; Brit. astronomer

ry·ot (rī′ət) *n.* ⟦Hindi *raiyat* < Ar *ra'īya,* flock, herd⟧ in India, a peasant or tenant farmer

Ry·u·kyu (rē yo͞o′kyo͞o′, rē o͞o′-) chain of Japanese islands in the W Pacific, between Kyushu & Taiwan: *c.* 1,800 sq mi (4,662 sq km): chief island, Okinawa

S

s[1] or **S** (es) ***n.****, pl.* **s's, S's** **1** the nineteenth letter of the English alphabet: from the Greek *sigma,* a borrowing from the Phoenician **2** any of the speech sounds that this letter represents, as, in English, the (s) of *soap* or (z) of *rise* **3** a type or impression for *s* or *S* **4** the nineteenth in a sequence or group **5** an object shaped like S —***adj.*** **1** of *s* or *S* **2** nineteenth in a sequence or group **3** shaped like S

s[2] *abbrev.* **1** school **2** second(s) **3** section **4** see **5** semi **6** series **7** shilling(s) **8** sign **9** silver **10** single **11** singular **12** sire **13** society **14** son **15** soprano **16** south **17** southern **18** substantive

S[1] *abbrev.* **1** Sabbath **2** *Football* safety (the player): sometimes written **s** **3** Saint **4** *Bible* Samuel **5** Saturday **6** Saxon **7** Seaman **8** Senate **9** September **10** siemens **11** Signor **12** single **13** slim (garment width) **14** small **15** Society **16** South **17** south **18** southern **19** Sunday **20** ⟦L *signa*⟧ *Pharmacy* write

S[2] *symbol* **1** *Physics* entropy **2** *Chem.* sulfur

-s ⟦alternate form of -ES, assimilated to preceding voiceless sounds as (s) and to preceding voiced sounds as (z) when those sounds are not sibilants⟧ *suffix* **1** forming the plural of most nouns *[hips, shoes]* **2** forming the 3d pers. sing., pres. indic., of certain verbs *[shouts, gives, runs]* **3** forming some adverbs *[betimes, days]*

-'s[1] ⟦assimilated contr. < ME *-es* < OE, masc. & neut. gen. sing. inflection⟧ *suffix* **1** forming the possessive singular of most nouns and noun phrases and of some pronouns [*a child's* game, the *defense attorney's* case, the *Senator from Maine's* bill, *one's* own ideas] **2** forming the possessive plural of nouns whose plural does not end in *s* [*a children's* dictionary] **3** forming the plural of letters and numbers [mind one's *p's* and *q's*; a pile of *10's* on the table]

-'s[2] *suffix* **1** is [*he's* here] **2** has [*she's* done it] **3** [Informal] does [*what's* it matter?] Used in contractions

-'s[3] *suffix* us: used with the verb *let* in the contraction *let's*

-s' *suffix* forming the possessive plural of most nouns [*cats'* whiskers, the *Johnsons'* children, *Americans'* eating habits]

sa *abbrev.* **1** semiannual **2** [Slang] sex appeal

Sa *abbrev.* **1** *Bible* Samuel **2** Saturday

SA *abbrev.* **1** Salvation Army **2** Seaman Apprentice **3** [Slang] sex appeal **4** South Africa **5** South America **6** South Australia **7** ⟦Ger *Sturmabteilung*⟧ storm troopers

s a *abbrev.* ⟦L *sine anno*⟧ without year or date

Saa·di (sä′dē) *alt. sp. of* SADI

Saa·mi (sä′mē) ***n.****, pl.* **-mi** or **-mis** *alt. sp. of* SAMI

Saa·nich (san′ich) ⟦prob. after the *Saanich,* a local Salish people⟧ city on SE Vancouver Island, British Columbia, Canada

Saar (sär, zär) **1** river flowing from the Vosges Mountains, NE France, north into the Moselle River, SW Germany: *c.* 150 mi (241 km) **2** rich coal-mining region in the valley of this river: administered by France (1919-35) & Germany (1935-47) until set up as an autonomous government having a customs union with France (1947-57): now roughly equivalent to the Ger. state SAARLAND: also **Saar Basin**

Saar·brück·en (sär′brook′ən, zär′-; *Ger* zär′brük′ən) city in SW Germany, on the Saar: capital of the Saarland

Saa·re·maa (sä′rə mä′) island of Estonia in the Baltic Sea, at the entrance to the Gulf of Riga: 1,048 sq mi (2,714 sq km)

Saa·ri·nen (sär′i nen′, -nən) **1 Ee·ro** (ā′rō) 1910-61; U.S. architect, born in Finland **2 (Gottlieb) E·liel** (ēl′yel) 1873-1950; Finn. architect, in the U.S. after 1923: father of Eero

Saar·land (sär′land′, zär′-; *Ger* zär′länt′) state of SW Germany, in the Saar Basin: 992 sq mi (2,569 sq km); cap. Saarbrücken: used with *the*

Sab *abbrev.* Sabbath

Sa·ba (sä′bə; *for 2* sā′bə, sab′ə) **1** island of the Leeward group, in the former Netherlands Antilles: 5 sq mi (13 sq km) **2** ancient kingdom in S Arabia in the region of modern Yemen: Biblical name SHEBA[2]

Sa·ba·dell (sä′bä del′) city in NE Spain, near Barcelona

sab·a·dil·la (sab′ə dil′ə) ***n.*** ⟦Sp *cebadilla,* dim. of *cebada,* barley < L *cibare,* to feed < *cibus,* food⟧ **1** a Mexican and Central American plant (*Schoenocaulon officinale*) of the lily family, with brown seeds used in insecticides and formerly in medicine **2** the seeds, containing the alkaloids veratrine, veratridine, etc.

Sa·bae·an (sə bē′ən) ***adj.*** of the ancient kingdom of Saba or its people, language, or culture —***n.*** **1** a member of the people of ancient Saba **2** the Semitic language spoken by the Sabaeans, known only from inscriptions

Sa·bah (sä′bä) state of Malaysia, occupying NE Borneo & several offshore islands, including Labuan: formerly, until 1963, a British colony (called *North Borneo*): 28,460 sq mi (73,711 sq km); cap. Kota Kinabalu

Sab·a·oth (sab′ā äth′, sab′ə ōth′; sə bā′ōth′) ***pl.n.*** ⟦ME < LL(Ec) < Gr(Ec) *Sabaōth* < Heb *tsevaot,* pl. of *tsava,* host, army⟧ *Bible* armies; hosts: in *the Lord of Sabaoth*: Rom. 9:29, James 5:4

Sa·ba·tier (sȧ bȧ tyā′), **Paul** (pôl) 1854-1941; Fr. chemist

sa·ba·yon (sä bä yōn′; *Fr* sȧ bȧ yōn′) ***n.*** ⟦Fr⟧ ZABAGLIONE

sab·bat (sab′ət) ***n.*** ⟦Fr, SABBATH⟧ [*sometimes* **S-**] WITCHES' SABBATH

Sab·ba·tar·i·an (sab′ə ter′ē ən) ***adj.*** ⟦LL(Ec) *sabbatarius*⟧ **1** of the Sabbath and its observance **2** of the beliefs and practices of the Sabbatarians —***n.*** **1** a person, esp. a Christian, who observes Saturday as the Sabbath **2** a Christian who favors rigid observance of Sunday as the Sabbath —**Sab′ba·tar′i·an·ism′** ***n.***

Sab·bath (sab′əth) ***n.*** ⟦ME *sabat* < OFr & OE, both < L *sabbatum* < Gr *sabbaton* < Heb *shabat* < *shavat,* to rest⟧ **1** the seventh day of the week (Saturday), set aside for rest and worship and observed as such by Jews (from Friday sunset to Saturday sunset) and some Christian denominations **2** Sunday as the usual Christian day of rest and worship **3** [*also* **s-**] a day or time set aside for rest or worship **4** [*also* **s-**] WITCHES' SABBATH —***adj.*** of the Sabbath

Sabbath school classes in religious instruction held on the Sabbath

Sab·bat·i·cal (sə bat′i kəl) ***adj.*** ⟦< Fr *sabbatique* < LL(Ec) *sabbaticus* < Gr *sabbatikos* < *sabbaton* (see SABBATH) + -AL⟧ **1** of or suited to the Sabbath **2** [**s-**] bringing a period of rest that recurs in regular cycles —***n.*** [**s-**] **1** a recurring period of rest **2** SABBATICAL LEAVE **3** SABBATICAL YEAR Also **Sab·bat′ic** —**Sab·bat′i·cal·ly** ***adv.***

sabbatical leave a period of paid leave from work given periodically for study, travel, etc., originally given to college faculty members so as to allow for independant research, writing, etc.

sabbatical year **1** among the ancient Jews, every seventh year, in which, according to Mosaic law, the land and vineyards were to remain fallow and debtors were to be released ☆**2** SABBATICAL LEAVE

Sa·be·an (sə bē′ən) ***adj.******, n.*** *alt. sp. of* SABAEAN

Sa·bel·li·an (sə bel′ē ən, -bel′yən) ***n.*** ⟦< L *Sabelli,* ancient name of the Sabines + -AN⟧ **1** a member of a group of ancient, pre-Roman peoples of Italy including the Sabines and Samnites **2** an extinct group of languages of the Italic branch of Indo-European, probably most closely related to Oscan

sa·ber (sā′bər) ***n.*** ⟦Fr *sabre* < Ger *sabel* < MHG < Pol & Hung: Pol *szabla* < Hung *szablya*⟧ **1** a heavy cavalry sword with a slightly curved blade **2** *Fencing* a type of weapon, heavier than a foil, used with a slashing as well as thrusting movement: a touch may be scored with the edge or point —***vt.*** to strike, wound, or kill with a saber

saber rattling a threatening of war, or a menacing show of armed force

☆**saber saw** a portable electric saw with a blade that is mounted vertically and moves up and down

sa·ber-toothed (-tōōtht′) ***adj.*** designating various animals with long, curved upper canine teeth

saber-toothed tiger any of various extinct cats, closely resembling the tiger, but with a more massive body, shorter legs and tail, and long, curved upper canine teeth: found from the Oligocene to the Pleistocene, and of wide distribution

☆**sa·bin** (sā′bin) ***n.*** ⟦after W. C. *Sabine* (1868-1919), U.S. physicist⟧ *Acoustics* the unit for absorption of sound equal to the absorption provided by one square foot of a completely absorbing material

Sa·bin (sā′bin), **Albert B(ruce)** 1906-93; U.S. physician & bacteriologist, born in Russia: developed an oral vaccine to prevent poliomyelitis

Sa·bine[1] (sā′bīn′) ***n.*** ⟦ME *Sabyn* < L *Sabinus* < Sabine **Safini* (pl.) < IE **swobho-,* var. of **s(w)ebh-*: see SIB⟧ **1** a member of an ancient people living chiefly in the Apennines of central Italy, conquered by the Romans in the 3d century B.C. **2** the Italic language of this people

Sa·bine[2] (sə bēn′) ⟦Fr < Sp *sabina,* red cedar: named for the trees along its banks⟧ river flowing from E Tex. south along the Tex.-La. border into the Gulf of Mexico: *c.* 550 mi (885 km): lower course is part of a system of channels (**Sabine-Neches Waterway**) connecting Beaumont, Tex., & Lake Charles, La., with the Gulf of Mexico

Sabine Lake shallow lake formed by the widening of the Sabine River just above its mouth: *c.* 17 mi (27 km) long

sa·ble (sā′bəl) ***n.****, pl.* **-bles** or **-ble** ⟦OFr < ML *sabelum* < MDu *sabel* < OHG *zobel* < Russ *sobol′*⟧ **1** any marten; esp., the stone marten or a darker American species (*Martes americana*) **2** *a)* the costly fur or pelt of the sable *b)* [*pl.*] a coat, neckpiece, etc. made of this **3** [*pl.*] [Now Rare] black mourning clothes **4** *Heraldry* the color black: indicated in engraving by crosshatching —***adj.*** **1** made of or with the fur of the sable **2** black or dark brown

Sa·ble (sā′bəl), **Cape** ⟦< Fr, sand < L *sabulum*, SAND⟧ **1** cape at the S tip of Fla.: southernmost point of the U.S. mainland: *c.* 20 mi (32 km) long **2** cape at the S tip of Nova Scotia

sable antelope a large antelope (*Hippotragus niger*) of South Africa, with long, scimitar-shaped, ringed horns

sa·ble·fish (sā′bəl fish′) ***n., pl.*** **-fish′** or **-fish′es** (see FISH) ☆any of a small family (Anoplopomatidae) of large fishes of the N Pacific, esp. an edible, dark species (*Anoplopoma fimbria*)

sa·bot (sa bō′, sab′ō) ***n.*** ⟦Fr < OFr *çabot*, altered (infl. by *bot*, BOOT[1]) < *savate*, shoe, via Turk < Ar *sabbāṭ*, sandal⟧ **1** *a)* a kind of shoe shaped and hollowed from a single piece of wood, traditionally worn by peasants in Europe *b)* a heavy leather shoe with a wooden sole **2** a bushing or similar device fitted around or in back of a projectile, as to make it fit the bore of the gun barrel or launching tube

sabot
(sense 1*a*)

sab·o·tage (sab′ə täzh′, sab′ə täzh′) ***n.*** ⟦Fr < *saboter*, to work badly, damage < *sabot*: see prec. & -AGE: from damage done to machinery by wooden shoes⟧ **1** intentional destruction of machines, waste of materials, etc., as by employees during labor disputes **2** destruction of railroads, bridges, machinery, etc., as by enemy agents or by an underground resistance **3** the deliberate obstruction of or damage to any cause, movement, activity, effort, etc. —***vt.*** **-taged′**, **-tag′ing** to injure or destroy by sabotage —***vi.*** to engage in sabotage

sab·o·teur (sab′ə tʉr′, -toor′) ***n.*** ⟦Fr⟧ one who engages in sabotage

sa·bra (sä′brə) ***n.*** ⟦ModHeb *sabra*, lit. (an obs. sense), prickly fruit of a regional cactus: in allusion to being viewed as tough outside but soft inside⟧ [*sometimes* **S-**] a native-born Israeli Jew

sa·bre (sā′bər) ***n., vt.*** **-bred**, **-bring** *alt. sp. of* SABER

sa·bre·tache (sā′bər tash′, sab′ər-) ***n.*** ⟦Fr < Ger *säbeltasche* < *säbel*, SABER + *tasche*, pocket < ML *tasca*: see TASK⟧ a square leather case hung from the saber belt of cavalrymen

sab·u·lous (sab′yoo ləs) ***adj.*** ⟦L *sabulosus* < *sabulum*, SAND⟧ sandy

sac (sak) ***n.*** ⟦Fr < L *saccus*: see SACK[1]⟧ a pouchlike part in a plant or animal, esp. one filled with fluid —**sac′like′** ***adj.***

Sac (sak, sôk) ***n., pl.*** **Sacs** or **Sac** *var. of* SAUK

SAC *abbrev.* Strategic Air Command

Sac·a·ga·we·a (sak′ə jə wē′ə, -wā′ə) 1787?-1812; Shoshone Indian woman: interpreter & guide for the Lewis & Clark expedition: see LEWIS[2], Meriwether: also **Sac′a·ja·we′a**

☆**sac·a·ton** (sak′ə tōn′) ***n.*** ⟦AmSp *zacatón* < *zacate*: see ZACATÓN⟧ a coarse native grass (*Sporobolus wrightii*), used for hay or pasture on dry ranges in the SW U.S. and Mexico

sac·cade (sa käd′) ***n.*** ⟦Fr, a jerk < obs. *saquer*, to shake, pull, dial. var. of OFr *sachier* < VL **saccare*, to pull from a sack < L *saccus*, SACK[1]⟧ any of the rapid, involuntary jumps made by the eyes from one fixed point to another, as in reading —**sac·cad·ic** (sa käd′ik) ***adj.***

sac·cate (sak′āt) ***adj.*** ⟦ML *saccatus* < L *saccus*: see SACK[1]⟧ **1** shaped like a sac; pouchlike **2** having a sac

sac·char- (sak′ər) *combining form* SACCHARO-: used before a vowel

sac·cha·rase (sak′ə rās′) ***n.*** ⟦prec. + -ASE⟧ SUCRASE

sac·cha·rate (-rāt′, -rit) ***n.*** ⟦SACCHAR- + -ATE[2]⟧ **1** a salt or ester of saccharic acid **2** a compound of sugar with the oxide of calcium, strontium, or a similar metal

sac·char·ic (sə kar′ik) ***adj.*** ⟦SACCHAR- + -IC⟧ of or derived from saccharine compounds

saccharic acid a diacid, $COOH(CHOH)_4COOH$, obtained by the oxidation of glucose and other hexoses by nitric acid

sac·cha·ride (sak′ə rīd′) ***n.*** ⟦SACCHAR- + -IDE⟧ **1** a compound of sugar with an organic base **2** any of the carbohydrates; esp., a monosaccharide

sac·char·i·fy (sə kar′ə fī′) ***vt.*** **-fied′**, **-fy′ing** ⟦SACCHAR- + -I- + -FY⟧ to convert (starch or dextrin) into sugar, as by chemical means —**sac·char′i·fi·ca′tion** ***n.***

sac·cha·rim·e·ter (sak′ə rim′ət ər) ***n.*** ⟦Fr *saccharimètre*: see SACCHARO- & -METER⟧ an instrument, as a form of polarimeter used to determine the amount of sugar in a solution

sac·cha·rin (sak′ə rin′) ***n.*** ⟦so named (1879) by its discoverers, I. Remsen & C. Fahlberg, U.S. chemists < ModL *saccharum*, sugar < L < Gr *sakcharon*, ult. < Sans *śarkarā*, pebble, sugar (> SUGAR) + -IN[1]⟧ ☆a white, crystalline coal-tar compound, $C_7H_5NO_3S$, about 500 times sweeter than cane sugar, used as a sugar substitute in diabetic diets, as a noncaloric sweetener, etc.

sac·cha·rine (-rin′, -rīn′) ***adj.*** ⟦< fol. + -INE[1]⟧ **1** of, having the nature of, containing, or producing sugar ☆**2** too sweet or syrupy [*a saccharine voice*] —☆***n.*** SACCHARIN —**sac′cha·rine′ly** ***adv.*** —**sac′cha·rin′i·ty** (-rin′ə tē) ***n.***

sac·cha·ro- (sak′ə rō′) ⟦< L *saccharum*, sugar: see SACCHARIN⟧ *combining form* sugar [*saccharometer*]

sac·cha·roi·dal (sak′ə roid′'l) ***adj.*** ⟦< prec. + -OID + -AL⟧ *Geol.* having a crystalline or granular texture: said esp. of some sandstones and marbles: often **sac′cha·roid′**

sac·cha·rom·e·ter (-räm′ət ər) ***n.*** ⟦SACCHARO- + -METER⟧ a form of hydrometer for determining the amount of sugar in a solution

sac·cha·rose (sak′ə rōs′) ***n.*** ⟦SACCHAR- + -OSE[1]⟧ SUCROSE

Sac·co (sak′ō, sä′kō), **Ni·co·la** (nē kô′lä) 1891-1927; It. anarchist in the U.S.: together with Bartolomeo VANZETTI, charged with murder & payroll theft in 1920: their conviction & execution aroused international protest, being regarded by many as the result of political bias

sac·cu·lar (sak′yə lər) ***adj.*** like a sac

sac·cu·late (-lāt′, -lit) ***adj.*** ⟦< fol. + -ATE[1]⟧ formed of or divided into saccules or a series of saclike expansions: also **sac′cu·lat′ed** —**sac′cu·la′tion** ***n.***

sac·cule (sak′yool) ***n.*** ⟦L *sacculus*, dim. of *saccus*, SACK[1]⟧ a small sac; esp., the smaller of the two divisions of the membranous labyrinth of the inner ear

sac·cu·lus (-yoo ləs) ***n., pl.*** **-li′** (-lī′) ⟦L⟧ SACCULE

sac·er·do·tal (sas′ər dōt′'l; *occas.* sak′-) ***adj.*** ⟦ME *sacerdotale* < MFr < L *sacerdotalis* < *sacerdos*, priest < *sacer*, SACRED + *-dos* < IE base **dhe-*, to DO[1]⟧ **1** of priests or the office of priest; priestly **2** characterized by belief in the divine authority of the priesthood —**sac′er·do′tal·ly** ***adv.***

sac·er·do·tal·ism (-iz′əm) ***n.*** ⟦prec. + -ISM⟧ **1** the existence, nature, system, or functions of priesthood **2** domination by or unwarranted or excessive dependence on a priesthood —**sac′er·do′tal·ist** ***n.***

sac fungus ⟦descriptive⟧ ASCOMYCETE

☆**sa·chem** (sā′chəm) ***n.*** ⟦< Algonquian languages of SE New England: cf. Massachusett *sontim*, Narragansett *sâchim*⟧ **1** among some North American Indian tribes, the chief (of the tribe or of a confederation) **2** any of the leaders of the Tammany Society

Sa·cher torte (sä′kər; *Ger* zä′khər) ⟦Ger *Sachertorte*, after the *Sacher* family of Vienna or their hotel + Ger *torte*, cake: see TORTE⟧ a usually dry, glazed chocolate cake, often filled with apricot jam: also **Sa·cher·torte** (sä′kər tôrt′) ***n.***

sa·chet (sa shā′) ***n.*** ⟦Fr < OFr, dim. of *sac*: see SAC⟧ **1** a small bag, pad, etc. filled with perfumed powder or dried herbs and placed in dresser drawers, closets, etc. to scent clothing **2** powder for such a bag: also **sachet powder**

Sachs (saks; *Ger* zäks), **Hans** 1494-1576; Ger. Meistersinger, a cobbler by trade

Sach·sen (zäk′sən) *Ger. name for* SAXONY[2]

sack[1] (sak) ***n.*** ⟦ME *sak* < OE *sacc*, akin to OHG *sac*, Goth *sakkus* < early Gmc borrowing < L *saccus*, bag, in LL(Ec), sackcloth garment < Gr *sakkos* < Sem: cf. Heb *sak*, Akkadian *shaqqu*, sackcloth⟧ **1** *a)* a bag, esp. a large one of coarse cloth, for holding grain, foodstuffs, etc. *b)* such a bag with its contents **2** the quantity contained in such a bag: a measure of weight of varying amounts **3** *a)* a short, loosefitting jacket worn by women *b)* SHIFT (***n.*** 7*b*) **4** [Slang] dismissal from a job; discharge: with *the* ☆**5** [Slang] a bed, bunk, etc. ☆**6** *Baseball* BASE[1] (***n.*** 9) ☆**7** *Football* the act of sacking a passer —***vt.*** **1** to put into a sack or sacks **2** [Slang] to dismiss (a person) from a job; discharge ☆**3** *Football* to tackle (a passer who is attempting a forward pass) —☆**sack in** [Slang] **1** HIT THE SACK **2** to stay in bed longer than usual —☆**hit the sack** [Slang] to go to bed: also **sack out**

USAGE—n. 4 & ***vt.*** 2 considered informal in Brit. usage

sack[2] (sak) ***n.*** ⟦MFr *sac* < It *sacco*, plunder, lit., bag < L *saccus*: see prec.⟧ the plundering or looting, esp. by soldiers, of a captured city or town —***vt.*** to plunder or loot (a captured city, etc.) —***SYN.*** RAVAGE

sack[3] (sak) ***n.*** ⟦earlier *(wyne)seck* < Fr *(vin)sec*, dry (wine) < L *siccus*, dry (see SICCATIVE); sp. infl. by ? Sp *(vino de) saca*, (wine for) export < *sacar*, to remove⟧ any of various dry white wines from Spain or the Canary Islands, popular in England during the 16th and 17th cent.

sack·but (sak′but′) ***n.*** ⟦MFr, *saquebute*, sackbut, earlier, hooked lance for fighting on horseback < OFr *saquer*, to draw, pull < VL **saccare*, to pull (from a sack) < L *saccus*, SACK[1] + OFr *bouter*, to push, BUTT[2]⟧ **1** a medieval wind instrument, forerunner of the trombone **2** ⟦incorrect transl. of Aram *sabecha*⟧ *Bible* a stringed instrument resembling a lyre: Dan. 3:5

sack·cloth (-klôth′, -kläth′) ***n.*** ⟦see SACK[1]⟧ **1** SACKING **2** coarse, rough cloth —**in sackcloth and ashes** ⟦in allusion to the orig. type, made of goats' hair and sometimes worn as a symbol of mourning or penitence, often with ashes sprinkled on the head⟧ in a state of great mourning or penitence

☆**sack coat** a man's loosefitting, straight-backed coat

sack·er[1] (sak′ər) ***n.*** a person who sacks; plunderer

sack·er[2] (sak′ər) ***n.*** a person who makes or fills sacks

sack·ful (sak′fool′) ***n., pl.*** **-fuls′** **1** the amount that a sack will hold **2** a large quantity

sack·ing (-iŋ) ***n.*** a cheap, coarse cloth, as burlap, woven of flax, hemp, jute, etc., used esp. for making sacks

sack race a race in which contestants, hobbled by having their feet and legs enclosed in a sack, move along by jumping

Sack·ville (sak′vil), **Thomas** 1st Earl of Dorset & Baron Buckhurst 1536-1608; Eng. statesman & poet

sacque (sak) ***n.*** ⟦pseudo-Fr for SACK[1]⟧ **1** SACK[1] (sense 3) ☆**2** a baby's jacket

sa·cral[1] (sā′krəl) ***adj.*** ⟦< L *sacrum*, neut. of *sacer*, SACRED + -AL⟧ of or for religious rites or observances

sa·cral[2] (sā′krəl) ***adj.*** ⟦ModL *sacralis*: see SACRUM & -AL⟧ of, or in the region of, the sacrum

sa·cral·ize (sā′krə līz′) ***vt.*** **-ized′**, **-iz′ing** to make sacred or holy —**sa′cral·i·za′tion** ***n.***

sac·ra·ment (sak′rə mənt) ***n.*** ⟦ME < OFr *sacrement* < LL(Ec) *sacramentum*, the gospel, a secret, sacrament (used as transl. of Gr *mystērion*) < L, an oath of allegiance, orig., sum deposited by the two parties to a suit < *sacrare*, to consecrate < *sacer*, SACRED⟧ **1** *Christianity* any of certain rites instituted by Jesus and believed to be means of grace: baptism, confirmation, the Eucharist, penance, holy orders, matrimony, and Anointing of the

Sick are the seven recognized by the Roman Catholic and Eastern Orthodox churches; Protestants generally recognize only baptism and the Lord's Supper (the Eucharist) 2 [*often* **S-**] the Eucharist, or Holy Communion; also, the consecrated bread and wine, or sometimes the bread alone, used in the Eucharist 3 something regarded as having a sacred character or mysterious meaning 4 [Archaic] *a)* a symbol or token *b)* a solemn oath or pledge

sac·ra·men·tal (sak′rə ment′'l) ***adj.*** ⟦ME *sacramentale* < LL *sacramentalis*⟧ 1 of or relating to a sacrament 2 being or resembling a sacrament —***n.*** *R.C.Ch.* something, as the use of holy water, instituted or approved by the Church as a pious means of petitioning divine help and favor —**sac′ra·men′tal·ly** ***adv.***

sac·ra·men·tal·ism (-iz′əm) ***n.*** belief in the efficacy of sacraments; esp., the doctrine that the sacraments are necessary to salvation —**sac′ra·men′tal·ist** ***n.***

sac·ra·men·tar·i·an (sak′rə men ter′ē ən) ***adj.*** ⟦ML *sacramentarius*⟧ 1 *a)* SACRAMENTAL *b)* of sacramentalism 2 [*also* **S-**] of the sacramentarians —***n.*** 1 [*also* **S-**] one holding that Christ is present only symbolically in the Eucharist 2 an adherent of sacramentalism; sacramentalist —**Sac′ra·men·tar′i·an·ism′** ***n.***

sac·ra·men·ta·ry (sak′rə ment′ə rē) ***n.***, *pl.* **-ries** a liturgical book containing rites and prayers of the Mass, ordinations, etc.

Sac·ra·men·to (sak′rə men′tō) ⟦Sp, sacrament⟧ 1 river in central Calif., flowing south into an E arm of San Francisco Bay: *c.* 400 mi (644 km) 2 capital of Calif., on this river

sa·crar·i·um (sə krer′ē əm) ***n.***, *pl.* **-i·a** (-ē ə) ⟦L < *sacer*, fol.⟧ a drain, usually in a sacristy, leading directly to the earth, for disposal of water used in washing altar linens, chalices, etc.

sa·cred (sā′krid) ***adj.*** ⟦ME < pp. of *sacren*, to consecrate < OFr *sacrer* < L *sacrare* < *sacer*, holy < ? IE base **sak-*, to sanctify, make a compact > ON *sättr*, reconciled, Hittite *šakliš*, law, ritual⟧ 1 consecrated to or belonging to the divinity or a deity; holy 2 of or connected with religion or religious rites [*a sacred song*] 3 regarded with the respect or reverence accorded holy things; venerated; hallowed 4 set apart for, and dedicated to, some person, place, purpose, sentiment, etc. [*sacred to his memory*] 5 secured as by a religious feeling or sense of justice against any defamation, violation, or intrusion; inviolate —***SYN.*** HOLY —**sa′cred·ly** ***adv.*** —**sa′cred·ness** ***n.***

sacred baboon HAMADRYAD (sense 3)

Sacred College COLLEGE OF CARDINALS

☆**sacred cow** ⟦in allusion to Hindu reverence for the cow⟧ any person or thing regarded as above criticism or attack

sac·ri·fice (sak′rə fīs′) ***n.*** ⟦OFr < L *sacrificium* < *sacer*, SACRED + *facere*, to make, DO[1]⟧ 1 *a)* the act of offering the life of a person or animal, or some object, in propitiation of or homage to a deity *b)* something so offered 2 *a)* the act of giving up, destroying, permitting injury to, or forgoing something valued for the sake of something having a more pressing claim *b)* a thing so given up, etc. 3 *a)* a selling or giving up of something at less than its supposed value *b)* the loss incurred ☆4 *Baseball* a sacrifice bunt or sacrifice fly —***vt.*** **-ficed′**, **-fic′ing** 1 to offer as a sacrifice to God or a god 2 to give up, destroy, permit injury to, or forgo (something valued) for the sake of something having a more pressing claim 3 to sell at less than the supposed value ☆4 *Baseball* to advance (a base runner) by means of a sacrifice —***vi.*** 1 to offer or make a sacrifice ☆2 *Baseball* to execute a sacrifice —**sac′ri·fic′er** ***n.***

☆**sacrifice bunt** *Baseball* a bunt made by the batter so that a base runner is advanced while the batter is put out: see also AT-BAT: also called **sacrifice hit**

☆**sacrifice fly** *Baseball* a fly ball that is caught for an out and that enables a runner to score from third base after the catch: see also AT-BAT

sac·ri·fi·cial (sak′rə fish′əl) ***adj.*** of, having the nature of, used in, or offering a sacrifice —**sac′ri·fi′cial·ly** ***adv.***

sac·ri·lege (sak′rə lij′) ***n.*** ⟦ME < MFr < L *sacrilegium* < *sacrilegus*, temple robber < *sacer*, SACRED + *legere*, to gather up, take away: see LOGIC⟧ 1 the act of appropriating to oneself or to secular use, or of violating, what is consecrated to God or religion 2 the intentional desecration or disrespectful treatment of a person, place, thing, or idea held sacred

SYN.—**sacrilege** implies a violation of something sacred, as by appropriating to oneself or to a secular use something that has been dedicated to a religious purpose; **profanation** suggests a lack of reverence or a positive contempt for things regarded as sacred; **desecration** implies a removal of the sacredness of some object or place, as by defiling or polluting it

sac·ri·le·gious (sak′rə lij′əs) ***adj.*** 1 that is or involves sacrilege 2 guilty of sacrilege —**sac′ri·le′gious·ly** ***adv.*** —**sac′ri·le′gious·ness** ***n.***

sa·cring (sā′kriŋ) ***n.*** ⟦ME < prp. of *sacren*: see SACRED⟧ [Archaic] consecration of the bread and wine of the Eucharist

sac·ris·tan (sak′ris tən) ***n.*** ⟦ME *sacristane* < ML(Ec) *sacristanus* < *sacrista*: see fol.⟧ a person in charge of a sacristy

sac·ris·ty (-tē) ***n.***, *pl.* **-ties** ⟦Fr *sacristie* < ML(Ec) *sacristia* < *sacrista*, sacristan < L *sacer*, SACRED⟧ a room in a church, usually adjoining the sanctuary, where the sacred vessels, vestments, etc. are kept; vestry

sac·ro- (sak′rō, sā′krō) ⟦ModL < SACRUM⟧ *combining form* sacrum, sacrum and [*sacroiliac*]

sac·ro·il·i·ac (sak′rō il′ē ak′, sā′krō-) ***adj.*** ⟦prec. + ILIAC⟧ of the sacrum and the ilium; esp., designating the joint between them —***n.*** the joint or cartilage between the sacrum and the ilium

sac·ro·sanct (sak′rō saŋkt′) ***adj.*** ⟦L *sacrosanctus* < *sacer*, SACRED + *sanctus*, holy: see SAINT⟧ very sacred, holy, or inviolable —**sac′ro·sanc′ti·ty** ***n.***

sac·ro·sci·at·ic (sak′rō sī at′ik, sā′krō-) ***adj.*** ⟦SACRO- + SCIATIC⟧ of the sacrum and the ischium

sac·rum (sak′rəm, sā′krəm) ***n.***, *pl.* **sac·ra** (sak′rə, sā′krə) or **-rums** ⟦ModL < LL *(os) sacrum*, lit., sacred (bone), transl. of Gr *hieron osteon* < *hieron*, sacred, ? last (< *hieros*: see HIERO-) + *osteon*: see OSSIFY⟧ a thick, triangular bone situated near the lower end of the spinal column, where it joins both innominate bones to form the dorsal part of the pelvis: it is formed in humans of five fused vertebrae

sad (sad) ***adj.*** **sad′der**, **sad′dest** ⟦ME < OE *sæd*, sated, full, hence having feelings assoc. with satiety, akin to Ger *satt*, sated < IE base **sā-*, satisfied, sated > L *satis*, enough, OIr *sāith*, satiety⟧ 1 having, expressing, or showing low spirits or sorrow; unhappy; mournful; sorrowful 2 causing or characterized by dejection, melancholy, or sorrow 3 dark or dull in color; drab 4 [Informal] very bad; deplorable 5 [Dial.] heavy or soggy [*a sad cake*] —**sad′ness** ***n.***

SYN.—**sad** is the simple, general term, ranging in implication from a mild, momentary unhappiness to a feeling of intense grief; **sorrowful** implies a sadness caused by some specific loss, disappointment, etc. [her death left him *sorrowful*]; **melancholy** suggests a more or less chronic mournfulness or gloominess, or, often, merely a wistful pensiveness [*melancholy* thoughts about the future]; **dejected** implies discouragement or a sinking of spirits, as because of frustration; **depressed** suggests a mood of brooding despondency, as because of fatigue or a sense of futility [the novel left him feeling *depressed*]; **doleful** implies a mournful, often lugubrious, sadness [the *doleful* look on a lost child's face] —***ANT.*** **happy, cheerful**

SAD *abbrev.* seasonal affective disorder

Sa·dat (sə dät′), **An·war (el-)** (än′wär′) 1918-81; president of Egypt (1970-81): assassinated

sad·den (sad′'n) ***vt., vi.*** to make or become sad

sad·dle (sad′'l) ***n.*** ⟦ME *sadel* < OE *sadol*, akin to Ger *sattel* < Gmc **sathula*, via ? OSlav **sedulo-* < IE base **sed-*, to SIT⟧ 1 a seat for a rider on a horse, bicycle, etc., usually padded and traditionally of leather, and generally straddled in riding 2 a padded part of a harness worn over a horse's back to hold the shafts 3 the part of an animal's back where a saddle is placed 4 anything suggesting a saddle, as in form, placement, etc. 5 a ridge between two peaks or summits 6 *a)* a cut of lamb, venison, etc., including part of the backbone and the two loins *b)* the rear part of the back of a fowl —***vt.*** **-dled**, **-dling** 1 to put a saddle upon 2 to load or encumber, as with a burden 3 to impose as a burden, obligation, etc. —***vi.*** to put a saddle on a horse and mount it: often with *up* —**back in the saddle** back performing one's job, being engaged in one's pursuits, etc. —**in the saddle** 1 seated on a saddle 2 in a position of control

sad·dle·back (-bak′) ***n.*** something saddle-backed

sad·dle-backed (-bakt′) ***adj.*** 1 having a low, hollow back curved like a saddle, as some horses 2 having a concave outline, as a ridge between peaks

sad·dle·bag (-bag′) ***n.*** 1 a large bag, usually one of a pair, carried on either side of the back of a horse, etc., just behind the saddle ☆2 a similar bag carried over the back wheel of a motorcycle or bicycle 3 [Informal] a deposit of fat forming a bulge at the top of the thigh: *usually used in the pl.*

☆**saddle block (anesthesia)** ⟦because affected areas are those that would be in contact with a saddle during horseback riding⟧ spinal anesthesia, often used during obstetric delivery, for anesthetizing the buttocks, perineum, and inner thighs

sad·dle·bow (-bō′) ***n.*** the arched front part, or bow, of a saddle, the top of which is the pommel

sad·dle·cloth (-klôth′, -kläth′) ***n.*** a thick cloth placed under a saddle on an animal's back

saddle horse 1 a horse trained or suitable for riding 2 any of a breed of medium-sized, dark-colored horse, often with a white face, characterized by a long, swanlike neck and a free, easy gait, frequently used as a show horse: in full **American saddle horse**

sad·dler (sad′lər) ***n.*** ⟦ME *sadelere*⟧ a person whose work is making, repairing, or selling saddles, harnesses, etc.

saddle roof a roof with two gables and a ridge

sad·dler·y (sad′lər ē) ***n.***, *pl.* **-dler·ies** ⟦ME *sadelarie*⟧ 1 the work or craft of a saddler 2 the articles, as saddles, harnesses, bridles, etc., made by a saddler 3 a shop where such articles are sold

saddle seat ⟦because its shape suggests the pommel of a *saddle*⟧ a concave wooden seat, esp. of a Windsor chair, often with a central ridge running from the front toward the back

☆**saddle shoes** ⟦because the band across the instep suggests a *saddle*⟧ white oxford shoes with a band of contrasting leather, usually black or brown, across the instep

saddle shoes

☆**saddle soap** a preparation, usually of mild soap and neat's-foot oil, for cleaning and softening leather

saddle sore a sore or irritation caused by friction of a saddle on a horse or rider

saddle stitch 1 a kind of stitch made of thread or with a STAPLE[2] (***n.*** 2), used as in binding magazines or booklets at the fold 2 *Sewing* a decorative stitch consisting of long stitches on the right side and short stitches on the underside

sad·dle·tree (sad′'l trē′) *n.* ⟦ME *sadeltre*⟧ the frame of a saddle

Sad·du·cee (saj′o͞o sē′, sad′yo͞o-) *n.* ⟦ME *Saducei* < OE *Sadduce* < LL(Ec) *Sadducaeus* < Gr(Ec) *Saddoukaios* < Heb *tsadoki,* prob. < *tsadok,* Zadok: see Ezek. 40:46⟧ a member of an ancient Jewish party, representing the ruling hierarchy, that accepted only the written law and rejected the oral, or traditional, law: opposed to PHARISEE —**Sad′du·ce′an** *adj.*

Sade (säd), Marquis **de** (full name Comte *Donatien Alphonse François de Sade*) 1740-1814; Fr. soldier & novelist, whose writings describe sexual aberrations

sa·dhe (sä′dē, tsä′-) *n.* ⟦Heb *tsādē*⟧ the eighteenth letter of the Hebrew alphabet (צ, ץ)

sa·dhu (sä′do͞o′) *n.* ⟦Sans < *sādhu,* straight, able < IE base **sēdh-*, to go straight to a goal > Gr *ithyein,* to go straight⟧ a Hindu ascetic or holy man, often one who travels from place to place begging

Sa·di (sä′dē) (born *Muslih-ud-Din*) 1184?-1291?; Pers. poet

Sa·die (sā′dē) *n.* a feminine name: see SARAH

sad·i·ron (sad′ī′ərn) *n.* ⟦SAD (sense 5) + IRON⟧ a heavy, solid flatiron, pointed at both ends

sad·ism (sā′diz′əm, sad′iz′əm) *n.* ⟦Fr, after the Marquis de SADE⟧ **1** the getting of sexual pleasure from dominating, mistreating, or hurting one's sexual partner **2** the getting of pleasure from inflicting physical or psychological pain on another or others Cf. MASOCHISM —**sad′ist** *n.* —**sa·dis·tic** (sə dis′tik) *adj.* —**sa·dis′ti·cal·ly** *adv.*

sad·ly (sad′lē) *adv.* **1** with sadness; in a sad or sorrowful way **2** unfortunately; regrettably [*sadly,* we must decline your invitation; his efforts were *sadly* overlooked]

sad·o·mas·o·chism (sā′dō mas′ə kiz′əm, sad′ō-) *n.* ⟦< SAD(ISM) + -O- + MASOCHISM⟧ the getting of pleasure, esp. sexual pleasure, from sadism or masochism, or both —**sad′o·mas′o·chist** *n.* —**sad′o·mas′o·chis′tic** *adj.*

Sa·do·vá (sä′dô vä′) village in the N Czech Republic: see HRADEC KRÁLOVÉ

☆**sad sack** ⟦shortened < mil. slang *sad sack of shit*⟧ [Slang] a person who means well but is incompetent, ineffective, etc. and is consistently in trouble

sae *abbrev.* [Brit.] stamped addressed envelope

SAE *abbrev.* Society of Automotive Engineers

sa·fa·ri (sə fär′ē) *n., pl.* **-ris** ⟦Swahili < Ar *safarī,* pertaining to a journey < *safar,* to journey⟧ **1** a journey or hunting expedition, esp. in E Africa **2** the caravan of such an expedition —*adj.* designating or of a style of clothing like that worn on safaris, esp. a belted jacket with pairs of pleated pockets above and below the belt

safe (sāf) *adj.* **saf′er, saf′est** ⟦ME *sauf* < OFr < L *salvus,* akin to *salus,* health, sound condition < IE base **solo-*, whole, well-preserved > Gr *holos,* whole, Sans *sarva,* unharmed, whole⟧ **1** *a)* free from damage, danger, or injury; secure *b)* having escaped danger or injury; unharmed **2** *a)* giving protection *b)* involving no risk, often, specif., because well-founded [it's *safe* to say his recklessness will get him in trouble some day] *c)* trustworthy **3** no longer dangerous; unable to cause trouble or damage [*safe* in jail] **4** taking no risks; prudent; cautious: said of persons ☆**5** *Baseball* having reached a base without being put out —*n.* ⟦altered (after the *adj.*) < earlier *save* < SAVE[1]⟧ **1** a container or box, capable of being locked and usually of metal, in which to store valuables **2** any compartment, box, etc. for storing food, etc. [a meat *safe*] **3** [Slang] a condom —**safe′ly** *adv.* —**safe′ness** *n.*

SYN.—**safe** implies freedom from damage, danger, or injury or from the risk of damage, etc. [is it *safe* to leave?]; **secure,** often interchangeable with **safe,** is now usually applied to something about which there is no need to feel apprehension [he is *secure* in his job] —*ANT.* **dangerous, precarious**

safe-con·duct (sāf′kän′dukt) *n.* ⟦ME *saufconduit* < OFr: see prec. & CONDUCT⟧ **1** permission to travel through a dangerous area, as in time of war, with protection against arrest or harm **2** a written pass giving such permission **3** the act of conducting in safety

safe·crack·ing (-krak′iŋ) *n.* the breaking open and robbing of safes —**safe′crack′er** *n.*

☆**safe-de·pos·it** (-di päz′it) *adj.* designating or of a box or vault, esp. in a bank, for storing jewels and other valuables, important documents, etc.: also **safe′ty-de·pos′it**

safe·guard (-gärd′) *n.* ⟦ME *saufgarde* < MFr *sauvegarde*: see SAVE[1] & GUARD⟧ any person or thing that protects or guards against loss or injury; specif., *a)* a precaution or protective stipulation *b)* a permit or pass allowing safe passage *c)* [Now Rare] a convoy or guard *d)* a safety device, as on machinery —*vt.* to protect or guard

safe house a house, apartment, etc. used as by an intelligence agency or underground organization as a refuge or hiding place for its agents

safe·keep·ing (-kēp′iŋ) *n.* a keeping or being kept in safety; protection or custody

safe·light (-līt′) *n. Photog.* a special light or lamp for a darkroom that does not affect the film, printing paper, etc.

safe sex sexual activity incorporating any of various safeguards, such as the use of a condom, that reduce the risk of spreading sexually transmitted diseases

safe·ty (sāf′tē) *n., pl.* **-ties** ⟦ME *sauvete* < MFr *sauveté* < OFr *salvetet* < ML *salvitas,* safety < L *salvus*: see SAFE⟧ **1** the quality or condition of being safe; freedom from danger, injury, or damage; security **2** any of certain devices for preventing an accident or an undesirable effect; specif., *a)* a catch or locking device on a firearm that prevents it from firing (also **safety catch** or **safety lock**) *b)* [Slang] a condom ☆**3** *Baseball* BASE HIT ☆**4** *Football a)* a play in which the defensive team is awarded two points as by tackling the offensive ball carrier behind the offensive team's goal line (distinguished from TOUCHBACK) *b)* a defensive back who is primarily responsible for covering pass receivers in the middle of the defensive backfield —*adj.* giving safety; reducing danger or harm

safety belt **1** a belt attaching a telephone lineman, window washer, etc. to a telephone pole, window sill, etc. to prevent falling **2** a restraining belt, as in an airplane or motor vehicle: see SEAT BELT, SHOULDER HARNESS

safety glass glass made to be shatterproof by fastening together two sheets of glass with a transparent, plastic substance between them

☆**safety island** SAFETY ZONE

safety lamp a miner's lamp designed to avoid explosion, fire, etc.: see also DAVY LAMP

safety match a MATCH[1] that will light only when it is struck on a prepared surface

safety net **1** a net suspended as beneath circus aerialists to catch them if they fall **2** any protection against failure or loss

safety pin a fastening device consisting of a wire pin curved so that the point at one end can be held by an attached guard at the other end

☆**safety razor** a razor with a detachable blade fitted into a holder provided with guards and set at an angle, designed to minimize the danger of cutting the skin

safety valve **1** an automatic valve for a steam boiler, pressure cooker, etc., which opens if the pressure becomes excessive **2** any outlet for the release of strong emotion, energy, etc.

☆**safety zone** a platform or marked area in a roadway, from which vehicular traffic is diverted, for protection of pedestrians as in boarding or leaving buses

saf·fi·an leather (saf′ē ən) ⟦Ger *saffian,* ult. < Pers *sāḫtiyān,* goatskin < *sāht,* hard, firm⟧ leather made of sheepskin or goatskin tanned with sumac and usually dyed a bright color

☆**Saf·fir-Simp·son Hurricane Scale** (saf′ər simp′sən, -sim′sən) ⟦developed (1969) by U.S. civil engineer H. *Saffir* & U.S. meteorologist R. *Simpson*⟧ a chart that categorizes hurricanes based on the potential damage caused by various levels of wind speed: see the Reference Supplement

saf·flow·er (saf′lou′ər) *n.* ⟦altered (< fol. & FLOWER) < Du or MFr: Du *saffloer* < MFr *saffleur* < It *saffiore* < Ar *aṣfar,* yellow⟧ **1** a thistlelike, annual plant (*Carthamus tinctorius*) of the composite family, with large, orange flower heads and seeds that yield a drying oil used in paints, foods, medicine, etc. **2** a dyestuff or drug prepared from its florets

saf·fron (saf′rən) *n.* ⟦ME *saffroun* < OFr *safran* < ML *safranum* < Ar *za'farān*⟧ **1** a perennial Old World plant (*Crocus sativus*) of the iris family, with funnel-shaped, purplish flowers having orange stigmas **2** the dried, aromatic stigmas of this plant, used in flavoring and coloring foods, and formerly in medicine **3** orange yellow: also **saffron yellow** —*adj.* orange-yellow

Sa·fi (sä fē′, saf′ē) seaport in W Morocco, on the Atlantic

S Afr *abbrev.* **1** South Africa: also **S Af** **2** South African

saf·ra·nine (saf′rə nēn′, -nin) *n.* ⟦Fr *safran,* SAFFRON + -INE[3]⟧ **1** a yellowish-red aniline dye, $C_{18}H_{15}N_4Cl$, or any of several dyes closely related in structure to this **2** any mixture of the various salts of the safranine dyes, used as a dye and as a stain in microscopy Also **saf′ra·nin** (-nin)

saf·role (saf′rōl) *n.* ⟦Fr *safran,* SAFFRON + *-ole,* for -OL[2]⟧ a clear, colorless oil, $C_3H_5C_6H_3O_2CH_2$, found in sassafras oil, camphor wood, etc., and used in perfumes, medicines, flavors, etc.: toxic when ingested and regarded as a possible carcinogen, its use in foods and beverages is forbidden in the U.S.

sag (sag) *vi.* **sagged, sag′ging** ⟦ME *saggen,* prob. < Scand, akin to Swed *sacka,* Norw dial. *sakka, sagga* < IE base **sengw-*, to SINK⟧ **1** to sink, bend, or curve, esp. in the middle, from weight or pressure **2** to hang down unevenly or loosely **3** to lose firmness, strength, or intensity; weaken through weariness, age, etc.; droop [*sagging* spirits] **4** to decline in price, value, sales, etc. **5** *Naut.* to drift [to *sag* to leeward] —*vt.* to cause to sag —*n.* **1** the act or an instance of sagging **2** the degree or amount of sagging ☆**3** a place of sagging; sunken or depressed place

SAG (sag) *abbrev.* Screen Actors Guild

sa·ga (sä′gə sag′ə) *n.* ⟦ON, thing said, tale, story, akin to OE *sagu* (> SAW[2]): see SAY⟧ **1** a medieval Icelandic or Scandinavian prose narrative dealing with the heroic exploits of legendary and historical kings and warriors or with the traditional history of an important family **2** any long story of adventure or heroic deeds **3** ROMAN-FLEUVE: in full **saga novel**

sa·ga·cious (sə gā′shəs) *adj.* ⟦< L *sagax* (gen. *sagacis*), wise, foreseeing; akin to *sagire,* to perceive acutely: see SAKE[1]⟧ **1** having or showing keen perception or discernment and sound judgment, foresight, etc. **2** [Obs.] having a keen sense of smell —*SYN.* SHREWD —**sa·ga′cious·ly** *adv.* —**sa·ga′cious·ness** *n.*

sa·gac·i·ty (sə gas′ə tē) *n., pl.* **-ties** ⟦Fr *sagacité* < L *sagacitas*⟧ the quality or an instance of being sagacious; penetrating intelligence and sound judgment

☆**sag·a·more** (sag′ə môr′) *n.* ⟦< Abenaki *sákəmα*⟧ a chief of second rank among certain tribes of North American Indians: sometimes equivalent to SACHEM (sense 1)

Sa·gan (sā′gən), **Carl (Edward)** 1934-96; U.S. astronomer & writer

sage[1] (sāj) *adj.* **sag′er, sag′est** ⟦OFr < VL **sapius* < L *sapiens*, wise, orig. prp. of *sapere*, to know, taste < IE base **sap-*, to taste > ON *safi*, sap, *sefi*, mind⟧ **1** wise, discerning, judicious, etc. **2** showing wisdom and good judgment [*a sage comment*] **3** [Obs.] grave or solemn —***n.*** a very wise person; esp., an elderly man, widely respected for his wisdom, experience, and judgment —**sage′ly** *adv.* —**sage′ness** *n.*

sage[2] (sāj) *n.* ⟦ME *sauge* < OFr < L *salvia* < *salvus*, SAFE: from its reputed healing powers⟧ **1** any of a genus (*Salvia*) of plants of the mint family, having a two-lipped corolla and two stamens: sages are cultivated for ornament, as the **scarlet sage** (*S. splendens*) with brilliant red flowers, or for flavoring, as the **garden sage** (*S. officinalis*) with aromatic leaves used, when dried, for seasoning meats, cheeses, etc. **2** any of various similar plants ☆**3** SAGEBRUSH

Sage (sāj), **Russell** 1816-1906; U.S. financier

☆**sage·brush** (sāj′brush′) *n.* ⟦SAGE[2] + BRUSH[1]⟧ any of a number of plants (genus *Artemisia*) of the composite family, common in the dry, alkaline areas of the W U.S.; esp., the **big sagebrush** (*A. tridentata*), with small, aromatic leaves and minute flower heads, important as a forage plant

☆**sage grouse** a large grouse (*Centrocercus urophasianus*) living on the sagebrush plains of W North America: also, esp. for the female, **sage hen**

sag·ger or **sag·gar** (sag′ər) *n.* ⟦dial. *saggard*, contr. < ? SAFEGUARD⟧ **1** a thin, protective box of fire clay for baking finer or more delicate ceramics in the kiln **2** the clay of which it is made

sag·gy (sag′ē) *adj.* **-gi·er, -gi·est** inclined to sag

Sag·i·naw (sag′ə nô′) ⟦< Ojibwa *sa·gi·na·ng*, lit., at the place of the Sauks⟧ city in central Mich.

Sa·git·ta (sə jit′ə) *n.* ⟦L, lit., arrow⟧ a small N constellation between Vulpecula and Aquila

sag·it·tal (saj′it′l) *adj.* ⟦ModL *sagittalis* < L *sagitta*, arrow⟧ **1** of or like an arrow or arrowhead **2** *Anat. a)* designating or of the suture between the two parietal bones along the length of the skull *b)* designating, of, or in the longitudinal plane of this suture, regarded as dividing the body into right and left halves *c)* of or in any plane parallel to this —**sag′it·tal·ly** *adv.*

Sag·it·tar·i·us (saj′ə ter′ē əs) *n.* ⟦ME < L *sagittarius*, archer < *sagitta*, arrow⟧ **1** a large S constellation in the brightest part of the Milky Way, beyond which lies the center of our galaxy; the Archer **2** the ninth sign of the zodiac, entered by the sun about November 21 **3** a person born under this sign: also **Sag′it·tar′i·an**

sag·it·tate (saj′ə tāt′) *adj.* ⟦ModL *sagittatus* < L *sagitta*, arrow⟧ in the shape of an arrowhead, as some leaves

sa·go (sā′gō) *n., pl.* **-gos** ⟦Malay *sagu*, flour from the pith of the sago palm⟧ **1** an edible starch, also used in sizing textiles, prepared from the pith of the trunk of certain palms, from the underground stems of certain cycads, as the coontie, or from some other plants **2** any of the palms that yield sago, esp. a Malayan tree (*Metroxylon sagu*): also **sago palm**

☆**sa·gua·ro** (sə gwär′ō, sə wär′ō) *n., pl.* **-ros** ⟦MexSp < Piman name⟧ a giant cactus (*Carnegiea gigantea*) with a thick, spiny stem and white flowers, native to the SW U.S. and N Mexico: also **sa·hua′ro** (-wä′-)

Sag·ue·nay (sag′ə nā′, sag′ə nā′) ⟦< ? AmInd⟧ **1** city in SC Quebec, Canada, on the Saguenay River: formed in 2002 by the merger of Jonquière, Chicoutimi, and several other cities **2** river in SC Quebec, Canada, flowing southeastward from Lake St. John into the Gulf of St. Lawrence: *c.* 120 mi (193 km); incl. principal headstream north of Lake St. John, 475 mi (764 km)

Sa·hap·ti·an (sä hap′tē ən) *n.* a family of North American Indian languages consisting of Sahaptin and Nez Percé

Sa·hap·tin (sä hap′tən) *n.* ⟦< Salish name for the Nez Percé⟧ **1** *pl.* **-tins** or **-tin** a member of any of several North American Indian groups living along the Columbia River in Washington and Oregon **2** the language of these groups

Sa·ha·ra (sə har′ə, -her′ə, -hä′rə) ⟦Ar *ṣaḥrā′* (pl. *ṣaḥārā*), desert⟧ vast desert region in N Africa, extending from the Atlantic to the Nile (or to the Red Sea): *c.* 3,500,000 sq mi (9,064,965 sq km) —**Sa·ha′ran** *adj.*

Sa·ha·ran·pur (sə här′ən poor′) city in NW Uttar Pradesh, N India

Sa·hel (sä hel′) region in NC Africa, south of the Sahara, characterized by periodic drought —**Sa·hel′ian** (-hel′yən, -hel′ē ən) *adj., n.*

Sahara

sa·hib (sä′ib′, -hib′; säb; sä′ēb′, -hēb′) *n.* ⟦Hindi *sāhib* < Ar *ṣāḥib*, master, lit., associate⟧ sir; master: title used in colonial India when speaking to or of a European, and later extended to any male as a sign of respect or formality

said (sed) *vt., vi. pt. & pp. of* SAY —***adj.*** aforesaid; named or mentioned before

Sa·i·da (sä′ē dä′) seaport in SW Lebanon, on the site of ancient Sidon

sai·ga (sī′gə) *n.* ⟦Russ *sajga*⟧ a small, stocky antelope (*Saiga tatarica*) with a broad, fleshy snout, native to the steppes of SE Russia and SW Siberia

Sai·gon (sī gän′, sī′gän′) *former name for* HO CHI MINH CITY

sail (sāl) *n.* ⟦ME *seil*, sail < OE *segl*, akin to Ger *segel*, prob. ult. < IE base **sek-*, to cut > L *secare*, to cut, *segmentum*, segment⟧ **1** any of the shaped sheets of canvas or other strong material spread to catch or deflect the wind, by means of which some vessels and some land vehicles are driven forward **2** sails collectively **3** a sailing vessel or vessels **4** a trip in a ship or boat, esp. one moved by sails **5** anything like a sail, as an arm of a windmill —***vi.*** ⟦ME *seilen* < OE *seglian* < the n.⟧ **1** *a)* to be moved forward by means of a sail or sails *b)* to be moved forward on water by mechanical means such as a propeller **2** to move upon or travel by water: said of a vessel or its passengers **3** to begin a trip by water **4** to manage a sailboat, as in racing or cruising **5** to glide, float, or move steadily through the air **6** to move smoothly and with dignity, like a ship in full sail **7** [Informal] to move or proceed quickly ☆**8** [Informal] to begin vigorously; throw oneself (*into*) with energy ☆**9** [Informal] to attack, criticize, or reprimand someone severely: with *into* —***vt.*** **1** to move through or upon (a body of water) in a boat or ship **2** to manage or navigate (a boat or ship) **3** to throw or otherwise propel (something) in a way that causes it to glide, float, or move steadily through the air —**make sail** SET SAIL (see phrase below) —**sail against the wind 1** to sail a course that slants slightly away from the true direction of the wind; sail closehauled **2** to work under difficulties or against direct opposition: also **sail near (to) the wind** —**sail close to the wind 1** to sail as nearly as possible straight against the wind **2** to be economical in one's affairs **3** to border on indecency, foolhardiness, etc. —**set sail 1** to hoist the sails in preparation for departure **2** to start out on a voyage by water —**take in sail** to lower sails, as in order to reduce the area of sail set —**under sail** sailing; with sails set

sail·board (sāl′bôrd′) *n.* a board similar to a surfboard, with a sail attached to a pivoting mast, used in windsurfing —**sail′board′er** *n.* —**sail′board′ing** *n.*

sailboard

sail·boat (-bōt′) *n.* a boat having a sail or sails by means of which it is propelled

sail·cloth (-klôth′, -kläth′) *n.* long-fibered canvas or other cloth used in making sails, tents, etc.

sail·er (sā′lər) *n.* a ship or boat, esp. one equipped with sails, specif. with reference to its sailing capability [*a swift sailer*]

sail·fish (-fish′) *n., pl.* **-fish′** or **-fish′es** (see FISH) any of a genus (*Istiophorus*, family Istiophoridae) of large, tropical marine billfishes with elongated scales, a sail-like dorsal fin, and a sword-shaped upper jaw

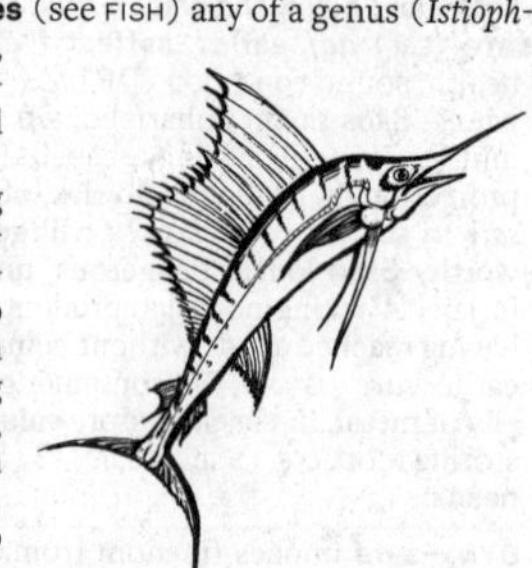

sailfish

sail·ing (sā′liŋ) *n.* **1** the act of a thing or person that sails **2** the art of navigation **3** the sport of managing a sailboat, as for racing **4** the start of a trip by water —***adj.*** **1** driven by wind on sails **2** relating to ships or shipping [*sailing orders*] —**smooth** (or **clear**, etc.) **sailing** progress that is free from interruptions, difficulties, etc.

sail·mak·er (-māk′ər) *n.* a person who makes or repairs sails; specif., one who designs and tests sails, esp. for racing

sail·or (sā′lər) *n.* ⟦ME *sailer*⟧ **1** a person who makes a living by sailing; mariner; seaman **2** *a)* an enlisted person in the navy *b)* any person in the navy **3** any person who engages in sailing for recreation **4** a straw hat with a low, flat crown and flat brim

sailor collar ⟦the collar worn by U.S. & some European sailors in the 19th and 20th c.⟧ **1** a V-neck collar having a squared piece hanging at the back of the shoulders **2** any of various collars suggestive of this

sail·or's-choice (sā′lərz chois′) *n., pl.* **sail′or's-choice′** any of several food fishes of the W Atlantic and the Gulf of Mexico; specif., a small grunt (*Haemulon parrai*)

sail·plane (sāl′plān′) *n.* a light glider especially designed for soaring —***vi.*** **-planed′, -plan′ing** to fly a sailplane

sai·min (sī′min′) *n.* ⟦prob. ult. < Chin *sai*, thin + *min*, noodle⟧ **1** long, thin noodles used in preparing various Japanese dishes **2** a soup made of broth and vegetables and served with such noodles

sain (sān) *vt.* ⟦ME *sainen* < OE *segnian* < L *signare*, to sign, make the sign of the cross on < *signum*: see SIGN⟧ [Now Chiefly Dial.] to make the sign of the cross over, or to bless, as a protection against evil

sain·foin (sān′foin′) *n.* ⟦Fr < *sain*, wholesome (< L *sanus*, healthy, confused in Fr with *saint*) + *foin* (< L *faenum*), hay⟧ a Eurasian perennial plant (*Onobrychis viciaefolia*) of the pea family, cultivated as a forage or cover crop

saint (sānt) *n.* ⟦OFr < LL(Ec) *sanctus*, saint < L, holy, consecrated, pp. of *sancire*, to consecrate, akin to *sacer*: see SACRED⟧ **1** a holy person **2** a person who is exceptionally meek, charitable, patient, etc. **3** [*pl.*] those, esp. holy persons, who have died and are believed to be with God **4** *a)* in the New Testament, any Christian *b)* [**S-**] a member of any of certain religious groups calling themselves *Saints* **5** in certain Christian churches, a person officially recognized as having lived an exceptionally holy life, and thus as being in heaven and capable of interceding for sinners; canonized person —*vt.* to make a saint of; canonize —**saint′like′** *adj.*

NOTE—For names of saints, see the given name (as JOHN[1], PAUL[1], etc.); also see entries beginning with St. and Saint

Saint Agnes's Eve the night of Jan. 20 when, in old superstition, a girl might have a vision of her future husband

Saint Andrew's cross ⟦from the traditional belief that *Saint* ANDREW was crucified on a cross of this type⟧ an X-shaped cross: see CROSS, illus.

Saint Anthony's cross ⟦after *Saint* ANTHONY[2], hermit of Egypt, said to have worn this type of cross on his chest⟧ TAU CROSS

Saint Anthony's fire ⟦after *Saint* ANTHONY[2] of Egypt (from the practice of praying for his intercession to relieve the illness) + FIRE (*n.* 8)⟧ any of several skin conditions or inflammations, as erysipelas or ergotism

Saint Ber·nard (bər närd′) ⟦after the traveler's hospice at the *Great St. Bernard Pass* in the Swiss Alps, named after *Saint* BERNARD OF MENTHON⟧ any of a breed of very large, reddish-brown and white dog, orig. bred and trained to rescue travelers lost in the snow

Sainte-Anne-de-Beau·pré (san tän də bō prā′) village in S Quebec, Canada, on the St. Lawrence: site of a Rom. Catholic shrine (established 1658)

Sainte-Beuve (sant böv′), **Charles Au·gus·tin** (shärl ō güs tan′) 1804-69; Fr. literary critic & writer

saint·ed (sānt′id) *adj.* **1** of, like, or suitable for a saint; saintly **2** regarded or venerated as a saint **3** holy; sacred; hallowed

Sainte-Foy (sant fwä′) former city in S Quebec, Canada, now part of Quebec City

Saint El·mo's fire (*or* **light)** (el′mōz) ⟦after *St. Elmo,* patron saint of sailors⟧ a visible electric discharge (*corona*) from charged, esp. pointed, objects, as the tips of masts, spires, trees, etc.: seen sometimes during electrical storms

Saint-Ex·u·pé·ry (san teg zü pā rē′), **An·toine de** (än twän′ də) 1900-44; Fr. aviator & writer

Saint-Gau·dens (sānt gôd′′nz), **Augustus** 1848-1907; U.S. sculptor, born in Ireland

saint·hood (sānt′hood′) *n.* **1** the status or rank of a saint: also **saint′ship′** (-ship′) **2** saints collectively

Saint-Hu·bert (san tü ber′) borough of Longueuil, near Montreal

Saint John ⟦named for the date of its discovery, June 24, 1604, the feast of *Saint* JOHN[1]⟧ river flowing from N Maine through New Brunswick, Canada, into the Bay of Fundy: 418 mi (673 km)

Saint-John Perse (purs) (pseud. of *Alexis Saint-Léger Léger*) 1887-1975; Fr. diplomat & poet

Saint-John's-wort (sānt jänz′wurt) *n.* ST. JOHNSWORT: also written **Saint John's wort**

Saint-Just (san zhüst′), **Louis An·toine Lé·on de** (lwē än twän′ lā ōn′ də) 1767-94; Fr. revolutionary

Saint-Lau·rent (san lō ran′) borough of Montreal

Saint-Lé·o·nard (san lā ō nar′) borough of Montreal

saint·ly (sānt′lē) *adj.* **-li·er, -li·est** of, like, or suitable for a saint —**saint′li·ness** *n.*

Saint Martin's summer [Chiefly Brit.] a period of mild, warm weather in late autumn, around the time of Martinmas

Saint Nicholas SANTA CLAUS: cf. NICHOLAS[2], Saint: also **Saint Nick**

Saint Patrick's Day March 17, observed by the Irish in honor of Saint Patrick, a patron saint of Ireland

Saint-Saëns (san säns′), **(Charles) Ca·mille** (kȧ mē′y′) 1835-1921; Fr. composer

Saints·bur·y (sānts′bər ē), **George (Edward Bateman)** 1845-1933; Eng. literary critic

Saint-Si·mon (san sē mōn′) **1** Comte **de** (*Claude Henri de Rouvroy*) 1760-1825; Fr. social philosopher **2** Duc **de** (*Louis de Rouvroy*) 1675-1755; Fr. courtier & writer

Saint Valentine's Day VALENTINE'S DAY

Saint Vi·tus' dance (vīt′əs) ⟦after *St. Vitus,* 3d-c. patron saint of persons having chorea⟧ CHOREA: also **St. Vitus's dance**

Sai·pan (sī pan′, -pän′) island in the W Pacific: seat of government of the Northern Mariana Islands: 47 sq mi (122 sq km)

Sa·ïs (sā′is) ancient city in the Nile delta: capital of Egypt (718-712 B.C.; 663-525 B.C.) —**Sa·ïte** (-īte′) *adj.*

saith (seth; *now also* sā′ith) *vt., vi. archaic 3d pers. sing., pres. indic., of* SAY

Sa·kai (sä′kī′) city in S Honshu, Japan

Sa·ka·ka·we·a (sä kä′kä wē′ə) *var. of* SACAGAWEA

sake[1] (sāk) *n.* ⟦ME < OE *sacu,* cause or suit at law, contention, akin to Ger *sache,* thing, affair < IE base **sāg-,* to investigate > SEEK, L *sagire,* to perceive, find, *sagax,* sharply discerning⟧ **1** purpose or reason; motive; cause [for the *sake* of harmony] **2** advantage; behalf; benefit [for my *sake*] —**for heaven's (***or* **gosh** *or* **Pete's,** etc.**) sake!** a mild exclamation of surprise, annoyance, etc.

sa·ke[2] (sä′kē) *n.* ⟦Jpn, ult. < ? *sakayu,* to prosper⟧ a Japanese alcoholic beverage made from fermented rice and usually warmed for serving: also sp. **sa′ki**

Sa·kha·lin (sak′ə lēn′, sä′kə-) island of Russia off the E coast of Siberia: formerly (1905-45) divided between Russia & Japan: *c.* 29,500 sq mi (76,405 sq km)

Sa·kha·rov (sä′kə rôf, sak′ə-), **An·drei (Dmitrievich)** (än′drā) 1921-89; Russ. nuclear physicist: political dissident & human rights activist

Sa·ki (sä′kē) (pseud. of *Hector Hugh Munro*) 1870-1916; Brit. short-story writer & novelist, born in Burma

Sak·kar·a (sə kär′ə) *alt. sp. of* SAQQARA

sal (sal) *n.* ⟦ME < L, SALT⟧ *Pharmacy* salt

sa·laam (sə läm′) *interj.* ⟦shortened < Ar *salām ʿalaykum,* peace (be) to you < *salām,* peace, health, akin to Heb *shalom,* peace⟧ peace: used as a greeting by Muslims: in full **salaam a·lei·kum** (ä lī′koom′), peace be with you —*n.* **1** this greeting **2** in the Near East, India, etc., a greeting or ceremonial compliment, made by bowing low with the palm of the right hand placed on the forehead **3** any obeisance or respectful greeting —*vt.* to greet with a salaam —*vi.* to make a salaam

sal·a·ble (sāl′ə bəl) *adj.* that can be sold; marketable

sa·la·cious (sə lā′shəs) *adj.* ⟦L *salax* (gen. *salacis*) < *salire,* to leap, (of animals) cover sexually: see SALIENT⟧ **1** [Archaic] lecherous; lustful **2** characterized by an excessive or improper emphasis on sexual matters [a *salacious* bit of gossip] —**sa·la′cious·ly** *adv.* —**sa·la′cious·ness** *n.*, **sa·lac′i·ty** (-las′ə tē)

sal·ad (sal′əd) *n.* ⟦ME *salat* < MFr *salade* < Prov *salada* < VL **salata* < fem. pp. of **salare,* to salt < L *sal,* SALT⟧ **1** a dish, usually cold, of raw or sometimes cooked vegetables or fruits in various combinations, served with a dressing, or molded in gelatin, and sometimes with seafood, poultry, eggs, etc. added **2** *a)* any green plant or herb used for such a dish or eaten raw *b)* [Dial.] lettuce ☆**3** a finely chopped or ground food mixed with mayonnaise, seasonings, etc. and served as on lettuce or in a sandwich [tuna *salad,* egg *salad* sandwich]

salad bar a buffet, as in a restaurant, at which diners may assemble a salad for themselves from an assortment of ingredients

salad days ⟦from Cleopatra's "My *salad days,* / When I was green in judgment": in Shakespeare's *Antony and Cleopatra,* I, v (1601)⟧ time of youth and inexperience

salad dressing any sauce for salads, made variously as with oil, vinegar, spices, etc.

sa·lade ni·çoise (sal′əd nē swäz′; *Fr* sȧ lȧd′ nē swȧz′) ⟦Fr < *salade,* salad + *niçoise,* fem. of *niçois,* of or from NICE⟧ [*occas.* **s- N-** *or* **S- N-**] a salad typically containing tuna, tomatoes, cooked green beans and potatoes, anchovies, hard-boiled eggs, and black olives, with or without greens, dressed with a garlic vinaigrette

Sal·a·din (sal′ə din) (born *Salah-ad-Din Yusuf ibn-Ayyub*) 1137-93; sultan of Egypt & Syria (1174-93): recaptured Jerusalem from the Crusaders (1187)

Sa·la·do (sä lä′thô) river in N Argentina, flowing from the Andes southeast into the Paraná: *c.* 1,100 mi (1,770 km)

sa·lal (sə lal′) *n.* ⟦< name in Chinook jargon⟧ a small, evergreen gaultheria shrub (*Gaultheria shallon*) native to the W coast of North America, having dark leaves, small clusters of white or pink flowers, and purple-black, edible berries

Sal·a·man·ca (sal′ə maŋ′kə; *Sp* sä′lä mäŋ′kä) **1** city in León, WC Spain **2** city in central Mexico

sal·a·man·der (sal′ə man′dər) *n.* ⟦ME *salamandre* < OFr < L *salamandra* < Gr⟧ **1** a mythological reptile, resembling the lizard, that was said to live in fire **2** a spirit supposed to live in fire: orig., a spirit in Paracelsus' alchemical system **3** any of various articles used in fire or able to produce or withstand heat, as a poker, portable oven, or a utensil for browning pastry **4** any of an order (Caudata) of limbed, tailed amphibians with a soft, moist skin —**sal′a·man′drine** (-drin) *adj.*

spotted salamander

sa·la·mi (sə lä′mē) *n.* ⟦It, pl. of *salame,* preserved meat, salt pork < VL **salamen,* for LL *salsamen,* salted food < L *salsus:* see SAUCE⟧ a highly spiced, salted sausage, orig. Italian, of pork and beef, or of beef alone

Sal·a·mis (sal′ə mis; *Gr* sä′lä mēs′) island of Greece, in the Saronic Gulf: 39 sq mi (101 sq km)

sal ammoniac ⟦ME *sal armoniak:* see SAL & AMMONIAC⟧ AMMONIUM CHLORIDE

sa·lar·i·at (sə ler′ē ət) *n.* ⟦Fr < *salaire,* salary + *prolétariat,* proletariat⟧ the class of workers receiving salaries, as distinguished from those receiving wages

sal·a·ried (sal′ə rēd, sal′rēd) *adj.* receiving or yielding a salary

sal·a·ry (sal′ə rē, sal′rē) *n., pl.* **-ries** ⟦ME *salarie* < L *salarium,* orig., money for salt (as part of Roman soldier's pay) < *sal,* SALT⟧ a fixed payment at regular intervals for services, esp. when clerical or professional —**SYN.** WAGE

sal·a·ry·man (-man′, -mən) *n., pl.* **-men′** (-men′, -mən) ⟦< Jpn < E prec. + MAN⟧ in Japan, a man who is a white-collar office worker, esp. an executive in a business organization

sal·at (sä lät′) *n.* ⟦Ar⟧ *Islam* the ritual of prayer performed five times a day

Sa·la·zar (sä′lə zär′), **An·to·nio de O·li·vei·ra** (än tô′nyoo dē ô′lē vā′rə) 1889-1970; prime minister & dictator of Portugal (1932-68)

sale (sāl) *n.* ⟦ME < OE *sala* < ON: for IE base see SELL⟧ **1** the act or an instance of selling; exchange of property of any kind, or of services, for an agreed sum of money or other valuable consideration **2** opportunity to sell or be sold; market **3** the act of offering goods to the highest bidder; auction **4** a special offering of goods at prices lower than usual **5** [*pl.*] receipts in business **6** [*pl.*] *a)* the business or work of selling a product or service *b)* the department, as of a company or branch, responsible for this work —**for sale** available for purchase: also **up for sale** —**on sale** available for purchase, esp. at a price lower than usual

Sa·lé (sa lā′) city & seaport in NW Morocco: suburb of Rabat

sale·a·ble (sāl′ə bəl) *adj. alt. sp. of* SALABLE

Sa·lem (sā′ləm) **1** ⟦after the biblical *Salem*: see Gen. 14:18, Ps. 76:2⟧ capital of Oreg., in the NW part, on the Willamette River **2** ⟦after the biblical *Salem*⟧ city in NE Mass., on Massachusetts Bay: suburb of Boston: site of witchcraft trials (1692) **3** city in N Tamil Nadu state, S India

sal·ep (sal′əp) *n.* ⟦Fr < Sp < informal Ar **sa*'*lab*, altered & contr. < *khuṣa al-tha*'*lab*, fox's testicles: see ORCHIS⟧ the starchy dried tubers of various orchids (esp. genera *Orchis* and *Eulophia*), ground up and used as food

☆**sal·e·ra·tus** (sal′ə rāt′əs) *n.* ⟦ModL *sal aeratus*, aerated salt⟧ sodium (or sometimes potassium) bicarbonate; baking soda, as used in cooking

Sa·ler·no (sə ler′nō, -lur′-) seaport in S Italy, on an inlet (**Gulf of Salerno**) of the Tyrrhenian Sea: ancient name **Sa·ler′num** (-nəm)

☆**sales·clerk** (sālz′klurk′) *n.* a person employed to sell goods in a retail store

sales·girl (-gurl′) *n.* [Informal] a girl or woman employed as a salesclerk

sales·la·dy (-lā′dē) *n., pl.* **-la′dies** [Informal] a saleswoman, esp. one employed as a salesclerk

sales·man (sālz′mən) *n., pl.* **-men** (-mən) **1** a man employed as a salesclerk ☆**2** SALES REPRESENTATIVE

sales·man·ship (-ship′) *n.* the ability, skill, or technique of selling

☆**sales·per·son** (sālz′pur′sən) *n., pl.* **-peo′ple** (-pē′pəl) a person employed to sell goods or services

☆**sales promotion** the use of publicizing methods other than paid advertising to promote a product, service, etc.

sales representative a salesperson, esp. one employed as a traveling agent for a manufacturer, distributor, etc.

☆**sales·room** (-ro͞om′) *n.* a room in which goods are shown and offered for sale

☆**sales slip** a receipt or bill of sale for a purchase from a retail store

☆**sales talk** **1** persuasion or argument used in an attempt to sell something **2** any argument aimed at persuading one to do or believe something

☆**sales tax** a tax on sales of goods and services, usually levied as a percentage of, and added to, the price paid by the consumer

sales·wom·an (-wo͝om′ən) *n., pl.* **-wom′en** (-wim′in) a woman salesclerk or sales representative

Sal·ford (sôl′fərd, sal′-) city in NW England, in Greater Manchester

Sa·li·an (sā′lē ən) *adj.* ⟦< LL *Salii*, Salian Franks, after the *Sala* (now IJssel) River⟧ of a group of Franks that settled along the IJssel River, in the Netherlands, in the 4th cent. —*n.* a Salian Frank

Sal·ic (sal′ik, sā′lik) *adj.* ⟦ML *Salicus*⟧ **1** of the Salian Franks **2** of the Salic law

sal·i·cin (sal′ə sin) *n.* ⟦Fr *salicine* < L *salix* (gen. *salicis*), willow, akin to *saliva*, saliva < IE **salik-* < base **sal-*, gray > OE *sol*, dark, dirty, *sealh*, willow⟧ a bitter, white, crystalline or powdery glucoside, $HOCH_2C_6H_4OC_6H_{11}O_5$, obtained from the bark of certain poplars and willows, and used as a reagent

Salic law **1** a code of laws of Germanic tribes, including the Salian Franks; esp., the provision of this code excluding women from inheriting land **2** the law excluding women from succeeding to the throne in the French and Spanish monarchies

sa·lic·y·late (sə lis′ə lāt′; sal′ə sil′āt′, -it) *n.* **1** a salt of salicylic acid containing the monovalent, negative radical HOC_6H_4COO **2** an uncharged ester of this acid

sal·i·cyl·ic acid (sal′ə sil′ik) ⟦*salicyl* (radical of the acid) < Fr *salicyle* < L *salix* (see SALICIN) + Fr *-yle*, -YL + -IC⟧ a white, crystalline compound, HOC_6H_4COOH, prepared from salicin or phenol and used in the manufacture of aspirin, as a food preservative and mild antiseptic, etc.

sa·lient (sāl′yənt, sā′lē ənt) *adj.* ⟦L *saliens*, prp. of *salire*, to leap < IE base **sel-*, to jump > Gr *halma*, a leap⟧ **1** *a)* leaping, jumping, or capering *b)* gushing or jetting forth **2** pointing outward; jutting or projecting, as an angle **3** standing out from the rest; noticeable; conspicuous; prominent **4** most important or notable —*n.* **1** the part of a battle line, trench, fort, etc. which projects farthest toward the enemy **2** a salient angle, part, etc. —**sa′lience** *n.*, **sa′lien·cy** *pl.* **-cies** —**sa′lient·ly** *adv.*

sa·li·en·ti·an (sā′lē en′shē ən, -shən) *n., adj.* ⟦< ModL *Salientia* (< L *saliens*: see prec.) + -AN⟧ ANURAN

sa·lif·er·ous (sə lif′ər əs) *adj.* ⟦< L *sal*, SALT + -FEROUS⟧ producing or containing salt

sal·i·fy (sal′ə fī′) *vt.* **-fied′**, **-fy′ing** ⟦Fr *salifier* < L *sal*, salt + *-ficare*, -FY⟧ to make salty; specif., *a)* to impregnate with salt *b)* to form a salt with; convert into a salt *c)* to combine with a salt

sa·lim·e·ter (sa lim′ət ər) *n.* ⟦SAL + -I- + -METER⟧ a hydrometer for determining the density of salt solutions

sa·li·na (sə lī′nə) *n.* ⟦Sp < L *salinae*, salt pits < *salinus*, saline, salty: see SALINE⟧ a salt marsh, pond, or lake

Sa·li·nas (sə lē′nəs) ⟦after the nearby *Salinas* River < Sp *salina* (see prec.): for the salt marshes at its mouth⟧ city in WC Calif., near Monterey

sa·line (sā′lēn′, -līn′; *for n. 1, also* sə lēn′) *adj.* ⟦LME *salyne* < L *salinus* < *sal*, SALT⟧ **1** of, characteristic of, or containing common salt, or sodium chloride **2** of or containing any of the salts of the alkali metals or magnesium —*n.* **1** a salt spring, lick, mine, etc. **2** a salt of magnesium or of an alkali metal, often used as a cathartic **3** a saline solution, esp. one that is isotonic, used in medical treatment or biological experiments —**sa·lin·i·ty** (sə lin′ə tē) *n.*

Sal·in·ger (sal′in jər), **J(erome) D(avid)** 1919-2010; U.S. novelist & short-story writer

sal·i·nize (sal′ə nīz′, sā′lə-) *vt.* **-nized′**, **-niz′ing** ⟦SALIN(E) + -IZE⟧ to contaminate (soil, etc.) with salts —**sal′i·ni·za′tion** *n.*

sal·i·nom·e·ter (sal′ə näm′ət ər) *n.* ⟦see SALINE & -METER⟧ any device for measuring the amount of dissolved salts in a solution, esp. one that measures the electrical conductivity of a water sample

Salis·bur·y[1] (sôlz′ber′e, -bə rē; salz′-), 3d Marquess of (*Robert Arthur Talbot Gascoyne-Cecil*) 1830-1903; Eng. statesman: prime minister (1885–1902)

Salis·bur·y[2] (sôlz′ber′ē, -bə rē; salz′-) ⟦OE *Searoburh*⟧ **1** city in Wiltshire, SC England: noted for its 13th-cent. cathedral **2** *former name for* HARARE

Salisbury Plain rolling plateau in Wiltshire, England: site of Stonehenge

☆**Salisbury steak** ⟦after J. H. *Salisbury* (1823-1905), U.S. nutritionist who advocated the consumption of ground beef to promote good health⟧ a patty consisting of ground beef mixed with egg, bread crumbs, onions, etc. and fried, broiled, or baked: now usually served in gravy

Sa·lish (sā′lish) *n.* ⟦Salish *sälst*, people⟧ **1** *pl.* **-lish** a member of a group of North American Indian peoples of NW North America **2** *a)* any of the languages of these peoples *b)* these languages as a group; Salishan —*adj.* of the Salish, their language group, or their culture

Sa·lish·an (-ən) *n.* a group or family of languages spoken by the Salish —*adj.* of the Salish or their languages

sa·li·va (sə lī′və) *n.* ⟦L: see SALICIN⟧ the thin, watery, slightly viscid fluid secreted by the salivary glands: it serves as an aid to swallowing and digestion by moistening and softening food, and contains enzymes which convert starch to dextrin and maltose

sal·i·var·y (sal′ə ver′ē) *adj.* of or relating to saliva; specif., designating or of three pairs of glands in the mouth that secrete saliva

sal·i·vate (-vāt′) *vt.* **-vat′ed**, **-vat′ing** ⟦< L *salivatus*, pp. of *salivare*, salivate⟧ to produce an excessive flow of saliva in —*vi.* to secrete saliva —**sal′i·va′tion** *n.*

Salk (sôlk), **Jo·nas E(dward)** (jō′nəs) 1914-95; U.S. physician & bacteriologist: developed a vaccine to prevent poliomyelitis

salle (sȧl) *n.* ⟦Fr < Frank or OHG *sal*, room, house: see SALOON⟧ a hall or room

sal·len·ders (sal′ən dərz) *pl.n.* ⟦Fr *solandres*, pl. of *solandre*⟧ a variety of eczema on the hock of a horse: see MALANDERS

sal·let (sal′it) *n.* ⟦ME < MFr *salade* < It *celata* < pp. of *celare*, to cover < L: see CONCEAL⟧ a rounded, metal helmet with a projecting guard for the neck and, often, a visor, worn in the 15th cent.

sal·low[1] (sal′ō) *adj.* ⟦ME *salou* < OE *salu*, sallow, dark, akin to OHG *salo* < IE base **sal-*, dirty gray: see SALICIN⟧ of a sickly, pale-yellow hue or complexion —*vt.* to make sallow —**sal′low·ness** *n.*

sal·low[2] (sal′ō) *n.* ⟦ME *salwe*, *sealh*: see SALICIN⟧ **1** a kind of willow (*Salix caprea*) with large catkins of flowers which appear before the leaves **2** a willow twig

Sal·lust (sal′əst) (L. name *Gaius Sallustius Crispus*) 86-35? B.C.; Rom. historian

sal·ly (sal′ē) *n., pl.* **-lies** ⟦MFr *saillie* < *saillir*, to come forth suddenly, rush out, leap < L *salire*, to leap, spring: see SALIENT⟧ **1** a sudden rushing forth, as of troops to attack besieging forces **2** any sudden start into activity **3** a quick witticism; bright retort; quip **4** an excursion or unusual side trip; jaunt —*vi.* **-lied**, **-ly·ing** **1** to make a sally **2** to rush out or come out suddenly **3** *a)* to come or go outdoors *b)* to set out on a trip Used with *forth* or *out*

Sal·ly (sal′ē) *n.* a feminine name: see SARAH

Sally Lunn (lun) ⟦said to be name of 18th-c. Eng woman who first made these at Bath⟧ [*also* **s- l-**] a variety of sweet tea cake, usually served hot

sal·ma·gun·di (sal′mə gun′dē) *n.* ⟦Fr *salmigondis*, earlier *salmigondin*, altered < ? It *salame conditi*, preserved pickled meat < *salame* (see SALAMI) + *conditi* < pp. of *condire*, to flavor, preserve < L, to preserve, pickle⟧ **1** a dish of chopped meat, eggs, etc. flavored with onions, anchovies, vinegar, and oil **2** any mixture or medley

sal·mi (sal′mē) *n.* ⟦Fr *salmis*, contr. < *salmigondis*: see prec.⟧ a highly seasoned dish of game or fowl, partly roasted, then stewed in wine

salm·on (sam′ən) *n., pl.* **-on** or **-ons** ⟦ME *salmoun* < MFr < OFr *saumon* < L *salmo* (gen. *salmonis*) < ?⟧ **1** any of several salmonoid food and game fishes (esp. genera *Oncorhynchus* and *Salmo*) of the Northern Hemisphere, with silver scales: salmon usually live in salt water and spawn in fresh water **2** the yellowish-pink or pale red color of the flesh of this fish: also **salmon pink**

Salm·on (sam′ən) river in central Ida., flowing into the Snake River: 420 mi (676 km)

☆**salm·on·ber·ry** (-ber′ē) *n., pl.* **-ries** **1** a tall, spineless raspberry (*Rubus spectabilis*) of the W coast of North America, having salmon-colored or reddish, edible fruit **2** its fruit

☆**sal·mo·nel·la** (sal′mə nel′ə) *n., pl.* **-lae** (-ē), **-la**, or **-las** ⟦ModL: so named after D. E. *Salmon* (1850-1914), U.S. pathologist⟧ any of a genus (*Salmonella*) of Gram-negative, rod-shaped bacteria that cause various diseases in people and domestic animals, including typhoid fever and food poisoning

☆**sal·mo·nel·lo·sis** (-nel ō′sis) *n.* ⟦< prec. + -OSIS⟧ a disease caused by various strains of salmonella and characterized by fever and intestinal disorders

sal·mo·nid (sal′mə nid) ***n.*** ⟦< ModL *Salmonidae*, pl., ult. < L *salmo*, SALMON⟧ any of a family (Salmonidae) of soft-finned fishes, including salmon, trout, and whitefish —***adj.*** of or having to do with a salmonid

sal·mo·noid (sal′mə noid′) ***adj.*** **1** like a salmon **2** of the suborder (Salmonoidei, order Salmoniformes) of bony fishes that includes the salmons, trouts, and most smelts —***n.*** a salmonoid fish

salmon trout any of various trouts, as the rainbow trout

Sa·lo·me (sə lō′mē, sal′ə mā′) ***n.*** ⟦name given by JOSEPHUS; LL(Ec) < Gr(Ec) *Salōmē* < Heb *shalom*, lit., peace⟧ the daughter of Herodias: in Matt. 14:8, her dancing pleased Herod so much that he granted her request for the head of John the Baptist

Sal·o·mon (sal′ə mən), **Haym** (hīm) 1740-85; Am. financier & patriot, born in Poland: helped finance the Am. Revolutionary War

sa·lon (sə län′, sal′än′; *Fr* sȧ lōn′) ***n.*** ⟦Fr: see SALOON⟧ **1** a large reception hall or social room, as in a hotel or on a ship; saloon **2** a drawing room of a private home in French-speaking countries **3** a regular gathering of eminent writers, artists, scientists, etc. in the home of a well-known, often wealthy and influential person **4** *a)* a room or gallery for the exhibition of works of art *b)* such an exhibition, esp. one held annually **5** a shop or business establishment specially furnished for performing some personal service [beauty *salon*]

Sa·lo·ni·ka (sə län′i kə, sal′ə nē′kə) **1** seaport in Macedonia, N Greece, at the head of the Gulf of Salonika: Gr. name THESSALONIKI **2 Gulf of** N arm of the Aegean Sea: *c.* 70 mi (113 km) long Also sp. **Salonica**

sa·loon (sə lo͞on′) ***n.*** ⟦Fr *salon* < It *salone* < *sala*, a room, hall < Langobardic **sala*, akin to OHG *sal*, a room, dwelling < IE base **sel-* > OSlav *selo*, village⟧ **1** [Old-fashioned] a large room or hall designed for receptions, exhibitions, entertainments, etc. **2** any interior public place used for some specific purpose; specif., *a)* a railway carriage or compartment used for a specific purpose [a dining *saloon*] *b)* the main social cabin of a passenger ship ☆**3** a place where alcoholic drinks are sold to be drunk on the premises; bar **4** [Brit.] *a)* SEDAN (sense 2) *b)* a luxurious parlor car

☆**sa·loon·keep·er** (-kēp′ər) ***n.*** a person who operates a SALOON (sense 3)

sa·loop (sə lo͞op′) ***n.*** ⟦var. of SALEP⟧ [Historical] a hot drink made from powdered salep or from sassafras

Sal·op (sal′əp) ⟦short for Early ME *Salopescira* < OE *Scropscir*, contr. < *Scrobbesbyrigscir*, Shropshire⟧ *former name* (1974-80) *for* SHROPSHIRE[2] —**Sa·lo·pi·an** (sə lō′pē ən) ***adj., n.***

salp (salp) ***n.***, *pl.* **salp** or **salps** ⟦ModL < L, kind of stockfish < Gr *salpē*⟧ any of an order (Salpida, class Thaliacea) of free-swimming tunicates characterized by a barrel-shaped body ringed with muscle and open at both ends: also called **sal·pa** (sal′pə) ***n.***, *pl.* **-pas** or **-pae** (-pē)

sal·pi·glos·sis (sal′pi gläs′is) ***n.*** ⟦ModL < Gr *salpinx*, a trumpet + *glōssis*, tongue: see GLOSS[2]⟧ a Chilean annual plant (*Salpiglossis sinuata*) of the nightshade family, cultivated for its long-stalked, trumpet-shaped flowers

sal·pin·gec·to·my (sal′pin jek′tə mē) ***n.***, *pl.* **-mies** ⟦SALPING(O)- + -ECTOMY⟧ the severing or excising of a fallopian tube, as in sterilizing a woman

sal·pin·gi·tis (sal′pin jīt′is) ***n.*** ⟦< fol. + -ITIS⟧ inflammation of a fallopian tube or eustachian tube

sal·pin·go- (sal piŋ′gō′) ⟦ModL < Gr *salpingos*, gen. of *salpinx*, a trumpet⟧ *combining form* **1** fallopian tube [*salpingectomy*] **2** eustachian tube [*salpingitis*] Also, before a vowel, **sal·ping′-**

sal·pinx (sal′piŋks′) ***n.***, *pl.* **sal·pin′ges** (-pin′jēz) ⟦ModL < Gr *salpinx*, a trumpet⟧ **1** FALLOPIAN TUBE **2** EUSTACHIAN TUBE —**sal·pin′gi·an** (-pin′jē ən) ***adj.***

☆**sal·sa** (säl′sə) ***n.*** ⟦AmSp < Sp, sauce < L: see SAUCE⟧ **1** a kind of Latin American dance music of Afro-Cuban and Puerto Rican origin, influenced by jazz and rock and usually played at fast tempos **2** a hot sauce made with chilies, tomatoes, onions, etc.

sal·si·fy (sal′sə fē′, -fī′) ***n.*** ⟦Fr *salsifis* < It *sassefrica* < ?⟧ a purple-flowered plant (*Tragopogon porrifolius*) of the composite family, with long, white, edible, fleshy roots having an oysterlike flavor; oyster plant

sal soda ⟦< L *sal*, fol.⟧ crystallized sodium carbonate, $Na_2CO_3 \cdot 10H_2O$

salt (sôlt) ***n.*** ⟦ME < OE *sealt*, akin to Ger *salz* < IE base **sal-*, salt > L *sal*, Gr *hals*, salt, Sans *salila*, salty⟧ **1** sodium chloride, NaCl, a white, crystalline substance with a characteristic taste, found in natural beds, in seawater, etc., and used for seasoning and preserving foods **2** a chemical compound derived from an acid by replacing hydrogen, wholly or partly, with a metal or an electropositive radical: the salt of an *-ous* acid is usually indicated by the suffix *-ite*, the salt of an *-ic* acid by the suffix *-ate* **3** that which lends a tang or piquancy; esp., sharp pungent humor or wit **4** SALTCELLAR **5** [*pl.*] any of various mineral salts used as a cathartic, as Epsom salts, or to soften bathwater, as a restorative, etc. **6** [Informal] a sailor, esp. an experienced one —***adj.*** **1** containing salt **2** preserved with salt **3** tasting or smelling of salt **4** [Now Rare] pungent or biting **5** *a)* flooded with salt water *b)* growing in salt water —***vt.*** **1** to sprinkle or season with salt **2** to preserve with salt or in a salt solution **3** to provide with salt **4** to treat with salt in chemical processes **5** to season or give a tang to [to *salt* a speech with wit] **6** to give artificial value to; specif., *a)* to alter (books, prices, etc.) in order to give false value ☆*b)* to scatter minerals or ores in (a mine), put oil in (a well), etc. in order to deceive prospective buyers —**above (or below) the salt** ⟦from the former practice of placing dinner guests at the upper or lower part of a table, with the saltcellar in the middle⟧ in a more honored (or less honored) position —**salt away (or down)** **1** to pack and preserve with salt ☆**2** [Informal] to store or save (money, etc.) —**salt out** to precipitate or separate (a substance) from its solution by the addition of a soluble salt —**with a grain (or pinch) of salt** ⟦Latinized as *cum grano salis*⟧ with some doubt, allowance for exaggeration, etc.; skeptically —**worth one's salt** ⟦from the former practice of paying wages in *salt* rather than money⟧ worth or, esp., well worth one's wages; skilled or competent in performing one's duties —**salt′like′** ***adj.*** —**salt′ness** ***n.***

☆**SALT** (sôlt) ***n.*** Strategic Arms Limitation Talks

Sal·ta (säl′tə) city in NW Argentina

☆**salt-and-pep·per** (sôlt′'n pep′ər) ***adj.*** dotted or speckled with contrasting colors, esp. black and white

sal·tant (sal′tənt) ***adj.*** ⟦L *saltans*, prp. of *saltare*, to leap, freq. of *salire*: see SALIENT⟧ [Now Rare] leaping; dancing

sal·ta·rel·lo (sal′tə rel′ō) ***n.*** ⟦It < *saltare*, to leap < L: see prec.⟧ **1** a lively Italian dance with a hopping, skipping step **2** music for this dance

sal·ta·tion (sal tā′shən) ***n.*** ⟦L *saltatio*, a dancing, dance < *saltatus*, pp. of *saltare*: see SALTANT⟧ **1** a leaping, jumping, or dancing **2** sudden change, movement, or development, as if by leaping **3** *Biol.* a sudden, major inherited change in an organism, usually caused by a mutation

sal·ta·to·ri·al (sal′tə tôr′ē əl) ***adj.*** **1** of saltation **2** *Zool.* of, characterized by, or adapted for leaping

sal·ta·to·ry (sal′tə tôr′ē) ***adj.*** ⟦L *saltatorius* < pp. of *saltare*: see SALTANT⟧ **1** of, characterized by, or adapted for leaping or dancing **2** proceeding by abrupt movements or changing by sudden variation

salt beef [Brit.] corned beef

salt·box (sôlt′bäks′) ***n.*** **1** a box for salt, with a sloping lid ☆**2** a house, as in colonial New England, shaped somewhat like this, having two stories in front and one at the rear, and a gable roof with a much longer slope at the rear

salt·bush (-bo͝osh′) ***n.*** any of various plants (genus *Atriplex*) of the goosefoot family, frequently growing in saline or alkaline soil, as in salt marshes or desert areas

salt cake impure sodium sulfate, used in making paper pulp, soaps, etc.

salt·cel·lar (-sel′ər) ***n.*** ⟦altered (infl. by CELLAR) < ME *salt saler* < *salt*, SALT + MFr *salière*, saltcellar < L *sal*, SALT⟧ a container, as a dish or saltshaker, for dispensing salt at the table

☆**salt dome** a domelike structure produced in stratified rocks by the intrusion of a mass of salt in a plastic state and frequently containing oil, gas, etc.

salt·er (sôl′tər) ***n.*** **1** a person who makes or sells salt **2** a person who salts meat, fish, etc.

salt·ern (-tərn) ***n.*** ⟦OE *sealtærn* < *sealt*, salt + *ærn*, house: see RANSACK⟧ SALTWORKS

☆**salt grass** any of various grasses growing in salt marshes or alkaline soils, esp., any of a genus (*Distichlis*) of North American perennial grasses

Sal·til·lo (säl tē′yô) city in N Mexico: capital of Coahuila

salt·i·ly (sôl′tə lē) ***adv.*** in a salty manner

sal·tim·boc·ca (sôl′təm bō′kə, säl′-) ***n.*** ⟦It, lit., jump into the mouth⟧ an Italian dish of thin slices of veal and ham flavored with sage, rolled together, and sautéed in butter

☆**salt·ine** (sôl tēn′) ***n.*** ⟦SALT + -INE[3]⟧ a flat, crisp cracker with grains of salt baked into its surface

salt·i·ness (sôl′tē nis) ***n.*** salty quality or state

salt·ing (sôl′tiŋ) ***n.*** ⟦< SALT, in ref. to the seawater⟧ [Brit.] grassy land regularly covered by tides: *usually used in pl.*

sal·tire (sal′tir) ***n.*** ⟦ME *sawtire* < MFr *sautoir*, stirrup loop < ML *saltatorium*, stirrup < L *saltatorius*: see SALTATORY⟧ *Heraldry* a bearing like a Saint Andrew's cross, formed by a bend and a bend sinister crossing: also sp. **sal′tier**

salt·ish (sôl′tish) ***adj.*** somewhat salty

Salt Lake City capital of Utah, near the SE end of Great Salt Lake

☆**salt lick** **1** an exposed natural deposit of mineral rock salt which animals come to lick **2** a block of rock salt placed in a pasture for cattle, etc. to lick

salt marsh grassland that is periodically flooded by salt water

salt of the earth ⟦see Matt. 5:13⟧ any person or persons regarded as representing the best or noblest of traditional values

Sal·ton Sea (sôlt′'n) ⟦prob. coined < SALT⟧ shallow saltwater lake, orig. a salt-covered depression (**Salton Sink**), in the Imperial Valley, S Calif., kept filled by runoff water from irrigation ditches fed by the Colorado River: *c.* 350 sq mi (906 sq km); *c.* 280 ft (85 m) below sea level

salt·pe·ter (sôlt′pēt′ər, sôlt′pēt′ər) ***n.*** ⟦altered (infl. by SALT) < ME *salpetre* < MFr < ML *sal petrae*, salt of rock < L *sal*, SALT + *petra*, rock⟧ POTASSIUM NITRATE: see CHILE SALTPETER: Brit. sp. **salt′pe′tre**

salt pork pork cured in salt; esp., fatty pork from the back, side, or belly of a hog

☆**salt-ris·ing bread** (-rīz′iŋ) bread that is leavened by a fermented, salted cornmeal batter

Salt River ⟦because the lower stream is salty⟧ river in SC Ariz., flowing into the Gila River: *c.* 200 mi (322 km)

☆**salt·shak·er** (sôlt′shāk′ər) ***n.*** a small container for salt, with a perforated top for shaking it out

salt·wa·ter (-wôt′ər, -wät′ər) ***adj.*** of, having to do with, or living in salt water or the sea

☆**saltwater taffy** ⟦orig. uncert., but prob. first so called at resorts in Atlantic City⟧ TAFFY (sense 1): name now assoc. esp. with taffy sold at fairs, amusement parks, etc.

salt·works (-wurks′) ***n., pl.*** **-works′** a place where salt is made, as by evaporation of natural brines

salt·wort (-wurt′) ***n.*** ⟦? based on Du *zoutkruid*⟧ any of a genus (*Salsola*) of plants of the goosefoot family, growing on seashores or saline soils, including the Russian thistle

salt·y (sôl′tē) ***adj.*** **salt′i·er, salt′i·est** **1** of, tasting of, or containing salt **2** smelling of or suggesting the sea **3** *a)* sharp; piquant; witty *b)* coarse or earthy *c)* cross or caustic —***n., pl.*** **salt′ies** [Informal] an oceangoing ship that operates on the Great Lakes

sa·lu·bri·ous (sə lo͞o′brē əs) ***adj.*** ⟦< L *salubris* (< *salus*, health: see SAFE) + -OUS⟧ promoting health or welfare; healthful, wholesome, salutary, etc. —**sa·lu′bri·ous·ly** ***adv.*** —**sa·lu′bri·ty** (-brə tē) ***n.***, **sa·lu′bri·ous·ness**

sa·lud (sä lo͞od′) ***interj.*** ⟦Sp, health⟧ to your health: used as a toast

Sa·lu·ki (sə lo͞o′kē) ***n.*** ⟦Ar *salūqī*, after *Salūq*, ancient S Arabian city⟧ [*often* **s-**] any of a breed of tall, slender dog, prob. of ancient Egyptian origin, resembling the greyhound, with a silky coat feathered on the legs and tail and long, hanging ears

sal·u·tar·y (sal′yo͞o ter′ē) ***adj.*** ⟦< Fr or L: Fr *salutaire* < L *salutaris* < *salus* (gen. *salutis*), health: see SAFE⟧ **1** promoting or conducive to health; healthful **2** promoting or conducive to some good purpose; beneficial —**sal′u·tar′i·ly** ***adv.*** —**sal′u·tar′i·ness** ***n.***

sal·u·ta·tion (sal′yo͞o tā′shən) ***n.*** ⟦ME *salutacion* < MFr < L *salutatio* < *salutatus*, pp. of *salutare*: see SALUTE⟧ **1** the act of greeting, addressing, or welcoming by gestures or words **2** a form of words serving as a greeting or, esp., as the opening of a letter, as "Dear Sir"

☆**sa·lu·ta·to·ri·an** (sə lo͞ot′ə tôr′ē ən) ***n.*** ⟦< fol. + -AN⟧ in some schools and colleges, the student, usually second highest in scholastic rank in the graduating class, who gives the salutatory: see also VALEDICTORIAN

sa·lu·ta·to·ry (sə lo͞ot′ə tôr′ē) ***adj.*** ⟦L *salutatorius*⟧ of or expressing a salutation —***n., pl.*** **-ries** ☆an opening or welcoming address, esp. at a school or college commencement exercise

sa·lute (sə lo͞ot′) ***vt.*** **-lut′ed, -lut′ing** ⟦ME *saluten* < L *salutare*, to salute, wish health to < *salus* (gen. *salutis*), health, greeting < *salvus*, SAFE⟧ **1** to greet or welcome with friendly words or ceremonial gesture, such as bowing, tipping the hat, etc. **2** to honor by performing a prescribed act or gesture, such as dipping the flag, firing cannons, or raising the right hand to the forehead, as a mark of military, naval, or official respect **3** to present itself to, as if in greeting **4** to acknowledge with praise; commend —***vi.*** to make a salute —***n.*** ⟦OFr *salut* < L *salus*⟧ **1** the act of saluting; salutation **2** *a)* a gesture or remark made in saluting *b)* the act of respect paid in saluting **3** something, as an event or ceremony, expressing respect, admiration, compliment, etc. [the benefit was a *salute* to the museum] **4** *Mil.* the position of the body, or of the hand, rifle, etc., assumed in saluting —**sa·lut′er** ***n.***

sal·va·ble (sal′və bəl) ***adj.*** ⟦ML *salvabilis*: see SAVE[1] & -ABLE⟧ that can be saved or salvaged

Sal·va·dor (sal′və dôr′; *Port* säl′və dôr′) seaport in E Brazil: capital of Bahia state

Sal·va·dor·an (sal′və dôr′ən) ***adj.*** of El Salvador or its people or culture —***n.*** a person born or living in El Salvador Also **Sal′va·dor′i·an** or **Sal′va·dor′e·an** (-dôr′ē ən)

sal·vage (sal′vij) ***n.*** ⟦Fr < MFr < *salver*, to SAVE[1]⟧ **1** *a)* the voluntary rescue of a ship or its cargo at sea from peril such as fire, shipwreck, capture, etc. *b)* compensation paid for such a rescue *c)* the ship or cargo so rescued *d)* the recovery of a sunken or wrecked ship or its cargo as by divers **2** *a)* the saving or rescue of any goods, property, etc. from destruction, damage, or waste *b)* any material, goods, etc. thus saved and sold or put to use *c)* the value, or proceeds from the sale, of such goods, specif. of damaged goods, as involved in insurance claim settlements —***vt.*** **-vaged, -vag·ing** to save or rescue from shipwreck, fire, flood, etc.; engage or succeed in the salvage of (ships, goods, etc.) —**sal′vage·a·bil′i·ty** ***n.*** —**sal′vage·a·ble** ***adj.*** —**sal′vag·er** ***n.***

sal·va·tion (sal vā′shən) ***n.*** ⟦ME *salvacioun* < OFr *salvation* < LL(Ec) *salvatio* < L *salvatus*, pp. of *salvare*, to SAVE[1]⟧ **1** a saving or being saved from danger, evil, difficulty, destruction, etc.; rescue **2** a person or thing that is a means, cause, or source of preservation or rescue **3** *Theol.* deliverance from sin and from the penalties of sin; redemption —**sal·va′tion·al** ***adj.***

Salvation Army an international Christian organization founded (1865) in England by William BOOTH for religious and philanthropic work among the very poor: name adopted in 1878

Sal·va·tion·ist (-ist) ***n.*** a member of the Salvation Army

salve[1] (sav, säv) ***n.*** ⟦ME < OE *sealf*, akin to Ger *salbe* < IE base **selp-*, fat, butter > Sans *sarpis-*, melted butter⟧ **1** any medicinal ointment applied to wounds, skin irritations, burns, etc. for purposes of soothing or healing **2** anything that soothes or heals; balm [a *salve* for one's conscience] —***vt.*** **salved, salv′ing** ⟦ME *salven* < OE *sealfian* < the n.⟧ **1** [Archaic] to apply salve to (wounds, etc.) **2** to soothe; smooth over; assuage

salve[2] (salv) ***vt.*** **salved, salv′ing** ⟦back-form. < SALVAGE⟧ [Archaic] SALVAGE

sal·ver (sal′vər) ***n.*** ⟦altered < Fr *salve* < Sp *salva*, the testing of food by a taster, hence tray on which food was placed, salver < *salvar*, to taste, save < L *salvare*: see SAVE[1]⟧ a tray on which refreshments, letters, visiting cards, etc. are presented

sal·ver·form (-fôrm′) ***adj.*** ⟦prec. + -FORM⟧ *Bot.* having a slender, tubular corolla with the lobes spreading at right angles to the tube, as in phlox: also **sal′ver-shaped′**

sal·vi·a (sal′vē ə) ***n.*** ⟦ModL, name of the genus < L: see SAGE[2]⟧ SAGE[2] (sense 1)

sal·vif·ic (sal vif′ik) ***adj.*** ⟦LL(Ec) *salvificus* < *salvificare*, to save < *salvus*, saved from sin (< L, SAFE) + L *-ficare*, -FY⟧ bringing salvation —**sal·vif′i·cal·ly** ***adv.***

sal·vo[1] (sal′vō) ***n., pl.*** **-vos** or **-voes** ⟦It *salva* < L *salve*, hail, imper. of *salvere*, to be safe < *salvus*, SAFE⟧ **1** a discharge of a number of pieces of artillery or small arms, in regular succession or at the same time, either as a salute or, esp. in naval battles, as a broadside **2** the release of a load of bombs or the launching of several rockets at the same time **3** a burst of cheers or applause

sal·vo[2] (sal′vō) ***n., pl.*** **-vos** ⟦< ML legal phr. *salvo jure*, right being reserved (< L *salvus*: see SAFE)⟧ *Law* a saving clause; reservation

sal vo·la·ti·le (vō lat′′l ē′) ⟦ModL, volatile salt⟧ **1** a mixture of ammonium bicarbonate and ammonium carbonate, esp. in aromatic solution for use as smelling salts **2** ammonium carbonate

sal·vor (sal′vər) ***n.*** ⟦SALV(E)[2] + -OR⟧ any of the persons or ships participating in the voluntary rescue of a ship at sea or its cargo

Sal·ween (sal wēn′) river in Southeast Asia, flowing from E Tibet through E Myanmar into the Gulf of Martaban: *c.* 1,750 mi (2,816 km)

Salz·burg (sôlz′bərg; *Ger* zälts′boork′) city in central Austria: scene of annual music festivals

Sam *abbrev. Bible* Samuel

SAM (sam) ***n.*** surface-to-air missile

sa·ma·dhi (sə mä′dē) ***n.*** *Buddhism, Hinduism, etc.* a state of concentration in yoga, preliminary to nirvana, in which there is no longer consciousness of self

Sa·man·tha (sə man′thə) ***n.*** a feminine name

Sa·mar (sä′mär) island of the EC Philippines, southeast of Luzon: 5,050 sq mi (13,079 sq km)

sam·a·ra (sam′ər ə, sə mer′ə) ***n.*** ⟦ModL < L, seed of the elm < Gaul < **samos*, SUMMER[1]⟧ a dry, one-seeded, winged fruit, as of the maple

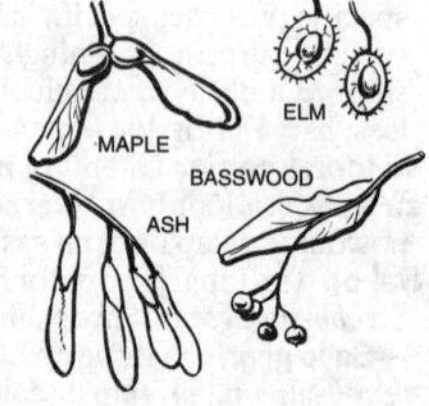

types of samara

Sa·ma·ra (sə mä′rə) city in SE European Russia, on the Volga: see KUIBYSHEV

Sa·mar·i·a (sə mer′ē ə, -mar′-) **1** region in W Jordan, west of the Jordan River **2** in ancient times, the N kingdom of the Hebrews; Israel **3** the capital of this kingdom **4** district of ancient Palestine between Galilee & Judea, later a part of the Roman province of Judea

Sa·mar·i·tan (sə mer′ə tən, -mar′-) ***n.*** ⟦ME < OE < LL(Ec) *Samaritanus* < Gr *Samareitēs* < *Samareia*, Samaria < Aram *shamerayin* < Heb *shomron*⟧ **1** a person born or living in Samaria **2** a person who comes to the aid of another: see GOOD SAMARITAN —***adj.*** of Samaria or its people or culture

sa·mar·i·um (sə mer′ē əm, -mar′-) ***n.*** ⟦ModL: so named (1879) by Boisbaudran (see GALLIUM) < Fr *samarskite* (see SAMARSKITE), in which it occurs + -IUM⟧ a chemical element, one of the rare-earth elements: symbol, Sm; at. no. 62: see the periodic table of elements in the Reference Supplement

Sam·ar·kand (sam′ər kand′; *Russ* sä mär känt′) city in E Uzbekistan: capital (as MARACANDA) of Tamerlane's empire (1370-1405)

sa·mar·skite (sə mär′skīt, sam′ər skīt′) ***n.*** ⟦< Fr, after Col. V. E. *Samarski-Bykhovets* (1803-70), Russ mining engineer⟧ a dark-colored, hard, radioactive, mineral, $(Y,Ce,U,Ca,Fe,Pb,Th)(Nb,Ta,Ti,Sn)_2O_6$, that is an ore of uranium or niobium

sam·ba (sam′bə, säm′-) ***n.*** ⟦Port, prob. of Afr orig.⟧ **1** a Brazilian dance of African origin, in duple time, with a syncopated rhythm **2** music for this dance —***vi.*** to dance the samba

sam·bal (säm′bäl) ***n.*** ⟦Malay⟧ in S Asian cooking, a condiment of chilies and various other ingredients

sam·bar (sam′bər, säm′-) ***n., pl.*** **-bars** or **-bar** ⟦Hindi *sābar* < Sans *śambara*⟧ a large Asian deer (*Cervus unicolor*) with coarse hair, a short, erectile mane, and three-pointed antlers: also sp. **sam′bur**

sam·bo (sam′bō′) ***n., pl.*** **-bos′** or **-boes′** ⟦< ? Fula *sambo*, uncle⟧ **1** a black person, esp. one who is dark-skinned and of African descent ☆**2** [*usually* **S-**] a racist stereotype of a U.S. black, variously depicted as foolish, shiftless, etc.

USAGE—an offensive term of contempt

sambo (wrestling) (sam′bō′, säm′-) ⟦Russ acronym for *sam(ozashchita) b(ez) o(ruzhiya)*, lit., self-defense without weapons⟧ [*often* **S-**] a Russian system of wrestling, combining traditional folk styles with judo: often written **SAMBO**

Sam Browne belt (sam′ broun′) ⟦after Brit Gen. Sir *Samuel J. Browne* (1824-1901)⟧ a military officer's belt with a diagonal strap across the right shoulder, designed to carry the weight of a pistol or sword

sam·bu·ca (sam bo͞o′kə) ***n.*** ⟦It < L *sambucus*: see ELDER[2], sense 1⟧ an Italian liqueur having the flavor of licorice

same (sām) ***adj.*** ⟦ME < ON *samr*, akin to Goth *sama*, OHG *samo*, OE *same* < IE **som-*, var. of base **sem-*, one, together, with > Sans *sam*, Gr *homos*, one and the same, L *simul*, at the same time, *similis*, like⟧ **1** being the very one; identical **2** alike in kind, quality, amount, or degree; corresponding: often prefixed to nouns or past participles to form adjectives **3** unchanged; not different [to look the *same* as ever] **4** before-mentioned; just spoken of ➥Usually used with *the* —***pron.*** the same person or thing: usually with *the, this,* or *that* —***adv.*** in the same way; in like manner: usually with *the*

SYN.—**same**, in one sense, agrees with **selfsame** and **very** in implying that what is referred to is one thing and not two or more distinct things [that is the *same*, or *selfsame* or *very*, house we once lived in] and, in another, implies reference to things that are really distinct but without any significant difference in kind, appearance, amount, etc. [I eat the *same* food every day]; **identical**, in one sense, also expresses the first idea [this is the *identical* bed where he slept] and, in another, implies exact correspondence in all details, as of quality, appearance, etc. [the signatures are *identical*]; **equal** implies the absence of any difference in quantity, size, value, degree, etc. [*equal* weights, an *equal* advantage]; **equivalent** implies of things that they amount to the same thing in value, force, meaning, etc. [$5 or its *equivalent* in merchandise] —ANT. **different**

sa·mekh or **sa·mech** (sä′mekh′, -mek′) ***n.*** ⟦Heb *samekh*, lit., support⟧ the fifteenth letter of the Hebrew alphabet (ס)

same·ness (sām′nis) ***n.*** **1** the state or quality of being the same; identity or uniformity **2** lack of change or variety; monotony

same-sex (sām′seks′) ***adj.*** **1** of, for, or relating to people of the same sex [*same-sex* schools] **2** of, for, or relating to homosexuals [*same-sex* marriage]

Sa·mhain (sou′ən) ***n.*** ⟦Ir < OIr *samain*⟧ the new year's festival of the ancient Celts, celebrated by modern pagans on Oct. 31 or Nov. 1

☆**Sam Hill** ⟦< ?⟧ [Slang] *euphemism for* HELL

Sa·mi (sä′mē) ***n., pl.*** **-mi** or **-mis** ⟦Lapp⟧ LAPP: for those in this ethnic group, now the preferred term

sam·i·sen (sam′ə sen′) ***n.*** ⟦Jpn *samisen, shamisen* < SinoJpn *san, sam,* three + *sen,* a line, string⟧ a Japanese musical instrument somewhat like a guitar, but with a long neck and three strings plucked with a large plectrum

sam·ite (sam′īt, sā′mīt) ***n.*** ⟦ME *samyte* < MFr *samit* < ML *samitum* < MGr *hexamiton* < *hexamitos,* woven with six threads < Gr *hex,* SIX + *mitos,* a thread⟧ a heavy silk fabric worn in the Middle Ages: it was sometimes interwoven with gold or silver

samisen

sam·iz·dat (säm′iz dät′) ***n.*** ⟦Russ < *sam(o)-,* self- (for IE base see SAME) + *izdat(el′stvo),* publishing < *izdat′,* publish⟧ [*also in roman type*] **1** a system by which manuscripts denied official publication in the Soviet Union were circulated clandestinely as in typescript or in mimeograph form, or were smuggled out for publication abroad **2** manuscripts distributed in this way

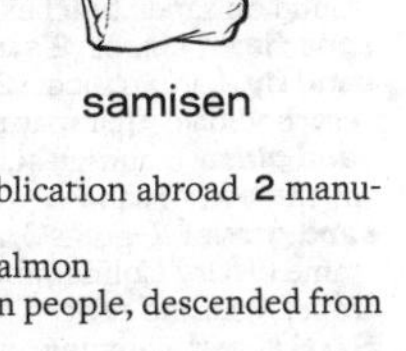

sam·let (sam′lit) ***n.*** ⟦< SALMON + -LET⟧ a young salmon

Sam·nite (sam′nīt′) ***n.*** a member of a pre-Roman people, descended from the Sabines, that lived in Samnium

Sam·ni·um (sam′nē əm) ⟦L < Sabine **Safiniom*: see SABINE[1]⟧ ancient country in SC Italy

Sa·mo·a (sə mō′ə) **1** group of islands in the South Pacific, north of Tonga: divided into AMERICAN SAMOA & Samoa **2** country in the South Pacific, consisting of two large islands (Savaii & Upolu) & several small ones: became independent in 1962 & a member of the Commonwealth in 1970: 1,137 sq mi (2,944 sq km); cap. Apia

Sa·mo·an (-ən) ***n.*** ⟦< prec. (ult. < Proto-Polynesian **ha′amoa,* ancient place name) + -AN⟧ **1** a person born or living in Samoa **2** the Austronesian language of the Samoans —***adj.*** of Samoa or its people, language, or culture

Samoa Standard Time a standard time used in the zone which includes American Samoa, corresponding to the mean solar time of the 165th meridian west of Greenwich, England: it is eleven hours behind Greenwich time

Sa·mos (sā′mäs′; *Gr* sä′mô̂s) Greek island in the Aegean, off W Turkey: *c.* 180 sq mi (466 sq km) —**Sa′mi·an** (-mē ən) ***adj., n.***

sa·mo·sa (sə mō′sə) ***n.*** ⟦Hindi & Urdu⟧ a small pastry turnover, orig. of India, filled with a spicy meat or vegetable mixture, as of potatoes and peas

Sam·o·thrace (sam′ə thrās′) Greek island in the NE Aegean: *c.* 70 sq mi (181 sq km): Gr. name **Sa·mo·thrá·ki** (sä′mô thrä′kē) —**Sam′o·thra′cian** (-thrā′shən) ***adj., n.***

sam·o·var (sam′ə vär′, säm′ə vär′) ***n.*** ⟦Russ, lit., self-boiler < *samo-,* self- (see SAMIZDAT) + *varit′,* to boil, akin to Lith *vìrti,* to boil < IE **(a)wer-* < base **awe-,* to moisten, flow > WATER⟧ a metal urn with a spigot and an internal tube for heating water in making tea: used esp. in Russia

Sam·o·yed (sam′ə yed′, sə moi′id) ***n.*** ⟦Russ *samoed* < self-designation of the *Sami,* or Lapps⟧ **1** a member of a group of peoples living in N Siberia and the Taimyr Peninsula **2** any of a group of Uralic languages spoken by the Samoyeds **3** any of a breed of strong working dog with a thick, white coat, erect ears, and a tail rolled over the back: developed in Siberia as a sled dog —***adj.*** of the Samoyeds or their languages or culture Also sp. (for ***n.*** 1-2 & ***adj.***) **Sam′o·yede′**

Sam·o·yed·ic (sam′ə yed′ik) ***n.*** the branch of the Uralic language family that includes Samoyed —***adj.*** **1** SAMOYED **2** of or relating to Samoyedic

samovar

☆**samp** (samp) ***n.*** ⟦< Narragansett *nasàump,* cornmeal mush⟧ **1** coarse meal of Indian corn **2** a porridge made from this

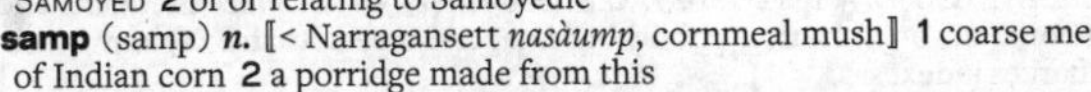

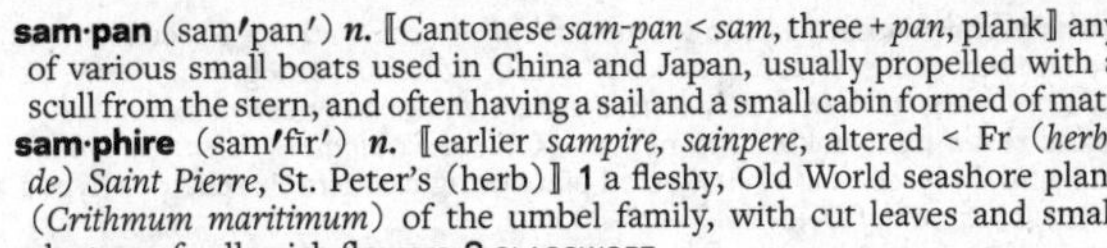

sam·pan (sam′pan′) ***n.*** ⟦Cantonese *sam-pan* < *sam,* three + *pan,* plank⟧ any of various small boats used in China and Japan, usually propelled with a scull from the stern, and often having a sail and a small cabin formed of mats

sam·phire (sam′fīr′) ***n.*** ⟦earlier *sampire, sainpere,* altered < Fr (*herbe de*) *Saint Pierre,* St. Peter's (herb)⟧ **1** a fleshy, Old World seashore plant (*Crithmum maritimum*) of the umbel family, with cut leaves and small clusters of yellowish flowers **2** GLASSWORT

sam·ple (sam′pəl, säm′-) ***n.*** ⟦ME, aphetic for *asample* < Anglo-Fr, for OFr *essample*: see EXAMPLE⟧ **1** a part, piece, or item taken or shown as representative of a whole thing, group, species, etc.; specimen; pattern [*samples* of wallpaper] **2** an illustration; example [a *sample* of his humor] **3** a small amount of sound, music, etc. taken from one context, digitized and recorded, edited, and used again in another context ☆**4** *Statistics* a selected segment of a population studied to gain knowledge of the whole —***vt.*** **-pled, -pling 1** to take a sample or samples of, as for testing quality **2** to digitize and record (small amounts of sound, music, etc.) for editing and using again in another context

sam·pler (-plər) ***n.*** ⟦senses 1 & 2 < prec. + -ER; sense 4 < ME *samplere,* aphetic < OFr *essamplaire* < LL *exemplarium* < L *exemplum*: see EXAMPLE⟧ **1** a person who prepares or selects samples for inspection **2** a collection or assortment of representative selections **3** an electronic device used to SAMPLE (***vt.*** 2) **4** a cloth embroidered with designs, mottoes, etc. in different stitches, to show a beginner's skill

sam·pling (-pliŋ) ***n.*** **1** the act or process of taking a small part or quantity of something as a sample for testing or analysis **2** the sample so taken **3** the practice or process of taking a SAMPLE (***n.*** 3) and reusing it in another context

sam·sa·ra (səm sä′rə) ***n.*** ⟦Sans *saṁsāra,* lit., running together < *sam-,* together (< IE **som-,* var. of base **sem-* > SAME) + *sara-,* fluid (< IE base **ser-,* to flow > SERUM)⟧ *Hinduism* the continuing cycle in which the same soul is repeatedly reborn

Sam·son (sam′sən) ***n.*** ⟦LL(Ec) < Gr(Ec) *Sampsōn* < Heb *shimshon* < ? *shemesh,* sun: interpretation of name uncert.⟧ **1** a masculine name: var. *Sampson* **2** *Bible* an Israelite judge, a Nazarite, noted for his feats of great strength: betrayed to the Philistines by Delilah: Judges 13-16

Sam·u·el (sam′yo͞o əl, -yool) ***n.*** ⟦LL(Ec) < Gr(Ec) *Samouēl* < Heb *shemuel,* lit., name of God⟧ **1** a masculine name: dim. *Sam, Sammy* **2** *Bible a)* a Hebrew judge and prophet *b)* either of the two books (1 Samuel, 2 Samuel) telling of Samuel, Saul, and David (abbrev. *S, Sa, Sam,* or *Sm*)

Sam·u·el·son (sam′yo͞o əl sən, -yool-), **Paul (Anthony)** 1915-2009; U.S. economist & educator

sam·u·rai (sam′ə rī′) ***n., pl.*** **-rai′** ⟦Jpn, var. of *saburai,* nominal form of *sabura(h)u,* to be in attendance, to serve⟧ **1** in feudal Japan, a member of a military class, consisting of the retainers of the daimyos: a samurai wore two swords and lived by the code of Bushido **2** later, used in English to designate a Japanese army officer or member of the military caste

-san (sän) ⟦Jpn, var. of *sama,* a directional suffix used as an honorific⟧ *suffix* a Japanese honorific title equivalent to *Mr., Mrs.,* etc., added to names as a mark of respect [Mishima-*san*]

Sa·naa (sä′nä, sä nä′) capital of Yemen, in the W part: also sp. **San′a** or **Sana**

☆**San An·dre·as fault** (san an drā′əs) ⟦after *San Andreas* valley, through which the fault runs: orig. Sp, *San Andrés,* Saint ANDREW⟧ active fault in the earth's crust extending northwest from S California for about 600 miles (966 km)

San An·to·ni·o (san′ an tō′nē ō′) ⟦Sp, Saint ANTHONY[2] (of Padua)⟧ city in SC Tex.: site of the Alamo

san·a·tive (san′ə tiv) ***adj.*** ⟦ME *sanatyf* < OFr *sanatif* < LL *sanativus* < L *sanatus,* pp. of *sanare,* to heal < *sanus*: see SANE⟧ having the power to heal or cure; curative

san·a·to·ri·um (san′ə tôr′ē əm) ***n., pl.*** **-ri·ums** or **-ri·a** (-ə) *chiefly Brit. var. of* SANITARIUM

san·be·ni·to (san′bə nēt′ō) ***n., pl.*** **-tos** ⟦Sp *sambenito,* after *San Benito,* Saint Benedict (see BENEDICT[2]): from resembling a Benedictine scapular⟧ **1** a yellow garment resembling a scapular in shape and having a red Saint Andrew's cross in front and in back, worn by a confessed, penitent heretic in the Spanish Inquisition **2** a similarly shaped black garment painted with flames, devils, etc., worn by a condemned heretic at an auto-da-fé

San Ber·nar·di·no (san′ bur′nər dē′nō, -nə-) ⟦Sp, after *Saint Bernardino* of Siena (1380-1444), It Franciscan priest⟧ city in S Calif.

San Bernardino Mountains mountain range in S Calif., south of the Mojave Desert: highest peak, 11,502 ft (3,506 m)

San·cerre (sän ser′) ***n.*** ⟦after *Sancerre,* town at the center of this wine region⟧ a dry, often fruity white wine from the upper Loire valley in central France

San·cho Pan·za (sän′chō pän′zə) the simple, credulous squire to Cervantes' Don Quixote: his practical, peasant common sense contrasts with the visionary idealism of his master

sanc·ti·fied (saŋk′tə fīd′) ***adj.*** **1** *a)* dedicated; consecrated *b)* made holy **2** affecting sanctity; sanctimonious

sanc·ti·fy (saŋk′tə fī′) ***vt.*** **-fied′, -fy′ing** ⟦ME *sanctifien,* altered (infl. by L) < OFr *saintifier* < LL(Ec) *sanctificare*: see SAINT & -FY⟧ **1** to make holy; specif., *a)* to set apart as holy; consecrate *b)* to make free from sin; purify **2** to make binding or inviolable by a religious sanction **3** to make seem morally right or binding [a practice *sanctified* by custom] —**sanc′ti·fi·ca′tion** ***n.*** —**sanc′ti·fi′er** ***n.***

sanc·ti·mo·ni·ous (saŋk′tə mō′nē əs) *adj.* ⟦< fol. + -OUS⟧ 1 pretending to be holy or pious; affecting sanctity 2 self-righteous, smug, etc. —*SYN.* DEVOUT —**sanc′ti·mo′ni·ous·ly** *adv.* —**sanc′ti·mo′ni·ous·ness** *n.*

sanc·ti·mo·ny (saŋk′tə mō′nē) *n.* ⟦OFr *sanctimonie* < L *sanctimonia* < *sanctus*, holy: see SAINT⟧ 1 affected piety or righteousness; religious hypocrisy 2 *obs. var. of* SANCTITY

sanc·tion (saŋk′shən) *n.* ⟦< Fr or L: Fr < L *sanctio* < *sanctus*: see SAINT⟧ 1 the act of a recognized authority confirming or ratifying an action; authorized approval or permission 2 support; encouragement; approval 3 something that gives binding force to a law, or secures obedience to it, as the penalty for breaking it, or a reward for carrying it out 4 something, as a moral principle or influence, that makes a rule of conduct, a law, etc. binding 5 *a)* a coercive measure, as a blockade of shipping, usually taken by several nations together, for forcing a nation considered to have violated international law to end the violation *b)* a coercive measure, as a boycott, taken by a group to enforce demands: *often used in pl.* 6 [Obs.] a formal decree; law —*vt.* to give sanction to; specif., *a)* to ratify or confirm *b)* to authorize or permit; countenance —*SYN.* APPROVE —**sanc′tion·a·ble** *adj.*

sanc·ti·ty (saŋk′tə tē) *n.* ⟦L *sanctitas* < *sanctus* (see SAINT) + *-itas*, -ITY⟧ 1 saintliness or holiness 2 the fact of being sacred or inviolable 3 *pl.* **-ties** anything held sacred: *usually used in pl.*

sanc·tu·ar·y (saŋk′cho͞o er′ē) *n., pl.* **-ar′ies** ⟦ME < MFr *saintuaire* < LL *sanctuarium* < L *sanctus*, sacred: see SAINT⟧ 1 a holy place, as a building set aside for worship of the divinity or of one or more deities; specif., *a)* the ancient Temple at Jerusalem *b)* a Christian church *c)* any church or temple *d)* a particularly holy place within a church or temple, as the part around the altar, the holy of holies in the Jewish Temple, etc. 2 *a)* a place of refuge or protection; asylum: orig., fugitives from justice were immune from arrest in churches or other sacred places *b)* immunity from punishment or the law, as by taking refuge in a church, etc. 3 a wildlife reservation where animals or birds are sheltered for breeding purposes and may not be hunted or trapped —*SYN.* SHELTER

sanc·tum (saŋk′təm) *n., pl.* **-tums** or **-ta** (-tə) ⟦L < neut. of *sanctus*, holy: see SAINT⟧ 1 a sacred place 2 a study or private room where one is not to be disturbed

sanctum sanc·to·rum (saŋk tôr′əm) ⟦LL(Ec), holy of holies (see prec.), used in Vulg. to transl. Gr(Ec) *to hagion tōn hagiōn* (in LXX), transl. of Heb *kodesh hakadashim*⟧ 1 HOLY OF HOLIES 2 a place of utmost privacy and inviolability

Sanc·tus (säŋk′to͝os, saŋk′təs) *n.* ⟦ME < LL(Ec), holy: see SAINT⟧ 1 an acclamation beginning "Holy, holy, holy Lord" that immediately follows the Preface of the Mass 2 a musical setting for this

Sanctus bell a small bell or set of bells rung at certain parts of the Mass (as at the Sanctus or after the consecration)

sand (sand) *n.* ⟦ME < OE, akin to Ger *sand*, ON *sandr* < IE base **bhes-*, to rub off, pulverize > Gr *psammos*, L *sabulum*⟧ 1 loose, gritty particles of eroded or weathered rock, varying in size from about 1/16 mm to 2 mm in diameter, usually deposited along the shores of bodies of water, in riverbeds, or in deserts 2 [*usually pl.*] a tract or area of sand; beach, etc. 3 ⟦with ref. to the sand in an hourglass⟧ [*usually pl.*] particles (of time); moments ☆4 [Slang] grit; courage; determination 5 any of the colors characteristic of sand, variously reddish yellow to grayish tan —*vt.* 1 to sprinkle or cover with sand 2 to smooth, polish, or clean with sand, sandpaper, or other abrasive substance 3 to fill with sand —*adj.* reddish-yellow to grayish-tan

Sand (sand; *Fr* sänd, sän), **George** (pseud. of *Amandine Aurore Lucie Dupin, Baronne Dudevant*) 1804-76; Fr. novelist

san·dal[1] (san′dəl) *n.* ⟦ME *sandalie* < L *sandalium* < Gr *sandalion*, dim. of *sandalon*⟧ 1 a kind of footwear consisting of a sole fastened in various ways to the foot by straps over the instep or toes, or around the ankle 2 any of various low slippers or shoes —**san′daled** *adj.*, **san′dalled**

san·dal[2] (san′dəl) *n.* SANDALWOOD

san·dal·wood (-wo͝od′) *n.* ⟦*sandal*, sandalwood < ME *sandell* < MFr *sandal* < ML *sandalum* < LGr *santalon* < Ar *ṣandal*, ult. < Sans *candana* < IE base **kand-*, to gleam, bright > L *candere*, to shine⟧ 1 *a)* the hard, light-colored, closegrained, sweet-smelling heartwood of any of several allied trees of Asia, used for carving and cabinetmaking or burned as incense; esp., the wood of a S Asian evergreen tree (*Santalum album*) of the sandalwood family *b)* any tree yielding such wood 2 *a)* any of a number of similar or related trees *b)* the wood of any of these —*adj.* designating a family (Santalaceae, order Santalales) of dicotyledonous plants, shrubs, and trees including the quandong

San·dal·wood (san′dəl wo͝od′) *former name for* SUMBA

san·da·rac (san′də rak′) *n.* ⟦L *sandaraca* < Gr *sandarakē*: prob. akin to Sans *candra-raga*, having the glow of the moon: for IE base see SANDALWOOD⟧ 1 a brittle, slightly aromatic, somewhat transparent, yellowish resin exuded from the bark of several African and Australian trees (genera *Tetraclinus* and *Callitris*) of the pine family, used esp. in varnishes and as incense 2 *a)* a N African tree (*Tetraclinus articulata*) yielding this resin and a mahogany-colored, durable wood used esp. in building (also **sandarac tree**) *b)* this wood

sand·bag (sand′bag′) *n.* 1 a bag filled with sand and used for ballast, in military fortifications, for levee protection against floods, etc. ☆2 a small, narrow bag filled with sand and used as a bludgeon —*vt.* **-bagged′**, **-bag′ging** 1 to place sandbags in or around ☆2 to strike or stun with a sandbag ☆3 [Informal] to force into doing something ☆4 [Informal] to deceive (someone, esp. an opponent), as by feigning friendship or by disguising one's skill or strength —**sand′bag′ger** *n.*

sand·bank (-baŋk′) *n.* ⟦SAND + BANK[2]⟧ 1 SANDBAR 2 a large mass of sand, as on a hillside

☆**sand·bar** (-bär′) *n.* a ridge or shoal of sand below high tide, formed in a river or along a shore by the action of currents or tides: also written **sand bar**

sand·blast (-blast′, -bläst′) *n.* 1 a current of air or steam carrying sand at a high velocity, used in etching glass and in cleaning or grinding hard surfaces, as of metals, stone, etc. 2 the machine used to apply this blast —*vt.* to engrave, clean, etc. with a sandblast —**sand′blast′er** *n.*

sand·box (-bäks′) *n.* ☆a box or pit containing sand for children to play in

sandbox tree a tropical American tree (*Hura crepitans*) of the spurge family, with small, woody fruit that bursts with a loud noise when ripe and scatters its seeds

☆**sand·bur** or **sand·burr** (-bur′) *n.* any of a genus (*Cenchrus*) of grasses, having their grains enclosed in spiny burs

Sand·burg (sand′bərg), **Carl** 1878-1967; U.S. poet, writer, & ballad collector

sand-cast (-kast′, -käst′) *vt.* **-cast′**, **-cast′ing** to make (a casting) by pouring metal in a mold of sand

sand·cas·tle (sand′kas′əl) *n.* a model, typically a crude one, of a castle or other structure, formed as a pastime from wet sand, as at the beach: cf. SAND SCULPTURE

sand·crack (-krak′) *n.* a perpendicular fissure in some part of the wall of an animal's hoof, esp. of a horse, often caused by sandy soil

sand dab 1 any of various small, edible flatfishes ☆2 any of several flounders (genus *Citharichthys*) found along North American coasts Also written **sand′dab′** *n.*

☆**sand dollar** any of an order (Clypeasteroida) of flat, round, disk-shaped echinoid echinoderms that live on sandy ocean beds

sand eel SAND LANCE

sand·er (san′dər) *n.* 1 a person who sands or sandpapers 2 a tool or machine for sanding or sandpapering

sand·er·ling (san′dər liŋ) *n.* ⟦< SAND + ? OE *yrthling*, farmer, kind of bird, lit., earthling⟧ a small, gray-and-white sandpiper (*Calidris alba*), often found on sandy beaches

sand flea 1 CHIGOE 2 SAND HOPPER

sand fly 1 BITING MIDGE 2 any of various other biting dipterous flies (family Psychodidae) that may transmit various diseases

sand·glass (sand′glas′, -gläs′) *n.* an hourglass used for measuring time by the flow of sand

sand·grouse (-grous′) *n.* any of a family (Pteroclididae) of birds in the same order (Columbiformes) as pigeons, found in sandy regions of S Europe, Asia, and Africa

S & H *abbrev.* shipping and handling

san·dhi (san′dē, sän′-, sun′-) *n.* ⟦< Sans *saṃdhi*, a linking, lit., placing together < IE **som-* < base **sem-*, together, SAME + **dhe-*, to place > DO[1]⟧ *Linguis.* modification of the sound of a morpheme in a given linguistic context (Ex.: the pronunciation of *the* [thə] in "the man" as opposed to *the* [thē] in "the old man", or of *am* as ['m] in "I am glad")

sand·hill crane (sand′hil′) a large North American crane (*Grus canadensis*) with grayish-brown plumage

☆**sand·hog** (sand′hôg′, -häg′) *n.* a laborer employed in underground or underwater construction projects as in a caisson or tunnel

sand hopper any of various small crustaceans (order Amphipoda), found on sea beaches, that jump like fleas

Sand·hurst (sand′hurst′) village in Berkshire, England: nearby is the Royal Military Academy Sandhurst

San Di·e·go (san′ dē ā′gō) ⟦after *San Diego* (St. Didacus), 15th-c. Sp friar⟧ seaport in S Calif.

sand·i·ness (san′dē nis) *n.* a sandy state or quality

San·di·nis·ta (san′də nēs′tə) *n.* ⟦after Gen. A. *Sandino* (1895-1934), Nicaraguan revolutionary leader + Sp *-ista*, -IST[1]⟧ a member of the socialist party that overthrew the government and took power in Nicaragua from 1979 until 1990

S & L *abbrev.* SAVINGS AND LOAN ASSOCIATION

sand lance any of a family (Ammodytidae) of small, eel-like, marine percoid fishes often found burrowing in coastal sands

☆**sand lily** a perennial spring plant (*Leucocrinum montanum*) of the lily family, native to the W U.S. and having grasslike leaves and umbels of white star-shaped flowers

☆**sand·lot** (sand′lät′) *adj.* ⟦orig. played on a sandy lot or field⟧ of or having to do with baseball as played by amateurs, now usually in organized leagues —**sand′lot′ter** *n.*

S&M *abbrev.* (sexual) sadism and masochism; sadomasochism: also **s&m** or **S and M**

sand·man (sand′man′) *n.* ⟦prob. < Ger *sandmann*: with ref. to the gritty residue in the eyes of sleepers⟧ *Folklore* a man, as in fairy tales, who makes children sleepy by dusting their eyes with sand

☆**sand myrtle** a small, evergreen, white-flowered plant (*Leiophyllum buxifolium*) of the heath family, native to the sand barrens of the SE U.S.

☆**S&P** ⟦(orig. two U.S. companies:) *Standard* Statistics + *Poor's* Publishing, after H. V. *Poor* (1812-1905), U.S. publisher⟧ *service mark* Standard and Poor's: an organization publishing financial research and various stock-market indexes

☆**sand painting** 1 in Navajo Indian healing ceremonies, the sprinkling of colored sands into designs made up of conventionalized symbolic figures 2 any similar design, painting, etc.

sand·pa·per (-pā′pər) ***n.*** strong paper with sand or other abrasive glued on one side, used for smoothing and polishing —***vt.*** to smooth or polish with sandpaper —**sand′pa′per·y** ***adj.***

sand·pip·er (-pī′pər) ***n.***, *pl.* **-pip′ers** or **-pip′er** any of a number of small shorebirds (family Scolopacidae) similar to the snipes but distinguished by a shorter, soft-tipped bill, including the **common sandpiper** (*Tringa hypoleucos*) of Europe and the **spotted sandpiper** (*Actitis macularia*) and **least sandpiper** (*Calidris minutilla*) of North America

spotted sandpiper

San·dra (san′drə, sän′-) ***n.*** a feminine name: dim. *Sandy*: see ALEXANDRA

sand sculpture a sculpture, typically an elaborate one, as of a building, animal or human figure, etc., fashioned from wet sand, as at the beach: cf. SANDCASTLE

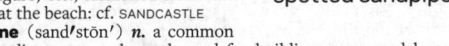

sand·stone (sand′stōn′) ***n.*** a common bedded sedimentary rock much used for building, composed largely of sand grains, mainly quartz, held together by silica, lime, etc.

sand·storm (-stôrm′) ***n.*** a windstorm in which large quantities of sand are blown about in the air in close proximity to the ground

☆**sand trap** a pit or trench filled with sand, serving as a hazard on a golf course

☆**sand verbena** any of a number of chiefly trailing plants (genus *Abronia*) of the four-o'clock family, with pink, white, or yellow flowers, found in sandy areas of the W U.S.

sand wedge *Golf* a type of wedge with a wide, heavy sole used for making shots from sand traps

sand·wich (sand′wich′, san′wich′) ***n.*** ⟦after John Montagu, 4th Earl of fol. (1718-92), said to have eaten these in order not to leave the gaming table for meals⟧ 1 two or more slices of bread with a filling of meat, fish, cheese, jam, etc. between them: now sometimes used of a single slice of bread covered with meat, gravy, etc. 2 anything in a layered arrangement like a sandwich —***vt.*** to place or squeeze between two other persons, places, things, materials, etc.

Sand·wich (sand′wich) ⟦OE *Sandwic* < *sand*, SAND + *wic*, WICK[2]⟧ town in Kent, SE England, near the Strait of Dover: one of the Cinque Ports

sandwich board a pair of signboards hung, one in front and one behind, from the shoulders of a person paid to walk the streets displaying them

☆**sandwich generation** ⟦see SANDWICH (***vt.***)⟧ a generation of people who are of an age to care for their elderly parents while also raising or supporting their own children

Sandwich Islands ⟦after the 4th Earl of *Sandwich*: see SANDWICH⟧ *former name for* the Hawaiian Islands: see HAWAII

sand·worm (sand′wurm′) ***n.*** any of various large, marine polychaetous worms usually living in burrows along sandy coastlines and commonly used as fishing bait, including the lugworm and nereis

sand·wort (sand′wurt′) ***n.*** any of a genus (*Arenaria*) of low, tufted, mat-forming plants of the pink family, growing in sandy soil

sand·y (san′dē) ***adj.*** **sand′i·er**, **sand′i·est** 1 composed of, full of, or covered with sand 2 like sand in texture; gritty 3 of the color of sand, specif., brownish or grayish blond [*sandy* hair]

Sandy Hook ⟦see HOOK (***n.*** *3a*)⟧ narrow, sandy peninsula in E N.J., at the S entrance to Lower New York Bay

sane (sān) ***adj.*** ⟦L *sanus*, healthy⟧ 1 having a normal, healthy mind; able to make sound, rational judgments 2 showing good sense; sensible [*a sane policy*] 3 [Rare] not diseased; healthy —**sane′ly** ***adv.*** —**sane′ness** ***n.***

San Fer·nan·do Valley (san′ fər nan′dō) ⟦after a mission named for *Ferdinand* III, 13th-c. king of Castile⟧ valley in SW Calif., partly in NW Los Angeles: *c.* 260 sq mi (673 sq km)

San·ford (san′fərd), **Mount** ⟦named (1885) by H. T. Allen for his ancestors, the *Sanford* family⟧ mountain in SE Alas.: 16,208 ft (4,940 m)

☆**San·for·ize** (san′fər īz′) ***vt.*** **-ized′**, **-iz′ing** ⟦back-form. from *Sanforized*, a trademark applied to fabrics so treated: after *Sanford* L. Cluett (1874-1968)⟧ to preshrink (cloth) permanently by a patented process before making garments

San Fran·cis·co (san′ frən sis′kō) ⟦Sp, name of old mission there, after Saint FRANCIS OF ASSISI⟧ seaport on the coast of central Calif., separated from Oakland by an inlet (**San Francisco Bay**) of the Pacific —**San′ Fran·cis′can** (-kən)

San Francisco Peaks ⟦Sp, after Saint FRANCIS OF ASSISI⟧ three peaks of an eroded volcano in NC Ariz.: highest peak, *c.* 12,700 ft (3,871 m)

sang (saŋ) ***vi.***, ***vt.*** *alt. pt. of* SING[1]

san·ga·ree (saŋ′gə rē′) ***n.*** ⟦earlier *sangre* < Sp *sangría*, SANGRIA⟧ a cold drink of sweetened, spiced wine or other alcoholic liquor, served over ice

Sang·er (saŋ′ər), **Margaret** (born *Margaret Higgins*) 1883-1966; U.S. nurse: leader in birth-control education

sang-froid (sän frwä′) ***n.*** ⟦Fr, lit., cold blood < L *sanguis* (see SANGUINE) + *frigidus* (see FRIGID)⟧ cool self-possession or composure —**SYN.** EQUANIMITY

San·greal (saŋ grāl′) ***n.*** ⟦ME *sangrayle* < MFr *Saint Graal*: see SAINT & GRAIL⟧ the Holy Grail: see GRAIL (sense 1)

San·gre de Cris·to Mountains (saŋ′grē də kris′tō) ⟦Sp, lit., blood of Christ⟧ range of the Rocky Mountains, in S Colo. & N N.Mex.: highest point, BLANCA PEAK

san·gri·a (san grē′ə, saŋ-) ***n.*** ⟦Sp *sangría*, lit., bleeding (so named from its color) < *sangre*, blood < L *sanguis*⟧ an iced punch made with red wine, fruit juice, and usually pieces of fruit and soda water

san·gui- (saŋ′gwi) ⟦< L *sanguis*, blood⟧ *combining form* blood

san·gui·na·ri·a (saŋ′gwi ner′ē ə) ***n.*** ⟦ModL < L < (*herba*) *sanguinaria*, (herb) that stanches blood < *sanguis*, blood⟧ 1 BLOODROOT 2 the dried rootstock of bloodroot, containing several alkaloids used in medicine

san·gui·nar·y (saŋ′gwi ner′ē) ***adj.*** ⟦L *sanguinarius* < *sanguis*, blood⟧ 1 accompanied by much bloodshed or carnage 2 flowing with blood; bloodstained 3 eager for bloodshed; bloodthirsty —**san′gui·nar′i·ly** ***adv.***

san·guine (saŋ′gwin) ***adj.*** ⟦ME *sanguin* < MFr < L *sanguineus* < *sanguis* (gen. *sanguinis*), blood⟧ 1 of the color of blood; ruddy: said esp. of complexions 2 in medieval physiology, having the warm, passionate, cheerful temperament and the healthy, ruddy complexion of one in whom the blood is the predominant humor of the four 3 cheerful and confident; optimistic; hopeful 4 *now rare var. of* SANGUINARY (sense 3) —**san′guine·ly** ***adv.*** —**san′guine·ness** ***n.***

san·guin·e·ous (saŋ gwin′ē əs) ***adj.*** ⟦L *sanguineus*: see prec. & -OUS⟧ 1 of or containing blood 2 having the color of blood; red 3 of bloodshed; sanguinary 4 sanguine; confident; hopeful

San·he·drin (san hē′drin, -he′-; san′ə drin′) ***n.*** ⟦TalmudHeb *sanhedrin* (*gedola*), (great) council < Gr *synedrion*, assembly < *syn-*, together + *hedra*, seat⟧ the highest court and council of the ancient Jewish nation, having religious and civil functions: it was abolished with the destruction of Jerusalem in A.D. 70: also [Chiefly Brit.] **San′he·drim′** (-drim′)

san·i·cle (san′i kəl) ***n.*** ⟦OFr < ML *sanicula*, prob. dim. < L *sanus*, healthy⟧ any of a genus (*Sanicula*) of plants of the umbel family, with long-stalked leaves and clusters of small, white or yellowish flowers: formerly regarded as having healing powers

sa·ni·es (sā′nē ēz′) ***n.*** ⟦L⟧ a thin, often greenish, serous discharge from a wound or ulcer —**sa′ni·ous** (-əs) ***adj.***

san·i·tar·i·an (san′ə ter′ē ən) ***adj.*** SANITARY —***n.*** a person who specializes in public health and sanitation

san·i·tar·i·um (san′ə ter′ē əm) ***n.***, *pl.* **-i·ums** or **-i·a** (-ə) ⟦ModL < L *sanitas*, health < *sanus*, healthy⟧ 1 a quiet resort, as in the mountains, where people go to rest and regain health 2 an institution for the care of invalids or convalescents, esp. one making use of local natural resources, as mineral springs, or one treating a specific disease, as tuberculosis

san·i·tar·y (san′ə ter′ē) ***adj.*** ⟦Fr *sanitaire* < L *sanitas*: see prec. & -ARY⟧ 1 of health or the rules and conditions of health; esp., promoting health and healthful conditions by the elimination of dirt and agents of infection or disease 2 in a clean, healthy condition; hygienic —**san′i·tar′i·ly** ***adv.*** —**san′i·tar′i·ness** ***n.***

☆**sanitary belt** a narrow elastic belt for holding a sanitary napkin in place

sanitary cordon CORDON SANITAIRE

sanitary engineering the branch of civil engineering having to do with sewage disposal, water supply, etc.

sanitary landfill LANDFILL (***n.*** 1 & 2)

☆**sanitary napkin** an absorbent pad of cotton, cellulose, etc. worn by women during menstruation

sanitary sewer a sewer or sewer system for carrying off wastewater and waste matter from a residence, business, etc.: cf. STORM SEWER

san·i·ta·tion (san′ə tā′shən) ***n.*** ⟦SANIT(ARY) + -ATION⟧ 1 the science and practice of effecting healthful and hygienic conditions; study and use of hygienic measures such as drainage, ventilation, pure water supply, etc. 2 drainage and disposal of sewage

san·i·tize (san′ə tīz′) ***vt.*** **-tized′**, **-tiz′ing** 1 to make sanitary, as by sterilizing 2 to make free of anything considered undesirable, offensive, etc. —**san′i·tiz′er** ***n.***

san·i·ty (san′ə tē) ***n.*** ⟦ME *sanite* < OFr < L *sanitas*, health⟧ 1 the condition of being sane; soundness of mind; mental health 2 soundness of judgment

San Ja·cin·to (san′ jə sin′tō) ⟦Sp, St. Hyacinth (13th c.)⟧ river in SE Tex., flowing into Galveston Bay: in a battle (1836) near its mouth, troops under Sam Houston won Tex. from Mexico: 100 mi (161 km)

San Joa·quin (san′ wô kēn′, wä-) ⟦Sp *San Joaquín*, Saint Joachim, father of the Virgin Mary⟧ river in central Calif., flowing from the Sierra Nevada into the Sacramento River: *c.* 350 mi (563 km)

San Jo·se (san′ hō zā′) ⟦Sp, *San José*, St. JOSEPH[1]⟧ city in WC Calif.

San Jo·sé (sän′ hô se′) capital of Costa Rica, in the central part

☆**San Jo·se scale** (san′ hō zā′) ⟦after SAN JOSE (Calif.), where first observed in the U.S.⟧ a scale insect (*Quadraspidiotus perniciosus*) that is very destructive to fruit trees and ornamental shrubs

San Juan (san′ hwän′, -wän′; *Sp* sän hwän′) ⟦Sp, St. JOHN[1]⟧ seaport & capital of Puerto Rico, on the Atlantic

San Juan Hill hill near Santiago de Cuba: captured by U.S. troops in a battle (1898) of the Spanish-American War

San Juan Islands group of islands in NW Wash., between the Strait of Georgia & Puget Sound

San Juan Mountains range of the Rocky Mountains in SW Colo. & N N.Mex.: highest peaks, over 14,000 ft (4,267 m)

sank (saŋk) ***vi.***, ***vt.*** *alt. pt. of* SINK

San·khya (säŋ′kyə) ***n.*** ⟦Sans *sāṁkhya* < *saṁkhyā*, calculation < *saṁkhyāti*, (he) counts up⟧ a major system of Hindu philosophy that assumes matter and spirit to be the two ultimate, completely distinct principles of reality

Sankt Mo·ritz (zäŋkt mō′rits) *Ger. name for* ST. MORITZ

Şan·liur·fa (shän lo͞o′fə) city in SE Turkey, near the Syrian border: cf. EDESSA

San Lu·is Po·to·sí (sän′ lwēs′ pô′tô sē′) 1 state of NC Mexico: 24,266 sq mi (62,849 sq km) 2 its capital, in the SW part

San Ma·ri·no (sän′ mä rē′nô; *E* san′ mə rē′nō) 1 independent country within E Italy: 24 sq mi (61 sq km) 2 its capital

San Mar·tín (sän′ mär tēn′), **Jo·sé de** (hô se′ de) 1778-1850; South American revolutionary leader, born in Argentina

San Ma·te·o (san′ mə tā′ō) ⟦Sp, St. MATTHEW⟧ city in W Calif., on San Francisco Bay: suburb of San Francisco

San Miguel de Tucumán *see* TUCUMÁN

☆**san·nup** (san′up′) ***n.*** ⟦Massachusett *sanomp*, younger man⟧ [Historical] a married North American Indian man

sann·ya·si (sun yä′sē) ***n.*** ⟦Hindi *sannyāsī* < Sans *saṁnyāsin*, casting away < *saṃ*, together (see SAME) + *ni*, down (for IE base see NETHER) + *asayati*, (he) casts⟧ 1 a Hindu holy man who is a homeless mendicant 2 a disciple of any of certain gurus Also **sann·ya′sin** (-sin)

S-A node (es′ā′) SINOATRIAL NODE

San Quentin a state prison in California, near San Francisco

San Re·mo (sän re′mô; *E* san rē′mō) resort town in Liguria, NW Italy, on the Riviera

sans (sanz; *Fr* sän) ***prep.*** ⟦ME *saun* < OFr *sanz* (Fr *sans*) < L *sine*, without: form infl. by L *absentia*, in the absence of, abl.: see ABSENCE⟧ without; lacking

Sans *abbrev.* Sanskrit

San Sal·va·dor (san sal′və dôr′; *Sp* sän säl′vä dôr′) ⟦Sp, Holy Savior⟧ 1 capital of El Salvador, in the central part 2 island of the E Bahamas: prob. the place of Columbus' landing (1492) in the New World: 63 sq mi (163 sq km)

San·scrit (san′skrit′) ***n., adj.*** *alt. sp. of* SANSKRIT

sans-cu·lotte (sanz′ko͝o lät′, -kyo͝o-; *Fr* sän kü lôt′) ***n.*** ⟦Fr, lit., without breeches: (see SANS & CULOTTES)⟧ 1 a revolutionary: term of contempt applied by the aristocrats to the republicans of the poorly clad French Revolutionary army, who substituted pantaloons for knee breeches 2 any radical or revolutionary —**sans′-cu·lot′tic** ***adj.***, **sans′-cu·lot′tish** —**sans′-cu·lot′tism′** ***n.***

sans doute (sän do͞ot′) ⟦Fr⟧ without doubt; certainly

San Se·bas·tián (sän′ se bäs tyän′; *E* san′ si bas′chən) seaport in The Basque Country, N Spain

☆**san·sei** (sän′sā′) ***n., pl.*** **-sei′** or **-seis′** ⟦Jpn < SinoJpn *san*, three + *sei*, generation⟧ [*also* **S-**] a native U.S. or Canadian citizen whose grandparents were Japanese immigrants: cf. ISSEI, KIBEI, NISEI

san·se·vie·ri·a (san′sə vir′ē ə) ***n.*** ⟦ModL, after the Prince of *Sanseviero* (1710-71), a learned Neapolitan⟧ any of a genus (*Sansevieria*) of succulent tropical plants of the agave family, with stiff, thick, lance-shaped leaves often yielding a strong, elastic fiber

Sansk *abbrev.* Sanskrit

San·skrit (san′skrit′) ***n.*** ⟦< Sans *saṃskṛta*, lit., made together, well arranged < *saṃ-*, together (see SAME) + *-kṛta*, made < IE base **kwer-*, to make > MIr *creth*, poetry: so called in distinction to *Prākrit*, lit., the common (spoken) language⟧ 1 the classical Old Indic literary language, as cultivated from the 4th cent. B.C. onward: because of the antiquity of its written expression and the detailed descriptive analysis it received in the Sutras of the Hindu grammarian Pānini (end of the 4th cent. B.C.), Sanskrit was used as a major source of data in the origin and development of Indo-European comparative linguistics 2 loosely, any written form of Old Indic, including Vedic —***adj.*** of or written in Sanskrit —**San·skrit′ic** ***adj.*** —**San′skrit·ist** (-skri tist) ***n.***

sans peur et sans re·proche (sän pėr′ ā sän rə prôsh′) ⟦Fr⟧ without fear and without reproach

sans-ser·if (san ser′if) ***n.*** ⟦see SANS & SERIF⟧ a style of printing type with no serifs

sans sou·ci (sän so͞o sē′) ⟦Fr⟧ without worry or care

San Ste·fa·no (sän ste′fä nô′) village in European Turkey: site of the signing of a peace treaty (1878) between Russia & Turkey at the end of the Russo-Turkish War

San·ta¹ (san′tə) ***n.*** ☆*short for* SANTA CLAUS

San·ta² (sän′tä, san′tə) ***adj.*** ⟦Sp or It, fem. of *santo* < L *sanctus*, holy: see SAINT⟧ holy —***n.*** saint: used before the given name of a female saint [*Santa Rosa*]

San·ta An·a¹ (san′tə an′ə) ⟦Sp, Saint ANNE¹⟧ hot desert wind from the east or northeast in S Calif.

San·ta An·a² (san′tə an′ə; *for 2, Sp* sän′tä ä′nä) ⟦Sp, Saint ANNE¹⟧ 1 city in SW Calif. 2 city in W El Salvador

San·ta An·na (sän′tä ä′nä), **An·to·nio Ló·pez de** (än tô′nyô lô′pes de) 1795?-1876; Mex. revolutionary leader & general: president (1833-35; 1841-44; 1846-47; 1853-55)

San·ta Bar·ba·ra (san′tə bär′brə, -bə rə) ⟦Sp *Santa Bárbara*, Saint Barbara, early Christian martyr⟧ city on the coast of SW Calif.

Santa Barbara Islands group of nine islands, & many islets, off the SW coast of Calif.

San·ta Cat·a·li·na (san′tə kat′ə lē′nə) ⟦Sp *Catalina*, Catherine: in honor of Saint CATHERINE² (of Alexandria)⟧ one of the Santa Barbara Islands; tourist resort: *c.* 20 mi (32 km) long

San·ta Cat·a·ri·na (sän′tə kä′tə rē′nə) state of S Brazil: 36,851 sq mi (95,444 sq km); cap. Florianópolis

San·ta Cla·ra (san′tə kler′ə; *for 1, Sp* sän′tä klä′rä) 1 city in central Cuba 2 ⟦Sp, *St. Clare* (of Assisi), 1194-1253⟧ city in W Calif., near San Jose

San·ta Cla·ri·ta (san′tə klə rēt′ə) city in SW Calif., near Los Angeles

☆**San·ta Claus** (san′tə klôz′) ⟦< Du dial. *Sinterklaas, Sante Klaas* < *Sant Nikolaas*, Saint NICHOLAS²⟧ *Folklore* a fat, white-bearded, jolly old man in a red suit, who lives at the North Pole, makes toys for children, and distributes gifts at Christmastime: also called *Father Christmas, Saint Nicholas, Saint Nick*

San·ta Cruz (san′tə kro͞oz′; *Sp* sän′tä kro͞os′) ⟦Sp, holy cross⟧ 1 city in central Bolivia 2 one of the Santa Barbara Islands: *c.* 23 mi (37 km) long 3 ST. CROIX

Santa Cruz de Te·ne·rife (də ten′ə rif′; *Sp* de te′ne rē′fe) seaport on Tenerife Island, Canary Islands

San·ta Fe (san′tə fā′) ⟦Sp, holy faith⟧ capital of N.Mex., in the NC part

San·ta Fé (sän′tä fe′) city in central Argentina

Santa Fe Trail trade route between Santa Fe, N.Mex., & Independence, Mo.: important from 1821 to 1880

Santa Fe Trail

☆**San·ta Ger·tru·dis** (san′tə gər tro͞o′dis) ⟦so named after a section of the King Ranch, in Texas⟧ any of a breed of hardy, red-colored beef cattle developed from a cross of shorthorned and Brahman stock

San·ta Is·a·bel (sän′tä ē sä bel′) *former name for* MALABO

San·ta Ma·ri·a (san′tə mə rē′ə) 1 active volcano in SW Guatemala: 12,362 ft (3,768 m) 2 city in WC Calif.

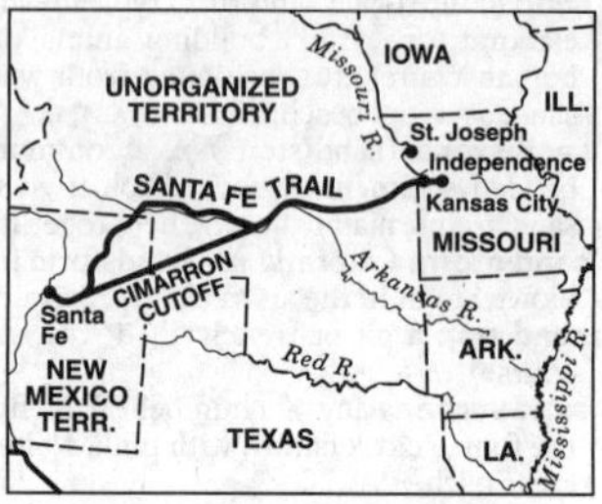

San·ta Mon·i·ca (san′tə män′i kə) ⟦Sp *Santa Mónica*, Saint Monica, mother of Saint AUGUSTINE² (of Hippo)⟧ city in SW Calif., on the Pacific: suburb of Los Angeles

San·tan·der (sän′tän der′) seaport in N Spain, on the Bay of Biscay

San·ta Ro·sa (san′tə rō′zə) ⟦Sp, St. Rose (of Lima) (1586-1617): 1st New World saint⟧ 1 one of the Santa Barbara Islands: 17 mi (27 km) long 2 city in W Calif., north of San Francisco

San·ta·ya·na (san′tē an′ə, -ä′nə; *Sp* sän′tä yä′nä), **George** (born *Jorge Agustín Nicolás de Santayana*) 1863-1952; U.S. philosopher & writer, born in Spain

San·tee (san tē′) ⟦prob. < name of a division of the Dakota Indians⟧ river in E S.C., flowing southeast into the Atlantic: 143 mi (230 km)

San·te·ri·a or **San·te·rí·a** (sän′tə rē′ə) ***n.*** ⟦< Sp *santería*, sanctity, holiness < *santo*, holy, saint < L *sanctus*: see SAINT⟧ a religion of the Caribbean region that originated in Cuba, based on Yoruban deities worshiped as Roman Catholic saints in rites that sometimes include the sacrifice of animals

San·ti·a·go (sän′tē ä′gō, san′-) capital of Chile, in the central part

Santiago de Cu·ba (de ko͞o′bä) seaport in SE Cuba, on the Caribbean

san·tims (sän′timz) ***n., pl.*** **-tim·i** (-ti mē) ⟦< Latvian *santims* < Fr *centime* (see CENTIME)⟧ a monetary unit of Latvia, equal to 1⁄100 of a lats

San·to Do·min·go (sän′tô dô miŋ′gô; *E* san′tō dō miŋ′gō) 1 seaport & capital of the Dominican Republic, on the S coast 2 *former name for* the DOMINICAN REPUBLIC 3 *former name for* HISPANIOLA

san·to·li·na (san′tə lē′nə) ***n.*** ⟦ModL, prob. altered < fol.⟧ any of a genus (*Santolina*) of Old World shrubs of the composite family; esp., a small, bushy, evergreen shrub (*S. chamaecyparissus*) with silvery gray, woolly, aromatic leaves and long-stalked, yellow flower heads, used in gardens and as a ground cover

san·ton·i·ca (san tän′i kə) ***n.*** ⟦ModL < L (*herba*) *santonica*, after the *Santoni*, a people of ancient Gaul⟧ 1 any of several European wormwoods (esp. *Artemisia cina*) 2 the unexpanded, dried flower heads of several European wormwoods, containing santonin

san·to·nin (san′tə nin) ***n.*** ⟦Fr *santonine* < ModL *santonica*: see prec.⟧ a colorless, poisonous, crystalline compound, $C_{15}H_{18}O_3$, obtained from certain species of wormwood and formerly used in medicine as a vermifuge

San·tos (sän′to͝os) seaport in S Brazil

san·tur (san to͝or′) ***n.*** ⟦< Pers & Turk name, via Ar; ult. < Gr *psaltērion*, harp: see PSALTER⟧ a Persian or Arabian dulcimer: also sp. **san·tour′**

São Fran·cis·co (soun′ frän sēs′ko͞o) river in E Brazil, flowing northeast and east into the Atlantic: *c.* 1,800 mi (2,897 km)

São Lu·ís (lwēs′) capital of Maranhão state, Brazil: seaport on an island off the N coast

São Mi·guel (mē gel′) largest island of the Azores: 293 sq mi (759 sq km); chief city, Ponta Delgada

Saône (sōn) river in E France, flowing south into the Rhone at Lyon: *c.* 280 mi (451 km)

São Pau·lo (soun pou′lo͞o) 1 state of SE Brazil: 96,066 sq mi (248,810 sq km) 2 its capital

São Sal·va·dor (soun säl′və dôr′) *var. of* SALVADOR

São Tomé (soun tô me′) 1 island of São Tomé and Príncipe, in the Gulf of Guinea, off the W coast of Africa: 332 sq mi (860 sq km) 2 capital of São Tomé and Príncipe, on this island

São To·mé and Prín·ci·pe (prin′sə pā′) country off the W coast of Africa, comprising two islands (*São Tomé* & *Príncipe*) & several islets in the Gulf of

Guinea: formerly a Portuguese territory, it became independent 1975: 386 sq mi (1,001 sq km); cap. São Tomé

sap[1] (sap) *n.* ⟦ME < OE *sæp*, akin to Ger *saft* < IE base **sab-*, var. of **sap-*, to taste, perceive > L *sapere*, to taste, know⟧ 1 the juice that circulates through a plant, esp. a woody plant, bearing water, food, etc. to the tissues 2 any fluid vital to the life or health of an organism 3 vigor; vitality 4 ⟦< SAPHEAD⟧ [Slang] a stupid person; fool —*vt.* **sapped, sap′ping** to drain of sap —**sap′less** *adj.*

sap[2] (sap) *n.* ⟦MFr *sappe* < the v.⟧ an extended, narrow trench for approaching or undermining an enemy position or fortification —*vt.* **sapped, sap′ping** ⟦MFr *sapper* < *sappe*, a hoe < VL *sappa*, orig. he-goat, prob. < Illyrian **zapp-*⟧ 1 to undermine by digging away foundations; dig beneath 2 to undermine in any way; weaken; exhaust —*vi.* 1 to dig saps 2 to approach an enemy's position by saps —**SYN.** WEAKEN

sap[3] (sap) [Slang] *n.* ⟦prob. orig. contr. < SAPLING⟧ ☆a blackjack, short club, etc. —☆*vt.* **sapped, sap′ping** to hit on the head, or knock out, with a sap

sap·a·jou (sap′ə jo͞o′) *n.* ⟦Fr < ?⟧ CAPUCHIN (sense 3)

sa·pan·wood (sə pan′wood′) *n. alt. sp. of* SAPPANWOOD

sap·head (sap′hed′) *n.* [Slang] a stupid person; fool —**sap′head′ed** *adj.*

sa·phe·na (sə fē′nə) *n.* ⟦ME < ML < Ar *ṣāfin*⟧ either of two large superficial veins of the leg —**sa·phe′nous** (-nəs) *adj.*

sap·id (sap′id) *adj.* ⟦L *sapidus* < *sapere*, to have a taste: see SAP[1]⟧ 1 having a taste, esp. a pleasing taste; savory 2 agreeable to the mind; interesting; engaging —**sa·pid·i·ty** (sə pid′ə tē) *n.*

sa·pi·ent (sā′pē ənt) *adj.* ⟦ME < L *sapiens*, prp. of *sapere*, to taste, know: see SAP[1]⟧ 1 full of knowledge; wise; sagacious; discerning 2 of or relating to the existing human species (*Homo sapiens*) —*n.* a sapient human —**sa′pi·ence** *n.* —**sa′pi·ent·ly** *adv.*

sa·pi·en·tial (sā′pē en′shəl) *adj.* ⟦LL *sapientialis* < L *sapiens*⟧ having, providing, or expounding wisdom

Sa·pir (sə pir′), **Edward** 1884-1939; U.S. linguist & anthropologist, born in Pomerania

sap·ling (sap′liŋ) *n.* ⟦ME *sappelynge*: see SAP[1] & -LING[1]⟧ 1 a young tree 2 a youth

sap·o·dil·la (sap′ə dil′ə) *n.* ⟦Sp *zapotillo*, dim. of *zapote* < Nahuatl *tzapotl*⟧ 1 a tropical American evergreen tree (*Achras zapota*) of the sapodilla family, yielding chicle and having a brown, rough-skinned fruit with a sweet, yellowish pulp 2 the fruit —*adj.* designating a large family (Sapotaceae, order Ebenales) of dicotyledonous, tropical trees and shrubs with a milky juice and sometimes edible fruits, including the balata, buckthorn, and marmalade tree

sap·o·na·ceous (sap′ə nā′shəs) *adj.* ⟦ModL *saponaceus* < L *sapo*, soap: see SAPONIFY⟧ soapy or soaplike

sa·pon·i·fi·ca·tion (sə pän′ə fi kā′shən) *n.* ⟦Fr < *saponifier*: see fol.⟧ the conversion of an ester heated with an alkali into the corresponding alcohol and acid salt; specif., this process carried out with fats (glyceryl esters) to produce soap

sa·pon·i·fy (sə pän′ə fī′) *vt.* **-fied′, -fy′ing** ⟦Fr *saponifier* < L *sapo* (gen. *saponis*), soap (< Gmc **saipo-* > OE *sape*, SOAP) + Fr *-fier*, -FY⟧ to subject to saponification; specif., to convert (a fat) into soap by reaction with an alkali —*vi.* to undergo conversion to soap —**sa·pon′i·fi′a·ble** *adj.* —**sa·pon′i·fi′er** *n.*

sap·o·nin (sap′ə nin) *n.* ⟦Fr *saponine* < L *sapo* (see prec.) + *-in*, -IN[1]⟧ any of a group of glycosides, found in soapbark, etc., which form a soapy foam when dissolved in water: used as detergents, etc.

sap·o·nite (-nīt′) *n.* ⟦Swed *saponit* < L *sapo*: see SAPONIFY & -ITE[1]⟧ a complex hydrous silicate of aluminum and magnesium, a light-colored, soft clay mineral, often found in veins and cavities in serpentine and basaltic rocks

sa·por (sā′pər) *n.* ⟦L < *sapere*, to taste: see SAP[1]⟧ that quality in a substance which produces taste or flavor; savor —**sap·o·rif·ic** (sap′ə rif′ik) *adj.*, **sa·por·ous** (sā′pər əs, sap′ər-)

sa·po·ta (sə pōt′ə) *n.* ⟦ModL < Sp *zapote*: see SAPODILLA⟧ SAPODILLA

sa·po·te (sə pōt′ē, -ā) *n.* ⟦Sp *zapote*: see SAPODILLA⟧ 1 any of several tropical American trees or their fruits 2 *a)* MARMALADE TREE *b)* SAPODILLA

sap·pan·wood (sə pan′wood′) *n.* ⟦partial transl. of Du *sapanhout* < Malay *sapang* + Du *hout*, wood, akin to OE *holt*: see HOLT⟧ 1 a wood yielding a red or blue dye, obtained from an East Indian tree (*Caesalpinia sappan*) of the caesalpinia family 2 the tree

sap·per (sap′ər) *n.* 1 a soldier employed in digging saps 2 a soldier employed in setting or disarming mines 3 a person or thing that saps (in various senses)

Sap·phic (saf′ik) *adj.* ⟦L *Sapphicus* < Gr *Sapphikos* < *Sapphō*⟧ 1 of Sappho 2 [*often* **s-**] designating or of certain meters or a form of stanza or strophe used by or named after Sappho, esp. a stanza of three lines, of five or six stresses each, followed by a short line 3 [*sometimes* **s-**] LESBIAN (*adj.* 2) —*n.* [*often* **s-**] a Sapphic verse

Sap·phi·ra (sə fī′rə) *n.* ⟦LL(Ec) *Saphira* < Gr(Ec) *Sappheirē* < Aram word meaning "beautiful"⟧ *Bible* the wife of Ananias, struck dead with her husband for lying: Acts 5:1-10

sap·phire (saf′īr) *n.* ⟦ME < OFr *saphir* < L *sapphirus* < Gr *sappheiros* < Heb *sapir* < Sans *śanipriya*, lit., dear to Saturn < *Śaniḥ*, Saturn (the planet) + *priya*, beloved < IE **prī-*, var. of base **prēi-*, to love > FRIEND⟧ 1 *a)* a clear, deep-blue variety of corundum, valued as a precious stone *b)* its deep-blue color 2 *a)* a translucent or transparent variety of corundum, varying in color *b)* a gem made of this [white, yellow, and purple *sapphires*] —*adj.* deep-blue

sap·phir·ine (saf′ər in, -ə rīn′) *adj.* of or like sapphire —*n.* a rare, blue or green, very hard, monoclinic mineral, $(Mg,Al)_8(Al,Si)_6O_{20}$, found in some metamorphic rocks

Sap·phism (saf′iz′əm) *n.* ⟦after fol. + -ISM: from the lesbianism attributed to the poet and her followers⟧ [*sometimes* **s-**] female homosexuality —**Sap′phist** *n.*

Sap·pho (saf′ō) fl. early 6th cent. B.C.; Gr. lyric poet of Lesbos

Sap·po·ro (sä pôr′ō) chief city on the island of Hokkaido, Japan, in the SW part

sap·py (sap′ē) *adj.* **-pi·er, -pi·est** ⟦ME *sapy* < OE *sæpig*⟧ 1 full of sap; juicy 2 ⟦< SAP[1], *n.* 4⟧ [Slang] foolish or silly, often, specif., in an overly sentimental way —**sap′pi·ness** *n.*

sa·pre·mi·a (sə prē′mē ə) *n.* ⟦ModL: see fol. & -EMIA⟧ a form of blood poisoning caused by toxic products resulting from the action of putrefactive microorganisms on dead tissue: also sp. **sa·prae′mi·a** —**sa·pre′mic** *adj.*

sap·ro- (sap′rō, -rə) ⟦< Gr *sapros*, rotten⟧ *combining form* dead, putrefying, decaying [*saprogenic*]: also, before a vowel, **sapr-**

sa·pro·bic (sa prō′bik) *adj.* ⟦< prec. + Gr *bios*, life + -IC⟧ *Biol.* 1 of or pertaining to organisms living in highly polluted waters 2 of or pertaining to saprophytes —**sa·probe** (sa′prōb′) *n.* —**sa·pro′bi·cal·ly** *adv.*

sap·ro·gen·ic (sap′rə jen′ik) *adj.* ⟦SAPRO- + -GENIC⟧ producing, or produced by, putrefaction: also **sa·prog·e·nous** (sə prä′jə nəs)

sap·ro·lite (sap′rə līt′) *n.* ⟦SAPRO- + -LITE⟧ *Geol.* completely decomposed rock lying in its original site —**sap′ro·lit′ic** (-lit′ik) *adj.*

sap·ro·pel (sap′rə pel′) *n.* ⟦< SAPRO- + Gr *pēlos*, mud, slime⟧ black, decaying, organic bottom deposits in some lakes, rivers, etc. that lack oxygen and are rich in hydrogen sulfide —**sap′ro·pel′ic** *adj.*

sa·proph·a·gous (sa präf′ə gəs) *adj.* ⟦SAPRO- + -PHAGOUS⟧ feeding on decaying organic matter

sap·ro·phyte (sap′rə fīt′) *n.* ⟦SAPRO- + -PHYTE⟧ any organism that lives on dead or decaying organic matter, as some fungi and bacteria —**sap′ro·phyt′ic** (-fit′ik) *adj.*

sap·ro·zo·ic (sap′rə zō′ik) *adj.* ⟦SAPRO- + ZO(O)- + -IC⟧ 1 absorbing simple organic material and dissolved salts for nourishment: said of certain animals 2 of a saprophyte, esp. an animal parasite lacking a functional digestive system, as the tapeworm

☆**sap·sa·go** (sap′sə gō′) *n.* ⟦altered < Ger *schabzieger* < *schaben*, to scrape (akin to SHAVE) + *zieger*, curds < Late OHG *ziger* < Rhaeto-Romanic *tšigrun* < Gaul **dwi-*, twice (< IE base **dwōu-*, TWO) + **ger-*, to heat (< IE **gwher-*, WARM); from being heated twice in processing⟧ a variety of hard, greenish cheese made orig. in Switzerland of skim milk flavored with melilot

☆**sap·suck·er** (sap′suk′ər) *n.* any of a genus (*Sphyrapicus*) of American woodpeckers that often drill holes in trees for the sap and the insects the sap attracts

sap·wood (sap′wood′) *n.* the soft wood between the inner bark of a tree and the heartwood, serving to conduct water and sap

Saq·qar·a (sə kär′ə) village in N Egypt, near the ruins of Memphis: site of many pyramids

SAR *abbrev.* Sons of the American Revolution

Sar·a (ser′ə, sar′-) *n.* a feminine name: see SARAH

sar·a·band (sar′ə band′) *n.* ⟦Fr *sarabande* < Sp *zarabanda* < ?⟧ 1 a graceful, stately, slow Spanish dance in triple time, developed from an earlier lively dance 2 a stylized dance of this type used as a movement in a classical suite

Sar·a·cen (sar′ə sən) [Historical] *n.* ⟦ME *Sarasene* < OFr & LL: OFr *Sarrazin* < LL *Saracenus* < LGr *Sarakēnos* < ? Ar *sharqīyīn*, easterners, pl. of *sharqī*, eastern < *sharq*, east⟧ 1 a member of any of the nomadic tribes of Syria and nearby regions 2 any Arab or any Muslim, esp. at the time of the Crusades —*adj.* of the Saracens or their culture —**Sar′a·cen′ic** (-sen′ik) *adj.*

Sa·ra·gos·sa (sar′ə gäs′ə) *Eng. name for* ZARAGOZA

Sar·ah (ser′ə, sar′-) *n.* ⟦Heb *sara*, lit., princess, fem. of *sar*, prince⟧ 1 a feminine name: dim. *Sadie, Sal, Sally;* var. *Sara* 2 *Bible* the wife of Abraham and mother of Isaac: see Gen. 17:15

Sa·rai (ser′ī′) *n. Bible* Sarah: so called before God's covenant with Abraham: Gen. 17:15

Sa·ra·je·vo (sar′ə yā′vō) capital of Bosnia and Herzegovina, in the central part

Sa·ra·ma·go (sä′rä mä′gô), **Jo·sé (de Sousa)** (zhô se′) 1922-2010; Port. novelist

☆**sa·ran** (sə ran′) *n.* ⟦< *Saran*, former trademark; arbitrary coinage⟧ any of various thermoplastic resins usually obtained by the polymerization of vinylidene chloride: it is used in extruded or molded form in making various fabrics, acid-resistant pipes and fittings, transparent wrapping material, etc.

Sar·a·nac Lake (sar′ə nak′) ⟦< ? Iroquoian name⟧ 1 any of three connected lakes (*Upper, Middle, & Lower*) in the Adirondacks, NE N.Y. 2 resort village on Lower Saranac Lake

Sa·ransk (sə ränsk′, -ransk′) city in central European Russia

☆**sa·ra·pe** (sə rä′pē, -pā) *n. alt. sp. of* SERAPE

Sar·a·so·ta (sar′ə sōt′ə) ⟦Sp *Sarazota* < unidentified AmInd language⟧ city on the W coast of Fla., near Tampa

Sar·a·to·ga (sar′ə tō′gə) ⟦prob. of Mohawk orig.⟧ *former name for* SCHUYLERVILLE: scene of two Revolutionary War battles (1777) in which American forces led by Gates defeated the British under Burgoyne

Saratoga Springs ⟦see prec.⟧ city in NE N.Y.: a resort with mineral springs

☆**Saratoga trunk** ⟦after prec.⟧ a kind of large trunk of elegant design, formerly used mainly by women when traveling

Sa·ra·tov (sä rä′tôf) city & port in SC European Russia, on the Volga

Sa·ra·wak (sə rä′wäk) state of Malaysia, occupying NC & NW Borneo: 48,050 sq mi (124,449 sq km); cap. Kuching

sar·casm (sär′kaz′əm) ***n.*** ⟦LL *sarcasmos* < Gr *sarkasmos* < *sarkazein*, to tear flesh like dogs, speak bitterly < *sarx* (gen. *sarkos*), flesh < IE base **twerk-*, to cut > Avestan *thwarəs-*, to cut, whittle⟧ **1** a taunting, sneering, cutting, or caustic remark; gibe or jeer, generally ironic **2** the making of such remarks **3** their characteristic quality

sar·cas·tic (sär kas′tik) ***adj.*** **1** of, having the nature of, or characterized by sarcasm; sneering, caustic, cutting, etc. **2** using, or fond of using, sarcasm —**sar·cas′ti·cal·ly** ***adv.***

SYN.—**sarcastic** implies intent to hurt by taunting with mocking ridicule, veiled sneers, etc. [a *sarcastic* reminder that work begins at 9:00 A.M.]; **satirical** implies as its purpose the exposing or attacking of the vices, follies, stupidities, etc. of others and connotes the use of ridicule, sarcasm, etc. [Swift's *satirical* comments]; **ironic** applies to a humorous or sarcastic form of expression in which the intended meaning of what is said is directly opposite to the usual sense ["My, you're early" was his *ironic* taunt to the latecomer]; **sardonic** implies disdainful or humorous sarcasm in a person, or, more often, in his or her expression, remarks, etc. [a *sardonic* smile]; **caustic** implies a cutting, biting, or stinging wit or sarcasm [a *caustic* tongue]

sarce·net (särs′net′) ***n.*** ⟦ME *sarsenet* < Anglo-Fr *sarzinett*, dim. < OFr *Sarrazin*: see SARACEN⟧ a soft silk cloth, formerly used for ribbons, linings, etc.

sar·co- (sär′kō, -kə) ⟦< Gr *sarx*, flesh: see SARCASM⟧ *combining form* flesh [*sarcology*]: also, before a vowel, **sarc-**

sar·co·carp (sär′kə kärp′) ***n.*** ⟦prec. + -CARP⟧ *Bot.* **1** the fleshy part of a stone fruit, as in the plum **2** loosely, any fleshy fruit

sar·coid·o·sis (sär′koi dō′sis) ***n.*** ⟦< Gr *sarkoeidēs*, fleshy (see SARCO- & -OID) + -OSIS⟧ a chronic disease of unknown cause, characterized by the development of lesions similar to tubercles in the lungs, bones, skin, eyes, etc.

sar·col·o·gy (sär käl′ə jē) ***n.*** ⟦SARCO- + -LOGY⟧ the branch of anatomy that deals with the soft tissues of the body

sar·co·ma (sär kō′mə) ***n.***, *pl.* **-mas** or **-ma·ta** (-mə tə) ⟦ModL < Gr *sarkōma* < *sarx*, flesh: see SARCASM & -OMA⟧ any of various malignant tumors that begin in connective tissue, or in tissue developed from the mesoderm —**sar·co′ma·to′sis** (-tō′sis) ***n.*** —**sar·co′ma·tous** (-təs, -käm′ə-) ***adj.***

sar·co·mere (sär′kō mir′) ***n.*** ⟦SARCO- + -MERE⟧ any of the segments making up the fibrils of striated muscles

sar·coph·a·gus (sär käf′ə gəs) ***n.***, *pl.* **-gi′** (-jī′) or **-gus·es** ⟦L < Gr *sarkophagos* < *sarx*, flesh (see SARCASM) + *phagein*, to eat (see -PHAGOUS): because the limestone caused rapid disintegration of the contents⟧ **1** among the ancient Greeks, Romans, and Egyptians, a limestone coffin or tomb, often inscribed and elaborately ornamented **2** any stone coffin, esp. one on display, as in a monumental tomb

sard (särd) ***n.*** ⟦ME *saarde* < L *sarda* < or akin to Gr *sardios*, sard, lit., ? Sardian stone < *Sardeis*, SARDIS⟧ **1** a very hard, deep orange-red variety of chalcedony, used in jewelry, etc. **2** a piece of this

sar·da·na (sär dä′nə) ***n.*** ⟦Sp < Catalan⟧ **1** a Spanish folk dance of Catalonia, danced in a circle **2** music for this

Sar·da·nap·a·lus (sär′də nap′ə ləs) legendary 7th-cent. B.C. king of Assyria: notorious for his decadence

sar·dine[1] (sär dēn′) ***n.***, *pl.* **-dines′** or **-dine′** ⟦ME *sardeyne* < MFr *sardine* < L *sardina* < *sarda*, kind of fish, prob. < Gr *Sardō*, SARDINIA⟧ any of various small ocean fishes preserved in tightly packed cans for eating, as a pilchard

sar·dine[2] (sär′din, -dīn′) ***n.*** SARD

Sar·din·i·a (sär din′ē ə, -din′yə) ⟦L < Gr *Sardō*⟧ **1** Italian island in the Mediterranean, south of Corsica: 9,194 sq mi (23,812 sq km) **2** region of Italy, comprising this island & small nearby islands: 9,301 sq mi (24,089 sq km); cap. Cagliari **3** former kingdom (1720-1860) including this region, Piedmont, Nice, Savoy (by which the kingdom was ruled), etc. It. name **Sar·de·gna** (sär dä′nyä)

Sar·din·i·an (-ē ən, -yən) ***n.*** **1** a person born or living in Sardinia **2** the Romance language of central and S Sardinia —***adj.*** of Sardinia or its people, language, or culture

Sar·dis (sär′dis) ⟦L < Gr *Sardeis*⟧ capital of ancient Lydia

sar·di·us (sär′dē əs) ***n.*** ⟦ME < LL(Ec) < Gr *sardios* < *Sardeis*, prec.⟧ **1** SARD **2** *Bible* one of the twelve precious stones in the breastplate of the Jewish high priest: Ex. 28:17

sar·don·ic (sär dän′ik) ***adj.*** ⟦Fr *sardonique* < L *sardonius* < Gr *sardonios*, altered after *Sardō*, SARDINIA⟧ disdainfully or humorously sneering or sarcastic [a *sardonic* smile] —SYN. SARCASTIC —**sar·don′i·cal·ly** ***adv.*** —**sar·don′i·cism′** (-ə siz′əm) ***n.***

sar·do·nyx (sär dän′iks, sär′də niks) ***n.*** ⟦ME < L < Gr *sardonyx* < *sardios*, SARD + *onyx*, ONYX⟧ a variety of onyx made up of alternating layers of white chalcedony and sard, used as a gem, esp. in making cameos

Sar·dou (sȧr do͞o′), **Vic·to·rien** (vēk tô ryan′) 1831-1908; Fr. dramatist

Sa·re·ma (sä′rə mä′) *alt. sp. of* SAAREMAA

Sa·re·ra Bay (sə rer′ə) large inlet on the NW coast of New Guinea: *c.* 200 mi (322 km) wide

Sar·gas·so Sea (sär gas′ō) ⟦Port *sargaço*: see fol.⟧ region of calms in the N Atlantic, northeast of the West Indies, noted for its abundance of sargassum

sar·gas·sum (sär gas′əm) ***n.*** ⟦ModL < Port *sargaço* < *sarga*, kind of grape⟧ any of a genus (*Sargassum*, family Sargassaceae) of floating brown algae (order Fucales) found in tropical seas and having a main stem with flattened outgrowths like leaves, and branches with berry-like air sacs; gulfweed: also **sar·gas′so** (-ō), *pl.* **-sos** or **sargasso weed**

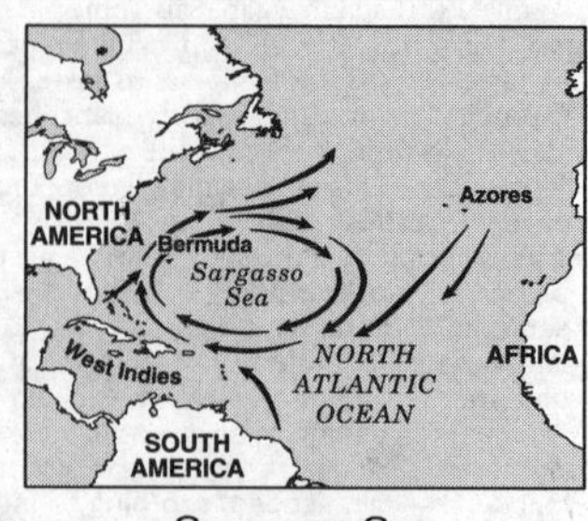

Sargasso Sea

☆**sarge** (särj) ***n.*** [Informal] *short for* SERGEANT

Sar·gent (sär′jənt), **John Singer** 1856-1925; U.S. painter in Europe

Sar·go·dha (sər gōd′ə) city in the Punjab region of NE Pakistan

Sar·gon (sär′gän′) **1** fl. *c.* 2300 B.C.; founder of the Akkadian kingdom **2** **Sargon II** died 705 B.C.; king of Assyria (722-705)

sa·ri (sä′rē) ***n.*** ⟦Hindi *sārī* < Sans *śāṭī*⟧ the principal outer garment of a woman of India, Pakistan, etc., consisting of a long piece of cloth worn wrapped around the body with one end forming an ankle-length skirt and the other end draped across the bosom, over one shoulder, and, sometimes, over the head: also sp. **sa′ree**

sari

sa·rin (sä′rin, ser′ən) ***n.*** ⟦Ger⟧ a highly toxic nerve gas, $C_4H_{10}FPO$, which attacks the central nervous system, quickly bringing on convulsions and death

sark (särk) ***n.*** ⟦ME *serke* < OE *serc* & ON *serkr*⟧ [Scot.] a shirt or chemise

sark·y (sär′kē) ***adj.*** **sark′i·er**, **sark′i·est** ⟦< SARC(ASTIC) + -Y²⟧ [Brit. Informal] sarcastic

Sar·ma·ti·a (sär mā′shə, -shē ə) ancient region in E Europe, between the Vistula & Volga rivers, occupied by the Sarmatians (*c.* 300 B.C.-*c.* A.D. 200)

Sar·ma·tian (-shən) ***adj.*** of ancient Sarmatia or its people, language, or culture —***n.*** a member of an ancient Indo-Iranian people related to the Scythians that lived in S Russia and the E Balkan Peninsula

sar·men·tose (sär men′tōs) ***adj.*** ⟦L *sarmentosus*, full of twigs < *sarmentum*, twig < *sarpere*, to trim, cut off < IE base **ser(p)-*, sickle > Gr *harpē*, Latvian *sirpis*⟧ producing long, slender stems which take root along the ground, as the strawberry plant does

sa·rod or **sa·rode** (sə rōd′) ***n.*** ⟦Hindi *sarod* < Pers⟧ a lutelike musical instrument of India, with many strings

sa·rong (sə rôŋ′, -räŋ′) ***n.*** ⟦Malay *sarung*, lit., sheath⟧ **1** the principal garment of men and women in the Malay Archipelago, the East Indies, etc., consisting of a long strip of cloth, often brightly colored and printed, worn like a skirt **2** cotton cloth for such garments

Sa·ron·ic Gulf (sə rän′ik) inlet of the Aegean Sea, in SE Greece, between Attica & the Peloponnesus: *c.* 50 mi (80 km) long

sar·os (ser′äs) ***n.*** ⟦Gr < Akkadian *shār* < Sumerian *shar*, multitude, large number⟧ *Astron.* the eclipse cycle of the sun and moon, recurring at intervals of 6,585.32 days (*c.* 18 years)

Sa·roy·an (sə roi′ən), **William** 1908-81; U.S. writer

Sar·pe·don (sär pēd′'n, -pē′dän′) ***n.*** ⟦L < Gr *Sarpēdōn*⟧ *Gr. Myth.* a son of Zeus and Europa, who becomes king of Lycia and is allowed to live three generations: in some versions, he is killed by Patroclus in the Trojan War

☆**sar·ra·ce·ni·a** (sar′ə sē′nē ə, -sēn′yə) ***n.*** ⟦ModL, after M. *Sarrazin*, Fr-Cdn physician who sent a specimen to botanists in France (*c.* 1700)⟧ any of a genus (*Sarracenia*) of perennial New World pitcher plants

SARS (särz) ***n.*** ⟦*s(evere) a(cute) r(espiratory) s(yndrome)*⟧ an acute, highly contagious, viral respiratory disease caused by a coronavirus and characterized by coughing, a high fever, and breathing difficulty

sar·sa·pa·ril·la (sas′pə ril′ə, särs′-; sär′sə-) ***n.*** ⟦Sp *zarzaparrilla* < *zarza*, bramble + *parrilla*, dim. of *parra*, vine⟧ **1** any of a number of tropical American, spiny, woody vines (genus *Smilax*) of the lily family, with large, fragrant roots and toothed, heart-shaped leaves **2** the dried roots of any of these plants, formerly used in medicine **3** an extract of these roots ☆**4** a sweetened, carbonated drink flavored with or as with sarsaparilla **5** any of several North American plants resembling sarsaparilla; esp., a woodland plant, **wild sarsaparilla** (*Aralia nudicaulis*), of the ginseng family

sarse·net (särs′net′) ***n.*** *alt. sp. of* SARCENET

Sar·to (sär′tō), **An·dre·a del** (än dre′ä del) (born *Andrea d'Agnolo di Francesco*) 1486-1531; Florentine painter

sar·to·ri·al (sär tôr′ē əl) ***adj.*** ⟦LL *sartor* (see fol.) + -IAL⟧ **1** of tailors or their work **2** of clothing or dress, esp. men's —**sar·to′ri·al·ly** ***adv.***

sar·to·ri·us (sär tō′rē əs, -tôr′ē-) ***n.*** ⟦ModL < LL *sartor*, a tailor (in ref. to the traditional cross-legged position of tailors at work) < L *sartus*, pp. of *sarcire*, to patch < IE base **serk-*, woven substance, to hedge in > Gr *herkos*, a hedge⟧ a narrow muscle of the thigh, the longest in the human body, that passes obliquely across the front of the thigh and helps rotate the leg to the cross-legged position

Sar·tre (sȧr′tr′; *E* sär′trə), **Jean-Paul** (zhän pôl) 1905-80; Fr. philosopher, playwright, & novelist —**Sar·tre·an** *adj.*, **Sar·tri·an** (sär′trē ən)

Sar·um use (ser′əm) ⟦< ML *Sarum*, prob. altered < abbrev. of OE *Saris-buria, Searobyrig*, Salisbury, seat of the bishopric (1075-1220)⟧ the form of the Latin Rite first used in the Salisbury diocese, the prevalent form in England before the Reformation

SASE *abbrev.* self-addressed, stamped envelope

Sa·se·bo (sä′se bô′) seaport in E Kyushu, Japan, on the East China Sea

sash¹ (sash) *n.* ⟦Ar *shāsh*, muslin⟧ an ornamental band, ribbon, or scarf worn over the shoulder or around the waist, often formally as a symbol of distinction

sash² (sash) *n.* ⟦taken as sing. of earlier *shashes* < Fr *châssis*, a frame: see CHASSIS⟧ **1** a frame holding the glass pane or panes of a window or door, esp. a sliding frame **2** such frames collectively —*vt.* to furnish with sashes

☆**sa·shay** (sa shā′) *vi.* ⟦altered < CHASSÉ⟧ **1** to do a chassé in a square dance **2** [Informal] *a)* to walk in an easy, casual manner *b)* to walk in a showy or affectedly casual manner, as with an exaggerated swaying of the hips and shoulders

sash cord a cord attached to either side of a sliding sash, having balancing weights (**sash weights**) so that the window can be raised or lowered easily

sa·shi·mi (sä shē′mē) *pl.n.* ⟦Jpn < *sashi*, nominal form of *sasu*, to pierce (used in place of *kiri*, to cut, formerly taboo) + *mi*, meat⟧ a Japanese dish consisting of thin slices of fresh raw fish served with soy sauce

Sask *abbrev.* Saskatchewan

Sas·katch·e·wan (sas kach′ə wän′, -wən) ⟦earlier *Keiskatchewan*, name of the river < Cree *kisiskatchewani sipi*, lit., swift-flowing river⟧ **1** river in central Saskatchewan flowing east into Lake Winnipeg: 340 mi (547 km): see also NORTH SASKATCHEWAN, SOUTH SASKATCHEWAN **2** province of SC Canada: 227,135 sq mi (588,276 sq km); cap. Regina: abbrev. *SK* or *Sask*

sas·ka·toon (sas′kə to͞on′) *n.* ⟦< Cree *misaaskwatoomin*, saskatoon berry < *misaaskwat*, the shrub, lit., that which is solid wood + *-min*, berry⟧ [Chiefly Cdn.] **1** a species of Juneberry (*Amelanchier alnifolia*) of the central and N North American plains **2** the edible fruit of this shrub

Sas·ka·toon (sas′kə to͞on′) city in central Saskatchewan, Canada, on the South Saskatchewan River

sas·quatch (sas′kwäch′) *n.* ⟦< Salish *saskehavas*, wild men⟧ [*also* **S-**] *Folklore* a huge, hairy, humanlike creature with long arms, living in the mountains of NW North America

sass (sas) *n.* ⟦var. of SAUCE⟧ **1** [Dial.] *a)* garden vegetables *b)* stewed fruit or preserves **2** [Informal] impudent talk —*vt.* [Informal] to talk impudently to

sas·sa·by (sas′ə bē′) *n.*, *pl.* **-bies′** ⟦< *tsèsèbè* in a local Bantu language⟧ a large, very swift, reddish South African antelope (*Damaliscus lunatus*) with a black back and face

☆**sas·sa·fras** (sas′ə fras′) *n.* ⟦Sp *sasafrás* < ?⟧ **1** a small E North American tree (*Sassafras albidum*) of the laurel family, having an aromatic bark, leaves with usually two or three fingerlike lobes, and small, bluish fruits **2** the dried root bark of this tree, used as a flavoring agent and yielding safrole

Sas·sa·nid (sas′ə nid) *n.*, *pl.* **Sas′sa·nids** or **Sas·san·i·dae** (sa san′ə dē′) ⟦< ML *Sassanidae*, pl., after *Sasan*, a Persian priest, the grandfather of the founder of the dynasty⟧ a member of the last dynasty of native rulers in Persia (A.D. 224-641): also **Sas·sa·ni·an** or **Sa·sa·ni·an** (sa sā′nē ən)

Sas·se·nach (sas′ə nak′) *n.* ⟦Ir *Sasanach* or Gael *Sasunnach* < Gael *Sasunn*, Saxon < Gmc, as in OE *Seaxan*, SAXON⟧ an English person or Lowlander: term used, often disparagingly, by the Irish and Scots

Sas·set·ta (säs set′tä) (born *Stefano di Giovanni*) 1400?-50?; It. painter

Sas·soon (sa so͞on′), **Siegfried (Lorraine)** 1886-1967; Eng. writer & poet

sass·y (sas′ē) *adj.* **sass′i·er**, **sass′i·est** ⟦dial. var. of SAUCY⟧ [Informal] impudent; saucy

sas·sy bark (sas′ē) ⟦prob. of Afr orig.⟧ **1** the bark of a leguminous African tree (*Erythrophleum guineense*) yielding an alkaloid, used as a substitute for digitalis, and a poison used in trial by ordeal **2** this tree: also called **sas′sy·wood′** (-wood′) *n.*

sas·tru·gi (sas tro͞o′gē) *pl.n.* ⟦< Russ *zastruga*, wind-formed furrow⟧ long, wavelike ridges of hard snow, formed perpendicular to the direction of the wind and common in polar regions

sat (sat) *vi.*, *vt. pt. & pp. of* SIT

Sat *abbrev.* **1** Saturday **2** Saturn

SAT *trademark* Scholastic Assessment Tests

Sa·tan (sāt′′n) *n.* ⟦ME < OE < LL(Ec) < Gr(Ec) < Heb *saṭan*, adversary, prob. < *śṭn*, to be adverse, plot against⟧ **1** *Judaism* any of various celestial beings functioning as accuser or critic of humanity **2** *Christian Theol.* the great enemy of humankind and of goodness; the Devil: usually identified with Lucifer, the chief of the fallen angels

sa·tang (sä taŋ′) *n.*, *pl.* **-tang′** ⟦Thai *satāṇ*⟧ a monetary unit of Thailand, equal to 1/100 of a baht

sa·tan·ic (sā tan′ik, sə-) *adj.* of, characteristic of, or like Satan; devilish; infernal; diabolic: also **sa·tan′i·cal** —**sa·tan′i·cal·ly** *adv.*

sa·tan·ism (sāt′′n iz′əm) *n.* ⟦< Fr *satanisme*⟧ [*also* **S-**] worship of Satan; esp., the principles and rites of a cult which travesties Christian ceremonies —**sa′tan·ist** *n.*

sa·tay or **sa·té** (sä tā′) *n.* ⟦Malay or Javanese < ?⟧ a dish of Southeast Asia, consisting of chunks of marinated meat, shrimp, etc., broiled on skewers and dipped in a spicy peanut sauce

satch·el (sach′əl) *n.* ⟦ME *sachel* < OFr < L *saccellus*, dim. of *saccus*, a bag, SACK¹⟧ a small bag for carrying clothes, books, etc., sometimes having a shoulder strap

sate¹ (sāt) *vt.* **sat′ed**, **sat′ing** ⟦prob. altered < dial. *sade*, akin to SAD, infl. by L *satiare*, to fill full: see SATIATE⟧ **1** to satisfy (an appetite, desire, etc.) to the full; gratify completely **2** to provide with more than enough, so as to weary or disgust; surfeit; glut —*SYN.* SATIATE

sate² (sat, sāt) *vi.*, *vt. archaic pt. & pp. of* SIT

sa·teen (sa tēn′, sə-) *n.* ⟦< SATIN, modeled on VELVETEEN⟧ a smooth, glossy cloth, as of cotton, made to imitate satin

sat·el·lite (sat′′l īt′) *n.* ⟦Fr < L *satelles* (gen. *satellitis*), an attendant, guard < Etr⟧ **1** *a)* a follower or attendant attached to a prince or other person of importance *b)* any obsequious or fawning follower or dependent **2** *a)* a celestial body that revolves around a larger celestial body *b)* a man-made object rocketed into orbit around the earth, the moon, etc.; specif., such an object containing electronic devices for originating or relaying communications, data, etc. **3** something subordinate or dependent; specif., a small state that is economically or politically dependent on, and hence adjusts its policies to, a larger, more powerful state

satellite dish a kind of dish antenna used for transmitting or receiving signals to or from a usually geostationary SATELLITE (*n.* 2*b*)

sa·tem (sä′təm) *adj.* ⟦< Avestan *satəm*, hundred < Sans *śátám*: see HUNDRED⟧: so named because the initial sound illustrates the typical development in this group of the IE palatal stop, which in the centum group is a velar stop⟧ designating or of the group of Indo-European languages, including Indo-Iranian, Slavic, Baltic, Albanian, and Armenian, in which a prehistoric change of certain original stops into sibilants sets these languages apart from those of the CENTUM group

sa·ti (sə tē′, sut′ē) *n. alt. sp. of* SUTTEE

sa·tia·ble (sā′shə bəl, sā′shē ə-) *adj.* that can be sated or satiated —**sa′tia·bil′i·ty** *n.* —**sa′tia·bly** *adv.*

sa·ti·ate (sā′shē āt′; *for adj., usually,* -it) *adj.* ⟦L *satiatus*, pp. of *satiare*, to fill full, satisfy < *satis*, enough: see SAD⟧ having had enough or more than enough; sated —*vt.* **-at′ed**, **-at′ing** **1** [Now Rare] to satisfy to the full; gratify completely **2** to provide with more than enough, so as to weary or disgust; glut; surfeit —**sa′ti·a′tion** *n.*

SYN.—**satiate** and **sate** in their basic sense mean to satisfy to the full, but in current use **satiate** almost always implies, as **sate** often does, a being filled or stuffed so full that all pleasure or desire is lost [*satiated*, or *sated*, with food, success, etc.]; **surfeit** implies a being filled or supplied to nauseating or disgusting excess [*surfeited* with pleasure]; **cloy** stresses the distaste one feels for something too sweet, rich, etc. that one has indulged in to excess [*cloying*, sentimental music]; **glut** implies an overloading by filling or supplying to excess [to *glut* the market]

Sa·tie (sȧ tē′), **E·rik (Alfred Leslie)** (e rēk′) 1866-1925; Fr. composer

sa·ti·e·ty (sə tī′ə tē) *n.* ⟦Fr *satiété* < OFr *sazieted* < L *satietas*⟧ the state of being satiated; surfeit

sat·in (sat′′n) *n.* ⟦ME < MFr < Sp *setuni* < Ar (*aṭlas*) *zaitūnī*, (satin) of *Zaitūn*, medieval name of Quanzhou, China⟧ a fabric of silk, nylon, rayon, or the like having a smooth finish, glossy on the face and dull on the back —*adj.* made of or like satin; smooth, soft, and glossy —**sat′in·y** *adj.*

sat·in·et or **sat·in·ette** (sat′′n et′) *n.* ⟦Fr < *satin*⟧ **1** thin or inferior satin **2** a strong cloth of cotton and wool, made to resemble satin

sat·in·wood (sat′′n wood′) *n.* **1** any of several very smooth, hard woods used in fine furniture, marquetry, veneers, etc. **2** any of a number of trees yielding such a wood; esp., *a)* the **East Indian satinwood** (*Chloroxylon swietenia*) of the rue family *b)* the **West Indian satinwood** (*Zanthoxylum flavum*) of the rue family

sat·ire (sa′tīr′) *n.* ⟦Fr < L *satira* or *satura*, satire, poetic medley < (*lanx*) *satura*, (dish) of various fruits, prob. < Etr, of Thracian orig.⟧ **1** *a)* a literary work in which vices, follies, abuses, etc. are held up to ridicule and contempt *b)* such literary works collectively **2** the use of ridicule, sarcasm, irony, etc. to expose, attack, or deride vices, follies, etc. —*SYN.* CARICATURE, WIT¹

sa·tir·i·cal (sə tir′i kəl) *adj.* **1** of, like, or containing satire **2** indulging in, or fond of indulging in, satire Also **sa·tir′ic** —*SYN.* SARCASTIC —**sa·tir′i·cal·ly** *adv.*

sat·i·rist (sat′ə rist) *n.* **1** a writer of satires **2** a person given to satirizing

sat·i·rize (-rīz′) *vt.* **-rized′**, **-riz′ing** ⟦Fr *satiriser*⟧ to attack, ridicule, or criticize with satire —**sat′i·riz′er** *n.*

sat·is·fac·tion (sat′is fak′shən) *n.* ⟦ME *satisfaccioun* < OFr *satisfaction* < L *satisfactio*⟧ **1** a satisfying or being satisfied **2** something that satisfies; specif., *a)* anything that brings gratification, pleasure, or contentment *b)* settlement of debt; discharge of obligation *c)* reparation for injury or insult *d)* *Theol.* atonement for sin —**give satisfaction** **1** to satisfy **2** to accept a challenge to duel

sat·is·fac·to·ry (-tə rē, -trē) *adj.* ⟦Fr *satisfactoire* < ML *satisfactorius*⟧ good enough to fulfill a need, wish, requirement, etc.; satisfying or adequate —**sat′is·fac′to·ri·ly** *adv.* —**sat′is·fac′to·ri·ness** *n.*

sat·is·fice (sat′is fīs′) *vi.* **-ficed′**, **-fic′ing** ⟦coined by H. A. SIMON² < fol. + (SUF)FICE⟧ ☆to select, accept, or provide a solution or outcome that is satisfactory rather than optimal

sat·is·fy (sat′is fī′) *vt.* **-fied′**, **-fy′ing** ⟦ME *satisfyen* < OFr *satisfier* < L *satisfacere* < *satis*, enough (see SAD) + *facere*, to make (see DO¹)⟧ **1** to fulfill the needs, expectations, wishes, or desires of (someone); content; gratify **2** to fulfill or answer the requirements or conditions of (something) **3** to comply with (rules, standards, or obligations) **4** *a)* to free from doubt or anxiety; convince *b)* to answer (a doubt, objection, etc.) adequately or convincingly; solve **5** *a)* to give what is due to *b)* to discharge (an obligation, debt, etc.); settle in full **6** to make reparation to or for —*vi.* to be satisfying, adequate, sufficient, etc. —**sat′is·fi′er** *n.*

SYN.—**satisfy** implies complete fulfillment of one's wishes, needs, expectations, etc.; **content** implies a filling of requirements to the degree that one is not disturbed by a desire for something more or different [some persons are *satisfied* only by great wealth, others are *contented* with a modest but secure income]

sat-nav (sat′nav′) *n.* ⟦*sat(ellite) nav(igation)*⟧ an electronic navigation system using satellites: also written **satnav, sat nav, SAT NAV**

sa·to·ri (sä tôr′ē) *n.* ⟦Jpn, nominal form of *satoru,* to understand the truth of⟧ spiritual enlightenment or illumination: term used esp. in Zen Buddhism

sa·trap (sā′trap′, sa′-) *n.* ⟦ME < L *satrapes* < Gr *satrapēs* < OPers *xšathrapāvan,* lit., protector of the land < *xšathra,* dominion (< IE base **kthēi-,* to gain dominion > Gr *ktēma,* possession) + **pā(y)-,* to protect < IE base **pō(i)-,* to herd sheep, protect, cover > OE *fothor,* sheath⟧ **1** the governor of a province in ancient Persia **2** a ruler of a dependency, esp. a despotic, subordinate official; petty tyrant

sa·trap·y (sā′trə pē, sa′-) *n., pl.* **-trap·ies** ⟦Fr *satrapie* < L *satrapia* < Gr *satrapeia*⟧ the government, authority, or province of a satrap

Sat·su·ma (sat′sə mä′, sat so͞o′mə) *n.* ⟦Jpn, after *Satsuma,* former province in S Kyushu, where the pottery was first made⟧ **1** a variety of Japanese pottery ☆**2** [**s-**] a small, loose-skinned variety of orange, grown in Florida and Alabama

sat·u·ra·ble (sach′ə rə bəl) *adj.* ⟦L *saturabilis*⟧ that can be saturated —**sat′u·ra·bil′i·ty** *n.*

sat·u·rant (-ə rənt) *adj.* ⟦L *saturans,* prp.⟧ that saturates; saturating —*n.* a substance that saturates

sat·u·rate (sach′ə rāt′; *for adj., usually,* -rit) *vt.* **-rat′ed, -rat′ing** ⟦< L *saturatus,* pp. of *saturare,* to fill up, saturate < *satur,* full; akin to *satis*: see SAD⟧ **1** to cause to be thoroughly soaked, imbued, or penetrated **2** to cause (something) to be filled, charged, supplied, etc. with the maximum that it can absorb **3** *Chem. a)* to cause (a substance) to combine to the full extent of its combining capacity with another; neutralize *b)* to dissolve the maximum amount of (a gas, liquid, or solid) in a solution at a given temperature and pressure —*adj.* SATURATED —SYN. SOAK —**sat′u·ra′tor** *n.*

sat·u·rat·ed (-rāt′id) *adj.* **1** filled to capacity; having absorbed all that can be taken up **2** soaked through with moisture; wet **3** undiluted with white: said of colors **4** *a) Chem.* designating or of an organic compound containing no double or triple bonds *b)* designating certain vegetable and animal fats and oils thought to cause unhealthy levels of cholesterol in the bloodstream **5** containing so much dissolved substance that no more can be dissolved at the given temperature: said of a solution **6** *Geol.* containing as much combined silica as is possible: said of rocks and minerals

sat·u·ra·tion (sach′ə rā′shən) *n.* ⟦LL *saturatio*⟧ **1** a saturating or being saturated **2** the degree of purity of a color, as measured by its freedom from mixture with white; intensity of hue **3** the condition of a magnetic substance that has been magnetized to the maximum

saturation bombing the practice of dropping an intense concentration of bombs in order to destroy virtually everything in a given target area

saturation point **1** the point at which the greatest possible amount of a substance has been absorbed **2** the limit beyond which something cannot be continued, endured, etc.

Sat·ur·day (sat′ər dā′; *occas.,* -dē′) *n.* ⟦ME *Saterdai* < OE *Sæterdæg,* akin to MDu *Saterdagh* < WGmc half-transl. of L *Saturni dies,* Saturn's day, transl. of Gr *Kronou hēmera,* Cronus' day⟧ the seventh and last day of the week: abbrev. *Sat, Sa,* or *S*

☆**Saturday night special** ⟦from their use in weekend crimes⟧ [Slang] any small, cheap, short-barreled handgun of a type that is readily available

Sat·ur·days (-dāz′; *occas.,* -dēz′) *adv.* during every Saturday or most Saturdays

Sat·urn (sat′ərn) *n.* ⟦ME *Saturne* < OE < L *Saturnus* < Etr⟧ **1** *Rom. Myth.* the god of agriculture: identified with the Greek Cronus **2** the second largest planet of the solar system and the sixth in distance from the sun: it has a thin, icy ring system around its equator: diameter, *c.* 120,540 km (*c.* 74,900 mi); period of revolution, 29.46 earth years; period of rotation, 10.66 hours; 62 satellites; symbol, ♄ **3** ⟦ML use of L *Saturnus*⟧ *Alchemy* LEAD[2] (sense 1)

Sat·ur·na·li·a (sat′ər nā′lē ə, -nāl′yə) *n., pl.* **-li·as** or **-li·a** ⟦L, neut. pl. of *Saturnalis,* of Saturn⟧ **1** the ancient Roman festival of Saturn, held about Dec. 17, with general feasting and revelry in celebration of the winter solstice **2** [**s-**] any period or occasion of unrestrained, often orgiastic, revelry

Sat·ur·na·li·an (-nā′lē ən, -nāl′yən) *adj.* **1** of the Saturnalia **2** [**s-**] riotously merry or orgiastic

Sa·tur·ni·an (sa tʉr′nē ən) *adj.* ⟦< L *Saturnius,* of Saturn + -AN⟧ **1** *a)* of the Roman god Saturn, whose reign was the GOLDEN AGE *b)* prosperous, peaceful, etc. (said of a period, age, etc.) **2** of the planet Saturn

sa·tur·ni·id (sə tʉr′nē id′) *n.* ⟦< ModL *Saturniidae* < L *Saturnia,* Juno, daughter of Saturn⟧ any of a family (Saturniidae) of large, brilliantly colored moths with a sunken head and hairy body

sat·ur·nine (sat′ər nīn′) *adj.* ⟦OFr *saturnin,* of Saturn < L *Saturnus,* Saturn⟧ **1** *Astrol.* born under the influence of the planet Saturn **2** sluggish or taciturn **3** of or having a gloomy manner **4** ⟦< ML *Saturnus,* alchemists' term for lead, which they considered to be very cold, like the planet⟧ having lead poisoning —**sat′ur·nine′ly** *adv.*

sat·ur·nism (sat′ər niz′əm) *n.* ⟦see prec.⟧ chronic lead poisoning

sat·ya·gra·ha (sut′yə gru′hə) *n.* ⟦< Hindi, lit., a grasping for truth < Sans *satyā,* truth + *graha,* grasping⟧ the doctrine of Mohandas Gandhi, emphasizing passive resistance and noncooperation

sa·tyr (sāt′ər, sat′-) *n.* ⟦ME *satir* < L *satyrus* < Gr *satyros*⟧ **1** *Gr. Myth.* any of a class of minor woodland deities, attendant on Dionysus, orig. represented as having the ears and tail of a horse, later as having pointed ears, short horns, the head and trunk of a man, and the hind legs of a goat, and as being fond of riotous merriment and lechery: cf. FAUN **2** a lustful or lecherous man **3** a man having satyriasis **4** any of a worldwide family (Satyridae) of butterflies with gray or brown wings, often with eyelike spots: also called **sa′ty·rid** (-ə rid) —**sa·tyr·ic** (sā tir′ik) *adj.*

sa·ty·ri·a·sis (sāt′ə rī′ə sis, sat′-) *n.* ⟦LL < Gr: see prec.⟧ excessive and uncontrollable desire by a man for sexual intercourse: cf. NYMPHOMANIA

satyr play a type of ancient Greek burlesque or comic play with a chorus represented as satyrs

sauce (sôs) *n.* ⟦ME < OFr *sause, saulse* < L *salsa,* salted food < *salsus,* pp. of *salire,* to salt < *sal,* SALT⟧ **1** *a)* a liquid or soft mixture served with food to add flavor or enhance its general appeal *b)* a flavored syrup used as a topping, as on ice cream ☆**2** stewed or preserved fruit **3** something that adds interest, zest, or flavor **4** [Dial.] garden vegetables eaten as a side dish **5** [Informal, Now Chiefly Brit.] impertinence; impudence ☆**6** [Slang] alcoholic liquor: usually with *the* —*vt.* **sauced, sauc′ing** **1** to flavor or season with a sauce **2** to give flavor or relish to **3** [Informal] to be impudent or impertinent to

sauce·boat (sôs′bōt′) *n.* GRAVY BOAT

sauce·box (-bäks′) *n.* [Old Informal] a saucy, rude child

sauced (sôst) *adj.* ⟦< ? SAUCE (*n.* 6) + -ED or < *soused*: see SOUSE[1]⟧ ☆[Slang] drunk; intoxicated

sauce·pan (sôs′pan′; *chiefly Brit* -pən) *n.* a small pot with a projecting handle, used for cooking

sau·cer (sô′sər) *n.* ⟦ME *sawsere* < MFr *saussier* < *sause,* SAUCE⟧ **1** a small, round, shallow dish, esp. one with an indentation designed to hold a cup **2** anything round and shallow like a saucer —**sau′cer·like′** *adj.*

sau·cier (sō syā′) *n.* ⟦Fr⟧ a chef's assistant who is in charge of preparing sauces

sau·cis·son (sō sē sōn′) *n., pl.* **-sons′** (-sōn′) ⟦Fr < *saucisse* + aug. suffix *-on*⟧ a large, cured French sausage of ground pork flavored with garlic

sau·cy (sô′sē) *adj.* **-ci·er, -ci·est** ⟦SAUC(E) + -Y[2]⟧ **1** rude; impudent **2** pert; sprightly [a *saucy* smile] **3** stylish or smart [her *saucy* new hat] —SYN. IMPERTINENT —**sau′ci·ly** *adv.* —**sau′ci·ness** *n.*

Sa·u·di (sou′dē, sô′dē; *occas.* sä o͞o′dē) *adj.* of Saudi Arabia or its people or culture —*n., pl.* **-dis** a person born or living in Saudi Arabia

Saudi Arabia kingdom occupying most of Arabia: 756,985 sq mi (1,960,582 sq km); cap. Riyadh —**Saudi Arabian**

☆**sau·er·bra·ten** (sou′ər brät′'n, zou′ər-) *n.* ⟦Ger < *sauer,* SOUR + *braten,* a roast < OHG *brato,* meat, flesh, akin to OE *bræd,* raw meat; sense infl. by OHG *bratan,* to fry, akin to OE *brædan,* to fry, *bread,* BREAD⟧ a dish made of beef marinated in vinegar with onion, spices, etc. before cooking

☆**sau·er·kraut** (sou′ər krout′) *n.* ⟦Ger < *sauer,* SOUR + *kraut,* cabbage⟧ chopped cabbage fermented in a brine of its own juice with salt

☆**sau·ger** (sô′gər) *n.* ⟦< ?⟧ a small American pikeperch (*Stizostedion canadense*) valued as a game or food fish

Sauk (sôk) *n., pl.* **Sauks** or **Sauk** ⟦earlier *Saukee* < Fr *Saki, Ousaki* < Ojibwa *ozaagii,* lit., person (or people) of the outlet⟧ **1** a member of a North American Indian people formerly living in the area of modern Green Bay, Wisconsin, and later on reservations in Oklahoma and Kansas **2** the Algonquian language of this people

Saul[1] (sôl) *n.* ⟦< LL(Ec) *Saul* < Gr(Ec) *Saoul* < Heb *shaul,* lit., asked (i.e., of God) < *shaal,* to ask⟧ (fl. 11th cent. B.C.) the first king of Israel (*c.* 1020-*c.* 1000): 1 Sam. 9

Saul[2] (sôl) ⟦LL(Ec) *Saulus* < Gr(Ec) *Saulos* < Heb *shaul*: see prec.⟧ *original name for* the Apostle PAUL[2]

Sault Ste. Ma·rie (so͞o′ sānt′ mə rē′) ⟦< Fr *Sault de Sainte Marie,* lit., falls of St. Mary⟧ city in SC Ontario, Canada, on the St. Marys River: site of international bridge to N Mich.: also **Sault Sainte Marie**

sau·na (sô′nə, sä′-) *n.* ⟦Finn⟧ **1** *a)* a Finnish bath in which sweating is induced by very hot, dry air produced by small amounts of water applied to heated stones, followed usually by a light beating of the skin or a brief plunge into cold water *b)* the enclosure for such a bath **2** *a)* any bath in which hot air or steam is used to induce sweating *b)* a room or establishment for such a bath

saun·ter (sôn′tər) *vi.* ⟦LME *santren,* to muse, meditate < ?⟧ to walk about idly; stroll —*n.* **1** a leisurely and aimless walk; stroll **2** a slow, leisurely gait —**saun′ter·er** *n.*

-saur (sôr) ⟦< Gr *sauros,* lizard⟧ *combining form* lizard [*dinosaur*]

sau·rel (sôr′əl) *n.* ⟦Fr < Prov < LL *saurus* < Gr *sauros,* horse mackerel, lizard⟧ HORSE MACKEREL (sense 2)

sau·ri·an (sôr′ē ən) *n.* ⟦< SAURO- + -IAN⟧ LIZARD —*adj.* of, or having the characteristics of, lizards

saur·is·chi·an (sô ris′kē ən, -rish′ē ən) *n.* ⟦< ModL *Saurischia* < Gr *sauros,* lizard + *ischion,* hip⟧ any of an order (Saurischia) of dinosaurs with, typically, a pelvic structure similar to that of modern reptiles, including the theropods and sauropods —*adj.* of the saurischians

sau·ro- (sôr′ə, -ō) ⟦ModL < Gr *sauros,* lizard⟧ *combining form* lizard [*saurian*]: also, before a vowel, **saur-**

sau·ro·pod (sôr′ə päd′) *n.* ⟦< ModL *Sauropoda:* see prec. & -PODA⟧ any of a superfamily (Sauropoda) of gigantic, plant-eating, four-footed saurischian dinosaurs with a long neck and tail, five-toed limbs, and a small head, as an apatosaurus —*adj.* of the sauropods

-sau·rus (sôr′əs) ⟦< Gr *sauros,* lizard⟧ *combining form Zool.* lizard: used to form the scientific names of certain genera of reptiles [*Brontosaurus*]

sau·ry (sôr′ē) *n., pl.* **-ries** ⟦prob. < ModL *saurus,* fish < Gr *sauros,* horse mackerel, lizard⟧ any of a family (Scomberesocidae, order Atheriniformes) of small bony fishes that live near the surface of temperate seas, with a long, slender body, a projecting beak, and a series of small fins behind the dorsal and anal fins

sau·sage (sô′sij) *n.* ⟦ME *sausige* < NormFr *saussiche,* for OFr *saulcisse* < VL *salsicia* < L *salsus:* see SAUCE⟧ **1** pork or other meat, chopped fine, highly seasoned, and either stuffed into membranous casings of varying size, as bologna or salami, or made into patties for cooking **2** a single patty or link of this mixture

Saus·sure (sō sür′), **Fer·di·nand de** (fer dē nän′ də) 1857-1913; Swiss linguist

sau·té (sô tā′, sō-) *adj.* ⟦Fr, pp. of *sauter,* to leap < L *saltare:* see SALTANT⟧ fried quickly in a little fat —*vt.* **-téed′**, **-té′ing** to fry quickly in a pan with a little fat —*n.* a sautéed dish

Sau·ternes (sō turn′; *Fr* sō tern′) *n.* ⟦Fr *sauternes,* after *Sauternes,* town in Gironde, France⟧ **1** a sweet white wine produced in SW France near the Bordeaux region **2** [*often* **s-**] any of various white wines, of varying sweetness, produced elsewhere: usually **Sau·terne** (sō turn′, -tern′; sô-)

sauve-qui-peut (sōv kē pö′) *n.* ⟦Fr < interjectional phr. *sauve qui peut,* (let him) save (himself) who can⟧ a frantic rush to escape: also written **sauve qui peut**

sau·vi·gnon blanc (sō′vēn yōn bläŋk′; *Fr* sō vē nyōn blän′) ⟦Fr⟧ **1** [*also* **S- B-**] a white grape of Bordeaux, used in making such wines as Graves and Sauternes **2** a dry white wine made entirely or mainly from this grape, esp. in California

Sa·va (sä′vä) river in S Europe, flowing from Slovenia eastward into the Danube: *c.* 450 mi (724 km)

sav·age (sav′ij) *adj.* ⟦ME *sauvage* < OFr *salvage* < VL *salvaticus,* wild < L *silvaticus,* belonging to a wood, wild < *silva,* a wood: see SYLVAN⟧ **1** wild, uncultivated, rugged, etc. [*a savage* jungle] **2** fierce; ferocious; untamed [*a savage* tiger] **3** without civilization; primitive; barbarous [*a savage* tribe] **4** lacking polish; crude; rude **5** cruel; pitiless **6** furious; ill-tempered —*n.* **1** a member of a preliterate culture, often having a tribal way of life: now often avoided as patronizing or offensive **2** a fierce, brutal person **3** a crude, boorish person —*vt.* **-aged**, **-ag·ing** to attack in a violent or brutal way —*SYN.* BARBARIAN —**sav′age·ly** *adv.* —**sav′age·ness** *n.*

sav·age·ry (-rē) *n., pl.* **-ries 1** the condition of being savage, or wild, primitive, uncultivated, etc. **2** savage act, behavior, or disposition; barbarity

Sa·vai·i (sä vī′ē) largest & westernmost island of Samoa: 659 sq mi (1,707 sq km)

sa·van·na or **sa·van·nah** (sə van′ə) *n.* ⟦Sp *sabana,* earlier *zavana* < the Taino name⟧ a treeless plain or a grassland characterized by scattered trees, esp. in tropical or subtropical regions having seasonal rains

Sa·van·nah (sə van′ə) ⟦< ? a name for the Shawnees in an unidentified Amerindian language⟧ **1** river forming the border between Ga. & S.C., flowing southeast into the Atlantic: 314 mi (505 km) **2** seaport in SE Ga., near the mouth of this river

sa·vant (sə vänt′, -vant′; sav′ənt; *Fr,* sȧ vän′) *n., pl.* **-vants′** (-vänts′, sav′ənts; *Fr,* sȧ vän′) ⟦Fr, orig. prp. of *savoir* < L *sapere:* see SAP[1]⟧ **1** a learned person; eminent scholar **2** a person with a severe developmental disorder or other major mental disability who possesses some remarkable aptitude, as for memorization, rapid mental calculation, art, or music

sav·a·rin (sav′ə rin) *n.* ⟦after A. BRILLAT-SAVARIN⟧ a light cake raised with yeast, baked in a ring-shaped mold, soaked in rum syrup, and filled with whipped cream or fruit

sa·vate (sə vät′, -vat′) *n.* ⟦Fr, orig., old shoe: see SABOT⟧ a form of boxing in which stiff-legged kicks as well as punches may be used

save[1] (sāv) *vt.* **saved**, **sav′ing** ⟦ME *saven* < OFr *sauver, salver* < L *salvare* < *salvus,* SAFE⟧ **1** to rescue or preserve from harm, danger, injury, etc.; make or keep safe **2** to keep in health and well-being: now only in certain formulas [God *save* the king!] **3** to preserve for future use; lay by: often with *up* **4** to prevent or guard against loss or waste of [to *save* time, to *save* a game] **5** to avoid, prevent, lessen, or guard against [to *save* wear and tear] **6** to treat or use carefully in order to preserve, lessen wear, etc. **7** *Comput.* to copy (data, a file, etc.) from random-access memory to a disk, tape, etc. for storage **8** *Theol.* to deliver from sin and its penalties —*vi.* **1** to avoid expense, loss, waste, etc.; be economical **2** to keep something or someone from danger, harm, etc. **3** to put by money or goods; hoard: often with *up* **4** to keep; last **5** *Comput.* to copy data, a file, etc. from random-access memory to a disk, tape, etc. for storage **6** *Theol.* to bring about deliverance from sin and its penalties —*n.* **1** *Sports* an action that keeps an opponent from scoring or winning ☆**2** *Baseball* an official credit given to a relief pitcher who enters a game for a team that is in the lead and preserves a lead for the remainder of the game —*SYN.* RESCUE —**sav′a·ble** *adj.,* **save′a·ble** —**sav′er** *n.*

save[2] (sāv) *prep.* ⟦ME *sauf* < OFr, lit., SAFE: sense developed from use in absolute constructions, e.g. *sauf le droit,* right (being) safe⟧ except; but —*conj.* **1** except; but **2** [Archaic] unless

save-all (sāv′ôl′) *n.* any of a number of devices which prevent waste or loss; specif., *a)* a sail placed to catch wind passing by the regular sails *b)* a net spread between a ship and pier while cargo is being loaded or unloaded

sav·e·loy (sav′ə loi′) *n.* ⟦altered < Fr *cervelas* < MFr *cervelat* < It *cervellata,* assoc. with *cervello,* the brains, used in making it (< L *cerebellum:* see CEREBELLUM); orig., however, prob. a deer-meat sausage < *cervo,* stag < L *cervus:* see CERVID⟧ a highly seasoned, dried English sausage

sav·in or **sav·ine** (sav′in) *n.* ⟦ME *savin* < OE *safene* & OFr *savine,* both < L (*herba*) *Sabina,* lit., Sabine (herb), savin⟧ **1** a low, spreading Eurasian juniper (*Juniperus sabina*) of E North America and Europe, whose leaves and tops yield an oil (**savin oil**) used in perfumery **2** RED CEDAR (sense 1*a*)

sav·ing[1] (sā′viŋ) *adj.* that saves; specif., *a)* rescuing; preserving *b)* economizing or economical *c)* containing an exception; making a reservation [*a saving* clause] —*n.* **1** the act of one that saves **2** [*often pl., with sing. v.*] any reduction in expense, time, labor, etc. [*a saving(s)* of 10% is effected] **3** *a)* anything saved *b)* [*pl.*] sums of money saved **4** *Law* a reservation; exception

sav·ing[2] (sā′viŋ) [Now Rare] *prep.* **1** with due respect for [*saving* your presence] **2** with the exception of; except; save —*conj.* except; save

saving grace a compensating or redeeming quality or feature

savings account an account in a bank on which interest is paid

☆**savings and loan association** a financial institution that chiefly accepts and holds the personal savings of depositors and makes mortgage loans on houses

savings bank 1 a bank in which savings may be deposited; esp., a banking establishment whose business is to receive and invest depositors' savings, on which it pays interest ☆**2** a small container with a slot for receiving coins to be saved

sav·ior or **sav·iour** (sāv′yər) *n.* ⟦ME *sauveour* < OFr < LL *salvator,* one who saves (< L *salvare,* to SAVE[1]), in LL(Ec), the Savior, Jesus, transl. of Gr(Ec) *sōtēr*⟧ **1** a person who saves: see SAVE[1] (*vi.* 2 & 6) **2** [**S-**] God **3** [**S-**] Jesus Christ

Sa·voie (sȧ vwȧ′) *Fr. name for* SAVOY

sa·voir-faire (sav′wär fer′; *Fr* sȧ vwȧr fer′) *n.* ⟦Fr < *savoir faire,* lit., to know (how) to do⟧ ready knowledge of the right thing to do or say in any social situation —*SYN.* TACT

sa·voir-vi·vre (sȧ vwȧr vē′vr′) *n.* ⟦Fr < *savoir vivre,* lit., to know (how) to live⟧ ability to live life well and with intelligent enjoyment, meeting every situation with poise, good manners, and elegance

Sa·vo·na·ro·la (sä′vô nä rô′lä; *E* sav′ə nə rō′lə), **Gi·ro·la·mo** (jē rô′lä mô′) 1452-98; It. monk: religious & political reformer: burned at the stake for heresy

sa·vor (sā′vər) *n.* ⟦ME < OFr *savour* < L *sapor,* akin to *sapere:* see SAP[1]⟧ **1** *a)* that quality of a thing which acts on the sense of taste or of smell *b)* a particular taste or smell **2** characteristic quality; distinctive property **3** perceptible trace; tinge **4** power to excite interest, zest, etc. **5** [Archaic] repute —*vi.* **1** to have the particular taste, smell, or quality; smack (*of*) **2** to show traces or signs (*of*) [*rudeness savoring* of contempt] —*vt.* **1** to be the source of the flavor or scent of; season **2** to taste or smell, esp. with relish **3** to enjoy with appreciation; dwell on with delight Brit. sp. **sa′vour** —**sa′vor·er** *n.* —**sa′vor·less** *adj.* —**sa′vor·ous** *adj.*

sa·vor·y[1] (sā′vər ē) *adj.* ⟦ME *savouri* < OFr *savouré,* pp. of *savourer,* to taste < *savour,* prec.⟧ **1** pleasing to the taste or smell; appetizing **2** *a)* pleasant, agreeable, attractive, etc. *b)* morally acceptable; respectable: often in negative constructions [*a less than savory* manner] **3** salty or piquant; not sweet [*a savory* relish] —*n., pl.* **-vor·ies** in England and Canada, a small, highly seasoned portion of food served at the end of a meal or as an appetizer Brit. sp. **sa′vour·y** —**sa′vor·i·ly** *adv.* —**sa′vor·i·ness** *n.*

sa·vor·y[2] (sā′vər ē) *n.* ⟦ME *saverey* < OFr *savoreie,* altered (prob. by assoc. with *savour,* SAVOR) < L *satureia,* savory⟧ any of a genus (*Satureja*) of aromatic mints; esp., **summer savory** (*S. hortensis*) and **winter savory** (*S. montana*), both native to Europe and used in cooking

sa·voy (sə voi′) *n.* ⟦Fr (*chou de*) *Savoie,* (cabbage of) Savoy⟧ a kind of cabbage with crinkled leaves and a compact head: also **savoy cabbage**

Sa·voy (sə voi′) region in SE France, on the borders of Italy & Switzerland: a former duchy & part of the kingdom of Sardinia: annexed by France (1860)

Sa·voy·ard (sə voi′ərd, sav′oi yärd′; *Fr* sȧ vwȧ yar′) *n.* **1** ⟦Fr < *Savoie,* prec. + *-ard,* personal suffix⟧ a person born or living in Savoy **2** ⟦after *Savoy* theater in London, where the operas were first produced⟧ an actor, producer, or enthusiastic admirer of Gilbert and Sullivan operas —*adj.* of Savoy or its people or culture

sav·vy (sav′ē) *vi.* **-vied**, **-vy·ing** ⟦< one or more varieties of Pidgin English < Portuguese *sabe,* 3rd pers. sing. of *saber,* to know < L *sapere:* see SAP[1]⟧ [Slang] to understand; get the idea —*n.* [Informal] **1** shrewdness or understanding **2** know-how —*adj.* **-vi·er**, **-vi·est** [Informal] shrewd or discerning

saw[1] (sô) *n.* ⟦ME *sawe* < OE *sagu,* akin to Ger *säge,* Du *zaag* < IE base **sek-,* to cut, > L *secare,* to cut, OE *seax,* knife⟧ **1** *a)* a cutting tool, of various shapes and sizes and worked by hand or machinery, consisting essentially of a thin blade or disk of metal, usually steel, the edge of which is a series of sharp teeth *b)* any of various tools or devices somewhat like this but with a sharp edge instead of teeth **2** a machine for operating a saw or saws —*vt.* **sawed**, **sawed** or [Chiefly Brit.] **sawn**, **saw′ing 1** to cut or divide with a saw **2** to shape or form with a saw **3** to make sawlike cutting motions through (the air, etc.) **4** to operate or produce with a to-and-fro motion suggestive of that used in working a saw [*to saw a knife through meat, to saw a tune on a fiddle*] —*vi.* **1** to cut with or as with a saw or as a saw does **2** to be cut with a saw [*wood that saws easily*] **3** to make sawlike cutting motions —☆**saw wood** ⟦in allusion to the rhythmic sound of snoring⟧ [Slang] to snore or sleep —**saw′er** *n.*

saw[2] (sô) *n.* ⟦ME *sawe* < OE *sagu*: see SAY⟧ an old saying, often repeated; maxim; proverb —*SYN.* SAYING

saw[3] (sô) *vt., vi. pt. of* SEE[1]

Sa·watch Mountains (sə wäch′) ⟦< ? AmInd name⟧ range of the Rocky Mountains, in central Colo.: highest peak, Mount ELBERT

saw·bones (sô′bōnz′) *n.* [Slang] a doctor; esp., a surgeon

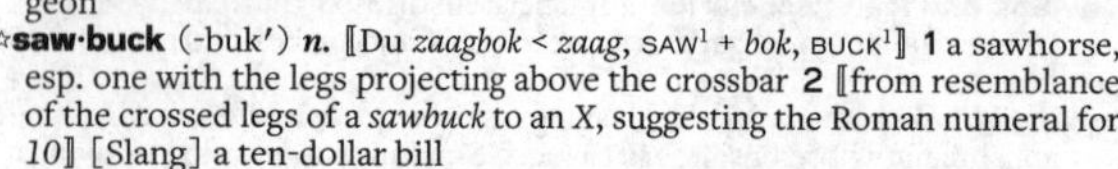

saws

☆**saw·buck** (-buk′) *n.* ⟦Du *zaagbok* < *zaag*, SAW[1] + *bok*, BUCK[1]⟧ **1** a sawhorse, esp. one with the legs projecting above the crossbar **2** ⟦from resemblance of the crossed legs of a *sawbuck* to an X, suggesting the Roman numeral for *10*⟧ [Slang] a ten-dollar bill

saw·dust (-dust′) *n.* minute particles of wood formed in sawing wood

sawed-off (sôd′ôf′) *adj.* ☆**1** designating a shotgun with the barrel cut off short ☆**2** [Informal] short in stature [*a skinny, sawed-off man*]

saw·fish (sô′fish′) *n., pl.* **-fish′** or **-fish′es** (see FISH) any of an order (Pristiformes) of large, tropical, sharklike rays, having the head prolonged into a flat, sawlike snout edged with large teeth on either side

saw·fly (-flī′) *n., pl.* **-flies′** any of various four-winged hymenopteran insects (esp. families Tenthredinidae and Cimbicidae): the abdomen of the female is provided with a pair of sawlike organs that cut into plants, the eggs being then deposited in the cuts

saw grass ⟦see SEDGE⟧ any of a number of related sedges with saw-edged leaves; esp., the **Jamaica saw grass** (*Cladium jamaicense*) found in the SE U.S.

saw·horse (-hôrs′) *n.* a rack consisting of a horizontal crosspiece and two pairs of spreading legs, used, usually one beside another, as to support wood while it is being sawed

☆**saw log** a log large enough for sawing into lumber

saw·mill (-mil′) *n.* a factory or place where logs are sawed into lumber

sawn (sôn) *vt., vi. chiefly Brit. pp. of* SAW[1]

☆**saw palmetto** a shrubby palm plant (*Serenoa repens*) with fan-shaped leaves and spiny leafstalks, native to the SE U.S.

saw set an instrument used to set, or bend slightly outward, the teeth of a saw

saw-toothed (sô′to͞otht′) *adj.* having notches along the edge like the teeth of a saw; serrate: also **saw′tooth′**

☆**saw-whet owl** (sô′hwet′, -wet′) ⟦echoic⟧ a very small North American forest owl (*Aegolius acadicus*) with brown-and-white plumage

saw·yer (sô′yər, soi′ər) *n.* ⟦ME *sawier* for *sawere*, with *-ier* < OFr suffix *-ier*: see CLOTHIER, LAWYER⟧ **1** a person whose work is sawing wood, as into planks and boards ☆**2** a log or tree caught in a river so that its branches saw back and forth with the water ☆**3** any of a genus (*Monochamus*) of brown-and-gray, long-horned beetles whose larvae burrow into wood

☆**sax** (saks) *n.* [Informal] *short for* SAXOPHONE

Sax *abbrev.* **1** Saxon **2** Saxony

Saxe (saks) *Fr. name for* SAXONY[2]: used in the names of several former duchies of the German Empire, now mostly in Thuringia

Saxe-Co·burg-Go·tha[1] (-kō′bərg gō′thə) *n.* ⟦after fol.: name changed by GEORGE V because of anti-German sentiment during WWI⟧ *former name* (1901-17) *for* the British royal house of Windsor

Saxe-Co·burg-Go·tha[2] (-kō′bərg gō′thə) duchy of central Germany, divided (1920) between Thuringia & Bavaria

sax·horn (saks′hôrn′) *n.* ⟦after A. J. *Sax* (1814-94), Belgian inventor⟧ any of a group of valved brass band instruments, with a full, even tone and a wide range

sax·ic·o·lous (sak sik′ə ləs) *adj.* ⟦< L *saxum*, a rock (see SAXATILE) + *colere*, to dwell + -OUS⟧ *Biol.* living on or among rocks: also **sax·ic′o·line′** (-līn′, -lin)

sax·i·frage (sak′sə frij′) *n.* ⟦ME < MFr < L *saxifraga* < *saxum*, a rock (see SAXATILE) + base of *frangere*, to BREAK: prob. from growing in rock crevices⟧ any of a genus (*Saxifraga*) of chiefly perennial plants of the saxifrage family, with small white, yellow, purple, or pinkish flowers, and with leaves massed usually at the base of the plant —*adj.* designating a family (Saxifragaceae, order Rosales) of dicotyledonous plants found chiefly in the North Temperate and Arctic zones, including the currants and gooseberries

sax·i·tox·in (sak′sə täk′sin) *n.* ⟦< ModL *Saxidomus*, name of a genus of clams (< L *saxum*, rock + -I- + L *domus*, home: see DOME) + TOXIN⟧ a powerful toxin that causes partial paralysis, sometimes found in shellfish that have fed on certain dinoflagellates (esp. genus *Gonyaulax*)

Sax·o Gram·mat·i·cus (sak′sō grə mat′i kəs) 1150?-1220?; Dan. historian

Sax·on (sak′sən) *n.* ⟦ME < LL *Saxo*, pl. *Saxones* < WGmc name > OE *Seaxan* < base akin to OHG *sahs*, sword, knife & L *saxum*, rock, stone, *secare*, to cut (see SAW[1]): hence, orig. ? knife bearers⟧ **1** a member of an ancient Germanic people of N Germany: some Saxons invaded and conquered parts of England in the 5th and 6th cent. A.D. **2** ANGLO-SAXON (*n.* 1 & 4) **3** a person born or living in modern Saxony **4** any of the Low German dialects of the Saxon peoples, as the dialect of modern Saxony —*adj.* **1** of the Saxons or their language or culture **2** English or Anglo-Saxon **3** of modern Saxony

Sax·on·ism (-iz′əm) *n.* a word, phrase, grammatical construction, or other feature originating in or peculiar to Anglo-Saxon

Sax·on·y[1] (sak′sə nē) *n.* ⟦because first produced in fol. (region in SE Germany)⟧ **1** a fine wool fabric with a soft finish **2** a closely twisted yarn used for knitting

Sax·on·y[2] (sak′sə nē) ⟦LL *Saxonia*⟧ **1** region of E Germany: formerly an electorate, kingdom, Prussian province, & state of the Weimar Republic **2** state of E Germany: 6,564 sq mi (17,000 sq km); cap. Dresden **3** medieval duchy at the base of the Jutland peninsula in what is now Lower Saxony

Sax·on·y-An·halt (-än′hält′) state of E Germany: 9,653 sq mi (25,001 sq km); cap. Magdeburg

sax·o·phone (sak′sə fōn′) *n.* ⟦Fr, after A. J. *Sax* (see SAXHORN) + -PHONE⟧ any of a group of keyed woodwind instruments having a single reed, conical bore, and metal body, usually curved —**sax′o·phon′ic** (-fän′ik) *adj.* —**sax′o·phon′ist** (-fōn′ist) *n.*

saxophone

sax·tu·ba (saks′to͞o′bə) *n.* ⟦SAX(HORN) + TUBA⟧ a large, bass saxhorn

say (sā) *vt.* **said**, **say′ing**; 3d pers. sing., pres. indic., **says** ⟦ME *seien* (< orig. 3d pers. sing., pres. indic.), *seggen* < OE *secgan*, akin to *sagu*, a saying, tale (ON *saga*), Ger *sagen*, to say < IE base **sekw-*, to note, see, show, say (> SEE[1], L *inseque* (imper.), tell!), orig., to follow > L *sequi*⟧ **1** to utter, pronounce, or speak **2** to express in words; state; declare; tell **3** to state positively, with assurance, or as an opinion [*who can say what will be?*] **4** to indicate or show [*the clock says ten*] **5** to recite; repeat [*to say one's prayers*] **6** to estimate; assume; hypothesize [*he is, I'd say, forty*] **7** to allege; report [*people say he's angry*] **8** to communicate (an idea, feeling, etc.) [*a painting that says nothing*] —*vi.* to make a statement; speak; express an opinion —*n.* **1** a chance to speak [*to have one's say*] **2** power or authority, as to make or help make a final decision: often with *the* **3** [Archaic] what a person says; dictum —*adv.* **1** for example [*any fish, say perch*] **2** about; nearly [*costing, say, 10 dollars*] —*interj.* used to express surprise, admiration, etc., or to get someone's attention —**go without saying** to be too obvious to need explanation; be self-evident —**not to say** though some might say: a rhetorical phrase used to introduce and acknowledge a more forceful or extreme characterization than the one just used [*a thorough, not to say pedantic, report*] —☆**say what?** [Informal] what did you say? —**say when!** [Informal] tell me when to stop!: said as when one is pouring another's drink —**that is to say** in other words; that means —**to say the least** to understate —**you can say that again!** [Informal] I agree with you! —**say′er** *n.*

Sa·yan Mountains (sä yän′) mountain system in central Asia, partially along the Mongolian-Russian border: highest peak, 11,453 ft (3,491 m)

Say·ers (sā′ərz, serz), **Dorothy L(eigh)** 1893-1957; Eng. writer, esp. of detective stories

say·ing (sā′iŋ) *n.* **1** the act of one who says **2** something said; esp., an adage, proverb, or maxim

SYN.—**saying** is the simple, direct term for any pithy expression of wisdom or truth; a **saw** is an old, homely saying that is well worn by repetition [*the preacher filled his sermon with wise saws*]; a **maxim** is a general principle drawn from practical experience and serving as a rule of conduct (Ex.: "Keep thy shop and thy shop will keep thee"); an **adage** is a saying that has been popularly accepted over a long period of time (Ex.: "Where there's smoke, there's fire"); a **proverb** is a piece of practical wisdom expressed in homely, concrete terms (Ex.: "A penny saved is a penny earned"); a **motto** is a maxim accepted as a guiding principle or as an ideal of behavior (Ex.: "Honesty is the best policy"); an **aphorism** is a terse saying embodying a general, more or less profound truth or principle (Ex.: "He is a fool that cannot conceal his wisdom"); an **epigram** is a terse, witty, pointed statement that gains its effect by ingenious antithesis (Ex.: "The only way to get rid of a temptation is to yield to it")

sa·yo·na·ra (sä′yô nä′rä) *interj., n.* ⟦Jpn, lit., if it is to be that way < *sayō*, that way + *nara*, if⟧ goodbye; farewell

says (sez) *vt., vi. 3d pers. sing., pres. indic., of* SAY

say-so (sā′sō′) *n.* [Informal] **1** a person's word, opinion, assurance, etc. [*based solely on her say-so*] **2** right of decision; authority [*who has the say-so in such matters?*]

say·yid or **say·id** (sä′yid) *n.* ⟦Ar *sayyid*⟧ a Muslim title of respect, specif. for certain descendants of Muhammad

sb *abbrev.* **1** *Baseball* stolen base(s): also **SB** **2** substantive

Sb ⟦L *stibium*⟧ *Chem. symbol for* antimony

SB or **S.B.** *abbrev.* 1 ⟦L *Scientiae Baccalaureus*⟧ Bachelor of Science 2 Senate Bill

SBA *abbrev.* Small Business Administration

SbE *abbrev.* south by east

'sblood (zblud) *interj.* [Obs.] *euphemism for* God's blood: used as a swearword

SbW *abbrev.* south by west

sc. *abbrev.* ⟦L *sculpsit*⟧ he (or she) carved it

sc *abbrev.* 1 scale 2 scene 3 science 4 scilicet 5 screw 6 scruple 7 *Printing* small capitals

Sc[1] *abbrev.* 1 Scotch 2 Scots 3 Scottish

Sc[2] *Chem. symbol for* scandium

SC *abbrev.* 1 Security Council (of the United Nations) 2 Signal Corps 3 South Carolina: also **S.C.** 4 Supreme Court

scab (skab) *n.* ⟦ME *scabbe* < ON *skabb*, akin to OE *sceabb* < IE base **(s)kep-*, to cut, split > L *scabies*, SCABIES, *scabere*, to SHAVE⟧ 1 a crust that forms over a sore or wound during healing 2 a mangy skin disease, as scabies, of animals, esp. sheep 3 *a)* any of various plant diseases characterized by roughened, scablike spots on leaves, stems, or fruits *b)* any such spot 4 *a)* [Old Slang] a low, contemptible fellow; scoundrel ☆*b)* a worker who refuses to join a union, or who works for lower wages or under different conditions than those accepted by the union *c)* a worker who refuses to strike, or who takes the place of a striking worker: usually a term of contempt or derision —*vi.* **scabbed**, **scab'bing** 1 to become covered with a scab; form a scab ☆2 to work or act as a scab

scab·bard (skab'ərd) *n.* ⟦ME *scabarde*, earlier *scauberc* < Anglo-Fr *escaubers* (pl.) < ? OHG *scar*, sword, cutting tool (akin to SHEAR) + *bergan*, to hide, protect: see BURY⟧ 1 a sheath or case to hold the blade of a sword, dagger, etc. 2 a sheath or holder for carrying a rifle —*vt.* to put into a scabbard; sheathe

scab·bard·fish (-fish') *n., pl.* **-fish'** or **-fish'es** (see FISH) any of several ocean fishes with an elongated, compressed, silvery body, as a cutlassfish: often written **scabbard fish**

scab·ble (skab'əl) *vt.* **-bled**, **-bling** ⟦earlier *scapple* < ME *scaplen*, aphetic < OFr *escapeler*, to dress timber < *es-* (< L *ex*), intens. + *chapler*, to cut < Gmc **kappan*, to split⟧ to dress or shape (stone) roughly, as with a hammer or pick

scab·by (skab'ē) *adj.* **-bi·er**, **-bi·est** 1 covered with or consisting of scabs 2 diseased with scab 3 low; base; mean —**scab'bi·ly** *adv.* —**scab'bi·ness** *n.*

sca·bies (skā'bēz, -bē ēz') *n.* ⟦L, roughness, itch: see SCAB⟧ a contagious skin disease caused by a parasitic mite (*Sarcoptes scabiei*) that burrows under the skin to deposit eggs, causing intense itching —**sca'bi·et'ic** (-bē et'ik) *adj.*

sca·bi·o·sa (skā'bē ō'sə) *n.* ⟦ModL; once considered a remedy for the itch: see fol.⟧ any of genus (*Scabiosa*) of plants of the teasel family, having showy, variously colored flowers in flattened or dome-shaped heads, as the **sweet scabiosa** (*S. atropurpurea*), often cultivated as a garden flower

sca·bi·ous[1] (skā'bē əs) *adj.* ⟦< Fr or L: Fr *scabieux* < L *scabiosus* < *scabies*: see SCAB⟧ 1 covered with scabs; scabby 2 of or like scabies

sca·bi·ous[2] (skā'bē əs) *n.* SCABIOSA

scab·rous (skab'rəs, skā'brəs) *adj.* ⟦LL *scabrosus* < L *scabere*, to scratch: see SCAB⟧ 1 *a)* rough with small points or knobs, like a file; scaly or scabby *b)* marked with or as with scabs; blotchy, encrusted, etc. 2 full of difficulties 3 indecent, shocking, improper, scandalous, etc. —**scab'rous·ly** *adv.* —**scab'rous·ness** *n.*

scad[1] (skad) *n., pl.* **scad** or **scads** ⟦akin to SHAD⟧ any of various edible jack fishes (esp. genus *Decapterus*)

scad[2] (skad) *n.* ⟦< ?⟧ [*usually pl.*] ☆[Informal] a very large number or amount [*scads of money*]

Sca·fell Pike (skô'fel) peak of a mountain in Cumbria, NW England, the highest in England: 3,210 ft (978 m)

scaf·fold (skaf'əld, -ōld') *n.* ⟦ME *scafald* < OFr *escafalt* < *es-* (L *ex-*, out) + VL **catafalicum*: see CATAFALQUE⟧ 1 a temporary wooden or metal framework for supporting workmen and materials during the erecting, repairing, or painting of a building, etc. 2 a raised platform on which criminals are executed, as by hanging 3 a temporary wooden stage or platform, as that on which medieval plays were presented 4 any raised framework —*vt.* to furnish or support with, or put on, a scaffold

scaf·fold·ing (-əl diŋ) *n.* 1 the poles, planks, etc. that form a scaffold 2 a scaffold or system of scaffolds

☆**scag** (skag) *n.* ⟦< ?⟧ [Slang] HEROIN

scagl·io·la (skal yō'lə) *n.* ⟦It *scagliuola*, dim. of *scaglia*, a chip, shell < Goth *skalja*, SCALE[2]⟧ an imitation marble made of gypsum and an adhesive, with colored stone dust or chips set into the surface

scal·a·ble (skāl'ə bəl) *adj.* that can be scaled

☆**scal·age** (skāl'ij) *n.* the percentage by which a figure, as for weight, price, etc., is scaled down to allow for shrinkage, etc.

sca·lar (skā'lər) *adj.* ⟦L *scalaris*, of a ladder < *scalae*, steps, ladder: see SCALE[1]⟧ 1 in, on, or involving a scale or scales 2 *Math.* designating or of a quantity that has magnitude but no direction in space, as volume or temperature —*n.* a scalar quantity: distinguished from VECTOR (*n. 2a*)

☆**sca·la·re** (skə ler'ē, -lär'-) *n.* ⟦ModL < L, neut. of *scalaris*, ladderlike (see prec.): from the lateral markings⟧ any of a genus (*Pterophyllum*) of freshwater cichlid fishes of N South America, having a flattened body and transparent pectoral fins; angelfish: popular as an aquarium fish

sca·lar·i·form (skə lar'ə fôrm') *adj.* ⟦< L *scalaris* (see SCALAR) + -FORM⟧ like a ladder; esp., having markings or transverse ridges like the rungs of a ladder

scalar product the product of the lengths of two vectors and the cosine of the angle between them

☆**scal·a·wag** (skal'ə wag', -ē-) *n.* ⟦< ?⟧ 1 [Informal] a scamp; rascal 2 a Southern white who supported the Republicans during the Reconstruction: an opprobrious term used by Southern Democrats

scald[1] (skôld, skäld) *vt.* ⟦ME *scalden* < NormFr *escalder*, for OFr *eschalder* < LL *excaldare*, to wash in warm water < L *ex-*, intens. + *calidus*, hot, akin to *calere*, to be warm: see CALORIE⟧ 1 to burn or injure with hot liquid or steam 2 to heat almost to the boiling point 3 to use boiling liquid on; specif., *a)* to sterilize by the use of boiling liquid *b)* to loosen the skin of (fruit, etc.), the feathers of (poultry), or the like, by the use of boiling water —*vi.* to be or become scalded —*n.* 1 a burn or injury caused by scalding 2 the act or an instance of scalding 3 *short for* SUNSCALD

scald[2] (skôld, skäld) *n. alt. sp. of* SKALD —**scald'ic** *adj.*

scale[1] (skāl) *n.* ⟦ME < LL *scala* (in Vulg., Jacob's ladder) < L, usually as pl., *scalae*, flight of stairs, ladder < **scandsla* < *scandere*, to climb: see DESCEND⟧ 1 [Obs.] *a)* a ladder or flight of stairs *b)* any means of ascent 2 *a)* a series of marks along a line, at regular or graduated intervals, used in measuring or registering something [*the scale of a thermometer*] *b)* any instrument or ruler marked in this manner 3 *a)* the proportion that a map, model, etc. bears to the thing that it represents; ratio between the dimensions of a representation and those of the object [*a scale of one inch to a mile*] *b)* a line marked off on a map to indicate this ratio or proportion 4 *a)* a system of grouping or classifying in a series of steps or degrees according to a standard of relative size, amount, rank, etc. [*the social scale, a wage scale*] *b)* a progressive graduated series, as of psychological or educational tests or scores *c)* a point, grade, level, or degree in such a series *d)* any relative degree or extent [*winter storm damage on a large scale*] 5 *Math.* a system of numerical notation [*the binary scale*] 6 *Music* a series of tones arranged in a sequence of rising or falling pitches in accordance with any of various systems of intervals; esp., all of such a series contained in one octave: see also CHROMATIC, DIATONIC, MAJOR SCALE, MINOR SCALE —*vt.* **scaled**, **scal'ing** 1 *a)* to climb up or over; go up by or as by a ladder or by clambering *b)* to reach or surmount (specified heights) 2 to regulate, make, or set according to a scale 3 to measure by or as by a scale ☆4 to estimate the amount of lumber that will be yielded by (a log, tree, etc.) —*vi.* 1 to climb; go up 2 to go up in a graduated series —**scale back** SCALE DOWN (see phrase below) —☆**scale down (or up)** to reduce (or increase), often according to a fixed ratio or proportion —**to scale** ⟦see *n. 3a*⟧ according to established, proportional dimensions [*a toy fighter plane built to scale*] —**scal'er** *n.*

scale[2] (skāl) *n.* ⟦ME, aphetic < OFr *escale*, husk, shell (< Frank *skala*) & *escaille*, shell (< Goth *skalja*): both < Gmc **skalja*, something split off < IE base **(s)kel-*, to cut > SHELL, HALF⟧ 1 any of the thin, flat, overlapping, rigid, horny plates forming the outer protective covering of the body in many fishes and reptiles and of the tails of a few mammals 2 any of the structurally similar thin plates on birds' legs or certain insects' wings 3 *a)* the single, round plate secreted by a scale insect *b)* SCALE INSECT 4 any thin, flaky or platelike layer or piece, as of dry skin, mail armor, etc. 5 a flaky film of oxide that forms on heated or rusted metals 6 a coating that forms on the inside of boilers, kettles, or other metal containers that heat liquids 7 any greatly reduced scalelike leaf or bract; esp., such a modified leaf covering and protecting the bud of a seed plant —*vt.* **scaled**, **scal'ing** 1 to strip or scrape scales from 2 to remove in thin layers; pare down 3 to cause scales to form on; cover with scales 4 to throw (a thin, flat object) so that its edge cuts the air or so that it skips along the surface of water 5 *Dentistry* to remove (tartar) from the teeth with a sharp instrument —*vi.* 1 to flake or peel off in scales 2 to become covered with scale or scales —**scale'less** *adj.*

scale[3] (skāl) *n.* ⟦ME < ON *skāl*, bowl, weighing balance; akin to OHG *scala*, OE *scealu*, SHELL: see prec.⟧ 1 either of the shallow dishes or pans of a balance 2 [*often pl.*] *a)* BALANCE (sense 1) *b)* any weighing machine —*vt.* **scaled**, **scal'ing** 1 to weigh in scales 2 to have a weight of —*vi.* to be weighed —**the Scales** Libra, the constellation and seventh sign of the Zodiac —**tip the scales** ⟦see TIP[3]⟧ to give an advantage to one possible outcome over another —**tip the scales at** ⟦see TIP[3]⟧ to weigh (a specified amount) —**turn the scales** to determine or decide something uncertain [*the arrival of fresh troops turned the scales*]

scale insect any of various families of small homopteran insects destructive to plants: the females secrete a round, wax scale under which they live and lay their eggs

sca·lene (skā'lēn', skā lēn') *adj.* ⟦LL *scalenus* < Gr *skalēnos*, uneven, odd < IE base **(s)kel-*, to bend, crooked > OE *sceolh*, squinting, L *coluber*, serpent⟧ 1 *Anat.* designating or of any of three deeply set muscles extending from the first two ribs to the cervical vertebrae, and serving to bend the neck 2 *Geom.* *a)* having unequal sides and angles (said of a triangle) *b)* having the axis not perpendicular to the base; oblique (said of a cone, etc.)

sca·le·nus (skā lē'nəs) *n.* ⟦LL⟧ a scalene muscle

sca·ler (skā'lər) *n.* 1 a person or thing that scales 2 *Electronics* a circuit designed to produce one output pulse after receiving a specific number of input pulses, usually two or ten, used as an electronic counter

scale·tail (skāl'tāl') *n.* any of a family (Anomaluridae) of African rodents that outwardly resemble flying squirrels and have scalelike structures on the lower surface of the tail

Sca·li·a (skə lē′ə), **An·to·nin** (an′tə nin) 1936-2016; associate justice, U.S. Supreme Court (1986-2016)

scal·i·ness (skā′lē nis) ***n.*** a scaly quality or condition

scaling circuit SCALER (sense 2)

scall (skôl) ***n.*** ⟦ME < ON *skalli*, bald head, akin to OE *scealu*, SHELL⟧ any scaly, or scabby, disease of the skin; scurf

☆**scal·la·wag** (skal′ə wag′, -ē-) ***n. alt. sp. of*** SCALAWAG

scal·lion (skal′yən) ***n.*** ⟦ME *scalon* < NormFr *escalogne* (for OFr *eschaloigne*) < VL **escalonia* < L (*caepa*) *Ascalonia*, (onion of) Ascalon (a city in Philistia)⟧ any of various onions or onionlike plants, as the shallot, green onion, or leek

scal·lop (skäl′əp, skal′-) ***n.*** ⟦ME *scalop* < OFr *escalope* < *escale*: see SCALE[2]⟧ **1** any of a family (Pectinidae) of bivalves with two deeply grooved, convex shells and an earlike wing on each side of the hinge, that swims by rapidly snapping its shells together to expel water in a jetlike manner **2** the edible large adductor muscle of such a mollusk **3** the single shell of such a mollusk; specif., *a)* one worn formerly as a badge by pilgrims returning from the Holy Land *b)* one, or a dish shaped like one, in which fish or other food is baked and served **4** any of a series of curves, circle segments, projections, etc. forming an ornamental edge on cloth, lace, etc. —***vt.*** **1** to cut the edge or border of in scallops **2** to bake until brown, as in a casserole, usually with a creamy sauce and a topping of bread crumbs —***vi.*** to gather scallops —**scal′lop·er** ***n.***

SHELL OF SCALLOP

SCALLOPED BORDER

☆**scal·ly·wag** (skal′ē wag′, -ə-) ***n.*** ⟦var. of SCALAWAG⟧ **1** [Informal] a scamp; rascal **2** SCALAWAG (sense 2)

scal·op·pi·ne (skäl′ə pē′nē, skal′-) ***n.*** ⟦It *scaloppini*, pl. of *scaloppino*, dim. of *scaloppo*, thin slice, scale, prob. < OFr *escalope*: see SCALLOP⟧ thin slices of meat, esp. veal, sautéed slowly with herbs and, usually, wine: also sp. **scal′lo·pi′ni** or **scal′lop·pe′ni**

scalp (skalp) ***n.*** ⟦ME < Scand, as in Dan dial. *skalp*, pod, shell, ON *skalpr*, sheath < IE **skelb-*, extension of base *(*s*)*kel-* > SCALE[2]⟧ **1** the skin on the top and back of the head, usually covered with hair **2** a part of this, cut or torn from the head of an enemy for a trophy, as formerly by certain North American Indians, frontiersmen, etc. **3** a symbol, indication, or recognition of victory, prowess, etc. **4** the skin on the top of the head of a dog, wolf, etc. ☆**5** [Informal] a small profit made by scalping —☆***vt.*** **1** to cut or tear the scalp from **2** *a)* to cheat or rob *b)* to defeat decisively **3** [Informal] to buy and sell in order to make small, quick profits **4** [Informal] to resell (tickets to the theater, a sports event, etc.) at a price higher than the regular price —☆***vi.*** [Informal] to scalp bonds, tickets, etc. —**scalp′er** ***n.***

scal·pel (skal′pəl) ***n.*** ⟦L *scalpellum*, dim. of *scalprum*, a knife < *scalpere*, to cut < IE base *(*s*)*kel-* > SCALE[2]⟧ a small, light, straight knife with a very sharp blade, used by surgeons and in anatomical dissections

☆**scalp lock** [Historical] a lock or tuft of hair left on the shaven crown of the head by certain North American Indian warriors

scal·y (skā′lē) ***adj.*** **scal′i·er**, **scal′i·est** **1** having, covered with, composed of, or resembling a scale or scales **2** shedding or yielding scales or flakes **3** full of or infested with scale insects

scaly anteater PANGOLIN

☆**scam** (skam) [Informal] ***n.*** ⟦prob. < obs. *scamp*, to roam, in cant sense, "to rob on the highway, steal by deceit": see SCAMP[1]⟧ a swindle or fraud; esp. a CONFIDENCE GAME —***vt.*** **scammed**, **scam′ming** to cheat or swindle, as in a confidence game —**scam′mer** ***n.***, **scam′ster**

Sca·man·der (skə man′dər) ***ancient name for*** MENDERES (river in NW Turkey)

scam·mo·ny (skam′ə nē) ***n.***, *pl.* **-nies** ⟦ME *skamonye* < L *scammonia* < Gr *skammōnia*⟧ **1** a climbing Asian convolvulus (*Convolvulus scammonia*) with thick roots, arrowhead-shaped leaves, and white or purplish flowers **2** *a)* any of several plants whose roots yield medicinal resins; specif., **Mexican scammony** (*Ipomoea orizabensis*) of the morning-glory family *b)* the resin from the roots of any of these plants

scamp[1] (skamp) ***n.*** ⟦< obs. *scamp*, to roam; akin to fol.⟧ a mischievous fellow; rascal —**scamp′ish** ***adj.***

scamp[2] (skamp) ***vt.*** ⟦akin to or < ON *skammr*, short < IE base *(*s*)*kem-*, stunted > OE *hamola*, man with cropped hair⟧ to make, do, or perform in a careless, inadequate way —**scamp′er** ***n.***

scam·per (skam′pər) ***vi.*** ⟦prob. < MFr *escamper*, to flee < It *scampare* < VL **excampare*, to decamp < L *ex*, out + *campus*, field of battle: see CAMPUS⟧ to run or go hurriedly or quickly —***n.*** the act of scampering —**scam′per·er** ***n.***

scam·pi (skam′pē) ***n.***, *pl.* **-pi** or **-pies** ⟦It, pl. of *scampo*, a prawn or shrimp⟧ **1** any of several large, greenish prawns, valued as food **2** a large shrimp broiled or fried with its tail on and served hot

scan (skan) ***vt.*** **scanned**, **scan′ning** ⟦ME *scannen* < L *scandere*, to climb, mount (in LL, to scan): see DESCEND⟧ **1** to analyze (verse) in terms of its rhythmic components, as by counting accents and syllables and marking the metrical feet **2** to look at closely or in a broad, searching way; scrutinize ☆**3** to glance at quickly; consider hastily **4** to examine, identify, or interpret (printed characters, video images, bar codes, etc.): said of an electronic device **5** *Comput.* to examine (items in a file) in sequence in order to find those that meet a particular criterion **6** *Electronics* to traverse (a region) with a succession of transmitted radar beams, usually radiated in a systematic pattern **7** *Radiology* to examine the structure or condition of (an internal bodily organ) with ultrasound, tomography, etc. **8** *TV* to traverse (a surface) rapidly and point by point with a beam of light or electrons in transmitting or reproducing the lights and shades of an image —***vi.*** **1** to scan verse **2** to conform to metrical principles: said of poetry —***n.*** **1** the act or an instance of scanning **2** scope of vision —***SYN.*** SCRUTINIZE

Scan or **Scand** ***abbrev.*** **1** Scandinavia **2** Scandinavian

scan·dal (skan′dəl) ***n.*** ⟦altered (infl. by Fr *scandale* or LL) < ME *scandle* < OFr *escandele* < LL(Ec) *scandalum*, cause for stumbling, temptation < Gr(Ec) *skandalon*, a snare: see DESCEND⟧ **1** *Christian Theol.* unseemly conduct of a religious person that discredits religion or causes moral lapse in another **2** any act, person, or thing that offends or shocks moral feelings of the community and leads to disgrace **3** a reaction of shame, disgrace, outrage, etc. caused by such an act, person, or thing **4** ignominy; disgrace **5** malicious gossip; defamatory or slanderous talk —***vt.*** **-daled** or **-dalled**, **-dal·ing** or **-dal·ling** **1** [Now Chiefly Dial.] to slander **2** [Obs.] to disgrace

scan·dal·ize (skan′də līz′) ***vt.*** **-ized′**, **-iz′ing** ⟦LME *scandalyzen* < OFr *scandaliser* < LL(Ec) *scandalizare* < Gr(Ec) *skandalizein*, to make stumble, give offense < *skandalon*: see prec.⟧ **1** [Now Rare] to slander; defame **2** to shock or outrage the moral feelings of; offend by some improper or unconventional conduct; shock —**scan′dal·i·za′tion** ***n.*** —**scan′dal·iz′er** ***n.***

scan·dal·mon·ger (skan′dəl muŋ′gər, -mäŋ′-) ***n.*** a person who gossips maliciously and spreads scandal

scan·dal·ous (skan′də ləs) ***adj.*** ⟦Fr *scandaleux* < ML *scandalosus*⟧ **1** causing scandal; offensive to a sense of decency or shocking to the moral feelings of the community; shameful **2** consisting of or spreading slander; libelous; defamatory —**scan′dal·ous·ly** ***adv.*** —**scan′dal·ous·ness** ***n.***

☆**scandal sheet** [Slang] a newspaper, magazine, etc. that features sensationalism, gossip, or the like

scan·dent (skan′dənt) ***adj.*** ⟦L *scandens*, prp. of *scandere*: see DESCEND⟧ climbing by attaching itself, as a vine

Scan·der·beg (skan′dər beg′) (born *George Castriota*) 1403?-68; Alb. leader & national hero

scan·di·a (skan′dē ə) ***n.*** ⟦ModL: see SCANDIUM⟧ the oxide of scandium, Sc_2O_3, a white, amorphous powder

Scan·di·an (skan′dē ən) ***adj.***, ***n.*** SCANDINAVIAN

Scan·di·na·vi·a (skan′də nā′vē ə, -nāv′yə) **1** region in N Europe, including Norway, Sweden, & Denmark and, sometimes, Finland, Iceland, & the Faroe Islands **2** SCANDINAVIAN PENINSULA

Scan·di·na·vi·an (-nā′vē ən, -nāv′yən) ***adj.*** of Scandinavia or its peoples, languages, or cultures —***n.*** **1** a person born or living in Scandinavia **2** the subbranch of the Germanic languages spoken by Scandinavians; North Germanic

Scandinavian Peninsula large peninsula in N Europe, consisting of Norway & Sweden

scan·di·um (skan′dē əm) ***n.*** ⟦ModL: so named (1879) by L. F. Nilson (1840-99), Swed chemist < ML *Scandia*, Scandinavia (source of the ore from which it was isolated) + -IUM⟧ a rare, silvery-white, metallic chemical element occurring with various rare-earth elements, used to produce high-intensity light sources, etc.: symbol, Sc; at. no. 21: see the periodic table of elements in the Reference Supplement

scan·na·ble (skan′ə bəl) ***adj.*** that can be scanned

scan·ner (skan′ər) ***n.*** a person or thing that scans; esp., any device used in television, OPTICAL CHARACTER RECOGNITION, etc. for scanning

scanning electron microscope a type of electron microscope in which a moving electron beam is used to scan an object causing it to emit secondary electrons which form a pattern that produces a three-dimensional image on the screen of a cathode-ray tube

scanning tunneling microscope ⟦see TUNNEL (*vi.* 2)⟧ a type of electron microscope capable of generating a three-dimensional image showing individual atoms: it consists of a moving electrode that scans an object by means of a line of tunneling electrons that flow between the tip of the electrode and the object

scan·sion (skan′shən) ***n.*** ⟦Fr < L *scansio*⟧ **1** the act of scanning, or analyzing, poetry in terms of its rhythmic components **2** the graphic representation, indicated by marked accents, feet, etc., of the rhythm of a line or lines of verse

scan·so·ri·al (skan sôr′ē əl) ***adj.*** ⟦< L *scansus*, pp. of *scandere*, to climb: see DESCEND⟧ *Zool.* **1** of or adapted for climbing, as a bird's feet **2** that climbs or can climb

scant (skant) ***adj.*** ⟦ME < ON *skamt* < *skammr*, short: see SCAMP[2]⟧ **1** inadequate in size or amount; not enough; meager [showing *scant* regard for the law] **2** not quite up to full measure [measuring a *scant* meter across] —***vt.*** **1** to limit in size or amount; stint **2** to fail to give full measure of **3** to furnish with an inadequate supply, short ration, etc. **4** to treat in an inadequate manner —***adv.*** scarcely; barely: dial. except in the phrase **scant few** [*scant few* details released to the press] —***SYN.*** MEAGER —**scant′ly** ***adv.*** —**scant′ness** ***n.***

scant·ies (skan′tēz) ***pl.n.*** ⟦orig. *scanty*, sing.n. < SCANTY⟧ very brief underpants, esp. for women

scant·ling (skant′liŋ) ***n.*** ⟦altered (as if < SCANT + -LING[1]) < ME *scantilone*, a carpenter's gauge, aphetic < NormFr *escantillon*, for OFr *eschandillon*, a measure < Prov *escandil*, a measure of volume < VL **scandaculum*, ladder, plumb < *scandere*: see DESCEND⟧ **1** [Archaic] a small amount or quantity **2** the size or dimensions of something; specif., the width and thickness of a piece of lumber **3** a small piece of lumber, as a two-by-four stud, used in the frame of a structure

scant·y (skan′tē) ***adj.*** **scant′i·er, scant′i·est** ⟦SCANT + -Y[2]⟧ **1** barely sufficient; not ample; meager **2** insufficient; not enough **3** narrow; small; close —***SYN.*** MEAGER —**scant′i·ly** ***adv.*** —**scant′i·ness** ***n.***

Scap·a Flow (skap′ə) sea basin in the Orkney Islands, off N Scotland: British naval base: *c.* 50 sq mi (129 sq km)

scape[1] (skāp) ***n.*** ⟦L *scapus:* see SHAFT⟧ **1** a leafless flower stalk growing from the crown of the root, as that of the narcissus or dandelion **2** something like a stalk, as the shaft of a feather or of an insect's antenna **3** *a)* the shaft of a column *b)* APOPHYGE

scape[2] (skāp) ***n., vt., vi.*** **scaped, scap′ing** ⟦ME *scapen,* aphetic < *escapen*⟧ [Archaic] ESCAPE: also written **'scape**

-scape (skāp) ⟦< (LAND)SCAPE⟧ *combining form* **1** a (specified) kind of view or scene *[seascape]* **2** a drawing, painting, etc. of such a view or scene

scape·goat (skāp′gōt′) ***n.*** ⟦coined by William TYNDALE (1530) < SCAPE[2] + GOAT, prob. from LL(Vulg.) *caper emissarius,* lit., emissary goat, transl. of Gr(Ec) *tragos aperchomenos,* departing goat, used as transl. of Heb *sair laazazel* < *sair,* he-goat + *l,* to + *azazel,* prob. name of a desert demon, but ? with folk-etym. meaning "goat that leaves," as if < *ez* (female) goat + *azal,* has left⟧ **1** a goat over the head of which the high priest of the ancient Jews confessed the sins of the people on the Day of Atonement, after which it was allowed to escape: Lev. 16:7-26 **2** a person, group, or thing upon whom the blame for the mistakes or crimes of others is thrust —***vt.*** to make a scapegoat of —**scape′goat′ing** ***n.***

scape·grace (skāp′grās′) ***n.*** ⟦SCAPE[2] + GRACE⟧ a graceless, unprincipled fellow; scamp; rogue; rascal

scape wheel escape wheel (see ESCAPEMENT, sense 2)

scaph·oid (skaf′oid′) ***adj., n.*** ⟦ModL *scaphoides* < Gr *skaphoeidēs* < *skaphos,* boat, hollow shell (< base of *skaptein,* to hollow out < IE base **(s)kap-,* to split, hollow out > SHAPE) + *-eides,* -OID⟧ NAVICULAR

scaph·o·pod (skaf′ə päd′) ***n.*** ⟦< Gr *skaphos,* a ship (see prec.) + -POD⟧ any of a class (Scaphopoda) of mollusks that live in muddy or sandy sea bottoms and have slightly curved, tubular shells open at both ends with a long, pointed, protrusile foot at the larger end

scap·o·lite (skap′ə līt′) ***n.*** ⟦< Gr *skāpos,* rod (see SHAFT) + -LITE⟧ any of a group of tetragonal minerals composed chiefly of silicates of aluminum, calcium, and sodium

sca·pose (skā′pōs) ***adj.*** ⟦< SCAPE[1] + -OSE[2]⟧ *Bot.* resembling, bearing, or consisting of a scape

scap·u·la (skap′yə lə) ***n., pl.*** **-lae′** (-lē′) or **-las** ⟦ModL < L (usually pl., *scapulae*), orig. prob. shovel (from use of the bone as a spade): for IE base see SCAPHOID⟧ either of two flat, triangular bones in the back of the shoulders of humans, or a similar bone in other vertebrates; shoulder blade

scap·u·lar (skap′yə lər) ***adj.*** ⟦ModL *scapularis* < L *scapula,* scapula (in LL, shoulder)⟧ of the shoulder, scapula, or scapulae —***n.*** **1** a sleeveless outer garment falling from the shoulders, worn as part of a monk's habit **2** two small pieces of cloth joined by strings, worn on the chest and back, under the clothes, by some Roman Catholics as a token of religious devotion or as a badge of some order **3** *Ornithology* a feather growing from a bird's scapular region **4** *Surgery* a bandage passed over the shoulder to support it or to keep another bandage in place

scapular medal *R.C.Ch.* a medal that has been blessed and may be substituted for a SCAPULAR (sense 2)

scar[1] (skär) ***n.*** ⟦ME, aphetic < MFr *escarre* < LL *eschara* < Gr, orig., fireplace, brazier⟧ **1** a mark left on the skin or other tissue after a wound, burn, ulcer, pustule, lesion, etc. has healed; cicatrix **2** a similar mark or cicatrix on a plant, as one on a stem where a leaf was attached **3** a marring or disfiguring mark on anything **4** the lasting mental or emotional effects of suffering or anguish —***vt.*** **scarred, scar′ring** to mark with or as with a scar —***vi.*** to form a scar in healing

scar[2] (skär) ***n.*** ⟦ME *skerre* < ON *sker:* for IE base see SHEAR⟧ [Brit.] **1** a precipitous rocky place or cliff **2** a projecting or isolated rock, as in the sea

scar·ab (skar′əb) ***n.*** ⟦Fr *scarabée* < L *scarabaeus,* altered < ? Gr *karabos,* a horned beetle, crayfish⟧ **1** any of a large family (Scarabaeidae) of mostly stout-bodied, often brilliantly colored beetles with antennae ending in flattened plates, including the June bugs, cockchafers, and dung beetles **2** *a)* the black, winged dung beetle (*Scarabaeus sacer*) held sacred by the ancient Egyptians *b)* an image of this beetle, cut from a stone or gem, often engraved with religious or historical inscriptions on the flat underside and, formerly, esp. in ancient Egypt, worn as a charm or used as a seal

TOP BOTTOM

scarab
(sense 2b)

scar·a·bae·id (skar′ə bē′id) ***n.*** ⟦< ModL < L *scarabaeus:* see prec.⟧ SCARAB (sense 1) —***adj.*** of the scarab beetles

Scar·a·mouch (skar′ə mo͞osh′, -mo͞och′) ***n.*** ⟦Fr *Scaramouche* < It *Scaramuccia,* lit., a SKIRMISH⟧ **1** a stock character in old Italian comedy, depicted as a braggart and poltroon **2** [**s-**] a boastful coward or rascal

Scar·bor·ough (skär′bur′ō, -ə; -bə rə) ⟦OE *Scartheborc* < ON *Skarthaborg* < *Skarthi* (lit., harelip, nickname of Thorgils, Norw founder of the town, *c.* 966) + *-borg;* akin to OE *burg,* BOROUGH⟧ **1** city & seaside resort in NE England, in North Yorkshire **2** former city in SE Ontario, Canada, now part of Toronto

scarce (skers) ***adj.*** **scarcer, scarcest** ⟦ME *scars* < NormFr *escars* (for OFr *eschars*) < VL **escarpsus,* for L *excerptus,* pp. of *excerpere,* to pick out, select (see EXCERPT); hence, that which is picked out and therefore scarce⟧ **1** not common; rarely seen **2** not plentiful; not sufficient to meet the demand; hard to get —***adv.*** [Literary] SCARCELY —**make oneself scarce** [Informal] to go or stay away —**scarce′ness** ***n.***

scarce·ly (skers′lē) ***adv.*** **1** hardly; not quite; only just **2** probably not or certainly not *[scarcely true]*

scarce·ment (skers′mənt) ***n.*** ⟦< obs. *scarce,* to make less < ME *scarsen* < *scars:* see SCARCE & -MENT⟧ a ledge or offset in a wall, etc.

scar·ci·ty (sker′sə tē) ***n., pl.*** **-ties** ⟦ME *scarsite* < NormFr *escarseté*⟧ **1** the condition or quality of being scarce; inadequate supply; dearth **2** rarity; uncommonness

scare (sker) ***vt.*** **scared, scar′ing** ⟦ME *skerren* < ON *skirra,* to scare, make timid < *skjarr,* timid, prob. < IE base **(s)ker-,* to jump > L *scurra,* buffoon⟧ to fill with fear or terror; esp., to frighten suddenly or startle; terrify —***vi.*** to become frightened, esp. suddenly *[a person who scares easily]* —***n.*** ⟦ME *skerre* < the v.⟧ **1** a sudden fear or panic; attack of fright, often unreasonable **2** a state of widespread fear or panic *[a war scare]* —***SYN.*** FRIGHTEN —**scare away (or off)** to drive away or off by frightening —☆**scare up** [Informal] to produce or gather quickly

scare·crow (sker′krō′) ***n.*** **1** anything set up in a field to scare birds away from crops, usually a figure of a man made with sticks, old clothes, etc. **2** anything that frightens but is actually not harmful **3** a person regarded as resembling a scarecrow in some way, as in being repellent or unattractive

scared·y-cat (sker′dē kat′) ***n.*** [Slang] a person who is unreasonably afraid: chiefly a child's term

☆**scare·head** (-hed′) ***n.*** [Informal] SCREAMER (sense 2)

scare·mon·ger (-muŋ′gər, -mäŋ′gər) ***n.*** a person who circulates alarming rumors —**scare′mon′ger·ing** ***n.***

scare quotes [Informal] quotation marks placed around a word or expression to indicate skepticism concerning its accuracy or appropriateness (Ex.: fresh concerns about the "freedom fighters")

scarf[1] (skärf) ***n., pl.*** **scarves** or sometimes **scarfs** ⟦NormFr *escarpe* (OFr *escharpe*), a purse suspended from the neck, wallet < ML *scirpa, scrippa,* earlier *scirpea,* rush pouch or basket < L *scirpeus,* of rushes < *scirpus,* a rush, bulrush⟧ **1** a long or broad piece of cloth worn about the neck, head, or shoulders for warmth or decoration; muffler, babushka, neckerchief, etc. **2** a long, narrow covering for a table, bureau top, etc.; runner **3** a sash worn by soldiers or officials —***vt.*** to cover or drape with a scarf

scarf[2] (skärf) ***n., pl.*** **scarfs** ⟦prob. < Scand, as in ON *skarfr,* obliquely cut beam-end < IE **skerp-* < base **(s)ker-,* to cut > SHEAR⟧ **1** a joint made by notching, grooving, or otherwise cutting the ends of two pieces and fastening them so that they lap over and join firmly into one continuous piece: also called **scarf joint** **2** the end of a piece cut in this fashion —***vt.*** **1** to join by a scarf **2** to cut so as to form a scarf on

☆**scarf**[3] (skärf) ***vt.*** ⟦var. of dial. *scaff,* eat voraciously < ?⟧ [Slang] to consume greedily: often with *down* or *up*

scarf·skin (skärf′skin′) ***n.*** ⟦SCARF[1] + SKIN⟧ the outermost layer of skin; epidermis or cuticle

scar·i·fi·ca·tion (sker′ə fi kā′shən) ***n.*** ⟦ME *scarificacioun* < LL *scarificatio*⟧ **1** the act of scarifying **2** scratches or cuts made by scarifying

scar·i·fi·ca·tor (sker′ə fi kāt′ər) ***n.*** ⟦ModL⟧ a surgical instrument for scarifying the skin

scar·i·fy[1] (sker′ə fī′) ***vt.*** **-fied′, -fy′ing** ⟦MFr *scarifier* < LL *scarificare,* altered < L *scarifare* < Gr *skariphasthai,* to scratch an outline, sketch < *skariphos,* pencil, stylus, akin to L *scribere,* to write: see SCRIBE⟧ **1** to make a series of small, superficial incisions or punctures in (the skin), as in surgery **2** to criticize sharply; make cutting remarks to or about **3** *Agric. a)* to loosen or stir (the topsoil) *b)* to make incisions in the coats of (seeds) in order to hasten germination —**scar′i·fi′er** ***n.***

scar·i·fy[2] (sker′ə fī′) ***vt.*** **-fied′, -fy′ing** ⟦formed irregularly < SCARE (***vt.***) + *-ify,* ? as in TERRIFY⟧ to frighten: usually in the present participle *[a scarifying experience]*

scar·i·ous (sker′ē əs) ***adj.*** ⟦ModL *scariosus* < L *scaria,* thorny shrub⟧ *Bot.* dry, thin, membranous, and not green, as some bracts

scar·la·ti·na (skär′lə tē′nə) ***n.*** ⟦ModL < ML (*febris*) *scarlatina,* scarlet (fever)⟧ *nontechnical term for* a mild form of SCARLET FEVER —**scar′la·ti′nal** ***adj.***

Scar·lat·ti (skär lät′tē) **1 A·les·san·dro** (ä′les sän′drô) 1660-1725; It. composer **2 (Giuseppe) Do·me·ni·co** (dô me′nē kô′) 1685-1757; It. composer: son of Alessandro

scar·let (skär′lit) ***n.*** ⟦ME, aphetic < OFr *escarlate* < ML *scarlatum* < Pers *säqirlät,* dress dyed crimson < ?⟧ **1** very bright red with a slightly orange tinge **2** cloth or clothing of this color —***adj.*** **1** of this color **2** of sin; sinful; specif., whorish

scarlet fever an acute contagious disease, esp. of children, caused by hemolytic streptococci and characterized by sore throat, fever, and a scarlet rash

scarlet hat a cardinal's hat: see RED HAT

☆**scarlet letter** ⟦< *The Scarlet Letter,* novel (1850) by Nathaniel HAWTHORNE⟧ [Historical] a red letter A worn by a person convicted of adultery

scarlet runner (bean) a climbing bean plant (*Phaseolus coccineus*) of tropical America, having pods with large, edible, red-and-black seeds and usually having scarlet flowers: often grown in cold climates as an ornamental

☆**scarlet tanager** a songbird (*Piranga olivacea*) native to the U.S., the male of which has a scarlet body and black wings and tail

scarp (skärp) ***n.*** ⟦It *scarpa*, a scarp, slope < Goth **skrapa*, akin to OE *scræf*, cave, hollow < IE **(s)kerb(h)-*, var. of base **(s)ker-*, to cut > SHEAR⟧ **1** a steep slope; specif., an escarpment or cliff extending along the edge of a plateau, mesa, etc. **2** the inner slope of a ditch below a rampart —***vt.*** **1** to make or cut into a steep slope **2** to provide with a scarp

scar·per (skär′pər) ***vi.*** ⟦ult. < It *scappare*, to run away, escape < LL **excappare*, ESCAPE⟧ [Brit. Slang] to run away or depart; decamp

Scar·ron (skå rōn′), **Paul** (pôl) 1610-60; Fr. poet & dramatist

scar tissue the dense, fibrous, contracted connective tissue of which a scar is composed

scarves (skärvz) ***n.*** *alt. pl. of* SCARF[1]

scar·y (sker′ē) ***adj.*** **scar′i·er**, **scar′i·est** [Informal] **1** causing alarm; frightening **2** easily frightened —**scar′i·ness** ***n.***

scat[1] (skat) ***vi.*** **scat′ted**, **scat′ting** ⟦? short for SCATTER⟧ [Informal] to go away: usually in the imperative

☆**scat**[2] (skat) ***adj.*** ⟦< ?⟧ *Jazz* designating or of singing in which meaningless syllables are improvised, often in imitation of the sounds of a musical instrument —***n.*** such singing —***vi.*** **scat′ted**, **scat′ting** to engage in scat singing

scat[3] (skat) ***n.*** ⟦< Gr *skōr*: see SCATO-⟧ excrement left by an animal, esp. a wild animal

☆**scat·back** (-bak′) ***n.*** ⟦SCAT[1] + BACK[1]⟧ [Slang] *Football* a halfback who is fast and agile

scathe (skāth) ***vt.*** **scathed**, **scath′ing** ⟦ME *scathen* < ON *skatha* < *skathi*, harm, akin to Ger *schaden*, to harm < IE base **skēth-*, to injure > Gr *(a)skēthēs*, (un)harmed⟧ **1** [Now Chiefly Dial.] *a)* to injure *b)* to wither; sear **2** to denounce fiercely —***n.*** [Now Chiefly Dial.] injury or harm

scath·ing (skā′*th*iŋ) ***adj.*** ⟦prp. of prec.⟧ searing; withering; harsh or caustic [*scathing* remarks] —**scath′ing·ly** ***adv.***

scat·o- (skat′ō, -ə) ⟦< Gr *skōr* (gen. *skatos*), excrement < IE base **sker-*, to defecate > ON *skarn*, OE *scearn*, dung⟧ *combining form* feces or excrement

sca·tol·o·gy (skə täl′ə jē) ***n.*** ⟦prec. + -LOGY⟧ **1** the study of feces or of fossil excrement **2** obscenity or obsession with the obscene, esp. with excrement or excretion, in literature —**scat·o·log·i·cal** (skat′ə läj′i kəl) ***adj.***

scat·ter (skat′ər) ***vt.*** ⟦ME *skateren*, ult. < IE **sked-*, to split, disperse < base **sek-*, to cut > L *secare*⟧ **1** *a)* to throw here and there or strew loosely; sprinkle *b)* to sprinkle over (*with*) something **2** to separate and drive in many directions; rout; disperse **3** [Archaic] to waste; dissipate **4** *Physics* to diffuse or deflect in an irregular, random manner —***vi.*** to separate and go off in several directions [the crowd *scattered*] —***n.*** **1** the act or process of scattering **2** that which is scattered about —**scat′ter·er** ***n.***

SYN.—scatter implies a strewing around loosely [to *scatter* seeds] or a forcible driving apart in different directions [the breeze *scattered* the papers]; **disperse** implies a scattering which completely breaks up an assemblage and spreads the individuals far and wide [a people *dispersed* throughout the world]; **dissipate** implies complete dissolution, as by crumbling, wasting, etc. [to *dissipate* a fortune]; **dispel** suggests a scattering that drives away something that obscures, confuses, troubles, etc. [to *dispel* fears] —***ANT.*** **assemble, gather, collect**

scat·ter·a·tion (skat′ər ā′shən) ***n.*** a scattering or being scattered; esp., the act or result of dispersing

scat·ter·brain (skat′ər brān′) ***n.*** a person who is incapable of concentrated or serious thinking; giddy, frivolous, flighty person —**scat′ter·brained′** ***adj.***

scat·ter·good (-good′) ***n.*** a wasteful person; spendthrift

scat·ter·ing (skat′ər iŋ) ***adj.*** **1** separating and going in various directions **2** distributed over a wide area, esp. at irregular intervals **3** distributed in small numbers among several or many candidates: said of votes —***n.*** **1** the act or process of one that scatters **2** a small amount of something spread out or interspersed in a medium **3** *Physics* the process by which the direction of motion of radiation or particles is changed randomly when passing through a medium, caused by collisions of the constituents of the radiation with particles in the medium —**scat′ter·ing·ly** ***adv.***

scatter plot *Math.* a graph consisting of points plotted along two axes, indicating the relationship between two data sets: also written **scat′ter·plot′** ***n.***

☆**scatter rug** a small rug for covering only a limited area

scat·ter·shot (-shät′) ***adj.*** **1** designating a shotgun shell that disperses the shot in a broad pattern **2** covering many points in a random way [*scattershot* criticism]

☆**scat·ter-site** (-sīt′) ***adj.*** designating or of inexpensive, publicly owned or financed housing units scattered throughout middle-class residential areas

scat·ty (skat′ē) ***adj.*** **-ti·er**, **-ti·est** ⟦contr. < ? SCATTERBRAINED⟧ [Brit. Slang] silly, foolish, or crazy

scaup (skôp) ***n.***, *pl.* **scaups** or **scaup** ⟦obs. var. of *scalp*, mussel bed: prob. so named from eating habits⟧ any of several wild ducks of the same genus (*Aythya*) as the redhead, canvasback, etc.: also **scaup duck**

scav·enge (skav′inj) ***vt.*** **-enged**, **-eng·ing** ⟦back-form. < fol.⟧ **1** to clean up (streets, alleys, etc.); remove rubbish, dirt, or garbage from **2** to salvage (usable goods) by rummaging through refuse or discards **3** to remove burned gases from (the cylinder of an internal-combustion engine) **4** *Metallurgy* to clean (molten metal) by using a substance that will combine chemically with the impurities present —***vi.*** **1** to act as a scavenger **2** to look for food

scav·eng·er (-in jər) ***n.*** ⟦ME *scavager* < Anglo-Fr *scawage*, inspection < NormFr *escauwer*, to inspect < Fl *scawen* or Frank *scouwon*, to peer at, observe, akin to OE *sceawian*, SHOW⟧ **1** a person who gathers things that have been discarded by others, as a junkman **2** any animal that eats refuse and decaying organic matter **3** anything that removes impurities, refuse, etc. **4** [Chiefly Brit.] a person employed to clean the streets, collect refuse, etc.

☆**scavenger hunt** a party game in which individual players or teams are sent out with the goal of bringing back as many of the items on a list of miscellaneous objects as they can acquire without buying them

ScB or **Sc.B.** *abbrev.* ⟦L *Scientiae Baccalaureus*⟧ Bachelor of Science

ScD or **Sc.D.** *abbrev.* ⟦L *Scientiae Doctor*⟧ Doctor of Science

sce·na (shā′nə) ***n.*** ⟦It⟧ **1** a dramatic section of an opera, for solo singers, that includes a recitative, arioso, and arias **2** an accompanied section of a libretto or a specially composed dramatic piece for a solo singer presented in concert

sce·nar·i·o (sə ner′ē ō′, -när′-) ***n.***, *pl.* **-i·os′** ⟦It < L *scaenarium* < *scaena*, stage, fol.⟧ **1** an outline or synopsis of a play, opera, or the like, indicating scenes, characters, etc. ☆**2** the script of a film **3** an outline for any proposed or planned series of events, real or imagined —☆**sce·nar′ist** ***n.***

scene (sēn) ***n.*** ⟦MFr *scène* < L *scena, scaena* < Gr *skēnē*, covered place, tent, stage < IE base **skai-*, to gleam softly > SHINE⟧ **1** in ancient Greece or Rome, a theater stage **2** the place in which any event, real or imagined, occurs [the *scene* of a battle] **3** the setting or locale of the action of a play, opera, story, etc. [the *scene* of *Hamlet* is Denmark] **4** a division of a play, usually part of an act, in which conventionally the action is continuous and in a single place **5** *a)* a part of a play, film, story, etc. that constitutes a unit of development or action, as a passage between certain characters *b)* *Film* a section of a film, usually made up of a number of shots, which is unified by time, setting, characters, etc. **6** SCENERY (sense 1) **7** a view of people or places; picture or spectacle **8** an awkward or embarrassing display of strong or excited feeling before others [to make a *scene* in court] **9** an episode, situation, or event, real or imaginary, esp. as described or represented **10** [Informal] the locale or environment for a specified activity [the poetry *scene*] —**behind the scenes** **1** backstage **2** in private or in secrecy; not for public knowledge —☆**make the scene** [Slang] **1** to be present **2** to participate, esp. in an effective or noticeable way

sce·ner·y (sē′nə rē) ***n.***, *pl.* **-er·ies** ⟦< obs. *scenary*, scenic < LL *scenarius* < L *scena*, prec.⟧ **1** painted screens, backdrops, hangings, etc., used on the stage to represent places and surroundings in a play, opera, etc. **2** the general appearance of a place; features of a landscape

sce·nic (sē′nik; *occas.* sen′ik) ***adj.*** ⟦MFr *scénique* < L *scenicus* < Gr *skēnikos* < *skēnē*, SCENE⟧ **1** *a)* of the stage; dramatic; theatrical *b)* relating to stage effects or stage scenery **2** *a)* having to do with natural scenery *b)* having beautiful scenery; affording beautiful views **3** representing an action, event, etc. Also [Now Rare] **sce′ni·cal** —**sce′ni·cal·ly** ***adv.***

☆**scenic railway** a small railway passing through areas with a scenic view, often artificially contrived, as at an amusement park

sce·nog·ra·phy (sē näg′rə fē) ***n.*** ⟦L *scaenographia* < Gr *skēnographia* < *skēnē*, SCENE + *graphein*: see GRAPHIC⟧ **1** the art of drawing or painting in perspective **2** *Theater* the design and painting of scenery —**sce·no·graph·ic** (sē′nə graf′ik, sen′ə-) ***adj.***, **sce′no·graph′i·cal**

scent (sent) ***vt.*** ⟦ME *senten* < OFr *sentir* < L *sentire*, to feel: see SEND⟧ **1** to smell; perceive by the olfactory sense **2** to get a hint or inkling of; suspect [to *scent* trouble] **3** to fill with an odor; give fragrance to; perfume —***vi.*** to hunt by the sense of smell —***n.*** **1** a smell; odor **2** the sense of smell **3** a manufactured fluid preparation used to give fragrance; perfume **4** an odor left by an animal, by which it is tracked in hunting **5** a track followed in hunting **6** any clue by which something is followed or detected **7** an intuitive capacity for discovering or detecting [a *scent* for news] —**scent′ed** ***adj.*** —**scent′less** ***adj.***

SYN.—scent, in this comparison, implies a relatively faint but pervasive smell, esp. one characteristic of a particular thing [the *scent* of apple blossoms]; **perfume** suggests a relatively strong, but usually pleasant, smell, either natural or manufactured [the rich *perfume* of gardenias]; **fragrance** always implies an agreeable, sweet smell, esp. of growing things [the *fragrance* of a freshly mowed field]; **bouquet** is specifically applied to the fragrance of a wine or brandy; **redolence** implies a rich, pleasant combination of smells [the *redolence* of a grocery] See also **smell** —***ANT.*** **stench, stink**

scep·ter (sep′tər) ***n.*** ⟦ME *sceptre* < OFr < L *sceptrum* < Gr *skēptron*, staff to lean on < base of *skēptesthai*, to prop oneself, lean on something < IE base **(s)kep-* > SHAFT⟧ **1** a rod or staff, highly ornamented, held by rulers on ceremonial occasions as a symbol of sovereignty **2** royal or imperial authority; sovereignty —***vt.*** to furnish with a scepter; invest with royal or imperial authority

scep·tic (skep′tik) ***n.***, ***adj.*** *chiefly Brit. sp. of* SKEPTIC —**scep′ti·cal** ***adj.*** —**scep′ti·cism′** ***n.***

scep·tre (sep′tər) ***n.***, ***vt.*** **-tred**, **-tring** *chiefly Brit. sp. of* SCEPTER

sch *abbrev.* **1** school **2** schooner

scha·den·freu·de (shäd′′n froi′də; *Ger*, -froi′-) ***n.*** ⟦Ger < *schaden*, to harm + *freude*, joy⟧ glee at another's misfortune

Schaff·hau·sen (shäf′hou′zən) canton of Switzerland, in the northernmost part: 115 sq mi (298 sq km)

schat·chen (shät′khən) ***n.*** *var. of* SHADCHAN

sched·ule (ske′jool, -əl; *Brit & often Cdn* shej′ool, shed′yool) ***n.*** ⟦altered (infl. by LL) < ME *sedule* < OFr *cedule* < LL *schedula*, dim. of L *scheda*, a strip of papyrus < Gr *schidē*, splinter of wood, split piece < *schizein*, to split: see

SCHIZO-] 1 [Obs.] a paper with writing on it 2 a list, catalog, or inventory of details, often as an explanatory supplement to a will, bill of sale, deed, tax form, etc. ☆3 *a)* a list of times of recurring events, projected operations, arriving and departing trains, etc.; timetable *b)* a sequence of such events, operations, etc. ☆4 a timed plan for a project or procedure —*vt.* **-uled, -ul·ing** 1 to place or include in a schedule 2 to make a schedule of ☆3 to plan for a certain time

Scheduled Castes the groups of people in India formerly belonging to the class of untouchables

scheel·ite (shā′līt′, shē′-) *n.* ⟦Ger *scheelit*, after K. W. *Scheele* (1742-86), Swed chemist⟧ a yellowish-white to brown, hard mineral, calcium tungstate, $CaWO_4$, that is an ore of tungsten

scheff·ler·a (shef lir′ə, -ler′-) *n.* ⟦ModL, after J. C. *Scheffler*, 19th-c. Ger botanist⟧ an ornamental plant (*Brassaia actinophylla*) of the ginseng family, with glossy, palmately arranged leaflets growing in an umbrellalike formation

Sche·he·ra·za·de (shə her′ə zäd′, -zä′də) *n.* ⟦Ger < Pers *Shīrazād*⟧ in *The Arabian Nights*, the Sultan's bride, who saves her life by suspensefully maintaining his interest in the tales she tells

Scheldt (skelt) river flowing from N France through Belgium and the Netherlands into the North Sea: *c.* 270 mi (435 km): Du. name **Schel·de** (skhel′də)

Schel·ling (shel′iŋ), **Frie·drich Wil·helm Jo·seph von** (frē′driH vil′helm yō′zef fôn) 1775-1854; Ger. philosopher

sche·ma (skē′mə) *n., pl.* **-mas** or, esp. for 2, **-ma·ta** (-mə tə) ⟦Gr *schēma*: see SCHEME⟧ 1 an outline, diagram, plan, or preliminary draft 2 *Psychol.* a mental image produced in response to a stimulus, that becomes a framework or basis for analyzing or responding to other related stimuli

sche·mat·ic (skē mat′ik, skə-) *adj.* ⟦ModL *schematicus*⟧ of, or having the nature of, a scheme, schema, plan, diagram, etc. —*n.* a schematic diagram, as of electrical wiring in a circuit —**sche·mat′i·cal·ly** *adv.*

sche·ma·tism (skē′mə tiz′əm) *n.* ⟦ModL *schematismus* < Gr *schēmatismos* < *schēmatizein*, to form: see SCHEME⟧ a set form for classification or exposition; arrangement of parts according to a scheme; design

sche·ma·tize (-tīz′) *vi., vt.* **-tized′, -tiz′ing** ⟦Gr *schēmatizein*⟧ to form, form into, or arrange according to, a scheme or schemes —**sche′ma·ti·za′tion** *n.*

scheme (skēm) *n.* ⟦L *schema* < Gr *schēma* (gen. *schēmatos*), a form, appearance, plan, akin to *schein, echein*, to hold, have < IE base **seĝh-*, to hold, hold fast, conquer > SCHOOL[1], Sans *sáhas*, power, victory, Goth *sigis*, Ger *sieg*, victory⟧ 1 *a)* a carefully arranged and systematic program of action for attaining some object or end *b)* a secret or underhanded plan; plot *c)* a visionary plan or project 2 an orderly combination of things on a definite plan; system [a color *scheme*] 3 an outline or diagram showing different parts or elements of an object or system 4 an analysis or summary in outline or tabular form 5 an astrological diagram —*vt.* **schemed, schem′ing** 1 to make a scheme for; plan as a scheme; devise 2 to plan in a deceitful way; plot —*vi.* 1 to make schemes; form plans 2 to plot; intrigue —*SYN.* PLAN —**schem′er** *n.*

schem·ing (skē′miŋ) *adj.* given to forming schemes or plots; crafty, tricky, deceitful, etc. —**schem′ing·ly** *adv.*

Sche·nec·ta·dy (skə nek′tə dē) ⟦Du *Schanhectade* < Mohawk *skahnéhtati*, Albany, lit., on the other side of the pines: the pines were between the communities; the Dutch transferred the name⟧ city in E N.Y., on the Mohawk River

scher·zan·do (sker tsän′dō, -tsan′-) *adj., adv.* ⟦It < prp. of *scherzare*, to play < *scherzo*: see fol.⟧ [*also in italics*] *Musical Direction* playful(ly)

scher·zo (sker′tsō) *n., pl.* **-zos** or **-zi** (-tsē) ⟦It, a jest, sport < Gmc, as in MHG *schërz*, pleasure, play, ult. < IE base **(s)ker-*, to leap, jump > SCARE, L *cardo*, a hinge, turning point⟧ *Music* 1 a lively, playful composition, usually in 3/4 time 2 such a piece serving as a movement, typically the third movement, of a sonata, symphony, or quartet

Schia·pa·rel·li (skyä′pä rel′lē), **Gio·van·ni Vir·gi·nio** (jô vän′nē vir jē′nyô) 1835-1910; It. astronomer

☆**Schick test** (shik) ⟦after Béla *Schick* (1877-1967), U.S. pediatrician, born in Hungary, who devised it⟧ a test to determine immunity to diphtheria, made by injecting dilute diphtheria toxin into the skin: if an area of inflammation results, the patient is not immune

Schie·le (shē′lə), **E·gon** (ā′gôn) 1890-1918; Austrian painter

Schiff's reagent (shifs) ⟦after H. *Schiff* (1834-1915), Ger chemist⟧ *Chem.* a colorless solution of fuchsin and sulfurous acid used as a reagent to identify an aldehyde from a ketone from the shade of reddish purple produced, to stain DNA, etc.

schil·ler (shil′ər) *n.* ⟦Ger, color play < *schillern*, to change color, akin to *schielen*, to blink, squint < OHG *scelah*, oblique < IE base **(s)kel-*, crooked > SCOLEX⟧ a peculiar bronzelike luster in certain minerals, often iridescent, caused by the diffraction of light in embedded crystals

Schil·ler (shil′ər), **(Johann Christoph) Frie·drich von** (frē′driH fôn) 1759-1805; Ger. dramatist & poet

schil·ling (shil′iŋ) *n.* ⟦Ger: see SHILLING⟧ the former basic monetary unit of Austria, superseded in 2002 by the EURO

schip·per·ke (skip′ər kē′) *n.* ⟦Fl, little skipper, dim. of *schipper* (see SKIPPER[2]): from earlier use of the breed as watchdogs on canalboats⟧ any of a breed of small dog with a dense, black coat forming a ruff about the neck, a foxlike head, and erect ears: traditionally the tail is docked

schism (siz′əm, skiz′-) *n.* ⟦ME *scisme* < OFr *cisme* < LL(Ec) *schisma* < Gr < *schizein*, to cleave, cut: see SCHIZO-⟧ 1 a split or division in an organized group or society, esp. a church, as the result of difference of opinion, of doctrine, etc. 2 the act of causing or trying to cause a split or division in a church 3 any of the sects, parties, etc. formed by such a split

schis·mat·ic (siz mat′ik, skiz-) *adj.* ⟦ME *scismatike* < MFr *scismatique* < LL(Ec) *schismaticus* < Gr *schismatikos*⟧ 1 of, characteristic of, or having the nature of, schism 2 tending to, causing, or guilty of schism Also **schis·mat′i·cal** —*n.* a person who causes or participates in schism —**schis·mat′i·cal·ly** *adv.*

schist (shist) *n.* ⟦Fr *schiste* < L *schistos (lapis)*, split (stone) < Gr *schistos*, easily cleft < *schizein*, to cleave: see SCHIZO-⟧ any of a group of metamorphic rocks containing parallel layers of flaky minerals, as mica or talc, and splitting easily into thin, parallel leaves —**schist′ose** (-ōs) *adj.*, **schist′ous** (-əs)

schis·to·some (shis′tə sōm′) *n.* ⟦< ModL < Gr *schistos*, cleft (see prec.) + *sōma*, body: see SOMATIC⟧ any of a genus (*Schistosoma*) of flukes that live as parasites in the blood vessels of birds and mammals, including humans

schis·to·so·mi·a·sis (shis′tə sō mī′ə sis) *n.* ⟦ModL: see prec. & -IASIS⟧ a chronic, usually tropical, disease, caused by schistosomes and characterized in humans by disorders of the liver, urinary bladder, lungs, or central nervous system

schiz·o (skit′sō, skiz′ō) *adj., n., pl.* **schiz′os** [Informal] *short for* SCHIZOPHRENIC

schiz·o- (skiz′ō, -ə; skit′sō, -sə) ⟦ModL < Gr *schizein*, to cleave, cut < IE **skeid-* < base **skei-*, to cut, separate > SHIN[1], L *scindere*, to cut⟧ *combining form* 1 split, cleavage, division [*schizocarp*] 2 schizophrenia [*schizoid*] Also, before a vowel, **schiz-**

schiz·o·af·fec·tive disorder (skit′sō ə fek′tiv, skiz′ō-) a psychiatric disorder characterized by symptoms of both schizophrenia and bipolar affective disorder

schiz·o·carp (skiz′ə kärp′, skit′sə-) *n.* ⟦SCHIZO- + -CARP⟧ *Bot.* a dry fruit, as of the maple, that splits at maturity into two or more one-seeded carpels which remain closed —**schiz′o·car′pous** (-kär′pəs) *adj.*, **schiz′o·car′pic** (-kär′pik)

schiz·o·gen·e·sis (skiz′ə jen′ə sis, skit′sə-) *n.* ⟦ModL: see SCHIZO- & -GENESIS⟧ *Biol.* reproduction by fission

schi·zog·o·ny (ski zäg′ə nē, skit säg′-) *n.* ⟦SCHIZO- + -GONY⟧ asexual reproduction by multiple fission, found in many sporozoans, as the malarial parasite

schiz·oid (skit′soid′, skiz′oid′) *adj.* ⟦SCHIZ(O)- + -OID⟧ 1 *Psychiatry* of, like, or having schizophrenia 2 designating a personality type characterized by quietness, seclusiveness, introversion, etc. —*n.* a schizoid person

schiz·ont (skiz′änt′, skit′sänt′) *n.* ⟦< SCHIZO- + Gr *ōn*, gen. *ontos*: see ONTO-⟧ a large cell in many sporozoans that multiplies by schizogony

schiz·o·phre·ni·a (skit′sə frē′nē ə, skiz′ə-; -fren′ē ə) *n.* ⟦ModL < SCHIZO- + Gr *phrēn*, the mind + -IA⟧ 1 a major mental disorder of unknown cause typically characterized by a separation between the thought processes and the emotions, a distortion of reality accompanied by delusions and hallucinations, a fragmentation of the personality, motor disturbances, bizarre behavior, etc., often with no loss of basic intellectual functions: this term has largely replaced *dementia praecox*, since it does not always result in deterioration (*dementia*) or always develop in adolescence or before maturity (*praecox*) 2 *nontechnical term for* MULTIPLE PERSONALITY DISORDER 3 [Informal] a situation, state of mind, etc. in which widely conflicting opinions, ideas, or practices coexist, often resulting in indecision, vacillation, wavering, etc.

schiz·o·phren·ic (-fren′ik, -frē′nik) *adj.* of, having, or characterized by SCHIZOPHRENIA —*n.* a person having SCHIZOPHRENIA: also **schiz′o·phrene′** (-frēn′) —**schiz′o·phren′i·cal·ly** *adv.*

schiz·o·phyte (skiz′ə fīt′, skit′sə-) *n.* ⟦SCHIZO- + -PHYTE⟧ in some systems of classification, any of a division (Schizophyta) of plants which consist of a single cell, or a chain or colony of cells, and reproduce only by simple fission or by asexual spores, including the bacteria and blue-green algae —**schiz′o·phyt′ic** (-fit′ik) *adj.*

schiz·o·pod (-päd′) *n.* ⟦< ModL *Schizopoda* < Gr *schizopous*, having parted toes: see SCHIZO- & -POD⟧ any of various shrimplike malacostracan crustaceans having thoracic appendages with two branches, including the mysids and krill —*adj.* of the schizopods: also **schi·zop·o·dous** (ski zäp′ə dəs)

schiz·o·thy·mi·a (skit′sə thī′mē ə, skiz′ə-) *n.* ⟦ModL < SCHIZO- + Gr *thymos*, spirit: see THYMUS⟧ an emotional condition characterized by schizoid tendencies: less severe than *schizophrenia* —**schiz′o·thy′mic** (-mik) *adj., n.*

schiz·zy or **schiz·y** (skit′sē, skiz′ē) *adj.* [Slang] SCHIZOPHRENIC

Schle·gel (shlā′gəl) 1 **Au·gust Wil·helm von** (ou′goost vil′helm fôn) 1767-1845; Ger. poet, critic, & translator 2 **(Karl Wilhelm) Frie·drich von** (frē′driH fôn) 1772-1829; Ger. critic & philosopher: brother of August

Schlei·er·ma·cher (shlī′ər mä′khər), **Frie·drich Ernst Da·ni·el** (frē′driH ernst dä′nē el) 1768-1834; Ger. theologian & philosopher

☆**schle·miel** (shlə mēl′) *n.* ⟦W Yiddish *shlemil* < Heb *shelumiel*, name of a tribal chief (see Num. 1:6), identified in the Talmud with a prince who met an unfortunate end⟧ [Slang] an ineffectual, bungling person who habitually fails or is easily victimized: also sp. **schle·mihl′**

☆**schlep** or **schlepp** (shlep) [Slang] *vt.* **schlepped, schlep′ping** ⟦< Yiddish *shlepn*, to drag < MHG dial. *sleppen* < LowG *slepen* < IE base **(s)leub-* > SLIP[3]⟧ to carry, take, haul, drag, etc. —*vi.* to go or move with effort; drag oneself —*n.* an ineffectual person

Schle·sing·er (shlā′ziŋ ər, shles′in jər) 1 **Arthur M(eier)** 1888-1965; U.S. historian 2 **Arthur M(eier), Jr.** 1917-2007; U.S. historian: son of Arthur

Schles·wig (shles′wig; *Ger* shläs′viH) region in the S Jutland peninsula, divided between Denmark & Germany: Dan. name SLESVIG

Schles·wig-Hol·stein (-hōl′stīn; *Ger*, -hôl′shtīn) state of N Germany: 6,077 sq mi (15,739 sq km); cap. Kiel

Schlie·mann (shlē′män), **Hein·rich** (hīn′riH) 1822-90; Ger. archaeologist

schlie·ren (shlir′ən) ***pl.n.***, *sing.* **-re** (-ə) ⟦Ger, lit., streaks; akin to SLUR⟧ **1** small streaks or masses in igneous rocks, differing in composition from the main rock but blending gradually into it **2** *Optics* regions in a translucent medium, as a fluid, that have a different density and consequently a different index of refraction than the medium and that can be photographed as shadows produced by the refraction of light passed through these regions

☆**schlock** (shläk) [Slang] ***n.*** ⟦< ? Ger *schlacke*, dregs, SLAG⟧ anything cheap or inferior; trash —***adj.*** cheap; inferior: also **schlock′y schlock′i·er, schlock′i·est**

☆**schlock·meis·ter** (-mīs′tər) ***n.*** ⟦prec. + Ger *meister* < L *magister*, MASTER: modeled on Ger *bürgermeister*, etc.⟧ [Slang] a person who deals in shoddy goods; specif., a writer, filmmaker, etc. who produces kitsch

☆**schlub** (shlub, shlo͝ob) ***n.*** ⟦Yiddish⟧ [Slang] a person who is ineffectual, inept, unkempt, boorish, etc.

☆**schlump** (shlump) [Slang] ***n.*** ⟦Yiddish < Ger *schlampe*, slut⟧ **1** a person who is stupid, foolish, inept, boring, etc. **2** one who is sloppily or poorly dressed —***vi.*** to go about lazily, sluggishly, or poorly dressed

☆**schmaltz** (shmälts, shmôlts) ***n.*** ⟦? via Yiddish < Ger *schmaltz*, lit., rendered fat, akin to *schmelzen*, to melt: see SMELT[2]⟧ [Informal] **1** highly sentimental and banal music, literature, etc. **2** banal or excessive sentimentalism Also sp. **schmalz** —**schmaltz′y** ***adj.*** **schmaltz′i·er, schmaltz′i·est**

schmaltz herring ⟦see prec.⟧ herring caught just before spawning, when it has much fat

☆***schmatte*** (shmät′ə) ***n., adj.*** ⟦Yiddish⟧ [Slang] *alt. sp. of* SHMATTE

schmear (shmir) ***n.*** ⟦E Yiddish *shmir*, lit., a smearing < *shmirn*, to smear < MHG *smir(we)n*⟧ [Slang] **1** some matter or activity with all its related features: usually **the whole schmear** **2** a bribe Also sp. **schmeer**

Schmidt system (shmit) ⟦after B. *Schmidt* (1879-1935), Ger optician, born in Estonia⟧ a wide-angle optical system having a concave, spherical mirror whose aberration is neutralized by a correcting lens: often used in special, photographic reflecting telescopes to obtain clear pictures of large areas of the celestial sphere: also called **Schmidt camera**

☆**schmo** (shmō) ***n.***, *pl.* **schmoes** or **schmos** ⟦< Yiddish, prob. altered < *shmok*: see SCHMUCK⟧ [Slang] a foolish or stupid person; dolt: also sp. **schmoe**

☆**schmooze** (shmo͞oz) [Slang] ***vi.*** **schmoozed, schmooz′ing** ⟦W Yiddish *shmuzn*, var. of Yiddish *shmuesn* < *shmues*, a chat, lit., rumors, gossip, pl. of *shmue* < Heb *shemua*, rumor, news < *shama*, to hear⟧ to chat or gossip —***n.*** an idle talk; chat Also **schmoos** (shmo͞os)

☆**schmuck** (shmuk) ***n.*** ⟦E Yiddish *shmok*, lit., penis < Old Pol *smok*, grass snake, dragon⟧ [Slang] a contemptible or foolish person; jerk

Schna·bel (shnä′bəl), **Ar·tur** (är′to͝or) 1882-1951; U.S. pianist & composer, born in Austria

schnapps (shnäps, shnaps) ***n.***, *pl.* **schnapps** ⟦Ger, a dram, nip < Du *snaps*, lit., a gulp, mouthful < *snappen*, to SNAP⟧ **1** HOLLANDS **2** any of various flavored liqueurs or brandies Also sp. **schnaps**

schnau·zer (shnou′zər) ***n.*** ⟦Ger < *schnauzen*, to snarl, growl < *schnauze*, SNOUT⟧ any member of three breeds of sturdily built dog with a wiry, pepper-and-salt or black coat, whiskers, and bushy eyebrows, orig. bred in Germany: the *standard schnauzer* is 17 to 23 in (43.2-58 cm) high at the shoulder; the *miniature schnauzer*, 12 to 14 in (30.5-35.5 cm); the *giant schnauzer*, over 23.5 in (59.7 cm)

schneck·en (shnek′ən) ***pl.n.***, *sing.* **schneck′e** (-ə) ⟦Ger, pl. of *schnecke*, lit., snail⟧ rich yeast rolls consisting of dough rolled around a filling as of nuts and cinnamon, sliced crosswise, and baked flat to produce a spiral shape

Schnitt·ke (shnit′ke), **Alfred** 1934-98; Russian composer

☆**schnit·zel** (shnit′səl) ***n.*** ⟦Ger, lit., a shaving, dim. of *schnitz*, a piece cut off < MHG *sniz*, akin to OE *snithan*, to cut, chop < IE base **sneit-* > Czech *snět*, a branch⟧ a cutlet, esp. of veal

Schnitz·ler (shnits′lər), **Arthur** 1862-1931; Austrian playwright & novelist

schnoo·dle (shno͞od′'l) ***n.*** ⟦< SCHNAUZER + POODLE⟧ a dog crossbred from a schnauzer and a poodle

☆**schnook** (shno͝ok) ***n.*** ⟦< Yiddish ? altered < SCHMUCK⟧ [Slang] a person easily imposed upon or cheated; pitifully meek person

schnor·rer (shnôr′ər) ***n.*** ⟦< Yiddish < Ger *schnurrer* < *schnurren*, to whir, purr (of echoic orig.): from the sound made by musical instruments carried by beggars⟧ [Slang] a person who lives by begging or by sponging off others

☆**schnoz** (shnäz) ***n.*** ⟦via Yiddish < Ger *schnauze*, akin to SNOUT⟧ [Slang] a nose, often, specif., a large or unattractive one: also **schnoz′zle** (shnäz′əl) or **schnozz**

schol·ar (skäl′ər) ***n.*** ⟦ME *scoler* < OE *scolere* or OFr *escoler*, both < ML < LL *scholaris*, relating to a school < L *schola*, SCHOOL[1]⟧ **1** *a)* a learned person *b)* a specialist in a particular branch of learning, esp. in the humanities *[a Mark Twain scholar]* **2** a student given scholarship aid **3** any student or pupil —***SYN.*** PUPIL[1]

schol·ar·ly (skäl′ər lē) ***adj.*** **1** of or characteristic of a SCHOLAR (sense 1); learned **2** having or showing much knowledge, accuracy, and critical ability **3** devoted to learning; studious

schol·ar·ship (skäl′ər ship′) ***n.*** **1** the quality of knowledge and learning shown by a student; standard of academic work **2** *a)* the systematized knowledge of a learned person, exhibiting accuracy, critical ability, and thoroughness; erudition *b)* the knowledge attained by scholars, collectively **3** a specific gift of money or other aid, as by a foundation, to help a student pay for instruction

scho·las·tic (skə las′tik) ***adj.*** ⟦L *scholasticus* < Gr *scholastikos* < *scholazein*, to devote one's leisure to study, be at leisure < *scholē*: see SCHOOL[1]⟧ **1** of schools, colleges, universities, students, teachers, and studies; educational; academic **2** [*also* **S-**] of or characteristic of scholasticism **3** pedantic, dogmatic, formal, etc. **4** of secondary schools *[scholastic football games]* Also **scho·las′ti·cal** —***n.*** **1** a student or scholar, esp. in a scholasticate **2** [*also* **S-**] SCHOOLMAN (sense 1) **3** a person who is devoted to logical subtleties and quibblings; pedant **4** [*also* **S-**] a person who favors Scholasticism —**scho·las′ti·cal·ly** ***adv.***

scho·las·ti·cate (-tə kāt′, -kit) ***n.*** *R.C.Ch.* a school for seminarians, esp. Jesuit seminarians

scho·las·ti·cism (skə las′tə siz′əm) ***n.*** **1** [*often* **S-**] the system of logic, philosophy, and theology of medieval university scholars, or schoolmen, from the 10th to the 15th century, based upon Aristotelian logic, the writings of the early Christian fathers, and the authority of tradition and dogma **2** insistence upon traditional doctrines and methods

scho·li·ast (skō′lē ast′, -əst) ***n.*** ⟦ModL *scholiasta* < MGr *scholiastēs* < *scholiazein*, to comment < Gr *scholion*, fol.⟧ one who writes marginal notes and comments; esp., an ancient interpreter and annotator of the classics —**scho′li·as′tic** ***adj.***

scho·li·um (skō′lē əm) ***n.***, *pl.* **-li·a** (-ə) or **-li·ums** ⟦ML < Gr *scholion* < *scholē*: see SCHOOL[1]⟧ a marginal note or commentary, esp. on the text of a Greek or Latin writer

Schön·berg (shurn′bərg, shōn′-; *Ger* shön′berk′), **Arnold** 1874-1951; U.S. composer, born in Austria: also sp. **Schoen′berg**

school[1] (sko͞ol) ***n.*** ⟦ME *scole* < OE *scol* < L *schola*, school < Gr *scholē*, leisure, that in which leisure is employed, discussion, philosophy, school < IE base **seĝh-*, to hold fast, overcome > SCHEME⟧ **1** a place or institution for teaching and learning; establishment for education; specif., *a)* an institution for teaching children *b)* a place for training and instruction in some special field, skill, etc. *[a dancing school]* ☆*c)* a college or university *d)* [**S-**] in the Middle Ages, a seminary of logic, metaphysics, and theology **2** the building or buildings, classrooms, laboratories, etc. of any such establishment **3** all the students, or pupils, and teachers at any such establishment **4** the period of instruction at any such establishment; regular session of teaching *[the date when school begins]* **5** *a)* attendance at a school *[to miss school for a week]* *b)* the process of formal training and instruction at a school; formal education; schooling **6** any situation, set of circumstances, or experience through which one gains knowledge, training, or discipline *[the school of hard knocks]* **7** a particular division of an institution of learning, esp. of a university *[the school of law]* **8** *a)* a group of people held together by the same teachings, beliefs, opinions, methods, etc.; followers or disciples of a particular teacher, leader, or creed *[the Impressionist school]* *b)* a group of artists associated with a specified place *[the Barbizon School]* **9** a way of life; style of customs, manners, etc. *[a gentleman of the old school]* —***vt.*** **1** to train, as at school; teach; instruct; educate **2** to discipline or control *[schooled herself in composure]* **3** [Archaic] to reprimand —***adj.*** **1** of a school or schools **2** [Obs.] of the Schoolmen (see SCHOOLMAN, sense 1) —***SYN.*** TEACH

school[2] (sko͞ol) ***n.*** ⟦Du, a crowd, school of fish: see SHOAL[1]⟧ a large number of fish or water animals of the same kind swimming or feeding together —***vi.*** to move together in a school, as fish, whales, etc.

school age **1** the age at which a child may or must begin to attend school **2** the years during which attendance at school is required or customary —**school′-age′** ***adj.***

school board a local board of education in charge of a public or private school or school system

school·book (sko͞ol′bo͝ok′) ***n.*** a book used for study in schools; textbook

school·boy (sko͞ol′boi′) ***n.*** a boy attending school

☆**school bus** a vehicle, owned and operated publicly or privately, used for transporting students to or from a school or on school-related trips

school·child (sko͞ol′chīld′) ***n.***, *pl.* **-chil′dren** (-chil′drən) a child attending school

School·craft (sko͞ol′kraft′), **Henry Rowe** (rō) 1793-1864; U.S. ethnologist

school (crossing) guard a person, either an adult or an older student, whose duty it is to help children cross streets near schools safely

school day **1** any day on which school is in session **2** the portion of any such day during which school is in session

☆**school district** a geographical division, with specified limits, whose school or schools are administered by a local board of education

school·fel·low (sko͞ol′fel′ō) ***n.*** SCHOOLMATE

school·girl (sko͞ol′gurl′) ***n.*** a girl attending school

school·house (sko͞ol′hous′) ***n.*** a building used as a school

school·ing (sko͞ol′iŋ) ***n.*** **1** training or education; esp., formal instruction at school **2** cost of instruction and living at school **3** [Archaic] disciplinary correction

school·man (sko͞ol′mən; *for 2, often*, -man′) ***n.***, *pl.* **-men** (-mən; *for 2, often*, -men′) **1** [*often* **S-**] any of the medieval university teachers of philosophy, logic, and theology; scholastic **2** a teacher, educator, or scholar

☆**school·marm** (sko͞ol′märm′, -mäm′) ***n.*** **1** [Old-fashioned] a woman schoolteacher **2** [Informal] any person whose attitudes and behavior resemble those often attributed to schoolmarms, as pedantry, priggishness, or prudishness —**school′marm′ish** ***adj.***

school·mas·ter (sko͞ol′mas′tər, -mäs′-) ***n.*** **1** [Old-fashioned] a man who teaches in a school **2** [Chiefly Brit.] a headmaster or master in a school **3** a person or thing that disciplines or instructs **4** a reddish-brown and orange snapper (*Lutjanus apodus*) with large scales, found in warm Atlantic waters

school·mate (-māt′) ***n.*** a companion or acquaintance at school

school·mis·tress (-mis′tris) ***n.*** [Old-fashioned] a woman who teaches in a school

school night the evening or night before a regular school day [students should go to bed earlier on *school nights*]

school·room (-ro͞om′) ***n.*** a room in which pupils are taught, as in a school

☆**school system** all the schools and support services under the jurisdiction of a board of education

school·teach·er (-tē′chər) ***n.*** a person whose work is teaching in a school

school tie OLD SCHOOL TIE

school·work (-wurk′) ***n.*** lessons worked on in classes at school or done as homework

school·yard (-yärd′) ***n.*** the ground around or near a school, used as a playground, playing field, etc.

school year the part of a year when school is in session, usually from September to June

☆**schoon·er** (sko͞o′nər) ***n.*** ⟦< ? Scot dial. *scun,* to skip a flat stone across water⟧ **1** a sailing vessel with two or more masts, rigged fore and aft **2** *short for* PRAIRIE SCHOONER **3** a large beer glass, usually holding a pint

Scho·pen·hau·er (shō′pən hou′ər), **Arthur** 1788-1860; Ger. pessimist philosopher —**Scho′pen·hau′er·ism′** ***n.***

schorl (shôrl) ***n.*** ⟦Ger *schörl*⟧ a black variety of tourmaline

schot·tische (shät′ish) ***n.*** ⟦< Ger *(der) schottische (tanz),* (the) Scottish (dance) < *Schotte* < OHG *Scotto* < LL *Scottus,* SCOT[1]⟧ **1** a form of round dance in 2/4 time, similar to the polka, but with a slower tempo **2** music for this —***vi.*** **-tisched, -tisch·ing** to dance a schottische

schrod (skräd) ***n.*** *alt. sp. of* SCROD

Schrö·ding·er (shrö′diŋ ər), **Er·win** (er′vēn) 1887-1961; Austrian physicist

☆**schtick** or **schtik** (shtik) ***n.*** *alt. sp. of* SHTICK

Schu·bert (sho͞o′bərt; *Ger* sho͞o′bert), **Franz (Peter)** (fränts) 1797-1828; Austrian composer

schul (sho͞ol) ***n.*** *alt. sp. of* SHUL

Schulz (sho͝olts), **Charles M(onroe)** 1922-2000; U.S. comic strip artist

Schu·mann (sho͞o′män), **Robert (Alexander)** 1810-56; Ger. composer

Schum·pe·ter (sho͝om′pā tər), **Joseph A(lois)** 1883-1950; U.S. economist, born in Austria

Schurz (sho͝orts), **Carl** 1829-1906; U.S. statesman, journalist, & Union general, born in Germany

schuss (sho͝os) ***n.*** ⟦Ger, lit., shot, rush: see SHOT[1]⟧ a straight run down a hill in skiing —***vi.*** to ski straight down a slope at full speed —**schuss′er** ***n.***

☆**schuss·boom·er** (sho͝os′bo͞om′ər) ***n.*** ⟦prec. + E *boom,* echoic of the sound of a sudden stop made by an expert skier + -ER⟧ a skier, esp. one who schusses expertly

Schütz (shüts), **Hein·rich** (hīn′riH) 1585-1672; Ger. composer

Schuy·ler (skī′lər), **Philip John** 1733-1804; Am. Revolutionary general & statesman

Schuy·ler·ville (skī′lər vil′) ⟦after prec.⟧ resort village in E N.Y., on the Hudson: cf. SARATOGA

Schuyl·kill (sko͝ok′əl; sko͞ol′kəl, -kil′) ⟦< Du *Schuilkil,* lit., hidden channel < *schuilen,* to hide, skulk + *kil,* stream, KILL[2]⟧ river in SE Pa., flowing southeast into the Delaware River at Philadelphia: 130 mi (209 km)

☆**schvart·ze** or **schwart·ze** (shvärt′sə) ***n.*** ⟦via Yiddish < Ger *schwarz,* black⟧ [Slang] a black person: a derogatory or contemptuous term

schwa (shwä, shvä) ***n.*** ⟦Ger < Heb *sheva,* a diacritic marking silence instead of a vowel sound⟧ **1** the neutral mid-central vowel sound of most unstressed syllables in English: the sound represented by *a* in *ago, e* in *agent, i* in *sanity,* etc. **2** the symbol (ə) for this sound, as in the International Phonetic Alphabet and this dictionary

Schwa·ben (shvä′bən) *Ger. name for* SWABIA

☆**schwag** (shwag) ***n.*** ⟦< SWAG (*n.* 3), ? infl. by Yiddish words such as *schnozzle*⟧ [Slang] **1** SWAG (*n.* 3*b*) **2** marijuana of inferior quality

Schwann cell (shwän) ⟦after T. *Schwann* (1810-82), Ger physiologist⟧ any of the cells covering the myelin sheath that surrounds and insulates an axon of a nerve cell: see also NODE OF RANVIER

Schwarz·wald (shvärts′vält′) *Ger. name for* the BLACK FOREST

Schweit·zer (shwīt′sər, shvīt′-), **Albert** 1875-1965; Alsatian medical missionary, theologian, & musicologist in Africa

Schweiz (shvīts) *Ger. name for* SWITZERLAND

Schwe·rin (shver′in; *Ger* shvā rēn′) city in N Germany: capital of the state of Mecklenburg-Western Pomerania

Schwyz (shvēts) canton of EC Switzerland, on Lake Lucerne: 351 sq mi (909 sq km)

sci *abbrev.* **1** science **2** scientific

sci·ae·nid (sī ē′nid) ***n.*** ⟦< ModL *Sciaena* (< L, a kind of fish < Gr *skiaina,* a dark-colored fish < *skia*: see fol.) + -ID⟧ DRUM[1] (*n.* 4) —**sci·ae′noid** (-noid) ***adj., n.***

sci·am·a·chy (sī am′ə kē) ***n., pl.*** **-chies** ⟦Gr *skiamachia* < *skia,* shadow (see SHINE) + *machein,* to fight (see -MACHY)⟧ a fighting with shadows or imaginary enemies

sci·at·ic (sī at′ik) ***adj.*** ⟦MFr *sciatique* < ML *sciaticus,* altered < L *ischiadicus* < Gr *ischiadikos* < *ischion,* the ISCHIUM⟧ of, in the region of, or affecting the hip or its nerves

sci·at·i·ca (sī at′i kə) ***n.*** ⟦ME < ML < *sciaticus*: see prec.⟧ any painful condition in the region of the hip and thigh; esp., neuritis of the long nerve (**sciatic nerve**) passing down the back of the thigh

sci·ence (sī′əns) ***n.*** ⟦OFr < L *scientia* < *sciens,* prp. of *scire,* to know, orig., to discern, distinguish < IE base **skei-,* to cut, separate > SHEATH, SHIN[1], SHIP, SKI, L *scindere,* to cut⟧ **1** [Archaic] the state or fact of knowledge; knowledge **2** systematized knowledge derived from observation, study, and experimentation carried on in order to determine the nature or principles of what is being studied **3** any specific branch of scientific knowledge, esp. one concerned with establishing and systematizing facts, principles, and methods, as by experiments and hypotheses [the *science* of mathematics] **4** *a)* the systematized knowledge of nature and the physical world *b)* any branch of this: see NATURAL SCIENCE **5** skill based upon systematized training [the *science* of cooking] ☆**6** [**S-**] *short for* CHRISTIAN SCIENCE

science fiction fiction of a highly imaginative or fantastic kind, typically involving some actual or projected scientific phenomenon

sci·en·tial (sī en′shəl) ***adj.*** **1** of or producing science, or knowledge **2** having knowledge

sci·en·tif·ic (sī′ən tif′ik) ***adj.*** ⟦ML *scientificus,* learned, lit., making knowledge (see SCIENCE & -FIC), orig. erroneous transl. of Gr *epistēmonikos,* pertaining to knowledge⟧ **1** of or dealing with science [*scientific* study] **2** used in or for natural science [*scientific* apparatus] **3** based on, using, or in accordance with, the principles and methods of science; systematic and exact [*scientific* classification] **4** *a)* done according to methods gained by systematic training [*scientific* boxing] *b)* having or showing such training —**sci′en·tif′i·cal·ly** ***adv.***

scientific method a method of research in which a hypothesis is tested by means of a carefully documented control experiment that can be repeated by any other researcher

scientific notation a mathematical expression used to represent any decimal number as a number between one and ten raised to a specific power of ten (Ex.: 4.1×10^0 for 4.1, 4.1×10^1 for 41, 4.1×10^2 for 410, 4.1×10^{-1} for 0.41, 4.1×10^{-2} for 0.041): often used for approximate computations with very large or small numbers

sci·en·tism (sī′ən tiz′əm) ***n.*** **1** the techniques, beliefs, or attitudes characteristic of scientists **2** the principle that scientific methods can and should be applied in all fields of investigation: often a disparaging usage —**sci′en·tis′tic** ***adj.***

sci·en·tist (sī′ən tist) ***n.*** **1** a specialist in science; esp., a person whose profession is investigating in one of the natural sciences, as biology, chemistry, physics, etc. ☆**2** [**S-**] *short for* CHRISTIAN SCIENTIST

☆**sci fi** (sī′ fī′) [Informal] *short for* SCIENCE FICTION: also written **sci-fi** ***n.*** —**sci′-fi′** ***adj.***

scil. *abbrev.* scilicet

scil·i·cet (sil′i set′) ⟦ME < L, contr. of *scire licet,* it is permitted to know: see SCIENCE & LICENSE⟧ ***adv.*** namely; to wit; that is to say

scil·la (sil′ə) ***n.*** ⟦ModL < L, SQUILL⟧ any of a genus (*Scilla*) of low, bulbous, perennial plants of the lily family, grown for their blue, pink, or white bell-shaped flowers

Scil·ly Isles (*or* Islands) (sil′ē) group of about 140 islets off Cornwall, England: *c.* 6 sq mi (16 sq km): also called **Isles of Scilly**

scim·i·tar (sim′ə tər, -tär′) ***n.*** ⟦It *scimitarra* < Pers *shimshir*⟧ any of various short, curved swords with an edge on the convex side, as used historically in the Near East

scin·coid (siŋ′koid′) ***adj.*** ⟦ModL *scincoides* < L *scincus*: see SKINK & -OID⟧ of or like the skinks —***n.*** a scincoid lizard

☆**scin·ti·gram** (sin′tə gram′) ***n.*** ⟦SCINTI(LLATION) + -GRAM⟧ a record made by scintigraphy

☆**scin·tig·ra·phy** (sin tig′rə fē) ***n.*** ⟦SCINTI(LLATION) + -GRAPHY⟧ a technique for recording with the aid of a scintiscanner the distribution of a radioactive tracer substance in bodily tissue

scin·til·la (sin til′ə) ***n.*** ⟦L⟧ **1** a spark **2** a particle; the least trace: used only fig.

scin·til·late (sint′'l āt′) ***vi.*** **-lat′ed, -lat′ing** ⟦< L *scintillatus,* pp. of *scintillare,* to sparkle < *scintilla,* a spark⟧ **1** to give off sparks; flash; sparkle **2** to sparkle intellectually; be brilliant and witty **3** to twinkle, as a star —***vt.*** to give off (sparks, flashes, etc.) —**scin′til·lant** ***adj.***

scin·til·la·tion (sint′'l ā′shən) ***n.*** ⟦L *scintillatio*⟧ **1** the act of scintillating; sparkling **2** a spark; flash **3** *Astron.* the twinkling of the stars caused by density changes in the atmosphere **4** *Nuclear Physics* the flash of light made by ionizing radiation upon striking a crystal detector or a phosphor

scintillation counter an instrument for detecting and measuring the scintillations induced by ionizing radiation in a crystal or phosphor

scin·til·la·tor (sint′'l āt′ər) ***n.*** **1** a person or thing that scintillates **2** *Physics* a crystal or phosphor capable of emitting scintillations

scin·til·lom·e·ter (sint′'l äm′ət ər) ***n.*** ⟦< L *scintilla,* a spark + -METER⟧ SCINTILLATION COUNTER

☆**scin·ti·scan·ner** (sin′tə skan′ər) ***n.*** ⟦SCINTI(LLATION) + SCANNER⟧ a type of scintillation counter used to locate and make a record (**scin′ti·scan′**) of radioactive substances

sci·o·lism (sī′ə liz′əm) ***n.*** ⟦< L *sciolus,* smatterer, dim. of *scius,* knowing < *scire,* to know: see SCIENCE⟧ superficial knowledge or learning —**sci′o·list** ***n.*** —**sci′o·lis′tic** ***adj.***

sci·on (sī′ən) ***n.*** ⟦ME *sioun, ciun* < OFr *cion,* earlier *chion* < Gmc **kijan-,* to sprout < IE base *ĝei-, ĝī- > OHG *chīnan*, to sprout, OE *kith*, sprig⟧ **1** a shoot or bud of a plant, esp. one for planting or grafting **2** a descendant; offspring

Scip·i·o (sip′ē ō, skip′-) **1** (*Publius Cornelius Scipio Africanus*) 237?-183? B.C.; Rom. general: defeated Hannibal (202) in the 2d Punic War: called *Major* or *the Elder* **2** (*Publius Cornelius Scipio Aemilianus Africanus Numantinus*) 185?-129? B.C.; Rom. general & statesman: destroyed Carthage (146): grandson (through adoption) of Scipio the Elder: called *Minor* or *the Younger*

sci·re fa·ci·as (sī′rē fā′shē as′) ⟦ME < L, that you cause to know⟧ *Law* **1** a writ, founded on a record, requiring the person against whom it is issued to appear and show cause why the record should not be enforced or annulled **2** a proceeding begun by issuing such a writ

scir·rhous (skir′əs, sir′-) *adj.* ⟦ModL *scirrhosus* < fol.⟧ of, or having the nature of, a scirrhus; hard and fibrous

scir·rhus (skir′əs, sir′-) *n., pl.* **-rhi′** (-ī′) or **-rhus·es** ⟦ModL < L *scirros* < Gr *skirrhos*, hardened swelling, tumor < *skiros*, hard⟧ a hard, cancerous tumor made up of much fibrous connective tissue —**scir′rhoid′** (-oid′) *adj.*

scis·sile (sis′il, -īl′) *adj.* ⟦L *scissilis* < *scissus*, pp. of *scindere*, to cut: see fol.⟧ that can be cut or split smoothly and easily, as into plates or laminae

scis·sion (sizh′ən, sish′-) *n.* ⟦Fr < LL *scissio* < L *scissus*, pp. of *scindere*, to cut < IE base *skei- > SCIENCE⟧ the act of cutting, dividing, or splitting, or the state of being cut, divided, or split; separation; fission

scis·sor (siz′ər) *vt.* ⟦< fol.⟧ to cut, cut off, or cut out with scissors —*n.* SCISSORS, esp. in attributive use

scis·sors (siz′ərz) *pl.n.* ⟦ME *sisoures* < OFr *cisoires* < LL *cisoria*, pl. of *cisorium*, cutting tool < L *caedere*, to cut: E sp. altered by assoc. with L *scissor*, one who cuts < *scissus*, pp. of *scindere*, to cut⟧ [*sometimes with sing. v.*] a cutting instrument with two opposing blades, each having a looped handle, which are pivoted together in the middle so that they work against each other as the instrument is closed on the paper, cloth, etc. to be cut: also called **pair of scissors** *sing.* —*n.* **1** a gymnastic feat or exercise in which the legs are moved in a way suggestive of the opening and closing of scissor blades **2** SCISSORS HOLD

scissors-and-paste (siz′ərz and pāst′) *adj.* [Informal] designating or of a piece of writing that has been assembled from a variety of sources rather than by original research, often in a hasty or uninspired way

scissors hold a wrestling hold in which one contestant clasps the other with the legs

scissors kick *Swimming* a kick, used esp. in the sidestroke, in which the motion of the legs is similar to the opening and closing of scissor blades

☆**scis·sor·tail** (siz′ər tāl′) *n.* a pale gray-and-pink tyrant flycatcher (*Muscivora forficata*) found in the S U.S. and Mexico, having a forked tail

sci·u·rid (sī yoor′id) *n.* ⟦< L *sciurus*, SQUIRREL + -ID⟧ any of a family (Sciuridae) of rodents including the squirrels, chipmunks, and marmots —**sci·u′roid′** *adj.*

sclaff (sklaf, skläf) *Golf vi.* ⟦< Scot *sclaf*, to shuffle: of echoic orig.⟧ to strike or scrape the ground before hitting the ball —*vt.* **1** to scrape (a club) along (the ground) before hitting the ball **2** to hit (the ball) in this way —*n.* a sclaffing stroke

SCLC *abbrev.* Southern Christian Leadership Conference

scler- (sklir, skler) *combining form* SCLERO-: used before a vowel

scle·ra (sklir′ə) *n., pl.* **-ras** or **-rae** ⟦ModL < Gr *sklēros*, hard < IE base *(s)kel-, to dry out > SHALLOW⟧ the tough, fibrous, white membrane covering all of the eyeball except the area covered by the cornea —**scle′ral** *adj.*

scle·ren·chy·ma (skli reŋ′kə mə) *n.* ⟦ModL < Gr *sklēros* (see prec.) + *enchyma*, infusion: see PARENCHYMA⟧ *Bot.* plant tissue of uniformly thick-walled, dead cells, as in a stem, the shell of a nut, etc. —**scle·ren·chym·a·tous** (sklir′eŋ kim′ə təs) *adj.*

scle·rite (sklir′īt′) *n.* ⟦SCLER(O)- + -ITE¹⟧ any of the hard plates forming the exoskeleton of arthropods

scle·ri·tis (skli rīt′is) *n.* ⟦< fol. + -ITIS⟧ inflammation of the sclera

scle·ro- (sklir′ō, skler′-; -ə) ⟦< Gr *sklēros*, hard: see SCLERA⟧ *combining form* **1** hard [*sclerometer*] **2** sclera [*scleritis*]

scler·o·der·ma (sklir′ə dur′mə, skler′-) *n.* ⟦ModL: see prec. & DERMA¹⟧ **1** hardening and thickening of the skin due to abnormal fibrous tissue growth **2** a disease in which this condition occurs

scler·o·der·ma·tous (-dur′mə təs) *adj. Zool.* covered with a hard outer tissue, as of horny scales or plates

scler·oid (sklir′oid′) *adj.* ⟦SCLER(O)- + -OID⟧ *Biol.* hard or hardened

scle·ro·ma (skli rō′mə) *n., pl.* **-ma·ta** (-mə tə) ⟦ModL < Gr *sklērōma*: see SCLERA & -OMA⟧ a hardening of bodily tissues; tumorlike induration

scle·rom·e·ter (-räm′ət ər) *n.* ⟦SCLERO- + -METER⟧ an instrument for measuring the relative hardness of a substance by determining the pressure needed to cause a diamond point to scratch its polished surface

scle·ro·pro·tein (sklir′ə prō′tēn′, skler′-; -prōt′ē in) *n.* any of a class of fibrous animal proteins insoluble in water, including the keratins and collagens

scle·rosed (skli rōst′, sklir′ōzd′) *adj.* hardened, or indurated, as by sclerosis

scle·ro·sis (skli rō′sis) *n., pl.* **-ses** (-sēz′) ⟦ME *sclirosis* < ML < Gr *sklērōsis*, a hardening < *sklēros*, hard: see SCLERA⟧ **1** *Bot.* a hardening of the cell wall of a plant, usually by an increase of lignin **2** *Med.* *a)* an abnormal hardening of body tissues or parts, esp. of the nervous system or the walls of arteries *b)* a disease characterized by this

scle·rot·ic (skli rät′ik) *adj.* ⟦ModL *scleroticus* < Gr *sklērotēs*, hardness: see SCLERA⟧ **1** hard; sclerosed **2** of, characterized by, or having sclerosis **3** of the sclera

scle·ro·ti·um (skli rō′shē əm) *n., pl.* **-ti·a** (-shē ə) ⟦ModL < Gr *sklēros*, hard: see SCLERA⟧ in various fungi, a hardened, black or reddish-brown mass of threads in which food material is stored and which is capable of remaining dormant for long periods —**scle·ro′tial** (-shəl) *adj.*

scle·rot·o·my (skli rät′ə mē) *n., pl.* **-mies** ⟦SCLERO- + -TOMY⟧ surgical incision into the sclera

scle·rous (sklir′əs) *adj.* ⟦< Gr *sklēros*, hard (see SCLERA) + -OUS⟧ **1** hard **2** bony

ScM or **Sc.M.** *abbrev.* ⟦L *Scientiae Magister*⟧ Master of Science

scoff¹ (skäf, skôf) *n.* ⟦ME *scof*, prob. < Scand: akin to OE *scop*, singer, OHG *skof*, poem, ridicule: for IE base see SHOVE⟧ **1** an expression of mocking contempt, scorn, or derision; jeer **2** an object of mocking contempt, scorn, etc. —*vt.* to mock at or deride —*vi.* to show mocking contempt, scorn, or derision, esp. by language; jeer: often with *at* —**scoff′er** *n.* —**scoff′ing·ly** *adv.*

scoff² (skäf, skôf; *Brit* skäf) *n.* ⟦< dial. *scaff* < ?⟧ [Slang, Chiefly Brit.] food or rations — *vt., vi.* [Slang] **1** to eat or devour **2** to plunder or seize

☆**scoff·law** (skäf′lô′) *n.* ⟦SCOFF¹ + LAW⟧ [Informal] a habitual or flagrant violator of laws, esp. traffic or liquor laws

scold (skōld) *n.* ⟦ME *scolde* < ON *skald*, poet (prob. of satirical verses)⟧ a person, esp. a woman, who habitually uses abusive language —*vt.* ⟦ME *scolden* < the n.⟧ to find fault with angrily; rebuke or chide severely —*vi.* **1** to find fault angrily **2** to use abusive language habitually —**scold′er** *n.* —**scold′ing** *adj., n.*

SYN.—**scold** is the common term meaning to find fault with or rebuke in angry, irritated, often nagging language [a mother *scolds* a naughty child]; **upbraid** implies bitter reproach or censure and usually connotes justification for this [she *upbraided* me for my carelessness]; **berate** suggests continuous, heated, even violent reproach, often connoting excessive abuse [the old shrew continued *berating* them]; **revile** implies the use of highly abusive and contemptuous language and often connotes deliberate defamation or slander [he *reviled* his opponent unmercifully]; **vituperate** suggests even greater violence in the attack [*vituperating* each other with foul epithets]

---

scol·e·cite (skäl′ə sīt′, skōl′-) *n.* ⟦Ger *scolezit* < Gr *skōlēx*, worm (see fol.): some forms curl when heated⟧ a colorless or white, monoclinic zeolite, $CaAl_2Si_3O_{10}{\cdot}3H_2O$, found in cavities or cracks, esp. in basalt, schist, or limestone; hydrous calcium aluminum silicate

sco·lex (skō′leks′) *n., pl.* **sco·le·ces** (skə lē′sēz′) or **sco·li·ces** (skōl′ə sēz′, skäl′-) ⟦ModL < Gr *skōlēx*, grub, worm < IE base *(s)kel-, to bend, twist > L *coluber*, serpent⟧ the head of a tapeworm, provided with hooks or suckers and acting as a holdfast in the intestine of a host

sco·li·o·sis (skō′lē ō′sis, skä′-) *n.* ⟦ModL < Gr *skoliōsis*, crookedness < *skolios*, crooked, akin to prec.⟧ lateral curvature of the spine —**sco′li·ot′ic** (-ät′ik) *adj.*

scol·lop (skäl′əp) *n., vt. var. of* SCALLOP

scom·broid (skäm′broid′) *adj.* ⟦< ModL *Scombridae* < L *scomber*, mackerel (< Gr *skombros*) + -OID⟧ **1** of a widely distributed family (Scombridae) of spiny-finned percoid food fishes, including the mackerels, bonitos, and tunas **2** like a mackerel —*n.* a fish of this family

sconce¹ (skäns) *n.* ⟦ME *sconse*, aphetic < OFr *esconse*, dark lantern < pp. of *escondre*, to hide < L *abscondere*: see ABSCOND⟧ a bracket attached to a wall for holding a candle, candles, or the like

sconce² (skäns) *n.* ⟦Du *schans*, fortress, orig., wickerwork, wicker basket < Ger *schanze* < It *scanso*, defense < *scansare*, to avoid < VL *excampsare < *ex-*, away + *campsare, to sail around < Gr *kampsai*, aorist of *kamptein*, to bend; akin to L *campus*: see CAMPUS⟧ **1** a small fort, bulwark, etc. **2** [Archaic] *a)* a hut, shed, or other shelter *b)* a helmet or the like *c)* the head or skull; also, brains; good sense —*vt.* **sconced**, **sconc′ing** [Obs.] **1** to provide with a SCONCE² (sense 1) **2** to shelter or protect

sconce³ (skäns) *vt.* **sconced**, **sconc′ing** ⟦< ?⟧ to fine; esp., at Oxford University, to fine lightly for a breach of manners —*n.* such a fine

scone (skōn, skän) *n.* ⟦Scot, contr. < ? MDu *schoonbrot*, fine bread < *schoon* (akin to Ger *schön*, OE *sciene*: see SHEEN), beautiful + *brot*, BREAD⟧ a kind of sweet BISCUIT (sense 2) made with baking powder, eggs, fruit, nuts, etc., orig. baked on a griddle, and served with butter

Scone (sko͞on, skōn) village in E Scotland northeast of Perth: site of an abbey that contained the stone (**Stone of Scone**) on which Scottish kings before 1296 were crowned: removed by Edward I and placed under the coronation chair at Westminster Abbey, the stone was returned to Scotland in 1996

☆**scooch** (sko͞och) *vi.* [Informal] **1** to hunch or draw oneself up and move (*through, down,* etc.); scrunch [she *scooched* through the window and unlocked the door; he *scooched* down in his chair] **2** to slide as with short, jerky movements, esp. while seated [*scooch* over and make room for me on the bench]

scoop (sko͞op) *n.* ⟦ME *scope* < MDu *schope*, bailing vessel, *schoppe*, a shovel, akin to Ger *schöpfen*, to dip out, create⟧ **1** any of various utensils shaped like a small shovel or a ladle; specif., *a)* a kitchen utensil used to take up sugar, flour, etc. *b)* a small utensil with a round bowl, for dishing up ice cream, mashed potatoes, etc. *c)* a small, spoonlike surgical instrument **2** the deep shovel of a dredge or power shovel, which takes up sand, dirt, etc. **3** the act or motion of taking up with or as with a scoop **4** the amount taken up at one time by a scoop **5** a hollowed-out place ☆**6** [Informal] *a)* the publication or broadcast of a news item before a competitor; beat *b)* such a news item *c)* current, esp. confidential, information —***adj.*** designating a rounded, somewhat low neckline in a dress, etc. —***vt.*** **1** to take up or out with or as with a scoop **2** to empty by bailing **3** to dig (*out*); hollow (*out*) **4** to make by digging out **5** to gather (*in* or *up*) as if with a scoop ☆**6** [Informal] to publish or broadcast a news item before (a competitor) —**scoop′er** ***n.***

scoop·ful (sko͞op′fo͝ol′) ***n.***, *pl.* **-fuls′** as much as a scoop will hold

scoot (sko͞ot) [Informal] ***vi.*** ⟦prob. via dial. < ON *skjōta*, to SHOOT[1]⟧ **1** to go or move quickly; hurry (off); dart **2** to slide as with short, jerky movements, esp. while seated: often with *over* [*scoot* over and make room for me on the bench] —***vt.*** to move or slide (something) quickly: often with *over* —***n.*** the act of scooting

☆**scootch** (sko͞och) ***vi.*** [Informal] *alt. sp. of* SCOOCH

scoot·er (sko͞ot′ər) ***n.*** ⟦< SCOOT⟧ **1** a child's toy for riding on, consisting of a low, narrow footboard with a wheel or wheels at each end, and a raised handlebar for steering: it is moved by a series of pushes made by one foot against the ground **2** *short for* MOTOR SCOOTER ☆**3** a sailboat with runners, for use on water or ice

scop (shôp, skäp) ***n.*** ⟦OE, poet, minstrel, lit., maker of taunting verses: see SCOFF[1]⟧ an Old English poet or bard

scope (skōp) ***n.*** ⟦It *scopo* < L *scopus*, goal, target < Gr *skopos*, a mark, spy, watcher < base of *skopein*, to see, altered by metathesis < IE base **spek-*, to peer, look carefully > SPY, L *specere*, to see⟧ **1** the extent of the mind's grasp; range of perception or understanding [a problem beyond his *scope*] **2** the range or extent of action, inquiry, etc., or of an activity, concept, etc. [the *scope* of a book] **3** room or opportunity for freedom of action or thought; free play **4** *short for* TELESCOPE, MICROSCOPE, RADARSCOPE, etc. **5** *Naut.* the length of chain attaching a vessel to an anchor or mooring buoy **6** [Now Rare] end; purpose —***vt.*** **scoped, scop′ing 1** [Slang] to look at or look into carefully; scrutinize; investigate; examine closely: often with *out* **2** [Informal] to perform arthroscopic surgery on —***SYN.*** RANGE

-scope (skōp) ⟦LL *-scopium* < Gr *-skopion* < *skopein*: see prec.⟧ *combining form forming nouns* an instrument, etc. for seeing or observing [*telescope, retinoscope, kaleidoscope*]

sco·pol·a·mine (skō päl′ə mēn′, -min) ***n.*** ⟦Ger *scopolamin* < ModL *Scopolia*, genus of plants in which the alkaloid appears (after G. A. *Scopoli* (1723-88), of Pavia, Italy) + Ger *amin*, AMINE⟧ an alkaloid, $C_{17}H_{21}NO_4$, obtained from various plants of the nightshade family, as belladonna, and used in medicine as a sedative or hypnotic, and sometimes with morphine to relieve pain

scop·u·la (skäp′yoo lə) ***n.***, *pl.* **-las** or **-lae′** (-lē′) ⟦ModL < L, broom twig, dim. of *scopa*, thin branch, shoot, akin to *scapus*, stalk: see SHAFT⟧ *Zool.* a brushlike tuft of hairs —**scop′u·late** (-lit) ***adj.***

-sco·py (skə pē) ⟦Gr *-skopia* < *skopein*: see SCOPE⟧ *combining form forming nouns* examination; observation [*bioscopy*]

scor·bu·tic (skôr byo͞ot′ik) ***adj.*** ⟦ModL *scorbuticus* < ML *scorbutus*, scurvy < ?⟧ of, like, or having scurvy: also **scor·bu′ti·cal**

scorch (skôrch) ***vt.*** ⟦ME *scorchen* < ? Scand, as in ON *scorpna*, to shrivel (< IE **(s)kerb(h)-*: see SHARP): sp. prob. infl. by OFr *escorcher*, to flay⟧ **1** *a)* to char, discolor, or damage the surface of by superficial burning *b)* to parch, shrivel, or spoil by too intense heat; wither **2** to make a caustic attack on; assail scathingly; excoriate **3** to burn and destroy everything in (an area) before yielding it to the enemy —***vi.*** **1** to become scorched **2** [Old Slang] to ride or drive at high speed —***n.*** **1** a superficial burning or burn **2** the browning and death of plant leaves or fruits, caused by too much heat, by fungi, etc. —***SYN.*** BURN[1]

scorched-earth (skôrcht′urth′) ***adj.*** ⟦apparently transl. < a Chin term for this practice⟧ having to do with a military strategy of burning or destroying everything in an area before yielding it to an enemy: often used fig.

scorch·er (skôr′chər) ***n.*** **1** anything that scorches **2** [Informal] *a)* a very hot day *b)* a withering remark

score (skôr) ***n.*** ⟦ME < OE *scoru* < ON *skor* < IE base **(s)ker-*, to cut > SHEAR⟧ **1** *a)* a scratch, mark, incision, etc. [*scores* made on ice by skates] *b)* a line drawn or scratched, often to mark a starting point, etc. *c)* notches made in wood, marks made as with chalk, etc., to keep tally or account **2** an amount or sum due; account; debt **3** a grievance or wrong one seeks to settle or get even for **4** anything offered as a reason or motive; ground [on the *score* of poverty] **5** the number of points made in a game or contest by a player or team, or the record of these points **6** *a)* a grade or rating, as on a test or examination *b)* a number indicative of quality, usually based on an arbitrary scale in which 100 means perfection in certain specified characteristics **7** *a)* twenty people or things; set of twenty *b)* [*pl.*] very many **8** [Informal] a successful move, stroke, remark, etc. ☆**9** [Informal] *a)* the way that life or a certain situation really is (chiefly in **know the score**) *b)* the pertinent facts; lowdown **10** [Slang] the victim of a swindle; mark **11** [Slang] the act of getting or stealing, as drugs **12** *Dancing* notation used to indicate dancers' movements, as in a ballet **13** *Music a)* a written or printed copy of a composition, showing all the parts for the instruments or voices *b)* the music for a stage production, film, etc., esp. as distinguished from the lyrics, dialogue, etc. —***vt.*** **scored, scor′ing** ⟦ME *scoren*⟧ **1** to mark with notches, scratches, cuts, lines, etc. **2** to crease or partly cut (cardboard, paper, etc.) for accurate folding or tearing **3** to cancel or mark *out* by lines drawn **4** to mark with lines or notches in keeping account **5** to keep account of by or as by lines or notches; reckon; tally; mark **6** *a)* to make (runs, hits, goals, etc.) in a game and so add to one's number of points *b)* to count toward the number of points [a touchdown *scores* 6] *c)* to record or enter the score of *d)* to record or add (points) to one's score ☆*e) Baseball* to bring (a runner) home as by getting a hit **7** to get by effort or merit; gain [to *score* a resounding success] **8** to grade (an examination, etc.); rate or evaluate, as in testing **9** to get (a specified grade) on a test **10** *a)* to raise welts on by lashing ☆*b)* to criticize severely; upbraid **11** [Slang] to get or steal (drugs, money, etc.) **12** *Cooking* to cut superficial gashes in (meat, etc.) **13** *Music, Dancing* to orchestrate, arrange, or write out in a score —***vi.*** **1** to make a point or points, as in a game **2** to keep the score, as of a game **3** to be rated by one's score on a test **4** *a)* to gain an advantage *b)* to win or enjoy credit, popularity, success, etc. **5** to make notches, lines, gashes, etc. **6** [Slang] to have sexual intercourse —**scor′er** ***n.***

score·board (skôr′bôrd′) ***n.*** ☆a large board for posting the score and other details of a game, as in a baseball stadium

☆**score card 1** a card for recording the score of a game, match, etc., as in golf **2** a card printed with the names, positions, etc. of the players of competing teams Also **score′card′** ***n.***

☆**score·keep·er** (-kēp′ər) ***n.*** a person keeping score, esp. officially, at a game, competition, etc.

score·less (-lis) ***adj.*** with no points having been scored

sco·ri·a (skôr′ē ə) ***n.***, *pl.* **-ri·ae′** (-ē′) ⟦ME < L < Gr *skōria*, refuse, dross < *skōr*, dung: see SCATO-⟧ **1** the slag or refuse left after metal has been smelted from ore **2** loose, cinderlike lava —**sco′ri·a′ceous** (-ā′shəs) ***adj.***

sco·ri·fy (skôr′ə fī′) ***vt.*** **-fied′**, **-fy′ing** to reduce to scoria, or slag —**sco′ri·fi·ca′tion** ***n.***

scorn (skôrn) ***n.*** ⟦ME < OFr *escharn* < *escharnir*, to scorn < Gmc base akin to OHG *skernon*, to mock, *scern*, a joke < IE base **(s)ker-*, to leap, jump about > Gr *skairein*, to jump, dance⟧ **1** extreme, often indignant, contempt for someone or something; utter disdain **2** expression of this in words or manner **3** the object of such contempt —***vt.*** **1** to regard with scorn; view or treat with contempt **2** to refuse or reject as wrong or disgraceful —***vi.*** [Obs.] to scoff —***SYN.*** DESPISE —**scorn′er** ***n.***

scorn·ful (skôrn′fəl) ***adj.*** filled with or showing scorn or contempt —**scorn′ful·ly** ***adv.*** —**scorn′ful·ness** ***n.***

scor·pae·nid (skôr pē′nid) ***n.*** ⟦< ModL *Scorpaenidae* < L *scorpaena*, kind of fish < Gr *skorpaina*, fem. of *skorpios*, spiny fish (see SCORPION) + -ID⟧ any of a family (Scorpaenidae, order Scorpaeniformes) of spiny-finned, marine bony fishes, including the scorpionfishes and the rockfishes —**scor·pae′noid** (-noid) ***adj., n.***

Scor·pi·o (skôr′pē ō′) ***n.*** ⟦L, SCORPION⟧ **1** *former name for* SCORPIUS **2** the eighth sign of the zodiac, entered by the sun about October 24 **3** a person born under this sign

scor·pi·oid (skôr′pē oid′) ***adj.*** ⟦Gr *skorpioeidēs*⟧ **1** like a scorpion **2** of the order consisting of the scorpions **3** with a curved end, like a scorpion's tail; circinate

scor·pi·on (skôr′pē ən) ***n.*** ⟦OFr < L *scorpio* < Gr *skorpios*, scorpion, kind of fish < IE base **(s)ker-*, to cut > SHEAR⟧ **1** any of an order (Scorpiones) of arachnids found in warm regions, with a front pair of nipping claws and a long, slender, jointed tail ending in a curved, poisonous sting **2** *Bible* a variety of whip or scourge —**the Scorpion** Scorpius, the constellation, or Scorpio, the eighth sign of the zodiac

scor·pi·on·fish (-fish′) ***n.***, *pl.* **-fish′** or **-fish′es** (see FISH) any of various small, marine scorpaenids (esp. genus *Scorpaena*) with poisonous spines in the dorsal, anal, and pelvic fins: often written **scorpion fish**

scorpion fly MECOPTERAN: the abdomen, in the male, curls up at the end and resembles a scorpion's sting

Scor·pi·us (skôr′pē əs) ***n.*** ⟦L, scorpion⟧ a S constellation in the Milky Way between Ophiuchus and Ara, containing the bright star Antares; the Scorpion

scot (skät) ***n.*** ⟦ME < ON *skot*, tribute, SHOT[1]⟧ money assessed or paid; tax; levy —**scot and lot 1** an old parish tax in Great Britain, assessed according to ability to pay **2** in full: in the phrase **pay scot and lot**

Scot[1] (skät) ***n.*** ⟦< ME *Scottes*, pl. < OE *Scottas* < LL *Scoti*, a people in N Britain, prob. < OIr *Scuit*, the Irish, pl. of *Scot*⟧ **1** a member of a Gaelic people of N Ireland that migrated to Scotland in the 5th cent. A.D. **2** a person born or living in Scotland: cf. SCOTSMAN, SCOTCHMAN

Scot[2] *abbrev.* **1** Scotch **2** Scotland **3** Scottish

scotch[1] (skäch) ***vt.*** ⟦ME *scocchen*, prob. < Anglo-Fr *escocher* < OFr *coche*, a notch, nick < VL **cocca*, knob at the end of a spindle (later, groove below this knob) < L *coccum*, berry < Gr *kokkos*⟧ **1** to cut; scratch; score; notch **2** ⟦< Theobald's emendation of *scorch* in Shakespeare's *Macbeth*, III, ii, 13⟧ to wound without killing; maim **3** to put an end to; stifle; stamp out [to *scotch* a rumor] —***n.*** a cut or scratch

scotch[2] (skäch) ***vt.*** ⟦earlier *scatch* < ? OFr *escachier*, to crush < *es-* (L *ex*) + VL **coacticare*: see CACHE⟧ to block (a wheel, log, etc.) with a wedge, block, etc. to prevent movement —***n.*** such a block, wedge, etc. used to prevent rolling, slipping, etc.

Scotch (skäch) ***adj.*** ⟦contr. < SCOTTISH⟧ of Scotland or its people, language, or culture; Scottish —***n.*** **1** SCOTTISH **2** [*often* **s-**] whiskey, often having a smoky flavor, distilled in Scotland from malted barley: in full **Scotch whisky** —**the Scotch** [Old-fashioned] the Scottish people

USAGE—See usage note at SCOTTISH

Scotch broth a broth of mutton and vegetables, thickened with barley

Scotch egg a British dish consisting of a hard-boiled egg encased in sausage meat, breaded, and fried

Scotch grain a coarse, pebble-grained finish given to heavy leather, esp. for men's shoes

☆**Scotch-I·rish** (-ī′rish) *adj.* of those people of N Ireland descended from Scottish settlers, esp. those who emigrated to America

Scotch·man (-mən) *n., pl.* **-men** (-mən) *var. of* SCOTSMAN

Scotch pine a hardy Eurasian pine (*Pinus sylvestris*), with yellow wood, cultivated for timber, Christmas trees, etc.

☆**Scotch tape** ⟦< *Scotch*, a trademark⟧ a thin, transparent cellulose adhesive tape

Scotch terrier SCOTTISH TERRIER

Scotch verdict a verdict in criminal cases of "not proved," rather than "not guilty": allowed notably in Scotland

Scotch woodcock eggs cooked and served on toast or crackers spread with anchovies or anchovy paste

sco·ter (skōt′ər) *n., pl.* **-ters** or **-ter** ⟦< ?⟧ any of several large, dark-colored sea ducks (genera *Oidemia* and *Melanitta*), found chiefly along the N coasts of Europe and North America

scot-free (skät′frē′) *adv., adj.* **1** free from payment of scot, or tax **2** without being punished or hurt; clear(ly); safe(ly)

sco·tia (skō′shə, -shē ə) *n.* ⟦L < Gr *skotia*, lit., darkness (from the shadow within the cavity) < *skotos*, darkness: see SHADE⟧ a deep concave molding, esp. at the base of a column

Sco·tia (skō′shə) ⟦LL⟧ *old poet. name for* SCOTLAND

Sco·tism (skōt′iz′əm) *n.* the scholastic philosophy of Duns Scotus and his followers —**Sco′tist** *adj., n.*

Scot·land (skät′lənd) division of the United Kingdom, occupying the N part of Great Britain & nearby islands: 30,418 sq mi (78,782 sq km); cap. Edinburgh

Scotland Yard ⟦so named because orig. the residence of the kings of Scotland when in London⟧ **1** short street in London, off Whitehall, orig. the site of police headquarters **2** headquarters of the metropolitan London police, on the Thames embankment since 1890: officially **New Scotland Yard** **3** the London police, esp. the detective bureau

sco·to·ma (skə tō′mə) *n., pl.* **-ma·ta** (-mə tə) or **-mas** ⟦ModL < LL, dimness of vision < Gr *skotōma* < *skotos*, darkness (see SHADE) + -OMA⟧ a dark area or gap in the visual field —**sco·tom′a·tous** (-täm′ə təs) *adj.*

sco·to·pi·a (skə tō′pē ə) *n.* ⟦ModL < Gr *skotos*, darkness (see SHADE) + -OPIA⟧ the normal visual perception or vision in dim light or twilight, or at night following dark adaptation, in which the light intensity fails to activate the retinal cones: cf. PHOTOPIA —**sco·to′pic** (-täp′ik) *adj.*

Scots (skäts) *adj., n.* ⟦ME (northern) *Scottis*, var. of *Scottissh*⟧ SCOTTISH

USAGE—See usage note at SCOTTISH

Scots Gaelic SCOTTISH GAELIC

Scots-Irish (skäts′ī′rish) *adj.* SCOTCH-IRISH

Scots·man (skäts′mən) *n., pl.* **-men** (-mən) a person born or living in Scotland, esp. a man: *Scotsman* or *Scot* is preferred to *Scotchman* in Scotland

Scots·wom·an (-woom′ən) *n., pl.* **-wom′en** (-wim′in) a woman born or living in Scotland

Scott[1] (skät) *n.* ⟦< the surname *Scott*, a Scottish person⟧ a masculine name: dim. *Scotty* —**great Scott!** [Old-fashioned] an exclamation of surprise or wonder

Scott[2] (skät) **1 Dred** (dred) 1795?-1858; U.S. black slave: his claim to be free as a result of living in free territory was denied in a controversial Supreme Court decision (1857) **2 Robert Fal·con** (fôl′kən) 1868-1912; Eng. naval officer & antarctic explorer **3** Sir **Walter** 1771-1832; Scot. poet & novelist **4 Win·field** (win′fēld′) 1786-1866; U.S. general

Scot·ti·cism (skät′ə siz′əm) *n.* a word, phrase, grammatical construction, or other feature originating in or peculiar to the English spoken in Scotland

Scot·tie (skät′ē) *n., pl.* **-ties** ⟦< fol. + -IE⟧ SCOTTISH TERRIER

Scot·tish (skät′ish) *adj.* ⟦ME *Scottissh* < Late OE *Scottisc*, for earlier *Scyttisc*⟧ of Scotland or its people, variety of English, or culture —*n.* the variety of English spoken by the people of Scotland —**the Scottish** the Scottish people

USAGE—*Scottish*, the original form, is preferred to *Scotch* and *Scots* in U.S. and British formal and literary usage with reference to the people, the country, etc., and in Scotland has replaced *Scotch*, the informal form prevailing in the U.S. and England; but with others, *Scotch* is almost invariably used (e.g., tweed, whisky), with others, *Scots* (e.g., law, mile)

Scottish deerhound any of a breed of tall, slender, swift hound resembling the greyhound but with a rough, wiry coat: orig. used in Scotland for hunting deer

Scottish fold any of a breed of domestic cat, originally bred in Scotland, with ears folded, or bent, forward, a coat of short, dense fur, and a stocky build

Scottish Gaelic GAELIC (*n.* 1)

Scottish rite a ceremonial system in Freemasonry

Scottish terrier any of a breed of terrier, originating in Scotland, with short legs, a squarish muzzle, a dense, wiry coat, and pointed, erect ears

Scotts·dale (skäts′dāl′) ⟦after Winfield *Scott* (1837-1910), early settler⟧ city in SC Ariz.: suburb of Phoenix

Scot·ty (skät′ē) *n., pl.* **-ties** *alt. sp. of* SCOTTIE

Scotus *see* DUNS SCOTUS, John

scoun·drel (skoun′drəl) *n.* ⟦prob. a disparaging dim. < Anglo-Fr *escoundre* (for OFr *escondre*), to abscond < VL **scondere*, aphetic for L *abscondere*, ABSCOND⟧ a mean, immoral, or wicked person; rascal —**scoun′drel·ly** *adj.*

scour[1] (skour) *vt.* ⟦ME *scouren* < MDu *scuren* < ? OFr *escurer* < VL **excurare*, to take great care of < L *ex-*, intens. + *curare*, to take care of < *cura*, care⟧ **1** to clean or polish by vigorous rubbing, as with abrasives, soap and water, etc.; make clean and bright **2** to remove dirt and grease from (wool, etc.) **3** *a)* to wash or clear as by a swift current of water; flush *b)* to wash away, or remove in this way **4** to clear the intestines of; purge **5** to clean (wheat) **6** to remove as if by cleaning; sweep away; get rid of —*vi.* **1** to clean things by vigorous rubbing and polishing **2** to become clean and bright by being scoured —*n.* **1** the act of scouring **2** a cleansing agent used in scouring **3** a scoured place, as a part of a channel where mud has been washed away **4** [*usually pl., with sing. v.*] dysentery in cattle, etc. —**scour′er** *n.*

scour[2] (skour) *vt.* ⟦ME *scouren* < ? OFr *escourre*, to run forth < VL **excurrere* < L *ex-*, out + *currere*, to run⟧ to range over or move through in a painstaking way, as in search or pursuit [*to scour a town for an escaped convict*] —*vi.* to run or range about, as in search or pursuit —**scour′er** *n.*

scourge (skurj) *n.* ⟦ME < OFr *escorgie* < L *ex*, off, from + *corrigia*, a strap, whip⟧ **1** a whip or other instrument for flogging **2** any means of inflicting severe punishment, suffering, or vengeance **3** any cause of serious trouble or affliction [*the scourge of war*] —*vt.* **scourged**, **scourg′ing** **1** to whip or flog **2** to punish, chastise, or afflict severely

☆**scour·ing rush** (skour′iŋ) ⟦so called because stems contain an abrasive substance and were formerly used for *scouring* and polishing⟧ HORSETAIL (sense 2)

scour·ings (skour′iŋz) *pl.n.* dirt, refuse, or remains removed by or as if by scouring

scouse (skous) *n. short for* LOBSCOUSE

scout[1] (skout) *n.* ⟦ME *scoute* < OFr *escoute* < *escouter*, *escolter*, to hear < VL *ascultare*, for L *auscultare*, to listen: see AUSCULTATION⟧ **1** a soldier, ship, or plane sent to spy out the strength, movements, etc. of the enemy ☆**2** a person sent out to observe the tactics of an opponent, to search out new talent, etc. [*a baseball scout*] **3** [**S-**] a member of the Boy Scouts or Girl Scouts **4** the act of reconnoitering **5** [Slang] fellow; guy —*vt.* **1** to follow closely so as to spy upon **2** to look for; watch **3** to find or get by looking around: often with *out*, *up* —*vi.* **1** to go out in search of information about the enemy; reconnoiter **2** to go in search of something; hunt [*scout around for some firewood*] ☆**3** to work as a SCOUT[1] (*n.* 2) —**scout′er** *n.*

scout[2] (skout) *vt.* ⟦prob. via dial. < ON *skuti*, a taunt, term of abuse, akin to SHOUT⟧ to reject as absurd; flout; scoff at —*vi.* to scoff (*at*); jeer

☆**scout car** an armored military reconnaissance car

scout·craft (skout′kraft′, -kräft′) *n.* **1** the practice of scouting **2** skills learned through participation in the Boy Scouts

scout·ing (-iŋ) *n.* **1** the act or process of a person that scouts **2** [*often* **S-**] participation in, or the activities of, the Boy Scouts or Girl Scouts

scout·mas·ter (-mas′tər, -mäs′-) *n.* the adult leader of a troop of Boy Scouts

☆**scow** (skou) *n.* ⟦Du *schouw*, lit., boat which is poled along, akin to LowG *schalde*, punt pole < IE **skoldha-*, pole, branch cut off < base **(s)kel-*, to cut > HALF⟧ a large, flat-bottomed boat with square ends, used for carrying coal, sand, etc. and often towed by a tug

scowl (skoul) *vi.* ⟦ME *scoulen*, prob. < Scand, as in Dan *skule*, in same sense, akin to MHG *schulen*, to be hidden, lurk < IE **(s)kulo-*, concealment < base **(s)keu-*, to cover⟧ **1** to contract the eyebrows and lower the corners of the mouth in showing displeasure; look angry, irritated, or sullen **2** to have a threatening look; lower —*vt.* to affect, influence, or express with a scowl or scowls —*n.* **1** the act or expression of scowling; angry frown **2** a threatening aspect —**scowl′er** *n.*

scrab·ble (skrab′əl) *vi.* **-bled**, **-bling** ⟦Du *schrabbelen* < *schrabben*, to scrape: for IE base see SCRAPE⟧ **1** to scratch, scrape, or paw as though looking for something **2** to struggle **3** to scribble; make meaningless marks —*vt.* **1** to scrape together quickly **2** *a)* to scribble *b)* to scribble on —*n.* **1** a scraping with the hands or paws **2** a scramble **3** a scribble; scrawl **4** a struggle —☆[**S-**] *trademark for* a word game played with lettered tiles placed on a board in arrangements like those in a crossword puzzle —**scrab′bler** *n.*

scrab·bly (-lē) *adj.* **-bli·er**, **-bli·est** [Informal] **1** having a scratching sound **2** scrubby, paltry, poor, etc.

scrag (skrag) *n.* ⟦prob. < ON, as in Norw *skragg*, feeble, stunted person, Dan *skrog*, ON *skröggr*, fox (nickname) < IE base **(s)ker-*, to shrivel, shrink⟧ **1** a lean, scrawny person or animal **2** a thin, stunted tree or plant **3** the neck, or back of the neck, of mutton, veal, etc. **4** [Slang] the human neck —*vt.* **scragged**, **scrag′ging** [Slang] to choke or wring the neck of; hang; throttle; garrote

scrag·gly (skrag′lē) *adj.* **-gli·er**, **-gli·est** ⟦see fol. & -LY[1]⟧ sparse, scrubby, irregular, uneven, ragged, etc. in growth or form [*a scraggly beard*] —**scrag′gli·ness** *n.*

scrag·gy (skrag′ē) *adj.* **-gi·er**, **-gi·est** ⟦< SCRAG + -Y[2]⟧ **1** rough or jagged **2** lean; bony; skinny —**scrag′gi·ly** *adv.*

☆**scram** (skram) *vi.* **scrammed**, **scram′ming** ⟦contr. of fol.⟧ [Slang] to leave or get out, esp. in a hurry: often used in the imperative —*vt.* to manually or automatically shut down (a nuclear reactor) usually by using the control rods —*n.* such a shutdown of a nuclear reactor

scram·ble (skram′bəl) *vi.* **-bled**, **-bling** ⟦< ? SCAMPER + SCRABBLE⟧ **1** to climb, crawl, or clamber hurriedly **2** to scuffle or struggle for something, as for coins scattered on the ground **3** to struggle or rush pell-mell, as to get something highly prized [*to scramble for political office*] **4** to get military aircraft into the air quickly ☆5 *Football* to maneuver about in the backfield while seeking an open receiver to whom to pass the ball; also, to run with the ball if unable to find a receiver —*vt.* **1** *a)* to throw together haphazardly; mix in a confused way; jumble *b) Electronics* to modify (transmitted auditory or visual signals) so as to make unintelligible without special receiving equipment **2** to gather haphazardly; collect without method: often with *up* ☆**3** to cook (eggs) while stirring the mixed whites and yolks **4** to order or get (military aircraft) into the air quickly —*n.* **1** a hard, hurried climb or advance, as over rough, difficult ground **2** a disorderly struggle or rush, as for something prized **3** a disorderly heap; jumble **4** a quick takeoff of military aircraft —**scram′bler** *n.*

☆**scram·jet** (skram′jet′) *n.* ⟦*s(upersonic) c(ombustion) ramjet*⟧ a high-altitude ramjet designed for speeds exceeding Mach 6

scran·nel (skran′əl) *adj.* ⟦< Scand, akin to Norw *skran*, wretched < IE base **(s)ker-*, to shrink, wrinkle > SCRAG⟧ [Archaic] **1** thin, lean, or slight **2** harsh and unmusical

Scran·ton (skrant′'n) ⟦family name of the founders of a local ironworks⟧ city in NE Pa.

scrap[1] (skrap) *n.* ⟦ME *scrappe* < ON *skrap*, scraps, trifles < *skrapa*, to SCRAPE⟧ **1** a small piece; bit; fragment; shred **2** a bit of something written or printed; brief extract **3** *a)* discarded metal in the form of machinery, auto parts, etc. suitable only for reprocessing *b)* discarded articles or fragments of rubber, leather, cloth, paper, etc. **4** [*pl.*] *a)* bits of leftover food *b)* the crisp remnants of animal fat after the oil has been removed by rendering —*adj.* **1** in the form of fragments, pieces, odds and ends, or leftovers **2** used and discarded —*vt.* **scrapped, scrap′ping 1** to make into scrap; break up **2** to get rid of or abandon as useless; discard; junk

scrap[2] (skrap) [Informal] *n.* ⟦< ? SCRAPE⟧ a fight or quarrel —*vi.* **scrapped, scrap′ping** to fight or quarrel

scrap·book (skrap′bo͝ok′) *n.* **1** a book of blank pages for mounting newspaper clippings, pictures, souvenirs, etc. **2** such a book containing a compilation of such memorabilia —*vi.* to compile memorabilia in a scrapbook, esp. as a hobby —**scrap′book′ing** *n.*

scrape (skrāp) *vt.* **scraped, scrap′ing** ⟦ME *scrapen* < ON *skrapa*, akin to Du *schrapen*, OE *screpan*, to scratch < IE base **(s)ker-*, to cut > SCURF, SHARP⟧ **1** to rub over the surface of with something rough or sharp **2** to make smooth or clean by rubbing with a tool or abrasive **3** to remove by rubbing with something sharp or rough: with *off, out,* etc. **4** to scratch or abrade by a rough, rubbing contact [to fall and *scrape* one's knee] **5** to rub with a harsh, grating sound [chalk *scraping* a blackboard] **6** to dig, esp. with the hands and nails **7** to collect or gather slowly and with difficulty [to *scrape* together some money] —*vi.* **1** to scrape something so as to remove dirt, etc. **2** to rub against something harshly; grate **3** to give out a harsh, grating noise **4** to collect or gather goods or money slowly and with difficulty **5** to manage to get by; survive: with *through, along, by* **6** to draw the foot back along the ground in bowing —*n.* **1** the act of scraping **2** a scraped place; abrasion or scratch **3** the noise of scraping; harsh, grating sound **4** a disagreeable or embarrassing situation; predicament, esp. when caused by one's own conduct **5** a fight or conflict —**scrap′er** *n.*

scrap·heap (skrap′hēp′) *n.* a pile of discarded material, as of scrap iron —**throw** (or **toss, cast,** etc.) **on the scrapheap** to discard or get rid of as useless

scrap·ie (skrā′pē) *n.* ⟦SCRAPE (*vi.*) + -IE: because affected animals rub against trees, fences, etc. to relieve the severe itching⟧ a fatal, degenerative nervous disease of sheep and goats

scrap·ing (skrā′piŋ) *n.* **1** the act of a person or thing that scrapes **2** the sound of this **3** [*usually pl.*] something scraped off, together, or up

scrap iron discarded or waste pieces of iron, to be recast or reworked

scrap·per[1] (skrap′ər) *n.* a person or thing that scraps

scrap·per[2] (skrap′ər) *n.* [Informal] a ready or effective fighter

☆**scrap·ple** (skrap′əl) *n.* ⟦dim. of SCRAP[1]⟧ cornmeal boiled with scraps of pork and allowed to set, then sliced and fried

scrap·py[1] (skrap′ē) *adj.* **-pi·er, -pi·est** ⟦< SCRAP[1] + -Y[2]⟧ **1** made of scraps; consisting of odds and ends **2** disconnected; disjointed [*scrappy* memories] —**scrap′pi·ly** *adv.* —**scrap′pi·ness** *n.*

scrap·py[2] (skrap′ē) *adj.* **-pi·er, -pi·est** ⟦< SCRAP[2] + -Y[2]⟧ [Informal] fond of fighting, arguing, etc.; aggressive —**scrap′pi·ly** *adv.* —**scrap′pi·ness** *n.*

scratch (skrach) *vt.* ⟦LME *scracchen*, prob. altered < *scratten*, to scratch, based on *cracchen* < or akin to MDu *cratsen*, to scratch < IE base **gred-* > Alb *gërij*, (I) scratch⟧ **1** to mark, break, or cut the surface of slightly with something pointed or sharp **2** to tear or dig with the nails or claws **3** *a)* to rub or scrape lightly, as with the fingernails, to relieve itching, etc. *b)* to chafe **4** to rub or scrape with a grating noise [to *scratch* a match on a wall] **5** to write or draw hurriedly or carelessly **6** to strike out or cancel (writing, etc.) **7** to gather or collect with difficulty; scrape (*together* or *up*) **8** *Sports* to withdraw (an entry) from a contest, specif. from a horse race —*vi.* **1** to use nails or claws in digging or wounding **2** to rub or scrape the skin lightly, as with the fingernails, to relieve itching, etc. **3** to manage to get by; scrape by **4** to make a harsh, scraping noise **5** to withdraw from a race or contest **6** in certain card games, to score no points **7** *Billiards, Pool* to make a scratch —*n.* **1** the act of scratching **2** a mark or tear made in a surface by something sharp or rough **3** a wound, usually superficial, inflicted by nails, claws, or something pointed pulled across the skin, etc. **4** a slight grating or scraping sound **5** a hasty mark, as of a pen; scribble **6** the starting line of a race **7** in certain card games, a score of zero ☆**8** [Slang] money **9** *Billiards, Pool* a shot that results in a penalty; specif., in pool, a shot in which the cue ball goes into a pocket **10** *Sports a)* the starting point or time of a contestant who receives no handicap *b)* such a contestant *c)* an entry withdrawn from a contest —*adj.* ☆**1** used for hasty notes, preliminary or tentative figuring, etc. [*scratch* paper] **2** skillful enough to require no handicap or special allowance in a contest [a *scratch* golfer] **3** put together in haste and without much selection [a *scratch* team] ☆**4** *Baseball* designating a chance hit credited to a batter for a ball not hit sharply, but on which the batter reaches base safely —**from scratch 1** from the start; from the very beginning **2** from nothing; without resources, advantage, etc. **3** without the use of components or ingredients commercially prepared, assembled, or mixed beforehand [a pie baked *from scratch*, a shed built *from scratch*] —**scratch one's head** ⟦from the common mannerism, as when pondering a question⟧ to puzzle over a question or problem —**scratch the surface** to do, consider, or affect something superficially —**up to scratch 1** toeing the mark; ready to start a race, contest, etc. **2** [Informal] ready to meet difficulties, start on an enterprise, etc. **3** [Informal] up to standard; acceptable; good —**scratch′er** *n.*

Scratch (skrach) *n.* ⟦altered (infl. by prec.) < ME *skratte* < ON *skratti*, monster, sorcerer, akin to OHG *scraz*, goblin < IE base **(s)ker-*, to shrink > SCRANNEL⟧ [*sometimes* **s-**] the Devil: usually *Old Scratch*

☆**scratch·board** (skrach′bôrd′) *n.* glossy, chalk-covered cardboard on which, after coating with ink, line drawings can be made by scratching through the ink to the white surface

scratch line 1 the starting line of a race ☆**2** a line that must not be overstepped in certain contests, as the long jump or javelin throw

scratch·pad (skrach′pad′) *n.* a pad of paper for jotting notes, doing simple calculations, etc.

☆**scratch sheet** a publication listing horses removed from the day's races at one or another racetrack

scratch test a test for determining substances to which a person is allergic, made by rubbing allergens into small scratches or punctures in the skin

scratch·y (skrach′ē) *adj.* **scratch′i·er, scratch′i·est 1** having the appearance of being drawn roughly, hurriedly, etc.; made with scratches **2** making a scratching or scraping noise **3** scratched together; haphazard **4** that scratches, scrapes, chafes, itches, etc. [*scratchy* cloth] —**scratch′i·ly** *adv.* —**scratch′i·ness** *n.*

scrawl (skrôl) *vt., vi.* ⟦< ? SCRATCH + SPRAWL⟧ to write, draw, or mark awkwardly, hastily, or carelessly; esp., to write with sprawling, poorly formed letters —*n.* **1** sprawling, often illegible handwriting **2** something scrawled —**scrawl′er** *n.* —**scrawl′y** *adj.* **scrawl′i·er, scrawl′i·est**

scraw·ny (skrô′nē) *adj.* **-ni·er, -ni·est** ⟦prob. var. of dial. *scranny*, lean, thin < Scand base > SCRANNEL⟧ **1** very thin; skinny and bony **2** stunted or scrubby —**scraw′ni·ness** *n.*

screak (skrēk) *vi.* ⟦ON *skraekja*, SCREECH⟧ to screech or creak —*n.* a screech or creak

scream (skrēm) *vi.* ⟦ME *screamen*, akin to Fl *schreemen*, to scream, Ger *schrei*, a cry < IE **skerei-* < echoic base **(s)ker-* > SHRIEK, RAVEN[1], RING[1]⟧ **1** *a)* to utter a shrill, loud, piercing cry in fright, pain, etc. *b)* to make or move with a shrill, piercing sound **2** to laugh loudly or hysterically **3** to have a startling effect; leave a vivid impression **4** to shout or yell in anger, hysteria, etc. —*vt.* **1** to utter with or as with a scream or screams **2** to bring into a specified state by screaming [to *scream* oneself hoarse] —*n.* **1** *a)* a sharp, piercing cry; shriek *b)* any shrill, piercing sound **2** [Informal] a person or thing considered hilariously funny

scream·er (skrēm′ər) *n.* **1** a person who screams ☆**2** [Slang] a sensational headline **3** [Slang] *Printing* an exclamation point **4** any of a primitive family (Anhimidae) of South American birds (order Anseriformes) having long toes and a bill like a chicken's

scream·ing (-iŋ) *adj.* **1** that screams **2** startling in effect **3** causing screams of laughter —**scream′ing·ly** *adv.*

☆**screaming mee·mies** (mē′mēz) ⟦< prec. + echoic redupl.: orig. used of Ger shells in WWI⟧ [Slang] extreme nervous tension

scree (skrē) *n.* ⟦back-form. < pl. *screes* < earlier *screethes* < ON *skritha*, landslide < *skritha*, to slide, creep, akin to Ger *schreiten*, to step < IE base **(s)ker-*, to turn, bend⟧ TALUS[2] (sense 2)

screech (skrēch) *vi.* ⟦ME *scrichen* < ON *skraekja*: for IE base see SCREAM⟧ to utter or make a shrill, high-pitched, harsh shriek or sound —*vt.* to utter with a screech —*n.* a shrill, high-pitched, harsh shriek or sound —**screech′er** *n.* —**screech′y** *adj.* **screech′i·er, screech′i·est** —**screech′i·ness** *n.*

screech owl ☆**1** any of various small New World owls (genus *Otus*) of a worldwide family (Strigidae), characterized by feathered ear tufts and an eerie, wailing cry rather than a hoot **2** [Brit.] any owl with such a cry

screed (skrēd) *n.* ⟦ME *screde*, var. of *schrede*, SHRED: sense from "long list on a strip of paper"⟧ **1** a long, tiresome speech or piece of writing **2** a strip of plaster or wood applied to a wall to serve as a guide to the desired thickness of plastering to be done later **3** [Brit.] a finishing layer of mortar laid over a concrete or other solid floor **4** [Scot.] a torn place; rent

screen (skrēn) *n.* ⟦ME *skrene*, sieve, curtain < OFr *escren* < Gmc, as in OHG *scerm* (Ger *shirm*), guard, protection, screen < IE base **(s)ker-*, to cut > SHEAR, SCORE⟧ **1** *a)* a light, movable, covered frame or series of frames hinged together, serving as a portable partition to separate, conceal, shelter, or protect *b)* any partition or curtain serving such a purpose **2** anything that functions to shield, protect, or conceal [a smoke *screen*] **3** a coarse mesh of wire, etc., used to sift out finer from coarser parts, as of sand or coal; sieve **4** a system for screening or selecting participants, candidates, etc. **5** a section of mesh held in a frame, for use as in a window or door to keep insects out, serve as a barrier, etc. 6 *a)* a flat, reflective or translucent surface, as a matte white sheet or one of beaded vinyl, upon which films, slides, etc. are projected *b)* the movie industry 7 the surface area of a television set, personal computer, radar receiver, etc. on which images or data are displayed 8 any protective military formation, as of troops or ships ☆9 *Basketball* an offensive maneuver or play in which a stationary player blocks or impedes the movement of a defensive player ☆10 *Football* SCREEN PASS 11 *Photoengraving* in the halftone process, a set of two glass plates cemented together so that parallel lines engraved in one plate are at right angles to the lines of the other plate 12 *Physics* a device used as a shield to prevent interference of some sort —*vt.* 1 to separate, conceal, shelter, or protect, with or as with a screen 2 to provide with a screen or screens 3 to sift through a coarse mesh so as to separate finer from coarser parts 4 *a)* to interview or test so as to separate according to skills, personality, aptitudes, etc. *b)* to select or discard in this way [to *screen* callers to a talk show] 5 *a)* to project (pictures, etc.) upon a screen, as with a film or slide projector *b)* to show (a film, etc.) to critics, the public, etc. —*vi.* to be screened or suitable for screening, as in films —**screen′a·ble** *adj.* —**screen′er** *n.* —**screen′less** *adj.*

screen door an outer door consisting of a frame covered with mesh, as of wire or plastic, used to keep insects out

screen·ing (skrēn′iŋ) *n.* 1 the act of a person or thing that screens 2 *a)* a screen or set of screens *b)* mesh used in a screen 3 [*pl.*] material separated out by a sifting screen 4 a special, often private, showing of a film as for critics, exhibitors, etc.

screen memory *Psychoanalysis* a memory from childhood that masks an allied memory that would be distressing if remembered

☆**screen pass** *Football* a pass thrown to a receiver who is near or behind the line of scrimmage and is protected by a screen of blockers

☆**screen·play** (-plā′) *n.* the script from which a film is produced

screen saver *Comput.* 1 a utility designed to interrupt a screen display during periods of inactivity by the user, as by causing the screen to go blank or by displaying moving objects or a succession of pictures: so called because such utilities were originally meant to prevent erosion in the CRT screen 2 the visual display of such a utility

screen·shot (-shät′) *n.* an image of a computer screen taken to show the display at a particular point in time

screen test 1 an audition, recorded on film, to determine a person's suitability as a film actor or for a particular film role 2 a short film made of such an audition

screen·writ·er (-rīt′ər) *n.* the writer of a script for a film —**screen′writ′ing** *n.*

screw (skrōō) *n.* ⟦ME *screwe* < MFr *escroue*, hole in which the screw turns < L *scrofa*, sow, infl. by *scrobis*, vulva⟧ 1 *a)* a mechanical device for fastening things together, consisting essentially of a cylindrical or conical piece of metal threaded evenly around its outside surface with an advancing spiral ridge and commonly having a slotted head: it penetrates only by being turned, as with a screwdriver (also called **male screw**) *b)* the internal thread, or helical groove, as of a nut, into which a male screw, bolt, etc. can be turned (also called **female screw**) *c)* the act or an instance of turning such a screw 2 any of various devices operating or threaded like a screw, as a jackscrew or screw propeller 3 *a)* anything that spirals or twists like the thread of a screw *b)* the act of spiraling, twisting, or moving like this 4 [Slang] a prison guard 5 [Chiefly Brit.] a small amount of tobacco, salt, etc. in a twist of paper 6 [Slang, Chiefly Brit.] *a)* a stingy person; miser *b)* a crafty bargainer *c)* a worn-out horse 7 [Brit. Slang] a salary 8 [Slang] *a)* an act or instance of sexual intercourse *b)* a person with whom one engages in sexual intercourse, often, specif., one of specified competence: somewhat vulgar —*vt.* 1 to twist; turn; tighten 2 *a)* to fasten, make secure, tighten, insert, etc. with or as with a screw or screws *b)* to put together or take apart with a screwlike motion 3 to twist out of natural shape; contort [to *screw* one's face up] 4 to make stronger; intensify: often with *up* 5 to force or compel, as if by using screws 6 [Slang] *a)* to cheat; swindle *b)* to treat unfairly 7 [Slang] to have sexual intercourse with: somewhat vulgar —*vi.* 1 to go together or come apart by being turned or twisted in the manner of a screw [a lid that *screws* on] 2 to twist; turn; wind; have a motion like that of a screw 3 [Slang] to engage in sexual intercourse: somewhat vulgar —**have a screw loose** [Slang] to be eccentric, odd, etc. —☆**put the screws on** (or **to**) ⟦< *screws*, var. of THUMBSCREW, instrument of torture⟧ [Informal] to subject to force; exert pressure on, as in exacting payment; coerce —**screw around** [Slang] to waste time —☆**screw up** [Informal] to make a mess (of), as by ineptness; bungle

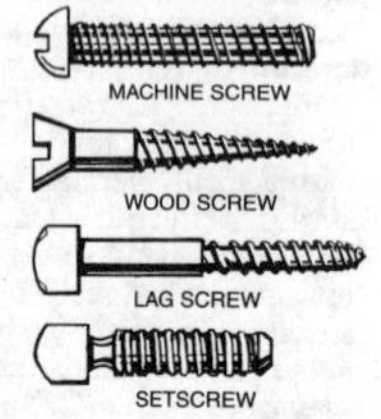

☆**screw·ball** (skrōō′bôl′) *n.* 1 *Baseball* a ball thrown by a right-handed pitcher that curves to the right, or one thrown by a left-handed pitcher that curves to the left 2 [Slang] a person who seems erratic, irrational, unconventional, or unbalanced —*adj.* [Slang] peculiar; irrational

☆**screw bean** 1 the spirally twisted pod growing on a mesquite tree (*Prosopis pubescens*) of the SW U.S., often used for fodder 2 this tree

screw·driv·er (-drī′vər) *n.* 1 a tool used for turning screws, having an end that fits into the slot in the head of the screw ☆2 a cocktail made of orange juice and vodka

screwed (skrōōd) *adj.* 1 having threads like a screw 2 twisted 3 [Slang] in a state of great trouble or distress, impending failure, etc. 4 [Slang, Chiefly Brit.] drunk

screw eye a screw with a loop for a head

screw hook a screw with a hook for a head

screw jack JACKSCREW

screw pine ⟦so named from the spirally arranged tufts of leaves⟧ any of a genus (*Pandanus*) of SE Asian trees and shrubs of the screw-pine family, often having edible starchy fruits

screw-pine (skrōō′pīn′) *adj.* designating a family (Pandanaceae, order Pandanales) of monocotyledonous trees, shrubs, and climbers, characterized by daggerlike leaves and prop roots

screw propeller *see* PROPELLER

screw thread the helical ridge of or for a screw

☆**screw-up** or **screw·up** (skrōō′up′) *n.* [Informal] 1 a serious mistake; blunder; mess 2 a person who screws up

☆**screw·worm** (skrōō′wurm′) *n.* the larva of an American blowfly (*Cochliomyia hominivorax*) that infests wounds, and the nostrils, navel, etc. of animals, often causing illness

screw·y (skrōō′ē) *adj.* **screw′i·er**, **screw′i·est** [Slang] ☆1 mentally unbalanced; crazy ☆2 peculiar, eccentric, or odd in a confusing way —**screw′i·ness** *n.*

Scria·bin (skryä′bēn; *E* skrē ä′bin), **A·lek·san·dr (Nikolayevich)** (ä′lyik sän′dr′) 1872-1915; Russ. composer & pianist

scrib·al (skrī′bəl) *adj.* 1 of scribes, or writers 2 arising from the process of writing [a *scribal* error]

scrib·ble (skrib′əl) *vt., vi.* **-bled**, **-bling** ⟦ME *scriblen* < ML *scribillare* < L *scribere*, to write: see SCRIBE⟧ 1 to write carelessly or illegibly 2 to make or cover with meaningless or illegible marks 3 to compose hastily, without regard to style —*n.* 1 illegible or careless handwriting 2 meaningless marks

scrib·bler (-lər) *n.* a person who scribbles; specif., *a)* a person who writes illegibly or carelessly *b)* a hack writer

scribe (skrīb) *n.* ⟦ME < L *scriba*, public writer, scribe, in LL(Ec), doctor of the Jewish law < *scribere*, to write < IE **skeribh-* < base **(s)ker-*, to cut, incise > SHEAR⟧ 1 a professional penman who copied manuscripts before the invention of printing 2 a writer or author 3 a person learned in the Jewish law who makes handwritten copies of the Torah 4 a person employed by the general public to write letters, etc. 5 SCRIBER —*vt.* **scribed**, **scrib′ing** 1 to score (wood, bricks, etc.) with a scriber 2 to mark (a line) with a scriber —*vi.* to work as a scribe

Scribe (skrēb), **Au·gus·tin Eu·gène** (ô güs tan′ ö zhen′) 1791-1861; Fr. dramatist & librettist

scrib·er (skrī′bər) *n.* a pointed tool for scoring wood, metal, etc. to show where it is to be cut

scrim (skrim) *n.* ⟦< ?⟧ 1 a light, sheer, loosely woven cotton or linen cloth, used for curtains, upholstery linings, etc. ☆2 a hanging of such cloth used in theatrical productions either as an opaque backdrop or as a semitransparent curtain, depending on the lighting

scrim·mage (skrim′ij) *n.* ⟦altered < SKIRMISH⟧ 1 a rough-and-tumble fight; tussle; confused struggle ☆2 *Football a) short for* LINE OF SCRIMMAGE *b)* play that begins with the snap from center, with both teams positioned on the line of scrimmage (usually with *from*) [yardage from *scrimmage*] 3 *Rugby* SCRUM ☆4 *Sports* a practice session or game between two different teams or two units of the same team — *vi., vt.* **-maged**, **-mag·ing** to take part in a scrimmage (against) —**scrim′mag·er** *n.*

scrimp (skrimp) *vt.* ⟦prob. < Scand, as in Swed *skrympa*, to shrink, akin to OE *scrimman*, Ger *schrumpfen* < IE base **(s)kremb-*, to turn, twist, shrink⟧ 1 to make too small, short, etc.; skimp 2 to treat stingily; stint —*vi.* to be sparing and frugal; try to make ends meet; economize —*adj.* [Archaic] curtailed; scanty —**scrimp′er** *n.*

scrimp·y (skrim′pē) *adj.* **scrimp′i·er**, **scrimp′i·est** 1 skimpy; meager 2 frugal or economical —**scrimp′i·ly** *adv.* —**scrimp′i·ness** *n.*

☆**scrim·shaw** (skrim′shô′) *n.* ⟦earlier also *scrimshander* < ?⟧ 1 intricate decoration and carving of bone, ivory, etc., as of whales and walruses, done esp. by sailors on long voyages 2 an article so made, or such articles collectively — *vt., vi.* to carve (shells, bone, etc.) in making scrimshaw

scrip[1] (skrip) *n.* ⟦ME *scrippe* < ML *scrippa*: see SCARF[1]⟧ [Archaic] a small bag, wallet, or satchel

scrip[2] (skrip) *n.* ⟦contr. < SCRIPT[1]⟧ 1 a brief writing, as a note, list, receipt, etc. 2 a small piece or scrap, esp. of paper 3 a certificate of a right to receive something; specif., *a)* a certificate representing a fraction of a share of stock *b)* a temporary paper to be exchanged for money, goods, land, etc. ☆*c)* a certificate of indebtedness, issued as currency, as by a local government during a financial depression ☆4 paper money in amounts of less than a dollar, formerly issued in the U.S.; fractional currency

Scripps (skrips), **Edward Wyl·lis** (wil′is) 1854-1926; U.S. newspaper publisher

scrip·sit (skrip′sit) *v.* ⟦L⟧ (he or she) wrote (it): placed after the author's name as on a manuscript

script[1] (skript) *n.* ⟦ME < MFr *escript* < L *scriptum* < neut. of *scriptus*, pp. of *scribere*, to write: see SCRIBE⟧ 1 *a)* handwriting; written words, letters, or figures *b)* a style of handwriting; manner or method of forming letters or figures *c) Printing* a typeface that looks like handwriting, with the letters seemingly connected when typeset (cf. CURSIVE) 2 a written document; original manuscript 3 the manuscript, or a copy of the text, of a stage, film, radio, or television show —*vt.* to write the script for (a film, etc.)

script[2] *abbrev.* 1 scriptural 2 scripture
scrip·to·ri·um (skrip tôr′ē əm) ***n.***, *pl.* **-ri·a** (-ə) ⟦ML < L *scriptus*: see SCRIPT[1]⟧ a writing room; esp., a room in a monastery for copying manuscripts, writing, and studying
scrip·ture (skrip′chər) ***n.*** ⟦ME < L *scriptura*, a writing, in LL(Ec), a Scripture, passage of Scripture < *scriptus*: see SCRIPT[1]⟧ 1 [Obs.] anything written 2 [S-] a Bible passage 3 *a)* any sacred writing or books *b)* any writing regarded as authoritative and inviolable 4 [S-] [*often pl.*] the sacred writings of the Jews, identical with the Old Testament of the Christians 5 [S-] [*often pl.*] the Christian Bible; Old and New Testaments —**scrip′tur·al** ***adj.***
script·writ·er (skript′rīt′ər) ***n.*** a person who writes scripts for films, television, etc.
scriv·en·er (skriv′ən ər) ***n.*** ⟦ME *scriveyner*, extended < *scrivein* < OFr *escrivain* < VL **scribanus* < L *scriba*, SCRIBE⟧ [Archaic] 1 a scribe, copyist, or clerk 2 a notary
scro·bic·u·late (skrō bik′yə lit, -lāt′) ***adj.*** ⟦< L *scrobiculus*, dim. of *scrobis*, a ditch (< IE **(s)kerb(h)-* > SHARP) + -ATE[1]⟧ *Biol.* pitted or furrowed
☆**scrod** (skräd) ***n.*** ⟦prob. < MDu *schrode*, piece cut off, strip < IE **(s)kreut-* > SHRED⟧ a young fish, as a cod or haddock, esp. one split and prepared for cooking
scrof·u·la (skräf′yə lə) ***n.*** ⟦ML < L *scrofulae*, pl., swellings of the neck glands < dim. of *scrofa*, a sow: prob. from the swollen condition of the glands⟧ tuberculosis of the lymphatic glands, esp. of the neck, characterized by the enlargement of the glands, suppuration, and scar formation
scrof·u·lous (-ləs) ***adj.*** 1 of, like, or having scrofula 2 morally corrupt; degenerate —**scrof′u·lous·ly** ***adv.***
scroll (skrōl) ***n.*** ⟦ME *scrowle*, altered (? by assoc. with *rowle*, var. of *rolle*, ROLL) < *scrowe* < OFr *escroue*: see ESCROW⟧ 1 a roll of parchment, paper, etc., usually with writing or pictures on it 2 an ancient book in the form of a rolled manuscript 3 a list of names; roll; roster [*the scroll of fame*] 4 anything having the form of a partly unrolled or loosely rolled sheet of paper, as the volute of an Ionic capital, or the ornamentally rolled end of the neck of a violin, etc. 5 the act or an instance of reading items in a scrolling display —***vi., vt.*** to display (lines of text, television credits, etc.) by moving them vertically or horizontally on a video screen —**scrolled** ***adj.***

scroll

scroll saw a saw with a narrow, fine-toothed blade, for cutting curves and ornamental designs; specif., fret saw or jigsaw
scroll·work (-wʉrk′) ***n.*** 1 ornamental work marked by scrolls 2 ornamental work done with a scroll saw
☆**scrooch** or **scrootch** (skrōōch) ***vt., vi.*** ⟦prob. alt. < SCROUGE⟧ [Informal] to crouch, hunch, huddle, squeeze, etc.
Scrooge (skrōōj) ***n.*** ⟦after Ebenezer *Scrooge*, character in Dickens' *A Christmas Carol* (1843)⟧ [*also* **s-**] a hardhearted, miserly misanthrope
scro·tum (skrōt′əm) ***n.***, *pl.* **-ta** (-ə) or **-tums** ⟦L < IE **(s)kreut-* > SHRED⟧ in most male mammals, the pouch of skin holding the testicles and related structures —**scro′tal** ***adj.***
scrouge (skrouj, skrōōj) ***vt.*** **scrouged**, **scroug′ing** ⟦earlier *scruze*: prob. echoic, suggested by SCREW, SQUEEZE⟧ [Dial.] to crowd, squeeze, press, etc.
scrounge (skrounj) ***vt.*** **scrounged**, **scroung′ing** ⟦prob. altered < prec.⟧ [Informal] 1 to manage to get or find by hunting around: usually with *up* 2 to get by begging or sponging; mooch 3 to take without permission; pilfer —***vi.*** [Informal] to seek (*around*) for something; forage —**scroung′er** ***n.***
scroung·y (skroun′jē) ***adj.*** **scroung′i·er**, **scroung′i·est** [Slang] shabby, dirty, unkempt, etc. —**scroung′i·ness** ***n.***
scrub[1] (skrub) ***n.*** ⟦ME, var. of *shrubbe*, SHRUB[1], infl. ? by ON *skroppa*, a lean creature⟧ 1 *a)* a scraggly, stunted tree or shrub *b)* short, stunted trees, bushes, or shrubs growing thickly together *c)* land covered with such growth 2 *a)* any animal or thing smaller than the usual, or inferior in quality, breed, etc. *b)* any small or insignificant person ☆3 *Sports a)* a player not on the varsity squad or regular team *b)* [*pl.*] a secondary or practice team made up of such players —***adj.*** 1 mean; poor; inferior 2 undersized, undernourished, or stunted ☆3 *Sports* of or for the scrubs
scrub[2] (skrub) ***vt.*** **scrubbed**, **scrub′bing** ⟦ME *scrobben*, prob. < Scand, as in Dan *skrubbe*, Norw dial. *skrubba*, to rub hard, akin to MLowG *schrubben* < IE base **(s)ker-*, to cut > SCRAPE⟧ 1 to clean or wash by rubbing or brushing hard 2 to remove (dirt, etc.) by brushing or rubbing 3 to rub hard 4 to cleanse (a gas) of impurities 5 [Informal] *a)* to cancel or call off (esp. a rocket launch before or during the countdown) *b)* to get rid of; eliminate —***vi.*** to clean something by rubbing, as with a brush —***n.*** 1 the act of scrubbing 2 a person who scrubs
scrub·ber (skrub′ər) ***n.*** ⟦prec. + -ER⟧ anything that scrubs or is used for scrubbing; specif., an apparatus that cleans the gases passing through a smokestack of a coal-burning power plant
scrub·by (skrub′ē) ***adj.*** **-bi·er**, **-bi·est** 1 stunted in growth; undersized or inferior 2 covered with or consisting of scrub, or brushwood 3 paltry, shabby, etc. —**scrub′bi·ly** ***adv.*** —**scrub′bi·ness** ***n.***
scrub·land (skrub′land′) ***n.*** land or a region characterized by scrub vegetation
☆**scrubs** (skrubz) ***pl.n.*** [Informal] sterile clothing worn as by doctors and nurses during surgery, childbirth, etc.
scrub typhus a disease of the Asian-Pacific area, transmitted to humans by the bite of the larva of a mite (esp. *Trombicula akamushi*) and caused by a rickettsia (*Rickettsia tsutsugamushi*): it is characterized by fever and a rash
scrub·wom·an (-woom′ən) ***n.***, *pl.* **-wom′en** (-wim′in) CHARWOMAN
scruff (skruf) ***n.*** ⟦< ON *skrufr*, a tuft of hair, forelock, var. of *skruf*, altered by metathesis < *skufr*, tuft < IE base **(s)keup-* > OE *scyfel*, woman's headdress⟧ 1 the back of the neck; nape 2 the loose skin at the back of the neck of some animals
scruff·y (skruf′ē) ***adj.*** **scruff′i·er**, **scruff′i·est** ⟦< dial. *scruff*, var. of SCURF + -Y[2]⟧ shabby, unkempt, or untidy; grubby —**scruff′i·ly** ***adv.*** —**scruff′i·ness** ***n.***
scrum (skrum) ***n.*** ⟦< fol.⟧ 1 *Rugby* a play in which the two sets of forwards, lined up facing each other in a compact formation, try to kick the ball, which has been thrown onto the ground between them, back to a teammate 2 [Informal] a disorderly group of people crowded together, often in pursuit of a person or thing: orig. Brit. —***vi.*** **scrummed**, **scrum′ming** to take part in a scrum: usually with *down*
scrum·mage (skrum′ij) ***n., vi.*** **-maged**, **-mag·ing** ⟦< dial. var. of SCRIMMAGE⟧ *Rugby* SCRUM
scrump·tious (skrump′shəs) ***adj.*** ⟦altered < SUMPTUOUS⟧ [Informal] very pleasing, attractive, etc., esp. to the taste; delicious —**scrump′tious·ly** ***adv.*** —**scrump′tious·ness** ***n.***
scrunch (skrunch) ***vt., vi.*** ⟦< CRUNCH, with emphatic initial *s-*⟧ 1 to crunch, crush, or crumple 2 to hunch, huddle, or squeeze —***n.*** a crunching or crumpling sound
scru·ple (skrōō′pəl) ***n.*** ⟦MFr *scrupule* < L *scrupulus*, small sharp stone (hence small weight, difficulty, doubt), dim. of *scrupus*, sharp stone < IE **skreup-* < base **(s)ker-*, to cut⟧ 1 a very small quantity, amount, or part 2 *a)* an ancient Roman unit of weight equal to 1/24 ounce *b)* a unit of weight equal to 1/3 dram apothecaries' weight or 20 grains (1.296 grams): abbrev. *sc* 3 a feeling of hesitancy, doubt, or uneasiness arising from difficulty in deciding what is right, proper, ethical, etc.; qualm or misgiving about something one thinks is wrong 4 [*pl.*] high ethical standards —***vt., vi.*** **-pled**, **-pling** to hesitate (at) from doubt or uneasiness; be unwilling because of one's conscience; have scruples (about) —***SYN.*** QUALM
scru·pu·lous (skrōōp′yə ləs) ***adj.*** ⟦< MFr or L: MFr *scrupuleux* < L *scrupulosus*⟧ 1 *a)* extremely careful to do the precisely right, proper, or correct thing in every last detail; most punctilious *b)* showing extreme care, precision, and punctiliousness 2 extremely conscientious 3 full of scruples; hesitant, doubtful, or uneasy, esp. constantly and obsessively, in deciding what is morally right or wrong —***SYN.*** CAREFUL —**scru′pu·los′i·ty** (-läs′ət ē) ***n.***, *pl.* **-ties** —**scru′pu·lous·ly** ***adv.*** —**scru′pu·lous·ness** ***n.***
scru·ta·ble (skrōōt′ə bəl) ***adj.*** ⟦LL **scrutabilis*: see INSCRUTABLE⟧ not inscrutable; open to being understood
scru·ti·nize (skrōōt′'n īz′) ***vt.*** **-nized′**, **-niz′ing** ⟦< fol. + -IZE⟧ to look at very carefully; examine closely; inspect minutely —**scru′ti·niz′er** ***n.***

SYN.—**scrutinize** implies a looking over carefully and searchingly in order to observe the minutest details [*he slowly scrutinized the bank note*]; **inspect** implies close, critical observation, esp. for detecting errors, flaws, etc. [*to inspect a building for fire hazards*]; **examine** suggests close observation or investigation to determine the condition, quality, validity, etc. of something [*examined thoroughly by a doctor*]; **scan**, in its earlier, stricter sense, implies close scrutiny, but in current usage, it more frequently connotes a quick, rather superficial survey [*to scan the headlines*]

scru·ti·ny (skrōōt′'n ē) ***n.***, *pl.* **-nies** ⟦LL *scrutinium* < L *scrutari*, to examine carefully, rummage through odds and ends < *scruta*, trash, prob. altered < Gr *grutē*, a miscellany, woman's vanity bag: for prob. IE base see CRUMB⟧ 1 close examination; minute inspection 2 a careful, continuous watch; surveillance 3 a lengthy, searching look
scry (skrī) ***vi.*** **scried**, **scry′ing** ⟦< DESCRY⟧ to practice crystal gazing
☆**scu·ba** (skōō′bə) ***n.*** ⟦*s(elf-)c(ontained) u(nderwater) b(reathing) a(pparatus)*⟧ 1 equipment worn by divers for breathing underwater, consisting typically of one or two compressed-air tanks strapped to the back and connected by a hose to a mouthpiece 2 SCUBA DIVING —***adj.*** of or for scuba diving [*scuba gear*]
scuba diving the act or recreation of swimming and exploring underwater with the aid of scuba gear —**scuba diver**
scud (skud) ***vi.*** **scud′ded**, **scud′ding** ⟦prob. < ON form akin to OE *scudan*, to hurry: see SHUDDER⟧ 1 to run or move swiftly; glide or skim along easily 2 to be driven or run before the wind —***n.*** 1 the act of scudding 2 spray, rain, or snow driven by the wind 3 a sudden gust of wind 4 *Meteorol.* very low, dark, patchy clouds moving swiftly, generally characteristic of bad weather
scu·do (skōō′dō) ***n.***, *pl.* **-di** (-dē) ⟦It, orig., a shield < L *scutum*, shield (prob. < IE **(s)keut-* > HIDE[2]): it bore a shield⟧ a former monetary unit and gold or silver coin of Italy and Sicily
scuff (skuf) ***vt.*** ⟦prob. < or akin to ON *skufa*, to SHOVE⟧ 1 to scrape (the ground, floor, etc.) with the feet 2 to wear a rough place or places on the surface of (a shoe, etc.) 3 to move (the feet) with a dragging motion —***vi.*** 1 to walk without lifting the feet; shuffle 2 to become scraped or worn in patches on the surface —***n.*** 1 a sound or act of scuffing 2 a worn or rough spot 3 a loosefitting house slipper, esp. one without a built-up heel or a counter
scuf·fle (skuf′əl) ***vi.*** **-fled**, **-fling** ⟦freq. of prec.⟧ 1 to struggle or fight in

rough confusion **2** to move in a confused hurry or bustle **3** to drag the feet; shuffle ☆**4** [Informal] to try hard but with little or no success; specif., to struggle to survive —*n.* **1** a rough, confused fight; close, haphazard struggle **2** the act or sound of feet shuffling

scuffle hoe a hoe with a flat blade, pushed back and forth through the surface soil, as to weed

scull (skul) *n.* ⟦ME *skulle*, prob. < Scand form akin to obs. Swed *skolle*, thin plate < IE base **(s)kel-*, to cut > HELM²⟧ **1** an oar mounted at the stern of a boat and worked from side to side to move the boat forward **2** either of a pair of light oars used, one on each side of a boat (now esp. a racing scull), by a single rower **3** a light, narrow racing boat for one, two, or four rowers using sculls — *vt., vi.* to propel (a boat) with a scull or pair of sculls —**scull′er** *n.*

scul·ler·y (skul′ər ē) *n., pl.* **-ler·ies** ⟦ME, room for care of plates, pans, and kitchen utensils < OFr *escuelerie* < *escuelle*, a dish < L *scutella*, salver, tray, dim. of *scutra*, platter⟧ [Now Rare] a room adjoining the kitchen, where pots and pans are cleaned and stored or where the rough, dirty kitchen work is done

scul·lion (skul′yən) *n.* ⟦LME *sculyon* < OFr *escouillon*, mop, cloth < *escouve*, broom < L *scopa*, broom, lit., twig, akin to *scapus*: see SHAFT⟧ [Archaic] a servant who does the rough, dirty work in a kitchen

sculp *abbrev.* **1** *sculpsit*: also **sculps** **2** sculptor **3** sculpture

scul·pin (skul′pin) *n., pl.* **-pin** or **-pins** ⟦prob. altered < Fr *scorpene* < L *scorpaena*: see SCORPION⟧ **1** any of a family (Cottidae) of small, generally scaleless, mostly marine percoid fishes with a spiny head and wide mouth ☆**2** a scorpionfish (*Scorpaena guttata*) of the S California coast

sculp·sit (skulp′sit) *v.* ⟦L⟧ (he or she) carved (it): placed after the artist's name as on a sculpture

sculpt (skulpt) *vt., vi.* ⟦Fr *sculpter*, altered (based on *sculpture*) < *sculper* < L *sculpere*: see fol.⟧ **1** to carve or model as a sculptor **2** to give sculpturelike form to (hair, fabric, etc.) Also **sculp**

sculp·tor (skulp′tər) *n.* ⟦L < *sculpere*, to carve in stone, akin to *scalpere*, to cut: see SCALPEL⟧ **1** a person, esp. an artist, who makes sculptures **2** [**S-**] a S constellation between Cetus and Phoenix containing the S galactic pole

sculp·tress (skulp′tris) *n.* a woman who sculpts: see -ESS

sculp·ture (skulp′chər) *n.* ⟦ME < L *sculptura* < *sculptus*, pp. of *sculpere*: see SCULPTOR⟧ **1** the art of carving wood, chiseling stone, casting or welding metal, molding clay or wax, etc. into three-dimensional representations, as statues, figures, forms, etc. **2** any work of sculpture, or such works collectively —*vt.* **-tured**, **-tur·ing** **1** to cut, carve, chisel, cast, weld, mold, etc. into statues, figures, etc. **2** to represent or portray by means of sculpture **3** to make or form as or like sculpture **4** to decorate with sculpture **5** to change in form by erosion [rock *sculptured* by a river] —*vi.* to work as a sculptor —**sculp′tur·al** *adj.* —**sculp′tur·al·ly** *adv.*

sculp·tur·esque (skulp′chər esk′) *adj.* like or suggesting sculpture

scum (skum) *n.* ⟦ME < MDu *schum*, akin to Ger *schaum*, foam, scum, prob. < IE base **(s)keu-*, to cover > SKY⟧ **1** a thin layer of impurities which forms on the top of liquids or bodies of water, often as the result of boiling or fermentation **2** the dross or refuse on top of molten metals **3** worthless parts or things; refuse **4** [Informal] a low, despicable person, or such people collectively; lowlife —*vi.* **scummed**, **scum′ming** to form scum; become covered with scum

☆**scum·bag** (skum′bag′) *n.* ⟦orig., a condom < slang use of prec., semen⟧ [Slang] a low, despicable person; lowlife

scum·ble (skum′bəl) *vt.* **-bled**, **-bling** ⟦freq. of SCUM⟧ **1** *a)* to soften the outlines or color of (a painting) by applying a thin coat of opaque color *b)* to apply (color) in this manner **2** to soften the outlines of (a drawing) by rubbing or blurring **3** to make by either of these processes —*n.* **1** a coat of color added in scumbling **2** the softening of outline produced by scumbling

scum·my (skum′ē) *adj.* **-mi·er**, **-mi·est** **1** of, like, or covered with scum **2** [Informal] despicable; low; mean

scun·gil·li (skun jē′lē, skuŋ gē′lē) *n.* ⟦It⟧ *Cooking* the edible part of a conch

scun·ner (skun′ər) *vi.* ⟦LME (Northern dial.) < ?⟧ [Scot. or North Eng.] to feel disgust or strong aversion —*n.* [Chiefly Brit.] a strong dislike: often in the phrase **take a scunner**

☆**scup** (skup) *n., pl.* **scup** or **scups** ⟦< earlier *scuppaug* < Narragansett *mishcuppaûog*, pl. of *mishcùp*⟧ a brown-and-white porgy (*Stenotomus chrysops*) found along the N Atlantic coast of the U.S.

scup·per (skup′ər) *n.* ⟦LME via ? Anglo-Fr < OFr *escopir*, lit., to spit < VL **skuppire*, of echoic orig.⟧ **1** an opening in a ship's side to allow water to drain from a weather deck **2** a similar outlet in a building, as for water to run off from a floor or roof —*vt.* [Brit. Informal] to wreck; ruin [our plans were *scuppered*]

☆**scup·per·nong** (skup′ər nôŋ′) *n.* ⟦after the *Scuppernong* River in N.C. < ? AmInd⟧ **1** a golden-green grape of the S U.S. **2** a sweet, light-colored wine made from this grape

scurf (skʉrf) *n.* ⟦ME < ON **skurfr*, akin to OE *sceorf*, Ger *schorf* < IE **(s)kerb(h)-* < base **(s)ker-*, to cut > SHEAR⟧ **1** little, dry scales shed by the skin, as dandruff **2** any scaly coating, as on some plants, sometimes indicating a diseased condition —**scurf′y** *adj.* **scurf′i·er**, **scurf′i·est**

scur·rile or **scur·ril** (skʉr′əl) *adj.* ⟦MFr *scurrile* < L *scurrilis* < *scurra*, buffoon, prob. of Etr orig.⟧ [Archaic] *var. of* SCURRILOUS (sense 1)

scur·ril·i·ty (skə ril′ə tē) *n.* ⟦L *scurrilitas*⟧ **1** the quality of being scurrilous **2** *pl.* **-ties** a scurrilous act or remark

scur·ri·lous (skʉr′ə ləs) *adj.* ⟦SCURRIL(E) + -OUS⟧ **1** [Archaic] characterized by indecent or abusive language; coarse; vulgar **2** maliciously insulting; slanderous, libelous, etc. —**scur′ri·lous·ly** *adv.* —**scur′ri·lous·ness** *n.*

scur·ry (skʉr′ē) *vi.* **-ried**, **-ry·ing** ⟦< *hurry-scurry*, redupl. of HURRY, prob. suggested by SCOUR²⟧ to run hastily; scamper —*vt.* to cause to scurry —*n.* **1** the act or sound of scurrying **2** a short run or race

scur·vy (skʉr′vē) *adj.* **-vi·er**, **-vi·est** ⟦< SCURF⟧ **1** *former var. of* SCURFY **2** low; mean; vile; contemptible —*n.* ⟦< the *adj.*⟧ a disease resulting from a deficiency of ascorbic acid in the body, characterized by weakness, anemia, spongy gums, bleeding from the mucous membranes, etc. —**scur′vi·ly** *adv.* —**scur′vi·ness** *n.*

scurvy grass an arctic plant (*Cochlearia officinalis*) of the crucifer family, with white flowers and a tarlike flavor, formerly used in treating scurvy: also **scurvy weed**

scut (skut) *n.* ⟦ME, hare, tail < ?⟧ **1** a short, stumpy tail, esp. of a hare, rabbit, or deer **2** a contemptible person

scu·ta (skyo͞ot′ə) *n. pl. of* SCUTUM

scu·tage (skyo͞ot′ij) *n.* ⟦ML *scutagium* < L *scutum*, a shield: see SCUTUM⟧ a tax paid by the holder of a knight's fee, usually in lieu of feudal military service

Scu·ta·ri (sko͞o′tä rē), **Lake** lake on the border of S Montenegro & NW Albania: 140-200 sq mi (363-518 sq km)

scu·tate (skyo͞o′tāt′) *adj.* ⟦ModL *scutatus* < L < *scutum*, shield: see SCUTUM⟧ **1** *Bot.* PELTATE **2** *Zool.* covered or protected by bony or horny plates or scales

scutch (skuch) *vt.* ⟦prob. < OFr **escoucher* < VL **excuticare*, to remove skin or rind < L *ex-*, out + *cutis*, skin: see HIDE²⟧ to free the fibers of (flax, cotton, etc.) from woody parts by beating —*n.* an instrument for doing this: also **scutch′er**

scutch·eon (skuch′ən) *n.* ⟦ME *scochoun*, aphetic for *escutcheon*⟧ *var. of* ESCUTCHEON

scute (skyo͞ot) *n.* ⟦L *scutum*, a shield: see SCUTUM⟧ *Zool.* **1** any external bony or horny plate, as on some fishes and many reptiles **2** any scalelike structure

scu·tel·late¹ (skyo͞ot′'l āt′, -it; skyo͞o tel′it) *adj.* ⟦ModL *scutellatus* < *scutellum*: see SCUTELLUM⟧ covered or protected with scutella, or small scales or plates

scu·tel·late² (skyo͞ot′'l āt′, -it; skyo͞o tel′it) *adj.* ⟦ModL *scutellatus* (see prec.), mistaken for L *scutulatus* < *scutulum*, dim. of *scutum*, a shield: see SCUTUM⟧ *Biol.* shaped like a shield or platter; round and nearly flat

scu·tel·la·tion (skyo͞ot′'l ā′shən) *n.* ⟦< SCUTELLATE¹⟧ *Zool.* the entire covering of small scales or plates, as on a bird's leg or certain fishes

scu·tel·lum (skyo͞o tel′əm) *n., pl.* **-tel′la** (-ə) ⟦ModL, mistaken for L *scutulum*: see SCUTELLATE²⟧ **1** *Bot.* any of various parts shaped like a shield **2** ⟦ModL < L *scutella*, a salver: see SCUTTLE¹⟧ *Zool.* a small, horny scale or plate

scu·ti·form (skyo͞ot′ə fôrm′) *adj.* ⟦ModL *scutiformis* < L *scutum*, a shield (see SCUTUM) + *-formis*, -FORM⟧ shaped like a shield; scutate

scut·ter (skut′ər) [Brit.] *vi.* ⟦var. of SCUTTLE²⟧ to scurry about; bustle —*n.* a scurrying or bustling about

scut·tle¹ (skut′'l) *n.* ⟦ME *scutel*, a dish < OE < L *scutella*, salver, dim. of *scutra*, flat dish⟧ **1** a broad, open basket for carrying grain, vegetables, etc. **2** a kind of bucket, usually with a wide lip, used for pouring coal on a fire: in full **coal scuttle**

scut·tle² (skut′'l) *vi.* **-tled**, **-tling** ⟦ME *scutlen*, prob. akin to SCUD⟧ to run or move quickly; scurry, esp. away from danger, trouble, etc. —*n.* a scurry or scamper; hasty flight

scut·tle³ (skut′'l) *n.* ⟦LME *skottelle* < MFr *escoutille*, trapdoor < Sp *escotilla*, an indentation, hollowing < *escote*, a notch, tuck, prob. < Goth *skauts*, seam, border; akin to OE *sceat*, SHEET¹⟧ **1** an opening in a wall or roof, fitted with a lid or cover **2** a small, covered opening in the hull or deck of a ship **3** the lid or cover for any such opening —*vt.* **-tled**, **-tling** **1** to sink (a ship or boat) intentionally by making holes in the hull below the waterline or by opening seacocks **2** to scrap or abandon (a plan, undertaking, etc.)

scut·tle·butt (skut′'l but′) *n.* ⟦orig. < *scuttled butt*, a cask or butt with an opening for a dipper⟧ **1** *Naut.* a drinking fountain on shipboard ☆**2** [Informal] rumor or gossip

scu·tum (skyo͞ot′əm) *n., pl.* for 1 & 3, **scu′ta** (-ə) ⟦L, prob. < IE base **(s)keut-*, to cover, skin < HIDE², L *cutis*, skin, Gr *skutos*, hide, leather⟧ **1** the long, wooden shield carried by infantrymen in the Roman legions **2** [**S-**] a small S constellation between Aquila and Sagittarius **3** *Zool.* a heavy, horny scale, as on certain reptiles and insects; scute

☆**scut·work** (skut′wʉrk′) *n.* ⟦< ? SCUT, sense 2⟧ [Informal] work that is regarded as tedious and routine or menial

☆**scuzz** (skuz) *n.* [Slang] **1** a scuzzy person: also **scuzz′ball′** (-bôl′) **2** filth, grime, etc.

☆**scuz·zy** (skuz′ē) *adj.* **-zi·er**, **-zi·est** ⟦< ?⟧ [Slang] dirty, shabby, disreputable, etc.

Scyl·la (sil′ə) *n.* ⟦L < Gr *Skylla*⟧ a dangerous rock on the Italian side of the Straits of Messina, opposite the whirlpool Charybdis: in classical mythology both Scylla and Charybdis were personified as female monsters —**between Scylla and Charybdis** between two perils or evils, neither of which can be evaded without risking the other

scy·phis·to·ma (sī fis′tə mə) *n., pl.* **-mae′** (-mē′) or **-mas** ⟦ModL < L *scyphus*, cup (see SCYPHUS) + Gr *stoma*, mouth (see STOMA)⟧ the small, attached polyp stage of the scyphozoan jellyfishes, preceding the strobila stage

scy·pho·zo·an (sī′fə zō′ən) *n.* ⟦< ModL *Scyphozoa* < Gr *skyphos*, a cup + *zōon*, an animal: see BIO-⟧ any of a class (Scyphozoa) of sea cnidarians, consisting of jellyfishes lacking a velum

scy·phus (sī′fəs) *n., pl.* **scy′phi′** (-fī′) ⟦L < Gr *skyphos*⟧ **1** a form of ancient Greek cup with two handles and a flat bottom **2** *Bot.* a cup-shaped part, as in some flowers

Scy·ros (sī′rəs) *Latin name for* SKÍROS

scythe (sīth) *n.* ⟦altered (infl. by L *scindere*, to cut) < ME *sithe* < OE *sithe*, *sigthe*, scythe, akin to LowG *seged* < IE base **sek-*, to cut > SAW[1], L *secare*, to cut⟧ a tool with a long, single-edged blade set at an angle on a long, curved handle, used in cutting long grass, grain, etc. by hand —*vt.* **scythed**, **scyth′ing** to cut with a scythe

scythe

Scyth·i·a (sith′ē ə) ancient region in SE Europe, centered about the N coast of the Black Sea

Scyth·i·an (-ən) *adj.* of ancient Scythia or its people, language, or culture —*n.* **1** a member of a warlike and nomadic Indo-Iranian people that lived in ancient Scythia **2** the extinct Iranian language of this people

SD *abbrev.* **1** sight draft **2** South Dakota: also **S.D.** or **S Dak** **3** *Statistics* standard deviation: also **sd**

s.d. *abbrev.* ⟦L *sine die*⟧ without date: see SINE DIE

'sdeath (zdeth) *interj.* [Obs.] *euphemism for* God's death: used as a swearword

SDI *abbrev.* Strategic Defense Initiative: a proposed (1983) defense system in which weapons based in space would intercept and destroy enemy missiles

SDR (es′dē′är′) *n., pl.* **SDRs** or **SDR's** ⟦S(PECIAL) D(RAWING) R(IGHT)⟧ a moneylike unit created by the International Monetary Fund to supplement gold and hard currencies in maintaining fixed exchange rates

Se *Chem. symbol for* selenium

SE *abbrev.* **1** southeast **2** southeastern **3** *Football* split end: sometimes written **se** **4** Standard English

sea (sē) *n.* ⟦ME *see* < OE *sæ*, akin to Du *zee*, Ger *see*⟧ **1** the continuous body of salt water covering the greater part of the earth's surface; ocean **2** a large body of salt water wholly or partly enclosed by land [the Red *Sea*, Irish *Sea*] **3** a large body of fresh water [the *Sea* of Galilee] **4** the state of the surface of the ocean with regard to waves or swells [a calm *sea*] **5** a heavy swell or wave **6** something like or suggesting the sea in extent or vastness; very great amount or number [lost in a *sea* of debt] **7** *Astron.* MARE[2] (sense 2) —*adj.* of, connected with, or for use at sea —**at sea** **1** on the open sea **2** uncertain; bewildered —**go to sea** **1** to become a sailor **2** to go on a voyage —**put (out) to sea** to sail away from land

sea anchor a large, canvas-covered device, often cone-shaped, designed to be dragged from a vessel in stormy weather to reduce drifting or to keep the vessel heading into the wind

sea anemone ⟦from its floral appearance⟧ any of an order (Actiniaria) of flowerlike, anthozoan sea polyps having a firm, gelatinous, often large, body without a skeleton, topped with petal-like tentacles: they are often brightly colored and live attached to rocks, pilings, etc.

sea bag a large, cylindrical canvas bag in which a sailor carries clothing and personal belongings

☆**sea bass** **1** any of a large family (Serranidae) of spiny-finned, predatory, marine percoid fishes; esp., a dark food fish (*Centropristes striata*) with large scales and a wide mouth, found along the Atlantic coast of the U.S. **2** any of various similar fishes, as a white drum (*Atractoscion nobilis*) of the warm waters along the California coast

sea·bed (sē′bed′) *n.* the ocean floor, esp. the areas with rich mineral or oil deposits

☆**Sea·bee** (sē′bē′) *n.* ⟦respelling of *CB*, short for *Construction Battalion*⟧ a member of any of the construction battalions of the Civil Engineer Corps of the United States Navy, that build harbor facilities, airfields, etc.

sea·bird (-burd′) *n.* a bird living on or near the sea, as a gull or tern

sea biscuit HARDTACK: also **sea bread**

sea·board (-bôrd′) *n.* ⟦SEA + BOARD⟧ land or coastal region bordering on the sea —*adj.* bordering on the sea

Sea·borg (sē′bôrg), **Glenn T(heodore)** 1912-99; U.S. nuclear chemist

sea·bor·gi·um (sē bôr′gē əm) *n.* ⟦ModL, after prec. + -IUM⟧ a radioactive chemical element with a very short half-life: a transactinide produced by bombarding californium or lead with high-energy nuclear particles: symbol, Sg; at. no. 106: see the periodic table of elements in the Reference Supplement

sea·borne (-bôrn′) *adj.* carried on or by seagoing ships

sea bream **1** any of various porgy fishes ☆**2** a porgy (*Archosargus rhomboidalis*) of the Atlantic coast of the U.S.

sea breeze a breeze blowing inland from the sea

sea captain the commander of a merchant ship

sea change ⟦used by SHAKESPEARE in *The Tempest*, I, ii (1610)⟧ an essential or notable transformation

sea·coast (-kōst′) *n.* land bordering on the sea; seashore

sea·cock (-käk′) *n.* a valve below the waterline in the hull of a ship, used to take in seawater as for ballast

sea cow any of an order (Sirenia), comprising the dugong and manatee, of large, herbivorous sea mammals with a cigar-shaped body, a blunt snout, large, mobile lips, flipperlike forelimbs, and a tail fluke

sea crawfish SPINY LOBSTER: also **sea crayfish**

sea cucumber ⟦so named from its shape and its dark, rough-textured outer covering⟧ HOLOTHURIAN

sea devil DEVILFISH

sea dog **1** an experienced sailor **2** ⟦transl. of Ger *seehund* (or Du *zeehond*), altered (as if < *see*, SEA) < earlier *seelhund* < **seel*, akin to SEAL[2] + *hund*, dog: from its bark⟧ any of various seals

sea eagle any of several fish-eating eagles of the same genus (*Haliaeetus*) as the bald eagle

sea elephant either of two very large, earless seals (genus *Mirounga*) that are hunted for oil: the male has a long proboscis

sea fan any of several gorgonians with the axial skeleton formed into a fanlike structure; esp., a horny coral (*Gorgonia flabellum*) of the West Indies and Florida Keys

sea·far·er (-fer′ər) *n.* a traveler by sea; esp., a sailor

sea·far·ing (-fer′iŋ) *adj.* traveling by sea, esp. as a sailor —*n.* travel by sea

sea feather any of several anthozoans with the skeleton branched into a featherlike form, as the sea pen

sea·floor (sē′flôr′) *n.* the ground along the bottom of the ocean: also written **sea floor**

☆**sea·food** (-fo͞od′) *n.* **1** food prepared from or consisting of saltwater fish or shellfish **2** loosely, food prepared from any fish

sea·fowl (-foul′) *n.* any bird living on or near the sea

sea·front (-frunt′) *n.* the part of a town or other built-up area facing on the sea

sea·girt (-gurt′) *adj.* surrounded by the sea

sea·go·ing (-gō′iŋ) *adj.* **1** made for use on the open sea [a *seagoing* schooner] **2** of or having to do with travel by sea

sea green a pale bluish-green color —**sea′-green′** *adj.*

sea gull GULL[1]; esp., any gull living along a seacoast

sea hare any of a family (Aplysiidae) of large, sluglike, gastropod sea mollusks, with a rudimentary internal shell and a prominent front pair of tentacles

sea holly a European eryngo (*Eryngium maritimum*) with leathery, bluish, spiny leaves and globular heads of small, bluish flowers

sea horse **1** any of a genus (*Hippocampus*) of small, semitropical, marine bony fishes of the same family (Syngnathidae, order Gasterosteiformes) as the pipefishes, having a slender prehensile tail, plated body, and a head and foreparts somewhat suggestive of those of a horse: it normally swims in an upright position, and the male incubates the eggs in a pouch in his abdomen: also written **sea′horse′** *n.* **2** WALRUS **3** a mythical sea creature, half fish and half horse

sea horse

☆**sea-is·land cotton** (sē′ī′lənd) a fine kind of long-fibered cotton (*Gossypium barbadense*) grown orig. in the Sea Islands

Sea Islands chain of islands off the coasts of S.C., Ga., & N Fla.

sea kale ⟦from its cabbagelike appearance⟧ a fleshy, European, coastal plant (*Crambe maritima*) of the crucifer family, whose edible young shoots are blanched and used like asparagus

sea king ⟦< ON *sækonungr* (OE *sækyning*)⟧ any of the Norse pirate chiefs of the Middle Ages

seal[1] (sēl) *n.* ⟦ME *seel* < OFr < L *sigillum*, a seal, mark, dim. of *signum*: see SIGN⟧ **1** a design, initial, or other device placed on a letter, document, etc., as a mark of genuineness or authenticity: letters were, esp. formerly, closed with a wafer of molten wax into which was pressed the distinctive seal of the sender **2** a stamp, signet ring, etc., or the signet itself, used in making such a design **3** a wax wafer, piece of paper, etc. bearing the impression of some official design and used as to authenticate a signature or document **4** *a)* something that seals, closes, or fastens tightly or securely; specif., a piece of metal, paper, etc. so placed over a lid, cap, etc. that it must be broken before the container can be opened *b)* a tight closure, as against the passage of air or water **5** anything that confirms, authenticates, or guarantees; pledge **6** an indication; sign; token [a handshake as a *seal* of friendship] **7** the standing water in the trap of a drainpipe, that seals off sewer gases ☆**8** an ornamental stamp placed on envelopes, packages, etc. [a Christmas *seal*] —*vt.* ⟦ME *selen* < OFr *seeler* < the n.⟧ **1** to mark with a seal; fix a seal to **2** to secure the contents of (a letter, envelope, etc.), orig. by closing with a sealed wax wafer, now usually with mucilage, tape, or a gummed flap **3** to confirm or authenticate (a document, etc.) by marking with a seal **4** to attest to or confirm the truth or genuineness of (a promise, bargain, etc.) **5** to certify as being accurate, exact, of a given size, quality, capacity, etc. by fixing a stamp or seal to **6** to grant, assign, or designate with a seal, pledge, etc. **7** to settle, determine, or decide finally or irrevocably [to *seal* one's fate] **8** *a)* to close, shut, or fasten with or as with a seal *b)* to close completely so as to make airtight or watertight *c)* to apply a nonpermeable coating to (a porous surface, as of wood) as before painting **9** *Elec.* to bring (a plug and jack) into full, interlocking contact **10** *Law* to bar public examination of [to *seal* the transcript of the testimony] ☆**11** *Mormon Ch.* to solemnize (a marriage) for eternity in a church rite —**seal off 1** to close completely **2** to enclose or surround (an area, etc.) with barriers, a cordon, etc. —**set one's seal to 1** to mark with one's seal **2** to endorse; approve —**under (one's) seal** in a document authenticated by one's seal

seal² (sēl) *n., pl.* **seals** or **seal** ⟦ME *sele* < OE *seolh*, akin to OHG *selah*, prob. < IE base **swelk-*, to pull, draw (with reference to the seal's labored movements on land) > L *sulcus*, furrow⟧ **1** any of two families (Otariidae and Phocidae) of sea carnivores with a doglike head, a torpedo-shaped body, and four webbed feet or flippers: they typically live in cold or temperate waters and usually eat fish: see EARED SEAL, EARLESS SEAL **2** *a)* the fur of a fur seal *b)* a similar fur used as a substitute for this **3** leather made from sealskin —*vi.* to hunt seals

fur seal

☆**SEAL** (sēl) *n., pl.* **SEALs** ⟦< *sea, air, land team*⟧ a member of a special U.S. Navy combat unit trained for sea, air, or land commando operations: also **Navy SEAL**

sea lamprey a parasitic lamprey (*Petromyzon marinus*) of the N Atlantic that ascends streams to spawn: now landlocked in the Great Lakes, where it is highly destructive to lake trout

sea lane a commonly used route for travel by sea

seal·ant (sēl′ənt) *n.* ⟦SEAL¹ + -ANT⟧ a substance, as a wax, plastic, silicone, etc., used for sealing a joint, opening, surface, etc.

sea lavender any of a genus (*Limonium*, family Plumbaginaceae) of stiff, dicotyledonous plants (order Plumbaginales) with white, pink, lavender, or yellow flowers and many branches: often dried for winter bouquets

sea lawyer [Informal] a contentious sailor, who habitually argues, questions orders and regulations, etc.

seal brown a rich, dark brown

sea legs the ability to walk steadily on board a ship at sea

seal·er¹ (sēl′ər) *n.* **1** a person or thing that seals; specif., a substance used to seal a porous surface, as before painting **2** an inspector who tests and certifies weights and measures

seal·er² (sēl′ər) *n.* **1** a hunter of seals **2** a ship used in seal hunting

sea lettuce any of a genus (*Ulva*) of marine green algae with edible, leaflike parts

sea level the level of the surface of the sea, esp. the mean level between high and low tide: used as a standard in measuring heights and depths

sea lily ⟦from its resemblance to a flower on a stalk⟧ any of several orders of stalked and attached crinoids

sealing wax a combination of resin and turpentine used for sealing letters, dry cells, etc.: it is hard at normal temperatures but softens when heated

sea lion any of several genera of large, eared seals without underfur, usually living in colonies along the Pacific coastline

seal ring SIGNET RING

seal·skin (sēl′skin′) *n.* **1** the skin or pelt of the fur seal, esp. with the coarse outer hair removed and the soft undercoat dyed dark-brown or black **2** a garment made of this —*adj.* made of sealskin

Sea·ly·ham terrier (sē′lē ham′; *also, chiefly Brit*, -lē əm) ⟦after *Sealyham*, an estate in Wales, where first bred⟧ any of a breed of small terrier with short legs, a long, white, bristly coat, a squarish muzzle, and an upright tail: traditionally the tail is docked

seam (sēm) *n.* ⟦ME *seme* < OE *seam*, akin to Ger *saum* < IE base **siw-*, **sū* > SEW⟧ **1** *a)* a joining of two pieces of material with a line of stitches *b)* the line of stitches [sew a fine *seam*] *c)* the material between the margin of each of the joined pieces and its outer edge [a one-inch *seam*] *d)* the line on the outside of a garment at the joining of two pieces of material **2** a line formed by the joining together of any separate pieces; line marking adjoining edges, as of boards **3** a mark, line, ridge, etc. like this, as a scar, wrinkle, mold line on glass, etc. **4** a thin layer or stratum of ore, coal, etc. —*vt.* **1** to join together so as to form a seam **2** to mark with a seamlike line, crack, wrinkle, etc. —*vi.* [Rare] to develop cracks or fissures —**burst at the seams** to be uncomfortably or dangerously full or overcrowded: a fig. use [an apartment *bursting at the seams* with guests] —**come apart at the seams** to fail to hold together; disintegrate, collapse, etc.: a fig. use [a trade agreement *coming apart at the seams*]

sea-maid (sē′mād′) *n.* **1** a mermaid **2** a sea nymph or sea goddess Also **sea′-maid′en**

sea·man (sē′mən) *n., pl.* **-men** (-mən) ⟦ME *seeman* < OE *sæman*: see SEA & MAN⟧ **1** a sailor; mariner **2** *U.S. Navy* an enlisted person ranking below a petty officer third class, whose general duties involve most ships' equipment other than boilers and engines

sea·man·like (-līk′) *adj.* like or characteristic of a competent seaman; showing seamanship: also **sea′man·ly**

sea·man·ship (-ship′) *n.* skill in operating, navigating, or handling a ship

sea·mark (sē′märk′) *n.* **1** a line marking the limit of the tide **2** any prominent object on shore, as a lighthouse, serving as a guide for ships

sea mew ⟦ME *semewe*: see MEW³⟧ [Brit.] SEA GULL

seam·less (sēm′lis) *adj.* **1** made without a seam or seams **2** smooth in texture, quality, transition, etc.; without discontinuities or disparities [a *seamless* blend of fact and fiction, a *seamless* adjustment to a new boss] —**seam′less·ly** *adv.*

sea·mount (sē′mount′) *n.* a mountain rising from the sea floor but not reaching the surface: cf. GUYOT

sea mouse ⟦from its bristles and general shape⟧ any of a genus (*Aphrodite*) of large, marine polychaetes with a flat, oval body covered with bristles

seam·ster (sēm′stər, sem′-) *n.* [Now Rare] TAILOR

seam·stress (sēm′stris, sem′-) *n.* ⟦ME *seamestre*, man or woman who sews < OE < *seam*, SEAM + additional fem. suffix -ESS⟧ a woman who is expert at sewing, esp. one who makes her living by sewing

seam·y (sēm′ē) *adj.* **seam′i·er, seam′i·est 1** having or showing seams, esp. with rough edges, as the underside of a garment **2** unpleasant or sordid [the *seamy* side of life] —**seam′i·ness** *n.*

Sean (shôn, shän) *n.* ⟦Ir, var. of JOHN¹⟧ a masculine name

sé·ance (sā′äns) *n.* ⟦Fr, lit., a sitting < *seoir* < L *sedere*, to SIT⟧ a meeting at which a medium seeks to communicate with the spirits of the dead

sea nettle ⟦so named from its ability to sting⟧ any large jellyfish

sea onion 1 the dried bulb of white varieties of a plant (*Urginea maritima*) of the lily family, formerly used in medicine **2** this plant

sea otter a marine otter (*Enhydra lutris*) with valuable dark-brown fur, found along the N Pacific coast

sea pen ⟦from a fancied resemblance to a quill pen⟧ any of an order (Pennatulacea) of mud-dwelling anthozoans that form feather-shaped colonies

sea·plane (sē′plān′) *n.* any airplane designed to land on and take off from water

sea·port (-pôrt′) *n.* **1** a port or harbor used by ocean ships **2** a town or city having such a port or harbor

sea power 1 naval strength **2** a nation having great naval strength

sea purse a horny egg case or egg capsule produced by certain rays and sharks

sea·quake (-kwāk′) *n.* an earthquake on the ocean floor

sear¹ (sir) *adj.* ⟦ME *seer* < OE *sear*, dry < IE base **saus* > Sans *śúṣyati*, (he) dries, withers, L *sudus*, dry⟧ *alt. sp. of* SERE² —*vt.* ⟦ME *seeren* < OE *searian* < the adj.⟧ **1** to dry up; wither **2** *a)* to scorch or burn the surface of *b)* to brown (meat) quickly at high heat **3** to brand or cauterize with a hot iron **4** to make callous or unfeeling; harden **5** to cause to quail or feel humiliated, as by a scornful glance —*vi.* [Archaic] to dry up; wither —*n.* a mark or condition caused by searing —**SYN.** BURN¹ —**sear′ing** *adj.*

sear² (sir) *n.* ⟦< MFr *serre*, a bolt < OFr *serrer*, to close, press < VL **serrare*, altered (infl. by L *serare*, to saw) < LL *serare*, to bolt, bar < L *sera*, a bar, bolt⟧ the catch in a gunlock that holds the hammer cocked or half-cocked

sea raven ☆a sculpin (*Hemitripterus americanus*) found in the N Atlantic

search (surch) *vt.* ⟦ME *searchen* < OFr *cercher* < LL *circare*, to go round, go about, explore < *circus*, a ring: see CIRCUS⟧ **1** to go over or look through for the purpose of finding something; explore; rummage; examine [to *search* a house for a lost article] **2** to examine (a person) for something concealed, as by running one's hands over the clothing, through the pockets, etc. **3** to examine closely and carefully; test and try; probe [to *search* one's conscience] **4** to look through (writings, records, etc.) to establish certain facts **5** to find out or uncover by investigation: usually with *out* —*vi.* **1** to try to find something; make a search **2** to examine data in a computer in order to locate items having a given property —*n.* **1** an act of searching; scrutiny, inquiry, or examination in an attempt to find something, gain knowledge, establish facts, etc. **2** the act of a belligerent in stopping and searching a neutral ship for contraband: see RIGHT OF SEARCH —**in search of** making a search for; trying to find, learn, etc. by searching —☆**search me!** [Slang] I do not know the answer to your query —**search′a·ble** *adj.* —**search′er** *n.*

search engine 1 software designed to examine documents, websites, etc. in order to locate items on a specified topic or having a given property **2** a website designed to search the internet in this manner, as a service to its customers

search·ing (surch′iŋ) *adj.* **1** examining or exploring thoroughly; scrutinizing; thorough **2** sharp; piercing; penetrating [the *searching* wind] —**search′ing·ly** *adv.*

search·light (surch′līt′) *n.* **1** an apparatus containing a light and reflector on a swivel, for projecting a strong, far-reaching beam in any direction **2** such a beam

search party a group of people taking part in a search, as for a lost or missing person

search warrant a legal document authorizing or directing an officer of the law to search a specified person, premises, etc., as for stolen or contraband articles, items to be used in evidence, etc.

☆**sea robin** any of a family (Triglidae) of spiny-finned, percoid sea fishes having a broad head covered with plates of bone, and large, winglike pectoral fins, esp. any of a genus (*Prionotus*) with reddish coloring: also written **sea′rob′in** *n.*

sea room enough open space for maneuvering a ship

sea rover a pirate or a pirate ship

sea salt salt obtained by the evaporation of sea water, used mainly for seasoning food

sea·scape (sē′skāp′) *n.* ⟦SEA + -SCAPE⟧ **1** a view of the sea **2** a drawing, painting, etc. of such a scene

sea scorpion any of an extinct order (Eurypterida, class Merostomata) of eurypterids

sea serpent 1 *Folklore* any large, unidentified or imaginary serpentlike animal reported to have been seen in the sea **2** *a)* OARFISH *b)* SEA SNAKE

sea·shell (-shel′) *n.* the shell of any marine mollusk

sea·shore (-shôr′) *n.* **1** land along the sea; seacoast **2** *Law* the land along the sea lying between the usual high-water and low-water marks
sea·sick (-sik′) *adj.* suffering from seasickness
sea·sick·ness (-sik′nis) *n.* nausea, dizziness, etc. caused by the rolling and pitching of a ship or boat
sea·side (sē′sīd′) *n.* land along the sea; seashore —*adj.* at or of the seaside
sea slug NUDIBRANCH
sea snake any of a large subfamily (Hydrophiinae) of poisonous elapine snakes with a flattened, oarlike tail, living in tropical seas
sea·son (sē′zən) *n.* ⟦ME *sesoun* < OFr *seson* < VL *satio*, season for sowing < L, a sowing, planting < base of *serere*, to sow: see SEED⟧ **1** any of the four arbitrary divisions of the year, characterized chiefly by differences in temperature, precipitation, amount of daylight, and plant growth; spring, summer, fall (or autumn), or winter **2** a time or part of the year during which a specified kind of agricultural work is done or a specified kind of weather prevails [the harvest *season*, the rainy *season*] **3** the time when something specified flourishes, develops, takes place, or is popular, permitted, or at its best [the opera *season*, the hunting *season*] **4** the period of time during which a sports league's games are played, often, specif., excluding the preseason and postseason **5** a period of time [a slack *season* in business] **6** the suitable, fitting, or convenient time **7** the period of time during which a specified festival or holiday occurs [the Christmas *season*] **8** ⟦< the v.⟧ [Obs.] something that seasons —*vt.* ⟦ME *sesonen*, aphetic < MFr *assaisonner*, to season, orig., to ripen < *a-* (< L *ad-*), to + *saison*⟧ **1** to make (food) more tasty by adding salt, spices, etc. **2** to add zest or interest to [to *season* a lecture with humor] **3** *a)* to make more suitable for use; improve the quality of, as by aging, drying, etc.; cure; mature [to *season* lumber] *b)* to give (an athlete, actor, etc.) experience to increase skill [many tours *seasoned* him as an actor] **4** to make used to; accustom; inure; acclimate [*seasoned* to a hard life] **5** to make less harsh or severe; temper; soften [discipline *seasoned* with kindness] **6** to prepare the surface of (a piece of cookware) for use, as by applying a coat of oil or lard and then heating —*vi.* to become seasoned, as wood by drying —**for a season** for a while —**in good season** early enough —**in season 1** available fresh for use as food: said of fruits, vegetables, seafood, etc. **2** at the legally established time for being hunted or caught: said of game **3** in or at the suitable or proper time **4** in good season; early enough **5** in heat: said of animals —**out of season** not in season —**sea′son·er** *n.*
sea·son·a·ble (-ə bəl) *adj.* ⟦ME *sesonable*⟧ **1** suitable to or usual for the time of year **2** coming or done at the right time; opportune; timely —**SYN.** TIMELY —**sea′son·a·ble·ness** *n.* —**sea′son·a·bly** *adv.*
sea·son·al (sē′zən əl) *adj.* of, characteristic of, or depending on the season or seasons —**sea′son·al·ly** *adv.*
seasonal affective disorder a disorder characterized by mental depression, the recurrence of which is associated with the shorter periods of daylight during the winter months
sea·son·ing (sē′zən iŋ) *n.* anything that adds zest; esp., salt, spices, etc. added to food to make it more flavorful
season's greetings used as a general expression of goodwill during the season of Hanukkah, Christmas, and New Year's
season ticket a ticket or set of tickets as for a series of concerts, sporting events, etc. or for transportation between fixed points for a limited time
sea spider ⟦so named from its overall body shape⟧ PYCNOGONID
sea squirt ⟦so named because it is able to draw in and *squirt* water from a body opening⟧ ASCIDIAN
sea swallow TERN
seat (sēt) *n.* ⟦ME *sete* < ON *sæti*: for IE base see SIT⟧ **1** the manner of sitting, as on horseback **2** *a)* a place or space to sit, or the right to such a place, esp. as evidenced by a ticket [to buy two *seats* to the opera] *b)* a thing to sit on; chair, bench, stool, etc. **3** *a)* the buttocks *b)* the part of a garment covering the buttocks *c)* the part of a chair, bench, etc. that supports the buttocks **4** the right to sit as a member; position of a member; membership [a *seat* on the stock exchange] **5** *a)* a part forming the base of something *b)* a part or surface on which another part rests or fits snugly **6** the place where something is carried on, settled, established, etc.; center; location; site [the *seat* of government, a *seat* of learning] **7** a part of the body in which some power, function, quality, etc. is or is thought to be centered **8** a home or residence; esp., a large house that is part of a country estate —*vt.* **1** to put or set in or on a seat **2** to lead to a seat or help to settle into a seat **3** to have seats for; accommodate with seats [a hall that *seats* 500] **4** to put a seat in or on; patch or renew the seat of; reseat **5** to put, fix, or establish in a particular place, position of authority, etc. —**be seated** to assume a seated position; sit down: also **take a seat** —**by the seat of one's (or the) pants** ⟦WWII pilots' term: prob. in ref. to experience gained while seated in the cockpit⟧ [Slang] relying on one's intuition and experience rather than on instruments or a predetermined plan
sea tangle any of various seaweeds
seat belt 1 a device consisting of an anchored strap or straps that buckle across the hips to hold a seated passenger safely in place as during a collision **2** such a device combined with a SHOULDER HARNESS, as in an automobile Also written **seat′belt′** *n.*
-seat·er (sēt′ər) *combining form* a vehicle, airplane, etc. having (a specified number of) seats [a two-*seater*]
seat·ing (sēt′iŋ) *n.* **1** the act of providing with or directing to a seat or seats **2** material for covering chair seats, etc. **3** the number or arrangement of seats or of persons seated **4** SEAT (*n.* 5*b*)
☆**seat·mate** (sēt′māt′) *n.* a person in an adjoining seat in an airplane, bus, etc.
SEATO (sēt′ō) *abbrev.* Southeast Asia Treaty Organization (1955-76)
seat-of-the-pants (sēt′ əv *th*ə pants′) *adj.* ⟦< BY THE SEAT OF ONE'S PANTS (see phr. under SEAT)⟧ [Slang] using or relying on intuition and experience rather than instruments, technology, or a predetermined plan
sea trout any of various saltwater drum fishes (genus *Cynoscion*) including several weakfishes
Se·at·tle (sē at′'l) ⟦city renamed (1852) after *Seathl* (1786?-1866), an Indian chief⟧ seaport in WC Wash., on Puget Sound —**Se·at′tle·ite′** *n.*
☆**seat·work** (sēt′wurk′) *n.* reading, writing, or other work on lessons, done in school by students at their desks
sea urchin ⟦so named because of its spines⟧ any of various orders of echinoid echinoderms having a somewhat globular body of fused skeletal plates studded with long, calcareous, movable spines

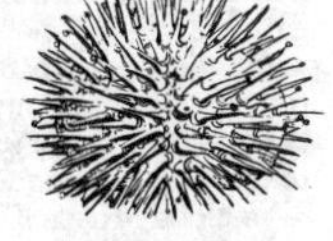
sea urchin

sea wall a wall or embankment made to break the force of the waves and to protect the shore from erosion: also written **sea′wall′** *n.*
sea walnut ⟦so named from its shape⟧ CTENOPHORE
sea·ward (sē′wərd) *n.* a direction or position away from the land and toward the sea —*adj.* directed, going, or situated toward the sea —*adv.* toward, or in the direction of, the sea: also **sea′wards**
sea·ware (-wer′) *n.* ⟦via dial. < OE *sæware*, seaweed < *sæ*, sea + *war*, alga⟧ seaweed; esp., large, coarse seaweed tossed up on shore, used as fertilizer
sea·wa·ter (sē′wôt′ər) *n.* the salty water of the ocean
sea·way (-wā′) *n.* **1** a route for travel on the sea **2** a moderate to rough sea **3** an inland waterway to the sea for ocean ships [St. Lawrence *Seaway*]
sea·weed (-wēd′) *n.* **1** any sea plant or plants; esp., any marine alga, as kelp: in full **marine seaweed 2** any similar freshwater plant: in full **freshwater seaweed**
sea whip any of several gorgonians with the axial skeleton branched, forming long, whiplike colonies
sea·wor·thy (-wur′*th*ē) *adj.* fit to travel in on the open sea; sturdy: said of a ship —**sea′wor′thi·ness** *n.*
sea wrack ⟦see WRACK[1]⟧ seaweed, esp. seaweed that has been cast ashore
se·ba·ceous (sə bā′shəs) *adj.* ⟦L *sebaceus* < *sebum*, tallow: see SOAP⟧ of or like fat, tallow, or sebum; esp., designating certain skin glands that secrete sebum
se·bac·ic acid (sə bas′ik, -bā′sik) ⟦< L *sebaceus* (see prec.) + -IC⟧ a white, crystalline acid, $COOH(CH_2)_8COOH$, obtained by the distillation of oleic acid or castor oil: used in making plasticizers, alkyd resins, etc.
Se·bas·tian[1] (sə bas′chən) *n.* ⟦L *Sebastianus* < Gr *Sebastianos*, lit., a man of *Sebastia*, ancient name of Sivas, or a man of *Sebaste*, name of Samaria after the time of Herod the Great⟧ a masculine name
Se·bas·tian[2] (sə bas′chən), Saint (died A.D. 288?); Christian martyr of Rome: his day is Jan. 20
Se·bas·to·pol (si bas′tə pōl′) *var. of* SEVASTOPOL
SEbE *abbrev.* southeast by east
se·bif·er·ous (sə bif′ər əs) *adj.* ⟦< L *sebum*, tallow (see SOAP) + -FEROUS⟧ *Biol.* secreting a fatty or waxlike substance; sebaceous: also **se·bip′a·rous** (-bip′ər əs)
seb·or·rhe·a or **seb·or·rhoe·a** (seb′ə rē′ə) *n.* ⟦ModL: see SEBUM & -RRHEA⟧ an excessive discharge from the sebaceous glands resulting in abnormally oily skin —**seb′or·rhe′ic** *adj.*, **seb′or·rhoe′ic**
SEbS *abbrev.* southeast by south
se·bum (sē′bəm) *n.* ⟦L, tallow: see SOAP⟧ the semiliquid, greasy secretion of the sebaceous glands
sec[1] (sek) *n.* [Informal] SECOND[3] (senses 1 & 3) [just wait a *sec*]
sec[2] (sek) *adj.* ⟦Fr: see SACK[3]⟧ dry; not sweet: said of wine
sec[3] *abbrev.* **1** secant **2** second(s) **3** secondary **4** secretary **5** section(s) **6** sector **7** *secundum* **8** security
SEC *abbrev.* Securities and Exchange Commission
se·cant (sē′kənt) *adj.* ⟦L *secans*, prp. of *secare*, to cut: see SAW[1]⟧ cutting; intersecting —*n.* **1** *Geom.* any straight line intersecting a curve at two or more points **2** *Trigonometry* the reciprocal of the cosine; specif., *a)* the ratio of the hypotenuse to the adjacent side of a given acute angle in a right triangle *b)* an equivalent, positive or negative ratio for certain related angles (Ex.: the secant of 57° or 303° is 1.8362, of 123° or 237° is −1.8362) or real numbers representing radians (Ex.: the secant of .9948 radians (57°) is 1.8362)
sec·a·teurs (sek′ə tərz) *pl.n.* ⟦< Fr *secateur* < L *secare*, to cut (see SAW[1]) + Fr *-ateur* < L *-ator*, -ATOR⟧ [Chiefly Brit.] shears used for pruning
Sec·chi disk (*or* disc) (sek′ē) ⟦after P. A. *Secchi* (1818-78), It astronomer⟧ a circular, white or colored disk lowered into a body of water to estimate the clarity of the water by measuring the depth at which it disappears
sec·co (sek′kô) *adj.* ⟦It < L *siccus*: see SICCATIVE⟧ dry —*n.* painting done on dry plaster
se·cede (si sēd′) *vi.* **-ced′ed**, **-ced′ing** ⟦L *secedere* < *se-*, *sed-*, apart (< IE base **se-*, **swe-*, apart, lone > OE *swæs*, special, dear) + *cedere*, to go: see CEDE⟧ to withdraw formally from membership in, or association with, a group, organization, etc., esp. a political group —**se·ced′er** *n.*
se·cern (si surn′) *vt.* ⟦L *secernere*, to sunder, separate < *se-* (see prec.) + *cernere*, to separate: see HARVEST⟧ to discriminate, or distinguish [to *secern* good from evil]

se·ces·sion (si sesh′ən) *n.* ⟦L *secessio*⟧ ☆1 an act of seceding; formal withdrawal or separation 2 [*often* **S-**] the withdrawal of the Southern states from the federal Union at the start of the Civil War —**se·ces′sion·al** *adj.*

☆**se·ces·sion·ist** (-ist) *n.* 1 a person who favors or takes part in secession, or upholds the right to secede 2 [*often* **S-**] one who favored the secession of the Southern states —**se·ces′sion·ism′** *n.*

☆**Seck·el (pear)** (sek′əl) ⟦after the Pa. fruit grower who originated it⟧ a small, sweet, juicy, reddish-brown pear

sec. leg. *abbrev.* ⟦L *secundum legum*⟧ according to law

se·clude (si klo͞od′) *vt.* **-clud′ed, -clud′ing** ⟦ME *secluden* < L *secludere* < *se-*, apart (see SECEDE) + *claudere*, to CLOSE[2]⟧ 1 to keep away or apart from others; bar or shut off from the view of or relations with others; isolate 2 to make private or hidden; screen

se·clud·ed (-klo͞od′id) *adj.* 1 shut off or kept apart from others; isolated; withdrawn 2 cut off from the public view; hidden, intimate, etc. [*a secluded garden*]

se·clu·sion (si klo͞o′zhən) *n.* ⟦ML *seclusio*⟧ 1 a secluding or being secluded; retirement; isolation; privacy 2 a secluded place —*SYN.* SOLITUDE

se·clu·sive (-siv) *adj.* ⟦< L *seclusus*, pp. of *secludere* (see SECLUDE) + -IVE⟧ 1 tending to seclude 2 fond of or seeking seclusion —**se·clu′sive·ly** *adv.* —**se·clu′sive·ness** *n.*

sec·o·bar·bi·tal (sek′ō bär′bi täl′, -tal′) *n.* a white, odorless, bitter powder, $C_{12}H_{18}N_2O_3$, used chiefly in the form of its water-soluble sodium salt as a sedative and hypnotic

Sec·o·nal (sek′ə nôl′, -nal) ⟦< arbitrary base + -AL⟧ *trademark for* SECOBARBITAL —*n.* [*also* **s-**] a capsule of this

sec·ond[1] (sek′ənd) *adj.* ⟦ME *secunde* < OFr < L *secundus*, following, second < *sequi*, to follow: see SEQUENT⟧ 1 coming next after the first in order of place or time; 2d or 2nd 2 another; other; additional; supplementary [to take a *second* helping] 3 being of the same kind as another; resembling a given original [a *second* Shakespeare] 4 alternate; other [every *second* day] 5 next below the first in rank, power, value, merit, excellence, etc. 6 inferior; subordinate; secondary 7 *Music* *a)* lower in pitch *b)* playing or singing a part that is lower in pitch —*n.* 1 the next after the first 2 any person, thing, class, place, etc. that is second 3 an article of merchandise that falls below the standard set for first quality: *usually used in pl.* 4 [*pl.*] *a)* a kind of coarse flour *b)* bread made from this 5 an aide or official assistant, esp. to one of the principals in a duel or boxing match 6 the second forward gear of a transmission: it provides more speed but less torque than first 7 the act or an instance of seconding 8 [*pl.*] a second helping of something to eat ☆9 *Baseball short for* SECOND BASE 10 *Music* *a)* the second tone of an ascending diatonic scale, or a tone one degree above or below any given tone in such a scale *b)* the interval between two such tones, or a combination of them *c)* the second part in a harmonized composition, esp. the alto *d)* an instrument or voice taking this part —*vt.* 1 to act as an aide or second to; assist 2 to give support or encouragement to; further; reinforce 3 to indicate formally one's approval or support of (a motion, nomination, etc.) as a necessary preliminary to discussion of or a vote on it —*adv.* 1 in the second place, rank, group, etc. 2 just before or just short of the last thing in a series [the *second*-last row] —**sec′ond·er** *n.*

se·cond[2] (si känd′) *vt.* ⟦< Fr *en second*, in second position⟧ [Brit.] 1 to transfer (a military officer) from regular service to special service, civil or military 2 to transfer (an official, employee, etc.) to a temporary assignment —**se·cond′ment** *n.*

sec·ond[3] (sek′ənd) *n.* ⟦ME *seconde* < ML (*pars minuta*) *secunda*, second (small part): from being a further division (i.e., beyond the minute) < L *secundus*: see SECOND[1]⟧ 1 *a)* 1⁄60 of a minute of time *b)* the basic unit of time in the SI, MKS, CGS, or FPS systems: redefined in 1967 so that it is now based on the periodic oscillations of an atomic clock which uses cesium atoms and has a resonance frequency of 9,192,631,770 hertz (abbrev. *s*) 2 1⁄60 of a minute of angular measurement: symbol, ″ 3 a very short period of time; moment; instant 4 a specific point in time

sec·ond·ar·y (sek′ən der′ē) *adj.* ⟦ME *secundary* < L *secundarius*⟧ 1 second, or below the first, in rank, importance, class, place, etc.; subordinate; minor; not primary 2 *a)* derived or resulting from something considered primary or original; dependent; derivative *b)* secondhand; not original [a *secondary* source of information] *c)* designating colors derived by mixing two primary colors: see COLOR (sense 3) 3 coming after that which is first in a series of processes, events, stages, etc., as of growth or development 4 coming next in sequence after the primary or elementary level [*secondary* education] 5 *Chem.* *a)* formed by the replacement of two atoms or radicals in the molecule [*secondary* sodium phosphate, Na_2HPO_4] *b)* characterized by or designating a carbon atom that is directly attached to two other carbon atoms in a closed or open chain 6 *Elec.* designating or of an induced current or its circuit in a transformer, induction coil, etc. 7 *Geol.* formed as a result of the alteration, disintegration, or erosion of preexisting rocks or minerals 8 *Linguis.* *a)* derived from a base that is itself a word, by the addition of a prefix or derivational suffix *b)* designating a form or a process that is historically relatively late; not original 9 *Ornithology* designating or of the long flight feathers attached to the second joint or segment of a bird's wing —*n., pl.* **-ar′ies** 1 a person or thing that is secondary, subordinate, or inferior 2 any of the secondary colors 3 *Elec.* an output winding of a transformer from which the power is taken 4 *Football* the defensive backfield 5 *Zool.* a secondary feather —**sec′ond·ar′i·ly** *adv.*

secondary cell *see* STORAGE BATTERY

secondary emission 1 the emission of electrons (**secondary electrons**) from a material, following impact by high-speed electrons 2 the emission of electrons or electromagnetic radiation from a liquid, solid, or gas, following impact by a charged particle or higher energy electromagnetic radiation

☆**secondary school** a school, esp. a high school, coming after elementary school

secondary sex (*or* sexual) characteristic any of the physical characteristics that differentiate male and female individuals, as distribution of hair or fat on the body, breast and muscle development, deepening of the voice, etc., that are not directly related to reproduction and usually appear at puberty

secondary stress (*or* accent) 1 *a)* any accent, or stress, that is weaker than the full, or primary, accent *b)* a mark (in this dictionary, ′) used to indicate this 2 *Linguis.* *a)* the second strongest of the four phonemic degrees of stress *b)* a mark indicating this

☆**second banana** ⟦see TOP BANANA⟧ [Slang] 1 a performer in show business, esp. burlesque, who plays a subordinate role, as straight man, to the top banana, or star comedian 2 any person in a subordinate, often servile, position

☆**second base** *Baseball* 1 the base located behind the pitcher, the second of the four bases that a base runner attempts to reach safely 2 the defensive position played by the second baseman

☆**second baseman** *Baseball* the infielder who plays on the right side of the infield near second base and frequently covers second base

second best something next in quality below the first; something next to the best —**sec′ond-best′** *adj.*

second childhood senility; dotage

Second City ⟦because it was *second* in population to New York City when so named (1890s)⟧ *name for* CHICAGO

sec·ond-class (sek′ənd klas′) *adj.* 1 of the class, rank, excellence, etc. next below the highest; of secondary quality 2 designating or of accommodations next below the best [a *second-class* railway carriage] ☆3 designating or of a former class of mail consisting of newspapers, periodicals, etc. 4 *a)* inferior, inadequate, etc. *b)* lacking or denied full rights, privileges, etc. [a *second-class* citizen] —*adv.* 1 with accommodations next below the best [to travel *second-class*] 2 as or by second-class mail

Second Coming *Christian Theol.* the expected return of Christ, at the Last Judgment: also **Second Advent**

second cousin the child of one's parent's first cousin; also, in some social traditions, the first cousin of one's parent

sec·ond-de·gree (sek′ənd di grē′) *adj.* designating either the second highest level or the second lowest level of damage, rank, etc.

second-degree burn *see* BURN[1] (*n.* 1)

Second Empire the government of France under Louis Napoleon, 1852-70

second estate *see* ESTATE (sense 2)

second fiddle the part played by the second violin section of an orchestra or by the second violin of a quartet, etc. —**play (or be) second fiddle** to have secondary status, as in the affection or attention of another

second floor ☆1 the floor above the ground floor of a building 2 in Europe and Great Britain, the floor two stories above the ground floor: sometimes used in this sense in hotels, etc. in the U.S.

second growth ☆tree growth on land stripped of virgin forest

sec·ond-guess (sek′ənd ges′) *vt., vi.* [Informal] to use hindsight in criticizing or advising (someone), re-solving (a past problem), remaking (a decision), etc. —**sec′ond-guess′er** *n.*

sec·ond·hand (-hand′) *adj.* 1 not direct from the original source; not original 2 used or worn previously by another; not new 3 of or dealing in merchandise that is not new —*adv.* not firsthand; not directly

second hand 1 the hand that marks seconds on the face of a watch or clock 2 an intermediate person or thing: now only in **(at) second hand**, indirectly

secondhand smoke smoke from a cigarette, cigar, etc., that is inhaled at a distance by persons other than the smoker

second lieutenant a commissioned officer of the lowest rank in the U.S. Army, Air Force, or Marine Corps

☆**second line** ⟦< name for the group of youngsters following and imitating the band in a New Orleans funeral procession⟧ a jaunty, syncopated rhythm in 2/4 time, often used in the rhythm and blues and jazz of New Orleans

sec·ond·ly (sek′ənd lē) *adv.* in the second place; second: used chiefly in enumerating topics

second mate a merchant ship's officer next in rank below the first mate: also **second officer**

second mortgage an additional mortgage placed on property already mortgaged: it ranks below the first mortgage in priority of claim

second nature habits, characteristics, etc. acquired and fixed so deeply as to seem part of a person's nature

se·con·do (se kôn′dô) *n., pl.* **-di** (-dē) ⟦It < L *secundus*, SECOND[1]⟧ *Music* the second, usually the lower, part in a piece arranged in parts, esp. in a piano duet

☆**second papers** *popular name for* the documents by which an alien formerly made application for U.S. citizenship after having earlier filed a declaration of intention

second person *Gram.* 1 *a)* the form of a pronoun (as *you*) or verb (as *do* or archaic *dost*) that refers to the person(s) or thing(s) spoken to in a given utterance *b)* a category consisting of such forms 2 narration characterized by the general use of such forms

sec·ond-rate (sek′ənd rāt′) *adj.* 1 second in quality, rank, etc.; second-class 2 inferior; mediocre; inadequate —**sec′ond-rate′ness** *n.* —**sec′ond-rat′er** *n.*

Second Republic the republic established in France in 1848, when Louis Philippe was deposed, lasting until 1852, when the Second Empire was established

second-run (-run′) *adj.* designating or of: *a)* a film, a TV program or series, etc. exhibited or telecast after the first-run showings *b)* a theater that shows second-run films

second self a person so intimately associated with another as to have taken on many of that person's personality traits, attitudes, beliefs, etc.

second sight the hypothesized ability to see things not physically present or to foretell events; clairvoyance

second-source (-sôrs′) *adj.* of or pertaining to a cooperative arrangement whereby the products of one company are also manufactured by another company —*vt.* **-sourced′, -sourc′ing** to manufacture (another company's products) under such an arrangement

☆**sec·ond-sto·ry man** (-stôr′ē) [Informal] a burglar who enters a building through an upstairs window

sec·ond-string (-striŋ′) *adj.* ⟦see STRING, *n.* 5⟧ [Informal] 1 *Sports* that is the second or a substitute choice for play at the specified position 2 subordinate or inferior in rank, importance, etc. —**sec′ond-string′er** *n.*

second thought a change in thought about a matter after reconsidering it: cf. SECOND THOUGHTS —**on second thought** after reconsideration

second thoughts misgivings, uncertainty, or a change of mind about a matter after reconsidering it: cf. SECOND THOUGHT

second wind 1 the return of relatively normal ease in breathing following the initial exhaustion that occurs during severe exertion or exercise, as while running 2 recovered capacity or renewed energy for continuing any sort of effort

Second World War WORLD WAR II

se·cre·cy (sē′krə sē) *n., pl.* **-cies** ⟦altered < ME *secretee* < *secre*, secret < OFr *secré* < L *secretus*: see fol.⟧ 1 the condition of being secret or concealed 2 a tendency to keep things secret; practice or habit of being secretive

se·cret (sē′krit) *adj.* ⟦OFr < L *secretus*, pp. of *secernere*, to set apart < *se-*, apart (see SECEDE) + *cernere*, to sift, distinguish: see HARVEST⟧ 1 kept from public knowledge or from the knowledge of a certain person or persons 2 withdrawn, remote, or secluded [*a secret* hideaway] 3 keeping one's affairs to oneself; secretive 4 beyond general knowledge or understanding; mysterious or esoteric 5 concealed from sight or notice; hidden [*a secret* drawer] 6 acting in secret [*a secret* society] —*n.* 1 something known only to a certain person or persons and purposely kept from the knowledge of others 2 something not revealed, understood, or explained; mystery [the *secret* of Stonehenge] 3 the true cause or explanation, regarded as not obvious [the *secret* of one's success] 4 [S-] a prayer said just before the Preface of the Mass —**in secret** without the knowledge of others; secretly —**se′cret·ly** *adv.*

SYN.—**secret**, the general term, implies a concealing or keeping from the knowledge of others, for whatever reason [my *secret* opinion of him]; **covert** implies a concealing as by disguising or veiling [*a covert* threat]; **clandestine** suggests that what is being kept secret is of an illicit, immoral, or proscribed nature [their *clandestine* meetings in the park]; **stealthy** implies a slow, quiet secrecy of action in an attempt to elude notice and often connotes deceit [the *stealthy* advance of the panther]; **furtive** adds to this connotations of slyness or watchfulness and suggests a reprehensible objective [the *furtive* movement of his hand toward my pocket]; **surreptitious** connotes a feeling of guilt in the one who is acting in a furtive or stealthy manner [she stole a *surreptitious* glance at him]; **underhanded** implies a stealthiness characterized by fraudulence or deceit [*underhanded* business dealings] —ANT. **open, obvious**

secret agent a person who carries on espionage or similar work of a secret nature, as for a government

sec·re·taire (sek′rə ter′) *n.* ⟦Fr⟧ a writing desk, esp. one with a hinged front panel that opens downward to become the writing surface; secretary

sec·re·tar·i·at (sek′rə ter′ē ət) *n.* ⟦Fr *secrétariat* < ML *secretariatus*⟧ 1 the office, position, or quarters of a secretary, esp. of an administrative secretary in a government or organization 2 a secretarial staff; specif., an administrative staff or department, headed by a secretary-general

sec·re·tar·y (sek′rə ter′ē) *n., pl.* **-tar′ies** ⟦ML *secretarius*, one entrusted with secrets < L *secretum*: see SECRET⟧ 1 *a)* a person whose work is keeping records, taking care of correspondence and other writing tasks, etc. as for an individual in a business office *b)* an officer of a company, club, etc. having somewhat similar functions ☆2 [*often* S-] an official in charge of a department of government 3 a writing desk, esp. one topped with a small bookcase —**sec′re·tar′i·al** *adj.* —**sec′re·tar′y·ship′** *n.*

secretary bird ⟦from the penlike feathers of its crest⟧ a large, black and grayish-blue African bird of prey (*Sagittarius serpentarius*), the only species in its family (Sagittariidae), with a long neck, long legs, and tufts of penlike feathers sticking out from the back of its head: it feeds on insects, snakes, etc.

sec·re·tar·y-gen·er·al (-jen′ər əl) *n., pl.* **-tar′ies-gen′er·al** the chief administrative officer of an organization, in charge of a secretariat

Secretary of State 1 in the U.S., the head of the State Department and senior official of the Cabinet, who is the President's chief foreign-policy advisor 2 a state official having various administrative duties

se·crete[1] (si krēt′) *vt.* **-cret′ed, -cret′ing** ⟦back-form. < SECRETION⟧ to form and release (a specified secretion), as a gland does

se·crete[2] (si krēt′) *vt.* **-cret′ed, -cret′ing** ⟦< earlier *secret*, to hide < L *secretus*, pp. of *secernere*: see SECRET⟧ to put or keep in a secret place; hide; conceal —SYN. HIDE[1]

se·cre·tin (si krēt′'n) *n.* ⟦< fol. + -IN[1]⟧ a hormone produced in the small intestine, that stimulates secretion of pancreatic juice, bile, etc.

se·cre·tion (si krē′shən) *n.* ⟦MFr < L *secretio*, separation < *secretus*: see SECRET⟧ 1 the act of hiding or concealing something 2 *a)* a process in which a gland, tissue, etc. produces a biochemical and releases it into the organism for special use by the organism or for excretion *b)* the substance thus released, including digestive juices, hormones, and perspiration

se·cre·tive (sē′krə tiv; *occas., and for 2 always,* si krēt′iv) *adj.* ⟦SECRET + -IVE⟧ 1 tending to conceal one's thoughts, feelings, affairs, etc. from others; reticent; not frank or open 2 SECRETORY —**se′cre·tive·ly** *adv.* —**se′cre·tive·ness** *n.*

se·cre·to·ry (sē′krə tôr′ē, si krēt′ə rē) *adj.* of, or having the function of, secretion; secreting —*n.* a secretory gland, etc.

secret police a police force that operates secretly, as for suppressing opposition to a dictator or totalitarian government

secret service 1 a government service organized to carry on secret investigation ☆2 [S- S-] a division of the U.S. Treasury Department concerned with the discovery and arrest of counterfeiters, protection of the President, etc.

secret society any organized group that conceals some of its ritual and other activities from nonmembers

sect[1] (sekt) *n.* ⟦ME *secte* < MFr < L *secta*, path, way, method, party, faction, in LL(Ec), doctrine, sect < *sequi*, to follow: see SEQUENT⟧ 1 a religious body or denomination, esp. a small group that has broken away from an established church 2 any group of people having a common leadership, set of opinions, philosophical doctrine, political principles, etc., specif. a faction of a larger group

sect[2] *abbrev.* section

-sect (sekt) ⟦< L *sectus*, pp. of *secare*, to cut: see SAW[1]⟧ *combining form forming adjectives* cut, separated [*pinnatisect*]

sec·tar·i·an (sek ter′ē ən) *adj.* ⟦< fol. + -AN⟧ 1 of or characteristic of a sect 2 devoted to, or prejudiced in favor of, some sect 3 narrow-minded; limited; parochial —*n.* 1 [Obs.] an apostate from an established church 2 a member of any religious sect 3 a person who is blindly and narrow-mindedly devoted to a sect —**sec·tar′i·an·ism′** *n.* —**sec·tar′i·an·ize′** (-īz′) *vt., vi.* **-ized′, -iz′ing**

sec·ta·ry (sek′tər ē) *n., pl.* **-ries** ⟦ML *sectarius* < L *secta*: see SECT[2]⟧ 1 a member of a sect 2 [*often* S-] a Dissenter; Nonconformist

sec·tile (sek′təl, -tīl′) *adj.* ⟦Fr < L *sectilis* < *secare*, to cut: see SAW[1]⟧ 1 capable of being cut smoothly with a knife 2 *Bot.* cut into small divisions —**sec·til′i·ty** (-til′ə tē) *n.*

sec·tion (sek′shən) *n.* ⟦L *sectio* < *sectus*, pp. of *secare*, to cut: see SAW[1]⟧ 1 the act or process of cutting or separating by cutting; specif., an incision in surgery 2 *a)* a part separated or removed by cutting; slice; division *b)* a very thin slice, as of tissue, used for microscopic study 3 *a)* a part or division of a book, newspaper, etc. *b)* a numbered paragraph of a writing, a law, etc. 4 any distinct, constituent part [a bookcase in five *sections*, various *sections* of society] 5 a segment of an orange, grapefruit, etc. 6 *a)* a part of a city, country, etc.; district or region [a hilly *section*, the business *section*] ☆*b)* a division of public lands, equal to 640 acres or one square mile (2.59 square kilometers or 259.005 hectares): see TOWNSHIP (sense 4) 7 a loose subdivision of a biological genus, group, family, etc. 8 a view or drawing of a thing as it would appear if cut straight through in a given plane 9 any of the distinct groups of instruments or voices in an orchestra or chorus [the woodwind *section*] 10 any of several tactical subdivisions of military, air, or naval forces ☆11 any of two or more buses, trains, or airplanes put into service for a particular route and schedule to accommodate extra passengers 12 *Educ.* any of the classes into which the students taking a course with a large enrollment are divided [Prof. Brown's *section* of Freshman English] 13 *Printing* a mark (§) used to indicate a section in a book, etc., or as a reference mark: in full **section mark** ☆14 *Railroading a)* part of a sleeping car containing an upper and lower berth *b)* a division of a railroad right of way, usually several miles of track under the care of a single maintenance crew —*vt.* 1 to cut or divide into sections 2 to represent in sections, as in mechanical drawing —SYN. PART[1]

sec·tion·al (sek′shən əl) *adj.* 1 of a section 2 of, characteristic of, or devoted to a given section or district; regional 3 made up of or divided into sections or parts that may be used as separate units, as a sofa —☆*n.* a sectional sofa, bookcase, etc. —**sec′tion·al·ly** *adv.*

☆**sec·tion·al·ism** (-iz′əm) *n.* narrow-minded concern for or devotion to the interests of one section of a country; sectional spirit, bias, etc. —**sec′tion·al·ist** *adj., n.*

sec·tion·al·ize (-īz′) *vt.* **-ized′, -iz′ing** 1 to make sectional 2 to divide into sections, esp. geographical sections —**sec′tion·al·i·za′tion** *n.*

☆**Section Eight** (*or* **8**) ⟦< section number of former U.S. Army regulation governing this⟧ 1 discharge from the armed forces because of military unsuitability, esp. psychological unfitness 2 [Informal] a person given such a discharge

☆**Section 8** (*or* **Eight**) ⟦< section number of the Federal Housing Act of 1974, under which this program originated⟧ designating or of a federal program in the U.S., providing the poor with rent subsidies and subsidizing the construction of low-income housing

☆**section gang** a crew of persons (**section hands**) who do the maintenance work on a railroad section

sec·tor (sek′tər; *occas.*, -tôr′) ***n.*** ⟦LL < L, cutter < *sectus*, pp. of *secare*, to cut: see SAW[1]⟧ **1** part of a circle bounded by any two radii and the arc included between them **2** a mathematical instrument consisting of two rulers marked with various scales and jointed together at one end, used in solving problems, measuring angles, etc. **3** any of the districts into which an area is divided for military operations **4** a distinct part of society or of an economy, group, area, etc.; section; segment **5** *Comput.* a segment of one of the concentric tracks on a hard disk or floppy disk —***vt.*** to divide into sectors —**sec′tor·al** ***adj.***

sec·to·ri·al (sek tôr′ē əl) ***adj.*** ⟦prec. + -IAL⟧ **1** of a sector **2** *Biol.* designating or of a chimera having two or more distinct types of tissue set apart as sectors **3** *Zool.* specialized for slicing or shearing; carnassial —***n.*** a sectorial tooth

sec·u·lar (sek′yə lər) ***adj.*** ⟦ME seculer < OFr < LL(Ec) *saecularis*, worldly, profane, heathen < L, of an age < *saeculum*, an age, generation < IE **seitlo-* < base **sei-*, to scatter, sow[2]⟧ **1** *a)* of or relating to worldly things as distinguished from things relating to church and religion; not sacred or religious; temporal; worldly [*secular* music, *secular* schools] *b)* of or marked by secularism; secularistic **2** ordained for a diocese **3** *a)* coming or happening only once in an age or century *b)* lasting for an age or ages; continuing for a long time or from age to age —***n.*** **1** a cleric ordained for a diocese **2** a person not a cleric; layman —**sec′u·lar·ly** ***adv.***

secular humanism **1** HUMANISM (sense 2, specif.) **2** SECULARISM, esp. when regarded as antagonistic toward organized religion —**secular humanist**

sec·u·lar·ism (-iz′əm) ***n.*** ⟦SECULAR + -ISM⟧ **1** a system of doctrines and practices that disregards or rejects any form of religious faith and worship **2** the belief that religion and ecclesiastical affairs should not enter into the functions of the state, specif., into public education —**sec′u·lar·ist** ***n., adj.*** —**sec′u·lar·is′tic** ***adj.***

sec·u·lar·i·ty (sek′yə ler′ə tē) ***n.*** ⟦ME seculerte < ML *saecularitas*⟧ **1** the state or quality of being secular **2** SECULARISM **3** *pl.* **-ties** a secular concern, matter, etc.

sec·u·lar·ize (sek′yə lə rīz′) ***vt.*** **-ized′**, **-iz′ing** ⟦Fr *séculariser* < LL(Ec) *saecularis*: see SECULAR⟧ **1** *a)* to change from religious to civil ownership or use *b)* to deprive of religious character, influence, or significance *c)* to convert to secularism **2** to release by church authority from religious vows and from connection with a monastery or similar religious institute; give secular status to —**sec′u·lar·i·za′tion** ***n.***

se·cund (sē′kənd, sek′ənd) ***adj.*** ⟦L *secundus*, following: see SECOND[1]⟧ *Bot.* growing on one side only, as the flowers in the lily of the valley

sec·un·dines (sek′ən dīnz′) ***pl.n.*** ⟦ME < LL *secundinae*, pl., the afterbirth < L *secundus*, following: see SECOND[1]⟧ AFTERBIRTH

se·cun·dum (si kun′dəm) ***prep.*** ⟦L, orig. neut. of *secundus*, following: see SECOND[1]⟧ according to

se·cure (si kyoor′) ***adj.*** ⟦L *securus* < *se-*, free from, apart (see SECEDE) + *cura*, care: see CURE⟧ **1** free from fear, care, doubt, or anxiety; not worried, troubled, or apprehensive **2** free from danger; not exposed to damage, attack, etc.; safe **3** in safekeeping or custody **4** not likely to fail or give way; firm; strong; stable [to make a knot *secure*] **5** reliable; dependable [a *secure* investment] **6** protected from unauthorized access [a *secure* phone line] **7** [Archaic] overconfident and careless —***vt.*** **-cured′**, **-cur′ing** **1** to make secure, or safe; guard; protect [to *secure* a position against attack] **2** to make sure or certain; guarantee; ensure, as with a pledge [to *secure* a loan with collateral] **3** *a)* to make firm, fast, tight, etc. [*secure* the bolt] *b)* to put under restraint; tie up **4** to get hold or possession of; obtain; acquire [to *secure* aid] **5** to take into custody; capture **6** to bring about; cause [to *secure* a laugh] **7** *Naut.* *a)* to relieve (personnel) from duty *b)* to bring to a halt; stop —***vi.*** **1** to give security [an insurance policy that *secures* against loss] **2** *Naut.* to stop working: said of personnel —***SYN.*** GET, SAFE —**se·cur′a·ble** ***adj.*** —**se·cur′ance** ***n.*** —**se·cure′ly** ***adv.*** —**se·cure′ness** ***n.*** —**se·cur′er** ***n.***

se·cu·ri·tize (si kyoor′ə tīz′) ***vt.*** **-tized′**, **-tiz′ing** to offer (assets) for sale through, or as collateral for, an issue of marketable securities —**se·cu′ri·ti·za′tion** ***n.***

se·cu·ri·ty (si kyoor′ə tē) ***n.***, *pl.* **-ties** ⟦ME securite < L *securitas* < *securus*: see SECURE⟧ **1** the state of being or feeling secure; freedom from fear, anxiety, danger, doubt, etc.; state or sense of safety or certainty **2** something that gives or assures safety, tranquillity, certainty, etc.; protection; safeguard **3** *a)* protection or defense against attack, interference, espionage, etc. [funds for national *security*] *b)* protection or defense against escape [a maximum-*security* prison] *c)* procedures to provide such protection or defense **4** an organization or department whose task is protection or safety, esp. a private police force hired to patrol or guard a building, park, or other area [if you see an intruder, call *security*] **5** *a)* something given as a pledge of repayment, fulfillment of a promise, etc.; guarantee *b)* a person who agrees to make good the failure of another to pay, perform a duty, etc.; surety **6** any evidence of debt or ownership; esp., a stock certificate or bond: *usually used in pl.* —***adj.*** of, designating, or serving as security [*security* precautions, *security* guard]

security blanket **1** a small blanket or other soft cloth, as clutched or stroked by a child for the feeling of comfort and security it affords **2** anything that gives a person a sense of safety or freedom from anxiety

Security Council the United Nations council responsible for maintaining international peace and security: it consists of five permanent members (China, France, Russia, the United Kingdom, and the U.S.) and ten nonpermanent members

secy or **sec'y** *abbrev.* secretary

se·dan (si dan′) ***n.*** ⟦? coined (1634) by Sir S. Duncombe, Eng holder of the patent, prob. < It *sedente*, sitting < *sedere*, to sit < L: see SIT⟧ **1** SEDAN CHAIR ☆**2** an automobile with two or four doors, a permanent rigid top, and a full-sized rear seat

Se·dan (si dan′; *Fr* sə dän′) city in N France, on the Meuse River: scene of a decisive French defeat (1870) in the Franco-Prussian War

sedan chair an enclosed chair for one person, with glass windows, carried on poles by two men, in use in Europe in the 17th and 18th cent.

sedan chair

se·date[1] (si dāt′) ***adj.*** ⟦L *sedatus*, pp. of *sedare*, to settle, caus. of *sedere*, to SIT⟧ calm, quiet, or composed; esp., serious and unemotional; staid; decorous —***SYN.*** SERIOUS —**se·date′ly** ***adv.*** —**se·date′ness** ***n.***

☆**se·date**[2] (si dāt′) ***vt.*** **-dat′ed**, **-dat′ing** ⟦back-form. < SEDATIVE⟧ **1** to dose with a sedative **2** to make calm or sleepy

se·da·tion (si dā′shən) ***n.*** ⟦L *sedatio*, a calming < *sedare*: see SEDATE[1]⟧ *Med.* **1** the act or process of reducing excitement, nervousness, or irritation, esp. by means of sedatives **2** the state so induced

sed·a·tive (sed′ə tiv) ***adj.*** ⟦MFr *sédatif* < ML *sedativus* < L *sedatus*: see SEDATE[1]⟧ **1** tending to soothe or quiet **2** *Med.* having the property of lessening excitement, nervousness, or irritation —***n.*** a sedative medicine

sed·en·tar·y (sed′'n ter′ē) ***adj.*** ⟦Fr *sédentaire* < L *sedentarius* < *sedens*, prp. of *sedere*, to SIT⟧ **1** *a)* of or marked by much sitting about and little travel *b)* keeping one seated much of the time [a *sedentary* job] **2** *a)* remaining in one locality; not migratory (said of birds, etc.) *b)* fixed to one spot, as a barnacle —**sed′en·tar′i·ly** ***adv.*** —**sed′en·tar′i·ness** ***n.***

Se·der (sā′dər) ***n.***, *pl.* **Se·ders** or **Se·dar·im** (sə där′im, sā dä rēm′) ⟦Heb *seder*, lit., order, arrangement < root *sdr*, to arrange, order⟧ [*also* **s-**] *Judaism* the feast commemorating the Exodus of the Jews from Egypt, observed in the home by the reading of the Haggada on the eve of the first day of Passover (and, by Orthodox Jews outside Israel, on the eve of the second day as well)

sedge (sej) ***n.*** ⟦ME *segge* < OE *secg*, akin to *sagu*, SAW[1]: from the shape of the leaves⟧ any of the plants of the sedge family often found on wet ground or in water, having usually triangular, solid stems, three rows of narrow, pointed leaves, and minute flowers borne in spikelets —***adj.*** designating a family (Cyperaceae, order Cyperales) of grasslike, monocotyledonous plants, including papyrus —**sedg′y** ***adj.*** **sedg′i·er**, **sedg′i·est**

se·dil·i·a (si dil′ē ə) ***pl.n.***, *sing.* **se·di′le** (-dī′lē) ⟦L, pl. of *sedile*, a seat < *sedere*, to SIT⟧ a set of seats, usually three, traditionally along the south side of a church, for the use of officiating clergy

sed·i·ment (sed′ə mənt) ***n.*** ⟦Fr *sédiment* < L *sedimentum* < *sedere*, to SIT⟧ **1** matter that settles to the bottom of a liquid **2** *Geol.* matter deposited by water or wind —**sed′i·men′tal** (-ment′'l) ***adj.***

sed·i·men·ta·ry (sed′ə men′tər ē, -men′trē; sed′ə mən ter′ē) ***adj.*** **1** of, having the nature of, or containing sediment **2** formed by the deposit of sediment or by evaporation or precipitation, as certain rocks —**sed′i·men′ta·ri·ly** ***adv.***

sed·i·men·ta·tion (sed′ə men tā′shən, -mən-) ***n.*** the depositing or formation of sediment

sed·i·men·tol·o·gy (sed′ə mən täl′ə jē) ***n.*** the branch of geology that deals with sediment and sedimentary rocks —**sed′i·men·tol′o·gist** ***n.***

se·di·tion (si dish′ən) ***n.*** ⟦ME *sedicion* < OFr < L *seditio* < *sed-*, apart (see SECEDE) + *itio*, a going < *ire*, to go: see YEAR⟧ **1** the stirring up of discontent, resistance, or rebellion against the government in power **2** [Archaic] revolt or rebellion —**se·di′tion·ar′y** ***n., adj.*** —**se·di′tion·ist** ***n.***

SYN.—**sedition** applies to anything regarded by a government as stirring up resistance or rebellion against it and implies that the evidence is not overt or absolute; **treason** implies an overt act in violation of the allegiance owed to one's state, specif. a levying war against it or giving aid or comfort to its enemies

se·di·tious (si dish′əs) ***adj.*** ⟦ME *cedicious* < MFr *seditieux* < L *seditiosus*⟧ **1** of, like, or constituting sedition **2** inclined toward or engaging in sedition —**se·di′tious·ly** ***adv.*** —**se·di′tious·ness** ***n.***

se·duce (si dōōs′, -dyōōs′) ***vt.*** **-duced′**, **-duc′ing** ⟦ME *seduisen* < LL(Ec) *seducere*, to mislead, seduce < L, to lead aside < *se-*, apart (see SECEDE) + *ducere*, to lead: see DUCT⟧ **1** *a)* to persuade to do something disloyal, disobedient, etc. *b)* to persuade or tempt to evil or wrongdoing; lead astray *c)* to persuade (someone) to engage, esp. for the first time, in illicit or unsanctioned sexual intercourse **2** to entice —***SYN.*** LURE —**se·duce′ment** ***n.*** —**se·duc′i·ble** ***adj.***

se·duc·er (-ər) ***n.*** a person or thing that seduces; esp., a man who seduces a woman sexually

se·duc·tion (si duk′shən) ***n.*** ⟦MFr < LL(Ec) *seductio* < L, a leading away⟧ **1** the act of seducing or the state of being seduced **2** something that seduces

se·duc·tive (-tiv) ***adj.*** ⟦< L *seductus*, pp. of *seducere* (see SEDUCE) + -IVE⟧ tending to seduce, or lead astray; tempting; enticing —**se·duc′tive·ly** ***adv.*** —**se·duc′tive·ness** ***n.***

se·duc·tress (-tris) ***n.*** a woman who seduces, esp. one who seduces a man sexually

se·du·li·ty (si dyo͞ol′ə tē, -do͞ol′-) ***n.*** ⟦L *sedulitas*⟧ the quality or fact of being sedulous

sed·u·lous (sej′o͞o ləs) ***adj.*** ⟦L *sedulus* < *sedulo*, diligently, orig., without guile < *se-*, apart (see SECEDE) + *dolus*, trickery < Gr *dolos*: see TALE⟧ **1** working hard and steadily; diligent **2** constant; persistent [*sedulous* attention to the task] —**SYN.** BUSY —**sed′u·lous·ly** ***adv.*** —**sed′u·lous·ness** ***n.***

se·dum (sē′dəm) ***n.*** ⟦ModL < L, houseleek⟧ any of a genus (*Sedum*) of mainly perennial plants of the orpine family, found on rocks and walls, with fleshy stalks and leaves and white, yellow, or pink flowers

see[1] (sē) ***vt.*** **saw, seen, see′ing** ⟦ME *seen* < OE *seon* (< **sehwan*), akin to Ger *sehen*, Goth *saihwan* < IE base **sekw-*, to observe, show, see, tell: see SAY⟧ **1** *a)* to get knowledge or an awareness of through the eyes; perceive visually; look at; view *b)* to visualize as though present; picture **2** *a)* to get a clear mental impression of; grasp by thinking; understand [to *see* the point of a joke] *b)* to accept as right, proper, or suitable [I can't *see* him as president] *c)* to consider to be; judge [*saw* it as his duty] **3** *a)* to learn; discover; find out [*see* what they want] *b)* to learn by reading, as in a newspaper **4** to have personal knowledge of; experience; witness; live through [to have *seen* two wars] **5** to look over; inspect; examine [let me *see* that burn] **6** to take care; make sure [*see* that he does it right] **7** *a)* to escort; accompany; attend [to *see* someone home] *b)* to keep company with; be dating regularly **8** *a)* to encounter; meet; come in contact with [have you *seen* John?] *b)* to recognize by sight **9** *a)* to call on; visit *b)* to have an interview with; consult [*see* a lawyer] **10** to admit to one's presence; receive [too ill to *see* anyone] **11** to be a spectator at; view or attend [to *see* a show] **12** *Poker* to equal (the preceding bet) or equal the bet of (the preceding bettor); call —***vi.*** **1** to have the power of sight **2** to discern objects, colors, etc. by using the eyes [to be able to *see* far] **3** *a)* to take a look [go and *see*] *b)* to investigate or inquire [*see* if he wants anything] **4** to comprehend; understand **5** to think over a given matter; reflect [let me *see*, where did I put it?] —***interj.*** look; behold —**(I'll) be seeing you** farewell; goodbye: a phrase used at parting —**see about 1** to investigate or inquire into **2** to attend to —**see after** to take care of; look after —**see double** to see two of every object through inability to focus the eyes, as from drunkenness —**see fit** to consider that it is desirable, proper, etc. [go if you *see fit*; he *saw fit* to sue them] —**see here!** used to express an objection —**see into 1** to investigate; look into **2** to perceive the true meaning, character, or nature of —**see off** to go with (another) to the place from which that person is to leave, as on a journey —**see out** [Rare] **1** to carry out; finish; go through with **2** to wait till the end of —**see through 1** to perceive the true meaning, character, or nature of [we *saw through* his smooth talk] **2** to carry out to the end; finish [to *see* a project *through*] **3** to help out or carry through a time of difficulty [*saw* her *through* her final exams] —**see to** to attend to —**see you (later)** [Informal] I'll be seeing you; goodbye —**see′a·ble** ***adj.***

SYN.—see, the most simple and direct of these terms, is the basic term for the use of the organs of sight; **behold** implies a directing of the eyes on something and holding it in view, usually stressing the strong impression made [he never *beheld* a sight more beautiful]; **espy** and **descry** both imply a catching sight of with some effort, **espy** suggesting the detection of that which is small, partly hidden, etc. [he *espied* the snake crawling through the grass] and **descry** the making out of something from a distance or through darkness, mist, etc. [he *descried* the distant steeple]; **view** implies a seeing or looking at what lies before one, as in inspection or examination [the jury *viewed* the evidence]

see[2] (sē) ***n.*** ⟦ME *se* < OFr *sie, sied* < L *sedes*, a seat (in ML(Ec), a see of a bishop) < *sedere*, SIT⟧ **1** the official seat, or center of authority, of a bishop **2** the position, authority, or jurisdiction of a bishop **3** [Obs.] a seat of authority, esp. a throne

See·beck effect (zā′bek′, sē′-) ⟦after T. J. *Seebeck* (1770-1831), Ger physicist⟧ *Elec.* **1** the production of a current in a circuit when junctions composed of unlike metals have different temperatures, as in a thermocouple **2** the current so produced

☆**see·catch** (sē′kach′) ***n.*** ⟦Russ *sekach, sekachi* < Ger *seekatze*, lit., sea cat, transl. of Russ *(morskoy) kot*, (sea) cat, term used in Kamchatka⟧ the adult male fur seal of Alaskan waters: also **see′catch′ie** (-ē)

seed (sēd) ***n.***, *pl.* **seeds** or **seed** ⟦ME *sede* < OE *sæd*, akin to Ger *saat* < IE base **sē(i)-*, to cast, let fall > L *serere*, to sow, plant, *sator*, sower, *semen*, seed⟧ **1** the part of a flowering plant that typically contains the embryo with its protective coat and stored food and that can develop into a new plant under the proper conditions; fertilized and mature ovule **2** loosely, *a)* any part, as a bulb, tuber, etc., from which a new plant can grow [a potato *seed*] *b)* a small, usually hard, seedlike fruit **3** seeds collectively **4** the source, origin, or beginning of anything [the *seeds* of revolt] **5** [Archaic] *a)* descendants; posterity *b)* ancestry **6** *a)* in the development of certain lower animals, a form suitable for transplanting, as spat *b)* the seed-bearing stage or condition [in *seed*] **7** SPORE (*n.* 2) **8** sperm or semen **9** something tiny, like a seed; esp., ☆*a)* a tiny crystal or other particle, as one added to a solution or liquid to start crystallization *b)* a tiny bubble, as a flaw in glassware ☆**10** *Sports* a seeded player, team, etc. —***vt.*** **1** to plant with seeds **2** to sow (seeds) **3** to remove the seeds from ☆**4** to inject, fill, or scatter with seeds (see SEED, sense 9*a*); esp., to sprinkle particles of dry ice, silver iodide, etc. into (clouds) in an attempt to induce rainfall **5** to provide with the means or stimulus for growing or developing **6** *Sports a)* to distribute the names of the ranking contestants in (the draw for position in a tournament) so that those with the greatest skill are not matched together in the early rounds *b)* to treat (a player) as a ranking contestant in this way —***vi.*** **1** to form seeds; specif., to become ripe and produce seeds **2** to go to seed; shed seeds **3** to sow seeds —**go (or run) to seed 1** to shed seeds after the time of flowering or bearing has passed **2** [Informal] to become weak, useless, unprofitable, etc.; deteriorate —**seed′ed** ***adj.*** —**seed′less** ***adj.***

seed·bed (sēd′bed′) ***n.*** a bed of soil, usually covered with glass, in which seedlings are grown for transplanting

seed beetle BEAN WEEVIL

seed cake 1 any cake or cookie containing seeds, typically caraway, sesame, or poppy seeds **2** OIL CAKE Also written **seed′cake′** ***n.***

seed·case (-kās′) ***n.*** SEED VESSEL

seed coat the outer layer or coating of a seed

seed coral fragments of coral used in ornaments

seed corn corn set aside for planting a new crop

seed·er (-ər) ***n.*** a person or thing that seeds; specif., *a)* one that sows or plants seeds *b)* a device for removing seeds, as from raisins

seed fern any of an extinct class (Pteridospermae) of Paleozoic, fernlike cycads that bore naked seeds upon their leaves

seed leaf COTYLEDON

seed·ling (-liŋ) ***n.*** **1** a plant grown from a seed, rather than from a cutting, etc. **2** any young plant; esp., a small, young tree

☆**seed money** money made available to begin the financing of, or to attract additional funds for, a long-term project

seed oysters oyster spat; very young oysters, esp. at the stage suitable for transplanting

seed pearl a very small pearl, often imperfect

seed plant any plant bearing seeds, as an angiosperm or a gymnosperm

seed·pod (-päd′) ***n.*** a carpel or pistil, enclosing ovules or seeds in angiosperms

seed shrimp OSTRACOD

seeds·man (sēdz′mən) ***n.***, *pl.* **-men** (-mən) **1** a sower of seeds **2** a dealer in seeds Also **seed·man** (sēd′mən), *pl.* **-men** (-mən)

seed·time (sēd′tīm′) ***n.*** the season for sowing seeds

seed vessel any fruit, esp. a dry, hollow pod, containing seeds

seed·y (sēd′ē) ***adj.*** **seed′i·er, seed′i·est 1** containing many seeds **2** gone to seed **3** having tiny bubbles: said of glass **4** shabby, run-down, etc. **5** feeling or looking physically bad or low in spirits —**seed′i·ly** ***adv.*** —**seed′i·ness** ***n.***

see·ing (sē′iŋ) ***n.*** **1** the sense or power of sight; vision **2** the act of using the eyes to see —***adj.*** having the sense of sight —***conj.*** in view of the fact; considering; inasmuch as

☆**Seeing Eye dog** ⟦< *Seeing Eye*, a trademark⟧ [*also* **s- e- d-**] a guide dog

seek (sēk) ***vt.*** **sought, seek′ing** ⟦ME *seken* < OE *secan*, akin to OS *sōkian*, Ger *suchen*, ON *sœkja* < IE base **sāg-*, to track down, trace > L *sagire*, to scent out, perceive⟧ **1** to try to find; search for; look for **2** to go to; resort to [to *seek* the woods for peace] **3** *a)* to try to get or find out by asking or searching [to *seek* the answer to a question] *b)* to request; ask for **4** to bend one's efforts toward; aim at; pursue [*seeking* perfection] **5** to try; attempt: used with an infinitive [to *seek* to please someone] **6** [Archaic] to explore —***vi.*** **1** *a)* to look for someone or something *b)* to make a search or investigation [to *seek* after something] **2** [Archaic] to resort (*to*) —**seek′er** ***n.***

seel (sēl) ***vt.*** ⟦LME *silen* < OFr *ciller* < *cil* < L *cilium*, lower eyelid⟧ **1** *Falconry* to sew together the eyelids of (a young hawk) **2** [Obs.] *a)* to close (the eyes) *b)* to blind

seem (sēm) ***vi.*** ⟦ME *semen*, prob. < ON *sœma*, to conform to (akin to OE *seman*, to bring to agreement) < IE base **sem-* > SAME⟧ **1** *a)* to appear to be; have the look of being [they *seemed* so happy together] *b)* to appear; give the impression (usually followed by an infinitive) [he *seems* to know the neighborhood well]: *seem* with an infinitive is also used to convey a person's impression or feeling [I *seem* to recall our conversation] **2** to appear to exist [there *seems* no point in going] **3** to be apparently true [it *seems* he was here ahead of us]

seem·ing (sēm′iŋ) ***adj.*** that seems real, true, etc. without necessarily being so; apparent [her *seeming* anger] —***n.*** outward appearance; semblance —**seem′ing·ly** ***adv.***

seem·ly (sēm′lē) ***adj.*** **-li·er, -li·est** ⟦ME *semlich* < ON *sœmiligr* < *sœmr*, fitting < *sœma*: see SEEM⟧ **1** pleasing in appearance; fair; handsome **2** suitable, proper, fitting, or becoming, esp. as regards conventional standards of conduct or good taste; decorous —***adv.*** [Archaic] in a seemly manner; properly, fittingly, etc. —**seem′li·ness** ***n.***

seen (sēn) ***vt., vi. pp. of*** SEE[1] —**have seen better days** [Informal] to have declined, deteriorated, etc.

seep (sēp) ***vi.*** ⟦ME **sipen* < OE *sipian*, to soak, akin to MLowG *sīpen*, to drip < IE base **seib-*, to run out, drip > SOAP⟧ to leak, drip, or flow out slowly through small openings or pores; ooze —***n.*** **1** a place where water, oil, etc. oozes from the ground to form a pool **2** SEEPAGE —**seep′y** ***adj.***

seep·age (-ij) ***n.*** **1** the act or process of seeping; leakage; oozing **2** liquid that seeps

seer[1] (sē′ər; *also, and for 2 usually*, sir) ***n.*** **1** a person who sees **2** a person with the supposed power to foretell events or a person's destiny; prophet

seer[2] (sir) ***n.*** ⟦Hindi *sēr*⟧ any of various units of weight used in certain countries of Asia, esp. a unit of weight of India equal to 1/40 maund or 2.06 lb (.933 kg)

seer·ess (sir′is, sē′ər is) ***n.*** a woman with the supposed power to foretell events or a person's destiny; prophetess

seer·suck·er (sir′suk′ər) ***n.*** ⟦Hindi *shirshaker* < Pers *shir u shakar*, lit., milk and sugar, also a kind of striped linen cloth⟧ a light, crinkled fabric of linen, cotton, etc., usually with a striped pattern

see·saw (sē′sô′) ***n.*** ⟦redupl. of SAW[1]: from the action of sawing⟧ **1** a plank balanced on a support at the middle, used by children at play, who ride the ends so that when one goes up, the other comes down **2** the act of riding a plank in this way **3** any up-and-down or back-and-forth movement or change, as in the lead in a competition —***adj.*** moving up and down or back and forth — ***vt., vi.*** to move on or as on a seesaw

seethe (sēth) ***vt.*** **seethed**, **seeth′ing** ⟦ME *sethen* < OE *sēothan*, akin to Ger *sieden* < IE base **sew-*, to cook, boil > Sans *hāvayan*, (they) stew⟧ **1** to cook by boiling **2** to soak, steep, or saturate in liquid —***vi.*** **1** to boil or to surge, bubble, or foam as if boiling **2** to be violently agitated or disturbed —***n.*** the act or condition of seething —**SYN.** BOIL[1]

see-through (sē′thro͞o′) ***adj.*** that can be seen through; more or less transparent or translucent [*see-through* fabric, *see-through* packages]

Se·fer·is (sə fer′əs), **George** (pseud. of *Georgios Stylianou Sepheriades*) 1900-71; Gr. poet, critic, & diplomat

☆**seg** (seg) ***n.*** [Slang] SEGREGATIONIST

seg·ment (seg′mənt; *for v.*, -ment) ***n.*** ⟦L *segmentum* < *secare*, to cut: see SAW[1]⟧ **1** any of the parts into which a body is separated or separable; division; section **2** *Geom. a)* a part of a figure, esp. of a circle or sphere, marked off or made separate by a line or plane, as a part of a circular area bounded by an arc and its chord *b)* any of the finite sections of a line **3** *Linguis.* a phone, or single sound, in the stream of speech **4** *Zool. a)* METAMERE *b)* the part of an arthropod appendage between joints —***vt., vi.*** to divide into segments —**SYN.** PART[1] —**seg′men·tar′y** ***adj.*** —**seg′ment·ed** ***adj.***

seg·men·tal (seg ment′'l) ***adj.*** **1** having the form of a segment of a circle **2** of, like, or made up of a segment or segments —**seg·men′tal·ly** ***adv.***

segmental phonemes phonemes consisting of sound segments; hence, the vowel, consonant, and semivowel sounds of a language: cf. SUPRASEGMENTAL PHONEMES

seg·men·ta·tion (seg′men tā′shən, -mən-) ***n.*** **1** a dividing or being divided into segments **2** *Biol.* the progressive growth and cleavage of a single cell into many others to form a new organism

segmentation cavity BLASTOCOELE

se·gno (sān′yō; *It* se′nyô) ***n.***, *pl.* **se′gni** (-yē; *It*, -nyē) ⟦It < L *signum*, a SIGN⟧ *Music* a sign; esp., the sign (𝄋 or :S:) used at the beginning or end of a repeat

☆**se·go** (sē′gō) ***n.***, *pl.* **-gos** ⟦< AmInd (Shoshonean), as in Ute *sígo*⟧ **1** a perennial bulb plant (*Calochortus nuttallii*) of the lily family, with trumpet-shaped flowers, found in W North America: in full **sego lily** **2** its edible bulb

Se·go·via (se gô′vyä; *E* sə gō′vē ə), **An·drés** (än dres′) 1893?-1987; Sp. guitarist & composer

seg·re·gate (seg′rə gāt′; *for adj. & n., usually*, -git) ***adj.*** ⟦ME *segregat* < L *segregatus*, pp. of *segregare*, to set apart, lit., to set apart from the flock < *se-*, apart (see SECEDE) + *grex* (gen. *gregis*), a flock: see GREGARIOUS⟧ separate; set apart; segregated —***vt.*** **-gat′ed**, **-gat′ing** to set apart from others or from the main mass or group; isolate; specif., to impose a system of segregation on (racial groups, social facilities, etc.) —***vi.*** **1** to separate from the main mass and collect together in a new body: said of crystals **2** to separate from others; be segregated **3** *Genetics* to undergo segregation —***n.*** a segregated person, thing, group, etc. —**seg′re·gat′ive** ***adj.***

seg·re·gat·ed (seg′rə gāt′id) ***adj.*** ☆conforming to a system that segregates racial groups [*a segregated* school district]

seg·re·ga·tion (seg′rə gā′shən) ***n.*** ⟦LL *segregatio*⟧ **1** a segregating or being segregated; specif., the policy or practice of compelling racial groups to live apart from each other, go to separate schools, use separate social facilities, etc. **2** *Genetics* the separation of allelic genes into different gametes during meiosis so that a particular gamete receives only one member of a pair of characters

seg·re·ga·tion·ist (-ist) ***n.*** a person who favors or practices segregation, esp. racial segregation —***adj.*** of, like, or favoring segregation or segregationists

se·gue (seg′wā′, sā′gwā′) ***vi.*** **-gued′**, **-gue′ing** ⟦It, 3d pers. sing., pres. indic., of *seguire*, to follow < VL *sequere*, for L *sequi*: see SEQUENT⟧ to continue without break (*to* or *into* the next part) —***n.*** an immediate transition from one part to another, as in music

se·gui·dil·la (seg′ə dēl′yə, sā′gə-; -dē′yə) ***n.*** ⟦Sp < *seguida*, a following < *seguir*, to follow < VL *sequere*: see prec.⟧ **1** a fast Spanish dance, to the accompaniment of castanets **2** the music for this dance, in 3/4 time **3** a stanza of four to seven short lines, partly assonant, with a distinctive rhythm, orig. sung to this music

Sehn·sucht (zān′zo͝okht′) ***n.*** ⟦Ger⟧ yearning; longing

sei·cen·to (sā chen′tō) ***n.*** ⟦It, six hundred: short for *mil seicento*, one thousand six hundred⟧ the 17th cent. as a period in Italian art and literature

seiche (sāsh) ***n.*** ⟦< Swiss-Fr⟧ a natural, standing wave in the water of a lake, bay, etc., caused by changes in atmospheric pressure, seismic disturbances, winds, waves, tides, etc.: it continues after the generating force stops

sei·del (zīd′'l, sīd′-) ***n.***, *pl.* **-dels** or **-del** ⟦Ger < MHG *sidelin* < L *situla*, bucket, dim. < *sinum*, large drinking vessel with bulging sides⟧ a large beer mug, sometimes with a hinged lid

Seid·litz powders (sed′lits) ⟦so named because their properties are said to resemble those of natural waters from the spring at Sedlčany (Ger *Seidlitz*), Czech Republic⟧ a laxative composed of two powders, one of sodium bicarbonate and Rochelle salt, the other of tartaric acid: the two are separately dissolved in water, combined, and drunk while effervescing: also **Seidlitz powder**

seif (sāf, sīf) ***n.*** an immense, long, curving, ridgelike sand dune, as of the Sahara

sei·gneur (sān yʉr′, sen-) ***n.*** ⟦Fr < MFr: see SEIGNIOR⟧ **1** SEIGNIOR (sense 1) **2** in French Canada, through the mid-19th cent., the owner of an estate orig. granted by royal decree to 17th-cent. French settlers —**sei·gneur′i·al** (-ē əl) ***adj.***

sei·gneur·y (sān′yər ē) ***n.***, *pl.* **-gneur·ies** **1** SEIGNIORY (sense 1) **2** in French Canada, through the mid-19th cent., the estate or manor of a seigneur

sei·gnior (sān′yər, sān yôr′) ***n.*** ⟦ME *segnour* < Anglo-Fr < OFr *seignor* < L *senior*: see SENIOR⟧ **1** a lord or noble; specif., the lord of a fee or manor **2** SEIGNEUR (sense 2)

sei·gnior·age (sān′yər ij) ***n.*** ⟦ME *seignorage* < OFr < *seignor*: see prec.⟧ **1** something claimed or taken by a sovereign or other superior as his or her just right or due **2** a government revenue that is the difference between the face value of coins and the costs of their mintage

sei·gnio·ri·al or **sei·gno·ri·al** (sān yôr′ē əl) ***adj.*** of, relating to, or characteristic of a seignior

sei·gnior·y (sān′yər ē) ***n.***, *pl.* **-gnior·ies** ⟦ME *seignorie* < OFr⟧ **1** the dominion or estate of a seignior **2** the rights or authority of a feudal lord **3** a body of lords, esp. those of a medieval Italian republic **4** SEIGNEURY (sense 2)

seine (sān) ***n.*** ⟦ME *seyne* < OE *segne* < early WGmc borrowing < L *sagena* < Gr *sagēnē* < IE base **twak-*, to enclose tightly⟧ a large fishing net with floats along the top edge and weights along the bottom — ***vt., vi.*** **seined**, **sein′ing** to fish with a seine —**sein′er** ***n.***

Seine (sān; *Fr* sen) river in N France, flowing northwest through Paris into the English Channel: 482 mi (776 km)

seise (sēz) ***vt.*** **seised**, **seis′ing** *alt. sp. of* SEIZE (sense 1)

sei·sin (sē′zin) ***n.*** *alt. sp. of* SEIZIN

seis·mic (sīz′mik, sīs′-) ***adj.*** ⟦< Gr *seismos*, earthquake < *seiein*, to shake < IE base **twei-*, to excite, shake, shock > Sans *tviṣ-*, to be excited, sparkle⟧ **1** of, having to do with, or caused by an earthquake or earthquakes or by man-made earth tremors **2** subject to earthquakes —**seis′mi·cal·ly** ***adv.***

seis·mic·i·ty (sīz mis′ə tē, sīs-) ***n.*** **1** the property or state of being seismic **2** the frequency, intensity, etc. of earthquake activity in a given region: also **seismic activity**

seis·mo- (sīz′mə, -mō; sīs′-) ⟦< Gr *seismos*: see SEISMIC⟧ *combining form* earthquake [*seismogram*]

seis·mo·gram (sīz′mə gram′, sīs′-) ***n.*** ⟦prec. + -GRAM⟧ the chart of an earthquake as recorded by a seismograph

seis·mo·graph (-graf′, -gräf′) ***n.*** ⟦SEISMO- + -GRAPH⟧ an instrument that records the intensity and duration of earthquakes and similar tremors —**seis·mog′ra·pher** (-mäg′rə fər) ***n.*** —**seis′mo·graph′ic** ***adj.*** —**seis·mog′ra·phy** ***n.***

seis·mol·o·gy (sīz mäl′ə jē, sīs-) ***n.*** ⟦SEISMO- + -LOGY⟧ a geophysical science dealing with earthquakes and related phenomena —**seis′mo·log′ic** (-mə läj′ik) ***adj.***, **seis′mo·log′i·cal** —**seis′mo·log′i·cal·ly** ***adv.*** —**seis·mol′o·gist** ***n.***

seis·mom·e·ter (-mäm′ə tər) ***n.*** ⟦SEISMO- + -METER⟧ a seismograph, esp. one that records actual earth movements —**seis′mo·met′ric** (-mə me′trik) ***adj.***, **seis′mo·met′ri·cal**

seis·mo·scope (sīz′mə skōp′, sīs′-) ***n.*** ⟦SEISMO- + -SCOPE⟧ an instrument indicating only the occurrence and time of earthquakes —**seis′mo·scop′ic** (-skäp′ik) ***adj.***

SEIU *abbrev.* Service Employees International Union

sei (whale) (sā) ⟦Norw *seihval* < *sei*, coalfish + *hval*, whale: from its arrival at fishing grounds with the coalfish⟧ a rorqual (*Balaenoptera borealis*) with a light-gray or bluish back, found in all seas

seize (sēz) ***vt.*** **seized**, **seiz′ing** ⟦ME *saisen* < OFr *saisir* < ML *sacire*, prob. < Frank **sakjan*, to lay claim to one's rights < IE base **sāg-* > SAKE[1]⟧ **1** *a)* [Historical] to put in legal possession of a feudal holding *b)* to put in legal possession of a particular thing; assign ownership to (in the passive voice) [*seized* of the lands] **2** *a)* to take forcible legal possession of; confiscate [to *seize* contraband] *b)* to capture and put into custody; arrest; apprehend [to *seize* a criminal suspect] **3** to take forcibly and quickly; grab [to *seize* power] **4** to take hold of suddenly or forcibly, with or as with the hand; clutch **5** *a)* to suddenly penetrate, illumine, or fill the mind of [an idea *seized* him] *b)* to grasp with the mind, esp. in a sudden or intuitive way [*seized* their intent] **6** to take quick advantage of (an opportunity, etc.) **7** to attack or afflict suddenly or severely [*seized* with a fit of sneezing] **8** *Naut.* to bind (large ropes) together with cords, small lines, etc. —***vi.*** **1** to stick or jam, esp. because of excessive heat or friction: said of a machine or its moving parts: often with *up* **2** to have a seizure, often, specif., an epileptic seizure —**SYN.** TAKE —**seize on** (or **upon**) **1** to take hold of suddenly and forcibly **2** to take possession of **3** to turn eagerly to (an idea, etc.) —**seiz′a·ble** ***adj.*** —**seiz′er** ***n.***

sei·zin (sē′zin) *n.* ⟦ME *seisine* < OFr *saisine* < *saisir*: see prec.⟧ *Law* legal possession, esp. of a freehold state

seiz·ing (sēz′iŋ) *n.* 1 SEIZURE (sense 1) 2 *Naut. a)* the act of binding or fastening together with cords, small lines, etc. *b)* the cords, small lines, etc. used for this *c)* a fastening made in this way

sei·zor (sē′zər, -zôr′) *n.* ⟦SEIZ(E) + -OR⟧ *Law* a person who takes possession of a freehold estate

sei·zure (sē′zhər) *n.* 1 *a)* the act of one who seizes, or an instance of this *b)* the state or an instance of being seized 2 *Med. a)* [Archaic] a sudden attack of illness, as a stroke *b)* a sudden surge in electrical brain activity, resulting in convulsions, loss of consciousness, etc.

se·jant or **se·jeant** (sē′jənt) *adj.* ⟦Anglo-Fr *seiant*, prp. of *seier* (OFr *seoir*), to sit < L *sedere*, to SIT⟧ *Heraldry* sitting erect with the forepaws resting on the ground *[a lion sejant]*

se·la·chi·an (si lā′kē ən) *n.* ⟦< ModL *Selachii* (< Gr *selachos*, cartilaginous fish, akin to *selas*, light, gleam: from its phosphorescent appearance: see SELENE) + -AN⟧ any shark or ray —*adj.* of the selachians

sel·a·gi·nel·la (sel′ə ji nel′ə) *n.* ⟦ModL, dim. < L *selago* (gen. *selaginis*), kind of plant⟧ any of a genus (*Selaginella*) of small-leaved lycopods, having two kinds of spores borne in cones at the tips of the branches

se·lah (sē′lə, -lä′; se lä′) *n.* ⟦Heb *sela*⟧ a Hebrew word of unknown meaning at the end of verses in the Psalms: perhaps a musical direction, but traditionally interpreted as a blessing meaning "forever"

Se·lan·gor (se läŋ′gôr) state of Malaysia, in SW Peninsular Malaysia: 3,072 sq mi (7,956 sq km)

Selassie *see* HAILE SELASSIE

sel·dom (sel′dəm) *adv.* ⟦ME *selden* < OE *seldan*, strange, rare, akin to Ger *selten* < Gmc base **selda-* < ? IE **selo-*: see SELF⟧ not often; rarely; infrequently —*adj.* rare; infrequent —**sel′dom·ness** *n.*

se·lect (sə lekt′) *adj.* ⟦L *selectus*, pp. of *seligere*, to choose, pick out < *se-*, apart + *legere*, to choose: see LOGIC⟧ 1 chosen in preference to another or others; picked out, esp. for excellence or some special quality; picked 2 choice; excellent; outstanding 3 limited to certain people or groups; exclusive —*vt.* to choose or pick out from among others, as for excellence, desirability, etc. —*vi.* to make a selection; choose —**se·lect′ness** *n.*

☆**se·lect·ee** (sə lek′tē′) *n.* a person inducted into the armed forces under selective service

se·lec·tion (sə lek′shən) *n.* ⟦L *selectio*⟧ 1 a selecting or being selected 2 *a)* a person or thing chosen *b)* a group or collection of these *c)* a variety from which to choose *[a selection of colors]* 3 *Biol.* any process, natural or artificial, by which certain organisms or characters are favored or perpetuated in, or as if in, preference to others: cf. NATURAL SELECTION —*SYN.* CHOICE

se·lec·tive (-tiv) *adj.* 1 of or characterized by selection 2 *a)* having the power of selecting; tending to select *b)* tending to select carefully; fastidious; discriminating 3 *Radio* excluding oscillations on all frequencies except the one desired —**se·lec′tive·ly** *adv.* —**se·lec′tive·ness** *n.*

☆**selective service** a system for enrolling persons in compulsory military service

se·lec·tiv·i·ty (sə lek′tiv′ə tē) *n.* 1 the state or quality of being selective 2 the degree to which a radio receiver will reproduce the signals of a given transmitter while rejecting the signals of the others

☆**se·lect·man** (sə lekt′mən; *locally, also* sē′lekt man′) *n., pl.* **-men** (-mən; *locally, also*, -men′) ⟦SELECT + MAN⟧ any of a board of officers elected in most New England towns to manage municipal affairs

se·lec·tor (sə lek′tər) *n.* a person or thing that selects

sel·e·nate (sel′ə nāt′) ⟦Swed *selenat* < *selen*, selenic + *-at*, -ATE[2]⟧ *n.* 1 a salt of selenic acid containing the divalent, negative radical SeO_4 2 an uncharged ester of this acid

Se·le·ne (si lē′nē) *n.* ⟦Gr *Selēnē* < *selēnē*, the moon < *selas*, light, gleam < ? IE base **swel-*, to burn, smolder > SWELTER⟧ *Gr. Myth.* the goddess of the moon: later identified with Artemis

se·le·nic (sə lē′nik, -len′ik) *adj.* ⟦SELEN(IUM) + -IC⟧ designating or of compounds in which selenium has a higher valence than in corresponding selenous compounds: usually containing tetravalent or hexavalent selenium

selenic acid a colorless, crystalline acid, H_2SeO_4, resembling sulfuric acid in its action

sel·e·nite (sel′ə nīt′) *n.* ⟦L *selenites* < Gr *selēnitēs (lithos)*, lit., moon (stone) < *selēnē*, the moon: once thought to wax and wane with the moon⟧ 1 a kind of gypsum found in transparent crystals 2 a salt of selenous acid containing the divalent, negative radical SeO_3

se·le·ni·um (sə lē′nē əm) *n.* ⟦ModL: so named (1818) by BERZELIUS < Gr *selēnē*, the moon (see SELENE) + -IUM, by analogy with TELLURIUM, with which it was assoc. in the ore⟧ a nonmetallic chemical element with several allotropic forms, used in photoelectric devices because its electrical conductivity varies with the intensity of light: also used in rectifiers, in certain electrostatic copying processes, etc.: symbol, Se; at. no. 34: see the periodic table of elements in the Reference Supplement

selenium cell a photoelectric cell using selenium as the photoconductive element

sel·e·no- (sel′ə nō) ⟦< Gr *selēnē*, the moon: see SELENE⟧ *combining form* moon *[selenography]*

sel·e·nod·e·sy (sel′ə näd′ə sē) *n.* ⟦prec. + *-desy*, based on GEODESY⟧ the branch of astronomy concerned with measuring, or determining the shape of, the moon or its surface features, by exactly locating various points on its surface, etc. —**sel′e·nod′e·sist** *n.*

sel·e·nog·ra·phy (-näg′rə fē) *n.* ⟦ModL *selenographia*: see SELENO- & -GRAPHY⟧ the study of the surface and physical features of the moon, esp. the mapping of the latitude and longitude —**sel′e·nog′ra·pher** *n.* —**se·le·no·graph·ic** (sə lē′nə graf′ik) *adj.*

sel·e·nol·o·gy (-näl′ə jē) *n.* ⟦SELENO- + -LOGY⟧ the branch of astronomy dealing with the moon in general —**se·le·no·log·i·cal** (sə lē′nə läj′i kəl) *adj.* —**sel′e·nol′o·gist** *n.*

se·le·nous (sə lē′nəs) *adj.* ⟦SELEN(IUM) + -OUS⟧ designating or of compounds in which selenium has a lower valence than in corresponding selenic compounds: usually containing divalent or tetravalent selenium: also **se·le′ni·ous** (-nē əs)

selenous acid a colorless, transparent, crystalline powder, H_2SeO_3, soluble in water and used as a reagent: also **selenious acid**

Se·leu·ci·a (sə lo͞o′shē ə, -shə) any of several ancient cities of SW Asia, founded by Seleucus I; esp., the chief city of the Seleucid Empire, on the Tigris

Se·leu·cid (sə lo͞o′sid) *n., pl.* **-cids** or **-ci·dae′** (-si dē′) ⟦< L *Seleucides* < Gr *Seleukidēs*⟧ a member of a dynasty founded by Seleucus I and ruling (312-64? B.C.) over S Asia Minor & the region between the Mediterranean Sea & the Indus River —*adj.* designating or of this dynasty: also **Se·leu′ci·dan**

Se·leu·cus I (sə lo͞o′kəs) died 280 B.C.; Macedonian general & founder of the Seleucid dynasty: called *Seleucus Nicator*

self (self) *n., pl.* **selves** ⟦ME < OE, prob. < IE **selo-* < base **se-*, refl. pron., orig. separate, apart (> L *sibi, se*) + **(o)lo-*, pron. suffix: basic sense "itself, by itself"⟧ 1 the identity, character, or essential qualities of any person or thing 2 one's own person as distinct from all others 3 one's own welfare, interest, or advantage; selfishness *[obsessed with self]* —*pron.* [Informal] myself, himself, herself, or yourself *[tickets for self and wife]* —*adj.* 1 being uniform or the same throughout 2 of the same kind, nature, color, material, etc. as the rest *[a self lining, self trim]*

self- (self) ⟦ME < OE < *self*: see prec.⟧ *prefix* 1 of oneself or itself: refers to the direct object of the implied transitive verb *[self-love, self-restraint]* 2 by oneself or itself: refers to the subject of the implied verb *[self-acting]* 3 in, within, or inherent in oneself or itself *[self-absorption, self-evident]* 4 to, for, or with oneself: often refers to the indirect object of the implied transitive verb *[self-addressed]* 5 automatic *[self-loading]* 6 of the same kind, color, material, etc. as the rest *[self-covered buttons on a plaid jacket]* Used in hyphenated compounds

self-a·base·ment (self′ə bās′mənt) *n.* a humbling or abasement of oneself

self-ab·ne·ga·tion (-ab′nə gā′shən) *n.* lack of consideration for oneself or one's own interest; self-denial

self-ab·sorp·tion (-ab sôrp′shən, -zôrp′-) *n.* 1 absorption in one's own interests, affairs, etc. 2 *Physics* the absorption of radiation by the substance emitting the radiation —**self′-ab·sorbed′** *adj.*

self-a·buse (-ə byo͞os′) *n.* 1 misuse of one's own abilities, talents, etc. 2 accusation, blame, or revilement of oneself 3 [Old-fashioned] MASTURBATION

self-act·ing (-ak′tiŋ) *adj.* acting without outside influence or stimulus; working by itself; automatic

self-ac·tu·al·i·za·tion (-ak′cho͞o əl i zā′shən) *n.* full development of one's abilities, ambitions, etc.

self-ad·dressed (-ə drest′) *adj.* addressed to oneself *[to enclose a self-addressed envelope]*

self-ad·he·sive (-əd hē′siv) *adj.* having a surface coated with an adhesive that will adhere to another surface without the application of moisture *[self-adhesive labels]*

self-ad·vance·ment (-əd vans′mənt) *n.* the act or process of advancing or promoting one's own interests

self-ag·gran·dize·ment (-ə gran′diz mənt) *n.* the act of making oneself more powerful, wealthy, etc., esp. in a ruthless way —**self′-ag·gran′diz′ing** (-dīz′iŋ) *adj.*

self-a·nal·y·sis (-ə nal′ə sis) *n.* analysis of one's own personality without the help of another

self-an·ni·hi·la·tion (-ə nī′ə lā′shən) *n.* loss of awareness of self, as in a mystical union with God

self-ap·point·ed (-ə point′id) *adj.* acting in a specified role, but not so recognized by others *[a self-appointed censor]*

self-as·ser·tion (-ə sur′shən) *n.* the act of demanding recognition for oneself or of insisting upon one's rights, claims, etc. —**self′-as·ser′tive** *adj.*, **self′-as·sert′ing**

self-as·sur·ance (-ə shoor′əns) *n.* confidence in oneself, or in one's own ability, talent, etc. —**self′-as·sured′** *adj.*

self-a·ware (-ə wer′) *adj.* characterized by self-awareness

self-a·ware·ness (-ə wer′nəs) *n.* awareness of oneself as an individual, esp. as a worthwhile person

self-cen·tered (-sent′ərd) *adj.* occupied or concerned only with one's own affairs; egocentric; selfish —**self′-cen′tered·ly** *adv.* —**self′-cen′tered·ness** *n.*

self-clean·ing (-klēn′iŋ) *adj.* designating or of an oven for cooking, whose interior is designed to be cleaned automatically as by a special high-temperature setting rather than by hand

self-clos·ing (-klō′ziŋ) *adj.* closing automatically

self-col·lect·ed (-kə lek′tid) *adj.* SELF-POSSESSED

self-col·ored (-kul′ərd) *adj.* 1 of only one color 2 of the natural or original color: said as of a fabric

self-com·mand (-kə mand′) ***n.*** SELF-CONTROL
self-com·pla·cent (-kəm plā′sənt) ***adj.*** self-satisfied, esp. in a smug way —**self′-com·pla′cen·cy** ***n.***
self-com·posed (-kəm pōzd′) ***adj.*** having or showing composure; calm; cool
self-con·ceit (-kən sēt′) ***n.*** too high an opinion of oneself; conceit; vanity —**self′-con·ceit′ed** ***adj.***
self-con·cept (-kän′sept′) ***n.*** SELF-IMAGE
self-con·fessed (-kən fest′) ***adj.*** being such by one's own admission [a *self-confessed* thief]
self-con·fi·dence (-kän′fə dəns) ***n.*** confidence in oneself, one's own abilities, etc. —*SYN.* CONFIDENCE —**self′-con′fi·dent** ***adj.*** —**self′-con′fi·dent·ly** ***adv.***
self-con·scious (-kän′shəs) ***adj.*** **1** *a)* conscious or, esp., unduly conscious of oneself as an object of notice [a *self-conscious* poet] *b)* awkward or embarrassed in the presence of others; ill at ease *c)* indicating embarrassment [a *self-conscious* cough] **2** *Philos., Psychol.* having or showing awareness of one's own existence, actions, etc.; conscious of oneself —**self′-con′scious·ly** ***adv.*** —**self′-con′scious·ness** ***n.***
self-con·sis·tent (-kən sis′tənt) ***adj.*** having all parts, ideas, actions, etc. consistent with one another
self-con·sti·tut·ed (-kän′stə to͞ot′id) ***adj.*** constituted as such by oneself or itself [a *self-constituted* arbiter]
self-con·tained (-kən tānd′) ***adj.*** **1** keeping one's affairs to oneself; reserved **2** showing self-command or self-control **3** having all working parts, complete with motive power, in an enclosed unit: said of machinery **4** having within oneself or itself all that is necessary; self-sufficient, as a community —**self′-con·tain′ment** ***n.***
self-con·tent·ed (-kən tent′id) ***adj.*** contented with what one is or has —**self′-con·tent′** ***n.***, **self′-con·tent′ment**
self-con·tra·dic·tion (-kän′trə dik′shən) ***n.*** **1** contradiction of oneself or itself **2** any statement or idea containing elements that contradict each other —**self′-con′tra·dict′ing** ***adj.*** —**self′-con′tra·dic′to·ry** ***adj.***
self-con·trol (-kən trōl′) ***n.*** control of oneself, or of one's own emotions, desires, actions, etc.
self-cor·rect·ing (-kə rek′tiŋ) ***adj.*** **1** correcting oneself or itself **2** designating or of a special device on a typewriter that allows the typist to correct an error by backspacing and retyping
self-crit·i·cism (-krit′ə siz′əm) ***n.*** criticism of one's own faults or shortcomings —**self′-crit′i·cal** ***adj.***
self-de·cep·tion (-di sep′shən) ***n.*** the deceiving of oneself as to one's true feelings, motives, circumstances, etc.: also **self′-de·ceit′** —**self′-de·ceiv′ing** ***adj.***
self-de·feat·ing (-di fēt′iŋ) ***adj.*** that defeats its own purpose or unwittingly works against itself
self-de·fense (-di fens′) ***n.*** **1** defense of oneself or of one's rights, beliefs, actions, etc. **2** the skill of boxing: used chiefly in the phrase **manly art of self-defense** **3** *Law* the right to defend oneself with whatever force is reasonably necessary against actual or threatened violence —**self′-de·fen′sive** ***adj.***
self-def·i·ni·tion (-def′ə nish′ən) ***n.*** the understanding or determination of one's own nature or basic qualities
self-de·lu·sion (-di lo͞o′zhən) ***n.*** SELF-DECEPTION
self-de·ni·al (-di nī′əl) ***n.*** denial or sacrifice of one's own desires or pleasures —**self′-de·ny′ing** ***adj.***
self-dep·re·cat·ing (-dep′rə kāt′iŋ) ***adj.*** belittling or poking fun at oneself [*self-deprecating* humor, a *self-deprecating* remark]: sometimes **self′-dep′re·ca·to′ry** (-kə tôr′ē) —**self′-dep′re·cat′ing·ly** ***adv.*** —**self′-dep′re·ca′tion** ***n.***
self-de·scribed (-di skrībd′) ***adj.*** described as being (something specified) by the person himself or herself [a *self-described* expert] —**self′-de·scrip′tion** ***n.***
self-des·ig·na·tion (-dez′ig nā′shən) ***n.*** a name taken for oneself or one's own people
☆**self-de·struct** (-di strukt′) ***vi.*** **1** to destroy itself automatically [a missile designed to *self-destruct*] **2** to greatly harm oneself or itself, specif. as the result of inherent or fundamental flaws
self-de·struc·tion (-di struk′shən) ***n.*** destruction of oneself or itself; specif., suicide
self-de·struc·tive (-di struk′tiv) ***adj.*** of, having to do with, or causing either damage to or the destruction of oneself or itself —**self′-de·struc′tive·ness** ***n.***
self-de·ter·mi·na·tion (-di tʉr′mə nā′shən) ***n.*** **1** the act or power of making up one's own mind about what to think or do, without outside influence or compulsion **2** the right of a people to decide upon its own political status or form of government, without outside influence —**self′-de·ter′mined** ***adj.*** —**self′-de·ter′min·ing** ***adj.***
self-de·vel·op·ment (-di vel′əp mənt) ***n.*** efforts toward self-fulfillment, either through formal study programs or on one's own
self-de·vo·tion (-di vō′shən) ***n.*** devotion of oneself to a cause or to others' interests
self-di·rect·ed (self′də rek′tid) ***adj.*** **1** directed at oneself [*self-directed* hostility] **2** guided by goals or principles determined by oneself [a *self-directed* course of study] —**self′-di·rec′tion** ***n.***
self-dis·ci·pline (-dis′ə plin) ***n.*** the disciplining or controlling of oneself or one's desires, actions, habits, etc. —**self′-dis′ci·plined** ***adj.***
self-dis·cov·er·y (-dis kuv′ər ē) ***n.*** a becoming aware of one's true potential, character, motives, etc.
self-doubt (-dout′) ***n.*** lack of confidence or faith in oneself
self-ed·u·cat·ed (-ej′ə kāt′id) ***adj.*** educated or trained by oneself, with little or no formal schooling
self-ef·face·ment (-i fās′mənt) ***n.*** the practice of keeping oneself in the background and minimizing one's own actions; modest, retiring behavior —**self′-ef·fac′ing** ***adj.***
self-em·ployed (-em ploid′) ***adj.*** working for oneself, with direct control over work, services, etc. undertaken and fees, charges, etc. set —**self′-em·ploy′ment** ***n.***
self-es·teem (-e stēm′) ***n.*** **1** belief in oneself; self-respect **2** undue pride in oneself; conceit —*SYN.* PRIDE
self-ev·i·dent (-ev′i dənt) ***adj.*** evident without need of proof or explanation —**self′-ev′i·dent·ly** ***adv.***
self-ex·am·i·na·tion (-ig zam′ə nā′shən) ***n.*** **1** the act or an instance of examining one's own qualities, conduct, motives, etc.; introspection **2** the act or an instance of examining one's own body, esp. manually as for a tumor or cyst: also **self′-ex·am′**
self-ex·cit·ed (-ek sīt′id) ***adj.*** *Elec.* excited by field current supplied from its own armature: said of a generator
self-ex·e·cut·ing (-ek′si kyo͞ot′iŋ) ***adj.*** coming into effect automatically when specified, without further provision being made, as a death clause in a contract
self-ex·ist·ent (-eg zis′tənt) ***adj.*** existing of or by itself without external cause or agency —**self′-ex·ist′ence** ***n.***
self-ex·plan·a·to·ry (-ek splan′ə tôr′ē) ***adj.*** explaining itself; obvious without explanation: also **self′-ex·plain′ing**
self-ex·pres·sion (-ek spresh′ən) ***n.*** expression of one's own personality or emotions, esp. in the arts
self-feed·ing (-fēd′iŋ) ***adj.*** **1** automatically supplying itself with what is needed, as a machine ☆**2** designating or of a system of supplying feed to animals so that they can eat the kind and amount they want when they want it
self-fer·til·i·za·tion (-fʉrt′'l i zā′shən) ***n.*** fertilization of a plant or animal by its own pollen or sperm
self-ful·fill·ing (-fəl fil′iŋ) ***adj.*** **1** bringing about self-fulfillment **2** brought to fulfillment chiefly as an effect of having been expected or predicted [a *self-fulfilling* prophecy]
self-ful·fill·ment (-fəl fil′mənt) ***n.*** fulfillment of one's aspirations, hopes, etc. through one's own efforts
self-gov·ern·ment (-guv′ərn mənt) ***n.*** government of a group by the action of its own members, as in electing representatives to make its laws —**self′-gov′ern·ing** ***adj.***
self-hard·en·ing (-härd′'n iŋ) ***adj.*** designating or of any steel that will harden if air-cooled after being heated above red heat
self-hate (-hāt′) ***n.*** hatred directed against oneself or one's own people, often in despair: also **self′-ha′tred**
self·heal (-hēl′) ***n.*** any of various plants supposed to have healing properties; esp., a common, Old World lawn and pasture weed (*Prunella vulgaris*) of the mint family
self-help (-help′) ***n.*** care for or betterment of oneself by one's own efforts —***adj.*** designating or of nontechnical books, magazines, videos, etc. designed to provide insight and guidance about one's health, psychology, family life, career, etc.
self·hood (-hood′) ***n.*** **1** all the things that make one what one is; personality or individuality **2** the condition of being self-centered; selfishness
self-hyp·no·sis (-hip nō′sis) ***n.*** AUTOHYPNOSIS
self-i·den·ti·fi·ca·tion (-ī den′tə fi kā′shən) ***n.*** the identification of oneself with another person or thing
self-i·den·ti·ty (-ī den′tə tē) ***n.*** **1** the identity of a thing with itself **2** awareness of one's individual identity
self·ie (sel′fē) ***n.*** ⟦SELF + -IE⟧ [Slang] a photograph that a person takes of himself or herself, as with a cell phone for posting on social media
self-im·age (-im′ij) ***n.*** one's conception of oneself and one's own identity, abilities, worth, etc.
self-im·mo·la·tion (-im′ə lā′shən) ***n.*** **1** suicide, usually by burning oneself in a public place **2** deliberate self-sacrifice
self-im·por·tant (-im pôrt′'nt) ***adj.*** having or showing an exaggerated opinion of one's own importance; pompous or officious —**self′-im·por′tance** ***n.***
self-im·posed (-im pōzd′) ***adj.*** imposed or inflicted on oneself by oneself
self-im·prove·ment (-im pro͞ov′mənt) ***n.*** improvement of one's status, mind, abilities, etc. by one's own efforts
self-in·clu·sive (-in klo͞o′siv) ***adj.*** including oneself or itself
self-in·crim·i·na·tion (-in krim′ə nā′shən) ***n.*** incrimination of oneself by one's own statements or answers —**self′-in·crim′i·nat′ing** ***adj.***
self-in·duced (-in do͞ost′) ***adj.*** **1** induced by oneself or itself **2** produced by self-induction
self-in·duc·tance (-in duk′təns) ***n.*** INDUCTANCE (sense 2)
self-in·duc·tion (-in duk′shən) ***n.*** the induction of a counter electromotive force in a circuit by the variation of current in that circuit
self-in·dul·gence (-in dul′jəns) ***n.*** indulgence of one's own desires, impulses, etc. —**self′-in·dul′gent** ***adj.***
self-in·flict·ed (-in flik′tid) ***adj.*** inflicted on oneself by oneself, as an injury

self-in·i·ti·at·ed (-i nish′ē āt′id) ***adj.*** initiated by oneself or itself

self-in·sur·ance (-in shoor′əns) ***n.*** insurance of oneself or one's property by setting apart one's own funds rather than by paying for an insurance policy

self-in·ter·est (-in′trist, -in′tər est′) ***n.*** **1** one's own interest or advantage **2** an exaggerated regard for this, esp. when at the expense of others

self-in·volved (-in välvd′, -vôlvd′) ***adj.*** self-centered; preoccupied with oneself —**self′-in·volve′ment** ***n.***

self·ish (sel′fish) ***adj.*** **1** too much concerned with one's own welfare or interests and having little or no concern for others; self-centered **2** showing or prompted by self-interest —**self′ish·ly** ***adv.*** —**self′ish·ness** ***n.***

self-justifying (self′jus′tə fī′iŋ) ***n.*** justifying or rationalizing one's actions, beliefs, motives, etc. —**self′-jus′ti·fi·ca′tion** (-fi kā′shən) ***n.***

self-knowl·edge (-näl′ij) ***n.*** knowledge of one's own qualities, character, abilities, etc.

self·less (self′lis) ***adj.*** **1** devoted to others' welfare or interests and not one's own; unselfish; altruistic **2** showing or prompted by unselfishness or altruism; self-sacrificing [a *selfless* act] —**self′less·ly** ***adv.*** —**self′less·ness** ***n.***

self-lim·it·ing (self′lim′it iŋ) ***adj.*** that terminates by the natural course of events [a *self-limiting* disease] —**self-lim′i·ta′tion** ***n.***

self-liq·ui·dat·ing (-lik′wə dāt′iŋ) ***adj.*** **1** that can be converted into cash over a certain period of time **2** having within itself the means of making up for, or yielding a profit on, the initial outlay [a *self-liquidating* investment]

self-load·ing (-lōd′iŋ) ***adj.*** loading again by its own action [a *self-loading* gun]

self-love (-luv′) ***n.*** **1** love of oneself **2** regard for oneself and one's own interests

self-made (-mād′) ***adj.*** **1** made by oneself or itself **2** successful, rich, etc. through one's own efforts [a *self-made* man] **3** being or having become such primarily through one's own efforts [a *self-made* millionaire]

self-med·i·cate (-med′ə kāt′) ***vi.*** **-cat′ed, -cat′ing** to medicate oneself without consulting a physician —**self′-med′i·ca′tion** ***n.***

self-mov·ing (-mo͞ov′iŋ) ***adj.*** moving or able to move under its own power, or of itself

self-op·er·at·ing (-äp′ə rāt′iŋ) ***adj.*** operating by itself; automatic: also **self′-op′er·at′ed**

self-o·pin·ion·at·ed (-ə pin′yə nāt′id) ***adj.*** **1** stubbornly holding to one's own opinions **2** conceited

self-per·pet·u·at·ing (-pər pech′o͞o āt′iŋ) ***adj.*** of a kind that causes or promotes indefinite continuation or renewal of itself or oneself [a *self-perpetuating* caste system]

self-pit·y (-pit′ē) ***n.*** pity for oneself, esp. pity that is self-indulgent or exaggerated

self-po·lic·ing (-pə lēs′iŋ) ***n.*** a process or procedure by which an industry, profession, or other cooperating group checks its own members to be sure they conform to established principles or agreements

self-pol·li·na·tion (-päl′ə nā′shən) ***n.*** the transfer of pollen from anthers to stigmas in the same flower, or to stigmas of another flower on the same plant or of a flower on a plant of the same clone —**self′-pol′li·nat′ed** ***adj.***

self-por·trait (-pôr′trit, -trāt′) ***n.*** a painting, drawing, etc. of oneself, done by oneself

self-pos·ses·sion (-pə zesh′ən) ***n.*** full possession or control of one's feelings, actions, etc.; self-command; composure —*SYN.* CONFIDENCE —**self′-pos·sessed′** ***adj.***

self-pres·er·va·tion (-prez′ər vā′shən) ***n.*** **1** preservation of oneself from danger, injury, or death **2** the urge to preserve oneself, regarded as an instinct

self-pro·claimed (-prō klāmd′) ***adj.*** so proclaimed or announced by oneself [a *self-proclaimed* ruler]

self-pro·duced (-prə do͞ost′) ***adj.*** produced by oneself or itself

self-pro·nounc·ing (-prə noun′siŋ) ***adj.*** showing pronunciation by accent marks or diacritical marks added to the original spelling instead of by phonetic transcription

self-pro·pelled (-prə peld′) ***adj.*** propelled by its own motor or power: also **self′-pro·pel′ling**

self-pro·tec·tion (-prə tek′shən) ***n.*** protection of oneself; self-defense

self-pub·lished (-pub′lisht) ***adj.*** issued directly to the public by the author rather than through a publishing company [a *self-published* novel]

self-ques·tion·ing (-kwes′chə niŋ) ***n.*** a querying or doubting of one's own beliefs, motives, etc.

self-re·al·i·za·tion (-rē′ə li zā′shən) ***n.*** complete fulfillment of the self or full development of one's own talents, capabilities, etc.

self-re·cord·ing (-ri kôrd′iŋ) ***adj.*** recording its own operations or reactions automatically, as a seismograph

self-re·crim·i·na·tion (-ri krim′ə nā′shən) ***n.*** a blaming of oneself, esp. a remorseful or persistent blaming

self-ref·er·en·tial (-ref′ə ren′shəl) ***adj.*** **1** making reference to itself or oneself **2** of, being, or related to a work of literature or art which exhibits the author's or artist's self-conscious awareness of the creative process, of the techniques he or she is using, etc. —**self′-ref′er·en·ti·al′i·ty** ***n.***

self-re·flex·ive (-ri flek′siv) ***adj.*** SELF-REFERENTIAL

self-re·gard (-ri gärd′) ***n.*** **1** regard or concern for oneself and one's own interests **2** SELF-RESPECT —**self′-re·gard′ing** ***adj.***

self-reg·u·lat·ing (-reg′yə lāt′iŋ) ***adj.*** regulating oneself or itself, so as to function automatically or without outside control —**self′-reg′u·la′tion** ***n.***

self-re·li·ance (-ri lī′əns) ***n.*** reliance on one's own judgment, abilities, etc. —**self′-re·li′ant** ***adj.***

self-re·nun·ci·a·tion (-ri nun′sē ā′shən) ***n.*** renunciation of one's own interests or desires, esp. for the benefit of others

self-rep·li·cat·ing (-rep′li kāt′iŋ) ***adj.*** having the ability to replicate, or produce copies of, itself —**self′-rep′li·ca′tion** ***n.***

self-re·proach (-ri prōch′) ***n.*** accusation or blame of oneself; guilt feeling —**self′-re·proach′ful** ***adj.***

self-re·spect (-ri spekt′) ***n.*** proper respect for oneself and one's worth as a person —**self′-re·spect′ing** ***adj.***

self-re·straint (-ri strānt′) ***n.*** restraint imposed on oneself by oneself; self-control —**self′-re·strained′** ***adj.***

self-re·veal·ing (-ri vēl′iŋ) ***adj.*** revealing or expressing one's innermost thoughts, emotions, etc.: also **self′-rev′e·la·to′ry** (-rev′ə lə tôr′ē) —**self′-rev′e·la′tion** ***n.***

self-right·eous (-rī′chəs) ***adj.*** filled with or showing a conviction of being morally superior, or more righteous than others; smugly virtuous —**self′-right′eous·ly** ***adv.*** —**self′-right′eous·ness** ***n.***

☆**self-ris·ing flour** (-rī′ziŋ) flour that has salt and baking powder mixed in so that it will rise in baking

self-rule (-ro͞ol′) ***n.*** SELF-GOVERNMENT

self-sac·ri·fice (-sak′rə fīs′) ***n.*** sacrifice of oneself or one's own interests for the benefit, or the supposed benefit, of others —**self′-sac′ri·fic′ing** ***adj.***

self·same (self′sām′) ***adj.*** exactly the same; identical; (the) very same —*SYN.* SAME —**self′same′ness** ***n.***

self-sat·is·fied (self′sat′is fīd′) ***adj.*** feeling or showing an often smug satisfaction with oneself or one's accomplishments —**self′-sat′is·fac′tion** ***n.***

self-sat·is·fy·ing (-sat′is fī′iŋ) ***adj.*** satisfying to oneself

self-seal·ing (-sēl′iŋ) ***adj.*** **1** containing, or composed of, a substance that automatically seals punctures, etc. [a *self-sealing* tire] **2** that can be sealed by pressure alone [a *self-sealing* envelope]

self-seek·er (-sē′kər) ***n.*** a person who seeks only or mainly to further his or her own interests —**self′-seek′ing** ***n., adj.***

self-se·lec·tion (-sə lek′shən) ***n.*** selection made by or for oneself

self-serve (-surv′) ***adj., n.*** *short for* SELF-SERVICE

☆**self-serv·ice** (-sur′vis) ***adj.*** designed so that customers serve themselves [a *self-service* carwash, cafeteria, gas station, etc.] —***n.*** this manner of doing business

self-serv·ing (-sur′viŋ) ***adj.*** serving one's own selfish interests, esp. at the expense of others

self-sown (-sōn′) ***adj.*** sown by wind, water, or other natural means, as some weeds, instead of by people or an animal

self-start·er (-stärt′ər) ***n.*** **1** STARTER (sense *e*) ☆**2** one who works on one's own initiative and without prodding

self-ster·ile (-ster′əl) ***adj.*** *Biol.* incapable of self-fertilization

self-stud·y (-stud′ē) ***n.*** **1** study by oneself, as through correspondence courses, without classroom instruction **2** study of oneself

self-styled (-stīld′) ***adj.*** considered and called (something specified) only by the individual himself or herself; alleged (to be such) only by the person concerned; pretended; professed [a *self-styled* expert]

self-suf·fi·cient (-sə fish′ənt) ***adj.*** having the necessary resources to get along without help; independent: also **self′-suf·fic′ing** (-fīs′iŋ) —**self′-suf·fi′cien·cy** ***n.***

self-sug·ges·tion (-səg jes′chən) ***n.*** AUTOSUGGESTION

self-sup·port (-sə pôrt′) ***n.*** support of oneself or itself without aid or reinforcement —**self′-sup·port′ing** ***adj.***

self-sur·rend·er (-sə ren′dər) ***n.*** surrender of oneself or one's will, as to an influence or emotion

self-sus·tain·ing (-sə stān′iŋ) ***adj.*** **1** supporting or able to support oneself or itself **2** able to continue once begun —**self′-sus·tained′** ***adj.***

self-taught (-tôt′) ***adj.*** **1** having taught oneself through one's own efforts; self-educated **2** learned by oneself without instruction

self-tor·ture (-tôr′chər) ***n.*** any mental or physical distress inflicted by oneself upon oneself

self·ward (self′wərd) ***adv.*** toward oneself: also **self′wards** —***adj.*** directed toward oneself

self-will (self′wil′) ***n.*** persistent carrying out of one's own will or wishes, esp. when in conflict with others; stubbornness; obstinacy —**self′-willed′** ***adj.***

self-wind·ing (self′wīn′diŋ) ***adj.*** wound automatically, as certain wristwatches with internal winding mechanisms activated by external motion, as by normal arm movements

self-worth (self′wurth′) ***n.*** one's worth as a person, as perceived by oneself

self·y (sel′fē) ***n.***, *pl.* **self′ies** [Slang] *alt. sp. of* SELFIE

Sel·juk (sel′jo͞ok′, sel jo͞ok′) ***n.*** ⟦after *Seljuk* (Turk *Selçuk*), a 10th-c. leader and ancestor of the dynasties⟧ a member of any of several Turkish dynasties that ruled much of W Asia in the 11th & 12th cent. —***adj.*** of or designating these dynasties or the peoples ruled by them Also **Sel·juk′i·an** (-jo͞o′kē ən)

Sel·kirk (sel′kurk′) former county of S Scotland: also **Sel′kirk′shire** (-shir, -shər)

Selkirk Mountains range of the Rocky Mountain system, in SE British Columbia: highest peak, 11,590 ft (3,533 m)

sell (sel) ***vt.*** **sold, sell′ing** ⟦ME *sellen* < OE *sellan*, to give, offer, akin to

Goth *saljan*, to offer (sacrifice): caus. formation in sense "to cause to take" < IE base *sel-, to take, grasp > SALE, Gr *helein*, to take⟧ **1** to give up, deliver, or exchange (property, goods, services, etc.) for money or its equivalent **2** *a)* to have or offer regularly for sale; deal in [a store that *sells* hardware, to *sell* real estate] *b)* to make or try to make sales in or to [to *sell* chain stores] **3** *a)* to give up or deliver (a person) to his or her enemies or into slavery, bondage, etc. *b)* to be a traitor to; betray (a country, cause, etc.) **4** to give up or dispose of (one's honor, one's vote, etc.) for profit or a dishonorable purpose **5** to bring about, help in, or promote, the sale of [television *sells* many products] ☆**6** [Informal] *a)* to establish faith, confidence, or belief in [to *sell* oneself to the public] *b)* to persuade (someone) of the value of something; convince (with *on*) [*sell* him on the idea] **7** [Slang] to cheat or dupe —*vi.* **1** to exchange property, goods, or services for money, etc. **2** to work or act as a salesman or salesclerk **3** to be sold; attract buyers: often used with reference to the rate of sale [to *sell* well, poorly, etc.] **4** to be sold (*for* or *at*) [belts *selling* for six dollars] **5** [Informal] to be accepted, approved, etc. [a scheme that won't *sell*] —*n.* **1** [Slang] a trick or hoax ☆**2** selling or salesmanship: cf. HARD SELL, SOFT SELL —**sell off** to get rid of by selling, esp. at low prices —**sell oneself 1** to exchange one's services for a price, esp. for a dishonorable purpose, as for prostitution ☆**2** [Informal] to convince another of one's worth —**sell out 1** to get rid of completely by selling ☆**2** [Informal] to betray (one's associates, cause, country, etc.) ☆**3** [Informal] to give up or be unfaithful to one's artistic aspirations or moral principles so as to achieve success, financial gain, etc. —☆**sell short 1** to sell securities, etc. not yet owned: see SHORT SALE **2** to value at less than its worth; underestimate —**sell up** [Brit.] to sell something, as a house or business, or everything that one owns [they *sold up* in London and moved to a village in Wales]

SYN.—**sell** implies a transferring of the ownership of something to another for money [to *sell* books, a house, etc.]; **barter** implies an exchange of goods or services without using money [to *barter* food for clothes]; **trade**, in transitive use, also implies the exchange of articles [let's *trade* neckties], and, intransitively, implies the carrying on of a business in which one buys and sells a specified commodity [to *trade* in wheat]; **auction** implies the public sale of items one by one, each going to the highest of the competing bidders [to *auction* off unclaimed property]; **vend** applies especially to the selling of small articles, as by peddling, slot machine, etc. [*vending* machines] —*ANT.* **buy**

sell·er (sel′ər) *n.* **1** a person who sells; vendor **2** something that sells: usually with reference to its rate of sale [a good *seller*]

seller's market a market favorable to sellers, with tight supply, high prices, etc.

selling point any quality or feature which arouses interest or is used to arouse interest in a product or service

selling race a claiming race immediately after which the winning horse is offered for sale at auction

sell-off (sel′ôf′) *n.* a period of heavy selling as on a stock exchange, resulting in a marked decline in prices

sel·lo·tape (sel′ō tāp′) [*also* **S-**] [Brit.] *n.* ⟦< *Sellotape*, Brit trademark, altered < CELLULOSE + -O- + TAPE⟧ a thin, transparent cellulose or plastic adhesive tape —*vt.* **-taped′**, **-tap′ing** to fasten or seal with this tape

☆**sell·out** (-out′) *n.* [Informal] **1** the act of selling out something or someone **2** an entertainment, lecture, etc. for which all the seats have been sold **3** a person who sells out: see phrase SELL OUT (sense 3) under SELL

Sel·ma[1] (sel′mə) *n.* ⟦< ? Gr *selma*, a ship⟧ a feminine name

Selma[2] (sel′mə) city in SC Ala.: site of a voter registration drive led by Martin Luther King, Jr., & starting point for a civil-rights march to Montgomery, Ala. (1965)

seltz·er (selt′sər) *n.* ⟦altered < Ger *Selterser (wasser)*, (water) from Selters, after *Niederselters*, village in WC Germany⟧ **1** [*often* **S-**] natural mineral water that is effervescent **2** any carbonated water, often flavored with fruit juices Also **seltzer water**

sel·va (sel′və) *n.* ⟦Sp & Port, forest < L *silva*: see SILVA⟧ a tropical rain forest, esp. in South America

sel·vage or **sel·vedge** (sel′vij) *n.* ⟦< SELF + EDGE, infl. by MDu *selfegge*⟧ **1** a specially woven edge that prevents cloth from raveling **2** any specially defined edge of fabric or paper, esp., such an edge that is to be trimmed off or covered **3** [Rare] the side plate of a lock through which the bolt passes

selves (selvz) *n. pl. of* SELF

Selz·nick (selz′nik), **David O(liver)** 1902-65; U.S. film producer

sem *abbrev.* **1** semester **2** semicolon

Sem *abbrev.* **1** Seminary **2** Semitic

se·mai·nier (sə men′yā) *n.* ⟦Fr, weekly⟧ a tall, narrow chest, typically with seven drawers, as for storing a week's supply of lingerie, shirts, etc.

se·man·tic (sə man′tik) *adj.* ⟦Gr *sēmantikos*, significant < *sēmainein*, to show, explain by a sign < *sēma*, a sign, symbol < IE *dhyāmṇ (> Sans *dhyāman*, thought) < base *dhyā-, to see, behold⟧ **1** of or pertaining to meaning, esp. meaning in language **2** of or according to semantics as a branch of linguistics or of semiotics Also **se·man′ti·cal** —**se·man′ti·cal·ly** *adv.*

se·man·ti·cist (-tə sist) *n.* a specialist in semantics

se·man·tics (-tiks) *n.* ⟦< SEMANTIC, based on Fr *sémantique*⟧ **1** the branch of linguistics concerned with the nature, the structure, and the development and changes of the meanings of speech forms, or with contextual meaning **2** *a)* SEMIOTICS *b)* the branch of semiotics dealing with relationships of signs and symbols to the things to which they refer, or with referential meaning **3** [*often with pl. v.*] the relationships between signs and symbols and the concepts, feelings, etc. associated with them in the minds of their interpreters; notional meaning **4** [*often with pl. v.*] the meanings of words, specif. in terms of their connotations, subtle distinctions, etc. **5** GENERAL SEMANTICS

sem·a·phore (sem′ə fôr′) *n.* ⟦Fr *sémaphore* < Gr *sēma*, sign (see SEMANTIC) + *-phoros*: see -PHORE⟧ **1** any apparatus for signaling, as the arrangement of lights, flags, and mechanical arms on railroads **2** a system of signaling by the use of two flags, one held in each hand: the letters of the alphabet are represented by the various positions of the arms **3** any system of signaling by semaphore — *vt., vi.* **-phored′**, **-phor′ing** to signal by semaphore —**sem′a·phor′ic** *adj.* —**sem′a·phor′ist** *n.*

Se·ma·rang (sə mär′äŋ) seaport in NC Java, Indonesia, on the Java Sea

se·ma·si·ol·o·gy (si mā′sē äl′ə jē) *n.* ⟦< Gr *sēmasia*, signification of a word (< *sēmainein*: see SEMANTIC) + -LOGY⟧ SEMANTICS (senses 1, 2, & 3) —**se·ma′si·o·log′i·cal** (-ə läj′i kəl) *adj.* —**se·ma′si·ol′o·gist** *n.*

se·mat·ic (si mat′ik) *adj.* ⟦< Gr *sēma* (gen. *sēmatos*), a sign (see SEMANTIC) + -IC⟧ *Zool.* serving as a sign of danger, as the coloration of some poisonous snakes

sem·bla·ble (sem′blə bəl) [Archaic] *adj.* ⟦ME < MFr < *sembler*: see fol.⟧ **1** similar **2** suitable **3** apparent —*n.* **1** something similar **2** likeness

sem·blance (sem′bləns) *n.* ⟦ME < OFr < *sembler*, to seem, appear < L *similare*, to make like < *similis*, like: see SAME⟧ **1** outward form or appearance; aspect **2** seeming likeness; resemblance **3** a likeness, image, or representation **4** false, assumed, or deceiving form or appearance **5** mere empty show; pretense —*SYN.* APPEARANCE

se·mé (sə mā′) *adj.* ⟦Fr, orig. pp. of *semer*, to sow < L *seminare* < *semen*, a SEED⟧ *Heraldry* having a design of many small figures; dotted, as with stars

Sem·e·le (sem′ə lē′) *n.* ⟦L < Gr *Semelē*⟧ *Gr. Myth.* a daughter of Cadmus and the mother of Dionysus: seeing Zeus in all his glory, she is consumed in his lightning

☆**sem·eme** (sem′ēm) *n.* ⟦coined (1933) by Leonard BLOOMFIELD < Gr *sēma*, a sign (see SEMANTIC) + -EME⟧ *Linguis.* the meaning of a morpheme

se·men (sē′mən) *n., pl.* **sem·i·na** (sem′ə nə) or **-mens** ⟦ModL < L, SEED⟧ the thick, whitish fluid secreted by the male reproductive organs and containing the spermatozoa

se·mes·ter (sə mes′tər) *n.* ⟦Ger < L *(cursus) semestris*, half-yearly (period) < *sex*, SIX + *mensis*, MONTH⟧ **1** a six-month period; half year **2** either of the two terms, of about eighteen weeks each, which usually make up a school or college year —**se·mes′tral** (-trəl) *adj.*

☆**sem·i** (sem′ī′) *n.* ⟦< SEMI(TRAILER)⟧ a semitrailer and the TRACTOR (sense 2) to which it is attached

sem·i- (sem′i; *also variously*, -ē, -ī, -ə) ⟦L < IE *semi- > Gr *hēmi-*, Sans *sāmi-*, OE *sām-*⟧ *prefix* **1** half [*semicircle*] **2** partly, not fully, imperfectly [*semicivilized*] **3** twice in a (specified period) [*semicentennial*]

sem·i·ab·stract (sem′ē ab strakt′) *adj.* designating or of a style of art in which an identifiable object is dealt with as an abstraction, as in some cubist works

sem·i·an·nu·al (-an′yoo əl) *adj.* done, happening, appearing, etc. every half year or twice a year —**sem′i·an′nu·al·ly** *adv.*

sem·i·a·quat·ic (-ə kwät′ik, -kwat′-) *adj. Biol.* **1** growing in or near water, as certain plants **2** spending some time in water, as muskrats

sem·i·ar·id (-ar′id) *adj.* characterized by little yearly rainfall and by the growth of short grasses and shrubs: said of a climate or region

sem·i·au·to·mat·ic (-ôt′ə mat′ik) *adj.* **1** partly automatic and partly hand-controlled: said of machinery **2** *Firearms* using the force of the explosion of a shell to eject and reload cartridges, as in an automatic, but requiring a trigger pull for each round fired —*n.* a semiautomatic firearm —**sem′i·au′to·mat′i·cal·ly** *adv.*

sem·i·au·ton·o·mous (-ô tän′ə məs) *adj.* granted autonomy with regard to internal affairs only, by a controlling nation, organization, etc.

sem·i·breve (sem′i brēv′) *n.* ⟦It⟧ [Chiefly Brit.] WHOLE NOTE

sem·i·cen·ten·ni·al (sem′i sen ten′ē əl) *adj.* ⟦SEMI- + CENTENNIAL⟧ of or ending a period of 50 years —*n.* a 50th anniversary or its commemoration

sem·i·cir·cle (sem′i sur′kəl) *n.* ⟦L *semicirculus*: see SEMI- & CIRCLE⟧ **1** a half circle **2** anything in the form of a half circle —**sem′i·cir′cu·lar** (-kyə lər) *adj.*

semicircular canal any of the three loop-shaped, tubular, fluid-filled structures of the inner ear that serve to maintain balance in the organism

sem·i·civ·i·lized (sem′i siv′ə līzd′) *adj.* partly civilized

sem·i·clas·si·cal (-klas′i kəl) *adj.* somewhat classical in form, quality, etc.; specif., designating or of music that is like classical music but is less complex in nature and has a more immediate appeal

sem·i·co·lon (sem′i kō′lən) *n.* a mark of punctuation (;) indicating a degree of separation greater than that marked by the comma and less than that marked by the period: used chiefly to separate units that contain elements separated by commas, and to separate closely related coordinate clauses

sem·i·con·duc·tor (sem′i kən duk′tər) *n.* **1** a substance, as germanium or silicon, whose conductivity is poor at low temperatures but is improved by minute additions of certain substances or by the application of heat, light, or voltage: used in transistors, rectifiers, etc. **2** CHIP (*n.* 8a)

sem·i·con·scious (sem′i kän′shəs) *adj.* not fully conscious or awake; half-conscious —**sem′i·con′scious·ness** *n.*

sem·i·dark·ness (-därk′nəs) *n.* partial darkness

sem·i·des·ert (-dez′ərt) *n.* a region somewhat like a desert, often located between a desert and grassland or woodland

sem·i·de·tached (-di tacht′) *adj.* partly separate or detached, as a pair of houses joined by a common wall —*n.* [Brit.] either of a pair of houses joined by a common wall

sem·i·di·am·e·ter (-dī am′ət ər) *n.* **1** half a diameter; radius **2** *Astron.* half the angular diameter of a celestial body with a visible disk, as the moon

sem·i·di·ur·nal (-dī ʉr′nəl) *adj.* **1** of, lasting, or performed in half a day **2** occurring twice a day, as the tides

sem·i·doc·u·men·ta·ry (-däk′yoo ment′ə rē) *n.* a film in which the technical style of a documentary is applied to a fictional subject, or, sometimes, to the dramatization of the story of a real person or situation, so as to add authenticity and realism

sem·i·dome (sem′i dōm′) *n.* a curved ceiling or roof covering a semicircular room, bay, etc.; half dome

sem·i·dou·ble (sem′i dub′əl) *adj.* having more than the normal numbers of petals, ray flowers, etc., but not enough to completely conceal the stamens and pistils

sem·i·el·lip·ti·cal (sem′ē i lip′ti kəl) *adj.* having the form of a half ellipse —**sem′i·el·lipse′** (-lips′) *n.*

sem·i·fi·nal (sem′i fī′nəl; *for n., usually* sem′i fī′nəl) *adj.* coming just before the final match, as of a tournament —*n.* **1** a semifinal match **2** [*pl.*] a semifinal round

sem·i·fi·nal·ist (-fī′nəl ist) *n.* a person taking part in a semifinal round, match, etc.

sem·i·fin·ished (-fin′isht) *adj.* designating or of a material, esp. a metal, that requires further processing to produce a finished product

sem·i·flu·id (-flōō′id) *adj.* heavy or thick but capable of flowing; viscous —*n.* a semifluid substance

sem·i·for·mal (-fôr′məl) *adj.* designating or requiring attire that is less than strictly formal but not informal

sem·i·gloss (sem′i glôs′, -gläs′) *adj.* having or producing a finish partway between glossy and flat: also written **semi-gloss**

sem·i·hard (-härd′) *adj.* somewhat hard, but easily cut

sem·i·leg·end·ar·y (-lej′ən der′ē) *adj.* having some historical basis, but legendary in part

sem·i·liq·uid (-lik′wid) *adj., n.* SEMIFLUID

sem·i·lit·er·ate (-lit′ər it) *adj.* knowing how to read and write a little or knowing only how to read

se·mil·lon or **sé·mil·lon** (sā mē yōn′; *Fr,* -yôn′) *n.* ⟦Fr *sémillon,* ult. < L *semen* (gen. *seminis*), a SEED⟧ **1** a white grape grown esp. in and near Bordeaux, used esp. in making Sauternes **2** a usually dry white wine made from this grape

sem·i·lu·nar (sem′i lōō′nər) *adj.* ⟦ModL *semilunaris:* see SEMI- & LUNAR⟧ shaped like a half-moon; crescent-shaped

semilunar valve either of two crescent-shaped heart valves that keep blood from flowing back into the ventricles: one, a pulmonary valve at the junction of the right ventricle and pulmonary artery, the other, an aortic valve at the junction of the left ventricle and aorta

sem·i·ma·jor axis (-mā′jər) *Astron.* one half of the longer axis of an elliptical orbit

sem·i·mi·nor axis (-mī′nər) *Astron.* one half of the shorter axis of an elliptical orbit

☆**sem·i·month·ly** (-munth′lē) *adj.* done, happening, published, etc. every half month or twice a month —*n., pl.* **-lies** something coming, appearing, etc. twice a month; esp., a magazine issued twice a month —*adv.* twice monthly; every half month

sem·i·nal (sem′ə nəl) *adj.* ⟦ME < MFr < L *seminalis* < *semen* (gen. *seminis*), a SEED⟧ **1** of or containing seed or semen **2** of reproduction *[seminal* power*]* **3** like seed in being a source or a first stage in development; germinal; originative *[*a *seminal* book*]* **4** being the first or earliest of something and later recognized as having been of primary influence *[*a *seminal* jazz band*]* **5** of essential importance; specif., *a)* basic; central; principal *b)* crucial; critical; pivotal —**sem′i·nal·ly** *adv.*

sem·i·nar (sem′ə när′) *n.* ⟦Ger < L *seminarium:* see SEMINARY⟧ **1** a group of supervised students doing research or advanced study, as at a university **2** *a)* a course for such a group, or any of its sessions *b)* the room where the group meets **3** any similar group discussion

sem·i·nar·i·an (sem′ə ner′ē ən) *n.* a student at a seminary (usually a theological seminary): also [Chiefly Brit.] **sem·i·nar·ist** (sem′ə nə rist)

sem·i·nar·y (sem′ə ner′ē) *n., pl.* **-nar′ies** ⟦ME, seed plot < L *seminarium,* seed plot, nursery, neut. of *seminarius,* of seed < *semen,* a SEED⟧ **1** [Now Rare] a place where something develops, grows, or is bred **2** [Old-fashioned] a school, esp. a private school for young women **3** a school or college where persons are trained to become priests, ministers, or rabbis

sem·i·na·tion (sem′ə nā′shən) *n.* ⟦L *seminatio* < *seminare,* to sow < *semen,* a SEED⟧ **1** propagation or dissemination **2** *Bot.* the act or process of sowing seeds

sem·i·nif·er·ous (-nif′ər əs) *adj.* ⟦< L *semen* (gen. *seminis*), a seed + -FEROUS⟧ **1** seed-bearing **2** containing or conveying semen *[seminiferous* tubules*]*

Sem·i·nole (sem′ə nōl′) *n.* ⟦< earlier *Seminolie* < Creek *simanó′li* wild, runaway, altered by metathesis < *simaló′ni* < New World Sp *cimarrón*⟧ **1** *pl.* **-noles′** or **-nole′** a member of any of the North American Indian groups that separated from the Creek Confederacy in the 18th cent. and migrated to Florida: now living in S Florida & Oklahoma **2** *a)* the variety of Creek spoken by the Florida Seminoles *b)* a related Muskogean language, usually called *Mikasuki*

sem·i·no·ma (sem′i nō′mə) *n., pl.* **-mas** or **-ma·ta** (-mə tə) ⟦ModL < Fr *séminome* < L *semen* (gen. *seminis*), a SEED, semen + *-ome, -*OMA⟧ a type of malignant tumor that forms in a testicle

sem·i·of·fi·cial (sem′ē ə fish′əl) *adj.* having some, but not full, official authority —**sem′i·of·fi′cial·ly** *adv.*

se·mi·ol·o·gy (sē′mē äl′ə jē, sem′ē-) *n.* ⟦< Gr *sēmeion* (see fol.) + -LOGY⟧ the science of signs in general —**se′mi·o·log′ic** (-ə läj′ik) *adj.*, **se′mi·o·log′i·cal** —**se′mi·ol′o·gist** *n.*

se·mi·ot·ics (sē′mē ät′iks, sem′ē-) *n.* ⟦Gr *sēmeiōtikos* < *sēmeion,* sign, akin to *sēma:* see SEMANTIC⟧ *Philos.* a general theory of signs and symbols; esp., the analysis of the nature and relationships of signs in language, usually including three branches, syntactics, semantics, and pragmatics —**se′mi·ot′ic** *adj.*, **se′mi·ot′i·cal** —**se′mi·o·ti′cian** (-ə tish′ən) *n.*

sem·i·o·vip·a·rous (sem′ē ō vip′ər əs) *adj.* ⟦SEMI- + OVIPAROUS⟧ *Zool.* producing living young whose natal development is incomplete, as marsupials

Se·mi·pa·la·tinsk (sye′mē pə lä′tinsk) city in NE Kazakhstan, on the Irtysh River

sem·i·pal·mate (sem′i pal′māt′) *adj.* with only a partial webbing of the anterior toes, as in some shorebirds: also **sem′i·pal′mat′ed** —**sem′i·pal·ma′tion** *n.*

sem·i·par·a·site (-par′ə sīt′) *n.* HEMIPARASITE

sem·i·per·me·a·ble (-pʉr′mē ə bəl) *adj.* allowing some substances to pass; permeable to smaller molecules but not to larger ones, as a membrane in osmosis

sem·i·po·lit·i·cal (-pə lit′i kəl) *adj.* political in some respects only; partly political

sem·i·por·ce·lain (-pôr′sə lən) *n.* a type of glazed earthenware that looks like porcelain but is opaque

sem·i·post·al (-pōs′təl) *n.* any stamp having a charge in addition to postage, to be used as for charity or a public monument

sem·i·pre·cious (-presh′əs) *adj.* designating gems of lower value than those classified as precious: said of the garnet, turquoise, etc.

sem·i·pri·vate (-prī′vət) *adj.* partly but not completely private; specif., designating or of a hospital room with two, three, or sometimes four beds

☆**sem·i·pro** (sem′i prō′) *adj., n. short for* SEMIPROFESSIONAL

sem·i·pro·fes·sion·al (sem′i prə fesh′ə nəl) *adj.* not fully professional; specif., *a)* engaging in a sport or other activity for pay but not as a regular occupation *b)* engaged in by semiprofessional players —*n.* a semiprofessional player, etc. —**sem′i·pro·fes′sion·al·ly** *adv.*

sem·i·pub·lic (-pub′lik) *adj.* partly public; public in some respects, as a private institution offering some public services or facilities

sem·i·qua·ver (sem′i kwā′vər) *n.* [Chiefly Brit.] SIXTEENTH NOTE

Se·mir·a·mis (si mir′ə mis) *n. Bab. Legend* a queen of Assyria noted for her beauty, wisdom, and sexual exploits: reputed founder of Babylon: based on a historical queen of the 9th cent. B.C.

sem·i·re·li·gious (sem′i ri lij′əs) *adj.* religious in some respects only; partly religious

sem·i·rig·id (-rij′id) *adj.* somewhat or partly rigid; specif., designating an airship having a rigid internal keel but no other supporting framework

sem·i·ru·ral (-roor′əl) *adj.* somewhat rural: used esp. of outlying areas adjacent to suburbs

sem·i·skilled (-skild′) *adj.* **1** partly skilled **2** of or doing manual work that requires only limited training

sem·i·soft (-sôft′) *adj.* soft but firm and easily cut, as Roquefort cheese, Edam cheese, etc.

sem·i·sol·id (-säl′id) *adj.* viscous and slowly flowing, as hot asphalt —*n.* a semisolid substance

sem·i·staged (-stājd′) *adj.* produced with the use of only a limited number of props, costumes, etc.: said as of an opera staged for an exhibition performance, in a concert hall, etc.

sem·i·sweet (-swēt′) *adj.* only slightly sweetened

Sem·ite (sem′īt′; *chiefly Brit* sē′mīt′) *n.* ⟦ModL *Semita* < LL(Ec) *Sem, Shem* < Gr (Ec) *Sem* < Heb *shem,* a son of Noah (Gen. 7:13)⟧ **1** a person regarded as descended from Shem **2** a member of any of the peoples speaking a Semitic language, including the Hebrews, Arabs, Assyrians, Phoenicians, etc. **3** JEW: a loose usage

Se·mit·ic (sə mit′ik) *adj.* ⟦Ger *semitisch* < ModL *Semiticus* < *Semita:* see prec.⟧ designating or of the Semites or their languages or cultures —*n.* a major subfamily of the Afroasiatic family of languages, including Arabic, Akkadian, Canaanite, Aramaic, Hebrew, and Ethiopic

Se·mit·ics (-iks) *n.* ☆the study of Semitic culture, languages, literature, etc.

Sem·i·tism (sem′ə tiz′əm) *n.* **1** a word, phrase, grammatical construction, or other feature originating in or peculiar to a Semitic language **2** the characteristics of the Semites; esp. the ideas, cultural qualities, etc. originating with the Jews

sem·i·tone (sem′i tōn′) *n. Music* the difference in pitch between any two immediately adjacent keys on the piano; half of a whole tone —**sem′i·ton′ic** (-tän′ik) *adj.*, **sem′i·ton′al** (-tōn′əl) —**sem′i·ton′al·ly** *adv.*

☆**sem·i·trail·er** (-trāl′ər) *n.* a detachable trailer designed to be attached to a coupling at the rear of a TRACTOR (sense 2), by which it is partly supported

sem·i·trans·par·ent (sem′i trans per′ənt) *adj.* not perfectly or completely transparent

sem·i·trop·i·cal (-träp′i kəl) *adj.* having some of the characteristics of the tropics: also **sem′i·trop′ic**

sem·i·vow·el (sem′i vou′əl) ***n.*** *Phonet.* a vowel-like sound occurring in consonantal positions in the same syllable with a true vowel, characterized by brief duration and rapid change from one position of articulation to another: the English glides (w) and (y) are semivowels

☆**sem·i·week·ly** (sem′i wēk′lē) ***adj.*** done, happening, published, etc. twice a week —***n.,*** *pl.* **-lies** a semiweekly publication —***adv.*** twice weekly

sem·i·year·ly (-yir′lē) ***adj.*** done, happening, appearing, etc. every half year or twice a year —***adv.*** twice yearly

sem·o·li·na (sem′ə lē′nə) ***n.*** ⟦It *semolino,* dim. of *semola,* bran < L *simila,* finest wheat flour < ?⟧ meal consisting of particles of coarsely ground durum (hard wheat), a byproduct in the manufacture of fine flour: used in making macaroni, puddings, breakfast cereals, etc.

sem·per (sem′pər) ***adv.*** ⟦L < IE base **sem-,* one, uniform, SAME + **per-* > PER[1]⟧ always

semper fi·de·lis (fi dā′lis) ⟦L⟧ always faithful: motto of the U.S. Marine Corps, often shortened to [Informal] **semper fi** (fī)

semper pa·ra·tus (pə rāt′əs, -rät′əs) ⟦L⟧ always prepared: motto of the U.S. Coast Guard

sem·per·vi·vum (sem′pər vī′vəm) ***n.*** ⟦ModL < L, neut. of *sempervivus,* ever living < *semper,* ever, always + *vivus,* living < *vivere,* to live: see BIO-⟧ any of a genus (*Sempervivum*) of plants of the orpine family, with yellow, pink, or red flowers and compact rosettes of thick, fleshy leaves

sem·pi·ter·nal (sem′pi tʉr′nəl) ***adj.*** ⟦ME < ML *sempiternalis* < L *sempiternus* < *semper,* always (see SEMPER) + *aeternus,* ETERNAL⟧ everlasting; perpetual; eternal —**sem′pi·ter′nal·ly** ***adv.*** —**sem′pi·ter′ni·ty** ***n.***

sem·pli·ce (sem′pli chā′) ***adj., adv.*** ⟦It, simple < L *simplex, simplic-:* see SIMPLEX⟧ *Musical Direction* with simplicity

sem·pre (sem′prā) ***adv.*** ⟦It, always < L *semper*⟧ *Musical Direction* without varying

semp·stress (sem′stris, semp′-) ***n. var. of*** SEAMSTRESS

sen (sen) ***n.,*** *pl.* **sen** ⟦Jpn < SinoJpn, coin < Chin *ch'ien,* money, coin⟧ **1** a monetary unit of Japan, equal to 1/100 of a yen: now used only as a money of account **2** a monetary unit, equal to 1/100 of the basic unit, of: *a)* Cambodia *b)* Indonesia *c)* Malaysia

Sen *abbrev.* **1** Senate **2** Senator **3** [*also* **s-**] senior

sen·a·ry (sen′ər ē) ***adj.*** ⟦L *senarius* < *seni,* six each < base of *sex,* six⟧ of six; on the basis of six

sen·ate (sen′it) ***n.*** ⟦ME *senat* < OFr < L *senatus* < *senex,* old, aged < IE base **sen(o)-,* old > Sans *sána-,* Gr *henos,* OIr *sen,* old⟧ **1** literally, a council of elders **2** the supreme council of the ancient Roman state, originally only of patricians but later including the plebeians **3** a lawmaking assembly; state council **4** [**S-**] ☆*a)* the upper house of the legislature of the U.S., or of most of the states of the U.S. *b)* a similar body in other countries **5** a governing or advisory council in a college or university [*the Faculty Senate*] **6** the building or hall where a senate meets

sen·a·tor (sen′ət ər) ***n.*** ⟦ME *senatour* < OFr *senateur* < L *senator*⟧ a member of a senate

sen·a·to·ri·al (sen′ə tôr′ē əl) ***adj.*** ⟦< L *senatorius* (< *senator*) + -IAL⟧ **1** of or suitable for a senator or a senate **2** composed of senators

senatorial courtesy a custom of the U.S. Senate whereby that body refuses to ratify a presidential nomination to an official position, as in a state, if the senators from that state or from the nominee's state do not approve

☆**senatorial district** any of the districts into which a state is divided for electing members to the state senate

send (send) ***vt.*** **sent, send′ing** ⟦ME *senden* < OE *sendan,* akin to Ger *senden,* Goth *sandjan,* caus. formation, "to cause to go" < IE base **sent-,* to go, find out, discover > L *sentire,* to feel, sense, OIr *sēt,* way⟧ **1** *a)* to cause to go or be carried; dispatch, convey, or transmit *b)* to dispatch, convey, or transmit (a letter, message, etc.) by mail, radio, etc. **2** to ask, direct, or command to go [*send the boy home*] **3** to arrange for the going of; enable to go or attend [*to send one's son to college*] **4** to cause or force to move, as by releasing, hitting, discharging, throwing, etc. [*he sent the ball over the fence*] **5** to bring or drive into some state or condition [*sent him to his ruin*] **6** to cause to happen, come, etc.; give [*a misfortune sent by the gods*] ☆**7** [Slang] to make very excited or exhilarated; thrill —***vi.*** **1** to send a message, messenger, emissary, etc. [*to send for help*] **2** to transmit, as by radio —**send around** to put into circulation —**send away** to dispatch or banish —**send down** [Brit.] to suspend or expel from a university —**send flying 1** to dismiss or cause to depart hurriedly **2** to stagger or repel, as with a blow **3** to put to flight; rout **4** to scatter abruptly in all directions —**send for 1** to ask for the arrival of; summon **2** to place an order for; make a request for delivery of —**send forth** to be a source of; cause to appear; give out or forth; produce, emit, utter, etc. —**send in 1** to dispatch, hand in, or send to a central point or to one receiving **2** to put (a player) into a game or contest —**send off 1** to mail or dispatch (a letter, gift, etc.) **2** to dismiss **3** to give a send-off to —**send out 1** to dispatch, distribute, issue, mail, etc. from a central point **2** to send forth **3** to send someone on an errand (*for* something) —**send out for** to place an order for (food, etc.) to be delivered —**send up 1** to cause to rise, climb, or go up ☆**2** [Informal] to sentence to prison **3** [Informal, Chiefly Brit.] to make seem ridiculous, esp. by parody —**send′er** ***n.***

Sen·dai (sen′dī′) seaport in NE Honshu, Japan

Sen·dak (sen′dak), **Maurice (Bernard)** 1928-2012; U.S. writer & illustrator

sen·dal (sen′dəl) ***n.*** ⟦ME *cendal* < OFr < ML *cendallum,* prob. ult. < Gr *sindōn,* fine linen of Sem orig; as in Heb *sadin,* linen undergarment⟧ a light silk fabric used in the Middle Ages for costumes, flags, etc.

☆**send-off** (send′ôf′) ***n.*** [Informal] **1** an expression or demonstration of friendly feeling toward someone starting out on a trip, career, etc. **2** a start given to someone or something

send·up (send′up′) ***n.*** [Informal, Chiefly Brit.] a mocking parody, esp. when done with seeming gravity; takeoff; spoof

se·ne (se′ne′) ***n.,*** *pl.* **se′ne′** ⟦Samoan < E CENT[1]⟧ a monetary unit of Samoa, equal to 1/100 of a tala

Sen·e·ca[1] (sen′i kə) ***n.*** ⟦< Du *Sennecas,* prob. < Mahican: orig. ref. to the Oneida, later including also the Onondaga, Cayuga, & Seneca⟧ **1** *pl.* **-cas** or **-ca** a member of a North American Indian people formerly living in W New York and now living chiefly in New York and Ontario: see FIVE NATIONS **2** the Iroquoian language of this people —***adj.*** of the Senecas or their language or culture

Sen·e·ca[2] (sen′i kə), **(Lucius Annaeus)** 4? B.C.-A.D. 65; Rom. philosopher, dramatist, & statesman —**Sen′e·can** ***adj.***

se·ne·ci·o (sə nē′shē ō′) ***n.,*** *pl.* **-ci·os** ⟦ModL, altered < L *senex,* old (from the white pappus): see SENATE⟧ GROUNDSEL

☆**sen·e·ga** (sen′i gə) ***n.*** ⟦< *Senega (root),* var. of SENECA[1]: from use by the Seneca against snake bites⟧ **1** an E North American milkwort (*Polygala senega*) with single racemes of white flowers **2** its dried root, formerly used as an expectorant Also **senega (snake) root**

Sen·e·gal (sen′i gôl′, -gäl′) **1** river flowing from W Mali northwest into the Atlantic: *c.* 1,000 mi (1,609 km) **2** country in W Africa, on the Atlantic: formerly a territory of French West Africa, it became independent in 1960: 75,749 sq mi (196,190 sq km); cap. Dakar: see MALI —**Sen′e·gal·ese′** (-gə lēz′) ***adj., n.,*** *pl.* **-ese′**

Sen·e·gam·bi·a (sen′i gam′bē ə) region in W Africa, comprising the basins of the rivers Senegal & Gambia

se·nes·cent (sə nes′ənt) ***adj.*** ⟦L *senescens,* prp. of *senescere,* to grow old < *senex,* old: see SENATE⟧ growing old; aging —**se·nes′cence** (-əns) ***n.***

sen·e·schal (sen′ə shəl) ***n.*** ⟦OFr < Frank *siniskalk,* oldest servant < **sini,* old (for IE base see SENATE) + *skalk,* servant (for IE base see MARSHAL)⟧ a steward or major-domo in the household of a medieval noble

Sen·ghor (sän gôr′), **Lé·o·pold Sé·dar** (lā ô pôld′ sā dȧr′) 1906-2001; Senegalese statesman & poet; president of Senegal (1960-80)

se·nhor (si nyôr′) ***n.,*** *pl.* **-nhor′es** (-nyôr′əsh, -əs) ⟦Port < L *senior:* see SENIOR⟧ **1** [**S-**] Mr.; Sir: Portuguese or Brazilian title of respect: abbrev. *Sr* **2** a man; gentleman

se·nho·ra (si nyôr′ə) ***n.,*** *pl.* **-nho′ras** (-nyôr′əsh, -əs) ⟦Port, fem. of prec.⟧ **1** [**S-**] Mrs.; Madam: Portuguese or Brazilian title of respect: abbrev. *Sra* **2** a married woman

se·nho·ri·ta (si′nyô rē′tə) ***n.,*** *pl.* **-tas** (-təsh, -təs) ⟦Port, dim. of prec.⟧ **1** [**S-**] Miss: Portuguese or Brazilian title of respect: abbrev. *Srta* **2** an unmarried woman or a girl

se·nile (sē′nīl′, sen′īl′) ***adj.*** ⟦L *senilis* < *senex,* old: see SENATE⟧ **1** *a)* of, typical of, or resulting from old age (now chiefly medical) *b)* showing the marked deterioration often accompanying old age, esp. mental impairment characterized by confusion, memory loss, etc. **2** *Geol.* nearing the end of an erosion cycle —**se·nile′ly** ***adv.*** —**se·nil·i·ty** (sə nil′ə tē) ***n.***

sen·ior (sēn′yər) ***adj.*** ⟦ME < L *senior,* compar. of *senex,* old: see SENATE⟧ **1** of the greater age; older: written *Sr.* after the name of a father whose son has been given exactly the same name: opposed to JUNIOR **2** of higher rank or standing, or longer in service ☆**3** of or for seniors in a high school or college **4** of or for senior citizens [*a senior center next to city hall*] **5** of or for competition among older athletes, often, specif., among older professional athletes [*a senior tennis circuit*] —***n.*** **1** a person older than another or others **2** a person of greater rank, standing, or length of service ☆**3** *a)* a student in the twelfth grade in high school *b)* a student in the final year of an undergraduate degree program **4** *short for* SENIOR CITIZEN —**one's senior** a person older than oneself

☆**senior chief petty officer** *U.S. Navy* an enlisted person ranking above a chief petty officer and below a master chief petty officer

senior citizen an elderly person, esp. one who is retired

☆**senior high school** a high school offering the last years of secondary education, usually consisting of grades 10, 11, and 12

sen·ior·i·ty (sēn yôr′ə tē, -yär′-) ***n.*** ⟦ML *senioritas*⟧ **1** the state or quality of being senior; precedence in birth, rank, etc. **2** status, priority, or precedence achieved by length of service, as in a given job

☆**senior master sergeant** *U.S. Air Force* a noncommissioned officer of the eighth grade, ranking above master sergeant and below chief master sergeant

sen·i·ti (sen′ə tē′) ***n.,*** *pl.* **sen′i·ti′** ⟦Tongan *sēniti* < E CENT[1]⟧ a monetary unit of Tonga, equal to 1/100 of a pa'anga

sen·na (sen′ə) ***n.*** ⟦ML *sene* < Ar *sanā*⟧ **1** any of a genus (*Cassia*) of plants of the caesalpinia family, with finely divided leaves and yellow flowers **2** the dried leaflets of various sennas, used, esp. formerly, as a laxative

Sen·nach·er·ib (sə nak′ər ib) died 681 B.C.; king of Assyria (705-681): son of Sargon II

sen·net (sen′it) ***n.*** ⟦prob. via Anglo-Fr < OFr *senet,* var. of *signet:* see SIGNET⟧ a trumpet call used as a signal for ceremonial entrances and exits in Elizabethan drama

Sen·nett (sen′it), **Mack** (mak) (born *Michael Sinnott*) 1884-1960; U.S. film producer & director, esp. of slapstick comedies, born in Canada

sen·night or **se′n·night** (sen′īt, -it) ***n.*** ⟦ME *sennyt* < OE *seofon nihta:* see SEVEN & NIGHT⟧ [Archaic] a week

sen·nit (sen′it) ***n.*** ⟦< ?⟧ **1** a flat braided material made by plaiting strands of rope yarn **2** plaited straw, grass, etc. used for making hats

se·ñor (se nyôr′) ***n.**, pl.* **-ño′res** (-nyô′res) ⟦Sp < L *senior*: see SENIOR⟧ **1** [**S-**] Mr.; Sir: Spanish title of respect: abbrev. *Sr* **2** a man; gentleman
se·ño·ra (se nyô′rä) ***n.**, pl.* **-ño′ras** (-räs) ⟦Sp, fem. of prec.⟧ **1** [**S-**] Mrs.; Madam: Spanish title of respect: abbrev. *Sra* **2** a married woman
se·ño·ri·ta (se′nyô rē′tä) ***n.**, pl.* **-tas** (-täs) ⟦Sp, dim. of prec.⟧ **1** [**S-**] Miss: Spanish title of respect: abbrev. *Srta* **2** an unmarried woman or a girl
sen·sate (sen′sāt′, -sit) ***adj.*** ⟦LL *sensatus*, intelligent < L *sensus*, SENSE⟧ **1** having the power of physical sensation **2** perceived by the senses **—sen′sate·ly** ***adv.***
sen·sa·tion (sen sā′shən) ***n.*** ⟦LL *sensatio* < *sensatus*: see prec.⟧ **1** the power or process of receiving conscious sense impressions through direct stimulation of the bodily organism [the *sensations* of hearing, seeing, touching, etc.] **2** an immediate reaction to external stimulation of a sense organ; conscious feeling or sense impression [a *sensation* of cold] **3** a generalized feeling or reaction, often vague and without reference to immediate stimulus [a *sensation* of happiness] **4** *a)* a state or feeling of general excitement and interest [the play caused such a *sensation*] *b)* the action, event, person, etc. causing such a feeling
sen·sa·tion·al (sen sā′shə nəl) ***adj.*** **1** of the senses or sensation **2** *a)* arousing intense interest and excitement; startling; exciting *b)* using or having effects intended to startle, shock, thrill, etc. **3** [Informal] exceptionally good, fine, etc. **—sen·sa′tion·al·ly** ***adv.***
sen·sa·tion·al·ism (-nə liz′əm) ***n.*** **1** the use of strongly emotional subject matter, or wildly dramatic style, language, or artistic expression, that is intended to shock, startle, thrill, excite, etc. **2** *Philos.* the belief that all knowledge is acquired through the use of the senses **—sen·sa′tion·al·ist** ***n.*** **—sen·sa′tion·al·is′tic** ***adj.***
sen·sa·tion·al·ize (-nə līz′) ***vt.*** **-ized′**, **-iz′ing** to make sensational; treat in a sensational and, often, exploitative way
sense (sens) ***n.*** ⟦Fr *sens* < L *sensus* < *sentire*, to feel, perceive: see SEND⟧ **1** the ability of the nerves and the brain to receive and react to stimuli, as light, sound, impact, constriction, etc.; specif., any of five faculties of receiving impressions through specific bodily organs and the nerves associated with them (sight, touch, taste, smell, and hearing) **2** the senses considered as a total function of the bodily organism, as distinguished from intellect, movement, etc. **3** *a)* feeling, impression, or perception through the senses [a *sense* of warmth, pain, etc.] *b)* a generalized feeling, awareness, or realization [a *sense* of longing] **4** an ability to judge, discriminate, or estimate external conditions, sounds, etc. [a *sense* of direction, pitch, etc.] **5** an ability to feel, appreciate, or understand some quality [a *sense* of humor, honor, etc.] **6** *a)* ability to think or reason soundly; normal intelligence and judgment, often as reflected in behavior *b)* soundness of judgment or reasoning [some *sense* in what he says] *c)* something wise, sound, or reasonable [to talk *sense*] *d)* [*pl.*] normal ability to reason soundly [to come to one's *senses*] **7** *a)* meaning; esp., any of several meanings conveyed by or attributed to the same word or phrase *b)* essential signification; gist [to grasp the *sense* of a remark] **8** the general opinion, sentiment, or attitude of a group **9** *Math.* either of two contrary directions that may be specified, as clockwise or counterclockwise for the circumference of a circle, positive or negative for a line segment, etc. **—*vt.*** **sensed**, **sens′ing** **1** to be or become aware of [to *sense* another's hostility] **2** to comprehend; understand **3** to detect automatically, as by sensors **—in a sense** **1** to a limited extent or degree **2** in one aspect **—make sense** to be intelligible or logical **—make sense of** to find meaning in; understand
sense datum that which is immediately perceived as the direct effect of stimulus on a sense organ
sense·less (sens′lis) ***adj.*** **1** unconscious **2** not having or showing good sense; stupid; foolish **3** having no real point or purpose; nonsensical; meaningless **—sense′less·ly** ***adv.*** **—sense′less·ness** ***n.***
sense organ any organ or structure, as an eye or a taste bud, containing afferent nerve terminals that are specialized to receive specific stimuli and transmit them to the brain; receptor
sense perception perception by sight, touch, etc.
sense strand *Genetics* that strand of a double-stranded DNA molecule which serves as the template from which RNA, esp. messenger RNA, is transcribed
sen·si·bil·i·ty (sen′sə bil′ə tē) ***n.*** ⟦ME < MFr < LL *sensibilitas* < L *sensibilis*: see fol.⟧ **1** the capacity for physical sensation; power of responding to stimuli; ability to feel **2** *pl.* **-ties** [*often pl.*] *a)* the capacity for being affected emotionally or intellectually, whether pleasantly or unpleasantly; receptiveness to impression *b)* the capacity to respond perceptively to intellectual, moral, or aesthetic values; delicate, sensitive awareness or responsiveness *c)* liability to be offended, repelled, etc.
sen·si·ble (sen′sə bəl) ***adj.*** ⟦ME < MFr < L *sensibilis* < *sensus*, pp. of *sentire*, to feel, SENSE⟧ **1** that can cause physical sensation; perceptible to the senses **2** perceptible to the intellect **3** easily perceived or noticed; marked; striking; appreciable **4** having senses; capable of receiving sensation; sensitive **5** having appreciation or understanding; emotionally or intellectually aware [*sensible* of another's grief] **6** having or showing good sense or sound judgment; intelligent; reasonable; wise **—*SYN.*** AWARE, PERCEPTIBLE, RATIONAL **—sen′si·bly** ***adv.***
sen·si·tive (sen′sə tiv) ***adj.*** ⟦ME *sensitife* < MFr *sensitif* < ML *sensitivus* < L *sensus*: see SENSE⟧ **1** of the senses or sensation; esp., connected with the reception or transmission of sense impressions; sensory **2** receiving and responding to stimuli from outside objects or agencies; having sensation **3** responding or feeling readily and acutely; very keenly susceptible to stimuli [a *sensitive* ear] **4** easily hurt; tender; raw **5** having or showing keen sensibilities; highly perceptive or responsive intellectually, aesthetically, etc. **6** easily offended, disturbed, shocked, irritated, etc., as by the actions of others; touchy **7** changing readily in the presence of some external force or condition; specif., *a)* readily affected by light (said of photographic film, etc.) *b)* readily receiving very weak radio signals *c)* operating readily in weak light (said of certain television camera tubes) **8** designed to indicate or measure small changes or differences **9** showing, or liable to show, unusual variation; fluctuating [a *sensitive* stock market] ☆**10** designating, of, or dealing with secret or delicate matters, esp. secret or delicate government matters **—*n.*** MEDIUM (*n.* 7) **—sen′si·tive·ly** ***adv.*** **—sen′si·tive·ness** ***n.***
sensitive plant a tropical American plant (*Mimosa pudica*) of the mimosa family, with a spiny stem, minute, purplish flowers in spherical clusters, and leaflets that fold and leafstalks that droop at the slightest touch
sen·si·tiv·i·ty (sen′sə tiv′ə tē) ***n.*** the condition or quality of being sensitive; specif., *a)* the responsiveness of an organ or organism to external stimuli *b)* *Radio, TV* the capacity of a receiver to respond to incoming signals
☆**sensitivity training** a kind of group therapy in which the members of the group, under the guidance of a leader, seek a deeper understanding of themselves and others through the exchange of intimate feelings and experiences, physical contact, etc.
sen·si·tize (sen′sə tīz′) ***vt.*** **-tized′**, **-tiz′ing** ⟦SENSIT(IVE) + -IZE⟧ to make sensitive or susceptible; specif., *a)* *Photog.* to make (a film or plate) sensitive to light, etc. *b)* *Immunology* to make (an individual) sensitive or hypersensitive to an antigen **—sen′si·ti·za′tion** ***n.*** **—sen′si·tiz′er** ***n.***
sen·si·tom·e·ter (sen′sə täm′ət ər) ***n.*** ⟦SENSIT(IVITY) + -O- + -METER⟧ an instrument used for measuring sensitivity, as of photographic film **—sen′si·to·met′ric** (-tə me′trik) ***adj.*** **—sen′si·tom′e·try** (-trē) ***n.***
sen·sor (sen′sər, -sôr′) ***n.*** ⟦< L *sensus*, pp. of *sentire*, SENSE + -OR⟧ any of various devices designed to detect, measure, or record physical phenomena, as radiation, heat, or blood pressure, and to respond, as by transmitting information, initiating changes, or operating controls
sen·so·ri·mo·tor (sen′sə rē mōt′ər) ***adj.*** ⟦< SENSORY + MOTOR⟧ **1** *Physiol.* of, pertaining to, or concerned with both the sensory and the motor impulses of an organism **2** *Psychol.* of or pertaining to motor responses initiated by sensory stimulation
sen·so·ri·neu·ral (-noor′əl, -nyoor′-) ***adj.*** of or having to do with sensory nerves, as in a hearing loss caused by faulty sensory nerves
sen·so·ri·um (sen sôr′ē əm) ***n.**, pl.* **-ri·ums** or **-ri·a** (-ə) ⟦LL < L *sensus*, SENSE⟧ **1** [Historical] the seat of physical sensation in the brain **2** the whole sensory apparatus of the body
sen·so·ry (sen′sər ē) ***adj.*** ⟦SENS(E) + -ORY⟧ **1** of the senses or sensation **2** connected with the reception and transmission of sense impressions Also **sen·so′ri·al** (-sôr′ē əl)
sensory neuron a type of neuron that carries impulses from a sense organ to the brain or spinal cord: see also MOTOR NEURON
sen·su·al (sen′shoo əl) ***adj.*** ⟦L *sensualis* < *sensus*, feeling, SENSE⟧ **1** of the body and the senses as distinguished from the intellect or spirit; bodily [*sensual* pleasures] **2** *a)* connected or preoccupied with bodily or sexual pleasures; voluptuous *b)* full of lust; licentious; lewd **3** resulting from, or showing preoccupation with, bodily or sexual pleasure [a *sensual* expression] **—*SYN.*** CARNAL, SENSUOUS **—sen′su·al·ly** ***adv.***
sen·su·al·ism (-iz′əm) ***n.*** **1** frequent or excessive indulgence in sensual pleasures **2** SENSATIONALISM (sense 2) **—sen′su·al·ist** ***n.*** **—sen′su·al·is′tic** ***adj.***
sen·su·al·i·ty (sen′shoo al′ə tē) ***n.*** **1** the state or quality of being sensual; fondness for or indulgence in sensual pleasures **2** lasciviousness; lewdness
sen·su·al·ize (sen′shoo əl īz′) ***vt.*** **-ized′**, **-iz′ing** to make sensual **—sen′su·al·i·za′tion** ***n.***
sen·su·ous (sen′shoo əs) ***adj.*** ⟦< L *sensus*, SENSE + -OUS⟧ **1** of, derived from, based on, affecting, appealing to, or perceived by the senses **2** readily susceptible through the senses; enjoying the pleasures of sensation **—sen′su·ous·ly** ***adv.*** **—sen′su·ous·ness** ***n.***

SYN.—**sensuous** suggests the strong appeal of that which is pleasing to the eye, ear, touch, etc. and, of a person, implies susceptibility to the pleasures of sensation [soft, *sensuous* music]; **sensual** refers to the gratification of the grosser bodily senses or appetites [*sensual* excesses]; **voluptuous** implies a tending to excite, or giving oneself up to the gratification of, sensuous or sensual desires [her *voluptuous* charms]; **luxurious** implies a reveling in that which lavishly provides a high degree of physical comfort or satisfaction [a *luxurious* feeling of drowsiness]; **epicurean** implies delight in luxury and sensuous pleasure, esp. that of eating and drinking

sent (sent) ***vt., vi.*** *pt. & pp. of* SEND
sen·te (sen′tē) ***n.**, pl.* **li·sen·te** (li sen′tē) ⟦< name in Sesotho (a Bantu language of Lesotho), ult. < E CENT[1]⟧ a monetary unit of Lesotho, equal to 1⁄100 of a loti
sen·tence (sent′'ns) ***n.*** ⟦OFr < L *sententia*, way of thinking, opinion, sentiment, prob. for *sentientia* < *sentiens*, prp. of *sentire*, to feel, SENSE⟧ **1** *a)* a decision or judgment, as of a court; esp., the determination by a court of the punishment of a convicted person *b)* the punishment itself **2** *Gram.* a word or a group of syntactically related words that states, asks, commands, or exclaims something; conventional unit of connected speech or writing, usually containing a subject and a predicate: in writing, a sentence

begins with a capital letter and concludes with an end mark (period, question mark, etc.), and in speech a sentence begins following a silence and concludes with any of various final pitches and a terminal juncture 3 [Archaic] a short moral saying; maxim 4 *Music* PERIOD —*vt.* **-tenced**, **-tenc·ing** to pronounce judgment or punishment upon (a convicted person); condemn (*to* a specified punishment) —**sen·ten·tial** (sen ten′shəl) *adj.*

sentence stress the arrangement of stresses on the syllables of the words making up a sentence, varying in distribution for emphasis, contrast, etc.

sentential function PROPOSITIONAL FUNCTION

sen·ten·tious (sen ten′shəs) *adj.* ⟦L *sententiosus* < *sententia*: see SENTENCE⟧ 1 expressing much in few words; short and pithy; pointed 2 full of, or fond of using, maxims, proverbs, etc., esp. in a way that is ponderously trite and moralizing —**sen·ten′tious·ly** *adv.* —**sen·ten′tious·ness** *n.*

sen·tience (sen′shəns, -shē əns) *n.* 1 a sentient state or quality; capacity for feeling or perceiving; consciousness 2 mere awareness or sensation that does not involve thought or perception Also **sen′tien·cy**

sen·tient (-shənt, -shē ənt) *adj.* ⟦L *sentiens*, prp. of *sentire*, to perceive by the senses: see SENSE⟧ of, having, or capable of feeling or perception; conscious —**sen′tient·ly** *adv.*

sen·ti·ment (sen′tə mənt) *n.* ⟦ME *sentement* < OFr < ML *sentimentum* < L *sentire*, to feel, SENSE⟧ 1 a complex combination of feelings and opinions as a basis for action or judgment; general emotionalized attitude [the *sentiment* of romantic love] 2 a thought, opinion, judgment, or attitude, usually the result of careful consideration, but often colored with emotion: *often used in pl.* 3 susceptibility to feeling or to emotional appeal; sensibility 4 appeal to the emotions in literature or art; expression of delicate, sensitive feeling 5 sentimentality; maudlin emotion 6 a short sentence or aphorism expressing some thought or wish, as in a toast 7 the thought or meaning behind something said, done, or given, as distinct from the literal statement, act, etc. —*SYN.* FEELING, OPINION

sen·ti·men·tal (sen′tə ment′'l) *adj.* 1 having or showing tender, gentle, or delicate feelings, as in aesthetic expression 2 having or showing such feelings in an excessive, superficial, or maudlin way; mawkish 3 influenced more by emotion than by reason; acting from feeling rather than from practical motives 4 of or resulting from sentiment [a *sentimental* reason] —**sen′ti·men′tal·ly** *adv.*

sen·ti·men·tal·ism (-iz′əm) *n.* 1 the habit, quality, or condition of being sentimental 2 any expression of this —**sen′ti·men′tal·ist** *n.*

sen·ti·men·tal·i·ty (sen′tə men tal′ə tē) *n.* 1 the quality or condition of being sentimental, esp. in a superficial or maudlin way 2 *pl.* **-ties** any expression of this

sen·ti·men·tal·ize (-ment′'l īz′) *vi.* **-ized′**, **-iz′ing** to be sentimental; think or behave in a sentimental way —*vt.* to regard or treat in a sentimental way [to *sentimentalize* war] —**sen′ti·men′tal·i·za′tion** *n.*

sen·ti·nel (sent′'n əl) *n.* ⟦Fr *sentinelle* < It *sentinella*, ult. < L *sentire*, to feel, SENSE⟧ a person or animal set to guard a group; specif., a sentry —*vt.* **-neled** or **-nelled**, **-nel·ing** or **-nel·ling** 1 to guard or watch over as a sentinel 2 to furnish or protect with a sentinel 3 to post as a sentinel

sen·try (sen′trē) *n.*, *pl.* **-tries** ⟦< ? obs. *centrinell*, var. of prec.⟧ 1 a sentinel; esp., any of the men of a military guard posted to guard against, and warn of, danger 2 [Now Rare] guard or watch [to keep *sentry*]

sentry box a small, boxlike structure serving as a shelter for a sentry on duty during bad weather

Se·nus·si or **Se·nu·si** (sə no͞o′sē, -nyo͞o′-) *n.*, *pl.* **-si** a member of a militant brotherhood of N African Muslims —**Se·nus′si·an** *adj.*, **Se·nu′si·an**

Seoul (sōl) capital of South Korea, in the NW part

sep *abbrev.* 1 separate 2 separated 3 separation

Sep *abbrev.* 1 September 2 Septuagint

SEP *abbrev.* simplified employee pension

se·pal (sē′pəl; *chiefly Brit* sep′əl) *n.* ⟦Fr *sépale* < ModL *sepalum*, arbitrary blend < Gr *skepē*, a covering + ModL *petalum*, PETAL⟧ *Bot.* any of the usually green, leaflike parts of the calyx —**se′paled** *adj.*, **se′palled**

se·pal·oid (sē′pə loid′, sep′ə-) *adj.* like or having the nature of a sepal

-sep·al·ous (sep′əl əs) ⟦< SEPAL + -OUS⟧ *combining form forming adjectives* having (a specified number or kind of) sepals [*gamosepalous*]

sep·a·ra·ble (sep′ə rə bəl, sep′rə bəl) *adj.* ⟦ME < L *separabilis*⟧ that can be separated —**sep′a·ra·bil′i·ty** *n.* —**sep′a·ra·bly** *adv.*

sep·a·rate (sep′ə rāt′; *for adj. & n.*, sep′ə rit, sep′rit) *vt.* **-rat′ed**, **-rat′ing** ⟦ME *separaten* < L *separatus*, pp. of *separare*, to separate < *se-*, apart (see SECEDE) + *parare*, to arrange, PREPARE⟧ 1 to set or put apart into sections, groups, sets, units, etc.; cause to part; divide; disunite; sever 2 to see the differences between; distinguish or discriminate between 3 to keep apart by being between; divide [a hedge that *separates* the yards] 4 to bring about a separation between (a husband and wife) 5 to single out or set apart from others for a special purpose; sort; segregate 6 to take away (a part or ingredient) from a combination or mixture 7 to discharge; specif., *a)* to release from military service ☆*b)* to dismiss from employment 8 to dislocate (a body joint) —*vi.* 1 to withdraw or secede [to *separate* from a party] 2 to part, come or draw apart, or become disconnected 3 to part company; go in different directions; cease to associate 4 to stop living together as husband and wife; enter into a legal SEPARATION (sense 4) 5 to become distinct or disengaged, as from a mixture 6 to become dislocated, as a shoulder —*adj.* 1 set apart or divided from the rest or others; not joined, united, or connected; severed 2 not associated or connected with others; having existence as an entity; distinct; individual 3 thought of or regarded as having individual form or function [the *separate* parts of the body] 4 of or for one only; not shared or held in common [*separate* beds] 5 [Archaic] withdrawn from others; solitary —*n.* 1 OFFPRINT 2 [*pl.*] coordinated articles of dress worn as a set or separately in various combinations —**sep′a·rate·ly** *adv.* —**sep′a·rate·ness** *n.*

SYN.—**separate** implies the putting apart of things previously united, joined, or assembled [to *separate* machine parts, a family, etc.]; **divide** implies a separation into parts, pieces, groups, etc. by or as by cutting, splitting, branching, etc., often for purposes of apportionment [to *divide* the profits into equal shares]; **part** is now usually applied to the separation of persons or things that have been closely connected or associated ["till death us do *part*"]; **sever** implies a forcible and complete separation, as by cutting off a part from a whole [to *sever* a branch from a tree]; **sunder**, now a literary term, implies a violent splitting, tearing, or wrenching apart —*ANT.* **unite, combine**

sep·a·ra·tion (sep′ə rā′shən) *n.* ⟦ME *separacion* < MFr < L *separatio*⟧ 1 a separating or being separated 2 the place where a separating occurs; break; division; gap 3 something that separates 4 a legal arrangement by which a husband and wife remain married but live apart

☆**separation center** a center where persons in the armed forces are discharged or released from active duty

sep·a·ra·tism (sep′ə rə tiz′əm) *n.* a condition or the advocacy of political, religious, or racial separation

sep·a·ra·tist (sep′ə rə tist, -ə rāt′ist) *n.* 1 a person who withdraws or secedes, esp. a member of a group that has seceded from a larger group; dissenter 2 a person who advocates political, religious, or racial separation —*adj.* of separatists or separatism

sep·a·ra·tive (sep′ə rāt′iv, -ə rə tiv′) *adj.* ⟦< Fr or LL: Fr *séparatif* < LL *separativus*⟧ tending to separate or cause separation: also **sep′a·ra·to′ry** (-ə rə tôr′ē)

sep·a·ra·tor (sep′ə rāt′ər) *n.* 1 a person or thing that separates 2 any of several devices for separating one substance from another, as cream from milk

Se·phar·di (sə fär′dē, -fär′dē′) *n.*, *pl.* **Se·phar·dim** (sə fär′dim, -fär′dēm′) ⟦Heb *sefaradi*, after *sefarad*, a region mentioned in Ob. 20, often identified with Spain, but prob. orig. an area in Asia Minor⟧ 1 a member of the group of Jews that lived in Spain and Portugal before the Inquisition and, after expulsion, in the Ottoman Empire, Middle East, and N Africa 2 a descendant of this group which has some traditions of ritual and prayer, culture and customs, and Hebrew pronunciation that differ from those of an Ashkenazi Distinguished from ASHKENAZI —**Se·phar′dic** *adj.*

se·pi·a (sē′pē ə) *n.* ⟦ModL, name of a genus of cuttlefishes < L, the cuttlefish < Gr *sēpia* < *sēpein*, to cause to rot (from the inky fluid emitted), akin to *sapros*, rotten⟧ 1 a dark-brown pigment prepared from the inky fluid secreted by cuttlefish 2 a dark reddish-brown color 3 a drawing or photographic print in this color —*adj.* 1 of sepia 2 dark reddish-brown

se·pi·o·lite (sē′pē ə līt′) *n.* ⟦Ger *sepiolith* < Gr *sēpion*, cuttlebone < *sēpia* (see prec.) + *-lith* (see -LITH)⟧ MEERSCHAUM (sense 1)

se·poy (sē′poi) *n.* ⟦Port *sipae* < Hindi & Pers *sipāhī* < *sipāh*, army⟧ [Historical] a native of India serving in a European army, esp. the British army

sep·pu·ku (se po͞o′ko͞o) *n.* ⟦Jpn < SinoJpn *setsu*, cut + *huku*, belly⟧ HARA-KIRI

sep·sis (sep′sis) *n.* ⟦ModL < Gr *sēpsis*, putrefaction < *sēpein*, to make putrid: see SEPIA⟧ a poisoned state caused by the absorption of pathogenic microorganisms and their products into the blood or other bodily tissue

sept (sept) *n.* ⟦var. of SECT[2] (prob. by confusion with L *septum*: see SEPTUM)⟧ 1 a clan or subdivision of a clan, as in ancient Ireland and Scotland 2 any similar group based on supposed descent from a common ancestor

Sept *abbrev.* 1 September 2 Septuagint

sept- (sept) *combining form* 1 SEPTI-[1] 2 SEPTI-[2] Used before a vowel

sep·ta (sep′tə) *n. alt. pl. of* SEPTUM

sep·tal (-təl) *adj.* of or forming a septum or septums

sep·tar·i·um (sep ter′ē əm) *n.*, *pl.* **-i·a** (-ē ə) ⟦ModL < L *septum*: see SEPTUM⟧ a cementlike mass, as of limestone, with fissures filled with some other material, as calcite —**sep·tar′i·an** *adj.*

sep·tate (sep′tāt′) *adj.* ⟦ModL *septatus*⟧ having or divided by a septum or septums

Sep·tem·ber (sep tem′bər) *n.* ⟦ME & OFr *Septembre* < L *September* < *septem*, seven (+ *-ber* < ?): so named as the seventh month of the ancient Roman year, which began with March⟧ the ninth month of the year, having 30 days: abbrev. *Sept*, *Sep*, or *S*

September massacre the massacre of Royalists in Paris, Sept. 2 to 6, 1792, during the French Revolution

Sep·tem·brist (sep tem′brist) *n.* a person who took part in the September massacre

sep·te·nar·y (sep′tə ner′ē, sep ten′ə rē) *adj.* ⟦L *septenarius* < *septem*, SEVEN⟧ 1 of the number seven 2 consisting of or forming a group of seven 3 SEPTENNIAL —*n.*, *pl.* **-nar′ies** a group or set of seven, esp. seven years

sep·ten·ni·al (sep ten′ē əl) *adj.* ⟦< L *septennium*, a period of seven years < *septem*, SEVEN + *annus*, year (see ANNUAL) + -AL⟧ 1 happening every seven years 2 lasting seven years —**sep·ten′ni·al·ly** *adv.*

sep·ten·tri·o·nal (sep ten′trē ə nəl) *adj.* ⟦ME < L *septentrionalis* < *septentriones*, the seven stars of Ursa Major, lit., seven plowing oxen < *septem*, SEVEN + *trio*, plow ox < base of *terere*, to rub: see THROW⟧ [Obs.] northern; boreal

sep·tet or **sep·tette** (sep tet′) ***n.*** ⟦Ger < L *septem*, SEVEN + Ger *(du)ett*⟧ **1** a group of seven persons or things **2** *Music a)* a composition for seven voices or seven instruments *b)* the seven performers of such a composition, or any group of seven musicians playing together

sep·ti-[1] (sep′tə, -ti) ⟦< L *septem*, SEVEN⟧ *combining form* seven *[septilateral]*

sep·ti-[2] (sep′tə, -ti) ⟦< SEPTUM⟧ *combining form* divider, septum *[septifragal]*

sep·tic (sep′tik) ***adj.*** ⟦L *septicus* < Gr *sēptikos* < *sēpein*, to make putrid: see SEPIA⟧ causing, or resulting from, sepsis or putrefaction —**sep′ti·cal·ly** ***adv.*** —**sep·tic′i·ty** (-tis′ə tē) ***n.***

sep·ti·ce·mi·a (sep′tə sē′mē ə) ***n.*** ⟦ModL *septicemia*: see prec. & -EMIA⟧ a systemic disease caused by the presence of pathogenic microorganisms and their toxic products in the blood —**sep′ti·ce′mic** (-mik) ***adj.***

sep·ti·ci·dal (sep′tə sīd′'l) ***adj.*** ⟦< SEPTI-[2] + -CIDE + -AL⟧ *Bot.* splitting open, or dehiscent, down the middle of the partitions uniting carpels —**sep′ti·ci′dal·ly** ***adv.***

septic tank an underground tank for receiving waste matter to be putrefied and decomposed through bacterial action

sep·tif·ra·gal (sep tif′rə gəl) ***adj.*** ⟦SEPTI-[2] + base of L *frangere*, to BREAK + -AL⟧ opening, or dehiscing, by the breaking away of the outer walls of the carpels from the partitions —**sep·tif′ra·gal·ly** ***adv.***

sep·til·lion (sep til′yən) ***n.*** ⟦Fr < L *septem*, SEVEN + Fr *(m)illion*⟧ ☆**1** the number represented by 1 followed by 24 zeros **2** [Brit.] the number represented by 1 followed by 42 zeros —***adj.*** amounting to one septillion in number —**sep·til′lionth** ***adj., n.***

sep·time (sep′tēm) ***n.*** ⟦< L *septimus*, seventh (< *septem*, SEVEN)⟧ a parrying position in fencing, the seventh of the eight positions

sep·tu·a·ge·nar·i·an (sep′to͞o ə jə ner′ē ən, -tyo͞o-) ***adj.*** ⟦< LL *(homo) septuagenarius*, (man) of seventy (< L *septuageni*, seventy each < *septuaginta*, seventy) + -AN⟧ 70 years old, or between the ages of 70 and 80 —***n.*** a septuagenarian person

Sep·tu·a·ges·i·ma (-jā′zi mə, -jes′i mə) ***n.*** ⟦ME *Septuagesme* < L, fem. of *septuagesimus*, seventieth, as in QUINQUAGESIMA: reason for name uncert.⟧ *former name for* the third Sunday before Lent: also **Septuagesima Sunday**

Sep·tu·a·gint (sep′to͞o ə jint, -tyo͞o-) ***n.*** ⟦< L *septuaginta*, seventy: because of the ancient tradition that it was completed in 70 (or 72) days by 72 Palestinian Jews for Ptolemy II of Egypt⟧ a translation into Greek of the Hebrew Scriptures made in the 3d & 2d cent. B.C.

sep·tum (sep′təm) ***n., pl.*** **-tums** or **-ta** (-tə) ⟦ModL < L, enclosure, hedge < *saepire*, to enclose, fence < *saepes*, a hedge < IE base **saip-*, hedge fence > Gr *haimos*, thicket⟧ *Biol.* a thin wall, membrane, etc. that separates two cavities or two masses of tissue, as in the nose or in a fruit

sep·tu·ple (sep′tə pəl, sep to͞o′pəl) ***adj.*** ⟦LL *septuplus* < L *septem*, SEVEN⟧ **1** consisting of seven **2** seven times as much or as many; sevenfold —***vt., vi.*** **-pled, -pling** to multiply by seven

sep·tu·plet (sep tup′lit, -to͞o′plit; sep′tə plet′) ***n.*** ⟦dim. of prec.⟧ **1** any of seven offspring from the same pregnancy **2** a collection or group of seven, usually of one kind

sep·ul·cher (sep′əl kər) ***n.*** ⟦ME < OFr *sepulcre* < L *sepulcrum* < *sepelire*, to bury < IE **sepel-*, veneration < base **sep-*, to honor > Sans *sápati*, (he) cultivates, cherishes⟧ **1** a vault for burial; grave; tomb **2** *R.C.Ch.* a small, sealed cavity, holding martyrs' relics, in a flat rectangular or square stone forming the top or part of the top of an altar —***vt.*** to place in a sepulcher; bury

se·pul·chral (sə pul′krəl) ***adj.*** ⟦L *sepulcralis*⟧ **1** of sepulchers, burial, etc. **2** suggestive of the grave or burial; dismal; gloomy **3** deep and melancholy: said of sound —**se·pul′chral·ly** ***adv.***

sep·ul·chre (sep′əl kər) ***n., vt.*** **-chred, -chring** *Brit. sp. of* SEPULCHER

sep·ul·ture (sep′əl chər) ***n.*** ⟦OFr < L *sepultura* < *sepelire*, to bury: see SEPULCHER⟧ **1** burial; interment **2** [Archaic] a burial place

seq *abbrev.* **1** sequence **2** sequential

seq. *abbrev.* ⟦L *sequentes* or *sequentia*⟧ the following

seqq. *abbrev.* ⟦L *sequentia*⟧ the following (ones)

se·qua·cious (si kwā′shəs) ***adj.*** ⟦L *sequax* < *sequi*, to follow (see SEQUENT) + -OUS⟧ easily influenced or led; servile; compliant —**se·qua′cious·ly** ***adv.*** —**se·quac′i·ty** (-kwas′ə tē) ***n.***

se·quel (sē′kwəl) ***n.*** ⟦ME *sequele* < MFr *sequelle* < L *sequela*: see fol.⟧ **1** something that follows; anything subsequent or succeeding; continuation **2** a result or consequence **3** a literary work, film, etc. complete in itself but continuing a story begun in an earlier work, film, etc.

se·que·la (si kwē′lə, -kwel′ə) ***n., pl.*** **-lae** (-kwē′lē, -kwel′ē) ⟦L < *sequi*, to follow: see SEQUENT⟧ **1** a thing that follows; consequence **2** *Med.* a diseased condition following, and usually resulting from, a previous disease

se·quence (sē′kwəns, -kwens′) ***n.*** ⟦MFr < LL, a following < L *sequens*: see SEQUENT⟧ **1** *a)* the following of one thing after another in chronological, causal, or logical order; succession or continuity *b)* the order in which this occurs **2** a continuous or related series, often of uniform things *[a sonnet sequence]* **3** three or more playing cards in unbroken order in the same suit; run **4** a resulting event; consequence; sequel **5** *Biochem.* the linear order of bases in a nucleic acid or of amino acids in a protein **6** *Math.* an ordered set of quantities or elements **7** *Film* a succession of scenes constituting a single, uninterrupted episode **8** *Music* the repetition of a melodic pattern in the same voice part but at different pitch levels **9** ⟦ME < ML *sequentia* < LL(Ec), used as transl. of Gr(Ec) *akolouthia*, a succession of notes on the last syllable of the alleluia: see ACOLYTE⟧ *R.C.Ch.* a hymn coming immediately before the Gospel in certain Masses —***vt.*** **-quenced, -quenc·ing** **1** to arrange in a sequence; put in order **2** *Biochem.* to find the unique order of (structural units of a gene, protein, etc.) by chemical analysis —*SYN.* SERIES

se·quenc·er (-kwən sər, -kwen′sər) ***n.*** ⟦< prec.⟧ **1** an electronic device or software program that allows a sequence of musical sounds, recorded in digital form, to be altered before being played back **2** *Biochem.* a complex device designed to automate the process of sequencing chemical base pairs in a strand of DNA

se·quent (-kwənt) ***adj.*** ⟦L *sequens*, prp. of *sequi*, to follow < IE base **sekw-*, to follow > OE *secg*, warrior⟧ **1** following in time or order; subsequent **2** following as a result or effect; consequent —***n.*** something that follows, esp. as a result; consequence

se·quen·tial (si kwen′shəl) ***adj.*** **1** SEQUENT **2** of, relating to, or forming a sequence —**se·quen′tial·ly** ***adv.***

se·ques·ter (si kwes′tər) ***vt.*** ⟦ME *sequestren* < MFr *sequestrer* < LL *sequestrare*, to remove, lay aside, separate < L *sequester*, trustee, akin to *sequi*: see SEQUENT⟧ **1** to set off or apart; separate; segregate; often, to segregate or isolate (the jury) during a trial **2** to take and hold (property) by judicial authority, for safekeeping or as security, until a legal dispute is resolved **3** to take over; confiscate; seize, esp. by authority **4** to withdraw; seclude: often used reflexively

se·ques·tered (-tərd) ***adj.*** removed from others; secluded

se·ques·trant (-trənt) ***n.*** *Chem.* an agent producing sequestration

se·ques·trate (si kwes′trāt′; sē′kwə strāt′, sek′wə-) ***vt.*** **-trat′ed, -trat′ing** ⟦< LL *sequestratus*, pp.: see SEQUESTER⟧ SEQUESTER —**se·ques′tra′tor** ***n.***

se·ques·tra·tion (sē′kwə strā′shən, si kwes′trā′-) ***n.*** ⟦ME *sequestracion* < MFr < LL *sequestratio*⟧ **1** a sequestering or being sequestered; seclusion; separation **2** *a)* the taking and holding of property pending resolution of a legal dispute *b)* confiscation of property, as by court or government action **3** the process by which a sequestrum forms **4** *Chem.* the close union of ions in solution with an added material so that a stable, soluble complex is produced

se·ques·trum (si kwes′trəm) ***n., pl.*** **-trums** or **-tra** (-trə) ⟦ModL < L, a deposit: see SEQUESTER⟧ *Med.* a piece of dead bone which has become separated from the surrounding healthy bone

se·quin (sē′kwin) ***n.*** ⟦Fr < It *zecchino* < *zecca*, a mint < Ar *sikka*, stamp, die⟧ **1** an obsolete gold coin of Italy and Turkey **2** a small, shiny ornament or spangle, as a metal disk, esp. one of many sewn on fabric for decoration

se·quined or **se·quinned** (-kwind) ***adj.*** adorned with sequins

☆**se·quoi·a** (si kwoi′ə, -koi′ə) ***n.*** ⟦ModL, genus name: after fol. (Cherokee *sikwo´ya*)⟧ **1** BIG TREE **2** REDWOOD (sense 1)

Se·quoy·ah (si kwoi′ə) 1760?-1843; Cherokee scholar and leader: created Cherokee syllabary: also sp. **Se·quoy′a**

ser[1] (sir) ***n.*** ⟦Hindi *sēr*⟧ *alt. sp. of* SEER[2]

ser[2] *abbrev.* **1** serial **2** series **3** sermon

ser- (sir) *combining form* SERO-: used before a vowel

se·ra (sir′ə) ***n.*** *alt. pl. of* SERUM

sé·rac (sə rak′, sā-) ***n.*** ⟦Swiss-Fr, orig., a type of white cheese < VL **seraceum*, soft cheese, whey < L *serum*: see SERUM⟧ a pointed mass or pinnacle of ice in or near a crevasse of a glacier

se·ra·glio (si ral′yō, -räl′-) ***n., pl.*** **-glios** ⟦It *serraglio*, enclosure, also (infl. by Turk *saray*, palace: see fol.), palace, seraglio < ML *serraculum*, a bolt, bar < LL *serare*, to lock, bar < L *sera*, a bolt, lock⟧ **1** the part of a Muslim household where wives or concubines live; harem **2** the palace of a Turkish sultan

se·ra·i (si rä′ē) ***n.*** ⟦Turk (modern sp. *saray*), palace, inn < Pers *sarāī*⟧ **1** in the Near East, an inn; caravansary **2** a Turkish palace

Se·ra·je·vo (ser′ə yā′vō) *alt. sp. of* SARAJEVO

ser·al (sir′əl) ***adj.*** *Ecol.* of or pertaining to a sere

Se·ram (si ram′) *alt. sp. of* CERAM

Seram Sea *alt. sp. of* CERAM SEA

☆**se·ra·pe** (sə rä′pē, -pā) ***n.*** ⟦MexSp⟧ a brightly colored wool blanket, used as an outer garment in Spanish-American countries

ser·aph (ser′əf) ***n., pl.*** **-a·phim′** (-ə fim′) or **-aphs** ⟦back-form. < LL(Ec) *seraphim*, pl. < Heb *serafim*, pl., sing. *saraf*, prob. < *saraf*, to burn⟧ **1** *Bible* one of the heavenly beings surrounding the throne of God, represented as having three pairs of wings: Isa. 6:2 **2** any of the highest order of angels, above the cherubim —**se·raph·ic** (sə raf′ik) ***adj.*** —**se·raph′i·cal·ly** ***adv.***

Se·ra·pis (sə rā′pis) ***n.*** ⟦L < Gr *osorāpis* < Egypt *wsyr-ḥp*, Osiris-Apis⟧ *Egypt. Myth.* a god of the lower world, whose cult spread to Greece and Rome

Serb[1] (surb) ***n.*** ⟦Serb *Srb*⟧ **1** a person born or living in Serbia; esp., a member of a Slavic people of Serbia and adjacent areas **2** SERBIAN (***n.*** 1) —***adj.*** SERBIAN

Serb[2] *abbrev.* **1** Serbia **2** Serbian

Ser·bi·a (sur′bē ə) country in the NW Balkan Peninsula: formerly a kingdom and (1946–2003) a constituent republic of Yugoslavia and (2003–06) of Serbia and Montenegro: 34,116 sq mi (88,361 sq km); cap. Belgrade

Serbia and Montenegro former country (2003–06) in the NW Balkan Peninsula, bordering on the Adriatic, consisting of the republics of Serbia & Montenegro: see YUGOSLAVIA

Ser·bi·an (-ən) ***adj.*** of Serbia or its people, language, or culture —***n.*** **1** the eastern variety of Serbo-Croatian, traditionally written in the Cyrillic alphabet **2** SERB[1] (***n.*** 1)

Ser·bo- (sur′bō) *combining form* Serbian, Serbian and *[Serbo-Croatian]*

Ser·bo-Cro·a·tian (sur′bō krō ā′shən) ***n.*** the South Slavic language spoken in the former Yugoslavia, and now in Serbia, Montenegro, Bosnia and Herzegovina, Croatia, and adjacent areas —***adj.*** of this language, the peoples that speak it, or their cultures

sere[1] (sir) ***n.*** ⟦back-form. < SERIES⟧ *Ecol.* the plant and animal communities that occur successively in a region and result in a CLIMAX (*n.* 3)

sere[2] (sir) ***adj.*** ⟦var. of SEAR[1]⟧ [Old Poet.] dried up; withered

Ser·em·ban (sur′əm bän′) city in SW Peninsular Malaysia, Malaysia: capital of Negri Sembilan

ser·e·nade (ser′ə nād′) ***n.*** ⟦Fr *sérénade* < It *serenata* < *sereno*, serene, open air < L *serenus*, clear, SERENE; meaning infl. by assoc. with L *sera*, evening < *serus*, late⟧ **1** a singing or playing of music outdoors at night, esp. by a lover under the window of his sweetheart **2** a piece of music suitable for this: cf. AUBADE **3** an instrumental composition somewhat like a suite —***vt., vi.*** **-nad′ed, -nad′ing** to play or sing a serenade (to) —**ser′e·nad′er** ***n.***

ser·e·na·ta (ser′ə nät′ə) ***n.***, *pl.* **-tas** or **-te** (-ā) ⟦It: see prec.⟧ **1** a type of 18th-cent. dramatic cantata for a special occasion, as a royal birthday **2** SERENADE

ser·en·dip·i·ty (ser′ən dip′ə tē) ***n.*** ⟦coined (*c.* 1754) by Horace Walpole after *The Three Princes of Serendip* (i.e., Sri Lanka), a Pers fairy tale in which the princes make such discoveries⟧ **1** a seeming gift for finding something good accidentally **2** luck, or good fortune, in finding something good accidentally **3** *pl.* **-ties** an instance of finding something good accidentally —**ser′en·dip′i·tous** ***adj.***

se·rene (sə rēn′) ***adj.*** ⟦L *serenus* < IE **ksero-*, dry (> Gr *xēros*, dry, OHG *serawēn*, to dry out) < base **ksā-*, to burn⟧ **1** clear; bright; unclouded [*a serene* sky] **2** not disturbed or troubled; calm, peaceful, tranquil, etc. **3** [**S-**] exalted; high-ranking: used in certain royal titles [*his Serene* Highness] —***n.*** [Old Poet.] a serene expanse, as of sky or water —***SYN.*** CALM —**se·rene′ly** ***adv.*** —**se·rene′ness** ***n.***

Ser·en·get·i (ser′ən get′ē) large plain in N Tanzania, part of which is set aside as a national wildlife sanctuary: usually with *the*

se·ren·i·ty (sə ren′ə tē) ***n.*** ⟦Fr *sérénité* < L *serenitas*⟧ the quality or state of being serene; calmness; tranquillity —***SYN.*** EQUANIMITY

serf (surf) ***n.*** ⟦OFr < L *servus*, slave, prob. of Etr orig.⟧ **1** [Obs.] a slave **2** a person in feudal servitude, bound to his or her master's land and transferred with it to a new owner **3** any person who is oppressed or without freedom —**serf′dom** ***n.***, **serf′hood′**

Serg *abbrev.* Sergeant

serge (surj) ***n.*** ⟦ME *sarge* < OFr < VL **sarica* < L *serica*, silken garments < *sericus*, silken, lit., of the *Seres*, a people of E Asia, prob. the Chinese < Gr *Sēres*, prob. ult. < Chin *se*, silk⟧ a strong twilled fabric with a diagonal rib, made of wool, silk, rayon, etc. and used for suits, coats, etc. —***vt.*** **serged, serg′ing** to finish (a cut edge, as of a garment seam) with overcast stitches to prevent raveling

ser·gean·cy (sär′jən sē) ***n.***, *pl.* **-cies** the position or rank of a sergeant: also **ser′geant·ship′**

ser·geant (sär′jənt) ***n.*** ⟦ME *serjaunt* < OFr *sergant* < L *serviens*, serving < *servire*, to SERVE⟧ **1** [Historical] a feudal servant who attends his master in battle **2** SERGEANT-AT-ARMS ☆**3** *a) U.S. Army, U.S. Marine Corps* a noncommissioned officer of the fifth grade, ranking above a corporal and below a staff sergeant *b) U.S. Air Force* a noncommissioned officer of the fourth grade, ranking above airman first class and below staff sergeant *c)* generally, any of the noncommissioned officers in the U.S. armed forces with *sergeant* as part of the title of their rank **4** *a)* in the U.S., a police officer ranking next below a captain or a lieutenant *b)* in England, a police officer ranking just below an inspector

ser·geant-at-arms (-ət ärmz′) ***n.***, *pl.* **ser′geants-at-arms′** an officer appointed to keep order in a legislature, court, social club, etc.

☆**sergeant first class** *U.S. Army* a noncommissioned officer of the seventh grade, ranking above staff sergeant and below master or first sergeant

☆**sergeant fish** **1** COBIA **2** SNOOK[1]

sergeant major *pl.* **sergeants major** **1** the chief administrative noncommissioned officer in a military headquarters: an occupational title and not a rank ☆**2** *U.S. Army, U.S. Marine Corps* the highest ranking noncommissioned officer **3** a small damselfish (*Abudefduf saxatilis*) with several dark, wide, vertical stripes on its bright-yellowish upper body

serg·er (surj′ər) ***n.*** any of various machines designed to serge a cut edge, as one on a piece of carpet or on a garment seam

Ser·gi·pe (sər zhē′pə) state of E Brazil: 8,514 sq mi (22,051 sq km); cap. Aracajú

Sergt *abbrev.* Sergeant

se·ri·al (sir′ē əl) ***adj.*** ⟦ModL *serialis* < L *series*, a row, order, SERIES⟧ **1** of, arranged in, or forming a series [*serial* numbers] **2** appearing, published, issued, etc. in a series or succession of continuous parts at regular intervals **3** of a serial or serials [*serial* rights to a novel] **4** committing an act, usually a criminal act, repeatedly and, typically, compulsively [*a serial* murderer] **5** *Comput. a)* of or for the transmission of a byte of data one bit at a time, over a single wire [*a serial* port] *b)* having to do with the performing of multiple operations one after the other [*serial* processing]: cf. PARALLEL (*adj.* 4) **6** *Music a)* designating or of a technique of composition in which various components of music, as pitch, rhythm, dynamics, etc., are arranged in an arbitrary order (a row or set) which serves as a basis for development *b)* loosely, TWELVE-TONE —***n.*** **1** *a)* a novel, story, film, etc. published or presented in serial form *b)* any of the separate parts or episodes **2** a periodical publication —**se′ri·al·ly** ***adv.***

se·ri·al·ism (-iz′əm) ***n.*** *Music* the twelve-tone system or technique of composition —**se′ri·al·ist** ***n.***

se·ri·al·ize (-īz′) ***vt.*** **-ized′, -iz′ing** to put or publish (a story, etc.) in serial form —**se′ri·al·i·za′tion** ***n.***

serial number a number that is one of a series, given for identification, as to armed forces personnel at enlistment or to engines at the time of manufacture

se·ri·ate (sir′ē it, -āt′) ***adj.*** ⟦ML *seriatus*, pp. of *seriare*, to arrange in a series⟧ arranged or occurring in a series —**se′ri·ate·ly** ***adv.*** —**se′ri·a′tion** ***n.***

se·ri·a·tim (sir′ē āt′im) ***adv., adj.*** ⟦ML < L *series*, based on *gradatim*, step by step⟧ one after another in order; point by point; serial(ly)

se·ri·ceous (sə rish′əs) ***adj.*** ⟦LL *sericeus* < L *sericum*, silken garment < *sericus*: see SERGE⟧ **1** of or like silk; silky **2** *Bot.* covered with fine, silky hairs

ser·i·cin (ser′ə sin) ***n.*** ⟦< L *sericus*, silk (see SERGE) + -IN[1]⟧ a resinous, amorphous substance that bonds the two gossamer filaments in a raw silk fiber

ser·i·cul·ture (ser′ə kul′chər) ***n.*** ⟦Fr *sériculture*, contr. < *sériciculture* < L *sericus* (see SERGE) + Fr *culture*⟧ the raising and keeping of silkworms for the production of raw silk —**ser′i·cul′tur·al** ***adj.*** —**ser′i·cul′tur·ist** ***n.***

ser·i·e·ma (ser′ə ē′mə, -ā′mə) ***n.*** ⟦ModL < Tupí *seriema*, lit., crested⟧ either of two South American, crested gruiform birds (family Cariamidae) with a long neck, one (*Cariama cristata*) with long, red legs and one (*Chunga burmeisteri*) with shorter, black legs

se·ries (sir′ēz) ***n.***, *pl.* **-ries** ⟦L < *serere*, to join or weave together < IE base **ser-*, to line up, join > Gr *eirein*, to join together, OE *searu*, a snare, armor, ON *sørvi*, necklace⟧ **1** a group or number of similar or related things arranged in a row [*a series* of arches] **2** a group or number of related or similar persons, things, or events coming one after another; sequence; succession **3** a number of things produced as a related group; set, as of books or television programs, related in subject, format, etc., or dealing with the same characters **4** *Bowling* a set of three consecutive games **5** *Elec.* an arrangement of devices in a circuit, in which the current flows sequentially through a series of components: used chiefly in the phrase **in series**: cf. PARALLEL (sense 7) **6** *Geol.* a subdivision of a system of stratified rocks, consisting of the rocks laid down during a geologic epoch **7** *Math.* the sum of a sequence, often infinite, of terms usually separated by plus signs or minus signs (Ex.: 1 + 3 + 5 + 7) **8** *Rhetoric* a group of successive coordinate elements of a sentence —***adj.*** *Elec.* designating or of a circuit in series

SYN.—**series** applies to a number of similar, more or less related things following one another in time or place [*a series* of concerts]; **sequence** emphasizes a closer relationship between the things, such as logical connection, numerical order, etc. [*the sequence* of events]; **succession** merely implies a following of one thing after another, without any necessary connection between them [*a succession* of errors]; **chain** refers to a series in which there is a definite relationship of cause and effect or some other logical connection [*a chain* of ideas]

series (*or* serial) comma *Gram.* a comma inserted before the conjunction, in a syntactic series made up of more than two items (Ex.: animal, vegetable, or mineral)

USAGE—in modern usage, the series comma is regarded as optional, but many careful writers still prefer it to avoid ambiguity (Ex.: in the sentence "choose one from among these lunch options: sandwich, omelet, soup and salad," is "soup and salad" one option or two?)

series winding the winding of an electric motor or generator in such a way that the field and armature circuits are connected in series —**se′ries-wound′** (-wound′) ***adj.***

ser·if (ser′if) ***n.*** ⟦Du *schreef*, a stroke, line < *schrijven*, to write < L *scribere*: see SCRIBE⟧ *Printing* a fine line projecting from a main stroke of a letter in common styles of type

ser·i·graph (ser′ə graf′, -gräf′) ***n.*** ⟦< L *sericum* (see SERICEOUS) + -GRAPH⟧ a color print made by the silk-screen process and printed by the artist personally —**se·rig·ra·pher** (sə rig′rə fər) ***n.*** —**se·rig′ra·phy** ***n.***

ser·in (ser′in) ***n.*** ⟦Fr, prob. < OProv *serena*, bee-eater, a green bird < LL *sirena*, for L *siren*, SIREN⟧ any of various small, yellow or yellowish-green Eurasian finches of a genus (*Serinus*) that includes the canary, esp. a European species (*S. serinus*)

ser·ine (ser′ēn′, sir′-; -in) ***n.*** ⟦< L *sericum*, silk (see SERICEOUS) + -INE[3]⟧ a nonessential amino acid, $HOCH_2CH(NH_2)COOH$, present in small quantities in many proteins: see AMINO ACID

se·rin·ga (sə riŋ′gə) ***n.*** ⟦Port < ModL *syringa*: see SYRINGA⟧ any of several Brazilian trees (genus *Hevea*) of the spurge family, yielding rubber

se·ri·o·com·ic (sir′ē ō käm′ik) ***adj.*** partly serious and partly comic —**se′ri·o·com′i·cal·ly** ***adv.***

se·ri·ous (sir′ē əs) ***adj.*** ⟦ME *seryows* < ML *seriosus* < L *serius*, grave, orig., prob. weighty, heavy < ? IE base **swer-* > OE *swær*, heavy, sad, Goth *swers*, important, orig., heavy⟧ **1** of, showing, having, or caused by earnestness or deep thought; earnest, grave, sober, or solemn [*a serious* person] **2** *a)* meaning what one says or does; not joking or trifling; sincere *b)* meant in earnestness; not said or done in play **3** concerned with grave, important, or complex matters, problems, etc.; weighty [*a serious* novel] **4** requiring careful consideration or thought; involving difficulty, effort, or considered action [*a serious* problem] **5** giving cause for concern; dangerous [*a serious* wound] —**se′ri·ous·ness** ***n.***

SYN.—**serious** implies absorption in deep thought or involvement in something really important as distinguished from something frivolous or merely amusing [*he takes a serious* interest in the theater]; **grave** implies the dignified weightiness of heavy responsibilities or cares [*a grave* expression on his face]; **solemn** suggests an impressive or awe-inspiring seriousness [*a solemn* ceremony]; **sedate** implies a dignified, proper, sometimes even prim seriousness [a *sedate* clergyman]; **earnest** suggests a seriousness of purpose marked by sincerity and enthusiasm [an *earnest* desire to help]; **sober** implies a seriousness marked by temperance, self-control, emotional balance, etc. [a *sober* criticism] **—ANT. frivolous, flippant**

se·ri·ous·ly (sir′ē əs lē) ***adv.*** **1** in a serious manner or to a serious degree [she looked at me *seriously*; to be *seriously* injured in an accident] **2** [Informal] *a)* really; actually; indeed [are you *seriously* going to drive in this weather?] *b)* sincerely [do you *seriously* believe he'll win?] **3** [Slang] to a great degree; very [*seriously* rich fudge brownies] **—*interj.*** [Informal] indeed; really: used for emphasis or to express surprise, skepticism, sarcasm, etc. **—take seriously** to regard or treat as important, serious, challenging, etc.

se·ri·ous-mind·ed (-mīn′did) ***adj.*** of, having, or showing earnestness or seriousness of purpose, method, etc.; not frivolous, jocular, etc.

ser·jeant (sär′jənt) ***n.*** *alt. Brit. sp. of* SERGEANT

ser·jeant-at-law (-at lô′) ***n.***, *pl.* **ser′jeants-at-law′** any of a former group of high-ranking British barristers

Ser·kin (sur′kin), **Rudolf** 1903-91; U.S. pianist, born in Bohemia

ser·mon (sur′mən) ***n.*** ⟦OFr < LL(Ec) *sermo* < L, a talk, discourse < IE base **swer-*, to speak > SWEAR⟧ **1** a lecture given as instruction in religion or morals, esp. by a priest, minister, or rabbi during services, using a text from Scripture **2** any serious talk on behavior, responsibility, etc., esp. a long, tedious one **—SYN.** SPEECH **—ser·mon′ic** (-män′ik) ***adj.***

ser·mon·ette (sur′mə net′) ***n.*** a short sermon

ser·mon·ize (sur′mə nīz′) ***vi.*** **-ized′, -iz′ing 1** to deliver a sermon or sermons **2** to preach, esp. in a dogmatic, moralizing fashion; lecture **—*vt.*** to preach to; exhort; lecture **—ser′mon·iz′er *n.***

Sermon on the Mount ⟦ult. a transl. of the L of St. AUGUSTINE of Hippo⟧ *Bible* the sermon delivered by Jesus to his disciples: Matt. 5-7, also Luke 6:20-49: it contains basic teachings of Christianity including the Lord's Prayer and the Beatitudes

se·ro- (sir′ə, -ō) ⟦< L *serum*: see SERUM⟧ *combining form* serum [*serology*]

se·ro·con·ver·sion (sir′ō kən vur′zhən) ***n.*** *Immunology* the process of producing antibodies in response to a specific antigen

se·rol·o·gy (si räl′ə jē) ***n.*** ⟦SERO- + -LOGY⟧ the science dealing with the properties and actions of serums **—se·ro·log·ic** (sir′ə läj′ik) ***adj.***, **se′ro·log′i·cal —se·rol′o·gist *n.***

se·ro·neg·a·tive (sir′ō neg′ə tiv) ***adj.*** being or having a negative test result for the presence of a specific antibody in the serum of the blood

se·ro·pos·i·tive (sir′ō päz′ə tiv) ***adj.*** being or having a positive test result for the presence of a specific antibody in the serum of the blood

se·ro·pu·ru·lent (sir′ō pyoor′ə lənt, -yoo lənt) ***adj.*** ⟦SERO- + PURULENT⟧ composed of pus and serum

se·ro·sa (si rō′sə, -zə) ***n.***, *pl.* **-sas** or **-sae** (-sē) ⟦ModL < L *serosus*, SEROUS⟧ **1** SEROUS MEMBRANE **2** CHORION **—se·ro′sal *adj.***

se·rot·i·nal (sə rät′n əl) ***adj.*** ⟦< L *serotinus* < *serus*, late < IE base **sē(i)-*, slow, let fall, neglect, stretch out > SEED, SIDE⟧ *Bot.* late or delayed in development: said esp. of late-flowering plants: also **se·rot′i·nous** (-əs)

se·ro·ton·in (sir′ə tō′nin, ser′-) ***n.*** ⟦SERO- + TON(IC) + -IN[1]⟧ a complex amine, $C_{10}H_{12}N_2O$, found in blood, the brain, etc. or produced synthetically: it constricts the blood vessels and contracts smooth muscle tissue, and is important as both a neurotransmitter and a hormone

se·ro·type (sir′ə tīp′) ***n.*** a strain of microorganisms having a set of antigens in common **—*vt.*** **-typed′, -typ′ing** to assign to a particular serotype

se·rous (sir′əs) ***adj.*** ⟦MFr *séreux* < *serum* < L: see SERUM⟧ **1** of or containing serum **2** like serum; thin and watery

serous fluid any of several serumlike fluids in the body cavities, esp. in those lined with serous membrane

serous membrane the thin membrane lining most of the closed cavities of the body and folded back over the enclosed organs, as the peritoneum or pericardium

se·ro·var (sir′ō ver′) ***n.*** ⟦SERO- + *-var*, as in CULTIVAR⟧ SEROTYPE

ser·ow (ser′ō) ***n.*** ⟦< *să-ro*, native name for long-haired goat in a language of Sikkim⟧ any of a genus (*Capricornis*) of dark-colored, sometimes maned, goat antelopes of E Asia

Ser·pens (sur′penz) ***n.*** ⟦L: see fol.⟧ an equatorial constellation split into two separate regions, **Serpens Ca·put** (kā′pət, kap′ət) (head) and **Serpens Cau·da** (kô′də) (tail), on opposite sides of Ophiuchus

ser·pent (sur′pənt) ***n.*** ⟦OFr < L *serpens* (gen. *serpentis*) < prp. of *serpere*, to creep < IE base **serp-*, to creep > Sans *sárpati*, (he) creeps, Gr *herpein*⟧ **1** a snake, esp. a large or poisonous one **2** [*often* **S-**] Satan, in the form he assumed to tempt Eve: Gen. 3:1-5 **3** a sly, sneaking, treacherous person **4** *Music* an early bass wind instrument, coiled in form, made of wood covered with leather

☆**ser·pen·tar·i·um** (sur′pən ter′ē əm) ***n.*** ⟦prec. + (AQU)ARIUM⟧ a place where snakes are kept, as for exhibition

ser·pen·tine (sur′pən tēn′, -tīn′) ***adj.*** ⟦ME *serpentyn* < OFr *serpentin* < LL(Ec) *serpentinus*⟧ of or like a serpent; esp., *a)* evilly cunning or subtle; treacherous *b)* coiled or twisted; winding **—*n.*** **1** something that twists or coils like a snake, as a coil of thin paper thrown out to unwind as a streamer **2** ⟦from resemblance of its markings to those on a serpent's skin⟧ a rock or mineral, as chrysotile, consisting chiefly of hydrous magnesium silicate and having a greenish, often mottled, coloring

ser·pi·go (sər pī′gō) ***n.*** ⟦ME < ML < L *serpere*, to creep: see SERPENT⟧ any spreading skin disease, as ringworm

Ser·ra (ser′ä), **Ju·ní·pe·ro** (hoo nē′pe rô′) (born *Miguel José Serra*) 1713-84; Sp. missionary in W North America

ser·ra·nid (ser′ə nid′) ***n.*** ⟦< ModL *Serranidae* < L *serra*, a saw⟧ SEA BASS (sense 1) **—*adj.*** designating or of the SEA BASS (sense 1) Also **ser′ra·noid′** (-noid′)

ser·ra·no (sə rä′nō) ***n.***, *pl.* **-nos** ⟦< MexSp *chile serrano* < Sp *chile*, chili (pepper) + *serrano* (adj.) < *sierra*, mountain range, lit., a saw < L *serra*, saw⟧ a kind of long, slender, very hot chili usually cooked while still green, used esp. in Mexican cooking: also **serrano chili (**or **pepper)**

ser·rate (ser′āt′, -it; *for v.*, ser′āt′, sə rāt′) ***adj.*** ⟦L *serratus* < *serra*, a saw⟧ having sawlike notches along the edge, as some leaves: also **ser′rat′ed —*vt.*** **-rat′ed, -rat′ing** to make serrate

ser·ra·tion (ser ā′shən) ***n.*** **1** the condition of being serrate **2** a single tooth or notch in a serrate edge **3** a formation of these Also **ser·ra·ture** (ser′ə chər)

ser·ried (ser′ēd) ***adj.*** ⟦pp. of obs. *serry* < Fr *serrer*, to crowd < LL *serare*, to lock: see SERAGLIO⟧ placed close together; crowded; compact, as soldiers in ranks

ser·ru·late (ser′yoo lit, ser′ə-; -lāt′) ***adj.*** ⟦ModL *serrulatus* < L *serrula*, dim. of *serra*, a saw⟧ having small, fine teeth or notches along the edge; finely serrate: also **ser′ru·lat′ed**

ser·ru·la·tion (ser′yoo lā′shən, ser′ə-) ***n.*** **1** the condition of being serrulate **2** a single tooth or notch in a serrulate edge **3** a formation of these

ser·tu·lar·i·an (sur′tyoo ler′ē ən) ***n.*** ⟦< ModL *Sertulariidae* (< L *sertula*, dim. of *serta*, garland < fem. pp. of *serere*, to join together: see SERIES) + -AN⟧ any of a family (Sertulariidae) of hydroids growing in colonies made up of double-rowed branches of cupped polyps

se·rum (sir′əm) ***n.***, *pl.* **-rums** or **-ra** (-ə) ⟦L, whey < IE **serom*, fluid < base **ser-*, to flow > Sans *sara-*, fluid, Gr *hormē*, an attack⟧ **1** *a)* a clear, watery animal fluid, as serous fluid *b)* the clear, yellowish fluid of the blood which separates from a blood clot after coagulation and shrinkage (in full **blood serum**) **2** blood serum containing agents of immunity, taken from an animal made immune to a specific disease by inoculation: it is used as an antitoxin and for diagnosis **3** the whey of milk **4** the thin, watery part of a plant fluid

serum albumin the most abundant protein of blood serum: it is synthesized by the liver and serves to regulate osmotic pressure and to carry certain metabolic products

serum globulin a component of blood serum consisting of proteins with larger molecular weights than serum albumin, including antibodies, lipoproteins, etc.

serum hepatitis HEPATITIS B

serv *abbrev.* **1** servant **2** service

ser·val (sur′vəl) ***n.***, *pl.* **-vals** or **-val** ⟦Fr < Port *(lobo) cerval* < L *(lupus) cervarius*, lynx, lit., deer wolf: see WOLF & CERVINE⟧ an African wildcat (*Leptailurus serval*) with a black-spotted, tawny coat, long legs, and no ear tufts

serv·ant (sur′vənt) ***n.*** ⟦ME < OFr < prp. of *servir* < L *servire*, to fol.⟧ **1** a person employed to perform services, esp. household duties, for another **2** a person employed by a government: cf. PUBLIC SERVANT, CIVIL SERVANT **3** a person devoted to another or to a cause, creed, etc.

serve (surv) ***vt.*** **served, serv′ing** ⟦ME *serven* < OFr *servir* < L *servire*, to serve < *servus*, servant, slave: see SERF⟧ **1** to work for as a servant **2** *a)* to do services or duties for; give service to; aid; assist; help *b)* to give obedience and reverent honor to (God, one's lord, etc.) *c)* [Archaic] to pay court to (a lady) **3** to do military or naval service for **4** to pass or spend (a term of imprisonment, military service, etc.) [to *serve* a year in prison] **5** *a)* to carry out the duties connected with (a position, office, etc.) *b)* to act as server for (Mass, Benediction, etc.) **6** *a)* to wait on (customers), as in a store *b)* to provide (customers, clients, or users) with goods or services, esp. professional services *c)* to provide (goods) for customers; supply **7** *a)* to prepare and offer (food, etc.) in a certain way [*serve* the beef with rice] *b)* to offer or set food, etc. before (a person) *c)* to give someone a portion or portions of (food, etc.) at the table **8** *a)* to meet the needs or satisfy the requirements of [a tool that *serves* many purposes] *b)* to promote or further [to *serve* the national interest] **9** to be used by [a library that *serves* the entire town] **10** to function or perform for [if memory *serves* me well] **11** to behave toward; treat [to be cruelly *served*] **12** *Animal Husbandry* to copulate with (a female): said of a male animal **13** *Law* *a)* to deliver (a legal instrument, as a summons) *b)* to deliver a legal instrument to; esp., to present with a writ **14** *Naut.* to wrap cords, twine, etc. around (a rope) to protect it **15** *Tennis, etc.* to hit (a tennis ball, etc.) to one's opponent in order to start play **—*vi.*** **1** to work as a servant **2** to be in service; do service [to *serve* in the navy] **3** *a)* to carry out the duties connected with a position, office, etc. *b)* to act as server for Mass, Benediction, etc. **4** to be used or usable; be of service; function **5** to meet needs or satisfy requirements **6** to provide guests with something to eat or drink, as by waiting on table **7** to be suitable or favorable: said of weather, wind, etc. **8** to start play by hitting the ball, etc. to one's opponent, as in tennis **—*n.*** the act or manner of serving the ball in tennis, etc., or one's turn to serve **—serve someone right** to be what someone deserves, for doing something wrong or foolish

serv·er (sur′vər) ***n.*** **1** a person who serves, as a waiter, a player who serves the ball, or an assistant to the celebrant at Mass **2** a thing used in serving, as a tray, cart, etc. **3** *Comput.* within a NETWORK (sense 3*a*), a computer that provides other computers access as to shared peripherals, programs, or databases

Ser·ve·tus (sər vēt′əs), **Michael** (Sp. name *Miguel Serveto*) 1511-53; Sp. theologian: burned at the stake for heresy

serv·ice¹ (sʉr′vis) ***n.*** ⟦ME *servise* < OFr < L *servitium*, servitude < *servus*, slave: see SERF⟧ **1** the occupation or condition of a servant **2** *a)* employment, esp. public employment [diplomatic *service*] *b)* a branch or department of this, including its personnel; specif., the armed forces, as army, navy, or air force **3** *a)* work done for a master or feudal lord *b)* work done or duty performed for another or others [repair *service*, public *service*] **4** the serving of God, as through good works, prayer, etc. **5** *a)* public worship *b)* any religious ceremony [the marriage *service*] *c)* [*sometimes pl.*] a similar, but nonreligious, ceremony, as for a burial or marriage [graveside *services*] *d)* a musical setting for a religious service **6** *a)* an act giving assistance or advantage to another *b)* the result of this; benefit; advantage *c)* [*pl.*] friendly help; also, professional aid or attention [the fee for his *services*] **7** the act or manner of serving food [a restaurant noted for its fine *service*] **8** a set of utensils or articles used in serving [silver tea *service*] **9** a system or method of providing people with the use of something, as electric power, water, transportation, mail delivery, etc. **10** installation, maintenance, repairs, etc., provided by a dealer or manufacturer to purchasers of equipment **11** the act or manner of serving the ball in tennis, etc., or one's turn to serve **12** [Archaic] devotion, as of a lover to his lady **13** *Animal Husbandry* the act of bringing a male animal to copulate with a female **14** *Law* notification of legal action, as by the serving of a writ **15** *Naut.* any material, as wire, used in serving (ropes, etc.) —***adj.*** **1** of, for, or in service; specif., *a)* of or relating to the armed forces *b)* providing repair, maintenance, supplies, etc. *c)* providing services, rather than goods **2** of, for, or used by servants, tradespeople, etc. [a *service* entrance] **3** *a)* for use during active service [a *service* uniform] *b)* serviceable; durable [*service* weight stockings] —***vt.*** **-iced, -ic·ing 1** to furnish with a service **2** to copulate with (a female): said of a male animal ☆**3** to make or keep fit for service, as by inspecting, adjusting, repairing, refueling, etc. **4** to make the periodic interest payments on (a debt) —**at someone's service 1** ready to serve or cooperate with someone **2** ready for someone's use —**be of service** be helpful or useful —**in service 1** in use; functioning: said esp. of an appliance, vehicle, etc. **2** in the armed forces **3** working as a domestic servant

serv·ice² (sʉr′vis) ***n.*** SERVICE TREE

Ser·vice (sʉr′vis), **Robert (William)** 1874-1958; Cdn. verse writer, born in England

serv·ice·a·ble (sʉr′vis ə bəl) ***adj.*** ⟦ME *servisable* < OFr⟧ **1** *a)* that can be of service; ready for use *b)* adequate for its purpose **2** that will give good service, esp. in hard use; durable [a *serviceable* fabric] **3** [Archaic] willing to serve —**serv′ice·a·bil′i·ty *n.*, serv′ice·a·ble·ness —serv′ice·a·bly *adv.***

serv·ice·ber·ry (-ber′ē) ***n.***, *pl.* **-ries** ☆**1** JUNEBERRY **2** the fruit of any service tree

service break *Tennis, etc.* the act or an instance of winning a game in which the opponent serves

service cap a military cap with a round, flat top and a visor

service ceiling the altitude at which a specified kind of aircraft cannot, because of reduced atmospheric pressure, climb faster than a specified rate

service charge a fee charged for a service, often in addition to a basic fee

☆**service club 1** any of various clubs, as Rotary, Kiwanis, etc., organized to provide certain services for its members and to promote the community welfare **2** an armed-services recreation center

☆**service elevator** an elevator intended for use not by the general public, but by maintenance personnel, deliverymen, etc. and for carrying freight, supplies, etc.

☆**service entrance** an entrance used by tradespeople, employees, etc. rather than by the general public

service line 1 *Handball* the line marking the front of the zone within which the server must stand **2** *Tennis* the line parallel to the net beyond which a served ball must not strike the court

serv·ice·man (sʉr′vis man′, -mən) ***n.***, *pl.* **-men′** (-men′, -mən) **1** a member of the armed forces **2** a person whose work is servicing or repairing something [a radio *serviceman*]: also written **service man**

☆**service mark** a symbol, design, word, letter, slogan, etc. used by a supplier of a service to distinguish the service from that of a competitor: usually registered and protected by law: cf. TRADEMARK

service module a component of certain spacecraft that contains various support systems and its own rocket engine: it is separated from the COMMAND MODULE before reentry

service plaza a service area along an expressway, with a restaurant, a gas station, restrooms, etc.

☆**service station 1** a place providing maintenance service, parts, supplies, etc. for mechanical or electrical equipment **2** a place providing such service, and selling gasoline, oil, etc., for motor vehicles

☆**service stripe** a stripe, or any of the parallel diagonal stripes, worn on the left sleeve of a uniform to indicate years spent in the service

service tree ⟦ME *serves*, pl. of obs. *serve* < OE *syrfe* < VL **sorbea* < L *sorbus* < IE base **sor-*, **ser-*, red, reddish⟧ **1** a European mountain ash (*Sorbus domestica*) having small, edible fruit **2** a European mountain ash, the **wild service tree** (*Sorbus torminalis*), similar to this

serv·ice·wom·an (-woom′ən) ***n.***, *pl.* **-wom′en** (-wim′in) a female member of the armed forces

ser·vi·ette (sʉr′vē et′) ***n.*** ⟦Fr < MFr < *servir*, to SERVE + *-ette*, -ET⟧ [Chiefly Brit.] a table napkin

ser·vile (sʉr′vəl, -vīl′) ***adj.*** ⟦ME < L *servilis* < *servus*, slave: see SERF⟧ **1** of a slave or slaves **2** like that of slaves or servants [*servile* employment] **3** like or characteristic of a slave; humbly yielding or submissive; cringing; abject **4** [Archaic] held in slavery; not free —**ser′vile·ly *adv.* —ser·vil·i·ty** (sər vil′ə tē) ***n.*** **—ser′vile·ness *n.***

serv·ing (sʉr′viŋ) ***n.*** **1** the act of one who serves **2** a helping, or single portion, of food —***adj.*** used for or suitable for giving food to a person or persons at the table [a *serving* dish]

ser·vi·tor (sʉr′və tər) ***n.*** ⟦ME *servitour* < OFr < LL *servitor* < pp. of L *servire*, to SERVE⟧ a person who serves another; servant, attendant, or, formerly, soldier

ser·vi·tude (sʉr′və to͞od′, -tyo͞od′) ***n.*** ⟦ME < MFr < L *servitudo* < *servus*, slave: see SERF⟧ **1** the condition of a slave, serf, or the like; subjection to a master; slavery or bondage **2** work imposed as punishment for crime **3** *Law* the burden placed upon the property of a person by a specified right another has in its use

SYN.—**servitude** refers to compulsory labor or service for another, often, specif., such labor imposed as punishment for crime; **slavery** implies absolute subjection to another person who owns and completely controls one; **bondage** originally referred to the condition of a serf bound to the master's land, but now implies any condition of subjugation or captivity —*ANT.* **freedom, liberty**

ser·vo (sʉr′vō) ***n.***, *pl.* **-vos** *short for:* **1** SERVOMECHANISM **2** SERVOMOTOR —***adj.*** of, pertaining to, incorporating, or controlled by a servomechanism

ser·vo·mech·a·nism (sʉr′vō mek′ə niz′əm) ***n.*** ⟦< fol. + MECHANISM⟧ an automatic control system in which the output is constantly or intermittently compared with the input through feedback so that the error or difference between the two quantities can be used to bring about the desired degree of control

ser·vo·mo·tor (sʉr′vō mōt′ər) ***n.*** ⟦< Fr *servo-moteur* < L *servus*, slave (see SERF) + Fr *moteur*, MOTOR⟧ a device, as an electric motor, hydraulic piston, etc., that is controlled by an amplified signal from a command device of low power, as in a servomechanism

ses·a·me (ses′ə mē′) ***n.*** ⟦altered (infl. by Gr) < earlier *sesama* < L *sesamum sesama* < Gr *sēsamon*, *sēsamē*, ult. < Akkadian *shaman shammī*, oil of plants⟧ **1** a plant (*Sesamum indicum*) of a family (Pedaliaceae, order Scrophulariales) of tropical, dicotyledonous herbs and shrubs, whose flat seeds yield an edible oil and are used for flavoring bread, rolls, etc. **2** its seeds See also OPEN SESAME

ses·a·moid (ses′ə moid′) ***adj.*** ⟦Gr *sēsamoeidēs* < *sēsamon* (see prec.) + *eidos*, -OID⟧ shaped like a sesame seed; specif., designating or of any of certain small bones located in tendons, as at a joint, or any of certain small cartilaginous nodules in the nose —***n.*** such a bone or cartilage

ses·qui- (ses′kwi, -kwə, -kwē) ⟦L, more by a half < *semis*, half (< *semi-*: see SEMI-) + *-que*, and < IE **kwe* (enclitic) > Sans *ca*, Gr *te*, OIr *-ch*, Goth *-h*⟧ *combining form* **1** one and a half [*sesquicentennial*] **2** *Chem.* containing two atoms of one radical or element combined with three of another [*sesquicarbonate*]

ses·qui·car·bon·ate (ses′kwi kär′bə nit, -nāt′) ***n.*** ⟦prec. + CARBONATE⟧ a carbonate in which there are three carbonate radicals for every two metal atoms

☆**ses·qui·cen·ten·ni·al** (-sen ten′ē əl, -ten′yəl) ***adj.*** of or ending a period of 150 years —***n.*** a 150th anniversary or its commemoration

ses·qui·ox·ide (ses′kwē äk′sīd′) ***n.*** ⟦SESQUI- + OXIDE⟧ an oxide in which three atoms or equivalents of oxygen are combined with two of some other element or radical

ses·qui·pe·da·li·an (ses′kwi pə dā′lē ən, -pə dāl′yən) ***adj.*** ⟦< L *sesquipedalis*, of a foot and a half < *sesqui-* (see SESQUI-) + *pedalis* < *pes* (gen. *pedis*), a FOOT⟧ **1** measuring a foot and a half **2** very long: said of words **3** using, or characterized by the use of, long words Also **ses·quip′e·dal** (-kwip′ə dəl) —***n.*** a long word **—ses′qui·pe·da′li·an·ism′ *n.***

ses·sile (ses′il, -īl′) ***adj.*** ⟦L *sessilis* < *sessus*, pp. of *sedere*, to SIT⟧ **1** *Biol.* *a)* attached directly by its base *b)* permanently fixed; immobile **2** *Bot.* having no pedicel or peduncle; attached directly to the main stem, as the flower and leaves of a trillium plant

ses·sion (sesh′ən) ***n.*** ⟦ME < L *sessio* < *sedere*, to SIT⟧ **1** *a)* the sitting together or meeting of a group; assembly, as of a court, legislature, council, etc. *b)* a continuous, day-to-day series of such meetings *c)* the term or period of such a meeting or meetings **2** *a)* a school term *b)* a day when school is open for classes **3** the governing body of a Presbyterian church, consisting of the minister and elders **4** a period of activity of any kind [a *session* with the dentist, a *session* on a computer] —**in session** officially meeting; assembled **—ses′sion·al *adj.***

Ses·sions (sesh′ənz), **Roger (Huntington)** 1896-1985; U.S. composer

ses·terce (ses′tərs) ***n.*** ⟦L *sestertius (nummus)*, for *semis tertius*, two and a half, because equal in value to two and a half asses: see NUMMULAR⟧ an old Roman coin, originally of silver, later of brass or copper, equal to ¼ denarius

ses·ter·ti·um (ses tʉr′shē əm, -shəm) ***n.***, *pl.* **-ti·a** (-shē ə, -shə) ⟦L < *(mille) sestertium*, gen. pl. of *sestertius*: see prec.⟧ a monetary unit of ancient Rome, equal to 1,000 sesterces

ses·tet (ses tet′, ses′tet′) ***n.*** ⟦It *sestetto*, dim. of *sesto*, sixth < L *sextus*, sixth < *sex*, SIX⟧ **1** *Music* SEXTET **2** *a)* the final six lines of a Petrarchan sonnet *b)* a poem or stanza of six lines

ses·ti·na (ses tē′nə) ***n.***, *pl.* **-nas** or **-ne** (-nā) ⟦It < *sesto*, sixth: see prec.⟧ an elaborate verse form of six six-line stanzas and a tercet: the end words of the first stanza are repeated in varying combinations in the other five stanzas and the tercet

Ses·tos (ses′täs) town in ancient Thrace, on the Hellespont opposite Abydos

set (set) ***vt.* set, set′ting** ⟦ME *setten* < OE *settan* (akin to Ger *setzen* & Goth *satjan* < Gmc **satjan*), caus. formation "to cause to sit" < base of SIT⟧ **1** to place in a sitting position; cause to sit; seat **2** *a)* to cause (a fowl) to sit on eggs in order to hatch them *b)* to put (eggs) under a fowl or in an incubator to hatch them **3** to put in a certain place or position; cause to be, lie, stand, etc. in a place [*set* the book on the table] **4** to put in the proper or designated place [to *set* a wheel on an axle] **5** to put or move (a part of the body) into or on a specified place [to *set* foot on land] **6** to bring (something) into contact with something else [to burn a paper by *setting* a match to it] **7** *a)* [Archaic] to put in writing; record *b)* to put or affix (one's signature, seal, etc.) to a document **8** to cause to be in some condition or relation; specif., *a)* to cause to be or become [to *set* a house on fire] *b)* to put in a certain physical position [to *set* a book on end] **9** to cause to be in working or proper condition; put in order; arrange; fix; adjust; specif., *a)* to fix (a net, trap, etc.) in a position to catch animals *b)* to fix (a sail) in a position to catch the wind *c)* to put (a part of a device) in position to work [to *set* a chuck on a lathe] *d)* to adjust so as to be in a desired position for use; regulate [to *set* a radio dial, a clock, a thermostat, etc.] *e)* to place (oneself) in readiness for action *f)* to adjust (a saw) by slightly deflecting alternate teeth in opposite directions *g)* to sink (the head of a nail) below, or level with, a surface *h)* to arrange (a table) with knives, forks, plates, etc. for a meal *i)* to put (a dislocated joint or fractured bone) into normal position for healing, mending, etc. **10** to cause to be in a settled or firm position; specif., *a)* to put or press into a fixed or rigid position [to *set* one's jaw] *b)* to cause (one's mind, purpose, etc.) to be fixed, unyielding, determined, etc. *c)* to cause to become firm or hard in consistency [pectin *sets* jelly] *d)* to make (a color) fast in dyeing *e)* to mount, embed, or fix (gems) in rings, bracelets, etc. *f)* to cover, encrust, or decorate (gold, watches, etc.) with gems *g)* to fix firmly in a frame [*set* the glass in the window] *h)* to arrange (hair) in the desired style with lotions, hairpins, etc. and let it dry *i)* to transplant (a shoot, etc.) **11** to cause to take a particular direction; specif., *a)* to cause to move as specified; propel [the current *set* them eastward] *b)* to point, direct, or face as specified [to *set* one's face toward home] *c)* to direct (one's desires, hopes, heart, etc.) with serious attention (*in* or *on* someone or something) **12** to appoint, establish, ordain, etc.; specif., *a)* to post or station for certain duties [to *set* sentries at a gate] *b)* to place in a position of authority *c)* to fix (limits or boundaries) *d)* to fix or appoint (a time) for something to happen [to *set* Friday as the deadline] *e)* to fix a time for (an event) *f)* to establish (a regulation, law, record, etc.) or prescribe (a form, order, etc.) *g)* to give or furnish (an example, pattern, etc.) for others *h)* to introduce (a fashion, style, etc.) *i)* to allot or assign (a task, lesson, etc.) for work or study *j)* to fix (a quota, as of work) for a given period *k)* to begin to apply (oneself) to a task, etc. **13** to estimate or fix; place mentally; specif., *a)* to fix (the amount of a price, fine, etc.) *b)* to fix (a price, fine, etc.) at a specified amount *c)* to estimate or value [to *set* at naught all that one has won] *d)* to fix or put as an estimate [to *set* little store by someone] **14** *Bridge* to prevent (one's opponents) from making their contract or prevent (a contract) from being made **15** *Cooking* to put aside (leavened dough) to rise **16** *Hunting* to point toward the position of (game): said of a dog **17** *Music* to write or fit (words *to* music or music *to* words) **18** *Printing a)* to arrange (type) for printing *b)* to produce or reproduce (printed matter) by computer or photocomposition *c)* to put (a piece of writing) into print **19** *Theater a)* to place (a scene) in a given locale *b)* to make up or arrange (scenery) on the stage *c)* to arrange the scenery and properties on (the stage) **—*vi.* 1** to sit on eggs: said of a fowl **2** to become firm or hard in consistency [cement *sets* after several hours] **3** to become fast: said of dye, color, etc. **4** *a)* to begin to move, travel, etc. (with *out, forth, on, off,* or *forward*) *b)* to begin or get started [to *set* to work] **5** to have a certain direction; tend **6** *a)* to make an apparent descent toward and below the horizon; go down [the sun was *setting* in the west] *b)* to wane; decline **7** to hang, fit, or suit in a certain way [a jacket that *sets* well] **8** to grow together; mend: said of a broken bone **9** [Now Dial.] to sit **10** *Bot.* to begin to develop into a fruit after pollination **11** *Hunting* to point toward the position of game: said of a dog **—*adj.* 1** fixed or appointed in advance [a *set* time] **2** established; prescribed, as by authority **3** deliberate; intentional; purposeful **4** conventional; stereotyped; not spontaneous [a *set* speech] **5** fixed; motionless; rigid; immovable **6** *a)* resolute; determined *b)* obstinate; unyielding **7** firm or hard in consistency **8** ready to begin some action or activity [get *set* to run] **9** formed; put together; built: now usually in comb. [*heavyset*] **—*n.* 1** a setting or being set; specif., *a)* the act of a dog in setting game *b)* a becoming hard or firm in consistency **2** the way or position in which a thing is set; specif., *a)* direction; course, as of a current *b)* tendency; inclination *c)* change of form resulting from pressure, twisting, strain, etc.; warp; bend *d)* sideways deflection in opposite directions of the alternate teeth of a saw *e)* the way in which an article of clothing fits or hangs *f)* the position or attitude of a limb or part of the body [the *set* of her head] *g)* *Psychol.* a readiness to respond or to prepare for a certain definite kind of activity **3** something which is set; specif., *a)* a twig or slip for planting or grafting *b)* a young plant; esp., a dwarfed bulb, as of an onion, dried and kept over winter for early spring planting *c)* a number of backdrops, flats, properties, etc. constructed and arranged for a scene in a play, film, etc. **4** *a)* the act or a style of setting hair *b)* the lotion, etc. used for this purpose (in full **hair set**) **5** a group of persons; specif., *a)* a company or group with common habits, occupation, interests, etc. [a *set* of smugglers] *b)* an exclusive or select group; clique; coterie *c)* the number of couples needed for a country or square dance **6** a collection of things belonging, issued, used, or growing together; specif., *a)* a number of magazines, books, etc., often in a similar format, by one author, on one subject, etc. *b)* a matching collection of china, silverware, etc. *c)* the complement of natural or artificial teeth of a person or animal *d)* a clutch of eggs *e)* the figures that make up a country or square dance ☆*f)* any of the segments of a performance as of jazz or dance music at a nightclub, concert, etc., usually separated from each other by an intermission; also, all of the musical pieces played during such a segment *g)* receiving equipment for radio or television assembled, as in a case or cabinet, for use *h)* *Tennis* a subdivision of a MATCH[2] (***n.*** 3), consisting of a series of at least six games: see also GAME[1] (***n.*** 2c) **7** *alt. sp. of* SETT **8** *Math.* a prescribed collection of points, numbers, or other objects that satisfy a given condition **9** *Printing* the width of the body of a piece of type **—*SYN.*** COTERIE **—☆all set** [Informal] prepared; ready **—set about** to begin; start doing **—set against 1** to balance **2** to compare **3** to make hostile toward; make an enemy of **—set apart** to separate and keep for a purpose; reserve **—set aside 1** to set apart **2** to discard; dismiss; reject **3** to annul; declare void **—set back 1** to put (a clock or its hands) to an earlier time, esp. to standard time **2** to reverse or hinder the progress of ☆**3** [Informal] to cost (a person) a specified sum of money **—set down 1** to place so as to rest upon a surface; put down **2** to land (an airplane) **3** to put in writing or print; record **4** to establish (rules, principles, etc.) **5** to consider, ascribe, attribute, etc. **—set forth 1** to publish **2** to express in words; state **—set in 1** to begin **2** to blow or flow toward the shore: said of wind, current, etc. **3** to insert **—set off 1** *a)* to start (a person) doing something *b)* to make begin; start going **2** to set in relief; make prominent by contrast **3** to show to advantage; enhance **4** to cause to explode **—set on 1** to incite or urge on, as to attack [to *set* dogs *on* intruders] **2** to attack **—set out 1** to limit; define; mark out **2** to plan; lay out (a town, garden, etc.) **3** to display, as for sale; exhibit **4** to plant **5** to take upon oneself; undertake [to *set out* to prove a theory] **6** to begin: with *on* [to *set out* on a long journey] **—set to 1** to make a beginning; get to work; begin **2** to begin fighting **—set up 1** *a)* to place in an upright position *b)* to place in a high position *c)* to raise to power *d)* to raise *e)* to present (oneself) as being something specified *f)* to present (something) as exemplary **2** to put together or erect (a tent, machine, etc.) **3** to establish; found **4** to make detailed plans for **5** to begin **6** to provide with money, etc., as for a business; fit out **7** to cause to feel stimulated, exhilarated, etc. **8** to make successful, well-to-do, etc. **9** to advance or propose (a theory, etc.) **10** to cause **11** *a)* to put (drinks, etc.) before customers ☆*b)* to pay for (food, drinks, etc.) for (another or others) ☆**12** [Informal] *a)* to put (someone) in a vulnerable situation or position, usually by deceit *b)* FRAME (***vt.*** 8) **13** to prepare the way for, lay the foundation for, make ready for, etc. **—set upon** to attack, esp. with violence

***USAGE*—set** and its inflections (**set, setting**), meaning putting or placing *something else* down, are commonly confused with **sit** and its inflections (**sat, sitting**), meaning being, or putting *oneself,* in a seated position

Set (set) ***n.*** ⟦Gr *Sēth* < Egypt *sth, štsh*⟧ *Egypt. Myth.* a god of evil, represented as having an animal's head with square-tipped ears

se·ta (sēt′ə) ***n.***, *pl.* **-tae** (-ē) ⟦ModL < L *seta, saeta,* a stiff hair < IE base **sei-*, cord > SINEW, OE *sal,* rope⟧ *Biol.* a bristle or bristlelike part or organ

se·ta·ceous (si tā′shəs) ***adj.*** ⟦ModL *setaceus* < *seta*: see prec.⟧ **1** having bristles **2** like a bristle or bristles; bristlelike **—se·ta′ceous·ly *adv.***

☆**set-a·side** (set′ə sīd′) ***n.*** something set aside or reserved, as by the government, for a specific purpose, for the use or benefit of a particular group, etc.

set·back (set′bak′) ***n.* 1** a reversal, check, or interruption in progress; relapse; upset **2** *a)* the required minimum distance between a building and a property line (often, specif., the front property line) established by local code or ordinance *b)* an upper part of a wall or building set back to form a steplike section **3** PITCH[2] (***n.*** 8)

se-ten·ant (sə ten′ənt, set′ə nän′) ***adj.*** ⟦Fr, lit., holding each other⟧ designating or of postage stamps joined together as pairs or larger sets, but differing in design, denomination, overprint, etc. **—*n.*** a se-tenant stamp Also written **setenant**

Seth[1] (seth) ***n.*** ⟦LL(Ec) < Gr(Ec) *Sēth* < Heb *shet*, lit., appointed < *shat*, to put⟧ **1** a masculine name **2** *Bible* the third son of Adam: Gen. 4:25

Seth[2] (sāt) ***n.*** *var. of* SET

SETI (set′ē) *abbrev.* search for extraterrestrial intelligence

se·ti- (sēt′i, -ə) ⟦< L *saeta*, a stiff hair: see SETA⟧ *combining form* bristle [*setiform*]

se·ti·fer·ous (sə tif′ər əs) ***adj.*** *Biol.* having setae (see SETA): also **se·tig·er·ous** (sə tij′ər əs)

se·ti·form (sēt′ə fôrm′) ***adj.*** ⟦SETI- + -FORM⟧ resembling a seta, or bristle, in shape

set-in (set′in′) ***adj.*** made as a separate unit to fit within another part [a *set-in* sleeve]

set·off (set′ôf′) ***n.* 1** a thing that makes up for or sets off something else;

counterbalance; compensation **2** *a)* a counterbalancing debt claimed by a debtor against a creditor *b)* a claim for this **3** OFFSET (*n.* 4 & 8)

Se·ton (sēt′'n) **1** Saint **Elizabeth Ann** (born *Elizabeth Ann Bayley*) (1774-1821); Am. Rom. Catholic leader: 1st native-born Am. saint: her day is Jan. 4 **2 Ernest Thompson** (born *Ernest Seton Thompson*) 1860-1946; U.S. naturalist, writer, & illustrator, born in England

se·tose (sē′tōs′) *adj.* ⟦L *saetosus*⟧ SETACEOUS

set piece **1** a carefully contrived work of literature, music, etc., or a discrete part of such a work, usually designed to produce an impressive effect and often employing a conventional method or form and a stylized manner **2** a scenic display of fireworks **3** a piece of stage scenery **4** any situation carefully planned beforehand, as in a military or diplomatic maneuver

set point *Tennis* **1** a situation in which the next point scored can decide the winner of the set **2** this point

set·screw (set′skrōō′) *n.* **1** a machine screw passing through one part and against or into another to prevent movement, as of a ring around a shaft **2** a screw used in regulating or adjusting the tension of a spring, etc.

☆**set shot** *Basketball* a shot attempted by a player while standing in place, rather than while jumping in the air

sett (set) *n.* ⟦ME, var. sp. of SET⟧ [Brit.] **1** the burrow of a badger **2** a rectangular stone, usually of granite, used for paving

set·tee (se tē′) *n.* ⟦prob. altered < SETTLE[1]⟧ **1** a seat or bench with a back, usually for two or three people **2** a small or medium-sized sofa

set·ter (set′ər) *n.* **1** a person who sets or a thing used in setting: often used in compounds *[pinsetter]* **2** ⟦< SET (*vt.* 16)⟧ a member of any of three breeds (ENGLISH SETTER, GORDON SETTER, IRISH SETTER) of long-haired bird dog trained to find game and point out its position while standing rigid

set theory the branch of mathematics that deals with the properties and relations of sets: see SET (*n.* 8)

set·ting (set′iŋ) *n.* **1** the act of one that sets **2** the position or adjustment of something, as a dial, that has been set **3** a thing in or upon which something is set; specif., the backing for a gem or gems, or the style or shape of this *[a marquise setting]* **4** the time, place, environment, and surrounding circumstances of an event, story, play, etc. **5** actual physical surroundings or scenery whether real or, as on a stage, artificial **6** the music or the composing of music for a set of words, as a poem **7** *a)* the eggs in the nest of a brooding hen *b)* a batch of eggs to be artificially incubated **8** PLACE SETTING

set·ting-up exercises (set′iŋ up′) CALISTHENICS

set·tle[1] (set′'l) *n.* ⟦ME *settel* < OE *setl* (akin to Ger *sessel*) < IE **sedla-* < base **sed-* > SIT⟧ a long wooden bench with a back, armrests, and sometimes a chest beneath the seat

set·tle[2] (set′'l) *vt.* **-tled, -tling** ⟦ME *setlen* < OE *setlan* < *setl*, a seat: see prec.⟧ **1** to put in order; arrange or adjust as desired *[to settle one's affairs]* **2** to set in place firmly or comfortably *[to settle oneself in a chair]* **3** to establish as a resident or residents *[he settled his family in London]* **4** to migrate to and set up a community in; colonize *[New York was settled by the Dutch]* **5** to cause to sink and become more dense and compact *[the rain settled the dust]* **6** to clarify (a liquid) by causing the sediment to sink to the bottom **7** to free (the mind, nerves, stomach, etc.) from disturbance; calm or quiet **8** to prevent from creating a disturbance or interfering, or from continuing in such action, as by a reprimand or a blow **9** to make stable or permanent; establish **10** to establish in business, office, work, marriage, etc. **11** to fix definitely; determine or decide (something in doubt) **12** to end (a dispute) **13** to pay (a bill, debt, account, etc.) **14** to make over (property, etc.) to someone by legal action: with *on* or *upon* **15** to resolve (a legal dispute) by agreement between the parties **16** to impregnate (a female): said of a male animal —*vi.* **1** to stop moving and stay in one place; come to rest **2** to cast itself, as darkness, fog, etc. over a landscape, or gloom or silence over a person or group; descend **3** to become localized in a given part of the body: said of pain or disease **4** to take up permanent residence; make one's home **5** to move downward; sink, esp. gradually *[the car settled in the mud]* **6** to become more dense or compact by sinking, as sediment or loose soil does when shaken **7** to become clearer by the settling of sediment or dregs **8** to become more stable or composed; stop fluctuating or changing **9** *a)* to reach an agreement or decision (usually with *with, on,* or *upon*) ☆*b)* to accept something in place of what is hoped for, demanded, etc. (with *for*) *[he'll settle for any kind of work]* **10** to pay a bill or debt —**SYN.** DECIDE —**settle down** **1** to take up permanent residence, a regular job, etc.; lead a more routine, stable life, as after marriage **2** to become less nervous, restless, or erratic **3** to become calm as by diminishing in force **4** to apply oneself steadily or attentively —**settle up** to determine what is owed and make the necessary adjustments

set·tle·ment (-mənt) *n.* **1** a settling or being settled (in various senses) **2** a new colony, or a place newly colonized **3** *a)* a small or isolated community; village *b)* a community established by the members of a particular religious or social group **4** an agreement, arrangement, or adjustment **5** *a)* the conveyance or disposition of property for the benefit of a person or persons *b)* the property thus conveyed **6** an institution in a depressed and congested neighborhood offering social services and educational and recreational activities: also **settlement house**

set·tler (set′lər) *n.* **1** a person or thing that settles ☆**2** a person who settles in a new country or colony

set·tlings (set′liŋz) *pl.n.* the solid matter that settles to the bottom of a liquid; sediment; dregs

set·tlor (set′lər) *n. Law* **1** a person who makes a settlement of property **2** a person who creates a trust by conveying property to a trustee; trustor

set-to (set′tōō′) *n., pl.* **-tos′** ⟦< SET TO (see phr. under SET)⟧ [Informal] **1** a fight or struggle; esp., a fist fight **2** any brisk or vigorous contest or argument; bout

set·up (set′up′) *n.* **1** the way in which something is set up; specif., *a)* the plan, makeup, or arrangement, as of equipment or an organization *b)* the details of a situation, plan of action, etc. ☆**2** bodily posture; carriage ☆**3** the glass, ice, soda water, etc. provided for preparing an alcoholic drink ☆**4** [Informal] *a)* a contest deliberately arranged as an uneven match to result in an easy victory *b)* the contestant marked for defeat in such a contest *c)* an undertaking that is, or is purposely made, very easy, or a goal or result that is easy to achieve *d)* a person who is easily tricked —*adj.* ☆*Baseball* of or having to do with a relief pitcher who specializes in pitching just before the closer

Seu·rat (sö rä′), **Georges (Pierre)** (zhôrzh) 1859-91; Fr. painter: noted for his use of pointillism

Seuss (sōōs), **Dr.** *pseudonym for* Theodor Seuss GEISEL

Se·vas·to·pol (sə vas′tə pōl′; *Russ* se′väs tô′pəl y′) seaport in SW Crimea, on the Black Sea

sev·en (sev′ən) *adj.* ⟦ME *seoven* < OE *seofon*, akin to Ger *sieben* < IE base **septṃ* > L *septem*, Gr *heptá*⟧ totaling one more than six —*n.* **1** the cardinal number between six and eight; 7; VII **2** any group of seven people or things **3** something numbered seven or having seven units, as a playing card or a throw of dice

Seven against Thebes *Gr. Myth.* the expedition of seven heroes, including Polynices, to recover his share of the throne of Thebes from his brother Eteocles: subject of a tragedy by Aeschylus

sev·en-card stud (sev′ən kärd′) a variety of stud poker in which seven cards are dealt to each player, the first two and the last face down, the others face up, the betting being done after each round of cards dealt face up and after the final round

sev·en·fold (sev′ən fōld′) *adj.* ⟦SEVEN + -FOLD⟧ **1** having seven parts **2** having seven times as much or as many —*adv.* seven times as much or as many

Seven Hills of Rome seven low hills on the E bank of the Tiber, on & about which Rome was originally built; Aventine, Caelian, Esquiline, Palatine (approximately in the center), Capitoline, Quirinal, & Viminal

seven seas all the oceans of the world

sev·en·teen (sev′ən tēn′) *adj.* ⟦ME *seventene* < OE *seofentyne*: see SEVEN & -TEEN⟧ totaling seven more than ten —*n.* the cardinal number between sixteen and eighteen; 17; XVII

sev·en·teenth (-tēnth′) *adj.* ⟦ME *sevententhe*: see prec. & -TH[2]⟧ **1** preceded by sixteen others in a series; 17th **2** designating any of the seventeen equal parts of something —*n.* **1** the one following the sixteenth **2** any of the seventeen equal parts of something; 1/17 —*adv.* in the seventeenth place, rank, group, etc.

Seven Hills of Rome
(A.D. 350)

☆**sev·en·teen-year locust** (sev′ən tēn′yir′) a cicada (*Magicicada septendecim*) which lives underground as a larva for from thirteen to seventeen years before emerging as an adult to live in the open for a brief period

sev·enth (sev′ənth) *adj.* ⟦ME *seventhe*, a new formation < *seoven* + *-th*, replacing OE *seofande* (akin to Ger *siebente*) & *seofotha*⟧ **1** preceded by six others in a series; 7th **2** designating any of the seven equal parts of something —*n.* **1** the one following the sixth **2** any of the seven equal parts of something; 1/7 **3** *Music* *a)* the seventh tone of an ascending diatonic scale, or a tone six degrees above or below any given tone in such a scale; leading tone; subtonic *b)* the interval between two such tones, or a combination of them *c)* the chord formed by any tone and the third, fifth, and seventh of which it is the fundamental (in full **seventh chord**) —*adv.* in the seventh place, rank, group, etc. —**sev′enth·ly** *adv.*

sev·enth-day (-dā′) *adj.* **1** of the seventh day (Saturday) **2** [*often* **Seventh-Day**] observing the Sabbath on Saturday *[Seventh-Day Adventists]*

seventh heaven **1** in certain ancient cosmological systems, the outermost of the concentric spheres viewed as enclosing the earth, in which God and the angels reside **2** a condition of perfect happiness

sev·en·ti·eth (sev′ən tē ith; *often*, -ən dē-) *adj.* ⟦ME *seventithe*: see fol. & -TH[2]⟧ **1** preceded by sixty-nine others in a series; 70th **2** designating any of the seventy equal parts of something —*n.* **1** the one following the sixty-ninth **2** any of the seventy equal parts of something; 1/70 —*adv.* in the seventieth place, rank, group, etc.

sev·en·ty (sev′ən tē; *often*, -ən dē) *adj.* ⟦ME *seofentig* < OE *(hund)seofontig*: see SEVEN & -TY[2]⟧ seven times ten —*n., pl.* **-ties** the cardinal number between sixty-nine and seventy-one; 70; LXX —**the seventies** the numbers or years, as of a century, from seventy through seventy-nine

☆**sev·en-up** (sev′ən up′) ***n.*** ⟦so called because *seven* points win a game⟧ ALL FOURS: name used in the U.S.

Seven Wonders of the World seven remarkable landmarks of ancient times: the Egyptian pyramids, the walls and hanging gardens of Babylon, the Mausoleum at Halicarnassus, the temple of Artemis at Ephesus, the Colossus of Rhodes, the statue of Zeus by Phidias at Olympia, and the Pharos (or lighthouse) at Alexandria

Seven Years' War a war (1756-63) in which England and Prussia defeated Austria, France, Russia, Sweden, and Saxony

sev·er (sev′ər) ***vt., vi.*** ⟦ME *severen* < OFr *sevrer, severer* < VL **seperare* < L *separare*, to SEPARATE⟧ **1** to separate; make or become distinct; divide [*severed* from his family by the war] **2** to part or break off, as by cutting or with force; cut in two [to *sever* a cable, *sever* all ties to an estranged wife] **—*SYN.*** SEPARATE

sev·er·a·ble (-ə bəl) ***adj.*** **1** that can be severed or divided **2** *Law* separable into distinct, independent obligations: said of a contract **—sev′er·a·bil′i·ty *n.***

sev·er·al (sev′ər əl, sev′rəl) ***adj.*** ⟦ME < Anglo-Fr < ML *separalis* < L *separ*, separate, back-form. < *separare*: see SEPARATE⟧ **1** existing apart; separate; distinct; individual **2** different; respective [parted and went their *several* ways] **3** more than two but not many; of an indefinite but small number; few **4** [Chiefly Dial.] quite a few; many **5** *Law* of or having to do with an individual person; not shared or joint **—*pl.n.*** an indefinite but small number (*of* persons or things) **—*pron.*** [*with pl. v.*] several persons or things; a few

sev·er·al·ly (-ē) ***adv.*** **1** separately; distinctly **2** respectively; individually

sev·er·al·ty (-tē) ***n.***, *pl.* **-ties** ⟦ME *severalte* < Anglo-Fr *severauté*: see SEVERAL & -TY[1]⟧ **1** the condition or character of being several or distinct **2** property owned by individual right, not shared with any other **3** the condition of property so owned

sev·er·ance (sev′ər əns, sev′rəns) ***n.*** ⟦ME < Anglo-Fr < OFr *sevrance*⟧ a severing or being severed **—*adj.*** of or having to do with extra compensation given to an employee dismissed from a job

se·vere (sə vir′) ***adj.*** **-ver′er, -ver′est** ⟦< MFr < OFr < L *severus*, prob. < *se-*, apart (see SECEDE) + IE base **wer-*, (to be) friendly > OE *wær*, faith, pledge, bond (of friendship)⟧ **1** harsh, strict, or highly critical, as in treatment; unsparing; stern **2** serious or grave; forbidding, as in expression or manner **3** serious or grievous [a *severe* wound] **4** conforming strictly to a rule, method, standard, etc.; rigidly accurate or demanding [a *severe* philosophy] **5** extremely plain or simple; unornamented; restrained [a dress with *severe* lines] **6** keen; extreme; intense [*severe* pain] **7** difficult; rigorous; trying [a *severe* test] **—se·vere′ly *adv.* —se·vere′ness *n.***

SYN.—**severe** applies to a person or thing that is strict and uncompromising and connotes a total absence of softness, laxity, frivolity, etc. [a *severe* critic, hairdo, etc.]; **stern** implies an unyielding firmness, esp. as manifested in a grim or forbidding aspect or manner [a *stern* guardian]; **austere** suggests harsh restraint, self-denial, stark simplicity [the *austere* diet of wartime], or an absence of warmth, passion, ornamentation, etc. [an *austere* bedroom]; **ascetic** implies extreme self-denial and self-discipline or even, sometimes, the deliberate self-infliction of pain and discomfort [an *ascetic* hermit] **—*ANT.* mild, lax, indulgent**

se·ver·i·ty (sə ver′ə tē) ***n.*** ⟦Fr *sévérité* < L *severitas*⟧ **1** the quality or condition of being severe; specif., *a)* strictness; harshness *b)* gravity, as of expression *c)* rigid accuracy *d)* extreme plainness or restraint, as in style *e)* keenness, as of pain; intensity *f)* rigorous or trying character **2** *pl.* **-ties** something severe, as a punishment

Sev·ern (sev′ərn) river flowing from central Wales through England & into the Bristol Channel: *c.* 200 mi (322 km)

Se·ver·na·ya Zem·lya (sev′ər nə yä′ zem lyä′) group of Russian islands in N Asian Russia north of the Taimyr Peninsula, between the Kara & Laptev seas: 14,175 sq mi (36,713 sq km)

Seversky, Alexander *see* DE SEVERSKY

Se·ver·us (sə vir′əs), **(Lucius Septimius)** A.D. 146-211; Rom. emperor (193-211)

se·vi·che (sə vē′chā, -chē) ***n.*** ⟦AmSp⟧ CEVICHE

Sé·vi·gné (sā vē nyā′), Marquise **de** (born *Marie de Rabutin-Chantal*) 1626-96; Fr. writer

Se·ville (sə vil′) city in SW Spain, on the Guadalquivir River: Spanish name **Se·vi·lla** (sā vē′lyä)

☆**Sev·in** (sev′in) ⟦so named from the groups of *seven* atoms in its molecular structure⟧ *trademark for* CARBARYL

Sè·vres (sev′rə; *Fr* se′vr′) ***n.*** ⟦after *Sèvres*, SW suburb of Paris, where made⟧ a type of fine French porcelain

sev·ru·ga (caviar) (sev ro͞o′gə) ⟦< Russ *sevrjuga*, this species of sturgeon⟧ caviar prepared from the small, grayish or black roe of a sturgeon chiefly from the Caspian Sea

sew (sō) ***vt.*** **sewed, sewn** or **sewed, sew′ing** ⟦ME *sewen* < OE *siwian*, akin to Goth *siujan* < IE base **siw-*, to sew > SEAM, L *suere* (pp. *sutus*), to sew, sew together⟧ **1** to join or fasten with stitches made with needle and thread **2** to make, mend, enclose, etc. by such means **—*vi.*** to work with needle and thread or at a sewing machine **—sew up 1** to close or bring together the edges of with stitches **2** to enclose in something by sewing ☆**3** [Informal] *a)* to get or have absolute control of or right to; monopolize *b)* to bring to a successful conclusion *c)* to make certain of success in [to *sew up* an election]

sew·age (so͞o′ij) ***n.*** ⟦SEW(ER)[1] + -AGE⟧ the waste matter carried off by sewers or drains

Sew·all (so͞o′əl), **Samuel** 1652-1730; Am. jurist, born in England: presided over witchcraft trials at Salem

☆**se·wan** (sē′wən) ***n.*** ⟦Du < unattested Delaware dial. word for unstrung wampum beads < root *se·w-*, to scatter⟧ shells used as money by the Algonquian Indians

Sew·ard (so͞o′ərd), **William Henry** 1801-72; U.S. statesman: secretary of state (1861-69)

Seward Peninsula ⟦after prec., who directed the purchase of Alaska from Russia (1867)⟧ peninsula of W Alas. on the Bering Strait: *c.* 200 mi (321 km) long

sew·er[1] (so͞o′ər) ***n.*** ⟦ME < MFr *esseweur* < *essever*, to drain off < VL **exaquare* < L *ex*, out + *aqua*, water: see ISLAND⟧ a pipe or drain, usually underground, used to carry off water and waste matter **—*vi.*** to maintain sewers

sew·er[2] (sō′ər) ***n.*** a person or thing that sews

sew·er[3] (so͞o′ər) ***n.*** ⟦ME, aphetic < Anglo-Fr *asseour* < OFr *asseoir*, to seat, cause to sit < L *assidere*, to sit by < *ad-*, to + *sedere*, to SIT⟧ a medieval servant of high rank in charge of serving meals and seating guests

sew·er·age (so͞o′ər ij) ***n.*** **1** removal of surface water and waste matter by sewers **2** a system of sewers **3** SEWAGE

sew·ing (sō′iŋ) ***n.*** **1** the act or occupation of a person who sews **2** material or items sewn or to be sewn

☆**sewing circle** a group of women who meet regularly to sew, as for some charitable purpose

☆**sewing machine** a machine with a mechanically driven needle, used for sewing and stitching

sewn (sōn) ***vt., vi. alt. pp. of*** SEW

sex (seks) ***n.*** ⟦ME < L *sexus* < ? *secare*, to cut, divide: see SAW[1]⟧ **1** either of the two divisions, male or female, into which persons, animals, or plants are divided, with reference to their reproductive functions **2** the character of being male or female; all the attributes by which males and females are distinguished **3** anything connected with sexual gratification or reproduction or the urge for these; esp., the attraction of those of one sex for those of the other **4** INTERCOURSE (sense 2) **5** the genitalia **—*adj.*** SEXUAL [*sex* education] **—*vt.*** to ascertain the sex of (chickens, etc.) **—sex up** [Slang] **1** to arouse sexually **2** to give appealing or titillating characteristics to

sex- (seks) ⟦< L *sex*, SIX⟧ *combining form* six

sex·a·ge·nar·i·an (sek′sə ji ner′ē ən) ***adj.*** ⟦< L *sexagenarius*, of sixty < *sexageni*, sixty each + -AN⟧ 60 years old, or between the ages of 60 and 70 **—*n.*** a sexagenarian person

Sex·a·ges·i·ma (sek′sə jā′zi mə, -jes′i mə) ***n.*** ⟦ME *sexagesime* < LL(Ec) *sexagesima (dies)* < fem. of L *sexagesimus*, sixtieth (+ *dies*, day), as in QUINQUAGESIMA, QUADRAGESIMA: reason for name uncert.⟧ *former name for* the second Sunday before Lent: also **Sexagesima Sunday**

sex·a·ges·i·mal (-jes′i məl) ***adj.*** ⟦ML *sexagesimalis* < L *sexagesimus*, sixtieth < *sexaginta*, sixty⟧ of or based on the number sixty

☆**sex appeal** the physical attractiveness and erotic charm that make a person sexually attractive

sex chromosome a sex-determining chromosome in the germ cells of most animals and a few plants: in most animals, including human beings, all the eggs carry an X chromosome and the spermatozoa either an X or a Y chromosome, and an egg receiving an X chromosome at fertilization will develop into a female (XX) while one receiving a Y will develop into a male (XY)

sexed (sekst) ***adj.*** **1** of or having sex or sexual differentiation **2** having (a specified degree of) sexuality

sex·en·ni·al (sek sen′ē əl) ***adj.*** ⟦< L *sexennium*, six years < *sex*, SIX + *annus* (see ANNUAL) + -AL⟧ **1** happening every six years **2** lasting six years **—sex·en′ni·al·ly *adv.***

sex hormone any hormone, as testosterone, estrogen, etc., influencing the development of, or having an effect upon, the reproductive organs, secondary sex characteristics, etc.

☆**sex hygiene** the branch of hygiene dealing with sex and sexual behavior: an earlier term for sex education

sex·i- (sek′sə) *combining form* SEX-

sex·i·ly (sek′sə lē) ***adv.*** [Informal] in a sexy manner

sex·i·ness (-sē nis) ***n.*** [Informal] a sexy state or quality

☆**sex·ism** (seks′iz′əm) ***n.*** ⟦SEX + (RAC)ISM⟧ discrimination against people on the basis of sex; specif., discrimination against, and prejudicial stereotyping of, women **—sex′ist *adj., n.***

☆**sex kitten** [Slang] a young woman who has much sex appeal

sex·less (seks′lis) ***adj.*** **1** lacking the characteristics of sex; asexual; neuter **2** lacking in normal sexual appetite or appeal; sexually cold **3** not involving sexual activity [a *sexless* marriage] **—sex′less·ly *adv.* —sex′less·ness *n.***

sex linkage *Genetics* the phenomenon by which inherited characters are determined by genes carried on one of the sex chromosomes and are consequently linked with the sex of an individual **—sex′-linked′** (-liŋkt′) ***adj.***

sex object a person regarded or valued mainly on the basis of his or her sexual attractiveness, exclusive of any other personal qualities or attributes: used mainly in reference to women

sex·ol·o·gy (sek säl′ə jē) ***n.*** the science dealing with human sexual behavior **—sex′o·log′i·cal *adj.* —sex·ol′o·gist *n.***

☆**sex·ploi·ta·tion** (seks′ploi tā′shən) ***n.*** ⟦SEX + (EX)PLOITATION⟧ the use of titillating sexual material, esp. in a film, to increase commercial appeal

☆**sex·pot** (seks′pät′) ***n.*** ⟦SEX + POT¹⟧ [Slang] a woman who has much sex appeal

☆**sex symbol** [Informal] a well-known person who is generally regarded as representative of sexual attractiveness

sext (sekst) ***n.*** ⟦ME *sexte* < ML(Ec) *sexta* < L *sexta (hora)*, sixth (hour), fem. of *sextus*, SIXTH⟧ [*often* **S-**] the fourth of the canonical hours, originally assigned to the sixth hour of the day (i.e., to noon, counting from 6 A.M.)

Sex·tans (seks′tənz) ***n.*** ⟦ModL: see fol.⟧ an equatorial constellation between Leo and Hydra

sex·tant (seks′tənt) ***n.*** ⟦ModL *sextans* (gen. *sextantis*), arc of a sixth part of a circle < L, a sixth part < *sextus*, SIXTH⟧ an instrument used by navigators for measuring the angular distance of the sun, a star, etc. from the horizon, as in finding the position of a ship

sex·tet or **sex·tette** (seks tet′) ***n.*** ⟦altered by assoc. with L *sex*, SIX < SESTET⟧ **1** a group of six persons or things **2** *Music a)* a composition for six voices or six instruments *b)* a group of six performers of such a composition, or any group of six musicians playing together

sex·tile (seks′təl) *Astrol.* ***n.*** ⟦L *sextilis* < *sextus*, SIXTH⟧ the aspect of two celestial bodies 60 degrees, or one sixth of a circle, apart —***adj.*** designating this aspect

sex·til·lion (seks til′yən) ***n.*** ⟦Fr < L *sextus*, sixth (< *sex*, SIX) + Fr *(m)illion*⟧ ☆**1** the number represented by 1 followed by 21 zeros **2** [Brit.] the number represented by 1 followed by 36 zeros —***adj.*** amounting to one sextillion in number —**sex·til′lionth** ***adj., n.***

sext·ing (seks′tiŋ) ***n.*** ⟦blend of SEX & TEXTING⟧ [Informal] the sending or exchanging of sexually explicit text messages or images by email or social media

sex·to·dec·i·mo (seks′tō des′ə mō′) ***n., pl.*** **-mos′** ⟦< L *(in) sextodecimo*, (in) sixteen, abl. of *sextusdecimus*, sixteenth⟧ SIXTEENMO

sex·ton (seks′tən) ***n.*** ⟦ME *sextein*, altered < *segerstane* < OFr *segrestain* < ML *sacristanus*: see SACRISTAN⟧ a church officer or employee in charge of the maintenance of church property: duties may include ringing the church bells and digging graves in the churchyard

sex·tu·ple (seks to͞o′pəl, seks′tə pəl) ***adj.*** ⟦< L *sextus*, SIXTH, after QUADRUPLE⟧ **1** consisting of or including six **2** six times as much or as many; sixfold **3** *Music* having six beats to a measure —***n.*** an amount six times as much or as many — ***vt., vi.*** **-pled**, **-pling** to make or become six times as much or as many; multiply by six

sex·tu·plet (seks to͞o′plit, -tup′lit; seks′tə plit) ***n.*** ⟦dim. of prec.⟧ **1** any of six offspring from the same pregnancy **2** a collection or group of six, usually of one kind **3** *Music* a group of six equal notes to be played in the same time as four of the same value would be played in the set rhythm

Sex·tus (seks′təs) ***n.*** ⟦L⟧ *Rom. History* a masculine praenomen

sex·u·al (sek′sho͞o əl) ***adj.*** ⟦LL *sexualis*⟧ **1** of, characteristic of, or involving sex, the sexes, the organs of sex and their functions, or the instincts, drives, behavior, etc. associated with sex **2** *Biol. a)* having sex *b)* designating or of reproduction involving the fertilization of a female gamete by a male gamete —**sex′u·al·ly** ***adv.***

sexual harassment inappropriate, unwelcome, and, typically, persistent behavior, as by an employer or co-worker, that is sexual in nature, specif. when actionable under federal or state statutes

sexual intercourse **1** a joining of the sexual organs of a male and a female, in which the erect penis of the male is inserted into the vagina of the female, usually with the ejaculation of semen into the vagina **2** INTERCOURSE (sense 2*b*)

sex·u·al·i·ty (sek′sho͞o al′ə tē) ***n.*** **1** the state or quality of being sexual **2** *a)* interest in or concern with sex *b)* sexual drive or activity **3** SEXUAL ORIENTATION

sex·u·al·ize (sek′sho͞o ə līz′) ***vt.*** **-ized′**, **-iz′ing** to make sexual; endow with sexual significance, feeling, etc.

sexual orientation a person's SEXUALITY (sense 2) with respect to his or her sexual desire; heterosexuality, homosexuality, bisexuality, etc.

sex worker any person paid to sexually gratify or arouse a customer, as a prostitute, a model in pornographic magazines, or a performer in pornographic films or nightclub acts —**sex work**

sex·y (sek′sē) ***adj.*** **sex′i·er**, **sex′i·est** **1** [Informal] exciting or intended to excite sexual desire **2** [Slang] exciting, glamorous, etc.

Sey·chelles (sā shel′, -shelz′) country on a group of islands in the Indian Ocean, northeast of Madagascar: formerly a British colony, it became independent as a republic within the Commonwealth (1976): 176 sq mi (455 sq km); cap. Victoria (on Mahé Island)

Sey·chell·ois (sā′shel wä′) ***n., pl.*** **-ois′** (-wäz′, -wä′) a person born or living in the Seychelles

☆**Sey·fert galaxy** (sē′fərt) ⟦after C. K. *Seyfert* (1911-60), U.S. astronomer who described the galaxies in 1943⟧ any of a number of spiral galaxies with a small, intensely bright nucleus and a spectrum with strong, broad spectral lines

Sey·mour¹ (sē′môr) ***n.*** ⟦orig. a surname, prob. < OE *sæ*, sea + *mor*, hill⟧ a masculine name

Sey·mour² (sē′môr), **Jane** 1509?-37; 3d wife of Henry VIII of England: mother of Edward VI

sf¹ or **SF** *abbrev.* **1** science fiction **2** square foot; square feet

sf² *abbrev.* sforzando

Sfax (sfäks) seaport on the E coast of Tunisia

SFC *abbrev.* Sergeant First Class

☆**sfer·ics** (sfer′iks, sfir′-) ***n.*** ⟦altered & shortened < ATMOSPHERICS⟧ **1** ATMOSPHERICS **2** the study of atmospherics; esp., the locating, tracking, and evaluating of natural electrical discharges

Sfor·za (sfôr′tsä) **1** Count **Car·lo** (kär′lô) 1873-1952; It. statesman & anti-Fascist leader **2 Fran·ces·co** (frän ches′kô) 1401-66; It. condottiere & duke of Milan **3 Lu·do·vi·co** (lo͞o′dô vē′kộ) 1451-1508; duke of Milan & patron of da Vinci: son of Francesco: also **Lo′do·vi′co** (lô′-)

sfor·zan·do (sfôr tsän′dō) [*also in italics*] *Music* ***adj., adv.*** ⟦It < *sforzare*, to force: *s-* (< L *ex-*, intens.) + VL **fortiare* < **fortia*, FORCE⟧ with sudden force or emphasis: a musical direction —***n., pl.*** **-dos** a sforzando note or chord

sfu·ma·to (sfo͞o mä′tō) ***n.*** ⟦It < pp. of *sfumare*, to evaporate⟧ an effect, as in oil painting, of the tones shading into one another so that there are no sharp outlines

sfz *abbrev.* sforzando

sg *abbrev.* specific gravity

Sg¹ *abbrev. Bible* Song of Solomon

Sg² *Chem. symbol for* seaborgium

sgd *abbrev.* signed

SGM *abbrev.* Sergeant Major

SGML *abbrev.* Standard Generalized Markup Language

sgraf·fi·to (skra fē′tō; *It* zgräf fē′tô) ***n., pl.*** **-ti** (-tē) ⟦It < *sgraffiare*, to scratch < *s-*, intens. (< L *ex-*) + *graffiare*, to scratch < L *graphium*, a writing style < Gr *graphion* < *graphein*: see GRAPHIC⟧ **1** a method of producing a design on ceramics, murals, etc. by incising the outer coating of slip or glaze to reveal a ground of a different color **2** such a design **3** an object bearing such a design

's Gra·ven·ha·ge (skhrä′vən hä′khə) *Du. name for* The HAGUE

Sgs *abbrev. Bible* Song of Solomon

Sgt *abbrev.* Sergeant

Sgt Maj *abbrev.* Sergeant Major

sh¹ (sh: *often a prolonged sound*) ***interj.*** *alt. sp. of* SHH

sh² *abbrev.* **1** share(s) **2** *Bookbinding* sheet **3** shilling(s)

sha (shô) ***interj.*** *alt. sp. of* SHAH²

Shaan·xi (shän′shē′) province of NC China: 75,599 sq mi (195,801 sq km); cap. Xi'an

Shab·bat (shä bät′) ***n., pl.*** **Shab·bat·ot′** (-bä tōt′) ⟦Heb *shabat*, SABBATH⟧ *Judaism* the Sabbath: also ⟦Yiddish *shabes* < Heb *shabat*⟧ **Shab′bos** (-bəs) or **Shab′bes** (-bəs)

shab·by (shab′ē) ***adj.*** **-bi·er**, **-bi·est** ⟦< dial. *shab*, scab, scoundrel < OE *sceabb*, scab, scale: see SCAB⟧ **1** run-down; dilapidated; deteriorated [*shabby* surroundings] **2** *a)* showing much wear; ragged; threadbare (said of clothing) *b)* wearing such clothing; seedy **3** beggarly; unworthy [a *shabby* offering] **4** disgraceful; shameful [*shabby* treatment of guests] —**shab′bi·ly** ***adv.*** —**shab′bi·ness** ***n.***

shab·by-gen·teel (-jen tēl′) ***adj.*** shabby but genteel in trying to keep up appearances

Sha·bu·oth (shä vo͞o′ōt, shə vo͞o′ōs) ***n.*** *var. of* SHAVUOT

Sha·che (shä′chu′) city in W Xinjiang, China; a trading center

☆**shack** (shak) ***n.*** ⟦< ? AmSp *jacal* < Nahuatl *xacalli*, wooden hut⟧ a small house or cabin that is crudely built and furnished; shanty —**shack up** [Slang] **1** to live or room (*in* a certain place) **2** to live (*with* one's lover)

shack·le (shak′əl) ***n.*** ⟦ME *schakel* < OE *sceacel*, akin to MDu *schakel*, chain link < ? IE base **(s)kenk-*, to gird, bind⟧ **1** a metal fastening, usually one of a linked pair, for the wrist or ankle of a prisoner; fetter; manacle **2** anything that restrains freedom of expression or action [the *shackles* of ignorance] **3** any of several devices used in fastening or coupling —***vt.*** **-led**, **-ling** **1** to put shackles on; fetter **2** to fasten or connect with a shackle or shackles **3** to restrain in freedom of expression or action —**shack′ler** ***n.***

Shack·le·ton (shak′əl tən), Sir **Ernest Henry** 1874-1922; Brit. antarctic explorer

shad (shad) ***n., pl.*** **shad** or **shads** ⟦OE *sceadd*, akin to Norw dial. *skadd*, prob. < IE base **skēt-*, to leap, spring up⟧ any of various marine or freshwater clupeid fishes; esp., *a)* an American coastal food fish (*Alosa sapidissima*) *b)* a species (*Dorosoma cepedianum*) widely introduced into fresh waters of the U.S. as food for other fish

☆**shad·ber·ry** (-ber′ē, -bər ē) ***n., pl.*** **-ries** JUNEBERRY

☆**shad·bush** (-bo͝osh′) ***n.*** ⟦from the fact that it flowers when shad appear in U.S. rivers⟧ JUNEBERRY (sense 1): also called **shad′blow′** (-blō′)

shad·chan (shäd′khən, shät′-) ***n.*** ⟦Yiddish *shatkhn* < Heb *shadechan* < *shidekh*, arrange a marriage⟧ a Jewish marriage broker or matchmaker

shad·dock (shad′ək) ***n.*** ⟦after Capt. *Shaddock*, who first carried this fruit from the East to the West Indies (late 17th c.)⟧ **1** a large, yellow, coarse-grained, pear-shaped citrus fruit resembling a grapefruit **2** the citrus tree (*Citrus grandis*) it grows on

shade (shād) ***n.*** ⟦ME *schade* < OE *sceadu* (gen. & dat. *sceadwe*), akin to Goth *skadus* < IE base **skot-*, darkness, shadow > Gr *skotos*, darkness⟧ **1** comparative darkness caused by a more or less opaque object cutting off rays of light, as from the sun **2** *a)* a place giving protection from the heat and light of the sun, as under a tree *b)* an area less brightly lighted than its surroundings **3** [Archaic] *a)* a shadow *b)* [*often pl.*] a retired or secluded place **4** an indication or representation of darkness in painting, drawing, photography, etc. **5** degree of darkness of a color; gradation of a color with reference to its mixture with black [various *shades* of blue]: cf. TINT (***n.*** 2) **6** *a)* a small difference or variation [*shades* of opinion] *b)* a slight amount or degree; trace; touch; suggestion [a *shade* of humor in his voice] **7** [Chiefly Literary] *a)* a ghost; specter *b)* anything lacking substance or reality; phantom **8** any of various devices used to protect or screen from light and heat; specif., *a)* LAMPSHADE ☆*b)* WINDOW SHADE ☆**9** [*pl.*] [Slang] sunglasses —*vt.* **shad′ed**, **shad′ing** **1** to protect or screen from light or heat **2** to provide with a shade **3** to hide or screen with or as with a shadow **4** to make dark, as with a shade or a shadow; darken; dim; obscure **5** *a)* to represent the effects of shade in (a painting, photograph, etc.) *b)* to depict in, or mark with, gradations of light or color **6** to change by very slight degrees or gradations ☆**7** to lessen or reduce (a price) slightly —*vi.* to change, move, or vary slightly or by degrees —**SYN.** COLOR —**in (**or **into) the shade** **1** in (or into) darkness or shadow **2** in (or into) comparative obscurity, or a position of minor importance —**shades of** *an exclamation used to refer to* something reminding one of something (or someone) past [*shades of* Prohibition!] —**the shades** **1** the increasing darkness, as of evening **2** *a)* the world of the dead; Hades *b)* the disembodied spirits of the dead, collectively —**shade′less** *adj.* —**shad′er** *n.*

shad·i·ly (shā′də lē) *adv.* in a shady manner

shad·i·ness (-dē nis) *n.* a shady state or quality

shad·ing (-diŋ) *n.* **1** protection or shielding against light or heat **2** the representation of light or shade in a picture **3** any small difference or variation, as in quality or kind

sha·doof (shä do͞of′) *n.* ⟦Ar *shādūf*⟧ a device consisting of a long, pivoted pole with a bucket on one end and a weight on the other, used in the Near East for raising water, esp. in irrigating land

shad·ow (shad′ō) *n.* ⟦ME *schadwe* < inflected forms (gen. & dat. *sceadwe*) of OE *sceadu*, SHADE⟧ **1** a definite area of shade on a surface, caused by a body blocking light rays **2** the dark image made by such a body **3** [*pl.*] the growing darkness after sunset **4** *a)* a feeling of gloom or depression, a suggestion of doubt, etc. *b)* anything causing gloom, doubt, etc. **5** a shaded area in a picture or X-ray **6** a dark area, as of a very short growth of beard **7** a mirrored image; reflection **8** *a)* something without reality or substance; imaginary vision *b)* a ghost; apparition **9** a vague indication or omen; prefiguration [*shadows* of things to come] **10** *a)* a faint suggestion or appearance; trace [not a *shadow* of hope] *b)* remnant; vestige [a mere *shadow* of his former self] **11** a close or constant companion ☆**12** a person who trails another closely, as a detective or spy **13** [Rare] protection or shelter —*vt.* **1** [Archaic] *a)* to shelter from light or heat *b)* to shelter; protect **2** to throw a shadow upon **3** to make dark or gloomy; cloud **4** to represent vaguely, mystically, or prophetically; prefigure: often with *forth* **5** to stay close to or follow, esp. in secret, so as to observe the movements and activities of —*vi.* **1** to change gradually **2** to become shadowy or clouded (*with* doubt, sorrow, etc.): said of the features —*adj.* **1** of or belonging to a SHADOW CABINET [a *shadow* minister] **2** darker, indistinct, not plainly perceived, etc. —**in (**or **under) the shadow of** **1** very close to; verging upon **2** under the influence or domination of —**under the shadow of** in danger of; apparently fated for —**shad′ow·er** *n.* —**shad′ow·less** *adj.*

shad·ow·box (-bäks′) *vi.* to spar with an imaginary opponent, esp. in training as a boxer —**shad′ow·box′ing** *n.*

☆**shadow box** a small, shallow case, usually having a glass front and hung on a wall, as for displaying small objects

shadow cabinet in the parliament of Great Britain and some other countries, those members of the opposition party who function as unofficial counterparts to the cabinet ministers of the party in power

shad·ow·graph (-graf′, -gräf′) *n.* an image or silhouette produced by throwing a shadow upon a lighted surface

shadow play a play produced by showing to the audience only the shadows of actors or puppets on a screen

shad·ow·y (shad′ō ē) *adj.* **1** that is or is like a shadow; specif., *a)* without reality or substance; illusory *b)* dim; indistinct **2** shaded or full of shadow —**shad′ow·i·ness** *n.*

Sha·drach (sha′drak′, shā′-) *n.* ⟦Heb *shadrach*: prob. a made-up name intended to sound Babylonian: see Dan. 1:7⟧ *Bible* one of the three captives who came out of the fiery furnace miraculously unharmed: Dan. 3:12-27

shad·y (shā′dē) *adj.* **shad′i·er**, **shad′i·est** **1** giving shade **2** shaded, as from the sun; full of shade **3** of darkness; secrecy, or concealment **4** [Informal] of questionable character or honesty

shaft (shaft, shäft) *n.* ⟦ME *schaft* < OE *sceaft*, akin to Ger *schaft* < IE base **(s)kap-*, to cut with a sharp tool > SHAVE, Gr *skapos*, rod, L *scapus*, shaft, stalk⟧ **1** *a)* the long stem or body of an arrow or spear *b)* an arrow or spear **2** a missile or something that seems to be hurled like a missile; bolt [*shafts* of lightning, derision, etc.] **3** a cone or column of light; ray; beam **4** a long, slender part or object; specif., *a)* [Rare] the trunk of a tree or stem of a plant *b)* the stem or rib of a feather *c)* the midsection of a long bone *d)* the supporting stem of a branched candlestick *e)* a column or obelisk; also, the main, usually cylindrical, part between the ends of a column or pillar *f)* a flagpole *g)* a tall, slender building or part of a building; spire *h)* a handle, as on some tools or implements *i)* either of the two poles between which an animal is harnessed to a vehicle; thill *j)* a bar, usually cylindrical, for supporting or transmitting motion to a wheel, pulley, gear, cam, etc. [the drive *shaft* of an engine] **5** a long, narrow, vertical or slanting passage sunk into the earth [a mine *shaft*] **6** a vertical opening passing through the floors of a building, as for an elevator **7** a conduit for air, as used in heating and ventilating —*vt.* [Slang] to cheat, trick, exploit, etc. —**get the shaft** [Slang] to be cheated, tricked, etc. —**give someone the shaft** [Slang] to cheat or trick someone

Shaftes·bur·y (shafts′ber′ē, shäfts′-; -bər ē), 1st Earl of (*Anthony Ashley Cooper*) 1621-83; Eng. statesman: lord chancellor (1672-73)

shaft·ing (shaf′tiŋ, shäf′-) *n.* **1** a system or group of shafts, as for transmitting motion or conveying air **2** material for making shafts

shag[1] (shag) *n.* ⟦ME **shagge* < OE *sceacga*, rough hair, akin to ON *skegg*, beard < IE base **skek-*, to spring forth > SHAKE, Ger *schicken*, to send⟧ **1** [Rare] heavily matted wool or hair **2** a haircut, short in front and longer in back, with multiple layers cut so as to produce a stylishly unkempt look **3** *a)* a heavy, rough nap, as on some woolen cloth *b)* cloth with such a nap **4** any disordered or tangled mass **5** coarse, shredded tobacco —*vt.* **shagged**, **shag′ging** to make shaggy or rough

shag[2] (shag) *n.* ⟦specialized use of prec. with ref. to the bird's rough crest⟧ any of several cormorants, esp. an American double-crested species (*Phalacrocorax auritus*) or a European species (*P. aristotelis*)

shag[3] (shag) *vt.* **shagged**, **shag′ging** ⟦< ?⟧ ☆to chase after and retrieve (baseballs hit in batting practice)

shag[4] (shag) [Brit. Slang] *vt.* **shagged**, **shag′ging** to have sexual intercourse with —*n.* an act of sexual intercourse Somewhat vulgar

shag·a·nap·pi (shag′ə nap′ē) *n.* ⟦altered < Cree dial. *piishaakanaapiy*, lit., leather string⟧ rawhide thongs or lacings, collectively

☆**shag·bark** (shag′bärk′) *n.* **1** a hickory tree (*Carya ovata*) with gray, loose, rough bark **2** its wood **3** its edible nut

shagged (shagd) *adj.* [Brit. Informal] exhausted; tired: often with *out*

shag·gy (shag′ē) *adj.* **-gi·er**, **-gi·est** **1** covered with or having long, coarse hair or wool **2** carelessly groomed; unkempt **3** of tangled, coarse growth; straggly; scrubby **4** having a rough nap or surface —**shag′gi·ly** *adv.* —**shag′gi·ness** *n.*

shaggy dog (story) ⟦as if from such an anecdote involving a *shaggy dog*⟧ a long, rambling joke or anecdote involving strange or absurd incidents and regarded as ultimately pointless

☆**shag·gy·mane** (-mān′) *n.* an edible inky cap mushroom (*Coprinus comatus*) with yellowish scales: also called **shaggy cap**

sha·green (shə grēn′) *n.* ⟦altered (as if from SHAG[1] & GREEN) < Fr *chagrin* < Turk *sağrı*, horse's back, hide from this area⟧ **1** rawhide with a rough, granular surface, made from the skin of the horse, seal, etc. **2** the hard, rough skin of the shark or dogfish, used as a polisher

shah[1] (shä, shô) *n.* ⟦Pers *šāh*, akin to Sans *kṣáyati*, (he) rules < IE base **kthē(i)-*, to acquire, gain power over > Gr *kteanon*, possessions⟧ the title of any of the former rulers of Iran

shah[2] (shô) *interj.* hush; be quiet: sometimes used to soothe a crying baby

Sha·hap·ti·an (shä hap′tē ən) *n. var. of* SAHAPTIAN

Shah Ja·han (shä′ jə hän′) 1592-1666; Mogul emperor of India (1628-58): builder of the Taj Mahal

Shahn (shän), **Ben(jamin)** 1898-1969; U.S. painter, born in Lithuania

shai·tan (shī tän′) *n.* ⟦Ar *šaiṭān*, akin to Heb *saṭan*: see SATAN⟧ [*often* **S-**] Satan, or the Devil, in Muslim usage

Shak *abbrev.* Shakespeare

shake (shāk) *vt.* **shook**, **shak′en**, **shak′ing** ⟦ME *schaken* < OE *sceacan*, akin to LowG *schaken* < IE **skeg-*, var. of base **skek-* > SHAG[1]⟧ **1** to cause to move up and down, back and forth, or from side to side with short, quick movements **2** to pivot (the head) from side to side, specif. as a sign of disagreement, disappointment, disapproval, etc. **3** to bring, force, mix, stir up, dislodge, rearrange, etc. by or as by abrupt, brisk movements [to *shake* a medicine before taking it] **4** *a)* to scatter by short, quick movements of the container [to *shake* pepper on a steak] *b)* to clean, empty, or straighten by short, quick movements (often with *out*) [to *shake* a rug] **5** to cause to quiver or tremble [chills that *shook* his body] **6** *a)* to cause to totter or become unsteady *b)* to unnerve; disturb; upset [he was *shaken* by the news] **7** to brandish; flourish; wave **8** to clasp (another's hand), as in greeting or agreement ☆**9** [Informal] to get away from or rid of [to *shake* one's pursuers] **10** *Music* TRILL —*vi.* **1** to move or be moved quickly and irregularly up and down, back and forth, or from side to side; vibrate **2** to tremble, quake, or quiver, as from cold or fear **3** to become unsteady; totter; reel **4** to clasp each other's hand, as in greeting or agreement **5** *Music* TRILL —*n.* **1** an act of shaking; back-and-forth movement **2** an unsteady or trembling movement; tremor **3** a natural split or fissure in rock or timber **4** a long, rough-hewn shingle split from a log **5** [Informal] an earthquake ☆**6** *short for* MILKSHAKE **7** [*pl.*] [Informal] a convulsive trembling, as from disease, fear, or alcoholism: usually with *the* **8** [Informal] a very short time; moment [be back in a *shake*] **9** [Informal] a particular kind of treatment; deal [to get a fair *shake*] **10** [Informal] HANDSHAKE **11** *Music* TRILL —☆**give someone (**or **something) the shake** [Slang] to avoid or get rid of an undesirable person (or thing) —**no great shakes** [Informal] not of outstanding ability, importance, etc.; ordinary —**shake down** **1** to bring down or cause to fall by shaking **2** to cause to settle by shaking **3** to test or condition (new equipment, etc.) ☆**4** [Slang] to extort money from, as by blackmail —**shake hands** to clasp each other's hand as a token of agreement or friendship, or in parting or greeting —**shake off** **1** to get away from or rid of (an undesirable person or thing) **2** to reject (a suggestion, request, etc.) —**shake up** **1** to shake, esp. so as to mix, blend, or loosen **2** to disturb or rouse by or as by shaking **3** to jar or shock **4** to redistribute or reorganize by or as by shaking —**shak′a·ble** *adj.*, **shake′a·ble**

shake·down (shāk′doun′) *n.* **1** a crude, makeshift bed, as a pallet of straw ☆**2** [Slang] an extortion of money, as by blackmail ☆**3** a thorough search of a person or place —☆*adj.* for testing the performance or operational characteristics or acclimating the personnel [the *shakedown* cruise of a new aircraft carrier]

shak·en (shā′kən) *vt., vi. pp. of* SHAKE

shake·out (-out′) *n.* ☆1 any movement in the market prices of securities that forces speculators to sell their holdings ☆2 any drop in economic activity that eliminates marginal or unprofitable businesses, products, etc.

shak·er (shā′kər) *n.* 1 a person or thing that shakes 2 a device used in shaking [a cocktail *shaker*] ☆3 ⟦short for earlier *Shaking Quaker*: so named because of trembling caused by emotional stress of devotions: see QUAKER⟧ [**S-**] a member of a religious sect that flourished in the 19th cent., practicing celibacy and owning common property for community living —*adj.* [*sometimes* **S-**] designating a sweater knitted in a ribbed stitch (**Shaker stitch**), using heavy yarn —**Shak′er·ism′** *n.*

shaker and mover MOVER AND SHAKER

Shake·speare (shāk′spir), **William** 1564-1616; Eng. poet & dramatist

Shake·spear·e·an or **Shake·spear·i·an** (shāk spir′ē ən) *adj.* of or like Shakespeare, his works, or his style —*n.* a scholar specializing in Shakespeare and his works

Shakespearean sonnet a sonnet composed of three quatrains, typically with the rhyme scheme *abab cdcd efef,* and a final couplet with the rhyme *gg;* English sonnet

shake-up (shāk′up′) *n.* 1 the act or an instance of shaking up ☆2 a reorganization of a drastic or extensive nature, as in policy or personnel

Shakh·ty (shäkh′tē) city in SW European Russia, in the Donets Basin

shaking palsy PARKINSON'S DISEASE

shak·o (shak′ō) *n., pl.* **shak′os** ⟦Fr *schako* < Hung *csákó* < ?⟧ a stiff, cylindrical military dress hat, usually with a flat top and a plume

shako

Shak·ti (shuk′tē) *n.* ⟦Sans *śakti*⟧ *Hinduism* divine power or energy worshiped in the person of the female consort of Siva or another god —**Shak′tism′** *n.*

sha·ku·ha·chi (shä′ko͞o hä′chē) *n.* ⟦Jpn⟧ a Japanese bamboo flute

shak·y (shā′kē) *adj.* **shak′i·er, shak′i·est** 1 not firm, substantial, or secure; weak, unsound, or unsteady: said as of a structure or belief 2 *a)* trembling or tremulous *b)* nervous or jittery 3 not dependable or reliable; questionable —**shak′i·ly** *adv.* —**shak′i·ness** *n.*

shale (shāl) *n.* ⟦< ME, lit., shell < OE *scealu,* SHELL⟧ a kind of fine-grained, thinly bedded sedimentary rock formed largely by the hardening of clay: it splits easily into thin layers: cf. MUDSTONE

shale oil a dark mineral oil produced by the destructive distillation of bituminous shale

shall (shal) *v.aux. pt.* **should** ⟦ME *schal,* pl. *schullen* < OE *sceal,* inf. *sceolan,* akin to Ger *sollen* < IE base *(*s*)*kel-,* to be indebted > Lith *skeliù,* to owe⟧ 1 used in the first person to indicate simple future time [I *shall* probably go tomorrow]: cf. WILL[2] (sense 1) 2 used in the second or third person, esp. in formal speech or writing, to express determination, compulsion, obligation, or necessity [you *shall* have to wait your turn] 3 used in the statement of laws or regulations [the fine *shall* not exceed $200] 4 used in questions about what to do [*shall* I invite them?] 5 used in formal conditional subordinate clauses [if any man *shall* hear, let him remember]

USAGE—See usage note at WILL[2]

shal·loon (sha lo͞on′, shə-) *n.* ⟦Fr *chalon,* after *Châlons-sur-Marne,* town in N France⟧ a twilled woolen fabric used largely for linings

shal·lop (shal′əp) *n.* ⟦Fr *chaloupe,* prob. < Du *sloep*(*e*), SLOOP⟧ [Historical] any of various small, open boats fitted with oars or sails or both

shal·lot (shə lät′, shal′ət) *n.* ⟦obs. Fr *eschalotte,* altered < OFr *eschaloigne*: see SCALLION⟧ 1 a small onion (*Allium ascalonicum*) whose clustered bulbs, like garlic but milder, are used for flavoring 2 GREEN ONION

shal·low (shal′ō) *adj.* ⟦ME *shalow* < OE **scealw* < IE base *(*s*)*kel-,* to dry out > SHOAL[2], Gr *skellein*⟧ 1 not deep [a *shallow* lake] 2 lacking depth of character, intellect, or meaning; superficial 3 slight; weak [*shallow* breathing] —*n.* [*usually pl., often with sing. v.*] a shallow place in a body of water; shoal — *vt., vi.* to make or become shallow —***SYN.*** SUPERFICIAL —**shal′low·ly** *adv.* —**shal′low·ness** *n.*

sha·lom (shä lōm′) *n., interj.* ⟦ModHeb *shalom,* lit., peace⟧ 1 hello 2 goodbye The traditional Jewish greeting or farewell

shalt (shalt) *v.aux. archaic 2d pers. sing., pres. indic., of* SHALL: used with *thou*

shal·y (shā′lē) *adj.* **shal′i·er, shal′i·est** of, like, or containing shale

sham (sham) *n.* ⟦prob. < N Eng dial. var. of SHAME⟧ 1 [Obs.] a trick or fraud 2 *a)* an imitation that is meant to deceive; counterfeit *b)* a hypocritical action, deceptive appearance, etc. 3 a person who is not what he or she pretends to be; fraud; impostor ☆4 *short for* PILLOW SHAM —*adj.* not genuine or real; false, counterfeit, pretended, etc. —*vt.* **shammed, sham′ming** to be or make an imitation or false show of; counterfeit —*vi.* to pretend to be what one is not —***SYN.*** FALSE

sha·man (shä′mən, shā′-; sham′ən) *n., pl.* **sha′mans** ⟦Russ *šaman* < Tungusic < Prakrit *śamana,* Buddhist monk < Sans *śramaṇa,* orig., ascetic, akin to *śram,* to fatigue⟧ a priest or medicine man, esp. among N Asian peoples, who is believed able to heal and to foretell the future through communication with good and evil spirits —**sha·man·ic** (shə man′ik) *adj.*

sha·man·ism (-iz′əm) *n.* the religion of certain peoples, esp. some indigenous to N Asia, based on a belief in good and evil spirits who can be influenced only by the shamans —**sha′man·ist** *n.* —**sha′man·is′tic** *adj.*

sha·mas (shä′məs) *n., pl.* **sha·mo′sim** (-môs′im) ⟦Yiddish < Heb *shamash,* servant, sexton < root *šmš,* to serve, minister⟧ 1 a synagogue official who provides various services, often one who manages day-to-day affairs 2 the candle used to light the other candles in a Hanukkah menorah Also sp. **sha′mos** or **sha′mes**

Sha·mash (shä′mäsh) *n.* ⟦< Akkadian *shamshu,* sun⟧ *Bab. & Assyr. Myth.* the sun god, responsible for summer warmth and the success of crops, and a symbol for justice

sham·ble (sham′bəl) *vi.* **-bled, -bling** ⟦< obs. adj. *shamble,* in *shamble legs,* prob. < fol., in obs. sense, "stool, bench"⟧ to walk in a lazy or clumsy manner, barely lifting the feet; shuffle —*n.* a shambling walk

sham·bles (-bəlz) *n.* ⟦ME *schamel,* bench, as for displaying meat for sale < OE *scamol,* bench or stool, akin to Ger *schemel* < early WGmc borrowing < L *scamellum,* dim. < *scamnum,* bench < IE base **skabh-,* **skambh-,* to prop up > Sans *skámbhana-,* a support⟧ 1 [Brit.] a place where meat is sold; butcher's stall or shop: now only a local usage, esp. in street names 2 a slaughterhouse 3 a scene of great slaughter, bloodshed, or carnage 4 any scene or condition of great destruction or disorder [rooms left a *shambles* by conventioneers]

sham·bol·ic (sham bäl′ik) *adj.* ⟦< prec.⟧ [Brit. Informal] confused, disorderly, chaotic, etc.

shame (shām) *n.* ⟦ME < OE *scamu,* akin to Ger *scham*⟧ 1 a painful feeling of having lost the respect of others because of the improper behavior, incompetence, etc. of oneself or of someone that one is close to or associated with 2 a tendency to have feelings of this kind, or a capacity for such feeling 3 dishonor or disgrace [to bring *shame* to one's family] 4 a person or thing that brings shame, dishonor, or disgrace 5 something regrettable, unfortunate, or outrageous [it's a *shame* that he wasn't told] —*vt.* **shamed, sham′ing** 1 to cause to feel shame; make ashamed 2 to dishonor or disgrace 3 to drive, force, or impel by a sense of shame [*shamed* into apologizing] —**for shame!** you ought to be ashamed! here is cause for shame! —**put to shame** 1 to cause to feel shame 2 to do much better than; surpass; outdo —**shame on** shame should be felt by; this is shameful of

shame·faced (shām′fāst′) *adj.* ⟦altered, by folk etym. < ME *schamfast* < OE *scamfæst* < *scamu,* shame + *fæst,* firm, FAST[1]⟧ 1 [Now Rare] very modest, bashful, or shy 2 showing a feeling of shame or embarrassment; ashamed Also [Archaic] **shame′fast′** (-fast′) —**shame·fac·ed·ly** (shām′ fās′id lē, shām′fāst′lē) *adv.* —**shame′fac′ed·ness** *n.*

shame·ful (-fəl) *adj.* 1 bringing or causing shame or disgrace; disgraceful 2 not just, moral, or decent; offensive —**shame′ful·ly** *adv.* —**shame′ful·ness** *n.*

shame·less (-lis) *adj.* having or showing no feeling of shame, modesty, or decency; brazen; impudent —**shame′less·ly** *adv.* —**shame′less·ness** *n.*

sham·mer (sham′ər) *n.* a person who shams

sham·mes or **sham·mas** (shä′məs) *n. alt. sp. of* SHAMAS

sham·my (sham′ē) *n., pl.* **sham′mies,** *adj., vt.* **-mied, -my·ing** *alt. sp. of* CHAMOIS (*n.* 2, *adj., vt.*)

sham·poo (sham po͞o′) *vt.* **-pooed′, -poo′ing** ⟦Hindi *chāmpo,* imper. of *chāmpnā,* to press, knead, shampoo⟧ 1 [Obs.] to massage 2 to wash (the hair and scalp), esp. with a shampoo 3 to wash the hair and scalp of 4 to clean or wash (a rug, upholstery, etc.) with a shampoo —*n.* 1 the act of washing hair, a rug, etc. 2 a cleaning preparation, esp. one in liquid form that produces suds —**sham·poo′er** *n.*

sham·rock (sham′räk′) *n.* ⟦Ir *seamrog,* dim. of *seamar,* clover⟧ any of certain clovers or cloverlike plants with leaflets in groups of three, used as the emblem of Ireland, as the red clover, white clover, wood sorrel, or black medic

☆**sha·mus** (shā′məs, shä′-) *n.* ⟦prob. blend of SHAMAS & Ir *Séamas,* James⟧ [Slang] 1 a policeman 2 a private detective

Shan (shän, shan) *n.* ⟦< Burmese⟧ 1 *pl.* **Shans** or **Shan** a member of a group of Asian peoples living esp. in NE Myanmar and S China 2 the Tai language of these peoples

Shan·dong (shän′do͝oŋ′) province of NE China, including a peninsula (**Shandong Peninsula**) which projects between the Yellow Sea & Bo Hai: 59,189 sq mi (153,299 sq km); cap. Jinan

shan·dy (shan′dē) *n.* ⟦< ?⟧ a beverage of ale or beer mixed with ginger ale, ginger beer, or lemonade: also **shan′dy·gaff′** (-gaf′)

Shane (shān) *n.* ⟦var. of SEAN⟧ a masculine name

shang·hai (shaŋ′hī′; *also for v.,* shaŋ hī′) *n.* ⟦after fol.⟧ [**S-**] any of a breed of large, dark-skinned chicken with white feathers and feathered shanks, imported from China in the 19th cent.: now known as the COCHIN —☆*vt.* **-haied′, -hai′ing** 1 ⟦orig. said of sailors thus kidnapped for crew duty on the China run⟧ to kidnap, usually by drugging, for service aboard ship 2 [Slang] to forcibly or deceitfully induce (another) to do something —**shang′hai′er** *n.*

Shang·hai (shaŋ′hī′, shäŋ′-) seaport in Jiangsu province, E China, near the mouth of the Chang

Shan·gri-La (shaŋ′gri lä′) *n.* ⟦after the fictional Tibetan lamasery that is the scene of *Lost Horizon* (1933) by James Hilton (1900-54), Brit novelist⟧ any imaginary, idyllic utopia or hidden paradise

shank (shaŋk) *n.* ⟦ME *shanke* < OE *scanca,* akin to Ger *schenkel,* thigh < IE base *(*s*)*keng-,* to limp > Gr *skazein,* Ger *hinken*⟧ 1 the lower part of the leg; part between the knee and ankle in humans or a part like this in animals 2 the whole leg 3 a cut of meat from the leg of an animal 4 a straight, narrow part between other parts, as *a)* the part of a tool or instrument between the handle and the working part; shaft *b)* the part of a tobacco pipe between the bowl and the stem *c)* the long central shaft of an anchor *d)* the narrow part of a shoe sole in front of the heel and beneath the instep **5** a projection or wire loop on some buttons by which they are sewn to fabric **6** the whole of a piece of type exclusive of the printing surface; body **7** *Bot.* FOOTSTALK —***vi.*** *Bot.* to decay and fall off a diseased footstalk: said of a flower —***vt.*** **1** *Golf* to hit (the ball) poorly by striking it with the heel of the club **2** *Sports* to hit or kick in an unintended direction —**shank of the evening 1** [Obs.] the latter part of the afternoon: see EVENING (sense 2) **2** now, the early part of the evening

Shan·kar (shaŋ′kär), **Ra·vi** (räv′ē) (born *Robindra Shankar Chowdhury*) 1920-2012; Indian composer & sitarist

shank's mare one's legs as a means of transportation: an old-fashioned usage [he went home on *shank's mare*]

Shan·non[1] (shan′ən) ***n.*** a masculine and feminine name

Shan·non[2] (shan′ən), **Claude El·wood** (el′wood) 1916-2001; U.S. mathematician

Shan·non[3] (shan′ən) river in WC Ireland, flowing southwestward into the Atlantic: *c.* 220 mi (354 km)

shan·ny (shan′ē) ***n., pl.*** **-nies** or **-ny** ⟦< Brit dial. *shan*⟧ any of several marine percoid fishes (family Stichaeidae), esp. a yellowish arctic species (*Lumpenus maculatus*) with dark spots

Shan·si (shän′shē′) *a former transliteration of* SHANXI

Shan State administrative division of EC Myanmar, occupying a plateau region (**Shan Plateau**), inhabited by Shans

shan't (shant, shänt) *contraction* shall not

Shan·tou (shän′tō′) seaport in Guangdong province, SE China, on the South China Sea

Shan·tung[1] (shan′tuŋ′) ***n.*** ⟦after fol.⟧ [*sometimes* **s-**] **1** a fabric with a slub filling, made from the silk of wild silkworms **2** a similar fabric of rayon, acetate, cotton, etc.

Shan·tung[2] (shan′tuŋ′) *a former transliteration of* SHANDONG

☆**shan·ty**[1] (shan′tē) ***n., pl.*** **-ties** ⟦< CdnFr *chantier*, workshop, applied to lumberers' living quarters < OFr: see GANTRY⟧ a small, shabby dwelling; shack; hut

shan·ty[2] (shan′tē, shän′-) ***n., pl.*** **-ties** *var. of* CHANTEY

☆**shan·ty·town** (shan′tē toun′) ***n.*** the section of a city where there are many shanties or ramshackle houses

Shan·xi (shän′shē′) province of NE China, between the Huang and Inner Mongolia: 60,657 sq mi (157,101 sq km); cap. Taiyuan

shape (shāp) ***n.*** ⟦ME *schap* < OE *(ge)sceap*, form, created thing, akin to *scieppan*, to create, form < IE **skeb-*, var. of base **(s)kep-*, to cut with a sharp tool > SHAFT, SHAVE⟧ **1** that quality of a thing which depends on the relative position of all points composing its outline or external surface; physical or spatial form **2** the form characteristic of a particular person or thing, or class of things **3** the contour of the body, exclusive of the face; figure **4** assumed or feigned appearance; guise [a foe in the *shape* of a friend] **5** an imaginary or spectral form; phantom **6** something having a particular shape, used as a mold or basis for shaping or fashioning **7** any of the forms, structures, etc. in which a thing may exist [dangers of every *shape*] **8** definite, regular, or suitable form; orderly arrangement [to begin to take *shape*] ☆**9** *a)* condition; state, esp. of health [a patient in poor *shape*] *b)* good physical condition [exercises that keep one in *shape*] —***vt.*** **shaped, shap′ing 1** to give definite shape to; make, as by cutting or molding material **2** to arrange, fashion, express, or devise (a plan, answer, etc.) in definite form **3** to adapt or adjust [to *shape* one's plans to one's abilities] **4** to direct or conduct (one's life, the course of events, etc.) **5** [Obs.] to appoint or decree —***vi.*** **1** [Obs.] to become suited; conform **2** [Rare] to happen **3** [Informal] to take shape or form: often with *into* or *up* —**SYN.** FORM, MAKE[1] —☆**shape up** [Informal] **1** to develop to a definite form, condition, etc. **2** to develop satisfactorily or favorably **3** to do what is expected of one; behave as required —**take shape** to begin to have definite form, condition, etc. —**shap′er *n.***

SHAPE (shāp) *abbrev.* Supreme Headquarters Allied Powers, Europe

☆**shaped charge** a charge arranged, in an armor-piercing projectile, in such a way as to concentrate its explosive force in a desired direction

shape·less (shāp′lis) ***adj.*** **1** without distinct or regular shape or form **2** without a pleasing or symmetrical shape; unshapely —**shape′less·ly *adv.*** —**shape′less·ness *n.***

shape·ly (-lē) ***adj.*** **-li·er, -li·est** having a pleasing or graceful shape or form; well-proportioned: used esp. of a woman with a full, rounded figure —**shape′li·ness *n.***

shape-shift·er (-shif′tər) ***n.*** *Folklore* a creature or thing that can change shape at will or that does so under certain conditions

☆**shape-up** (-up′) ***n.*** a method of selecting a daily work crew, as of longshoremen, from an assembled group of those available

Shap·ley (shap′lē), **Har·low** (här′lō) 1885-1972; U.S. astronomer

shard (shärd) ***n.*** ⟦ME < OE *sceard*, akin to *scieran*, to SHEAR⟧ **1** a fragment or broken piece, esp. of pottery; potsherd **2** *Zool.* a hard covering, as a shell, plate, scale, or elytron

share[1] (sher) ***n.*** ⟦ME < OE *scearu*, akin to *scieran*, to SHEAR⟧ **1** a part or portion that belongs or is allotted to an individual, or the part contributed by an individual **2** a just, due, reasonable, or full part or quota [to do one's *share* of work] **3** *a)* any of the parts or portions into which the ownership of a piece of property is divided *b)* any one of the equal parts into which the capital stock of a corporation is divided —***vt.*** **shared, shar′ing 1** to distribute in shares; give out a portion or portions of; apportion **2** to receive, use, experience, etc. in common with another or others —***vi.*** **1** to have or take a share; participate: often with *in* **2** to share or divide something equally: often with *with* —**go shares** to take part jointly, as in an enterprise —☆**on shares** with each person concerned taking a share of the profit or loss —**share and share alike** with each having an equal share —**share′a·ble *adj.***, **shar′a·ble** —**shar′er *n.***

SYN.—**share** means to use, enjoy, or possess in common with others and generally connotes a giving or receiving a part of something [to *share* expenses]; **participate** implies a taking part with others in some activity or enterprise [to *participate* in the talks]; **partake** implies a taking one's share, as of a meal or responsibility [to *partake* of a friend's hospitality]

share[2] (sher) ***n.*** ⟦ME *schar* < OE *scear*, akin to *scieran*, to SHEAR⟧ the part of a plow or other agricultural tool that cuts the soil; plowshare

☆**share·crop** (sher′kräp′) ***vi., vt.*** **-cropped′, -crop′ping** to work (land) for a share of the crop, esp. as a tenant farmer —**share′crop′per *n.***

share·hold·er (sher′hōl′dər) ***n.*** a person who holds or owns a share or shares, esp. in a corporation

share·ware (sher′wer′) ***n.*** ⟦SHARE[1] + -WARE⟧ copyrighted computer software that typically is available free of charge for trial use but that must be paid for by anyone who uses it regularly

Sha·ri (shä′rē) river in central Africa, flowing northwest through the Central African Republic & Chad into Lake Chad: *c.* 500 mi (805 km)

sha·ri·a (shə rē′ə) ***n.*** ⟦Ar *sharī'a*⟧ [*also* **S-**] [*also in italics*] Islamic law as derived from the Koran and the traditions of Islam: also sp. **sha·ri′ah**

sha·rif (shə rēf′) ***n.*** *var. of* SHERIF

shark[1] (shärk) ***n.*** ⟦prob. < Ger *schurke*, scoundrel, rogue, sharper < MHG *schurgen*, to push, mislead < IE **skēu-* < base **sek-*, to cut > SAW[1]⟧ **1** a person who victimizes others, as by swindling or cheating ☆**2** [Slang] a person with great ability in a given activity; adept; expert —***vt., vi.*** [Archaic] to get or live by fraud or stratagems

white shark

shark[2] (shärk) ***n.*** ⟦? akin to prec.⟧ any of various orders of cartilaginous fishes that are usually large and mostly marine, having a tough, spiny, usually slate-gray skin, separate lateral gill openings, and a slender, rounded body with the mouth on the underside: most sharks are fish-eaters, and some will attack humans

shark·skin (shärk′skin′) ***n.*** **1** leather made from the skin of a shark ☆**2** a cloth of cotton, wool, rayon, etc. with a smooth, silky surface, used for suits, etc. **3** a fabric woven with a pebbly pattern

shark·suck·er (-suk′ər) ***n.*** REMORA (sense 1)

Shar·on[1] (sher′ən) ***n.*** ⟦? contr. < ROSE OF SHARON⟧ a feminine name

Shar·on[2] (sher′ən), **Plain of** ⟦Heb *Shārōn*, region of Israel (see S. of Sol. 2:1), aphetic for *yesharon*, lit., the plain < *yashav*, adj., level⟧ coastal plain in W Israel, extending from Tel Aviv to Mount Carmel

sharp (shärp) ***adj.*** ⟦ME < OE *scearp*, akin to Ger *scharf*, ON *skarpr* < IE **(s)kerb(h)-* < base **(s)ker-*, to cut > SHEAR, HARVEST, L *caro*, flesh⟧ **1** suitable for use in cutting or piercing; having a very thin edge or fine point; keen **2** having a point or edge; not rounded or blunt; peaked [a *sharp* ridge, *sharp* features] **3** not gradual; abrupt; acute [a *sharp* turn] **4** clearly defined; distinct; clear [a *sharp* contrast] **5** made up of hard, angular particles, as sand **6** quick, acute, or penetrating in perception or intellect; specif., *a)* acutely sensitive in seeing, hearing, etc. *b)* clever; shrewd **7** showing or having a keen awareness; attentive; vigilant [a *sharp* lookout] **8** crafty; designing; underhanded **9** harsh, biting, or severe [a *sharp* temper, *sharp* criticism] **10** violent or impetuous; sudden and forceful [a *sharp* attack] **11** brisk; active; vigorous [a *sharp* run] **12** having a keen effect on the senses or feelings; specif., *a)* severe; intense; acute; keen [a *sharp* pain, grief, appetite, etc.] *b)* strong; biting; pungent, as in taste or smell *c)* high-pitched; shrill [a *sharp* sound] *d)* brilliant; intense [a *sharp* flash of light] *e)* cold and cutting [a *sharp* wind] **13** [Slang] attractively or stylishly dressed or groomed **14** *Music a)* higher in pitch by a half step [C *sharp* (C♯)] *b)* out of tune by being above the true or proper pitch —***adv.*** **1** in a sharp manner; specif., *a)* abruptly or briskly *b)* attentively or alertly *c)* so as to have a sharp point or edge *d)* keenly; piercingly *e) Music* above the true or proper pitch **2** precisely; exactly: used postpositively [one o'clock *sharp*] —***n.*** **1** a sewing needle with an extremely fine point **2** [Informal] an expert or adept **3** [Informal] SHARK[1], SHARPER **4** [Slang] any sharp medical device, as a hypodermic needle: *usually used in pl.* **5** *Music a)* a note or tone one half step above another *b)* the sign (♯) indicating such a note —***vt.*** *Music* to make sharp; raise a half step —***vi.*** *Music* to sing or play above the true or proper pitch —**sharp′ly *adv.*** —**sharp′ness *n.***

SYN.—**sharp** and **keen** both apply to that which is cutting, biting, incisive, or piercing, as because of a fine edge, but **sharp** more often implies a harsh cutting quality [a *sharp* pain, tongue, flavor, etc.] and **keen**, a pleasantly biting or stimulating quality [*keen* wit, delight, etc.]; **acute** literally implies sharp-pointedness and figuratively suggests a penetrating or poignant quality [*acute* hearing, distress, etc.]

sharp-eared (shärp′ird′) ***adj.*** having keenly sensitive hearing

Shar-Pei (shär pā′) ***n.*** ⟦< Chin, sand fur or sand skin⟧ a breed of dog having loose skin with a wrinkled appearance: it originated in China

sharp·en (shär′pən) *vt., vi.* to make or become sharp or sharper —**sharp′en·er** *n.*

sharp·er (shär′pər) *n.* a person, esp. a gambler, who is dishonest in dealing with others; cheat; swindler

sharp-eyed (shärp′īd′) *adj.* having keen sight or perception

☆**sharp·ie** (shär′pē) *n.* ⟦< SHARP: in sense 1, referring to its *sharp* lines⟧ **1** a long, narrow, flat-bottomed boat with a centerboard and one or two masts, each rigged with a triangular sail **2** [Informal] *a)* a shrewd, cunning person *b)* a cheat; swindler

sharp-nosed (shärp′nōzd′) *adj.* **1** having a thin, pointed nose **2** having a keen sense of smell

sharp-set (-set′) *adj.* **1** having a keen desire or appetite, as for food **2** set so as to be sharp or at an acute angle

☆**sharp-shinned hawk** (-shind′) a small North American hawk (*Accipiter striatus*) with a dark-gray back and a barred, reddish-and-white breast, feeding mainly on small birds

☆**sharp·shoot·er** (-sho͞ot′ər) *n.* a person who shoots with great accuracy; good marksman —**sharp′shoot′ing** *n.*

sharp-sight·ed (-sīt′id) *adj.* **1** having keen sight; sharp-eyed **2** keenly observant or perceptive; sharp-witted —**sharp′-sight′ed·ly** *adv.* —**sharp′-sight′ed·ness** *n.*

sharp-tongued (-tuŋd′) *adj.* using or characterized by severe, sharp, or harshly critical language

sharp-wit·ted (-wit′id) *adj.* having or showing keen intelligence or discernment; thinking quickly and effectively —**sharp′-wit′ted·ly** *adv.* —**sharp′-wit′ted·ness** *n.*

shash·lik (shäsh′lik) *n.* ⟦Russ *šašlyk*, ult. < Turk *şiş*, skewer, spit⟧ kebabs of meat, esp. lamb, skewered and broiled

Shas·ta (shas′tə), **Mount** ⟦< name of a local North American Indian people < ?⟧ volcanic mountain in the Cascade Range, N Calif.: 14,162 ft (4,317 m)

☆**Shasta daisy** ⟦after prec.⟧ any of several varieties of a daisylike chrysanthemum (*Chrysanthemum maximum*) having large flowers

shat (shat) *vt., vi. alt. pt. & pp. of* SHIT: somewhat vulgar

Shatt-al-A·rab (shat′äl är′äb) river in SE Iraq, formed by the confluence of the Tigris & Euphrates rivers & flowing southeast into the Persian Gulf: 120 mi (193 km)

shat·ter (shat′ər) *vt.* ⟦ME *schateren*, var. of *scateren*, to SCATTER⟧ **1** [Obs.] to scatter; strew **2** to break or burst into pieces suddenly, as with a blow **3** to damage severely; destroy or wreck [the accident *shattered* her peace of mind] —*vi.* to break or burst into pieces; smash —*n.* [*pl.*] broken pieces: chiefly in **in** (or **into**) **shatters** —*SYN.* BREAK

☆**shatter cone** a cone-shaped fragment of rock, probably formed by violent shock waves, as from meteoritic impact or atomic explosions

shat·ter·proof (-pro͞of′) *adj.* that will resist shattering

shave (shāv) *vt.* **shaved**, **shaved** or **shav′en**, **shav′ing** ⟦ME *schaven* < OE *sceafan*, akin to Ger *schaben* < IE base *(*s*)*kab-*, to cut > L *scabere*, to shave⟧ **1** to cut or scrape away a thin slice or slices from [to *shave* the edge of a door] **2** to cut or scrape into thin sections or slices [*shaved* ham] **3** *a)* to cut off (hair, esp. the beard) at the surface of the skin (often with *off* or *away*) *b)* to cut the hair to the surface of [to *shave* the chin, the legs, etc.] *c)* to cut the beard of (a person) **4** to barely touch or just miss touching in passing; graze **5** to cut short or trim (grass, etc.) closely ☆**6** to deliberately limit the number of (points) scored by one's team in a game (esp. a basketball game) in an effort to affect the result for gambling purposes ☆**7** [Informal] to purchase (a note, bill, etc.) at a discount greater than the legal or customary rate ☆**8** [Informal] to lower (a price, rate, etc.) by a slight margin —*vi.* to cut off hair or the beard with a razor or shaver; shave oneself —*n.* **1** a tool used for cutting thin slices, as of wood, from a surface **2** the act or an instance of shaving the beard See also CLOSE SHAVE

shave·ling (shāv′liŋ) *n.* **1** [Now Rare] a priest or monk with a tonsured head: used contemptuously **2** a youth; stripling

shav·en (shā′vən) *vt., vi. alt. pp. of* SHAVE —*adj.* **1** shaved or tonsured **2** closely trimmed

shav·er (-vər) *n.* **1** a person who shaves **2** an instrument used in shaving, esp. a device with a small electric motor that operates a set of vibrating or rotating cutters **3** [Informal] a boy; lad **4** [Archaic] a person who is hard or grasping in bargaining

☆**shave·tail** (shāv′tāl′) *n.* ⟦orig. an unbroken mule; ? in allusion to the untrained mules, with closely cropped tails, formerly sent to the Quartermaster Corps⟧ [Slang] a second lieutenant, esp. one recently appointed

Sha·vi·an (shā′vē ən) *adj.* ⟦ModL *Shavianus* < *Shavius*, Latinized < SHAW⟧ of or characteristic of George Bernard Shaw or his work —*n.* an admirer of Shaw or his work

shav·ing (shā′viŋ) *n.* **1** the action of a person or thing that shaves **2** something shaved off, esp. a thin slice of wood or metal

Sha·vu·ot (shä vo͞o′ōt, shə vo͞o′ōs) *n.* ⟦< Heb (*chag-ha*) *shavuot*, (the Feast of) Weeks < *shavua*, week < *sheva*, seven; akin to IE **septṃ*, seven⟧ a Jewish holiday, the Feast of Weeks, or Pentecost, originally celebrating the spring harvest, now chiefly commemorating the revelation of the Law at Mount Sinai: celebrated on the 6th & 7th days of Sivan

shaw (shô) *n.* ⟦ME *shawe* < OE *sceaga*, akin to ON *skagi*: for IE base see SHAG[1]⟧ [Dial.] a thicket; copse

Shaw (shô) **1 George Bernard** 1856-1950; Brit. dramatist & critic, born in Ireland **2 Henry Wheeler** *see* BILLINGS[1], Josh **3 Thomas Edward** *see* LAWRENCE[2], T(homas) E(dward)

shawl (shôl) *n.* ⟦prob. via Urdu < Pers *shāl*, after ? *Shāliāt*, town in India where produced⟧ an oblong or square cloth worn, esp. by women, as a covering for the head or shoulders

shawl collar a wide collar, as on a sweater or robe, that extends downward across the chest and meets or laps at or near the waist

shawm (shôm) *n.* ⟦ME *schalme* < MFr *chalemie*, altered < OFr *chalamel* < LL *calamellus*, dim. of L *calamus*, reed: see CALAMUS⟧ an early double-reed wind instrument resembling the oboe

Shawn[1] (shôn) *n.* ⟦var. of SEAN⟧ a masculine name

Shawn[2] (shôn), **Ted** (born *Edwin Myers Shawn*) 1891-1972; U.S. dancer & choreographer: husband of Ruth ST. DENIS

Shaw·nee (shô nē′, shô′nē) *n.* ⟦back-form. < *Shawnese*, taken as pl. < earlier *Shawanoes*, ult. < Shawnee *shaawanooki*, lit., people of the south⟧ **1** *pl.* **-nees′** or **-nee′** a member of a North American Indian people living at various times in the East and Midwest, and now chiefly in Oklahoma **2** the Algonquian language of this people

shay (shā) *n.* ⟦back-form. < CHAISE, assumed as pl.⟧ [Dial.] a light carriage; chaise

Shays (shāz), **Daniel** 1747?-1825; Am. Revolutionary soldier: leader of an insurrection (**Shays' Rebellion**) in W Mass. (1786-87) in reaction to high land taxes

☆**sha·zam** (shə zam′) *interj.* [Slang] used to signify, or seemingly command as if by magic, a sudden and surprising change or occurrence

shd. *abbrev.* should

she (shē) *pron., pl.* **they** ⟦ME *sche*, *scho*, prob. developed (infl. by OE *seo*, fem. def. article) < OE *hēo*, she⟧ **1** the woman, girl, or female animal (or, sometimes, the thing regarded as female) previously mentioned: feminine personal pronoun in the third person singular: *she* is the nominative form, *her* the objective, *hers* the possessive, and *herself* the reflexive and intensive; *her* is the possessive pronominal adjective **2** *a)* the person; the one; anyone *b)* the person just mentioned: used occasionally as an alternative to the generic *he* [every child needs to feel that *she* is loved] —*n., pl.* **shes** a woman, girl, or female animal

s/he (shē′ər hē′, shē′hē′) *pron.* she or he: used in writing to avoid the masculine implications of the generic *he*

she- (shē) *combining form* female: used in hyphenated compounds [*she-bear*]

shea (shē, shē′ə; *also, and for sense 2 usually*, shā) *n.* ⟦Mandingo *si*, *se*⟧ **1** an African tree (*Butyrospermum parkii*) of the sapodilla family: in full **shea tree** **2** a thick, white fat extracted from the seeds of the shea tree: used as a food, in soap, etc.: in full **shea butter**

sheaf (shēf) *n., pl.* **sheaves** ⟦ME *schefe* < OE *sceaf*, akin to Ger *schaub* < IE base **skeup-*, **skeubh-*, a bundle, clump > SHOP⟧ **1** a bunch of cut stalks of grain, etc. bound up in a bundle **2** a collection of things gathered together; bundle, as of papers —*vt.* SHEAVE[2]

shear (shir) *vt.* **sheared**, **sheared** or **shorn**, **shear′ing** ⟦ME *scheren* < OE *scieran*, akin to Ger *scheren* < IE base *(*s*)*ker-*, to cut > HARVEST⟧ **1** to cut with shears or a similar sharp-edged instrument **2** *a)* to remove (the hair, wool, etc.) by cutting or clipping *b)* to cut or clip the hair, wool, etc. from **3** to tear or wrench (*off*) by shearing stress **4** to move through as if cutting **5** to strip or divest (someone) *of* a power, right, etc. **6** [Dial.] to reap with a sickle —*vi.* **1** *a)* to use a cutting tool, as shears, in trimming or cutting wool, shrubbery, metal, etc. *b)* [Dial.] to use a sickle in reaping **2** to come apart or break under the action of shearing stress **3** to move by or as if by cutting —*n.* ⟦ME *schere* < OE *scear*⟧ **1** *a)* *rare var. of* SHEARS *b)* a single blade of a pair of shears **2** a machine used in cutting metal, esp. sheet metal **3** the action, process, or result of shearing; specif., the shearing of wool from an animal: used in designating a sheep's age [a sheep of three *shears*] **4** *a)* SHEARING STRESS *b)* any strain or distortion in shape resulting from the action of shearing stress —**shear′er** *n.*

sheared (shird) *adj.* subjected to shearing; esp., designating fur trimmed to give it an even surface [*sheared* beaver]

shear·ing (shir′iŋ) *n.* **1** the action or process of cutting with or as with shears **2** something cut off with shears, as the amount of wool cut from sheep

shearing stress a force causing two contacting parts or layers to slide upon each other, in opposite directions parallel to the plane of their contact

shear·ling (-liŋ) *n.* ⟦see SHEAR & -LING[1]⟧ **1** a sheep that has been sheared once, usually a yearling **2** tanned sheepskin or lambskin from an animal killed not long after being sheared

shears (shirz) *pl.n.* **1** *a)* a pair of scissors, typically a large pair *b)* any of a number of cutting tools with two pivoted, opposing blades, typically one used as in gardening for pruning or trimming: also called **pair of shears** *sing.* **2** any of several large tools or machines used to cut metal, etc. by the scissors action of two opposed cutting edges **3** a device used in hoisting, consisting of two or more guyed poles or legs spread at the base and joined at the top to hold hoisting tackle: also **shear·legs** (shir′legz′)

shear·wa·ter (shir′wôt′ər, -wät′-) *n.* ⟦SHEAR + WATER⟧ any of a genus (*Puffinus*, family Procellariidae) of black-and-white tubenose sea birds that skim the water in flight

sheat·fish (shēt′fish′) *n., pl.* **-fish′** or **-fish′es** (see FISH) ⟦earlier *sheath-fish* < fol. + FISH⟧ any silurid catfish, esp. a very large species (*Silurus glanis*)

sheath (shēth) *n., pl.* **sheaths** (shēthz, shēths) ⟦ME *schethe* < OE *sceath*, akin to Ger *scheide* < IE base **skei-*, to cut, split, divide (> L *scire*, to know): the earliest form of sheath was prob. a split stick⟧ **1** a contoured holder for the blade of a knife, sword, etc. 2 a covering or receptacle resembling this, as the membrane around a muscle, a leaf base enveloping a stem of grass, etc. 3 a woman's closefitting dress 4 [Brit.] CONDOM —*vt.* SHEATHE

sheath·bill (shēth′bil′) *n.* any of a family (Chionidae) of white-plumed antarctic shorebirds distinguished by a horny sheath at the base of the upper part of the bill

sheathe (shēth) *vt.* **sheathed, sheath′ing** ⟦ME *schethen* < *schethe*⟧ 1 to put into a sheath or scabbard 2 to enclose in or protect with a case or covering [wood *sheathed* with tin] 3 to thrust (a sword, knife, etc.) into flesh 4 to retract (claws)

sheath·ing (shē′thiŋ) *n.* 1 the act of one that sheathes 2 something that sheathes or encases; casing; specif., the inner covering of boards or waterproof material on the roof or outside wall of a frame house

sheath knife a knife carried in a sheath

sheave[1] (shēv, shiv) *n.* ⟦ME *sheve*, var. of *schive* < OE **scife*, akin to Ger *scheibe*, disk < IE **skeip-* < base **skei-*, to cut > SHEATH⟧ a wheel with a grooved rim, such as is mounted in a pulley block to guide the rope or cable; pulley wheel

sheave[2] (shēv) *vt.* **sheaved, sheav′ing** ⟦< SHEAF⟧ to gather and fix (grain, papers, etc.) in a sheaf or sheaves

sheaves[1] (shēvz) *n. pl. of* SHEAF

sheaves[2] (shēvz, shivz) *n. pl. of* SHEAVE[1]

Sheba[1] (shē′bə), **Queen of** *Bible* the queen who visited King Solomon to investigate his reputed wisdom: 1 Kings 10:1-13

She·ba[2] (shē′bə) *Biblical name for* SABA (the ancient kingdom)

☆**she·bang** (shə baŋ′) *n.* ⟦prob. var. of SHEBEEN⟧ 1 a shack or hut 2 [Informal] an affair, business, contrivance, thing, etc.: chiefly in **the whole shebang**

She·bat (shə vät′) *n. var. of* SHEVAT

she·been (shi bēn′) *n.* ⟦Anglo-Ir < Ir *sībīn*, little mug⟧ esp. in Ireland, Scotland, and South Africa, an establishment where liquor is sold without a license

She·boy·gan (shi boi′gən) ⟦< Menomini *saapiiweehekaneh*, lit., at a hearing distance through the woods⟧ city & port in E Wis., on Lake Michigan

shed[1] (shed) *n.* ⟦< ME *shadde*, var. of *shade* < OE *scead*, shelter, protection, SHADE⟧ 1 a small, rough building or lean-to, used for shelter or storage, as a workshop, etc. 2 a large, strongly built, barnlike or hangarlike structure, often with open front or sides

shed[2] (shed) *vt.* **shed, shed′ding** ⟦ME *scheden* < OE *sceadan*, to separate, distinguish, akin to Ger *scheiden*, to cut, separate: for IE base see SHEATH⟧ 1 to pour out; give off; emit; diffuse 2 to cause to flow in a stream or fall in drops [to *shed* tears] 3 to cause to flow off without penetrating; repel [oilskin *sheds* water] 4 *a)* to cast off or lose (a natural growth or covering, as leaves, skin, hair, etc.) *b)* to get rid of (something unwanted) [to *shed* a few pounds] —*vi.* 1 to shed a natural growth or covering, as hair 2 to drop off or fall out: said of leaves, seeds, etc. —*n.* ⟦ME *schede*, division⟧ 1 a ridge of high ground; specif., WATERSHED 2 an opening in the warp threads of a loom for the shuttle to pass through —**shed blood** to kill in a violent or bloody way

she'd (shēd) *contraction* 1 she had 2 she would

shed·der (shed′ər) *n.* 1 a person or thing that sheds ☆2 a lobster, crab, etc. that is shedding or has just shed its shell

Sheel·er (shē′lər), **Charles** 1883-1965; U.S. painter & photographer

sheen (shēn) *n.* ⟦< the *adj.*⟧ 1 brightness; shininess; luster 2 bright or shining attire —*adj.* ⟦ME *schene* < OE *sciene*, beautiful, splendid, akin to Ger *schön* (< IE base *(s)keu-*, to observe, heed > HEAR): sense infl. by assoc. with SHINE⟧ [Archaic] of shining beauty; bright —*vi.* [Dial.] to shine; gleam —**sheen′y** *adj.* **sheen′i·er, sheen′i·est**

shee·ny or **shee·nie** (shē′nē) *n., pl.* **-nies** ⟦< ?⟧ [*also* **S-**] [Slang] a Jewish person: a somewhat old-fashioned term of disparagement or contempt

sheep (shēp) *n., pl.* **sheep** ⟦ME *schep* < OE *sceap, scæp*, akin to Ger *schaf*: known only in WGmc⟧ 1 any of a wide variety of bovid ruminants, with horns in both sexes; esp., the domesticated sheep (*Ovis aries*), having heavy wool, edible flesh called *mutton*, and skin used in making leather, parchment, etc. 2 leather made from the skin of the sheep, as for bookbinding 3 a person who is meek, stupid, timid, submissive, etc. —**make** (or **cast**) **sheep's eyes at** to look shyly but amorously at

☆**sheep·ber·ry** (shēp′ber′ē) *n., pl.* **-ries** 1 a tall North American viburnum shrub or small tree (*Viburnum lentago*) with white flowers and juicy, blue-black berries 2 this berry

sheep·cote (-kōt′) *n.* ⟦see COTE[1]⟧ *chiefly Brit. var. of* SHEEPFOLD: also **sheep′cot′** (-kät′)

sheep-dip (-dip′) *n.* any chemical preparation used as a bath to free sheep from vermin and sheep scab or to clean the fleece and skin before shearing

sheep·dog (-dôg′, -däg′) *n.* any dog trained to herd and protect sheep, specif., the OLD ENGLISH SHEEPDOG

sheep fescue a widespread perennial grass (*Festuca ovina*) of temperate climates, growing in small, grayish-green tufts

sheep·fold (-fōld′) *n.* ⟦ME < OE *sceapa fald*: see FOLD[2]⟧ a pen or enclosure for sheep

☆**sheep·herd·er** (-hʉr′dər) *n.* a person who herds or takes care of a large flock of grazing sheep —**sheep′herd′ing** *n.*

sheep·ish (-ish) *adj.* ⟦ME *shepisse*, like a sheep⟧ 1 *a)* embarrassed as because of feeling chagrin *b)* awkwardly shy or bashful 2 resembling sheep in meekness, timidity, etc. —**sheep′ish·ly** *adv.* —**sheep′ish·ness** *n.*

sheep ked (ked) ⟦*ked* < ?⟧ SHEEP TICK

☆**sheep laurel** a small E North American plant (*Kalmia angustifolia*) of the heath family, with pinkish flowers and evergreen leaves poisonous to sheep and other animals

sheep·man (-man′, -mən) *n., pl.* **-men′** (-men′, -mən) ☆a person who raises sheep for the market

sheep-run (-run′) *n.* [Austral.] a large property for raising sheep: also **sheep′-sta′tion** (-stā′shən)

sheep·shank (-shaŋk′) *n.* a knot used for shortening a rope

sheeps·head (shēps′hed′) *n.* ☆1 *pl.* **-head′** or **-heads′** *a)* a large, edible, marine porgy fish (*Archosargus probatocephalus*) with a massive head, a striped body, and sheeplike incisor and molar teeth: found along the Atlantic and Gulf coasts of the U.S. *b)* the freshwater drum (*Aplodinotus grunniens*) common in the Great Lakes and Mississippi watershed *c)* a red wrasse (*Semicossyphus pulcher*) of the California coast 2 [Archaic] a stupid person

sheep·shear·ing (shēp′shir′iŋ) *n.* 1 the act of shearing sheep 2 the time when sheep are sheared 3 a traditional feast held at this time —**sheep′shear′er** *n.*

sheep·skin (-skin′) *n.* 1 the skin of a sheep, esp. one dressed with the fleece on it, as for a coat 2 parchment or leather made from the skin of a sheep: the parchment is often used for documents, as diplomas ☆3 [Informal] DIPLOMA

sheep sorrel a low-growing sorrel (*Rumex acetosella*) with reddish or yellowish flowers, often found on dry soils

sheep tick a wingless, flattened, leathery dipterous fly (*Melophagus ovinus*) that is an external parasite on sheep

sheep·walk (-wôk′) *n.* [Chiefly Brit.] a range for sheep

sheer[1] (shir) *vi.* ⟦var. of SHEAR, prob. infl. by Du or LowG *scheren*, to cut, deviate, warp away⟧ to turn aside sharply from a course; swerve —*vt.* to cause to sheer —*n.* 1 a sudden change of course; abrupt turn; swerve 2 the oblique heading or position of a ship riding at a single bow anchor 3 the upward curve of a ship's deck toward the bow and stern, as seen from the side

sheer[2] (shir) *adj.* ⟦ME *schere*, prob. var. of *scere*, free, exempt < ON *skærr*, bright, clear, akin to Ger *schier*: for IE base see SHINE⟧ 1 very thin; transparent; diaphanous: said of textiles 2 not mixed or mingled with anything else; pure [*sheer* ice] 3 absolute; downright; unqualified; utter [*sheer* persistence] 4 perpendicular or extremely steep, as the face of a cliff —*adv.* 1 completely; utterly; outright 2 perpendicularly or very steeply —*n.* thin, fine material, or a curtain, etc. made of it —**SYN.** STEEP[1] —**sheer′ly** *adv.* —**sheer′ness** *n.*

sheer·legs (shir′legz′, -lāgz′) *pl.n.* SHEARS (sense 3)

sheesh (shēsh) *interj.* ⟦prob. var. of JEEZ⟧ used variously to express disbelief, surprise, annoyance, etc.

sheet[1] (shēt) *n.* ⟦ME *schete* < OE *sceat*, piece of cloth, lappet, region, akin to Ger *schoss*, lap, ON *skaut*, lappet: for prob. IE base see SHOOT[1]⟧ 1 a large, rectangular piece of cotton, linen, etc., used to cover a bed, usually in pairs, with one under and one over the sleeper's body 2 *a)* a rectangular piece of paper, esp. one of a number of pieces cut to a definite, uniform size, as for use in writing, printing, etc. *b)* a large piece of such paper with a number of pages printed on it, to be folded into a signature for binding into a book (*usually used in pl.*) *c)* [Informal] a newspaper [a scandal *sheet*] 3 a broad, continuous surface, layer, or expanse, as of flame, water, ice, etc. 4 a broad, thin, usually rectangular piece of any material, as glass, plywood, metal, etc. 5 a flat baking pan [a cookie *sheet*] 6 [Old Poet.] a sail 7 *Geol.* any layer or deposit of rock, gravel, soil, ice, etc. that is broad in extent and comparatively thin 8 *Philately a)* the unseparated stamps printed on a piece of paper by a single impression of a plate *b)* PANE (sense 4a) —*vt.* to cover or provide with, or form into, a sheet or sheets —*adj.* in the form of a sheet [*sheet* iron] —**sheet′like′** *adj.*

sheet[2] (shēt) *n.* ⟦ME *shete*, as if < OE *sceata*, lower corner of a sail (akin to prec.) but actually short for *sceatline*, line attached to that part of a sail⟧ 1 a rope or chain attached to a lower corner of a sail: it is shortened or slackened to control the set of the sail 2 [*pl.*] the spaces not occupied by thwarts, or cross seats, at the bow and stern of an open boat —**sheet home** to tighten the sheets of (a square sail) until it is set as flat as possible —**three sheets in** (or **to**) **the wind** ⟦by analogy between the staggering as of a drunken sailor and the erratic motion of a ship whose sails are not controllable because some of their *sheets* have come loose⟧ [Slang] very drunk

sheet anchor ⟦ME *shute anker* < ? *schuten*, to SHOOT[1] + *anker*, ANCHOR: reason for name uncert.⟧ 1 [Historical] the heaviest anchor on a sailing ship, located amidships and used in emergencies 2 a person or thing to be relied upon in danger

sheet bend *Naut.* a knot used in fastening a rope to the bight of another rope or to an eye

sheet·ing (shēt′iŋ) *n.* 1 cotton or linen material used for making sheets 2 material used in covering or lining a surface [copper *sheeting*] 3 the action or process of covering with or forming into sheets

sheet lightning a sheetlike flash of light in the sky, caused by lightning reflected and diffused by thunderclouds

sheet metal metal rolled thin in the form of a sheet

sheet music music printed on unbound sheets of paper

Sheet·rock (-räk′) *trademark for* a kind of plasterboard —*n.* [*often* **s-**] such plasterboard

Shef·field (shef′ēld) city in NC England, in South Yorkshire

she/he (shē′hē′, shē′ôr hē′, shē′slash′hē′) *pron.* she or he: used to avoid the masculine implication of the generic use of *he*

sheik or **sheikh** (shēk; *also, for 1 & 2,* shāk) ***n.*** ⟦Ar *shaikh*, lit., old man < *shākha*, to grow old⟧ **1** the chief of an Arab family, tribe, or village **2** a Muslim religious or community leader **3** ⟦< *The Sheik*, novel (1921) by E. M. Hull (1880-1947), Brit novelist⟧ [Old Slang] a masterful man to whom women are irresistibly attracted

sheik·dom (shēk′dəm, shāk′-) ***n.*** a political unit ruled by a sheik: also sp. **sheikh′dom**

Shei·la (shē′lə) ***n.*** ⟦Ir⟧ **1** a feminine name: see CECILIA[1] **2** [**s-**] [Austral. & N.Z. Informal] a girl or young woman

shek·el (shek′əl) ***n.*** ⟦Heb < *shakal*, to weigh⟧ **1** an ancient unit of weight used by Hebrews, Babylonians, etc., equal to about half an ounce **2** a half-ounce gold or silver coin of the ancient Hebrews **3** the basic monetary unit of Israel: see the table of monetary units in the Reference Supplement **4** [*pl.*] [Slang] money

She·ki·nah (shə kē′nə, -kī′-; *Heb* shə khē nä′) ***n.*** ⟦TalmudHeb *shechina* < root *škn*, to dwell⟧ *Judaism* the manifestation of the Divine Presence

shel·drake (shel′drāk′) ***n., pl.*** **-drakes′** or **-drake′** ⟦ME *sheldedrake*, prob. < a ME cognate of MDu *schillede*, variegated < *schillen*, to make different + *drake*, DRAKE[1]⟧ **1** SHELDUCK **2** MERGANSER

shel·duck (-duk′) ***n., pl.*** **-ducks′** or **-duck′** any of a genus (*Tadorna*) of brightly colored wild ducks that feed on fish, etc. and nest in burrows

shelf (shelf) ***n., pl.*** **shelves** ⟦ME, prob. < MLowG *schelf*, akin to OE *scylf*, shelf, ledge < IE **skelp* < base **(s)kel-*, to cut > HALF⟧ **1** a thin, flat length of wood, metal, etc. fixed horizontally at right angles to a wall and used for holding things **2** a similar support, usually one of a set, built into a frame, as in a bookcase or cupboard **3** the contents or capacity of a shelf **4** something like a shelf; specif., *a)* a flat ledge jutting out from a cliff *b)* a sandbar or sandy reef **5** a layer of bedrock, as under deposits of soil or gravel —**on the shelf** out of use, activity, or circulation —**shelf′like′** ***adj.***

shelf fungus ⟦so named from its shape⟧ BRACKET FUNGUS

shelf ice ICE SHELF

shelf life **1** the length of time a packaged food, chemical preparation, etc. can be stored without deteriorating **2** figuratively, the length of time something remains popular, well-known, etc.

shell (shel) ***n.*** ⟦ME *schelle* < OE *sciel*, akin to MDu *schelle* < IE base **(s)kel-*: see SHELF⟧ **1** a hard outer covering, as of a turtle, mollusk, insect, egg, fruit, seed, etc. **2** something like or suggestive of a shell in being hollow, empty, or simply a covering or framework, as the hull of a boat, a hollow pastry or unfilled pie crust, the framework of a building, a structure with an arched or hemispherical roof or back, a tapered beer glass, etc. **3** a shy, reserved, or uncommunicative attitude or manner [to come out of one's *shell*] ☆**4** a woman's simple sleeveless blouse or sweater ☆**5** a long, narrow, thin-hulled racing boat rowed usually by a team of oarsmen **6** an explosive artillery projectile containing high explosives and sometimes shrapnel, chemicals, etc. ☆**7** a cartridge for small arms or small artillery, consisting of a metal, paper, or plastic case holding the primer, powder charge, and shot or bullet **8** a pyrotechnic cartridge which explodes high in the air **9** *a)* a mollusk *b)* [*pl.*] shellfish **10** *Chem., Physics a)* any of the spherical or elliptical orbits of electrons around the nucleus of an atom, each with the same principal quantum number and about the same energy *b)* the space taken up by such an orbit *c)* a grouping of like nucleons of approximately the same energy in the nucleus —***vt.*** **1** to remove the shell or covering from; take out of the shell [to *shell* peas, oysters, etc.] **2** to separate kernels or grains of (corn, wheat, etc.) from the cob or ear **3** to fire shells at from a large gun or guns; bombard —***vi.*** **1** to separate from the shell or covering [peanuts *shell* easily] **2** to fall, slough, or peel off ☆**3** to gather or collect shells —**shell out** [Informal] to pay out (money) —**shell′-like′** ***adj.*** —**shell′y** ***adj.***

she'll (shēl, shil) *contraction* **1** she will **2** she shall

shel·lac or **shel·lack** (shə lak′) ***n.*** ⟦SHEL(L) + LAC, used as transl. of Fr *laque en écailles*, lac in fine sheets⟧ **1** refined lac, a resinous substance usually produced in thin, flaky layers or shells and used in making varnish, phonograph records, insulating materials, etc. **2** a thin, usually clear kind of varnish containing this resin and alcohol —***vt.*** **-lacked′**, **-lack′ing** **1** to apply shellac to; cover or varnish with shellac ☆**2** [Slang] *a)* to beat *b)* to defeat decisively

shel·lack·ing (-iŋ) ***n.*** [Slang] ☆**1** a whipping; flogging; beating ☆**2** a thorough defeat

shell·back (shel′bak′) ***n.*** ⟦SHELL + BACK[1], in allusion to the shell of the sea turtle⟧ **1** an old, experienced sailor **2** anyone who has crossed the equator by ship

☆**shell·bark** (-bärk′) ***n.*** SHAGBARK

☆**shell bean** any bean, as the lima bean, whose seeds but not pods are used as food

shell company (*or* corporation) a company existing as a legal entity but having no significant assets, independent business operations, etc., often owned or controlled by another company and used for various, often illegal, purposes

-shelled (sheld) *combining form* having a (specified kind of) shell [hard-*shelled* crab]

shell·er (shel′ər) ***n.*** a collector of seashells

Shel·ley[1] (shel′ē) ***n.*** a feminine name: var. *Shelly*

Shel·ley[2] (shel′ē) **1 Mary Woll·stone·craft** (wool′stən kraft′) 1797-1851; Eng. novelist: daughter of Mary Wollstonecraft & William Godwin: second wife of Percy **2 Percy Bysshe** (bish) 1792-1822; Eng. poet

shell·fire (shel′fīr′) ***n.*** the firing of large shells

shell·fish (-fish′) ***n., pl.*** **-fish′** or **-fish′es** (see FISH) ⟦ME *shellfyssche* < OE *scilfisc* < *sciel*, SHELL + *fisc*, FISH⟧ any aquatic animal with a shell, esp. an edible animal such as the clam or lobster

☆**shell game** **1** a game, typically a swindle, in which spectators are challenged to bet on the location of a small object ostensibly concealed under one of three cups or nutshells manipulated by sleight of hand **2** any scheme for tricking and cheating people

shell jacket a closefitting semiformal jacket; mess jacket

shell·proof (-proōf′) ***adj.*** proof against damage from shells or bombs

shell shock *former term for* COMBAT FATIGUE: now used fig. —**shell′shocked′** (-shäkt′) ***adj.***

shell steak a cut of steak from the short loin

Shel·ta (shel′tə) ***n.*** ⟦earlier *sheldru, shelter* < ? OIr *bēlre*, speech⟧ [*also* **s-**] a traditional jargon, based on Irish Gaelic, spoken as by tinkers in some parts of Ireland and England

shel·ter (shel′tər) ***n.*** ⟦prob. < ME *scheltroun*, earlier *scheltrum* < OE *sceldtruma*, lit., shield troop, body of men protected by interlocked shields < *scield* (see SHIELD) + *truma*, an array, troop; akin to *trum*, strong: (see TRIM)⟧ **1** something that covers or protects; protection, or place affording protection, as from the elements or danger **2** the state of being covered or protected; protection; refuge **3** any of various places for providing food and lodging on a temporary or emergency basis, as one for the homeless or one for stray pets —***vt.*** to provide shelter or refuge for; protect —***vi.*** to find protection or refuge —**shel′ter·er** ***n.*** —**shel′ter·less** ***adj.***

SYN.—**shelter** implies the protection of something that covers, as a roof or other structure that shields one from the elements or danger [to find *shelter* from the rain]; **refuge** suggests a place of safety that one flees to in escaping danger or difficulties [he sought political *refuge* in France]; **retreat** implies retirement from that which threatens one's peace, and withdrawal to a safe, quiet, or secluded place [a country *retreat*]; **asylum** is applied to a refuge where one is immune from seizure or harm, as because it is beyond a particular legal jurisdiction [the convict sought *asylum* abroad]; a **sanctuary** is an asylum that has a sacred or inviolable character [the former right of *sanctuary* in churches]

☆**shel·ter·belt** (-belt′) ***n.*** a barrier zone of trees or shrubs planted to protect crops, soil, etc. against strong winds and storms

sheltered workshop a workshop and training center for handicapped persons, where they can earn wages but are free from the competitive stress of the usual job

☆**shelter tent** a small, portable tent that shelters two persons: it is made by fastening together two sections (**shelter halves**)

shel·tie or **shel·ty** (shel′tē) ***n., pl.*** **-ties** ⟦prob. < Orkney pronun. of ON *hjalti*, SHETLANDER⟧ [Informal] **1** SHETLAND SHEEPDOG **2** SHETLAND PONY

shelve (shelv) ***vi.*** ⟦< SHELF⟧ **shelved**, **shelv′ing** to incline or slope gradually —***vt.*** ⟦< pl. of SHELF⟧ **1** to equip with shelves **2** to put on a shelf or shelves **3** *a)* to lay aside as if on a shelf; defer [to *shelve* a discussion] *b)* to dismiss or retire from active service

shelves (shelvz) ***n.*** *pl. of* SHELF

shelv·ing (shel′viŋ) ***n.*** **1** material for shelves **2** shelves collectively **3** the condition or degree of sloping

Shem (shem) ***n.*** ⟦Heb *shem*⟧ *Bible* the eldest of Noah's three sons: Gen. 5:32

She·ma (shə mä′) ***n.*** ⟦< Heb *shma* < *shma yisroel*, Hear, O Israel (the opening words): see Deut. 6:4-9⟧ a declaration of the basic principle of Jewish belief, proclaiming the absolute unity of God

☆**she-male** (shē′māl′) ***n.*** ⟦pun on FEMALE⟧ **1** [Old Slang] an aggressive or masculine woman **2** a transgender person who was born male and who has some female characteristics, as enlarged breasts, from hormone therapy but has not undergone sex-change surgery: an offensive term of contempt

Shem·ite (shem′īt′) ***n.*** *rare var. of* SEMITE

Shen·an·do·ah (shen′ən dō′ə) ⟦prob. of Iroquoian orig.⟧ river in N Va., flowing through a valley (**Shenandoah Valley**) between the Blue Ridge & Allegheny mountains, into the Potomac: *c.* 200 mi (322 km)

☆**she·nan·i·gans** (shi nan′i gənz) ***pl.n.*** ⟦altered < ? Ir *sionnachuighim*, I play the fox⟧ [Informal] **1** [*also sing.*] [Old-fashioned] trickery; mischief **2** *a)* treacherous or deceitful tricks *b)* playful or mischievous tricks

Shen·si (shen′sē′; *Chin* shun′shē′) *a former transliteration of* SHAANXI

Shen·yang (shun′yäŋ′) city in NE China; capital of Liaoning province

She·ol (shē′ōl) ***n.*** ⟦Heb < ? *shaal*, to dig⟧ *Bible* a place in the depths of the earth conceived of as the dwelling of the dead

Shep·ard (shep′ərd), **Alan (Bartlett)** 1923-98; U.S. astronaut: 1st American in space (1961)

shep·herd (shep′ərd) ***n.*** ⟦ME *shephirde* < OE *sceaphyrde*: see SHEEP & HERD[2]⟧ **1** a person who herds and takes care of sheep **2** a leader of a group; esp., a minister **3** GERMAN SHEPHERD —***vt.*** to tend, herd, guard, or lead as or like a shepherd

shep·herd·ess (shep′ər dis) ***n.*** a girl or woman shepherd, esp. as a stock character in pastoral poetry: see -ESS

shepherd's check (*or* plaid) **1** a pattern of small checks formed by stripes of black and white **2** fabric woven in this pattern Also **shepherd check**

shepherd's pie a meat pie baked with a layer of mashed potatoes serving as a top crust

shepherd's purse a small weed (*Capsella bursa-pastoris*) of the crucifer family, with triangular, pouchlike pods

Sher·a·ton (sher′ə tən) ***adj.*** ⟦after Thomas *Sheraton* (1751-1806), Eng cabinetmaker] designating or of an 18th-cent. Eng. style of furniture characterized by simplicity of form, straight lines, and classically chaste decoration

sher·bet (shur′bət) ***n.*** ⟦Turk *şerbet* < Ar *sharba(t)*, a drink, var. of *sharāb*: see SYRUP⟧ **1** [Brit.] a beverage, originally from Asia, made of watered fruit juice and sugar and served cold **2** a frozen dessert like an ice but with gelatin and, often, milk added: also, erroneously, **sher·bert** (shur′bərt)

Sher·brooke (shur′brook′) city in S Quebec, Canada

sherd (shurd) ***n.*** *var. of* SHARD (sense 1)

Sher·i·dan (sher′i dən) **1 Philip Henry** 1831-88; Union general in the Civil War **2 Richard Brins·ley** (brinz′lē) 1751-1816; Brit. dramatist & politician, born in Ireland

she·rif (shə rēf′) ***n.*** ⟦Ar *sharīf*, noble⟧ **1** a descendant of Muhammad through his daughter Fatima **2** an Arab prince or chief **3** the chief magistrate of Mecca

sher·iff (sher′if) ***n.*** ⟦ME *schirreve* < OE *scirgerefa* < *scir*, SHIRE + *gerefa*, REEVE[1]⟧ **1** in England, esp. formerly, any of various officers of a shire, or county ☆**2** in the U.S., the chief law-enforcement officer of a county, charged in general with the keeping of the peace and the execution of court orders —**sher′iff·dom** ***n.***

Sher·lock Holmes (shur′läk′ hōmz′, hōlmz′) a fictitious Brit. detective with great powers of deduction: the main character in many stories by Arthur Conan DOYLE, most of which are ostensibly narrated by Holmes's partner, Dr. Watson

Sher·man (shur′mən) **1 John** 1823-1900; U.S. statesman: brother of William **2 Roger** 1721-93; Am. statesman: signer of the Declaration of Independence **3 William Tecumseh** 1820-91; Union general in the Civil War

Sher·pa (shur′pə, sher′-) ***n.*** **1** *pl.* **-pas** or **-pa** a member of a Tibetan people living on the S slopes of the Himalaya Mountains in Nepal, known for their endurance at high elevations and often serving as guides for foreign mountain climbers **2** [**s-**] a fabric with a woolly pile of polyester, cotton, etc., often used for linings of winter clothing

sher·ris (sher′is) ***n.*** *archaic var. of* SHERRY

sher·ry (sher′ē) ***n.***, *pl.* **-ries** ⟦taken as sing. of earlier *sherris*, after *Xeres* (now *Jerez*), Spain, where first made⟧ **1** a Spanish fortified wine varying in color from light yellow to dark brown and in flavor from very dry to sweet **2** any similar wine made elsewhere

's Her·to·gen·bosch (ser′tō khən bôs′) city in SC Netherlands: capital of North Brabant province

Sher·wood (shur′wood), **Robert (Emmet)** 1896-1955; U.S. playwright

Sher·wood Forest (shur′wood) forest in Nottinghamshire, England, made famous in the Robin Hood legends

she's (shēz) *contraction* **1** she is **2** she has

Shet·land[1] (shet′lənd) ***n.*** **1** *a)* SHETLAND PONY *b)* SHETLAND SHEEPDOG **2** [*also* **s-**] *a)* SHETLAND WOOL *b)* a fabric made from Shetland wool

Shet·land[2] (shet′lənd) ⟦ON *Hjaltland*⟧ administrative division of NE Scotland, consisting of a group of islands (**Shetland Islands**) in the Atlantic, northeast of the Orkney Islands: 566 sq mi (1,466 sq km) —**Shet′land·er** ***n.***

Shetland pony any of a breed of hardy pony (typically 38-40 in, 96.5-101.5 cm, in height), originally from the Shetland Islands, with a full mane and tail and a shaggy coat in winter

Shetland sheepdog any of a breed of dog closely resembling the rough collie but smaller: developed in the Shetland Islands for herding cattle and sheep: see COLLIE

Shetland wool **1** fine wool from the undercoat of sheep from Shetland **2** a soft, fine wool yarn made from this wool

She·vat (shə vät′) ***n.*** ⟦Heb *shebhāṭ*⟧ the fifth month of the Jewish year: see the Jewish calendar in the Reference Supplement

shew (shō) ***n., vt., vi.*** **shewed**, **shewn** or **shewed**, **shew′ing** *archaic sp. of* SHOW

shew·bread (shō′bred′) ***n.*** *archaic var. of* SHOWBREAD

SHF or **shf** *abbrev.* superhigh frequency

shh (sh: *often a prolonged sound*) ***interj.*** used to urge or request silence

Shi·a (shē′ə) ***n.***, *pl.* **Shi′as** or **Shi′a** *var. of* SHIITE: often **Shi′ah**, *pl.* **Shi′ah**

shi·at·su (shē ät′sōō) ***n.*** ⟦contr. of Jpn *shiatsuryōhō*, lit., finger pressure treatment < *shi*, finger + *atsu-*, pressure + *ryōhō*, treatment⟧ [*sometimes* **S-**] ACUPRESSURE (sense 1): occas. sp. **shi·at′zu**

shib·bo·leth (shib′ə leth′, -ləth) ***n.*** ⟦ME *sebolech*, after LL(Ec) *sciboleth* < Heb *shibolet*, a stream: pres. meaning from the use of the word as a test word⟧ **1** the test word used by the men of Gilead to distinguish the escaping Ephraimites, who pronounced the initial (sh) as (s): Judg. 12:4-6 **2** any test word or password **3** any phrase, custom, etc. distinctive of a particular party, class, etc.

Shi·be·li (shə bel′ē) river in E Africa, flowing from SE Ethiopia through Somalia into a swamp near the Juba River: *c.* 1,200 mi (1,931 km)

shick·er (shik′ər) [Slang] ***adj.*** ⟦Yiddish *shiker* < Heb *shikor*: see CIDER⟧ DRUNK (sense 1) —***n.*** DRUNKARD

shied (shīd) ***vi., vt.*** *pt. & pp. of* SHY[1], SHY[2]

shield (shēld) ***n.*** ⟦ME *schelde* < OE *scield*, akin to Ger *schild* < Gmc **skild-* < IE base **(s)kel-* > SHELF⟧ **1** a flat, usually broad, piece of metal, wood, etc., carried in the hand or worn on the forearm to ward off blows or missiles **2** any person or thing that guards, protects, or defends **3** a heraldic escutcheon **4** anything shaped like a triangular shield, broad at the top and with curved sides, as an escutcheon, plaque, trophy, badge, or emblem **5** a heavy metal screen attached to an artillery piece for the protection of the gunners **6** *a)* a guard or safety screen, as over the moving parts of machinery *b)* an insulating covering on electric wires, etc. *c)* any material or structure used for protection against radiation **7** DRESS SHIELD **8** *Zool.* a hard surface covering or shell; protective plate, as on a turtle —***vt.*** **1** to be or provide a shield for; defend; protect; guard **2** to hide from view; screen —***vi.*** to serve as a shield, or protection —**shield′er** ***n.***

shield
(sense 3)

shiel·ing (shē′liŋ) ***n.*** ⟦< Scot *shiel*, shieling (< ME *schele*, a shelter, akin to ON *skjol*, ult. < IE base **(s)keu-*, to cover > HOUSE, HIDE[1]) + -ING⟧ [Scot.] **1** a pasture **2** a shepherd's rude hut or cottage

shi·er[1] (shī′ər) ***n.*** a horse that tends to shy

shi·er[2] (shī′ər) ***adj.*** *alt. compar. of* SHY[1]

shi·est (-əst) ***adj.*** *alt. superl. of* SHY[1]

shift (shift) ***vt.*** ⟦ME *schiften* < OE *sciftan*, to divide, separate < IE **skeib-* > SHIP⟧ **1** to move or transfer from one person, place, or position to another [to *shift* the blame] **2** to replace by another or others; change or exchange **3** to change (gears) from one arrangement to another in driving a motor vehicle **4** to change phonetically, as by Grimm's law **5** [Now Chiefly Dial.] to change (clothes) —***vi.*** **1** *a)* to change position, direction, form, character, etc. *b)* to undergo phonetic change **2** to get along; manage [to *shift* for oneself] **3** to use tricky, evasive, or expedient methods ☆**4** to change from one gear arrangement to another **5** in typing, to change from small letters, etc. to capitals, etc. by depressing a key (**shift key**) **6** [Now Chiefly Dial.] to change one's clothing —***n.*** **1** the act of shifting from one person, place, position, etc. to another; change; transfer; substitution **2** a means or plan of conduct, esp. one followed in an emergency or difficulty; expedient; stratagem **3** a deceitful scheme or method; evasion; trick ☆**4** *short for* GEARSHIFT **5** *a)* a group of people working in relay with another or other groups [the night *shift*] *b)* the regular work period of such a group **6** a change in direction, as of the wind **7** *a)* [Now Rare] a chemise, or woman's slip *b)* a loose dress that hangs straight with no waistline **8** [Now Chiefly Dial.] a change of clothing ☆**9** *Football* a regrouping of offensive or defensive players before the ball is put in play **10** *Linguis.* a phonetic change or series of changes that alters the system of sounds in a language: see GREAT VOWEL SHIFT **11** *Mining* a fault or displacement, as in a vein **12** *Music* a change in the position of the hand, as on the fingerboard of a violin **13** *Physics* a change in the observed frequency of a wave, as of light or sound —**make shift** to manage or do the best one can (*with* whatever means are at hand) —**shift′a·ble** ***adj.*** —**shift′er** ***n.***

shift·less (shift′lis) ***adj.*** **1** lacking the will or ability to do or accomplish; incapable, inefficient, lazy, etc. **2** showing such lack —**shift′less·ly** ***adv.*** —**shift′less·ness** ***n.***

shift·y (shif′tē) ***adj.*** **shift′i·er**, **shift′i·est** **1** [Now Rare] full of shifts or expedients; resourceful **2** [Informal] having or showing a tricky or deceitful nature; evasive —**shift′i·ly** ***adv.*** —**shift′i·ness** ***n.***

shi·gel·la (shi gel′ə) ***n.***, *pl.* **-lae** (-ē) or **-las** ⟦ModL, after Kiyoshi *Shiga* (1870-1957), Jpn bacteriologist⟧ any of a genus (*Shigella*) of Gram-negative bacilli, certain species of which cause dysentery

shig·el·lo·sis (shig′ə lō′sis) ***n.*** ⟦< prec. + -OSIS⟧ dysentery caused by various strains of shigella

Shih Tzu (shēd′zōō′, shēt′sōō′) *pl.* **Shih Tzus** or **Shih Tzu** ⟦Mandarin *shihtzu*, lion⟧ any of a breed of toy dog, developed in China, with long, silky hair, short legs, a short, square muzzle, and a plumed tail curved over the back

shii·ta·ke (shē tä′kē) ***n.*** ⟦Jpn < *shii*, name for any of several trees + *take*, mushroom⟧ an edible Japanese mushroom (*Lentinus edodes*) from a family (Agaricaceae) of basidiomycetous fungi

Shi·ite (shē′īt′) ***n.*** ⟦Ar *shī'a*, followers, faction, sect < *shā'a*, to spread, circulate⟧ a member of one of the two great sects of Muslims: Shiites consider Ali, Muhammad's son-in-law and the fourth of the caliphs, as the first Imam and the rightful successor of Muhammad, and do not accept the Sunna as authoritative: cf. SUNNI —**Shi′ism′** ***n.*** —**Shi·it′ic** (-it′ik) ***adj.***

Shi·jia·zhuang (shu′jyä′jwäŋ′) city in NE China; capital of Hebei province: former transliteration **Shih′chia′chuang′**

shi·kar (shi kär′) ***n.*** ⟦Pers *shikār*⟧ in India, hunting as a sport

shi·ka·ri or **shi·ka·ree** (shi kä′rē) ***n.*** ⟦Hindi *shikāri* < Pers *shikār*, a hunt⟧ in India, a hunter, esp. a native hunter who serves as a guide

shik·ker (shik′ər) ***adj.*** [Slang] *alt. sp. of* SHICKER

Shi·ko·ku (shē′kô kōō′) one of the four main islands of Japan, south of Honshu: 7,258 sq mi (18,798 sq km); chief city, Matsuyama

shik·sa (shik′sə) ***n.*** a woman or girl who is not Jewish: term of mild contempt: also sp. **shik′se** or **shik′seh**

shill (shil) [Slang] ***n.*** ⟦contr. < *shillaber* < ?⟧ **1** the confederate of a gambler, pitchman, auctioneer, etc. who pretends to buy, bet, or bid so as to lure onlookers into participating **2** a person who works energetically to sell or promote something —***vi.*** to act or work as a shill

shil·le·lagh or **shil·la·lah** (shi lā′lē, -lə) ***n.*** ⟦after *Shillelagh*, village in County Wicklow, Ireland, famous for its oaks and blackthorns⟧ a club or cudgel: term used chiefly of or by the Irish: also sp. **shil·le′lah**

shil·ling (shil′iŋ) ***n.*** ⟦ME *schilling* < OE *scylling*, akin to Ger *schilling* < Gmc **skildling*, prob. < **skild-* (see SHIELD) + *-*ling*, -LING[1]⟧ **1** *a)* a former monetary unit of the United Kingdom, equal to $\frac{1}{20}$ of a pound or 12 pence *b)* a cupronickel coin worth one shilling: coinage discontinued in 1971 *c)* a former monetary unit of various other countries in or formerly in the Commonwealth, equal to $\frac{1}{20}$ of a pound or 12 pence **2** the basic monetary unit of: *a)* Kenya *b)* Somalia *c)* Tanzania *d)* Uganda: see the table of monetary units in the Reference Supplement **3** any of several coins of colonial America

Shil·luk (shi lo͝ok′) ***n.*** **1** *pl.* **-luks′** or **-luk′** a member of a Nilotic people of Sudan living principally on the west bank of the White Nile **2** the Eastern Sudanic language of this people

shil·ly-shal·ly (shil′ē shal′ē) ***adv.*** ⟦redupl. of *shall I?* meaning "shall I or shall I not?"⟧ [Now Rare] in a vacillating manner; irresolutely **—*n.*** [Now Rare] vacillation or irresolution, esp. over a trivial matter **—*vi.*** **-lied, -ly·ing** to be irresolute; vacillate, esp. over trifles

Shi·loh (shī′lō) ⟦after an ancient town in Israel: see Josh. 18:1⟧ national military park in SW Tenn., on the Tennessee River: scene of a Civil War battle (1862)

shim (shim) ***n.*** ⟦< ?⟧ ☆a thin, usually wedge-shaped piece of wood, metal, or stone typically inserted under some part so as to level it or make it flush with another part **—☆*vt.*** **shimmed, shim′ming** to fit with a shim or shims

shim·mer (shim′ər) ***vi.*** ⟦ME *schimeren* < OE *scymrian*, freq. formation on base of *scima*, ray, light < IE base **skāi-* > SHINE⟧ **1** to shine with an unsteady light; glimmer **2** to form a wavering image, as by reflection from waves of water or heat **—*n.*** a shimmering light; glimmer **—SYN.** FLASH **—shim′mer·y *adj.***

shim·my (shim′ē) ***n.*** **1** ⟦< CHEMISE misunderstood as pl.⟧ [Old Slang] a chemise ☆**2** ⟦< phr. *to shake a shimmy*⟧ *a)* a jazz dance, popular in the 1920s, characterized by much shaking of the body *b)* a marked shaking, vibration, or wobble, as in the front wheels of an automobile **—☆*vi.*** **-mied, -my·ing** **1** to dance the shimmy **2** to shake, vibrate, or wobble

Shi·mo·no·se·ki (shē′mô nô sä′kē) seaport at the SW tip of Honshu, Japan

shin[1] (shin) ***n.*** ⟦ME *schine* < OE *scinu*, akin to Ger *schiene*, thin plate, *schien-*, shin < IE base **skei-* > SHEATH⟧ **1** the front part of the leg between the knee and the ankle **2** a cut of beef from the lower foreleg **—*vi.*** **shinned, shin′ning** to climb a rope, pole, etc. by using both hands and legs for gripping: usually with *up* or *down*

shin[2] (shēn) ***n.*** ⟦Heb *sīn, shīn*, lit., tooth⟧ the twenty-second letter of the Hebrew alphabet (ש)

Shi·nar (shī′när) region mentioned in the Bible, prob. corresponding to Sumer, in Babylonia

shin·bone (shin′bōn′) ***n.*** TIBIA (sense 1)

☆**shin·dig** (shin′dig′) ***n.*** ⟦folk-etym. form of fol., as if *shin-dig*, a jovial kick in the shin⟧ [Informal] a dance, party, entertainment, or other gathering, esp. of an informal kind

shin·dy (shin′dē) ***n.***, *pl.* **-dies** ⟦< ?⟧ [Old Informal] **1** a noisy disturbance; commotion; row **2** SHINDIG

shine (shīn) ***vi.*** **shone** or (& for *vt.* 2 only) **shined, shin′ing** ⟦ME *schinen* < OE *scinan*, akin to Ger *scheinen* < IE base **skāi-*, to glimmer > Gr *skia*, shadow⟧ **1** to emit or reflect light; be radiant or bright with light; gleam; glow **2** to be eminent, conspicuous, or brilliant; stand out; excel **3** to exhibit itself clearly or conspicuously *[love shining from her face]* **—*vt.*** **1** to direct the light of *[to shine a flashlight]* **2** to make shiny or bright by polishing *[to shine shoes]* **—*n.*** **1** brightness; radiance **2** luster; polish; gloss ☆**3** *short for* SHOESHINE **4** splendor; brilliance; show **5** sunshine; fair weather *[the outdoor concert will be held rain or shine]* ☆**6** [Old Informal] a trick or prank: *usually used in pl.* ☆**7** [Slang] BLACK (*n.* 5): an offensive term of hostility and contempt **—SYN.** POLISH **—☆shine up to** *pt. & pp.* **shined** [Slang] to try to ingratiate oneself with; curry favor with **—☆take a shine to** [Slang] to take a liking to (someone)

shin·er (shī′nər) ***n.*** **1** a person or thing that shines ☆**2** *pl.* **-ers** or **-er** any of a number of freshwater minnows (esp. genus *Notropis*) with silvery scales ☆**3** [Slang] BLACK EYE (sense 2)

shin·gle[1] (shiŋ′gəl) ***n.*** ⟦prob. < Scand, as in Norw *singel*, akin to MDu *singele*, coastal detritus < ?⟧ [Chiefly Brit.] **1** large, coarse, waterworn gravel, as found on a beach **2** an area, as a beach, covered with this **—shin′gly *adj.***

shin·gle[2] (shiŋ′gəl) ***n.*** ⟦ME *schingel*, prob. altered < OE *scindel*, akin to OS *scindula* < WGmc borrowing < L *scindula*, later form of *scandula*, shingle < IE **(s)k(h)end-*, to split, extension of base **sek-*, to cut > SAW[1]⟧ **1** a thin, wedge-shaped piece of wood, asphaltic material, slate, etc. laid with others in a series of overlapping rows as a covering for roofs and the sides of houses ☆**2** a woman's short haircut in which the hair over the nape is shaped close to the head ☆**3** [Informal] a small signboard, esp. that which a physician or lawyer hangs outside his or her office **—*vt.*** **-gled, -gling** **1** to cover (a roof, etc.) with shingles ☆**2** to cut (hair) in shingle style

shin·gle[3] (shiŋ′gəl) ***vt.*** **-gled, -gling** ⟦< Fr dial. (Picardy) *chingler*, var. of Fr *cingler*, to strike with a flexible rod, ult. < L *cingula*: see CINGULUM⟧ to work on (puddled iron) by hammering and squeezing it to remove impurities

shin·gles (shiŋ′gəlz) ***n.*** ⟦ME *schingles*, altered < ML *cingulus* < L *cingulum*, a belt, girdle < *cingere*, to gird (see CINCH): used in ML as transl. of Gr *zōnē*, girdle, shingles, prob. from occurrence of the blisters around the middle of the body in many cases of the illness⟧ *nontechnical name for* HERPES ZOSTER

shin·guard (shin′gärd′) ***n.*** one of a pair of padded guards worn to protect the shins, as by a baseball catcher or hockey goalkeeper

shin·i·ness (shī′nē nis) ***n.*** the state or quality of being shiny; luster; polish

shin·ing (shī′niŋ) ***adj.*** **1** giving off or reflecting light; radiant; bright **2** brilliant; splendid *[a shining example]* **—SYN.** BRIGHT

☆**shin·leaf** (shin′lēf′) ***n.*** ⟦reason for name uncert.⟧ any of a genus (*Pyrola*) of plants of the heath family, with slender stalks having small, rounded evergreen leaves at the base and racemes of globular flowers

shin·ny[1] (shin′ē) ***n.***, *pl.* **-nies** ⟦prob. < SHIN[1]⟧ **1** a simple form of hockey, esp. as played by children **2** the curved stick or club used in this game **—*vi.*** **-nied, -ny·ing** to play shinny Also sp. **shin′ney**

☆**shin·ny**[2] (shin′ē) ***vi.*** **-nied, -ny·ing** ⟦< SHIN[1] + -Y[4]⟧ to climb a rope, pole, etc. by using both hands and legs for gripping: usually with *up* or *down*

☆**shin·plas·ter** (shin′plas′tər, -pläs′tər) ***n.*** **1** a plaster or poultice for use on sore shins **2** [Old Slang] *a)* a piece of paper money of small face value, usually less than a dollar, as any issued by the U.S. government between 1862 and 1878 *b)* a piece of paper money made almost worthless, as by inflation or inadequate security

shin·splints (-splints′) ***pl.n.*** ⟦< SHIN[1] & SPLINT, *n.* 4⟧ [*with sing. or pl. v.*] painful strain of extensor muscles in the lower leg, typically caused by excessive running on a hard surface

Shin·to (shin′tō) ***n.*** ⟦Jpn *shintō, shindō* < SinoJpn *shin*, god (< Chin *shen*) + *tō, dō*, way⟧ a principal religion of Japan, with emphasis upon the worship of nature and of ancestors and ancient heroes and upon the divinity of the emperor: prior to 1945, the state religion: also **Shin′to·ism′** **—Shin′to·ist** ***n., adj.*** **—Shin′to·is′tic *adj.***

shin·y (shī′nē) ***adj.*** **shin′i·er, shin′i·est** **1** full of, or reflecting, light; bright; shining **2** highly polished; glossy **3** worn or rubbed smooth, and having a glossy finish

ship (ship) ***n.*** ⟦ME < OE *scip*, akin to Ger *schiff*, ON *skip* < IE **skeib-* < **skei-*, to cut, separate (> L *scindere*, to cut), extension of base **sek-*, to cut (> SAW[1]): basic sense "hollowed-out tree trunk"⟧ **1** any large seagoing vessel **2** a sailing vessel with a bowsprit and at least three square-rigged masts, each composed of three sections, a lower mast, a topmast, and a topgallant mast **3** a ship's officers and crew **4** an aircraft **—*vt.*** **shipped, ship′ping** ☆**1** to send or transport by any carrier *[to ship cattle by rail]* **2** to take in (water) over the gunwale or side, as in a heavy sea **3** to put or fix (an object) in its proper place on a ship or boat *[ship the oars]* **4** [Informal] to send (*away, out*, etc.); get rid of **—*vi.*** [Now Rare] **1** to go aboard ship; embark **2** to engage to serve on a ship **—ship over** ☆to reenlist in the U.S. Navy **—ship out** **1** to go to sea: said of a sailor or traveler **2** to leave, esp. because of not doing as well as expected: in ☆**shape up or ship out** **—the Ship** the constellation ARGO **—when (or if, etc.) one's ship comes in (or home)** when (or if, etc.) one becomes rich

-ship (ship) ⟦ME < OE *-scipe* (akin to Ger *-schaft*, Du *-scap*) < base of *scieppan*, to create: see SHAPE⟧ *a suffix forming nouns* **1** the quality, condition, or state of being *[hardship, friendship]* **2** *a)* the rank or office of *[professorship]* *b)* a person having the rank or status of *[lordship]* **3** ability or skill as *[statesmanship]* **4** all individuals (of the specified class) collectively *[readership]*

ship biscuit HARDTACK

ship·board (ship′bôrd′) ***n.*** **1** a ship: chiefly in **on shipboard**, aboard a ship **2** [Obs.] the side of a ship **—*adj.*** done, happening, used, etc. on a ship *[a shipboard romance]*

ship·build·er (-bil′dər) ***n.*** a person whose business is the designing and building of ships **—ship′build′ing *n.***

ship chandler a person who deals in ship supplies

ship·fit·ter (-fit′ər) ***n.*** a person whose work is to lay out, fabricate, and position plates, bulkheads, etc. inside the hull of a ship in readiness for riveting or welding

ship·lap (-lap′) ***n.*** **1** siding consisting of boards with rabbets cut in their long edges so that adjoining boards will fit together to form a flush joint **2** such a joint

ship·load (-lōd′) ***n.*** the full load of a ship

ship·man (-mən) ***n.***, *pl.* **-men** (-mən) [Archaic] **1** SEAMAN (sense 1) **2** SHIPMASTER

ship·mas·ter (-mas′tər, -mäs′-) ***n.*** the officer in command of a merchant ship; master; captain

ship·mate (-māt′) ***n.*** a fellow sailor on the same ship

ship·ment (-mənt) ***n.*** **1** the shipping or transporting of goods **2** goods shipped or consigned

ship money a former tax levied on English ports, maritime counties, etc. to provide money for warships

ship of the line [Historical] a sailing warship of the largest class, with guns mounted on three or more decks

ship·own·er (-ō′nər) ***n.*** an owner of a ship or ships

ship·pa·ble (-ə bəl) ***adj.*** that can be shipped

ship·per (-ər) ***n.*** a person or agent who ships goods by any carrier; also, the carrier to whom they are consigned for transporting

ship·ping (-iŋ) ***n.*** **1** the act or business of sending or transporting goods **2** ships, esp. commercial ships, collectively, as those belonging to a certain nation or using a certain port

shipping clerk an employee who prepares goods for shipment, as by packing boxes, affixing postage, etc., and keeps records of shipments made

shipping room a room or department, as in a warehouse, where goods are made ready for shipment, and from which they are taken by a carrier

ship·shape (-shāp′) ***adj.*** having everything neatly in place, as on board ship; trim **—*adv.*** in a neat and orderly manner

ship·side (-sīd′) ***n.*** the area on a dock, pier, etc. alongside a moored ship

ship's papers all the documents that a merchant ship must carry to meet the requirements of port authorities, international law, etc.

ship·way (ship′wā′) ***n.*** the ways used in shipbuilding: see WAY (*n.* 21)

ship·worm (-wurm′) ***n.*** any of a family (Teredinidae) of marine, bivalve mollusks with wormlike bodies: they burrow into and damage submerged wood, as of ships, pilings, etc.

ship·wreck (-rek′) ***n.*** **1** the remains of a wrecked ship; wreckage **2** the loss or destruction of a ship through storm, collision, going aground, etc. **3** any ruin, failure, or destruction —***vt.*** **1** to cause to undergo shipwreck **2** to cause, as a result of a shipwreck, to be stranded in some desolate place, as a desert island **3** to destroy, ruin, or wreck

ship·wright (-rīt′) ***n.*** a man, esp. a carpenter, whose work is the construction and repair of ships

ship·yard (-yärd′) ***n.*** a place where ships are built and repaired

shi·raz (shi räz′) ***n.*** ⟦prob. after fol.⟧ SYRAH: name used mainly in Australia and sometimes in the U.S.

Shi·raz (shi räz′) city in SC Iran

shire (shīr) ***n.*** ⟦ME < OE *scir*, office, charge, akin to OHG *scīra*, official charge⟧ **1** any of the former districts or regions in Great Britain **2** any of the counties of England, esp. one with a name ending in *-shire* **3** any of a breed of large, powerful draft horse with feathery fetlocks, originally raised in the Shires and much used in the Middle Ages as a war horse —**the Shires** the counties of EC England, esp. Cambridgeshire and Lincolnshire

Shi·re (shē′re) river in SE Africa, flowing from Lake Malawi south into the Zambezi: *c.* 250 mi (402 km)

shirk (shurk) ***vt.*** ⟦? akin to Ger *schurke*, scoundrel, rascal⟧ to neglect or evade doing (something that should be done) —***vi.*** to neglect or evade work, duty, etc. —**shirk′er** ***n.***

Shir·ley (shur′lē) ***n.*** ⟦orig. a surname < the E place name *Shirley* < OE *scire*, SHIRE + *leah*, meadow, LEA[1]: hence, lea where the shire moot was held⟧ a feminine name

☆**Shirley Temple** ⟦after Shirley TEMPLE⟧ any of various drinks mixed to resemble a cocktail but containing no alcohol and often garnished with a maraschino cherry

☆**shirr** (shur) ***n.*** ⟦< ?⟧ SHIRRING —***vt.*** **1** to make shirring in (cloth or a garment) **2** to bake (eggs) in small buttered dishes, often with crumbs, cheese, etc.

☆**shirr·ing** (shur′iŋ) ***n.*** **1** a gathering made in cloth by drawing the material up on parallel rows of short running stitches **2** any trimming made by this method

shirt (shurt) ***n.*** ⟦ME *shert* < OE *scyrte* (akin to Ger *schürze*, apron, ON *skyrta*, shirt) < base of *scort*, SHORT⟧ **1** *a)* the usual sleeved garment worn by men on the upper part of the body, often under a coat or jacket, typically having a collar and a buttoned opening down the front *b)* a similar garment for women **2** UNDERSHIRT —☆**keep one's shirt on** [Slang] to remain patient or calm —**lose one's shirt** [Slang] to suffer the loss of all one's money, all one's investment, etc. —**shirt′less** ***adj.***

shirt·dress (shurt′dres′) ***n.*** a dress having trim, simple lines, with the bodice styled like a shirt

shirt·ing (-iŋ) ***n.*** material used in making shirts

shirt·jack·et (shurt′jak′it) ***n.*** a jacket styled like a shirt

shirt·sleeve (-slēv′) ***n.*** either sleeve, esp. a long sleeve, of a shirt: *often used in pl.* —☆***adj.*** **1** in one's shirtsleeves: usually **shirt′sleeved′** **2** suitable for being in one's shirtsleeves [*shirtsleeve* weather] **3** plain, direct, and informal [*shirtsleeve* philosophy] —**in (one's) shirtsleeves** not wearing a coat, jacket, etc. over one's shirt

☆**shirt·tail** (shurt′tāl′) ***n.*** **1** the part of a shirt extending below the waist, often, specif., either of the long parts at the front or back that extend below the hips **2** [Slang] information added, often by a different writer, at the end of a newspaper article —☆***adj.*** [Informal] being only distantly related [a *shirttail* cousin]

☆**shirt·waist** (-wāst′) ***n.*** **1** [Archaic] a woman's blouse or bodice tailored more or less like a shirt **2** a dress with a bodice like this: in full **shirtwaist dress**

shirt·y (shur′tē) ***adj.*** **shirt′i·er, shirt′i·est** ⟦< SHIRT, as in phr. *to have one's* (or *get someone's*) *shirt out*, to become (or make someone) angry + -Y[2]⟧ [Slang, Chiefly Brit.] ill-tempered, cross, angry, etc.

shish ke·bab (shish′ kə bäb′) ⟦Arm *shish kabab* < Ar *shīsh*, skewer + *kabāb*, kebab⟧ a dish consisting of small chunks of marinated meat, esp. lamb, placed on skewers alternately with tomatoes, onions, green peppers, etc., and broiled: also sp. **shish kabob** or **shish kebob**

shit (shit) ***vi.*** **shit, shit′ted,** or, occas., **shat, shit′ting** ⟦earlier *shite* < OE *scītan*, akin to Du *schijten* (MLowG *schīten*), Ger *scheissen* (OHG *skīzan*) < Gmc **skīt-*, **skit-*⟧ to discharge excrement; defecate —***vt.*** **1** to discharge (excrement) **2** to soil by defecation [to *shit* one's pants] **3** [Slang] to tease or try to fool —***n.*** **1** *a)* excrement; feces *b)* [Slang] the act of discharging excrement **2** [Slang] *a)* anyone or anything thought of as being bad, disgusting, foolish, worthless, etc. *b)* the smallest or least thing, amount, etc. (usually in negative constructions) [they didn't do *shit* to help us; the wrecked auto isn't worth *shit*] *c)* nonsense; foolishness *d)* trouble *e)* things in general; stuff *f)* an intoxicant or narcotic, esp. marijuana or heroin —***interj.*** [Informal] used variously to express surprise, anger, disgust, strong disagreement, etc. ➥Considered by many to be at least somewhat vulgar in all uses —**beat** (or **kick,** etc.) **the shit out of** [Slang] to give a severe beating to —**eat shit** [Slang] to be humble or undergo humiliation —**get** (or **have**) **one's shit together** [Slang] to become (or be) organized; put (or have) one's affairs in order —**give a shit** [Slang] to be concerned or interested; care: usually in negative constructions [I just don't *give a shit!*] —**no shit!** [Slang] I can hardly believe it!: an exclamation of doubt or surprise: often used sarcastically —**not worth a shit** [Slang] useless, valueless, etc. —**shit on** [Slang] to behave contemptuously or disparagingly toward —**take a shit** [Slang] to defecate —**tough shit!** [Slang] too bad! —**when the shit hits the fan** [Slang] at the time that a crisis point is reached or disaster takes place —[Slang] **shit′ty** ***adj.*** **-ti·er, -ti·est**

shite (shīt) ***n., interj.*** [Slang] *Brit. var. of* SHIT: somewhat vulgar

shit-eating grin (shit′ēt′iŋ) [Slang] a sly, knowing, or self-satisfied grin: somewhat vulgar

☆**shit·faced** (shit′fāst′) ***adj.*** [Slang] drunk; intoxicated: somewhat vulgar

shit·house (-hous′) ***n.*** [Slang] **1** an outhouse for defecating and urinating **2** any filthy place Somewhat vulgar

☆**shit·kick·er** (-kik′ər) [Slang] ***n.*** a poor, rural person, esp. one from the S or SW U.S. —***adj.*** **1** rural or rustic **2** of or having to do with country music Somewhat vulgar

☆**shit list** [Slang] those people or things regarded by someone with particular contempt, disfavor, etc.: usually in the phrase **on someone's shit list**, in someone's particular disfavor: somewhat vulgar: also sp. **shit′list′** ***n.***

☆**shit·load** (shit′lōd′) ***n.*** [Slang] a very great amount or number: somewhat vulgar [a *shitload* of trouble]

shit·tah (shit′ə) ***n., pl.*** **shit′tahs** or **shit′tim** (-im) ⟦Heb *shita*, pl. *shitim*⟧ a tree mentioned in the Bible, now generally identified as an Asian acacia (*Acacia seyal* or *A. tortils*) with closegrained, yellowish-brown wood

shit·tim (wood) (shit′im) ⟦Heb: see prec.⟧ **1** the wood of the shittah, used in making the ark of the covenant and parts of the Jewish tabernacle: Ex. 25:10, 13, 23, etc. ☆**2** a small tree or shrub (*Bumelia lanuginosa*) of the sapodilla family, growing in the S U.S.

shiv (shiv) ***n.*** ⟦earlier *chiv*, prob. < Romany *chiv*, blade⟧ [Slang] a knife, esp. one used as a weapon

shi·va (shi′və) ***n.*** ⟦< Heb *shiva*, seven⟧ [*often not in italics*] *Judaism* the formal mourning period of seven days, observed as in the home of the deceased, during which friends visit and comfort the bereaved: often in the phrase **sit shiva**, to observe the period of *shiva*: also sp. ***shi′vah***

Shi·va (shē′və) ***n.*** *Hinduism var. of* SIVA

shiv·a·ree (shiv′ə rē′, shiv′ə rē′) ***n.*** ⟦altered < CHARIVARI⟧ a noisy demonstration or celebration; esp., a mock serenade with kettles, horns, etc. to a couple on their wedding night; charivari —***vt.*** **-reed′, -ree′ing** to serenade with a shivaree

shive (shīv) ***n.*** ⟦ME *shive* < OE **scife*, akin to Ger *scheibe*, disk, slice < IE **skeip-* < **skei-*, to cut: see SHIP⟧ a broad, shallow cork, as for a wide-mouthed bottle

shiv·er[1] (shiv′ər) ***n.*** ⟦ME *schievere*, freq. formation < base of prec.⟧ a fragment or splinter of something broken, as glass — ***vt., vi.*** ⟦ME *schiveren*⟧ to break into many fragments or splinters; shatter

shiv·er[2] (shiv′ər) ***vi.*** ⟦ME *sheveren*, altered < *cheveren*, altered < ? *chivelen* in same sense < OE *ceafl*, jaw (see JOWL[1]): prob. basic sense "to have chattering teeth"⟧ to shake, quiver, or tremble, as from fear or cold —***n.*** a shaking, quivering, or trembling, as from fear or cold —**the shivers** a fit of shivering

shiv·er·y[1] (shiv′ər ē) ***adj.*** easily broken into shivers, or fragments

shiv·er·y[2] (shiv′ər ē) ***adj.*** **1** shivering or inclined to shiver; suffering from cold, fear, etc. **2** causing or likely to cause shivering; chilling; terrifying

Shi·zu·o·ka (shē′zo͞o ô′kä) city on the S coast of Honshu, Japan

☆**shlep** or **shlepp** (shlep) ***n., vt., vi.*** **shlepped, shlep′ping** [Slang] *alt. sp. of* SCHLEP

☆**shlock** (shläk) ***n., adj.*** [Slang] *alt. sp. of* SCHLOCK

☆**shlump** (shlump) ***n., vi.*** [Slang] *alt. sp. of* SCHLUMP —**shlump′y** ***adj.***

☆**shmaltz** (shmôlts, shmälts) ***n.*** [Slang] *alt. sp. of* SCHMALTZ —**shmaltz′y** ***adj.*** **shmaltz′i·er, shmaltz′i·est**

shmatte (shmät′ə) ***n.*** ⟦Yiddish⟧ [Slang] **1** a rag **2** a piece of clothing, esp. cheap, old, or tattered clothing **3** a piece of junk

☆**shmooze** (shmo͞oz) ***vi., vi.*** **shmoozed, shmooz′ing,** ***n.*** [Slang] *alt. sp. of* SCHMOOZE

☆**shmuck** (shmuk) ***n.*** [Slang] *alt. sp. of* SCHMUCK

☆**shnook** (shno͝ok) ***n.*** [Slang] *alt. sp. of* SCHNOOK

Sho·ah (shō′ə) ***n.*** ⟦ModHeb *šo'ah* < Heb, devastation, catastrophe⟧ THE HOLOCAUST with ref. to European Jews: usually with *the*

shoal[1] (shōl) ***n.*** ⟦via dial. < OE *scolu*, multitude, school of fish, akin to Du *school* < IE **skel-* < base **(s)kel-*, to cut > SHIELD⟧ **1** a large group; mass; crowd **2** a large school of fish —***vi.*** to come together in or move about as a shoal or school

shoal[2] (shōl) ***n.*** ⟦< earlier adj. *shoal*, shallow < ME *scholde* < OE *sceald*, shallow; akin to OE **scealw*, SHALLOW⟧ **1** a shallow place in a river, sea, etc.; a shallow **2** a sandbar or piece of rising ground forming a shallow place that is a danger to navigation, esp. one visible at low water —***vi.*** to become shallow or shallower —**shoal′y** ***adj.***

SYN.—**shoal** applies to any place in a sea, river, etc. where the water is shallow and difficult to navigate; **bank**, in this connection, applies to a shallow place, formed by an elevated shelf of ground, that is deep enough to be safely navigated by lighter vessels; a **reef** is a ridge of rock, coral, etc. lying at or very close to the surface of the sea, just offshore; **bar** applies to a ridge of sand, etc. silted up across the mouth of a river or harbor and hindering navigation

shoat (shōt) ***n.*** ⟦ME *schote*, akin to Fl < ?⟧ a young, weaned pig

shock[1] (shäk) ***n.*** ⟦Fr *choc* < *choquer*: see the ***vt.***⟧ **1** the impact of persons, forces, etc. in combat or collision **2** *a)* a sudden, powerful concussion; violent blow, shake, or jar [the *shock* of an earthquake] *b)* the result or effect of such concussion **3** *a)* any sudden disturbance or agitation of the mind or emotions, as through great loss or surprise *b)* something causing this **4** an extreme stimulation of the nerves, muscles, etc. accompanying the passage of electric current through the body **5** *short for* SHOCK ABSORBER **6** *Med.* a disorder resulting from ineffective circulation of the blood, produced by hemorrhage, severe infection, disturbance of heart function, etc., and characterized by a marked decrease in blood pressure, a weak, rapid pulse, decreased kidney function, etc. —*vt.* ⟦MFr *choquer*, prob. < MDu *schokken*, to collide < IE **skeug-*, to push, shoot, var. of base **skeub(h)-*, SHOVE⟧ **1** to disturb the mind or emotions of; affect with great surprise, distress, disgust, etc. **2** to affect with physical shock **3** to produce electrical shock in (a body) —*vi.* **1** [Archaic] to come together violently; collide **2** to be shocked, distressed, disgusted, etc. [she doesn't *shock* easily] —*adj.* [Informal] of or characterized by content that is intentionally shocking, offensive, vulgar, etc. [*shock* art, *shock* radio]: see also SHOCK JOCK

shock[2] (shäk) *n.* ⟦ME *schokke*, prob. via MDu or MLowG *schok* < IE **(s)keug-* < base **keu-*, to bend, arch > Russ *kuča*, a pile, HEAP: basic sense, "rounded heap"⟧ a pile of grain sheaves, as of corn or wheat, stacked together on end to cure and dry — *vt., vi.* to gather and pile in shocks

shock[3] (shäk) *n.* ⟦< ? prec.⟧ a thick, bushy or tangled mass, as of hair —*adj.* bushy or shaggy, as hair

shock absorber a device that absorbs the force of sudden jarring actions; esp., the hydraulic or pneumatic tubes used in the suspension systems of motor vehicles, aircraft, etc.

shock·er (shäk′ər) *n.* **1** a person or thing that shocks **2** a startling or shocking story, play, etc.

shocks of corn

shock·ing (shäk′iŋ) *adj.* **1** having an effect like that of a heavy blow or shock; staggering [the *shocking* news of his death] **2** *a)* highly offensive to good taste, propriety, etc.; extremely revolting *b)* very bad —**shock′ing·ly** *adv.*

shocking pink vivid or glaring pink

shock jock ⟦SHOCK[1] (*adj.*) + JOCK[2]⟧ [Slang] a radio talk-show host who features material that is deliberately offensive, vulgar, etc.

Shock·ley (shäk′lē), **William (Bradford)** 1910-89; U.S. physicist, born in Great Britain

☆**shock probation** ⟦from the theory that the shock of even a brief confinement may have a deterrent effect⟧ the release on probation of a criminal after brief imprisonment

☆**shock·proof** (-pro͞of′) *adj.* able to absorb shock without being damaged [a *shockproof* watch]

shock therapy *nontechnical term for* ELECTROCONVULSIVE THERAPY: also **shock treatment**

shock troops troops especially chosen, trained, and equipped to lead an attack: often used fig.

shock wave **1** a surface of discontinuity in a flow of air, sound, etc. set up when the flow suddenly changes from subsonic to supersonic, characterized by marked increases in temperature, pressure, and density of the flow, as in supersonic flow about an airplane wing **2** BLAST (*n.* 6c)

shod (shäd) *vt. alt. pt. & pp. of* SHOE

shod·dy (shäd′ē) *n., pl.* **shod′dies** ⟦19th c. < ?⟧ **1** *a)* an inferior woolen yarn made from fibers taken from used fabrics and reprocessed *b)* cheap woolen cloth made from this **2** anything of less worth or quality than it seems to have; esp., an inferior imitation —*adj.* **-di·er**, **-di·est** **1** *a)* made of shoddy *b)* made of any cheap, inferior material *c)* poorly done or made **2** counterfeit; sham [*shoddy* gentility] **3** contemptible; mean; low [a *shoddy* trick] —**shod′di·ly** *adv.* —**shod′di·ness** *n.*

shoe (sho͞o) *n.* ⟦ME *sho* < OE *sceoh*, akin to Ger *schuh* < IE base **(s)keu-*, to cover > SKY, HIDE[1]⟧ **1** an outer covering for the human foot, made of leather, canvas, etc. and usually having a stiff or thick sole and a heel: sometimes restricted to footwear that does not cover the ankle, as distinguished from a BOOT[1] **2** *short for* HORSESHOE **3** something like a shoe in shape or use; specif., *a)* a metal cap or ferrule fitted over the end of a cane, pole, staff, etc. *b) short for* BRAKE SHOE *c)* a part forming a base for the supports of a superstructure, as of a roof or bridge *d)* the metal strip along the bottom of a sled runner *e)* the casing of a pneumatic tire *f)* the sliding contact plate by which an electric train picks up current from the third rail *g)* a metal protecting plate upon which a mechanical part moves —*vt.* **shod** or **shoed**, **shoe′ing** **1** to furnish or fit with a shoe or shoes **2** to cover, tip, or sheathe (a stick, wearing surface, etc.) with a metal plate, ferrule, etc. —**fill someone's shoes** to take over someone's responsibilities —**in another's shoes** in another's position —☆**the shoe is on the other foot** the situation is reversed for the persons involved —**where the shoe pinches** the source of trouble, grief, difficulty, etc.

shoe·bill (sho͞o′bil′) *n.* a large wading bird (*Balaeniceps rex*), the only member of its family (Balaenicipitidae), with long legs and a heavy, shoelike bill: found along the White Nile in central Africa

shoe·horn (-hôrn′) *n.* an implement of metal, horn, plastic, etc. with a curved blade, inserted inside the back of a shoe to aid the wearer in slipping his or her heel in —*vt.* to force or squeeze into a narrow space

shoe·lace (-lās′) *n.* a length of cord, leather, etc. used for lacing and fastening a shoe

shoe·mak·er (-māk′ər) *n.* a person whose business is making or repairing shoes —**shoe′mak′ing** *n.*

☆**shoe·pac** (-pak′) *n.* ⟦altered by folk etym. (infl. by SHOE) < 17th-c. Delaware trade language *seppock*, shoe, shoes < Delaware *čípahko*, shoes, moccasins (sing. *čí·p·akw*)⟧ PAC (sense 2)

sho·er (sho͞o′ər) *n.* a person who shoes horses

shoe·shine (-shīn′) *n.* **1** the cleaning and polishing of a pair of shoes **2** the shiny surface of polished shoes

shoe·string (-striŋ′) *n.* **1** SHOELACE ☆**2** a small or barely adequate amount of capital [a business started on a *shoestring*] —*adj.* **1** like a shoestring; long and narrow ☆**2** of, operating on, or characterized by a small amount of money [a *shoestring* budget] ☆**3** *Sports* at, near, or around the ankles [a *shoestring* catch, a *shoestring* tackle]

☆**shoestring potatoes** ⟦descriptive⟧ potatoes cut into long, very narrow strips and fried crisp in deep fat

shoe tree a tapered, oval block, as of wood or metal, inserted in a shoe to stretch it or preserve its shape

sho·far (shō′fər, -fär′; *Heb* shô fär′) *n., pl.* **-fars** or Heb. **-frot′** (-frōt′) ⟦Heb *shofar*⟧ a ram's horn used in ancient times as a signaling trumpet, and still blown in synagogues on Rosh Hashana and at the end of Yom Kippur

shofar

sho·gun (shō′gun′, -go͝on′, -go͞on′) *n.* ⟦SinoJpn *shōgun*, military leader < Chin *chiang-chun*⟧ any of the hereditary governors of Japan who, until 1867, constituted a quasi-dynasty exercising absolute rule and relegating the emperors to a nominal position —**sho′gun·al** *adj.* —**sho′gun·ate** (-gə nit, -nāt′) *n.*

sho·ji (shō′jē) *n., pl.* **-ji** or **-jis** ⟦SinoJpn *shōji*, partition⟧ **1** a translucent sliding panel of rice paper on a wooden frame, used in Japanese homes as a partition or door **2** any panel, screen, etc. like this Also **shoji screen**

Sho·la·pur (shō′lə po͝or′) city in S Maharashtra, W India

Sho·lo·khov (shô′lə kôf′), **Mi·kha·il (Aleksandrovich)** (mi khä ēl′) 1905-84; Russ. novelist

sho·lom (shä lōm′) *n., interj. alt. sp. of* SHALOM

Sho·lom A·leich·em *see* ALEICHEM, Sholom

shone (shōn; *chiefly Brit* shän) *vi., vt. alt. pt. & pp. of* SHINE

shoo (sho͞o) *interj.* ⟦echoic⟧ go away; get out: used as in driving away chickens, flies, etc. —*vi.* **shooed**, **shoo′ing** to cry "shoo" —*vt.* to drive away abruptly, by or as by waving the hand or arm and crying "shoo"

☆**shoo·fly** (sho͞o′flī′) *n.* **1** ⟦< phr. *shoo, fly, don't bother me*, in a Civil War nonsense song⟧ [Historical] a kind of shuffling dance **2** a child's rocker with a seat mounted between supports typically designed in the form of horses, swans, etc. **3** ⟦said to be so named from attracting flies which must be shooed away⟧ an open pie with a filling of molasses and brown sugar: in full **shoofly pie**

☆**shoo-in** (sho͞o′in′) *n.* ⟦SHOO + IN[2]⟧ [Informal] someone or something expected to win easily in an election, a race, etc.

shook[1] (sho͝ok) *n.* ⟦prob. var. of SHOCK[2]⟧ ☆**1** a set of the pieces used in assembling a single box, cask, etc. **2** a shock of grain sheaves

shook[2] (sho͝ok) *vt., vi. pt. and dial. pp. of* SHAKE —☆**shook up** [Informal] upset; disturbed; agitated

shoon (sho͞on) *n. archaic or dial. pl. of* SHOE

shoot[1] (sho͞ot) *vt.* **shot**, **shoot′ing** ⟦ME *shoten* < OE *sceotan*, akin to ON *skjōta*, Ger *schiessen* < IE base **(s)keud-*, to throw, shoot > SHUT, OSlav *iskydati*, to throw out⟧ **1** *a)* to move swiftly over, by, across, etc. [to *shoot* the rapids in a canoe] *b)* to make move with great speed or sudden force [to *shoot* an elevator upward] **2** to pour, empty out, or dump, as down a chute **3** *a)* to throw or hurl out or forth [volcanoes *shooting* molten rock into the air] *b)* to cast (an anchor, fish net, etc.) ☆*c)* to throw away or spoil (an opportunity, chance, etc.) *d)* [Informal] to use up or waste (time, money, etc.) **4** to slide (a door bolt) into or out of its fastening **5** *a)* to variegate, streak, fleck, etc. (*with* another color or substance) [a blue sky *shot* with white clouds] *b)* to vary (*with* something different) [a story *shot* with humor] **6** *a)* to thrust out suddenly [snakes *shooting* out their tongues] *b)* to put forth (a branch, leaves, etc.) **7** *a)* to send forth (a missile or projectile); discharge or fire (a bullet, arrow, etc.) *b)* to discharge or emit (rays) with force **8** to send forth (a question, reply, glance, fist, etc.) swiftly, suddenly, or with force or feeling **9** *a)* to discharge or fire (a gun, bow, charge of explosive, etc.) *b)* to hit, wound, kill, or destroy with a bullet, arrow, etc. *c)* to make by firing a bullet [to *shoot* a hole in a door] **10** to hunt game in or on (a tract of land) **11** to take the altitude of (a star) with a transit, sextant, etc. **12** *a)* to take a picture of with a camera; photograph; film *b)* to photograph (a FILM, *n.* 5a) *c)* to make an electronic recording of (an image or images), as with a digital camera **13** to inject (a narcotic drug, etc.) intravenously **14** to straighten (the edge of a board) with a plane ☆**15** [Slang] to send, hand, or give in a swift or hasty way **16** *Games, Sports* *a)* to hit, kick, throw, drive, or propel (a ball, marble, etc.) toward the objective ☆*b)* to throw (dice) as in a game of craps *c)* to make or score (a goal, points, total strokes, etc.) *d)* to play (golf, pool, craps, etc.) *e)* to make (a specified bet), as in craps —*vi.* **1** *a)* to move swiftly; rush; dart [a cat *shot* out of the room] *b)* to spurt or gush [water *shot* from the hose] **2** to be felt suddenly and keenly [pain *shot* through his arm] **3** to grow or sprout, esp. rapidly **4** to jut out; project **5**

to send forth a missile or projectile; discharge bullets, arrows, etc.; go off; fire **6** *a)* to use guns, bows and arrows, etc., as in hunting *b)* to have skill in using a gun, etc. ☆**7** *a)* to photograph or record electronically a scene or subject *b)* to start the cameras working in photographing a scene or FILM (*n.* 5*a*) **8** *Games, Sports a)* to propel a ball, marble, etc. toward the objective *b)* to throw dice —***n.*** **1** *a)* the act of shooting *b)* a shooting trip, party, or contest [a turkey *shoot*] *c)* a round of shots in a shooting contest **2** the action of growing or sprouting **3** a new growth; sprout or twig **4** action or motion like that of something shot, as of water from a hose **5** the launching of a rocket, guided missile, etc. ☆**6** a sloping trough or channel; chute **7** a body of ore in a vein, usually elongated and vertical or steeply inclined **8** a twinge or spasm of pain **9** a period of photographing, filming, or recording electronically, esp. away from the studio [a fashion *shoot*, a three-month *shoot* in Rome] —***interj.*** [Slang] used to tell a person to begin talking [now I'm ready—*shoot!*] —**shoot at** (or **for**) [Informal] to try to reach, gain, or accomplish; strive for —**shoot down 1** to bring down by hitting with a shot or shots **2** [Informal] to destroy, reject, etc., esp. forcefully —**shoot from the hip** to act or talk in a rash, impetuous way —☆**shoot oneself in the foot** to hurt inadvertently oneself or one's own interests or chances for success —☆**shoot off one's** (or **at the**) **mouth** [Slang] **1** to speak without caution or discretion; blab **2** to boast; brag —**shoot up 1** to grow or rise rapidly **2** to hit with several or many shots ☆**3** [Informal] to spread terror and destruction throughout by lawless and wanton shooting ☆**4** [Slang] to inject a narcotic drug, esp. heroin, intravenously

☆**shoot**[2] (sho͞ot) ***interj.*** ⟦euphemism for SHIT⟧ [Slang] used to express anger, disgust, disappointment, etc.

☆**shoot'em-up** (sho͞ot′'m up′) ***n.*** [Slang] a book, film, TV show, video game, etc. characterized by much violent content, gunplay, etc.

shoot·er (sho͞ot′ər) ***n.*** **1** a person or thing that shoots **2** having bullet chambers of a (specified) number: used in hyphenated compounds [a six-*shooter*] ☆**3** [Slang] a shot of whiskey or other liquor

shoot·ing (sho͞ot′iŋ) ***n.*** the act or an instance of shooting a gun, specif., one that results in wounding or killing

shooting box (*or* **lodge**) [Chiefly Brit.] a small house or lodge used by hunters during hunting season

shooting gallery 1 a place, as a booth at an amusement park, for practice shooting at targets ☆**2** [Slang] a place, as an apartment, where a narcotics addict can prepare and inject an illicit drug, as heroin, with equipment usually provided on the premises

☆**shooting iron** [Old Slang, Chiefly West] a pistol, esp. a six-shooter

☆**shooting script** the final version of a movie or TV script as it is to be filmed or taped

shooting star 1 METEOR[1] (sense 1) **2** any of a genus (*Dodecatheon*) of North American plants of the primrose family, with clusters of flowers whose petals are turned back

shooting stick a canelike stick with a spike at one end and a narrow, folding seat at the top for resting on

☆**shoot·out** or **shoot-out** (sho͞ot′out′) ***n.*** **1** [Informal] *a)* a battle with handguns, etc., as between police and criminals *b)* any confrontation to settle a conflict **2** *Sports* any of various tiebreakers at the end of a game, as, in soccer, one in which each team is given penalty kicks

☆**shoot-the-chute** (sho͞ot′*thə* sho͞ot′) ***n.*** CHUTE-THE-CHUTE

shop (shäp) ***n.*** ⟦ME *schoppe* < OE *sceoppa*, booth, stall, akin to Ger *schopf*, porch < IE base *(*s*)*keup-*, a bundle, sheaf of straw: prob. basic meaning "roof made of straw thatch"⟧ **1** *a)* a place where certain goods or services are offered for sale; esp., a small store *b)* a specialized department in a large store [the gourmet *shop*] **2** a place where a particular kind of work is done [a printing *shop*] ☆**3** in some schools, an industrial arts course, class, or department —***vi.*** **shopped**, **shop′ping** to visit a shop or shops so as to look at and buy or price things for sale —***vt.*** ☆**1** [Informal] to shop at (a specified store) **2** [Brit. Slang] *a)* to inform on, esp. to the police *b)* to arrest or imprison **3** [Informal] to offer for sale: often with *around* —**set up shop** to open or start a business —☆**shop around 1** to go from shop to shop, looking for bargains or special items **2** to search about for a good or better job, idea, etc. —**shut up shop 1** to close a place of business, as for the night **2** to go out of business —**talk shop** to discuss one's work

shop·a·hol·ic (shäp′ə hôl′ ik; -häl′-) ***n.*** ⟦SHOP + -AHOLIC⟧ a person who exhibits an excessive need for, or a preoccupation with, shopping

shop floor 1 the part of a factory where the products are manufactured **2** the workers who are engaged in production there

shop·girl (-gurl′) ***n.*** [Old-fashioned] a female clerk in a store

sho·phar (shō′fər, -fär′; *Heb* shô fär′) ***n.*** *alt. sp. of* SHOFAR

shop·keep·er (shäp′kēp′ər) ***n.*** a person who owns or operates a shop, or small store —**shop′keep′ing *n.***

shop·lift (-lift′) ***vt., vi.*** to steal (articles) from a store during shopping hours —**shop′lift′er** (-lif′tər) ***n.***

shoppe (shäp) ***n.*** *alt. sp. of* SHOP (sense 1): early sp. now used faddishly, esp. in the names of such shops

shop·per (shäp′ər) ***n.*** **1** a person who shops **2** a person hired, as by a store, to shop for others **3** a person hired by a store to compare competitors' merchandise and prices ☆**4** a handbill containing advertisements of local stores

shopping bag a large paper or plastic bag with handles, for carrying purchases

shopping center a complex of stores, movie theaters, restaurants, etc. grouped together and having a common parking area

☆**shopping mall** MALL (sense 3*b*)

shop steward a person elected by co-workers in a union shop to represent them in dealing with the employer

shop·talk (shäp′tôk′) ***n.*** **1** the specialized or technical vocabulary and idioms of those in the same work, profession, etc.: see SLANG **2** conversation about one's work or business, esp. after hours

shop·worn (-wôrn′) ***adj.*** **1** soiled, faded, etc. from having been displayed in a shop **2** drab, dull, trite, etc.

shore[1] (shôr) ***n.*** ⟦ME *schore* < OE **score* (akin to MLowG *schore*) < or akin to *scorian*, to jut out < IE base *(*s*)*ker-*, to cut > HARVEST⟧ **1** land at or near the edge of a body of water, esp. along an ocean, large lake, etc. **2** land as opposed to water **3** *Law* SEASHORE

SYN.—**shore** is the general word applied to an edge of land directly bordering on the sea, a lake, a river, etc.; **coast** applies only to land along the sea; **beach** applies to a level stretch of sandy or pebbly seashore or lake shore, usually one that is washed by high water; **strand** is a poetic word for **shore** or **beach**; **bank** applies to rising or steep land at the edge of a stream

shore[2] (shôr) ***n.*** ⟦ME *schore*, akin to MDu, ON *skortha*, a prop, stay: for IE base see prec.⟧ a prop, as a beam, placed under or against something as a support or stabilizer; specif., any of the timbers used to support a boat or ship that is out of water —***vt.*** **shored**, **shor′ing** to support or make stable with or as if with a shore or shores; prop: usually with *up*

shore[3] (shôr) ***vt., vi.*** *archaic or dial. pt. & pp. of* SHEAR

shore·bird (shôr′burd′) ***n.*** any of various birds that live, feed, or nest near the shore, esp. any of a suborder (Charadrii, order Charadriiformes) of birds that includes plovers, snipes, sandpipers, and avocets

☆**shore dinner** a meal that features a variety of seafood dishes

shore leave leave granted to a member of a ship's company for going ashore: term no longer used in the U.S. Navy

shore·less (-lis) ***adj.*** having no shore; boundless

shore·line (-līn′) ***n.*** the edge of a body of water

☆**shore patrol** a detail of U.S. Navy personnel assigned to police duties ashore

shore·ward (-wərd) ***adv.*** toward the shore: also **shore′wards** —***adj.*** moving toward the shore

shor·ing (shôr′iŋ) ***n.*** **1** the act of supporting with or as with shores **2** a system of shores used for support

shorn (shôrn) ***vt., vi.*** *alt. pp. of* SHEAR

short (shôrt) ***adj.*** ⟦ME < OE *scort*, akin to ON *skort*, short piece of clothing, OHG *scurz*, short < IE *(*s*)*kerd-* < base *(*s*)*ker-*, to cut, SHEAR < CURT⟧ **1** not extending far from end to end; not long or not long enough **2** not great in span, range, or scope [a *short* distance, journey, throw, view, etc.] **3** low or relatively low in height; not tall **4** *a)* lasting only a little time; brief *b)* passing quickly [a few *short* weeks] **5** not retentive for long [a *short* memory] **6** condensed or concise, as a literary style, story, speech, etc. **7** brief or abrupt to the point of rudeness; curt **8** quickly angered or irked **9** less than or lacking a sufficient or correct amount, amount of time, etc. [a *short* measure, *short* on money, *short* notice] **10** not far enough to reach the mark, objective, etc. [the shot fell *short*] **11** having a tendency to break or crumble; friable; specif., *a)* crisp or flaky, as pastry made from dough rich in shortening *b)* brittle and inductile when cold (**cold short**) or hot (**hot short**) (said of metal) **12** designating a historical period considered in terms of a briefer duration than typically would be ascribed to it ["the *short* 20th century" (1914-2000) begins with WWI]: cf. LONG[1] (***adj.*** 11) ☆**13** *a)* not having in possession at the time of sale the commodity or security one is selling in anticipation of a decline in price *b)* designating or of a sale of commodities or securities not in the possession of the seller (see also SHORT SALE) **14** *Phonet. a)* articulated for a relatively short time; brief in duration (said of a speech sound) *b)* popularly, not diphthongized [the *short a* in "pan"] (opposed to LONG[1], *adj.* 12*b*) **15** *Prosody a)* requiring a relatively short time to pronounce (said of syllables in quantitative verse) *b)* unstressed (said of syllables in accentual verse) —***n.*** **1** something that is short; specif., *a)* a short sound or syllable, contrasted with one that is long *b)* a film usually less than 30 min. in length *c)* a fish or lobster below the size that may be legally taken *d)* a shot that falls short of the target or objective **2** a variation of clothing size shorter than the average for that size **3** *a)* [*usually pl.*] short, loose trousers reaching partway to the knee, worn in sports, etc. ☆*b)* [*pl.*] men's undershorts **4** [*pl.*] items needed to make up a shortage or deficiency **5** [*pl.*] a byproduct of wheat milling that consists of bran, germ, and coarse meal **6** [*pl.*] trimmings, clippings, etc. left over in the manufacture of various products **7** *short for:* ☆*a)* SHORTSTOP *b)* SHORT CIRCUIT **8** one who has not yet covered the short sale of a stock, commodity, etc. —***adv.*** **1** abruptly; suddenly **2** rudely; curtly **3** briefly; concisely **4** so as to be short in length **5** by surprise; unawares [caught *short*] **6** by a short sale —***vt.*** **1** to give less than what is needed, wanted, or usual **2** to take a short position in (a stock, commodity, etc.) **3** *short for: a)* SHORTCHANGE *b)* SHORT-CIRCUIT —***vi.*** *short for* SHORT-CIRCUIT —SYN. BRIEF —**for short** by way of abbreviation or contraction —**in short 1** in summing up; to summarize **2** in a few words; briefly —**run short** to have or be less than enough —**short and sweet** agreeably or expeditiously brief —**short for** being a shortened form of, or an abbreviation or nickname for —**short of 1** not equaling; less than **2** without a sufficient or correct amount of; lacking **3** not far enough to reach (the mark, objective, etc.) **4** without actually resorting to **5** *see* NOTHING SHORT OF (at NOTHING) —☆**the short end of the stick** the worst of a deal —**short′ness *n.***

☆**short·age** (-ij) *n.* a deficiency in the quantity or amount needed or expected, or the extent of this; deficit

short·bread (-bred′) *n.* a rich, crumbly cake or cookie made with much shortening

short·cake (-kāk′) *n.* 1 *a)* a crisp, light biscuit traditionally served with fruit, whipped cream, etc. as a dessert *b)* any sweet cake, as spongecake, served thus as a dessert 2 such a dessert [strawberry *shortcake*]

short·change (-chānj′) *vt.* **-changed′**, **-chang′ing** 1 to give (someone) less money than is due in change 2 to cheat by depriving of something due —**short′chang′er** *n.*

short circuit 1 a usually accidental low-resistance connection between two points in an electric circuit, resulting in either excessive current flow that often causes damage or in a new shorter circuit that draws current away from the original pathways and components 2 popularly, a disrupted electric circuit resulting from this

short-cir·cuit (-sʉr′kit) *vt.* 1 *Elec.* to make a short circuit in 2 to bypass (an obstruction, custom, etc.) 3 to cause a sudden break in; impede; thwart —*vi.* to develop a short circuit

short·com·ing (-kum′iŋ) *n.* a falling short of what is expected or required; defect or deficiency

☆**short covering** the buying of securities or commodities to close out a short sale

short·cut (-kut′) *n.* 1 a shorter way to get to the same place 2 any way of saving time, effort, expense, etc. —*vt.* **-cut′**, **-cut′ting** to make shorter, as by using a shortcut —*vi.* to take or use a shortcut

short-day (-dā′) *adj. Bot.* maturing and blooming under short periods of light and long periods of darkness

short division the process of dividing a number by another, ordinarily a single digit, without putting down the steps of the process in full

short·en (shôrt′'n) *vt.* 1 to make short or shorter; reduce in length, amount, or extent 2 to reef or furl (a sail) so that less canvas is exposed to the breeze 3 to add shortening in making (pastry, etc.) for crispness or flakiness —*vi.* to become short or shorter

SYN.—**shorten** implies reduction in length, extent, or duration [to *shorten* a rope, a visit, one's life, etc.]; **curtail** implies a making shorter than was originally intended, as because of necessity or expediency [expenditures *curtailed* because of a reduced income]; **abridge** implies reduction in compass by condensing, omitting parts, etc. but usually connotes that what is essential is kept [to *abridge* a dictionary]; **abbreviate** usually refers to the shortening of a word or phrase by contraction or by substitution of a symbol, but also has extended, sometimes jocular applications [an *abbreviated* costume] —*ANT.* **lengthen, extend**

short·en·ing (shôrt′'n iŋ, shôrt′niŋ) *n.* 1 the act of making or becoming short or shorter 2 edible fat, esp. as used to make pastry, etc. crisp or flaky

short·fall (-fôl′) *n.* the act or an instance of falling short, or the amount of the shortage

☆**short fuse** [Slang] a tendency to become angry readily; quick temper

short·grass (shôrt′gras′) *n.* any grass that grows to a height of only a couple of feet above the ground; esp., any of the various grasses, as buffalo grass or grama, that grow in somewhat dry areas of the W Great Plains

short·hair (shôrt′her′) *n.* any member of either of two breeds of short-haired domestic cat: the **American shorthair** has a slightly oblong head and a tapering tail; the **British shorthair** has a round head and a shorter, thick tail: see also COLORPOINT SHORTHAIR, EXOTIC SHORTHAIR, ORIENTAL SHORTHAIR

short·hand (-hand′) *n.* 1 any system of abbreviated writing using quickly made symbols to represent letters, words, and phrases; stenography 2 *a)* a concise way of describing or referring to something *b)* any word, phrase, etc. used in this way —*adj.* using or written in shorthand

short-hand·ed (-han′did) *adj.* short of workers or helpers —**short′-hand′ed·ness** *n.*

short·head (shôrt′hed′) *n.* a brachycephalic person —**short′head′ed** *adj.* —**short′head′ed·ness** *n.*

short·horn (-hôrn′) *n.* any of a breed of beef cattle, orig. from England, with short, inward-curving horns and a heavy, low-set body, typically red, white, and roan in color: they are raised for both beef and milk

☆**short-horned grasshopper** (-hôrnd′) any of a family (Acrididae) of grasshoppers with antennae much shorter than the body, including most common grasshoppers

☆**shor·ti·a** (shôrt′ē ə) *n.* ⟦ModL, after C. W. *Short* (1794-1863), U.S. horticulturist + -IA⟧ any of a genus (*Shortia*, family Diapensiaceae, order Diapensiales) of evergreen, dicotyledonous plants with nodding, bell-shaped, white flowers on long stalks; esp., an American species (*S. galacifolia*) native to the mountains of the Carolinas

short·ie (shôrt′ē) *n.* [Informal] *alt. sp. of* SHORTY

short interest the sum of the short sales in a security, commodity, etc., or on an exchange, which have not been covered as of a given date: see also SHORT SALE

short·ish (-ish) *adj.* rather short

short·list (shôrt′list′) *n.* a list of those candidates for a position, award, etc. not eliminated in the preliminary selection process, from which the final choice will be made: also **short list** —*vt.* [Chiefly Brit.] to place on a shortlist: often in the pp.

short-lived (-livd′, -līvd′) *adj.* having or tending to have a short life span or existence

short loin the front part of a loin of beef, from the ribs to the sirloin

short·ly (-lē) *adv.* 1 in a few words; briefly 2 in a short time; soon 3 abruptly and rudely; curtly

short novel a prose narrative midway between the novel and the short story in length and scope

short order any food that can be cooked or served quickly when ordered, as at a lunch counter —**short′-or′der** *adj.*

☆**short position** 1 the position of one who has not yet covered a short sale 2 SHORT INTEREST

short-range (shôrt′rānj′) *adj.* 1 designating or of a gun, aircraft, missile, etc. that has only a relatively short range 2 not looking far into the future [*short-range* plans]

short ribs the rib ends of beef from the forequarter, next to the plate

short-run (shôrt′run′) *adj.* lasting for a short period of time; short-term

☆**short sale** a sale of securities or commodities which the seller does not yet have but expects to cover later at a lower price

short shrift ⟦orig., a brief time granted a condemned person for religious confession and absolution before execution: see SHRIFT⟧ very little care or attention, as from lack of patience or sympathy —**make short shrift of** to make short work of; dispose of quickly and impatiently

short·sight·ed (-sīt′id) *adj.* 1 NEARSIGHTED 2 having or showing a lack of foresight —**short′sight′ed·ly** *adv.* —**short′sight′ed·ness** *n.*

short-spo·ken (-spōk′ən) *adj.* 1 using only a few words; laconic 2 brief to the point of rudeness; curt

☆**short·stop** (-stäp′) *n. Baseball* 1 the infielder who plays on the left side of the infield near second base and often covers second base 2 the defensive position played by this infielder

short story a kind of story shorter than the novel or novelette, characteristically developing a single central theme and limited in scope and number of characters

short subject a film short, as that shown with a feature film

short-tem·pered (-tem′pərd) *adj.* having a tendency to lose one's temper; easily or quickly angered

short-term (-tʉrm′) *adj.* 1 for or extending over a short time 2 designating or of a bond, capital gain, etc. that involves a relatively short period of time, usually less than a year, for maturity, repayment, amortization, etc. or for computing tax liability 3 designating memory involving recent facts or events —*adv.* over or for a short period of time

short ton *see* TON[1] (sense 1): abbrev. *st*

short-waist·ed (-wās′tid) *adj.* unusually short between shoulders and waistline; with a high waistline

short·wave (-wāv′) *n.* 1 an electromagnetic wave that is shorter than those used in commercial broadcasting, usually a radio wave 60 meters or less in length 2 a radio or radio band for broadcasting or receiving shortwaves: in full **shortwave radio** 3 *a)* the band of frequencies (approximately 1.7 to 30 megahertz) used for shortwave transmissions by international broadcasters, licensed amateurs and other operators *b)* the transmissions that are broadcast

short-wind·ed (-win′did) *adj.* 1 easily put out of breath by exertion 2 breathing with quick, labored breaths 3 brief, often overly or undesirably so: said of speech or writing

short·y (-ē) *n., pl.* **short′ies** [Informal] a person or thing of less than average height or size

Sho·sho·ne[1] (shō shō′nē) *n.* ⟦< ? Shoshonean *tsosoni*, curly head, in allusion to their hairdo⟧ 1 *pl.* **-nes** or **-ne** a member of a group of North American Indians scattered over Idaho, Nevada, Utah, Wyoming, and California 2 the Shoshonean language of this people Also sp. **Sho·sho′ni**

Sho·sho·ne[2] (shō shō′nē) river in NW Wyo., flowing northeast into the Bighorn River: *c.* 100 mi (161 km)

Sho·sho·ne·an (shō shō′nē ən, shō′shə nē′ən) *adj.* designating or of a branch of the Uto-Aztecan language family, including Shoshone, Comanche, Ute, Paiute, and Hopi —*n.* this branch of the Uto-Aztecan language family

Shoshone Falls waterfall on the Snake River, in S Ida.: *c.* 200 ft (61 m)

Sho·sta·ko·vich (shô′stä kô′vich; *E* shäs′tə kō′vich), **Dmi·tri (Dmitrievich)** (d′mē′trē) 1906-75; Russ. composer

shot[1] (shät) *n.* ⟦ME < OE *sceot* < *sceotan* (akin to ON *skot*, Ger *schuss*): see SHOOT[1]⟧ 1 the act of shooting; discharge of a missile, esp. from a gun 2 *a)* the distance over which a missile travels *b)* range; reach; scope 3 an attempt to hit with a missile 4 *a)* any attempt or try *b)* a guess or conjecture 5 a pointed, critical remark 6 *a)* in various games, the flight or path of a ball, puck, etc. after it is shot toward a goal or other object *b)* a stroke, as in tennis or golf *c)* an attempt to score, as in basketball or hockey 7 *a)* a solid projectile designed for discharge from a firearm or cannon, as distinguished from an explosive shell *b)* such projectiles collectively 8 *a)* lead or steel in small pellets, of which a quantity is used for a single charge of a shotgun *b)* a single pellet of this kind 9 the heavy metal ball used in the SHOT PUT 10 a blast, or the amount of explosive used for a blast, as in mining 11 a marksman [a fair *shot*] ☆12 *a)* the act of taking a single photograph *b)* a single photograph *c)* a continuous succession of images as taken on film, videotape, or by a live TV camera 13 ⟦cf. SCOT⟧ an amount due, esp. for drinks or entertainment 14 a hypodermic injection, as of vaccine ☆15 a drink of liquor; specif., JIGGER[2] 16 [Informal] something to bet on, considered from the standpoint of odds or chances of winning [a horse that is a ten-to-one *shot*] 17 *Naut.* a 90-foot length of chain, esp. for an anchor —*vt.* **shot′ted**, **shot′ting** to load or weight with shot —**a shot in the arm** ⟦see *n.* 14⟧ something that bolsters up, reinvigorates, encourages, etc., esp. in a difficult situation —**call the shots** [Informal] **1** to give orders **2** to control what is done or what happens —**have (or take) a shot at** [Informal] to make a try at —**like a shot** **1** quickly; rapidly **2** suddenly

shot² (shät) *vt., vi. pt. & pp. of* SHOOT¹ —*adj.* **1** variegated, streaked, flecked, etc. with another color or substance **2** woven with threads of different colors so as to appear iridescent **3** varied with something different [a novel *shot* through with pathos] ☆**4** [Informal] ruined or worn out

☆**shot clock** *Basketball* a timing device that indicates the number of seconds a team has in which to attempt a shot or else lose possession of the ball

☆**shot glass** a small drinking glass for serving a single jigger, or shot, of liquor

shot·gun (shät′gun′) *n.* **1** a smoothbore gun, usually used for firing a charge of shot at short range, as in hunting small game **2** *Football* an offensive formation, esp. for passing, in which the quarterback takes the snap while standing several yards behind the line of scrimmage: often **shotgun formation** — *vt., vi.* to shoot, force, or threaten with a shotgun —*adj.* **1** done or made under duress; specif., designating a wedding or marriage into which one or both partners are forced, as because of pregnancy **2** covering many points in a random, hit-or-miss way **3** designating a long, narrow house, apartment, etc. with rooms arranged one behind the other —**ride shotgun** **1** [Historical] in the W U.S., to go along as an armed guard, esp. with the driver of a stagecoach **2** [Slang] to ride in the front passenger seat of a motor vehicle

shot hole **1** a drilled hole in which an explosive charge is put for blasting **2** a hole bored in timber by an insect

shot in the dark **1** any attempt that must depend mainly upon luck to succeed **2** a guess based on little or no evidence

shot put *Track & Field* **1** a contest in which a heavy metal ball is propelled for distance with an overhand thrust from the shoulder **2** a single put of the shot —**shot′-put′ter** *n.* —**shot′-put′ting** *n.*

shott (shät) *n.* ⟦Fr *chott* < Ar *shaṭṭ*, orig., river bank⟧ in N Africa, a closed basin, often containing a temporary, shallow, brackish lake

shot·ten (shät′'n) *vt., vi. obs. pp. of* SHOOT¹ —*adj.* ⟦in specialized sense (esp. applied to herrings), prob. infl. by Du *schoten*⟧ **1** that has recently spawned and so become of inferior food value: said of fish **2** [Archaic] undesirable

should (shood) *v.aux.* ⟦ME *scholde* < OE *sceolde*, pt. of *sceal, scal*, I am obliged: see SHALL⟧ **1** *pt. of* SHALL [I had hoped I *should* see you] **2** used to express obligation, duty, propriety, or desirability [you *should* ask first; the plants *should* be watered weekly] **3** used to express expectation or probability [he *should* be here soon; I *should* know by tomorrow] **4** used to express a future condition [if I *should* die tomorrow, if you *should* be late] **5** used in polite or tentative expression of opinion [I *should* think they will be pleased] See usage note at WILL²

shoul·der (shōl′dər) *n.* ⟦ME *schuldere* < OE *sculdor*, akin to Ger *schulter* < IE **skl̥dhrā*, shoulder blade used as a spade < base **(s)kel-*, to cut > SHELL, SHILLING, SKULL⟧ **1** *a)* the joint connecting the arm or forelimb with the body *b)* the part of the body including this joint and extending to the base of the neck **2** [*pl.*] the two shoulders and the part of the back between them: often used fig. with reference to this region as a place where burdens are often carried **3** a cut of meat consisting of the upper foreleg and attached parts **4** the part of a garment that covers the shoulder **5** something like a shoulder in shape or position; shoulderlike projection **6** that part of the top of a piece of type which extends beyond the base of the raised character ☆**7** the strip of land along the edge of a paved road; berm —*vt.* **1** to push or thrust along or through, with or as with the shoulder [to *shoulder* one's way through a crowd] **2** to take or carry upon the shoulder **3** to assume the burden of —*vi.* to push with the shoulder or shoulders —**cry on someone's shoulder** to tell one's troubles to someone in seeking comfort or sympathy —**put one's shoulder to the wheel** to set to work vigorously; put forth vigorous effort —**shoulder arms** *Mil.* **1** to rest a rifle against the (right or left) shoulder, supporting the butt with the hand on the same side **2** *a)* this position *b)* the command to assume it —**shoulder to shoulder** **1** side by side and close together **2** working together; with common effort —**straight from the shoulder** **1** moving straight forward from the shoulder: said of a blow **2** without reserve or evasion; frankly —**turn (or give) a cold shoulder to** **1** to treat with disdain; snub **2** to avoid or shun

shoulder bag a bag of leather, cloth, etc. hung from the shoulder by a long strap, as for carrying personal effects

shoulder blade SCAPULA

☆**shoulder board (***or* **mark)** either of a pair of oblong pieces of stiffened cloth worn on the shoulders of certain uniforms and showing insignia of rank

shoulder girdle PECTORAL GIRDLE

☆**shoulder harness** a restraining device consisting of an anchored strap passing diagonally across the chest, used with a seat belt, as in an automobile: also called **shoulder belt**

shoulder holster a holster attached to a shoulder strap and usually worn under the arm, allowing a handgun to be concealed beneath a jacket or coat

shoulder knot **1** a knot of ribbon or lace formerly worn as an ornament on the shoulder **2** a detachable ornament of braided cord worn on the shoulders of full-dress uniforms

☆**shoulder patch** a cloth insignia identifying the wearer's unit, branch of service, etc., worn on the sleeve of a uniform, just below the shoulder

shoulder strap **1** a strap, usually one of a pair, worn over the shoulder to support a garment **2** a strap worn over the shoulder for carrying a purse, camera, etc.

should·n't (shood′'nt, shoont) *contraction* should not

shouldst (shoodst) *v. archaic 2d pers. sing. pt. of* SHALL: used with *thou*: also **should·est** (shood′ist)

should've (shood′əv) *contraction* should have

shout (shout) *n.* ⟦ME *schoute*, prob. < an OE cognate of ON *skūta*, a taunt, prob. < IE **(s)kud-*, to cry out > SCOUT²⟧ **1** a loud cry or call **2** any sudden, loud outburst or uproar **3** ⟦orig. uncert.⟧ [Brit. Informal] one's turn to buy a round of drinks, etc. —*vt.* **1** to utter or express in a shout **2** [Austral. & N.Z. Informal] to treat (someone) to (a round of drinks, etc.) —*vi.* to utter a shout; cry out loudly —**shout down** to silence or overwhelm by loud shouting; shout louder than —**shout′er** *n.*

☆**shout-out** (shout′out′) *n.* [Slang] a public acknowledgment of recognition, gratitude, or respect, given as in a recorded song or on live TV

shove (shuv) *vt., vi.* **shoved, shov′ing** ⟦ME *shoven* < OE *scufan*, akin to ON *skufa*, Ger *schieben* < IE base **skeubh-*, to throw, shove > SCOFF¹⟧ **1** to push or thrust, as along a surface **2** to push roughly or hastily —*n.* the act or an instance of shoving; a push or thrust —**shove off** **1** to push a boat away from shore, a dock, etc. ☆**2** [Informal] to start off; leave —**shov′er** *n.*

shov·el (shuv′əl) *n.* ⟦ME *schovele* < OE *scofl* < base of *scufan*: see prec.⟧ **1** *a)* a tool with a broad, deep scoop or blade and a long handle: used in lifting and moving loose material, as earth, snow, gravel, etc. *b)* any machine, as a STEAM SHOVEL, equipped with a large scoop or blade for lifting and moving loose material **2** SHOVELFUL —*vt.* **-eled** or **-elled**, **-el·ing** or **-el·ling** **1** to lift and move with a shovel **2** to clean or dig out (a path, etc.) with a shovel **3** to put or throw, in large quantities —*vi.* to use a shovel

shov·el·er or **shov·el·ler** (shuv′əl ər, shuv′lər) *n.* **1** a person or thing that shovels **2** a freshwater duck (*Anas clypeata*) with a very long, broad, flattened bill, living in the Northern Hemisphere mainly in marshes: also called **northern shoveler**

shov·el·ful (shuv′əl fool′) *n., pl.* **-fuls′** as much as a shovel will hold

shovel hat a stiff, low-crowned hat with a broad brim turned up at the sides, worn by some clergymen

☆**shov·el·head** (-hed′) *n.* a small hammerhead shark (*Sphyrna tiburo*) with a narrow head resembling the blade of a shovel

shov·el-nosed (-nōzd′) *adj.* having a broad, flattened nose, head, or bill

shov·el·nose sturgeon (-nōz′) any of a genus (*Scaphirhynchus*) of freshwater sturgeons with a broad, shovel-like snout

☆**shov·el-read·y** (-red′ē) *adj.* designating or of a construction project requiring little more than funding and approval to get underway [federal funding for 5,000 *shovel-ready* jobs]

show (shō) *vt.* **showed, shown** or **showed, show′ing** ⟦ME *schewen* < OE *sceawian*, akin to Ger *schauen*, to look at < IE base **(s)keu-*, to notice, heed > L *cavere*, to beware, OE *hieran*, to HEAR⟧ **1** to bring or put in sight or view; cause or allow to appear or be seen; make visible; exhibit; display **2** *a)* to enter (animals, flowers, etc.) in a competitive show *b)* to exhibit (paintings, sculpture, etc.), as in a gallery **3** to guide; conduct [to *show* a guest to a room] **4** to direct to another's attention; point out [to *show* the sights to visitors] **5** to reveal, manifest, or make evident (an emotion, condition, quality, etc.) by behavior or outward sign **6** to exhibit or manifest (oneself or itself) in a given character, condition, etc. [to *show* oneself to be reliable] **7** to open (a house, apartment, etc.) to prospective buyers or renters **8** to make evident by logical procedure; explain or prove [to *show* that something is right] **9** to make clear by going through a procedure; demonstrate [to *show* how to tie a bowknot] **10** to register; indicate [a clock *shows* the time] **11** to grant or bestow (favor, kindness, mercy, etc.) **12** *Law* to allege; plead [to *show* cause] —*vi.* **1** to be or become seen or visible; appear **2** *a)* to be apparent or noticeable [a scratch that hardly *shows*] *b)* to be visibly pregnant [five months pregnant and still not *showing*] **3** to have a given appearance; appear [to *show* to good effect] ☆**4** to finish third or better in a horse race or dog race **5** [Informal] to come or arrive as expected; make an appearance **6** *Theater* to give a performance; appear —*n.* **1** a showing, demonstration, or manifestation [a *show* of passion] **2** a display or appearance, specif. a colorful or striking one **3** spectacular, pompous display; ostentation **4** an indication of the presence of metal, coal, oil, etc. in the earth; trace **5** something false or superficial; semblance; pretense [sorrow that was mere *show*] **6** a person or thing looked upon as peculiar, ridiculous, laughable, etc.; spectacle; sight **7** a public display or exhibition centered around a particular activity or industry [a trade *show*] **8** a presentation of entertainment, as a theatrical production, TV program, film, etc. ☆**9** third position at the finish of a horse race or dog race **10** [Informal] any undertaking, matter, or affair —*adj.* of or having to do with a SHOW (*n.* 7 or 8), specif. a Broadway or Hollywood musical [a medley of *show* tunes] —**for show** in order to attract notice or attention —**get (or put) the show on the road** [Informal] to set things in operation; start an activity, venture, etc. —**good show!** [Chiefly Brit.] an exclamation of appreciation and congratulations on another's accomplishment —**show someone in (or out)** to usher someone into (or out of) a given place —**show off** **1** to make a display of; exhibit in a showy manner **2** to behave in a manner intended to attract attention —**show up** **1** to bring or come to light; expose or be exposed, as faults **2** to be clearly seen; stand out **3** to come; arrive; make an appearance —**show someone up** [Informal] to behave in a way that deliberately calls attention to the failure or shortcoming of (a rival, opponent, etc.) —**steal the show** to become the main focus of attention, plaudits, etc., esp. if in a subordinate role or position

---

SYN.—**show** implies a putting or bringing something into view so that it can be seen or looked at [show us the garden]; to **display** something is to spread it out so that it is shown to advantage [jewelry *displayed* on a sales counter]; **exhibit** implies prominent display, often for the purpose of attracting public attention or inspection [to *exhibit* products at a fair]; **expose** implies the laying open and displaying of something that has been covered or concealed [this bathing suit *exposes* the scar]; **flaunt** implies an ostentatious, impudent, or defiant display [to *flaunt* one's riches, vices, etc.]

show and tell an elementary-school activity in which a student brings in an object of interest, shows it to the class, and talks about it: also **show′-and-tell′** ***n.***

show bar a nightclub or bar, typically upscale, that features an array of exotic dancers

show bill a sheet or poster containing a notice or advertisement: also **show card**

show·biz (shō′biz′) ***n.*** [Informal] SHOW BUSINESS —**show′biz′zy** ***adj.***, **show′-biz′zy**

☆**show·boat** (-bōt′) ***n.*** **1** a boat, esp. a steamboat, containing a theater and carrying a troupe of actors who play river towns **2** [Slang] a showoff; exhibitionist —***vi.*** [Slang] to show off

show·bread (-bred′) ***n.*** ⟦< earlier *shewbread* < SHEW + BREAD, after Ger *schaubrot*, Luther's transl. of Heb *lechim panim*, lit., bread of the (divine) face, or presence⟧ *Judaism* the twelve loaves of unleavened bread placed at the altar in the ancient Temple as a token offering every Sabbath by the priests

☆**show business** the theater, films, TV, etc. as a business or industry

☆**show·case** (-kās′) ***n.*** **1** a glass-enclosed case for protecting things on display, as in a store or exhibition **2** anything displaying someone or something to good advantage [the revue was a *showcase* for new talent] —***vt.*** **-cased′**, **-cas′ing** to display to good advantage

☆**show·down** (-doun′) ***n.*** [Informal] **1** *Poker* the displaying, faceup on the table, of the hands of all of the players who have not withdrawn as of the final round of betting, to determine who wins the pot **2** any action or confrontation that brings matters to a climax or settles them

show·er[1] (shō′ər) ***n.*** a person who shows, exhibits, etc.

show·er[2] (shou′ər) ***n.*** ⟦ME *schoure* < OE *scur*, akin to Ger *schauer*, shower, squall < IE base **(s)keu-*, to cover > SHOE, HIDE[1]⟧ **1** a brief fall of rain, or sometimes of hail, sleet, or snow **2** a sudden, abundant fall or discharge, as of tears, meteors, rays, sparks, etc. **3** an abundant flow; rush [a *shower* of compliments] ☆**4** a party at which a number of gifts are presented to the guest of honor [a bridal *shower*] ☆**5** *a)* a way of bathing in which the body is sprayed with fine streams of water from a perforated nozzle, usually fixed overhead (sometimes **shower bath**) *b)* an apparatus, as in a bathtub, or a room or enclosure used for this —***vt.*** **1** to make wet as with a spray of water; sprinkle; spray **2** to pour forth or scatter in or as in a shower [*showered* with praise] —***vi.*** **1** to fall or come as a shower **2** to bathe under a shower —**show′er·y** ***adj.***

☆**show·girl** (shō′gurl′) ***n.*** **1** CHORUS GIRL **2** a female EXOTIC DANCER

show·i·ly (shō′ə lē) ***adv.*** in a showy manner

show·i·ness (-ē nis) ***n.*** the quality or condition of being showy

show·ing (-iŋ) ***n.*** **1** the act of presenting or bringing to view or notice **2** an exhibition; formal display ☆**3** a performance, appearance, etc. [a good *showing* in the contest]

show·man (shō′mən) ***n.***, *pl.* **-men** (-mən) **1** a person whose business is producing or presenting shows **2** a person skilled at this or at presenting anything in an exciting way —**show′man·ship′** ***n.***

Show Me State *name for* MISSOURI[2]

shown (shōn) ***vt., vi.*** *alt. pp. of* SHOW

show·off (shō′ôf′) ***n.*** [Informal] **1** the act of showing off; vain or showy display **2** a person who shows off

show of hands a raising of hands, as in voting or volunteering

show·piece (shō′pēs′) ***n.*** **1** something displayed or exhibited **2** something that is a fine example of its kind

show·place (-plās′) ***n.*** any place that is beautiful, lavishly furnished, etc., esp. such a place that is open to the public

show·room (-ro͞om′) ***n.*** a room where merchandise is displayed, as for advertising or sale

show·stop·per (-stäp′ər) ***n.*** **1** a song or sequence in a musical theater production, show, etc. so exciting or impressive that applause from the audience interrupts the performance **2** anything so exciting, impressive, showy, etc. that it attracts much attention —**show′stop′ping** ***adj.***, **show′-stop′ping**

show·time (-tīm′) ***n.*** the time when a show begins

show trial a trial, widely publicized and seemingly open and fair, of a person regarded as a political subversive or ideological dissident, in which a verdict of guilty is assured by means of false evidence, a forced confession, etc.

☆**show window** a store window in which merchandise is displayed

show·y (-ē) ***adj.*** **show′i·er**, **show′i·est** **1** of striking or attractive appearance **2** attracting attention in a gaudy or flashy way

sho·yu (shō′yo͞o) ***n.*** ⟦Jpn⟧ SOY SAUCE

shp *abbrev.* shaft horsepower

shpt *abbrev.* shipment

shr *abbrev.* share(s)

shrank (shraŋk) ***vt., vi.*** *alt. pt. of* SHRINK

shrap·nel (shrap′nəl) ***n.*** ⟦after H. *Shrapnel* (1761-1842), Brit general who invented it⟧ **1** an artillery shell filled with an explosive charge and many small metal balls, designed to explode in the air over the objective **2** the balls scattered by such an explosion **3** any fragments scattered by an exploding shell, bomb, etc.

shred (shred) ***n.*** ⟦ME *schrede* < OE *screade*, akin to Ger & MDu *schrot* < IE **(s)kreu(t)-* (> L *scrotum*, SCROTUM) < base **(s)ker-*, to cut > SHEAR, HARVEST⟧ **1** a long, narrow strip or piece made by cutting or tearing **2** a very small piece or amount; fragment; particle [not a *shred* of evidence] —***vt.*** **shred′ded** or **shred**, **shred′ding** to cut or tear into shreds —**shred′da·ble** ***adj.***

shredded wheat partly cooked wheat that is shredded, formed into biscuits, toasted in an oven, and used as breakfast cereal

shred·der (shred′ər) ***n.*** **1** a person or thing that shreds **2** an apparatus for cutting large quantities of paper into thin strips: used as to destroy confidential documents or to convert waste paper into packing material

Shreve·port (shrēv′pôrt′) ⟦after H. M. *Shreve* (1785-1851), Mississippi River steamboat captain⟧ city in NW La.

shrew (shro͞o) ***n.*** ⟦ME *schrewe*, a malicious person < OE *screawa*, shrewmouse, akin to OHG *scrawaz*, dwarf, goblin, MHG *schröuwel*, devil < IE **(s)ker-*: see SHRED⟧ **1** any of a number of small, slender, mouselike, insectivorous mammals (esp. family Soricidae) with soft fur and a long, pointed snout **2** a scolding, bad-tempered woman

shrewd (shro͞od) ***adj.*** ⟦ME *schrewed*, pp. of *schrewen*, to curse < *schrewe*: see prec.⟧ **1** [Obs.] *a)* evil, bad, wicked, mischievous, shrewish, etc. *b)* artful, cunning, wily, etc. in one's dealings with others **2** keen-witted, clever, or sharp in practical affairs; astute: the usual current sense **3** [Archaic] keen; piercing; sharp —**shrewd′ly** ***adv.*** —**shrewd′ness** ***n.***

SYN.—**shrewd** implies keenness of mind, sharp insight, and a cleverness in practical matters [a *shrewd* comment, businessman, etc.]; **sagacious** implies keen discernment and farsighted judgment [a *sagacious* counselor]; **perspicacious** suggests the penetrating mental vision or discernment that enables one clearly to see and understand what is obscure, hidden, etc. [a *perspicacious* judge of character]; **astute** implies shrewdness combined with sagacity and sometimes connotes, in addition, artfulness or cunning [an *astute* politician] See also **clever**

shrew·die (shro͞od′ē) ***n.*** [Informal] a person who is shrewd

shrew·ish (shro͞o′ish) ***adj.*** like a shrew in disposition; evil-tempered —**shrew′ish·ly** ***adv.*** —**shrew′ish·ness** ***n.***

shrew·mouse (-mous′) ***n.***, *pl.* **-mice′** (-mīs′) SHREW (sense 1)

shriek (shrēk) ***vi.*** ⟦ME *schriken*, var. of *scriken*, prob. < ON **skrīka*, to cry, akin to *skrikja*, cry of birds: for IE base see SCREAM⟧ to make a loud, sharp, piercing cry or sound, as certain animals, or a person in terror, pain, or laughter; screech —***vt.*** to utter with a shriek —***n.*** a loud, piercing cry or sound —**shriek′er** ***n.***

shriev·al·ty (shrēv′əl tē) ***n.***, *pl.* **-ties** in England, esp. formerly, *a)* a sheriff's office or term of office *b)* the district served by a sheriff

shrieve (shrēv) ***n.*** *obs. var. of* SHERIFF —**shriev′al** ***adj.***

shrift (shrift) ***n.*** ⟦ME *schrift* < OE *scrift* < *scrifan*, to SHRIVE⟧ [Archaic] **1** confession to and absolution by a priest **2** the act of shriving See also SHORT SHRIFT

shrike (shrīk) ***n.*** ⟦via dial. < OE *scric*, thrush, shrike, akin to ME *schriken*, SHRIEK⟧ any of a family (Laniidae) of predatory, shrill-voiced passerine birds with hooked beaks, gray, black, and white plumage, and long tails: most types feed on insects, some on small birds, frogs, etc., which they may impale on thorns before eating

shrill (shril) ***adj.*** ⟦ME *shrille*, akin to LowG *schrell*, Ger *schrill*: echoic, prob. akin to SHRIEK⟧ **1** having or producing a high, thin, piercing tone; high-pitched **2** characterized or accompanied by shrill sounds **3** unrestrained and irritatingly insistent **4** [Archaic] keen; sharp; biting; poignant —***adv.*** [Rare] in a shrill manner —***vi.*** to make a shrill noise or sound —***vt.*** to utter shrilly —**shril′ly** ***adv.*** —**shrill′ness** ***n.***

shrimp (shrimp) ***n.***, *pl.* **shrimps** or **shrimp** ⟦ME *schrimpe*, shrimp, puny person < base of OE *scrimman* (akin to obs. Ger *schrimpfen*, to shrink, dry up) < IE **(s)kremb-*, to turn, twist, shrink < base **(s)ker-*, to turn⟧ **1** any of a large number of small, slender, long-tailed decapods, mostly marine: many are highly valued as food **2** [Informal] a small or insignificant person —***vi.*** to fish for shrimp —**shrimp′er** ***n.***

shrimp plant ⟦from the fancied resemblance of the spike to the tail of a shrimp⟧ a widely grown tropical American plant (*Beloperone guttata*) of the acanthus family, with long, curving spikes of tiny, white flowers

shrine (shrīn) ***n.*** ⟦ME *schrin* < OE *scrin* < L *scrinium*, chest, box, orig., a round container < IE **(s)krei-* < base **(s)ker-*, to turn: see fol.⟧ **1** *a)* RELIQUARY *b)* a niche or other setting for a statue, picture, or other object arousing or designed to arouse devotion *c)* a small area or structure arranged for private devotion **2** *a)* a place revered as the place of death or burial of a saint or other venerable personage *b)* a place revered as the site of a reported supernatural apparition, miraculous occurrence, etc. *c)* any of certain churches or chapels often visited by pilgrims, specif. by those seeking special spiritual help, cures, etc. **3** any site or structure used in worship or devotion; esp., an area or a temple or templelike structure used in the worship of one or more deities **4** *a)* a place or structure esteemed for its importance or centrality as in history or the arts *b)* a place or structure designed as a memorial to someone or something —***vt.*** **shrined**, **shrin′ing** ENSHRINE

shrink (shriŋk) ***vi.*** **shrank** or **shrunk**, **shrunk** or **shrunk′en**, **shrink′ing** ⟦ME *schrynken* < OE *scrincan*, akin to Swed *skrynka*, to wrinkle < IE **(s)kreng-* < base **(s)ker-*, to bend, turn > SHRIMP, Gr *kirkos*, a ring, L *curvus*, curved⟧ **1** to become or seem to become smaller, more compact, etc.; contract, as from heat, cold, moisture, etc. **2** to lessen, as in amount, worth, etc. **3** to draw back; turn away; cower, as from fear **4** to hold back, as from taking action; hesitate or recoil *[to shrink from doing one's duty]* —*vt.* to cause to shrink or contract; specif., to cause (fabric) to shrink by a special process in manufacturing so as to minimize later shrinkage —*n.* **1** a shrinking; shrinkage ☆**2** ⟦< (HEAD)SHRINK(ER)⟧ [Slang] a clinical psychiatrist or psychologist —*SYN.* CONTRACT —**shrink′a·ble** *adj.*

shrink·age (shriŋ′kij) *n.* **1** the act or process of shrinking; contraction in size, as of a fabric in washing **2** decrease in value; depreciation **3** the total loss in weight of livestock from the time of shipment to the final processing as meat **4** the amount of such shrinking, decrease, etc.

shrinking violet a very shy or unassuming person

shrink-wrap (shriŋk′rap′) *vt.* **-wrapped′**, **-wrap′ping** to wrap (a commodity) in a tough, transparent plastic material which is then shrunk by heating to form a sealed, tightfitting package —*n.* a wrapping of such material

shrive (shrīv) [Archaic] *vt.* **shrived** or **shrove**, **shriv·en** (shriv′ən) or **shrived**, **shriv′ing** ⟦ME *shriven* < OE *scrifan*, akin to Ger *schreiben*, to write < early WGmc borrowing < L *scribere*, to write: see SCRIBE⟧ **1** to hear the confession of and absolve **2** to get absolution for oneself by confessing —*vi.* **1** to make one's confession **2** to hear confessions

shriv·el (shriv′əl) *vt., vi.* **-eled** or **-elled**, **-el·ing** or **-el·ling** ⟦Early ModE, prob. < Scand, as in Swed dial. *skryvla*, to wrinkle⟧ **1** to shrink and make or become wrinkled or withered **2** to make or become helpless, useless, or inefficient

shroff (shräf) *n.* ⟦Anglo-Ind *sharaf* < Hindi *sarrāf* < Ar *ṣarrāf*, money-changer < *ṣarafa*, to issue, disburse⟧ in Asia *a)* a banker or money-changer *b)* an expert in testing coins —*vt.* to examine (coins) to separate the genuine from the counterfeit

Shrop·shire[1] (shräp′shir) *n.* any of a breed of medium-sized, dark-faced sheep, orig. developed in Shropshire

Shrop·shire[2] (shräp′shir) county in W England: 1,347 sq mi (3,488 sq km)

shroud (shroud) *n.* ⟦ME *schroude* < OE *scrud*, akin to ON *skrud*, accouterments, cloth, OE *screade*, SHRED⟧ **1** a cloth used to wrap a corpse for burial; winding sheet **2** something that covers, protects, or screens; veil; shelter **3** any of a set of ropes or wires stretched from a ship's side to a masthead to offset lateral strain on the mast **4** any of the set of lines from the canopy of a parachute to the harness: in full **shroud line** —*vt.* **1** to wrap (a corpse) in a shroud **2** to hide from view; cover; screen **3** [Archaic] to shelter and protect —*vi.* [Archaic] to take shelter

shrove (shrōv) *vt., vi. alt. pt. of* SHRIVE

Shrove·tide (shrōv′tīd′) *n.* ⟦ME *schroffetide* < *shriven*, to SHRIVE + TIDE[1]⟧ *former name for* the time, esp. the Tuesday (**Shrove Tuesday**: cf. MARDI GRAS), just before Ash Wednesday: so called from the custom of preparing for Lent by sacramental confession esp. during this period

shrub[1] (shrub) *n.* ⟦Early ME *schrubbe* < OE *scrybb*, brushwood, akin to SCRUB[1], Dan *skrubbe*⟧ a low, woody plant with several permanent stems instead of a single trunk; bush —**shrub′like′** *adj.*

shrub[2] (shrub) *n.* ⟦Ar *sharāb*, a drink: see SYRUP⟧ **1** a drink made of fruit juice, sugar, and, usually, rum or brandy **2** an iced drink made with slightly acid fruit juice and water

shrub·ber·y (shrub′ər ē) *n.* **1** shrubs collectively **2** *pl.* **-ber·ies** [Brit.] a place where many shrubs are grown

shrub·by (-ē) *adj.* **-bi·er**, **-bi·est** **1** covered with shrubs **2** like a shrub —**shrub′bi·ness** *n.*

shrug (shrug) *vt., vi.* **shrugged**, **shrug′ging** ⟦ME *schruggen*, orig., to shiver (as with cold)⟧ to draw up (the shoulders), as in expressing indifference, doubt, disdain, contempt, etc. —*n.* **1** the gesture so made **2** a woman's short jacket or sweater with wide, loose sleeves —**shrug off** to dismiss or disregard in a carefree way

shrunk (shruŋk) *vi., vt. alt. pt. & pp. of* SHRINK

shrunk·en (shruŋ′kən) *vi., vt. alt. pp. of* SHRINK —*adj.* contracted in size; shriveled

sht *abbrev.* sheet

shtet·l (shtet′'l) *n., pl.* **shtet′lach′** or Eng. **shtet′ls** ⟦Yiddish, dim. of *shtot*, city < MHG *stat*, city⟧ *[also in roman type]* any of the former Jewish village communities of E Europe, esp. in Russia

shtg *abbrev.* shortage

☆**shtick** (shtik) *n.* ⟦< E Yiddish *shtik*, pl., pranks, interpreted as sing. < *shtik*, lit., piece < MHG *stücke*⟧ [Slang] **1** a comic scene or piece of business, as in a vaudeville act **2** an attention-getting device **3** a special trait, talent, etc. Also sp. **shtik**

shuck (shuk) *n.* ⟦< ?⟧ **1** a shell, pod, or husk; esp., the husk of an ear of corn ☆**2** the shell of an oyster or clam ☆**3** [*pl.*] [Informal] something valueless *[not worth shucks]* ☆**4** [Slang] *a)* a hoax or fraud *b)* a fraudulent person or thing; phony —*vt.* **1** to remove shucks from (corn, clams, etc.) **2** to remove like a shuck *[to shuck one's clothes]* ☆**3** [Slang] to fool or hoax —*vi.* [Slang] to fool or deceive, often in a playful way —**shuck′er** *n.*

☆**shucks** (shuks) *interj.* ⟦prob. < prec.⟧ [Slang] used to express mild disappointment, embarrassment, etc.

shud·der (shud′ər) *vi.* ⟦ME *schoderen*, akin to Ger *schaudern*, to feel dread, OFris *skedda*, to shake < IE base **(s)kut-*, to shake > Lith *kutù*, to shake up⟧ to shake or tremble suddenly and violently, as in horror or extreme disgust —*n.* the act of shuddering; a convulsive tremor of the body —**the shudders** a feeling of horror, repugnance, etc. —**shud′der·ing·ly** *adv.* —**shud′der·y** *adj.*

shuf·fle (shuf′əl) *vt.* **-fled**, **-fling** ⟦Early ModE, prob. < or akin to LowG *schuffeln*, to walk clumsily, shuffle cards < base of SHOVE⟧ **1** *a)* to move (the feet) with a dragging or shoving gait *b)* to perform (a dance) with such steps **2** to mix (playing cards) so as to change their order, as before dealing **3** to push or mix together in a jumbled or disordered mass **4** to shift (things) about from one place to another **5** to bring, put, or thrust (*into* or *out of*) clumsily or trickily —*vi.* **1** to move by dragging or scraping the feet, as in walking or dancing **2** to get (*into* or *out of* a situation or condition) by trickery, evasion, lies, etc. **3** to act in a shifty, dishonest manner; practice deceit, trickery, evasion, etc. **4** to change or shift repeatedly from one position or place to another **5** to shuffle playing cards **6** to move clumsily (*into* or *out of* clothing) —*n.* **1** the act of shuffling **2** a tricky or deceptive action; evasion; trick **3** *a)* a shuffling of the feet *b)* a gait, dance, etc. characterized by this **4** *a)* the act of shuffling playing cards *b)* a player's turn or right to shuffle —☆**lose in the shuffle** to leave out or disregard in the confusion of things —**shuffle off** to get rid of —**shuf′fler** *n.*

shuf·fle·board (shuf′əl bôrd′) *n.* ⟦< earlier *shovel board*: so named because of the shape of the cues⟧ **1** a game in which large disks are pushed with a cue along a smooth lane toward numbered areas of a diagram **2** the marked surface on which it is played

shul (shōōl) *n.* ⟦Yiddish, lit., school < MHG *schuol*, school < L *schola*, SCHOOL[1]⟧ SYNAGOGUE

Shu·lam·ite (shōō′lə mīt′) *n.* the name of the maiden in the Song of Solomon, 6:13

shun (shun) *vt.* **shunned**, **shun′ning** ⟦ME *schunien* < OE *scunian*⟧ to keep away from; avoid scrupulously or consistently, often, specif., as a practice by a group against a co-worker, coreligionist, etc. who has fallen out of favor —**shun′ner** *n.* —**shun′ning** *n.*

☆**shun·pike** (shun′pīk′) *n.* a secondary road used to avoid turnpikes and expressways —**shun′pik′er** *n.* —**shun′pik′ing** *n.*

shunt (shunt) *vt., vi.* ⟦ME *schunten* < ? or akin to SHUN⟧ **1** to move or turn to one side; turn aside or out of the way **2** to shift or switch, as a train, car, etc. from one track to another **3** *Elec.* to divert or be diverted by a shunt: said of a current **4** to provide or connect with a shunt —*n.* **1** the act of shunting **2** SWITCH (*n.* 6*a*) **3** *Elec.* a conductor connecting two points in a circuit in parallel so that an additional pathway is created for the current **4** *Med.* an abnormal natural channel or a surgically created one allowing flow from one organ or pathway to another —**shunt′er** *n.*

shunt winding the winding of an electric motor or generator in such a way that the field and armature circuits are connected in parallel —**shunt′-wound′** (-wo͝ond′) *adj.*

shush (shush) *interj.* ⟦echoic⟧ hush; be quiet —*vt.* to say "shush" to; tell (another) to be quiet; hush

Shu·shan (shōō′shän′) *Biblical name for* SUSA

shut (shut) *vt.* **shut**, **shut′ting** ⟦ME (W Midland) *schutten* < OE *scyttan* < base of *sceotan*, to cast: see SHOOT[1]⟧ **1** *a)* to move (a door, window, lid, etc.) into a position that closes the opening to which it is fitted *b)* to close by so moving its lid, cover, etc. *[shut a cash box, one's eyes, etc.]* *c)* to fasten (a door, etc.) securely, as with a bolt or catch **2** to close (an opening, passage, container, etc.) **3** *a)* to prevent or forbid entrance to or exit from; close or bar *b)* to confine or enclose *in* a room, cage, building, etc. **4** to fold up or bring together the parts of (an umbrella, a book, the mouth, etc.) **5** to stop or suspend the operation of (a business, school, etc.) —*vi.* to move to a closed position; be or become shut —*adj.* closed, fastened, or secured —*n.* **1** the act or time of shutting or closing; close **2** the connecting line between two pieces of welded metal —**shut down** **1** to close by lowering **2** to descend and envelop or darken a place: said of night, fog, etc. **3** to cease or cause to cease operating; close (a factory, etc.) ☆**4** [Informal] to bring to an end or restrict severely (with *on* or *upon*) —**shut in** to surround or enclose; hem in —**shut of** [Dial.] rid of; free from —**shut off** **1** to prevent the passage of (electricity, steam, etc.) **2** to prevent passage through (a road, faucet, etc.) **3** to separate; isolate —**shut out** **1** to deny entrance or admission to; exclude (sound, a view, etc.) ☆**2** to prevent (an opposing side or team) from scoring in a game or from winning even one game in a series of games —**shut up** **1** to enclose, confine, or imprison **2** to close all the entrances to **3** [Informal] *a)* to stop or cause to stop talking *b)* to prevent from speaking or writing freely; silence or censor

☆**shut·down** (shut′doun′) *n.* a stoppage or suspension of work or activity, as in a factory

shut-eye (-ī′) *n.* [Slang] sleep

shut-in (-in′) *adj.* **1** confined to one's home, an institution, etc. by illness or infirmity **2** inclined to shun others; withdrawn —☆*n.* an invalid who is shut-in

shut-off (-ôf′) *n.* **1** something that shuts off a flow or movement, as a valve **2** a stoppage or interruption

shut·out (-out′) *n.* ☆**1** the act of preventing the opposing team from scoring in a game ☆**2** a game or series of games in which one team is shut out

shut·ter (shut′ər) *n.* **1** a person or thing that shuts **2** *a)* a movable screen or cover, typically one of a pair, for a window: shutters are usually hinged

shutters

and often fitted with louvers *b)* an ornamental detail, typically one of a pair, resembling this but fixed in place beside a window **3** anything used to cover an opening, as a slide or door on a lantern **4** *Photog.* a device that controls the duration of an exposure by opening and closing, allowing light to reach the film or plate for a specified amount of time —*vt.* to close or furnish with or as with a shutter or shutters

☆**shut·ter·bug** (-bug′) *n.* ⟦prec. + BUG¹⟧ [Slang] a person whose hobby is photography

shut·tle (shut′'l) *n.* ⟦ME *schutylle* < OE *scytel*, missile < base of *sceotan*, to SHOOT¹: so called because shot to and fro with the thread in weaving⟧ **1** *a)* an instrument containing a reel or spool of the woof thread, used in weaving to carry the thread back and forth between the warp threads *b)* a smaller but similar thread holder used in tatting, etc. *c)* a device that carries the lower thread back and forth in making a lock stitch on a sewing machine *d)* any of several devices having a similar to-and-fro action ☆**2** *a)* a traveling back and forth over an often short route, as by an airplane, train, bus, etc. *[kept the planes in a 24-hour shuttle]* *b)* the route so traveled *c)* a shuttle service offered by an airline, esp. one for which reservations are not required *[the New York–Washington shuttle]* *d)* an airplane, train, bus, etc. used in a shuttle **3** SPACE SHUTTLE **4** *short for* SHUTTLECOCK — ***vt., vi.* -tled, -tling 1** to move or go back and forth rapidly or frequently ☆**2** to move or go by or as by means of a shuttle

shut·tle·cock (-käk′) *n.* **1** in badminton or other similar games, a rounded piece of cork having a flat end stuck with feathers or, now, a piece of plastic formed to resemble this: it is struck back and forth across a net with rackets or paddles **2** the game of battledore and shuttlecock: cf. BATTLEDORE — *vt., vi.* to go, send, or bandy back and forth

☆**shuttle diplomacy** diplomacy between hostile countries or groups conducted by a mediator who travels back and forth between the parties involved

shvart·ze (shvärt′sə) *n.* [Slang] *alt. sp. of* SCHVARTZE: a derogatory term

shy¹ (shī) *adj.* **shy′er** or **shi′er**, **shy′est** or **shi′est** ⟦ME *schei*, dial. development < OE *sceoh*, akin to Ger *scheu*, shy, prob. < IE **skeuk-*, harassed (> OSlav *ščuti*, to pursue); akin to **skeub-* > SCOFF¹⟧ **1** easily frightened or startled; timid **2** not at ease with other people; extremely self-conscious; bashful **3** showing distrust or caution; wary **4** not bearing or breeding well, as some plants; unproductive ☆**5** [Slang] *a)* not having paid money due, as one's poker ante *b)* lacking; short (*on* or *of*) —***vi.* shied, shy′ing 1** to move suddenly as when startled; jump; start; recoil *[the horse shied at the gunshot]* **2** to react negatively; be or become cautious or unwilling; draw back: often with *at* or *from* —***n., pl.* shies** an act of shying; start, as of a horse —**fight shy of** to keep from; avoid; evade —**shy′er *n.*** —**shy′ly *adv.*** —**shy′ness *n.***

SYN.—**shy** implies a shrinking from the notice of others and a reticence in approaching them, either as an inherent trait or as resulting from inexperience; **bashful** implies such shyness as is displayed in awkward behavior and embarrassed timidity; **diffident** implies a self-distrust and lack of self-confidence that makes one reluctant to assert oneself; **modest** implies an unassuming manner in one who, because of ability, achievements, etc., might be expected to assert himself or herself strongly; **demure**, in current usage, suggests a decorously modest manner, often one that is affectedly so —*ANT.* **bold, confident**

shy² (shī) ***vt., vi.* shied, shy′ing** ⟦< ?⟧ to throw or fling, esp. sideways with a jerk *[shying stones at a target]* —***n., pl.* shies 1** the act of shying; fling **2** [Informal] a try or attempt **3** [Informal] a gibe

Shy·lock (shī′läk′) *n.* **1** the Jewish moneylender in Shakespeare's *Merchant of Venice* **2** [**s-**] a person who is without pity in business dealings; exacting creditor **3** [**s-**] [Slang] LOAN SHARK

USAGE—because of the Shakespearean character's associations with traditional anti-Semitic stereotypes, senses 2 & 3 are often regarded as anti-Semitic

☆**shy·ster** (shī′stər) *n.* ⟦earlier *shuyster*, prob. altered (? after *barrister*) < Ger *scheisser*, defecator⟧ [Slang] a person, esp. a lawyer, who uses unethical or tricky methods; pettifogger

si (sē) *n.* ⟦< ML *S(ancte) I(ohannes)*: see GAMUT⟧ *Music* TI¹: see also SOLFEGGIO

SI *abbrev.* ⟦Fr *S(ystème) I(nternational d'Unités)*, International System of Units⟧ International System of weights and measures, using the metric system augmented by scientific units used in technology: see the table of weights and measures in the Reference Supplement

Si¹ *abbrev. Bible* Sirach (Ecclesiasticus)

Si² *Chem. symbol for* silicon

sì (sē) *adv., interj.* ⟦It⟧ yes

sí (sē) *adv., interj.* ⟦Sp⟧ yes

si·al (sī′al′) *n.* ⟦SI(LICA) + AL(UMINA)⟧ *Geol.* the upper layer of the crust of the earth, consisting of rocks rich in silica and alumina —**si·al′ic *adj.***

si·al·a·gogue (sī al′ə gäg′) *n.* ⟦ModL *sialagogus* < Gr *sialon*, saliva + ModL *-agogus*, -AGOGUE⟧ any substance that stimulates the flow of saliva —**si·al′a·gog′ic** (-gä′jik) *adj.*

si·a·lid (sī′ə lid) *adj.* ⟦< ModL *Sialidae* < Gr *sialis*, a kind of bird⟧ of an alderfly —*n.* an alderfly Also **si·al·i·dan** (sī al′i dən)

Si·al·kot (sē äl′kōt) city in the Punjab region of NE Pakistan

si·a·loid (sī′ə loid′) *adj.* ⟦< Gr *sialon*, saliva + -OID⟧ resembling saliva

Si·am (sī am′) **1** *former name for* THAILAND **2 Gulf of** *former name for* the Gulf of THAILAND

si·a·mang (sī′ə maŋ′, sē′-) *n.* ⟦Malay⟧ a very agile black gibbon (*Symphalangus syndactylus*) of the Malay Peninsula and Sumatra

Si·a·mese (sī′ə mēz′, -mēs′; *for adj., usually* sī′ə mēz′, -mēs′) ***n., pl.* -mese′ 1** *former name for* THAI **2** any of a breed of domestic cat, thought to have originated in Siam, with blue eyes and a light-colored coat that is darker on the face, ears, legs, and tail: also **Siamese cat** —***adj.* 1** *former term for* THAI **2** ⟦< fol.⟧ [*also* **s-**] designating or of a pipe coupling or joint in the form of a Y, for joining two pipes or hoses to one pipe

Siamese twins ⟦after a pair of twins so joined, Chang and Eng (1811-74), born in SIAM⟧ any pair of twins born with bodies joined together in some way

Si·an (shē′än′) *a former transliteration of* XI'AN

Siang (shyäŋ) *a former transliteration of* XIANG

sib (sib) *n.* ⟦ME *sibb* < OE, kinsman, kinship, akin to Ger *sippe*, kinship < IE **s(w)ebh-*, of the same kind (> OHG *Swaba*, Swabian) < base **se-*, apart > L *se*⟧ **1** blood relatives; kin **2** a blood relative; kinsman or kinswoman; esp., a brother or sister **3** *Anthrop.* a group of persons tracing their descent unilineally from a traditional or actual common ancestor **4** *Zool.* any of the offspring of the same parents in relation to one another —*adj.* related by blood; akin

Si·be·li·us (si bā′lē oos; *E* sə bāl′yəs), **Jean** (zhän) (born *Johan Julius Christian Sibelius*) 1865-1957; Finn. composer

Si·ber·i·a (sī bir′ē ə) region in N Asia, between the Urals & the Pacific: Asian section of Russia: *c.* 5,208,000 sq mi (13,488,667 sq km): notorious for its harsh climatic conditions & isolated location —**Si·ber′i·an *adj., n.***

Siberian husky ⟦see HUSKY¹⟧ any of a breed of medium-sized dog, originating in Siberia, with erect ears and a soft, thick coat, used especially for pulling sleds

sib·i·lant (sib′ə lənt) *adj.* ⟦L *sibilans* < *sibilare*, to hiss⟧ **1** having or making a hissing sound **2** *Phonet.* articulated with such a sound, as (s), (z), (sh), (zh), (ch), and (j) —*n.* a sibilant consonant: a type of fricative —**sib′i·lance *n.***, **sib′i·lan·cy**, *pl.* **-cies** —**sib′i·lant·ly *adv.***

sib·i·late (-lāt′) ***vt., vi.* -lat′ed, -lat′ing** ⟦< L *sibilatus*, pp.: see prec.⟧ to hiss, or pronounce with a hissing sound —**sib′i·la′tion *n.***

Si·biu (sē byoo̅′) city in central Romania

sib·ling (sib′liŋ) *n.* ⟦20th-c. revival of OE, a relative: see SIB & -LING¹⟧ one of two or more persons born of the same parents or, sometimes, having one parent in common; brother or sister

sib·yl (sib′əl) *n.* ⟦ME *sibille* < L *sibylla* < Gr⟧ **1** any of certain women consulted as prophetesses by the ancient Greeks and Romans **2** a fortuneteller

Sib·yl (sib′əl) *n.* ⟦L *Sibylla*: see prec.⟧ a feminine name: var. *Sybil*

sib·yl·line (sib′ə līn′, -lēn′, -lin) *adj.* ⟦L *sibyllinus*⟧ of or like the sibyls; prophetic: also **si·byl′ic** or **si·byl·lic** (si bil′ik)

Sibylline Books a number of oracular manuscripts consulted regularly by the ancient Romans and thought to have been written by the sibyl of Cumae

sic¹ (sik) *adj. Scot. var. of* SUCH

sic² (sik) *vt.* **sicced** or **sicked**, **sic′cing** or **sick′ing** ⟦var. of SEEK⟧ **1** to set upon; pursue and attack: said esp. of or to a dog **2** to urge or incite to attack *[to sic a dog on someone]*

sic³ (sik, sēk) *adv.* ⟦L⟧ thus; so: used within brackets, [*sic*], to show that a quoted passage, esp. one containing some error or something questionable, is reproduced accurately

sic·ca·tive (sik′ə tiv) *adj.* ⟦LL *siccativus* < L *siccatus*, pp. of *siccare*: see DESICCATE⟧ causing to dry; drying —*n.* a substance that promotes drying, esp. a DRIER (sense 1)

Si·chuan (sē′chwän′) province of SC China: 219,692 sq mi (569,000 sq km); cap. Chengdu

Si·ci·lia (sē chē′lyä) *It. name for* SICILY

Si·cil·i·an (si sil′yən, -ē ən) *adj.* of Sicily or its people, language, or culture —*n.* **1** a person born or living in Sicily **2** the variety of Italian spoken in Sicily

Sicilies, Two *see* TWO SICILIES

Sic·i·ly (sis′ə lē) **1** island of Italy, off its S tip **2** region of Italy, comprising this island & small nearby islands: 9,926 sq mi (25,708 sq km); cap. Palermo

sick¹ (sik) *adj.* ⟦ME *sik*, *seke* < OE *seoc*, akin to Ger *siech* < IE base **seug-*, to be troubled or grieved > Arm *hiucanim*, (I) am weakening⟧ **1** suffering from disease or illness; unwell; ill: in this sense, now rare or literary in England **2** having nausea; about to vomit or in the act of vomiting: the predominant sense in England **3** characteristic of or accompanying sickness *[a sick expression]* **4** of or for sick people *[sick leave]* **5** deeply disturbed or distressed; extremely upset, as by grief, disappointment, disgust, failure, etc. **6** disgusted by reason of excess; annoyed or exasperated: usually with *of [sick of such excuses]*: often **sick and tired 7** in poor condition; impaired; unsound **8** having a great longing or nostalgia (*for*) *[sick for the hills]* **9** of sickly color; pale **10** having a discharge of the menses; menstruating **11** mentally ill or emotionally disturbed **12** [Informal] sadistic, morbid, or abnormally unwholesome *[a sick joke]* ☆**13** *Agric. a)* incapable of producing an adequate yield of a certain crop *[wheatsick soil]* *b)* infested with harmful microorganisms *[a sick field]* —**sick to one's** (or **the**) **stomach** having nausea; about to vomit or in the act of vomiting: also **sick at the stomach** —**the sick** sick or ill people collectively

SYN.—**sick** and **ill** both express the idea of being in bad health, affected with disease, etc. (for differences in American and British usage, see definition above), but **sick** is more commonly used than **ill**, which is somewhat formal [he's a *sick* person; he is *sick*, or *ill*, with the flu]; **ailing** usually suggests prolonged or even chronic poor health [she has been *ailing* ever since her operation]; **indisposed** suggests a slight, temporary illness or feeling of physical discomfort [*indisposed* with a headache] —ANT. **well, healthy**

sick² (sik) ***vt.*** *alt. sp. of* SIC²

sick bay a hospital and dispensary, esp. on board ship

sick·bed (sik′bed′) ***n.*** ⟦ME *seke bed*⟧ the bed to which a sick person is confined

sick building syndrome a condition affecting occupants of a particular building and characterized variously by headaches, fatigue, respiratory ailments, dermatitis, etc.: often attributed to bacteria or other contaminants circulated by air-conditioning systems: also written **sick′-build′ing syndrome**

sick call *Mil.* **1** a daily formation made up of personnel who wish to receive medical attention **2** a signal for or the time of such a formation

sick·en (sik′ən) ***vt., vi.*** ⟦ME *sekenen*⟧ to make or become sick, ill, disgusted, distressed, etc. —**sick′en·er** ***n.***

sick·en·ing (-iŋ) ***adj.*** **1** causing sickness or nausea **2** disgusting or revolting —**sick′en·ing·ly** ***adv.***

Sick·ert (sik′ərt), **Walter Richard** 1860-1942; Brit. painter & etcher

sick headache **1** any headache accompanied by or resulting from nausea **2** MIGRAINE

☆**sick·ie** (sik′ē) ***n.*** [Slang] a sick person, esp. one who is emotionally disturbed, sadistic, etc.

sick·ish (sik′ish) ***adj.*** **1** somewhat sick or nauseated **2** somewhat sickening or nauseating —**sick′ish·ly** ***adv.***

sick·le (sik′əl) ***n.*** ⟦ME *sikel* < OE *sicol* (akin to Ger *sichel*) < early WGmc borrowing < L *secula* < *secare*, to cut: see SAW¹⟧ a tool consisting of a crescent-shaped blade with a short handle: used for cutting down tall grasses and weeds

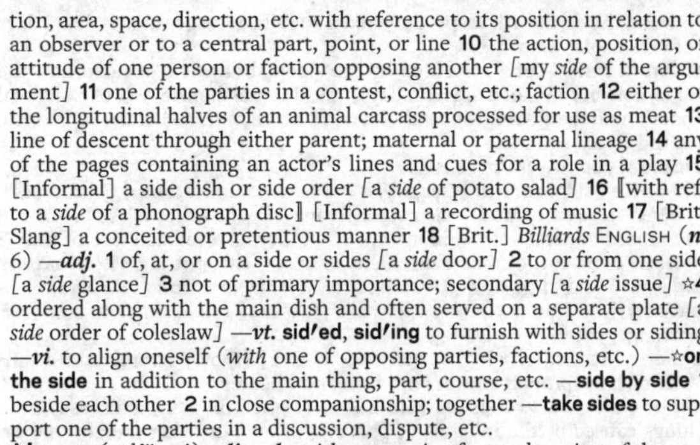

sickle

sick leave leave from work granted for illness, often with pay (**sick pay**), for a limited number of days

☆**sickle bar** a mowing device, as in a harvesting machine, consisting of a heavy bar which supports and protects the cutting blade or blades

☆**sick·le·bill** (-bil′) ***n.*** any bird with a sharply curved bill resembling a sickle, as a curlew or thrasher

☆**sickle cell anemia** an inherited chronic anemia found chiefly among black people, characterized by an abnormal red blood cell (**sickle cell**) containing a defective form of hemoglobin that causes the cell to become sickle-shaped when deprived of oxygen: also **sickle cell disease**

☆**sickle cell trait** the heterozygous condition of having one gene for sickle cell hemoglobin and one for normal hemoglobin: ordinarily this does not cause anemia or sicklemia

sickle feather any long, curving feather, as in the tail of a rooster

☆**sick·le·mi·a** (sik lē′mē ə, sik′əl ē′mē ə) ***n.*** ⟦SICKLE (CELL) + -(E)MIA⟧ the presence of sickle cells in the blood, with or without accompanying anemia

sick·ly (sik′lē) ***adj.*** **-li·er, -li·est** ⟦ME *sekly*⟧ **1** in poor health; chronically sick or prone to sickness; not strong or robust **2** of or produced by sickness [a *sickly* pallor] **3** characterized by the prevalence of disease or sickness; unhealthful **4** sickening; nauseating [a *sickly* odor] **5** faint; feeble [a *sickly* light] **6** weak; mawkish [a *sickly* smile] —**sick′li·ness** ***n.***

sick·ness (-nis) ***n.*** **1** the condition of being sick or diseased; illness **2** a malady or disease **3** nausea

☆**sick·o** (sik′ō) ***n., pl.*** **sick′os** [Slang] SICKIE

☆**sick·out** (-out′) ***n.*** a joint action by a group of employees claiming illness and not reporting for work in order to force the granting of certain demands; specif., such an action by a group forbidden by law to strike

sick·room (-ro͞om′) ***n.*** the room to which a sick person is confined

sic pas·sim (sik pas′im) ⟦L, so everywhere⟧ thus throughout (the book, etc.): said of a word, phrase, etc.

sic trans·it glo·ri·a mun·di (sik tran′sit glôr′ē ə mun′dē, -mo͞on′dē) ⟦L⟧ thus passes away the glory of the world

Sid·dhar·tha (sid där′tə) *see* BUDDHA²

Sid·dons (sid′'nz), **Sarah** (born *Sarah Kemble*) 1755-1831; Eng. actress

sid·dur (sid′ər) ***n., pl.*** **-durs** or **sid·du·rim** (si do͝or′im) ⟦Yiddish *sider* < MHeb *sidur*, shortening of Heb *sefer sidur hatefila*, lit., book of the order of prayer < root *sdr*: see SEDER⟧ the Jewish prayer book that contains the daily and Sabbath liturgy: cf. MAHZOR

side (sīd) ***n.*** ⟦ME < OE *side*, akin to Ger *seite*, side, OE *sīd*, ample, broad < IE base **sē(i)-*, to throw, let fall, reach for, let go, rest > SOW²⟧ **1** the right or left half of a human or animal body, esp. either half of the trunk **2** a position or space beside one **3** *a)* any of the lines or surfaces that bound or limit something [a square has four *sides*, a cube six] *b)* any bounding line or surface of an object other than the ends or top and bottom *c)* either of the two bounding surfaces of an object that are distinguished from the front, back, top, and bottom **4** either of the two surfaces of a thing having no appreciable thickness, as paper, cloth, etc. **5** a surface or part of a surface having a specified aspect [the visible *side* of the moon] **6** any aspect or phase as contrasted with another or others [his cruel *side*] **7** a slope of a hill, bank, etc. **8** the shore of a river or other body of water **9** any location, area, space, direction, etc. with reference to its position in relation to an observer or to a central part, point, or line **10** the action, position, or attitude of one person or faction opposing another [my *side* of the argument] **11** one of the parties in a contest, conflict, etc.; faction **12** either of the longitudinal halves of an animal carcass processed for use as meat **13** line of descent through either parent; maternal or paternal lineage **14** any of the pages containing an actor's lines and cues for a role in a play **15** [Informal] a side dish or side order [a *side* of potato salad] **16** ⟦with ref. to a *side* of a phonograph disc⟧ [Informal] a recording of music **17** [Brit. Slang] a conceited or pretentious manner **18** [Brit.] *Billiards* ENGLISH (***n.*** 6) —***adj.*** **1** of, at, or on a side or sides [a *side* door] **2** to or from one side [a *side* glance] **3** not of primary importance; secondary [a *side* issue] ☆**4** ordered along with the main dish and often served on a separate plate [a *side* order of coleslaw] —***vt.*** **sid′ed, sid′ing** to furnish with sides or siding —***vi.*** to align oneself (*with* one of opposing parties, factions, etc.) —☆**on the side** in addition to the main thing, part, course, etc. —**side by side** **1** beside each other **2** in close companionship; together —**take sides** to support one of the parties in a discussion, dispute, etc.

☆**side·arm** (sīd′ärm′) ***adj., adv.*** with a sweeping forward motion of the arm from the side of the body at or below shoulder level [a *sidearm* pitch]

side arm a weapon of the kind that may be worn at the side or at the waist, as a sword, dagger, or pistol: *often used in pl.*

side·band (-band′) ***n.*** *Radio* the frequency or frequencies on either side of a carrier frequency that are generated by the process of modulation of the carrier

side·bar (-bär′) ***n.*** **1** a short article dealing with a sidelight of a major news story and printed alongside it **2** a discussion at the bench between the lawyers and the judge, conducted outside the hearing of the jury: also **sidebar conference** **3** a small GUI window, typically positioned at the side of a larger window or of the user screen, that displays, variously, information, a menu, a browser tool, etc.

side·board (-bôrd′) ***n.*** **1** a piece of dining-room furniture for holding linen, silver, china, etc. **2** a board that forms or is part of a side [the *sideboards* of a wagon] **3** [*pl.*] *Ice Hockey* the solid wooden fence surrounding the rink

☆**side·burns** (-burnz′) ***pl.n.*** ⟦reversed < BURNSIDES⟧ **1** BURNSIDES **2** the hair on a man's face, just in front of the ears, esp. when the rest of the beard is cut off

side·car (-kär′) ***n.*** **1** a small car attached to the side of a motorcycle, for carrying a passenger ☆**2** a cocktail of brandy, an orange-flavored liqueur, and lemon juice

side chain *Chem.* a chain of atoms attached to a closed chain

side chair a chair without arms, usually one of a set used at a dining table

☆**side check** a checkrein passing back to the saddle from the side of a horse's head

-sid·ed (sīd′id) *combining form* having (a specified number or kind of) sides [six-*sided*]

side dish any food served along with the main course, usually in a separate dish

side effect **1** something that occurs incidentally **2** an incidental and, often, undesirable effect resulting from a medication or medical treatment

side horse POMMEL HORSE

☆**side·kick** (sīd′kik′) ***n.*** [Informal] **1** a companion; close friend **2** a partner; confederate

side·light (sīd′līt′) ***n.*** **1** a light coming from the side **2** a bit of incidental knowledge or information on a subject **3** a window or opening in or at the side of a wall, door, etc. **4** either of two running lights carried on the side of a ship or boat, a red one on the port side and a green one on the starboard

side·line (sīd′līn′) ***n.*** a line at or along the side; specif., *a)* either of two lines marking the side limits of a playing area, as in football or tennis *b)* [*pl.*] the areas just outside these lines ☆*c)* a line, as of merchandise or work, in addition to one's main line —***vt.*** **-lined′, -lin′ing** ☆to remove from active participation [*sidelined* by an injury] —☆**on the sidelines** **1** in the area along the sidelines **2** outside the main sphere of action **3** not actively participating —**side′lin′er** ***n.***

side·ling (sīd′liŋ) ***adv.*** ⟦ME *sydelinge*: see SIDE & -LING²⟧ sidelong; sideways; obliquely —***adj.*** **1** directed or moving to the side [a stealthy, *sideling* approach] **2** inclined; sloping

side·long (sīd′lôŋ′) ***adv.*** ⟦altered (based on ALONG) < prec.⟧ **1** toward the side; laterally; obliquely **2** on the side; side downward —***adj.*** **1** inclined; slanting; sloping **2** directed to the side, as a glance **3** indirect; subtle or devious [a *sidelong* remark]

☆**side·man** (sīd′man′) ***n., pl.*** **-men′** (-men′) ⟦as distinguished from the *front man*, or leader⟧ a member of a jazz or dance band other than the leader or a featured soloist

☆**side meat** [Dial.] meat from the side of a pig; specif., bacon or salt pork

side·piece (sīd′pēs′) ***n.*** a piece forming or attached to the side of something

sider-¹ (sid′ər) *combining form* SIDERO-¹: used before a vowel

sider-² (sid′ər) *combining form* SIDERO-²: used before a vowel

si·de·re·al (sī dir′ē əl) ***adj.*** ⟦< L *sidereus* < *sidus* (gen. *sideris*), a star < IE base **sweid-*, to gleam > Lith *svidù*, to gleam⟧ **1** of or pertaining to the stars **2** expressed in reference to the stars —**si·de′re·al·ly** ***adv.***

sidereal day the time between two successive passages of the vernal equinox across the meridian: it measures one rotation of the earth and equals 23 hours, 56 minutes, 4.1 seconds of mean solar time

sidereal month the time required for the moon to complete one revolution around the earth with respect to a fixed star: its average value is 27.32 days of mean solar time

sidereal time 1 time measured by the sidereal day: it is divided into the **sidereal hour** (1/24 of a sidereal day), the **sidereal minute** (1/60 of a sidereal hour), and the **sidereal second** (1/60 of a sidereal minute) 2 the hour angle of the vernal equinox

sidereal year *see* YEAR (sense 3)

sid·er·ite (sid′ə rīt′) *n.* ⟦Ger *siderit* < L *siderites*, lodestone < Gr *siderītēs* < *sidēros*, iron: Early ModE *siderite*, lodestone < L⟧ 1 a yellowish to brownish, semihard mineral, iron carbonate, $FeCO_3$, that is a valuable ore of iron 2 [Obs.] a meteorite consisting chiefly of iron —**sid′er·it′ic** (-rit′ik) *adj.*

sid·er·o-[1] (sid′ər ō, -ə) ⟦< Gr *sidēros*⟧ *combining form* iron [*siderolite*]

sid·er·o-[2] (sid′ər ō, -ə) ⟦< L *sidus*: see SIDEREAL⟧ *combining form* star [*sideromancy*]

sid·er·o·lite (sid′ər ə līt′) *n.* ⟦SIDERO-[1] + -LITE⟧ [Obs.] any meteorite containing large proportions of both iron and silicates

sid·er·o·sis (sid′ə rō′sis) *n.* ⟦ModL: see SIDERO-[1] & -OSIS⟧ a disease of the lungs caused by the inhaling of particles of iron or other metal —**sid′er·ot′ic** (-rät′ik) *adj.*

side·sad·dle (sīd′sad′'l) *n.* a saddle, designed esp. for women riders in skirts, upon which the rider sits with both legs on the same side of the animal —*adv.* on or as if on a sidesaddle

☆**side·show** (-shō′) *n.* 1 a small, separate show in connection with the main show, as of a circus or carnival 2 something of minor importance; subordinate event

side·slip (-slip′) *vi.* **-slipped′**, **-slip′ping** 1 to slip or skid sideways, as on skis 2 *Aeron.* to move in a sideslip —*vt.* to cause to sideslip —*n.* 1 a slip or skid to the side 2 *Aeron. a)* a lateral slide or yaw during flight, caused by crosswinds, etc. *b)* a downward, lateral slide during a sharp bank, caused by gravity (see SKID, *vi.* 4)

side·split·ting (-split′iŋ) *adj.* 1 very hearty: said of laughter 2 causing hearty laughter [*a sidesplitting* comedy]

☆**side·step** (-step′) *vt.* **-stepped′**, **-step′ping** to avoid by or as by stepping aside; dodge [to *sidestep* a difficulty] —*vi.* to step to one side; take a side step or side steps

side step a step to one side, as to avoid something, or a step taken sideways

side·stroke (sīd′strōk′) *n.* *Swimming* a stroke performed, while lying sideways in the water, by working the arms alternately backward and forward while executing a scissors kick with the legs

☆**side·swipe** (-swīp′) *vt.* **-swiped′**, **-swip′ing** to hit along the side in passing —*n.* a glancing blow of this kind

☆**side·track** (-trak′) *vt., vi.* 1 to switch from a main line to a siding: said of a train, etc. 2 to turn away from the main issue or course; divert or be diverted —*n.* a railroad siding

☆**side·walk** (-wôk′) *n.* a path for pedestrians, usually paved, along the side of a street

☆**side·wall** (-wôl′) *n.* the side of a tire between the tread and the bead

side·ward (-wərd) *adv., adj.* directed or moving toward one side: also **side′wards** *adv.*

side·ways (-wāz′) *adv.* 1 from the side 2 so as to present a side; with one side forward 3 toward one side; laterally; obliquely —*adj.* turned or moving toward or from one side Also **side′way′** or **side′wise′** (-wīz′)

☆**side-wheel** (sīd′hwēl′, -wēl′) *adj.* designating a steamboat having a paddle wheel on each side —**side′-wheel′er** *n.*

side whiskers whiskers growing at the side of the face

side·wind·er (sīd′wīn′dər) *n.* ☆1 a small desert rattlesnake (*Crotalus cerastes*) of the SW U.S. that moves over shifting sand by looping its body sideways 2 [Informal] a hard, swinging blow of the fist, delivered from the side ☆3 [S-] an air-to-air missile that homes in on a target by a heat-seeking device

Si·di-bel-Ab·bès (sē′dē bel′ä bes′) city in NW Algeria, near Oran

sid·ing (sīd′iŋ) *n.* ☆1 a covering for an outside wall, as of a frame building, consisting generally of overlapping shingles, boards, aluminum panels, etc. 2 a short railroad track connected with a main track by a switch and used for unloading, bypassing, etc.; sidetrack

si·dle (sīd′'l) *vi.* **-dled**, **-dling** ⟦back-form. < SIDELING⟧ to move sideways, as in an unobtrusive, stealthy, or shy manner —*vt.* to make go sideways —*n.* a sidling movement

Sid·ney[1] (sid′nē) *n.* ⟦< the surname *Sidney*, prob. reduced < *St. Denis*⟧ a masculine and feminine name: dim. *Sid*

Sid·ney[2] (sid′nē), Sir **Philip** 1554-86; Eng. poet, soldier, & statesman

Si·don (sīd′'n) ⟦L < Gr *Sidōn* < Heb *tsidon* or Phoen *ṣdn*, prob. < or akin to Sem root *ṣyd, to hunt, fish⟧ chief city of ancient Phoenicia: site of modern SAIDA —**Si·do′ni·an** (-dō′nē ən) *adj., n.*

Sid·ra (sid′rə), **Gulf of** inlet of the Mediterranean, on the NC coast of Libya

SIDS (sidz) *abbrev.* SUDDEN INFANT DEATH SYNDROME

siè·cle (sye′kl') *n., pl.* **-cles** (-kl') ⟦Fr⟧ 1 a century 2 an era

siege (sēj) *n.* ⟦ME *sege* < OFr *siege*, aphetic < **assiege* < VL **absedium*, for L *obsidium*, siege, blockade, ambush < *obsidere*, to besiege < *ob-*, against + *sedere*, to SIT⟧ 1 the encirclement of a fortified place by an opposing armed force intending to take it, usually by blockade and bombardment 2 any persistent attempt to gain control, overcome opposition, etc. ☆3 a long, distressing or wearying period [a *siege* of illness] 4 ⟦ME *sege* < OFr < VL **sedicum* < **sedicare*, to set < L *sedere*, to SIT⟧ [Obs.] a seat; throne —*vt.* **sieged**, **sieg′ing** BESIEGE —**lay siege to** to subject to a siege; attempt to win, gain, overcome, etc.

siege mentality an attitude or state of mind in which one feels surrounded or under attack by enemies, opposition, etc.

Siege Perilous *Arthurian Legend* a seat at the Round Table, fatal to any occupant except the knight destined to find the Holy Grail

Sieg·fried (sig′frēd, sēg′-; *Ger* zēk′frēt′) *n.* ⟦Ger < Gmc **segu-*, power, victory + **frith-*, peace, protection⟧ *Gmc. Legend* a hero who wins the treasure of the Nibelungs, kills a dragon, and helps Gunther win Brunhild for a wife

Siegfried line a system of heavy fortifications built before WWII on the W frontier of Germany

Sieg Heil (zēk′ hīl′) ⟦Ger⟧ hail to victory: a Nazi salute

sie·mens (sē′mənz) *n., pl.* **-mens** ⟦after either Sir William SIEMENS or his brother, E. W. von *Siemens* (1816-92), Ger engineer & inventor⟧ the basic unit of electric conductance in the SI system, equal to one ampere per volt: abbrev. *S*

Sie·mens (sē′mənz; *Ger* zē′məns), Sir **William** (born *Karl Wilhelm von Siemens*) 1823-83; Brit. engineer & inventor, born in Germany

Si·en·a (sē en′ə; *It* sye′nä) commune in Tuscany, central Italy —**Si·en·ese** (sē′ə nēz′, -nēs′) *adj., n.*

Sien·kie·wicz (shen kye′vich), **Hen·ryk** (hen′rik) 1846-1916; Pol. novelist

si·en·na (sē en′ə) *n.* ⟦It *terra di Siena*, lit., earth of SIENA, where first obtained⟧ 1 an earth pigment containing iron and manganese oxides, yellowish-brown in the natural state and reddish-brown when burnt: cf. BURNT SIENNA 2 either of these colors

si·er·ra (sē er′ə) *n.* ⟦Sp < L *serra*, a saw⟧ 1 a range of hills or mountains having a saw-toothed appearance from a distance 2 any of several marine scombroid fishes (genus *Scomberomorus*), valued for sport and as food

Si·er·ra Le·one (sē er′ə lē ōn′) country in W Africa, on the Atlantic, between Guinea & Liberia: formerly a British colony, it became independent & a member of the Commonwealth in 1961; a republic since 1971: 27,699 sq mi (71,740 sq km); cap. Freetown

Si·er·ra Ma·dre (sē er′ə mä′drā; *Sp* sye′rä mä′dre) mountain system of Mexico, consisting of three ranges bordering the central plateau: highest peak, Orizaba

Si·er·ra Ne·vad·a (sē er′ə nə vad′ə, -vä′də) ⟦Sp, lit., snowy range⟧ mountain range in E Calif.: highest peak, Mt. Whitney: also **the Sierras**

si·es·ta (sē es′tə) *n.* ⟦Sp < L *sexta (hora)*, sixth (hour), noon⟧ a brief nap or rest taken after the noon meal, esp. in Spain and some Latin American countries

sieur (syër) *n.* ⟦OFr, inflected form of *sire*, SIRE⟧ SIR: archaic Fr. title of respect

sieve (siv) *n.* ⟦ME *sive* < OE *sife*, akin to Ger *sieb* < IE base **seip-*, to drip > SEEP⟧ a utensil having many small meshed or perforated openings, used to strain solids from liquids, to separate fine particles of loose matter from coarser ones, etc.; sifter; strainer — *vt., vi.* **sieved**, **siev′ing** to put or pass through a sieve; sift

sie·vert (sē′vərt) *n.* ⟦after R. M. *Sievert* (1896-1966), Swed radiologist⟧ the basic unit in the SI system that is used to measure the amount of biological damage caused by various types of ionizing radiation, equal to the dose that produces the same amount of damage in human tissue as one gray of X-rays (100 rem or 8.38 roentgens): abbrev. *Sv*

sieve tube *Bot.* a longitudinal tube in the phloem of flowering plants, consisting of a connected series of individual cells (**sieve cells**) and serving to conduct organic food materials through the plant

sift (sift) *vt.* ⟦ME *siften* < OE *siftan* < *sife*, SIEVE⟧ 1 to pass through a sieve so as to separate the coarse from the fine particles, or to break up lumps, as of flour 2 to scatter (a pulverized substance) by or as by the use of a sieve 3 to inspect or examine with care, as by testing or questioning; weigh (evidence, etc.) 4 to separate; screen; distinguish [to *sift* fact from fable] —*vi.* 1 to sift something 2 to pass through or as through a sieve —**sift′er** *n.*

sift·ings (sif′tiŋz) *pl.n.* 1 something sifted or having fallen as if sifted [*siftings* of snow] 2 something removed by sifting; residue

sig *abbrev.* 1 ⟦L *signa* or *signetur*⟧ label it; let it be labeled 2 signal 3 signature

Sig. or **Sig** *abbrev.* 1 *Signor* 2 *Signore* 3 *Signori*

sigh (sī) *vi.* ⟦ME *sighen*, back-form. < *sihten*, pt. of *siken* < OE *sican*, to sigh: prob. echoic⟧ 1 to take in and let out a long, deep, audible breath, esp. in expressing sorrow, relief, fatigue, longing, etc. 2 to make a sound like that of a sigh [trees *sighing* in the wind] 3 to feel longing or grief; yearn or lament (*for*) —*vt.* 1 to express with a sigh 2 to spend in sighing [to *sigh* the day away] 3 [Rare] to lament with sighing —*n.* the act or sound of sighing —**sigh′er** *n.*

sight (sīt) *n.* ⟦ME *siht* < OE *(ge)siht* < base of *seon*, to SEE[1]⟧ 1 *a)* something seen; view *b)* a remarkable or spectacular view; spectacle *c)* a thing worth seeing (*usually used in pl.*) [the *sights* of the city] 2 the act of seeing; perception by the eyes 3 a view; look; glimpse 4 [*often pl.*] any of various devices used to aid the eyes in lining up a gun, optical instrument, etc. on its objective: often used fig., as in the phrase SET ONE'S SIGHTS ON (see phrase below) 5 aim or an observation taken with mechanical aid, as on a sextant or gun 6 the faculty or power of seeing; vision; eyesight 7 mental vision or perception 8 range or field of vision 9 mental view; opinion; judgment [a hero in our *sight*] 10 [Informal] any person or thing of a strikingly unpleasant or unusual appearance 11 [Dial.] a large amount; great deal [a *sight* better than fighting] 12 *obs. var. of* INSIGHT —*vt.* 1 to observe or examine by taking a sight 2 to catch sight of; see ☆3 to bring into the sights of a rifle, etc.; aim at 4 *a)* to furnish with sights or a sighting device *b)* to adjust the sights of **5** to aim (a gun, etc.) using the sights —*vi.* **1** to take aim or an observation with a sight **2** to look carefully in a specified direction [*sight* along the line] —*adj.* **1** read, done, understood, etc. quickly and easily as soon as seen ☆**2** due or payable when presented [a *sight* draft] —**a sight for sore eyes** [Informal] a person or thing that is pleasant to see; welcome sight —**at first sight** when seen or considered for the first time —**at** (or **on**) **sight** **1** when or as soon as seen **2** *Commerce* upon demand or presentation —**by sight** by appearance; by recognizing but not through being acquainted —**catch sight of** **1** to make out by means of the eyes; discern; see **2** to see briefly; glimpse —**lose sight of** **1** to fail to keep in sight; see no longer **2** to fail to keep in mind; forget —**not by a long sight** **1** not nearly **2** not at all —**out of sight** **1** not in sight **2** far off; remote **3** [Informal] beyond reach; unattainable; extremely high, as in standards, price, etc. **4** [Slang] excellent; wonderful —**out of sight of** **1** not in sight of **2** not close or near to; remote from —**set one's sights on** to aim to achieve or attain [to *set your sights on* a college diploma] —**sight unseen** without seeing (the thing mentioned) beforehand

sight·ed (sīt′id) *adj.* **1** having sight; not blind **2** having (a specified kind of) sight: used in comb. [*farsighted*]

☆**sight gag** a bit of comic business, as in a play or show, whose effect depends on action rather than speech

sight·ing (-iŋ) *n.* an observation, often of something rare or unusual

sight·less (-lis) *adj.* **1** blind **2** unseen; invisible —**sight′less·ly** *adv.* —**sight′less·ness** *n.*

sight·line (-līn′) *n.* any of the straight lines of unimpeded vision from various points, as in a theater to the stage: *usually used in pl.*

sight·ly (-lē) *adj.* **-li·er**, **-li·est** **1** pleasant to the sight; comely **2** providing a fine view —**sight′li·ness** *n.*

sight reading the act or skill of performing unfamiliar written music, or of translating something written in a foreign language, readily on sight, without previous study —**sight′-read′** *vt., vi.* —**sight reader**

sight·see·ing (-sē′iŋ) *n.* the act of visiting places and things of interest, for pleasure, education, etc. —*adj.* for or engaged in seeing sights —**sight′seer** (-sē′ər) *n.*

sig·il (sij′əl) *n.* ⟦L *sigillum*, dim. of *signum*, a SIGN⟧ **1** a seal; signet **2** an image or sign having some mysterious power in magic or astrology

sigill. *abbrev.* ⟦L *sigillum*⟧ signet; seal

Sig·is·mund (sij′is mənd, sig′-; *Ger* zē′gis moont′) 1368-1437; Holy Roman emperor (1411-37)

sig·la (sig′lə) *pl.n., sing.* **sig′lum** (-ləm) abbreviations, symbols, etc. used in the scholarly edition of a text as to indicate manuscript sources

sig·ma (sig′mə) *n.* ⟦Gr⟧ the eighteenth letter of the Greek alphabet (Σ, σ, ς)

sig·mate (sig′māt′) *adj.* shaped like a sigma or an S

sig·moid (-moid′) *adj.* ⟦Gr *sigmoeidēs*: see SIGMA & -OID⟧ **1** *a)* having a double curve like the letter S *b)* curved like the letter C (uncial form of sigma) **2** of the sigmoid flexure of the colon Also **sig·moi′dal** —**sig·moi′dal·ly** *adv.*

sigmoid flexure **1** *Anat.* the last curving part of the colon, ending in the rectum: also **sigmoid colon** **2** *Zool.* an S-shaped curve

sig·moid·o·scope (sig moid′ə skōp′) *n.* ⟦SIGMOID + -O- + -SCOPE⟧ an illuminated, tubular instrument for the direct examination of the rectum, colon, and sigmoid flexure —**sig·moid′o·scop′ic** (-skäp′ik) *adj.* —**sig′moid·os′co·py** (-äs′kə pē) *n., pl.* **-pies**

Sig·mund (sig′mənd) *n.* ⟦< Ger *Siegmund* & ON *Sigmundr* < Gmc **sig*-, victory + **mund*-, hand, protection: see MANUAL⟧ a masculine name

sign (sīn) *n.* ⟦ME *signe* < OFr < L *signum*, a mark, token, prob. < base of *secare*, to cut (see SAW[1]): orig. sense prob. "incised mark"⟧ **1** something that indicates a fact, quality, etc.; indication; token [black as a *sign* of mourning] **2** *a)* a gesture or motion that conveys information, gives a command, etc. [a nod as a *sign* of approval] *b)* any of the gestures used in sign language *c)* SIGN LANGUAGE (sense 2) **3** a mark or symbol having an accepted and specific meaning [¢ is the *sign* for cent(s)] **4** any linguistic unit, as a word, letter, etc., that is the symbol of an idea, function, etc. **5** a publicly displayed board, placard, etc. bearing information, advertising, a warning, etc. ☆**6** anything marking the trail of an animal, as footprints **7** any visible trace or indication [the *signs* of spring] **8** *a)* an act or happening regarded as a manifestation of divine will or power *b)* an omen; portent **9** SIGN OF THE ZODIAC **10** *Med.* an objective indication or symptom of a disease —*vt.* **1** to mark with a sign, esp. with the sign of the cross, as in blessing **2** to write one's name on, as in acknowledging authorship, authorizing action, etc. **3** to write (one's name) as a signature **4** to engage by written contract; sign on **5** [Now Rare] to indicate or express by a sign; signal **6** to communicate (thoughts, ideas, etc.) by using SIGN LANGUAGE —*vi.* **1** to write one's signature, as in attesting or confirming something **2** to make a sign; signal; also, specif., to use the sign language of the deaf —**sign away** (or **over**) to abandon or transfer title to (something) by or as by signing a document; convey —**sign in** (or **out**) to sign a register upon arrival (or departure) —**sign off** **1** to announce the end of broadcasting, as for the day, and stop transmitting **2** SIGN OFF ON (see phrase below) —**sign off on** to indicate approval or acceptance of (a plan, statement, etc.) by, or as if by, signing or initialing it [the mayor *signed off on* the budget figures] —**sign on** **1** to engage (oneself or others) for employment; hire or be hired, esp. by a signed agreement **2** [Informal] to go along with a plan, etc., as in the capacity of a partner or participant **3** to announce the beginning of broadcasting, as for the day, and start transmitting —**sign up** **1** SIGN ON **2** to enlist, enroll, etc. —**under the sign** (or **Sign**) **of** *Astrol.* during that portion of the year when the sun passes through (a specified sign of the zodiac), thus making a person subject to its influence [born *under the sign of* Leo] —**sign′er** *n.*

sign·age (sī′nij) *n.* the signs, collectively, displayed as in a community, often, specif., when graphically coordinated

sig·nal (sig′nəl) *n.* ⟦OFr < VL *signale* < neut. of LL *signalis* < L *signum*, a SIGN⟧ **1** [Now Rare] a token or indication **2** a sign or event fixed or understood as the occasion for prearranged combined action [a bugle *signal* to attack] **3** anything which occasions a certain action or response **4** *a)* a sign given by gesture, sound or call, flashing light, etc. *b)* an object or device, as a red flag, flashing light, etc., providing such a sign **5** in some card games, a bid or play designed to guide one's partner **6** in radio, television, cell phones, etc., the electrical impulses, sound or picture elements, etc. transmitted or received **7** [*pl.*] *Football* code words, numbers, etc. called out, esp. by the quarterback, to indicate which play or defense to use next —*adj.* **1** not average or ordinary; remarkable; notable **2** used as a signal or in signaling —*vt.* **-naled** or **-nalled**, **-nal·ing** or **-nal·ling** **1** to make a signal or signals to **2** to make known or communicate (information) by signals —*vi.* to make a signal or signals —**sig′nal·er** *n.*, **sig′nal·ler**

signal corps the part of an army in charge of communications, as by radio

sig·nal·ize (sig′nə līz′) *vt.* **-ized′**, **-iz′ing** **1** to make remarkable or noteworthy [a career *signalized* by great achievement] **2** to make clearly known; draw attention to [the cheers which *signalized* his arrival] —**sig′nal·i·za′tion** *n.*

sig·nal·ly (sig′nə lē) *adv.* in a signal manner; remarkably

sig·nal·man (sig′nəl mən, -man′) *n., pl.* **-men** (-mən, -men′) a person responsible for signaling or receiving signals

sig·nal·ment (-mənt) *n.* ⟦Fr *signalement* < *signaler*, to signal⟧ a description giving distinguishing or identifying marks, as of someone wanted by the police

sig·na·to·ry (sig′nə tôr′ē) *adj.* ⟦L *signatorius*, of sealing, of a signer < *signator*, one who seals or signs < *signare*, to set a seal upon, sign: see SIGN⟧ that has joined in the signing of something —*n., pl.* **-ries** any of the persons, states, etc. that have signed a document

sig·na·ture (sig′nə chər) *n.* ⟦LL *signatura* < L *signare*: see prec.⟧ **1** a person's name written by that person; also, a representation of this in a mark, stamp, deputy's handwriting, etc. **2** the act of signing one's name **3** an identifying characteristic or mark **4** that part of a doctor's prescription telling the patient how to use the medicine prescribed: usually marked *S* or *Sig.* **5** THEME SONG (sense 2) **6** *Music* *a)* KEY SIGNATURE *b)* TIME SIGNATURE **7** *Printing* *a)* a large sheet upon which are printed a number of pages in some multiple of four, and which, when folded to page size, forms one section of a book *b)* a letter or number at the bottom of the first page in such a sheet showing in what order that section is to be gathered for binding —*adj.* ☆**1** designating or of a product, as clothing, which is distinguished by a label bearing the stylized signature of its designer **2** typical of or identified with a person, place, etc. [an actor's *signature* mannerism, a restaurant's *signature* entree]

sign·board (sīn′bôrd′) *n.* a board bearing a sign or notice, esp. one advertising a business, product, etc.

Signed English a form of sign language based on English and using English syntax rather than the syntax of American Sign Language

☆**sign·ee** (sī nē′, sī′nē) *n.* a signer, esp. of a petition, contract, etc.

sig·net (sig′nit) *n.* ⟦ME < MFr, dim. of *signe*, a SIGN⟧ **1** a seal, esp. one used as a signature in marking documents as official, etc. **2** a mark or impression made by or as by a signet —*vt.* to stamp or make official with a signet

signet ring a finger ring containing a signet, often in the form of an initial or monogram

sig·nif·i·cance (sig nif′ə kəns) *n.* ⟦LME < L *significantia* < *significans*: see fol.⟧ **1** that which is signified; meaning **2** the quality of being significant; suggestiveness; expressiveness **3** importance; consequence; moment Also **sig·nif′i·can·cy** —**SYN.** IMPORTANCE

sig·nif·i·cant (-kənt) *adj.* ⟦L *significans*, prp. of *significare*, to SIGNIFY⟧ **1** *a)* having or expressing a meaning *b)* full of meaning **2** important; momentous **3** having or conveying a special or hidden meaning; suggestive **4** of or pertaining to an observed departure from a hypothesis too large to be reasonably attributed to chance [a *significant* statistical difference] —*n.* [Archaic] something that has significance; sign —**sig·nif′i·cant·ly** *adv.*

☆**significant other** **1** a person having importance in, or influence on, another's life **2** a person with whom one has an intimate, often long-term and usually sexual, relationship

sig·ni·fi·ca·tion (sig′nə fi kā′shən) *n.* ⟦ME *significacion* < OFr < L *significatio*⟧ **1** significance; meaning **2** the act of signifying; indication

sig·nif·i·ca·tive (sig nif′ə kāt′iv) *adj.* SIGNIFICANT

sig·ni·fied (sig′nə fīd′) *n.* *Linguis.* the object or concept represented by a SIGNIFIER (sense 2)

sig·ni·fi·er (sig′nə fī′ər) *n.* **1** a person or thing that signifies **2** *Linguis.* a sound or group of sounds, an image, or a symbol that stands for an object or concept: cf. SIGNIFIED

sig·ni·fy (sig′nə fī′) *vt.* **-fied′**, **-fy′ing** ⟦ME *signifien* < OFr *signifier* < L *significare* < *signum*, a SIGN + *facere*, to make, DO[1]⟧ **1** to be a sign or indication of; mean [the rags that *signify* their poverty] **2** to show or make known, as by a sign, words, etc. [to *signify* approval by saying "aye"] —*vi.* to have meaning or importance; be significant; matter —**sig′ni·fi′a·ble** *adj.*

☆**sig·ni·fy·ing** (sig′nə fī′iŋ) *n.* [Slang] verbal play, esp. as engaged in by urban African-Americans, involving boastful taunts, witty insults, indirect threats, etc.

si·gnior (sēn′yôr′) *n. Eng. sp. of* SIGNOR

sign language 1 communication of thoughts or ideas by means of manual signs and gestures, esp. between two people who have no language in common 2 a language used as by the deaf, consisting of a system of signs and gestures

sign manual a personal signature, esp. that of a monarch on an official document

sign of peace the liturgical practice of exchanging a handshake, embrace, etc., as a sign of peace, union, or friendship, at some point in a Christian service, esp. in a Mass or Communion service

sign of the cross 1 [*often* **S- of the C-**] an outline of a CROSS (sense 5*a*) made symbolically by a movement of the hand or fingers 2 [*usually* **S- of the C-**] a short Trinitarian prayer recited while performing this movement, beginning with the words "In the name of the Father"

sign of the zodiac any of the twelve divisions or houses of the zodiac, each represented by a symbol: see ZODIAC

si·gnor (sē nyôr′; *E* sēn′yôr′) *n., pl.* **si·gno′ri** (-nyô′rē) or Eng. **si′gnors′** ⟦It, reduced form of *signore*: see SIGNORE⟧ 1 [**S-**] Mr.: Italian title of respect, used before the name 2 a man; gentleman

si·gno·ra (sē nyô′rä; *E* sēn yôr′ə) *n., pl.* **si·gno′re** (-re) or Eng. **si·gno′ras** ⟦It, fem. of prec.⟧ 1 [**S-**] Mrs.; Madam: Italian title of respect 2 a married woman

si·gno·re (sē nyô′re; *E* sēn yôr′ā) *n., pl.* **si·gno·ri** (sē nyô′rē; *E* sēn yôr′ē) or Eng. **si·gno′res** ⟦It < ML *senior*, lord < L: see SENIOR⟧ 1 [**S-**] sir: Italian title of respect, used in direct address without the name 2 a man; gentleman

si·gno·ri·na (sē′nyô rē′nä; *E* sēn′yə rē′nə) *n., pl.* **si′gno·ri′ne** (-nē) or Eng. **si′gno·ri′nas** ⟦It, dim. of *signora*⟧ 1 [**S-**] Miss: Italian title of respect 2 an unmarried woman or a girl

si·gno·ri·no (sē′nyô rē′nô; *E* sēn′yə rē′nō) *n., pl.* **si′gno·ri′ni** (-nē) or Eng. **si′gno·ri′nos** ⟦It, dim. of *signore*⟧ 1 [**S-**] Master: Italian title of courtesy for a young man or a boy 2 a young man or a boy

si·gno·ry (sēn′yər ē) *n., pl.* **-ries** *alt. sp. of* SEIGNIORY (senses 1, 2, & 3)

sign·post (sīn′pōst′) *n.* 1 a post bearing a sign; guidepost 2 a clear indication; obvious clue, etc. —*vt.* to put or provide a signpost at, for, etc.

Si·gurd (sig′ərd) *n. Norse Myth.* a hero who kills a dragon and awakens Brynhild: identified with the Germanic Siegfried

si·ka (sē′kə) *n.* ⟦< Jpn, deer⟧ a small, reddish deer (*Cervus nippon*) with white spots, native to China, Japan, etc.: often **sika deer**

Sikh (sēk, sik) *n.* ⟦Hindi, a disciple⟧ a member of a religion founded by the guru Nanak about 1500 in N India and based on monotheism and the rejection of the caste system and of idolatry —*adj.* of or relating to Sikhs or Sikhism —**Sikh′ism′** *n.*

Sik·kim (sik′im) state, formerly a protectorate, of India, in the E Himalayas: 2,740 sq mi (7,097 sq km); cap. Gangtok —**Sik′kim·ese′** (-ēz′, -ēs′) *adj., n., pl.* **-ese′**

Si·kor·sky (si kôr′skē), **I·gor (Ivanovich)** (ē′gôr) 1889-1972; U.S. aeronautical engineer, born in Russia

si·lage (sī′lij) *n.* ⟦contr. (based on SILO) < ENSILAGE⟧ green fodder preserved in a silo; ensilage

Si·las (sī′ləs) *n.* ⟦LL(Ec) < Gr(Ec) < Aram *sh'îlâ*, lit., asked for⟧ a masculine name: dim. *Si*

Si·las·tic (si las′tik) ⟦SIL(ICONE RUBBER) + (EL)ASTIC⟧ *trademark for* a soft, flexible, inert silicone rubber, used esp. in prosthetic medicine

sild (sild) *n., pl.* **sild** or **silds** ⟦Norw, herring⟧ any of several small or young herrings canned as Norwegian sardines

si·lence (sī′ləns) *n.* ⟦OFr < L *silentium* < *silens*: see SILENT⟧ 1 the state or fact of keeping silent; a refraining from speech or from making noise 2 absence of any sound or noise; stillness 3 a withholding of knowledge or omission of mention [*to note an author's silence on a point*] 4 failure to communicate, write, keep in touch, etc. 5 oblivion or obscurity —*vt.* **-lenced**, **-lenc·ing** 1 to cause to be silent; still; quiet 2 to put down; repress 3 to put (enemy guns) out of action —*interj.* be silent

si·lenc·er (sī′lən sər) *n.* 1 a person or thing that silences ☆2 a device attached to the muzzle of a firearm to muffle the report 3 [Brit.] MUFFLER (sense 2)

si·lent (sī′lənt) *adj.* ⟦L *silens* < prp. of *silere*, to be silent, still, prob. < IE base **sē(i)*-, **sī*-, to rest > SEED, SIDE, Goth *(ana)silan*, to cease (of the wind)⟧ 1 making no vocal sound; not speaking; speechless; mute 2 seldom speaking; saying little; not talkative 3 free from, or not making, sound or noise; quiet; still; noiseless 4 *a)* not spoken, uttered, or expressed [*silent longing*] *b)* included in the spelling of a word but with no part of the word's pronunciation corresponding directly to it (said of a letter or group of letters) [*silent b* in "debt" and *gh* in "thought"] 5 withholding knowledge or omitting mention; uncommunicative 6 not active [*factories silent for months*] 7 designating or of films without a synchronized soundtrack 8 not having noticeable symptoms [*a silent heart attack*] —*n.* [*pl.*] silent films: often preceded by *the* —**si′lent·ly** *adv.*

silent auction an auction in which sealed bids are submitted beforehand

☆**silent butler** a dish with a hinged cover and a handle, in which to empty ashtrays, brush crumbs, etc.

☆**silent partner** a partner who shares in financing but not in managing a business, firm, etc.

Si·le·nus (sī lē′nəs) *n.* ⟦L < Gr *Seilēnos*⟧ *Gr. Myth.* 1 the foster father and tutor of Dionysus and leader of the satyrs, traditionally pictured as a fat, drunken, jovial old man with pointed ears 2 *pl.* **-ni** (-nī) or Gr. **-noi** (-noi) [**s-**] any of a group of woodland deities resembling the satyrs

si·le·sia (sī lē′shə, si-; -zhə) *n.* 1 [Archaic] a linen cloth made in Silesia 2 a strong, lightweight, twilled cotton cloth used for linings and pockets

Si·le·sia (sī lē′shə, si-; -zhə) region in E Europe, on both sides of the upper Oder, mainly in what is now SW Poland —**Si·le′sian** *adj., n.*

si·lex (sī′leks′) *n.* ⟦L (gen. *silicis*), dissimilated < **scilec*- < **scelic*- < IE base **(s)kel*-, to cut > SHELF, SHIELD⟧ 1 silica, esp. in the form of flint or quartz 2 heat-resistant glass made of fused quartz

sil·hou·ette (sil′ə wet′) *n.* ⟦Fr, after Étienne de *Silhouette* (1709-67), Fr minister of finance, in derogatory reference to his fiscal policies and to such amateur portraits by him, both regarded as inept⟧ 1 *a)* an outline, esp. a profile portrait, made either by cutting from black paper and fixing on a light background, or by drawing and then filling in with a solid color *b)* any dark shape or figure seen against a light background 2 the outline of a figure, garment, etc.; contour —*vt.* **-et′ted**, **-et′ting** to show or project in silhouette —*SYN.* OUTLINE

silhouette

silic- *combining form* SILICO-: used before a vowel

sil·i·ca (sil′i kə) *n.* ⟦ModL < L *silex*, flint: see SILEX⟧ a glassy, very hard mineral, silicon dioxide, SiO_2, found in a variety of forms, including quartz, opal, chalcedony, sand, or chert

silica gel an amorphous, highly adsorbent form of silica used as a drying agent in air-conditioning equipment, as a carrier of catalysts in chemical reactions, etc.

silica glass a very clear, strong glass produced when pure silica is fused at high temperature, used as in optical instruments: see MOHS SCALE

sil·i·cate (sil′i kit, -kāt′) *n.* a salt or ester derived from silica or a silicic acid

si·li·ceous (sə lish′əs) *adj.* ⟦L *siliceus*⟧ 1 of, containing, or like silica 2 growing in soil that has a large proportion of silica Also sp. **si·li′cious**

si·lic·ic (sə lis′ik) *adj.* ⟦SILIC(A) + -IC⟧ of, like, or derived from silica or silicon

silicic acid 1 any of several jellylike masses, $SiO_2 \cdot nH_2O$, precipitated by acidifying sodium silicate solution 2 any of several hypothetical acids of which the different mineral silicates may be regarded as salts

sil·i·cide (sil′i sīd′) *n.* a binary compound of silicon and another element, usually a metal

sil·i·cif·er·ous (sil′ə sif′ər əs) *adj.* ⟦< L *silex* (see SILEX) + -FEROUS⟧ containing or producing silica

si·lic·i·fy (sə lis′ə fī′) *vt.* **-fied′**, **-fy′ing** ⟦< L *silex* (see SILEX) + -FY⟧ to convert into or impregnate with silica; specif., PETRIFY (*vt.* 1) —*vi.* to become silicified, as wood —**si·lic′i·fi·ca′tion** *n.*

si·li·ci·um (sə lish′ē əm, -lis′-) *n.* ⟦ModL: so named (1808) by Sir Humphry DAVY < L *silex*, flint (see SILEX) + -IUM⟧ *former name for* SILICON

sil·i·cle (sil′i kəl) *n.* ⟦< Fr or L: Fr *silicule* < L *silicula*, dim. of *siliqua*, pod: for IE base see SILEX⟧ *Bot.* a short, broad silique: also **si·lic·u·la** (sə lik′yoo lə), *pl.* **-lae′** (-lē′)

sil·i·co- (sil′i kō, -kə) ⟦< fol.⟧ *combining form* silicon, silica [*silicosis*]

sil·i·con (sil′i kän′, -kən) *n.* ⟦ModL: altered (1817, by T. Thomson (1773-1852), Scot chemist, modeled on BORON, CARBON, because of chemical resemblances) < SILICIUM⟧ a nonmetallic chemical element occurring in several forms, found always in combination, and more abundant in nature than any other element except oxygen, with which it combines to form silica: used in the manufacture of transistors, solar cells, rectifiers, silicones, ceramics, etc.: symbol, Si; at. no. 14: see the periodic table of elements in the Reference Supplement

silicon carbide a bluish-black, crystalline substance, SiC, produced in an electric furnace: see CARBORUNDUM, MOHS SCALE

sil·i·cone (-kōn′) *n.* ⟦SILIC(O)- + -ONE⟧ any of a group of polymerized, organic silicon compounds containing a basic structure of alternate oxygen and silicon atoms, usually with various organic groups attached to the chain: characterized by relatively high resistance to heat, water, etc. and used in oils, polishes, etc.

silicone rubber a rubberlike polymer prepared from certain silicones: it maintains its elasticity over a wide range of temperatures and is used in gaskets, insulation, etc.

☆**Silicon Valley** ⟦< SILICON, the principal material used in computer chips⟧ *name for* a valley in California, southeast of San Francisco, a center of high-technology activities, esp. those involving microelectronics

sil·i·co·sis (sil′i kō′sis) *n.* ⟦ModL: see SILICO- & -OSIS⟧ a chronic disease of the lungs, characterized by diffuse fibrosis and caused by the continued inhalation of silica dust

si·lic·u·lose (sə lik′yoo lōs′) *adj.* ⟦ModL *siliculosus*⟧ 1 having silicles 2 having the form of a silicle

si·lique (si lēk′, sil′ik) *n.* ⟦Fr < L *siliqua*: see SILICLE⟧ the pod of plants of the crucifer family, with two valves that fall away from a thin membrane bearing the seeds —**sil·i·quose** (sil′ə kwōs′) *adj.*, **sil′i·quous** (-kwəs)

silk (silk) *n.* ⟦ME *silke* < OE *seoluc*, prob. via Slav (as in OPrus *silkas*) < ? L *sericus* (or Gr *sērikos*), silken: see SERGE⟧ 1 the fine, soft, shiny fiber produced by silkworms to form their cocoons 2 thread or fabric made from this fiber 3 *a)* a garment or other article made of this fabric *b)* [*pl.*] a distinctive silk uniform, as of a jockey 4 *a)* the silk gown worn by a King's (or Queen's) Counsel in British law courts *b)* [Informal] KING'S (or QUEEN'S) COUNSEL 5 any silklike filament or substance, as that produced by spiders, or that within a milkweed pod, on the end of an ear of corn, etc. —*adj.* of or like silk; silken —☆*vi.* to develop silk: said of Indian corn —**hit the silk** [Slang] to parachute from an aircraft

silk cotton KAPOK

silk-cot·ton tree (silk′kät′'n) any of several large, tropical trees (genera *Bombax* and *Ceiba*) of the bombax family that have capsular fruits with silky hairs around the seeds

silk·en (sil′kən) *adj.* ⟦ME < OE *seolcen:* see SILK & -EN⟧ **1** [Literary] made of silk **2** like silk in appearance, texture, quality, etc.; specif., *a)* soft or smooth *b)* lustrous; glossy *c)* smooth and ingratiating [*silken* flattery] *d)* [Literary] elegant; luxurious [*silken* ease] *e)* delicate or gentle [*silken* caresses]

silk hat a tall, cylindrical, narrow-brimmed hat covered with silk or satin, worn by men in formal dress

Silk Road ⟦from the fact that *silk* was China's primary export⟧ ancient caravan route extending from China to the Mediterranean: often **Silk Route**

silk-screen print (silk′skrēn′) a print made by the silk-screen process: cf. SERIGRAPH

silk-screen process a stencil method of printing a flat color design through a piece of silk or other fine cloth on which all parts of the design not to be printed have been stopped out by an impermeable film —**silk′-screen′** *vt.*

silk-stock·ing (-stäk′iŋ) *adj.* **1** fashionably or richly dressed; elegant **2** wealthy, aristocratic, or upper-class —*n.* ☆a member of the wealthy or aristocratic class

☆**silk·weed** (-wēd′) *n.* MILKWEED (*n.* 1)

silk·worm (-wurm′) *n.* any of certain moth caterpillars (esp. family Bombycidae) that produce cocoons of silk fiber: they feed chiefly on mulberry leaves, and some species (esp. *Bombyx mori*) are cultivated as the source of commercial silk

silk·y (sil′kē) *adj.* **silk′i·er, silk′i·est 1** like silk in appearance, texture, quality, etc.; specif., *a)* soft or smooth *b)* lustrous; glossy *c)* smooth and ingratiating [a *silky* voice] *d)* delicate or gentle [a *silky* touch] **2** having fine, soft, silklike hairs, as some leaves —**silk′i·ly** *adv.* —**silk′i·ness** *n.*

silky terrier any of a breed of toy dog with a long, silky, bluish-gray and tan coat, erect ears, and general terrierlike qualities

sill (sil) *n.* ⟦ME *sille* < OE *syll,* akin to Dan *sville,* Ger *schwelle* < IE base **sel-,* **swel-,* beam, plank > Gr *selma,* beam⟧ **1** a heavy, horizontal timber or line of masonry supporting a house wall, etc. **2** a horizontal piece forming the bottom frame of the opening into which a window or door is set **3** *Geol.* a flattened piece of igneous rock forced between beds of stratified rocks

sil·la·bub (sil′ə bub′) *n. alt. sp. of* SYLLABUB

☆**sil·li·man·ite** (sil′ə mə nīt′) *n.* ⟦after B. Silliman (1779-1864), U.S. chemist and geologist + -ITE[1]⟧ a very hard, mineral, aluminum silicate, Al_2SiO_5, usually found in metamorphic rock as long, slender crystals of various colors

sil·ly (sil′ē) *adj.* **-li·er, -li·est** ⟦ME *seli, sili* (with shortened vowel), good, blessed, innocent < OE *sælig,* happy, prosperous, blessed (akin to Ger *selig,* blessed) < *sæl,* happiness < IE base **sel-,* favorable, in good spirits (> Gr *hilasia,* propitiation, *hilaros,* cheerful, merry, L *solari,* to comfort); sense development: happy → blissful → unaware of reality → foolish⟧ **1** [Obs.] *a)* simple; plain; innocent *b)* feeble; infirm; helpless **2** [Now Rare] feebleminded; imbecile **3** having or showing little sense, judgment, or sobriety; foolish, stupid, absurd, ludicrous, irrational, etc.: often used in a weakened sense to mean "unreasonably concerned" [don't be *silly,* it's no bother] **4** frivolous or trivial **5** [Informal] dazed or senseless, as from a blow —*n., pl.* **-lies** a silly person —**sil′li·ly** *adv.,* **sil′ly** —**sil′li·ness** *n.*

SYN.—**silly** implies ridiculous or irrational behavior that seems to demonstrate a lack of common sense, good judgment, or sobriety [it was *silly* of you to dress so lightly]; **stupid** implies a slow-wittedness or lack of normal intelligence [he is *stupid* to believe that]; **fatuous** suggests stupidity, inanity, or obtuseness coupled with a smug complacency [a *fatuous* smile]; **asinine** implies the extreme stupidity conventionally attributed to an ass [an *asinine* argument] See also **absurd** —*ANT.* **wise, intelligent**

☆**Silly Putty** *trademark for* a rubbery substance of silicone oil and boric acid, used as a plaything: it stretches, snaps apart into pieces, bounces, shapes easily, etc.

si·lo (sī′lō) *n., pl.* **-los** ⟦Fr < Sp < L *sirus* < Gr *siros,* an underground granary, pit⟧ **1** an airtight pit or tower in which green fodder is preserved ☆**2** a large, underground facility for the control, storage, and launching of a long-range ballistic missile —*vt.* **-loed, -lo·ing** to store in a silo

Si·lo·am (si lō′əm, sī-) *n.* ⟦LL(Ec) < Gr(Ec) *Silōam* < Heb *shiloach,* lit., sending forth < *shalach,* to send⟧ *Bible* a spring and pool outside Jerusalem: John 9:7

Si·lo·ne (sē lô′ne; *E* sə lō′nē), **Ig·na·zio** (ē nyä′tsyô) (born *Secondo Tranquilli*) 1900-78; It. writer

si·lox·ane (si läk′sān) *n.* ⟦SIL(ICON) + OX(YGEN) + -ANE⟧ any of a class of compounds, varying from liquids to hard resins, whose molecules are composed of chains of alternate silicon and oxygen atoms, usually with hydrogen or hydrocarbon groups attached to the free valences of the silicon atoms

silt (silt) *n.* ⟦ME *cylte,* prob. < Scand, as in Norw & Dan dial. *sylt,* salt marsh, akin to OHG *sulza,* brine: for IE base see SALT⟧ **1** sediment suspended in stagnant water or carried by moving water, that often accumulates on the bottom of rivers, bays, etc., esp. such sediment with particles smaller than sand and larger than clay **2** soil composed of 80 percent or more silt and less than 12 percent clay —*vt., vi.* to fill, cover, or choke up with silt —SYN. WASH —**sil·ta·tion** (sil tā′shən) *n.*

silt·y (sil′tē) *adj.* **silt′i·er, silt′i·est** of, like, or full of silt

Sil·u·res (sil′yə rēz′, sī lo͝or′ēz) *pl.n.* ⟦L⟧ members of an ancient people of SE Wales, conquered (*c.* A.D. 80) by the Romans

Si·lu·ri·an (si lo͝or′ē ən, sī-) *adj.* **1** of the Silures **2** ⟦because the rocks were first found in an area in SE Wales: see prec.⟧ [*sometimes* **s-**] designating or of the third geologic period of the Paleozoic Era, characterized by the development of coral reefs and small land plants, the first fish with jaws, and the first land arthropods —**the Silurian** the Silurian Period or its rocks: see the geologic time chart in the Reference Supplement

si·lu·rid (si lo͝or′id, sī-) *n.* ⟦< ModL *Siluridae* < L *silurus,* a kind of river fish < Gr *silouros*⟧ any of a family (Siluridae) of freshwater catfishes found in Europe and Asia, with anal and caudal fins fused —*adj.* of or pertaining to this family

sil·va (sil′və) *n.* ⟦ModL < L, forest, prob. < IE *(*k*)*selwa-;* akin to Gr *xylon,* wood⟧ **1** the forest trees of a certain area **2** *pl.* **-vas** or **-vae** (-vē) a book or treatise describing the trees of a certain area

sil·van (sil′vən) *adj., n. alt. sp. of* SYLVAN

Sil·va·nus (sil vā′nəs) *n. Rom. Myth.* the god of fields and woods

sil·ver (sil′vər) *n.* ⟦ME *selver* < OE *seolfer,* akin to Ger *silber,* Goth *silubr,* prob. a loanword < a non-IE source⟧ **1** a soft, white, metallic chemical element that is extremely ductile and malleable, an excellent reflector of light, and the best metallic conductor of heat and electricity: it is a precious metal and is used in the manufacture of coins, jewelry, alloys, etc.: symbol, Ag; at. no. 47: see the periodic table of elements in the Reference Supplement **2** *a)* silver coin *b)* money; riches; wealth **3** something, esp. tableware, made of or plated with silver; silverware **4** the lustrous, grayish-white color of silver **5** something having this color, as the material used in coating the back of a mirror **6** a salt of silver as used in photography, etc. **7** *short for* SILVER MEDAL —*adj.* **1** made of, containing, or plated with silver [*silver* thread] **2** of, based on, or having to do with silver [the *silver* standard] ☆**3** of or advocating the adoption of silver as a standard of currency **4** having the color or luster of silver; silvery **5** having a silvery tone or sound **6** eloquent [a *silver* tongue] **7** marking or celebrating the 25th anniversary —*vt.* **1** to cover or coat with silver or something like silver **2** to make silvery in color [hair *silvered* with age] —*vi.* to become silvery in color

Silver Age 1 *Class. Myth.* the second age of the world, inferior to the earlier Golden Age **2** [**s- a-**] any period of progress, prosperity, etc. of a lesser degree than that of a corresponding golden age

sil·ver·back (sil′vər bak′) *n.* a mature male gorilla with a saddle-shaped patch of silver-gray hair on its back

☆**silver bell** any of a genus (*Halesia*) of small trees of the storax family, with drooping, bell-shaped, white flowers, native to the E U.S. and to China: also **sil·ver-bell tree** (sil′vər bel′)

☆**sil·ver·ber·ry** (-ber′ē) *n., pl.* **-ries** a shrub (*Elaeagnus commutata*) of the oleaster family, with silvery leaves and fruit, native to the N U.S. and to Canada

☆**silver birch** PAPER BIRCH

silver bromide a yellow-white, crystalline compound, AgBr, which becomes dark when exposed to light: the main salt used in photographic emulsions

silver bullet any simple but sweeping solution to a complex or virtually insurmountable problem [the legislation was no *silver bullet* for crime]

☆**silver certificate** [Historical] a type of U.S. paper currency redeemable in silver

silver chloride a white crystalline compound, AgCl, which becomes dark when exposed to light: used in photography and as lenses in infrared spectroscopy

sil·ver·fish (-fish′) *n.* **1** *pl.* **-fish′** or **-fish′es** (see FISH) any of various fishes of a silvery color, as the tarpon or silverside **2** *pl.* **-fish′** any of various families of primitive, wingless thysanuran insects with silvery scales, long feelers, and a bristly tail: they thrive in dampness and darkness and are often injurious to books and other paper products

silver foil silver beaten into thin sheets

silver fox 1 a variety of North American red fox with black fur having individual hairs that are silvery white near the tips, often bred for its pelt **2** the fur of this fox

silver frost *var. of* SILVER THAW

silver gilt 1 gilded silver, or an imitation of this **2** silver leaf, used for decoration

sil·ver-gray (-grā′) *adj., n.* gray with a silvery luster

☆**silver hake** an edible hake fish (*Merluccius bilinearis*) of the Atlantic coast of the U.S.

sil·ver·ing (-iŋ) *n.* **1** the act of covering with silver or a silvery substance **2** a coating of silver or a silvery substance **3** a silvery sheen or appearance

silver iodide a yellow powder, AgI, which becomes dark when exposed to light: used in photography, medicine, and in seeding clouds to make rain

silver leaf very thin sheets of silver foil

silver lining ⟦< the proverb, "Every cloud has a silver lining"; alluded to by John MILTON[2] in *Comus* (1634) and by W. S. GILBERT[2] in *The Mikado* (1885)⟧ some basis for hope or some comforting aspect in the midst of despair, misfortune, etc.

sil·ver·ly (-lē) *adv.* with a silvery appearance or sound

silver medal a medal, typically silver in color or composition, given as an award to the person coming in second in a competition, race, etc.

sil·vern (sil′vərn) ***adj.*** ⟦ME *silveren* < OE *seolfren:* see SILVER & -EN⟧ [Archaic] of or like silver

silver nitrate a colorless, crystalline salt, $AgNO_3$, prepared by dissolving silver in dilute nitric acid and used in silver-plating and photography, as an antiseptic, etc.

☆**silver perch** **1** a common drum fish (*Bairdiella chrysoura*) of the Atlantic coast of the U.S., with a silvery body and yellow fins **2** any of various silvery, perchlike fishes

silver plate tableware made of, or plated with, silver

sil·ver-plate (-plāt′) ***vt.*** **-plat′ed, -plat′ing** to coat with silver, esp. by electroplating

sil·ver·point (-point′) ***n.*** **1** a method of drawing on specially prepared paper with an instrument tipped with silver **2** a drawing so made

silver protein any of several colloidal silver solutions containing silver and a protein, as albumin: formerly used in treating inflammation of mucous membranes

☆**silver salmon** COHO

silver screen **1** a screen on which films are projected in theaters ☆**2** films collectively: with *the*

☆**sil·ver·side** (sil′vər sīd′) ***n.*** any of a family (Atherinidae, order Atheriniformes) of small, mostly marine bony fishes with silver stripes along the sides: also **sil′ver·sides′**

sil·ver·smith (-smith′) ***n.*** a craftsman who makes and repairs articles of silver —**sil′ver·smith′ing** ***n.***

silver standard a monetary standard solely in terms of silver, in which the basic currency unit is made equal to and redeemable by a specified quantity of silver

☆**Silver Star Medal** a U.S. military decoration in the form of a bronze star with a small silver star at the center, awarded for gallantry in action

silver thaw glitter ice (see GLITTER, *n.* 4)

sil·ver·tone or **sil·ver-tone** (sil′vər tōn′) ***adj.*** made to resemble silver in color, sheen, etc. [*a silvertone* buckle]

sil·ver-tongued (-tuŋd′) ***adj.*** eloquent; persuasive

☆**sil·ver·ware** (sil′vər wer′) ***n.*** **1** articles, esp. tableware, made of or plated with silver **2** any metal tableware

silver wedding a 25th wedding anniversary

sil·ver·weed (sil′vər wēd′) ***n.*** **1** a trailing perennial cinquefoil (*Potentilla anserina*) with pinnately compound leaves which are silvery beneath **2** any of a genus (*Argyreia*) of tropical, shrubby, climbing plants of the morning-glory family, with silvery leaves

sil·ver·y (sil′vər ē) ***adj.*** **1** *a)* resembling silver, as in color or luster *b)* covered with or containing silver **2** soft and clear, like the sound of a silver bell —**sil′ver·i·ness** ***n.***

Sil·ves·ter (sil ves′tər) ***n.*** a masculine name: see SYLVESTER

sil·vex (sil′veks) ***n.*** ⟦< L *silva* (see SILVA) + *-ex,* arbitrary suffix⟧ a restricted, toxic herbicide, $C_9H_7Cl_3O_3$, used esp. for weed control

Sil·vi·a (sil′vē ə) ***n.*** a feminine name: see SYLVIA

sil·vics (sil′viks) ***n.*** ⟦SILV(A) + -ICS⟧ the study of forests and their ecology, including the application of soil science, botany, zoology, etc. to forestry

sil·vi·cul·ture (sil′vi kul′chər) ***n.*** ⟦Fr *sylviculture* < L *silva,* forest (see SILVA) + *cultura,* CULTURE⟧ the art of cultivating a forest; forestry —**sil′vi·cul′tur·al** ***adj.*** —**sil′vi·cul′tur·ist** ***n.***

s'il vous plaît (sē vo͞o ple′, sēl-) ⟦Fr, if it pleases you⟧ if you please; please

si·ma (sī′mə) ***n.*** ⟦Ger < *si(licium),* SILICIUM + *ma(gnesium),* MAGNESIUM⟧ *Geol.* the heavy igneous rock material of the earth's inner crust, forming a continuous shell and underlying the sial and also the ocean floors

si·mar (si mär′) ***n.*** ⟦Fr *simarre* < It *cimarra* or Sp *zamarra* < Ar *sammūr,* sable⟧ a flowing robe or long, loose jacket formerly worn by women, orig. in the late medieval period

SIM (card) (sim) ⟦*S*(*ubscriber*) *I*(*dentity*) *M*(*odule*)⟧ a small electronic card containing an INTEGRATED CIRCUIT, inserted in a GSM cell phone, that stores data identifying the user and allows connection to a cellular network

Si·me·non (sēm nōn′; *E* sē′mə nōn′), **Georges (Joseph Christian)** (zhôrzh) 1903-89; Fr. novelist, born in Belgium

Sim·e·on (sim′ē ən) ***n.*** ⟦LL(Ec) *Symeon* < Gr(Ec) *Symeōn* < Heb *shim'on,* lit., heard < *sham'a,* to hear⟧ **1** a masculine name **2** *Bible a)* the second son of Jacob and Leah, or the tribe of Israel descended from him: Gen. 29:33; Num. 1:22 *b)* a pious man who, on seeing the infant Jesus in the Temple, spoke the words later set to the canticle "Nunc Dimittis": Luke 2:25-32

Simeon Sty·li·tes (stī līt′ēz), Saint ⟦< LGr(Ec) *stylitēs:* see STYLITE⟧ A.D. 390?-459?; Syrian monk who preached from & lived atop a pillar near Antioch for over 30 years: his day is Jan. 5

Sim·fe·ro·pol (sim′fe rô′pôl y′) capital of the republic of Crimea

Sim·hat To·rah (sim khät′ tō rä′, sim′khäs tō′rə) ⟦Heb *simchat-tora,* lit., rejoicing in the law < *simchat* (< root *śmḥ,* to rejoice) + *tora,* TORAH⟧ a Jewish festival, celebrated on the 23d day of Tishri, that marks the end of the annual cycle of Torah readings and the beginning of the next cycle: also sp. **Sim·chath′ Torah**

sim·i·an (sim′ē ən) ***adj.*** ⟦< L *simia,* an ape, prob. < *simus,* flat-nosed < Gr *simos* < ? IE base **swei-,* to bend⟧ of or like an ape or monkey —***n.*** an ape or monkey

sim·i·lar (sim′ə lər) ***adj.*** ⟦Fr *similaire* < L *similis:* see SAME⟧ **1** nearly but not exactly the same or alike; having a resemblance **2** *Geom.* having the same shape, but not the same size or position —**sim′i·lar·ly** ***adv.***

sim·i·lar·i·ty (sim′ə ler′ə tē) ***n.*** ⟦prec. + -ITY⟧ **1** the state or quality of being similar; resemblance or likeness **2** *pl.* **-ties** a point, feature, or instance in which things are similar —***SYN.*** LIKENESS

sim·i·le (sim′ə lē′) ***n.*** ⟦ME < L, a likeness < neut. of *similis,* SIMILAR⟧ a figure of speech in which one thing is likened to another, dissimilar thing by the use of *like, as,* etc. (Ex.: a heart as big as a whale, her tears flowed like wine): distinguished from METAPHOR

si·mil·i·tude (sə mil′ə to͞od′, -tyo͞od′) ***n.*** ⟦ME < MFr < L *similitudo*⟧ **1** a person or thing resembling another; counterpart; facsimile **2** the form or likeness (*of* some person or thing) **3** similarity; likeness; resemblance **4** [Obs.] *a)* a simile *b)* a parable or allegory

Si·mi Valley (sē′mē) ⟦prob. < a Hokan place name⟧ city in SW Calif., northwest of Los Angeles

Sim·la (sim′lə) city in N India: resort & former summer capital

Sim·men·tal (zim′ən täl′) ***n.*** ⟦after *Simme* Valley, Switzerland, where orig. bred⟧ any of a breed of beef and dairy cattle with a white face and a reddish body with white markings

sim·mer (sim′ər) ***vi.*** ⟦earlier *simper* < LME *simperen:* orig. echoic⟧ **1** to remain at or just below the boiling point, usually forming tiny bubbles with a low, murmuring sound **2** to be about to break out, as in anger, revolt, etc. —***vt.*** **1** to keep (a liquid) at or just below the boiling point **2** to cook in such a liquid —***n.*** the state of simmering —***SYN.*** BOIL[1] —**simmer down** **1** to condense by simmering, as a liquid ☆**2** to become calm; cool off

sim·nel (sim′nəl) ***n.*** ⟦ME *simenel* < OFr < L *simila,* finest wheat flour: see SEMOLINA⟧ in England, *a)* a kind of bread or roll formerly prepared by boiling, or boiling and baking *b)* a rich fruitcake traditionally eaten in mid-Lent or at Easter or Christmas

☆**si·mo·le·on** (sə mō′lē ən) ***n.*** ⟦prob. < obs. *simon,* a dollar, by assoc. with NAPOLEON⟧ [Old Slang] a dollar

Si·mon[1] (sī′mən) ***n.*** ⟦ME < LL(Ec) < Gr(Ec) *Simōn, Seimōn* < Heb *shim'on,* lit., heard: see SIMEON⟧ **1** a masculine name: dim. *Si* **2** *Bible a)* one of the twelve Apostles, called *Peter* or **Simon Peter** (see PETER[1]) *b)* one of the twelve Apostles, called **Simon the Canaanite (or the Zealot)**: Mark 3:18: his day is Oct. 28 (also **Saint Simon**) *c)* a brother or relative of Jesus: Mark 6:3

Si·mon[2] (sī′mən), **Herbert A(lexander)** 1916-2001; U.S. social scientist & economist

si·mo·ni·ac (si mō′nē ak′) ***n.*** ⟦ME *symoniak* < ML *simoniacus*⟧ a person guilty of simony —**si·mo·ni·a·cal** (sī′mə nī′ə kəl, sim′ə-) ***adj.***

Si·mon·i·des (sī män′ə dēz′) 556?-468? B.C.; Gr. lyric poet: also **Simonides of Keos**

☆**si·mon·ize** (sī′mə nīz′) ***vt.*** **-ized′, -iz′ing** ⟦< *SIMONIZ,* a trademark for a metal polish⟧ to polish (an automobile, etc.) with or as with wax

Simon Le·gree (lə grē′) **1** the villainous slave overseer in the novel *Uncle Tom's Cabin* (1852) by Harriet Beecher STOWE **2** [*occas.* **s- l-**] any cruel taskmaster

Simon Ma·gus (mā′gəs) *Bible* a Samaritan magician whose offer of money to learn how to impart the Holy Ghost to others angered Peter: Acts 8:9-24

si·mon-pure (sī′mən pyoor′) ***adj.*** ⟦after *Simon Pure,* a Quaker in Susanna Centlivre's play *A Bold Stroke for a Wife* (1718), who must prove his identity against an impostor's claims⟧ genuine; real; authentic

si·mo·ny (sī′mə nē, sim′ə-) ***n.*** ⟦ME *simonie* < OFr < ML(Ec) *simonia,* after SIMON MAGUS⟧ the impious buying or selling of sacraments, church benefices, etc.

si·moom (si mo͞om′, sī-) ***n.*** ⟦Ar *samūm* < *samma,* to poison⟧ a hot, violent, sand-laden wind of the African and Asian deserts: also called **si·moon′** (-mo͞on′)

☆**simp** (simp) ***n.*** [Slang] *short for* SIMPLETON

sim·pa·ti·co (sim pät′i kō′, -pat′-) ***adj.*** ⟦< It *simpatico* or Sp *simpático,* both ult. < L *sympathia,* SYMPATHY + *-icus,* -IC⟧ that gets along well with or goes well with another or others; compatible or congenial

sim·per (sim′pər) ***vi.*** ⟦Early ModE, akin to Dan dial., MDu *simperlijc,* dainty, affected⟧ to smile in a silly, affected, or self-conscious way —***vt.*** to say or express with a simper —***n.*** a silly, affected, or self-conscious smile —**sim′per·er** ***n.*** —**sim′per·ing·ly** ***adv.***

sim·ple (sim′pəl) ***adj.*** **-pler, -plest** ⟦OFr < L *simplus* < IE **sm̥plos* < bases **sem-,* one + **-plo-,* -fold: see DOUBLE⟧ **1** having or consisting of only one part, feature, substance, etc.; not compounded or complex; single **2** having few parts or features; not complicated or involved [*a simple* pattern] **3** easy to do, solve, or understand, as a task, question, etc. **4** without additions or qualifications; mere; bare [the *simple* facts] **5** *a)* not ornate; unembellished; unadorned [*simple* clothes] *b)* not luxurious or elegant; plain [*simple* tastes] **6** pure; unadulterated **7** without guile or deceit; innocent; artless **8** *a)* without ostentation or affectation; natural *b)* lacking sophistication; naive **9** of low rank or position; specif., *a)* humble; lowly *b)* common; ordinary **10** lacking significance; unimportant **11** *a)* having or showing little sense or reasoning ability; easily misled or deceived; stupid or foolish *b)* uneducated or ignorant **12** *Bot. a)* consisting of one piece; whole *b)* not branched *c)* developing from a single pistil or carpel [*a simple* fruit] **13** *Chem. a)* elementary *b)* unmixed **14** *Law* unconditional; absolute [in fee *simple*] **15** *Zool.* not divided into or made up of parts; not compounded [*a simple* eye] —***n.*** **1** a person who is ignorant or easily misled **2** something having only one part, substance, etc. **3** [Archaic] *a)* a medicinal herb *b)* a medicine made from such a plant **4** [Archaic] a person of humble position —***SYN.*** EASY —**sim′ple·ness** ***n.***

simple equation LINEAR EQUATION

simple fraction COMMON FRACTION

simple fracture a bone fracture in which the broken ends of bone do not pierce the skin

sim·ple-heart·ed (-härt′id) *adj.* artless or unsophisticated

simple interest interest computed on principal alone, and not on principal plus interest: cf. COMPOUND INTEREST

simple machine any of the basic mechanical devices, including the lever, wheel and axle, pulley, wedge, screw, and inclined plane, one or more of which are essential to any more complex machine

simple majority 1 a share of votes that exceeds half of the total number cast 2 [Brit.] PLURALITY (sense 4*a*)

simple meter *Music* any time signature in which the upper figure indicates two, three, or four beats per measure, as 2/8, 3/2, or 4/4

sim·ple-mind·ed (-mīnd′id) *adj.* 1 artless; unsophisticated; simple-hearted 2 foolish; stupid 3 mentally retarded —**sim′ple-mind′ed·ly** *adv.* —**sim′ple-mind′ed·ness** *n.*

simple protein a protein composed only of amino acids

simple sentence *Gram.* a sentence consisting of a single independent clause (Ex: The dog barked loudly)

simple sugar MONOSACCHARIDE

sim·ple·ton (-tən) *n.* ⟦< SIMPLE, after proper names ending in *-ton*⟧ a person who is stupid or easily deceived; fool

simple vow *R.C.Ch.* a vow made with canonical effects less strict than those of a SOLEMN VOW: e.g., a simple vow of chastity, broken by entering marriage while the vow is still in effect, makes the marriage illicit but not invalid

sim·plex (sim′pleks′) *adj.* ⟦L, simple < IE base **sem-*, one + **plak-*: see DUPLEX⟧ 1 having only one part; not complex or compounded 2 designating or of a system of telegraphy, telephony, etc. in which a signal can be transmitted in only one direction at a time —*n., pl.* **-plex·es** or **-pli·ces′** (-plə sēz′) *Math.* an element or figure contained within a Euclidean space of a specified number of dimensions and having one more boundary point than the number of dimensions (Ex.: a *simplex* of zero dimensions is a point, of one dimension is a line segment, of two dimensions is a triangle and its interior, of three dimensions is a tetrahedron and its interior)

sim·plic·i·ty (sim plis′ə tē) *n., pl.* **-ties** ⟦ME *simplicite* < OFr *simplicité* < L *simplicitas*⟧ 1 a simple state or quality, as of form or composition; freedom from intricacy or complexity 2 absence of elegance, embellishment, luxury, etc.; plainness 3 freedom from affectation, subtlety, etc.; artlessness 4 lack of sense; foolishness

sim·pli·fy (sim′plə fī′) *vt.* **-fied′**, **-fy′ing** ⟦Fr *simplifier* < ML *simplificare*: see SIMPLE & -FY⟧ to make simpler, less complex, etc.; make easier —**sim′pli·fi·ca′tion** *n.* —**sim′pli·fi′er** *n.*

sim·plist (sim′plist) *n.* a person given to simplistic explanations, theories, etc. —*adj.* SIMPLISTIC —**sim′plism′** (-pliz′əm) *n.*

sim·plis·tic (sim plis′tik) *adj.* making complex problems unrealistically simple; oversimplifying or oversimplified —**sim·plis′ti·cal·ly** *adv.*

Sim·plon (sim′plän′; *Fr* san plōn′) 1 mountain pass in the Alps of S Switzerland: 6,589 ft (2,008 m) 2 railway tunnel near this pass: 12 mi (19 km) long

sim·ply (sim′plē) *adv.* 1 in a simple manner; with simplicity 2 merely; only; just [*simply* trying to help] 3 absolutely; completely [I was *simply* furious]

sim·u·la·crum (sim′yə lā′krəm, -lak′rəm) *n., pl.* **-la′cra** (-lā′krə, -lak′rə) ⟦L < *simulare*: see SIMULATE⟧ 1 an image; likeness 2 a vague representation; semblance 3 a mere pretense; sham

sim·u·lant (sim′yə lənt) *adj.* ⟦L *simulans*, prp.: see SIMULATE⟧ that simulates; simulating —*n.* one that simulates; simulator

sim·u·lar (sim′yə lər) *adj., n. archaic var. of* SIMULANT

sim·u·late (sim′yə lāt′) *vt.* **-lat′ed**, **-lat′ing** ⟦< L *simulatus*, pp. of *simulare*, to feign < *simul*, together with, at the same time: see SAME⟧ 1 to give a false indication or appearance of; pretend; feign [to *simulate* an interest] 2 to have or take on the external appearance of; look or act like [an insect *simulating* a twig] 3 to achieve or imitate the characteristics or effect of [to *simulate* the feel of fine leather] 4 to use computer simulation to represent (a system, physical process, etc.) —*adj.* [Archaic] pretended; mock —**SYN.** ASSUME

sim·u·la·tion (sim′yə lā′shən) *n.* ⟦ME *simulacion* < MFr < L *simulatio*⟧ 1 the act of simulating; pretense; feigning 2 *a)* a simulated resemblance *b)* an imitation or counterfeit 3 the use of a computer to calculate, by means of extrapolation, the effect of a given physical process 4 the duplicating or reproducing of certain characteristics or conditions, as of a system or physical process, by the use of a model or representation, for study, training, etc. —**sim′u·la′tive** *adj.*

sim·u·la·tor (sim′yə lāt′ər) *n.* 1 one that simulates; specif., a training device that duplicates artificially the conditions likely to be encountered in some operation, as in a spacecraft [a flight *simulator*] 2 a computer that performs simulation

☆**si·mul·cast** (sī′məl kast′) *vt.* **-cast′** or **-cast′ed**, **-cast′ing** ⟦< fol. + -CAST⟧ to broadcast (a program, event, etc.) simultaneously by radio and television —*n.* a program, etc. so broadcast

si·mul·ta·ne·ous (sī′məl tā′nē əs, -tān′yəs; *chiefly Brit & Cdn,* sim′əl-) *adj.* ⟦ML *simultaneus* < *simultas*, simultaneity < L, competition, rivalry < *simul*: see SAME⟧ occurring, done, existing, etc. together or at the same time —**SYN.** CONTEMPORARY —**si′mul·ta·ne′i·ty** (-tə nē′ə tē, -nā′-) *n.*, **si′mul·ta′ne·ous·ness** —**si′mul·ta′ne·ous·ly** *adv.*

simultaneous equations two or more equations used together in the same problem and having common solutions

sin¹ (sēn) *n.* ⟦Heb⟧ the twenty-first letter of the Hebrew alphabet (שׁ)

sin² (sin) *n.* ⟦ME (East Midland) *sinne* < OE *synne* (for **sunjo*), akin to Ger *sünde*, prob. < early Gmc borrowing < L *sous* (gen. *sontis*), guilty, technical legal term, orig. part. form of *esse*, to be (see IS¹), in sense, "(he) being (the one)"⟧ 1 *a)* an offense against God, religion, or good morals *b)* the condition of being guilty of continued offense against God, religion, or good morals 2 an offense against any law, standard, code, etc. [a *sin* against good taste] —*vi.* **sinned**, **sin′ning** to commit a sin —**live in sin** to live together as spouses although not legally married; cohabit: now somewhat old-fashioned and sometimes used humorously

sin³ *abbrev. Trigonometry* sine

SIN (sin) *abbrev.* Social Insurance Number: in Canada, an individual number containing nine digits and used by the government to identify a person for the paying of taxes and the receipt of pensions and other government benefits

Si·nai (sī′nī′), **Mount** the mountain (probably in the S Sinai Peninsula but not identified) where Moses received the law from God: Ex. 19

Sinai Peninsula broad peninsula in NE Egypt, between the Gulf of Suez & the Gulf of Aqaba

Si·na·it·ic (sī′nā it′ik) *adj.* of or from Mount Sinai or the Sinai Peninsula: also **Si·na·ic** (sī nā′ik)

Si·na·lo·a (sē′nä lô′ä) state of NW Mexico, on the Gulf of California: 22,429 sq mi (58,091 sq km); cap. Culiacán

Sin·an·thro·pus (si nan′thrə pəs, sī-) *n.* ⟦ModL: see SINO- & ANTHROPO-⟧ *former name for* PEKING MAN

sin·a·pism (sin′ə piz′əm) *n.* ⟦L *sinapismus* < Gr *sinapismos* < *sinapi*, mustard⟧ MUSTARD PLASTER

Si·na·tra (si nä′trə), **Frank** (born *Francis Albert Sinatra*) 1915-98; U.S. popular singer & film actor

Sin·bad (the Sailor) (sin′bad′) a merchant in *The Arabian Nights* who makes seven adventurous voyages

since (sins) *adv.* ⟦ME *syns*, contr. < *sithens*, adv. gen. of *sithen* < OE *siththan*, for earlier **siththon* < *sith*, after, since (for IE base see SIDE) + *thon*, instrumental form of *thæt*, THAT⟧ 1 from then until now [she arrived Tuesday and has been here ever *since*] 2 at some or any time between then and now; subsequently [he was ill last week but has *since* recovered] 3 before the present time; before now; ago [they are long *since* gone] —*prep.* 1 continuously from (the time given) until now [out walking *since* one o'clock] 2 during the period between (the time given) and now; subsequently to [many achievements *since* his election] —*conj.* 1 during the period from the specified time or event until the present [I haven't seen him *since* we were in high school] 2 continuously from the time when [I've been lonely *since* he left] 3 inasmuch as; because [*since* you are finished, let's go]

sin·cere (sin sir′) *adj.* **-cer′er**, **-cer′est** ⟦MFr *sincère* < L *sincerus*, clean, pure, sincere⟧ 1 without deceit, pretense, or hypocrisy; truthful; straightforward; honest [*sincere* in his desire to help] 2 being the same in actual character as in outward appearance; genuine; real [*sincere* grief] 3 [Archaic] not adulterated [*sincere* wine] 4 [Obs.] uninjured; whole —**sin·cere′ly** *adv.* —**sin·cere′ness** *n.*

sin·cer·i·ty (sin ser′ə tē) *n.* ⟦MFr *sincérité* < L *sinceritas*⟧ the quality or state of being sincere; honesty, genuineness, good faith, etc.

sin·ci·put (sin′si put′) *n.* ⟦L, half a head < *semi*, half (see SEMI-) + *caput*, HEAD⟧ the upper part of the skull or head; esp., the forehead —**sin·cip′i·tal** (-sip′ət′l) *adj.*

Sin·clair (sin kler′), **Up·ton (Beall, Jr.)** (up′tən) 1878-1968; U.S. novelist & socialist

Sind (sind) province of Pakistan, in the lower Indus River valley: 54,407 sq mi (140,914 sq km); cap. Karachi

Sind·bad (the Sailor) (sin′bad, sind′-) *n. var. of* SINBAD (THE SAILOR)

Sin·dhi (sin′dē) *n.* ⟦Ar *Sindī*, after *Sind*, Sind < Hindi < Sans *sindhu*, river⟧ 1 a member of a chiefly Muslim people of Sind and adjacent parts of India 2 the Indo-Aryan language of this people

sine¹ (sīn) *n.* ⟦ML *sinus* (< L, a bend, curve, hanging fold of a toga), used as transl. of Ar *jaib*, sine, bosom of a garment⟧ *Trigonometry* the reciprocal of the cosecant; specif., *a)* the ratio of the opposite side of a given acute angle in a right triangle to the hypotenuse *b)* an equivalent, positive or negative ratio for certain related angles (Ex.: the sine of 57° or 123° is .8387, of 237° or 303° is -.8387) or real numbers representing radians (Ex.: the sine of .9948 radians (57°) is .8387)

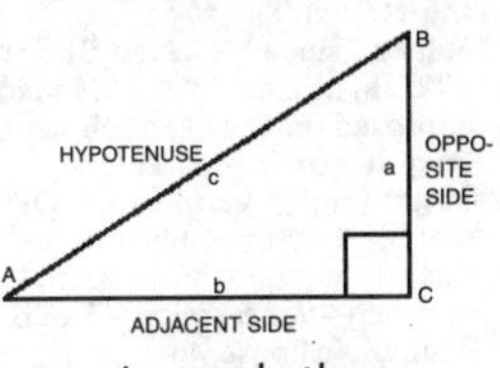

sine and other trigonometric functions
sine of angle A = a/c
cosine of A = b/c
tangent of A = a/b
cotangent of A = b/a
secant of A = c/b
cosecant of A = c/a

si·ne² (sī′nē, sin′ā) *prep.* ⟦L⟧ without

si·ne·cure (sī′nə kyoor′, sin′ə-) *n.* ⟦< ML(Ec) (*beneficium*) *sine cura*, (benefice) without a CURE (*n.* 5) < L *sine*, without + *cura*, care: see CURE⟧ 1 [Obs.] a church benefice not involving the care of souls 2 any office or position providing an income or other advantage but requiring little or no work

sine curve a graphic representation of the sine function; specif., the graph of $y = \sin x$, with x denoting radian measure of an angle periodically changing from 0° to 360°

si·ne di·e (sī′nē dī′ē, sin′ā dē′ā) ⟦LL⟧ without (a) day (being set for meeting again); for an indefinite period [to adjourn an assembly *sine die*]

si·ne pro·le (sī′nē prō′lē, sin′ā prō′lā) ⟦L⟧ *Law* without offspring; childless

si·ne qua non (sī′nē kwā nän′, sin′ā kwā nōn′) ⟦L, without which not⟧ an essential condition, qualification, etc.; indispensable thing; absolute prerequisite

sin·ew (sin′yo͞o) ***n.*** ⟦ME < OE *seonwe*, oblique form < nom. *seonu*, akin to OHG *senawa*, ON *sin* < IE base **sēi-*, to bind, a band > L *saeta*, bristle, Sans *sinâti*, (he) ties⟧ **1** a tendon **2** muscular power; strength **3** any source of power or strength; means of supplying strength: *usually used in pl.* **—*vt.*** to strengthen as with sinews

sine wave a waveform described by the sine function: complex waveforms can be regarded as a combination of several sine waves that differ in wavelength

sin·ew·y (sin′yo͞o ē) ***adj.*** **1** of or like sinew; tough; strong **2** having many or large sinews, as a cut of meat **3** having good muscular development [*sinewy* shoulders] **4** vigorous; powerful; robust [a *sinewy* style of writing]

sin·fo·ni·a (sin′fə nē′ə) ***n.*** ⟦It < L *symphonia*, SYMPHONY⟧ any of various early Italian instrumental works; esp., a type of overture, as to an opera

sinfonia con·cer·tan·te (kän′sər tän′tā, -chər-) a type of concerto for two or more solo instruments accompanied by an orchestra

sin·fo·niet·ta (sin′fən yet′ə) ***n.*** ⟦It, dim. of *sinfonia*: see SINFONIA⟧ a brief symphony, usually for a small orchestra

sin·ful (sin′fəl) ***adj.*** full of or characterized by sin; wicked; immoral **—sin′ful·ly *adv.*** **—sin′ful·ness *n.***

sing[1] (siŋ) ***vi.* sang, sung, sing′ing** ⟦ME *singen* < OE *singan*, akin to Ger *singen* < IE base **sengwh-* > Gr *omphē*, a voice, oracle⟧ **1** *a)* to produce musical sounds or notes with the voice, esp. in a connected series, as in giving voice to a song *b)* to perform musical selections vocally, esp. as a professional **2** to use song or verse in description, praise, etc. [of thee I *sing*] **3** *a)* to make musical sounds like those made by the human voice, as a violin or songbird *b)* to make a sound of whistling, buzzing, humming, etc., as a steaming teakettle, a bee, a strong wind, etc. **4** to have a sensation of ringing, humming, buzzing, etc., as the ears **5** to admit of being sung **6** to be exultant; rejoice [a sight to make one's heart *sing*] **7** [Slang] to confess to a crime, esp. so as to implicate others **—*vt.*** **1** to render or deliver (a song, musical role, etc.) by singing **2** to chant or intone (part of a church service, etc.) **3** to describe, proclaim, extol, celebrate, etc. in or as in song or verse [to *sing* someone's praises] **4** to bring to a given state or place by or with singing [to *sing* a baby to sleep] **—*n.*** **1** [Informal] singing by a group gathered for the purpose **2** such a gathering of people **—sing out** [Informal] to speak or call out loudly; shout **—sing′a·ble *adj.***

sing[2] *abbrev.* singular

sing·a·long (siŋ′ə lôŋ′) ***n.*** **1** an informal gathering of people to join in the singing of songs **2** a form of entertainment in which the audience or patrons, as of a nightclub or bar, sing familiar songs along with the entertainer or performer

Sin·ga·pore (siŋ′ə pôr′, siŋ′gə-) **1** island off the S tip of the Malay Peninsula **2** country comprising this island & nearby islets: a former British colony, it became a state of Malaysia (1963-65) & an independent republic & member of the Commonwealth (1965): 268 sq mi (693 sq km) **3** its capital, a seaport on the S coast **4 Strait of** channel between Singapore & a group of Indonesian islands to the south: 65 mi (105 km) long: also **Singapore Strait** **—Sin′ga·por′e·an *adj., n.***

singe (sinj) ***vt.* singed, singe′ing** ⟦ME *sengen* < OE *sengan*, akin to Ger *sengen* < IE base **senk-*, to burn, dry out > OSlav *isočiti*, to dry, *sęcilo*, oven⟧ **1** to burn superficially or slightly **2** to expose (the carcass of an animal or fowl) to flame in removing bristles or feathers **3** to burn the nap from (cloth) as a process of manufacture **4** to burn the tips of (hair), as after a haircut **—*n.*** **1** the act of singeing **2** a superficial burn **—*SYN.*** BURN[1]

sing·er[1] (siŋ′ər) ***n.*** **1** a person who sings, esp. professionally **2** a bird that sings **3** [Old Poet.] a poet

sing·er[2] (sin′jər) ***n.*** a person or thing that singes

Sing·er (siŋ′ər) **1 Isaac Ba·shev·is** (bä shev′is) 1904-91; U.S. writer in Yiddish, born in Poland **2 Isaac Mer·ritt** (mer′it) 1811-75; U.S. inventor: improved the sewing machine

Sin·gha·lese (siŋ′gə lēz′, -lēs′) ***adj., n., pl.* -lese′** *var. of* SINHALESE

sin·gle (siŋ′gəl) ***adj.*** ⟦ME < OFr *sengle* < L *singulus*, single: for IE base see SIMPLE⟧ **1** *a)* one only; one and no more; individual *b)* separate and distinct from others of the same kind [every *single* time] **2** without another or others; alone; solitary **3** of or for one person, as a bed or room, or one family, as a house **4** between two persons only; with only one on each side [*single* combat] **5** *a)* unmarried *b)* of or characteristic of the unmarried state **6** having only one part; not double, compound, multiple, etc. **7** the same for all; uniform [a *single* scale of pay] **8** being a whole, or unbroken [forming a *single* front] **9** having only one row or set of petals: said of flowers **10** honest; sincere **11** seeing justly [to judge with a *single* eye] **12** [Rare] unique; singular **13** [Archaic] weak; inferior: said of beer, ale, etc. **—*vt.* -gled, -gling** **1** to select or distinguish from others: now usually with *out* ☆**2** *Baseball* to advance (a runner) by hitting a single **—*vi.*** ☆*Baseball* to hit a single **—*n.*** **1** a single person or thing; specif., *a)* a hotel room, travel space, etc. for one person *b)* [*pl.*] unmarried people collectively ☆*c)* a one-dollar bill *d)* a phonograph record, usually recorded at 45 rpm, with one short performance on each side **2** TWIN BED ☆**3** *Baseball* a hit on which the batter reaches first base **4** *Cricket* a hit by which one run is scored **5** *Golf* a match between two players **6** [*pl.*] *Racket Sports* a match with only one player on each side **—sin′gle·ness *n.***

sin·gle-act·ing (-ak′tiŋ) ***adj.*** acting in or impelled from one direction only, as an engine; not reciprocating

sin·gle-ac·tion (-ak′shən) ***adj.*** ☆designating a firearm whose trigger serves to fire the weapon but not to cock it

sin·gle-blind (-blīnd′) ***adj.*** designating or of a technique used to test objectively the effects of a drug, course of treatment, etc. in which the researchers but not the subjects know during the testing who is actually receiving the drug, treatment, etc.: cf. DOUBLE-BLIND

single bond *Chem.* the sharing of two electrons between two atoms, represented in formulas as C:C or C-C

sin·gle-breast·ed (-bres′tid) ***adj.*** overlapping the front of the body just enough to fasten with a single row of buttons or a single button: said as of a coat

single entry a system of bookkeeping in which the only account kept is a single one consisting usually of a record of cash and of debts owed to and by the concern in question **—sin′gle-en′try *adj.***

single file **1** a single line of people or things placed or moving one directly behind another **2** in such a line [to walk *single file*]

☆**sin·gle-foot** (-fo͝ot′) ***n.*** the gait of a horse in which the legs move in lateral pairs, each foot falling separately **—*vi.*** to move with this gait

sin·gle-hand·ed (-han′did) ***adj.*** **1** having only one hand **2** using or requiring the use of only one hand [a *single-handed* sword] **3** without help; done or working alone; unaided **—*adv.*** **1** by means of only one hand **2** without help **—sin′gle-hand′ed·ly *adv.*** **—sin′gle-hand′ed·ness *n.***

sin·gle-heart·ed (-härt′id) ***adj.*** honest; faithful; sincere **—sin′gle-heart′ed·ly *adv.*** **—sin′gle-heart′ed·ness *n.***

sin·gle-lens reflex (siŋ′gəl lenz′) a reflex camera having a viewing system that allows the photographer to see the subject through the same lens that brings the image to the film or digital sensor

single malt designating Scotch whisky that is produced by a single distiller in a single batch and not blended

sin·gle-mind·ed (-mīn′did) ***adj.*** **1** SINGLE-HEARTED **2** with only one aim or purpose **—sin′gle-mind′ed·ly *adv.*** **—sin′gle-mind′ed·ness *n.***

sin·gle-pay·er (-pā′ər) ***adj.*** designating or of a system of healthcare provided as by private hospitals and paid for by a single entity, usually the government

sin·gle-phase (-fāz′) ***adj.*** powered either by a single AC voltage or current or by several equal AC voltages or currents that are either in phase or out of phase by one half a cycle (180°)

singles bar a bar which serves as a meeting place for unmarried people, esp. young ones in search of social, often specif. sexual, relationships

sin·gle-side·band (-sīd′band′) ***adj.*** of or pertaining to a system of radio transmission in which one of the two sidebands produced during modulation is suppressed

sin·gle-space (-spās′) ***vt., vi.* -spaced′, -spac′ing** to type (copy) so as to leave no blank space between lines

☆**single standard** MONOMETALLISM

sin·gle·stick (-stik′) ***n.*** **1** a swordlike stick fitted with a guard and formerly used for fencing **2** the sport of fencing with such sticks

☆**sin·gle-stick·er** (-stik′ər) ***n.*** [Old Informal] a sailboat, esp. a sloop, having only one mast

sin·glet (siŋ′glit) ***n.*** ⟦< SINGLE, modeled on DOUBLET⟧ **1** [Brit.] a man's undershirt, esp. a sleeveless one **2** [Austral. & N.Z.] a short-sleeved or sleeveless knit top, as a T-shirt or tank top **3** an atom that is freed from combination by being raised to a higher energy level

☆**single tax** **1** a system of taxation in which all revenue is to be derived from a tax on a single thing, specif. on the value of land **2** such a tax **—sin′gle-tax′ *adj.***

sin·gle·ton (siŋ′gəl tən) ***n.*** ⟦< SINGLE, after proper names ending in *-ton*⟧ **1** a playing card that is the only one of its suit in a hand dealt to a player **2** something occurring or existing singly and not as one of a pair or of a group

☆**sin·gle-track** (-trak′) ***adj.*** ONE-TRACK

sin·gle·tree (-trē′) ***n.*** ⟦altered (as if < SINGLE) < *swingletree* < ME *swingle*, rod, whip + *tre*, TREE⟧ a wooden bar swung at the center from a hitch on a plow, wagon, etc. and hooked at either end to the traces of a horse's harness

sin·gly (siŋ′glē) ***adv.*** **1** as a single, separate person or thing; alone **2** individually and in sequence; one by one **3** single-handed; unaided

Sing Sing (siŋ′ siŋ′) ⟦< Du *Sintsing* < *Ossinsing*, earlier form of the village name, apparently < a Delaware word meaning "at the small stones"⟧ a penitentiary at Ossining, a village in SE N.Y.

sing·song (siŋ′sôŋ′, -säŋ′) ***n.*** **1** *a)* a monotonous rise and fall of tone, as in speaking *b)* speech, tones, etc. marked by this **2** *a)* monotonous, stereotyped rhyme or rhythm in verse *b)* verse marked by this **3** [Brit.] SING[1] **—*adj.*** in or like a singsong

Sing·spiel (ziŋ′shpēl′) ***n., pl.* -spiel′en** (-ən) ⟦Ger, lit., sing-play⟧ an 18th-cent. German musical play of a popular type

sin·gu·lar (siŋ′gyə lər) ***adj.*** ⟦ME *singuler* < OFr < L *singularis* < *singulus*, SINGLE⟧ **1** being the only one of its kind; single; unique [a *singular* specimen] **2** exceptional; extraordinary; remarkable [*singular* beauty] **3** peculiar; strange; odd [what a *singular* remark!] **4** [Archaic] existing apart from others; separate; individual **5** *Gram.* designating or of the category of number that refers to only one person or thing **6** *Logic* *a)* of an individual thing considered by itself *b)* used to designate such a thing **—*n.*** **1** *Gram.* *a)* the singular number *b)* the singular form of a word *c)* a word in singular form **2** *Logic* a thing considered apart from all others —**sin′gu·lar·ly** *adv.*

sin·gu·lar·i·ty (siŋ′gyə ler′ə tē) *n., pl.* **-ties** ⟦ME *singularite* < OFr < LL *singularitas*⟧ **1** the condition or quality of being singular **2** a unique, distinct, or peculiar feature or thing **3** *Physics* a point or region at the center of a black hole, where, it is theorized, the force of gravity compresses an object such that it has infinite density and almost no volume

sin·gu·lar·ize (siŋ′gyə lər īz′) *vt.* **-ized′**, **-iz′ing** to make singular

Sin·ha·la (sin hä′lə) *adj.* SINHALESE (*adj.*) —*n.* SINHALESE (*n.* 2)

Sin·ha·lese (sin′hə lēz′, sin′ə-; -lēs′) *adj.* ⟦< Sans *Siṅhala*, Sri Lanka + -ESE⟧ of Sri Lanka or its principal people, language, or culture —*n.* **1** *pl.* **-lese′** a member of the principal people of Sri Lanka **2** the Indo-Aryan language of this people

Sin·i·cism (sin′i siz′əm, sī′ni-) *n.* ⟦< ML *Sinicus*, Chinese (< LL *Sinae*, an Asian people < Gr *Sinai*) + -ISM⟧ a custom, language trait, etc. originating with or peculiar to the Chinese

Si·ning (shē′niŋ′) *a former transliteration of* XINING

sin·is·ter (sin′is tər) *adj.* ⟦ME *sinistre* < L *sinister*, left-hand, or unlucky (side), orig. lucky (side) < IE base **sene-*, to prepare, achieve > Sans *sánīyān*, more favorable: early Roman augurs faced south, with the east (lucky side) to the left, but the Greeks (followed by later Romans) faced north⟧ **1** *a)* [Archaic] on, to, or toward the left-hand side; left *b)* *Heraldry* on the left side of a shield (the right as seen by the viewer) (opposed to DEXTER) **2** threatening harm, evil, or misfortune; ominous; portentous [*sinister* storm clouds] **3** wicked, evil, or dishonest, esp. in some dark, mysterious way [*a sinister* plot] **4** most unfavorable or unfortunate; disastrous [met a *sinister* fate] —**sin′is·ter·ly** *adv.* —**sin′is·ter·ness** *n.*

SYN.—**sinister**, in this connection, applies to that which can be interpreted as presaging imminent danger or evil [a *sinister* smile]; **baleful** refers to that which is inevitably deadly, destructive, pernicious, etc. [a *baleful* influence]; **malign** is applied to that which is regarded as having an inherent tendency toward evil or destruction [a *malign* doctrine]

sin·is·tral (sin′is trəl) *adj.* ⟦OFr < L *sinistra*, left hand: see prec.⟧ **1** on the left-hand side; left **2** left-handed **3** having whorls that rise to the apex in clockwise spirals from the opening at the lower left: said of the shells of some gastropods Opposed to DEXTRAL —**sin′is·tral′i·ty** (-tral′ə tē) *n.* —**sin′is·tral·ly** *adv.*

sin·is·tro- (sin′is trō, -trə) ⟦< L *sinister*: see SINISTER⟧ *combining form* of, at, or toward the left [*sinistrodextral*]: also, before a vowel, **sin′is·tr-**

sin·is·tro·dex·tral (sin′is trō deks′trəl) *adj.* ⟦prec. + DEXTRAL⟧ going or directed from left to right

sin·is·trorse (sin′is trôrs′) *adj.* ⟦ModL *sinistrorsus* < L, contr. of *sinistrovorsus* < *sinister*, to the left (see SINISTER) + *versus, vorsus* (see VERSE)⟧ *Bot.* twining upward while constantly turning to the left, as the stems of some vines do: opposed to DEXTRORSE —**sin′is·trorse′ly** *adv.*

sin·is·trous (sin′is trəs) *adj.* [Archaic] SINISTER

Si·nit·ic (sī nit′ik, si-) *n.* ⟦see SINO-, -ITE[1], & -IC⟧ a branch of the Sino-Tibetan family of languages, including the languages of China —*adj.* of China or its people, languages, or culture

sink (siŋk) *vi.* **sank** or **sunk**, **sunk**, **sink′ing** ⟦ME *sinken* < OE *sincan*, akin to Ger *sinken* < IE base **sengw-*, to fall, sink > Gr *heaphthē*, (he) sank⟧ **1** to go beneath the surface of water, deep snow, soft ground, etc. so as to be partly or completely covered **2** to go down slowly; fall or descend gradually **3** to appear to fall or descend [the sun *sinking* in the west] **4** *a)* to become lower in level; diminish in height or depth [a lake that has *sunk* three inches] *b)* to slope downward (*from, to,* etc.) **5** to diminish or decrease in degree, volume, or strength; subside, as wind, flames, a sound, spirits, etc. **6** to become lower in value or amount; lessen, as prices, funds, etc. **7** to seem or become hollow or shrunken; recede, as the cheeks or eyes **8** to pass gradually (*into* sleep, despair, lethargy, etc.) **9** to become increasingly and dangerously ill; approach death; fail **10** *a)* to lose position, wealth, prestige, dignity, etc. *b)* to lose or abandon one's moral values and stoop (*to* some unworthy action) **11** to become absorbed; penetrate —*vt.* **1** to cause to submerge or go beneath the surface [to *sink* a boat, to *sink* the blade of a shovel into the ground] **2** to cause or allow to fall or go down; lower **3** to make (a well, mine, engraved design, etc.) by digging, drilling, or cutting **4** to cause to penetrate or become absorbed **5** to reduce in volume, amount, degree, or intensity **6** *a)* to invest (money, capital, etc.) *b)* to lose by investing **7** to hold back, suppress, or conceal (evidence, identity, personal interests, etc.) **8** to pay up (a debt) **9** *a)* to cause to lose courage, strength, etc. or position, dignity, etc. *b)* to debase (character, dignity, etc.) **10** to defeat; undo; ruin ☆**11** *Games, Sports* to put (a basketball, golf ball, pool ball, etc.) through the net, into the cup, into a pocket, etc. —*n.* ⟦ME *sinke* < the v.⟧ **1** a cesspool or sewer **2** any place or thing considered morally filthy or corrupted **3** any of various basins, as in a kitchen, connected with a drainpipe and, usually, a water supply **4** a repository or device for collecting, removing, or absorbing energy, heat, a specific substance, etc. from a system and then disposing of or dissipating it ☆**5** *Geol.* *a)* an area of slightly sunken land, esp. one in which water collects, often forming a salt lake, or disappears by evaporation or percolation into the ground *b)* SINKHOLE (sense 2) —**sink in** [Informal] to be grasped by the mind, esp. with difficulty; be recognized or understood in full —**sink′a·ble** *adj.*

sink·age (siŋ′kij) *n.* **1** the act of sinking **2** the degree to which something has sunk or been sunk **3** an area or part sunk below the surrounding level; depression

sink·er (-kər) *n.* **1** a person or thing that sinks **2** a lead weight used in fishing ☆**3** [Informal] a doughnut ☆**4** *Baseball* a pitched ball that drops downward sharply as it reaches home plate: sometimes called **sink′er·ball′** (-bôl′)

sink·hole (siŋk′hōl′) *n.* **1** CESSPOOL ☆**2** a saucer-shaped surface depression produced when underlying material, such as limestone or salt, dissolves or when caves, mines, etc. collapse

Sin·kiang (sin′kyaŋ′; *Chin* shin′jyäŋ′) *a former transliteration of* XINJIANG

sinking fund a fund made up of sums of money set aside at intervals, usually invested at interest, in order to meet a specified future obligation, as the retirement of bonds at maturity

sin·less (sin′lis) *adj.* without sin; innocent —**sin′less·ly** *adv.* —**sin′less·ness** *n.*

sin·ner (-ər) *n.* a person who sins; wrongdoer

Sinn Fein (shin′ fān′) ⟦Ir, we ourselves⟧ an Irish nationalist organization and political party formed in 1905: the present-day organization is regarded as the political wing of the IRISH REPUBLICAN ARMY

Si·no- (sī′nō, sin′ō) ⟦Fr < LL *Sinae* < Gr *Sinai*, an Asian people⟧ *combining form* Chinese, Chinese and [*Sinology*]

si·no·a·tri·al node (sī′nō ā′trē əl) ⟦< SINUS + ATRIAL⟧ PACEMAKER (sense 2*a*): sometimes called **si′no·au·ric′u·lar node** (-ô rik′yə lər)

Si·no-Jap·a·nese (sī′nō jap′ə nēz′) *adj.* having to do with both China and Japan

Si·nol·o·gist (sī näl′ə jist, si-) *n.* a specialist in Sinology: also **Si·no·logue** (sī′nə lôg′, sin′ə-)

Si·nol·o·gy (sī näl′ə jē, si-) *n.* ⟦SINO- + -LOGY⟧ the study of the Chinese language or of Chinese literature, art, customs, etc. —**Si·no·log·i·cal** (sī′nə läj′i kəl) *adj.*

Si·no-Ti·bet·an (sī′nō ti bet′'n) *n.* a family of languages spoken in central and Southeast Asia, including the Sinitic and Tibeto-Burman languages

sin·se·mil·la (sin′sə mil′ə) *n.* ⟦AmSp < Sp *sin*, without + *semilla*, seed⟧ a potent form of marijuana produced by preventing the female plant from being pollinated

sin tax a tax on an activity or on a product associated with behavior thought of as being sinful or harmful, esp. such a tax on gambling, alcoholic beverages, tobacco, etc.

sin·ter (sin′tər) *n.* ⟦Ger: see CINDER⟧ **1** *Geol.* a concretionary sediment of silica or calcium carbonate deposited near the mouth of a mineral spring, geyser, etc. **2** *Metallurgy* a bonded mass of metal particles shaped and partially fused by pressure and heating below the melting point — *vi., vt.* to become or make into a SINTER (*n.* 2)

Sin·tra (sēn′trə, sin′-) city in W Portugal, northwest of Lisbon

sin·u·ate (sin′yo͞o it, -āt′; *for v.*, -āt′) *adj.* ⟦L *sinuatus*, pp. of *sinuare*, to bend < *sinus*, a bend⟧ **1** SINUOUS **2** *Bot.* having an indented, wavy margin, as some leaves —*vi.* **-at′ed**, **-at′ing** to bend or wind in and out; be sinuous or wavy —**sin′u·ate·ly** *adv.* —**sin′u·a′tion** *n.*

sin·u·os·i·ty (sin′yo͞o äs′ə tē) *n.* ⟦Fr *sinuosité*⟧ **1** the state or quality of being sinuous **2** *pl.* **-ties** a sinuous turn or movement; undulation

sin·u·ous (sin′yo͞o əs) *adj.* ⟦L *sinuosus* < *sinus*, a bend⟧ **1** bending, winding, or curving in and out; wavy; serpentine **2** not straightforward; devious; crooked **3** SINUATE (*adj.* 2) —**sin′u·ous·ly** *adv.*

si·nus (sī′nəs) *n.* ⟦L, a bend, curve, fold⟧ **1** a bend or curve **2** any cavity or hollow formed by a bending or curving **3** *Anat., Zool.* any of various cavities, hollows, or passages; esp., *a)* any of the air cavities in the skull opening into the nasal cavities *b)* a large channel for venous blood *c)* a dilated part in a blood vessel, etc. **4** *Bot.* a rounded depression between two consecutive lobes, as of a leaf **5** *Med.* a channel leading from a pus-filled cavity

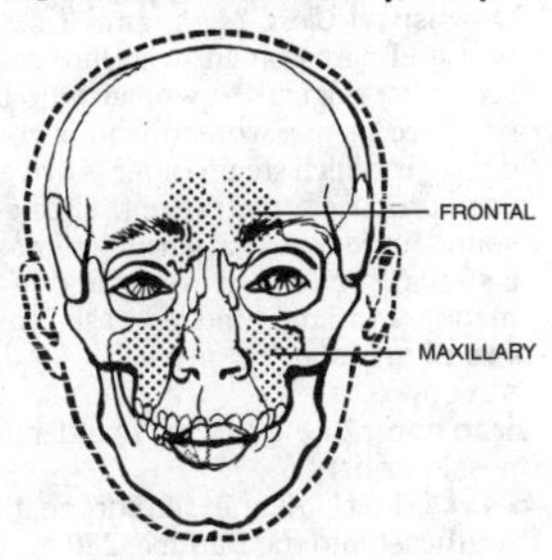

sinuses
(sense 3*a*)

si·nus·i·tis (sī′nəs īt′is) *n.* ⟦ModL: see prec. & -ITIS⟧ inflammation of a sinus or sinuses, esp. those of the skull

si·nus·oid (sī′nəs oid′) *n.* SINE CURVE —**si′nus·oi′dal** *adj.*

sinusoidal projection an equal-area map projection showing the entire surface of the earth with all lines of latitude as straight lines and all lines of longitude as curved lines

Si·on (sī′ən) *var. of* Zion

Siou·an (so͞o′ən) *n.* a family of North American Indian languages formerly spoken in the WC U.S., central Canada, and parts of Virginia and the Carolinas: it includes Iowa, Mandan, Dakota, Crow, Hidatsa, Osage, etc. —*adj.* designating or of this family of languages

Sioux (so͞o) *n., pl.* **Sioux** (so͞o, so͞oz) ⟦Fr, contr. < *Nadouessioux*, pl. < Ottawa dialect of *nadowe-is-iw*, *naadoweesiwag*, an ethnic name, lit., adder: applied in variant forms in different Algonquian languages to a number of non-Algonquian groups⟧ DAKOTA[1] (*n.* 1 & 2) —*adj.* DAKOTA[1] (*adj.* 1)

Sioux City ⟦after the *Sioux* Indians, whose members gave help to settlers in the 1850s⟧ city in W Iowa, on the Missouri River

Sioux Falls ⟦named for the *falls* on the Big *Sioux* River, on which it is situated⟧ city in SE S.Dak.

sip (sip) *vt., vi.* **sipped**, **sip′ping** ⟦ME *sippen*, akin to LowG *sippen*: for IE base see SUP[1]] to drink very little, or a little at a time —*n.* **1** the act of sipping **2** a small quantity sipped at one time —**sip′per** *n.*

si·phon (sī′fən) *n.* ⟦Fr < L *sipho* (gen. *siphonis*) < Gr *siphōn*, tube, siphon⟧ **1** a bent tube used for carrying liquid from a reservoir over the top edge of its container to a point below the surface of the reservoir: the tube must be filled, as by suction, before flow will start **2** SIPHON BOTTLE **3** a tubelike organ in some animals, as cuttlefishes, used for drawing in or ejecting liquids —*vt.* to draw off or carry through or as through a siphon —*vi.* to pass through a siphon —**si′phon·al** (-əl) *adj.*, **si·phon·ic** (sī fän′ik)

siphon

si·phon·age (-ij) *n.* the act of siphoning

siphon bottle a heavy, sealed bottle with a tube on the inside connected at the top with a nozzle and valve which, when opened, allows the flow of pressurized, carbonated water contained within

si·pho·no·phore (sī′fə nə fôr′, sī fän′ə-) *n.* ⟦< Gr *siphōn*, tube + -PHORE⟧ any of an order (Siphonophora) of small, transparent, often colored, swimming or floating sea hydrozoans composed of several kinds of polyps and including the Portuguese man-of-war

si·pho·no·stele (-stēl′, -stē′lē) *n.* ⟦< Gr *siphōn*, tube + STELE⟧ *Bot.* a type of vascular system consisting of a ring of vascular bundles surrounding a central pith —**si′pho·no·ste′lic** (-stē′lik) *adj.*

sip·pet (sip′it) *n.* ⟦prob. dim. of SOP⟧ **1** a small piece of toasted or fried bread used as a garnish, dipped in gravy, etc. **2** any small piece; fragment

Si·quei·ros (sē ke′rôs), **(José) Da·vid Al·fa·ro** (dä vēd′ äl fä′rô) 1896-1974; Mex. painter, esp. of murals

sir (sʉr) *n.* ⟦ME < *sire*: see SIRE⟧ **1** a man of rank; lord **2** [*sometimes* **S-**] a respectful term of address used to a man: not followed by the given name or surname and often used in the salutation of a letter [*Dear Sir*] **3** [**S-**] the title used before the given name or full name of a knight or baronet [*Sir* Walter Ralegh] **4** [Archaic] a term of address used with the title of a man's office, rank, or profession [*sir* priest, *sir* judge, *sir* knight]

Sir *abbrev. Bible* Sirach

Si·rach (sī′rak) *n.* a book of proverbs in the Old Testament Apocrypha: in some versions called *Ecclesiasticus*: abbrev. *Si* or *Sir*

Si·ra·cu·sa (sē′rä ko͞o′zä) *It. name for* SYRACUSE (the seaport in Sicily)

sir·dar (sər där′) *n.* ⟦Urdu < Pers, leader < *sar*, the head + *dār*, holding⟧ **1** in India, Pakistan, and Afghanistan, *a)* a chief or noble *b)* a high military officer **2** in India, a person, esp. a Sikh, holding an important position **3** any Sikh man

sire (sīr) *n.* ⟦ME < OFr, a master < L *senior*: see SENIOR⟧ **1** *a)* [Archaic] a person of authority; man of high rank *b)* [**S-**] a title of respect used in addressing a king, equivalent to "your majesty" **2** [Old Poet.] a father or forefather **3** the male parent of an animal, esp. of a four-legged mammal —*vt.* **sired**, **sir′ing** to beget: said esp. of animals

sir·ee (sə rē′) *interj. alt. sp. of* SIRREE

si·ren (sī′rən) *n.* ⟦ME *syrene* < OFr < LL *Sirena*, for L *Siren* < Gr *Seirēn* < ? *seira*, cord, rope (hence, orig. ? one who snares, entangles) < IE base **twer-*, to grasp⟧ **1** *Class. Myth.* any of several sea nymphs, represented as part bird and part woman, who lure sailors to their death on rocky coasts by seductive singing **2** a woman who uses her sexual attractiveness to entice or allure men; a woman who is considered seductive **3** *a)* an acoustical device in which steam or air is driven against a rotating, perforated disk so as to produce sound; specif., such a device producing a loud, often wailing sound, used esp. as a warning signal *b)* an electronic device that produces a similar sound **4** any of a family (Sirenidae) of slender, eel-shaped salamanders without hind legs; esp., the mud eel

si·re·ni·an (sī rē′nē ən) *n.* ⟦< ModL *Sirenia* < L *Siren* (see prec.) + -AN⟧ SEA COW

siren song ⟦see SIREN, *n.* 1⟧ a dangerously attractive, esp. seductive, proposal or offer

Si·ret (si ret′) river in SE Europe, flowing from the Carpathian Mountains southeast into the Danube: 280 mi (451 km)

Sir·i·us (sir′ē əs) *n.* ⟦ME < L < Gr *Seirios*, lit., scorcher: so named by the ancients because it rises and sets with the sun during the hottest part of the year⟧ a binary, variable star in the constellation Canis Major, the brightest star in the sky; Dog Star: magnitude, -1.44

sir·loin (sʉr′loin′) *n.* ⟦Early ModE *surloyn* < MFr *surlonge* < OFr *sur*, over (see SUR-[1]) + *loigne*, LOIN⟧ a choice cut of meat, esp. of beef, from the loin end just in front of the rump

si·roc·co (sə räk′ō, shə-) *n.*, *pl.* **-cos** ⟦It < Ar *sharq*, the east < *sharaqa*, to rise (of the sun)⟧ **1** a hot, steady, oppressive wind blowing from the Libyan deserts across the Mediterranean into S Europe, often bringing dust and sometimes accompanied by rain **2** any hot, oppressive wind, esp. one blowing toward a center of low barometric pressure

sir·rah or **sir·ra** (sir′ə) *n.* ⟦< SIR⟧ [Archaic] a contemptuous term of address used, as in anger, to a man

☆**sir·ree** (sə rē′) *interj.* ⟦< SIR⟧ used to provide emphasis after *yes* or *no*

sir-rev·er·ence (sʉr′rev′ər əns) *interj.* ⟦confused form for *sa'reverence*, contr. < *save reverence*, saving (your) reverence, transl. of ML *salva reverentia*⟧ [Obs.] begging your pardon: an expression of apology formerly used before a word or remark that might be regarded as indelicate

sir·up (sʉr′əp, sir′-) *n. alt. sp. of* SYRUP —**sir′up·y** *adj.*

sir·ventes (sir vent′; *Fr* sēr vänt′) *n.*, *pl.* **-ventes** (sir vents′; *Fr* sēr vänt′) ⟦Prov < *sirvent*, serving (< L *serveint-*, root of *serveins*, prp. of *servire*, to SERVE) + *-es*, *-esc* < It *-esco*: (see -ESQUE)⟧ a Provençal form of verse or troubadour song, usually satirical

☆**sis** (sis) *n.* [Informal] *short for* SISTER (*n.* 1-5): a familiar term of address

si·sal (sī′səl, sis′əl) *n.* ⟦after *Sisal*, Yucatán, a former seaport (< Maya, lit., cold waters)⟧ **1** a strong fiber, similar to the related henequen, obtained from the leaves of an agave (*Agave sisalana*) native to S Mexico and now cultivated throughout the tropics, used for making rope, sacking, insulation, etc. **2** the plant yielding this fiber Also **sisal hemp**

Sis·er·a (sis′ər ə) *n.* ⟦Heb *sisera*; prob. of Hittite orig.⟧ *Bible* a military leader of the Canaanites who was defeated by the Israelites, murdered by Jael: Judg. 4:17-22

sis·kin (sis′kin) *n.* ⟦via Fl or Du < Ger *zeischen*, dim. of *zeizig* < Czech *čížek*, dim. of *číž* (akin to Pol *czyz*, Russ *čiž*), of echoic orig.⟧ **1** a Eurasian finch (*Carduelis spinus*) with yellow-green plumage and black markings **2** PINE SISKIN

Sis·ley (sēs lā′; *E* sis′lē), **Al·fred** (àl fred′) 1839-99; Eng. painter; born & lived in France

Sis·mon·di (sēs môn dē′; *E* sis män′dē), **Jean Charles Lé·o·nard Si·monde de** (zhän shàrl lā ô nàr′ sē mônd′ də) 1773-1842; Swiss historian & economist

☆**sis·si·fied** (sis′ə fīd′) *adj.* [Informal] SISSY

☆**sis·sy** (sis′ē) *n.*, *pl.* **-sies** ⟦dim. of SIS⟧ **1** [Informal] *a)* an effeminate boy or man *b)* a timid person or coward **2** [Slang] a homosexual: term of mild contempt —*adj.* **-si·er**, **-si·est** [Informal] of or like a sissy —**sis′sy·ish** *adj.*

☆**sissy bar** [Slang] a metal bar shaped like an inverted U, attached behind the seat of a motorcycle or bicycle as a kind of roll bar or a backrest, or to prevent a rider from sliding backward

sis·ter (sis′tər) *n.* ⟦ME < ON *systir* (akin to OE *sweoster* > dial. *suster*), akin to Ger *schwester* < IE **swesor-*, sister (> Sans *svasar*, L *soror*, OIr *siur*) < **sewe-*, (one's) own, refl. pron. (see SUICIDE) + **sor-*, woman: hence, lit., woman of our (family)⟧ **1** a woman or girl as she is related to the other children of her parents: sometimes also used of animals **2** a woman or girl related to one by having a parent in common; half sister **3** a stepsister **4** a foster sister **5** a close female friend who is like a sister **6** *a)* a female fellow member of the same race, church, profession, organization, etc. [*a sorority* sister] *b)* [Slang] a fellow black who is female *c)* [Slang] a black woman or girl **7** [*often* **S-**] a member of a female religious community, usually one with simple vows: often a term of address **8** something associated with another of the same kind, model, etc. **9** [Brit.] a nurse, esp. a head nurse: often a term of address **10** [Informal] any woman: often used as a familiar term of address —*adj.* related or seeming to be related as sisters

sis·ter·hood (-ho͝od′) *n.* ⟦ME *sisterhod*, *sosterhode*: see prec. & -HOOD⟧ **1** the state of being a sister or sisters **2** an association of women united in a common interest, work, creed, etc. **3** a belief in or feeling of unity and cooperation among women

sis·ter-in-law (-in lô′) *n.*, *pl.* **sis′ters-in-law′** **1** the sister of one's husband or wife **2** the wife of one's sibling **3** the wife of a sibling of one's husband or wife

sis·ter·ly (-lē) *adj.* **1** of a sister **2** having traits considered typical of sisters; friendly, kind, helpful, etc. —*adv.* [Archaic] as a sister —**sis′ter·li·ness** *n.*

Sis·tine (sis′tēn′, -tin) *adj.* ⟦It *Sistino* < *Sisto* (< ML *Sixtus*, for L *Sextus*, lit., SIXTH)⟧ of or having to do with any pope named Sixtus

Sistine Chapel ⟦built by order of *Sixtus IV*: see prec.⟧ the principal chapel in the Vatican at Rome, famous for its frescoes by Michelangelo and other artists

sis·troid (sis′troid′) *adj.* ⟦< ?⟧ *Math.* designating the angle formed by the convex sides of two intersecting curves: opposed to CISSOID

sis·trum (sis′trəm) *n.*, *pl.* **-trums** or **-tra** (-trə) ⟦ME < L < Gr *seistron* < *seiein*, to shake < IE **tweisō-* < base **twei-*, to shake⟧ a metal rattle or noisemaker consisting of a handle and a frame fitted with loosely held rods: orig. used by the ancient Egyptians in religious worship

Sis·y·phe·an (sis′ə fē′ən) *adj.* ⟦< L *Sisypheius* < Gr *Sisypheios* < *Sisyphos* + -AN⟧ **1** of or like Sisyphus **2** endless and toilsome, useless, etc. [a *Sisyphean* task]

Sis·y·phus (sis′ə fəs) *n.* ⟦L < Gr *Sisyphos*⟧ *Gr. Myth.* a greedy king of Corinth doomed in Hades to roll a heavy stone uphill continually, only to have it always roll back down

sit (sit) *vi.* **sat**, **sit′ting** ⟦ME *sitten* < OE *sittan*, akin to ON *sitja*, Ger *sitzen* < IE base **sed-*, to sit > L *sedere*, Gr *hizein*, Welsh *seddu*, to sit⟧ **1** *a)* to rest the weight of the body upon the buttocks and the back of the thighs, as on a chair; be seated *b)* to rest on the haunches with the forelegs braced (said of quadrupeds) *c)* to perch or roost (said of birds) **2** to cover and warm eggs for hatching; set; brood **3** *a)* to occupy a seat in the capacity of judge, legislator, etc. *b)* to be in session, as a court or legislature **4** to pose for one's portrait or as a model **5** [Chiefly Brit.] to take an examination (*for* a degree, scholarship, etc.) **6** to be or remain inactive **7** to be located or have a place [a house *sitting* up on the hill] **8** to fit or hang on the wearer [a coat that *sits* loosely] **9** to rest or lie as specified [cares *sit* lightly upon him] ☆**10** *a)* BABYSIT *b)* to watch over or care for a person or thing for a short time (often used in comb.) [*housesit*, *dogsit*] *c)* to stay *with* a person so as to provide companionship for a short time; keep someone company [to *sit* with a dying patient] **11** to have a certain direction; set: said of the wind —*vt.* **1** to place in a seat; cause to sit; seat: often used reflexively [to *sit* oneself down] 2 to keep one's seat on (a horse, etc.) 3 to have seats or seating space for ☆4 BABYSIT —*n.* [Informal] 1 the time spent in a seated position, esp. while waiting 2 the way a coat, dress, etc. hangs when put on —**sit back** 1 to relax 2 to remain passive: also **sit by** —**sit down** 1 to lower oneself to a sitting position; take a seat 2 to settle down for or as for a siege —**sit in** to attend a meeting, etc. without actively participating: often with *on* [to *sit in* on a professor's class] —**sit in for** to take over someone's role or duties temporarily —**sit on (**or **upon)** 1 to serve as a member of (a jury, committee, etc.) 2 to confer on or investigate 3 [Informal] to suppress, repress, or squelch 4 [Informal] to hold (something) back from being considered or acted on —☆**sit on one's hands** 1 to fail to applaud 2 to fail to do what is needed or expected —**sit out** 1 to stay until the end of 2 to stay longer than (another); outsit 3 to remain seated during or take no part in (a dance or other activity) —**sit up** 1 to rise to a sitting position 2 to sit erect 3 to sit solely on the haunches, as with the forelegs upright or the front paws held up in front of the chest: said of four-legged animals 4 to put off going to bed 5 [Informal] to become suddenly alert —**sit well with** to be agreeable to

USAGE—See usage note at SET

si·tar (si tär′, si′tär′) ***n.*** ⟦Hindi *sitār*⟧ a lutelike instrument of India with a long, fretted neck, a resonating gourd or gourds, and three to seven playing strings and a number of strings that vibrate sympathetically —**si·tar′ist** ***n.***

sitar

sit·com (sit′käm′) ***n.*** [Informal] *short for* SITUATION COMEDY

☆**sit-down** (sit′doun′) ***n.*** 1 a strike, usually illegal, in which the strikers stay inside a factory, etc., refusing to work or leave until agreement is reached: in full **sit-down strike** 2 SIT-IN 3 a meeting or conference —***adj.*** served to persons, esp. guests, who are seated at a table [a *sit-down* dinner for twelve]

site (sīt) ***n.*** ⟦ME < L *situs,* position, situation < pp. of *sinere,* to put down, permit, allow < IE base **sei-,* to cast out, let fall: see SIDE⟧ 1 a piece of land considered from the standpoint of its use for some specified purpose [a good *site* for a town] 2 the place where something is, was, or is to be; location or scene [the *site* of a battle] 3 *Comput.* a location on the internet that is accessible at a single address; often, specif., a WEBSITE —***vt.* sit′ed, sit′ing** to locate or position on a site

sith (sith) ***adv., conj., prep.*** ⟦ME < OE *siththa,* contr. form of *siththan:* see SINCE⟧ [Archaic] since

sit-in (sit′in′) ***n.*** a method of protesting the policy of a government, business, etc., in which demonstrators sit in, and refuse to leave, a public place, thus blocking traffic, disrupting operations, etc.

Sit·ka (sit′kə) ⟦Tlingit *sheet′ka* < *šiˑ-t′i-ka,* on the seaward side of Baranof Island⟧ city in SE Alas., on Baranof Island

si·to- (sī′tō, -tə) ⟦< Gr *sitos,* food, grain⟧ *combining form* 1 food [*sitology*] 2 grain [*sitosterol*]

si·tol·o·gy (sī täl′ə jē) ***n.*** ⟦prec. + -LOGY⟧ the study of foods, food values, nutrition, diet, etc.; dietetics

si·tos·ter·ol (sī täs′tə rôl′, -rōl′) ***n.*** ⟦SITO- + (CHOLE)STEROL⟧ any of a group of crystalline alcoholic sterols resembling cholesterol in their properties

sit·ter (sit′ər) ***n.*** a person or thing that sits; specif., ☆*a)* *short for* BABYSITTER *b)* a brooding hen

sit·ting (sit′iŋ) ***n.*** 1 the act or position of one that sits, as for a portrait 2 a session or meeting, as of a court 3 a period of being seated at some activity [to read a book in two *sittings*] 4 *a)* a brooding upon eggs, as by a hen *b)* the number of eggs upon which a hen sits for a single hatching 5 a space in which to be seated 6 one of two or more successive periods when a meal is served, as aboard a ship [assigned to the second *sitting*] —***adj.*** 1 that sits; seated 2 in office [a *sitting* president]

Sitting Bull 1834?-90; a principal chief of the Dakota Indians: fought in the Battle of the Little Bighorn

sitting duck ☆[Informal] a person or thing especially vulnerable to attack; easy target

sitting room 1 LIVING ROOM 2 any room, esp. a small one next to a bedroom, used as a living room

Sit·twe (sit′wē′) seaport in W Myanmar

sit·u·ate (sich′o͞o it, -āt′; *for v.,* -āt′) ***adj.*** ⟦ML *situatus,* pp. of *situare,* to place < L *situs:* see SITE⟧ *rare or archaic var. of* SITUATED —***vt.* -at′ed, -at′ing** to put in a certain place or position; place; locate

sit·u·at·ed (-āt′id) ***adj.*** ⟦pp. of prec.⟧ 1 placed as to site or position; located 2 placed as to circumstances [comfortably *situated* for retirement]

sit·u·a·tion (sich′o͞o ā′shən) ***n.*** ⟦LME *setuacyon* < ML *situatio:* see SITUATE⟧ 1 manner in which a thing is situated in relation to its surroundings; location; position 2 a place; locality 3 position or condition with regard to circumstances 4 *a)* the combination of circumstances at any given time *b)* a difficult or critical state of affairs *c)* any significant combination of circumstances developing in the course of a novel, play, etc. *d)* *Psychol.* the objective conditions immediately affecting an individual 5 a position of employment —***SYN.*** POSITION, STATE —**sit′u·a′tion·al** ***adj.***

situation comedy a comic television series made up of episodes involving the same group of characters dealing with various problems, awkward situations, etc.

situation ethics a theory of ethics according to which moral rules are not absolutely binding but may be modified in the light of specific situations

situation room a room or suite from which a political or military crisis is managed

☆**sit-up** or **sit·up** (sit′up′) ***n.*** an exercise in which a person lying flat on the back rises to a sitting position without using the hands: sit-ups are usually done in a series

si·tus (sīt′əs) ***n.*** ⟦L: see SITE⟧ position or location; esp., the normal position, as of an organ of the body or a plant part

Sit·well (sit′wəl, -wel), Dame **Edith** 1887-1964; Eng. poet & critic

sitz bath (sits, zits) ⟦partial transl. of Ger *sitzbad* < *sitz,* a seat, sitting (< *sitzen,* SIT) + *bad,* BATH[1]⟧ 1 a bath in which only the hips and buttocks are immersed, usually for therapy 2 a tub or basin used for such a bath

sitz·mark (sits′märk′, zits′-) ***n.*** ⟦< Ger *sitzmarke* < *sitz,* seat (< *sitzen,* SIT) + *marke,* MARK[1]⟧ the depression made in snow by a skier who has fallen backward

Si·va (sē′və, shē′-) ***n.*** ⟦Hindi < Sans, auspicious⟧ Hindu god of destruction and reproduction, a member of the supreme Hindu trinity: see BRAHMA[1], VISHNU

Si·va·ism (-iz′əm) ***n.*** worship of Siva —**Si′va·is′tic** ***adj.***

Si·van (sē vän′, siv′ən) ***n.*** ⟦Heb *siwan,* akin to Akkadian *simānu,* name of 3d Babylonian month⟧ the ninth month of the Jewish year: see the Jewish calendar in the Reference Supplement

Si·vas (sē väs′) city in central Turkey

six (siks) ***adj.*** ⟦ME < OE *sex,* akin to Ger *sechs,* ON *sex,* Goth *saihs* < IE base **seks,* **sweks* > L *sex,* Gr *hex,* Sans *ṣáṭ*⟧ totaling one more than five —***n.*** 1 the cardinal number between five and seven; 6; VI 2 any group of six people or things; half a dozen 3 *a)* something numbered six or having six units, as a playing card, domino, face of a die, etc. *b)* an engine with six cylinders or an automobile with such an engine —**at sixes and sevens** 1 in confusion or disorder 2 at odds; disagreeing

six·fold (siks′fōld′) ***adj.*** ⟦prec. + -FOLD⟧ 1 having six parts 2 having six times as much or as many —***adv.*** six times as much or as many

☆**Six Nations** the Five Nations plus the Tuscaroras, constituting a later confederacy of Iroquoian peoples

☆**six-pack** (-pak′) ***n.*** 1 a package containing six units of a product, as six cans of beer 2 ⟦from the appearance of two vertical muscles crossed by tendons⟧ [Slang] a set of well-defined muscles in a trim abdomen

six·pence (-pəns) ***n.*** 1 [Brit.] the sum of six (old) pennies: see PENNY (sense 1*b*) 2 a former British coin equal to this sum

six·pen·ny (-pen′ē, -pə nē) ***adj.*** 1 worth or costing sixpence 2 of small worth; cheap 3 *Carpentry* designating a size of nail, usually two inches long

☆**six-shoot·er** (-sho͞ot′ər) ***n.*** [Informal] a revolver having a cylinder that holds six cartridges; specif., such a revolver with a long barrel and of relatively large caliber of the kind used in the W U.S. in the second half of the 19th cent.: also **six′-gun′**

666 a number variously associated with Satan, the Antichrist, the emperor Nero, etc. (Rev. 13:18)

six·teen (siks′tēn′) ***adj.*** ⟦ME *sixtene* < OE *syxtene:* see SIX & -TEEN⟧ totaling six more than ten —***n.*** the cardinal number between fifteen and seventeen; 16; XVI

six·teen·mo (siks tēn′mō) ***n., pl.* -mos** ⟦prec. + *-mo,* as in SEXTODECIMO⟧ 1 the page size of a book made up of printer's sheets folded into sixteen leaves, each leaf being approximately 4½ by 6¾ inches 2 a book consisting of pages of this size Usually written *16mo* or *16°* —***adj.*** consisting of pages of this size

six·teenth (siks′tēnth′) ***adj.*** ⟦ME *sixtenthe,* replacing OE *syxteotha:* see SIXTEEN & -TH[2]⟧ 1 preceded by fifteen others in a series; 16th 2 designating any of the sixteen equal parts of something —***n.*** 1 the one following the fifteenth 2 any of the sixteen equal parts of something; 1/16 —***adv.*** in the sixteenth place, rank, etc.

sixteenth note *Music* a note having one sixteenth the duration of a whole note

sixth (siksth) ***adj.*** ⟦ME *sixth* < OE *sixta,* akin to Ger *sechste,* L *sextus:* see SIX & -TH[2]⟧ 1 preceded by five others in a series; 6th 2 designating any of the six equal parts of something —***n.*** 1 the one following the fifth 2 any of the six equal parts of something; 1/6 3 *Music a)* the sixth tone of an ascending diatonic scale, or a tone five degrees above or below any given tone in such a scale; submediant; superdominant *b)* the interval between two such tones, or a combination of them *c)* the chord formed by a triad in which the fundamental tone is raised an octave, creating a new interval of a sixth, as E-G-C (in full **sixth chord**) —***adv.*** in the sixth place, rank, group, etc. —**sixth′ly** ***adv.***

sixth form ⟦see FORM (*n.* 15)⟧ a senior section in some British, Australian, and New Zealand secondary schools, in which students continue preparation for college, do specialized work, study for A levels, etc. —**sixth′-form′er** (-fôr′mər) ***n.***

sixth sense a power of perception thought of as a sense in addition to the commonly accepted five senses; intuitive power

six·ti·eth (siks′tē ith) ***adj.*** ⟦ME *sixtithe* < OE *sixteogotha* < *sixtig:* see SIXTY & -TH[2]⟧ 1 preceded by fifty-nine others in a series; 60th 2 designating any of the sixty equal parts of something —***n.*** 1 the one following the fifty-ninth 2 any of the sixty equal parts of something; 1/60 —***adv.*** in the sixtieth place, rank, group, etc.

Six·tine (siks′tēn′, -tin) *adj. var. of* SISTINE

six·ty (siks′tē) *adj.* ⟦ME *sixti* < OE *sixtig*: see SIX & -TY[2]⟧ six times ten —*n., pl.* **-ties** the cardinal number between fifty-nine and sixty-one; 60; LX —**the sixties** the numbers or years, as of a century, from sixty through sixty-nine

six·ty-fourth note (-fôrth′) *Music* a note having one sixty-fourth the duration of a whole note

sixty-nine (siks′tē nīn′) *n.* ⟦transl. of Fr *soixante-neuf*: from the notion that sex partners, lying so positioned, resemble the juxtaposed numerals 6 and 9⟧ [Slang] a sexual activity involving two individuals and consisting of simultaneous oral stimulation of the genitals: somewhat vulgar: often written **69**

siz·a·ble (sī′zə bəl) *adj.* quite large or bulky: also sp. **size′a·ble** —**siz′a·ble·ness** *n.* —**siz′a·bly** *adv.*

siz·ar (sī′zər) *n.* ⟦< fol. + -AR⟧ a student receiving a scholarship allowance at Trinity College, Dublin, or at Cambridge University: also, earlier, **siz′er**

size[1] (sīz) *n.* ⟦ME < OFr *sise*, aphetic for *assise*: see ASSIZE⟧ **1** that quality of a thing which determines how much space it occupies; dimensions or magnitude of a thing **2** any of a series of graded classifications of measure into which merchandise is divided [jumbo-*size* peanuts, *size* nine shoes] **3** *a)* extent, magnitude, amount, etc. [an undertaking of great *size*] *b)* relatively large amount, dimensions, etc. **4** character of a person with regard to ability to meet requirements **5** [Informal] actual condition; true state of affairs [that's the *size* of it] **6** [Obs.] standard ration or allowance, as of food —*vt.* **sized**, **siz′ing 1** to make of a certain size **2** to arrange or grade according to size —**of a size** of one or the same size —☆**size up** [Informal] to make an estimate or judgment of —**siz′er** *n.*

size[2] (sīz) *n.* ⟦ME *syse*, prob. < MFr *sise*, a setting: see prec.⟧ any thin, pasty or gluey substance used as a glaze or filler on porous materials, as on plaster, paper, or cloth —*vt.* **sized**, **siz′ing** to apply size to; fill, stiffen, or glaze with size

-size (sīz) *combining form* -SIZED [life-*size*]

-sized (sīzd) *combining form* having a (specified) size: usually used in hyphenated compounds [medium-*sized*, *undersized*]

siz·ing (sī′ziŋ) *n.* **1** SIZE[2] **2** the act or process of applying such size

siz·zle (siz′əl) *vi.* **-zled**, **-zling** ⟦echoic⟧ **1** to make a hissing sound when in contact with heat, as a drop of water on hot metal **2** to be extremely hot **3** to be in a state of suppressed emotion or passion; esp., to simmer with rage —*vt.* to make sizzle —*n.* a sizzling sound

☆**siz·zler** (siz′lər) *n.* [Informal] something hot (in various senses), as a very hot day

SJ *abbrev.* Society of Jesus

Sjæl·land (shel′län) *Dan. name for* ZEALAND

sjam·bok (sham′bäk) *n.* ⟦Afrik < Malay *cambuk*, a large whip < Hindi *cābuk*⟧ in South Africa, a whip traditionally made of rhinoceros or hippopotamus hide —*vt.* to strike or flog with a sjambok

SK *abbrev.* Saskatchewan

ska (skä) *n.* a form of dance music, originally from Jamaica, characterized by the use of saxophones and brass, a heavily accented offbeat, and the influence of New Orleans rhythm and blues, jazz, and calypso

☆**skag** (skag) *n. alt. sp. of* SCAG

Ska·gen (skä′yən), **Cape** The SKAW

Skag·er·rak (skag′ə rak′) arm of the North Sea, between Norway & Denmark: 150 mi (241 km) long; 70-90 mi (113-145 km) wide

skald (skôld, skäld) *n.* ⟦ON *skāld*: see SCOLD⟧ any of the ancient Scandinavian poets, specif. of the Viking period —**skald′ic** *adj.*

Skan·da (skun′də) *n.* the Hindu god of war, typically depicted as a boy

☆**skank** (skaŋk) *n.* ⟦< ?⟧ [Slang] a skanky person; specif., a woman or girl considered sleazy, sluttish, etc.

☆**skank·y** (skaŋ′kē) *adj.* **skank′i·er**, **skank′i·est** ⟦< ?⟧ [Slang] sleazy, sluttish, disreputable, etc. in appearance or character: a derogatory or insulting term

skat (skat, skät) *n.* ⟦Ger < It *scarto*, discard < *scartare*, to discard < *s-* (< L *ex-*, out) + *carta*, card (< L *charta*: see CARD[1])⟧ a card game for three people, played with thirty-two cards

skate[1] (skāt) *n.* ⟦taken as sing. of earlier *skates* < Du *schaats*, a skate, stilt < NormFr *escache* < OFr *eschace*, stilt, crutch < Frank **skatja*, stilt⟧ **1** *a)* a bladelike metal runner mounted in a frame having clamps and straps for fastening it to the sole of a shoe and used for gliding on ice *b)* a shoe with such a runner permanently attached: also *ice skate* **2** a similar frame or shoe with a pair of small wheels near the toe and another pair at the heel, for gliding on a hardwood floor, sidewalk, etc.: also *roller skate* **3** IN-LINE SKATE **4** the act or a period of skating —*vi.* **skat′ed**, **skat′ing 1** to glide or move along on, or as on, skates **2** to ride or perform stunts on a skateboard —**skat′er** *n.*

skate[2] (skāt) *n., pl.* **skates** or **skate** ⟦ME *scate* < ON *skata*⟧ any ray fish (esp. order Rajiformes): often used of the larger commercial species

skate[3] (skāt) *n.* ⟦< ?⟧ [Old Slang] ☆**1** a broken-down horse; nag **2** a person: now only in **good skate**, a congenial, likable person: see also CHEAPSKATE

☆**skate·board** (skāt′bôrd′) *n.* a short, oblong board having a pair of small wheels at each end, on which a person rides by pushing against the ground with the foot and then coasting while standing or crouching, often performing stunts —*vi.* to ride or perform stunts on a skateboard —**skate′board′er** *n.* —**skate′board′ing** *n.*

skate park a recreation area designed with ramps, rails, etc. for skateboarding: also written **skate′park′** *n.*

skat·ole (skat′ōl) *n.* ⟦< Gr *skōr* (gen. *skatos*), dung (see SCATO-) + -OL[2]⟧ a foul-smelling, colorless, crystalline compound, C_9H_9N, formed by the decomposition of proteins, as in the intestine

Skaw (skô), **The** cape at the N tip of the Jutland peninsula, Denmark

skean (shkēn, skēn) *n.* ⟦Gael *sgian*, akin to MIr *scïan*, a knife < IE base **skei-*, to cut > L *scire*⟧ a kind of dirk formerly used in Scotland and Ireland

Skeat (skēt), **W(alter) W(illiam)** 1835-1912; Eng. philologist & lexicographer

ske·dad·dle (ski dad′'l) [Informal] *vi.* **-dled**, **-dling** ⟦popularized in military slang of Civil War period: prob. a fanciful formation⟧ to run off or away; leave in a hurry —*n.* a running or scurrying away

☆**skeet** (skēt) *n.* ⟦20th-c. adoption and alteration of ON *skeyti*, projectile, akin to *skjōta*, to SHOOT[1]⟧ trapshooting in which the shooter fires from different stations, usually eight, at clay disks thrown from traps to simulate birds in flight —**skeet′er** *n.*

☆**skee·ter** (skēt′ər) *n.* ⟦phonetic sp. of dial. pronun. of MOSQUITO⟧ *dial. or slang var. of* MOSQUITO

skeg (skeg) *n.* ⟦Du *schegge* < ON *skegg*, beard (basic sense "a projection"): see SHAG[1]⟧ *Naut.* the after part of the keel, or an extension of this upon which the rudderpost is mounted

skein (skān) *n.* ⟦ME *skeyn* < MFr *escaigne*⟧ **1** *a)* a quantity of thread or yarn wound in a coil *b)* something like this, as a coil of hair **2** a flock of wild fowl **3** a sequence of events, esp. a series of games won or lost by a team [a 20-game winning *skein*]

skel·e·ton (skel′ə tən) *n.* ⟦ModL < Gr < *skeleton (sōma)*, dried (body), mummy < *skeletos*, dried up, akin to *sklēros*, dry, hard < IE base **(s)kel-* > SHALLOW⟧ **1** the hard framework of an animal body, supporting the tissues and protecting the organs; specif., all the bones collectively, or the bony framework, of a human being or other vertebrate animal **2** anything like a skeleton in any of various ways *a)* a very lean or emaciated person or animal *b)* a supporting framework, as of a building or ship *c)* an outline or preliminary sketch, as of a novel *d)* the meager or devitalized remains of something —*adj.* **1** of or like a skeleton; specif., of, or having the nature of, the main or essential outline, framework, etc. [a *skeleton* plan] **2** greatly reduced [a *skeleton* force] —**skeleton at the feast** ⟦in allusion to a memento mori offered near the end of many ancient Egyptian banquets, as described by PLUTARCH, in which a servant carried in a *skeleton* and exclaimed to the guests, "Eat, drink, and be merry; for, tomorrow you die!"⟧ a person or event that brings gloom or sadness to an occasion of joy or celebration —**skeleton in the closet** ⟦phr. popularized by W. M. THACKERAY, but in use earlier⟧ some fact, as about one's family, kept secret because of shame or fear of disgrace —**skel′e·tal** (-təl) *adj.*

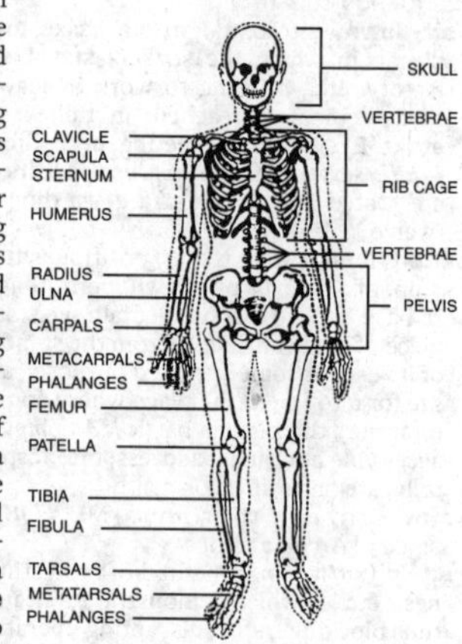

skeleton of a woman

skel·e·ton·ize (-īz′) *vt.* **-ized′**, **-iz′ing 1** to reduce to a skeleton or a bare framework **2** to outline or sketch (a story, report, etc.) briefly **3** to reduce (a workforce, etc.) greatly in number or size

skeleton key a key having a large part of the bit filed away so that it can be used to open any of various simple locks

skel·lum (skel′əm) *n.* ⟦Early ModE < Du *schelm*, akin to OHG *skelmo*, one deserving to die < IE base **(s)kel-*, to cut > SHELL, HELM[2]⟧ [Chiefly Brit.] a rascal; rogue; scamp: term now common only in South Africa: also **skelm** (skelm)

skelp (skelp) [Brit. Dial.] *vt.* ⟦ME *shelpen*, to beat, flog⟧ to slap or spank —*vi.* to hurry along; hustle —*n.* a slap; blow

Skel·ton (skelt′'n), **John** 1460?-1529; Eng. poet

skene (skēn) *n. var. of* SKEAN

skep (skep) *n.* ⟦ME *skeppe* < OE *sceppe* < ON *skeppa*, a measure, bushel < IE base **(s)kep-* > SHAPE⟧ **1** [Archaic] a round, wooden or wicker basket **2** a beehive, esp. one of straw

skep·tic (skep′tik) *adj.* ⟦L *scepticus* < Gr *skeptikos*, thoughtful, inquiring < *skeptesthai*, to consider: altered by metathesis < IE base **spek-*, to peer > SPY⟧ *var. of* SKEPTICAL: used esp. in philosophy —*n.* **1** [**S-**] a member of any of the ancient Greek philosophical schools that denied the possibility of any certain knowledge **2** a person who believes in or practices philosophical skepticism **3** a person who habitually doubts, questions, or suspends judgment upon matters generally accepted **4** a person who doubts religious doctrines

skep·ti·cal (skep′ti kəl) *adj.* **1** of or characteristic of skeptics or skepticism **2** not easily persuaded or convinced; doubting; questioning **3** doubting the fundamental doctrines of religion —**skep′ti·cal·ly** *adv.*

skep·ti·cism (-siz′əm) *n.* **1** [**S-**] the doctrines of the ancient Greek Skeptics **2** the critical philosophical position that neither truth nor sure and certain knowledge are humanly attainable, whether through reason, the senses, or any other means **3** skeptical or doubting attitude or state of mind **4** doubt about fundamental religious doctrines —**SYN.** UNCERTAINTY

sker·ry (sker′ē) ***n., pl.* -ries** ⟦via Orkney dial. < ON *sker*, reef (< IE base **sker-*, to cut > SHEAR) + *ey*, ISLAND⟧ [Scot.] an isolated rock or reef in the sea

sketch (skech) ***n.*** ⟦earlier *schitz* < Du *schets* < It *schizzo* < L *schedium*, extempore poem < Gr *schedios*, extempore, sudden < *schein*, to hold: see SCHEME⟧ **1** a simple, rough drawing or design, done rapidly and without much detail **2** a brief plan or description of major parts or points; outline **3** a short, light, informal story, description, play, skit, or piece of music —***vt.*** **1** to draw quickly or in outline **2** to give a brief description of; outline: usually with *out* —***vi.*** to make a sketch or sketches —**sketch′er** ***n.***

sketch·book (skech′boo͝k′) ***n.*** a book of drawing paper for making sketches: also written **sketch book**

sketch·y (-ē) ***adj.*** **sketch′i·er, sketch′i·est** **1** having the form of a sketch; presenting only major parts or points; not detailed **2** lacking completeness; rough; inadequate —**sketch′i·ly** ***adv.*** —**sketch′i·ness** ***n.***

skew (skyo͞o) ***vi.*** ⟦ME *skewen* < NormFr *eskiuer*, altered < OFr *eschiver*: see ESCHEW⟧ **1** to take a slanting or oblique course or direction; swerve or twist **2** to squint or glance sideways (*at*) —***vt.*** **1** to make slanting or oblique; set at a slant **2** to bias, distort, or pervert —***adj.*** **1** turned aside or to one side; slanting; oblique **2** having a part or arrangement that is so turned, as in gearing having the shafts neither parallel nor intersecting **3** not symmetrical —***n.*** **1** a slant or twist **2** a slanting part or movement —**skewed** ***adj.***

skew arch an arch with jambs not at right angles with the face, as in a vault or tunnel which narrows or widens from its opening

skew·back (skyo͞o′bak′) ***n.*** **1** the slanting surface supporting either end of a segmental arch **2** a supporting piece, as a stone, with such a surface

skew·bald (skyo͞o′bôld′) ***adj.*** ⟦< ME *skewed*, piebald + BALD⟧ having large patches of white and brown or any other color except black —***n.*** a skewbald horse

skew·er (skyo͞o′ər) ***n.*** ⟦var. of *skiver* < ON *skifa*, a slice < v., to slice: see SKIVE[1]⟧ **1** *a)* a long pin used to hold meat together while cooking *b)* a similar but longer pin used as a brochette **2** any of several things shaped or used like a meat skewer —***vt.*** **1** to fasten or pierce with or as with skewers **2** to criticize sharply

skew lines *Math.* two or more lines that lie in different planes, are not parallel, and do not intersect

skew·ness (skyo͞o′nis) ***n.*** **1** the fact or condition of being skew, or, esp., unsymmetrical **2** *Statistics* the lack of symmetry of the curve for a frequency distribution

skew polygon the figure formed by joining four or more points, not all in one plane, by the same number of lines

ski (skē) ***n., pl.* skis** ⟦Norw < ON *skith*, snowshoe, strip of wood, akin to OE *scid*, OHG *scit*, thin piece of wood, shingle < IE base **skei-* > SHEATH⟧ **1** a long, thin runner of wood, metal, or now usually fiberglass, that is fastened to a kind of boot (**ski boot**) and used in pairs to glide over snow **2** *short for* WATER SKI —***vi.*** **skied** (skēd), **ski′ing** **1** to travel on skis by gliding over the snow **2** to engage in the sport of gliding down snow-covered inclines on skis **3** *short for* WATER-SKI —***vt.*** to travel over on skis

ski·a·graph (skī′ə graf′, -gräf′) ***n.*** ⟦Gr *skia*, shadow (see SHINE) + -GRAPH⟧ RADIOGRAPH: also **ski′a·gram′** (-gram′) —**ski·ag·ra·phy** (skī ag′rə fē) ***n.***

skid (skid) ***n.*** ⟦Early ModE, prob. < ON *skith*: see SKI⟧ ☆**1** a plank, log, etc., often one of a pair or set, used as a support or as a track upon which to slide or roll a heavy object **2** a low, movable wooden platform for holding loads or stacks **3** a runner used in place of a wheel on aircraft landing gear **4** a sliding wedge or drag used to check the motion of a vehicle by pressure against a wheel **5** the act of skidding —***vt.*** **skid′ded, skid′ding** **1** to brake or lock (a wheel) with a skid **2** to support with or slide on a skid or skids ☆**3** to haul, roll, or drag (logs) along a special track or trail, as through a forest **4** to cause (a wheel, vehicle, etc.) to slide or slip —***vi.*** **1** to slide without turning, as a wheel when skids or brakes are applied on a slippery surface **2** to slide or slip sideways, as a vehicle when not gripping the road on ice **3** to slide sharply downward **4** *Aeron.* to slide outward while turning, as a result of failing to bank sufficiently —☆**be on** (or **hit**) **the skids** [Slang] to be on the decline or downgrade; meet with failure —☆**put the skids under** (or **on** or **to**) [Slang] to thwart or cause to fail —**skid′der** ***n.***

☆**skid·doo** (ski do͞o′) ***vi.*** ⟦prob. < SKEDADDLE⟧ [Old Slang] to go away; leave: usually in the imperative

skid·dy (skid′ē) ***adj.*** **-di·er, -di·est** having a slippery surface on which vehicles are liable to skid

skid·proof (skid′pro͞of′) ***adj.*** that resists or prevents skidding, as some automobile tires, road surfaces, etc.

☆**skid road** **1** in lumbering, a trail along which newly cut logs are skidded **2** *a)* [Historical] a section of town frequented by loggers *b)* SKID ROW

☆**skid row** ⟦altered < prec.⟧ a usually run-down section of a city frequented by indigent alcoholics, vagrants, derelicts, etc.

ski·er (skē′ər) ***n.*** a person who skis

skiff (skif) ***n.*** ⟦MFr *esquif* < It *schifo* < Langobardic **skif*, akin to SHIP⟧ any of various small, light, open boats propelled by oars, sail, or motor

☆**skif·fle** (skif′əl) ***n.*** ⟦orig. uncert.⟧ **1** a former primitive style of jazz played by bands using some nonstandard or homemade instruments **2** a kind of up-tempo popular music played as by jug bands, esp. in the United Kingdom in the 1950s, characterized by elements of jazz, blues, country, folk, etc.

☆**ski·jor·ing** (skē′jôr′iŋ, skē jôr′-) ***n.*** ⟦Norw *skikjøring* < *ski*, SKI + *kjøre*, to ride, drive⟧ a sport in which skiers are drawn over snow or ice by a horse, tractor, etc.

☆**ski jump** **1** a jump made by a skier after gaining momentum by a glide down a long, usually artificial incline or track **2** such an incline or track

skil·ful (skil′fəl) ***adj.*** *chiefly Brit. sp. of* SKILLFUL —**skil′ful·ly** ***adv.*** —**skil′ful·ness** ***n.***

☆**ski lift** a motor-driven, endless cable, typically with seats attached, for carrying skiers up a ski slope

skill (skil) ***n.*** ⟦ME, discernment, reason < ON *skil*, distinction, akin to *skilja*, to cut apart, separate < IE base **(s)kel-*, to cut (> SHIELD, SHELL): basic sense "ability to separate," hence "discernment"⟧ **1** great ability or proficiency; expertness that comes from training, practice, etc. **2** *a)* an art, craft, or science, esp. one involving the use of the hands or body *b)* ability in such an art, craft, or science **3** [Obs.] knowledge, understanding, or judgment —***vi.*** [Archaic] to matter, avail, or make a difference —**SYN.** ART[1]

skilled (skild) ***adj.*** **1** having skill; skillful **2** having or requiring an ability, as in a particular industrial occupation, gained by special experience or training

skil·let (skil′it) ***n.*** ⟦ME *skelett* < ? OFr *escuellette*, dim. of *escuelle*, porringer, basin < L *scutella*, dim. of *scutra*, dish⟧ **1** [Chiefly Brit.] a pot or kettle with a long handle and, sometimes, feet **2** FRYING PAN

skill·ful (skil′fəl) ***adj.*** having or showing skill; accomplished; expert —**skill′ful·ly** ***adv.*** —**skill′ful·ness** ***n.***

skil·ling (skil′iŋ, shil′-) ***n.*** ⟦Norw, Dan, Swed, akin to SHILLING⟧ any of various former Scandinavian copper coins and units of value

skim (skim) ***vt.*** **skimmed, skim′ming** ⟦ME *skimen*, prob. akin to SCUM⟧ **1** *a)* to clear (a liquid) of floating matter *b)* to remove (floating matter) from a liquid **2** to coat or cover with a thin layer [*a pond skimmed with ice*] **3** to look at hastily or carelessly; glance through (a book, etc.) without reading word for word **4** *a)* to glide or pass swiftly and lightly over *b)* to throw so as to cause to bounce or ricochet swiftly and lightly [*to skim a flat stone across a pond*] **5** [Informal] to refrain from reporting for tax purposes (a percentage of income, gambling gains, etc.) —***vi.*** **1** to move along swiftly and lightly over a surface, through space, etc.; glide; sail **2** to make a rapid or careless examination, as of a book: usually with *over* or *through* **3** to become thinly coated, as with scum —***n.*** **1** something that has been skimmed **2** the act of skimming **3** a thin coating or film —***adj.*** **1** that has been skimmed **2** *Plastering* designating or of a thin coat that serves as a final or leveling coat

ski mask a knitted article of apparel that covers the head and has openings for the eyes and mouth, worn as by skiers for protection in cold weather

skim·mer (skim′ər) ***n.*** **1** a person or thing that skims **2** any utensil used in skimming liquids **3** any of a family (Rynchopidae) of long-winged shorebirds that use their elongated lower bill to scoop up food while skimming over water **4** any of a family (Libellulidae) of large dragonflies that hover low over ponds, ditches, etc. ☆**5** a hat, usually of straw, with a flat crown and a wide, straight brim

skim milk milk from which the cream has been removed: also **skimmed milk**

skim·ming (skim′iŋ) ***n.*** [*usually pl.*] anything that has been skimmed from a liquid

ski·mo·bile (skē′mō bēl′) ***n., vi.*** **-biled′, -bil′ing** SNOWMOBILE

skimp (skimp) [Informal] ***adj.*** ⟦prob. altered < SCRIMP⟧ SCANTY —***vi.*** **1** to give or allow too little; be stingy **2** to keep expenses very low —***vt.*** **1** to do poorly or carelessly **2** to be stingy in or toward; specif., to make too small, too short, etc.

skimp·y (skim′pē) ***adj.*** **skimp′i·er, skimp′i·est** barely or not quite enough; somewhat less in size, fullness, etc. than is needed; scanty —**skimp′i·ly** ***adv.*** —**skimp′i·ness** ***n.***

skin (skin) ***n.*** ⟦ME *skinn* < ON, akin to Ger *schinden*, to flay, peel < IE **(s)ken(d)-*, to split off (< base **sek-*, to cut: see SAW[1]) > OIr *ceinn*, a scale, scurf⟧ **1** the outer covering or integument of the animal body **2** such a covering, esp. that of a small animal, when removed from the body and prepared for use; pelt **3** something like skin in appearance or function; any outer layer, as fruit rind, the shell or plating of a ship, a film or scum, the outermost nacreous layer in a pearl, etc. **4** a container made of animal skin, used for holding liquids ☆**5** [*pl.*] [Slang] *Jazz, etc.* a set of drums ☆**6** [Slang] a dollar —***vt.*** **skinned, skin′ning** **1** to cover with or as with skin; grow skin on **2** to remove skin from **3** to strip or peel off, as or like skin **4** to injure by scraping or abrading (one's knee, elbow, etc.) **5** [Slang] *a)* to defraud or cheat; swindle ☆*b)* to criticize or scold severely ☆**6** [Informal] to drive

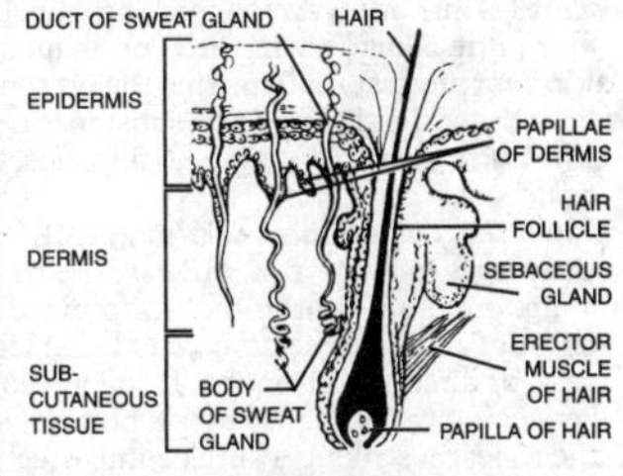

human skin (cross section)

or urge on (a mule, ox, etc.) —*vi.* 1 to become covered with skin 2 [Informal] to climb (*up* or *down*) 3 to move (*through*), pass (*by*), succeed, etc. by a very narrow margin —*adj.* [Informal] depicting and exploiting nudity and sex [*a skin* magazine] —☆**be no skin off someone's nose** (or **back**, etc.) [Informal] to affect someone not at all; be of no direct concern to someone —**by the skin of one's teeth** by the smallest possible margin; barely —☆**get under someone's skin** [Informal] to anger or irritate someone —**have a thick** (or **thin**) **skin** to be insensitive (or acutely sensitive) to blame, criticism, insults, etc. —**save someone's skin** [Informal] to save someone from harm or injury or, often, specif., from death —**skin someone alive** [Informal] ☆1 to scold or punish someone severely 2 to defeat someone decisively —**skin and bones** (the condition of being) extremely lean and bony

SYN.—**skin** is the general term for the outer covering of the animal body and for the covering, especially if thin and tight, of certain fruits and vegetables [human *skin*, the *skin* of a peach]; **hide** is used of the tough skins of certain large animals, as of a horse, cow, elephant, etc.; **pelt** refers to the skin, esp. the untanned skin, of a fur-bearing animal, as of a mink, fox, sheep, etc.; **rind** applies to the thick, tough covering of certain fruits, as of a watermelon, or of cheeses, bacon, etc.; **peel** is used of the skin or rind of fruit that has been removed, as by stripping [potato *peel*, lemon *peel*]; **bark** applies to the hard covering of trees and woody plants

skin-deep (skin′dēp′) *adj.* 1 penetrating no deeper than the skin 2 without real depth or significance; superficial; shallow —*adv.* so as to be only skin-deep; superficially Also written **skin deep**

skin diving underwater swimming in which the swimmer, without air lines to the surface, is variously equipped with a face mask, flipperlike footgear, scuba equipment, etc. —**skin′-dive′** (-dīv′) *vi.* **-dived′**, **-div′ing** —**skin diver**

skin effect the tendency of alternating current to concentrate at or near the surface of a conductor

☆**skin·flick** (-flik′) *n.* [Slang] a film characterized by nudity and explicit sexual activity

skin·flint (-flint′) *n.* ⟦< thieves' slang: lit., one who would *skin* (that is, chip or abrade) a worn *flint* rather than pay for a new one⟧ a niggardly person; miser

skin·ful (-fool′) *n., pl.* **-fuls′** 1 as much as a skin container can hold 2 [Informal] *a)* as much as the stomach can hold *b)* enough alcoholic liquor to make one drunk

☆**skin game** [Informal] a cheating, swindling trick

skin grafting the surgical transplanting of skin (**skin graft**) to replace skin destroyed, as by burning

skin·head (-hed′) *n.* 1 [Slang] a person who is bald or whose hair has been shaved off or closely cropped 2 *a)* any of a group of working-class youths, orig. in England in the 1960s, with closely cropped hair, often engaging in rowdyism *b)* any of a similar group of alienated youths in the U.S., Europe, etc. who variously affect a rough appearance, advocate fascist and racist policies, and engage in hostile and violent activity

skink (skiŋk) *n.* ⟦L *scincus* < Gr *skinkos*⟧ any of a family (Scincidae) of widely distributed lizards having an elongated, shiny body, smooth scales, and short legs

skin·less (skin′lis) *adj.* 1 with the skin removed [*skinless* chicken] 2 without a covering or casing [*skinless* sausages]

-skinned (skind) *combining form* having (a specified kind of) skin: used in hyphenated compounds [dark-*skinned*]

skin·ner (skin′ər) *n.* 1 a person who strips skins or processes them for market ☆2 [Slang] a mule driver: now chiefly historical

Skin·ner (skin′ər), **B(urrhus) F(rederic)** 1904-90; U.S. psychologist

skin·ny (skin′ē) *adj.* **-ni·er**, **-ni·est** 1 of or like skin 2 without much flesh; very thin 3 of inadequate size, growth, etc. —*n.* [Slang] inside or confidential information; gossip —**skin′ni·ness** *n.*

☆**skin·ny-dip** (-dip′) [Informal] *vi.* **-dipped′**, **-dip′ping** to swim in the nude —*n.* a swim in the nude

☆**skin-pop** (skin′päp′) *vt.* **-popped′**, **-pop′ping** [Slang] to inject (a narcotic drug) subcutaneously: cf. MAINLINE —**skin′-pop′per** *n.*

skint (skint) *adj.* ⟦var. (or dial. pronun.) of *skinned*, pp. of SKIN (*vt.*), used fig.⟧ [Brit. Slang] having little or no money; broke

skin test any test for detecting the presence of a disease or allergy from the reaction of the skin to a test substance

skin·tight (skin′tīt′) *adj.* clinging closely to the body; tightfitting [*skin-tight* jeans]

skip[1] (skip) *vi.* **skipped**, **skip′ping** ⟦ME *skippen*, prob. < Scand form akin to ON *skopa*, to jump, run < IE **skeub-*, to shoot, throw > SHOVE⟧ 1 to leap, jump, or spring lightly; specif., to move along by hopping lightly on first one foot and then the other 2 to be deflected from a surface; ricochet 3 to pass, or direct the attention, from one point to another, omitting what lies between 4 to fail to play back a portion of the recording, esp. as a result of the tonearm striking a surface imperfection: said of a phonograph record ☆5 to be promoted in school beyond the next regular grade 6 [Informal] to leave hurriedly, esp. under questionable circumstances; abscond —*vt.* 1 to jump or leap lightly over 2 to pass over or omit, either deliberately or inadvertently 3 to omit attending a session or sessions of (school, church, etc.) 4 to cause to skip or ricochet ☆5 *a)* to promote (a student) to the grade beyond the next regular one in school *b)* to pass over (the next regular grade) ☆6 [Informal] to leave (a town, country, etc.) hurriedly —*n.* 1 *a)* an act of skipping; leap; spring *b)* a skipping gait alternating light hops on each foot 2 a passing over or omitting —☆**skip it!** [Informal] never mind! it doesn't matter!

SYN.—**skip** suggests a springing forward lightly and quickly, leaping on alternate feet, and, of inanimate things, deflection from a surface in a series of jumps; **bound** implies longer, more vigorous leaps, as in running, or by an elastic object thrown along the ground; **hop** suggests a single short jump, as on one leg, or a series of short, relatively jerky jumps; **ricochet** is used of an inanimate object that has been thrown or shot and that bounds or skips in glancing deflection from a surface

skip[2] (skip) *n.* 1 [Informal] *short for* SKIPPER[2] 2 the captain of a lawn bowling team or curling team —*vt.* **skipped**, **skip′ping** to act as captain for (a bowling or curling team)

ski pants pants that fit snugly at the ankles, worn for skiing and other winter sports

skip·jack (skip′jak′) *n., pl.* **-jacks′** or **-jack′** any of various fishes that leap out of, or play at the surface of, the water, as the bluefish or a saury

ski·plane (skē′plān′) *n.* an airplane with skis instead of wheels for landing on, and taking off from, snow

ski pole either of a pair of light poles with a sharp metal tip surmounted by a projecting ring: used by skiers to gain speed and as a help in climbing and keeping their balance

skip·per[1] (skip′ər) *n.* 1 a person or thing that skips 2 SAURY 3 any of a family (Hesperiidae) of mostly small, heavy-bodied butterflies, having threadlike antennae usually ending in a hook, and characterized by short, erratic bursts of flight 4 any skipping insect

skip·per[2] (skip′ər) *n.* ⟦ME < MDu *schipper* < *schip*, a SHIP⟧ 1 the captain of a ship, esp. of a small ship or boat 2 [Informal] any leader, director, or captain —*vt.* to act as skipper of

skirl (skʉrl) *vt., vi.* ⟦ME (northern) *skrille*, *skyrle*, prob. < Scand, as in Norw dial. *skrylla*, to scream: for IE base see SHRILL⟧ [Scot.] to sound out in shrill, piercing tones, as a bagpipe does —*n.* a shrill sound, as of a bagpipe

skir·mish (skʉr′mish) *n.* ⟦ME *scarmoch* < MFr *escharmuche* < It *scaramuccia* < *schermire*, to fight < Gmc, as in OHG **skirmjan*, to protect < *skirm*, a guard: see SCREEN⟧ 1 a brief fight or encounter between small groups, usually an incident of a battle 2 any slight, unimportant conflict; brush —*vi.* ⟦ME *scarmishen*⟧ to take part in a skirmish —*SYN.* BATTLE[1] —**skir′mish·er** *n.*

Skí·ros (skē′rôs) Greek island of the N Sporades, in the Aegean Sea: 80 sq mi (207 sq km)

skirr (skʉr) *vi.* ⟦of echoic orig.⟧ to move, run, fly, etc. swiftly and, occas., with a whirring sound —*vt.* 1 to cover in searching; scour 2 to throw and cause to skim —*n.* a whirring sound

skirt (skʉrt) *n.* ⟦ME < ON *skyrt*, shirt, kirtle, akin to OE *scyrte*, SHIRT⟧ 1 that part of a dress, coat, robe, etc. that hangs below the waist 2 a woman's or girl's garment of varying length that hangs down from the waist 3 something like a skirt, as a flap hanging from the side of a saddle or one covering the legs of a sofa, chair, etc. 4 [*pl.*] the outer or bordering parts; outskirts, as of a city 5 [Slang] a girl or woman: often considered mildly offensive —*vt.* 1 to lie along or form the border or edge of 2 *a)* to move along the edge of or pass around rather than through *b)* to miss narrowly 3 to avoid (something controversial, difficult, etc.) 4 to border or edge with something —*vi.* to be on, or move along, the edge or border [a path *skirting* along the pond] —**skirt′er** *n.*

skirt-chas·er (skʉrt′chās′ər) *n.* [Slang] a man who aggressively flirts with or pursues casual sexual relationships with many different women —**skirt′-chas′ing** *n., adj.*

skirt steak a thin cut of beef taken from the plate or, sometimes, from the diaphragm

ski run a slope or course used for skiing

skit (skit) *n.* ⟦< dial., v., to be skittish, taunt, prob. < Scand var. of ON *skjōta*, SHOOT[1]⟧ 1 [Now Rare] a taunt; gibe 2 a short piece of satirical or humorous writing 3 a brief, comic performance piece, typically of an informal nature, as for two or more actors

☆**ski touring** the sport of cross-country skiing

☆**ski tow** a kind of ski lift for pulling skiers up a slope on their skis

skit·ter (skit′ər) *vi.* ⟦freq. of dial. *skite*, to dart about < Scand, akin to SHOOT[1]⟧ 1 to skip, scamper, or move along quickly and lightly ☆2 to draw a fish lure over the water with a skipping motion —*vt.* to cause to skitter

skit·ter·y (skit′ər ē) *adj.* SKITTISH

skit·tish (skit′ish) *adj.* ⟦ME: see SKIT & -ISH⟧ 1 lively or playful, esp. in a coy manner 2 easily frightened; jumpy [a *skittish* horse] 3 fickle or undependable —**skit′tish·ly** *adv.* —**skit′tish·ness** *n.*

skit·tle (skit′'l) *n.* ⟦prob. < Scand cognate of SHUTTLE (as in Dan *skyttel*, a shuttle, marble)⟧ 1 [*pl., with sing. v.*] a British form of ninepins in which a wooden disk or ball is used to knock down the pins 2 any of these pins —**(not) all beer and skittles** (not) pure pleasure and enjoyment

skive[1] (skīv) *vt.* **skived**, **skiv′ing** ⟦ON *skifa;* akin to SHIVE⟧ to slice off (leather, rubber, etc.) in thin layers; shave

skive[2] (skīv) *vi.* **skived**, **skiv′ing** ⟦orig. uncert.⟧ [Brit. Informal] to avoid work by leaving; play truant: often with *off*

skiv·er[1] (skī′vər) *n.* 1 a soft, thin leather made from the outer half of split sheepskin and used for bookbindings, hat linings, etc. 2 a person who skives leather 3 a tool used in skiving leather

skiv·er[2] (skī′vər) ***n.*** ⟦see SKIVE[2]⟧ [Brit. Informal] a person who skives

skiv·vy[1] (skiv′ē) ***n., pl.*** **-vies** ⟦< ?⟧ [Slang] **1** a man's, esp. a sailor's, short-sleeved undershirt: usually **skivvy shirt** **2** [*pl.*] men's underwear

skiv·vy[2] (skiv′ē) [Informal] ***n., pl.*** **-vies** ⟦< ?⟧ **1** [Brit.] HOUSEMAID **2** any person hired to do menial work; drudge —***vi.*** **-vied, -vy·ing** [Brit.] to do menial work

skoal (skōl) ***interj.*** ⟦Dan & Norw *skaal*, a cup < ON *skāl*, bowl: for base see SCALE[3]⟧ to your health: used as a toast

☆**skoo·kum** (sko͞o′kəm) ***adj.*** ⟦Chinook jargon, evil spirit⟧ [Northwest & Cdn.] strong, big, excellent, etc.

Sko·pje (skô′pye) capital of Macedonia (the country), in the N part: also **Skop·lje** (skôp′lye)

Skr, Skrt, *or* **Skt** ***abbrev.*** Sanskrit

SKU (skyo͞o) ***n.*** ⟦*s(tock-)k(eeping) u(nit)*⟧ **1** a number by which a retail merchant identifies the brand, style, size, etc. of an item of merchandise **2** an item of merchandise so identified Also written **sku**

sku·a (skyo͞o′ə) ***n.*** ⟦ModL, adapted (*c.* 1604) < Faroese *skūgver* < ON *skūfr*, tuft, sheaf (akin to SHOP)⟧ **1** a large, brown-and-white, predatory shorebird (*Catharacta skua*, family Stercorariidae) found in cold seas **2** [Brit.] JAEGER (sense 2)

☆**skul·dug·ger·y** or **skull·dug·ger·y** (skul dug′ər ē) ***n.*** ⟦obs. Scot *sculdudrie* < ?⟧ [Informal] sneaky, dishonest behavior; trickery

skulk (skulk) ***vi.*** ⟦ME *sculken*, prob. < LowG *schulken*, to play truant, or Dan *skulke*, to skulk⟧ **1** to move or lurk about in a stealthy, craven, or sinister manner; slink **2** [Chiefly Brit.] to avoid work or responsibility; shirk; malinger —***n.*** **1** a person who skulks **2** [Obs.] a pack (*of* foxes) —**skulk′er** ***n.***

skull (skul) ***n.*** ⟦ME *scolle* < Scand, as in Swed *skulle*, skull, akin to SCALE[3], SHELL⟧ **1** the entire bony or cartilaginous framework of the head of a vertebrate, enclosing and protecting the brain and sense organs, including the bones of the face and jaw **2** the human cranium regarded as the seat of thought or intelligence: usually with humorous or derogatory implication [a thick *skull*, an empty *skull*] —***vt.*** **1** to hit on the head **2** to hit the top of (a golf ball) causing it to go too far —**out of one's skull** [Slang] insane; crazy

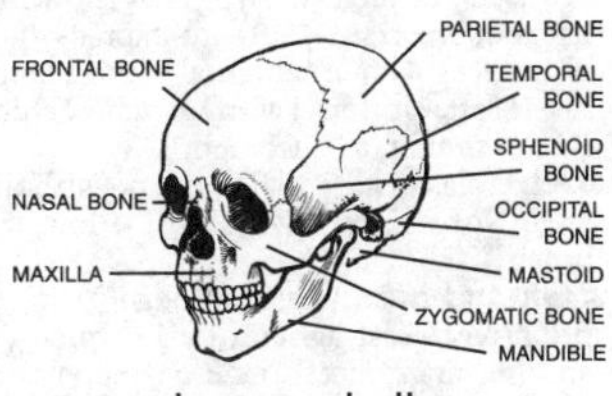

human skull

skull and crossbones a human skull facing forward with CROSSBONES beneath, as traditionally pictured on pirates' flags and now used as a warning sign as on poisons

skull·cap (skul′kap′) ***n.*** **1** a light, closefitting, brimless cap, usually worn indoors; specif., a zucchetto or a yarmulke **2** any of a genus (*Scutellaria*) of mints with a closed, helmet-shaped calyx

☆**skull practice** (*or* **session**) [Slang] **1** a meeting of a sports team with its coaches to discuss plays and strategy **2** any meeting at which ideas, plans, strategies, etc. are discussed

☆**skunk** (skuŋk) ***n., pl.*** **skunks** or **skunk** ⟦< New England Algonquian cognate of Abenaki *segôgw*⟧ **1** *a)* any of several bushy-tailed carnivores (family Mustelidae) of the New World, about the size of a house cat: it has glossy black fur, usually with white stripes or spots down the back, and ejects a foul-smelling, musky liquid when disturbed or frightened *b)* its fur **2** [Informal] a despicable, offensive person —***vt.*** [Slang] to defeat overwhelmingly in a game or contest; often, specif., to keep (an opponent) from scoring any points

skunk

☆**skunk cabbage** **1** a perennial E North American plant (*Symplocarpus foetidus*) of the arum family, growing in wet soil and having large, cabbagelike leaves, a spadix of small flowers concealed in a purple, hooded spathe, and a disagreeable smell **2** a similar plant (*Lysichitum americanum*) of the arum family of W North America

☆**skunk·weed** (-wēd′) ***n.*** any of several plants, as joe-pye weed, that have a disagreeable smell

skunk·y (skuŋ′kē) ***adj.*** **skunk′i·er, skunk′i·est** ⟦< SKUNK⟧ [Informal] having a foul or rancid smell or taste [*skunky* beer]

sky (skī) ***n., pl.*** **skies** ⟦ME < ON, a cloud, akin to OE *sceo*, a cloud, OHG *scuwo*, shadow < IE base **(s)keu-*, a cloud, OHG *scuwo*, shadow < IE base **(s)keu-*, to cover, hide > HIDE[1], L *cutis*, skin, Gr *skytos*, leather⟧ [*often pl.*] **1** the upper atmosphere, esp. with reference to its appearance [blue *skies*, a cloudy *sky*] **2** the expanse of the heavens that forms an apparent arch over the earth; firmament **3** *a)* heaven, or the celestial regions *b)* climate or weather [the balmy southern *sky*] —***vt.*** **skied** or **skyed, sky′ing** **1** to hit, throw, shoot, etc. high in the air **2** to hang (a picture) so high on a wall that it is not easily viewed —**out of a** (or **the**) **clear** (**blue**) **sky** without warning; suddenly —**the sky's the limit** the prospects are vast or seemingly boundless —**to the skies** without reserve; extravagantly [praised her *to the skies*]

sky blue a blue color like that of the sky on a clear day

☆**sky·box** (skī′bäks′) ***n.*** a privately owned or leased, enclosed luxury unit located in the higher levels of a sports stadium or arena

☆**sky·cap** (-kap′) ***n.*** a porter, or redcap, at an airport terminal

☆**sky·div·ing** (-dīv′iŋ) ***n.*** the sport of jumping from an airplane and executing free-fall maneuvers before opening the parachute, often at the last possible moment —**sky′dive′** (-dīv′) ***vi.*** **-dived′, -div′ing** —**sky′div′er** ***n.***

Skye (skī), **Isle of** island off the W coast of Scotland: largest of the Inner Hebrides: 643 sq mi (1,665 sq km)

Skye terrier ⟦after prec., where the breed originated⟧ any of a breed of small terrier with a long body, short legs, and a profuse coat of long, straight hair

sky·ey (skī′ē) ***adj.*** **1** of or like the sky, as a shade of blue **2** of great height; lofty

sky-high (skī′hī′) ***adj.*** of or to a great height, amount, degree, etc. —***adv.*** to a great height, amount, degree, etc.

☆**sky·jack** (-jak′) ***vt.*** to hijack (an aircraft) —**sky′jack′er** ***n.***

sky·lark (-lärk′) ***n.*** a lark (*Alauda arvensis*) that is found chiefly in Eurasia, famous for the song it utters as it soars upward and flies about high in the sky —***vi.*** ⟦< SKY + LARK[2]: orig. naut., of playing in the rigging⟧ to play about boisterously; frolic

sky·light (-līt′) ***n.*** a window in a roof or ceiling

sky·line (-līn′) ***n.*** **1** the line along which the sky seems to touch the earth; visible horizon **2** the outline, as of a city, seen against the sky

sky·lit (-lit′) ***adj.*** illuminated by means of a skylight: often **sky′light′ed**

☆**sky marshal** a federal officer assigned to guard against the hijacking of commercial airliners

sky pilot [Slang] a member of the clergy; esp., a CHAPLAIN (sense 2)

sky·rock·et (-räk′it) ***n.*** a fireworks rocket that explodes in midair in a shower of colored sparks —☆***vi., vt.*** to rise or cause to rise rapidly [meat prices *skyrocketed*]

Ský·ros (skē′rôs) *alt. sp. of* SKÍROS

sky·sail (skī′sāl′, -səl) ***n.*** a small sail set above a royal at the top of a square-rigged mast

sky·scrap·er (-skrā′pər) ***n.*** ☆a very tall building

sky·walk (-wôk′) ***n.*** a walkway suspended one or more stories above street level and usually enclosed or covered

sky·ward (-wərd) ***adv., adj.*** toward the sky: also **sky′wards** ***adv.***

sky wave a radio wave that is reflected back to earth from one of the layers of the ionosphere

sky·way (-wā′) ***n.*** **1** AIR LANE **2** an elevated highway **3** SKYWALK

sky·writ·ing (-rīt′iŋ) ***n.*** the act or result of tracing words, figures, etc. in the sky by trailing smoke from an airplane in flight —**sky′write′** ***vi., vt.*** **-wrote′, -writ′ten** —**sky′writ′er** ***n.***

s.l. ***abbrev.*** ⟦L *sine loco*⟧ without place (of publication)

slab[1] (slab) ***n.*** ⟦ME *sclabbe*⟧ **1** a piece that is flat, broad, and fairly thick [a *slab* of concrete, a *slab* of bread] **2** any of the rough, outer pieces cut from a log, as in sawing it into lumber —***vt.*** **slabbed, slab′bing** **1** to make into a slab or slabs **2** to cut the slabs from (a log) **3** to pave or cover with slabs

slab[2] (slab) ***adj.*** ⟦< Scand, as in Swed dial. *slabb*, muddy water: for IE base see SLAVER[1]⟧ [Archaic] thick and heavy; viscid [*slab* porridge]

slab·ber (slab′ər) ***vi., vt., n.*** *var. of* SLOBBER

slab-sid·ed (slab′sīd′id) ***adj.*** [Informal] **1** flat-sided **2** tall and slender; lank

slack[1] (slak) ***adj.*** ⟦ME *slakke* < OE *slæc*, akin to Du *slak* < IE base **(s)lēg-*, loose, slack > L *laxus*, lax⟧ **1** slow; idle; sluggish **2** barely moving: said of a current, as of air or water **3** characterized by little work, trade, or business; not busy or active; dull [a *slack* period] **4** loose; relaxed; not tight, taut, or firm **5** easily changed or influenced; weak; lax **6** careless or negligent [a *slack* workman] —***vt.*** **1** to make slack; slacken **2** to slake —***vi.*** **1** to be or become slack; slacken **2** to be idle, careless, or negligent —***adv.*** in a slack manner; so as to be slack —***n.*** **1** a part that is slack or hangs loose **2** a lack of tension or tautness; looseness **3** a stoppage of movement, as in a current **4** a period of lessened activity, production, etc.; lull —***SYN.*** REMISS —☆**cut someone some slack** [Slang] to be less demanding of someone; ease up on someone —**pick** (or **take**) **up the slack** [Informal] to address or remedy a lag, underperformance, etc. —**slack off** to slacken —**slack′ly** ***adv.*** —**slack′ness** ***n.***

slack[2] (slak) ***n.*** ⟦ME *sleck*, akin to Fl *slecke*, dross, Du *slak*: for IE base see SLAY⟧ a mixture of small pieces of coal, coal dust, and dirt left from the screening of coal

slack[3] (slak) ***n.*** ⟦ME *slak* < ON **slakki* < IE base **sl̥ēk-*, wet, sprinkle⟧ [Scot. or North Eng.] a small valley or surface depression

slack·en (slak′ən) ***vi.*** ⟦< SLACK[1]⟧ **1** to become less active, intense, brisk, etc. [*slackening* trade] **2** to become less tense; loosen, as rope —***vt.*** **1** to reduce the intensity or severity of; retard; abate; moderate **2** to reduce the tension of; relax; loosen [to *slacken* one's grip] —**slack′en·er** ***n.***

slack·er (-ər) ***n.*** **1** a person who shirks work or duty **2** a person who evades military service in wartime ☆**3** [Informal] a young person, typically in his or her twenties, variously regarded as idle, lazy, unambitious, etc. —**slack′er·dom** ***n.***

slacks (slaks) ***pl.n.*** trousers for men or women; esp., trousers that are not part of a suit

slack water **1** the period between tides when the water is neither in ebb nor flood **2** any stretch of water having little or no current

slag (slag) ***n.*** ⟦< MLowG *slagge* (> Ger *schlacke*) < *slagen*, to strike: for IE base see SLAY⟧ **1** the fused refuse or dross separated from a metal in the process of smelting **2** lava resembling this **3** [Slang, Chiefly Brit.] *a)* a worthless, contemptible person *b)* a sexually promiscuous woman: a derogatory or insulting term —*vt.* **slagged**, **slag′ging 1** to form into slag **2** ⟦see SLAG (*n.* 3)⟧ [Slang, Chiefly Brit.] to criticize, disparage, or insult: often with *off* —*vi.* to form into slag —**slag′gy** *adj.* **-gi·er**, **-gi·est**

slain (slān) *vt. pp. of* SLAY

sláin·te (slän′chə) *interj.* ⟦Ir, health⟧ to your health: used as a toast

slake (slāk) *vt.* **slaked**, **slak′ing** ⟦ME *slakien* < OE *slacian* < *slæc*, SLACK[1]⟧ **1** to allay or make (thirst, desire, etc.) less active or intense by satisfying; assuage; satisfy **2** to cause (a fire) to die down or go out **3** to produce a chemical change in (lime) by combination with water [*slaked* lime is calcium hydroxide] **4** [Obs.] to lessen, reduce, or relieve **5** [Obs.] to lessen the tension of —*vi.* to become slaked: said of lime

sla·lom (slä′ləm) *n.* ⟦Norw, ski track with an even slope < dial. *slad*, sloping gently + *lom*, trail⟧ *Skiing* **1** a timed Alpine race downhill over a zigzag course marked by flag-topped poles, or gates: see GATE[1] (*n.* 8): cf. GIANT SLALOM **2** any race over a zigzag course similarly marked —*vi.* to take part in a slalom

slam[1] (slam) *vt.* **slammed**, **slam′ming** ⟦prob. < Scand, as in Norw dial. *slamra, slemma*⟧ **1** to shut or allow to shut with force and noise [to *slam* a door] **2** to hit, throw, or put in place or action with force and noise [to *slam* a baseball over the fence] ☆**3** [Informal] to criticize or disparage severely —*vi.* to shut, go into place, etc. with force and noise —*n.* **1** *a)* a heavy, noisy impact, shutting, etc. *b)* the noise made by this ☆**2** an informal poetry competition in which the participants read their work aloud and are judged by the audience **3** any fast-moving or violent shot, action, etc., as in sports ☆**4** [Informal] a severe criticism ☆**5** [Slang] *short for* SLAMMER

slam[2] (slam) *n.* ⟦< ?⟧ *Bridge short for:* **1** GRAND SLAM (sense 1*a*) **2** SMALL SLAM

slam-bang (slam′baŋ′) [Informal] *adv.* **1** swiftly or abruptly and recklessly **2** with loud noise —*adj.* characterized by liveliness, noise, etc.

slam dancing a kind of dancing to punk rock, grunge, etc. in which the dancers hurl themselves at each other: also written **slam′-danc′ing** *n.* —**slam′-dance′** *vi.* **-danced′**, **-danc′ing**

slam-dunk (-duŋk′) *n.* **1** *Basketball* a dunk shot in which the ball is slammed through the basket ☆**2** [Informal] a certainty; sure thing Also written **slam dunk** —*vt. Basketball* to slam (the ball) through the basket

slam·mer (slam′ər) *n.* **1** a person or thing that slams ☆**2** [Slang] a prison or jail

☆**slam·ming** (slam′iŋ) *n.* the practice of switching someone's telephone service, usually long-distance service, from one company to another without the customer's permission

slan·der (slan′dər) *n.* ⟦ME *sclaunder* < Anglo-Fr *esclaundre* (OFr *esclandre, escandle*) < LL(Ec) *scandalum*: see SCANDAL⟧ **1** the utterance in the presence of another person of a false statement or statements, damaging to a third person's character or reputation: usually distinguished from *libel*, which is written **2** such a spoken statement —*vt.* to utter a slander about —**slan′der·er** *n.*

slan·der·ous (-əs) *adj.* ⟦ME *sclaunderous*⟧ **1** characterized by or constituting slander **2** uttering slander

slang (slaŋ) *n.* ⟦18th-c. cant < ?⟧ **1** [Obs.] the specialized vocabulary and idioms as of criminals and tramps, the purpose of which was to disguise from outsiders the meaning of what was said: now usually called CANT[1] **2** the specialized vocabulary and idioms of those in the same work, way of life, etc.: now usually called SHOPTALK, ARGOT, JARGON[1] **3** highly informal speech that is outside conventional or standard usage and consists both of coined words and phrases and of new or extended meanings attached to established terms: slang develops from the attempt to find fresh and vigorous, colorful, pungent, or humorous expression, and generally either passes into disuse or comes to have a more formal status —*vi.* [Brit.] to use slang or abusive talk —*vt.* [Brit. Informal] to address with abusive talk

slang·y (slaŋ′ē) *adj.* **slang′i·er**, **slang′i·est 1** of, like, or containing slang **2** given to using slang —**slang′i·ly** *adv.* —**slang′i·ness** *n.*

slant (slant) *vt., vi.* ⟦ME *slenten*, to glide, slope < Scand, as in ODan *slente*, to slip < IE *(*s*)*lend*(*h*)- < base *(*s*)*leidh*-, slippery, to glide > SLIDE⟧ **1** to incline or turn from a direct line or course, esp. one that is perpendicular or level; slope ☆**2** *a)* to write or tell so as to appeal to a particular interest *b)* to distort in writing or telling so as to express a particular bias —*n.* **1** *a)* an oblique or inclined surface, line, direction, etc.; slope; incline *b)* VIRGULE ☆**2** *a)* a point of view, attitude, or opinion *b)* a distortion or bias in narration **3** [Informal] a quick, oblique look; glance —*adj.* ⟦prob. aphetic < ME *aslonte*, aslant⟧ oblique; sloping; inclined —**slant′ing·ly** *adv.* — [Informal] **slant′y** *adj.*

slant rhyme rhyme in which there is close but not exact correspondence of sounds (Ex.: *lid, lad; wait, made*)

slant·wise (-wīz′) *adv.* so as to slant or slope; obliquely: also **slant′ways′** (-wāz′) —*adj.* slanting; oblique

slap (slap) *n.* ⟦LowG *sklapp*: of echoic orig.⟧ **1** *a)* a blow or smack, esp. with something flat, specif. the palm of the hand *b)* the sound of this, or a sound like it **2** an injury to pride, self-respect, etc., as an insult or rebuff —*vt.* **slapped**, **slap′ping 1** to strike with something flat, specif. the palm of the hand **2** to put, throw, hit, etc. carelessly or with force [to *slap* a hat on one's head] **3** [Informal] *a)* to penalize (a person, business, etc.) *with* a fine, lawsuit, etc. *b)* to impose (a fine, etc.) *on* a person, business, etc. —*vi.* to make a sudden, sharp noise, as upon impact —*adv.* [Informal] directly and abruptly [I ran *slap* into the wall] —**slap down** [Informal] to rebuke, suppress, or rebuff harshly —**slap′per** *n.*

slap and tickle [Brit. Informal] playful sexual activity: also written **slap′-and-tick′le** *n.*

slap-bang (slap′baŋ′) *adv.* [Informal, Chiefly Brit.] suddenly; violently

slap·dash (-dash′) *n.* something done carelessly and hastily —*adv.* in a hasty, careless manner —*adj.* hasty, careless, impetuous, etc.

☆**slap-hap·py** (-hap′ē) *adj.* [Slang] **1** dazed or mentally impaired by or as by blows to the head; punch-drunk **2** silly or giddy

☆**slap·jack** (-jak′) *n.* FLAPJACK

slap shot *Ice Hockey* a hard shot made with a full swing, usually causing the puck to leave the ice

☆**slap·stick** (-stik′) *n.* **1** an implement made of two flat pieces of wood that slap together loudly when hit against something: sometimes used by clowns to strike others with loud, harmless slaps **2** crude comedy in which the humor depends upon violent activity, horseplay, etc. —*adj.* characterized by such comedy

slap-up (-up′) *adj.* [Brit. Informal] **1** stylish; lavish **2** first-rate

slash[1] (slash) *vt.* ⟦ME *slaschen* < ? OFr *esclachier*, to break, prob. < *es*- (< L *ex*-), intens. + Gmc **klakjan*, to crack, of echoic orig.⟧ **1** to cut or wound with a sweeping stroke or strokes, as of a knife **2** to whip viciously; lash; scourge **3** to cut slits in (a fabric, dress, etc.), esp. so as to expose underlying material, usually of another color **4** to reduce drastically [to *slash* prices] **5** to criticize severely —*vi.* **1** to make a sweeping stroke or strokes with or as with something sharp **2** to criticize or rebuke harshly **3** to move through or penetrate something quickly and precisely [a speeding car *slashing* through traffic] —*n.* **1** a sweeping stroke made as with a knife **2** a cut made by or as by such a stroke; gash; slit **3** a short diagonal line (/) used between two words to show that either is applicable (and/or), in dates or fractions (3/8), to express "per" (feet/second), etc.; virgule: cf. BACKSLASH **4** an ornamental slit in a fabric, dress, etc. ☆**5** *a)* an open place in a forest, cluttered with branches, chips, or other debris, as from the cutting of timber *b)* such debris

☆**slash**[2] (slash) *n.* ⟦< dial. *slash*, boggy hollow, *slashy*, swampy, prob. < Scand, as in Norw *slask*, mud, slush⟧ a low, swampy area, usually covered with brush

slash-and-burn (slash′ən burn′) *adj.* **1** of or having to do with a type of primitive forest agriculture in which fields are cleared by cutting down and burning vegetation **2** characterized by indiscriminate or destructive recklessness

slash·er (slash′ər) *n.* a person or thing that slashes —*adj.* designating or of a horror film characterized by graphic bloodletting and, typically, a serial killer as villain

slash·ing (-iŋ) *adj.* **1** severe; merciless; violent **2** dashing; spirited **3** [Informal] huge [a *slashing* success] —*n.* **1** the act of one that slashes **2** SLASH[1] (*n.* 4) **3** *Forestry a)* SLASH[1] (*n.* 5*a*) *b)* [*usually pl.*] SLASH[1] (*n.* 5*b*) **4** *Sports* the illegal act of swinging the stick at an opponent, as in ice hockey —**slash′ing·ly** *adv.*

☆**slash pine 1** a common pine (*Pinus caribaea*) growing in slashes, or swamps, in the SE U.S., the West Indies, and Central America **2** the hard wood of this tree

slash pocket a pocket in a garment, having a finished, usually diagonal slit for an opening

slat[1] (slat) *n.* ⟦ME *sclat* < OFr *esclat*, a fragment < *esclater*, to splinter < Langobardic *slaitan*, to tear apart, split, akin to OHG *slizzan*, OE *slitan*: see SLIT⟧ **1** a thin, narrow strip of wood, metal, etc. [*slats* of a Venetian blind] ☆**2** [*pl.*] [Slang] *a)* the ribs *b)* the buttocks —*vt.* **slat′ted**, **slat′ting** to provide or make with slats

slat[2] (slat) *vt.* **slat′ted**, **slat′ting** ⟦ME *sclatten*, prob. < ON *sletta*, to throw: infl. by prec.⟧ [Brit. Dial.] **1** to throw forcefully **2** to beat; strike

slate[1] (slāt) *n.* ⟦ME *sclate* < OFr *esclate*, fem. of *esclat*: see SLAT[1]⟧ **1** a hard, fine-grained, metamorphic rock, typically formed from shale, that cleaves naturally into thin, smooth-surfaced layers **2** *a)* a thin piece of slate or slatelike material, esp. one used as a roofing tile or as a tablet for writing on with chalk *b)* slates collectively; slating **3** the bluish-gray color of most slate: also **slate blue** ☆**4** a list of candidates proposed for nomination or election —*vt.* **slat′ed**, **slat′ing 1** to cover with slate ☆**2** to put on a list or designate, as for candidacy, appointment, engagement, etc.; choose or schedule —**a clean slate** a record showing no marks of discredit, dishonor, etc.

slate[2] (slāt) *vt.* **slat′ed**, **slat′ing** ⟦prob. < ON *sleita*, strife (akin to OE *slætan*, to bait, torment)⟧ [Informal, Chiefly Brit.] **1** to punish severely, as by thrashing **2** to scold or criticize harshly

slat·er (slāt′ər) *n.* **1** a person who slates **2** any of various isopod crustaceans; esp., a sow bug

slath·er (slath′ər) [Informal or Dial.] *n.* ⟦< ?⟧ [*usually pl.*] a large amount; a lot —*vt.* **1** to cover or spread thickly **2** to use or use up in a lavish or wasteful way

slat·ing (slāt′iŋ) *n.* **1** the act of one who slates **2** slates collectively, as a material for roofing

slat·tern (slat′ərn) *n.* ⟦< dial. *slatter*, to spill, slop < or akin to ON *slattari*, idler⟧ **1** a woman who is careless and sloppy in her habits, appearance, work, etc. **2** [Old-fashioned] a sexually promiscuous woman

slat·tern·ly (-lē) *adj.* **1** having the habits of a slattern; dirty; slovenly; untidy **2** characteristic of or fit for a slattern —*adv.* in a slatternly manner —**slat′tern·li·ness** *n.*

slat·ting (slat′iŋ) *n.* **1** slats collectively **2** material for making slats
slat·y (slāt′ē) *adj.* **slat′i·er, slat′i·est 1** of or like slate **2** having the bluish-gray color of slate
slaugh·ter (slôt′ər) *n.* ⟦ME *slahter* < ON *slātr*, lit., slain flesh, contr. < *slattr*, akin to OE *sleaht*, slaughter, death: for IE base see SLAY⟧ **1** the killing of an animal or animals for food; butchering **2** the killing of a human being, esp. in a brutal manner **3** the killing of people in large numbers, as in battle **4** [Informal] a complete defeat or victory —*vt.* **1** to kill (an animal or animals) for food; butcher **2** to kill (people), esp. brutally or in large numbers **3** [Informal] to conquer or defeat completely —**slaugh′ter·er** *n.*

SYN.—**slaughter**, as applied to people, suggests extensive and brutal killing, as in battle or by deliberate acts of wanton cruelty; **massacre** implies the indiscriminate and wholesale slaughter of those who are defenseless or helpless to resist; **butchery** adds implications of extreme cruelty and of such coldblooded heartlessness as one might display in the slaughtering of animals; **carnage** stresses the result of bloody slaughter and suggests the accumulation of the bodies of the slain; **pogrom** refers to an organized, often officially inspired, massacre of a minority group, specifically of the Jews in czarist Russia

slaugh·ter·house (-hous′) *n.* a place where animals are butchered for food
slaugh·ter·ous (-əs) *adj.* brutally destructive or murderous
Slav[1] (släv, slav) *n.* ⟦ME *Sclave* < ML *Slavus*: see SLAVE⟧ a member of any of a group of Slavic-speaking peoples of E, SE, and central Europe, generally divided into **Eastern Slavs, Southern Slavs,** and **Western Slavs**: see SLAVIC (*n.*) —*adj.* [Rare] *var. of* SLAVIC
Slav[2] *abbrev.* Slavic
slave (slāv) *n.* ⟦ME *sclave* < OFr or ML: OFr *esclave* < ML *sclavus*, slave, orig., Slav < LGr *Sklabos*, ult. < OSlav *Slovēne*, native name of a Slavic people: first used of captives of Slavic orig. in SE Europe⟧ **1** a human being who is owned as property by, and is absolutely subject to the will of, another; bondservant divested of all freedom and personal rights **2** a person who is completely dominated by some influence, habit, person, etc. [*a slave to fashion*] **3** a person who slaves; drudge **4** SLAVE ANT **5** a device actuated or controlled by another, similar device —*vi.* **slaved, slav′ing 1** to work like a slave; drudge **2** to deal in slaves; be a slaver —*vt.* [Archaic] to enslave
slave ant any ant enslaved by a SLAVE-MAKING ANT
Slave Coast W African coast between the Volta & Niger rivers, on the Bight of Benin: its ports were the former centers of the African slave trade 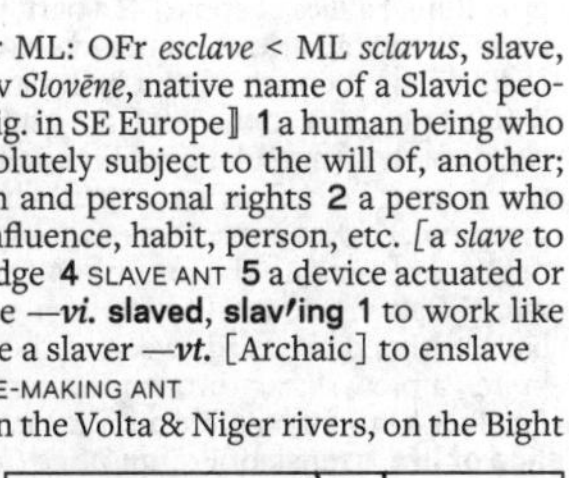
☆**slave driver 1** a person who directs or oversees the work of slaves **2** any merciless taskmaster
slave·hold·er (slāv′hōl′dər) *n.* a person who owns slaves —**slave′hold′ing** *adj., n.*
slave-mak·ing ant (-māk′iŋ) an ant of any of several species that enslave ants of other species, as by raiding their nests to carry off pupae that are kept until they become useful as workers
slav·er[1] (slav′ər, släv′-) *vi.* ⟦ME *slaveren* < Scand, as in Ice *slafra*, to slobber < IE **slep-* < base **(s)lāp-* > LIP, SLEEP⟧ to let saliva run or dribble from the mouth; drool —*vt.* [Archaic] to slobber on or cover with saliva —*n.* saliva drooling from the mouth

Slave Coast

slav·er[2] (slāv′ər) *n.* **1** SLAVE SHIP **2** a person who deals in slaves
Slave River river in NE Alberta & S Northwest Territories, Canada, flowing from Lake Athabasca northwest into Great Slave Lake: 258 mi (415 km)
slav·er·y (slā′vər ē, slāv′rē) *n.* **1** the owning or keeping of slaves as a practice or institution; slaveholding **2** the condition of being a slave; bondage; servitude **3** a condition of submission to or domination by some influence, habit, etc. **4** hard work or toil like that done by slaves; drudgery —SYN. SERVITUDE
slave ship a ship for transporting slaves, esp. one used in the African slave trade
slave state [*often* **S- S-**] any of the states in which slavery was legal before the Civil War: Ala., Ark., Del., Fla., Ga., Ky., La., Md., Miss., Mo., N.C., S.C., Tenn., Tex., & Va.
slave trade traffic in slaves; specif., the former transportation of black people from Africa to America for sale as slaves
slav·ey (slā′vē, slav′ē) *n., pl.* **-eys** [Brit. Informal] a female domestic servant, esp. one who does hard, menial work
Slav·ic (släv′ik, slav′-) *n.* a principal branch of the Indo-European family of languages, generally divided into **East Slavic** (Russian, Ukrainian, Belorussian), **South Slavic** (Old Church Slavonic, Bulgarian, Serbo-Croatian, Slovenian, Macedonian), and **West Slavic** (Polish, Lusatian, Czech, Slovak)
slav·ish (slā′vish) *adj.* **1** of or characteristic of a slave or slaves; specif., *a)* hopelessly submissive; servile *b)* [Now Rare] involving drudgery; laborious **2** blindly dependent or imitative [*slavish adherence to a model*] —**slav′ish·ly** *adv.* —**slav′ish·ness** *n.*
Slav·ism (släv′iz′əm, slav′-) *n.* characteristics, interests, culture, etc. of Slavs collectively
Slav·ist (släv′ist, slav′-) *n.* a specialist in the study of Slavic languages, cultures, etc.: also **Slav′i·cist** (-ə sist)
Slav·kov (släf′kôf) *Czech name for* AUSTERLITZ
Slav·o- (släv′ō, slav′-; -ə) *combining form* Slav [*Slavophile*]
☆**slav·oc·ra·cy** (slāv äk′rə sē) *n.* ⟦SLAV(E) + -O- + -CRACY⟧ slaveholders and pro-slavery forces as a dominant or powerful class in the U.S. before 1865
Sla·vo·ni·a (slə vō′nē ə, -nyə) region in S Europe bounded by the Sava, Drava, & Danube rivers —**Sla·vo′ni·an** *adj., n.*
Sla·von·ic (slə vän′ik) *adj., n.* SLAVIC
Slav·o·phile (släv′ə fīl′, slav′ə-) *n.* ⟦SLAVO- + -PHILE⟧ a person who strongly admires the Slavs or their customs, culture, influence, etc.: also **Slav′o·phil** (-fil) —**Sla·voph·i·lism** (slə väf′ə liz′əm; släv′ə fil′iz′əm, slav′-) *n.*
☆**slaw** (slô) *n. short for* COLESLAW
slay (slā) *vt.* **slew** or for 2 **slayed, slain, slay′ing** ⟦ME *slean* < OE < **slahan*, akin to Ger *schlagen*, Du *slagen* < IE base **slak-*, to hit > MIr *slacc*, sword⟧ **1** to kill or destroy in a violent way **2** [Slang] to impress, delight, amuse, etc. with overwhelming force **3** [Obs.] to strike or hit —SYN. KILL[1] —**slay′er** *n.*
SLBM *abbrev.* submarine-launched ballistic missile
SLCM *abbrev.* sea-launched cruise missile
sld *abbrev.* **1** sailed **2** sealed
sleave (slēv) *n.* ⟦< OE *-slǣfan*, to separate; akin to *slifan*: see SLIVER⟧ **1** [Obs.] *a)* a fine silk thread separated from a large thread *b)* untwisted silk that tends to mat or tangle; floss **2** [Rare] any tangle, as of ravelings —*vt.* **sleaved, sleav′ing** [Obs.] to separate or pull apart (twisted or tangled threads)
sleaze (slēz) *n.* ⟦back-form. < SLEAZY⟧ [Slang] **1** the quality or condition of being sleazy; sleaziness **2** anything cheap, vulgar, shoddy, etc. **3** a shady, coarse, or immoral person: also **sleaze′bag′** (-bag′) or **sleaze′ball′** (-bôl′)
slea·zoid (slē′zoid′) [Slang] *adj.* ⟦< prec. + -OID⟧ SLEAZY (*adj.* 2) —*n.* SLEAZE (*n.* 3)
slea·zy (slē′zē) *adj.* **-zi·er, -zi·est** ⟦< *slesia*, var. of SILESIA⟧ **1** flimsy or thin in texture or substance; lacking firmness [*a sleazy rayon fabric*] **2** [Informal] shoddy, shabby, cheap, vulgar, etc. —**slea′zi·ly** *adv.* —**slea′zi·ness** *n.*
sled (sled) *n.* ⟦ME *sledde* < MLowG or MDu, akin to Ger *schlitten*: for IE base see SLIDE⟧ any of several types of vehicle mounted on runners for use on snow, ice, etc.: small sleds are used in the sport of coasting, large ones (also called *sledges*), for carrying loads —☆*vt.* **sled′ded, sled′ding** to carry on a sled —☆*vi.* to ride or coast on a sled —**sled′der** *n.*
☆**sled·ding** (-iŋ) *n.* **1** a riding or carrying on a sled **2** the condition of the ground with reference to the use of sleds: often used fig. [*the work was hard sledding*]
sled dog a husky, malamute, or other dog trained to pull a dog sled
sledge[1] (slej) *n., vt., vi.* **sledged, sledg′ing** ⟦ME *slegge* < OE *slecge* < base of *slean*, to strike, SLAY⟧ *var. of* SLEDGEHAMMER
sledge[2] (slej) *n.* ⟦MDu *sleedse*, akin to *sledde*, SLED⟧ a sled or sleigh for carrying loads over ice, snow, etc. — *vi., vt.* **sledged, sledg′ing** to go or take by sledge
sledge·ham·mer (slej′ham′ər) *n.* ⟦see SLEDGE[1]⟧ a long, heavy hammer, usually held with both hands — *vt., vi.* to strike with or as with a sledgehammer —*adj.* crushingly powerful
sleek (slēk) *adj.* ⟦var. of SLICK, with Early ModE vowel lengthening⟧ **1** smooth and shiny; glossy, as a highly polished surface, well-kept hair or fur, etc. **2** of well-fed or well-groomed appearance [*fat, sleek pigeons*] **3** polished in speech and behavior, esp. in a specious way; unctuous **4** highly fashionable, or stylish; elegant **5** having a smooth, elegant contour [*a sleek automobile*] —*vt.* to make sleek; smooth: also **sleek′en** —**sleek′ly** *adv.* —**sleek′ness** *n.*
sleek·it (slēk′it) *adj.* ⟦Scot var. of pp. of prec.⟧ [Scot.] **1** sleek, or smooth and shiny **2** sly, crafty, or sneaky
sleep (slēp) *n.* ⟦ME *slep* < OE *slǣp*, akin to Ger *schlaf*, sleep, *schlaff*, loose, lax < IE **slab* < base **(s)leb-*, **(s)lab-*, loose, slack > LIP, LIMP[1], L *labor*, to slip, sink⟧ **1** *a)* a natural, regularly recurring condition of rest for the body and mind, during which the eyes are usually closed and there is little or no conscious thought or voluntary movement, but there is intermittent dreaming *b)* a spell of sleeping **2** any state of inactivity thought of as like sleep, as death, unconsciousness, hibernation, etc. **3** the gritty or gummy residue in or around the eyes after a period of sleep: usually in the phrase **rub the sleep from one's eyes 4** *Bot.* NYCTITROPISM —*vi.* **slept, sleep′ing 1** to be in the state of sleep; slumber **2** to be in a state of inactivity like sleep, as that of death, quiescence, hibernation, inattention, etc. **3** to have sexual intercourse (*with, together,* etc.): a euphemism **4** *Bot.* to assume a nyctitropic position at night, as petals or leaves —*vt.* **1** to slumber in (a specified kind of sleep) [*to sleep the sleep of the just*] **2** to provide sleeping accommodations for [*a boat that sleeps four*] —**put to sleep 1** to make (someone) weary and bored to, or as if to, the point of inducing sleep **2** to put (a pet) to death in a humane manner —**sleep around** [Informal] to have promiscuous sexual relations —**sleep away 1** to spend in sleeping; sleep during **2** to get rid of by sleeping —**sleep in 1** to sleep at the place where one is employed as a household servant **2** to sleep much later into the morning than one usually does —**sleep it off** to rid oneself of the effects of some excess, overindulgence, etc., specif. of the aftereffects of drinking much alcoholic liquor, by sleeping —**sleep like a log** (or **top**) to sleep undisturbed and very deeply —**sleep on it** [Informal] to postpone making a decision until the next day —**sleep out** to sleep outdoors —**sleep over** [Informal] to spend the night at another's home

sleep apnea a chronic disorder in which breathing is briefly suspended repeatedly during sleep

sleep disorder any of various chronic psychological or physiological disorders associated with sleep, as insomnia, sleep apnea, snoring, sleepwalking, etc.

sleep·er (slē′pər) *n.* ⟦ME *slepere* < OE *slæpere*⟧ **1** a person or animal that sleeps, esp. as specified *[a sound sleeper]* **2** *a)* a timber or beam laid horizontally, as on the ground, to support something above it *b)* any of a number of strips of wood, laid as on a concrete subfloor, to which finished flooring is attached **3** [Chiefly Brit.] a tie supporting a railroad track ☆**4** SLEEPING CAR **5** a sofa or upholstered chair designed to convert easily to a bed, typically by means of a built-in foldout cot beneath its cushions ☆**6** a previously disregarded person or thing that unexpectedly achieves success, assumes importance, etc. **7** *a)* MOLE[2] (sense 2) *b)* a terrorist who infiltrates a society, a government agency, etc. long before taking action ☆**8** *a)* [*often pl.*] a kind of pajamas for infants and young children, that enclose the feet *b)* BUNTING[1] (sense 3) ☆**9** *Bowling* a pin standing directly behind, and hidden by, another after the first bowl of a frame —*adj.* of or having to do with a SLEEPER (sense 7) *[a sleeper cell]*

sleep·i·ly (-pə lē) *adv.* in a sleepy or drowsy manner

sleep·i·ness (-pē nis) *n.* a sleepy quality or state

☆**sleeping bag** a large, warmly lined, zippered bag, often waterproof, in which a person can sleep, esp. outdoors

Sleeping Beauty the title character of a fairy tale, a princess who is put to sleep by an evil fairy, to be awakened only by the kiss of a prince

☆**sleeping car** a railroad car equipped with berths, compartments, etc. for passengers to sleep in

sleeping partner *Brit. term for* SILENT PARTNER

☆**sleeping pill** a pill or capsule containing a drug, esp. a barbiturate, for inducing sleep

sleeping policeman [Brit.] SPEED BUMP

sleeping sickness **1** an infectious disease, esp. common in tropical Africa, caused by either of two trypanosomes (*Trypanosoma gambiense* or *T. rhodesiense*) that are transmitted by the bite of a tsetse fly: it is characterized by fever, drowsiness, and coma, usually ending in prolonged coma and death **2** inflammation of the brain, caused by a virus and characterized by drowsiness and lethargy

sleep·less (slēp′lis) *adj.* **1** unable to sleep; wakeful; restless **2** marked by absence of sleep *[a sleepless night]* **3** constantly moving, active, or alert —**sleep′less·ly** *adv.* —**sleep′less·ness** *n.*

sleep mode an energy-saving mode of operation in certain computers, in which the screen display and some programs are rendered temporarily inactive after a period of disuse

sleep·o·ver (-ō′vər) *n.* **1** an instance of spending the night at a friend's house **2** a party for young people at which the guests spend the night at the host's home

sleep·walk·ing (-wôk′iŋ) *n.* the act or practice of walking about while asleep; somnambulism —**sleep′walk′** *vi.* —**sleep′walk′er** *n.*

sleep·wear (-wer′) *n.* NIGHTCLOTHES

sleep·y (slē′pē) *adj.* **sleep′i·er, sleep′i·est** **1** ready or inclined to sleep; drowsy **2** not very active; dull; quiet *[a sleepy little town]* **3** of, causing, or showing drowsiness

SYN.—**sleepy** applies to a person who is nearly overcome by a desire to sleep and, figuratively, suggests either the power to induce sleepiness or a resemblance to this state *[a sleepy lullaby]*; **drowsy** stresses the sluggishness or lethargic heaviness accompanying sleepiness *[the drowsy sentry fought off sleep through the watch]*; **somnolent** is a formal equivalent of either of the preceding *[the somnolent voice of the speaker]*; **slumberous**, a poetic equivalent, in addition sometimes suggests latent powers in repose *[a slumberous city]*

sleep·y·head (-hed′) *n.* a sleepy person: an affectionate or playful use

sleet (slēt) *n.* ⟦ME *slete* < OE **sliete*, akin to Ger *schlosse*, hail < IE base **(s)leu-*, loose, lax > SLUR, SLUG[1]⟧ **1** partly frozen rain, or rain that freezes as it falls **2** transparent or translucent precipitation in the form of pellets of ice that are smaller than 5 mm (.2 in) **3** the icy coating formed when rain freezes on trees, streets, etc. —*vi.* to shower in the form of sleet —**sleet′y** *adj.*

sleeve (slēv) *n.* ⟦ME *sleve* < OE *sliefe*, akin to Du *sloof*, apron: for IE base see SLIP[3]⟧ **1** that part of a garment that covers an arm or part of an arm **2** a tube or tubelike part fitting over or around another part **3** a thin paper or plastic cover for protecting a phonograph record, usually within a JACKET (*n.* 2*b*) **4** a drogue towed by an airplane for target practice **5** [Slang] tattooing covering much or most of the arm: in full **sleeve tattoo** or **tattoo sleeve** —*vt.* **sleeved, sleev′ing** to provide or fit with a sleeve or sleeves —**roll up one's sleeves** to prepare to work, esp. at a difficult task requiring prolonged effort —**up one's sleeve** hidden or secret but ready at hand

sleeved (slēvd) *adj.* fitted with sleeves: often in hyphenated compounds *[short-sleeved]*

sleeve·less (slēv′lis) *adj.* without sleeves *[a sleeveless sweater]*

sleeve·let (-lit) *n.* a covering fitted over the lower part of a garment sleeve, as to protect it from soiling

☆**sleigh** (slā) *n.* ⟦Du *slee*, contr. of *slede*, a SLED⟧ a light vehicle on runners, usually horse-drawn, for carrying persons over snow and ice —*vi.* to ride in or drive a sleigh

☆**sleigh bell** any of a number of small, spherical bells fixed to the harness straps of an animal drawing a sleigh: *usually used in pl.*

sleight (slīt) *n.* ⟦ME < ON *slægth* < *slægr*, crafty, clever: see SLY⟧ **1** cunning or craft used in deceiving **2** skill or dexterity

sleight of hand **1** skill with the hands, esp. in confusing or deceiving onlookers, as in doing magic tricks; legerdemain **2** a trick or tricks thus performed

slen·der (slen′dər) *adj.* ⟦ME *slendre, sclendre* < ?⟧ **1** small in width or girth; narrow *[a slender waist]* **2** having a slim, trim figure *[a slender girl]* **3** small or limited in amount, size, extent, etc.; meager *[a student living on slender means]* **4** of little force or validity; having slight foundation; feeble *[slender hope]* —**slen′der·ly** *adv.* —**slen′der·ness** *n.*

slen·der·ize (-īz′) *vt.* **-ized′**, **-iz′ing** to make slender or cause to seem slender —*vi.* to become slender

slept (slept) *vi., vt. pt. & pp. of* SLEEP

Sles·vig (sles′vikh) *Dan. name for* SCHLESWIG

sleuth (slo͞oth) *n.* ⟦ME, a trail, spoor < ON *slóth*, akin to *slothra*, to drag (oneself) ahead: for IE base see SLUG[1]⟧ **1** [Archaic] SLEUTHHOUND (sense 1) ☆**2** DETECTIVE (*n.* 2) —☆*vi.* [Informal] to act as a detective

sleuth·hound (slo͞oth′hound′) *n.* **1** [Archaic] a dog, as a bloodhound, able to follow a trail by scent **2** [Informal] a keen detective or investigator

☆**slew[1]** (slo͞o) *n. alt. sp. of* SLOUGH[2] (sense 4)

slew[2] (slo͞o) *n., vt., vi. alt. sp. of* SLUE[1]

☆**slew[3]** (slo͞o) *n.* ⟦Ir *sluagh*, a host⟧ [Informal] a large number, group, or amount *[a slew of reporters at the crime scene]*

slew[4] (slo͞o) *vt. pt. of* SLAY

slice (slīs) *n.* ⟦ME < OFr *esclice* < *esclicier*, to slice < Frank *slizzan*, akin to SLIT⟧ **1** a relatively thin, broad piece cut from an object having some bulk or volume *[a slice of apple]* **2** a part, portion, or share *[a slice of one's earnings]* **3** any of various implements with a flat, broad blade, as a spatula **4** *Golf, etc.* *a)* the path of a hit ball that curves away to the right from a right-handed player or to the left from a left-handed player *b)* a ball that follows such a path *c)* a tendency to hit a ball in this manner —*vt.* **sliced, slic′ing** **1** to cut into slices **2** *a)* to cut off as in a slice or slices (often with *off, from, away*, etc.) *b)* to cut across or through like a knife **3** to separate into parts or shares *[sliced up the profits]* **4** to use a SLICE (*n.* 3) to spread, remove, etc. **5** *Golf, etc.* to hit (a ball) in a SLICE (*n.* 4*a*) **6** *Tennis, etc.* to hit (the ball) with a downward sweep of the racket —*vi.* **1** to cut (*through*) like a knife *[a plow slicing through the earth]* **2** *Golf, etc.* *a)* to be hit in a SLICE (*n.* 4*a*) *b)* to hit a ball in a SLICE (*n.* 4*a*) —**slic′er** *n.*

slice of life ⟦transl. of Fr *tranche de (la) vie*, prob. coined by dramatist Jean Jullien (1854-1919)⟧ **1** the realistic description or representation, in literature, film, journalism, etc., of events and situations from everyday life **2** such an event or situation —**slice′-of-life′** *adj.*

slick (slik) *vt.* ⟦ME *slikien* < OE *slician*, to make smooth, akin to ON *slikr*, smooth < IE **(s)leig-*, slimy, to smooth, glide < base **(s)lei-*: see SLIDE⟧ **1** to make sleek, glossy, or smooth **2** [Informal] to make smart, neat, or tidy: usually with *up* —*adj.* ⟦ME *slike* < the v.⟧ **1** sleek; glossy; smooth **2** slippery; oily: said as of a surface **3** accomplished; adept; clever; ingenious **4** [Informal] clever in deception or trickery; deceptively plausible; smooth *[a slick alibi]* **5** [Informal] having or showing skill in composition or technique but little depth or literary significance *[a slick style of writing]* **6** [Slang] excellent, fine, enjoyable, attractive, etc. —*n.* ☆**1** *a)* a smooth area on the surface of water, as resulting from a layer of oil *b)* an oily layer on the surface of water *c)* a slippery, oily area on the surface of a road **2** something used for smoothing and polishing, as any of various tools with broad, flat blades ☆**3** [Informal] a magazine printed on paper with a glossy finish: distinguished from PULP (*n.* 7) —*adv.* smoothly, cleverly, deftly, easily, etc. —**slick′ly** *adv.* —**slick′ness** *n.*

slick·en·side (slik′ən sīd′) *n.* ⟦dial. *slicken*, var. of prec. + SIDE⟧ *Geol.* a smooth, polished rock surface produced by friction, pressure, or cleavage

slick·er (slik′ər) *n.* ⟦SLICK, *adj.* + -ER⟧ ☆**1** a loose, waterproof coat made of oil-treated cloth ☆**2** [Old Informal] a tricky, cleverly deceptive person: see also CITY SLICKER

slid·den (slid′'n) *vi., vt. archaic or dial. pp. of* SLIDE

slide (slīd) *vi.* **slid** (slid), **slid′ing** ⟦ME *sliden* < OE *slidan* < IE **(s)leidh-*, slippery < base **(s)lei-*, slimy, slippery > LIME[1], SLICK, SLIME⟧ **1** to move along in constant frictional contact with some surface or substance *[windows that slide open]* **2** to move in this manner on a sled, the feet, etc. in contact with a smooth surface, esp. snow or ice **3** to move quietly and smoothly; glide **4** to move stealthily or unobtrusively **5** to shift from a position; slip *[the wet cup slid from his hand]* **6** to pass gradually (*into* or *out of* some condition) *[to slide into bad habits]* **7** *Baseball* to drop down and slide along the ground toward a base to avoid being tagged out —*vt.* **1** to cause to slide; make move with a smooth, gliding motion **2** to move, place, or slip quietly, deftly, or stealthily (*in* or *into*) —*n.* **1** an act of sliding **2** a smooth, usually inclined track, surface, or chute down which to slide, as on a playground **3** something that works by sliding; part that slides or is slid on **4** a photographic transparency mounted for use with a viewer or projector **5** a small glass plate used as a mounting for objects to be examined under a microscope **6** *a)* the fall of a mass of rock, snow, earth, etc. down a slope ☆*b)* the mass that falls **7** ⟦so called because the wearer's foot can *slide* into it easily⟧ a heelless and, often, toeless shoe, usually for casual wear **8** *Music* *a)* PORTAMENTO *b)* an ornament made up of two or more notes ascending or descending to a principal note *c)* a U-shaped section of tubing which is moved to change the pitch of certain brass instruments, esp. the trombone —*adj.* ☆BOTTLENECK —**let something slide** [Informal] to fail to take some expected or required action on something

☆**slide fastener** a zipper or a zipperlike device having two grooved plastic edges joined or separated by a sliding tab, or pull

slide knot a kind of slipknot

slid·er (slīʹdər) ***n.*** **1** a person or thing that slides ☆**2** *Baseball* a type of pitch with the speed of a fastball and the movement of a curve

slide rule a once-common manual device like a ruler but with a central sliding piece, both parts being marked with various number scales: used to find square roots, logarithms, quotients, etc.

slide show **1** a sequential display of a series of photographic transparencies, using a slide projector **2** any sequential display of a series of still images, as on a computer screen

slide trombone *see* TROMBONE

slide valve a valve which opens and closes a passageway, as the cylinder port of a steam engine, by sliding back and forth across it

slid·ing (slīʹdiŋ) ***adj.*** **1** varying in accordance with given conditions **2** operating or moving on a track or groove, as a door or panel

sliding scale a standard or schedule, as of costs, wages, fees, tariff rates, etc., that varies in accordance with given conditions or standards, as cost of living, level of income, etc.

slight (slīt) ***adj.*** ⟦ME (northern dial.) *sliht* < OE, kin to OHG *sleht*, straight, smooth: for IE base see SLICK⟧ **1** *a)* light in form or build; not stout or heavy; slender *b)* frail; fragile **2** having little weight, strength, substance, or significance [a *slight* criticism] **3** small in amount or extent; not great or intense [a *slight* fever] —***vt.*** **1** to do carelessly or poorly; neglect **2** to treat with disrespect or indifference; be discourteous toward **3** to treat as unimportant —***n.*** a slighting or being slighted by pointedly indifferent, disrespectful, or supercilious treatment —**SYN.** NEGLECT —**slightʹly** ***adv.*** —**slightʹness** ***n.***

slight·est (slītʹist) ***adj.*** *superl. of* SLIGHT —**not in the slightest** not in the least; not at all

slight·ing (slītʹiŋ) ***adj.*** constituting a slight; disdainful; disparaging [a *slighting* remark] —**slightʹing·ly** ***adv.***

Sli·go (sliʹgō) county in Connacht province, NW Ireland: 693 sq mi (1,795 sq km)

sli·ly (slīʹlē) ***adv.*** *alt. sp. of* SLYLY

slim (slim) ***adj.*** **slimʹmer, slimʹmest** ⟦orig., useless, bad, weak < Du, crafty, bad, akin to Ger *schlimm*, bad⟧ **1** small in girth in proportion to height or length; slender **2** small in amount, degree, or extent; slight; scant; meager [*slim* pickings, a *slim* hope] — ***vt., vi.*** **slimmed, slimʹming** to make or become slim or slimmer: usually with *down* —***n.*** [**S-**] a nickname for a slim or lanky person —**slimʹly** ***adv.*** —**slimʹness** ***n.***

slime (slīm) ***n.*** ⟦ME < OE *slim*, akin to Ger *schleim* < IE base *(*s*)*lei-*, slimy: see SLIDE⟧ any soft, moist, slippery, sometimes sticky matter, as soft mud, the mucous coating on fish, etc.; specif., moist or sticky matter considered filthy or disgusting —***vt.*** **slimed, slimʹing** **1** to cover with slime **2** to clean slime from —***vi.*** to become slimy Often used fig.

slime·ball (slīmʹbôlʹ) ***n.*** [Slang] a disgusting, despicable person

slime mold (*or* fungus) MYXOMYCETE

☆**slim·sy** (slimʹzē) ***adj.*** **-si·er, -si·est** ⟦SL(IM) + (FL)IMSY⟧ [Old Informal] slight; flimsy

slim·y (slīmʹē) ***adj.*** **slimʹi·er, slimʹi·est** **1** of or like slime **2** covered with or full of slime **3** [Informal] disgusting, repulsive, despicable, etc. —**slimʹi·ly** ***adv.*** —**slimʹi·ness** ***n.***

sling[1] (sliŋ) ***n.*** ⟦ME *slinge* < the v.⟧ **1** *a)* a primitive instrument for throwing stones, etc., consisting of a piece of leather tied to cords that are whirled by hand for releasing the missile ☆*b)* SLINGSHOT **2** the act of throwing with or as with a sling; cast; throw; fling **3** *a)* a looped or hanging band, strap, etc. used in raising and lowering a heavy object or for carrying, supporting, or steadying something [a rifle *sling*] *b)* a wide piece of cloth suspended from the neck and looped under an injured arm for support **4** SLINGBACK —***vt.*** **slung, slingʹing** ⟦ME *slingen*, prob. < ON *slyngva*, to throw, akin to OE & OHG *slingan*, to twist oneself, worm along < IE base **slenk-*, to twist, turn, creep > SLINK[1], Lith *slenkù*, to creep⟧ **1** to throw (stones, etc.) with a sling **2** to throw, cast, fling, or hurl **3** to place, carry, raise, lower, etc. in a sling **4** to hang (something) with or as with a sling or slings [to *sling* a hammock between two trees] ☆**5** [Slang] to cook or serve (a specified food), as at a lunch counter or fast-food restaurant: a dismissive or humorous usage [*slinging* hash at a diner]

sling[2] (sliŋ) ***n.*** ⟦< ?⟧ an alcoholic drink made with gin, rum, brandy, whiskey, etc., water or soda water, sugar, and, usually, lemon juice

sling·back (sliŋʹbakʹ) ***n.*** a woman's open-heeled shoe held in place with a strap around the back of the ankle

sling·er (sliŋʹər) ***n.*** **1** a man using a sling for throwing missiles, as in ancient warfare **2** a person who throws or slings **3** a person operating, or supervising the use of, a sling, as in loading

slinger ring a ring-shaped tube, fitted around the hub of an airplane propeller, through which alcohol or some other de-icing fluid is applied to the blades by centrifugal force

☆**sling·shot** (sliŋʹshätʹ) ***n.*** a Y-shaped piece of wood, metal, etc. with an elastic band or bands attached to the upper tips for shooting stones, etc.

slink[1] (sliŋk) ***vi.*** **slunk, slinkʹing** ⟦ME *slinken* < OE *slincan*, to creep, crawl along, akin to LowG *slinken* < IE **sleng-*, var. of base **slenk-*, to wind, twist, turn > SLING[1]⟧ to move in a quiet, furtive, or sneaking manner, as from fear, guilt, etc.; sneak —**slinkʹing·ly** ***adv.***

slink[2] (sliŋk) ***vt.*** **slinked** or **slunk, slinkʹing** ⟦prob. < SLING[1]⟧ to expel (a fetus) prematurely: said of animals —***n.*** an animal, esp. a calf, born prematurely —***adj.*** born prematurely

slink·y (sliŋʹkē) ***adj.*** **slinkʹi·er, slinkʹi·est** ⟦SLINK[1] + -Y[2]⟧ **1** sneaking; stealthy; furtive **2** [Informal] attractively sleek and revealing, as by being, variously, brief, contoured, gauzy, etc.: said esp. of women's clothing [a *slinky* nightgown] **3** [Informal] sinuous and graceful in movement, outline, etc. —**slinkʹi·ness** ***n.***

slip[1] (slip) ***vi.*** **slipped, slipʹping** ⟦ME *slippen* < MLowG, akin to OHG *slifan* < IE *(*s*)*leib-*, to glide, slip < base *(*s*)*lei-*, slimy: see SLIDE⟧ **1** to go quietly or secretly; move without attracting notice [to *slip* out of a room] **2** *a)* to go, move, pass, etc. smoothly, quickly, or easily *b)* to get (*into* or *out of* clothes) quickly *c)* to go imperceptibly; pass unmarked [time *slipped* by] **3** to pass gradually into or out of some condition, activity, habit, opinion, etc. [to *slip* off to sleep] **4** to escape or pass from a person's memory, mind, power, grasp, etc. [to let a chance *slip* by] **5** to move out of place by sliding; shift or slide from position [a napkin *slipping* from one's lap] **6** to slide accidentally on a slippery surface, lose footing, etc. **7** to make a mistake; fall into error; err **8** to become worse; lose strength, ability, mental keenness, etc. **9** to decline slightly; fall off [a *slipping* market] **10** *Aeron.* SIDESLIP —***vt.*** **1** to cause to slip or move with a smooth, sliding motion **2** to put (*on*) or take (*off*) quickly or easily, as an article of clothing **3** to put, pass, insert, etc. quickly, deftly, or stealthily [to *slip* a pill into one's mouth, to *slip* in a cutting remark] **4** *a)* to escape or pass from (the mind or memory) *b)* [Now Rare] to let pass unheeded; overlook; miss **5** to get loose or away from (a restraint, pursuer, etc.); become free of [the dog *slipped* its leash] **6** to let loose (hounds) to pursue game **7** to transfer (a stitch) from one needle to another without knitting it, as in forming patterns in, or decreasing the width of, a knitted piece **8** to slink (a fetus) **9** to put out of joint; dislocate **10** *Naut.* to free an anchored ship from (the anchor) by parting or unshackling the cable —***n.*** **1** *a)* SLIPWAY ☆*b)* a water channel between piers or wharves, used for the docking of ships **2** a leash for a dog made so that it can be released quickly **3** *a)* a woman's sleeveless undergarment the same length as a dress, usually suspended from shoulder straps *b)* a petticoat or HALF SLIP **4** a cloth cover for a pillow **5** an act of slipping, sliding, or falling down **6** a deviation or turning aside, esp. from a practice, course of conduct, etc. considered right **7** an error or mistake, esp. one made inadvertently in speaking, writing, etc. **8** an accident or mishap **9** the amount or degree of operative inefficiency of a mechanical device, expressed in terms of the difference between theoretical and actual output **10** movement of one part upon another, usually where no movement is meant to exist; play **11** *Aeron.* SIDESLIP **12** *Cricket* a fielder placed behind the wickets on the off side of the batter **13** *Geol.* *a)* any movement displacing parts of rock or soil masses in relation to one another; small fault or landslide *b)* a smooth surface or joint where such movement has taken place **14** *Metallurgy* the process by which plastic deformation is produced in metal crystals by one part of a crystal moving in relation to another, usually in a particular crystallographic plane —**SYN.** ERROR —**give someone the slip** [Slang] to evade or escape from someone —**let slip** to say or reveal without intending to —☆**slip one over on** [Informal] to trick; hoodwink; cheat —☆**slip up** [Informal] to make a mistake, esp. a careless one

slip[2] (slip) ***n.*** ⟦ME *slippe* < MDu < *slippen*, to cut⟧ **1** a stem, root, twig, etc. cut or broken off a plant and used for planting or grafting; cutting; scion **2** a young, slim person: archaic except in the phrase **slip of a** [a mere *slip* of a girl] **3** a long, thin piece or strip, as of cloth **4** a small piece of paper, esp. one prepared for a specific use [an order *slip*] ☆**5** a narrow church pew —***vt.*** **slipped, slipʹping** to take a slip from (a plant) for planting or grafting

slip[3] (slip) ***n.*** ⟦ME < OE *slyppe, slypa*, paste, slime, dropping < IE base *(*s*)*leub-*, to glide, slip > SLEEVE, L *lubricus*, slippery⟧ *Ceramics* clay thinned to the consistency of cream for use in decorating or casting, or as a cement or coating

slip·case (slipʹkāsʹ) ***n.*** a boxlike container for a book or set of books, open at one end to expose the spine or spines —**slipʹcasedʹ** ***adj.***

slip·cov·er (-kuvʹər) ***n.*** a removable, fitted cloth cover for an armchair, sofa, etc. —***vt.*** **-covʹered, -covʹer·ing** to cover (a chair, etc.) with a slipcover

slip-joint (-jointʹ) ***adj.*** **1** designating or of pliers having an adjustable pivot for expanding the angle of the jaws **2** designating or of a FOLDING KNIFE with a pivot that does not lock into place

slip·knot (-nätʹ) ***n.*** a knot made so that it will slip along the rope, etc. around which it is tied

slip noose a noose made with a slipknot

slip-on (-änʹ) ***adj.*** easily put on or taken off, as shoes without laces, or a garment to be slipped on or off over the head —***n.*** a slip-on shoe or garment

slip·o·ver (-ōʹvər) ***adj., n.*** PULLOVER

slip·page (slipʹij) ***n.*** **1** the act or an instance of slipping, as in meshing gear teeth **2** the amount of this **3** the resulting loss of motion or power, as in a chain or belt drive

slipped disk a ruptured disk between two vertebrae, esp. of the lumbar spine, often causing sciatica

slip·per (slipʹər) ***n.*** a light, low shoe easily slipped onto the foot, esp. one for indoor wear —**slipʹpered** ***adj.***

slipper sock a SOCK[1] (*n.* 3) with a sole of leather, etc. or with nonskid ridges, for wearing indoors like a slipper

slip·per·y (slipʹər ē, slipʹrē) ***adj.*** **-per·i·er, -per·i·est** ⟦altered < ME *sliper*, slippery < OE *slipor*, akin to MHG *slupferic*: for IE base see SLIP[1]⟧ **1** causing or liable to cause sliding or slipping, as a wet, waxed, or greasy surface **2**

tending to slip away, as from a grasp **3** not reliable or trustworthy; deceitful **4** subject to change [*a slippery* situation] **5** [Obs.] immoral —**slip′per·i·ness** *n.*

☆**slippery elm 1** a wide-branching North American elm (*Ulmus rubra*) with fragrant, mucilaginous inner bark and hard wood **2** the wood or bark

slippery slope a course or situation regarded as easily or inevitably leading to further decline or deterioration

slip·py (slip′ē) *adj.* **1** [Informal or Dial.] SLIPPERY **2** [Brit. Informal] alert; sharp; quick

slip ring *Elec.* a metal ring mounted on, and insulated from, the rotor shaft of a generator or motor, designed to lead current into or away from the coils through a stationary brush pressing on the ring

slip·sheet (slip′shēt′) *n.* a blank sheet of paper inserted between freshly printed sheets to prevent offset — *vt., vi.* to insert slipsheets between (printed sheets)

slip·shod (-shäd′) *adj.* ⟦SLIP[1] + SHOD < dial. or obs. *slip-shoe*, slipper⟧ **1** [Archaic] wearing shoes with worn-down heels **2** careless, as in appearance or workmanship [*a slipshod* job]

slip·slop (-släp′) *n.* ⟦redupl. of SLOP⟧ [Old Informal] **1** sloppy or watery food or drink **2** shallow, pointless talk or writing

slip·sole (-sōl′) *n.* **1** a half sole between the bottom sole and the insole **2** INSOLE (sense 2)

slip stitch 1 *Sewing* a continuous stitch for a folded edge, especially a hem, in which the fabric is fastened together by a series of extra long stitches in the back and small, widely spaced stitches in the front that are intended to be nearly invisible **2** *a) Knitting* a stitch that is passed from one needle to the other without being worked *b)* in crocheting, a short stitch made by passing the yarn through one or more loops, usually used to connect chains of stitches, join pieces, finish an edge, etc.

slip·stream (-strēm′) *n.* the current of air thrust backward by the spinning propeller of an aircraft; propeller wash

slipt (slipt) *vi., vt. archaic or old poetic pt. of* SLIP[1]

☆**slip-up** (slip′up′) *n.* [Informal] **1** an error or oversight **2** an unlucky happening; mishap Also written **slipup**

slip·ware (slip′wer′) *n.* pottery decorated by the surface application of SLIP[3], which may be carved, painted, etc.

slip·way (-wā′) *n.* an inclined plane leading down into the water, on which ships are built or repaired

slit (slit) *vt.* **slit, slit′ting** ⟦ME *slitten* < OE **slittan*, akin to MHG *slitzen* < WGmc **slitjan* < base of Gmc **slitan* (> OE *slitan*) < IE base **(s)kel-*, to cut > SHIELD, SHELL⟧ **1** to cut or split open, esp. by a straight incision **2** to cut into strips **3** to cut (*off*); sever —*n.* **1** a cut or tear, esp. one that is long and straight **2** a long, narrow opening or crack —**slit′ter** *n.*

slith·er (slith′ər) *vi.* ⟦ME *slitheren*, var. of *slideren* < OE *sliderian*, freq. < base of *slidan*, to SLIDE⟧ **1** to slip or slide on or as on a slope with a loose or broken surface **2** *a)* to move along by sliding or gliding, as a snake *b)* to walk with a sliding motion —*vt.* to cause to slither or slide —*n.* a sliding, slithering motion

slith·er·y (-ē) *adj.* **1** slippery **2** like or characterized by a slither [*a slithery* walk]

slit trench a narrow, relatively shallow trench for protecting a soldier from shellfire, bombs, etc.

sliv·er (sliv′ər) *n.* ⟦ME *slivere* < *sliven*, to cut, cleave < OE *slifan*, to split < IE **skleip-* < base **(s)kel-*: see SLIT⟧ **1** a thin, sharp piece that has been cut, split, or broken off something; splinter **2** any slender fragment or portion [the cresecent moon was a *sliver* of light] **3** a loose, thin, continuous fiber or strand, as of wool or flax after carding, ready to be drawn and twisted —*vt., vi.* to cut or break into slivers

sliv·o·vitz (sliv′ə vits′) *n.* ⟦Serb *sljivovica* < *sliva*, plum < OSlav: see LIVID⟧ a usually colorless plum brandy made esp. in E Europe

Sloan (slōn), **John (French)** 1871-1951; U.S. painter & etcher

slob (släb) *n.* ⟦Ir *slab*, mud < Scand: see SLAB[2]⟧ [Informal] a sloppy, coarse, or gross person —**slob′by** *adj.*

slob·ber (släb′ər) *vi.* ⟦ME *sloberen*, prob. < or akin to LowG *slubberen*, to swig, lap: for IE base see SLOVEN⟧ **1** to let saliva, food, etc. run from the mouth; slaver **2** to speak, write, etc. in a mawkish or maudlin way —*vt.* to wet, smear, or dribble on with saliva —*n.* **1** saliva, etc. running from the mouth **2** mawkish talk or writing —**slob′ber·er** *n.* —**slob′ber·y** *adj.*

slob ice a dense mass of sludge or floating ice

sloe (slō) *n.* ⟦ME *slo* < OE *sla*, akin to Ger *schlehe*, Russ & OSlav *sliva*, plum: see LIVID⟧ **1** BLACKTHORN (sense 1) **2** the small, blue-black, plumlike fruit of the blackthorn **3** any of various wild plums

sloe-eyed (slō′īd′) *adj.* **1** having large, dark eyes **2** having almond-shaped eyes

☆**sloe gin** a red liqueur made of dry gin flavored with sloes

slog[1] (släg) *vt., vi.* **slogged, slog′ging** ⟦var. of SLUG[4]⟧ to hit hard; slug —**slog′ger** *n.*

slog[2] (släg) *vt., vi.* **slogged, slog′ging** ⟦ME *sluggen*: see SLUGGARD⟧ **1** to make (one's way) with great effort; plod **2** to work hard (*at something*); toil [*slogging* away at her work] —*n.* **1** hard work done persistently **2** an arduous, lengthy, and, sometimes, boring trip, effort, or task [*a slog* through deep snow] —**slog′ger** *n.*

slo·gan (slō′gən) *n.* ⟦Gael *sluggh-ghairm* < *sluagh*, a host + *gairm*, a call⟧ **1** [Historical] a cry used by Scottish Highland and Irish clans in battle or as an assembly signal **2** a catchword or rallying motto distinctly associated with a political party or other group **3** a catchphrase used to advertise a product

☆**slo·gan·eer** (slō′gə nir′) *vi.* to coin or make use of slogans —*n.* a person who coins or uses slogans

☆**slo·gan·ize** (slō′gə nīz′) *vt.* **-ized′, -iz′ing** to express or generalize in the form of a slogan —**slo′gan·is′tic** *adj.*

slo-mo (slō′mō′) [Informal] *n.* SLOW MOTION —*adj.* SLOW-MOTION

sloop (slo͞op) *n.* ⟦Du *sloep* < LowG *sluup* < *slupen* (akin to OE *slupan*), to glide: for IE base see SLIP[3]⟧ a fore-and-aft-rigged, single-masted sailing vessel with a mainsail and a jib

sloop of war [Historical] a small sailing warship with guns mounted on one deck only

slop (släp) *n.* ⟦ME *sloppe* < OE (only in comp.) < base of *slypa*: see SLIP[3]⟧ **1** watery snow or mud; slush **2** a splash or puddle of spilled liquid **3** any liquid or semiliquid food that is unappetizing or of poor quality **4** [*often pl.*] *a)* liquid waste of any kind ☆*b)* kitchen waste or swill, used for feeding pigs, etc. **5** [Informal] excessively sentimental speech or writing See also SLOPS —*vi.* **slopped, slop′ping 1** to spill or splash **2** to walk or splash through slush or mud —*vt.* **1** to spill liquid on **2** to spill ☆**3** to feed swill or slops to (pigs, etc.) —**slop over 1** to overflow or spill, as a liquid when its container is tilted ☆**2** [Informal] to make a display of sentimentality; gush

slop bowl (*or* basin) [Chiefly Brit.] a bowl into which the dregs from tea cups are emptied at table

slope (slōp) *n.* ⟦ME < *aslope*, sloping (mistaken as *a slope*) < OE *aslopen*, pp. of *aslupan*, to slip away < *slupan*, to glide: see SLOOP⟧ **1** a piece of ground that is not flat or level; rising or falling ground; specif., a portion of the side of a hill or mountain [*a ski slope*] **2** any inclined line, surface, position, etc.; slant **3** *a)* deviation from the horizontal or vertical *b)* the amount or degree of this **4** ⟦from the notion that the epicanthus of East Asians makes the eye appear slanted⟧ [Slang] a native of East Asia, often, specif., of Vietnam: an offensive term of hostility and contempt ☆**5** the land area that drains into a given ocean **6** *Math, a)* the trigonometric tangent of the positive angle formed between a given straight line and the x-axis of a pair of Cartesian coordinates *b)* the slope of the tangent line to a given curve at a designated point —*vi.* **sloped, slop′ing 1** to have an upward or downward inclination; take an oblique direction; incline; slant **2** [Informal, Chiefly Brit.] to go or move (*off, away*, etc.), esp. in a leisurely or furtive way —*vt.* to cause to slope —*adj.* [Old Poet.] that slopes; slanting; inclined —**the slopes** an area used or reserved for downhill skiing —**slop′er** *n.*

slo pitch (slō) *alt. sp. of* SLOW PITCH: also written **slo′-pitch′** *n.*

slop·py (släp′ē) *adj.* **-pi·er, -pi·est 1** consisting of or covered with slop; wet and splashy; muddy; slushy **2** splashed or spotted with liquids **3** *a)* very untidy; showing lack of care; slovenly or messy *b)* careless; slipshod **4** [Informal] gushingly sentimental —**slop′pi·ly** *adv.* —**slop′pi·ness** *n.*

☆**sloppy Joe** [*also* **s- j-**] a dish consisting of ground meat cooked with tomato sauce, spices, etc. and served on a bun: also **sloppy Joes (or joes)**

slops (släps) *pl.n.* ⟦ME *sloppes*, pl. of *slop, sloppe* < OE *-slop* (as in *oferslop*, loose outer garment); akin to *sliefe*, SLEEVE⟧ **1** loosefitting outer garments; specif., *a)* [*sing.*] a smock, coveralls, or the like *b)* [Archaic] baggy trousers or breeches **2** clothing, bedding, etc. issued or sold to sailors **3** cheap, ready-made clothing

☆**slop sink** a deep sink for filling and emptying scrub pails, washing out mops, etc.

slop·work (släp′wurk′) *n.* **1** the manufacture of cheap clothing **2** work that is carelessly done —**slop′work′er** *n.*

slosh (släsh) *vt.* ⟦var. of SLUSH⟧ **1** to shake or agitate (a liquid or something in a liquid) **2** to apply (a liquid) lavishly or carelessly —*vi.* **1** to splash or move clumsily through water, mud, etc. **2** to splash about: said of a liquid —*n.* **1** SLUSH (*n.* 1) **2** the sound of liquid splashing about —**slosh′y** *adj.*

sloshed (släsht) *adj.* [Slang] drunk

slot[1] (slät) *n.* ⟦ME, a bar, bolt < OFr *esclot* < Frank **sclot*; akin to Ger *schliessen*, to lock: see CLOSE[2]⟧ **1** a narrow notch, groove, or opening, as a keyway in a piece of machinery, a slit for a coin in a vending machine, etc. **2** any of various openings in the wing or tail surface of an airplane used in connection with a high-lift or control device; specif., an air gap between the wing and an auxiliary airfoil, as an aileron or flap, providing for a smooth flow of air on the upper surface ☆**3** a position in a group, series, sequence, etc. **4** [Informal] *short for* SLOT MACHINE: *often used in pl.* —*vt.* **slot′ted, slot′ting 1** to make a slot or slots in ☆**2** to place in a particular position within a series or sequence —*vi.* to fit into place readily or easily in a SLOT[1] (*n.* 1 & 3): with *into* or *in*

slot[2] (slät) *n.* ⟦OFr *esclot* < ? ON *sloth*: see SLEUTHHOUND⟧ a track or trail of an animal, esp. a deer —*vt.* **slot′ted, slot′ting** to follow the trail of

☆**slot·back** (slät′bak′) *n.* *Football* an offensive back positioned just behind and between an offensive tackle and a split end

☆**slot car** a miniature, electrically driven, toy race car, raced against other such cars over a slotted track: each car is remotely controlled as by a hand-held rheostat

sloth (slôth, släth; *also, and chiefly Brit,* slōth) *n.* ⟦ME *slouthe* < *slou*, slow, used for older *slewthe, sleuthe* < OE *slæwth*, sloth < *slaw*, slow: see SLOW & -TH[1]⟧ **1** disinclination to work or exert oneself; indolence; laziness; idleness **2** [Now

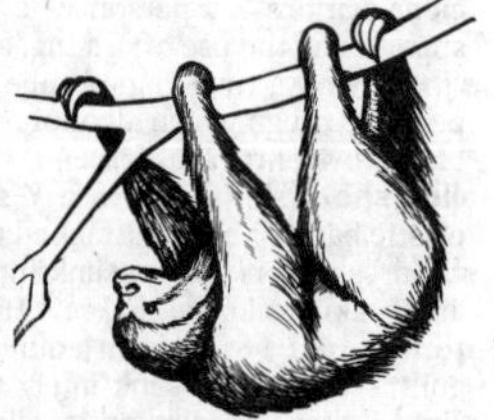

three-toed sloth

Rare] slowness; delay **3** *a)* any of a family (Bradypodidae) of slow-moving, tree-dwelling edentate mammals of tropical Central and South America that hang, back down, from branches and feed on fruits and vegetation, including a three-toed species (genus *Bradypus*) and a two-toed species (genus *Choloepus*) *b)* any of various families of extinct, ground-dwelling edentate mammals

sloth bear a bear (*Melursus ursinus*) with shaggy, black fur, a flexible snout, and long, white claws: it is found in India and Sri Lanka and feeds chiefly on fruits and insects

sloth·ful (-fəl) *adj.* characterized by sloth; indolent; lazy —**sloth′ful·ly** *adv.* —**sloth′ful·ness** *n.*

slot machine a machine worked or started by inserting a coin or token in a slot; specif., *a)* a vending machine *b)* a gambling device having a lever that is pulled to spin disks and turn up symbols, various combinations of which indicate the results

slouch (slouch) *n.* ⟦< ? dial. *slouk*, a lazy fellow < ON *slōkr* < *slōka*, to hang down, droop < IE *(s)leug-, var. of base *(s)leu-, to hang limply > SLUG¹, SLEET⟧ ☆**1** *a)* a person who is awkward or lazy *b)* [Informal] a person who is incompetent (usually with a negative) [she's no *slouch* at golf] **2** *a)* a drooping or bending forward of the head and shoulders *b)* slovenly posture in general **3** a hanging down or drooping, as of a hat brim —*vi.* **1** to sit, stand, walk, etc. in a slouch **2** to droop, as a hat brim —*vt.* to cause to slouch

slouch hat a soft hat with a broad, drooping brim

slouch·y (slou′chē) *adj.* **slouch′i·er, slouch′i·est** slouching, esp. in posture —**slouch′i·ly** *adv.* —**slouch′i·ness** *n.*

slough¹ (sluf) *n.* ⟦ME *slouh*, akin to Ger *schlauch*, a skin, bag < IE base *sleuĝ-, to glide, slip > Latvian *sl'užât*, to slide⟧ **1** the skin of a snake, esp. the outer layer that is periodically cast off **2** any castoff layer, covering, etc.: often used fig. **3** *Med.* a mass of dead tissue in, or separating from, living tissue or an ulceration —*vi.* ⟦< the *n.*⟧ **1** *a)* to be shed, cast off, or discarded; come off *b)* to drop off; become fewer or less **2** to shed skin or other covering **3** *Med.* to separate from the surrounding tissue: said of dead tissue Often with *off* —*vt.* **1** to shed or throw *off* (slough); get rid of **2** *Bridge* to get rid of (a card); discard —**slough over** to gloss over; minimize —**slough′y** *adj.*

slough² (slou; *for 4* sloo) *n.* ⟦ME *slowe* < OE *sloh*, akin to MLowG *slōch*, swamp < IE base *slĕk, wet > SLACK³⟧ **1** a place, as a hollow, full of soft, deep mud **2** ⟦after *Slough of Despond*, a deep swamp in Bunyan's *Pilgrim's Progress*⟧ deep, hopeless dejection or discouragement **3** moral degradation **4** a swamp, bog, or marsh, esp. one that is part of an inlet or backwater —**slough′y** *adj.*

Slo·vak (slō′väk′, -vak′) *n.* **1** a member of a Slavic people living chiefly in Slovakia **2** the West Slavic language of this people, closely related to Czech —*adj.* of Slovakia or its people, language, or culture

Slo·va·ki·a (slō vä′kē ə, -vak′ē ə) country in central Europe: formerly the E constituent republic of Czechoslovakia: 18,859 sq mi (48,845 sq km); cap. Bratislava —**Slo·va′ki·an** (-vä′kē ən, -vak′-) *adj., n.*

slov·en (sluv′ən) *n.* ⟦ME *slovein*, prob. < MDu *slof*, lax, limp (< IE base *(s)leubh-, to hang loosely > SLOBBER, Lith *slùbnas*, limp) + Anglo-Fr *-ain*, *-ein*, -AN⟧ a person who is careless in appearance, habits, work, etc.; dirty or untidy person

Slo·ve·ni·a (slō vē′nē ə, -vēn′yə) country in the NW Balkan Peninsula: formerly a constituent republic of Yugoslavia (1946-91): 7,827 sq mi (20,273 sq km); cap. Ljubljana

Slo·ve·ni·an (slō vē′nē ən, -vēn′yən) *n.* **1** a member of a Slavic people living chiefly in Slovenia **2** the South Slavic language of this people —*adj.* of Slovenia or its people, language, or culture Also **Slo·vene** (slō′vēn′, slō vēn′)

slov·en·ly (sluv′ən lē) *adj.* **1** characteristic of a sloven **2** careless in appearance, habits, work, etc.; untidy; slipshod —*adv.* in a slovenly manner —**slov′en·li·ness** *n.*

Slo·ven·sko (slô′ven skô′) *Czech name for* SLOVAKIA

slow (slō) *adj.* ⟦ME *slowe* < OE *slaw*, akin to Du *sleeuw*, ON *slær*, dull < ?⟧ **1** not quick or clever in understanding; dull; obtuse **2** *a)* taking a longer time than is expected or usual to act, move, go, happen, etc. *b)* not hasty, quick, ready, or prompt [a *slow* retort, *slow* to anger] **3** making relatively little progress for the time spent; marked by low speed, rate of rhythm, etc.; not fast or rapid **4** holding back fast progress, development, etc.; making speed or progress difficult [a *slow* growing season, a *slow* track] **5** showing a time that is behind the correct time: said of a timepiece **6** *a)* passing slowly or tediously [a *slow* afternoon] *b)* not lively or interesting; dull or boring [a *slow* town] **7** characterized by little activity; slack [*slow* trading] **8** lacking in energy; sluggish **9** behind the times; out of fashion **10** burning so as to give off a low or moderate heat [a *slow* fire] **11** gradual, as growth **12** *Photog.* *a)* having less sensitivity to light than other film, etc.: such film may require a longer exposure period *b)* allowing less light to enter than other lenses —*vt.* **1** to make slow or slower **2** to retard; delay Often with *up* or *down* —*vi.* to go or become slow or slower: often with *up* or *down* —*adv.* in a slow manner or at a slow speed; slowly —**SYN.** STUPID —**slow′ly** *adv.* —**slow′ness** *n.*

slow burn ☆[Slang] a gradual working up or show of anger: often in the phrase **do a slow burn**

slow·down (slō′doun′) *n.* a slowing down, as of production

slow match a match, or fuse, that burns slowly, used for setting off blasting charges

slow motion **1** slow-motion movement or action **2** an effect using slow-motion photography or video techniques

slow-mo·tion (-mō′shən) *adj.* **1** moving or operating below usual or normal speed **2** designating a film or taped TV sequence in which the action is made to appear slower than the actual action by exposing more frames per second than is usual and projecting the film at normal speed or by filming or taping at normal speed and projecting or replaying at a lower than usual speed

slow-mov·ing (-mōōv′iŋ) *adj.* **1** moving slowly; showing little progress or activity **2** selling in a relatively small quantity or at a slow rate, as merchandise, stocks, etc.

slow oven an oven heated to a relatively low temperature, for slow, or gradual, cooking

slow pitch a variety of softball in which the ball is pitched with an underhand motion at moderate speed in an arc that rises at least six feet above the ground: cf. FAST PITCH

☆**slow·poke** (-pōk′) *n.* [Slang] a person who acts or moves slowly

slow time [Informal] standard time, as distinguished from daylight saving time

slow virus any of a number of viruses or viruslike infective agents that incubate for months or years before the manifestation of symptoms

slow-wit·ted (-wit′id) *adj.* having a mind that works slowly and ineffectively; not bright or alert; dull —**slow′-wit′ted·ly** *adv.* —**slow′-wit′ted·ness** *n.*

slow·worm (-wurm′) *n.* ⟦altered (by assoc. with SLOW) < ME *slaworme* < OE *slawyrm* < *sla-*, akin to Norw *slo*, slowworm, ult. < IE base *(s)lei-, slimy (> LIME¹, Gr *leimax*, snail) + OE *wyrm*, WORM⟧ BLINDWORM

SLR (es′el′är′) *n.* ⟦*s*(ingle) *l*(ens) *r*(eflex)⟧ SINGLE-LENS REFLEX

slub (slub) *n.* ⟦< ?⟧ **1** a roll of fiber, as of wool or cotton, twisted slightly for use in spinning **2** a soft lump or thick irregular place in yarn or fabric —*vt.* **slubbed, slub′bing** to draw out (fibers of wool, cotton, etc.) and twist slightly for use in spinning

sludge (sluj) *n.* ⟦var. of *slutch*, sludge, mud: akin to ME *sluchched*, muddy, prob. ult. < IE base *(s)leu-, to hang limply > SLEET, MHG *slote*, mud, ooze⟧ **1** mud, mire, or ooze covering the ground or forming a deposit at the bottom of bodies of water **2** spongy lumps of drift ice **3** any heavy, slimy deposit, sediment, or mass, as the waste resulting from oil refining, the mud brought up by a mining drill, the precipitate in a sewage tank, the sediment in a steam boiler or crankcase, etc. —**sludg′y** *adj.* **sludg′i·er, sludg′i·est**

sludge·worm (sluj′wurm′) *n.* a small, freshwater tubifex worm (*Tubifex tubifex*) able to live in very low oxygen concentrations, as in sewage sludges and other bottom muds rich in organic matter

slue¹ (slōō) *vt., vi.* **slued, slu′ing** ⟦< ?⟧ to turn or swing around as on a pivot or fixed point —*n.* **1** the act of sluing **2** the position to which a thing has been slued

slue² (slōō) *n. alt. sp. of* SLOUGH² (sense 4)

slue³ (slōō) *n. alt. sp. of* SLEW³

sluff (sluf) *n., vi., vt. alt. sp. of* SLOUGH¹

slug¹ (slug) *n.* ⟦ME *slugge*, slow, clumsy person or thing < Scand, as in Swed dial. *slogga*, to be sluggish < IE base *(s)leu-, to hang loosely, lax > SLUDGE⟧ **1** any of a large number of small, gastropod mollusks, esp. the ones resembling a land snail, but having only a rudimentary internal shell buried in the mantle **2** a smooth, soft moth (family Eucleidae) or sawfly larva, resembling a slug **3** a person, vehicle, etc. that moves sluggishly

slug² (slug) *n.* ⟦prob. < prec.⟧ **1** a small piece or lump of metal; specif., a bullet ☆**2** a piece of metal shaped like and used in place of a coin in automatic coin machines; esp., such a substitute coin when used illegally ☆**3** *Printing* *a)* a strip of metal used to add space between lines of type *b)* a line of type made in one piece or strip, as by a linotype machine *c)* a short heading, often a single word, indicating the subject of copy **4** *Physics* a unit of mass, equal to *c.* 14.6 kg (*c.* 32.2 lb), to which a force of one pound imparts an acceleration of one foot per second per second —*vt.* **slugged, slug′ging** *Printing* to insert (a slug) between lines

slug³ (slug) *n.* ⟦prob. < Dan *sluge*, to gulp; akin to Ger *schlucken*, to swallow < IE base *(s)leug- > OIr *slucim*, (I) swallow⟧ [Slang] a single drink, esp. of straight alcoholic liquor

slug⁴ (slug) [Informal] *vt.* **slugged, slug′ging** ⟦< dial. (Shetland) *slog*, *slag*, a blow < ON *slag*, akin to OE *slean*, to strike: see SLAY⟧ to hit hard [to *slug* someone in the nose, to *slug* a baseball over the fence] —*n.* a hard blow or hit

slug·a·bed (slug′ə bed′) *n.* ⟦< ME *sluggen* (see SLUGGARD) + BED⟧ [Old-fashioned] a lazy person who stays in bed when he or she should be up

☆**slug·fest** (slug′fest′) *n.* ⟦SLUG⁴ + -FEST⟧ [Informal] **1** a fight or boxing match characterized by much heavy punching **2** a baseball game in which many hits are made

slug·gard (slug′ərd) *n.* ⟦ME *slogarde* < *sluggen*, to be lazy, go slowly, prob. < Scand, as in Swed dial. *slogga*, to be slow: see SLUG¹ & -ARD⟧ a habitually lazy or idle person —*adj.* lazy or idle: also **slug′gard·ly**

☆**slug·ger** (slug′ər) *n.* [Informal] a person who slugs; specif., *a)* a prizefighter who punches hard *b)* a baseball player with a high percentage of home runs

☆**slugging percentage** *Baseball* a number expressing a player's average effectiveness in making extra-base hits, calculated by dividing the total number of bases (from all singles, doubles, triples, and home runs) by the number of official at bats: also **slugging average**

slug·gish (slug′ish) *adj.* ⟦< SLUG[1] + -ISH⟧ **1** lacking energy, alertness, or vigor; indisposed to exertion; slothful **2** not active; slow or slow-moving; dull **3** not functioning with normal vigor —**slug′gish·ly** *adv.* —**slug′gish·ness** *n.*

sluice (slo͞os) *n.* ⟦ME *scluse* < OFr *escluse* & LL *exclusa* < fem. pp. of L *excludere*, to shut out, EXCLUDE⟧ **1** an artificial channel or passage for water, having a gate or valve at its head to regulate the flow, as in a canal or millstream **2** the water held back by or passing through such a gate **3** a gate or valve used in opening or closing a sluice; floodgate: also **sluice gate** **4** any channel, esp. one for excess water ☆**5** a sloping trough or flume through which water is run, as in washing gold ore, carrying logs, etc. —*vt.* **sluiced, sluic′ing** **1** to draw off by or as by means of a sluice **2** *a)* *Mining* to wash with water flowing in or from a sluice *b)* to wash off with a rush of water [to *sluice* a deck with hoses] ☆**3** to carry (logs, etc.) in a sluice —*vi.* to run or flow in or as in a sluice

☆**sluice·way** (slo͞os′wā′) *n.* an artificial channel for water, with or without a floodgate; sluice

slum (slum) *n.* ⟦*c.* 1800 < cant: orig. sense, "a room" < ?⟧ **1** a usually heavily populated area of a city, characterized by poverty, poor housing, etc. **2** something considered to be like a slum, as in being dilapidated or dirty —*vi.* **slummed, slum′ming** [Informal] **1** to visit a slum or other place condescendingly regarded as inferior to what one is accustomed to **2** to deal with conditions or engage in an activity condescendingly regarded as inferior to what one is accustomed to Often in the phrase **slum it** —[Informal] **slum′mer** *n.* — [Informal] **slum′my** *adj.* **-mi·er, -mi·est**

slum·ber (slum′bər) *vi.* ⟦ME *slumeren* < OE *slumerian* < *sluma*, slumber: for IE base see SLUG[1]⟧ **1** to sleep **2** to be dormant, negligent, or inactive —*vt.* to spend in sleeping —*n.* **1** sleep **2** an inactive state —**slum′ber·er** *n.*

slum·ber·land (-land′) *n.* the state of being asleep: a jocular term

slum·ber·ous (slum′bər əs) *adj.* **1** inclined to slumber; sleepy; drowsy **2** suggestive of or characterized by slumber **3** causing sleep or drowsiness; soporific **4** tranquil; calm; quiet [a *slumberous* little town] Also **slum′brous** (-brəs) —*SYN.* SLEEPY

☆**slumber party** a SLEEPOVER (sense 2) for girls, esp. teenage girls

☆**slum·gul·lion** (slum′gul′yən) *n.* ⟦< ?⟧ [Informal] any inexpensive stew or hash

☆**slum·lord** (slum′lôrd′) *n.* ⟦SLUM + (LAND)LORD⟧ [Slang] an absentee landlord of slum dwellings, esp. one who charges inflated rents and neglects upkeep

slump (slump) *vi.* ⟦prob. < or akin to MLowG *slumpen*, to come about by accident: for IE base see LIMP[1]⟧ **1** to fall, sink, or collapse, esp. suddenly or heavily **2** to decline suddenly, as in value, activity, etc. **3** to have a drooping posture or gait —*n.* **1** a sudden or sharp fall **2** a decline in business activity, prices, etc. **3** a drooping posture or gait ☆**4** an extended period during which a player, team, worker, etc. is below normal in performance

slung (sluŋ) *vt. pt. & pp. of* SLING[1]

☆**slung shot** a small, heavy weight attached to a strap or thong, used like a blackjack

slunk[1] (sluŋk) *vi. pt. & pp. of* SLINK[1]

slunk[2] (sluŋk) *vt. alt. pt. & pp. of* SLINK[2]

slur (slʉr) *vt.* **slurred, slur′ring** ⟦prob. < MDu *sleuren*, to drag, move slowly, trail in mud: for IE base see SLUG[1]⟧ **1** to pass over quickly and carelessly; make little of: often with *over* **2** to pronounce rapidly and indistinctly, as by combining or dropping sounds **3** [Dial.] to stain, smirch, or sully **4** to blur or smear, as in printing **5** to disparage or discredit; cast aspersions on **6** *Music a)* to sing or play (different and successive notes) by gliding from one to another without a break *b)* to mark (notes) with a slur —*n.* **1** the act or process of slurring **2** something slurred, as a pronunciation **3** a blot, stain, or smear **4** any remark or action that harms or is meant to harm someone's reputation; aspersion, reproach, stigma, etc. **5** *Music a)* a curved line written above or below two or more successive notes of different pitch that are to be sounded without a noticeable break *b)* a group of such notes

slurp (slʉrp) [Informal] *vt., vi.* ⟦Du *slurpen*, to sip, lap, akin to Ger *schlürfen*; prob. ult. < IE echoic base **serbh-*, to slurp > L *sorbere*, to suck in⟧ to drink or eat noisily —*n.* a loud sipping or sucking sound

slur·ry (slʉr′ē) *n., pl.* **-ries** ⟦ME *slory* < *slore*, thin mud < MDu, akin to SLUR⟧ a thin, watery mixture of a fine, insoluble material, as clay or cement

slush (slush) *n.* ⟦prob. < Scand, as in Dan *sluske*, ult. < IE base **(s)leu-* > SLEET⟧ **1** a heavy, wet mixture of snow, ice, and water **2** soft mud; mire **3** any of several greasy compounds used as lubricants or rust preventives for machinery ☆**4** overly sentimental talk or writing; drivel ☆**5** a confection consisting of shaved or crushed ice with a syrup, usually fruit-flavored, poured over it **6** [Informal] SLUSH PILE —*vt.* **1** to splash or cover with slush, esp. in lubricating or protecting **2** to fill with mortar —*vi.* to walk or move through slushy snow, ice, or mud —**slush′i·ness** *n.* —**slush′y** *adj.* **slush′i·er, slush′i·est**

☆**slush fund** ⟦orig. a fund established aboard ship from the sale of refuse cooking grease (*slush*), used to buy small luxuries⟧ money set aside for bribery, political pressure, or other corrupt purposes

slush pile [Informal] a publisher's accumulation of unsolicited manuscripts

slut (slut) *n.* ⟦ME *slutte*, prob. < Scand or LowG form akin to MLowG *slote*, ditch, mud puddle, Ice *sluta*, to dangle: for IE base see SLUG[1]⟧ **1** a careless, dirty, slovenly woman; slattern **2** a sexually promiscuous person, esp. a woman: a derogatory or insulting term —**slut′tish** *adj.* —**slut′tish·ly** *adv.* —**slut′tish·ness** *n.* —**slut′ty** *adj.* **slut′ti·er, slut′ti·est**

sly (slī) *adj.* **sli′er** or **sly′er, sli′est** or **sly′est** ⟦ME *sley* < ON *slœgr*, clever, cunning, lit., able to strike < base of *slā* & OE *slean*, to strike: see SLAY⟧ **1** [Dial.] skillful or clever **2** skillful at trickery or deceit; crafty; wily **3** showing a secretive, crafty, or wily nature; cunningly underhanded **4** mischievous in a playful way; roguish —**on the sly** secretly; stealthily —**sly′ly** *adv.* —**sly′ness** *n.*

SYN.—**sly** implies a working to achieve one's ends by evasiveness, insinuation, furtiveness, duplicity, etc. [a *sly* bargain]; **cunning** implies a cleverness or shrewd skillfulness at deception and circumvention [a *cunning* plot]; **crafty** implies an artful cunning in contriving stratagems and subtle deceptions [a *crafty* diplomat]; **tricky** suggests a shifty, unreliable quality rather than cleverness at deception [*tricky* subterfuges]; **foxy** suggests slyness and craftiness that have been sharpened by experience [a *foxy* old trader]; **wily** implies the deceiving or ensnarement of others by subtle stratagems and ruses [*wily* blandishments]

sly·boots (-bo͞ots′) *n.* ⟦prec. + BOOTS, in Brit informal sense, "a fellow"⟧ [Informal] a person who is clever or crafty in an appealing or engaging way

Sm[1] *abbrev.* **1** *Bible* Samuel **2** small: also **sm**

Sm[2] *Chem. symbol for* samarium

SM *abbrev.* **1** ⟦L *Scientiae Magister*⟧ Master of Science: also **S.M.** **2** service mark

S/M or **S-M** *abbrev.* (sexual) sadism and masochism; sadomasochism

smack[1] (smak) *n.* ⟦ME *smac* < OE *smæc*, akin to Ger *(ge)schmack* < IE base **smeg(h)-*, to taste > Lith *smaguriáuti*, to nibble⟧ **1** a distinctive taste or flavor, esp. one that is faint or slight **2** *a)* a small amount; bit *b)* a touch, trace, or suggestion —*vi.* to have a smack (*of*) [diction that *smacks* of the stage]

smack[2] (smak) *n.* ⟦< ? or akin to MDu *smack*, LowG *smacke*, of echoic orig.⟧ **1** a sharp noise made by pressing the lips together and parting them suddenly, as in showing enjoyment of a taste **2** [Informal] a loud kiss **3** *a)* a sharp blow with the hand or any flat object; slap *b)* the sound of such a blow —*vt.* **1** to press (the lips) together and part them suddenly so as to make a smack **2** [Informal] to kiss loudly **3** to slap loudly **4** to collide with or strike suddenly and forcefully —*vi.* **1** to make a loud, sharp noise, as on impact **2** to collide or strike suddenly and forcefully [two cars *smacked* against each other] —*adv.* [Informal] **1** with or as with a smack; violently; sharply **2** directly; precisely; squarely: also **smack′-dab′** (-dab′) —**smack down** [Slang] ☆to humble or reprimand (someone who is overstepping bounds)

smack[3] (smak) *n.* ⟦prob. < Du *smak* (> Dan *smakke*, Sp *zumaca*) < *smacken*, to slap, SMACK[1]: from the flapping sail⟧ **1** [Historical] a small sailboat, typically rigged as a sloop ☆**2** a fishing boat with a well for keeping fish alive

☆**smack**[4] (smak) *n.* ⟦prob. < Yiddish *shmek*, a sniff⟧ [Slang] heroin

smack·er (smak′ər) *n.* **1** a person or thing that smacks **2** [Slang] a loud kiss ☆**3** [Old Slang] a dollar: *usually used in pl.*

smack·ing (-iŋ) *adj.* ⟦prp. of SMACK[2]⟧ brisk; sharp; lively

small (smôl) *adj.* ⟦ME *smal*, narrow, slender < OE *smæl*, akin to Ger *schmal*, narrow < IE base **(s)mēlo-*, smaller animal: see MAL-⟧ **1** little in size, esp. when compared with others of the same kind; not large or big; limited in size **2** *a)* little in quantity, extent, numbers, value, duration, etc. [a *small* income] *b)* of slight intensity; of limited degree or scope *c)* consisting of relatively few units; numerically low **3** of little importance or significance; trivial **4** young [a book for *small* children] **5** having relatively little investment, capital, etc. [a *small* business] **6** small-minded; mean; petty **7** *a)* of low or inferior rank; ordinary; not notable *b)* modest or humble **8** gentle and low; soft: said of sound or the voice **9** diluted; light; weak [*small* ale] **10** LOWERCASE —*adv.* **1** in small pieces **2** in a low, faint tone; softly **3** in a small manner —*n.* **1** the small or narrow part [the *small* of the back] **2** [*pl.*] small things or articles collectively **3** [*pl.*] [Brit. Informal] *a)* [Archaic] SMALLCLOTHES *b)* UNDERCLOTHES —**feel small** to feel shame or humiliation —**small′ness** *n.*

SYN.—**small** and **little** are often used interchangeably, but **small** is preferred with reference to something concrete of less than the usual quantity, size, amount, value, importance, etc. [a *small* man, tax, audience, matter, etc.] and **little** more often applies to absolute concepts [he has his *little* faults], in expressing tenderness, indulgence, condescension, etc. [the *little* woman], and in connoting insignificance, meanness, pettiness, etc. [of *little* importance]; **diminutive** implies extreme, sometimes delicate, smallness or littleness [the *diminutive* Lilliputians]; **minute** and the more informal **tiny** suggest that which is extremely diminutive, often to the degree that it can be discerned only by close scrutiny [a *minute*, or *tiny*, difference]; **miniature** applies to a copy, model, representation, etc. on a very small scale [*miniature* painting]; **petite** has specific application to a girl or woman who is small and trim in figure —*ANT.* **large, big, great**

small arms firearms of small caliber, held in the hand or hands when fired, as pistols, rifles, etc.

small beer **1** [Brit. Archaic] weak or inferior beer **2** [Informal] a person or thing of little importance

small calorie CALORIE (sense 1)

small capital a capital letter of smaller size than the regular capital letter used: the regular capitals used in this dictionary are A, B, C, D, etc.; the small capitals are A, B, C, D, etc.

small change **1** coins, esp. those of low denomination **2** something of little value or importance

small·clothes (smôl′klōthz′, -klōz′) *pl.n.* closefitting knee breeches worn during the 18th cent.

☆**small forward** *Basketball* that one of the two forwards whose function is primarily to score and who is therefore usually quicker and more agile

small fry ☆1 children ☆2 people or things regarded as insignificant *Sometimes used in sing.*

small game small wild animals, and sometimes birds, hunted as game

small·hold·er (smôl′hōl′dər) *n.* [Brit.] a person who owns or works a smallholding

small·hold·ing (smôl′hōl′diŋ) *n.* [Brit.] a relatively small tract of land that is bought or rented for cultivation, sometimes as a source of extra income

small hours ⟦because designated by low numbers⟧ the first few hours after midnight

small intestine the narrow, convoluted section of the intestines, extending from the pyloric end of the stomach to the large intestine and including the duodenum, jejunum, and ileum

small·ish (smôl′ish) *adj.* somewhat small; not large

small letter the form of an alphabetical letter used when a CAPITAL LETTER is not called for; lowercase letter (Ex.: a, b, c, etc. are small letters; A, B, C, etc. are capital letters)

small-mind·ed (-mīn′did) *adj.* blindly selfish, prejudiced, vindictive, etc.; petty; mean; narrow —**small′-mind′ed·ly** *adv.* —**small′-mind′ed·ness** *n.*

☆**small·mouth bass** (-mouth′) a black North American sunfish (*Micropterus dolomieui*) found in cool, clear fresh waters

☆**small potatoes** [Informal] a petty or insignificant person (or people) or thing (or things)

small·pox (-päks′) *n.* ⟦so called to distinguish it from syphilis, the "great pox"⟧ an acute, highly contagious disease caused by a poxvirus and characterized by prolonged fever, vomiting, and pustular eruptions that often left pitted scars, or pockmarks, when healed: eradicated in the 1970s: see also VARIOLA

small-scale (-skāl′) *adj.* 1 drawn to a small scale and showing few details: said of a map, etc. 2 of limited scope; not extensive [*small-scale* business operations]

small screen, the [Informal] television

small slam *Bridge* the winning of all but one trick in a deal by the declarer; little slam

small stores *U.S. Navy* small miscellaneous articles stocked by a store on a ship or naval base, for sale to naval personnel

small·sword (-sôrd′) *n.* a light, tapering, straight sword, used esp. in fencing

small talk light conversation about common, everyday things; chitchat

☆**small-time** (-tīm′) *adj.* [Informal] of little importance or significance; minor or petty

☆**small-town** (-toun′) *adj.* of or characteristic of a small town; easygoing, unsophisticated, provincial, etc.

smalt (smôlt) *n.* ⟦Fr < It *smalto* < Frank **smalt* < WGmc base of OHG *smelzan,* to melt: see SMELT[2]⟧ 1 deep-blue glass prepared from silica, potash, and oxide of cobalt: used, in pulverized form, as a pigment 2 pigment made in this way 3 its deep-blue color

smalt·ite (smôl′tīt′) *n.* ⟦prec. + -ITE[1]⟧ a white to gray, natural, isometric, cobalt-nickel arsenide, $(Co,Ni)As_{3-x}$

smal·to (smäl′tō; *It* zmäl′tô) *n., pl.* **-tos** or **-ti** (-tē) ⟦It: see SMALT⟧ 1 a kind of colored glass or enamel used in mosaics 2 a piece of this

smar·agd (smar′agd′) *n.* ⟦ME *smaragde* < OFr < L *smaragdus:* see EMERALD⟧ *now rare var. of* EMERALD (sense 1) —**sma·rag·dine** (smə rag′din) *adj.*

sma·rag·dite (smə rag′dīt′) *n.* ⟦Fr: see prec. & -ITE[1]⟧ a bright-green kind of amphibole

smarm (smärm) *n.* ⟦back-form. < fol.⟧ [Informal, Chiefly Brit.] 1 a smarmy thing or quality 2 smarmy behavior, words, etc. collectively

smarm·y (smär′mē) *adj.* **smarm′i·er, smarm′i·est** ⟦< *smarm, smalm,* to bedaub, smear (< ?) + -Y[2]⟧ [Informal] flattering in an oily, insincere manner; unctuous —**smarm′i·ly** *adv.* —**smarm′i·ness** *n.*

smart (smärt) *vi.* ⟦ME *smerten* < OE *smeortan,* akin to Ger *schmerzen* < IE **mer-d* < base **mer-,* to rub away, fret > L *mordere,* to bite, sting, Gr *smerdnos,* frightful⟧ 1 *a)* to cause sharp, stinging pain, as a slap *b)* to be the source of such pain, as a wound *c)* to feel such pain 2 to feel mental distress or irritation, as in resentment, remorse, etc. —*vt.* to cause to smart —*n.* ⟦ME *smerte* < base of v.⟧ 1 a smarting sensation, pain or distress ☆2 [*pl.*] [Slang] shrewdness, intelligence, or acumen —*adj.* ⟦ME *smerte* < OE *smeart* < base of v.⟧ 1 causing sharp or stinging pain [*a smart* slap] 2 sharp or stinging, as pain 3 brisk; vigorous; lively [walking at a *smart* pace] 4 *a)* intelligent, alert, clever, witty, etc. *b)* shrewd or sharp, as in one's dealings 5 neat; trim; spruce 6 *a)* in keeping with the current fashion; stylish *b)* characteristic of or used by those who follow the current fashions 7 [Informal] insolent, flippant, etc. 8 [Dial.] quite strong, intense, numerous, etc.; considerable [a right *smart* rain] 9 *Comput. a)* INTELLIGENT (sense 3) *b)* aimed, guided, and controlled precisely, through the use of computer technology [*smart* weapons] *c)* programmed in advance with certain features, as navigation information or sensing and self-correcting functions [*smart* cars, *smart* guns] —*adv.* in a smart way —**SYN.** INTELLIGENT —**smart off** [Slang] to be impertinent or flippant —**smart′ly** *adv.* —**smart′ness** *n.*

Smart (smärt), **Christopher** 1722-71; Eng. poet

☆**smart al·eck** or **smart al·ec** (al′ik) ⟦SMART + *Aleck,* dim. of ALEXANDER[1]⟧ [Informal] a person who is annoyingly conceited, insolent, flippant, etc. —**smart′-al′eck** *adj.*, **smart′-al′eck·y**

☆**smart·ass** or **smart-ass** (smärt′as′) [Slang] *n.* a person who is annoyingly or obnoxiously cocky, knowing, flippant, etc.; wiseguy —*adj.* annoyingly cocky, knowing, etc.: also **smart′-assed′** Regarded as mildly vulgar by some

☆**smart bomb** [Informal] an extremely accurate guided missile directed to its target by any of various electronic means, as by a reflected laser beam

smart card a plastic card with memory provided by an embedded integrated circuit, used for banking transactions, identification, etc.

smart drink a nonalcoholic drink, with a base such as fruit juice, containing one or more smart drugs

smart drug a substance, as a legal drug, botanical, vitamin, or mineral, believed by some to enhance a person's memory, concentration, and general cognitive ability

smart·en (smärt′'n) *vt., vi.* to make or become smart or smarter; specif., *a)* to make or become neater or more stylish *b)* to make or become more alert, knowing, aware, etc.: usually with *up*

smart money ☆1 ⟦< SMART, *adj.* 4⟧ money bet or invested by those in the best position to know what might be advantageous ☆2 ⟦< SMART, *n.*⟧ *Law* EXEMPLARY DAMAGES

smart-mouth (-mouth′) *n.* [Informal] a person who is insolent, flippant, etc. —**smart′-mouthed′** (-mouthd′) *adj.*

smart·phone (smärt′fōn′) *n.* ⟦SMART (*adj.* 9) + -PHONE⟧ a cellular phone equipped with various additional features and services, as text messaging, information storage, and internet access

☆**smart set** sophisticated, fashionable people, collectively

smart·weed (-wēd′) *n.* any of various knotgrasses (genus *Polygonum*) whose acrid juice may cause skin irritation

☆**smart·y** (smärt′ē) *n., pl.* **smart′ies** [Informal] SMART ALECK: also [Slang] **smart′y-pants′** (-pants′)

smash (smash) *vt.* ⟦prob. < *s-*, intens. + MASH⟧ 1 to break or shatter into pieces with noise or violence 2 to hit (a tennis ball, badminton bird, etc.) with a hard overhand stroke 3 to hit with a hard, heavy blow or impact 4 to ruin completely; defeat utterly; wreck —*vi.* 1 to break into pieces 2 to be destroyed; come to ruin 3 to collide with crushing force 4 to move by smashing or with force —*n.* 1 a hard, heavy hit or blow; specif., a hard overhand stroke, as in tennis, that is difficult to return 2 *a)* a violent, noisy breaking or shattering *b)* the sound of this 3 *a)* a violent collision *b)* a wreck 4 complete ruin or defeat; total failure, esp. in business 5 an iced drink made of bruised mint leaves, sugar, soda water, and an alcoholic liquor ☆6 [Informal] an overwhelming popular success —☆*adj.* [Informal] that is a SMASH (*n.* 6) —**SYN.** BREAK

smashed (smasht) *adj.* [Slang] drunk; intoxicated

smash·er (smash′ər) *n.* 1 a person or thing that smashes 2 [Informal, Chiefly Brit.] a handsome, attractive, or beautiful person or thing

smash·ing (-iŋ) *adj.* 1 that smashes 2 [Informal] outstandingly good; extraordinary —**smash′ing·ly** *adv.*

☆**smash-mouth** (smash′mouth′) *adj.* [Slang] designating or of a style of football characterized by rough, aggressive play and, typically, strong offensive rushing

smash·up (-up′) *n.* [Informal] 1 a wreck or collision, esp. one that does great damage 2 complete defeat or failure; ruin 3 any disaster or catastrophe

smat·ter (smat′ər) *vt.* ⟦ME *smateren,* to chatter, prob. akin to MHG *smetern,* to chatter, gossip, of echoic orig.⟧ [Now Rare] 1 to speak or utter (a language, words, etc.) with only slight knowledge 2 to study or learn (a subject) superficially —*n.* SMATTERING

smat·ter·ing (-iŋ) *n.* ⟦prec. + -ING⟧ 1 a slight or superficial knowledge [a *smattering* of Latin] 2 a small number or amount

☆**smaze** (smāz) *n.* ⟦SM(OKE) + (H)AZE⟧ a mixture of smoke and haze

smear (smir) *vt.* ⟦ME *smerien* < OE *smerian,* to anoint, akin to Ger *schmieren* < IE base **smeru-,* grease > OIr *smir,* marrow & (prob.) L *medulla,* marrow⟧ 1 to cover, daub, or soil with something greasy, sticky, or dirty 2 *a)* to apply or daub so as to leave a coating, mark, etc. *b)* [Informal] to apply (a SPREAD, *n.* 6) to 3 to make an unwanted mark or streak on, or to obscure, by rubbing [to *smear* a fresh signature] 4 to make a smear with [to *smear* one's hand across a surface] 5 to harm the reputation of; malign; slander 6 [Slang] to overwhelm or defeat decisively —*vi.* to be or become smeared —*n.* ⟦ME *smere* < OE *smeoru,* grease⟧ 1 a spot or mark made by smearing 2 a small quantity of some substance, as blood, smeared on a slide for microscopic study, etc. 3 the act or an instance of smearing, or slandering, someone 4 *a)* [Obs.] ointment *b)* a substance to be smeared on something

☆**smear·case** (smir′kās′) *n.* ⟦Ger *schmierkäse* < *schmieren,* to spread (see prec.) + *käse,* CHEESE[1]⟧ COTTAGE CHEESE

smear·y (smir′ē) *adj.* **smear′i·er, smear′i·est** 1 covered with or having smears; smeared 2 tending to smear, as wet ink —**smear′i·ness** *n.*

smec·tic (smek′tik) *adj.* ⟦< L *smecticus,* cleansing < Gr *smēktikos* < *smēktos,* smeared (< *smēchein,* to wipe off: for IE base see SMITE) + *-ikos,* -IC⟧ designating or of a kind of liquid crystal in which the molecules form layers, with the molecules ordered or disordered within each layer

smeg·ma (smeg′mə) *n.* ⟦ModL < L, detergent < Gr *smēgma* < *smēchein,* to wipe off: see prec.⟧ a cheesy sebaceous secretion that may accumulate under the foreskin or around the clitoris

smell (smel) *vt.* **smelled** or [Chiefly Brit.] **smelt, smell′ing** ⟦ME *smellen* < OE **smyllan* < IE base **smel-,* to burn slowly > SMOLDER: basic sense "to give off smoke"⟧ 1 to be or become aware of by means of the nose and the olfactory nerves; detect the scent or odor of **2** to sense the presence or existence of [to *smell* trouble] **3** to test by the scent or odor; sniff [*smell* the milk to tell if it's sour] —*vi.* **1** to use the sense of smell; sniff: often with *at* or *of* **2** *a)* to have or emit a scent or odor [flowers that do not *smell*] *b)* to have or emit an unpleasant odor; stink **3** to have the odor or a suggestion (*of*) [breath that *smells* of garlic] **4** [Informal] *a)* to lack ability, worth, etc.; be of poor quality *b)* to be foul, corrupt, mean, etc. —*n.* ⟦ME *smel*⟧ **1** that one of the five senses of the body by which a substance is perceived through the chemical stimulation of the olfactory nerves in the nasal cavity by particles given off by that substance **2** the characteristic stimulation of any specific substance upon the olfactory nerves; odor; scent **3** an act of smelling **4** that which suggests the presence or existence of something; trace; suggestion —**smell out** to look for or find by or as by smelling —**smell up** [Informal] to cause to stink —**smell'er** *n.*

SYN.—**smell** is the most general word for any quality perceived through the olfactory sense [foul and fresh *smells*]; **scent** refers to the emanation from the thing smelled, often implying that it can be discriminated only by a sensitive sense of smell [the *scent* of a hunted animal]; **odor** suggests a heavier emanation and, therefore, one that is more generally perceptible and more clearly recognizable [chemical *odors*]; **aroma** suggests a pervasive, pleasant, often spicy odor [the *aroma* of fine tobacco]

smelling salts an aromatic mixture of carbonate of ammonium with some fragrant scent, used as an inhalant in relieving faintness, headaches, etc.

smell·y (smel'ē) *adj.* **smell'i·er, smell'i·est** having an unpleasant smell —**smell'i·ness** *n.*

smelt¹ (smelt) *n., pl.* **smelts** or **smelt** ⟦ME < OE, akin to Norw *smelt*, whiting, Du *smelt*, Ger *schmelte*, sand eel⟧ any of various fishes (order Salmoniformes); esp., any of a family (Osmeridae) of small, silvery, salmonoid food fishes found in northern seas or lakes: most run up rivers to spawn

smelt² (smelt) *vt.* ⟦MDu or MLowG *smelten*, akin to Ger *schmelzen* < IE *(*s*)*mel*-, to crush, grind fine > MELT, MALT⟧ **1** to melt or fuse (ore, etc.) so as to separate impurities from pure metal **2** to refine or extract (metal) in this way —*vi.* to undergo fusing or smelting

smelt³ (smelt) *vt., vi. chiefly Brit. pt. & pp. of* SMELL

smelt·er (smel'tər) *n.* **1** one engaged in the work or business of smelting **2** a place where smelting is done: also **smelt'er·y**, *pl.* **-er·ies**

Sme·ta·na (sme'tä nä; *E* smet''n ə), **Be·dřich** (bed'ər zhikh) 1824-84; Czech composer

smew (smyo͞o) *n.* ⟦var. of *smee*, akin to obs. Du *sme(ente)*, MHG *smiche*, kind of small duck⟧ a small Eurasian merganser (*Mergus albellus*), the male of which has a white crest

smidge (smij) *n.* [Informal] *short for* SMIDGEN

smidg·en (smij'ən) *n.* ⟦prob. < dial. *smidge*, var. of *smitch*, particle⟧ [Informal] a small amount; bit: also sp. **smidg'in** or **smidg'eon**

smi·lax (smī'laks') *n.* ⟦L < Gr, bindweed⟧ **1** GREENBRIER **2** a twining greenhouse vine (*Asparagus asparagoides*) of the lily family, with bright-green foliage

smile (smīl) *vi.* **smiled, smil'ing** ⟦ME *smilen*, akin to Norw *smile*, Swed *smila*, prob. via MLowG **smilen* < IE base *(*s*)*mei*-, to smile, be astonished > L *mirus*, wonderful, OE *smearcian*, to smile⟧ **1** to have or take on a facial expression showing usually pleasure, amusement, affection, friendliness, etc., or, sometimes, irony, derision, etc. and characterized by an upward curving of the corners of the mouth and a sparkling of the eyes **2** to look (*at, on,* or *upon* someone) with a pleasant expression of this kind **3** to regard with favor or approval: with *on* or *upon* **4** to have a favorable, pleasing, or agreeable appearance —*vt.* **1** to express with a smile **2** to change or affect by smiling —*n.* **1** the act of smiling **2** the facial expression made in smiling **3** a favorable, pleasing, or agreeable appearance —**all smiles** [Informal] smiling brightly and for a time, as from delight or happiness —**smile away** to drive away or get rid of by a smile or smiling —**smil'er** *n.* —**smil'ing·ly** *adv.*

smil·ey (smī'lē) *adj.* characterized by smiling, esp. bright or frequent smiling —*n.* SMILEY FACE

smiley face **1** a stylized representation of a smiling face, typically a yellow circle with dots for eyes and a curved line for a smile **2** EMOTICON

smirch (smurch) *vt.* ⟦ME *smorchen*, prob. < OFr *esmorcher*, to hurt < *es*- (< L *ex*), intens. + *pp.* of *mordre*, to bite, hurt: see MORDANT⟧ **1** to make dirty or discolor as by smearing or staining with grime **2** to sully or dishonor (a reputation, good name, etc.) —*n.* **1** a smudge; smear; stain **2** a stain on a reputation, etc.

smirk (smurk) *vi.* ⟦ME *smirken* < OE *smearcian*, to SMILE⟧ to smile in a conceited, knowing, or annoyingly complacent way —*n.* a smile of this kind —**smirk'er** *n.* —**smirk'ing·ly** *adv.* —**smirk'y** *adj.*

smite (smīt) *vt.* **smote, smit'ten, smit'ing** ⟦ME *smiten* < OE *smitan*, akin to Ger *schmeissen*, to throw < IE base **smē*-, to smear, smear on, stroke on⟧ **1** [Archaic or Literary] *a)* to hit or strike hard *b)* to bring into a specified condition by or as by a blow [to *smite* someone dead] **2** *a)* to strike or attack with powerful or disastrous effect [*smitten* by the flu] *b)* to inspire strong and sudden love or devotion [he saw her and was immediately *smitten*]: now archaic or literary except in the pp. —**smit'er** *n.*

smith (smith) *n.* ⟦ME < OE, akin to Ger *schmied* (older *schmid*) < IE base **smēi*-, to work with a sharp tool > Gr *smilē*, knife⟧ **1** a person who makes or repairs metal objects, esp. by shaping the metal while it is hot and soft; metalworker: usually in comb. [*silversmith*] **2** *short for* BLACKSMITH

Smith (smith) **1 Adam** 1723-90; Scot. economist **2 Alfred E(manuel)** (called *Al Smith*) 1873-1944; U.S. politician **3 Bes·sie** (bes'ē) 1894?-1937; U.S. blues singer **4 David (Roland)** 1906-65; U.S. sculptor & painter **5** Captain **John** 1580?-1631; Eng. colonist in America: cf. POCAHONTAS **6 Joseph** 1805-44; U.S. founder of the Mormon Church **7 Sydney** 1771-1845; Eng. clergyman & essayist **8 Wayland** *see* WAYLAND **9 William** 1769-1839; Eng. geologist

-smith (smith) *combining form used to form nouns meaning* a skilled maker, composer, or user of a (specified) thing [*songsmith, wordsmith*]

smith·er·eens (smith'ər ēnz') *pl.n.* ⟦Ir *smidirīn*⟧ [Informal] small fragments or broken pieces; bits

smith·er·y (smith'ər ē) *n., pl.* **-er·ies** **1** the work or craft of a smith **2** SMITHY

Smith·so·ni·an Institution (smith sō'nē ən) ⟦founded (1846) by a bequest of James *Smithson* (1765?-1829), Eng scientist⟧ institution & museum in Washington, D.C.: branches of the Institution cover a wide range of fields in the arts and sciences: also, unofficially, **Smithsonian Institute**

smith·son·ite (smith'sə nīt') *n.* ⟦after James *Smithson* (see prec.) + -ITE¹⟧ ☆a hard, variously colored, rhombohedral mineral, $ZnCO_3$, an ore of zinc; zinc carbonate

smith·y (smith'ē, smith'ē) *n., pl.* **smith'ies** ⟦ME *smithi* < OE *smiththe* (< *smith*) or ON *smithja* (< *smithr*, smith)⟧ **1** the workshop of a smith, esp. a blacksmith ☆**2** BLACKSMITH

smit·ten (smit''n) *vt. pp. of* SMITE

smock (smäk) *n.* ⟦ME *smoc* < OE *smoc* or ON *smokkr* < IE *(*s*)*meugh* < base **meug*-, slippery, to slip, slip on > SMUGGLE, MEEK, L *mucus*⟧ **1** a long, loose, shirtlike outer garment worn to protect the clothes **2** [Archaic] a chemise, or sliplike undergarment **3** a loose-fitting woman's or girl's dress or top having smocking at the bust —*vt.* **1** to dress in a smock **2** to decorate with smocking

smock frock a heavy smock, esp. of the kind formerly worn by European farm laborers

smock·ing (smäk'iŋ) *n.* shirred, decorative stitching used in gathering cloth, as to make it hang in even folds

smog (smäg, smôg) *n.* ⟦fol. + (F)OG⟧ **1** [Archaic] a noxious mixture of fog and smoke **2** a low-lying, perceptible layer of polluted air —SYN. MIST —**smog'gy** *adj.* **-gi·er, -gi·est**

smoke (smōk) *n.* ⟦ME < OE *smoca*, akin to Ger *schmauch* < IE base **smeukh*-, to smoke > Gr *smychein*, to smolder, Ir *mūch*, smoke⟧ **1** *a)* vaporous matter arising from something burning and made visible by minute particles of carbon suspended in it *b)* a mass or cloud of this **2** any vapor, fume, mist, etc. resembling smoke **3** [Informal] ☆*a)* an act or period of smoking tobacco, etc. [time out for a *smoke*] *b)* something to smoke, as a cigarette or pipeful of tobacco **4** something without substance, significance, or lasting reality **5** something that beclouds or obscures **6** a dusky gray **7** *Chem.* a suspension of solid particles in a gas —*vi.* **smoked, smok'ing** **1** to give off smoke or a smokelike substance **2** to discharge smoke in the wrong place, esp. into a room: said of a furnace, fireplace, etc. **3** to give off too much smoke: said of a lamp, type of fuel, etc. **4** [Informal] to move or operate very rapidly **5** *a)* to draw the smoke of tobacco, etc. into the mouth, and often lungs, and blow it out again *b)* to be a habitual smoker —*vt.* **1** to stain or color with smoke **2** to treat (meat, fish, etc.) with smoke, as in flavoring or curing **3** to fumigate as with smoke **4** to drive or force into the open with or as with smoke; force out of hiding, secrecy, etc.: often with *out* **5** to stupefy or stun (bees, etc.) with smoke **6** to draw the smoke of or from (tobacco, a pipe, etc.) into the mouth, and often lungs, and blow it out again **7** [Archaic] to detect or be suspicious of **8** [Obs.] to tease or mock ☆**9** [Slang] to hit or throw with great force [the batter *smoked* the ball over the fence] —**go up in smoke** **1** to be consumed by fire **2** to come to nothing; fail utterly —**smok'a·ble** *adj.*, **smoke'a·ble**

smoke and mirrors elaborate deception or pretense: so called after the use of smoke, mirrors, etc. by professional magicians to create an illusion

smoke bomb a kind of bomb containing chemicals which when ignited give off dense clouds of smoke

smoke detector a usually battery-operated warning device that sets off a loud signal when excessive smoke or heat is detected

smoke-free (smōk'frē') *adj.* of or having a policy of not permitting smoking [a *smoke-free* restaurant]

smoke·house (smōk'hous') *n.* ☆a building, esp. an outbuilding on a farm, where meats, fish, etc. are cured by smoke

smoke·jack (-jak') *n.* ⟦SMOKE + JACK⟧ a device which turns a fireplace roasting spit, taking its power from a wheel rotated by the heated air rising in the chimney

☆**smoke jumper** an employee of the forest service who is parachuted to strategic spots in fighting forest fires

smoke·less (-lis) *adj.* **1** having or making little or no smoke [a *smokeless* fire] **2** designating or of tobacco products, as chewing tobacco and snuff, intended to be consumed without smoking

smokeless powder a propellant or explosive that consists mainly of nitrocellulose and makes little or no smoke when it is fired

smok·er (smō'kər) *n.* **1** a person or thing that smokes; specif., a person who habitually smokes cigarettes, a pipe, etc. ☆**2** a railroad car or compartment reserved esp. for smoking: also **smoking car** ☆**3** [Old-fashioned] an informal social gathering for men only

smoke·screen (smōk'skrēn') *n.* **1** a cloud of smoke spread to screen the movements of troops, ships, etc. **2** anything said or done to conceal or mislead Also written **smoke screen**

smoke signal [*often pl.*] a signal, consisting of a column of smoke, that is visible across great distances

☆**smoke·stack** (smōk′stak′) ***n.*** a pipe for the discharge of smoke from a steamship, locomotive, factory, etc. —***adj.*** designating or of heavy manufacturing industries, such as those producing steel, automobiles, or rubber

smoke tree 1 a small, bushy, Old World tree (*Cotinus coggygria*) of the cashew family, with filmy, feathery flower clusters resembling smoke 2 a tree (*Cotinus americanus*) of the cashew family, growing in the SW U.S. and having brilliant orange and scarlet coloring in the fall

smok·ey (smō′kē) ***adj.*** *alt. sp. of* SMOKY

Smok·ies (smō′kēz) GREAT SMOKY MOUNTAINS

☆**smoking gun** [Informal] any conclusive evidence that proves guilt or fault

smoking jacket a man's lounging jacket for wear at home

smoking room a room or lounge set apart for smoking

smok·y (smō′kē) ***adj.*** **smok′i·er, smok′i·est** 1 giving off smoke, esp. excessive smoke 2 like, of, or as of smoke [*a smoky haze*] 3 filled with smoke 4 having the color of smoke 5 having a flavor suggestive of smoke or smoked food 6 darkened or soiled by smoke —**smok′i·ly** ***adv.*** —**smok′i·ness** ***n.***

Smoky Hill ⟦named for the haze on the nearby hills⟧ river flowing from E Colo. eastward through Kans., joining the Republican River to form the Kansas River: 540 mi (869 km)

Smoky Mountains GREAT SMOKY MOUNTAINS

smoky quartz CAIRNGORM

smol·der (smōl′dər) ***vi.*** ⟦ME *smoldren* < Gmc **smul-*: for IE base see SMELL⟧ 1 to burn and smoke without flame; be consumed by slow combustion 2 to exist in a suppressed state or with activity stifled 3 to have or show feelings of suppressed anger, hate, passion, etc. —***n.*** the act or condition of smoldering

Smo·lensk (smō lensk′, smä-; *Russ* smô lyensk′) city in W European Russia, on the Dnieper

Smol·lett (smäl′it), **Tobias (George)** 1721-71; Brit. novelist, born in Scotland

smolt (smōlt) ***n.*** ⟦LME (Scot): prob. akin to SMELT[1]⟧ a young salmon when it first leaves fresh water and descends to the sea

smooch[1] (smōōch) ***vt., n.*** *var. of* SMUTCH

smooch[2] (smōōch) [Slang] ***n.*** ⟦var. of dial. *smouch*, akin to Ger dial. (Westphalian) *smuck*: ult. akin to SMACK[2]⟧ a kiss — ***vi., vt.*** 1 to kiss 2 to hug, kiss, and caress in making love —**smooch′er** ***n.*** —**smooch′y** ***adj.***, **smooch′ie**

☆**smoosh** (smoosh) ***vt.*** [Informal] *alt. sp. of* SMUSH

smooth (smōōth) ***adj.*** ⟦ME *smothe* < OE *smoth*, for earlier *smethe* < Gmc **smanthi* < IE **som-*, together < base **sem-*, together, SAME⟧ 1 *a)* having an even or level surface; having no roughness or projections that can be seen or felt *b)* having its projections leveled by wear [*a smooth tire*] 2 having an even consistency; without lumps [*a smooth paste*] 3 even, calm, or gentle in flow or movement [*a smooth voyage*] 4 free from interruptions, obstacles, difficulties, etc. [*smooth progress*] 5 not easily agitated or ruffled; calm; serene [*a smooth temper*] 6 free from hair, beard, etc. 7 pleasing to the taste; not sharp or harsh; bland 8 having an easy, gentle, flowing rhythm or sound ☆9 suave, polished, or ingratiating, esp. in a flattering, insincere way ☆10 [Informal] polished; competent [*a smooth dancer*] 11 [Slang] very pleasant, attractive, or enjoyable 12 *Mech.* having relatively little friction 13 *Phonet.* articulated without aspiration —***vt.*** 1 to make level or even 2 to remove the lumps from 3 to remove wrinkles from by pressing 4 to free from interruptions, difficulties, etc.; make easy 5 to make calm or serene; soothe 6 to make less crude; polish or refine —***vi.*** to become smooth —***adv.*** in a smooth manner —***n.*** 1 something smooth; smooth part 2 an act of smoothing —**SYN.** EASY, LEVEL —**smooth away** to remove (difficulties, obstacles, etc.) —**smooth down** to make or become smooth, or even, level, calm, etc. —**smooth over** to relieve or resolve the tension in (a conflict or situation) —**smooth′er** ***n.*** —**smooth′ly** ***adv.*** —**smooth′ness** ***n.***

☆**smooth·bore** (-bôr′) ***adj.*** having no grooves or ridges on the inner surface of the barrel; not rifled: said of certain guns —***n.*** a smoothbore gun

smooth breathing ⟦transl. of L *spiritus lenis*⟧ 1 in written Greek, the mark (’) placed over an initial vowel to show that in ancient Greek it was pronounced without a preceding (h) sound, or aspirate 2 the lack of aspiration thus indicated

☆**smooth dogfish** a requiem shark (*Mustelus canis*) without spines in front of the dorsal fin, common in the Atlantic

smoothe (smōōth) ***vt., vi.*** **smoothed, smooth′ing** *alt. sp. of* SMOOTH

smooth·en (-ən) ***vt., vi.*** to make or become smooth

smooth-faced (smōōth′fāst′) ***adj.*** 1 having no beard or mustache; beardless or smooth-shaven 2 having a smooth face, or surface [*a smooth-faced tile*] 3 having a false semblance of sincerity; plausibly ingratiating

smooth fox terrier *see* FOX TERRIER

smooth·hound (-hound′) ***n.*** any of several requiem sharks (esp. genus *Mustelus*) common in the Atlantic and Pacific

☆**smooth·ie** (smōō′thē) ***n.*** 1 [Informal] a suave, glib, attractive person, esp. a man 2 a drink made from fruits, juices, vegetables, crushed ice, and usually milk or yogurt, whipped in a blender until smooth Also sp. **smooth′y**, *pl.* **smooth′ies**

smooth muscle a contractile type of muscle tissue controlled by the involuntary nervous system, occurring in the walls of the uterus, stomach, intestines, blood vessels, etc., and characterized by nonstriated, spindle-shaped cells

smooth-shav·en (smōōth′shāv′ən) ***adj.*** having recently been shaved

smooth-spo·ken (-spō′kən) ***adj.*** speaking in a pleasing, persuasive, or polished manner

smooth-tongued (-tuŋd′) ***adj.*** smooth-spoken, esp. in a plausible or flattering way

☆**s'more** (smôr) ***n.*** ⟦prob. contr. of *some more*⟧ a dessert, made as at a campfire, consisting of a toasted marshmallow and a piece of chocolate between two graham crackers: often sp. **smore**

☆**smor·gas·bord** or **smör·gås·bord** (smôr′gəs bôrd′, smur′-) ***n.*** ⟦Swed *smörgåsbord* < *smörgås*, buttered bread < *smör*, butter (akin to SMEAR) + dial. *gås*, a clump (of butter), lit., goose (akin to GOOSE) + *bord*, table (akin to BOARD)⟧ 1 *a)* a wide variety of appetizers along with such foods as cheeses, fishes, meats, salads, etc., served buffet style *b)* a meal selected from these 2 a restaurant serving smorgasbord 3 any widely varied assortment or collection from which to choose

smør·re·brød (smur′ə brüth) ***n.*** ⟦Dan < *smør*, butter + *brød*, bread⟧ 1 an assortment of open-faced sandwiches consisting as of fish, meat paste, or vegetables on slices of buttered bread, as served in Denmark and other Scandinavian countries 2 one such sandwich Also **smor′re·brod**

smor·zan·do (smôr tsän′dô) ***adj., adv.*** ⟦It⟧ *Musical Direction* dying away

smote (smōt) ***vt.*** *pt. & archaic pp. of* SMITE

smoth·er (smuth′ər) ***vt.*** ⟦ME *smorthren* < *smorther*, dense smoke < base of OE *smorian*, to suffocate, akin to MLowG *smoren*, to smoke < var. of IE base **smel-* > SMELL⟧ 1 *a)* to keep from getting enough air to breathe; stifle *b)* to kill in this way; suffocate 2 to cover (a fire), excluding air from it and causing it to smolder or die down 3 to cover over thickly [*liver smothered in onions*] 4 to hide or suppress by or as by covering; stifle [*to smother a yawn*] 5 to overwhelm, dominate, suppress, or impede in a manner regarded as suffocating [*a child smothered with affection*] —***vi.*** 1 *a)* to be kept from getting enough air to breathe *b)* to die in this way; be suffocated 2 to be hidden, stifled, or suppressed —***n.*** 1 dense, suffocating smoke or any thick cloud of dust, steam, fog, etc. 2 a confused turmoil; welter 3 [Archaic] a smoldering fire 4 [Archaic] a smoldering state or condition —**smoth′er·er** ***n.*** —**smoth′er·y** ***adj.***

smoul·der (smōl′dər) ***vi., n.*** *Brit. sp. of* SMOLDER

smudge (smuj) ***n.*** ⟦Early ModE, prob. < the v.⟧ 1 a stain, blur, or smear; dirty spot 2 *a)* a fire made to produce dense smoke *b)* such smoke produced by burning a material in containers (**smudge pots**), esp. for driving away insects or protecting plants from frost —***vt.*** **smudged, smudg′ing** ⟦ME *smogen*, akin to Du *smotsen*, to besmirch: for IE base see SMUT⟧ 1 to protect (an orchard, etc.) with smudge 2 to make dirty; soil; smutch —***vi.*** 1 to blur or smear 2 to become smudged

smudg·y (smuj′ē) ***adj.*** **smudg′i·er, smudg′i·est** covered with smudges; stained, blurred, etc. —**smudg′i·ly** ***adv.*** —**smudg′i·ness** ***n.***

smug (smug) ***adj.*** **smug′ger, smug′gest** ⟦prob. < LowG *smuk*, trim, neat, akin to Ger *schmuck*, neat: for IE base see SMOCK⟧ 1 [Archaic] neat, spruce, trim, etc. 2 narrowly contented with one's own accomplishments, beliefs, morality, etc.; self-satisfied to an annoying degree; complacent —**smug′ly** ***adv.*** —**smug′ness** ***n.***

smug·gle (smug′əl) ***vt.*** **-gled, -gling** ⟦< LowG *smuggeln*, akin to OE *smugan*, to creep: for IE base see SMOCK⟧ 1 to bring into or take out of a country secretly, under illegal conditions or without paying the required import or export duties 2 to bring, take, carry, etc. secretly or stealthily —***vi.*** to practice smuggling; be a smuggler —**smug′gler** ***n.***

smush (smoosh) ☆***vt.*** [Informal] to press, smash, or squeeze into a soft or flat mass; squash

smut (smut) ***n.*** ⟦< or akin to LowG *smutt*, akin to Ger *schmutz*, dirt < IE **(s)meud-* < base **meu-*, wet, musty > MUD, MOSS⟧ 1 *a)* sooty matter *b)* a particle of this 2 a mark made by something dirty; soiled spot 3 pornographic or indecent talk, writing, etc. 4 *Bot. a)* any of various plant diseases, esp. of cereal grasses, characterized by the appearance of masses of black spores which usually break up into a fine powder *b)* any of an order (Ustilaginales) of basidiomycetous fungi causing smut —***vt.*** **smut′ted, smut′ting** ⟦later var. of ME *smoten*, besmirch⟧ to mark or affect with smut —***vi.*** to be marked or affected by smut

smutch (smuch) ***vt.*** ⟦akin to prec.⟧ to make dirty; smudge —***n.*** 1 a dirty spot or mark; smudge 2 soot, smut, grime, or dirt —**smutch′y** ***adj.*** **smutch′i·er, smutch′i·est**

Smuts (smuts), **Jan Chris·ti·aan** (yän′ kris′tē än) 1870-1950; South African general: prime minister (1919-24; 1939-48)

smut·ty (smut′ē) ***adj.*** **-ti·er, -ti·est** 1 soiled with smut 2 affected with plant smut 3 pornographic or indecent —**smut′ti·ly** ***adv.*** —**smut′ti·ness** ***n.***

Smyr·na (smur′nə) *former name for* IZMIR

Sn ⟦L *stannum*⟧ *Chem. symbol for* tin

SN *abbrev.* U.S. Navy Seaman

S/N or **s/n** *abbrev.* signal-to-noise ratio: the difference, in decibels, between the level of a specific signal and that of unwanted noise

snack (snak) ***n.*** ⟦ME *snake*, a bite < *snaken*, to bite, snap, prob. < MDu *snacken*, to snap⟧ 1 [Archaic] a share or part 2 a small quantity of food; light meal or refreshment taken between regular meals 3 [*pl.*] foods commonly eaten between regular meals, specif. such prepared foods as pretzels, popcorn, chips, dips, etc.: also **snack food** —***vi.*** to eat a snack or snacks

snack bar a lunch counter, cafeteria, etc. serving snacks

snaf·fle (snaf′əl) ***n.*** ⟦short for *snaffle piece*, prob. < Du *snavel*, horse's muzzle < ODu **snabel*, dim. of **snabbe*, bill of a bird, akin to Ger *schnabel*: see SNAP⟧ a bit, usually light and jointed, attached to a bridle and having no curb —*vt.* **-fled, -fling 1** to fit with or control by a snaffle **2** [Brit. Informal] to purloin or snitch

☆**sna·fu** (sna fo͞o′, snaf′o͞o) [Slang] *adj.* ⟦orig. mil. slang for *s(ituation) n(ormal), a(ll) f(ucked) u(p)*⟧ in characteristic disorder or confusion; mixed up as usual —*vt.* **-fued′, -fu′ing** to throw into confusion —*n.* a mix-up, mishap, mistake, etc.

snag (snag) *n.* ⟦< Scand, as in ON *snagi*, wooden peg, Norw *snage*, sharp point, projection, akin to Ger *schnake*⟧ **1** a piece, part, or point that sticks out, esp. one that is sharp or rough, as the broken end of a tree limb ☆**2** an underwater tree stump or branch dangerous to navigation **3** a broken or irregular tooth **4** a small branch of an antler **5** *a)* a break or tear, as in cloth, made by a splinter, snag, etc. *b)* a pulled thread in knitted material, causing a loop at the point where it is caught ☆**6** an unexpected or hidden obstacle, difficulty, etc. —*vt.* **snagged, snag′ging 1** to catch, tear, etc. on a snag **2** to impede with or as with a snag **3** to catch or grab quickly —*vi.* **1** to become caught or impeded by a sharp projection, a difficulty, etc. ☆**2** to strike or become caught on a snag in water **3** to form or develop a snag

snag·gle·tooth (snag′əl to͞oth′) *n., pl.* **-teeth′** ⟦< prec.⟧ **1** a tooth that sticks out beyond the others **2** a crooked or broken tooth —**snag′gle·toothed′** (-to͞otht′, -to͞othd′) *adj.*

snag·gy (snag′ē) *adj.* **-gi·er, -gi·est 1** of, or having the nature of, a snag **2** full of snags, as a body of water **3** having snags

snail (snāl) *n.* ⟦ME *snaile* < OE *snægl*, akin to Ger dial. *schnägel*, ON *snigill* < IE base **sneg-*, to creep > SNAKE, SNEAK⟧ **1** any of a large number of slow-moving gastropods living on land or in water and having a spiral protective shell: some kinds are used as food **2** any lazy, slow-moving person or animal —**snail′like′** *adj.*

☆**snail darter** a very small freshwater fish (*Percina tanasi*) of the perch family: now nearly extinct

snail fever ⟦so named because the schistosome causing the disease in humans makes use of a *snail* as its intermediate host⟧ SCHISTOSOMIASIS

snail mail ⟦in allusion to the slowness of the *snail*⟧ [Informal] mail or mail delivery by means of a traditional postal service rather than by fax, email, etc.: a humorous or dismissive use

snail-paced (snāl′pāst′) *adj.* very slow-moving

snake (snāk) *n.* ⟦ME < OE *snaca*, akin to ON *snakr*, MLowG *snake*: for IE base see SNAIL⟧ **1** any of a limbless suborder (Serpentes, order Squamata) of reptiles with an elongated, scaly body, lidless eyes, and a tapering tail: some species have a poisonous bite **2** a treacherous or deceitful person **3** a plumber's tool consisting of a long, sturdy, very flexible wire or cable, used to remove obstructions from pipes, etc. —*vi.* **snaked, snak′ing** to move, curve, twist, or turn like a snake —*vt.* **1** to clear obstructions from (a pipe, drain, etc.) by means of a SNAKE (*n.* 3) ☆**2** [Informal] to drag or pull, esp. lengthwise and with force **3** [Informal] to pull quickly —**snake′like′** *adj.*

☆**snake·bird** (snāk′burd′) *n.* ANHINGA

snake·bit (snāk′bit′) *adj.* ☆[Informal] having or characterized by bad luck; marked by a series of misfortunes, mistakes, etc.: occas. **snake′bit′ten** (-ən)

snake·bite (-bīt′) *n.* a bite by a snake, esp. a poisonous one, or the condition caused by it

snake charmer an entertainer who seems to hypnotize snakes by means of movements or music

☆**snake dance 1** a ceremonial dance by American Indians involving the handling, imitation, etc. of snakes; esp., a ceremony performed every two years by the Hopi Indians, in which live rattlesnakes are handled **2** an informal parade in which those taking part move along behind each other in a long, winding line

snake doctor ☆**1** DRAGONFLY ☆**2** HELLGRAMMITE

☆**snake eyes** ⟦descriptive⟧ *Craps* a throw of two (two ones)

☆**snake fence** ⟦from its undulating form⟧ VIRGINIA (RAIL) FENCE

☆**snake·head** (-hed′) *n.* TURTLEHEAD

snake in the grass a treacherous or deceitful person

☆**snake·mouth** (-mouth′) *n.* POGONIA

☆**snake oil** a liquid substance with no real medicinal value sold as a cure-all or nostrum, esp. in a medicine show

snake pit 1 a pit where snakes are kept ☆**2** [Slang] a place of horror and confusion ☆**3** ⟦< the title of a novel (1946) by M. J. Ward⟧ a crowded mental hospital where patients are improperly cared for

☆**snake plant** SANSEVIERIA

Snake River ⟦transl. (prob. erroneous) of earlier *Shoshone River*⟧ river in the NW U.S., flowing from Yellowstone National Park into the Columbia River in Wash.: 1,038 mi (1,670 km)

☆**snake·root** (-ro͞ot′, -root′) *n.* **1** any of a number of plants reputed to be remedies for snakebites, as the **black snakeroot** (genus *Sanicula*) of the umbel family or the **white snakeroot** (*Eupatorium rugosum*) of the composite family **2** the roots of any of these plants

snake·skin (-skin′) *n.* **1** the skin of a snake **2** leather made from this

snake·weed (-wēd′) *n.* any of several plants supposedly resembling snakes or reputedly a cure for snakebites; specif., *a)* any of various plants (genus *Gutierrezia*) of the composite family, with small, yellow flower heads *b)* BISTORT ☆*c)* SNAKEROOT

snak·y (snā′kē) *adj.* **snak′i·er, snak′i·est 1** of or like a snake or snakes **2** having a snakelike form; serpentine; winding; twisting **3** cunningly treacherous or evil **4** full of or infested with snakes **5** formed of or entwined with snakes [a Gorgon's *snaky* hair] —**snak′i·ly** *adv.* —**snak′i·ness** *n.*

snap (snap) *vi.* **snapped, snap′ping** ⟦< MDu or MLowG *snappen*, akin to Ger *schnappen* < Gmc base **snab-*⟧ **1** to bring the jaws together sharply; bite suddenly: often with *at* [a fish *snaps* at bait] **2** to snatch or grasp quickly or eagerly: with *at* [to *snap* at a chance] **3** to speak sharply, abruptly, or irritably: often with *at* **4** to break, part, or be released suddenly, esp. with a sharp, cracking sound **5** to give way suddenly under strain, as nerves, resistance, etc. **6** to make a sudden, sharp cracking or clicking sound, as a whip **7** *a)* to close, fasten, go into place, etc. with a snapping sound [the lock *snapped* shut] *b)* to become closed or fastened by means of a SNAP (*n.* 6) **8** to move or act suddenly and smartly [to *snap* to attention] **9** to appear to flash or sparkle, as in anger: said of the eyes —*vt.* **1** to grasp or get suddenly with or as with a bite; snatch: often with *up* **2** to break or sever suddenly or with a snapping sound **3** to speak or utter sharply or harshly, as in anger: often with *out* **4** to cause to make a snapping sound [to *snap* one's fingers] **5** to close, fasten, put into place, etc. with a snapping sound [to *snap* a lid shut] **6** to strike sharply by releasing one end of something held under tension [to *snap* someone with a rubber band] **7** to cause to move suddenly and smartly [*snap* the ball to first base] ☆**8** [Informal] *a)* to take a snapshot of *b)* to take (a snapshot) ☆**9** *Football* to put (the ball) into play by passing or handing it back between the legs to a member of the offensive backfield: said of the center —*n.* ⟦MDu *snap*⟧ **1** a sudden bite, grasp, snatch, catch, etc. **2** a sudden breaking or parting **3** a sudden, sharp cracking or clicking sound [the *snap* of a whip] **4** a short, angry manner of speaking **5** a brief period or spell of cold weather **6** any clasp or fastening that closes with a click or snap **7** a hard, thin cookie [*gingersnap*] ☆**8** *short for* SNAPSHOT ☆**9** [Informal] alertness, vigor, or energy ☆**10** [Informal] an easy task, job, problem, etc. ☆**11** *Football* the act of snapping the ball —*adj.* ☆**1** made or done quickly or on the spur of the moment without deliberation; impulsive [a *snap* decision] **2** that fastens with a snap ☆**3** [Slang] simple; easy [a *snap* assignment] —*adv.* with, or as with, a snap —☆**in a snap** [Informal] quickly and easily —**snap back** to recover quickly from an illness, disappointment, etc. —**snap one's fingers at** to show lack of concern for; be careless of or indifferent toward —☆**snap out of it** [Informal] to change suddenly from a bad condition to a better one; recover quickly or regain one's senses

SNAP (snap) *n.* ⟦*s(ystems for) n(uclear) a(uxiliary) p(ower)*⟧ a small nuclear power source designed to provide electricity for satellites, remote automatic weather stations, etc.

☆**snap·back** (snap′bak′) *n.* [Old-fashioned] *Football* SNAP (*n.* 11)

snap bean ⟦so named because it is *snapped* into pieces for cooking⟧ any of various green beans or wax beans

snap-brim hat (snap′brim′) a man's hat with the crown creased lengthwise and the brim turned down in front

snap·drag·on (-drag′ən) *n.* ⟦SNAP + DRAGON: from the mouth-shaped flowers⟧ **1** any of a genus (*Antirrhinum*) of perennial plants of the figwort family, with showy white, yellow, red, or purplish flowers; esp., a common garden species (*A. majus*) with white, purple, crimson, etc., saclike, two-lipped, closed flowers **2** ⟦in allusion to a fire-breathing dragon⟧ [Historical] *a)* a game in which raisins or the like are snatched from a bowl of burning brandy *b)* that which is so snatched

snap·per (snap′ər) *n.* **1** a person or thing that snaps **2** *pl.* **-pers** or **-per** ☆*a)* SNAPPING TURTLE *b)* any of a family (Lutjanidae) of percoid fishes inhabiting most warm seas; esp., the red snapper ☆**3** *a)* PUNCHLINE *b)* the climactic, often surprising or shocking part of a story, speech, etc.

☆**snapping beetle** CLICK BEETLE

☆**snapping turtle** any of a family (Chelydridae) of large freshwater turtles of North America, with a small shell and powerful jaws which snap with great force, esp., a common species (*Chelydra serpentina*)

snap·pish (snap′ish) *adj.* **1** likely to snap or bite **2** cross or irritable, uncivil; sharp-tongued —**snap′pish·ly** *adv.* —**snap′pish·ness** *n.*

snap·py (snap′ē) *adj.* **-pi·er, -pi·est 1** snappish; cross **2** that snaps; snapping **3** [Informal] *a)* brisk, vigorous, or lively [a *snappy* reply, pace, etc.] *b)* sharply chilly [*snappy* weather] **4** [Informal] stylish; smart [a *snappy* dresser] —☆**make it snappy** [Slang] be quick; hurry —**snap′pi·ly** *adv.* —**snap′pi·ness** *n.*

snap roll a maneuver in which an airplane makes one complete fast roll about its longitudinal axis while maintaining its general horizontal direction

snap·shot (snap′shät′) *n.* **1** a hurried shot fired with little or no aim **2** an informal photograph, usually intended for private use, taken with a small camera **3** *a)* a brief, often informal, explanation or summary *b)* anything regarded as typifying something larger or more encompassing [a neighborhood that is a *snapshot* of Middle America]

snare (sner) *n.* ⟦ME < OE *sneare* < ON *snara*, akin to OHG *snarha* < IE **(s)nerk-* < base **(s)ner-*, to twist: see NARCOTIC⟧ **1** a kind of trap for small animals, usually consisting of a noose which jerks tight upon the release of a spring trigger **2** anything dangerous, risky, etc. that tempts or attracts; thing by which a person is entangled; trap **3** *a)* any of a set of spiraled wires or of lengths of gut, strung across the bottom of a snare drum for added vibration *b)* [*sometimes pl.*] a snare drum **4** *Surgery* a wire noose for removing tumors, polyps, etc. —*vt.* **snared, snar′ing** ⟦< Du *snaar*, akin to Ger *schnur*⟧ **1** to catch in a trap or snare **2** to tempt or attract into a situation, esp. one that is dangerous, risky, etc. —***SYN.*** CATCH, TRAP[1] —**snar′er** *n.*

snare drum a small, double-headed drum with snares

snare drum

snarf (snärf) *vt.* ⟦? echoic⟧ [Slang] to eat or ingest very quickly: often with *down* or *up*

snark·y (snär′kē) *adj.* **snark′i·er, snark′i·est** ⟦< dial. *snark,* to grumble, find fault with⟧ [Informal] **1** ill-humored, short-tempered, etc. **2** critical, derisive, sarcastic, etc. —**snark′i·ness** *n.*

snarl[1] (snärl) *vi.* ⟦extended from earlier *snar,* to growl, akin to Swed *snarra,* MHG, MDu, MLowG *snarren,* to growl < IE echoic base **(s)ner-, *(s)nur-* > SNEER, SNORE, OIce *norn,* NORN⟧ **1** to growl fiercely, baring the teeth, as a threatening dog does **2** to speak harshly and sharply, as in anger, impatience, etc. —*vt.* to utter or give vent to with a snarl [*to snarl one's contempt*] —*n.* **1** a fierce, harsh growl **2** a harsh utterance expressing anger, impatience, etc. —**snarl′er** *n.* —**snarl′ing·ly** *adv.*

snarl[2] (snärl) *vt.* ⟦ME *snarlen* < *snare* (see SNARE) + *-len,* -LE⟧ **1** to make (thread, hair, etc.) knotted or tangled **2** to make disordered or confused; complicate [*to snarl traffic*] **3** to ornament (metalwork) with a raised design, as by hammering —*vi.* to become knotted or tangled —*n.* ⟦ME *snarle*⟧ **1** a knotted or tangled mass or tuft; tangle [*hair full of snarls*] **2** a confused, disordered state or situation; complication; confusion

snarl·y[1] (snär′lē) *adj.* **snarl′i·er, snarl′i·est** snarling; bad-tempered; cross

snarl·y[2] (snär′lē) *adj.* **snarl′i·er, snarl′i·est** snarled; tangled; confused

snatch (snach) *vt.* ⟦ME *snacchen,* prob. var. of *snakken,* to seize; akin to *snaken:* see SNACK⟧ **1** to grasp or seize suddenly, eagerly, or without right, warning, etc.; grab **2** to remove abruptly or hastily **3** to take, get, or avail oneself of hastily or while there is a chance [*to snatch some rest*] ☆**4** [Slang] to kidnap —*vi.* **1** to try to grasp or seize a thing suddenly; grab (*at*) **2** to accept or take advantage of a chance, etc. eagerly: with *at* —*n.* ⟦ME *snacche*⟧ **1** the act of snatching; a grab **2** a brief period; short time or spell [*to sleep in snatches*] **3** a small portion, esp. one that is incomplete or disconnected; fragment; bit [*snatches of gossip*] **4** [Vulgar Slang] the vulva ☆**5** [Slang] an act of kidnapping **6** *Weight Lifting* a lift in which the barbell is raised in one continuous motion from the floor to a position directly overhead with the arms completely extended —*SYN.* TAKE —**snatch′er** *n.*

snatch block *Naut.* a block so designed that it can be readily opened for the insertion of the bight (as distinct from the end) of a rope

snatch·y (snach′ē) *adj.* **snatch′i·er, snatch′i·est** done in snatches; not complete or continuous; disconnected

snath (snath) *n.* ⟦altered (infl. by dial. *snathe,* to lop, prune < ON *sneitha,* to cut; akin to OE *snithan:* see SCHNITZEL) < OE *snæd*⟧ the curved shaft or handle of a scythe: also **snathe** (snāth)

☆**snaz·zy** (snaz′ē) *adj.* **-zi·er, -zi·est** ⟦< ? SN(APPY) + (J)AZZY⟧ [Slang] stylishly or showily attractive; flashy

☆**SNCC** (snik) *abbrev.* Student Nonviolent (*later* National) Coordinating Committee

sneak (snēk) *vi.* **sneaked** or ☆**snuck, sneak′ing** ⟦prob. < OE **snecan,* akin to *snican,* to crawl: for IE base see SNAIL⟧ **1** to move quietly and stealthily so as to avoid being seen or heard; go furtively **2** to be a sneak; behave in a stealthy, underhanded, or cowardly manner —*vt.* to give, put, carry, take, etc. secretly or in a stealthy, sneaking manner —*n.* **1** a person who sneaks; stealthy, underhanded, contemptible person **2** an act of sneaking ☆**3** *short for* SNEAKER (sense 2): *usually used in pl.* —*adj.* without warning; stealthy [*a sneak attack*] —**sneak up (on)** to approach (someone) by or as by stealth
USAGE—See usage note at SNUCK

sneak·er (snē′kər) *n.* **1** a person or animal that sneaks ☆**2** ⟦because the soft sole allows movement with little or no sound⟧ a shoe with an upper of, typically, canvas or nylon, and a continuous sole and heel as of soft rubber: for recreation and informal wear

sneak·ing (-kiŋ) *adj.* **1** cowardly, stealthy, underhanded, or furtive [*a sneaking manner*] **2** not admitted or made known to others; secret [*a sneaking fondness for candy*] **3** slight, or slight but increasing [*a sneaking suspicion*] —**sneak′ing·ly** *adv.*

☆**sneak preview** a single advance showing of a film, as for evaluating audience reaction or for increasing interest in the film, prior to the regular showing

☆**sneak thief** a person who commits thefts in a sneaking way, without the use of force or violence

sneak·y (snē′kē) *adj.* **sneak′i·er, sneak′i·est** of or like a sneak; underhanded —**sneak′i·ly** *adv.* —**sneak′i·ness** *n.*

☆**sneaky Pete** (pēt) [Slang] very cheap wine

sneer (snir) *vi.* ⟦ME *sneren,* akin to Fris *sneere,* to scorn, Dan *snaere,* to grin like a dog: see SNARL[1]⟧ **1** to smile derisively; show scorn or contempt as by curling the upper lip **2** to express derision, scorn, or contempt in speech or writing —*vt.* to utter with a sneer or in a sneering manner —*n.* **1** an act of sneering **2** a sneering expression, insinuation, etc. —**sneer′er** *n.* —**sneer′ing·ly** *adv.*

sneeze (snēz) *vi.* **sneezed, sneez′ing** ⟦ME *snesen,* prob. echoic alteration of *fnesen* < OE *fneosan:* for IE base see PNEUMA⟧ to exhale breath from the nose and mouth in a sudden, involuntary, explosive action, as a result of an irritation of the nasal mucous membrane —*n.* an act of sneezing —**not to be sneezed at** not to be considered lightly or disregarded —**sneez′er** *n.* —**sneez′y** *adj.*

☆**sneeze·weed** (snēz′wēd′) *n.* any of a genus (*Helenium*) of plants of the composite family; esp., a North American perennial (*H. autumnale*) said to cause sneezing

☆**sneeze·wort** (-wʉrt′) *n.* a strong-smelling, white-flowered plant (*Achillea ptarmica*) of the composite family, with leaves and flowers formerly used in medicine

snell[1] (snel) *adj.* ⟦ME < OE, akin to Ger *schnell*⟧ [Dial.] **1** quick; active **2** clever; smart; acute **3** severe; extreme; harsh **4** keen; sharp

☆**snell**[2] (snel) *n.* ⟦U.S. dial. < ?⟧ a short length of gut, nylon, etc. used to attach a fishhook to a fish line —*vt.* to attach (a fishhook) to a snell

SNF (snif) *abbrev.* skilled nursing facility

SNG (es′en′jē′) *n.* ⟦*s(ubstitute) n(atural) g(as)* or *s(ynthetic) n(atural) g(as)*⟧ any manufactured fuel gas with properties similar to natural gas, produced from organic material such as coal or naphtha

snick[1] (snik) *n.* ⟦prob. back-form. < *snick or snee:* see SNICKERSNEE⟧ **1** a small cut or notch; nick **2** *Cricket* a glancing blow —*vt.* **1** to cut slightly; nick **2** *Cricket* to hit (the ball) a glancing blow

snick[2] (snik) *n.* ⟦echoic⟧ a click or clicking sound —*vi.* to make a click —*vt.* to cause to click

snick·er (snik′ər) *vi.* ⟦echoic⟧ **1** to laugh in a sly or derisive, partly stifled manner **2** to neigh; nicker —*vt.* to utter with a snicker —*n.* a sly or derisive, partly stifled laugh —*SYN.* LAUGH —**snick′er·ing·ly** *adv.*

snick·er·snee (snik′ər snē′) *n.* ⟦< *snick or snee,* earlier *stick or snee,* combat with knives < Du *steken,* to thrust, stab + *snijden,* to cut⟧ [Rare] a large knife, designed for use as a thrusting and cutting weapon

snide (snīd) *adj.* ⟦orig., counterfeit, bogus < thieves' slang, prob. of Du dial. or Ger orig. < base of Ger *schneiden,* to cut, with reference to coin clipping and, later, to cutting remarks⟧ slyly malicious or derisive [*a snide remark*] —**snide′ly** *adv.* —**snide′ness** *n.*

sniff (snif) *vi.* ⟦ME *sniffen,* akin to Dan *snive,* of echoic orig.⟧ **1** to draw in air through the nose with enough force to be heard, as in clearing the nose, smelling something, or expressing contempt or skepticism **2** to say in a curt and disdainful way, with or as if with a sniff [*I don't believe it," she sniffed.*] —*vt.* **1** to breathe in forcibly through the nose; draw in or inhale nasally **2** to smell (a substance) by sniffing **3** to detect, perceive, or get a suspicion of by or as by sniffing: often with *out* —*n.* **1** an act or sound of sniffing **2** something sniffed —**not to be sniffed at** worthy of consideration or acceptance —**sniff′er** *n.*

snif·fle (snif′əl) *vi.* **-fled, -fling** ⟦freq. of prec.⟧ to sniff repeatedly, as in checking mucus running from the nose —*n.* an act or sound of sniffling —**the sniffles** [Informal] a condition of continual sniffling, as one resulting from a head cold or from an allergy —**snif′fler** *n.*

sniff·y (snif′ē) *adj.* **sniff′i·er, sniff′i·est** [Informal] **1** characterized by or having a tendency to sniff **2** contemptuous; disdainful Also **sniff′ish** —**sniff′i·ly** *adv.* —**sniff′i·ness** *n.*

snif·ter (snif′tər) *n.* ⟦< *snift,* var. of SNIFF⟧ ☆**1** [Brit. Informal] a small drink of alcoholic liquor ☆**2** a footed goblet that tapers to a small opening to concentrate the aroma, as of brandy

snig·ger (snig′ər) *vi., vt., n.* ⟦echoic⟧ SNICKER (*vi.* 1, *vt.*, *n.*)

snig·gle (snig′əl) *vi.* **-gled, -gling** ⟦< dial. *snig,* eel < ME *snygge,* young eel, prob. akin to *snegge,* snail, akin to Ger *schnecke:* for IE base see SNAIL⟧ to fish for eels by putting a baited hook into their hiding holes —*vt.* to catch (eels) by this method

snip (snip) *vt.* **snipped, snip′ping** ⟦Du *snippen,* akin to SNAP⟧ **1** to cut with scissors or shears in a short, quick stroke or strokes **2** to remove by or as by such cutting —*vi.* to make a short, quick cut or cuts —*n.* **1** a small cut made with scissors, etc. **2** the sound of this **3** *a)* a small piece cut off *b)* any small piece; bit **4** [*pl.*] heavy hand shears used esp. for cutting sheet metal **5** [Informal] a young, small, or insignificant person, esp. one regarded as impudent or insolent —**snip′per** *n.*

snipe (snīp) *n.* ⟦ME *snype* < ON *snipa* (akin to Ger *schnepfe*) < Gmc **sneb-,* beak < base seen in prec., SNAP⟧ **1** *pl.* **snipes** or **snipe** any of various shorebirds (family Scolopacidae) with a long, slender, flexible bill used in probing for food, esp. a genus (*Gallinago*) living chiefly in marshy places **2** a shot from a hidden position ☆**3** [Slang] the butt of a cigar or cigarette —*vi.* **sniped, snip′ing** **1** to hunt or shoot snipe **2** to shoot from a hidden position, as at individuals of an enemy force **3** to direct an attack (*at* someone) in a sly or underhanded way

snip·er (snī′pər) *n.* a person, esp. a soldier, who snipes

☆**snip·er·scope** (-skōp′) *n.* a snooperscope for mounting on a rifle or carbine

snip·pet (snip′it) *n.* ⟦dim. of SNIP⟧ a small piece, scrap, or portion, specif. of information from a book, report, etc.

snip·pet·y (-ē) *adj.* **1** made up of scraps or snippets **2** [Informal] SNIPPY

snip·py (snip′ē) *adj.* **-pi·er, -pi·est** **1** made up of small scraps or snips; fragmentary **2** [Informal] curt, sharp, or snappish, esp. in an insolent manner —**snip′pi·ly** *adv.* —**snip′pi·ness** *n.*

☆**snit** (snit) *n.* ⟦< ? prec. + (F)IT⟧ a fit of anger, pique, etc.: usually in the phrase **in (or into) a snit**

snitch (snich) [Slang] *vt.* ⟦< 18th-c. thieves' slang: orig. sense "a nose"⟧ to steal (usually something of little value); pilfer —*vi.* to be an informer; tattle (*on*) —*n.* an informer: also **snitch′er**

sniv·el (sniv′əl) *vi.* **-eled** or **-elled, -el·ing** or **-el·ling** ⟦ME *snivelen* < OE **snyflan* < base seen in *snofl,* mucus, prob. ult. < IE base **sneu-,* to flow⟧ **1** to have mucus running from the nose **2** to sniff repeatedly, as from a head cold, crying, etc.; sniffle **3** to cry and sniffle **4** to fret or complain in a whining, tearful manner **5** to make a whining, tearful, often false display of grief, sympathy, disappointment, etc. —*n.* **1** nasal mucus **2** the act of sniveling **3** a sniveling display of grief, etc. —**sniv′el·er** *n.*

snob (snäb) *n.* ⟦orig. dial. "boy, cobbler's boy" < ?⟧ **1** [Obs.] a person having no wealth or social rank; one of the common people **2** a person who attaches great importance to wealth, social position, etc., having or displaying contempt for his or her inferiors and admiration for superiors **3** a person who feels and acts smugly superior about his or her particular tastes or interests [an intellectual *snob*] —**snob′bish** ***adj.*** —**snob′bish·ly** ***adv.*** —**snob′bish·ness** ***n.***

snob·ber·y (snäb′ə rē) ***n., pl.*** **-ber·ies** snobbish behavior or character, or an instance of this: also **snob′bism′** (-iz′əm)

snob·by (snäb′ē) ***adj.*** of, like, or characteristic of a snob

snock·ered (snäk′ərd) ***adj.*** ⟦ult. < ? dial. *snock,* a knock or blow⟧ [Slang] drunk

☆**sno-cone** (snō′kōn′) ***n.*** ⟦perhaps infl. by *Sno-Kone,* a trademark⟧ *alt. sp. of* SNOW CONE

snog (snäg) ***vi., vt.*** ⟦< ?⟧ [Brit. Slang] to kiss, cuddle, or fondle

snood (sno͞od) ***n.*** ⟦via ME dial. < OE *snod,* ult. < IE base *sne-, to twist threads, spin > NEEDLE⟧ **1** a tie or ribbon for the hair, esp. as formerly worn by young unmarried women in Scotland **2** a baglike net worn at the back of a woman's head to hold the hair **3** a hat or part of a hat resembling this **4** SNELL[2] —***vt.*** to bind or hold up (the hair) with a snood

snook[1] (snook) ***n., pl.*** **snook** or **snooks** ⟦Du *snoek,* pike < MDu *snoec,* akin to ON *snokr,* small shark & OE *snacc,* small vessel⟧ any of a family (Centropomidae) of percoid fishes of warm seas; esp., a large game and food fish (*Centropomus undecimalis*) of the tropical Atlantic

snook[2] (snook) ***n.*** ⟦< ?⟧ [Informal, Chiefly Brit.] *used only in the phrase* **cock a snook**, THUMB ONE'S NOSE (see phrase at THUMB)

snook·er (snook′ər) ***n.*** ⟦< ?⟧ a variety of the game of pool played with fifteen red balls and six other balls —***vt.*** **1** to make a direct shot impossible for (an opponent in snooker) **2** [Informal] to thwart or defeat ☆**3** [Slang] to deceive, trick, or cheat

☆**snoop** (sno͞op) [Informal] ***vi.*** ⟦Du *snoepen,* to eat snacks on the sly⟧ to look about in a sneaking, prying way —***n.*** **1** a person who snoops: also **snoop′er 2** the act of snooping —**snoop′y** ***adj.*** **snoop′i·er, snoop′i·est**

☆**snoop·er·scope** (sno͞o′pər skōp′) ***n.*** ⟦see prec. & -SCOPE⟧ an electronic viewing device using infrared radiation that allows an observer to see objects, areas, etc. in the dark

snoot (sno͞ot) [Informal] ***n.*** ⟦ME *snute:* see SNOUT⟧ **1** the nose **2** the face **3** a grimace —***vt.*** to snub

☆**snoot·y** (sno͞ot′ē) ***adj.*** **snoot′i·er, snoot′i·est** ⟦prec. + -Y[2]: from the image of haughty people with their noses in the air⟧ [Informal] haughty; snobbish —**snoot′i·ly** ***adv.*** —**snoot′i·ness** ***n.***

snooze (sno͞oz) [Informal] ***n.*** ⟦< 18th-c. cant < ? or akin to LowG *snusen* (Dan *snuse*), to sniff, snore⟧ a brief sleep; nap; doze —***vi.*** **snoozed, snooz′ing** to take a brief sleep; nap; doze —**snooz′er** ***n.***

Sno·qual·mie Falls (snō kwäl′mē) ⟦< Salish tribal name⟧ waterfall in WC Wash., on a river (**Snoqualmie**) that flows west out of the Cascade Range: 270 ft (82 m)

snore (snôr) ***vi.*** **snored, snor′ing** ⟦ME *snoren:* see SNARL[1]⟧ to breathe, while asleep, with harsh sounds caused by vibration of the soft palate, usually with the mouth open —***n.*** the act or sound of snoring —**snor′er** ***n.***

☆**snor·kel** (snôr′kəl) ***n.*** ⟦Ger *schnorchel,* inlet, breathing tube, lit., snort, akin to *schnarchen,* to snore, akin to prec.⟧ **1** a device for submarines, having air intake and exhaust tubes: it makes long periods of underwater operation possible **2** a breathing tube extending above the surface of the water, used in swimming just below the surface **3** a hydraulic crane with a bucketlike aerial platform, mounted on a truck for firefighting, etc. —***vi.*** **-keled, -kel·ing** to move or swim underwater using a snorkel —**snor′kel·er** ***n.***

snorkel

Snor·ri Stur·lu·son (snôr′rē stur′lə sən) 1179?-1241; Icelandic historian & poet

snort (snôrt) ***vi.*** ⟦ME *snorten,* prob. < or akin to *snoren,* to SNORE⟧ **1** to force breath suddenly and violently through the nostrils so as to make a harsh sound **2** to express anger, contempt, or the like by a snort **3** to make a noise like a snort, as in laughing boisterously ☆**4** [Slang] to take a narcotic drug into the nose by sniffing —***vt.*** **1** to express or utter with a snort **2** to expel by or as by a snort ☆**3** [Slang] to take (a narcotic drug) into the nose by sniffing —***n.*** **1** the act or sound of snorting ☆**2** [Slang] a quick drink of straight liquor ☆**3** [Slang] a dose of a drug, esp. cocaine or heroin, that is snorted —**snort′er** ***n.***

snot (snät) ***n.*** ⟦ME < OE *(ge)snot,* mucus, akin to Ger dial. *schnutz:* for IE base see SNOUT⟧ [Informal] **1** nasal mucus: sometimes considered mildly vulgar **2** a person, esp. a young person, who is impudent, insolent, etc.

snot·ty (snät′ē) ***adj.*** **-ti·er, -ti·est** [Informal] **1** of, like, or dirtied with snot: sometimes considered mildly vulgar **2** impudent, insolent, etc. —**snot′ti·ly** ***adv.*** —**snot′ti·ness** ***n.***

snout (snout) ***n.*** ⟦ME *snoute,* prob. < MDu *snute,* akin to Ger *schnauze* < IE base *snā-, *sneu-, to drip fluid, wetness > L *natare,* to swim, *nutrire,* to nurse⟧ **1** *a)* the projecting nose and jaws, or muzzle, of an animal *b)* an anterior prolongation of the head resembling this, as in a weevil **2** a projecting part **3** [Informal] a large nose

☆**snout beetle** WEEVIL

snow (snō) ***n.*** ⟦ME < OE *snaw,* akin to Ger *schnee* < IE base *sneigwh-, to snow, *snoigwhos, snow > OIr *snechta,* Russ *sneg,* L *nix* (gen. *nivis*)⟧ **1** particles of water vapor which when frozen in the upper air fall to earth as soft, white, crystalline flakes **2** *a)* a falling of snow *b)* snowy weather **3** a mass or accumulation of fallen snow **4** [Old Poet.] whiteness **5** something like snow in whiteness, texture, etc. ☆**6** fluctuating spots appearing on a television screen as a result of a weak signal, shot effect, etc. ☆**7** [Slang] cocaine or heroin —***vi.*** ⟦ME *snowen* < OE *sniwian*⟧ to fall as or like snow —***vt.*** **1** to shower or let fall as or like snow ☆**2** to cover, obstruct, etc. with or as with snow: usually with *in, under,* etc. ☆**3** [Slang] to deceive, mislead, or win over by glib talk, flattery, etc. —☆**snow under 1** to weigh down or overwhelm with work, etc. **2** to defeat decisively

Snow (snō), **C(harles) P(ercy)** Baron Snow of Leicester 1905-80; Eng. novelist & physicist

snow·ball (snō′bôl′) ***n.*** **1** a mass of snow packed together into a ball, esp. one made by hand as for throwing in fun ☆**2** any of various plants with snowball-like flowers; esp., a cultivated European cranberry bush (*Viburnum opulus* var. *roseum*) with spherical clusters of sterile, white or pinkish flowers —***vi.*** **1** to increase or accumulate rapidly and uncontrollably, like a ball of snow rolling down a snow-covered hill **2** to throw snowballs —***vt.*** **1** to throw snowballs at **2** to cause to increase or accumulate rapidly

snow·bank (-baŋk′) ***n.*** a large mass of snow, esp. a drift on a hillside, in a gully, etc.

☆**snow·bell** (-bel′) ***n.*** any of several shrubby, white-flowered plants (genus *Styrax*) of the storax family, native to the E U.S. and E Asia

☆**snow·belt** (snō′belt′) ***n.*** [*often* **S-**] any region characterized by relatively large snowfalls: also written **snow belt** or **Snow Belt** —**the Snowbelt** that part of the U.S., including states of the Northeast and those bordering the Great Lakes, characterized by cold, snowy winters

snow·ber·ry (snō′ber′ē) ***n., pl.*** **-ries 1** a hardy, shrubby North American plant (*Symphoricarpos albus*) of the honeysuckle family, with tubular, small, pink flowers and soft, white berries **2** any of various other plants having white berries **3** any of these berries

snow·bird (-burd′) ***n.*** **1** a widely distributed junco (*Junco hyemalis*) commonly seen in the winter ☆**2** ⟦see SNOW, 7 & BIRD, 5⟧ [Slang] a person addicted to the use of cocaine or heroin ☆**3** [Slang] a northern tourist who vacations in the South during the winter

snow-blind (-blīnd′) ***adj.*** blinded temporarily by ultraviolet rays reflected from snow —**snow blindness**

snow·blink (-bliŋk′) ***n.*** a bright reflection of sunlight, esp. in polar regions, on the bottom of a low cloud, caused by a distant snowfield: cf. ICEBLINK: also written **snow blink**

snow·blow·er (-blō′ər) ***n.*** a motorized, hand-guided machine on wheels, for removing snow as from sidewalks: also written **snow blower**

snow·board (-bôrd′) ***n.*** a board somewhat similar to a small surfboard, on which a person stands and descends snowy hills for sport —***vi.*** to engage in the sport of descending snowy hills on a snowboard —**snow′board′er** ***n.***

snow·bound (-bound′) ***adj.*** shut in or blocked off by snow or snowy weather

snow bunting a small bunting (*Plectrophenax nivalis*) inhabiting cold regions in the Northern Hemisphere: the male is white in summer with black streaks on the back

☆**snow·bush** (-boosh′) ***n.*** a California shrub (*Ceanothus cordulatus*) of the buckthorn family, with white flowers

snow·cap (-kap′) ***n.*** a cap of snow, as on a mountain, the top of a tree, etc. —**snow′capped′** ***adj.***

☆**snow cone** a confection consisting of crushed ice and a flavored syrup, served in a paper cone

snow crab an edible spider crab (*Chionoecetes opilio*) of the N Pacific

Snow·don (snōd′'n) mountain in NW Wales: highest peak, 3,560 ft (1,085 m)

snow·drift (snō′drift′) ***n.*** **1** a smooth heap of snow blown together by the wind **2** snow blown along by the wind

snow·drop (-dräp′) ***n.*** any of a genus (*Galanthus*) of low-growing, bulbous perennials of the lily family; esp., the **common snowdrop** (*G. nivalis*) of the Mediterranean region, with small, bell-shaped, white flowers

snow·fall (-fôl′) ***n.*** **1** a fall of snow **2** the amount of snow that falls in a given area or period of time

snow fence a light fence of lath and wire erected to control the drifting of snow

snow·field (-fēld′) ***n.*** a large expanse of snow

snow·flake (-flāk′) ***n.*** **1** a single, feathery crystal of snow **2** SNOW BUNTING **3** any of a genus (*Leucojum*) of European bulbous plants of the lily family with drooping white flowers

snow goose a wild, medium-sized, white goose (*Anser caerulescens*) with a reddish bill and black wing tips, that breeds in the Arctic and has a bluish-gray color phase if it migrates farther south

☆**snow job** [Slang] the act or an instance of deceiving, persuading, etc. with glib talk, flattery, etc.

snow leopard a large, whitish cat (*Panthera uncia*) of the mountains of central Asia, having many dark blotches on its long, thick fur

snow line (*or* limit) the boundary between a region of permanent snow and a region where the snow melts in the summer

snow·man (-man′) ***n., pl.*** **-men′** (-men′) a figure of packed snow suggestive of a human form, traditionally composed of two or three large spheres stacked one upon the other, made as an outdoor activity in the winter

snow·melt (-melt′) ***n.*** meltwater from snow, esp. in the spring

snow·mo·bile (-mō bēl′) ***n.*** ⟦SNOW + -MOBILE⟧ any of various motor vehicles for traveling over snow, usually with steerable runners at the front and tractor treads at the rear —***vi.*** **-biled′, -bil′ing** to travel by snowmobile —**snow′mo·bil′er** ***n.***

snow·mold (-mōld′) *n.* a fungus disease of grasses and grains, appearing in lawns as gray patches near the edge of melting snow

snow-on-the-moun·tain (snō′än *thə* mount′'n) *n.* ☆a spurge (*Euphorbia marginata*) of the W U.S., with small flowers and the margins of the upper leaves white

snow·pack (-pak′) *n.* the accumulated snow covering an area, that melts in the spring and provides water for irrigation, electric power, etc., usually estimated in millions of acre-feet

snow pea a variety of pea with crisp, edible seedpods

snow plant ☆a red, fleshy, saprophytic plant (*Sarcodes sanguinea*) of the heath family, with hanging red flowers and no leaves, growing in the pine forests of the Sierra Nevada: often found in spring before the snow has melted

☆**snow·plow** (snō′plou′) *n.* **1** any device, machine, or vehicle used to clear snow off a road, railroad, etc. **2** *Skiing* a stemming of both skis, as for stopping, with the inside ski edges dug into the snow, and the tips of the skis pointed at each other —*vi.* to stem with both skis

snow pudding a kind of fluffy pudding made with beaten egg whites, sugar, and gelatin or cornstarch

☆**snow·shed** (-shed′) *n.* a long shed to protect a section of railroad track against snow

☆**snow·shoe** (-sho͞o′) *n.* either of a pair of racket-shaped frames of wood, etc. fitted with crosspieces and crisscrossed with strips of leather, etc., worn on the feet to prevent sinking in deep snow —*vi.* **-shoed′**, **-shoe′ing** to use snowshoes in walking —**snow′sho′er** *n.*

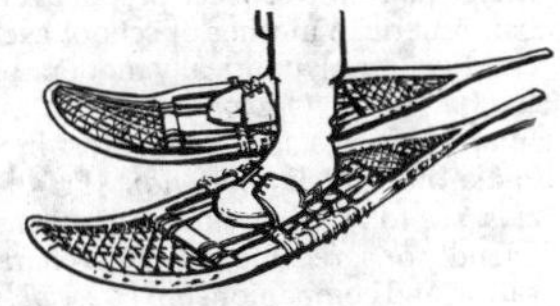
snowshoes

snowshoe hare ⟦so named from its broad feet, which are heavily furred in winter⟧ a large hare (*Lepus americanus*) of N North America whose coloration changes from brown in summer to white in winter: also **snowshoe rabbit**

☆**snow·slide** (-slīd′) *n.* an avalanche consisting mostly of snow

☆**snow·storm** (-stôrm′) *n.* a storm with a heavy snowfall

☆**snow·suit** (-so͞ot′) *n.* a heavily lined one-piece garment or set of pants and jacket, often with a hood, worn in cold weather; esp., such a garment or suit made for children

snow thrower SNOWBLOWER

☆**snow tire** a tire with a deep tread, and sometimes protruding studs, for added traction on snow or ice

Snow White ⟦transl. of LowG *Schneewittchen*, character so named because of her fair skin⟧ the title character of a fairy tale, a princess who flees her jealous stepmother, finds refuge with seven dwarfs, and is awakened from a sleeping spell by a prince

snow-white (-hwīt′, -wīt′) *adj.* white as snow

snow·y (snō′ē) *adj.* **snow′i·er**, **snow′i·est** ⟦ME *snawi* < OE *snawig*⟧ **1** characterized by snow or, esp., by much snow **2** covered or filled with snow [a *snowy* valley] **3** like or suggestive of snow; specif., *a)* pure; unsoiled; spotless *b)* white **4** of or consisting of snow —**snow′i·ly** *adv.* —**snow′i·ness** *n.*

snowy egret a white, medium-sized, migratory egret (*Egretta thula*) with black legs and yellow feet, usually living in colonies in marshland ranging from the U.S. to Chile and Argentina

snowy owl a large, white owl (*Nyctea scandiaca*) of northern tundras that usually feeds on small mammals, esp. lemmings

snub (snub) *vt.* **snubbed**, **snub′bing** ⟦ME *snubben* < ON *snubba*, to chide, snub⟧ **1** [Obs.] to check or interrupt with sharp or slighting words **2** to treat with scorn, contempt, disdain, etc.; behave coldly toward; slight or ignore **3** *a)* to check suddenly the outward movement of (a rope, cable, etc.) by turning it around a fixed object, as a post *b)* to make (a horse, boat, etc.) held fast by such an action ☆**4** to put out (a cigarette): usually with *out* —*n.* **1** scornful, slighting action or treatment; affront **2** a snubbing, or checking —*adj.* short and turned up; pug: said of the nose —**snub′ber** *n.*

snub·by (snub′ē) *adj.* **-bi·er**, **-bi·est** **1** turned up; snub **2** tending to snub or slight

snub-nosed (-nōzd′) *adj.* **1** having a snub nose **2** designating or of a handgun with a very short barrel

☆**snuck** (snuk) *vi., vt. alt. pt. & pp. of* SNEAK
USAGE—this form is still regarded by some as nonstandard

snuff[1] (snuf) *n.* ⟦ME < ?⟧ the charred end of a candlewick —*vt.* ⟦ME *snuffen* < the *n.*⟧ **1** to trim off the charred end of (a candlewick) **2** to put out (a candle) with snuffers or by pinching **3** [Slang] to kill; murder —*adj.* designating or of a kind of pornographic film that purports to show someone being murdered as the climax of sexual activity —**snuff out 1** to put out (a candle, etc.); extinguish **2** to bring to an end suddenly; destroy

snuff[2] (snuf) *vt.* ⟦< MDu *snuffen* < Gmc **snuf-* < IE **sneup* < base **sneu-*: see SNOUT⟧ **1** to draw in through the nose; inhale strongly; sniff **2** to smell, sniff, or sniff at —*vi.* to sniff or snort —*n.* **1** the act or sound of snuffing; sniff **2** a preparation of powdered tobacco that is inhaled by sniffing, chewed, or rubbed on the gums **3** smell; scent —**up to snuff 1** [Informal] up to the usual standard, as in health, quality, etc. **2** [Brit. Informal] not easily deceived; alert

snuff·box (snuf′bäks′) *n.* a small, often ornamental box for holding snuff

snuff·er (-ər) *n.* **1** a device with a cone on the end of a handle, for extinguishing a burning candle: in full **candle snuffer** **2** [*usually pl.*] an instrument designed to open and close like a pair of scissors, for snuffing a candle: also **pair of snuffers**

snuf·fle (snuf′əl) *vi.* **-fled**, **-fling** ⟦freq. of SNUFF[2], v.⟧ **1** to breathe audibly and with difficulty or by constant sniffing, as a dog in trailing; sniff or sniffle **2** to speak or sing in a nasal tone **3** [Rare] to whine —*vt.* to utter by snuffling —*n.* **1** the act or sound of snuffling **2** a nasal tone or twang —**the snuffles** [Informal] THE SNIFFLES —**snuf′fler** *n.*

snuff·y (snuf′ē) *adj.* **snuff′i·er**, **snuff′i·est** **1** like snuff, as in color or texture **2** having the habit of taking snuff **3** soiled with snuff **4** disagreeable; unattractive

snug (snug) *adj.* **snug′ger**, **snug′gest** ⟦Early ModE < naut. language, prob. via E Fris *snugge*, Du *snugger*, smooth, neat < Scand, as in ON *snøggr*, short-haired, short (hence, tight, taut) < IE **ksneu-* < base **kes-*, to comb, shear (hair) > Gr *xainein*, to comb⟧ **1** protected from the weather or the cold; warm and cozy **2** small but well arranged; compact and convenient; neat; trim [a *snug* cottage] **3** large enough to provide ease and comfort: said of an income **4** tight or close in fit [a *snug* coat, a *snug* joint] **5** trim and well-built; seaworthy **6** hidden or concealed [to lie *snug*] —*adv.* **snug′ger**, **snug′gest** so as to be snug —*vi.* **snugged**, **snug′ging** [Dial.] SNUGGLE —*vt.* to make snug or secure —*n.* [Brit.] SNUGGERY —*SYN.* COMFORTABLE —**snug down** *Naut.* to make ready for a storm by reducing sail, securing movable gear, etc. —**snug′ly** *adv.* —**snug′ness** *n.*

snug·ger·y (snug′ər ē) *n., pl.* **-ger·ies** [Chiefly Brit.] a snug or comfortable place, room, etc.; esp., a small private room or booth in a public house

☆**snug·gies** (-ēz) *pl.n.* women's long, warm underwear

snug·gle (snug′əl) *vi.* **-gled**, **-gling** ⟦freq. of SNUG⟧ to lie closely and comfortably; nestle; cuddle, as for warmth, in affection, etc. —*vt.* to hold or draw close or in a comfortable position; cuddle; nestle —**snug′gly** (snug′əl ē) *adj.*

so[1] (sō) *adv.* ⟦ME *so*, *swo* < OE *swa*, so, as, akin to Goth *swa*, OHG *so* < IE base **se-*, **swe-*, refl. particle⟧ **1** in the way or manner shown, expressed, indicated, understood, etc.; as stated or described; in such a manner [hold the bat just *so*] **2** *a)* to the degree expressed or understood; to such an extent [why are you *so* late?] *b)* to an unspecified but limited degree, amount, number, etc. [to go *so* far and no further] *c)* to a very high degree; very [they are *so* happy] *d)* used with *that* or *as* when providing a result, implication, or comparison [she was *so* late that she missed dessert; he went *so* far as to accuse them of treason; sales were not *so* brisk as they were a year ago] **3** for the reason specified; therefore [they were tired, and *so* left] **4** also; likewise [she enjoys music, and *so* does he] **5** then [and *so* to bed] **6** [Informal] very much [she *so* wants to go]: also used in contradicting a negative statement [I did *so* tell the truth!] —*conj.* **1** in order that; with the purpose that: usually followed by *that* [talk louder *so* (that) everyone can hear] **2** with the result that; because of this [she smiled, *so* I did too] **3** [Archaic] if only; as long as; provided (*that*) ➡The conjunction *so* is also used as a superfluous element for connecting clauses, introducing comments, or resuming a conversation —*pron.* that which has been specified or named [they are friends and will remain *so*] —*interj.* used to express surprise, approval or disapproval, triumph, etc. —*adj.* true; in reality [is that *so?*] —**and so on (or forth)** and others; and the rest; and in like manner; et cetera (etc.) —**just so** in precise or proper order [when it comes to housecleaning, everything must be *just so*] —**or so** approximately that number, amount, etc.; more or less [fifty dollars *or so*] —**so as to** in order to: followed by an infinitive —**so be it** a phrase used to express acceptance or acquiescence —**so long!** [Informal] goodbye! farewell! —**so much** to an unspecified but limited degree, amount, etc. [paid *so much* per day]: often used as an intensifier [*so much* the worse for us!] —**so much for** no more need be said about [*so much for* my problems] —**so there!** a phrase used to accompany a defiant or spiteful gesture, action, remark, etc. —☆**so what?** [Informal] even if so, what then?: used to express disregard, challenge, contempt, etc.: often reduce to **so?**

so[2] (sō) *n. Music* SOL[2]

so[3] *abbrev.* **1** south **2** southern

SO *abbrev.* strikeout(s)

soak (sōk) *vt.* ⟦ME *soken* < OE *socian* < base of *sucan*: see SUCK⟧ **1** to make thoroughly wet; drench or saturate [*soaked* to the skin by the rain] **2** to submerge or keep in a liquid, as for thorough wetting, softening, for hydrotherapy, etc. **3** *a)* to take in (liquid) by sucking or absorbing *b)* to expose oneself to (something) and take it in as if through absorption [to *soak* up sunshine, *soak* up their praise]: usually with *up* **4** *a)* to take in mentally, esp. with little effort (usually with *up*) [to *soak* up knowledge] *b)* to immerse (oneself) in some study or branch of learning ☆**5** [Slang] to charge heavily or too dearly; overcharge —*vi.* **1** to stay immersed in water or other liquid for wetting, softening, etc. **2** to pass or penetrate as a liquid does; permeate [rain *soaking* through his coat] **3** to become absorbed mentally [the fact *soaked* into his head] —*n.* **1** the act or process of soaking **2** the state of being soaked **3** liquid used for soaking or steeping **4** [Slang] a drunkard —**soak out** to draw out (dirt, etc.) by or as by soaking —**soak′er** *n.*

SYN.—**soak** implies immersion in a liquid, etc. as for the purpose of absorption, thorough wetting, softening, etc. [to *soak* bread in milk]; **saturate** implies absorption to a point where no more can be taken up [air *saturated* with moisture]; **drench** implies a thorough wetting as by a downpour [a garden *drenched* by the rain]; **steep** usually suggests soaking for the purpose of extracting the essence of something [to *steep* tea]; **impregnate** implies the penetration and permeation of one thing by another [wood *impregnated* with creosote]

soak·age (sōk′ij) *n.* **1** a soaking or being soaked **2** liquid that has seeped out or been absorbed

soak·ing (sōk′iŋ) *n.* the act or an instance of making or becoming soaked —*adj.* very wet; drenched: also **soaking wet**

so-and-so (sō′ən sō′) *n., pl.* **so′-and-sos′** [Informal] some person or thing whose name is either not specified or not known: often used euphemistically in place of a strong or vulgar, disparaging epithet

soap (sōp) *n.* ⟦ME *sope* < OE *sape,* akin to Ger *seife* < Gmc **saipo-* < IE base **seib-*, to trickle, run out > L *sebum,* tallow⟧ **1** a substance used with water to produce suds for washing or cleaning: soaps are usually sodium or potassium salts of fatty acids, produced by the action of an alkali, as caustic soda or potash, on fats or oils **2** any metallic salt of a fatty acid ☆**3** [Slang] SOAP OPERA: also **soap′er** —*vt.* to lather, scrub, etc. with soap —☆**no soap** [Slang] **1** the offer, idea, etc. is not acceptable **2** to no avail

soap·bark (sōp′bärk′) *n.* **1** *a)* a South American tree (*Quillaja saponaria*) of the rose family, with leathery leaves and white flower clusters *b)* its inner bark, used in cleansing preparations for its saponin content **2** any of several tropical American trees (genus *Pithecellobium*) of the mimosa family, whose bark contains saponin

soap·ber·ry (-ber′ē) *n., pl.* **-ries 1** any of a genus (*Sapindus*) of trees of the soapberry family, with fruits containing saponin **2** the globular fruit, with yellowish flesh and a large, round seed —*adj.* designating a family (Sapindaceae, order Sapindales) of chiefly tropical, dicotyledonous trees and shrubs, including the litchi and longan

soap·box (-bäks′) *n.* **1** a box or crate for soap ☆**2** any improvised platform used by a person (**soapbox orator**) making an informal, often impassioned speech to a street audience, as on a current, controversial issue

soap bubble 1 a filmy bubble of soapy water, specif. one blown up, as from a pipe **2** something short-lived, insubstantial, or ephemeral

☆**soap opera** ⟦so called because many of the original sponsors were manufacturers of soaps or detergents⟧ a radio or television serial drama of a highly melodramatic, sentimental nature

☆**soap plant** any of various plants some parts of which can be used as soap; esp., a tall W North American plant (*Chlorogalum pomeridianum*) of the lily family

soap·stone (-stōn′) *n.* ⟦so named because it is waxy to the touch⟧ a compact, usually impure, massive variety of talc, used to make electrical insulators, stove linings, etc.

soap·suds (-sudz′) *pl.n.* **1** soapy water, esp. when stirred into a foam **2** the foam on soapy water

soap·wort (-wurt′) *n.* any of a genus (*Saponaria*) of plants of the pink family, with bright, colorful flowers and sap that forms a lather with water, including the bouncing Bet

soap·y (sō′pē) *adj.* **soap′i·er, soap′i·est 1** covered with or containing soap; lathery **2** of, like, or characteristic of soap **3** [Informal] of, like, or characteristic of a soap opera **4** [Slang] suave; unctuous; oily —**soap′i·ly** *adv.* —**soap′i·ness** *n.*

soar (sôr) *vi.* ⟦ME *soren* < OFr *essorer,* to expose (wings) to the air, hence soar, as a falcon < VL **exaurare* < L *ex-*, out + *aura,* air: see AURA⟧ **1** to rise or fly high into the air **2** to fly, sail, or glide along high in the air **3** to glide along without engine power, maintaining or gaining altitude on currents of air: said of an aircraft, esp. a glider **4** to rise well above the usual or ordinary level or bounds; be elevated [*soaring* prices, *soaring* spirits] —*vt.* [Old Poet.] to reach by soaring —*n.* **1** soaring range or height **2** the act of soaring —**soar′er** *n.* —**soar′ing** *adj.*

So·a·ve (sə wä′vā, swä′-; *It* sô ä′ve) *n.* ⟦It, after town where made⟧ [*occas.* **s-**] a dry white wine of N Italy

sob (säb) *vi.* **sobbed, sob′bing** ⟦ME *sobben*⟧ **1** to weep aloud with a catch or break in the voice and short, gasping breaths **2** to make a sound like that of sobbing, as the wind —*vt.* **1** to bring (oneself) into a given state, esp. sleep, by sobbing **2** to utter with sobs —*n.* the act or sound of one that sobs —*SYN.* CRY —**sob′bing·ly** *adv.*

SOB (es′ō′bē′) *n., pl.* **SOB's** [Slang] SON OF A BITCH (sense 1): a euphemism: also written **s.o.b.** or **S.O.B.**

so·ba (noodles) (sō′bə) ⟦Jpn *soba*⟧ Japanese noodles containing buckwheat flour

so·be·it (sō bē′it) *conj.* ⟦*so be it*⟧ [Archaic] provided; if it should be that

so·ber (sō′bər) *adj.* ⟦ME *sobre* < OFr < L *sobrius* < *so(d)-*, var. of *se(d)-*, without + *ebrius,* drunk⟧ **1** temperate or sparing in the use of alcoholic liquor **2** not drunk **3** temperate in any way; not extreme or extravagant **4** serious, solemn, grave, or sedate **5** not bright, garish, or flashy; quiet; plain: said of color, clothes, etc. **6** not exaggerated or distorted [the *sober* truth] **7** characterized by reason, sanity, or self-control; showing mental and emotional balance — *vt., vi.* to make or become sober: often with *up* or *down* —*SYN.* SERIOUS —**so′ber·ly** *adv.* —**so′ber·ness** *n.*

so·ber-mind·ed (-mīn′did) *adj.* sensible and serious —**so′ber-mind′ed·ly** *adv.* —**so′ber-mind′ed·ness** *n.*

so·ber·sides (-sīdz′) *n., pl.* **-sides′** a sedate, serious-minded person

So·bies·ki (sō byes′kē), **John** *see* JOHN III

so·bri·e·ty (sə brī′ə tē, sō-) *n.* ⟦ME *sobrete* < OFr *sobriete* < L *sobrietas* < *sobrius,* SOBER⟧ the state or quality of being sober; specif., *a)* temperance or moderation, esp. in the use of alcoholic liquor *b)* seriousness; sedateness

so·bri·quet (sō′brə kā′, -ket′; sō′brə kā′, -ket′) *n.* ⟦Fr < MFr *soubriquet,* chuck under the chin < ?⟧ **1** a nickname **2** an assumed name

☆**sob sister** [Old Slang] a journalist, esp. a woman, who writes sentimental human-interest stories

☆**sob story** [Informal] a very sad story, esp. an account of personal troubles that is meant to arouse sympathy

soc *abbrev.* **1** social **2** socialist **3** society

so·ca (sō′kə) *n.* ⟦< SO(UL) + CA(LYPSO)⟧ a popular dance music, a blend of calypso and SOUL (*n.* 9c), that originated in Trinidad

soc·age (säk′ij) *n.* ⟦ME: see SOKE & -AGE⟧ a medieval English system of land tenure in which a tenant held land in return for a fixed payment or for certain stated nonmilitary services to his lord

SoCal (sō′kal′) *abbrev.* Southern California

so-called (sō′kôld′) *adj.* **1** popularly known or called by this term [the *so-called* nuclear powers] **2** inaccurately or questionably designated as such [a *so-called* liberal]

soc·cer (säk′ər) *n.* ⟦altered < (AS)SOC(IATION FOOTBALL)⟧ a game played with a round ball by two teams, usually of eleven players, on a field with a goal at either end: the ball is moved chiefly by kicking or by using any part of the body except the hands and arms

☆**soccer mom** ⟦from the notion that such women spend much time driving their children to soccer practice, etc.⟧ [Informal] a middle-class, suburban American mother of school-age children, regarded as being, typically, child-centered, politically moderate, civic-minded, etc.

So·che (sō′che′) *a former transliteration of* SHACHE

So·chi (sô′chē) seaport & resort in S Russia, on the Black Sea

so·cia·ble (sō′shə bəl) *adj.* ⟦Fr < L *sociabilis* < *sociare,* to associate < *socius:* see fol.⟧ **1** enjoying or requiring the company of others; gregarious **2** friendly or agreeable; affable **3** characterized by pleasant, informal conversation and companionship [a *sociable* evening] —*n.* ☆a social, esp. a church social —**so′cia·bil′i·ty** *n., pl.* **-ties** —**so′cia·ble·ness** *n.* —**so′cia·bly** *adv.*

so·cial (sō′shəl) *adj.* ⟦< Fr or L: Fr < L *socialis* < *socius,* companion, akin to *sequi,* to follow < IE base **sekw-*, to follow > OE *secg,* man, warrior⟧ **1** of or having to do with human beings living together as a group in a situation in which their dealings with one another affect their common welfare [*social* consciousness, *social* problems] **2** living in this way; gregarious [man as a *social* being] **3** of or having to do with the ranks or activities of society, specif. the more exclusive or fashionable of these [a *social* event] **4** getting along well with others; sociable [a *social* nature] **5** of, for, or involving friends, companionship, or sociability [a *social* club] **6** offering material aid, counseling services, group recreational activities, etc. to those who need it; of or engaged in welfare work [a *social* worker or agency] **7** living or associating in groups or communities [the ant is a *social* insect] **8** *Bot.* growing in clumps or masses —*n.* an informal gathering of people for recreation or amusement; party —**so′cial·ly** *adv.*

☆**social climber** a person who associates with socially prominent people in an attempt to gain higher social status

social contract (*or* compact) in the theories of certain political philosophers, as Locke and Rousseau, the implicit agreement among individuals, by which organized society was begun and sets of regulations are instituted to govern interrelations

social dancing BALLROOM DANCING

social Darwinism 1 the application, chiefly in the late 19th cent., of Darwinism to the understanding of human society **2** any belief or theory that attempts to explain human society in terms of NATURAL SELECTION, specif., the theory that individuals, ethnic groups, etc. achieve success or dominance because of inherent genetic superiority and a resultant competitive advantage —**social Darwinist**

social democrat 1 [**S- D-**] a member or adherent of a Social Democratic Party **2** a person who advocates a moderately socialist government or society —**social democracy**

Social Democratic Party any of various political parties, as in Europe, advocating moderate socialism within a democratic system

social disease [Old-fashioned] a sexually transmitted disease: a euphemistic usage

social drinker someone who drinks alcoholic beverages only or primarily when socializing with others and not to excess —**social drinking**

social engineering the application of methods regarded as similar to engineering techniques in their emphasis on practicality, efficiency, and moral neutrality in an effort to solve a social problem or improve the condition of society —**social engineer**

Social Gospel a movement among some U.S. Protestants beginning around 1870, seeking to eliminate poverty, ignorance, etc. by reforming society according to Christian principles

social insurance any insurance program undertaken by a government to provide income or payments to persons who are unemployed, disabled, elderly, etc.

so·cial·ism (sō′shəl iz′əm) *n.* **1** any of various theories or systems of the ownership and operation of the means of production and distribution by society or the community rather than by private individuals, with all members of society or the community sharing in the work and the products **2** [*often* **S-**] *a)* a political movement for establishing such a system *b)* the doctrines, methods, etc. of the Socialist parties **3** in Marxist doctrine, the stage of society coming between the capitalist and the communist stages: see COMMUNISM (sense 2)

so·cial·ist (-ist) ***n.*** 1 an advocate or supporter of socialism 2 [**S-**] a member of a Socialist Party —***adj.*** 1 of or like socialism or socialists 2 advocating or supporting socialism 3 [**S-**] of or having to do with a Socialist Party Also **so′cial·is′tic** —**so′cial·is′ti·cal·ly** ***adv.***

Socialist Party a political party based on the principles of socialism advocated by Marx and Engels

socialist realism a style of writing, painting, etc., established in the Soviet Union in the 1930s, typically depicting laborers and other members of a communist society in a heroic or idealized fashion —**socialist realist**

☆**so·cial·ite** (sō′shə līt′) ***n.*** a person who is prominent in fashionable society

so·ci·al·i·ty (sō′shē al′ə tē) ***n.*** ⟦L *socialitas*⟧ 1 the quality or state of being social or sociable; sociability 2 *pl.* **-ties** the tendency in individuals to join together in groups and associate with one another

so·cial·ize (sō′shə līz′) ***vt.*** **-ized′**, **-iz′ing** 1 to make social; adjust to or make fit for cooperative group living 2 to adapt or make conform to the common needs of a social group 3 to subject to governmental ownership and control; nationalize 4 to cause to become socialist —☆***vi.*** to take part in social activity —**so′cial·i·za′tion** ***n.*** —**so′cial·iz′er** ***n.***

socialized medicine any system supplying complete medical and hospital care, through public funds, for all the people in a community, district, or nation

social media SOCIAL NETWORKING applications regarded collectively as a type of communciations media

social networking open, Web-based networking in which users are able to informally share, variously, messages, videos, digital photographs, etc. —**social network**

social psychology the study of the behavior of people in social groups

social realism a style or movement in art, fiction, film, etc., in which the everyday lives of ordinary, typically poor or working-class, people are depicted in realistic settings —**social realist**

☆**social register** ⟦< the title of such a directory, later trademarked⟧ a directory or list of people prominent in the fashionable society of a given area

social science 1 the study of people living together in groups, families, etc., and their customs, activities, etc. 2 any of several fields of study, as economics, political science, or anthropology, dealing with the structure of society and the activity of its members —**social scientist**

social secretary a secretary employed by an individual to handle his or her social appointments and correspondence

☆**social security** 1 any system by which a society or community provides for those of its members who may be in need 2 [*usually* **S- S-**] in the U.S., a federal system of social-insurance and welfare programs, including Medicare and Medicaid, paying benefits to eligible persons who are retired, unemployed, disabled, indigent, etc. 3 benefits paid by this system, esp., the monthly check issued to eligible retirees

social service SOCIAL WORK —**so′cial-serv′ice** ***adj.***

☆**social studies** a course of study, esp. in elementary and secondary schools, including history, civics, geography, etc.

social welfare 1 the welfare of society, esp. of those segments of society that are underprivileged or disadvantaged because of poverty, poor education, unemployment, etc. 2 SOCIAL WORK

social work 1 any service or activity designed to promote the welfare of the community and the individual, as through counseling services, health clinics, recreation halls and playgrounds, or aid for the needy, the aged, the physically handicapped, etc. 2 such services and activities collectively

social worker a person trained to perform the tasks of social work, esp. one with a college or university degree in social work

so·ci·e·tal (sə sī′ə təl) ***adj.*** pertaining to society; social

so·ci·e·ty (sə sī′ə tē) ***n.***, *pl.* **-ties** ⟦MFr *société* < L *societas* < *socius*, companion: see SOCIAL⟧ 1 a group of persons regarded as forming a single community, esp. as forming a distinct social or economic class 2 the system or condition of living together as a community in such a group [an agrarian *society*] 3 all people, collectively, regarded as constituting a community of related, interdependent individuals [a law for the good of *society*] 4 company or companionship [to seek another's *society*] 5 one's friends or associates 6 any organized group of people joined together because of work, interests, etc. in common [a medical *society*] 7 *a)* a group of persons regarded or regarding itself as a dominant class, usually because of wealth, birth, education, etc. [her debut into *society*] *b)* the conduct, standards, activities, etc. of this class 8 a group of animals or plants living together in a single environment and regarded as constituting a homogeneous unit or entity —***adj.*** of or characteristic of SOCIETY (***n.*** 7*a*) [the *society* page of a newspaper]

Society Islands ⟦so named (1769) by James COOK[1]⟧ group of islands in the South Pacific, constituting a division of French Polynesia: *c.* 613 sq mi (1,588 sq km); chief town, Papeete

Society of Friends a Christian denomination, founded in England *c.* 1650 by George Fox, that has no formal creed, liturgy, or priesthood and rejects violence in human relations, esp. warfare: cf. QUAKER

Society of Jesus *see* JESUIT

So·cin·i·an·ism (sō sin′ē ən iz′əm) ***n.*** the teachings of Faustus Socinus (1539-1604), It. rationalistic religious reformer, denying the Trinity, the divinity of Christ, etc., and holding that salvation is attained solely by practicing the virtues exemplified by Christ —**So·cin′i·an** ***n., adj.***

so·ci·o- (sō′sē ō, -shē-; -ə) ⟦Fr < L *socius*, companion: see SOCIAL⟧ *combining form* social, society, sociological (and) [*socioeconomic, sociometry*]

☆**so·ci·o·bi·ol·o·gy** (sō′sē ō bī äl′ə jē, -shē-) ***n.*** the scientific study of the biological basis for animal and human social behavior: it is based on the theory that some or much of such behavior is genetically determined —**so′ci·o·bi′o·log′i·cal** ***adj.*** —**so′ci·o·bi·ol′o·gist** ***n.***

so·ci·o·cul·tu·ral (sō′sē ō kul′chər əl, sō′shē-) ***adj.*** of or involving both social and cultural factors

☆**so·ci·o·e·co·nom·ic** (-ē′kə näm′ik, -ek′ə-) ***adj.*** of or involving both social and economic factors

so·ci·o·gram (sō′sē ə gram′, sō′shē-) ***n.*** *Sociology* a diagram designed to indicate from answers to sociometric questions how individuals in a group feel toward each other

sociol *abbrev.* 1 sociological 2 sociology

so·ci·o·lin·guis·tics (sō′sē ō liŋ gwis′tiks, -shē-) ***n.*** the branch of linguistics that analyzes the effects of social and cultural factors within a speech community upon its language patterns —**so′ci·o·lin′guist** ***n.*** —**so′ci·o·lin·guis′tic** ***adj.***

so·ci·o·log·i·cal (sō′sē ə lä′ji kəl, -shē-) ***adj.*** 1 of or having to do with human society, its organization, needs, development, etc. 2 of sociology Also **so′ci·o·log′ic** —**so′ci·o·log′i·cal·ly** ***adv.***

so·ci·ol·o·gy (sō′sē äl′ə jē, -shē-) ***n.*** ⟦Fr *sociologie* (coined in 1830 by A. COMTE): see SOCIO- & -LOGY⟧ 1 the science of human society and of social relations, organization, and change; specif., the study of the beliefs, values, etc. of societal groups and of the processes governing social phenomena 2 SYNECOLOGY —**so′ci·ol′o·gist** ***n.***

so·ci·om·e·try (-äm′ə trē) ***n.*** 1 the quantitative study of group relationships ☆2 a technique for measuring what members of a group perceive, think, and feel about other members of the group —**so′ci·o·met′ric** (-ə me′trik) ***adj.***

so·ci·o·path (sō′sē ə path′, -shē-) ***n.*** ⟦SOCIO- + (PSYCHO)PATH⟧ a person suffering from psychopathic personality, whose behavior is aggressively antisocial —**so′ci·o·path′ic** ***adj.***

so·ci·o·po·lit·i·cal (sō′sē ō pə lit′i kəl, -shē-) ***adj.*** of or involving both social and political factors

sock[1] (säk) ***n.*** ⟦ME *socke* < OE *socc* < L *soccus*, type of light, low-heeled shoe < Gr *sukchis*, prob. of Phrygian orig.; akin to Avestan *haxa-*, sole of the foot⟧ 1 a light shoe worn by comic characters in ancient Greek and Roman drama 2 comedy or the muse of comedy 3 *pl.* **socks** or **sox** a knitted covering for the foot and ankle, like a short stocking, sometimes extending to just below the knee 4 *short for* WINDSOCK —☆**sock away** [Informal] to set aside (money), esp. as savings —☆**sock in** to ground (an aircraft) or close (an airfield) as because of fog: usually in the passive voice

sock[2] (säk) [Slang] ***vt.*** ⟦Early ModE < cant⟧ to hit or strike with force, esp. with the fist —***n.*** a blow —***adv.*** directly; squarely —☆**sock it to** to confront, rebuke, attack, or otherwise treat harshly or severely

sock cymbal ⟦< prec.⟧ HIGH-HAT

☆**sock·dol·a·ger** or **sock·dol·o·ger** (säk däl′ə jər) ***n.*** ⟦metathetic alteration (infl. by SOCK[2]) < DOXOLOGY (in sense of "conclusion") + -ER⟧ [Old Slang] 1 something final or decisive, as a heavy blow 2 something outstanding

sock·et (säk′it) ***n.*** ⟦ME *soket*, spearhead shaped like a plowshare < Anglo-Fr, dim. < OFr *soc*, plowshare < Gaul **soccus*, plowshare, orig., pig's snout (hence, that which roots out) < IE **suk-*, var. of base **su-*, SOW[1]⟧ a hollow piece or part into which something fits [the *socket* for a lightbulb, of the eye, of the hipbone, etc.] —***vt.*** to furnish with or fit into a socket

socket wrench a wrench with a cylindrical socket that fits over a nut or bolt of a specific size and shape

sock·eye salmon (säk′ī′) ⟦altered < Salish *suk-kegh*⟧ a red-fleshed salmon (*Oncorhynchus nerka*) of the N Pacific: it is an endangered species

sock hop [Informal] an informal dance where participants dance in their socks, popular esp. in the 1950s among high-school students

☆**sock·o** (säk′ō) ***adj.*** ⟦< SOCK[2]⟧ [Slang] very popular, impressive, or successful

sock puppet 1 a HAND PUPPET consisting of a sock, typically having a simple or crude face 2 a false identity, esp. one assumed online for participating anonymously in social networking websites, making comments on blogs or forums, etc.

so·cle (säk′əl, sōk′-) ***n.*** ⟦Fr < It *zoccolo*, pedestal, wooden shoe < L *socculus*, dim. of *soccus*, SOCK[1]⟧ *Archit.* a projecting foundation piece, as for a column, wall, or statue

So·co·tra (sō kō′trə) island of Yemen, in the Indian Ocean, off the E tip of Africa: 1,351 sq mi (3,499 sq km)

Soc·ra·tes (säk′rə tēz′) 470?-399 B.C.; Athenian philosopher & teacher: principal figure in the Platonic dialogues —**So·crat·ic** (sə krat′ik, sō-) ***adj., n.***

Socratic irony ⟦so called from its use by Socrates as part of the fol.⟧ pretense of ignorance in a discussion to expose the fallacies in the opponent's logic

Socratic method a method of teaching or discussion, like that used by Socrates, in which by means of a series of questions and answers the logical soundness of a definition is tested, the meaning of a concept examined, etc.

sod[1] (säd) ***vt., vi.*** *obs. pt. of* SEETHE

sod[2] (säd) ***n.*** ⟦ME, prob. < MDu or MLowG *sode*, akin to OFris *sada, satha*⟧ 1 a surface layer of earth containing grass plants with their matted roots; turf; sward 2 a piece of this layer —***vt.*** **sod′ded**, **sod′ding** to cover with sod or sods —**the old sod** one's native land: used esp. by the Irish —**under the sod** dead and buried

sod[3] (säd) [Brit. Slang] ***n.*** ⟦shortened < *sodomite*: see SODOMITE, sense

2]] 1 a sodomite 2 a person; often, specif., one who is objectionable or contemptible —*vt.* to damn; curse: used only in the imperative [*sod* all!] ➥Still considered somewhat vulgar by some in all senses —**sod off!** go away! get lost!

so·da (sō′də) *n.* ⟦ML (or It or Sp) < Ar *suwayd*, burnt plant (from which soda was produced), dim. of *'aswad*, black⟧ 1 *a)* sodium oxide, Na_2O *b)* SODIUM BICARBONATE *c)* SODIUM CARBONATE *d)* SODIUM HYDROXIDE 2 *a)* SODA WATER ☆*b)* a flavored, carbonated soft drink, esp. as sold in bottles or cans ☆*c)* a confection of soda water flavored with syrup, fruit, etc. and served with ice cream in it ☆3 in faro, the card turned up in the dealing box before play starts

soda ash crude SODIUM CARBONATE (sense 1)

☆**soda biscuit** 1 a biscuit made with baking soda and sour milk or buttermilk 2 [Chiefly Brit.] SODA CRACKER

☆**soda cracker** a cracker, usually salted, prepared from dough made of flour, water, and leavening, orig. baking soda and cream of tartar

☆**soda fountain** a counter with equipment for making and serving soft drinks, sodas, sundaes, etc.

☆**soda jerk** [Old Slang] a person who works at a soda fountain: also **soda jerk′er**

soda lime a white, powdery mixture of sodium hydroxide and calcium oxide, used as a chemical reagent and as an absorbent for moisture and acid gases

so·da·lite (sō′də līt′) *n.* ⟦SODA + -LITE⟧ a usually blue, hard mineral, $Na_4(AlSiO_4)_3Cl$, used in making jewelry; sodium aluminum silicate chloride

so·dal·i·ty (sō dal′ə tē) *n., pl.* **-ties** ⟦L *sodalitas* < *sodalis*, companion < IE base **swedh-* > ETHICAL⟧ 1 fellowship; companionship 2 an association or brotherhood 3 *R.C.Ch.* a lay society for devotional or charitable activity

☆**soda pop** ⟦see POP[1], *n.* 3⟧ a flavored, carbonated soft drink, esp. as sold in bottles or cans; soda

soda water 1 [Historical] an effervescent solution of water, acid, and sodium bicarbonate 2 *a)* water charged under pressure with carbon dioxide gas, used in ice-cream sodas or as a chaser or mix *b)* SODA POP

☆**sod·bust·er** (säd′bus′tər) *n.* [Old Slang, Chiefly West] a farmer: a disparaging term

sod·den (säd′'n) *adj.* ⟦obs. pp. of SEETHE⟧ 1 [Archaic] boiled or steeped 2 filled with moisture; soaked through 3 heavy or soggy from improper baking or cooking: said as of bread 4 dull or stupefied, as from liquor —*vt., vi.* to make or become sodden —**sod′den·ly** *adv.*

Sod·dy (säd′ē), **Frederick** 1877-1956; Brit. chemist

so·di·um (sō′dē əm) *n.* ⟦ModL: so named (1807) by Sir Humphry DAVY < SODA (because isolated from caustic soda) + -IUM⟧ 1 a soft, silver-white, metallic chemical element, one of the alkali metals, having a waxlike consistency: it is found in nature only in combined form and is extremely actively chemically: symbol, Na; at. no. 11: see the periodic table of elements in the Reference Supplement 2 *short for* SODIUM CHLORIDE

sodium benzoate a sweet, odorless, white powder, C_6H_5COONa, the sodium salt of benzoic acid, used as a food preservative, antiseptic, etc.

sodium bicarbonate BAKING SODA

sodium bromide a white, crystalline compound, NaBr, used in medicine as a sedative and in photography to produce silver bromide

sodium carbonate 1 the anhydrous sodium salt of carbonic acid, Na_2CO_3 2 any of the hydrated carbonates of sodium; esp., SAL SODA

sodium chlorate a colorless, crystalline salt, $NaClO_3$, used as an oxidizing agent in matches, explosives, etc.

sodium chloride common salt, NaCl

sodium citrate a white, crystalline powder, $Na_3C_6H_5O_7{\cdot}2H_2O$, that dissolves in water but not alcohol, with a salty taste, used as a food additive, esp. in soft drinks, as an anticoagulant, etc.

sodium cyanide a white, highly poisonous salt, NaCN, used in electroplating, as an insecticide, etc.

sodium dichromate a red, crystalline salt, $Na_2Cr_2O_7$, used as an oxidizing agent, corrosion inhibitor, antiseptic, etc.

sodium fluoride a colorless, toxic, crystalline powder, NaF, with many uses, esp. as an insecticide, in making glass, and, in minute quantities, in toothpaste and to fluoridate public water supplies

sodium flu·o·ro·ac·e·tate (flôr′ō as′ə tāt, floor′-) a powder, $CH_2FCOONa$, used as a rodent poison

sodium hydroxide a white, deliquescent substance, NaOH, in the form of a powder, flakes, sticks, etc.: it is a strong caustic base, widely used in chemistry, oil refining, etc.

sodium hypochlorite a greenish, unstable salt, NaOCl, usually stored in solution, used esp. as a bleaching agent and disinfectant

sodium hy·po·sul·fite (hī′pō sul′fīt′) SODIUM THIOSULFATE

sodium nitrate a clear, odorless, crystalline salt, $NaNO_3$, used in manufacturing nitric acid, sodium nitrite, explosives, fertilizers, etc., and as an oxidizing agent

sodium nitrite a yellowish or white powder, $NaNO_2$, used to make dyes, preserve meats, counteract cyanide poisoning, etc.

sodium pentothal ⟦< *Pentothal*, trademark for this substance: see PENTOTHAL SODIUM⟧ THIOPENTAL SODIUM

sodium perborate a white, odorless, crystalline compound, $NaBO_3{\cdot}4H_2O$, used chiefly as a bleaching and oxidizing agent and in germicides, deodorants, etc.

sodium peroxide a yellowish-white powder, Na_2O_2, used as an antiseptic, bleaching and oxidizing agent, etc.

sodium phosphate any of various clear, crystalline sodium salts of phosphoric acid, widely used in industry

sodium propionate a transparent, deliquescent, crystalline compound, $C_3H_5O_2Na$, used to prevent mold, esp. in foods

sodium sulfate a white, crystalline salt, Na_2SO_4, used in medicine and in the making of dyes, glass, etc.

sodium thiosulfate a white, crystalline salt, $Na_2S_2O_3$, used as an antichlor, as a fixing agent in photography, etc.: popularly called *sodium hyposulfite* or *hypo*

so·di·um-va·por lamp (sō′dē əm vā′pər) a discharge lamp used for street lighting, fitted with two electrodes and filled with neon and sodium vapor, giving off a soft, yellow light

Sod·om (säd′əm) *n.* ⟦LL(Ec) *Sodoma* < Gr(Ec) < Heb *sedom*⟧ *Bible* a city destroyed by fire together with a neighboring city, Gomorrah, because of the sinfulness of the people: Gen. 18-19

Sod·om·ite (säd′ə mīt′) *n.* ⟦OFr < LL(Ec) *Sodomita* < Gr(Ec)⟧ 1 a person living in ancient Sodom 2 [**s-**] a person who practices sodomy

sod·om·ize (-mīz′) *vt.* **-ized′**, **-iz′ing** ⟦fol. + -IZE⟧ to engage in sodomy with; specif., to forcibly subject to sodomy

sod·om·y (-mē) *n.* ⟦ME *sodomie* < *Sodome*, SODOM⟧ any sexual intercourse held to be abnormal; specif., *a)* bestiality *b)* anal intercourse, esp. between two male persons

Sod's law (sädz) [Brit. Informal] MURPHY'S LAW

so·ev·er (sō ev′ər) *adv.* ⟦see SO[1] & EVER⟧ [Archaic] 1 in any way; to any extent or degree: usually following *how* and an adjective [how dark *soever* the night may be] 2 of any kind; at all [no rest *soever*]

-so·ev·er (sō ev′ər) *combining form* any (person, thing, time, place, manner, etc.) of all those possible: added, for emphasis or generalization, to *who, what, when, where, how*, etc.

so·fa (sō′fə) *n.* ⟦Fr < Ar *ṣuffa*, a platform covered with rugs & cushions⟧ an upholstered couch, usually of spring construction, with fixed back and arms

sofa bed a sofa that can be opened into a bed

☆**so·far** (sō′fär′) *n.* ⟦< *so(und) f(ixing) a(nd) r(anging)*⟧ system for locating the site of an underwater explosion by calculations of the time the sound vibrations take to reach several shore stations

sof·fit (säf′it) *n.* ⟦Fr *soffite* < It *soffitto* < VL **suffictus*, for L *suffixus*: see SUFFIX⟧ 1 the horizontal underside of an eave, cornice, etc. 2 the intrados of an arch or vault

So·fi·a (sō′fē ə, sō fē′ə; *Bulg* sô′fē yä′) capital of Bulgaria, in the W part: also sp. **So′fi·ya′**

S of S *abbrev.* Song of Songs: see SONG OF SOLOMON

soft (sôft, säft) *adj.* ⟦ME < OE *softe*, gentle, quiet < *sefte*, akin to Ger *sanft* < IE base **sem-*, together, together with > SMOOTH, SAME: basic sense "fitting, friendly, suited to"⟧ 1 giving way easily under pressure, as a feather pillow or moist clay 2 easily cut, marked, shaped, or worn away, as pine wood or pure gold 3 not hard for its kind; not as hard as is normal, desirable, etc. [*soft* butter] 4 smooth or fine to the touch; not rough, harsh, or coarse 5 *a)* bland; not acid, sour, or sharp *b)* easy to digest because free from roughage (said of a diet) 6 nonalcoholic: said of drinks 7 having in solution few or none of the mineral salts that interfere with the lathering and cleansing properties of soap: said of water 8 mild, gentle, or temperate, as a breeze, the weather, climate, etc. 9 *a)* weak or delicate; not strong or vigorous; esp., not able to endure hardship, as because of easy living *b)* having flabby muscles 10 requiring little effort; easy [a *soft* job] 11 showing, or done with, little force or strength [a *soft*, underhand toss] 12 *a)* kind or gentle, esp. to the point of weakness; lenient or compassionate *b)* easily impressed, influenced, or imposed upon 13 not bright, intense, or glaring; subdued: said of color or light 14 showing little contrast or distinctness; not sharp in lines, tones, focus, etc., as a photograph 15 gentle; low; not loud or harsh: said of sound 16 based on data from interviews, surveys, etc., rather than from controlled, repeatable experiments [*soft* evidence] 17 replenished by nature, or capable of being used with relatively little damage to the natural environment [solar power is a *soft* energy source] 18 designating news reports concerned with relatively trivial or less serious subjects or events 19 *Finance a)* unstable and declining (said of a market, prices, etc.) *b)* not readily accepted as foreign exchange (said of certain currencies) *c)* having very favorable terms (said of a loan) 20 *Mil.* above ground and vulnerable: said of targets or bases 21 *Phonet. a)* designating *c* sounded as in *voice* or *g* sounded as in *age b)* voiced *c)* palatalized, as certain consonants in Slavic languages are: not used in these ways as a technical term by phoneticians 22 *Radiology* of low penetrating power: said of X-rays —*adv.* softly; gently; quietly —*n.* something soft —*interj.* [Archaic] 1 be quiet; hush 2 slow up; stop —**be soft on** 1 to treat gently 2 [Informal] to feel affectionate or amorous toward —**soft in the head** stupid or foolish —**soft′ly** *adv.* —**soft′ness** *n.*

SYN.—**soft**, in this connotation, implies an absence or reduction of all that is harsh, rough, too intense, etc., so as to be pleasing to the senses [*soft* colors, a *soft* voice]; **bland** implies such an absence of irritation, stimulation, pungency, etc. in something as to make it soothing, unexciting, and hence, sometimes, uninteresting [*bland* foods, climate, etc.]; **mild** applies to that which is not as rough, harsh, irritating, etc. as it might be [a *mild* cigarette, criticism, etc.]; **gentle**, often equivalent to **mild**, carries a more positive connotation of being pleasantly soothing or tranquil [a *gentle* breeze, voice, etc.] —*ANT.* **harsh, rough**

☆**soft·ball** (sôft′bôl′, säft′-) ***n.*** **1** a kind of baseball played with underhand pitching, a small infield, and usually four outfielders **2** the ball used in playing softball: it is larger than a hardball
soft-boiled (-boild′) ***adj.*** cooked in simmering water only a short time so that the yolk is still soft: said of an egg
☆**soft·bound** (-bound′) ***adj.*** SOFTCOVER
soft chancre CHANCROID
soft coal BITUMINOUS COAL
soft-core (sôft′kôr′, säft′-) ***adj.*** portraying sexual acts in a manner that is highly suggestive rather than explicit: also written **softcore**
☆**soft·cov·er** (-kuv′ər) ***adj.*** **1** designating any book bound in a flexible cover, as vinyl plastic or imitation leather **2** PAPERBACK **—*n.*** a softcover book
soft drink a nonalcoholic drink, esp. one that is carbonated
soft drug a relatively mild drug, such as marijuana, generally regarded as being nonaddictive
soft·en (sôf′ən, säf′-) ***vt., vi.*** ⟦ME *softnen*: see SOFT & -EN⟧ **1** to make or become soft or softer **2** to weaken the resistance or opposition of (someone): often with *up*
soft·en·er (-ər) ***n.*** something that softens; specif., *a)* a positively charged compound added to water in treating fabrics to make them softer and fluffier (in full **fabric softener**) *b) short for* WATER SOFTENER
softening of the brain [Old-fashioned] **1** degeneration of the brain tissues **2** dementia
soft-finned (sôft′find′, säft′-) ***adj.*** *Zool.* having fins with soft rays instead of hard spines
soft·gel (-jel′) ***n.*** ⟦< SOFT + GEL(ATIN)⟧ a dose of medicine, vitamin supplement, etc. suspended in a liquid and enclosed in a mass of soft gelatin
soft·goods (-good̸z′) ***pl.n.*** goods that last a relatively short time, esp. textile products: also **soft goods**
soft·head·ed (-hed′id) ***adj.*** stupid or foolish **—soft′head′ed·ly *adv.*** **—soft′head′ed·ness *n.***
soft·heart·ed (-härt′id) ***adj.*** **1** full of compassion or tenderness **2** not strict or severe, as in discipline or authority **—soft′heart′ed·ly *adv.*** **—soft′heart′ed·ness *n.***
soft·ie (sôf′tē, säf′-) ***n.*** [Informal] *alt. sp. of* SOFTY
☆**soft landing** a landing of a spacecraft on a planet or moon without damage to the craft or its contents
soft money money given as a donation to a political party but not designated for a particular candidate
soft palate the soft part at the rear of the roof of the mouth; velum
soft pedal a pedal used to soften or dampen the tone of a piano or any of certain other musical instruments
soft-ped·al (sôft′ped′'l, säft′-) ***vt.*** **-aled** or **-alled**, **-al·ing** or **-al·ling** **1** to soften or dampen the tone of (a musical instrument) by use of a special pedal **2** [Informal] to make less emphatic, less obtrusive, less conspicuous, etc.; tone down; play down
soft porn [Slang] soft-core pornography
soft rot any of various plant diseases, characterized by watery decay of rhizomes, roots, fruits, etc. and caused by any of numerous fungi or bacteria
soft science ⟦see SOFT, *adj.* 16⟧ BEHAVIORAL SCIENCE: opposed to HARD SCIENCE
soft sculpture sculpture, as of human or animal forms, made of fabric, stuffing, plastic, foam, etc.
☆**soft sell** selling that relies on subtle suggestion rather than high-pressure salesmanship **—soft′-sell′ *adj.***
soft serve FROZEN CUSTARD
☆**soft-shell** (-shel′) ***adj.*** **1** having a soft shell **2** having an unhardened shell as the result of recent molting Also **soft′-shelled′** **—*n.*** a soft-shell animal; esp., a crab that has recently molted
☆**soft-shell clam** any of a family (Myidae) of edible clams of the coasts of North America, having elongated siphons and a chalky, white shell
☆**soft-shelled turtle** any of a family (Trionychidae) of aquatic turtles of North America, Asia, and Africa, with a soft, oval, leathery shell; esp., a North American genus (*Trionyx*) common in the Mississippi drainage
soft-shoe (-sho͞o′) ***adj.*** designating a kind of tap-dancing done without metal taps on the shoes
☆**soft shoulder** soft ground along the edge of a highway
soft soap **1** soap in liquid or semifluid form **2** [Informal] flattery or smooth talk
soft-soap (-sōp′) ***vt.*** [Informal] to flatter **—soft′-soap′er *n.***
soft-spo·ken (-spō′kən) ***adj.*** **1** speaking or spoken with a soft, low voice **2** smooth; ingratiating; suave
☆**soft touch** [Slang] a person who is easily persuaded, esp. to give or lend money
soft·ware (-wer′) ***n.*** ⟦SOFT + (HARD)WARE⟧ ☆the programs, routines, etc. for a computer or computer system: cf. HARDWARE (sense 3*b*)
soft wheat wheat with low protein content and soft kernels, yielding a flour used as in pastries
soft·wood (-wood̸′) ***n.*** **1** *a)* any light, easily cut wood *b)* any tree yielding such wood **2** *Forestry* the wood of any conifer
soft·y (sôf′tē, säf′-) ***n., pl.*** **soft′ies** [Informal] **1** a person who is overly sentimental or trusting **2** a person who lacks physical stamina or vigor
Sog·di·an (säg′dē ən) ***n.*** **1** a member of a people that lived in Sogdiana **2** the extinct Iranian language of this people
Sog·di·a·na (säg′dē an′ə) ancient region in central Asia, between the Oxus & Jaxartes rivers
sog·gy (säg′ē, sôg′ē) ***adj.*** **-gi·er**, **-gi·est** ⟦< obs. *sog*, damp, boggy place, prob. < or akin to ON *sea*, lit., a sucking < base of SUCK⟧ **1** saturated with moisture or liquid; soaked **2** moist and heavy; sodden *[soggy* cake*]* **3** dull, heavy, and boring **—sog′gi·ly *adv.*** **—sog′gi·ness *n.***
So·ho (sō′hō′, sō hō′) district in Westminster, central London
So·Ho (sō′hō′) ⟦< *so*(*uth of*) *Ho*(*uston*) (street in Manhattan), prob. echoing *Soho* (see prec.)⟧ district in the lower west side of Manhattan: noted as a center for artists, art galleries, etc.
soi-di·sant (swȧ dē zän′) ***adj.*** ⟦Fr, lit., self-saying⟧ SELF-STYLED
soi·gné (swän yā′) ***adj.*** ⟦see fol.⟧ **1** dressed and groomed elegantly and with great care: used in referring to a man **2** *occas. sp. of* SOIGNÉE (with reference to a woman) **3** manifesting elegance, sophistication, care, good taste, etc. *[*a *soigné* silk suit, *soigné* manners*]*
soi·gnée (swän yā′) ***adj.*** ⟦Fr, fem. of *soigné*, pp. of *soigner*, to take care of, attend to < ML (Gallic) *soniare* < *sonium*, care < Frank **sunnja*⟧ dressed and groomed elegantly and with great care: used in referring to a woman
soil[1] (soil) ***n.*** ⟦ME *soile* < Anglo-Fr *soil*, for OFr *suel* < L *solum*, floor, ground, soil⟧ **1** the surface layer of earth, supporting plant life **2** any place for growth or development **3** land; country; territory *[*native *soil]* **4** ground or earth *[*barren *soil]* **—the soil** life and work on a farm **—soil′less *adj.***
soil[2] (soil) ***vt.*** ⟦ME *soilen* < OFr *souiller* < VL **suculare* < L *suculus*, dim. of *sus*, pig: see SOW[1]⟧ **1** to make dirty, esp. on the surface **2** to smirch or stain **3** to bring disgrace upon **4** to corrupt or defile; sully **—*vi.*** to become soiled or dirty **—*n.*** ⟦ME *soile* < OFr *soil*, pig sty < L *suile* < *sus*⟧ **1** a soiled spot; stain; smirch **2** manure used for fertilizing **3** excrement, sewage, refuse, etc. **4** a soiling or being soiled **—*SYN.*** DIRTY
soil[3] (soil) ***vt.*** ⟦altered < ? OFr *saoler* < L *satullare*, to satiate < *satullus*, filled (with food), dim. of *satur*: see SATURATE⟧ **1** to feed (livestock) on soilage **2** to purge (livestock) by means of green food
soil·age (-ij) ***n.*** ⟦prec. + -AGE⟧ green crops cultivated for fodder
☆**soil bank** a U.S. federal program under which subsidies are paid to farmers to stop growing certain surplus crops and to enrich the idle land by various methods
soil conservation the protection of fertile topsoil from erosion by wind and water and the replacement of nutrients in the soil, as by means of cover crops, terracing, contour farming, crop rotation, etc.
soil pipe a pipe for carrying off liquid waste from toilets
soil·ure (soil′yoor) ***n.*** ⟦ME *soylure* < MFr *soilleure* < *soillier*: see SOIL[2]⟧ [Archaic] **1** a soiling, dirtying, or sullying **2** a stain; blot
soi·ree or **soi·rée** (swä rā′) ***n.*** ⟦Fr *soirée* < *soir*, evening < L *sero*, at a late hour < *serus*, late⟧ a party or gathering in the evening
so·journ (sō′jurn′; *also, for v.,* sō jurn′) ***vi.*** ⟦ME *sojournen* < OFr *sojorner* < VL **subdiurnare* < L *sub-*, under + *diurnus*, of a day: see JOURNEY⟧ to live somewhere temporarily, as on a visit; stay for a while **—*n.*** a brief or temporary stay; visit **—so′journ′er *n.***
soke (sōk) ***n.*** ⟦ME < ML *soca* < OE *socn*, jurisdiction, prosecution < base of *secan* (< **sokjan*), to SEEK⟧ *Eng. History* **1** the right to hold court and dispense justice within a given territory **2** the territory under the jurisdiction of a court
So·kol (sō′kôl′) ***n.*** ⟦Czech, lit., falcon⟧ an international organization promoting physical health, esp. in gymnastics
So·ko·tra (sō kō′trə) *alt. sp. of* SOCOTRA
sol[1] (sōl; *Sp* sôl) ***n., pl.*** **sols** or Sp. **so·les** (sô′les) ⟦Sp, lit., sun: from the radiant sun used as a device on one side⟧ the basic monetary unit of Peru: see the table of monetary units in the Reference Supplement
sol[2] (sōl) ***n.*** ⟦< ML *sol(ve)*: see GAMUT⟧ *Music* a syllable representing the fifth tone of the diatonic scale: see SOLFEGGIO
sol[3] (säl, sōl) ***n.*** ⟦< *-sol* < SOL(UTION), as in HYDROSOL⟧ a colloidal dispersion in a liquid
sol[4] *abbrev.* ⟦L *solutio*⟧ *Pharmacy* solution
Sol[1] (säl) ***n.*** ⟦ME < L < **sawol*, **saol* < IE base **sāwel-*, **swen-* > SUN[1], Gr *hēlios*, Goth *sauil*, sun⟧ *1 Rom. Myth.* the sun god: identified with the Greek Helios **2** the sun personified
Sol[2] *abbrev.* Solicitor
so·la[1] (sō′lə) ***adj.*** ⟦L⟧ alone: a stage direction, used of a woman
so·la[2] (sō′lə) ***n.*** *alt. pl. of* SOLUM
sol·ace (säl′is) ***n.*** ⟦ME < OFr *solaz* < L *solacium* < *solari*, to comfort < IE base **sel-*, favorable, in good spirits > SILLY⟧ **1** an easing of grief, loneliness, discomfort, etc. **2** something that eases or relieves; comfort; consolation; relief Also **sol′ace·ment** (-mənt) **—*vt.*** **-aced**, **-ac·ing** **1** to give solace to; comfort; console **2** to lessen or allay (grief, sorrow, etc.) **—*SYN.*** COMFORT **—sol′ac·er *n.***
so·lan (goose) (sō′lən) ⟦Scot < ME *soland* < ON *sūla*, gannet + *-and*, *-ǫnd*, a duck, akin to OE *ænid*, Ger *ente* < IE **anet-* > L *anas*⟧ GANNET
so·la·nine (sō′lə nēn′, -nin) ***n.*** ⟦Fr < L *solanum*, nightshade (see fol.) + Fr *-ine*, -INE[3]⟧ a complex glycosidic alkaloid, $C_{45}H_{73}NO_{15}$, found in potato sprouts and various plants of the nightshade family: also **so′la·nin** (-nin)
so·la·num (sō lā′nəm) ***n.*** ⟦L, nightshade, orig., sun plant < *sol*: see SOL[1]⟧ any of a large genus (*Solanum*) of trees, vines, shrubs, and plants of the nightshade family: most are poisonous, but a few are cultivated for food, as the potato and eggplant
so·lar (sō′lər) ***adj.*** ⟦L *solaris* < *sol*, the sun: see SOL[1]⟧ **1** of or having to do with the sun **2** produced by or coming from the sun *[solar* energy*]* **3** depending upon the sun's light or energy *[solar* heating*]* **4** fixed or measured by the earth's motion with relation to the sun *[*mean *solar* time*]* **5** [Archaic] *Astrol.* under the influence of the sun

☆**solar battery** *n.* an assembly of one or more photovoltaic cells (**solar cells**) used to convert the radiant energy of sunlight into electric power

solar constant the average amount of solar radiation received normally by a unit area just outside the earth's atmosphere, equal to *c.* 1.37 x 10^6 ergs per cm^2 per second

solar cooker any of various devices designed to focus the sun's rays so as to provide heat for cooking, as at a campsite

solar cycle a period of time, averaging *c.* 11 years, during which certain phenomena, as maximum sunspot activity, recur on the sun

solar day *Law* the period from sunrise to sunset

solar eclipse *see* ECLIPSE (*n.* 1)

solar flare a sudden, short-lived increase of intensity in the light of the sun, usually near sunspots, often accompanied by a large increase in cosmic rays, X-rays, etc. and by resultant magnetic storms

solar furnace a furnace for heating, smelting, etc. that uses concave mirrors to concentrate the sun's rays

so·lar·i·um (sō ler′ē əm, sə-) *n., pl.* **-i·a** (-ē ə) ⟦L, sundial, place exposed to the sun < *sol*, the sun: see SOL[1]⟧ a glassed-in porch, room, etc. where people sun themselves, as in treating illness

so·lar·ize (sō′lər īz′) *vt.* **-ized′**, **-iz′ing** 1 to affect by exposing to the light and heat of the sun 2 to overexpose (a photographic film or plate) deliberately during developing to create special effects —*vi.* to become injured by such overexposure —**so′lar·i·za′tion** *n.*

solar panel a large, thin panel consisting of an array of solar cells, often attached to artificial satellites, rooftops, etc. to generate electricity directly from sunlight

solar plexus ⟦< SOLAR, in extended use (by analogy between the rays of the sun & the radiating pattern of nerve fibers) + PLEXUS⟧ 1 a network of nerves in the abdominal cavity behind the stomach and in front of the aorta, containing ganglia that send nerve impulses to the abdominal viscera 2 the area of the belly just below the sternum: not a technical term

solar pond a shallow, stagnant pool of, usually, salt water, that is heated by the sun and used to store solar energy, to extract salts from seawater, etc.

solar prominence PROMINENCE (sense 3)

solar still any system for the purification of salt water in which a shallow pool of salt water evaporates within a greenhouselike structure, causing the formation on the ceiling of droplets of fresh water, which drip down into collection pools

solar system 1 that portion of our galaxy which is subject to the gravity of the sun 2 all the matter within this portion, including interplanetary dust or gas; esp., the sun itself and its planets 3 any similar system consisting of a star, its planets, etc.

solar wind streams of ionized gas particles constantly emitted by the sun in all directions at speeds of *c.* 300 to 1,000 km per second (*c.* 186 to 620 mi per second): cf. STELLAR WIND

solar year *see* YEAR (sense 2)

sol·ate (säl′āt′) *vi.* **-at′ed**, **-at′ing** ⟦SOL[3] + -ATE[1]⟧ *Chem.* to convert into a sol —**sol·a′tion** *n.*

so·la·ti·um (sō lā′shē əm) *n., pl.* **-ti·a** (-shē ə) ⟦LL < L, SOLACE⟧ compensation or damages, esp. for injury to the feelings

sold (sōld) *vt., vi. pt. & pp. of* SELL

sol·der (säd′ər; *Brit* säl′dər) *n.* ⟦ME *soudre* < OFr *souldure* < *soulder*, to make solid < L *solidare* < *solidus*, SOLID⟧ 1 a metal alloy that is heated and used to join or patch metal parts or surfaces: **soft solders** of tin-lead alloys melt easily; **hard (or brazing) solders** of copper-zinc alloys melt only at red heat 2 anything that joins or fuses; bond —*vt.* 1 to join, patch, etc. with solder 2 to act as a bond between; unite —*vi.* 1 to become joined or united as by solder 2 to join things with solder —**sol′der·er** *n.*

sol·der·ing iron (säd′ər iŋ) a pointed metal tool heated for use in melting and applying solder

sol·dier (sōl′jər) *n.* ⟦ME *soldiour* < OFr *soldier* < *solde*, coin, pay < LL *solidus*: see SOLIDUS⟧ 1 a person serving in an army; member of an army 2 *a)* an enlisted person, as distinguished from one holding a warrant or commission *b)* any low-ranking member of a Mafia family 3 one who has much military experience or military skill 4 a person who works zealously for a specified cause 5 an ant or termite of a caste having an enlarged head and jaws and serving as fighters in defense of the colony —*vi.* 1 to serve as a soldier 2 to proceed stubbornly or doggedly: usually with *on* 3 to shirk one's duty, as by making a pretense of working, feigning illness, etc.

sol·dier·ly (-lē) *adj.* of, like, or characteristic of a good soldier —**sol′dier·li·ness** *n.*

soldier of fortune 1 a mercenary soldier, esp. one seeking adventure or excitement 2 any adventurer

☆**Soldier's Medal** a U.S. Army decoration awarded for deeds of heroism outside of combat

sol·dier·y (-ē) *n.* 1 soldiers collectively 2 a group of soldiers 3 the profession, skill, or training of a soldier

sol·do (säl′dō; *It* sôl′dô) *n., pl.* **-di** (-dē) ⟦It < LL *solidus*, SOLIDUS⟧ a former Italian copper coin and unit of money, equal to $\frac{1}{20}$ of a lira

sold-out (sōld′out′) *adj.* having all tickets or accommodations sold, esp. in advance

sole[1] (sōl) *n.* ⟦OFr < VL **sola*, for L *solea*, sandal, sole, kind of fish < *solum*, sole, base, ground, bottom⟧ 1 the bottom surface of the foot 2 the part of a shoe, boot, sock, etc. corresponding to this 3 the bottom surface of any of several objects, as a golf club —*vt.* **soled**, **sol′ing** to furnish (a shoe, etc.) with a sole

sole[2] (sōl) *adj.* ⟦ME < OE *sol* < L *solus*, alone < ? IE **sōlo-* < base **se-*, **s(e)wo-*, apart > L *suus*, one's own⟧ 1 *a)* without another or others; single; one and only *b)* acting, working, etc. alone without help 2 of or having to do with only one (specified) person or group 3 given or belonging to no other; not shared or divided; exclusive [the *sole* rights to a patent] 4 [Archaic] alone; solitary 5 *Law* unmarried: cf. FEME SOLE

sole[3] (sōl) *n., pl.* **sole** or **soles** ⟦OFr < VL **sola*, for L *solea* (see SOLE[1]): so named from its shape⟧ any of various flatfishes (esp. family Soleidae) usually highly valued as food

sol·e·cism (säl′ə siz′əm) *n.* ⟦L *soloecismus* < Gr *soloikismos* < *soloikos*, speaking incorrectly, after *Soloi*, city in Cilicia, whose dialect was a corrupt form of Attic⟧ 1 a violation of the conventional usage, grammar, etc. of a language; ungrammatical use of words (Ex.: "We done it" for "We did it"): see also BARBARISM, IMPROPRIETY 2 a violation of good manners; breach of etiquette 3 a mistake or impropriety —**sol′e·cist** *n.* —**sol′e·cis′tic** *adj.* —**sol′e·cis′ti·cal·ly** *adv.*

sole·ly (sōl′lē) *adv.* 1 without another or others; alone [to be *solely* to blame] 2 only, exclusively, merely, or altogether [to read *solely* for pleasure]

sol·emn (säl′əm) *adj.* ⟦ME *solemne* < OFr < L *sollemnis*, *sollennis*, yearly, annual, hence religious, solemn (from assoc. with annual religious festivals) < *sollus*, all, entire < Oscan, akin to L *salvus* (see SAFE) + ? *annus*, year⟧ 1 *a)* observed or done according to ritual or tradition (said esp. of religious holidays, rites, etc.) *b)* sacred in character 2 according to strict form; formal [a *solemn* ceremony] 3 *a)* serious or grave [a *solemn* face] *b)* deeply earnest; very sincere [a *solemn* oath] 4 very impressive or arousing feelings of awe because of its great importance or seriousness [a *solemn* occasion] 5 somber because dark in color —*SYN.* SERIOUS —**sol′emn·ly** *adv.* —**sol′emn·ness** *n.*

Solemn (High) Mass a highly ceremonial Mass with parts of the text sung by the celebrant, with a deacon and subdeacon assisting at the ceremonies, and with choir singing and organ music

so·lem·ni·fy (sə lem′nə fī′) *vt.* **-fied′**, **-fy′ing** to make solemn

so·lem·ni·ty (sə lem′nə tē) *n., pl.* **-ties** ⟦ME *solempnete* < OFr *solempneté* < L *sollemnitas*⟧ 1 solemn ceremony, ritual, observance, etc. 2 solemn feeling, character, or appearance; serious or awesome quality; gravity 3 *Law* the formality needed to validate an act, contract, etc.

sol·em·nize (säl′əm nīz′) *vt.* **-nized′**, **-niz′ing** ⟦ME *solempnisen* < OFr *solemniser* < ML(Ec) *solemnizare* < L *sollemnis*, SOLEMN⟧ 1 to celebrate with formal ceremony or according to ritual 2 to perform the ceremony of (marriage, etc.) 3 to make solemn, or serious, grave, etc. —*SYN.* CELEBRATE —**sol′em·ni·za′tion** *n.* —**sol′em·niz′er** *n.*

solemn vow *R.C.Ch.* a vow made with canonical effects stricter than those of a SIMPLE VOW: e.g., a solemn vow of chastity, broken by attempting marriage while the vow is still in effect, makes the marriage both illicit and invalid

so·le·no·cyte (sə lē′nə sīt′) *n.* ⟦< Gr *sōlēn*, a channel + -CYTE⟧ an elongated, tubular flame cell with one or more long flagella, occurring in certain annelids, cephalochordates, etc.

so·le·no·glyph (-glif′) *n.* ⟦< ModL *Solenoglypha*, a former suborder < Gr *sōlēn*, a channel (in reference to the tubular fangs) + *glyphein*, to carve: for IE base see CLEAVE[1]⟧ any poisonous snake of the viper family with hollow, paired, erectile fangs

so·le·noid (sō′lə noid′, säʹ-) *n.* ⟦Fr *solénoïde* < Gr *sōlēn*, a tube, channel (< IE **tul-* < base **twō-* > Sans *tūṇa*, a quiver) + *eidos*, -OID⟧ a coil of wire, usually surrounding a movable iron core, that acts as a magnet when carrying a current: used as an electromagnetic switch or relay —**so′le·noi′dal** *adj.*

So·lent (sō′lənt), **The** W portion of the channel separating the Isle of Wight from the mainland of Hampshire, England: *c.* 15 mi (24 km) long: the E portion of the channel is called *Spithead*

sole·plate (sōl′plāt′) *n.* ⟦SOLE[1] + PLATE⟧ the ironing surface of a flatiron or steam iron

so·les (sô′les) *n. Sp. pl. of* SOL[1]

So·leure (sô lër′) *Fr. name for* SOLOTHURN

sol-fa (sōl′fä′) *n.* ⟦It *solfa* < *sol* + *fa*: see GAMUT⟧ 1 the syllables *do* (formerly *ut*), *re*, *mi*, *fa*, *sol* (or *so*), *la*, *ti* (or *si*), *do* (or *ut*), used to represent the tones of a scale, regardless of its key 2 the use of these syllables, as in vocal exercises; solfeggio — *vt., vi.* **-faed′** (-fäd′), **-fa′ing** to sing (a scale, phrase, or song) to the sol-fa syllables —**sol′-fa′ist** *n.*

sol·fa·ta·ra (sōl′fə tä′rə) *n.* ⟦It < *solfo*, sulfur < L *sulfur*⟧ a volcanic vent or fissure giving off only vapors, esp. sulfurous gases

sol·fège (säl fezh′) *n.* ⟦Fr < It *solfeggio*: see fol.⟧ 1 SOLFEGGIO 2 the teaching of the essentials of music theory, including tonality, tempo, rhythm, etc.

sol·feg·gio (säl fej′ō) *n., pl.* **-feg′gios** or **-feg′gi** (-ē) ⟦It < *solfa*: see SOL-FA⟧ 1 voice practice in which scales are sung to the sol-fa syllables; solmization 2 the use of these syllables in singing, esp. in reading a song, etc. at sight

so·lic·it (sə lis′it) *vt.* ⟦ME *soliciten* < MFr *solliciter* < L *sollicitare* < *sollicitus*: see SOLICITOUS⟧ 1 to ask or seek earnestly or pleadingly; appeal to or for [to *solicit* aid, to *solicit* members for donations] 2 to tempt or entice (someone) to do wrong 3 to approach for some immoral purpose, as a prostitute does —*vi.* to solicit someone or something —*SYN.* BEG —**so·lic′i·tant** (-i tənt) *n., adj.* —**so·lic′i·ta′tion** *n.*

so·lic·i·tor (-ər) *n.* ⟦ME *solycitour* < MFr *solliciteur*⟧ 1 a person who solicits; esp., one who seeks trade, asks for contributions, etc. 2 in England, a member of the legal profession who is not a barrister: solicitors are not members of the bar and may not plead cases in superior courts ☆3 in the U.S., a lawyer serving as official law officer for a city, department, etc. —**SYN.** LAWYER

☆**solicitor general** *pl.* **solicitors general** or **solicitor generals** 1 the law officer in the U.S. Department of Justice ranking next below the attorney general: the U.S. solicitor general represents the U.S. in cases before the Supreme Court 2 a law officer of similar rank in certain U.S. states and in England

so·lic·i·tous (sə lis′ə təs) ***adj.*** ⟦L *sollicitus* < *sollus*, whole (see SOLEMN) + *citus*, pp. of *ciere*, to set in motion: see CITE⟧ 1 showing care, attention, or concern [*solicitous* for her welfare] 2 showing anxious desire; eager [*solicitous* to make friends] 3 full of anxiety or apprehension; troubled —**so·lic′i·tous·ly** ***adv.*** —**so·lic′i·tous·ness** ***n.***

so·lic·i·tude (-to͞od′, -tyo͞od′) ***n.*** ⟦ME < L *sollicitudo*⟧ 1 the state of being solicitous; care, concern, etc.; sometimes, excessive care or concern 2 [*pl.*] causes of care or concern —**SYN.** CARE

sol·id (säl′id) ***adj.*** ⟦ME *solide* < MFr < L *solidus* < *sollus*, whole: see SOLEMN⟧ 1 tending to keep its form rather than to flow or spread out like a liquid or gas; relatively firm or compact 2 filled with matter throughout; not hollow 3 *a)* having the three dimensions of length, breadth, and thickness [prisms and other *solid* figures] *b)* dealing with bodies or figures in three dimensions 4 *a)* firm, strong, and dependable [a *solid* structure] *b)* substantial, sound, and reliable [*solid* reasoning] *c)* sturdy or vigorous [a *solid* build, a *solid* punch] 5 serious; not superficial or trivial [*solid* scholarship] 6 complete, thoroughgoing, or genuine [*solid* satisfaction] 7 *a)* having no breaks or divisions [a *solid* line of fortifications] *b)* written or printed without a hyphen [a *solid* compound] 8 characterized by no pauses or interruptions [to talk for a *solid* hour] 9 *a)* of one or the same color, material, or consistency throughout [a *solid* walnut table] *b)* consisting of one unalloyed metal throughout; also, containing no more alloy than is necessary to insure hardness (said of gold, etc.) ☆10 characterized by or showing complete unity; unanimous [a *solid* vote] 11 thick or dense in appearance or texture [a *solid* fog] 12 firm or dependable [a *solid* friendship] ☆13 [Informal] having a firmly favorable or good relationship [to be in *solid* with someone] 14 [Informal] healthful and filling [a *solid* meal] ☆15 [Slang] very good; excellent [a *solid* dance band] 16 *Printing* set without spaces between the lines of type —***n.*** 1 a substance that is solid, not a liquid or gas 2 an object or figure having or represented as having length, breadth, and thickness —**SYN.** FIRM[1] —**sol′id·ly** ***adv.*** —**sol′id·ness** ***n.***

sol·i·da·go (säl′ə dā′gō) ***n.***, *pl.* **-gos** ⟦ModL < ML, goldenrod < L *solidare*, to strengthen (see SOLDER): in reference to its supposed healing powers⟧ GOLDENROD

solid angle the angle formed by three or more planes meeting in a common point or formed at the vertex of a cone

sol·i·dar·i·ty (säl′ə dar′ə tē) ***n.***, *pl.* **-ties** ⟦Fr *solidarité* < *solidaire*: see SOLID & -ARY⟧ combination or agreement of all elements or individuals, as of a group; complete unity, as of opinion, purpose, interest, or feeling —**SYN.** UNITY

solid fuel any of various rocket fuels and oxidizers that are mixed and solidified into a storable mass: also called **solid propellant**

solid geometry the branch of geometry dealing with solid, or three-dimensional, figures

so·lid·i·fy (sə lid′ə fī′) ***vt., vi.*** **-fied′**, **-fy′ing** ⟦Fr *solidifier*: see SOLID & -FY⟧ 1 to make or become solid, firm, hard, compact, etc. 2 to crystallize 3 to make or become strong, or united —**so·lid′i·fi·ca′tion** ***n.***

so·lid·i·ty (-tē) ***n.*** ⟦L *soliditas*⟧ the quality or condition of being solid; firmness, soundness, hardness, etc.

solid rocket any of various rockets using solid fuel

sol·id-state (säl′id stāt′) ***adj.*** 1 designating or of the branch of physics dealing with the fundamental properties of solids, as structure, binding forces, electrical, magnetic, and optical properties, etc., and with their effects 2 designating, of, or equipped with electronic devices, as semiconductors, that can control current without heated filaments, moving parts, etc.

sol·i·dus (säl′i dəs) ***n.***, *pl.* **sol′i·di′** (-dī′) ⟦ME < LL < L *solidus (nummus)*, lit., SOLID (coin): see NUMMULAR⟧ 1 a gold coin of the Late Roman Empire 2 a medieval money of account worth twelve denarii: abbreviated *s* in £ s.d. 3 *a)* a slant line (/), orig. the old long s (ſ), used to separate shillings from pence (Ex.: 7/6) *b)* VIRGULE

sol·i·fluc·tion (säl′ə fluk′shən, sō′li-) ***n.*** ⟦< L *solum*, soil + *fluctio*, a flowing < pp. of *fluere*, to flow: see FLUCTUATE⟧ a more rapid form of soil creep, often found near a glacier, in which saturated soil slips over hard or frozen layers

so·lil·o·quize (sə lil′ə kwīz′) ***vi.*** **-quized′**, **-quiz′ing** to deliver a soliloquy; talk to oneself —***vt.*** to utter in or as a soliloquy —**so·lil′o·quist** (-kwist) ***n.***

so·lil·o·quy (-kwē) ***n.***, *pl.* **-quies** ⟦LL *soliloquium* < L *solus*, alone, SOLE[2] + *loqui*, to speak⟧ 1 an act or instance of talking to oneself 2 lines in a drama in which a character reveals his or her thoughts to the audience, but not to the other characters, by speaking as if to himself or herself

So·li·mões (sô′li moins′) the upper Amazon, between the Peruvian border & the Negro River

So·ling·en (zō′liŋ ən) city in W Germany, in the Ruhr Basin, in the state of North Rhine-Westphalia

sol·ip·sism (säl′ip siz′əm) ***n.*** ⟦< L *solus*, alone, SOLE[2] + *ipse*, self + -ISM⟧ 1 the theory that the self can be aware of nothing but its own experiences and states 2 the theory that nothing exists or is real but the self —**sol′ip·sis′tic** ***adj.*** —**sol′ip·sist** ***n.***

sol·i·taire (säl′ə ter′) ***n.*** ⟦Fr *solitaire* < L *solitarius*: see fol.⟧ 1 [Archaic] a hermit or recluse 2 a diamond or other gem set by itself, as in a ring 3 any of many card games played by one person

sol·i·tar·y (säl′ə ter′ē) ***adj.*** ⟦ME < OFr *solitaire* < L *solitarius* < *solus*, alone, SOLE[2]⟧ 1 living or being alone 2 without others; single; only [a *solitary* example] 3 characterized by loneliness or lack of companions 4 lonely; remote; unfrequented [a *solitary* place] 5 done in solitude 6 *Bot.* occurring singly, as a flower 7 *Zool.* living alone or in pairs; not colonial, social, etc. —***n.***, *pl.* **-tar′ies** 1 a person who lives alone; esp., a hermit 2 [Informal] SOLITARY CONFINEMENT —**SYN.** ALONE —**sol′i·tar′i·ly** ***adv.*** —**sol′i·tar′i·ness** ***n.***

solitary confinement confinement of a prisoner in isolation from all other prisoners, often in a dungeonlike cell: a form of extra punishment for misconduct

sol·i·ton (säl′i tän′) ***n.*** ⟦SOLIT(ARY) + -ON⟧ *Physics* a solitary wavelike disturbance that maintains its shape and velocity despite collisions with other such disturbances

sol·i·tude (säl′ə to͞od′, -tyo͞od′) ***n.*** ⟦ME < MFr < L *solitudo* < *solus*, alone, SOLE[2]⟧ 1 the state of being solitary, or alone; seclusion, isolation, or remoteness 2 a lonely or secluded place —**sol′i·tu′di·nous** (-to͞od′'n əs, -tyo͞od′-) ***adj.***

SYN.—**solitude** refers to the state of one who is completely alone, cut off from all human contact, and sometimes stresses the loneliness of such a condition [the *solitude* of a hermit]; **isolation** suggests physical separation from others, often an involuntary detachment resulting from the force of circumstances [the *isolation* of a forest ranger]; **seclusion** suggests retirement from intercourse with the outside world, as by confining oneself to one's home, a remote place, etc.

sol·ler·et (säl′ər et′, säl′ər et′) ***n.*** ⟦MFr *soleret*, dim. of *soler*, shoe < ML *subtelaris (calceus)*, (shoe) under the arch of the foot < LL *subtel*, the hollow of the foot < L *sub*, under (see UP[1]) + *talus*, ankle⟧ a kind of shoe worn with a suit of armor, made of hinged steel plates

sol·mi·za·tion (säl′mi zā′shən) ***n.*** ⟦Fr *solmisation* < *solmiser*, to sol-fa < *sol* + *mi*: see GAMUT⟧ the system or practice of identifying musical tones by syllables: often used as an aid in teaching music

so·lo (sō′lō) ***n.***, *pl.* **-los**; for 1, sometimes, **-li** (-lē) ⟦It < L *solus*, alone, SOLE[2]⟧ 1 *a)* a musical piece or passage played or sung by one person, with or without accompaniment *b)* a performance of such a piece or passage *c)* a dance, pantomime, etc., for performance by one person 2 an airplane flight made by a pilot alone, without an assistant, instructor, etc. 3 any performance by one person alone 4 any of several card games in which each person plays, or a person may choose to play, alone against the others, without a partner —***adj.*** 1 designed for or performed by a single voice, person, or instrument 2 performing a solo —***adv.*** without another or others; alone —***vi.*** **-loed**, **-lo·ing** 1 to perform a solo 2 to make a solo flight

so·lo·ist (-ist) ***n.*** a person who performs a solo

So·lo man (sō′lō) ⟦after *Solo* River in central Java⟧ a type of early human (*Homo sapiens soloensis*) known from fossil remains found in Upper Pleistocene deposits in central Java: see JAVA MAN

Sol·o·mon (säl′ə mən) ***n.*** ⟦LL(Ec) *Solomon, Salomon* < Gr(Ec) *Solomōn, Salōmōn* < Heb *shelomo*, lit., peaceful < *shalom*, peace⟧ 1 a masculine name: dim. *Sol* 2 (fl. 10th cent. B.C.) a king of Israel (*c.* 970-*c.* 931): he built the first temple and was noted for his wisdom: son & successor of DAVID[1]: 2 Sam. 12:24 3 a very wise man; sage —**Sol′o·mon′ic** (-män′ik) ***adj.***

Solomon Islands 1 country on a group of islands in the SW Pacific, east of New Guinea: formerly a British protectorate, it became independent & a member of the Commonwealth in 1978: 10,985 sq mi (28,450 sq km); cap. Honiara 2 group of islands including the islands of this country, Bougainville, and other islands belonging to Papua New Guinea: *c.* 16,000 sq mi (41,440 sq km)

Solomon's seal 1 a mystical symbol in the form of a six-pointed star: cf. STAR OF DAVID 2 ⟦transl. of ModL *sigillum Salomonis*: so named prob. from starlike markings on the rootstock⟧ any of a genus (*Polygonatum*) of perennial plants of the lily family, with broad, waxy leaves, drooping, greenish flowers, and blue or black berries

so·lon (sō′lən, -län′) ***n.*** ⟦after fol.⟧ [*sometimes* **S-**] a lawmaker or legislator, esp. a wise one

So·lon (sō′lən, -län′) 640?-559? B.C.; Athenian statesman & lawgiver: framed the democratic laws of Athens

so long [Informal] GOODBYE

So·lo·thurn (zō′lō to͝orn′) 1 canton of NW Switzerland: 305 sq mi (790 sq km) 2 its capital

sol·stice (säl′stis, sōl′-) ***n.*** ⟦ME < MFr < L *solstitium* < *sol*, the sun (see SOL[1]) + *sistere*, caus. of *stare*, to STAND⟧ 1 the moment or date when the sun in its apparent annual movement along the ecliptic reaches its maximum distance north or south of the celestial equator: in the Northern Hemisphere, the day of the **summer solstice** (about June 21, marking the beginning of summer) is the time of the sun's maximum elevation and, thus, has the longest period of sunlight; the day of the **winter solstice** (about Dec. 21, marking the beginning of winter) is the time of the sun's minimum elevation and, thus, has the shortest period of sunlight 2 either of the two points on the celestial sphere where the sun's path reaches its maximum distance north or south of the celestial equator —**sol·sti·tial** (säl sti′shəl, sōl′-) ***adj.***

sol·u·bil·i·ty (säl′yoo bil′ə tē) ***n.***, *pl.* **-ties** 1 the quality, condition, or extent of being soluble; capability of being dissolved 2 the amount of a substance that can be dissolved in a given solvent under specified conditions

sol·u·bi·lize (säl′yə bə līz′) ***vt., vi.*** **-lized′, -liz′ing** to make or become soluble; dissolve —**sol′u·bi·li·za′tion** ***n.***

sol·u·ble (säl′yə bəl) ***adj.*** ⟦ME < MFr < L *solubilis* < *solvere*: see SOLVE⟧ **1** that can be dissolved; able to pass into solution **2** capable of being solved —**sol′u·bly** ***adv.***

soluble glass WATER GLASS (sense 3)

so·lum (sō′ləm) ***n., pl.*** **-lums** or **-la** (-lə) ⟦ModL < L, base, soil⟧ the altered soil or material overlying the parent material, often including the A-horizon and the B-horizon

so·lus (sō′ləs) ***adj.*** ⟦L, SOLE²⟧ alone: a stage direction

sol·ute (säl′yo͞ot′) ***n.*** ⟦< L *solutus*, pp. of *solvere*, to loosen: see SOLVE⟧ the substance dissolved in a solution

so·lu·tion (sə lo͞o′shən) ***n.*** ⟦ME *solucion* < OFr < L *solutio* < *solutus*: see prec.⟧ **1** *a)* the act, method, or process of solving a problem *b)* the answer to a problem *c)* an explanation, clarification, etc. [the *solution* of a mystery] **2** *a)* the act or process of dispersing one or more liquid, gaseous, or solid substances in another, usually a liquid, so as to form a homogeneous mixture *b)* the state or fact of being dissolved *c)* a homogeneous molecular mixture, usually a liquid, so produced **3** a breaking up or coming to an end; dissolution; break; breach **4** *Med. a)* the termination of a disease *b)* the crisis of a disease *c)* a drug in solution; liquid medicine

solution set *Math.* the roots or values satisfying a given equation or inequality, or a set of simultaneous equations or inequalities

So·lu·tre·an or **So·lu·tri·an** (sə lo͞o′trē ən) ***adj.*** ⟦after *Solutre*, village in France where artifacts were found⟧ designating or of an Upper Paleolithic culture of Europe, characterized by delicate, laurel-leaf flint points

solv·a·ble (säl′və bəl, sôl′-) ***adj.*** **1** that can be solved **2** [Now Rare] that can be dissolved —**solv′a·bil′i·ty** ***n.***

sol·vate (säl′vāt′, sôl′-) ***n.*** ⟦SOLV(ENT) + -ATE¹⟧ *Chem.* a complex formed by the combining of molecules or ions of a solvent and solute —***vt.*** **-vat′ed, -vat′ing** to convert (molecules or ions) into a solvate —**sol·va′tion** ***n.***

Sol·vay process (säl′vā) ⟦developed by Ernest *Solvay* (1838-1922), Belgian chemist⟧ a process for making soda (sodium carbonate) by treating common salt (sodium chloride) with ammonia and carbon dioxide

solve (sälv, sôlv) ***vt.*** **solved, solv′ing** ⟦ME *solven* < L *solvere* (for *se-luere*), to loosen, release, free < *se-*, apart (see SECEDE) + *luere*, to let go, set free: see LOSE⟧ **1** to find or provide a satisfactory answer or explanation for; make clear; explain **2** to find or provide the correct or a satisfactory solution to (a problem) —**solv′er** ***n.***

sol·ven·cy (säl′vən sē, sôl′-) ***n.*** a solvent state or quality

sol·vent (-vənt) ***adj.*** ⟦L *solvens*, prp. of *solvere*, to loosen: see SOLVE⟧ **1** able to pay all one's debts or meet all financial responsibilities **2** that dissolves or can dissolve another substance —***n.*** **1** a substance, usually liquid, that dissolves or can dissolve another substance **2** something that solves or explains; solution

sol·vol·y·sis (säl väl′ə sis, sôl-) ***n.*** ⟦< prec. + -O- + -LYSIS⟧ a chemical interaction, as hydrolysis, between a solute and solvent, with the production of new compounds

Sol·way Firth (säl′wā) arm of the Irish Sea, between England & Scotland: *c.* 40 mi (64 km) long

Sol·y·man (säl′i mən) *var. of* SULEIMAN

Sol·zhe·ni·tsyn (sōl′zhə nēt′sin), **Al·ek·san·dr (Isayevich)** (al′ig zan′dər) 1918-2008; Russ. writer, esp. of novels: in the U.S. 1976-94

som (säm) ***n.*** **1** ⟦Kirghiz⟧ the basic monetary unit of Kyrgyzstan: see the table of monetary units in the Reference Supplement **2** ⟦Uzbek *sŭm*⟧ the basic monetary unit of Uzbekistan: see the table of monetary units in the Reference Supplement

so·ma¹ (sō′mə) ***n., pl.*** **so′ma·ta** (-mə tə) ⟦ModL < Gr *sōma*, body < IE **twōmn̥*, something compact, sturdy < base **tēu-*, to swell, thick > THUMB, L *tumor*, Gr *sōros*, a heap⟧ the entire body of an animal or plant, with the exception of the germ cells

so·ma² (sō′mə) ***n.*** ⟦Sans < IE base **seu-*, juice > SUCK, OE *seaw*, sap, L *sucus*, juice⟧ **1** an intoxicating plant juice referred to in the literature of Vedic ritual **2** ⟦so called as a supposed source of this juice⟧ an E Indian plant (*Sarcostemma acidum*) of the milkweed family

So·ma·li (sō mä′lē, sə-) ***n.*** ⟦< ?⟧ **1** *pl.* **-lis** or **-li** a member of a people of Somalia and neighboring regions **2** the Eastern Cushitic language of this people **3** *pl.* **-lis** or **-li** any of a breed of domestic cat developed from the Abyssinian and similar to members of that breed except for the coat, which is of medium length

So·ma·li·a (sō mä′lē ə, sə-; -mäl′yə) country of E Africa, on the Indian Ocean & the Gulf of Aden: formed by the merger of British Somaliland & Italian Somaliland (1960): 246,201 sq mi (637,657 sq km); cap. Mogadishu —**So·ma′li·an** ***adj., n.***

So·ma·li·land (-land′) region in E Africa, including NE Somalia, Djibouti, & E Ethiopia

somat- *combining form* SOMATO-: used before a vowel

so·mat·ic (sō mat′ik) ***adj.*** ⟦Gr *sōmatikos* < *sōma* (gen. *sōmatos*), body: see SOMA¹⟧ **1** of the body, as distinguished from the soul, mind, or psyche; corporeal; physical **2** *Biol.* of the soma **3** *Anat., Zool.* of the outer walls of the body, as distinguished from the viscera —*SYN.* BODILY —**so·mat′i·cal·ly** ***adv.***

somatic cell any of the cells of an organism that become differentiated into the tissues, organs, etc. of the body: opposed to GERM CELL

so·ma·to- (sō′mə tō, -tə; sō mat′ə) ⟦< Gr *sōma* (gen. *sōmatos*), body: see SOMA¹⟧ *combining form* body [*somatoplasm*]

so·ma·tol·o·gy (sō′mə täl′ə jē) ***n.*** ⟦prec. + -LOGY⟧ **1** the science concerned with the properties of organic bodies **2** *former term for* the branch of anthropology that deals with the physical nature and characteristics of people —**so′ma·to·log′ic** (-tə läj′ik) ***adj.***, **so′ma·to·log′i·cal** —**so′ma·tol′o·gist** ***n.***

so·ma·to·me·din (sə mat′ə mēd′ən, sō′mə tə-) ***n.*** ⟦SOMATO- + (INTER)MED(IARY) + -IN¹⟧ any of a group of protein hormones produced in the liver and regulating the activity of growth hormones in building muscle and cartilage

so·ma·to·plasm (sō′mə tə plaz′əm, sō mat′ə-) ***n.*** ⟦SOMATO- + -PLASM⟧ tissue cells collectively, as distinguished from germ cells —**so′ma·to·plas′tic** ***adj.***

so·ma·to·pleure (-plo͝or′) ***n.*** ⟦SOMATO- + Gr *pleura*, a side⟧ *Embryology* a mass of tissue formed from the fusion of the ectoderm and the outer of the two layers of the mesoderm, forming much of the body wall and the amnion and chorion —**so′ma·to·pleu′ral** ***adj.***

so·ma·to·stat·in (sō′mə tə stat′'n) ***n.*** ⟦SOMATO- + -STAT + -IN¹⟧ a hormone produced mainly in the hypothalamus and pancreas, or prepared synthetically, that inhibits the release of glucagon and insulin from the pancreas: used in treating diabetes

so·ma·to·trop·in (sə mat′ə trō′pən, sō′mə tə-) ***n.*** GROWTH HORMONE (sense 1): also **so·ma′to·troph′in** (-trō′fən)

so·ma·to·type (-tīp′) ***n.*** body type; specif., any of the three main body types (*ectomorph, endomorph, mesomorph*) in a system for typing the human physique

som·ber (säm′bər) ***adj.*** ⟦Fr *sombre* < LL **subumbrare*, to shade < L *sub*, under + *umbra*, shade⟧ **1** dark and gloomy or dull **2** mentally depressed or depressing; melancholy **3** earnest and solemn; grave Also [Chiefly Brit.] **som′bre** —**som′ber·ly** ***adv.*** —**som′ber·ness** ***n.***

☆**som·bre·ro** (säm brer′ō, səm-) ***n., pl.*** **-ros** ⟦Sp, hat < *sombra*, shade: see prec.⟧ a broad-brimmed, tall-crowned felt or straw hat of a kind worn in Mexico, the Southwest, etc.

some (sum) ***adj.*** ⟦ME *som* < OE *sum*, a certain one, akin to Goth *sums* < IE **som-* > SAME⟧ **1** being a certain one or ones not specified or known [open *some* evenings] **2** being of a certain unspecified (but often considerable) number, quantity, degree, etc. [to have *some* fear, married for *some* years] **3** about [*some* ten of them] ☆**4** [Informal] remarkable, striking, etc. [it was *some* fight]: often used ironically or sarcastically [he didn't even thank me—that's *some* gratitude!] —***pron.*** **1** certain ones not specified or known [*some* agree] **2** a certain indefinite or unspecified number, quantity, etc. as distinguished from the rest [take *some*] —***adv.*** **1** approximately; about [*some* ten men] **2** [Informal] to some extent; somewhat [slept *some*] ☆**3** [Informal] to a great extent or at a great rate [must run *some* to catch up] —☆**and then some** [Informal] and more than that

-some¹ (səm) ⟦ME *-som* < OE *-sum*, akin to prec.⟧ *suffix* like, tending to, tending to be [*toilsome, tiresome, lonesome*]

-some² (səm) ⟦ME *-sum* < *sum, som*, SOME⟧ *suffix* a group of (a specified number of) members [*threesome*]

-some³ (sōm) ⟦< Gr *sōma*, body: see SOMA¹⟧ *combining form* **1** body [*chromosome*] **2** chromosome [*monosome*]

some·bod·y (sum′bäd′ē, -bud′ē, -bəd ē) ***pron.*** a person unknown or not named; someone —***n., pl.*** **-bod′ies** a person of importance

some·day (-dā′) ***adv.*** at some future day or time

some·how (-hou′) ***adv.*** in a way or by a method not known, stated, or understood [was *somehow* completed]: often in the phrase **somehow or other**

some·one (-wun′) ***pron.*** a person unknown or not named; somebody

some·place (-plās′) [Informal] ***adv.*** in, to, or at some place: somewhere —***n.*** SOMEWHERE

som·er·sault (sum′ər sôlt′) ***n.*** ⟦altered < MFr *sombresault, soubresault* < L *supra*, over + *saltus*, a leap < pp. of *saltare*: see SALTANT⟧ an acrobatic stunt performed by turning the body one full revolution forward or backward, heels over head: often used fig., as of a complete reversal of opinion, sympathies, etc. —***vi.*** to perform a somersault or a series of somersaults Also **som′er·set′** (-set′)

Som·er·set (sum′ər set′) ⟦OE *Sumersaete*, contr. < *Sumortun sæte*, lit., the people of Somerton (< *sumor*, SUMMER¹ + *tun*, TOWN) + *sæte*, residents, pl. of *sæta*, akin to *sæti*, SEAT⟧ county in SW England, on Bristol Channel: 1,333 sq mi (3,452 sq km): also **Som′er·set·shire′** (-shir′)

some-such (sum′such′) [Informal or Dial.] ***adj.*** of like or similar kind; suchlike [a wrench or *some-such* thing as will fix the leak] —***pron.*** a thing (or things) or person (or persons) of such a kind or of similar kind

some·thing (sum′thiŋ) ***pron.*** **1** a thing that is not definitely known, understood, or identified; some undetermined thing [*something* went wrong] **2** some thing or things, definite but unspecified [have *something* to eat] **3** a bit; a little [*something* over an hour] —***n.*** [Informal] an important or remarkable person or thing [that party was really *something!*] —***adv.*** **1** a little; somewhat [she looks *something* like me] **2** [Informal] really; quite [sounds *something* awful] —☆**something else** [Slang] a remarkable person or thing *USAGE*—also used after a figure to indicate a fraction beyond [the bus leaves at six *something*]

-some·thing (sum′thiŋ) *combining form forming adjectives* **1** of, relating to, being, or for a person of an age one to nine years more than (a specified multiple of ten) [*fortysomething*, or in one's forties] **2** of a quantity one to nine more than (a specified multiple of ten) [*60-something* people at the party]

some·time (sum′tīm′) ***adv.*** **1** at some time not known or specified **2** at some unspecified time in the future **3** [Archaic] *a)* sometimes *b)* formerly —*adj.* 1 former; erstwhile [her *sometime* friend] 2 merely occasional; sporadic [his wit is a *sometime* thing]

some·times (-tīmz′) *adv.* 1 at times; on various occasions; occasionally 2 [Obs.] formerly

some·way (-wā′) *adv.* in some way or manner; somehow or other: also **some′ways′**

some·what (-hwut′, -hwät′, -wut′, -wət) *pron.* some degree, amount, portion, or part; a bit: often followed by *of* [*somewhat* of a surprise] —*adv.* to some extent or degree; a little; rather [*somewhat* late]

some·where (-hwer′, -wer′) *adv.* 1 in, to, or at some place not known or specified [lives *somewhere* nearby] 2 at some time, degree, age, figure, etc. (with *about, around, near, in, between,* etc.) [*somewhere* about ten o'clock] —*n.* an unspecified or undetermined place Also [Chiefly Dial.] **some′wheres′**

some·whith·er (-hwith′ər) *adv.* [Archaic] to some place

so·mite (sō′mīt′) *n.* ⟦< SOMA[1] + -ITE[1]⟧ 1 METAMERE 2 a blocklike segment of mesodermal tissue in the vertebrate embryo, giving rise to muscle, bone, etc. —**so·mit′ic** (-mit′ik) *adj.*, **so′mi·tal** (-mit′l)

Somme (sum; *Fr* sôm) river in N France: *c.* 150 mi (241 km)

☆**som·me·lier** (sum′əl yā′; *Fr* sô mə lyā′) *n., pl.* **-liers′** (-yāz′; *Fr,* -lyā′) ⟦Fr < MFr, orig., person in charge of pack animals (hence, steward) < OFr *sommerier* < *sommier* < LL *sagmarius:* see SUMMER[2]⟧ the person in a restaurant, club, etc. who is responsible for the selection of, and for serving, the wines, esp. with a French cuisine; wine steward

som·nam·bu·late (säm nam′byoo͞ lāt′, səm-) *vi.* **-lat′ed, -lat′ing** ⟦< L *somnus,* sleep (see SOMNUS) + *ambulatus,* pp. of *ambulare,* to walk: see AMBLE⟧ to get up and move about in a trancelike state while asleep —**som·nam′bu·lant** *adj.* —**som·nam′bu·la′tion** *n.* —**som·nam′bu·la′tor** *n.*

som·nam·bu·lism (-liz′əm) *n.* 1 the act or practice of somnambulating; sleepwalking 2 the trancelike state of one who somnambulates —**som·nam′bu·list** *n.* —**som·nam′bu·lis′tic** *adj.* —**som·nam′bu·lis′ti·cal·ly** *adv.*

som·nif·er·ous (säm nif′ər əs, səm-) *adj.* ⟦L *somnifer* < *somnus,* sleep (see SOMNUS) + *ferre,* to bring, BEAR[1] + -OUS⟧ inducing sleep; soporific —**som·nif′er·ous·ly** *adv.*

som·nil·o·quy (-nil′ə kwē) *n.* ⟦< L *somnus,* sleep (see SOMNUS) + *loqui,* to speak⟧ 1 the act or habit of talking while asleep 2 the words so spoken —**som·nil′o·quist** *n.*

som·no·lent (säm′nə lənt) *adj.* ⟦LME *sompnolent* < MFr < L *somnolentus* < *somnus,* sleep: see fol.⟧ 1 sleepy; drowsy 2 inducing drowsiness —**SYN.** SLEEPY —**som′no·lence** *n.*, **som′no·len·cy** —**som′no·lent·ly** *adv.*

Som·nus (säm′nəs) *n.* ⟦L, sleep < IE **swopnos* < base **swep-,* to sleep > Gr *hypnos,* sleep, Sans *svapiti,* (he) sleeps, OE *swefan,* to sleep⟧ *Rom. Myth.* the god of sleep: identified with the Greek Hypnos

so·mo·ni (sō′mō nē′) *n., pl.* **-nis′** ⟦Tajik⟧ the basic monetary unit of Tajikistan: see the table of monetary units in the Reference Supplement

son (sun) *n.* ⟦ME *sone* < OE *sunu,* akin to Ger *sohn,* Goth *sunus* < IE **sūnus* < base **seu-,* to give birth to > Sans *sūyatē,* (she) bears, OIr *suth,* birth⟧ 1 a boy or man as he is related to either or both parents: sometimes also used of animals 2 a male descendant 3 *a)* a stepson *b)* an adopted son *c)* a son-in-law 4 a male thought of as having been formed by some influence, as a child is by a parent [*sons* of France] 5 an affectionate or familiar form of address to a boy or man, as used by an older person —**the Son** *Christian Theol.* Jesus Christ, as the second person of the Trinity

so·nance (sō′nəns) *n.* 1 [Obs.] *a)* a sound *b)* a tune 2 the quality or state of being sonant

so·nant (sō′nənt) *adj.* ⟦L *sonans,* sounding, prp. of *sonare,* to SOUND[1]⟧ 1 of sound 2 having sound; sounding —*n. Phonet.* 1 a syllabic consonant 2 a voiced sound

so·nar (sō′när′) *n.* ⟦*so(und) n(avigation) a(nd) r(anging)*⟧ an apparatus that transmits high-frequency sound waves through water and registers the vibrations reflected from an object, used in finding submarines, depths, etc.

so·na·ta (sə nät′ə) *n.* ⟦It, lit., a sounding < L *sonare,* to SOUND[1]: orig., an instrumental composition as opposed to CANTATA, lit., something sung⟧ a composition for one or two instruments, usually consisting of several movements: some modern sonatas have single movements

sonata form a type of musical composition, often serving as the first movement of a sonata or symphony, consisting of an exposition which contrasts two distinct keys, followed by a development of the exposition, and a recapitulation which returns to the original key or tonality: in full **sonata-allegro (*or* sonata allegro) form**

so·na·ti·na (sän′ə tē′nə) *n.* ⟦It, dim. of *sonata*⟧ a short or simplified sonata

☆**sonde** (sänd) *n.* ⟦Fr, a sounding line < *sonder:* see SOUND[4]⟧ any of various devices, esp. a radiosonde, for measuring and usually telemetering meteorological and other physical conditions at high altitudes

☆**sone** (sōn) *n.* ⟦< L *sonus,* SOUND[1]⟧ a unit of loudness, subjectively determined, equal to the loudness of a sound of one kilohertz at 40 decibels above the threshold of hearing of a given listener

son et lu·mière (sōn ā lü myer′) ⟦Fr, sound and light⟧ 1 a technique of presenting a historical spectacle, esp. at night before a monument, etc., using special lighting effects and live or recorded narration, music, etc. 2 such a spectacle

song (sôŋ) *n.* ⟦ME < OE *sang:* for IE base see SING[2]⟧ 1 the act or art of singing [to break into *song*] 2 a piece of music sung or composed for singing 3 *a)* [Old Poet.] poetry; verse *b)* a relatively short metrical composition for, or suitable for, singing, as a ballad or simple lyric 4 a musical sound like singing [the *song* of the lark] —**for a song** [Informal] for very little money; cheap —**song′ful** *adj.* —**song′less** *adj.*

Song *abbrev. Bible* Song of Solomon

☆**song and dance** 1 singing and dancing, esp. in vaudeville 2 [Informal] talk, esp. an explanation, that is pointless, devious, or evasive

song·bird (sôŋ′burd′) *n.* a passerine bird that makes vocal sounds that are like music

song·book (sôŋ′book′) *n.* 1 a book containing a collection of songs, usually including lyrics as well as music 2 the popular songs of a particular composer, period, etc., thought of as a body of work

song cycle a series of songs by a single composer that are poetically related to form a unified work

☆**song·fest** (sôŋ′fest′) *n.* ⟦SONG + -FEST⟧ an informal gathering of people for singing, esp. folk songs

Song·hua (sooŋ′hwä′) river in Manchuria, NE China, flowing into the Amur River: 1,149 mi (1,849 km)

Song of Solomon *Bible* a book consisting of a love poem, dramatic and lyrical in character, traditionally ascribed to Solomon: also called **Song of Songs** or (in the Douay Bible) *Canticle of Canticles*: abbrev. *Sg, Sgs, S of S, Song, Song of Sol*

song·smith (sôŋ′smith′) *n.* [Informal] a songwriter

☆**song sparrow** a common North American sparrow (*Melospiza melodia*) with a striped breast, noted for its sweet song

song·ster (sôŋ′stər) *n.* ⟦ME < OE *sangestre:* see SONG & -STER⟧ 1 a singer or writer of songs, esp. popular songs 2 SONGBIRD

song·stress (-stris) *n.* a female singer or writer of songs, esp. popular songs: see -ESS

song thrush a mostly Eurasian songbird (*Turdus philomelos*) with brown wings and a white breast with many large, dark spots

song·writ·er (-rīt′ər) *n.* a person who writes the words or music or both for songs, esp. popular songs

Son·ia (sōn′yə, sôn′-) *n.* a feminine name: var. *Sonja*

son·ic (sän′ik) *adj.* ⟦< L *sonus,* SOUND[1] + -IC⟧ 1 of or having to do with sound 2 designating or of a speed equal to the speed of sound (about 1,220 km per hour, or 760 mph, through air at sea level at room temperature) —**son′i·cal·ly** *adv.*

son·i·cate (sän′ə kāt′) *vt.* **-cat′ed, -cat′ing** ⟦prec. + -ATE[1]⟧ to subject (a cell, virus, etc.) to the energy produced by sound waves —**son′i·ca′tion** *n.* —**son′i·ca′tor** *n.*

sonic barrier the large increase of aerodynamic resistance encountered by some aircraft when flying near the speed of sound; sound barrier

sonic boom an explosive sound resulting from a shock wave caused by an object, as an airplane, traveling at supersonic speed

sonic depth finder FATHOMETER

so·nif·er·ous (sō nif′ər əs) *adj.* ⟦< L *sonus,* a SOUND[1] + -FEROUS⟧ carrying or producing sound

son-in-law (sun′in lô′) *n., pl.* **sons′-in-law′** the husband of one's daughter or, now sometimes, of one's son

son·net (sän′it) *n.* ⟦Fr < It *sonnetto* < Prov *sonet,* dim. of *son,* a sound, song < L *sonus,* a SOUND[1]⟧ a poem normally of fourteen lines in any of several fixed verse and rhyme schemes, typically in rhymed iambic pentameter: sonnets characteristically express a single theme or idea: see PETRARCHAN SONNET, SHAKESPEAREAN SONNET — *vt., vi.* SONNETIZE

son·net·eer (sän′ə tir′) *n.* ⟦prec. + -EER⟧ 1 a person who writes sonnets 2 any minor or inferior poet: used contemptuously

son·net·ize (sän′ə tīz′) *vi., vt.* **-ized′, -iz′ing** to write sonnets (about)

son·ny (sun′ē) *n., pl.* **-nies** little son: used as a familiar term of address to any young boy

son·o·buo·y (sän′ə boo͞′ē, sō′nə-; -boi′) *n.* ⟦< L *sonus,* SOUND[1] + BUOY⟧ a buoy equipped to detect underwater sounds and transmit them by radio

son of a bitch [Slang] 1 a person or thing regarded with anger, contempt, etc. 2 an interjection used to express surprise, annoyance, etc. Considered offensive by some Also written **son·of·a·bitch** (sun′əv ə bich′; *for interj., usually* sun′əv ə bich′) *n., interj.*

son of Adam any man or boy

son of a gun [Slang] a euphemistic alteration of SON OF A BITCH: a much milder term, with overtones of indulgence, familiarity, etc. when used of a person

Son of God (*or* Man) *Christian Theol. name for* Jesus Christ

son·o·gram (sän′ə gram, sō′nə-) *n.* ⟦< L *sonus,* SOUND[1] + -GRAM⟧ 1 ECHOGRAM 2 a visual pattern representing the sound waves of a voice, call, or noise —**so·nog·ra·phy** (sə näg′rə fē) *n.*

So·no·ra (sô nô′rä) state of NW Mexico, on the Gulf of California & the S Ariz. border: 71,403 sq mi (184,933 sq km); cap. Hermosillo

so·no·rant (sə nôr′ənt, sō-) *n.* ⟦SONOR(OUS) + (CONSON)ANT⟧ *Phonet.* a voiced consonant that is less sonorous than a vowel but more sonorous than an unvoiced plosive and that may occur as a syllabic [English *sonorants* are (l), (r), (w), (y), (m), (n), and (ŋ)]

so·nor·i·ty (-ə tē) *n., pl.* **-ties** ⟦< Fr or LL: Fr *sonorité* < LL *sonoritas*⟧ quality, state, or instance of being sonorous; resonance

so·no·rous (sə nôr′əs, sän′ər əs) *adj.* ⟦L *sonorus* < *sonor,* a sound, din, akin to *sonus,* a SOUND[1]⟧ 1 producing or capable of producing sound, esp. sound of full, deep, or rich quality; resonant 2 full, deep, or rich: said of sound 3 having a powerful, impressive sound; high-sounding [*sonorous* prose] 4 *Phonet.* having a degree of resonant tonality: said esp. of vowels, semivowels, and nasals —**so·no′rous·ly** *adv.* —**so·no′rous·ness** *n.*

son·ship (sun′ship) ***n.*** the fact or state of being a son

son·sy or **son·sie** (sän′sē) ***adj.*** ⟦< dial. *sonse*, prosperity, plenty < Gael *sonas*, good fortune + -Y[2]⟧ [Chiefly Scot.] **1** buxom or plump **2** good-natured

Son·tag (sän′tag), **Susan** (born *Susan Rosenblatt*) 1933-2004; U.S. writer

Soo (so͞o) ⟦alteration of *Sault*⟧ region in N Mich. & SC Ontario, Canada, at the St. Marys Falls Canals, including the city of Sault Ste. Marie: often with *the*

Soo·chow (so͞o′chou′; *Chin* so͞o′jō′) *a former transliteration of* SUZHOU

sook (so͝ok) ***n.*** *alt. sp. of* SOUK

Soo Locks locks of St. Marys Falls Canals

soon (so͞on) ***adv.*** ⟦ME *sone* < OE *sona*, at once, akin to OHG *sān*, Goth *suns*⟧ **1** in a short time (after a time specified or understood); shortly; before long [will *soon* be there] **2** promptly; quickly [as *soon* as possible] **3** ahead of time; early [we left too *soon*] **4** readily; willingly [I would as *soon* go as stay] **5** [Obs.] at once; immediately —**had sooner** would rather; would prefer to —**sooner or later** inevitably; eventually

☆**soon·er** (so͞on′ər) ***n.*** ⟦< compar. of prec.⟧ **1** a person occupying homestead land, as formerly in the W U.S., before the authorized time for doing so, thus gaining an unfair advantage in choice of location **2** [**S-**] [Informal] a person born or living in Oklahoma

soot (so͝ot, so͞ot) ***n.*** ⟦ME < OE *sot*, akin to MDu *soet* < IE base **sed-*, to SIT: basic sense "what settles"⟧ a black substance consisting chiefly of carbon particles formed by the incomplete combustion of burning matter —***vt.*** to cover, soil, or treat with soot

sooth (so͞oth) ***adj.*** ⟦ME *soth* < OE, akin to Goth *sunja*, truth, ON *sannr*, true < IE base **es-*, to be (> AM, IS[1]): basic sense "that is"⟧ **1** [Archaic] true or real **2** [Old Poet.] soothing; smooth —***n.*** [Archaic] truth; fact —**in sooth** [Archaic] in truth; truly —**sooth′ly** ***adv.***

soothe (so͞oth) ***vt.*** **soothed**, **sooth′ing** ⟦ME *sothen* < OE *sothian*, to bear witness to, prove true < *soth*: see prec.⟧ **1** to make calm or composed, as by gentle treatment, flattery, etc.; appease; mollify **2** to allay or relieve (pain, an ache, etc.); assuage —***vi.*** to have a soothing effect —***SYN.*** COMFORT —**sooth′er** ***n.*** —**sooth′ing** ***adj.*** —**sooth′ing·ly** ***adv.***

sooth·fast (so͞oth′fast′, -fäst′) ***adj.*** ⟦ME *sothfast* < OE *sothfæst*⟧ [Archaic] **1** truthful or loyal **2** true or real

sooth·say (so͞oth′sā′) ***vi.*** **-said′**, **-say′ing** [Historical] to make predictions; foretell —**sooth′say′ing** ***n.***

sooth·say·er (-ər) ***n.*** ⟦ME *sothseyere*, one who speaks the truth⟧ **1** [Historical] a person who professes to foretell the future **2** MANTIS

soot·y (so͝ot′ē, so͞ot′ē) ***adj.*** **soot′i·er**, **soot′i·est** ⟦ME < OE *sotig*: see SOOT & -Y[2]⟧ **1** of, like, or covered with, soot **2** dark or black like soot —**soot′i·ness** ***n.***

sop (säp) ***n.*** ⟦ME *soppe* < OE *sopp* < base of *supan*: see SUP[1]⟧ **1** a piece of food, as bread, soaked in milk, gravy, etc. **2** *a)* something given by way of concession or appeasement *b)* a bribe —***vt.*** **sopped**, **sop′ping** ⟦OE *soppian* < the n.⟧ **1** to soak, steep, or saturate in or with liquid **2** to take up (liquid) by absorption: usually with *up* —***vi.*** **1** to soak (*in*, *into*, or *through* something) **2** to be or become thoroughly wet

SOP *abbrev.* standard operating procedure

☆**so·pai·pil·la** or **so·pa·pil·la** (sō′pə pē′ə) ***n.*** ⟦MexSp *sopaipilla*, dim. of Sp *sopaipa*, sweet fritter⟧ a dessert consisting of a piece of deep-fried, puffed pastry, usually covered with honey or syrup

☆**soph** (säf) ***n.*** [Informal] *short for* SOPHOMORE

So·phi·a (sō fē′ə, -fī′ə) ***n.*** ⟦< Gr *sophia*, skill, wisdom < *sophos*, wise⟧ a feminine name: dim. *Sophie*, *Sophy*

soph·ism (säf′iz′əm) ***n.*** ⟦altered (infl. by L) < ME *sophime* < OFr *soffime* < L *sophisma* < Gr < *sophizesthai*, to play the sophist < *sophos*, clever, skillful, wise⟧ a clever and plausible but fallacious argument or form of reasoning, esp. one intended to deceive

soph·ist (-ist) ***n.*** ⟦L *sophista* < Gr *sophistēs*, wise man: see prec.⟧ **1** [*often* **S-**] in ancient Greece, any of a group of teachers of rhetoric, politics, philosophy, etc., some of whom were notorious for their clever, specious arguments **2** any person practicing clever, specious reasoning

so·phis·ti·cal (sə fis′ti kəl) ***adj.*** ⟦ML *sophisticalis* < L *sophisticus* < Gr *sophistikos* < *sophistēs*, wise man, sophist⟧ **1** of or characteristic of sophists or sophistry **2** clever and plausible, but unsound and tending to mislead [a *sophistical* argument] **3** using sophistry Also **so·phis′tic** —**so·phis′ti·cal·ly** ***adv.***

so·phis·ti·cate (sə fis′tə kāt′; *for n., usually*, -kit) ***vt.*** **-cat′ed**, **-cat′ing** ⟦ME *sophisticaten* < ML *sophisticatus*, pp. of *sophisticare* < L *sophisticus*: see prec.⟧ **1** to change from being natural, simple, artless, etc. to being artificial, worldly-wise, urbane, etc. **2** to bring to a more developed, complex, or refined form, technique, level, etc. **3** [Now Rare] to make impure by mixture or adulteration **4** [Archaic] to corrupt or mislead —***n.*** a sophisticated person

so·phis·ti·cat·ed (-kāt′id) ***adj.*** **1** not simple, artless, naive, etc.; urbane, worldly-wise, etc. or knowledgeable, perceptive, subtle, etc. **2** designed for or appealing to sophisticated people **3** highly complex, refined, or developed; characterized by advanced form, technique, etc. [*sophisticated* equipment] —**so·phis′ti·cat′ed·ly** ***adv.***

so·phis·ti·ca·tion (sə fis′tə kā′shən) ***n.*** ⟦ME *sophisticacioun* < ML *sophisticatio*⟧ **1** [Archaic] the use of sophistry **2** *a)* the act or process of sophisticating *b)* the state, quality, or character of being sophisticated

soph·ist·ry (säf′is trē) ***n.*** ⟦ME *sophistrie* < ML *sophistria*⟧ **1** unsound or misleading but clever, plausible, and subtle argument or reasoning **2** *pl.* **-tries** SOPHISM

Soph·o·cles (säf′ə klēz′) 496?-406 B.C.; Gr. writer of tragic dramas

soph·o·more (säf′môr′, säf′ə môr′) ***n.*** ⟦altered (< Gr *sophos*, wise + *mōros*, foolish) < older *sophumer* < *sophum*, sophism, prob. < ME *sophime*, SOPHISM⟧ **1** a student in the second year of college or the tenth grade in high school ☆**2** a person in his or her second year in some enterprise —***adj.*** of or for sophomores

☆**soph·o·mor·ic** (säf môr′ik, säf′ə môr′ik) ***adj.*** **1** of, like, or characteristic of sophomores **2** juvenile, pretentious, silly, etc.: also **soph′o·mor′i·cal** —**soph′o·mor′i·cal·ly** ***adv.***

-so·phy (sə fē) ⟦< Gr *sophia*, skill, wisdom⟧ *combining form* knowledge or thought [*theosophy*]

so·por (sō′pər) ***n.*** ⟦L: for IE base see SOMNUS⟧ an unnaturally deep sleep; stupor

sop·o·rif·ic (säp′ə rif′ik, sō′pə-) ***adj.*** ⟦Fr *soporifique*: see prec. & -FIC⟧ **1** causing or tending to cause sleep: also **sop′o·rif′er·ous** (-rif′ər əs) **2** of or characterized by sleep or sleepiness —***n.*** something, as a drug, that causes sleep

sop·ping (säp′iŋ) ***adj.*** thoroughly wet; drenched

sop·pres·sa·ta (so͞o′prə sät′ə) ***n.*** ⟦It⟧ a type of dried Italian salami, usually of pork

sop·py (säp′ē) ***adj.*** **-pi·er**, **-pi·est** **1** very wet; sopping **2** rainy **3** [Informal] sentimental

so·pra·ni·no (sō′prə nē′nō) ***adj.*** ⟦It, dim. of *soprano*⟧ designating or of any musical instrument smaller and of a higher pitch than the soprano of that family —***n.*** a sopranino instrument, esp. a recorder

so·pra·no (sə pran′ō, -prä′nō) ***n.***, *pl.* **-nos** or **-ni** (-prä′nē) ⟦It < *sopra*, above < L *supra*⟧ **1** the range of the highest voice of women or boys, usually from middle C to two or more octaves above **2** *a)* a voice or singer with such a range *b)* an instrument with a similar range within its family, as a soprano recorder *c)* a part for such a voice or instrument **3** in four-part harmony, the highest part —***adj.*** of, for, or having the range of a soprano

☆**so·ra** (sôr′ə) ***n.*** ⟦< ?⟧ a small rail (*Porzana carolina*) with a short, yellow bill: the most common rail of North America

sorb (sôrb) ***n.*** ⟦Fr *sorbe* < L *sorbum*, serviceberry, *sorbus*, SERVICE TREE⟧ **1** any of a number of European trees of the rose family, as the rowan and the service tree **2** the fruit of any of these trees

Sorb (sôrb) ***n.*** ⟦Ger *Sorbe* < Serb *Srb*⟧ LUSATIAN (***n.*** 1)

sorb·ent (sôr′bənt) ***n.*** ⟦< E *sorb*, to gather by absorption or adsorption, altered back-form. < SORPTION⟧ any substance or process that adsorbs, absorbs, or desorbs

sor·bet (sôr bā′, sôr′bət) ***n.*** ⟦Fr < It *sorbetto* < Ar *sharba(t)*: see SHERBET⟧ a tart ice, as of fruit juice, served as a dessert or, sometimes, between courses of a meal to refresh the palate

Sor·bi·an (sôr′bē ən) ***n.***, ***adj.*** LUSATIAN

sor·bic acid (sôr′bik) ⟦SORB + -IC⟧ a white, crystalline solid, $CH_3CH{:}CHCH{:}CHCOOH$, isolated from the berries of mountain ash or made synthetically: used in drying oils, and as a food preservative, fungicide, etc.

sor·bi·tol (sôr′bi tôl′, -tōl′) ***n.*** ⟦SORB + -IT(E) + -OL[1]⟧ a sweet, white, odorless, crystalline alcohol, $C_6H_8(OH)_6$, found in certain berries and fruits, used as a moistening agent in lotions or creams, as a sugar substitute, etc.

Sor·bonne (sôr bän′; *Fr* sôr bôn′) ***n.*** ⟦Fr, after the founder, Robert de *Sorbon* (1201-74), chaplain of Louis IX⟧ **1** a former theological college in Paris, established about the middle of the 13th cent. **2** the University of Paris; specif., the seat of the faculties of letters and science

sor·bose (sôr′bōs′) ***n.*** ⟦SORB(ITOL) + -OSE[1]⟧ a white, crystalline hexose, $C_6H_{12}O_6$, obtained by fermenting sorbitol: it is used in the manufacture of vitamin C

sor·cer·er (sôr′sər ər) ***n.*** ⟦extended < ME *sorcer* < OFr *sorcier*, sorcerer < *sorz*, lot, chance < L *sors* (gen. *sortis*), lot, share: see SORT⟧ a person who practices sorcery; wizard

sor·cer·ess (sôr′sər əs) ***n.*** a woman who practices sorcery; witch

sor·cer·y (-ē) ***n.***, *pl.* **-cer·ies** ⟦ME < OFr *sorcerie* < *sorcier*: see SORCERER⟧ **1** the use of an evil supernatural power to control or influence people and their affairs or the natural world; black magic **2** magical power or influence —***SYN.*** MAGIC —**sor′cer·ous** ***adj.*** —**sor′cer·ous·ly** ***adv.***

sor·did (sôr′did) ***adj.*** ⟦Fr *sordide* < L *sordidus* < *sordes*, filth < IE base **swordo(s)-*, black, dirty > SWARTHY, Ger *schwarz*⟧ **1** *a)* dirty; filthy *b)* squalid; depressingly wretched **2** *a)* base; ignoble; mean *b)* mercenary, avaricious, grasping, or meanly selfish —***SYN.*** BASE[2] —**sor′did·ly** ***adv.*** —**sor′did·ness** ***n.***

sor·di·no (sôr dē′nō) ***n.***, *pl.* **-ni** (-nē) ⟦It < *sordo*, deaf, silent < L *surdus*: see SURD⟧ MUTE (***n.*** 4)

sor·dor (sôr′dər) ***n.*** ⟦ModL < L *sordes*, filth: see SORDID⟧ wretchedness or squalor; sordidness

sore (sôr) ***adj.*** **sor′er**, **sor′est** ⟦ME *sor* < OE *sar*, akin to Ger *sehr*, very, lit., sore < IE base **sai-*, pain, sickness > L *saevus*, raging, terrible, OIr *sāeth*, illness⟧ **1** *a)* giving physical pain; painful; tender [a *sore* throat] *b)* feeling physical pain, as from wounds, bruises, etc. [to be *sore* all over] **2** *a)* filled with sadness, grief, or sorrow; distressed [with a *sore* heart] *b)* causing sadness, grief, misery, or distress [a *sore* hardship] *c)* distressingly intense or bitter; extreme [a *sore* lack] **3** provocative of irritation or disagreeable feelings [a *sore* point] ☆**4** [Informal] angry; offended; feeling hurt or resentful —***n.*** ⟦OE *sar*, pain⟧ **1** a sore, usually infected spot on the body, as an ulcer, boil, or blister **2** a source of pain, irritation, grief, distress, etc. —***adv.*** **sor′er**, **sor′est** [Archaic] sorely; greatly —***vt.*** **sored**, **sor′ing** ☆to inflict soring on (a horse) —**sore′ness** ***n.***

sore·head (sôr′hed′) *n.* [Informal] a person who is angry, resentful, vindictive, etc., or one easily made so

So·rel (sô rel′; *E* sə rel′), **Georges (Eugène)** (zhôrzh) 1847-1922; Fr. social philosopher

sore·ly (sôr′lē) *adv.* ⟦ME *sorelie* < OE *sarlice*: see SORE & -LY[2]⟧ **1** grievously; painfully [*sorely* vexed] **2** urgently; greatly; extremely [*sorely* needed]

sor·ghum (sôr′gəm) *n.* ⟦ModL < It *sorgo* < dial. *soreg* < L *syricus*, Syrian: hence, orig., Syrian grass⟧ **1** any of a genus (*Sorghum*) of tropical grasses that have solid stems bearing large panicles of spikelets with numerous small, glossy grains: grown for grain, syrup, fodder, etc. ☆**2** syrup made from the sweet juices of a sorgo

sor·go (sôr′gō) *n., pl.* **-gos** ⟦It: see prec.⟧ any of several varieties of sorghum with sweet, watery juice, grown for syrup, fodder, or silage: also sp. **sor′gho**, *pl.* **-ghos**

so·ri (sō′rē) *n. pl. of* SORUS

sor·i·cine (sôr′ə sīn′, -sin) *adj.* ⟦L *soricinus* < *sorex* (gen. *soricis*), shrew < IE echoic base **swer-*, to buzz > SWARM[1]⟧ of or like the shrews; shrewlike

sor·ing (sôr′iŋ) *n.* ☆the practice of making the front feet of a show horse sore, as by bruising or blistering, so as to force it to take high, exaggerated steps in exhibitions

so·ri·tes (sō rīt′ēz) *n., pl.* **-tes** ⟦L < Gr *sōreitēs* (*syllogismos*), heaped up (syllogism) < *sōros*, a heap: see SOMA[1]⟧ *Logic* a series of premises followed by a conclusion, arranged so that the predicate of the first premise is the subject of the next, and so forth, the conclusion uniting the subject of the first with the predicate of the last in an elliptical series of syllogisms

so·ror·al (sə rôr′əl) *adj.* of or characteristic of a sister or sisters; sisterly —**so·ror′al·ly** *adv.*

so·ror·ate (sə rôr′it, -āt) *n.* ⟦ModL < L *soror*, SISTER + -ATE[2]⟧ the custom in some cultures of marrying the younger sister of one's wife, esp. after the wife's death

so·ror·i·cide (sə rôr′ə sīd′) *n.* **1** ⟦LL *sororicidium* < L *soror*, SISTER + *caedere*, to strike, kill⟧ the act of murdering one's own sister **2** ⟦L *sororicida*⟧ a person who does this —**so·ror′i·ci′dal** *adj.*

so·ror·i·ty (sə rôr′ə tē) *n., pl.* **-ties** ⟦ML *sororitas*, sisterhood < L *soror*, SISTER⟧ **1** a group of women or girls joined together by common interests, for fellowship, etc. ☆**2** a Greek-letter college organization for women

so·ro·sis (sə rō′sis) *n., pl.* **-ses** (-sēz) ⟦ModL < Gr *sōros*, a heap: see SOMA[1]⟧ a multiple fruit formed by the merging of many flowers into a fleshy mass, as in the mulberry

sorp·tion (sôrp′shən) *n.* ⟦back-form. < ABSORPTION & ADSORPTION⟧ absorption or adsorption

sor·rel[1] (sôr′əl, sär′-) *n.* ⟦ME *sorel* < OFr *surele* < Frank **sur*; akin to OHG *sur*, SOUR⟧ **1** any of various short, coarse weeds (genus *Rumex*) of the buckwheat family, with sour, edible leaves: see DOCK[3] **2** WOOD SORREL

sor·rel[2] (sôr′əl, sär′-) *n.* ⟦LME < OFr *sorel* < *sor, sore*, light brown < ML *saurus* < Gmc **saur*, light brown, color of dry leaves, orig., dry, akin to SEAR[1]⟧ **1** a light reddish-brown color **2** a horse or other animal of this color —*adj.* light reddish-brown

☆**sorrel tree** SOURWOOD

Sor·ren·to (sə ren′tō; *It* sôr ren′tô) resort town in S Italy, on the Bay of Naples

sor·row (sär′ō, sôr′ō) *n.* ⟦ME *sorwe* < OE *sorg*, akin to Ger *sorge* < IE base **swergh-*, to worry, be ill > Sans *sūrkṣati*, he worries about, Lith *sergù*, to be sick⟧ **1** mental suffering caused by loss, disappointment, etc.; sadness, grief, or regret **2** that which produces such suffering; trouble, loss, affliction, etc. **3** the outward expression of such suffering; mourning; lamentation **4** earnest repentance; contrition [*sorrow* for sin] —*vi.* to feel or show sorrow; grieve —**sor′row·er** *n.*

sor·row·ful (-ə fəl) *adj.* ⟦ME *soruful* < OE *sorgful*⟧ full of sorrow; feeling, causing, or expressing sorrow —*SYN.* SAD —**sor′row·ful·ly** *adv.* —**sor′row·ful·ness** *n.*

sor·ry (sär′ē, sôr′ē) *adj.* **-ri·er, -ri·est** ⟦ME *sorie* < OE *sarig* < *sar*, SORE⟧ **1** full of sorrow, pity, or sympathy: also used as an expression of apology or mild regret **2** *a)* inferior in worth or quality; poor [a *sorry* exhibit] *b)* wretched; miserable [a *sorry* tenement] —**sor′ri·ly** *adv.* —**sor′ri·ness** *n.*

sort (sôrt) *n.* ⟦ME < MFr < VL **sorta* < L *sors* (gen. *sortis*), lot, chance, fate, akin to *serere*, to join together, arrange: see SERIES⟧ **1** any group of persons or things related by having something in common; kind; class **2** quality or type; nature [remarks of that *sort*] **3** [Archaic] manner or way **4** *Comput.* the act or an instance of sorting **5** [*usually pl.*] *Printing* any of the kinds of characters in a font of type —*vt.* to place, separate, or arrange according to class or kind: often with *out* —*vi.* **1** [Archaic] to associate; consort **2** [Archaic] to harmonize or agree; suit **3** *Comput.* to arrange data or a group of records in a particular way, as chronologically or alphabetically, for more efficient access —**after a sort** in some way but not very well —**of sorts** **1** of various kinds **2** of a poor or inferior kind: also **of a sort** —**out of sorts** **1** *Printing* lacking certain sorts of type **2** [Informal] *a)* not in a good humor; cross *b)* not feeling well; slightly ill —**sort of** [Informal] somewhat —**sort out** to analyze or resolve (difficulties, a problem, etc.) —**sort′a·ble** *adj.* —**sort′er** *n.*

sort·a (sôrt′ə) *adv. phonetic sp. of* SORT OF (in informal pronunciation) (see phrase under SORT)

sor·tie (sôrt′ē, sôr tē′) *n.* ⟦Fr < *sortir*, to issue, go out < VL **sortire*, prob. < L *sortitus*, chosen, selected by lot, pp. of *sortiri* < *sors*: see SORT⟧ **1** *a)* a sudden rushing forth; sally; specif., a quick raid on besiegers by those besieged *b)* the forces making such a raid **2** one mission by a single military plane

sor·ti·lege (sôrt′ə lij) *n.* ⟦ME < ML *sortilegium* < LL *sortilegus*, fortuneteller < L *sors*, lot (see SORT) + *legere*, to read: see LOGIC⟧ **1** divination or prophecy by casting lots **2** sorcery; black magic

so·rus (sō′rəs, sôr′əs) *n., pl.* **-ri** (-ī) ⟦ModL < Gr *sōros*, a heap: see SOMA[1]⟧ a cluster of spore cases, esp. the ones on the undersurface of a fern frond

SOS (es′ō′es′) *n.* **1** a signal of distress in code (· · · – – – · · ·) used internationally in wireless telegraphy, as by ships **2** [Informal] any call for help

s.o.s. *abbrev.* ⟦L *si opus sit*⟧ *Pharmacy* if necessary

Sos·no·wiec (sôs nô′vyets) city in SW Poland

so-so (sō′sō′) *adv.* ⟦redupl.⟧ indifferently; just tolerably or passably —*adj.* neither very good nor very bad; only fair Also written **so so**

sos·te·nu·to (säs′tə no͞ot′ō; *It* sôs′te no͞o′tô) [*also in italics*] *Music adj., adv.* ⟦It, pp. of *sostenere* < L *sustinere*, to SUSTAIN⟧ (performed) at a slower but sustained tempo, with each note held for its full value: often used as a musical direction —*n., pl.* **-tos** or **-ti** (-tē) a sostenuto passage

sot (sät) *n.* ⟦ME < Late OE *sott*, a fool, or OFr *sot*, a fool < ML *sottus*, prob. < Heb *shote*, a fool⟧ a drunkard

so·te·ri·ol·o·gy (sō tir′ē äl′ə jē) *n.* ⟦< Gr *sōtēria*, deliverance (in LXX & N.T., salvation) < *sōtēr*, deliverer (in N.T., Savior) < *sōzein*, to save < *sōs*, *saos*, safe, sound, prob. < IE **twewos* < base **tēu-*, to swell, be strong > L *tumere* + -LOGY⟧ *Theol.* study of the divine accomplishment of the salvation of humanity; specif., in Christian theology, study of this as effected through Jesus Christ —**so·te·ri·o·log·i·cal** (sō tir′ē ə läj′i kəl) *adj.*

So·thic (sō′thik, säth′ik) *adj.* ⟦Gr *Sōthiakos* < *Sōthis*, the Dog Star < Egypt *Spdt*⟧ **1** of or having to do with Sirius, the Dog Star **2** designating or of an ancient Egyptian cycle or period based on a fixed year of 365¼ days (**Sothic year**) and equal to 1,460 such years

So·tho (sō′thō, -tō) *n.* **1** *pl.* **So′thos** or **So′tho** a member of a group of peoples living in S Africa **2** the group of Bantu languages of these peoples

☆**so·tol** (sō′tōl′, sō tōl′) *n.* ⟦AmSp < Nahuatl *tzotolli*⟧ any of a genus (*Dasylirion*) of yuccalike desert plants of the agave family, with dense clusters of whitish, lilylike flowers, growing in the SW U.S. and N Mexico

So·to·ma·yor (sō′tō mī yôr′), **Sonia (Maria)** 1954-   ; associate justice, U.S. Supreme Court (2009-   )

sot·tish (sät′ish) *adj.* **1** of or like a sot **2** stupid or foolish from or as from too much drinking —**sot′tish·ly** *adv.*

sot·to vo·ce (sät′ō vō′chē; *It* sôt′tô vô′che) ⟦It, under the voice⟧ in an undertone, so as not to be overheard

sou (so͞o) *n., pl.* **sous** (so͞oz; *Fr* so͞o) ⟦Fr < OFr *sol* < LL *solidus*: see SOLIDUS⟧ any of several former French coins, esp. one equal to five centimes

sou·a·ri (so͞o är′ē) *n.* ⟦Fr *saouari* < Carib *sawarra*⟧ any of a genus (*Caryocar*) of trees of N South America having durable timber (**souari wood**) and large, edible nuts (**souari nuts**) that yield an oil used in cooking, etc.

sou·bise (so͞o bēz′) *n.* ⟦Fr, after Charles de Rohan, Prince de *Soubise* (1715-87), Marshal of France⟧ a sauce containing onions and melted butter, or purée of onions

sou·brette (so͞o bret′) *n.* ⟦Fr < Prov *soubreto* < *soubret*, affected, sly < *soubra*, to put aside, exceed < L *superare*, to be above: see SUPER-⟧ **1** in a play, light opera, etc., the role of a lady's maid, esp. one involved in intrigue, or of any pretty, flirtatious, or frivolous young woman **2** an actress who plays such roles

sou·bri·quet (so͞o′brə kā′, -ket′, sō′-; so͞o′brə kā′, -ket′, sō′-) *n. var. of* SOBRIQUET

sou·chong (so͞o′chôŋ′, -shôŋ′) *n.* ⟦< Mandarin *hsiao*, small or young + *chung*, kind⟧ a black tea with large leaves

souf·fle (so͞o′fəl) *n.* ⟦Fr < *souffler*, to blow: see fol.⟧ *Med.* a soft, blowing sound heard on auscultation

souf·flé (so͞o flā′, so͞o′flā) *adj.* ⟦Fr < pp. of *souffler*, to blow < L *sufflare*, to inflate, blow up, puff out < *sub-* (see SUB-) + *flare*, to BLOW[1]⟧ made light and puffy in the process of being cooked or baked: also **souf·fléed′** (-flād′) —*n.* any of several baked foods, as a dish prepared with white sauce and egg yolks and some additional ingredient, as cheese, made light and puffy by beaten egg whites added before baking

sough (sou, suf) *n.* ⟦19th c. < Northern dial. < ME *swough* < OE *swogan*, to sound < ? IE base *(*s*)*wāgh-*: see ECHO⟧ a soft, low, murmuring, sighing, or rustling sound —*vi.* ⟦ME *swowen, soghen* < OE *swogan*, to sound⟧ to make a sough

sought (sôt) *vt., vi. pt. & pp. of* SEEK

souk (so͞ok) *n.* ⟦Ar *sūq*⟧ an open-air marketplace in N Africa and the Middle East

sou·kous (so͞o′ko͞os′) *n.* ⟦< name of the dance (in ? Lingala), altered < Fr *secouer*, to shake or *secousse*, a shake, jolt⟧ a popular African dance music that originated in the Democratic Republic of the Congo, emphasizing modified rumba rhythms and a complex blend of melodies played on guitars, etc.

soul (sōl) *n.* ⟦ME *soule* < OE *sawol*, akin to Ger *seele*, Goth *saiwala* < Gmc **saiwalo*, lit., ? that belonging to the sea (< **saiwa-* > SEA): from the early Gmc belief that souls originate in and return to the sea⟧ **1** an entity which is regarded as being the immortal or spiritual part of a person and which, having no physical or material reality, is credited with the functions of thinking, willing, and choosing **2** the moral or emotional nature of a human being **3** spiritual or emotional warmth, force, etc., or evidence of this [a cold painting, without *soul*] **4** vital or essential part, quality, or principle ["brevity is the *soul* of wit"] **5** the person who leads or dominates; central figure [Daniel Boone, *soul* of the frontier] **6** embodiment; personification [the very *soul* of kindness] **7** a person [a town of 1,000 *souls]* **8** the spirit of a dead person, thought of as separate from the body and leading an existence of its own ☆**9** *a)* the deep spiritual and emotional quality of black American culture and heritage *b)* strong expression of this quality in a musical performance *c)* a form of rhythm and blues characterized by a more deliberate beat, emotionally intense vocals, and elements of U.S. gospel music —☆***adj.*** of, for, like, or characteristic of American blacks —**upon my soul!** an exclamation of surprise

☆**soul food** items of food popular originally in the South, esp. among blacks, such as chitterlings, ham hocks, yams, corn bread, and collard greens

soul·ful (sōl′fəl) ***adj.*** full of or showing deep feeling —**soul′ful·ly** ***adv.*** —**soul′ful·ness** ***n.***

☆**soul kiss** FRENCH KISS —**soul′-kiss′** ***vt., vi.***

soul·less (-lis) ***adj.*** lacking soul, sensitivity, or depth of feeling; without spirit or inspiration

soul mate [Informal] a person, esp. a romantic partner, with whom one feels an uncommon intimacy or compatibility: also written **soul′mate′** ***n.***

☆**soul music** [Informal] SOUL (*n.* 9c)

soul-search·ing (-surʹchiŋ) ***n.*** close, honest examination of one's true feelings, motives, etc.

sound[1] (sound) ***n.*** ⟦< ME *soun* (+ unhistoric *-d*) < OFr *son* < L *sonus* < IE **swonos,* a sound, noise < base **swen-,* to sound > OE *swinsian,* to sing, make music⟧ **1** *a)* vibrations in air, water, etc. that stimulate the auditory nerves and produce the sensation of hearing: although the speed of sound varies considerably, the standard is *c.* 331 meters per second (*c.* 740 mph), which is the speed in dry air at STP *b)* the auditory sensation produced by such vibrations **2** *a)* any auditory effect that is distinctive or characteristic of its source; identifiable noise, tone, vocal utterance, etc. [the *sound* of a violin, a speech *sound]* *b)* such effects as transmitted by or recorded for radio, TV, films, or on phonograph records *c)* the volume or quality of transmitted or recorded sound **3** the distance within which a given sound may be heard; earshot [within *sound* of the bells] **4** the mental impression produced by the way something is worded; tenor; drift [the *sound* of his report] **5** meaningless noise; racket **6** [Archaic] *a)* report; rumor *b)* meaning; significance —***vi.*** ⟦ME *sounen* < OFr *soner* < L *sonare*⟧ **1** to make a sound or sounds **2** to have a particular tone or quality of sound [your voice *sounds* hoarse] **3** to seem, from the sound or manner of utterance [to *sound* troubled] **4** to seem to be or appear to be, based on information one has heard [their plan *sounds* crazy] —***vt.*** **1** *a)* to cause to sound [to *sound* a gong] *b)* to produce the sound of [to *sound* a C on a piano] *c)* to utter distinctly; articulate [to *sound* one's r's] **2** to express, signal, indicate, or announce [the clock *sounds* the hour] **3** to make widely known; proclaim [to *sound* someone's praises] **4** to examine (the chest) by auscultation or percussion —**sound off** ☆**1** *a)* to speak in turn, as in counting off for a military formation *b)* to count cadence in marching ☆**2** [Informal] *a)* to give voice freely to opinions, complaints, etc. *b)* to speak in a loud or offensive way, as in boasting

sound[2] (sound) ***adj.*** ⟦ME < OE *(ge)sund,* akin to Dan *sund,* Ger *(ge)sund* < Gmc **swintha-,* strong > OE *swith*⟧ **1** free from defect, damage, or decay; whole and in good condition [*sound* timber] **2** normal and healthy; not weak, diseased, or impaired [a *sound* body and mind] **3** *a)* firm and safe; stable; secure [a *sound* alliance] *b)* safe and secure financially [a *sound* bank] **4** based on truth or valid reasoning; accurate, reliable, judicious, sensible, etc. [*sound* advice] **5** agreeing with established views or beliefs; not heterodox [*sound* doctrine] **6** thorough, solid, substantial, forceful, etc. [a *sound* defeat] **7** deep and undisturbed: said of sleep **8** morally strong; honest, honorable, loyal, etc. **9** legally valid [a *sound* title to a property] —***adv.*** completely; deeply [*sound* asleep] —***SYN.*** VALID —**sound′ly** ***adv.*** —**sound′ness** ***n.***

sound[3] (sound) ***n.*** ⟦ME < OE *sund,* a swimming, water, strait & ON *sund,* both < base **swem-* > SWIM[1]⟧ **1** a wide channel or strait linking two large bodies of water or separating an island from the mainland **2** a long inlet or arm of the sea **3** the swim bladder of certain fishes

sound[4] (sound) ***vt.*** ⟦ME *sounden* < MFr *sonder* < VL *subundare,* to submerge < L *sub,* under + *unda,* a wave: see WATER⟧ **1** *a)* to measure the depth or various depths of (water or a body of water), esp. with a weighted line *b)* to measure (depth) in this way *c)* to investigate or examine (the bottom of the sea, etc.) with a weighted line that brings up adhering particles *d)* to probe (the atmosphere or space) so as to gain data **2** *a)* to investigate, examine, or try to find out (a person's opinions) *b)* to try to find out the opinions or feelings of (a person), as by roundabout questioning (often with *out*) **3** *Med.* to examine with a sound, or probe —***vi.*** **1** to sound water or a body of water **2** to dive suddenly downward through the water: said esp. of whales or large fish **3** to try to find out something, as by roundabout questioning —***n.*** *Med.* a long probe used in examining body cavities

Sound (sound), **The** ÖRESUND

sound-a·like (sound′ə līk′) ***n.*** a person or thing that resembles another in sound [he is a Bogart *sound-alike]* —***adj.*** sounding like another or each other [*sound-alike* names] Also written **sound′a·like′**

sound barrier SONIC BARRIER

sound bite a brief, quotable remark, or excerpt from a speech, made as by a politician and suitable for use on TV or radio newscasts: often a dismissive term implying superficiality

sound·board (sound′bôrd′) ***n.*** **1** a thin plate, as of wood, built into a musical instrument to increase its resonance or serve as a resonator **2** SOUNDING BOARD (sense 1*b*)

sound effects sounds, as of thunder, blows, animals, traffic, etc., produced artificially or by recording to supply sounds called for in the script of a radio, stage, film, or TV production

sound·er[1] (soun′dər) ***n.*** **1** a person or thing that makes a sound or sounds **2** a telegraphic device that converts electric code impulses into sound

sound·er[2] (soun′dər) ***n.*** a person or thing that sounds the depth of water, etc.

sound·ing[1] (-diŋ) ***adj.*** **1** making or giving forth sound **2** resonant; sonorous **3** high-sounding; bombastic

sound·ing[2] (-diŋ) ***n.*** **1** *a)* the act of measuring the depth or examining the bottom of a body of water, etc. with or as with a weighted line *b)* depth so measured *c)* [*pl.*] a place, usually less than 100 fathoms (*c.* 180 m) in depth, where a sounding line will touch bottom **2** *a)* an examination of the atmosphere at or to a given height, as with a radiosonde *b)* a probe of space, as with a rocket **3** [*pl.*] measurements learned or data acquired by sounding **4** [*often pl.*] an exploratory sampling, as of public opinion

sounding board **1** *a)* SOUNDBOARD (sense 1) *b)* a structure over or behind a rostrum, stage, etc. designed to reflect sound toward the audience **2** *a)* a person or thing used for spreading ideas around *b)* a person on whom one tests one's ideas, opinions, etc.

sounding line LEAD LINE

sound·less[1] (sound′lis) ***adj.*** without sound; quiet; noiseless —**sound′less·ly** ***adv.*** —**sound′less·ness** ***n.***

sound·less[2] (-lis) ***adj.*** so deep as to be incapable of being sounded; unfathomable: now rare, found mostly in old poetry [the *soundless* ocean] or used fig.

sound·proof (-pro͞of′) ***adj.*** that keeps sound from coming through —***vt.*** to make soundproof

sound spectrograph an electronic instrument that graphically displays a sound wave or voiceprint on a monitor or makes a record (**sound spectrogram**) of it on graph paper

sound·stage (sound′stāj′) ***n.*** an enclosed soundproof area, esp. one in a STUDIO (*n.* 3*b*), equipped for producing films or TV shows

sound·track (-trak′) ***n.*** **1** the area along one side of a film, carrying its recorded sound portion **2** *a)* the sound portion of a film *b)* a recording of this, esp. of the music, on disc, tape, etc. Also written **sound track**

☆**sound truck** a truck or van with amplifiers, loudspeakers, etc., used on the streets for disseminating political statements or appeals, advertising announcements, etc.

sound wave *Physics* a longitudinal pressure wave stimulated by a mechanical disturbance of an elastic medium, as air, at some source and propagated by the action of disturbed particles on adjacent particles; esp., any of such waves within the range of those audible to the human ear (*c.* 15 cycles to 20,000 cycles per second)

soup (so͞op) ***n.*** ⟦Fr *soupe* < OFr, soup: see SUP[2]⟧ **1** a liquid food, with or without solid particles, made by cooking meat, vegetables, fish, etc. in water, milk, or the like **2** [Slang] a heavy fog ☆**3** [Slang] nitroglycerin —☆**from soup to nuts** ⟦with ref. to the first and last courses of a meal⟧ [Informal] from beginning to end; completely or exhaustively —**in the soup** [Slang] in trouble —**soup up** [Slang] to increase the power, capacity for speed, etc. of (an engine, etc.)

soup·çon (so͞op sōn′, so͞op′sōn′) ***n.*** ⟦Fr < OFr *sospeçon* < VL *suspectio,* for L *suspicio:* see SUSPICION⟧ **1** literally, a suspicion **2** a slight trace, as of a flavor; hint; suggestion **3** a tiny amount; bit

soup du jour (so͞op′do͞o zhoor′; *Fr* so͞op dü zho͞or′) ⟦< Fr *soupe du jour,* soup of the day⟧ the special, sometimes the only, soup served in a restaurant on any particular day: also, Fr. sp., ***soupe du jour***

soup kitchen a place where hot soup or the like is given to people in dire need

soup·spoon (so͞op′spo͞on′) ***n.*** a large-bowled spoon for eating soup

soup·y (so͞o′pē) ***adj.*** **soup′i·er, soup′i·est** **1** watery like soup **2** [Informal] *a)* thick and dank [a *soupy* fog] *b)* quite foggy [*soupy* weather] ☆**3** [Slang] sloppily sentimental; mawkish

sour (sour) ***adj.*** ⟦ME *soure* < OE *sur,* akin to Ger *sauer,* ON *sūrr* < IE **suro-,* sour, salty > Latvian *sũrs,* salty, bitter⟧ **1** having the sharp, acid taste of lemon juice, vinegar, green fruit, etc. **2** made acid or rank by or as by fermentation [*sour* milk] **3** *a)* cross, bad-tempered, peevish, morose, etc. [a *sour* mood] *b)* ill-disposed and bitter [*sour* toward former associates] **4** below what is usual or normal; poor; bad [his game has gone *sour]* **5** distasteful or unpleasant **6** gratingly wrong or off pitch [a *sour* note] **7** excessively acid: said of soil **8** tainted with sulfur compounds: said of gasoline, etc. —***n.*** **1** that which is sour; something sour ☆**2** a cocktail made with lemon or lime juice, sugar, and, usually, soda water [a whiskey *sour]* —***vt., vi.*** to make or become sour [the milk will *sour, soured* on life] —**sour′ly** ***adv.*** —**sour′ness** ***n.***

SYN.—**sour** usually implies an unpleasant sharpness of taste and often connotes fermentation or rancidity [*sour* milk]; **acid** suggests a sourness that is normal or natural [a lemon is an *acid* fruit]; **acidulous** suggests a slightly sour or acid quality [*acidulous* spring water]; **tart** suggests a slightly stinging sharpness or sourness and usually connotes that this is pleasant to the taste [a *tart* cherry pie] —***ANT.*** **sweet**

sour·ball (sour′bôl′) ***n.*** a small ball of tart, hard candy

source (sôrs) ***n.*** ⟦ME *sours* < OFr *sourse* < pp. of *sourdre,* to rise < L *surgere:* see SURGE⟧ **1** a spring, fountain, etc. that is the starting point of a stream **2** that from which something comes into existence, develops, or derives [the sun is our *source* of energy; the *source* of a difficulty] **3** *a)* any person, place, or thing by which something is supplied [a *source* of pleasure] *b)* a person, book, document, etc. that provides information [to consult various *sources*] **4** the point or thing from which light rays, sound waves, etc. emanate —*adj.* of or constituting a source [letters, journals, etc. are a biographer's *source* materials] — *vt., vi.* **sourced, sourc′ing** [Informal] ☆**1** to obtain (parts, materials, etc.) from a source of supply ☆**2** to identify the source of (information, quotations, etc.) —SYN. ORIGIN

☆**source·book** (sôrs′bo͝ok′) *n.* a collection of documents or a diary, journal, etc. used as basic information in studying, evaluating, and writing about a person, period, etc.

source language the language from which a text is to be translated into another language: cf. TARGET LANGUAGE (sense 1)

sour cherry **1** a cherry tree (*Prunus cerasus*) bearing acid fruits that are usually used in cooking, preserves, etc. **2** this fruit

sour cream cream soured and thickened naturally or by addition of a lactobacillus culture, for use as a topping or in sauces, dressings, dips, etc.

sour·dine (so͝or dēn′) *n.* ⟦Fr < It *sordina* < *sordo,* deaf: see SORDINO⟧ SORDINO

sour·dough (sour′dō′) *n.* **1** [Dial.] leaven **2** *a)* fermenting dough saved from one baking to be used for producing fermentation in a later one, thus avoiding the need for fresh yeast *b)* bread made with such dough (in full **sourdough bread**) **3** [Historical] a prospector or settler in the W U.S. or Canada, esp. one living alone: so called because sourdough bread was a staple

sour gourd **1** an Australian tree (*Adansonia gregorii*) of the bombax family with a gourdlike fruit **2** its woody fruit, with acid pulp and large seeds **3** BAOBAB

sour grapes ⟦from Aesop's fable in which the fox, after futile efforts to reach some grapes, scorns them as being sour⟧ the act or an instance of disparaging something desirable, simply because one does not have it or cannot do it

☆**sour-gum** (sour′gum′) *adj.* designating a family (Nyssaceae, order Cornales) of dicotyledonous trees and shrubs, including the tupelos

☆**sour mash** a grain mash made with some mash from an earlier run, used in distilling some whiskeys

sour orange **1** an orange tree (*Citrus aurantium*) widely grown as a rootstock for grafting other citrus trees **2** its fruit, used in making marmalade

☆**sour·puss** (sour′po͝os′) *n.* ⟦< PUSS[2]⟧ [Slang] a person who has a gloomy or disagreeable expression or nature

☆**sour salt** crystals of citric acid or tartaric acid, used in flavoring foods, in pharmaceuticals, etc.

sour·sop (sour′säp′) *n.* ⟦SOUR + SOP: from the flavor & texture of the fruit⟧ **1** a tropical American tree (*Annona muricata*) of the custard-apple family, with large, pulpy, acid fruit **2** this fruit

☆**sour·wood** (-wo͝od′) *n.* a North American tree (*Oxydendrum arboreum*) of the heath family, with thick, fissured bark, small, white flowers, grayish fruit, and sour leaves

Sou·sa (so͞o′zə, -sə), **John Philip** 1854-1932; U.S. bandmaster & composer of marches

☆**sou·sa·phone** (so͞o′zə fōn′, so͞o′sə-) *n.* ⟦after prec., who suggested its form⟧ a brass instrument of the tuba family, with a large, movable bell: it was developed from the helicon and is used esp. in military bands

sousaphone

sous-chef (so͞o′shef′) *n.* ⟦Fr, lit., under-chef⟧ a chef's assistant

souse (sous) *n.* ⟦ME *sows* < OFr *souz* < OHG *sulza,* brine, akin to *salz,* SALT⟧ **1** a pickled food, esp. the feet, ears, and head of a pig **2** liquid used for pickling; brine **3** the act of plunging into a liquid, esp. into brine for pickling ☆**4** [Slang] a drunkard — *vt., vi.* **soused, sous′ing** **1** to pickle **2** to plunge or steep in a liquid **3** to make or become soaking wet ☆**4** [Slang] to make or become intoxicated

sou·tache (so͞o tash′) *n.* ⟦Fr < Hung *sujtás,* pendant⟧ a narrow, flat braid used for trimming

sou·tane (so͞o tan′, -tän′) *n.* ⟦Fr < It *sottana* < *sotto,* under < L *subtus,* under, beneath < *sub,* under⟧ CASSOCK

south (south) *n.* ⟦ME < OE *suth,* akin to OHG *sund-,* ON *suthr* < Gmc **suntha-* (understood as sun side < IE **sun-,* SUN[1]), prob. < **swintha-,* strong, SOUND[2], to the right side, in reference to the east-facing position during prayer⟧ **1** the direction to the left of a person facing the sunset; direction of the South Pole from any other point on the earth's surface **2** the point on a compass at 180°, directly opposite north **3** a region or district in or toward this direction **4** [*often* **S-**] the southern part of the earth, esp. the antarctic regions —*adj.* **1** in, of, to, toward, or facing the south **2** from the south [a *south* wind] **3** [**S-**] designating the southern part of a continent, country, etc. [*South* Asia] —*adv.* in or toward the south; in a southerly direction —☆**go south** [Informal] to decline, deteriorate, fail, etc. [stock prices *went south*] —**south of** ⟦fig. use, from the traditional "lower" position of south on a map or globe⟧ [Informal] fewer or less than; below [a salary *south of* $90,000] —**the South** ☆**1** that part of the U.S. which is bounded on the north by the S border of Pa., the Ohio River, and the E and N borders of Mo.; specif., in the Civil War, the Confederacy **2** the Southern Hemisphere, esp. as the region comprising the majority of the poor, underdeveloped nations on earth

South Africa country in southernmost Africa: formerly the *Union of South Africa,* it became a republic in 1961; member of the Commonwealth: 471,011 sq mi (1,219,912 sq km); caps. Cape Town (legislative), Pretoria (administrative), & Bloemfontein (judicial)

South African **1** of S Africa **2** of South Africa **3** a person born or living in South Africa; esp., AFRIKANER

South African Dutch [Rare or Chiefly Brit.] **1** the Boers **2** AFRIKAANS

South African Republic *former name for* TRANSVAAL

South America S continent in the Western Hemisphere: *c.* 6,880,000 sq mi (17,819,000 sq km) —**South American**

South·amp·ton (south amp′tən, -hamp′-) **1** seaport in S England, on an inlet (**Southampton Water**) of The Solent or Spithead **2** ⟦after Henry Wriothesley (1573-1624), 3d Earl of *Southampton*⟧ island in N Hudson Bay, Canada: 15,700 sq mi (40,663 sq km)

South Australia state of SC Australia: 379,724 sq mi (983,480 sq km); cap. Adelaide

South Bend ⟦so named from its location at the *bend* that is farthest *south* on the St. Joseph River⟧ city in N Ind.

☆**south·bound** (south′bound′) *adj.* bound south; going southward

south by east the direction, or the point on a mariner's compass, halfway between due south and south-southeast; 11°15′ east of due south

south by west the direction, or the point on a mariner's compass, halfway between due south and south-southwest; 11°15′ west of due south

South Carolina ⟦see CAROLINA[1]⟧ state of the SE U.S., on the Atlantic: one of the 13 original states: 30,109 sq mi (77,983 sq km); cap. Columbia: abbrev. *SC* or *S.C.*

South Carolinian **1** of South Carolina: usually used in the predicate **2** a person born or living in South Carolina

South China Sea arm of the W Pacific, touching Taiwan, the Philippines, Borneo, the Malay Peninsula, Indochina, & China: *c.* 1,148,500 sq mi (2,974,604 sq km)

South Dakota ⟦see DAKOTA[2]⟧ Midwestern state of the NC U.S.: admitted 1889; 75,885 sq mi (196,540 sq km); cap. Pierre: abbrev. *SD, S.D.,* or *S Dak*

South Dakotan **1** of South Dakota: usually used in the predicate **2** a person born or living in South Dakota

South·down (south′doun′) *n.* ⟦after SOUTH DOWNS⟧ any of a breed of small, thickset sheep yielding a high-quality short-staple wool, but raised esp. for food

South Downs *see* DOWNS

south·east (south′ēst′; *naut.* sou′-) *n.* **1** the direction, or the point on a mariner's compass, halfway between south and east; 45° east of due south **2** a district or region in or toward this direction —*adj.* **1** in, of, to, toward, or facing the southeast **2** from the southeast [a *southeast* wind] —*adv.* in or toward the southeast —☆**the Southeast** the SE part of the U.S.

Southeast Asia region comprising the Malay Archipelago, the Malay Peninsula, & Indochina

southeast by east the direction, or the point on a mariner's compass, halfway between southeast and east-southeast; 11°15′ east of southeast

southeast by south the direction, or the point on a mariner's compass, halfway between southeast and south-southeast; 11°15′ south of southeast

☆**south·east·er** (south′ēs′tər; *naut.* sou′-) *n.* a storm or strong wind from the southeast

south·east·er·ly (-tər lē) *adj., adv.* **1** in or toward the southeast **2** from the southeast, as a wind

south·east·ern (-tərn) *adj.* **1** in, of, to, toward, or facing the southeast **2** from the southeast [a *southeastern* wind] ☆**3** [**S-**] of or characteristic of the Southeast —**South′east′ern·er** *n.*

south·east·ward (-wərd) *adv., adj.* toward the southeast —*n.* a southeastward direction, point, or region

south·east·ward·ly (-wərd lē) *adj., adv.* **1** toward the southeast **2** from the southeast [a *southeastwardly* wind]

south·east·wards (-wərdz) *adv. var. of* SOUTHEASTWARD

South·end-on-Sea (south′end′än sē′) seaport in Essex, SE England, on the Thames estuary

south·er (south′ər) *n.* a storm or strong wind from the south

south·er·ly (suth′ər lē) *adj., adv.* **1** in or toward the south **2** from the south, as a wind —*n., pl.* **-lies** a wind from the south

south·ern (suth′ərn) *adj.* ⟦ME < OE *suthern*⟧ **1** in, of, to, toward, or facing the south **2** from the south [a *southern* wind] ☆**3** [*usually* **S-**] of or characteristic of the South ☆**4** [**S-**] designating a dialect of American English spoken in the Delmarva Peninsula, the Va. Piedmont, E N.C. and S.C., Ga., Fla., Ark., Tenn., and the states along the Gulf of Mexico —*n.* [*also* **S-**] *dial. var. of* SOUTHERNER (sense 2)

Southern Alps mountain range on South Island, New Zealand: highest peak, Mt. Cook

Southern Cross, the the constellation Crux

Southern Crown, the the constellation Corona Australis

south·ern·er (suth′ər nər, -ə nər) *n.* **1** a person born or living in the south ☆**2** [*also* **S-**] a person born or living in a U.S. state of THE SOUTH (see the phrase at SOUTH)

☆**Southern Gothic** a literary genre depicting life in the S U.S. and featuring grotesque characters and often macabre themes and imagery

Southern Hemisphere that half of the earth south of the equator
south·ern·ism (suth′ərn iz′əm) ***n.*** 1 a word, expression, or practice peculiar to the south ☆2 an idiom peculiar to the southern U.S.
southern lights [*also* **S- L-**] AURORA AUSTRALIS
south·ern·most (suth′ərn mōst′) ***adj.*** farthest south
Southern Ocean 1 that part of the Indian Ocean south of Australia: name used by Australians 2 ANTARCTIC OCEAN
Southern Rhodesia *former name for* ZIMBABWE
Southern Sporades SPORADES (islands along Turkish coast)
Southern Up·lands (up′ləndz) hilly moorland region in S Scotland, between the English border & the Lowlands
south·ern·wood (suth′ərn wood′) ***n.*** ⟦ME *suthernewode* < OE *sutherne wudu:* it is native to southern Europe⟧ a shrubby European wormwood (*Artemisia abrotanum*) with yellowish flowers and fragrant leaves
Sou·they (sou′thē, suth′ē), **Robert** 1774-1843; Eng. poet & writer: poet laureate (1813-43)
South Frigid Zone *see* FRIGID ZONE
South Georgia island under British control in the South Atlantic: former dependency of the Falkland Islands: 1,450 sq mi (3,755 sq km)
South Glamorgan county in S Wales: 161 sq mi (417 sq km)
South Holland province of the W Netherlands, on the North Sea: 1,330 sq mi (3,445 sq km); cap. The Hague
south·ing (sou′thiŋ, -thiŋ) ***n.*** 1 *Naut.* the distance due south covered by a vessel traveling on any southerly course 2 a southerly direction
South Island S island of the two main islands of New Zealand: 58,384 sq mi (151,214 sq km)
South Korea *see* KOREA
south·land (south′land′, -lənd) ***n.*** [*also* **S-**] 1 the southern region of a country 2 land in the south —**south′land′er** ***n.***
South Orkney Islands group of British islands in the South Atlantic, southeast of South America: 240 sq mi (622 sq km)
☆**south·paw** (-pô′) [Informal] ***n.*** ⟦SOUTH + PAW[1]: the ballpark in Chicago (*c.* 1885) was so situated that the pitcher's left arm was toward the south⟧ a person who is left-handed; esp., a left-handed baseball pitcher —***adj.*** left-handed
South Platte river flowing from central Colo. through W Nebr., joining the North Platte to form the Platte: 424 mi (682 km)
south pole 1 the place where the southern rotational axis intersects the surface of a planet, moon, etc. 2 the zenith of such a place; esp., the zenith (**south celestial pole**) of this place on earth 3 that end of a straight magnet that points to the south when the magnet hangs free 4 [**S- P-**] the place on earth where its southern rotational axis intersects its surface: in full **South Terrestrial Pole**
south·ron (suth′rən) ***n.*** ⟦LME *sothron,* altered (prob. modeled on BRITON, SAXON) < *southren,* dial. var. of *southern*⟧ [Archaic] a southerner: applied in Scottish dialect to an Englishman and, formerly, in the U.S. to a Southerner
South Saskatchewan river flowing from SW Alberta, Canada, east & northeast through Saskatchewan, joining the North Saskatchewan to form the Saskatchewan: 865 mi (1,392 km)
South Sea Islands islands in temperate or tropical parts of the South Pacific —**South Sea Islander**
South Seas 1 the South Pacific 2 all the seas south of the equator
South Shetland Islands group of British islands in the South Atlantic, south of South America: 1,800 sq mi (4,662 sq km)
south-south·east (south′south′ēst′; *naut.,* sou′sou′-) ***n.*** the direction, or the point on a mariner's compass, halfway between due south and southeast; 22°30′ east of due south — ***adj., adv.*** 1 in or toward this direction 2 from this direction, as a wind
south-south·west (-west′) ***n.*** the direction, or the point on a mariner's compass, halfway between due south and southwest; 22°30′ west of due south — ***adj., adv.*** 1 in or toward this direction 2 from this direction, as a wind
South Sudan country in NC Africa, south of Sudan: formerly part of Sudan, it became independent in 2011: 239,285 sq mi (619,745 sq km); cap. Juba
South Temperate Zone *see* TEMPERATE ZONE
south·ward (south′wərd; *naut.* suth′ərd) ***adv., adj.*** toward the south —***n.*** a southward direction, point, or region
south·ward·ly (-wərd lē) ***adv., adj.*** 1 toward the south 2 from the south [*a southwardly* wind]
south·wards (-wərdz) ***adv.*** SOUTHWARD
South·wark (suth′ərk) borough of Greater London, England
south·west (south′west′; *naut.* sou′-) ***n.*** 1 the direction, or the point on a mariner's compass, halfway between south and west; 45° west of due south 2 a district or region in or toward this direction —***adj.*** 1 in, of, to, toward, or facing the southwest 2 from the southwest [*a southwest* wind] —***adv.*** in or toward the southwest —☆**the Southwest** the SW part of the U.S., esp. Okla., Tex., N.Mex., Ariz., and S Calif.
South West Africa *former name for* NAMIBIA
southwest by south the direction, or the point on a mariner's compass, halfway between southwest and south-southwest; 11°15′ south of southwest
southwest by west the direction, or the point on a mariner's compass, halfway between southwest and west-southwest; 11°15′ west of southwest
south·west·er (south′wes′tər; *naut.* sou′-) ***n.*** 1 a storm or strong wind from the southwest 2 a sailor's waterproof coat or hat of oilskin, canvas, etc.: the hat has a brim that broadens in the back to protect the neck
south·west·er·ly (-ter lē) ***adj., adv.*** 1 in or toward the southwest 2 from the southwest, as a wind
south·west·ern (-tərn) ***adj.*** 1 in, of, to, toward, or facing southwest 2 from the southwest [*a southwestern* wind] ☆3 [**S-**] of or characteristic of the Southwest —**South′west′ern·er** ***n.***
south·west·ward (south′west′wərd) ***adv., adj.*** toward the southwest —***n.*** a southwestward direction, point, or region
south·west·ward·ly (-wərd lē) ***adv., adj.*** 1 toward the southwest 2 from the southwest [*a southwestwardly* wind]
south·west·wards (-wərdz) ***adv.*** *var. of* SOUTHWESTWARD
South Yorkshire county in N England: 602 sq mi (1,559 sq km)
Sou·tine (soo tēn′), **Cha·im** (khī′im) 1894-1943; Fr. painter, born in Lithuania
sou·ve·nir (soo′və nir′, soo′və nir′) ***n.*** ⟦Fr, orig. inf., to remember < L *subvenire,* to come to mind: see SUBVENE⟧ something kept or serving as a reminder of a place, person, or occasion; keepsake; memento
souvenir sheet (*or* card) a sheet (or card) with one or more commemorative postage stamps or reproductions, with an inscription to mark a philatelic or historical event
sou·vla·ki·a (soo vlä′kē ə) ***n.*** ⟦< ModGr *soubla,* skewer < Gr, awl; akin to L *subula* < IE **siūdhla* < base **siw-,* SEW⟧ a Greek version of shish kebab, for which the meat is marinated before broiling: also **sou·vla′ki** (-kē)
sou′west·er (sou′wes′tər) ***n.*** SOUTHWESTER
sov·er·eign (säv′rən, -ər in; *occas.* suv′-) ***adj.*** ⟦ME *soveraine* < OFr < VL **superanus* < L *super,* above, OVER⟧ 1 above or superior to all others; chief; greatest; supreme 2 supreme in power, rank, or authority 3 of or holding the position of ruler; royal; reigning 4 independent of all others [*a sovereign* state] 5 excellent; outstanding 6 very effectual, as a cure or remedy 7 *Finance* of or having to do with the economy or finances of a national government [Greece's *sovereign* debt] —***n.*** 1 a person who possesses sovereign authority or power; specif., a monarch or ruler 2 a British gold coin valued at 20 shillings or one pound sterling, no longer minted for circulation —**sov′er·eign·ly** ***adv.***
sov·er·eign·tist (-tist) [Chiefly Cdn.] ***adj.*** of or expressing support for making the province of Quebec essentially independent from Canada —***n.*** a person who supports such independence for Quebec
sov·er·eign·ty (-tē) ***n., pl.*** **-ties** ⟦ME *soverainete* < Anglo-Fr *sovereyneté,* OFr *souveraineté*⟧ 1 the state or quality of being sovereign 2 the status, dominion, rule, or power of a sovereign 3 supreme and independent political authority 4 a sovereign state or governmental unit
so·vi·et (sō′vē it, -et′) ***n.*** ⟦Russ *sovet,* council, advice⟧ 1 *a)* any of the various governing councils that performed executive and legislative functions in the Soviet Union: in structure the soviets formed a pyramid, with the village and town soviets as its base and the SUPREME SOVIET as its apex *b)* any similar council in a socialist governing system 2 [**S-**] [*pl.*] the government officials or the people of the Soviet Union, Russia, or Uzbekistan —***adj.*** 1 of a soviet or soviets or government by soviets 2 [**S-**] of or connected with the Soviet Union
so·vi·et·ism (sō′vē ə tiz′əm) ***n.*** [*often* **S-**] 1 government by soviets or the Soviets 2 the system, principles, practices, etc. of such government
so·vi·et·ize (sō′vē ə tīz′) ***vt.*** **-ized′, -iz′ing** [*often* **S-**] 1 to change to a soviet form of government 2 to make conform with the system, principles, practices, etc. of the Soviets —**so′vi·et·i·za′tion** ***n.***
So·vi·et·ol·o·gy (sō′vē ə täl′ə jē) ***n.*** ⟦SOVIET + -OLOGY⟧ the study of the political and economic policies, practices, etc. of the Soviet Union —**So′vi·et·ol′o·gist** ***n.***
Soviet Union UNION OF SOVIET SOCIALIST REPUBLICS: also **Soviet Russia**
sov·khoz (säf kôz′, -käz′) ***n., pl.*** **-khoz′y** (-kô′zē, -kä′-) ⟦Russ *sovxoz* < *sovetskoe xozjajstvo,* soviet farm⟧ a state-owned farm in the Soviet Union
sow[1] (sou) ***n.*** ⟦ME *sowe* < OE *sugu,* akin to Ger *sau* (OHG *su*) < IE base **sū-,* pig > SWINE, L *sus*⟧ 1 *a)* an adult female pig *b)* an adult female of certain other mammals, as the bear 2 *a)* a channel or sluice carrying molten metal from a blast furnace to the molds in which pig bars are cast *b)* a large mass of metal that has solidified in this channel
sow[2] (sō) ***vt.*** **sowed, sown** (sōn) or **sowed, sow′ing** ⟦ME *sowen* < OE *sawan,* akin to Ger *säen* < IE base **sē(i)* > SEED⟧ 1 to scatter or plant (seed) for growing 2 to plant seed in or on (a field, ground, earth, etc.) 3 to spread or scatter; broadcast, disseminate, or propagate [to *sow* hate] 4 to implant; inculcate [to *sow* suspicion] —***vi.*** to sow seed for growing —**sow′er** ***n.***
☆**sow·bel·ly** (sou′bel′ē) ***n.*** [Informal] SALT PORK
sow bug (sou) any of several small terrestrial isopods (esp. genus *Oniscus*) living in damp places, as under rocks
sow thistle (sou) ⟦ME *sowethistel* (parallel with Ger *saudistel*): see SOW[1] & THISTLE⟧ any of several weeds (genus *Sonchus*) of the composite family, with yellow flower heads and spiny leaves
sox (säks) ***n.*** *alt. pl. of* SOCK[1] (sense 3)
soy (soi) ***n.*** ⟦Jpn, prob. dial. var. of SinoJpn *shōyu* < *shō,* rice, wheat, or beans fermented & steeped in brine + *yu,* oil⟧ 1 SOY SAUCE 2 the soybean plant or its seeds Also [Chiefly Brit.] **soy·a** (soi′ə)
soy·bean (soi′bēn′) ***n.*** ⟦prec. + BEAN⟧ 1 an annual crop plant (*Glycine max*) of the pea family, native to China and Japan but widely grown for its seeds, which contain much protein and oil, and as a forage and cover crop 2 its seed

Soy·er (soi′ər) **1 Moses** 1899-1974; U.S. painter, born in Russia **2 Raphael** 1899-1987; U.S. painter, born in Russia: twin brother of Moses

soy sauce a dark, salty sauce made from soybeans fermented and steeped in brine, used esp. as a flavoring in Chinese and Japanese dishes

☆**soy·uz** (sä′yo͞oz; *Russ* su yo͞os′) *n.* ⟦Russ *sojuz,* lit., union⟧ any of a series of Russ. manned spacecraft capable of docking in space

soz·zled (säz′əld) *adj.* ⟦pp. of dial. *sozzle, sossle,* to mix in a sloppy manner, splash⟧ [Informal] drunk; intoxicated

sp *abbrev.* **1** special **2** species **3** specific **4** spelling

Sp *abbrev.* **1** Spain **2** Spaniard **3** Spanish

SP *abbrev.* **1** Shore Patrol **2** Specialist **3** standard play (tape, disc, etc.) **4** Submarine Patrol

s.p. *abbrev.* ⟦L *sine prole*⟧ without issue; childless

spa (spä) *n.* ⟦after *Spa,* Belgian health resort town known for its mineral springs⟧ **1** a mineral spring **2** any place, esp. a health resort, having a mineral spring **3** any fashionable resort **4** a commercial establishment with exercise rooms, sauna baths, etc. **5** a large whirlpool bath, with ledges for seating several people

space (spās) *n.* ⟦ME < OFr *espace* < L *spatium* < IE base *spēi-, to flourish, expand, succeed > SPEED, L *spes,* hope, ON *sparr,* OE *spær,* thrifty⟧ **1** *a)* the three-dimensional, continuous expanse extending in all directions and containing all matter: variously thought of as boundless or indeterminately finite *b)* OUTER SPACE **2** *a)* a continuous, unoccupied area, as between, over, within, etc. things *b)* area or room sufficient for or allotted to something [a parking *space*] **3** an interval or period of time, often one of specified length ☆**4** reserved accommodations [to buy *space* on a ship] ☆**5** room in a newspaper or magazine, or time on radio or TV, available for use by advertisers **6** [Informal] independence, privacy, and freedom to follow one's own interests **7** *Math.* a set of points or elements assumed to satisfy a given set of postulates (Ex.: *space* of one dimension is a line and of two dimensions is a plane) **8** *Music* the open area between any two lines of a staff **9** *Printing a)* a blank piece of type metal used to separate characters or words *b)* the area left vacant by this or by mechanical or electronic means on a printed or typed line **10** *Telegraphy* an interval when the key is open, or not in contact, during the sending of a message —*adj.* of or pertaining to space, esp. to outer space —*vt.* **spaced, spac′ing** to arrange with space or spaces between; divide into or by spaces: often with *out* —**space out 1** to insert more space between letters, words, or lines so as to extend to the required length **2** to be or seem to be in a daze, distracted, inattentive, etc. —**spac′er** *n.*

Space Age [*also* **s- a-**] the period characterized by the launching of artificial satellites and manned space vehicles: regarded as beginning with the launching of the first sputnik on October 4, 1957 —**space′-age′** *adj.*

space bar a bar at the bottom of a typewriter or keyboard, pressed to leave a blank space or spaces rather than to produce a character

☆**space cadet** [Slang] a person regarded as silly, flighty, irresponsible, etc.

☆**space capsule** *see* CAPSULE (*n.* 3*b*)

space charge *Electronics* the negative electric charge within a cloud of electrons that is located in one of the spaces between electrodes, usually the cathode and first grid, in a vacuum tube

space·craft (spās′kraft′, -kräft′) *n., pl.* **-craft′** any vehicle, satellite, etc. designed to orbit the earth or travel through the solar system: often called, esp. if unmanned, **space capsule**

☆**spaced-out** (spāst′out′) *adj.* [Slang] **1** under or as if under the influence of a drug **2** distracted, inattentive, dazed, etc. Also **spaced**

☆**space·flight** (spās′flīt′) *n.* **1** flight in a spacecraft **2** a trip by spacecraft

space heater a small heating unit for warming the air of a single confined area, as a room

space lattice any array of points formed by the exact repetition in three dimensions of the structural units of a crystal

space·less (-lis) *adj.* **1** having no spatial limits **2** occupying no space

space·man (-man′, -mən) *n., pl.* **-men′** (-men′, -mən) an astronaut or any of the crew of a spaceship

☆**space medicine** a branch of medicine concerned with diseases and disorders incident to flight in outer space: cf. AEROMEDICINE

☆**space opera** ⟦prob. after HORSE OPERA, SOAP OPERA⟧ [Informal] a highly melodramatic science-fiction novel, film, etc. about adventures in space travel

space·port (-pôrt′) *n.* a center where spacecraft are assembled, tested, and launched and are sometimes landed

space·ship (-ship′) *n.* a spacecraft, esp. if manned

☆**space shuttle** a manned, airplanelike spacecraft designed for shuttling back and forth, as between the earth and a space station, transporting personnel and equipment

space station (*or* **platform)** an artificial satellite designed to serve as a station from which to launch other spacecraft, as a research center, etc.

☆**space·suit** (-so͞ot′) *n.* a pressure suit used in space travel

space telescope a satellite put in orbit around the earth and equipped with an extremely accurate reflecting telescope, cameras, etc.: it is designed to relay astronomical data to the earth

space-time (-tīm′) *n.* **1** a four-dimensional continuum with four coordinates, the three dimensions of space and that of time, in which any event can be located: also called **space-time continuum 2** the physical reality inherent in such a continuum

☆**space·walk** (-wôk′) *n.* the act of an astronaut in moving about in space outside a spacecraft —*vi.* to engage in a spacewalk —**space′walk′er** *n.*

☆**space writer** a journalist or other writer paid according to the amount of space occupied by copy used

☆**space·y** or **spac·y** (spā′sē) *adj.* **spac′i·er, spac′i·est** [Slang] **1** SPACED-OUT **2** *a)* very eccentric or unconventional *b)* not in touch with reality; flighty, irresponsible, neurotic, etc. —**spac′i·ness** *n.*

spa·cial (spā′shəl) *adj. alt. sp. of* SPATIAL

spac·ing (spā′siŋ) *n.* **1** the arrangement of spaces **2** space or spaces, as between printed words **3** the act of a person or thing that spaces

spa·cious (spā′shəs) *adj.* ⟦ME < OFr *spacieux* < L *spatiosus*⟧ **1** having or giving more than enough space or room; vast; extensive **2** great; large; not confined or limited —**spa′cious·ly** *adv.* —**spa′cious·ness** *n.*

☆**Spack·le** (spak′əl) ⟦prob. adapted < Ger *spachtel,* spatula, *spachteln,* to fill or smooth (a surface), ult. < L *spatula:* see SPATULA⟧ *trademark for* a powdery substance mixed with water to form a paste that dries hard, used to fill holes, cracks, etc. in wallboard, wood, etc. —*n.* [**s-**] this substance —*vt.* **-led, -ling** [**s-**] to fill, or cover the holes, etc. in, with spackle

☆**spack·ling compound** (spak′liŋ) spackle: see SPACKLE, *vt.*

spade[1] (spād) *n.* ⟦ME < OE *spadu,* akin to Ger *spaten* < IE base *spē-, long flat piece of wood > SPOON, Gr *spathē,* broad blade, paddle of an oar, sword blade⟧ **1** a heavy, flat-bladed, long-handled tool used for digging by pressing the metal blade into the ground with the foot **2** any of several tools resembling a spade **3** a part of the trail of a gun carriage which digs into the ground, so as to brace the gun during recoil — *vt., vi.* **spad′ed, spad′ing** to dig or cut with or as with a spade —**call a spade a spade** to call something by its right name; use plain, blunt words —**spade′ful** *n.* —**spad′er** *n.*

spade[2] (spād) *n.* ⟦Sp *espada,* sword (the sign used on Spanish cards) < L *spatha,* flat blade < Gr *spathē:* see prec.⟧ **1** any of a suit of playing cards marked with black figures shaped like this: ♠ **2** [*pl., with sing. or pl. v.*] this suit of cards **3** [Slang] BLACK (*n.* 5): an offensive term of hostility and contempt —☆**in spades** ⟦from the fact that spades are the highest suit in bridge, etc.⟧ [Informal] in an extreme or emphatic way

spade[3] (spād) *vt.* **spad′ed, spad′ing** *dial. var. of* SPAY

spade·fish (spād′fish′) *n., pl.* **-fish′** or **-fish′es** (see FISH) **1** any of a family (Ephippidae) of edible, disk-shaped percoid fishes of the Atlantic and Pacific, having sharp-spined fins **2** PADDLEFISH

spade·foot toad (-fo͝ot′) any of several toads (family Pelobatidae) with a hornlike projection on the hind foot that is used in digging burrows

spade·work (-wurk′) *n.* preparatory work for some main project, esp. when tiresome or difficult

spa·dix (spā′diks) *n., pl.* **-dix·es** or **-di·ces** (spā′də sēz′, spā dī′sēz) ⟦ModL < L, a palm branch broken off together with the fruit, date-brown color < Gr < IE base *spē-, to pull > SPAN[1]⟧ a fleshy spike of tiny flowers, usually enclosed in a spathe

spaet·zle (shpet′slə, -səl, -slē) *n.* ⟦< Ger dial. *spätzle,* lit., little sparrows < Ger *spatz,* sparrow⟧ **1** a dish consisting of irregularly shaped egg noodles or dumplings, made usually by pressing the dough through a colander or coarse sieve into boiling water **2** *pl.* **-zles** such a noodle or dumpling

spa·ghet·ti (spə get′ē) *n.* ⟦It, pl. of *spaghetto,* dim. of *spago,* small cord⟧ **1** pasta in the form of long, thin strings, cooked by boiling or steaming and served with a sauce **2** *Elec.* an insulating tubing somewhat resembling macaroni, used for sheathing a bare wire or several insulated wires

spa·ghet·ti·ni (spə ge′tē′nē) *n.* ⟦It, dim. of *spaghetti*⟧ pasta thicker than vermicelli but thinner than spaghetti

spaghetti squash a large, round squash (*Cucurbita pepo*) with flesh that forms spaghettilike strands when cooked

☆**spaghetti strap** ⟦descriptive⟧ a very thin shoulder strap on a woman's garment

☆**spaghetti western** [Informal] a WESTERN (*n.* 2), esp. from the 1960s, produced by the Italian film industry

spa·hi or **spa·hee** (spä′hē′) *n.* ⟦Fr < Turk *sipahi* < Pers: see SEPOY⟧ **1** a member of a corps of Turkish professional cavalry **2** a member of a corps of native Algerian cavalry in the French armed forces

Spain (spān) ⟦ME *Spaine,* aphetic < Anglo-Fr *Espaigne* < OFr < LL *Spania,* for L *Hispania* (prob. infl. by Gr *Spania*)⟧ country in SW Europe, on the Iberian peninsula: 194,897 sq mi (504,782 sq km); cap. Madrid: Sp. name ESPAÑA

spake (spāk) *vi., vt. archaic pt. of* SPEAK

☆**spal·deen** (spôl dēn′, späl-) *n.* ⟦altered < *Spalding,* manufacturer's name, printed on the ball, after A. G. *Spalding* (1850-1915), Boston baseball player who founded the company (1876)⟧ [*often* **S-**] a small, pink, hollow rubber ball used in playing stickball, stoopball, etc.

spall (spôl) *n.* ⟦ME *spalle,* prob. < or akin to *spalden,* to chip, split, akin to Ger *spalten,* to split: see SPOOL⟧ a flake or chip, esp. of stone — *vt., vi.* **1** to break up or split **2** to break off in layers parallel to a surface

spall·a·tion (spô lā′shən) *n.* ⟦< prec.⟧ a nuclear reaction produced by high-energy projectiles in which two or more fragments or particles, as neutrons or protons, are ejected from the target nucleus

spal·peen (spal pēn′) *n.* ⟦Ir *spailpīn*⟧ [Irish] a scamp or rascal

spam (spam) *Comput. n.* ⟦prob. ult. < fol.⟧ unsolicited email, often advertisements, sent out over a computer network to many addresses, usually indiscriminately — *vt., vi.* **spammed, spam′ming** to send such email to (a user or users) —**spam′mer** *n.*

☆**Spam** (spam) ⟦prob. < *sp*(*iced h*)*am*⟧ *trademark for* a kind of canned luncheon meat made from pieces of seasoned pork and ham pressed into a loaf

Sp Am *abbrev.* **1** Spanish America **2** Spanish-American

span[1] (span) *n.* ⟦ME *spanne* < OE *sponn*, akin to Ger *spanne* < IE **(s)pen(d)-*, to pull, draw (> SPIN, Gr *span*, to pull) < base **spe-*, to pull, extend⟧ **1** a unit of linear measure equal to nine inches: originally based on the distance between the tips of a man's extended thumb and little finger **2** *a)* the full amount or extent between any two limits *b)* the distance between ends or supports [the *span* of an arch] *c)* the full duration (often with *of*) [a time *span*, the short *span* of human existence] **3** a part between two supports [a bridge of four *spans*] **4** *short for* WINGSPAN ☆**5** ⟦borrowed in U.S. < Du *span*, in same sense⟧ a team of two animals used together —*vt.* **spanned**, **span′ning** ⟦ME *spannen* < OE *spannan*, join: see *n.*⟧ **1** to measure, esp. by the hand with the thumb and little finger extended **2** to encircle with the hand or hands, in or as in measuring **3** to extend, stretch, reach, or pass over or across [the bridge that *spans* the river] **4** to furnish with something that extends or stretches over [to *span* an aisle with an arch] —*SYN.* PAIR

span[2] (span) *vt., vi. archaic pt. of* SPIN

Span *abbrev.* **1** Spaniard **2** Spanish

spa·na·ko·pi·ta (spä′nə kō′pē tə, span′ə-; -pə tə) *n.* ⟦ModGr < *spanaki*, spinach + *pita*, pie⟧ a Greek dish consisting of a small, triangular shell of phyllo that is filled with spiced spinach and feta cheese and baked

span·cel (span′səl) *n.* ⟦LowG *spansel* < *spannen*, to stretch, tie: see SPAN[1]⟧ a rope for fettering or hobbling cattle, etc. —*vt.* **-celed** or **-celled**, **-cel·ing** or **-cel·ling** to fetter or hobble as with a spancel

☆**span·dex** (span′deks′) *n.* ⟦arbitrary metathesis of EXPAND⟧ an elastic fiber, chiefly a synthetic polymer of polyurethane, used in girdles, swimsuits, etc.

span·drel (span′drəl) *n.* ⟦ME *spaundrell*, dim. of Anglo-Fr *spaundre* < OFr *espandre*, to expand < L *expandere*, EXPAND⟧ **1** either of the triangular spaces between the exterior curve of an arch and a rectangular frame or mold enclosing it **2** any of the spaces between a series of arches and a straight cornice running above them

spang (spaŋ) *adv.* ⟦< dial. *spang*, with a leap⟧ [Informal] abruptly, directly, or exactly

span·gle (spaŋ′gəl) *n.* ⟦ME *spangel*, dim. of *spang*, a buckle, clasp < OE, akin to Ger *spange*: for IE base see SPAN[1]⟧ **1** a small piece of bright metal, esp. any of a number of these sewn on fabric for decoration **2** any small, bright object that glitters —*vt.* **-gled**, **-gling** to cover or decorate with spangles or other bright objects —*vi.* to glitter with or as with spangles —**span′gly** *adj.* **-gli·er**, **-gli·est**

Spang·lish (spaŋ′glish) *n.* ⟦blend of SPANISH & ENGLISH⟧ [Slang] Spanish that contains many English words and phrases, esp. as spoken among bilingual people of Hispanic background

Span·iard (span′yərd) *n.* ⟦ME *Spaignard* < OFr *Espaignart* < *Espaigne*, SPAIN⟧ a person born or living in Spain

span·iel (span′yəl) *n.* ⟦ME *spainel* < MFr *espagnol*, lit., Spanish < Sp *español* < *España*, Spain < L *Hispania*⟧ **1** any member of several breeds of medium-sized hunting dog with large, drooping ears and a dense, wavy coat **2** a servile, fawning person

Span·ish (span′ish) *adj.* of Spain or its people, language, or culture —*n.* the Romance language spoken in Spain and Spanish America: cf. CASTILIAN —**the Spanish** the people of Spain

Spanish America Mexico and those countries in Central and South America and islands in the Caribbean in which Spanish is the chief language

Span·ish-A·mer·i·can (-ə mer′i kən) *adj.* **1** of both Spain and America **2** of Spanish America or its people or culture —*n.* a person born or living in Spanish America, esp. one of Spanish descent

Spanish-American War the war between the U.S. and Spain (1898)

Spanish Armada *see* ARMADA

Spanish bayonet any of a number of yuccas, esp. any of two species (*Yucca aloifolia* or *Y. gloriosa*) with stiff, sword-shaped leaves: also called **Spanish dagger**

Spanish cedar **1** a West Indian tree (*Cedrela odorata*) of the mahogany family, yielding a light, aromatic wood used in making cigar boxes, etc. **2** its wood

Spanish Civil War the civil war in Spain (1936-39), fought primarily between the Republicans, or Loyalists, and the Nationalists (including the Falangists) and ending with the fascist dictatorship of Francisco Franco

Spanish fly **1** a bright-green blister beetle (*Lytta vesicatoria*) of S Europe **2** CANTHARIDES (sense 2) Also **Span′ish·fly′** *n.*

Spanish Guinea *former name for* EQUATORIAL GUINEA

Spanish Inquisition the Inquisition as reorganized in Spain in 1478: notorious for its cruel and extreme practices against those accused of heresy and against Marranos

Spanish mackerel any of a genus (*Scomberomorus*) of edible marine scombroid fishes; esp., an Atlantic species (*S. maculatus*)

Spanish Main **1** [Historical] the coastal region of the Americas along the Caribbean Sea; esp., the N coast of South America between the Isthmus of Panama & the mouth of the Orinoco: an earlier usage **2** later, the Caribbean Sea itself, or that part of it adjacent to the N coast of South America, traveled in the 16th-18th cent. by Spanish merchant ships, which were often harassed by pirates

Spanish Morocco the former Spanish zone of Morocco, constituting a coastal strip along the Mediterranean

☆**Spanish moss** a rootless epiphytic plant (*Tillandsia usneoides*) of the pineapple family, often found growing in long, graceful strands from the branches of trees in the SE U.S. and tropical America

☆**Spanish needles** **1** a bur marigold (*Bidens bipinnata*) of the E U.S. **2** its barbed fruit

☆**Spanish omelet** an omelet folded around a sauce of chopped onion, green pepper, and tomato

Spanish onion any of several large, globe-shaped, mild-flavored onions, often eaten raw

Spanish paprika paprika made from a variety of mild red pepper grown in Spain

☆**Spanish rice** boiled rice cooked with tomatoes and chopped onions, green peppers, etc.

Spanish Sahara *former name for* WESTERN SAHARA

Spanish Succession, **War of the** a war (1701-14) between European powers disputing the succession to the Spanish throne

spank (spaŋk) *vt.* ⟦echoic⟧ to strike with something flat, as the open hand, esp. on the buttocks, as in punishment —*vi.* ⟦< SPANKING, *adj.*⟧ to move along swiftly or smartly —*n.* a smack given in spanking

spank·er (spaŋ′kər) *n.* **1** a person or thing that spanks **2** [Old Informal] an exceptionally fine, large, etc. person or thing **3** *Naut. a)* a fore-and-aft sail, usually hoisted on a gaff, on the after mast of a square-rigged vessel ☆*b)* the after mast and its sail on a vessel of more than three masts rigged fore and aft

spank·ing (-kiŋ) *adj.* ⟦< intens. use of prp. of SPANK⟧ **1** swiftly moving; rapid **2** brisk: said of a breeze **3** [Informal] exceptionally fine, large, vigorous, etc. —*adv.* [Informal] altogether; completely [*spanking* new] —*n.* a series of smacks, esp. on the buttocks, as in punishing a child

span·ner (span′ər) *n.* ⟦Ger < *spannen*, to stretch: see SPAN[1]⟧ **1** a person or thing that spans **2** [Chiefly Brit.] WRENCH (sense 4)

span-new (span′no͞o′, -nyo͞o′) *adj.* ⟦ME *span-newe* < ON *spān-nȳr* < *spānn*, a chip (akin to SPOON) + *nȳr*, NEW⟧ [Now Rare] perfectly new

☆**Span·sule** (span′so͝ol, -syo͝ol) ⟦SPAN[1] + (CAP)SULE⟧ *trademark for* a medicinal capsule containing many tiny beads of medicine that dissolve at spaced intervals for long-acting medication —*n.* [*often* **s-**] such a capsule

☆**span·worm** (span′wurm′) *n.* MEASURING WORM

spar[1] (spär) *n.* ⟦< MDu or MLowG, akin to OE *spær(stan)*, gypsum, chalk⟧ any shiny, crystalline, nonmetallic mineral that cleaves easily into chips or flakes: often in comb. [*calcspar*]

spar[2] (spär) *n.* ⟦ME *sparre* < ON *sparri* or MDu *sparre* < IE base **sper-*, pole, rod > SPEAR, L *sparus*, short spear⟧ **1** any pole, as a mast, yard, boom, or gaff, supporting or extending a sail of a ship **2** any of the main structural beams attached to the fuselage of an airplane to support the wings

spar[3] (spär) *vi.* **sparred**, **spar′ring** ⟦ME *sparren*, prob. < MFr *esparer* < It *sparare*, to fling out the hind legs, kick < *s-* (< L *ex-*, intens.) + *parare*, to PARRY⟧ **1** to fight with the feet and spurs: said of a fighting cock **2** to box with jabbing or feinting movements, landing few heavy blows, as in exhibition or practice matches **3** to wrangle or dispute —*n.* **1** a sparring match or movement **2** a dispute

☆**Spar** or **SPAR** (spär) *n.* ⟦< *s(emper) par(atus)*, always prepared, L motto of the U.S. Coast Guard⟧ a woman member of the U.S. Coast Guard

spar·a·ble (spar′ə bəl) *n.* ⟦altered < *sparrow bill*: from its shape⟧ a small, headless nail used by shoemakers

spar buoy a buoy in the form of a pole shaped like a spar, anchored at one end so as to float perpendicularly or obliquely

spar deck the upper deck running a ship's full length

spare (sper) *vt.* **spared**, **spar′ing** ⟦ME *sparien* < OE *sparian*, akin to *spær*, thrifty, Ger *sparen*, to save: see SPACE⟧ **1** to treat with mercy or leniency; refrain from killing, injuring, troubling, or distressing; save **2** to save or free (a person) from something [to *spare* him further inconvenience] **3** to refrain from, omit, avoid using, or use frugally [to *spare* no effort] **4** to give up the use or possession of; part with or give up conveniently [able to *spare* a cup of sugar] —*vi.* **1** to practice close economy; be frugal or sparing **2** to be merciful or restrained, as in punishing —*adj.* **spar′er**, **spar′est** **1** not in regular use or immediately needed; extra [a *spare* room, a *spare* tire] **2** not taken up by regular work or duties; free [*spare* time] **3** frugal; meager; scanty [to live on *spare* rations] **4** not fleshy; lean; thin **5** economical in style; using simple language and a minimum of words; restrained —*n.* **1** a spare, or extra, part, thing, etc. ☆**2** *Bowling a)* the act of knocking down all the pins with two consecutive rolls of the ball *b)* a score so made —*SYN.* MEAGER —**something to spare** a surplus of something —**spare′ly** *adv.* —**spare′ness** *n.* —**spar′er** *n.*

spare·ribs (sper′ribz′) *pl.n.* ⟦altered (infl. by prec.) < MLowG *ribbesper*, cured pork ribs roasted on a spit < *ribbe*, RIB + *sper*, a spit, SPEAR⟧ a cut of meat, esp. pork, consisting of the thin end of the ribs with most of the meat cut away

spare tire **1** an extra tire and wheel for a motor vehicle, stored in the vehicle for use in an emergency ☆**2** [Slang] a bulging layer of fat around the waist

sparge (spärj) *vt., vi.* **sparged**, **sparg′ing** ⟦MFr *espargier* < L *spargere*: see SPARK[1]⟧ to splash or sprinkle —**sparg′er** *n.*

spar·ing (sper′iŋ) *adj.* **1** that spares **2** careful in spending or using; frugal **3** scanty or meager —*SYN.* THRIFTY —**spar′ing·ly** *adv.* —**spar′ing·ness** *n.*

spark[1] (spärk) *n.* ⟦ME *sperke* < OE *spearca*, akin to MDu *sparke* < IE base **sp(h)er(e)-g-*, to strew, sprinkle > SPRINKLE, L *spargere*⟧ **1** a glowing bit of matter, esp. one thrown off by a fire **2** any flash or sparkle of light like this **3** a tiny beginning or vestige, as of life, interest, excitement, etc.; particle or trace **4** liveliness; vivacity **5** *Elec. a)* a very brief flash of light accompanying an electric discharge through air or some other insulating material, as between the electrodes of a spark plug *b)* such a discharge

☆6 [*pl., with sing. v.*] [Slang] a ship's radio operator —*vi.* 1 to make or throw off sparks 2 to come forth as or like sparks 3 to produce the sparks properly: said of the spark plug in an internal combustion engine —*vt.* to serve as the activating or animating influence of or in; stir up; activate [to *spark* interest] —**spark′er** *n.*

spark² (spärk) *n.* ⟦ON *sparkr,* lively: for IE base see prec.⟧ [Old-fashioned] 1 a dashing, gallant young man 2 a beau or lover —☆*vt., vi.* [Old Informal] to court, woo, pet, etc. —**spark′er** *n.*

Spark (spärk), Dame **Muriel (Sarah)** (born *Muriel Sarah Camberg*) 1918-2006; Brit. writer

☆**spark arrester** any device used to prevent sparks from escaping, specif. one placed in the flue at the top of a chimney

spark chamber any of several devices for detecting charged subatomic particles, etc., consisting usually of a group of closely spaced, oppositely charged metal plates between which sparks will jump through an inert gas, as neon, along the ionized path created by the passage of radiation

spark coil an induction coil producing high voltage for a sparking device, as a spark plug

spark gap a space between two electrodes through which a spark discharge may take place

spar·kle (spär′kəl) *vi.* **-kled, -kling** ⟦ME *sparklen,* freq. of *sparken,* to SPARK¹⟧ 1 to throw off sparks 2 to gleam or shine in flashes; glitter or glisten, as jewels, sunlit water, etc. 3 to be brilliant and lively [*sparkling* wit] 4 to effervesce or bubble: said of soda water and some wines —*vt.* to cause to sparkle —*n.* 1 a spark or glowing particle 2 a sparkling, or glittering 3 brilliance; liveliness; vivacity —*SYN.* FLASH —**spar′kly** *adj.*

spar·kler (-klər) *n.* a person or thing that sparkles; specif., *a)* a thin stick of pyrotechnic material that burns with bright sparks *b)* [*pl.*] [Informal] clear, brilliant eyes *c)* [Informal] a diamond or similar gem

sparkling wine wine that is effervescent, as champagne

☆**spark plug** 1 an electrical device threaded into the cylinder of an internal-combustion engine to ignite the fuel mixture by producing timed sparks between electrodes 2 [Informal] a person or thing that inspires, activates, or advances something —**spark′plug′** *vt.* **-plugged′, -plug′ging**

spark transmitter an early type of radio transmitter that uses the oscillatory discharge of a capacitor through an inductor in series with a spark gap to generate its high-frequency power

spark·y (spär′kē) *adj.* 1 giving off sparks 2 lively; animated

spar·ling (spär′liŋ) *n., pl.* **-ling** or **-lings** ⟦ME *sperlynge* < MFr *esperlinge* < MDu *spirlinc,* orig. dim. of *spīr,* a small point, grass shoot: see SPIRE²⟧ a European smelt (*Osmerus eperlanus*)

sparring partner any person with whom a professional boxer spars or practices while training

spar·row (spar′ō) *n.* ⟦ME *sparwe* < OE *spearwa,* akin to MHG *sparwe* < IE base **sper-,* bird name, esp. for sparrow > Gr *sporgilos,* sparrow, *psar,* starling⟧ 1 any of a family (Passeridae) of Old World passerine birds, including the English sparrow 2 any of various New World passerine birds (family Emberizidae), including the song sparrow and white-throated sparrow 3 any of several other similar birds, as the hedge or Java sparrows

spar·row·grass (spar′ō gras′) *n.* ⟦altered by folk etym. < ASPARAGUS⟧ *dial. var. of* ASPARAGUS

sparrow hawk ⟦ME *sparowhawke:* so named from preying on sparrows⟧ 1 any of certain Eurasian hawks; esp., a small hawk (*Accipiter nisus*) with short, rounded wings ☆2 AMERICAN KESTREL

spar·ry (spär′ē) *adj.* **-ri·er, -ri·est** of, like, or rich in mineral spar

sparse (spärs) *adj.* **spars′er, spars′est** ⟦L *sparsus,* pp. of *spargere,* to scatter: see SPARK¹⟧ thinly spread or distributed; not dense or crowded —*SYN.* MEAGER —**sparse′ly** *adv.* —**sparse′ness** *n.,* **spar′si·ty** (-sə tē)

Spar·ta (spärt′ə) ancient city in the S Peloponnesus, Greece: a powerful military city in Laconia

Spar·ta·cus (spärt′ə kəs) died 71 B.C.; Thracian slave & gladiator in Rome: leader of a slave revolt

Spar·tan (spärt′'n) *adj.* ⟦L *Spartanus*⟧ 1 of ancient Sparta or its people or culture 2 like or characteristic of the Spartans, who were famous for being warlike, brave, stoical, severe, frugal, and highly disciplined 3 not luxurious or ornate; plain; austere [*Spartan* furnishings] —*n.* 1 a person born or living in Sparta 2 a person with Spartan traits —**Spar′tan·ism′** *n.*

spar·te·ine (spär′tē ēn′, -tē in) *n.* ⟦< ModL *Spartium* (< L *spartum,* broom (see ESPARTO) + -INE³⟧ a clear, oily, poisonous, liquid alkaloid, $C_{15}H_{26}N_2$, obtained from a broom (*Spartium scoparium*)

spar varnish a varnish that forms a hard, durable finish, used on outdoor surfaces to protect them against the weather

spasm (spaz′əm) *n.* ⟦ME *spasme* < MFr < L *spasmus* < Gr *spasmos* < *span,* to draw, pull, wrench: see SPAN¹⟧ 1 a sudden, convulsive, involuntary muscular contraction: a **tonic spasm** is persistent and sustained, and a **clonic spasm** is one of a series of relatively brief contractions alternating with relaxations 2 any sudden, violent, temporary activity, feeling, etc. —*vi.* to undergo a spasm

spas·mod·ic (spaz mäd′ik) *adj.* ⟦ModL *spasmodicus* < Gr *spasmōdēs* < *spasmos:* see prec. & -OID⟧ 1 of, having the nature of, like, or characterized by a spasm or spasms; sudden, violent, and temporary; fitful; intermittent 2 [Rare] highly emotional or excitable Also **spas·mod′i·cal** —**spas·mod′i·cal·ly** *adv.*

spas·tic (spas′tik) *adj.* ⟦L *spasticus* < Gr *spastikos,* drawing, pulling < *span:* see SPASM⟧ 1 of, characterized by, affected with, or produced by a spasm [*spastic* colon] 2 afflicted with or involving spastic paralysis —*n.* a person with spastic paralysis: now often considered an insulting usage —**spas′ti·cal·ly** *adv.* —**spas·tic′i·ty** (-tis′ə tē) *n.*

spastic paralysis a condition, as in cerebral palsy, in which certain muscles are in a state of continuous contraction, causing rigidity of a normally movable part, accompanied by exaggerated tendon reflexes

spat¹ (spat) *n.* ⟦prob. echoic⟧ 1 [Rare] a slap 2 a quick, slapping sound 3 [Informal] a brief, petty quarrel or dispute —*vi.* **spat′ted, spat′ting** 1 [Rare] to slap 2 to strike with a quick, slapping sound ☆3 [Informal] to engage in a spat, or quarrel —*vt.* [Rare] to slap —*SYN.* QUARREL²

spat² (spat) *n.* ⟦contr. < SPATTERDASH⟧ a gaiterlike covering for the instep and ankle, usually of heavy cloth

spat³ (spat) *vt., vi. alt. pt. & pp. of* SPIT²

spat⁴ (spat) *n.* ⟦Anglo-Fr < ?⟧ a young oyster or young oysters collectively

spatch·cock (spach′käk′) [Brit.] *vt.* 1 to split open and broil (a fowl) 2 [Informal] *a)* to interpolate (a word or words) *in* or *into* a text, often hastily or inappropriately *b)* to put together so as to form a unit or whole, often a clumsy or incongruous one

spate (spāt) *n.* ⟦ME (northern dial.) < ?⟧ 1 [Chiefly Brit.] *a)* a flash flood *b)* a sudden, heavy rain 2 an unusually large outpouring, as of words 3 a great number or quantity [a *spate* of forest fires]

spa·tha·ceous (spə thā′shəs) *adj.* 1 having a spathe 2 of, or having the nature of, a spathe

spathe (spāth) *n.* ⟦ModL *spatha* < L, a flat blade: see SPADE²⟧ a large, leaflike part or pair of such parts enclosing a flower cluster (esp. a spadix) —**spathed** (spāthd) *adj.*

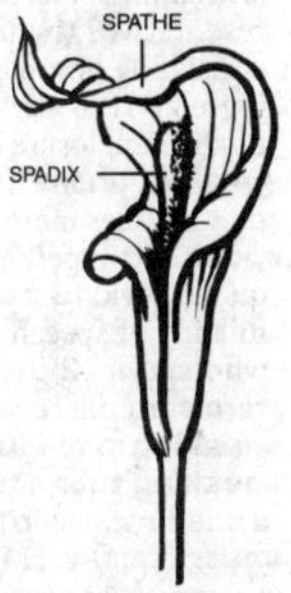

SPATHE
SPADIX

spath·ic (spath′ik) *adj.* ⟦Ger *spath,* obs. sp. for *spat,* SPAR¹ < MHG *spat* (for IE base see SPADE¹) + -IC⟧ *Mineralogy* of or like spar

spa·those¹ (spā′thōs, spath′ōs) *adj.* SPATHACEOUS

spath·ose² (spath′ōs) *adj.* SPATHIC

spath·u·late (spath′yoo lit) *adj.* SPATULATE (sense 1)

spa·tial (spā′shəl) *adj.* ⟦< L *spatium,* SPACE + -AL⟧ 1 of space 2 happening or existing in space —**spa′ti·al′i·ty** (-shē al′ə tē) *n.* —**spa′tial·ly** *adv.*

spa·ti·o·tem·po·ral (spā′shē ō tem′pər əl) *adj.* 1 existing in both space and time 2 of space-time —**spa′ti·o·tem′po·ral·ly** *adv.*

spat·ter (spat′ər) *vt.* ⟦akin to Fris *spateren,* freq. of *spatten,* to splash, spurt⟧ 1 to scatter in drops or small blobs [to *spatter* red paint over blue] 2 to splash, spot, or soil with such drops or blobs 3 to defame or slander —*vi.* 1 to emit or spurt out in drops or small blobs, as fat in frying 2 to fall or strike in or as in a shower, as raindrops or pellets —*n.* 1 *a)* the act or an instance of spattering *b)* the sound of this 2 a mark or wet spot caused by spattering 3 a small amount or number

spat·ter·dash (-dash′) *n.* ⟦prec. + DASH¹⟧ a long legging formerly worn to protect the stocking or trouser leg, as in wet weather

☆**spat·ter·dock** (-däk′) *n.* any of several waterlilies; esp., a North American species (*Nuphar advena*) with thick roots, heart-shaped leaves, and yellow flowers

spat·u·la (spach′ə lə) *n.* ⟦L, dim. of *spatha,* flat blade: see SPADE²⟧ any of various implements with a broad, flat, flexible blade, used for spreading or blending substances, as foods or paints, for scraping, etc. —**spat′u·lar** *adj.*

spat·u·late (-lit, -lāt′) *adj.* ⟦ModL *spatulatus*⟧ 1 *Bot.* spoon-shaped in outline and attached at the narrow end, as some leaves 2 *Zool.* spoon-shaped or spatula-shaped

spät·zle (shpet′slə, -səl, -slē) *n., pl.* **-zles** *alt. sp. of* SPAETZLE

spav·in (spav′in) *n.* ⟦ME *spaveine* < MFr *esparvain* < ?⟧ a disease of horses in which a deposit of bone (**bone spavin**) or an infusion of lymph (**bog spavin**) develops in the hock joint, usually causing lameness

spav·ined (-ind) *adj.* afflicted with spavin; lame

spawn (spôn) *vt., vi.* ⟦ME *spaunnen* (for **spaunden*) < Anglo-Fr *espaundre* < OFr *espandre,* to shed < L *expandere:* see EXPAND⟧ 1 to produce or deposit (eggs, sperm, or young) 2 to bring forth or be the source of (esp. something regarded with contempt and produced in great numbers) 3 *Hort.* to plant with spawn, or mycelium —*n.* 1 the mass of eggs or young produced by fish, mollusks, crustaceans, amphibians, etc. 2 something produced, esp. in great quantity; specif., numerous offspring or progeny: usually contemptuous 3 the mycelium of fungi, esp. of mushrooms grown to be eaten

spay (spā) *vt.* ⟦ME *spayen,* aphetic < Anglo-Fr *espeier* < OFr *espeer,* to cut with a sword < *espee,* sword < L *spatha:* see SPADE²⟧ to sterilize (a female animal) by removing the ovaries

☆**spaz** (spaz) *n.* ⟦altered < SPASTIC⟧ [Slang] someone regarded as being clumsy, awkward, stupid, odd, etc.: a dismissive or contemptuous term

SPCA *abbrev.* Society for the Prevention of Cruelty to Animals

speak (spēk) *vi.* **spoke, spo′ken, speak′ing** ⟦ME *speken* < OE *specan,* earlier *sprecan,* akin to Ger *sprechen* < IE base **sp(h)er(e)-g-,* to strew, sprinkle > SPARK¹, L *spargere,* to sprinkle: basic sense "to scatter (words)"⟧ 1 to utter words with the ordinary voice; talk 2 to express or communicate opinions, feelings, ideas, etc. by or as by talking [*speak* in our behalf, actions *speak* louder than words] 3 to make a request or reservation (*for*): usually in the passive voice [a seat not yet *spoken* for] 4 to make a speech; deliver an address or lecture; discourse 5 to be a spokesman (*for*) 6 to talk with another or others; converse 7 to make or give out sound, as a gun firing or a dog barking —*vt.* 1 to express or make known by or as by speaking 2 to use or be able to use (a given language) in speaking **3** to utter (words) orally **4** [Archaic] to speak to; address **5** [Archaic] to declare or show to be; reveal **6** *Naut.* to hail (a passing ship) **—so to speak** in a manner of speaking; that is to say **—speak for itself** to be self-evident **—speak out (or up) 1** to speak audibly or clearly **2** to speak freely or forcefully **—speak to** to respond to, deal with, fulfill, etc. [the decision *speaks to* the needs of everyone involved] **—speak well for** to say or indicate something favorable about **—to speak of** worthy of mention [no gains *to speak of*] **—speak′a·ble** *adj.*

SYN.—speak and **talk** are generally synonymous, but **speak** often connotes formal address to an auditor or audience [who will *speak* at the dinner?] and **talk** often suggests informal conversation [we were *talking* at dinner]; **converse** suggests a talking together by two or more people so as to exchange ideas and information [they are *conversing* in the parlor]; **discourse** suggests a somewhat formal, detailed, extensive talking to another or others [she was *discoursing* to us on Keats]

-speak (spēk) *combining form* ⟦< *Newspeak*, possibly also *Oldspeak*, in the novel *1984*: see NEWSPEAK⟧ jargon, language [*computerspeak, doublespeak*]

☆**speak-eas·y** (-ē′zē) *n., pl.* **-eas′ies** ⟦SPEAK + EASY: so named from the relaxed atmosphere⟧ [Slang] a place where alcoholic drinks are sold illegally, esp. such a place in the U.S. during Prohibition

speak·er (spē′kər) *n.* **1** a person who speaks; esp., *a)* a person who makes a speech or speeches in public *b)* the officer presiding over any of various lawmaking bodies ☆*c)* [**S-**] the presiding officer of the U.S. House of Representatives (in full **Speaker of the House**) **2** ⟦(LOUD)SPEAKER⟧ *a)* a device consisting of a magnet and a diaphragm of paper, plastic, etc., for converting electrical signals to sound waves that are radiated into the air *b)* a boxlike enclosure holding one or more such devices **—speak′er·ship′** *n.*

☆**speak·er·phone** (-fōn′) *n.* a telephone with a speaker and microphone that enables more than one person to take part in a call

speak·ing (spē′kiŋ) *adj.* **1** that speaks or seems to speak; expressive; eloquent; vivid [a *speaking* likeness] **2** used in or for speech **3** allowing or admitting of speech [within *speaking* range] **—*n.* 1** the act or art of a person who speaks **2** that which is spoken; utterance; discourse **—on speaking terms** friendly enough to exchange greetings or carry on conversation

speaking in tongues GLOSSOLALIA (sense 1)

speaking tube a tube or pipe made to carry the voice, as from one part of a building or ship to another

spear (spir) *n.* ⟦ME *spere* < OE (akin to Ger *speer*) < IE base **sper-* > SPAR², L *sparus*⟧ **1** a weapon consisting of a long wooden shaft with a sharp point, usually of metal or stone, for thrusting or throwing **2** any spearlike, often forked, implement used for thrusting, as in one kind of fishing **3** *short for* SPEARMAN **4** ⟦var. of SPIRE²; ? infl. by *n.* 1 above⟧ a long blade or shoot, as of grass **—*vt.* 1** to pierce or stab with something pointed, as a spear **2** to catch (fish, etc.) with a spear **3** [Informal] to extend the arm so as to make a one-handed catch of (a baseball, etc.) **—*vi.* 1** to pierce or shoot like a spear **2** ⟦cf. *n.* 4⟧ to sprout into a long stem **—spear′er** *n.*

spear carrier ⟦so called in allusion to the role of soldier, a typical walk-on part in grand opera⟧ **1** [Informal] an actor with a walk-on role **2** a person having a minor or insignificant role in an organization, activity, etc.

☆**spear·fish** (spir′fish′) *n., pl.* **-fish′** or **-fish′es** (see FISH) any billfish; esp., any of a genus (*Tetrapturus*, family Istiophoridae) of large, percoid, food and game fishes of the open seas **—*vi.*** to fish with a spear or spear-thrusting device (**spear gun**)

spear grass any of several perennial grasses (genus *Stipa*) having hard, sharp-pointed, bearded fruits

spear·head (-hed′) *n.* **1** the pointed head of a spear **2** the leading person, part, or group in an endeavor, esp. in a military attack **—*vt.*** to take the lead in (an attack, etc.)

spear·man (-mən) *n., pl.* **-men** (-mən) a warrior armed with a spear

spear·mint (-mint′) *n.* ⟦prob. from the appearance of the flowers on the stem⟧ **1** a fragrant perennial plant (*Mentha spicata*) of the mint family **2** the pungent oil it yields, used for flavoring **3** the flavor of the oil **—*adj.*** flavored with spearmint

spec¹ (spek) *n.* [Informal] *short for:* **1** SPECIFICATION (sense 2) **2** SPECULATION (sense 2) **—on spec** [Informal] **1** according to specification(s) **2** as a speculation or gamble

spec² *abbrev.* **1** special **2** specifically

spe·cial (spesh′əl) *adj.* ⟦ME < OFr *especial* < L *specialis* < *species*, kind, sort: see SPECIES⟧ **1** of a kind different from others; distinctive, peculiar, or unique **2** exceptional; extraordinary [a *special* treat] **3** highly regarded or valued [a *special* friend] **4** of or for a particular person, occasion, purpose, etc. [by *special* permission, a *special* edition] **5** not general or regular; specific or limited [*special* legislation] **6** having a physical or mental disability **—*n.* 1** a special person or thing; specif., a special train, edition, sale offer or item, etc. ☆**2** a single TV program, not part of a regular series

SYN.—special and **especial** both imply that the thing so described has qualities, aspects, or uses which differentiate it from others of its class, and the choice of word generally depends on euphony, but **especial** is usually preferred where preeminence is implied [a matter of *especial* interest to you]; **specific** and **particular** are both applied to something that is singled out for attention, but **specific** suggests the explicit statement of an example, illustration, etc. [he cited *specific* cases], and **particular** emphasizes the distinctness or individuality of the thing so described [in this *particular* case] **—*ANT.* general**

special assessment a special tax levied on a property to pay for a local public improvement, as a sewer, that will presumably benefit that property

special court-martial a military court for judging offenses less grave than those judged by a general court-martial

☆**special delivery** a postal service through which, for an extra fee, mail is delivered by a special messenger

Special Drawing Right *see* SDR

special education educational programs and practices designed for students, as handicapped or gifted students, whose mental ability, physical ability, emotional functioning, etc. requires special teaching approaches, equipment, or care within or outside a regular classroom

special effects 1 artificial visual effects, either realistic or fantastic, used to create illusions in films **2** the art or work of creating these illusions **3** the complex mechanical devices and photographic techniques used to produce the effects

☆**Special Forces** small detachments of U.S. Army personnel who train and direct non-U.S. forces in guerrilla operations: full name **U.S. Army Special Forces**

☆**special handling** a postal service which, for an extra fee, provides extra care in the handling of unusual mail and packages, as of certain live animals

special interest any interest group, esp. one thought of as placing its own objectives ahead of the public interest, having undue influence on public officials and legislation, etc.: also **spe′cial-in′ter·est group**

spe·cial·ism (spesh′əl iz′əm) *n.* concentration on or specialization in a branch or field of a study, profession, etc.

spe·cial·ist (-ist) *n.* **1** a person who specializes in a particular field of study, professional work, etc. ☆**2** *U.S. Army* any of six grades for enlisted personnel with technical training and duties, corresponding to the grades of corporal through sergeant major **—*adj.*** of a specialist or specialism: also **spe′cial·is′tic**

spe·ci·al·i·ty (spesh′ē al′ə tē) *n., pl.* **-ties** ⟦ME *specialite* < OFr *specialité*⟧ *chiefly Brit. var. of* SPECIALTY

spe·cial·ize (spesh′əl īz′) *vt.* **-ized′, -iz′ing** ⟦Fr *spécialiser*⟧ **1** to make special, specific, or particular; specify **2** to direct toward or concentrate on a specific end **3** *Biol.* to adapt (parts or organs) to a special condition, use, or requirement **—*vi.* 1** to make a special study of something or work only in one part or branch of a subject, profession, etc. [to *specialize* in medieval history] **2** *Biol.* to become adapted to meet a special condition, use, etc. **—spe′cial·i·za′tion** *n.*

special jury *Law* STRUCK JURY

spe·cial·ly (spesh′əl ē) *adv.* **1** in a special manner; particularly **2** for a special purpose

special needs the particular requirements of a person with a physical or mental disability, as for additional assistance or accommodation **—spe′cial-needs′** *adj.*

special pleading 1 *Law* a pleading which is more than a mere denial of the charges or allegations, as one introducing new matter justifying an otherwise culpable act **2** an argument or presentation that leaves out what is unfavorable and develops only what is favorable to the case

☆**special team** *Football* any of various units of players used only in certain special situations, primarily ones involving place kicks or punts: *usually used in pl.* **—spe′cial-team′er** *n.*

special theory of relativity *see* RELATIVITY (sense 4): also called **special relativity**

spe·cial·ty (spesh′əl tē) *n., pl.* **-ties** ⟦ME *specialte* < OFr *especialté*⟧ **1** a special quality, feature, point, characteristic, etc. **2** a thing specialized in; special interest, field of study or professional work, etc. **3** the state of being special **4** an article or class of article characterized by special features, superior quality, novelty, etc. [a bakery whose *specialty* is pie] **5** *Law* a special contract, obligation, agreement, etc. under seal, or a contract by deed **—*adj.* 1** designating or of a store or stores that specialize in selling certain types of goods or to certain types of customers **2** of such goods or customers

☆**spe·ci·a·tion** (spē′shē ā′shən, -sē-) *n.* ⟦SPECI(ES) + -ATION⟧ *Biol.* the natural development of new species through evolution **—spe′ci·ate′** (-āt′) *vi.* **-at′ed, -at′ing**

spe·cie (spē′shē, -sē) *n.* ⟦abl. of L *species:* used in E from occurrence in the phrase *(paid) in specie*⟧ coin, as distinguished from paper money; also, coin made of precious, as distinguished from base, metal **—in specie 1** in kind **2** in coin

spe·cies (-shēz, -sēz) *n., pl.* **-cies** ⟦L, a seeing, appearance, shape, kind, or quality < base of *specere*, to see: see SPY⟧ **1** a distinct kind; sort; variety; class [a *species* of bravery] **2** [Obs.] outward form, appearance, or mental image **3** *obs. var. of* SPECIE **4** *Biol.* a naturally existing population of similar organisms that usually interbreed only among themselves, and are given a unique, latinized binomial name to distinguish them from all other creatures: see GENUS (sense 2) **5** *Logic* a class of individuals or objects having certain distinguishing attributes in common, given a common name, and comprised with other similar classes in a more comprehensive grouping called a GENUS: cf. DIFFERENTIA **6** *Physics a)* a specific kind of atomic nucleus *b)* NUCLIDE **7** *R.C.Ch. a)* the totality of natural physical characteristics (appearance, taste, etc.) of bread or wine, these characteristics remaining the same in the consecrated bread or wine of the Eucharist *b)* the consecrated bread or wine of the Eucharist **—the species** the human race

spe·cies·ism (spē′shēz iz′əm, -sēz-) *n.* discrimination against or exploitation of animals based on the assumption that humans are superior to and more important than all other species

specif *abbrev.* 1 specific 2 specifically

spec·i·fi·a·ble (spes′ə fī′ə bəl) *adj.* that can be specified

spe·cif·ic (spə sif′ik) *adj.* ⟦LL *specificus* < L *species* (see SPECIES) + *-ficus,* -FIC⟧ 1 limiting or limited; specifying or specified; precise; definite; explicit [no *specific* plans] 2 of or constituting a species 3 peculiar to or characteristic of something [*specific* traits] 4 of a special, or particular, sort or kind 5 *Med. a)* specially indicated as a cure for a particular disease [a *specific* remedy] *b)* produced by a particular microorganism [a *specific* disease] 6 *Physics* designating a certain constant characteristic of a substance or phenomenon measured against some arbitrary, fixed standard of reference or expressed as an amount per unit area, unit volume, etc. Also [Rare] **spe·cif′i·cal** —*n.* 1 something specially suited for a given use or purpose 2 a specific cure or remedy 3 a distinct item or detail; particular —*SYN.* EXPLICIT, SPECIAL —**spe·cif′i·cal·ly** *adv.*

-spe·cif·ic (spə sif′ik) *combining form* limited or specific to, characteristic of (a specified thing or person) [species-*specific*]

spec·i·fi·ca·tion (spes′ə fi kā′shən) *n.* ⟦ML *specificatio*⟧ 1 the act of specifying; detailed mention or definition 2 [*usually pl.*] *a)* a detailed description of the parts of a whole *b)* a statement or enumeration of particulars, as to actual or required size, quality, performance, terms, etc. [*specifications* for a new building] 3 something specified; specified item, particular, etc.

specific characters the persistent features that distinguish one species from all others

specific gravity the ratio of the weight or mass of a given volume of a substance to that of an equal volume of another substance (water for liquids and solids, air or hydrogen for gases) used as a standard

specific heat 1 the number of calories needed to raise the temperature of one gram of a given substance 1°C 2 the ratio of the amount of heat required to raise the temperature of a given mass of a substance one degree to the amount of heat required to raise the temperature of an equal mass of water one degree

spec·i·fic·i·ty (spes′ə fis′ə tē) *n.* the fact, condition, or quality of being specific

specific performance *Law* the exact performance of a contract or an order compelling it

spec·i·fy (spes′ə fī′) *vt.* **-fied′**, **-fy′ing** ⟦ME *specifien* < OFr *specifier* < LL *specificare* < *specificus,* SPECIFIC⟧ 1 to mention, describe, or define in detail; state definitely [to *specify* the time and place] 2 to include as an item in a set of specifications 3 to state explicitly as a condition —**spec′i·fi′er** *n.*

spec·i·men (spes′ə mən) *n.* ⟦L, a mark, token, example < *specere,* to see: see SPY⟧ 1 a part of a whole, or one individual of a class or group, used as a sample or example of the whole, class, or group; typical part, individual, etc. 2 [Informal] a (specified kind of) individual or person [an unsavory *specimen*] 3 *Med.* a sample, as of urine, sputum, or blood, for analysis

spe·cious (spē′shəs) *adj.* ⟦ME, fair, beautiful < L *speciosus,* showy, beautiful, plausible < *species,* look, show, appearance: see SPECIES⟧ 1 seeming to be good, sound, correct, logical, etc. without really being so; plausible but not genuine [*specious* logic] 2 [Obs.] pleasing to the sight —*SYN.* PLAUSIBLE —**spe′cious·ly** *adv.* —**spe′cious·ness** *n.*, **spe′ci·os′i·ty** (-shē äs′ə tē)

speck (spek) *n.* ⟦ME *specke* < OE *specca:* for IE base see SPARK[1]⟧ 1 a small spot, mark, or stain 2 a very small bit; particle —*vt.* to mark with specks

speck·le (spek′əl) *n.* ⟦ME *spakle,* dim. of *specke,* prec.⟧ a small mark of contrasting color; speck —*vt.* **-led**, **-ling** to mark with speckles

☆**speckled trout** any of various fishes, as the sea trout or brook trout

specs (speks) *pl.n.* [Informal] 1 spectacles; eyeglasses ☆2 specifications: see SPECIFICATION (sense 2)

spec·ta·cle (spek′tə kəl) *n.* ⟦OFr < L *spectaculum* < *spectare,* to behold, freq. of *specere,* to see: see SPY⟧ 1 something to look at, esp. some strange or remarkable sight; unusual display 2 a public show or exhibition on a grand scale 3 [*pl.*] [Old-fashioned] a pair of eyeglasses 4 [*usually pl.*] something like a pair of eyeglasses in shape, use, etc. —**make a spectacle of oneself** to behave foolishly or improperly in public

spec·ta·cled (-kəld) *adj.* 1 wearing spectacles 2 having markings that resemble spectacles

spec·tac·u·lar (spek tak′yə lər) *adj.* ⟦< L *spectaculum* (see SPECTACLE) + -AR⟧ 1 of or like a spectacle, or show 2 unusual to a striking degree; characterized by a great display, as of daring —*n.* an elaborate show or display —**spec·tac′u·lar·ly** *adv.*

spec·tate (spek′tāt′) *vi.* **-tat′ed**, **-tat′ing** ⟦back-form. < fol.⟧ to be a spectator at some event, esp. an athletic contest

spec·ta·tor (spek′tāt′ər, spek tāt′-) *n.* ⟦L < pp. of *spectare,* to behold: see SPECTACLE⟧ 1 a person who sees or watches something without taking an active part; onlooker 2 a woman's shoe having two contrasting colors and with the toe and heel characteristically ornamented with perforations —**spec′ta′tor·ship′** *n.*

spec·ta·to·ri·al (spek′tə tôr′ē əl) *adj.* of, or being that of, a spectator or onlooker [their purely *spectatorial* role in the conflict]

spec·ter (spek′tər) *n.* ⟦Fr *spectre* < L *spectrum,* an appearance, apparition < *spectare,* to behold: see SPECTACLE⟧ 1 a ghost; apparition 2 any object of fear or dread Brit. sp. **spec′tre**

spec·ti·no·my·cin (spek′tə nō mī′sin) *n.* ⟦< ModL *spectabilis,* species name of source bacterium (< L, visible < *spectare,* to behold: see SPECTACLE) + (ACT)INOMYCIN⟧ an antibiotic, $C_{14}H_{24}N_2O_7$, made synthetically or obtained from an actinomycete (*Streptomyces spectabilis*) and used esp. in treating cases of gonorrhea that are resistant to penicillin

spec·tra (spek′trə) *n. alt. pl. of* SPECTRUM

spec·tral (-trəl) *adj.* ⟦< SPECTER + -AL⟧ 1 of, having the nature of, or like a specter; phantom; ghostly 2 of or caused by a spectrum or spectra —**spec·tral′i·ty** (-tral′ə tē) *n.*, **spec′tral·ness** —**spec′tral·ly** *adv.*

spectral line any of a number of lines in a spectrum produced by the emission of electromagnetic radiation from an excited atom: a spectral line represents the energy difference between two energy levels

spec·tro- (spek′trō, -trə) ⟦< SPECTRUM⟧ *combining form* 1 of radiant energy as exhibited in a spectrum [*spectrogram*] 2 of or by a spectroscope [*spectroheliogram*]

spec·tro·chem·is·try (spek′trō kem′is trē) *n.* the branch of chemistry dealing with the analysis of the spectra of substances —**spec′tro·chem′i·cal** *adj.*

spec·tro·gram (spek′trə gram′) *n.* a photograph or other visual representation of a spectrum

spec·tro·graph (-graf′, -gräf′) *n.* any of various instruments that record various types of spectra, esp. one that uses a camera to record a spectrum of light —**spec′tro·graph′ic** *adj.* —**spec′tro·graph′i·cal·ly** *adv.*

☆**spec·tro·he·li·o·gram** (spek′trə hē′lē ə gram′) *n.* a monochromatic image of the sun's chromosphere produced by a spectroheliograph

☆**spec·tro·he·li·o·graph** (-graf′, -gräf′) *n.* an instrument acting like a filter, for photographing the sun using light from only one spectral line, usually from hydrogen (red) or calcium (violet)

☆**spec·tro·he·li·o·scope** (-skōp′) *n.* a spectroheliograph adapted for visual use

spec·trom·e·ter (spek träm′ət ər) *n.* ⟦Ger *spektrometer:* see SPECTRO- & -METER⟧ an instrument used for measuring spectral wavelengths —**spec′tro·met′ric** (-trō me′trik) *adj.* —**spec·trom′e·try** (-ə trē) *n.*

spec·tro·pho·tom·e·ter (spek′trə fō täm′ət ər) *n.* an instrument used for measuring the transmission or reflection of light by comparing various wavelengths of the light —**spec′tro·pho′to·met′ric** (-fōt′ə me′trik) *adj.* —**spec′tro·pho·tom′e·try** *n.*

spec·tro·scope (spek′trə skōp′) *n.* ⟦Ger *spektroskop:* see SPECTRO- & -SCOPE⟧ an optical instrument used for forming spectra for study —**spec′tro·scop′ic** (-skäp′ik) *adj.* —**spec′tro·scop′i·cal·ly** *adv.*

spec·tros·co·py (spek träs′kə pē) *n.* the study of spectra by use of the spectroscope —**spec·tros′co·pist** (-pist) *n.*

spec·trum (spek′trəm) *n., pl.* **-tra** (-trə) or **-trums** ⟦ModL, special use (by Sir Isaac NEWTON[2], 1671) of L *spectrum:* see SPECTER⟧ 1 the series of colored bands or lines dispersed and arranged in the order of their respective wavelengths by the passage of white light through a prism or other dispersing device and shading continuously from red (produced by the longest wave visible) through violet (produced by the shortest): the six main colors of the spectrum are red, orange, yellow, green, blue, and violet, with a seventh color (indigo) sometimes specified, between blue and violet 2 the intensity of any radiation or motion displayed as a function of frequency, or wavelength 3 an afterimage 4 a continuous range or the entire extent [a wide *spectrum* of opinion] 5 *a)* RADIO SPECTRUM *b)* ELECTROMAGNETIC SPECTRUM

spectrum analysis analysis of substances or bodies through study of their spectra

spec·u·lar (spek′yə lər) *adj.* ⟦L *specularis*⟧ of, like, or by means of, a speculum —**spec′u·lar·ly** *adv.*

spec·u·late (spek′yə lāt′) *vi.* **-lat′ed**, **-lat′ing** ⟦< L *speculatus,* pp. of *speculari,* to view < *specula,* watchtower < *specere,* to see: see SPY⟧ 1 to think about the various aspects of a given subject; meditate; ponder; esp., to conjecture 2 to buy or sell stocks, commodities, land, etc., usually in the face of higher than ordinary risk, hoping to take advantage of an expected rise or fall in price; also, to take part in any risky venture on the chance of making huge profits —*SYN.* THINK[1] —**spec′u·la′tor** *n.*

spec·u·la·tion (spek′yə lā′shən) *n.* 1 *a)* the act of speculating, or meditating *b)* a thought or conjecture 2 *a)* the act of speculating in stocks, land, etc. *b)* a speculative business venture

spec·u·la·tive (spek′yə lə tiv, -lāt′iv) *adj.* ⟦ME *speculatif* < MFr < LL *speculativus*⟧ 1 of, characterized by, or having the nature of, speculation or meditation, conjecture, etc. 2 theoretical, not practical 3 of or characterized by financial speculation 4 uncertain; risky 5 indulging in or fond of speculation —**spec′u·la·tive·ly** *adv.*

spec·u·lum (spek′yə ləm) *n., pl.* **-la** (-lə) or **-lums** ⟦L, a mirror < *specere,* to look: see SPY⟧ 1 *a)* a mirror, esp. one of polished metal *b)* [Historical] such a mirror in a reflecting telescope 2 *Med.* an instrument for dilating a passage or cavity to facilitate its examination 3 *Ornithology* a distinctive patch of color on the wings of certain birds, esp. ducks

speculum metal an alloy of copper and tin that will take a mirrorlike polish, used for making mirrors

sped (sped) *vi., vt. alt. pt. & pp. of* SPEED

speech (spēch) *n.* ⟦ME *speche* < OE *spæc, spræc* < base of *sprecan,* to speak: see SPEAK⟧ 1 the act of speaking; expression or communication of thoughts and feelings by spoken words 2 the power or ability to speak 3 the manner of speaking [her lisping *speech*] 4 that which is spoken; utterance, remark, statement, talk, conversation, etc. 5 a talk or address given to an audience 6 the language used by a certain group of people; dialect or tongue 7 the study of the theory and practice of oral expression and communication 8 [Archaic] rumor; report

SYN.—**speech** is the general word for a discourse delivered to an audience, whether prepared or impromptu; **address** implies a formal, carefully prepared speech and usually attributes importance to the speaker or the speech [an *address* to a legislature]; **oration** suggests an eloquent, rhetorical, sometimes merely bombastic speech, esp. one delivered on some special occasion [political *orations* at the picnic]; a **lecture** is a carefully prepared speech intended to inform or instruct the audience [a *lecture* to a college class]; **talk** suggests informality and is applied either to an impromptu speech or to an address or lecture in which the speaker deliberately uses a simple, conversational approach; a **sermon** is a lecture by a clergyman intended to give religious or moral instruction and usually based on Scriptural text

speech clinic a clinic for treating speech disorders

speech community all the people speaking a particular language or dialect, in a single geographical area or dispersed throughout various regions

speech disorder any conspicuous speech imperfection, or variation from accepted speech patterns, caused either by a physical defect in the speech organs or by a mental disorder, as aphasia, stuttering, etc.

speech form LINGUISTIC FORM

speech·i·fy (spē′chə fī′) *vi.* **-fied′**, **-fy′ing** to make a speech: used humorously or contemptuously —**speech′i·fi′er** *n.*

speech·less (spēch′lis) *adj.* 1 incapable of speech; lacking the ability to speak 2 temporarily unable to speak; silent, as from shock 3 not expressed or expressible in words [*speechless* terror] —**speech′less·ly** *adv.* —**speech′less·ness** *n.*

speech·mak·er (-māk′ər) *n.* a person who makes a speech or speeches; orator —**speech′mak′ing** *n.*

speech·writ·er (-rīt′ər) *n.* a person whose work is writing speeches as for a political candidate or officeholder

speed (spēd) *n.* ⟦ME *sped* < OE *spœd,* wealth, power, success, akin to *spowan,* to prosper, succeed < IE base **spēi-*, to flourish, expand > SPACE, SPARE⟧ 1 [Archaic] luck; success; prosperity [to wish someone good *speed*] 2 the act or state of moving rapidly; swiftness; quick motion 3 *a)* the rate of movement or motion; VELOCITY (sense 2*a*) *b)* the magnitude of a VELOCITY (sense 2*b*) *c)* the rate or rapidity of any action [reading *speed*] 4 a gear or arrangement of gears for the drive of an engine or bicycle [a truck with five forward *speeds*] 5 [Informal] one's kind or level of taste, capability, etc. ☆6 [Slang] any of various amphetamine compounds, esp. methedrine 7 *Photog. a)* the sensitivity of film to light, expressed in various numerical scales *b)* the widest effective aperture of a camera lens (see also F-NUMBER) *c)* the length of time the shutter is opened for an exposure —*adj.* of or having to do with speed —*vi.* **sped** or **speed′ed**, **speed′ing** 1 to move rapidly, esp. more rapidly than is safe or allowed by law 2 [Archaic] *a)* to get along; fare *b)* to have fortune, good or bad *c)* to have good fortune; prosper; succeed —*vt.* 1 to help (a project) to succeed; aid; promote 2 to wish Godspeed to [to *speed* the parting guest] 3 to send, convey, or cause to move, go, etc. swiftly [to *speed* a letter on its way] 4 to cause or design (a machine, etc.) to operate at a certain speed or speeds 5 [Archaic] to cause to succeed or prosper —*SYN.* HASTE —**at speed** [Chiefly Brit.] quickly; rapidly —**speed up** to increase in speed; go or make go faster; accelerate —**up to speed** 1 working or operating at full speed, maximum efficiency, etc. 2 [Informal] fully informed or having enough information

speed bag a small PUNCHING BAG typically suspended at eye level and so as to swing freely, designed to be punched rapidly as the bag rebounds

☆**speed·ball** (spēd′bôl′) *n.* [Slang] a dose of a depressant mixed with a stimulant, as heroin or morphine mixed with cocaine or an amphetamine

speed·boat (-bōt′) *n.* a motorboat built for speed

speed brake an airplane flap designed to decrease flight speed, esp. when landing

☆**speed bump** a raised ridge, as in a parking lot, to discourage fast driving by jolting a motor vehicle driving over it

speed dial a function on a telephone that automatically dials stored telephone numbers

speed·er (-ər) *n.* ☆a person or thing that speeds; esp., a motorist who drives faster than is safe or legal

speed·ing (-iŋ) *n.* ☆the act of driving a motor vehicle at a higher speed than is safe or legal

speed limit the legal maximum speed that traffic may go on a particular stretch of road, highway, etc.

Speed·o (spē′dō′) ⟦so named because its styling allows for rapid movement through the water⟧ *trademark for* a kind of men's very brief, legless swimsuit

speed·om·e·ter (spi däm′ət ər) *n.* ⟦< SPEED + -METER⟧ a device, often combined with an odometer, attached to a motor vehicle, etc. to indicate speed, as in miles per hour: it is usually connected to the transmission by a flexible drive shaft

speed-read·ing (spēd′rēd′iŋ) *n.* a technique for reading texts at an extremely rapid rate with adequate comprehension —**speed′-read′** *vi., vt.* —**speed′-read′er** *n.*

speed·skat·ing (spēd′skāt′iŋ) *n.* competitive racing on ice skates: also written **speed skating** —**speed′skat′er** *n.*

☆**speed·ster** (spēd′stər) *n.* 1 a very fast driver, runner, vehicle, etc. 2 SPEEDER

☆**speed trap** a stretch of road where speeders are frequently apprehended, as by concealed police or through radar

speed·up (-up′) *n.* an increase in speed; esp., an increase in the rate of output, as required by an employer without any increase in pay

☆**speed·way** (-wā′) *n.* 1 a track for racing automobiles or motorcycles 2 a road for high-speed traffic

speed·well (-wel′) *n.* ⟦< SPEED (v.) + WELL[2]: orig. sense prob., "prosper well"⟧ any of a genus (*Veronica*) of plants of the figwort family, with white or bluish flower spikes

speed·y (spēd′ē) *adj.* **speed′i·er**, **speed′i·est** 1 characterized by speed of motion; rapid; swift 2 without delay; quick; prompt [a *speedy* reply] —*SYN.* FAST[1] —**speed′i·ly** *adv.* —**speed′i·ness** *n.*

speiss (spīs) *n.* ⟦Ger *speise,* amalgam, lit., food < ML *spesa,* cost, expense, earlier *spensa* < L *expensa* (*pecunia*), (money) spent < pp. of *expendere,* to EXPEND⟧ a mixture of metallic arsenides produced during the smelting of copper, iron, and certain other ores

spe·lae·an or **spe·le·an** (spi lē′ən) *adj.* ⟦< L *spelaeum* < Gr *spēlaion,* cave + -AN⟧ 1 of or like a cave 2 dwelling in caves

spe·le·ol·o·gy (spē′lē äl′ə jē) *n.* ⟦< L *spelaeum* (see prec.) + -LOGY⟧ the scientific study and exploration of caves —**spe′le·o·log′i·cal** *adj.* —**spe′le·ol′o·gist** *n.*

spe·le·o·them (spē′lē ə them′) *n.* ⟦ult. < Gr *spēlaion,* cave + *thema,* what is laid down, deposit⟧ a mineral deposit formed in caves by the evaporation of mineral-rich water, as a stalactite, stalagmite, or helictite

spell[1] (spel) *n.* ⟦ME < OE, a saying, tale, charm, akin to Goth *spill,* tale < ? IE base *(*s*)*pel-*, to speak loudly⟧ 1 a word, formula, or form of words having some magic power; incantation 2 seemingly magical power or irresistible influence; charm; fascination 3 a trance —**cast a spell on** 1 to put into, or as into, a trance 2 to win the complete affection of —**under a spell** held in a spell or trance; enchanted

spell[2] (spel) *vt.* **spelled** or **spelt**, **spell′ing** ⟦ME *spellen* < OFr *espeller,* to explain, relate < Frank **spellōn,* akin to prec.⟧ 1 to name, write, or signal the letters which make up (a word, syllable, etc.), esp. the right letters in the right order, together with any required hyphens, apostrophes, accents, etc. 2 to make up, or form (a word, etc.): said of specified letters 3 to signify; mean [hard work *spelled* success] —*vi.* to spell a word, words, etc.; esp., to do so correctly —**spell out** 1 to read letter by letter or with difficulty 2 to make out, or discern, as if by close reading ☆3 to explain exactly and in detail

spell[3] (spel) *vt.* **spelled**, **spell′ing** ⟦ME *spelien* < OE *spelian,* to substitute for, akin to *spala,* a substitute⟧ 1 [Informal] to serve or work in place of (another), esp. so as to give a period of rest to; relieve 2 [Chiefly Austral.] to give a period of rest to —*vi.* [Chiefly Austral.] to take a period of rest or relief —*n.* 1 a turn of serving or working in place of another 2 a period or turn of work, duty, etc. [a two-year *spell* as reporter] 3 a turn, period, or fit of something [a *spell* of brooding] 4 a period of a specified sort of weather [a cold *spell*] 5 [Informal] a period of time that is indefinite, short, or of a specified character ☆6 [Dial.] a short distance 7 [Informal] a period or fit of some illness, indisposition, etc. 8 [Chiefly Austral.] a period of rest or relief from activity

spell·bind (spel′bīnd′) *vt.* **-bound′**, **-bind′ing** ⟦back-form. < SPELLBOUND⟧ to hold by or as by a spell; fascinate; enchant

☆**spell·bind·er** (-bīn′dər) *n.* a speaker, esp. a politician, who can sway an audience with eloquence

spell·bound (-bound′) *adj.* ⟦SPELL[1] + BOUND[2]⟧ held or affected by or as by a spell; fascinated; enchanted

spell check the act or an instance of using a SPELL-CHECKER

spell-check·er (spel′chek′ər) *n.* a word-processing program that reviews words in a document for misspellings: also **spelling checker**

☆**spell·down** (spel′doun′) *n.* SPELLING BEE

spell·er (spel′ər) *n.* 1 a person with respect to his or her ability to spell words [a poor *speller*] ☆2 a book of exercises for teaching spelling

spell·ing (-iŋ) *n.* 1 the act of one who spells words 2 the way in which a word is spelled; orthography

☆**spelling bee** a spelling contest, esp. one in which a contestant is eliminated after misspelling a word

spelling pronunciation a pronunciation of a word that is influenced by its spelling and does not follow standard usage [(fôr′kas′əl) is a *spelling pronunciation* of *forecastle* (fōk′səl)]

spelt[1] (spelt) *vt., vi. alt. pt. & pp. of* SPELL[2]

spelt[2] (spelt) *n.* ⟦ME < OE < LL *spelta* < Gmc **speltō* < IE base *(*s*)*p*(*h*)*el-*, to split off > SPILL[1]⟧ a primitive species (*Triticum spelta*) of wheat with grains that do not thresh free of the chaff: now seldom cultivated

spel·ter (spel′tər) *n.* ⟦< or akin to MDu *speauter,* LowG *spialter:* akin to PEWTER⟧ crude zinc from the smelter, esp. as used in galvanizing

☆**spe·lunk·er** (spi luŋ′kər, spē′luŋ′-) *n.* ⟦< obs. *spelunk,* cave (< ME *spelunke* < L *spelunca* < Gr *spēlynx,* akin to *spēlaion,* cave) + -ER⟧ a person who explores caves as a hobby —**spe·lunk′ing** *n.*

spence (spens) *n.* ⟦ME < ML *spensa,* aphetic for *dispensa* < L, fem. pp. of *dispendere,* to weigh out: see DISPENSE⟧ [Now Chiefly Dial.] a larder or pantry

spen·cer[1] (spen′sər) *n.* ⟦after the 2d Earl *Spencer* (1758-1834)⟧ a short jacket of an early 19th-cent. style

spen·cer[2] (spen′sər) *n.* ⟦< pers. name: see fol.⟧ a fore-and-aft sail attached to a gaff and set on a foremast or mainmast

Spen·cer[1] (spen′sər) *n.* ⟦< the surname *Spencer* < ME *spenser,* butler, steward < OFr *despencier* < *despense,* larder, buttery < ML *dispensa:* see SPENCE⟧ a masculine name: var. *Spenser*

Spen·cer[2] (spen′sər), **Herbert** 1820-1903; Eng. philosopher

spend (spend) ***vt.*** **spent, spend′ing** ⟦ME *spenden* < OE *spendan* (in comp.) < ML *spendere* < L *expendere:* see EXPEND⟧ **1** to use up, exhaust, consume, or wear out [*his fury was spent*] **2** to pay out (money); disburse **3** to give or devote (time, labor, thought, or effort) to some enterprise or for some purpose **4** to pass (a period of time) [*spending* hours together] **5** to waste; squander —***vi.*** **1** to pay out or use up money, etc. **2** [Obs.] to be or become consumed, wasted, etc. —**spend′a·ble** ***adj.***

spend·er (-ər) ***n.*** a person who spends, esp. lavishly

Spen·der (spen′dər), Sir **Stephen** 1909-95; Eng. poet & critic

spending money money for small personal expenses

spend·thrift (spend′thrift′) ***n.*** a person who spends money carelessly or wastefully; squanderer —***adj.*** wasteful; extravagant

Speng·ler (shpeŋ′lər, speŋ′-), **Oswald** 1880-1936; Ger. philosopher of history —**Speng·le′ri·an** (-lir′ē ən) ***adj.***

Spen·ser[1] (spen′sər) ***n.*** a masculine name: see SPENCER[1]

Spen·ser[2] (spen′sər), **Edmund** 1552?-99; Eng. poet

Spen·se·ri·an (spen sir′ē ən) ***adj.*** of or characteristic of Edmund Spenser or his writing —***n.*** **1** a follower or imitator of Spenser **2** a Spenserian stanza, or poem in such stanzas

Spenserian stanza a stanza consisting of eight lines of iambic pentameter and a final line of iambic hexameter (an alexandrine), with a rhyme scheme *ababbcbcc*, used by Spenser in *The Fairie Queene*

spent (spent) ***vt., vi. pt. & pp. of*** SPEND —***adj.*** **1** tired out; physically exhausted; without energy **2** used up; worn out; without power **3** exhausted of sperm or spawn

sperm[1] (spurm) ***n.*** ⟦ME *sperme* < MFr *esperme* < LL *sperma* < Gr, seed, germ < *speirein,* to sow, scatter: for IE base see SPARK[1]⟧ **1** the male generative fluid; semen **2** *pl.* **sperm** or **sperms** a male gamete, esp. a spermatozoon rather than a spermatozoid

sperm[2] (spurm) ***n.*** *short for:* **1** SPERMACETI **2** SPERM OIL **3** SPERM WHALE

-sperm (spurm) ⟦see SPERM[1]⟧ *combining form forming nouns* seed [*gymnosperm*]

sper·ma·ce·ti (spur′mə sēt′ī′, -sēt′ē; -set′-) ***n.*** ⟦ML *sperma ceti,* lit., whale sperm < LL *sperma,* SPERM[1] + L *ceti,* gen. of *cetus,* whale < Gr *kētos*⟧ a white, waxlike substance taken from the oil in the head of a sperm whale or dolphin, used in making cosmetics, ointments, candles, etc.

sper·ma·go·ni·um (-gō′nē əm) ***n., pl.*** **-ni·a** (-nē ə) ⟦ModL < LL *sperma,* SPERM[1] + ModL *-gonium,* -GONIUM⟧ *Bot.* a flasklike structure found in certain fungi and lichens, which produces small, nonmotile sperm cells (*spermatia*)

-sper·mal (spur′məl) *combining form* -SPERMOUS

sper·ma·ry (spur′mə rē) ***n., pl.*** **-ries** ⟦ModL *spermarium* < LL *sperma,* SPERM[1]⟧ an organ in which male germ cells are formed; male gonad; testis

sper·ma·the·ca (spur′mə thē′kə) ***n.*** ⟦ModL: see SPERM[1] & THECA⟧ a small, saclike structure in the female reproductive tract in many invertebrates, esp. insects, for receiving and storing sperm

sper·mat·ic (spər mat′ik) ***adj.*** ⟦MFr *spermatique* < LL *spermaticus* < Gr *spermatikos*⟧ **1** of, like, or having to do with sperm or sperm cells; generative or seminal **2** of or having to do with a spermary

spermatic cord the cord that suspends a testicle within the scrotum, consisting of a vas deferens, nerves, blood and lymphatic vessels, and connective tissue

sper·ma·tid (spur′mə tid) ***n.*** ⟦SPERMAT(O)- + -ID⟧ *Zool.* any of the four haploid cells formed by the two consecutive meiotic divisions of a primary spermatocyte, each of which develops into a spermatozoon

sper·ma·ti·um (spər mā′shē əm) ***n., pl.*** **-ti·a** (-shē ə) ⟦ModL < Gr *spermation,* dim. of *sperma,* a seed: see SPERM[1]⟧ *Bot.* **1** a nonmotile male sex cell in red algae **2** a very small, nonmotile male gamete, found in some lichens and fungi

sper·ma·to- (spur′mə tō, -tə; spər mat′ō, -ə) ⟦< Gr *sperma* (gen. *spermatos*), a seed, SPERM[1]⟧ *combining form* seed or sperm [*spermatogenesis*]: also, before a vowel, **spermat-**

sper·ma·to·cyte (spur′mə tə sīt′, spər mat′ə-) ***n.*** ⟦prec. + -CYTE⟧ **1** *Bot.* a cell that develops into a spermatozoid **2** *Zool.* a stage in the development of the male sex cell, originating by growth from a spermatogonium

sper·ma·to·gen·e·sis (spur′mə tə jen′ə sis, spər mat′ə-) ***n.*** ⟦ModL: see SPERMATO- & -GENESIS⟧ the production and development of spermatozoa —**sper′ma·to·ge·net′ic** ***adj.***

sper·ma·to·go·ni·um (-gō′nē əm) ***n., pl.*** **-ni·a** (-nē ə) ⟦ModL < SPERMATO- + Gr *gonē,* seed: see GONAD⟧ *Zool.* a primitive male germ cell which divides into spermatocytes or more spermatogonia —**sper′ma·to·go′ni·al** ***adj.***

sper·ma·to·phore (spur′mə tə fôr′, spər mat′ə-) ***n.*** ⟦SPERMATO- + -PHORE⟧ *Zool.* a case or capsule containing a number of spermatozoa, expelled whole by the male of certain animals, as in many copepods or leeches —**sper·ma·toph·o·ral** (spur′mə täf′ər əl) ***adj.***

sper·ma·to·phyte (-fīt′) ***n.*** ⟦SPERMATO- + -PHYTE⟧ any seed-bearing plant —**sper′ma·to·phyt′ic** (-fit′ik) ***adj.***

sper·ma·tor·rhe·a (spur′mə tə rē′ə, spər mat′ə-) ***n.*** ⟦SPERMATO- + -RRHEA⟧ the too frequent involuntary discharge of semen without an orgasm

sper·ma·to·zo·id (-zō′id) ***n.*** ⟦< fol. + -ID⟧ *Bot.* in certain mosses, ferns, etc., a male gamete that moves by means of flagella: it is usually produced in an antheridium

sper·ma·to·zo·on (-zō′än′, -ən) ***n., pl.*** **-zo′a** (-zō′ə) ⟦ModL < SPERMATO- + Gr *zōion,* animal: see BIO-⟧ the male germ cell, found in semen, which penetrates the ovum, or egg, of the female to fertilize it: typically it consists of a head containing a large nucleus, a small midsection, and a whiplike tail used for locomotion —**sper′ma·to·zo′al** ***adj.,*** **sper′ma·to·zo′an,** or **sper′ma·to·zo′ic**

sperm·i·cide (spur′mə sīd′) ***n.*** ⟦SPERM[1] + *-i-* + -CIDE⟧ an agent that kills spermatozoa —**sperm′i·cid′al** ***adj.***

sperm·ine (spur′mēn′, -min) ***n.*** ⟦SPERM[1] + -INE[3]⟧ a basic substance, $C_{10}H_{26}N_4$, associated with nucleic acids and cell membranes, found in nearly all animal tissues: first found in human semen

sper·mi·o·gen·e·sis (spur′mē ō jen′ə sis) ***n.*** ⟦ModL < *spermium* (< Gr *spermeion,* sperm < *sperma:* see SPERM[1]) + -GENESIS⟧ **1** *Zool.* the changing of a spermatid into a spermatozoon **2** SPERMATOGENESIS

sper·mo- (spur′mə, -mō) *combining form* SPERMATO-

sper·mo·go·ni·um (spur′mə gō′nē əm) ***n., pl.*** **-ni·a** (-nē ə) ⟦ModL⟧ *alt. sp. of* SPERMAGONIUM

sperm oil oil obtained from the sperm whale, used as a lubricant

sper·mo·phile (spur′mə fil′, -fil) ***n.*** ⟦< Gr *sperma,* a seed (see SPERM[1]) + -PHILE⟧ any of several squirrel-like rodents, as the ground squirrels, that live in burrows, feed on vegetation, and sometimes damage crops

sper·mous (spur′məs) ***adj.*** of or like sperm

-spermous (spur′məs) *combining form forming adjectives* having (a specified number or kind of) seed [*monospermous*]

sperm whale any of a family (Physeteridae) of toothed whales; esp., a large species (*Physeter catodon*) inhabiting warm seas: a closed cavity in its roughly square head contains sperm oil

sper·ry·lite (sper′i līt′) ***n.*** ⟦after its Cdn discoverer, F. L. *Sperry* + -LITE⟧ a rare, silvery-white, granular or crystalline mineral, $PtAs_2$, that is an ore of platinum; platinum arsenide

spes·sar·tite (spes′ər tīt′) ***n.*** ⟦Fr, after *Spessart,* mountain range in Bavaria + *-ite,* -ITE[1]⟧ a usually dark-red type of garnet, $Mn_3Al_2(SiO_4)_3$; manganese aluminum silicate: also called **spes′sar·tine′** (-tēn′)

spew (spyo͞o) ***vt., vi.*** ⟦ME *spewen* < OE *spiwan,* akin to Ger *speien,* Goth *speiwan* < IE base **(s)p(h)yēu-* > L *spuere,* to vomit, Gr *ptyein,* to spit⟧ **1** to throw up (something) from or as from the stomach; vomit **2** to flow or cause to flow plentifully; gush —***n.*** something spewed; vomit —**spew′er** ***n.***

Spezia *see* LA SPEZIA

SPF *abbrev.* sun protection factor

sp gr *abbrev.* specific gravity

sphac·e·late (sfas′ə lāt′) ***vt., vi.*** **-lat′ed, -lat′ing** ⟦< ModL *sphacelatus,* pp. of *sphacelare,* to mortify < *sphacelus,* gangrene < Gr *sphakelos*⟧ to make or become gangrenous; mortify —**sphac′e·la′tion** ***n.***

sphag·num (sfag′nəm) ***n.*** ⟦ModL < Gr *sphagnos,* kind of moss⟧ **1** any of a genus (*Sphagnum*) of highly absorbent, spongelike, grayish peat mosses found in bogs **2** a mass of such peat mosses, used to improve soil, to pack and pot plants, etc. —**sphag′nous** (-nəs) ***adj.***

sphal·er·ite (sfal′ər īt′, sfāl′-) ***n.*** ⟦Ger *sphalerit* < Gr *sphaleros,* deceptive (< *sphallein,* to trip, deceive: for IE base see SPOIL) + *-it,* -ITE[1]: so named from being mistaken for other ores⟧ a usually brownish mineral, (Zn,Fe)S, the chief ore of zinc; zinc iron sulfide

sphene (sfēn) ***n.*** ⟦Fr *sphène* < Gr *sphēn,* a wedge (for IE base see SPOON): so named from the shape of its crystals⟧ a variously colored mineral, $CaTiSiO_5$, that is an ore of titanium; calcium titanium silicate

sphe·no- (sfē′nō, -nə) ⟦< Gr *sphēn:* see prec.⟧ *combining form* **1** shaped like a wedge [*sphenogram*] **2** of the sphenoid bone Also, before a vowel, **sphen-**

sphe·no·don (sfē′nə dän′) ***n.*** ⟦< prec. + Gr *odōn,* TOOTH⟧ TUATARA

sphe·no·gram (sfē′nə gram′) ***n.*** ⟦SPHENO- + -GRAM⟧ a cuneiform, or wedge-shaped, character

sphe·noid (sfē′noid′) ***adj.*** ⟦ModL *sphenoides* < Gr *sphēnoeides:* see SPHENE & -OID⟧ **1** wedge-shaped **2** *Anat.* designating or of the wedge-shaped compound bones of the skull Also **sphe·noi′dal** —***n.*** **1** the sphenoid bone **2** *Mineralogy* a wedge-shaped crystal form having four triangular faces

spher·al (sfir′əl) ***adj.*** ⟦LL *sphaeralis*⟧ **1** of or like a sphere **2** rounded in form; spherical **3** symmetrical

sphere (sfir) ***n.*** ⟦ME *spere* < OFr *espere* < L *sphaera* < Gr *sphaira*⟧ **1** any round body or figure having the surface equally distant from the center at all points; globe; ball **2** a star, planet, etc. **3** the visible heavens; sky **4** *short for* CELESTIAL SPHERE **5** any of a series of hypothetical spherical shells, transparent, concentric, and postulated as revolving one within another, in which the stars, planets, sun, moon, etc. are supposedly set: a concept of ancient astronomy **6** a place, range, or extent of knowledge, experience, influence, etc. **7** social stratum; place in society; walk of life —***vt.*** **sphered, spher′ing** [Old Poet.] **1** to put in or as in a sphere **2** to put among the heavenly spheres **3** to form into a sphere

-sphere (sfir) *combining form* **1** something, esp. a cell or body part, resembling a sphere [*oosphere*] **2** any of the atmospheric layers surrounding a planet or star [*chromosphere*]

sphere of influence a region in which political and economic influence or control is exerted by one nation over another or others

spher·i·cal (sfer′i kəl, sfir′-) ***adj.*** ⟦< LL *sphaericus* < Gr *sphairikos* + -AL⟧ **1** shaped like a sphere; globular **2** of a sphere or spheres **3** of the celestial spheres: sometimes with astrological reference Also **spher′ic** —***SYN.*** ROUND[1] —**spher′i·cal·ly** ***adv.***

spherical aberration optical distortion resulting from the spherical shape of a lens or mirror

spherical angle an angle formed by the intersecting arcs of two great circles on a sphere

spherical coordinate *Math.* any of three coordinates for locating a point in three-dimensional space by reference to the length of its radius vector and the two polar angles that determine the position of this vector

spherical geometry the study of the geometry of figures drawn on a sphere

spherical polygon a closed figure on the surface of a sphere bounded by the arcs of three or more great circles

spherical triangle a closed figure on the surface of a sphere bounded by the arcs of three great circles: the sum of the angles exceeds 180°

spherical trigonometry the application of trigonometry to spherical triangles

sphe·ric·i·ty (sfi ris′ə tē) ***n.*** ⟦ML *sphaericitas*⟧ the state of being spherical; round form; roundness

spher·ics[1] (sfer′iks, sfir′-) ***n.*** ⟦< *spheric* (adj.: see SPHERICAL) + -ICS: mathematical study of the sphere⟧ **1** SPHERICAL GEOMETRY **2** SPHERICAL TRIGONOMETRY

spher·ics[2] (sfer′iks, sfir′-) ***n.*** *alt. sp. of* SFERICS

sphe·roid (sfir′oid) ***n.*** ⟦L *sphaeroides* < Gr *sphairoeidēs*: see SPHERE & -OID⟧ a body that is almost but not quite a sphere, esp. one generated by the rotation of an ellipse about one of its axes —***adj.*** of this shape: also **sphe·roi′dal**

sphe·rom·e·ter (sfi räm′ət ər) ***n.*** ⟦Fr *sphéromètre*: see SPHERE & -METER⟧ an instrument used for measuring the curvature of a surface, as of a lens

spher·ule (sfer′o͞ol, sfir′-; -yo͞ol) ***n.*** ⟦L *sphaerula*, dim. of *sphaera*: see SPHERE⟧ a small sphere or spherical body; globule —**spher′u·lar** ***adj.***

spher·u·lite (-ə līt′, -yə līt′) ***n.*** ⟦prec. + -ITE[1]⟧ a rounded or spherical crystalline body found in some glassy volcanic rocks —**spher′u·lit′ic** (-lit′ik) ***adj.***

spher·y (sfir′ē) ***adj.*** **spher′i·er, spher′i·est** [Old Poet.] **1** of or like a sphere **2** of the heavenly spheres

sphinc·ter (sfiŋk′tər) ***n.*** ⟦LL < Gr *sphinktēr* < *sphingein*, to draw close < IE **spheig-* < base **spēi-*, to flourish, grow thick > SPEED, SPARE⟧ *Anat.* a ring-shaped muscle that surrounds a natural opening in the body and can open or close it by expanding or contracting —**sphinc′ter·al** ***adj.***

sphin·gid (sfin′jid) ***n.*** ⟦< ModL *Sphingidae*, family name < *sphinx* (gen. *sphingis*), type genus < L: see fol. & -IDAE⟧ HAWK MOTH

sphinx (sfiŋks) ***n.***, *pl.* **sphinx′es** or **sphin·ges** (sfin′jēz′) ⟦ME *spynx* < L *sphinx* < Gr, lit., the strangler < *sphingein*: see SPHINCTER⟧ **1** *Gr. Myth. a)* a winged monster with a lion's body and the head and breasts of a woman *b)* [**S-**] a sphinx at Thebes that strangles passersby who are unable to guess its riddle **2** *a)* any ancient Egyptian statue or figure having, typically, the body of a lion and the head of a man, ram, or hawk *b)* [**S-**] a huge statue having the body of a lion and the head of a man, at Gîza, near Cairo, Egypt **3** a person who is difficult to know or understand **4** *Zool.* HAWK MOTH

sp ht *abbrev.* specific heat

sphyg·mic (sfig′mik) ***adj.*** ⟦ModL *sphygmicus* < Gr *sphygmikos* < *sphygmos*, the pulse < *sphyzein*, to throb⟧ *Physiol.* of the pulse

sphyg·mo- (sfig′mō, -mə) ⟦< Gr *sphygmos*: see prec.⟧ *combining form* the pulse [*sphygmograph*]: also, before a vowel, **sphygm-**

sphyg·mo·gram (sfig′mə gram′) ***n.*** ⟦prec. + -GRAM⟧ the record or tracing made by a sphygmograph

sphyg·mo·graph (-graf′, -gräf′) ***n.*** ⟦SPHYGMO- + -GRAPH⟧ an instrument for recording the rate, force, and variations of the pulse —**sphyg′mo·graph′ic** ***adj.*** —**sphyg·mog′ra·phy** (-mä′grə fē) ***n.***

sphyg·mo·ma·nom·e·ter (sfig′mō mə näm′ət ər) ***n.*** ⟦SPHYGMO- + MANOMETER⟧ an instrument for measuring arterial blood pressure, consisting of an inflatable band wrapped around the upper arm to compress the artery, and an attached manometer

sphyg·mom·e·ter (sfig mäm′ət ər) ***n.*** ⟦SPHYGMO- + -METER⟧ an instrument for measuring the force and rate of the pulse

☆**spic** (spik) ***n.*** ⟦< (HI)SP(AN)IC⟧ [Slang] a person from a Spanish-speaking country of Latin America or from a Spanish-speaking community in the U.S.: an offensive term of contempt and derision

spi·ca (spī′kə) ***n.*** ⟦L, ear of grain, orig., a point: see SPIKE[2]⟧ **1** *pl.* **-cae** (-sē) *Bot.* a spike, as of a flower **2** *Med.* a kind of bandage wrapped back and forth with spiral overlapping around parts of a joint **3** ⟦so named because it marks a sheaf of grain in the virgin's hand in ancient diagrams of the constellation⟧ [**S-**] a binary, variable star, the brightest star in the constellation Virgo: magnitude, 0.98

spi·cate (spī′kāt′) ***adj.*** ⟦L *spicatus*, pp. of *spicare*, to provide with spikes < *spica*, a point, SPIKE[2]⟧ **1** *Biol.* spikelike in form **2** arranged in a spike or spikes

spic·ca·to (spi kät′ō) ***adj.*** ⟦It, pp. of *spiccare*, to detach⟧ *Musical Direction* played with the bow wrist relaxed so that the bow of the violin, viola, etc. rebounds rapidly between notes

spice (spīs) ***n.*** ⟦ME < OFr *espice* < L *species* (see SPECIES): in LL, wares, assorted goods, esp. spices and drugs⟧ **1** *a)* any of several vegetable substances, as cloves, cinnamon, nutmeg, or pepper, used to season food; spices are usually dried for use and have distinctive flavors and aromas *b)* such substances collectively or as a material **2** a spicy fragrance or aroma **3** that which adds zest, piquancy, or interest **4** [Archaic] a small bit; trace —***vt.*** **spiced, spic′ing 1** to season or flavor with spice **2** to add zest, piquancy, or interest to: usually with *up*

☆**spice·ber·ry** (spīs′ber′ē) ***n.***, *pl.* **-ries 1** *a)* a Caribbean tree (*Eugenia rhombea*) of the myrtle family, having orange or black fruit *b)* this fruit **2** any of several aromatic plants, esp. WINTERGREEN (sense 1)

☆**spice·bush** (-bo͝osh′) ***n.*** **1** an aromatic E North American plant (*Lindera benzoin*) of the laurel family, with leathery leaves, small yellowish flowers, and red fruit formerly dried for use as a spice **2** CAROLINA ALLSPICE

Spice Islands *former name for* the MOLUCCAS

spic·er·y (spīs′ər ē) ***n.***, *pl.* **-er·ies** ⟦ME *spicerie* < MFr *espicerie* < *espice*: see SPICE⟧ **1** spices **2** spicy quality, flavor, or aroma **3** [Obs.] a place to keep spices

☆**spick** (spik) ***n.*** [Slang] *alt. sp. of* SPIC

spick-and-span (spik′'n span′) ***adj.*** ⟦short for *spick-and-span-new* < *spick*, var. of SPIKE[1] + SPAN-NEW < ME *spon-neowe* < ON *spān-nýr* < *spánn*, a chip, shaving + *nýr*, NEW⟧ **1** new or fresh **2** neat and clean

spic·u·late (spik′yə lāt′) ***adj.*** ⟦L *spiculatus*⟧ **1** shaped like a spicule; needlelike **2** covered with or consisting of spicules Also **spic′u·lar** (-lər)

spic·ule (spik′yo͞ol′) ***n.*** ⟦< ModL & L: ModL *spicula* < ML, head of a lance or arrow < L *spiculum*, dim. of *spica*, a point, ear, SPIKE[2]⟧ **1** *Astron.* any of the short-lived, bright, dense gas jets continuously spurting up through the chromosphere of the sun: thought to be extensions of the photosphere's granules **2** *Bot.* a small spike; spikelet **3** *Zool.* a small, hard, needlelike piece or process, esp. of bony or calcareous material, as in the skeleton of the sponge

spic·u·lum (spik′yə ləm) ***n.***, *pl.* **-la** (-lə) ⟦L⟧ a spicule; esp., any of several spinelike organs found in lower animals, as the starfish

spic·y (spī′sē) ***adj.*** **spic′i·er, spic′i·est 1** containing or abounding in spices **2** having the flavor or aroma of spice; fragrant, aromatic, or pungent **3** piquant or zestful; lively, interesting, etc. **4** risqué; racy —**spic′i·ly** ***adv.*** —**spic′i·ness** ***n.***

spi·der (spī′dər) ***n.*** ⟦ME *spithre* < OE *spithra* < **spinthra* < *spinnan*, to SPIN⟧ **1** any of an order (Araneae) of small, chiefly land arachnids having a body composed of a cephalothorax bearing the legs and an abdomen bearing two or more pairs of spinnerets that spin the silk threads from which are made nests, cocoons for the eggs, or webs for trapping insects ☆**2** a cast-iron frying pan, originally one with legs for use on a hearth **3** any of various devices or frameworks with several leglike extensions

spider crab any of a family (Majidae) of sea crabs with a pear-shaped body and long, slender legs: they are often overgrown with algae, hydroids, etc.

spider flower ⟦so called prob. from the spidery visual effect of its long stamens⟧ CLEOME

spider mite any of a family (Tetranychidae, order Acariformes) of plant-eating mites that resemble spiders

spider monkey any of a genus (*Ateles*, family Cebidae) of New World monkeys with long, spidery limbs, a long, prehensile tail, and the thumb rudimentary or absent

spider plant ⟦so named from fancied resemblance, prob. likening the young plants on their runners to *spiders* descending on their silk threads⟧ an African plant (*Chlorophytum comosum*) of the lily family, with long, narrow leaves often streaked with white and long runners with small, white flowers that develop into new plants: often used as a houseplant

spi·der·web (-web′) ***n.*** a web made by a spider

spi·der·wort (-wurt′) ***n.*** any of a genus (*Tradescantia*) of fleshy perennial plants of the spiderwort family, having grasslike leaves and showy purplish, white, or pink flowers —***adj.*** designating a family (Commelinaceae, order Commelinales) of monocotyledonous plants, including the dayflower and wandering Jew

spi·der·y (-ē) ***adj.*** **1** like a spider **2** long and thin like a spider's legs **3** infested with spiders

spie·gel·ei·sen (spē′gəl ī′zən) ***n.*** ⟦Ger < *spiegel*, mirror (< OHG *spiagal* < L *speculum*: see SPECULUM) + *eisen*, IRON⟧ a hard, white pig iron containing 15 to 32% manganese: also **spie·gel** (spē′gəl) or **spiegel iron**

☆**spiel** (spēl, shpēl) [Informal] ***n.*** ⟦Ger, play, game⟧ a talk, speech, or harangue, as in persuading or selling —***vi.*** ⟦Ger *spielen*, to play⟧ to give a spiel —**spiel off** [Slang] to recite by or as if by rote —**spiel′er** ***n.***

spi·er (spī′ər) ***n.*** a person who spies

spiff (spif) ***vt.*** ⟦see fol.⟧ [Slang] to make spiffy; spruce (*up*)

spiff·y (spif′ē) ***adj.*** **spiff′i·er, spiff′i·est** ⟦< 19th-c. cant term *spiff*, well-dressed person < ?⟧ [Slang] spruce, smart, or dapper —**spiff′i·ness** ***n.***

spig·ot (spig′ət; *also* spik′ət) ***n.*** ⟦ME *spigote*, prob. akin (? via OFr) to OIt dial. *spigorare*, to tap (a cask) < L *spiculum*: see SPICULE⟧ **1** a plug used to stop the hole in a barrel **2** *a)* a faucet *b)* the valve or plug in a faucet **3** the end of a pipe that is inserted into an enlarged end of another pipe to form a joint

spike[1] (spīk) ***n.*** ⟦ME < ON *spīkr*, a nail, spike, or < MDu & MLowG *spīker*, both ult. < IE base **(s)p(h)ei-*, sharp, pointed splinter > SPIT[1], SPOKE[1], L *spica*, ear of grain, *spina*, SPINE⟧ **1** a long, heavy nail **2** a sharp-pointed part or projection, usually slender and of metal, as along the top of an iron fence, etc. **3** any long, slender, pointed object, as the unbranched antler of a young deer **4** *a)* any of a number of sharp or pointed metal projections on the soles, and often on the heels, of shoes used for baseball, golf, track, etc. to prevent slipping *b)* [*pl.*] a pair of such shoes *c)* STILETTO (*n.* 3) (also **spike heel**) ☆**5** a young mackerel not more than six inches long **6** *a)* a transient wave or variation in potential difference that propagates along a nerve axon *b)* a graphic recording or tracing of this, as any of the jagged peaks in an electroencephalogram **7** a sudden, rapid rise in something measurable, as blood pressure —***vt.*** **spiked, spik′ing 1** to fasten or fit with or as with a spike or spikes **2** to mark, pierce, cut, etc. with a spike or spikes, or impale on a spike **3** [Historical] to make (a cannon) unusable by driving a spike into the touchhole **4** *a)* to experience a sudden or rapid rise or increase in (something) [the baby *spiked* a fever] *b)* to cause a sudden or rapid rise or increase in (something) [the new film version *spiked* book sales] **5** to thwart, frustrate, or block (a scheme, etc.)

☆6 [Informal] to add a substance, as a narcotic or other drug, to (a drink, food, etc.); specif., to add alcoholic liquor to (a drink) 7 *Baseball* to injure with the spikes on one's shoes 8 *Football* to throw (the football) to the ground, esp. in celebration of scoring a touchdown ☆9 *Volleyball* to leap into the air while close to the net and slam (the ball) into the opponents' court —*vi.* to rise suddenly and rapidly —**hang up one's spikes** to retire, as from a professional sport

spike[2] (spīk) *n.* ⟦ME *spik* < L *spica:* see prec.⟧ 1 an ear of grain 2 an unbranched flower cluster with stalkless flowers attached directly to the central axis —**spiked** *adj.*

spike lavender a European lavender mint (*Lavandula latifolia*) that yields an oil used in making perfumes, food flavorings, etc.

spike·let (spīk′lit) *n.* a small spike; esp., an individual unit of a flower cluster of a grass

spike·nard (-närd′, -nərd) *n.* ⟦ME < LL(Ec) *spica nardi* < L *spica,* an ear of grain (see SPIKE[2]) + *nardus,* NARD⟧ 1 a fragrant ointment used in ancient times 2 an Asian plant (*Nardostachys jatamansi*) of the valerian family that yielded this ointment ☆3 a perennial North American plant (*Aralia racemosa*) of the ginseng family, with whitish flowers, purplish berries, and fragrant roots

spike-tooth harrow (-to͞oth′) a harrow with sharp teeth

spik·y (spī′kē) *adj.* **spik′i·er, spik′i·est** 1 shaped like a spike; long and pointed 2 having spikes 3 [Informal, Chiefly Brit.] not amiable or companionable; bristling, irascible, etc. —**spik′i·ness** *n.*

spile (spīl) *n.* ⟦MDu, splinter, skewer, bar, spindle: for IE base see SPIKE[1]⟧ 1 a plug or spigot, as for a barrel ☆2 a tap or spout driven into a maple tree to draw off sap 3 a heavy stake or timber driven into the ground as a foundation or support; pile —*vt.* **spiled, spil′ing** 1 to set a spile into (a tree, barrel, etc.) 2 to stop up (a hole) with a spile, or plug

spill[1] (spil) *vt.* **spilled** or [Chiefly Brit.] **spilt, spill′ing** ⟦ME *spillen* < OE *spillan,* to destroy, squander, akin to MHG *spillen,* to split < IE base **(s)p(h)el-,* to split, split off > SPALL, L *spolium*⟧ 1 to allow or cause, esp. unintentionally or accidentally, to run, fall, or flow over from a container, usually so as to result in loss or waste [who *spilled* the milk?] 2 to shed (blood) 3 to lessen the pressure of (wind) on (a sail) as by reducing the area of sail being acted upon 4 to scatter at random from a receptacle or container 5 to cause or allow (a rider, load, etc.) to fall off; throw off 6 [Informal] to let (something secret) become known; divulge 7 [Obs.] *a)* to kill *b)* to destroy or ruin *c)* to squander; waste —*vi.* to be spilled from a container; overflow; run out —*n.* 1 the act of spilling 2 the amount spilled 3 SPILLWAY 4 a fall or tumble, as from a horse or from a vertical position —☆**spill one's guts** [Slang] to divulge everything one knows or reveal all one's personal problems —**spill over** to overflow in superabundance or excess

spill[2] (spil) *n.* ⟦ME *spille,* prob. via dial. *spil* < ON *spila,* a splinter, akin to SPILE⟧ 1 a splinter, thin roll of paper, etc., set on fire and used to light a pipe, candle, etc. 2 a paper cone or roll used as a container

spill·age (-ij) *n.* the act of spilling or the amount spilled

spil·li·kin (spil′i kən) *n.* ⟦< MDu *spilleken,* dim. of *spille:* see SPILE⟧ [Chiefly Brit.] 1 any of the strips used in jackstraws 2 [*pl., with sing. v.*] the game of jackstraws Also sp. **spil′i·kin**

spill·o·ver (spil′ō′vər) *n.* 1 the act of spilling over 2 that which spills over; excess or overabundance

☆**spill·way** (-wā′) *n.* ⟦SPILL[1] + WAY⟧ a passageway or channel to carry off excess water, as around a dam

spilt (spilt) *vt., vi. chiefly Brit. pt. & pp. of* SPILL[1]

spilth (spilth) *n.* ⟦SPIL(L) + -TH[1]⟧ [Obs.] 1 the act of spilling 2 that which is spilled, esp. profusely

spin (spin) *vt.* **spun, spin′ning** ⟦ME *spinnen* < OE *spinnan,* akin to Ger *spinnen* < IE base **(s)pen(d)-,* to pull, draw, spin > Lith *spéndžiu,* to lay a snare & (prob.) L *pendere,* to hang⟧ 1 *a)* to draw out and twist fibers of (wool, cotton, etc.) into thread *b)* to make (thread, yarn, etc.) by this process 2 to make (a web, cocoon, etc.) from a filament of a viscous fluid that is extruded from the body and hardens on exposure to the air: said of spiders, silkworms, etc. 3 to make or produce in a way suggestive of spinning [to *spin* a tale] 4 to draw *out* (a story, etc.) to a great length; prolong; protract 5 to cause to whirl or rotate swiftly [to *spin* a top] 6 to cause (wheels of a vehicle) to rotate freely without traction, as on ice or in sand 7 to extract water from (clothes) in a washer by the centrifugal force of swift rotation ☆8 *a)* to present (information) with a slant or emphasis, as in an attempt to persuade or deceive someone *b)* to attempt to persuade or deceive (someone) in this way —*vi.* 1 to spin thread or yarn 2 to form a thread, web, etc.: said of spiders, etc. 3 to fish with a spinning reel 4 to whirl or rotate swiftly 5 to go into or descend in a spin: said of an aircraft 6 to seem to be spinning from dizziness 7 to move along swiftly and smoothly 8 to rotate freely without traction [wheels *spinning* on ice] —*n.* 1 the act of spinning or rotating something 2 a spinning or rotating movement 3 a moving along swiftly and smoothly 4 a ride or pleasure trip in a motor vehicle 5 any descent in which an airplane comes down nose first along a spiral path of large pitch and small radius 6 any sudden, steep downward movement ☆7 ⟦from the fact that the spin imparted to a ball in certain games affects its direction, bounce, etc.⟧ *a)* a particular emphasis or slant imparted to information in order to create a desired effect, such as a favorable public image for a politician *b)* the presenting of information in this way 8 *Physics a)* the intrinsic angular momentum of an elementary particle or photon, produced by rotation about its own axis *b)* the total angular momentum of a nuclide —**spin off** 1 to produce as an outgrowth or secondary benefit, product, development, etc. 2 to get rid of —☆**spin out** [Informal] to slide with a spinning or rotating movement: said of a vehicle that is out of control

spi·na bi·fi·da (spī′nə bif′ə də) ⟦ModL < L *spina* (see SPINE) + *bifida,* fem. of *bifidus,* BIFID⟧ a congenital defect or opening in the spinal column through which the spinal membranes or spinal cord may protrude, often resulting in hydrocephalus, paralysis, etc.

spin·ach (spin′ich) *n.* ⟦< MFr *espinach* < (? via ML *spinachia*) OSp *espinaca* < Ar *isbānakh* < Pers *aspanākh*⟧ 1 a plant (*Spinacia oleracea*) of the goosefoot family, with large, dark-green, juicy, edible leaves, usually eaten cooked 2 the leaves of this plant

spi·nal (spī′nəl) *adj.* ⟦LL *spinalis*⟧ 1 of or having to do with the spine or spinal cord 2 of a spine or needle-shaped process —*n.* a spinal anesthetic —**spi′nal·ly** *adv.*

spinal anesthesia *Surgery* anesthesia of the lower part of the body by the injection of an anesthetic into the spinal cord, usually in the lumbar region —**spinal anesthetic**

spinal canal the canal, or tube, formed by the vertebral arches, containing the spinal cord

spinal column the series of joined vertebrae forming the axial support for the skeleton; spine; backbone

spinal cord the thick cord of nerve tissue of the central nervous system, extending down the spinal canal from the medulla oblongata

spin casting SPINNING (*n.* 2) —**spin-cast** (spin′kast′) *vi.*

spin·dle (spin′dəl) *n.* ⟦ME (with intrusive *-d-*) < OE *spinel* < *spinnan,* to SPIN⟧ 1 a slender rod or pin used in spinning; specif., *a)* in hand spinning, a rounded rod, usually wooden, tapering toward each end, for twisting into thread the fibers pulled from the material on the distaff, and notched at one end so as to hold the thread *b)* on a spinning wheel, the rod by which the thread is twisted and on which it is then wound *c)* in a spinning machine, any of the rods holding the bobbins on which the spun thread is wound 2 a measure for yarn, equal to 14,400 yards in linen or 15,120 yards in cotton 3 a short turned piece or decorative rod, as a baluster or element in some chair backs 4 any rod, pin, or shaft that revolves or serves as an axis for a revolving part, as an axle, arbor, or mandrel 5 in a lathe, a shaftlike part (**live spindle**) that rotates while holding the thing to be turned, or a similar part (**dead spindle**) that does not rotate ☆6 a metal spike on a base, on which papers are impaled for temporary filing: also **spindle file** 7 *Biol.* the spindle-shaped bundle of nuclear fibers formed during one stage of mitosis 8 *Lockmaking* the small, square shaft passing through a door lock, to which the doorknobs are attached 9 *Physics* HYDROMETER —*adj.* of or like a spindle or spindles —*vi.* **-dled, -dling** 1 to grow in a long, slender shape 2 to grow into a long, slender stalk or stem —*vt.* 1 to form into a spindle 2 to fit or equip with a spindle ☆3 to impale (papers, etc.) on a SPINDLE (sense 6)

spin·dle-leg·ged (-leg′id, -legd′; -lā′gid, -lāgd′) *adj.* having thin legs: also **spin′dle-shanked′** (-shaŋkt′)

spin·dle·legs (-legz′, -lāgz′) *pl.n.* thin legs —*n.* [Informal] a person with thin legs

spindle tree EUONYMUS

spin·dling (spind′liŋ) *adj.* SPINDLY

spin·dly (spind′lē) *adj.* **-dli·er, -dli·est** long or tall and very thin or slender, often to such a degree as to be or seem frail or weak

☆**spin doctor** [Slang] a person employed, as by a politician, to use SPIN (*n.* 7) in interpreting information or events

spin·drift (spin′drift′) *n.* ⟦earlier *spenedrift,* Scot var. of *spoondrift* < *spoon,* to scud (< ?) + DRIFT⟧ spray blown from a rough sea or surf

spine (spīn) *n.* ⟦ME < OFr *espine* < L *spina,* thorn, prickle, backbone: see SPIKE[1]⟧ 1 any of the stiff, sharp-pointed, superficial emergences on a plant, as on a rose, thistle, or cactus 2 *a)* a sharp process of bone *b)* any of the sharp, stiff projections on the bodies of certain animals, as the quill of a porcupine or a ray of a fish's fin *c)* anything resembling either of these projections 3 the spinal column; backbone 4 anything regarded as resembling a backbone, as *a)* a ridge of ground, crest of a hill, etc. *b)* the part of a bound book covering the backbone, and usually bearing the title and author's name ☆5 courage, willpower, etc.

spine-chill·ing (spīn′chil′iŋ) *adj.* inspiring a feeling of sudden fear or apprehension

spi·nel (spi nel′, spin′əl) *n.* ⟦Early ModE *spynel* < MFr *spinelle* < It *spinella,* dim. of *spina,* thorn, spine < L: see SPINE⟧ a variously colored, crystalline mineral, $MgAlO_4$, used as a gem; magnesium aluminum oxide

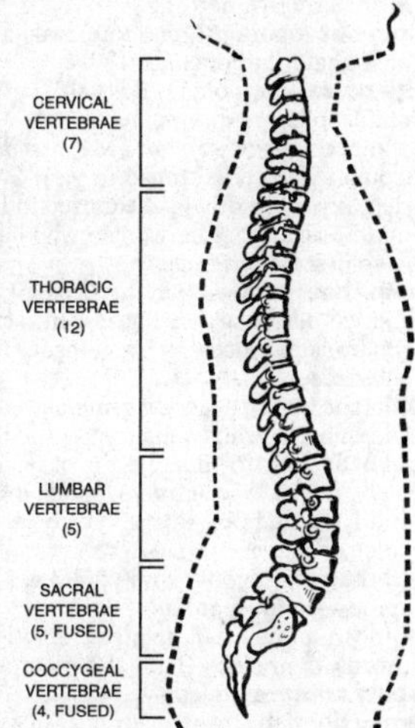

human spinal column

spine·less (spīn′lis) *adj.* 1 having no backbone; invertebrate 2 having a weak or flexible backbone 3 lacking courage, resistance, willpower, etc. 4 without spines, or thorny processes —**spine′less·ly** *adv.* —**spine′less·ness** *n.*

spi·nes·cent (spī nes′ənt) *adj.* ⟦LL *spinescens,* prp. of *spinescere,* to grow spiny < L *spina,* SPINE⟧ 1 spiny; having spines 2 becoming spiny or spinelike

spin·et (spin′it, spi net′) *n.* ⟦MFr *espinete* < It *spinetta,* said to be after its alleged inventor, G. *Spinetti,* but prob. < *spina,* thorn (< L, SPINE): so named from the pointed quills used to pluck the strings⟧ 1 an early, small variety of harpsichord with a single keyboard 2 *a)* a small upright piano of relatively low height *b)* a small electronic organ of similar design

spine-tin·gling (spīn′tiŋ′gliŋ) *adj.* very moving, thrilling, or terrifying

spin fishing SPINNING (*n.* 2)

spi·nif·er·ous (spī nif′ər əs) *adj.* ⟦L *spinifer* < *spina,* SPINE + -FEROUS⟧ bearing spines

spin·i·fex (spin′i feks′) *n.* ⟦ModL < L *spina,* SPINE + *facere,* to make, DO[1]⟧ any of a genus (*Spinifex*) of Australian grasses with pointed leaves and bristly seed heads

spin·i·ness (spī′nē nis) *n.* a spiny quality or condition

spin·na·ker (spin′ə kər) *n.* ⟦said to be < *spinx,* altered after *Sphinx,* name of a yacht which carried the sail⟧ a large, triangular, baggy headsail set on a boom, used on some racing yachts when running before the wind

spin·ner (spin′ər) *n.* a person or thing that spins; specif., *a)* a fishing lure with attached blades that revolve or flutter when drawn through the water; also, any of these blades *b)* a domelike cap that fits over the hub of an airplane propeller and rotates with it

spin·ner·et (spin′ə ret′) *n.* ⟦dim. of prec.⟧ 1 the organ in spiders, caterpillars, etc., that spins thread for webs or cocoons 2 a thimblelike device or metal plate with tiny holes through which a solution is forced in the making of synthetic fibers

spin·ney (spin′ē) *n., pl.* **-neys** ⟦ME *spenne,* thorn hedge < OFr *espinei* < VL **spinēta,* for L *spinetum* < *spina,* thorn, SPINE⟧ [Chiefly Brit.] a small wood; copse

spin·ning (spin′iŋ) *n.* 1 the act of making thread or yarn from fibers or filaments 2 the act of fishing with a rod that has a fixed spool, a light line, and light lures —*adj.* that spins or is used in spinning

spinning jenny ⟦orig. uncert.⟧ an early spinning machine with several spindles, for spinning more than one thread at a time

spinning mule MULE[1] (sense 3)

spinning reel a type of fishing reel with a nonrevolving spool and a bail for controlling the unwinding and rewinding of the line

spinning wheel a simple spinning machine for making thread or yarn, fitted with a single spindle that is driven by the rotation of a large wheel spun by a foot treadle or by hand

spin·off (spin′ôf′) *n.* 1 *a)* the divestiture by a corporation of some of its assets or operations, accomplished by distributing to its stockholders shares of a new company formed to assume control over the divested parts *b)* the divestiture of a subsidiary by distributing its shares in this way *c)* the new company or subsidiary so divested 2 a secondary benefit, product, development, etc., as a television series built around a character, situation, etc. from another series

spi·nose (spī′nōs′) *adj.* ⟦L *spinosus* < *spina,* SPINE⟧ full of or covered with spines —**spi′nose·ly** *adv.*

spi·nos·i·ty (spī näs′ə tē) *n., pl.* **-ties** ⟦LL *spinositas*⟧ 1 the condition of being spinose 2 something spinose, or thorny, nettling, etc.

spi·nous (spī′nəs) *adj.* ⟦L *spinosus*⟧ 1 SPINOSE 2 like a spine or thorn in form 3 thorny; nettling

☆**spin·out** (spin′out′) *n.* [Informal] a spinning slide or skid by a motor vehicle that is out of control

Spi·no·za (spi nō′zə), **Ba·ruch** (bə ro͞ok′) (Eng. *Benedict*) 1632-77; Du. philosopher

spin·ster (spin′stər) *n.* ⟦ME < *spinnen,* to SPIN + -STER⟧ 1 [Archaic] a woman who spins thread or yarn 2 [Archaic] a woman who is not married, divorced, or widowed: used in legal documents 3 [Old-fashioned] a middle-aged or older woman who has never married —**spin′ster·hood′** *n.* —**spin′ster·ish** *adj.*

spin·thar·i·scope (spin thar′ə skōp′) *n.* ⟦< Gr *spintharis,* a spark + -SCOPE⟧ a small device with a fluorescent screen, for visually observing the scintillations produced by the impact of alpha rays given off by a radioactive substance

☆**spin the bottle** a kissing game played by young people, in which a bottle is laid on its side and spun to point to the one to be kissed

spin·to (spēn′tô) *adj.* ⟦It, pp. of *spingere,* to push, spur on < VL *expingere* < L *ex-,* intens. + *pangere,* to fasten, drive in: see FANG⟧ *Music* both dramatic and lyric: said of a singer's voice [*a spinto* soprano] —*n., pl.* **-tos** a spinto voice or singer

spi·nule (spī′nyo͞ol′, spin′yo͞ol′) *n.* ⟦L *spinula,* dim. of *spina,* SPINE⟧ a small spine —**spi′nu·lose′** *adj.*

spin·y (spī′nē) *adj.* **spin′i·er, spin′i·est** 1 covered with or having spines, thorns, or prickles 2 full of difficulties; thorny 3 spine-shaped

spiny anteater ECHIDNA

spiny dogfish any of an order (Squaliformes) of sharks having a sharp single spine in front of each dorsal fin; esp., a small shark (*Squalus acanthias*)

spin·y-finned (spī′nē find′) *adj.* having fins in which the membrane is supported by spines

spin·y-head·ed worm (-hed′id) ACANTHOCEPHALAN

spiny lobster any of a family (Palinuridae) of lobsters lacking large pincers and having a spiny shell

spin·y-rayed (-rād′) *adj.* 1 having pointed, stiff rays: said of a fin 2 SPINY-FINNED

spir- *combining form* SPIRO-[2]: used before a vowel

spi·ra·cle (spir′ə kəl, spī′rə-) *n.* ⟦ME < L *spiraculum* < *spirare,* to breathe: see SPIRIT⟧ 1 a small opening allowing the outer air to come through into a confined space; air hole 2 *Geol.* a small vent formed on the surface of a thick lava flow 3 *Zool.* an aperture for breathing, as *a)* any of the small external openings of the tracheal respiratory system in most terrestrial arthropods, ordinarily along the sides of certain thoracic and abdominal segments; stigma *b)* any of various similar openings for the passage of air or respiratory water, as in tadpoles *c)* BLOWHOLE (sense 1) —**spi·rac·u·lar** (spī rak′yo͞o lər, spi-) *adj.*

spi·rae·a (spī rē′ə) *n. alt. sp. of* SPIREA

spi·ral (spī′rəl) *adj.* ⟦ML *spiralis* < L *spira,* a coil < Gr *speira:* see SPIRE[1]⟧ 1 circling around a central point in a flat, two-dimensional curve that constantly increases (or decreases) in size 2 circling around a central axis in a conical or cylindrical, three-dimensional curve —*n.* 1 a spiral curve occurring in a single plane 2 a spiral curve occurring in a series of planes; helix 3 something having a spiral form, as a wire for holding sheets in some notebooks 4 a spiral path or flight [the descending *spiral* of a falling leaf] 5 a section or segment of a spiral 6 a general course or trend that gains continuously in strength, momentum, etc. [an inflationary *spiral* ending in financial collapse] ☆7 *Football* a kick or pass in which the ball rotates on its longer axis as it moves through the air —*vi.* **-raled** or **-ralled, -ral·ing** or **-ral·ling** to move in or form a spiral —*vt.* to cause to move in or form a spiral —**spi′ral·ly** *adv.*

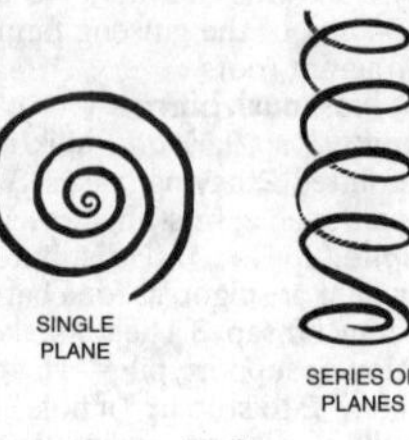

spirals

spiral galaxy a galaxy having the visible form of a spiral: also **spiral nebula**

spi·rant (spī′rənt) *n.* ⟦< L *spirans,* prp. of *spirare,* to breathe: see SPIRIT⟧ *Phonet.* a consonantal sound, as (sh) or (v), produced by the passage of breath through the partially closed oral cavity; fricative —*adj.* having the nature of a spirant; fricative

spire[1] (spīr) *n.* ⟦Fr < L *spira* < Gr *speira* < IE base **sper-,* to turn, wrap > Latvian *sprangāt,* to lace up⟧ 1 a spiral or coil 2 any of the convolutions of a spiral or coil 3 *Zool.* the upper part of a spiral shell of a gastropod

spire[2] (spīr) *n.* ⟦ME < OE *spir,* akin to ON *spíra:* for IE base see SPIKE[1]⟧ 1 a sprout, spike, or stalk of a plant, a blade of grass, etc. 2 the top part of a pointed, tapering object or structure, as a mountain peak 3 anything that tapers to a point, as a pointed structure capping a tower or steeple —*vi.* **spired, spir′ing** to extend upward, tapering to a point; shoot up or rise in, or put forth, a spire or spires —**spired** *adj.*

spi·re·a (spī rē′ə) *n.* ⟦< ModL *Spiraea* < L *spiraea,* meadowsweet < Gr *speiraia* < *speira:* see SPIRE[1]⟧ any of a genus (*Spiraea*) of shrubs of the rose family, with dense clusters of small, pink or white flowers

spi·reme (spī′rēm) *n.* ⟦Gr *speirēma,* a coil < *speira:* see SPIRE[1]⟧ *Biol.* a thin, threadlike tangle of chromatin at the beginning of the prophase in mitosis

spi·rif·er·ous (spī rif′ər əs) *adj.* ⟦< ModL *spirifer:* see SPIRE[1] & -FEROUS⟧ *Zool.* characterized by a spire, or spiral structure, as some shells, or by spiral appendages, as a brachiopod

spi·ril·lum (spī ril′əm) *n., pl.* **-la** (-ə) ⟦ModL, dim. of L *spira:* see SPIRE[1]⟧ 1 any of a genus (*Spirillum*) of bacteria having the form of a spiral thread and characterized by flagella 2 any of various similar microorganisms

spir·it (spir′it) *n.* ⟦ME < OFr *espirit* < L *spiritus,* breath, courage, vigor, the soul, life, in LL(Ec), spirit < *spirare,* to blow, breathe < IE base **(s)peis-,* to blow > (prob.) Norw *fisa,* to puff, blow, OSlav *piskati,* to pipe, whistle⟧ 1 *a)* the life principle, esp. in human beings, originally regarded as inherent in the breath or as infused by a deity *b)* SOUL (sense 1) 2 the thinking, motivating, feeling part of a person, often as distinguished from the body; mind; intelligence 3 [*also* **S-**] life, will, consciousness, thought, etc., regarded as separate from matter 4 a supernatural being, esp., *a)* one haunting or possessing a person, house, etc., as a ghost, or thought of as inhabiting a certain region *b)* one of a certain good (or evil) character or influence, as an angel, demon, fairy, or elf 5 an individual person or personality thought of as showing or having some specific quality [the brave *spirits* who pioneered] 6 [*usually pl.*] frame of mind; disposition; mood; temper [in high *spirits*] 7 vivacity, courage, vigor, enthusiasm, etc. [to answer with *spirit*] 8 enthusiasm and loyalty [school *spirit*] 9 real meaning; true intention [to follow the *spirit* if not the letter of the law] 10 a pervading animating principle, essential or characteristic quality, or prevailing tendency or attitude [the *spirit* of the Renaissance] 11 a divine animating influence or inspiration 12 [*usually pl.*] strong alcoholic liquor produced by distillation 13 [Obs.] *a)* any of certain substances or fluids thought of as permeating organs of the body *b)* *Alchemy* sulfur, sal ammoniac, mercury, or orpiment 14 [*often pl.*] *Chem.* *a)* any liquid produced by distillation, as from wood, shale, etc. [*spirits* of turpentine] *b)* ALCOHOL (sense 1) 15 *Dyeing* a solution of a tin salt, etc., used as a mordant 16 [*often pl.*] *Pharmacy* an alcoholic solution of a volatile or essential substance [*spirits* of camphor] —*vt.* 1 to inspirit, animate, encourage, cheer, etc.: (often with *up*) **2** to carry (*away, off*, etc.) secretly and swiftly, or in some mysterious way —***adj.*** **1** *a)* of spirits or spiritualism ☆*b)* believed to be manifested by spirits [*spirit* rapping] **2** operating by the burning of alcohol [*a spirit* lamp] —**in spirit** furnishing inspiration or moral support, but otherwise not physically present [he could not attend, but he's here with us *in spirit*] —**out of spirits** sad; depressed —**the Spirit** HOLY SPIRIT

spir·it·ed (-id) ***adj.*** **1** full of spirit; lively; energetic; animated **2** having a (specified) character, mood, or disposition: used in comb. [public-*spirited*, mean-*spirited*] —**spir′it·ed·ly** ***adv.*** —**spir′it·ed·ness** ***n.***

☆**spirit gum** a solution of gum arabic in ether, etc. used as in the theater to attach false hair, whiskers, etc. to the face

spir·it·ism (-iz′əm) ***n.*** SPIRITUALISM —**spir′it·ist** ***n., adj.*** —**spir′it·is′tic** ***adj.***

spir·it·less (-lis) ***adj.*** lacking spirit, energy, or vigor; listless; depressed —**spir′it·less·ly** ***adv.*** —**spir′it·less·ness** ***n.***

spirit level ⟦so named because it often contains alcohol, to prevent freezing in cold weather⟧ LEVEL (***n.*** 1)

spi·ri·to·so (spir′i tō′sō; *It* spē′rē tô′sô) ***adj., adv.*** ⟦It⟧ *Musical Direction* (in a) lively or spirited (manner)

spir·it·ous (spir′i təs) ***adj.*** **1** SPIRITUOUS **2** [Obs.] lively; high-spirited

spirits of ammonia a 10% solution of ammonia in alcohol: also **spirit of ammonia**

spirits of hartshorn *old-fashioned term for* AMMONIUM HYDROXIDE: also **spirit of hartshorn**

spirits of turpentine TURPENTINE (sense 3): also **spirit of turpentine**

spirits of wine ALCOHOL (sense 1): also **spirit of wine**

spir·it·u·al (spir′i chə wəl; *also*, spir′i chəl) ***adj.*** ⟦ME *spirituel* < OFr < LL(Ec) *spiritualis* < L, of breathing or air⟧ **1** of the spirit or the soul as distinguished from the body or material matters **2** of, from, or concerned with the intellect; intellectual **3** of or consisting of spirit; not corporeal **4** characterized by the ascendancy of the spirit; showing much refinement of thought and feeling **5** of religion or the church; sacred, devotional, or ecclesiastical; not lay or temporal **6** spiritualistic or supernatural —***n.*** ☆**1** any of a type of American folk hymn; specif., any of such songs originating among S U.S. blacks in the 18th and 19th cent. combining African and European musical elements **2** [*pl.*] religious or church matters —**spir′it·u·al·ly** ***adv.*** —**spir′it·u·al·ness** ***n.***

spir·it·u·al·ism (-iz′əm) ***n.*** ☆**1** *a)* the belief that the dead survive as spirits that can communicate with the living, esp. with the help of a third party (*medium*) *b)* any practice arising from this belief **2** [Archaic] the philosophical doctrine that all reality is in essence spiritual; idealism **3** spirituality; spiritual quality —**spir′it·u·al·ist** ***n.*** —**spir′it·u·al·is′tic** ***adj.*** —**spir′it·u·al·is′ti·cal·ly** ***adv.***

spir·it·u·al·i·ty (spir′i cho͞o al′ə tē) ***n., pl.*** **-ties** **1** spiritual character, quality, or nature **2** religious devotion or piety **3** [*often pl.*] the rights, jurisdiction, tithes, etc. belonging to the church or to an ecclesiastic **4** the fact or state of being incorporeal

spir·it·u·al·ize (spir′i chə wəl īz′; *also*, -chəl īz′) ***vt.*** **-ized′**, **-iz′ing** **1** to make spiritual; deprive of materiality or worldliness **2** to give a spiritual sense or meaning to —**spir′it·u·al·i·za′tion** ***n.***

spir·it·u·al·ty (spir′i chə wəl tē; *also*, -chəl tē) ***n., pl.*** **-ties** **1** the clergy **2** [*often pl.*] SPIRITUALITY (sense 3)

spi·ri·tu·el (spē rē tü el′) ***adj.*** ⟦Fr: see SPIRITUAL⟧ having or showing a refined nature or, esp., a quick, graceful wit or mind

spir·it·u·ous (spir′i cho͞o əs) ***adj.*** ⟦< L *spiritus*, SPIRIT + -OUS⟧ of, like, or containing alcohol: said esp. of distilled as opposed to fermented beverages —**spir′it·u·os′i·ty** (-äs′ə tē) ***n.***

spi·ro-[1] (spī′rō, -rə) ⟦< L *spirare*, to breathe: see SPIRIT⟧ *combining form* respiration [*spirograph*]

spi·ro-[2] (spī′rō, -rə) ⟦< Gr *speira*, a coil: see SPIRE[1]⟧ *combining form* spiral or coil [*spirochete*]

spi·ro·chete (spī′rō kēt′) ***n.*** ⟦< ModL *Spirochaeta*, genus name < Gr *speira*, SPIRE[1] + *chaitē*, hair⟧ any of an order (Spirochaetales) of slender, flexible, spiral-shaped bacteria, including some species that cause disease, some that are parasitic, and some that are free-living: also sp. **spi′ro·chaete′** —**spi′ro·chet′al** (-kēt′'l) ***adj.***

spi·ro·chet·o·sis (spī′rō kē tō′sis) ***n.*** ⟦ModL < *Spirochaeta*, genus name (see prec.) + -OSIS⟧ any disease, as syphilis or relapsing fever, caused by spirochetes

spi·ro·gy·ra (spī′rō jī′rə) ***n.*** ⟦ModL < Gr *speira*, SPIRE[1] + *gyros*, a ring: see GYRATE⟧ any of a genus (*Spirogyra*, family Zygnemataceae) of freshwater green algae containing spiral chlorophyll bands in their cylindrical cells

spi·roid (spī′roid′) ***adj.*** ⟦ModL *spiroides*: see SPIRE[1] & -OID⟧ like a spiral; having a spiral form

spi·rom·e·ter (spī räm′ət ər) ***n.*** ⟦SPIRO-[1] + -METER⟧ an instrument for measuring the breathing capacity of the lungs —**spi′ro·met′ric** (-rə me′trik) ***adj.*** —**spi·rom′e·try** (-räm′ə trē) ***n.***

spirt (spurt) ***vt., vi., n.*** *archaic sp. of* SPURT

spir·u·la (spir′yə lə, spī′ro͝o lə) ***n., pl.*** **-lae′** (-lē′) ⟦ModL, name of the genus, dim. of L *spira*: see SPIRE[1]⟧ any of a genus (*Spirula*) of two-gilled, deep-water cephalopods, having a flat spiral shell with a series of chambers

spi·ru·li·na (spī′rə lī′nə, -lē′-) ***n.*** ⟦ModL < *spirula*, small coil < L *spira*, a coil: see SPIRE[1]⟧ [*sometimes* **S-**] **1** any of a genus (*Spirulina*) of blue-green algae, some of which are dried and used as a food or a nutritional supplement **2** this food or supplement

spir·y[1] (spīr′ē) ***adj.*** **spir′i·er**, **spir′i·est** [Old Poet.] spiral; coiled; curled

spir·y[2] (spīr′ē) ***adj.*** **spir′i·er**, **spir′i·est** **1** of, or having the form of, a spire, steeple, etc. **2** having many spires

spit[1] (spit) ***n.*** ⟦ME *spite* < OE *spitu*, akin to OHG *spizzi*, sharp: for IE base see SPIKE[1]⟧ **1** a thin, pointed rod or bar on which meat is impaled for broiling or roasting over a fire or before other direct heat **2** a narrow point of land, or a narrow reef or shoal, extending into a body of water —***vt.*** **spit′ted**, **spit′ting** to fix or impale on or as on a spit —**spit′ter** ***n.***

spit[2] (spit) ***vt.*** **spit** or **spat**, **spit′ting** ⟦ME *spitten* < OE *spittan*, akin to Dan *spytte*: for IE base see SPEW⟧ **1** to eject from within the mouth **2** to eject, throw (*out*), emit, or utter explosively [to *spit* out an oath] **3** to light (a fuse) —***vi.*** **1** to eject saliva from the mouth; expectorate **2** to rain or snow lightly or briefly **3** to make an explosive hissing noise, as an angry cat **4** to express contempt or hatred by or as if by spitting saliva (*on* or *at*) **5** to sputter, as frying fat —***n.*** **1** the act of spitting **2** saliva; spittle **3** something like saliva, as the frothy secretion of certain insects **4** a light, brief shower of rain or fall of snow **5** ⟦< earlier phr., *as like (someone) as if spit out of (his) mouth*⟧ [Old Informal] a perfect likeness or exact image, as of a person: with *the* —**spit up** to regurgitate or cough up

spit·al (spit′'l) ***n.*** ⟦respelling (based on HOSPITAL) of earlier *spittle* < ME *spitel* < ML *hospitale*⟧ [Obs.] **1** a hospital, esp. one for the poor or for lepers, etc. **2** a travelers' wayside shelter

spit and polish precise attention to orderliness, neatness, etc., as in the military

☆**spit·ball** (spit′bôl′) ***n.*** **1** a small piece of paper chewed up into a wad for throwing as a schoolboy prank **2** *Baseball* a pitch, now illegal, thrown with the fingers or a portion of the ball moistened to affect its flight

☆**spit curl** a curled lock of hair dampened, as with spit, and pressed flat against the forehead or temple

spite (spīt) ***n.*** ⟦ME, aphetic < *despite*: see DESPITE⟧ **1** *a)* a mean or evil feeling toward another, characterized by the inclination to hurt, humiliate, annoy, frustrate, etc.; ill will; malice *b)* [Archaic] an instance of this; a grudge **2** [Obs.] something annoying or irritating —***vt.*** **spit′ed**, **spit′ing** to behave in a spiteful manner toward; vent one's spite upon by hurting, annoying, frustrating, etc. —**in spite of** in defiance of; regardless of; notwithstanding

spite·ful (spīt′fəl) ***adj.*** full of or showing spite; purposefully annoying; malicious —**SYN.** VINDICTIVE —**spite′ful·ly** ***adv.*** —**spite′ful·ness** ***n.***

spit·fire (spit′fīr′) ***n.*** a person, esp. a woman or girl, who is easily aroused to outbursts of anger

Spit·head (spit′hed′) *see* SOLENT, The

Spits·ber·gen (spits′bur′gən) **1** group of Norwegian islands in the Arctic Ocean, constituting the major part of Svalbard: 23,641 sq mi (61,230 sq km) **2** SVALBARD

spit·ter (spit′ər) ***n.*** **1** a person or animal that spits saliva, etc. ☆**2** [Informal] SPITBALL (sense 2)

spitting cobra any of various cobras, esp. the ringhals and a small, black-necked African cobra (*Naja nigricollis*), that spray jets of venom at the eyes of an aggressor

spitting image ⟦altered < earlier *spit and image* < SPIT[2] (***n.*** 5)⟧ [Informal] a perfect likeness or exact image: typically a hyperbolic use: often with *the* [a son who is the *spitting image* of his father]

spit·tle (spit′'l) ***n.*** ⟦earlier *spettle* < ME *spetil* < OE *spætl*, var. of *spatl*: for IE base see SPEW⟧ **1** saliva; spit **2** the frothy secretion of larval spittlebugs

☆**spit·tle·bug** (-bug′) ***n.*** any of a family (Cercopidae) of small, leaping homopteran insects whose nymphs produce white frothy masses on plants

☆**spit·toon** (spi to͞on′) ***n.*** ⟦< SPIT[2]⟧ a lidless pot for spitting into; cuspidor

spitz (spits) ***n.*** ⟦Ger < *spitz*, pointed < OHG *spizzi*: see SPIT[1]⟧ in the U.S., any of several dogs, as the chow, Samoyed, or Eskimo dog, characterized by a long, dense coat, erect, pointed ears, and a tail that curls over the back; esp., a variety of Pomeranian, usually white

spiv (spiv) ***n.*** ⟦prob. var. of *spiff*: see SPIFFY⟧ [Brit. Slang] a man who lives by his wits, without doing any regular or honest work, esp. one engaged in petty, shady dealings

splanch·nic (splaŋk′nik) ***adj.*** ⟦ModL *splanchnicus* < Gr *splanchnikos* < *splanchnon*, gut: for IE base see SPLEEN⟧ of the viscera; visceral

splanch·no- (splaŋk′nō) ⟦< Gr *splanchnon*: see prec.⟧ *combining form* the viscera [*splanchnology*]: also, before a vowel, **splanchn-**

splash (splash) ***vt.*** ⟦intens. extension of PLASH[2]⟧ **1** to cause (a liquid substance) to scatter and fall in drops or blobs **2** to dash or scatter a liquid substance, mud, etc. on, so as to wet or soil **3** to cause to splash a liquid [to *splash* one's feet in puddles] **4** to make (one's way) by splashing **5** to mark or spot by or as by splashing [a glade *splashed* with sunlight] **6** to display conspicuously [scandal *splashed* all over the front page] —***vi.*** **1** to dash or scatter a liquid substance about **2** to fall, strike, or scatter with a splash or splashes [rain *splashing* against the window] **3** to move with splashes —***n.*** **1** the act or sound of splashing **2** a mass of splashed water, mud, etc. **3** a spot or mark made by or as by splashing **4** a patch of color, light, etc. **5** a small amount of a liquid [a whiskey with a *splash* of soda water] **6** [Informal] a conspicuous or ostentatious display —**make a splash** [Informal] to attract great, often brief attention by doing something striking or ostentatious —**splash′er** ***n.***

splash·board (splash′bôrd′) ***n.*** **1** any screen or board protecting riders on a vehicle from being splashed in wet weather **2** a trap for closing a sluice or spillway **3** BACKSPLASH

☆**splash·down** (-doun′) ***n.*** a spacecraft's soft landing on the sea, permitting the recovery of rockets, instruments, etc.

☆**splash guard** any piece or device designed to protect against or deflect splashing liquid, specif., one behind a wheel of a motor vehicle for stopping water, mud, etc. from splashing against the vehicle body

splash·y (-ē) *adj.* **splash′i·er, splash′i·est** 1 splashing; making splashes 2 liable to splash; wet, muddy, etc. 3 covered or marked with splashes 4 [Informal] attracting much notice or attention; spectacular; striking —**splash′i·ly** *adv.* —**splash′i·ness** *n.*

splat¹ (splat) *n.* ⟦via dial. < base of SPLIT⟧ a thin, flat piece of wood, esp. one forming the central, upright element in the back of a chair

splat² (splat) *n., interj.* ⟦echoic⟧ (used to suggest) a splattering or wet, slapping sound —*vi.* **splat′ted, splat′ting** 1 to make such a sound 2 to flatten on impact

splat·ter (splat′ər) *n., vt., vi.* ⟦altered (infl. by SPLASH) < SPATTER⟧ spatter or splash

splay (splā) *vt., vi.* ⟦ME *splaien,* aphetic < *displaien,* to DISPLAY⟧ 1 to spread out or apart; expand; extend: often with *out* 2 to make or be beveled or sloping —*n.* ⟦< the v.⟧ 1 a sloping or beveled surface or angle, as of the side of a doorway 2 a spreading; expansion; enlargement —*adj.* 1 sloping, spreading, or turning outward 2 broad and flat 3 awkwardly awry

splay·foot (splā′foot′) *n., pl.* **-feet′** 1 a foot that is flat and turned outward 2 the condition of having feet of this kind —*adj.* of or having splayfoot: also **splay′foot′ed**

spleen (splēn) *n.* ⟦ME *splen* < OFr *esplen* < L *splen* < Gr *splēn,* spleen < IE **sp(h)elĝh-* > Sans *plīhan,* OSlav *slězena,* spleen⟧ 1 a large, vascular, lymphatic organ in the upper left part of the abdominal cavity of vertebrates, near the stomach: it has various functions in modifying the structure of the blood, and was formerly regarded as the seat of certain emotions 2 *a)* malice; spite; bad temper *b)* [Archaic] melancholy; low spirits *c)* [Obs.] a whim or caprice

spleen·ful (splēn′fəl) *adj.* full of spleen; irritable, peevish, spiteful, etc.

spleen·wort (-wurt′) *n.* any of a genus (*Asplenium,* family Aspleniaceae) of ferns with simple or compound fronds and elongated sori

splen- (splēn, splen) *combining form* SPLENO-: used before a vowel

splen·dent (splen′dənt) *adj.* ⟦LME < L *splendens,* prp. of *splendere:* see fol.⟧ *archaic var. of* RESPLENDENT

splen·did (splen′did) *adj.* ⟦L *splendidus* < *splendere,* to shine < IE **splend-* < base **(s)p(h)el-,* to gleam, shine > Sans *sphulinga,* a spark, Gr *splēndos,* ashes, Ger *flink,* lively⟧ 1 having or showing splendor; specif., *a)* shining; lustrous; brilliant *b)* magnificent; gorgeous 2 worthy of high praise; grand; glorious; illustrious [*a splendid* accomplishment] 3 very good; excellent; fine [*splendid* weather] —**splen′did·ly** *adv.* —**splen′did·ness** *n.*

splen·dif·er·ous (splen dif′ər əs) *adj.* ⟦prob. a mod. recoinage (< fol. + -FEROUS) of obs. *splendiferous* < ME < ML *splendiferus,* for LL *splendorifer* < L *splendor* + *-fer,* -FER⟧ [Informal] gorgeous; splendid: a jocularly pretentious usage —**splen·dif′er·ous·ly** *adv.* —**splen·dif′er·ous·ness** *n.*

splen·dor (splen′dər) *n.* ⟦ME *splendure* < OFr *splendeur* < L *splendor* < *splendere,* to shine: see SPLENDID⟧ 1 great luster or brightness; brilliance 2 magnificent richness or glory; pomp; grandeur —**splen′dor·ous** (-dər əs) *adj.,* **splen′drous** (-drəs)

splen·dour (splen′dər) *n. Brit. sp. of* SPLENDOR

sple·nec·to·my (spli nek′tə mē) *n., pl.* **-mies** ⟦SPLEN- + -ECTOMY⟧ the surgical removal of the spleen

sple·net·ic (spli net′ik) *adj.* ⟦LL *spleneticus*⟧ 1 of the spleen; splenic 2 bad-tempered, irritable, peevish, spiteful, etc.; spleenful 3 [Obs.] melancholy Also **sple·net′i·cal** —*n.* a spleenful person —**SYN.** IRRITABLE —**sple·net′i·cal·ly** *adv.*

splen·ic (splen′ik, splēn′-) *adj.* ⟦L *splenicus* < Gr *splēnikos*⟧ 1 of or having to do with the spleen 2 in or near the spleen

sple·ni·us (splē′nē əs) *n., pl.* **-ni·i′** (-nē ī′) ⟦ModL < L *splenium,* a patch, plaster < Gr *splēnion,* dim. of *splēn,* SPLEEN⟧ either of two large, flat muscles at the back of the neck, serving to rotate and extend the head and rotate and flex the neck —**sple′ni·al** *adj.*

sple·no- (splē′nō, splen′ə) ⟦< Gr *splēn* (gen. *splēnos*), SPLEEN⟧ *combining form* the spleen [*splenomegaly*]

sple·no·meg·a·ly (splē′nə meg′ə lē, splen′ə-) *n.* ⟦ModL: see prec., MEGALO- & -Y³⟧ enlargement of the spleen

splice (splīs) *vt.* **spliced, splic′ing** ⟦MDu *splissen,* akin to *splitten,* to SPLIT⟧ 1 to join or unite (ropes or rope ends) by weaving together the end strands 2 to join the ends of (pieces of lumber) by overlapping and binding or bolting together 3 to fasten the ends of (wire, film, audiotape, etc.) together, as by twisting, soldering, cementing, etc. 4 *Genetics* in fashioning recombinant DNA, to insert (a gene, DNA, etc.) into genetic material that has had some portion of its DNA removed —*n.* a joint or joining made by splicing —**splic′er** *n.*

splices

spliff (splif) *n.* ⟦< ?⟧ [Slang] a marijuana cigarette

spline (splīn) *n.* ⟦< E Anglian dial., prob. akin to Norw dial. *splindra,* a large, flat splinter: for IE base see SPLIT⟧ 1 a long, flat, pliable strip, as of wood or metal, esp. one used in drawing curves 2 *a)* a flat key or strip that fits into a groove or slot between parts *b)* the groove or slot into which it fits —*vt.* **splined, splin′ing** to fit with a spline

splint (splint) *n.* ⟦ME *splente* < MDu or MLowG *splinte:* for IE base see SPLIT⟧ 1 a thin strip of wood or cane woven together with others to make baskets, chair seats, etc. 2 a thin strip of metal used in overlapping construction with others to make medieval armor 3 a thin, rigid strip of wood, metal, etc. set along a broken bone to keep the pieces in place or used to keep a part of the body in a fixed position 4 a bony growth or tumor on the cannon bone of a horse, mule, etc. —*vt.* to fit, support, or hold in place with or as with a splint or splints

splint bone in horses and similar animals, either of two small bones, one on each side of the cannon bone

splin·ter (splin′tər) *vt., vi.* ⟦ME < MDu, akin to *splinte,* SPLINT⟧ 1 to break or split into thin, sharp pieces 2 to break into small parts or into groups with divergent views; fragment —*n.* 1 a thin, sharp piece of wood, bone, etc., made by splitting or breaking; sliver 2 a splinter group —*adj.* designating a group that separates from a main party, church, etc. because of divergent views —**SYN.** BREAK

splin·ter·y (-ē) *adj.* 1 easily splintered 2 of or like a splinter 3 resulting in splinters, as a fracture 4 full of splinters; splintered

split (split) *vt.* **split, split′ting** ⟦MDu *splitten,* akin to MHG *splīzen* < IE base **(s)plei-,* to split, crack > FLINT⟧ 1 to separate, cut, or divide into two or more parts; cause to separate along the grain or length; break into layers 2 to break or tear apart by force; burst; rend 3 to divide into parts or shares; portion out [*to split* the cost] ☆4 to cast (one's vote) or mark (one's ballot) for candidates of more than one party 5 to cause (a group, political party, etc.) to separate into divisions or factions; disunite 6 *Chem., Physics a)* to break (a molecule) into atoms or into smaller molecules *b)* to produce nuclear fission in (an atom) 7 *Finance* to divide (stock) by substituting some multiple of the original shares that will usually have the same aggregate par value as the old, but a proportionately lower value per share —*vi.* 1 to separate lengthwise into two or more parts; separate along the grain or length 2 to break or tear apart; burst; rend 3 to separate or break up through failure to agree, etc.: often with *up* 4 [Informal] to divide something with another or others, each taking a share [*winners split*] ☆5 [Slang] to leave a place; depart 6 [Brit. Slang] to inform (*on* an accomplice) —*n.* 1 the act or process of splitting 2 the result of splitting; specif., *a)* a break; fissure; crack; tear *b)* a breach or division in a group, between persons, etc. 3 a splinter; sliver 4 a single thickness of hide split horizontally 5 a flexible strip of wood, as osier, used in basket making ☆6 a confection made of a split banana or other fruit with ice cream, nuts, sauces, whipped cream, etc. 7 [*often pl.*] the feat, esp. in gymnastics, of spreading the legs apart until they lie flat on the floor, etc. in a straight line, the body remaining upright 8 [Informal] *a)* a small bottle of carbonated water, wine, etc., usually about six ounces *b)* a drink or portion half the usual size 9 [Informal] a share, as of loot or booty 10 *Bowling* an arrangement of pins, after the first bowl of a frame, in which the pins are so widely separated as to make a spare extremely difficult —*adj.* 1 divided or separated along the length or grain 2 divided, separated, or disunited —**SYN.** BREAK —**split off** to break off or separate as by splitting

Split (splēt) seaport in Croatia, on the Adriatic

☆**split decision** a decision in a boxing match that is not one made unanimously by the judges and referee

split end 1 a tip of human hair that has split apart, as from excessive dryness: *usually used in pl.* ☆2 *Football* an offensive end positioned away from the other linemen, often as a wide receiver: cf. TIGHT END

☆**split-fin·ger fastball** (split′fiŋ′gər) *Baseball* a type of fastball that sinks abruptly as it nears home plate, thrown with the grip used for a forkball: also **split′-fin′gered fastball**

split infinitive *Gram.* an infinitive with an adverb or other modifier placed between *to* and the verb form (Ex.: he decided *to gradually change* his methods): although some object to this construction, many writers use split infinitives where ambiguity or wrong emphasis would otherwise result

split-lev·el (-lev′əl) *adj.* designating or of a type of house with floor levels staggered in such a way that each level is about a half story above or below the adjacent one, with stairs between —*n.* a house having such a configuration of floors

☆**split pea** a green or yellow pea that has been shelled, dried, and split: used esp. for making soup

split personality 1 SCHIZOPHRENIA (sense 1) 2 *nontechnical term for* MULTIPLE PERSONALITY DISORDER

split-rail (split′rāl′) *adj.* designating or of a fence made with rails split from logs

split screen *Film, TV* the technique of showing two or more images simultaneously and separately on the screen —**split′-screen′** *adj.*

split second a fraction of a second: often a hyperbolic use —**split′-sec′ond** *adj.*

☆**split shift** a shift, or work period, divided into two parts that are separated by an interval longer than that of the usual meal or rest period

☆**splits·ville** (splits′vil′) *n.* [*also* **S-**] [Slang] the ending of an intimate relationship; esp., a divorce

split·ter (split′ər) *n.* 1 a person or thing that splits ☆2 [Informal] *Baseball* SPLIT-FINGER FASTBALL

☆**split ticket** a ballot cast for candidates of more than one party: opposed to STRAIGHT TICKET

split·ting (split′iŋ) *adj.* 1 that splits 2 *a)* aching severely: said of the head *b)* severe, as a headache

☆**split-up** (-up′) *n.* a breaking up or separating into two or more parts, units, groups, etc.

splodge (spläj) *n., vt.* **splodged, splodg′ing** [Brit.] *var. of* SPLOTCH

splotch (spläch) *n.* ⟦prob. blend of SPOT + BLOTCH⟧ a spot, splash, or stain, esp. one that is irregular — *vt., vi.* to mark or soil, or be marked or soiled, with a splotch or splotches —**splotch′y** *adj.* **splotch′i·er, splotch′i·est**

☆**splurge** (splurj) *n.* ⟦echoic blend of SPLASH & SURGE⟧ **1** [Old Informal] any very showy or self-indulgent display or effort **2** [Informal] a spell of extravagant spending —*vi.* **splurged, splurg′ing 1** [Old Informal] to make a showy display or effort **2** [Informal] to spend money extravagantly —**splurg′er** *n.*

splut·ter (splut′ər) *vi.* ⟦var. of SPUTTER⟧ **1** to make hissing or spitting sounds, or to throw off particles in an explosive way, as something frying; sputter **2** to speak hurriedly and confusedly, as when excited or embarrassed —*vt.* **1** to utter hurriedly and confusedly; sputter **2** to spatter —*n.* **1** a spluttering sound or utterance **2** a loud sputtering or splash —**splut′ter·er** *n.* —**splut′ter·y** *adj.*

Spock (späk), **Benjamin (McLane)** 1903-98; U.S. pediatrician, writer of books on child care, & social activist: called *Dr. Spock*

Spode (spōd) ⟦after Josiah *Spode* (1754-1827), Eng potter⟧ *trademark for* a type of fine china and earthenware

spod·u·mene (späj′o͞o mēn′) *n.* ⟦< Gr *spodumenos,* prp. of *spodousthai,* to be burned to ashes < *spodos,* ashes: from being reduced to an ashlike form before the blowpipe⟧ a variously colored, monoclinic mineral, $LiAl(Si_2O_6)$, that is an ore of lithium and is used as a gem; lithium aluminum silicate

spoil (spoil) *vt.* **spoiled** or [Brit.] **spoilt, spoil′ing** ⟦ME *spoilen* < MFr *espoillier* < L *spoliare,* to plunder < *spolium,* arms taken from a defeated foe, plunder, orig., hide stripped from an animal < IE base **(s)p(h)el-,* to split, tear off > SPALL, SPILL[1]⟧ **1** to damage or injure in such a way as to make useless, valueless, etc.; destroy **2** to mar or impair the enjoyment, quality, or functioning of [rain *spoiled* the picnic] **3** to overindulge so as to cause to demand or expect too much **4** [Archaic] *a)* to strip (a person) of goods, money, etc. by force *b)* to rob; pillage; plunder *c)* to seize (goods) by force —*vi.* **1** to be damaged or injured in such a way as to become useless, valueless, etc.; specif., to decay, as food **2** [Archaic] to pillage; plunder —*n.* ⟦ME *spoile* < MFr *espoille* < L *spolia,* pl.⟧ **1** [*usually pl.*] *a)* goods, territory, etc. taken by force in war; plunder; loot; booty ☆*b)* public offices to which the successful political party has the power of appointment **2** an object of plunder; prey **3** waste material removed in making excavations, etc. **4** [Archaic] the act of plundering; spoliation **5** [Obs.] damage; impairment —☆**be spoiling for a fight** to be aggressively eager for a fight or confrontation —**spoil′a·ble** *adj.*

SYN.—**spoil** (now, more commonly, **spoils**) refers to any property, territory, etc. taken in war by the conqueror; **pillage** suggests violence and destructiveness in the taking of spoils; **plunder** is equivalent to **pillage** but also applies to property taken by bandits, highwaymen, etc.; **booty** suggests plunder taken by a band or gang, to be divided among the members; **prize** refers specifically to spoils taken at sea, esp. the taking of an enemy warship or its cargo; **loot**, a more derogatory equivalent for any of the preceding, emphasizes the immorality or predatory nature of the act See also **decay, indulge, injure**

spoil·age (spoil′ij) *n.* **1** a spoiling or being spoiled **2** something spoiled or the amount spoiled

spoil·er (-ər) *n.* **1** a person or thing that spoils **2** a contestant, sports team, etc. having no chance of succeeding, but spoiling another's chances for success **3** any projecting device serving to break up airflow around a body; specif., *a)* a movable flap on the upper side of an airplane wing for increasing drag and decreasing lift *b)* a rigid, oblong fixture attached to an automobile to reduce drag **4** an instance of revealing, as in a review, a key part of the plot of a new book or movie

☆**spoils·man** (spoilz′mən) *n., pl.* **-men** (-mən) a person who aids a political party in order to share in the spoils, or one who advocates the spoils system

spoil·sport (spoil′spôrt′) *n.* a person who behaves in such a way as to ruin the pleasure of others

☆**spoils system** the system or practice of regarding and treating appointive public offices as the booty of the successful party in an election, to be distributed, with their opportunities for profit, among party workers

spoilt (spoilt) *vt., vi.* [Brit.] *pt. & pp. of* SPOIL

Spo·kane (spō kan′, -kān′; spō′kan′) ⟦< ? Salish *spokanee,* sun⟧ city in E Wash.

spoke[1] (spōk) *n.* ⟦ME < OE *spaca,* akin to Ger *speiche*: see SPIKE[1]⟧ **1** any of the braces or bars extending between the hub and the rim of a wheel **2** any of the grips or handholds projecting from the rim of a ship's steering wheel —*vt.* **spoked, spok′ing** to equip with or as with spokes

spoke[2] (spōk) *vi., vt. pt. & archaic pp. of* SPEAK

spo·ken (spō′kən) *vi., vt. pp. of* SPEAK —*adj.* **1** uttered; oral **2** characterized by or uttered in a (specified) kind of voice: used in comb. [*soft-spoken*] —**spoken for** claimed, reserved, set aside, etc.; specif., married or engaged

spoke·shave (spōk′shāv′) *n.* a cutting or planing tool consisting of a blade with a curved handle at either end; orig. used to shape spokes, but now used for trimming and smoothing rounded surfaces

spokes·man (spōks′mən) *n., pl.* **-men** (-mən) ⟦irregularly formed < SPOKE[2]⟧ a person who speaks for another or for a group

spokes·per·son (-pur′sən) *n.* SPOKESMAN: used to avoid the masculine implication of *spokesman*

spokes·wom·an (spōks′wo͝om′ən) *n., pl.* **-wom′en** (-wim′in) a woman who speaks for another or for a group

spo·li·ate (spō′lē āt′) *vt.* **-at′ed, -at′ing** ⟦back-form. < fol.⟧ to rob, plunder, or despoil

spo·li·a·tion (spō′lē ā′shən) *n.* ⟦ME *spoliacioun* < L *spoliatio*: see SPOIL⟧ **1** a spoliating or being spoliated; robbery; plundering **2** the act of spoiling or damaging **3** *Law* the destruction or alteration of a document by an unauthorized person

spon·dee (spän′dē) *n.* ⟦ME *sponde* < L *spondeum* < *spondeus,* of a libation < Gr *spondeios* < *spondē,* solemn libation (such libations were accompanied by a solemn melody) < *spendein,* to present a libation: see SPONSOR⟧ a metrical foot of two long or accented syllables —**spon·da·ic** (spän dā′ik) *adj.*

☆**spon·du·lix** or **spon·du·licks** (spän do͞o′liks, -dyo͞o′-) *n.* ⟦< ?⟧ [Brit. Slang] money

spon·dy·li·tis (spän′də līt′is) *n.* ⟦< fol. + -ITIS⟧ inflammation of the vertebrae

spon·dy·lo- (spän′də lō, -lə) ⟦< Gr *spondylos,* vertebra < IE base **sp(h)e(n)d-,* to jerk, dangle > Sans *spandatē,* (he) jerks⟧ *combining form* vertebra [*spondylitis*]: also, before a vowel, **spondyl-**

sponge (spunj) *n.* ⟦ME < OE < L *spongia* < Gr *spongia, spongos*⟧ **1** any of a phylum (Porifera) of simple, aquatic, sessile animals having a porous structure and a tough, often siliceous or calcareous, skeleton **2** the elastic skeleton, or a piece of the skeleton, of certain sponges, light in weight and highly absorbent, used for washing surfaces, in bathing, etc. **3** any substance like this; specif., *a)* a piece of spongy plastic, cellulose, rubber, etc., used like natural sponge *b)* a pad of gauze or cotton, as used in surgery *c)* a vaginal contraceptive device consisting of a round piece of spongy material infused with a spermicide *d)* a light dessert made of whipped gelatin and beaten egg whites or whipped cream *e)* raised dough, as for bread *f)* any of several metals, as platinum, found in a porous mass **4** *a)* a person having a spongelike capacity, as for drink, knowledge, etc. *b)* [Informal] SPONGER (sense 3) —*vt.* **sponged, spong′ing** ⟦ME *spongen* < the *n.*⟧ **1** to use a sponge on so as to dampen, wipe clean, etc. **2** to remove or obliterate with or as with a damp sponge: usually with *out, off, away,* etc. **3** to absorb with, as with, or like a sponge: often with *up* **4** [Informal] to get without cost, as by begging, imposition, etc. —*vi.* **1** to gather sponges from the sea **2** to take up liquid like a sponge **3** [Informal] to be a SPONGER (sense 3): often with *off* or *on* —**throw (**or **toss, etc.) in the sponge** [Informal] to admit defeat; give up: from the practice by a boxer's second of throwing a sponge into the ring to concede defeat

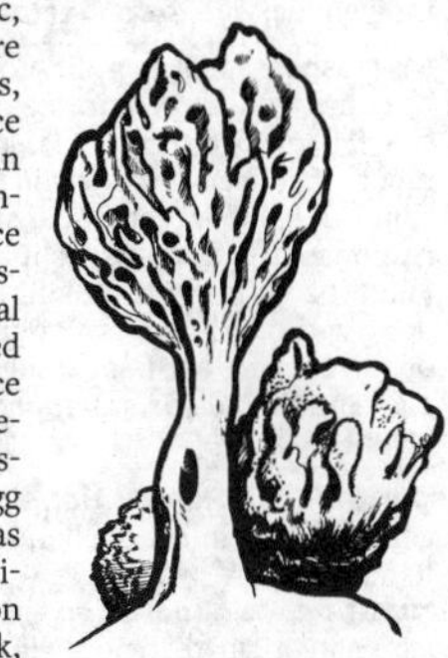
sponges (*n.* 1)

sponge bath a bath taken by using a wet sponge or cloth without getting into water or under a shower

sponge·cake (spunj′kāk′) *n.* a light, spongy cake made of flour, eggs, sugar, etc., but no shortening: also written **sponge cake**

spong·er (spun′jər) *n.* **1** a person or vessel that gathers sponges **2** a person who cleans, etc. with a sponge **3** [Informal] a person who, though able to work, depends on others for food, money, etc.

sponge rubber rubber processed so that it has a spongelike texture that is firmer and denser than foam rubber: used for gaskets, rubber balls, etc.

sponge·ware (spunj′wer′) *n.* a kind of earthenware on which patterns have been made by using a sponge to dab on pigment: it was popular in the late 19th cent.

spon·gin (spun′jin) *n.* ⟦Ger < L *spongia,* SPONGE + Ger *-in,* -INE[3]⟧ a sulfur-containing protein making up the resilient fibrous network that forms the skeleton in many sponges

spon·gy (-jē) *adj.* **-gi·er, -gi·est 1** of or like a sponge; specif., *a)* light, soft, and elastic *b)* porous *c)* absorbent **2** soft and thoroughly soaked with moisture [*spongy* ground] —**spon′gi·ness** *n.*

spon·sion (spän′shən) *n.* ⟦L *sponsio* < *spondere,* to promise solemnly: see SPONSOR⟧ **1** a formal promise or pledge, esp. one made on behalf of another person, as by a godparent **2** in international law, an act done or engagement made for a state by an unauthorized agent

spon·son (spän′sən) *n.* ⟦altered < ? EXPANSION: orig. applied to the platforms on each side of a steamer's paddle wheels⟧ **1** a structure that projects from the side of a ship or boat; specif., *a)* a projecting gun platform *b)* an air chamber built into the gunwale of a canoe **2** a short, winglike piece attached to the hull of a seaplane just above water level to give stability in the water

spon·sor (spän′sər) *n.* ⟦L, surety < *spondere,* to promise solemnly < IE base **spend-,* to bring a libation, vow > Gr *spendein,* to promise, *spondē,* libation⟧ **1** a person or agency that undertakes certain responsibilities in connection with some other person or some group or activity, as in being a proponent, endorser, advisor, underwriter, surety, etc. **2** *a)* a godfather or godmother; person who answers for a child, as at baptism, making the profession of faith and the promises prescribed *b)* in some Christian denominations, a person who acts as patron for someone being confirmed ☆3 a business firm or other agency that alone or with others pays the costs of a radio or television program on which it advertises or promotes something —*vt.* to act as sponsor for —**spon·so′ri·al** (-sôr′ē əl) *adj.* —**spon′sor·ship′** *n.*

SYN.—a **sponsor** is one who assumes a certain degree of responsibility for another in any of various ways [the *sponsors* of a television program assume the costs of production]; a **patron** is one who assumes the role of protector or benefactor, now usually in a financial capacity as of an artist, an institution, etc.; a **backer** is one who lends support, esp. financial support, to someone or something but does not necessarily assume any responsibilities [the magazine failed when it lost its *backers*]; **angel** is an informal term for the backer of a theatrical enterprise

spon·ta·ne·i·ty (spän′tə nē′ə tē; -nā′-) *n.* 1 the state or quality of being spontaneous 2 *pl.* **-ties** spontaneous behavior, movement, action, etc.

spon·ta·ne·ous (spän tā′nē əs) *adj.* ⟦LL *spontaneus* < L *sponte,* of free will < IE base *(s)pen(d)-, to pull > SPIN⟧ 1 acting in accordance with or resulting from a natural feeling, impulse, or tendency, without any constraint, effort, or premeditation 2 having no apparent external cause or influence; occurring or produced by its own energy, force, etc. or through internal causes; self-acting 3 growing naturally without being planted or tended; indigenous; wild —**spon·ta′ne·ous·ly** *adv.* —**spon·ta′ne·ous·ness** *n.*

SYN.—**spontaneous** applies to that which is done so naturally that it seems to come without prompting or premeditation [a *spontaneous* demonstration]; **impulsive** applies to that which is prompted by some external incitement or sudden inner inclination rather than by conscious rational volition [an *impulsive* retort]; **instinctive** suggests an instantaneous, unwilled response to a stimulus, as if prompted by some natural, inborn tendency [he took an *instinctive* liking to her]; **involuntary** refers to that which is done without thought or volition, as a reflex action [an *involuntary* flicker of the eyelid]; **automatic** suggests an unvarying, machinelike reaction to a given stimulus or situation [an *automatic* response] —*ANT.* **deliberate, voluntary**

spontaneous combustion the process of catching fire as a result of heat generated by internal chemical action, and not from an exterior spark, flame, etc.

spontaneous generation the theory, now discredited, that living organisms can originate in nonliving matter independently of other living matter

spon·toon (spän to͞on′) *n.* ⟦Fr *sponton* < It *spuntone* < *s-* (< L *ex-*) + *punto* < L *punctum,* a POINT⟧ a short pike or halberd carried by 18th-cent. infantry officers

spoof (spo͞of) *n.* ⟦orig. a game involving hoaxing and nonsense, invented (*c.* 1889) by Arthur Roberts (1852-1933), Brit comedian⟧ 1 [Informal] a trick or ruse 2 a light parody or satire — *vt., vi.* 1 [Informal] to fool; deceive 2 to satirize in a playful, amiable manner —**spoof′er** *n.*

☆**spook** (spo͞ok) *n.* ⟦Du, akin to Ger *spuk*⟧ 1 [Informal] a specter; ghost 2 [Slang] a spy or secret agent —*vt.* [Informal] 1 to haunt (a person or place) 2 to startle, frighten, make nervous, annoy, etc. —*vi.* [Informal] to become frightened or startled [a horse that *spooks* easily]

☆**spook·y** (spo͞o′kē) *adj.* **spook′i·er, spook′i·est** [Informal] 1 of, like, or suggesting a spook or spooks; weird; eerie 2 easily spooked; nervous, apprehensive, fearful, jumpy, etc. —**spook′i·ly** *adv.* —**spook′i·ness** *n.*

spool (spo͞ol) *n.* ⟦ME *spole* < MFr *espole* < MDu *spoele,* akin to Ger *spule* < IE base *(s)p(h)el-, to split, split off > SPALL, SPILL[1], SPOIL⟧ 1 a cylinder or roller, usually with a hole for a spindle from end to end and a rim at either end, upon which thread, wire, etc. is wound 2 something like a spool, as a bobbin, reel, etc. 3 the material wound on a spool —*vt.* to wind on a spool

spoon (spo͞on) *n.* ⟦ME *spon* < OE a chip: sense infl. by cognate ON *spōnn,* spoon: see SPADE[1]⟧ 1 a utensil consisting of a small, shallow, usually oval-shaped bowl and a handle, used for picking up or stirring food, etc. as in eating or cooking 2 something shaped like a spoon; specif., a shiny, curved fishing lure, usually made of metal, set above a hook or hooks so as to wobble when drawn through the water 3 *Golf former term for* number 3 wood: see WOOD[1] —*vt.* 1 to take up with or as with a spoon and, usually, move from one place to another [to *spoon* custard into a baby's mouth] 2 to push, lift, or hit (a ball) with a scooping motion instead of a direct blow —*vi.* 1 [Old Informal] to embrace, kiss, and caress: said of lovers 2 ⟦allusion to spoons arranged compactly together⟧ [Informal] to nestle against each other, on the sides and front to back —**born with a silver spoon in one's mouth** born rich —**spoon′er** *n.*

spoon·bill (spo͞on′bil′) *n.* 1 any of several wading birds (family Threskiornithidae) with a broad, flat bill that is spoon-shaped at the tip; esp., the **roseate spoonbill** (*Ajaia ajaja*) of North and South America 2 any of a number of other birds with a bill like this, as a shoveler duck ☆3 PADDLEFISH

☆**spoon bread** [Chiefly South] a soft, light, moist bread made of cornmeal, eggs, milk, shortening, and, usually, baking powder: served with a spoon

spoon·er·ism (spo͞o′nər iz′əm) *n.* ⟦after Rev. W. A. *Spooner* (1844-1930), Oxford scholar famous for such slips⟧ an unintentional or intentional interchange of sounds, usually initial sounds, in two or more words (Ex.: "a well-boiled icicle" for "a well-oiled bicycle")

spoon-feed (spo͞on′fēd′) *vt.* **-fed′, -feed′ing** 1 to feed with a spoon 2 to pamper; coddle 3 to treat, instruct, or inform in a manner that destroys initiative or curbs independent thought and action

spoon·ful (-fo͝ol′) *n., pl.* **-fuls′** as much as a spoon will hold

spoon·y or **spoon·ey** (spo͞o′nē) *adj.* **spoon′i·er, spoon′i·est** [Old Informal] silly or foolish; esp., foolishly sentimental or amorous

spoor (spo͝or) *n.* ⟦Afrik < MDu, akin to OE *spor,* Ger *spur:* for IE base see SPUR⟧ the track or trail of an animal, esp. of a wild animal hunted as game — *vt., vi.* to trace or track by a spoor

Spo·ra·des (spôr′ə dēz′; *Gr* spô rä′thes) 1 all the Greek islands in the Aegean Sea except the Cyclades 2 the Greek islands along the W coast of Turkey, esp. the Dodecanese: also *Southern Sporades* See also NORTHERN SPORADES

spo·rad·ic (spə rad′ik) *adj.* ⟦ML *sporadicus* < Gr *sporadikos* < *sporas,* scattered: for IE base see SPORE⟧ 1 happening from time to time; not constant or regular; occasional 2 widely separated from others, scattered, or isolated in occurrence; appearing singly, apart, or in isolated instances —**spo·rad′i·cal·ly** *adv.*

spo·ran·gi·um (spə ran′jē əm) *n., pl.* **-gi·a** (-ə) ⟦ModL < *spora* (see fol.) + Gr *angeion,* vessel⟧ *Bot.* an organ or single cell producing spores —**spo·ran′gi·al** *adj.*

spore (spôr, spōr) *n.* ⟦ModL *spora* < Gr, a sowing, seed, akin to *speirein,* to sow < IE base *(s)p(h)er-, to strew, sow > SPREAD, SPROUT⟧ 1 *Biol.* any of various small reproductive bodies, usually consisting of a single cell, produced by bacteria, algae, mosses, ferns, certain protozoans, etc., either asexually (**asexual spore**) or by the union of gametes (**sexual spore**): they are capable of giving rise to a new adult individual, either immediately or after an interval of dormancy 2 any small organism or cell that can develop into a new individual; seed, germ, etc. —*vi.* **spored, spor′ing** to bear or develop spores

spore case SPORANGIUM

spore fruit any specialized structure, as an ascocarp, in which spores are formed

spore mother cell a cell from which a spore is produced

spo·rif·er·ous (spô rif′ər əs) *adj.* bearing spores

☆**spork** (spôrk) *n.* ⟦SP(OON) + (F)ORK⟧ an eating utensil, typically of plastic, concave like a spoon but with wedge-shaped tines

spo·ro- (spôr′ō, spôr′ə; spō′rō, -rə) ⟦< ModL *spora,* SPORE⟧ *combining form* spore [*sporocarp*]: also, before a vowel, **spor-**

spo·ro·carp (spôr′ə kärp′) *n.* ⟦prec. + -CARP⟧ *Bot.* a many-celled body produced from a fertilized archicarp, serving for the development of spores in red algae, lichens, etc.

spo·ro·cyst (-sist′) *n.* ⟦SPORO- + -CYST⟧ 1 *Bot.* a resting cell giving rise to asexual spores 2 *Zool.* *a)* a saclike larval stage of many trematodes which produces rediae by asexual development from germinal cells *b)* a protective cyst produced by some protozoans before sporulation, or a protozoan in such encystment

spo·ro·gen·e·sis (spôr′ə jen′ə sis) *n.* ⟦ModL: see SPORO- & -GENESIS⟧ *Biol.* 1 reproduction by means of spores 2 the formation of spores —**spo′ro·gen′ic** *adj.* —**spo·rog·e·nous** (spô räj′ə nəs) *adj.*

spo·ro·go·ni·um (-gō′nē əm) *n., pl.* **-ni·a** (-nē ə) ⟦ModL: see SPORO- & -GONIUM⟧ the sporophyte in mosses and liverworts, usually a spore-bearing capsule on a stalk that never separates from the mother plant

spo·rog·o·ny (spô räg′ə nē) *n.* ⟦SPORO- + -GONY⟧ the process by which a large number of sporozoites are produced by cell divisions from a single zygote

spo·ro·phore (spôr′ə fôr′) *n.* ⟦SPORO- + -PHORE⟧ *Bot.* an organ or structure in various fungi that bears spores —**spo·roph·o·rous** (spō räf′ər əs) *adj.*

spo·ro·phyll (-fil) *n.* ⟦SPORO- + -PHYLL⟧ a leaf, modified leaf, or leaflike part producing one or more sporangia —**spo·roph·yl·lar·y** (spō rä′fi ler′ē) *adj.*

spo·ro·phyte (-fīt′) *n.* ⟦SPORO- + -PHYTE⟧ in certain plants and algae, the spore-bearing generation that is diploid and reproduces by spores: the sporophyte generation begins with the fertilized egg and ends with meiosis: distinguished from GAMETOPHYTE —**spo′ro·phyt′ic** (-fit′ik) *adj.*

-spor·ous (spō′rəs, spôr′əs, spər əs) ⟦SPOR(O)- + -OUS⟧ *combining form forming adjectives* having (a special number or kind of) spores [*homosporous*]

spo·ro·zo·an (spôr′ə zō′ən) *n.* ⟦< ModL *Sporozoa* (see SPORO- & -ZOA) + -AN⟧ any of a class (Sporozoa) of parasitic protozoans, including the organisms that cause malaria and Texas fever, that usually pass through phases of both sexual and asexual generation, frequently in different hosts, during which sporogenesis takes place: also **spo′ro·zo′on** (-zō′än, -ən), *pl.* **-zo′a** (-zō′ə) —*adj.* of the sporozoans: also **spo′ro·zo′ic** —**spo′ro·zo′al** *adj.*

spo·ro·zo·ite (-īt′) *n.* ⟦< ModL *Sporozoa* (see prec.) + -ITE[2]⟧ an infective body or group of cells released from spores in many sporozoans and formed by the division of a zygote: it is the infective stage of the malaria parasite

spor·ran (spôr′ən, spär′-) *n.* ⟦Gael *sporan*⟧ a leather pouch or purse, usually covered with fur or hair, worn hanging from the front of the belt in the dress costume of Scottish Highlanders

sport (spôrt) *n.* ⟦ME *sporte,* aphetic for DISPORT⟧ 1 any activity or experience that gives enjoyment or recreation; pastime; diversion 2 such an activity, esp. when competitive, requiring more or less vigorous bodily exertion and carried on, sometimes as a profession, according to some traditional form or set of rules, whether outdoors, as football, golf, etc., or indoors, as basketball, bowling, etc. 3 fun or play 4 [Informal] *a)* a person who is sportsmanlike, easygoing, or companionable [be a *sport!*] *b)* a person judged according to his or her ability to take loss, defeat, teasing, etc. [a good (or poor) *sport*] ☆5 [Informal] a pleasure-loving, showy person **6** [Obs.] amorous trifling or sexual play **7** *Biol.* a plant or animal showing some marked variation from the normal type, usually as a result of mutation —*vt.* [Informal] to wear or display, esp. with unnecessary show [*to sport a loud tie*] —*vi.* **1** to play or frolic **2** to engage in a sport or sports **3** *a)* to joke or jest *b)* to trifle, dally, or play (*with*) **4** *Biol.* to vary markedly from the normal type; mutate —*adj.* **1** SPORTING (sense 1) **2** suitable for informal or casual wear; not dressy [*a sport shirt*] —**in** (or **for**) **sport** in joke or jest; not in earnest —**make sport of** to mock or ridicule; poke fun at —**sport′er** *n.* —**sport′ful** *adj.* —**sport′ful·ly** *adv.*

sport coat a men's hip-length, long-sleeved jacket, typically having a notched lapel and buttons down the front, for informal wear

spor·tif (spôr tēf′) *adj.* ⟦Fr⟧ **1** athletic or fond of sports **2** [*also in roman type*] of, having to do with, or characteristic of sportswear; casual

sport·ing (spôrt′iŋ) *adj.* **1** of, having to do with, or for sports, or athletic games, etc. **2** interested in or taking part in sports, or athletic games, etc. **3** sportsmanlike; fair ☆**4** interested in or having to do with games, races, etc. characterized by gambling or betting **5** *Biol.* inclined to mutate —**sport′ing·ly** *adv.*

sporting chance a fair or even chance

sporting house [Old Informal] ☆**1** a gambling house ☆**2** a house of prostitution; brothel

spor·tive (-iv) *adj.* **1** *a)* fond of or full of sport or merriment; playful *b)* done in fun or play, not in earnest **2** of, or having the nature of, sport, esp. outdoor sport **3** [Obs.] amorous or erotic —**spor′tive·ly** *adv.* —**spor′tive·ness** *n.*

sport jacket *var. of* SPORT COAT: also **sports jacket**

sports (spôrts) *adj.* **1** SPORT (*adj.* 2) [*sports clothes*] **2** of or having to do with athletic games, esp. professional ones [*a TV sports reporter*]

sports bar a bar or tavern featuring numerous television screens for viewing sporting events

sports car a small car, often with only two seats, offering above-average speed, acceleration, and handling

☆**sports·cast** (spôrts′kast′, -käst′) *n.* ⟦SPORTS + -CAST⟧ a sports broadcast, esp. of sports news, on radio or television —**sports′cast′er** *n.*

sports coat *var. of* SPORT COAT: also written **sports′coat′** *n.*

sports·man (-mən) *n., pl.* **-men** (-mən) **1** a person, esp. a man, who is interested in or takes part in sports, esp. in hunting, fishing, etc. **2** a person who can take loss or defeat without complaint, or victory without gloating, and who treats opponents with fairness, generosity, courtesy, etc. —**sports′man·like′** *adj.*, **sports′man·ly**

sports·man·ship (-mən ship′) *n.* **1** skill in or fondness for sports **2** qualities and behavior befitting a sportsman

sports medicine a branch of medicine concerned with athletic conditioning and nutrition and the treatment and prevention of athletic injuries

sports·wear (spôrts′wer′) *n.* clothing designed for recreation and other informal occasions

sports·wom·an (-woom′ən) *n., pl.* **-wom′en** (-wim′in) a woman who is interested in or takes part in sports, esp. in hunting, fishing, etc.

sports·writ·er (-rīt′ər) *n.* a reporter who writes about sports

sport utility vehicle a passenger vehicle similar to a station wagon but with the chassis of a small truck and, usually, four-wheel drive

sport·y (spôrt′ē) *adj.* **sport′i·er, sport′i·est** [Informal] **1** characteristic of a sport or sportsman **2** casually stylish: said as of clothing **3** like or like that of a SPORTS CAR in design, power, etc. —**sport′i·ly** *adv.* —**sport′i·ness** *n.*

spor·u·late (spôr′yoo lāt′) *vi.* **-lat′ed, -lat′ing** ⟦SPORUL(E) + -ATE[1]⟧ to undergo sporulation

spor·u·la·tion (spôr′yoo lā′shən) *n.* ⟦< fol. + -ATION⟧ **1** *Bot.* the formation of spores **2** *Zool.* a type of multiple fission in certain protozoans by which a parent spore becomes almost completely broken up into buds

spor·ule (spôr′yool′) *n.* ⟦ModL *sporula,* dim. of *spora,* SPORE⟧ a small spore or, sometimes, any spore

spot (spät) *n.* ⟦ME < or akin to MDu *spotte,* akin to ON *spotti,* small piece (of ground)⟧ **1** a small area of different color or texture from the main area of which it is a part; often, a mark made by some foreign matter; stain, blot, speck, patch, etc. **2** *a)* any of the pips used on playing cards, dice, etc. *b)* a playing card having (a specified number of) pips that indicate its rank [*the ten spot of spades*] **3** a flaw or defect, as in character or reputation; something blameworthy; fault **4** *a)* a locality; place [*a good fishing spot*] *b)* any small area or space **5** *short for* SPOTLIGHT **6** a small, edible, silvery, marine drum fish (*Leiostomus xanthurus*) of the W Atlantic with a black spot behind the gill cover **7** [Informal, Chiefly Brit.] a small quantity; bit [*a spot of tea*] **8** [Informal] position; situation; job **9** [Informal] position or place in a schedule or listing **10** [Informal] a spot advertisement or announcement **11** [Informal] *a)* the number of points, strokes, etc. added to or subtracted from a competitor's score as a handicap *b)* the number of points, etc. assigned by gamblers to one side in a contest, in an attempt to equalize betting on both sides ☆**12** [Slang] a nightclub ☆**13** [Slang] a piece of paper money of a specified value [*a ten spot*] —*vt.* **spot′ted, spot′ting 1** to mark with spots **2** to sully; stain; blemish **3** to mark for future consideration **4** *a)* to place in or on a given spot or spots; locate [*to spot men at strategic points*] *b)* [Informal] to put in a spot in a schedule or listing **5** to be located at various places in or on **6** to shine a spotlight on **7** to remove (individual spots, marks, etc.) as in dry cleaning **8** *a)* to pick out; detect; see; recognize [*to spot someone in a crowd*] *b)* to determine the location of (a target, the enemy, etc.) *c)* to correct the accuracy of (gunfire) for a gun crew **9** to observe and report on (plays) as a spotter in sports ☆**10** [Informal] to give a numeric scoring advantage to (the weaker side in a contest) [*to spot the beginner five points*] —*vi.* **1** to become marked with spots **2** to cause a spot or spots; make a stain, as ink, water, etc. **3** to act as a spotter, esp. for a gun crew or in sports —*adj.* **1** *a)* that can be paid out or delivered immediately; ready [*spot cash*] *b)* involving immediate payment of cash *c)* involving cash transactions only **2** made at random or according to an arbitrary sampling procedure [*a spot survey*] **3** inserted between regular radio or television programs [*a spot advertisement or announcement*] —**change one's spots** ⟦in allusion to a leopard's distinctive coat⟧ to alter one's fundamental or distinguishing beliefs, behavior, etc. —☆**hit the high spots** [Informal] to treat only the main points of a topic, as in a cursory discussion —**hit the spot** [Informal] to satisfy a craving or need —☆**in a (bad) spot** [Informal] in a bad situation; in trouble —**on the spot 1** on or at the place mentioned **2** at once; immediately ☆**3** [Informal] in trouble or difficulty **4** [Informal] in a position where an immediate response to a difficult question or situation is expected

spot-check (spät′chek′) *vt.* to check or examine at random or by sampling —*n.* an act or instance of such checking

spot·less (-lis) *adj.* **1** having no spots; perfectly clean **2** having no faults or defects, as in character; irreproachable —**spot′less·ly** *adv.* —**spot′less·ness** *n.*

☆**spot·light** (-līt′) *n.* **1** *a)* a strong beam of light used to illuminate prominently a particular person, thing, or group, as on a stage, in a window display, etc. *b)* a lamp used to project such a beam of light **2** a lamp with a strong, focused beam, as on an automobile, that can be directed on a small area **3** the condition of being well-known and subject to public scrutiny: with *the* —*vt.* to illuminate or draw attention to by, or as by, a spotlight

spot on [Brit. Informal] precisely accurate or thoroughly appropriate: also written **spot′-on′**

☆**spot pass** *Sports* a pass of the ball, puck, etc. to a prearranged spot at which the receiver is expected to arrive at the same time as the ball, puck, etc.

spot·ted (spät′id) *adj.* **1** marked with spots **2** stained, blemished

☆**spotted adder** MILK SNAKE

spotted fever any of various febrile diseases accompanied by skin eruptions; esp., Rocky Mountain spotted fever

spotted owl a dark-brown owl (*Strix occidentalis,* family Strigidae) with scattered white spots and dark eyes, sometimes seen in the forests of W North America: it is an endangered species

spot·ter (spät′ər) *n.* a person or thing that spots; specif., *a)* a person whose work is removing spots, etc. in dry cleaning ☆*b)* a person hired to watch for dishonesty, etc. among employees, as in a store *c)* a person who watches for, and reports, enemy aircraft *d)* a person who determines, as for a gun crew, the position of a target and the closeness to it of the projectiles fired ☆*e)* a football coach's assistant in the stands who reports on the plays to the bench by phone ☆*f)* an assistant to a sports announcer who helps identify the players for the announcer *g)* a person, esp. a trainer, who assists weight lifters, gymnasts, etc. in their training, as to prevent injury

spot·ty (-ē) *adj.* **-ti·er, -ti·est 1** having, occurring in, or marked with spots **2** not uniform or consistent; irregular, as in quality; uneven —**spot′ti·ly** *adv.* —**spot′ti·ness** *n.*

spot welding a welding process in which overlapping metal pieces are held under great pressure between two electrodes, between which a brief, powerful current is passed, effecting the weld —**spot′-weld′** *vt., vi.* —**spot′-weld′er** *n.*

spous·al (spou′zəl) *n.* ⟦see ESPOUSAL⟧ [*often pl.*] [Now Rare] a marriage ceremony —*adj.* **1** [Now Rare] of marriage **2** of or relating to a spouse [*spousal benefits*]

spouse (spous; *also, esp. for vt.,* spouz) *n.* ⟦ME *spus* < OFr *espous* < L *sponsus,* betrothed, pp. of *spondere:* see SPONSOR⟧ a partner in marriage; (one's) husband or wife —*vt.* **spoused, spous′ing** [Archaic] to marry; wed

spout (spout) *n.* ⟦ME *spute, spoute* < the v.⟧ **1** a lip, orifice, or projecting tube, as on a teapot, in a drinking fountain, etc., by which a liquid is poured or discharged **2** *a)* a stream, jet, or discharge of or as of liquid from a spout *b)* the stream of air and water rising from the blowhole of a whale **3** *a)* DOWNSPOUT *b)* WATERSPOUT **4** a chute for conveying substances, as grain or flour, or articles **5** ⟦from the chute formerly used as a conveyance in such a shop⟧ [Old Brit. Slang] a pawnshop —*vt.* ⟦ME *spouten,* to spout, vomit, akin to MDu *spuiten,* to spout: prob. < base of SPEW⟧ **1** to shoot out (liquid, etc.) from or as from a spout **2** to speak or utter in a loud, pompous manner or in a ready, rapid flow of words —*vi.* **1** to flow or shoot out with force in a jet: said of liquid, etc. **2** to discharge liquid, etc. from or as from a spout **3** to spout words —**spout off** [Informal] to spout words in a way that is hasty, irresponsible, etc. —**up the spout** [Brit. Slang] **1** bankrupt; ruined **2** pregnant —**spout′er** *n.* —**spout′less** *adj.*

spp *abbrev.* species (*pl. of* SPECIES)

SPQR *abbrev.* ⟦L *S(enatus) P(opulus)q(ue) R(omanus),* the Senate and people of Rome⟧ the government of ancient Rome, specif. of the Roman Republic

Sprach·ge·fühl (shpräk′gə fül) *n.* ⟦Ger⟧ a seemingly innate understanding of what is idiomatic or grammatical in a given language

sprad·dle (sprad′'l) *vt., vi.* **-dled, -dling** ⟦blend of SPREAD & STRADDLE⟧ [Informal or Dial.] to spread (the legs) in a sprawling or straddling way

sprag (sprag) *n.* ⟦prob. < Scand, as in Dan *sprag,* twig < base of *sprage,* to crack, crackle: for IE base see SPARK¹⟧ **1** a roof prop used in a coal mine ☆**2** a device for preventing a vehicle from rolling backward on a grade

sprain (sprān) *vt.* ⟦< ? OFr *espreindre,* to force out, strain < VL **expremere,* for L *exprimere:* see EXPRESS⟧ to wrench or twist a ligament or muscle of (a joint, as the ankle) without dislocating the bones —*n.* **1** an act of spraining **2** the resulting condition, characterized by swelling, pain, and disablement of the joint

sprang (spraŋ) *vi., vt. alt. pt. of* SPRING

sprat (sprat) *n.* ⟦< ME *sprotte* < OE *sprott:* for IE base see SPROUT⟧ any of a genus (*Sprattus*) of small, silvery herrings of temperate seas, esp. a European species (*S. sprattus*) often canned as food

sprawl (sprôl) *vi.* ⟦ME *spraulen* < OE *spreawlian,* to move convulsively: see SPROUT⟧ **1** *a)* to spread the limbs in a relaxed, awkward, or unnatural position *b)* to sit or lie in such a position [to *sprawl* in a chair] **2** to crawl in an awkward, ungainly way **3** to spread out in an awkward or uneven way, esp. so as to take up more space than is necessary, as handwriting, a line of men, etc. —*vt.* to cause to sprawl —*n.* **1** a sprawling movement or position **2** *a)* the unchecked, uncoordinated spread of real-estate development into areas on the outskirts of a city, regarded as undesirable *b)* the buildings and infrastructure resulting from this —**sprawl′er** *n.* —**sprawl′y** *adj.* **sprawl′i·er, sprawl′i·est**

spray¹ (sprā) *n.* ⟦< or akin to MDu *spraeien,* to spray, akin to Ger *sprühen:* see SPREAD⟧ **1** a cloud or mist of fine liquid particles, as of water from breaking waves **2** *a)* a jet of fine liquid particles, or mist, as from an atomizer or spray gun *b)* a device for shooting out such a jet *c)* any liquid for spraying from such a device **3** something likened to a spray of liquid particles [a *spray* of bullets] —*vt.* **1** to direct a spray onto; treat with or subject to a spray **2** to direct a spray of onto something —*vi.* **1** to shoot out a spray **2** to be shot out as a spray **3** to mark territory by urinating: said as of a male cat —**spray′a·ble** *adj.* —**spray′er** *n.*

spray² (sprā) *n.* ⟦ME: for IE base see SPARK¹⟧ **1** a small branch or sprig of a tree or plant, with leaves, berries, flowers, etc. **2** a design or ornament like this

spray can a can in which gas under pressure is used to disperse the contents in the form of a spray

☆**spray gun** a device that shoots out a spray of liquid, as paint or insecticide, by air pressure from a compressor

spray paint paint in or from a SPRAY CAN —**spray′-paint′** *vi., vt.*

spread (spred) *vt.* **spread, spread′ing** ⟦ME *spreden* < OE *sprædan,* akin to Ger *spreiten* < IE **sprei-d-,* to sprinkle, strew < base **(s)p(h)er-,* to strew, spray, burst (of buds) > SPRAY¹, SPRAWL, SPROUT⟧ **1** to draw out so as to display more fully; open or stretch out so as to cover more space; unfold or unfurl **2** to lay out in display; exhibit **3** to move apart (the fingers, arms, legs, wings, etc.) **4** *a)* to distribute over a surface or area; scatter; disperse *b)* to distribute among a group [to *spread* the wealth] **5** *a)* to distribute in a thin layer; smear [to *spread* butter on toast] *b)* to cover by smearing (*with* something) [to *spread* bread with jelly] **6** to extend or prolong in time [to *spread* payments over a two-year period] **7** to cause to be widely or more widely known, felt, existent, etc.; disseminate; propagate; diffuse [to *spread* news, a disease, etc.] **8** to cover, overlay, or deck (*with* something) **9** *a)* to set (a table) for a meal *b)* to set (food) on a table **10** to push apart or farther apart ☆**11** to record in full; enter (*on a record*) **12** to flatten out (a rivet, etc.) by hammering —*vi.* **1** to extend itself; be extended or expanded **2** to become distributed or dispersed **3** to be made widely or more widely known, felt, existent, etc.; be disseminated, propagated, or diffused **4** to be pushed apart or farther apart **5** to be of such consistency that it can be distributed in a thin layer, as butter; be capable of being smeared —*n.* **1** the act of spreading; extension; expansion; diffusion **2** *a)* the extent to which something is spread or can be spread *b)* the interval or difference between the highest and lowest figures of a set, as of the scores of a test *c)* the difference between related prices, rates, etc., as that between the prices at which a broker buys and sells shares of a stock *d)* in betting, the number of points by which a team, esp. a football team, is expected to defeat its opponent **3** an expanse; extent; stretch; compass ☆**4** *a)* two facing pages of a newspaper, magazine, etc., treated as a single continuous sheet, as in advertising *b)* printed matter set across a page, or across several columns, of a newspaper, magazine, etc. ☆**5** BEDSPREAD ☆**6** any soft substance, as jam or margarine, used for spreading on bread or crackers **7** a broadening, as of a weight-gainer's hips and waistline [middle-age *spread*] **8** [Informal] a lavish meal, esp. one with a wide variety of food ☆**9** a ranch, or any large farm or estate —☆**spread oneself thin** to try to do too many things at once —**spread′a·bil′i·ty** *n.* —**spread′a·ble** *adj.*

spread eagle **1** the figure of an eagle with wings and legs spread, used as an emblem of the U.S. **2** something suggesting this, as an acrobatic figure in skating

spread-ea·gle (spred′ē′gəl) *adj.* **1** having the figure of an eagle with wings and legs spread **2** having the legs and, often, the arms spread wide: also **spread′-ea′gled** ☆**3** [Old Informal] boastful or jingoistic about the U.S. —*vi.* **-gled, -gling** to perform a spread eagle: see SPREAD EAGLE (sense 2)

spread·er (-ər) *n.* a person or thing that spreads; specif., *a)* a small, dull knife for spreading butter, etc. *b)* a contrivance for scattering or applying something [a fertilizer *spreader*] *c)* a device, as a bar, for keeping wires, stays, etc. apart

spreading factor a substance, as hyaluronidase, that promotes the diffusion of a material through bodily tissues

spread·sheet (-shēt′) *n.* ⟦*spread,* adj. (< pp. of SPREAD, *vt.*) + SHEET¹⟧ **1** *Bookkeeping* a financial worksheet with multiple rows and columns, used in preparing an income statement, balance sheet, etc. **2** a computer program that organizes numerical data into rows and columns, for computing desired calculations and making overall adjustments based on new data

Sprech·ge·sang (shpreH′gə zäŋ′) *n.* ⟦Ger, lit., speech song⟧ *var. of* SPRECHSTIMME

Sprech·stim·me (shpreH′shtim′ə) *n.* ⟦Ger, lit., speaking voice⟧ a form of vocal performance partly like speech and partly like song

spree (sprē) *n.* ⟦late 18th-c. slang, for earlier *spray* < ?⟧ **1** a lively, noisy frolic **2** a period of drunkenness **3** a period of uninhibited activity [a shopping *spree*]

Spree (shprā) river in E Germany, flowing northwest through Berlin into the Havel: c. 250 mi (402 km)

sprez·za·tu·ra (spret′tsä tōō′rä) *n.* ⟦It⟧ a seeming effortlessness or ease, esp. in art or literature; careless grace

sprig (sprig) *n.* ⟦ME *sprigge,* prob. akin to MDu *sprik,* dry twig: for IE base see SPARK¹⟧ **1** *a)* a little twig or spray *b)* a design or ornament like this **2** a small, headless brad **3** a young fellow; stripling **4** a person as the offspring or scion of a family, institution, class, etc.: used humorously —*vt.* **sprigged, sprig′ging** **1** to remove sprigs from (a bush, tree, etc.) **2** to decorate with a design of sprigs **3** to fasten with small, headless brads —**sprig′gy** *adj.* **-gi·er, -gi·est**

spright·ly (sprīt′lē) *adj.* **-li·er, -li·est** ⟦< *spright,* var. of SPRITE + -LY¹⟧ full of energy and spirit; lively, brisk, etc. —*adv.* **-li·er, -li·est** in a sprightly manner —*SYN.* AGILE, LIVELY —**spright′li·ness** *n.*

spring (spriŋ) *vi.* **sprang** or **sprung, sprung, spring′ing** ⟦ME *springen* < OE *springan,* akin to Du & Ger *springen* < IE **sprenĝh-,* to move quickly (< base **sper-,* to jerk) > Sans *spṛhayati,* (he) strives for⟧ **1** to move suddenly and rapidly; specif., *a)* to move upward or forward from the ground, etc. by suddenly contracting the muscles; leap; bound; also, to make a series of such leaps *b)* to rise suddenly and quickly from or as from a sitting or lying position [to *spring* to one's feet] *c)* to come, appear, etc. suddenly and quickly [curses *springing* to his lips] *d)* to move as a result of resilience; bounce **2** to come or arise as from some source; specif., *a)* to grow or develop [the plant *springs* from a seed] *b)* to come into existence, usually quickly [towns *sprang* up] *c)* to be descended *d)* [Archaic] to begin to appear, as day; dawn **3** to become warped, bent, split, loose, etc. [the door has *sprung*] **4** to rise up above surrounding objects; tower [a steeple *springing* high above the town] ☆**5** [Informal] to bear the cost for someone else; treat (with *for*) **6** *Archit.* to rise from the impost with an outward curve ➥In many senses of the *vi., spring* is often followed by *up* —*vt.* **1** to cause (a game bird) to leap or come forth suddenly [to *spring* a covey of quail] **2** [Rare] to leap over; vault **3** to cause to close or snap shut, as by a spring [to *spring* a trap] **4** *a)* to cause to warp, bend, strain, split, etc., as by force *b)* to stretch (a spring, etc.) beyond the point where it will spring back fully **5** to explode (a military mine) **6** to make known or cause to appear suddenly or unexpectedly [to *spring* a surprise on someone] **7** ⟦< the *n.,* sense 3⟧ to equip with springs ☆**8** [Slang] to get (someone) released from jail or custody, as by paying bail —*n.* ⟦ME & OE *springe*⟧ **1** the act or an instance of springing; specif., *a)* a jump or leap forward or upward, or the distance covered by this *b)* a sudden darting or flying back **2** *a)* the quality of elasticity; resilience *b)* energy or vigor, as in one's walk **3** a device, typically a coil of wire, that returns to its original form after being forced out of shape; specif., *a)* any of various devices on an automobile chassis, designed to absorb shock *b)* any of the coils providing the motive power in traditional clocks and watches *c)* a bedspring or box spring (*usually used in pl.*) **4** *a)* a flow of water from the ground, often a source of a stream, pond, etc. *b)* any source, origin, or motive **5** *a)* that season of the year in which plants begin to grow after lying dormant all winter: in the North Temperate Zone, generally regarded as including the months of March, April, and May: in the astronomical year, that period between the vernal equinox and the summer solstice *b)* any period of beginning or newness **6** [Scot.] a lively song or dance **7** *Archit.* the line or plane in which an arch or vault rises from its impost —*adj.* **1** of, for, appearing in, or planted in the spring **2** of or acting like a spring; elastic; resilient **3** having, or supported on, a spring or springs [a *spring* mattress] **4** coming from a spring (see *n.* 4a) [*spring* water] —*SYN.* RISE —**spring a leak** ☆to begin to leak suddenly or unexpectedly —**spring′less** *adj.*

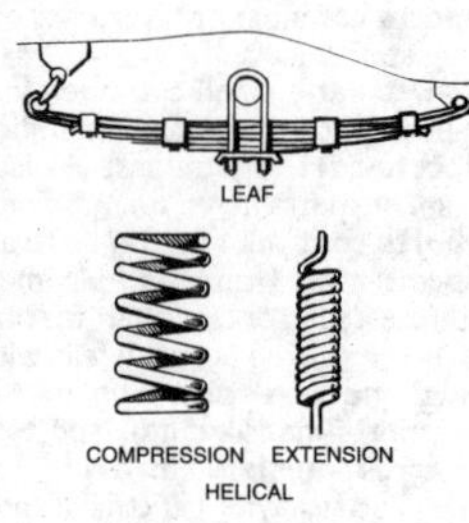

springs

spring·al (spriŋ′əl) *n.* ⟦< ME *sprynhold,* prob. < *springen:* see prec.⟧ [Archaic] an active young man; youth: also **spring′ald** (-əld)

☆**spring beauty** CLAYTONIA

spring·board (spriŋ′bôrd′) *n.* **1** a flexible, springy board used by acrobats, gymnasts, etc. as a takeoff in performing various feats of leaping **2** DIVING BOARD **3** anything serving as the starting point or providing the impetus for something else

spring·bok (-bäk′) *n., pl.* **-bok′** or **-boks′** ⟦Afrik < Du *springen,* to SPRING + *bok,* BUCK[1]⟧ a graceful gazelle (*Antidorcas marsupialis*) of S Africa, noted for its tendency to leap high in the air, as when startled: also **spring′buck′** (-buk′)

☆**spring chicken** 1 a young chicken, esp. one used for broiling or frying 2 [Slang] a young or inexperienced person

spring-clean·ing (-klēn′iŋ) *n.* a thorough cleaning of the interior of a house, etc. as conventionally done in the spring

springe (sprinj) *n.* ⟦ME *sprenge* < *sprengen* < OE *sprengan,* to cause to spring, caus. of *springan,* to SPRING⟧ a snare consisting of a noose attached to something under tension, as a bent tree branch —*vt.* **springed, springe′ing** to snare in a springe

spring·er (spriŋ′ər) *n.* 1 a person or thing that springs 2 *short for* SPRINGER SPANIEL ☆3 SPRING CHICKEN (sense 1) 4 *Archit.* either of the lowest voussoirs of an arch

spring·er·le (spriŋ′ər lə, shpriŋ′-) *pl.n.* anise-flavored cookies, orig. of Germany: often used as a modifier [a plate of *springerle* cookies]

springer spaniel ⟦so named because orig. used for *springing* game birds: see SPRING (*vt.* 1)⟧ any dog of either of two breeds of spaniel: see ENGLISH SPRINGER SPANIEL, WELSH SPRINGER SPANIEL

☆**spring fever** the laziness or restlessness that many people feel during the first warm, sunny days of spring

Spring·field (spriŋ′fēld′) ⟦first sense after *Springfield,* village in Essex, England: others prob. after first sense⟧ 1 city in SW Mass., on the Connecticut River 2 city in SW Mo. 3 capital of Ill., in the central part

☆**Springfield rifle** ⟦after prec., Mass., location of a U.S. armory⟧ a .30-caliber magazine-fed rifle, operated by a bolt, adopted for use by the U.S. Army in 1903 and replaced as the standard infantry weapon by the Garand rifle in 1936

spring·form pan (spriŋ′fôrm′) a circular baking pan, esp. for cakes, with the side held in place by clamps, which are released to free the baked contents

spring·halt (spriŋ′hôlt′) *n.* STRINGHALT

spring·head (-hed′) *n.* a source or fountainhead

☆**spring·house** (-hous′) *n.* a small structure built over a spring or brook, used for cooling milk, etc.

spring·let (-lit) *n.* a small spring of water

spring lock a lock in which the bolt is shot automatically by a spring

☆**spring peeper** a small tree frog (*Hyla crucifer*) of the E U.S., that makes shrill, peeping sounds in early spring

spring roll an East Asian dish similar to an EGG ROLL but having a thinner wrapper that develops a crisper texture when fried

spring·tail (-tāl′) *n.* any of an order (Collembola) of small, primitive, wingless insects, able to leap great distances by the sudden release of a forklike, abdominal appendage

spring tide 1 a type of tide that occurs at the time of a new moon or full moon: at these times the high tides are higher and the low tides are lower than the corresponding tides during neap tide because of the gravitational effects of the straight-line alignment of the moon, earth, and sun 2 any great flow, rush, or flood

spring·time (-tīm′) *n.* 1 the season of spring 2 a period resembling spring; earliest period: also [Obs. or Old Poet.] **spring′tide′**

Spring Valley town in SE Nev., near Las Vegas

spring·wood (-wood′) *n.* the first-formed woody portion of the annual growth ring of a shrub or tree

spring·y (-ē) *adj.* **spring′i·er, spring′i·est** 1 having spring; elastic, resilient, etc. 2 having many springs of water —**spring′i·ly** *adv.* —**spring′i·ness** *n.*

sprin·kle (spriŋ′kəl) *vt.* **-kled, -kling** ⟦ME *sprinklen,* akin to Ger *sprenkeln:* see SPARK[1]⟧ 1 to scatter (water, sand, etc.) in drops or particles 2 *a)* to scatter drops or particles upon; cover or strew with a sprinkling *b)* to dampen before ironing 3 to distribute at random or in a pattern 4 to water (a lawn, etc.) with a SPRINKLER —*vi.* 1 to scatter something in drops or particles 2 to fall in drops or particles 3 to rain lightly or infrequently —*n.* 1 the act of sprinkling 2 a small quantity; sprinkling 3 a light rain 4 [*pl.*] tiny pieces of candy, variously flavored and shaped, used for decorating cookies, servings of ice cream, etc.

sprin·kler (spriŋ′klər) *n.* a person or thing that sprinkles; specif., *a)* a device for distributing water over a lawn, garden, etc. as a spray of droplets *b)* a device for spraying water, etc. to extinguish a building fire See also SPRINKLER SYSTEM

sprinkler system 1 a system of pipes and attached nozzles carrying water or other fluid throughout a building, for extinguishing or limiting the spread of fires: it usually operates automatically when exposed to abnormal heat 2 a system of pipes and nozzles, often underground, for watering a lawn, golf course, etc.: also **sprinkling system**

sprin·kling (-kliŋ) *n.* 1 a small number, quantity, or amount, esp. one that is sprinkled, scattered, or thinly distributed 2 the act of one that sprinkles

sprint (sprint) *vi.* ⟦ME *sprenten,* to leap, run < Scand, as in Swed dial. *sprinta,* ON *spretta,* to run⟧ to run or race at full speed, esp. for a short distance —*n.* 1 the act of sprinting 2 a short run or race at full speed; dash 3 a brief period of intense activity —**sprint′er** *n.*

sprit (sprit) *n.* ⟦ME *spret* < OE *spreot,* a sprout, pole, akin to Du *spriet:* for IE base see SPREAD⟧ a spar extended diagonally upward from a mast to the topmost corner of a fore-and-aft sail, serving to extend the sail

sprite (sprīt) *n.* ⟦ME *sprit* < OFr *esprit* < L *spiritus,* SPIRIT⟧ 1 *archaic var. of* SPIRIT 2 *Folklore* an imaginary being or spirit, as a fairy, elf, or goblin 3 a person regarded as elfin in some way

sprit·sail (sprīt′sāl′, -səl) *n.* a sail extended by a sprit

spritz (sprits, shprits) *vt., vi., n.* ⟦PaGer *spritz* (< Ger *spritze(n)*) & Yiddish *shprits,* both < MHG *sprütze* < *sprützen,* to spray: for IE base see SPROUT⟧ [Informal] squirt or spray

spritz·er (-ər) *n.* a drink consisting of wine, usually white, and soda water

sprock·et (spräk′it) *n.* ⟦Early ModE < ?⟧ 1 any of a number of teeth or points, as on the rim of a wheel, arranged to fit into the links of a chain 2 a wheel fitted with sprockets on its outer rim, used in a chain drive: in full **sprocket wheel**

sprout (sprout) *vi.* ⟦ME *sprouten* < OE *sprutan,* akin to Ger *spriessen* < IE **spreud-* < base **(s)p(h)er-*: see SPREAD⟧ 1 to begin to grow or germinate; give off shoots or buds 2 to grow or develop rapidly —*vt.* to grow or to cause to sprout —*n.* ⟦ME *sprute* < the v.⟧ 1 a young growth on a plant, as a stem or branch; shoot 2 *a)* a new growth from a bud, rootstock, germinating seed, etc. *b)* such a growth from the germinating seed of any of various plants, as alfalfa or mung beans, eaten as a vegetable, as in salads or Asian dishes 3 something like or suggestive of a sprout, as an offshoot or young person 4 [*pl.*] Brussels sprouts

spruce[1] (sprōōs) *n.* ⟦ME *Spruce,* for *Pruce,* Prussia < OFr < ML *Prussia:* prob. because the tree was first known as a native of Prussia⟧ 1 any of a genus (*Picea*) of evergreen trees of the pine family, having slender needles that are rhombic in cross section 2 the soft, light wood of any of these trees 3 any of several evergreen trees, as the Douglas fir, resembling the spruces

spruce[2] (sprōōs) *adj.* **spruc′er, spruc′est** ⟦< ME *Spruce* (see prec.), esp. in the phr. *Spruce leather,* fine leather imported from Prussia⟧ neat and trim in a smart, dapper way —*vt.* **spruced, spruc′ing** to make spruce: usually with *up* —*vi.* to make oneself spruce: usually with *up* —**spruce′ly** *adv.* —**spruce′ness** *n.*

spruce beer a fermented beverage made with an extract of spruce needles and twigs

☆**spruce grouse** a gray, black, and brown grouse (*Canachites canadensis*) of the spruce forests of N North America

☆**spruce pine** 1 a pine (*Pinus glabra*) of the SE U.S. 2 any of several similar pines, spruces, or hemlocks

sprue[1] (sprōō) *n.* ⟦Du *spruw*⟧ a chronic, chiefly tropical disease characterized by defective absorption of food, anemia, gastrointestinal disorders, etc.

sprue[2] (sprōō) *n.* ⟦< ?⟧ 1 an opening through which molten material, as metal or plastic, is poured into a mold 2 the waste piece of metal, etc. cast in such an opening

sprung (spruŋ) *vi., vt. pp. & alt. pt. of* SPRING —*adj.* 1 having the springs broken, overstretched, or loose 2 having the parts warped, bent, etc. so that they no longer fit together properly 3 provided with or mounted on springs

sprung rhythm ⟦term coined by G. M. HOPKINS⟧ a kind of rhythm in English poetry, based on the normal rhythms of speech and made up of a mixture of feet, each foot consisting of either a single stressed syllable or a stressed syllable followed by one or more unstressed syllables

spry (sprī) *adj.* **spri′er** or **spry′er, spri′est** or **spry′est** ⟦< Brit dial. *sprey* < Scand, as in Swed *sprygg,* lively⟧ full of life; active, nimble, brisk, etc., esp. though elderly —SYN. AGILE —**spry′ly** *adv.* —**spry′ness** *n.*

spud (spud) *n.* 1 ⟦ME *spudde,* prob. < Scand, as in ON *spjōt,* a spear: for IE base see SPIKE[1]⟧ any of various sharp, spadelike or chisel-like tools used for rooting out weeds, stripping off bark, etc. 2 ⟦from the use of this tool to dig potatoes⟧ [Informal] a potato — *vt., vi.* **spud′ded, spud′ding** to dig, strip, drill, etc. with or as with a spud —**spud′der** *n.*

spue (spyōō) *n., vt., vi.* **spued, spu′ing** *alt. sp. of* SPEW

spume (spyōōm) *n.* ⟦ME < MFr *espume* < L *spuma:* see FOAM⟧ foam or froth, as on waves — *vt., vi.* **spumed, spum′ing** to foam or froth —**spu′mous** *adj.* or **spum′y, -i·er, -i·est**

spu·mes·cent (spyōō mes′ənt) *adj.* ⟦L *spumescens,* prp. of *spumescere,* to grow frothy < *spuma:* see prec.⟧ 1 like froth or foam 2 frothing; foaming —**spu·mes′cence** *n.*

spu·mo·ni (spə mō′nē) *n.* ⟦It, pl. of *spumone,* aug. of *spuma,* foam (< L: see FOAM)⟧ an Italian frozen dessert made of variously flavored and colored layers of smooth ice cream, often containing candied fruits and pistachio nuts: also sp. **spu·mo′ne**

spun (spun) *vt., vi. pt. & pp. of* SPIN —*adj.* formed by or as if by spinning

spun glass fine glass fiber, made by forming liquid glass into a thread

spunk (spuŋk) *n.* ⟦Ir *sponc,* tinder, touchwood, sponge < L *spongia,* SPONGE⟧ 1 a kind of wood or fungus that smolders when ignited; punk 2 [Informal] courage; spirit 3 [Slang] semen: a somewhat vulgar usage

spunk·y (spuŋ′kē) *adj.* **spunk′i·er, spunk′i·est** [Informal] having spunk; courageous; spirited —**spunk′i·ly** *adv.* —**spunk′i·ness** *n.*

spun silk a kind of yarn made from silk floss or waste

spun sugar COTTON CANDY

spun yarn 1 yarn spun from staple fibers 2 *Naut.* a line made of several rope yarns twisted together

spur (spur) *n.* ⟦ME *spure* < OE *spura,* akin to Ger *sporn* < IE base **sp(h)er-,* to jerk, push with the foot > SPURN, Sans *sphurāti,* (he) kicks away, L *spernere,* lit., to push away⟧ 1 any of various pointed devices worn on the heel by the rider of a horse and used to urge the horse forward 2 anything that urges, impels, or incites; stimulus to action 3 something like a spur; specif., *a)* a spinelike process, as on the wings or legs of certain birds *b)* a spinelike outgrowth of bone, as on the human heel, resulting from injury, disease, etc. *c)* CLIMBING IRON *d)* a sharp metal device attached as a weapon to the leg of a gamecock in a cockfight *e)* a short, stunted, or projecting branch or shoot of a tree, etc. **4** a range or ridge projecting in a lateral direction from the main mass of a mountain or mountain range **5** *a)* GRIFFE *b)* a buttress, as of masonry, or any similar structure *c)* a short wooden reinforcing piece; brace; strut **6** SPUR TRACK **7** *Bot.* a slender, tubelike structure formed by a basal extension of one or more petals or sepals, often serving as a nectar receptacle; calcar *—vt.* **spurred, spur′ring 1** to strike or prick with a spur or spurs **2** to urge, incite, or stimulate to action, greater effort, etc.: often with *on* **3** to provide with a spur or spurs **4** to strike or injure as with a SPUR (sense *3d*) *—vi.* to spur one's horse —**on the spur of the moment** hastily and abruptly; without forethought or preparation —**win one's spurs** to attain distinction or honor, esp. for the first time; establish one's reputation —**spur′rer** *n.*

spurge (spurj) *n.* ⟦ME < MFr *espurge* < *espurger,* to purge < L *expurgare:* see EXPURGATE⟧ any of a genus (*Euphorbia*) of plants of the spurge family, with milky juice and minute, simplified flowers borne in cuplike inflorescences *—adj.* designating a family (Euphorbiaceae, order Euphorbiales) of dicotyledonous plants, usually with milky juice and diclinous flowers, including the poinsettia, cassava, and rubber tree

spur gear 1 a gear having radial teeth parallel to the axle: also **spur wheel 2** a system of gearing having this kind of gear: also **spur gearing**

spurge laurel a Eurasian evergreen shrub (*Daphne laureola*) of the mezereum family, with yellowish-green flowers, oblong leaves, and poisonous berries

spu·ri·ous (spyoor′ē əs, spur′-) *adj.* ⟦L *spurius,* illegitimate (in LL, false), orig., a bastard < Etr⟧ **1** [Now Rare] illegitimate; bastard **2** not true or genuine; false; counterfeit **3** *Bot.* like in appearance but unlike in structure or function **4** *Radio* designating or of an unwanted signal transmitted or received at other than the desired frequency —*SYN.* ARTIFICIAL —**spu′ri·ous·ly** *adv.* —**spu′ri·ous·ness** *n.*

spurn (spurn) *vt.* ⟦ME *spurnen* < OE *spurnan,* to spurn, kick: see SPUR⟧ **1** [Archaic] to push or drive away contemptuously with or as with the foot **2** to refuse or reject with contempt or disdain; scorn *—vi.* to show contempt or disdain in refusing or rejecting *—n.* **1** [Archaic] a kick **2** scornful treatment or rejection —*SYN.* DECLINE —**spurn′er** *n.*

spurred (spurd) *adj.* having, wearing, or fitted with spurs or spurlike parts

spur·ri·er (spur′ē ər) *n.* a person who makes spurs

spur·ry or **spur·rey** (spur′ē) *n.* ⟦Du *spurrie* < ML *spergula* < L *spargere,* to strew (see SPARK[1]): so named from scattering its seeds⟧ any of a genus (*Spergula*) of European plants of the pink family; esp., the **common corn spurry** (*S. arvensis*) with small white flowers, now a weed in North America (*S. arvensis*) with small white flowers, now a weed in North America

spurt (spurt) *vt.* ⟦prob. altered by metathesis < ME *sprutten,* to sprout, spring forth < OE *spryttan* < base of *sprutan:* see SPROUT⟧ to expel suddenly in a stream or gushing flow; squirt; jet *—vi.* **1** to gush forth in a stream or jet **2** to show a sudden, brief burst of energy, increased activity, etc., as near the end of a race *—n.* **1** a sudden gushing or shooting forth; jet **2** a sudden, brief burst of energy, speed, activity, etc.

spur track a short track connected with the main track of a railroad

sput·nik (spoot′nik, sput′-) *n.* ⟦< Russ, lit., co-traveler < *s(o)-,* with + *put′,* way + *-nik,* -NIK⟧ [*often* **S-**] any of a series of man-made satellites put into orbit by the U.S.S.R. beginning in October, 1957

sput·ter (sput′ər) *vi.* ⟦Du *sputteren,* freq. < MDu *spotten,* to spit: for base see SPEW⟧ **1** to spit out drops of saliva, bits of food, etc. in an explosive manner, as when talking excitedly; splutter **2** to speak hastily in a confused, explosive manner **3** to make sharp, sizzling or spitting sounds, as burning wood, frying fat, etc. *—vt.* **1** to spit or throw out (bits or drops) in an explosive manner **2** to utter by sputtering *—n.* **1** the act or noise of sputtering **2** matter thrown out in sputtering **3** hasty, confused, explosive utterance —**sput′ter·er** *n.*

spu·tum (spyoot′əm) *n., pl.* **spu′ta** (-ə) ⟦L, that which is spit out < *sputus,* pp. of *spuere,* to SPIT[2]⟧ saliva, usually mixed with mucus from the respiratory tract, ejected from the mouth

Spuy·ten Duy·vil (spīt′′n dī′vəl) ⟦Du, lit., spouting devil, nickname for a dangerous ford⟧ ship canal between N Manhattan Island & the mainland, connecting the Hudson & Harlem rivers

spy (spī) *vt.* **spied, spy′ing** ⟦ME *spien* < OFr *espier* < OHG *spehōn,* to search out, examine (< IE base **spek-,* to spy, watch closely > L *specere,* to see, Sans *spaśati,* (he) sees, Gr *skopein,* to observe⟧ **1** to watch or observe closely and secretly, usually with unfriendly purpose: often with *out* **2** to catch sight of; make out; perceive; see *—vi.* **1** to watch or observe closely and secretly; specif., to act as a spy: often with *on* **2** to make a close examination or careful inspection *—n., pl.* **spies 1** a person who keeps close and secret watch on another or others ☆**2** a person employed by a government to get secret information about or monitor the affairs, plans, armed forces, etc. of another government **3** a person employed by a company, as in industry or commerce, to discover the business secrets of another company **4** [Now Rare] an act of spying *—adj.* **1** of or about spies or espionage **2** used for purposes of military espionage [*spy* plane, *spy* satellite] —**spy out** to discover or seek to discover by close observation, inspection, etc.

spy·glass (spī′glas′, -gläs′) *n.* a small telescope

spy·hole (-hōl′) *n.* [Chiefly Brit.] PEEPHOLE

spy·ware (spī′wer′) *n.* ⟦SPY + -WARE⟧ unauthorized software that collects and transmits information over the internet about a computer user without the user's knowledge or consent

sq *abbrev.* **1** sequence **2** squadron **3** square

sq. *abbrev.* ⟦L *sequens*⟧ the following one

sqq. *abbrev.* ⟦L *sequentes; sequentia*⟧ the following ones; what follows

squab (skwäb) *n.* ⟦prob. < Scand, as in Swed *sqvabb,* loose flesh⟧ **1** a nestling pigeon, still unfledged **2** a short, stout person **3** [Chiefly Brit.] *a)* a thick cushion *b)* a sofa or couch *—adj.* **1** newly hatched or not fully fledged **2** short and stout

squab·ble (skwäb′əl) *vi.* **-bled, -bling** ⟦< Scand as in Swed *skvabbel,* a dispute⟧ to quarrel noisily over a small matter; wrangle *—n.* a noisy, petty quarrel or dispute; wrangle —*SYN.* QUARREL[2] —**squab′bler** *n.*

squab·by (skwäb′ē) *adj.* **-bi·er, -bi·est** short and stout

squad (skwäd) *n.* ⟦Fr *escouade* < Sp *escuadra* or It *squadra,* a square, both < VL **exquadrare,* to form into a square: see SQUARE, *vt.*⟧ **1** *a)* a small group of soldiers assembled for inspection, duty, etc. *b)* the smallest military tactical unit, often a subdivision of a platoon ☆**2** *a)* any small group of people working together [a police *squad*] *b)* an athletic team [a football *squad*] *—vt.* **squad′ded, squad′ding 1** to form into squads **2** to assign to a squad

☆**squad car** PATROL CAR

squad·ron (skwäd′rən) *n.* ⟦It *squadrone* < *squadra,* a square < L *quadra,* fem. of *quadrus,* SQUARE⟧ **1** a group of warships, usually of the same type, assigned to some special duty; specif., a naval unit consisting of two or more divisions **2** a unit of armored cavalry composed of from two to four troops, a headquarters, and auxiliary units **3** *a)* a military flight formation *b)* the basic tactical and administrative air-force unit, smaller than an air group and larger than a flight **4** a large or organized group

squa·lene (skwā′lēn′) *n.* ⟦< ModL *Squalus,* a genus of sharks (< L, a kind of sea-fish: see WHALE[1]) + -ENE⟧ an unsaturated hydrocarbon, $C_{30}H_{50}$, found in shark livers, etc. that is a precursor of cholesterol in biosynthesis

squal·id (skwäl′id, skwôl′-) *adj.* ⟦L *squalidus* < *squalere,* to be foul or filthy⟧ **1** foul or unclean, esp. as the result of neglect or unsanitary conditions **2** wretched; miserable; sordid —**squal′id·ly** *adv.* —**squal′id·ness** *n.*

squall[1] (skwôl) *n.* ⟦< Scand, as in Swed *sqval,* a sudden shower, downpour: for prob. base see fol.⟧ **1** a brief, violent windstorm, usually with rain or snow **2** [Informal] trouble or disturbance *—vi.* to storm briefly; blow a squall —**squall′y** *adj.* **squall′i·er, squall′i·est**

squall[2] (skwôl) *vi., vt.* ⟦< ON *skvala,* to cry out, yell: see SQUEAL⟧ to cry or scream loudly and harshly *—n.* a harsh, shrill cry or loud scream —**squall′er** *n.*

squal·or (skwäl′ər, skwôl′-) *n.* ⟦L, foulness, akin to *squalere,* to be filthy⟧ the quality or condition of being squalid; filth and wretchedness

squa·ma (skwā′mə, skwä′-) *n., pl.* **-mae** (-mē) ⟦L, a scale, husk⟧ a scale or scalelike part of an animal or plant

squa·mate (skwā′māt′, skwä′-) *adj.* ⟦LL *squamatus* < L *squama,* a scale⟧ having or covered with scales; scaly

squa·ma·tion (skwā mā′shən, skwə-) *n.* **1** the condition of being squamate **2** epidermal scale arrangement

squa·mo- (skwā′mō, -mə) ⟦< L *squama,* a scale⟧ *combining form* squama: also, before a vowel, **squam-**

squa·mo·sal (skwə mō′səl) *adj.* **1** SQUAMOUS **2** *Zool.* designating or of a bone in the skull of lower vertebrates analogous to the squamous portion of the temporal bone in humans *—n.* a squamosal bone

squa·mous (skwā′məs) *adj.* ⟦L *squamosus* < *squama,* a scale⟧ **1** like, formed of, or covered with scales **2** *Anat.* designating or of a thin, scalelike cell, structure, etc., esp. an epithelial cell or a platelike structure in the upper anterior portion of the temporal bone Also **squa·mose** (skwā′mōs)

squam·u·lose (skwam′yə lōs′, skwā′myə-) *adj.* ⟦ModL *squamulosus* < L *squamula,* dim. of *squama,* a scale⟧ having, covered with, or consisting of small scales

squan·der (skwän′dər) *vt.* ⟦prob. a specialized use of dial. *squander,* to scatter, popularized after Shakespeare's *Merchant of Venice,* I, iii⟧ to spend or use wastefully or extravagantly *—vi.* to be wasteful or extravagant *—n.* [Rare] a squandering; extravagant expenditure

square (skwer) *n.* ⟦ME < OFr *esquarre* < VL **exquadra* < **exquadrare,* to make square < L *ex,* out + *quadrare,* to square < *quadrus,* a square < base of *quattuor,* FOUR⟧ **1** a plane figure having four equal sides and four right angles **2** *a)* anything having or approximating this shape [a *square* of cloth] *b)* any of the spaces on a board for chess, checkers, etc. ☆**3** BLOCK (*n.* 11) **4** *a)* an open area bounded by, or at the intersection of, several streets, usually used as a park, plaza, etc. *b)* buildings surrounding such an area **5** an instrument having two sides that form an angle of 90 degrees, used for drawing or testing right angles **6** a solid piece with at least one face that is a square [to cut a cake into *squares*] **7** the product of a number or quantity multiplied by itself [9 is the *square* of 3] ☆**8** [Informal] a square meal [three *squares* a day]: see SQUARE (*adj.* 11) ☆**9** [Informal] a person who is SQUARE (*adj.* 12) *—vt.* **squared, squar′ing** ⟦ME *squaren* < OFr *es-*

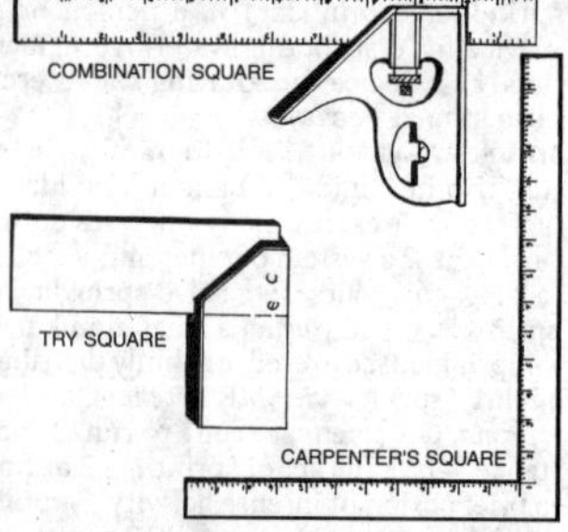

quarrer < VL **exquadrare*⟧ 1 *a)* to make into a square; make square *b)* to make into any sort of rectangle: often with *off* 2 to test or adjust with regard to straightness or evenness [to *square* a surface with a straightedge] 3 to bring into a position or arrangement that is straight, upright, perpendicular, even across, etc. [to *square* one's shoulders] 4 *a)* to settle; adjust; make right or even [to *square* accounts] *b)* to adjust or settle the accounts of [to *square* oneself with another] 5 to make equal [to *square* the score of a game] 6 to bring into agreement; make conform [to *square* a statement with the facts] 7 to mark off (a surface) in a series of connected squares 8 to bring into the correct position, as with reference to a line, course, etc. 9 to multiply (a number or quantity) by itself 10 to determine the square that is equal in area to (a figure) 11 [Old Slang] to bribe —*vi.* ⟦ME < OFr *esquarre,* pp. of *esquarrer*⟧ to fit; agree; accord (*with*) —*adj.* **squar′er, squar′est** 1 *a)* having four equal sides and four right angles *b)* more or less cubical; rectangular and three-dimensional, as a box 2 forming a right angle, or having a rectangular part or parts 3 correctly adjusted, positioned, or arranged; level, even, shipshape, etc. 4 *a)* leaving no balance or advantage; even *b)* even in score; tied 5 just; fair; honest 6 clear; direct; straightforward; unequivocal [a *square* refusal] 7 *a)* designating or of a unit of surface measure in the form of a square having sides of a specified length *b)* given or stated in terms of such surface measure 8 having a shape broad for its length or height, with a solid, sturdy appearance, and somewhat rectangular or rectilinear [a *square* jaw] 9 square or rectangular in cross section, as some files 10 designating a number that is the product of another number multiplied by itself ☆11 [Informal] satisfying; solid; substantial: now only in **square meal** ☆12 [Informal] not conversant with the current fads, styles, slang, etc.; old-fashioned, unsophisticated, conservative, etc. 13 *Naut.* at right angles to the keel and to the mast, as the yards of a square-rigged ship —*adv.* **squar′er, squar′est** 1 honestly; fairly; justly 2 so as to be or form a square; at right angles 3 directly; exactly 4 so as to face 5 firmly; solidly —**on the square** 1 at right angles (to something specified) 2 [Informal] honest(ly), fair(ly), genuine(ly), etc. —**out of square** 1 not at right angles (with something specified) 2 [Informal] not in harmony, order, or agreement —**square around** to turn so as to face squarely someone or something —**square away** 1 to bring a ship's yards around so as to sail directly before the wind 2 SQUARE OFF 3 [Informal] to get ready; put in order —☆**square off** 1 to assume a stance of attack or self-defense, as in boxing 2 [Informal] to fight —☆**square oneself** [Informal] to make amends for damage, a wrong, hurt, etc. done by oneself to another —**square the circle** 1 to construct or find a square equal in area to a given circle: an insoluble problem in Euclidean geometry 2 to do or attempt something that seems impossible —**square up** 1 to make a settlement, as by paying or by balancing accounts 2 to assume a posture of opposition (*to* an adversary) —**square′ness** *n.*

square bracket either of a pair of signs [ ]: see BRACKET (*n.* 5)

square dance a lively American folk dance in which, traditionally, sets of four couples are arranged in a series of squares and prompted through various steps and movements by a caller —**square′-dance′** *vi.* **-danced′, -danc′ing**

☆**square deal** [Informal] any dealing or transaction that is honest and fair

square knot a double knot in which the free ends run parallel to the parts that have been made fast

square·ly (skwer′lē) *adv.* in a square manner, or so as to be square (in various senses) [to look someone *squarely* in the eye, to strike a nail *squarely* with a hammer, a post seated *squarely* in its hole]

square measure a system of measuring area, esp. the system in which 144 square inches = 1 square foot or that in which 10,000 square centimeters = 1 square meter: see the table of weights and measures in the Reference Supplement

square one ⟦in allusion to the penalty, in certain board games, of returning to the starting square⟧ the point from which someone or something started: usually in the phrase **back to** (or **at**) **square one**, back to the beginning and with all progress erased

square-rigged (-rigd′) *adj.* rigged with square sails as the principal sails

square-rig·ger (-rig′ər) *n.* a square-rigged ship

square root the number or quantity which when squared will produce a given number or quantity [3 is the *square root* of 9]

square sail a four-sided sail rigged on a yard suspended horizontally across the mast and at right angles to the keel

☆**square shooter** [Informal] an honest, just person

square-shoul·dered (-shōl′dərd) *adj.* having a build or posture in which the shoulders jut out squarely from the main axis of the body

square-toed (-tōd′) *adj.* 1 having a broad, square toe: said of a shoe 2 [Now Rare] old-fashioned

square-rigged ship

squar·ish (skwer′ish) *adj.* somewhat square

squar·rose (skwar′ōs, skwə rōs′) *adj.* ⟦L *squarrosus*⟧ 1 *Biol.* rough or scaly 2 *Bot.* having tips projecting at right angles, or having spreading bracts —**squar′rose·ly** *adv.*

squash[1] (skwôsh, skwäsh) *vt.* ⟦OFr *esquasser* < VL **exquassare* < L *ex-*, intens. + *quassus*: see QUASH[2]⟧ 1 *a)* to squeeze or crush into a soft or flat mass *b)* to press or squeeze tightly or too tightly 2 to suppress or bring to an abrupt end; quash [to *squash* a rebellion] 3 [Informal] to silence or disconcert (another) in a crushing manner —*vi.* 1 to be squashed, as by a heavy fall, pressure, etc. 2 to make a sound of squashing or splashing 3 to force one's way; crowd; squeeze —*n.* 1 a squashing or being squashed 2 the sound of squashing 3 either of two similar games combining elements of both tennis and handball; specif., *a)* one played in a four-walled court with a small, long-handled racket and a small rubber ball (in full **squash racquets**) *b)* one played in a similar court, but with a larger racket and a larger, livelier ball (in full **squash tennis**) 4 [Brit.] a drink made of sweetened fruit juice or fruit-flavored syrup diluted with water [lemon *squash*] —*adv.* 1 so as to squash 2 with a squashing sound

☆**squash**[2] (skwôsh, skwäsh) *n.* ⟦shortened < *isquoutersquashes, squontersquashes*, pl. < S New England Algonquian: cf. Narragansett *askútasquash*, pl.⟧ 1 the fleshy fruit of any of various plants (genus *Cucurbita*) of the gourd family, eaten as a vegetable 2 a plant, usually a vine, bearing this fruit

☆**squash bug** a large, dark-colored hemipteran insect (*Anasa tristis*) that attacks squash vines and similar plants

squash·y (-ē) *adj.* **squash′i·er, squash′i·est** 1 soft and wet; mushy 2 easily squashed or crushed, as overripe fruit —**squash′i·ly** *adv.* —**squash′i·ness** *n.*

squat (skwät) *vi.* **squat′ted, squat′ting** ⟦ME *squatten* < MFr *esquatir* < *es-* (L *ex-*), intens. + *quatir*, to press flat < VL **coactire* < L *coactus*, pp. of *cogere*, to force, compress: see COGENT⟧ 1 to crouch so as to sit on the heels with the knees bent and the weight resting on the balls of the feet 2 to crouch or cower close to the ground: said of an animal ☆3 to settle on land, esp. public or unoccupied land, without right or title ☆4 to settle on public land under regulation by the government, in order to get title to it 5 to occupy illegally an empty, abandoned, or condemned house, building, apartment, etc. —*vt.* to cause to squat: usually reflexive —*adj.* **squat′ter, squat′test** 1 crouched in a squatting position 2 short and heavy or thick —*n.* 1 the act of squatting 2 the position taken in squatting; crouching posture 3 a dwelling used by a squatter ☆4 ⟦shortened < DIDDLY SQUAT⟧ [Slang] *a)* anything: used in a negative construction signifying "nothing or a very small amount" [he doesn't know *squat* about it] *b)* nothing 5 *Weight Lifting* a type of exercise in which a person holding a barbell at shoulder height squats, then stands erect —**squat′ly** *adv.* —**squat′ness** *n.*

squat·ter (skwät′ər) *n.* 1 a person or animal that squats, or crouches ☆2 a person who settles on public or unoccupied land: see SQUAT (*vi.* 3 & 4) 3 a person who occupies illegally a vacant house, building, etc.

squat·ty (-ē) *adj.* **-ti·er, -ti·est** squat; thickset

☆**squaw** (skwô) *n.* ⟦< Massachusett *squa*, younger woman⟧ 1 a North American Indian woman or wife 2 [Old Slang] any woman or wife: often a mild term of contempt

USAGE—now mostly a disparaging term, but still used descriptively within historical contexts

☆**squaw·fish** (skwô′fish′) *n., pl.* **-fish′** or **-fish′es** (see FISH) any of a genus (*Ptychocheilus*) of very long, slender cyprinoid fishes, found in rivers of the W U.S. and Canada

squawk (skwôk) *vi.* ⟦echoic⟧ 1 to utter a loud, harsh cry, as a parrot or chicken does ☆2 [Informal] to complain or protest, esp. in a loud or raucous voice —*vt.* to utter in a squawk —*n.* 1 a loud, harsh cry ☆2 [Informal] a loud, raucous complaint or protest ☆3 the black-crowned night heron —**squawk′er** *n.*

squawk box [Slang] 1 INTERCOM 2 SPEAKERPHONE

☆**squaw man** [Historical] a white man married to a North American Indian woman, esp. when they live with her tribe: this term is considered offensive

☆**squaw·root** (skwô′ro͞ot′) *n.* 1 an E North American yellowish-brown, scaly, leafless plant (*Conopholis americana*) of the broomrape family, parasitic on the roots of some trees, esp. oaks 2 a purple trillium (*Trillium erectum*)

Squaw Valley ⟦< ?⟧ valley in the Sierra Nevada Mountains, E Calif., near Lake Tahoe: a ski resort

squeak (skwēk) *vi.* ⟦ME *squeken*, prob. akin to ON *skvakka*, to gurgle⟧ 1 to make or utter a short, sharp, high-pitched sound or cry 2 [Informal, Chiefly Brit.] to act as an informer; squeal —*vt.* 1 to utter or produce in a squeak 2 to cause (a door, etc.) to squeak —*n.* a thin, sharp, usually short sound or cry —**narrow** (or **close** or **near**) **squeak** [Informal] a narrow escape —**squeak through** (or **by**, etc.) [Informal] to succeed, get through, survive, etc. by a narrow margin or with difficulty —**squeak′y** *adj.* **squeak′i·er, squeak′i·est** —**squeak′i·ly** *adv.*

squeak·er (skwē′kər) *n.* 1 a person, animal, or thing that squeaks ☆2 [Informal] a narrow escape, victory, etc.

squeak·y-clean (skwē′kē klēn′) *adj.* ⟦from the sound produced when fingers are rubbed through wet hair, over a clean window, etc.⟧ [Informal] 1 very clean 2 having no faults or defects; wholesome, unsullied, irreproachable, etc. Also **squeaky clean**

squeal (skwēl) *vi.* ⟦ME *squelen*, prob. akin to ON *skvala*, to cry out, yell < IE *(s)kwel-*, var. of base **kel-* > L *calare*, to cry out, *clamor*, a cry⟧ 1 to utter or make a long, shrill cry or sound 2 [Slang] to act as an informer; betray a secret: often with *on* —*vt.* to utter in a squeal —*n.* a long, shrill cry or sound —**squeal′er** *n.*

squeam·ish (skwē′mish) *adj.* ⟦ME *squaymysch,* earlier *squaimous* < Anglo-Fr *escoimous,* orig., disdainful, shy⟧ **1** having a digestive system that is easily upset; easily nauseated; queasy **2** easily shocked or offended; prudish **3** excessively fastidious; oversensitive —**SYN.** DAINTY —**squeam′ish·ly** *adv.* —**squeam′ish·ness** *n.*

squee·gee (skwē′jē) *n.* ⟦prob. < *squeege,* intens. form of fol.⟧ **1** a T-shaped tool with a blade of rubber, etc. set across the handle, used to scrape water from a flat surface, as in washing windows **2** a tool with a rubber blade, roller, etc. used to remove surface liquid, apply ink, etc. —*vt.* **-geed, -gee·ing** to scrape or treat with a squeegee

squeeze (skwēz) *vt.* **squeezed, squeez′ing** ⟦intens. of ME *queisen* < OE *cwysan,* to squeeze, dash against, bruise, akin to Goth *quistjan,* to destroy < IE base *gweye-, to overpower > Sans *jināti,* (he) conquers⟧ **1** to press hard or closely; exert pressure on, esp. from two or more sides; compress **2** *a)* to press in order to extract liquid, juice, etc. [to *squeeze* oranges] *b)* to get, bring forth, or extract by pressure [to *squeeze* water from a sponge] **3** to force (*into, out, through,* etc.) by or as by pressing **4** to get, extract, or extort by force or unfair means **5** to oppress with exactions, burdensome taxes, etc. **6** to put pressure or bring influence to bear upon (someone) to do a certain thing, as to pay money, etc. **7** to embrace closely; hug ☆**8** *Baseball* to score (a run) or cause (a runner) to score by a squeeze play ☆**9** *Bridge* to force (an opponent) to discard a card needed to defeat the contract —*vi.* **1** to yield or give way to pressure [a wet sponge *squeezes* easily] **2** to exert pressure **3** to force one's way by pushing or pressing (*in, out, through,* etc.) —*n.* **1** a squeezing or being squeezed; hard or close pressure **2** *a)* a close embrace; hug *b)* a firm pressing or grasping of another's hand in one's own **3** the state of being closely pressed or packed; crush **4** a period or situation marked by scarcity, hardship, insecurity, etc. **5** a facsimile impression made by pressing a soft substance onto something, as a coin or inscription **6** a quantity of something extracted by squeezing **7** [Informal] pressure or influence brought to bear, as in extortion: used esp. in the phrase ☆**put the squeeze on** ☆**8** *short for* SQUEEZE PLAY **9** [Slang] a sweetheart or lover: used esp. in the expression **main squeeze** —**squeeze through** (or **by,** etc.) [Informal] to succeed, survive, get through, etc. by a narrow margin or with difficulty —**squeez′a·ble** *adj.* —**squeez′er** *n.*

☆**squeeze bottle** a flexible plastic container which is squeezed to eject its contents through a tiny hole or holes

squeeze·box or **squeeze-box** (skwēz′bäks) *n.* [Informal] an accordion or concertina

☆**squeeze play** **1** *Baseball* a play in which the batter bunts in an effort to allow a runner on third base to score **2** *Bridge* any play that forces an opponent to discard a card needed to defeat the contract **3** pressure or coercion exerted to achieve some goal

squelch (skwelch) *n.* ⟦prob. echoic⟧ **1** the sound of liquid, mud, slush, etc. moving under pressure or suction, as in wet shoes **2** a crushed mass of something **3** [Informal] the act of suppressing or silencing; esp., a crushing retort, answer, rebuke, etc. —*vt.* **1** to crush or smash by or as by falling or stamping upon; squash **2** to suppress or silence completely and with a crushing effect —*vi.* **1** to walk heavily, as through mud, making a sucking sound **2** to make such a sound —**squelch′er** *n.*

squelch circuit a circuit which disconnects a receiver in order to eliminate output noise when no signal or an extremely weak signal is received

☆**sque·teague** (skwē tēg′) *n., pl.* **sque·teague′** ⟦< Algonquian name: a pl. form⟧ WEAKFISH

squib (skwib) *n.* ⟦prob. echoic⟧ **1** a type of firecracker that burns with a hissing, spurting noise before exploding **2** a short, sharp, usually witty attack in words **3** a short news item; filler — *vt., vi.* **squibbed, squib′bing** **1** to shoot off (a squib) **2** [Archaic] to write or utter a squib or squibs (against) **3** to explode with the sound of a squib

squid (skwid) *n., pl.* **squids** or **squid** ⟦prob. < *squit,* dial. for SQUIRT⟧ any of a number of long, slender, carnivorous cephalopod sea mollusks (esp. order Teuthoidea) having eight arms and two long tentacles: small squid are used as food and for fish bait —☆*vi.* **squid′ded, squid′ding** **1** to take on an elongated squidlike shape due to strong air pressure: said of a parachute **2** to fish for squid or with squid as bait

squid

SQUID (skwid) *n.* ⟦*s(uperconducting) qu(antum) i(nterference) d(evice)*⟧ an electronic device for detecting and measuring very weak magnetic fields and currents, esp. the minute ones in and around the brain and heart

squif·fy (skwif′ē) *adj.* **-fi·er, -fi·est** ⟦< dial. *skew-whiff,* askew, tipsy + -Y[3]⟧ [Informal, Chiefly Brit.] drunk; intoxicated: also **squiffed** (skwift)

squig·gle (skwig′əl) *n.* ⟦SQU(IRM) + (W)IGGLE⟧ **1** a short curved or wavy line; curlicue **2** an illegible or meaningless scribble or scrawl —*vt.* **-gled, -gling** **1** to form into squiggles **2** to write as a squiggle or scrawl —*vi.* **1** to make squiggles **2** to move with a squirming motion; wriggle —**squig′gly** *adj.* **squig′gli·er, squig′gli·est**

squil·gee (skwē′jē, skwil′-) *n.* ⟦? blend of SWILL & SQUEEGEE⟧ *Naut.* a squeegee for use on a ship's deck

squill (skwil) *n.* ⟦ME < L *squilla, scilla* < Gr *skilla*⟧ **1** SEA ONION **2** SCILLA

squil·la (skwil′ə) *n., pl.* **-las** or **-lae** (-ē) ⟦L *squilla, scilla,* prawn, shrimp, sea onion: see prec.⟧ STOMATOPOD

squinch[1] (skwinch) *n.* ⟦var. of *scunch,* contr. < LME *scuncheon* < OFr *escoinson* < *es-* (< L *ex-*) + *coin,* corner: see COIN⟧ an interior corner support, as a small arch, corbeling, or lintel, supporting a weight, as of a spire, resting upon it

☆**squinch**[2] (skwinch) *vt.* ⟦< fol. + (P)INCH⟧ **1** *a)* to squint (the eyes) *b)* to pucker or screw up (the face, nose, brow, etc.) **2** to squeeze or compress —*vi.* **1** to squint, pucker, or contort **2** to crouch down or draw oneself together so as to seem smaller **3** to flinch Often with *up, down,* or *away*

squint (skwint) *vi.* ⟦aphetic for ASQUINT⟧ **1** to look or peer with the eyes partly closed, as when the light is too strong **2** to look with the eyes turned to the side; look obliquely or askance **3** to be cross-eyed **4** to incline or have a tendency (*toward* a given direction, belief, etc.) **5** to deviate from a given line, tendency, etc. —*vt.* **1** to cause to squint **2** to keep (the eyes) partly closed in peering at something —*n.* **1** the act of squinting **2** an inclination or tendency **3** an oblique or perverse tendency or bent **4** the condition of being cross-eyed; strabismus **5** [Informal] a look or glance, often sidelong or casual —*adj.* **1** squinting; looking askance or sidelong **2** characterized by strabismus [*squint* eyes] —**squint′er** *n.* —**squint′ing·ly** *adv.* —**squint′y** *adj.*

squint·eyed (skwint′īd′) *adj.* squinting; specif., *a)* cross-eyed *b)* looking askance; malicious; prejudiced; spiteful

☆**squint·ing** (-iŋ) *adj. Gram.* designating a modifier, as an adverb, that can be interpreted as modifying either the preceding or the following part of the construction in which it appears (Ex.: *often* in "those who lie often are found out"); also, designating the construction itself

squire (skwīr) *n.* ⟦ME *squier* < OFr *escuier:* see ESQUIRE⟧ **1** a young man of high birth who served a medieval knight as an attendant or armorbearer **2** in England, a country gentleman or landed proprietor, esp. the main landowner in a district ☆**3** a title of respect for a justice of the peace or similar local dignitary, as in a rural district —*vt.* **squired, squir′ing** to act as a squire to

squire·ar·chy (skwīr′är kē) *n.* ⟦prec. + -ARCHY, after HIERARCHY⟧ country gentry or landed proprietors collectively: also sp. **squir′ar·chy**

squir·een (skwīr ēn′) *n.* ⟦SQUIR(E) + *-een,* Ir dim. suffix < Gael *-in*⟧ [Irish] a small landowner; petty squire

squirm (skwʉrm) *vi.* ⟦prob. suggestive of the action of the v., infl. by WORM⟧ **1** to twist and turn the body in a snakelike movement; wriggle; writhe **2** to show or feel distress, as from painful embarrassment, humiliation, etc. —*n.* the act of squirming; a squirming motion —**squirm′y** *adj.* **squirm′i·er, squirm′i·est**

squir·rel (skwʉr′əl, skwʉrl) *n., pl.* **-rels** or **-rel** ⟦ME *squirel* < OFr *escuriuel* < VL **scuriolus,* dim. of **scurius,* for L *sciurus* < Gr *skiouros,* squirrel < *skia,* shadow (see SHINE) + *oura,* tail: see URO-[2]⟧ **1** any of a family (Sciuridae) of small rodents living in trees, on the ground, or in burrows and usually having a long, bushy tail, including flying squirrels, chipmunks, and marmots; esp., a tree squirrel **2** the fur of some of these animals —*vt.* **-reled** or **-relled, -rel·ing** or **-rel·ling** ⟦from the fact that squirrels store up nuts and seeds for the winter⟧ to store, hide, or hoard: usually with *away*

squirrel cage a cage for a squirrel, hamster, etc. containing a drum that revolves when the animal runs inside it: often used fig.

☆**squirrel corn** ⟦so named from resemblance of yellow tuberous roots to kernels of *corn* (maize)⟧ an E North American woodland, spring wildflower (*Dicentra canadensis*) of the fumitory family, having racemes of spurred, whitish flowers

☆**squir·rel·ly** or **squir·rel·y** (skwʉr′ə lē, skwʉr′lē) *adj.* ⟦in allusion to a squirrel's diet of nuts: see NUT, *n.* 7*a*⟧ [Slang] **1** odd, crazy, etc. **2** nervous, restless, keyed up, etc.

squirrel monkey any of a genus (*Saimiri*) of small, tropical, New World monkeys (family Cebidae) characterized by naked black skin around the nose and mouth, white fur around the eyes and ears, and a long tail that is not prehensile

squirt (skwʉrt) *vt.* ⟦LME *squyrten,* prob. altered < or akin to LowG & Du *swirtjen,* to squirt⟧ **1** to shoot out (a liquid) in a jet or narrow stream **2** to wet with liquid so shot out —*vi.* to be squirted out; spurt —*n.* **1** something used to squirt liquid, as a syringe **2** the act of squirting **3** a small amount of squirted liquid; jet or narrow stream **4** [Informal] a small or young person, esp. one who is impudent; whippersnapper —**squirt′er** *n.*

☆**squirt gun** a toy gun that shoots a stream of water

squirting cucumber a sprawling vine (*Ecballium elaterium*) of the gourd family, with a small, fleshy fruit that separates from its stalk and squirts out its seeds when ripe

squish (skwish) *vi.* ⟦echoic var. of SQUASH[1]⟧ to make a soft, splashing sound when walked on, squeezed, etc. —*vt.* [Informal] to squeeze into a soft mass; squash —*n.* **1** a squishing sound **2** [Informal] the act of squashing; squash

squish·y (skwish′ē) *adj.* **squish′i·er, squish′i·est** **1** soft and pliable; yielding to pressure **2** making a squishing sound

squoosh (skwoosh) *vt.* ⟦altered < SQUASH[1]⟧ [Informal] **1** to squeeze or crush into a soft, liquid mass **2** SLOSH —**squoosh′y** *adj.* **squoosh′i·er, squoosh′i·est**

sr *abbrev.* steradian(s)

Sr[1] *abbrev.* **1** ⟦Port⟧ *Senhor* **2** Senior: also **sr** **3** ⟦Sp⟧ *Señor* **4** Sister

Sr[2] *Chem. symbol for* strontium

Sra *abbrev.* **1** ⟦Port⟧ *Senhora* **2** ⟦Sp⟧ *Señora*

Sre·bre·ni·ca (sreb′rə nēt′sə) town in E Bosnia and Herzegovina: site of a massacre (1995) largely of Bosnian Muslims by Serbian forces

sri (shrē) *n.* ⟦Hindi, lit., glorious < Sans *śrī* < IE base **k̂rei-,* to shine forth > Gr *kreiōn,* noble⟧ in India, a title of respect equivalent to English *Mr.*

Sri Lan·ka (srē läŋ′kə) country comprising an island off the SE tip of India: a former British colony (as *Ceylon*), it became independent & a member of the Commonwealth in 1948: renamed and made a republic in 1972: 25,332 sq mi (65,610 sq km); cap. Colombo —**Sri Lan′kan**

Sri·nag·ar (srē nug′ər) city in N India, on the Jhelum River: summer capital of Jammu and Kashmir

SRO *abbrev.* **1** single room occupancy **2** standing room only

Srta *abbrev.* **1** ⟦Port⟧ *Senhorita* **2** ⟦Sp⟧ *Señorita*

ss *abbrev.* **1** *Baseball* shortstop: also **SS** **2** ⟦L *supra scriptum*⟧ written above

SS[1] (es′es′) *n.* ⟦Ger abbrev. of *Schutzstaffel,* lit., protective rank⟧ a quasi-military unit of the Nazi party, used as a special police

SS[2] *abbrev.* **1** Social Security **2** steamship **3** *Football* strong safety: sometimes written **ss** **4** Sunday school

SS. *abbrev.* **1** ⟦L *scilicet*⟧ namely **2** ⟦L *Sancti*⟧ Saints

SSA *abbrev.* Social Security Administration

SSB *abbrev.* single sideband

SSE *abbrev.* south-southeast

SSG or **SSgt** *abbrev.* Staff Sergeant

SSI *abbrev.* Supplemental Security Income

SSN *abbrev.* Social Security number

SSR or **S.S.R.** *abbrev.* Soviet Socialist Republic: used to designate a republic of the U.S.S.R. other than the R.S.F.S.R.

SSS *abbrev.* Selective Service System

SST *abbrev.* supersonic transport

SSW *abbrev.* south-southwest

st *abbrev.* **1** short ton(s) **2** stanza **3** state **4** statute(s) **5** stet **6** stitch **7** stone(s) (unit of weight)

St *abbrev.* **1** Saint: terms beginning with *St.* are entered in this dictionary as if spelled *St-* **2** stoke(s) (the unit) **3** Strait **4** Street

-st *suffix* -EST (sense 2) *[didst]*

Sta *abbrev.* **1** Santa **2** Station

stab (stab) *n.* ⟦ME *stabbe,* prob. < *stobbe,* var. of *stubbe,* STUB⟧ **1** a wound made by piercing with a knife, dagger, or other pointed weapon **2** a thrust, as with a knife or dagger **3** a sudden sensation of anguish or pain —*vt.* **stabbed, stab′bing** **1** to pierce or wound with or as with a knife, etc. **2** to thrust or plunge (a knife, etc.) into something **3** to go into in a sharp, thrusting way —*vi.* **1** to make a thrust or piercing wound with or as with a knife **2** to feel like a knife stabbing: said of pain —☆**make (**or **take) a stab at** [Informal] to make an attempt at —**stab in the back** **1** to harm (a friend, partner, etc.) by treachery **2** an act of betrayal —**stab′ber** *n.*

Sta·bat Ma·ter (stä′bät mät′ər) ⟦ML, lit., the mother was standing (the opening words of the text)⟧ **1** a Latin hymn about the sorrows of the Virgin Mary at the crucifixion of Jesus **2** any musical setting of this hymn

sta·bile (stā′bəl, -bil; *also, and for n. usually,* -bēl, -bīl′) *adj.* ⟦L *stabilis:* see STABLE[1]⟧ **1** stable; stationary; fixed in position **2** resistant to chemical change —*n.* a large stationary abstract sculpture, usually a construction of metal, wire, wood, etc.: the analogue of MOBILE

sta·bil·i·ty (stə bil′ə tē) *n., pl.* **-ties** ⟦ME *stablete* < OFr *stableté* < L *stabilitas*⟧ **1** the state or quality of being stable, or fixed; steadiness **2** firmness of character, purpose, or resolution **3** *a)* resistance to change; permanence *b)* resistance to chemical decomposition **4** *a)* composure; self-possession *b)* mental soundness; sanity **5** the capacity of an object to return to equilibrium or to its original position after having been displaced **6** *R.C.Ch.* a vow binding Benedictine monks until death to the monastery where they join the order

sta·bi·lize (stā′bə līz′) *vt.* **-lized′, -liz′ing** ⟦Fr *stabiliser* < L *stabilis:* see STABLE[1] & -IZE⟧ **1** to make stable, or firm **2** to keep from changing or fluctuating, as in price **3** to give stability to (an airplane, ship, etc.) with a stabilizer —*vi.* to become stabilized —**sta′bi·li·za′tion** *n.*

sta·bi·liz·er (-lī′zər) *n.* a person or thing that stabilizes; specif., *a)* any of the fixed airfoils or vanes that keep an airplane steady in flight, as the components of the tail section *b)* a device used to steady a ship in rough waters, esp. a gyrostabilizer *c)* any additive used in substances and compounds to keep them stable, retard deterioration, etc.

sta·ble[1] (stā′bəl) *adj.* **-bler, -blest** ⟦ME < OFr *estable* < L *stabilis* < *stare,* to STAND⟧ **1** *a)* not easily moved or thrown off balance; firm; steady *b)* not likely to break down, fall apart, or give way; fixed **2** *a)* firm in character, purpose, or resolution; steadfast *b)* reliable, dependable **3** not likely to change or be affected adversely; lasting; enduring **4** *a)* emotionally steady; composed; self-possessed *b)* mentally sound; sane; rational **5** capable of returning to equilibrium or original position after having been displaced **6** *Chem., Physics* *a)* not readily decomposing or changing from one state of matter to another *b)* not undergoing spontaneous change **7** *Nuclear Physics* incapable of radioactive decay —**sta′bly** *adv.*

sta·ble[2] (stā′bəl) *n.* ⟦ME < OFr *estable* < L *stabulum* < *stare,* to STAND⟧ **1** *a)* a building in which horses or cattle are sheltered and fed *b)* a group of animals kept or belonging in such a building **2** *a)* all the racehorses belonging to one owner *b)* the people employed to take care of and train such a group of racehorses **3** [Informal] all the athletes, writers, performers, etc. under one management, with one agent, etc. —*vt., vi.* **-bled, -bling** to lodge, keep, or be kept in or as in a stable

sta·ble·boy (-boi′) *n.* a boy who works in a stable

sta·ble·man (-mən, -man′) *n., pl.* **-men** (-mən, -men′) a man who works in a stable

sta·ble·mate (-māt′) *n.* **1** any of the horses sharing a stable **2** one belonging to a stable

sta·bling (stā′bliŋ′) *n.* **1** a stable or stables **2** accommodations in a stable or stables, for horses, etc.

stab·lish (stab′lish) *vt. archaic var. of* ESTABLISH

stac·ca·to (stə kät′ō) *adj.* ⟦It, pp. of *staccare,* aphetic for *distaccare,* to detach < *di(s)-* (< L, DIS-) + Frank **stakka:* see STICK⟧ **1** *[also in italics] Musical Direction* with distinct breaks between successive tones: usually indicated by a dot (**staccato mark**) placed over or under each note to be so produced: cf. LEGATO **2** made up of abrupt, distinct elements or sounds *[a staccato outburst of gunfire]* —*adv.* [*also in italics*] so as to be staccato; in a staccato manner —*n., pl.* **-tos** something, as a speech pattern, that is staccato

stack (stak) *n.* ⟦ME *stac* < ON *stakkr,* akin to MLowG *stack,* barrier of slanting stakes: for IE base see STICK⟧ **1** a large pile of straw, hay, etc., esp. one neatly arranged, as in a conical form, for outdoor storage **2** any somewhat orderly pile or heap, as of boxes, books, poker chips, etc. **3** a number of arms, esp. three rifles, leaning against one another on end so as to form a pyramid **4** [Brit.] a unit of measure for firewood or coal, equal to 108 cubic feet **5** *a)* a number of chimney flues or pipes arranged together *b)* SMOKESTACK ☆**6** [*pl.*] *a)* an extensive series of bookshelves *b)* the main area where books are shelved in a library **7** *a)* the part of a computer memory used to store data temporarily: retrieval of data from it is in reverse order to its storage *b)* the data so stored **8** [Informal] a large number or amount —*vt.* **1** to pile or arrange in a stack **2** to load with stacks of something **3** to assign (aircraft) to various altitudes for circling while awaiting a turn to land **4** to arrange in advance underhandedly so as to predetermine the outcome *[to stack a jury]* —*vi.* to form a stack —☆**stack the cards (**or **deck)** **1** to arrange the order of playing cards secretly so that certain cards are dealt to certain players **2** to prearrange circumstances, usually secretly and unfairly —**stack up** **1** to add up; accumulate **2** to stand in comparison (*with* or *against*); measure up —**stack′a·ble** *adj.* —**stack′er** *n.*

stacked (stakt) *adj.* ☆[Slang] having a full, shapely figure; curvaceous; specif., having large breasts: said of a woman

☆**stacked (**or **stack) heel** a heel on a shoe composed of several layers, as of leather, of alternating shades

stack·up (stak′up′) *n.* an arrangement of circling aircraft at various altitudes, each awaiting its turn to land

stac·te (stak′tē) *n.* ⟦ME *stacten* < acc. of L *stacte,* oil of myrrh < Gr *staktē* < *stazein,* to drip: see STAGNATE⟧ a spice used by the ancient Hebrews in preparing incense: Ex. 30:34

Sta·cy (stā′sē) *n.* a feminine and masculine name: var. *Stacey*

stad·dle (stad′'l) *n.* ⟦ME *stadel* < OE *stathol,* akin to Ger *stadel,* barn: for IE base see STAND⟧ [Now Chiefly Dial.] a lower part or support; specif., the base or framework of a stack, as of hay

stade (stād) *n.* ⟦Fr < L *stadium,* STADIUM⟧ STADIUM (sense 1*b*)

stad·hold·er (stad′hōl′dər) *n.* ⟦< Du *stadhouder* < *stad,* a place (akin to STEAD) + *houder,* holder < *houden,* to HOLD[1]⟧ [Historical] **1** the governor or viceroy of a province of the Netherlands **2** the chief magistrate of the 16th-17th cent. Netherlands republic Also **stadt′hold′er** (stat′-)

sta·di·a[1] (stā′dē ə) *n.* ⟦It, prob. < L, pl. of *stadium:* see STADIUM⟧ a method of surveying in which distances and elevations are obtained by observing the interval on a graduated, upright rod (**stadia rod**) intercepted by two parallel horizontal lines (**stadia hairs** or **stadia wires**) in a surveyor's transit set up at a distance from the rod

sta·di·a[2] (stā′dē ə) *n. alt. pl. of* STADIUM

sta·di·um (stā′dē əm) *n., pl.* **-di·a** (-dē ə); also, and for sense 2 usually, **-di·ums** ⟦ME < L < Gr *stadion,* fixed standard of length, altered (infl. by *stadios,* standing) < earlier *spadion* < *span,* to draw, pull: see SPAN[1]⟧ **1** in ancient Greece and Rome, *a)* a unit of linear measure, equal to about 607 feet (185 meters) *b)* a straight track for footraces, typically one stadium in length, with tiers of seats for spectators on each side (see HIPPODROME) **2** a large, usually open structure with tiers of seats for spectators, as for athletic events **3** *Biol.* a period or stage in the life history of an animal or plant

Staël (stäl), Madame **de** Baronne de Staël-Holstein (born *Anne Louise Germaine Necker*) 1766-1817; Fr. writer: presided over an influential literary salon

staff[1] (staf) *n., pl.* **staffs**; also, for senses 1 & 5, **staves** (stāvz) ⟦ME *staf* < OE *stæf,* akin to Ger *stab,* < IE base **steb(h)-,* post, pole > STEM[1], STAMP⟧ **1** a stick, rod, or pole; specif., *a)* a stick used as a support in walking *b)* a pole or club used as a weapon *c)* a pole for supporting a banner or flag *d)* a rod, wand, crosier, etc. used as a symbol of authority *e)* [Archaic] a shaft, as of a lance *f)* any of several graduated sticks or rules used for measuring, as in surveying **2** a group of people assisting a chief, manager, president, or other leader **3** a group of officers serving a military or naval commanding officer in an advisory and administrative capacity without combat duties or command **4** a specific group of workers or employees *[a teaching staff, newspaper staff, maintenance staff]* **5** *Music* the horizontal lines on and between which notes are written or printed: the placement of a note on the staff indicates its pitch —*adj.* of, by, for, or on a staff; specif., employed full-time, as on a magazine staff, rather than as a freelance writer —*vt.* to provide with a staff, as of workers

☆**staff**[2] (staf) *n.* ⟦< Ger *staffieren,* to fill out, decorate; via Du < OFr *estoffe,* STUFF⟧ a building material of plaster and fiber, used as for decorative moldings or as a finish on temporary buildings

staff·er (-ər) *n.* a member of a staff, as of a newspaper

staff officer **1** an officer serving on a staff ☆**2** *U.S. Navy* a commissioned officer with nonmilitary duties, as a surgeon or chaplain

staff of life bread, regarded as the basic food

Staf·ford (staf′ərd) 1 county seat of Staffordshire, WC England 2 STAFFORDSHIRE
Staf·ford·shire (-shir′) county in WC England: 1,048 sq mi (2,714 sq km)
Staffordshire terrier any of either of two breeds of stocky, muscular terrier with a broad skull and short hair, developed by crossing the bulldog and an English terrier: the breeds (**American Staffordshire terrier** and **Staffordshire bull terrier**) are distinguished principally by size, the former being heavier
staff sergeant ☆1 *U.S. Army* a noncommissioned officer of the sixth grade, ranking above sergeant and below sergeant first class ☆2 *U.S. Air Force* a noncommissioned officer of the fifth grade, ranking above sergeant and below technical sergeant ☆3 *U.S. Marine Corps* a noncommissioned officer of the sixth grade, ranking above sergeant and below gunnery sergeant
staff-tree (staf′trē′) ***n.*** any of a genus (*Celastrus*) of shrubby, usually climbing, plants of the staff-tree family, growing in Asia, Australia, and North America, including bittersweet —***adj.*** designating a family (Celastraceae, order Celastrales) of widely distributed dicotyledonous trees and twining shrubs bearing red seeds in pods, including khat and euonymus
stag (stag) ***n.***, *pl.* **stags** or **stag** ⟦ME < OE *stagga,* akin to ON *(andar)steggi,* drake < IE base **stegh-,* to stick, pierce⟧ 1 a full-grown male deer, esp. a hart or a caribou 2 a male animal, esp. a hog, castrated in maturity ☆3 *a)* a man who attends a social gathering unaccompanied by a woman *b)* a social gathering attended by men only —***adj.*** ☆for men only [a *stag* dinner] —***vt.*** **stagged, stag′ging** [Brit. Slang] to observe or follow secretly or furtively; spy on —***vi.*** ☆to go to a party, etc. as a STAG (sense 3*a*) —☆**go stag** [Informal] 1 to go as a STAG (sense 3*a*) 2 to go unescorted by a man
stag beetle any of a family (Lucanidae) of large beetles: the male has long, branched, antlerlike mandibles
stage (stāj) ***n.*** ⟦ME < OFr *estage* < VL **staticum* < L *status,* pp. of *stare,* to STAND⟧ 1 a platform or dock 2 a scaffold for workmen 3 a level, floor, or story 4 *a)* a platform on which plays, speeches, etc. are presented *b)* any area, as in an arena theater, in which actors perform *c)* the whole working section of a theater, including the acting area, the backstage area, etc. *d)* the theater, drama, or acting as a profession (with *the*) 5 *a)* the scene of an event or series of events *b)* the center of attention 6 a place where a stop is made on a journey, esp., formerly, a regular stopping point for a stagecoach 7 the distance or a part of a route between two stopping places; leg of a journey 8 *short for* STAGECOACH 9 a shelf attached to a microscope for holding the object to be viewed 10 a period, level, or degree in a process of development, growth, or change [the larval *stage* of an insect] 11 any of two or more propulsion units used, in sequence, as the launch vehicle of a missile, spacecraft, etc.: when no longer operational or useful, the lower stages usually separate and fall back to earth 12 *Electronics* a component, circuit, etc. that does one specific job, as amplification, while being a part of a larger, more complex system 13 *Geol.* a subdivision of a series of stratified rocks consisting of the rocks laid down during a geologic age —***vt.*** **staged, stag′ing** 1 to present, represent, or exhibit on or as on a stage ☆2 *a)* to plan, arrange, and carry out [to *stage* a counteroffensive] *b)* to create or manage (an elaborate ruse or pretense) [to *stage* one's own death and flee the country] —***vi.*** to be suitable for presentation on the stage [a play that *stages* well] —**by** (or **in**) **easy stages** 1 traveling only a short distance at a time 2 working or acting unhurriedly, with stops for rest
stage·coach (stāj′kōch′) ***n.*** a horse-drawn coach that formerly carried passengers, parcels, and mail on scheduled trips over a regular route
stage·craft (-kraft′, -kräft′) ***n.*** skill in, or the art of, writing or staging plays
stage direction 1 an instruction in the script of a play, directing the movements of the actors, the arrangement of scenery, etc. 2 the art or practice of directing the production of a play
stage door an outside door leading to the backstage part of a theater, used by actors, production staff, etc.
stage effect an effect or impression created on the stage as by lighting, scenery, or sound
stage fright nervousness felt when appearing as a speaker or performer before an audience
stage·hand (-hand′) ***n.*** a person who helps to set and remove scenery and furniture, operate the curtain, etc. for a performance, as of a stage play
stage-man·age (-man′ij) ***vt.*** **-aged, -ag·ing** ⟦back-form. < fol.⟧ 1 to serve as stage manager for 2 to arrange or manipulate, esp. as if from behind the scenes —**stage′-man′age·ment** ***n.***
stage manager an assistant to the director of a play, in overall charge backstage during the actual performances
stage mother a woman who aggressively attempts to advance her child's career in show business —**stage parent**
stage name a professional pseudonym assumed by a performer, esp. by an actor
stag·er (stā′jər) ***n.*** ⟦STAG(E) + -ER⟧ 1 a person or animal of much experience; old hand; veteran: usually with *old* 2 [Archaic] an actor
stage-struck (stāj′struk′) ***adj.*** having an intense desire to be associated with the theater, esp. to be an actor or actress
stage whisper 1 the delivery of a line or lines in a loud whisper by an actor on stage, to be regarded as unheard by the other characters 2 any similar loud whisper meant to be overheard
stage·y (stā′jē) ***adj.*** **stag′i·er, stag′i·est** *alt. sp. of* STAGY
stag·fla·tion (stag flā′shən) ***n.*** ⟦STAG(NATION) + (IN)FLATION⟧ condition of continuing economic inflation together with a decline in business activity and an increase in unemployment
stag·gard (stag′ərd) ***n.*** ⟦ME *stagard:* see STAG & -ARD⟧ a hart in its fourth year
stag·ger (stag′ər) ***vi.*** ⟦ME *stakeren* < ON *stakra,* to totter, intens. of *staka,* to push (for IE base see STAKE): akin to & prob. infl. in form by MDu *staggeren*⟧ 1 to move unsteadily, as though about to collapse; totter, sway, or reel, as from a blow, fatigue, drunkenness, etc. 2 to lose determination, strength of purpose, etc.; hesitate; waver —***vt.*** 1 to cause to stagger, as with a blow 2 to affect strongly with astonishment, horror, grief, etc.; overwhelm 3 to set, arrange, or incline alternately, as on either side of a line; make zigzag or alternating [to *stagger* the teeth of a saw] 4 to arrange (periods of activity, duties, etc.) so as to avoid crowding, provide for continuity of expertise, etc. [to *stagger* employees' vacations or board members' terms] 5 *Aeron.* to set or arrange (airfoils, rotors, etc.) so that one is slightly ahead of another —***n.*** 1 the act of staggering, or reeling, tottering, etc. 2 a staggered or zigzag arrangement 3 [*pl., with sing. or pl. v.*] any of several diseases or toxic conditions of horses, cattle, etc., characterized by a loss of coordination, and by staggering, falling, etc.: often with *the* —**stag′ger·er** ***n.***
☆**stag·ger·bush** (-boosh′) ***n.*** an E North American shrub (*Lyonia mariana*) of the heath family, with white or pinkish flowers, poisonous to livestock
stag·ger·ing (-iŋ) ***adj.*** 1 that staggers 2 that causes one to stagger; astonishing; overwhelming; specif., astonishingly great [a *staggering* sum] —**stag′ger·ing·ly** ***adv.***
stag·horn coral (stag′hôrn′) any stony coral (esp. *Madrepore cervicornis*) having a structure that somewhat resembles the antlers of a stag
stag·horn fern any of a genus (*Platycerium,* family Polypodiaceae) of epiphytic ferns with antler-shaped fronds and smaller, round barren fronds that cling to branches, wood, etc. for support
stag·hound (stag′hound′) ***n.*** any of various large hounds, similar to the greyhound, but heavier, used in coursing the stag and other large game animals
stag·ing (stā′jiŋ) ***n.*** 1 a temporary structure used for support; scaffolding 2 the business of operating stagecoaches 3 travel by stagecoach 4 the act, process, or manner of presenting a play on the stage
staging area *Mil.* an area where troops are assembled and processed, as for regrouping, transportation, etc.
Stag·i·rite (staj′ə rīt′) ⟦< L *Stagirites* < Gr *Stageiritēs,* person born or living in *Stageira* (L *Stagira*), city in Macedonia⟧ *name for* ARISTOTLE: with *the*
stag·nant (stag′nənt) ***adj.*** ⟦L *stagnans,* prp. of *stagnare:* see fol.⟧ 1 not flowing or moving 2 foul from lack of movement: said of water, etc. 3 not active, alert, etc.; sluggish [a *stagnant* mind] —**stag′nan·cy** (-nən sē) ***n.*** —**stag′nant·ly** ***adv.***
stag·nate (-nāt′) ***vi.*** **-nat′ed, -nat′ing** ⟦< L *stagnatus,* pp. of *stagnare,* to stagnate < *stagnum,* pool, swamp, standing water < IE base **stag-,* to trickle, seep > Gr *stazein,* to drip⟧ to be or become stagnant —***vt.*** to make stagnant —**stag·na′tion** ***n.***
stag·y (stā′jē) ***adj.*** **stag′i·er, stag′i·est** 1 of or characteristic of the stage; theatrical: usually in an unfavorable sense 2 affected; not real [*stagy* diction] —**stag′i·ly** ***adv.***
staid (stād) ***vi., vt.*** *archaic pt. & pp. of* STAY[3] —***adj.*** 1 [Rare] resisting change; fixed 2 sober; sedate; settled and steady —**staid′ly** ***adv.*** —**staid′ness** ***n.***
stain (stān) ***vt.*** ⟦ME *stainen,* aphetic < *disteinen,* DISTAIN: sense and form infl. by ON *steinn,* color, lit., STONE (hence, mineral pigment)⟧ 1 to spoil the appearance of by patches or streaks of color or dirt; discolor; spot 2 to bring shame upon (someone's character, reputation, etc.); taint; disgrace; dishonor 3 to change the appearance of (wood, glass, etc.) by applying a dye, pigment, etc. 4 to treat (material for microscopic study) with a coloring matter that facilitates study, as by making transparent parts visible or by producing a different effect upon different structures or tissues —***vi.*** to impart or take a color or stain —***n.*** 1 a discoloration, streak, or spot resulting from staining 2 a moral blemish; dishonor; guilt; taint [a *stain* on one's reputation] 3 a substance used to impart color in staining; specif., *a)* a dye or pigment in solution, esp. one that penetrates a wood surface *b)* a dye used to stain material for microscopic study —**stain′a·ble** ***adj.*** —**stain′er** ***n.***
stained glass glass used as for church windows that has been colored in any of various ways, as by fusing metallic oxides into it, by enameling, or by burning pigments into its surface —**stained′-glass′** ***adj.***
stain·less (stān′lis) ***adj.*** 1 without a mark or stain 2 that resists staining, rusting, etc. 3 made of stainless steel —***n.*** flatware made of stainless steel —**stain′less·ly** ***adv.***
stainless steel steel alloyed with chromium, etc., virtually immune to rust and corrosion
stair (ster) ***n.*** ⟦ME *steire* < OE *stæger* < base of *stigan,* to climb: see STILE[1]⟧ 1 [*usually pl.*] a flight of steps; stairway 2 a single step, esp. one of a series forming a stairway

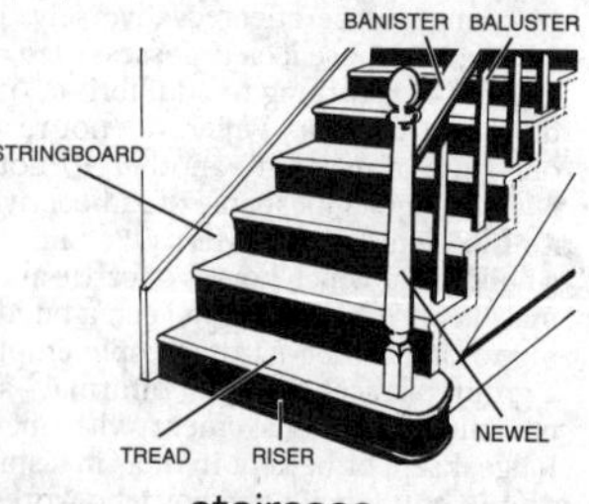

staircase

stair·case (ster′kās′) ***n.*** a stairway, esp. one constructed for access between the floors of a building, and usually having a handrail or balustrade

stair·way (-wā′) *n.* a means of access, as from one level of a building to another, consisting of a series of stairs, with or without a balustrade, etc.

stair·well (-wel′) *n.* a vertical shaft (in a building) containing a staircase

staithe (stāth) *n.* ⟦ME *stathe* < OE *stæth,* shore, infl. by ON *stǫth,* landing place: for IE base see STAND⟧ [Brit. Archaic] a stage or wharf equipped to load and unload (coal, etc.) from railroad cars into vessels

stake (stāk) *n.* ⟦ME < OE *staca,* akin to Frank **stakka:* see STICK⟧ **1** a length of wood or metal pointed at one end for driving into the ground, as for marking a boundary, supporting a plant, etc. **2** *a)* the post to which a person was tied for execution by burning *b)* execution by burning (with *the*) **3** a pole or post fitted upright into a socket, as at the edge of a railway flatcar, truck bed, etc. to help hold a load **4** [*often pl.*] something, esp. money, bet, as in a wager, game, or contest **5** [*often pl.*] a reward given a winner, as in a race; prize **6** [*pl., with sing. v.*] a race in which a prize is offered **7** a share or interest, as in property, a person, or a business venture ☆**8** *Mormon Ch.* a geographical area made up of a number of wards ☆**9** [Informal] *short for* GRUBSTAKE —*vt.* **staked, stak′ing** ☆**1** *a)* to mark the location or boundaries of with or as with stakes *b)* to establish (a claim) in this way (often with *out*) **2** to support (a plant, etc.) by tying to a stake **3** to hitch or tether to a stake **4** ⟦infl. by MDu *staken,* to fix, place⟧ to risk or hazard; gamble; bet **5** [Informal] to furnish with money or resources ☆**6** [Informal] *short for* GRUBSTAKE —**at stake** being risked or hazarded; in danger of being lost, injured, etc. —☆**pull up stakes** [Informal] to change one's place of residence, business, etc. —**stake out 1** to station (police officers, detectives, etc.) for surveillance of a suspected criminal, a place, etc. **2** to put (a suspected criminal, a place, etc.) under such surveillance —**stake up** (or **in**) to close up (or in) with a fence of stakes

☆**stake body** a flat truck body having sockets into which stakes may be fitted, as to support railings

Staked Plain *see* LLANO ESTACADO

stake·hold·er (stāk′hōl′dər) *n.* **1** one who holds money bet by others and pays it to the winner **2** a person or group having a stake, or interest, in the success of an enterprise, business, movement, etc.

☆**stake·out** (-out′) *n.* **1** the staking out of police, etc. in a surveillance of a location, suspected criminal, etc. **2** an area so staked out

☆**stake truck** a truck having a stake body

Sta·kha·nov·ism (stə khä′nə viz′əm) *n.* ⟦after Aleksei *Stakhanov,* Soviet miner whose efforts inspired it (1935)⟧ in the Soviet Union, a system whereby teams of workers sought to increase their production by improving efficiency and, if successful, were rewarded with bonuses and privileges —**Sta·kha′nov·ite′** (-vīt′) *adj., n.*

sta·lac·ti·form (stə lak′tə fôrm′) *adj.* having the form of a stalactite

sta·lac·tite (stə lak′tīt, stal′ək tīt′) *n.* ⟦ModL *stalactites* < Gr *stalaktos,* trickling or dropping < *stalassein,* to let fall drop by drop: see STALE²⟧ an icicle-shaped, secondary mineral deposit, usually calcite, that hangs from the roof of a cave and is formed by the evaporation of dripping water that is full of minerals —**stal·ac·tit·ic** (stal′ək tit′ik) *adj.*

STALACTITE

STALAGMITE

Sta·lag (shtä′läk; *E* stä′läg) *n.* ⟦Ger < *sta(mm)-lag(er)* < *stamm,* a base, lit., STEM¹ + *lager,* a camp: see LAIR⟧ a German prisoner-of-war camp, esp. in WWII

sta·lag·mite (stə lag′mīt, stal′əg mīt′) *n.* ⟦ModL *stalagmites* < Gr *stalagmos,* a dropping < *stalassein,* to drop or drip: see STALE²⟧ a secondary mineral deposit, typically cylindrical with a somewhat conical top, built up on the floor of a cave by dripping water, often from a stalactite above —**stal·ag·mit·ic** (stal′əg mit′ik) *adj.*

St. Al·bans (ôl′bənz) city in Hertfordshire, SE England

stale¹ (stāl) *adj.* **stal′er, stal′est** ⟦ME, prob. via Anglo-Norm < OFr *estale,* quiet, stagnant < Gmc **stall:* for IE base see STILL¹⟧ **1** having lost freshness; made musty, dry, bad, etc. by having been kept too long; specif., *a)* flat; vapid; tasteless [*stale* beer] *b)* hard and dry (said of bread, etc.) *c)* low in oxygen content; stagnant [*stale* air] **2** having lost originality or newness; lacking in interest through familiarity or overuse; hackneyed; trite [a *stale* joke, *stale* gossip] **3** out of condition, ineffective, enervated, bored, etc. from either too much or too little activity **4** *Law* having lost legal force or effect through lack of use or action, as a claim or lien —*vt., vi.* **staled, stal′ing** [Now Rare] to make or become stale —**stale′ly** *adv.* —**stale′ness** *n.*

stale² (stāl) *vi.* **staled, stal′ing** ⟦ME, akin to MLowG *stal,* urine < IE base **(s)tel-,* to let flow, urinate > Gr *stalassein,* to drip, *telma,* puddle⟧ to urinate: said as of horses and cattle —*n.* urine, as of horses or cattle

stale·mate (stāl′māt′) *n.* ⟦obs. *stale,* stalemate < ME < OFr *estal,* fixed location, safe place < Gmc, as in OHG *stal* (see STALL¹) + MATE²⟧ **1** *Chess* any situation in which a player, whose king is not currently in check, cannot move without placing that king in check: it results in a draw **2** any unresolved situation in which further action is impossible or useless; deadlock; draw —*vt.* **-mat′ed, -mat′ing** to bring into a stalemate

Sta·lin (stä′lin), **Joseph** (born *Iosif Vissarionovich Dzhugashvili*) 1878-1953; Soviet premier (1941-53): general secretary of the Communist party of the U.S.S.R. (1922-53) —**Sta′lin·ism′** *n.* —**Sta′lin·ist** *adj., n.*

Sta·lin·a·bad (stä′li nä bät′) *former name for* DUSHANBE

Sta·lin·grad (stä′lin grät′; *E* stä′lin grad′) *name* (1925-61) *for* VOLGOGRAD

Sta·li·no (stä′li nô′) *former name for* DONETSK

Sta·linsk (stä′linsk) *former name for* NOVOKUZNETSK

stalk¹ (stôk) *vi.* ⟦ME *stalken* < OE *stealcian* (in comp.) < *stealc,* high, steep < IE **stelg-* < base **stel-,* to place, set up > STILL¹, Gr *stellein*⟧ **1** *a)* to walk in a stiff, haughty, or grim manner *b)* to advance or spread grimly [plague *stalks* across the land] **2** to pursue or approach game, an enemy, etc. stealthily, as from cover **3** [Obs.] to walk or move along stealthily or furtively —*vt.* **1** to pursue or approach (game, prey, etc.) stealthily **2** to move through grimly or menacingly [terror *stalked* the streets] **3** to follow or pursue (another person) persistently in a harassing and, typically, obsessive way —*n.* **1** a slow, stiff, haughty, or grim stride **2** the act of stalking game, an enemy, etc. —**stalk′er** *n.* —**stalk′ing** *n.*

stalk² (stôk) *n.* ⟦ME *stalke,* akin to OE *stealc,* high, steep < IE **stelg-* < base **stel-:* see STILL¹⟧ **1** any stem or stemlike part, as a slender rod, shaft, or support **2** *Bot. a)* the main stem or axis of a plant *b)* a lengthened part of a plant on which an organ grows or is supported, as the petiole of a leaf, the peduncle of a flower, etc. **3** *Zool. a)* a lengthened support for an animal organ *b)* a similar structure supporting a whole animal body, as the peduncle of a goose barnacle —**stalked** *adj.* —**stalk′less** *adj.*

stalk-eyed (stôk′īd′) *adj.* having eyes on short, movable stalks, as crabs do

stalk·ing-horse (stô′kiŋ hôrs′) *n.* **1** a horse, or a figure of a horse, used as cover by a hunter stalking game **2** anything used to disguise or conceal intentions, schemes, or activities; blind **3** *Politics* a person whose candidacy is advanced temporarily to conceal the actual choice or to divide the opposition

stalk·y (stô′kē) *adj.* **stalk′i·er, stalk′i·est 1** like a stalk; long and slender **2** having, or consisting mainly of, stalks —**stalk′i·ness** *n.*

stall¹ (stôl) *n.* ⟦ME *stal* < OE *steall,* place, station, stall, stable, akin to OHG *stal* < IE base **stel-,* to place, set up, stiff, stem > STILL¹⟧ **1** *a)* [Obs.] a stable *b)* a compartment for one animal in a stable **2** any of various compartments, booths, separate sections, etc.; specif., *a)* a booth, table, or counter, as at a market or fair, at which goods are sold *b)* a pew or enclosed seat in the main part of a church or in the choir *c)* a small, enclosed space, as a compartment in which one showers or a compartment enclosing a toilet in a public restroom ☆*d)* any of the spaces marked off, as in a garage, for parking individual automobiles **3** [Brit.] *a)* an orchestra seat in a theater, esp. one in the front part *b)* [*pl.*] ORCHESTRA (sense 3*a*); also, the people sitting in these seats **4** a protective sheath, as of rubber, for a finger or thumb; cot **5** the condition of being brought to a stop or standstill, as through some malfunction **6** *Aeron.* a condition in which an improper angle of attack and a lack of airspeed combine to disrupt the airflow around an airfoil enough to result in a loss of lift which forces the aircraft to drop, possibly going out of control —*vt., vi.* ⟦ME *stallen* < the n. & < OFr *estaler* < Gmc, as in OHG *stal*⟧ **1** to put, keep, or be kept in a stall **2** to cause to stick fast or to be stuck fast, as in mud **3** to bring or be brought to a stop or standstill, esp. unintentionally **4** to stop or cause to stop through some malfunction: said of a motor or engine **5** *Aeron.* to put or go into a stall

stall² (stôl) *vi.* ⟦< *stall,* decoy, var. of obs. *stale,* one who lures < Anglo-Fr *estale* < OFr *estaler:* see prec.⟧ to act or speak evasively or hesitantly so as to deceive or delay [to *stall* for time] —*vt.* to put off or delay by stalling: usually with *off* [to *stall* off creditors] —*n.* any action, device, etc. used to deceive or delay; evasive trick

stall-feed (stôl′fēd′) *vt.* **-fed′** (-fed′), **-feed′ing** to feed (an animal kept inactive in a stall) for fattening

stal·lion (stal′yən) *n.* ⟦ME *stalon* < OFr *estalon* < Gmc *stal:* see STALL¹⟧ an uncastrated male horse, esp. one used as a stud

stal·wart (stôl′wərt) *adj.* ⟦ME *stalworthe* < OE *stælwyrthe,* short for *stathol-wyrthe,* firm < *stathol,* foundation (see STADDLE) + *wyrthe,* worth: hence, lit., having a firm foundation⟧ **1** strong and well-built; sturdy; robust **2** brave; valiant **3** resolute; firm; unyielding —*n.* **1** a stalwart person **2** a person supporting a cause, esp. that of a political party, with firm partisanship —**stal′wart·ly** *adv.* —**stal′wart·ness** *n.*

Stam·boul or **Stam·bul** (stäm bo͞ol′) **1** *former name for* ISTANBUL **2** the old section of Istanbul

sta·men (stā′mən) *n., pl.* **-mens** or **stam·i·na** (stam′ə nə, stā′mə-) ⟦ModL < L, thread, orig., warp (in an upright loom), akin to Gr *stēmōn* < IE **stamen-,* a standing < base **sta-,* STAND⟧ a pollen-bearing organ in a flower, made up of a slender stalk (*filament*) and a pollen sac (*anther*); microsporophyll of a flowering plant

Stam·ford (stam′fərd) ⟦after *Stamford,* town in NE England⟧ city in SW Conn.

stam·i·na¹ (stam′ə nə) *n.* ⟦L, pl. of *stamen:* see STAMEN⟧ resistance to fatigue, illness, hardship, etc.; endurance

stam·i·na² (stam′ə nə, stā′mə-) *n. alt. pl. of* STAMEN

stam·i·nal¹ (stam′ə nəl) *adj.* of or having to do with stamina

stam·i·nal² (stam′ə nəl, stā′mə-) *adj.* of or having to do with a stamen or stamens

stam·i·nate (-nit, -nāt′) *adj.* ⟦ModL *staminatus* < L, consisting of threads⟧ **1** bearing stamens but no pistils, as male flowers do **2** having or bearing a stamen or stamens

stam·i·ni- (stam′ə ni) ⟦< L *stamen* (gen. *staminis*)⟧ *combining form* stamen [*staminiferous*]: also, before a vowel, **stamin-**

stam·i·nif·er·ous (stam′ə nif′ər əs) *adj.* ⟦prec. + -FEROUS⟧ having or bearing a stamen or stamens

stam·i·node (stam′ə nōd′) *n.* ⟦ModL *staminodium* < *stamen* + *-odium:* see

-ODE[2]⟧ an abortive or sterile stamen: also **stam′i·no′di·um** (-nō′dē əm), *pl.* **-di·a** (-dē ə)

stam·i·no·dy (-nō′dē) ***n.*** ⟦< STAMIN(I)- + Gr *-ōdia,* a becoming like < *-ōdēs:* see -ODE[2]⟧ the change of other organs of a flower into stamens

stam·mel (stam′əl) ***n.*** ⟦prob. < MFr *estamel* < OFr *estame,* woolen thread < L *stamen:* see STAMEN⟧ **1** a type of rough woolen cloth used by some medieval ascetics for undergarments **2** a red color like that usually used in dyeing such cloth

stam·mer (stam′ər) ***vt., vi.*** ⟦ME *stameren* < OE *stamerian,* akin to Du *stameren,* freq. formation < IE base **stem-,* to stumble in speech, halt > STEM[2], STUMBLE, Ger *stumm,* dumb⟧ to speak or say with involuntary pauses or blocks, often with rapid repetitions of syllables or initial sounds, as temporarily from excitement, embarrassment, etc. or chronically —***n.*** act, instance, or habit of stammering —**stam′mer·er** ***n.*** —**stam′mer·ing·ly** ***adv.***

stamp (stamp) ***vt.*** ⟦ME *stampen,* akin to OHG *stampfon* < Gmc **stampon,* **stampjan,* to press to pieces < IE **stembh-,* to crush < base **steb(h)-,* a post, pole > STAFF[1], STEP, STUMP⟧ **1** to bring (the foot) down forcibly on the ground, a floor, etc. **2** *a)* to strike down on forcibly with the foot [to *stamp* the floor in anger] *b)* to beat, crush, etc. in a specified way by treading on heavily [to *stamp* the grass down to the earth] *c)* to remove by stamping the foot or feet [to *stamp* the snow from one's boots] *d)* to pulverize (ore, etc.) by grinding or crushing **3** *a)* to imprint or cut out (a mark, design, lettering, etc.) by bringing a form forcibly against a material [to *stamp* initials in leather] *b)* to cut out, form, or make as by applying a die to metal (often with *out*) [to *stamp* auto bodies] **4** to impress, mark, or imprint with some design, characters, etc., as to decorate or to show authenticity, ownership, sanction, or the like **5** to impress or mark distinctly or indelibly [the incident was *stamped* in her memory] **6** to put an official seal or a stamp on (a document, letter, etc.) **7** to characterize or reveal distinctly, as if by imprinting [the courage that *stamped* him as a hero] —***vi.*** **1** to bring the foot down forcibly on the ground, a floor, etc. **2** to walk with loud, heavy steps, as in anger, etc. —***n.*** **1** the act of stamping **2** a machine, tool, etc. used for stamping or crushing ore, etc. **3** *a)* any tool or implement, as a die, used by being forcibly brought against something to mark or shape it *b)* a mark or form made by such a tool or implement **4** a mark, seal, impression, etc. used to show officially that a tax has been paid, authority given, etc. **5** *a)* a small piece of paper, distinctively imprinted on the face and usually gummed on the back, issued by a government for a specified price and required to be affixed to a letter, parcel, document, commodity subject to duty, etc. as evidence that the prescribed fee, as for carrying mail, has been paid *b)* any piece of paper similar to a stamp, issued by an organization, business firm, etc. [trading *stamps*] **6** any characteristic sign or impression; indication [the *stamp* of truth] **7** character; kind; class; type —**stamp out** **1** to beat, crush, or put out by treading on forcibly [to *stamp out* a fire, a cigarette, etc.] **2** to crush, suppress, or squelch

Stamp Act a law passed by the British Parliament in 1765 to raise revenue, requiring that stamps be used for all legal and commercial documents, newspapers, etc. in the American colonies: it was repealed in March, 1766, because of strong colonial opposition

☆**stam·pede** (stam pēd′) ***n.*** ⟦AmSp *estampida* < Sp, a crash, uproar < *estampar,* to stamp < Gmc **stampjan,* STAMP⟧ **1** a sudden, headlong running away of a group of frightened animals, esp. horses or cattle **2** a confused, headlong rush or flight of a large group of people **3** any sudden, impulsive, spontaneous mass movement [a *stampede* to support a candidate] —***vi.*** **-ped′ed, -ped′ing** to move, or take part, in a stampede —***vt.*** **1** to cause to stampede **2** to make a headlong charge at or upon as a group [panicked patrons *stampeded* the exits] —**stam·ped′er** ***n.***

stamp·er (stam′pər) ***n.*** a person or thing that stamps; specif., *a)* a worker who stamps (something specified) [a metal *stamper*] *b)* any of various machines or tools for stamping, as for pulverizing ore

☆**stamping ground** [Informal] a regular or favorite gathering place, resort, or haunt: *also used in pl.*

stamp mill a mill or machine for pulverizing ore

stance (stans) ***n.*** ⟦OFr *estance* < VL **stantia* < L *stans* (gen. *stantis*), prp. of *stare,* to STAND⟧ **1** the way a person or animal stands; standing posture, with special reference to placement of the feet, as the posture of a golfer, baseball batter, etc. ☆**2** the attitude adopted in confronting or dealing with a particular situation [a belligerent political *stance*] —***SYN.*** POSTURE

stanch (stänch, stanch, stônch) ***vt., vi., adj.*** *see* STAUNCH

stan·chion (stan′chən, -shən) ***n.*** ⟦ME *stanchon* < OFr *estanson, estanchon* < *estance:* see STANCE⟧ **1** an upright bar, beam, or post used as a support ☆**2** a restraining device fitted loosely around the neck of a cow to confine it to its stall —***vt.*** **1** to provide or support with stanchions ☆**2** to confine (a cow) with a stanchion

stand (stand) ***vi.*** **stood, stand′ing** ⟦ME *standen* < OE *standan;* akin to MDu *standen,* Goth *standan* < IE base **stā-,* to stand, be placed > L *stare,* to stand, Gr *histanai,* to set, cause to stand⟧ **1** *a)* to be or remain in a generally upright position, supported on the feet (or foot) *b)* to be or remain in an upright position, supported on its base, bottom, pedestal, etc. (said of physical objects) *c)* to grow upright or erect (said of plants) **2** to rise to an upright position, as from a sitting, lying, or crouching position **3** *a)* to take, move into, or be in a (specified) upright position [*stand* straight!] *b)* to take, maintain, or be in a (specified) position, attitude, or course, as of support, antagonism, responsibility, sponsorship, etc. [to *stand* opposed to an act] **4** to have a (specified) height when standing [he *stands* six feet] **5** to POINT (*vi.* 4): said of a dog **6** *a)* to be placed; be situated *b)* to remain where situated, built, etc. **7** to gather and remain: said of a liquid [sweat *stood* on his brow] **8** *a)* to remain unchanged, intact, effective, or valid [the law still *stands*] *b)* to be or remain in a printed or written form **9** to be in a (specified) condition, relation, or circumstance: used with a phrase, infinitive, or adverb [they *stood* in awe; he *stands* to lose ten dollars] **10** to be of a (specified) rank, degree, or the like [to *stand* first in one's class] **11** to maintain one's opinion, viewpoint, adherence, etc.; remain resolute or firm **12** to make resistance, as to hostile action **13** *a)* to come to a stop; halt *b)* to be or remain stationary **14** to show the (specified) relative position of those involved [the score *stands* at 28 to 20] ☆**15** to be available for breeding: said of a stallion **16** [Chiefly Brit.] to be a candidate, as for an office; run **17** *Naut.* to take or hold a course [a ship *standing* out of the harbor] **18** *Printing* to remain set: said of type or printed matter —***vt.*** **1** to make stand; set or place upright **2** to go on enduring; put up with; bear; tolerate [to *stand* pain] **3** to remain uninjured or unaffected by; withstand [*stood* the trip quite well] **4** to be subjected to; undergo [to *stand* trial] **5** to do the duty of [to *stand* watch] **6** [Informal] *a)* to bear the cost of (a dinner, etc.) as when treating *b)* to treat (a person) to food, drink, etc. **7** *Mil.* to stand in formation at (reveille, retreat, etc.) —***n.*** ⟦OE *stand* < *standan,* to stand⟧ **1** the act or position of standing (in various senses); esp., a stopping; halt or stop; specif., *a)* a stopping to counterattack, resist, etc., as in a retreat ☆*b)* a halt made by a touring theatrical company to give a performance; also, the place stopped at **2** the place where a person stands or is supposed to stand; position; station [to take one's *stand* at the rear] **3** a view, opinion, or position, as on an issue [to make one's *stand* clear] **4** a structure for a person or persons to stand or sit on, or to stand at; specif., *a)* a raised platform, as for a band or for spectators along a parade route *b)* [*often pl.*] a set of steplike tiers of benches, as for the spectators at a ballgame *c)* the place where a witness testifies in a courtroom *d)* a lectern, pulpit, reading desk, etc. ☆**5** a place of business; specif., *a)* a booth, stall, etc. where goods are sold *b)* a parking space along the side of a street, reserved as for taxicabs *c)* a business site or location **6** a rack, small table, etc. for holding something [a music *stand*] ☆**7** a growth of trees or plants **8** [Now Dial.] a group, set, etc. —***SYN.*** BEAR[1] —**it stands to reason** it is logical or reasonable —**make a stand** **1** to take a position for defense or opposition **2** to support a definite position, opinion, etc. **3** to come to a stop —**stand a chance** to have a chance (*of* winning, surviving, etc.) —**stand by** **1** *a)* to be near and ready to act if or when needed *b)* to wait to go aboard **2** to aid or support **3** *a)* to make good (a promise, etc.) *b)* to maintain (a policy) **4** to be near or present, esp. in a passive manner or as a mere onlooker **5** *Radio, TV* to remain tuned in, as for continuance of a program, or to remain ready to transmit without actually doing so —**stand down** **1** *Law* to leave the witness stand, as after testifying **2** to withdraw from a post, position, confrontation, etc. **3** [Chiefly Brit.] to withdraw one's candidacy for a public office **4** *Mil.* *a)* to withdraw from military operations or active service *b)* to reduce or order a reduction in military activity —**stand for** **1** to be a symbol for or sign of; represent; mean ☆**2** [Informal] to put up with; endure; tolerate —**stand in** ☆[Informal] to be on good terms; be friendly: usually followed by *with* —**stand in for** to substitute for —**stand off** **1** to keep at a distance ☆**2** to put off, stave off, or evade (a creditor or assailant) **3** *Naut.* to take or hold a course away from shore —**stand on** **1** to be based or founded upon; depend on **2** to insist upon; demand due observance of (ceremony, one's dignity or rights, etc.) **3** *Naut.* to hold the same course or tack —**stand out** **1** to stick out; project **2** to show up clearly; be distinct in appearance **3** to be prominent, notable, or outstanding; have distinction **4** to refuse to give in; be firm in resistance **5** *Naut.* to take or hold a course away from shore —**stand over** **1** to hover over (someone) **2** to postpone or be postponed; hold over —**stand up** **1** to rise to or be in a standing position **2** to prove valid, satisfactory, durable, etc. ☆**3** [Informal] to fail to keep an engagement with —**stand up for** **1** to take the side of; defend **2** to serve as a ceremonial advocate or supporter, as in a wedding [the best man *stands up for* the groom] —**stand up to** to confront fearlessly; refuse to be cowed or intimidated by —**stand up with** to act as a wedding attendant to —☆**take the stand** to sit (or stand) in the designated place in a courtroom and give testimony —**stand′er** ***n.***

stand-a·lone (stand′ə lōn′) ***adj.*** **1** designating or of a computer device or program that can perform functions independently **2** designating or of anything that is a separate unit, independent of a larger structure, organization, etc. [a *stand-alone* fax machine, business, novel, sculpture, etc.] —***n.*** a stand-alone device, unit, structure, etc.

stand·ard (stan′dərd) ***n.*** ⟦ME < OFr *estendard* < Frank **standord,* place of formation < Gmc **standan,* to STAND + **ort,* a place, orig., a point, akin to OE *ord* (see ODD): hence, orig., a standing place⟧ **1** any figure or object, esp. a flag or banner, used as an emblem or symbol of a leader, people, military unit, etc.; specif., *a)* *Heraldry* a long, tapering flag used as an ensign, as by a king *b)* *Mil.* the colors of a cavalry unit **2** something established for use as a rule or basis of comparison in measuring or judging capacity, quantity, content, extent, value, quality, etc. [*standards* of weight and measure] **3** *a)* the proportion of pure gold or silver and base metal prescribed for use in coinage *b)* the basis for the measure of value in a given monetary system (see GOLD STANDARD, SILVER STANDARD) **4** the type, model, or example commonly or generally accepted or adhered to; criterion set for usages or practices [moral *standards*] **5** a level of excellence, attainment, etc. regarded as a measure of adequacy **6** any upright object used as a support, often a part of the thing it supports; supporting piece; base; stand **7** a piece of popular music that continues to be included in the repertoire of many bands, singers, etc. through the years **8** *Bot.* *a)* the large, upper petal of a butterfly-shaped flower; vexillum *b)* any of the three erect petals in the flower of an iris **9** *Hort.* *a)* a tree or shrub with a tall, erect stem, that stands alone without support *b)* a plant grafted on a single erect stem to grow in tree form —*adj.* **1** used as, or meeting the requirements of, a standard, rule, model, etc. **2** generally accepted as reliable or authoritative [*standard* reference books] **3** conforming to what is usual; ordinary; not special or extra [*standard* procedure] **4** *Linguis.* *a)* of or in accord with the level of usage of most educated speakers of a language and established as the prestigious form of that language *b)* [**S-**] designating the prestigious dialect of a given language [*Standard* American English] **5** *Mech.* designating or of an automotive transmission that is MANUAL (*adj.* 3)

SYN.—**standard** applies to some measure, principle, model, etc. with which things of the same class are compared in order to determine their quantity, value, quality, etc. [*standard* of purity for drugs]; **criterion** applies to a test or rule for measuring the excellence, fitness, or correctness of something [mere memory is no accurate *criterion* of intelligence]; **gauge** literally applies to a standard of measurement [a wire *gauge*], but figuratively it is equivalent to **criterion** [sales are an accurate *gauge* of a book's popularity]; **yardstick** refers to a test or criterion for measuring genuineness or value [time is the only true *yardstick* of a book's merit] See also **model**

stand·ard-bear·er (-ber′ər) *n.* **1** the person assigned to carry the standard, or flag, of a group, esp. of a military organization **2** the leader or chief representative of a movement, political party, etc.

☆**Stand·ard·bred** (-bred′) *n.* any of a breed of light horse developed from the Thoroughbred and specially trained for trotting or pacing in harness races

standard deviation *Statistics* a measure of variability equal to the square root of the arithmetic average of the squares of the deviations from the mean in a frequency distribution

standard error *Statistics* a measure of the dispersion in the distribution of differences between expected and observed values of a statistic: the standard error of the mean is equal to the standard deviation of the original frequency distribution divided by the square root of the sample size

standard gauge **1** a width of 56.5 in (143.5 cm) between the rails of a railroad track, established as standard **2** a railroad having such a gauge **3** a locomotive or car for tracks of such a gauge —**stand′ard-gauge′** *adj.*

stand·ard·ize (stan′dər dīz′) *vt.* **-ized′**, **-iz′ing** **1** to make standard or uniform; cause to be without variations or irregularities **2** to compare with, test by, or adjust to a standard —**stand′ard·i·za′tion** *n.* —**stand′ard·iz′er** *n.*

Standard Model *Particle Physics* a theory based on the interactions of leptons, quarks, and bosons, that is used to explain the basic structure of matter, electricity, magnetism, radioactivity, etc. but not of gravity

standard of living a level of subsistence, as of a nation, social class, or person, with reference to the adequacy of necessities and comforts in daily life

standard pitch CONCERT PITCH

☆**standard time** **1** the time in any of the 24 time zones, each an hour apart, into which the earth is divided: it is based on distance east or west of Greenwich, England; the 8 zones of North America (*Atlantic, Eastern, Central, Mountain, Pacific, Alaska, Hawaii-Aleutian*, and *Samoa*) use the mean solar times of the 60th, 75th, 90th, 105th, 120th, 135th, 150th, and 165th meridians, respectively: see TIME ZONE, map **2** the official time, whether mean solar time or daylight saving time, in any given region

stand·by (stand′bī′) *n., pl.* **-bys′** **1** a person or thing that can always be depended on, is always effective, etc. **2** a person or thing ready to serve or be put into service on an emergency basis or as a substitute **3** a person waiting to board an airplane, etc. if space becomes available, as through a cancellation —*adj.* of, for, or functioning as a standby —**on standby** ready or waiting as a standby

stand-down (stand′doun′) *n.* the act or an instance of standing down (see the phrase STAND DOWN under STAND)

☆**stand·ee** (stan dē′) *n.* a person who stands, usually because there are no vacant seats, as on a bus

☆**stand-in** (stand′in′) *n.* **1** a person who serves as a substitute for a film or television actor or actress as while lights and cameras are being adjusted **2** any substitute for another

stand·ing (stan′diŋ) *n.* **1** the act, state, or position of a person or thing that stands **2** a place to stand; standing room **3** *a)* status, position, rank, or reputation [in good *standing*] *b)* [*pl.*] a list showing rank or order, as in achievement, resources, etc. [team *standings* in a league] **4** duration or length of service, existence, membership, etc. [a record of long *standing*] —*adj.* **1** upright or erect [a *standing* position] **2** done or made in or from a standing position [a *standing* jump] **3** not flowing; stagnant: said as of water **4** going on regularly without change; lasting; permanent [a *standing* order] **5** stationary; not movable **6** not in use; idle: said as of a machine **7** *Printing* set and stored for future use: said as of type

standing army an army maintained on a permanent basis, in peacetime as well as in time of war

standing O [Slang] *short for* STANDING OVATION

standing order **1** an order remaining in effect indefinitely until canceled or modified **2** [*pl.*] in parliamentary procedure, the rules which continue in force through all sessions until changed or repealed

standing ovation an enthusiastic outburst of applause in which some or all members of the audience rise to their feet

standing rigging the permanently positioned parts of a vessel's rigging, as stays and shrouds, used to support sails, masts, etc.: cf. RUNNING RIGGING

standing room room in which to stand, esp. when there are no vacant seats, as in a theater

standing wave an oscillatory motion with a definite wavelength, frequency, and amplitude and having stationary, regularly spaced points where there is no motion: all the movement of the wave is contained between these nodes, thus providing for no net transport of energy

stand·ish (stan′dish) *n.* ⟦< ? STAND + DISH⟧ [Archaic] a stand for writing materials; inkstand

Stan·dish (stan′dish), **Miles** (or **Myles**) 1584?-1656; Eng. colonist: military leader of Plymouth Colony

stand·off (stand′ôf′) *n.* **1** a standing off or being stood off **2** a counterbalancing or equalizing effect **3** a tie or draw in a game or contest —*adj.* that stands off

stand·off·ish (stand′ôf′ish) *adj.* reserved and cool; aloof —**stand′off′ish·ly** *adv.* —**stand′off′ish·ness** *n.*

stand oil ⟦so called because orig. prepared from linseed oil left to *stand* in sunlight⟧ linseed oil thickened by heat treatment

stand·out (stand′out′) *n.* ⟦< STAND OUT (see phr. under STAND)⟧ a person or thing conspicuously superior or notable in performance, quality, etc. —*adj.* outstanding

☆**stand·pat** (-pat′) *adj.* [Informal] of or characterized by a tendency to stand pat, or resist change; conservative —**stand′pat′ter** (-pat′ər) *n.* —**stand·pat·tism** (stand′pat iz′əm) *n.*

stand·pipe (-pīp′) *n.* a high vertical pipe or cylindrical tank for storing water and keeping it at a desired pressure, esp. such a large tank used in the water-supply system for a town, etc.

stand·point (-point′) *n.* ⟦calque < Ger *standpunkt*⟧ **1** a position from which something is or may be viewed **2** the mental position from which things are judged; point of view

stand·still (-stil′) *n.* a stop, halt, or cessation

stand-up (-up′) *adj.* **1** standing upright or erect **2** done, taken, etc. in a standing position [a *stand-up* lunch] **3** high, stiff, and without folds: said of a collar ☆**4** ⟦< *adj.* 2⟧ designating or of a comedian who delivers monologues, tells a series of jokes, etc., as in nightclubs **5** [Slang] designating or having to do with a loyal, courageous person who will stand up resolutely for friends, principles, etc. [a *stand-up* guy] —*n.* **1** a stand-up comedian **2** stand-up comedy

stane (stān) *n., vt., adj. Scot. var. of* STONE

☆**Stan·ford-Bi·net test** (stan′fərd bi nā′) a revision of the Binet-Simon test: developed at Stanford University, it covers a wider range and offers more tests than the original scale: also called **Stanford revision**

stang[1] (staŋ) *vt., vi. archaic pt. & pp. of* STING

stang[2] (staŋ) *vt., vi., n.* ⟦< ME *stangen* < ON *stanga*, to prick, goad: for IE base see STING⟧ *Scot. or North Eng. var. of* STING

stan·hope (stan′hōp′, stan′əp) *n.* ⟦after Fitzroy *Stanhope* (1787-1864), Brit clergyman for whom the first one was built⟧ a light, open carriage drawn by one horse, with two low wheels and one seat, popular in 19th-cent. England and the U.S.

Stan·hope (stan′əp), **Philip Dor·mer** (dôr′mər) *see* CHESTERFIELD, 4th Earl of

sta·nine (stā′nīn′) *n.* ⟦STA(NDARD) + NINE⟧ any of nine statistical units based on a standardized distribution of results, used in grading psychological or educational tests

Stan·i·slav·sky (stan′i släf′skē, stän′-), **Kon·stan·tin** (kän′stən tēn′) (born *Konstantin Sergeyevich Alekseyev*) 1863-1938; Russ. actor, director, & teacher of acting

stank (staŋk) *vi. alt. pt. of* STINK

Stan·ley[1] (stan′lē) *n.* ⟦< the surname *Stanley* < the place name *Stanley* < OE *stan leah*, stone lea⟧ a masculine name: dim. *Stan*

Stan·ley[2] (stan′lē), Sir **Henry Morton** (born *John Rowlands*) 1841-1904; Brit. journalist & explorer in Africa

Stan·ley[3] (stan′lē), **Mount** mountain in EC Africa: highest peak of the Ruwenzori group: 16,795 ft (5,119 m)

Stanley Falls series of seven cataracts of the upper Congo River, just south of Kisangani

Stanley Pool *another name for* MALEBO POOL

Stan·ley·ville (stan′lē vil′) *former name for* KISANGANI

stan·na·ry (stan′ər ē) *n., pl.* **-ries** ⟦ML *stannaria* < LL *stannum, stagnum*, tin, prob. < Celt⟧ a region of tin mines and tinworks —**the Stannaries** such a region in Devon & Cornwall, England

stan·nic (stan′ik) *adj.* ⟦< LL *stannum* (see prec.) + -IC⟧ of or containing tin, specif. tetravalent tin

stan·nite (stan′īt′) *n.* ⟦< LL *stannum*, tin + -ITE[1]⟧ a dark-colored, tetragonal mineral, Cu_2FeSnS_4, an ore of tin; copper iron tin sulfide

stan·nous (stan′əs) *adj.* ⟦< LL *stannum*, tin + -OUS⟧ of or containing tin, specif. divalent tin

Stan·ton (stant′'n) **1 Edwin Mc·Mas·ters** (mək mas′tərz) 1814-69; U.S. statesman: secretary of war (1862-68) **2 Elizabeth Ca·dy** (kā′dē) 1815-1902; U.S. reformer & suffragist leader

stan·za (stan′zə) *n.* ⟦It, lit., stopping place, room < VL **stantia*: see STANCE⟧ a group of lines of verse forming one of the divisions of a poem or song: it is usually made up of four or more lines and often has a regular pattern in the number of lines and the arrangement of meter and rhyme —**stan·za′ic** (-zā′ik) *adj.*

sta·pe·dec·to·my (stā′pə dek′tə mē) *n., pl.* **-mies** ⟦ModL *staped-*, stem of STAPES + -ECTOMY⟧ a surgical operation of the middle ear, in which the stapes is removed and, usually, replaced with an artificial part, as to restore hearing

sta·pe·di·al (stə pē′dē əl) ***adj.*** ⟦< ModL *staped-*, stem of STAPES⟧ of the stapes

sta·pe·li·a (stə pē′lē ə, -pēl′yə) ***n.*** ⟦ModL, after Jan Bode van *Stapel* (died 1636), Du botanist and physician⟧ any of a genus (*Stapelia*) of cactuslike African plants of the milkweed family, with large, star-shaped, bad-smelling, yellowish or purple flowers

sta·pes (stā′pēz′) ***n., pl.*** **sta′pes′** or **sta·pe·des** (stə pē′dēz′) ⟦ModL < ML, a stirrup, prob. < Gmc, as in MDu *stap*, a STEP, Langobardic *staffa*, step, stirrup⟧ *Anat.* a small, stirrup-shaped bone, the innermost of a chain of three bones in the middle ear of mammals; stirrup

staph (staf) ***n.*** *short for* STAPHYLOCOCCUS

staph·y·lo- (staf′ə lō, -lə) ⟦< Gr *staphylē*, bunch of grapes⟧ *combining form* **1** uvula *[staphylorrhaphy]* **2** grapelike *[staphylococcus]* Also, before a vowel, **staphyl-**

staph·y·lo·coc·cus (staf′ə lō käk′əs) ***n., pl.*** **-coc′ci′** (-käk′sī′) ⟦ModL: see prec. & -COCCUS⟧ any of a genus (*Staphylococcus*) of spherical, Gram-positive bacteria that generally occur in irregular clusters or short chains: the pathogenic species (esp. *S. aureus*) are the cause of pus formation in boils, abscesses, etc. —**staph′y·lo·coc′cal** (-käk′əl) ***adj.***, **staph′y·lo·coc′cic** (-käk′sik)

staph·y·lor·rha·phy (staf′ə lôr′ə fē) ***n., pl.*** **-phies** ⟦< STAPHYLO- + Gr *rhaphē*, a sewing, suture < *rhaptein*, to sew: see RHAPSODY⟧ the operation of uniting a cleft palate by plastic surgery

sta·ple[1] (stā′pəl) ***n.*** ⟦ME *stapel* < OFr *estaple* < MDu *stapel*, mart, emporium, post, orig. support, akin to fol.⟧ **1** the chief commodity, or any of the most important commodities, made, grown, or sold in a particular place, region, country, etc. **2** a chief item, part, material, or element in anything **3** any chief item of trade, regularly stocked and in constant demand *[flour, sugar, and salt are staples]* **4** the fiber of cotton, wool, flax, etc., with reference to length and fineness —***adj.*** **1** regularly found on the market or in stock as a result of a constant demand **2** produced, consumed, or exported regularly and in quantity **3** most important; leading; principal *[staple industries]* —***vt.*** **-pled, -pling** to sort (wool, cotton, etc.) according to the nature of its staple

sta·ple[2] (stā′pəl) ***n.*** ⟦ME *stapel* < OE *stapol*, post, pillar, akin to Ger *stapel*, stake, beam: for IE base see STAMP⟧ **1** a U-shaped piece of metal with sharp, pointed ends, driven into a surface to keep a hook, hasp, wire, etc. firmly in place **2** a similar piece of thin wire driven through papers and clinched over as a binding —***vt.*** **-pled, -pling** to fasten or bind with a staple or staples

sta·pler[1] (stā′plər) ***n.*** **1** a person who deals in staple goods **2** a person who staples (wool, etc.)

sta·pler[2] (stā′plər) ***n.*** **1** any of various devices or machines for driving staples through paper, etc., as for binding pamphlets **2** a heavier device for stapling insulation, upholstery fabric, etc. in place: also called **staple gun**

star (stär) ***n.*** ⟦ME *sterre* < OE *steorra*, akin to Goth *stairnō*, Cornish *sterenn* < IE base **ster-*, a star > Gr *astēr*, L *stella* (dim. < **ster-ela*), star⟧ **1** any of the luminous celestial objects seen as points of light in the sky; esp., any self-luminous celestial body having continuous nuclear reactions which send heat, light, etc. in all directions **2** a conventionalized flat figure having (usually five or six) symmetrical projecting points, regarded as a representation of a star of the sky **3** any mark, shape, emblem, or the like resembling such a figure, often used as an award, symbol of rank or authority, etc. **4** ASTERISK **5** *[often pl.]* *a)* *Astrol.* a zodiacal constellation or a planet regarded as influencing human fate or destiny *b)* [Obs.] fate; destiny; fortune **6** a person who excels or performs brilliantly in a given activity, esp. a sport **7** a prominent actor or actress, esp. one playing a leading role and having special billing in a given production —***vt.*** **starred, star′ring** **1** to mark or set with stars as a decoration **2** to mark with one or more stars as a grade of quality **3** to mark with an asterisk **4** to present or feature (an actor or actress) in a leading role —***vi.*** **1** to perform brilliantly; excel **2** to perform as a star, as in a theatrical production —***adj.*** **1** having exceptional skill and talent; outstanding; excelling others; leading *[a star performer]* **2** of a star or stars —**see stars** [Informal] to experience the sensation of lights brightly flashing before the eyes, as from a blow on the head —**thank one's (lucky) stars** to be thankful for what appears to be good luck

star apple **1** a tropical American evergreen tree (*Chrysophyllum cainito*) of the sapodilla family, with shiny leaves, whitish flowers, and applelike fruit showing a starlike figure inside when cut across **2** its fruit

Sta·ra Za·go·ra (stä′rä zä gô′rä) city in central Bulgaria

star·board (stär′bərd, -bôrd′) ***n.*** ⟦ME *sterbord* < OE *steorbord* < *steoran*, to STEER[1] (the old rudder being a large oar used on the right side of the ship) + *bord:* see BOARD⟧ the right-hand side of a ship, boat, or airplane as one faces forward: opposed to PORT[4] —***adj.*** **1** of or on this side **2** designating a sailing tack on which the wind passes over the starboard side — ***vt., vi.*** to move or turn (the helm) to the right

star·burst (-burst′) ***n.*** a pattern or design characterized by lines radiating from a central point

starburst galaxy a galaxy exhibiting a relatively high degree of star formation

starch (stärch) ***n.*** ⟦ME *starche* < *sterchen*, to stiffen < OE **stercan* < *stearc*, rigid, stiff, akin to Ger *stark*, strong: see STARK⟧ **1** a white, tasteless, odorless substance found in potatoes, rice, corn, wheat, cassava, and many other vegetables: it is a granular solid, chemically a complex carbohydrate, $(C_6H_{10}O_5)_n$, and is used in adhesives, sizes, cooking, cosmetics, medicine, etc. **2** a powdered form of this, used in laundering for stiffening cloth, fabrics, etc. **3** *[pl.]* starchy foods **4** formal, unbending manner or behavior; stiffness ☆**5** [Informal] energy; vigor —***vt.*** to stiffen with or as if with starch —**starch′less** ***adj.***

Star Chamber ⟦ME, earlier *Sterred Chambre:* said to be so called because the ceiling was ornamented with stars⟧ **1** a royal English court or tribunal abolished in 1641, notorious for its secret sessions without jury, and for its harsh and arbitrary judgments and its use of torture to force confessions **2** *[also* **s- c-***]* any similar tribunal or inquisitorial body

starch·y (stär′chē) ***adj.*** **starch′i·er, starch′i·est** **1** of, containing, or like starch **2** stiffened with starch **3** stiff; formal; unbending —**starch′i·ly** ***adv.*** —**starch′i·ness** ***n.***

star-crossed (stär′krôst′) ***adj.*** ⟦see STAR, ***n.*** 5⟧ destined to an unhappy fate; sure to end up in misfortune; unlucky

star·dom (-dəm) ***n.*** **1** the status of a STAR (***n.*** 6 & 7) **2** stars of films, TV, etc., collectively

star·dust (-dust′) ***n.*** **1** a cluster of stars too distant to be seen separately with the naked eye **2** [Informal] an enchanting, dreamlike state or mood; starry-eyed quality

stare (ster) ***vi.*** **stared, star′ing** ⟦ME *staren* < OE *starian*, akin to ON *stara* < Gmc **stara-*, having fixed eyes, rigid < IE base **(s)ter-*, rigid, stiff > STARK, Gr *strēnēs*, hard⟧ **1** to gaze or look steadily with eyes wide open, as in fear, admiration, wonder, incomprehension, etc. **2** [Now Rare] *a)* to stand out conspicuously *[staring bones]* *b)* to stand on end, as hair —***vt.*** **1** to look fixedly at *[to stare a person up and down]* **2** to affect in a given way by staring *[to stare someone into confusion]* —***n.*** the act of staring; steady or vacant look or gaze —**stare down** to stare at (another) boldly until he or she looks away —**stare someone in the face** **1** to look at someone steadily and intently **2** to be imminent, pressing, or inescapable —**star′er** ***n.***

sta·re de·ci·sis (stär′ē di sī′sis, ster′-) ⟦L, to stand by things decided⟧ a policy of law that requires courts to abide by laws and precedents previously laid down as applicable to a similar set of facts

sta·rets (stär′yəts) ***n., pl.*** **star·tsy** (stärt′sē) ⟦Russ *starec*, an elder, venerable old man < *staryj*, old⟧ *Eastern Orthodox Ch.* a spiritual advisor

star·fish (stär′fish′) ***n., pl.*** **-fish′** or **-fish′es** (see FISH) any of a subclass (Asteroidea) of echinoderms with a hard, spiny skeleton and five or more arms or rays arranged like the points of a star; asteroid

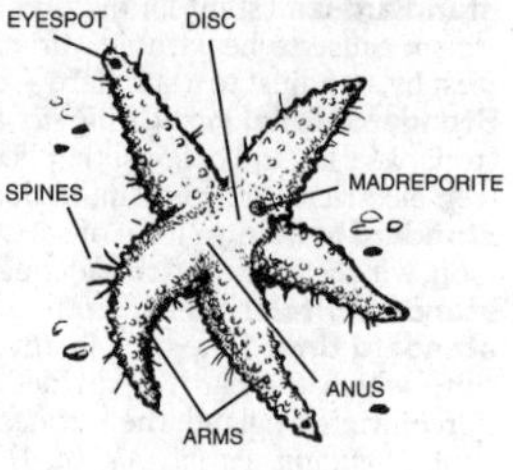

EYESPOT DISC SPINES MADREPORITE ANUS ARMS

starfish

star·flow·er (-flou′ər) ***n.*** **1** any of a genus (*Trientalis*) of small woodland plants of the primrose family, with white or pink, five-petaled, star-shaped flowers **2** any of various other plants with star-shaped flowers, as the star-of-Bethlehem

star fruit ⟦so named because its cross section is shaped like a *star*⟧ CARAMBOLA (sense 2)

star·gaze (-gāz′) ***vi.*** **-gazed′, -gaz′ing** ⟦back-form. < fol.⟧ **1** to gaze at the stars **2** to indulge in dreamy, fanciful, or visionary musing; daydream

star·gaz·er (-gā′zər) ***n.*** **1** a person who stargazes, as an astrologer or astronomer **2** any of a family (Uranoscopidae) of tropical, marine percoid fishes having eyes at the top of the head and electrical organs behind the eyes

star grass any of a number of grasslike plants with star-shaped flowers, including two genera (*Hypoxis* and *Aletris*) of the lily family

stark (stärk) ***adj.*** ⟦ME *starc* < OE *stearc:* see STARE⟧ **1** *a)* [Archaic] physically stiff or rigid *b)* rigorous; harsh; severe *[stark discipline]* **2** sharply outlined or prominent *[one stark tree]* **3** bleak; desolate; barren *[stark wasteland]* **4** *a)* emptied; stripped *[stark shelves]* *b)* [Archaic] totally naked; bare **5** grimly blunt; unsoftened, unembellished, etc. *[stark realism]* **6** sheer; utter; downright; unrelieved *[stark terror]* **7** [Archaic] strong; powerful —***adv.*** in a stark manner; esp., utterly; wholly *[stark mad]* —**stark′ly** ***adv.*** —**stark′ness** ***n.***

stark·ers (stär′kərz) ***adj.*** [Informal, Chiefly Brit.] **1** wearing no clothes; naked **2** insane; crazy

stark-na·ked (stärk′nā′kid) ***adj.*** ⟦altered (infl. by STARK) < ME *stertnaked*, lit., tail-naked < *stert-* < OE *steort*, tail, rump < IE **(s)terd-:* see START⟧ absolutely naked: also written **stark naked**

star·less (stär′lis) ***adj.*** **1** without stars **2** with no stars visible *[a starless sky]*

star·let (-lit) ***n.*** **1** a small star ☆**2** a young actress being promoted as a possible future star

star·light (-līt′) ***n.*** light given by the stars

star·like (-līk′) ***adj.*** **1** like a star in brilliance **2** star-shaped; having radial points

star·ling (stär′liŋ) ***n.*** ⟦ME < OE *stærlinc*, dim. of *stær*, starling < IE **stor(n)os*, starling, bird with similar cry > L *sturnus*⟧ any of an Old World family (Sturnidae) of dark-colored passerine birds with a short tail, long wings, and a sharp, pointed bill; esp., the **common starling** (*Sturnus vulgaris*) with iridescent plumage, introduced into the U.S.

star·lit (stär′lit′) ***adj.*** lighted by the stars

☆**star-nosed mole** (-nōzd′) a brownish-black, long-tailed, North American mole (*Condylura cristata*) having a ring of fleshy tentacles around its nose

star of Bethlehem *Bible* the bright star over Bethlehem at the birth of Jesus, guiding the Magi: Matt. 2:1-10

star-of-Beth·le·hem (-əv beth′lə hem′, -lē əm) *n., pl.* **stars′-of-Beth′le·hem′** a bulbous plant (*Ornithogalum umbellatum*) of the lily family, with white, star-shaped flowers and long, narrow leaves

Star of David ⟦transl. < Heb *magen david*, lit., shield of David⟧ a six-pointed star formed of two, often interlaced, equilateral triangles: a symbol of Judaism and now of the State of Israel: as a mystic symbol in the Middle Ages, called *Solomon's Seal*

Star of David

starred (stärd) *adj.* **1** marked or decorated with or as with a star or stars **2** thought, as in astrology, to be influenced by the stars [*ill-starred*]

☆**star route** ⟦so named from the *star*, or asterisk, designating such routes in postal records⟧ a route between one city or town and another over which mail is transported by a private carrier under contract

star·ry (stär′ē) *adj.* **-ri·er, -ri·est 1** set or marked with stars **2** shining like stars; bright **3** shaped like a star **4** lighted by or full of stars **5** of or coming from the stars —**star′ri·ness** *n.*

☆**star·ry-eyed** (-īd′) *adj.* **1** with the eyes sparkling in a glow of happiness, dreams, wonder, romance, etc. **2** impractical, unrealistic, overly optimistic, etc. [*a starry-eyed* reformer]

☆**Stars and Bars** *name for* the original flag (1861) of the American Confederacy, with a white horizontal bar between two parallel red ones and at the upper left, on a blue field, a circle of seven white stars, one for each seceded state

☆**Stars and Stripes** *name for* the flag of the United States, with seven horizontal red stripes and six white ones, the colors alternating, and in the upper left corner a blue field with white stars (now 50), one for each state

star sapphire a type of sapphire that reflects light in a star-shaped pattern when cut as a cabochon

star shell *Mil.* a shell timed to burst in midair in a shower of bright particles that light up the surrounding terrain

star·ship (stär′ship′) *n.* in science fiction, a spaceship capable of traveling to various stars or galaxies

star-span·gled (stär′spaŋ′gəld) *adj.* studded or spangled with stars

☆**Star-Spangled Banner** ⟦with reference to the U.S. flag⟧ the United States national anthem: the words were written by Francis Scott Key during the War of 1812

star-struck or **star·struck** (stär′struk′) *adj.* ⟦< STAR (*n.* 6 & 7)⟧ drawn to or fascinated by famous or eminent people, esp. those in the theater, films, music, etc.

start (stärt) *vi.* ⟦ME *sterten* < OE *styrtan* & ON *sterta*, akin to Ger *stürzen*, to overthrow < IE **sterd-* < base **(s)ter-*, stiff, walk stiffly > STARE, STARVE, STORK⟧ **1** to make a sudden, involuntary or unexpected movement, as when surprised; jump, leap, jerk, etc. in a startled way **2** to be displaced; become loose, warped, etc. **3** to stick out or seem to stick out [eyes *starting* in fear] **4** *a)* to begin to do something or go somewhere; go into action or motion *b)* to make or have a beginning; commence **5** to be among the beginning entrants, as in a race; be a starter **6** to spring into being, activity, view, or the like —*vt.* **1** to cause to jump or move suddenly; rouse or flush (game) **2** to displace, loosen, warp, etc. **3** *a)* to enter upon; begin to perform, play, do, etc. *b)* to cause or enable to begin; set into motion, action, or operation **4** to introduce (a subject, topic, or discussion) **5** to open and make the contents flow from (a receptacle); tap **6** *a)* to give the starting signal for (a race) or to (the contestants in a race) *b)* to cause to be an entrant in a race, etc. *c)* to put (a player) into a game at the beginning *d)* to play in (a game) at the beginning (said of a player) **7** [Now Chiefly Dial.] to cause to start, or move involuntarily; startle —*n.* **1** a sudden, brief shock or fright; startled reaction **2** a sudden, startled movement; jump, leap, jerk, etc. **3** [*pl.*] sudden, usually brief bursts of activity: usually in the phrase *by fits and starts* **4** *a)* a part that is loosened, warped, etc. *b)* a break or gap resulting from this **5** a starting, or beginning; a getting into action or motion; commencement; specif., the fact of being part of the team that starts a game [a pitcher with 30 *starts* for the season] **6** *a)* a place where, or a time when, a beginning is made, as in a race; starting point [ahead from the *start*] *b)* a lead or other advantage, as at the beginning of a race or contest *c)* a signal to begin, as in a race **7** an opportunity of beginning or entering upon a career, etc. **8** [Archaic] an outburst or fit, as of emotion, or a sally, as of wit —*SYN.* BEGIN —**start a hare** [Chiefly Brit.] to bring forward an issue, question, etc. for consideration —☆**start in** to begin a task, activity, etc. —**start out** (or **off**) **1** to start a journey **2** to make a start on some course of action or procedure —**start something** to cause a disturbance or trouble —**start up 1** to rise up or stand suddenly, as in fright **2** to come into being suddenly; spring up **3** to cause (a motor, etc.) to begin running

☆**START** (stärt) *abbrev.* Strategic Arms Reduction Talks

start·er (-ər) *n.* a person or thing that starts; specif., *a)* the first in a series *b)* a person or animal that starts in a race or game *c)* a person who gives the signal to start, as in a race *d)* a person who supervises the departure of commercial trucks, buses, etc. *e)* any of various devices for initiating motion in an internal-combustion engine; specif., an electric motor briefly activated by the ignition switch and powered by the battery to turn the flywheel *f)* a device within a fluorescent lamp or other discharge lamp, for initiating high voltage across the electrodes *g)* a pure culture used to start fermentation of cream, etc. *h)* the first course of a meal; appetizer ☆*i)* *Baseball* a pitcher who starts a game —**for starters** [Informal] to begin with

star thistle any of several European plants (genus *Centaurea*) of the composite family; esp., an annual weed (*C. maculosa*) now common in NE U.S.

starting blocks *Track & Field* the rigid blocks, mounted on a track and set at various angles, against which a runner's shoes are placed to aid in starting

starting gate a movable set of stalls with gates that open simultaneously at the start of a horse race

star·tle (stärt′'l) *vt.* **-tled, -tling** ⟦ME *stertlen*, to rush, stumble along, freq. of *sterten*: see START⟧ to surprise, frighten, or alarm suddenly or unexpectedly; esp., to cause to start, or move involuntarily, as from sudden fright —*vi.* to be startled —*n.* a start or shock, as of surprise or fright —**star′tler** *n.* —**star′tling** *adj.* —**star′tling·ly** *adv.*

start-up (stärt′up′) *n.* **1** a starting or starting up **2** a new business venture —*adj.* of or for a new business venture [*start-up* capital] Also **start′up′**

star turn ⟦see TURN (*n.* IV, 6)⟧ the best or most important performer or performance in a program, achievement in a group or series, etc.

star·va·tion (stär vā′shən) *n.* **1** the act of starving **2** the state of being starved —*adj.* likely to cause starving [a *starvation* diet]

starve (stärv) *vi.* **starved, starv′ing** ⟦ME *sterven* < OE *steorfan*, to die, perish, akin to Ger *sterben*: see START⟧ **1** *a)* to die from lack of food *b)* to suffer or become weak from hunger *c)* [Informal] to be ravenously hungry **2** to suffer great need: with *for* [*starving* for affection] **3** [Now Dial.] to suffer and die slowly from any cause, esp. from extreme cold —*vt.* **1** to cause to starve by depriving of food **2** to force by starvation [to *starve* an enemy into submission] **3** to cause to suffer from a lack or need of something specified **4** [Now Dial.] to cause to die from extreme cold

starve·ling (stärv′liŋ) [Now Literary] *n.* ⟦prec. + -LING[1]⟧ a person or animal that is thin or weak from lack of food —*adj.* **1** starving; weak and hungry **2** suffering, showing, or caused by extreme deprivation; impoverished

☆**Star Wars** ⟦from the title of a 1977 science-fiction film⟧ [Informal] SDI

☆**stash** (stash) [Informal] *vt.* ⟦< ?⟧ to put or hide away (money, valuables, etc.) in a secret or safe place, as for future use —*n.* **1** a place for hiding things **2** something hidden away; specif., a hidden supply of an illegal drug

sta·sis (stā′sis, stas′is) *n., pl.* **-ses′** (-sēz′) ⟦ModL < Gr, a standing < *histanai*, to STAND⟧ **1** *a)* a stoppage of the flow of some fluid in the body, as of blood *b)* reduced peristalsis of the intestines resulting in the retention of feces **2** a state of equilibrium, balance, or stagnancy

stat[1] (stat) *n.* [Informal] *short for* STATISTIC

stat[2] (stat) *adv.* ⟦see STAT.⟧ at once; immediately: orig. a medical term

stat[3] *abbrev.* **1** statuary **2** statute(s)

stat. *abbrev.* ⟦L *statim*⟧ *Pharmacy* at once

-stat (stat) ⟦prob. < Gr *-statēs*, that which stops or makes steady < *sta-*, root of *histanai*, to cause to stand: see STAND⟧ *combining form* an instrument or agent that keeps something (specified) stable or stationary [*thermostat, heliostat*]

state (stāt) *n.* ⟦ME < OFr & L: OFr *estat* < L *status*, state, position, standing < pp. of *stare*, to STAND⟧ **1** a set of circumstances or attributes characterizing a person or thing at a given time; way or form of being; condition [a *state* of poverty] **2** a particular mental or emotional condition [a *state* of bliss] **3** condition as regards physical structure, constitution, internal form, stage or phase of existence, etc. [liquid *state*] **4** *a)* condition or position in life; social status, rank, or degree *b)* high rank or position *c)* the style of living characteristic of people having high rank and wealth; rich, imposing, ceremonious display [drove up in *state*] **5** [*sometimes* **S-**] *a)* the power or authority represented by a body of people politically organized under one government, esp. an independent government, within a territory or territories having definite boundaries *b)* such a body of people; body politic ☆**6** [*often* **S-**] any of the territorial and political units that together constitute a federal government, as in the U.S. ☆**7** the territory of a STATE (senses 5*b* & 6) **8** the political organization constituting the basis of civil government [church and *state*] **9** the sphere of highest governmental authority and administration [matters of *state*] **10** [**S-**] foreign policy: used in titles [Secretary of *State*] —*adj.* **1** of, for, or characteristic of occasions of great ceremony; formal; ceremonial **2** [*sometimes* **S-**] of or controlled, maintained, etc. by the government or a state —*vt.* **stat′ed, stat′ing 1** to fix or establish by specifying [at the *stated* hour] **2** *a)* to set forth in words, esp. in a specific, definite, or formal way [to *state* one's objectives] *b)* to express or present in a nonverbal way [to *state* a musical theme in the first three measures] —**in** (or **into**) **a state** [Informal] in (or into) a condition of agitation or excitement —**lie in state** to be displayed formally to the public before burial —**the States** the United States —**stat′a·ble** *adj.*

SYN.—**state** and **condition** both refer to the set of circumstances surrounding or characterizing a person or thing at a given time [what is his mental *state*, or *condition?*], but **condition** more strongly implies some relationship to causes or circumstances which may be temporary [his *condition* will not permit him to travel]; **situation** implies a significant interrelationship of the circumstances, and connection between these and the person involved [to be in a difficult *situation*]; **status**, basically a legal term, refers to one's state as determined by such arbitrary factors as age, sex, training, mentality, service, etc. [his *status* as a veteran exempts him]

☆**state bank** a bank chartered by a state of the U.S. and subject to its regulations

state capitalism an economic system in which much of the capital, industry, etc. is controlled by the state: a loose term sometimes equivalent to STATE SOCIALISM

state church ESTABLISHED CHURCH

state·craft (stat′kraft′, -kräft′) *n.* STATESMANSHIP

stat·ed (stāt′id) *adj.* **1** fixed or set, as by agreement **2** declared, esp. in specific terms; expressed —**stat′ed·ly** *adv.*

stated clerk an administrative official in the Presbyterian Church and certain other Protestant churches

☆**State Department** the department of the executive branch of the U.S. government in charge of relations with foreign countries

stateful (stāt′fəl) *adj.* capable of retaining information about transactions or sessions: said of software

☆**state·hood** (stāt′hood′) *n.* **1** the condition or status of being a state **2** [*sometimes* **S-**] the condition or status of being a state of the U.S.

state·house (-hous′) *n.* ☆[*often* **S-**] in the U.S., the building in which a state legislature meets

state·less (stāt′lis) *adj.* **1** having no state or nationality **2** incapable of retaining information about transactions or sessions: said of software

state·ly (stāt′lē) *adj.* **-li·er, -li·est 1** imposing; dignified; majestic **2** slow, dignified, and deliberate [*a stately* pace] —*SYN.* GRAND —**state′li·ness** *n.*

state·ment (stāt′mənt) *n.* **1** *a)* an act of stating *b)* the thing stated; account, declaration, assertion, etc. **2** *a)* an abstract, usually itemized, of a financial account [a bank *statement*] *b)* a listing of charges for goods or services; bill

Stat·en Island (stat′'n) ⟦< Du *Staaten Eylandt,* States Island, referring to the States-General of the Dutch Republic⟧ **1** island in New York Bay: 60 sq mi (155 sq km) **2** borough of New York City, comprising this island & small nearby islands

state of the art the current level of sophistication of a developing technology —**state′-of-the-art′** *adj.*

☆**State of the Union (address)** an annual speech delivered in January by the sitting U.S. president to a joint session of Congress

state of war a condition or period of hostilities between nations, either undeclared or officially declared

stat·er (stāt′ər) *n.* ⟦ME < LL(Ec) < Gr *statēr,* orig., a weight⟧ any of various gold and silver coins of ancient Greece

state·room (stāt′room′) *n.* ⟦see STATE (*adj.* 1): orig. used of a richly furnished ceremonial room as in a palace, and later of the spacious cabin of a ship's captain or officer⟧ **1** a private cabin on a ship ☆**2** a private sleeping room in a railroad car

☆**State's attorney** a lawyer appointed or elected to prepare cases for a U.S. state and represent it in court

☆**state's evidence** *Law* evidence given by or for the prosecution in a criminal case, usually evidence given by a criminal against his or her associates —**turn state's evidence** to give evidence for the prosecution in a criminal case

States-Gen·er·al (stāts′jen′ər əl) *n.* ⟦transl. of Fr *états généraux,* Du *staaten generaal*⟧ **1** the legislative body in France before the Revolution of 1789, made up of representatives of the clergy, the nobility, and the third estate **2** the legislative assembly of the Netherlands Also **States General**

☆**state·side** (stāt′sīd′) [Informal] *adj.* of or characteristic of the U.S. (as viewed from abroad) —*adv.* in, to, or toward the U.S.

states·man (stāts′mən) *n., pl.* **-men** (-mən) ⟦*state's,* gen. of STATE + MAN, based on Fr *homme d'état*⟧ a person who shows wisdom, skill, and vision in conducting state affairs and dealing with public issues, or one engaged in the business of government —**states′man·like′** *adj.,* **states′man·ly**

states·man·ship (-ship′) *n.* ⟦see -SHIP⟧ the ability, character, or methods of a statesman; skill and vision in managing public affairs

state socialism the theory, doctrine, or practice of an economy planned and controlled by the state, based on state ownership of public utilities, basic industries, etc.

States of the Church PAPAL STATES

☆**states' rights** [*sometimes* **S- r-**] all the rights and powers which the Constitution neither grants to the federal government nor denies to the state governments —**states' right′er**

states·wom·an (stāts′woom′ən) *n., pl.* **-wom′en** (-wim′in) a female statesman

☆**state university** a university supported and controlled by a U.S. state as part of its public educational system

☆**state·wide** (stāt′wīd′) *adj.* extending throughout a state —*adv.* throughout a state

stat·ic (stat′ik) *adj.* ⟦ModL *staticus* < Gr *statikos,* causing to stand < *histanai,* to cause to STAND⟧ **1** of bodies, masses, or forces at rest or in equilibrium: opposed to DYNAMIC **2** not moving or progressing; at rest; inactive; stationary **3** *Comput.* designating or of memory that retains stored data as long as power is supplied **4** *Elec.* of or producing stationary electrical charges, as those resulting from friction [*static* electricity] **5** *Radio* of or having to do with static Also **stat′i·cal** —*n.* ☆**1** *a)* electrical discharges in the atmosphere that interfere with radio or television reception, etc. *b)* interference or noises produced by such discharges **2** [Slang] adversely critical remarks —**stat′i·cal·ly** *adv.* —☆**stat′ick·y** *adj.*

stat·i·ce (stat′ə sē′) *n.* ⟦ModL < L, an astringent herb < Gr *statikē* < fem. of *statikos,* causing to stand, astringent: see prec.⟧ **1** SEA LAVENDER **2** THRIFT (sense 3)

stat·ics (stat′iks) *n.* ⟦see STATIC & -ICS⟧ the branch of mechanics dealing with bodies, masses, or forces at rest or in equilibrium

static tube a tube with openings in its walls, inserted in a fluid in motion so that the flow is across the openings and used to measure the static pressure of the fluid: see also PITOT-STATIC TUBE

stat·in (stat′'n) *n.* ⟦prob. < -STAT + -IN[1]⟧ any of a class of drugs, as lovastatin, that lower the levels of LDL and cholesterol in the blood, commonly used in treating heart disease

sta·tion (stā′shən) *n.* ⟦ME *stacioun* < OFr *station* < L *statio,* a standing, post, station < *status,* pp. of *stare,* to STAND⟧ **1** the place where a person or thing stands or is located, esp. an assigned post, position, or location; specif., *a)* the place where a person, as a guard, stands while on duty *b)* the post, building, base, or headquarters assigned to a group of people working together, as in providing a service, making scientific observations, etc. [a police *station,* service *station*] *c)* in Australia, a sheep or cattle ranch *d)* a place or region to which a naval fleet, ship, etc. is assigned for duty *e)* a post-office subdivision in a community with a main post office (distinguished from BRANCH, *n.* 6e) **2** *a)* a regular stopping place, with a shelter, platform, etc., as on a bus line or railroad *b)* the building or buildings at such a place, for passengers, etc. **3** social standing, position, or rank **4** *a)* a place equipped to transmit or receive radio waves; esp., the studios, offices, and technical installations collectively of an establishment for radio or television transmission *b)* such an establishment *c)* a broadcasting frequency or channel assigned to such an establishment **5** a fixed point from which measurements are made in surveying **6** one of the divisions of the STATIONS OF THE CROSS **7** [Archaic] the fact or condition of being stationary **8** *Biol.* a habitat, esp. the exact location of a given plant or animal —*vt.* to assign to or place in a station; post

sta·tion·ar·y (stā′shə ner′ē) *adj.* ⟦ME *stacionarye* < L *stationarius* < *statio:* see prec.⟧ **1** not moving or not movable; fixed or still **2** unchanging in condition, value, etc.; not increasing or decreasing **3** not migratory or itinerant —*n., pl.* **-ar′ies** a person or thing that is stationary

stationary bike (*or* **bicycle)** EXERCISE BIKE

stationary engineer a person who operates and maintains stationary engines and mechanical equipment

stationary front *Meteorol.* a front that is not moving or is moving at a speed of less than about five miles per hour

stationary wave STANDING WAVE: also called **stationary vibration**

☆**station break** a pause in radio and television programs for station identification and, usually, commercials

sta·tion·er (stā′shə nər) *n.* ⟦ME *stacionere* < ML *stationarius,* tradesman with a fixed station or shop (by contrast with a peddler) < L, STATIONARY⟧ **1** [Obs.] a bookseller or publisher **2** a person who sells office supplies, greeting cards, some books, etc.

sta·tion·er·y (stā′shə ner′ē) *n.* ⟦see prec. & -ERY⟧ writing materials; specif., paper and envelopes used for letters

station house a building used as a station, esp. by a company of police or firefighters

☆**sta·tion·mas·ter** (stā′shən mas′tər, -mäs′tər) *n.* an official in charge of a railroad station

Stations of the Cross 1 a series of fourteen pictures, statues, etc., as along the walls of a church, depicting the stages of Jesus' final sufferings and of his death and burial: a prayer is said at each station in succession as a devotional exercise **2** the devotional exercise itself

☆**station wagon** an automobile capable of carrying more passengers or cargo than a conventional sedan: it has a large interior with a tailgate, but no trunk

stat·ism (stāt′iz′əm) *n.* the doctrine or practice of vesting economic control, economic planning, etc. in a centralized state government —**stat′ist** (-ist) *n., adj.*

sta·tis·tic (stə tis′tik) *adj. rare var. of* STATISTICAL —*n.* a statistical item or element

sta·tis·ti·cal (-ti kəl) *adj.* ⟦< ModL *statisticus,* of politics < L *status* (see STATE) + -AL⟧ of, having to do with, consisting of, or based on statistics —**sta·tis′ti·cal·ly** *adv.*

stat·is·ti·cian (stat′is tish′ən) *n.* an expert or specialist in statistics

sta·tis·tics (stə tis′tiks) *pl.n.* ⟦< Ger *statistik* < ModL *statisticus:* see STATISTICAL⟧ facts or data of a numerical kind, assembled, classified, and tabulated so as to present significant information about a given subject —*n.* the branch of mathematics dealing with the calculation, description, manipulation, and interpretation of the mathematical attributes of sets or populations too numerous or extensive for exhaustive measurements

Sta·ti·us (stā′shē əs, stā′shəs), **Publius Pa·pin·i·us** (pə pin′ē əs) A.D. 45?-96?; Rom. poet

sta·tive (stāt′iv) *adj. Gram.* of or designating a class of verbs that express a state or condition (Ex.: I have the keys; Sue is a lawyer; I know the facts), rather than an action

stat·o·blast (stat′ə blast′) *n.* ⟦< Gr *statos,* standing (see fol.) + -BLAST⟧ *Zool.* a bud, enclosed in a hard covering, produced by most freshwater bryozoans, able to survive freezing, drying, etc. to germinate and form a new colony

stat·o·cyst (-sist′) *n.* ⟦< Gr *statos,* standing < *histanai,* to STAND + -CYST⟧ **1** *Bot.* a plant cell containing plastids, starch grains, or other statoliths **2** *Zool.* a sense organ found in many invertebrate animals, consisting typically of a fluid-filled sac lined with small sensory hairs and containing one or more tiny, free, sandlike grains, or statoliths: it functions as an organ of balance or equilibrium —**stat′o·cys′tic** (-sis′tik) *adj.*

stat·o·lith (-lith′) *n.* ⟦< Gr *statos,* standing (see prec.) + -LITH⟧ **1** *Bot.* any of the small, freely moving concretions, often a starch grain, found in statocysts **2** *Zool.* OTOLITH (sense 2) —**stat′o·lith′ic** *adj.*
sta·tor (stāt′ər) *n.* ⟦ModL < L, one who stands < pp. of *stare,* to STAND⟧ a fixed part forming the pivot or housing for a revolving part (*rotor*), as in a motor, dynamo, etc.
stat·o·scope (stat′ə skōp′) *n.* ⟦< Gr *statos,* standing (see STATOCYST) + -SCOPE⟧ **1** a highly sensitive aneroid barometer **2** such a barometer adapted for use as an altimeter to indicate slight variations in the altitude of an aircraft
stats (stats) *pl.n.* [Informal] *short for* STATISTICS
stat·u·ar·y (stach′o͞o er′ē) *n.* ⟦L *statuaria* < *statuarius,* of statues < *statua,* fol.⟧ **1** statues collectively **2** *pl.* **-ar′ies** a group or collection of statues **3** the art of making statues —*adj.* of or suitable for statues
stat·ue (stach′o͞o) *n.* ⟦OFr < L *statua* < *statuere,* to set, place < pp. of *stare,* to STAND⟧ the figure of a person or animal, or an imagined or abstract form, carved in stone, wood, etc., modeled in a plastic substance, or cast in plaster, bronze, etc., esp. when done in the round rather than in relief
stat·ued (stach′o͞od) *adj.* ornamented with or represented in a statue or statues
☆**Statue of Liberty** a colossal copper statue personifying Liberty in the form of a crowned woman holding a torch in her upraised hand: it was given to the U.S. by France and is located on Liberty Island in New York harbor: official name *Liberty Enlightening the World*
stat·u·esque (stach′o͞o esk′) *adj.* ⟦STATU(E) + -ESQUE⟧ **1** of or like a statue **2** tall and well-proportioned, with a stately grace and dignity —**stat′u·esque′ly** *adv.* —**stat′u·esque′ness** *n.*
stat·u·ette (-et′) *n.* ⟦Fr, dim. of *statue*⟧ a small statue
stat·ure (stach′ər) *n.* ⟦ME < OFr *estature* < L *statura,* height or size of body < *statuere:* see STATUE⟧ **1** the height of a person, or sometimes an animal, in a natural standing position **2** development, growth, or level of attainment, esp. as worthy of esteem [*moral stature*] —*SYN.* HEIGHT
sta·tus (stat′əs, stāt′-) *n., pl.* **-tus·es** ⟦L: see STATE⟧ **1** condition or position with regard to law [*the status of a minor*] **2** *a)* position; rank; standing [*high status*] *b)* high position; prestige [*seeking status*] **3** state or condition, as of affairs [*economic status*] —*SYN.* STATE
status quo (kwō) ⟦L, lit., the state in which⟧ the existing state of affairs (at a particular time): also **status in quo**
status quo an·te (an′tē) ⟦L⟧ the state of affairs existing prior to a given event
status symbol a possession, practice, etc. regarded as a mark of social status, esp. high social status
sta·tus·y or **sta·tus-y** (stat′əs ē, stāt′-) *adj.* [Informal] revealing, conferring, or having high status, or prestige [*statusy cars, designer labels, or vacation spots*]
stat·u·ta·ble (stach′o͞o tə bəl) *adj.* STATUTORY
stat·ute (stach′o͞ot) *n.* ⟦ME < OFr *statut* < LL *statutum,* neut. of L *statutus,* pp. of *statuere:* see STATUE⟧ **1** an established rule; formal regulation **2** *a)* a law passed by a legislative body and set forth in a formal document *b)* such a document —*SYN.* LAW
statute book a book or other record of the body of statutes of a particular jurisdiction
statute law law established by a legislative body
statute mile MILE
statute of limitations **1** a statute limiting the period within which a specific legal action may be taken **2** the period itself
stat·u·to·ry (stach′o͞o tôr′ē) *adj.* **1** of, or having the nature of, a statute or statutes **2** fixed, authorized, or established by statute **3** declared by statute to be such, and hence legally punishable: said of an offense
statutory rape the crime of having sexual intercourse with a person below the AGE OF CONSENT (sense 2)
St. Au·gus·tine (ô′gəs tēn′) ⟦after *Saint* AUGUSTINE[2] (of Hippo)⟧ seaport in NE Fla.; oldest city (founded 1565) in the U.S.
staunch (stônch, stänch) *vt.* ⟦ME *stanchen* < OFr *estanchier* < VL **stanticare,* to bring to a stop < L *stans:* see STANCE⟧ **1** to stop or check (the flow of blood or of tears, etc.) from (a wound, opening, etc.) **2** *a)* to stop or lessen (the flow or drain of funds, resources, etc.) *b)* to stop up or close off (a source of draining or leakage) **3** [Now Chiefly Dial.] *a)* to quench; quell *b)* to allay; appease —*vi.* to cease flowing or draining out or away —*adj.* ⟦OFr *estanche,* fem. of *estanc,* akin to v.⟧ **1** [Archaic] watertight; seaworthy [*a staunch ship*] **2** firm; steadfast; loyal [*a staunch supporter*] **3** strong; solidly made; substantial Also **stanch** —*SYN.* FAITHFUL —**staunch′ly** *adv.* —**staunch′ness** *n.*
USAGE—for the *adj.*, *staunch* is now the prevailing form; for the *v.*, usage is about evenly divided between *staunch* and *stanch*
stau·ro·lite (stôr′ə līt′) *n.* ⟦Fr < Gr *stauros,* a cross, post (< IE **steur-* > ON *staurr,* post: see STEER[1]) + *-lite,* -LITE⟧ a dark-colored mineral, $(Fe,Mg)_2Al_9Si_4O_{23}(OH)$, a silicate of iron and aluminum: the crystals are often found twinned in the form of a cross —**stau′ro·lit′ic** (-lit′ik) *adj.*
Sta·vang·er (stä vaŋ′ər) seaport in SW Norway, on the North Sea
stave (stāv) *n.* ⟦ME, taken as sing. of *staves,* pl. of *staf,* STAFF[1]⟧ **1** *a)* any of the thin, shaped strips of wood or metal that are set edge to edge to form or strengthen the wall of a barrel, bucket, etc. *b)* any similar slat, bar, rung, stay, etc. **2** a stick or staff **3** a set of verses, or lines, of a song or poem; stanza **4** *Music* STAFF[1] (sense 5) —*vt.* **staved** or **stove**, **stav′ing** **1** to puncture or smash, esp. by breaking in a stave or staves **2** to beat as with a staff —**stave in** to break or crush inward —**stave off** to ward off, hold off, or put off, as by force, guile, etc.
staves (stāvz) *n.* **1** *alt. pl. of* STAFF[1] **2** *pl. of* STAVE
staves·a·cre (stāvz′ā′kər) *n.* ⟦ME *staphisagre* < ML *staphisagria* < Gr *staphis,* raisin + *agrios,* wild; akin to *agros:* see ACRE⟧ **1** a tall, purple-flowered delphinium (*Delphinium staphisagria*) of Europe and Asia, with poisonous seeds having strongly emetic and cathartic properties **2** its seeds
Stav·ro·pol (stäv′rō pôl′y′) city in Russia, in the N Caucasus
stay[1] (stā) *n.* ⟦ME *staie* < OE *stæg,* akin to Du *stag* < IE **stăk-,* to stand, place < base **sta-:* see STAND⟧ a heavy rope or cable, usually of wire, used as a brace or support, as for a mast of a ship; guy —*vt.* to brace or support with a stay or stays —**in stays** IN IRONS (see phrase under IRON)
stay[2] (stā) *n.* ⟦MFr *estaie* < Frank **stakka:* see STICK⟧ **1** anything used as a support, or prop **2** a strip of stiffening material used in a corset, the collar of a shirt, etc. **3** [*pl.*] [Chiefly Brit.] a corset stiffened as with whalebone —*vt.* **1** to support, or prop up **2** to strengthen, comfort, or sustain in mind or spirit **3** to cause (something) to rest *on, upon,* or *in* for support
stay[3] (stā) *vi.* **stayed**, **stay′ing** ⟦ME *staien* < Anglo-Fr *estaier* < OFr *ester* < L *stare,* to STAND⟧ **1** to continue in the place or condition specified; remain; keep [*to stay at home, to stay healthy*] **2** to live, dwell, or reside, esp. temporarily (*for* the time specified) **3** to stand still; stop; halt **4** to pause; tarry; wait; delay **5** [Informal] to continue or endure; last [*to stay with a project*] **6** [Informal] to keep up (*with* another contestant in a race, etc.) **7** [Archaic] to cease doing something **8** [Archaic] to make a stand ☆**9** *Poker* to remain in a hand by equaling the preceding bet —*vt.* **1** to stop, halt, or check **2** to hinder, impede, restrain, or detain **3** to postpone or delay (legal action or proceedings) **4** [Rare] to quell or allay (strife, etc.) **5** to satisfy or appease for a time the pangs or cravings of (thirst, appetite, etc.) **6** *a)* to remain through or during (often with *out*) [*to stay the week (out)*] *b)* to be able to last through [*to stay the distance in a long race*] **7** [Archaic] to await —*n.* **1** *a)* a stopping or being stopped *b)* a stop, halt, check, or pause **2** a postponement or delay in legal action or proceedings [*a stay of execution*] **3** *a)* the action of remaining or continuing in a place for a time *b)* time spent in a place [*a long stay in the hospital*] **4** [Informal] ability to continue or endure —☆**stay put** [Informal] to remain in place or unchanged —**stay the course** to continue in some effort or course of action to its end, in spite of difficulties or obstacles; persevere

SYN.—**stay**, the general term, implies a continuing in a specified place [*stay there until you hear from me*]; **remain** specifically suggests a staying behind while others go [*he alone remained at home*]; **wait** suggests a staying in anticipation of something [*wait for me at the library*]; **abide**, now somewhat archaic, implies a staying fixed for a relatively long period, as in a settled residence [*he came for a visit and has been abiding here since*]; **tarry** and **linger** imply a staying on after the required or expected time for departure, **linger** esp. implying that this is deliberate, as from reluctance to leave [*we tarried in town two days; he lingered at his sweetheart's door*] —*ANT.* **go, leave, depart**

stay·ca·tion (stā kā′shən) *n.* ⟦blend of prec. & VACATION⟧ [Informal] a relatively inexpensive vacation spent at or near one's home, rather than in travel
staying power ability to last or endure; endurance
stay·sail (stā′sāl′; *naut.*, -səl) *n.* a triangular, fore-and-aft headsail fastened to a stay
STB or **S.T.B.** *abbrev.* ⟦L *Sacrae Theologiae Baccalaureus*⟧ Bachelor of Sacred Theology
stbd *abbrev.* starboard
St. Bernard **1** *var. of* SAINT BERNARD (dog) **2** *see* GREAT ST. BERNARD PASS and LITTLE ST. BERNARD PASS
St. Cath·ar·ines (kath′ə rinz, kath′rinz) city in SE Ontario, Canada, on the Welland Canal
St. Christopher *another name for* ST. KITTS
St. Clair ⟦after Fr *Sainte Claire* (St. Clare of Assisi, 1194-1253)⟧ **1** river between Mich. & Ontario, Canada, connecting Lake St. Clair & Lake Huron: 40 mi (64 km) **2** **Lake** lake between SE Mich. & Ontario, Canada: 460 sq mi (1,191 sq km)
St. Croix (kroi) ⟦< Fr *saint croix,* holy cross⟧ **1** largest island of the Virgin Islands of the U.S.: 83 sq mi (215 sq km) **2** river flowing from NW Wis. south along the Wis.-Minn. border into the Mississippi: *c.* 165 mi (266 km)
std *abbrev.* standard
STD[1] (es′tē′dē′) *n., pl.* **STDs** ⟦*s*(*exually*) *t*(*ransmitted*) *d*(*isease*)⟧ any disease capable of being transmitted by sexual contact
STD[2] *abbrev.* ⟦L *Sacrae Theologiae Doctor*⟧ Doctor of Sacred Theology: also **S.T.D.**
St-De·nis (sand nē′) capital of Réunion Island
St. Den·is (sānt′ den′is), **Ruth** (born *Ruth Dennis*) 1877?-1968; U.S. dancer & choreographer: wife of Ted Shawn
Ste *abbrev.* **1** ⟦< Fr *Sainte*⟧ Saint (female) **2** Suite
stead (sted) *n.* ⟦ME *stede* < OE, akin to Ger *statt,* a place, *stadt,* town < IE base **stă-,* to STAND⟧ **1** the place or position of a person or thing as filled by a replacement, substitute, or successor [*to send another in one's stead*] **2** advantage, service, or avail: now only in **stand someone in good stead**, to give someone good use, service, or advantage **3** [Obs.] a place, site, or locality —*vt.* [Archaic] to be of advantage, service, or avail to
stead·fast (sted′fast′) *adj.* ⟦ME *stedefast* < OE *stedefæste:* see prec. & FAST[1]⟧ **1** firm, fixed, settled, or established **2** not changing, fickle, or wavering; constant —**stead′fast′ly** *adv.* —**stead′fast′ness** *n.*

stead·ing (sted′iŋ) ***n.*** ⟦ME *steding:* see STEAD & -ING⟧ *Brit. var. of* FARMSTEAD

stead·y (sted′ē) ***adj.*** **stead′i·er, stead′i·est** ⟦STEAD + -Y[2]⟧ **1** that does not shake, tremble, totter, etc.; firm; fixed; stable **2** constant, regular, uniform, or continuous; not changing, wavering, or faltering [a *steady* gaze, a *steady* diet, a *steady* rhythm] **3** not given to sudden changes in behavior, loyalty, disposition, etc. **4** habitual or regular; by habit [a *steady* customer] **5** not easily agitated, excited, or upset; calm and controlled [*steady* nerves] **6** grave; sober; staid; reliable; not frivolous or dissipated **7** staying headed in the same direction: said of a ship —***interj.*** **1** stay calm; control yourself **2** proceed carefully: used as an order or warning **3** *Naut.* keep the ship or boat on its present course: used as an order to the helmsman — ***vt., vi.*** **stead′ied, stead′y·ing** to make or become steady —***n.*** ☆[Informal] a person whom one dates regularly and exclusively; sweetheart —***adv.*** **stead′i·er, stead′i·est** in a steady manner —☆**go steady** [Informal] **1** to date someone regularly and exclusively **2** to date each other regularly and exclusively —**stead′i·ly** ***adv.*** —**stead′i·ness** ***n.***

SYN.—**steady** implies a fixed regularity or constancy, esp. of movement, and an absence of deviation, fluctuation, faltering, etc. [a *steady* breeze]; **even**, often interchangeable with **steady**, emphasizes the absence of irregularity or inequality [an *even* heartbeat]; **uniform** implies a sameness or likeness of things, parts, events, etc., usually as the result of conformity with a fixed standard [a *uniform* wage rate]; **regular** emphasizes the orderliness or symmetry resulting from evenness or uniformity [*regular* features, attendance, etc.]; **equable** implies that the quality of evenness or regularity is inherent [an *equable* temper] —*ANT.* **changeable, jerky**

stead·y-state (-stāt′) ***adj.*** designating or of a system, operation, mixture, rate, etc. that does not change with time or that maintains a state of relative equilibrium even after undergoing fluctuations or transformations

steady-state theory a theory of cosmology, no longer favored, holding that new matter is continuously being created, thus keeping the density of the expanding universe constant: see BIG-BANG THEORY

steak (stāk) ***n.*** ⟦ME *steike* < ON *steik* < base of *steikja,* to roast on a spit: for IE base see STICK⟧ **1** a slice of meat, esp. beef, or of a large fish, cut thick for broiling or frying **2** ground beef formed into a patty for broiling or frying

☆**steak·house** (stāk′hous′) ***n.*** a restaurant that specializes in beefsteaks

☆**steak knife** a table knife with a sharp, often serrated blade

☆**steak tartare** *see* TARTARE

steal (stēl) ***vt.*** **stole, stol′en, steal′ing** ⟦ME *stelen* < OE *stælan,* akin to Ger *stehlen,* prob. altered < IE base **ster-,* to rob > Gr *sterein,* to rob⟧ **1** to take or appropriate (another's property, ideas, etc.) without permission, dishonestly, or unlawfully, esp. in a secret or surreptitious manner **2** to get, take, or give slyly, surreptitiously, or without permission [to *steal* a look, to *steal* a kiss] **3** to take or gain insidiously or artfully [to *steal* someone's heart, a defenseman *stealing* the puck] **4** to be the outstanding performer in (a scene, act, etc.), esp. in a subordinate role **5** to move, put, carry, or convey surreptitiously or stealthily (*in, into, from, away,* etc.) ☆**6** *Baseball* to gain (a base) safely without the help of a hit, walk, or error, usually by running to it from another base while the pitch is being delivered —***vi.*** **1** to be a thief; practice theft **2** to move, pass, etc. stealthily, quietly, gradually, or without being noticed **3** *Baseball* to steal or attempt to steal a base —***n.*** [Informal] **1** an act of stealing **2** something stolen **3** something obtained at a cost so low as to be regarded as excessively favorable to the buyer: a hyperbolic use —**steal′er** ***n.***

stealth (stelth) ***n.*** ⟦ME *stelthe* < base of *stelen,* to steal: see prec.⟧ **1** secret, furtive, or artfully sly action or behavior **2** [Obs.] theft —***adj.*** **1** of or incorporating technology designed to prevent military aircraft, etc. from being detected by enemy radar **2** calculated to achieve some aim by going undetected or by being disregarded

stealth·y (stel′thē) ***adj.*** **stealth′i·er, stealth′i·est** characterized by stealth; secret, furtive, or sly —*SYN.* SECRET —**stealth′i·ly** ***adv.*** —**stealth′i·ness** ***n.***

steam (stēm) ***n.*** ⟦ME *steme* < OE *steam,* akin to Du *stoom,* WFris *steam*⟧ **1** [Obs.] a vapor, fume, or exhalation **2** *a)* water as converted into an invisible vapor or gas by being heated to the boiling point; vaporized water: it is used for heating, cooking, cleaning, and, under pressure, as a source of power *b)* the power supplied by steam under pressure *c)* condensed water vapor, seen as the mist condensed on windows or in the air above boiling water **3** [Informal] driving force; vigor; energy —***adj.*** **1** using steam; heated, operated, propelled, etc. by steam **2** containing or conducting steam [a *steam* pipe] **3** treated with, or exposed to the action of, steam —***vi.*** **1** to give off steam or a steamlike vapor, esp. condensed water vapor **2** to rise or be given off as steam **3** to become covered with condensed steam: usually with *up* [when the hot bath was drawn, the bathroom mirror *steamed* up] **4** to generate steam **5** to move or travel by or as if by steam power **6** [Informal] to seethe with anger, vexation, etc.; fume —***vt.*** **1** to treat with, or expose to the action of, steam; cook, soften, remove, open, etc. by using steam **2** to give off (vapor) or emit as steam —**let (or blow) off steam** [Informal] to express strong feeling; release pent-up emotion —**steam up** [Informal] to make excited or angry —**under one's own steam** [Informal] by means of one's own power, efforts, or resources

steam bath **1** the act of bathing by exposing oneself to steam, as to induce sweating **2** a room or establishment for such bathing

☆**steam·boat** (stēm′bōt′) ***n.*** a steamship, esp. a relatively small one for use on inland waterways

steam boiler a tank used to produce steam by heating water and to hold the steam under pressure

steam chest a compartment in a steam engine through which steam passes from the boiler to the cylinder

steamed (stēmd) ***adj.*** **1** cooked by exposure to steam [*steamed* clams] ☆**2** [Slang] angry; upset

steam engine **1** an engine using steam under pressure to supply mechanical energy, usually through the action of a piston sliding in a cylinder **2** a locomotive powered by steam

steam·er (stēm′ər) ***n.*** **1** something operated by steam power, as a steamship or, formerly, a steam-powered automobile **2** a container in which things are cooked, cleaned, etc. with steam **3** a person or thing that steams **4** SOFT-SHELL CLAM

☆**steamer chair** DECK CHAIR

☆**steamer rug** a heavy woolen blanket used by passengers in deck chairs on shipboard to cover the lap and legs

☆**steamer trunk** a broad, low, rectangular trunk, originally designed to fit under a bunk on shipboard

steam·fit·ter (stēm′fit′ər) ***n.*** a mechanic whose work is installing and maintaining boilers, pipes, etc. in steam-pressure systems —**steam′fit′ting** ***n.***

steam heat heat given off by steam in a closed system of pipes and radiators

☆**steam iron** an electric iron that forms steam from water and releases it through the soleplate onto the material being pressed

steam·roll·er (stēm′rōl′ər) ***n.*** **1** a heavy, originally steam-driven, machine with rollers, used in building and repairing roads **2** an overwhelming power or influence, esp. when used relentlessly to force acceptance of a policy, override opposition, etc. —***vt.*** **1** to bring overwhelming force to bear upon; crush or override as if with a steamroller **2** to cause the passage or defeat of (a legislative bill, etc.), or make (one's way, etc.), by crushing opposition or overriding obstacles —***vi.*** to move with overwhelming force, or use steamroller tactics —***adj.*** relentlessly overpowering Also, for ***vt.*** & ***vi.***, **steam′roll′**

steam room a room for taking a steam bath

steam·ship (-ship′) ***n.*** a ship driven by steam power

☆**steam shovel** **1** a large, mechanically operated digger powered by steam **2** loosely, any POWER SHOVEL

steam table a serving table or counter, as in a restaurant, having a metal top with compartments heated by steam or hot water below, to keep foods warm

steam turbine a turbine turned by steam moving under great pressure

steam·y (stēm′ē) ***adj.*** **steam′i·er, steam′i·est** **1** of or like steam **2** covered or filled with steam **3** giving off steam or steamlike vapor **4** [Informal] erotic —**steam′i·ly** ***adv.*** —**steam′i·ness** ***n.***

ste·ap·sin (stē ap′sin) ***n.*** ⟦< Gr *stea(r),* fat (see STONE) + (PE)PSIN⟧ *Biochem.* the lipase present in pancreatic juice

ste·a·rate (stē′ə rāt′, stir′āt′) ***n.*** a salt or ester of stearic acid

ste·ar·ic (stē ar′ik, stir′ik) ***adj.*** ⟦Fr *stéarique* < Gr *stear,* tallow: see STONE⟧ **1** of, derived from, or like stearin or fat **2** of or pertaining to stearic acid

stearic acid **1** a colorless, odorless, waxlike fatty acid, $CH_3(CH_2)_{16}COOH$, found in many animal and vegetable fats, and used in making candles, stearates, soaps, etc. **2** a commercial mixture of palmitic and stearic acids

ste·a·rin (stē′ə rin, stir′in) ***n.*** ⟦Fr *stéarine:* see STEARIC & -INE[3]⟧ a white, crystalline substance, glyceryl stearate, $(C_{18}H_{35}O_2)_3C_3H_5$, found in the solid portion of most animal and vegetable fats and used in soaps, adhesives, textile sizes, etc.: also **ste·a·rine** (stē′ə rin, -rēn′; stir′in, -ēn)

ste·a·rop·tene (stē′ə räp′tēn) ***n.*** ⟦STEAR(IC) + (ELE)OPTENE⟧ the oxygenated, chiefly solid part of an essential oil

ste·a·tite (stē′ə tīt′) ***n.*** ⟦L *steatitis* < Gr *stear,* tallow: see STONE⟧ SOAPSTONE —**ste′a·tit′ic** (-tit′ik) ***adj.***

ste·a·tol·y·sis (stē′ə täl′ə sis) ***n.*** ⟦ModL < Gr *stear,* gen. *steatos,* tallow (see STONE) + -LYSIS⟧ the hydrolysis of a fat into glycerol and fatty acids

ste·a·to·pyg·i·a (stē′ə tō pij′ē ə, -pī′jē ə) ***n.*** ⟦ModL < Gr *stear* (see prec.) + *pygē,* buttocks < IE base **pu-,* to swell > L *pustula:* see PUSTULE⟧ the condition of having a heavy deposit of fat in the buttocks or thighs, as in some Hottentot women: sometimes called **ste′a·to′py·gy** (-tä′pə jē) —**ste′a·to·pyg′ic** ***adj.***, **ste′a·to·py′gous** (-pī′gəs)

ste·a·tor·rhe·a (stē′ə tə rē′ə) ***n.*** ⟦ModL < Gr *stear* (see STONE) + -RRHEA⟧ an excessive amount of fat in the feces

sted·fast (sted′fast′) ***adj.*** *former var. of* STEADFAST —**sted′fast′ly** ***adv.*** —**sted′fast′ness** ***n.***

steed (stēd) ***n.*** ⟦ME *stede* < OE *steda,* stud horse, stallion < base of *stod,* STUD[2]⟧ a horse, esp. a high-spirited riding horse: literary term

steel (stēl) ***n.*** ⟦ME *stel* < OE *stiele, stæli,* akin to Ger *stahl* < IE **stak-,* to stand: see STAY[1]⟧ **1** a hard, tough metal composed of iron alloyed with various small percentages of carbon and often variously with other metals, as nickel, chromium, manganese, etc., to produce hardness, resistance to rusting, etc. **2** something made of steel; specif., *a)* [Old Poet.] a sword or dagger *b)* a piece of steel used with flint for making sparks *c)* a steel strip used for stiffening *d)* a roughened steel rod on which to sharpen knives **3** great strength, hardness, or toughness **4** [*often pl.*] shares of stock in steel-making companies **5** [Informal] STEEL GUITAR —***adj.*** of or like steel —***vt.*** **1** to cover or edge with steel **2** to make hard, tough, unfeeling, etc.

steel band a percussion band, of a kind originated in Trinidad, using as instruments steel oil drums (**steel drums**) modified to produce varying pitches when struck

steel blue a metallic blue color like that of tempered steel —**steel′-blue′** ***adj.***

Steele (stēl), Sir **Richard** 1672-1729; Brit. essayist & dramatist, born in Ireland

steel engraving 1 an engraving made on a steel plate 2 a print from this 3 the process used for this
steel gray a bluish-gray color —**steel′-gray′** *adj.*
steel guitar a type of guitar mounted horizontally upon legs or designed to be held flat across the lap of a seated player: the metal strings are plucked while a steel bar is slid across them to alter the pitch
☆**steel·head** (stēl′hed′) *n., pl.* **-head′** or **-heads′** a rainbow trout that has returned from the sea
steel mill a mill where iron ore is processed into steel
steel wool long, hairlike shavings of steel in a pad or ball, used for scouring, smoothing, and polishing
steel·work (stēl′wʉrk′) *n.* 1 articles or parts made of steel 2 [*pl., often with sing. v.*] STEEL MILL
steel·work·er (-wʉr′kər) *n.* a worker in a steel mill
steel·y (stēl′ē) *adj.* **steel′i·er, steel′i·est** 1 of or like steel, as in hardness 2 severe; stern [*a steely* glare] —**steel′i·ness** *n.*
steel·yard (stēl′yärd′, stil′yərd) *n.* ⟦STEEL + YARD[1] (in obs. sense of "rod, bar")⟧ a balance, or scale, consisting of a metal arm suspended from above by a pivot close to one end: the object to be weighed is hung from the shorter end and a sliding weight is moved along the graduated longer end until the whole arm balances
Steen (stān), **Jan** (yän) 1626-79; Du. painter
steen·bok (stēn′bäk′, stān′-) *n., pl.* **-bok′** or **-boks′** ⟦Afrik < Du *steen,* STONE + *bok,* BUCK[1]⟧ STEINBOK: also **steen′buck′** (-buk′)
steep[1] (stēp) *adj.* ⟦ME < OE *steap,* lofty, high, akin to OFris *steep,* MHG *stouf,* cliff (as in Ger *Hohenstaufen*) < IE **steup-* < base **(s)teu-,* to strike, butt > STOCK, STUB, L *tundere,* to strike⟧ 1 having a sharp rise or highly inclined slope; precipitous [*a steep* incline] 2 [Informal] *a)* unreasonably high or great; exorbitant; excessive [*steep* demands, a *steep* price] *b)* extreme; exaggerated [a rather *steep* statement] 3 [Obs.] high; lofty —*n.* a steep slope or incline —**steep′ly** *adv.* —**steep′ness** *n.*

SYN.—**steep** suggests such sharpness of rise or slope as to make ascent or descent very difficult [a *steep* hill]; **abrupt** implies a sharper degree of inclination in a surface breaking off suddenly from the level [an *abrupt* bank at the river's edge]; **precipitous** suggests the abrupt and headlong drop of a precipice [a *precipitous* height]; **sheer** applies to that which is perpendicular, or almost so, and unbroken throughout its length [cliffs falling *sheer* to the sea]

steep[2] (stēp) *vt.* ⟦ME *stepen,* akin to ON *steypa,* to overturn, cast (metals), plunge into: for prob. IE base see prec.⟧ 1 to soak in liquid, so as to soften, clean, extract the essence of, etc. 2 to immerse, saturate, absorb, or imbue [*steeped* in folklore] —*vi.* to be steeped: said as of tea leaves —*n.* 1 a steeping or being steeped 2 liquid in which something is steeped —**SYN.** SOAK
steep·en (stēp′ən) *vt., vi.* to make or become steep or steeper
stee·ple (stē′pəl) *n.* ⟦ME *stepel* < OE < base of *steap,* lofty: see STEEP[1]⟧ 1 a tower rising above the main structure of a building, esp. of a church, usually capped with a spire 2 a church tower with a spire; also, the spire
☆**stee·ple·bush** (-boosh′) *n.* ⟦from the shape of its flower cluster, seen as resembling a *steeple*⟧ a shrub (*Spiraea tomentosa*) of the rose family, with clusters of pink, purple, or sometimes white flowers and hairy leaves, native to the E U.S.
stee·ple·chase (-chās′) *n.* ⟦because such a race orig. had as its goal a distant, visible *steeple*⟧ 1 [Obs.] a cross-country horse race 2 a horse race run over a prepared course with artificial obstructions, such as ditches, hedges, and walls 3 a cross-country footrace or one run over a prepared course with ditches and other obstacles —*vi.* **-chased′, -chas′ing** to ride or run in a steeplechase —**stee′ple·chas′er** *n.*
stee·ple·jack (-jak′) *n.* a person whose work is building, painting, or repairing steeples, smokestacks, etc.
steer[1] (stir) *vt.* ⟦ME *steren* < OE *stieran,* akin to Ger *steuern,* ON *styra* < IE **steur-,* a support, post (> Gr *stauros,* ON *staurr,* post) < base **stā-,* to STAND⟧ 1 to guide (a ship or boat) by means of a rudder 2 to direct the course or movement of [to *steer* an automobile] 3 to oversee, direct, or guide [to *steer* a team to victory] 4 to set and follow (a course) —*vi.* 1 to steer a ship, automobile, etc. 2 to be steered or guided [a car that *steers* easily] 3 to set and follow a course or way —*n.* ☆[Informal] a suggestion on how to proceed; tip —**steer clear of** to avoid —**steer′a·ble** *adj.*
steer[2] (stir) *n.* ⟦ME *ster* < OE *steor,* akin to Ger *stier* < IE **steu-ro* (> MPers *stor,* horse, draft animal) < base **stā-,* to STAND⟧ a castrated male ox, esp. one raised for beef
steer·age (stir′ij) *n.* 1 [Archaic] the act of steering (a ship, etc.) 2 ⟦orig. located near the steering mechanism⟧ [Historical] a section in some ships, with the poorest accommodations, occupied by the passengers paying the lowest fare
steer·age·way (-wā′) *n.* ⟦prec. + WAY (*n.* 20)⟧ the lowest forward speed at which a ship will respond to the helmsman's guidance
☆**steering committee** a committee, as of a legislative body, appointed to arrange the order of business
steering gear any mechanism used for steering, as in a ship, automobile, airplane, etc.
steering wheel a wheel that is turned by hand to operate a steering gear
steers·man (stirz′mən) *n., pl.* **-men** (-mən) a person who steers a ship or boat; helmsman
steeve (stēv) *vt.* **steeved, steev′ing** ⟦< ? or akin to OFr *estive,* tail of a plow < L *stiva,* plow handle⟧ to set (a bowsprit) so that it inclines upward above the line of the horizon or of the keel —*vi.* to be set so that it inclines upward in this way: said of a bowsprit —*n.* the angle a bowsprit so set forms with the horizon or the keel
Ste·fans·son (stef′ən sən), **Vil·hjal·mur** (vil′hyoul′mər) 1879-1962; U.S. arctic explorer, born in Canada
☆**steg·o·sau·rus** (steg′ə sôr′əs) *n., pl.* **-ri** (-ī) ⟦ModL < Gr *stegos,* roof (see THATCH) + -SAURUS⟧ any of a suborder (Stegosauria) of large ornithischian dinosaurs of the Upper Jurassic having a small head and heavy bony plates with sharp spikes down the backbone: also **steg′o·saur′**
Stei·chen (stī′kən), **Edward** 1879-1973; U.S. photographer, born in Luxembourg
Stei·er·mark (shtī′ər märk′) *Ger. name for* STYRIA
stein (stīn) *n.* ⟦Ger < *steingut,* stoneware < *stein,* STONE + *gut,* goods⟧ 1 an earthenware beer mug, or a similar mug of pewter, glass, etc. 2 the amount that a stein will hold, about a pint
Stein (stīn), **Gertrude** 1874-1946; U.S. writer in France
Stein·beck (stīn′bek′), **John (Ernst)** 1902-68; U.S. novelist & short-story writer
stein·bok (stīn′bäk′) *n., pl.* **-bok′** or **-boks′** ⟦Ger *steinbock* < *stein,* STONE + *bock,* BUCK[1]⟧ a small, reddish antelope (*Raphicerus campestris*) found in grassy areas of S and E Africa
Stein·er (stī′nər), **Max(imilian Raoul Walter)** 1888-1971; U.S. composer of film scores, born in Austria
Stein·metz (stīn′mets), **Charles Proteus** 1865-1923; U.S. electrical engineer & inventor, born in Germany
ste·la (stē′lə) *n., pl.* **-lae** (-lē) STELE (senses 1 & 2)
☆**Stel·a·zine** (stel′ə zēn′) ⟦< *stela-,* arbitrary prefix + (THI)AZINE⟧ *trademark for* a synthetic drug, $C_{21}H_{24}F_3N_3S{\cdot}2HCl$, used as a tranquilizer in treating certain mental disorders
ste·le (stē′lē; *also, & for 2 & 3 usually,* stēl) *n.* ⟦L *stela* < Gr *stēlē,* post, slab < IE base **stel-* > STILL[1]⟧ 1 an upright stone slab or pillar engraved with an inscription or design and used as a monument, grave marker, etc. 2 *Archit.* a prepared surface, as on a facade, having an inscription, carved design, etc. 3 *Bot.* a central cylinder of vascular tissues in the stems and roots of plants
St. Elias 1 range of the Coast Ranges, in SW Yukon Territory & SE Alas.: highest peak, Mt. Logan 2 **Mount** mountain in this range, on the Canadian-Alaskan border: 18,008 ft (5,489 m)
Stel·la (stel′ə) *n.* ⟦see fol.⟧ a feminine name: see ESTELLE
stel·lar (stel′ər) *adj.* ⟦LL *stellaris* < L *stella,* a STAR⟧ 1 of the stars or a star 2 like a star, as in shape 3 by or as by a star performer; excellent; outstanding 4 leading; chief [a *stellar* role]
☆**stel·lar·a·tor** (stel′ə rāt′ər) *n.* ⟦prec. + -ATOR⟧ *Physics* a device shaped like the figure 8 used to investigate the production of a controlled thermonuclear reaction by using changeable magnetic fields to confine a plasma
stellar wind streams of ionized gas particles constantly emitted in all directions by a star: cf. SOLAR WIND
stel·late (stel′āt′, -it) *adj.* ⟦L *stellatus,* pp. of *stellare,* to cover with stars < *stella,* a STAR⟧ shaped like a star; coming out in rays or points from a center: also **stel′lat′ed** —**stel′late′ly** *adv.*
stel·li·form (stel′ə fôrm′) *adj.* ⟦ModL *stelliformis* < L *stella,* STAR + *-formis,* -FORM⟧ shaped like a star
Stel·lite (stel′īt′) ⟦prob. < L *stella,* STAR + -ITE[1]: so named from its luster⟧ *trademark for* any of a group of cobalt-chromium superalloys characterized by great hardness and resistance to corrosion at high temperatures, used in making jet engine parts, cutting blades, etc. —*n.* [**s-**] any such superalloy
stel·lu·lar (-yoo lər) *adj.* ⟦< LL *stellula,* dim. of L *stella,* STAR + -AR⟧ 1 shaped like a small star or stars 2 covered with small stars or starlike spots
stem[1] (stem) *n.* ⟦ME < OE *stemn, stefn,* akin to Ger *stamm,* tree trunk < IE base **stebh-,* post, pole > STEP, STAFF[1]⟧ 1 the main upward-growing axis of a plant, having nodes and bearing leaves, usually extending in a direction opposite to that of the root and above the ground, and serving to support the plant and to transport and store food materials; specif., the main stalk or trunk of a tree, shrub, or other plant, from which leaves, flowers, and fruit develop 2 *a)* any stalk or part supporting leaves, flowers, or fruit, as a pedicel, petiole, or peduncle *b)* a stalk of bananas 3 a piece or part like a stem; specif., *a)* the slender part of a tobacco pipe between the bowl and the bit, esp. the part between the shank and the bit *b)* a narrow supporting part between the foot and the bowl, as of a wineglass *c)* the cylindrical shaft projecting from a watch, with a knurled knob at its end for winding the spring, setting the hands, etc. *d)* the rounded rod in some locks, about which the key fits and is turned *e)* the main or thick stroke of a letter, as in printing *f)* the vertical line forming part of a musical note (other than a whole note) *g)* the shaft of a feather or hair 4 *a)* the upright piece to which the side timbers or plates are attached to form the prow of a ship *b)* the forward part of a ship; prow; bow 5 main line of descent of a family; ancestry; stock 6 *Linguis.* the part of a word, consisting of a root or a root with one or more affixes, to which inflectional endings are added or in which inflectional phonetic changes are made [the present *stem* "bring" is the base to which *-s* may be added to form "brings"] —*vt.* **stemmed, stem′ming** 1 to remove the stem or stems from (a fruit, etc.) 2 to provide (artificial flowers, etc.) with stems 3 ⟦< *n.* 4⟧ to make headway or progress against [to row upstream, *stemming* the current] —*vi.* to originate, derive, or be descended —**SYN.** RISE —**from stem to stern** 1 from one end of a ship to the other 2 through the entire length of anything —**stem′less** *adj.* —**stem′like′** *adj.*

stem[2] (stem) ***vt.* stemmed, stem′ming** ⟦ME < ON *stemma* (akin to Ger *stemmen*), to stop: see STAMMER⟧ **1** to stop or check; esp., to dam up (a river, etc.), or to stop or check as if by damming up **2** to stop up, plug, or tamp (a hole, etc.) **3** to turn (a ski) in stemming —***vi.*** to stop or slow down in skiing by turning one ski (**single stemming**) or both skis (**double stemming**) with the heel thrust outward and the tip of the ski(s) turned in —***n.*** an act or manner of stemming on skis

stem cell *Biol.* any of a number of rudimentary cells that replicate repeatedly, providing a continuous source of new cells that differentiate into specialized cells

stem·ma (stem′ə) ***n.,*** *pl.* **stem·ma·ta** (stem′ə tə) or **stem′mas** ⟦L < Gr, garland, wreath < *stephein,* to crown: see STEPHANOTIS⟧ **1** FAMILY TREE (sense 1) **2** a record or diagram showing the connections between manuscripts of a given literary work —**stem·mat·ic** (stem at′ik) ***adj.***

stemmed (stemd) ***adj.*** **1** having a stem, usually of a specified kind [*a thin-stemmed* goblet] **2** with the stem or stems removed

stem·mer (stem′ər) ***n.*** a person or thing that stems; specif., one that removes stems as from fruit or tobacco

stem turn a turn made in skiing by stemming with one of the skis and bringing the other parallel

☆**stem·ware** (stem′wer′) ***n.*** goblets, wineglasses, etc. having stems

☆**stem·wind·er** (stem′wīn′dər) ***n.*** **1** a stem-winding watch **2** ⟦slang meaning, "first-rate", from the time when such watches were an innovation⟧ a rousing speech

☆**stem-wind·ing** (-wīn′diŋ) ***adj.*** wound by turning a knurled knob at the outer end of the stem [a *stem-winding* wristwatch]

stench (stench) ***n.*** ⟦ME < OE *stenc* < base of *stincan,* to STINK⟧ an offensive smell or odor; stink

sten·cil (sten′səl) ***vt.*** **-ciled** or **-cilled, -cil·ing** or **-cil·ling** ⟦< ME *stansilen,* to ornament with spangles < OFr *estenceler* < *estencele,* spangle, spark < VL **stincilla,* for L *scintilla,* spark: see SCINTILLATE⟧ to make, mark, or paint with a stencil —***n.*** **1** a thin sheet, as of paper, metal, or impermeable film, with holes cut through in the shape of letters or designs: when ink, paint, etc. is spread over the stencil, the letters or designs are marked on the surface beneath **2** a pattern, design, letter, etc. made by stenciling —**sten′cil·er *n.*, sten′cil·ler**

Sten·dhal (sten däl′) (pseud. of *Marie Henri Beyle*) 1783-1842; Fr. novelist and essayist

☆**sten·o** (sten′ō) ***n.,*** *pl.* **sten′os** *short for:* **1** STENOGRAPHER **2** STENOGRAPHY

sten·o- (sten′ō, -ə) ⟦< Gr *stenos,* narrow < IE base **sten-* > OE *stith,* hard, austere⟧ *combining form* narrow, thin, small [*stenography*]

sten·o·bath (sten′ə bath′) ***n.*** ⟦prec. + Gr *bathos,* depth⟧ *Biol.* an organism that can live only in a narrow range of water depths: opposed to EURYBATH —**sten′o·bath′ic *adj.***

Sten·o·graph (sten′ə graf′) ⟦< fol.⟧ *trademark for* a keyboard machine used to produce shorthand letters in stenotypy —***n.*** [**s-**] such a machine —***vt.*** [**s-**] to write in shorthand

☆**ste·nog·ra·pher** (stə näg′rə fər) ***n.*** a person skilled in stenography

ste·nog·ra·phy (stə näg′rə fē) ***n.*** shorthand writing; specif., the skill or work of writing down dictation, testimony, etc. in shorthand and later transcribing it, as on a typewriter —**sten·o·graph·ic** (sten′ə graf′ik) ***adj.*,** **sten′o·graph′i·cal** —**sten′o·graph′i·cal·ly *adv.***

sten·o·ha·line (sten′ə hā′līn′, -hal′īn′) ***adj.*** ⟦STENO- + HAL(O)- + -INE[3]⟧ *Biol.* able to exist only in waters with a very narrow range in their salt content: opposed to EURYHALINE

sten·o·hy·gric (-hī′grik) ***adj.*** ⟦STENO- + HYGR- + -IC⟧ *Biol.* able to withstand only a narrow range of humidity: opposed to EURYHYGRIC

ste·noph·a·gous (stə näf′ə gəs) ***adj.*** *Biol.* eating only a limited variety of foods: opposed to EURYPHAGOUS

ste·nosed (stə nōst′, -nōzd′) ***adj.*** that has undergone stenosis; narrowed; constricted

ste·no·sis (stə nō′sis) ***n.,*** *pl.* **-ses′** (-sēz′) ⟦ModL < Gr *stenōsis:* see STENO- & -OSIS⟧ *Med.* a narrowing, or constriction, of a passage, duct, opening, etc. —**ste·not′ic** (-nät′ik) ***adj.***

sten·o·therm (sten′ə thurm′) ***n.*** *Biol.* an organism that can live only in a narrow range of temperatures: opposed to EURYTHERM —**sten′o·ther′mal** (-thur′məl) ***adj.*,** **sten′o·ther′mous** (-məs), or **sten′o·ther′mic** (-mik)

☆**sten·o·top·ic** (sten′ə täp′ik) ***adj.*** ⟦< Ger *stenotop,* stenotopic (< *steno-,* STENO- + *-top* < Gr *topos,* place: see TOPIC) + -IC⟧ *Biol.* able to withstand only a limited range of variations in environmental conditions: opposed to EURYTOPIC

☆**sten·o·type** (sten′ə tīp′) ***n.*** **1** a letter or combination of letters representing a sound, word, or phrase in stenotypy **2** a keyboard machine that produces such letters and combinations —***vt.*** **-typed′, -typ′ing** to record by stenotype

sten·o·typ·y (-tī′pē) ***n.*** a form of shorthand based on a phonetic system in which letters and combinations of letters representing sounds, words, or phrases are produced on a keyboard machine: used primarily by court reporters —**sten′o·typ′ist *n.***

stent (stent) ***n.*** ⟦after Charles R. *Stent* (died 1901), Brit dentist who invented a substance later used to make molds for holding skin grafts in place⟧ *Surgery* any of a various materials or devices used to hold tissue in place; esp., a tubular device implanted inside a blood vessel to keep the vessel open

Sten·tor (sten′tôr′) ***n.*** ⟦L < Gr *Stentōr,* akin to *stenein,* to rumble, roar < IE base **(s)ten-* > L *tonare,* to THUNDER⟧ **1** *Gr. Myth.* a Greek herald in the Trojan War, described in the *Iliad* as having the voice of fifty men **2** [*usually* **s-**] a person having a very loud voice **3** [**s-**] any of a genus (*Stentor*) of large, trumpet-shaped, ciliated protozoans, found in stagnant fresh waters

sten·to·ri·an (sten tôr′ē ən) ***adj.*** ⟦prec. + -IAN⟧ very loud [the *stentorian* voice of a drill sergeant]

step (step) ***n.*** ⟦ME *steppe* < OE *stepe,* akin to Ger *stapf* < IE base **steb(h)-,* post (> STAMP): basic sense "to stamp feet"⟧ **1** the act of moving and placing the foot forward, backward, sideways, up, or down, as in walking, dancing, or climbing **2** *a)* the distance covered by such a movement *b)* [*pl.*] the path covered by a series of such movements [to retrace one's *steps*] **3** a short distance **4** *a)* a manner of stepping; gait *b)* any of various paces or strides in marching [the goose *step*] *c)* a sequence of movements in dancing, usually repeated in a set pattern **5** the sound of stepping; tread; footfall **6** a mark or impression made by stepping; footprint **7** a rest for the foot in climbing; specif., *a)* any of the parts of a stairway formed by a tread supported by a riser *b)* the tread itself **8** [*pl.*] *a)* a stairway *b)* [Brit.] a stepladder **9** something resembling a stair step; specif., *a)* a bend or angle, as in a supply pipe, for passing around an obstruction *b)* a shelf or ledge cut in mining or quarrying *c) Naut.* a raised frame or platform for supporting the butt end of a mast *d)* any of a series of angled surfaces on the underside of the hull of a hydroplane or seaplane **10** a degree; rank; level; stage [one *step* nearer victory] **11** any of a series of acts, processes, etc. [explain the next *step*] **12** *Music a)* a degree of the staff or scale *b)* the interval between two consecutive degrees —***vi.*** **stepped, step′ping** ⟦ME *steppen* < OE *steppan*⟧ **1** to move by executing a step or steps **2** to walk, esp. a short distance [*step* outside] **3** to move with measured steps, as in dancing **4** to move quickly or briskly: often with *along* **5** to come or enter (*into* a situation, condition, etc.) [to *step* into a fortune] **6** *a)* to put the foot down (*on* or *in* something) *b)* to press down with the foot (*on* something) [to *step* on the brake] —***vt.*** **1** to take (one or more strides or paces) **2** *a)* to set (the foot) down *b)* to move across or over on foot **3** to execute the steps of (a dance) **4** to measure by taking steps: usually with *off* [*step* off ten paces] **5** to provide with steps; specif., to arrange in a series of degrees or grades [to *step* tests] **6** *Naut.* to set and fix (a mast) in its step —**break step** to stop marching in cadence —**in step** **1** conforming to a rhythm or cadence as in marching or dancing; esp., conforming to the cadence of another marcher or other marchers **2** in conformity or agreement —**keep step** to stay in step —**out of step** not in step —**step by step** **1** gradually or slowly **2** by marking or noting, or by explaining, each stage in a process —**step down** ☆**1** to resign or abdicate (*from* an office, position, etc.) ☆**2** to decrease or reduce, as in rate, by or as by one or more steps, or degrees —**step in** to intervene —**step it** to dance —**step on it** [Informal] to go faster; hurry; hasten —**step out** **1** to leave a room or building for a short time **2** to start to walk briskly, esp. with long strides ☆**3** [Informal] to go out for a good time **4** [Informal] to be unfaithful to: with *on* —**step up** **1** to go or come near; approach **2** to advance or progress ☆**3** to increase or raise, as in rate, by or as by one or more steps, or degrees ☆**4** [Informal] STEP UP TO THE PLATE (sense 2) (see phrase below) —☆**step up to the plate** **1** *Baseball* to take one's position in the batter's box **2** [Informal] to meet one's responsibility or challenge; rise to the occasion —**take steps** to adopt certain means or measures in order to facilitate, hinder, or modify something —☆**watch one's step** **1** to exercise care in walking or stepping **2** [Informal] to be careful or cautious

step- (step) ⟦ME < OE *steop-,* orphaned (akin to Ger *stief-,* ON *stjup-*) < base of *stiepan,* to bereave, prob. < IE **(s)teub-,* to strike (hence "cut off") > STUMP, STEEP[1]: orig. used of orphaned children⟧ *combining form* related through the remarriage of a parent [*stepchild, stepparent*]

step·broth·er (step′bruth′ər) ***n.*** ⟦prec. + BROTHER⟧ one's stepparent's son by a former marriage

step·child (-chīld′) ***n.,*** *pl.* **-chil′dren** (-chil′drən) ⟦ME < OE *steopcild:* see STEP- & CHILD⟧ **1** a child that one's husband or wife had by a former marriage **2** someone or something regarded as unpopular, neglected, etc.

step dance a dance emphasizing special, often intricate, steps and sometimes characterized by limited movement of the torso and arms —**step dancing**

step·daugh·ter (-dôt′ər) ***n.*** a female stepchild

step-down (-doun′) ***adj.*** that steps down, or decreases; specif., *a)* designating a transformer in which the output voltage is less than the input voltage *b)* designating a gear that reduces the speed —***n.*** a decrease, as in amount, intensity, etc.

step·fam·i·ly (-fam′ə lē, -fam′lē) ***n.*** a family having a stepparent

step·fa·ther (-fä′thər) ***n.*** a male stepparent

☆**Step·ford** (step′fərd) ***adj.*** ⟦after the title characters in *The Stepford Wives* (1972), science-fiction novel by Ira Levin, programmed to be traditional, perfectly compliant helpmates⟧ resembling an automaton in being conformist and submissive, unemotional, mechanical, etc.

Steph·a·nie (stef′ə nē) ***n.*** ⟦var. of *Stephana,* fem. of *Stephanus:* see STEPHEN[1]⟧ a feminine name

steph·a·no·tis (stef′ə nōt′is) ***n.*** ⟦ModL < Gr *stephanōtis,* fit for a crown < *stephanos,* that which surrounds, a crown < *stephein,* to encircle, crown, prob. < IE base **steb(h)-,* post, support, restrict > STAMP⟧ any of a genus (*Stephanotis*) of climbing plants of the milkweed family; esp., a woody vine (*S. floribunda*) grown for its white, waxy, sweet-scented flowers

Ste·phen¹ (stē′vən) ⟦L *Stephanus* < Gr *Stephanas* < *stephanos,* a crown: see prec.⟧ **1** *n.* a masculine name: dim. *Steve*; var. *Steven*; equiv. L. *Stephanus,* Fr. *Étienne,* Ger. *Stephan,* It. *Stefano,* Sp. *Esteban,* Russ. *Stepen*; fem. *Stephanie* **2** *Bible* one of the seven chosen to assist the Apostles (Acts 6 & 7); the 1st Christian martyr: his day is Dec. 26: called **Saint Stephen**

Ste·phen² (stē′vən) **1** (sometimes *Stephen of Blois*) 1097?-1154; king of England (1135-54): grandson of William the Conqueror **2 Stephen I** A.D. 975-1038; king of Hungary (1001-38): as **Saint Stephen,** his day is Aug. 16 **3** Sir **Leslie** 1832-1904; Eng. editor & critic: father of Virginia Woolf

Ste·phens (stē′vənz) **1 Alexander Hamilton** 1812-83; U.S. statesman: vice president of the Confederacy (1861-65) **2 James** 1882-1950; Ir. poet & novelist **3 John Lloyd** 1805-52; U.S. explorer & archaeologist

Ste·phen·son (stē′vən sən) **1 George** 1781-1848; Eng. engineer: developed the steam locomotive **2 Robert** 1803-59; Eng. engineer & bridge builder: son of George

step-in (step′in′) *adj.* put on by being stepped into [*a step-in* dress] —*n.* **1** a step-in garment **2** [*pl.*] [Old-fashioned] short underpants worn by women

step·lad·der (-lad′ər) *n.* a ladder with broad, flat steps, typically consisting of two frames joined at the top, usually with a hinge, so that it stands on four legs

step·moth·er (-muth′ər) *n.* a female stepparent

Step·ney (step′nē) former metropolitan borough of E London, now part of Tower Hamlets

step·par·ent (-per′ənt, -par′-) *n.* ⟦STEP- + PARENT⟧ the person who has married one's parent after the death of or divorce from the other parent; stepfather or stepmother

step·par·ent·ing (-per′ənt iŋ, -par′-) *n.* parenting within a stepfamily

steppe (step) *n.* ⟦Russ *step′*⟧ **1** any of the great plains of SE Europe and Asia, having few trees **2** any similar plain

☆**stepped-up** (stept′up′) *adj.* increased, as in tempo; accelerated

step·per (step′ər) *n.* a person or animal that steps, usually in a specified manner, as a dancer or a horse

step·ping·stone (step′iŋ stōn′) *n.* **1** a stone, usually one of a series, that a person may step on, as in crossing a stream or soft turf **2** something used to better one's position or situation; means of advancement Also **stepping stone**

step·sis·ter (step′sis′tər) *n.* ⟦STEP- + SISTER⟧ one's stepparent's daughter by a former marriage

step·son (-sun′) *n.* a male stepchild

step stool a portable step or set of steps, as a short stepladder or low platform, used for reaching high cupboards, shelves, etc.: sometimes written **step′stool′** *n.*

step-up (-up′) *adj.* that steps up, or increases; specif., *a)* designating a transformer in which the output voltage is greater than the input voltage *b)* designating a gear that increases the speed —*n.* an increase, as in amount, intensity, etc.

step·wise (-wīz′) *adv.* like a series of steps

ster *abbrev.* sterling

-ster (stər) ⟦ME < OE *-estre,* orig. a fem. agent suffix⟧ *suffix* **1** a person who is, does, or creates (something specified): often derogatory [*oldster, punster; rhymester, trickster*] **2** a person associated with (something specified) [*gangster*]

ste·ra·di·an (stə rā′dē ən) *n.* ⟦STE(REO)- + RADIAN⟧ the basic unit of solid angular measure in the SI system, equal to the solid angle subtended at the center of a sphere by an area, on its surface, that is equal to the square of its radius: one sphere equals 4π steradians: abbrev. *sr*

ster·co·ra·ceous (stur′kə rā′shəs) *adj.* ⟦< L *stercus* (gen. *stercoris*), dung < IE base *(*s*)*ter-* > ON *threkkr,* Ger *dreck,* dirt, filth + -ACEOUS⟧ of, like, or containing feces, or dung

ster·co·ric·o·lous (stur′kə rik′ə ləs) *adj.* ⟦< L *stercus* (see prec.) + -COLOUS⟧ *Biol.* living in dung: said of certain insects

ster·cu·li·a (stur kyōō′lē ə) *adj.* ⟦< L *Sterculius,* the deity presiding over manuring < *stercus:* see STERCORACEOUS⟧ designating a family (Sterculiaceae) of tropical, dicotyledonous plants (order Malvales), mostly shrubs and trees, including the cacao and cola

stere (stir) *n.* ⟦Fr *stère* < Gr *stereos,* solid, cubic: see STEREO-⟧ a cubic meter

ster·e·o (ster′ē ō′, stir′-) *n., pl.* **-os′** ☆**1** *a)* a stereophonic high-fidelity sound reproduction device [*turn on the stereo*] *b)* a stereophonic system or effect [*to record in stereo*] **2** *a)* a stereoscopic system or effect *b)* a stereoscopic picture, film, etc. —*adj. short for* STEREOPHONIC

ster·e·o- (ster′ē ō, stir′-; -ē ə) ⟦< Gr *stereos,* hard, firm, solid < IE base **ster-,* stiff > STARE⟧ *combining form* **1** solid, firm [*stereotomy*] **2** three-dimensional [*stereoscope*]

ster·e·o·bate (ster′ē ə bāt′, stir′-) *n.* ⟦L *stereobata* < Gr *stereobatēs* < *stereos,* solid (see prec.) + *batēs,* that which steps or treads < *bainein,* to COME⟧ a foundation, as of a building, or a solid substructure or platform of masonry

ster·e·o·chem·is·try (ster′ē ō kem′is trē, stir′-) *n.* ⟦STEREO- + CHEMISTRY⟧ the branch of chemistry dealing with the spatial arrangement of atoms or groups of atoms that make up molecules

ster·e·o·gram (ster′ē ə gram′, stir′-) *n.* **1** a stereographic diagram or picture **2** STEREOGRAPH

ster·e·o·graph (-graf′) *n.* a picture or a pair of pictures prepared for use with a stereoscope

ster·e·og·ra·phy (ster′ē äg′rə fē, stir′-) *n.* the representation or projection of a three-dimensional form onto a plane surface, as in cartography —**ster′e·o·graph′ic** (-ə graf′ik) *adj.,* **ster′e·o·graph′i·cal**

ster·e·o·i·so·mer (ster′ē ō ī′sə mər, stir′-) *n.* any of two or more isomers containing the same atoms linked in an identical manner in the molecule and differing from each other only in the spatial arrangement of the atoms or groups of atoms —**ster′e·o·i′so·mer′ic** (-mer′ik) *adj.* —**ster′e·o·i·som′er·ism′** (-ī säm′ər iz′əm) *n.*

ster·e·om·e·try (ster′ē äm′ə trē, stir′-) *n.* the art of determining the dimensions and volume of solids —**ster′e·o·met′ric** (-ə me′trik) *adj.,* **ster′e·o·met′ri·cal** —**ster′e·o·met′ri·cal·ly** *adv.*

ster·e·o·phon·ic (ster′ē ə făn′ik, stir′-) *adj.* designating or of sound reproduction, as in films, records, tapes, or broadcasting, using two or more channels to carry and reproduce through separate speakers a blend of sounds from separate sources —**ster′e·o·phon′i·cal·ly** *adv.* —**ster′e·oph′o·ny** (-äf′ə nē) *n.*

ster·e·op·sis (-äp′sis) *n.* ⟦ModL: see STEREO- & -OPSIS⟧ stereoscopic vision

☆**ster·e·op·ti·con** (-äp′ti kən, -kän′) *n.* ⟦< Gr *stereos,* solid (see STEREO-) + *optikon,* neut. of *optikos,* of sight, OPTIC⟧ **1** a kind of slide projector designed to allow one view to fade out while the next is fading in **2** STEREOSCOPE

ster·e·o·scope (ster′ē ə skōp′, stir′-) *n.* a hand-held device with two eyepieces through which a pair of photographs of the same scene or subject, taken at slightly different angles, are viewed side by side: the two photographs are seen as a single picture apparently having depth, or three dimensions

ster·e·o·scop·ic (ster′ē ə skäp′ik, stir′-) *adj.* **1** of or relating to stereoscopy **2** of or made by a stereoscope **3** 3-D —**ster′e·o·scop′i·cal·ly** *adv.*

ster·e·os·co·py (ster′ē äs′kə pē, stir′-) *n.* **1** the science of stereoscopic effects and techniques **2** the viewing of things as in three dimensions

ster·e·o·tax·is (-ə tak′sis) *n.* **1** *Biol.* the positive (or negative) response of a freely moving organism to cling to (or avoid) a solid object after contact **2** *Surgery* STEREOTAXY —**ster′e·o·tac′tic** (-tak′tik) *adj.*

ster·e·o·tax·y (ster′ē ə tak′sē, stir′-) *n.* ⟦STEREO- + *-taxy,* an arranging < Gr *-taxia* < *taxis:* see TAXIS⟧ brain surgery that makes use of measurement in three dimensions for positioning an electrode, needle, etc. precisely —**ster′e·o·tax′ic** (-tak′sik) *adj.*

ster·e·o·type (ster′ē ə tīp′, stir′-) *n.* ⟦Fr adj. *stéréotype:* see STEREO- & -TYPE⟧ **1** a one-piece printing plate cast in type metal from a mold (*matrix*) taken of a printing surface, as a page of set type **2** STEREOTYPY **3** a fixed or conventional notion or conception, as one regarding a social or ethnic group —*vt.* **-typed′**, **-typ′ing** **1** to make a stereotype of **2** to print from stereotype plates **3** to perceive in terms of, or relegate to, a STEREOTYPE (*n.* 3) —**ster′e·o·typ′er** *n.,* **ster′e·o·typ′ist**

ster·e·o·typed (-tīpt′) *adj.* **1** relegated to a STEREOTYPE (*n.* 3) **2** hackneyed; trite —**SYN.** TRITE

ster·e·o·typ·i·cal (ster′ē ə tip′i kəl, stir′-) *adj.* **1** of or produced by stereotypy **2** conforming to a STEREOTYPE (*n.* 3) [*a stereotypical* college nerd] **3** hackneyed; trite Also **ster′e·o·typ′ic**

ster·e·o·typ·y (ster′ē ə tī′pē, stir′-) *n.* ⟦Fr *stéréotypie*⟧ **1** the process of making or printing from stereotype plates **2** abnormal repetition of an action, speech phrase, etc., or abnormal sustained maintenance of a position or posture, as seen in some phases of schizophrenia

ster·ic (ster′ik, stir′-) *adj.* ⟦STER(EO)- + -IC⟧ *Chem.* having to do with the spatial arrangement of the atoms in a molecule —**ster′i·cal·ly** *adv.*

steric hindrance the prevention or retardation of a chemical reaction, caused by the arrangement of atoms in a molecule

ster·i·lant (ster′ə lənt) *n.* a sterilizing agent, as great heat

ster·ile (ster′əl; *Brit & Cdn, usually,* -īl′) *adj.* ⟦L *sterilis* < IE **ster-,* barren (> Gr *steira,* barren, OE *stierc,* calf), special use of base **ster-,* stiff, rigid > STARE⟧ **1** incapable of producing others of its kind; barren **2** producing little or nothing; unfruitful [*sterile* soil, a *sterile* policy] **3** lacking in interest or vitality; not stimulating or effective [*a sterile* style] **4** free from living microorganisms; esp., aseptic **5** *Bot.* *a)* unable or failing to bear fruit or spores, as a plant, or to germinate, as a seed *b)* having stamens only, as a male flower, or having neither pistils nor stamens —**ste·ril·i·ty** (stə ril′ə tē) *n.*

SYN.—sterile and **infertile** imply incapability of producing offspring or fruit, as because of some disorder of the reproductive system; **barren** and **unfruitful** are specifically applied to a sterile woman or to plants or soil; **impotent** is specif. applied to a man who cannot engage in sexual intercourse because of an inability to have an erection. All of these words have figurative uses [*sterile* thinking, an *infertile* mind, a *barren* victory, *unfruitful* efforts, *impotent* rage] —**ANT. fertile**

ster·i·lize (ster′ə līz′) *vt.* **-lized′**, **-liz′ing** to make sterile; specif., *a)* to make incapable of producing others of its kind, as by removing the organs of reproduction or preventing them from functioning effectively *b)* to make (land) unproductive *c)* to make free of living microorganisms, as by subjecting to great heat or chemical action —**ster′i·li·za′tion** *n.* —**ster′i·liz′er** *n.*

ster·let (stur′lit) *n.* ⟦Russ *sterljad′*⟧ a small sturgeon (*Acipenser ruthenus*) found in the Caspian Sea and used as food and as a source of caviar

ster·ling (stur′liŋ) *n.* ⟦ME *sterlinge,* Norman silver penny < OFr *esterlin* < Frank **esterling,* dim. < VL *istater* < LL(Ec) *stater,* STATER⟧ **1** an early English silver penny: a pound weight of these pennies was later standardized as a money of account **2** English money having the fineness of quality of the standard silver penny **3** sterling silver or articles made of it **4** the standard of fineness of legal British coinage: for silver, 0.500; for gold, 0.91666 **5** British money —*adj.* **1** of standard quality; specif., designating a silver alloy that is at least 92.5 percent pure silver **2** of or payable in British money **3** made of sterling silver **4** of genuinely high quality; excellent [*sterling* principles]

sterling area a former group of countries that pegged the value of their currencies to that of the British pound sterling

Sterling Heights ⟦after A. W. *Sterling*, early settler⟧ city in SE Mich.: suburb of Detroit

stern[1] (sturn) *adj.* ⟦ME *sterne* < OE *styrne* < IE base **ster-*, stiff, rigid > STARE, STARVE⟧ **1** hard; severe; unyielding; strict [*stern* measures] **2** grim; forbidding [a *stern* face] **3** relentless; inexorable [*stern* reality] **4** unshakable; firm [*stern* determination] —*SYN.* SEVERE —**stern′ly** *adv.* —**stern′ness** *n.*

stern[2] (sturn) *n.* ⟦ME *steorne*, stern, rudder < ON *stjorn*, steering < *styra*, to STEER[1]⟧ **1** the rear end of a ship or boat **2** the rear end of anything

Stern (sturn) **1 Isaac** 1920-2001; U.S. violinist, born in Russia **2 Otto** 1888-1969; U.S. physicist, born in Germany

ster·na (stur′nə) *n. alt. pl. of* STERNUM

ster·nal (stur′nəl) *adj.* of or near the sternum

stern chaser [Historical] a gun mounted on the stern of a ship, used for firing to the rear

Sterne (sturn), **Laurence** 1713-68; Brit. novelist, born in Ireland

stern·fore·most (sturn′fôr′mōst) *adv.* with the stern foremost; backward

stern·most (sturn′mōst′) *adj.* **1** nearest the stern **2** last in a line of ships; farthest astern

☆**Ster·no** (stur′nō) *trademark for* gelatinized methyl alcohol with nitrocellulose, sold in cans as a fuel for small stoves or chafing dishes

ster·no- (stur′nō, -nə) ⟦< STERNUM⟧ *combining form* sternum, sternum and [*sternalgia*]: also, before a vowel, **stern-**

stern·post (sturn′pōst′) *n.* the main, upright piece at the stern of a vessel, usually supporting the rudder

stern sheets the space at the stern of an open boat

ster·num (stur′nəm) *n., pl.* **-nums** or **-na** ⟦ModL < Gr *sternon*, the breastbone < IE base **ster-*, to spread out, STREW⟧ the thin, flat structure of bone and cartilage to which most of the ribs are attached in the front of the chest in most vertebrates; breastbone

ster·nu·ta·tion (stur′nyo͞o tā′shən) *n.* ⟦L *sternutatio* < *sternutare*, freq. of *sternuere*, to sneeze < IE echoic base **pster-*, to sneeze > Gr *ptarnysthai*⟧ a sneeze or the act of sneezing

ster·nu·ta·tor (stur′nyo͞o tāt′ər) *n.* a gas designed to incapacitate by severely irritating the respiratory passages

ster·nu·ta·to·ry (stər nyo͞ot′ə tôr′ē) *adj.* **1** of or causing sternutation **2** being, or having the effect of, a sternutator Also **ster·nu·ta·tive** (stur′nyo͞o tāt′iv) —*n., pl.* **-ries** a sternutatory substance

stern·ward (sturn′wərd) *adv.* toward the stern; astern: also **stern′wards**

stern·way (-wā′) *n.* backward movement of a ship or boat

☆**stern-wheel·er** (-hwēl′ər, -wēl′ər) *n.* a steamboat propelled by a paddle wheel at the stern

ster·oid (stir′oid′, ster′-) *n.* ⟦< fol. + -OID⟧ **1** any of a group of compounds including the sterols, bile acids, and sex hormones, characteristically having the carbon-atom ring structure of the sterols; specif., an ANABOLIC STEROID **2** [*often pl.*] a drug consisting of, or a regimen involving, a compound from this group —**on steroids** ⟦in allusion to the characteristic effects of anabolic steroids⟧ [Informal] augmented or strengthened, often, to an extreme or unnatural degree —**ste·roi′dal** *adj.*

ster·ol (stir′ôl′, ster′-; -ōl′) *n.* ⟦< (CHOLE)STEROL⟧ any of a group of solid cyclic unsaturated alcohols, as cholesterol, found in plant and animal tissues

ster·tor (stur′tər) *n.* ⟦ModL < L *stertere*, to snore⟧ snoring or loud, raspy, labored breathing, caused by obstructed respiratory passages —**ster′to·rous** *adj.* —**ster′to·rous·ly** *adv.* —**ster′to·rous·ness** *n.*

stet (stet) *v. imper.* ⟦L, 3d pers. sing., pres. subj., of *stare*, to STAND⟧ let it stand: a printer's term used to indicate that matter previously marked for deletion or revision is to remain unchanged —*vt.* **stet′ted**, **stet′ting** to cancel a change in or a marked deletion of (a word, character, passage, etc., as in a proof or manuscript), as by writing "stet" in the margin and underlining stetted matter with a row of dots

steth·o- (steth′ō, -ə) ⟦Gr *stētho-* < *stēthos*, the chest, breast⟧ *combining form* chest, breast [*stethoscope*]: also, before a vowel, **steth-**

steth·o·scope (steth′ə skōp′) *n.* ⟦Fr *stéthoscope*: see prec. & -SCOPE⟧ *Med.* a simple medical instrument for listening to sounds made by, or occurring within, the heart, lungs, etc., typically consisting of a resonating disk connected to earpieces by tubing —**steth′o·scop′ic** (-skäp′ik) *adj.*, **steth′o·scop′i·cal** —**steth′o·scop′i·cal·ly** *adv.* —**ste·thos·co·py** (ste thäs′kə pē) *n.*

St-É·tienne (san tā tyen′) city in SE France

☆**Stet·son** (stet′sən) ⟦after John B. *Stetson* (1830-1906), who originated it⟧ *trademark for* hats of various kinds —*n.* [*sometimes* **s-**] a hat, usually of felt, with a broad brim and a high, soft crown, associated typically with cowboys and the Old West

Stet·tin (shte tēn′) *Ger. name for* SZCZECIN

Steu·ben (sto͞o′bən; *Ger* shtoi′bən), Baron **Frederick William Augustus von** 1730-94; Prus. military officer: served as Am. general in the American Revolution

☆**ste·ve·dore** (stē′və dôr′) *n.* ⟦Sp *estivador* < *estivar*, to stow, ram tight: see STEEVE[1]⟧ a person whose work is loading and unloading ships; longshoreman — *vt., vi.* **-dored′**, **-dor′ing** to load or unload the cargo of (a ship)

Ste·ven (stē′vən) *n.* a masculine name: dim. *Steve*: see STEPHEN[1]

Ste·vens (stē′vənz) **1 John Paul** 1920-   ; associate justice, U.S. Supreme Court (1975-2010) **2 Thaddeus** 1792-1868; U.S. statesman & abolitionist **3 Wallace** 1879-1955; U.S. poet

Ste·ven·son (stē′vən sən), **Robert Louis (Balfour)** 1850-94; Scot. novelist, poet, & essayist

ste·vi·a (stē′vē ə) *n.* ⟦ModL, after P. J. *Esteve*, 16th-c. Sp botanist⟧ **1** any of a genus of New World plants of the sunflower family, esp., an herb (*Stevia rebaudiana*) with sweet leaves **2** a sugar substitute made from these leaves

stew (sto͞o, styo͞o) *vt.* ⟦ME *stuen* < MFr *estuver*, to stew, bathe < VL **extufare* < L *ex*, out + Gr *typhos*, steam, smoke < IE **dheubh-* < base **dheu-*, blow, be turbid > DULL⟧ to cook by simmering or boiling slowly for a long time —*vi.* **1** to undergo cooking in this way **2** to be oppressed with heat, crowded conditions, etc. **3** to fret, fume, or worry; be vexed or troubled —*n.* ⟦ME *stewe* < MFr *estuve*⟧ **1** ⟦< obs. sense, "a public room for hot baths"⟧ *former term for* BROTHEL: *usually used in pl.* **2** a dish, esp. a mixture of meat and vegetables, cooked by stewing **3** a state of vexation or worry —*SYN.* BOIL[1] —**stew in one's own juice** to suffer from one's own actions

stew·ard (sto͞o′ərd, styo͞o′-) *n.* ⟦ME *stiward* < OE *stiweard* < *stig*, enclosure, hall, STY[1] + *weard*, keeper, WARD⟧ **1** a person put in charge of the affairs of a large household or estate, whose duties include supervision of the kitchen and the servants, management of household accounts, etc. **2** one who acts as a supervisor or administrator, as of finances and property, for another or others **3** a person variously responsible for the food and drink, the service personnel, etc. in a club, restaurant, etc. **4** a person, usually one of a group, in charge of arrangements for a ball, race, meeting, etc. **5** *a)* an attendant, as on a ship, train, etc., employed to look after the passengers' comfort *b)* FLIGHT ATTENDANT **6** *short for* SHOP STEWARD **7** a person morally responsible for the careful use of money, time, talents, or other resources, esp. with respect to the principles or needs of a community or group [our responsibility as *stewards* of the earth's resources] —*vi.* to act as a steward —*vt.* to be the steward of (something); manage —**stew′ard·ship′** *n.*

stew·ard·ess (-ər dis) *n.* **1** a woman STEWARD (*n.* 5*a*) **2** a woman FLIGHT ATTENDANT

Stew·art[1] (sto͞o′ərt, styo͞o′-) *n.* ⟦var. of STUART[1]⟧ a masculine name: see STUART[1]

Stew·art[2] (sto͞o′ərt, styo͞o′-) **1 James (Maitland)** (called *Jimmy Stewart*) 1908-97; U.S. film actor **2 Potter** 1915-85; associate justice, U.S. Supreme Court (1958-81)

Stew·art[3] (sto͞o′ərt, styo͞o′-) island of New Zealand, just south of South Island: 674 sq mi (1,746 sq km)

stewed (sto͞od, styo͞od) *adj.* **1** cooked by stewing [*stewed* tomatoes] **2** [Slang] drunk; intoxicated

stew·pan (sto͞o′pan′, styo͞o′-) *n.* a pan used for stewing

stg *abbrev.* sterling

St. Gal·len (gäl′ən) **1** canton of NE Switzerland, on the Rhine: 782 sq mi (2,025 sq km) **2** its capital, in the N part Fr. name **St-Gall** (san gål′)

stge *abbrev.* storage

St. George's capital of Grenada, on the SW coast

St. George's Channel strait between Ireland & Wales, connecting the Irish Sea with the Atlantic: *c.* 100 mi (161 km) long

St. Gott·hard (gät′ərd, gäth′-) **1** mountain group in the Lepontine Alps, SC Switzerland: highest peak, 10,490 ft (3,197 m) **2** pass through these mountains: *c.* 6,935 ft (2,114 m) high Fr. name **St-Got·hard** (san gô tår′)

St. He·le·na (hə lē′nə, hel′ə nə) **1** British island in the South Atlantic, *c.* 1,200 mi (1,931 km) from Africa: site of Napoleon's exile (1815-21): 47 sq mi (122 sq km) **2** British colony including this island, Ascension, & the Tristan da Cunha group: *c.* 119 sq mi (308 sq km); cap. Jamestown

St. Hel·ens (hel′ənz), **Mount** ⟦after Baron A. F. *St. Helens* (1753-1839), Brit diplomat⟧ volcanic mountain in the Cascade Range, SW Wash.: dormant since 1857, it erupted in 1980: 8,364 ft (2,549 m)

sthen·ic (sthen′ik) *adj.* ⟦< Gr *sthenos*, strength + -IC⟧ **1** *former term for* MESOMORPHIC (sense 2) **2** designating or of feelings or symptoms marked by excessive excitement, strength, or activity

STI *abbrev.* sexually transmitted infection

stib·ine (stib′ēn, -in; *chiefly Brit,* -īn) *n.* ⟦< L *stibium*, antimony < Gr *stibi*, *stimi* < Egypt *sdm* + -INE[3]⟧ antimonous hydride, SbH_3, a colorless, poisonous gas

stib·nite (-nīt′) *n.* ⟦< prec. + -ITE[1]⟧ a soft, shiny, metallic-gray, orthorhombic mineral, Sb_2S_3, often found in long, pointed crystals; antimony sulfide

stich (stik) *n.* ⟦Gr *stichos*: see STILE[1]⟧ *Prosody* a line of prose or, esp., of verse

stich·o·myth·i·a (stik′ə mith′ē ə) *n.* ⟦Gr < *stichos*, a line (see STILE[1]) + *mythos*, speech, MYTH[1]⟧ dialogue in brief, alternate lines, as in ancient Greek drama: also **sti·chom·y·thy** (sti käm′ə thē) —**stich′o·myth′ic** *adj.*

-stich·ous (stik′əs) ⟦< Gr *stichos*, a line (see STILE[1]) + -OUS⟧ *combining form forming adjectives* having (a specified number or kind of) rows

stick (stik) *n.* ⟦ME *stikke* < OE *sticca*, akin to Du *stek*, ON *stik* < IE base **steig-*, a point > STAKE, Frank **stakka*, Gr *stigma*, L *instigare*, INSTIGATE⟧ **1** a long, usually slender piece of wood; specif., *a)* a twig or small branch broken off or cut off, esp. a dead and dry one *b)* a tree branch of any size, used for fuel, etc. *c)* a long, slender, and usually tapering piece of wood shaped for a specific purpose, as a wand, staff, club, baton, cane, rod, etc. **2** a stalk, as of celery **3** something that comes in narrow or oblong pieces [a *stick* of chewing gum, of butter, of dynamite, etc.] **4** a separate item; article [every *stick* of furniture] **5** an implement used for striking a ball, puck, etc. [a hockey *stick]* 6 something made of sticks, as a racing hurdle 7 a sticking, as with a pointed weapon; stab 8 anything, as a threat, used in compelling another 9 *a)* *short for* STICK SHIFT *b)* GEARSHIFT 10 a number of bombs, parachutists, etc. dropped from the air in such a way as to fall in a line across a target area 11 [Archaic] a stoppage, delay, or obstacle 12 [Informal] a dull, stupid, or spiritless person ☆13 [Slang] a marijuana cigarette 14 *Aeron.* JOYSTICK (sense 1) 15 [Now Rare] *Naut.* a mast or a part of a mast 16 *Printing* a composing stick or its contents —*vt.* **stuck** or, for *vt.* 9, **sticked, stick′ing** ⟦combination of ME *steken,* to prick, fasten (< OE *stecan*) & ME *stikien* < OE *stician,* to stick, stab, prick: both akin to the n.⟧ 1 to pierce or puncture, as with a pointed instrument 2 to kill by piercing; stab 3 to pierce something with (a knife, pin, etc.) 4 to thrust or push (*in, into, out,* etc.) [*to stick* one's finger into a hole] 5 to set with piercing objects [a cushion *stuck* with pins] 6 *a)* to fasten or attach as by gluing, pinning, etc. [to *stick* a poster on a wall] *b)* to decorate with things fastened in this way 7 *a)* to transfix or impale *b)* to impale (insect specimens, etc.), as on a pin, and mount for exhibit 8 to obstruct, entangle, bog down, etc.; also, to detain, delay, etc.: usually used in the passive [the wheels were *stuck*; we were *stuck* in town] 9 ⟦< the *n.*⟧ *a)* to prop (a vine, etc.) with a stick or sticks *b)* *Printing* to set type in a composing stick 10 [Informal] to place; put; set 11 [Informal] to make sticky by smearing 12 [Informal] to puzzle; baffle [to be *stuck* by a question] 13 [Slang] *a)* to make pay, often exorbitantly *b)* to impose a disagreeable task, burden, expense, etc. upon *c)* to cheat or defraud 14 [Informal, Chiefly Brit.] to endure or tolerate —*vi.* 1 to be or remain fixed or embedded by a pointed end, as a nail 2 to be or remain attached by adhesion; adhere; cleave 3 *a)* to remain in the same place; stay; abide [they *stick* at home] *b)* to remain fixed in the memory *c)* to remain in effect [to make the charges *stick*] 4 to remain in close association; be fixed; cling [friends *stick* together; the nickname *stuck*] 5 to keep close [to *stick* to a trail] 6 to persevere; persist [to *stick* at a job] 7 to remain firm and resolute; endure [they *stuck* through thick and thin] 8 to become fixed, blocked, lodged, etc. as by an obstacle; specif., *a)* to become embedded and immovable [a shoe *stuck* in the mud] *b)* to become unworkable; jam [the gears *stuck*] *c)* to become stopped or delayed; come to a standstill [a bill *stuck* in committee] 9 to be puzzled 10 to be reluctant; hesitate; scruple [a person who will *stick* at nothing] 11 to protrude, project, or extend (*out, up, through,* etc.) —☆**on the stick** [Slang] alert, efficient, etc. —**stick around** [Slang] to stay near at hand; not go away —**stick by (or to)** to remain faithful or loyal to —**stick it out** [Slang] to carry on or endure something until it is ended —**stick it to someone** [Slang] to harshly criticize, punish, or retaliate against someone —☆**stick to someone's ribs** to be nourishing and satisfying: said of food —**stick up** [Slang] to commit armed robbery upon —**stick up for** [Informal] to support; uphold; defend —☆**the sticks** [Informal] the rural districts; hinterland

SYN.—**stick** is the simple, general term here, implying attachment by gluing or fastening together in any way, by close association, etc. [to *stick* a stamp on a letter, to *stick* to a subject]; **adhere** implies firm attachment and, of persons, denotes voluntary allegiance or devotion as to an idea, cause, or leader [to *adhere* to a policy]; **cohere** implies such close sticking together of parts as to form a single mass [glue made the particles of sawdust *cohere*]; **cling** implies attachment by embracing, entwining, or grasping with the arms, tendrils, etc. [a vine *clinging* to the trellis]; **cleave** is a poetic or lofty term implying a very close, firm attachment [my tongue *cleaved* to the roof of my mouth] —*ANT.* **part, detach, separate**

stick·a·bil·i·ty (stik′ə bil′ə tē) *n.* ⟦prec. + ABILITY⟧ the ability to endure something or persevere in something

☆**stick·ball** (stik′bôl′) *n.* a game like baseball played by children, as on city streets, with improvised equipment such as a broom handle and a soft rubber ball

stick-built (-bilt′) *adj.* designating or of a house or other structure that is constructed on-site rather than prefabricated

stick·er (-ər) *n.* 1 a person or thing that sticks; specif., ☆*a)* a bur, barb, or thorn ☆*b)* a gummed label 2 [Informal] STICKLER 3 [Slang] a knife used as a weapon

sticker price ⟦so called because it is displayed as on an affixed sticker⟧ the manufacturer's suggested retail price, as of a new automobile, usually subject to a negotiated discount

sticker shock [Informal] the surprise and dismay supposedly experienced by consumers when confronted with high or greatly increased prices, esp. the sticker price of a new automobile

stick figure 1 a simple drawing, as by a child, of a human or animal figure, of which the torso and limbs are depicted by mere straight lines 2 a character, as in a novel, portrayed in a superficial or shallow way

stick·han·dle (stik′han′dəl) *vt.* **-dled, -dling** to maneuver (a hockey puck, lacrosse ball, etc.) with one's stick —**stick′han′dler** *n.*

stick·i·ly (-ə lē) *adv.* in a sticky manner

stick·i·ness (-ē nis) *n.* the quality or condition of being sticky

sticking plaster [Brit.] an adhesive bandage or band-aid for covering a slight wound

sticking point 1 a point beyond which someone or something will not budge 2 a point or issue that delays or hinders progress or resolution

stick insect a sticklike phasmid insect

stick-in-the-mud (stik′'n *thə* mud′) *n.* [Informal] a person who resists change or progress, new ideas, etc.

stick·le (stik′əl) *vi.* **-led, -ling** ⟦prob. < ME *stightlen,* to rule, order, dispose, freq. of *stighten,* to dispose, destine < OE *stihtan,* prob. akin to Ger *stiften,* to arrange, establish: for prob. IE base see STIFF⟧ 1 to raise objections, haggle, or make difficulties, esp. in a stubborn, narrow manner and usually about trifles 2 to have objections; scruple (*at*)

stick·le·back (stik′əl bak′) *n.* ⟦ME *stykylbak* < OE *sticel,* a prick, sting < base of *sticca* (see STICK) + ME *bak,* BACK[1]⟧ any of a family (Gasterosteidae, order Gasterosteiformes) of small, bony-plated, marine and freshwater bony fishes with two to eleven sharp spines in front of the dorsal fin: the male builds a nest for the female's eggs

stick·ler (stik′lər) *n.* ⟦see STICKLE⟧ 1 a person who insists on the strict observance of something specified: usually with *for* [a *stickler* for discipline] ☆2 [Informal] something puzzling or difficult to solve

stick·man (stik′man′) *n., pl.* **-men′** (-men′) [Slang] ☆1 an employee of a gambling house who oversees the play, esp. at a dice table, raking in the dice and chips, as with a stick 2 *Hockey, etc.* a player who uses a stick: often with reference to that player's skill with the stick [a good *stickman*] 3 STICK FIGURE (sense 1)

☆**stick·pin** (-pin′) *n.* 1 a long, straight pin with a jeweled or decorated head, worn to hold a cravat or necktie in place 2 such a pin now often worn by women, as on the lapel of a jacket as an ornament

☆**stick·seed** (-sēd′) *n.* any of several plants with barbs or prickles on the seeds or fruit; esp., any of a genus (*Lappula*) of the borage family with small, blue or whitish flowers

☆**stick shift** a type of motor vehicle transmission requiring manual shifting of the gears by means of a metal rod or bar mounted typically in the floor or in a center console and coordinated with a clutch pedal; manual transmission

☆**stick·tight** (stik′tīt′) *n.* 1 *a)* BUR MARIGOLD *b)* STICKSEED 2 the barbed achene of any of these plants

☆**stick-to-it·ive·ness** (stik to͞o′it iv nis) *n.* [Informal] pertinacity; persistence; perseverance

☆**stick·um** (stik′əm) *n.* ⟦STICK + *'em,* short for THEM⟧ [Informal] any sticky, or adhesive, substance

stick·up (-up′) *n. slang term for* HOLDUP (sense 2)

☆**stick·weed** (-wēd′) *n.* any of various North American plants with barbed seeds, as the ragweed or stickseed

stick work the use of a stick or sticks, as in playing hockey or playing the drums: also written **stick′work′** *n.*

stick·y (stik′ē) *adj.* **stick′i·er, stick′i·est** 1 *a)* that sticks; adhesive; tending to cling to anything touched *b)* not moving easily [*sticky* valves] 2 covered with an adhesive or viscous substance [a *sticky* countertop] 3 [Informal] hot and humid [a *sticky* climate] ☆4 [Informal] difficult to deal with; troublesome [a *sticky* problem] ☆5 [Informal] overly sentimental

☆**sticky fingers** [Slang] an inclination or tendency to steal or pilfer —**stick′y-fin′gered** *adj.*

sticky rice a short-grain rice that sticks together when cooked, used esp. in Southeast and East Asian cuisines

sticky wicket 1 *Cricket* the playing area between the wickets when it is damp and hence sticky and slow 2 [Informal, Chiefly Brit.] a difficult or awkward situation

Stieg·litz (stēg′lits), **Alfred** 1864-1946; U.S. photographer

stiff (stif) *adj.* ⟦ME *stif* < OE, akin to Ger *steif* < IE **stip-,* a pole, stick together (var. of base **steib(h)-,* rod) > L *stipes,* stem, stake, log, *stipare,* to crowd, cram⟧ 1 hard to bend or stretch; rigid; firm; not flexible or pliant 2 hard to move or operate; not free or limber 3 stretched tight; taut; tense 4 *a)* sore or limited in movement (said of joints and muscles) *b)* having such joints or muscles, as from exertion, cold, etc. 5 not fluid or loose; viscous; thick; dense; firm [to beat egg whites until *stiff*] 6 strong; specif., *a)* moving swiftly, as a breeze or current *b)* containing much alcohol (said of a drink) *c)* of high potency [a *stiff* dose of medicine] *d)* done or delivered with great force; powerful 7 harsh [*stiff* punishment] 8 difficult to do or deal with [a *stiff* climb, *stiff* competition] 9 excessively formal, constrained, or awkward; not easy, natural, or graceful 10 resolute, stubborn, or uncompromising, as a person, a fight, etc. 11 [Informal] high or excessive [a *stiff* price] 12 [Slang] drunk; intoxicated 13 *Naut.* not tending to lean or tilt to one side even in strong winds or when carrying much sail: opposed to TENDER[1] (*adj.* 11) —*adv.* 1 to a stiff condition 2 [Informal] completely; thoroughly [scared *stiff*] —*n.* [Slang] ☆1 a corpse ☆2 a drunken person 3 an excessively formal or constrained person ☆4 an awkward or rough person ☆5 a hobo ☆6 a man [a working *stiff*] 7 a person who gives a small tip or no gratuity at all —☆*vt.* **stiffed, stiff′ing** [Slang] 1 to cheat (someone), as by not paying 2 to fail to leave a tip for —*SYN.* FIRM[1] —**stiff′ish** *adj.* —**stiff′ly** *adv.* —**stiff′ness** *n.*

stiff-arm (stif′ärm′) ☆*vt.* to push away (an opponent, as a would-be tackler in football) with one's arm outstretched —☆*n.* the act of stiff-arming

stiff·en (stif′ən) *vt., vi.* to make or become stiff or stiffer —**stiff′en·er** *n.*

stiff-necked (stif′nekt′) *adj.* stubborn; obstinate

sti·fle[1] (stī′fəl) *vt.* **-fled, -fling** ⟦altered (prob. infl. by ON *stīfla,* to stop up: for IE base see STIFF) < ME *stuflen,* freq. formation < MFr *estouffer,* to smother < VL **stuppare,* to stuff up (see STOP), infl. by **extufare,* to quench, smother, steam, STEW⟧ 1 to kill by cutting off the supply of air from; suffocate; smother; choke 2 to suppress or repress; hold back; check, stop, inhibit, etc. [to *stifle* a sob, to *stifle* protests] —*vi.* 1 to die from lack of air 2 to suffer from lack of fresh, cool air —**sti′fler** *n.*

sti·fle[2] (stī′fəl) *n.* ⟦ME⟧ the kneelike joint above the hock in the hind leg of a horse, dog, etc.: also **stifle joint**

sti·fling (stī′fliŋ) *adj.* so close as to be oppressive; suffocating —**sti′fling·ly** *adv.*

stig·ma (stig′mə) *n., pl.* **stig′mas**; also, and for 4, 5, 7, & 8 usually, **stig·ma·ta** (stig mät′ə, stig′mə tə) ⟦L < Gr, lit., a puncture made with a pointed instrument < *stizein,* to prick: for IE base see STICK⟧ **1** [Archaic] a distinguishing mark burned or cut into the flesh, as of a slave or criminal **2** something that detracts from the character or reputation of a person, group, etc.; mark of disgrace or reproach **3** a mark, sign, etc. indicating that something is not considered normal or standard **4** a small mark, scar, opening, etc. on the surface of a plant or animal, as a pore or eyespot, etc. **5** a spot on the skin, esp. one that bleeds as the result of certain nervous tensions: see also STIGMATA **6** *Bot.* the free upper tip of the style of a flower, on which pollen falls and develops **7** *Med.* any sign characteristic of a specific disease **8** *Zool.* SPIRACLE (sense 3*a*) —**stig′mal** *adj.*

stig·mas·ter·ol (stig mas′tər ôl′, -ōl′) *n.* ⟦contr. < ModL *Physostigma* (see PHYSOSTIGMINE) + STEROL⟧ a sterol, $C_{29}H_{48}O$, isolated from soy or Calabar beans

stig·ma·ta (stig mät′ə, stig′mə tə) *n. alt. pl. of* STIGMA —*pl.n.* [*often* **S-**] [*with pl. or sing. v.*] marks resembling the crucifixion wounds of Jesus, appearing on some devout persons in a state of intense religious fervor

stig·mat·ic (stig mat′ik) *adj.* **1** of, like, or having a stigma, stigmas, or stigmata: also **stig·mat′i·cal** **2** of or having STIGMATISM (sense 2) —*n.* a person marked with stigmata: also **stig′ma·tist** (-mə tist) —**stig·mat′i·cal·ly** *adv.*

stig·ma·tism (stig′mə tiz′əm) *n.* **1** the condition characterized by the presence of stigmas or stigmata **2** the condition of a lens, and the normal condition of the eye, in which rays of light from a single point are focused upon a single point

stig·ma·tize (stig′mə tīz′) *vt.* **-tized′**, **-tiz′ing** ⟦ML *stigmatizare:* see STIGMA & -IZE⟧ **1** to mark with a stigma, stigmas, or stigmata **2** to characterize or mark as disgraceful —**stig′ma·ti·za′tion** *n.*

stil·bene (stil′bēn′) *n.* ⟦< Gr *stilbein,* to glitter + -ENE⟧ a crystalline hydrocarbon, $C_6H_5CH{:}CHC_6H_5$, used in the manufacture of dyes and as a crystal scintillation detector

stil·bes·trol (stil bes′trôl′, -trōl′) *n.* ⟦< prec. + ESTR(ONE) + -OL[2]⟧ DIETHYLSTILBESTROL

stil·bite (stil′bīt′) *n.* ⟦Fr < Gr *stilbein,* to glitter: see -ITE[1]⟧ a usually white, semihard, monoclinic zeolite, $NaCa_2Al_5Si_{13}O_{36}\cdot 14H_2O$, usually found in sheaflike crystals; hydrous sodium calcium aluminum silicate

stile[1] (stīl) *n.* ⟦ME < OE *stigel* < *stigan,* to climb < IE base **steigh-,* to step, climb > STAIR, Sans *stighnoti,* (he) climbs, Gr *stichos,* a row, line⟧ **1** a set of steps used in climbing over a fence or wall **2** *short for* TURNSTILE

stile[2] (stīl) *n.* ⟦Du *stijl,* doorpost⟧ a vertical piece in a panel or frame, as of a door or window

sti·let·to (sti let′ō) *n., pl.* **-tos** or **-toes** ⟦It, dim. of *stilo,* dagger < L *stilus:* see STYLE⟧ **1** a small dagger, having a slender, tapering blade **2** a small, sharp-pointed instrument used for making eyelet holes in cloth, etc. **3** a high, very thin heel on a woman's shoe: in full **stiletto heel** —*vt.* **-toed**, **-to·ing** to stab, or kill by stabbing, with a stiletto

still[1] (stil) *adj.* ⟦ME < OE *stille,* akin to Ger *still* < IE **stelnu-* < base **stel-,* to place, set up, standing, immobile > STALK[1], STALL[1], L *locus,* place, Gr *stēlē,* a post⟧ **1** without sound; quiet; silent **2** hushed, soft, or low in sound **3** not moving; stationary; at rest; motionless: following *stand, sit, lie,* etc., sometimes regarded as an adverb **4** characterized by little or no commotion or agitation; tranquil; calm; serene [the *still* water of the lake] **5** not effervescent or bubbling: said of wine **6** *Film* designating or of a single posed photograph or a photograph made from a single frame of a filmed sequence or scene, for use as in publicity —*n.* **1** silence; quiet [in the *still* of the night] **2** *Film* a still photograph —*adv.* **1** at or up to the time indicated, whether past, present, or future [does she *still* work here?] **2** even; yet: used as an intensifier with a comparative form, etc. [cold yesterday, but *still* colder today] **3** nevertheless; even then [he's rich but *still* he's unhappy]; often used as a conjunctive adverb [he failed; *still,* he never stopped trying] **4** [Archaic] ever; constantly —*vt.* to make still; quiet; specif., *a)* to make silent *b)* to make motionless *c)* to calm; relieve —*vi.* to become still —**still and all** [Informal] nevertheless —**still′ness** *n.*

still[2] (stil) *n.* ⟦< obs. *still,* to distill < L *stillare,* to drop, drip, trickle < *stilla,* a drop < **stir(a)la,* dim. of *stiria,* a drop: see STONE⟧ **1** an apparatus used for distilling liquids, esp. alcoholic liquors **2** DISTILLERY —*vt., vi.* **1** to distill **2** [Dial.] to distill (alcoholic liquor) illegally

still·birth (stil′burth′) *n.* **1** the birth of a stillborn fetus **2** a stillborn fetus

still·born (-bôrn′) *adj.* **1** dead when delivered from the womb **2** unsuccessful from the beginning; abortive

☆**still hunt** a stealthy hunt for game, as by stalking or using cover —**still′-hunt′** *vt., vi.*

still life **1** *pl.* **still lifes** a painting, drawing, etc. having as its subject an arrangement of inanimate objects, as fruit, bottles, flowers, and books **2** such works of art collectively, regarded as a genre, or kind —**still′-life′** *adj.*

☆**Still·son wrench** (stil′sən) ⟦after Daniel *Stillson,* its U.S. inventor (1869)⟧ a wrench having a ridged jaw that moves through a collar pivoted loosely to the shaft, used for turning pipes, etc.: the jaw tightens as pressure is applied to the handle

still·y (stil′ē; *for adv.,* stil′lē) *adj.* **still′i·er**, **still′i·est** ⟦ME *stillich* < OE *stillic*⟧ [Literary] still; silent; calm —*adv.* ⟦ME *stilleli* < OE *stillice*⟧ in a still manner; silently; calmly

stilt (stilt) *n.* ⟦ME *stilte,* prob. < MLowG or MDu *stelte,* akin to Ger *stelze:* for base see STILL[1]⟧ **1** either of a pair of poles, each with a footrest somewhere along its length, used for walking with the feet above the ground, as by children at play, by acrobats, etc. **2** any of a number of long posts or piles used to hold a building, etc. above the ground or out of the water **3** *pl.* **stilts** or **stilt** any of several shorebirds (family Recurvirostridae) with a long, slender bill, long legs, and three-toed feet; esp., the **black-necked stilt** (*Himantopus mexicanus*), living chiefly in marshes and ponds of temperate North America and N South America

stilt·ed (stil′tid) *adj.* **1** raised or elevated on or as on stilts **2** so formal or high-sounding as to seem pompous, unnatural, or old-fashioned: said of writing or speech —**stilt′ed·ly** *adv.* —**stilt′ed·ness** *n.*

Stil·ton (cheese) (stilt′'n) ⟦orig. sold at *Stilton,* village in EC England⟧ a rich, crumbly cheese with veins of blue-green mold

Stim·son (stim′sən), **Henry L(ewis)** 1867-1950; U.S. statesman: secretary of state (1929-33): secretary of war (1911-13; 1940-45)

stim·u·lant (stim′yə lənt) *adj.* ⟦L *stimulans,* prp.⟧ that stimulates; stimulating —*n.* anything that stimulates; specif., *a)* any drug, medicine, etc., as an amphetamine, caffeine, nicotine, or cocaine, that temporarily increases the activity of some vital process, organ, or system, esp. the nervous system *b)* popularly, an alcoholic drink: alcohol is physiologically a depressant

stim·u·late (-lāt′) *vt.* **-lat′ed**, **-lat′ing** ⟦< L *stimulatus,* pp. of *stimulare,* to prick, goad, excite < *stimulus:* see fol.⟧ **1** to rouse or excite to action or increased action; animate; spur on **2** to invigorate or seem to invigorate, as by an alcoholic drink **3** *Med., Physiol.* to excite (an organ, part, etc.) to activity or increased activity —*vi.* to act as a stimulant or stimulus —*SYN.* ANIMATE, PROVOKE —**stim′u·la′tor** *n.*, **stim′u·lat′er** —**stim′u·la′tion** *n.* —**stim′u·la′tive** *adj., n.*

stim·u·lus (-ləs) *n., pl.* **-u·li′** (-lī′) ⟦L, a goad, sting, torment, pang, spur, incentive: see STYLE⟧ **1** something that rouses or incites to action or increased action; incentive **2** *Physiol., Psychol.* any action or agent that causes or changes an activity in an organism, organ, or part, as something that excites an end organ, starts a nerve impulse, or activates a muscle

sti·my (stī′mē) *n., pl.* **-mies** STYMIE —*vt.* **-mied**, **-my·ing**

sting (stiŋ) *vt.* **stung**, **sting′ing** ⟦ME *stingen* < OE *stingan,* akin to ON *stinga* < IE base **stegh-,* to pierce, sharp > STAG⟧ **1** to prick or wound with a sting: said of plants and insects **2** to cause sharp, sudden, smarting pain to, by or as by pricking with a sharp point [the cold wind *stinging* their cheeks] **3** to cause to suffer emotionally; make unhappy [to be *stung* by one's conscience] **4** to stir up or stimulate suddenly and sharply [*stung* into action by her words] **5** [Slang] to cheat; esp., to overcharge —*vi.* **1** to use a sting; prick or wound with a sting **2** to cause or feel sharp, smarting pain, either physical or mental [his arm *stinging* from the blow] —*n.* ⟦OE *sting*⟧ **1** the act of stinging **2** a pain or wound resulting from or as from stinging **3** a thing that urges or stimulates; goad **4** the ability or power to sting or wound [criticism with much *sting* in it] **5** a sharp-pointed organ in insects and certain other animals, used to prick, wound, or inject poison **6** any of the hollow, stinging hairs on some plants, as nettles **7** [Informal] *a)* an elaborate CONFIDENCE GAME *b)* an elaborately planned operation engaged in by law-enforcement agents to entrap criminals —**sting′less** *adj.*

☆**sting·a·ree** (stiŋ′ə rē′, stiŋ′ə rē′) *n. var. of* STINGRAY

sting·er (stiŋ′ər) *n.* **1** a person or thing that stings; specif., *a)* an animal or plant that stings *b)* a sharp-pointed organ used for stinging; sting *c)* [Informal] a blow, reply, etc. that stings **2** a cocktail made with white crème de menthe, brandy, and ice **3** [Informal] any of various injuries characterized by sudden, brief pain, as stinging or burning, in the neck, shoulder, or arm

stinging hair STING (*n.* 6)

☆**sting·ray** (stiŋ′rā′) *n.* any of a family (Dasyatidae, order Myliobatiformes) of large rays having a long, whiplike tail with one or more usually poisonous spines that can inflict painful wounds

stin·gy[1] (stin′jē) *adj.* **stin′gi·er**, **stin′gi·est** ⟦< **stinge,* dial. form of STING⟧ **1** giving or spending grudgingly or only through necessity; mean; miserly **2** less than needed or expected; scanty —**stin′gi·ly** *adv.* —**stin′gi·ness** *n.*

SYN.—**stingy** implies a grudging, mean reluctance to part with anything belonging to one; **close** suggests the keeping of a tight hold on what one has accumulated; **niggardly** implies such closefistedness that one grudgingly spends or gives the least amount possible; **parsimonious** implies unreasonable economy or frugality, often to the point of niggardliness; **penurious** implies such extreme parsimony and niggardliness as to make one seem poverty-stricken or destitute; **miserly** implies the penuriousness of one who is meanly avaricious and hoarding —*ANT.* **generous, bountiful**

sting·y[2] (stiŋ′ē) *adj.* stinging or capable of stinging

stink (stiŋk) *vi.* **stank** or **stunk**, **stunk**, **stink′ing** ⟦ME *stinken* < OE *stincan,* akin to Ger *stinken*⟧ **1** to give off a strong, unpleasant smell **2** to be very offensive; be hateful or abhorrent **3** [Informal] to be of low standard or quality; be no good **4** [Slang] to have much or an excess: with *of* or *with* —*n.* **1** a strong, unpleasant smell; stench **2** [Informal] a strong public reaction, as one of outrage, censure, protest, etc. —**stink up (**or **out)** [Informal] to cause to stink —**stink′y** *adj.* **stink′i·er**, **stink′i·est**

stink bomb a device made to burn or explode and give off an offensive smell

☆**stink bug** any of various foul-smelling insects; esp., any of a family (Pentatomidae) of hemipterous bugs with a broad, shield-shaped body

stink·er (stiŋk′ər) *n.* **1** a person or thing that stinks **2** [Slang] *a)* a contemptible, obnoxious, or disgusting person *b)* a very difficult task, problem, etc. *c)* something of very low standard or quality

stink·horn (-hôrn′) *n.* any of an order (Phallales) of foul-smelling basidiomycetous fungi
stink·ing (-iŋ) *adj.* 1 that stinks; bad-smelling 2 [Slang] *a)* very bad, unsatisfactory, etc. *b)* offensive, disgusting, etc. —*adv.* [Slang] to an excessive or offensive degree —**stink′ing·ly** *adv.*
☆**stinking smut** BUNT[2]
☆**stink·o** (stiŋk′ō) *adj.* [Slang] 1 very bad; inferior in quality; lousy 2 drunk; intoxicated
stink·pot (stiŋk′pät′) *n.* 1 a kind of stink bomb formerly used in naval warfare ☆2 a small musk turtle (*Sternotherus odoratus*) of the E and S U.S. 3 [Slang] STINKER (sense 1)
stink·stone (-stōn′) *n.* a variety of stone, esp. limestone, that gives off a foul smell when rubbed or struck, as from decayed organic matter contained in it
stink·weed (-wēd′) *n.* any of various plants, as the jimson weed or dog fennel, having a foul or strong smell
stink·wood (-wood′) *n.* 1 any of several trees whose wood has an offensive odor; esp., a South African tree (*Ocotea bullata*) of the laurel family, yielding a hard, durable wood 2 the wood of any such tree
stint[1] (stint) *vt.* ⟦ME *stinten,* to stint, cease, stop < OE *styntan,* to blunt or dull, akin to *stunt,* blunt, dull: see STUNT[1]⟧ 1 to restrict or limit to a certain quantity, number, share, or allotment, often small or scanty 2 [Archaic] to stop —*vi.* 1 to be sparing or grudging in giving or using 2 [Archaic] to stop —*n.* 1 restriction; limit; limitation 2 [Now Rare] a limited or fixed quantity, allotment, share, etc. 3 *a)* an assigned task or quantity of work *b)* a specified period of time spent doing something —*SYN.* TASK —**stint′er** *n.*
stint[2] (stint) *n.* ⟦LME *stynte* < ?⟧ any of various small sandpipers, as the **little stint** (*Calidris minuta*)
stipe (stīp) *n.* ⟦Fr < L *stipes,* log, stock, trunk of a tree: see STIFF⟧ 1 *Bot.* a usually short, thick stem, as *a)* the stalk of a mushroom *b)* the petiole of a fern frond *c)* a stalklike extension of the receptacle of a spermatophyte *d)* the stemlike part supporting the thallus in certain algae 2 *Zool.* STIPES
sti·pel (stī′pəl) *n.* ⟦ModL, dim. of *stipula,* STIPULE⟧ a small or secondary stipule at the base of a leaflet —**sti·pel·late** (stī pel′it, -āt) *adj.*
sti·pend (stī′pənd, -pend′) *n.* ⟦ME *stipende* < L *stipendium,* tax, impost, tribute, contr. < **stipipendum* < *stips,* small coin or a contribution in small coin (< ?) + *pendere,* to hang, weigh out, pay: see PENDANT⟧ 1 a regular or fixed payment for services, as a salary 2 any periodic payment, as a pension or allowance —*SYN.* WAGE
sti·pen·di·ar·y (stī pen′dē er′ē) *adj.* ⟦L *stipendiarius*⟧ 1 receiving, or performing services for, a stipend 2 paid for by a stipend [*stipendiary* services] 3 of, or having the nature of, a stipend —*n., pl.* **-ar′ies** a person who receives a stipend
sti·pes (stī′pēz′) *n., pl.* **stip·i·tes** (stip′ə tēz′) ⟦L: see STIPE⟧ *Zool.* a stalklike part or peduncle, as an eyestalk or the basal portion of the typical maxilla in insects —**stip·i·tate** (stip′ə tāt′) *adj.*
stip·ple (stip′əl) *vt.* **-pled, -pling** ⟦Du *stippelen* < *stippel,* a speckle, dim. of *stip,* a point, akin to *stippen,* to prick: for IE base see STIFF⟧ 1 to paint, draw, engrave, or apply in small points or dots rather than in lines or solid areas 2 to cover or mark with dots or quick dabs; fleck —*n.* 1 *a)* the art or method of painting, drawing, or engraving in dots *b)* the effect produced by this, or an effect, as in nature, resembling it 2 stippled work —**stip′pler** *n.*
stip·u·lar (stip′yoo lər) *adj.* 1 of or like a stipule or stipules 2 growing on or near a stipule
stip·u·late[1] (stip′yə lāt′) *vt.* **-lat′ed, -lat′ing** ⟦< L *stipulatus,* pp. of *stipulari,* to bargain < or akin to Umbrian *stiplo,* to stipulate; akin to L *stips:* see STIPEND⟧ to specify in the terms of an agreement, a contract, etc. —*vi.* to make a specific demand (*for* something) as a condition of or requirement in an agreement —**stip′u·la′tor** *n.* —**stip′u·la·to′ry** (-lə tôr′ē) *adj.*
stip·u·late[2] (stip′yoo lit, -lāt′) *adj.* ⟦ModL *stipulatus*⟧ having stipules: also **stip′u·lat′ed**
stip·u·la·tion (stip′yə lā′shən) *n.* ⟦L *stipulatio*⟧ 1 the act of stipulating 2 something stipulated, as a condition in a contract
stip·ule (stip′yool′) *n.* ⟦ModL *stipula* < L, a stalk, straw, dim. of *stipes,* trunk: see STIPE⟧ either of a pair of small, leaflike parts at the base of some leaf petioles, as on a bean, pea, or rose plant

STIPULE

stir[1] (stur) *vt.* **stirred, stir′ring** ⟦ME *stirien* < OE *styrian:* see STORM⟧ 1 to move, shake, agitate, etc., esp. slightly 2 to change the position of slightly; displace [to *stir* a log in a fireplace] 3 to rouse from sleep, lethargy, indifference, etc. 4 to put (oneself, one's limbs, etc.) into motion or activity, esp. briskly 5 *a)* to move an implement, the hand, etc. through (a liquid or loose substance) with an agitated motion so that the particles change position with relation to one another *b)* to mix by or as by imparting such a motion to 6 to excite the feelings of; move strongly 7 to incite or provoke: often with *up* [to *stir* up trouble] 8 to evoke, or call up [to *stir* memories] —*vi.* 1 to move or change position, esp. only slightly [not a leaf *stirred*] 2 to be up and about; be busy and active 3 to be taking place, going on, happening, etc. 4 to begin to show signs of activity; begin to come to life 5 to impart an agitated motion to a liquid, mixture, etc. as with a spoon 6 to be stirred [a mixture that *stirs* easily] —*n.* 1 the act, an instance, or the sound of stirring 2 movement; activity; agitation 3 a state of excitement; commotion; tumult —**stir′rer** *n.*

SYN.—**stir** (in this sense, often **stir up**) implies a bringing into action or activity by exciting or provoking [the colonies were *stirred* to rebellion]; **arouse** and **rouse** are often used interchangeably, but **arouse** usually implies merely a bringing into consciousness, as from a state of sleep [she was *aroused* by the bell], and **rouse** suggests an additional incitement to vigorous action [the rifle shot *roused* the sleeping guard]; **awaken** and **waken** literally mean to arouse from sleep, but figuratively they suggest the elicitation of latent faculties, emotions, etc. [it *awakened,* or *wakened,* her maternal feelings]; **rally** implies a gathering of the component elements or individuals so as to stir to effective action [to *rally* troops, one's energy, etc.]

stir[2] (stur) *n.* ⟦19th-c. thieves' slang, prob. contr. < Romany *steripen*⟧ [Slang] a prison
☆**stir-cra·zy** (stur′krā′zē) *adj.* ⟦< prec.⟧ [Slang] anxious, tense, etc. from long, close confinement, as in prison
stir-fry (stur′frī′) *vt.* **-fried′, -fry′ing** in Chinese cooking, to fry (diced or sliced vegetables, meat, etc.) very quickly in a wok, with a little oil, while stirring constantly —*n., pl.* **-fries′** a dish prepared in this way
stirk (sturk) *n.* ⟦ME < OE *stierc,* akin to Goth *stairo,* barren: see STERILE⟧ [Brit.] a bullock or heifer, esp. one between one and two years old
Stir·ling (stur′liŋ) administrative division of central Scotland: formerly a county & district: also, for the county, **Stir′ling·shire′** (-shir′)
Stir·ling engine (stur′liŋ) ⟦after R. *Stirling* (1790-1878), Scot engineer who developed the operating principle⟧ an external-combustion engine in which the heat released from the burning fuel is transferred to a confined gas, as hydrogen, which activates the pistons
stirps (sturps) *n., pl.* **stir·pes** (stur′pēz′) ⟦L, lit., a stalk, trunk, root < IE base **ster-,* rigid, stiff, STARE⟧ 1 family or branch of a family 2 *Law* the person from whom a family or branch of a family is descended
stir·ring (stur′iŋ) *adj.* 1 active; busy 2 that stirs one's feelings; rousing [*stirring* music] —**stir′ring·ly** *adv.*
stir·rup (stur′əp, stir′-) *n.* ⟦ME *stirop* < OE *stigrap,* akin to Ger *stegreif:* for IE bases see STILE[2] & ROPE⟧ 1 a ring with a flat bottom hung by a strap, usually on each side of a saddle and used as a footrest in mounting and riding 2 any of various supports, clamps, etc. resembling or suggesting such a ring 3 *a)* [*usually pl.*] an apparatus attached to a chair or examining table, consisting of a pair of supports for the feet and enabling the knees to be raised and positioned well apart during a gynecological exam or procedure *b)* either of the foot supports 4 *Naut.* a short rope hung from a yard for use in supporting a footrope 5 the stapes, one of the three bones of the middle ear: also **stirrup bone**
stirrup cup [Archaic] a farewell drink taken by a rider mounted to depart
stirrup leather (*or* **strap**) a strap connecting a stirrup with the saddle
stirrup pants close-fitting pants with a stirruplike strap, at the end of each leg, to be positioned under the arch of the foot
stirrup pump a hand pump for putting out fires, set in a bucket and held firm by a stirrup, or bracket, for one foot
stish·ov·ite (stish′ə vīt′) *n.* ⟦after S. *Stishov,* Soviet mineralogist who discovered it + -ITE[1]⟧ a very dense, tetragonal form of silica that is colorless and transparent
stitch (stich) *n.* ⟦ME *stiche* < OE *stice,* a puncture, stab: for IE base see STICK⟧ 1 *a)* a single complete in-and-out movement of the threaded needle in sewing *b)* SUTURE (sense 4c) 2 a single loop of yarn worked off a needle in knitting, crocheting, etc. 3 the piece of thread worked in, or a loop, knot, etc. made, by stitching 4 a particular kind of stitch or style of stitching 5 a sudden, sharp pain in the side or back 6 a bit or piece; specif., an article of clothing [wearing not a *stitch*] —*vi.* to make stitches; sew —*vt.* 1 to fasten, join, repair, adorn, or operate upon with or as with stitches; sew 2 to fasten or unite (cartons, booklets, etc.) with staples —**in stitches** in a state of uproarious laughter —**stitch′er** *n.*
stitch·er·y (-ər ē) *n.* 1 the art of ornamental needlework, as embroidery, crewelwork, etc. 2 *pl.* **-er·ies** something made or decorated in this way
stitch·ing (-iŋ) *n. Sewing* a row or series of stitches
stitch·wort (-wurt′) *n.* ⟦ME *stichwurt:* see STITCH & WORT[2]⟧ any of several chickweeds; esp., an Old World perennial (*Stellaria holostea*) with grasslike leaves
stith·y (stith′ē, stith′ē) *n., pl.* **stith′ies** ⟦ME *stethie* < ON *stethi,* anvil: for IE base see STEAD⟧ [Now Chiefly Dial.] an anvil or smithy
sti·ver (stī′vər) *n.* ⟦Du *stuiver* < MDu *stūver* < *stūf,* stumpy, cut short: for IE base see STEEP[1]⟧ 1 a former Dutch coin equal to $\frac{1}{20}$ of a guilder 2 a trifling sum
St. James's Palace palace in Westminster, London: the royal residence from 1697 to 1837
St. John[1], **Henry** *see* BOLINGBROKE, 1st Viscount
St. John[2] 1 island of the Virgin Islands of the U.S.: 20 sq mi (52 sq km) 2 **Lake** lake in SC Quebec, Canada: 321 sq mi (831 sq km): Fr. name **Lac St-Jean** (läk san zhän′)
St. Johns river in E & NE Fla., flowing into the Atlantic near Jacksonville: 276 mi (444 km)
St. John's 1 seaport & capital of Newfoundland and Labrador, Canada, on the SE coast 2 seaport & capital of Antigua and Barbuda; chief town of Antigua, on the N coast

St. Johns·wort (jänz′wurt) ⟦after *Saint* JOHN[1] + WORT[2]: reason for name uncert.⟧ any of a genus (*Hypericum*) of ornamental plants of the St. Johnswort family, with usually yellow flowers and numerous stamens — designating a family (Guttiferae, order Theales) of dicotyledonous trees, shrubs, and plants used for timber, in drugs, etc. Also written **St-John's-wort** or **St. John's wort**

St. Joseph ⟦after *St. Joseph,* husband of Mary⟧ city in NW Mo., on the Missouri River

St. Kitts (kits) island of the country St. Kitts and Nevis: 65 sq mi (168 sq km)

St. Kitts and Nevis country in the Leeward Islands of the West Indies, consisting of two islands (St. Kitts & Nevis): formerly a British colony, it became an independent state (1983) & a member of the Commonwealth: *c.* 101 sq mi (261 sq km); cap. Basseterre

St. Lau·rent (san lô rän′), **Louis Stephen** 1882-1973; Cdn. statesman: prime minister (1948-57)

St. Lawrence ⟦< Fr, after *St Laurent* (died A.D. 258), Roman martyr⟧ **1** river flowing from Lake Ontario northeast into the Gulf of St. Lawrence: *c.* 750 mi (1,207 km) **2 Gulf of** large inlet of the Atlantic in E Canada: *c.* 100,000 sq mi (259,000 sq km)

St. Lawrence Seaway inland waterway for oceangoing ships, connecting the Great Lakes with the Atlantic: operated jointly by the U.S. & Canada, it consists of the Welland Canal, the St. Lawrence River, & several locks & canals between Montreal & Lake Ontario

St. Lou·is (lo͞o′is, lo͞o′ē) ⟦prob. after LOUIS IX⟧ city & port in E Mo., on the Mississippi

St. Lu·ci·a (lo͞o′shē ə, -shə; lo͞o sē′ə) country on an island of the Windward group, West Indies, south of Martinique: formerly a British colony, it became independent & a member of the Commonwealth in 1979: 238 sq mi (616 sq km); cap. Castries

STM or S.T.M. *abbrev.* ⟦L *Sacrae Theologiae Magister*⟧ Master of Sacred Theology

St-Ma·lo (san mȧ lō′) **1** seaport & resort town on an island in the Gulf of St-Malo, NW France **2 Gulf of** inlet of the English Channel, on the N coast of Brittany, NW France: *c.* 60 mi (97 km) wide

St. Martin island of the Leeward group, West Indies, south of Anguilla: the N part belongs to France, the S part is now an independent nation associated with the Kingdom of the Netherlands: 34 sq mi (88 sq km): Fr. name **St-Mar·tin** (san mȧr tan′); Du. name **St. Maar·ten** (sint märt′′n)

St. Mar·y·le·bone (mer′i lə bōn′) former metropolitan borough of London: since 1965, part of Westminster

St. Marys 1 river flowing from the Okefenokee Swamp along the Ga.-Fla. border into the Atlantic: *c.* 180 mi (290 km) **2** river flowing from Lake Superior into Lake Huron, between NE Mich. & Ontario, Canada: 63 mi (101 km)

St. Marys Falls Canals three ship canals (two U.S., one Canadian) bypassing a rapids of the St. Marys River at Sault Ste. Marie

St. Mo·ritz (sānt′ mō rits′; *Fr* san mô rēts′) mountain resort town in SE Switzerland

sto·a (stō′ə) ***n., pl.*** **sto′ae** (-ē) or **sto′as** ⟦Gr < IE **stōu-* < base **stā-* > STAND⟧ a portico, as in ancient Greece, having a wall on one side and pillars on the other

stoat (stōt) ***n., pl.*** **stoats** or **stoat** ⟦ME *stote*⟧ a large European ermine (*Mustela erminea*), esp. in its brown summer coat

stob (stäb) ***n.*** ⟦ME, var. of STUB⟧ [Dial.] **1** a stake or short post **2** a stump

stoc·ca·do (stə kä′dō) ***n.*** ⟦OIt *stoccata* < *stocca,* dagger, sword point < MFr *estoc* < OFr *estoquier,* to strike with the point < LowG *stoken,* to stick: for IE base see STOCK⟧ [Archaic] a stab or thrust with a pointed weapon

sto·chas·tic (stō kas′tik, stə-) ***adj.*** ⟦< Gr *stochastikos,* proceeding by guesswork, lit., skillful in aiming < *stochazesthai,* to aim at < *stochos,* a target: for IE base see STING⟧ **1** of, pertaining to, or arising from chance; involving probability; random **2** *Math.* designating a process in which a sequence of values is drawn from a corresponding sequence of jointly distributed random variables

stock (stäk) ***n.*** ⟦ME *stocke* < OE *stocc,* akin to Ger *stock,* Du *stok,* a stick < IE base **(s)teu-,* to strike, chop > STUMP, STUB⟧ **1** the trunk of a tree **2** [Archaic] *a)* a tree stump *b)* a wooden block or log **3** *a)* a blockhead *b)* anything lacking life, motion, or feeling **4** *a)* a plant stem into which a graft is inserted *b)* a plant from which cuttings are taken **5** an underground plant stem; rhizome or rootstock **6** any of a number of plants of the crucifer family, as **evening stock** (*Mathiola bicornis*), or **Virginian stock** (*Malcomia maritima*) **7** *a)* the first of a line of descent *b)* a line of descent; lineage *c)* a strain, race, or other related group of animals or plants *d)* an ethnic group or other major subdivision of human beings *e)* a group of related languages or language families **8** a supporting or main part, as the handle of an implement, weapon, etc., to which the working parts are attached; specif., *a)* a bitstock or brace *b)* the butt or handle of a whip, fishing rod, etc. *c)* the block of a plane, in which the cutting blade is inserted *d)* the frame of a plow, to which the share, handles, etc. are attached *e)* the handle, usually wooden, to which the barrel of a rifle, shotgun, etc. is attached **9** DIESTOCK **10** the crosspiece near the top of the shank on some anchors **11** [*pl.*] a framework; specif., *a)* a former instrument of punishment consisting of a heavy wooden frame with holes for confining the ankles and, sometimes, the wrists of an offender *b)* a frame of timbers supporting a ship during construction ☆*c)* a frame in which an animal is held, as for shoeing **12** something out of which other things are made; specif., *a)* raw material *b)* water in which meat, fish, etc. has been boiled, used as a base for soup or gravy **13** a specified kind of paper [*heavy stock*] **14** a store or supply; specif., *a)* all the animals, equipment, etc. kept and used on a farm *b) short for* LIVESTOCK *c)* the total amount of goods on hand in a store, etc.; inventory *d)* the portion of a deck of cards remaining after the hands have been dealt, available for use later in the hand **15** *a)* [Archaic] the part of a tally given to the creditor *b)* a debt represented by a tally or tallies *c)* the capital invested in a company or corporation through the buying of shares, each of which entitles the buyer to a share in the ownership and, usually, dividends, voting rights, etc. *d)* the proportionate share in the ownership held by an individual stockholder *e)* the shares of a particular company, industry, etc. or shares, collectively *f) short for* STOCK CERTIFICATE *g)* [Informal] a part interest in something **16** a STOCK COMPANY (sense 2), or its repertoire **17** a former type of large, wide, stiff cravat **18** STOCK CAR (sense 2) **19** [Obs.] a stocking —***vt.*** **1** to provide with or attach to a stock [*to stock a firearm, plow, etc.*] **2** *a)* to furnish (a farm) with stock or (a shop, etc.) with a stock *b)* to supply with [*to stock a pond with fish*] **3** to keep or put in a supply of, as for sale or for future use ☆**4** to sow (land) with grass, clover, etc. —***vi.*** **1** to put forth new shoots: said of a plant **2** to put in a stock, or supply: often with *up* —***adj.*** **1** continually kept in stock [*stock sizes*] **2** of the nature of something kept in stock; common, ordinary, hackneyed, or trite [*a stock excuse*] **3** that deals with stock **4** *Finance* relating to stock or a stock company **5** *a)* of or having to do with a theatrical STOCK COMPANY or its repertoire *b)* designating or of a character, as in a play or TV show, of a conventionalized type **6** for breeding [*a stock mare*] **7** of, or for the raising of, livestock [*stock farming*] —**in stock** available for sale or use; on hand —**on the stocks** being built: said of a ship, etc. —**out of stock** not immediately available for sale or use; not on hand —**take stock 1** to inventory the amount of stock on hand **2** to make an estimate or appraisal, as of available resources, probabilities, etc. —☆**take stock in** to have faith in, give credence to, or attribute real significance to: also **put stock in**

stock·ade (stä kād′) ***n.*** ⟦Fr *estacade* (also *estocade,* by assoc. with OFr *estoc,* trunk, log < Frank **stock,* akin to Ger *stock:* see prec.) < Prov *estacado* < *estaca,* post, stake < Gmc base akin to STAKE⟧ **1** a barrier of stakes driven into the ground side by side, for defense against attack ☆**2** an enclosure, as a fort, made with such stakes ☆**3** an enclosure for military prisoners —***vt.*** **-ad′ed, -ad′ing** to surround, protect, or fortify with a stockade

stock boy a boy or man who handles stock, as in a stockroom or warehouse

stock·breed·er (stäk′brēd′ər) ***n.*** a person who breeds and raises livestock —**stock′breed′ing *n.***

stock·bro·ker (-brō′kər) ***n.*** a person who acts as an agent in buying and selling stocks, bonds, etc.

stock·bro·ker·age (-brō′kər ij) ***n.*** a stockbroker's work or business: also [Brit.] **stock′bro′king**

☆**stock car 1** a railroad car built to carry livestock **2** a passenger automobile of standard make, modified in various ways for use in racing

stock certificate a certificate issued as written evidence of ownership to one who buys shares of stock

stock company 1 a company or corporation whose capital is divided into shares **2** a commercial theatrical company that presents a repertoire of plays, usually at one theater

stock dividend a dividend paid by a corporation to its shareholders in the form of additional shares of stock

stock dove ⟦ME *stockdowe:* see STOCK, *n.* 1 & DOVE[1]: it nests in hollow trees⟧ a European pigeon (*Columba oenas*)

stock·er (stäk′ər) ***n.*** **1** a person who handles stock, as in a stockroom or warehouse ☆**2** [Informal] STOCK CAR

stock exchange 1 a place where stocks and bonds are regularly bought and sold **2** an association whose members meet together for the business of buying and selling stocks and bonds according to regulations

stock farm a farm for raising livestock —**stock farming**

stock·fish (stäk′fish′) ***n., pl.*** **-fish′** or **-fish′es** (see FISH) ⟦ME *stokfysshe* < MDu *stokvisch* < *stok,* stick (see STOCK) + *visch,* FISH⟧ any fish cured by being split and hung in the open air to dry without salt, as cod, haddock, etc.

Stock·hau·sen (shtôk′hou′zən), **Karl·heinz** (kärl′hīnts) 1928-2007; Ger. composer

stock·hold·er (-hōl′dər) ***n.*** **1** a person owning stock in a given company **2** in Australia, a person who raises livestock

Stock·holm (stäk′hōm′, -hōlm′) seaport & capital of Sweden, on the Baltic Sea

Stockholm syndrome ⟦after prec., site of a 1973 bank robbery in which the hostages reacted in this way⟧ [*also* **S- S-**] a psychological condition in which a person taken hostage sympathizes with or becomes emotionally involved with his or her captors

stock·i·ness (stäk′ē nis) ***n.*** the quality of being stocky

stock·i·nette or **stock·i·net** (stäk′ə net′) ***n.*** ⟦prob. for earlier *stocking net*⟧ **1** an elastic, machine-knitted cloth used for making stockings, underwear, etc. **2** a knitting stitch fashioned by alternating rows of knitting and purling

stock·ing (stäk′iŋ) ***n.*** ⟦< STOCK, in obs. sense, "leg covering" + -ING⟧ **1** a closefitting covering, usually knitted, for the foot and, usually, most of the leg; specif., a women's garment, usually made of sheer nylon or silk, covering the leg to the thigh **2** something resembling a stocking or sock, as a patch of color on the leg of an animal **3** CHRISTMAS STOCKING —**in one's stocking feet** wearing stockings or socks but no shoes —**stock′inged *adj.***

stocking cap a long, tapered knitted cap, often with a tassel or pompon at the end of the tapered part

stocking mask a nylon stocking worn over the head, as by a robber, so as to distort the features and make identification difficult

☆**stocking stuffer** [Informal] a small gift of the kind typically given in a Christmas stocking

stock in trade 1 goods kept available for sale at a store or shop 2 tools, materials, etc. used in carrying on a trade or a business 3 any resources, practices, or devices characteristically employed by a given person or group

stock·ish (stäk′ish) *adj.* ⟦see STOCK, *n.* 2-3⟧ [Now Rare] stupid; dull; thickheaded —**stock′ish·ly** *adv.*

stock·job·ber (-jäb′ər) *n.* ☆1 a stockbroker, esp. one engaged in irregular trading: often used contemptuously 2 [Brit.] until the late 1980s, a member of a stock exchange who dealt only with brokers, and not the general public —**stock′job′ber·y** *n.*, **stock′job′bing**

stock·man (-mən; *also, esp. for 3,* -man′) *n., pl.* **-men** (-mən, -men′) 1 a person who owns or raises livestock 2 [Chiefly Austral.] a person who has charge of livestock 3 STOCKER (sense 1)

stock market 1 STOCK EXCHANGE 2 a system or program by which the buying and selling of stocks is conducted [an over-the-counter *stock market*] 3 the activity of buying and selling stocks [to play the *stock market*] 4 the general level of stock prices [the *stock market* is up today]

☆**stock option** an option to buy or sell shares of stock at a specified price within a specified time; specif., an option to buy a company's stock for less than the market price, given to an employee as a form of remuneration

stock·pile (-pīl′) *n.* a reserve supply of goods, raw material, etc., accumulated esp. in anticipation of future shortage or emergency —*vt., vi.* **-piled′**, **-pil′ing** to accumulate a stockpile (of) —**stock′pil′er** *n.*

Stock·port (stäk′pôrt′) city in Greater Manchester, NW England

stock·pot (-pät′) *n.* 1 a pot used for preparing soup stock 2 a soup containing various kinds of meat and vegetables

☆**stock raising** the raising of livestock —**stock raiser**

stock·room (-ro͞om′) *n.* a room in which a store of goods, materials, etc. is kept: also **stock room**

stock split the act or result of splitting stock: see SPLIT (*vt.* 7)

stock-still (stäk′stil′) *adj.* perfectly motionless

stock·tak·ing (stäk′tāk′iŋ) *n.* ⟦< TAKE STOCK (sense 2) (see phr. under STOCK)⟧ appraisal, esp. self-appraisal, for the purpose of assessing accomplishments, prospects, etc.

Stock·ton (stäk′tən) ⟦after R. F. *Stockton* (1795-1866), U.S. naval officer⟧ city in central Calif.

Stock·ton-on-Tees (-än tēz′) city in Durham, N England, on the Tees

stock·y (stäk′ē) *adj.* **stock′i·er**, **stock′i·est** ⟦STOCK, *n.* 2 + -Y[2]⟧ 1 heavily built; sturdy; short and thickset 2 having a strong, often thick, stem: said of a plant

stock·yard (stäk′yärd′) *n.* 1 an enclosure for stock on a farm ☆2 an enclosure with pens, sheds, etc. where cattle, hogs, sheep, or horses are kept temporarily before slaughtering or shipment: *usually used in pl.*

stodge (stäj) [Informal] *n.* ⟦< ?⟧ [Chiefly Brit.] 1 heavy, filling food, often unpalatable 2 anything boring or hard to learn

stodg·y (stä′jē) *adj.* **stodg′i·er**, **stodg′i·est** ⟦< prec. + -Y[2]⟧ 1 heavy and unpalatable: said of food 2 heavily built; bulky and slow in movement 3 dull; tedious; uninteresting 4 drab, unfashionable, or unattractive 5 stubbornly old-fashioned; narrow and conventional —**stodg′i·ly** *adv.* —**stodg′i·ness** *n.*

☆**sto·gie** or **sto·gy** (stō′gē) *n., pl.* **-gies** ⟦said to be so named because favored by drivers of Conestoga wagons⟧ 1 *a)* a long, thin, usually inexpensive cigar *b)* loosely, any cigar 2 a heavy, roughly made shoe or boot

Sto·ic (stō′ik) *n.* ⟦ME *Stoycis* (pl.) < L *stoicus* < Gr *stōikos* < *stoa,* porch, colonnade (see STOA): because Zeno taught under a colonnade at Athens⟧ 1 a member of a Greek school of philosophy founded by Zeno about 308 B.C., holding that all things are governed by unvarying natural laws, and that the wise man is led by reason to live virtuously and free from passion, accepting calmly whatever happens 2 [**s-**] a stoical person —*adj.* 1 of the Stoics or their philosophy 2 [**s-**] STOICAL

sto·i·cal (stō′i kəl) *adj.* ⟦ME: see prec. & -AL⟧ 1 showing austere indifference to joy, grief, pleasure, or pain; calm and unflinching under suffering, bad fortune, etc. 2 [**S-**] STOIC —*SYN.* IMPASSIVE —**sto′i·cal·ly** *adv.*

stoi·chi·om·e·try (stoi′kē äm′ə trē) *n.* ⟦< Gr *stoicheion,* a first principle, element, base, akin to *steichein,* to step, go (for IE base see STILE[1]) + -METRY⟧ 1 the determination of the proportions in which chemical elements combine or are produced and the weight relations in any chemical reaction 2 the branch of chemistry dealing with the relationships of elements entering into and resulting from combination, esp. with quantitative relationships Alt. Brit. sp. **stoi′chei·om′e·try** —**stoi′chi·o·met′ric** (-ə met′rik) *adj.*

Sto·i·cism (stō′i siz′əm) *n.* 1 the philosophical system of the Stoics 2 [**s-**] indifference to pleasure or pain; stoical behavior —*SYN.* PATIENCE

stoke[1] (stōk) *vt., vi.* **stoked**, **stok′ing** ⟦back-form. < STOKER⟧ 1 to stir up and feed fuel to (a fire, furnace, etc.) 2 to tend (a furnace, boiler, etc.) 3 to feed or eat large quantities of food; fill (*up*)

stoke[2] (stōk) *n.* ⟦after Sir George *Stokes* (1819-1903), Irish-born physicist & mathematician⟧ a basic unit in the CGS system, equal to the viscosity of a fluid, measured in poises, divided by the density of the fluid, measured in grams per cubic centimeter (0.0001 square meter per second): abbrev. *St*

stoke·hold (stōk′hōld′) *n.* a room in which the boilers are stoked on a ship

stoke·hole (-hōl′) *n.* ⟦STOKE[1] + HOLE: in part transl. of Du *stookgat* < *stoken,* to stoke + *gat,* hole⟧ 1 the opening in a furnace or boiler through which the fuel is put 2 a space in front of a furnace or boiler from which the fire is tended, as on a ship 3 STOKEHOLD

Stoke New·ing·ton (stōk no͞o′iŋ tən) former metropolitan borough of London, now part of Hackney

Stoke-on-Trent (stōk′än trent′) city in Staffordshire, WC England, on the Trent

stok·er (stō′kər) *n.* ⟦Du < *stoken,* to poke, stir up < *stok,* a stick: see STOCK⟧ 1 a person who tends a furnace, specif. of a steam boiler, as formerly on a ship or locomotive 2 a mechanical device that stokes a furnace

Sto·ker (stō′kər), **Bram** (bram) (born *Abraham Stoker*) 1847-1912; Ir. writer: author of *Dracula*

Stokes (stōks), Sir **George Gabriel** 1819-1903; Brit. physicist & mathematician

☆**sto·ke·si·a** (stō kē′zhē ə, -sē ə) *n.* ⟦after Jonathan *Stokes* (1755-1831), Eng botanist⟧ a perennial plant (*Stokesia laevis*) of the composite family, native to the SE U.S.: cultivated for its large, blue or purple flowers

Sto·kow·ski (stə kôf′skē, -kou′-), **Leopold (Boleslawowicz Stanislaw Antoni)** 1882-1977; U.S. orchestra conductor, born in England

☆**STOL** (stōl) *adj.* ⟦*s(hort) t(ake)o(ff and) l(anding)*⟧ designating, of, or for an aircraft that can take off and land on a relatively short airstrip —*n.* a STOL aircraft, airstrip, etc.

stole[1] (stōl) *n.* ⟦ME < OE < L *stola* < Gr *stolē,* garment, orig., array, equipment < base of *stellein,* to place, array: for IE base see STALK[1]⟧ 1 a long, robe-like outer garment worn by matrons in ancient Rome 2 a long, decorated strip of cloth worn around the neck or over one shoulder by officiating clergy of various churches 3 a woman's long scarf of cloth or fur worn around the shoulders

stole[2] (stōl) *vt., vi. pt. of* STEAL

stol·en (stō′lən) *vt., vi. pp. of* STEAL

stol·id (stäl′id) *adj.* ⟦L *stolidus,* firm, slow, stupid: for IE base see STILL[1]⟧ having or showing little or no emotion or sensitivity; unexcitable; impassive —*SYN.* IMPASSIVE —**sto·lid·i·ty** (stə lid′ə tē) *n.*, **stol′id·ness**—**stol′id·ly** *adv.*

☆**stol·len** (stō′lən; *Ger* shtô′lən) *n., pl.* **-len** or **-lens** ⟦Ger, lit., post (in reference to shape) < OHG *stollo* < IE base **stel-,* to place > STILL[1]⟧ a sweet, yeast-raised, German bread containing fruit and nuts

sto·lon (stō′län′) *n.* ⟦ModL *stolo* (gen. *stolonis*) < L, a shoot, twig, scion: for IE base see STILL[1]⟧ 1 *Bot.* a creeping stem that lies on or above the soil surface and bears foliage leaves, as in the strawberry or creeping bent grass 2 *Zool.* a stemlike, cylindrical structure, as in certain hydroids and tunicates, giving rise to buds from which new individuals grow

stol·port (stōl′pôrt′) *n.* an airport designed for STOL aircraft

sto·ma (stō′mə) *n., pl.* **-ma·ta** (-mə tə) or **-mas** ⟦ModL < Gr, mouth < IE **stomen,* mouth > Avestan *staman-,* (dog's) mouth⟧ 1 *Bot.* a microscopic opening in the epidermis of plants, surrounded by guard cells and serving for gaseous exchange 2 *Zool.* a mouth or mouthlike opening; esp., an ingestive opening in lower invertebrates

stom·ach (stum′ək, -ik) *n.* ⟦ME *stomak* < OFr *estomac* < L *stomachus,* gullet, esophagus, stomach < Gr *stomachos,* throat, gullet < *stoma,* mouth: see prec.⟧ 1 *a)* the large, saclike organ of vertebrates into which food passes from the esophagus or gullet for storage while undergoing the early processes of digestion *b)* any of the separate sections of such a digestive organ, as in ruminants, or all these sections collectively (see RUMINANT, illus.) 2 any enlarged storage portion of the digestive cavity, as in invertebrates 3 the abdomen, or belly 4 appetite for food 5 desire or inclination of any kind 6 an ability to tolerate or endure something [a strong *stomach* for violent movies] 7 [Archaic] character or disposition 8 [Obs.] *a)* spirit *b)* pride *c)* resentment —*vt.* 1 to be able to eat or digest 2 to tolerate; bear; endure 3 [Obs.] to resent —**on a full (or an empty) stomach** after having consumed much (or little or no) food or drink —**stom′ach·ful′** *n.*

stom·ach·ache (-āk′) *n.* pain in the stomach or abdomen

stom·ach·er (-ər) *n.* ⟦ME *stomachere:* see STOMACH & -ER⟧ a richly ornamented, triangular piece of cloth formerly worn, esp. by women, as a covering for the chest and abdomen

stomach flu acute gastroenteritis with vomiting and diarrhea, typically caused by a virus but not related to influenza: a nontechnical term

sto·mach·ic (stə mak′ik) *adj.* ⟦L *stomachicus* < Gr *stomachikos*⟧ of or having to do with the stomach or digestion —*n.* a digestive tonic

stomach pump a suction pump with a flexible tube fed into the stomach through the mouth and esophagus to remove its contents, as in cases of poisoning

sto·ma·tal (stō′mə təl) *adj.* of or having a stoma

sto·mat·ic (stō mat′ik) *adj.* ⟦ModL *stomaticus* < Gr *stomatikos* < *stomata,* pl. of *stoma,* mouth: see STOMA⟧ 1 of the mouth 2 of, or having the nature of, a stoma

sto·ma·ti·tis (stō′mə tīt′is, stäm′ə-) *n.* ⟦ModL: see fol.⟧ inflammation of the mouth

sto·ma·to- (stō′mə tə, stäm′ə tə) ⟦< Gr *stoma* (gen. *stomatos*), mouth: see STOMA⟧ *combining form* of, like, or relating to a mouth [*stomatology*]: also **stomat-**

sto·ma·tol·o·gy (stō′mə täl′ə jē) *n.* ⟦prec. + -LOGY⟧ the branch of medicine dealing with the mouth and its diseases —**sto′ma·to·log′i·cal** (-tə läj′i kəl) *adj.*

sto·ma·to·pod (stō′mə tə päd′, stäm′ə tə-) *n.* ⟦< ModL *Stomatopoda:* see STOMATO- & -POD⟧ any of an order (Stomatopoda) of crustaceans having strong, clasping claws on the second pair of legs and gills on the abdominal appendages; squilla

sto·ma·tous (stō′mə təs, stäm′ə-) ***adj.*** having a stoma

-stome (stōm) ⟦< Gr *stoma,* mouth: see STOMA⟧ *combining form forming nouns* mouth or mouthlike opening [*cyclostome*]

sto·mo·dae·um or **sto·mo·de·um** (stō′mə dē′əm, stäm′ə-) ***n.,*** *pl.* **-dae′a** (-ə) or **-de′a** (-ə) ⟦ModL < Gr *stoma,* mouth (see STOMA) + *hodios,* on the way < *hodos,* way, road < IE **sed-,* to go < base **sed-,* SIT⟧ the anterior portion of the digestive tract of an embryo, lined with ectoderm and including the mouth area

-sto·mous (stə məs) ⟦< Gr *stoma* (see STOMA) + -OUS⟧ *combining form forming adjectives* having a (specified kind of) mouth [*monostomous*]

stomp (stämp) ***vt., vi.*** *var. of* STAMP (*vt.* 1, 2*a-c, vi.*); esp., to injure or crush as by stamping (on) —☆***n.*** [Historical] **1** a jazz tune with a lively rhythm and a strong beat **2** a dance to this music —**stomp′er** ***n.***

stomping ground [Informal] STAMPING GROUND: *also used in pl.*

-sto·my (stə mē) ⟦Gr *-stomia* < *stoma,* mouth: see STOMA⟧ *combining form forming nouns* a surgical operation making an opening into a (specified) part or organ [*colostomy*]

stone (stōn) ***n.*** ⟦ME < OE *stan,* akin to Du *steen,* Ger *stein* < IE base **stāi-,* to become thick, compress, stiffen > L *stiria,* a drop (< *stilla*), Gr *stear,* tallow⟧ **1** the hard, solid, nonmetallic mineral matter of which rock is composed **2** a piece of rock of relatively small size **3** a piece of rock shaped or finished for some purpose; specif., *a)* a large, solid piece used in building; also, such pieces collectively *b)* a paving block *c)* a gravestone or memorial *d)* a boundary mark or milestone *e)* a grindstone or whetstone **4** something that resembles a small stone; specif., *a)* a hailstone *b)* the stonelike seed of certain fruits, as of a date *c)* the hard endocarp and the enclosed seed of a drupe, as of a peach *d)* [Archaic] a testicle **5** *short for* PRECIOUS STONE **6** *pl.* **stone** [Brit.] a unit of weight, equal to 14 pounds (6.3503 kilograms): abbrev. *st* **7** *Med.* an abnormal stony mass formed in the body, esp. in a kidney or gallbladder **8** *a) Printing* a table with a smooth top, originally of stone, on which page forms are composed *b)* a surface incised or engraved with a design or text to be lithographed —***vt.*** **stoned, ston′ing 1** to throw stones at; esp., to kill by pelting with stones **2** to furnish, pave, line, etc. with stones **3** to remove the stone from (a peach, cherry, etc.) —***adj.*** **1** of stone or stoneware **2** ⟦cf. STONE-⟧ [Slang] complete, utter, thoroughgoing, etc. [*a stone* genius] —***adv.*** completely, thoroughly, etc. [*stone* sober] —**carve** (or **write, set,** etc.) **in stone** to make official, permanent, or final [an unsigned contract means that nothing is *carved in stone* yet] —**cast** (or **throw**) **the first stone** ⟦in allusion to Jesus's words to those about to stone a woman for adultery (John 8:7)⟧ to be the first one to rebuke or punish another: phrase used as an appeal for mercy, with the implication that no one is blameless —**leave no stone unturned 1** to search everywhere **2** to do everything possible

Stone (stōn) **1 Edward Du·rell** (də rel′) 1902-78; U.S. architect **2 Harlan Fiske** (fisk) 1872-1946; chief justice of the U.S. (1941-46) **3 Lucy** (Mrs. *Henry Brown Blackwell*) 1818-93; U.S. reformer & suffragist

stone- (stōn) ⟦< STONE, with the sense "like or as a stone"⟧ *combining form* very, completely: used in hyphenated compounds [*stone*-blind, *stone*-broke]

Stone Age a period in human culture during which stone implements are used; specif., the time of the Paleolithic, Mesolithic, and Neolithic periods of the Old World: often used fig. [an outmoded business model right out of the *Stone Age*]

stone-blind (stōn′blīnd′) ***adj.*** ⟦see STONE-⟧ completely blind

stone·chat (-chat′) ***n.*** ⟦from its cry, like the sound of pebbles knocked together⟧ any of certain small, insect-eating Old World thrushes (esp. *Saxicola torquata*) with a black head and back and a white rump

stone china a kind of stoneware containing a variety of feldspar found in England

stone crab ☆a large, common, edible, dark-bluish crab (*Menippe mercenaria*) found in the coastal mud flats of the SE U.S. and in the Caribbean

stone·crop (-kräp′) ***n.*** ⟦ME *stoncroppe* < OE *stancrop* < *stan,* STONE + *crop,* a sprout⟧ SEDUM

stone·cut·ter (-kut′ər) ***n.*** a person or machine that cuts and dresses stone —**stone′cut′ting** ***n.***

stoned (stōnd) ***adj.*** **1** having the stones removed [*stoned* prunes] ☆**2** [Informal] *a)* drunk; intoxicated *b)* under the influence of a narcotic, hallucinogen, etc.

stone-deaf (stōn′def′) ***adj.*** ⟦see STONE-⟧ completely deaf

stone·fish (stōn′fish′) ***n.,*** *pl.* **-fish′** or **-fish′es** (see FISH) any of a family (Synanceiidae, order Scorpaeniformes) of tropical, marine bony fishes having venomous spines, a scaleless body, and a stonelike appearance

stone·fly (-flī′) ***n.,*** *pl.* **-flies′** any of an order (Plecoptera) of soft-bodied, winged insects whose nymphs live under stones in swift streams: often used as bait in fishing

stone fruit any fruit, as a plum, having a stone; drupe

stone-ground (stōn′ground′) ***adj.*** ground between millstones [*stone-ground* wheat]

Stone·henge (stōn′henj′) ***n.*** ⟦ME *stonheng* < *ston,* STONE + OE *henge,* (something) hanging: for IE base see HANG⟧ a circular arrangement of prehistoric megaliths on Salisbury Plain, England, probably set up in the Neolithic period

stone lily a fossil crinoid

stone marten 1 a light-colored European sable (*Martes foina*) **2** its fur

stone·ma·son (-mā′sən) ***n.*** a person who cuts stone to shape and uses it in making walls, buildings, etc. —**stone′ma′son·ry** ***n.***

Stone Mountain ⟦descriptive⟧ mountain near Atlanta, Ga., on which a huge Confederate memorial is carved: *c.* 2,000 ft (610 m) high

ston·er (stōn′ər) ***n.*** **1** a person or thing that stones ☆**2** ⟦< STONED, sense 2⟧ [Slang] a habitual user of marijuana

☆**stone roller 1** any of a genus (*Campostoma*) of North American freshwater cyprinoid fishes that hollow out a nest in gravelly stream beds **2** any of a genus (*Hypentelium*) of sucker fishes of rocky streams

Stones River (stōnz) river in central Tenn., flowing into the Cumberland: *c.* 60 mi (97 km)

stone's throw a relatively short distance

stone·wall (stōn′wôl′) ***vi.*** **1** *Cricket* to play only a defensive game in order to gain a draw: said of a batsman **2** [Chiefly Brit.] to obstruct a debate, negotiation, etc.; esp., to filibuster **3** [Informal] to behave in an obstructive, uncooperative manner, as by refusing to answer, withholding information, etc. when questioned —***vt.*** [Informal] to impede or obstruct, esp. by refusing to comply or cooperate with

stone·ware (stōn′wer′) ***n.*** a dense, opaque, glazed or unglazed pottery containing clay, silica, and feldspar and fired at a high heat

stone·washed (stōn′wôsht′, -wäsht′) ***adj.*** washed with small, abrasive stones in manufacturing to cause fading and make softer [*stonewashed* bluejeans]: also written **stone-washed**

stone·work (-wurk′) ***n.*** **1** the art or process of working in stone, as in masonry or jewelry **2** something made or built of stone **3** [*pl.*] a place where masonry stone is cut and dressed

stone·wort (-wurt′) ***n.*** any of a class (Charophyceae) of green algae with jointed axes and whorled branches, usually covered with lime

ston·y (stō′nē) ***adj.*** **ston′i·er, ston′i·est** ⟦ME < OE *stanig*⟧ **1** covered with or having many stones **2** of or like stone; specif., *a)* hard *b)* unfeeling; pitiless *c)* cold; fixed; rigid **3** petrifying Also sp. **ston′ey** —**ston′i·ly** ***adv.*** —**ston′i·ness** ***n.***

stony coral any coral having a dense, calcareous external skeleton (esp. order Scleractinia)

ston·y·heart·ed (-härt′id) ***adj.*** unfeeling; pitiless; cruel —**ston′y·heart′ed·ness** ***n.***

Stony Point ⟦descriptive⟧ village in SE N.Y., on the Hudson: site of a British fort in the Revolutionary War

stood (stood) ***vi., vt.*** *pt. & pp. of* STAND

☆**stooge** (stōōj) ***n.*** ⟦< ?⟧ **1** a comic actor who assists a comedian by feeding him lines and by being the butt of jokes and pranks **2** any person who acts as an underling or puppet of another: term of contempt —***vi.*** **stooged, stoog′ing** [Informal] to be a stooge (*for* someone)

stook (stook) ***n., vt., vi.*** ⟦ME *stouke,* prob. < or akin to MLowG *stūke,* a shock, stump < IE **(s)teug-* < base **(s)teu-,* to strike > STOCK⟧ *Brit. term for* SHOCK[2]

stool (stōōl) ***n.*** ⟦ME < OE *stol,* akin to Ger *stuhl* < IE **stal-* (> OSlav *stolŭ,* throne, seat) < base **sta-,* to STAND⟧ **1** *a)* a piece of furniture for one person to sit on, typically having a round seat, three or four legs or a central post, and no back or arms *b)* FOOTSTOOL **2** the inside ledge at the bottom of a window **3** a toilet, or water closet **4** fecal matter eliminated in a single bowel movement **5** *a)* a root or tree stump sending out shoots *b)* a cluster of such shoots ☆**6** *a)* a perch to which a bird is fastened as a decoy for others *b)* a bird or other object used as a decoy —***vi.*** **1** to put out shoots in the form of a stool ☆**2** [Slang] to act as an informer

☆**stool pigeon** ⟦see STOOL (*n.* 6)⟧ **1** [Old Informal] one serving as a decoy **2** [Informal] a spy or informer, esp. for the police: also [Slang] **stool·ie** (stōō′lē) ***n.***

stoop[1] (stōōp) ***vi.*** ⟦ME *stupen* < OE *stupian,* akin to ON *stūpa* < IE **(s)teup-* < base **(s)teu-,* to strike > STOCK⟧ **1** to bend the body forward or in a crouch **2** to carry the head and shoulders or the upper part of the body habitually bent forward **3** *a)* to condescend, or deign *b)* to demean or degrade oneself **4** to pounce or swoop down, as a bird of prey **5** [Archaic] to yield or submit —***vt.*** **1** to bend (the head, etc.) forward **2** [Archaic] to humble or debase —***n.*** **1** the act or position of stooping the body, esp. habitually **2** the act of condescending **3** a swoop, as by a hawk at prey —**stoop′er** ***n.*** —**stoop′ing·ly** ***adv.***

SYN.—**stoop,** in this connection, implies a descending in dignity, as by committing some shameful or immoral act [to *stoop* to cheating]; **condescend** implies a voluntary descent by one high in rank, power, etc. to act graciously or affably toward one regarded as his inferior [the general *condescended* to talk with the private]; **deign** is usually used in negative constructions or with such qualifications as *hardly, barely,* etc. and, hence, connotes unwilling or arrogant condescension [she scarcely *deigned* to answer me]

☆**stoop**[2] (stōōp) ***n.*** ⟦Du *stoep,* akin to Ger *stufe:* for IE base see STEP⟧ a small porch or platform with steps, at the door of a house or apartment building

☆**stoop·ball** (stōōp′bôl′) ***n.*** ⟦< prec.⟧ a game somewhat like baseball, in which a rubber ball is thrown against a step or wall rather than batted, and is fielded on the rebound

☆**stoop labor** work done by stooping, as in picking fruit from low-growing plants

stop (stäp) ***vt.*** **stopped, stop′ping** ⟦ME *stoppen* < OE *-stoppian* (in comp.) < WGmc *stoppōn* < VL **stuppare,* to stop up, stuff < L *stuppa* < Gr *styppē,* tow < IE *stewe-, to thicken, contract > Gr *styphein*, to contract, Sans *stuka*, tuft⟧ I. *to close by filling, shutting off, covering, etc.* 1 to staunch (a cut, wound, etc.) 2 to block up (a passage, road, pipe, etc.) so as to make impassable; obstruct: often with *up* 3 to fill in, plug up, or cover (a hole, cavity, opening, mouth, etc.): often with *up* 4 to close (a bottle, jug, etc.) as with a cork or cap 5 *a)* to close (a finger hole of a wind instrument) so as to produce a desired tone *b)* to produce (a tone) in this way II. *to cause to cease motion, activity, etc.* 1 to prevent the passage or further passage of (water, light, etc.); block; intercept 2 to prevent the movement or further movement of; specif., *a)* to halt the progress of (a person, animal, vehicle, etc.) *b)* to check (a blow, stroke, or thrust); parry; counter *c)* to defeat (an opponent) *d)* to intercept (a letter, etc.) in transit *e)* to baffle; perplex; nonplus 3 to cease; desist from (with a gerund) [*stop* talking] 4 *a)* to cause to cease or end [*stop* that racket] *b)* to bring to an end; discontinue [to *stop* a subscription] *c)* to kill *d)* to defeat, as by knocking out 5 to cause (an engine, machine, etc.) to cease operation 6 to press down (a violin string, etc.) against the fingerboard to produce a desired tone 7 to place a stop order on (a stock or other security) 8 *Bridge* to hold a card or cards that will prevent an opponent from running (a suit) 9 [Chiefly Brit.] to insert punctuation marks in III. *to keep from beginning, acting, happening, etc.; prevent* 1 to keep (a person) from doing something contemplated 2 to prevent the starting, advent, etc. of; preclude 3 to notify one's bank to withhold payment on (one's check) —*vi.* 1 to cease moving, walking, proceeding, etc.; halt 2 to leave off doing something; desist from continuing 3 to cease operating or functioning 4 to be able to go no further; come to an end 5 to become clogged or choked 6 to tarry or stay for a while, esp. as a customer or guest: often with *at* or *in* —*n.* 1 a stopping or being stopped; check; arrest; cessation; halt; specif., a pause in speech or at the end of a sense unit in verse 2 a coming to an end; finish; end 3 a stay or sojourn 4 a place stopped at, as on a bus route 5 an indentation in the face of an animal, esp. a dog, between the forehead and the nose or muzzle 6 something that stops; obstruction; obstacle; specif., *a)* a plug or stopper *b)* STOP ORDER *c)* an order to withhold payment on a check *d)* a mechanical part that stops, limits, or regulates motion, as a pawl *e)* [Chiefly Brit.] a punctuation mark, esp. a period 7 *a)* pressure, as of a finger, on a string of a violin, etc. to produce a desired tone *b)* a fret on a guitar, etc. 8 *a)* the closing of a finger hole of a wind instrument to produce a desired tone *b)* such a hole 9 *a)* a tuned set of organ pipes, reeds, or electronic devices of the same specific type and tone quality *b)* a pull, lever, or key for putting such a set or sets into or out of operation 10 *Naut.* a piece of line used to secure something, as a sail 11 *Phonet.* *a)* the complete stopping of the outgoing breath, as with the lips, tongue, or velum *b)* a consonant formed in this way, as (p), (b), (t), (d), (k), and (g) (distinguished from CONTINUANT) 12 *Photog.* *a)* the aperture, usually adjustable, of a lens *b)* the f-number —*adj.* ☆that stops or is meant to stop [a *stop* signal] —**pull out all (the) stops** ⟦with ref. to the *stops* of an organ⟧ [Informal] to apply maximum effort; use every means possible —**put a stop to** to cause to cease; stop; end —**stop at nothing** to be ruthlessly resolute in pursuing an end —**stop down** *Photog.* to reduce the lens aperture by adjustment of the diaphragm —☆**stop off** to stop for a short stay en route to a place —☆**stop out** 1 to interrupt one's education as in order to work 2 to block out (areas not to be printed or painted) as of a silk-screen design —☆**stop over** 1 to visit for a while: also **stop in** (or **by**) 2 to break a journey, as for rest

SYN.—**stop** implies a suspension or ending of some motion, action, or progress [my watch *stopped*]; **cease** implies a suspension or ending of some state or condition or of an existence [the war had *ceased*]; **quit** is equivalent to either **stop** or **cease** [to *quit* working means either to stop working, as for the day, or to cease working, i.e., to retire]; **discontinue** suggests the suspension of some action that is a habitual practice, an occupation, etc. [he has *discontinued* the practice of law]; **desist** implies a ceasing of some action that is annoying, harmful, futile, etc. [*desist* from further bickering] —*ANT.* **begin, start, commence**

stop-ac·tion (stäp′ak′shən) *n.* STOP-MOTION: also used attributively

stop-and-go (stäp′ən gō′) *adj.* characterized by or involving frequent stopping and restarting [*stop-and-go* traffic at rush hour]

stop·bank (-baŋk′) *n.* [Austral. & N.Z.] LEVEE[1] (sense 1)

stop bath *Photog.* a weak solution of acetic acid used to stop development of photographic prints or film before fixing

stop·cock (-käk′) *n.* a valve or faucet for stopping or regulating the flow of a fluid, as through a pipe; cock

stope (stōp) *n.* ⟦< MLowG *stōpe*, akin to STEP⟧ a steplike excavation formed by the removal of ore from around a mine shaft — *vt., vi.* **stoped, stop′ing** to mine in stopes

stop·gap (stäp′gap′) *n.* a person or thing serving as a temporary substitute for another; makeshift —*adj.* used as a stopgap —*SYN.* RESOURCE

☆**stop·light** (-līt′) *n.* 1 a traffic light, specif. when red (signaling vehicles to stop) 2 [Now Rare] BRAKE LIGHT

stop-mo·tion (stäp′mō′shən) *n.* an animation technique in which inanimate figures, as of clay, are shot one frame at a time: the figures are moved slightly between frames, resulting in simulated motion when the film is run: also used attributively

stop order an order to a broker to buy or sell a certain stock when a specified price is reached

☆**stop·o·ver** (-ō′vər) *n.* 1 a brief stop or stay at a place in the course of a journey 2 a place for such a stop Also **stop′-off′**

stop·page (stäp′ij) *n.* 1 a stopping or being stopped 2 an obstructed condition; blockage

stop·per (stäp′ər) *n.* 1 a person or thing that stops or causes a stoppage 2 something inserted to close an opening; plug ☆3 *Baseball* *a)* that starting pitcher regarded as best able to prevent his or her team from having a long losing streak *b)* CLOSER (sense 3) 4 *Bridge* a card or cards that will prevent an opponent from running a suit —*vt.* to close with a plug or stopper

stop·ple (stäp′əl) *n.* ⟦ME *stoppel*, dim. < *stoppen*, to STOP⟧ a stopper, or plug —*vt.* **-pled, -pling** to close with a stopple

☆**stop street** a street on which all vehicles must come to a complete stop at a given intersection

stopt (stäpt) *vt., vi. old poet. pt. & pp. of* STOP

stop-time (stäp′tīm′) *n. Jazz* a technique or effect in which the rhythm section stops playing for one or more beats each measure, usually for a chorus, while a soloist continues to play

stop·watch (stäp′wäch′) *n.* a watch with a hand or a digital readout that can be started and stopped instantly so as to indicate seconds or fractions of seconds, as for timing races

stor·age (stôr′ij) *n.* 1 a storing or being stored 2 *a)* a place or space for storing goods *b)* the cost of keeping goods stored 3 the charging of a storage battery so as to make possible the subsequent generation of electricity 4 *Comput.* MEMORY (sense 8*b*); esp., memory of a disk, tape, etc.

storage battery a battery of electrochemical cells (*secondary cells*) for generating electric current: the cells can be recharged by passing a current through them in the direction opposite to the discharging flow of current

sto·rax (stôr′aks) *n.* ⟦ME < L *storax, styrax* < Gr *styrax*, of Sem orig., as in Heb *tsori*, terebinth resin⟧ 1 the aromatic balsam exuded by liquidambar trees, used in medicine and perfumery 2 a fragrant, solid resin obtained from a small, E Mediterranean tree (*Styrax officinalis*) of the storax family, formerly used as incense 3 any of a genus (*Styrax*) of chiefly tropical trees and shrubs of the storax family, with drooping clusters of showy white flowers —*adj.* designating a family (Styracaceae, order Ebenales) of widely distributed dicotyledonous trees or shrubs, as the snowbell

store (stôr) *vt.* **stored, stor′ing** ⟦ME *storen* < OFr *estorer*, to erect, furnish, store < L *instaurare*, to repair, restore, erect < *in-*, IN-[1] + *-staurare* < IE base *stā-, to STAND⟧ 1 to put aside, or accumulate, for use when needed 2 to fill or furnish with a supply or stock [a mind *stored* with trivia] 3 to put, as in a warehouse, for safekeeping 4 to be a place for the storage of 5 *Comput.* to put or keep (information) on a disk, tape, etc. —*vi.* to undergo storage in a specified manner —*n.* ⟦ME < OFr *estor* < the v.⟧ 1 a supply (*of* something) for use when needed; reserve; stock 2 [*pl.*] supplies, esp. of food, clothing, arms, etc. ☆3 a retail establishment where goods are regularly offered for sale 4 a place where supplies are kept; storehouse; warehouse 5 a great amount or number; abundance —*adj.* of a kind sold in stores; being a commercial or mass-produced article —**in store** set aside for, or awaiting one in, the future; in reserve or in prospect —☆**mind the store** [Informal] to tend to business —**set** (or **put** or **lay**) **store by** to have regard or esteem for; value —**stor′a·ble** *adj.*

store-bought (stôr′bôt′) *adj.* [Informal] produced commercially and not homemade [*store-bought* cookies]

☆**store·front** (-frunt′) *n.* 1 the front of a store 2 a room at the ground front of a building, usually with display windows, designed for use as a retail store —*adj.* housed in or as in a storefront [a *storefront* church]

store·house (-hous′) *n.* a place where things are stored; esp., a warehouse

store·keep·er (-kē′pər) *n.* 1 a person in charge of stores, esp. military or naval stores ☆2 a retail merchant

store·room (-ro͞om′) *n.* a room where things are stored

☆**store·wide** (-wīd′) *adj.* throughout a store, including many or all departments [a *storewide* sale]

sto·rey (stôr′ē) *n., pl.* **-reys** *Brit. sp. of* STORY[2]

sto·ried[1] (stôr′ēd) *adj.* 1 [Archaic] ornamented with designs showing scenes as from history [a *storied* tapestry] 2 famous in story or history

sto·ried[2] (stôr′ēd) *adj.* having stories, or floors: usually in hyphenated compounds [many-*storied*]

stork (stôrk) *n., pl.* **storks** or **stork** ⟦ME < OE *storc*, akin to Ger *storch* < IE *sterg- < base *(*s*)*ter-*, stiff > STARE: so named from its stiff-legged walk⟧ any of a family (Ciconiidae) of large, long-legged, mostly Old World wading birds having a long neck and bill; esp., the European **white stork** (*Ciconia ciconia*) that nests on rooftops and in trees: a symbol of childbirth, from the notion in euphemistic tales to children that it brings newborn babies

stork's-bill (stôrks′bil′) *n.* any of various geraniums with beak-shaped fruit, as a pelargonium or heronsbill

storm (stôrm) *n.* ⟦ME < OE, akin to Ger *sturm* < IE base *(*s*)*twer-*, to whirl, move or turn quickly > STIR[1], L *turbare*, to agitate⟧ 1 an atmospheric disturbance characterized by a strong wind, usually accompanied by rain, snow, sleet, or hail, and, often, thunder and lightning 2 any heavy fall of snow, rain, or hail 3 anything resembling a storm; specif., *a)* a heavy shower or volley of things [a *storm* of bullets] *b)* a strong outburst of emotion, passion, excitement, etc. *c)* a strong disturbance or upheaval of a political or social nature 4 a sudden, strong attack on a fortified place: now mainly in the phrase **take by storm**, to conquer, overwhelm, or win over suddenly and forcefully 5 *short for:* *a)* STORM WINDOW *b)* STORM DOOR: *usually used in pl.* 6 *Meteorol.* a wind whose speed is 64 to 72 miles per hour: see the Beaufort scale in the Reference Supplement —*vi.* 1 to be stormy; blow violently, rain, snow, etc. 2 to be violently angry; rage; rant 3 to rush or move violently and tumultuously [to *storm* into a room] —*vt.* **1** to attack or direct something at (someone) in a vigorous or angry outburst [to *storm* a speaker with questions] **2** to capture or attempt to capture (a fortified place) with a sudden, strong attack —*SYN.* ATTACK —**up a storm** [Informal] in a highly adept, enthusiastic, or spectacular fashion: said of a specified action [the children's chorus danced *up a storm*]

storm·bound (stôrm′bound′) *adj.* halted, delayed, or cut off by storms

☆**storm cellar** a deep cellar for shelter during heavy windstorms

storm center **1** the shifting center of a cyclone, an area of lowest barometric pressure and comparative calm **2** a center or focus of trouble, turmoil, or disturbance

☆**storm door** a door, typically lighter weight, placed outside a regular entrance door as added protection against severe, esp. winter, weather

storm petrel any of a family (Hydrobatidae) of petrels; esp., a black-and-white species (*Hydrobates pelagicus*) of the N Atlantic and the Mediterranean

storm·proof (-pro͞of′) *adj.* **1** that can withstand a storm **2** giving protection against storms

storm sewer a sewer or sewer system for carrying off wastewater and, esp., rainwater from city streets, roofs, etc.: cf. SANITARY SEWER

storm trooper a member of Hitler's Nazi party militia, notorious for their brutal and terroristic methods

☆**storm window** a window placed outside a regular window as added protection against severe, esp. winter, weather: also **storm sash**

storm·y (stôr′mē) *adj.* **storm′i·er, storm′i·est** ⟦ME *stormi* < OE *stormig*⟧ **1** of, characteristic of, or affected by storms **2** having or characterized by storms **3** violent, raging, turbulent, etc. —**storm′i·ly** *adv.* —**storm′i·ness** *n.*

stormy petrel STORM PETREL

sto·ry[1] (stôr′ē) *n., pl.* **-ries** ⟦ME *storie* < OFr *estoire* < L *historia*: see HISTORY⟧ **1** the telling of a happening or connected series of happenings, whether true or fictitious; account; narration **2** an anecdote or joke **3** *a)* a fictional composition in prose or poetry, shorter than a novel; narrative; tale; specif., SHORT STORY *b)* the form of literature represented by such compositions **4** the plot of a novel, play, film, etc. **5** *a)* a report or rumor *b)* [Informal] a falsehood or fib **6** romantic legend or history ☆**7** *a)* a news event or a report of it *b)* [Informal] the pertinent facts or circumstances relating to a particular person, situation, etc., esp. such facts not widely known or not previously revealed [what's his *story*? what's the *story* on your firing?] —*vt.* **-ried, -ry·ing** **1** [Archaic] to tell the story of **2** to decorate with paintings, etc. representing scenes from history or legend

SYN.—**story**, the broadest in scope of these words, refers to a series of connected events, true or fictitious, that is written or told with the intention of entertaining or informing; **narrative** is a more formal word, referring to the kind of prose that recounts happenings; **tale**, a somewhat elevated or literary term, usually suggests a simple, leisurely story, more or less loosely organized, especially a fictitious or legendary one; **anecdote** applies to a short, entertaining account of a single incident, usually personal or biographical

sto·ry[2] (stôr′ē) *n., pl.* **-ries** ⟦ME < ML *historia*, a picture (< L: see HISTORY): prob. from use of "storied" windows or friezes marking the outside of different floors⟧ **1** a section or horizontal division of a building, extending from the floor to the ceiling or roof lying directly above it; floor [a hotel ten *stories* high] **2** all the rooms on the same level of a building **3** any horizontal section or division

Sto·ry (stôr′ē), **Joseph** 1779-1845; associate justice, U.S. Supreme Court (1811-45)

sto·ry·board (stôr′ē bôrd′) *n.* **1** a large board on which a series of sketches of shots or scenes are arranged in sequence for outlining the action of a film, video, etc. **2** such a series of sketches, often accompanied with captions containing dialogue, narrations, etc. —*vt.* to make a storyboard of (a shot or scene) for (a film, video, etc.) —**sto′ry·board′ing** *n.*

sto·ry·book (-bo͝ok′) *n.* a book of stories, esp. one for children —*adj.* typical of romantic, idealized tales, as those in children's storybooks [their love affair had a *storybook* ending]

story line STORY[1] (*n.* 4): often written **sto′ry·line′** *n.*

sto·ry·tell·er (-tel′ər) *n.* **1** a person who narrates stories; sometimes, specif., one who tells stories to children as in a school or library **2** [Informal] a fibber or liar —**sto′ry·tell′ing** *n.*

☆**stoss** (stäs, stôs; *Ger* shtōs) *adj.* ⟦Ger < *stossen*, to push < OHG *stozan* < IE base *(*s*)*teu-*, to push, beat > STOCK, L *tundere*, to strike⟧ facing or located in the direction from which a glacier moves: opposed to LEE

sto·tin·ka (stô tiŋ′kə) *n., pl.* **-tin′ki** (-kē) ⟦Bulg < *sto*, hundred⟧ a monetary unit of Bulgaria, equal to 1/100 of a lev

stound (stound) *n.* ⟦ME *stunde* < OE *stund*, akin to Ger *stunde*, ON *stund*, hour, while: for IE base see STAND⟧ [Now Brit. Dial] **1** a short time **2** a pain or pang; shock —*vi.* [Scot. or North Eng.] to ache or pain

stoup (sto͞op) *n.* ⟦ME *stowpe*, bucket < ON *staup*: for IE base see STEEP[1]⟧ **1** [Now Scot. or North Eng.] a drinking cup; tankard **2** [Now Scot.] a pail or bucket **3** FONT[1] (sense 1*b*)

stour (sto͞or) *n.* ⟦ME *stoure* < OFr *estour* < OHG *sturm*, STORM⟧ [Now Chiefly Dial.] **1** combat or conflict **2** turmoil **3** a storm **4** wind-blown dust

stout (stout) *adj.* ⟦ME < OFr *estout*, bold, prob. < Frank *stolt*, proud, bold, akin to MDu *stelte*, STILT⟧ **1** courageous; brave; undaunted **2** *a)* strong in body; sturdy *b)* strong in construction; firm; substantial [a *stout* wall] **3** powerful; forceful **4** fat; thickset; corpulent —*n.* **1** a fat person **2** a garment in a size for a fat man **3** a dark-brown beer like porter, but heavier and sweeter and containing a higher percentage of hops —**stout′ish** *adj.* —**stout′ly** *adv.* —**stout′ness** *n.*

stout·heart·ed (-härt′id) *adj.* courageous; brave; undaunted —**stout′heart′ed·ly** *adv.* —**stout′heart′ed·ness** *n.*

stove[1] (stōv) *n.* ⟦ME < MDu, heated room, akin to Ger *stube*, sitting room, OE *stofa*, hot air bath < early borrowing < VL **extufa*, back-form. < **extufare*, to steam, STEW⟧ **1** an apparatus using fuel or electricity for heating a room **2** an appliance using fuel or electricity for cooking; specif., *a)* RANGE (*n.* 12) *b)* STOVE-TOP **3** any heated chamber or room, as a kiln for drying manufactured articles

stove[2] (stōv) *vt., vi. alt. pt. & pp. of* STAVE

stove·pipe (stōv′pīp′) *n.* **1** a metal pipe used to carry off smoke or fumes from a stove, as into a chimney flue ☆**2** ⟦descriptive of its shape⟧ a man's tall silk hat: in full **stovepipe hat**

sto·ver (stō′vər) *n.* ⟦ME, aphetic < OFr *estover*: see ESTOVERS⟧ ☆**1** cured stalks of grain, without the ears, used as fodder for animals **2** [Brit. Dial.] any fodder

stove-top (stōv′täp′) *n.* the top surface of a stove, now typically containing gas or electric burners: also written **stove top**

stow (stō) *vt.* ⟦ME *stowen* < *stowe*, a place < OE < IE base **stā-*, to STAND⟧ **1** to pack or store away; esp., to pack in an orderly, compact way **2** to fill by packing in an orderly way **3** to hold or receive: said of a room, container, etc. **4** [Obs.] to provide lodging for **5** [Slang] to stop; cease [*stow* the chatter!] —**stow away** **1** to put or hide away, as in a safe place **2** to be a stowaway **3** to consume (food or drink), esp. in large amounts

stow·age (stō′ij) *n.* **1** a stowing or being stowed **2** place for stowing **3** something stowed **4** charges for stowing

stow·a·way (-ə wā′) *n.* a person who hides aboard a ship, airplane, etc. to get free passage, evade port officials, etc.

Stowe (stō), **Harriet (Elizabeth) Beecher** 1811-96; U.S. novelist: sister of Henry Ward Beecher

STP *abbrev.* standard temperature (0°C) and air pressure (760 mm of mercury)

St. Paul ⟦after the Apostle PAUL[2]⟧ capital of Minn., on the Mississippi: see MINNEAPOLIS

St. Pe·ters·burg (pēt′ərz burg′) **1** seaport in NW Russia, on the Gulf of Finland: former capital of the Russian Empire (1712-1917): see LENINGRAD, PETROGRAD **2** ⟦after the Russian city⟧ city in WC Fla., on Tampa Bay

St-Pierre (san pyer′) town in NW Martinique, West Indies, on the site of a city destroyed (1902) by eruption of Mount Pelée

St-Pierre and Mi·que·lon (san pē er′ən mik′ə län′) group of islands in the Atlantic, south of Newfoundland, constituting a political unit of France: includes the islands of **St-Pierre** (*c.* 10 sq mi, 26 sq km) & MIQUELON & several islets: 93 sq mi (241 sq km)

str *abbrev.* **1** steamer **2** *Music* string(s)

stra·bis·mus (strə biz′məs) *n.* ⟦ModL < Gr *strabismos* < *strabizein*, to squint < *strabos*, twisted < IE **streb-* < base *(*s*)*ter-*, stiff, taut > START, STARE⟧ a disorder of the muscles of the eyes, as cross-eye, in which both eyes cannot be focused on the same point at the same time —**stra·bis′mal** *adj.*, **stra·bis′mic** —**stra·bis′mal·ly** *adv.*

Stra·bo (strā′bō) 63? B.C.-A.D. 21?; Gr. geographer

Stra·chey (strā′chē), **(Giles) Lyt·ton** (lit′n) 1880-1932; Eng. biographer

Strad (strad) *n. short for* STRADIVARIUS

strad·dle (strad′'l) *vt.* **-dled, -dling** ⟦freq. of STRIDE⟧ **1** to place oneself with a leg on either side of; stand or sit astride of **2** to spread (the legs) wide apart ☆**3** to take or appear to take both sides of (an issue); avoid committing oneself on —*vi.* **1** to sit, stand, or walk with the legs wide apart **2** to be spread apart: said of the legs ☆**3** to straddle an issue, argument, etc.; refuse to commit oneself; hedge —*n.* **1** the act or position of straddling **2** the distance straddled ☆**3** a refusal to commit oneself definitely to either side of an issue, argument, etc. ☆**4** in hedging or speculating, a position consisting of a put and a call on the same stock or commodity, with each option having the same strike price and expiration date **5** a salvo of artillery rounds, in which some fall on opposite sides of the target, indicating a hit on or near the target —**strad′dler** (-lər) *n.*

Stra·di·va·ri (strä′dē vä′rē), **An·to·nio** (än tô′nyô) (L. name *Antonius Stradivarius*) 1644-1737; It. violin maker

Strad·i·var·i·us (strad′ə ver′ē əs) *n.* a string instrument, esp. a violin, made by A. Stradivari or his sons

strafe (strāf; *chiefly Brit*, sträf) *vt.* **strafed, straf′ing** ⟦< Ger phr. *Gott strafe England* (God punish England) used in World War I⟧ to attack with gunfire; esp., to attack (ground positions, troops, etc.) with machine-gun fire from low-flying aircraft —**straf′er** *n.*

Straf·ford (straf′ərd), 1st Earl of (*Thomas Wentworth*) 1593-1641; Eng. statesman: advisor of Charles I: beheaded

strag·gle (strag′əl) *vi.* **-gled, -gling** ⟦ME *straglen*, prob. for **straklen*, freq. of *straken*, to go about, wander, roam⟧ **1** to stray from the path or course, or wander from the main group **2** to wander or be scattered over a wide area; ramble **3** to leave, arrive, or occur at irregular intervals **4** to hang in a disheveled manner, as hair, clothes, etc. —*n.* a straggly group —**strag′gler** *n.*

strag·gly (-lē) *adj.* **-gli·er, -gli·est** spread out in a straggling, irregular way

straight (strāt) *adj.* ⟦ME *streght*, pp. of *strecchen*, to STRETCH⟧ **1** having the same direction throughout its length; having no curvature or angularity [a *straight* line] 2 not crooked, bent, bowed, wavy, curly, etc. [*straight* hair] 3 upright; erect [*straight* posture] 4 level; even [a *straight* hemline] 5 with all cylinders in a direct line; in-line: said of some internal-combustion engines 6 direct; undeviating, uninterrupted, etc. [to hold a *straight* course] ☆7 following strictly the principles, slate of candidates, etc. of a political party: see also STRAIGHT TICKET 8 following a direct or systematic course of reasoning, etc.; methodical; accurate 9 in order; properly arranged, etc. [to put a room *straight*] 10 *a)* honest; sincere; upright *b)* reliable; factual [*straight* information] 11 outspoken; frank ☆12 *a)* without anything added or mixed in; undiluted [a *straight* shot of whiskey] *b)* not blended with neutral grain spirits 13 not qualified, modified, slanted, etc. [a *straight* denial] ☆14 at a fixed price per unit regardless of the quantity bought or sold [apples at ten cents *straight*] ☆15 [Slang] *a)* normal or conventional, as in one's lifestyle; also, SQUARE (*adj.* 12) *b)* HETEROSEXUAL *c)* not using drugs, alcohol, etc. —*adv.* 1 in a straight line or direction; unswervingly 2 upright; erectly 3 *a)* without detour, delay, etc. [go *straight* to bed] *b)* without equivocation, circumlocution, etc.; directly [tell it *straight*] *c)* without alteration, addition, etc. [play the role *straight*] 4 in an honest, law-abiding manner [a convict pledging to go *straight*] —*n.* 1 the quality or condition of being straight 2 something straight; specif., *a)* the straight part of a racetrack between the last turn and the winning post ☆*b) Poker* a hand consisting of five cards in sequence, but not all in the same suit: it ranks just above three of a kind and below a flush (cf. STRAIGHT FLUSH) 3 [Slang] *a)* a straight, or conventional, person *b)* a HETEROSEXUAL —**set someone straight** [Informal] to give the correct facts to, specif., so as to disabuse him or her —**set the record straight** to make the truth known, esp., so as to correct a misconception —**straight off** at once; without delay —**straight up** [Informal] served without ice: said of alcoholic beverages —**the straight and narrow (path)** a morally strict code of behavior —**straight′ly** *adv.* —**straight′ness** *n.*

straight-a·head (strāt′ə hed′) *adj.* 1 not complex; straightforward; uncomplicated 2 characterized by a typical or standard approach or style [*straight-ahead* rock music] 3 *Jazz* designating or of a style of playing strongly influenced by bop and not combined with elements of rock, pop, etc.

straight angle an angle of 180 degrees

☆**straight-arm** (-ärm′) *vt.* to push away (an opponent, as a would-be tackler in football) with the arm outstretched —*n.* the act or an instance of straight-arming

☆**straight arrow** [Informal] a person who is straight-arrow

☆**straight-ar·row** (-ar′ō, -er′ō) *adj.* ⟦< *Straight Arrow*, heroic title character in 1950s radio serial⟧ [Informal] proper, righteous, conscientious, etc.: often used with connotations of conservatism, stodginess, dullness, or the like

straight·a·way (strāt′ə wā′; *for adv.* strāt′ə wā′) *adj.* extending in a straight line —*n.* 1 a racetrack, or part of a track, that extends in a straight line 2 a straight and level stretch of highway —*adv.* at once; without delay

straight chain *Chem.* a chain of atoms, usually carbon, without any branches: see OPEN CHAIN

straight chair a chair with a back that is straight, or almost vertical, and not upholstered

straight·edge (strāt′ej′) *n.* a piece or strip of wood, etc. having a perfectly straight edge used in drawing straight lines, testing plane surfaces, etc.

straight·en (strāt′′n) *vt., vi.* to make or become straight —**straighten out** 1 to make or become less confused, easier to deal with, etc. ☆2 to make or become more correct or moral in behavior; reform —**straighten up** to put in good order; make tidy [*straighten up* your room before leaving] —**straight′en·er** *n.*

straight face a facial expression showing no amusement or other emotion —**straight′-faced′** *adj.*

straight flush *Poker* a hand consisting of five cards in sequence and all of the same suit: it is the highest hand, ranking just above four of a kind

straight·for·ward (strāt′fôr′wərd) *adj.* 1 moving or leading straight ahead; direct 2 *a)* honest; frank; open *b)* not ambiguous or obscure; clear [a *straightforward* explanation] —*adv.* in a straightforward manner; directly; openly: also **straight′for′wards** —**straight′for′ward·ly** *adv.* —**straight′for′ward·ness** *n.*

straight·jack·et (strāt′jak′it) *n., vt. alt. sp. of* STRAITJACKET

straight-laced (-lāst′) *adj. alt. sp. of* STRAIT-LACED (sense 2)

straight-line (-līn′) *adj.* 1 composed of straight lines 2 *Finance* designating or of a method of allocating costs to given time periods at a fixed rate [*straight-line* depreciation] 3 *Mech.* *a)* designating or of a device, mechanism, etc. whose main parts are positioned or move in a straight line *b)* designating a device designed to transmit or cause motion in a straight line

☆**straight man** that member of a comedy team who serves as a foil for, and feeds lines to, the comedian delivering the quips and punchlines

straight-out (-out′) *adj.* [Informal] 1 straightforward; direct 2 unrestrained ☆3 thoroughgoing; unqualified

straight pin PIN (*n.* 2)

☆**straight razor** a razor with a long, unguarded blade that can be folded into the handle

☆**straight shooter** [Informal] a person who is honest, sincere, ethical, etc.

straight-shoot·ing (-shōōt′iŋ) *adj.* [Informal] characterized by candor, honesty, ethical behavior, etc.

☆**straight ticket** a ballot cast for candidates of only one party: opposed to SPLIT TICKET

☆**straight time** 1 the number of working hours fixed as a standard for a given work period 2 the rate of pay for work during these hours

straight·way (-wā′) *adv.* [Now Chiefly Literary] *var. of* STRAIGHTAWAY

strain[1] (strān) *vt.* ⟦ME *streinen* < OFr *estraindre*, to strain, wring hard < L *stringere*, to draw tight: see STRICT⟧ 1 to draw or stretch tight 2 to exert, use, or tax to the utmost [to *strain* every nerve] 3 to overtax; injure by overexertion; wrench [to *strain* a muscle] 4 to injure or weaken by force, pressure, etc. [the wind *strained* the roof] 5 to stretch or force beyond the normal, customary, or legitimate limits [to *strain* a rule to one's own advantage] 6 to change the form or size of, by applying external force 7 *a)* to pass through a screen, sieve, filter, etc.; filter *b)* to remove or free by filtration, etc. 8 to hug or embrace: now only in **strain to one's bosom** (or **heart**, etc.) 9 [Obs.] to force; constrain —*vi.* 1 to make violent or continual efforts; strive hard 2 to be or become strained 3 to be subjected to great stress or pressure 4 to pull or push with force 5 to filter, ooze, or trickle 6 ⟦from a misunderstanding of "strain at a gnat" (Matt. 23:24)⟧ to hesitate or be unwilling; balk (*at*) —*n.* 1 a straining or being strained 2 great effort, exertion, or tension 3 an injury to a part of the body as a result of great effort or overexertion [muscle *strain*] 4 *a)* change in form or size, or both, resulting from stress or force *b)* stress or force 5 a great or excessive demand on one's emotions, resources, etc. [a *strain* on the imagination]

strain[2] (strān) *n.* ⟦ME *stren* < OE *streon*, gain, procreation, stock, race < base *strynan, streonan*, to produce: for IE base see STREW⟧ 1 [Obs.] *a)* a begetting *b)* offspring 2 ancestry; lineage; descent 3 the descendants of a common ancestor; race; stock; line; breed; variety 4 an inherited or natural characteristic or tendency 5 a trace; streak 6 the manner, style, or tone of a speech, book, action, etc. [to write in an angry *strain*] 7 [*often pl.*] a passage of music; tune; air 8 a passage of poetry, esp. of a lyric sort 9 a flight or outburst of eloquence, profanity, etc. 10 *Genetics, Taxonomy* a line of individuals of a certain species or race, differentiated from the main group by certain qualities, often, specif., superior qualities resulting from artificial breeding

strained (strānd) *adj.* 1 not natural or relaxed; forced [a *strained* smile] 2 characterized by a loss of closeness, cordiality, etc. [*strained* relations between siblings]

strain·er (strān′ər) *n.* a person or thing that strains; specif., a device for straining, sifting, or filtering; sieve, filter, colander, etc.

strain·ing piece (strān′iŋ) a horizontal brace or beam connected at either end to opposite rafters in a roof truss: also **straining beam**

strait (strāt) *adj.* ⟦ME *streit* < OFr *estreit* < L *strictus*: see STRICT⟧ 1 [Archaic] restricted or constricted; narrow; tight; confined 2 [Archaic] strict; rigid; exacting 3 [Now Rare] straitened; difficult; distressing —*n.* 1 [Rare] a narrow passage 2 [*often pl.*] a narrow waterway connecting two large bodies of water 3 [*usually pl.*] difficulty; distress 4 [Rare] an isthmus —***SYN.*** EMERGENCY

strait·en (strāt′′n) *vt.* 1 [Now Rare] *a)* to make strait or narrow *b)* to hem in closely *c)* to restrict or confine in scope, range, etc.; hamper 2 to bring into difficulties; cause to be in distress or want: usually in the phrase **in straitened circumstances**, lacking sufficient money

strait·jack·et (strāt′jak′it) *n.* 1 a jacketlike device with sleeves that bind the arms tight against the body: used, as in a psychiatric ward, to restrain persons in a violent state 2 anything that confines or limits —*vt.* to confine or restrict with or as with a straitjacket

strait-laced (-lāst′) *adj.* 1 [Archaic] *a)* tightly laced, as a corset *b)* wearing tightly laced garments 2 narrowly strict or severe in behavior or moral views

Straits Settlements former British crown colony in Southeast Asia, comprising Singapore, Malacca, Penang, Labuan, Christmas Island, & the Cocos Islands

strake (strāk) *n.* ⟦ME, akin to *strecchen*, to STRETCH⟧ a single line of planking or metal plating extending along the hull of a ship or boat from stem to stern

stra·mo·ni·um (strə mō′nē əm) *n.* ⟦ModL⟧ 1 JIMSON WEED 2 the dried leaves and flowering top of this plant, formerly used in medicine as an antispasmodic

strand[1] (strand) *n.* ⟦ME < OE, akin to ON *strǫnd*, Ger *strand*, prob. < IE base **ster-*, to extend, stretch out > STREW⟧ land at the edge of a body of water; shore, esp. ocean shore —*vt., vi.* 1 to run or drive aground [a ship *stranded* by the storm] 2 to leave in, or be put into, a difficult, helpless position [*stranded* penniless in a strange city] —***SYN.*** SHORE[1]

strand[2] (strand) *n.* ⟦ME *stronde* < ?⟧ 1 *a)* any one of the threads, fibers, wires, etc. that are twisted together to form a length of string, rope, or cable *b)* any of the individual bundles of thread or fiber so twisted together 2 a ropelike length of anything [a *strand* of pearls, a *strand* of hair] 3 any of the parts that are bound together to form a whole [the *strands* of one's life] —*vt.* 1 to form (rope, etc.) by twisting together strands 2 to break a strand or strands of (a rope, etc.) —**strand′er** *n.*

strand·line (strand′līn′) *n.* a shoreline, esp. a former one from which the water has receded: often written **strand line**

strange (strānj) *adj.* **strang′er, strang′est** ⟦ME < OFr *estrange* < L *extraneus*, EXTRANEOUS⟧ 1 of another place or locality; foreign; alien 2 not previously known, seen, heard, or experienced; unfamiliar 3 quite unusual or uncommon; extraordinary 4 queer; peculiar; odd 5 [Archaic] reserved, distant, or cold in manner 6 lacking experience; unaccustomed [a new employee who is *strange* to the job] —*adv.* **strang′er, strang′est** in a strange manner —**strange′ly** *adv.*

SYN.—strange, the term of broadest application here, refers to that which is unfamiliar, as because of being uncommon, unknown, new, etc. [a *strange* voice, idea, device, etc.]; **peculiar** applies either to that which puzzles or to that which has unique qualities [a *peculiar* smell, pattern, etc.]; **odd** suggests that which differs from the ordinary or conventional, sometimes to the point of being bizarre [*odd* behavior]; **queer** emphasizes an element of eccentricity, abnormality, or suspicion [a *queer* facial expression]; **quaint** suggests an oddness, esp. an antique quality, that is pleasing or appealing [a *quaint* costume]; **outlandish** suggests an oddness that is decidedly, often outrageously, fantastic or bizarre [*outlandish* customs] —**ANT. familiar, ordinary**

strange attractor in the mathematics of CHAOS (*n.* 4), a set of values that tends to reoccur periodically, as the data describing the particular climate of a certain region: often represented by a butterfly-shaped graph

strange·ness (strānj′nis) *n.* 1 the state or quality of being strange 2 *Particle Physics* a property of quarks and certain other elementary particles that explains the longer lifetimes of these particles and is expressed as a quantum number with −1 meaning a particle (**strange particle**) has strangeness and 0 meaning a particle does not have strangeness

strange quark *Particle Physics* a type of quark with a mass of *c.* 0.1 to 0.3 GeV/c^2, a negative charge that is ⅓ the charge of an electron, zero charm, and −1 strangeness: see FLAVOR (sense 5)

strang·er (strān′jər) *n.* ⟦ME < MFr *estranger* < OFr *estrange:* see STRANGE⟧ 1 an outsider, newcomer, or foreigner 2 [Now Rare] a guest or visitor 3 a person not known or familiar to one; person who is not an acquaintance 4 a person unaccustomed (*to* something specified); novice [an athlete who is no *stranger* to physical pain] 5 *Law* a person who is not party (*to* an act, agreement, title, etc.) —***SYN.*** ALIEN

stran·gle (straŋ′gəl) *vt.* **-gled, -gling** ⟦ME *stranglen* < OFr *estrangler* < L *strangulare* < Gr *strangalan* < *strangalē,* halter < *strangos,* twisted: see STRONG⟧ 1 to kill by squeezing the throat as with the hands, a noose, etc., so as to shut off the breath; throttle; choke 2 to suffocate or choke in any manner 3 to suppress, stifle, or repress [free speech *strangled* by tyranny] —*vi.* to be strangled —**stran′gler** *n.*

stran·gle·hold (-hōld′) *n.* 1 an illegal wrestling hold that chokes off an opponent's breath 2 any force that restricts or suppresses freedom or progress

stran·gles (straŋ′gəlz) *n.* a disease of young horses caused by a bacterial infection (*Streptococcus equi*) and characterized by inflammation of the mucous membrane of the respiratory tract and by the formation of abscesses in the adjacent lymph nodes

stran·gu·late (straŋ′gyə lāt′) *vt.* **-lat′ed, -lat′ing** ⟦< L *strangulatus,* pp. of *strangulare*⟧ 1 STRANGLE 2 *Med.* to constrict (a tube, herniated organ, etc.) so as to cut off a flow, esp. so as to cut off circulation of the blood —*vi. Med.* to become constricted —**stran′gu·la′tion** *n.*

stran·gu·ry (straŋ′gyə rē) *n.* ⟦ME < L *stranguria* < Gr *strangouria* < *stranx* (gen. *strangos*), a drop, akin to *strangos,* twisted (see STRONG) + *ouron,* URINE⟧ slow and painful urination

strap (strap) *n.* ⟦dial. form of STROP⟧ 1 a narrow strip or band of leather or other flexible material, often with a buckle or similar fastener at one end, for binding or securing things 2 any flat, narrow piece, as of metal, used as a fastening 3 any of several straplike parts or things, as a shoulder strap, a loop for pulling on boots, a razor strop, etc. —*vt.* **strapped, strap′ping** 1 to fasten with a strap 2 to beat with a strap 3 to strop (a razor)

strap·hang·er (strap′haŋ′ər) *n.* ⟦from the hanging straps designed to serve as supports⟧ [Informal] a standing passenger, as on a crowded bus or subway car

strap hinge a hinge with long, usually triangular, parts by which it is fastened

strap·less (-lis) *adj.* having no strap or straps; specif., having no shoulder straps [a *strapless* bra]

strap·pa·do (strə pā′dō, -pä′-) *n., pl.* **-does** ⟦It *strappata* < *strappare,* to pull < Gmc, as in Ger dial. (Swiss) *strapfen,* to pull tight (akin to Ger *strafen,* to punish) < IE **strep-* < base **(s)ter-,* stiff > STARE⟧ 1 a kind of torture in which the victim is lifted in the air by a rope fastened to the wrists, then suddenly dropped part way to the ground 2 the instrument used in this torture

☆**strapped** (strapt) *adj.* ⟦< pp. of STRAP, in dial. or slang sense, "give credit to", orig., lit., to place name on list of debtors⟧ [Informal] in great need of money: often in such phrases as **strapped for cash, strapped for funds,** etc.

strap·per (strap′ər) *n.* 1 a person or thing that straps 2 [Informal] a strapping person

strap·ping (-iŋ) *adj.* ⟦prp. of STRAP, used (like *thumping, whopping,* expressing violent action) to denote large size⟧ [Informal] large and robust

Stras·berg (stras′burg), **Lee** (born *Israel Strassberg*) 1901-82; U.S. drama teacher & stage director, born in Austria-Hungary

Stras·bourg (stras′burg; *Fr* strȧz bo͞or′) city & port in NE France, on the Rhine

strass (stras) *n.* ⟦Fr & Ger < ?: said to be after J. Strass (or *Strasser*), Ger jeweler⟧ PASTE (*n.* 7*a*)

stra·ta (strāt′ə, strat′ə) *n. alt. pl. of* STRATUM

strat·a·gem (strat′ə jəm) *n.* ⟦LME *stratageme* < L *strategema* < Gr *stratēgēma,* device or act of a general < *stratēgos,* a general < *stratos,* army (for IE base see STREW) + *agein,* to lead: see ACT[1]⟧ 1 a trick, scheme, or plan for deceiving an enemy in war 2 any trick or scheme for achieving some purpose —***SYN.*** TRICK

stra·tal (strāt′'l) *adj.* of a stratum or strata

stra·te·gic (strə tē′jik) *adj.* 1 of or having to do with strategy 2 characterized by sound strategy; favorable; advantageous 3 *a)* essential to effective military strategy ☆*b)* operating or designed to operate directly against the military, industrial, etc. installations of an enemy [the *Strategic* Air Command] 4 required for the effective conduct of a war [*strategic* materials] Also **stra·te′gi·cal** —**stra·te′gi·cal·ly** *adv.*

strat·e·gist (strat′ə jist) *n.* one using strategy; esp., one skilled in strategy

strat·e·gize (-jīz′) *vi.* **-gized′, -giz′ing** to plan a strategy or strategies

strat·e·gy (-jē) *n., pl.* **-gies** ⟦Fr *stratégie* < Gr *stratēgia,* generalship < *stratēgos,* a general: see STRATAGEM⟧ 1 *a)* the science of planning and directing large-scale military operations, specif. (as distinguished from TACTICS) of maneuvering forces into the most advantageous position prior to actual engagement with the enemy *b)* a plan or action based on this 2 a stratagem or the artful use of stratagems 3 any carefully devised plan of action [a marketing *strategy*] Sometimes, esp. for sense 1, **stra·te·gics** (strə tē′jiks) *n.*

Strat·ford-up·on-A·von (strat′fərd ə pän ā′vän′) town in S Warwickshire, England, on the Avon: birthplace & burial place of Shakespeare: county district called **Stratford-on-Avon**

strath (strath) *n.* ⟦< Gael *srath*⟧ a wide river valley

Strath·clyde (strath klīd′) former administrative region of SW Scotland, on the Firth of Clyde

strath·spey (strath spā′) *n.* ⟦after *Strathspey,* valley of Spey River, N Scotland: see STRATH⟧ 1 a Scottish dance resembling, but slower than, the reel 2 the music for this

strat·i·fi·ca·tion (strat′ə fi kā′shən) *n.* 1 the process of stratifying or the state of being stratified 2 a stratified arrangement or appearance 3 *Geol.* a structure characterized by a succession of tabular layers, beds, strata, etc. —**strat′i·fi·ca′tion·al** *adj.*

strat·i·form (strat′ə fôrm′) *adj.* ⟦< STRATUM + -FORM⟧ having the form of a stratum; showing stratification

strat·i·fy (-fī′) *vt.* **-fied′, -fy′ing** ⟦Fr *stratifier* < ModL *stratificare* < L *stratum,* layer + *facere,* to make: see STRATUM & DO[1]⟧ 1 to form or arrange in layers or strata 2 to preserve (seeds) by placing them between layers of moisture-retaining soil, peat moss, etc. 3 to classify or separate (people) into groups graded according to status as variously determined by birth, income, education, etc. —*vi.* to become stratified

stra·tig·ra·phy (strə tig′rə fē) *n.* ⟦< STRATUM + -GRAPHY⟧ 1 the arrangement of rocks in layers or strata 2 the branch of geology dealing with the study of the nature, distribution, and relations of the stratified rocks of the earth's crust —**stra·tig′ra·pher** *n.* —**strat·i·graph·ic** (strat′ə graf′ik) *adj.* —**strat′i·graph′i·cal·ly** *adv.*

stra·toc·ra·cy (strə täk′rə sē) *n., pl.* **-cies** ⟦< Gr *stratos,* army (see STRATAGEM) + -CRACY⟧ government by the military

stra·to·cu·mu·lus (strāt′ō kyo͞om′yə ləs, strat′-) *n., pl.* **-li′** (-lī′) ⟦ModL: see STRATUS & CUMULUS⟧ the type of white or gray cloud found at low altitudes and consisting of large, smooth or patchy layers of water droplets and possibly some hail or snow: see CLOUD

strat·o·pause (strat′ə pôz′) *n.* ⟦< fol. + PAUSE (*n.*)⟧ an atmospheric transition zone or shell, located between the stratosphere and the mesosphere at an altitude of *c.* 50 to 55 km (*c.* 31 to 34 mi), in which temperatures begin to drop with increasing altitude

strat·o·sphere (strat′ə sfir′) *n.* ⟦Fr *stratosphère* < ModL *stratum,* fol. + Fr *sphère,* SPHERE⟧ 1 the atmospheric zone or shell located above the tropopause at an altitude of *c.* 20 to 50 km (*c.* 12 to 31 mi) and characterized by an increase in temperature with increasing altitude 2 any extremely high point, place, or level —**strat′o·spher′ic** (-sfer′ik, -sfir′-) *adj.*

stra·tum (strāt′əm, strat′-) *n., pl.* **stra′ta** (-ə) or **-tums** ⟦ModL < L, a covering, blanket < *stratus,* pp. of *sternere,* to spread, stretch out, cover: for IE base see STREW⟧ 1 a horizontal layer or section of material, esp. any of several lying one upon another; specif., *a) Biol.* a layer of tissue *b) Geol.* a single layer of sedimentary rock 2 a section, level, or division, as of the atmosphere or ocean, regarded as like a stratum 3 any of the socioeconomic groups of a society as determined by birth, income, education, etc.

stra·tus (strāt′əs) *n., pl.* **stra′ti** (-ī) ⟦L, a strewing: see prec.⟧ the type of gray cloud found at low altitudes and consisting of a uniform layer of water droplets and sometimes ice crystals

Straus (strous; *Ger* shtrous), **Oscar** (or **Oskar**) 1870-1954; Fr. composer, born in Austria

Strauss (shtrous; *E* strous) 1 **Jo·hann, II** (yō′hän′) 1825-99; Austrian composer, esp. of waltzes 2 **Rich·ard** (riH′ärt) 1864-1949; Ger. composer & conductor

stra·vage (strə vāg′) *vi.* **-vaged′, -vag′ing** ⟦aphetic contr. < ML *extravagari,* to stray: see EXTRAVAGANT⟧ [Scot., Irish, or North Eng.] to wander about aimlessly; roam: also sp. **stra·vaig′**

Stra·vin·sky (strə vin′skē), **I·gor (Feodorovich)** (ē′gôr) 1882-1971; Russ. composer & conductor, in the U.S. after 1940

straw (strô) *n.* ⟦ME *stra* < OE *streaw,* akin to *streawian:* see STREW⟧ 1 hollow stalks or stems of grain after threshing, collectively: used for fodder, for bedding, for making hats, etc. 2 a single one of such stalks 3 such a stalk or, now esp., a tube of waxed paper, plastic, etc., used for sucking beverages 4 something, as a hat, made of straw 5 something of little or no value; worthless trifle 6 *short for* STRAW MAN (sense 4) 7 *see* LAST STRAW

—*adj.* 1 straw-colored; yellowish 2 made of straw 3 of little or no value or significance; worthless; meaningless ☆4 of or having to do with a STRAW VOTE [a *straw* ballot] —**a straw in the wind** an indication of what may happen —**grasp (or clutch or catch) at a straw (or straws)** to try any measure, however unlikely, that offers even the slightest hope —**straw′y** *adj.*

straw·ber·ry (strô′ber′ē, -bər ē) *n., pl.* **-ries** ⟦ME *strawberi* < OE *streawberie* < *streaw,* straw + *berige,* berry: prob. from the appearance of the achenes, like bits of straw or chaff on the red surface⟧ 1 the small, red, fleshy accessory fruit of a stolon-bearing plant (genus *Fragaria*) of the rose family 2 this plant 3 [Slang] a reddish abrasion of the skin: see also STRAWBERRY MARK

☆**strawberry blond** 1 reddish blond 2 a person with hair of this color —**straw′ber′ry-blond′** *adj.*

☆**strawberry bush** an E American euonymus (*Euonymus americana*) with red pods and seeds with a red covering

strawberry mark a small, red birthmark: see also STRAWBERRY (sense 3)

strawberry roan reddish roan

☆**strawberry shrub** CAROLINA ALLSPICE

☆**strawberry tomato** a ground-cherry, esp. an E American species (*Physalis pruinosa*) with a small, edible, yellow fruit

strawberry tree 1 a European evergreen tree (*Arbutus unedo*) of the heath family, with small, white flowers and red, berrylike fruit ☆2 STRAWBERRY BUSH

straw·board (strô′bôrd′) *n.* a coarse cardboard made of straw and used in making boxes, etc.

☆**straw boss** ⟦orig. uncert.⟧ [Informal] 1 a person having subordinate authority, as a foreman's assistant 2 a supervisor who has little or no authority to enforce his or her orders

straw color a pale-yellow color —**straw′-col′ored** *adj.*

straw·flow·er (-flou′ər) *n.* an annual Australian plant (*Helichrysum bracteatum*) of the composite family, whose brightly colored flower heads are dried for winter bouquets

☆**straw-hat** (-hat′) *adj.* ⟦from the practice, esp. formerly, of wearing straw hats in summer⟧ designating, of, or having to do with a summer theater or summer theaters

straw man 1 SCARECROW 2 a person of little importance; nonentity 3 a deliberately weak and easily refuted argument put forward, as by a politician or debater, as the argument of the opposition 4 a person used to disguise another's intentions, activities, etc.; blind

☆**straw vote (*or* poll)** ⟦< ? A STRAW IN THE WIND (see phrase at STRAW)⟧ an unofficial vote or poll taken to determine general group opinion on a given issue

straw wine a sweet, rich wine made from grapes that have been dried in the sun, as on a bed of straw

straw·worm (-wurm′) *n.* any of several hymenopteran insect larvae (family Eurytomidae) which damage the stalks of grain

stray (strā) *vi.* ⟦ME *straien* < OFr *estraier* < *estrée,* road, street < LL *strata,* STREET⟧ 1 to wander from a given place, limited area, direct course, etc., esp. aimlessly; roam; rove 2 to go wrong; be in error; deviate (*from* what is right) 3 to fail to concentrate; be inattentive or digress —*n.* 1 a person or thing that strays; esp., a domestic animal wandering at large 2 [*usually pl.*] static interfering with radio reception —*adj.* 1 having strayed or wandered; lost 2 occurring alone or infrequently; isolated; incidental [a few *stray* words] —**stray′er** *n.*

streak (strēk) *n.* ⟦ME *streke* < OE *strica:* for IE base see STRIKE⟧ 1 a line or long, thin mark; stripe or smear, generally differing in color or texture from the surrounding area 2 a ray of light or a flash, as of lightning 3 a vein or stratum of a mineral 4 a layer, as of fat in meat 5 a strain, element, or tendency in behavior, temperament, etc.; trait [a jealous *streak*] ☆6 a period, spell, or series [a *streak* of bad luck, a *streak* of losses] 7 *Bacteriology* an inoculum placed, as in a line, on a solid culture medium 8 *Mineralogy* a colored line of powder produced by rubbing a mineral over a hard, white surface (**streak plate**): it serves as a distinguishing character —*vt.* 1 to make streaks on or in; mark with streaks 2 to make usually lighter streaks in (hair) with a coloring agent —*vi.* 1 to form streaks; become streaked 2 to move at high speed; go fast; hurry ☆3 to dash naked in public as a prank —☆**like a streak** [Informal] at high speed; swiftly —**streak′er** *n.*

streak·y (strē′kē) *adj.* **streak′i·er, streak′i·est** 1 marked with or showing streaks 2 occurring in streaks 3 uneven or variable, as in quality —**streak′i·ly** *adv.* —**streak′i·ness** *n.*

stream (strēm) *n.* ⟦ME *strem* < OE *stream,* akin to Ger *strom* < IE base **sreu-,* to flow > Gr *rheein,* to flow⟧ 1 a current or flow of water or other liquid, esp. one running along the surface of the earth; specif., a small river 2 *a)* a steady movement or flow of any fluid [a *stream* of cold air] *b)* a steady movement or flow of rays of energy [a *stream* of light] 3 a continuous series or succession [a *stream* of cars] 4 a trend or course [the *stream* of events] 5 [Brit.] *Educ.* any of the sections formed when students within a grade level are grouped, as according to their abilities: see also STREAMING (sense 2) —*vi.* 1 to flow in or as in a stream 2 to give off a stream; flow (*with*) [eyes *streaming* with tears] 3 to move steadily or continuously 4 to move swiftly; rush [fire *streamed* up the wall] 5 to extend or stretch out; float; fly, as a flag in the breeze 6 to transmit data by STREAMING (sense 1) —*vt.* 1 to cause to stream 2 to transmit by STREAMING (sense 1)

stream·bed (strēm′bed′) *n.* the channel in which a stream flows or has flowed

stream·er (strēm′ər) *n.* 1 something that streams 2 a long, narrow, ribbonlike flag or banner 3 any long, narrow strip of cloth, colored paper, ribbon, etc., hanging loose at one end 4 a ray or stream of light extending up from the horizon 5 a newspaper headline across the full page; banner

stream·ing (strēm′iŋ) *n.* 1 a method of sequentially transmitting an audio or video presentation, as over the internet: the data is playable as it is being received, rather than only after it is completely downloaded 2 [Chiefly Brit.] *Educ.* the practice of classifying students according to ability and placing them in groups with distinct curricula, career expectations, etc.; tracking

stream·let (strēm′lit) *n.* a small stream; rivulet

stream·line (-līn′) *n.* 1 the path, or a section of the path, of a fluid moving past a solid object 2 a contour with reference to its resistance, as to air —*vt.* **-lined′, -lin′ing** to make streamlined —*adj.* STREAMLINED

stream·lined (-līnd′) *adj.* 1 having a contour designed to offer the least resistance in moving through air, water, etc. ☆2 arranged or organized so as to be simpler or more efficient 3 with no excess, as of fat, decoration, etc.; trim [a *streamlined* figure or design]

streamline flow LAMINAR FLOW

stream of consciousness ⟦term popularized by William JAMES[2]⟧ *Psychol.* individual conscious experience regarded as a continuous series of occurrences rather than as separate, disconnected events

stream-of-con·scious·ness (-əv kän′shəs nis) *adj.* designating, of, or using a narrative technique whereby the thoughts, percepts, etc. of one or more of the characters of a novel, short story, etc. are rendered in a direct, free-flowing manner

street (strēt) *n.* ⟦ME < OE *stræt,* akin to Ger *strasse* < early WGmc loanword < LL *strata* < L *strata (via),* paved (road), fem. of *stratus:* see STRATUM⟧ 1 a public road in a town or city; esp. a paved thoroughfare with sidewalks and buildings along one or both sides 2 such a road apart from its sidewalks [children playing in the *street*] 3 the people living, working, etc. in the buildings along a given street 4 [*often pl.*] figuratively, the general public, common people, etc. [taking the issue to the *streets*] 5 [*usually pl.*] figuratively, an urban environment characterized by poverty, crime, etc. —*adj.* 1 of, in, on, or near the street 2 suitable for everyday wear in public [*street* clothes] 3 of, relating to, or characterized by urban life and culture, urban crime, homelessness, etc. [a *street* artist, the current *street* value of heroin] —**the Street** ☆WALL STREET

street Arab [Archaic] a homeless or neglected child left to roam the streets: also **street urchin**

☆**street·car** (strēt′kär′) *n.* a large coach or car on rails that provides public transportation along certain streets

street cred (kred) ⟦*street cred(ibility)*: see STREET (*n.* 4)⟧ [Slang] popularity with or acceptance by the common people [a political candidate who lacks *street cred*]

street·light (strēt′līt′) *n.* a light mounted on a high pole, used to illuminate a street or road: also **street′lamp′** (-lamp′)

street·scape (-skāp′) *n.* ⟦STREET + -SCAPE⟧ a street or portion of a street, including the sidewalks, streetlights, buildings, etc., considered in terms of its visual effect

street-smart (-smärt′) *adj.* [Informal] 1 STREETWISE 2 knowledgeable or shrewd in any given field, social setting, etc. as a result of practical experience

street smarts [Informal] 1 cunning or shrewdness needed to live in, or to deal with people living in, an urban environment characterized by poverty, crime, etc. 2 experience in and shrewdness about any given field, social setting, etc.

☆**street theater** an amateur theatrical production performed in a street, park, etc. or indoors, usually for a nonpaying audience, with an improvised script generally on a social or political theme

street·walk·er (-wôk′ər) *n.* a prostitute who solicits customers along the streets —**street′walk′ing** *n.*

☆**street·wise** (-wīz′) *adj.* [Informal] knowledgeable and shrewd, as a result of practical experience, about life in urban areas where vice and crime are prevalent

strength (streŋkth, streŋth; *often* strenth) *n.* ⟦ME *strengthe* < OE *strengthu* < **strang-ithu:* see STRONG & -TH[1]⟧ 1 the state or quality of being strong; force; power; vigor 2 the power to resist strain, stress, etc.; toughness; durability 3 the power to resist attack; impregnability 4 legal, moral, or intellectual force or effectiveness 5 *a)* capacity for producing a reaction or effect *b)* potency or concentration [a cleaning fluid used at full *strength*] *c)* great effectiveness or high potency 6 intensity, as of sound, color, odor, etc. 7 force as measured in numbers [a battalion at full *strength*] 8 vigor or force of feeling or expression 9 a source of strength or support 10 a tendency to rise or remain firm in prices —**from strength to strength** from one accomplishment or peak to another, often in an increasing progression —**on the strength of** based or relying on

SYN.—**strength** refers to the inherent capacity to act upon or affect something, to endure, to resist, etc. [the *strength* to lift something, tensile *strength*]; **power**, somewhat more general, applies to the ability, latent or exerted, physical or mental, to do something [the *power* of the press, of a machine, etc.]; **force** usually suggests the actual exertion of power, esp. in producing motion or overcoming opposition [the *force* of gravity]; **might** suggests great or overwhelming strength or power [with all one's *might*]; **energy** specifically implies latent power for doing work or affecting something [the *energy* in an atom]; **potency** refers to the inherent capacity or power to accomplish something [the *potency* of a drug] —*ANT.* **weakness, impotence**

strength·en (-ən) *vt., vi.* to increase in strength; make or become stronger —**strength'en·er** *n.*

stren·u·ous (stren'yo͞o əs) *adj.* ⟦L *strenuus,* vigorous, active < IE base **(s)ter-,* rigid > STARE, Gr *strēnēs,* strong⟧ **1** requiring or characterized by great effort or energy *[a strenuous* game of handball*]* **2** vigorous, arduous, zealous, etc. *[strenuous* efforts*]* —**SYN.** ACTIVE —**stren'u·ous·ly** *adv.* —**stren'u·ous·ness** *n.*

strep (strep) *n. short for:* **1** STREPTOCOCCUS **2** STREP THROAT

☆**strep throat** a sore throat caused by a streptococcus and characterized by inflammation and fever

strep·to- (strep'tō, -tə) ⟦< Gr *streptos,* twisted: see STREPTOMYCES⟧ *combining form* **1** twisted chain **2** streptococcus

strep·to·coc·cus (strep'tə käk'əs) *n., pl.* **-coc'ci'** (-käk'sī') ⟦ModL < Gr *streptos,* twisted (see STREPTOMYCES) + COCCUS⟧ any of a genus (*Streptococcus*) of spherical, Gram-positive bacteria that divide in only one plane and occur generally in chains: some species cause various serious diseases —**strep'to·coc'cal** (-käk'əl) *adj.,* **strep'to·coc'cic** (-käk'sik)

strep·to·ki·nase (-kī'nās', -kin'ās') *n.* ⟦< prec. + KINASE⟧ a proteolytic enzyme derived from certain hemolytic streptococci, used in dissolving blood clots

strep·to·my·ces (-mī'sēz') *n., pl.* **-ces'** ⟦ModL < Gr *streptos,* twisted < *strephein,* to turn (see STROPHE) + *mykēs,* fungus (see MYCO-)⟧ any of a genus (*Streptomyces*) of funguslike, chiefly soil bacteria: several species yield antibiotics

☆**strep·to·my·cin** (-mī'sin) *n.* ⟦< prec. + -IN[1]⟧ an antibiotic, $C_{21}H_{39}N_7O_{12}$, obtained from a soil bacterium (*Streptomyces griseus*) and used in treating various bacterial diseases, as tuberculosis

strep·to·thri·cin (-thrī'sin) *n.* ⟦< ModL *Streptothrix,* name of the fungus < Gr *streptos,* twisted (see STREPTOMYCES) + *thrix,* hair + -IN[1]⟧ an antibiotic derived from an actinomycete (*Actinomyces lavendulae*) and used in the treatment of various bacterial infections

stress (stres) *n.* ⟦ME *stresse* < OFr *estresse* < VL **strictia* < L *strictus,* STRICT; also, in some senses, aphetic < DISTRESS⟧ **1** strain or straining force; specif., *a)* force exerted upon a body, that tends to strain or deform its shape *b)* the intensity of such force, usually measured in pounds per square inch *c)* the opposing reaction or cohesiveness of a body resisting such force **2** emphasis; importance; significance **3** *a)* mental or emotional tension or strain characterized by feelings of anxiety, fear, etc. *b)* a factor or combination of factors that causes such tension or strain, as an urgent need or perceived threat *c) Psychol.* a condition typically characterized by symptoms of mental and physical tension or strain, as depression or hypertension, that can result from a reaction to a situation in which a person feels threatened, pressured, etc. **4** *Music* ACCENT (senses 13 & 14) **5** *Phonet. a)* the relative force or loudness with which a syllable is uttered *b)* an accented syllable (for stress marks, see PRIMARY STRESS, SECONDARY STRESS) **6** *Prosody a)* the relative force of utterance given a syllable or word according to the meter *b)* an accented syllable —*vt.* ⟦OFr *estrecer* < VL **strictiare*⟧ **1** *a)* to put stress, pressure, or strain on *b)* [Informal] to subject to mental or emotional stress **2** to give stress or accent to **3** to emphasize —**stress'ful** *adj.* —**stress'ful·ly** *adv.*

-stress (stris) ⟦< -STER + -ESS⟧ *suffix* **1** a female person who is, does, or creates (something specified) *[songstress]* **2** a female person associated with (something specified) Cf. -STER: see also -ESS

stressed-out (strest'out') *adj.* [Informal] tired, nervous, or depressed as a result of overwork, mental pressure, etc.

stress fracture a fracture near the muscle attachments on the leg bones caused by repetitive stress, as from intensive exercise

stress·or (stres'ər) *n.* ⟦STRESS, *vt.* + -OR⟧ any stimulus producing mental or physical stress in an organism

stress test **1** a controlled medical test in which a cardiac patient exercises vigorously, often on a treadmill, while connected to an electrocardiograph **2** any test designed to challenge the integrity of a complex system, a piece of equipment, etc. —**stress'-test'** *vt.*

stretch (strech) *vt.* ⟦ME *strecchen* < OE *streccan,* akin to Ger *strecken* < IE **sterg-* < base **(s)ter-,* to be stiff, rigid > STARE⟧ **1** to hold out or reach out; extend *[to stretch* out a helping hand*]* **2** to cause (the body or limbs) to reach out to full length, as in yawning, relaxing, or reclining, or in preparing to exercise **3** to pull or spread out to full extent or to greater size *[to stretch* sheets out to dry*]* **4** to cause to reach or extend over a given space, distance, or time *[to stretch* pipelines across a continent*]* **5** *a)* to cause to reach or extend farther or too far; force or strain *b)* to strain in interpretation, application, scope, etc. to questionable or unreasonable limits *[to stretch* a rule, to *stretch* the truth*]* **6** to make tense or tight with effort; strain (a muscle, etc.) **7** [Slang] to knock down, esp. so as to cause to lie at full length —*vi.* **1** *a)* to spread or be spread out to full extent or beyond normal limits *b)* to extend or continue over a given space, distance, direction, or time **2** *a)* to extend the body or limbs to full length, as in yawning, reaching for something, or preparing to exercise *b)* to lie down at full length (usually with *out*) **3** to become stretched or be capable of being stretched to greater size, as any elastic substance **4** *Jazz* to perform a lengthy improvised solo: with *out* —*n.* **1** a stretching or being stretched **2** *a)* an unbroken period; continuous space (*of* time) *[over a stretch* of ten days*]* *b)* [Informal] a term served in prison under a sentence **3** the extent to which something can be stretched **4** an unbroken length, tract, or space; continuous extent or distance *[a long stretch* of beach*]* **5** *a)* any of the sections of a course or track for racing *b) short for* HOMESTRETCH (sense 1) **6** a course or direction **7** [Informal] a stretch limousine, airliner, etc. **8** an action or effort that exceeds someone's normal limits or powers; specif., a dramatic role regarded as beyond an actor's normal range or abilities **9** [Informal] anything regarded as far-fetched or as an exaggeration *[*likening him to Einstein is a bit of a *stretch]* ☆**10** *Baseball* the act of bringing the hands together, as before the chest, and then lowering them and pausing before pitching the ball or attempting to pick off a base runner: cf. WINDUP (*n.* 2) —*adj.* **1** made of elasticized fabric so as to stretch easily and fit closely *[stretch* pants*]* **2** designating or of a vehicle, esp. a limousine, that has been customized by extending the passenger section to enlarge seating capacity —**stretch'a·bil'i·ty** *n.* —**stretch'a·ble** *adj.*

stretch·er (strech'ər) *n.* **1** a person or thing that stretches; specif., *a)* a brace or tie used to extend or support a framework; crosspiece *b)* a brick or stone laid lengthwise in a wall *c)* any of several framelike devices used for stretching and shaping cloth, garments, curtains, etc. **2** *a)* a light frame covered with canvas, etc. and used for carrying the sick, injured, or dead; litter *b)* any similar device, as a wheeled cot used in ambulances —*vt.* to move or remove by means of a stretcher *[*the injured player was *stretchered* off the field*]*

stretch·er-bear·er (-ber'ər) *n.* a person who helps carry a stretcher, esp. in military combat

stretch mark a streak or wrinkle that forms in the skin, esp. of the abdomen, hips, or thighs, after the dermis has been stretched excessively in a short period of time due to pregnancy, obesity, etc.: *usually used in pl.*

☆**stretch·out** (strech'out') *n.* a stretching or extending; specif., in business or industry, *a)* the practice of requiring workers to do more work with little or no increase in pay *b)* the practice of extending the time allotted for producing a given output

stretch·y (-ē) *adj.* **stretch'i·er, stretch'i·est** **1** that can be stretched; elastic **2** tending to stretch too far

stret·to (stret'ō) *n., pl.* **-tos** or **-ti** (-ē) ⟦It < L *strictus,* tight, narrow: see STRICT⟧ *Music* **1** in a fugue, the following of the voices in close succession, esp. in the closing section **2** any concluding passage performed with a climactic increase in speed: also **stret'ta** (-ə), *pl.* **-tas** or **-te** (-ā)

streu·sel (stro͞o'səl, stroi'-; -zəl) *n.* ⟦Ger, lit., something strewn < MHG *ströusel* < *ströuwen,* to strew < OHG *strewen:* see fol.⟧ a crumbly topping, as for coffeecake, made with flour, butter, sugar, and cinnamon

strew (stro͞o) *vt.* **strewed, strewn** or **strewed, strew'ing** ⟦ME *strewen* < OE *streawian,* akin to Ger *streuen* < IE **streu-* < base **ster-,* to extend, stretch out, strew > STRAW, L *struere,* to pile up⟧ **1** to cover over (a surface) *with* something **2** to scatter (things) over or about a surface **3** to lie scattered over or about (a surface)

stri·a (strī'ə) *n., pl.* **stri'ae** (-ē) ⟦L: for IE base see STRIKE⟧ **1** a narrow groove or channel **2** any of a number of parallel lines, stripes, bands, furrows, etc.; specif., *a)* any of the cylindrical fibers in voluntary muscles *b)* any of the parallel lines on glaciated surfaces or crystal faces *c)* any of the luminous bands in an electric discharge through a gas

stri·ate (strī'āt'; *for adj., usually,* -it) *vt.* **-at'ed, -at'ing** ⟦< L *striatus,* grooved, furrowed, pp. of *striare,* to groove, channel < *stria:* see prec.⟧ to mark with striae; stripe, band, furrow, etc. —*adj.* marked with striae: said esp. of muscles which control the skeleton: usually **stri'at'ed**

stri·a·tion (strī ā'shən) *n.* **1** the condition of having striae **2** the arrangement of striae **3** STRIA

strick (strik) *n.* ⟦ME *strik,* prob. < MDu or LowG: MDu *stric* (or MLowG *strik*), rope⟧ any of the bast fibers, as of flax or hemp, made ready to be drawn into sliver form

strick·en (strik'ən) *vt., vi. alt. pp. of* STRIKE —*adj.* **1** struck or wounded, as by a missile **2** afflicted or affected, as by something painful or very distressing *[a child stricken* with polio, a *stricken* conscience*]* **3** having the contents level with the top of a container

strick·le (strik'əl) *n.* ⟦ME *strikile* < OE *stricel* < base in *strican,* to STRIKE⟧ **1** a stick used to level the top of a measure of grain **2** a tool used for sharpening a scythe, etc. **3** *Metallurgy* a bevel-edged finishing tool used in shaping molds —*vt.* **-led, -ling** to use a strickle on

strict (strikt) *adj.* ⟦L *strictus,* pp. of *stringere,* to draw tight, compress < IE **streig-,* stiff, taut, a rope < base **(s)ter-,* rigid > STARE⟧ **1** exact or precise; not loose, vague, or broad *[a strict* translation*]* **2** perfect; absolute; entire *[*the *strict* truth*]* **3** *a)* following or enforcing a rule or rules with great care; punctilious *b)* closely enforced or rigidly maintained *c)* disciplining rigorously or severely **4** [Obs.] *a)* close; tight *b)* narrow **5** *Bot.* stiff and upright; erect —**strict'ly** *adv.* —**strict'ness** *n.*

strict construction judicial interpretation of a law based on a literal reading of it or on faithfulness to its original intent; specif., ORIGINALISM —**strict constructionist**

stric·tion (strik'shən) *n.* ⟦L *strictio:* see STRICT⟧ the act of drawing tight; constriction

strict liability absolute liability of a manufacturer or seller of a defective product causing injury or damage, despite showing exercise of due care

stric·ture (strik'chər) *n.* ⟦ME *strictture* < L *strictura* < *strictus:* see STRICT⟧ **1** sharp adverse criticism; censure **2** a limiting or restricting condition; restriction **3** [Obs.] strictness **4** *Med.* an abnormal narrowing of a passage in the body; stenosis —**stric'tured** *adj.*

stride (strīd) *vi.* **strode, strid'den, strid'ing** ⟦ME *striden* < OE *stridan,* akin to Ger *streiten,* to quarrel < IE **streidh-* < base **(s)ter-,* to be stiff, rigid > STARE, STARVE⟧ **1** to walk with long steps, esp. in a vigorous or swaggering manner **2** to take a single, long step (esp. *over* something) —*vt.* **1** to take a single, long step in passing over (an obstacle, etc.) **2** to walk with long steps along or through [to *stride* the street] **3** [Obs.] to sit or stand astride of; straddle —*n.* **1** the act of striding **2** *a)* a long step in walking or running *b)* the distance covered by such a step **3** *a)* any single forward movement by a four-legged animal, completed when the legs return to their original relative positions *b)* the distance covered in such a movement **4** a manner of running; gait **5** [*usually pl.*] progress; advancement [to make rapid *strides*] —*adj. Jazz* designating or of a style of piano playing in which the left hand alternates rhythmically between a strong bass note and middle-range chords —☆**hit one's stride** to reach one's normal speed or level of efficiency —**take in (one's) stride** to cope with (a difficult task or challenge) without hesitation, disruption, overreaction, etc. —**strid′er** *n.*

stri·dent (strīd′'nt) *adj.* ⟦L *stridens,* prp. of *stridere,* to make a grating noise, rasp < IE echoic base *(s)trei- > Gr *trizein,* to chirp, screech, L *strix,* screech owl⟧ **1** harsh-sounding; shrill; grating **2** characterized by harsh, irritating insistence —**SYN.** VOCIFEROUS —**stri′den·cy** *n.* —**stri′dent·ly** *adv.*

stri·dor (strī′dər, -dôr′) *n.* ⟦L < *stridere:* see prec.⟧ **1** a strident sound **2** *Med.* a harsh, high-pitched whistling sound, produced in breathing by an obstruction in the bronchi, trachea, or larynx

strid·u·late (strij′ə lāt′) *vi.* **-lat′ed, -lat′ing** ⟦< ModL *stridulatus,* pp. of *stridulare* < L *stridulus:* see fol.⟧ to make a shrill grating or chirping sound by rubbing certain body parts together, as certain insects do —**strid′u·la′tion** *n.* —**strid′u·la·to′ry** (-lə tôr′ē) *adj.*

strid·u·lous (-ləs) *adj.* ⟦L *stridulus* < *stridere:* see STRIDENT⟧ making a shrill grating or chirping sound: also **strid′u·lant**

strife (strīf) *n.* ⟦ME *strif* < OFr *estrif:* see STRIVE⟧ **1** the act of striving or vying with another; contention or competition **2** the act or state of fighting or quarreling, esp. bitterly; struggle; conflict **3** [Archaic] strong endeavor —**SYN.** DISCORD

strig·il (strij′əl) *n.* ⟦L *strigilis:* see STRIKE⟧ an instrument of bone, metal, etc. used by the ancient Greeks and Romans for scraping the skin during a bath

stri·gose (strī′gōs′, stri gōs′) *adj.* ⟦ModL *strigosus* < *striga,* stiff bristle < L, furrow: for IE base see fol.⟧ **1** *Bot.* having stiff hairs or bristles, as some leaves **2** *Zool.* having fine, close-set grooves or streaks

strike (strīk) *vt.* **struck, struck** or occas. (but for *vt.* 11 commonly and for *vt.* 8 & 15 usually) **strick′en, strik′ing** ⟦ME *striken,* to proceed, flow, strike with rod or sword < OE *strican,* to go, proceed, advance, akin to Ger *streichen* < IE *streig- < base *ster-, a streak, strip, to stroke > L *stringere,* to couch, *strigilis,* scraper, Ger *strahl,* ray⟧ **1** to hit with the hand or a tool, weapon, etc.; smite; specif., *a)* to give a blow to; hit with force [to *strike* a nail with a hammer] *b)* to give (a blow, etc.) *c)* to remove, knock off, etc. by or as by a blow [to *strike* a gun from someone's hand] *d)* to make or impress by stamping, punching, printing, etc. [to *strike* coins in a mint] *e)* to pierce or penetrate [*struck* in the head by a bullet] *f)* to harpoon or shoot (a whale) *g)* to hook (a fish that has risen to the bait) by a pull on the line *h)* to seize (the bait) (said of a fish) **2** *a)* to produce (a tone or chord) by hitting a key or keys or touching a string or strings on a musical instrument *b)* to touch the strings of (a musical instrument) *c)* to make contact with (a key on a typewriter, computer keyboard, etc.) **3** to signal (a particular time, esp. the moment when a new hour begins): said of a clock [the clock *struck* twelve] **4** to cause to come into violent or forceful contact; specif., *a)* to cause to hit something [to *strike* one's head on a beam] *b)* to thrust (a weapon, implement, etc.) in or into something *c)* to bring forcefully into contact [to *strike* cymbals together] *d)* to cause to ignite by friction [to *strike* a match] **5** *a)* to produce (a light, etc.) by friction *b)* to make (an arc) in an arc lamp **6** to come into violent or forceful contact with; crash into; hit [the stone *struck* a head] **7** *a)* to wound with the fangs (said of snakes) *b)* to attack **8** to afflict, as with disease, pain, or death **9** to come into contact with; specif., *a)* to fall on; shine on [light *striking* the wall] *b)* to catch or reach (the ear) (said of a sound) ☆*c)* to come upon; arrive at [the bus *struck* the main road] *d)* to make (a path, trail, etc.) as one goes along *e)* to notice, find, or hit upon suddenly or unexpectedly ☆*f)* to discover, as after drilling or prospecting [to *strike* oil] *g)* to appear to [the sight that *struck* my eyes] **10** to affect as if by contact, a blow, etc.; specif., *a)* to come into the mind of; occur to [an idea *struck* me] *b)* to be attractive to or impress (someone's fancy, sense of humor, etc.) *c)* to seem to [an idea that *strikes* me as silly] *d)* to cause to become suddenly [to be *struck* dumb] *e)* to influence, inspire, or overcome suddenly with strong feeling [to be *struck* with amazement] *f)* to cause (a feeling, emotion, etc.) to come suddenly; arouse [to *strike* terror to the heart] **11** to remove or expunge (*from* a list, minutes, record, etc.) **12** *a)* to make and ratify (a bargain, agreement, truce, etc.) *b)* to arrive at by figuring, estimating, etc. [to *strike* a balance] **13** *a)* to lower or haul down (a sail, flag, etc.), as in surrendering (sailors formerly *struck* sails in protest of grievances) *b)* to take down (a tent, etc.) *c)* to abandon (a camp) as by taking down tents **14** ⟦from *vt.* 13*a* via obs. sense "to put (tools) out of use" in protest of grievances⟧ to refuse to continue to work at (a factory, company, etc.) until certain demands are met **15** *a)* [Obs.] to stroke or smooth *b)* to level (a measure of grain, sand mold, etc.) by stroking the top with a straight instrument; strickle **16** to assume (an attitude, pose, etc.) **17** *a)* to send down or put forth (roots) (said of plants, etc.) *b)* to cause (cuttings, etc.) to take root **18** [Obs.] to wage (battle) **19** ⟦cf. *vt.* 13⟧ *Theater a)* to dismantle and remove (scenery or a set) *b)* to remove the scenery of (a play) *c)* to turn (a light) down or off —*vi.* **1** to deliver a blow or blows **2** to aim a blow or blows [to *strike* in vain at a ball] **3** *a)* to attack [the enemy *struck* at dawn] *b)* to take part in a fight or struggle (*for* some objective) **4** *a)* to make a sound or sounds as by being struck (said of a bell, clock, etc.) *b)* to be announced by the striking of a bell, chime, etc. (said of the time) **5** *a)* to make sudden and violent contact; hit; collide (*against, on,* or *upon*) *b)* to be noticed; have an effect **6** to ignite or be capable of igniting, as a match **7** to seize or snatch at a bait: said of a fish **8** to make a darting movement in an attempt to inflict a wound: said of a snake, tiger, etc. **9** to penetrate or pierce (*to, through,* etc.) **10** to come suddenly or unexpectedly; fall, light, etc. (*on* or *upon*) [to *strike* on the right combination] **11** to haul down one's flag in token of surrender **12** to refuse to continue to work until certain demands are met; go on strike **13** to send out roots; take root: said of a plant **14** to begin, advance, or proceed, esp. in a new way or direction; turn **15** to move or pass quickly; dart ☆**16** *U.S. Navy* to be in training to qualify for (*for* a specified rating) —*n.* **1** the act of striking; blow; specif., a military attack [an air *strike*] **2** STRICKLE **3** *a)* a concerted refusal by employees to go on working, in an attempt to force an employer to grant certain demands, as for higher wages, better working conditions, etc. *b)* any similar refusal by a person or group of people to do something, undertaken as a form of protest [a prisoner's hunger *strike,* a buyers' *strike*] **4** the discovery of a rich deposit of oil, coal, minerals, etc. ☆**5** any sudden success, esp. one bringing large financial return **6** ☆*a)* the pull on the line by a fish seizing or snatching at bait *b)* the pull that a fisherman gives the line to engage a baited hook in a fish's mouth **7** the number of coins, medals, etc. struck at one time **8** the part of a timepiece that strikes **9** the metal piece on a doorjamb, into which the latch fits when the door is shut: also **strike plate** ☆**10** *Baseball* a pitched ball that is struck at but missed, declared within the strike zone but not struck at, or hit foul but not caught: the batter is out after three strikes but the third strike cannot be a foul ball unless it was on a bunt attempt or unless it was a foul tip that was caught by the catcher ☆**11** *Bowling a)* the act of knocking down all the pins on the first bowl *b)* the score made in this way **12** *Geol., Mining* the trace of a rock bed, fault, or vein on the horizontal, at right angles to the direction of dip —**be struck with** to be attracted to or impressed by —☆**have two strikes against one** [Informal] to be at a decided disadvantage: from the three strikes permitted a batter in baseball —**(out) on strike** striking: see STRIKE (*vi.* 12) —**strike down 1** to cause to fall by a blow, etc.; knock down **2** to do away with; undo, cancel, etc. **3** to have a disastrous or disabling effect upon: said of illness, etc. —**strike dumb** to amaze; astound; astonish —**strike hands** [Archaic] **1** to show agreement by clasping hands **2** to make a bargain, contract, etc. —**strike home 1** to deliver an effective or crippling blow **2** to achieve a desired or significant effect —☆**strike it rich 1** to discover a rich deposit of ore, oil, etc. **2** to become rich or successful suddenly —**strike off 1** to separate, or remove, by or as by a blow or cut **2** to remove from a record, list, etc.; erase; expunge **3** to print —**strike out 1** to make by hitting or striking **2** to originate; produce; devise **3** to aim or strike a blow; hit out **4** to remove from a record, etc.; erase; expunge **5** to begin moving or acting; start out ☆**6** *Baseball a)* to be put out as the result of three strikes *b)* to put (a batter) out by pitching three strikes ☆**7** [Informal] to be a failure —**strike up 1** to begin or cause to begin playing, singing, sounding, etc. **2** to begin (a friendship, conversation, etc.) **3** to emboss (metal, decorative figures, etc.)

strike·bound (strīk′bound′) *adj.* closed or hampered because of striking employees [a *strikebound* plant]

strike·break·er (-brāk′ər) *n.* **1** a person who is active in trying to break up a workers' strike, as by intimidating strikers **2** SCAB (*n.* 4*b*) —**strike′break′ing** *n.*

strike fault *Geol.* a fault running parallel to the strike of the strata that it cuts

☆**strike·out** (-out′) *n. Baseball* an out made by a batter charged with three strikes

strike price in an option contract, the specified price at which a stock, commodity, etc. may be bought or sold; the price at which a call or put can be exercised profitably: also **striking price**

strik·er (strī′kər) *n.* **1** a person who strikes; specif., a worker who is on strike **2** a thing that strikes, as the clapper in a bell, the striking device in a clock, etc. ☆**3** *a) U.S. Army* an enlisted person doing extra-duty work for an officer for extra pay *b) U.S. Navy* an enlisted person who is in training to qualify for a rating **4** *Soccer* the forward and main scorer of a soccer team

☆**strike zone** *Baseball* the area over home plate, by rule between the batter's knees and armpits, through which the ball must be pitched for a strike to be called by the umpire

strik·ing (strī′kiŋ) *adj.* **1** that strikes or is on strike **2** very noticeable or impressive; specif., very attractive in appearance [a *striking* blonde] —**SYN.** NOTICEABLE —**strik′ing·ly** *adv.*

Stri·mon (strē môn′) *Gr. name for* STRUMA

Strind·berg (strind′bərg, strin′-; *Swed* strin′bar′y'), **(Johan) August** 1849-1912; Swed. dramatist & novelist

Strine (strīn) *n.* ⟦< (AU)STRALIAN: phonetic sp. of caricatured Austral dial. pronun.⟧ [Austral. & N.Z. Informal] the variety of English spoken in Australia

string (striŋ) *n.* ⟦ME *streng* < OE, akin to Ger *strang:* see STRONG⟧ **1** *a)* fiber twisted into a thin line, used for tying, pulling, fastening, etc.; a type of slender cord or thick thread *b)* a length of this *c)* a narrow strip of leather or cloth for fastening shoes, clothing, etc.; lace [apron *strings*] **2** a length or loop of like things threaded, strung, or hung on a string [a *string* of pearls] 3 *a)* a number of things arranged in a line or row [a *string* of houses] *b)* any series of things in close or uninterrupted succession [a *string* of victories] 4 *a)* a number of racehorses belonging to one owner *b)* a number of business enterprises under one ownership or management [a *string* of gift shops] ☆5 any of the groupings of players on a team according to ability: the **first string** is more skilled than the **second string**, etc. 6 *a)* a slender cord of wire, gut, nylon, etc. stretched on a musical instrument and bowed, plucked, or struck to make a musical sound *b)* [*pl.*] all the stringed instruments of an orchestra, quintet, etc. played with a bow *c)* [*pl.*] the players of such instruments 7 a strong, slender organ, structure, etc. resembling a string; specif., *a)* [Archaic] an animal nerve or tendon *b)* a fiber of a plant, esp. one connecting the two halves of a bean pod ☆8 [Informal] a condition, limitation, or proviso, typically an undesirable one, attached to a plan, offer, donation, etc.: *usually used in pl.* [his "favors" always come with *strings* attached] 9 *Archit.* *a)* one of the inclined boards under a staircase, notched to support the treads and risers *b)* STRINGCOURSE ☆10 *Billiards* *a)* a line indicated but unmarked across the table at one end, from behind which the cue ball must be played after being out of play (in full **string line**) *b)* the act of stroking the cue ball so that it rebounds from the far cushion to stop as close as possible to the string line, for determining the order of play 11 *Particle Physics* in string theory, any of various extremely tiny, one-dimensional, vibrating stringlike particles thought to be the basic units of matter —*vt.* **strung, string′ing** 1 to fit or provide with a string or strings [to *string* a longbow, a violin, etc.] 2 to thread or bead on a string 3 to tie, pull, fasten, hang, lace, etc. with a string or strings 4 to adjust or tune the strings of (a musical instrument) by tightening, etc. 5 to make tense, nervous, or keyed (*up*) 6 to remove the strings from (beans, etc.) 7 to arrange or set forth in a row or successive series 8 to stretch or extend like a string [to *string* a cable] —*vi.* 1 to form into a string or strings 2 to stretch out in a line; extend; stretch; move or progress in a string 3 to serve as a stringer (*for* a newspaper, magazine, etc.) 4 *Billiards* LAG[1] (*vi.* 4) —*adj.* *Music* 1 of or composed for stringed instruments [*string* quartet] 2 STRINGED —**on a (or the) string** completely under someone's control or subject to someone's whims —**pull strings** 1 to get someone to use influence in one's behalf, often secretly 2 to direct action of others, often secretly —☆**string along** [Informal] to go along or agree —☆**string someone along** [Informal] to dupe or keep in an uncertain state, as by continual encouragement or false promises —**string up** [Slang] to kill by hanging —**string′less** *adj.*

string band a band of musicians playing folk or country music on such stringed instruments as the guitar, banjo, and violin —**string′-band′** *adj.*

string bass DOUBLE BASS

☆**string bean** 1 SNAP BEAN 2 [Informal] a tall, skinny person

string bikini a bikini having minimal covering parts held in place by thin, stringlike ties

string·board (striŋ′bôrd′) *n.* a board placed along the side of a staircase to cover the ends of the steps

string·course (-kôrs′) *n.* a decorative, horizontal course of brick or stone set in the wall of a building

stringed (striŋd) *adj.* designating a musical instrument, as the violin, guitar, zither, or harp, often made of wood, in which the tone or tones are produced by a vibrating string or strings: cf. STRING (*n.* 6)

strin·gen·cy (strin′jən sē) *n., pl.* **-cies** the quality or state of being stringent; strictness; severity

strin·gen·do (strin jen′dō) *adj., adv.* ⟦It < *stringere,* to tighten, bind < L: see STRICT⟧ *Musical Direction* with accelerated tempo, as toward a climax

strin·gent (strin′jənt) *adj.* ⟦L *stringens,* prp. of *stringere,* to draw tight: see STRICT⟧ 1 rigidly controlled, enforced, etc.; strict; severe ☆2 tight in loan or investment money [a *stringent* money market] 3 compelling; convincing [*stringent* reason] —**strin′gent·ly** *adv.* —**strin′gent·ness** *n.*

string·er (striŋ′ər) *n.* 1 a person or thing that strings 2 *a)* a long, heavy piece of lumber used as a horizontal connector of posts in a framework, often, specif., one that supports a floor *b)* STRING (*n.* 9*a*) *c)* STRINGPIECE 3 a long, lightweight structural member of an airplane fuselage, rocket, etc. ☆4 a string or metal line with clips on which caught fish are strung ☆5 a person serving as a part-time, local correspondent for a newspaper, magazine, etc. ☆6 ⟦see STRING, *n.* 5⟧ a person of a specified ranked: used in comb. [second-*stringer*]

string·halt (striŋ′hôlt′) *n.* a condition in horses causing one or both hind legs to jerk spasmodically in walking —**string′halt′ed** *adj.*

string·piece (-pēs′) *n.* any long, heavy piece of lumber used horizontally in building or shoring

string quartet 1 a quartet of players on stringed instruments, usually first and second violins, a viola, and a violoncello 2 a composition for such a group

☆**string theory** *Particle Physics* any theory in which a STRING (*n.* 11) is considered to be the basic unit of matter

☆**string tie** 1 a very narrow necktie, usually tied in a bow 2 BOLO TIE 3 any string or lace used to hold a garment in place

string·y (striŋ′ē) *adj.* **string′i·er, string′i·est** 1 like a string or strings; long, thin, wiry, sinewy, etc. 2 consisting of strings or fibers 3 having tough fibers [*stringy* meat, celery, etc.] 4 forming strings; viscous; ropy [*stringy* molasses] —**string′i·ness** *n.*

strip[1] (strip) *vt.* **stripped, strip′ping** ⟦ME *strepen* < OE *stripan,* akin to *streifen,* to strip off < IE **streub-* < base **ster-,* to streak, stroke > STRIKE⟧ 1 to remove (the clothing or covering) of or from (a person); make naked; undress 2 to deprive or dispossess (a person or thing) of (honors, titles, attributes, etc.) 3 to despoil of wealth, property, etc.; plunder; rob 4 *a)* to pull, tear, or take off (a covering, skin, etc.) from (a person or thing) *b)* to pull or tear (an object) away from (someone) [to *strip* an opponent of the football] 5 to make bare or clear by removing fruit, growth, removable parts, etc. [to *strip* a room of furniture] 6 to take apart (a firearm, etc.) piece by piece, as for cleaning; dismantle 7 to break or damage the thread of (a nut, bolt, or screw) or the teeth of (a gear) 8 to remove the last milk from (a cow) with a stroking movement of the thumb and forefinger 9 to remove the large central rib from (tobacco leaves) or the leaf from (the stalk) —*vi.* 1 to take off all clothing; undress ☆2 to perform a striptease —☆*n.* *short for* STRIPTEASE

SYN.—**strip** implies the pulling or tearing off of clothing, outer covering, etc. and often connotes forcible or even violent action and total deprivation [to *strip* paper off a wall, *stripped* of sham]; **denude** implies that the thing stripped is left exposed or naked [land *denuded* of vegetation]; **divest** implies the taking away of something with which one has been clothed or invested [an official *divested* of authority]; **bare** simply implies an uncovering or laying open to view [to *bare* one's head in reverence]; **dismantle** implies the act of stripping a house, ship, etc. of all of its furniture or equipment [a *dismantled* factory]

strip[2] (strip) *n.* ⟦altered (infl. by prec.) < STRIPE⟧ 1 a long, narrow piece, as of land, ribbon, wood, etc. ☆2 an area of dense commercial development, often of a specified kind, along a thoroughfare [a fast-food *strip*] ☆3 *short for* COMIC STRIP 4 *short for* AIRSTRIP 5 *Philately* a vertical or horizontal row of three or more attached stamps —*vt.* to cut or tear into strips

strip cropping crop planting in which wide rows of heavy-rooted plants are alternated with loose-rooted plants so as to lessen erosion, as on a hillside

stripe (strīp) *n.* ⟦< MLowG & MDu *strīpe* < IE **streib-* < base **ster-* > STRIP[2]⟧ 1 a long, narrow band, mark, or streak, differing in color, texture, or material from the surrounding area 2 [*often pl.*] a fabric or garment with a pattern of parallel stripes 3 a strip of cloth or braid, as a chevron, bar, or curve, worn on the sleeve as of a military uniform to indicate rank or length of service 4 a distinctive type, kind, or sort [graduates of all *stripes* are entering the workforce] 5 [Archaic] *a)* a stroke with a whip, etc. *b)* a long welt on the skin —*vt.* **striped, strip′ing** to mark with a stripe or stripes —☆**earn one's stripes** ⟦see *n.* 3⟧ [Informal] to earn, through experience and accomplishments, one's position of authority, one's fame, etc.

striped (strīpt, strī′pid) *adj.* having a stripe or stripes

☆**striped bass** (bas) a silvery, dark-striped, food and game bass (*Morone saxatilis*) of the same family (Percichthyidae) as white bass, found along the coasts of North America: it goes up rivers to spawn

strip·er (strī′pər) *n.* 1 [Mil. Slang] any enlisted person, or a naval officer, who wears a STRIPE (*n.* 3) or stripes: usually in hyphenated compounds referring to a specified number of stripes [a four-*striper*] 2 STRIPED BASS

strip·ling (strip′liŋ) *n.* ⟦ME *strypling,* lit., one slim as a strip⟧ a grown boy; youth passing into manhood

☆**strip mall** a kind of shopping center consisting of a series of adjoining shops typically with direct access to each from a common parking area in front

☆**strip mining** a method of mining, esp. for coal, by laying bare a mineral deposit near the surface of the earth: cf. OPEN-PIT MINING

stripped-down (stript′doun′) *adj.* reduced to the essential elements; specif., *a)* basic; minimal *b)* simple; unadorned

strip·per (strip′ər) *n.* 1 a person or thing that strips ☆2 a person who does a striptease

strip-search (strip′surch′) *vt.* to search (a person) by requiring removal of the clothes —*n.* such a search Also **strip search**

strip steak a porterhouse steak with no bone or filet

stript (stript) *vt., vi. rare pt. & pp. of* STRIP[1]

☆**strip·tease** (strip′tēz′) *n.* an erotic performance, as in a burlesque show, in which the performer undresses slowly, usually to the accompaniment of music —**strip′tease′** *vi.* **-teased′, -teas′ing** —**strip′teas′er** *n.*

strip·y (strī′pē) *adj.* **strip′i·er, strip′i·est** characterized by, like, or marked with stripes

strive (strīv) *vi.* **strove** or **strived, striv·en** (striv′ən) or **strived, striv′ing** ⟦ME *striven* < OFr *estriver,* to quarrel, contend < *estrif,* effort < Gmc, as in MHG *striben,* obs. Du *strijven,* to strive, struggle < IE **streibh-* (> Gr *striphnos,* hard, solid) < base **(s)ter-,* rigid > STARE⟧ 1 to make great efforts; try very hard [to *strive* to win] 2 to be in conflict; struggle; contend; fight [to *strive* against oppression] 3 [Obs.] to compete; vie —*SYN.* TRY —**striv′er** *n.*

strobe (strōb) *n.* 1 *short for* STROBOSCOPE (sense 1) 2 an electronically regulated discharge tube that can emit extremely rapid, brief, and brilliant flashes of light: used in photography, the theater, etc.: also **strobe light** —*adj.* STROBOSCOPIC

stro·bi·la (strō bī′lə) *n., pl.* **-lae** (-lē) ⟦ModL < Gr *strobilē,* plug of lint twisted into oval shape < *strobilos:* see fol.⟧ *Zool.* 1 the main, jointed body of a tapeworm 2 the attached stage of polyp scyphozoan jellyfishes during which the immature jellyfishes are released by transverse budding —**stro·bi′lar** *adj.* —**stro′bi·la′tion** (-bə lā′shən) *n.*

stro·bile (strō′bil′, -bil; strä′bil) *n.* ⟦< Fr or LL: Fr < LL *strobilus* < Gr *strobilos,* anything twisted, pine cone < base of *strephein,* to twist: see STROPHE⟧ *Bot.* CONE (*n.* 3)

stro·bi·lus (strō bī′ləs) *n., pl.* **-li′** (-lī′) ⟦ModL < LL: see prec.⟧ 1 CONE (*n.* 3) 2 STROBILA (sense 1)

stro·bo·scope (strō′bə skōp′; *occas.* sträb′ə-) ***n.*** ⟦< Gr *strobos*, a twisting around (for IE base see STROPHE) + -SCOPE⟧ **1** an instrument for studying periodic or varying motion; specif., a device using a strobe light to illuminate a moving body, machine, etc. very briefly at frequent intervals **2** STROBE (sense 2) —**stro′bo·scop′ic** (-skäp′ik) ***adj.*** —**stro′bo·scop′i·cal·ly** ***adv.***

strode (strōd) ***vi., vt.*** *pt. of* STRIDE

stro·ga·noff (strō′gə nôf′, strô′-) ***adj.*** ⟦prob. after Count S. *Stroganov* (1794-1881), Russ official & gourmet⟧ cooked with sour cream, onions, mushrooms, etc.: used postpositively [beef *stroganoff*] —***n.*** a dish cooked this way

stroke (strōk) ***n.*** ⟦ME, akin to Ger *streich*, a stroke, OE *strican:* see STRIKE⟧ **1** a striking of one thing against another; blow or impact of an ax, whip, etc. **2** *a)* a sudden action resulting in a powerful or destructive effect, as if from a blow [a *stroke* of lightning] *b)* a sudden occurrence, often a pleasant one [a *stroke* of luck] **3** a sudden cerebrovascular failure usually caused by arteriosclerosis, hypertension, embolism, or hemorrhage and resulting variously in impaired vision and speech, coma, convulsions, paralysis, etc. **4** *a)* a single effort to do, produce, or accomplish something, esp. a successful effort *b)* something accomplished by such an effort; feat *c)* a distinctive effect or touch in an artistic, esp. literary, work **5** the sound of striking, as of a clock **6** *a)* a single movement, as with some tool, club, racquet, etc. [a *stroke* of the pen, a backhand *stroke* in tennis] *b)* any of a series of repeated rhythmic motions made against water, air, etc. [the *stroke* of a swimmer, rower, etc.] *c)* a type, manner, or rate of such movement [a slow *stroke*] **7** a mark made by or as by a pen or similar marking tool **8** a beat of the heart **9** a gentle, caressing motion with the hand **10** [*pl.*] [Informal] praise, flattery, etc. offered to reassure, influence, persuade, etc. **11** *Golf* a scoring unit used to record each time the ball is hit with the head of a club **12** *Mech.* any of a series of continuous, often reciprocating, movements; specif., a single movement of a piston from one end of its range to the other, constituting a half revolution of the engine **13** *Rowing a)* the rower who sits nearest the stern and sets the rate of rowing for the others *b)* the position occupied by this rower —***vt.*** **stroked**, **strok′ing** ⟦ME *stroken* < OE *stracian*, akin to *strican:* see STRIKE⟧ **1** to draw one's hand, a tool, etc. gently over the surface of, as in caressing or smoothing **2** to mark with strokes or draw a line through: often with *out* **3** to hit; esp., to hit (a ball) in playing tennis, golf, pool, etc. **4** [Informal] to flatter, pay special attention to, etc. in an effort to influence, reassure, persuade, etc. **5** [Slang] to manipulate in masturbation: somewhat vulgar **6** *Rowing* to set the rate of rowing for (a crew) or for the crew of (a boat) —***vi.*** **1** to hit a ball in playing tennis, golf, etc. **2** *Rowing* to act as stroke (*for*) —***adj.*** [Slang] of or for masturbating: somewhat vulgar [a *stroke* magazine] —**keep stroke** to make strokes in rhythm

stroke oar **1** the oar set nearest the stern of a boat **2** STROKE (*n.* 13)

stroke play *Golf* the most common form of competitive play, in which the score is calculated by counting the total number of strokes taken; medal play: distinguished from MATCH PLAY

stroll (strōl) ***vi.*** ⟦Early ModE *strowl*, prob. < Swiss Ger dial. *strolen*, var. of *strolchen*, to stroll < Ger *strolch*, vagabond, rascal, altered < It *astrologo*, astrologer⟧ **1** to walk in an idle, leisurely manner; saunter **2** to go from place to place; wander —***vt.*** to stroll along or through (a street, the countryside, etc.) —***n.*** the act of strolling; leisurely walk

stroll·er (strō′lər) ***n.*** **1** a person who saunters **2** *a)* a wanderer; esp., an itinerant actor *b)* a vagrant ☆**3** a light, chairlike baby carriage, usually collapsible, with openings for the legs at the front

stro·ma (strō′mə) ***n.***, *pl.* **-ma·ta** (-tə) ⟦ModL < L, coverlet, bed covering < Gr *strōma*, mattress, bed: for IE base see STREW⟧ **1** *Anat. a)* the connective tissue forming the framework or matrix of an organ or part *b)* the colorless framework of a red blood corpuscle or other cell **2** *Bot.* in some fungi, a cushionlike mass of hyphae, frequently having fruiting bodies embedded in it —**stro′mal** ***adj.***, **stro·mat′ic** (-mat′ik)

stro·mat·o·lite (strō mat′ə līt′) ***n.*** ⟦< Ger *stromatolith* < ModL *stromat-*, prec.: see -LITE⟧ a laminated, sedimentary rock structure formed primarily in Precambrian shallow pools by mats of sticky, blue-green algae which trapped layers of silt, esp. of calcium carbonate: these wavy or round formations serve as evidence for dating the first life forms on earth —**stro·mat′o·lit′ic** (-lit′ik) ***adj.***

strom·bo·li (sträm bō′lē) ***n.*** ⟦< ?⟧ ☆an Italian-American dish consisting of meat, cheese, etc. rolled into flattened bread dough, baked, and served typically in slices

Strom·bo·li (strôm′bô lē′) **1** northernmost of the Lipari Islands, north of Sicily, *c.* 5 sq mi (13 sq km) **2** active volcano on this island: 3,040 ft (927 m)

strong (strôŋ) ***adj.*** ⟦ME < OE *strang*, akin to ON *strangr*, strong, severe, Ger *streng*, severe < IE base **strenk-*, **streng-*, tense, taut > STRING, Gr *strangos*, twisted, L *stringere*, to draw taut⟧ **1** *a)* physically powerful; having great muscular strength; robust *b)* in a healthy and sound condition; hale; hearty **2** *a)* performing well or in a normal manner [a *strong* heart] *b)* not easily affected or upset [a *strong* stomach] **3** morally powerful; having strength of character or will **4** *a)* intellectually powerful; able to think vigorously and clearly *b)* having special competence or ability (*in* or *on* a specified area) [a student who is *strong* in botany] **5** governing or leading with firm authority; authoritarian **6** *a)* powerfully made, built, or constituted; tough; firm; durable [a *strong* wall, a *strong* fabric] *b)* holding firmly; tenacious [a *strong* grip] *c)* binding tightly [*strong* glue] **7** *a)* hard to capture; able to resist and endure attack [a *strong* fort] *b)* not easily defeated; formidable [a *strong* opponent] *c)* not easily dislodged; deep-rooted [*strong* prejudice] **8** having many resources; powerful in wealth, numbers, supplies, etc. [a *strong* nation] **9** of a specified number; reaching a certain degree in number or strength [a task force 6,000 *strong*] **10** having a powerful effect; drastic [*strong* measures] **11** having a large amount of its essential quality; not weak or diluted [*strong* coffee] **12** affecting the senses powerfully; intense [a *strong* light, *strong* smell, etc.] **13** having an offensive taste or smell; rank [*strong* butter] **14** firm and loud [a *strong* voice] **15** intense in degree or quality; not mild; specif., *a)* ardent; passionate; warm [*strong* affection] *b)* forceful; persuasive; cogent [*strong* reasons] *c)* felt deeply; pronounced; decided [a *strong* opinion] *d)* vigorously active; zealous [a *strong* socialist] *e)* vigorous, forthright, and unambiguous, often offensively so [*strong* language] *f)* clear; distinct; marked [a *strong* resemblance] *g)* receiving or showing emphasis or stress [a *strong* accent or beat] **16** moving rapidly and with force [a *strong* wind] **17** having high powers of magnification [*strong* lenses] **18** tending toward higher prices: said of a stock or stock market **19** *Chem.* having a high ion concentration, as certain acids and bases **20** *Gram.* in English and other Germanic languages, designating or of verbs that express variation in tense chiefly by internal change of a syllabic vowel rather than by the addition of inflectional endings; irregular (Ex.: *swim, swam, swum; drive, drove, driven*): cf. WEAK (sense 15) —***adv.*** in a strong manner; greatly, severely, vigorously, etc. —☆**come on strong** [Informal] to be socially assertive or aggressive —**going strong** [Informal] thriving; flourishing [a family business still *going strong*] —**strong′ish** ***adj.*** —**strong′ly** ***adv.***

☆**strong-arm** (strôŋ′ärm′) [Informal] ***adj.*** using physical force or violence —***vt.*** to use physical force or violence upon, esp. in robbing

strong·box (-bäks′) ***n.*** a heavily made box or safe for storing valuables

strong breeze a wind whose speed is 25 to 31 miles per hour: see the Beaufort scale in the Reference Supplement

strong drink alcoholic liquor

strong force STRONG INTERACTION

☆**strong forward** *Basketball* POWER FORWARD

strong gale a wind whose speed is 47 to 54 miles per hour: see the Beaufort scale in the Reference Supplement

strong·hold (-hōld′) ***n.*** **1** a place having strong defenses; fortified place **2** a place where a group having certain views, attitudes, etc. is concentrated

strong interaction *Particle Physics* the short-range interaction between hadrons responsible for the force that binds the nucleus of an atom together: it is the strongest of all known forces: see WEAK INTERACTION, ELECTROMAGNETIC INTERACTION

strong·man (-man′) ***n.***, *pl.* **-men′** (-men′) **1** one who performs feats of strength, as in a circus **2** [Informal] one who rules a country with absolute power; dictator

strong-mind·ed (-mīn′did) ***adj.*** having a strong, unyielding mind or will —**strong′-mind′ed·ly** ***adv.*** —**strong′-mind′ed·ness** ***n.***

strong nuclear force STRONG INTERACTION

strong·room (-ro͞om′) ***n.*** a fortified room used for the safekeeping of valuables

☆**strong safety** *Football* a safety positioned opposite the STRONG SIDE and typically covering the tight end

☆**strong side** **1** *Basketball* the side of the court with more players **2** *Football a)* the side of an offensive formation, either left or right of the center, on which the tight end lines up *b)* the side of a defensive formation that is across the line of scrimmage from the offensive strong side —**strong′ side′** ***adj.***

strong-willed (-wild′) ***adj.*** having a strong, resolute, or obstinate will

stron·gyle (strän′jil, -jīl′) ***n.*** ⟦< ModL *Strongylus* < Gr *strongylos*, round, turned: for IE base see STRONG⟧ any of a superfamily (Strongyloidea) of nematode worms living as parasites in animals, esp. horses

stron·gy·lo·sis (strän′jə lō′sis) ***n.*** ⟦ModL: see prec. & -OSIS⟧ the condition of being infested by strongyles

stron·ti·a (strän′shə, -shē ə) ***n.*** ⟦ModL < fol.⟧ **1** the oxide of strontium, SrO, a white powder somewhat like lime **2** loosely, strontium hydroxide, $Sr(OH)_2$

stron·ti·an (-shən, -shē ən) ***n.*** ⟦after *Strontian*, Scotland, in whose lead mines it was first found⟧ strontium, esp. in the form of a compound

stron·ti·an·ite (-īt′) ***n.*** ⟦prec. + -ITE[1]⟧ a light-colored, semihard mineral, strontium carbonate, $SrCO_3$, that is an ore of strontium

stron·tic (strän′tik) ***adj.*** of strontium

stron·ti·um (strän′shəm, -shē əm; stränt′ē əm) ***n.*** ⟦ModL: see STRONTIA & -IUM; so named (1808) by Sir Humphry DAVY, who first isolated it⟧ a pale-yellow, metallic chemical element, one of the alkaline-earth metals, resembling calcium in properties and found only in combination: strontium compounds burn with a red flame and are used in fireworks: symbol, Sr; at. no. 38: a deadly radioactive isotope (**strontium-90**) is present in the fallout of nuclear explosions: see the periodic table of elements in the Reference Supplement

strop (sträp) ***n.*** ⟦ME, a band, thong, noose < OE, akin to MHG *strupfe* < early WGmc loanword < L *struppus* < Gr *strophos*, a twisted band: for IE base see STROPHE⟧ **1** *var. of* STRAP **2** a device, esp. a thick leather band, used for putting a fine edge on razors —***vt.*** **stropped**, **strop′ping** to sharpen on a strop —**strop′per** ***n.***

stro·phan·thin (strō fan′thin) ***n.*** ⟦ModL *Strophanthus*, type genus < Gr *strophos* (see prec.) + *anthos*, flower (see ANTHO-) + -IN[1]⟧ a glycoside or mixture of glycosides obtained from a tropical plant (*Strophanthus kombé*) of the dogbane family, used as a heart stimulant

stro·phe (strō′fē) ***n.*** ⟦Gr *strophē*, lit., a turning, twist < *strephein*, to turn < IE **strebh-* < base **(s)ter-*, rigid, taut > STARE⟧ **1** in the ancient Greek theater, *a)* the movement of the chorus in turning from right to left of the stage (cf. ANTISTROPHE) *b)* the part of the choric song performed during this **2** in a Pindaric ode, the stanza which is answered by the antistrophe, in the same metrical pattern **3** a stanza; esp., any of the irregular divisions of a poem —**stroph·ic** (sträf′ik, strō′fik) ***adj.***, **stroph′i·cal**

strop·py (sträp′ē) ***adj.*** **-pi·er**, **-pi·est** ⟦? shortened & altered < OBSTREPEROUS⟧ [Brit. Informal] hard to deal with or control; angry, unruly, impudent, etc.

strove (strōv) ***vi.*** *alt. pt. of* STRIVE

strow (strō) ***vt.*** **strowed**, **strown** (strōn) or **strowed**, **strow′ing** *archaic form of* STREW

struck (struk) ***vt., vi.*** *pt. & pp. of* STRIKE —***adj.*** closed or affected in some other way by a labor strike

struck jury a jury of 12 drawn from the panel of names remaining after each side has been permitted to strike out a certain number of the original list of names

struc·tur·al (struk′chər əl) ***adj.*** **1** of, having, associated with, or characterized by structure [*structural* complexity] **2** used in or suitable for construction, as of buildings [*structural* steel] **3** of, or in accordance with, structural linguistics **4** *Geol.* of or related to the structure of the earth's crust and the changes produced in it by movement; geotectonic —**struc′tur·al·ly** ***adv.***

structural formula a formula which illustrates the arrangement of the atoms and bonds in a molecule

structural gene any gene that determines the amino acid sequence of a polypeptide

struc·tur·al·ism (-iz′əm) ***n.*** **1** a movement for determining and analyzing the basic, relatively stable structural elements of a system, esp. in the behavioral sciences **2** STRUCTURAL LINGUISTICS

struc·tur·al·ist (-ist) ***n.*** a follower or advocate of structuralism, as in the analysis or application of social, economic, or linguistic theory —***adj.*** of or relating to structuralists or their theories

struc·tur·al·ize (-īz′) ***vt.*** **-ized′**, **-iz′ing** to form or organize into a structure —**struc′tur·al·i·za′tion** ***n.***

structural linguistics [*with sing. v.*] language study based on the assumptions that a language is a coherent system of formal units and that the task of linguistic study is to inquire into the nature of those units and their peculiar systematic arrangement, without reference to historical antecedents or comparison with other languages —**structural linguist**

struc·ture (struk′chər) ***n.*** ⟦ME < L *structura* < *structus*, pp. of *struere*, to heap together, arrange: see STREW⟧ **1** manner of building, constructing, or organizing **2** something built or constructed, as a building or dam **3** the arrangement or interrelation of all the parts of a whole; manner of organization or construction [the *structure* of the atom, the *structure* of society] **4** something composed of interrelated parts forming an organism or an organization —***vt.*** **-tured**, **-tur·ing** to put together systematically; construct; organize —***SYN.*** BUILDING —**struc′ture·less** ***adj.***

stru·del (strōōd′'l) ***n.*** ⟦Ger, lit., whirlpool < OHG *stredan*, to rush, bubble up < IE **sret-* < base **ser-*, to flow, gush > SERUM⟧ a kind of pastry made of a very thin sheet of dough covered as with apple slices, cherries, or a cheese mixture, then rolled up and baked

strug·gle (strug′əl) ***vi.*** **-gled**, **-gling** ⟦ME *strogelen* < ?⟧ **1** to contend or fight violently with an opponent **2** to make great efforts or attempts; strive; labor **3** to make one's way with difficulty [to *struggle* through a thicket] —***vt.*** [Rare] **1** to bring, put, do, etc. by struggling **2** to make (one's way) with difficulty —***n.*** **1** great effort or a series of efforts; violent exertion **2** conflict; strife; contention —***SYN.*** CONFLICT, TRY —**strug′gler** ***n.***

strum (strum) ***vt., vi.*** **strummed**, **strum′ming** ⟦echoic⟧ **1** to play (a guitar, banjo, etc.), esp. with long strokes across the strings and often in a casual or aimless way, or without much skill **2** to play (a tune) in this way —***n.*** the act or sound of this —**strum′mer** ***n.***

stru·ma (strōō′mə) ***n., pl.*** **-mae** (-mē) ⟦L, a scrofulous tumor < IE **streu-*: see STRUT⟧ **1** *Bot.* a cushionlike swelling on a plant organ, esp. on one side at the base of the capsule of a moss **2** *Med. a)* GOITER *b)* [Archaic] SCROFULA —**stru′mose′** (-mōs′) ***adj.***

Stru·ma (strōō′mä) river in SE Europe, flowing from W Bulgaria across NE Greece into the Aegean Sea: *c.* 220 mi (354 km)

strum·pet (strum′pit) ***n.*** ⟦ME < ?⟧ [Old-fashioned] a prostitute; harlot: now usually used with a humorous connotation

strung (struŋ) ***vt., vi.*** *pt. & pp. of* STRING —☆**strung out** [Slang] **1** suffering from the physical or mental effects of addiction to a narcotic drug **2** mentally exhausted or extremely nervous

strut (strut) ***vi.*** **strut′ted**, **strut′ting** ⟦ME *strouten*, to spread out, swell out < OE *strutian*, to stand rigid < IE **streu-* < base **(s)ter-*, stiff, rigid > STARE⟧ to walk in a vain, stiff, swaggering manner —***vt.*** **1** to provide with a strut or brace **2** to make a display of; show off —***n.*** **1** the act of strutting; vain, swaggering walk or gait **2** a brace fitted into a framework to resist pressure in the direction of its length and thereby stabilize a structure **3** a device that combines a shock absorber and its mounting plates in one assembly, used in the suspension system of a motor vehicle —**strut′ter** ***n.***

stru·thi·ous (strōō′thē əs) ***adj.*** ⟦< L *struthio* (< Gr *strouthiōn*, sparrow, ostrich) + -OUS⟧ designating or of an ostrich or ostrichlike bird

strych·nine (strik′nīn′, -nin, -nēn′) ***n.*** ⟦Fr < ModL *Strychnos* < L < Gr *strychnos*, nightshade⟧ a highly poisonous, colorless, crystalline alkaloid, $C_{21}H_{22}N_2O_2$, obtained from nux vomica and other similar plants

strych·nin·ism (-iz′əm) ***n.*** a diseased condition resulting from ingestion of strychnine

St. Thomas second largest island of the Virgin Islands of the U.S.: 31 sq mi (80 sq km)

St-Tro·pez (san trō pā′) commune and seaside resort in SE France, on the Mediterranean

Stu·art[1] (stōō′ərt, styōō′-) ***n.*** ⟦< the surname *Stuart* < ? OE *stiweard*: see STEWARD⟧ **1** a masculine name **2** name of the ruling family of Scotland (1371-1603) & of England & Scotland (1603-1714) except during the Commonwealth (1649-60)

Stu·art[2] (stōō′ərt, styōō′-) **1 Charles Edward** 1720-88; Eng. prince: grandson of James II: called *The Young Pretender, Bonnie Prince Charlie* **2 Gilbert (Charles)** 1755-1828; U.S. portrait painter **3 J(ames) E(well) B(rown)** (called *Jeb Stuart*) 1833-64; Confederate general **4 James Francis Edward** 1688-1766; Eng. prince: son of James II: called *The Old Pretender*

stub (stub) ***n.*** ⟦ME < OE *stybb*, akin to ON *stubbr*: for IE base see STOCK⟧ **1** the stump of a tree or plant **2** a short piece or length remaining after the main part has been removed or used up [the *stub* of a tail, cigar, pencil, etc.] **3** any short projection [a mere *stub* of a horn] **4** a pen having a short, blunt point **5** a short, thick nail ☆**6** the part of a ticket, bank check, etc. kept as a record after the rest has been torn off —***vt.*** **stubbed**, **stub′bing** **1** to dig or pull (weeds, etc.) out by the roots **2** to cut down, leaving only a stump **3** to clear (land) of stubs, or stumps **4** to strike (one's foot, toe, etc.) accidentally against something **5** to put out (a cigarette, cigar, etc.) by pressing the end against a surface: often with *out*

stubbed (stubd) ***adj.*** **1** like a stub; short; stubby **2** covered with stubs or stumps

stub·ble (stub′əl) ***n.*** ⟦ME *stobil* < OFr *estouble*, *stuble* < VL *stupula*, for L *stipula*, stalk, stem: see STIPULE⟧ **1** the short stumps of grain, corn, etc., collectively, left standing after harvesting **2** any short, bristly growth suggestive of this [a *stubble* of beard] —**stub′bly** ***adj.***

stub·born (stub′ərn) ***adj.*** ⟦ME *stoburn*, prob. < OE *stubb*, var. of *stybb*, STUB⟧ **1** refusing to yield, obey, or comply; resisting doggedly or unreasonably; resolute or obstinate **2** done or carried on in an obstinate or doggedly persistent manner [a *stubborn* campaign] **3** hard to handle, treat, or deal with; intractable [a *stubborn* cold] —**stub′born·ly** ***adv.*** —**stub′born·ness** ***n.***

SYN.—**stubborn** implies an innate fixedness of purpose, course, condition, etc. that is strongly resistant to change, manipulation, etc. [a *stubborn* child, belief, etc.]; **obstinate** applies to one who adheres persistently, and often unreasonably, to a purpose, course, etc., against argument or persuasion [a panel hung by an *obstinate* juror]; **dogged** implies thoroughgoing determination or, sometimes, sullen obstinacy [the *dogged* pursuit of a goal]; **pertinacious** implies a strong tenacity of purpose that is regarded unfavorably by others [a *pertinacious* critic] —*ANT.* **compliant, tractable**

Stubbs (stubz), **George** 1724-1806; Eng. painter

stub·by (stub′ē) ***adj.*** **-bi·er**, **-bi·est** **1** covered with stubs or stubble **2** short and heavy or dense [*stubby* bristles] **3** short and thickset —**stub′bi·ly** ***adv.*** —**stub′bi·ness** ***n.***

stuc·co (stuk′ō) ***n., pl.*** **-coes** or **-cos** ⟦It, prob. < Langobardic **stukki*, akin to OHG *stucki*, rind, crust, orig., piece: for IE base see STOCK⟧ plaster or cement, either fine or coarse, used for surfacing inside or outside walls or for molding relief ornaments, cornices, etc. —***vt.*** **-coed**, **-co·ing** to cover or decorate with stucco

stuc·co·work (-wurk′) ***n.*** work done in stucco

stuck (stuk) ***vt., vi.*** *pt. & pp. of* STICK —**stuck on** ☆[Informal] infatuated with

stuck-up (stuk′up′) ***adj.*** [Informal] snobbish; conceited

stud[1] (stud) ***n.*** ⟦ME *stode* < OE *studu*, column, pillar, post, akin to ON *stoth*, Ger *stützen*, to prop < IE **stūt-* < base **stā-*, to STAND⟧ **1** any of a series of small knobs or rounded nailheads used to ornament a surface, as of leather **2** a small, buttonlike device with a smaller button or shank on the back, inserted in a shirt front as an ornament or fastener **3** any of a number of upright pieces in the outer or inner walls of a building, to which panels, siding, laths, etc. are nailed **4** a metal crossbar bracing a link, as in a chain cable **5** a projecting pin or peg used as a support, pivot, stop, etc. or, as in an automobile tire, to increase traction on ice **6** a screw threaded at each end, used in fastening metal to metal or concrete **7** an earring consisting of a small ornament, as a gem, on a metal post that passes through a hole in the ear lobe, held in place by a fastener that attaches behind the ear: in full **stud earring** —***vt.*** **stud′ded**, **stud′ding** **1** to set or decorate with studs or studlike objects [a crown *studded* with jewels] **2** to be set thickly on; be scattered over [rocks *stud* the hillside]

stud[2] (stud) ***n.*** ⟦ME *stod* < OE, akin to Ger *stute*, mare (OHG *stuot*, stud of horses) < IE **stādh-* < base **sta-*, to STAND⟧ **1** *a)* a number of horses, or sometimes other animals, esp. as kept for breeding *b)* the place where these are kept ☆**2** *a)* STUDHORSE *b)* any male animal used esp. for breeding **3** [Slang] *a)* a virile, sexually promiscuous man *b)* HUNK (*n.* 2) **4** *short for* STUD POKER: see also FIVE-CARD STUD, SEVEN-CARD STUD —***adj.*** **1** of or having to do with a stud [a *stud* farm] **2** kept for breeding —**at stud** available for breeding: said of male animals

stud·book (stud′book′) ***n.*** a register of purebred animals, esp. racehorses: also **stud book**

stud·ding (stud′iŋ) ***n.*** **1** studs collectively, esp. for walls **2** material used for or as studs

stud·ding·sail (stud′iŋ sāl′; *naut.* stun′səl) ***n.*** ⟦< ?⟧ an auxiliary sail set outside the edge of a principal square sail in light weather by means of an extensible boom: also **studding sail**

stu·dent (sto͞od′'nt, styo͞od′-) ***n.*** ⟦ME *studiante, studente* < OFr & L: OFr *estudiant* < L *studens,* prp. of *studere,* to STUDY⟧ **1** a person who studies, or investigates [a *student* of human behavior] **2** a person who is enrolled for study at a school, college, etc. **—SYN.** PUPIL[1]

☆**student lamp** any of various lamps for use on a desk, as one with a gooseneck or, orig., one with a shaded light that can be moved up and down or sideways on a slender pole

stu·dent·ship (-ship′) ***n.*** **1** the state of being a student **2** [Brit.] a grant for study; scholarship

☆**student teacher** a college or university student who teaches school under the supervision of an experienced teacher as a requirement for a degree in education **—student teaching**

student union a building on a college or university campus used for student activities and usually having meeting and recreation rooms, offices, a snack bar, etc.

stud·horse (stud′hôrs′) ***n.*** a stallion kept for breeding

stud·ied (stud′ēd) ***adj.*** **1** prepared or planned by careful study [a *studied* reply] **2** deliberate; premeditated [in *studied* disarray] **3** [Now Rare] learned; well-informed **—stud′ied·ly** ***adv.*** **—stud′ied·ness** ***n.***

stu·di·o (sto͞o′dē ō′, styo͞o′-) ***n., pl.*** **-os′** ⟦It < L *studium,* a STUDY⟧ **1** a room or rooms where an artist, photographer, or musician works ☆**2** a room or rooms where dancing lessons, music lessons, etc. are given **3** *a)* a business establishment engaged in producing and, usually, distributing films *b)* a physical facility, as one belonging to such an establishment, where films are made **4** a room or rooms where radio or television programs are produced or where recordings are made **5** STUDIO APARTMENT

studio apartment a one-room apartment with kitchen facilities and a separate bathroom

☆**studio couch** a kind of couch that can be made into a full-sized bed, as by sliding out the spring frame fitted beneath it

stu·di·ous (sto͞o′dē əs, styo͞o′-) ***adj.*** ⟦ME < L *studiosus*⟧ **1** of, given to, or engaged in study **2** characterized by close attention; thoughtful [a *studious* inspection] **3** zealous; wholehearted [*studious* efforts] **4** [Now Rare] studied; deliberate **5** [Old Poet.] conducive to study **—stu′di·ous·ly** ***adv.*** **—stu′di·ous·ness** ***n.***

☆**stud poker** ⟦< STUD[2]⟧ any of several varieties of poker in which each player is dealt some cards face up: see FIVE-CARD STUD, SEVEN-CARD STUD

stud·y (stud′ē) ***n., pl.*** **stud′ies** ⟦ME *studie* < OFr *estudie* < L *studium,* zeal, study < *studere,* to busy oneself about, apply oneself to, study, orig., prob., to aim toward, strike at, akin to *tundere,* to strike, beat < IE **(s)teud-* < base **(s)teu-,* to beat > STOCK, STEEP[1]⟧ **1** the act or process of applying the mind so as to acquire knowledge or understanding, as by reading, investigating, etc. **2** careful attention to, and critical examination and investigation of, any subject, event, etc. **3** *a)* [*usually pl., with sing. v.*] a branch of learning or knowledge [urban *studies* is a popular major] *b)* any subject of study **4** [*pl.*] formal education; schooling **5** a product of studying; specif., *a)* an essay or thesis embodying the results of a particular investigation *b)* a work of literature or art treating a subject in careful detail and typically done as an exercise in technique, etc. *c)* a first sketch for a story, picture, etc. *d)* ÉTUDE **6** an earnest effort or intention **7** a state of mental absorption; reverie **8** a room, as in a house, designed for study, writing, reading, etc. **9** a person with reference to the ability to memorize, comprehend, etc. [a quick *study*] **—*vt.*** **stud′ied, stud′y·ing** **1** to apply one's mind to attentively; try to learn or understand by reading, thinking, etc. [to *study* history] **2** *a)* to examine or investigate carefully [to *study* the problem of air pollution] *b)* to look at carefully; scrutinize [to *study* a map] **3** *a)* to read (a book, lesson, etc.) so as to know and understand it *b)* to concentrate on so as to memorize **4** to take a course in, as at a school or college **5** to give attention, thought, or consideration to [*studying* possible changes] **—*vi.*** **1** to study something **2** to be a student; take a regular course (*at* a school or college) **3** to make earnest efforts; try hard **4** to meditate; ponder **—SYN.** CONSIDER **—**☆**study up on** [Informal] to make a careful study of

☆**study hall** **1** any room in a school used for studying and doing homework **2** a class period reserved for study

stuff (stuf) ***n.*** ⟦ME *stoffe* < OFr *estoffe* < *estoffer,* prob. < Gr *styphein,* to pull together, tighten < *styppē,* tow, coarse cloth of flax or hemp: see STOP⟧ **1** the material or substance out of which anything is or can be made; raw material **2** constituent elements or basic nature; essence; character [a man made of stern *stuff*] **3** matter or substance of an unspecified or generalized kind **4** cloth, esp. woolen cloth **5** *a)* household goods *b)* personal belongings *c)* things in general; objects *d)* things grouped together or viewed in a certain way **6** [Old-fashioned] something to be drunk, swallowed, etc.; specif., *a)* a medicine ☆*b)* [Slang] a drug, as heroin **7** worthless objects; refuse; junk **8** *a)* anything said, done, written, composed, etc.; talk or action of a specified kind *b)* foolish or worthless ideas, words, actions, etc. [*stuff* and nonsense!] **9** [Informal] *a)* basic ability; capability *b)* superior ability; exceptional capability ☆*c)* special skill or knowledge; specialty [to do or know one's *stuff*] ☆**10** [Informal] *a)* ability of a baseball pitcher, billiards player, etc. to control the ball, esp. to make it curve or spin *b)* such control, or speed, a curve, spin, etc. given to a ball ☆**11** [Slang] *Basketball* *a)* a dunk shot *b)* a shot that is completely blocked **—*vt.*** ⟦ME *stoffen* < OFr *estoffer*⟧ **1** to fill the inside of (something); pack; specif., *a)* to fill (a cushion, chair, toy, etc.) with padding or stuffing *b)* to fill the skin of (a dead animal, bird, etc.) in taxidermy *c)* to fill (a chicken, turkey, etc.) with a seasoned mixture as of bread crumbs, chopped vegetables, and herbs before roasting **2** *a)* to fill too full; cram; overload *b)* to fill to excess with food **3** to pack, cram, or crowd (something) into a container, etc. **4** to fill with information, ideas, etc. [to *stuff* one's head with facts] ☆**5** to put fraudulent votes into (a ballot box) **6** *a)* to plug; block *b)* to choke up or stop up, as with phlegm **7** to force or push [to *stuff* money into a wallet] **8** to treat (leather) with a preparation designed to soften and preserve it **9** [Slang] to stop or defeat (an opponent) decisively **—*vi.*** to eat too much or too quickly **—stuff it** [Slang] used as a generalized expression of contempt, anger, disdain, etc.

☆**stuffed shirt** [Slang] a pompous, pretentious person

stuff·er (stuf′ər) ***n.*** **1** a person or thing that stuffs ☆**2** something, as a piece of advertising, inserted in an envelope along with a bill, statement, paycheck, etc.

stuff·ing (-iŋ) ***n.*** **1** the action of filling, packing, or gorging **2** something used to fill or stuff; specif., *a)* soft, springy material used as padding in cushions, upholstered furniture, etc. *b)* a seasoned mixture for stuffing fowl, roasts, etc.

stuffing box a chamber that holds packing tightly around a moving part, as a piston rod, boat propeller shaft, etc., to prevent leakage of fluid along the part

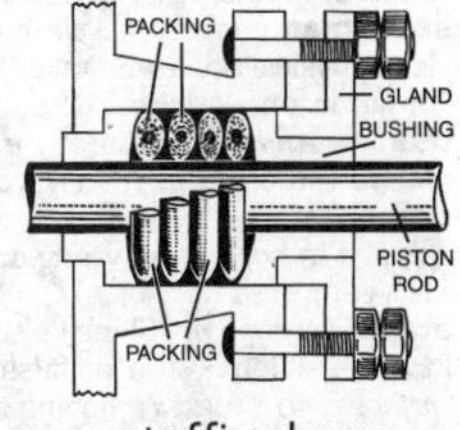

stuffing box

stuff·y (stuf′ē) ***adj.*** **stuff′i·er, stuff′i·est** ⟦STUFF + -Y[2]⟧ **1** *a)* poorly ventilated; having little fresh air; close *b)* stale or oppressive [the *stuffy* air] **2** having the nasal passages stopped up, as from a cold **3** [Informal] *a)* dull or stodgy; not interesting or stimulating *b)* conservative, conventional, old-fashioned, etc. *c)* prim; strait-laced *d)* pompous; pretentious **—stuff′i·ly** ***adv.*** **—stuff′i·ness** ***n.***

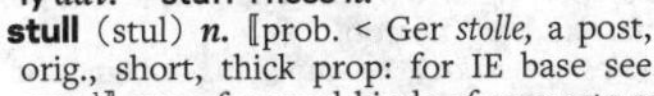

stull (stul) ***n.*** ⟦prob. < Ger *stolle,* a post, orig., short, thick prop: for IE base see STILL[1]⟧ any of several kinds of supports or frameworks used in mines to prevent cave-ins, support a platform, etc.

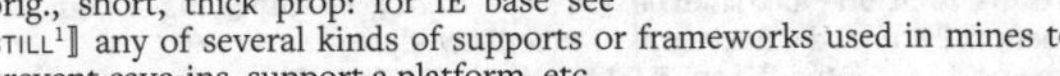

stul·ti·fy (stul′tə fī′) ***vt.*** **-fied′, -fy′ing** ⟦LL *stultificare* < L *stultus,* foolish, akin to *stolidus,* STOLID + *facere,* to make, DO[1]⟧ **1** *a)* to make seem foolish, stupid, inconsistent, etc.; make absurd or ridiculous *b)* to make dull or torpid **2** to render worthless, useless, or futile **3** *Law* to allege to be of unsound mind and therefore not legally responsible **—stul′ti·fi·ca′tion** ***n.*** **—stul′ti·fi′er** ***n.***

stum (stum) ***n.*** ⟦Du *stom,* must, new wine < *stom,* dumb: see fol.⟧ **1** grape juice that is unfermented or only partly fermented **2** wine revived by adding stum to it so as to produce new fermentation **—*vt.*** **stummed, stum′ming** to revive (wine) by adding stum

stum·ble (stum′bəl) ***vi.*** **-bled, -bling** ⟦ME *stumblen* < Scand, as in Norw dial. *stumba,* ON *stumra* < IE base **stem-,* to bump against, hamper > STAMMER, Ger *stumm,* Du *stom,* mute⟧ **1** to trip or miss one's step in walking, running, etc. **2** to walk or go in an unsteady or awkward manner, as from age, weakness, etc. **3** to speak, act, or proceed in a confused, blundering manner [to *stumble* through a speech] **4** to fall into sin or error; do wrong **5** to come by chance; happen [to *stumble* across a clue] **—*vt.*** **1** to cause to stumble **2** to puzzle or perplex; confound **—*n.*** **1** the act of stumbling **2** a blunder, error, or sin **—stum′bler** ***n.*** **—stum′bling·ly** ***adv.***

☆**stum·ble·bum** (-bum′) ***n.*** [Slang] BUM[1] (senses 1, 2, & 4)

stumbling block an obstacle, hindrance, or difficulty standing in the way of progress or understanding

stump (stump) ***n.*** ⟦ME *stumpfe,* prob. < or akin to MLowG *stump* < IE **stomb-* < base **steb(h)-* > STAMP, STAFF[1]⟧ **1** the lower end of a tree or plant remaining in the ground after most of the stem or trunk has been cut off **2** anything like a stump; specif., *a)* the part of a limb or tooth left after the rest has been cut off, broken off, etc. *b)* the part of anything left after the main part is gone; butt; stub [the *stump* of a pencil] ☆**3** ⟦from earlier use of tree stumps as speakers' platforms⟧ the place where a political speech is made; political rostrum: a fig. usage **4** *a)* the sound of a heavy, clumsy, tramping step *b)* such a step **5** a pointed roll of leather or paper used for shading drawings in charcoal, pencil, crayon, pastel, etc. **6** [*pl.*] [Slang] the legs **7** *Cricket* any of the three upright sticks of a wicket **—*vt.*** **1** to reduce to a stump; lop **2** to remove stumps from (land) ☆**3** to travel over (a district), making political speeches; canvass **4** to tone down or soften with a STUMP (sense 5) **5** [Informal] to stub (one's toes, etc.) ☆**6** [Informal] to puzzle, perplex, or baffle **7** *Cricket* to put (a batsman) out by striking a bail from the wicket with the ball while the batsman is out of his or her ground: said of the wicketkeeper **—*vi.*** **1** to walk with a heavy, clumsy, thumping step, as with a wooden leg ☆**2** to travel about, making political speeches **—**☆**up a stump** [Informal] unable to act, think, answer, etc.; in a dilemma; perplexed **—stump′er** ***n.***

stump·age (stum′pij) ***n.*** **1** standing timber or its value **2** the right to cut such timber

stump·y (stum′pē) ***adj.*** **stump′i·er, stump′i·est** ☆**1** covered with stumps **2** like a stump; short and thickset; stubby

stun (stun) ***vt.*** **stunned, stun′ning** ⟦ME *stonien* < OFr *estoner,* to stun: see ASTONISH⟧ **1** to make senseless or unconscious, as by a blow **2** to daze or stupefy; shock deeply; astound; overwhelm [he was *stunned* by the news] **3** to overpower or bewilder as by a loud noise or explosion —*n.* the effect or condition of being stunned

stung (stuŋ) *vt., vi. pt. & pp. of* STING

stun gun a hand-held, battery-operated device that delivers a powerful electric shock upon contact: used as for law enforcement

stunk (stuŋk) *vi. pp. & alt. pt. of* STINK

stun·ner (stun′ər) *n.* **1** one that stuns **2** [Informal] a remarkably attractive, excellent, etc. person or thing

stun·ning (-iŋ) *adj.* **1** that stuns **2** [Informal] remarkably attractive, excellent, etc. —**stun′ning·ly** *adv.*

stun·sail or **stun·s'l** (stun′səl) *n.* studdingsail: phonetic spellings

stunt[1] (stunt) *vt.* ⟦< dial., short and thick, stunted < ME, dull, stupid (with sense infl. by ON *stuttr,* short) < OE < IE **(s)teud-* < base **(s)teu-,* to strike > STOCK⟧ **1** to check the growth or development of; dwarf **2** to hinder (growth or development) —*n.* **1** the act or process of stunting or dwarfing **2** a stunted creature or thing **3** any of various plant diseases causing stunting

☆**stunt**[2] (stunt) *n.* ⟦< ?⟧ **1** a display of skill or daring; feat; trick **2** something done for a thrill, to attract attention, etc. ☆**3** *Football* any of various maneuvers involving different sets of defensive players, usually used to confuse the blockers while blitzing the quarterback —*vi.* to perform a stunt or stunts

☆**stunt·man** (-man′) *n., pl.* **-men′** (-men′) *Film, TV* a person with specialized physical skills who takes the place of an actor in scenes involving risky or hazardous activity

stunt·wom·an (-woom′ən) *n., pl.* **-wom′en** (-wim′in) a female stuntman

stu·pa (sto͞o′pə) *n.* ⟦Sans⟧ a dome-shaped Buddhist shrine

stupe[1] (sto͞op) *n.* ⟦< L *stupa, stuppa,* TOW[2]: see STOP⟧ *Med.* a soft cloth dipped in hot water, wrung dry, often medicated, and applied to the body as a compress

stupe[2] (sto͞op) *n.* [Slang] a stupid person

stu·pe·fa·cient (sto͞o′pə fā′shənt, styo͞o′-) *adj.* ⟦L *stupefaciens,* prp. of *stupefacere,* to STUPEFY⟧ having a stupefying or narcotic effect: also **stu′pe·fac′tive** (-fak′tiv) —*n.* a stupefacient drug; narcotic

stu·pe·fac·tion (-fak′shən) *n.* ⟦Fr *stupéfaction*⟧ **1** a stupefying or being stupefied **2** stunned amazement or utter bewilderment

stu·pe·fy (sto͞o′pə fī′, styo͞o′-) *vt.* **-fied′**, **-fy′ing** ⟦Fr *stupéfier* < L *stupefacere* < *stupere,* to be stunned (see STUPID) + *facere,* to make, DO[1]⟧ **1** to bring into a state of stupor; stun; make dull or lethargic **2** to astound, amaze, or bewilder —**stu′pe·fi′er** *n.*

stu·pen·dous (sto͞o pen′dəs, styo͞o-) *adj.* ⟦L *stupendus,* ger. of *stupere,* to be stunned: see fol.⟧ **1** astonishing; overwhelming [a *stupendous* development] **2** astonishingly great or large [a *stupendous* success] —**stu·pen′dous·ly** *adv.*

stu·pid (sto͞o′pid, styo͞o′-) *adj.* ⟦L *stupidus* < *stupere,* to be stunned or amazed < IE **steup-,* to strike: see STEEP[1]⟧ **1** in a state of stupor; dazed; stunned; stupefied **2** lacking normal intelligence or understanding; slow-witted; dull **3** showing or resulting from a lack of normal intelligence; foolish; irrational [a *stupid* idea] **4** dull and boring; tiresome [a *stupid* party]: also used informally as a generalized term of disapproval [a *stupid* hat] —*n.* a stupid person —**stu′pid·ly** *adv.* —**stu′pid·ness** *n.*

SYN.—**stupid** implies such lack of intelligence or incapacity for perceiving, learning, etc. as might be shown by one in a mental stupor [a *stupid* idea]; **dull** implies a mental sluggishness that may be constitutional or may result from extreme fatigue, disease, etc. [the fever left me *dull* and listless]; **dense** suggests obtuseness, or an irritating failure to understand quickly or to react intelligently [too *dense* to take a hint]; **slow** suggests that the quickness to learn, but not necessarily the capacity for learning, is below average [a pupil *slow* in most studies] See also **silly** —*ANT.* **intelligent, bright**

stu·pid·i·ty (sto͞o pid′ə tē, styo͞o-) *n.* ⟦L *stupiditas*⟧ **1** the quality or condition of being stupid **2** *pl.* **-ties** something stupid; foolish remark, irrational act, etc.

stu·por (sto͞o′pər, styo͞o′-) *n.* ⟦ME < L *stupere:* see STUPID⟧ **1** a state in which the mind and senses are dulled; partial or complete loss of sensibility, as from the use of a narcotic or from shock **2** mental or moral dullness or apathy —**stu′por·ous** *adj.*

stur·dy[1] (stur′dē) *adj.* **-di·er**, **-di·est** ⟦ME, defiant, refractory, hardy < OFr *estourdi,* stunned, reckless (the basic sense being "hard to influence or control") < VL **exturdire,* to be dizzy (? from too much chattering) < L *ex-,* intens. + *turdus,* a THRUSH[1]⟧ **1** that will not yield or compromise; firm; resolute [*sturdy* defiance] **2** physically strong; vigorous; hardy **3** strongly built or constructed —**stur′di·ly** *adv.* —**stur′di·ness** *n.*

stur·dy[2] (stur′dē) *n.* ⟦OFr *estourdi,* giddiness: see prec.⟧ GID —**stur′died** *adj.*

stur·geon (stur′jən) *n., pl.* **-geons** or **-geon** ⟦ME *sturgiun* < OFr *esturjon* < Frank **sturjo,* akin to OE *styria,* Ger *stör*⟧ any of a family (Acipenseridae, order Acipenseriformes) of large, edible, primitive bony fishes having rows of spiny plates along the body and a projecting snout: valuable as a source of caviar and isinglass

Sturm und Drang (shtoorm′ oont drăŋ′) ⟦Ger < *Wirrwarr, oder Sturm und Drang,* lit., Confusion, or Storm and Stress, play by F. M. v. Klinger (1752-1831), Ger dramatist⟧ an early Romantic movement in 18th-cent. German literature and music

stut·ter (stut′ər) *vt., vi.* ⟦freq. of dial. *stut,* to stutter < ME *stutten,* akin to Ger *stossen,* to knock, push < IE **(s)teud-:* see STUDY⟧ **1** STAMMER **2** to make (a series of repeated sounds) [*stuttering* machine guns] —*n.* the act or an instance of stuttering —**stut′ter·er** *n.*

stut·ter-step (stut′ər step′) *vi.* **-stepped′**, **-step′ping** ⟦descriptive of the action⟧ to move in sudden stops and starts so as to deceive or evade an opponent, as in sports —*n.* the act or practice of moving in such a way: also written **stutter step**

Stutt·gart (sto͞ot′gärt′, stut′-; *Ger* shto͞ot′gärt′) city in SW Germany: capital of the state of Baden-Württemberg

Stuy·ve·sant (stī′və sənt), **Peter** 1592-1672; last Du. governor of New Netherland (1646-64)

St. Vincent island of the Windward group in the West Indies: 133 sq mi (344 sq km)

St. Vincent and the Grenadines country consisting of St. Vincent & the N Grenadines: formerly a British colony, it became independent & a member of the Commonwealth (1979): 150 sq mi (389 sq km); cap. Kingstown

sty[1] (stī) *n., pl.* **sties** ⟦ME *stie* < OE *sti, stig,* hall, enclosure, prob. < IE base **stāi-,* to stop up, thicken > STONE⟧ **1** a pen for pigs **2** any foul or filthy place —*vt., vi.* **stied**, **sty′ing** to lodge in or as in a sty

sty[2] or **stye** (stī) *n., pl.* **sties** or **styes** ⟦< obs. dial. *styany* (taken as *sty on eye*) < dial. *styan,* rising < OE *stigend,* prp. of *stigan,* to climb, rise: see STILE[1]⟧ a small, inflamed swelling of a sebaceous gland on the rim of an eyelid

Styg·i·an (stij′ē ən, stij′ən) *adj.* ⟦< L *Stygius* (< Gr *Stygios* < *Styx:* see STYX) + -AN⟧ **1** of or characteristic of the river Styx and the infernal regions **2** [*also* **s-**] *a)* infernal or hellish *b)* dark or gloomy *c)* inviolable; completely binding, as an oath sworn by the river Styx

sty·lar (stī′lər) *adj.* of or like a style, stylus, etc.

style (stīl) *n.* ⟦ME < L *stilus* (sp. infl. by unrelated Gr *stylos,* pillar) < IE base **(s)tei-,* pointed > L *stimulus*⟧ **1** a sharp, slender, pointed instrument used by the ancients in writing on wax tablets **2** any of several devices, etc. similar in shape or use; specif., *a)* [Obs.] a pen *b)* an etching needle *c)* an engraving tool *d)* the pointer on a dial, chart, etc. *e)* the gnomon of a sundial *f) Bot.* the slender, stalklike part of a carpel between the stigma and the ovary *g) Zool.* a small, pointed projection or bristlelike process, as on some insects **3** *a)* manner or mode of expression in language, as distinct from the ideas expressed; way of using words to express thoughts *b)* specific or characteristic manner of expression, execution, construction, or design, in any art, period, work, employment, etc. [the Byzantine *style,* modern *style*] **4** distinction, excellence, originality, and character in any form of artistic or literary expression [an author who lacks *style*] **5** the way in which anything is made or done **6** *a)* the current, fashionable way of dressing, speaking, acting, etc. *b)* something stylish; esp., a garment of current, smart design *c)* a fashionable, luxurious existence [to live in *style*] **7** distinction and elegance of manner and bearing **8** form of address; title [entitled to the *style* of Mayor] **9** sort; kind; variety; type **10** a way of reckoning time, dates, etc.: see OLD STYLE (sense 1), NEW STYLE **11** *Printing* a particular manner of dealing with spelling, punctuation, word division, etc., as by a specific publisher, newspaper, etc. —*vt.* **styled**, **styl′ing** **1** to name; call [Abraham Lincoln, *styled* the Great Emancipator] ☆**2** to design the style of **3** to treat (hair) by cutting, blow-drying, coloring, etc. in order to achieve a desired, usually fashionable, style **4** to bring into accord with an accepted style, as of a publisher; normalize spelling, punctuation, etc. of —*SYN.* FASHION —**style′less** *adj.* —**styl′er** *n.*

style·book (stīl′book′) *n.* a book consisting of examples or rules of STYLE (esp. sense 11)

sty·let (stī′lit) *n.* ⟦Fr < It *stiletto:* see STILETTO⟧ **1** a slender, pointed weapon; esp., a stiletto **2** *Surgery a)* a slender probe *b)* a wire inserted into a soft catheter to keep it rigid **3** *Zool.* STYLE (*n.* 2g)

sty·li·form (stī′lə fôrm′) *adj.* ⟦ModL *stiliformis:* see STYLE⟧ shaped like a style or stylus

styl·ish (stī′lish) *adj.* **1** conforming to current style in dress, decoration, behavior, etc.; smart; fashionable **2** characterized by an elegant or lofty style —**styl′ish·ly** *adv.* —**styl′ish·ness** *n.*

styl·ist (stī′list) *n.* ⟦< STYLE + -IST[1]; analogous with Fr *styliste,* Ger *stilist*⟧ **1** a writer, musician, etc. who takes great pains in matters of expression, execution, etc. and who has a distinctive style or one regarded as excellent or exemplary **2** a person who designs, creates, or advises on current styles, as in dress **3** a person who styles hair

sty·lis·tic (stī lis′tik) *adj.* ⟦< STYLE, modeled on Ger *stilistisch*⟧ of or having to do with style, esp. literary style —**sty·lis′ti·cal·ly** *adv.*

sty·lis·tics (-tiks) *n.* the study of style as a means of analyzing works of literature and their effect; now often, specif., such study using mathematical and statistical methods

sty·lite (stī′līt′) *n.* ⟦LGr(Ec) *stylitēs* < Gr, dwelling on a pillar < *stylos,* pillar < IE **st(h)ū-* < base **stā-,* to STAND⟧ any of various Christian ascetics who lived on the tops of pillars —**sty·lit′ic** (-lit′ik) *adj.* —**sty′lit·ism′** *n.*

styl·ize (stīl′īz′, stī′ə līz′) *vt.* **-ized′**, **-iz′ing** ⟦< STYLE + -IZE, modeled on Ger *stilisiren*⟧ to make conform to a given style; specif., to design or represent according to the rules of a style rather than according to nature; conventionalize —**styl′i·za′tion** *n.* —**styl′iz·er** *n.*

sty·lo- (stī′lō, -lə) ⟦< L *stylus,* for *stilus,* pointed instrument: see STYLE⟧ *combining form* pointed, sharp [*stylograph*]: also, before a vowel, **styl-**

sty·lo·bate (stī′lə bāt′) *n.* ⟦L *stylobates* < Gr *stylobatēs* < *stylos* (see STYLITE) + *bainein,* to go: see COME⟧ *Archit.* a continuous base or coping for a row of columns

sty·lo·graph (-graf′, -gräf′) *n.* ⟦STYLO- + -GRAPH⟧ a fountain pen having a pierced conical point, rather than a nib, through which the ink flows

sty·lo·graph·ic (stī′lə graf′ik) *adj.* **1** of or like a stylograph **2** of or used in stylography —**sty′lo·graph′i·cal·ly** *adv.*

sty·log·ra·phy (stī läg′rə fē) *n.* ⟦STYLO- + -GRAPHY⟧ drawing, writing, or engraving done with a style or stylus

sty·loid (stī′loid′) *adj.* **1** resembling a style; styliform **2** *Anat.* designating or of any of various long, slender processes, esp. that at the base of the temporal bone

sty·lo·lite (stī′lə līt′) *n.* ⟦*stylo-* < Gr *stylos* (see STYLITE) + -LITE⟧ a small, columnlike formation in a rock deposit, having grooved or scratched sides and usually composed of limestone

sty·lo·po·di·um (stī′lə pō′dē əm) *n., pl.* **-di·a** (-dē ə) ⟦ModL: see STYLO- & -PODIUM⟧ a disk or swelling at the base of the style in plants of the umbel family

sty·lus (stī′ləs) *n., pl.* **-lus·es** or **-li** (-lī) ⟦L, for *stilus,* pointed instrument: see STYLE⟧ **1** a style or other needlelike marking device **2** any of various pointed tools, as one used for marking mimeograph stencils or one used in Braille embossing **3** *a)* a sharp, pointed device for cutting the grooves of a phonograph record *b)* the short, pointed piece, tipped usually with a sapphire or diamond, that moves in such grooves and transmits vibrations to the cartridge in the pickup of a phonograph **4** *Comput.* a hand-held, pen-shaped device used to draw lines, to select keys and icons, etc. on the display of a TOUCH SCREEN

sty·mie (stī′mē) *n.* ⟦prob. a use of earlier Scot, a person partially blind < *styme* < ME *stime* (sense obscure): the reference is to the blind shot caused by a stymie⟧ **1** *Golf* the condition that exists on a putting green when an opponent's ball lies in a direct line between the player's ball and the hole: since 1951, the obstructing ball may be picked up to permit a putt to be made **2** any situation in which one is obstructed or frustrated —*vt.* **-mied, -mie·ing 1** to hinder or obstruct as with a stymie **2** to block; impede

sty·my (stī′mē) *n., pl.* **-mies,** *vt.* **-mied, -my·ing** *alt. sp. of* STYMIE

styp·sis (stip′sis) *n.* ⟦LL < Gr: see fol.⟧ the action or use of a styptic

styp·tic (-tik) *adj.* ⟦LME *stiptik* < L *stypticus* < Gr *styptikos,* astringent < *styphein,* to contract: see STOP⟧ tending to halt bleeding by contracting the tissues or blood vessels; astringent —*n.* any styptic substance —**styp·tic′i·ty** (-tis′ə tē) *n.*

styptic pencil a small stick of a styptic substance, as alum, used to stop bleeding, as from razor nicks

Styr (stir) river in NW Ukraine & S Belarus, flowing north into the Pripet River: *c.* 290 mi (467 km)

sty·rene (stī′rēn′, stir′ēn′) *n.* ⟦< L *styrax* (see STORAX) + -ENE⟧ a colorless or yellowish, easily polymerized, aromatic liquid, $C_6H_5CH{:}CH_2$, used in organic synthesis, esp. in manufacturing synthetic rubber and plastics

Styr·i·a (stir′ē ə) region of central & SE Austria; Ger. name STEIERMARK

☆**Sty·ro·foam** (stī′rə fōm′) ⟦(POLY)STYR(ENE) + -O- + FOAM⟧ *trademark for* rigid, lightweight, cellular polystyrene, used in boat construction, insulation, commercial displays, etc. —*n.* [*also* **s-**] this substance, or one like it

Sty·ron (stī′rən), **William** 1925-2006; U.S. writer

Styx (stiks) *n.* ⟦L < Gr, lit., the Hateful, orig., icy cold⟧ *Gr. Myth.* the river encircling Hades over which Charon ferries the souls of the dead

Su *abbrev.* Sunday

su·a·ble (so͞o′ə bəl, syo͞o′-) *adj.* liable to suit in a court; that may be sued —**su′a·bil′i·ty** *n.*

sua·sion (swā′zhən) *n.* ⟦ME < L *suasio* < *suasus,* pp. of *suadere,* to persuade: see SWEET⟧ PERSUASION: now chiefly in **moral suasion,** the act of persuading someone by appealing to his or her sense of morality —**sua′sive** (-siv) *adj.* —**sua′sive·ly** *adv.* —**sua′sive·ness** *n.*

suave (swäv) *adj.* **suaver, suavest** ⟦MFr < L *suavis,* SWEET⟧ smoothly gracious or polite; polished; blandly ingratiating; urbane —**suave′ly** *adv.* —**suave′ness** *n.*

SYN.—**suave** suggests the smoothly gracious social manner of one who deals with people easily and tactfully [*a suave* sophisticate]; **urbane** suggests the social poise of one who is highly cultivated and has had much worldly experience [an *urbane* cosmopolite]; **diplomatic** implies adroitness and tactfulness in dealing with people and handling delicate situations, sometimes in such a way as to gain one's own ends [a *diplomatic* answer]; **politic** also expresses this idea, often stressing the expediency or opportunism of a particular policy pursued [a *politic* move]; **bland** is the least complex of these terms, simply implying a gentle or ingratiating pleasantness [a *bland* disposition]

suav·i·ty (swäv′ə tē, swav′-) *n.* ⟦ME *suavitee* < OFr *suavité* < L *suavitas*⟧ **1** the quality of being suave; graceful politeness **2** *pl.* **-ties** a suave action, speech, etc.

sub[1] (sub) [Informal] *n. short for:* **1** SUBMARINE **2** SUBSCRIPTION **3** SUBSTITUTE **4** SUBMARINE SANDWICH —*vi.* **subbed, sub′bing** to be a substitute (*for* someone)

sub[2] *abbrev.* **1** subaltern **2** substitute(s) **3** suburb(an)

sub- (sub, səb) ⟦< L *sub,* under, below: see UP[1]⟧ *prefix* **1** under, beneath, below, from beneath [*submarine, subsolar*] **2** lower in rank, position, or importance than; inferior or subordinate to [*subaltern, subhead*] **3** to a lesser degree than, somewhat, slightly [*subhuman, subaquatic*] **4** *a)* so as to form a division into smaller or less important parts [*subdivide*] *b)* forming such a division [*subspecies*] **5** *a)* near, bordering on [*subalpine*] *b)* nearly, almost [*subteen*] **6** *Chem. a)* with less than the normal amount of (the specified substance) [*suboxide*] *b)* basic [*subcarbonate*] In words of Latin origin, *sub-* becomes *suc-* before *c; suf-* before *f; sug-* before *g; sum-* before *m; sup-* before *p; sur-* before *r;* and, often, *sus-* before *c, p,* or *t*

sub·ac·e·tate (sub as′ə tāt′) *n.* a basic acetate

sub·ac·id (-as′id) *adj.* ⟦L *subacidus*⟧ **1** slightly acid or sour, as certain fruits **2** slightly sharp or biting, as a remark —**sub′a·cid′i·ty** (-ə sid′ə tē) *n.* —**sub·ac′id·ly** *adv.*

sub·a·cute (sub′ə kyo͞ot′) *adj.* **1** somewhat acute; nearly pointed [*subacute* angle] **2** between acute and chronic [a *subacute* disease] —**sub′a·cute′ly** *adv.*

sub·a·dult (sub′ə dult′, sub′ad′ult′) *Zool. n.* a developing animal that has some adult characteristics but is not sexually mature —*adj.* of or being a subadult

sub·a·gent (sub ā′jənt) *n.* a person representing an agent; agent of an agent

sub·al·pine (-al′pīn′, -pin) *adj.* ⟦L *subalpinus,* lit., lying near the Alps: see SUB- & ALPINE⟧ **1** designating or of regions at the foot of the Alps **2** designating, of, or growing in mountain regions just below the timberline or on a tundra or paramo; alpestrine

sub·al·tern (səb ôl′tərn; *chiefly Brit* sub′əl tərn) *adj.* ⟦Fr *subalterne* < LL *subalternus* < L *sub-,* SUB- + *alternus,* ALTERNATE⟧ **1** subordinate; of lower rank **2** [Brit.] holding an army commission below that of captain **3** *Logic* designating a proposition that is implied by another proposition but does not imply it [a particular proposition is *subaltern* to a corresponding universal proposition] —*n.* **1** a subordinate **2** [Brit.] a subaltern officer **3** *Logic* a subaltern proposition

sub·al·ter·nate (səb ôl′tər nit) *adj.* ⟦ME < LL *subalternatus,* pp. of *subalternare* < *subalternus:* see prec.⟧ **1** following in order; successive **2** *Bot.* in an alternate arrangement, but tending to become opposite: said of leaves —**sub·al′ter·nate·ly** *adv.* —**sub·al′ter·na′tion** *n.*

sub·ant·arc·tic (sub′ant ärk′tik, -är′-) *adj.* designating or of the area immediately surrounding the Antarctic Circle

sub·a·quat·ic (sub′ə kwät′ik, -kwat′-) *adj.* partly aquatic

sub·a·que·ous (sub ā′kwē əs, -ak′wē-) *adj.* ⟦SUB- + AQUEOUS⟧ **1** adapted for underwater use or existence; underwater **2** formed, living, or occurring under water

sub·a·rach·noid (sub′ə rak′noid′) *adj.* ⟦SUB- + ARACHNOID⟧ located in the space between the arachnoid and the pia mater membranes of the brain and spinal cord, which contains cerebrospinal fluid [a *subarachnoid* hemorrhage]

sub·arc·tic (sub ärk′tik, -är′-) *adj.* designating or of the area immediately surrounding the Arctic Circle

sub·ar·id (-ar′id) *adj.* slightly arid; moderately dry

☆**sub·as·sem·bly** (sub′ə sem′blē) *n., pl.* **-blies** an assembled unit designed to be fitted to a larger unit of which it is a component [a *subassembly* of an electronic circuit]

sub·at·om (sub at′əm) *n.* a constituent part of an atom

sub·a·tom·ic (sub′ə täm′ik) *adj. Particle Physics* of or pertaining to the inner part of an atom or to a particle, as an elementary particle or hadron, that is smaller than an atom

sub·au·di·tion (sub′ô dish′ən) *n.* ⟦LL *subauditio* < *subaudire,* to understand or supply a word omitted < L *sub-,* under + *audire,* to hear: see AUDIENCE⟧ **1** the act or process of understanding or mentally filling in a word or thought implied but not expressed **2** something thus understood or filled in

sub·au·ric·u·lar (sub′ô rik′yə lər) *adj.* situated below the auricle of the ear

sub·base (sub′bās′) *n.* the lowest section of a base or pedestal that is divided horizontally

sub·base·ment (-bās′mənt) *n.* any floor or room below the principal basement

sub·branch (-branch′) *n.* a division of a branch

sub·cal·i·ber (sub kal′ə bər) *adj.* **1** smaller than the caliber of the gun from which it is fired: said of a projectile fired, as in practice, through a tube of proper caliber inserted in or slipped on the barrel **2** of or having to do with a subcaliber projectile

sub·ce·les·tial (sub′sə les′chəl) *adj.* ⟦< ML *subcaelestis* (see SUB- & CELESTIAL) + -AL⟧ beneath the heavens; terrestrial or mundane

sub·cel·lar (sub′sel′ər) *n.* a cellar beneath the principal cellar

sub·cen·ter (sub′sent′ər) *n.* a subsidiary, or secondary, center of commercial activity

sub·cen·tral (sub sen′trəl) *adj.* close to or beneath the center —**sub′cen′tral·ly** *adv.*

sub·chas·er (sub′chā′sər) *n. short for* SUBMARINE CHASER

sub·chlo·ride (sub klôr′īd) *n.* a chloride containing a relatively small proportion of chlorine

sub·class (sub′klas′) *n.* **1** a subdivision of a class; specif., any main natural subdivision of a class of plants or animals **2** *Math.* SUBSET

sub·cla·vi·an (sub klā′vē ən) *adj.* situated under the clavicle —*n.* a subclavian vein, artery, etc.

subclavian groove either of two grooves in the first rib, one for the main artery (**subclavian artery**) and the other for the main vein (**subclavian vein**) of the arm

sub·cli·max (sub klī′maks) *n. Ecol.* the successional stage just preceding a climax formation

sub·clin·i·cal (-klin′i kəl) *adj.* without obvious clinical symptoms, as a disease in its early stages

sub·com·mit·tee (sub′kə mit′ē) *n.* a subordinate committee chosen from among the members of a main committee to carry out special assignments

sub·com·pact (sub käm′pakt′) ***n.*** a model of automobile smaller than a compact

sub·com·po·nent (sub′kəm pō′nənt) ***n.*** a componentlike part within a component part, used esp. to build electronic equipment

sub·con·scious (sub kän′shəs) ***adj.*** **1** occurring without conscious perception, or with only slight perception, on the part of the individual: said of mental processes and reactions **2** not fully conscious; imperfectly aware —**the subconscious** subconscious mental activity: a term, now obs. in psychiatry, that was formerly used to include *the preconscious* and *the unconscious* —**sub·con′scious·ly** ***adv.*** —**sub·con′scious·ness** ***n.***

sub·con·ti·nent (sub′känt′'n ənt) ***n.*** a large land mass, smaller than that usually called a continent; often, a subdivision of a continent, regarded as a geographic or political entity

sub·con·tract (sub′kän′trakt; *also, for v.,* sub′kən trakt′) ***n.*** a secondary contract undertaking some or all of the obligations of a primary or previous contract: construction companies often let subcontracts for the electrical work, plumbing, etc. — ***vt., vi.*** to make a subcontract (for)

sub·con·trac·tor (sub′kän′trak tər; sub′kən trak′-) ***n.*** a person or company that assumes by secondary contract some or all of the obligations of an original contractor

sub·con·tra·ry (sub kän′trer′ē) ***n.***, *pl.* **-ries** *Logic* either of two propositions so related that both can be true but both cannot be false

sub·cor·tex (sub′kôr′teks) ***n.*** the part of the brain beneath the cerebral cortex

sub·cor·ti·cal (sub kôr′ti kəl) ***adj.*** of or having to do with the region or tissue below a cortex, esp. the brain tissue below the cerebral cortex

sub·cos·tal (sub käs′təl, -kôs′-) ***adj.*** ⟦SUB- + COSTAL⟧ lying beneath the ribs —***n.*** a subcostal muscle, etc.

sub·crit·i·cal (-krit′i kəl) ***adj.*** **1** less than critical **2** unable to sustain a fission chain reaction: said of a nuclear reactor, device, etc.

sub·cul·ture (sub′kul′chər) ***n.*** **1** *a)* a group (within a society) of persons who are of the same age, social or economic status, ethnic background, etc. and who share the same distinctive interests, goals, etc. *b)* the distinct cultural patterns of such a group **2** a culture, as of bacteria, grown on a fresh medium from a previous culture —**sub·cul′tur·al** ***adj.***

sub·cu·ta·ne·ous (sub′kyo͞o tā′nē əs) ***adj.*** ⟦LL *subcutaneus:* see SUB- & CUTANEOUS⟧ being, used, or introduced beneath the skin —**sub′cu·ta′ne·ous·ly** ***adv.***

sub·dea·con (sub′dē′kən) ***n.*** ⟦ME *subdecon* (< *sub-,* SUB- + *deken,* DEACON) based on LL(Ec) *subdiaconus*⟧ **1** [Historical] *R.C.Ch.* a cleric ranking just below a deacon **2** in the Eastern Church, a cleric ranking just above a lector

☆**sub·deb** (sub′deb′) ***n.*** ⟦SUB- + DEB(UTANTE)⟧ **1** a girl in the years just preceding her debut into upper-class society **2** any girl of such age: see DEBUTANTE —***adj.*** of or suitable for a subdeb

sub·der·mal (sub dur′məl) ***adj.*** situated or occurring beneath the skin

sub·di·ac·o·nate (sub′dī ak′ə nit) ***n.*** ⟦ML(Ec) *subdiaconatus* < LL(Ec)⟧ the office or position of a subdeacon

sub·dis·trict (sub′dis′trikt) ***n.*** a subdivision of a district

sub·di·vide (sub′di vīd′, sub′di vīd′) ***vt., vi.*** **-vid′ed, -vid′ing** ⟦ME *subdividen* < LL *subdividere:* see SUB- & DIVIDE⟧ **1** to divide further after previous division has been made **2** to divide (land) into small parcels for sale, as by a real-estate firm —**sub′di·vid′er** ***n.***

sub·di·vi·sion (sub′di vizh′ən; *also, and for 3 always,* sub′di vizh′ən) ***n.*** ⟦LL(Ec) *subdivisio*⟧ **1** a subdividing or being subdivided **2** one of the parts resulting from subdividing **3** a piece of land resulting from this; esp., a large tract subdivided into small parcels for sale

sub·dom·i·nant (sub däm′ə nənt) ***adj.*** less than or only partly dominant —***n.*** **1** something that is subdominant **2** *Ecol.* a species having considerable importance in a community but much less influence than the dominant species **3** *Music* the fourth tone of a diatonic scale; tone next below the dominant

sub·duce (səb do͞os′, -dyo͞os′) ***vt.*** **-duced′, -duc′ing** ⟦L *subducere* < *sub-,* from + *ducere,* to lead: see DUCT⟧ [Obs.] to withdraw; take away

sub·duc·tion (səb duk′shən) ***n.*** a process of pulling something down; esp., *a)* the muscular action needed to aim an eye downward *b) Geol.* the sinking of one crustal plate under another as they collide —**sub·duct′** (-dukt′) ***vt., vi.***

sub·due (-do͞o′, -dyo͞o′) ***vt.*** **-dued′, -du′ing** ⟦ME *subdewen* (altered in sense and form by assoc. with L *subdere,* to put under, subject) < OFr *soduire,* to withdraw, seduce < L *subducere:* see SUBDUCE⟧ **1** to bring into subjection; conquer; vanquish **2** to overcome, as by persuasion or training; control **3** to make less intense; reduce; diminish; soften; allay **4** to repress (emotions, passions, etc.) **5** to bring (land) under cultivation —***SYN.*** CONQUER —**sub·du′a·ble** ***adj.*** —**sub·du′al** ***n.*** —**sub·du′er** ***n.***

sub·dued (-do͞od′, -dyo͞od′) ***vt. pt. & pp. of*** SUBDUE —***adj.*** **1** reduced or low in intensity; muted [*subdued* lighting] **2** quiet or withdrawn

sub·du·ral (səb do͝or′əl, -dyo͝or′-) ***adj.*** ⟦< SUB- + DURA MATER⟧ located between the dura mater and the arachnoid membranes of the brain and spinal cord [a *subdural* hematoma]

sub-ed·i·tor or **sub·ed·i·tor** (sub ed′it ər) ***n.*** [Brit.] COPY EDITOR —**sub-ed′it** ***vt.***

☆**sub·em·ployed** (sub′əm ploid′) ***adj.*** designating or of those workers who are unemployed, underemployed, or employed at wages below a subsistence level —**sub′em·ploy′ment** ***n.***

sub·en·try (sub′en′trē) ***n.***, *pl.* **-tries** an entry listed under a main entry

su·ber·ic acid (so͞o ber′ik) ⟦Fr *subérique* < L *suber,* cork tree⟧ a dibasic acid, $HOOC(CH_2)_6COOH$, obtained by the oxidation of cork and from other sources

su·ber·in (so͞o′bər in, so͞o ber′in) ***n.*** ⟦Fr *subérine* < L *suber,* cork + Fr *-ine,* -INE[3]⟧ a waxy or fatty substance contained in cork

su·ber·ize (-bər īz′) ***vt.*** **-ized′, -iz′ing** ⟦L *suber,* cork + -IZE⟧ *Bot.* to make impermeable by the formation of suberin in the cell walls, changing them into cork —**su′ber·i·za′tion** ***n.***

sub·fam·i·ly (sub′fam′ə lē, -fam′lē) ***n.***, *pl.* **-lies** **1** any main natural subdivision of a family of plants or animals **2** a major division of a language family, above a branch [the Indo-Iranian *subfamily* of Indo-European]

sub·floor (sub′flôr′) ***n.*** a rough floor upon which a finished floor is laid

sub·freez·ing (sub′frē′ziŋ) ***adj.*** below freezing

sub·fusc (sub′fusk′, sub fusk′) [Chiefly Brit.] ***adj.*** ⟦L *subfuscus,* brownish, dusky < *sub-,* below (see SUB-) + *fuscus,* FUSCOUS⟧ having a dull or dark, often drab, color —***n.*** subfusc clothing, esp. as academic dress at Oxford or Cambridge university

sub·ge·nus (sub′jē′nəs) ***n.***, *pl.* **-gen′er·a** (-jen′ər ə) or **-ge′nus·es** any main natural subdivision of a genus of plants or animals

sub·gla·cial (sub glā′shəl) ***adj.*** currently or formerly at the bottom of, or deposited beneath, a glacier [a *subglacial* stream, a *subglacial* deposit] —**sub·gla′cial·ly** ***adv.***

sub·grade (sub′grād′) ***n.*** a layer of rock or earth leveled and graded for a foundation, as of a road

sub·group (-gro͞op′) ***n.*** **1** a subdivision of a group; subordinate group **2** *Chem.* a vertical subdivision of a group in the periodic table of chemical elements **3** *Math.* a group whose elements form a subset of another group

☆**sub·gum** (sub′gum′) ***adj.*** ⟦< Cantonese *sahp gám,* fancy mixed vegetables < *sahp,* ten, diverse + *gám,* brocade⟧ designating any of various Chinese-American dishes, as chow mein, prepared with water chestnuts, mushrooms, almonds, etc.

sub·head (sub′hed′) ***n.*** **1** the title of a subdivision of a chapter, article, etc. **2** a subordinate heading or title, as of a magazine article Also **sub′head′ing**

sub·hu·man (sub hyo͞o′mən) ***adj.*** **1** below the human race in development; less than human **2** regarded as unfit for use, habitation, etc. by human beings [*subhuman* living conditions]

sub·in·ci·sion (sub′in sizh′ən) ***n.*** the practice, as among Australian Aboriginal peoples, of slitting the underside of the penis all or part of the length of the urethra as a puberty rite

sub·in·dex (sub′in′deks) ***n.***, *pl.* **-dex·es** or **-di·ces′** (-də sēz′) **1** an index to a subdivision of a main category **2** *Math.* SUBSCRIPT

sub·in·feu·da·tion (sub in′fyo͞o dā′shən) ***n.*** **1** the transfer of feudal lands by a vassal lord to a subtenant with all the privileges and responsibilities falling to the new holder **2** tenure so established **3** the lands or fief so held

☆**sub·ir·ri·gate** (sub ir′ə gāt′) ***vt.*** **-gat′ed, -gat′ing** to irrigate (land) by a system of underground pipes —**sub′ir·ri·ga′tion** ***n.***

su·bi·to (so͞o′bi tō′) ***adv.*** ⟦It < L, suddenly < pp. of *subire,* to approach, spring up: see SUDDEN⟧ [*also in italics*] *Musical Direction* suddenly; quickly; abruptly

subj *abbrev.* **1** subject **2** subjective **3** subjunctive

sub·ja·cent (sub jā′sənt) ***adj.*** ⟦L *subjacens,* prp. of *subjacere,* to lie under < *sub-,* under + *jacere,* to lie, throw: see SUB- & JET[1]⟧ **1** situated directly under or below; underlying **2** being lower but not directly beneath —**sub·ja′cen·cy** ***n.***

sub·ject (sub′jikt, -jekt′; *for v.* səb jekt′) ***adj.*** ⟦ME *suget* < OFr < L *subjectus,* pp. of *subjicere,* to place under, put under, subject < *sub-,* under + *jacere,* to throw: see JET[1]⟧ **1** under the authority or control of, or owing allegiance to, another [*subject* peoples] **2** having a disposition or tendency; liable (to) [*subject* to fits of anger] **3** liable to receive; exposed (to) [*subject* to censure] **4** contingent or conditional upon (with *to*) [*subject* to your approval] —***n.*** ⟦ME *suget* < OFr < L *subjectus:* see the ***adj.***⟧ **1** a person under the authority or control of another; esp., a person owing allegiance to a particular ruler, government, etc. **2** someone or something made to undergo a treatment, experiment, analysis, dissection, etc. **3** ⟦L *subjectum,* foundation, subject (transl. of Gr *to hypokeimenon*) < neut. of *subjectus:* see the ***adj.***⟧ something dealt with in discussion, study, writing, painting, etc.; theme **4** the main theme or melody of a musical composition or movement, esp., the opening theme in a fugue **5** originating cause, reason, or motive **6** any of the various courses of study in a school or college; branch of learning **7** *Gram.* the noun or other substantive that is one of the two immediate constituents of a sentence and about which something is said in the predicate **8** *Logic* that part of a proposition about which something is said; that which is affirmed or denied **9** *Philos.* *a)* the actual substance of anything as distinguished from its qualities and attributes *b)* the mind, or ego, that thinks and feels, as distinguished from everything outside the mind —***vt.*** **1** [Obs.] to place under or below **2** to bring under the authority or control of; cause to owe allegiance **3** to make liable or vulnerable [to *subject* oneself to the contempt of others] **4** to cause to experience or receive some action or treatment [to *subject* someone to interrogation, *subject* a new drug to rigorous testing] **5** [Rare] to place before; submit [a plan *subjected* for approval] —**sub·jec′tion** ***n.***

sub·jec·tive (səb jek′tiv) ***adj.*** ⟦ME < LL *subjectivus,* of the subject < *subjectus:* see prec.⟧ **1** of, affected by, or produced by the mind or a particular state of mind; of or resulting from the feelings or temperament of the subject, or person thinking; not objective; personal [a *subjective* judgment] **2**

determined by and emphasizing the ideas, thoughts, feelings, etc. of the artist or writer, not just rigidly transcribing or reflecting reality 3 *Gram.* NOMINATIVE 4 *Philos.* of or having to do with the perception or conception of a thing by the mind as opposed to its reality independent of the mind 5 *Med.* designating or of a symptom or condition perceptible only to the patient 6 *Psychol.* *a)* existing or originating within the observer's mind or sense organs and, hence, incapable of being checked externally or verified by other persons *b)* introspective —**sub·jec′tive·ly** *adv.* —**sub·jec·tiv·i·ty** (sub′jek tiv′ə tē) *n.*, **sub·jec′tive·ness**

sub·jec·tiv·ism (səb jek′tiv iz′əm) *n.* 1 the philosophic theory that all knowledge is subjective and relative, never objective 2 any philosophic theory that restricts knowledge in some way to the subjective elements, as by limiting external reality to what can be known or inferred by subjective standards of truth 3 an ethical theory holding that personal attitudes and feelings are the sole determinants of moral values —**sub·jec′tiv·ist** *adj., n.* —**sub·jec′ti·vis′tic** *adj.*

subject matter the thing or things considered in a book, course of instruction, discussion, etc.

sub·join (səb join′) *vt.* ⟦MFr *subjoindre* < L *subjungere:* see SUB- & JOIN⟧ to add (something) at the end of what has been stated; append —[Rare] **sub·join′der** *n.*

sub ju·di·ce (sub jo͞o′də sē′) ⟦L, lit., under judgment⟧ before the court; under judicial consideration

sub·ju·gate (sub′jə gāt′) *vt.* **-gat′ed, -gat′ing** ⟦ME *subiugaten* < L *subjugatus,* pp. of *subjugare,* to bring under the yoke < *sub-,* under + *jugum,* YOKE⟧ 1 to bring under control or subjection; conquer 2 to cause to become subservient; subdue —*SYN.* CONQUER —**sub′ju·ga′tion** *n.* —**sub′ju·ga′tor** *n.*

sub·junc·tive (səb juŋk′tiv) *adj.* ⟦LL *subjunctivus* < L *subjunctus,* pp. of *subjungere,* to SUBJOIN⟧ *Gram.* designating or of the mood of a verb that is used to express supposition, desire, hypothesis, possibility, etc., rather than to state an actual fact (Ex.: the mood of *were* in "if I were you"): cf. INDICATIVE, IMPERATIVE —*n.* 1 the subjunctive mood 2 a verb in this mood

sub·king·dom (sub′kiŋ′dəm) *n.* any main natural subdivision of the plant or animal kingdom

sub·lap·sar·i·an (sub′lap ser′ē ən) *n., adj.* ⟦ModL *sublapsarius* < L *sub-,* below + *lapsus,* LAPSE, fall⟧ INFRALAPSARIAN —**sub′lap·sar′i·an·ism′** *n.*

sub·late (səb lāt′) *vt.* **-lat′ed, -lat′ing** ⟦< L *sublatus* (suppletive pp. of *tollere,* to lift up, take away, annul) < *sub-,* up (see SUB-) + *latus,* suppletive pp. of *ferre,* to BEAR[1]⟧ *Logic* to deny, contradict, or negate

sub·lease (sub′lēs′; *for v.* sub lēs′) *n.* a lease granted by a lessee to another person —*vt.* **-leased′, -leas′ing** to grant, obtain, or hold a sublease of —**sub′les·see′** (-les ē′) *n.* —**sub·les·sor** (sub les′ôr′, sub′les ôr′) *n.*

sub·let (sub let′; *also, and for n. always,* sub′let′) *vt.* **-let′, -let′ting** 1 to let to another (property which one is renting) 2 to let out (work) to a subcontractor —*n.* an apartment, condominium, etc. that has been sublet

sub·le·thal (sub lē′thəl) *adj.* not quite lethal; insufficient to cause death [a *sublethal* dose of poison]

sub·lieu·ten·ant (sub′lo͞o ten′ənt; *Brit,* -lef ten′-) *n.* [Brit.] a naval officer ranking below a lieutenant

sub·li·mate (sub′lə māt′; *for adj. & n., also,* -mit) *vt.* **-mat′ed, -mat′ing** ⟦< L *sublimatus,* pp. of *sublimare:* see fol.⟧ 1 to cause to change directly from a solid to a gas, or from a gas to a solid, without becoming a liquid 2 to have a purifying or ennobling influence or effect on 3 to express (socially or personally unacceptable impulses, specif. sexual impulses) in constructive, acceptable forms, often unconsciously —*vi.* to undergo sublimating —*adj.* sublimated —*n.* a substance that is the product of sublimating —**sub′li·ma′tion** *n.*

sub·lime (sə blīm′) *adj.* ⟦L *sublimus* < *sub-,* up to + *limen,* lintel (hence, orig., up to the lintel): see LIMEN⟧ 1 noble; exalted; majestic 2 inspiring awe or admiration through grandeur, beauty, etc. 3 outstandingly or supremely such [a man of *sublime* taste] 4 [Archaic] *a)* elated; joyful *b)* proud; lofty; haughty *c)* upraised; aloft —*vt.* **-limed′, -lim′ing** ⟦ME *sublimen* < MFr *sublimer* < ML *sublimare* < L, to lift high < the adj.⟧ 1 to make sublime 2 SUBLIMATE (*vt.* 1) —*vi.* SUBLIMATE —**the sublime** sublime quality; sublimity —**sub·lime′ly** *adv.* —**sub·lime′ness** *n.*

sub·lim·i·nal (sub lim′ə nəl) *adj.* ⟦see SUB- & LIMEN & -AL⟧ below the threshold of consciousness or apprehension; specif., involving or using stimuli intended to take effect subconsciously by repetition —**sub·lim′i·nal·ly** *adv.*

sub·lim·i·ty (sə blim′ə tē) *n.* ⟦L *sublimitas*⟧ 1 the state or quality of being sublime, majestic, noble, etc. 2 *pl.* **-ties** something sublime

sub·lin·gual (sub liŋ′gwəl) *adj.* ⟦ML *sublingualis:* see SUB- & LINGUAL⟧ situated under the tongue

sub·lu·nar·y (sub lo͞on′ər ē, sub′lo͞o ner′ē) *adj.* ⟦ML *sublunaris* < L *sub-,* under + *luna,* the moon: see LIGHT[1]⟧ 1 situated beneath the moon; terrestrial 2 earthly; mundane Also **sub·lu′nar**

sub·lux·a·tion (sub′lək sā′shən) *n.* ⟦< ModL *subluxatio:* see SUB- (sense 3) & LUXATE⟧ a partial dislocation of a bone from a joint

☆**sub·ma·chine gun** (sub′mə shēn′) a portable, automatic or semiautomatic firearm with a stock and a short barrel, taking pistol ammunition and fired from the shoulder or hip

sub·mar·gin·al (sub mär′jə nəl) *adj.* 1 below minimum requirements or standards [*submarginal* housing] 2 not yielding a satisfactory return; not profitable [*submarginal* land] 3 *Biol.* near the margin of an organ or part —**sub·mar′gin·al·ly** *adv.*

sub·ma·rine (sub′mə rēn′, sub′mə rēn′) *adj.* ⟦SUB- + MARINE⟧ being, living, used, or carried on beneath the surface of the water, esp. of the sea —*n.* 1 a submarine plant or animal 2 a watercraft designed to operate underwater; esp., a naval warship so designed, armed with torpedoes, etc. 3 ⟦short for SUBMARINE SANDWICH⟧ HERO SANDWICH

submarine chaser a small, fast naval patrol vessel equipped for use against submarines

sub·ma·rin·er (sub′mə rēn′ər, sub′mə rēn′ər, sub mer′ə nər) *n.* a member of the crew of a submarine

☆**submarine sandwich** ⟦so named because its shape resembles that of a modern SUBMARINE (*n.* 2)⟧ HERO SANDWICH

sub·max·il·la (sub′mak sil′ə) *n., pl.* **-lae** (-ē) or **-las** ⟦ModL: see SUB- & MAXILLA⟧ the lower jaw or jawbone

sub·max·il·lar·y (sub mak′sə ler′ē) *adj.* designating, of, or below the lower jaw; esp., designating or of either of two salivary glands, one on each side, below the inside edge of the lower jaw

sub·me·di·ant (-mē′dē ənt) *n.* ⟦SUB- + MEDIANT⟧ the sixth tone of a diatonic scale; tone just above the dominant and below the subtonic; superdominant

sub·merge (səb murj′) *vt.* **-merged′, -merg′ing** ⟦L *submergere* < *sub-,* under + *mergere,* to plunge: see MERGE⟧ 1 to place under or cover with water or the like; plunge into water, inundate, etc. 2 to cover over; suppress; hide 3 to cause to sink below a decent level of life [the *submerged* people of the slums] —*vi.* to sink or plunge beneath the surface of water, etc. —**sub·mer′gence** (-mur′jəns) *n.* —**sub·mer′gi·ble** (-jə bəl) *adj.*

sub·merse (səb murs′) *vt.* **-mersed′, -mers′ing** ⟦< L *submersus,* pp. of *submergere*⟧ SUBMERGE —**sub·mer′sion** (-mur′zhən, -shən) *n.*

sub·mersed (-murst′) *adj. Bot.* growing under water

sub·mers·i·ble (səb mur′sə bəl) *adj.* that can function while submerged —*n.* a vessel designed to operate underwater, esp. in carrying out research or exploration

sub·mi·cron (sub mī′krän) *adj.* being shorter or smaller than a micron [a *submicron* particle]

sub·mi·cro·scop·ic (sub′mī krə skäp′ik) *adj.* too small to be seen through a microscope: see ULTRAMICROSCOPIC

sub·min·i·a·ture (sub min′ē ə chər) *adj.* designating or of a very small camera, electronic component, etc., smaller than one described as "miniature"

sub·min·i·a·tur·ize (-īz′) *vt., vi.* **-ized′, -iz′ing** to construct (something) on a subminiature scale —**sub·min′i·a·turi·za′tion** *n.*

sub·miss (səb mis′) *adj.* [Archaic] submissive; humble

sub·mis·sion (səb mish′ən) *n.* ⟦OFr < L *submissio* < *submissus,* pp. of *submittere:* see SUBMIT⟧ 1 the act of submitting, yielding, or surrendering 2 the quality or condition of being submissive; resignation; obedience; meekness 3 *a)* the act of submitting something to another for decision, consideration, etc. *b)* something thus submitted, as an article or photograph to a publisher 4 *Law* an agreement whereby parties to a dispute submit the matter to arbitration and agree to be bound by the decision

sub·mis·sive (səb mis′iv) *adj.* ⟦< L *submissus,* pp. of *submittere* (see fol.) + -IVE⟧ having or showing a tendency to submit without resistance; docile; yielding —**sub·mis′sive·ly** *adv.* —**sub·mis′sive·ness** *n.*

sub·mit (səb mit′) *vt.* **-mit′ted, -mit′ting** ⟦ME *submitten* < L *submittere* < *sub-,* under, down + *mittere,* to send: see MISSION⟧ 1 to present or refer to others for decision, consideration, etc. 2 to yield to the action, control, power, etc. of another or others; also, to subject or allow to be subjected to treatment, analysis, etc. of some sort: often used reflexively 3 to offer as an opinion; suggest; propose —*vi.* 1 *a)* to yield to the power, control, etc. of another or others; give in *b)* to allow oneself to be subjected (*to* treatment, analysis, etc.) 2 to defer to another's judgment or decision 3 to be submissive, obedient, humble, etc. —**sub·mit′ta·ble** *adj.* —**sub·mit′tal** *n.* —**sub·mit′ter** *n.*

sub·mon·tane (sub män′tān, sub′män tān′) *adj.* ⟦< SUB- + L *montanus:* see MOUNTAIN⟧ 1 located at the foot of a mountain or mountain range 2 of or characteristic of foothills

sub·mul·ti·ple (sub mul′tə pəl) *n.* ⟦SUB- + MULTIPLE⟧ a number that will divide another with no remainder; exact divisor (of a specified number) [3 is a *submultiple* of 12]

sub·nor·mal (-nôr′məl) *adj.* below the normal; less than normal, esp. in intelligence —*n.* a subnormal person —**sub′nor·mal′i·ty** (-mal′ə tē) *n.* —**sub·nor′mal·ly** *adv.*

sub·nu·cle·ar (-no͞o′klē ər, -nyo͞o′-) *adj.* designating or of any of the particles within the nuclei of atoms

sub·o·ce·an·ic (sub′ō shē an′ik) *adj.* situated or occurring on or beneath the ocean floor

sub·op·ti·mal (sub äp′tə məl) *adj.* being less than optimal

sub·or·bit·al (sub ôr′bit′l) *adj.* 1 designating or of a flight in which a rocket, spacecraft, etc. follows a ballistic trajectory of less than one orbit 2 beneath the orbit of the eye

sub·or·der (sub′ôr′dər) *n.* any natural subdivision of an order of plants or animals —**sub·or′di·nal** (-ôrd′'n əl) *adj.*

sub·or·di·nate (sə bôrd′'n it; *for v.,* -bôr′də nāt′) *adj.* ⟦ME < ML *subordinatus,* pp. of *subordinare* < L *sub-,* under + *ordinare,* to order: see ORDAIN⟧ 1 inferior to or placed below another in rank, power, importance, etc.; secondary 2 under the power or authority of another 3 subservient or submissive 4 *Gram.* having the function of a noun, adjective, or adverb within a sentence [a *subordinate* clause] —*n.* a subordinate person or thing —*vt.* **-nat′ed, -nat′ing** 1 to place in a subordinate position; treat as less important or inferior (*to*) **2** to make obedient or subservient (*to*); control; subdue —**sub·or′di·nate·ly** ***adv.*** —**sub·or′di·na′tive** ***adj.***

subordinate clause *Gram.* DEPENDENT CLAUSE

subordinating conjunction a conjunction (as *if, as, so, unless, although,* or *when*) that connects subordinate words, phrases, or clauses to some other sentence element: also **subordinate conjunction**

sub·or·di·na·tion (sə bôrd′′n ā′shən) ***n.*** **1** a subordinating or being subordinated **2** [Now Rare] subjection or submission to rank, power, or authority; obedience

sub·orn (sə bôrn′) ***vt.*** ⟦L *subornare,* to furnish or supply, instigate, incite secretly < *sub-,* under + *ornare,* to furnish, adorn: see ORNAMENT⟧ **1** to get or bring about through bribery or other illegal methods **2** to induce or instigate (another) to do something illegal, esp. to commit perjury —**sub·orn′er** ***n.***

sub·or·na·tion (sub′ôr nā′shən) ***n.*** ⟦ML *subornatio*⟧ a suborning or being suborned; esp., the crime of inducing another to commit perjury (**subornation of perjury**)

sub·os·cine (səb äs′in, -īn′) ***adj.*** of or having to do with any passerine bird that is not in the suborder of the oscines —***n.*** any such bird characterized by a vocal organ that is less developed than that of an oscine

sub·ox·ide (sub äk′sīd) ***n.*** an oxide containing a relatively small proportion of oxygen

sub·phy·lum (sub′fī′ləm) ***n., pl.*** **-la** (-lə) any main natural subdivision of a phylum

sub·plot (-plät′) ***n.*** a secondary plot in a play, novel, etc.

sub·poe·na (sə pē′nə) ***n.*** ⟦ME *suppena* < ML *subpena* < L *sub poena,* lit., under penalty: see SUB- & PAIN⟧ a written legal order directing a person to appear in court to give testimony, show specified records, etc. —***vt.*** **-naed, -na·ing 1** to summon with such an order ☆**2** to order that (specified records, documents, etc.) be brought to a court Also sp. **sub·pe′na**

sub·pop·u·la·tion (sub′päp yə lā′shən) ***n.*** a subdivision of a population, with common, distinguishing characteristics

sub·prime (sub′prīm′) ***adj.*** ⟦orig. referring to the high-risk borrowers, their credit ratings, etc.⟧ designating or of mortgage loans made to higher-risk borrowers, as those with poor credit ratings, who typically pay higher interest rates

sub·prin·ci·pal (sub′prin′sə pəl) ***n.*** an assistant principal in a school, etc.

☆**sub·pro·fes·sion·al** (sub′prō fesh′ə nəl) ***n.*** PARAPROFESSIONAL

sub·re·gion (sub′rē′jən) ***n.*** any of the divisions of a region, esp. with reference to plant and animal distribution

sub·ro·gate (sub′rə gāt′) ***vt.*** **-gat′ed, -gat′ing** ⟦< L *subrogatus, surrogatus:* see SURROGATE⟧ to substitute (one person) for another

sub·ro·ga·tion (sub′rō gā′shən, -rə-) ***n.*** ⟦ME *subrogacioun* < ML *subrogatio* < L *subrogatus*⟧ a subrogating; esp., the substitution of one creditor for another, along with a transference of the claims and rights of the old creditor

sub ro·sa (sub rō′zə) ⟦L, lit., under the rose, an ancient symbol of secrecy⟧ secretly; privately; confidentially

sub·rou·tine (sub′ro͞o tēn′) ***n.*** a set of instructions, appearing once within a computer program but available for repeated use, for performing a specific task

sub-Sa·ha·ran (sub′sə har′ən) ***adj.*** designating or of the part of the African continent south of the Sahara desert

sub·sam·ple (sub′sam′pəl) ***n.*** a selected sample of a total sampling —***vt.*** **-sam′pled, -sam′pling** to take a subsample of

sub·scribe (səb skrīb′) ***vt.*** **-scribed′, -scrib′ing** ⟦ME *subscriben* < L *subscribere:* see SUB- & SCRIBE⟧ **1** to sign (one's name) at the end of a document, etc. **2** to write one's signature on (a document, etc.) as an indication of consent, approval, attestation, etc. **3** to support; consent to; favor; sanction **4** to promise to contribute (a sum of money), esp. by signing a pledge —***vi.*** **1** to sign one's name at the end of a document, etc. **2** to give support, sanction, or approval; consent or agree (*to*) [to *subscribe* to certain measures] **3** to promise to contribute, or to give, a sum of money **4** to register or be registered to pay for and receive a periodical, service, theater tickets, etc. for a specified period of time (with *to*) —**sub·scrib′er** ***n.***

sub·script (sub′skript′) ***adj.*** ⟦L *subscriptus,* pp. of *subscribere,* to prec.⟧ written below; esp., INFERIOR (***adj.*** 8) —***n.*** a figure, letter, or symbol written below and to the side of another [in Y_3 and X_a, 3 and a are *subscripts*]

sub·scrip·tion (səb skrip′shən) ***n.*** ⟦ME *subscripcion* < L *subscriptio*⟧ **1** the act of subscribing **2** something subscribed; specif., *a)* a written signature *b)* a signed document, etc. *c)* consent or sanction, esp. in writing *d)* an amount of money subscribed *e)* a formal agreement to receive and pay for a periodical, books, theater tickets, etc. for a specified period of time *f)* the right to receive a periodical, etc., as by payment of a fixed sum **3** that part of a doctor's prescription giving directions to the pharmacist: cf. SIGNATURE (***n.*** 4) **4** *Eccles.* assent to certain doctrines for promoting uniformity; specif., in the Anglican Church, acceptance of the Thirty-nine Articles of Faith

sub·sec·tion (sub′sek′shən) ***n.*** a subdivision of any of the sections into which a group, document, etc. is divided

sub·se·quence (sub′si kwəns, -kwens′; *for 3* sub′sē′kwəns) ***n.*** ⟦ML *subsequentia*⟧ **1** the fact or condition of being subsequent **2** a subsequent happening **3** *Math.* a sequence within a sequence

sub·se·quent (-kwənt, -kwent′) ***adj.*** ⟦ME < L *subsequens,* prp. of *subsequi,* to follow close after: see SUB- & SEQUENT⟧ coming after; following in time, place, or order —**subsequent to** after; following —**sub′se·quent·ly** ***adv.***

sub·sere (sub′sir′) ***n.*** ⟦SUB- + SERE[1]⟧ *Ecol.* a secondary succession occurring after all or part of the vegetation in an area has been destroyed, as by humans or fire

sub·serve (səb surv′) ***vt.*** **-served′, -serv′ing** ⟦L *subservire* < *sub-,* under + *servire,* to SERVE⟧ to be useful or helpful to (a purpose, cause, etc.); serve; promote; aid

sub·ser·vi·ence (səb sur′vē əns) ***n.*** **1** the state or quality of being subservient **2** subservient behavior or manner; obsequiousness; servility Also **sub·ser′vi·en·cy**

sub·ser·vi·ent (-ənt) ***adj.*** ⟦L *subserviens,* prp. of *subservire,* to SUBSERVE⟧ **1** that is useful, helpful, or of service, esp. in an inferior or subordinate capacity **2** willing to obey or serve because of being in a lower position; submissive —**sub·ser′vi·ent·ly** ***adv.***

sub·set (sub′set′) ***n.*** **1** a mathematical set in which every element in the set is also contained in a larger set or in an equal set [the even numbers are a *subset* of the whole numbers] **2** any group that is part of a larger group [a small but vocal *subset* of the city's dog owners]

sub·shrub (-shrub′) ***n.*** a partly shrubby plant that has woody stems growing new shoots annually at the tips

sub·side (səb sīd′) ***vi.*** **-sid′ed, -sid′ing** ⟦L *subsidere* < *sub-,* under + *sidere,* to settle < *sedere,* to SIT⟧ **1** to sink or fall to the bottom; settle, as sediment **2** to sink to a lower level **3** to become less active, intense, etc.; abate —*SYN.* WANE —**sub·sid·ence** (səb sīd′'ns, sub′si dəns) ***n.***

sub·sid·i·ar·y (səb sid′ē er′ē, -ē ər ē) ***adj.*** ⟦L *subsidiarius* < *subsidium:* see SUBSIDY⟧ **1** giving aid, support, service, etc.; serving to supplement; auxiliary **2** being in a secondary or subordinate relationship **3** of, constituting, or maintained by a subsidy or subsidies —***n., pl.*** **-ar′ies** a person or thing that is subsidiary; specif., *a)* a company controlled by another company which owns all or a majority of its shares (in full **subsidiary company**) *b)* *Music* a subordinate theme —**sub·sid′i·ar′i·ly** ***adv.***

sub·si·dize (sub′sə dīz′) ***vt.*** **-dized′, -diz′ing** ⟦< fol. + -IZE⟧ **1** to support with a subsidy **2** to buy the aid or support of with a subsidy, often as a kind of bribe —**sub′si·di·za′tion** ***n.*** —**sub′si·diz′er** ***n.***

sub·si·dy (sub′sə dē) ***n., pl.*** **-dies** ⟦ME < Anglo-Fr *subsidie* < L *subsidium,* auxiliary forces, reserve troops, aid, support < *subsidere,* to sit down, remain: see SUBSIDE⟧ a grant of money; specif., *a)* a grant of money from one government to another, as for military aid *b)* a government grant to a private enterprise considered of benefit to the public *c)* [Historical] in England, money granted by Parliament to the Crown

sub·sist (səb sist′) ***vi.*** ⟦L *subsistere,* to stand still, stay, abide < *sub-,* under + *sistere,* to place, stand, redupl. of base of *stare,* to STAND⟧ **1** *a)* to continue to be or exist; have existence as a reality, entity, etc. *b)* to continue to be in use, force, etc. **2** to continue to live; remain alive (*on* sustenance, *by* specific means, etc.); be sustained **3** to consist or inhere (*in*) **4** *Philos.* to be logically conceivable and have being as a conceptual entity that may be the subject of true statements —***vt.*** to maintain with sustenance; support

sub·sist·ence (-sis′təns) ***n.*** ⟦ME < LL(Ec) *subsistentia* < L *subsistere:* see prec.⟧ **1** existence; being; continuance **2** the act of providing sustenance **3** means of support or livelihood; often, specif., the barest means in terms of food, clothing, and shelter needed to sustain life **4** the quality of being inherent **5** *Philos.* *a)* the status of something that exists in itself as an individual whole *b)* the status of something whose very act of existing is its essence, as God *c)* the quality of being logically conceivable —**sub·sist′ent** ***adj.***

sub·soil (sub′soil′) ***n.*** the layer of soil beneath the topsoil —***vt.*** to stir or turn up the subsoil of —**sub′soil′er** ***n.***

sub·so·lar (sub sō′lər) ***adj.*** ⟦SUB- + SOLAR⟧ **1** located under the sun **2** having the sun in the zenith

sub·son·ic (-sän′ik) ***adj.*** ⟦SUB- + SONIC⟧ **1** designating, of, or moving at a speed in a surrounding fluid less than that of sound in the same fluid **2** INFRASONIC

sub·space (sub′spās′) ***n.*** *Math.* a space which forms a proper subset of some larger space

sub spe·ci·e ae·ter·ni·ta·tis (sub spē′shi ē′ ē tur′ni tät′is) ⟦L, lit., under the aspect of eternity⟧ from the standpoint of eternity; from a universal perspective

sub·spe·cies (sub′spē′shēz) ***n.*** ⟦ModL: see SUB- & SPECIES⟧ any natural subdivision of a species that exhibits small, but persistent, morphological variations from other subdivisions of the same species living in different geographical regions or times: the subspecies name is usually the third term (not capitalized) in a trinomial (Ex.: the scientific name for *Neanderthal man* is *Homo sapiens neanderthalensis*) —**sub′spe·cif′ic** (-spə sif′ik) ***adj.***

subst *abbrev.* **1** substantive **2** substitute

sub·stage (sub′stāj′) ***n.*** **1** any subdivision or part of a stage **2** the part of a microscope located below the stage to which a mirror, light, etc. can be attached

sub·stance (sub′stəns) ***n.*** ⟦OFr < L *substantia* < *substare,* to be present < *sub-,* under + *stare,* to STAND⟧ **1** the real or essential part or element of anything; essence, reality, or basic matter **2** *a)* the physical matter of which a thing consists; material *b)* matter of a particular kind or chemical composition **3** *a)* solid quality; substantial character *b)* consistency; body **4** the real content, meaning, or gist of something said or written **5** material possessions; property; resources; wealth ☆**6** a drug: see CONTROLLED SUBSTANCE **7** *Philos.* *a)* something that has independent existence and is acted upon by causes *b)* that part of a thing in which its properties inhere —**in substance 1** with regard to essential elements **2** actually; really

substance abuse excessive use of alcohol, opiates, stimulants, hallucinogens, etc., esp. without prescription

sub·stand·ard (sub stan′dərd) *adj.* below standard; specif., *a)* below a standard established as by law *b) Linguis.* NONSTANDARD (*substandard,* not widely used by linguists, is a usually pejorative designation for dialects or linguistic forms that differ from the standard dialect)

sub·stan·tial (səb stan′shəl) *adj.* ⟦ME *substancial* < ML *substantialis* < LL⟧ **1** of or having substance **2** real; actual; true; not imaginary **3** strong; solid; firm; stout **4** considerable; ample; large **5** of considerable worth or value; important **6** having property or possessions; wealthy **7** with regard to essential elements; in substance **8** *Philos.* of, or having the nature of, substance —*n.* a substantial thing: *usually used in pl.* —**sub·stan′ti·al′i·ty** (-shē al′ə tē) *n.*, **sub·stan′tial·ness** —**sub·stan′tial·ly** *adv.*

sub·stan·ti·a ni·gra (səb stan′shē ə nī′grə) *pl.* **sub·stan·ti·ae ni·grae** (səb stan′shē ē′ nī′grē) or **sub·stan′ti·a ni′gras** ⟦ModL, black substance⟧ a layer of dark cells in the midbrain that produce dopamine

sub·stan·ti·ate (səb stan′shē āt′) *vt.* **-at′ed, -at′ing** ⟦< ModL *substantiatus,* pp. of *substantiare* < L *substantia,* SUBSTANCE⟧ **1** to give substance or true existence to **2** to give concrete form or body to; convert into substance; embody **3** to show to be true or real by giving evidence; prove; confirm —*SYN.* CONFIRM —**sub·stan′ti·a′tion** *n.* —**sub·stan′ti·a′tive** *adj.* —**sub·stan′ti·a′tor** *n.*

sub·stan·tive (sub′stən tiv, səb stan′tiv) *adj.* ⟦LME < LL *substantivus* < L *substantia:* see SUBSTANCE⟧ **1** existing independently; not dependent upon or subordinate to another **2** of considerable amount or quantity; substantial **3** having a real existence; actual **4** *a)* of, containing, or dealing with the essential elements; essential *b)* having direct bearing on a matter **5** of or relating to legal rights and principles as distinguished from legal procedures **6** becoming fixed without the use of a mordant: said of a dye **7** *Gram.* *a)* expressing existence [the *substantive* verb "to be"] *b)* of or used as a substantive —*n.* **1** something substantive **2** *Gram.* a noun or any other word or group of words that functions as a noun; nominal —**sub′stan·ti′val** (-tī′vəl) *adj.* —**sub′stan·ti′val·ly** *adv.*, **sub′stan·tive·ly** —**sub′stan·tive·ness** *n.*

substantive right a basic human right, as life, liberty, etc., regarded as having authoritative standing and importance independent of man-made laws

sub·sta·tion (sub′stā′shən) *n.* a lesser station or a division of a station; specif., *a)* a small post-office station, as in a retail store *b)* a subsidiary station in an electric power grid, equipped, variously, with transformers, capacitors, circuit breakers, etc.

sub·stel·lar (sub stel′ər) *adj. Astron.* of a size much smaller than that of a typical star

sub·stit·u·ent (sub stich′o͞o ənt) *n.* ⟦< L *substituens,* prp. of *substituere:* see fol.⟧ *Chem.* an atom or group of atoms replacing another atom or group in a compound

sub·sti·tute (sub′stə to͞ot′, -tyo͞ot′) *n.* ⟦ME < L *substitutus,* pp. of *substituere,* to put instead of < *sub-,* under + *statuere,* to put, place: see STATUE⟧ **1** a person or thing serving or used in place of another **2** *Gram.* any word or word group, as a pronoun, the verb *to do,* etc., used in place of another word or words (Ex.: *did* for *shouted* in "she shouted, and he did, too") —*vt.* **-tut′ed, -tut′ing 1** to put or use in place of another **2** [Now Rare] to take the place of **3** *Chem.* to replace as a substituent —☆*vi.* to act or serve in place of another: often with *for* —*adj.* being a substitute or substitutes —**sub′sti·tut′a·ble** *adj.*

sub·sti·tu·tion (sub′stə to͞o′shən, -tyo͞o′-) *n.* the substituting of one person or thing for another —**sub′sti·tu′tion·al** *adj.*, **sub′sti·tu′tion·ar′y**

sub·sti·tu·tive (sub′stə to͞ot′iv, -tyo͞ot′-) *adj.* ⟦LL *substitutivus*⟧ **1** of or having to do with substitution **2** being or capable of being a substitute —**sub′sti·tu′tive·ly** *adv.*

sub·strate (sub′strāt′) *n.* **1** SUBSTRATUM **2** *Biochem.* a substance acted upon, as by an enzyme **3** *Bacteriology, Biol.* MEDIUM (*n.* 6)

sub·strat·o·sphere (sub strat′ə sfir′) *n.* loosely, the highest part of the troposphere

sub·stra·tum (sub′strāt′əm, -strat′-) *n.*, *pl.* **-ta** (-ə) or **-tums** ⟦ModL < L, neut. of *substratus,* pp. of *substernere,* to strew beneath < *sub-,* under + *sternere,* to spread out < IE base **ster-* > STREW⟧ **1** *a)* a part, substance, element, etc. which lies beneath and supports another; foundation *b)* any basis or foundation **2** SUBSTRATE (senses 2 & 3) **3** loosely, SUBSOIL **4** *Bot.* the base or material to which a plant is attached and from which it gets nutriment **5** *Philos.* SUBSTANCE (sense 7*b*) **6** *Photog.* a thin layer of material on a photographic film or plate serving as a base for the sensitive emulsion **7** *Zool.* the ground or other solid material on which an animal moves or is fastened

sub·struc·ture (sub′struk′chər) *n.* a part or structure acting as a support, base, or foundation: also [Archaic] **sub′struc′tion** (-shən) —**sub·struc′tur·al** *adj.*

sub·sume (səb so͞om′, -syo͞om′) *vt.* **-sumed′, -sum′ing** ⟦ModL *subsumere* < L *sub-,* under + *sumere,* to take: see CONSUME⟧ **1** to include within a larger class, group, order, etc. **2** to show (an idea, instance, etc.) to be covered by a rule, principle, etc.

sub·sump·tion (səb sump′shən) *n.* ⟦ModL *subsumptio* < *subsumptus,* pp. of *subsumere*⟧ a subsuming or being subsumed —**sub·sump′tive** *adj.*

sub·sur·face (sub′sʉr′fis) *adj.* lying below the surface, esp. of the earth, the oceans, etc. —*n.* a subsurface part

sub·sys·tem (sub′sis′təm) *n.* any system that is part of a larger system; component system

sub·tan·gent (sub tan′jənt) *n. Geom.* the segment of the x-axis included between the ordinate of a given point on a curve and the tangent at that point

☆**sub·teen** (sub′tēn′) *n.* a child who is nearly a teenager

sub·tem·per·ate (sub tem′pər it) *adj.* of or occurring in the colder areas of the temperate zones

sub·ten·ant (sub′ten′ənt) *n.* a person who rents from a tenant; tenant of a tenant —**sub·ten′an·cy** *n.*

sub·tend (səb tend′) *vt.* ⟦L *subtendere* < *sub-,* under + *tendere,* to stretch: see TEND[2]⟧ **1** to extend under or be opposite to in position [each side of a triangle *subtends* the opposite angle] **2** *Bot.* to enclose in an angle, as between a leaf and its stem

sub·ter- (sub′tər) ⟦L < *subter,* below < *sub* (see SUB-) + *-ter,* compar. suffix⟧ *prefix* below, under, less than, secretly

sub·ter·fuge (sub′tər fyo͞oj′) *n.* ⟦LL *subterfugium* < L *subterfugere,* to flee secretly, escape < *subter-,* secretly (< *subter,* below) + *fugere,* to flee: see FUGITIVE⟧ any plan, action, or device used to hide one's true objective, evade a difficult or unpleasant situation, etc.; stratagem; artifice —*SYN.* DECEPTION

sub·ter·ra·ne·an (sub′tə rā′nē ən) *adj.* ⟦L *subterraneus* < *sub-* (see SUB-) + *terra,* earth: see TERRAIN⟧ **1** lying beneath the earth's surface; underground **2** secret; hidden Also **sub′ter·ra′ne·ous** —*n.* one who lives underground —**sub′ter·ra′ne·an·ly** *adv.*

sub·text (sub′tekst′) *n.* **1** the complex of feelings, motives, etc. conceived of by an actor as underlying the actual words and actions of the character being portrayed **2** an underlying meaning, theme, etc. —**sub·tex′tu·al** *adj.*

sub·tile (sut′'l, sub′til) *adj.* ⟦ME < MFr *subtil,* altered (infl. by L) < OFr *soutil:* see SUBTLE⟧ *var. of* SUBTLE —**sub′tile·ly** *adv.* —**sub′tile·ness** *n.* —**sub′til·ty** *n.*, *pl.* **-ties**

sub·til·ize (sut′'l īz′, sub′til-) *vt.*, *vi.* **-ized′, -iz′ing** ⟦ML *subtilizare* < L *subtilis,* SUBTLE⟧ **1** to make or become subtle **2** to discuss or argue with subtle distinctions —**sub′til·i·za′tion** *n.*

sub·ti·tle (sub′tīt′'l) *n.* **1** a secondary or explanatory title, as of a book or play **2** one or more lines of text, as a translation of dialogue in a foreign language, appearing usually at the bottom of a film or video image —*vt.* **-ti′tled, -ti′tling** to add a subtitle or subtitles to

sub·tle (sut′'l) *adj.* **sub′tler** (-lər, -'l ər), **sub′tlest** ⟦ME *sotil* < OFr *soutil* < L *subtilis,* fine, thin, precise, orig., closely woven < *sub-* (see SUB-) + *tela,* web < **texla* < *texere,* to weave: see TECHNIC⟧ **1** thin; rare; tenuous; not dense or heavy [a *subtle* gas] **2** *a)* capable of making or noticing fine distinctions in meaning, etc. [a *subtle* thinker] *b)* marked by or requiring mental keenness [*subtle* reasoning] **3** delicately skillful or clever; deft or ingenious [a *subtle* filigree] **4** not open or direct; crafty; sly **5** delicately suggestive; not grossly obvious [a *subtle* hint] **6** working insidiously; not easily detected [a *subtle* poison] —**sub′tle·ness** *n.* —**sub′tly** *adv.*

sub·tle·ty (-tē) *n.* ⟦ME *sutelte* < OFr *sotillete* < L *subtilitas*⟧ **1** the quality or condition of being subtle; esp., the ability or tendency to make fine distinctions **2** *pl.* **-ties** something subtle; esp., a fine distinction

sub·ton·ic (sub tän′ik) *n. Music* the seventh tone of a diatonic scale; tone next below the upper tonic

sub·top·ic (sub′täp′ik) *n.* a topic that is a division of a main topic

sub·to·tal (sub′tōt′'l) *n.* a total that forms part of a final, complete total — *vt.*, *vi.* **-taled** or **-talled**, **-tal·ing** or **-tal·ling** to add up so as to form a subtotal

sub·tract (səb trakt′) *vt.*, *vi.* ⟦< L *subtractus,* pp. of *subtrahere,* to draw away underneath, subtract < *sub-,* SUB- + *trahere,* to DRAW⟧ **1** to take away (a part from a whole) **2** to take away or deduct (one number or quantity from another) —**sub·tract′er** *n.*

sub·trac·tion (səb trak′shən) *n.* ⟦ML *subtractio* < LL(Ec), a drawing back⟧ a subtracting or being subtracted; esp., the mathematical process of finding the difference between two numbers or quantities

sub·trac·tive (-tiv) *adj.* ⟦ML *subtractivus*⟧ **1** tending to subtract **2** capable of or involving subtraction **3** that is to be subtracted; marked with the minus sign (−)

sub·tra·hend (sub′trə hend′) *n.* ⟦L *subtrahendus,* ger. of *subtrahere:* see SUBTRACT⟧ a number or quantity to be subtracted from another (the *minuend*)

☆**sub·treas·ur·y** (sub′trezh′ər ē) *n.*, *pl.* **-ur·ies** a branch treasury

sub·trop·i·cal (sub träp′i kəl) *adj.* **1** designating or of regions bordering on the tropical zone **2** characteristic of such regions; nearly tropical Also **sub·trop′ic**

sub·trop·ics (sub′träp′iks) *pl.n.* subtropical regions

su·bu·late (so͞o′byo͞o lit, -lāt′) *adj.* ⟦ModL *subulatus* < L *subula,* an awl < **sudhla* < *suere,* SEW⟧ *Biol.* slender and tapering to a point; awl-shaped

sub·um·brel·la (sub′um brel′ə) *n.* ⟦SUB- + UMBRELLA⟧ *Zool.* the concave lower, or oral, surface of a jellyfish

sub·urb (sub′ərb) *n.* ⟦ME < L *suburbium* < *sub-,* under, near + *urbs* (gen. *urbis*), town⟧ **1** a usually residential district or separately incorporated city or town, on or near the outskirts of a larger city **2** [*pl.*] a region made up of such districts: with *the*

sub·ur·ban (sə bʉr′bən) *adj.* ⟦L *suburbanus*⟧ **1** of, in, or residing in a suburb or the suburbs **2** characteristic of the suburbs or suburbanites

sub·ur·ban·ite (-bə nīt′) *n.* a person living in a suburb

sub·ur·ban·ize (-nīz′) *vt.*, *vi.* **-ized′, -iz′ing** to make or become suburban —**sub·ur′ban·i·za′tion** *n.*

sub·ur·bi·a (sə bʉr′bē ə) *n.* the suburbs or suburbanites collectively: usually used to connote the values, attitudes, and activities regarded as characteristic of suburban life

sub·vene (səb vēn′) *vi.* **-vened′, -ven′ing** ⟦L *subvenire,* to come to one's assistance, lit., to come up < *sub-,* under + *venire,* to COME⟧ [Rare] to happen or come, so as to help

sub·ven·tion (-ven′shən) *n.* ⟦ME < *subvencioun* < OFr *subvencion* < LL *subventio*⟧ 1 [Obs.] the act of subvening 2 money granted, as by a government, in support of a study, institution, etc.; subsidy —**sub·ven′tion·ar′y** *adj.*

sub ver·bo (sub vur′bō, -ver′bō, -wer′bō) ⟦L⟧ under the word (specified): with reference to an entry in a dictionary, index, etc.

sub·ver·sion (səb vur′zhən, -shən) *n.* ⟦OFr < L *subversio*⟧ a subverting or being subverted; ruin; overthrow

sub·ver·sive (-siv) *adj.* ⟦ML *subversivus* < L *subversus,* pp. of *subvertere:* see fol.⟧ tending or seeking to subvert, overthrow, or destroy (an established government, institution, belief, etc.) —*n.* a person regarded as subversive —**sub·ver′sive·ly** *adv.* —**sub·ver′sive·ness** *n.*

sub·vert (səb vurt′) *vt.* ⟦ME *subverten* < MFr *subvertir* < L *subvertere* < *sub-,* SUB- + *vertere,* to turn: see VERSE⟧ 1 to overthrow or destroy (something established) 2 to undermine or corrupt, as in morals —**sub·vert′er** *n.*

sub vo·ce (sub vō′sē, -vō′kā, -wō′kā) ⟦L, under the voice, i.e., utterance or term⟧ SUB VERBO

sub·way (sub′wā′) *n.* 1 *a)* an underground way or passage *b)* [Chiefly Brit.] an underpass for pedestrians ☆2 an underground, metropolitan electric railway or the tunnel through which it runs

sub·woof·er (sub′woof′ər) *n.* a large, high-fidelity speaker for reproducing sounds with very low frequencies, esp. those in the range 25 to 180 hertz

suc- (suk, sək) *prefix* SUB-: used before *c* [*succumb*]

suc·ce·da·ne·um (suk′si dā′nē əm) *n., pl.* **-ne·a** (-nē ə) ⟦ModL < neut. sing. of L *succedaneus,* substituted < *succedere:* see fol.⟧ *rare var. of* SUBSTITUTE

suc·ceed (sək sēd′) *vi.* ⟦ME *succeden* < L *succedere,* to go beneath or under, follow after < *sub-,* under + *cedere,* to go: see CEDE⟧ 1 *a)* to come next after another; follow; ensue *b)* to follow another into office, possession, etc., as by election, appointment, or inheritance (often with *to*) *c)* [Obs.] to devolve, as an estate 2 to happen or turn out as planned or attempted [*a plan that succeeded*] 3 to achieve or accomplish something planned or attempted [*to succeed in persuading someone*] 4 to have or enjoy success; realize a goal or goals, esp. in becoming wealthy, winning fame or approval, etc. [*to succeed in business*] —*vt.* 1 to take the place left by; follow into office, etc. 2 to come or occur after; follow —*SYN.* FOLLOW —**suc·ceed′er** *n.*

suc·cès de scan·dale (sük se də skän dȧl′) ⟦Fr, success of scandal⟧ 1 notoriety gained by something scandalous, as a shocking play, film, novel, etc. 2 something that causes such notoriety

suc·cès d'es·time (sük se des tēm′) ⟦Fr, success of esteem⟧ 1 the gaining of acclaim from professional critics; critical success 2 an artistic work receiving such acclaim, often without being a financial success

suc·cès fou (sük se fo͞o′) ⟦Fr, mad success⟧ an extraordinary success, esp. financially

suc·cess (sək ses′) *n.* ⟦L *successus* < pp. of *succedere:* see SUCCEED⟧ 1 [Obs.] result; outcome 2 *a)* a favorable or satisfactory outcome or result *b)* something having such an outcome 3 the gaining of wealth, fame, rank, etc. 4 a successful person

suc·cess·ful (-fəl) *adj.* 1 coming about, taking place, or turning out to be as was hoped for [*a successful mission*] 2 having achieved success; specif., having gained wealth, fame, etc. —**suc·cess′ful·ly** *adv.* —**suc·cess′ful·ness** *n.*

suc·ces·sion (sək sesh′ən) *n.* ⟦OFr < L *successio* < *succedere:* see SUCCEED⟧ 1 the act of succeeding or coming after another in order or sequence or to an office, estate, throne, etc. 2 the right to succeed to an office, estate, etc. 3 a number of persons or things coming one after another in time or space; series; sequence [*a succession of delays*] 4 *a)* a series of heirs or rightful successors of any kind *b)* the order or line of such a series 5 *Ecol.* the slow, regular sequence of changes in the regional development of communities of plants and associated animals, culminating in a climax characteristic of a specific geographical environment —*SYN.* SERIES —**in succession** one after another in a regular series or sequence; successively —**suc·ces′sion·al** *adj.* —**suc·ces′sion·al·ly** *adv.*

suc·ces·sive (sək ses′iv) *adj.* ⟦ME < LL *successivus*⟧ 1 coming in succession; following one after another in sequence; consecutive 2 of or involving succession —**suc·ces′sive·ly** *adv.* —**suc·ces′sive·ness** *n.*

suc·ces·sor (-ər) *n.* ⟦ME < OFr *successour* < L *successor* < *successus,* pp. of *succedere:* see SUCCEED⟧ a person or thing that succeeds, or follows, another; esp., one who succeeds to an office, title, etc.

suc·ci·nate (suk′sə nāt′) *n.* a salt or ester of succinic acid

suc·cinct (sək siŋkt′) *adj.* ⟦ME, girdled, girded < L *succinctus,* prepared, short, contracted, pp. of *succingere,* to gird, tuck up, prepare < *sub-,* SUB- + *cingere,* to gird: see CINCH⟧ 1 clearly and briefly stated; terse 2 characterized by brevity and conciseness of speech 3 [Archaic] *a)* enclosed as by a girdle *b)* closefitting —*SYN.* CONCISE —**suc·cinct′ly** *adv.* —**suc·cinct′ness** *n.*

suc·cin·ic acid (sək sin′ik) ⟦Fr *succinique* < L *succinum,* amber⟧ a colorless, crystalline dibasic acid, $HOOC(CH_2)_2COOH$, found in amber, lignite, and many plants, and produced synthetically or during alcoholic fermentation: it is used in medicine and organic synthesis

suc·cin·yl·cho·line chloride (suk′sə nəl kō′lēn) a powerful muscle relaxant, $C_{14}H_{30}Cl_2N_2O_4$, used in surgery, electroconvulsive therapy, etc.: it briefly paralyzes the voluntary and respiratory muscles

suc·cor (suk′ər) *vt.* ⟦ME *socouren* < OFr *sucurre, socorre* < L *succurrere* < *sub-,* SUB- + *currere,* to run: see COURSE⟧ to give assistance to in time of need or distress; help; aid; relieve —*n.* ⟦ME *socur,* assumed sing. of *socours* < OFr *sucurs* < ML *succursus* < L, pp.: see the *vt.*⟧ 1 aid; help; relief 2 a person or thing that succors Brit. sp. **suc′cour** —*SYN.* HELP

suc·cor·y (suk′ər ē) *n.* ⟦altered < MLowG *suckerie* < older *sycory,* early form of CHICORY⟧ CHICORY

☆**suc·co·tash** (suk′ə tash′) *n.* ⟦< Narragansett *msíckquatash,* boiled whole kernels of corn⟧ a dish consisting of lima beans and kernels of corn cooked together

Suc·coth (so͞o kōt′; sook′ōt′, -ōs′) *n. alt. sp. of* SUKKOT

suc·cu·bus (suk′yo͞o bəs) *n., pl.* **-bi′** (-bī′) ⟦ME < ML (altered by assoc. with INCUBUS) < LL *succuba,* strumpet < L *succubare,* to lie under < *sub-,* SUB- + *cubare,* to lie: see CUBE[1]⟧ *Folklore* a female evil spirit or demon who has sexual intercourse with sleeping men: cf. INCUBUS: also **suc′cu·ba** (-bə), *pl.* **-bae′** (-bē′)

suc·cu·lent (suk′yo͞o lənt) *adj.* ⟦L *succulentus* < *sucus,* juice: see SUCK⟧ 1 full of juice; juicy 2 full of interest, vigor, etc.; not dry or dull 3 *Bot.* having thick, fleshy tissues for storing water, as a cactus —*n.* a succulent plant —**suc′cu·lence** *n.,* **suc′cu·len·cy** —**suc′cu·lent·ly** *adv.*

suc·cumb (sə kum′) *vi.* ⟦L *succumbere* < *sub-,* SUB- + *cumbere,* nasalized form of *cubare,* to lie: see CUBE[1]⟧ 1 to give way (*to*); yield; submit [*to succumb to persuasion*] 2 to die [*half the population of the town succumbed to the plague*] —*SYN.* YIELD

suc·cuss (sə kus′) *vt.* ⟦< L *succussus,* pp. of *succutere,* to toss up < *sub-,* under + *quatere,* to shake: see QUASH[2]⟧ to shake forcibly; esp. formerly, to shake (a patient) from side to side in order to detect a liquid in some body cavity, esp. in the thorax —**suc·cus′sion** *n.*

such (such) *adj.* ⟦ME *suche* < OE *swilc, swelc,* akin to Ger *solch,* Goth *swaleiks* < PGmc **swalika-:* for components see SO[1] & LIKE[1]⟧ 1 *a)* of the kind mentioned or implied [*a man such as his father*] *b)* of the same or a similar kind; like [*pens, pencils, crayons, and such supplies*] 2 certain but not specified; whatever [*at such time as you go*] 3 so extreme, so much, so great, etc.: used, according to the context, for emphasis [*embarrassed by such praise*] ➥*Such* is a term of comparison, although that with which comparison is made is not always expressed; when it is expressed, *as* or *that* is used as a correlative with *such* [*such love as his is seldom experienced*]. *Such* is not preceded by an article, although the article may occur between it and the noun it modifies [*such a fool!*] —*adv.* to so great a degree; so [*such good news*] —*pron.* 1 other persons or things of the kind mentioned [*a buffet of soup, appetizers, and such*] 2 the person or thing mentioned or implied [*such was her nature*] —**as such** 1 as being what is indicated or suggested 2 in itself [*a name, as such, means nothing*] —**such as** 1 for example 2 like or similar to (something specified) —**such as it is** (or **was,** etc.) being the kind it is (or was, etc.): used in referring to something in either an apologetic or a derogatory way —**such that** in such a way that [*divided such that each subgroup had at least 3 members*]

such and such (being) something particular but not named or specified [*we went to such and such a place*]

such·like (such′līk′) *adj.* of such a kind; of like or similar kind —*pron.* a thing (or things) or person (or persons) of such a kind or of similar kind

Su·chow (sho͞o′jō′) *a former transliteration of* XUZHOU

suck (suk) *vt.* ⟦ME *suken* < OE *sucan,* akin to Ger *saugen* < IE **seuk-, *seug-* < base **seu-,* damp, juice > SUP[1], L *sucus,* juice, *sugere,* to suck⟧ 1 *a)* to draw (liquid) into the mouth by creating a vacuum or partial vacuum with the lips, cheeks, and tongue *b)* to draw up (water, oil, etc.) by the action of a pump 2 to take up or in by or as by sucking; absorb, inhale, etc. [*to suck air into the lungs*] 3 to suck liquid from (a breast, fruit, etc.) 4 to hold (candy, ice, etc.) in the mouth and lick so as to dissolve and consume 5 to place (the thumb, a pencil, etc.) in the mouth and draw on as if sucking 6 to bring into a specified state by sucking [*to suck an orange dry*] 7 [Vulgar Slang] to perform fellatio on —*vi.* 1 to draw in water, air, etc. by creating a partial vacuum 2 to suck milk from the breast or udder 3 to hold something in the mouth and lick or draw on it: used with *on* or *at* [*to suck on a piece of ice, sucking away at his pipe*] 4 to make a sound or movement of sucking 5 to draw in air instead of liquid: said of a faulty pump 6 ⟦see *vt.* 7⟧ [Slang] to be contemptible or very unsatisfying, as because of low quality: considered mildly vulgar by some [*this show sucks*] —*n.* 1 the act of sucking; sucking action or force; suction 2 a sound or movement of sucking 3 *a)* something drawn in by sucking *b)* [Informal] the amount sucked at one time; sip —**suck in** 1 to compress and pull inward [*to suck in one's belly*] 2 [Slang] to take advantage of; swindle, etc. —☆**suck it up** [Slang] to respond to hardship, pain, etc. calmly and without complaint —**suck up (to)** [Slang] to flatter or fawn (on) ingratiatingly

suck·er (suk′ər) *n.* 1 a person or thing that sucks ☆2 any of a family (Catostomidae, order Cypriniformes) of bony fishes with a mouth adapted for sucking, found in freshwater of E Asia and North America 3 a part or device used for sucking; specif., *a)* a pipe or conduit through which something is sucked *b)* the piston or piston valve of a suction pump *c)* an organ used by the leech, fluke, remora, etc. for sucking or holding fast to a surface by suction ☆4 LOLLIPOP ☆5 [Slang] *a)* a person easily cheated or taken in; dupe *b)* a person highly susceptible to the attractions of something specified [*a sucker for old horror movies*] *c)* any person or thing (often used humorously or affectionately, or to express mild annoyance) 6 *Bot.* a subordinate shoot from a bud on the root or stem of a plant —*vt.* 1 to remove suckers, or shoots, from ☆2 [Slang] to make a dupe of; trick —*vi.* to bear suckers, or shoots

suck·er·fish (-fish′) ***n.***, *pl.* **-fish′** or **-fish′es** (see FISH) REMORA (sense 1)

☆**sucker punch** [Slang] 1 a quick punch delivered without warning; an unexpected blow 2 to punch (someone) unexpectedly: sometimes written **suck′er-punch′** ***vt.***

sucking louse LOUSE (*n.* 1*a*)

suck·le (suk′əl) ***vt.*** **-led**, **-ling** ⟦ME *sokelen*, prob. back-form. < *sokelynge*, SUCKLING⟧ 1 to cause to suck at the breast or udder; nurse 2 to bring up; rear; foster —*vi.* to suck at the breast or udder

suck·ler (-lər) ***n.*** 1 an animal that suckles its young; mammal 2 SUCKLING

suck·ling (-liŋ) ***n.*** ⟦ME *sokelynge:* see SUCK & -LING[1]⟧ 1 an unweaned young animal 2 [Archaic] an unweaned child

Suck·ling (suk′liŋ), Sir **John** 1609-42; Eng. poet

su·crase (so͞o′krās′) ***n.*** ⟦< Fr *sucre*, SUGAR + -ASE⟧ an enzyme present in certain plant and animal tissues that catalyzes the hydrolysis of sucrose into glucose and fructose

su·cre (so͞o′kre) ***n.*** ⟦AmSp, after fol.⟧ the former basic monetary unit of Ecuador

Su·cre[1] (so͞o′kre), **An·to·nio Jo·sé de** (än tô′nyô hô se′ de) 1795-1830; South American liberator: 1st president of Bolivia (1826-28)

Su·cre[2] (so͞o′kre) city in SC Bolivia: legal capital & seat of the judiciary: cf. LA PAZ

su·crose (so͞o′krōs′) ***n.*** ⟦< Fr *sucre*, SUGAR + -OSE[1]⟧ *Chem.* a pure crystalline disaccharide extracted from sugar cane or sugar beets and consisting of glucose and fructose joined together in the molecule

suc·tion (suk′shən) ***n.*** ⟦L *suctio* < *suctus*, pp. of *sugere*, to SUCK⟧ 1 the act or process of sucking 2 the production of a vacuum or partial vacuum in a cavity or over a surface so that the external atmospheric pressure forces the surrounding fluid, particulate solid, etc. into the cavity or causes something to adhere to the surface 3 the suction force created in this way —***adj.*** 1 causing suction 2 operating by suction

suction cup a rubber cup that will stick to a surface by creating a vacuum in the area it covers

suction pump a pump that draws liquid up by suction created by pistons fitted with valves

suc·to·ri·al (suk tôr′ē əl) ***adj.*** ⟦< ModL *suctorius* < L *suctus* (see SUCTION) + -AL⟧ 1 of or adapted for sucking or suction 2 having organs used for sucking

Su·dan (so͞o dan′, -dän′) 1 vast semiarid region in NC Africa, south of the Sahara, extending from the Atlantic to the Red Sea 2 country in the E part of this region, south of Egypt: formerly a British & Egyptian condominium called ANGLO-EGYPTIAN SUDAN, it became an independent republic in 1956: 728,215 sq mi (1,886,068 sq km); cap. Khartoum Often preceded by *the* —**Su·da·nese** (so͞o′də nēz′) ***adj.***, ***n.***, *pl.* **-nese′**

☆**Sudan grass** ⟦after prec., where it is cultivated⟧ a tall annual grass (*Sorghum sudanense*) grown for summer pasture and hay

Su·dan·ic (so͞o dan′ik) ***adj.*** 1 of or pertaining to Sudan 2 designating or of either of two branches (**Eastern Sudanic** and **Central Sudanic**) of the Chari-Nile subfamily of languages, including various languages spoken in Sudan

su·dar·i·um (so͞o der′ē əm) ***n.***, *pl.* **-i·a** (-ə) ⟦L < *sudor*, SWEAT⟧ in ancient Rome, a cloth for wiping sweat from the face: also **su·da·ry** (so͞o′də rē), *pl.* **-ries**

su·da·to·ri·um (so͞o′də tôr′ē əm) ***n.***, *pl.* **-ri·a** (-ə) ⟦L, neut. of *sudatorius:* see fol.⟧ a heated room, as in a bath, for inducing sweating

su·da·to·ry (so͞o′də tôr′ē) ***adj.*** ⟦L *sudatorius* < *sudor*, SWEAT⟧ 1 of a sudatorium 2 SUDORIFIC —***n.***, *pl.* **-ries** SUDATORIUM

Sud·bur·y (sud′ber′ē, -bər ē) city in SE Ontario, Canada

sudd (sud) ***n.*** ⟦Ar⟧ floating masses of weeds, reeds, etc. that often obstruct navigation on the White Nile

sud·den (sud′'n) ***adj.*** ⟦ME *sodain* < OFr < VL **subitanus*, for L *subitaneus*, sudden, extended < *subitus*, pp. of *subire*, to approach, go stealthily < *sub-*, under + *ire*, to go or come: see YEAR⟧ 1 *a)* happening or coming unexpectedly; not foreseen or prepared for [*a sudden* storm came up] *b)* sharp or abrupt [*a sudden* turn in the road] 2 done, coming, or taking place quickly or abruptly; hasty —**all of a sudden** suddenly; unexpectedly —**sud′den·ly** ***adv.*** —**sud′den·ness** ***n.***

SYN.—**sudden** implies extreme quickness or hastiness and, usually, unexpectedness [*a sudden* outburst of temper]; **precipitate** adds the implication of rashness or lack of due deliberation [*a precipitate* decision]; **abrupt** implies a breaking in or off suddenly and, hence, suggests the lack of any warning or a curtness, lack of ceremony, etc. [*an abrupt* dismissal]; **impetuous** implies vehement impulsiveness or extreme eagerness [*an impetuous* suitor] —**ANT.** **deliberate**

sudden death *Sports* an additional period, game, etc. added to break a tie, the play ending when one side or participant scores

sudden infant death syndrome a syndrome of unknown cause, characterized by the sudden death of an apparently healthy infant, usually during sleep

Su·de·ten[1] (so͞o dāt′'n; *Ger* zo͞o dā′tən) ***n.***, *pl.* **-tens** or **-ten** a person born or living in the Sudetenland —***adj.*** of the Sudetenland or its people or culture

Su·de·ten[2] (so͞o dāt′'n; *Ger* zo͞o dā′tən) 1 SUDETES MOUNTAINS 2 SUDETENLAND

Su·de·ten·land (-land′; *Ger*, -länt′) region in the Sudetes Mountains, N Czech Republic: annexed by Germany (1938): returned to Czechoslovakia (1945)

Su·de·tes Mountains (so͞o dēt′ēz) mountain range along the borders of the N Czech Republic & SW Poland: highest peak, 5,259 ft (1,603 m)

Su·do·ku (so͞o dō′ko͞o) ***n.*** ⟦Jpn < *sū*, number + *doku*, single: shortened < *sūji wa dokushin ni kagiru*, numbers must be single, name orig. used in Japan (1980s) for "Number Place," puzzle originating in the U.S. (1979)⟧ a puzzle typically consisting of a large grid of 81 squares (9 across and 9 down) subdivided into 9 smaller grids of 9 squares (3 across and 3 down), with each of the squares to be filled in with the numbers 1 through 9 without repeating a number in any of the large grid's rows, columns, or smaller grids: the puzzle originates with some squares already filled in, with the number of filled-in squares determining the level of difficulty

su·dor·if·er·ous (so͞o′də rif′ər əs) ***adj.*** ⟦ModL *sudoriferus* < L *sudor* (gen. *sudoris*): see SWEAT & -FEROUS⟧ secreting sweat

su·dor·if·ic (-rif′ik) ***adj.*** ⟦ModL *sudorificus* < L *sudor*, SWEAT + *facere*, to make, DO[1]⟧ causing or increasing sweating —***n.*** a sudorific drug

Su·dra (so͞o′drə) ***n.*** ⟦Sans *śūdra*⟧ a member of the fourth and lowest Hindu caste, that of menial laborers

suds (sudz) ***pl.n.*** ⟦prob. (via East Anglian dial.) < MDu *sudse*, marsh, marsh water: for IE base see SEETHE⟧ 1 soapy water with a froth or foam on the surface 2 froth or foam ☆3 [Slang] beer or ale —☆*vi.* to produce suds —☆*vt.* [Informal] to wash in suds

suds·er (sud′zər) ***n.*** ⟦(SOAP)SUDS + -ER⟧ [Informal] SOAP OPERA

☆**suds·y** (sud′zē) ***adj.*** **suds′i·er**, **suds′i·est** full of or like suds or froth; foamy

sue (so͞o) ***vt.*** **sued**, **su′ing** ⟦ME *suen* < OFr *sivre*, *suir* < VL **sequere*, for L *sequi*, to follow: see SEQUENT⟧ 1 to appeal to; petition; beseech 2 [Archaic] to be a suitor of; woo 3 *Law a)* to petition (a court) for legal redress *b)* to bring civil action against or prosecute in a court of law in seeking justice or redress of wrongs *c)* to carry (an action) through to its final decision —*vi.* 1 to make an appeal; petition; plead (*for* or *to*) 2 [Archaic] to pay suit; woo 3 to institute legal proceedings in court; bring suit —**SYN.** APPEAL —**sue out** to apply for and receive from a court (a writ or other legal process) —**su′er** ***n.***

suede or **suède** (swād) ***n.*** ⟦Fr *Suède*, Sweden, in *gants de Suède*, Swedish gloves⟧ 1 tanned leather of calf, kid, cowhide, etc., with the flesh side buffed into a nap 2 a kind of cloth made to resemble this: also **suede cloth**

sued·ed or **suèd·ed** (swā′did) ***adj.*** made to resemble suede

su·et (so͞o′it) ***n.*** ⟦ME dim. < Anglo-Fr *sue* < OFr *sieu*, *seu* < L *sebum*, tallow: see SOAP⟧ the hard fat deposited around the kidneys and loins of cattle and sheep: used in cooking and as a source of tallow —**su′et·y** ***adj.***

Sue·to·ni·us (swi tō′nē əs) (*Gaius Suetonius Tranquillus*) A.D. 69?-140?; Rom. biographer & historian

Su·ez (so͞o ez′, so͞o′ez) 1 seaport in NE Egypt, on the Suez Canal 2 **Gulf of** N arm of the Red Sea: *c.* 180 mi (290 km) long 3 **Isthmus of** strip of land connecting Asia & Africa, between the Mediterranean & the Gulf of Suez: narrowest point, 72 mi (116 km)

Suez Canal ship canal across the Isthmus of Suez, joining the Mediterranean & the Gulf of Suez: *c.* 107 mi (172 km) long

suf or **suff** *abbrev.* 1 sufficient 2 suffix

suf- (suf) *prefix* SUB-: used before *f* [*suffix*]

suf·fer (suf′ər) ***vt.*** ⟦ME *suffren* < Anglo-Fr *suffrir* < OFr *sofrir* < VL **sufferire*, for L *sufferre*, to undergo, endure < *sub-*, SUB- + *ferre*, to BEAR[1]⟧ 1 to undergo (something painful or unpleasant, as injury, grief, a loss, etc.); be afflicted with 2 to undergo or experience (any process, esp. change) 3 to allow; permit; tolerate 4 to bear up under; endure: now chiefly in negative constructions [they could not *suffer* opposition] —*vi.* 1 to experience pain, harm, loss, a penalty, etc. 2 to be at a disadvantage [my grades *suffer* by comparison with yours] 3 [Archaic] to tolerate or endure evil, injury, etc. —**SYN.** BEAR[1], LET[1] —**suf′fer·er** ***n.***

suf·fer·a·ble (-ə bəl) ***adj.*** that can be suffered, endured, or allowed —**suf′fer·a·bly** ***adv.***

suf·fer·ance (suf′ər əns, suf′rəns) ***n.*** ⟦ME < Anglo-Fr *souffrance* < OFr < LL(Ec) *sufferentia* < L *sufferens*, prp.: see SUFFER⟧ 1 the power or capacity to endure or tolerate pain, distress, etc. 2 consent, permission, or sanction implied by failure to interfere or prohibit; toleration 3 [Archaic] suffering —**on sufferance** allowed or tolerated but not supported or encouraged

suf·fer·ing (suf′ər iŋ, suf′riŋ) ***n.*** 1 the bearing or undergoing of pain, distress, or injury 2 something suffered; pain, distress, or injury —**SYN.** DISTRESS

suf·fice (sə fīs′, -fīz′) ***vi.*** **-ficed′**, **-fic′ing** ⟦ME *sufficen* < stem of OFr *soufire* < L *sufficere*, to provide, suffice < *sub-*, SUB- + *facere*, to make, DO[1]⟧ 1 to be enough; be sufficient or adequate 2 [Obs.] to be competent or able —*vt.* [Archaic] to be enough for; meet the needs of; satisfy —**suffice (it) to say** probably it is enough simply to state: used as an introduction suggesting that what follows is plainly evident or merits only brief comment

suf·fi·cien·cy (sə fish′ən sē) ***n.*** 1 sufficient means, ability, or resources; specif., *a)* an adequate amount or quantity (*of* what is needed) *b)* enough wealth or income 2 the state or quality of being sufficient or adequate; adequacy

suf·fi·cient (-ənt) ***adj.*** ⟦ME < L *sufficiens*, prp. of *sufficere:* see SUFFICE⟧ 1 as much as is needed; equal to what is specified or required; enough 2 competent; well-qualified; able —**suf·fi′cient·ly** ***adv.***

SYN.—**sufficient** and **enough** agree in describing that which satisfies a requirement exactly and is neither more nor less in amount than is needed [a word to the wise is *sufficient; enough* food for a week]; **adequate** suggests the meeting of an acceptable (sometimes barely so) standard of fitness or suitability [the supporting players were merely *adequate*] —*ANT.* **deficient, inadequate**

sufficient condition 1 *Logic* an antecedent whose validity entails the validity of the consequent 2 something whose existence or occurrence by itself guarantees that a given thing will exist or occur Cf. NECESSARY CONDITION

suf·fix (suf′iks; *also, for v.,* sə fiks′) ***n.*** ⟦ModL *suffixum* < neut. of L *suffixus,* pp. of *suffigere,* to fasten on beneath < *sub-,* SUB- + *figere,* to FIX⟧ 1 a letter, syllable, or group of syllables added at the end of a word or word base to change its meaning, give it grammatical function, or form a new word (Ex.: *-ish* in *smallish, -ed* in *walked, -ness* in *darkness*) 2 anything added to the end of something else —***vt.*** to add as a suffix —**suf′fix·al** ***adj.*** —**suf′fix·a′tion** ***n.*** —**suf·fix′ion** ***n.***

suf·fo·cate (suf′ə kāt′) ***vt.*** **-cat′ed, -cat′ing** ⟦< L *suffocatus,* pp. of *suffocare,* to choke < *sub-,* SUB- + *fauces,* gullet, throat: see FAUCES⟧ 1 to kill by cutting off the supply of oxygen to the lungs, gills, etc. 2 to hinder the free breathing of; deprive of fresh air; stifle; choke 3 to smother, suppress, extinguish, etc. by or as by cutting off the supply of air —***vi.*** 1 to die by being suffocated 2 to be unable to breathe freely; choke; stifle; smother 3 to be unable to develop properly as because of a repressive or dulling environment —**suf′fo·cat′ing·ly** ***adv.*** —**suf′fo·ca′tion** ***n.*** —**suf′fo·ca′tive** ***adj.***

Suf·folk[1] (suf′ək) ***n.*** 1 any of a breed of hornless, hardy sheep, native to the Suffolk area of EC England, having a black face and black legs and raised for mutton 2 any of a breed of medium-sized, thickset draft horse, chestnut in color and native to Suffolk county, England

Suf·folk[2] (suf′ək) county in E England, on the North Sea: 1,466 sq mi (3,797 sq km)

suf·fra·gan (suf′rə gən) ***n.*** ⟦ME < MFr < ML(Ec) *suffraganus* < L *suffragari,* to vote for, support, favor < *suffragium,* ballot: see fol.⟧ 1 a bishop appointed to assist the bishop of a diocese 2 any bishop in his capacity as a subordinate to his archbishop —***adj.*** 1 designating or of such a bishop 2 subordinate to a larger see

suf·frage (suf′rij) ***n.*** ⟦ME < MFr < ML(Ec) < L *suffragium,* decision, vote, suffrage < *sub-* (see SUB-) + *fragor,* loud applause, orig., din, a crashing < IE base **bhreĝ-,* to crash, BREAK⟧ 1 a prayer or act of intercession or supplication 2 a vote or voting; esp., a vote in favor of some candidate or issue ☆3 the right to vote, esp. in political elections; franchise

suf·fra·gette (suf′rə jet′) ***n.*** ⟦< prec. + -ETTE⟧ a woman who militantly advocates the right of women to vote: this term is objected to by some, who prefer *suffragist* —**suf′fra·get′tism′** ***n.***

suf·fra·gist (suf′rə jist) ***n.*** a person who believes in extending political suffrage, esp. to women

suf·fuse (sə fyo͞oz′) ***vt.*** **-fused′, -fus′ing** ⟦< L *suffusus,* pp. of *suffundere,* to pour beneath, diffuse beneath or upon < *sub-,* under + *fundere,* to pour: see FOUND[3]⟧ to overspread as so as to fill with a glow, color, fluid, etc.: said of light, a blush, air, etc. —**suf·fu′sion** (-fyo͞o′zhən) ***n.*** —**suf·fu′sive** (-siv) ***adj.***

Su·fi (so͞o′fē) ***n.*** ⟦Ar *ṣūfī,* ascetic, lit., (a man) of wool < *ṣūf,* wool⟧ a Muslim following the teachings and traditions of an ancient form of Islamic mysticism —**Su·fism** (so͞o′fiz′əm) ***n.***

sug- (sug) *prefix* SUB-: used before *g* [*suggest*]

sug·ar (sho͝og′ər) ***n.*** ⟦ME *sucre* < OFr < OSp *azúcar* or OIt *zucchero,* both < Ar *sukkar* < Pers *šakar* < Sans *śárkarâ,* akin to *śarkaraḥ,* pebble⟧ 1 any of a class of sweet, soluble, crystalline carbohydrates, as the disaccharides and the monosaccharides 2 sucrose, esp. when prepared as a crystalline or powdered substance used as a food and sweetening agent 3 a sugar bowl, specif. as forming a set with a creamer 4 flattery; honeyed words 5 *short for* SUGAR DIABETES 6 darling; sweetheart: a term of endearment 7 [Slang] money —***vt.*** 1 to mix, cover, sprinkle, or sweeten with sugar 2 *short for* SUGARCOAT —***vi.*** ☆1 to form sugar ☆2 to boil down maple syrup to form maple sugar: usually with *off* —**sug′ar·like′** ***adj.***

sugar apple SWEETSOP

sugar beet a variety or cultivar of the common beet (*Beta vulgaris*) having a root with white flesh and a high sugar content, grown commercially as a source of sugar

☆**sug·ar·ber·ry** (-ber′ē) ***n.,*** *pl.* **-ries** HACKBERRY

sug·ar·bush (-bo͝osh′) ***n.*** a grove of sugar maples

sugar cane a very tall, perennial, tropical grass (*Saccharum officinarum*) cultivated as the main source of sugar: also written **sug′ar·cane′** ***n.***

sug·ar·coat (-kōt′) ***vt.*** 1 to cover or coat with sugar 2 to make (something disagreeable) seem more acceptable or less unpleasant, as by using flattery, euphemism, etc.

☆**sug·ar-cured** (-kyo͝ord′) ***adj.*** treated with a pickling preparation of sugar, salt, and nitrate or nitrite, as ham, bacon, etc.

☆**sugar daddy** [Slang] a rich, esp. older, man who supports or spends lavishly on a usually much younger girlfriend, mistress, etc.

sugar diabetes *nontechnical term for* DIABETES MELLITUS

sug·ar·house (-hous′) ***n.*** 1 a place where sugar is processed ☆2 a building where maple sap is boiled for producing maple syrup and sugar

sug·ar·less (-lis) ***adj.*** having no sugar; specif., prepared with synthetic sweeteners

sugar loaf 1 a conical mass of crystallized sugar 2 a similarly shaped hill, mountain, etc.

Sugar Loaf Mountain granite mountain at the entrance to the harbor of Rio de Janeiro: 1,296 ft (395 m)

☆**sugar maple** an E North American maple (*Acer saccharum*), valued for its hard wood and for its sap, which yields maple syrup and maple sugar

sugar of lead LEAD ACETATE

sugar of milk LACTOSE

☆**sugar pine** a giant pine (*Pinus lambertiana*) of the Pacific coast, with soft, reddish-brown wood, large cones, sugarlike resin, and needles in groups of five

sug·ar·plum (-plum′) ***n.*** 1 a round or oval piece of sugary candy; bonbon ☆2 JUNEBERRY

sugar snap pea a variety of tall pea plant with thick, edible pods containing large smooth peas

sugar tongs small tongs for serving lumps of sugar

sug·ar·y (sho͝og′ər ē) ***adj.*** 1 of, like, or containing sugar; sweet, granular, etc. 2 cloyingly or mawkishly sweet or sentimental —**sug′ar·i·ness** ***n.***

sug·gest (səg jest′; *also, & Brit usually,* sə jest′) ***vt.*** ⟦< L *suggestus,* pp. of *suggerere,* to carry or lay under, furnish < *sub-,* SUB- + *gerere,* to carry⟧ 1 to mention as something to think over, act on, etc.; bring to the mind for consideration 2 to bring or call to mind through association of ideas [objects *suggested* by the shapes of clouds] 3 to propose as a possibility [to *suggest* a course of study] 4 to show indirectly; imply; intimate [a silence that *suggested* agreement] 5 to serve as a motive for; prompt [a success that *suggested* further attempts] —**sug·gest′er** ***n.***

SYN.—**suggest** implies a putting of something into the mind either intentionally, as by way of a proposal [I *suggest* you leave now], or unintentionally, as through association of ideas [the smell of ether *suggests* a hospital]; **imply** stresses the putting into the mind of something involved, but not openly expressed, in a word, a remark, etc. and suggests the need for inference [the answer *implied* a refusal]; **hint** connotes faint or indirect suggestion that is, however, intended to be understood [he *hinted* that he would come]; **intimate** suggests a making known obliquely by a very slight hint [she only dared to *intimate* her feelings]; **insinuate** implies the subtle hinting of something disagreeable or of that which one lacks the courage to say outright [are you *insinuating* that I am dishonest?]

sug·gest·i·ble (-jes′tə bəl) ***adj.*** 1 readily influenced by suggestion, often, specif., through hypnosis 2 that can be suggested —**sug·gest′i·bil′i·ty** ***n.***

sug·ges·tion (-jes′chən) ***n.*** ⟦ME < OFr *suggestioun* < L *suggestio*⟧ 1 a suggesting or being suggested 2 something suggested 3 the process by which an idea is brought to the mind through its connection or association with another idea already in the mind 4 a faint hint or indication; small amount; trace [a *suggestion* of boredom in her tone] 5 *Psychol. a)* inducing of an idea that is accepted or acted on readily and uncritically, as in hypnosis *b)* the idea induced or the stimulus used to induce it

sug·ges·tive (-jes′tiv) ***adj.*** 1 that suggests or tends to suggest thoughts or ideas 2 tending to suggest something considered improper or indecent; risqué —**sug·ges′tive·ly** ***adv.*** —**sug·ges′tive·ness** ***n.***

Su·har·to (so͞o här′tō) 1921-2008; president of Indonesia (1967-98)

su·i·ci·dal (so͞o′ə sīd′'l, so͞o′ə sīd″'l) ***adj.*** 1 of, involving, or leading to suicide 2 having an urge to commit suicide 3 rash to the point of being very dangerous —**su′i·ci′dal·ly** ***adv.***

su·i·cide (so͞o′ə sīd′) ***n.*** ⟦L *sui,* of oneself (< IE **sewe-,* refl. pron. < base **se-,* apart > OE *swæs,* own) + -CIDE⟧ 1 the act of killing oneself intentionally 2 ruin of one's interests or prospects through one's own actions, policies, etc. 3 a person who commits suicide —***vi.*** **-cid′ed, -cid′ing** [Rare] to commit suicide —***adj.*** 1 of or relating to the act or an instance of suicide [a *suicide* note] 2 of or relating to a terrorist act intended to result in the death of the person carrying it out [a *suicide* bomber]

☆**su·i·ci·dol·o·gy** (so͞o′ə sī däl′ə jē) ***n.*** the study of suicide, its causes, and its prevention, and of the behavior of those who threaten or attempt suicide

su·i ge·ne·ris (so͞o′ē jen′ər is, so͞o′ī) ⟦L, lit., of his (or her or its) own kind⟧ without a counterpart or equal; unique

su·i ju·ris (jo͝or′is) ⟦L, of one's own right⟧ *Law* legally competent to manage one's own affairs, in that one is of legal age and sound mind

su·int (so͞o′int, swint) ***n.*** ⟦Fr < *suer,* to sweat < L *sudare:* see SWEAT⟧ the natural grease found in sheep's wool

Suisse (swēs) *Fr. name for* SWITZERLAND

suit (so͞ot) ***n.*** ⟦ME *sute,* a pursuit, action of suing, garb, set of garments, sequence < OFr *suite* < VL **sequita,* fem. pp. of *sequere,* to follow < L *sequi,* to follow: see SEQUENT⟧ 1 *a)* a set of clothes to be worn together; now, esp., a coat and trousers (or skirt), and sometimes a vest, usually all of the same material *b)* any complete outfit [a *suit* of armor] 2 [Slang] a person wearing a suit; specif., a business executive or a bureaucrat: usually a term of mild derision 3 a group of similar things forming a set or series; specif., any of the four sets of thirteen playing cards each (*spades, clubs, hearts,* and *diamonds*) that together make up a pack 4 [Historical] attendance at the court or manor of a feudal lord 5 a legal action brought by one or several parties against another or others, as to recover a right, make a claim for a loss or injury, etc. 6 *a)* an act of suing, pleading, or requesting *b)* a petition 7 the act of wooing; courtship —***vt.*** 1 to meet the requirements of; be right for or appropriate to; befit 2 to make right or appropriate; fit; adapt 3 to please; satisfy [anything that *suits* your fancy] 4 to furnish with clothes, esp. with a suit —***vi.*** 1 [Archaic] to correspond or harmonize: usually with *to* or *with* 2 to be fit, suitable, convenient, or satisfactory —**bring suit** to institute legal, civil action; sue —**follow suit** 1 to play a card of the same suit as the card led **2** to follow the example set —**someone's strong** (or **strongest**) **suit** a person's greatest talent, most conspicuous character trait, etc. [patience is *my strong suit*] —**suit oneself** to act according to one's own wishes —☆**suit up** [Informal] to put on an athletic uniform, spacesuit, etc. in preparation for a particular activity

suit·a·ble (so͞ot′ə bəl) ***adj.*** that suits a given purpose, occasion, condition, propriety, etc.; fitting; appropriate; apt —***SYN.*** FIT¹ —**suit′a·bil′i·ty *n.*, suit′a·ble·ness** —**suit′a·bly *adv.***

suit·case (-kās′) ***n.*** a travel case for clothes, etc., esp. a rectangular one that opens into two hinged compartments

suit coat (*or* **jacket**) a jacket intended to be worn with a matching pair of trousers or skirt as part of a suit

suite (swēt; *for 2b, also* so͞ot) ***n.*** ⟦Fr: see SUIT⟧ **1** a group of attendants or servants; train; retinue; staff **2** a set or series of related things; specif., *a)* a group of connected rooms used as a unit, such as an apartment *b)* a set of pieces of matched furniture for a given room [a bedroom *suite*] **3** *Music a)* an early form of instrumental composition consisting of a series of dances in the same key or in related keys *b)* a modern instrumental composition in a number of movements

suit·ing (so͞ot′iŋ) ***n.*** cloth used for making suits

suit·or (so͞ot′ər) ***n.*** ⟦ME *sutere* < Anglo-Fr *seutor* < L *secutor* < *secutus,* pp. of *sequi,* to follow: see SEQUENT⟧ **1** a person who requests, petitions, or entreats **2** a person who sues at law **3** a man courting or wooing a woman **4** a corporation, investor group, etc. seeking to acquire a company, as by a takeover

Su·kar·na·pu·ra (so͞o kär′nə po͝or′ə) *former name for* JAYAPURA

Su·kar·no (so͞o kär′nō) 1902?-70; Indonesian statesman: president of Indonesia (1945-67)

Su·khu·mi (so͞o′ko͞o mē′) city in NW Georgia: capital of Abkhazia region

☆**su·ki·ya·ki** (so͞o′kē yä′kē, so͝ok′ē-; skē yä′kē) ***n.*** ⟦Jpn, prob. < *sukimi,* thinly sliced meat (< *suku,* to slice thinly + *mi,* meat) + *yaki,* nominal form of *yaku,* to broil⟧ a Japanese dish of thinly sliced meat, onions, and other vegetables cooked quickly, often at table, with soy sauce, sake, sugar, etc.

suk·kah (so͝ok′ə, -ä) ***n.,*** *pl.* **-kahs** or **-kot** (-ōt, -ōs) ⟦see fol.⟧ a temporary structure with a roof of leafy boughs, bamboo sticks, etc., built by Jews for Sukkot to commemorate the tabernacles of the Exodus

Suk·kot or **Suk·koth** (so͞o kōt′; so͝ok′ōt′, -ōs′) ***n.*** ⟦Heb *sukot,* pl. of *suka,* tabernacle; earlier, booth < root *skk,* to cover, screen⟧ a Jewish festival, the Feast of Tabernacles, celebrating the fall harvest and commemorating the desert wandering of the Israelites during the Exodus: observed from the 15th to the 22d day of Tishri: also **Suk·kos** (so͝ok′ōs′)

Su·la·we·si (so͞o′lä wā′sē) island of Indonesia, in the Malay Archipelago, east of Borneo: 74,005 sq mi (191,671 sq km)

sul·cate (sul′kāt′) ***adj.*** ⟦L *sulcatus,* pp. of *sulcare,* to furrow < *sulcus,* a furrow < IE base **swelk-,* to pull > OE *sulh,* a furrow⟧ *Biol.* having deep, parallel furrows or grooves; grooved; fluted: also **sul′cat′ed**

sul·cus (sul′kəs) ***n.,*** *pl.* **-ci** (-sī) ⟦L: see prec.⟧ **1** a groove or furrow **2** *Anat.* any of the shallow grooves separating the convolutions of the brain

Su·lei·man (I) (so͞o′lā män′) 1494?-1566; sultan of the Ottoman Empire (1520-66): called *the Magnificent*

sulf- (sulf) *combining form* of or containing sulfur [*sulfinyl*]

sul·fa (sul′fə) ***adj.*** ⟦contr. < SULFANILAMIDE⟧ designating or of a family of drugs of the sulfanilamide type, used in combating certain bacterial infections

sul·fa·di·a·zine (sul′fə dī′ə zēn′, -zin) ***n.*** ⟦prec. + DIAZINE⟧ a sulfa drug, $C_{10}H_{10}N_4O_2S$, used in treating certain pneumococcal, streptococcal, and staphylococcal infections

sul·fa·mer·a·zine (-mer′ə zēn′) ***n.*** ⟦SULFA + *-mer* (as in ISOMER) + AZINE⟧ a sulfa drug, $C_{11}H_{12}N_4O_2S$, a methyl derivative of sulfadiazine that is more rapidly absorbed

sul·fa·nil·a·mide (-nil′ə mīd′, -mid) ***n.*** ⟦< fol. + AMIDE⟧ a white, crystalline compound, $C_6H_8N_2O_2S$, formerly used in treating gonorrhea, streptococcal infections, etc.: a synthetic coal-tar product

sul·fa·nil·ic acid (sul′fə nil′ik) ⟦SULF(O)- + ANIL(INE) + -IC⟧ a colorless, crystalline acid, $H_2NC_6H_4SO_3H$, prepared by heating aniline with sulfuric acid: used in dyes and medicines

sul·fate (sul′fāt′) ***n.*** ⟦Fr < L *sulphur,* sulfur + Fr *-ate,* -ATE²⟧ **1** a salt of sulfuric acid containing the divalent, negative radical SO_4 **2** an uncharged ester of this acid —***vt.*** **-fat′ed, -fat′ing 1** to treat with sulfuric acid or a sulfate **2** to convert into a sulfate **3** to cause a deposit of lead sulfate to form on (the negative plates of a storage battery) —***vi.*** to become sulfated —**sul·fa′tion *n.***

sul·fide (sul′fīd′) ***n.*** a compound of sulfur with another element or a radical

sul·fi·nyl (sul′fə nil′) ***n.*** ⟦SULF(O)- + -IN¹ + -YL⟧ the SO group, present in certain organic compounds

sul·fite (sul′fīt′) ***n.*** **1** a salt of sulfurous acid containing the divalent, negative radical SO_3: commonly used as a preservative in wine, dried fruit, etc. **2** an uncharged ester of this acid

sul·fo- (sul′fō, -fə) *combining form* **1** containing sulfur, esp. divalent sulfur **2** replacing oxygen with sulfur: see THIO- **3** having the sulfonic or sulfonyl group

sul·fon·a·mide (sul fän′ə mīd′, -mid) ***n.*** ⟦SULFON(YL) + AMIDE⟧ any of the sulfa drugs, as sulfadiazine, containing the group or the monovalent, negative radical SO_2NH_2

sul·fo·nate (sul′fə nāt′) ***n.*** a salt or ester of a sulfonic acid —***vt.*** **-nat′ed, -nat′ing** to introduce the sulfonic group into (an aromatic hydrocarbon) by treating with sulfuric acid

sul·fone (sul′fōn′) ***n.*** ⟦Ger *sulfon* < *sulfur* (< L *sulphur,* sulfur) + *-on,* -ONE⟧ any of a group of organic compounds containing the group or the divalent radical SO_2, the sulfur atom of which is linked chemically with a carbon atom of each of two alkyl groups

sul·fon·ic (sul fän′ik) ***adj.*** ⟦< prec. + -IC⟧ designating or of the monovalent acid group SO_3H

sulfonic acid any of numerous organic acids containing the sulfonic group SO_3H, derived from sulfuric acid by the replacement of an OH group: used in the manufacture of dyes, drugs, phenols, etc.

sul·fo·ni·um (sul fō′nē əm) ***n.*** ⟦ModL: see SULFO- & -ONIUM⟧ a monovalent radical containing three alkyl radicals and one atom of sulfur, as the triethyl sulfonium radical $(C_2H_5)_3S$

sul·fon·meth·ane (sul′fōn meth′ān, -fän-) ***n.*** ⟦SULFON(E) + METHANE⟧ a colorless, crystalline compound, $C_7H_{16}O_4S_2$, used in medicine as a soporific and hypnotic

sul·fo·nyl (sul′fə nil′) ***n.*** ⟦SULFON(E) + -YL⟧ the divalent radical SO_2

sul·fo·nyl·u·re·a (sul′fə nil yo͞o rē′ə) ***n.*** any of a group of oral drugs, as tolbutamide, that stimulate the pancreas to secrete more insulin, used to treat diabetes

sulf·ox·ide (sulf äk′sīd′) ***n.*** ⟦SULF(O)- + OXIDE⟧ any of a group of organic compounds containing the group or the divalent radical SO: see THIONYL

sul·fur (sul′fər) ***n.*** ⟦ME *sulphur* < L⟧ **1** a pale-yellow, nonmetallic chemical element found in crystalline or amorphous form: it burns with a blue flame and a stifling odor and is used in vulcanizing rubber and in making matches, paper, gunpowder, insecticides, sulfuric acid, etc.: symbol, S; at. no. 16: see the periodic table of elements in the Reference Supplement **2** any of numerous small to medium-sized butterflies (family Pieridae) having yellow or orange wings with dark borders: in full **sulfur butterfly 3** yellow with a greenish tinge: often **sulfur yellow** —***vt.*** SULFURIZE

sul·fu·rate (sul′fyo͞o rāt′, -fə-) ***vt.*** **-rat′ed, -rat′ing** SULFURIZE —**sul′fu·ra′tion *n.***

sul·fur-bot·tom (sul′fər bät′əm) ***n.*** BLUE WHALE

sulfur dioxide a heavy, colorless, suffocating gas, SO_2, easily liquefied and used as a bleach, disinfectant, preservative, etc.

sul·fu·re·ous (sul fyo͝or′ē əs) ***adj.*** ⟦L *sulfureus*⟧ **1** of, like, or containing sulfur **2** greenish-yellow

sul·fu·ret (sul′fyo͞o ret′, -fə-) ***n.*** ⟦ModL *sulphuretum*⟧ SULFIDE —***vt.*** **-ret′ed** or **-ret′ted, -ret′ing** or **-ret′ting** SULFURIZE

sul·fu·ric (sul fyo͝or′ik) ***adj.*** ⟦Fr *sulfurique*⟧ **1** of or containing sulfur, esp. hexavalent sulfur **2** of or derived from sulfuric acid

sulfuric acid an oily, colorless, corrosive liquid, H_2SO_4, used in making dyes, paints, explosives, fertilizers, etc.

sul·fu·rize (sul′fyo͞o rīz′, -fə-) ***vt.*** **-rized′, -riz′ing** ⟦Fr *sulfuriser:* see SULFUR & -IZE⟧ to combine, treat, or impregnate with sulfur or a compound of sulfur, esp. with sulfur dioxide fumes in bleaching or disinfecting —**sul′fu·ri·za′tion *n.***

sul·fu·rous (sul′fər əs, sul fyo͝or′əs) ***adj.*** ⟦L *sulphurosus*⟧ **1** of or containing sulfur, esp. tetravalent sulfur **2** like burning sulfur in odor, color, etc. **3** of or suggesting the fires of hell; infernal; hellish **4** violently emotional; heated; fiery —**sul′fu·rous·ly *adv.*** —**sul′fu·rous·ness *n.***

sulfurous acid a colorless acid, H_2SO_3, known only in the form of its salts or in aqueous solution and used as a chemical reagent, a bleach, in medicine, etc.

sul·fur·y (sul′fər ē) ***adj.*** of or like sulfur

sul·fur·yl (sul′fə ril′) ***n.*** SULFONYL

sulk (sulk) ***vi.*** ⟦back-form. < fol.⟧ to be sulky —***n.*** **1** a sulky mood or state: also **the sulks 2** a sulky person

sulk·y (sul′kē) ***adj.*** **sulk′i·er, sulk′i·est** ⟦prob. < OE *-solcen* (in comp.), idle, sluggish, pp. of *-seolcan,* to become slack < IE base **selĝ-,* to let go, let loose > Sans *sarjati,* (he) releases⟧ **1** showing resentment or dissatisfaction by petulant or peevish withdrawal **2** gloomy; dismal; sullen [a *sulky* day] —***n.,*** *pl.* **sulk′ies** ⟦prob. < the ***adj.,*** in the sense, "keeping aloof", because the vehicle seats only one person⟧ a light, two-wheeled, one-horse carriage having a seat for only one person, esp. now, one used in harness races —**sulk′i·ly *adv.*** —**sulk′i·ness *n.***

Sul·la (sul′ə) (*Lucius Cornelius Sulla Felix*) 138-78 B.C.; Rom. general: dictator of Rome (82-79)

sul·lage (sul′ij) ***n.*** ⟦prob. < Fr *souiller,* to SULLY + -AGE⟧ **1** filth or refuse; sewage **2** silt or sediment deposited by running water **3** *Metallurgy* scoria on the surface of molten metal in a ladle

sul·len (sul′ən) ***adj.*** ⟦ME *solein,* alone, solitary < VL **solanus,* alone < L *solus,* alone, SOLE²⟧ **1** showing resentment and ill humor by morose, unsociable withdrawal **2** gloomy; dismal; sad; depressing **3** somber; dull [*sullen* colors] **4** slow-moving; sluggish **5** [Obs.] baleful; threatening —**sul′len·ly *adv.*** —**sul′len·ness *n.***

Sul·li·van (sul′ə vən) **1** Sir **Arthur Seymour** 1842-1900; Eng. composer: see also GILBERT², Sir William Schwenck **2 John L(awrence)** 1858-1918; U.S. prizefighter **3 Louis Hen·ri** (hen′rē) 1856-1924; U.S. architect

sul·ly (sul′ē) ***vt.*** **-lied, -ly·ing** ⟦prob. < Fr *souiller* < OFr *soillier:* see SOIL²⟧ to soil, stain, tarnish, or besmirch, now esp. by disgracing —***vi.*** [Obs.] to become sullied —***n.,*** *pl.* **-lies** [Archaic] a stain or tarnish; defilement

Sul·ly (sul′ē; *also, for 1, Fr* sü lē′) **1** Duc **de** (*Maximilien de Béthune*) 1560-1641; Fr. statesman **2 Thomas** 1783-1872; U.S. painter, born in England

Sul·ly-Pru·dhomme (sü lē prü dôm′), **Re·né Fran·çois Ar·mand** (rə nā′ frän swȧ′ ȧr män′) 1839-1907; Fr. poet & critic

sulph- (sulf) [Chiefly Brit.] SULF-

sul·phur (sul′fər) *n. chiefly Brit. sp. of* SULFUR —**sul·phu·ric** (sul fyoor′ik) *adj.* —**sul′phu·rous** *adj.*

sul·tan (sult′'n) *n.* ⟦Fr < Ar *sulṭān,* ruler, prince, orig., dominion⟧ 1 a Muslim ruler 2 [S-] the former monarch of Turkey

sul·tan·a (sul tan′ə, -tä′nə) *n.* ⟦It < Ar *sulṭāna,* fem. of *sulṭān:* see prec.⟧ 1 *a)* the wife of a sultan *b)* the mother, sister, or daughter of a sultan: also **sul·tan·ess** (sult′'n is) 2 a mistress, esp. of a king, prince, etc. 3 *a)* a small, white, seedless grape used for raisins and in wine making *b)* [Brit.] such a raisin

sul·tan·ate (sult′'n it, -āt′) *n.* 1 the land ruled by a sultan 2 the authority, office, or reign of a sultan

sul·try (sul′trē) *adj.* **-tri·er, -tri·est** ⟦var. of SWELTRY⟧ 1 oppressively hot and moist; close; sweltering 2 extremely hot; fiery 3 *a)* hot or inflamed, as with passion or lust *b)* suggesting or expressing smoldering passion —**sul′tri·ly** *adv.* —**sul′tri·ness** *n.*

su·lu (so͞o′lo͞o) *n.* ⟦Fijian, clothes⟧ a garment similar to a sarong, worn by Melanesians, as in the Fiji Islands

Sulu Archipelago (so͞o′lo͞o) group of islands in the Philippines, southwest of Mindanao: 1,038 sq mi (2,688 sq km)

Sulu Sea arm of the W Pacific, between the SW Philippines & NE Borneo

sum[1] (sum) *n.* ⟦ME *somme* < MFr < L *summa,* fem. of *summus,* highest, superl. < base of *super:* see SUPER-⟧ 1 an amount of money [*a sum* paid in reparation] 2 the whole amount; totality; aggregate [*the sum* of our experience] 3 the gist or a summary of something said, done, etc.: usually in **sum and substance** 4 *a)* the result obtained by adding numbers or quantities; total *b)* [Old-fashioned] a series of numbers to be added together, or any problem in arithmetic *c)* the limit of the sum of the first *n* terms of an infinite series as *n* grows indefinitely *d)* the set containing every element belonging to one or both of two original sets and no other elements *e)* in Boolean algebra, DISJUNCTION (sense 2) 5 [Archaic] the highest degree; height; summit —*vt.* **summed, sum′ming** 1 to determine the sum of by adding 2 to summarize or review briefly; sum up —*vi.* to get, or come to, a total —**in sum** to put it briefly; in short —**sum up** 1 to add up or collect into a whole or total 2 to review briefly; summarize

SYN.—**sum** refers to the number or amount obtained by adding individual units [the *sum* of 3 and 5 is 8]; **amount** applies to the result obtained by combining all the sums, quantities, measures, etc. that are involved [we paid the full *amount* of the damages]; **aggregate** refers to the whole group or mass of individual items gathered together [the *aggregate* of our experiences]; **total** stresses the wholeness or inclusiveness of a sum or amount [the collection reached a *total* of $200]

sum[2] (so͞om) *n., pl.* **sum** *var. of* SOM (sense 2)

sum- (sum) *prefix* SUB-: used before *m*

su·mac or **su·mach** (so͞o′mak′, sho͞o′-) *n.* ⟦ME *sumac* < MFr < Ar *summāq*⟧ 1 any of various shrubs and small trees (genus *Rhus*) of the cashew family, including poison sumac and several nonpoisonous plants 2 the pulverized dried leaves of some of these nonpoisonous plants (esp. *Rhus coriaria*), used in tanning and dyeing 3 the wood of any of these plants

Su·ma·tra (so͞o mä′trə) large island of Indonesia, just south of the Malay Peninsula: 185,656 sq mi (480,847 sq km) —**Su·ma′tran** *adj., n.*

Sum·ba (so͞om′bə) island of Indonesia, west of Timor & south of Flores: 4,306 sq mi (11,152 sq km)

Sum·ba·wa (so͞om bä′wä) island of Indonesia, between Lombok & Flores: 5,965 sq mi (15,449 sq km)

Su·mer (so͞o′mər) ancient region in the lower valley of the Euphrates River

Su·mer·i·an (so͞o mir′ē ən, -mer′-) *adj.* 1 of Sumer 2 of the people of Sumer, an ancient non-Semitic people of S Mesopotamia —*n.* 1 a member of this people 2 the language of the Sumerians, extinct as a spoken language since *c.* 2000 B.C. although it continued to be written until the abandonment of the cuneiform writing system: its tablets and inscriptions date back to 3000 B.C.: no clear relationship to any other language has been established

su·mi (so͞o′mē) ⟦Jpn⟧ *n.* an instrument, consisting of a stick made of soot mixed with glue, that is dipped in water to produce an inky substance applied in lines in a style of Japanese writing and painting

sum·ma (so͝om′ə) *n., pl.* **-mae** (-ē) ⟦ML < L: see SUM[1]⟧ a comprehensive treatise or exposition, as by a medieval scholastic

sum·ma cum lau·de (so͝om′ə ko͝om lou′de, sum′ə kum lô′dē) ⟦L, lit., with the greatest praise⟧ phrase signifying the highest category of academic standing at the time of graduation from a college or university: see also CUM LAUDE, MAGNA CUM LAUDE

sum·ma·rist (sum′ə rist) *n.* a person who summarizes

sum·ma·rize (sum′ə rīz′) *vt.* **-rized′, -riz′ing** 1 to make a summary of; state briefly 2 to be a summary of —**sum′ma·ri·za′tion** *n.* —**sum′ma·riz′er** *n.*

sum·ma·ry (sum′ə rē) *adj.* ⟦ME < ML *summarius* < L *summa,* SUM[1]⟧ 1 that presents the substance or general idea in brief form; summarizing; concise; condensed 2 *a)* prompt and without formality; expeditious [*summary* punishment] *b)* hasty and arbitrary [*a summary* dismissal] —*n., pl.* **-ries** ⟦L *summarium:* see the *adj.*⟧ a brief statement or account covering the substance or main points; digest; abridgment; compendium —**SYN.** ABRIDGMENT —**sum·mar·i·ly** (sə mer′ə lē) *adv.* —**sum′ma·ri·ness** *n.*

summary court-martial the least formal military court, consisting of one officer, for judging minor offenses

summary judgment judgment rendered without a trial, as when there is agreement among the parties as to the material facts and only a question of law needs to be resolved

sum·ma·tion (sə mā′shən) *n.* ⟦ModL *summatio*⟧ 1 the act or process of summing up, or of finding a total 2 a total or aggregate 3 the final summing up of arguments, as in a court trial or debate, before the decision is given

sum·mer[1] (sum′ər) *n.* ⟦ME *sumer* < OE *sumor,* akin to Ger *sommer* < IE base **sem-,* summertime > Sans *sámā,* half year, season⟧ 1 the warmest season of the year: in the North Temperate Zone, generally regarded as including the months of June, July, and August: in the astronomical year, that period between the summer solstice and the autumnal equinox 2 a year as reckoned by this season [a youth of sixteen *summers*] 3 any period of growth, development, fulfillment, perfection, etc. —*adj.* 1 of or typical of summer 2 designed for or taking place during summer [*summer* activities] —*vi.* to pass the summer —*vt.* to keep, feed, or maintain during the summer

sum·mer[2] (sum′ər) *n.* ⟦ME < OFr *somier,* pack horse < LL *sagmarius,* pack horse < *sagma,* pack saddle < Gr < base of *sattein,* to stuff⟧ 1 a large, horizontal, supporting beam or girder 2 LINTEL 3 the capstone of a column supporting an arch or lintel

summer cypress an annual plant (*Kochia scoparia*) of the goosefoot family, cultivated for its brilliant red or purplish fall foliage

sum·mer·house (sum′ər hous′) *n.* a small, open structure in a garden, park, etc., for providing a shady rest

summer house a house or cottage, as in the country, used during the summer

sum·mer·sault (sum′ər sôlt′) *n., vi. alt. sp. of* SOMERSAULT

☆**summer sausage** a type of hard, dried or smoked sausage that does not spoil easily

☆**summer school** a school or college session held during the regular summer vacation

summer solstice *see* SOLSTICE

☆**summer squash** any of a variety (*Cucurbita pepo melopepo*) of small garden squashes grown in summer and eaten before fully ripe

summer theater a theater that puts on plays or musicals during the summer

sum·mer·time (sum′ər tīm′) *n.* the season of summer

summer triangle a group of three first-magnitude stars (Deneb, Vega, and Altair) visible during the summer in the N skies

☆**sum·mer·wood** (-wo͝od′) *n.* the last-formed woody portion of the annual growth ring of a shrub or tree, usually containing more fibers and fewer vessels than springwood

sum·mer·y (-ē) *adj.* of or like summer; warm, pleasant, etc.

sum·mit (sum′it) *n.* ⟦ME *sommete* < OFr, dim. of *som,* summit < L *summum,* highest part < *summus,* highest: see SUM[1]⟧ 1 the highest point, part, or elevation; top or apex 2 the highest degree or state; acme ☆3 *a)* the highest level of officials; specif., in connection with diplomatic negotiations, the level restricted to heads of government [a meeting at the *summit*] *b)* a conference at the summit —*adj.* ☆of the heads of government [a *summit* parley] — *vt., vi.* to climb to the summit of (a mountain)

SYN.—**summit** literally refers to the topmost point of a hill or similar elevation and, figuratively, to the highest attainable level, as of achievement; **peak** refers to the highest of a number of high points, as in a mountain range or, figuratively, in a graph; **climax** applies to the highest point, as in interest, force, excitement, etc., in a scale of ascending values; **acme** refers to the highest possible point of perfection in the development or progress of something; **apex** suggests the highest point (literally, of a geometric figure such as a cone; figuratively, of a career, process, etc.) where all ascending lines, courses, etc. ultimately meet; **pinnacle,** in its figurative uses, is equivalent to **summit** or **peak,** but sometimes connotes a giddy or unsteady height; **zenith** literally refers to the highest point in the heavens and hence figuratively suggests fame or success reached by a spectacular rise

☆**sum·mit·eer** (sum′i tir′) *n.* any of the participants in a summit conference

sum·mit·ry (sum′i trē) *n., pl.* **-ries** the use of, or reliance upon, summit conferences to resolve problems of international diplomacy

sum·mon (sum′ən) *vt.* ⟦ME *somonen* < OFr *somondre* < VL **submonere,* for L *summonere,* to remind privily < *sub-,* under, secretly + *monere,* to advise, warn: see MONITOR⟧ 1 to call together; order to meet or convene 2 to order to come or appear; call for or send for with authority or urgency 3 to order, as by a summons, to appear in court 4 to call upon to do something 5 to call forth; rouse: often with *up* [*summon* up your courage] —**SYN.** CALL —**sum′mon·er** *n.*

sum·mons (-ənz) *n., pl.* **-mons·es** ⟦ME *somounce* < Anglo-Fr *somonse* < OFr *sumunse* < pp. of *somondre:* see prec.⟧ 1 *a)* an order or command to come, attend, appear, or perform some action *b)* *Law* an official order to appear in court, specif. to respond as a defendant to a charge; also, the writ containing such an order 2 a call, command, knock, or other signal that summons —*vt.* [Informal] to serve a court summons upon

sum·mum bo·num (so͝om′əm bō′nəm) ⟦L⟧ the highest, or supreme, good

Sum·ner (sum′nər) 1 **Charles** 1811-74; U.S. statesman & abolitionist 2 **William Graham** (grā′əm) 1840-1910; U.S. sociologist & economist

su·mo (wrestling) (so͞o′mō) ⟦Jpn *sumō,* to compete⟧ [*sometimes* S-] a highly stylized Japanese form of wrestling engaged in by large, extremely heavy men

sump (sump) *n.* ⟦ME *sompe,* SWAMP⟧ **1** *a)* a pit, tank, etc. for collecting liquid, specif. one into which waste or excess liquid drains and from which it is evacuated mechanically *b)* [Brit.] OIL PAN **2** *Mining a)* a pit or pool at the bottom of a shaft or mine, in which water collects and from which it is pumped *b)* an excavation at the head of a tunnel or shaft

sump pump a pump for removing liquid from a sump

sump·ter (sump′tər) *n.* ⟦ME *sompter,* pack horse, orig., driver of a pack horse < OFr *sometier* < LL **sagmatarius* < LL *sagma* (gen. *sagmatis*), pack-saddle: see SUMMER²⟧ a pack animal

sump·tu·ar·y (sump′cho͞o er′ē) *adj.* ⟦L *sumptuarius* < *sumptus,* expense < pp. of *sumere,* to take: see CONSUME⟧ of or regulating expenses or expenditures; specif., seeking to regulate extravagance on religious or moral grounds

sump·tu·ous (sump′cho͞o əs) *adj.* ⟦ME < OFr *sumptueux* < L *sumptuosus* < *sumptus:* see prec.⟧ **1** involving great expense; costly; lavish **2** magnificent or splendid, as in furnishings, etc. **—sump′tu·ous·ly** *adv.* **—sump′tu·ous·ness** *n.*

Sumter, Fort *see* FORT SUMTER

sum total **1** the total arrived at by adding up a sum or sums **2** everything involved or included

sum-up (sum′up′) *n.* [Informal] the act or result of summarizing

sun¹ (sun) *n.* ⟦ME *sunne* < OE, akin to Ger *sonne,* Goth *sunnō* < IE **sun-, *swen-,* var. of base **sāwel-* > L *sol,* Gr *hēlios*⟧ **1** [*often* **S-**] the self-luminous, gaseous central star of the solar system: magnitude, −26.74; mean distance from the earth, *c.* 149.6 million km (*c.* 93 million mi); diameter, *c.* 1.4 million km (*c.* 864,000 mi); mass, *c.* 332,000 times that of the earth; volume, *c.* 1.3 million times that of the earth; mean density, *c.* 0.25 times that of the earth; central temperature, *c.* 15 to 28 million degrees K; surface temperature, *c.* 6,000°K; rotational period, *c.* 27 earth days: with *the* **2** the heat or light of the sun [*to lie in the sun*] **3** any star, esp. one that is the center of a planetary system **4** something like the sun, as in warmth or brilliance **—*vt.* sunned, sun′ning** to expose to the sun's rays; warm, dry, bleach, tan, etc. in or as in the sunlight **—*vi.*** to sun oneself **—from sun to sun** [Archaic] from sunrise to sunset **—place in the sun** a prominent or favorable position **—under the sun** on earth; in the world

sun² (sun) *n.* ⟦Hindi *san* < Sans *śaṇa,* hempen⟧ **1** an East Indian annual plant (*Crotalaria juncea*) of the pea family, grown for its bast fiber used in making rope, bagging, cigarette papers, etc. **2** its fiber Also **sun hemp**

Sun *abbrev.* Sunday

sun·baked (sun′bākt′) *adj.* **1** baked by the heat of the sun, as bricks **2** dried, cracked, etc. by the heat of the sun

sun bath exposure of the body to sunlight or a sunlamp, as for the purpose of getting a tan

sun·bathe (-bāth′) *vi.* **-bathed′, -bath′ing** to take a sun bath **—sun′bath′er** *n.*

sun·beam (-bēm′) *n.* a ray or beam of sunlight

☆**Sun·belt** (sun′belt′) that part of the U.S. comprising most of the states of the South and the Southwest, characterized by a warm, sunny climate: also **Sun Belt**

sun·bird (sun′burd′) *n.* any of a family (Nectariniidae) of small, brightly colored, tropical Old World passerine birds, somewhat resembling the hummingbirds

sun bittern a tropical American wading bird (*Eurypyga helias*) of a gruiform family (Eurypygidae) having only one species, with a slim body and long neck

sun·block (sun′bläk′) *n.* **1** a substance, as para-aminobenzoic acid, used in lotions, cosmetics, etc. to block certain ultraviolet rays of the sun and reduce the danger of sunburn; sunscreen **2** a lotion, cosmetic, etc. containing this Also written **sun block**

sun·bon·net (-bän′it) *n.* a bonnet with a large brim and back flap for shading the face and neck from the sun, worn, esp. formerly, by women and girls

sun·bow (-bō′) *n.* a rainbow formed by sunlight refracted in fine spray, as from a waterfall or fountain

sun·burn (-burn′) *n.* inflammation of the skin resulting from prolonged exposure to the sun's rays or to a sunlamp **—*vi., vt.* -burned′** or **-burnt′, -burn′ing** to get or cause to get a sunburn

sun·burst (-burst′) *n.* **1** the sudden appearance of sunlight, as through a break in clouds ☆**2** a decorative device representing the sun with spreading rays

sun·choke (sun′chōk′) *n.* JERUSALEM ARTICHOKE

☆**sun-cured** (-kyoord′) *adj.* cured, as meat or fruit, by drying in the sun

☆**sun·dae** (sun′dā; *occas.,* -dē) *n.* ⟦prob. < SUNDAY¹, from being orig. sold only on this day⟧ a serving of ice cream covered with a syrup, fruit, nuts, whipped cream, etc.

Sunda Islands (sun′də; *Du* so͞on′dä) group of islands in the Malay Archipelago, consisting of two smaller groups: **Greater Sunda Islands** (Sumatra, Java, Borneo, Sulawesi, & small nearby islands) & **Lesser Sunda Islands** (Bali & islands stretching east through Timor)

☆**sun dance** a religious dance in worship of the sun performed at the summer solstice by certain Plains Indians

Sun·day¹ (sun′dā; *occas.,* -dē) *n.* ⟦ME < OE *sunnandœg,* lit., sun day, akin to ON *sunnudagr,* Ger *Sonntag* < 3d-c. transl. of LL *dies solis,* day of the sun, transl. of LGr *hēmera hēlion*⟧ the first day of the week: it is observed by most Christian denominations as the Sabbath **—*adj.* 1** of, having to do with, or characteristic of Sunday **2** done, worn, performing, etc. usually or only on Sunday [*Sunday* suit, *Sunday* golfer] Abbrev. *Sun, Su, S*

Sun·day² (sun′dē, -dā), **Billy** (born *William Ashley Sunday*) 1862-1935; U.S. Christian evangelist

Sunday best [Informal] one's best clothes

☆**Sunday driver** ⟦implying that such a motorist drives infrequently⟧ [Old Informal] an unskilled or tentative motorist

☆**Sun·day-go-to-meet·ing** (-gō′tə mēt′iŋ, -mēt′'n) *adj.* [Dial. or Old Informal] best or most presentable, and hence appropriate for Sunday church services [one's *Sunday-go-to-meeting* clothes]

☆**Sunday punch** [Slang] **1** a boxer's hardest punch **2** any measure most effective against an opponent

Sun·days (-dāz; *occas.,* -dēz) *adv.* on every Sunday or most Sundays

Sunday school **1** a school, usually affiliated with some church or synagogue, giving religious instruction on Sunday **2** the teachers and pupils of such a school

sun deck any open porch, deck, etc. for taking sun baths

sun·der (sun′dər) *vt., vi.* ⟦ME *sundren* < OE *sundrian* < *sundor,* asunder, akin to Ger *sonder* < IE **sn̥ter-* < base **seni-,* away from, separate > L *sine,* without⟧ to break apart; separate; part; split **—*SYN.*** SEPARATE **—in sunder** into parts or pieces **—sun′der·a·ble** *adj.*

Sun·der·land (sun′dər lənd) seaport in Tyne and Wear, N England, on the North Sea

sun·dew (sun′do͞o′, -dyo͞o′) *n.* ⟦transl. of ML *ros solis* < L *ros,* dew (see RACE¹) + *solis,* gen. of *sol,* SUN¹⟧ any of a genus (*Drosera*) of small plants of the sundew family, having leaves covered with adhesive hairs that trap insects, which are digested by the plant **—*adj.*** designating a family (Droseraceae, order Nepenthales) of dicotyledonous plants, including the Venus' flytrap

sun·di·al (-dī′əl) *n.* an instrument that indicates time by the position of a gnomon's shadow cast by the sun on the face of a dial marked in hours

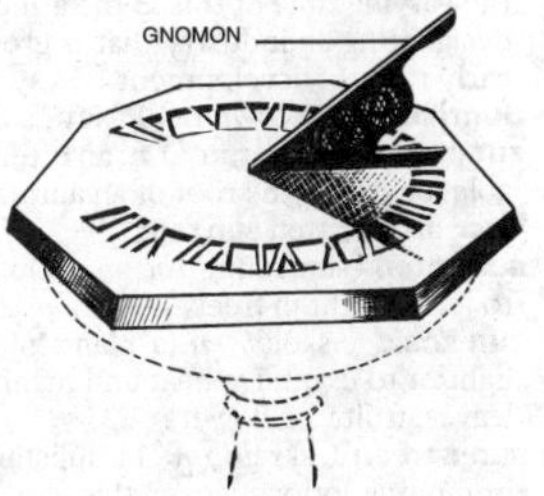

sundial

sun disk a disk flanked by two serpents and set in a pair of outspread wings: a symbol of the Egyptian sun god, Ra

sun·dog (-dôg′) *n.* PARHELION

sun·down (-doun′) *n.* ⟦contr. < ? *sun go(ing) down*⟧ SUNSET (esp. sense 1*b*)

sun·down·er (-dou′nər) *n.* **1** ⟦prec. + -ER: from habitually arriving at a stock farm too late for work but early enough to receive a night's lodging and food⟧ [Austral. Informal] a tramp or vagrant **2** [Brit. Informal] an alcoholic drink taken at sunset

sun·dress (-dres′) *n.* a lightweight, sleeveless dress with a scoop neckline or, sometimes, shoulder straps, for wear in warm weather

sun-dried (-drīd′) *adj.* dried by the sun

sun·dries (sun′drēz) *pl.n.* sundry, esp. minor, items

☆**sun·drops** (sun′dräps′) *n., pl.* **-drops′** any of various evening primroses, usually having large, yellow flowers

sun·dry (sun′drē) *adj.* ⟦ME *sundri* < OE *syndrig,* separate < *sundor,* apart: see SUNDER & -Y²⟧ various; miscellaneous; divers [*sundry* items of clothing] **—*pron.*** [*with pl. v.*] sundry persons or things: used mainly in the phrase **all and sundry,** everybody; one and all

sun·fast (sun′fast′, -fäst′) *adj.* not fading in sunlight

sun·fish (-fish′) *n., pl.* **-fish′** or **-fish′es** (see FISH) ☆**1** any of a large family (Centrarchidae) of North American, percoid, freshwater fishes, including the bluegill and black bass **2** OCEAN SUNFISH

sun·flow·er (-flou′ər) *n.* any of a genus (*Helianthus*) of tall plants of the composite family, having large, yellow, daisylike flowers with yellow, brown, purple, or almost black disks containing edible seeds that yield an oil

Sunflower State *name for* KANSAS

sung (suŋ) *vi., vt. pp. & rare pt. of* SING¹

Sung (so͞oŋ) Chin. dynasty (A.D. 960-1279), noted for achievement in art & literature

Sun·ga·ri (so͞oŋ′gä rē′) *a former transliteration of* SONGHUA

sun·glass (sun′glas′, -gläs′) *n.* **1** BURNING GLASS **2** [*pl.*] eyeglasses with special lenses, usually tinted, to protect the eyes from the sun's glare

sun·glow (-glō′) *n.* a colored glow seen in the sky at sunrise or sunset as a result of the diffraction of the sun's rays by particles in the air

sun god **1** the sun personified and worshiped as a god **2** any god associated or identified with the sun

sun-grebe (sun′grēb′) *n.* any of a gruiform family (Heliornithidae) of shy, long-necked tropical birds living along streams, lakes, etc.

sunk (suŋk) *vi., vt. pp. & alt. pt. of* SINK **—*adj.* 1** SUNKEN **2** [Informal] utterly ruined; undone

sunk·en (suŋ′kən) *vi., vt. obs. pp. of* SINK **—*adj.* 1** submerged [*a sunken* ship] **2** below the level of the surrounding or adjoining area [*a sunken* patio] **3** fallen in; hollow [*sunken* cheeks] **4** depressed; dejected [*sunken* spirits]

☆**sun·lamp** (sun′lamp′) *n.* an electric lamp that radiates ultraviolet rays, used for tanning the body and therapeutically as a substitute for sunlight

sun·less (sun′lis) *adj.* without sun or sunlight; dark

sun·light (-līt′) *n.* the light of the sun

sun·lit (-lit′) *adj.* lighted by the sun
sunn (sun) *n. alt. sp. of* SUN²: also **sunn hemp**
Sun·na or **Sun·nah** (soon′ə) *n.* ⟦Ar *sunna,* lit., a form, course, tradition⟧ Muslim law based, according to tradition, on the teachings and practices of Muhammad and observed by orthodox Muslims: a supplement to the Koran
Sun·ni (soon′ē) *n., pl.* **Sun′ni** a member of one of the two great sects of Muslims: Sunni approve the historical order of the first four caliphs as the rightful line of succession to Muhammad and accept the Sunna as an authoritative supplement to the Koran: cf. SHIITE —**Sun′nism′** *n.*
Sun·nite (soon′īt′) *n.* ⟦< Ar *sunna* (see SUNNA) + -ITE¹⟧ SUNNI
sun·ny (sun′ē) *adj.* **-ni·er, -ni·est 1** shining or bright with sunlight; full of sunshine **2** bright and cheerful [a *sunny* smile] **3** of or suggestive of the sun [a *sunny* radiance] —**sun′ni·ly** *adv.* —**sun′ni·ness** *n.*
sunny side 1 the side exposed to sunlight **2** the more pleasant or cheerful aspect —☆**on the sunny side of** somewhat younger than (a specified age) —☆**sunny side up** fried with the yolk unbroken and without being turned over [two eggs *sunny side up*]
Sun·ny·vale (sun′ē vāl′) ⟦descriptive⟧ city in WC Calif.: suburb of San Jose
☆**sun parlor** (*or* **porch**) a sitting room (or an enclosed porch) with large windows to let sunlight in freely
sun·proof (sun′proof′) *adj.* impervious to or unaffected by sunlight
sun protection factor a number indicating the relative effectiveness of a sunblock in preventing certain ultraviolet rays from burning the skin: a higher number indicates a greater degree of protection
sun·rise (sun′rīz′) *n.* ⟦SUN¹ + RISE, v., prob. in such phrases as *before the sun rise*⟧ **1** the daily appearance of the sun above the eastern horizon **2** the varying time of this **3** the atmospheric phenomena at this time —*adj.* designating an industry that is growing rapidly, esp. one that is still in an early stage of development
Sunrise Manor town in SE Nev.: suburb of Las Vegas
sun·roof (-roof′, -roof′) *n.* an often transparent panel, movable or removable, built into the roof of an automotive vehicle to provide light, fresh air, etc.: also written **sun roof**
sun·room (sun′room′) *n.* an enclosed porch or a room with large windows to let sunlight in freely
sun·scald (-skôld′) *n.* a plant injury caused by exposure to bright sunlight or to excessive heat and manifested by whitening or browning of the leaves, fruits, or flowers
sun·screen (-skrēn′) *n.* **1** a substance, esp. para-aminobenzoic acid, used in tanning lotions, cosmetics, etc. to block certain ultraviolet rays of the sun so as to reduce the danger of sunburn **2** such a preparation
sun·set (-set′) *n.* ⟦ME *sunne set, sonsette:* see SUNRISE⟧ **1** *a)* the daily disappearance of the sun below the western horizon *b)* the varying time of this *c)* the atmospheric phenomena at this time, specif., the display of coloration visible in the western sky **2** the final phase or decline (*of* a period) —*adj.* ☆**1** designating or of a law, bill, etc. requiring that certain government agencies, programs, etc. come to an end after a specified period unless they get legislative approval again **2** having to do with a final phase or decline [a retiree's *sunset* years]
sun·shade (-shād′) *n.* a parasol, awning, broad hat, etc. used for protection against the sun's rays
sun·shine (-shīn′) *n.* **1** *a)* the shining of the sun *b)* the light and heat from the sun *c)* a sunny place or part **2** *a)* cheerfulness, happiness, etc. *b)* a source of this —*adj.* ☆designating or of a law, bill, etc., requiring that certain meetings, records, etc. of public bodies be open to the public —**sun′shin′y** (-shīn′ē) *adj.*
Sunshine State *name for* FLORIDA
sun·spot (-spät′) *n.* any of the temporarily cooler regions appearing cyclically as dark spots on the surface of the sun, accompanied by increased geomagnetic disturbances
sun·stone (-stōn′) *n.* ⟦descriptive⟧ a reddish or orange aventurine feldspar often used as a gem
sun·stroke (-strōk′) *n.* a form of heatstroke caused by excessive exposure to the sun —**sun′struck′** (-struk′) *adj.*
sun·suit (-soot′) *n.* a one-piece garment with short legs, often sleeveless or with shoulder straps, worn by babies and young children
sun·tan (-tan′) *n.* **1** a darkened condition of the skin resulting from exposure to the sun or a sunlamp **2** a reddish-brown color **3** [*pl.*] *a)* the shirt and trousers of lightweight tan or khaki fabric that make up the summer uniform of some branches of the military *b)* these trousers; also, similar ones worn by civilians —**sun′-tanned′** *adj.*
sun·up (-up′) *n.* SUNRISE
sun visor a visorlike shade for the eyes, worn at the brow and held in place by a strap
sun·ward (-wərd) *adv.* toward the sun: also **sun′wards** —*adj.* facing the sun
Sun Yat-sen (soon′yät′sen′) 1866-1925; Chin. political & revolutionary leader: see CHINESE REVOLUTION
su·o ju·re (soo′ō joor′ē, -joor′ā) ⟦L⟧ in or by one's own right
su·o lo·co (lō′kō) ⟦L⟧ in one's or its own (i.e., proper) place
Suo·mi (swô′mē) *Finn. name for* FINLAND
sup¹ (sup) *n., vt., vi.* **supped, sup′ping** ⟦ME *soupen* < OE *supan,* to sup, drink, akin to Ger *saufen:* see SUCK⟧ [Dial.] SIP
sup² (sup) *vi.* **supped, sup′ping** ⟦ME *soupen* < OFr *souper* < *soupe,* soup, orig., a sop < VL *suppa* < WGmc **suppa* < IE **seub-,* var. of base **seu-* > SUCK⟧ [Old-fashioned] to eat the evening meal; have supper —**sup on** (or **upon**) to eat a supper featuring or consisting of [to *sup on* leftovers]
sup³ *abbrev.* **1** superior **2** superlative **3** supine **4** supplement **5** supplementary **6** supply
sup. *abbrev.* ⟦L *supra*⟧ above
sup- (sup) *prefix* SUB-: used before *p* [*supply*]
su·per¹ (soo′pər) *n.* ⟦< SUPER- as used in numerous E comp.⟧ **1** *short for: a)* SUPERNUMERARY (esp. *n.* 2) *b)* SUPERINTENDENT (esp. *n.* 2) **2** [Informal] a product of superior grade, extra-large size, etc.: a trade term **3** *Bookbinding* a kind of starched cotton gauze used to reinforce the spine of a book —*adj.* **1** [Informal] outstanding; exceptionally fine **2** great, extreme, or excessive —*adv.* [Informal] very, extremely, or excessively —*vt. Bookbinding* to reinforce with super
super² *abbrev.* **1** superfine **2** superior
su·per- (soo′pər) ⟦L < *super,* above < IE **eksuper* (> Gr *hyper*) < **eghs* (> EX-¹) + **uper,* OVER⟧ *prefix* **1** over, above, on top of [*superstructure, superscribe*] **2** higher in rank or position than; superior to [*superintendent*] **3** *a)* greater in quality, amount, or degree than; surpassing [*superfine, superabundant*] *b)* greater or better than others of its kind [*supermarket*] **4** to a degree greater than normal [*supersaturate*] **5** extra, additional [*supertax*] **6** *Chem.* with a large amount of (the specified substance) [*superphosphate*]: now usually replaced by BI-¹, DI-¹, PER-, etc.
su·per·a·ble (soo′pər ə bəl) *adj.* ⟦L *superabilis* < *superare,* to overcome < *super:* see prec.⟧ [Rare] that can be overcome or conquered; surmountable —**su′per·a·bly** *adv.*
su·per·a·bound (soo′pər ə bound′) *vi.* ⟦ME *superhabounden* < LL *superabundare:* see SUPER- & ABOUND⟧ to be greatly or excessively abundant
su·per·a·bun·dant (-ə bun′dənt) *adj.* ⟦ME *superhabundaunt* < LL *superabundans,* prp. of *superabundare:* see SUPER- & ABOUND⟧ being more than is usual or needed; surplus; excess; overly abundant —**su′per·a·bun′dance** *n.* —**su′per·a·bun′dant·ly** *adv.*
su·per·add (-ad′) *vt.* ⟦L *superaddere:* see SUPER- & ADD¹⟧ to put in as extra; add to what has already been added —**su′per·ad·di′tion** (-ə dish′ən) *n.*
su·per·al·loy (-al′oi) *n.* an alloy that resists oxidation and can withstand high temperatures and stresses
su·per·al·tern (-ôl′tərn) *n.* ⟦SUPER- + (SUB)ALTERN⟧ *Logic* a universal proposition that is the basis for immediate inference to a corresponding subaltern
su·per·an·nu·ate (-an′yoo āt′) *vt., vi.* **-at′ed, -at′ing** ⟦back-form. < fol.⟧ **1** to set aside as, or become, old-fashioned or obsolete **2** to retire from service, esp. with a pension, because of old age or infirmity —**su′per·an′nu·a′tion** (-wā′shən) *n.*
su·per·an·nu·at·ed (-an′yoo āt′id) *adj.* ⟦< ML *superannuatus,* pp. of *superannuari,* to be too old < L *super* (see SUPER-) + *annus,* year (see ANNUAL)⟧ **1** *a)* too old or worn for further work, service, etc. *b)* retired, esp. with a pension, because of old age or infirmity **2** obsolete; old-fashioned; outdated
su·perb (sə purb′, soo-) *adj.* ⟦L *superbus,* proud, haughty, delicate < *super* (see SUPER-) + *-bus* < IE **bhwos* < base **bhū-,* var. of **bheu-,* to grow > BE⟧ **1** noble or majestic **2** rich or splendid **3** extremely fine; excellent —**su·perb′ly** *adv.* —**su·perb′ness** *n.*
☆**su·per·block** (soo′pər bläk′) *n.* an urban area of several acres, usually closed to through traffic, having interrelated residences and industries along with commercial, social, and recreational facilities
☆**Super Bowl** *trademark for* the annual championship game of the National Football League
su·per·bug (soo′pər bug′) *n.* ⟦SUPER- + BUG¹, *n.* 4⟧ [Informal] any strain of bacteria that has become particularly resistant to antibiotics, esp. one that is also highly virulent
su·per·cal·en·der (soo′pər kal′ən dər) *n.* ⟦SUPER- + CALENDER¹⟧ a series of polished rollers used in papermaking to give an extra-high gloss to the paper —*vt.* to process with a supercalender
su·per·car·go (soo′pər kär′gō) *n., pl.* **-goes** or **-gos** ⟦earlier *supracargo* < Sp *sobrecargo* < *sobre,* over (< L *super:* see SUPER-) + *cargo,* CARGO⟧ an officer on a merchant ship who has charge of the cargo and the business dealings of the voyage
su·per·cede (soo′pər sēd′) *vt.* **-ced′ed, -ced′ing** *disputed sp. of* SUPERSEDE
su·per·charge (soo′pər chärj′) *vt.* **-charged′, -charg′ing 1** to increase the power of (an engine), as with a supercharger **2** PRESSURIZE (sense 1)
su·per·charg·er (-chär′jər) *n.* an engine-driven compressor used in some motor vehicles and airplanes to improve power by increasing the flow of air and fuel into the cylinders: also used in airplanes to pressurize cabins and to maintain adequate air pressure in the engine at higher altitudes
su·per·cil·i·ar·y (soo′pər sil′ē er′ē) *adj.* ⟦ModL *superciliarius* < L *supercilium:* see fol.⟧ of or near the eyebrow
su·per·cil·i·ous (-sil′ē əs) *adj.* ⟦L *superciliosus* < *supercilium,* eyebrow, hence (with reference to facial expression with raised brows) haughtiness < *super-,* above + *cilium,* eyelid (see CILIA)⟧ disdainful or contemptuous; full of or characterized by pride or scorn; haughty —*SYN.* PROUD —**su′per·cil′i·ous·ly** *adv.* —**su′per·cil′i·ous·ness** *n.*
☆**su·per·cit·y** (soo′pər sit′ē) *n., pl.* **-cit′ies** MEGALOPOLIS
su·per·class (soo′pər klas′, -kläs′) *n.* a natural subdivision that includes a group of related classes within a zoological phylum or a botanical division
su·per·clus·ter (soo′pər klus′tər) *n.* a massive group of neighboring clusters of galaxies

su·per·col·lid·er (so͞o′pər kə līd′ər) ***n.*** *Nuclear Physics* an accelerator that produces very high-energy collisions of subatomic particles

☆**su·per·co·los·sal** (so͞o′pər kə läs′əl) ***adj.*** [Informal] extremely great, large, impressive, etc.: a hyperbolic term

su·per·com·put·er (so͞o′pər kəm pyo͞ot′ər) ***n.*** an extremely fast and expensive computer, typically used for such complex tasks as scientific simulations, weather forecasting, etc.

su·per·con·duc·tiv·i·ty (-kän′dək tiv′ə tē) ***n.*** *Physics* the phenomenon, exhibited by various metals, alloys, and compounds, of conducting electrical current without resistance when cooled to low temperatures: sometimes called **su′per·con·duc′tion** (-kən duk′shən) —**su′per·con·duct′ing** ***adj.***, **su′per·con·duc′tive**

su·per·con·duc·tor (so͞o′pər kən duk′tər) ***n.*** any material that exhibits superconductivity

su·per·con·ti·nent (so͞o′pər känt″n ənt) ***n.*** a massive formation of land, as Pangea, that existed for some period of time in geologic history

su·per·cool (so͞o′pər ko͞ol′) ***vt.*** to cool (a liquid) below its freezing point without causing solidification —***vi.*** to become supercooled

su·per·crit·i·cal (so͞o′pər krit′i kəl) ***adj.*** **1** *Chem.* designating or of a fluid at a temperature greater than its critical temperature **2** *Nuclear Physics* designating or of a highly unstable mass of fissionable material in which the total number of free neutrons and the rate of fission increase with time

☆**su·per·del·e·gate** (so͞o′pər del′ə git) ***n.*** a delegate to a political party convention held to nominate a presidential candidate, who attends by virtue of being a party official or elected officeholder rather than as a regular elected delegate: superdelegates are not obligated to vote for a particular candidate

su·per·dom·i·nant (so͞o′pər däm′ə nənt) ***n.*** SUBMEDIANT

☆**su·per-du·per** (so͞o′pər do͞o′pər) ***adj.*** ⟦redupl. of SUPER[1]⟧ [Slang] extremely great, large, impressive, etc.

su·per·e·go (so͞o′pər ē′gō, so͞o′pər ē′gō) ***n.***, *pl.* **-gos** *Psychoanalysis* that part of the psyche which is critical of the self or ego and enforces moral standards: at an unconscious level it blocks unacceptable impulses of the id

su·per·em·i·nent (so͞o′pər em′ə nənt) ***adj.*** ⟦LL *supereminens* < prp. of L *supereminere,* to rise above: see SUPER- & EMINENT⟧ *now rare var. of* PREEMINENT —**su′per·em′i·nence** ***n.*** —**su′per·em′i·nent·ly** ***adv.***

su·per·er·o·gate (-er′ə gāt′) ***vi.*** **-gat′ed, -gat′ing** ⟦< LL *supererogatus,* pp. of *supererogare,* to pay out beyond what is expected < *super-* (see SUPER-) + *erogare,* to pay out (after consent by the people) < *e-* (for *ex-*), out + *rogare,* to ask: see ROGATION⟧ [Obs.] to do more than is required or expected

su·per·er·o·ga·tion (-er′ə gā′shən) ***n.*** ⟦LL *supererogatio* < *supererogatus:* see prec.⟧ the act of doing more than is required or expected

su·per·e·rog·a·to·ry (-i räg′ə tôr′ē) ***adj.*** ⟦ML *supererogatorius:* see SUPEREROGATE & -ORY⟧ **1** done or observed beyond the degree required or expected **2** superfluous

☆**su·per·ette** (so͞o′pər et′, so͞o′pər et′) ***n.*** ⟦SUPER(MARKET) + -ETTE⟧ a small self-service grocery store

su·per·fam·i·ly (so͞o′pər fam′ə lē) ***n.***, *pl.* **-lies** **1** a natural subdivision ranking above a family and below an order, usually less extensive than a suborder **2** *Linguis.* a category of language classification that is above the family, often proposed as a grouping of families that are believed to be related because of some similar characteristics

☆**su·per·fec·ta** (so͞o′pər fek′tə) ***n.*** ⟦SUPER- + (PER)FECTA⟧ a bet or betting procedure in which one wins if one correctly picks the first four finishers in a horse race in the order in which they finish

☆**su·per·fe·cun·da·tion** (so͞o′pər fē′kən dā′shən, -fek′ən-) ***n.*** ⟦SUPER- + FECUNDATION⟧ the fertilization of two ova at separate times during the same ovulation period

su·per·fe·ta·tion (-fē tā′shən) ***n.*** ⟦ML *superfetatio* < L *superfetatus,* pp. of *superfetare* < *super-* (see SUPER-) + *fetare,* to bring forth, impregnate < *fetus,* FETUS⟧ the fertilization of an ovum during a pregnancy already in existence

su·per·fi·cial (so͞o′pər fish′əl) ***adj.*** ⟦ME *superficyall* < L *superficialis* < *superficies:* see fol.⟧ **1** *a)* of or being on the surface [a *superficial* burn] *b)* of or limited to surface area; plane [*superficial* measurements] **2** concerned with and understanding only the easily apparent and obvious; not profound; shallow **3** quick and cursory [a *superficial* reading] **4** seeming such only at first glance; merely apparent [a *superficial* resemblance] —**su′per·fi′ci·al′i·ty** (-ē al′ə tē) ***n.***, *pl.* **-ties** —**su′per·fi′cial·ly** ***adv.*** —**su′per·fi′cial·ness** ***n.***

SYN.—**superficial** implies concern with the obvious or surface aspects of a thing [*superficial* characteristics] and, in a derogatory sense, lack of thoroughness, profoundness, significance, etc. [*superficial* judgments]; **shallow**, in this connection always derogatory, implies a lack of depth of character, intellect, meaning, etc. [*shallow* writing]; **cursory**, which may or may not be derogatory, suggests a hasty consideration of something without pausing to note details [a *cursory* inspection] —**ANT. deep, profound**

su·per·fi·ci·es (so͞o′pər fish′ē ēz′, -fish′ēz) ***n.***, *pl.* **-ci·es** ⟦L < *super-* (see SUPER-) + *facies,* FACE⟧ **1** a surface; outer area **2** the outward form or aspect

su·per·fine (so͞o′pər fīn′, so͞o′pər fīn′) ***adj.*** ⟦ME *superfyne:* see SUPER- & FINE[1]⟧ **1** too subtle, delicate, or refined; overnice [a *superfine* distinction] **2** of exceptionally fine quality [*superfine* glassware] **3** extremely fine-grained [*superfine* sugar]

su·per·fix (so͞o′pər fiks′) ***n.*** ⟦SUPER- + (AF)FIX⟧ *Linguis.* a pattern of stress, pitch, or juncture superposed on the segmental phonemes, as for indicating grammatical function (Ex.: *in′sert, n.,* and *in·sert′, v.*)

su·per·flu·id·i·ty (so͞o′pər flo͞o id′ə tē) ***n.*** the phenomenon, exhibited by liquid helium at temperatures below 2.18°K, of flowing without friction and having very high thermal conductivity —**su′per·flu′id** (-flo͞o′id) ***n., adj.***

su·per·flu·i·ty (-flo͞o′ə tē) ***n.***, *pl.* **-ties** ⟦ME *superfluite* < OFr *superfluité* < L *superfluitas*⟧ **1** the state or quality of being superfluous **2** a quantity or number beyond what is needed; excess; superabundance **3** something superfluous; thing not needed

su·per·flu·ous (sə pur′flo͞o əs, so͞o-) ***adj.*** ⟦L *superfluus* < *superfluere,* to overflow: see SUPER- & FLUCTUATE⟧ **1** being more than is needed, useful, or wanted; surplus; excessive **2** not needed; unnecessary; irrelevant [a *superfluous* remark] **3** [Obs.] extravagant; prodigal —**su·per′flu·ous·ly** ***adv.*** —**su·per′flu·ous·ness** ***n.***

☆**Su·per·fund** (so͞o′pər fund′) ***n.*** [*also* **s-**] a U.S. government fund created for the cleanup or eradication of sites at which toxic waste, hazardous to the environment, has been dumped

su·per·gi·ant (so͞o′pər jī′ənt) ***n.*** an immense and extremely luminous star, as Betelgeuse or Antares, that has a diameter at least 100 times that of the sun and that is 100 to more than 10,000 times as bright

su·per·graph·ics (so͞o′pər graf′iks) ***pl.n.*** [*with sing. or pl. v.*] very large, usually brightly colored, graphic images of simple design

su·per·grav·i·ty (so͞o′pər grav′ə tē) ***n.*** *Physics* any unified field theory that attempts to combine the force of gravity with the other fundamental forces of nature

su·per·group (so͞o′pər gro͞op′) ***n.*** **1** a rock-music group made up of members of other well-known groups **2** a highly successful rock group

su·per·heat (so͞o′pər hēt′; *for n.,* so͞o′pər hēt′) ***vt.*** **1** OVERHEAT **2** to heat (a liquid) above its boiling point without vaporizing it **3** to heat (steam not in contact with water) beyond its saturation point, so that a drop in temperature will not cause reconversion to water —***n.*** the number of degrees by which the temperature of superheated steam exceeds the temperature of the steam at its saturation point —**su′per·heat′er** ***n.***

su·per·he·ro (so͞o′pər hir′ō) ***n.***, *pl.* **-roes** **1** a heroic fictional character, of a kind found in comic books, who has physical and mental abilities, skills, etc. that are either superhuman or superior to those of ordinary human beings **2** any person regarded as having extraordinary ability in some field

su·per·het·er·o·dyne (so͞o′pər het′ər ə dīn′) ***adj.*** ⟦SUPER(SONIC) + HETERODYNE⟧ designating or of a form of radio reception in which part of the amplification prior to demodulation is carried out at an intermediate supersonic frequency produced by beating the frequency of the received carrier waves with that of locally generated oscillations —***n.*** a radio set for this method of reception

su·per·high frequency (so͞o′pər hī′) any radio frequency between 3,000 and 30,000 megahertz

☆**su·per·high·way** (so͞o′pər hī′wā′) ***n.*** EXPRESSWAY

su·per·hu·man (so͞o′pər hyo͞o′mən) ***adj.*** **1** having powers or a nature above that of a human being **2** greater than that of a normal human being: often hyperbolic [a *superhuman* effort will be required from everyone] —**su′per·hu′man·ly** ***adv.*** —**su′per·hu′man·ness** ***n.***

su·per·im·pose (-im pōz′) ***vt.*** **-posed′, -pos′ing** **1** to put or lay on top of something else, esp. so that both remain visible, audible, etc. **2** to add as a dominant or unassimilated feature —**su′per·im′po·si′tion** (-im′pə zish′ən) ***n.***

su·per·in·cum·bent (-in kum′bənt) ***adj.*** ⟦L *superincumbens,* prp. of *superincumbere:* see SUPER- & INCUMBENT⟧ **1** *a)* lying or resting on something else *b)* brought to bear from above (said of pressure) **2** arching over or overhanging —**su′per·in·cum′bence** ***n.***, **su′per·in·cum′ben·cy**

su·per·in·duce (-in do͞os′, -dyo͞os′) ***vt.*** **-duced′, -duc′ing** ⟦L *superinducere:* see SUPER- & INDUCE⟧ to introduce or bring in as an addition to an existent condition, effect, etc. —**su′per·in·duc′tion** (-duk′shən) ***n.***

su·per·in·fec·tion (-in fek′shən) ***n.*** an additional infection occurring during the course of an existing infection, usually caused by opportunistic microorganisms resistant to the antimicrobial agents used in treating the first infection

su·per·in·tend (-in tend′) ***vt.*** ⟦LL(Ec) *superintendere:* see SUPER- & INTEND⟧ to act as superintendent of; direct; supervise; manage —**su′per·in·tend′ence** ***n.***, **su′per·in·tend′en·cy**

su·per·in·tend·ent (-in ten′dənt) ***n.*** ⟦< LL(Ec) *superintendens,* prp. of *superintendere,* to superintend⟧ **1** a person in charge of a department, institution, etc.; director; supervisor **2** a person responsible for the maintenance of a building; custodian —***adj.*** that superintends

su·pe·ri·or (sə pir′ē ər) ***adj.*** ⟦OFr < L, compar. of *superus,* that is above < *super:* see SUPER-⟧ **1** higher in space; placed higher up; upper **2** high or higher in order, status, rank, etc. **3** greater in quality or value than: with *to* **4** above average in quality; excellent **5** refusing to give in to or be affected by: with *to* [a person *superior* to temptation] **6** showing a feeling of being better than others; haughty **7** more comprehensive or inclusive; generic: said of terms, concepts, etc. **8** *Anat.* located above or directed upward **9** *Astron.* *a)* farther from the sun than the earth is (said of five planets) *b)* designating that conjunction which occurs when the sun is directly between the earth and an inferior planet **10** *Bot.* *a)* attached above some other organ, as the ovary of a hypogynous flower *b)* of the upper or adaxial petal of an axillary flower **11** *Printing* placed above the type line (Ex.: 2 in x^2) —***n.*** **1** a superior person or thing **2** the head of a religious community —**su·pe′ri·or·ly** ***adv.***

Su·pe·ri·or (sə pir′ē ər), **Lake** ⟦orig. so called in Fr (*Supérieur*), from its position above Lake Huron⟧ largest & westernmost of the Great Lakes, between Mich. & Ontario, Canada: 31,700 sq mi (82,103 sq km)

☆**superior court** in some U.S. states, either a lower court of general jurisdiction or a court of appeals below the highest appellate court

su·pe·ri·or·i·ty (sə pir′ē ôr′ə tē) *n.* **1** the state or quality of being superior, or higher, greater, better, etc. **2** *pl.* **-ties** an instance of this

superiority complex popularly, a feeling of superiority or exaggerated self-importance, often accompanied by excessive aggressiveness, arrogance, etc. which are compensation for feelings of inferiority: cf. INFERIORITY COMPLEX

su·per·ja·cent (so͞o′pər jā′sənt) *adj.* ⟦LL *superjacens,* prp. of *superjacere* < *super-,* over (see SUPER-) + *jacere,* to lie, be thrown down, throw: see JET[1]⟧ lying or resting above or upon

su·per·king·dom (so͞o′pər kiŋ′dəm) *n. Biol.* in some taxonomic systems, the highest classification category, ranking above a kingdom

superl *abbrev.* superlative

su·per·la·tive (sə pʉr′lə tiv, so͞o-) *adj.* ⟦ME < MFr *superlatif* < LL *superlativus* < L *superlatus,* excessive < *super-,* above, beyond + *latus,* pp. of *ferre,* to BEAR[1]⟧ **1** superior to or excelling all other or others; of the highest kind, quality, degree, etc.; supreme **2** excessive or exaggerated **3** *Gram.* designating or of the extreme degree of comparison of adjectives and adverbs; expressing the greatest degree of the quality or attribute expressed by the positive degree: usually indicated by the suffix -EST *(hardest)* or by the use of *most* with the positive form *(most beautiful)* —*n.* **1** the highest or utmost degree; acme; height; peak **2** something superlative **3** *Gram. a)* the superlative degree *b)* a word or form in this degree —**su·per′la·tive·ly** *adv.* —**su·per′la·tive·ness** *n.*

su·per·lu·na·ry (so͞o′pər lo͞on′ər ē) *adj.* ⟦< SUPER- + L *luna,* moon (see LIGHT[1]) + -ARY⟧ located above or beyond the moon: also **su′per·lu′nar**

su·per·ma·jor·i·ty (so͞o′per mə jôr′ə tē, -jär′-) *n.* a specified number or percentage of votes, exceeding the minimum needed to produce a majority, required to pass certain legislative bills, ballot issues, etc.

su·per·man (so͞o′pər man′) *n., pl.* **-men′** (-men′) ⟦calque < Ger *übermensch* (< *über,* over + *mensch,* person), Nietzsche's term⟧ **1** in the philosophy of Nietzsche, an idealized superior, dominating human being, regarded as the goal of the evolutionary struggle for survival **2** ⟦often in allusion to *Superman,* a trademark for a superhero first appearing in U.S. comic books in 1938⟧ [*often* **S-**] a man having apparently superhuman powers

☆**su·per·mar·ket** (-mär′kit) *n.* a large, self-service, retail food store or market, often one of a chain

su·per·max (so͞o′pər maks′) *n.* ⟦< *super-max(imum-security prison)*⟧ a maximum-security prison or prison wing in which prisoners are kept in solitary confinement and under constant surveillance

super middleweight a boxer between a middleweight and a light heavyweight, with a maximum weight of 168 pounds (76.20 kg)

su·per·mod·el (-mäd′'l) *n.* a very prominent and highly paid fashion model

su·per·nal (so͞o pʉr′nəl) *adj.* ⟦LME < MFr < L *supernus,* upper < *super,* above: see SUPER-⟧ of, from, or as though from the heavens or the sky; celestial, heavenly, or divine —**su·per′nal·ly** *adv.*

su·per·na·tant (so͞o′pər nāt′'nt) *adj.* ⟦L *supernatans,* prp. of *supernatare,* to swim above < *super-* (see SUPER-) + *natare,* to swim (see NATANT)⟧ **1** floating on the surface or over something **2** *Chem.* designating or of a liquid standing above a precipitate

su·per·nat·u·ral (so͞o′pər nach′ər əl) *adj.* ⟦ML *supernaturalis:* see SUPER- & NATURAL⟧ **1** existing or occurring outside the normal experience or knowledge of man; not explainable by the known forces or laws of nature; specif., of, involving, or attributed to God or a god **2** of, involving, or attributed to ghosts, spirits, the occult, etc. **3** exceeding normal bounds; extreme [skating with *supernatural* grace] —**the supernatural** supernatural beings, forces, happenings, etc., esp. ghosts, spirits, and the like —**su′per·nat′u·ral·ly** *adv.*

su·per·nat·u·ral·ism (-iz′əm) *n.* **1** the quality or state of being supernatural **2** belief in the supernatural, esp. a belief that some supernatural, or divine, force controls nature and the universe —**su′per·nat′u·ral·ist** *n., adj.* —**su′per·nat′u·ral·is′tic** *adj.*

su·per·nat·u·ral·ize (-īz′) *vt.* **-ized′**, **-iz′ing** **1** to make supernatural **2** to think of or treat as supernatural

su·per·nor·mal (so͞o′pər nôr′məl) *adj.* **1** above normal **2** PARANORMAL —**su′per·nor′mal·ly** *adv.*

su·per·no·va (-nō′və) *n., pl.* **-vas** or **-vae** (-vē) ⟦ModL: see SUPER- & NOVA⟧ a rare, extremely bright nova that suddenly increases up to a billion times in brightness and reaches an absolute magnitude of *c.* -16

su·per·nu·mer·ar·y (-no͞o′mə rer′ē, -nyo͞o′-) *adj.* ⟦LL *supernumerarius* < L *super,* above (see SUPER-) + *numerus,* NUMBER⟧ **1** that exceeds or is beyond the regular or prescribed number; extra **2** that is beyond the number or quantity needed or desired; superfluous —*n., pl.* **-ar′ies** **1** a supernumerary person or thing **2** *Theater* a person with a small, nonspeaking part, as in a mob scene

su·per·or·der (so͞o′pər ôr′dər) *n.* a natural subdivision between an order and a class or subclass of plants or animals

su·per·or·di·nate (so͞o′pər ôrd′'n it) *adj.* ⟦SUPER- + (SUB)ORDINATE⟧ of a superior kind, rank, status, etc.

su·per·or·gan·ism (-ôr′gə niz′əm) *n.* a colony of interdependent organisms, as in the social insects, regarded as an organic unit

su·per·ov·u·la·tion (-äv′yə lā′shən, -ō′vyə-) *n.* the release of a larger-than-normal number of eggs for fertilization, esp. when artificially induced by injected hormones to produce embryos for transplantation, frozen storage, etc. —**su′per·ov′u·late′** (-lāt′) *vt., vi.* **-lat′ed**, **-lat′ing**

su·per·ox·ide (-äk′sīd) *n.* ⟦SUPER- (sense 6) + OXIDE⟧ a compound containing the paramagnetic, monovalent, negative free radical O_2

☆**super PAC** (pak) ⟦see PAC⟧ a type of political action committee having no official affiliation with a particular candidate or party and, hence, no limits on its spending

su·per·par·a·site (-par′ə sīt′) *n.* an organism that lives as a parasite upon another parasite

su·per·pa·tri·ot (-pā′trē ət) *n.* a person who is or professes to be a devout patriot, often to the point of fanaticism —**su′per·pa′tri·ot′ic** (-pā′trē ät′ik) *adj.* —**su′per·pa′tri·ot·ism′** *n.*

su·per·phos·phate (-fäs′fāt) *n.* an acid phosphate, esp. a mixture mainly of monobasic calcium phosphate and gypsum, made by treating bone, phosphate rock, etc. with sulfuric acid and used as fertilizer

su·per·phys·i·cal (-fiz′i kəl) *adj.* beyond the physical or the known laws of physics; hyperphysical

su·per·plas·tic·i·ty (-plas tis′ə tē) *n.* the phenomenon, exhibited by certain metals and alloys usually at high temperatures, of stretching to extreme lengths without breaking —**su′per·plas′tic** (-tik) *adj., n.*

su·per·pose (-pōz′) *vt.* **-posed′**, **-pos′ing** ⟦Fr *superposer* < L *superpositus,* pp. of *superponere,* to place over: see SUPER- & POSE[1]⟧ **1** to lay or place on, over, or above something else **2** *Geom.* to make (one figure) coincide with another in all parts, by or as if by placing one on top of the other —**su′per·pos′a·ble** *adj.* —**su′per·po·si′tion** (-pə zish′ən) *n.*

su·per·posed (-pōzd′) *adj.* ⟦pp. of prec.⟧ *Bot.* growing or lying directly above another part or organ

su·per·pow·er (so͞o′pər pou′ər) *n.* **1** power that is superior or very great **2** a very powerful nation, having great influence in international affairs

su·per·sat·u·rate (so͞o′pər sach′ə rāt′) *vt.* **-rat′ed**, **-rat′ing** ⟦SUPER- + SATURATE, after Fr *sursaturer*⟧ to make more highly concentrated than in normal saturation at a given temperature —**su′per·sat′u·ra′tion** *n.*

su·per·scribe (so͞o′pər skrīb′) *vt.* **-scribed′**, **-scrib′ing** ⟦L *superscribere:* see SUPER- & SCRIBE⟧ to write, mark, or engrave (an inscription, name, etc.) at the top or on an outer surface of (something); specif., to write (a name, address, etc.) on (an envelope, parcel, etc.)

su·per·script (-skript′) *adj.* ⟦L *superscriptus,* pp.: see prec.⟧ written above; esp., SUPERIOR (*adj.* 11) —*n.* a figure, letter, or symbol written above and to the side of another [in y^2 and x^n, 2 and n are *superscripts*]

su·per·scrip·tion (so͞o′pər skrip′shən) *n.* ⟦ME *superscripcioun* < L *superscriptio*⟧ **1** the act of superscribing **2** something superscribed; esp., an address on a letter, etc. **3** *Pharmacy* the Latin word *recipe* (meaning "take") or its symbol, ℞, on a prescription

su·per·sede (-sēd′) *vt.* **-sed′ed**, **-sed′ing** ⟦MFr *superseder,* to leave off, give over < L *supersedere,* lit., to sit over, preside over, forbear: see SUPER- & SIT⟧ **1** to cause to be set aside or dropped from use as inferior or obsolete and replaced by something else **2** to take the place of in office, function, etc.; succeed **3** to remove or cause to be removed so as to make way for another; supplant —*SYN.* REPLACE —**su′per·sed′er** *n.* —☆**su′per·se′dure** (-sē′jər) *n.,* **su′per·sed′ence** (-sē′dəns)

su·per·se·de·as (-sē′dē as′) *n.* ⟦ME < L, you shall desist < *supersedere:* see prec.⟧ a legal document issued to halt or delay the action of some process of law

su·per·sen·si·ble (-sen′sə bəl) *adj.* outside or beyond the range of perception by the senses —**su′per·sen′si·bly** *adv.*

su·per·sen·si·tive (-sen′sə tiv) *adj.* extremely sensitive —**su′per·sen′si·tiv′i·ty** *n.*

su·per·sen·so·ry (-sen′sə rē) *adj.* SUPERSENSIBLE

su·per·ses·sion (-sesh′ən) *n.* ⟦ML *supersessio* < L *supersessus,* pp. of *supersedere*⟧ a superseding or being superseded —**su′per·ses′sive** (-ses′iv) *adj.*

su·per·size (so͞o′pər sīz′) [Informal] *adj.* extra-large or excessively large: also **su′per·sized′** —*vt.* **-sized′**, **-siz′ing** to make extra-large or excessively large

su·per·son·ic (so͞o′pər sän′ik) *adj.* ⟦SUPER- + SONIC⟧ **1** designating, of, or moving at a speed in a surrounding fluid greater than that of sound in the same fluid **2** ULTRASONIC —**su′per·son′i·cal·ly** *adv.*

su·per·son·ics (-sän′iks) *n.* ⟦see prec. & -ICS⟧ the science dealing with supersonic phenomena: specif., the study of the aerodynamics of supersonic speeds

☆**su·per·star** (so͞o′pər stär′) *n.* a very prominent performer, as in sports or the entertainment industry, often one considered to have exceptional skill and talent

su·per·sta·tion (-stā′shən) *n.* a local TV station whose broadcasts are relayed via electronic satellite to cable TV systems over a large geographical area

su·per·sti·tion (so͞o′pər stish′ən) *n.* ⟦ME *supersticion* < MFr < L *superstitio,* excessive fear of the gods, superstition, orig., a standing still over < *superstare,* to stand over < *super-,* SUPER- + *stare,* to STAND⟧ **1** any belief, based on fear or ignorance, that is inconsistent with the known laws of science or with what is considered as true and rational; esp., such a belief in charms, omens, the supernatural, etc. **2** any action or practice based on such a belief **3** such beliefs collectively

su·per·sti·tious (-əs) *adj.* **1** of, characterized by, or resulting from superstition **2** having superstitions —**su′per·sti′tious·ly** *adv.* —**su′per·sti′tious·ness** *n.*

su·per·store (so͞o′pər stôr′) *n.* a very large retail store offering a very wide selection of merchandise [a computer *superstore*]

su·per·stra·tum (so͞o′pər strāt′əm, -strat′-) ***n., pl.*** **-stra′ta** (-ə) or **-stra′tums** a stratum lying over another

su·per·string (so͞o′pər striŋ′) ***n.*** *Physics* a theoretical object analogous to an elementary particle, consisting of a curve of finite length but only one dimension, which vibrates within a framework of ten dimensions

su·per·struc·ture (-struk′chər) ***n.*** **1** a structure built on top of another: sometimes used fig. **2** that part of a building above the foundation **3** that part of a ship above the main deck

su·per·sub·tle (so͞o′pər sut′'l) ***adj.*** extremely subtle or too subtle —**su′per·sub′tle·ty** ***n.***

su·per·sym·me·try (so͞o′pər sim′ə trē) ***n.*** *Nuclear Physics* any of various mathematical theories that attempt to unify all the forces and subatomic particles of nature —**su′per·sym·met′ric** (-si me′trik) ***adj.***

su·per·tank·er (so͞o′pər taŋ′kər) ***n.*** an extremely large tanker, of about 300,000 tons or more

su·per·tax (so͞o′pər taks′) ***n.*** an additional tax; esp., a surtax

su·per·ti·tle (-tīt′'l) ***n.*** ⟦< SUPER- (sense 1), by analogy with SUBTITLE (*n.* 2)⟧ one or more lines of a translation of the lyrics of an opera, oratorio, etc. in a foreign language, displayed above the stage during a performance

su·per·ton·ic (so͞o′pər tän′ik) ***n.*** *Music* the second tone of a diatonic scale, next above the tonic

☆**Super Tuesday** a Tuesday early in a presidential election year, on which many states hold primary elections

su·per·vene (so͞o′pər vēn′) ***vi.*** **-vened′**, **-ven′ing** ⟦L *supervenire,* to come over or upon, follow < *super-* (see SUPER-) + *venire,* to COME⟧ **1** to come or happen as something extraneous or unexpected **2** to take place; ensue —**su′per·ven′ient** (-vēn′yənt) ***adj.*** —**su′per·ven′tion** (-ven′shən) ***n.***, **su′per·ven′ience** (-vēn′yəns)

su·per·vise (so͞o′pər vīz′) ***vt., vi.*** **-vised′**, **-vis′ing** ⟦< ML *supervisus,* pp. of *supervidere* < L *super-* (see SUPER-) + *videre,* to see: see VISION⟧ to oversee, direct, or manage (work, workers, a project, etc.); superintend —**su′per·vi′sion** (-vizh′ən) ***n.***

su·per·vi·sor (so͞o′pər vī′zər) ***n.*** **1** a person who supervises; superintendent; manager; director ☆**2** in certain school systems, an official in charge of the courses of study for a particular subject and of all teachers of that subject —**su′per·vi′so·ry** ***adj.***

su·per·wom·an (so͞o′pər wo͝om′ən) ***n., pl.*** **-wom′en** (-wim′in) an extremely accomplished woman, specif., one equally successful in dealing with the demands of work and family

su·pi·nate (so͞o′pə nāt′) ***vt., vi.*** **-nat′ed**, **-nat′ing** ⟦< L *supinatus,* pp. of *supinare,* to lay backward < *supinus,* SUPINE⟧ to rotate (the hand or forearm) so that the palm faces upward or forward: see PRONATE —**su′pi·na′tion** ***n.***

su·pi·na·tor (so͞o′pə nāt′ər) ***n.*** the muscle in the forearm by which supination is effected

su·pine (so͞o pīn′; *also, and for n. always,* so͞o′pīn′) ***adj.*** ⟦L *supinus,* prob. akin to *sub-*: see SUB-⟧ **1** lying on the back, face upward **2** with the palm upward or away from the body: said of the hand **3** [Old Poet.] leaning or sloping backward **4** mentally or morally inactive; sluggish; listless; passive —***n.*** *Gram.* **1** a Latin verbal noun formed from the stem of the past participle and having only an accusative and an ablative form **2** an infinitive in English preceded by *to* —**SYN.** PRONE —**su′pine′ly** ***adv.*** —**su′pine′ness** ***n.***

supp or **suppl** ***abbrev.*** **1** supplement **2** supplementary

sup·per (sup′ər) ***n.*** ⟦ME *souper* < OFr, orig. inf., to SUP²⟧ **1** an evening meal; specif., *a)* one that is the chief meal of the day *b)* one eaten on a day when the chief meal (called *dinner*) is served during the middle of the day *c)* a late, usually light, evening meal ☆**2** an evening social affair at which a meal is served [a church *supper*]

supper club an intimate, expensive nightclub

sup·plant (sə plant′, -plänt′) ***vt.*** ⟦ME *supplanten* < OFr *supplanter* < L *supplantare,* to put under the sole of the foot, trip up < *sub-,* under (see SUB-) + *planta,* sole of the foot: see PLANT⟧ **1** to take the place of; supersede, esp. through force or plotting **2** to remove or uproot in order to replace with something else —**SYN.** REPLACE —**sup·plan·ta·tion** (sup′lan tā′shən) ***n.*** —**sup·plant′er** ***n.***

sup·ple (sup′əl) ***adj.*** **-pler**, **-plest** ⟦ME *souple* < OFr < L *supplex,* humble, submissive, akin to *supplicare:* see SUPPLICATE⟧ **1** easily bent or twisted; flexible; pliant **2** able to bend and move easily and nimbly; lithe; limber [a *supple* body] **3** easily changed or influenced **4** adaptable, as to changes [a *supple* mind] — ***vt., vi.*** **-pled**, **-pling** to make or become supple —**SYN.** ELASTIC —**sup′ple·ly** ***adv.*** —**sup′ple·ness** ***n.***

sup·ple·jack (-jak′) ***n.*** ☆**1** a twining, woody, North American vine (*Berchemia scandens*) of the buckthorn family, with tough stems, greenish-white flowers, and dark-purple fruit **2** *a)* a tropical American woody vine (*Paullinia curassavica*) of the soapberry family, the wood of which is used for walking sticks *b)* such a walking stick

sup·ple·ment (sup′lə mənt; *for v.,* -ment′) ***n.*** ⟦ME < L *supplementum* < *supplere:* see SUPPLY¹⟧ **1** something added, esp. to make up for a lack or deficiency **2** a section added to a book or the like to give additional information, correct errors in the body of the work, etc. ☆**3** a separate section containing feature stories, comic strips, or the like, issued with a newspaper **4** the amount to be added to a given angle or arc to make 180° or a semicircle —***vt.*** to provide a supplement to; add to, esp. so as to make up for a lack or deficiency —**sup′ple·men′tal** ***adj.*** —**sup′ple·men·ta′tion** (-mən tā′shən) ***n.***

sup·ple·men·ta·ry (sup′lə men′tər ē, -men′trē) ***adj.*** supplying what is lacking; additional —***n., pl.*** **-ries** a supplementary person or thing

supplementary angle either of two angles that together equal 180°

sup·ple·tion (sə plē′shən) ***n.*** ⟦ME *supplecioun* < ML *suppletio* < L *suppletus:* see fol.⟧ *Linguis.* **1** *a)* the occurrence of an allomorph of a morpheme which has no phonological similarity to the other allomorphs (Ex.: the *-en* of *oxen,* as opposed to a form ending in *-s*) *b)* the use of an unrelated word (*suppletive form*) in a paradigm (Ex.: *went* for the past tense of *go*) **2** the morphological process by which such replacement occurs —**sup·ple·tive** (sup′lə tiv, sə plēt′iv) ***adj.***

sup·ple·to·ry (sup′lə tôr′ē) ***adj.*** ⟦LL *suppletorius* < L *suppletus,* pp. of *supplere,* to SUPPLY¹⟧ SUPPLEMENTARY: archaic except in legal usage

sup·pli·ance (sup′lē əns) ***n.*** ⟦< fol.⟧ SUPPLICATION

sup·pli·ant (sup′lē ənt) ***n.*** ⟦ME *suppliaunt:* see the ***adj.***⟧ a person who supplicates; petitioner —***adj.*** ⟦MFr, prp. of *supplier* < L *supplicare,* to SUPPLICATE⟧ **1** asking humbly; supplicating; entreating **2** expressing supplication [*suppliant* words] —**sup′pli·ant·ly** ***adv.***

sup·pli·cant (sup′lə kənt) ***adj.*** that supplicates; supplicating —***n.*** a person who supplicates; suppliant

sup·pli·cate (sup′lə kāt′) ***vt.*** **-cat′ed**, **-cat′ing** ⟦ME *supplicaten* < L *supplicatus,* pp. of *supplicare,* to kneel down, pray < *sub-,* SUB- + *plicare,* to fold, double up: see PLY¹⟧ **1** to ask for humbly and earnestly, as by prayer **2** to make a humble request of; petition earnestly —***vi.*** to make a humble request or supplication, esp. in prayer —**SYN.** APPEAL —**sup′pli·ca·to′ry** (-kə tôr′ē) ***adj.*** —**sup′pli·ca′tor** ***n.***

sup·pli·ca·tion (sup′lə kā′shən) ***n.*** **1** the act of supplicating **2** a humble request, prayer, petition, etc.

sup·ply¹ (sə plī′) ***vt.*** **-plied′**, **-ply′ing** ⟦ME *supplyen* < MFr *supplier* < L *supplere,* to fill up < *sub-,* SUB- + *plere,* to fill: see FULL¹⟧ **1** to give, furnish, or provide (what is needed or wanted) [to *supply* tools to workers] **2** to meet the needs or requirements of; furnish, provide, or equip *with* what is needed or wanted [to *supply* workers with tools] **3** to compensate for; make good [to *supply* a deficiency] **4** to act as a substitute in; fill or serve in temporarily [to *supply* another's pulpit] —***vi.*** to serve as a temporary substitute —***n., pl.*** **-plies′** **1** the act of supplying **2** an amount or quantity available for use; stock; store **3** [*pl.*] materials, provisions, etc. for supplying an army, expedition, a business, etc.; sometimes, specif., provisions for an army other than materiel, vehicles, etc. **4** [*often pl.*] [Chiefly Brit.] an amount of money granted for government expenses; appropriation **5** a temporary substitute, as for a minister **6** [Obs.] *a)* aid; assistance *b)* reinforcements **7** *Econ.* the amount of a commodity available for purchase at a given price: opposed to DEMAND (*n.* 6) —***adj.*** **1** having to do with a supply or supplies **2** serving as a substitute —**sup·pli′er** ***n.***

sup·ply² (sup′lē) ***adv.*** in a supple manner; supplely

☆**sup·ply-side** (sə plī′sīd′) ***adj.*** designating or of a theory that economic growth can be achieved by stimulating investment, with the money for investment coming chiefly through tax reductions

☆**sup·ply-sid·er** (-sīd′ər) ***n.*** one who advocates or puts into practice supply-side economic theory

sup·port (sə pôrt′) ***vt.*** ⟦ME *supporten* < MFr *supporter* < LL(Ec) *supportare,* to endure, bear < L, to carry, bring to a place < *sub-,* SUB- + *portare,* to carry: see PORT³⟧ **1** *a)* to carry or bear the weight of; keep from falling, slipping, or sinking; hold up *b)* to carry or bear (a specified weight, strain, pressure, etc.) **2** to give courage, faith, or confidence to; help or comfort **3** to give approval to or be in favor of; subscribe to; uphold **4** to maintain or provide for (a person, institution, etc.) with money, or subsistence **5** to show or tend to show to be true; help prove, vindicate, or corroborate [evidence to *support* a claim] **6** to bear; endure; submit to; tolerate **7** to keep up; maintain; sustain; specif., to maintain (the price of a specified commodity) as by government purchase of surpluses **8** *Comput.* to be compatible with: see COMPATIBLE (sense 5) **9** *Theater* to act a subordinate role in the same play with (a specified star) —***n.*** **1** a supporting or being supported **2** a person or thing that supports; specif., *a)* a prop, base, brace, etc. *b)* a means of subsistence *c)* an elastic, girdlelike device to support or bind a part of the body *d)* maintenance and service, as for a computer system's software or hardware [technical *support*] —***adj.*** providing or having to do with support [*support* staff for a company's computer system] —**sup·port′a·ble** ***adj.*** —**sup·port′a·bly** ***adv.***

SYN.—**support**, the broadest of these terms, suggests a favoring of someone or something, either by giving active aid or merely by approving or sanctioning [to *support* a candidate for office]; **uphold** suggests that what is being supported is under attack [to *uphold* civil rights for all]; **sustain** implies full active support so as to strengthen or keep from failing [*sustained* by his hope for the future]; **maintain** suggests a supporting so as to keep intact or unimpaired [to *maintain* the law, a family, etc.]; **advocate** implies support in speech or writing and sometimes connotes persuasion or argument [to *advocate* a change in policy]; **back** (often **back up**) suggests support, as financial aid, moral encouragement, etc., given to prevent failure [I'll *back* you *up* in your demands]

sup·port·er (-ər) ***n.*** **1** a person who supports; advocate; adherent; partisan **2** a thing that supports; esp., *a)* an elastic, girdlelike device worn to support the back, abdomen, etc. ☆*b)* *short for* ATHLETIC SUPPORTER ☆*c)* GARTER **3** *Heraldry* either of a pair of figures, as of animals or men, standing one on either side of a shield —**SYN.** FOLLOWER

support group a group formed to provide its members with support in dealing with and information regarding a specific problem, as coping with a serious disease or overcoming an addiction

sup·port·ing (-iŋ) *adj.* *Film, Theater* designating or of an actor or role that is subordinate to or of lesser importance than that of a lead or principal

sup·port·ive (-iv) *adj.* that gives support, help, or approval

sup·pose (sə pōz′) *vt.* **-posed′, -pos′ing** ⟦ME *supposen* < MFr *supposer,* to suppose, imagine, altered (infl. by *poser:* see POSE¹) < ML *supponere,* to suppose, assume < L, to put under, substitute < *sub-,* SUB- + *ponere:* see POSITION⟧ **1** to assume to be true, as for the sake of argument or to illustrate a proof [*suppose* A equals B] **2** to believe, think, guess, etc. [I *suppose* you're right] **3** PRESUPPOSE (sense 2) **4** to consider as a proposed or suggested possibility: used in the imperative [*suppose* they don't come] **5** to expect or obligate: always in the passive [you're *supposed* to telephone] —*vi.* to make a supposition; conjecture —**sup·pos′a·ble** *adj.* —**sup·pos′a·bly** *adv.* —**sup·pos′er** *n.*

sup·posed (sə pōzd′, -pō′zid) *adj.* **1** regarded as true, genuine, etc., without actual knowledge **2** merely imagined

sup·pos·ed·ly (sə pō′zid lē) *adv.* according to what is, was, or may be supposed

sup·pos·ing (sə pō′ziŋ) *conj.* assuming that; on the assumption that

sup·po·si·tion (sup′ə zish′ən) *n.* ⟦OFr < L *suppositio* < *suppositus,* pp. of *supponere:* see SUPPOSE⟧ **1** the act of supposing **2** something supposed; assumption; hypothesis Also **sup·pos·al** (sə pō′zəl) —**sup′po·si′tion·al** *adj.* —**sup′po·si′tion·al·ly** *adv.*

sup·po·si·tious (-əs) *adj.* SUPPOSITITIOUS

sup·pos·i·ti·tious (sə päz′ə tish′əs) *adj.* ⟦L *suppositicius* < *suppositus:* see SUPPOSITION⟧ **1** substituted with intent to deceive or defraud; spurious; counterfeit **2** suppositional; hypothetical —**sup·pos′i·ti′tious·ly** *adv.*

sup·pos·i·tive (sə päz′ə tiv) *adj.* ⟦LL *suppositivus*⟧ having the nature of, based on, or involving supposition —*n.* *Gram.* a conjunction introducing a supposition, as *if, assuming,* or *provided*

sup·pos·i·to·ry (sə päz′ə tôr′ē) *n., pl.* **-ries** ⟦ME *suppositorie* < ML *suppositorium* < neut. of L *suppositorius,* placed underneath < *suppositus:* see SUPPOSITION⟧ a small piece of medicated substance, usually conical, ovoid, or cylindrical, introduced into a body passage, as the rectum or vagina, where body heat causes it to melt

sup·press (sə pres′) *vt.* ⟦ME *suppressen* < L *suppressus,* pp. of *supprimere,* to press under, suppress < *sub-,* SUB- + *premere,* to PRESS¹⟧ **1** *a)* to put down by force; subdue; quell; crush *b)* to abolish by authority **2** to keep from appearing or being known, published, etc. [to *suppress* a news story, a book, etc.] **3** to keep back; restrain; check [to *suppress* a laugh, a cough, etc.] **4** to check or stop (a natural flow, secretion, or excretion) **5** *Electronics* to eliminate or weaken (an unwanted oscillation, echo, etc.) in a circuit **6** *Psychiatry* to consciously dismiss from the mind (unacceptable ideas, impulses, etc.): cf. REPRESS —**sup·press′i·ble** *adj.* —**sup·pres′sive** *adj.* —**sup·pres′sive·ly** *adv.* —**sup·pres′sor** *n.*

sup·pres·sant (-ənt) *n.* something, esp. a drug, that tends to suppress an action, condition, etc. [a cough *suppressant*]

sup·pres·sion (sə presh′ən) *n.* ⟦L *suppressio*⟧ **1** a suppressing or being suppressed **2** *Psychiatry a)* the mechanism by which unacceptable ideas, impulses, etc. are suppressed *b)* something suppressed in this way

sup·pu·rate (sup′yoo rāt′) *vi.* **-rat′ed, -rat′ing** ⟦< L *suppuratus,* pp. of *suppurare,* to form pus underneath < *sup-,* SUB- + *pus* (gen. *puris*), PUS⟧ to form or discharge pus; fester —**sup′pu·ra′tion** *n.* —**sup′pu·ra′tive** *adj.*

su·pra (soo′prə) *adv.* ⟦L⟧ above (in the book, etc.)

su·pra- (soo′prə) ⟦< L *supra,* above, over, akin to *super:* see SUPER-⟧ *prefix* above, over, beyond, or before [*suprarenal*]

su·pra·lap·sar·i·an (soo′prə lap ser′ē ən) *n.* ⟦< prec. + L *lapsus,* a fall (see LAPSE) + -ARIAN⟧ any of a group of Calvinists who held that God's plan of salvation for some people preceded the fall of humanity from grace, which had been predestined: opposed to INFRALAPSARIAN —*adj.* of this doctrine —**su′pra·lap·sar′i·an·ism′** *n.*

su·pra·lim·i·nal (-lim′i nəl) *adj.* ⟦SUPRA- + LIMINAL⟧ above the threshold of consciousness; at a conscious level

su·pra·mo·lec·u·lar (-mə lek′yə lər) *adj.* composed of more than one molecule

su·pra·na·tion·al (-nash′ə nəl) *adj.* of, for, involving, or over all nations or a number of nations [*supranational* authority]

su·pra·or·bit·al (-ôr′bit′l) *adj.* *Anat.* situated above the orbit of the eye

su·pra·re·nal (-rē′nəl) *adj.* ⟦ModL *suprarenalis:* see SUPRA- & RENAL⟧ situated on or above the kidney; specif., designating or of an adrenal gland —*n.* an adrenal gland

su·pra·seg·men·tal phonemes (-seg ment′'l) phonemes or features of speech, as pitch, stress, and juncture, that may extend over and modify series of SEGMENTAL PHONEMES

su·prem·a·cist (sə prem′ə sist, soo-) *n.* a person who believes in or promotes the supremacy of a particular group

su·prem·a·cy (-prem′ə sē) *n., pl.* **-cies** ⟦< fol. + -ACY⟧ **1** the quality or state of being supreme **2** supreme power or authority

su·preme (-prēm′) *adj.* ⟦L *supremus,* superl. of *superus,* that is above < *super:* see SUPER-⟧ **1** highest in rank, power, authority, etc.; dominant **2** highest in quality, achievement, performance, etc.; most excellent **3** highest in degree; utmost [a *supreme* fool] **4** final; ultimate —**su·preme′ly** *adv.* —**su·preme′ness** *n.*

Supreme Being God

Supreme Court ☆**1** the highest U.S. federal court, consisting of nine judges: its decisions are final and take precedence over those of all other judicial bodies in the country ☆**2** the highest court in most states

supreme sacrifice the sacrifice of one's life

Supreme Soviet **1** the legislative body of the Soviet Union: it consisted of two equal chambers, the Soviet of the Union (whose members were elected on the basis of population) and the Soviet of Nationalities (whose members were elected by the various nationality groups) **2** *a)* a part of the legislative body of Russia *b)* the legislative body of Uzbekistan

su·prem·o (soo prēm′ō, syoo-, sə-) *n., pl.* **-os** [Informal, Chiefly Brit.] the person having the greatest power or authority

Supt *abbrev.* Superintendent

sur-¹ (sur) ⟦ME < OFr *sur-, sour-* < L *super, supra,* over: see SUPER-⟧ *prefix* over, upon, above, beyond [*surcoat, surface*]

sur-² (sur) *prefix* SUB-: used before *r* [*surrogate*]

su·ra (soo′rə, soor′ə) *n.* ⟦Ar *sūra,* lit., enclosure⟧ any of the main divisions, or chapters, of the Koran

Su·ra·ba·ya or **Su·ra·ba·ja** (soor′ə bī′ə) seaport in NE Java, Indonesia, opposite Madura

su·rah (soor′ə) *n.* ⟦after SURAT: orig. used of coarse cotton goods made there⟧ a soft, twilled fabric of silk or rayon

Su·ra·kar·ta (soor′ə kär′tə) city in central Java, Indonesia

su·ral (soo′rəl, soor′əl) *adj.* ⟦ModL *suralis* < L *sura,* calf of the leg⟧ *Anat.* of the calf of the leg

Su·rat (soo rat′, soor′ət) seaport in Gujarat state, W India, on the Arabian Sea

sur·base (sur′bās′) *n.* a molding along the top of a base, as of a pedestal, baseboard, etc.

sur·based (-bāst′) *adj.* **1** ⟦< prec. + -ED⟧ having a surbase **2** ⟦< Fr *surbaissé* < *sur-* (see SUR-¹) + *baissé,* pp. of *baisser,* to lower < VL **bassiare* < *bassus:* see BASE²⟧ designating an arch whose rise is less than half its span

sur·cease (sur sēs′; *for n., usually* sur′sēs′) *vt., vi.* **-ceased′, -ceas′ing** ⟦ME *sursessen* < OFr *sursis,* pp. of *surseoir,* to pause, delay < L *supersedere,* to refrain from: see SUPERSEDE⟧ [Archaic] to stop; end —*n.* an end, or cessation

sur·charge (sur′chärj′) *vt.* **-charged′, -charg′ing** ⟦ME *surchargen* < OFr *surcharger:* see SUR-¹ & CHARGE⟧ **1** to overcharge **2** to overload; overburden **3** to fill to excess or beyond normal capacity **4** to mark (a postage stamp) with a surcharge **5** *Law* to show an omission, as of a credit, in (an account) —*n.* **1** *a)* an additional amount added to the usual charge *b)* an overcharge **2** an extra or excessive load, burden, etc. **3** a new valuation overprinted on a postage stamp, etc., to change its denomination **4** *Law* the act of surcharging

sur·cin·gle (sur′siŋ′gəl) *n.* ⟦ME *surcengle* < MFr < OFr *sur-,* SUR-¹ + L *cingulum,* a belt: see CINGULUM⟧ **1** a strap passed around a horse's body to bind on a saddle, blanket, pack, etc. **2** [Historical] the belt of a cassock

sur·coat (-kōt′) *n.* ⟦ME *surcote* < MFr: see SUR-¹ & COAT⟧ an outer coat or gown; esp. in the Middle Ages, a loose, short cloak worn over armor

sur·cu·lose (sur′kyoo lōs′) *adj.* ⟦ModL *surculosus* < L, woody < *surculus,* twig, graft, sucker, dim. of *surus,* twig, branch < IE base **swer-,* a stake > OE *swier,* a post⟧ *Bot.* having suckers

surd (surd) *adj.* ⟦L *surdus,* deaf, dull, mute: used to transl. Gr *alogos,* irrational, lit., without reason⟧ **1** *Math.* IRRATIONAL **2** *Phonet.* VOICELESS (*adj.* 6) —*n.* **1** *Math.* an irrational number or quantity; specif., a root which can be expressed only approximately [$\sqrt{5}$ is a *surd*] **2** *Phonet.* a voiceless sound

sure (shoor) *adj.* **sur′er, sur′est** ⟦OFr *seur* < L *securus:* see SECURE⟧ **1** [Obs.] secure or safe **2** that will not fail; always effective [a *sure* method] **3** that can be relied upon; trustworthy [a *sure* friend] **4** that cannot be doubted, questioned, or disputed; absolutely true; certain **5** having or showing no doubt; positive; confident [to be *sure* of one's facts] **6** that can be counted on to be or happen [a *sure* defeat] **7** bound or destined to do, experience, or be something specified [*sure* to be elected] **8** never missing; unerring [a *sure* aim] —*adv.* **sur′er, sur′est** [Informal] **1** surely; inevitably **2** certainly; indeed: an intensive, often used as an affirmative answer to questions —*interj.* [Informal] of course; I understand; OK —**for sure** certain(ly); without doubt —**make sure** to be or cause to be certain —**sure enough** [Informal] certainly; without doubt —**to be sure** surely; certainly —**sure′ness** *n.*

SYN.—**sure**, the simple word, suggests merely an absence of doubt or hesitancy [I'm *sure* you don't mean it]; **certain** usually suggests conviction based on specific grounds or evidence [this letter makes me *certain* of his innocence]; **confident** stresses the firmness of one's certainty or sureness, esp. in some expectation [she's *confident* she'll win]; **positive** suggests unshakable confidence, esp. in the correctness of one's opinions or conclusions, sometimes to the point of dogmatism [he's too *positive* in his beliefs] —ANT. **doubtful**

☆**sure-e·nough** (shoor′i nuf′) *adj.* [Informal] real; actual

sure·fire or **sure-fire** (shoor′fīr′) *adj.* [Informal] sure to be successful or as expected; that will not fail

sure-foot·ed (-foot′id) *adj.* **1** not likely to stumble, slip, or fall **2** not likely to err; skillful, competent, etc. Also written **sure′foot′ed** —**sure′-foot′ed·ly** *adv.* —**sure′-foot′ed·ness** *n.*

sure·ly (-lē) *adv.* **1** with assurance or confidence; in a sure, unhesitating manner **2** without a doubt; assuredly; certainly: often used as an intensive emphasizing a supposition [*surely* you don't believe that!] **3** without risk of failing: chiefly in **slowly but surely**

☆**sure thing** [Informal] **1** something considered certain to win, succeed, etc. **2** all right; OK: used interjectionally

sur·e·ty (shoor′ə tē, shoor′tē) ***n., pl.*** **-ties** ⟦ME *seurte* < OFr < L *securitas* < *securus,* sure, SECURE⟧ 1 the state of being sure; sureness; assurance 2 something sure; certainty 3 something that makes sure or gives assurance, as against loss, damage, or default; security; guarantee 4 *a)* a person who takes responsibility for another *b)* *Law* one who accepts liability for another's debts, defaults of obligations, etc. —**sur′e·ty·ship′** ***n.***

surf (surf) ***n.*** ⟦earlier *suffe,* prob. var. of SOUGH⟧ 1 the waves or swell of the sea breaking on the shore or a reef 2 the foam or spray caused by this —***vi.*** 1 to engage in the sport of surfing 2 [Informal] to browse or sample a succession of TV channels, Web pages, etc. —***vt.*** [Informal] to browse or sample a succession of (TV channels, Web pages, etc.) on (a TV, the internet, etc.) —**surf′er** ***n.***

sur·face (sur′fis) ***n.*** ⟦Fr < *sur-* (see SUR-[1]) + *face,* FACE, based on L *superficies*⟧ 1 *a)* the outer face, or exterior, of an object *b)* any of the faces of a solid *c)* the area or extent of such a face 2 superficial features, as of a personality; outward appearance 3 AIRFOIL 4 *Geom.* an extent or magnitude having length and breadth, but no thickness —***adj.*** 1 of, on, or at the surface 2 intended to function or be carried on land or sea, rather than in the air or under water [*surface* forces, *surface* mail] 3 merely apparent; external; superficial —***vt.*** **-faced, -fac·ing** 1 to treat the surface of, esp. so as to make smooth or level 2 to give a surface to, as in paving 3 to bring to the surface; esp., to bring (a submarine) to the surface of the water —***vi.*** 1 to work at or near the surface, as in mining 2 to rise to the surface of the water 3 to appear or become known, esp. after having been concealed; come to light —**sur′fac·er** ***n.***

sur·face-ac·tive (-ak′tiv) ***adj.*** *Chem.* designating or of a substance, as a detergent or wetting agent, that lowers the surface tension of the solvent in which it is dissolved or the tension at the interface between two immiscible liquids

surface noise noise produced by the friction of a phonograph stylus moving in the grooves of a record

☆**surface structure** in transformational grammar, the formal structure of a sentence as it actually occurs in speech and as distinguished from the abstract, underlying deep structure

surface tension a property of liquids in which the exposed surface tends to contract to the smallest possible area because of unequal molecular cohesive forces near the surface: measured by the force per unit of length

☆**sur·face-to-air** (-to͞o er′) ***adj.*** designating a missile launched from the surface of the earth and directed at a target in the air

☆**sur·face-to-sur·face** (-to͞o sur′fis) ***adj.*** designating a missile launched from the surface of the earth and directed at a target elsewhere on the surface

sur·fac·tant (sur fak′tənt) ***n.*** ⟦*surf*(*ace-*)*act*(*ive agent*) + -ANT⟧ any substance that is SURFACE-ACTIVE

☆**surf and turf** ⟦so called in allusion to ocean & grassland, sources of the two kinds of food included⟧ [Informal] a dinner entree that includes both lobster or other seafood and beefsteak

☆**surf·bird** (surf′burd′) ***n.*** a shorebird (*Aphriza virgata*) of the same family as the sandpiper, found on the Pacific coast of the Americas during the winter: it has a short, square tail, white at the base and black at the tip

surf·board (-bôrd′) ***n.*** a long, narrow board used in the sport of surfing —***vi.*** to engage in this sport —**surf′board′er** ***n.*** —**surf′board′ing** ***n.***

surf·boat (-bōt′) ***n.*** a light, sturdy boat used in heavy surf

☆**surf-cast** (-kast′, -käst′) ***vi.*** **-cast′, -cast′ing** to fish by casting into the surf from or near the shore —**surf′-cast′er** ***n.***

☆**surf clam** any of various large clams (genera *Mactra* and *Spisula*) living in habitats influenced by the surf

sur·feit (sur′fit) ***n.*** ⟦ME *surfet* < OFr *sorfait* < *sorfaire,* to overdo < LL **superficere* < L *super* (see SUPER-) + *facere,* to make, DO[1]⟧ 1 too great an amount or supply; excess (*of*) [*a surfeit* of compliments] 2 overindulgence, esp. in food or drink 3 discomfort, disgust, nausea, etc. resulting from any kind of excess; satiety —***vt.*** ⟦ME *sorfeten*⟧ to feed or supply to satiety or excess —***vi.*** [Now Rare] to indulge or be supplied to satiety or excess; overindulge —***SYN.*** SATIATE —**sur′feit·er** ***n.***

☆**surf fish** any of various fishes living in shallow water along the Pacific coast of North America, as the surfperches

sur·fi·cial (sər fish′əl) ***adj.*** ⟦(SURF)ACE + *-icial,* as in SUPERFICIAL⟧ *Geol.* of or having to do with the surface of the earth, surface deposits, etc.

surf·ing (sur′fiŋ) ***n.*** the sport of riding in toward shore on the crest of a wave, esp. while balancing standing up on a surfboard

☆**surf·perch** (surf′purch′) ***n., pl.*** **-perch′** or **-perch′es** any of a family (Embiotocidae) of percoid sea fishes that bear living young and live in shallow water along the Pacific coast of North America

surf scoter an American sea duck (*Melanitta perspicillata*) living in northern waters: the males are black with white-marked faces and necks, the females are grayish-brown

surf·y (sur′fē) ***adj.*** **surf′i·er, surf′i·est** 1 of, like, or forming surf 2 having surf, esp. heavy surf

surg *abbrev.* 1 surgeon 2 surgery 3 surgical

surge (surj) ***n.*** ⟦LME *sourge,* fountain, stream, prob. < OFr *sourgeon* < stem of *sourdre,* to rise < L *surgere,* to rise, spring up < **subsregere* < *subs-,* var. of *sub-* (see SUB-) + *regere,* to direct (see RIGHT)⟧ 1 *a)* a large mass of or as of moving water; wave; swell; billow *b)* such waves or billows collectively or in a series 2 a movement of or like that of a mass of water; violent rolling, sweeping, or swelling motion [the *surge* of the sea] 3 a sudden, sharp increase of electric current or voltage in a circuit 4 any sudden, strong increase, as of energy, enthusiasm, etc. 5 *Naut.* *a)* the concave part of a capstan or windlass, upon which the rope surges, or slips *b)* such a surging, or slipping —***vi.*** **surged, surg′ing** ⟦< OFr *sourg-,* stem of *sourdre:* see the ***n.***⟧ 1 to have a heavy, violent swelling motion; move in or as in a surge or surges 2 to rise and fall or be tossed about on waves, as a ship 3 to increase suddenly or abnormally: said of electric current or voltage 4 to slip: said esp. of a rope or cable on a capstan or windlass —***vt.*** to cause (a rope or cable) to slacken or slip

sur·geon (sur′jən) ***n.*** ⟦ME *surgien* < OFr *cirurgien* < *cirurgie,* SURGERY⟧ a doctor who specializes in surgery, as distinguished from a physician

☆**sur·geon·fish** (-fish′) ***n., pl.*** **-fish′** or **-fish′es** (see FISH) any of a family (Acanthuridae) of edible, usually brightly colored, tropical percoid sea fishes with one or more movable, lancelike spines on either side of the base of the tail

☆**Surgeon General** *pl.* **Surgeons General** or **Surgeon Generals** 1 the chief general officer or admiral in charge of the medical department of the U.S. Army, Air Force, or Navy 2 the chief medical officer in the U.S. Public Health Service or in some state health services Abbrev. **Surg Gen**

surgeon's knot any of several knots used as by surgeons in tying ligatures

surge protector a portable device containing one or more electrical outlets that protects equipment plugged into it from a surge in current

sur·ger·y (sur′jər ē) ***n., pl.*** **-ger·ies** ⟦ME < OFr *cirurgie,* contr. of *cirurgerie* < L *chirurgia* < Gr *cheirourgia,* a working with the hands, handicraft, skill < *cheir* (gen. *cheiros*), the hand + *ergein,* to WORK⟧ 1 *a)* the treatment of disease, injury, or deformity by manual or instrumental operations, as the removal of diseased parts or tissue by cutting *b)* an operation of this kind *c)* the branch of medicine dealing with this 2 the operating room of a surgeon or hospital 3 [Brit.] a doctor's office

sur·gi·cal (-ji kəl) ***adj.*** 1 of surgeons or surgery 2 used in or connected with surgery 3 resulting from or after surgery 4 of or like surgery or a surgical procedure in being regarded as very accurate, precisely targeted, etc. [a *surgical* air strike] —**sur′gi·cal·ly** ***adv.***

sur·gi·cen·ter (sur′jə sent′ər) ***n.*** ⟦< *Surgicenter,* a service mark⟧ a medical facility that offers various types of minor surgery for outpatients

su·ri·cate (soor′i kāt′) ***n.*** ⟦< Fr *suricate* or Ger *surikate* < native name in S Africa⟧ a small, four-toed, burrowing carnivore (*Suricata suricatta*) of S Africa, of the same family (Viverridae) as the civet and mongoose

su·ri·mi (so͞o rē′mē) ***n.*** ⟦Jpn⟧ a fish paste prepared from pollock or other inexpensive fish: used as the basis for imitation crab or lobster

Su·ri·name (soor′i näm′, -nam′; soor′i näm′, -nam′) country in NE South America: a former territory of the Netherlands, it became an independent republic in 1975: 63,039 sq mi (163,270 sq km); cap. Paramaribo: formerly **Su′ri·nam′**

sur·ly (sur′lē) ***adj.*** **-li·er, -li·est** ⟦earlier *sirly,* masterful, imperious < *sir,* SIR⟧ 1 bad-tempered; sullenly rude; hostile and uncivil 2 gloomy and threatening: said of weather 3 [Obs.] haughty; arrogant —**sur′li·ly** ***adv.*** —**sur′li·ness** ***n.***

sur·mise (sər mīz′; *for n., also* sur′mīz′) ***n.*** ⟦ME *surmyse* < OFr *surmise,* accusation, fem. of *surmis,* pp. of *surmettre,* lit., to put upon, hence to accuse < *sur-* (see SUR-[1]) + *mettre,* to put < L *mittere,* to send (see MISSION)⟧ 1 an idea or opinion formed from evidence that is neither positive nor conclusive; conjecture; guess 2 the act or process of surmising; conjecture in general — ***vt., vi.*** **-mised′, -mis′ing** to imagine or infer (something) without conclusive evidence; conjecture; guess —***SYN.*** GUESS

sur·mount (sər mount′) ***vt.*** ⟦ME *surmounten* < OFr *surmonter:* see SUR-[1] & MOUNT[2]⟧ 1 [Obs.] to surpass or exceed; go beyond 2 to get the better of; conquer; overcome 3 to be or lie at the top of; be or rise above 4 to climb up and across (a height, obstacle, etc.) 5 to place something above or on top of —**sur·mount′a·ble** ***adj.***

sur·mul·let (sər mul′it) ***n., pl.*** **-lets** or **-let** ⟦Fr *surmulet* < OFr *sormulet* < *sor,* red (see SORREL[2]) + *mulet,* MULLET[1]⟧ GOATFISH

sur·name (sur′nām′) ***n.*** ⟦ME < *sur-* (see SUR-[1]) + *name,* infl. by earlier *surnoun* < OFr *surnom* < *sur-* + *nom* < L *nomen,* NAME⟧ 1 the family name, or last name, as distinguished from a given name 2 a name or epithet added to a person's given name (Ex.: Ivan *the Terrible*) —***vt.*** **-named′, -nam′ing** to give a surname to

sur·pass (sər pas′, -päs′) ***vt.*** ⟦MFr *surpasser* < *sur-* (see SUR-[1]) + *passer,* to PASS[2]⟧ 1 to excel or be superior to 2 to exceed in quantity, degree, amount, etc. 3 to go beyond the limit, capacity, range, etc. of [riches *surpassing* belief] —***SYN.*** EXCEL

sur·pass·ing (-iŋ) ***adj.*** that surpasses the average or usual; exceeding or excelling; unusually excellent —***adv.*** [Archaic] exceedingly —**sur·pass′ing·ly** ***adv.***

sur·plice (sur′plis) ***n.*** ⟦ME *surplis* < Anglo-Fr *surpliz* < OFr < ML *superpelliceum* < L *super-,* above (see SUPER-) + *pelliceum,* fur robe, neut. of L *pelliceus,* made of skins < *pellis,* skin (see FELL[4])⟧ a loose, white, wide-sleeved outer ecclesiastical vestment for some services, ranging from hip length to knee length —**sur′pliced** ***adj.***

surplice

sur·plus (sur′plus′, -pləs) ***n.*** ⟦ME < OFr < *sur-,* above (see SUR-[1]) + L *plus,* more (see PLUS)⟧ 1 a quantity or amount over and above what is needed or used; something left over; excess 2 *a)* the excess of the assets of a business over its liabilities for a given period *b)* the excess of the total accumulated assets of a business over its liabilities and capital stock outstanding —*adj.* 1 forming a surplus; excess; extra ☆2 designating or of commodities (specif., certain excess farm products) bought, stored, distributed, etc. by the government under the Federal price-support program: cf. PRICE SUPPORT

sur·plus·age (-ij) *n.* ⟦ME: see prec. & -AGE⟧ 1 surplus; excess 2 *a)* irrelevant or superfluous words or matter *b)* *Law* such matter in the pleading of a case

surplus value in Marxist economics, the amount by which the value of the worker's product exceeds the wage the worker is paid, viewed as the source of capitalist profit

sur·print (sur′print′) *vt., n.* OVERPRINT

sur·pris·al (sər prī′zəl) *n.* [Now Rare] *var. of* SURPRISE

sur·prise (sər prīz′, sə prīz′) *vt.* **-prised′, -pris′ing** ⟦ME *surprysen* < OFr *surpris,* pp. of *sorprendre,* to surprise, take napping < *sur-* (see SUR-[1]) + *prendre,* to take (see PRIZE[2])⟧ 1 to come upon suddenly or unexpectedly; take unawares 2 to attack or capture suddenly and without warning 3 *a)* to cause to feel wonder or astonishment by being unexpected *b)* to present (someone) unexpectedly with a gift, etc. 4 *a)* to cause by some unexpected action to do or say something unintended [to *surprise* someone into an admission] *b)* to bring out or elicit by such means [to *surprise* an admission from someone] —*n.* 1 [Now Rare] the act of surprising or taking unawares 2 an unexpected seizure or attack 3 the state of being surprised; a feeling aroused by something unusual or unexpected; wonder or astonishment 4 something that surprises because unexpected, unusual, etc. —**take by surprise** 1 to come upon suddenly or without warning 2 to amaze; astound —**sur·pris′ed·ly** *adv.* —**sur·pris′er** *n.*

SYN.—**surprise**, in this connection, implies an affecting with wonder because of being unexpected, unusual, etc. [I'm *surprised* at your concern]; **astonish** implies a surprising with something that seems unbelievable [to *astonish* with sleight of hand]; **amaze** suggests an astonishing that causes bewilderment or confusion [*amazed* at the sudden turn of events]; **astound** suggests a shocking astonishment that leaves one helpless to act or think [I was *astounded* by the proposal]; **flabbergast** is an informal term suggesting an astounding to the point of speechlessness

Sur·prise (sər prīz′, sə-) city in SC Ariz.: suburb of Phoenix

sur·pris·ing (-prī′ziŋ) *adj.* causing surprise; amazing —**sur·pris′ing·ly** *adv.*

sur·re·al (sə rē′əl) *adj.* ⟦back-form. < fol.⟧ 1 of, related to, or characteristic of surrealism 2 of or like a dream; fantastic, hallucinatory, bizarre, etc.

sur·re·al·ism (-iz′əm) *n.* ⟦Fr *surréalisme:* see SUR-[1] & REALISM⟧ a modern movement in art and literature, in which an attempt is made to portray or interpret the workings of the unconscious mind as manifested in dreams: it is characterized by an irrational, fantastic arrangement of material —**sur·re′al·is′tic** *adj.* —**sur·re′al·ist** *adj., n.* —**sur·re′al·is′ti·cal·ly** *adv.*

sur·re·but·ter (sur′ri but′ər) *n.* *Law* a plaintiff's reply to a defendant's rebutter

sur·re·join·der (-ri join′dər) *n.* *Law* a plaintiff's reply to a defendant's rejoinder

sur·ren·der (sə ren′dər) *vt.* ⟦ME *surrendren* < MFr *surrendre* < *sur-,* up (see SUR-[1]) + *rendre,* to RENDER⟧ 1 to give up possession of or power over; yield to another on demand or compulsion 2 to give up claim to; give over or yield, esp. voluntarily, as in favor of another 3 to give up or abandon [*surrendering* all hope] 4 to yield or resign (oneself) to an emotion, influence, etc. —*vi.* 1 to give oneself up to another's power or control, esp. as a prisoner 2 to give in (*to*) [to *surrender* to temptation] —*n.* ⟦LME < MFr *surrendre,* inf. used as n.⟧ 1 the act of surrendering, yielding, or giving up, over, or in 2 *Insurance* the voluntary abandonment of a policy by an insured person in return for a cash payment (**surrender value**), thus freeing the company of liability

sur·rep·ti·tious (sur′əp tish′əs) *adj.* ⟦ME *surrepticious* < L *surrepticius* < *surreptus,* pp. of *surripere,* to take away secretly < *sub-* (see SUB-) + *rapere,* to seize (see RAPE[1])⟧ 1 done, gotten, made, etc. in a secret, stealthy way; clandestine 2 acting in a secret, stealthy way —SYN. SECRET —**sur′rep·ti′tious·ly** *adv.* —**sur′rep·ti′tious·ness** *n.*

sur·rey (sur′ē) *n., pl.* **-reys** ⟦< *Surrey (cart),* a light pleasure cart first built in SURREY[2], England⟧ ☆a light, four-wheeled pleasure carriage of the late 19th and early 20th cent., usually drawn by two horses and typically having two seats and a flat top

surrey

Sur·rey[1] (sur′ē), Earl of (*Henry Howard*) 1517?-47; Eng. poet & courtier: executed for treason

Sur·rey[2] (sur′ē) 1 county in SE England: 647 sq mi (1,676 sq km) 2 ⟦after the county in England⟧ city in SW British Columbia, Canada, near Vancouver

sur·ro·ga·cy (sur′ə gə sē) *n., pl.* **-cies** 1 the fact or condition of being a surrogate 2 the act or practice of utilizing a surrogate mother to conceive and bear a child

sur·ro·gate (sur′ə git, -gāt′; *for v.,* -gāt′) *n.* ⟦L *surrogatus,* pp. of *surrogare,* to elect in place of another, substitute < *sub-* (see SUB-) + *rogare,* to ask: see ROGATION⟧ 1 someone appointed to act in place of another ☆2 in some states, probate court, or a judge of this court 3 *Psychiatry* a substitute figure, esp. a person of some authority, who replaces a father or mother in one's feelings 4 a woman who, by prior agreement, becomes pregnant and bears a child for another woman or a couple, who will then raise it —*adj.* of or acting as a surrogate —*vt.* **-gat′ed, -gat′ing** to put in another's place as a substitute or deputy

sur·round (sə round′) *vt.* ⟦ME *surrounden,* altered (as if < *sur-,* SUR-[1] + *round*) < *surunden,* to overflow < OFr *suronder* < LL *superundare* < L *super-* (see SUPER-) + *undare,* to move in waves, rise < *unda,* a wave (see WATER)⟧ 1 to cause to be enclosed or encircled [to *surround* a field with barbed wire] 2 *a)* to form an enclosure around; encompass [a wall *surrounds* the city] *b)* to be present on all or nearly all sides of; encircle [lush fields *surround* the cottage] 3 to enclose with or as with troops, so as to cut off communication or retreat —*n.* [Chiefly Brit.] something serving as a border, etc.

sur·round·ing (-roun′diŋ) *n.* 1 that which surrounds 2 [*pl.*] the things, conditions, influences, etc. that surround a given place or person; environment —*adj.* that surrounds

sur·sum cor·da (sur′səm kôr′də) ⟦L, lift up (your) hearts: opening words of the Preface of the Mass⟧ an incitement to fervor, joy, etc.

sur·tax (sur′taks′) *n.* ⟦SUR-[1] + TAX, based on Fr *surtaxe*⟧ an extra tax on something already taxed; esp. a graduated tax on the amount by which an income exceeds a given figure —*vt.* to levy a surtax on

sur·ti·tle (sur′tīt′'l) *n.* ⟦SUR-[1] + TITLE⟧ [Brit.] SUPERTITLE

sur·tout (sər to͞o′, -to͝ot′; *Fr* sür to͞o′) *n.* ⟦Fr, lit., overall < *sur-* (see SUR-[1]) + *tout* < L *totus,* all: see TOTAL⟧ a man's long, closefitting overcoat of the late 19th cent.

surv *abbrev.* 1 survey 2 surveying 3 surveyor

sur·veil (sər vāl′) *vt.* **-veilled′, -veil′ling** ⟦back-form. < fol.⟧ to engage in surveillance of; keep watch over

sur·veil·lance (sər vā′ləns; *occas.,* -vāl′yəns) *n.* ⟦Fr < *surveiller,* to watch over < *sur-* (see SUR-[1]) + *veiller* < L *vigilare,* to watch, WAKE[1]⟧ 1 *a)* close watch kept over someone, esp. a suspect *b)* constant observation of a place or process 2 supervision or inspection

sur·veil·lant (-vā′lənt; *occas.,* -vāl′yənt) *n.* a person who watches, observes, or supervises

sur·vey (sur′vā′; *for v., also* sər vā′) *vt.* ⟦ME *surveien* < Anglo-Fr *surveier* < OFr *surveoir* < *sur-* (see SUR-[1]) + *veoir* < L *videre,* to see: see VISION⟧ 1 to examine for some specific purpose; inspect or consider carefully; review in detail 2 to look at or consider, esp. in a general or comprehensive way; view 3 to determine the location, form, or boundaries of (a tract of land) by measuring the lines and angles in accordance with the principles of geometry and trigonometry 4 to make a survey of —*vi.* to survey land —*n., pl.* **-veys′** 1 a detailed study or inspection, as by gathering information through observations, questionnaires, etc. and analyzing it 2 a general view; comprehensive study or examination [a *survey* of Italian art] 3 *a)* the process of surveying a tract of land *b)* a tract surveyed *c)* a plan or written description of this

sur·vey·ing (sər vā′iŋ) *n.* 1 the act of one who surveys 2 the science or work of making land surveys

sur·vey·or (-ər) *n.* ⟦ME *surveior* < OFr *surveour*⟧ a person who surveys, esp. one whose work is surveying land

surveyor's level an instrument consisting of a revolving telescope mounted on a tripod and fitted with cross hairs and a spirit level, used by surveyors in finding points of identical elevation

surveyor's measure a system of measurement used in surveying, based on the chain (**surveyor's chain**) as a unit: see CHAIN (*n.* 5*a*)

sur·viv·a·ble (sər vīv′ə bəl) *adj.* capable of being survived [a *survivable* auto accident] —**sur·viv′a·bil′i·ty** *n.*

sur·viv·al (sər vī′vəl) *n.* 1 the act, state, or fact of surviving 2 someone or something that survives, esp. an ancient belief, custom, usage, etc.

sur·viv·al·ist (-ist) *n.* 1 someone strongly determined to survive 2 a person who takes measures, as storing food and weapons, living in a wilderness, etc., to ensure survival after an expected economic collapse, nuclear war, etc.

survival of the fittest ⟦coined by Herbert SPENCER[2] in his book *Principles of Biology* (1864)⟧ 1 *nontechnical term for* NATURAL SELECTION 2 the concept that, in a society, industry, corporation, etc., those individuals or groups who are superior or best suited will succeed in the competitive struggle for success or dominance

sur·vive (sər vīv′) *vt.* **-vived′, -viv′ing** ⟦ME *surviven* < OFr *survivre* < L *supervivere* < *super-,* above (see SUPER-) + *vivere,* to live (see BIO-)⟧ 1 to live or exist longer than or beyond the life or existence of; outlive 2 to continue to live after or in spite of [to *survive* a wreck] —*vi.* to continue living or existing, as after an event or after another's death

sur·vi·vor (sər vī′vər) *n.* 1 a person or thing that survives; specif., a person who has survived an ordeal or great misfortune 2 a person regarded as resilient or courageous enough to be able to overcome hardship, misfortune, etc.

sur·vi·vor·ship (sər vī′vər ship′) *n.* 1 the state of being a survivor 2 *Law* the right of a surviving owner or owners of property held as under joint tenancy to undivided ownership upon the death of either or any of them

Sur·ya (so͞or′yə) *n.* ⟦Sans, sun⟧ Hindu sun god

sus- (sus, səs) *prefix* SUB-: used before *c, p,* and *t* [*susceptible, suspend, sustain*]

Su·sa (sōō′sä) capital of ancient Elam, now a ruined city in W Iran

Su·san (sōō′zən) ***n.*** ⟦Fr *Susanne* < LL(Ec) *Susanna* < Gr(Ec) *Sousanna* < Heb *shoshana,* lily⟧ a feminine name: dim. *Sue, Susie, Suzy;* var. *Susanna, Susannah, Suzanne;* equiv. Fr. *Susanne, Suzanne*

Su·san·nah or **Su·san·na** (sōō zan′ə) ***n.*** **1** a feminine name: see SUSAN **2** *Bible a)* a woman falsely accused of adultery by two elders whose advances she had spurned *b)* the book of the O.T. Apocrypha that tells her story (abbrev. *Sus*)

sus·cep·tance (sə sep′təns) ***n.*** ⟦< fol. + -ANCE⟧ *Elec.* a component of admittance, measured in siemens: it is the reciprocal of reactance

sus·cep·ti·bil·i·ty (sə sep′tə bil′ə tē) ***n.,*** *pl.* **-ties** ⟦ML *susceptibilitas*⟧ **1** the quality or state of being susceptible **2** [*pl.*] sensibilities; feelings **3** a susceptible temperament or disposition; capacity for receiving impressions **4** *Physics* the ratio of electric or magnetic polarization in a material to the strength of the field producing that polarization

sus·cep·ti·ble (sə sep′tə bəl) ***adj.*** ⟦ML *susceptibilis* < L *susceptus,* pp. of *suscipere,* to receive, undertake < *sus-* (see SUB-), under + *capere,* to take (see HAVE)⟧ easily affected emotionally; having a sensitive nature or feelings —**susceptible of** that gives a chance for; admitting; allowing [testimony *susceptible of* error] —**susceptible to** easily influenced by or affected with [*susceptible to* disease] —**sus·cep′ti·ble·ness** ***n.*** —**sus·cep′ti·bly** ***adv.***

sus·cep·tive (sə sep′tiv) ***adj.*** ⟦ML *susceptivus*⟧ **1** SUSCEPTIBLE **2** RECEPTIVE —**sus·cep·tiv·i·ty** (sus′ep tiv′ə tē) ***n.,*** **sus·cep′tive·ness**

su·shi (sōō′shē) ***n.*** ⟦Jpn⟧ a Japanese dish consisting of small cakes of cold cooked rice flavored with vinegar, typically garnished with strips of raw or cooked fish, cooked egg, vegetables, etc.

sus·lik (sus′lik) ***n.*** ⟦Russ, gopher, akin to OSlav *sysati,* to whistle, buzz < IE echoic base **sūs-* > Ger *sausen,* to whistle⟧ **1** a small ground squirrel (*Citellus citellus*) of NC Eurasia **2** its fur

sus·pect (sə spekt′; *for adj. usually, & for n. always,* sus′pekt′) ***vt.*** ⟦LME *suspecten* < L *suspectus,* pp. of *suspicere,* to look under, look up to, admire, also to mistrust < *sus-* (see SUB-), under + *specere,* to look (see SPY)⟧ **1** to believe (someone) to be guilty of something specified, on little or no evidence **2** to believe to be bad, wrong, harmful, questionable, etc.; distrust **3** to think it probable or likely; guess; surmise; suppose —***vi.*** to be suspicious; have suspicion —***adj.*** viewed with suspicion; suspected —***n.*** a person who is suspected, esp. one suspected of a crime, etc.

sus·pend (sə spend′) ***vt.*** ⟦ME *suspenden* < OFr *suspendre* < L *suspendere,* to hang up < *sus-,* for *sub-,* SUB- + *pendere,* to hang: see PEND⟧ **1** to bar or exclude as a penalty from an office, school, position, etc., usually for a specified time; debar **2** to cause to cease or become inoperative for a time; stop temporarily [to *suspend* train service, to *suspend* a rule] **3** *a)* to defer or hold back (judgment), as until more is known *b)* to hold in abeyance or defer action on (a sentence, etc.) **4** to hang by a support from above so as to allow free movement **5** to hold or keep (dust in the air, particles in a liquid, etc.) in suspension **6** [Now Rare] to keep in suspense, wonder, etc. **7** *Music* to continue (a note) into the following chord —***vi.*** **1** to stop temporarily **2** to withhold payment of debts or obligations, as through inability to pay —**SYN.** ADJOURN, EXCLUDE

sus·pend·ed animation (sə spen′did) **1** a temporary cessation of some vital functions, as in hibernation **2** in science fiction, a state resembling hibernation, induced artificially as to ensure survival over a long period of time

sus·pend·ers (-dərz) ***pl.n.*** **1** a pair of straps or bands passed over the shoulders to hold up trousers or a skirt **2** [Brit.] garters for holding up stockings

sus·pense (sə spens′) ***n.*** ⟦ME < MFr *suspens, suspense,* delay, deferring < ML *suspensum* < L *suspensus,* suspended, uncertain, lit., hung up, pp. of *suspendere,* to SUSPEND⟧ **1** the state of being undecided or undetermined **2** a state of usually anxious uncertainty, as in awaiting a decision **3** the growing interest and excitement felt while awaiting a climax or resolution, as of a novel, play, series of events, etc. **4** [Rare] suspension or interruption, as of a legal right —**sus·pense′ful** ***adj.***

suspense account *Bookkeeping* an account in which items are temporarily entered until their disposition can be determined

☆**sus·pens·er** (sə spen′sər) ***n.*** [Informal] a suspenseful novel, film, etc.

sus·pen·sion (sə spen′shən) ***n.*** ⟦ML *suspensio* < LL, an arching < L *suspensus:* see SUSPENSE⟧ **1** a suspending or being suspended; specif., *a)* a temporary barring from an office, school, etc. *b)* a temporary stoppage of payment, service, etc. *c)* a temporary canceling, as of rules *d)* a deferring of action on a sentence *e)* a holding back of a judgment, etc. **2** a supporting device or framework upon or from which something is suspended **3** the system of springs, shocks, etc. supporting a vehicle upon its undercarriage or axles **4** the act or means of suspending the balance or pendulum in a timepiece **5** *Chem. a)* the condition of a substance whose particles are dispersed through a fluid but not dissolved in it, esp. the condition of one having relatively large particles that will separate out on standing (cf. COLLOID) *b)* a substance in this condition **6** *Music a)* the continuing of one or more tones of one chord into a following chord while the other tones are changed, so that a temporary dissonance is created *b)* the tone or tones so continued

suspension bridge

suspension bridge a bridge suspended from chains or cables which are anchored at either end and supported by towers at regular intervals

suspension point any of a series of dots, typically three, indicating the omission of a word, phrase, sentence, etc., as from something quoted: cf. ELLIPSIS POINTS

sus·pen·sive (sə spen′siv) ***adj.*** ⟦ML *suspensivus*⟧ **1** that suspends, defers, or temporarily stops something **2** tending to suspend judgment; undecided **3** of, characterized by, expressing, or in suspense **4** [Rare] of or characterized by physical suspension —**sus·pen′sive·ly** ***adv.***

sus·pen·soid (-soid′) ***n.*** ⟦SUSPENS(ION) + (COLL)OID⟧ a system of solid, colloidal particles suspended in a liquid

sus·pen·sor (-sər) ***n.*** ⟦ML⟧ **1** SUSPENSORY **2** *Bot.* a cell or group of cells that forces the embryo of a higher plant into its food supply, the endosperm

sus·pen·so·ry (-sə rē) ***adj.*** ⟦< L *suspensus* (see SUSPENSE) + -ORY⟧ **1** suspending, supporting, or sustaining [a *suspensory* muscle or bandage] **2** suspending or delaying, esp. so as to leave something undecided —***n.,*** *pl.* **-ries** **1** a suspensory muscle or bandage **2** a mesh fabric pouch for supporting the scrotum, on a band around the hips

suspensory ligament any of various ligaments supporting bodily organs; esp., a ligament supporting the lens of the eye

sus·pi·cion (sə spish′ən) ***n.*** ⟦ME *suspecion* < Anglo-Fr *suspecioun* < OFr *sospeçon* < LL *suspectio,* orig., a looking up to, esteeming, later with sense and sp. of L *suspicio,* suspicion < L *suspectus,* pp. of *suspicere,* to look up at, admire, look secretly at, mistrust, SUSPECT⟧ **1** the act or an instance of suspecting guilt, a wrong, harmfulness, etc. with little or no supporting evidence **2** the feeling or state of mind of a person who suspects **3** a very small amount or degree; suggestion; inkling; trace —☆***vt.*** [Informal or Dial.] to suspect —**above suspicion** not to be suspected; honorable —**on suspicion** on the basis of suspicion; because suspected —**under suspicion** suspected

sus·pi·cious (-əs) ***adj.*** ⟦ME *suspecious* < OFr < L *suspiciosus*⟧ **1** arousing or likely to arouse suspicion in others **2** showing or expressing suspicion **3** *a)* feeling suspicion *b)* tending habitually to suspect, esp. to suspect evil —**sus·pi′cious·ly** ***adv.*** —**sus·pi′cious·ness** ***n.***

sus·pire (sə spīr′) ***vi.*** **-pired′, -pir′ing** ⟦ME *suspiren* < L *suspirare,* to breathe out < *sub-,* SUB- + *spirare: see* SPIRIT⟧ [Rare] to take a long, deep breath; esp., to sigh —**sus·pi·ra·tion** (sus′pi rā′shən) ***n.***

Sus·que·han·na (sus′kwi han′ə) ⟦< earlier *Sasquesahanough,* name of an Iroquoian people in an unidentified Eastern Algonquian language < name of the river: meaning of name unknown⟧ river flowing from central N.Y. through Pa. & Md. into Chesapeake Bay: 444 mi (715 km)

suss (sus) ***vt.*** ⟦shortened < SUSPECT⟧ [Slang, Chiefly Brit.] to figure out; grasp, as a result of investigation, study, or intuition: often with *out*

Sus·sex[1] (sus′iks) ***n.*** any of a breed of domestic chicken, originating in Sussex, with speckled or reddish feathers, usually raised for its meat

Sus·sex[2] (sus′iks) ⟦ME *Suth-sæxe* < OE *Suth-Seaxe,* South Saxon (land or people): see SOUTH & SAXON⟧ **1** former Anglo-Saxon kingdom in SE England: see HEPTARCHY **2** former county of SE England, on the English Channel: now divided into two counties, EAST SUSSEX & WEST SUSSEX

Sussex spaniel any of a breed of spaniel, originating in Sussex, with short legs and a coat that is golden liver in color: traditionally the tail is docked

sus·tain (sə stān′) ***vt.*** ⟦ME *susteinen* < OFr *sustenir* < L *sustinere* < *sus-* (see SUB-), under + *tenere,* to hold (see THIN)⟧ **1** to keep in existence; keep up; maintain or prolong [to *sustain* a mood] **2** to provide for the support of; specif., to provide sustenance or nourishment for **3** to support from or as from below; carry the weight or burden of **4** to strengthen the spirits, courage, etc. of; comfort; buoy up; encourage **5** to bear up against; endure; withstand **6** to undergo or suffer (an injury, loss, etc.) **7** to uphold the validity or justice of [to *sustain* a verdict] **8** to confirm; corroborate —**SYN.** SUPPORT —**sus·tain′er** ***n.*** —**sus·tain′ment** ***n.***

sus·tain·a·ble (sə stān′ə bəl) ***adj.*** **1** capable of being sustained **2** *a)* designating, of, or characterized by a practice that sustains a given condition, as economic growth, or a human population without destroying or depleting natural resources, polluting the environment, etc. [*sustainable* agriculture] *b)* governed or maintained by, or produced as a result of, such practices [*sustainable* growth] —**sus·tain′a·bil′i·ty** ***n.*** —**sus·tain′a·bly** ***adv.***

sus·te·nance (sus′tə nəns) ***n.*** ⟦ME < OFr *soustenance* < LL *sustinentia,* patience, endurance < L *sustinere:* see SUSTAIN⟧ **1** a sustaining or being sustained **2** one's means of livelihood; maintenance; support **3** that which sustains life; nourishment

sus·ten·ta·tion (-tā′shən) ***n.*** ⟦ME < MFr < L *sustentatio* < *sustentare,* freq. of *sustinere,* to SUSTAIN⟧ **1** a sustaining or being sustained; maintenance, support, or preservation **2** something that sustains or supports; sustenance —**sus·ten·ta·tive** (sus′ten tāt′iv, səs ten′tə tiv′) ***adj.***

Su·su (sōō′sōō′) ***n.*** **1** *pl.* **Su′sus′** or **Su′su′** a member of a people living chiefly in Guinea and Sierra Leone **2** the Mande language of this people

su·sur·rant (sə sur′ənt) ***adj.*** ⟦L *susurrans,* prp. of *susurrare,* to whisper: see SWARM[1]⟧ whispering; murmuring; rustling

su·sur·rate (-āt′) ***vi.*** **-rat′ed, -rat′ing** ⟦L *susurratus,* pp.: see prec.⟧ to whisper; murmur; rustle —**su·sur·ra·tion** (sus′ə rā′shən) ***n.***

su·sur·rus (-əs) ***n.*** ⟦L < *susurrare:* see SUSURRANT⟧ a whispering, murmuring, or rustling sound

Suth·er·land[1] (suth′ər lənd), Dame **Joan (Alston)** 1926-2010; Austral. operatic soprano

Suth·er·land[2] (suth′ər lənd) former county & former district of N Scotland

Sut·lej (sut′lej) river flowing from SW Tibet across the Punjab into the Indus River in Pakistan: *c.* 900 mi (1,448 km)

sut·ler (sut′lər) ***n.*** ⟦16th-c. Du *soeteler* < *soetelen,* to do dirty work, akin to Ger *sudeln,* to do in a slovenly way < IE base **seu-,* damp, juice > SUCK⟧ [Historical] a person following an army to sell food, liquor, etc. to its soldiers

su·tra (so͞o′trə) ***n.*** ⟦Sans *sūtra,* a thread, string < IE base **siw-,* to SEW⟧ **1** *Hinduism a)* a precept or maxim *b)* a collection of these **2** *Buddhism* a scriptural narrative; esp., an account of a dialogue or sermon of the Buddha Also **sut·ta** (so͝ot′ə)

sut·tee (sə tē′, sut′ē) ***n.*** ⟦Hindi *sattī* < Sans *satī,* chaste and virtuous wife < *sat,* good, pure, prp. of *as,* to be: for IE base see IS[1]⟧ **1** a Hindu widow who allowed herself to be cremated alive on the funeral pyre of her husband's body **2** the former Hindu custom of such self-immolation

Sut·ter's Mill (sut′ərz) a mill, owned by John Sutter (1803-80), northeast of Sacramento, Calif.: discovery of gold near there led to the gold rush of 1849

Sut·ton (sut′'n) borough of S Greater London, England

su·ture (so͞o′chər) ***n.*** ⟦L *sutura* < *sutus,* pp. of *suere,* to SEW⟧ **1** *a)* the act of joining together by or as by sewing *b)* the line along which such a joining is made **2** *Anat.* the joining together, or the irregular line of junction, of certain vertebrate bones, esp. of the skull **3** *Bot. a)* a seam formed when two parts unite *b)* a line of dehiscence along which a fruit, as a pod or capsule, splits **4** *Surgery a)* the act or method of joining together the two edges of a wound or incision by stitching or similar means *b)* any material, as gut, thread, wire, etc., so used *c)* a single loop or knot of such material made in suturing —***vt.* -tured, -tur·ing** to join together with or as with sutures —**su′tur·al** ***adj.***

SUV (es′yo͞o′vē′) ***n.,*** *pl.* **SUVs** SPORT UTILITY VEHICLE

Su·va (so͞o′vä) capital of Fiji: seaport on Viti Levu Island

Su·vo·rov (so͞o vô′rôf), Count **A·lek·san·dr (Vasilievich)** (ä′lyik sän′dr′) 1729-1800; Russ. field marshal

Su·wan·nee (sə wä′nē, swä′-) ⟦< Creek < Sp *San Juan,* name of a Sp mission on the river⟧ river flowing from the Okefenokee Swamp across N Fla. into the Gulf of Mexico: *c.* 250 mi (402 km)

Su·zanne (so͞o zan′) ***n.*** a feminine name: see SUSAN

su·ze·rain (so͞o′zə rin′, -rān′) ***n.*** ⟦Fr < *sus,* above (< L *su(r)sum,* upward, above, contr. < *subversum* < *sub-,* SUB- + *versum,* a turning < pp. of *vertere:* see VERSE) + ending *-erain,* as in *souverain,* SOVEREIGN⟧ **1** a feudal lord **2** a state in its relation to a semiautonomous state over which it exercises political control

su·ze·rain·ty (-tē) ***n.,*** *pl.* **-ties** ⟦Fr *suzeraineté* < MFr *suserenete*⟧ the position or power of a suzerain

Su·zhou (so͞o′jō′) city in S Jiangsu province, E China, on the Grand Canal

Sv *abbrev.* sievert(s)

s.v. *abbrev.* **1** ⟦L *sub verbo*⟧ under the word specified **2** ⟦L *sub voce*⟧ under the word specified

Sval·bard (sväl′bär) group of Norwegian islands, including Spitsbergen, in the Arctic Ocean, between Greenland & Franz Josef Land: 24,209 sq mi (62,701 sq km)

svc or **svce** *abbrev.* service

Sved·berg (unit) (sfed′bərg) ⟦after T. *Svedberg* (1884-1971), Swed chemist⟧ a unit of time, equal to 10^{-13} second, used in determining the rate of sedimentation of a macromolecule in an ultracentrifuge

svelte (svelt, sfelt) ***adj.*** ⟦Fr < It *svelto,* pp. of *svegliere,* to pull out, hence, to free < VL **exvellere,* for L *evellere,* to pluck out < *e-,* out + *vellere,* to pluck: see VELLICATE⟧ **1** slender and graceful; lithe **2** suave, polished, sophisticated, etc. *[his svelte singing style]*

Sven·ga·li (sven gä′lē, sfen-) ***n.*** ⟦after the evil hypnotist, *Svengali,* in the novel *Trilby* (1894) by George DU MAURIER⟧ a person who dominates or manipulates another, esp. with evil intentions

Sverd·lovsk (sferd lôfsk′) *name* (1924-91) *for* YEKATERINBURG

Sve·ri·ge (sve′rē ə) *Swed. name for* SWEDEN

svgs *abbrev.* savings

Sw *abbrev.* **1** Sweden **2** Swedish

SW *abbrev.* **1** southwest **2** southwestern

swab (swäb) ***n.*** ⟦contr. < fol.⟧ **1** a yarn mop, usually used wet, for cleaning decks, floors, etc. **2** *a)* a small piece of cotton, cloth, or sponge, often fixed to a small stick, used to clean a wound, the ears, etc. or to apply medicine to wounds *b)* matter collected in this way **3** a brush, wad of cloth, etc. on a long handle, for cleaning the barrel of a gun **4** [Slang] a clumsy, loutish person **5** [Slang] *a)* a sailor ☆*b)* an enlisted person in the U.S. Navy: also, and for *b* usually, **swab′bie** or **swab′by** (-ē) —***vt.* swabbed, swab′bing** to use a swab on; clean, medicate, etc. with a swab

swab·ber (-ər) ***n.*** ⟦< or akin to 16th-c. Du *zwabber* < *zwabben,* to do dirty work, splash, akin to Ger *schwappen* < IE base **swep-,* to throw, pour out > L *supare,* to throw around⟧ **1** a person who uses a swab **2** a device for swabbing

Swa·bi·a (swā′bē ə) region in SW Germany, formerly a duchy: Ger. name SCHWABEN —**Swa′bi·an** ***adj., n.***

swacked (swakt) ***adj.*** ☆[Slang] drunk; intoxicated

swad·dle (swäd′'l) ***vt.* -dled, -dling** ⟦ME *swathlen,* prob. altered (infl. by *swathen,* to SWATHE[1]) < *swethlen* < OE *swethel,* swaddling band, akin to *swathian,* to SWATHE[1]⟧ **1** to wrap (a newborn baby) in swaddling clothes, a blanket, etc., as to calm it **2** to bind in or as in bandages; swathe —***n.*** ⟦ME *swathil* < OE *swethel:* see the ***vt.***⟧ a cloth, bandage, etc. used for swaddling

swaddling clothes the long, narrow bands of cloth wrapped around a newborn baby in former times

swag (swag) ***vi.* swagged, swag′ging** ⟦< or akin to Norw *svagga,* to sway (in walking), SWAGGER⟧ **1** to sway or lurch **2** to hang down; sag —***vt.*** **1** to decorate with swags **2** to hang in a swag —***n.*** **1** a swaying or lurching **2** a valance, garland, chain, etc. hanging decoratively in a loop or curve; festoon **3** [Slang] *a)* stolen money or property; loot; plunder *b)* products that are given away free, typically for promotional purposes **4** [Austral.] *a)* a bundle containing personal belongings, as of an itinerant worker *b)* [Informal] a large number or amount *[a swag of essays to mark]*

swage (swāj) ***n.*** ⟦ME < OFr *souage*⟧ **1** a kind of tool for bending or shaping metal **2** a die or stamp for shaping or marking metal by hammering —***vt.* swaged, swag′ing** to use a swage on; shape, bend, etc. with a swage

swage block a block of metal made with grooves and perforations, used as a form in hammering out bolt heads, etc.

swag·ger (swag′ər) ***vi.*** ⟦prob. < Norw dial. *svagra,* to sway in walking, freq. of *svagga,* to sway < IE base **swek-,* to bend, turn⟧ **1** to walk with a bold, arrogant, or lordly stride; strut **2** to boast, brag, or show off in a loud, superior manner —***vt.*** [Rare] to influence, force, etc. by blustering —***n.*** (a) swaggering walk, manner, or behavior —*SYN.* BOAST[2] —**swag′ger·er** ***n.*** —**swag′ger·ing·ly** ***adv.***

swagger stick a short stick or cane as carried by some army officers, etc.: also [Brit.] **swagger cane**

swag·man (swag′mən) ***n.,*** *pl.* **-men** (-mən) ⟦with ref. to carrying a SWAG (*n.* 4*a*)⟧ [Austral.] **1** an itinerant worker **2** a tramp

Swa·hi·li (swä hē′lē) ***n.*** ⟦< Ar *sawāḥil,* pl. of *sāḥil,* coast + *-i,* belonging to⟧ **1** *pl.* **-lis** or **-li** a member of a people living on Zanzibar and the nearby mainland **2** the Northern Bantu language of this people, characterized by a vocabulary with many Arabic roots and used as a lingua franca in EC Africa and parts of the Democratic Republic of the Congo

swain (swān) ***n.*** ⟦ME *swein* < ON *sveinn,* boy, servant, akin to OE *swan,* shepherd, peasant, youth < IE **swe-,* one's own, apart⟧ [Archaic] **1** a country youth **2** a young rustic lover or gallant **3** a lover or suitor —**swain′ish** ***adj.*** —**swain′ish·ness** ***n.***

SWAK or **swak** *abbrev.* sealed with a kiss: written on a letter, as from a lover or a child

swale (swāl) ***n.*** ⟦ME, shade, prob. < ON *svalr,* cool, akin to OE *swelan,* to burn, ignite < IE base **swel-* > SWELTER⟧ **1** a hollow, depression, or low area of land ☆**2** such a place in a wet, marshy area

swal·low[1] (swä′lō) ***n.*** ⟦ME *swalwe* < OE *swealwe,* akin to Ger *schwalbe,* ON *svala,* swallow, & prob. Russ *solovej,* Czech *slavík,* nightingale⟧ **1** any of a family (Hirundinidae) of small, swift-flying, insect-eating passerine birds with long, pointed wings and a forked tail, including the barn swallow and purple martin: most species migrate, often between widely separated summer and winter homes **2** any of various birds resembling swallows, as certain swifts

barn swallow

swal·low[2] (swä′lō) ***vt.*** ⟦ME *swolwen* < OE *swelgan,* akin to Ger *schwelgen* < IE base **swel-,* to devour > SWILL⟧ **1** to pass (food, drink, etc.) from the mouth through the gullet or esophagus into the stomach, usually by a series of muscular actions in the throat **2** to take in; absorb; engulf; envelop: often with *up* **3** to take back (words said); retract; withdraw **4** to put up with; tolerate; bear humbly *[to swallow an insult]* **5** to refrain from expressing; hold back; suppress *[to swallow one's pride]* **6** to utter (words) indistinctly **7** [Informal] to accept as true without question; receive gullibly —***vi.*** to move the muscles of the throat as in swallowing something; specif., to do so under stress of emotion —***n.*** **1** the act of swallowing **2** the amount swallowed at one time **3** [Now Chiefly Brit.] the throat or gullet **4** *Naut.* the space between the wheel and the frame of a pulley block, through which a line passes —**swal′low·er** ***n.***

swallow dive [Brit.] SWAN DIVE

swal·low·tail (-tāl′) ***n.*** **1** something having a forked shape like that of a swallow's tail **2** any of a large family (Papilionidae) of brightly colored butterflies found worldwide, having the hind wings extended in taillike points **3** TAILCOAT

swal·low-tailed (-tāld′) ***adj.*** having a tail or end extended in forked points like the tail of a swallow

swallow-tailed coat TAILCOAT

swal·low·wort (-wurt′) ***n.*** **1** CELANDINE (sense 1) **2** any of several plants of the milkweed family, as **black swallowwort** (*Cynanchum nigrum*), a twining European vine with purplish-brown flowers, now wild in the E U.S.

swam (swam) ***vi., vt.*** *pt. of* SWIM[1] & SWIM[2]

swa·mi (swä′mē) ***n.,*** *pl.* **-mis** ⟦Hindi *svāmī* < Sans *svāmin,* lord⟧ **1** lord; master: a Hindu title of respect, esp. for a Hindu religious teacher **2** a learned man; pundit Also sp. **swa′my,** *pl.* **-mies**

swamp (swämp, swômp) ***n.*** ⟦< dial. var. (or LowG cognate) of ME *sompe,* akin to MLowG *swamp,* Goth & OE *swamm,* fungus, mushroom < IE base **swomb(h)os,* spongy, porous > Gr *somphos,* spongy⟧ a piece of wet, spongy land that is permanently or periodically covered with water, characterized by growths of shrubs and trees; marsh; bog —***adj.*** of or native to a swamp —***vt.*** **1** to plunge or sink in a swamp, deep water, etc. **2** to flood or submerge with or as with water **3** to overcome or overwhelm; ruin [*swamped* by debts] **4** to sink (a boat) by filling with water ☆**5** to make (a path) or clear (an area) by removing underbrush and slash, as in logging —***vi.*** to become swamped; sink in or as in a swamp —**swamp′ish *adj.***

☆**swamp buggy** an automotive vehicle, often amphibious and equipped with very large tires, for traveling over swampy or muddy terrain

☆**swamp·er** (swäm′pər, swôm′-) ***n.*** **1** a person who lives in a swamp **2** a person who works at swamping: see SWAMP (*vt.* 5) **3** [Old Informal] a handyman or helper

☆**swamp fever** **1** MALARIA **2** EQUINE INFECTIOUS ANEMIA

swamp gas MARSH GAS

☆**swamp·land** (-land′) ***n.*** a swamp, or land in a swamp, esp. when cultivable

swamp·y (swäm′pē, swôm′-) ***adj.*** **swamp′i·er, swamp′i·est** **1** of or consisting of a swamp or swamps **2** like a swamp; wet and spongy; marshy —**swamp′i·ness *n.***

swan[1] (swän, swôn) ***n.*** ⟦ME < OE, akin to Ger *schwan* < IE base **swen-,* to sound, sing > L *sonus,* SOUND[1]⟧ **1** *pl.* **swans** or **swan** any of several large-bodied, web-footed waterfowl (family Anatidae, esp. genus *Cygnus*) with a long, graceful neck and, typically, pure white feathers: swans are graceful swimmers and strong flyers **2** a person who resembles or is thought to resemble a swan in some way; sometimes, specif., a great poet or singer —***vi.*** [Informal, Chiefly Brit.] to move slowly or majestically, with a calm, serene air —**the Swan** the constellation Cygnus

☆**swan**[2] (swän, swôn) ***vi.*** ⟦< ? Brit dial. *Is' wan,* I'll warrant⟧ [Dial.] to swear: usually in the exclamation **I swan!**, used to express surprise, impatience, etc.

☆**swan dive** a forward dive in which the legs are held straight and together, the back is arched, and the arms are stretched out to the sides: the arms are brought forward and together just before entering the water

Swa·nee (swä′nē) *var. of* SUWANNEE

swang (swaŋ) ***vi., vt.*** [Now Chiefly Dial.] *pt. of* SWING

swan·herd (swän′hurd′, swôn′-) ***n.*** a person who tends swans

swank[1] (swaŋk) ***n.*** ⟦orig. slang < dial. vi., akin to OE *swancor,* pliant, supple, with notion of swinging the body: for IE base see SWING⟧ [Informal] **1** stylish display or ostentation in dress, etc. **2** swaggering, ostentatious behavior, speech, etc. —***adj.*** [Informal] ostentatiously stylish —***vi.*** [Slang] to act in a showy manner; swagger

swank[2] (swaŋk) ***vi.*** *alt. pt. of* SWINK

swank·y (swaŋ′kē) ***adj.*** **swank′i·er, swank′i·est** ⟦SWANK[1] + -Y[2]⟧ [Informal] ostentatiously stylish; expensive and showy —**swank′i·ly *adv.*** —**swank′i·ness *n.***

swan·ner·y (swän′ər ē, swôn′-) ***n., pl.*** **-ner·ies** a place where swans are kept or bred

Swans·combe man (swänz′kəm) ⟦after *Swanscombe,* town in Kent, England, where the remains were found⟧ a type of early human (*Homo sapiens steinheimensis*) known from fossil remains and believed to be from the late Lower Paleolithic

swan's-down (swänz′doun′, swônz′-) ***n.*** **1** the soft, fine under-feathers, or down, of the swan, used for trimming clothes, etc. **2** a soft, thick fabric of wool and silk, rayon, or cotton, used for making baby clothes, etc. **3** a cotton fabric with a satin weave and a heavy napped finish **4** a very soft cotton flannel Also **swans′down′**

Swan·sea (swän′sē, -zē) seaport in West Glamorgan, S Wales, on the Bristol Channel

swan·skin (swän′skin′, swôn′-) ***n.*** **1** the skin of a swan with feathers on it **2** a closely woven flannel with a twill weave, used for work clothes

swan song **1** the sweet song supposed in ancient fable to be sung by a dying swan **2** the last act, final creative work, etc. of a person, as before retirement or death

swan-up·ping (-up′iŋ) ***n.*** ⟦< SWAN[1] + UP[1], v.⟧ the practice in England of marking young swans with a notch in the upper beak as a sign of ownership

swap (swäp, swôp) ***vt., vi.*** **swapped, swap′ping** ⟦ME *swappen,* to strike (prob. echoic): from the striking of hands on concluding a bargain⟧ to exchange, trade, or barter —***n.*** **1** an exchange, trade, or barter **2** *Finance* a negotiated contract as between two corporations for a mutually beneficial exchange of currencies, loans, etc. —**swap out** [Informal] to exchange or substitute for another of the same kind —**swap′per *n.***

swap meet a gathering of persons for the purpose of selling, buying, or bartering collectibles, used items, etc.

sward (swôrd) ***n.*** ⟦ME *swarde* < OE *sweard,* a skin, hide, akin to Ger *schwarte,* rind, hard skin, ON *svǫrthr,* skin⟧ grass-covered soil; turf —***vt.*** to cover with sward

sware (swer) ***vi., vt.*** *archaic pt. of* SWEAR

swarf (swôrf) ***n.*** ⟦prob. < OE *gesweorf,* filings < *sweorfan,* to file away, scour: see SWERVE⟧ the fine bits and shavings that accumulate in the grinding or cutting of metal

swarm[1] (swôrm) ***n.*** ⟦ME < OE *swearm,* akin to Ger *schwarm,* prob. < IE base **swer-,* to buzz > L *susurrare,* to hiss, whisper, *sorex,* Gr *hyrax,* shrew⟧ **1** *a)* a large number of bees, led by a queen, leaving one hive for another to start a new colony *b)* a colony of bees in a hive *c)* any large number of social insects moving in a group [a *swarm* of ants] **2** a moving mass, crowd, or throng [a *swarm* of onlookers] —***vi.*** **1** to gather and fly off in a swarm: said as of bees **2** to move, collect, be present, etc. in large numbers; throng; abound **3** to be filled or crowded; teem —***vt.*** **1** to fill with a swarm; crowd; throng **2** to act as a swarm in surrounding, attacking, dealing with, etc. [to *swarm* the quarterback, researchers *swarming* a problem] —**SYN.** CROWD[1], GROUP —**swarm′er *n.***

swarm[2] (swôrm) ***vi., vt.*** ⟦orig. naut. word < ?⟧ to climb (a tree, mast, pole, etc.) using the hands and feet; shin (*up*)

swarm spore *Biol.* ZOOSPORE

swart (swôrt) ***adj.*** ⟦ME < OE *sweart,* akin to Ger *schwarz,* black < IE **swordos,* dirty, black > L *sordidus,* SORDID⟧ *old poet. var. of* SWARTHY

swarth (swôrth) ***n.*** *dial. var. of* SWARD —***adj.*** *var. of* SWARTHY

swarth·y (swôr′thē, -thē) ***adj.*** **swarth′i·er, swarth′i·est** ⟦< dial. *swarth,* var. of SWART + -Y[2]⟧ having a dark complexion —**SYN.** DUSKY —**swarth′i·ly *adv.*** —**swarth′i·ness *n.***

Swart·krans ape-man (svärt′kränz′) ⟦after *Swartkrans,* near Johannesburg, South Africa, where the remains were found⟧ an early hominid (*Australopithecus robustus crassidens*) known from fossil remains and thought to be from the Middle Pleistocene

swash (swäsh, swôsh) ***vi.*** ⟦echoic⟧ **1** to dash, strike, wash, etc. with a splashing sound; splash **2** [Archaic] to swagger or bluster —***vt.*** to splash (a liquid), as in a container —***n.*** **1** a body of swift, dashing water; specif., a channel cutting through or behind a sandbank **2** a bar washed over by the sea **3** the splashing of water or the sound of this **4** [Archaic] a swaggering or blustering person

swash·buck·ler (-buk′lər) ***n.*** ⟦pejorative for one who noisily strikes a shield < prec. + BUCKLER⟧ a person, esp. a man, engaged in swashbuckling

swash·buck·ling (-buk′liŋ) ***n.*** **1** [Archaic] loud boasting or bullying **2** daring, flamboyant adventures of a kind typical of romantic historical novels and movies —***adj.*** of or typical of swashbuckling [*swashbuckling* buccaneers]

swash·ing (-iŋ) ***adj.*** **1** SWASHBUCKLING **2** splashing or dashing —**swash′ing·ly *adv.***

swash letters ⟦< ?⟧ italic capital letters formed with long tails and flourishes

swas·ti·ka (swäs′ti kə) ***n.*** ⟦Sans *svastika* < *svasti,* well-being, benediction < *su,* well (< IE base **su-,* var. of **swe-,* **sewe-:* see SUICIDE) + *asti,* he is: for IE base see IS[1]⟧ **1** a design or ornament of ancient origin in the form of a cross with four equal arms, each bent in a right-angle extension: a mystic symbol found in both the Old World and the New World **2** this design with the arms bent back clockwise, used in Nazi Germany and by other Nazi fascists as a party emblem and symbol of anti-Semitism

swastikas

swat (swät) ***vt.*** **swat′ted, swat′ting** ⟦echoic⟧ to hit with a quick, sharp blow —***n.*** a quick, sharp blow, as with a bat or swatter

Swat[1] (swät) ***n., pl.*** **Swa·ti** (swä′tē) *var. of* SWATI

Swat[2] (swät) region in NE Pakistan, on the Indus River: former princely state of India

☆**SWAT** (swät) ***n.*** ⟦*S(pecial) W(eapons) a(nd) T(actics)*⟧ a special unit of a law enforcement agency, trained to deal with violence, riots, terrorism, etc.: in full **SWAT team**

swatch (swäch) ***n.*** ⟦orig., a cloth tally < ?⟧ **1** a sample piece of cloth or other material **2** a small amount or number in a cluster, bunch, or patch

swath (swäth, swôth) ***n.*** ⟦ME *swathe* < OE *swathu,* a track, akin to Ger *schwade,* space covered by a scythe swing: for IE base see fol.⟧ **1** the space or width covered with one cut of a scythe or other mowing device **2** [Rare] a stroke with a scythe **3** a line or row of grass, wheat, etc. cut in one course by a scythe, mower, etc. **4** a long strip, streak, or zone of any kind [a red scarf providing a *swath* of color] —☆**cut a wide swath** to make an ostentatious display or forceful impression

swathe[1] (swāth, swäth) ***vt.*** **swathed, swath′ing** ⟦ME *swathen* < OE *swathian,* akin to ON *svatha,* to glide, prob. < IE base **swei-,* to turn, bend > SWAY⟧ **1** to wrap or bind up in a long strip or bandage **2** to wrap (a bandage, etc.) around something **3** to surround or envelop; enclose —***n.*** a bandage or wrapping —**swath′er *n.***

swathe[2] (swāth) ***n.*** *var. of* SWATH

Swa·ti (swä′tē) ***n., pl.*** **-ti** or **-tis** a member of a people of Muslim faith living in SWAT[2]

Swat·ow (swä′tou′) *a former transliteration of* SHANTOU

swat·ter (swät′ər) ***n.*** **1** a person who swats **2** a device, as of fine mesh on a handle, for swatting flies, etc.: in full **fly swatter**

S wave ⟦< *s(econdary) wave*⟧ wave motion in a solid medium in which the particles of the medium oscillate in a direction perpendicular to the direction of travel of the wave: it cannot be transmitted through a fluid

sway (swā) ***vi.*** ⟦ME *sweyen* < ON *sveigja,* to turn, bend: for IE base see SWATHE[1]⟧ **1** *a)* to swing or move from side to side or to and fro *b)* to vacillate or alternate between one position, opinion, etc. and another **2** *a)* to lean or incline to one side; veer *b)* [Obs.] to incline or tend in judgment or opinion **3** [Old Poet.] to rule; reign; hold sway —***vt.*** **1** *a)* to cause to swing or move from side to side *b)* to cause to vacillate **2** *a)* to cause to lean or incline to one side *b)* to cause (a person, an opinion, actions, etc.) to be inclined a certain way or be turned from a given course; influence or divert [*swayed* by promises] 3 [Archaic] *a)* to wield (a scepter, etc.) *b)* to rule over or control; dominate 4 *Naut.* to hoist (a mast, yard, etc.) into place: usually with *up* —*n.* 1 a swaying or being swayed; movement to the side; a swinging, leaning, fluctuation, etc. 2 influence, force, or control [moved by the *sway* of passion] 3 sovereign power or authority; rule; dominion —SYN. AFFECT[1], POWER, SWING —**hold sway** to reign or prevail —**sway′er** *n.*

sway·backed (swā′bakt′) *adj.* ⟦prob. < (or transl. of) Dan *sveibaget* or *sveirygget* < ON *sveigja,* to bend, prec. + *bak,* BACK[1] or *rygg,* back, RIDGE⟧ having an abnormal sagging of the spine, usually as a result of strain or overwork, as some horses, etc. —**sway′back′** *n.*

Swa·zi (swä′zē) *n.* 1 *pl.* **Swa′zis** or **Swa′zi** a member of a farming people of Swaziland 2 the Bantu language of this people

Swa·zi·land (-land′) country in SE Africa, surrounded on three sides by South Africa: a former British protectorate, it became an independent kingdom & member of the Commonwealth (1968): 6,704 sq mi (17,363 sq km); cap. Mbabane

SWbS *abbrev.* southwest by south

SWbW *abbrev.* southwest by west

swear (swer) *vi.* **swore**, **sworn**, **swear′ing** ⟦ME *swerien* < OE *swerian,* akin to Ger *schwören* < IE base **swer-,* to speak > OSlav *svariti,* to revile⟧ 1 to make a solemn declaration with an appeal to God or to something held sacred for confirmation [to *swear* on one's honor] 2 to make a solemn promise; vow 3 to use profane or obscene language; curse 4 *Law* to give evidence under oath —*vt.* 1 to declare solemnly in the name of God or of something held sacred 2 to pledge or vow on oath 3 to assert or promise with great conviction or emphasis 4 to take (an oath) by swearing 5 to administer an oath to [to *swear* someone to secrecy; the witness has been *sworn*] —SYN. BLASPHEMY —**swear by** 1 to name (something held sacred) in taking an oath 2 to have great faith or confidence in —**swear for** to give assurance for; guarantee —**swear in** to administer an oath to (a person taking office, a witness in a legal proceeding, etc.) —**swear off** to promise to give up, leave off, or renounce —☆**swear out** to obtain (a warrant for someone's arrest) by making a charge under oath —**swear′er** *n.*

☆**swear·word** (swer′wurd′) *n.* a word or phrase used in swearing or cursing; profane or obscene word or phrase

sweat (swet) *vi.* **sweat** or **sweat′ed**, **sweat′ing** ⟦ME *sweten* < OE *swǣtan* < *swat,* sweat, akin to Ger *schweissen* < IE base **sweid-,* to sweat > Gr *hidrōs,* L *sudor,* sweat⟧ 1 to give forth a characteristic salty moisture through the pores of the skin; perspire 2 *a)* to give forth moisture in droplets on its surface, as a ripening cheese does *b)* to collect and condense water in droplets on its surface, as a glass of ice water does in a warm room 3 to ferment: said of tobacco leaves, etc. 4 to come forth in drops through pores or a porous surface; ooze 5 to work hard enough to cause sweating 6 [Informal] to suffer distress, anxiety, etc. —*vt.* 1 *a)* to give forth (moisture) through pores or a porous surface *b)* to collect and condense (moisture) on the surface 2 to cause to sweat, or perspire, as by drugs, exercise, heat, etc. 3 to cause to give forth moisture; esp., to ferment [to *sweat* tobacco leaves] 4 to make wet with sweat, or perspiration 5 to heat (a metal) in order to extract an easily fusible constituent 6 to unite (metal parts) by pressing them together, usually with solder between them, and heating the point of contact until fusion is effected 7 to remove particles of metal from (a coin) illegally, as by abrading 8 *a)* to cause to work so hard as to sweat; overwork *b)* to cause (employees) to work long hours at low wages under poor working conditions; exploit (workers) ☆9 [Informal] *a)* to get information from by torture or by long, grueling questioning *b)* to get (information) in this way 10 [Slang] to try hard or too hard to get or achieve 11 [Slang] to worry or be annoyed about —*n.* ⟦altered < the v. < ME *swat* < OE⟧ 1 the clear, alkaline, salty liquid given forth in drops through the pores of the skin; perspiration 2 moisture given forth or collected in droplets on the surface of something 3 *a)* the act or condition of sweating or being sweated *b)* an artificially induced sweating 4 a condition of eagerness, anxiety, impatience, etc. 5 hard work; drudgery 6 exercise, as a run, given a horse before a race 7 [*pl.*] clothes worn for exercising, warming up, etc.; specif., a sweat suit —☆**no sweat** [Slang] no trouble or difficulty at all; easily done: often used interjectionally —**sweat blood** [Slang] 1 to work very hard; overwork 2 to be impatient, apprehensive, anxious, etc. —**sweat it** [Slang] to be worried or annoyed about something —**sweat off** to get rid of (weight) by sweating —☆**sweat out** [Informal] 1 to get rid of or try to get rid of by sweating [to *sweat out* a cold] 2 to wait or suffer through (some ordeal, nuisance, etc.) 3 to anticipate or wait anxiously or impatiently for

☆**sweat·band** (-band′) *n.* 1 a band, as of leather, inside a hat to protect the hat against damage from sweat 2 a band of absorbent cloth worn around the wrist or head to absorb perspiration

sweat bee any of a family (Halictidae) of small bees that usually nest in vertical tunnels in the ground: some species drink animal or human perspiration

sweat·box (-bäks′) *n.* 1 a box in which hides, dried fruits, etc. are sweated 2 a place in which one sweats profusely, as because of close confinement, heat, etc.

☆**sweat equity** [Informal] 1 hard work put into a house, business, etc. to increase its value 2 the increased value so produced

☆**sweat-eq·ui·ty** (swet′ek′wit ē) *adj.* [Informal] designating or of a kind of plan for renovating houses, neighborhoods, etc. in which houses are offered free or at low prices to persons promising to make the necessary repairs

sweat·er (swet′ər) *n.* 1 a person or thing that sweats, esp. to excess 2 a knitted or crocheted outer garment for the upper part of the body, with or without sleeves, styled as either a pullover or a jacket

sweater dress a knitted dress that is shaped like a long, straight-sided pullover sweater: also written **sweat′er·dress′** *n.*

sweat gland any of the very small, coiled, tubular glands in the subcutaneous tissue that secrete sweat

sweating sickness an acute, infectious, rapidly fatal disease, epidemic in Europe in the 15th and 16th cent., characterized by high fever and profuse sweating

sweat lodge a dome-shaped tent constructed by Indian peoples of the Great Plains and W North America, used for ritual cleansing and purification by means of steam produced by pouring water over hot stones

sweat·pants (-pants′) *pl.n.* loosefitting pants, usually made of a soft, absorbent cloth, with a drawstring or elastic waistband and, often, closefitting at the ankles, worn during exercise or as loungewear: also written **sweat pants**

☆**sweat·shirt** (-shurt′) *n.* a loosefitting, long-sleeved pullover, usually made of a soft, absorbent cloth, worn during exercise or as loungewear

☆**sweat·shop** (-shäp′) *n.* a shop, factory, etc. where employees work long hours at low wages under poor working conditions

sweat suit an outfit, consisting of a sweatshirt and sweatpants, worn for exercise or as loungewear: also written **sweat′suit′** *n.*

sweat·y (-ē) *adj.* **sweat′i·er**, **sweat′i·est** 1 *a)* sweating; covered with sweat *b)* damp with or smelling of sweat 2 of or like that of sweat [a *sweaty* odor] 3 causing sweat [a hot, *sweaty* day] 4 laborious or labored —**sweat′i·ly** *adv.* —**sweat′i·ness** *n.*

Swed *abbrev.* 1 Sweden 2 Swedish

Swede (swēd) *n.* 1 a person born or living in Sweden 2 ⟦< SWEDISH TURNIP⟧ [**s-**] [Chiefly Brit.] RUTABAGA

Swe·den (swēd′'n) country in N Europe, in the E part of the Scandinavian Peninsula: 173,732 sq mi (449,964 sq km); cap. Stockholm: Swed. name SVERIGE

Swe·den·borg (swēd′'n bôrg′; *Swed* svād′'n bôr′y′), **Emanuel** (born *Emanuel Swedberg*) 1688-1772; Swed. scientist, mystic, & religious philosopher

Swe·den·bor·gi·an (swēd′'n bôr′jē ən, -gē-) *n.* any of the followers of Swedenborg; specif., any member of his Church of the New Jerusalem —*adj.* of Swedenborg, his doctrines, or his followers —**Swe′den·bor′gi·an·ism′** *n.*, **Swe′den·borg′ism′** (-bôr′giz′əm)

Swed·ish (swē′dish) *adj.* of Sweden or its people, language, or culture —*n.* the North Germanic language spoken in Sweden —**the Swedish** the people of Sweden

Swedish ivy any of various trailing plants (genus *Plectranthus*) of the mint family, often used as houseplants, esp. one (*P. oertendahlii*) that became very popular in Sweden

Swedish massage massage combined with a set of exercises (**Swedish movements**), used in treating certain diseases

Swedish turnip [Chiefly Brit.] RUTABAGA

☆**swee·ny** (swē′nē) *n.* ⟦altered (prob. via PaGer *schwinne*) < Ger dial. *schweine,* atrophy < *schweinen,* to atrophy, shrink < OHG *suinan,* to decrease, akin to ON *svina,* to disappear < IE base **swi-,* to disappear, decrease⟧ atrophy of the shoulder muscles of horses

sweep (swēp) *vt.* **swept**, **sweep′ing** ⟦ME *swepen,* akin to (or ? altered <) OE *swapan:* see SWOOP⟧ 1 to clear or clean (a surface, room, etc.) as by brushing with a broom 2 to remove or clear away (dirt, debris, etc.) as with a broom or brushing movement 3 to clear (a space, path, etc.) with or as with a broom 4 to strip, clear, carry away, remove, or destroy with a forceful movement or movements 5 to move or carry along with a sweeping movement [to *sweep* one's hand through one's hair] 6 to touch or brush in moving across [hands *sweeping* the keyboard] 7 to pass swiftly over or across; traverse [searchlights *sweeping* the sky, a fad that is *sweeping* the nation] 8 to direct (the eyes, a glance, etc.) over something swiftly 9 to drag (a river, pond, etc.) with a net, grapple, etc. 10 to direct gunfire along; rake 11 *a)* to win all the games or events of (a series, set, or match) *b)* to win overwhelmingly [to *sweep* an election] —*vi.* 1 to clean a surface, room, etc. with or as with a broom or the like 2 to move, pass, or progress steadily or smoothly, esp. with speed, force, or gracefulness [planes *sweeping* across the sky, music *sweeping* to a climax] 3 to trail, as skirts or the train of a gown 4 to reach or extend in a long, graceful curve or line [a road *sweeping* up the hill] —*n.* 1 the act of sweeping, as with a broom 2 *a)* a continuous sweeping or driving movement [the *sweep* of a scythe] *b)* a stroke or blow resulting from this 3 a trailing, as of skirts 4 range or scope [within the *sweep* of their guns] 5 extent or range; stretch; reach [a long *sweep* of meadow] 6 a line, contour, curve, etc. that gives an impression of flow or movement 7 a person whose work is sweeping; specif., CHIMNEY SWEEP 8 [*usually pl.*] things swept up; sweepings 9 *a)* the taking or winning of all; complete victory or success, as in a series of contests *b)* in casino, the taking of all the cards on the board, by pairing or combining 10 SWEEPS 11 a long oar 12 a long pole mounted on a pivot, with a bucket at one end, used for raising water, as from a well ☆13 a blade or plow-point of various widths, used in the shallow cultivation of row crops 14 a sail of a windmill 15 *Electronics* one transit of an electron beam across the screen of a cathode-ray tube, moving either horizontally from line to line, as in a picture tube, or circularly around a center point, as in a radarscope **16** *Football* a play in which the ball carrier runs a relatively long way toward a sideline before turning toward the line of scrimmage

sweep·back (swēp′bak′) ***n.*** **1** a backward slant of an airfoil, esp. of a wing **2** the angle formed by some reference line along an airplane wing and the lateral axis of the airplane

sweep·er (swē′pər) ***n.*** **1** a person who sweeps **2** *a)* a device for sweeping ☆*b)* *short for* CARPET SWEEPER **3** *Soccer* a defensive back who plays in front of the goalkeeper

sweep hand SECOND HAND (sense 1): also **sweep second hand**

sweep·ing (swē′piŋ) ***adj.*** **1** that sweeps; cleansing or carrying away with or as with a broom **2** reaching in a long curve or line **3** extending over the whole range or a great space **4** *a)* extensive; comprehensive; thoroughgoing *b)* complete; decisive *c)* indiscriminate [a *sweeping* generalization] —***n.*** **1** [*pl.*] things swept up, as litter, refuse, etc. swept from a floor **2** the act, work, etc. of a person or thing that sweeps —**sweep′ing·ly** ***adv.***

sweeps (swēps) ***n., pl.*** **sweeps** **1** SWEEPSTAKES **2** *a)* a national rating survey of local radio and TV stations for determining advertising rates *b)* the period during which such a survey is conducted

sweep·stakes (swēp′stāks′) ***n., pl.*** **-stakes′** ⟦because the winner "*sweeps* in" all of the *stakes*⟧ **1** a lottery in which each participant puts up money in a common fund which is given as the prize to the winner or in shares to several winners **2** *a)* a contest, esp. a horse race, the result of which determines the winner or winners of such a lottery *b)* the prize or prizes won in such a lottery **3** any of various other lotteries Also **sweep′stake′** (-stāk′)

sweet (swēt) ***adj.*** ⟦ME *swete* < OE, akin to *swot,* sweetness, Ger *süss,* sweet < IE base *swad-, pleasing to taste > Gr *hēdys,* sweet, L *suadere,* to persuade & *suavis,* sweet⟧ **1** *a)* having a taste of, or like that of, sugar *b)* containing sugar in some form [*sweet* wines] **2** *a)* having a generally agreeable taste, smell, sound, appearance, etc.; pleasant *b)* agreeable to the mind; gratifying [*sweet* praise] *c)* having a friendly, pleasing disposition; characterized by kindliness and gentleness [a *sweet* old lady] *d)* endearing because of one's innocence, vulnerability, etc. [a *sweet* baby] *e)* dear (formerly a polite form of address) [*sweet* sir] *f)* sentimental, saccharine, or cloying *g)* [Slang] good, delightful, etc. (a generalized epithet of approval) **3** *a)* not rancid, spoiled, sour, or fermented [*sweet* milk, *sweet* cider] *b)* not salty or salted (said of water or butter) *c)* free from sourness or acidity (said of soil) **4** *Chem. a)* free from unpleasant odors and gases *b)* purified and free from acid, corrosive elements, etc. **5** *Jazz* designating or of music or playing characterized by more or less strict adherence to melody, sentimentality or blandness in tone and rhythm, and a moderate tempo —***n.*** **1** the quality of being sweet; sweetness **2** *a)* [*pl.*] sweet foods *b)* [Chiefly Brit.] a piece of candy or a sweet dessert *c)* something, as an experience, that gives delight or satisfaction (*usually used in pl.*) [the *sweets* of victory] ☆*d)* *short for* SWEET POTATO **3** a sweet, or beloved, person; darling —***adv.*** in a sweet manner —**be sweet on** [Informal] to be in love with —**sweet′ly** ***adv.*** —**sweet′ness** ***n.***

Sweet (swēt), Henry 1845-1912; Eng. linguist

sweet alyssum a short garden plant (*Lobularia maritima*) of the crucifer family, with small spikes of tiny flowers

sweet-and-sour (swēt′'n sour′) ***adj.*** cooked with or incorporating both sugar and a sour substance, as vinegar or lemon juice

sweet basil a basil (*Ocimum basilicum*): see BASIL

sweet bay **1** LAUREL (***n.*** 1) ☆**2** a North American magnolia (*Magnolia virginiana*) with fragrant, white flowers, common along the coast from Maine to Texas

sweet·bread (swēt′bred′) ***n.*** ⟦Early ModE < SWEET + BREAD, in OE sense, morsel⟧ the thymus (**heart sweetbread** or **throat sweetbread**) or sometimes the pancreas (**stomach sweetbread**) of a calf, lamb, etc., when used as food: *usually used in pl.*

sweet·bri·er or **sweet·bri·ar** (-brī′ər) ***n.*** EGLANTINE

sweet cherry **1** an Old World cherry (*Prunus avium*) whose fruits have a sweet pulp and juice: many varieties have been derived from this tree **2** its fruit See BIGARREAU, HEART CHERRY

sweet cicely ☆**1** any of several perennial North American herbs (genus *Osmorhiza*) of the umbel family, with compound leaves and clusters of small, white flowers **2** a European perennial herb (*Myrrhis odorata*) of the umbel family, with anise-scented leaves formerly used in flavoring

sweet clover any of a genus (*Melilotus*) of annual or biennial plants of the pea family, with small, white or yellow flowers, leaflets in groups of three, and single-seeded pods: grown for hay, forage, or green manure

☆**sweet corn** **1** any of various strains of Indian corn with kernels rich in sugar, eaten as a table vegetable in the unripe, or milky, stage **2** an ear of such corn

sweet·en (swēt′'n) ***vt.*** **1** to make sweet with or as with sugar **2** to make pleasant or agreeable, as to the sense of smell **3** to counteract the acidic condition of (the soil, the stomach, etc.) **4** *a)* to mollify; appease *b)* [Now Rare] to alleviate; ease **5** [Informal] *Business a)* to increase the value of (collateral for a loan) by pledging additional securities *b)* to increase the value of (an offer) in order to induce acceptance, promote sales, etc. **6** *Poker* to increase the stakes in (a pot) by anteing again following a round when no bet was made —***vi.*** to become sweet

sweet·en·er (swēt′'n ər, swēt′nər) ***n.*** a sweetening agent, esp. a synthetic substance such as saccharin

sweet·en·ing (swēt′'n iŋ, swēt′niŋ) ***n.*** **1** the process of making sweet **2** something that sweetens

☆**sweet fern** a flowering shrub (*Comptonia peregrina*) of the bayberry family, with fragrant, fernlike leaves

sweet flag a perennial marsh plant (*Acorus calamus*) of the arum family, with sword-shaped leaves, small, green flowers, and a sweet-scented rhizome

sweet gale a fragrant marsh plant (*Myrica gale*) of the bayberry family, with bitter leaves and yellowish flowers

sweet grass any of various sweet-smelling grasses, esp. a perennial (*Hierochloe odorata*) traditionally used as a food flavoring and in Native American rituals

☆**sweet gum** **1** a large North American tree (*Liquidambar styraciflua*) of the witch hazel family, with alternate maplelike leaves, spiny fruit balls, and fragrant juice **2** the wood of this tree **3** STORAX (***n.*** 1)

sweet·heart (-härt′) ***n.*** **1** *a)* someone with whom one is in love and by whom one is loved; lover *b)* darling (a term of endearment) **2** [Slang] a very agreeable person or an excellent thing —***adj.*** designating or of any agreement, deal, contract, etc. involving collusion between the parties to it; specif., of such a contract or arrangement between union officials and an employer with terms disadvantageous to union members

sweetheart neckline a neckline on a woman's or girl's garment with the front cut low and shaped to resemble the top half of a conventionalized heart

☆**sweet·ie** (swēt′ē) ***n.*** [Informal] SWEETHEART: also **sweetie pie**

sweet·ing (-iŋ) ***n.*** **1** a variety of sweet apple **2** [Archaic] SWEETHEART

sweet·ish (-ish) ***adj.*** rather sweet

sweet marjoram an annual marjoram (*Origanum majorana*) grown for its aromatic leaves used in cooking

sweet·meat (-mēt′) ***n.*** ⟦LME *sweit meit* < OE *swetmete:* see SWEET & MEAT⟧ any sweet food or delicacy prepared with sugar or honey, as a cake, confection, preserve, etc.; specif., a candy, candied fruit, etc.

sweet nothings [Informal] murmured words of endearment, as between sweethearts

sweet oil any mild, edible oil, as olive oil

sweet pea a climbing annual plant (*Lathyrus odoratus*) of the pea family, with butterfly-shaped flowers

sweet pepper **1** any of various large, mild peppers, esp. any of various red, bell-shaped varieties: see CAPSICUM (sense 1) **2** a plant on which these grow

☆**sweet potato** **1** a tropical, trailing plant (*Ipomoea batatas*) of the morning-glory family, with purplish flowers and a fleshy, brownish, tuberlike root used as a vegetable **2** its root **3** [Informal] OCARINA

☆**sweet science, the** [Now Literary] the sport of boxing, esp. professional boxing

sweet·sop (-säp′) ***n.*** **1** a tropical American tree (*Annona squamosa*) of the custard-apple family, having green fruit with a sweet pulp and black seeds **2** its edible fruit

☆**sweet spot** **1** *Sports* that particular area on the striking surface of a racket, golf club, baseball bat, etc. that, if struck against the ball, will generate the most power and afford the best control **2** the optimum location in a room, etc. for experiencing the full effects of the multi-channel sound of a film soundtrack or musical recording

☆**sweet-talk** (-tôk′) ***vi., vt.*** [Informal] to talk in a flattering or blandishing way (to)

sweet tooth [Informal] a fondness or craving for sweets

sweet william [*also* **s- W-**] a perennial pink (*Dianthus barbatus*) with dense, flat clusters of small flowers

swell (swel) ***vi.*** **swelled, swelled** or **swol′len, swell′ing** ⟦ME *swellen* < OE *swellan;* akin to Ger *schwellen,* ON *svella*⟧ **1** to increase in volume or become larger as a result of pressure from within; expand; dilate **2** to become larger at a particular point; curve out; bulge; protrude; specif., to become distended from an abnormal accumulation of fluid in bodily tissue, as from infection or injury **3** to extend beyond or above the normal or surrounding level **4** to form swells, or large waves: said of the sea **5** to be or become filled (*with* pride, indignation, self-importance, etc.) **6** to increase within a person, as a feeling [the anger *swelling* in him] **7** to increase in size, force, intensity, degree, etc. [membership *swelled* to a thousand] **8** to increase in volume or loudness —***vt.*** to cause to swell; specif., *a)* to cause to increase in size, volume, extent, degree, etc. *b)* to cause to bulge or protrude *c)* to fill with pride, indignation, etc.; inflate; puff *d)* to cause (a tone, chord, etc.) to increase in loudness —***n.*** **1** a part that swells, bulge; curve; protuberance; specif., *a)* a large wave that moves steadily without breaking *b)* a piece of rising ground; rounded hill or slope **2** a swelling or being swollen **3** an increase in size, amount, extent, degree, etc. **4** [Informal] *a)* a person who is strikingly stylish, esp. in dress *b)* a person of social prominence **5** an increase in loudness of sound **6** *Music a)* a gradual increase in volume (*crescendo*), usually followed by a gradual decrease (*decrescendo*) *b)* a device for controlling the loudness of tones, as in an organ —***adj.*** ⟦ME *swelle,* tumid, proud⟧ **1** [Old Informal] stylish; very fashionable **2** [Slang] first-rate; excellent: a generalized epithet of approval —**SYN.** EXPAND

swell box a chamber enclosing one or more sets of organ pipes or reeds and fitted with movable shutters that regulate the loudness of tone

swelled head [Informal] an exaggerated notion of one's own worth

☆**swell·fish** (swel′fish′) ***n., pl.*** **-fish′** or **-fish′es** (see FISH) PUFFER (sense 2)

swell·head (-hed′) ***n.*** [Informal] a vain or conceited person; egotist —**swell′head′ed** ***adj.*** —**swell′head′ed·ness** ***n.***

swell·ing (-iŋ) *n.* **1** an increasing or being increased in size, volume, etc. **2** something swollen; esp., an abnormally swollen part of the body

swel·ter (swel′tər) *vi.* ⟦freq. of ME *swelten,* to die, swoon away, faint < OE *sweltan,* to die < IE base **swel-,* to burn > Gr *heilē,* sun's heat⟧ to be or feel uncomfortably hot; sweat, feel weak, etc. from great heat —*vt.* **1** to cause to swelter **2** [Archaic] to exude (venom or poison) —*n.* **1** the condition of sweltering **2** oppressive heat

swel·ter·ing (-iŋ) *adj.* **1** that swelters or suffers from the heat **2** very hot; sultry Also **swel·try** (swel′trē), **-tri·er, -tri·est** —**swel′ter·ing·ly** *adv.*

swept (swept) *vt., vi. pt. & pp. of* SWEEP

swept·back (swept′bak′) *adj.* **1** having a sweepback: said of the wing of an aircraft **2** having sweptback wings: said of an aircraft

swept·wing (-wiŋ′) *n. Aeron.* a sweptback wing

swerve (swʉrv) *vi., vt.* **swerved, swerv′ing** ⟦ME *swerven* < OE *sweorfan,* to file away, scour < IE base **swerbh-,* to turn, wipe, sweep > Gr *syrphetos,* sweepings, litter⟧ to turn aside or cause to turn aside sharply or suddenly from a straight line, course, etc. —*n.* the act or degree of swerving —*SYN.* DEVIATE —**swerv′er** *n.*

swev·en (swev′ən) *n.* ⟦ME < OE *swefn,* a dream, sleep < IE **swepnos* < base **swep-* > L *somnus,* Gr *hypnos,* sleep⟧ [Archaic] a dream or vision

SWG *abbrev.* standard wire gauge

swid·den (swid′'n) *adj.* ⟦ult. < obs. or dial. *swithen,* to burn, scorch⟧ SLASH-AND-BURN

swift (swift) *adj.* ⟦ME < OE < IE **sweip-* < base **swei-,* to bend, turn > SWATHE[1], SWOOP⟧ **1** moving or capable of moving with great speed; rapid; fast **2** coming, happening, or done quickly or suddenly **3** acting or responding quickly; prompt; ready —*adv.* in a swift manner —*n.* **1** a cylinder in a carding machine **2** an expanding reel used to hold skeins of silk, etc. that are being wound off **3** any of a large family (Apodidae, order Apodiformes) of aerial-feeding, insectivorous, swift-flying, swallowlike birds with long, stiff wings and a small, weak bill, as the chimney swift **4** any of several swift-moving North American iguanas (genera *Sceloporus* and *Uta*) living esp. in arid or desert regions **5** a small fox (*Vulpes velox*) of the plains of W U.S. and S Canada: in full **swift fox** —*SYN.* FAST[1] —**swift′ly** *adv.* —**swift′ness** *n.*

Swift (swift), **Jonathan** 1667-1745; Eng. satirist, born in Ireland

swift-foot·ed (swift′foot′id) *adj.* that can run swiftly

Swift·i·an (swif′tē ən) *adj.* **1** of or relating to Jonathan Swift **2** like Swift's writings in tone or outlook; often, specif., sardonic, caustic, pessimistic, etc.

swig (swig) [Informal] *vt., vi.* **swigged, swig′ging** ⟦< ?⟧ to drink, esp. in great gulps or quantities —*n.* an instance of swigging; deep draft, esp. of liquor —**swig′ger** *n.*

swill (swil) *vt.* ⟦ME *swilen* < OE *swilian* < IE base **swel-,* to devour > SWALLOW[2]⟧ **1** to flood with water so as to wash or rinse **2** to drink greedily or in large quantity **3** to feed swill to (pigs, etc.) —*vi.* to drink, esp. liquor, in large quantities —*n.* **1** garbage, table scraps, etc. mixed with liquid and used for feeding pigs, etc.; wash **2** garbage or slop **3** the act of swilling **4** a deep draft of liquor; swig —**swill′er** *n.*

swim[1] (swim) *vi.* **swam, swum, swim′ming** ⟦ME *swimmen* < OE *swimman,* akin to Ger *schwimmen* < IE base **swem-,* to move vigorously, be in motion > Welsh *chwyfio,* to move⟧ **1** to move through water by movements of the arms and legs, or of flippers, fins, tail, etc. **2** to move with a smooth, gliding motion, as though swimming **3** to float on the surface of a liquid **4** to be covered or saturated with or as with a liquid **5** to overflow; be flooded [eyes *swimming* with tears] **6** [Informal] *a)* to have far too many or far too much [an employer *swimming* in job applications] *b)* to have too much room, as within an ill-fitting item of apparel [a child *swimming* in an adult's overcoat]: with *in* —*vt.* **1** to move across (a body of water) by swimming **2** to cause to swim or float **3** to perform (a specified stroke) in swimming —*n.* **1** the act or motion of swimming **2** a period of swimming for sport [a short *swim* before lunch] **3** a distance swum or to be swum **4** *short for* SWIM BLADDER —*adj.* [Informal] of or for swimming [*swim* trunks] —**in the swim** conforming to the current fashions, or active in the main current of affairs —**swim′ma·ble** *adj.* —**swim′mer** *n.*

swim[2] (swim) *n.* ⟦ME *swime* < OE *swima,* akin to Du *zwijmen,* to faint < IE base **swei-,* to bend, turn > SWIFT⟧ the condition of being dizzy; dizzy spell —*vi.* **swam, swum, swim′ming 1** to be dizzy [the excitement made my head *swim*] **2** to have a hazy, reeling, or whirling appearance [the room *swam* before me]

swim bladder a gas-filled sac in the dorsal portion of the body cavity of most bony fishes, giving buoyancy to the body and used as an accessory, lunglike organ in lungfishes

☆**swim fin** FLIPPER (sense 2)

swim·mer·et (swim′ər et′) *n.* any of the small, abdominal appendages, or pleopods, in certain crustaceans, used primarily in swimming and for carrying eggs

swim·ming[1] (swim′iŋ) *n.* ⟦see SWIM[1]⟧ the act, practice, sport, etc. of a person or animal that swims —*adj.* **1** that swims **2** of, for, or used in swimming

swim·ming[2] (swim′iŋ) *n.* ⟦see SWIM[2]⟧ dizziness —*adj.* affected with a dizzy, whirling sensation

☆**swimming hole** a pond or a deep place in a river, creek, etc. used for swimming

swim·ming·ly (-lē) *adv.* easily and with success

☆**swimming pool** a pool of water used for swimming, esp., an artificially created pool, or tank, either indoors or outdoors and usually with water-filtering equipment

swim·suit (swim′so͞ot′) *n.* a garment worn for swimming

swim·wear (-wer′) *n.* garments worn for swimming

Swin·burne (swin′bərn), **Algernon Charles** 1837-1909; Eng. poet & critic

swin·dle (swin′dəl) *vt.* **-dled, -dling** ⟦back-form. < fol.⟧ **1** to get money or property from (another) under false pretenses; cheat; defraud **2** to get by false pretenses or fraud —*vi.* to engage in swindling others —*n.* an act of swindling; trick; cheat; fraud —*SYN.* CHEAT

swin·dler (swind′lər) *n.* ⟦Ger *schwindler* < *schwindeln,* to be dizzy, defraud, cheat < OHG *swintilon,* freq. of *swintan,* to disappear, wither, prob. < IE base *(*s*)*wendh-,* to disappear > OSlav *uvędati,* to wither⟧ a person who swindles; cheat

swine (swīn) *n., pl.* **swine** ⟦ME *swin* < OE, akin to Ger *schwein* < IE base **su-,* pig, sow > Gr *hys,* SOW[1], L *sus*⟧ **1** any of a family (Suidae) of omnivorous, artiodactylous mammals with a bristly coat and elongated, flexible snout; esp., a domesticated pig or hog: usually used collectively **2** a vicious, contemptible, or disgusting person

swine flu a virulent, highly contagious influenza infecting humans and swine

swine·herd (swīn′hʉrd′) *n.* a person who tends swine

swing (swiŋ) *vi.* **swung, swing′ing** ⟦ME *swingen* < OE *swingan,* akin to Ger *schwingen,* to brandish < IE base **sweng-,* to curve, swing⟧ **1** to sway or move backward and forward with regular movement, as a freely hanging object or a ship at anchor; oscillate **2** to walk, trot, etc. with freely swaying, relaxed movements of the limbs **3** to deliver or aim a blow; strike (*at*) **4** to turn or pivot, as on a hinge or swivel [the door *swung* open] **5** *a)* to move in a curve, esp. in order to go around something [the car *swung* around to avoid the obstacle in the road] *b)* [Informal] to move, travel, or come (*by, over to, around to,* etc.) in a casual manner, as by automobile [they *swung* by to pick us up] **6** *a)* to hang; be suspended *b)* [Informal] to be put to death by hanging **7** to move backward and forward on a SWING (*n.* 10) ☆**8** to have an exciting rhythmic quality [music that really *swings*] **9** *a)* to move or alternate, often rapidly, between extremes, or from one position or condition to another [his moods *swinging* between joy and despair, stock prices that *swung* wildly] *b)* to arrive at a final point in this way [oil prices finally *swung* into a tolerable range] ☆**10** [Slang] to be ultra-fashionable, sophisticated, active, etc., esp. in the pursuit of pleasure **11** [Slang] *a)* to engage in casual sexual relations, esp. in an open, deliberate way *b)* to exchange partners with other couples and engage in sexual activity (said esp. of married couples) —*vt.* **1** *a)* to move or wave (a weapon, tool, bat, etc.) with a sweeping motion; flourish; brandish *b)* to lift or hoist with a sweeping motion **2** to cause (a hanging object) to sway backward and forward; specif., to cause (a person on a swing) to move backward and forward by pushing or pulling the swing **3** to cause to turn or pivot, as on a hinge or swivel [to *swing* a door open] **4** to cause to hang freely, so as to be capable of easy movement [to *swing* a hammock] **5** to cause to move in a curve [to *swing* a car around a corner] **6** to head (a ship or aircraft) toward each of the points of the compass in order to determine compass error resulting from deviation ☆**7** *a)* [Slang] to cause to come about successfully; manage with the desired results [I'll take a vacation this summer if I can *swing* it] *b)* to sway; influence [bribery allegations were likely to *swing* voters' opinion] ☆**8** to play (music) in the style of swing —*n.* **1** the act or process of swinging **2** the arc, or the length of the arc, through which something swings [the *swing* of a pendulum] **3** the manner of swinging; specif., the manner of striking with a golf club, baseball bat, the arm, etc. **4** freedom to do as one wishes or is naturally inclined [given full *swing* in the matter] **5** a free, relaxed motion, as in walking **6** a sweeping blow or stroke **7** the course, development, or movement of some activity, business, etc. **8** the power, or force, behind something swung or thrown; impetus **9** rhythm, as of poetry or music **10** a device, as a seat hanging from ropes or chains, on which one can sit and swing backward and forward as a form of amusement **11** a trip or tour [a *swing* around the country] ☆**12** a style of jazz, esp. in its development from about 1935 to 1945, characterized by the use of large bands, fast tempos, and written arrangements for ensemble playing ☆**13** [Informal] *Business* regular upward and downward change in the price of stocks or in some other business activity —☆*adj.* **1** of, in, or playing swing (music) **2** ⟦see *vt.* 7b⟧ of or having the ability to sway an election or vote [independents were the majority of the *swing* vote] —**in full swing 1** in complete and active operation **2** going on without reserve or restraint —**swing′y** *adj.* **swing′i·er, swing′i·est**

SYN.—**swing** suggests the to-and-fro motion of something that is suspended, hinged, pivoted, etc. so that it is free to turn or swivel at the point or points of attachment [a *swinging* door]; **sway** describes the swinging motion of something flexible or self-balancing, whether attached or unattached, in yielding to pressure, weight, etc. [branches *swaying* in the wind]; to **oscillate** is to swing back and forth, within certain limits, in the manner of a pendulum; **vibrate** suggests the rapid, regular, back-and-forth motion of a plucked, taut string and is applied in physics to a similar movement of the particles of a fluid or elastic medium [sound *vibrating* through an amphitheater]; **fluctuate** implies continual, irregular alternating movements and is now most common in its extended sense [*fluctuating* prices]; **undulate** implies a gentle wavelike motion or form [*undulating* land]

swing bridge a bridge that can be swung back in a horizontal plane to allow tall vessels, etc. to pass

☆**swing·by** (swiŋ′bī′) *n.* a flight path of a spacecraft using the gravitational field of an intermediate planet or the destination planet to achieve a desired change in course or orbit

swinge (swinj) *vt.* **swinged, swinge′ing** ⟦ME *swengen* < OE *swengan,* caus. of *swingan,* to SWING⟧ [Archaic] to punish with blows; beat; whip

swinge·ing (swin′jiŋ) *adj.* ⟦prp. of prec.: cf. STRAPPING⟧ [Brit.] **1** forceful, often in a negative way; severe *[a swingeing* attack*]* **2** [Now Rare] huge; very large

swing·er (swiŋ′ər) *n.* **1** one that swings ☆**2** [Slang] a person who is sophisticated, ultra-fashionable, active, uninhibited, etc., esp. in the pursuit of pleasure **3** [Slang] *a)* a person who swings (see SWING, *vi.* 11*a*) *b)* either one of a couple that swings (see SWING, *vi.* 11*b*)

swing·ing (swiŋ′iŋ) *adj.* **1** that swings **2** done with a swing ☆**3** [Slang] lively, sophisticated, ultra-fashionable, etc. **4** [Slang] engaging in casual or group sexual relations —**swing′ing·ly** *adv.*

swinging door a door hung so that it can be opened in either direction and swings shut by itself

swin·gle[1] (swiŋ′gəl) *vt.* **-gled, -gling** ⟦ME *swinglen* < MDu *swinghelen* < *swinghel,* a swingle: see the *n.*⟧ to clean (flax or hemp) by beating or scraping with a swingle —*n.* ⟦ME < OE *swingele* < MDu *swinghel:* for IE base see SWING⟧ **1** a wooden, swordlike tool used to clean flax or hemp by beating or scraping **2** the swiple of a flail

☆**swin·gle**[2] (swiŋ′gəl) *n.* ⟦blend of SWINGER & SINGLE⟧ [Slang] an unmarried person who engages in casual sexual relations

swin·gle·tree (-trē′) *n.* SINGLETREE

☆**swing·man** (swiŋ′man′) *n., pl.* **-men** (-men′) *Basketball* a player able to play either of two positions effectively, esp. guard and forward

swing pass *Football* a pass thrown to a receiver, usually a running back, who is running toward a sideline

☆**swing shift** the work shift between the day and the night shifts, commonly from 4:00 P.M. to midnight

swin·ish (swīn′ish) *adj.* ⟦ME *swinisch*⟧ of, like, fit for, or characteristic of swine; beastly, piggish, coarse, etc. —**swin′ish·ly** *adv.* —**swin′ish·ness** *n.*

swink (swiŋk) *n., vi.* **swinked** or **swank, swink′ing** ⟦ME *swinken* < OE *swincan:* for IE base see SWING⟧ [Archaic] labor; toil

swipe (swīp) *n.* ⟦prob. var. of SWEEP⟧ **1** a lever or handle **2** *a)* a hard, sweeping blow *b)* [Informal] a sweeping motion, as in wiping *[give* the table a *swipe* with a rag*]* **3** [Informal] a groom for horses, esp. at a racetrack **4** the act or an instance of swiping a magnetically encoded card —*vt.* **swiped, swip′ing** ⟦< ? ON *svipa,* to whip, make a swift motion, akin to SWOOP⟧ **1** [Informal] *a)* to hit with a hard, sweeping blow *b)* to wipe (a rag, cloth, etc.) over (a surface) with a sweeping motion ☆**2** [Slang] to steal; pilfer **3** to pass (a credit card or other magnetically encoded card) across or through an electronic device that reads it —*vi.* to make a sweeping blow, stroke, or motion

swipes (swīps) *pl.n.* ⟦< prec., in obs. sense, "gulp down"⟧ [Brit. Slang] beer, esp. weak or inferior beer

swi·ple or **swip·ple** (swip′əl) *n.* ⟦ME *swepyl* < *swepen,* to SWEEP⟧ the part of a flail that strikes the grain in threshing

swirl (swurl) *vi.* ⟦ME (Scot) *swyrl,* prob. < Norw dial. *svirla,* freq. of *sverra,* to whirl: for IE base see SWARM[1]⟧ **1** to move with a twisting, whirling motion; eddy **2** to swim, or be dizzy: said of the head —*vt.* to cause to swirl; whirl —*n.* **1** a swirling motion; whirl; eddy **2** something having a twisting, curving form; twist; curl; whirl; whorl **3** dizzy confusion —**swirl′ing·ly** *adv.*

swirl·y (swur′lē) *adj.* **1** full of swirls; swirling **2** [Scot.] tangled

swish (swish) *vi.* ⟦echoic⟧ **1** to move with a sharp, hissing sound, as a cane swung through the air **2** to move with a light, brushing sound, as skirts in walking **3** *Basketball* to pass through the basket without hitting the hoop or backboard: said of a ball —*vt.* **1** to cause to swish **2** to move (liquid), esp. in the mouth, with a light, hissing or gurgling sound *[swish* the mouthwash around*]* **3** *Basketball* to cause (a ball) to swish —*n.* **1** a hissing or rustling sound **2** a movement, etc. that makes this sound ☆**3** [Slang] an effeminate male homosexual: a term of contempt and hostility —*adj.* **1** [Informal, Chiefly Brit.] fashionable ☆**2** [Slang] of, like, or for effeminate male homosexuals: a term of contempt and hostility

swish·y (-ē) *adj.* **swish′i·er, swish′i·est 1** making a hissing or rustling sound ☆**2** [Slang] designating, of, like, or for effeminate male homosexuals: a term of contempt and hostility

Swiss (swis) *adj.* ⟦Fr *Suisse* < MHG *Swiz*⟧ of Switzerland or its people or culture —*n.* **1** *pl.* **Swiss** a person born or living in Switzerland **2** [**s-**] a type of sheer fabric: see DOTTED SWISS **3** SWISS CHEESE —**the Swiss** the people of Switzerland

Swiss chard CHARD

Swiss cheese ⟦so named because orig. made in Switzerland⟧ [*sometimes* **s- c-**] a hard cheese, white or pale-yellow, with many large holes

Swiss Guards a corps of Swiss mercenary soldiers, esp. those hired as Vatican bodyguards to the pope

☆**Swiss steak** a thick cut of steak, esp. round steak, pounded with flour, browned, and cooked slowly, usually with tomatoes, onions, etc.

switch (swich) *n.* ⟦Early ModE *swits,* prob. < MDu or LowG, as in MDu *swick,* a whip, akin to ON *sveigr,* flexible stalk: for IE base see SWIFT⟧ **1** a thin, flexible twig, rod, stick, etc., esp. one used for whipping **2** the bushy part of the tail in some animals, as the cow **3** a separate tress or plait of natural or synthetic hair bound at one end and used by women as part of a coiffure **4** an abrupt, sharp, lashing movement, as with a switch **5** a device that controls the flow of current in an electric circuit, esp. by turning the current on or off or diverting it to a particular part of the circuit **6** *a)* a movable section of railroad track used in transferring a train from one set of tracks to another ☆*b)* SIDING (sense 2) **7** a shift, transference, or change, esp. if sudden or unexpected —*vt.* **1** to whip or beat with or as with a switch **2** to jerk or swing sharply; lash *[*a cow *switching* its tail*]* **3** to shift; transfer; change; turn aside; divert **4** *a)* to operate the switch of (an electric circuit) so as to connect, disconnect, or divert *b)* to turn (an electric light or appliance) *on* or *off* in this way ☆**5** to transfer (a railroad train or car) from one set of tracks to another by use of a switch; shunt **6** to change or exchange *[*to *switch* places*]* —*vi.* ☆**1** to move from or as from one set of tracks to another **2** to shift; transfer; change **3** to swing sharply; lash —**switch′er** *n.*

☆**switch·back** (swich′bak′) *n.* **1** a road or railroad following a zigzag course up a steep grade **2** [Brit.] ROLLER COASTER

☆**switch·blade (knife)** (-blād′) a large jackknife that snaps open when a release button on the handle is pressed

☆**switch·board** (-bôrd′) *n.* a board or panel equipped with apparatus for controlling the operation of a system of electric circuits, as in a telephone exchange

☆**switch cane** a small bamboo (*Arundinaria tecta*) native to the SE U.S.

☆**switch·er·oo** (swich′ə ro͞o′) *n.* ⟦SWITCH (*n.* 7) + -EROO⟧ [Slang] a sudden or unexpected shift or change, often a deliberately deceptive one

switch grass ⟦altered < *quitch grass:* see QUITCH⟧ a type of tall panic grass (*Panicum virgatum*), usually found in the North American prairie and used for fodder or as an ornamental: also written **switch′grass′** *n.*

☆**switch-hit·ter** (swich′hit′ər) *n.* **1** a baseball player who can bat from either side of home plate, usually batting right-handed against a left-handed pitcher and left-handed against a right-handed pitcher **2** [Informal] a person who is competent in two different jobs, specialties, roles, etc. **3** [Slang] a person who engages in sexual activities with both sexes; bisexual: a humorous usage

switch·man (-mən) *n., pl.* **-men** (-mən) a railroad employee who operates switches

☆**switch·yard** (-yärd′) *n.* a railroad yard where cars are shifted from one track to another by means of a system of switches, as in making up trains

Swith·in or **Swith·un** (swith′ən, swith′-), Saint (A.D. 800?-862?); Eng. prelate: his day is July 15

Switz *abbrev.* Switzerland

Swit·zer (swit′sər) *n.* ⟦MHG < *Switz, Swiz,* Switzerland⟧ **1** [Archaic] a person born or living in Switzerland **2** a Swiss mercenary soldier

Swit·zer·land (swit′sər lənd) country in WC Europe, in the Alps: 15,942 sq mi (41,290 sq km); cap. Bern: Ger. name SCHWEIZ, Fr. name SUISSE

swive (swīv) *vi., vt.* **swived, swiv′ing** [Archaic] to have sexual intercourse (with)

swiv·el (swiv′əl) *n.* ⟦ME *swiuel* < base of OE *swifan,* to revolve, turn: for IE base see SWIFT⟧ a coupling device that allows free turning of the parts attached to it; specif., a chain link made in two parts, one piece fitting like a collar below the bolt head of the other and turning freely about it —*vt.* **-eled** or **-elled, -el·ing** or **-el·ling 1** to cause to turn or rotate on or as if on a swivel **2** to fit, fasten, or support with a swivel —*vi.* to turn on or as if on a swivel

☆**swivel chair** a chair whose seat turns horizontally on a pivot in the base

swiv·et (swiv′it) *n.* ⟦< ?⟧ [Informal or Dial.] a condition of irritation, exasperation, annoyance, etc.

swiz·zle (swiz′əl) *n.* ⟦< ?⟧ any of several chilled alcoholic drinks containing liquor, sugar, lime juice, etc. mixed together as with a swizzle stick

swizzle stick a small rod for stirring mixed drinks

swol·len (swōl′ən) *vi., vt. alt. pp. of* SWELL —*adj.* increased in volume or size, as from inner pressure; blown up; distended; bulging

swoon (swo͞on) *vi.* ⟦ME *swounen,* prob. back-form. < *swoweninge,* swooning, prp. of *iswowen* < OE *geswogen,* unconscious, pp. of **swogan* < ?⟧ **1** to faint **2** to feel strong, esp. rapturous, emotion —*n.* **1** an act or instance of swooning **2** [Informal] a period of poor performance *[*a summer *swoon* in the economy*]* —**swoon′er** *n.* —**swoon′ing·ly** *adv.*

swoop (swo͞op) *vt.* ⟦ME *swopen* < OE *swapan,* to sweep along, rush, akin to Ger *schweifen,* ON *sveipa:* see SWIFT⟧ to snatch or seize suddenly, with a sweeping movement: often with *up, off,* or *away* —*vi.* to descend suddenly and swiftly, as a bird in hunting; pounce or sweep (*down* or *upon*) —*n.* the act of swooping or pouncing; sudden, violent descent

swoosh (swo͝osh, swo͞osh) *vi., vt.* ⟦echoic intens. of SWISH⟧ to move, pour, etc. with or as with a sharp rushing or whistling sound —*n.* such a sound

swop (swäp) *vt., vi., n.* **swopped, swop′ping** [Chiefly Brit.] *alt. sp. of* SWAP

sword (sôrd) *n.* ⟦ME < OE *sweord,* akin to Ger *schwert,* prob. < IE base **swer-,* to cut, pierce⟧ **1** a hand weapon having a long, sharp-pointed blade, usually

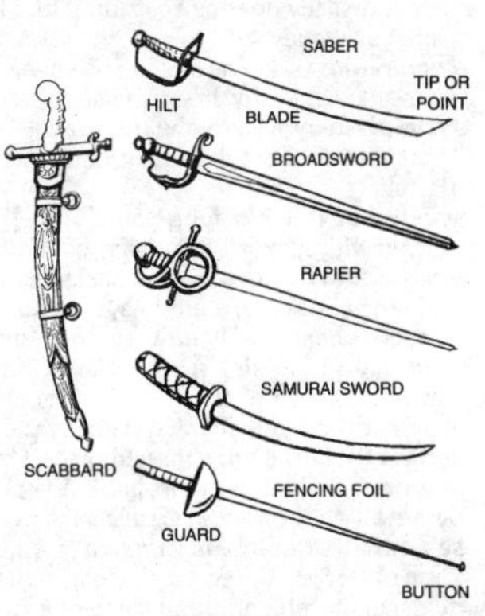

swords

with a sharp edge on one or both sides, set in a hilt; broadsword, rapier, saber, scimitar, etc. **2** *a)* the sword regarded as an instrument of death, destruction, etc. *b)* power; esp., military power *c)* the military class or profession *d)* war or warfare —**at swords' points** ready to quarrel or fight —**cross swords** **1** to fight **2** to argue violently —**put to the sword** **1** to kill with a sword or swords **2** to slaughter, esp. in war —**sword′like′** *adj.*

sword bayonet a short sword that can be mounted on a rifle for use as a bayonet

sword belt a belt from which a sword is hung

sword cane a weapon consisting of a sword or dagger concealed within a walking stick: also **sword′stick′** (-stik′) *n.*

sword dance any dance, esp. by men, involving the use of swords, esp. one performed around bare swords laid on the ground —**sword dancer**

☆**sword fern** any of various ferns with sword-shaped leaves; esp., a giant fern (*Nephrolepis biserrata*) of S Florida, with pinnate leaves

sword·fish (sôrd′fish′) *n., pl.* **-fish′** the only species of a family (Xiphiidae) of percoid fishes, a large, marine, food and game fish (*Xiphias gladius*) having a sail-like dorsal fin and a long, flat, swordlike upper jawbone

sword grass any of a number of sedges or grasses with toothed or sword-shaped leaves

sword knot a loop, now ornamental, of leather, ribbon, etc., attached to a sword hilt and worn around the wrist

sword·play (-plā′) *n.* the act or skill of using a sword in fencing or fighting

swords·man (sôrdz′mən) *n., pl.* **-men** (-mən) **1** a person who uses a sword in fencing or fighting **2** a person skilled in using a sword Also [Obs.] **sword·man** (sôrd′mən), *pl.* **-men** (-mən) —**swords′man·ship′** *n.*

sword·tail (sôrd′tāl′) *n.* any of a genus (*Xiphophorus*) of livebearers: the male has the lower caudal fin rays drawn out in a swordlike process

swore (swôr) *vi., vt. pt. of* SWEAR

sworn (swôrn) *vi., vt. pp. of* SWEAR —*adj.* bound, pledged, promised, etc. by or as by an oath

swot (swät) [Brit. Informal] *vi., vt.* **swot′ted, swot′ting** ⟦dial. var. of SWEAT⟧ to study hard; cram: often used with *up* —*n.* a person who studies hard; grind: often contemptuous —**swot′ter** *n.*

swound (swound, swo͞ond) *n., vi.* ⟦ME *swounde, swounden* < *swounen,* SWOON, with unhistoric *-d*⟧ [Archaic] swoon; faint

swum (swum) *vi., vt. pp. of* SWIM[1] & SWIM[2]

swung (swuŋ) *vi., vt. pp. & pt. of* SWING

swung dash ⟦descriptive of its shape, produced with a sweeping motion⟧ a mark (~) used, as in dictionaries, to indicate a repetition of a word or a part of a word

-sy (sē, zē) *suffix* forming adjectives and nouns with diminutive, and often mocking or pejorative, force *[artsy, cutesy]*

Syb·a·ris (sib′ə ris) ancient Greek city in S Italy, famed as a center of luxury: destroyed 510 B.C.

Syb·a·rite (-rīt′) *n.* ⟦L *Sybarita* < Gr *Sybaritēs*⟧ **1** a person born or living in ancient Sybaris **2** [**s-**] anyone very fond of self-indulgence and luxury; voluptuary —**Syb′a·rit′ic** *adj.*, **syb′a·rit′ic** (-rit′ik) —**syb′a·rit′i·cal·ly** *adv.* —**syb′a·rit′ism′** (-rīt′iz′əm) *n.*

Syb·il (sib′əl) *n.* a feminine name: see SIBYL

syc·a·mine (sik′ə min, -mīn′) *n.* ⟦L *sycaminus* < Gr *sykaminos* < Sem, as in Heb *shikma,* mulberry⟧ a tree mentioned in the Bible (Luke 17:6), believed to be a mulberry (*Morus nigra*) with dark fruit

syc·a·more (sik′ə môr′) *n.* ⟦ME *sicomore* < OFr *sicamor* < L *sycomorus* < Gr *sykomoros,* prob. altered (after *sykon,* fig + *moron,* black mulberry) < Heb *shikma,* mulberry⟧ **1** a fig tree (*Ficus sycamorus*) native to Egypt and Asia Minor, with edible fruit: the sycamore of the Bible **2** a tall maple tree (*Acer pseudoplatanus*) with yellow flowers, found in Europe and Asia ☆**3** PLANE[1], esp. a species (*P. occidentalis*) found chiefly in the E U.S.

syce (sīs) *n.* ⟦Ar *sā'is,* groom, manager < *sāsa,* to govern, administer⟧ in India, a groom (for horses)

sy·cee (sī sē′) *n.* ⟦Cantonese < Mandarin *hsi ssŭ,* fine silk: so called because it may, when heated, be spun into fine threads⟧ silver in the form of ingots, usually bearing the stamp of a banker or assayer, formerly used in China as money

sy·co·ni·um (sī kō′nē əm) *n., pl.* **-ni·a** (-nē ə) ⟦ModL < Gr *sykon,* fig⟧ *Bot.* a pear-shaped, fleshy, hollow false fruit, as of the fig

syc·o·phan·cy (sik′ə fən sē, -fan′-) *n., pl.* **-cies** ⟦L *sycophantia* < Gr *sykophantia*⟧ the behavior or character, or an act, of a sycophant; servile flattery

syc·o·phant (sik′ə fənt, -fant′) *n.* ⟦L *sycophanta* < Gr *sykophantēs,* informer, lit., maker of the sign of the fig < *sykon,* fig + *phainein,* to show: see FANTASY⟧ a person who seeks favor by flattering people of wealth or influence; parasite; toady —**syc′o·phan′tic** (-fan′tik) *adj.*, **syc′o·phant′ish** —**syc′o·phan′ti·cal·ly** *adv.*, **syc′o·phant′ish·ly** —**syc′o·phant·ism′** *n.*

sy·co·sis (sī kō′sis) *n.* ⟦ModL < Gr *sykōsis* < *sykon,* fig + *-ōsis,* -OSIS⟧ a chronic disease of the hair follicles, esp. of the beard, caused by certain staphylococci and characterized by the formation of papules and pustules

Syd·ney[1] (sid′nē) *n.* a masculine and feminine name: see SIDNEY[1]

Syd·ney[2] (sid′nē) seaport in SE Australia: capital of New South Wales

Sy·e·ne (sī ē′nē) *ancient name for* ASWAN

sy·e·nite (sī′ə nīt′) *n.* ⟦Fr *syénite* < L *Syenites (lapis),* Syenite (stone) < *Syene* < Gr *Syēnē,* prec.⟧ a grayish, intrusive igneous rock usually containing feldspar, hornblende, and some quartz —**sy′e·nit′ic** (-nit′ik) *adj.*

syl or **syll** *abbrev.* syllable

syl- (sil) *prefix* SYN-: used before *l*

syl·la·bar·y (sil′ə ber′ē) *n., pl.* **-bar′ies** ⟦ModL *syllabarium* < L *syllaba:* see SYLLABLE⟧ **1** a set or table of syllables **2** a set of written signs or characters representing the syllables that are the units in a language that uses syllabic, rather than alphabetic, writing

syl·la·bi (sil′ə bī′) *n. alt. pl. of* SYLLABUS

syl·lab·ic (si lab′ik) *adj.* ⟦LL *syllabicus* < Gr *syllabikos*⟧ **1** of a syllable or syllables **2** forming a syllable or the nucleus of a syllable; specif., *a)* being the most prominent sound in a phonemic syllable (said of a vowel) *b)* constituting the more heavily stressed part of a diphthong, as the sound of *o* in *boy* *c)* standing by itself as the nucleus of a syllable without an accompanying vowel (said of a consonant, as the sound of *l* in *tattle*) **3** designating or of a form of verse whose structure is based on the number of syllables in a line rather than on rhythm, stress, or quantity **4** pronounced with the syllables distinct —*n.* **1** a syllabic sound **2** [*pl.*] syllabic verse —**syl·lab′i·cal·ly** *adv.*

syl·lab·i·cate (si lab′i kāt′) *vt.* **-cat′ed, -cat′ing** SYLLABIFY —**syl·lab′i·ca′tion** *n.*

syl·lab·i·fy (si lab′ə fī′) *vt.* **-fied′, -fy′ing** ⟦back-form. < *syllabification* < L *syllaba,* SYLLABLE + -FICATION⟧ to form or divide into syllables —**syl·lab′i·fi·ca′tion** *n.*

syl·la·bism (sil′ə biz′əm) *n.* ⟦< L *syllaba,* fol. + -ISM⟧ **1** the use of syllabic characters, rather than letters, in writing **2** division into syllables

syl·la·ble (sil′ə bəl) *n.* ⟦ME *sillable* < OFr *sillabe* < L *syllaba* < Gr *syllabē,* a syllable, lit., that which holds together < *syllambanein,* to join < *syn-,* together + *lambanein,* to hold < IE base *(*s*)*lagw-,* to grasp > LATCH⟧ **1** a word or part of a word pronounced with a single, uninterrupted sounding of the voice; unit of pronunciation, consisting of a single sound of great sonority (usually a vowel) and generally one or more sounds of lesser sonority (usually consonants) **2** any of the parts into which a written word is often divided, as at the end of a line, in approximate conformity to the spoken syllables **3** the least bit of expression; slightest detail, as of something said —*vt.* **-bled, -bling** to pronounce in or as in syllables

syl·la·bub (sil′ə bub′) *n.* ⟦Early ModE *solybubbe* < ?⟧ **1** a dessert or beverage made of sweetened milk or cream mixed with wine or cider and beaten to a froth **2** a kind of eggnog made of cream and beaten egg whites whipped with brandy, rum, etc., often thickened for use as a topping or dessert

syl·la·bus (sil′ə bəs) *n., pl.* **-bus·es** or **-bi′** (-bī′) ⟦ModL < LL(Ec), a list, register (prob. false form for *syllaba,* SYLLABLE), mistaken reading of L *sillybus,* altered < *sittybus,* strip of parchment used as a label < Gr *sittybos,* strip of leather⟧ **1** a summary or outline, esp. of a course of study **2** *Law* brief notes preceding and explaining the decision or points of law in the written report of an adjudged case

syl·lep·sis (si lep′sis) *n., pl.* **-ses′** (-sēz′) ⟦L < Gr *syllēpsis,* a putting together < *syllambanein:* see SYLLABLE⟧ a grammatical construction in which a single word is used in a syntactic relationship with two or more words in the same sentence, though it can agree with only one of them in gender, number, or case (Ex.: either they or I am wrong) —**syl·lep′tic** *adj.*

syl·lo·gism (sil′ə jiz′əm) *n.* ⟦ME *silogisme* < MFr < L *syllogismus* < Gr *syllogismos,* a reckoning together < *syllogizesthai,* to reckon together, sum up < *syn-,* together + *logizesthai,* to reason < *logos,* word: see LOGIC⟧ **1** an argument or form of reasoning in which two statements or premises are made and a logical conclusion is drawn from them (Ex.: All mammals are warmblooded [*major premise*]; whales are mammals [*minor premise*]; therefore, whales are warmblooded [*conclusion*]) **2** reasoning from the general to the particular; deductive logic —**syl′lo·gis′tic** *adj.*, **syl′lo·gis′ti·cal** —**syl′lo·gis′ti·cal·ly** *adv.*

syl·lo·gize (sil′ə jīz′) *vi., vt.* **-gized′, -giz′ing** ⟦ME *sylogysen* < ML *syllogizare*⟧ to reason or infer by the use of syllogisms

sylph (silf) *n.* ⟦ModL *sylphus,* coined (prob. by PARACELSUS) < ? L *sylva, silva* (see SYLVAN) + *nympha,* NYMPH⟧ **1** in Paracelsus's alchemical system, any of a class of mortal, soulless beings that inhabit the air **2** a slender, graceful woman or girl —**sylph′like′** *adj.*

sylph·id (sil′fid) *n.* ⟦Fr *sylphide:* see prec. & -ID⟧ a small or young sylph —**sylph′id·ine** (-fi din, -dīn′) *adj.*

syl·va (sil′və) *n., pl.* **-vas** or **-vae** (-vē) *alt. sp. of* SILVA

syl·van (sil′vən) *n.* ⟦Fr *sylvan,* forest deity < L *Silvanus* < *silva,* forest, prob. < IE *(*k*)*selwa-* > Gr *xylon,* wood⟧ one who lives in the woods —*adj.* **1** of or characteristic of the woods or forest **2** living or found in the woods or forest **3** wooded

syl·van·ite (sil′və nīt′) *n.* ⟦after (TRAN)SYLVAN(IA), where first found + -ITE[1]⟧ a gray or silvery telluride of gold and silver $(Ag,Au)Te_2$, crystallizing in the monoclinic system

syl·vat·ic (sil vat′ik) *adj.* ⟦L *silvaticus* < *silva:* see SYLVAN⟧ of or having to do with a disease present in a population of animals in the wild *[sylvatic plague]*

Syl·ves·ter (sil ves′tər) *n.* ⟦L *Silvester* < *silvestris,* of a wood or forest < *silva,* wood⟧ a masculine name

Syl·vi·a (sil′vē ə) *n.* ⟦L *Silvia* < *silva:* see SYLVAN⟧ a feminine name: dim. *Sylvie*

syl·vi·cul·ture (sil′vi kul′chər) *n. alt. sp. of* SILVICULTURE

syl·vite (sil′vīt′) *n.* ⟦earlier *sylvine* < Fr < ModL *sal digestivus sylvii,* lit., digestive salt of Sylvius (after Franz de la Boë *Sylvius,* 1614-72, physician at Leyden)⟧ a white or colorless mineral, KCl, that is the chief ore of the potassium used to make fertilizers

sym *abbrev.* **1** symbol **2** symphony

sym- (sim) *prefix* SYN-: used before *b, m,* or *p [symmetalism, sympodium]*

sym·bi·ont (sim′bī änt′, -bē-) ***n.*** ⟦Ger < Gr *symbiountos,* prp. of *symbioun:* see fol.⟧ an organism living in a state of symbiosis —**sym′bi·on′tic** ***adj.***

sym·bi·o·sis (sim′bī ō′sis, -bē-) ***n.*** ⟦ModL < Gr *symbiōsis* < *symbioun,* to live together < *syn-,* together + *bios,* life: see BIO-⟧ **1** *Biol.* the intimate living together of two kinds of organisms, esp. if such association is of mutual advantage: see COMMENSALISM, MUTUALISM, PARASITISM **2** a similar relationship of mutual interdependence —**sym′bi·ot′ic** (-ät′ik) ***adj.***

sym·bol (sim′bəl) ***n.*** ⟦< Fr & L: Fr *symbole* < L *symbolus, symbolum* < Gr *symbolon,* token, pledge, sign by which one infers a thing < *symballein,* to throw together, compare < *syn-,* together + *ballein,* to throw: see BALL[2]⟧ **1** something that stands for, represents, or suggests another thing; specif., *a)* an object used to represent something abstract [the dove is a *symbol* of peace] *b)* a stylized emblem [an upside-down Y is a peace *symbol*] *c)* a person who represents a quality, movement, etc. [a sex *symbol*] **2** a written or printed mark, letter, abbreviation, etc. standing for an object, quality, process, quantity, etc., as in music, mathematics, or chemistry **3** *Psychoanalysis* an act or object representing an unconscious desire that has been repressed —***vt.*** **-boled** or **-bolled**, **-bol·ing** or **-bol·ling** SYMBOLIZE

sym·bol·ic (sim bäl′ik) ***adj.*** ⟦LL *symbolicus* < Gr *symbolikos*⟧ **1** of or expressed in a symbol or symbols **2** that serves as a symbol (*of* something) **3** characterized by symbolism Also **sym·bol′i·cal** —**sym·bol′i·cal·ly** ***adv.***

symbolic logic a modern type of formal logic using special symbols for propositions, quantifiers, and relationships among propositions and concerned with the elucidation of permissible operations upon such symbols

sym·bol·ism (sim′bə liz′əm) ***n.*** **1** the representation of things by use of symbols, esp. in art or literature **2** a system of symbols **3** symbolic meaning **4** [*usually* **S-**] the theories or practices of the Symbolists

sym·bol·ist (-list) ***n.*** **1** a person who uses symbols, as in art or literature **2** [*usually* **S-**] any of a group of French and Belgian writers and artists of the late 19th cent. who rejected realism and tried to express ideas, emotions, and attitudes by the use of symbolic words, figures, objects, etc. **3** a person who studies or is expert in interpreting symbols or symbolism —**sym′bol·is′tic** ***adj.*** —**sym′bol·is′ti·cal·ly** ***adv.***

sym·bol·ize (-līz′) ***vt.*** **-ized′**, **-iz′ing** ⟦Fr *symboliser* < ML *symbolizare*⟧ **1** to be a symbol of; typify; stand for **2** to represent by a symbol or symbols —***vi.*** to use symbols —**sym′bol·i·za′tion** ***n.*** —**sym′bol·iz′er** ***n.***

sym·bol·o·gy (sim bäl′ə jē) ***n.*** ⟦SYMBO(L) + -LOGY⟧ **1** the study or interpretation of symbols **2** representation or expression by means of symbols; symbolism

sym·met·al·lism (sim met′'l iz′əm) ***n.*** ⟦< SYM- (var. of SYN-) + METAL + -ISM⟧ the use of two or more metals as a monetary standard

sym·met·ri·cal (si me′tri kəl) ***adj.*** ⟦SYMMETR(Y) + -ICAL⟧ having or showing symmetry; specif., *a) Bot.* that can be divided into similar halves by a plane passing through the center; also, having the same number of parts in each whorl of leaves (said of a flower) *b) Chem.* exhibiting a regular repeated pattern of atoms in the structural formula; specif., designating a compound (benzene derivative) in which substitution takes place at the alternate carbon atoms *c) Logic, Math.* designating an equation, relation, etc. whose terms can be interchanged without affecting its validity *d) Med.* affecting corresponding parts of the body simultaneously in the same way (said of a disease, infection, etc.) Also **sym·met′ric** —**sym·met′ri·cal·ly** ***adv.***

sym·me·trize (sim′ə trīz′) ***vt.*** **-trized′**, **-triz′ing** to make symmetrical —**sym′me·tri·za′tion** ***n.***

sym·me·try (sim′ə trē) ***n.***, *pl.* **-tries** ⟦< MFr or L: MFr *symmetrie* (Fr *symétrie*) < L *symmetria* < Gr < *symmetros,* measured together < *syn-,* together + *metron,* a MEASURE⟧ **1** condition of being symmetrical; specif., *a)* similarity of form or arrangement on either side of a dividing line or plane *b)* correspondence of opposite parts in size, shape, position, etc. **2** balance or beauty of form or proportion, esp. as resulting from such correspondence

SYN.—**symmetry**, with reference to the interrelation of parts to form an aesthetically pleasing whole, strictly implies correspondence in the form, size, arrangement, etc. of parts on either side of a median line or plane; **proportion** implies a gracefulness that results from the measured fitness in size or arrangement of parts to each other or to the whole; **harmony** implies such agreement or proportionate arrangement of parts in size, color, form, etc. as to make a pleasing impression; **balance** suggests the offsetting or contrasting of parts so as to produce an aesthetic equilibrium in the whole

Sym·onds (sim′ənz, -əndz), **John Ad·ding·ton** (ad′iŋ tən) 1840-93; Eng. poet, writer, & scholar

sym·pa·thec·to·my (sim′pə thek′tə mē) ***n.***, *pl.* **-mies** ⟦< fol. + -ECTOMY⟧ the interruption by surgical means of part of the sympathetic nervous system

sym·pa·thet·ic (sim′pə thet′ik) ***adj.*** ⟦ModL *sympatheticus* < Gr *sympatheia,* SYMPATHY, infl. by Gr *pathētikos,* PATHETIC⟧ **1** of, expressing, resulting from, feeling, or showing sympathy; sympathizing **2** in agreement with one's tastes, mood, feelings, disposition, etc.; congenial **3** showing favor, approval, or agreement [to be *sympathetic* to a plan] **4** *Physiol.* designating or of that part of the autonomic nervous system whose nerves originate in the lumbar and thoracic regions of the spinal cord and that is especially concerned with mediating the involuntary response to alarm, as by speeding the heart rate, raising the blood pressure, and dilating the pupils of the eyes: these nerves oppose the parasympathetic nerves in the regulation of many body processes **5** *Acoustics, Physics* designating or of vibrations, sounds, etc. caused by other vibrations of the same period transmitted from a neighboring vibrating body —**SYN.** TENDER[1] —**sym′pa·thet′i·cal·ly** ***adv.***

sympathetic ink INVISIBLE INK

sym·pa·thize (sim′pə thīz′) ***vi.*** **-thized′**, **-thiz′ing** ⟦Fr *sympathiser*⟧ **1** to share or understand the feelings or ideas of another **2** to feel or express sympathy, esp. in pity or compassion; commiserate **3** [Now Rare] to be in harmony or accord —**sym′pa·thiz′ing·ly** ***adv.***

sym·pa·thiz·er (-thī′zər) ***n.*** one who sympathizes with another or others; specif., one who approves of or agrees with an idea, cause, etc. of others [Confederate *sympathizers* in Northern states]

sym·pa·tho·lyt·ic (sim′pə thō lit′ik) ***adj.*** ⟦SYMPATH(ETIC) + -O- + -LYTIC⟧ having the effect of decreasing the activity of the sympathetic nervous system: said of certain drugs, chemicals, etc.

sym·pa·tho·mi·met·ic (-mi met′ik, -mī-) ***adj.*** ⟦SYMPATH(ETIC) + -O- + MIMETIC⟧ having an effect similar to that produced when the sympathetic nervous system is stimulated: said of certain drugs, chemicals, etc.

sym·pa·thy (sim′pə thē) ***n.***, *pl.* **-thies** ⟦L *sympathia* < Gr *sympatheia* < *syn-,* together + *pathos,* feeling: see PATHOS⟧ **1** sameness of feeling; affinity between persons or of one person for another **2** [Now Rare] agreement in qualities; harmony; accord **3** a mutual liking or understanding arising from sameness of feeling **4** *a)* an entering into, or the ability to enter into, another person's mental state, feelings, emotions, etc. *b)* pity or compassion felt for another's trouble, suffering, etc. **5** [*often pl.*] a feeling of approval of or agreement with an idea, cause, etc. **6** *Physics* a relation or harmony between bodies of such a nature that vibrations in one cause sympathetic vibrations in the other or others **7** *Physiol.* a relation between body parts of such a nature that a disorder, pain, etc. in one induces a similar effect in another —**SYN.** PITY

sympathy card a greeting card bearing a message of condolence, sent usually to relatives of a recently deceased person

sympathy strike a strike by a group of workers in support of another group on strike

sym·pa·ti·co (sim pät′i kō, -pat′-) ***adj.*** *alt. sp. of* SIMPATICO

sym·pat·ric (sim pa′trik) ***adj.*** ⟦SYM- (var. of SYN-) + PATR(I)- + -IC⟧ *Ecol.* of or pertaining to closely related species of organisms occurring in the same geographic area —**sym·pat′ri·cal·ly** ***adv.*** —**sym·pat·ry** (sim′pə trē) ***n.***

sym·pet·al·ous (sim pet′'l əs) ***adj.*** ⟦SYM- (var. of SYN-) + PETALOUS⟧ *Bot.* GAMOPETALOUS

sym·phon·ic (sim fän′ik) ***adj.*** **1** of, like, or for a symphony or symphony orchestra **2** of or having to do with harmony of sound —**sym·phon′i·cal·ly** ***adv.***

symphonic poem a musical composition for symphony orchestra, usually in one movement and based on a literary, historical, or other nonmusical subject

sym·pho·ni·ous (sim fō′nē əs) ***adj.*** ⟦< L *symphonia,* harmony (see SYMPHONY) + -OUS⟧ [Now Rare] harmonious, esp. in sound —**sym·pho′ni·ous·ly** ***adv.***

sym·pho·nist (sim′fə nist) ***n.*** **1** a composer of symphonies **2** a member of a symphony orchestra

sym·pho·ny (sim′fə nē) ***n.***, *pl.* **-nies** ⟦ME *symfonye* < OFr *simphonie* < L *symphonia* < Gr *symphōnia* < *syn-,* together + *phōnē,* a sound: see PHONO-⟧ **1** harmony of sounds, esp. of instruments **2** harmony of any kind, esp. of color **3** anything, as a picture, characterized by harmonious composition **4** *Music a)* an extended composition for full orchestra, usually having several movements *b)* [Historical] an instrumental passage in a composition that is largely vocal or choral *c) short for* SYMPHONY ORCHESTRA *d)* [Informal] a concert by a symphony orchestra

symphony orchestra a large orchestra comprising string, woodwind, brass, and percussion sections for playing symphonic works

sym·phy·sis (sim′fə sis) ***n.***, *pl.* **-ses′** (-sēz′) ⟦ModL < Gr, a growing together < *syn-,* with + *phyein,* to grow: see BE⟧ a growing together or fusing; specif., *a) Anat.* the growing together of bones originally separate, as of the two halves of the lower jaw or the two pubic bones; also, the line of junction and fusion of such bones *b) Bot.* the growing together of similar parts of a plant; coalescence —**sym·phys′e·al** (-fiz′ē əl) ***adj.***, **sym·phys′i·al**

sym·po·di·um (sim pō′dē əm) ***n.***, *pl.* **-di·a** (-ə) ⟦ModL: see SYM- & -PODIUM⟧ *Bot.* an apparent stem actually made up of a series of axillary branches growing one from another, giving the effect of a simple stem, as in the grape —**sym·po′di·al** ***adj.***

sym·po·si·ac (sim pō′zē ak′) ***adj.*** ⟦L *symposiacus,* belonging to a banquet, convivial < Gr *symposiakos*⟧ of, having the nature of, or appropriate to a symposium

sym·po·si·arch (-ärk′) ***n.*** ⟦Gr *symposiarchos,* master of a feast: see SYMPOSIUM & -ARCH⟧ the master or director of a symposium, esp. in ancient Greece

sym·po·si·ast (-ast′) ***n.*** ⟦< fol. + *-ast,* as in ENTHUSIAST⟧ a person participating in a symposium

sym·po·si·um (-əm) ***n.***, *pl.* **-si·ums** or **-si·a** (-ə) ⟦L < Gr *symposion* < *syn-,* together + *posis,* a drinking < IE base **pō-,* to drink > L *potio*⟧ **1** in ancient Greece, a drinking party at which there was intellectual conversation **2** any meeting or social gathering at which ideas are freely exchanged **3** a conference organized for the discussion of some particular subject **4** a collection of opinions, esp. a published group of essays, on a given subject

symp·tom (simp′təm) ***n.*** ⟦altered (infl. by LL or Gr) < ME *symthoma* < ML *sinthoma* < LL *symptoma* < Gr *symptōma,* anything that has befallen one, casualty < *sympiptein,* to fall together, happen < *syn-,* together + *piptein,* to fall: see FEATHER⟧ **1** any circumstance, event, or condition that accompanies something and indicates its existence or occurrence; sign; indication **2** *Med.* any condition accompanying or resulting from a disease or a physical disorder and serving as an aid in diagnosis

symp·to·mat·ic (simp′tə mat′ik) ***adj.*** ⟦Fr *symptomatique* < Gr *symptōmatikos,* accidental⟧ **1** of or having to do with symptoms **2** that constitutes a symptom, as of a disease; indicative (*of*) **3** in accordance with symptoms [*a symptomatic* treatment] —**symp′to·mat′i·cal·ly** ***adv.***

symp·tom·a·tize (simp′te mə tīz′) ***vt.*** **-tized′**, **-tiz′ing** to be a symptom or sign of; indicate: also **symp′tom·ize′** (-təm īz′)

symp·tom·a·tol·o·gy (simp′tə mə täl′ə jē) ***n.*** ⟦ModL *symptomatologia* < Gr *symptōma* (gen. *symptomatos*), SYMPTOM + *-logia,* -LOGY⟧ **1** symptoms of disease, collectively **2** all the symptoms of a given disease

syn *abbrev.* **1** synonym **2** synonymous **3** synonymy

syn- (sin) ⟦Gr < *syn,* with, earlier *xyn*⟧ *prefix* with, together, at the same time [*synesthesia, syncarpous*]: it becomes, by assimilation, *syl-* before *l*; *sym-* before *b, m,* or *p*; and *sys-* before *s* or in words in which it reflects original combining with a word containing an initial aspirate, or (h) sound

syn·aes·the·sia (sin′əs thē′zhə, -zhē ə, -zē ə) ***n.*** *alt. sp. of* SYNESTHESIA —**syn′aes·thet′ic** (-thet′ik) ***adj.***

syn·a·gogue (sin′ə gäg′, -gôg′) ***n.*** ⟦ME *sinagoge* < OFr < LL(Ec) *synagoga* < Gr(Ec) *synagōgē* < Gr, a bringing together, assembly < *synagein,* to bring together < *syn-,* together + *agein,* to do: see ACT[1]⟧ **1** an assembly of Jews for worship and religious study **2** a building or place used by Jews for worship, religious study, and, often, community activity **3** the Jewish religion as organized in such local congregations Also **syn′a·gog′** —**syn′a·gog′al** (-gäg′əl, -gôg′-) ***adj.***

syn·apse (sin′aps′, si naps′) ***n.*** ⟦ModL *synapsis:* see fol.⟧ the minute space between a nerve cell and another nerve cell, a muscle cell, etc., through which nerve impulses are transmitted from one to the other

syn·ap·sis (si nap′sis) ***n.,*** *pl.* **-ses′** (-sēz′) ⟦ModL < Gr, junction, connection < *syn-,* together + *apsis,* a joining < *haptein,* to join⟧ **1** *Genetics* the association side by side of homologous maternal and paternal paired chromosomes in the early stages of meiosis **2** *Physiol.* SYNAPSE —**syn·ap′tic** (-tik) ***adj.***

syn·ap·to·some (si nap′tə sōm′) ***n.*** ⟦see prec. & -SOME[3]⟧ a tiny sac of special cellular materials found at a synapse —**syn·ap′to·so′mal** ***adj.***

syn·ar·thro·sis (sin′är thrō′sis) ***n.,*** *pl.* **-ses′** (-sēz′) ⟦ModL < Gr *synarthrōsis,* a being jointed together < *synarthroun,* to link together < *syn-,* with + *arthron,* a joint: see ART[1]⟧ *Anat.* any of various immovable articulations, or joints —**syn′ar·thro′di·al** (-dē əl) ***adj.***

sync or **synch** (siŋk) [Informal] ***vt., vi.*** *short for* SYNCHRONIZE —***n.*** *short for* SYNCHRONIZATION —**in sync** (or **synch**) **1** in synchronization (*with*) **2** in harmony (*with*); compatible —**out of sync** (or **synch**) **1** out of synchronization (*with*) **2** discordant; incompatible

syn·car·pous (sin kär′pəs) ***adj.*** ⟦see SYN- & -CARPOUS⟧ *Bot.* composed of carpels growing together —**syn′car·py** ***n.***

syn·chro (siŋ′krō, sin′-) ***n.,*** *pl.* **-chros** ⟦< fol.⟧ a system consisting of a generator and one or more motorlike devices connected electrically so that, upon receipt of a signal from the generator, the rotors of the synchronous motors always assume positions identical with that of the generator rotor

syn·chro- (siŋ′krō, sin′-) *combining form* synchronized, synchronous [*synchromesh*]

☆**syn·chro·cy·clo·tron** (siŋ′krō sī′klə trän′, sin′-) ***n.*** a modified cyclotron in which the frequency of the accelerating voltage is modulated to take into account the increase in the relativistic mass of the particle as it reaches high energies

syn·chro·mesh (siŋ′krə mesh′, sin′-) ***adj.*** ⟦SYNCHRO- + MESH⟧ a device in a transmission system that automatically brings the gears to be meshed to about the same speed of rotation before a shift occurs

syn·chro·nal (siŋ′krə nəl, sin′-) ***adj.*** SYNCHRONOUS

syn·chron·ic (sin krän′ik) ***adj.*** **1** SYNCHRONOUS **2** of or concerned with language, mores, etc. at a given time, without reference to historical antecedents: cf. DIACHRONIC —**syn·chron′i·cal·ly** ***adv.***

syn·chro·nic·i·ty (siŋ′krə nis′ə tē, sin′-) ***n.,*** *pl.* **-ties** ⟦prec. + -ITY: used extensively, and perhaps coined, by C. G. JUNG⟧ the fact or state of being synchronous; simultaneous occurrence

synchronic linguistics the branch of linguistics that analyzes the structure of a language at a given point in its history

syn·chro·nism (siŋ′krə niz′əm, sin′-) ***n.*** ⟦ModL *synchronismus* < Gr *synchronismos* < *synchronos:* see fol.⟧ **1** the fact or state of being synchronous; simultaneous occurrence **2** a chronological, usually tabular, listing of persons or events in history, showing synchronous existence or occurrence —**syn′chro·nis′tic** ***adj.*** —**syn′chro·nis′ti·cal·ly** ***adv.***

syn·chro·nize (siŋ′krə nīz′, sin′-) ***vi.*** **-nized′**, **-niz′ing** ⟦Gr *synchronizein,* to be contemporary with < *synchronos,* contemporary < *syn-,* together + *chronos,* time⟧ to move or occur at the same time or rate; be synchronous —***vt.*** **1** to cause to agree in time or rate of speed; regulate (clocks, a flash gun and camera shutter, etc.) so as to make synchronous **2** to assign (events, etc.) to the same date or period; represent as or show to be coincident or simultaneous **3** *Film* to align (the picture and soundtrack) —**syn′chro·ni·za′tion** ***n.*** —**syn′chro·niz′er** ***n.***

synchronized swimming a sport in which the movements of one or more swimmers are synchronized to musical accompaniment

syn·chro·nous (-nəs) ***adj.*** ⟦LL *synchronus* < Gr *synchronos:* see SYNCHRONIZE⟧ **1** happening at the same time; occurring together; simultaneous **2** having the same period between movements, occurrences, etc.; having the same rate and phase, as vibrations **3** *Elec.* designating or of a machine, specif. an alternating-current motor, generator, or converter, whose normal operating speed is exactly proportional to the frequency of the current in the circuit to which it is connected —**SYN.** CONTEMPORARY —**syn′chro·nous·ly** ***adv.*** —**syn′chro·nous·ness** ***n.***

syn·chro·ny (siŋ′krə nē, sin′-) ***n.*** SYNCHRONISM (sense 1)

syn·chro·scope (siŋ′krə skōp′, sin′-) ***n.*** ⟦SYNCHRO(NISM) + -SCOPE⟧ an electronic device for measuring the degree to which two or more systems, machines, or parts are synchronous or synchronized

☆**syn·chro·tron** (-trän′) ***n.*** ⟦SYNCHRO- + (ELEC)TRON⟧ a circular machine for accelerating charged particles to very high energies through the use of a magnetic field in combination with a high-frequency electrostatic field

synchrotron radiation the electromagnetic radiation given off by high-energy particles, as electrons, as they spiral at a speed close to the speed of light in a strong magnetic field, as in a synchrotron or in a galaxy

syn·cli·nal (sin klī′nəl) ***adj.*** ⟦< Gr *synklinein,* to incline together < *syn-,* together + *klinein,* to LEAN[1]⟧ **1** sloping downward in opposite directions so as to meet **2** of, formed by, or forming a syncline

syn·cline (sin′klīn′) ***n.*** ⟦back-form. < prec.⟧ *Geol.* a down fold in stratified rocks from whose central axis the beds rise upward and outward in opposite directions: opposed to ANTICLINE

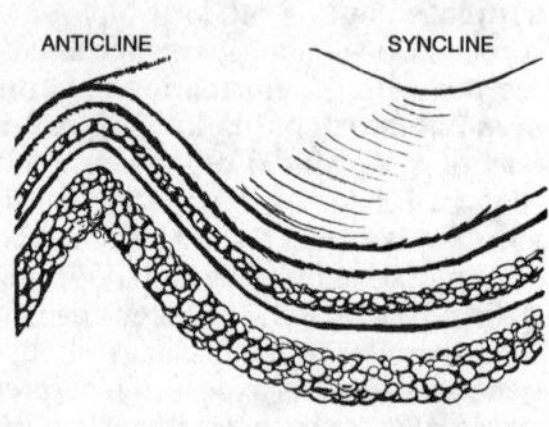

syn·cli·no·ri·um (sin′klī nôr′ē əm, siŋ′-) ***n.,*** *pl.* **-ri·a** (-ə) ⟦ModL < prec. + Gr *oros,* mountain < IE **or-,* var. of base **er-,* to set in motion, raise > RUN⟧ *Geol.* a large, generally synclinal structure consisting of a succession of subordinate synclines and anticlines: opposed to ANTICLINORIUM

syn·co·pate (siŋ′kə pāt′, sin′-) ***vt.*** **-pat′ed**, **-pat′ing** ⟦< ML *syncopatus,* pp. of *syncopare,* to cut short < LL, to swoon < *syncope:* see SYNCOPE⟧ **1** to shorten (a word) by syncope **2** *Music a)* to shift (the regular accent) as by beginning a tone on an unaccented beat and continuing it through the next accented beat, or on the last half of a beat and continuing it through the first half of the following beat *b)* to use such shifted accents in (a musical composition, passage, rhythmic pattern, etc.) —**syn′co·pa′tor** ***n.***

syn·co·pa·tion (siŋ′kə pā′shən, sin′-) ***n.*** **1** a syncopating or being syncopated **2** syncopated music, a syncopated rhythm, etc. **3** *Gram.* SYNCOPE

syn·co·pe (siŋ′kə pē, sin′-) ***n.*** ⟦LL < Gr *synkopē* < *syn-,* together + *koptein,* to cut < IE base **(s)kep-* > CAPON⟧ **1** loss of sounds or letters from the middle of a word, as in the pronunciation of *Gloucester* (gläs′tər) **2** temporary loss of consciousness, caused by an inadequate flow of blood to the brain —**syn′co·pal** ***adj.***

syn·cre·tism (siŋ′krə tiz′əm, sin′-) ***n.*** ⟦Fr *syncrétisme* < ModL *syncretismus* < Gr *synkrētismos,* union of two parties against a third, orig., a joining of Cretans < *syn-,* with, together + *Krētes,* pl. of *Krēs,* Cretan⟧ **1** the combination or reconciliation of differing beliefs or practices in religion, philosophy, etc. **2** *Linguis. a)* the merging into one of two or more differently inflected forms *b)* the resulting identity between two or more inflected forms of a word (Ex.: past tense *twisted* in "She twisted the handle" and past participle *twisted* in "the twisted vine") —**syn·cret·ic** (sin kret′ik) ***adj.,*** **syn·cre·tis·tic** (siŋ′krə tis′tik, sin′-) —**syn′cre·tist** ***n., adj.***

syn·cre·tize (siŋ′krə tīz′, sin′-) ***vt., vi.*** **-tized′**, **-tiz′ing** ⟦ModL *syncretizare* < Gr *synkrētizein,* back-form. < *synkrētismos:* see prec.⟧ to join together in a syncretic way

syn·cy·ti·um (sin sish′ē əm) ***n.,*** *pl.* **-ti·a** (-ə) ⟦SYN- + CYT(O)- + -IUM⟧ a mass of protoplasm containing scattered nuclei that are not separated into distinct cells, as in striated muscle fibers —**syn·cy′ti·al** (-əl) ***adj.***

syn·dac·tyl or **syn·dac·tyle** (sin dak′təl) ***adj.*** ⟦Fr *syndactyle* < Gr *syn-,* together + *daktylos,* finger, toe: see DACTYL⟧ having two or more digits united, as by webbing —***n.*** a syndactyl mammal or bird —**syn·dac′tyl·ism′** ***n.***

syn·des·mo·sis (sin′des mō′sis) ***n.,*** *pl.* **-ses′** (-sēz′) ⟦ModL < Gr *syndesmos,* ligament < *syndein,* to bind together: see fol.⟧ the joining of adjacent bones as by ligaments —**syn′des·mot′ic** (-mät′ik) ***adj.***

syn·det·ic (sin det′ik) ***adj.*** ⟦Gr *syndetikos* < *syndein,* to tie up < *syn-,* together + *dein,* to bind: see DIADEM⟧ connecting or connected by means of conjunctions; connective

syn·dic (sin′dik) ***n.*** ⟦Fr < LL *syndicus,* representative of a corporation < Gr *syndikos,* helping in a court of justice, hence, defendant's advocate, judge < *syn-,* together + *dikē,* justice < IE base **deik-,* to point out > DICTION, TOKEN⟧ **1** [Brit.] a business agent or manager, esp. of a university **2** any of various government officials in some European countries; esp., a civil magistrate or the like

syn·di·cal (sin′di kəl) ***adj.*** **1** of a syndic **2** of syndicalism

syn·di·cal·ism (-iz′əm) ***n.*** ⟦Fr *syndicalisme* < *syndical,* of a syndic or labor union (*chambre syndicale*) < *syndic:* see SYNDIC⟧ a movement in trade unionism, esp. in Europe between 1890 and 1920, that sought to bring the means of production under the control of federations of labor unions by means of general strikes and other forms of direct action —**syn′di·cal·ist** ***adj., n.*** —**syn′di·cal·is′tic** ***adj.***

syn·di·cate (sin′də kit; *for v.*, -kāt′) ***n.*** ⟦Fr *syndicat* < *syndic*, SYNDIC⟧ **1** a group or council of syndics **2** *a)* an association of individuals or corporations formed to carry out some large-scale project requiring much capital *b)* any group organized to further some undertaking ☆*c)* an informal association of criminals controlling a network of vice, gambling, etc. ☆*d)* a group of newspapers, owned as a chain ☆**3** an organization that sells special articles or features for publication by many newspapers or periodicals —***vt.*** **-cat′ed**, **-cat′ing** **1** to manage as or form into a syndicate ☆**2** *a)* to sell (an article, feature, etc.) through a syndicate for publication in many newspapers or periodicals *b)* to sell (a program, series, etc.) to a number of radio or TV stations —***vi.*** to form a syndicate —**SYN.** MONOPOLY —**syn′di·ca′tion** ***n.*** —**syn′di·ca′tor** ***n.***

syn·drome (sin′drōm′) ***n.*** ⟦ModL < Gr *syndromē* < *syn-*, with + *dramein*, to run: see DROMEDARY⟧ **1** a number of symptoms occurring together and characterizing a specific disease or condition **2** any set of characteristics regarded as identifying a certain type, condition, etc. —**syn·drom′ic** (-drō′mik, -dräm′ik) ***adj.***

syne (sīn) [Scot.] ***adv.*** ⟦Scot < ME *sithen:* see SINCE⟧ since; ago — ***conj.***, ***prep.*** since

syn·ec·do·che (si nek′də kē) ***n.*** ⟦LME, altered (infl. by L) < *synodoche* < ML *sinodoche*, for L *synecdoche* < Gr *synekdochē*, lit., a receiving together < *synekdechesthai*, to receive together < *syn-*, together + *ekdechesthai*, to receive < *ek-*, from + *dechesthai*, to receive < IE base **dek̑-* > DECENT⟧ a figure of speech in which a part is used for a whole, an individual for a class, a material for a thing, or the reverse of any of these (Ex.: *bread* for *food, the army* for *a soldier*, or *copper* for *a penny*) —**syn·ec·doch·ic** (sin′ek däk′ik) ***adj.***, **syn′ec·doch′i·cal**

syn·e·col·o·gy (sin′i käl′ə jē) ***n.*** ⟦Ger *synökologie* < *syn-*, SYN- + *ökologie*, ECOLOGY⟧ the ecological study of different natural communities or ecosystems: cf. AUTECOLOGY

syn·er·e·sis (si ner′ə sis) ***n.***, *pl.* **-ses′** (-sēz′) ⟦ModL < Gr *synairesis*, a taking or drawing together < *syn-*, together + *hairein*, to take⟧ **1** the drawing together of two consecutive vowels or syllables into one syllable, esp. so as to form a diphthong **2** SYNIZESIS **3** *Chem.* contraction of a gel so that liquid is exuded at the surface, as in the separation of serum from a blood clot

syn·er·get·ic (sin′ər jet′ik) ***adj.*** ⟦Gr *synergētikos* < *synergein*, to work together: see SYNERGY⟧ working together; cooperating; synergic —**syn′er·get′i·cal·ly** ***adv.***

syn·er·gid (si nur′jid, sin′ər-) ***n.*** ⟦ModL *synergida* < Gr *synergein*, to work together (see SYNERGY) + ModL *-ida*, sing. of *-idae* (see -IDAE)⟧ either of the two cells that lie alongside of the egg cell in the embryo sac of flowering plants

syn·er·gism (sin′ər jiz′əm) ***n.*** ⟦ModL *synergismus* < Gr *synergos*, working together: see SYNERGY⟧ **1** the simultaneous action of separate agencies which, together, have greater total effect than the sum of their individual effects: said esp. of drugs **2** the combined or correlated action of different organs or parts of the body, as of muscles working together —**syn′er·gis′tic** ***adj.***

syn·er·gist (sin′ər jist) ***n.*** a synergistic organ, drug, etc.

syn·er·gy (sin′ər jē) ***n.*** ⟦ModL *synergia* < Gr, joint work < *synergein*, to work together < *syn-*, together + *ergon*, WORK⟧ **1** combined or cooperative action or force **2** SYNERGISM —**syn·er·gic** (si nur′jik) ***adj.***

syn·e·sis (sin′ə sis) ***n.*** ⟦ModL < Gr, sagacity, quick perception < *synienai*, to perceive, lit., to bring together < *syn-*, together + *hienai*, to set in motion: see JET[1]⟧ a grammatical construction which conforms to the meaning rather than to strict syntactic agreement or reference (Ex.: Has *everyone* washed *their* hands?)

syn·es·the·sia (sin′əs thē′zhə, -zhē ə, -zē ə) ***n.*** ⟦ModL *synaesthesia:* see SYN- & ESTHESIA⟧ **1** *Physiol.* sensation felt in one part of the body when another part is stimulated **2** *Psychol.* a process in which one type of stimulus produces a secondary, subjective sensation, as when some color evokes a specific smell —**syn′es·thet′ic** (-thet′ik) ***adj.***

☆**syn·fu·el** (sin′fyo͞o′əl, -fyo͞ol′) ***n.*** ⟦SYN(THETIC) + FUEL⟧ a fuel, as oil or gas produced from coal, or methane produced from plant cellulose, used as a substitute as for petroleum or natural gas

syn·ga·my (siŋ′gə mē, sin′-) ***n.*** ⟦SYN- + -GAMY⟧ sexual reproduction; union of gametes to form a fertilized ovum —**syn·gam·ic** (sin gam′ik) ***adj.***, **syn·ga·mous** (siŋ′gə məs)

Synge (siŋ), **(Edmund) John Mil·ling·ton** (mil′iŋ tən) 1871-1909; Ir. dramatist

syn·ge·ne·ic (sin′jə nē′ik) ***adj.*** ⟦< SYN- + Gr *genos*, race, kind + -IC⟧ designating or of genetically identical, or nearly identical, tissue, cells, etc.: cf. ALLOGENEIC: sometimes called **syn·gen·ic** (sin jen′ik)

syn·gen·e·sis (sin jen′ə sis) ***n.*** ⟦ModL: see SYN- & -GENESIS⟧ sexual reproduction —**syn·ge·net·ic** (sin′jə net′ik) ***adj.***

syn·i·ze·sis (sin′ə zē′sis) ***n.***, *pl.* **-ses′** (-sēz′) ⟦LL < Gr *synizēsis* < *synizanein*, to sink in, collapse < *syn-*, with + *hizein*, to SIT⟧ **1** the contraction of two adjacent vowels into a single syllable, without the formation of a diphthong **2** *Biol.* the massing of the chromatin in meiosis during synapsis

syn·kar·y·on (sin kar′ē än′, -ən) ***n.*** ⟦ModL < *syn-*, SYN- + Gr *karyon*, nut⟧ the nucleus resulting from the fusion of male and female nuclei during fertilization

syn·od (sin′əd) ***n.*** ⟦ME, altered (after LL) < OE *sinoth* < LL(Ec) *synodus* < LGr(Ec) *synodos*, church synod < Gr, a meeting, lit., a coming together < *syn-*, together + *hodos*, way: see -ODE[1]⟧ **1** an ecclesiastical council; specif., *a)* *R.C.Ch.* a regional or international meeting of bishops; also, a meeting of diocesan priests, the diocesan bishop presiding *b)* *Eastern Orthodox Ch.* HOLY SYNOD **2** a high governing body in certain Christian churches; specif., *a)* a Presbyterian governing body ranking between the general assembly and presbytery *b)* a national or district organization of Lutheran or certain other Protestant churches **3** a district governed or represented by a Protestant synod **4** any assembly or council —**syn′od·al** ***adj.***

syn·od·i·cal (si näd′i kəl) ***adj.*** ⟦LL *synodicus* < Gr *synodikos* < *synodos:* see prec.⟧ **1** of a synod; synodal **2** *Astron.* of or having to do with conjunction, esp. with the interval (**synodic period**) between two successive conjunctions of the same celestial bodies: also **syn·od′ic** —**syn·od′i·cal·ly** ***adv.***

syn·o·nym (sin′ə nim′) ***n.*** ⟦ME *sinonyme* < L *synonymum* < Gr *synōnymon*, of like meaning or like name < *syn-*, together + *onyma*, a NAME⟧ **1** a word having the same or nearly the same meaning in one or more senses as another in the same language: opposed to ANTONYM **2** METONYM **3** an incorrect taxonomic name —**syn′o·nym′ic** ***adj.***, **syn′o·nym′i·cal** —**syn′o·nym′i·ty** ***n.***

syn·on·y·mize (si nän′ə mīz′) ***vt.*** **-mized′**, **-miz′ing** to furnish a synonym or synonyms for (a word)

syn·on·y·mous (-məs) ***adj.*** ⟦ML *synonymus* < Gr *synōnymos:* see SYNONYM⟧ of, or having the nature of, a synonym; equivalent or similar in meaning —**syn·on′y·mous·ly** ***adv.***

syn·on·y·my (-mē) ***n.***, *pl.* **-mies** ⟦LL *synonymia* < Gr *synōnymia*⟧ **1** the study of synonyms **2** a list or listing of synonyms, esp. one in which the terms are discriminated from one another **3** *a)* the scientific names used in different nomenclature systems to designate the same species, genus, etc. *b)* a list of such names **4** the quality of being synonymous; identity or near identity of meaning

syn·op·sis (si näp′sis) ***n.***, *pl.* **-ses′** (-sēz′) ⟦LL < Gr < *syn-*, together + *opsis*, a seeing, visual image < *ōps*, EYE⟧ a statement giving a brief, general review or condensation; summary —**SYN.** ABRIDGMENT

☆**syn·op·size** (-sīz′) ***vt.*** **-sized′**, **-siz′ing** to make a synopsis of; summarize

syn·op·tic (-tik) ***adj.*** ⟦ModL *synopticus* < Gr *synoptikos*⟧ **1** of or constituting a synopsis; presenting a general view or summary **2** [*often* **S-**] giving an account from the same point of view: said of the first three Gospels, as distinguished from the fourth **3** *Meteorol.* presenting or involving data on weather and atmospheric conditions over a wide area at a given time [*a synoptic chart*] Also **syn·op′ti·cal** —**syn·op′ti·cal·ly** ***adv.***

syn·o·vi·a (si nō′vē ə) ***n.*** ⟦ModL: coined by PARACELSUS < ?⟧ the clear, albuminous lubricating fluid secreted by the membranes of joint cavities, tendon sheaths, etc. —**syn·o′vi·al** ***adj.***

syn·o·vi·tis (sin′ə vīt′is) ***n.*** inflammation of a synovial membrane

syn·tac·tic (sin tak′tik) ***adj.*** ⟦< ModL *syntacticus* < Gr *syntaktikos* < *syntaxis:* see SYNTAX⟧ of or in accordance with the rules of syntax: also **syn·tac′ti·cal** —**syn·tac′ti·cal·ly** ***adv.***

syntactic foam ⟦so named because its elements are arranged in a structure having a high degree of regularity: see SYNTAX (*n.* 1)⟧ any of several buoyant materials made up of tiny hollow spheres embedded in a surrounding plastic: used in submersibles, spacecraft, etc.

syn·tac·tics (-tiks) ***n.*** the branch of semiotics dealing with the formal interrelationships of signs and symbols apart from their users or external reference

syn·tag·ma (sin tag′mə) ***n.***, *pl.* **-ma·ta** (-mə tə) or **-mas** ⟦Fr *syntagme* < Gr *syntagma*, that which is put together in order < *syntassein:* see SYNTAX⟧ *Linguis.* a unit in a sequential linguistic structure: also **syn′tagm′** (-tam′)

syn·tag·mat·ic (sin′tag mat′ik) ***adj.*** ⟦Fr *syntagmatique*⟧ of or relating to the sequential syntactic relationship between units in a linguistic structure

syn·tax (sin′taks′) ***n.*** ⟦Fr *syntaxe* < LL *syntaxis* < Gr < *syntassein*, to join, put together < *syn-*, together + *tassein*, to arrange: see TAXIS⟧ **1** [Now Rare] orderly or systematic arrangement **2** *Gram., Linguis.* *a)* the arrangement of and relationships among words, phrases, and clauses forming sentences; sentence structure *b)* the study of this **3** *Comput.* *a)* the structure of statements in a computer language *b)* the rules governing this structure **4** *Logic* syntactics as applied to language in the abstract with no meaning attached either to the symbols or to the expressions constructed from these symbols

synth (sinth) ***n.*** [Informal] *short for* SYNTHESIZER (sense 2)

syn·the·sis (sin′thə sis) ***n.***, *pl.* **-ses′** (-sēz′) ⟦Gr < *syn-*, together + *tithenai*, to place, DO[1]⟧ **1** the putting together of parts or elements so as to form a whole **2** a whole made up of parts or elements put together **3** *Chem.* the formation of a complex compound by the combining of two or more simpler compounds, elements, or radicals **4** *Philos.* in Hegelian philosophy, the unified whole in which opposites (thesis and antithesis) are reconciled

syn·the·sist (-sist) ***n.*** **1** a person or thing that synthesizes **2** a person who plays an electronic synthesizer

syn·the·size (-sīz′) ***vt.*** **-sized′**, **-siz′ing** **1** to bring together into a whole by synthesis **2** to form by bringing together separate parts **3** *Chem.* to produce by synthesis rather than by extraction, refinement, etc.

syn·the·siz·er (-sī′zər) ***n.*** **1** a person or thing that synthesizes ☆**2** an electronic device containing filters, oscillators, and voltage-control amplifiers, used to produce sounds unobtainable from ordinary musical instruments or to imitate instruments and voices

syn·the·tase (sin′thə tās′, -tāz′) ***n.*** LIGASE

syn·thet·ic (sin thet′ik) ***adj.*** ⟦Fr *synthétique* < Gr *synthetikos*⟧ **1** of, involving, or using synthesis **2** produced by synthesis; specif., produced by chemical synthesis, rather than of natural origin **3** not real or genuine; artificial or insincere [*synthetic* enthusiasm] **4** *Linguis.* characterized by the use of inflection to express grammatical relationships [Russian is a *syn-*

thetic language] **5** *Logic* true not by virtue of the meaning of its component terms alone but by virtue of observation, and with its denial not resulting in self-contradiction: opposed to ANALYTIC Also **syn·thet′i·cal** —*n.* something synthetic; specif., a substance produced by chemical synthesis —**SYN.** ARTIFICIAL —**syn·thet′i·cal·ly** *adv.*

synthetic resin **1** any of a large class of complex organic liquids or solids formed from simpler molecules by condensation or polymerization, used esp. in making plastics **2** any of various chemically modified natural resins

synthetic rubber any of several elastic substances resembling natural rubber, prepared by polymerization of butadiene, isoprene, and other unsaturated hydrocarbons

synth-pop (sinth′päp′) *n.* a kind of popular music, esp. of the 1980s, emphasizing the use of synthesizers and often characterized by blandly monotonous rhythms and optimistic lyrics: also written **synth′pop′**

syn·ton·ic (sin tän′ik) *adj.* ⟦< Gr *syntonos,* in harmony < *syn-,* with + *tonos,* voice, TONE⟧ *Psychol.* in emotional equilibrium and responsive to the environment

syph·i·lis (sif′ə lis) *n.* ⟦ModL < *Syphilis sive Morbus Gallicus,* lit., Syphilis or the French disease, title of a poem (1530) by Girolamo Fracastoro: after the hero *Syphilus,* a shepherd⟧ an infectious disease caused by a spirochete (*Treponema pallidum*) and transmitted usually by sexual intercourse or acquired congenitally: if untreated, it can ultimately lead to the degeneration of the heart, bones, nerve tissue, etc. —**syph′i·lit′ic** *adj., n.*

sy·phon (sī′fən) *n., vt., vi. alt. sp. of* SIPHON

Syr *abbrev.* **1** Syria **2** Syriac **3** Syrian

Syr·a·cuse (sir′ə kyo͞os′, -kyo͞oz′) **1** ⟦after the seaport in Sicily⟧ city in central N.Y. **2** seaport on the SE coast of Sicily: in ancient times, a Greek city-state: It. name SIRACUSA

sy·rah (sē rä′) *n.* ⟦Fr⟧ **1** a red grape grown esp. in the Rhone Valley in France and now also in the U.S. and Australia **2** a full-bodied red wine made from this grape

Syr Dar·ya (sir där′yə) river in central Asia, flowing from the Tian Shan Mountains into the Aral Sea: *c.* 1,700 mi (2,736 km)

☆**syr·ette** (si ret′) *n.* ⟦SYR(INGE) + -ETTE⟧ a small, collapsible tube fitted with a hypodermic needle and filled with a single dose of medication

Syr·i·a (sir′ē ə) **1** region of ancient times at the E end of the Mediterranean **2** country in the NW part of this region, south of Turkey: formerly a French mandate, it became an independent republic (1944-58); united with Egypt to form the UNITED ARAB REPUBLIC (1958-61); union dissolved (1961): 71,498 sq mi (185,180 sq km); cap. Damascus —**Syr′i·an** *adj., n.*

Syr·i·ac (sir′ē ak′) *n.* an Aramaic dialect that became the literary and liturgical language of the ancient Syrian Christian churches

sy·rin·ga (sə riŋ′gə) *n.* ⟦ModL, name of the genus < Gr *syrinx* (gen. *syringos*), a pipe, tube (see fol.): from the use of the plants for making pipes⟧ **1** LILAC (senses 1 & 2) **2** MOCK ORANGE

sy·ringe (sə rinj′, sir′inj) *n.* ⟦ME *siringe* < ML *sirynga* < Gr *syrinx* (gen. *syringos*), a reed, pipe, prob. < IE base **two-,* a tube > Sans *tūṇa,* a quiver⟧ **1** a device consisting of a narrow tube fitted at one end with a rubber bulb or piston by means of which a liquid can be drawn in and then ejected in a stream: used to inject fluids into, or extract fluids from, body cavities, to cleanse wounds, etc. **2** *short for* HYPODERMIC SYRINGE —*vt.* **-ringed′**, **-ring′ing** to cleanse, inject, etc. by using a syringe

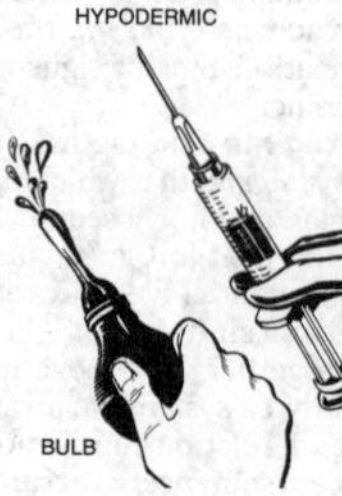

syringes

sy·rin·ge·al (sə rin′jē əl) *adj.* of the syrinx

sy·rin·go·my·e·li·a (sə riŋ′gō mī ē′lē ə) *n.* ⟦ModL < Gr *syrinx* (see SYRINGE) + *myelos,* marrow⟧ a chronic, progressive disease characterized by the formation of cavities filled with liquid within the spinal cord

syr·inx (sir′iŋks) *n., pl.* **sy·rin·ges** (sə rin′jēz′) or **syr′inx·es** ⟦ModL < Gr, a pipe: see SYRINGE⟧ **1** *Ornithology* the vocal organ of birds, usually located at the base of the trachea and sometimes in the bronchi or trachea **2** PANPIPE

syr·phus fly (sur′fəs) ⟦ModL *Syrphus* < Gr *syrphos,* gnat⟧ any of a family (Syrphidae) of dipterous flies, many of which mimic bees or wasps: the adults feed on nectar and pollen, and the larvae of various species feed on plant lice, plants, etc.: also **syr′phid** (-fid) *n.*

syr·up (sur′əp, sir′-) *n.* ⟦ME *sirupe* < OFr *sirop* < ML *sirupus* < Ar *sharāb,* a drink < *shariba,* to drink⟧ any sweet, thick liquid; specif., *a)* a solution of sugar and water boiled together, to which flavoring is often added *b)* any solution of sugar used in pharmacy as a vehicle for medicines *c)* the sweet, thick liquid obtained in the process of manufacturing cane sugar or glucose *d) short for* MAPLE SYRUP, CORN SYRUP, etc.

syr·up·y (sur′ə pē, sir′-) *adj.* **1** resembling syrup in some way **2** overly sentimental; cloyingly sweet, as in tone or manner

sys- (sis) *prefix* SYN-: used before *s,* or, sometimes, to reflect original combining with a word containing an initial aspirate, or (h) sound

sys·op (sis′äp′) *n.* ⟦< *sys(tem) op(erator)*⟧ a person who manages a computer network, bulletin board, etc.

syst *abbrev.* system

sys·tal·tic (sis tal′tik, -tôl′-) *adj.* ⟦LL *systalticus* < Gr *systaltikos,* drawing together < *systellein,* to draw together < *syn-,* together + *stellein,* to set up, order < IE base **stel-* > STILL¹⟧ characterized by alternate contraction and dilatation, as the action of the heart

sys·tem (sis′təm) *n.* ⟦LL *systema* < Gr *systēma* (gen. *systēmatos*) < *synistanai,* to place together < *syn-,* together + *histanai,* to set: see STAND⟧ **1** a set or arrangement of things so related or connected as to form a unity or organic whole [a solar *system,* school *system, system* of highways] **2** a set of facts, principles, rules, etc. classified or arranged in a regular, orderly form so as to show a logical plan linking the various parts **3** a method or plan of classification or arrangement **4** *a)* an established way of doing something; method; procedure *b)* orderliness or methodical planning in one's way of proceeding **5** *a)* the body considered as a functioning organism *b)* a number of bodily organs acting together to perform one of the main bodily functions [the digestive *system*] **6** a related series of natural objects or elements, as cave passages, rivers, etc. **7** *Chem.* a group of substances in or approaching equilibrium: a system with two components, phases, or variables is called binary, one with three, ternary, etc. **8** *Comput. a)* an organization of hardware and software, often together with personnel, that function together as a unit *b)* OPERATING SYSTEM: often in the pl. form when used attributively [a *system* programmer, *systems* software] **9** *Crystallography* any of the seven divisions (cubic, tetragonal, hexagonal, rhombohedral, orthorhombic, monoclinic, and triclinic) in which all crystal forms can be placed, based on the degree of symmetry of the crystals **10** *Geol.* a major division of stratified rocks consisting of the rocks laid down during a geologic period —**get something out of one's system** [Informal] to free oneself as from an emotional attachment to or obsession with something

sys·tem·at·ic (sis′tə mat′ik) *adj.* ⟦Gr *systēmatikos*⟧ **1** forming or constituting a system **2** based on or involving a system **3** made or arranged according to a system, method, or plan; regular; orderly **4** characterized by the use of method or orderly planning; methodical **5** of or having to do with classification; taxonomic Also **sys′tem·at′i·cal** —**sys′tem·at′i·cal·ly** *adv.*

sys·tem·at·ics (-iks) *n. Biol.* the science or a method of classification; esp., taxonomy

sys·tem·a·tism (sis′tə mə tiz′əm) *n.* the practice or process of systematizing

sys·tem·a·tist (-tist) *n.* **1** a person who works according to a system **2** a taxonomist

sys·tem·a·tize (sis′tə mə tīz′) *vt.* **-tized′**, **-tiz′ing** to form into a system; arrange according to a system; make systematic —**sys′tem·a·ti·za′tion** *n.* —**sys′tem·a·tiz′er** *n.*

sys·tem·ic (sis tem′ik) *adj.* **1** of or affecting a system, specif. an entire system **2** *Physiol.* of or affecting the entire organism or bodily system —☆*n.* any of a group of pesticides that are absorbed into the tissues of plants, which in consequence become poisonous to insects, etc. that feed on them —**sys·tem′i·cal·ly** *adv.*

sys·tem·ize (sis′təm īz′) *vt.* **-ized′**, **-iz′ing** SYSTEMATIZE —**sys′tem·i·za′tion** (-mə zā′shən, -mī′-) *n.*

☆**systems analysis** **1** an engineering technique that breaks down complex technical, social, etc. problems into basic elements whose interrelations are evaluated and programmed, with the aid of mathematics, into a complete and integrated system **2** the designing of an efficient computer system for a particular business, project, etc. —**systems analyst**

sys·to·le (sis′tə lē′) *n.* ⟦ModL < Gr *systolē* < *systellein,* to draw together: see SYSTALTIC⟧ the usual rhythmic contraction of the heart, esp. of the ventricles, following each dilatation (*diastole*), during which the blood is driven onward from the chambers: opposed to DIASTOLE —**sys·tol·ic** (sis täl′ik) *adj.*

Syz·ran (siz′rən) city in SE European Russia, on the Volga, near Samara

syz·y·gy (siz′ə jē) *n., pl.* **-gies** ⟦LL *syzygia* < Gr < *syn-,* together + *zygon,* YOKE⟧ **1** a pair of things, esp. a pair of opposites **2** *Astron.* a configuration of three celestial bodies, as of the sun, earth, and moon during an eclipse, in an approximately straight line **3** *Gr. & Latin Prosody* a measure of two feet, as a dipody —**sy·zyg·i·al** (sə zij′ē əl) *adj.*

Szcze·cin (shche tsēn′) river port in NW Poland, on the Oder

Sze·chwan¹ or **Sze·chuan** (sech′wän′) *adj.* ⟦after fol.⟧ designating or of a tradition of Chinese cuisine originating in the Sichuan province

Sze·chwan² or **Sze·chuan** (sech′wän′) *a transliteration of* SICHUAN

Sze·ged (se′ged) city in SE Hungary, at the junction of the Mureş & Tisza rivers

Szell (sel, zel), **George** 1897-1970; U.S. orchestra conductor & pianist, born in Hungary

Szi·lard (zē′lärd′, zi lärd′), **Leo** 1898-1964; U.S. nuclear physicist, born in Hungary

Szold (zōld), **Henrietta** 1860-1945; U.S. Zionist leader

T

t[1] or **T** (tē) ***n., pl.*** **t's, T's** **1** the twentieth letter of the English alphabet: from the Greek *tau,* derived from the Hebrew *tav* **2** any of the speech sounds that this letter represents, as, in English, the (t) of *time* **3** a type or impression for *t* or *T* **4** the twentieth in a sequence or group **5** an object shaped like T —***adj.*** **1** of *t* or *T* **2** twentieth in a sequence or group **3** shaped like T —**to a T** to perfection; exactly

t[2] *abbrev.* **1** ⟦L *tempore*⟧ in the time (of) **2** tare **3** target **4** teaspoon(s) **5** telephone **6** temperature **7** tempo **8** tenor **9** tense **10** time **11** ton(s) **12** town **13** township **14** transit **15** transitive **16** troy **17** ⟦L *tomus*⟧ volume

T[1] (tē) ***n., pl.*** **T's** or **Ts** *short for* T-SHIRT

T[2] *abbrev.* **1** absolute (Kelvin) temperature **2** tablespoon(s) **3** *Football* tackle: sometimes written **t** **4** Technician **5** temperature **6** tension **7** tera- **8** Territory **9** tesla(s) **10** Testament **11** Thursday **12** thymine **13** time (of firing or launching) **14** *Rom. History* Titus (the praenomen) **15** ton(s) **16** *Physics* torque **17** *Chem.* triple bond **18** Tuesday

T[3] *Physics symbol* half-life

-t *suffix* forming past participles and adjectives derived from them *[slept, burnt]*: see -ED

't- *prefix* it: used with verbs in contractions, chiefly in poetry *['twas]*

-'t *suffix* it: used with verbs in contractions, chiefly in poetry *[do't]*

ta (tä) ***interj.*** ⟦orig. a child's term⟧ [Brit. Informal] thank you

Ta *Chem. symbol for* tantalum

TA (tē′ā′) ***n., pl.*** **TA's** [Informal] TEACHING ASSISTANT

tab[1] (tab) ***n.*** ⟦< ?⟧ **1** a small, flat loop, strap, or metal ring fastened to something for pulling it, hanging it up, etc. **2** a small, often ornamental, flap or piece fastened to the edge or surface as of a dress, coat, etc. **3** an attached or projecting piece as of a file folder, often with a label, used in filing **4** *Aeron.* an auxiliary airfoil set into the trailing edge of a larger control surface, such as an aileron —***vt.*** **tabbed, tab′bing** **1** to provide with tabs **2** to choose or select

tab[2] (tab) ☆***n.*** ⟦prob. short for TABULATION⟧ [Informal] **1** a bill or check, as for expenses **2** total cost or expenses —☆**keep tabs (or a tab) on** [Informal] to keep a check on; follow or watch every move of —☆**pick up the tab** [Informal] to pay the bill or total cost

tab[3] (tab) ***n.*** *short for:* **1** TABLET **2** TABLOID **3** TAB KEY —***vi.*** **tabbed, tab′bing** *Comput.* to move a cursor with a TAB KEY

tab[4] *abbrev.* **1** table(s) **2** ⟦L *tabella*⟧ *Pharmacy* tablet(s)

tab·a·nid (tab′ə nid) ***n.*** ⟦< L *tabanus,* horsefly + -ID⟧ any of a family (Tabanidae) of large, bloodsucking dipterous flies, consisting of horse flies and deer flies

tab·ard (tab′ərd) ***n.*** ⟦ME < OFr *tabart*⟧ **1** a loose jacket of heavy material, sleeved or sleeveless, worn outdoors as by peasants in the Middle Ages **2** a short-sleeved, emblazoned cloak worn by a knight over his armor **3** a herald's official coat emblazoned with his king's or lord's arms

tabard

☆**Ta·bas·co**[1] (tə bas′kō) ⟦after fol.⟧ *trademark for* a very hot sauce made from a tropical American hot red pepper

Ta·bas·co[2] (tə bas′kō; *Sp* tä bäs′kô) state of SE Mexico, west of Yucatán: 9,522 sq mi (24,662 sq km); cap. Villahermosa

tab·bou·leh (tə bo͞o′lē, -le) ***n.*** ⟦Ar *tabbūla*⟧ a Middle Eastern salad of soaked bulgur wheat and finely chopped parsley, tomatoes, scallions, and mint leaves, with an olive oil and lemon juice dressing

tab·by (tab′ē) ***n., pl.*** **-bies** ⟦Fr *tabis,* earlier *atabis* < ML *attabi* < Ar *al-ʿattābīya* < *ʿattābī,* the quarter of Baghdad where it was manufactured: after a prince *ʿAttāb,* of the Omayyad dynasty⟧ **1** a silk taffeta with stripes or wavy markings; watered silk **2** a light-colored cat with darker stripes, sometimes of another color **3** any domestic cat, esp. a female **4** [Old Brit. Informal] *a)* an old maid *b)* a malicious woman gossip —***adj.*** **1** made of, or like, tabby **2** having dark stripes over gray or brown; brindled —***vt.*** **-bied, -by·ing** to make wavy markings in (silk, etc.)

tab·er·nac·le (tab′ər nak′əl) ***n.*** ⟦ME < LL(Ec) *tabernaculum,* the Jewish tabernacle (transl. of Heb *ohel* in *ohel-moed,* tent of meeting) < L, tent, dim. of *taberna,* hut, shed, TAVERN⟧ **1** [Archaic] *a)* a temporary shelter, as a tent *b)* a dwelling place **2** the human body considered as the dwelling place of the soul **3** a shrine, niche, etc. with a canopy **4** a place of worship, esp. one with a large seating capacity **5** [T-] the portable sanctuary carried by the Jews during the Exodus: Ex. 25, 26, 27 **6** *Eccles.* a cabinetlike enclosure for consecrated Hosts, usually at the center of an altar —***vi.*** **-led, -ling** to dwell temporarily —***vt.*** to place in or as in a tabernacle —**tab′er·nac′u·lar** (-yə lər) ***adj.***

ta·bes (tā′bēz′) ***n.*** ⟦L, a wasting away < *tabere,* to waste away < IE base **ta-,* to melt > THAW⟧ *Med.* **1** any wasting or atrophy due to disease **2** *short for* TABES DORSALIS —**ta·bet·ic** (tə bet′ik) ***adj., n.***

tabes dor·sa·lis (dôr sā′lis, -sal′is) ⟦ModL, tabes of the back: see prec. & DORSAL[1]⟧ a chronic disease of the nervous system, usually caused by syphilis and characterized by disturbances of sensations, loss of reflexes and of muscular coordination, functional disorders of organs, etc.

Tab·i·tha (tab′i thə) ***n.*** ⟦LL(Ec) < Gr(Ec) *Tabeitha* < Aram *tavita,* lit., roe, gazelle⟧ a feminine name

tab key **1** *see* TABULATOR (subsense *a)*) **2** *Comput.* a key on a computer keyboard that moves the cursor a preset number of spaces or that moves the cursor from one field, icon, etc. to another

tab·la (täb′lä) ***n.*** ⟦Hindustani < Ar *ṭabla,* drum⟧ a set of two small drums whose pitch can be varied, used esp. in India and played with the hands

tab·la·ture (tab′lə chər) ***n.*** ⟦Fr < ML *tabulatura* < *tabulatus,* tablet < LL *tabulare,* to provide with a table < L *tabula:* see fol.⟧ **1** a method of notation for guitar or ukulele in which vertical lines represent the strings, horizontal lines represent the frets, and dots on these lines indicate finger placement **2** [Archaic] a flat surface or tablet with an inscription, painting, or design on it

ta·ble (tā′bəl) ***n.*** ⟦OFr < L *tabula,* a board, painting, tablet < ? IE **taldhla* < base **tel-,* flat, a board > OE *thille,* thin board, flooring⟧ **1** [Obs.] a thin, flat tablet or slab of metal, stone, or wood, used for inscriptions **2** *a)* a piece of furniture consisting of a flat, horizontal top usually set on legs *b)* such a table set with food for a meal *c)* food served at table; feasting as entertainment *d)* the people seated at a table to eat, talk, etc. *e)* a location, as a site for a meeting, an opportunity, setting, etc. thought of as being like a table on which issues may be placed for discussion or consideration *[they brought fresh offers to the table]* **3** any of various large, flat-topped pieces of furniture or equipment used for games, as a working surface, etc. *[pool table, examining table]* **4** *a)* a compact, systematic list of details, contents, etc. *b)* a compact arrangement of related facts, figures, values, etc. in orderly sequence, and usually in parallel rows and columns, for convenience of reference *[the multiplication table]* **5** TABLELAND **6** the flat upper surface of certain styles of faceted gems **7** *Anat.* the hard inner or outer layer of the bony tissue of the skull **8** *Archit.* *a)* any horizontal, projecting piece, as a molding or cornice; stringcourse *b)* a plain or decorated rectangular piece set into or raised on a wall; panel **9** *Backgammon* *a)* either of the two hinged leaves of a backgammon board *b)* either half of either of these leaves —***adj.*** **1** of, for, or on a table **2** fit for serving at table *[table salt]* —***vt.*** **-bled, -bling** **1** [Obs.] to make a list or compact arrangement of; tabulate **2** to put on a table ☆**3** to postpone indefinitely the discussion or consideration of (a legislative bill, motion, etc.) **4** [Brit.] to submit for discussion or consideration —**at table** at a meal —**drink someone under the table** [Informal] to outlast someone, as in a drinking competition, esp., to the point where he or she becomes unconscious —**on the table** ☆**1** postponed or shelved: said of a bill, etc. **2** presented or open for discussion, consideration, etc. —**the tables** laws, as the Ten Commandments or ancient Roman codes, inscribed on flat stone slabs —**turn the tables** to reverse completely a situation as it affects two opposing persons or groups —**under the table** [Informal] covertly: said as of a bribe

tab·leau (ta blō′) ***n., pl.*** **-leaux′** (-blōz′) or **-leaus′** ⟦Fr < OFr *tablel,* dim. of *table:* see prec.⟧ **1** a striking, dramatic scene or picture **2** TABLEAU VIVANT

tab·leau vi·vant (tä blō vē vän′) *pl.* ***tab·leaux vi·vants*** (tä blō vē vän′) ⟦Fr, living tableau⟧ a representation of a scene, picture, etc. by a person or group in costume, posing silently without moving

ta·ble·cloth (tā′bəl klôth′) ***n.*** a cloth for covering a table, esp. at meals

ta·ble d'hôte (tä′bəl dōt′, tab′əl-) *pl.* ***ta′bles d'hôte′*** (tä′bəlz-, tab′əlz-) ⟦Fr, lit., table of the host⟧ a complete meal with courses as specified on the menu, served at a restaurant or hotel for a set price: distinguished from A LA CARTE

☆**ta·ble-hop** (tā′bəl häp′) ***vi.*** **-hopped′, -hop′ping** to leave one's table in a restaurant, nightclub, etc. and visit at other tables —**ta′ble-hop′per** ***n.***

ta·ble·land (-land′) ***n.*** a high, broad, level region; plateau

table linen tablecloths, napkins, etc.

ta·ble·mount (-mount′) ***n.*** GUYOT

Table Mountain flat-topped mountain in S Western Cape province, South Africa: 3,549 ft (1,082 m)

table saw a circular saw mounted on the underside of a table through which its blade projects: work to be sawed is placed on the table

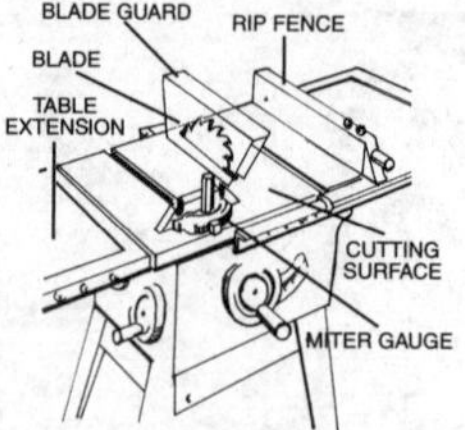

table saw

ta·ble·spoon (tā′bəl spo͞on′) *n.* **1** a large spoon used for serving at table **2** *a)* a measuring unit in cookery, equal to about half a fluid ounce or 3 teaspoons (abbrev. *tbs* or *tbsp*) *b)* a spoon for eating, shaped like a teaspoon but larger, able to hold about half a fluid ounce **3** TABLESPOONFUL
ta·ble·spoon·ful (-spo͞on′fo͝ol) *n., pl.* **-fuls** as much as a tablespoon will hold
tab·let (tab′lit) *n.* ⟦ME *tablette* < MFr *tablete,* dim. of *table:* see TABLE⟧ **1** a thin, flat piece of stone, wood, metal, etc. shaped for a specific purpose **2** such a piece with an inscription, used as a memorial wall panel; plaque **3** *a)* a smooth, flat leaf made of wood, ivory, metal, etc. and used to write on *b)* a set of such leaves fastened together **4** a writing or drawing pad consisting of sheets of paper glued together at one edge **5** any of various small, lightweight laptop computers characterized by a touch screen and a representation of a keyboard that is part of its GUI interface: some tablets consist of a single, thin rectangular unit, others consist of a screen that can swivel so as to expose an additional, standard keyboard beneath: in full **tablet computer** **6** a small, flat piece of solid or compressed material, as of medicine, soap, etc.
table talk informal conversation, as that taking place at meals
table tennis a game somewhat like tennis in miniature, played on a large, rectangular table, with a small, hollow celluloid or plastic ball and short-handled, wooden paddles
ta·ble·top (tā′bəl täp′) *n.* the flat upper part or upper surface of a table —*adj.* **1** relatively compact, so as to fit on the top of a table **2** suitable for display on the top of a table [*tabletop* sculpture]
ta·ble·ware (tā′bəl wer′) *n.* dishes, glassware, silverware, etc. for use at table
table wine a still and usually dry wine for serving with meals, usually containing no more than 14 percent alcohol by volume
tab·loid (tab′loid′) *n.* ⟦TABL(ET) + -OID: a trademark for a medicine tablet; from the idea that the newspaper presents news in concentrated form, as the tablet contains concentrated medicine⟧ **1** a size of newspaper page, about 14 inches high by 12 inches wide, half the size of a standard page: cf. BROADSHEET (sense 2) **2** a newspaper using such a page size, esp. one with many pictures and short, often sensational, news stories —*adj.* **1** condensed; short **2** of or characterized by the sensationalism regarded as typical of tabloids [*tabloid* talk shows]
ta·boo (tə bo͞o′, ta-) *n., pl.* **-boos′** ⟦< a Polynesian language: cf. Tongan, Samoan, Maori, etc. *tapu*⟧ **1** *a)* among some Polynesian peoples, a sacred prohibition put upon certain people, things, or acts which makes them untouchable, unmentionable, etc. *b)* the highly developed system or practice of such prohibitions **2** *a)* any social prohibition or restriction that results from convention or tradition *b)* *Linguis.* the substitution of one word or phrase for another because of such restriction —*adj.* **1** sacred and prohibited by taboo **2** restricted by taboo: said of people **3** prohibited or forbidden by tradition, convention, etc. —*vt.* **-booed′**, **-boo′ing** **1** to put under taboo **2** to prohibit or forbid because of tradition, convention, etc.
ta·bor (tā′bər) *n.* ⟦ME < OFr *tabur* < Pers *tabīr,* drum⟧ a small drum, formerly used by a pipe player to beat out his own rhythmic accompaniment —*vi.* to beat on or as on a tabor Also sp. **ta′bour**
Ta·bor (tā′bər), **Mount** mountain in N Israel, east of Nazareth: *c.* 1,900 ft (579 m)
tab·o·ret (tab′ə ret′, tab′ə ret′) *n.* ⟦OFr, a stool, lit., little drum, dim. of *tabur:* see TABOR⟧ **1** a small tabor **2** a low, upholstered footstool Also sp. **tab′ou·ret′**
tab·o·rin (tab′ə rin) *n.* ⟦MFr *tabourin,* dim. of *tabur:* see TABOR⟧ a small tabor played with only one stick: also **tab′o·rine′** (-ə rēn′)
ta·bou·li (tə bo͞o′lē) *n. var. of* TABBOULEH
Ta·briz¹ (tə brēz′) *n.* ⟦after fol.⟧ a Persian rug usually having a stiff pile and a medallion center with an arabesque border
Ta·briz² (tä brēz′) city in NW Iran
ta·bu (tə bo͞o′, ta-) *n., adj., vt. alt. sp. of* TABOO
tab·u·lar (tab′yə lər) *adj.* ⟦L *tabularis* < *tabula,* a board, tablet: see TABLE⟧ **1** having a tablelike surface; flat [*tabular* rock] **2** *a)* of or arranged in a table or tabulated scheme *b)* computed from or calculated by such a table or tables —**tab′u·lar·ly** *adv.*
ta·bu·la ra·sa (tab′yə lə rä′zə, -rä′sə) *pl.* **ta·bu·lae ra·sae** (tab′yə lē rä′zē, -rä′sē) ⟦ML < L *tabula* (see TABLE) + *rasa,* fem. pp. of *radere,* to scrape, ERASE⟧ a blank tablet; clean slate: used esp. of the mind when regarded as blank until impressions are recorded upon it by experience
tab·u·late (tab′yə lāt′; *for adj.,* -lit, -lāt′) *vt.* **-lat′ed**, **-lat′ing** ⟦< LL *tabulatus,* pp. of *tabulare:* see TABLATURE⟧ to put (facts, statistics, etc.) in a table or columns or otherwise arrange systematically —*adj.* **1** having a flat surface **2** having or made of thin, horizontal plates, as some corals —**tab′u·la′tion** *n.*
tab·u·la·tor (-lāt′ər) *n.* a person or thing that tabulates; specif., *a)* a device on a typewriter activated by a key (**tab key**), used to move the carriage a given number of spaces, as in making columns *b)* a machine for automatically compiling lists, tabulations, etc. from information encoded on punch cards
ta·bu·li (tə bo͞o′lē) *n. var. of* TABBOULEH
ta·bun (tä′bo͝on) *n.* ⟦Ger < ?⟧ a highly toxic nerve gas, $(CH_3)_2NPO(C_2H_5O)CN$
TAC *abbrev.* Tactical Air Command
tac·a·ma·hac (tak′ə mə hak′) *n.* ⟦Sp *tacamahaca,* earlier *tecomahaca* < Nahuatl *tecomahca,* lit., stinking copal⟧ **1** a strong-smelling gum resin used in ointments and incenses **2** any of several trees, as the balsam poplar, yielding this resin Also **tac′a·ma·hac′a** (-ə)
ta·cet (tā′set′) *v.impersonal* ⟦L, 3d pers. sing., pres. indic., of *tacere,* to be silent: see TACIT⟧ *Musical Direction* it is silent: a note to the performer to be silent for the indicated time
tach (tak) *n. short for* TACHOMETER
tache or **tach** (tach) *n.* ⟦ME < MFr, a nail < OFr *estache:* see ATTACH⟧ [Archaic] a device, as a buckle, hook and eye, etc., for fastening two parts together
tach·i·na fly (tak′i nə) ⟦ModL < Gr *tachinos* < *tachys,* swift: see TACHY-⟧ any of a large family (Tachinidae) of bristly, gray and black, dipterous flies, whose larvae are parasitic on caterpillars and other insects: also **tach′i·nid** (-nid) *n.*
tach·isme (tash′iz′əm; *Fr* tȧ shēz′m′) *n.* ⟦Fr < *tache,* a spot (< OFr *teche:* see TETCHY) + *isme,* -ISM⟧ a method of action painting in which the paint is splashed, dribbled, etc. upon the canvas in apparently random patterns —**tach′iste** (-ist; *Fr,* -shēst′) *adj.*
ta·chis·to·scope (tə kis′tə skōp′) *n.* ⟦< Gr *tachistos,* superl. of *tachys,* swift (see TACHY-) + -SCOPE⟧ an apparatus that exposes words, pictures, etc. for a measured fraction of a second, used to increase reading speed or to test memory, perception, etc. —**ta·chis′to·scop′ic** (-skäp′ik) *adj.*
ta·chom·e·ter (ta käm′ət ər, tə-) *n.* ⟦< Gr *tachos,* speed (< *tachys:* see TACHY-) + -METER⟧ a device that indicates or measures the rotational speed of a spinning shaft
ta·chom·e·try (-ə trē) *n.* the use of a tachometer
tach·y- (tak′i) ⟦Gr < *tachys,* swift < IE **dhengh-,* to reach, strong, fast > Sans *daghnōti,* (he) reaches⟧ *combining form* rapid, swift, fast [*tachymeter*]
tach·y·car·di·a (tak′i kär′dē ə) *n.* ⟦ModL < Gr *tachys* (see prec.) + *kardia,* HEART⟧ an abnormally fast heartbeat
tach·y·graph (tak′i graf′) *n.* ⟦Fr *tachygraphe* < Gr *tachygraphos,* swift writer: see TACHY- & -GRAPH⟧ **1** something written in tachygraphy **2** a person skilled in tachygraphy: also **ta·chyg·ra·pher** (ta kig′rə fər, tə-)
ta·chyg·ra·phy (ta kig′rə fē, tə-) *n.* ⟦TACHY- + -GRAPHY⟧ the art or use of rapid writing; esp., ancient Greek and Roman shorthand or the medieval cursive writing, with abbreviations, etc., in these languages —**tach·y·graph·ic** (tak′ə graf′ik) *adj.*, **tach′y·graph′i·cal**
tach·y·lyte or **tach·y·lite** (tak′ə līt′) *n.* ⟦Ger *tachylit* < Gr *tachys,* swift (see TACHY-) + *lytos,* soluble < *lyein,* to dissolve (see LYSIS): from its rapid decomposition in acids⟧ a kind of dark-colored, basaltic volcanic glass —**tach′y·lyt′ic** (-lit′ik) *adj.*
ta·chym·e·ter (ta kim′ət ər, tə-) *n.* ⟦TACHY- + -METER⟧ a surveying instrument for rapid determination of distances, elevations, etc. —**ta·chym′e·try** *n.*
tach·y·on (tak′ē än′) *n.* ⟦TACHY- + -ON⟧ a theoretical subatomic particle conceived of as traveling faster than the speed of light: see also TARDYON
ta·chys·ter·ol (ta kis′tər ôl′, -ōl′) *n.* ⟦TACHY- + STEROL⟧ an isomer of ergosterol, $C_{28}H_{44}O$, formed during the production of calciferol by the irradiation of ergosterol
tac·it (tas′it) *adj.* ⟦< Fr or L: Fr *tacite* < L *tacitus,* pp. of *tacere,* to be silent < IE base **takē-,* to be silent > Goth *thahan,* ON *thegja*⟧ **1** [Now Rare] saying nothing; still **2** unspoken; silent **3** not expressed or declared openly, but implied or understood [*tacit* approval] **4** *Law* happening without contract but by operation of law —**tac′it·ly** *adv.* —**tac′it·ness** *n.*
tac·i·turn (tas′ə tʉrn′) *adj.* ⟦< Fr or L: Fr *taciturne;* L *taciturnus* < *tacere:* see prec.⟧ almost always silent; not liking to talk; uncommunicative —**tac′i·tur′ni·ty** (-tʉr′nə tē) *n.* —**tac′i·turn′ly** *adv.*
Tac·i·tus (tas′ə təs), **(Publius Cornelius)** A.D. 55?-120?; Rom. historian
tack (tak) *n.* ⟦ME *takke* < MDu *tacke,* twig, point, akin to Ger *zacke* < ? IE base **dek-,* to tear > TAIL¹⟧ **1** a short nail or pin, with a narrow shaft that is not tapered and a relatively large, flat head **2** *a)* the act of fastening, esp. in a slight or temporary way *b)* *Sewing* a stitch for marking darts, etc. from a pattern, clipped and later removed (in full **tailor's tack**) *c)* stickiness; adhesiveness **3** a zigzag course, or movement in such a course **4** a course of action or policy, esp. one differing from another or a preceding course **5** ⟦< ?⟧ food; foodstuff [*hardtack*] **6** *Naut.* *a)* a rope for securing the lower forward corner of a fore-and-aft sail *b)* this corner *c)* the direction in which a vessel is moving in relation to the position of the sails *d)* a change of direction in which the sail or sails shift from one side of the vessel to the other *e)* a course against the wind *f)* any of a series of zigzag movements in such a course **7** equipment for riding a horse, as saddles, bridles, etc.; saddlery —*vt.* **1** to fasten or attach with tacks **2** to attach temporarily, as by sewing with long stitches **3** to attach as a supplement; add [to *tack* an amendment onto a bill] **4** *Horsemanship* to

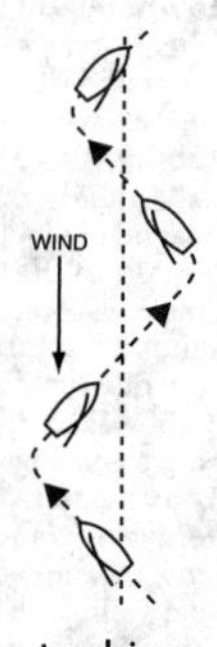

tacking

put a saddle, bridle, etc. on (a horse): often with *up* **5** *Naut.* *a)* to change the course of (a vessel) by turning its bow into and across the wind (opposed to WEAR²) *b)* to maneuver (a vessel) against the wind by a series of tacks —*vi.* **1** *Naut.* *a)* to tack a sailing vessel *b)* to change its course by being tacked, or sail against the wind by a series of tacks (said of a sailing vessel) **2** to go in a zigzag course **3** to change suddenly one's policy or course of action —**tack′er** *n.*

tack·le (tak′əl; *for n. 2 & 5, naut.* tā′kəl) *n.* ⟦ME *takel* < MDu, pulley, rope, equipment in general, prob. akin to MLowG *tacken*, to touch, press, ? akin to TAKE⟧ **1** apparatus; equipment; gear [*fishing tackle*] **2** a rope and pulley block, or a system of ropes and pulleys, used to lower, raise, or move various objects **3** the act or an instance of tackling, as in football ☆**4** *Football* *a)* an offensive lineman who is primarily a blocker, usually positioned just outside an offensive guard *b)* a defensive lineman usually positioned near the offensive center *c)* a type of football in which the defensive players tackle the ballcarrier: cf. TOUCH FOOTBALL: in full **tackle football** **5** *Naut.* *a)* [Archaic] a ship's rigging *b)* later, the running rigging and pulleys to operate the sails —*vt.* **tack′led**, **tack′ling** **1** to fasten by means of tackle **2** to harness (a horse) **3** to take hold of; seize **4** *a)* to undertake to do or solve (something difficult) [*to tackle a job*] *b)* to deal with (a difficult person) **5** *Football* to stop (an opponent carrying the ball), esp. by knocking or throwing him or her to the ground **6** to knock or throw to the ground [*a policeman tackled the fleeing robber*] —*vi.* **1** *Football* to stop an opponent who is carrying the ball, esp. by knocking or throwing the opponent to the ground **2** to knock or throw someone to the ground —**tack′ler** *n.*

tack room a room near a stable, in which tack is kept

tack·y¹ (tak′ē) *adj.* **tack′i·er**, **tack′i·est** ⟦TACK (*n.* 2c) + -Y²⟧ sticky: said as of varnish before it is fully dry —**tack′i·ness** *n.*

☆**tack·y²** (tak′ē) *adj.* **tack′i·er**, **tack′i·est** ⟦< *tacky*, hillbilly < ?⟧ [Informal] **1** dowdy or shabby, as in dress or appearance **2** in poor taste; inelegant —**tack′i·ly** *adv.* —**tack′i·ness** *n.*

Tac·na (täk′nə, tak′-) **1** city in S Peru **2** region in S Peru which, with an adjacent region (ARICA²) in Chile, was divided between the two countries in 1929

☆**ta·co** (tä′kō) *n., pl.* **-cos** ⟦AmSp < Sp, a plug, wadding, light lunch⟧ a Mexican dish consisting of a fried and folded or rolled tortilla filled with chopped meat, shredded lettuce, etc.

Ta·co·ma (tə kō′mə) ⟦< ? AmInd⟧ seaport in W Wash., on Puget Sound

☆**tac·o·nite** (tak′ə nīt′) *n.* ⟦< *Taconic*, old name for rock formations first identified in the Taconic Range (in Vt. and Mass.) + -ITE¹⟧ an iron-bearing chert containing from 25 to 35 percent hematite and magnetite: it is a low-grade iron ore that is pelletized for blast-furnace reduction

tact (takt) *n.* ⟦Fr < L *tactus*, pp. of *tangere*, to touch < IE base **tag-*, to touch, grasp > OE *thaccian*, to stroke⟧ **1** [Archaic] the sense of touch **2** delicate perception of the right thing to say or do without offending; skill in dealing with people **3** delicate sensitivity, esp. in aesthetics

SYN.—**tact** implies the skill in dealing with persons or difficult situations of one who has a quick and delicate sense of what is fitting and thus avoids giving offense [*it will require tact to keep him calm*]; **poise** implies composure in the face of disturbing or embarrassing situations [*despite the social blunder, she maintained her poise*]; **diplomacy** implies a smoothness and adroitness in dealing with others, sometimes in such a way as to gain one's own ends [*his lack of diplomacy lost him the contract*]; **savoir-faire** implies sophistication in knowing the right thing to do or say in any situation

tact·ful (takt′fəl) *adj.* having or showing tact —**tact′ful·ly** *adv.* —**tact′ful·ness** *n.*

tac·tic¹ (tak′tik) *adj.* ⟦ModL *tacticus* < Gr *taktikos*: see TACTICS⟧ *Biol.* of, showing, or characteristic of taxis

tac·tic² (tak′tik) *n.* ⟦ModL *tactica* < Gr *taktikē* (*technē*), (art) of arranging: see TACTICS⟧ **1** TACTICS **2** a detail or branch of tactics —*adj.* of arrangement or system

tac·ti·cal (tak′ti kəl) *adj.* **1** of or having to do with tactics, esp. in military or naval maneuvers **2** characterized by or showing cleverness and skill in tactics —**tac′ti·cal·ly** *adv.*

tac·ti·cian (tak tish′ən) *n.* an expert in tactics

tac·tics (tak′tiks) *pl.n.* ⟦Gr (*ta*) *taktika*, lit., (the) matters of arrangement < *taktikos*, fit for arranging < *tassein*, to arrange, put in order < IE base **tāg-*, to set aright > Gr *taxis*, order⟧ **1** *a)* [*with sing. v.*] the science of arranging and maneuvering military and naval forces in action or before the enemy, esp. (as distinguished from STRATEGY) with reference to short-range objectives *b)* actions in accord with this science **2** any methods used to gain an end; esp., skillful methods or procedure

tac·tile (tak′təl; *chiefly Brit*, -tīl′) *adj.* ⟦Fr < L *tactilis* < *tangere*, to touch: see TACT⟧ **1** that can be perceived by the touch; tangible **2** of, having, or related to the sense of touch —**tac·til′i·ty** (-til′ə tē) *n.*

tactile corpuscle any of various small, epidermal structures with nerve endings sensitive to touch or pressure

tact·less (takt′lis) *adj.* not having or showing tact —**tact′less·ly** *adv.* —**tact′less·ness** *n.*

tac·tu·al (tak′cho͞o əl) *adj.* ⟦< L *tactus* (see TACT) + -AL⟧ TACTILE

☆**tad** (tad) *n.* ⟦prob. < TADPOLE⟧ **1** a little child, esp. a boy **2** a small amount or extent: often used with *a* and having adverbial force [*a tad tired*]

ta-da (tä dä′) *interj.* ⟦echoic⟧ [Informal] used to suggest the sound of a fanfare: an exclamation of triumph or pride accompanying an announcement, a bow, etc.: also sp. **ta da**, **ta-dah**, etc.

tad·pole (tad′pōl′) *n.* ⟦ME *taddepol* < *tadde*, toad + *poll*, head, hence, toad that seems all head⟧ **1** the larva of certain amphibians, as frogs and toads, having gills and a tail and living in water: as it matures, the gills usually are lost and legs develop **2** the free-swimming larval stage of tunicates, having gill slits and a notochord

Ta·dzhik (tä jik′, -jēk′) *n. alt. sp. of* TAJIK

Ta·dzhik·i (tä jik′ē, -jē′kē) *n. alt. sp. of* TAJIKI

Tadzhik Soviet Socialist Republic a republic of the U.S.S.R.: now TAJIKISTAN

tae·di·um vi·tae (tē′dē əm vī′tē, -vē′tī) ⟦L, weariness of life⟧ a feeling that life is wearisome and boring

tae kwon do (tī′kwän′dō′) ⟦Kor < *tae*, kick + *kwon*, fist + *do*, way, method⟧ a Korean self-defense system much like karate

tael (tāl) *n.* ⟦Port < Malay *tahil*, a unit of weight for measuring gold, silver, or opium⟧ **1** any of various units of weight of E Asia **2** [Historical] a Chinese unit of money equal in value to a tael of silver

ta'en (tān) *vt., vi.* [Old Poet.] TAKEN

tae·ni·a (tē′nē ə) *n., pl.* **-ni·ae′** (-ē′) ⟦L < Gr *tainia*, ribbon, tape, akin to *teinein*, to stretch: see THIN⟧ **1** an ancient Greek headband or fillet **2** *Anat.* a ribbonlike part or structure, as of muscle or nerve tissue **3** *Archit.* a band between the frieze and the architrave of a Doric entablature **4** *Zool.* a tapeworm (esp. genus *Taenia*)

tae·ni·a·cide (tē′nē ə sīd′) *n.* ⟦prec. + -CIDE⟧ a drug, etc. that destroys tapeworms —**tae′ni·a·ci′dal** *adj.*

tae·ni·a·sis (tē nī′ə sis) *n.* ⟦ModL: see TAENIA & -IASIS⟧ infestation with tapeworms

☆**TAF** or **T.A.F.** (tē′ā′ef′) *n.* ⟦< *t*(*umor*) *a*(*ngiogenesis*) *f*(*actor*)⟧ a substance, consisting of protein and nucleic acid developed in a malignant tumor, that stimulates the formation of capillaries for nourishing the tumor and carrying off its waste matter

taf·fe·ta (taf′i tə) *n.* ⟦ME *taffata* < OFr *taffetas* < It *taffetà* < Pers *tāftah*, woven < *tāftan*, to weave, spin, shine⟧ a fine, rather stiff fabric of silk, nylon, acetate, etc., with a sheen —*adj.* like or made of taffeta

taff·rail (taf′rāl′) *n.* ⟦altered (infl. by RAIL¹) < *tafferel*, archaic term for the upper part of a ship's stern < Du *tafereel*, a panel, picture, for **tafeleel*, dim. of *tafel*, table < L *tabula*, tablet or slab for inscriptions (see TABLE): the *tafferel* was so named from its carved panels⟧ a protective rail around the weather deck at the stern of a ship

taf·fy (taf′ē) *n.* ⟦< ?⟧ **1** a chewy candy made of sugar or molasses boiled down and pulled: cf. TOFFEE ☆**2** [Old Informal] flattery or cajolery

☆**taffy pull** a party at which taffy is made

☆**taf·i·a** or **taf·fi·a** (taf′ē ə) *n.* ⟦Fr < or akin to *ratafia*: see RATAFIA⟧ a low-grade rum made in the West Indies

Taft (taft) **1 Lo·ra·do** (lə rā′dō) 1860-1936; U.S. sculptor **2 William Howard** 1857-1930; 27th president of the U.S. (1909-13): chief justice of the U.S. (1921-30)

tag (tag) *n.* ⟦ME *tagge*, prob. < Scand, as in Swed *tagg*, a point, spike, Norw, a point; akin to Ger *zacke*, a point, jag: see TACK⟧ **1** [Archaic] a hanging end or rag, as on a torn skirt **2** any small part or piece hanging from or loosely attached to the main piece **3** a hard-tipped end, as of metal, on a cord or lace, to give stiffness for drawing through holes; aglet **4** a piece of bright material tied next to the fly on a fishhook ☆**5** a card, ticket, plastic marker, etc. tied or attached to something as a label or worn as identification, etc. [*a price tag, a name tag*] **6** a word or phrase that describes a person or thing; epithet **7** *a)* an ornamental, instructive, or strikingly effective ending for a speech, story, etc. *b)* a short, familiar quotation, often, specif., one used as such an ending **8** TAG LINE **9** the last part of any proceeding **10** a loop on a garment for hanging it up, or on a boot for pulling it on **11** a flourish or decorative stroke in writing **12** *a)* a lock of hair *b)* a matted lock of wool **13** a children's game in which one player, called "it," chases the others with the object of touching, or tagging, one of them and making that one "it" in turn **14** a tiny amount of radioactive isotope incorporated into a compound so that it can be readily traced through a chemical reaction, physiological cycle, etc. **15** [Obs.] the rabble: cf. RAGTAG **16** *Baseball* the act of tagging **17** *Comput.* *a)* a label assigned to identify data in memory *b)* a sequence of characters in a markup language used to provide information, such as formatting specifications, about a document —*vt.* **tagged**, **tag′ging** **1** to provide with a tag; fasten a tag to; label **2** to apply a descriptive name to; call by an epithet **3** to choose or select ☆**4** to overtake and touch in or as in the game of tag ☆**5** to print (a postage stamp) with luminescent ink so that ultraviolet light can locate the stamp for cancellation and sorting: chiefly in the past participle **6** [Informal] to strike or hit hard **7** [Informal] to follow close behind ☆**8** [Informal] *a)* to put a parking ticket on (a vehicle) *b)* to charge with lawbreaking [*he was tagged for speeding*] ☆**9** *Baseball* to touch (a base runner) with the ball or to touch (a base) with the ball or while holding the ball, with the aim of putting the runner out —*vi.* [Informal] to follow close behind a person or thing: usually with *along, after*, etc. —☆**tag up** *Baseball* to return to the base and touch it before taking another lead or running: said of a base runner —**tag′ger** *n.*

Ta·ga·log (tä gä′lôg′) *n.* ⟦< ?⟧ **1** *pl.* **-logs′** or **-log′** a member of the ethnic group that is indigenous to Manila and the surrounding region in the Philippines **2** the Western Austronesian language of this ethnic group, an official language of the Republic of the Philippines: cf. PILIPINO

Ta·gan·rog (tä′gən räg′; *Russ* tä′gän rôk′) seaport in SW Russia, on the Sea of Azov, near Rostov

☆**tag·board** (tag′bôrd′) ***n.*** sturdy cardboard used for tags, posters, mountings, etc.

tag end 1 any loosely attached or hanging end 2 the last part of something; remnant

tag·gant (tag′ənt) ***n.*** ⟦< TAG (v.) + -ANT⟧ a substance, usually a chemical, added to a product, esp. an explosive, so that the product is traceable back to its origin or is easily detectable by specially trained security dogs, electronic detectors, etc.

ta·glia·tel·le (täl′yə tel′ē) ***n.*** ⟦It, pl.n. < *tagliato,* pp. of *tagliare,* to cut < VL *taliare:* see TAILOR⟧ pasta in the form of wide (approximately ¾ in), flat noodles

tag line 1 the last line of a play, joke, story, etc., often providing some point in a dramatic or humorous way, as a PUNCHLINE 2 SLOGAN (*n.* 2 & 3): also written **tag′line′** ***n.***

☆**tag·meme** (tag′mēm′) ***n.*** ⟦coined (1933) by Leonard BLOOMFIELD < Gr *tagma,* a rank, arrangement (< *tassein,* to arrange: see TACTICS) + -EME⟧ *Linguis.* the smallest meaningful unit of grammatical form —**tag·me′mic** (-mē′mik) ***adj.***

☆**tag·me·mics** (tag mē′miks) ***n.*** ⟦< prec. + -ICS⟧ a theory of language viewing the tagmeme as the basic unit of grammar and emphasizing the function of structured grammatical units

Ta·gore (tə gôr′), Sir **Ra·bin·dra·nath** (rə bēn′drə nät′) 1861-1941; Indian (Bengali) poet

tag question a brief question with the general meaning "Is it not so?", added to a declarative or imperative sentence: it is negative in construction when the original sentence is affirmative, and vice versa (Ex.: It isn't raining, *is it?* Hurry now, *won't you?*)

tag sale a sale of items that have price tags, as one of used items held in a garage or yard or of new items in a store

tag team ⟦so named because a wrestler must *tag,* or touch, a teammate before replacing him or her in the ring: see TAG (*vt.* 4)⟧ a two-member team in TAG-TEAM wrestling

tag-team (tag′tēm′) ***adj.*** 1 designating or having to do with a form of professional wrestling in which two-member teams compete, with teammates alternating in the ring 2 [Informal] of or having to do with any activity in which participants work together alternately

ta·gua (tä′gwə) ***n.*** ⟦AmSp < Quechua *tawa*⟧ a South American palm (*Phytelephas macrocarpa*) whose ivorylike seed is used to make buttons, ornaments, etc.; vegetable ivory

Ta·gus (tā′gəs) river flowing west across central Spain & Portugal into the Atlantic through a broad estuary: *c.* 600 mi (966 km): Sp. name TAJO; Port. name TEJO

ta·hi·ni (tä hē′nē) ***n.*** ⟦< Ar *ṭaḥīnī,* mealy < *ṭaḥīn,* flour, meal < *ṭaḥana,* to grind⟧ a food paste made from ground sesame seeds

Ta·hi·ti (tə hēt′ē) ⟦< Proto-Polynesian **tafiti,* distant, remote⟧ one of the Society Islands, in the South Pacific: 402 sq mi (1,041 sq km); chief town, Papeete

Ta·hi·ti·an (tə hēsh′ən, tä-; -hēt′ē ən) ***adj.*** of Tahiti or its people, language, or culture —***n.*** 1 a person born or living on Tahiti 2 the Polynesian language spoken on Tahiti

Ta·hoe (tä′hō′), **Lake** ⟦< Washo (a Hokan language) *dá′aw,* lake⟧ lake between Calif. & Nev.: resort area: 193 sq mi (500 sq km)

tahr (tär) ***n.*** ⟦< name in a language of the W Himalayas⟧ a short-horned, wild goat (genus *Hemitragus*) of Arabia, India, and the Himalayas

Tai (tī) ***n.*** 1 *a)* a subbranch of the Sino-Tibetan language family, including Thai, Laotian, and Shan *b)* a member of any of the Southeast Asian peoples speaking these languages 2 *a)* a member of a people of N Vietnam that speaks a Tai language *b)* the language of this people —***adj.*** of these peoples or their languages or cultures

tai chi (tī′ jē′, tī′ chē′) ⟦< Mandarin *t'ai-chi,* lit., grand ultimate; *t'ai-chi ch'uan* < Mandarin *ch'uan,* fist, boxing⟧ a form of exercise or martial art developed in China and characterized by slow, rhythmic, circular movements: in full **t'ai chi ch'uan** (chwän)

Tai·chung (tī′choon′) city in WC Taiwan

tai·ga (tī′gə) ***n.*** ⟦Russ *tajga*⟧ *Ecol.* a type of transitional plant community that is located between the arctic tundra and the boreal coniferous forests, having scattered trees: often it is considered to include the N regions of the boreal forests

tail[1] (tāl) ***n.*** ⟦ME < OE *tægel,* akin to OHG *zagel* < IE base **dek̂-,* to tear, tear off > Sans *saśā,* fringe⟧ 1 *a)* the rear end of an animal's body, esp. when forming a distinct, flexible appendage to the trunk *b)* such an appendage 2 anything like an animal's tail in form or position *[the tail of a shirt]* 3 a luminous train behind a comet or meteor 4 the hind, bottom, last, or inferior part of anything 5 [*often pl.*] the reverse side of a coin 6 a long braid or tress of hair 7 a train of followers or attendants; retinue 8 the lower end of a pool or stream 9 *a)* the rear or back section of an aircraft *b)* a set of stabilizing planes at the rear of an airplane *c)* the rear part of a rocket or missile ☆10 [*pl.*] *a)* TAILCOAT *b)* full-dress attire for men that includes a tailcoat 11 [Informal] a person or vehicle that follows another, esp. in surveillance 12 [Slang] the buttocks 13 [Slang] *a)* sexual intercourse with a woman *b)* a woman regarded as a sexual partner: somewhat vulgar 14 *Printing* the bottom of a page 15 *Prosody* the short line or lines ending certain stanzas or verse forms —***adj.*** 1 at the rear or rear end 2 from the rear *[a tail wind]* —***vt.*** 1 to provide with a tail 2 to cut or detach the tail or taillike part from 3 to form the tail or end of, as of a group or procession; be at the rear or end of 4 to fasten or connect at or by the tail 5 to fasten one end of (a brick, board, etc.) into a wall, etc.: usually used with *in* ☆6 [Informal] to follow stealthily; shadow —***vi.*** 1 to straggle 2 to become gradually smaller or fainter: with *off* or *away* 3 to be fastened into a wall, etc. by one end: said of a brick or board ☆4 [Informal] to follow close behind —☆**on someone's tail** [Informal] following or shadowing someone closely —**turn tail** to run from danger, difficulty, hardship, etc. —**with one's tail between one's legs** in defeat or in escape from expected defeat, esp. with fear or dejection —**tail′less** ***adj.*** —**tail′like′** ***adj.***

tail[2] (tāl) ***n.*** ⟦ME *taile* < OFr *taille,* a cutting < *taillier:* see TAILOR⟧ ENTAIL (*n.* 2 & 3) —***adj.*** limited in a specific way, as to certain heirs or order of succession

☆**tail·back** (tāl′bak′) ***n.*** 1 *Football* the running back farthest from the line of scrimmage 2 [Brit.] a long line of slow-moving traffic; traffic jam

tail·board (tāl′bôrd′) ***n.*** [Brit.] TAILGATE

tail·bone (tāl′bōn′) ***n.*** COCCYX

tail·coat (tāl′kōt′) ***n.*** a man's full-dress coat, with long, tapering tails at the back

tail covert any of the small feathers covering the basal parts of the large tail feathers of a bird

tailed (tāld) ***adj.*** having a (specified kind of) tail: usually in comb. *[bobtailed]*

tail end 1 the rear or bottom end of anything 2 the concluding part of anything 3 [Informal] the buttocks

tail·fan (tāl′fan′) ***n.*** the fanlike structure at the rear of a crayfish or lobster, used for swimming backward

tail fin 1 a fixed or adjustable fin on the rear of a rocket, car, etc.: sometimes written **tail′fin′** ***n.*** 2 *Zool.* a movable fin that forms the tail of a fish, the fluke of a whale, etc.

☆**tail·gate** (-gāt′) ***n.*** a board or gate at the back of a wagon, truck, station wagon, etc., designed to be removed or swung open on hinges for loading or unloading —***vt.*** **-gat′ed, -gat′ing** to drive too closely behind (another vehicle) —***vi.*** 1 to drive too closely behind another vehicle 2 ⟦so called because the meal was orig. served on the tailgate⟧ to picnic at or near one's automobile or in a parking lot, as before a sporting event —**tail′gat′er** ***n.***

tail·ing (tā′liŋ) ***n.*** ⟦TAIL[1], V. + -ING⟧ 1 [*pl.*] waste or refuse left in various processes of milling, mining, distilling, etc. 2 the part of a projecting brick, stone, etc. fastened into a wall

tail·lamp (tāl′lamp′) ***n.*** [Chiefly Brit.] *var. of* TAILLIGHT

taille (tāl; *Fr* tä′y′) ***n.*** ⟦OFr < *taillier,* to cut: see TAILOR⟧ a French feudal tax imposed by the king or a lord

tail·leur (tä yʉr′) ***n.*** ⟦Fr, lit., tailor < OFr *tailleor,* cutter: see TAILOR⟧ a woman's tailored suit

tail·light (tāl′līt′) ***n.*** a light, usually red, at the rear of a vehicle to warn vehicles coming from behind

tai·lor (tā′lər) ***n.*** ⟦ME < OFr *tailleor,* cutter < *taillier,* to cut, decide, fix < VL *taliare,* to split, cut, orig. prob. to prune < L *talea,* a stick, twig, scion < IE base **tal-,* to grow, sprout > ON *thǫll,* young fir⟧ a person who makes, repairs, or alters clothes, esp. suits and coats —***vi.*** to work as a tailor —***vt.*** 1 *a)* to make (clothes) by tailor's work *b)* to fit or provide (a person) with clothes made by a tailor 2 *a)* to make by cutting and sewing to fit a particular thing *b)* to cut, form, or alter so as to meet certain conditions *[a novel tailored to popular taste]* 3 to fashion (women's garments) with trim, simple lines like those of men's clothes

tai·lor·bird (-burd′) ***n.*** any of several small Old World warblers that stitch leaves together to make a camouflaged holder for their nests

tai·lored (tā′lərd) ***adj.*** 1 having trim, simple lines: said as of some women's garments 2 specially fitted: said as of slipcovers

tai·lor·ing (-lər iŋ) ***n.*** 1 the occupation of a tailor 2 the workmanship or skill of a tailor

tai·lor-made (tā′lər mād′) ***adj.*** made by or as by a tailor; specif., *a)* having trim, simple lines; tailored *b)* custom-made *c)* as if made to meet particular conditions *[we found a sofa tailor-made for our small apartment]*

tail·piece (tāl′pēs′) ***n.*** 1 a piece or part added to, or forming the end of, something 2 the small triangular piece of wood at the lower end of a violin, cello, etc., to which the strings are attached 3 a short beam or rafter with one end tailed in a wall and the other supported by a header 4 *Printing* an ornamental design put at the end of a chapter or at the bottom of a page

☆**tail·pipe** (-pīp′) ***n.*** 1 the exhaust pipe coming from the muffler of a motor vehicle 2 the exhaust duct of a jet engine

tail·race (-rās′) ***n.*** 1 the lower part of a millrace 2 a water channel to carry away tailings from a mine

tail·spin (-spin′) ***n.*** 1 SPIN (*n.* 5): also **tail spin** 2 a state of rapidly increasing depression or confusion

tail·stock (-stäk′) ***n.*** *Mech.* the adjustable part of a lathe, containing the dead center which holds the work

tail wind a wind blowing in the same direction as the course of an aircraft, etc.

Tai·myr Peninsula (tī mir′) large peninsula in N Asian Russia, between the Kara & Laptev seas: *c.* 700 mi (1,127 km) wide at its base: also sp. **Taymyr, Taimir,** or **Taymir**

Tai·nan (tī′nän′) city in SW Taiwan

Taí·na·ron (tā′nə rôn′), **Cape** *Gr. name for* Cape MATAPAN

Taine (ten; *E* tān), **Hip·po·lyte A·dolphe** (ē pô lēt′ à dôlf′) 1828-93; Fr. literary critic & historian

Tai·no (tī′nō) ***n.,*** *pl.* **-nos** or **-no** ⟦< Taino *nitayno,* the first, the good⟧ 1 a member of an aboriginal Indian people of the West Indies, extinct since the 16th cent. 2 the Arawakan language of this people

taint (tānt) ***vt.*** ⟦prob. a merging of ME *taynten*, to touch (aphetic < *ataynten*, ATTAINT) + Anglo-Fr *teinter*, to color < *teint*, pp. of OFr *teindre* < L *tingere*, to wet, moisten: see TINGE⟧ **1** *a)* to affect with something physically injurious, unpleasant, etc.; infect, poison, etc. *b)* to affect with putrefaction or decay; spoil **2** to make morally corrupt **3** [Obs.] to sully or stain ***—vi.*** to become tainted ***—n.*** **1** a trace of corruption, disgrace, evil, etc. **2** an infectious or contaminating trace; infection, decay, etc. **—SYN.** CONTAMINATE

t'ain't (tānt) *contraction* [Dial.] it ain't

tai·pan (tī pan′) ***n.*** ⟦< name in a language of Australia⟧ a deadly venomous snake (*Oxyuranus scutellatus*) of the cobra family, found mainly in Australia

Tai·pei (tī′pā′) capital of Taiwan, in the N part: also sp. **Tai′peh′**

Tai·wan (tī′wän′) **1** island of China, off the SE coast: a Japanese territory (1895-1945) **2** political unit consisting of this island, the Pescadores, Quemoy, Matsu, and other small island groups, governed as a separate country since 1949 and officially called the *Republic of China:* regarded as a province of China by the People's Republic of China: 13,892 sq mi (35,980 sq km); cap. Taipei —**Tai·wan·ese** (tī′wə nēz′, -nēs′) ***adj., n., pl.*** **-ese′**

Taiwan Strait strait between Taiwan & Fujian province, China, joining the East & South China seas: *c.* 100 mi (161 km) wide

Tai·yu·an (tī′yo͞o än′) city in N China; capital of Shanxi province

Ta·jik (tä jik′, -jēk′) ***n.*** **1** *pl.* **-jiks′** or **-jik′** a member of a people of Iranian stock living in Afghanistan, Tajikistan, and parts of Uzbekistan **2** the Iranian language of this people ***—adj.*** of the Tajiks or their language or culture

Ta·jik·i (tä jik′ē, -jē′kē) ***n.*** TAJIK (*n.* 2)

Ta·jik·i·stan (tä jik′i stan′, -stän′) country in WC Asia: became independent upon the breakup of the U.S.S.R. (1991): 55,251 sq mi (143,100 sq km); cap. Dushanbe: formerly, *Tadzhik Soviet Socialist Republic*

Taj Ma·hal (täzh′ mə häl′, täj′-) ⟦Pers, best of buildings⟧ famous mausoleum at Agra, India, built (1630?-48?) by Shah Jahan for his favorite wife

Ta·jo (tä′hō′) *Sp. name for* TAGUS

ta·ka (tä′kä) ***n.,*** *pl.* **-ka** ⟦Beng < Sans *ṭŏṅkŏ*, silver coins⟧ the basic monetary unit of Bangladesh: see the table of monetary units in the Reference Supplement

take (tāk) ***vt.*** **took, tak′en, tak′ing** ⟦ME *taken* < OE *tacan* < ON *taka* < ? IE base **dēg-*, to lay hold of⟧ **I.** *to get possession of by force or skill; seize, grasp, catch, capture, win, etc.* **1** to get by conquering; capture; seize **2** to trap, snare, or catch (a bird, animal, or fish) **3** *a)* to win (a game, a trick at cards, etc.) *b)* to capture (an opponent's piece in chess or checkers) **4** to get hold of; grasp or catch **5** to hit (a person) *in* or *on* some part **6** to affect; attack [*taken* with a fit] **7** to catch in some act, esp. a moral fault [*taken* in adultery] **8** to capture the fancy of; charm **II.** *to get by action not involving force or skill; obtain, acquire, assume, etc.* **1** to get into one's hand or hold; transfer to oneself **2** to eat, drink, swallow, etc. for nourishment or as medicine **3** to admit; let in [the bus *takes* 20 riders] **4** to get benefit from by exposure to (the air, sun, etc.) **5** to enter into a special relationship with [to *take* a wife] **6** to have sexual intercourse with **7** to buy [he *took* the first suit he tried on] **8** to rent, lease, or pay for so as to occupy or use [to *take* a cottage] **9** to get regularly by paying for [to *take* a daily newspaper] **10** to assume as a responsibility, task, etc. [to *take* a job] **11** to assume or adopt (a symbol of duty or office) [the president *took* the chair] **12** to obligate oneself by [to *take* a vow] **13** to join or associate oneself with (one party or side in a contest, disagreement, etc.) **14** to assume as if granted or due one [to *take* the blame, to *take* deductions] **15** [Slang] to cheat; trick **16** *Gram.* to have or admit of according to usage, nature, etc.; be used with in construction [a transitive verb *takes* an object] **III.** *to get, adopt, use, etc. by selection or choice* **1** to choose; select **2** to use or employ; resort to [to *take* a mop to the floor] **3** *a)* to travel by [to *take* a bus] *b)* to set out on; follow [to *take* the old path] **4** to go to (a place) for shelter, safety, etc. [to *take* cover] **5** to deal with; consider [to *take* a matter seriously] **6** *a)* to occupy [*take* a chair] *b)* to use up; consume [to *take* all day] **7** to require; demand; need: often used impersonally [it *takes* money; to *take* a size ten] ☆**8** *Baseball* to allow (a pitched ball) to pass without swinging one's bat **IV.** *to get from a source* **1** to derive, inherit, or draw (a name, quality, etc.) from something or someone specified **2** to extract, as for quotation; excerpt [to *take* a verse from the Bible] **3** to obtain or ascertain by observation, query, or experiment [to *take* a poll, to *take* one's temperature] **4** to study; specif., to be enrolled as a student in [to *take* an art course] **5** to write down; copy [*take* notes] **6** *a)* to make (a photograph, picture, etc.) *b)* to draw, photograph, etc. a likeness of [*take* the scene in color] **7** to make an impression of [*take* his fingerprints] **V.** *to get as offered or due; receive, accept, suffer, etc.* **1** to win (a prize, reward, etc.) **2** to be the object of; specif., *a)* to undergo [to *take* a beating] *b)* to withstand; endure; hold up against [a tire designed to *take* punishment; she can't *take* a joke] **3** to occupy oneself in; enjoy [*take* a nap] **4** to accept (something offered) [to *take* a bet, to *take* advice] **5** to have a specified reaction to [to *take* a joke in earnest] **6** to confront and get over, through, etc. [the horse *took* the jump] **7** to be affected by (a disease, etc.) [to *take* cold] **8** to absorb; become impregnated or treated with (a dye, polish, etc.) **VI.** *to receive mentally* **1** *a)* to understand the remarks of (a person) *b)* to comprehend the meaning of (words or remarks) *c)* to understand or interpret in a specified way **2** to suppose; presume [he *took* her to be a teacher] **3** to have or feel (an emotion or mental state) [*take* pity, *take* notice] **4** to hold and act upon (an idea, point of view, etc.) **VII.** *to make or complete by action* **1** to do; perform (an act) [to *take* a walk] **2** to make or put forth (a resolution or objection) as the result of thought **3** [Informal] to aim and execute (a specified action) at an object [to *take* a jab at someone] **VIII.** *to move, remove, etc.* **1** to be the way or means of going to (a place, condition, etc.); conduct; lead [the path *takes* you to the river] **2** to escort or accompany [to *take* a friend to dinner] **3** to carry or transport [to *take* a book with one] **4** to remove from a person, thing, or place; specif., to steal **5** to remove by death; bring to an end [cancer *takes* many lives] **6** to subtract [to *take* two from ten] **7** to direct or move (oneself) ***—vi.*** **1** to get possession **2** to hook or engage with another part: said of a mechanical device **3** to take root; begin growing: said of a plant **4** to lay hold; catch [the fire *took* rapidly] **5** to gain public favor; be popular **6** to be effective in action, operation, desired result, etc. [the vaccination *took*; the dye *takes* well] **7** to remove a part; detract (*from*) [nothing *took* from the scene's beauty] **8** to be made or adapted to be taken (*up, down, apart,* etc.) **9** [Informal] to be photographed in a specified way [she *takes* well in profile] **10** *Law* to take possession of property ***—n.*** **1** the act or process of taking **2** something that has been taken **3** *a)* the amount or quantity of something taken [the day's *take* of fish] *b)* [Slang] money received; receipts or profit **4** a vaccination that takes **5** *Film* *a)* an uninterrupted shot photographed by a camera *b)* the process of photographing such a shot **6** *a)* any of a series of recordings or tapes of a performance, from which one will be made for release to the public *b)* the process of so recording **7** [Informal] opinion; evaluation; assessment: followed by *on* [what's your *take* on the new tax?] **8** *Printing* the amount of copy sent to the compositor at one time —☆**on the take** [Slang] willing or seeking to take bribes or illicit income —**take after** **1** to resemble (a parent, etc.) in some way **2** [Informal] to run after or pursue —☆**take a meeting** [Slang] to attend a business conference —**take amiss** **1** [Archaic] to be wrong concerning; mistake **2** to misunderstand the reason behind (an act), esp. so as to become offended —**take back** **1** to regain use or possession of **2** to retract (something said, promised, etc.) **3** to return (something), as to be exchanged —**take down** **1** to remove from a higher place and put in a lower one; pull down **2** to unfasten; take apart **3** to make less conceited; humble **4** to put in writing; record —☆**take five (or ten, etc.)** [Informal] take a break for five (or ten, etc.) minutes, as from working —**take for** **1** to consider to be; regard as **2** to mistake for —**take hold** to take effect or become firmly established [the new fad *took hold* quickly] —**take hold of** to seize; grasp —**take ill (or sick)** to become ill (or sick) —**take in** **1** to admit; receive **2** to reef or furl (a sail) **3** to make smaller or more compact **4** to include; comprise **5** to understand; comprehend **6** to cheat; trick; deceive ☆**7** to visit, see, experience, etc. [to *take in* all the sights] **8** to receive into one's home for pay [to *take in* boarders] —**take it** **1** to suppose; believe ☆**2** [Slang] to withstand difficulty, criticism, hardship, ridicule, etc. —**take it or leave it** accept it or not —**take it out of** [Informal] **1** to exhaust; tire **2** to obtain payment or satisfaction from —☆**take it out on** [Informal] to make (another) suffer for one's own anger, irritation, bad temper, etc. —**take off** **1** to remove (a garment, etc.) **2** to draw or conduct away **3** *a)* to go away; depart *b)* to absent oneself, as from work **4** to deduct; subtract **5** to kill **6** to make a copy or likeness of **7** to leave the ground or water in flight **8** [Informal] to start **9** [Informal] to imitate in a burlesque manner; parody: with *on* **10** [Informal] to become very popular and successful **11** [Slang] to rob —**take off (or out) after** [Informal] to run after or pursue —**take on** **1** to acquire; assume (form, quality, etc.) **2** to employ; hire **3** to begin to do (a task, etc.); undertake **4** to compete or play against; oppose **5** [Informal] to show violent emotion, especially anger or sorrow —**take one's time** to be slow or unhurried; delay —**take out** **1** *a)* to remove; extract *b)* to deduct **2** to obtain by application to the proper authority **3** [Informal] to escort, as on a date **4** [Slang] to kill; specif., to assassinate —**take over** to assume control or possession of —**take to** **1** to develop a habit or practice of doing, using, etc. **2** to apply oneself to (one's studies, work, etc.) **3** to become fond of; care for; be attracted to **4** *a)* to go to or withdraw to [to *take to* the hills, *take to* one's bed with the flu] *b)* to travel on or proceed by [to *take to* the open road] —**take up** **1** to raise; lift **2** to make tighter or shorter **3** to pay off; recover by buying (a mortgage, note, etc.) **4** to absorb (a liquid) **5** *a)* to accept (a challenge, bet, etc.) *b)* to accept the challenge, offer, etc. of (with *on*) [to *take* him *up* on his generous offer] **6** to assume protection or custody of **7** to interrupt in disapproval or rebuke: with *on* **8** to resume (something interrupted) **9** *a)* to become interested in or devoted to (an occupation, study, hobby, belief, etc.) *b)* to adopt (an idea) **10** to occupy or fill (space or time) —**take upon (or on) oneself** **1** to take the responsibility for; accept as a charge **2** to begin (to do something) —**take up with** [Informal] to become a friend or companion of —**tak′a·ble** ***adj.,*** **take′a·ble**

SYN.—take is the general word meaning to get hold of by or as by the hands [to *take* a book, the opportunity, etc.]; to **seize** is to take suddenly and forcibly [he *seized* the gun from the robber; to *seize* power]; **grasp** implies a seizing and holding firmly [to *grasp* a rope, an idea, etc.]; **clutch** implies a tight or convulsive grasping of that which one is eager to take or keep hold of [she *clutched* his hand in terror]; **grab** implies a roughness or unscrupulousness in seizing [the child *grabbed* all the candy; to *grab* credit]; **snatch** stresses an abrupt quickness and, sometimes, a surreptitiousness in seizing [she *snatched* the letter from my hand; to *snatch* a purse] See also **bring, receive**

---

take-a·way or **take·a·way** (tāk′ə wā′) [Chiefly Brit.] ***adj.*** TAKEOUT (*adj.* 1) ***—n.*** **1** TAKEOUT (*n.* 2) **2** a restaurant, store, etc. that sells takeout food

take-charge (tāk′chärj′) ***adj.*** ⟦see CHARGE (*n.* II, 1)⟧ [Informal] responsible, authoritative, and forceful

take·down (tāk′doun′) ***n.*** **1** the act or process of taking down, esp. of disassembling mechanically **2** the act of bringing an opponent in an amateur wrestling match to the mat from a standing position, a maneuver for which points are awarded **3** [Informal] humiliation —*adj.* made to be easily taken apart [a *takedown* firearm]

☆**take-home (pay)** (tāk′hōm′) wages or salary after deductions for income tax, social security, etc. have been made

tak·en (tāk′ən) *vt., vi. pp. of* TAKE

take·off (tāk′ôf′) *n.* **1** the act of leaving the ground from any angle, as in jumping, launching, or flight: cf. LIFTOFF **2** the place from which one leaves a surface ☆**3** *a)* the starting point or launching stage *b) Econ.* the early stages of rapid, self-sustained growth and development **4** [Informal] an amusing or mocking imitation; caricature; burlesque Also **take′-off′**

take·out (-out′) *n.* **1** the act of taking out **2** prepared food bought to be taken away and eaten at home, etc. —*adj.* ☆**1** designating of or prepared food sold as by a restaurant to be eaten away from the premises **2** *Bridge* designating a double intended, not to penalize one's opponents, but to force one's partner to bid: cf. BUSINESS (*adj.* 3) Also **take′-out′**

take·o·ver (-ō′vər) *n.* the act or an instance of assuming control or possession; esp., *a)* the usurpation of power in a nation, organization, etc. ☆*b)* the assumption of ownership or control of a corporation, esp. through the acquisition of its stock Also **take′-o′ver**

tak·er (tāk′ər) *n.* **1** a person who takes something; esp., an available buyer, bettor, etc. **2** a person who is characterized by selfishness

take·up (-up′) *n.* **1** the act or process of taking up, making tight, etc. **2** a mechanical device to tighten something Also **take′-up′**

ta·kin (tä′kin, tā′-) *n.* ⟦< name in Mishmi, a Tibeto-Burman language⟧ a goatlike bovid ruminant (*Budorcas taxicolor*) of the Himalayan forests

tak·ing (tāk′iŋ) *adj.* **1** that captures interest; attractive; winning **2** [Obs.] contagious: said of disease —*n.* **1** the act of one that takes **2** something taken **3** an expropriation of private property by eminent domain: *usually used in pl.* **4** [*pl.*] earnings; profits; receipts **5** [Old Brit. Informal] a state of agitation or excitement —**tak′ing·ly** *adv.*

ta·la[1] (tä′lə) *n.* ⟦< Sans *tāla*, lit., the slapping or clapping of hands together⟧ any of the various repeating rhythmic patterns of stressed and unstressed units, played on a percussion instrument in the music of India

ta·la[2] (tä′lä′) *n., pl.* **ta′la′** ⟦Samoan < E DOLLAR⟧ the basic monetary unit of Samoa: see the table of monetary units in the Reference Supplement

ta·lar·i·a (tə ler′ē ə, -lar′-) *pl.n.* ⟦L < *talaris*, of the ankles < *talus*, ankle⟧ winged sandals or wings on the ankles, represented in mythology as an attribute, esp. of Hermes, or Mercury

talc (talk) *n.* ⟦Fr < Ar *ṭalq*⟧ **1** a soft, light-colored, monoclinic mineral, $Mg_3Si_4O_{10}(OH)_2$, with a greasy feel, used to make talcum powder, lubricants, etc.; magnesium silicate: see MOHS SCALE **2** *short for* TALCUM (POWDER) —*vt.* **talcked** or **talced**, **talck′ing** or **talc′ing** to use talc on

Tal·ca (täl′kä′) city in central Chile

Tal·ca·hua·no (täl′kä wä′nō) seaport in SC Chile, near Concepción

talc·ose (tal′kōs′) *adj.* of or containing talc: occas. **talc′ous** (-kəs)

tal·cum (powder) (tal′kəm) ⟦ML < Ar *ṭalq*, talc⟧ a powder for the body and face made of powdered, purified talc, usually perfumed

tale (tāl) *n.* ⟦ME < OE *talu*, speech, number, akin to Ger *zahl*, number, Du *taal*, speech < IE base *del-, to aim, reckon, trick > Gr *dolos*, L *dolus*, guile, artifice⟧ **1** something told or related; relation or recital of happenings **2** *a)* a story or account of true, legendary, or fictitious events; narrative *b)* a literary composition in narrative form, often, specif., an unsophisticated, somewhat digressive one **3** a piece of gossip **4** a falsehood; lie **5** [Archaic] a tally; count **6** [Obs.] the act of telling —*SYN.* STORY[1]

tale·bear·er (-ber′ər) *n.* a person who spreads scandal or tells secrets; gossip —**tale′bear′ing** *adj., n.*

tal·ent (tal′ənt) *n.* ⟦ME < OE *talente* < L *talentum*, a coin, orig., unit of weight < Gr *talanton*, a unit of money, weight, orig., a balance < IE base **tel-*, to lift up, weigh, bear > TOLERATE: senses 2-4 from the parable of the talents (Matt: 25:14-30)⟧ **1** any of various large units of weight or of money (the value of a talent weight in gold, silver, etc.) used in ancient Greece, Rome, the Middle East, etc. **2** any natural ability or power; natural endowment **3** a superior, apparently natural ability in the arts or sciences or in the learning or doing of anything **4** people collectively, or a person, with talent [to encourage young *talent*] —**tal′ent·ed** *adj.*

SYN.—**talent** implies an apparently native ability for a specific pursuit and connotes either that it is or can be cultivated by the one possessing it [a *talent* for drawing]; **gift** suggests that a special ability is bestowed upon one, as by nature, and not acquired through effort [a *gift* for making plants grow]; **aptitude** implies a natural inclination for a particular work, specif. as pointing to special fitness for, or probable success in, it [*aptitude* tests]; **faculty** implies a special ability that is either inherent or acquired, as well as a ready ease in its exercise [the *faculty* of judgment]; **knack** implies an acquired faculty for doing something cleverly and skillfully [the *knack* of rhyming]; **genius** implies an inborn mental endowment, specif. of a creative or inventive kind in the arts or sciences, that is exceptional or phenomenal [the *genius* of Edison]

☆**talent scout** a person whose work is seeking out persons of superior ability in a certain field, as in the theater

ta·ler (tä′lər) *n., pl.* **ta′ler** ⟦Ger: see DOLLAR⟧ any of various former silver coins issued by various German states between the 15th and 19th cent.

ta·les (tā′lēz′) *pl.n.* ⟦ME < ML *tales (de circumstantibus)*, such (of those standing about), phr. in writ summoning them < L, pl. of *talis*, such: see THAT⟧ *Law* **1** people summoned to fill jury vacancies when the regular panel has become deficient in number, as by challenge **2** [*with sing. v.*] the writ that summons them

ta·les·man (tālz′mən, tā′lēz-) *n., pl.* **ta′les·men** (-mən) a person summoned as one of the TALES

tale·tell·er (tāl′tel′ər) *n.* **1** STORYTELLER **2** TALEBEARER

ta·li (tā′lī′) *n. pl. of* TALUS[1]

Tal·ib (tä lēb′, tal′ēb) *n.* ⟦Ar or Pers, seeker, student⟧ a member of the Taliban

Tal·i·ban (tal′ə ban′, tä′lə bän′) *n.* ⟦< Ar or Pers, pl. of prec.⟧ a militant fundamentalist-Islamic movement, chiefly in Afghanistan and Pakistan: Brit. sp. **Tal′e·ban′**

Ta·lien (täl yen′, däl-) *a former transliteration of* DALIAN

tal·i·on (tal′ē ən) *n.* ⟦ME *talioun* < MFr *talion* < L *talio* (gen. *talionis*) < *talis*, such: see THAT⟧ punishment that exacts a penalty corresponding in kind to the crime

tal·i·ped (tal′i ped′) *adj.* having talipes; clubfooted

tal·i·pes (tal′i pēz′) *n.* ⟦ModL < L *talus*, ankle + *pes* (gen. *pedis*), FOOT⟧ CLUBFOOT

tal·i·pot (tal′i pät′) *n.* ⟦Beng *tālipāt*, palm leaf < Sans *tālī*, fan palm + *pattra*, leaf: for IE bases see TAILOR & FEATHER⟧ a fan palm (*Corypha umbraculifera*) of the East Indies, with gigantic leaves used for fans, umbrellas, etc., and seeds used for buttons: also **talipot palm**

tal·is·man (tal′is mən, -iz-) *n., pl.* **-mans** ⟦Fr < Ar *ṭilasm*, magic figure, horoscope < MGr *telesma*, consecrated object (hence, one with power to avert evil) < LGr, religious rite < Gr *telein*, to initiate, orig., to complete < *telos*, an end: see TELO-[2]⟧ **1** something, as a ring or stone, bearing engraved figures or symbols thought to bring good luck, keep away evil, etc.; amulet **2** anything thought to have magic power; a charm —**tal′is·man′ic** *adj.*, **tal′is·man′i·cal**

talk (tôk) *vi.* ⟦ME *talken* (akin to Fris, to chatter), prob. freq. based on OE *talian*, to reckon, akin to *talu*, TALE⟧ **1** *a)* to put ideas into, or exchange ideas by, spoken words; speak; converse *b)* to express something in words; make a statement (*of, on, about*, etc. something) **2** to express ideas by speech substitutes [to *talk* by signs] **3** to speak emptily or trivially; chatter **4** to gossip **5** to confer; consult **6** to make noises suggestive of speech **7** to reveal secret information; esp., to confess or inform on someone **8** to make a speech, esp. a somewhat informal one —*vt.* **1** to put into spoken words; utter **2** to use in speaking [to *talk* Spanish, to *talk* slang] **3** *a)* to speak about; discuss [to *talk* sports] *b)* [Informal] to speak of (something impressive, remarkable, expensive, etc.) (usually in prp.) [we're *talking* high prices] **4** to put into a specified condition, state of mind, etc. by talking [to *talk* oneself hoarse] —*n.* **1** *a)* the act of talking; speech *b)* conversation, esp. of an informal nature **2** a speech, esp. a somewhat informal one **3** [*often pl.*] a formal discussion; conference **4** rumor; gossip **5** the subject of conversation, gossip, etc. **6** empty or frivolous remarks, discussion, or conversation **7** a particular kind of speech; dialect; lingo **8** sounds, as by an animal, suggestive of speech —*SYN.* SPEAK, SPEECH —**big talk** [Slang] bragging or boasting talk —**have a talk with** to admonish or caution —**make talk 1** to talk idly, as in an effort to pass time **2** to cause gossip —**talk around** to talk (a person) over; persuade —**talk at** to speak to in a way that indicates a response is not really desired —**talk away 1** to pass (a period of time) by talking **2** to talk continuously; chatter —☆**talk back** to answer impertinently or rudely —**talk big** [Slang] to boast; brag —**talk down 1** to silence by talking louder, longer, or more effectively than **2** to aid (a pilot) in landing by giving spoken instructions —**talk down to** to talk in a patronizing way to, as by using pointedly simple speech —**talk someone's ear off** [Slang] to talk to someone at great length or without pause —**talk into** to persuade (someone) to do something —**talk out** to discuss (a problem, etc.) at length in an effort to reach an understanding —**talk out of** to dissuade (someone) from doing something —**talk over 1** to have a conversation about; discuss **2** to win (a person) over to one's view by talking; persuade —**talk up** ☆**1** to promote or praise in discussion **2** to speak loudly and clearly ☆**3** to speak boldly, frankly, etc. —**talk′er** *n.*

☆**talk·a·thon** (tôk′ə thän′) *n.* ⟦prec. + -ATHON⟧ any prolonged period of talking; extended speech, debate, etc.

talk·a·tive (-tiv) *adj.* talking, or fond of talking, a great deal; loquacious —**talk′a·tive·ly** *adv.* —**talk′a·tive·ness** *n.*

SYN.—**talkative**, implying a fondness for talking frequently or at length, is perhaps the least derogatory of these words [a jolly, *talkative* girl]; **loquacious** usually implies a disposition to talk incessantly or to keep up a constant flow of chatter [a *loquacious* mood]; **garrulous** implies a wearisome loquacity about trivial matters [a *garrulous* old man]; **voluble** suggests a continuous flow of glib talk [a *voluble* oration]

talk·ie (tôk′ē) *n.* ⟦TALK (*vi.*) + (MOV)IE⟧ [Old Informal] TALKING PICTURE

talk·ing (tôk′iŋ) *n.* the act of a person who talks; discussion; conversation —*adj.* that talks; talkative

☆**talking book** a recording of a person reading a book, magazine, etc. aloud, for use as by the blind

talking cure [Informal] PSYCHOTHERAPY: usually with *the*

☆**talking head** a person on television or in a film who is shown merely speaking, as in an interview: term suggesting a dull or unimaginative presentation

talking picture [Old-fashioned] a film with a synchronized soundtrack

☆**talking point** a persuasive point to be emphasized, as in presenting an argument

talk·ing-to (tôk′iŋ to͞o′) *n.* [Informal] a rebuke; scolding

talk radio a radio format emphasizing talk and discussion instead of music

talk show *Radio, TV* a program featuring informal conversation, often on a particular topic or range of topics, between a host and, variously, guest celebrities and experts, members of a studio audience, or listeners or viewers telephoning from their homes

talk therapy [Informal] PSYCHOTHERAPY —**talk therapist**

talk·y (tôk′ē) *adj.* **talk′i·er**, **talk′i·est** 1 talkative 2 containing too much talk, or dialogue [a *talky* novel] —**talk′i·ness** *n.*

tall (tôl) *adj.* ⟦ME *tal,* dexterous, seemly < OE *(ge)tæl,* swift, prompt, akin to OHG *gizal,* swift < IE base **del-,* to aim > TALE, TELL[1]⟧ 1 of more than normal height or stature [a *tall* man, a *tall* building] 2 having a specified height [five feet *tall*] ☆3 [Informal] hard to believe because exaggerated or untrue: see also TALL TALE ☆4 [Informal] large; of considerable size [a *tall* drink] ☆5 [Informal] high-flown; pompously eloquent [*tall* talk] 6 [Obs.] *a)* handsome *b)* brave —*adv.* in an upright, dignified manner [to stand *tall,* ride *tall* in the saddle] —**tall′ness** *n.*

tal·lage (tal′ij) *n.* ⟦ME *taillage* < OFr: see TAIL[2] & -AGE⟧ in feudalism *a)* a tax levied by kings upon towns and crown lands *b)* a tax levied by a feudal lord upon his tenants —*vt.* **-laged**, **-lag·ing** to levy a tallage upon; tax

Tal·la·has·see (tal′ə has′ē) ⟦< Creek *talwahasi* < *talwa,* town + *hasi,* old⟧ capital of Fla., in the N part

tall·boy (tôl′boi′) *n.* [Brit.] HIGHBOY

Tal·ley·rand (tal′i rand′; *Fr* tȧl rän′, tȧ le-) (born *Charles Maurice de Talleyrand-Périgord*) Prince of Benevento 1754-1838; Fr. statesman & diplomat

tall·grass (tôl′gras′) *n.* any grass that grows to a height of five feet or more; esp., any such grass growing in the eastern region of the Great Plains

Tal·linn (täl′in) capital of Estonia, on the Gulf of Finland: also sp. **Tal′lin**

Tal·lis (tal′is), **Thomas** 1510?-85; Eng. composer

tall·ish (tôl′ish) *adj.* somewhat tall

tal·lit (tä lēt′, täl′is) *n.* ⟦TalmudHeb *talit,* lit., cloak < ? root *tll,* to cover⟧ *Judaism* the prayer shawl with fringes (*zizit*) on each of its four corners, worn over the shoulders or head by men during morning prayer: cf. Deut. 22:12: also **tal·lith** (täl′ith, -is) or **tal·lis** (täl′is)

☆**tall oil** ⟦half-transl. of Ger *tallöl,* half-transl. of Swed *tallolja,* lit., pine oil < *tall,* pine < ON *thǫll,* young fir (< IE base **tal-,* to sprout > TAILOR) + Swed *olja,* oil < MLowG *olie* < VL *olium,* for L *oleum,* OIL⟧ a resinous liquid obtained as a byproduct in the manufacture of chemical wood pulp: it is used in the manufacture of soap, varnishes, linoleum, etc.

tal·low (tal′ō) *n.* ⟦ME *talgh,* prob. < MLowG *talg,* akin to OE *tælg,* a color, *telgan,* to color, prob. < IE base **del-,* to drip > MIr *delt,* dew⟧ the nearly colorless and tasteless solid fat extracted from the natural fat of cattle, sheep, etc., used in making candles, soaps, lubricants, etc.: see VEGETABLE TALLOW —*vt.* to cover or smear with tallow —**tal′low·y** *adj.*

tallit

tall ship a large, typically square-rigged sailing ship with tall masts, as a clipper

☆**tall tale** a kind of story or folk tale characterized by intentionally ludicrous exaggeration and incredible incidents

tal·ly (tal′ē) *n., pl.* **-lies** ⟦ME *talye* < Anglo-L *talia* < L *talea,* a stick, cutting: see TAILOR⟧ 1 *a)* [Obs.] a stick with cross notches representing the amount of a debt owing or paid: usually the stick was split lengthwise, half for the debtor and half for the creditor *b)* anything used as a record for an account, reckoning, or score 2 an account, reckoning, or score 3 *a)* either of two corresponding parts of something; counterpart *b)* agreement; correspondence 4 any number of objects used as a unit in counting 5 an identifying tag or label —*vt.* **-lied**, **-ly·ing** 1 to put on or as on a tally; record 2 to count; add: usually with *up* 3 to put a label or tag on 4 [Archaic] to make (two things) agree or correspond —*vi.* 1 to tally something 2 to score a point or points in a game 3 to agree; correspond —**SYN.** AGREE

tal·ly·ho (tal′ē hō′) *interj.* ⟦altered < Fr *taïaut*⟧ in fox hunting, used by a hunter to signify that he or she has sighted the fox —*n., pl.* **-hos′** 1 a cry of "tallyho" 2 a coach drawn by four horses

tal·ly·man (tal′ē mən) *n., pl.* **-men** (-mən) 1 a person who tallies something 2 [Brit.] a person who sells goods door to door on the installment plan and calls regularly to collect the payments

Tal·mud (täl′mo͝od, tal′-; -məd) *n.* ⟦Talmud Heb *talmud,* lit., learning, instruction (akin to Aram *talmuda*) < root *lmd:* see MELAMED⟧ the collection of writings constituting the Jewish civil and religious law: it consists of two parts, the Mishna (text) and the Gemara (commentary), but the term is sometimes restricted to the Gemara: cf. HALAKHA and HAGGADA —**Tal·mud′ic** *adj.,* **Tal·mud′i·cal** —**Tal′mud·ism′** *n.*

Tal·mud·ist (-ist) *n.* 1 any of the compilers of the Talmud 2 a student of or expert in the Talmud 3 a person who accepts the authority of the Talmud

tal·on (tal′ən) *n.* ⟦ME, talon, claw < OFr, heel, spur < VL **talo* < L *talus,* ankle⟧ 1 the claw of a bird of prey or, sometimes, of an animal 2 a human finger or hand when like a claw in appearance or grasp 3 the part of the bolt of a lock upon which the key presses as it is turned 4 *a)* in games of solitaire, the cards laid aside either as unplayable discards or for possible use later *b)* STOCK (*n.* 14*d*) 5 *Archit.* an ogee molding —**tal′oned** *adj.*

Ta·los (tā′läs′) *n. Gr. Myth.* 1 an inventor killed because of jealousy by Daedalus, his uncle 2 a man of brass given by Zeus to Minos, King of Crete, as a watchman

ta·lus[1] (tā′ləs) *n., pl.* **-lus·es** or **-li′** (-lī′) ⟦ModL < L, ankle⟧ 1 the bone of the ankle that joins with the ends of the fibula, tibia, and calcaneus to form the ankle joint; anklebone 2 the entire ankle

ta·lus[2] (tā′ləs) *n., pl.* **-lus·es** ⟦Fr < OFr *talu* < L *talutium,* surface indications of the presence of subterranean gold, prob. of Iberian orig.⟧ 1 a slope 2 *Geol. a)* a pile of rock debris at the foot of a cliff *b)* a mantle of rock fragments on a slope below a rock face

☆**Tal·win** (tal′win) ⟦arbitrary name chosen in a contest for naming the product⟧ *trademark for* PENTAZOCINE

tam (tam) *n.* 1 *short for* TAM-O'-SHANTER 2 [Cdn.] BERET

☆**ta·ma·le** (tə mä′lē) *n.* ⟦MexSp *tamal,* pl. *tamales* < Nahuatl *tamalli*⟧ a Mexican dish consisting of cornmeal dough around a filling as of minced meat and red peppers, the whole then wrapped in corn husks or plantain leaves and cooked by baking, steaming, etc.

ta·man·dua (tä′män dwä′) *n.* ⟦Port *tamanduá* < Tupí < *ta* (contr. of *tacy,* ant) + *monduar,* hunter⟧ a small, tree-dwelling species (*Tamandua tetradactyla,* family Myrmecophagidae) of edentate anteaters of tropical America, with a naked tail and large ears

tam·a·rack (tam′ə rak′) *n.* ⟦CdnFr *tamarac:* presumed to be of Algonquian orig.⟧ 1 an American larch tree (*Larix laricina*), usually found in swamps 2 the wood of this tree

ta·ma·rau (tä′mə rou′) *n.* ⟦Tagalog⟧ a small, black, wild buffalo (*Bubalus mindorensis*), native to Mindoro in the Philippines and now rare: also sp. **ta′ma·rao′**

ta·ma·ri (tə mä′rē) *n.* ⟦Jpn⟧ a Japanese soy sauce, made by natural methods and often aged: also **tamari (soy) sauce**

tam·a·rin (tam′ə rin) *n.* ⟦Fr < Galibi⟧ any of several South American marmosets having long, silky fur, esp. any of a species (*Saguinus tamarin*) having black hands and feet

tam·a·rind (tam′ə rind) *n.* ⟦Sp *tamarindo* < Ar *tamr hindī,* date of India⟧ 1 a tropical leguminous tree (*Tamarindus indica*) of the caesalpinia family, with yellow flowers and brown pods with an acid pulp 2 its fruit, used in foods, beverages, etc.

tam·a·risk (tam′ə risk) *n.* ⟦ME *tamarisc* < LL *tamariscus,* for L *tamarix*⟧ any of a genus (*Tamarix*) of small trees or shrubs of the tamarisk family with slender branches and feathery flower clusters, common near salt water and often grown for a windbreak —*adj.* designating a family (Tamaricaceae, order Violales) of small, dicotyledonous shrubs and trees

ta·ma·sha (tə mä′shə) *n.* ⟦Hindustani < Ar *tamāsha,* a walking around⟧ in India, a spectacle; show; entertainment

Ta·mau·li·pas (tä′mou lē′päs) state of NE Mexico, on the Texas border & the Gulf of Mexico: 30,822 sq mi (79,829 sq km); cap. Ciudad Victoria

Ta·ma·yo (tä mä′yô), **Ru·fi·no** (ro͞o fē′nô) 1899-1991; Mex. painter

tam·ba·la (täm bä′lä) *n., pl.* **ma′tam·ba′la** (mä′-) ⟦lit., rooster, in a Bantu language of Malawi⟧ a monetary unit of Malawi, equal to $\frac{1}{100}$ of a kwacha

tam·bour (tam′bo͝or′) *n.* ⟦ME < MFr < OFr *tambor,* a drum, prob. via Sp < Ar *ṭunbūr* (colloq. form *ṭanbūr*), stringed instrument < Pers *tabīrah,* drum⟧ 1 a drum 2 *a)* an embroidery frame of two closely fitting, concentric hoops that hold the cloth stretched between them *b)* embroidery worked on such a frame ☆3 a door, panel, etc., as in a cabinet, consisting of narrow, wooden slats glued to a flexible base, as canvas, that slides in grooves, as around curves — *vt., vi.* to embroider on a tambour

tam·bour·a (täm bo͝or′ə) *n.* ⟦Pers *ṭambūra*⟧ a lutelike instrument of India, etc., usually with four strings, used to give a drone or ostinato accompaniment

tam·bou·rin (tam′bə rin′; *Fr* tän bo͞o ran′) *n.* ⟦Fr, dim. of *tambour:* see TAMBOUR⟧ 1 a long drum used in Provence 2 a sprightly dance of Provence, or music for it

tam·bou·rine (tam′bə rēn′) *n.* ⟦Fr *tambourin:* see prec.⟧ a shallow, single-headed hand drum having jingling metal disks in the rim: it is played by shaking, hitting with the knuckles, etc. —**tam′bou·rin′ist** *n.*

Tam·bov (täm bôf′) city in central European Russia, southeast of Moscow

tam·bur·a (täm bo͝or′ə) *n. alt. sp. of* TAMBOURA

tam·bu·rit·za (tam′bə rit′sə, täm′-; täm bo͝or′it-, tam-) *n.* ⟦Serb, ult. < Ar *ṭunbūr,* a stringed instrument: see TAMBOUR⟧ any of a family of plucked stringed instruments of South Slavic regions, somewhat resembling the mandolin

tame (tām) *adj.* **tam′er**, **tam′est** ⟦ME < OE *tam* < IE **dom-,* var. of base **dem-,* to tame, subdue > L *domare,* Gr *daman,* to tame⟧ 1 changed from a wild to a domesticated state: said as of animals trained for use by humans or as pets 2 like a domesticated animal in nature; gentle and easy to control; docile 3 crushed by or as by domestication; submissive; servile 4 without spirit or force; dull [a *tame* boxing match] 5 cultivated: said of plants or land —*vt.* **tamed**, **tam′ing** 1 to make tame, or domestic 2 to overcome the wildness or fierceness of; make gentle, docile, obedient, or spiritless; subdue 3 to make less intense; soften; dull —*vi.* to become tame —**tam′a·ble** *adj.,* **tame′a·ble** —**tame′ly** *adv.* —**tame′ness** *n.* —**tam′er** *n.*

tame·less (tām′lis) *adj.* 1 not tamed 2 not tamable

Tam·er·lane (tam′ər lān′) ⟦after *Timur lenk,* Timur the lame⟧ 1336?-1405; Mongol warrior whose conquests extended from the Black Sea to the upper Ganges

Tam·il (tam′əl, täm′-, tum′-) *n.* 1 *pl.* **-ils** or **-il** a member of a people living chiefly in S India and N Sri Lanka 2 the Dravidian language, ancient or modern, of this people: official language of the state of Tamil Nadu

Tamil Na·du (tam′əl nä′do͞o, nä do͞o′; täm′-, tum′-) state of S India: 50,216 sq mi (130,059 sq km); cap. Chennai

☆**Tam·ma·ny** (tam′ə nē) *n.* ⟦after *Tamanen(d)*, a 17th-c. Delaware chief renowned for his superior qualities: meaning of his name unknown⟧ a powerful Democratic political organization of New York City, incorporated in 1789 and historically often associated with bossism and other political abuses: also **Tammany Society** or **Tammany Hall**

Tam·muz (tä′mo͞oz) *n.* ⟦Heb *tammūz* < Akkadian *tamūz*, a god of fertility < Sumerian *Dumu-zi* (lit., true son), god & legendary king⟧ the tenth month of the Jewish year: see the Jewish calendar in the Reference Supplement

Tam·my (tam′ē) *n.* a feminine name

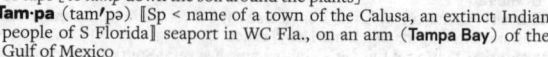

tam-o'-shan·ter (tam′ə shan′tər) *n.* ⟦< the name of the main character of Robert Burns's poem "Tam o' Shanter"⟧ a Scottish cap with a wide, round, flat top and, often, a center pompom

tam-o'-shanter

ta·mox·i·fen (tə mäk′sə fen′) *n.* ⟦altered < T(RANS)- + AM(INE) + OXY-[1] + PHEN(OL), portions of the technical name⟧ a synthetic hormone, $C_{32}H_{37}NO_{10}$, used as an estrogen-blocking drug to inhibit the growth of certain types of tumors, esp. in cases of advanced breast cancer: in full **tamoxifen citrate**

tamp (tamp) *vt.* ⟦? back-form. < *tampin*, var. of TAMPION⟧ **1** in blasting, to pack clay, sand, etc. around the charge in (the drill hole) **2** to pack more tightly or make more compact by a series of blows or taps [to *tamp* down the soil around the plants]

Tam·pa (tam′pə) ⟦Sp < name of a town of the Calusa, an extinct Indian people of S Florida⟧ seaport in WC Fla., on an arm (**Tampa Bay**) of the Gulf of Mexico

tam·pal·a (tam pal′ə) *n.* ⟦< native name in India⟧ a cultivated strain of pigweed (*Amaranthus gangeticus*)

tam·per[1] (tam′pər) *n.* a person or thing that tamps; specif., any of various instruments or tools for tamping

tam·per[2] (tam′pər) *vi.* ⟦var. of TEMPER⟧ [Archaic] to contrive something secretly; plot; scheme —**tamper with 1** to make secret, illegal arrangements with, as by bribing **2** to interfere with or meddle with, esp. so as to damage, corrupt, etc. —**tam′per·er** *n.*

Tam·pe·re (täm′pə re′) city in SW Finland

Tam·pi·co (täm pē′kō) seaport in E Mexico, in Tamaulipas state

tam·pi·on (tam′pē ən) *n.* ⟦Fr *tampon*, nasalized form of *tapon* < Frank **tappo*, akin to TAP[2]⟧ a plug or stopper put in the muzzle of a gun not in use

tam·pon (tam′pän′) *n.* ⟦Fr: see prec.⟧ a plug of cotton or other absorbent material put into a body cavity, wound, etc. to stop bleeding or absorb secretions; esp., such a plug for absorbing the menses —*vt.* to put a tampon into

tam·pon·ade (tam′pə näd′) *n.* ⟦< prec. + -ADE⟧ **1** use of a tampon, as in surgery **2** an accumulation of fluid in the sac surrounding the heart, resulting in severe restriction of blood circulation

tam-tam (tum′tum′, tam′tam′, täm′täm′) *n.* ⟦Hindi *ṭamṭam*, generic term for a tabor, drum, or gong: of echoic orig.⟧ **1** a large gong of indefinite pitch, sounded with a soft-headed mallet **2** *var. of* TOM-TOM

tan[1] (tan) *n.* ⟦MFr < ML *tanum*, prob. < Gaul⟧ **1** TANBARK **2** tannin or a solution made from it, used to tan leather **3** a yellowish-brown color **4** a darkening of the skin as by exposure to the sun or a sunlamp —*adj.* **tan′ner, tan′nest** yellowish-brown; tawny —*vt.* **tanned, tan′ning** ⟦ME *tannen* < Late OE *tannian* < ML *tannare* < the n.⟧ **1** to change (hide) into leather by soaking in tannin **2** to produce a tan color in, as by exposure to the sun **3** [Informal] to whip severely; flog —*vi.* to become tanned —**tan someone's hide** [Informal] to flog someone severely

tan[2] *abbrev.* tangent

Ta·na (tä′nə) **1** river in E Kenya, flowing southeast into the Indian Ocean: *c.* 500 mi (805 km) **2 Lake** lake in N Ethiopia: source of the Blue Nile: *c.* 1,400 sq mi (3,626 sq km)

Ta·nach (tä näkh′) *n.* ⟦< Heb *tanakh*, acronym formed from *tora* (the Pentateuch), *neviim* (the Prophets), & *ketuvim* (the *Hagiographa*)⟧ the Holy Scriptures of Judaism

tan·a·ger (tan′ə jər) *n.* ⟦ModL *tanagra* < Port *tángara* < Tupí *tangara*⟧ any of a large family (Thraupidae) of small, New World passerine birds: the males usually are brilliantly colored

Tan·a·gra (tan′ə grə, tə näg′rə) ancient Greek town in Boeotia, known for the terra cotta figurines made there

Tan·a·na (tan′ə nä′, -nô′) river in E Alas., flowing northwest into the Yukon River: 800 mi (1,287 km)

Ta·na·na·rive (tə nan′ə rēv′; *Fr* tȧ nȧ nȧ rēv′) *former name for* ANTANANARIVO

tan·bark (tan′bärk′) *n.* any bark containing tannin, used to tan hides and, after the tannin has been extracted, to cover racetracks, circus rings, etc.

Tan·cred (taŋ′krid) 1078?-1112; Norman leader of the 1st Crusade

☆**T&A** (tē′ənd ā′) *n.* ⟦< *t(its) and a(ss)*⟧ [Informal] entertainment, as TV programs or movies, that is characterized by the deliberately titillating display of the female form: also written **T and A**

tan·dem (tan′dəm) *adv.* ⟦orig. punning use of L *tandem*, at length, finally < *tam*, so much (< IE **tam*, acc. sing. fem. of pron. < base **to-* > THE) + *-dem*, demonstrative particle⟧ one behind another; in single file —*n.* **1** a two-wheeled carriage drawn by horses harnessed tandem **2** a team, as of horses, harnessed tandem **3** a bicycle with two seats and sets of pedals placed tandem **4** a relationship between two persons or things involving cooperative action, mutual dependence, etc. [to work in *tandem*] —*adj.* having two parts or things placed tandem

tan·door (tän do͝or′, tän′do͝or′) *n.* ⟦Hindi, clay oven < Turk *tandur* < Ar *tannūr*, portable oven, ult. < Akkadian *tinūru*⟧ an oven, originally in India, made of clay and capable of high temperatures, for fast cooking or baking

tan·door·i (tän do͝or′ē) *adj.* ⟦Hindi < prec.⟧ of or cooked in a tandoor [*tandoori* chicken]

Ta·ney (tô′nē), **Roger B(rooke)** 1777-1864; chief justice of the U.S. (1836-64)

tang[1] (taŋ) *n.* ⟦ME *tange* < ON *tangi*, a sting, point, dagger, nasalized form of base seen in TACK⟧ **1** a projecting point or prong on a chisel, file, knife, etc., that fits into a handle, shaft, etc. **2** a strong and penetrating taste or odor **3** a touch or trace (*of* some quality) **4** a special or characteristic flavor, quality, etc. ☆**5** SURGEONFISH —*vt.* to provide (a knife, etc.) with a tang

tang[2] (taŋ) *n.* ⟦echoic⟧ a loud, ringing sound; twang — *vt., vi.* to sound with a loud ringing

Tang (täŋ) *n.* 618-906 A.D.; Chin. dynasty under which literature & art flourished & printing was developed

Tan·gan·yi·ka (tan′gən yē′kə, taŋ′gə nē′kə) **1** mainland region of Tanzania, on the E coast of Africa: a former British territory, it became a member of the Commonwealth as an independent republic in 1961: united with Zanzibar to form Tanzania (1964) **2 Lake** lake in EC Africa, between Tanganyika & the Democratic Republic of the Congo: 12,700 sq mi (32,893 sq km) —**Tan′gan·yi′kan** *adj., n.*

☆**tan·ge·lo** (tan′jə lō′) *n., pl.* **-los′** ⟦TANG(ERINE) + (POM)ELO⟧ a fruit produced by crossing a tangerine with a grapefruit

tan·gent (tan′jənt) *adj.* ⟦L *tangens*, prp. of *tangere*, to touch: see TACT⟧ **1** that touches; touching **2** *Geom.* touching and not intersecting a curve or curved surface at one and only one point: said of a line or plane —*n.* ⟦< ModL (*linea*) *tangens*, tangent (line)⟧ **1** *Geom. a)* a tangent line, curve, or surface *b)* the length of a straight line tangent to a curve, measured from the point of tangency to the intersection of the tangent line with the x-axis **2** *Trigonometry* the reciprocal of the cotangent; specif., *a)* the ratio of the opposite side of a given acute angle in a right triangle to the adjacent side *b)* an equivalent, positive or negative ratio for certain related angles (Ex.: the tangent of 57° or 237° is 1.5399, of 123° or 303° is -1.5399) or real numbers representing radians (Ex.: the tangent of .9948 radians (57°) is 1.5399) —*SYN.* ADJACENT —**go (or fly) off at (or on) a tangent** to break off suddenly from a line of action or train of thought and pursue another course —**tan′gen·cy** *n.*

tan·gen·tial (tan jen′shəl) *adj.* **1** of, like, or in the direction of a tangent **2** drawn as a tangent **3** going off at a tangent; diverging or digressing **4** merely touching a subject, not dealing with it at length —**tan·gen′tial·ly** *adv.*

tan·ge·rine (tan′jə rēn′, tan′jə rēn′) *n.* ⟦< Fr *Tanger*, TANGIER + -INE[1]⟧ **1** a variety of mandarin orange with a deep reddish-yellow color and segments that are easily separated **2** a deep reddish-yellow color

tan·gi·ble (tan′jə bəl) *adj.* ⟦LL *tangibilis* < L *tangere*, to touch: see TACT⟧ **1** that can be touched or felt by touch; having actual form and substance **2** corporeal and able to be appraised for value [*tangible* assets] **3** that can be understood; definite; objective —*n.* [*pl.*] property that can be appraised for value; assets having real substance; material things —*SYN.* PERCEPTIBLE —**tan′gi·bil′i·ty** *n.*, **tan′gi·ble·ness** —**tan′gi·bly** *adv.*

Tan·gier (tan jir′) seaport in N Morocco, on the Strait of Gibraltar: formerly part of an internationalized zone: Fr. name **Tan·ger** (tän zhā′)

tan·gle (taŋ′gəl) *vt.* **-gled, -gling** ⟦ME *tanglen*, prob. nasalized var. of *taglen*, to entangle, akin to Swed dial. *taggla*, to disarrange⟧ **1** to hinder, obstruct, or confuse by or as by covering, circling, entwining, etc. **2** to catch in or as in a net or snare; trap **3** to make a knot or snarl of; intertwist —*vi.* **1** to become tangled **2** [Informal] to fight, quarrel, or argue —*n.* **1** an intertwisted, confused mass of things, as string, branches, etc.; snarl **2** a jumbled, confused condition **3** a perplexed state **4** [Informal] a fight, quarrel, or argument —**tan′gler** *n.*

☆**tan·gle·foot** (-fo͝ot′) *n.* [West Slang] cheap whiskey

tan·gly (taŋ′glē) *adj.* **-gli·er, -gli·est** full of tangles; snarled

tan·go (taŋ′gō) *n., pl.* **-gos** ⟦AmSp⟧ **1** a dance for couples, originated in South America, with long gliding steps and dips **2** music for this dance in 2/4 or 4/4 time —*vi.* to dance the tango

tan·gram (taŋ′grəm; tan′gram′) *n.* ⟦prob. arbitrary coinage on analogy of ANAGRAM⟧ a Chinese puzzle made by cutting a square into five triangles, a square, and a rhomboid, and using these pieces to form various figures and designs

tangram

Tang·shan (täŋ shän′, däŋ-) city in Hebei province, NE China, near Tianjin

Tan·guy (tän gē′), **Yves** (ēv) 1900-55; U.S. painter, born in France

tang·y (taŋ′ē) *adj.* **tang′i·er, tang′i·est** having a tang, or pleasantly sharp flavor —**tang′i·ness** *n.*

Ta·nis (tā′nis) city in ancient Egypt, in the Nile delta: probable capital of the Hyksos kings

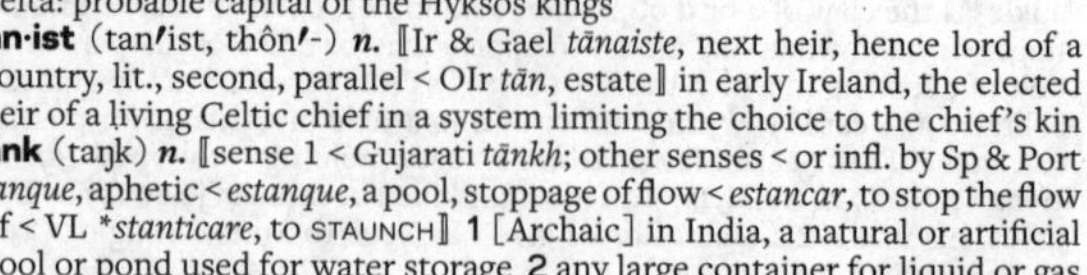

tan·ist (tan′ist, thôn′-) *n.* ⟦Ir & Gael *tānaiste*, next heir, hence lord of a country, lit., second, parallel < OIr *tān*, estate⟧ in early Ireland, the elected heir of a living Celtic chief in a system limiting the choice to the chief's kin

tank (taŋk) *n.* ⟦sense 1 < Gujarati *tānkh*; other senses < or infl. by Sp & Port *tanque*, aphetic < *estanque*, a pool, stoppage of flow < *estancar*, to stop the flow of < VL **stanticare*, to STAUNCH⟧ **1** [Archaic] in India, a natural or artificial pool or pond used for water storage **2** any large container for liquid or gas [a gasoline *tank*, a swimming *tank*] **3** *short for: a)* TANK TOP *b)* TANK SUIT **4** ⟦name orig. used for purpose of secrecy during manufacture⟧ a heavily armored, self-propelled combat vehicle armed with guns and moving on full tractor treads ☆**5** [Slang] a jail cell, esp. one for new prisoners charged with misdemeanors —*vt.* **1** to put, store, or process in a tank **2** [Slang] to lose (a game, match, etc.) deliberately or due to a lack of effort —*vi.* [Slang] **1** to fail or go into a sharp decline **2** to lose, esp. as a result of a lack of effort —☆**go in the tank** ☆[Slang] to lose or fail badly or on purpose —**tank up** [Informal] **1** to supply with or get a full tank of fuel ☆**2** to drink much liquor

tan·ka (täŋ′kə) *n.* ⟦SinoJpn < *tan,* short + *ka,* poem, song⟧ **1** a Japanese verse form of 31 syllables in five unrhymed lines, the first and third having five syllables each and the others seven **2** a poem in this form

tank·age (taŋ′kij) *n.* **1** the capacity of a tank or a number of tanks collectively **2** *a)* the storage of fluids, gases, etc. in tanks *b)* the charge for such storage ☆**3** slaughterhouse waste from which the fat has been rendered in tanks: the residue is dried and ground for use as fertilizer or feed

tank·ard (taŋ′kərd) *n.* ⟦ME < OFr *tanquart,* prob. < *tant,* as much as (< L *tantus* < *tam:* see TANDEM) + *quart,* QUART[1]⟧ a large drinking cup with a handle and, often, a hinged lid

☆**tank car** a large tank on wheels, for carrying liquids and gases by rail

tank destroyer a highly mobile, armored vehicle on tractor treads, on which an antitank gun is mounted

☆**tanked** (taŋkt) *adj.* [Informal] drunk: also **tanked up**

tank·er (taŋ′kər) *n.* **1** a ship with large tanks in the hull for carrying a cargo of oil or other liquids ☆**2** *a)* TANK CAR *b)* a truck, semitrailer, or trailer with a tank for transporting liquids, as gasoline, or dry commodities in bulk ☆**3** an aircraft designed to carry liquids, as chemicals, fuels, etc., for dumping on fires, refueling other aircraft in flight, etc.

☆**tank farm** an expanse of land on which a number of fuel oil storage tanks are located

tank farming HYDROPONICS

tank·ful (taŋk′fo͝ol) *n.* as much as a tank will hold

tank suit ⟦so called from orig. being worn in swimming *tanks,* or pools⟧ a contoured, one-piece woman's swimsuit with shoulder straps and, often, a scoop neck

☆**tank top** ⟦so called from resembling the top part of a prec.⟧ a casual shirt having wide shoulder straps and, usually, a scoop neck

☆**tank town** a small, unimportant town: originally applied to such a town at which railroad locomotives stopped to have their boilers filled with water

☆**tank truck** a motor truck built to be used as a TANKER (sense 2*b*)

tan·nage (tan′ij) *n.* **1** the act or process of tanning **2** something that has been tanned

tan·nate (tan′āt′) *n.* a salt of tannic acid

tan·ner[1] (tan′ər) *n.* a person whose work is tanning hides

tan·ner[2] (tan′ər) *n.* ⟦< ?⟧ [Brit. Informal] a sixpence

tan·ner·y (tan′ər ē) *n., pl.* **-ner·ies** a place where hides are tanned

Tann·häu·ser (tän′hoi′zər, tan′-; -hou′-) ⟦Ger⟧ a German knight and minnesinger of the 13th cent., dealt with in legend as a knight who seeks absolution after giving himself up to revelry in Venusberg

tan·nic (tan′ik) *adj.* ⟦Fr *tannique* < *tanin,* TANNIN + *-ique,* -IC⟧ **1** of, like, or obtained from tanbark or a tannin **2** tasting of tannins absorbed from grape skins and seeds and from oak barrels; somewhat bitter or astringent: said of some red wines

tannic acid **1** a yellowish, astringent substance, $C_{14}H_{10}O_9$, derived from oak bark, gallnuts, etc. and used in tanning hides, in medicine, etc. **2** any of a number of similar substances

tan·nin (tan′in) *n.* ⟦Fr *tanin* < *tan,* TAN[1] + *-in,* -IN[1]⟧ any of a group of naturally occurring phenolic compounds that precipitate proteins, alkaloids, and glucosides from solution, and convert hide into leather, including tannic acid: some are present in coffee and tea

tan·ning (tan′iŋ) *n.* **1** the art or process of making leather from hides **2** the act of making fair skin brown, as by exposure to the sun **3** [Informal] a severe whipping; flogging

☆**tanning bed** a narrow bedlike device having a clamshell lid and equipped with sunlamps, on which a person lies in order to acquire a tan

tan·nish (tan′ish) *adj.* somewhat tan in color

tan·noy (ta′noi) *n.* ⟦< *Tannoy,* a trademark⟧ [*also* **T-**] [Brit.] PUBLIC-ADDRESS SYSTEM

Ta·no·an (tä′nō ən) *n.* ⟦coined (1891) by J. W. Powell < Sp *Tano,* Tano or Tewa Indian < Tewa *tʰaánu*⟧ a family of North American Indian languages including those of the Kiowas and of a number of Pueblo villages in New Mexico and Arizona

tan·sy (tan′zē) *n., pl.* **-sies** ⟦ME < OFr *tanesie* < VL **tanaceta* < LL *tanacetum* < ?⟧ any of a genus (*Tanacetum*) of plants of the composite family; esp., a poisonous weed (*T. vulgare*) with strong-smelling foliage and flat-topped clusters of small, yellow, rayless flower heads

Tan·ta (tän′tə) city in N Egypt, in the center of the Nile delta

tan·ta·late (tan′tə lāt′) *n.* a salt of tantalic acid

tan·tal·ic (tan tal′ik) *adj.* **1** of, derived from, or containing tantalum, esp. pentavalent tantalum **2** designating any of several colorless, crystalline, acidic, hydrated tantalum pentoxides, $Ta_2O_5 \cdot xH_2O$, that form salts with bases

tantalic acid a colorless, crystalline acid, $HTaO_3$, that forms complex salts

tan·ta·lite (tan′tə līt′) *n.* ⟦Ger *tantalit:* see TANTALUM & -ITE[1]⟧ a black, orthorhombic mineral, $(Fe,Mn)(Ta,Nb)_2O_6$, that is an ore of tantalum and niobium

tan·ta·lize (tan′tə līz′) *vt.* **-lized′**, **-liz′ing** ⟦< TANTALUS + -IZE⟧ to tease or excite by promising or showing something desirable and then withholding it —**tan′ta·li·za′tion** *n.* —**tan′ta·liz′er** *n.*

tan·ta·liz·ing (tan′tə līz′iŋ) *adj.* **1** that tantalizes **2** tempting; enticing [the *tantalizing* aroma of freshly baked bread] —**tan′ta·liz′ing·ly** *adv.*

tan·ta·lous (tan′tə ləs) *adj.* of, derived from, or containing tantalum, esp. trivalent tantalum

tan·ta·lum (tan′tə ləm) *n.* ⟦ModL: so named (1802) by its discoverer, A. G. Ekeberg (1767-1813), Swed chemist < Gr *Tantalos,* fol. (its insolubility in most acids made extraction from the mineral *tantalizing*) + -(I)UM⟧ a hard, gray, ductile, corrosion-resistant, metallic chemical element found in various minerals and used in making nuclear reactors, chemical equipment, missiles, electronic components, etc.: symbol, Ta; at. no. 73: see the periodic table of elements in the Reference Supplement

Tan·ta·lus (tan′tə ləs) *n.* ⟦L < Gr *Tantalos*⟧ *Gr. Myth.* a king, son of Zeus, doomed in the lower world to stand in water that always recedes when he tries to drink it and under branches of fruit that always remain just out of reach

tan·ta·mount (tant′ə mount′) *adj.* ⟦< Anglo-Fr *tant amunter,* to amount to as much < OFr *tant* (< L *tantus,* so much: see TANDEM) + *amonter* (see AMOUNT)⟧ having equal force, value, effect, etc.; equal or equivalent (*to*)

tan·ta·ra (tan′tə rə; tan tar′ə, -tä′rə) *n.* ⟦echoic⟧ **1** a trumpet blast or fanfare **2** a sound like this

tant·e (tänt′ə) *n.* ⟦Ger & Yiddish⟧ aunt

tan·tiv·y (tan tiv′ē) *adv.* ⟦prob. echoic of sound of a horse galloping⟧ at full gallop; headlong —*n., pl.* **-tiv′ies** a gallop; rapid movement

tant mieux (tän myö′) ⟦Fr⟧ so much the better

tan·to (tän′tô) *adv.* ⟦It < L *tantum,* so much⟧ *Musical Direction* so much (Ex.: *allegro ma non tanto,* fast, but not so much or not too much)

tant pis (tän pē′) ⟦Fr⟧ so much the worse

tan·tra (tun′trə, tän′-) *n.* ⟦Sans, a doctrine, lit., warp, akin to *tanti,* cord, string < IE base **ten-,* to stretch > THIN⟧ [*often* **T-**] a form of yoga that teaches the attainment of ecstasy through esoteric, sometimes erotic, techniques —**tan′tric** *adj.*

tan·trum (tan′trəm) *n.* ⟦< ?⟧ a violent, willful outburst of annoyance, rage, etc.; childish fit of bad temper

Tan-tung (tän to͝oŋ′, dän do͝oŋ′) *a former transliteration of* DANDONG

Tan·ya (tän′yə) *n.* a feminine name

Tan·za·ni·a (tan′zə nē′ə) country in E Africa, formed by the merger of Tanganyika & Zanzibar (1964); member of the Commonwealth: 364,900 sq mi (945,087 sq km); cap. Dodoma —**Tan′za·ni′an** *adj., n.*

tan·za·nite (tan′zə nīt′) *n.* ⟦prec. + -ITE[1]⟧ a deep-blue variety of zoisite, used as a semiprecious stone

Tao (dou, tou) *n.* ⟦Chin *tao,* (the) way⟧ **1** in Chinese philosophy and religion, esp. in Taoism, the central or organizing principle of the universe, moral life, etc. **2** the governing creative principle of an art, craft, or other purposeful activity: often with *the* [the *Tao* of fashion design]

taoi·seach (tē′shəkh) *n., pl.* **-sigh** (-shē) ⟦Ir, leader, chief⟧ the prime minister of the Republic of Ireland

Tao·ism (dou′iz′əm, tou′-) *n.* ⟦TAO + -ISM⟧ a Chinese religion and philosophy reputedly founded by Laotzu, that advocates simplicity, selflessness, etc., in conformity with the Tao —**Tao′ist** *n., adj.* —**Tao·is′tic** *adj.*

Ta·os (tä′ōs, tous) ⟦Sp (orig. pl.) < Taos (a Tanoan language) *tôotʰo,* pueblo name, lit., in the village⟧ resort town in N N.Mex.

tap[1] (tap) *vt.* **tapped, tap′ping** ⟦ME *tappen* < OFr *taper,* prob. of echoic orig.⟧ **1** to strike lightly and rapidly **2** to strike something lightly, and often repeatedly, with **3** to make or do by tapping [to *tap* a message with the fingers] ☆**4** to choose or designate, as for membership in a club **5** to repair (a shoe) by adding a thickness of leather, etc. to the heel or sole —*vi.* **1** to strike a light, rapid blow or a series of such blows **2** to perform a tap dance **3** to move with a tapping sound —*n.* **1** a light, rapid blow, or the sound made by it **2** the leather, etc. added in tapping a shoe **3** *a)* a small, metal plate attached to the heel or toe of a shoe, as for tap-dancing *b)* the act or skill of tap-dancing —**tap′per** *n.*

tap[2] (tap) *n.* ⟦ME *tappe* < OE *tæppa,* akin to Ice *tappi* < IE **dāp-* < base **da-,* to divide > TIDE[1]⟧ **1** a device for starting or stopping the flow of liquid in a pipe, barrel, etc.; faucet **2** a plug, cork, etc. for stopping a hole in a container holding a liquid **3** liquor of a certain kind or quality, as drawn from a certain tap **4** *short for* TAPROOM **5** the act or an instance of draining liquid, as from a body cavity **6** a tool used to cut threads inside a nut, pipe, etc. ☆**7** the act or an instance of wiretapping **8** *Elec.* a place in a circuit where a connection can be made —*vt.* **tapped, tap′ping** ⟦ME *tappen* < OE *tæppian* < the n.⟧ **1** to put a tap or spigot on **2** to make a hole in for drawing off liquid [to *tap* a sugar maple] **3** to pull out the tap or plug from **4** to draw (liquid) from a container, cavity, etc. **5** to draw upon; make use of [to *tap* new resources] **6** *a)* to make a connection with (a water main, electrical circuit, etc.) ☆*b)* to make a secret connection with (a telephone line) in order to overhear or record private conversations **7** to cut threads on the inner surface of (a nut, pipe, etc.) **8** [Slang] to borrow or get money from —*vi.* to use, draw upon, make a connection with, etc.: with *into* —**on tap** **1** in a tapped or open cask (of liquor) and ready to be drawn; on draft **2** [Informal] ready for consideration or action —**tap′per** *n.*

ta·pa[1] (tä′pä) *n.* ⟦Tahitian⟧ an unwoven cloth made by people in the Pacific islands from the inner bark of the paper mulberry tree

ta·pa[2] (tä′pä) *n., pl.* **ta′pas** (-päs) ⟦Sp, lit., lid or cover, referring to the small plate holding a tidbit that is set on top of a glass of sherry⟧ [*also in* *roman type*] in Spain, an appetizer or snack as served in a bar with sherry, beer, etc.: *usually used in pl.*

Ta·pa·jós or **Ta·pa·joz** (tä′pə zhôsh′, -zhôs′) river in N Brazil, flowing northeast into the Amazon: *c.* 500 mi (805 km): with principal headstream, *c.* 1,200 mi (1,931 km)

tap dance 1 a dance performed with sharp, loud taps of the foot, toe, or heel at each step 2 [Informal] a statement or action meant to evade or distract attention from a concern, question, etc. —**tap′-dance′** *vi.* **-danced′**, **-danc′ing** —**tap′-danc′er** *n.*

tape (tāp) *n.* ⟦ME < OE *tæppe*, a fillet, akin to *tæppa*: see TAP²⟧ 1 a strong, narrow, woven strip of cotton, linen, etc. used to bind seams in garments, tie bundles, etc. 2 a narrow strip or band of steel, paper, etc. 3 a strip of cloth stretched between posts above the finishing line of a race 4 *short for* TAPE MEASURE 5 *short for* ADHESIVE TAPE, FRICTION TAPE, MAGNETIC TAPE, TICKER TAPE, etc. —*vt.* **taped**, **tap′ing** 1 to put tape on or around, as for binding or tying 2 to measure by using a tape measure 3 to record (sound, video material, computer data, etc.) on magnetic tape —**tap′er** *n.*

☆**tape deck** 1 a magnetic recording device consisting of a tape transport, heads, and preamplifiers, but not amplifiers or speakers 2 a component of an audio system containing such a mechanism and used to record and play back magnetic tapes, usually using an external amplifier and speakers

tape delay 1 an electronic system or process for recording a live event, as a sports competition, on magnetic tape or digitally in order to be able to delay the broadcast of the event until a later, typically more convenient time 2 the act or an instance of using such a system —**tape′-de·layed′** *adj.*

☆**tape grass** any of several submerged, freshwater, flowering plants (genus *Vallisneria*) of the frog's-bit family, with elongated, ribbonlike leaves

tape loop LOOP¹ (*n.* 5)

tape measure a tape with marks in inches, feet, centimeters, meters, etc. for measuring: also **tape′line′** (-līn′) *n.*

tap·e·nade (tä′pə näd′, tap′ə-) *n.* ⟦Fr *tapénade* < Prov *tapenado* < *tapeno*, caper⟧ a Provençal spread, used mainly in appetizers, consisting of black olives, capers, anchovies, seasonings, and olive oil

ta·per (tā′pər) *n.* ⟦ME < OE *tapur*, prob. by dissimilation < L *papyrus* (see PAPER): from use of papyrus pith as wick⟧ 1 a wax candle, esp. a long, slender one 2 a long wick coated with wax, used for lighting candles, lamps, etc. 3 any feeble light 4 *a)* a gradual decrease in width or thickness [the *taper* of a pyramid] *b)* a gradual decrease in action, power, etc. 5 something that tapers —*adj.* gradually decreased in breadth or thickness toward one end — *vt., vi.* 1 to decrease gradually in width or thickness 2 to lessen; diminish —**taper off** 1 to become smaller gradually toward one end 2 to diminish or stop gradually

tape-re·cord (tāp′ri kôrd′) *vt.* to record on magnetic tape

tape recorder a device for recording on magnetic tape and for playing back what has been recorded: see MAGNETIC RECORDING

tap·es·try (tap′əs trē) *n., pl.* **-tries** ⟦LME *tapsterie*, earlier *tapicerie* < MFr *tapisserie* < OFr *tapis*, a carpet < MGr *tapētion* < Gr, dim. of *tapēs* (gen. *tapētos*), a carpet, prob. < Iran, as in Pers *tāftan*, to twist, spin < IE **temp-* < base **ten-*, to stretch > THIN⟧ a heavy cloth woven by hand or machinery with decorative designs and pictures and used as a wall hanging, furniture covering, etc. —*vt.* **-tried**, **-try·ing** to decorate as with a tapestry: usually in the pp.

tape transport the mechanism consisting of motors, pulleys, etc. that moves magnetic tape past the heads of a tape deck or recorder

ta·pe·tum (tə pēt′əm) *n., pl.* **-pe′ta** (-ə) ⟦ModL < L < *tapete*, a carpet < Gr *tapēs*: see TAPESTRY⟧ 1 *Anat., Zool.* any of various membranous layers; esp., *a)* the iridescent choroid membrane in the eye of certain animals, as the cat *b)* a layer of fibers from the corpus callosum forming a portion of the roof of each lateral ventricle of the brain 2 *Bot.* a nutritive layer of cells lining the inner wall of a fern sporangium or of an anther —**ta·pe′tal** *adj.*

tape·worm (tāp′wurm′) *n.* ⟦so named from the shape of its flattened body⟧ any of various cestode flatworms that live in the adult stage as parasites in the intestines of humans and other vertebrates and in the larval stage usually in various intermediate hosts

ta·phon·o·my (ta făn′ə mē) *n.* ⟦ult. < Gr *taphos*, tomb (see EPITAPH) + *nomos*, law (see -NOMY): coined (1940) by I. A. Efremov (1908-72), Russ paleontologist & author⟧ the branch of paleontology that deals with the process of fossilization —**taph·o·nom·ic** (taf′ə näm′ik) *adj.*, **taph′o·nom′i·cal** (-i kəl) —**ta·phon′o·mist** (-mist) *n.*

tap·house (tap′hous′) *n.* ⟦TAP² + HOUSE⟧ a tavern or inn

tap·i·o·ca (tap′ē ō′kə) *n.* ⟦Port & Sp < Tupí & Guaraní *typyoca* < *tipi*, dregs + *ok*, to squeeze out⟧ 1 a starchy, granular substance prepared from the root of the cassava plant, used to make puddings, thicken soups, etc. 2 pudding made from this substance

ta·pir (tā′pər) *n., pl.* **ta′pirs** or **ta′pir** ⟦Sp < Tupí *tapyra*, large mammal, tapir⟧ any of a family (Tapiridae) of large, hoofed, hoglike perissodactylous mammals of tropical America and the Malay Peninsula: tapirs have flexible snouts, feed on plants, and are active at night

Baird's tapir

tap·is (tap′ē, -is; ta pē′) *n.* ⟦MFr < OFr: see TAPESTRY⟧ tapestry used as a curtain, tablecloth, carpet, etc.: now only in **on (or upon) the tapis**, under consideration

tap pants ⟦so named because they resemble in style the shorts formerly worn by *tap*-dancers⟧ women's underpants cut loose and full, and wide in the legs, somewhat like shorts

tapped out [Slang] ☆1 having no ready money; broke ☆2 exhausted or depleted

tap·pet (tap′it) *n.* ⟦TAP¹ + -ET⟧ a sliding rod in an engine or machine moved by intermittent contact with a cam and used to move another part, as a valve

tap·ping (tap′iŋ) *n.* 1 the act of a person or thing that taps 2 [*pl.*] that which is drawn by tapping

tap·room (tap′ro͞om′) *n.* ⟦TAP² + ROOM⟧ BARROOM

tap·root (tap′ro͞ot′) *n.* ⟦TAP² + ROOT¹⟧ a main root, growing almost vertically downward, from which small branch roots spread out

taps (taps) *n.* ⟦< TAP¹, because orig. a drum signal⟧ [*with sing. or pl. v.*] ☆a bugle call to put out lights in retiring for the night, as in an army camp: also sounded at a military funeral

tap·ster (tap′stər) *n.* ⟦ME < OE *tæppestre*, barmaid < *tæppa*: see TAP²⟧ [Archaic] a bartender

tap water water taken directly from the tap, or faucet, as for drinking or cooking

tar¹ (tär) *n.* ⟦ME *terre* < OE *teru* < PGmc **terw(i)a-*, substance from trees < IE base **deru-*, TREE⟧ 1 a thick, sticky, brown to black liquid with a pungent odor, obtained by the destructive distillation of wood, coal, peat, shale, etc.: tars are composed of hydrocarbons and their derivatives, and are used for protecting and preserving surfaces, in making various organic compounds, etc. 2 loosely, any of the solids in smoke, as from tobacco —*vt.* **tarred**, **tar′ring** to cover or smear with or as with tar —*adj.* 1 of or like tar 2 covered with tar; tarred —☆**tar and feather** to cover (a person) with tar and feathers as in punishment by mob action —**tarred with the same brush (or stick)** having similar faults or obnoxious traits

tar² (tär) *n.* ⟦< TAR(PAULIN)⟧ [Old Informal] a sailor

tar·a·did·dle (tar′ə did′'l) *n.* ⟦fanciful elaboration of DIDDLE²⟧ [Informal, Chiefly Brit.] 1 a petty lie; fib 2 nonsense; twaddle

ta·ra·ma (tä′rä mä) *n. short for* TARAMASALATA

ta·ra·ma·sa·la·ta (tä′rä mä sä lä′tä) *n.* ⟦ModGr *taramosalata* < *taramas*, roe + *salata*, salad⟧ a Greek appetizer consisting of a thick paste made from salted fish roe, onion, and lemon juice, pureed with bread or potato: also sp. **ta′ra·mo·sa·la′ta**

tar·an·tel·la (tar′ən tel′ə) *n.* ⟦It, dim. of TARANTO: popularly assoc. with fol. because of its lively character⟧ 1 a fast, whirling S Italian dance for couples, in 6/8 time 2 music for this

tar·ant·ism (tar′ən tiz′əm) *n.* ⟦It *tarantismo*: because formerly epidemic in the vicinity of fol.; popularly assoc. with the *tarantula*, by whose bite it was erroneously said to be caused⟧ a nervous disease characterized by hysteria and popularly believed to be curable by dancing or manifested by a mania for dancing: prevalent in S Italy during the 16th and 17th cent.

Ta·ran·to (tə ran′tō, tär′ən tō′) ⟦L *Tarentum* < Gr *Taras*, said to be named after *Taras*, son of Poseidon⟧ 1 seaport in SE Italy, on the Gulf of Taranto 2 **Gulf of** arm of the Ionian Sea, in SE Italy: *c.* 85 mi (137 km) long

ta·ran·tu·la (tə ran′cho͞o lə) *n., pl.* **-las** or **-lae′** (-lē′) ⟦ML < It *tarantola* < prec., near which the wolf spider was found⟧ 1 a wolf spider (*Lycosa tarentula*) of S Europe, whose bite was popularly but wrongly supposed to cause tarantism 2 any of numerous large, hairy spiders with a poisonous bite that usually has little effect on warmblooded animals; specif., any of a family (Theraphosidae) found in the SW U.S. and tropical America

hairy tarantula

Ta·ra·wa (tə rä′wə; tär′ə wə) coral atoll in the WC Pacific, near the equator: capital of Kiribati: 9 sq mi (23.3 sq km)

☆**tar baby** ⟦after a small, sticky tar figure in a story by Joel Chandler HARRIS¹⟧ something that is a persistent encumbrance

Tar·bell (tär′bel′, -bəl), **Ida M(inerva)** 1857-1944; U.S. journalist & writer

tar·boosh (tär bo͞osh′) *n.* ⟦Ar *ṭarbūsh*⟧ a brimless cap of cloth or felt shaped like a truncated cone, worn by Muslim men, sometimes as the inner part of a turban

Tar·de·noi·si·an (tär′də noi′zē ən) *adj.* ⟦after *Fère-en-Tardenois*, town in NE France, where implements were found⟧ designating or of a Mesolithic culture characterized by microliths

tar·di·grade (tär′di grād′) *n.* ⟦Fr < L *tardigradus*, slow-paced: see TARDY & GRADE⟧ any of a phylum (Tardigrada) of minute water animals with segmented bodies and four pairs of unsegmented legs, often regarded as primitive arthropods

tar·dive dyskinesia (tär′div) ⟦*tardive*, developing late (< Fr, fem. of *tardif*, TARDY) + DYSKINESIA⟧ a neuromuscular disorder, characterized by involuntary movements of the face, mouth, etc., believed to be induced by long-term use of certain tranquilizers or dopamine

tar·do (tär′dō) *adj.* ⟦It < L *tardus*: see fol.⟧ *Musical Direction* slow

tar·dy (tär′dē) *adj.* **-di·er**, **-di·est** ⟦LME *tardyve* < OFr *tardif* < VL **tardivus* < L *tardus*, slow, prob. < IE base **ter-*, delicate, weak > Gr *terēn*, tender⟧ 1 slow in moving, acting, etc. 2 behind time; late, delayed, or dilatory —**tar′di·ly** *adv.* —**tar′di·ness** *n.*

tar·dy·on (tär′dē än′) *n.* ⟦prec. + -ON⟧ any subatomic particle traveling slower than the speed of light: see also TACHYON

tare¹ (ter) *n.* ⟦ME, small seed, vetch < or akin to MDu *tarwe*, wheat < IE base **derwā-*, kind of grain > Sans *dūrvā*, millet grass: used in ME and Early ModE versions of N.T. to transl. LL(Ec) *zizania*, darnel⟧ 1 any of several vetches, esp. the common vetch (*Vicia sativa*) 2 the seed of any of these plants 3 *Bible* a noxious weed, thought to be darnel: Matt. 13:25-40

tare[2] (ter) ***n.*** ⟦LME < MFr < It *tara*, prob. < Ar *ṭaraḥa*, to reject, throw, cast⟧ 1 the weight of a container, wrapper, vehicle, etc. deducted from the total weight to determine the weight of the contents or load 2 the deduction of this —***vt.* tared, tar′ing** to find out, allow for, or mark the tare of

tare[3] (ter) ***vt., vi.*** *archaic or dial. pt. & pp. of* TEAR[1]

Ta·ren·tum (tə rent′əm) *ancient name for* TARANTO

targe (tärj) ***n.*** ⟦ME < OE < ON *targa*, akin to OHG *zarga*, a rim, frame < IE base **dergh-*, to grip > Gr *drakhmē*: see DRACHMA⟧ [Obs. or Old Poet.] a shield or buckler

tar·get (tär′git) ***n.*** ⟦ME < MFr *targette*, dim. of *targe*, a shield < Frank **targa*, akin to prec.⟧ 1 [Historical] a small shield, esp. a round one 2 *a)* a round, flat board, straw coil, etc., often one marked with concentric circles, set up to be aimed at, as in archery or rifle practice *b)* any object that is shot at, thrown at, etc. 3 *a)* an objective; goal *b)* a date aimed at, as for the completion of a project (also ☆**target date**) 4 someone or something that is the focus of attention, interest, etc. 5 a ship, building, site, etc. that is the object of a military attack 6 an object of verbal attack, criticism, or ridicule 7 something resembling a target in shape or use; specif., ☆*a)* the sliding sight on a surveyor's leveling rod ☆*b)* a disk-shaped signal on a railroad switch *c)* a metallic insert, usually of tungsten or molybdenum, in the anode of an X-ray tube, upon which the stream of cathode rays impinges and from which X-rays emanate *d)* a surface, object, etc. subjected to irradiation or to bombardment as by nuclear particles —***vt.*** to establish as a target, goal, etc. —**on target** completely accurate; precise

target language 1 the language into which a text in a given language is to be translated: cf. SOURCE LANGUAGE (sense 1) 2 a language other than one's own that one is learning

Tar·gum (tär′goom, tär gōōm′) ***n.***, *pl.* **Tar′gums** or **Tar·gu·mim** (tär gōōm′ im) ⟦MHeb < Aram *targūm*, lit., interpretation⟧ any of several translations or paraphrases of parts of the Jewish Scriptures, written in the vernacular (Aramaic) of Judea

☆**Tar·heel** (tär′hēl′) ***n.*** [Informal] a person born or living in North Carolina, called the **Tarheel State**

tar·iff (tar′if) ***n.*** ⟦It *tariffa* < Ar *ta'rīf*, information, explanation < *'arafa*, to know, inform⟧ 1 a list or system of taxes placed by a government upon exports or, esp., imports 2 a tax of this kind, or its rate 3 any list or scale of prices, charges, etc. ☆4 [Informal] any bill, charge, fare, etc. —***vt.*** 1 to make a schedule of tariffs on; set a tariff on 2 to fix the price of according to a tariff

Ta·rim (tä′rēm′, dä′-) river in NW China flowing from the Tian Shan into E Xinjiang region: *c.* 1,300 mi (2,092 km)

tar·la·tan or **tar·le·tan** (tär′lə tən) ***n.*** ⟦Fr *tarlatane*, earlier *tarnatane* < ?⟧ a thin, stiff, open-weave muslin

tar·mac (tär′mak′) ***n.*** ⟦< fol.⟧ 1 TARMACADAM 2 [Chiefly Brit.] an airport runway or apron 3 [Chiefly Brit.] a paved road

tar·ma·cad·am (tär′mə kad′əm) ***n.*** ⟦TAR[1] + MACADAM⟧ a mixture of small broken stones and a tar or asphalt binder, used to pave roads: cf. MACADAM

tarn (tärn) ***n.*** ⟦ME *terne* < or akin to ON *tjörn*, tarn, lit., hole filled with water⟧ a small lake, esp. one that fills a cirque

tar·na·tion (tär nā′shən) ***n., interj.*** ⟦prob. < *'tarnal* (short dial. form of ETERNAL) + (DAM)NATION⟧ *dial. var. of* DAMNATION: also used as an intensifier [what in *tarnation* is that?]

tar·nish (tär′nish) ***vt.*** ⟦< Fr *terniss-*, inflectional stem of *ternir*, to make dim < MFr, prob. < OHG *tarnjan*, to conceal < *tarni*, hidden⟧ 1 to dull the luster of or discolor the surface of (a metal) as by exposure to air 2 *a)* to besmirch or sully (a reputation, honor, etc.) *b)* to spoil, mar, or debase [to *tarnish* a memory] —***vi.*** 1 to lose luster; grow dull; discolor, as from oxidation 2 to become sullied, soiled, spoiled, marred, etc. —***n.*** 1 the condition of being tarnished; dullness 2 the film of discoloration on the surface of tarnished metal 3 a stain; blemish —**tar′nish·a·ble *adj.***

ta·ro (ter′ō, tär′ō) ***n.***, *pl.* **-ros** ⟦< a Polynesian language < Proto-Polynesian **talo*⟧ 1 a large, tropical Asian plant (*Colocasia esculenta*) of the arum family, with shield-shaped leaves: it is cultivated for its edible corms, which are the source of poi 2 the tuber of this plant

ta·roc or **ta·rok** (tə räk′) ***n.*** ⟦< OIt *tarocco*: see fol.⟧ an old card game of Italy, Austria, etc. played with a deck of, usually, 78 cards that includes the tarot cards as trumps

tar·ot (tar′ō, -ət; ta rō′) ***n.*** ⟦Fr < MFr < OIt *tarocco*, prob. < Ar *ṭaraḥa*, to reject > TARE[2]⟧ [*often* **T-**] any of a set of 22 cards bearing pictures of certain traditional allegorical figures, used in fortunetelling: sometimes used in combination with other cards

☆**tarp** (tärp) ***n.*** *short for* TARPAULIN

☆**tar paper** a heavy paper impregnated with tar, used as a base for roofing, etc.

tar·pau·lin (tär pô′lin, tär′pə lin) ***n.*** ⟦TAR[1] + *-paulin*, prob. < *palling* < PALL[2], a covering⟧ 1 a sheet of waterproof material, specif. canvas coated or impregnated with a waterproofing compound, for spreading over something to protect it as from weather damage 2 [Archaic] a sailor; tar

Tar·pe·ia (tär pē′ə) ***n.*** *Rom. Myth.* a girl who treacherously opens the Capitoline citadel to the invading Sabines, who then crush her to death with their shields

Tar·pe·ian (-ən) ***adj.*** ⟦L *Tarpeianus*, after *Tarpeia*: see prec.⟧ designating or of a cliff on the Capitoline Hill in Rome from which traitors to the state were hurled to their death

tar·pon (tär′pən, -pän′) ***n.***, *pl.* **-pons** or **-pon** ⟦< ?⟧ any of a family (Megalopidae, order Elopiformes) of bony fishes; esp., a large, silvery game fish (*Megalops atlanticus*) with very large scales, found in the warmer parts of the W Atlantic

Tar·quin (tär′kwin) (*Lucius Tarquinius Superbus*) semilegendary Etruscan king of Rome (534?-510? B.C.)

tar·ra·did·dle (tar′ə did′'l) ***n.*** *alt. sp. of* TARADIDDLE

tar·ra·gon (tar′ə gän′) ***n.*** ⟦Sp *taragona* < Ar *ṭarkhūn* < ? Gr *drakōn*, DRAGON⟧ 1 an Old World wormwood (*Artemisia dracunculus*) whose fragrant leaves are used for seasoning, esp. in vinegar 2 the leaves of this plant

tar·ri·ance (tar′ē əns) ***n.*** [Archaic] 1 the act of tarrying; delay 2 a sojourn; stay

tar·ry[1] (tar′ē) ***vi.* -ried, -ry·ing** ⟦ME *tarien*, to delay, vex, hinder < OE *tergan*, to vex, provoke, prob. infl. by ME *targen*, to retard < OFr *targer* < VL **tardicare* < L *tardare*, to delay < *tardus*, slow > TARDY⟧ 1 to delay, linger, be tardy, etc. 2 to stay for a time, esp. longer than originally intended; remain temporarily 3 to wait —***vt.*** [Archaic] to wait for —***n.*** [Now Rare] a sojourn; stay —**SYN.** STAY[3] —**tar′ri·er *n.***

tar·ry[2] (tär′ē) ***adj.* -ri·er, -ri·est** 1 of or like tar 2 covered or smeared with tar —**tar′ri·ness *n.***

tars- (tärs) *combining form* TARSO-: used before a vowel

tar·sal (tär′səl) ***adj.*** ⟦< ModL *tarsus* (see TARSUS) + -AL⟧ of the tarsus of the foot or the tarsi of the eyelids —***n.*** a tarsal bone or plate

tar sands *Geol.* sands or sandstone deposits containing tarry, viscous, bituminous oil

Tar·shish (tär′shish′) ***n.*** seaport or maritime region of uncertain location, mentioned in the Bible: cf. 1 Kings 10:22

tar·si (tär′sī′) ***n.*** *pl. of* TARSUS

tar·si·er (tär′sē ər) ***n.*** ⟦Fr, so named by BUFFON < *tarse*, TARSUS, from the foot structure⟧ any of a family (Tarsiidae) of small arboreal primates of the East Indies and the Philippines, with very large, gogglelike eyes, and a long, tufted tail: tarsiers are active at night and feed esp. on lizards and insects

tar·so- (tär′sō, -sə) ⟦< ModL *tarsus*⟧ *combining form* tarsus or tarsal [*tarsometatarsus*]

tar·so·met·a·tar·sus (tär′sō met′ə tär′səs) ***n.*** ⟦prec. + METATARSUS⟧ *Ornithology* the large bone in the lower part of a bird's leg, connecting the tibia with the toes

tar·sus (tär′səs) ***n.***, *pl.* **tar′si′** (-sī′) ⟦ModL < Gr *tarsos*, flat of the foot, any flat surface, orig. a wickerwork frame for drying fruits or cheeses < IE base **ters-*, to dry > THIRST, L *torridus*⟧ 1 *Anat.* *a)* the human ankle, consisting of seven bones between the tibia and metatarsus *b)* the small plate of connective tissue stiffening the eyelid 2 *Zool.* *a)* a group of bones in the ankle region of the hind limbs of tetrapods *b)* TARSOMETATARSUS *c)* the fifth segment from the base of an insect leg

Tar·sus (tär′səs) city in S Turkey, near the Mediterranean: in ancient times, the capital of Cilicia & birthplace of the Apostle Paul

tart[1] (tärt) ***adj.*** ⟦ME < OE *teart* < PGmc **trat-* < IE base **der-* > TEAR[1]⟧ 1 sharp in taste; sour; acid; acidulous 2 sharp in meaning or implication; cutting [a *tart* answer] —**SYN.** SOUR —**tart′ly *adv.*** —**tart′ness *n.***

tart[2] (tärt) ***n.*** ⟦ME *tarte* < OFr, prob. var. of *tourte* < LL(Ec) *torta*, twisted loaf < L *tortus*: see TORT⟧ 1 a small shell of pastry filled with jam, jelly, etc. 2 in England, a small pie filled with fruit or jam and often having a top crust

tart[3] (tärt) ***n.*** ⟦< prec., orig., slang term of endearment⟧ [Informal] a prostitute or any promiscuous woman —**tart up** [Slang, Chiefly Brit.] to clothe, furnish, or decorate in a showy and, often, vulgar way —**tart′y *adj.***

tar·tan (tärt′'n) ***n.*** ⟦prob. < MFr *tiretaine*, a cloth of mixed fibers < OFr *tiret*, a kind of cloth < *tire*, cloth (of silk) from the East < ML *tyrius*, material from Tyre < L *Tyrus*, TYRE; sp. infl. by ME *tartarin*, a rich material < MFr (*drap*) *tartarin*, Tartar (cloth)⟧ 1 woolen cloth with a woven pattern of straight lines of different colors and widths crossing at right angles, esp. as traditionally worn in the Scottish Highlands, with each clan having its own pattern 2 any plaid cloth like this 3 any tartan pattern 4 a garment made of tartan —***adj.*** of, like, or made of tartan

tar·tar (tärt′ər) ***n.*** ⟦ME < ML *tartarum* < MGr *tartaron* < ?⟧ 1 cream of tartar, esp. the crude form present in grape juice and forming a reddish or whitish, crustlike deposit (*argol*) in wine casks 2 a hard deposit on the teeth, consisting of saliva proteins, food deposits, various salts, as calcium phosphate, etc.; dental calculus

Tar·tar (tärt′ər) ***n.*** ⟦ME *Tartre* < ML *Tartarus*, a Tatar, altered (after TARTARUS) < Pers *Tātār*⟧ 1 TATAR 2 [*usually* **t-**] an irritable, violent, intractable person —***adj.*** TATAR

tar·tare (tär tär′) ***adj.*** ⟦< *steak tartare* < Fr *tartare*, prec.: hence, in Tartar style⟧ that is ground up or diced, mixed with seasonings, and served raw: usually used postpositively [tuna *tartare*]

Tar·tar·e·an (tär ter′ē ən, -tar′-) ***adj.*** of Tartarus; infernal

tartar emetic antimony potassium tartrate, $K(SbO)C_4H_4O_6 \cdot \frac{1}{2}H_2O$, a poisonous, odorless, white salt used in medicine to cause expectoration, vomiting, and perspiration, and in dyeing as a mordant

Tar·tar·i·an (tär ter′ē ən) ***adj.*** TATAR

tar·tar·ic (tär tar′ik, -tär′-) ***adj.*** of, containing, or derived from tartar or tartaric acid

tartaric acid an acid, $HOOC(CHOH)_2COOH$, a clear, colorless crystal or a white, crystalline powder, found in vegetable tissues and fruit juices and obtained commercially from tartar: it is used in dyeing, photography, medicine, etc.

tar·tar·ous (tärt′ər əs) *adj.* of, like, or containing tartar

tar·tar sauce (tärt′ər) ⟦Fr *sauce tartare*⟧ a sauce, as for seafood, consisting of mayonnaise with chopped pickles, olives, capers, etc.: also sp. **tar′tare sauce**

tartar steak STEAK TARTARE: see TARTARE

Tar·ta·rus (tärt′ə rəs) *n.* ⟦L < Gr *Tartaros*⟧ *Gr. Myth.* **1** an infernal abyss below Hades, where Zeus hurls the rebel Titans, later a place of punishment for the wicked after death **2** HADES (sense 1*a*)

Tar·ta·ry (tärt′ər ē) *var. of* TATARY

Tar·ti·ni (tär tē′nē), **Giu·sep·pe** (jo͞o zep′pe) 1692-1770; It. violinist, composer, & musical theoretician

tart·let (tärt′lit) *n.* ⟦MFr *tartelette*: see TART[1] & -LET⟧ a small pastry tart

tar·trate (tär′trāt′) *n.* ⟦Fr < *tartre*, TARTAR + *-ate*, -ATE[2]⟧ **1** a salt of tartaric acid containing the divalent, negative radical $C_4H_4O_6$ **2** an uncharged ester of this acid

tar·trat·ed (-trāt′id) *adj.* **1** derived from or containing tartar **2** combined with tartaric acid

Tar·tu (tär′to͞o) city in E Estonia

Tar·tuffe (tär to͞of′; *Fr* tȧr tüf′) *n.* ⟦Fr < It *Tartufo*, lit., a truffle⟧ **1** the title character, a religious hypocrite, of a satirical comedy (1664-69) by Molière **2** [**t-**] a hypocrite

☆**Tar·zan** (tär′zən, -zan′) *n.* ⟦after *Tarzan*, hero raised by jungle apes in stories by Edgar Rice BURROUGHS⟧ [*also* **t-**] any very strong, virile, and agile man: often used ironically or humorously

☆**tase** (tāz) *vt.* **tased, tas′ing** ⟦back-form. < fol.⟧ [*also* **T-**] [Slang] to stun with a Taser

☆**Tas·er** (tā′zər) ⟦arbitrary coinage < *T(om) S(wift's) e(lectric) r(ifle)* (on the pattern of LASER & MASER), after *Tom Swift*, hero of a series of science fiction stories⟧ *trademark for* a hand-held, battery-operated device used to deliver a powerful electric shock either by direct contact or by firing electrically charged darts: used for self-defense and law enforcement —*n.* [*often* **t-**] such a device —*vt.* [*often* **t-**] to stun with a Taser

Tash·kent (tash kent′, täsh-) capital of Uzbekistan, on a branch of the Syr Darya

Ta·si·an (tä′sē ən) *adj.* ⟦after *Deir Tasa*, village in upper Egypt, where artifacts were found⟧ designating or of the earliest known Neolithic farming culture of Egypt, preceding the Badarian

task (task, täsk) *n.* ⟦ME *taske* < NormFr *tasque* (OFr *tasche*) < ML *tasca*, for *taxa*, a tax < L *taxare*, to rate, value, TAX⟧ **1** a piece of work assigned to or demanded of a person **2** any piece of work **3** an undertaking involving labor or difficulty —*vt.* **1** to assign a task to; require or demand a piece of work of **2** to put a burden on; strain; overtax —**take someone to task** to reprimand or scold someone

SYN.—**task** refers to a piece of work assigned to or demanded of someone, as by another person, by duty, etc., and usually implies that this is difficult or arduous work [he has the *task* of answering letters]; **chore** applies to any of the routine domestic activities for which one is responsible [his *chore* is washing the dishes]; **stint** refers to a task that is one's share of the work done by a group and usually connotes a minimum to be completed in the allotted time [we've all done our daily *stint*]; **assignment** applies to a specific, prescribed task allotted by someone in authority [classroom *assignments*]; **job**, in this connection, refers to a specific piece of work, as in one's trade or as voluntarily undertaken for pay [the *job* of painting our house]

☆**task force** **1** a specially trained, self-contained military unit assigned a specific mission or task, as the raiding of enemy installations **2** any group assigned to a specific project

task·mas·ter (task′mas′tər) *n.* a person, esp. a strict or demanding person, who assigns tasks or hard work to others

Tas·man (täs′män′; *E* taz′mən), **A·bel Jans·zoon** (ä′bəl yän′sōn) 1603?-59; Du. navigator who discovered Tasmania & New Zealand

Tas·ma·ni·a (taz mā′nē ə, -mān′yə) **1** island south of Victoria, Australia: 24,497 sq mi (63,447 sq km) **2** state of Australia comprising this island & smaller nearby islands: 26,409 sq mi (68,400 sq km); cap. Hobart —**Tas·ma′ni·an** *adj., n.*

Tasmanian devil a stout, extremely voracious, flesh-eating species (*Sarcophilus harrisii*, family Dasyuridae) of Tasmanian marsupial, having black fur with white patches and a large head

Tasmanian wolf (*or* **tiger**) a fierce, flesh-eating, possibly extinct species (*Thylacinus cynocephalus*, family Thylacinidae) of Tasmanian marsupial with dark stripes on the back

Tas·man Sea (taz′mən) section of the South Pacific, between SE Australia & New Zealand

tass (tas, täs) *n.* ⟦LME *tasse* < MFr < OFr < Ar *ṭāsa*, shallow metal cup < Pers *tast*, a cup⟧ [Now Scot.] **1** a small drinking cup or goblet **2** its contents; a small draft

Tass (täs) *n.* ⟦Russ *TASS* < *Telegrafnoe Agentstvo Sovetskogo Sojuza*, Telegraph Agency of the Soviet Union⟧ a Soviet agency for gathering and distributing news

tasse (tas) *n.* ⟦MFr, purse, pouch⟧ any of a series of jointed, metal plates forming a skirtlike protection of armor for the lower trunk and thighs: also **tas′set** (-ət)

tas·sel[1] (tas′əl) *n.* ⟦ME < OFr, knob, knot, button < VL *tassellus, altered < L *taxillus*, a small die (akin to *talus*, ankle), based on L *tessella*, small cube, piece of mosaic⟧ **1** [Obs.] a clasp or fibula **2** an ornamental tuft of threads, cords, etc. of equal length, hanging loosely from a knob or from the knot by which they are tied together **3** something resembling this; specif., the tassel-like inflorescence of some plants, as corn —*vt.* **-seled** or **-selled, -sel·ing** or **-sel·ling** to ornament with tassels —☆*vi.* to grow tassels: said as of corn

tas·sel[2] (tas′əl) *n.* [Obs.] TIERCEL

Tas·so (täs′sô; *E* tas′ō), **Tor·qua·to** (tôr kwä′tô) 1544-95; It. epic poet

taste (tāst) *vt.* **tast′ed, tast′ing** ⟦ME *tasten* < OFr *taster*, to handle, touch, taste < VL *tastare, prob. < *taxitare, freq. of L *taxare*, to feel, touch sharply, judge of, freq. of *tangere*: see TACT⟧ **1** [Obs.] to test by touching **2** to test the flavor of by putting a little in one's mouth **3** to detect or distinguish the flavor of by the sense of taste [to *taste* sage in a dressing] **4** to eat or drink, esp. a small amount of **5** to receive the sensation of, as for the first time; experience; have [to have *tasted* freedom at last] **6** [Archaic] to appreciate; like —*vi.* **1** to discern or recognize flavors by the sense of taste; have the sense of taste **2** to eat or drink a small amount (*of*) **3** to have the specific taste or flavor: sometimes with *of* [the milk *tastes* sour; the salad *tastes* of garlic] **4** to have a sensation, limited experience, or anticipating sense (*of* something) —*n.* ⟦ME < OFr *tast* < the v.⟧ **1** [Obs.] *a)* a test; trial *b)* the act of tasting **2** that one of the five senses that is stimulated by contact of a substance with the taste buds and is capable of distinguishing basically among sweet, sour, salt, and bitter: the flavor of any specific substance is usually recognized by its combined taste, smell, and texture **3** the quality of a thing that is perceived through the sense of taste; flavor; savor **4** a small amount put into the mouth to test the flavor **5** the distinguishing flavor of a substance [a chocolaty *taste*] **6** a slight experience of something; sample [to get a *taste* of another's anger] **7** a small amount; bit; trace; suggestion; touch **8** *a)* the ability to notice, appreciate, and judge what is beautiful, appropriate, or harmonious, or what is excellent in art, music, decoration, clothing, etc. *b)* a specific preference; partiality; predilection [a *taste* for red ties] *c)* an attitude or a style reflecting such ability or preferences on the part of a group of people of a particular time and place **9** a liking; inclination; fondness; bent [to have no *taste* for business] —**in (good, poor,** etc.**) taste** in a form, style, or manner showing a (good, poor, etc.) sense of beauty, excellence, fitness, propriety, etc. —**in taste** in good taste —**to one's taste** **1** pleasing to one **2** so as to please one —**to taste** so that the flavor is pleasing: phrase used as in recipes [simmer, and season *to taste*]

taste bud an oval cluster of cells embedded principally in the epithelium of the tongue and functioning as the sense organ of taste

taste·ful (tāst′fəl) *adj.* having or showing good taste [*tasteful* decor] —**taste′ful·ly** *adv.* —**taste′ful·ness** *n.*

taste·less (tāst′lis) *adj.* **1** *a)* without taste or flavor; flat; insipid *b)* dull; uninteresting **2** lacking good taste or showing poor taste —**taste′less·ly** *adv.* —**taste′less·ness** *n.*

taste·mak·er (tāst′māk′ər) *n.* a person or group that influences fashionable or popular taste

tast·er (tās′tər) *n.* ⟦ME *tastour* < Anglo-Fr⟧ **1** a person who tastes; specif., *a)* a person employed to test the quality of wines, teas, etc. by tasting *b)* a servant who tastes food and drink prepared as for a sovereign, to detect poisoning **2** any of several devices used for tasting, sampling, or testing **3** [Informal] a slight experience of something; sample; taste

tast·ing (tās′tiŋ) *n.* the process of, or an event for, tasting and evaluating a number of wines or other beverages or foods

tast·y (tās′tē) *adj.* **tast′i·er, tast′i·est** **1** that tastes good; flavorful; savory **2** [Now Rare] TASTEFUL —**tast′i·ly** *adv.* —**tast′i·ness** *n.*

tat[1] (tat) *vt.* **tat′ted, tat′ting** ⟦prob. back-form. < TATTING⟧ to make by tatting —*vi.* to do tatting

tat[2] (tat) *n.* ⟦< ? TAP[1]⟧ *see* TIT FOR TAT

tat[3] (tat) *n.* [Informal] *short for* TATTOO[1] (*n.*)

TAT *abbrev.* THEMATIC APPERCEPTION TEST

ta-ta (tä tä′; *Brit* ta tä′, tə-) *interj.* ⟦orig. a child's term⟧ [Brit. Informal] goodbye

ta·ta·mi (tə tä′mē) *n.* ⟦Jpn < nominal form of *tatamu*, to fold up, pile up⟧ **1** flooring material of woven straw, used traditionally in Japanese homes **2** *pl.* **-mi** or **-mis** a floor mat of this material, typically of a standard size for modular use

Ta·tar (tät′ər) *n.* ⟦Pers⟧ **1** a member of any of the Mongolian and Turkic peoples that took part in the invasion of central and W Asia and E Europe in the Middle Ages **2** a member of a Turkic people living in a region of EC European Russia, the Crimea, and parts of Asia **3** any of the Turkic languages of these peoples; esp., a language (**Kazan Tatar**) spoken around Kazan —*adj.* of Tatary or its peoples, languages, or cultures: also **Ta·tar·i·an** (tä ter′ē ən) or **Ta·tar′ic**

Ta·tar Strait strait between Sakhalin Island & the Asia mainland: *c.* 350 mi (563 km) long

Ta·ta·ry (tät′ə rē) vast region in Europe & Asia under the control of Tatar tribes in the late Middle Ages: its greatest extent was from SW Russia to the Pacific

Tate (tāt) **1 (John Orley) Allen** 1899-1979; U.S. poet & critic **2 Nahum** 1652-1715; Brit. poet & dramatist, born in Ireland: poet laureate (1692-1715)

ta·ter (tāt′ər) *n. dial. form of* POTATO

Ta·tra Mountains (tä′trə) range of the Carpathian Mountains in N Slovakia & S Poland: highest peak, 8,737 ft (2,663 m)

tat·ter (tat′ər) *n.* ⟦ME, prob. < ON *töturr*, rags, tatters, akin to Ger *zotte*, tuft < IE base **dā(i)-*, to cut out, divide > TIDE[1]⟧ **1** a torn and hanging shred or piece, as of a garment **2** a separate shred or scrap; rag **3** [*pl.*] torn, ragged clothes —***vt.*** to reduce to tatters; make ragged —***vi.*** to become ragged

tat·ter·de·mal·ion (tat′ər di māl′yən, -ē ən; -mal′-) *n.* ⟦< prec. + ?⟧ a person in torn, ragged clothes; ragamuffin

tat·tered (tat′ərd) *adj.* ⟦ME *tatered*⟧ **1** in tatters; torn and ragged **2** wearing torn and ragged clothes

tat·ter·sall (tat′ər sôl′) *n.* ⟦after *Tattersall's*, a London horse market and gamblers' rendezvous, founded (1766) by Richard Tattersall⟧ a checkered pattern of dark lines on a light background —***adj.*** having such a pattern

tat·ting (tat′iŋ) *n.* ⟦prob. < Brit dial. *tat*, to tangle⟧ **1** a fine lace made by looping and knotting thread that is wound on a hand shuttle: used for edging, trimming, etc. **2** the act or process of making this

tat·tle (tat′'l) *vi.* **-tled**, **-tling** ⟦LME *tattlen*, prob. < MDu *tatelen*, of echoic orig.⟧ **1** to talk idly; chatter; gossip **2** to reveal other people's secrets; tell tales **3** to inform against someone —***vt.*** to reveal (a secret) through gossiping —***n.*** idle talk; chatter; tattling

tat·tler (tat′lər) *n.* **1** a person who tattles; gossip or informer ☆**2** a grayish-brown sandpiper (*Heteroscelus incanus*) of the Pacific coastal region, known for its loud cry

☆**tat·tle·tale** (tat′'l tāl′) *n.* an informer or talebearer: now chiefly a child's term

tat·too[1] (ta to͞o′) *vt.* **-tooed′**, **-too′ing** ⟦< a Polynesian language < Proto-Polynesian **tatau*⟧ **1** to leave permanent marks or designs on (a person or a part of the body) by puncturing the skin with a needle and inserting ink or other indelible pigments **2** to make (marks or designs) on a person or part of the body in this way —***n.***, *pl.* **-toos′** a tattooed mark or design —**tat·too′er** ***n.***, **tat·too′ist**

tat·too[2] (ta to͞o′) *n.*, *pl.* **-toos′** ⟦earlier *taptoo* < Du *taptoe* < *tap toe*, tap to (shut): a signal for closing barrooms⟧ **1** *a)* a signal on a drum or bugle, summoning military personnel to their quarters at night *b)* in Great Britain, a military spectacle featuring music, marching, and military exercises **2** any continuous drumming or rapping — ***vt.***, ***vi.*** **-tooed′**, **-too′ing** to beat or tap on (a drum or other surface)

tat·ty (tat′ē) *adj.* **-ti·er**, **-ti·est** ⟦prob. < OE *taetteca*, a rag, akin to ON *töturr*, TATTER⟧ [Chiefly Brit.] shabby, decrepit, or tawdry —**tat′ti·ly** ***adv.*** —**tat′ti·ness** ***n.***

Ta·tum (tāt′əm), **Art(hur)** 1910-56; U.S. jazz pianist

tau (tou, tô) *n.* ⟦ME *taw*, *tau* (esp. with ref. to the tau cross) < L *tau* < Gr < Sem, as in Heb *tav*, TAV⟧ the nineteenth letter of the Greek alphabet (Τ, τ)

tau cross a cross shaped like a capital tau

taught (tôt) *vt.*, *vi. pt. & pp. of* TEACH

taunt (tônt, tänt) *vt.* ⟦< ? Fr *tant pour tant*, tit for tat⟧ **1** to reproach in scornful or sarcastic language; jeer at; mock **2** to drive or provoke (a person) by taunting —***n.*** a scornful or jeering remark; gibe —**SYN.** RIDICULE —**taunt′er** ***n.*** —**taunt′ing·ly** ***adv.***

Taun·ton (tônt′'n, tänt′'n) county seat of Somerset, SW England

tau particle ⟦< TAU, first letter of Gr *tritos*, THIRD: because it was the third charged lepton to be discovered⟧ *Particle Physics* an unstable, negatively charged lepton with a mass of *c.* 1,777 MeV/c^2 (or *c.* 3,490 times that of an electron) and a mean lifetime of 2.2 $\times 10^{-13}$ second: also called **tau lepton** or **tau·on** (tou′än′)

taupe (tōp) *n.* ⟦Fr < L *talpa*, mole⟧ a dark, brownish gray, the color of moleskin —***adj.*** of such a color

Tau·re·an (tôr′ē ən) *n. var. of* TAURUS (sense 3)

tau·rine[1] (tôr′īn′, -in) *adj.* ⟦L *taurinus* < *taurus*, bull: see TAURUS⟧ **1** of or like a bull **2** [T-] of TAURUS (sense 2)

tau·rine[2] (tôr′ēn′, -in) *n.* ⟦< L *taurus* (see TAURUS) + -INE[3]: because first obtained (1826) from ox bile⟧ a colorless, crystalline amino acid, $NH_2CH_2CH_2SO_3H$, which is found in the free form in invertebrates and as a constituent of taurocholic acid in the bile of mammals

tau·ro·cho·lic acid (tôr′ō kō′lik) ⟦< prec. + CHOL(O)- + -IC⟧ a colorless, crystalline acid, $NC_{26}H_{45}O_7S$, that occurs in the bile of mammals as the sodium salt and promotes the intestinal absorption of lipids, as cholesterol

tau·rom·a·chy (tô räm′ə kē) *n.* ⟦Gr *tauromachia*, bullfight < *tauros*, bull (see fol.) + *machē*, a battle⟧ *literary term for* BULLFIGHTING

Tau·rus (tôr′əs) *n.* ⟦ME < L, bull, ox, prob. < IE **tauros* < base **tēu-*, to swell > THUMB, L *tumere*, to swell⟧ **1** a N constellation between Aries and Orion containing the Hyades and the Pleiades star clusters, the Crab nebula, and the bright star Aldebaran; the Bull **2** the second sign of the zodiac, entered by the sun about April 21 **3** a person born under this sign

Taurus Mountains mountain range along the S coast of Asia Minor, Turkey: highest peak, *c.* 12,250 ft (3,734 m)

taut (tôt) *adj.* ⟦ME *toght*, tight, firm, prob. < pp. of *togen* (< OE *togian*), to pull, TOW[1]⟧ **1** tightly stretched: said as of a rope **2** showing strain; tense [*a taut smile*] **3** trim, orderly, and characterized by strict enforcement of discipline: said of a ship —**SYN.** TIGHT —**taut′ly** ***adv.*** —**taut′ness** ***n.***

taut·en (tôt′'n) *vt.*, *vi.* to make or become taut

tau·to- (tôt′ō, -ə) ⟦Gr < *tauto* < *to auto*, the same⟧ *combining form* the same [*tautology*]

☆**tau·tog** (tô täg′) *n.* ⟦Narragansett *tautaũog*, pl. of *taut*⟧ an edible, black and greenish wrasse fish (*Tautoga onitis*) of the Atlantic coast of the U.S.

tau·to·log·i·cal (tôt′ə läj′i kəl) *adj.* of, involving, or using tautology —**tau′to·log′i·cal·ly** ***adv.***

tau·tol·o·gous (tô täl′ə gəs) *adj.* **1** TAUTOLOGICAL **2** ANALYTIC (sense 5) —**tau·tol′o·gous·ly** ***adv.***

tau·tol·o·gy (tô täl′ə jē) *n.*, *pl.* **-gies** ⟦LL *tautologia* < Gr: see TAUTO- & -LOGY⟧ **1** *a)* needless repetition of an idea in different words; redundancy; pleonasm (Ex.: "necessary essentials") *b)* an instance of such repetition **2** *Logic* a proposition that is ANALYTIC (sense 5)

tau·to·mer (tôt′ə mər) *n.* ⟦back-form. < fol.⟧ a substance exhibiting tautomerism

tau·tom·er·ism (tô täm′ər iz′əm) *n.* ⟦< TAUTO- + Gr *meros*, a part + -ISM⟧ *Chem.* the property of some substances of being in a condition of equilibrium between two isomeric forms and of reacting readily to form either —**tau·to·mer·ic** (tôt′ə mer′ik) ***adj.***

tau·to·nym (tôt′ə nim′) *n.* ⟦< TAUT(O)- + Gr *onyma*, NAME⟧ *Biol.* **1** a scientific name consisting of two terms, in which the generic name and specific name are the same (Ex.: *Vulpes vulpes*, the red fox): this kind of name is no longer used in botany, but is common in zoology **2** a scientific name consisting of three terms, in which the name of the typical subdivision of the species repeats the specific name (Ex.: *Lama glama glama*, a domesticated llama) —**tau′to·nym′ic** ***adj.*** —**tau·ton·y·my** (tô tän′ə mē) ***n.***

tav (täf, täv) *n.* ⟦Heb *tāw*⟧ the twenty-third letter of the Hebrew alphabet (ת)

tav·ern (tav′ərn) *n.* ⟦ME *taverne* < OFr < L *taberna*, tavern, booth, stall made of boards, altered by dissimilation < **traberna* < *trabs*, a beam, roof < IE base **treb-*, beamed structure, building > THORP⟧ **1** a place where liquors, beer, etc. are sold to be drunk on the premises; saloon; bar **2** [Archaic] an inn

ta·ver·na (tä ver′nə) *n.* ⟦ModGr *taberna* < L: see prec.⟧ a small, inexpensive tavern or restaurant in Greece, often with music and dancing

tav·ern·er (tav′ər nər) *n.* [Archaic] the proprietor of a tavern

Tav·ern·er (tav′ər nər), **John** (*c.* 1490-1545) Eng. composer

taw[1] (tô) *n.* ⟦< ?⟧ **1** in a game of marbles, *a)* a fancy marble that a player shoots *b)* the line from which the players shoot **2** a game of marbles in which players attempt to drive marbles out of a marked circle

taw[2] (tô) *vt.* ⟦ME *tawen* < OE *tawian*, to prepare, akin to Goth *taujan*, to do, make < ? IE base **deu-*, to work on, process (something)⟧ to prepare (a natural product) for further treatment or use; specif., to make (skins) into leather by treating with alum, salt, etc.

taw[3] (täf, täv) *n. alt. sp. of* TAV

taw·dry (tô′drē) *adj.* **-dri·er**, **-dri·est** ⟦by syllabic merging of *St. Audrey*, esp. in *St. Audrey laces*, women's neckpieces sold at St. Audrey's fair in Norwich, England⟧ **1** cheap and showy; gaudy; sleazy **2** shameful or indecent —**taw′dri·ness** ***n.***

taw·ny (tô′nē) *adj.* **-ni·er**, **-ni·est** ⟦ME *tauny* < OFr *tanné*, pp. of *tanner*, to TAN[1]⟧ brownish-yellow; tan —***n.*** tawny color —**SYN.** DUSKY —**taw′ni·ness** ***n.***

tawse (tôz) *n.*, *pl.* **tawse** ⟦prob. pl. of obs. *taw*, thong, tawed leather < TAW[2]⟧ [*sometimes with pl. v.*] a leather thong split into strips at the end, used as a whip: also sp. **taws**

tax (taks) *vt.* ⟦ME *taxen* < MFr *taxer*, to tax < L *taxare*, to appraise, tax, censure < base of *tangere*, to touch (see TACT): used interchangeably with *tasken* (see TASK) in ME⟧ **1** [Obs.] to determine the value of; assess **2** *a)* to require to pay a percentage of income, property value, etc. for the support of a government *b)* to require to pay a special assessment, as in a society, labor union, etc. **3** to assess a tax on (income, property, purchases, etc.) **4** to impose a burden on; put a strain on [*such babbling taxes one's patience*] **5** to accuse; charge [*to be taxed with negligence*] —***n.*** ⟦ME⟧ **1** *a)* a compulsory payment, usually a percentage, levied on income, property value, sales price, etc. for the support of a government *b)* a special assessment, as in a society, labor union, etc. **2** a heavy demand; burden; strain —**tax′a·bil′i·ty** ***n.*** —**tax′a·ble** ***adj.*** —**tax′er** ***n.***

tax·a (tak′sə) *n. pl. of* TAXON

tax·a·tion (tak sā′shən) *n.* ⟦ME *taxacion* < MFr *taxation* < L *taxatio* < pp. of *taxare*: see TAX⟧ **1** a taxing or being taxed **2** a tax or tax levy **3** revenue from taxes

Tax·co (täs′kō) city in Guerrero state, S Mexico: resort & silver manufacturing center

tax-de·duct·i·ble (taks′dē dukt′ə bəl) *adj.* that is allowed as a deduction in computing income tax

☆**tax duplicate** **1** the certification of real-estate assessments to the taxing authorities **2** the basis upon which the tax collector prepares tax bills and for which the collector is accountable to the auditor

tax·eme (tak′sēm′) *n.* ⟦coined (1933) by Leonard BLOOMFIELD < Gr *taxis*, arrangement (see TAXIS) + -EME⟧ any of the minimal features in grammatical construction, as word selection, word order, or modulation in stress and pitch —**tax·e·mic** (tak sē′mik) ***adj.***

tax-ex·empt (taks′eg zempt′) *adj.* **1** exempt from taxation; that may not be taxed **2** producing income that is exempt from taxation [*tax-exempt bonds*]

tax-free (taks′frē′) *adj.* **1** having no taxes [*a tax-free state*] **2** TAX-EXEMPT

☆**tax·i** (tak′sē) *n.*, *pl.* **tax′is** **1** *short for* TAXICAB **2** any craft for ferrying passengers, as across a river or between the islands of an archipelago [*a water taxi, an air taxi*] —***vi.*** **tax′ied**, **tax′i·ing** or **tax′y·ing** **1** to go in a taxicab **2** to move slowly along the ground or on the water as before taking off or after landing: said of an airplane —***vt.*** **1** to carry in a taxicab **2** to cause (an airplane) to taxi

☆**tax·i·cab** (-kab′) *n.* ⟦< *taxi(meter) cab*⟧ an automobile in which passengers are carried for a fare

☆**taxi dancer** ⟦so called (based on prec.) because hired to dance⟧ a woman employed at a dance hall to dance with patrons, who pay a fee

tax·i·der·my (tak′si dur′mē) ***n.*** ⟦< Gr *taxis* (see TAXIS) + *derma,* skin⟧ the art of preparing, stuffing, and mounting the skins of animals, so as to create lifelike replicas —**tax′i·der′mic** ***adj.*** —**tax′i·der′mist** ***n.***

tax·i·me·ter (tak′sē mēt′ər) ***n.*** ⟦Fr *taximètre,* altered (infl. by Gr *taxis:* see fol.) < *taxamètre* < Ger *taxameter* < ML *taxa,* TAX + *-meter,* -METER⟧ an automatic device in taxicabs that computes and registers the fare due

tax·is (tak′sis) ***n.*** ⟦Gr, arrangement, division: see TACTICS⟧ **1** in ancient Greece, a unit of troops of varying size **2** ⟦ModL < Gr⟧ *Biol.* the movement of a free-moving cell or organism toward or away from some external stimulus **3** *Surgery* the act of replacing a displaced part, as in a dislocation, manually and without cutting any tissue

-tax·is (tak′sis) ⟦ModL < Gr < *taxis:* see prec.⟧ *combining form* **1** arrangement, order *[phyllotaxis]* **2** TAXIS (sense 2) *[phototaxis]*

☆**taxi stand** a place where taxicabs are stationed for hire

tax·i·way (tak′sē wā′) ***n.*** any of the paved strips at an airport for use by airplanes in taxiing to and from the runways

tax-loss carryforward (taks′lôs′) CARRYFORWARD

tax·man (taks′man′) ***n., pl.*** **-men′** (-men′) [Informal] a collector of taxes

tax·ol (tak′sôl) ***n.*** ⟦< taxonomic name of the tree⟧ a substance, $C_{47}H_{51}NO_{14}$, obtained from a small yew tree (*Taxus brevifolia*) of W North America, used in treating certain kinds of cancer

tax·on (tak′sän′) ***n., pl.*** **tax′a** (-sə) ⟦back-form. < fol.⟧ a taxonomic category or unit, as a species or family

tax·on·o·my (tak sän′ə mē) ***n., pl.*** **-mies** ⟦Fr *taxonomie* < Gr *taxis* (see TAXIS) + *nomos,* law (see -NOMY)⟧ **1** the science of classification; laws and principles covering the classifying of objects **2** *Biol.* a system of arranging animals and plants into natural, related groups based on some factor common to each, as structure, embryology, or biochemistry: the basic taxa now in use are, in descending order from most inclusive, *domain, kingdom, phylum* (in botany, *division*), *class, order, family, genus,* and *species* —**tax′o·nom′ic** (-sə näm′ik) ***adj.*** —**tax′o·nom′i·cal·ly** ***adv.*** —**tax·on′o·mist** ***n.***

tax·pay·er (taks′pā′ər) ***n.*** any person who pays taxes or is subject to taxation

tax rate the percentage of income, property value, etc. assessed as tax

☆**tax shelter** any financial investment made in order to acquire expenses, depreciation allowances, etc. or to defer income, as in an IRA or Keogh plan, so as to reduce one's income tax

tax stamp a stamp that shows that a tax has been paid

☆**tax title** the title conveyed to the purchaser of property sold for nonpayment of taxes

tax·us (tak′səs) ***n., pl.*** **tax′us** ⟦ModL < L, akin ? to Gr *toxon,* a bow < Scythian **tachša:* akin to Pers *tachš,* bow, arrow⟧ YEW (***n.*** 1)

Tay (tā) **1** river in EC Scotland, flowing into the North Sea: *c.* 120 mi (193 km) **2 Firth of** estuary of this river: 25 mi (40 km)

Tay·lor (tā′lər) **1 (James) Bay·ard** (bī′ərd, bā′ärd′) 1825-78; U.S. poet, journalist, & translator **2 Edward** 1644?-1729; Am. poet **3 Jeremy** 1613-67; Eng. bishop & theological writer **4 Zachary** 1784-1850; U.S. general: 12th president of the U.S. (1849-50)

☆**Tay-Sachs disease** (tā′saks′) ⟦after W. *Tay* (1843-1927), Eng physician, & B. *Sachs* (1858-1944), U.S. neurologist, who described it⟧ a hereditary condition, found chiefly among descendants of some Eastern European Jews, caused by an enzyme deficiency and characterized by intellectual disability, paralysis, and death in early childhood

Tay·side (tā′sīd′) former administrative region of EC Scotland, on the Firth of Tay

☆**taze** (tāz) ***vt.*** **tazed, taz′ing** ⟦phonetic sp., back-form. < TASER⟧ [*also* **T-**] [Slang] to stun with a Taser

taz·za (tät′sə) ***n.*** ⟦It < Ar *ṭāsa:* see TASS⟧ a shallow, ornamental cup or vase, usually with a pedestal

tb *abbrev.* **1** trial balance **2** tubercle bacillus

Tb[1] *abbrev. Bible* Tobit

Tb[2] *Chem. symbol for* terbium

TB[1] (tē′bē′) ***n.*** TUBERCULOSIS

TB[2] *abbrev. Football* tailback: sometimes written **tb**

TBA, t.b.a., *or* **tba** *abbrev.* to be announced

☆**T-ball** (tē′bôl′) ***n.*** a type of baseball for young children in which the ball is not pitched, but instead is placed on a tall TEE[3] (***n.*** *2b*) and struck with a bat

T-bar (tē′bär′) ***n.*** ☆a T-shaped bar suspended from the moving cable of a ski lift, used to pull two skiers at a time uphill as they stand on their skis

TBD *abbrev.* to be determined: sometimes written **tbd**

Tbi·li·si (tə bə lē′sē, tə bil′i sē′) capital of the country of Georgia, on the Kura River

☆**T-bill** (tē′bil′) ***n.*** *short for* TREASURY BILL

☆**T-bone** (tē′bōn′) ***n.*** a beefsteak from the short loin, with a T-shaped bone, containing some tenderloin: in full **T-bone steak** —***vt.*** **T′-boned′, T′-bon′ing** [Informal] to ram (something) broadside *[T-boned* by another car after running a red light*]*

tbs or **tbsp** *abbrev.* **1** tablespoon(s) **2** tablespoonful(s)

tc *abbrev.* tierce(s)

Tc *Chem. symbol for* technetium

TCDD (tē′sē′dē′dē′) ***n.*** ⟦*(2,3,7,8-)t(etra)c(hloro)d(ibenzo-p-)d(ioxin)*⟧ a highly poisonous contaminant, $C_{12}H_4O_2Cl_4$, found in some herbicides: see DIOXIN

TCE *abbrev.* trichloroethylene

T cell ⟦< *t(hymus)*⟧ any of the lymphocytes that are affected by the thymus and are involved in rejecting foreign tissue, regulating cellular immunity, and controlling the production of antibodies in the presence of an antigen: cf. B CELL

Tchai·kov·sky (chī kôf′skē), **Peter Il·ich** (il′yich) 1840-93; Russ. composer

Tche·kov (chek′ôf) *alt. sp. of* CHEKHOV: also **Tche′khov**

☆**tchotch·ke** (chäch′kə, -kē) ***n.*** ⟦Yiddish *tshatshke* < Slav⟧ [Informal] a knickknack, collectible, trinket, etc.

TD *abbrev.* **1** *Football* touchdown: sometimes written **td 2** Treasury Department

TDD *abbrev.* telecommunications device for the deaf

TDE *abbrev.* DDD

TDY *abbrev.* temporary duty

Te *Chem. symbol for* tellurium

TE *abbrev. Football* tight end: sometimes written **te**

tea (tē) ***n.*** ⟦Amoy Chin *t'e* (Mandarin *ch'a*)⟧ **1** a white-flowered, evergreen plant (*Camellia sinensis*) of the tea family, grown in China, India, Japan, etc. **2** its dried and prepared leaves, used to make a beverage **3** the beverage made by soaking such leaves in boiling water **4** any of several plants resembling or used as tea **5** a tealike beverage made from such a plant or from a meat extract *[mint tea,* beef *tea]* **6** [Chiefly Brit.] *a)* a light meal, esp. in the late afternoon, at which tea is the usual beverage *b)* a more substantial, early evening meal that is often the main meal of the day (in Britain usually called *high tea*) **7** a reception or other social gathering in the afternoon, at which tea, coffee, etc. are served ☆**8** [Slang] marijuana —***adj.*** designating a family (Theaceae, order Theales) of evergreen dicotyledonous trees, shrubs, or vines, often with showy flowers, found in warm regions and including the camellias and loblolly bay

☆**tea bag** a small, porous bag, as of paper, containing tea leaves and used in making an individual cup of tea

☆**tea ball** a hollow, perforated metal ball used to hold tea leaves in making tea

tea·ber·ry (tē′ber′ē) ***n., pl.*** **-ries 1** WINTERGREEN (sense 1) **2** the berry of the wintergreen

tea biscuit [Chiefly Brit.] any of a variety of crackers or cookies often served with tea

☆**tea cart** a small table on wheels for holding a tea service, extra dishes at a dinner, etc.; serving cart

teach (tēch) ***vt.*** **taught, teach′ing** ⟦ME *techen* < OE *tæcan* < base of *tacn,* a sign, symbol (see TOKEN); basic sense "to show, demonstrate," as in Ger *zeigen*⟧ **1** to show or help (a person) to learn (*how*) to do something *[*to *teach* a child (how) to swim*]* **2** to give lessons to (a student, pupil, or class); guide the studies of; instruct **3** to give lessons in (a subject) to someone; help someone to develop (a skill or trait) *[teaches* French, *taught* him self-discipline*]* **4** *a)* to provide (a person) with knowledge, insight, etc. *[*the accident that *taught* her to be careful*]* *b)* to attempt to cause someone to understand or accept (a precept or philosophy), esp. by one's own example or preaching *[*her life itself *teaches* nonviolence*]* **5** to give instruction at or in (a place) *[*to *teach* school*]* —***vi.*** to give lessons or instruction; be a teacher, esp. in a school or college —**teach′a·bil′i·ty** ***n.***, **teach′a·ble·ness** —**teach′a·ble** ***adj.*** —**teach′a·bly** ***adv.***

SYN.—**teach** is the basic, inclusive word for the imparting of knowledge or skills and usually connotes some individual attention to the learner *[*he *taught* her how to skate*]*; **instruct** implies systematized teaching, usually in some particular subject *[*she *instructs* in chemistry*]*; **educate** stresses the development of latent faculties and powers by formal, systematic teaching, esp. in institutions of higher learning *[*he was *educated* in European universities*]*; **train** implies the development of a particular faculty or skill, or instruction toward a particular occupation, as by methodical discipline, exercise, etc. *[*he was *trained* as a mechanic*]*; **school**, often equivalent to any of the preceding, sometimes specifically connotes a disciplining to endure something difficult *[*he had to *school* himself to obedience*]*

Teach (tēch), **Edward** *see* BLACKBEARD

teach·er (tē′chər) ***n.*** a person who teaches, esp. as a profession; instructor —**teach′er·ship′** ***n.***

teachers college a college, usually having a four-year curriculum and granting a bachelor's degree, for training teachers for elementary and secondary schools

☆**teach-in** (tēch′in′) ***n.*** ⟦see TEACH & -IN[2]⟧ a special, extended meeting, as at a college or university, with lectures, discussion, and debate on a controversial issue, esp. such a meeting held to protest against some policy

teach·ing (tē′chiŋ) ***n.*** **1** the action of a person who teaches; profession of a teacher **2** something taught; precept, doctrine, or instruction: *usually used in pl.*

teaching assistant a student in a graduate school who assists a professor with teaching duties in return for compensation, as tuition credit or a small stipend

☆**teaching fellow** a student in a graduate school under a grant that requires the performance of some teaching duties

teaching hospital a hospital, often affiliated with a medical school, in which medical students, residents, and other health professionals receive supervised clinical training

☆**teaching machine** a computer or mechanical device used for programmed instruction, which provides immediate corrective feedback and, often, extra practice if needed

tea·cup (tē′kup′) *n.* **1** a cup for drinking tea, etc. **2** TEACUPFUL —*adj.* designating an especially small variety of a small breed of dog [a *teacup* Chihuahua]

tea·cup·ful (-fo͝ol′) *n., pl.* **-fuls′** as much as a teacup will hold, about four fluid ounces

☆**tea dance** a dance held in the late afternoon, at teatime

tea·house (tē′hous′) *n.* a place, as in the Far East, where tea and other refreshments are served

teak (tēk) *n.* ⟦Port *teca* < Malayalam *tēkka* < Sans *śāka*⟧ **1** a tall SE Asian tree (*Tectona grandis*) of the verbena family, with white flowers and hard, yellowish-brown wood used for shipbuilding, furniture, etc. **2** its wood: also **teak′wood′**

tea·ket·tle (tē′ket′′l) *n.* a covered kettle with a spout and handle, for boiling water to make tea, etc.

teal (tēl) *n.* ⟦ME *tele,* akin to Du *taling,* MLowG *telink,* teal⟧ **1** *pl.* **teals** or **teal** any of several small, short-necked, freshwater wild ducks (genus *Anas*) **2** a dark greenish-blue or grayish-blue color: also **teal blue**

team (tēm) *n.* ⟦ME < OE, offspring, brood, team of draft animals (akin to Ger *zaum,* bridle, rein) < base of *tēon,* to draw < IE base **deuk-,* to pull > DUCT⟧ **1** *a)* [Obs.] progeny, race, or lineage *b)* [Dial.] a brood of young animals, esp. of ducks or pigs **2** two or more horses, oxen, etc. harnessed to the same vehicle or plow **3** *a)* two or more draft animals and their vehicle *b)* one draft animal and its vehicle **4** *a)* a group of people constituting one side in a contest or competition *b)* a group of people working together in a coordinated effort —*vt.* **1** *a)* to harness or yoke together in a team *b)* to join together in a cooperative activity **2** to haul with a team —*vi.* **1** to drive a team ☆**2** to join in cooperative activity: often with *up* [to *team* up on a research project] —*adj.* of or done by a team

team·mate (tēm′māt′) *n.* a fellow member on a team

team player one who subordinates personal aspirations and works in a coordinated effort with other members of a group, or team, in striving for a common goal

☆**team·ster** (tēm′stər) *n.* **1** a person whose occupation is driving teams or trucks for hauling goods **2** [T-] a member of the International Brotherhood of Teamsters, a labor union

☆**team teaching** classroom instruction in which two or more teachers, often from different disciplines, collaborate —**team′-taught′** (-tôt′) *adj.*

team·work (tēm′wurk′) *n.* ☆**1** joint action by a group of people, in which individual interests are subordinated to group unity and efficiency; coordinated effort, as of an athletic team **2** work done by or with a team

tea party a social gathering at which tea is served, usually in the late afternoon

tea·pot (tē′pät′) *n.* a pot with a spout, handle, and lid, for brewing and pouring tea

tea·poy (tē′poi′) *n.* ⟦Hindi *tipāī* < *tin, tir* (< Sans *tri,* THREE) + Pers *pāī* (akin to Sans *pad-,* FOOT): sp. infl. by assoc. with *tea*⟧ **1** a small, three-legged stand **2** a small table for holding a tea service

tear[1] (ter) *vt.* **tore, torn, tear′ing** ⟦ME *teren* < OE *teran,* to rend, akin to Ger *zehren,* to destroy, consume < IE base **der-,* to skin, split > DRAB[1], DERMA[1]⟧ **1** to pull apart or separate into pieces by force; rip or rend (cloth, paper, etc.) **2** to make or cause by tearing or puncturing [to *tear* a hole in a dress] **3** to wound by tearing; lacerate [skin *torn* and bruised] **4** to force apart or divide into factions; disrupt; split [ranks *torn* by dissension] **5** to divide with doubt, uncertainty, etc.; agitate; torment [a mind *torn* between duty and desire] **6** to remove by or as by tearing, pulling, etc.: with *up, out, away, off,* etc. [to *tear* a plant up by its roots, to *tear* oneself away] —*vi.* **1** to be torn **2** to move violently or with speed; dash —*n.* **1** the act of tearing **2** the result of a tearing; torn place; rent **3** a rushing pace; great hurry **4** *see* WEAR AND TEAR ☆**5** [Slang] a carousal; spree —**tear at** to make violent, pulling motions at in an attempt to tear or remove —**tear down** **1** to wreck or demolish (a building, etc.) **2** to dismantle or take apart [to *tear down* an engine] **3** to cause to disintegrate **4** to controvert or disprove (an argument, etc.) point by point —**tear into** [Informal] to attack impetuously and, often, devastatingly —**tear it** [Slang] to be that which brings about final failure, defeat, frustration, loss of patience, etc. [that *tears it!*] —**tear′er** *n.*

SYN.—**tear** implies a pulling apart by force, so as to lacerate or leave ragged edges [to *tear* wrapping paper]; **rip** suggests a forcible tearing, especially along a seam or in a straight line [to *rip* a hem]; **rend,** a somewhat literary term, implies a tearing with violence [the tree was *rent* by a bolt of lightning]

tear[2] (tir) *n.* ⟦ME *tere* < OE *tēar, teagor,* akin to Ger *zähre* < IE **dakru,* tear > OL *dacrima* (> L *lacrima*), Gr *dakryon*⟧ **1** a drop of the salty fluid secreted by the lacrimal gland to lubricate the eyeball, kill bacteria, etc.: in humans, tears may flow for emotional reasons due to the tightening of muscles near the glands **2** anything resembling this, as a drop of transparent gum; tearlike mass **3** [*pl.*] sorrow; grief —*vi.* to fill with tears —**in tears** crying; weeping

tear·a·way (ter′ə wā′) *adj.* designed to be easily opened, separated, etc., as by tearing —*n.* [Brit.] a nonconformist, rebel, or bohemian person

tear·drop (tir′dräp′) *n.* a tear —*adj.* shaped like a falling tear

tear·ful (tir′fəl) *adj.* **1** *a)* in tears; crying *b)* on the verge of tears **2** tending to shed tears; weepy **3** causing tears or apt to cause tears; sad; pathetic —**tear′ful·ly** *adv.* —**tear′ful·ness** *n.*

tear gas (tir) a volatile liquid or gas that causes irritation of the eyes, a heavy flow of tears, and temporary blindness: used as in warfare or by the police —**tear′-gas′** *vt.* **-gassed′, -gas′sing**

tear·ing (ter′iŋ) *adj.* violent; impetuous; rushing

☆**tear-jerk·er** (tir′jur′kər) *n.* [Slang] a play, film, etc. that is sad in a very maudlin way

tear·less (tir′lis) *adj.* **1** without tears; not weeping **2** unable to weep —**tear′less·ly** *adv.* —**tear′less·ness** *n.*

tea·room (tē′ro͞om′) *n.* a restaurant that serves tea, coffee, light lunches, etc.

tea rose **1** a species of Chinese rose (*Rosa odorata*) with a sweet scent, producing a hybrid tea rose when crossed with various hybrid roses **2** a yellowish-pink color

☆**tear sheet** (ter) a page cut or torn, or taken before binding, as from a magazine or journal, for special distribution

tear·y (tir′ē) *adj.* **tear′i·er, tear′i·est** TEARFUL: often used to suggest excessive or maudlin sentimentality —**tear′i·ly** *adv.* —**tear′i·ness** *n.*

Teas·dale (tēz′dāl′), **Sara** 1884-1933; U.S. poet

tease (tēz) *vt.* **teased, teas′ing** ⟦ME *tesen* < OE *tæsan,* to pull about, pluck, tease, akin to Du *teezen* < IE **di-s* < base **dā(i)-,* to cut apart, divide > TIDE[1]⟧ **1** *a)* to separate the fibers of; card or comb (flax, wool, etc.) *b)* to fluff (the hair) by brushing or combing in strokes from the hair ends toward the scalp *c)* to gently shred or pull apart (tissues, etc.) for microscopic examination, cellular research, etc. ☆*d)* to reveal, extract, obtain, etc. by painstaking effort (often with *out*) [it took hours to *tease* out the meaning of the story] **2** to raise a nap on (cloth) by brushing with teasels; teasel **3** to annoy or harass by persistent mocking or poking fun, playful fooling, etc. **4** to urge persistently; importune **5** *a)* to tantalize *b)* to excite sexually without intending to satisfy the desire aroused —*vi.* to indulge in teasing —*n.* **1** a teasing or being teased **2** a person who teases —SYN. ANNOY —**teas′ing·ly** *adv.*

tea·sel (tē′zəl) *n.* ⟦ME *tasel* < OE *tæsel* < base of *tæsan,* to TEASE⟧ **1** any of a genus (*Dipsacus*) of bristly plants of the teasel family, with prickly, cylindrical heads of yellowish or purplish flowers, esp. the **fuller's teasel** (*D. fullonum*) with flower heads having sharp, spinelike bracts **2** a flower head of the fuller's teasel, used when dried for raising a nap on cloth **3** any device for raising a nap on cloth —*adj.* designating a family (Dipsacaceae, order Dipsacales) of dicotyledonous plants bearing dense flower heads covered with stiff bracts, including scabiosa and teasel —*vt.* **tea′seled** or **tea′selled, tea′sel·ing** or **tea′sel·ling** to raise a nap on (cloth) by means of teasels —**tea′sel·er** *n.*, **tea′sel·ler**

teas·er (tē′zər) *n.* **1** a person or thing that teases **2** an annoying or puzzling problem

tea set (*or* **service**) a set, as of china or silver, for serving tea, including a teapot, creamer, sugar bowl, etc.

tea·spoon (tē′spo͞on′) *n.* **1** a spoon for stirring tea, coffee, etc. and for eating some soft foods **2** a measuring unit in cookery, equal to about ⅓ of a tablespoon or about 1⅓ fluid drams: abbrev. *tsp* **3** TEASPOONFUL

tea·spoon·ful (-fo͝ol′) *n., pl.* **-fuls′** as much as a teaspoon will hold

teat (tēt) *n.* ⟦ME *tete* < OFr < Gmc base akin to OE *tit*⟧ **1** NIPPLE (sense 1) **2** any small projection like a teat

tea table a table, typically small, for serving tea

tea·tast·er (tē′tās′tər) *n.* a person whose work is tasting tea for grading

tea·time (tē′tīm′) *n.* the time of day when TEA (*n.* 6*a*) is customarily served

tea towel ⟦from being used to dry the pieces of a *tea* service after they have been washed⟧ [Chiefly Brit.] DISH TOWEL

tea tray a tray for carrying cups, plates, spoons, etc. in serving tea or other light refreshment

tea wagon TEA CART

tea·zel or **tea·zle** (tē′zəl) *n., vt. alt. sp. of* TEASEL

Te·bet or **Te·beth** (tā vāt′, tā′vəs) *n. var. of* TEVET

tech *abbrev.* **1** technical **2** technically **3** technology

tech·ie (tek′ē) *n.* [Informal] **1** TECHNICIAN (sense 3) **2** a person with training or expertise in a technology, esp. computer technology

tech·ne·ti·um (tek nē′shē əm, -shəm) *n.* ⟦ModL < Gr *technētos,* artificial (< *technasthai,* to contrive by art < *technē*: see TECHNIC) + -IUM: so named (1947) by E. G. Segré (1905-89), It-American physicist, and C. Perrier (1886-1948), It physicist, who discovered it (1937)⟧ a silver-gray, metallic chemical element obtained by the irradiation of molybdenum with deuterons and in the fission of uranium: it does not exist in nature and all its isotopes are radioactive: it is a superconductor, an inhibitor of metal corrosion, and a medical tracer: symbol, Tc; at. no. 43: see the periodic table of elements in the Reference Supplement

☆**tech·ne·tron·ic** (tek′ni trän′ik) *adj.* ⟦< TECHNOLOGY + ELECTRONIC⟧ characterized by the application of technology and electronics to the solution of social, political, and economic problems [a *technetronic* society]

tech·nic (tek′nik; *for n. 1, also* tek nēk′) *adj.* ⟦Gr *technikos* < *technē,* art, artifice < IE base **tekth-,* to weave, build, join > Gr *tektōn,* carpenter, L *texere,* to weave, build⟧ TECHNICAL —*n.* **1** TECHNIQUE **2** [*pl., with sing. or pl. v.*] the study or principles of technology, an art, or the arts

tech·ni·cal (tek′ni kəl) *adj.* ⟦prec. + -AL⟧ **1** having to do with the practical, industrial, or mechanical arts or the applied sciences [a *technical* school] **2** of, used in, or peculiar to a specific science, art, profession, craft, etc.; specialized [*technical* vocabulary] **3** skilled in a particular science, art, etc. [a *technical* assistant] **4** of, in, or showing technique [*technical* skill] **5** in terms of some science, art, etc.; according to principles or rules [a *technical* difference] 6 concerned with or making use of technicalities or minute, formal points 7 *Finance* caused by factors within the market, not by external economic factors [a shortage of available shares led to a *technical* rally in stocks] —*n. short for* TECHNICAL FOUL —**tech′ni·cal·ly** *adv.*

technical foul in certain team games, esp. basketball, a foul other than a personal foul charged against a player, a team, or a coach, usually for misconduct or a rule infraction not involving active play

tech·ni·cal·i·ty (tek′ni kal′ə tē) *n., pl.* **-ties** 1 the state or quality of being technical 2 the use of technical terms, methods, etc. 3 a point, detail, term, method, etc. of or peculiar to an art, science, code, or skill, esp. one that only a technical expert would likely be aware of 4 a minute formal point, detail, etc. brought to bear upon a main issue [convicted on a *technicality*]

technical knockout *Boxing* a victory won when the opponent, though not knocked out, is so badly hurt that the referee stops the match

☆**technical sergeant** *U.S. Air Force* a noncommissioned officer of the sixth grade, ranking above staff sergeant and below master sergeant

tech·ni·cian (tek nish′ən) *n.* 1 a person skilled in the technicalities of some subject 2 an artist, writer, musician, etc. who has great technical skill or knowledge 3 a person providing technological or technical assistance or support

☆**Tech·ni·col·or** (tek′ni kul′ər) *trademark for* a process of making color films by combining several separate, synchronized negatives each of which is sensitive to a single color —*n.* [t-] 1 this process 2 bright, intense colors —**tech′ni·col′ored** *adj.*

tech·nique (tek nēk′) *n.* ⟦Fr < Gr *technikos:* see TECHNIC⟧ 1 the manner in which the details of an artistic work or of a scientific or mechanical operation are executed or performed 2 the degree of expertness in following this [a pianist with good *technique* but poor expression] 3 any method or manner of accomplishing something

tech·no (tek′nō) *n.* ⟦shortened < TECHNOLOGICAL, with ref. to the electronic equipment⟧ a form of popular dance music of the 1980s and 1990s characterized by a fast, driving rhythm and the use of computers and keyboard synthesizers to produce electronic sounds

tech·no- (tek′nō, -nə) ⟦< Gr *technē:* see TECHNIC⟧ *combining form* 1 art, science, skill [*technography*] 2 technical, technological [*technocracy*]

☆**tech·noc·ra·cy** (tek näk′rə sē) *n.* ⟦prec. + -CRACY⟧ government by technicians; specif., the theory or doctrine of a proposed system of government in which all economic resources, and hence the entire social system, would be controlled by scientists and engineers —**tech′no·crat′** (-nə krat′) *n.* —**tech′no·crat′ic** *adj.*

tech·nog·ra·phy (tek näg′rə fē) *n.* ⟦TECHNO- + -GRAPHY⟧ the historical description or study of arts and applied sciences in relationship to their geographical distribution

tech·no·log·i·cal (tek′nə läj′i kəl) *adj.* 1 of or having to do with technology 2 due to developments in technology; resulting from technical progress in the use of machinery and automation in industry, agriculture, etc. [*technological* productivity, *technological* unemployment] Also **tech′no·log′ic** —**tech′no·log′i·cal·ly** *adv.*

tech·nol·o·gy (tek näl′ə jē) *n., pl.* **-gies** ⟦Gr *technologia,* systematic treatment: see TECHNIC & -LOGY⟧ 1 the science or study of the practical or industrial arts, applied sciences, etc. 2 the terms used in a science, etc.; technical terminology 3 applied science 4 a method, process, etc. for handling a specific technical problem 5 the system by which a society provides its members with those things needed or desired —**tech·nol′o·gist** *n.* —**tech·nol′o·gize′** *vt., vi.* **-gized′, -giz′ing**

tech·no·phile (tek′nə fīl′) *n.* a person who is enthusiastic about advanced technology or about high-tech equipment or devices —**tech′no·phil′ic** *adj.*

tech·no·pho·bi·a (tek′nə fō′bē ə) *n.* dislike or fear of advanced technology or of high-tech equipment or devices —**tech′no·phobe′** *n.* —**tech′no·pho′bic** *adj.*

tech·no-pop (tek′nō päp′) *n.* a form of popular dance music of the 1980s and 1990s combining elements of TECHNO with live instrumentation, pop lyrics, etc.

tech·no-thrill·er (tek′nō thril′ər) *n.* a THRILLER (sense 2a) containing detailed accounts of technologically advanced weapons, electronic devices, etc.

tech·y (tech′ē) *adj.* **tech′i·er, tech′i·est** *alt. sp. of* TETCHY

tec·tite (tek′tīt′) *n. alt. sp. of* TEKTITE

tec·ton·ic (tek tän′ik) *adj.* ⟦LL *tectonicus* < Gr *tektonikos* < *tektōn,* carpenter, builder: see TECHNIC⟧ 1 of or having to do with building; constructional 2 architectural 3 designating, of, or pertaining to changes in the structure of the earth's crust, the forces responsible for such deformation, or the external forms produced

tec·ton·ics (-iks) *pl.n.* ⟦see prec.⟧ 1 the constructive arts in general; esp., the art of making things that have both beauty and usefulness 2 [*with sing. v.*] *Geol.* the study of the earth's crustal structure and the forces that produce changes in it

tec·ton·ism (tek′tə niz′əm) *n.* DIASTROPHISM

tec·trix (tek′triks′) *n., pl.* **-tri·ces′** (-tri sēz′) ⟦ModL, fem. of L *tector,* one who covers < *tectus,* pp. of *tegere,* to cover: see THATCH⟧ WING COVERT

tec·tum (tek′təm) *n., pl.* **tec′ta** (-tə) ⟦ModL < L, a roof < *tectus:* see prec.⟧ *Biol.* a rooflike structure or covering —**tec′tal** *adj.*

Te·cum·seh (ti kum′sə) 1768?-1813; chief of the Shawnee Indians: attempted to unite the W Indian tribes

ted (ted) *vt.* **ted′ded, ted′ding** ⟦ME *tedden,* prob. < ON *tethja,* to spread manure < IE base *dā(i)- > TIDE¹⟧ to spread or scatter (newly cut grass) for drying as hay —**ted′der** *n.*

Ted (ted) *n. nickname for:* 1 EDWARD¹ 2 THEODORE Also **Ted′dy**

☆**ted·dy** (ted′ē) *n., pl.* **-dies** ⟦prob. < the nickname *Teddy*⟧ a woman's one-piece undergarment, combining a chemise top with panties

☆**teddy bear** ⟦after *Teddy,* nickname for Theodore ROOSEVELT²: first used (1902) after a cartoon by C. K. Berryman, containing a small cub in jocular allusion to his fondness for big-game hunting⟧ a child's stuffed toy made to look like a bear cub

Teddy boy ⟦< *Teddy,* nickname for EDWARD¹⟧ 1 a British youth of the 1950s or early 1960s who affected flashy dress, esp. of a neo-Edwardian style 2 [Brit. Informal] any rough or delinquent youth

Te De·um (tē dē′əm, tā dā′oom) ⟦ME < LL(Ec)⟧ 1 an ancient Christian hymn beginning *Te Deum laudamus* (We praise thee, O God) 2 music for this hymn 3 a service of thanksgiving at which this hymn is used

te·di·ous (tē′dē əs; *occas.* tē′jəs) *adj.* ⟦ME < LL *taediosus*⟧ full of tedium; long or verbose and wearisome; tiresome; boring —**te′di·ous·ly** *adv.* —**te′di·ous·ness** *n.*

te·di·um (tē′dē əm) *n.* ⟦L *taedium* < *taedet,* it disgusts, offends⟧ the condition or quality of being tiresome, wearisome, boring, or monotonous; tediousness

tee¹ (tē) *n., pl.* **tees** 1 the letter T 2 something shaped like T 3 *short for* T-SHIRT —*adj.* shaped like T

tee² (tē) *n.* ⟦< prec.: the mark was orig. T-shaped⟧ a mark aimed at in quoits, curling, etc.

tee³ (tē) *n.* ⟦prob. contr. < Scot dial. *teaz* (< ?), but now assoc. with prec. in form and sense⟧ 1 *Golf a)* [Historical] a small, cone-shaped mound as of sand, on which a golf ball was placed to be driven *b)* a small, slender, pointed piece wood, plastic, etc. designed to support a golf ball just above the ground during a drive: the pointed end is inserted into the ground *c)* the designated starting area of each hole, where a golfer is permitted to use a tee ☆2 *a)* a small holder on which a football is positioned for a kickoff *b)* a tall device for holding a ball up for a hitter in T-ball —*vt., vi.* **teed, tee′ing** to place (a ball) on a tee: usually with *up* —**tee off** 1 to play a golf ball from a tee 2 to begin; start ☆3 [Slang] to make angry or disgusted

tee-hee (tē′hē′) *interj., n.* ⟦ME: echoic⟧ (used to suggest the sound of) a titter or snicker —*vi.* **-heed′, -hee′ing** to titter or snicker

teel (tēl) *n.* ⟦< Hindi *til* < Sans *tila*⟧ 1 SESAME 2 the oil of sesame seed

teem¹ (tēm) *vi.* ⟦ME *temen* < OE *tieman,* to produce, bear < base of *team,* progeny: see TEAM⟧ 1 [Obs.] to produce offspring; bear 2 to be full, as though ready to bring forth young; abound; swarm: often in the prp. [a river *teeming* with fish]

teem² (tēm) *vt.* ⟦ME *temen* < ON *tœma,* to empty⟧ [Now Rare] to empty; pour out —*vi.* to pour [a *teeming* rain]

teen¹ (tēn) *n.* ⟦see -TEEN⟧ 1 [*pl.*] *a)* the years from thirteen through nineteen (of a century or of a person's age) *b)* the numbers from thirteen through nineteen 2 TEENAGER —*adj.* TEENAGE

teen² (tēn) *n.* ⟦ME *tene* < OE *teona,* akin to OFris *tiona,* ON *tjōn,* injury < IE base *du-, to injure, destroy > Sans *dū,* pain⟧ [Now Chiefly Dial.] 1 injury or harm 2 anger; wrath 3 grief or suffering

-teen (tēn) ⟦ME *-tene* < OE *-tene, -tyne,* inflected form of *tien,* TEN⟧ *suffix* ten and: used to form the cardinal numbers from *thirteen* to *nineteen*

teen·age (tēn′āj′) *adj.* 1 in one's teens 2 of, characteristic of, or for persons in their teens

☆**teen·ag·er** (tēn′ā′jər) *n.* a person in his or her teens

tee·ny (tē′nē) *adj.* **-ni·er, -ni·est** *informal var. of* TINY: also **teen·sy** (tēn′zē, -sē), **-si·er, -si·est**

☆**teen·y-bop·per** (tē′nē bäp′ər) *n.* ⟦< TEEN¹ + -Y¹ + BOP² + -ER⟧ [Slang] a young teenager, esp. a girl, following the latest fads in fashion, popular music, etc.

tee·ny-wee·ny (tē′nē wē′nē) *adj.* ⟦redupl. of TEENY⟧ [Informal] very small; tiny: a facetious imitation of child's talk: also **teen·sy-ween·sy** (tēn′zē wēn′zē, tēn′sē wēn′sē)

☆**tee·pee** (tē′pē) *n. alt. sp. of* TEPEE

Tees (tēz) river in N England, flowing into the North Sea: 70 mi (113 km)

☆**tee shirt** *var. of* T-SHIRT

tee·ter (tēt′ər) *vi.* ⟦dial. *titter* < ME *titeren* < ON *titra,* to tremble, akin to Ger *zittern* < redupl. of IE base *drā-, to step > TRAP¹, TRIP⟧ to totter, wobble, waver, etc. —*n. short for* TEETER-TOTTER

☆**tee·ter·board** (-bôrd′) *n.* SEESAW

tee·ter-tot·ter (-tät′ər) *n., vi.* ⟦redupl. of TEETER⟧ SEESAW

teeth (tēth) *n. pl. of* TOOTH —**armed (or dressed) to the teeth** as armed (or dressed up) as one can be —**get (or sink) one's teeth into** to become fully occupied or absorbed with —**in the teeth of** 1 directly against; in the face of 2 in opposition to; defying —**set one's teeth** to prepare to meet firmly something difficult or unpleasant —**show one's teeth** to show hostility; threaten angrily —**throw something in someone's teeth** 1 to reproach someone for something 2 to hurl (a challenge, taunt, etc.) at someone

teethe (tēth) *vi.* **teethed, teeth′ing** ⟦ME *tethen* < *tethe,* teeth⟧ to grow teeth; cut one's teeth

☆**teething ring** a ring of plastic, rubber, etc., for teething babies to bite on

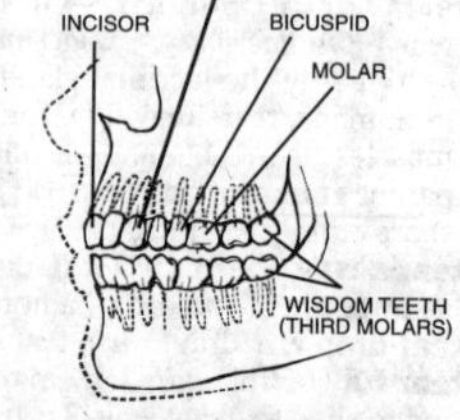

teeth of human adult

teeth·ridge (tēth′rij′) *n.* the ridge of gum along the inside of the upper front teeth

tee time the time scheduled to begin a round of golf

tee·to·tal (tē′tōt′'l, tē′tōt′'l) *adj.* ⟦redupl., for emphasis, of initial letter of TOTAL⟧ **1** [Informal] entire; complete **2** of or advocating teetotalism —**tee′to′tal·er** *n.*, **tee′to′tal·ler** —**tee′to′tal·ly** *adv.*

tee·to·tal·ism (-iz′əm) *n.* ⟦prec. + -ISM⟧ the principle or practice of never drinking any alcoholic liquor —**tee′to′tal·ist** *n.*

tee·to·tum (tē tōt′əm) *n.* ⟦earlier *T totum* < the T (for *totum*) marked on one side + *totum,* the name of the toy < L *totum,* neut. of *totus* (see TOTAL): the four sides were orig. marked *T* (*totum,* all) *A* (*aufer,* take), *D* (*depone,* put), *N* (*nihil,* nothing)⟧ a small top spun with the fingertips, esp. one with four lettered sides used in a game of chance

te·fil·lin (tə fil′in) *n., pl.* **-lin** ⟦var. sp. of Heb *tefilin*: see PHYLACTERY⟧ either of two small, boxlike leather cases holding slips inscribed with certain Scriptural passages, fastened, using leather thongs, one to the forehead and the other to the arm, by Orthodox or Conservative Jewish men during weekday morning prayer: see Deut. 6:4-9: usually used in the pl., referring to the pair of cases containing the slips together with the straps

tefillin

TEFL *abbrev.* teaching English as a foreign language

☆**Tef·lon** (tef′län′) ⟦< *(poly)te(tra)fl(uoro-ethylene)* + *-on,* arbitrary suffix for synthetic products⟧ *trademark for* a tough, insoluble polymer, used in making nonsticking coatings, as for cookware, and in gaskets, bearings, electrical insulators, etc. —*n.* this substance, esp. as a coating —*adj.* [Informal] regarded as having the ability to maintain one's standing or reputation in spite of scandal, wrongdoing, etc.

Teg·a·kwith·a (teg′ə kwith′ə) *var. of* TEKAKWITHA: also **Teg′a·koui′ta** (-kwēt′ə)

teg·men (teg′mən) *n., pl.* **teg′mi·na** (-mi nə) ⟦L < *tegere,* to cover: see THATCH⟧ **1** a covering; integument **2** *Bot.* the inner coat of a seed **3** *Zool.* *a)* a beetle elytron *b)* a hardened forewing in some insects —**teg′mi·nal** *adj.*

Te·gu·ci·gal·pa (te goo̅′sē gäl′pä) capital of Honduras, in the SC part

teg·u·lar (teg′yoo̅ lər, -yə-) *adj.* ⟦< L *tegula,* a tile < *tegere,* to cover (see THATCH) + -AR⟧ **1** of or like a tile or tiles **2** arranged like tiles —**teg′u·lar·ly** *adv.*

teg·u·ment (teg′yoo̅ mənt, -yə-) *n.* ⟦L *tegumentum* < *tegere,* to cover: see THATCH⟧ INTEGUMENT —**teg′u·men′tal** (-ment′'l) *adj.*, **teg′u·men′ta·ry** (-tə rē)

te-hee (tē′hē′) *interj., n., vi.* **-heed′**, **-hee′ing** *alt. sp. of* TEE-HEE

Teh·ran (te rän′, tā-; -ran′) capital of Iran, in the NC part: also **Te·he·ran** (te rän′, tə-; te′ə rän′, te′he rän′; -ran′)

Te·huan·te·pec (tə wänt′ə pek′) **1 Gulf of** arm of the Pacific, off the S coast of Mexico: *c.* 300 mi (483 km) wide **2 Isthmus of** narrowest part of Mexico, between this gulf & the Gulf of Campeche: *c.* 125 mi (201 km) wide

Te·huel·che (te wel′che) *n., pl.* **-ches** or **-che** ⟦Araucanian *cheu(ù)lche,* lit., fearless & elusive⟧ a member of a South American Indian people of Patagonia, famous in older European literature for their tall stature and great strength

Tei·de (tā′də), **Pi·co de** (pē′kō də) volcanic mountain on Tenerife, Canary Islands: *c.* 12,200 ft (3,719 m)

Teil·hard de Char·din (te yȧr də shȧr dan′), **Pierre** (pyer) 1881-1955; Fr. paleontologist, philosopher, & Jesuit priest

☆**Te·ja·no** (te hä′nō, tə-) *n.* ⟦AmSp, Texan⟧ **1** *pl.* **-nos** a Texan of Mexican descent **2** a style of dance music combining elements of Mexican folk music, German polka music featuring the accordion, and variously country music, jazz, rock, etc.

Te·jo (te′zhoo̅) *Port. name for* TAGUS

Tek·a·kwith·a (tek′ə kwith′ə), **Catherine** (also called *Kateri Tekakwitha*) 1656-80; North American Indian ascetic; beatified: called *Lily of the Mohawks*

☆**tek·tite** (tek′tīt′) *n.* ⟦< Gr *tēktos,* molten (< *tēkein,* to melt < IE base **tā-* > THAW) + -ITE[1]⟧ any of certain small, yellowish-green to black glassy bodies of various shapes, found in isolated locations around the world and thought to have originated as meteorites or from meteorite impacts

tel[1] (tel) *n. alt. sp. of* TELL[2]

tel[2] *abbrev.* **1** telegram **2** telegraph **3** telephone

tel- (tel) *combining form* **1** TELE- *[TelAutograph]* **2** TELO-[2] *[telangiectasis]*

tel·a·mon (tel′ə män′) *n., pl.* **tel′a·mo′nes′** (-mō′nēz′) ⟦L < Gr *telamōn,* bearer < *telassai,* to bear < IE base **tel-* > TOLERATE⟧ *Archit.* a supporting column in the form of a man's figure: see also ATLANTES, CARYATID

tel·an·gi·ec·ta·sis (te lan′jē ek′tə sis) *n., pl.* **-ses′** (-sēz′) ⟦ModL < Gr *telos,* an end (see TELO-[2]) + *angeion,* receptacle (see ANGIO-) + *ektasis,* extension, dilatation⟧ *Med.* chronic dilatation of capillaries and small arterial branches, producing small, reddish tumors in the skin, as of the face, thighs, etc.: also **tel·an′gi·ec·ta′sia** (-ek tā′zhə, -zhē ə) —**tel·an′gi·ec·tat′ic** (-tat′ik) *adj.*

Tel A·viv (tel′ ə vēv′) seaport in W Israel, incorporating the former city of Jaffa —**Tel A·viv·an** (ə vē′vən)

tel·e- (tel′ə) *combining form* **1** ⟦Gr *tēle-* < *tēle,* far off < IE base **kwel-,* distant, remote > Welsh *pell,* distant⟧ at, over, from, or to a distance *[telegraph]* **2** ⟦< TELE(VISION)⟧ of, in, or by television *[telecast]* **3** ⟦< TELE(PHONE)⟧ by telephone, on the telephone, etc.: often in nonce compounds *[telemarketing, telenuisance]*

tel·e·cast (tel′ə kast′) *vt., vi.* **-cast′** or **-cast′ed**, **-cast′ing** ⟦prec. + -CAST⟧ to broadcast by television —*n.* a television broadcast —**tel′e·cast′er** *n.*

tel·e·com (tel′ə käm′) *n.* **1** *short for* TELECOMMUNICATION: also [Chiefly Brit.] **tel′e·coms′** **2** a company involved in the telecommunication industry

tel·e·com·mu·ni·ca·tion (tel′ə kə myoo̅′ni kā′shən) *n.* ⟦TELE- + COMMUNICATION, after Fr *télécommunication*⟧ [*also pl., with sing. or pl. v.*] communication by electronic or electric means, as through radio, telephone, telegraph, television, or computers

tel·e·com·mute (tel′ə kə myoo̅t′) *vi.* **-mut′ed**, **-mut′ing** ⟦< TELE- + COMMUTE, *vi.* 2⟧ to use a microcomputer, fax, etc. to perform work in one's home that traditionally has been done in the office —**tel′e·com·mut′er** *n.*

☆**tel·e·con·fer·ence** (tel′ə kän′fər əns) *n.* a conference of individuals in different locations, as by speakerphone or closed-circuit TV —*vi.* **-enced**, **-enc·ing** to hold such a conference

☆**tel·e·course** (tel′ə kôrs′) *n.* a course of televised lectures for credit or for auditing, offered by a college or other school

tel·e·du (tel′ə doo̅′) *n.* ⟦Malay⟧ a small, badgerlike, burrowing carnivore (*Mydaus javanensis*) related to the skunk and native to Java, Borneo, and Sumatra: it ejects a vile-smelling fluid when disturbed or frightened

☆**tel·e·film** (tel′ə film′) *n.* a film made to be broadcast on television

teleg *abbrev.* **1** telegram **2** telegraph **3** telegraphy

tel·e·gen·ic (tel′ə jen′ik) *adj.* ⟦TELE- + -GENIC⟧ looking or likely to look attractive on television: said of a person

te·leg·o·ny (tə leg′ə nē) *n.* ⟦Ger *telegonie:* see TELE- & -GONY⟧ the supposed transmission of characters of one sire to offspring subsequently born to other sires by the same female —**tel·e·gon·ic** (tel′ə gän′ik) *adj.*

☆**tel·e·gram** (tel′ə gram′) *n.* ⟦TELE- + -GRAM⟧ a message transmitted by telegraph

tel·e·graph (tel′ə graf′) *n.* ⟦Fr *télégraphe:* see TELE- & -GRAPH: orig. used of a semaphore⟧ **1** [Obs.] any signaling apparatus **2** an apparatus or system that converts a coded message into electric impulses and sends it to a distant receiver: originally, Morse code signals were sent using a key that opened and closed the circuit to activate an electromagnetic sounder, but now teletypewriters, computers, radio and microwave signals, satellites, and lasers are used —*vt.* **1** to send (a message) by telegraph **2** to send a telegram to **3** [Informal] to signal (an intended action, decision, etc.) unintentionally to another, as by a gesture or look —*vi.* to send a telegram —**te·leg·ra·pher** (tə leg′rə fər) *n.*, **te·leg′ra·phist**

tel·e·graph·ic (tel′ə graf′ik) *adj.* **1** of or transmitted by telegraph **2** in the concise style of a telegram —**tel′e·graph′i·cal·ly** *adv.*

telegraph plant a tick trefoil (*Desmodium gyrans*) of tropical Asia: so called because the two lateral leaflets of each leaf move like a railroad semaphore signal

te·leg·ra·phy (tə leg′rə fē) *n.* **1** the operation of telegraph apparatus or the study of this **2** the transmission of messages by telegraph

Tel·e·gu (tel′ə goo̅′) *n. alt. sp. of* TELUGU

tel·e·ki·ne·sis (tel′ə ki nē′sis) *n.* ⟦ModL < *tele-,* TELE- + Gr *kinēsis,* motion < *kinein,* to move: see CITE⟧ *Parapsychology* the act or process of causing an object to move by means of psychic forces, as directed by a spiritualistic medium, and not by means of any physical force —**tel′e·ki·net′ic** (-net′ik) *adj.*

Te·lem·a·chus (tə lem′ə kəs) *n.* ⟦L < Gr *Tēlemachos*⟧ *Gr. Legend* the son of Odysseus and Penelope: he helps his father slay his mother's suitors

Te·le·mann (te′lə män′), **Ge·org Phi·lipp** (gā ôrk′ fē′lip) 1681-1767; Ger. composer

tel·e·mark (tel′ə märk′) *n.* ⟦after *Telemark,* region in S Norway⟧ *Skiing* a slow turning movement in which the outer ski is advanced and turned in at a widening angle until the turn is accomplished

☆**tel·e·mar·ket·ing** (tel′ə mär′kət iŋ) *n.* ⟦TELE- (sense 3) + MARKETING⟧ the practice of making unsolicited telephone calls for the purpose of selling, promotion, market research, etc. —**tel′e·mar′ket·er** *n.*

tel·e·me·ter (tel′ə mēt′ər, tə lem′ət ər) *n.* ⟦TELE- + -METER⟧ **1** an instrument for determining the distance to a remote object; range finder **2** any device for transmitting measurements of physical phenomena, as temperature, radiation, etc., to a distant recorder or observer: used in satellites, spacecraft, etc. — *vt., vi.* to transmit by telemeter —**tel′e·met′ric** (-me′trik) *adj.* —**tel′e·met′ri·cal·ly** *adv.* —**te·lem·e·try** (tə lem′ə trē) *n.*

tel·en·ceph·a·lon (tel′en sef′ə län′) *n., pl.* **-la** (-lə) ⟦ModL: see TELE- & ENCEPHALON⟧ the most anterior part of the forebrain, including the cerebral hemispheres and olfactory lobes —**tel′en·ce·phal′ic** (-sə fal′ik) *adj.*

te·le·no·ve·la (tā′lā nô vā′lä; *E* tel′ə nō vel′ə) *n., pl.* **-las** (-läs) ⟦AmSp < *tele(visión),* television + *novela,* novel⟧ [*often not in italics*] in Latin America, a TV soap opera, often one having a limited number of episodes

te·le·ol·o·gy (tē′lē äl′ə jē, tel′ē-) *n.* ⟦ModL *teleologia* < Gr *telos, teleos,* an end (see TELO-[2]) + *-logia* (see -LOGY)⟧ **1** the study of final causes **2** the fact or quality, attributed to natural processes, of being directed toward a definite end or of having an ultimate purpose **3** *a)* the doctrine that natural phenomena are determined by an overall design or purpose in nature *b)* the study of evidence for this belief —**te′le·o·log′i·cal** *adj.* —**te′le·ol′o·gist** *n.*

te·le·on·o·my (tē′lē än′ə mē, tel′ē-) *n.* ⟦*teleo-* (as in prec.) + -NOMY⟧ the concept that an organism's structures or functions must have given it an evolutionary advantage —**te′le·o·nom′ic** (-ə näm′ik) ***adj.***

tel·e·op·er·a·tor (tel′ə äp′ər āt′ər) ***n.*** ⟦< TELE- (sense 1) + OPERATOR⟧ a robotic device controlled from a distance by a human operator, as in working with radioactive materials

tel·e·ost (tel′ē äst′, tē′lē-) ***n.*** ⟦< Gr *teleos,* complete < *telos* (see TELO-[2]) + *osteon,* bone: see OSSIFY⟧ any of many orders of bony fishes having a consolidated internal skeleton, swim bladder, thin cycloid scales, etc. —***adj.*** of or belonging to the teleosts Also **tel′e·os′te·an** (-äs′tē ən)

te·lep·a·thy (tə lep′ə thē) ***n.*** ⟦TELE- + -PATHY: coined (1882) by F. W. Myers (1843-1901), Eng writer⟧ *Parapsychology* communication between minds by some means other than the normal sensory channels; transference of thought —**tel·e·path** (tel′ə path′) ***n.*** —**tel′e·path′ic** ***adj.*** —**tel′e·path′i·cal·ly** ***adv.*** —**te·lep′a·thist** ***n.***

tel·e·phone (tel′ə fōn′) ***n.*** ⟦TELE- (sense 1) + -PHONE: term adopted by A. G. BELL (1876) after use for other sound instruments⟧ ☆**1** a system for transmitting speech or computerized information over distances, usually by converting sounds into electric impulses that are sent through a network of wires and cables: some systems transmit by means of radio waves **2** any device having a transmitter, receiver, and dialing mechanism, used in a telephone system —☆***vi.*** **-phoned′**, **-phon′ing 1** to converse or communicate by telephone **2** to try to make a connection by dialing a telephone number —***vt.*** **1** to convey (a message) by telephone **2** to speak to or reach (a person) by telephone; call —**tel′e·phon′er** ***n.*** —**tel′e·phon′ic** (-fän′ik) ***adj.*** —**tel′e·phon′i·cal·ly** ***adv.***

☆**telephone book** a book in which are listed alphabetically the names of persons, businesses, etc. having telephones in a specified area, along with their addresses and telephone numbers: also **telephone directory**

☆**telephone booth** a booth in a public place containing a telephone, usually operated by inserting coins

☆**telephone receiver** *see* RECEIVER (sense 2*b*)

telephone tag PHONE TAG

tel·e·phon·ist (tel′ə fōn′ist, tə lef′ə nist) ***n.*** [Chiefly Brit.] a telephone switchboard operator

te·leph·o·ny (tə lef′ə nē) ***n.*** **1** the science of telephonic transmission **2** the making or operation of telephones

tel·e·pho·to (tel′ə fōt′ō) ***n.*** ⟦< *Telephoto,* former trademark⟧ a TELEPHOTOGRAPH (sense 2) —***adj.*** designating or of a camera lens for photographing or filming distant objects so as to produce a larger image

tel·e·pho·to·graph (tel′ə fōt′ə graf′) ***n.*** **1** a photograph taken with a telephoto lens **2** a photograph transmitted by telephotography

tel·e·pho·tog·ra·phy (tel′ə fə täg′rə fē) ***n.*** **1** photography of distant objects using a telephoto lens **2** a method for transmitting photographs as over a telephone line by converting the images to electrical signals —**tel′e·pho′to·graph′ic** (-fōt′ə graf′ik) ***adj.***

☆**tel·e·play** (tel′ə plā′) ***n.*** a play or screenplay written for, or produced on, television

tel·e·por·ta·tion (tel′ə pôr tā′shən) ***n.*** ⟦TELE- + (TRANS)PORTATION⟧ the theoretical transportation of matter through space by converting it into energy and then reconverting it at the terminal point —**tel′e·port′** ***vt.***

tel·e·print·er (tel′ə print′ər) ***n.*** TELETYPEWRITER

tel·e·pro·cess·ing (tel′ə prä′səs iŋ) ***n.*** data processing with computer terminals, over communication lines

☆**tel·e·promp·ter** (tel′ə prämp′tər) ***n.*** ⟦< *TelePrompTer,* orig., name of the device (not trademarked), now a trademark of TelePrompTer Corp., supplier of cable & TV services⟧ an electronic device that, unseen by the audience, scrolls a prepared speech, script, etc. line by line, as a prompting aid to a speaker or actor

☆**tel·e·ran** (tel′ə ran′) ***n.*** ⟦*tele(vision) r(adar) a(ir) n(avigation)*⟧ an electronic aid to aerial navigation by which data received by radar, maps of the terrain, etc. are transmitted to aircraft by television

tel·e·scope (tel′ə skōp′) ***n.*** ⟦It *telescopio* (coined by GALILEO, 1611) < ModL *telescopium* < Gr *tēleskopos,* seeing from a distance: see TELE- & -SCOPE⟧ an optical instrument for making distant objects, as the stars, appear nearer and consequently larger: it consists of two or more lenses or mirrors: see also RADIO TELESCOPE, REFLECTING TELESCOPE, REFRACTING TELESCOPE —***adj.*** having parts that slide one inside another —***vi.*** **-scoped′**, **-scop′ing 1** to have one part slide into another part like the concentric tubes of a small, collapsible telescope **2** to come into contact with such force that the colliding parts become compressed —***vt.*** **1** to cause to telescope **2** to condense; shorten, as by combining parts, compressing, etc.

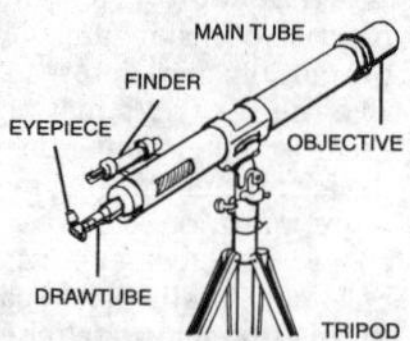

refracting telescope

tel·e·scop·ic (tel′ə skäp′ik) ***adj.*** **1** of a telescope or telescopes **2** seen or obtained by a telescope **3** visible only with the aid of a telescope **4** having distant vision: said esp. of a sight or lens that apparently enlarges distant objects **5** having sections that slide one inside another [*a telescopic* drinking tumbler] Also **tel′e·scop′i·cal** —**tel′e·scop′i·cal·ly** ***adv.***

Tel·e·sco·pi·um (tel′ə skō′pē əm) ***n.*** ⟦ModL, TELESCOPE⟧ a S constellation between Sagittarius and Pavo

te·les·co·py (tə les′kə pē) ***n.*** the art or practice of using a telescope —**te·les′co·pist** ***n.***

tel·e·screen (tel′ə skrēn′) ***n.*** any of various televisionlike screens used in communication, broadcasting, surveillance, etc., esp. as in science fiction

☆**tel·e·sis** (tel′ə sis) ***n.*** ⟦ModL < Gr *telein,* to fulfill, complete < *telos,* an end: see TELO-[2]⟧ the purposeful use of natural and social forces; planned progress

tel·e·spec·tro·scope (tel′ə spek′trə skōp′) ***n.*** an instrument combining a telescope and a spectroscope, for producing the spectra of stars

tel·es·the·si·a (tel′es thē′zhə, -zē ə) ***n.*** ⟦ModL: see TELE- & ESTHESIA⟧ *Parapsychology* extrasensory perception of distant objects, events, etc. —**tel′es·thet′ic** (-thet′ik) ***adj.***

te·les·tich or **te·les·tic** (tə les′tik, tel′ə stik′) ***n.*** ⟦< Gr *telos,* an end (see TELO-[2]) + *stichos,* a line (see STICH), modeled on ACROSTIC⟧ an acrostic in which the last letters of the lines spell a word or words when taken in order

Tel·e·stra·tor (tel′ə strāt′ər) ⟦? blend of TELE- & ILLUSTRATOR⟧ *trademark for* an electronic device that allows the user to draw line illustrations, with a finger or stylus, that are superimposed over images on a TV or computer screen, as to indicate movement or to highlight content

tel·e·text (tel′ə tekst′) ***n.*** a communications service in which information, as news, is superimposed onto a television signal and broadcast to home television sets

☆**tel·e·thon** (tel′ə thän′) ***n.*** ⟦TELE(VISION) + (MARA)THON⟧ a campaign, as on a lengthy telecast, seeking support for a cause, as by pledged donations made by telephone

☆**tel·e·type** (tel′ə tīp′) ***n.*** ⟦< *Teletype,* former trademark⟧ [*also* **T-**] a former kind of telegraphic apparatus that printed messages typed on the keyboard of the transmitter

☆**tel·e·type·writ·er** (tel′ə tīp′rīt′ər) ***n.*** a form of telegraph in which the receiver prints messages typed on the keyboard (like that of a typewriter) of the transmitter: the striking of the keys produces electrical impulses that activate the corresponding keys on the receiver

☆**tel·e·van·ge·list** (tel′ə van′jə list) ***n.*** a minister who uses TV broadcasts or cablecasts to spread an evangelistic message, solicit donations, etc. —**tel′e·van′ge·lism′** (-liz′əm) ***n.***

tel·e·vise (tel′ə vīz′) ***vt., vi.*** **-vised′**, **-vis′ing** ⟦back-form. < fol.⟧ to put (something) on, or transmit (something) by, television —**tel′e·vi′sor** ***n.***

tel·e·vi·sion (tel′ə vizh′ən) ***n.*** ⟦TELE- + VISION⟧ **1** the practice, science, or medium of transmitting moving images by radio waves, cable wires, or satellite to receivers consisting of a display monitor, tuner, and electronic circuitry: images may be produced by means of a camera tube, such as an image orthicon or vidicon, or a CCD device that converts light rays into electrical signals that are sent to a receiver for reproduction of the image, as by reconverting the signals into electron beams that are projected against the fluorescent screen of the kinescope, or picture tube, or by the use of LCD or plasma, flat-panel displays **2** *a)* broadcasting by television as an industry, entertainment, art, etc. *b)* all the facilities and related activities of such broadcasting **3** a television receiver **4** a television program or programs [they watched *television* last night] —***adj.*** of, using, used in, or sent by television

tel·e·vis·u·al (tel′ə vizh′o͞o əl) ***adj.*** ⟦< prec., infl. by VISUAL⟧ of or having to do with television, esp. the visual aspect of a television program or broadcast

tel·ex (tel′eks′) ***n.*** ⟦TEL(ETYPEWRITER) + EX(CHANGE)⟧ **1** a teletypewriter using a telephone dial to establish connections **2** a message sent in this way —***vt.*** to send (a message) by telex

te·li·al (tē′lē əl, tel′ē-) ***adj.*** **1** of a telium **2** designating or of the final stage in the life cycle of the rust fungi

te·lic (tē′lik, tel′ik) ***adj.*** ⟦Gr *telikos* < *telos,* an end: see TELO-[2]⟧ **1** directed toward an end; purposeful **2** *Linguis.* PERFECTIVE Opposed to ATELIC

te·li·o·spore (tē′lē ō spôr′, tel′ē ō-) ***n.*** ⟦< fol. + SPORE⟧ a thick-walled resting spore that develops in late summer during the telial stage of the rust fungi and germinates the next spring —**te′li·o·spor′ic** ***adj.***

te·li·um (tē′lē əm, tel′ē-) ***n., pl.*** **-li·a** (-ə) ⟦ModL < Gr *teleios,* complete < *telos,* an end: see TELO-[2]⟧ the teliospore-bearing sorus of the rust fungi

tell[1] (tel) ***vt.*** **told, tell′ing** ⟦ME *tellen* < OE *tellan,* lit., to calculate, reckon < Gmc **taljan* > Ger *zahl,* number: see TALE⟧ **1** to enumerate; count; reckon [*to tell* time] **2** to give an account of (a story, etc.) in speech or writing **3** to express in words; utter; say [*to tell* the truth] **4** to report; announce; publish **5** to reveal; disclose; make known [a smile that *told* her joy] **6** to recognize; distinguish; discriminate [unable to *tell* one from the other] **7** to decide; know [one can't *tell* what will happen] **8** to let know; inform; acquaint [*tell* me about the game] **9** to request; direct; order; command [*tell* him to leave] **10** to state emphatically to [it's there, I *tell* you] —***vi.*** **1** to give an account or description (*of* something) **2** to give evidence or be an indication (*of* something) **3** to carry tales; reveal secrets [to kiss and *tell*] **4** to produce a result; be effective; have a marked effect [efforts that are beginning to *tell*] —***n.*** **1** *Poker* an unconscious movement, gesture, mannerism, etc., such as repeatedly checking one's cards or behaving nervously in some way, which unintentionally reveals information about one's hand to other players **2** [Informal] any behavior that unintentionally reveals one's unspoken thoughts or motivations —**SYN.** REVEAL[1] —☆**do tell!** [Informal] is that a fact?: often used sarcastically —**tell off 1** to count (persons, etc.) and separate them from the total number **2** [Informal] to rebuke severely —**tell on 1** to have a marked, usually adverse, effect on **2** [Informal] to inform against or gossip about

tell[2] (tel) ***n.*** ⟦Ar *tall,* a mound⟧ *Archaeol.* esp. in the Middle East, a large mound or hill, built up gradually, covering the successive remains of ancient communities

Tell (tel), **William** *see* WILLIAM TELL
tell·a·ble (tel′ə bəl) ***adj.*** 1 that can be told 2 worth being told
tell-all (tel′ôl′) ***adj.*** designating or of a book, magazine article, interview, etc., esp. an autobiographical one, that reveals personal, often scandalous, information
tell·er (tel′ər) ***n.*** 1 a person who tells (a story, etc.); narrator 2 a person who counts; specif., *a)* one who counts votes, as in a legislative body *b)* a bank clerk who pays out or receives money
Tel·ler (tel′ər), **Edward** 1908-2003; U.S. nuclear physicist, born in Hungary
tell·ing (tel′iŋ) ***adj.*** 1 having an effect; forceful; striking [a *telling* retort] 2 that tells or reveals much —**SYN.** VALID —**tell′ing·ly** ***adv.***
tell·tale (tel′tāl′) ***n.*** 1 a person who tells secrets or informs; talebearer; tattler 2 an outward indication of something secret 3 any of various devices for indicating or recording information; indicator; specif., ☆*a)* a row of dangling ropes, etc. hung over a railroad track to warn trainmen, riding on top of a car, of an approaching low bridge, tunnel, etc. *b)* a ribbon, piece of yarn, etc. attached to a sail, shroud, etc. on a sailboat to indicate wind direction *c)* a time clock *d)* a gauge on a pipe organ showing the air pressure —***adj.*** revealing or indicating that which is hidden or meant to be secret [the *telltale* smell of alcohol on his breath]
tel·lu·ri·an (te loor′ē ən, tə-) ***adj.*** ⟦< L *tellus,* gen. *telluris,* the earth (< IE base **telo-,* flat surface > THILL, DEAL[3]) + -AN⟧ of the earth; terrestrial —***n.*** 1 an inhabitant of the earth 2 an apparatus for demonstrating how the earth's position and movement (diurnal rotation, annual revolution, etc.) cause day and night and the cycle of the seasons: also **tel·lu′ri·on′** (-än′, -ən)
tel·lu·ric[1] (te loor′ik, tə-) ***adj.*** of, derived from, or containing tellurium, esp. in a higher valence than in the corresponding tellurous compounds
tel·lu·ric[2] (te loor′ik, tə-) ***adj.*** 1 terrestrial; tellurian 2 of or arising from the earth, or soil
telluric acid a heavy, white, crystalline acid, H_2TeO_4
tel·lu·ride (tel′yoo rīd′, -yə-) ***n.*** a compound of tellurium combined with an electropositive element or with a radical
tel·lu·rite (tel′yoo rīt′, -yə-) ***n.*** 1 a salt of tellurous acid 2 native tellurium dioxide, TeO_2
tel·lu·ri·um (te loor′ē əm, tə-) ***n.*** ⟦ModL: coined (1798) by M. H. Klaproth (1743-1817), Ger chemist < L *tellus,* earth (see TELLURIAN) + -IUM, in contrast to URANIUM⟧ a rare, tin-white, brittle, nonmetallic chemical element, belonging to the same family of elements as sulfur and selenium and occurring naturally in mineral tellurite and tellurides: it is used as a glass tint, as an alloying material, and in thermoelectric converters: symbol, Te; at. no. 52: see the periodic table of elements in the Reference Supplement
tel·lu·rize (tel′yoo rīz′, -yə-) ***vt.*** **-rized′**, **-riz′ing** to combine or treat with tellurium
tel·lu·rous (tel′yoo rəs, -yə-; te loor′əs, tə-) ***adj.*** of, derived from, or containing tellurium, esp. in a lower valence than in the corresponding telluric compounds
tellurous acid a white, crystalline powder, H_2TeO_3
Tel·lus (tel′əs) ***n.*** ⟦L: see TELLURIAN⟧ *Rom. Myth.* the goddess of the earth: identified with the Greek Gaea
tel·ly (tel′ē) ***n., pl.*** **-lies** ⟦altered < TELE(VISION)⟧ *Brit. informal term for* TELEVISION
tel·o-[1] (tel′ə, -ō) *combining form* TELE- (sense 1)
tel·o-[2] (tel′ə, -ō) ⟦< Gr *telos,* an end, completion, orig. prob. "turning point" < IE base **kwel-,* to turn > WHEEL⟧ *combining form* end [*telophase*]
te·lome (tē′lōm′) ***n.*** ⟦Ger *telom* < *tel-* (< Gr *telos:* see prec.) + *-om* (< ModL *-oma,* a stem, mass: see -OMA)⟧ *Bot.* the terminal branchlet of a primitive vascular plant
tel·o·mer·ase (te lä′mə rāz′, -rās′) ***n.*** ⟦< fol. + -ASE⟧ an enzyme found in cancer cells that protects or repairs the cells' telomeres, allowing the cells to reproduce indefinitely: used in medical research to extend the life of noncancerous cells
tel·o·mere (tel′ə mir′) ***n.*** ⟦TELO-[2] + -MERE⟧ any of the specialized structures, consisting of a set of nucleotides, that form the terminal sections of a eukaryotic chromosome and that are essential for cellular replication
tel·o·phase (tel′ə fāz′) ***n.*** ⟦TELO-[2] + PHASE[1]⟧ *Biol.* the final stage of mitosis, in which the parent cell becomes completely divided into two cells, each having a reorganized nucleus
te·los (tel′äs) ***n., pl.*** **-loi** (-oi) ⟦Gr: see TELO-[2]⟧ [*also in roman type*] an end or goal; ultimate purpose
tel·pher (tel′fər) ***n.*** ⟦< TEL(E)- + Gr *pherein,* to BEAR[1]⟧ an electrically driven car suspended from and run on overhead cables
tel·pher·age (-ij) ***n.*** a transportation system using telphers
tel·son (tel′sən) ***n.*** ⟦ModL < Gr, a limit, boundary, prob. akin to *telos,* end: see TELO-[2]⟧ the last, stinging segment of the body of a scorpion, or a projection of the last body segment, as in many decapod crustaceans
☆**Tel·star** (tel′stär′) ***n.*** ⟦TEL(E)- + STAR⟧ either of two experimental communications satellites used between July 10, 1962, and May, 1965, to amplify and relay various signals, esp. television, across the oceans
Tel·u·gu (tel′ə goo′) ***n.*** ⟦< the Telugu name⟧ 1 *pl.* **-gus′** or **-gu′** a member of a people living in Andhra Pradesh, India 2 the Dravidian language of this people —***adj.*** of the Telugus or their language or culture
☆**tem·blor** (tem′blôr′, -blər) ***n.*** ⟦< Sp *temblor (de tierra),* lit., trembling (of the earth) < *temblar,* to tremble < VL **tremulare:* see TREMBLE⟧ EARTHQUAKE
Te·mec·u·la (tə mek′yoo lə) ⟦Sp < a Native American name⟧ city in SW Calif.
tem·er·ar·i·ous (tem′ər er′ē əs) ***adj.*** ⟦L *temerarius* < *temere:* see fol.⟧ reckless; rash —**tem′er·ar′i·ous·ly** ***adv.***
te·mer·i·ty (tə mer′ə tē) ***n.*** ⟦ME *temeryte* < L *temeritas* < *temere,* rashly, blindly < IE base **tem-,* dark > OS *thimm,* dark, L *tenebrae,* darkness⟧ foolish or rash boldness; foolhardiness; recklessness

SYN.—**temerity** refers to a rashness or foolish boldness that results from underrating the dangers or failing to evaluate the consequences [he had the *temerity* to criticize his employer]; **audacity** suggests either great presumption or defiance of social conventions, morals, etc. [shocked at the *audacity* of his proposal]; **effrontery**, always derogatory in usage, connotes shamelessness or insolence in defying the rules of propriety, courtesy, etc. [his *effrontery* in addressing the teacher by her first name]; **nerve**, **cheek**, and **gall** are informal equivalents of **effrontery**, but **nerve** and **cheek** usually suggest mere impudence or sauciness and **gall**, unmitigated insolence

temp[1] (temp) [Informal] ***n.*** *short for* TEMPORARY (***n.***) —***vi.*** to work as a temporary
temp[2] *abbrev.* 1 temperature 2 temporary
temp. *abbrev.* ⟦L *tempore*⟧ in the time of: used in historical references
Tem·pe (tem pē′, tem′pē; *for 2* tem′pē) 1 ⟦after the sacred Greek valley⟧ city in SC Ariz., on the Salt River: suburb of Phoenix 2 **Vale of** valley of the Piniós River in NE Thessaly, Greece, between Mounts Olympus & Ossa: anciently regarded as sacred to Apollo
tem·peh (tem′pā) ***n.*** ⟦Indonesian *tempe*⟧ a cheeselike, high-protein food, originally of Indonesia, made of cooked soybeans fermented with a rhizopus fungus and used as a meat substitute, in salads, etc.
tem·per (tem′pər) ***vt.*** ⟦ME *tempren* < OE *temprian* & OFr *temprer,* both < L *temperare,* to observe proper measure, mix, regulate, forbear < *tempus* (gen. *temporis*), time, period, orig., a span < IE **tempos,* a span < **temp-,* to pull < base **ten-,* to stretch > THIN⟧ 1 to make suitable, desirable, or free from excess by mingling with something else; reduce in intensity, esp. by the admixture of some other quality; moderate; assuage; mollify [to *temper* criticism with reason] 2 *a)* to bring to the proper texture, consistency, hardness, etc. by mixing with something or treating in some way [to *temper* paints with oil, to *temper* steel by heating and sudden cooling, to *temper* clay by moistening and kneading] *b)* to toughen, as by rigors or trying experiences 3 [Rare] to fit; adapt 4 [Archaic] to mix in proper proportions 5 *Music* to adjust the pitch of (a note) or tune (an instrument) according to some temperament —***vi.*** to be or become tempered —***n.*** 1 the state of being tempered; specif., *a)* [Archaic] a properly proportioned mixture *b)* the state of a metal with regard to the degree of hardness and resilience 2 frame of mind; disposition; mood [in a bad *temper*] 3 calmness of mind; composure: now only in the phrases **lose one's temper** and **keep one's temper** 4 a tendency to become angry readily [to have a *temper*] 5 anger; rage [to go into a *temper*] 6 something used to temper a mixture, etc. 7 the trend in thought and feeling (of an era, period, etc.); character [the *temper* of the times, the modern *temper*] 8 [Archaic] a middle course; mean 9 [Obs.] character; quality —**SYN.** DISPOSITION, MOOD[1] —**tem′per·a·bil′i·ty** ***n.*** —**tem′per·a·ble** ***adj.*** —**tem′per·er** ***n.***
tem·per·a (tem′pər ə) ***n.*** ⟦It < *temperare* < L: see prec.⟧ 1 *a)* a process of painting in which pigments are mixed with size, casein, or egg, esp. egg yolk, to produce a dull finish *b)* the paint used in this process 2 POSTER COLOR
tem·pera·ment (tem′prə mənt, -pər mənt; -pər ə-) ***n.*** ⟦ME < L *temperamentum,* proper mixing < *temperare:* see TEMPER⟧ 1 [Obs.] the act or an instance of tempering; proportionate mixture or balance of ingredients 2 in medieval physiology, any of the four conditions of body and mind (*sanguine, phlegmatic, choleric* or *bilious,* and *melancholic*) attributed to an excess of one of the four corresponding humors: see HUMOR 3 one's customary frame of mind or natural disposition; nature [a man of even *temperament*] 4 a nature that is excitable, moody, capricious, volatile, etc. [the *temperament* of a prima donna] 5 [Obs.] *a)* climate *b)* temperature 6 *Music* a system of adjustment of the intervals between the tones of an instrument of fixed intonation: it may be **pure temperament**, in which the intervals are set exactly according to theory, or **equal temperament**, as in a piano, in which the pitch of the tones is adjusted slightly to make them suitable for all keys —**SYN.** DISPOSITION
tem·pera·men·tal (tem′prə ment′'l, -pər ment′'l; -pər ə-) ***adj.*** 1 of or caused by temperament 2 having an excitable temperament; easily upset 3 erratic in behavior; unpredictable —**tem′pera·men′tal·ly** ***adv.***
tem·per·ance (tem′pər əns, -prəns) ***n.*** ⟦ME < MFr < L *temperantia,* moderation, sobriety < prp. of *temperare:* see TEMPER⟧ 1 the state or quality of being temperate; self-restraint in conduct, expression, indulgence of the appetites, etc.; moderation 2 moderation in drinking alcoholic beverages or total abstinence from alcoholic beverages
tem·per·ate (tem′pər it, -prit) ***adj.*** ⟦ME *temperat* < L *temperatus,* pp. of *temperare,* to TEMPER⟧ 1 moderate in indulging the appetites; not self-indulgent; abstemious, esp. in the use of alcoholic beverages 2 moderate in one's actions, speech, etc.; self-restrained 3 moderate or restrained [a *temperate* reply] 4 *a)* neither very hot nor very cold (said of climate, etc.) *b)* having a temperate climate —**SYN.** MODERATE —**tem′per·ate·ly** ***adv.*** —**tem′per·ate·ness** ***n.***
Temperate Zone either of the two zones of the earth (**North Temperate Zone** and **South Temperate Zone**) between the tropics and the polar circles
tem·per·a·ture (tem′pər ə chər, -prə chər, -pər-, -pə-) ***n.*** ⟦L *temperatura* < *temperatus,* TEMPERATE⟧ 1 a measure of the quantity of heat in an object,

usually as measured on a thermometer; specif., *a)* the degree of heat of a living body *b)* an excess of this over the normal (*c.* 37°C or *c.* 98.6°F in humans); fever *c)* the degree of heat of the atmosphere **2** [Obs.] temperament

temperature gradient the rate of temperature change, esp. with increase in altitude

tem·pered (tem′pərd) *adj.* **1** having been given the desired temper, consistency, hardness, etc. [*tempered* steel] **2** modified by addition of or mixture with other qualities, ingredients, etc. [the mercy in a *tempered* justice] **3** having a (specified kind of) temper [bad-*tempered*] **4** *Music* adjusted to a temperament, esp. equal temperament

tem·pest (tem′pist) *n.* ⟦ME < OFr *tempeste* < VL **tempesta,* for L *tempestas,* portion of time, weather, a calamity, storm, tempest < *tempus,* time: see TEMPER⟧ **1** a violent storm with high winds, esp. one accompanied by rain, hail, or snow **2** a violent outburst; tumult —*vt.* [Old Poet.] to agitate violently —☆**tempest in a teapot** a great commotion over a small problem

tem·pes·tu·ous (tem pes′cho͞o əs, -tyo͞o əs) *adj.* ⟦MFr *tempestueus* < LL *tempestuosus* < L *tempestas:* see prec.⟧ **1** of, involving, or like a tempest **2** violent; turbulent —**tem·pes′tu·ous·ly** *adv.* —**tem·pes′tu·ous·ness** *n.*

tem·pi (tem′pē) *n. alt. pl. of* TEMPO

Tem·plar (tem′plər) *n.* ⟦ME *templer* < OFr *templier* < ML *templarius* < L *templum:* see TEMPLE[1]: so named from having quarters near the site of Solomon's Temple in Jerusalem⟧ **1** KNIGHT TEMPLAR **2** [**t-**] a barrister or law student of the Temple in London

tem·plate (tem′plit, -plāt′) *n.* ⟦altered (infl. by PLATE) < earlier *templet* < Fr, dim. of *temple* < L *templum,* small timber, purlin, akin to fol.⟧ **1** a pattern, usually in the form of a thin plate of metal, wood, plastic, etc., for forming an accurate copy of an object or shape **2** *Archit.* *a)* a short piece of stone, timber, or metal placed under a beam to help distribute the pressure *b)* a beam for supporting joists over an open space, as a doorway **3** *Biochem.* any complex molecular structure, as DNA or RNA, that serves as a pattern in the synthesis of another complex molecular structure

tem·ple[1] (tem′pəl) *n.* ⟦ME < OE *tempel* & OFr *temple,* both < L *templum,* temple, sanctuary, orig., space marked out: for IE base see TEMPER⟧ **1** *a)* a building for the worship of a divinity or divinities *b)* anything viewed as the dwelling place of God or a divinity **2** *a)* [**T-**] any of the Jewish sacred edifices for worshiping Jehovah, successively built in ancient Jerusalem *b)* a synagogue, esp. of a Reform or Conservative congregation **3** a church **4** [**T-**] either of two sets (**Inner Temple** and **Middle Temple**) of London buildings housing two of England's four principal law societies: their site was formerly occupied by the London branch of the Knights Templars: see also INNS OF COURT **5** a building, usually of imposing size, etc., serving the public or an organization in some special way [a *temple* of art, a Masonic *temple*] —**tem′pled** *adj.*

tem·ple[2] (tem′pəl) *n.* ⟦OFr < VL *tempula,* altered < L *tempora,* the temples, pl. of *tempus,* akin to *tempus,* time (in reference to pulse): see TEMPER⟧ **1** either of the flat surfaces alongside the forehead, in front of each ear ☆**2** either of the sidepieces of a pair of glasses that fit across the temples and over the ears

tem·ple[3] (tem′pəl) *n.* ⟦LME < MFr: see TEMPLATE⟧ *Weaving* a device for keeping the cloth in a loom stretched to its correct width

Tem·ple (tem′pəl) **1 Shirley (Jane)** 1928-2014; U.S. child film actress **2 Sir William** 1628-99; Brit. diplomat & writer

Temple Bar a former London gateway before the Temple buildings: the heads of executed traitors and criminals were exhibited on it: see TEMPLE[1] (sense 4)

tem·plet (tem′plit) *n. alt. sp. of* TEMPLATE

tem·po (tem′pō) *n., pl.* **-pos** or **-pi** (-pē) ⟦It < L *tempus,* time: see TEMPER⟧ **1** the speed at which a musical composition is, or is supposed to be, performed: it is indicated by such notations as *allegro, andante,* etc. or by reference to metronome timing **2** rate of activity; pace [the *tempo* of modern living] —**in tempo** conforming to the speed at which a piece of music is, or should be, played —**out of tempo 1** not in tempo **2** *Jazz* deliberately deviating from the regular tempo; rubato

tem·po·ral[1] (tem′pə rəl, -prəl) *adj.* ⟦ME < L *temporalis* < *tempus,* time: see TEMPER⟧ **1** [Now Rare] lasting only for a time; transitory; temporary, not eternal **2** of this world; worldly, not spiritual **3** civil or secular rather than ecclesiastical **4** of or limited by time **5** *Gram.* expressing distinctions in time; pertaining to tense —**tem′po·ral·ly** *adv.*

tem·po·ral[2] (tem′pə rəl, -prəl) *adj.* ⟦LL *temporalis* < L *tempora:* see TEMPLE[2]⟧ of or near the temple or temples (of the head)

temporal bone either of a pair of compound bones forming the sides of the skull

tem·po·ral·i·ty (tem′pə ral′ə tē) *n., pl.* **-ties** ⟦ME *temporalite* < LL(Ec) *temporalitas*⟧ **1** the quality or state of being temporal **2** [*usually pl.*] secular properties or revenues of a church

tem·po·rar·y (tem′pə rer′ē) *adj.* ⟦L *temporarius* < *tempus,* time: see TEMPER⟧ lasting, enjoyed, used, etc. for a time only; not permanent —*n.* an employee, esp. an office worker, hired for temporary service —**tem′po·rar′i·ly** *adv.* —**tem′po·rar′i·ness** *n.*

SYN.—**temporary** applies to a post held (or to the person holding such a post) for a limited time [a *temporary* clerical position]; **provisional** is specifically applied to a government established for the time being, as in a newly formed nation, until a permanent government can be formed; **interim** refers to an appointment for an intervening period, as between the death of an official and the election of a successor; **acting** is applied to one who temporarily takes over the powers of a regular official during the latter's absence [a vice-president often serves as *acting* president] —*ANT.* **permanent**

tem·po·rize (tem′pə rīz′) *vi.* **-rized′**, **-riz′ing** ⟦Fr *temporiser* < ML *temporizare* < L *tempus,* time: see TEMPER⟧ **1** to suit one's actions to the time, occasion, or circumstances, without reference to principle **2** *a)* to give temporary compliance or agreement, evade immediate decision, etc., so as to gain time or avoid argument *b)* to parley or deal (*with* a person, etc.) so as to gain time **3** to effect a compromise (*with* a person, etc., or *between* persons or parties); negotiate —**tem′po·ri·za′tion** *n.* —**tem′po·riz′er** *n.*

tem·po·ro·man·dib·u·lar (tem′pə rō man dib′yo͞o lər) *adj.* ⟦< TEMPORAL[2] + -O- + MANDIBULAR⟧ designating or of either of two joints connecting the lower jaw with the temporal bones

temporomandibular joint disorder a syndrome caused by a dislocation, injury, etc. of the temporomandibular joint, characterized variously by headache, facial pain, dizziness, partial loss of hearing, etc.

tempt (tempt) *vt.* ⟦ME *tempten* < OFr *tempter* < LL(Ec) *temptare* < L, to try the strength of, urge < IE **temp-:* see TEMPER⟧ **1** [Archaic] to test; try **2** to try to persuade; induce or entice, esp. to something immoral or sensually pleasurable **3** to rouse desire in; be inviting to; attract **4** to provoke or run the risk of provoking (fate, etc.) **5** to incline strongly [to be *tempted* to accept] —*SYN.* LURE —**tempt′a·ble** *adj.*

temp·ta·tion (temp tā′shən) *n.* ⟦OFr < LL(Ec) *temptatio* < L, an attack, trial⟧ **1** a tempting or being tempted **2** something that tempts; enticement

tempt·er (temp′tər) *n.* ⟦ME *temptour* < MFr *tempteur* < L *temptator,* tempter, in LL(Ec), Satan⟧ a person who tempts —**the Tempter** the Devil; Satan

tempt·ing (-tiŋ) *adj.* that tempts; alluring; attractive; seductive —**tempt′ing·ly** *adv.*

tempt·ress (-tris) *n.* a woman who tempts, esp. sexually

tem·pu·ra (tem po͝or′ə, tem′po͝or ə) *n.* ⟦Jpn < ? Port *tempero,* condiment, flavor⟧ a Japanese dish consisting of shrimp, fish, vegetables, etc. dipped in an egg batter, deep-fried to produce a light, crisp crust, and served with a piquant dipping sauce

tem·pus fu·git (tem′pəs fyo͞o′jit, -fo͞o′git) ⟦L⟧ time flies

ten (ten) *adj.* ⟦ME < OE *ten, tyn, tene,* akin to Ger *zehn* < IE **dékm̥,* ten > Sans *dáça,* Gr *deka,* L *decem*⟧ totaling one more than nine —*n.* **1** the cardinal number between nine and eleven; 10; X **2** any group of ten people or things **3** something numbered ten or having ten units, as a playing card or a throw of dice ☆**4** ⟦from the practice of using an informal 1-10 scale; popularized by the movie *10* (1979)⟧ [Informal] something or someone regarded as worthy of the highest rating; specif., a person regarded as possessing exceptional sexual attractiveness ☆**5** [Informal] a ten-dollar bill

ten- (ten) TENO-: used before a vowel

ten·a·ble (ten′ə bəl) *adj.* ⟦Fr < OFr < *tenir,* to hold: see TENANT⟧ that can be held, defended, or maintained —**ten′a·bil′i·ty** *n.*, **ten′a·ble·ness** —**ten′a·bly** *adv.*

ten·ace (ten′ās′, -əs) *n.* ⟦< Sp *tenaza,* lit., tongs, pincers < L *tenaces,* things that hold fast < *tenax:* see fol.⟧ *Bridge* an imperfect sequence of high cards in the same suit, as the ace and queen without the king

te·na·cious (tə nā′shəs) *adj.* ⟦L *tenax* (gen. *tenacis*) < *tenere,* to hold: see TENANT⟧ **1** holding firmly [a *tenacious* grip] **2** that retains well; retentive [a *tenacious* memory] **3** that holds together strongly; cohesive **4** that clings; adhesive **5** persistent; stubborn [*tenacious* courage] —**te·na′cious·ly** *adv.* —**te·na′cious·ness** *n.*

te·nac·i·ty (tə nas′ə tē) *n.* ⟦L *tenacitas*⟧ the quality or state of being tenacious

te·nac·u·lum (tə nak′yo͞o ləm, -yə-) *n., pl.* **-la** (-lə) ⟦LL, instrument for holding < L *tenere,* to hold: see TENANT⟧ *Surgery* a pointed, hooked instrument for lifting and holding parts such as blood vessels

te·naille or **te·nail** (te nāl′) *n.* ⟦Fr *tenaille,* lit., pincers, tongs < VL **tenacula,* for LL *tenaculum:* see prec.⟧ an outwork before the curtain between two bastions

ten·an·cy (ten′ən sē) *n., pl.* **-cies 1** *a)* the condition of being a tenant; occupation of land, a building, etc. by rental or lease *b)* [Obs.] property occupied by a tenant *c)* the duration of such an occupancy **2** possession or occupation of property, an office, etc. by any kind of title or right

ten·ant (ten′ənt) *n.* ⟦ME *tenaunt* < OFr *tenant,* orig. prp. of *tenir,* to hold < L *tenere,* to hold < IE base **ten-,* to pull, stretch > THIN⟧ **1** a person who pays rent to occupy or use land, a building, etc. **2** an occupant of or dweller in a specified place **3** a person who possesses lands, etc. by any kind of title —*vt.* to hold as a tenant; occupy —**ten′ant·a·ble** *adj.* —**ten′ant·less** *adj.*

tenant farmer a person who farms land owned by another and pays rent in cash or in a share of the crops

ten·ant·ry (ten′ən trē) *n., pl.* **-ries** ⟦ME: see TENANT & -RY⟧ **1** the tenants collectively, as of an estate **2** the condition of being a tenant

☆**ten-cent store** (ten′sent′) *short for* FIVE-AND-TEN-CENT STORE

tench (tench) *n., pl.* **tench′es** or **tench** ⟦ME & OFr *tenche* < LL *tinca*⟧ a small, European, freshwater cyprinoid fish (*Tinca tinca*) now established in North America

Ten Commandments *Bible* the ten laws constituting the fundamental moral code of Israel, given to Moses by God on Mount Sinai; Decalogue: Ex. 20:2-17; Deut. 5:6-22

tend[1] (tend) *vt.* ⟦ME *tenden,* aphetic < *attenden:* see ATTEND⟧ **1** to take care of; minister to; watch over; look after; attend to [to *tend* plants or animals, to *tend* the sick] **2** to be in charge of or at work at; manage or operate [to *tend* a store] **3** *Naut.* to watch over (a rope, diver's air line, etc.) carefully to keep it from becoming tangled, being snagged, etc. —*vi.* to pay attention; attend —**tend on** to wait upon; serve

tend[2] (tend) *vi.* ⟦ME *tenden* < OFr *tendre* < L *tendere,* to stretch, extend, tend: see THIN⟧ **1** to be directed; proceed or extend [the road *tends* south] **2** to have an inclination, tendency, bias, etc. to do something; incline [*tending* to overeat] **3** to lead or be directed (*to* or *toward* a specified result)

tend·ance (ten′dəns) *n.* **1** a tending, attention, or care **2** [Obs.] attendants collectively

tend·en·cy (ten′dən sē) *n., pl.* **-cies** ⟦ML *tendentia* < L *tendens,* prp. of *tendere,* to TEND[2]⟧ **1** an inclination to move or act in a particular direction or way; constant disposition to some action or state; leaning; bias; propensity; bent **2** a course or apparent course toward some purpose, object, or result; drift **3** a definite purpose or point of view in something said or written

SYN.—**tendency** refers to an inclination or disposition to move in a particular direction or act in a certain way, esp. as a result of some inherent quality or habit [he has a *tendency* toward exaggeration]; **trend** suggests a general direction, without a definite course or goal, subject to change or fluctuation by some external force [a recent *trend* in literature]; **current** differs from **trend** in connoting a clearly defined course, but one also subject to change [the *current* of one's life]; **drift** refers to the course along which something is being carried or driven [the *drift* toward absolute conformity] or to a course taken by something that has unstated implications [what is the *drift* of this argument?]; **tenor**, equivalent in this connection to **drift**, connotes more strongly the clarity or purport of the unstated purpose or objective [the general *tenor* of the Bill of Rights]

ten·den·tious (ten den′shəs) *adj.* ⟦Ger *tendenziös* < *tendenz* (< ML *tendentia*), prec.⟧ advancing a definite point of view; often, specif., biased or slanted [*tendentious* writings] —**ten·den′tious·ly** *adv.* —**ten·den′tious·ness** *n.*

ten·der[1] (ten′dər) *adj.* ⟦ME *tendre* < OFr < L *tener,* soft, delicate, tender, prob. altered (infl. by *tenuis,* THIN) < Sabine *terenum,* soft, akin to Gr *terēn,* tender < IE **ter-,* tender, weak, orig., rubbed, worn down < base **ter-,* to rub > THROW⟧ **1** soft or delicate and easily chewed, broken, cut, etc.; fragile, succulent, etc. **2** weak of constitution or physique; unable to endure pain, hardship, etc.; feeble; frail **3** having weakness due to youth; immature; young [the *tender* years] **4** of soft quality or delicate tone; subdued [*tender* colors] **5** that requires careful handling; ticklish; delicate [a *tender* question] **6** gentle, mild, or light; not rough or heavy [a *tender* touch] **7** *a)* that has or expresses affection, love, consideration, etc. [a *tender* smile] *b)* careful; considerate [*tender* of another's feelings] **8** sparing; chary [*tender* of one's praise] **9** *a)* acutely sensitive, as to pain, insult, etc. *b)* sensitive to impressions, emotions, moral influences, etc.; impressionable [a *tender* conscience] *c)* sensitive to others' feelings; sympathetic; compassionate [a *tender* heart] **10** giving physical pain, as from overuse or when not fully healed; painful; hurting [a *tender* pitching arm] **11** *Naut.* tending to lean to one side too easily when under sail: opposed to STIFF (*adj.* 13) —*vt.* **1** to make tender **2** [Archaic] to treat with tenderness —**ten′der·ly** *adv.* —**ten′der·ness** *n.*

SYN.—**tender**, in this connection, implies a softness or gentleness in one's relations with others that is expressive of warm affection, concern, etc. [a *tender* caress]; **compassionate** is applied to one who is easily affected by another's troubles or pains and is quick to show pity or mercy [a *compassionate* judge]; **sympathetic** implies the ability or disposition to enter into another's mental state or emotions and thus to share sorrows, joys, desires, etc. [a *sympathetic* interest in a colleague's career]; **warm** and **warmhearted** suggest a sympathetic interest or affection characterized by cordiality, generosity, etc. [*warm,* or *warmhearted,* hospitality]

ten·der[2] (ten′dər) *vt.* ⟦Fr *tendre* < L *tendere,* to stretch, extend, TEND[2]⟧ **1** to offer in payment of an obligation **2** to present for acceptance; offer [to *tender* an invitation, apology, etc.] **3** to submit as a tender [to *tender* a bid] —*n.* **1** an offer of money, services, etc. made to satisfy an obligation, avoid legal action, etc. **2** a formal offer, as a proposal of marriage, a bid stating terms of a contract, or a bid on a printed form submitted to buy securities at a certain price ☆**3** something offered in payment, esp. money: cf. LEGAL TENDER —**ten′der·er** *n.*

tend·er[3] (ten′dər) *n.* **1** a person who tends, or has charge of, something **2** *a)* an auxiliary ship for supplying or servicing another ship or a submarine, lighthouse, etc. *b)* a boat for carrying passengers, etc. to or from a ship close to shore **3** a railroad car carrying fuel and water for a steam locomotive, to the rear of which it is attached

ten·der[4] (ten′dər) *n.* ⟦< TENDER(LOIN)⟧ a strip of meat, as from the tenderloin; esp., a strip of chicken breast, often served breaded and fried or baked

☆**ten·der·foot** (ten′dər foot′) *n., pl.* **-foots′** or **-feet′** **1** a newcomer to the ranching and mining country of the West, unused to the hardships of the life **2** any newcomer, novice, or beginner **3** a beginner in the Boy Scouts

ten·der·heart·ed (ten′dər härt′id) *adj.* having a tender heart; quick to feel pity; sympathetic —**ten′der·heart′ed·ly** *adv.* —**ten′der·heart′ed·ness** *n.*

ten·der·ize (ten′dər īz′) *vt.* **-ized′**, **-iz′ing** to make (meat) tender by using a process or adding a substance that softens tissues —**ten′der·i·za′tion** *n.* —**ten′der·iz′er** *n.*

☆**ten·der·loin** (ten′dər loin′) *n.* **1** the tenderest part of a loin of beef, pork, etc., located on either side of the backbone and consisting of the psoas muscle **2** [*usually* **T-**] any urban district similar to the TENDERLOIN

Ten·der·loin (ten′dər loin′), **the** former district in New York City, in which there was much graft and corruption: so called because regarded as a choice assignment for police seeking graft

tender offer ⟦see TENDER[2]⟧ a public offer to purchase a block of stock in a corporation, often the controlling interest, within a specified period and at a stipulated price, usually well above the existing market price

ten·di·ni·tis (ten′də nīt′is) *n.* ⟦< ModL or ML *tendo,* TENDON + *-itis,* -ITIS⟧ inflammation of a tendon: also sp. **ten′don·i′tis**

ten·di·nous (ten′də nəs) *adj.* ⟦Fr *tendineux* < ML *tendinosus*⟧ **1** of or like a tendon **2** consisting of tendons

ten·don (ten′dən) *n.* ⟦ML *tendo,* altered (infl. by L *tendere,* to stretch) < Gr *tenōn,* sinew < *teinein,* to stretch: see THIN⟧ any of the inelastic cords of tough, fibrous connective tissue in which muscle fibers end and by which muscles are attached to bones or other parts; sinew

ten·dresse (tän dres′) *n.* ⟦Fr⟧ **1** tenderness; delicacy **2** tender feeling; fondness

ten·dril (ten′drəl) *n.* ⟦earlier *tendrell,* prob. altered < ME *tendron,* young tender shoot < OFr *tendrum,* ult. < L *tener,* TENDER[1]⟧ **1** a threadlike part of a climbing plant, often in a spiral form, supporting it by clinging to or coiling around an object **2** a wispy or curly strand of hair, often clinging to the face or neck

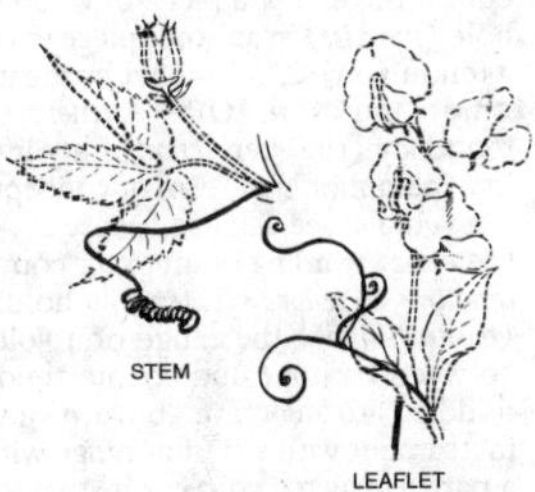

tendrils

Ten·e·brae (ten′ə brā′, -brē′) *pl.n.* ⟦L, pl., shadows, darkness: see TEMERITY⟧ [*with sing. or pl. v.*] a Holy Week night service (Wednesday through Friday), formerly widely observed in the Western Church, consisting of group recitation of Matins and Lauds of the following day in commemoration of Christ's death and burial

ten·e·brif·ic (ten′ə brif′ik) *adj.* ⟦< L *tenebrae* (see prec.) + -FIC⟧ making dark; obscuring

ten·e·brous (ten′ə brəs) *adj.* ⟦ME *tenebrus* < OFr < L *tenebrosus* < *tenebrae:* see TEMERITY⟧ dark; gloomy: also **te·neb·ri·ous** (tə neb′rē əs)

Ten·e·dos (ten′ə däs′) *ancient name for* BOZCAADA

1080 (ten′āt′ē) *n.* ⟦the manufacturer's laboratory serial number⟧ SODIUM FLUOROACETATE

ten·e·ment (ten′ə mənt) *n.* ⟦ME < OFr, a holding < ML *tenementum* < L *tenere,* to hold: see TENANT⟧ **1** *Law* land, buildings, offices, franchises, etc. held of another by tenure **2** a dwelling house **3** a room or set of rooms tenanted as a separate dwelling; apartment; flat **4** TENEMENT HOUSE **5** [Old Poet.] a dwelling place; abode —**ten′e·men′tal** *adj.*, **ten′e·men′ta·ry**

☆**tenement house** a building divided into tenements, or apartments, now specif. one in the slums that is run-down, overcrowded, etc.

Te·ne·ri·fe (ten′ə rē′fā, -rēf′; *Sp* te′ne rē′fe) largest island of the Canary Islands: 795 sq mi (2,059 sq km)

te·nes·mus (ti nez′məs, -nes′-) *n.* ⟦ML < L *tenesmos* < Gr *teinesmos* < *teinein,* to stretch: see THIN⟧ *Med.* a feeling of urgent need to defecate or urinate, with a straining but unsuccessful effort to do so

ten·et (ten′it) *n.* ⟦L, he holds < *tenere:* see TENANT⟧ a principle, doctrine, or belief held as a truth, as by some group —*SYN.* DOCTRINE

ten·fold (ten′fōld′) *adj.* ⟦TEN + -FOLD⟧ **1** having ten parts **2** having ten times as much or as many —*adv.* ten times as much or as many

☆**ten-gal·lon hat** (ten′gal′ən) a wide-brimmed felt hat with a high, round crown, originally worn by American cowboys

ten·ge (teŋ′gə) *n.* **1** the basic monetary unit of Kazakhstan **2** a monetary unit of Turkmenistan, equal to $\frac{1}{100}$ of a manat See the table of monetary units in the Reference Supplement

Teng·ri Nor (teŋ′rē nôr′) *another name for* NAM CO

te·ni·a (tē′nē ə) *n. alt. sp. of* TAENIA

Ten·iers (ten′yərz; *Fl* tə nirs′) **1 David** 1582-1649; Fl. painter: called *the Elder* **2 David** 1610-90; Fl. painter: son of Teniers the Elder: called *the Younger*

Tenn *abbrev.* Tennessee

ten·ner (ten′ər) *n.* [Informal] **1** a ten-dollar bill **2** [Brit.] a ten-pound note

Ten·nes·se·an (ten′ə sē′ən) *adj.* of the state of Tennessee: usually used in the predicate —*n.* a person born or living in Tennessee

Ten·nes·see (ten′ə sē′) ⟦< *Tanasi,* Cherokee village name⟧ **1** state of the EC U.S.: admitted 1796; 41,217 sq mi (106,752 sq km); cap. Nashville: abbrev. *TN* or *Tenn* **2** river flowing from NE Tenn. through N Ala. & W Tenn. into the Ohio River: 652 mi (1,049 km)

☆**Tennessee Valley Authority** a federal corporation organized in 1933 to provide cheap electric power, flood control, irrigation, etc. by developing the entire basin of the Tennessee River, esp. by building dams and reservoirs

☆**Tennessee walking horse** any of a breed of saddle or light utility horse with an easy, ambling gait

Ten·niel (ten′yəl), Sir John 1820-1914; Eng. illustrator & caricaturist

☆**ten·nies** (ten′ēz′) ***pl.n.*** [Slang] tennis shoes

ten·nis (ten′is) ***n.*** ⟦ME *tenetz,* prob. < Anglo-Fr *tenetz,* receive, hold (imper. for OFr *tenez*) < OFr *tenir,* to hold (see TENANT): a cry by the server before play⟧ **1** a game, usually played outdoors, in which two players or two pairs of players using rackets hit a fabric-covered, hollow rubber ball back and forth over a net stretched across a marked, level, rectangular area (**tennis court**): in full **lawn tennis** **2** a similar but more complex old indoor game (**court tennis**) in which the ball is bounced against the walls of a specially constructed court as well as hit over a net

tennis bracelet ⟦so named in ref. to such a bracelet that fell from the wrist of U.S. tennis champion Chris Evert during a match in 1987⟧ a bracelet consisting of a single strand of small stones, usually diamonds, in a plain setting

tennis elbow painful inflammation of the elbow, esp. of its tendons, caused by strain in rotating the forearm, as in using a tennis racket

tennis shoe SNEAKER (sense 2)

Ten·ny·son (ten′i sən), **Alfred** 1st Baron Tennyson 1809-92; Eng. poet: poet laureate (1850-92): called *Alfred, Lord Tennyson* —**Ten′ny·so′ni·an** (-sō′nē ən) ***adj.***

ten·o- (ten′ō, -ə) ⟦< Gr *tenōn,* TENDON⟧ *combining form* tendon *[tenotomy]*

ten·on (ten′ən) ***n.*** ⟦ME < MFr < *tenir,* to hold: see TENANT⟧ a projecting part cut on the end of a piece of wood, etc. for insertion into a corresponding hole (*mortise*) in another piece in order to form a joint — ***vt., vi.*** **1** to make a tenon (on) **2** to connect by means of a tenon and mortise

ten·or (ten′ər) ***n.*** ⟦OFr < L *tenere,* to hold: see TENANT⟧ **1** general course or tendency *[*the even *tenor* of my life*]* **2** general meaning; drift; purport **3** in a metaphor, that term or concept that is described in a figurative way by the vehicle: see VEHICLE (sense 3) **4** [Obs.] general character or nature **5** the exact wording or an exact copy of a legal document **6** *a)* ⟦ME < MFr *tenour* < It *tenore* < L *tenor,* a holding: the tenor voice "held" the melody (*canto fermo*)⟧ the range of a voice, often, specif., an adult male voice, between baritone and countertenor, usually from about an octave below middle C to an octave above *b)* a voice or singer with such a range *c)* an instrument with a similar range within its family, as a tenor saxophone *d)* a part for such a voice or instrument **7** in four-part harmony, the second lowest part **8** in a set of bells for ringing changes, the bell with the lowest tone —***adj.*** of, for, or having the range of a tenor **—*SYN.*** TENDENCY

tenor clef a C clef on the fourth line of a staff, used in notation for the upper range of the cello, bassoon, tenor trombone, etc.

☆**ten·or·ist** (ten′ər ist) ***n.*** *Jazz* a person who plays the tenor saxophone

ten·o·rite (ten′ə rīt′) ***n.*** ⟦It, after M. *Tenore* (1780-1861), It botanist + *-ite,* -ITE[1]⟧ a dark-colored, triclinic mineral, CuO, an ore of copper; cupric oxide

te·nor·rha·phy (tə nôr′ə fē) ***n., pl.*** **-phies** ⟦TENO- + Gr *rrhaphia,* a suturing < *rhaphē,* seam⟧ *Surgery* the joining of a divided tendon by sutures

te·no·syn·o·vi·tis (ten′ō sin′ə vīt′is) ***n.*** ⟦TENO- + SYNOVITIS⟧ inflammation of the membrane that surrounds and cushions any of certain tendons passing over a bone or through a joint

te·not·o·my (tə nät′ə mē) ***n., pl.*** **-mies** ⟦TENO- + -TOMY⟧ *Surgery* the cutting or dividing of a tendon

ten·pen·ny (ten′pen′ē, -pə nē) ***adj.*** **1** worth ten (esp. Brit.) pennies **2** *Carpentry* designating a nail three inches long

ten·pin (-pin′) ***n.*** a pin used in the game of tenpins

ten·pins (-pinz′) ***n.*** the game of bowling in which ten pins are used

ten·pound·er (ten′poun′dər) ***n.*** any of a family (Elopidae, order Elopiformes) of marine or freshwater bony fishes, including the ladyfish and machete

ten·rec (ten′rek′) ***n.*** ⟦Fr *tanrac, tenrec* < Malagasy *tràndraka, tàndeke*⟧ any of a family (Tenrecidae) of small, burrowing insectivores of Madagascar and the Comoro Islands

tense[1] (tens) ***adj.*** **tens′er, tens′est** ⟦L *tensus,* pp. of *tendere,* to stretch < IE **tend-* < base **ten-,* to stretch > THIN⟧ **1** stretched tight; strained; taut **2** feeling, showing, or causing mental strain; anxious **3** *Phonet.* articulated with the jaw and tongue muscles relatively rigid: said of certain vowels, as (ē) and (o͞o): opposed to LAX — ***vt., vi.*** **tensed, tens′ing** to make or become tense **—*SYN.*** TIGHT —**tense′ly** ***adv.*** —**tense′ness** ***n.***

tense[2] (tens) ***n.*** ⟦ME < OFr *tens* < L *tempus,* time: see TEMPER⟧ **1** a characteristic of verbs that indicates the time of the action or state of being that a verb expresses; also, an analytic category based on this characteristic **2** any of the forms a verb takes to indicate this characteristic **3** a set of such forms for a given time reference *[*the present *tense* of "be"*]*

USAGE—tenses in English are usually listed as *present, past, future, present perfect, past perfect (pluperfect),* and *future perfect,* in accordance with Latin models; English tenses other than the simple present and simple past are formed by the use of an auxiliary verb with a participle

ten·sile (ten′səl; *chiefly Brit,* -sīl′) ***adj.*** ⟦ModL *tensilis* < L *tensus:* see TENSE[1]⟧ **1** of, undergoing, or exerting tension **2** capable of being stretched —**ten·sil′i·ty** (-sil′ə tē) ***n.***

tensile strength resistance to lengthwise stress, measured (in force per unit of cross-sectional area) by the greatest load pulling in the direction of length that a given substance can bear without tearing apart

ten·sim·e·ter (ten sim′ət ər) ***n.*** ⟦TENSI(ON) + -METER⟧ an instrument that measures the difference in vapor pressure of two liquids

ten·si·om·e·ter (ten′sē äm′ət ər) ***n.*** ⟦< fol. + -METER⟧ any instrument for measuring tautness or tension, as of a stretched wire or fabric or of the surface of a fluid

ten·sion (ten′shən) ***n.*** ⟦< MFr or L: MFr < L *tensio* < *tensus:* see TENSE[1]⟧ **1** a tensing or being tensed **2** mental or nervous strain, often accompanied by muscular tautness **3** a state of strained relations; uneasiness due to mutual hostility **4** a device for regulating tension or tautness, as of thread in a sewing machine **5** VOLTAGE *[*a high-*tension* cable*]* **6** loosely, the expansive force, or pressure, of a gas or vapor **7** *a)* stress on a material produced by the pull of forces tending to cause extension *b)* a force or combination of forces exerting such a pull against the resistance of the material **8** a balancing of forces or elements in opposition —***vt.*** to subject to tension —**ten′sion·al** ***adj.***

ten·si·ty (ten′sə tē) ***n.*** a tense state or quality

ten·sive (-siv) ***adj.*** ⟦Fr *tensif*⟧ relating to or causing tension

ten·sor (ten′sər, -sôr′) ***n.*** ⟦ModL < L *tensus:* see TENSE[1]⟧ **1** any muscle that stretches, or tenses, some part of the body **2** *Math.* an abstract object representing a generalization of the vector concept and having a specified system of components that undergo certain types of transformation under changes of the coordinate system

ten-speed (-spēd′) ***n.*** a bicycle equipped with a derailleur of ten speeds, or gear arrangements

☆**ten-strike** (ten′strīk′) ***n.*** **1** *Bowling* STRIKE **2** [Informal] any entirely successful action

tent[1] (tent) ***n.*** ⟦ME < OFr *tente* < L *tenta,* fem. pp. of *tentus,* alt. pp. of *tendere,* to stretch: see THIN⟧ **1** a portable shelter consisting of canvas, skins, etc. stretched over poles and attached to stakes **2** anything suggestive of a tent, as an oxygen tent —***adj.*** of or like a tent —***vi.*** to live in a tent; encamp —***vt.*** **1** to lodge in tents **2** to cover with or as if with a tent

tent[2] (tent) ***n.*** ⟦ME *tente* < OFr, a probe < *tenter,* to try, test < L *tentare,* var. of *temptare:* see TEMPT⟧ *Med.* a plug of gauze, lint, etc. placed into an opening or wound to dilate it or keep it open —***vt.*** to insert such a plug in

ten·ta·cle (ten′tə kəl) ***n.*** ⟦ModL *tentaculum* < L *tentare,* to touch: see prec.⟧ **1** any of a variety of long, slender, flexible growths, as about the head or mouth of some invertebrate animals, used variously for grasping, feeling, moving, etc. **2** *Bot.* any of various sensitive hairs on the leaves of some plants, as those used in capturing insects —**ten′ta·cled** ***adj.*** —**ten·tac·u·lar** (ten tak′yo͞o lər) ***adj.***

ten·ta·tive (ten′tə tiv) ***adj.*** ⟦LL *tentativus* < pp. of L *tentare,* to touch, try: see TENT[2]⟧ **1** made, done, proposed, etc. experimentally or provisionally; not definite or final *[tentative* plans, a *tentative* explanation*]* **2** indicating timidity, hesitancy, or uncertainty *[*a *tentative* caress*]* —**ten′ta·tive·ly** ***adv.*** —**ten′ta·tive·ness** ***n.***

☆**tent caterpillar** any of various caterpillars (esp. genus *Malacosoma,* family Lasiocampidae) that usually live in colonies in large, tentlike webs spun among the branches of trees, which they defoliate

tent dress a dress that is fitted in the shoulders and widens considerably down to the hem

tent·ed (tent′id) ***adj.*** **1** covered by or sheltered in a tent or tents **2** shaped like a tent

ten·ter (ten′tər) ***n.*** ⟦ME *tentoure,* altered (infl. by *tent,* TENT[1]) < MFr *tendëure* < *tendre,* to stretch: see TEND[2]⟧ **1** a frame on which cloth is stretched after having been milled, so as to dry evenly without shrinking: in full **tenter frame** **2** [Obs.] a tenterhook —***vt.*** ⟦ME *tenteren*⟧ to stretch (cloth) on a tenter or tenters

ten·ter·hook (ten′tər ho͝ok′) ***n.*** any of the hooked nails that hold cloth stretched on a tenter —**on tenterhooks** in suspense; filled with anxiety

tenth (tenth) ***adj.*** ⟦Early ME *tenthe,* replacing OE *teogotha, teotha:* see TEN & -TH[2]⟧ **1** preceded by nine others in a series; 10th **2** designating any of the ten equal parts of something —***n.*** **1** the one following the ninth **2** any of the ten equal parts of something; $\frac{1}{10}$ **3** a tenth of a gallon —***adv.*** in the tenth place, rank, group, etc. —**tenth′ly** ***adv.***

tent show a show, as a circus, given in a tent

tent stitch ⟦< ? TENT[1]⟧ an embroidery stitch that forms a series of parallel slanting lines

ten·u·is (ten′yo͞o is) ***n., pl.*** **-u·es′** (-yo͞o ēz′) ⟦ML < L, THIN: used as transl. of Gr *psilos,* bare, unaspirated (so applied by Aristotle)⟧ *Phonet.* an unaspirated voiceless stop

te·nu·i·ty (tə no͞o′ə tē, -nyo͞o′-) ***n., pl.*** **-ties** ⟦MFr *tenuité* < L *tenuitas*⟧ the quality or state of being tenuous; specif., *a)* thinness; slenderness; fineness *b)* lack of substance; rarity, as of air *c)* faintness, as of light or voice *d)* meagerness; slightness

ten·u·ous (ten′yo͞o əs, -yə wəs) ***adj.*** ⟦< L *tenuis,* THIN + -OUS⟧ **1** slender or fine, as a fiber **2** rare, as air at high altitudes; not dense **3** not substantial; slight; flimsy *[tenuous* evidence*]* —**ten′u·ous·ly** ***adv.*** —**ten′u·ous·ness** ***n.***

ten·ure (ten′yər, -yoor) ***n.*** ⟦ME < MFr < *tenir,* to hold: see TENANT⟧ **1** the act or right of holding property, an office, a position, etc. **2** the length of time, or the conditions under which, something is held **3** the status of holding one's position on a permanent basis, granted to teachers, civil service personnel, etc. on the fulfillment of specified requirements —**ten′ured** ***adj.*** —**ten·u·ri·al** (ten yoor′ē əl) ***adj.***

te·nu·to (tā no͞o′tō) ***adj., adv.*** ⟦It, pp. of *tenere,* to hold < L *tenere:* see THIN⟧ *Musical Direction* held for the full value: usually indicated by a short line over the note or chord —***n., pl.*** **-ti** (-tē) *[also in roman type] Music* a note or chord to be played *tenuto*

te·o·cal·li (tē′ō kal′ē; *Sp* te′ô kä′yē) ***n., pl.*** **-cal′lis** (-ēz; *Sp,* -yēs) ⟦Nahuatl *teo:kalli,* temple < *teo:ƛ,* god + *kalli,* house⟧ an ancient Mexican or Central American temple of the Aztecs, usually a building on a truncated pyramid

te·o·sin·te (tē′ō sin′tē) ***n.*** ⟦AmSp < Nahuatl *teo:sinƛi, teo:senƛi,* lit., divine maize < *teo:ƛ,* god + *sinƛi, senƛi,* maize⟧ a tall, cornlike fodder grass (*Zea mexicana*) native to Mexico and Central America, having a tassel and small, hard ears: presumed to be the wild ancestor of maize

Te·o·ti·hua·cán (tā′ō tē′wä kän′) largest city in ancient Mesoamerica, near present-day Mexico City: site of extensive archaeological ruins

tep·a·ry bean (tep′ə rē) ⟦< ?⟧ **1** a twining, drought-resistant bean plant (*Phaseolus acutifolius* var. *latifolius*) cultivated in the SW U.S., Mexico, etc. **2** the edible seed of this plant

☆**te·pee** (tē′pē) ***n.*** ⟦Dakota *tʰípi*, dwelling < *tʰi*-, to dwell + -*pi*, suffix indicating pl., indefinite, or abstract form⟧ **1** a cone-shaped tent of animal skins or bark used by North American Indian peoples of the plains and Great Lakes regions **2** a similarly shaped Indian dwelling of other materials, such as canvas

tepee

teph·ra (tef′rə) ***pl.n.*** ⟦< Gr: see fol.⟧ [*with sing. or pl. v.*] clastic volcanic materials, as dust, ashes, or pumice, ejected during an eruption and carried through the air before deposition

teph·rite (tef′rīt′) ***n.*** ⟦< Gr *tephra*, ashes < IE base **dhegwh*-, to burn (> FEVER) + -ITE[1]⟧ an extrusive igneous rock resembling basalt and consisting essentially of plagioclase, nepheline, etc. —**teph·rit′ic** (-rit′ik) ***adj.***

Te·pic (tā pēk′) city in W Mexico: capital of Nayarit

tep·id (tep′id) ***adj.*** ⟦ME *teped* < L *tepidus* < *tepere*, to be slightly warm < IE base **tep*-, to be warm > Sans *tapati*, (it) burns⟧ **1** barely or moderately warm; lukewarm: said of liquids **2** lacking warmth of feeling or enthusiasm —**te·pid·i·ty** (tə pid′ə tē) ***n.***, **tep′id·ness** —**tep′id·ly** ***adv.***

te·poy (tē′poi′) ***n.*** *alt. sp. of* TEAPOY

☆**te·qui·la** (tə kē′lə) ***n.*** ⟦AmSp < Nahuatl *Tuiquila*, region in Mexico (orig. the name of a people), where orig. produced⟧ **1** a strong alcoholic liquor of Mexico, distilled esp. from a mash made from the core of certain agaves **2** a Mexican agave (*Agave tequilana*) that is a source of tequila and mescal

☆**tequila sunrise** ⟦from the colorful appearance of the unstirred ingredients in a glass⟧ a cocktail made of tequila, orange juice, and grenadine

ter *abbrev.* **1** terrace **2** territory

ter- (ter, tʉr) ⟦< L *ter*, third; akin to *tres*, THREE⟧ *combining form* three, three times

ter·a- (ter′ə) ⟦< Gr *teras*, monster: see TERATO-⟧ *combining form* one trillion; the factor 10^{12} [*terahertz*]

ter·a·byte (ter′ə bīt′) ***n.*** ⟦prec. + BYTE⟧ **1** a unit of storage capacity in a computer system, equal to 1,099,511,627,776 (2^{40}) bytes **2** loosely, one trillion bytes Abbrev. *TB*

ter·a·flops (-fläps′) ***n.***, *pl.* **-flops′** a unit of processing speed in a computer, equal to one trillion flops

ter·a·hertz (-hʉrts′) ***n.***, *pl.* **-hertz′** one trillion hertz: abbrev. *THz*

te·rai (tə rī′) ***n.*** ⟦after *Terai*, region in NW India, where first worn by travelers⟧ a soft, broad-brimmed, double-crowned hat of felt, worn for protection against the sun

ter·a·phim (ter′ə fim′) ***pl.n.***, *sing.* **ter′aph** (-əf) ⟦ME *theraphym* < LL(Ec) *theraphim* < Gr(Ec) *theraphin* < Heb *terafim*⟧ small images or other things representing household gods, used among ancient Semitic peoples

ter·a·tism (ter′ə tiz′əm) ***n.*** ⟦< fol. + -ISM⟧ malformation of a fetus

ter·a·to- (ter′ə tō, -tə) ⟦< Gr *teras* (gen. *teratos*), a wonder, monster < IE base **kwer*-, to cast a spell upon, orig. prob. to form, make > Sans *karōti*, (he) makes⟧ *combining form* monster, monstrosity [*teratology*]: also, before a vowel, **terat-**

ter·a·to·gen (ter′ə tə jən) ***n.*** ⟦prec. + -GEN⟧ an agent, as a chemical or disease, that causes malformation of a fetus —**ter′a·to·gen′ic** (-jen′ik) ***adj.***

ter·a·toid (ter′ə toid′) ***adj.*** ⟦TERAT(O)- + -OID⟧ *Biol.* malformed or abnormal

ter·a·tol·o·gy (ter′ə täl′ə jē) ***n.*** ⟦TERATO- + -LOGY⟧ the scientific study of congenital abnormalities and malformations —**ter′a·to·log′i·cal** (-tə läj′i kəl) ***adj.***

ter·a·to·ma (ter′ə tō′mə) ***n.*** ⟦TERAT(O)- + -OMA⟧ a tumor containing various kinds of embryonic tissue, as of hair and teeth

ter·a·watt (ter′ə wät′) ***n.*** one trillion watts: abbrev. *TW*

ter·bi·a (tʉr′bē ə) ***n.*** ⟦ModL < fol.⟧ terbium oxide, Tb_2O_3, a white powder soluble in dilute acids

ter·bi·um (tʉr′bē əm) ***n.*** ⟦ModL: so named (1843) by K. G. Mosander, its discoverer, after *Ytterby*: see ERBIUM⟧ a soft, silver-gray, ductile chemical element, one of the rare-earth elements, found in gadolinite and other minerals: symbol, Tb; at. no. 65: see the periodic table of elements in the Reference Supplement

terbium metals a series of closely related rare-earth elements, including terbium, gadolinium, europium, and, sometimes, dysprosium

Ter Borch (tər bôrkh′), **Ge·rard** (gā′rärt) 1617-81; Du. painter: also written **Terborch**

terce (tʉrs) ***n.*** ⟦see TIERCE⟧ [*often* **T-**] *Eccles.* the third of the seven canonical hours; midmorning prayer

Ter·cei·ra (tər sā′rə) island of the central Azores: 147 sq mi (381 sq km)

ter·cel (tʉr′səl) ***n.*** *var. of* TIERCEL

ter·cen·te·nar·y (tʉr′sen ten′ər ē, tər sen′tə ner′ē) ***adj., n.***, *pl.* **-nar·ies** ⟦L *ter*, three times (akin to *tres*, THREE) + CENTENARY⟧ TRICENTENNIAL: also **ter′cen·ten′ni·al** (-ten′ē əl)

ter·cet (tʉr′sit, tər set′) ***n.*** ⟦Fr < It *terzetto*, dim. of *terzo* < L *tertius*, THIRD⟧ a group of three lines that rhyme with one another or are connected by rhyme with an adjacent triplet or triplets

ter·e·bene (ter′ə bēn′) ***n.*** ⟦Fr *térébène* < *térébinthe*, TEREBINTH + -*ène*, -ENE⟧ a mixture of terpenes obtained by the action of sulfuric acid on spirits of turpentine, used as an expectorant, deodorant, and inhalant

te·reb·ic acid (tə reb′ik, -rē′bik) ⟦< fol. + -IC⟧ a white, crystalline acid, $C_7H_{10}O_4$, a product of the oxidation of spirits of turpentine

ter·e·binth (ter′ə binth′) ***n.*** ⟦ME *terebint* < MFr *therebint(he)* < L *terebinthus* < Gr *terebinthos*, earlier *terminthos*⟧ a small European tree (*Pistacia terebinthus*) of the cashew family, whose cut bark yields a turpentine

ter·e·bin·thine (ter′ə bin′thin, -thēn′, -thīn′) ***adj.*** **1** of the terebinth tree **2** of or like turpentine

te·re·do (tə rē′dō) ***n.***, *pl.* **-dos** or **-di·nes′** (-də nēz′) ⟦ME < L < Gr *terēdōn*, borer, akin to *teirein*, to rub: see THROW⟧ any of a genus (*Teredo*) of long shipworms that feed on wood

Ter·ence[1] (ter′əns) ***n.*** ⟦L *Terentius*, name of a Roman gens⟧ a masculine name: dim. *Terry*

Ter·ence[2] (ter′əns) (L. name *Publius Terentius Afer*) 195?-159? B.C.; Rom. writer of comedies

Te·reng·ga·nu (te reŋ gä′no͞o) state of Malaysia, on the E coast of Peninsular Malaysia: 5,002 sq mi (12,955 sq km)

ter·eph·thal·ic acid (ter′ef thal′ik-) ⟦TERE(BENE) + PHTHALIC ACID⟧ a white, crystalline powder, $C_6H_4(COOH)_2$, produced by the oxidation of certain xylene hydrocarbons and used in making plastics, polyester fiber, etc.

Te·re·sa[1] (tə rē′sə, -zə) ***n.*** a feminine name: see THERESA

Te·re·sa[2] (*for 1* tə rā′sə; *for 2* tə rē′sə *or Sp* te re′sä) **1** Mother (born *Agnes Gonxha Bojaxhiu*) 1910-97; Rom. Catholic missionary in India, born in Skopje, Albania (now in the country Macedonia) **2** Saint (1515-82); Sp. Carmelite nun: her day is Oct. 12: called **Teresa of Ávila** (ä′vē lä′)

Te·re·si·na (tā′rā zē′nä, ter′ə zē′nə) city in NE Brazil, on the Parnaíba River: capital of Piauí state

te·rete (te rēt′, ter′ēt′) ***adj.*** ⟦L *teres* (gen. *teretis*), round, smooth, orig., rubbed < *terere*, to rub: see THROW⟧ *Biol.* of or having a circular shape when cross-sectioned or a cylindrical shape that tapers at each end

Te·re·us (tē′rē əs) ***n.*** ⟦L < Gr *Tēreus*⟧ *Gr. Myth.* a king of Thrace: see PHILOMELA

ter·gi·ver·sate (tʉr′ji vər sāt′, tʉr jiv′ər sāt′) ***vi.*** **-sat′ed**, **-sat′ing** ⟦< L *tergiversatus*, pp. of *tergiversari*, to turn one's back, decline, shift < *tergum*, the back (see fol.) + *versari*, to turn < *versus*: see VERSE⟧ **1** to desert a cause, party, etc.; become a renegade; apostatize **2** to use evasions or subterfuge; equivocate —**ter′gi·ver·sa′tion** ***n.*** —**ter′gi·ver·sa′tor** ***n.***

ter·gum (tʉr′gəm) ***n.***, *pl.* **-ga** (-gə) ⟦L, the back, prob. akin to Gr *terphos*, back skin, shell, hide < IE base **(s)ter*-, stiff > START⟧ the longitudinal, dorsal surface of a body segment of most arthropods

ter·i·ya·ki (ter′ē yä′kē) ***n.*** ⟦Jpn < *teri*, nominal form of *teru*, to shine + *yaki*, nominal form of *yaku*, to broil: so called because the sauce makes the meat or fish shiny⟧ a Japanese dish consisting of meat or fish marinated or dipped in spiced soy sauce and broiled, grilled, or barbecued

term[1] (tʉrm) ***n.*** ⟦ME *terme* < OFr < L *terminus*, a limit, boundary, end < IE **termn̥*, a boundary stake < base **ter*-, to cross over, go beyond > TRANS-, Gr *terma*, goal⟧ **1** [Archaic] a point of time designating the beginning or end of a period **2** a set date, as for payment, termination of tenancy, etc. **3** a set period of time; duration; specif., *a)* a division of a school year, as a semester or quarter, during which a course of studies is given ☆*b)* the stipulated duration of an appointment to a particular office [elected to a four-year *term*] *c)* the normal elapsed period for birth after conception; also, delivery at the end of this period; parturition **4** [*pl.*] conditions of a contract, agreement, sale, etc. **5** [*pl.*] mutual relationship between or among persons; footing [on speaking *terms*] **6** a word or phrase having a limiting and definite meaning in some science, art, etc. ["tergum" is a zoological *term*] **7** any word or phrase used in a definite or precise sense; expression [a technical *term*] **8** [*pl.*] words that express ideas in a specified way [to speak in derogatory *terms*] **9** *a)* [Now Rare] a limit; boundary; extremity *b)* [*pl.*] [Obs.] conditions; circumstances **10** *Archit.* a boundary post, esp. one consisting of a pedestal topped by a bust, as of the god Terminus **11** *Law a)* the time a court is in session *b)* the length of time for which an estate is granted *c)* the estate itself *d)* time allowed a debtor to pay **12** *Logic a)* either of two concepts that have a stated relation, as the subject and predicate of a proposition *b)* any of the three elements (MAJOR TERM, MINOR TERM, MIDDLE TERM) which function variously as subjects and predicates in a syllogism **13** *Math. a)* either of the two quantities of a fraction or a ratio *b)* each of the quantities in a series or sequence *c)* each of the quantities connected by plus or minus signs in an algebraic expression —***vt.*** to call by a term; name —**bring to terms** to reduce to submission; force to agree —**come to terms** to arrive at an agreement or accommodation —**in terms of** **1** by means of **2** with reference to

term[2] *abbrev.* **1** terminal **2** termination

ter·ma·gant (tʉr′mə gənt) ***n.*** ⟦ME *Tervagant* < OFr, name of an imaginary Muslim deity prob. introduced by the Crusaders⟧ **1** [**T-**] an imaginary deity believed by medieval Christians to be worshiped by Muslims and represented in morality plays as a boisterous, overbearing figure **2** a boisterous, quarrelsome, scolding woman; shrew —***adj.*** of the nature of a termagant; quarrelsome; scolding —**ter′ma·gan·cy** ***n.*** —**ter′ma·gant·ly** ***adv.***

term·er (tʉr′mər) ***n.*** a person serving a specified term, esp. in prison: usually in hyphenated compounds [third-*termer*]

ter·mi·na·ble (tʉr′mi nə bəl) ***adj.*** **1** that can be terminated **2** that terminates after a specified time, as a contract —**ter′mi·na·bil′i·ty** ***n.***, **ter′mi·na·ble·ness** —**ter′mi·na·bly** ***adv.***

ter·mi·nal (tʉr′mə nəl) ***adj.*** ⟦L *terminalis*⟧ **1** of, at, or forming the end, extremity, or terminus of something [*terminal* feathers] **2** occurring at the end of a series; concluding; closing; final [a *terminal* payment] **3** designating, of, or having a fatal disease in its final stages [*terminal* cancer, to be diagnosed as *terminal*] **4** [Informal] extreme or excessive [*terminal* cuteness] **5** having to do with a term or established period of time; occurring regularly in each term **6** of, at, or forming the end of a transportation line **7** *Bot.* growing at the end of a stem or branch [a *terminal* bud] —*n.* **1** a terminating part; end; extremity; limit **2** a connective device or point in or attached to an electric circuit or conductor ☆**3** *a)* either end of a transportation line, as for an airplane, bus, or railroad, including servicing facilities, etc. *b)* a station or city located there *c)* a station at any important point or junction of a transportation line **4** *Archit.* an ornamental carving at the end of a structural element **5** *Comput.* a device, usually with a typewriter keyboard and a video screen, for putting information into, or getting it from, a computer, as over communication lines —**ter′mi·nal·ly** *adv.*

terminal juncture *Linguis.* any of several kinds of pause, differing in duration and sometimes very brief, occurring after various types of utterance endings [rising, falling, or sustained *terminal juncture*]

☆**terminal leave** the final leave granted to a member of the armed forces immediately before discharge, equal in duration to accumulated unused leave

terminal moraine *see* MORAINE

terminal velocity *Physics* the unchanging velocity reached by a falling body when the frictional resistance of the enveloping medium is equal to the force of gravity

ter·mi·nate (tʉr′mə nāt′) *vt.* **-nat′ed, -nat′ing** ⟦< L *terminatus,* pp. of *terminare,* to end, limit < *terminus:* see TERM[1]⟧ **1** to bring to an end in space or time; form the end or conclusion of; limit, bound, finish, or conclude **2** to put an end to; stop; cease ☆**3** to dismiss from employment; fire ☆**4** to assassinate: a euphemistic usage —*vi.* **1** to come to an end in space or time; stop; end **2** to have its end (*in* something) [a road *terminating* in woods] —**SYN.** CLOSE[2] —**ter′mi·na′tive** *adj.*

ter·mi·na·tion (tʉr′mə nā′shən) *n.* ⟦L *terminatio*⟧ **1** a terminating or being terminated **2** the end of something in space or time; limit, bound, conclusion, or finish **3** *Linguis.* the end of a word; final sound, morpheme, or syllable; specif., an inflectional ending **4** a thing's outcome or result [friendly *termination* of a dispute] —**ter′mi·na′tion·al** *adj.*

ter·mi·na·tor (tʉr′mə nāt′ər) *n.* ⟦LL(Ec)⟧ **1** a person or thing that terminates **2** the line dividing the illuminated and dark parts of the disk of the moon or a planet

ter·mi·nol·o·gy (tʉr′mə näl′ə jē) *n., pl.* **-gies** ⟦Ger *terminologie* < ML *terminus,* a term < L (see TERM[1]) + Ger *-logie,* -LOGY⟧ **1** the terms or system of terms used in a specific science, art, etc.; nomenclature [lexicographer's *terminology*] **2** the systematic study of terms —**ter′mi·no·log′i·cal** (-nə läj′i kəl) *adj.* —**ter′mi·no·log′i·cal·ly** *adv.*

term insurance life insurance which expires at the end of a specified period of time: in full **term life insurance**

ter·mi·nus (tʉr′mə nəs) *n., pl.* **-ni′** (-nī′) or **-nus·es** ⟦L: see TERM[1]⟧ **1** a boundary or limit **2** a boundary stone or marker **3** an end; final point; extremity or goal **4** [Chiefly Brit.] either end of a transportation line, or a station or town located there; terminal **5** [**T-**] *Rom. Myth.* the deity presiding over boundaries and landmarks

ter·mi·nus ad quem (tʉr′mi nəs ad kwem′, -äd-) ⟦L, end toward which⟧ a destination; conclusion; end

terminus a quo (ā kwō′, ä-) ⟦L, end from which⟧ a starting point; point of origin; beginning

ter·mi·tar·i·um (tʉr′mi ter′ē əm) *n., pl.* **-i·a** (-ē ə) ⟦< LL *termes* (gen. *termitis*), fol. + -ARIUM⟧ a termite nest, often consisting of bits of earth and vegetable matter cemented together into a large mound: often called **ter′mi·tar′y** (-ē), *pl.* **-ies**

ter·mite (tʉr′mīt′) *n.* ⟦< LL *termes* (gen. *termitis*) < L *tarmes,* wood-boring worm < base of *terere,* to rub, bore: see THROW⟧ any of an order (Isoptera) of pale-colored social insects having a soft body and living in colonies composed of winged forms that mate and wingless workers and soldiers that are usually sterile or immature: they are very destructive to wooden structures and are found in the temperate zones and esp. in the tropics

term·less (tʉrm′lis) *adj.* **1** limitless **2** unconditional

term of art a word or phrase having a particular meaning specific to an occupation or field

term·or (tʉr′mər) *n.* ⟦ME < Anglo-Fr *termer* < *terme:* see TERM[1] & -ER⟧ *Law* a person holding an estate for a certain period of years or for life

☆**term paper** a long paper or report assigned to be written by a student in a course during a school or college term

tern (tʉrn) *n.* ⟦< ON *therna,* via E Anglian dial.; akin to OE *stearna*⟧ any of several shorebirds (family Laridae) with webbed feet, a deeply forked tail, a straight bill, and a slender body; sea swallow

ter·na·ry (tʉr′nə rē) *adj.* ⟦ME < L *ternarius* < *terni,* three each < *tres,* THREE⟧ **1** made up of three parts or things; threefold; triple **2** third in order or rank **3** *Chem.* of or containing three different atoms, elements, radicals, etc. **4** *Math. a)* having three as a base *b)* involving three variables **5** *Metallurgy* of an alloy of three elements —*n., pl.* **-ries** [Rare] a group or set of three

ter·nate (tʉr′nāt′) *adj.* ⟦ModL *ternatus* < L *terni* (see prec.) + *-atus,* -ATE[1]⟧ **1** consisting of three **2** arranged in threes **3** *Bot. a)* having three leaflets *b)* growing in groups or whorls of three, as some leaves

terne·plate (tʉrn′plāt′) *n.* ⟦Fr *terne,* dull (< OHG *tarni,* hidden) + PLATE⟧ steel plate coated with an alloy of lead and a small amount of tin

Ter·ni (ter′nē) commune in central Italy, northeast of Rome

ter·pene (tʉr′pēn′) *n.* ⟦Ger *terpen* < *terp(entin),* turpentine + *-en,* -ENE⟧ **1** any of a series of isomeric, unsaturated hydrocarbons of the general formula $C_{10}H_{16}$, found in resins, essential oils, etc.: they are used in perfumes, medicines, etc. **2** any of various derivatives of the terpene hydrocarbons

ter·pin·e·ol (tər pin′ē ôl′, -ōl′) *n.* ⟦< *terpine,* $C_{10}H_{18}(OH)_2$ (< prec. + -INE[3]) + -OL[1]⟧ any of three isomeric alcohols, $C_{10}H_{17}OH$, with a lilac odor, found in certain volatile oils and used in perfumes

ter·pin hydrate (tʉr′pin) ⟦< *terpine:* see prec.⟧ a colorless, crystalline powder, $C_{10}H_{20}O_2 \cdot H_2O$, used chiefly, in the form of an elixir, as an expectorant or cough syrup

Terp·sich·o·re (tərp sik′ə rē′) *n.* ⟦Gr *Terpsichorē* < *terpsichoros,* delighting in the dance < *terpein,* to delight in + *choros,* a dance⟧ *Gr. Myth.* the Muse of the dance

terp·si·cho·re·an (tʉrp′si kə rē′ən, tʉrp′si kôr′ē ən) *adj.* **1** [**T-**] of Terpsichore **2** having to do with dancing —*n.* a dancer: now only in facetious use

terr *abbrev.* **1** terrace **2** territory

Ter·ra (ter′ə) *n.* ⟦L < IE **tersa* < base **ters-:* see THIRST⟧ *name for* the planet earth, as in science fiction

ter·ra al·ba (ter′ə al′bə) ⟦L, lit., white earth⟧ any of several white mineral substances, as *a)* finely ground gypsum, used in making paints, paper, etc. *b)* pulverized kaolin, used in ceramics *c)* MAGNESIA (sense 1)

ter·race (ter′əs) *n.* ⟦OFr, walled platform, orig., mound of earth < It *terrazzo* < *terra* < L, TERRA⟧ **1** *a)* a raised, flat mound of earth with sloping sides *b)* any of a series of flat platforms of earth with sloping sides, rising one above the other, as on a hillside *c)* a geologic formation of this nature **2** an unroofed, paved area, immediately adjacent to a house, etc. and usually overlooking a lawn or garden **3** *a)* a gallery, portico, or colonnade *b)* a usually spacious veranda; piazza **4** a small, usually roofed balcony, as outside an apartment **5** a flat roof, esp. of a house of Spanish or Middle Eastern architecture **6** *a)* a line of houses, esp. of row houses, on ground raised from the street *b)* a street in front of such houses (often used in street names) ☆**7** a parklike strip in the middle of a boulevard, etc. **8** [*usually pl.*] [Brit.] in a soccer stadium, etc., a cheaper section for standing spectators, consisting of wide, terrraced steps —*vt.* **-raced, -rac·ing** to form into, lay out in, or surround with a terrace or terraces

ter·ra cot·ta (ter′ə kät′ə) ⟦It, lit., baked earth < L *terra cocta:* see TERRA & COOK⟧ **1** a hard, brown-red, usually unglazed earthenware used for pottery, sculpture, etc. **2** its brown-red color **3** an object made of terra cotta —**ter′ra-cot′ta** *adj.*

ter·ra fir·ma (ter′ə fʉr′mə) ⟦L⟧ firm earth; solid ground

ter·rain (tə rān′) *n.* ⟦Fr < L *terrenum* < *terrenus,* of earth, earthen < *terra,* TERRA⟧ **1** ground or a tract of ground, esp. with regard to its natural or topographical features or fitness for some use **2** prevailing conditions; setting; milieu [the political *terrain* of prewar Europe] **3** *Geol.* TERRANE (sense 1)

ter·ra in·cog·ni·ta (ter′ə in käg′ni tə; *also* -in′käg nē′tə) *pl.* **ter·rae in·cog·ni·tae** (ter′ē in käg′ni tē′; *also* -in′käg nē′tē) ⟦L⟧ **1** an unknown land; unexplored territory **2** an unknown or unexplored field of knowledge

☆**Ter·ra·my·cin** (ter′ə mī′sin) ⟦< L *terra,* TERRA + MYC(O)- + -IN[1]⟧ *trademark for* OXYTETRACYCLINE

ter·rane (tə rān′, ter′ān′) *n.* ⟦Fr *terrain:* see TERRAIN⟧ *Geol.* **1** *a)* a geologic formation or series of related formations *b)* a region where a specific rock or group of rocks predominates **2** TERRAIN (sense 1)

☆**ter·ra·pin** (ter′ə pin) *n.* ⟦< dim. of earlier *torope,* tortoise < Virginia Algonquian⟧ **1** any of a family (Emydidae) of North American, terrestrial, freshwater or tidewater turtles, esp. the diamondback **2** its edible flesh

ter·ra·que·ous (ter ā′kwē əs) *adj.* ⟦< L *terra,* TERRA + AQUEOUS⟧ consisting of land and water

ter·rar·i·um (tə rer′ē əm) *n., pl.* **-i·ums** or **-i·a** (-ə) ⟦ModL < L *terra,* TERRA + *-arium,* as in *aquarium*⟧ **1** an enclosure in which to keep small land animals **2** a glass container enclosing a garden of small plants

ter·raz·zo (tə raz′ō, tə rät′sō) *n.* ⟦It, lit., TERRACE⟧ flooring made of small chips of marble set in cement and polished

Terre Haute (ter′ə hōt′) ⟦Fr, lit., high land⟧ city in W Ind., on the Wabash

ter·rene (tə rēn′, ter′ēn′) *adj.* ⟦ME < L *terrenus:* see TERRAIN⟧ **1** of earth; earthy **2** worldly; mundane —*n.* **1** the earth **2** a land or territory

terre·plein (ter′plān′) *n.* ⟦Fr < It *terrepieno* < *terrapienare,* to fill with earth, terrace < *terra* (see TERRACE) + *pienare,* to fill < L *plenus,* full: see PLENTY⟧ a level platform behind a parapet, rampart, etc., where guns are mounted

ter·res·tri·al (tə res′trē əl) *adj.* ⟦ME *terrestrialle* < L *terrestris* < *terra,* TERRA⟧ **1** of this world; worldly; earthly; mundane **2** of, constituting, or representing the earth [a *terrestrial* globe] **3** consisting of land as distinguished from water **4** living on land rather than in water, in the air, in trees, etc. **5** growing on land or in the soil **6** of the four small, rocky inner planets of the solar system, specif. Mercury, Venus, Earth, and Mars: cf. JOVIAN (sense 3) —*n.* an inhabitant of the earth —**SYN.** EARTHLY —**ter·res′tri·al·ly** *adv.*

ter·ret (ter′it) *n.* ⟦ME *teret* < OFr *toret,* dim. of *tour,* a turn < *torn* < *torner, turner,* TURN⟧ **1** a ring for attaching a chain or leash, as on a dog collar **2** any of the rings on a harness, through which the reins pass

terre-verte (ter′vert′) *n.* ⟦Fr < *terre* (< L *terra,* TERRA) + *verte,* green (see VERT[1])⟧ any of several green earths or clays containing iron silicates, used as a green pigment by artists

ter·ri·ble (ter′ə bəl) *adj.* ⟦OFr < L *terribilis* < *terrere,* to frighten: see TERROR⟧ **1** causing terror; fearful; frightful; dreadful **2** extreme; intense;

severe 3 very bad, unpleasant; disagreeable, etc.: a general term of disapproval —**ter′ri·ble·ness** *n.*

ter·ri·bly (ter′ə blē) *adv.* 1 in a terrible manner 2 extremely; very [*a terribly funny man*]

ter·ric·o·lous (te rik′ə ləs, tə-) *adj.* ⟦< L *terricola,* earth dweller < *terra,* TERRA + *colere,* to dwell, till (see CULT) + -OUS⟧ *Biol.* living in or on the ground

ter·ri·er (ter′ē ər) *n.* ⟦ME *terrere* < MFr *(chien) terrier,* hunting (dog) < *terrier,* hillock, burrow < ML *terrarius,* of earth < L *terra,* TERRA⟧ any member of several breeds of generally small and typically aggressive dog, orig. bred to rout vermin and small game animals from their lairs

Australian terrier

ter·rif·ic (tə rif′ik) *adj.* ⟦L *terrificus* < base of *terrere,* to frighten: see TERROR & -FIC⟧ 1 [Archaic] causing great fear or dismay; terrifying; dreadful; appalling 2 unusually great in degree, intensity, severity, etc. [*a terrific explosion*] 3 [Informal] unusually fine, admirable, enjoyable, etc.: a general term of approval —**ter·rif′i·cal·ly** *adv.*

ter·ri·fy (ter′ə fī′) *vt.* **-fied′**, **-fy′ing** ⟦L *terrificare* < *terrificus,* prec.⟧ to fill with terror; frighten greatly; alarm —*SYN.* AFRAID, FRIGHTEN —**ter′ri·fy′ing·ly** *adv.*

ter·rig·e·nous (te rij′ə nəs, tə-) *adj.* ⟦L *terrigenus* < *terra,* TERRA + *gignere,* to be born: see GENUS⟧ 1 earthborn 2 designating or of sea-bottom sediment derived from the erosion of land

ter·rine (te rēn′, tə-) *n.* ⟦Fr: see TUREEN⟧ 1 an earthenware dish or casserole in which a pâté or any of various similar meat or vegetable mixtures is cooked and served 2 the food so prepared

ter·ri·to·ri·al (ter′ə tôr′ē əl) *adj.* ⟦LL *territorialis*⟧ 1 of territory or land 2 of, belonging to, or limited to a specific territory, district, or jurisdictional area [*territorial waters*] ☆3 [*often* **T-**] of a Territory or Territories 4 [*often* **T-**] organized in regional groups for home defense [*the Territorial Army of Great Britain*] 5 *Zool.* characterized by or displaying territoriality —*n.* 1 a member of a territorial force 2 [**T-**] a member of the British Territorial Army —**ter′ri·to′ri·al·ly** *adv.*

ter·ri·to·ri·al·ism (-iz′əm) *n.* any territorial system —**ter′ri·to′ri·al·ist** *n.*

ter·ri·to·ri·al·i·ty (ter′ə tôr′ē al′ə tē) *n.* 1 the state or quality of being territorial 2 *Zool.* the behavior pattern exhibited by an animal in defending its territory

ter·ri·to·ri·al·ize (ter′ə tôr′ē əl īz′) *vt.* **-ized′**, **-iz′ing** 1 to add territory to 2 to establish as a territory 3 to make territorial —**ter′ri·to′ri·al·i·za′tion** *n.*

ter·ri·to·ry (ter′ə tôr′ē) *n., pl.* **-ries** ⟦ME < L *territorium* < *terra,* TERRA⟧ 1 the land and waters under the jurisdiction of a nation, state, ruler, etc. 2 a part of a country or empire that does not have the full status of a principal division; specif., ☆*a)* [*also* **T-**] a part of the U.S. having its own legislature but without the status of a state and under the administration of an appointed governor *b)* [*also* **T-**] a similar region, as in Canada or Australia, without the status of a province or state: see also TRUST TERRITORY 3 any large tract of land; region; district ☆4 an assigned area, as of a traveling salesman or franchised dealer 5 any specified area or region [*foul territory in a ballpark*] 6 a sphere or province of action, existence, thought, etc. 7 the particular area occupied by an animal or group of animals; esp., the specific area appropriated by an animal or pair of animals, usually for breeding, nesting, and foraging purposes, and forcibly defended against by any intruders 8 *Football, Hockey, etc.* that half of the playing area defended by a specified team

ter·ror (ter′ər) *n.* ⟦ME *terrour* < MFr *terreur* < L *terror* < *terrere,* to frighten < IE **ters-,* to tremble (> Gr *trein,* to tremble, flee) < base **ter-,* to wriggle⟧ 1 intense fear 2 *a)* a person or thing causing intense fear *b)* the quality of causing such fear; terribleness 3 a program of terrorism or a party, group, etc. resorting to terrorism 4 [Informal] a very annoying or unmanageable person, esp. a child; nuisance; pest —*SYN.* FEAR —**the Terror** REIGN OF TERROR

ter·ror·ism (ter′ər iz′əm) *n.* ⟦Fr *terrorisme*⟧ 1 the act of terrorizing; use of force or threats to demoralize, intimidate, and subjugate, esp. such use as a political weapon or policy 2 the demoralization and intimidation produced in this way —**ter′ror·ist** *n., adj.* —**ter′ror·is′tic** *adj.*

ter·ror·ize (ter′ər īz′) *vt.* **-ized′**, **-iz′ing** 1 to fill with terror; terrify 2 to coerce, make submit, etc. by filling with terror, as by the use or threat of violence —*SYN.* FRIGHTEN —**ter′ror·i·za′tion** *n.*

ter·ror-strick·en (-strik′ən) *adj.* overcome with terror

ter·ry (ter′ē) *n., pl.* **-ries** ⟦prob. < Fr *tiré,* pp. of *tirer,* to draw < VL **tirare*⟧ 1 uncut loops forming the pile of some fabrics 2 cloth having a pile of such loops; esp., cotton cloth used for toweling: also **terry cloth**

Ter·ry[1] (ter′ē) *n.* 1 a masculine name: see TERENCE[1] 2 a feminine name: var. *Terri:* see THERESA

Ter·ry[2] (ter′ē), Dame **Ellen (Alice** or **Alicia)** 1848-1928; Eng. actress

terse (turs) *adj.* **ters′er**, **ters′est** ⟦L *tersus,* wiped off, clean, pp. of *tergere,* to wipe < IE **terg-* < base **ter-,* to rub, turn: see THROW⟧ 1 free of superfluous words; concise in a polished, smooth way; succinct 2 brief or concise to the point of rudeness; curt —*SYN.* CONCISE —**terse′ly** *adv.* —**terse′ness** *n.*

ter·tial (tur′shəl) *adj.* ⟦< L *tertius,* THIRD + -AL⟧ designating or of the flight feathers, forming the third row, on the basal part of a bird's wing —*n.* a tertial feather

ter·tian (tur′shən) *adj.* ⟦ME *tercian* < L *(febris) tertiana,* tertian (fever) < *tertius,* THIRD⟧ occurring every other day so that it happens on the first and third days: usually applied to fever or a disease causing it, esp. any of certain forms of malaria —*n.* a tertian fever or disease

ter·ti·ar·y (tur′shē er′ē, -shə rē) *adj.* ⟦L *tertiarius* < *tertius,* THIRD⟧ 1 of the third rank, order, formation, stage, etc.; third 2 *Chem. a)* third in order or type; involving the substitution of three atoms or radicals *b)* characterized by or designating a carbon atom or group attached to three other carbon atoms or groups in a chain or ring 3 [*usually* **T-**] *Geol.* designating or of the former first geologic period of the Cenozoic Era, characterized by the formation of major mountain ranges, the first grasses and grasslands, and the development of mammals as the dominant animal: now divided into the Paleogene and Neogene periods 4 *Linguis. a)* designating, of, or being the third strongest of the four phonemic degrees of stress *b)* a mark used to indicate this 5 *R.C.Ch.* of a Third Order: see THIRD ORDER 6 *Zool.* TERTIAL —*n., pl.* **-ar′ies** 1 *R.C.Ch.* a member of a Third Order 2 *Zool.* TERTIAL —**the Tertiary** the Tertiary Period or its rocks: see the geologic time chart in the Reference Supplement

ter·ti·um quid (tur′shē əm kwid′) ⟦L, lit., third something⟧ something of uncertain or unclassifiable nature, related to, but distinct from, two, usually opposite, things

Ter·tul·li·an (tər tul′ē ən, -tul′yen) (L. name *Quintus Septimius Florens Tertullianus*) A.D. 160?-230?; Rom. church father, born in Carthage

ter·va·lent (tər vā′lənt) *adj.* ⟦L *ter,* thrice (akin to *tres,* THREE) + -VALENT⟧ TRIVALENT: see -VALENT

Ter·y·lene (ter′i lēn′) ⟦former trademark; arbitrary blend of *terephthalate* (< TEREPHTHALIC ACID + -ATE[2]) & POLYETHYLENE⟧ *trademark for* a synthetic, polyester textile fiber, used in making suits, shirts, rainwear, etc. —*n.* [*also* **t-**] this fiber, or fabric made from it

ter·za ri·ma (tert′sə rē′mə) ⟦It, lit., third rhyme⟧ a verse form of Italian origin, made up of tercets, the second line of each tercet rhyming with the first and third lines of the next one (*aba, bcb, cdc,* etc.)

TESL *abbrev.* teaching English as a second language

tes·la (tes′lə) *n.* ⟦after fol.⟧ the basic unit of magnetic flux density in the SI and MKS systems, equal to one weber per square meter (10,000 gauss): abbrev. *T*

Tes·la (tes′lə), **Ni·ko·la** (nik′ə lə) 1856-1943; U.S. inventor, born in Croatia

tes·sel·late (tes′ə lāt′; *for adj.,* -lit, -lāt′) *vt.* **-lat′ed**, **-lat′ing** ⟦< L *tessellatus* < *tessella,* little square stone, dim. of *tessera,* a square: see fol.⟧ to lay out, inlay, or pave in a mosaic pattern of small, square blocks —*adj.* arranged in a mosaic pattern; tessellated —**tes′sel·la′tion** (-lā′shən) *n.*

tes·ser·a (tes′ər ə) *n., pl.* **-ser·ae′** (-ē′) ⟦L, square piece, cube < Gr (Ionic) *tesseres* (for *tessares*), four: see TETRA-⟧ 1 in ancient Rome, a small tablet of wood, ivory, etc. used as a token, ticket, label, etc. 2 any of the small pieces used in mosaic work

Tes·sin (*Fr* tā san′; *Ger* te sēn′) *Fr. & Ger. name for* TICINO

tes·si·tu·ra (tes′i toor′ə; *It* tes′sē tōō′rä) *n., pl.* **-ras** ⟦It, lit., texture < L *textura,* TEXTURE⟧ *Music* the register that encompasses most of the notes of a specific composition or part, esp. for the voice; also, a voice in relation to such a register

test[1] (test) *n.* ⟦ME, a cupel < OFr, a pot, cupel < L *testum,* earthen vessel < *testa,* piece of burned clay, shell < IE base **tekth-,* to weave, join > Sans *tašta,* cup, Gr *tektōn,* carpenter: mod. meaning from use of the cupel in examining metals⟧ 1 [Archaic] CUPEL (sense 1) 2 an examination, experiment, or trial, as to prove the value or ascertain the nature of something 3 *a)* a method, process, or means used in making such an examination or trial *b)* a standard or criterion by which the qualities of a thing are tried *c)* an oath or declaration required as proof of one's orthodoxy, loyalty, etc. 4 an event, set of circumstances, etc. that proves or tries a person's qualities [*the delay was a test of our patience*] 5 a set of questions, problems, or exercises for determining a person's knowledge, abilities, aptitude, or qualifications; examination 6 *Chem. a)* a trial or reaction for identifying a substance or ingredient *b)* the reagent used in the procedure *c)* a positive indication obtained by it —*vt.* 1 to refine (metal), as in a cupel 2 to subject to a test; try 3 *Chem.* to examine by means of a reagent or reagents —*vi.* 1 to give or undergo a diagnostic test or a test of quality, function, etc.: usually with *for* [*to test for blood sugar*] 2 to be rated as the result of a test [*to test high in comprehension*] —*SYN.* TRIAL —**test′a·ble** *adj.*

test[2] (test) *n.* ⟦L *testa:* see prec.⟧ the hard outer covering of certain invertebrate animals, as the shell of clams

Test *abbrev.* Testament

tes·ta (tes′tə) *n., pl.* **-tae** (-tē) ⟦ModL < L: see TEST[1]⟧ *Bot.* the hard outer covering or integument of a seed

tes·ta·ceous (tes tā′shəs) *adj.* ⟦L *testaceus,* consisting of brick, tile, or shell < *testa:* see TEST[1]⟧ 1 of, like, or from shells 2 having a hard shell 3 *Biol.* of the color of unglazed earthenware; light reddish-brown

tes·ta·cy (tes′tə sē) *n.* *Law* the state of being testate

tes·ta·ment (tes′tə mənt) *n.* ⟦OFr < LL(Ec) *testamentum,* Testament (in N.T., transl. of Gr *diathēkē,* covenant) < L, a will < *testari,* to testify, make a will < *testis,* a witness: see TESTIFY⟧ 1 [Obs.] a covenant, esp. one between God and man 2 [**T-**] *a)* either of the two parts of the Christian Bible, the *Old Testament* and the *New Testament* *b)* [Informal] a copy of the New Testament 3 *a)* a statement, act, etc. testifying to the fact, validity, or worth of something; testimonial [a *testament* to liberty] *b)* an affirmation of beliefs or convictions; profession [a freethinker's *testament*] **4** *Law* a will: now rare except in the phrase **last will and testament** —**tes′ta·men′ta·ry** (-men′tə rē) *adj.*, **tes′ta·men′tal**

tes·tate (tes′tāt′) *adj.* ⟦LME < L *testatus,* pp. of *testari:* see prec.⟧ having made and left a legally valid will —*n.* a person who has died testate

tes·ta·tor (tes′tāt′ər, tes tāt′-) *n.* ⟦ME *testatour* < L *testator* < pp. of *testari:* see TESTAMENT⟧ a person who has made a will, esp. one who has died leaving a valid will

tes·ta·trix (tes tā′triks) *n., pl.* **-tri·ces′** (-tri sēz′) a female testator

test ban an agreement between or among nuclear powers to forgo tests of nuclear weapons, esp. in the atmosphere

test case *Law* **1** a case that, after its determination, is likely to be used as a precedent ☆**2** a case entered into with the intention of testing the constitutionality of a particular law

test-drive (test′drīv′) *vt.* **-drove′** (-drōv′), **-driv′en** (-driv′ən), **-driv′ing 1** to drive (a motor vehicle) under actual operating conditions for the purpose of evaluation, as before a purchase **2** to test the performance of under actual operating conditions —*n.* any testing under actual operating conditions Also written **test drive**

test·ee (tes tē′) *n.* ⟦TEST[1] + -EE[1]⟧ a person who has been or is being tested

test·er[1] (tes′tər) *n.* a person or thing that tests

tes·ter[2] (tes′tər) *n.* ⟦ME *testere* < OFr *testiere,* headpiece, crown of a hat < *teste,* the head < L *testa:* see TEST[1]⟧ a canopy, as over a bed

tes·ter[3] (tes′tər) *n.* ⟦altered < MFr *testart* < *teston,* TESTON + *-art,* -ARD⟧ TESTON (sense *b*)

tes·tes (tes′tēz′) *n. pl. of* TESTIS

tes·ti·cle (tes′ti kəl) *n.* ⟦L *testiculus,* dim. of *testis,* testicle, lit., witness (to virility): see TESTIFY⟧ either of two oval sex glands in the male that are suspended in the scrotum and secrete spermatozoa; testis —**tes·tic′u·lar** (-tik′yoo lər) *adj.*

tes·tic·u·late (tes tik′yoo lit, -lāt′) *adj.* ⟦< L *testiculus* (see prec.) + -ATE[1]⟧ *Bot.* **1** shaped like a testicle **2** having two testicle-shaped tubers, as certain orchids

tes·ti·fy (tes′tə fī′) *vi.* **-fied′**, **-fy′ing** ⟦ME *testifien* < L *testificari* < *testis,* a witness (prob. < **tri-sto-,* standing as a third < *tri-,* TRI- + base of *stare,* STAND) + *facere,* to make, DO[1]⟧ **1** to make a serious declaration to substantiate a fact; bear witness or give evidence, esp. under oath in court **2** to be evidence or an indication [a look *testifying* to his impatience] —*vt.* **1** to bear witness to; affirm; declare, esp. under oath in court **2** to be evidence of; indicate **3** [Archaic] to profess or proclaim publicly —**tes′ti·fi·ca′tion** *n.* —**tes′ti·fi′er** *n.*

tes·ti·mo·ni·al (tes′tə mō′nē əl) *n.* ⟦OFr < LL *testimonialis* < *testimonium:* see fol.⟧ **1** a statement testifying to a person's qualifications, character, etc. or to the merits of some product, service, etc.; letter or statement of recommendation **2** something given or done as an expression of gratitude or appreciation —*adj.* of or having to do with testimony or a testimonial

tes·ti·mo·ny (tes′tə mō′nē) *n., pl.* **-nies** ⟦ME < L *testimonium* < *testis,* a witness: see TESTIFY⟧ **1** a declaration or statement made under oath or affirmation by a witness in a court, often in response to questioning, to establish a fact **2** any affirmation or declaration **3** any form of evidence, indication, etc.; proof [the smile that was *testimony* of disbelief] **4** public avowal, as of faith or of a religious experience **5** *Bible a)* the tablet bearing the Mosaic law; Decalogue: Ex. 25:16 *b)* [*pl.*] the precepts of God —**SYN.** PROOF

tes·tis (tes′tis) *n., pl.* **-tes′** (-tēz′) ⟦L⟧ TESTICLE

test-mar·ket (test′mär′kit) *vt.* to test potential sales of (a product) by offering it in a limited number of small markets

test match any of a series of cricket or rugby matches played by a team representing one nation against a team representing another nation

tes·ton (tes′tən) *n.* ⟦Fr < It *testone* < *testa,* the head < L *testa:* see TEST[1]⟧ any of several old European coins with the image of a head on one side; specif., *a)* a silver French coin of the 16th century *b)* an English coin with the head of Henry VIII Also **tes·toon′** (-to͞on′)

tes·tos·ter·one (tes täs′tər ōn′) *n.* ⟦TEST(IS) + -O- + STER(OL) + -ONE⟧ a steroidal male sex hormone, $C_{19}H_{28}O_2$, produced as a white, crystalline substance by isolation from animal testes, or synthesized: used in medicine

test paper 1 a paper on which a test has been written **2** paper, as litmus paper, prepared with a reagent for making chemical tests

test pattern a standard pattern of lines, colors, etc. broadcast by a TV station, used to evaluate or adjust individual TV receivers for image quality

test pilot a pilot who tests new or newly designed airplanes in flight, to determine their fitness for use

test tube a tube of thin, transparent glass closed at one end, used in chemical experiments, etc.

test-tube (test′to͞ob′, -tyo͞ob′) *adj.* **1** made in or as in a test tube; experimental **2** produced by in vitro fertilization [a *test-tube* baby]

tes·tu·di·nal (tes to͞od′'n əl, -tyo͞od′-) *adj.* ⟦< L *testudineus* < *testudo* (see TESTUDO) + -AL⟧ of or like a tortoise or its shell; testudinate: also **tes·tu′di·nar′i·ous** (-er′ē əs)

tes·tu·di·nate (tes to͞od′'n it, -tyo͞od′'n-; -āt′) *adj.* ⟦LL *testudinatus:* see fol.⟧ **1** arched or vaulted like a tortoise shell **2** having a protective bony shell, as the turtle —*n.* a turtle

tes·tu·do (tes to͞o′dō, -tyo͞o′-) *n., pl.* **-di·nes′** (-di nēz′) ⟦L, tortoise, tortoise shell, hence protective covering, shed < *testa,* shell: see TEST[2]⟧ **1** a movable shelter or screen with a strong arched roof, used as a protection by ancient Roman soldiers **2** a protective covering over a group of ancient Roman soldiers, formed by overlapping their shields above their heads

tes·ty (tes′tē) *adj.* **-ti·er**, **-ti·est** ⟦ME *testif* < Anglo-Fr < OFr *teste,* the head < L *testa:* see TEST[1]⟧ irritable; touchy; peevish —**tes′ti·ly** *adv.* —**tes′ti·ness** *n.*

tet (tet) *n. alt. sp. of* TETH

Tet (tet) *n.* ⟦Vietnamese *tết*⟧ Vietnamese lunar New Year's festival, celebrated in late January or early February

te·tan·ic (te tan′ik) *adj.* ⟦L *tetanicus* < Gr *tetanikos* < *tetanos,* a spasm: see TETANUS⟧ of, like, characterized by, or producing tetanus —*n.* any drug, as strychnine, capable of producing tetanic spasms of the muscles

tet·a·nize (tet′'n īz′) *vt.* **-nized′**, **-niz′ing** to produce tetanic spasms in (a muscle)

tet·a·nus (tet′'n əs, tet′nəs) *n.* ⟦L < Gr *tetanos,* spasm (of muscles), lit., stretched < base of *teinein:* see THIN⟧ **1** an acute infectious disease, often fatal, caused by the specific toxin of a bacterium (*Clostridium tetani*) which usually enters the body through wounds: it is characterized by spasmodic contractions and rigidity of some or all of the voluntary muscles, esp. of the jaw, face, and neck; lockjaw **2** *Physiol.* the state of continuous contraction of a muscle, esp. when caused experimentally by a series of rapidly repeated stimuli

tet·a·ny (tet′'n ē) *n.* ⟦ModL *tetania:* see prec.⟧ an abnormal condition characterized by tetanic spasms of voluntary muscles, esp. in the extremities

te·tar·to- (tə tärt′ə) ⟦< Gr *tetartos,* fourth, akin to *tetra:* see TETRA-⟧ *combining form* **1** one fourth part of [*tetartohedral*] **2** the fourth of a set, as the fourth cusp on an upper molar [*tetartocone*]

te·tar·to·he·dral (tə tärt′ə hē′drəl) *adj.* ⟦prec. + -HEDRAL⟧ having one fourth of the planes needed for crystallographic symmetry of the system

tetched (techt) *adj.* ⟦LME *techyd,* prob. altered (infl. by *teche,* a quality, mark: see fol.) < *touchede,* pp. of *touchen,* TOUCH⟧ [Dial.] touched; slightly demented: also used humorously

tetch·y (tech′ē) *adj.* **tetch′i·er**, **tetch′i·est** ⟦< LME *teche,* touchy, prob. < ME, a mark, quality < OFr, spot, mark < VL **tecca* < Frank **tekka* < **tēkan;* akin to OE *tacn,* TOKEN⟧ touchy; irritable; peevish —**tetch′i·ly** *adv.* —**tetch′i·ness** *n.*

tête-à-tête (tāt′ə tāt′, tet′ə tet′; *Fr* te tȧ tet′) *n.* ⟦Fr, lit., head-to-head⟧ **1** a private or intimate conversation between two people ☆**2** a usually S-shaped seat on which two people can sit so as to face each other —*adj.* for or of two people in private —*adv.* together privately [to speak *tête-à-tête*]

tête-bêche (tet′besh′) *adj.* ⟦Fr < *tête,* head + *bêche,* contr. < *béchevet,* the head of one at the feet of the other (in bed)⟧ designating a pair of postage stamps printed, purposely or in error, so that one is inverted in relation to the other

teth (tet) *n.* ⟦Heb *ṭēth*⟧ the ninth letter of the Hebrew alphabet (ט)

teth·er (teth′ər) *n.* ⟦ME < ON *tjōthr,* akin to OHG *zeotar,* wagon shaft⟧ **1** a rope, cord, etc. fastened to something to prevent drifting, escape, etc.; specif., a rope or chain fastened to an animal so as to keep it within certain bounds **2** the limit of one's abilities, resources, etc. —*vt.* to fasten or confine with a tether —**at the end of one's tether** at the end of one's endurance, resources, etc.

☆**teth·er·ball** (teth′ər bôl′) *n.* **1** a game played by two people who, using the hand or a paddle, hit from opposite directions at a ball hanging by a length of a cord from a pole: the object of the game is to make the cord coil completely around the pole **2** the ball so used

Te·thys[1] (tē′this) *n.* ⟦L < Gr *Tēthys*⟧ **1** *Gr. Myth.* a daughter of Uranus and wife of Oceanus, by whom she is the mother of the Oceanides **2** a satellite of Saturn having long trenchlike valleys and sharing its orbit with other satellites

Te·thys[2] (tē′this) any of various ancient seas and geosynclines, esp. any of those of the Mesozoic and early Cenozoic eras that separated Laurasia from Gondwana

Te·ton (tē′tän′) *n., pl.* **-tons′** or **-ton′** ⟦Dakota *tʰitʰuⁿwaⁿ*⟧ **1** LAKOTA (*n.* 1) **2** LAKOTA (*n.* 2)

Te·tons (tē′tänz′, -tənz) *see* GRAND TETONS

tet·ra (te′trə) *n.* ⟦contr. < ModL *Tetragonopterus,* old genus designation < *tetragonum,* TETRAGON + *-pterus,* -PTEROUS⟧ any of a number of brightly colored, tropical American, characin fishes, often kept in aquariums

tet·ra- (te′trə) ⟦Gr *tetra-* < base of *tettares, tessares,* four < IE base **kwetwer-* > FOUR⟧ *combining form* four [*tetrachord*]: also, before a vowel, **tetr-**

tet·ra·bas·ic (te′trə bā′sik) *adj.* ⟦prec. + BASIC⟧ designating or of an acid having four replaceable hydrogen atoms per molecule

tet·ra·bran·chi·ate (te′trə braŋ′kē it, -āt′) *adj.* ⟦ModL *tetrabranchiatus:* see TETRA-, BRANCHIAE, & -ATE[1]⟧ having two pairs of gills: said of nautiloid cephalopods: opposed to DIBRANCHIATE

tet·ra·chlo·ride (te′trə klôr′īd′) *n.* any chemical compound with four chlorine atoms to the molecule

tet·ra·chord (te′trə kôrd′) *n.* ⟦Gr *tetrachordon,* musical instrument < *tetrachordos,* four-stringed: see TETRA- & CHORD[2]⟧ *Music* a series of four tones contained in the interval of a perfect fourth —**tet′ra·chor′dal** *adj.*

te·trac·id (te tras′id) *n.* ⟦TETR(A)- + ACID⟧ **1** a base that can react with four molecules of a monobasic acid to form a salt **2** an alcohol having four OH groups per molecule

tet·ra·cy·cline (te′trə sī′klēn′, -klin) *n.* ⟦TETRA- + CYCL(IC) + -INE[3]⟧ a yellow, odorless, crystalline powder, $C_{22}H_{24}N_2O_8$, prepared synthetically or obtained from certain streptomyces: it is a broad-spectrum antibiotic

tet·rad (te′trad′) ***n.*** ⟦Gr *tetras* (gen. *tetrados*), four: see TETRA-⟧ **1** a group or set of four **2** *Bot.* a group of four cells formed by division within a spore mother cell during meiosis **3** *Chem.* an atom, radical, or element that is tetravalent **4** *Genetics* a group of four similar chromatids formed by the longitudinal division of a pair of homologous chromosomes during meiotic prophase

te·trad·y·mite (te trad′i mīt′) ***n.*** ⟦Ger *tetradymit* < Gr *tetradymos,* fourfold (because it occurs in compound twin crystals) + Ger *-it,* -ITE[1]⟧ a pale steel-gray mineral, Bi_2Te_2S, consisting chiefly of tellurium and bismuth

☆**tet·ra·eth·yl lead** (te′trə eth′əl) a heavy, colorless, poisonous compound of lead, $Pb(C_2H_5)_4$, added to gasoline to increase power and prevent engine knock

tet·ra·gon (te′trə gän′) ***n.*** ⟦LL *tetragonum* < Gr *tetragōnon:* see TETRA- & -GON⟧ a plane figure with four angles and four sides; quadrangle

te·trag·o·nal (te trag′ə nəl) ***adj.*** **1** of, or having the form of, a tetragon; quadrangular **2** designating or of a crystal system having three axes that intersect at right angles with one another, two of which are of equal length: see CRYSTAL SYSTEM

tet·ra·gram (te′trə gram′) ***n.*** ⟦Gr *tetragrammon:* see TETRA- & -GRAM⟧ a word of four letters

Tet·ra·gram·ma·ton (te′trə gram′ə tän′) ***n.*** ⟦ME < Gr *tetragrammaton* < *tetra-,* four + *gramma,* a letter: see GRAM[1]⟧ the four consonants of the ancient Hebrew name for God (variously transliterated JHVH, IHVH, JHWH, YHVH, YHWH), that was considered too sacred to be spoken aloud: the word *Adonai* (Lord) is substituted for this name when spoken by Orthodox Jews, and the vowels of *Adonai* or *Elohim* (God) are inserted in Hebrew texts, thus prompting the modern reconstructions *Yahweh, Jehovah,* etc.

tet·ra·he·dral (te′trə hē′drəl) ***adj.*** of, or having the form of, a tetrahedron —**tet′ra·he′dral·ly** ***adv.***

tet·ra·he·drite (te′trə hē′drīt′) ***n.*** ⟦Ger *tetraëdrit* < LGr *tetraedros* (see fol.) + *-it,* -ITE[1]⟧ a gray to black, semihard, cubic mineral, copper iron antimony sulfide, $(Cu,Fe)_{12}Sb_4S_{13}$, that is a main ore of copper

tet·ra·he·dron (te′trə hē′drən) ***n.,*** *pl.* **-drons** or **-dra** (-drə) ⟦ModL < neut. of LGr *tetraedros,* four-sided: see TETRA- & -HEDRON⟧ a solid figure with four triangular faces

tet·ra·hy·dro·can·na·bi·nol (te′trə hī′drō kə nab′i nôl′) ***n.*** ⟦TETRA- + HYDRO- + CANNABIN + -OL[1]⟧ the hallucinatory chemical, $C_{21}H_{30}O_2$, that is the principal and most active ingredient in marijuana; THC

te·tral·o·gy (te tral′ə jē) ***n.,*** *pl.* **-gies** ⟦Gr *tetralogia:* see TETRA- & -LOGY⟧ **1** a series of four dramas, three tragic and one satirical, performed in sequence at the ancient Athenian festival of Dionysus **2** any series of four related plays, novels, etc.

te·tram·er·ous (te tram′ər əs) ***adj.*** ⟦TETRA- + -MEROUS⟧ *Biol.* made up of four parts or divisions; in multiples of four

te·tram·e·ter (te tram′ət ər) ***n.*** ⟦LL *tetrametrus* < Gr *tetrametros:* see TETRA- & METER[1]⟧ **1** a line of verse containing four metrical feet or measures **2** verse consisting of tetrameters —***adj.*** having four metrical feet or measures

tet·ra·pet·al·ous (te′trə pet′′l əs) ***adj.*** four-petaled

tet·ra·ploid (te′trə ploid′) ***adj.*** ⟦TETRA- + -PLOID⟧ *Biol.* having four times the haploid number of chromosomes —***n.*** a tetraploid cell or organism —**tet′ra·ploi′dy** ***n.***

tet·ra·pod (te′trə päd′) ***n.*** ⟦TETRA- + -POD⟧ any vertebrate having four legs or limbs, including the mammals, birds, and reptiles: snakes, whales, etc. are included in this group because they evolved from four-legged animals

te·trap·ter·ous (te trap′tər əs) ***adj.*** ⟦Gr *tetrapteros:* see TETRA- & -PTEROUS⟧ *Zool.* having four wings

te·trarch (te′trärk′, tē′-) ***n.*** ⟦ME *tetrarche* < LL(Ec) *tetrarcha* < L *tetrarches* < Gr *tetrarchēs:* see TETRA- & -ARCH⟧ **1** in the ancient Roman Empire, the ruler of part (orig. a fourth part) of a province **2** a subordinate prince, governor, etc. —**te·trar′chic** (-trär′kik) ***adj.***

te·trar·chy (te′trär′kē, tē′-) ***n.,*** *pl.* **-chies** ⟦L *tetrarchia* < Gr⟧ **1** the rule or territory of a tetrarch **2** government by four persons Also **te·trar·chate** (te′trär kāt′, tē′-; -kit)

tet·ra·spo·ran·gi·um (te′trə spō ran′jē əm) ***n.,*** *pl.* **-gi·a** (-ə) *Bot.* a sporangium containing four haploid spores

tet·ra·spore (te′trə spôr′) ***n.*** *Bot.* any of the asexual algal spores produced in groups of four by meiosis in a tetrasporangium

tet·ra·stich (te′trə stik′) ***n.*** ⟦L *tetrastichon* < Gr: see TETRA- & STICH⟧ a poem or stanza of four lines

te·tras·ti·chous (te tras′ti kəs) ***adj.*** ⟦Gr *tetrastichos,* in four rows: see TETRA- & STICH⟧ *Bot.* in four vertical rows, as the flowers on some spikes

tet·ra·syl·la·ble (te′trə sil′ə bəl) ***n.*** a word of four syllables —**tet′ra·syl·lab′ic** (-si lab′ik) ***adj.***

tet·ra·tom·ic (te′trə täm′ik) ***adj.*** **1** designating or of a molecule consisting of four atoms **2** having four replaceable atoms or groups

tet·ra·va·lent (te′trə vā′lənt) ***adj.*** **1** having four valences **2** having a valence of four See -VALENT

te·traz·zi·ni (te′trə zē′nē) ***adj.*** ⟦after L. *Tetrazzini* (1871-1940), Ital soprano⟧ [*also* **T-**] diced and combined with noodles, mushrooms, and cream sauce, then topped with grated Parmesan cheese and browned in the oven [*turkey tetrazzini*]

tet·ri (tet′rē) ***n.,*** *pl.* **-ri** or **-ris** ⟦Georgian⟧ a monetary unit of Georgia, equal to 1/100 of a lari

tet·rode (te′trōd′) ***n.*** ⟦TETR(A)- + -ODE[1]⟧ an electron tube that has four electrodes (a cathode, anode, and two grids), used to generate, amplify, modulate, or demodulate electrical signals

tet·ro·do·tox·in (te′trə dō täk′sin) ***n.*** ⟦< ModL *Tetrodon,* a genus of fishes (short for *tetraodon* < *tetra-,* TETRA- + Gr *odōn,* TOOTH) + TOXIN⟧ an extremely poisonous neurotoxin, $C_{11}H_{17}N_3O_8$, found in the puffer fishes and a genus (*Taricha*) of newts, that blocks the conduction of nerve signals

te·trox·ide (te träk′sīd′) ***n.*** any oxide with four atoms of oxygen in each molecule

tet·ryl (te′trəl) ***n.*** ⟦*tetr(anitrometh)yl(aniline)*⟧ a yellow powder, $C_7H_5N_5O_8$, used as a primer and as an explosive, esp. in detonators

tet·ter (tet′ər) ***n.*** ⟦ME *tetere* < OE *teter,* akin to Sans *dadru,* skin disease < IE **dedru-,* redupl. of base **der-,* to skin > TEAR[1]⟧ any of various skin diseases, as eczema, characterized by itching

Te·tu·án (te′to͞o än′, -twän′) seaport in NE Morocco, on the Mediterranean: former cap. of Spanish Morocco

Tet·zel (tet′səl), **Jo·hann** (yō′hän′) 1465?-1519; Ger. Dominican monk & inquisitor: opposed by Luther

Teut *abbrev.* **1** Teuton **2** Teutonic

Teu·to·burg Forest (to͞ot′ə bʉrg′, tyo͞ot′-) region of low, forested mountains, mostly in North Rhine-Westphalia, Germany: highest point, *c.* 1,500 ft (457 m): Ger. name **Teu·to·bur·ger Wald** (toi′tô bo͝or′gər vält′)

Teu·ton (to͞ot′′n, tyo͞ot′′n; to͞o′tän′, tyo͞o′-) ***n.*** **1** a member of the Teutones **2** a member of any Teutonic people; esp., a German

Teu·to·nes (to͞ot′′n ēz′, tyo͞ot′-) ***pl.n.*** ⟦L < IE **teutonos,* ruler < **teutā,* people, crowd: see DEUTSCHLAND⟧ the members of an ancient people, variously thought to have spoken a Germanic or a Celtic language, that lived north of the Elbe in Jutland

Teu·ton·ic (to͞o tän′ik, tyo͞o-) ***adj.*** **1** of the ancient Teutones **2** of the Germans; German **3** GERMANIC (*adj.* 2) **4** *Linguis. former term for* GERMANIC —**Teu·ton′i·cal·ly** ***adv.***

Teutonic Order a military and religious order of German knights (**Teutonic Knights**) organized in 1191 for service in the Crusades and later active in the military conquests by Germany of Baltic and Slavic lands

Teu·ton·ism (to͞ot′′n iz′əm, tyo͞ot′-) ***n.*** **1** belief in the supposed racial superiority of the Teutons, esp. of the Germans **2** Teutonic culture **3** a Germanism Also **Teu·ton·i·cism** (to͞o tän′ə siz′əm, tyo͞o-) —**Teu′ton·ist** ***n.***

Teu·ton·ize (-īz′) ***vt., vi.*** **-ized′, -iz′ing** to make or become Teutonic or German —**Teu′ton·i·za′tion** ***n.***

TeV or **Tev** *abbrev.* tera-electron-volt

Te·ve·re (te′ve re) *It. name for the* TIBER

Te·vet (tā vāt′, tā′vəs) ***n.*** ⟦Heb *tēbhēth*⟧ the fourth month of the Jewish year: see the Jewish calendar in the Reference Supplement

Te·wa (tē′wə, tā′-) ***n.*** ⟦self-designation in Tewa⟧ **1** *pl.* **-was** or **-wa** a member of any of seven North American Indian groups living in pueblo villages (six in New Mexico and one in Arizona) **2** the Tanoan language of the Tewas

Tewkes·bur·y (to͞oks′ber′ē, tyo͞oks′-; -bə rē) town in N Gloucestershire, England, on the Severn: site of a battle (1471) in the Wars of the Roses, reestablishing Edward IV on the English throne

Tex *abbrev.* Texas

Tex·an (tek′sən) ***adj.*** of Texas: usually used in the predicate —***n.*** a person born or living in Texas

Tex·ar·kan·a (tek′sär kan′ə, tek′sər-) ⟦< TEX(AS), ARK(ANSAS), (LOUISI)ANA⟧ city on the Texas-Arkansas border, having a separate municipal government in each state

tex·as (tek′səs) ☆***n.*** ⟦after fol.: from the name given to officers' quarters on Mississippi steamboats because they were the largest cabins, as Texas was the largest state⟧ a structure on the hurricane deck of a river steamboat, containing the officers' quarters and having the pilothouse atop or immediately in front of it

Tex·as (tek′səs) ⟦Sp *Texas,* earlier pronounced (te′shäs), orig. an ethnic name < Caddo *tayša,* friends, allies⟧ state of the SW U.S., on the Gulf of Mexico & the Mexican border: admitted 1845; 261,797 sq mi (678,052 sq km); cap. Austin: abbrev. *TX* or *Tex*

☆**Texas fever** an infectious disease of cattle caused by various sporozoans (genus *Babesia*) that invade the red blood cells and are carried by various ticks (esp. genus *Boophilus*); babesiosis

☆**Texas hold 'em** a variety of poker in which each player forms the best possible hand from any combination of two cards dealt face down to that player and five cards dealt face up and shared by all players

☆**Texas leaguer** ⟦after the *Texas* (baseball) *League*⟧ *Baseball* a fly ball that falls in fair territory between the infield and outfield

☆**Texas Ranger** any member of a division (**Texas Rangers**) of the Texas state police

☆**Texas tower** ⟦so named after such structures, orig. for oil drilling, off the coast of TEXAS⟧ an offshore platform erected on firm foundations or steel legs planted deeply in the sea bottom: used for supporting radar installations, navigation beacons, etc.

☆**Tex-Mex** (teks′meks′) ***adj.*** characterized by both Mexican and SW American (esp. Texan) elements, influences, etc. [*Tex-Mex* cooking]

text (tekst) ***n.*** ⟦ME < OFr *texte* < L *textus,* fabric, structure, text < pp. of *texere,* to weave: see TECHNIC⟧ **1** the actual structure of words in a piece of writing; wording **2** *a)* the actual or original words used by an author, as distinguished from notes, commentary, paraphrase, translation, etc. *b)* the exact or original words of a speaker **3** any of the forms, versions, or editions in which a written work exists **4** the principal matter on a printed or written page, as distinguished from notes, headings, illustrations, etc. **5** the main body of a book, excluding front and back matter **6** the body, or substance, of an item of computer data, esp. nonnumerical data, as opposed to the accompanying information necessary for storage, retrieval, etc. **7** *a)* letters, numbers, or symbols forming words, phrases, etc., used chiefly in a text message *b) short for* TEXT MESSAGE **8** the words of a song, oratorio, etc. **9** *a)* a Biblical passage quoted as authority for a belief or as the topic of a sermon *b)* any passage, book, etc. used to support one's stand or as thematic material, etc. *c)* any topic or subject dealt with **10** something, usually a piece of writing, regarded as an object of analysis or interpretation **11** TEXT HAND **12** any of several black-letter styles of type **13** *short for* TEXTBOOK **14** any of various versions or recensions of all or part of the Scriptures, taken to represent the authentic reading —*vt., vi.* to send a text message (to)

text·book (tekst′bo͝ok′) *n.* a book giving instructions in the principles of a subject of study, specif. one used as the basis or partial basis of a course of study —*adj.* so typical as to be suitable for inclusion in a textbook; providing a model; classic [*a textbook* case of medical malpractice]

text edition that edition of a book prepared for use in schools or colleges: cf. TRADE EDITION

tex·tile (teks′tīl′, -təl) *adj.* ⟦L *textilis* < *textus:* see TEXT⟧ **1** having to do with weaving or with woven fabrics **2** that has been or can be woven [*textile* material] —*n.* **1** a fabric made by weaving, knitting, etc.; cloth **2** raw material suitable for this, as cotton, wool, nylon, etc.

text·ing (tekst′iŋ) *n.* the act or practice of sending or receiving a text message

text message a short communication in the form of TEXT (*n.* 7*a*) sent or received by a portable electronic device, esp. a cell phone —**text messaging**

tex·tu·al (teks′cho͞o əl) *adj.* ⟦ME *textuel* < L *textus:* see TEXT⟧ of, in, based on, or conforming to a text —**tex′tu·al·ly** *adv.*

textual criticism the scholarly study of the text of a written work, often, specif., in an effort to determine the original or most authoritative form of that work

tex·tu·al·ism (-iz′əm) *n.* strict adherence to the text, esp. of the Scriptures

tex·tu·ar·y (teks′cho͞o er′ē) *adj.* TEXTUAL

tex·ture (teks′chər) *n.* ⟦ME < L *textura* < *texere,* to weave: see TECHNIC⟧ **1** [Archaic] a woven fabric **2** the character of a woven fabric as determined by the arrangement, size, quality, etc. of the fabric's threads [coarse *texture,* twilled *texture*] **3** the arrangement of the particles or constituent parts of any material or substance as it affects the appearance or feel of the surface; structure, composition, consistency, grain, etc. **4** *a)* the tactile surface quality of a work of art, resulting from the artist's technique *b)* the melodic and harmonic relationships of musical materials **5** basic structure [the *texture* of society] —*vt.* **-tured, -tur·ing** to cause to have a particular texture —**tex′tur·al** *adj.* —**tex′tur·al·ly** *adv.*

tex·tured (teks′chərd) *adj.* having a particular kind of texture, esp. one that is uneven, not smooth, etc. [*textured* wallpaper]

tex·tur·ize (teks′chər īz′) *vt.* **-ized′, -iz′ing** to give a particular texture to

tex·tur·ized (teks′chər īzd′) *adj.* that has been given a particular texture; specif., designating a synthetic fabric, as polyester, whose filaments have been processed to give them added bulk and resilience

Tey·de (tā′də), **Pi·co de** (pē′kō də) *alt. sp. of* Pico de TEIDE

TF *abbrev.* Teaching Fellow

☆**T formation** ⟦so named because *T*-shaped on the field⟧ *Football* an offensive formation with the quarterback behind the center, the fullback behind the quarterback, and a halfback at each side of the fullback

tg *abbrev.* type genus

TG *abbrev.* transformational grammar

☆**TGIF** (tē′jē′ī′ef′) *interj.* Thank God It's Friday: used to express relief at the end of the workweek

☆**T-group** (tē′gro͞op′) *n.* ⟦*t(raining) group*⟧ a group engaging in sensitivity training

Th[1] *abbrev.* **1** *Bible* Thessalonians **2** Thursday

Th[2] *Chem. symbol for* thorium

-th[1] ⟦ME *-th, -the* < OE *-thu, -tho, -th,* akin to Goth *-itha* (< IE **-ita* > L *-ta,* Sans *-tā*): in words such as *height, sleight,* the *-th* has become *-t*⟧ *suffix forming nouns* **1** the act of ____ing [*growth*] **2** the state or quality of being or having [*wealth, depth*]

-th[2] ⟦ME *-the* < OE *-tha, -the, -otha, -othe* < IE **-tos* > Gr *-tos,* L *-tus;* in *fifth, sixth, eleventh, twelfth,* it replaced the orig. OE *-ta, -te*⟧ *suffix* forming ordinal numerals [*fourth, ninth*] Also, after a vowel, **-eth**

-th[3] ⟦ME < OE: see -ETH[2]⟧ *suffix* -ETH[2]

Thack·er·ay (thak′ər ē), **William Make·peace** (māk′pēs′) 1811-63; Eng. novelist

Thad·de·us or **Thad·e·us** (thad′ē əs, tha dē′əs) *n.* ⟦ME < LL(Ec) *Thaddaeus* < Gr(Ec) *Thaddaios*⟧ a masculine name: dim. *Tad, Thad*

Thai (tī) *n.* **1** *pl.* **Thais** or **Thai** a person born or living in Thailand **2** the official language of Thailand, belonging to the Tai subbranch of the Sino-Tibetan languages **3** *alt. sp. of* TAI —*adj.* of Thailand or its people, language, or culture

Thai·land (tī′land′, -lənd) **1** country in Southeast Asia, on the Indochinese & Malay peninsulas: 198,457 sq mi (514,000 sq km); cap. Bangkok: abbrev. **Thai 2 Gulf of** arm of the South China Sea, between the Malay & Indochinese peninsulas

thal·a·mus (thal′ə məs) *n., pl.* **-mi′** (-mī′) ⟦ModL < L, an inner chamber < Gr *thalamos*⟧ **1** *Anat.* a mass of gray matter forming the lateral walls of the diencephalon and involved in the transmission and integration of certain sensations **2** *Bot.* RECEPTACLE (sense 3*a*) —**tha·lam·ic** (thə lam′ik) *adj.*

thal·as·se·mi·a (thal′ə sē′mē ə) *n.* ⟦ModL < Gr *thalassa,* sea + -EMIA⟧ an inherited chronic anemia, initially found among Mediterranean peoples, resulting from faulty hemoglobin production

tha·las·sic (thə las′ik) *adj.* ⟦Fr *thalassique* < Gr *thalassa,* sea⟧ **1** of the sea or ocean; marine **2** of bays, gulfs, etc. and inland seas, as distinguished from the ocean

tha·ler (tä′lər) *n. alt. sp. of* TALER

Tha·les (thā′lēz′) 636?-546? B.C.; Gr. philosopher

Tha·li·a (thā′lē ə, thāl′yə; *for 2, usually* thə lī′ə) *n.* ⟦L < Gr *Thaleia* < *thallein,* to flourish, bloom < IE base **dhal-,* to blossom > Alb *dal,* (I) sprout⟧ *Gr. Myth.* **1** the Muse of comedy and pastoral poetry **2** Bloom, one of the three Graces

tha·lid·o·mide (thə lid′ə mīd′) *n.* ⟦< fol. + (IM)IDO- + *(glutari) mide* < GLUT(EN) + (TART)AR(IC) + IMIDE⟧ a crystalline solid, $C_{13}H_{10}N_2O_4$, formerly used as a sedative and hypnotic: found to be responsible for severe birth deformities when taken during pregnancy

thal·lic (thal′ik) *adj.* designating or of a chemical compound containing trivalent thallium

thal·li·um (thal′ē əm) *n.* ⟦ModL: so named by Sir William CROOKES, its discoverer < Gr *thallos,* young, green shoot (< *thallein:* see THALIA) because of its green spectral line⟧ a rare, poisonous, bluish-gray, soft, metallic chemical element, used in making photoelectric cells, rat poisons, etc.: symbol, Tl; at. no. 81: see the periodic table of elements in the Reference Supplement

thal·lo·phyte (thal′ə fīt′) *n.* ⟦< Gr *thallos,* young shoot (see prec.) + -PHYTE⟧ any of a former subkingdom (Thallobionta) of nonvascular plantlike organisms showing no clear distinction of roots, stem, or leaves and not producing flowers or seeds: it included the fungi, lichens, and most algae —**thal′lo·phyt′ic** (-fit′ik) *adj.*

thal·lous (thal′əs) *adj.* designating or of a chemical compound containing monovalent thallium

thal·lus (thal′əs) *n., pl.* **thal′li′** (-ī′) or **thal′lus·es** ⟦ModL < Gr *thallos,* young shoot: see THALIA⟧ the nonvascular plant body of a thallophyte —**thal′loid′** (-oid′) *adj.*

Thames (temz; *for 3* thāmz, tāmz, temz) **1** river in S England, flowing from Gloucestershire east through London into the North Sea: 210 mi (338 km) **2** ⟦after the English river⟧ river in SE Ontario, Canada, flowing southwest into Lake St. Clair: 163 mi (262 km) **3** ⟦after the English river⟧ estuary in SE Conn., flowing south into Long Island Sound: 15 mi (24 km)

than (*th*an) *conj.* ⟦ME *than, thene, thonne* < OE *thenne, thanne, thonne,* orig., then: for IE base see THAT⟧ **1** introducing the second element in a comparison, following an adjective or adverb in the comparative degree: if the first element is a subject, object, predicate nominative, etc., the second element is construed in the same way: [he is taller *than* I; she arrived earlier *than* the others; Mom liked you better *than* me]: sometimes, informally, this use of *than* is construed as a preposition and the second element as its object [he is taller *than* me] **2** expressing exception, following an adjective or adverb [none other *than* Sam] **3** when: used esp. following an inverted construction introduced by *scarcely, hardly, barely,* etc. [scarcely had I seen her *than* she spoke to me] **4** indicating difference or distinction, as: *a)* introducing an adverbial clause [Paris was different *than* I'd thought it would be] *b)* linking nouns or pronouns [her story is different *than* his]: this mainly informal use of *than* with *different* and *differently* is objected to by some —*prep.* compared with: chiefly in the phrase **than whom (or which)**, compared or in comparison with whom (or which) [a writer *than whom* there is none finer]

than·a·to- (than′ə tō, -tə) ⟦< Gr *thanatos,* death < IE **dhwen-,* dark, clouded < base **dheu-,* to be smoky, stormy > DULL⟧ *combining form* death [*thanatophobia*]: also, before a vowel, **thanat-**

than·a·tol·o·gy (than′ə täl′ə jē) *n.* ⟦prec. + -LOGY⟧ the study of death, esp. of the medical, psychological, and social problems associated with dying —**than′a·tol′o·gist** *n.*

than·a·to·pho·bi·a (than′ə tə fō′bē ə) *n.* ⟦THANATO- + -PHOBIA⟧ an abnormally great fear of death

☆**than·a·top·sis** (than′ə täp′sis) *n.* ⟦coined by William Cullen BRYANT: see THANATO- & -OPSIS⟧ a view of or musing upon death

Than·a·tos (than′ə täs′) *n.* ⟦Gr: see THANATO-⟧ **1** *Gr. Myth.* death personified as a god: identified with the Roman Mors **2** [*also* **t-**] DEATH INSTINCT

thane (thān) *n.* ⟦ME *thayne* < OE *thegen,* akin to ON *thegn* < IE base **tek-,* to engender, beget > Sans *takman-,* child: basic sense "freeborn man"⟧ **1** in early England, a member of a class of freemen who held land of the king or a lord in return for military services **2** in early Scotland, a person of rank, often a clan chief, who held land of the king —**than′age** (-ij) *n.*

thank (thaŋk) *vt.* ⟦ME *thankien* < OE *thancian,* akin to Ger *danken* < IE base **tong-,* to think > THINK[1], L *tongere,* to know⟧ **1** to show or express appreciation or gratitude to, as by saying "thank you" **2** to hold responsible; blame: an ironic use [we have them to *thank* for our failure]

thank·ful (thaŋk′fəl) *adj.* feeling or expressing thanks; grateful —**thank′ful·ness** *n.*

thank·ful·ly (thaŋk′fə lē) *adv.* **1** in a thankful way **2** one is or should be thankful (that) [*thankfully,* the child was found]

thank·less (-lis) *adj.* **1** not feeling or expressing thanks; ungrateful **2** not producing nor likely to produce thanks; unappreciated —**thank′less·ly** *adv.* —**thank′less·ness** *n.*

thanks (thaŋks) ***pl.n.*** ⟦pl. of ME *thank* < OE *thanc,* thanks: see THANK⟧ an expression of gratitude; grateful acknowledgment of something received by or done for one —***interj.*** thank you —**thanks to** **1** thanks be given to **2** on account of; because of

thanks·giv·ing (thaŋks'giv'iŋ) ***n.*** **1** *a)* the act of giving thanks *b)* an expression of this; esp., a formal, often public, expression of thanks to God in the form of a prayer, etc. ☆**2** [**T-**] *a)* an annual U.S. holiday observed on the fourth Thursday of November as a day of giving thanks and feasting: it commemorates the Pilgrims' celebration of the good harvest of 1621 *b)* a similar Canadian holiday on the second Monday of October: in full **Thanksgiving Day**

thank·wor·thy (thaŋk'wur'thē) ***adj.*** worthy of thanks

thank you *short for* I thank you: the usual expression of appreciation in use today

thank-you (-yo͞o') ***n.*** THANKS

Thant (thänt, tänt, thant), **U** (o͞o) 1909-74; Burmese statesman & diplomat: secretary-general of the United Nations (1962-71)

Thap·sus (thap'səs) ancient town in N Africa: its site is on the NE coast of Tunisia

Thar Desert (tär, tur) desert in NW India & E Pakistan

Tha·sos (thā'säs', thä'sôs') island of Greece in the N Aegean: 146 sq mi (378 sq km)

that (that) ***pron., pl.*** **those** ⟦ME < OE *thæt,* nom. & acc. neut. of the def. article (nom. masc. *se,* nom. fem. *seo*), akin to Ger neut. nom. & acc. *das* < IE demonstrative base **-to-,* **-tā-* > THERE, THITHER, L *istud,* that, *talis,* such⟧ **I.** *as a demonstrative* **1** the person or thing mentioned or understood [*that* is John; *that* tastes good] **2** the thing farther away than another referred to as "this" [this is larger than *that*] **3** the more remote in thought of two contrasted things [of the two possibilities, this is more likely than *that*] **4** [*pl.*] certain people [*those* who know] **II.** *as a relative pronoun, now often omitted, esp. in sense* 1 **1** who, whom, or which [the road (*that*) we took] **2** where; at which; on which [the place *that* I saw her] **3** when; in which; on which [the year *that* I was born] —***adj., pl.*** **those** **1** designating the person or thing mentioned or understood [*that* woman is Mary; *that* pie tastes good] **2** designating the thing farther away than the one referred to as "this" [this house is larger than *that* one] **3** designating the more remote in thought of two contrasted things [of the two, this possibility is more likely than *that* one] **4** designating something or someone not described but well known or easily recognizable: sometimes with implications of disparagement [*that* certain feeling, there comes *that* smile!, *that* George!] —***conj.*** a subordinating conjunction used to introduce: *a)* a noun clause expressing a supposed or actual fact [*that* she's gone is obvious; the truth was *that* we never saw her; it was true *that* we never saw her] *b)* an adverbial clause expressing purpose [they died *that* we might live] *c)* an adverbial clause expressing result [you ran so fast *that* I couldn't catch up] *d)* an adverbial clause expressing cause [I'm sorry *that* I caused you such annoyance] *e)* an elliptical sentence expressing surprise, indignation, or desire [*that* you should say such a thing! oh, *that* this day would be over!] —***adv.*** **1** to that extent; so [I can't see *that* far ahead]: also used informally before an adjective modified by a clause of result [I'm *that* tired I could drop] ☆**2** [Informal] very; so very: used in negative constructions [I didn't like the book *that* much] —**all that** [Informal] **1** so very: used in negative constructions [they aren't *all that* rich] **2** everything of the same or related sort [romance and *all that*] —☆**at that** **1** at that point; with no further discussion, etc.: also **with that** **2** moreover; even so —**that is** **1** to be specific **2** in other words —**that's that!** that is settled!

that·a·way (that'ə wā') ***adv., n.*** [Dial. or Informal] that way; there

thatch (thach) ***n.*** ⟦altered (based on the v.) < older *thack* < ME *thac* < OE *thæc,* a thatch, roof: for base see the ***vt.***⟧ **1** *a)* a covering, as the roof of a house, made of straw, rushes, palm leaves, etc. *b)* material for such a covering **2** any of a number of palms whose leaves are used for thatch: also **thatch palm** **3** anything suggestive of thatch on a roof as *a)* the hair growing on the head *b)* a matted layer of partly decayed leaves, stems, etc. between growing vegetation and the soil —***vt.*** ⟦ME *thecchen* < OE *thec-c(e)an,* akin to Ger *decken,* to cover < IE base **(s)teg-,* to cover > Gr *stegos,* roof, L *tegere,* to cover⟧ **1** to cover with or as with thatch **2** DETHATCH —**thatch'y** ***adj.*** **thatch'i·er, thatch'i·est**

Thatch·er (thach'ər), **Margaret (Hilda)** Baroness Thatcher of Kesteven (born *Margaret Hilda Roberts*) 1925-2013; Brit. politician: prime minister (1979-90)

thatch·ing (thach'iŋ) ***n.*** **1** the act of a person who thatches **2** material used to thatch a roof, etc.

that'll (*that'*'l) *contraction* that will

that's (thats) *contraction* **1** that is **2** that has

that·ta·way (that'ə wā') ***adv., n.*** [Dial. or Informal] *alt. sp. of* THATAWAY

thau·ma·trope (thô'mə trōp') ***n.*** ⟦Gr *thauma* (see THAUMATOLOGY) + -TROPE⟧ a device consisting of a card or disk with different designs on either side, which, when the card or disk is twirled, appear to blend into one: it demonstrates the persistence of vision

thau·ma·turge (-turj') ***n.*** ⟦Fr < ML *thaumaturgus* < Gr *thaumaturgos,* working wonders < *thauma,* miracle (see THEATER) + *-ergos,* working < *ergon,* WORK⟧ a person who works supernatural miracles: also **thau'ma·turg'ist**

thau·ma·tur·gy (-tur'jē) ***n.*** ⟦Gr *thaumatourgia:* see prec.⟧ the working of supernatural miracles; magic —**thau'ma·tur'gic** ***adj.,*** **thau'ma·tur'gi·cal**

thaw (thô) ***vi.*** ⟦ME *thawen* < OE *thawian,* akin to Du *dooien,* Ger *(ver)-dauen,* to digest < IE base **tā-,* to melt, dissolve, flow > L *tabere,* to melt, vanish⟧ **1** *a)* to become liquid or semiliquid; melt (said of ice, snow, etc.) *b)* to pass to an unfrozen state (said of frozen foods) *c)* to have its contents melt [underground water pipes *thaw* in the spring] **2** to rise in temperature above the freezing point, so that snow, etc. melts: said of weather conditions, with impersonal *it* [it will *thaw* tomorrow] **3** *a)* to get rid of the chill, stiffness, etc. resulting from extreme cold (often with *out*) *b)* to lose coldness or reserve of manner —***vt.*** to cause to thaw —***n.*** **1** the act of thawing **2** a spell of weather warm enough to allow thawing **3** a becoming less reserved in manner **4** a mutual softening of hardline stances by opposed countries, factions, etc., as through a resumption of dialogue or negotiation —***SYN.*** MELT

Thay·er (thā'ər, ther), **Syl·va·nus** (sil vā'nəs) 1785-1872; U.S. army officer & educator: reorganized the U.S. Military Academy at West Point

ThB or **Th.B.** *abbrev.* ⟦L *Theologiae Baccalaureus*⟧ Bachelor of Theology

THC (tē'āch'sē') ***n.*** tetrahydrocannabinol

ThD or **Th.D.** *abbrev.* ⟦L *Theologiae Doctor*⟧ Doctor of Theology

the (*thə; before vowels* thē, thi) ***adj., definite article*** ⟦ME, indeclinable article < OE *se* (nom. masc. article) with *th-* < other case & gender forms (*thone, thæs, thære, thæm, thy*): for IE base see THAT; the meaning is controlled by the basic notion "previously recognized, noticed, or encountered" in distinction to A[2], AN[1]⟧ **I.** *referring to a particular person, thing, or group (as opposed to* a, an), *as:* **1** that (one) being spoken of or already mentioned [*the* story ended] **2** that (one) which is present, close, nearby, etc., as distinguished from all others viewed as remote [*the* day is starting out warm; *the* heat is oppressive] **3** that (one) designated or identified, as by a title [*the* President (of the U.S.), *the* Mississippi (River)] **4** that (one) considered outstanding, most fashionable, etc.: usually italicized in print [that's *the* restaurant in town] **5** that (one) belonging to a person previously mentioned or understood [take me by *the* hand; rub into *the* face] **6** one specified period of time, esp. a decade [*the* Dark Ages, *the* seventies] **7** [Informal] that (one) who has a specific family relationship to one [*the* wife, *the* kid sister] **II.** *referring to that one of a number of persons or things which is identified by a modifier, as by:* **1** an attributive adjective [*the* front door] **2** a relative clause [*the* man who answered] **3** a prepositional phrase [*the* hit of the week] **4** an infinitive phrase [*the* right to strike] **5** a participle [follow *the* directions given] **III.** *referring to a person or thing considered generically or universally, as:* **1** one taken as the representative of the entire genus or type [learn to use *the* typewriter; *the* cow is a domestic animal] **2** an adjective used as a noun [*the* good, *the* beautiful, *the* true] —***adv.*** **1** that much; to that extent [*the* better to see you with] **2** by how much . . . by that much; to what extent . . . to that extent: used in a correlative construction expressing comparison [*the* sooner *the* better] —***prep.*** to each; in each; for each; per [at five dollars *the* half ton]

the·a·ter or **the·a·tre** (thē'ə tər) ***n.*** ⟦ME *theatre* < OFr < L *theatrum* < Gr *theatron* < base of *theasthai,* to see, view < IE base **dhāu-,* to see > Gr *thauma,* miracle⟧ **1** a place where plays, operas, films, etc. are presented; esp., a building or outdoor structure expressly designed for such presentations **2** any place resembling a theater, esp. a lecture hall, surgical clinic, etc., having the floor of the seating space raked **3** any place where events take place; scene of operations; specif., an area of military operations, as in a war [a commander in the Southern Pacific *theater*] **4** *a)* the dramatic art or dramatic works; drama *b)* the theatrical world; people engaged in theatrical activity *c)* the legitimate theater, as distinguished from films, TV, etc. (often with *the*) **5** theatrical technique, production, etc. with reference to its effectiveness [a play that is good *theater*] **6** a showy, affected, or melodramatic display, situation, etc. thought of as being like a theatrical performance

the·a·ter·go·er or **the·a·tre·go·er** (-gō'ər) ***n.*** a person who attends the theater, esp. one who goes often —**the'a·ter·go'ing** ***adj., n.***

☆**the·a·ter-in-the-round** (thē'ə tər in *thə* round') ***n.*** ARENA THEATER

theater of the absurd avant-garde, mid-20th-cent. drama made up of apparently absurd, incongruous, or pointless situations and dialogue, typically expressing the existential nature of self-isolation, anxiety, frustration, etc.

the·at·ri·cal (thē a'tri kəl) ***adj.*** ⟦< LL *theatricus* (< Gr *theatrikos*) + -AL⟧ **1** having to do with the theater, the drama, a play, actors, etc. **2** characteristic of the theater; dramatic; esp. (in disparagement), melodramatic, histrionic, showy, or affected **3** designating or of a film, usually a FEATURE (*n.* 6), produced for first exhibition in a commercial theater as distinguished from one made for showing first on TV, as home video, etc. Also, for 1 and 2, **the·at'ric** —**the·at'ri·cal·ism'** ***n.,*** **the·at'ri·cal'i·ty** (-kal'ə tē) —**the·at'ri·cal·ly** ***adv.***

the·at·ri·cal·ize (-īz') ***vt.*** **-ized', -iz'ing** **1** to make theatrical; give a dramatic, sometimes overly dramatic, quality to **2** to put into a theatrical setting —**the·at'ri·cal·i·za'tion** (-i zā'shən) ***n.***

the·at·ri·cals (thē a'tri kəlz) ***pl.n.*** performances of stage plays, esp. by amateurs

the·at·rics (thē a'triks) ***n.*** the art of the theater —***pl.n.*** something done or said for theatrical effect; histrionic actions, manners, devices, etc.

the·ba·ine (thē'bə ēn', thi bā'in) ***n.*** ⟦< L *Thebae* (< Gr *Thēbai*), Thebes + -INE[3]: after an opium from Thebes⟧ a colorless, crystalline, poisonous alkaloid, $C_{19}H_{21}NO_3$, obtained from opium and used in medicine

the·be (te'be) ***n., pl.*** **the'be** ⟦native Bantu term, lit., shield⟧ a monetary unit of Botswana, equal to $\frac{1}{100}$ of a pula

Thebes (thēbz) **1** ancient city in S Egypt, on the Nile, on the site of modern Luxor and Karnak **2** chief city of ancient Boeotia, EC Greece —**The·ban** (thē'bən) ***adj., n.***

the·ca (thē′kə) ***n., pl.*** **-cae** (-sē) ⟦ModL < L < Gr *thēkē,* a case < IE **dhēkā* < base **dhē-,* to place, put > DO¹, L *facere*⟧ **1** *Bot.* a spore case, sac, or capsule **2** *Anat., Zool.* any sheath or sac enclosing an organ or a whole organism, as the covering of an insect pupa —**the′cal** ***adj.***

the·cate (thē′kit, -kāt′) ***adj.*** having a theca; sheathed

the·co·dont (thē′kə dänt′) ***n.*** ⟦ModL < Gr *thēkē* (see THECA) + *odous* (gen. *odontos*), TOOTH: so named because its teeth grew in sockets in the jaw⟧ any of an order (Thecodontia) of reptiles of the Permian and Triassic periods, believed to be ancestors of the dinosaurs and crocodilians

thé dan·sant (tā dän sän′) *pl.* ***thés dan·sants*** (tā dän sän′) ⟦Fr⟧ TEA DANCE

thee (*th*ē) ***pron.*** ⟦ME *the* < OE, dat. & acc. of *thu,* THOU¹⟧ **1** [Archaic] *objective form of* THOU¹ [they will help *thee;* to *Thee* we pray; did he give *thee* the book?] **2** THOU¹ (nominative case): used as the subject, with the verb in the third person singular, by some members of the Society of Friends (Quakers) [*thee* speaks harshly]

theft (theft) ***n.*** ⟦ME *thefte* < OE *thiefth:* see THIEF & -TH¹⟧ the act or an instance of stealing; larceny

SYN.—**theft** is the general term and **larceny** the legal term for the unlawful or felonious taking away of another's property without his or her consent and with the intention of depriving the person of it; **robbery** in its strict legal sense implies the felonious taking of another's property from that person or in his or her immediate presence by the use of violence or intimidation; **burglary** in legal use implies a breaking into a house with intent to commit theft or other felony and is often restricted to such an act accomplished at night

thegn (thān) ***n.*** ⟦OE⟧ *alt. sp. of* THANE

the·ine (thē′ēn′, -in) ***n.*** ⟦ModL *theina* < *thea:* see THEOPHYLLINE⟧ CAFFEINE, esp. that in tea

their (*th*er) ***possessive pronominal adj.*** ⟦ME *theyr* < ON *theirra,* gen. pl. of the demonstrative pron. replacing ME *here,* OE *hira:* see THEY⟧ of, belonging to, made by, or done by them: often used with a singular antecedent (as *everybody, somebody, everyone*) to avoid the masculine implications of the traditional use of *he* without distinction as to gender, although this usage is objected to by some [did everybody finish *their* lunch?]

theirs (*th*erz) ***pron.*** ⟦ME *theires* < *theyr* (see prec.) + *-es* by analogy with *his,* HIS⟧ that or those belonging to them: the possessive form of THEY, used without a following noun, often after *of* [that house is *theirs; theirs* are better; I am a friend of *theirs*]: often used with a singular antecedent (as *everybody, somebody, everyone*) to avoid the masculine implications of the traditional use of *he* without distinction as to gender, although this usage is objected to by some [she'll bring her husband if everyone else brings *theirs*]

the·ism (thē′iz′əm) ***n.*** ⟦THE(O)- + -ISM⟧ **1** belief in a god or gods **2** belief in one God; monotheism: opposed to PANTHEISM, POLYTHEISM **3** belief in one God viewed as creator and ruler of the universe and known by revelation: distinguished from DEISM —**the′ist** ***n., adj.*** —**the·is′tic** ***adj.,*** **the·is′ti·cal** —**the·is′ti·cal·ly** ***adv.***

Thel·ma (thel′mə) ***n.*** ⟦< ?, but often a var. of SELMA¹⟧ a feminine name

them (*th*em) ***pron.*** ⟦ME *theim* < ON, dat. of the demonstrative pron.: see THEY⟧ *objective form of* THEY: [help *them;* give *them* the books]

USAGE—*them* is also used as a predicate complement with a linking verb [it's *them*] and in certain comparative constructions [we run faster than *them,* but we're not as agile as *them*], although both usages are objected to by some: see also the note at THEY (sense 3)

the·mat·ic (thē mat′ik) ***adj.*** **1** of or constituting a theme or themes **2** *Linguis.* of or relating to the stem of a word or to a vowel ending a stem that precedes an inflectional ending **3** [Brit.] *Philately* of stamps collected according to a theme, or topic —***n.*** [Brit.] any stamp of a thematic collection —**the·mat′i·cal·ly** ***adv.***

☆**Thematic Apperception Test** *Psychol.* a test used to analyze personality that consists of a series of standard pictures of ambiguous social situations about which a person makes up stories that are assumed to reveal elements of his or her psychological makeup

theme (thēm) ***n.*** ⟦ME < OFr & L: OFr *teme* < L *thema* < Gr, what is laid down < base of *tithenai,* to put, place: see DO¹⟧ **1** *a)* a topic or subject, as of a lecture, sermon, essay, etc. *b)* a recurring, unifying subject or idea; motif **2** a short essay, esp. one written as an assignment in a school course: also **theme paper** **3** *a)* a short melody used as the subject of a musical composition *b)* a musical phrase upon which variations are developed ☆**4** *short for* THEME SONG —***vt.*** **themed, them′ing** to give a theme to; specif., to plan according to a central theme [a *themed* restaurant]

☆**theme park** an amusement park whose decor, rides, etc. are designed to reflect a central theme, such as a particular period in history or the world of the future

☆**theme song** **1** a recurring song or melody in a film, musical, etc.; esp., such a song or melody intended to be identified with the work as a whole **2** an identifying song or melody used by a dance band, singer, etc. or for a radio or television series; signature

The·mis (thē′mis) ***n.*** *Gr. Myth.* a goddess of law and justice, daughter of Uranus and Gaea: represented as holding aloft a scale for weighing opposing claims

The·mis·to·cles (thə mis′tə klēz′) 525?-460? B.C.; Athenian statesman & naval commander

them·selves (*th*em selvz′) ***pron.*** ⟦Late (Northern) ME *thaim selfe* for ME *hemselve(n)* (see THEY) + *-s,* pl. suffix⟧ a form of THEY, used: *a)* as an intensifier [they saw it *themselves*] *b)* as a reflexive [they hurt *themselves*] *c)* with the meaning "their real, true, or normal selves" [they are not *themselves* today] (in this construction *them* functions as an adjective and *selves* as a noun; when they are separated, the form *their* is used [*their* own sweet selves])

USAGE—*themselves* is often used with a sing. antecedent (as *everybody, somebody, everyone*) [everyone expressed *themselves* at the town meeting]

then (*th*en) ***adv.*** ⟦ME: see THAN⟧ **1** at that time [he was young *then*] **2** soon afterward; next in time [he took his hat and *then* left] **3** next in order [first comes alpha and *then* beta] **4** in that case; therefore; accordingly: used with conjunctive force [if it rains, *then* there will be no picnic] **5** besides; moreover [he enjoys walking, and *then* there are the benefits of exercise] **6** at another time or at other times: used as a correlative with *now, sometimes,* etc. [now it's warm, *then* it's freezing] —***adj.*** of that time; being such at that time: often in comb. [the *then*-director] —***n.*** that time [by *then,* they were gone] —**but then** but on the other hand; but at the same time —**then again** from the opposed point of view; on the other hand —**then and there** at that time and in that place; at once —**what then?** what would happen in that case?

the·nar (thē′när′) ***n.*** ⟦ModL < Gr < IE base **dhen-,* palm of the hand, level place > DEN⟧ **1** the palm of the hand or, sometimes, the sole of the foot **2** the bulge at the base of the thumb —***adj.*** of a thenar

thence (*th*ens; *occas.* thens) ***adv.*** ⟦ME *thens, thannes* (with adv. gen. suffix *-es*) < OE *thanan,* thence: for IE base see THAT⟧ **1** [Archaic or Literary] from that place; therefrom: often with *from* **2** from that time; thenceforth **3** on that account; therefore

thence·forth (*th*ens′fôrth′) ***adv.*** from that time onward; after that; thereafter: also **thence·for′ward** (-fôr′wərd)

the·o- (thē′ō, -ə) ⟦< Gr *theos,* god < ? IE **dhewes-,* to storm, breathe > L *furere,* to rage⟧ *combining form* God or a god [*theocentric*]: also, before a vowel, **the-**

the·o·bro·mine (thē′ō brō′mēn′, -min) ***n.*** ⟦< ModL *Theobroma,* a genus of trees of the sterculia family < Gr *theos,* god (see prec.) + *brōma,* food + -INE³⟧ a bitter, crystalline alkaloid, $C_7H_8N_4O_2$, extracted from the leaves and seeds of the cacao plant, used in medicine as a diuretic and nerve stimulant: it is closely related to caffeine and is also found in cola nuts and tea

the·o·cen·tric (thē′ō sen′trik) ***adj.*** ⟦THEO- + CENTRIC⟧ centering on or directed toward God or a god as a focus of interest, source of authority, etc. —**the′o·cen′tri·cal·ly** ***adv.*** —**the′o·cen·tric′i·ty** (-tris′ə tē) ***n.*** —**the′o·cen′trism′** (-triz′əm) ***n.***

the·oc·ra·cy (thē äk′rə sē) ***n., pl.*** **-cies** ⟦Gr *theokratia:* see THEO- & -CRACY⟧ **1** government by a person or persons claiming to rule with divine authority **2** a country governed in this way —**the·o·crat** (thē′ō krat′) ***n.*** —**the′o·crat′ic** ***adj.,*** **the′o·crat′i·cal** —**the′o·crat′i·cal·ly** ***adv.***

The·oc·ri·tus (thē ä′kri təs) 3d cent. B.C.; Gr. poet

the·od·i·cy (thē äd′ə sē) ***n., pl.*** **-cies** ⟦Fr *théodicée:* coined by LEIBNIZ (1710) < Gr *theos,* god + *dikē,* justice⟧ a theological argument or doctrine that seeks to explain how the existence of evil in the world can be reconciled with the justice and goodness of God

the·od·o·lite (thē äd′ə līt′) ***n.*** ⟦ModL *theodelitus:* prob. invented (*c.* 1571) by Leonard Digges, Eng mathematician⟧ a surveying instrument used to measure vertical and horizontal angles —**the·od′o·lit′ic** (-ə lit′ik) ***adj.***

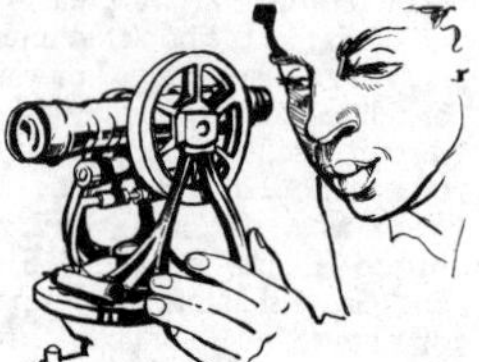
transit theodolite

The·o·dor·a (thē′ə dôr′ə) ***n.*** ⟦Gr *Theodōra:* see fol.⟧ a feminine name: dim. *Dora*

The·o·dore (thē′ə dôr′) ***n.*** ⟦L *Theodorus* < Gr *Theodōros* < *theos,* god + *dōron,* gift⟧ a masculine name: dim. *Ted, Teddy;* var. *Theodor;* fem. *Theodora*

The·od·o·ric (thē äd′ə rik) ⟦LL *Theodoricus,* altered (after *Theodorus,* Theodore) < Goth **Thiudoreiks* < *thiuda,* folk, akin to OHG *thioda* (see DEUTSCHLAND) + *reiks,* ruler, leader: for IE base see RIGHT⟧ A.D. 454?-526; king of the Ostrogoths (474-526)

The·o·do·si·us I (thē′ə dō′shəs, -shē əs) (*Flavius Theodosius*) A.D. 346?-395; Rom. general: emperor of Rome (379-395): called *the Great* —**The′o·do′sian** ***adj.***

the·og·o·ny (thē äg′ə nē) ***n., pl.*** **-nies** ⟦Gr *theogonia:* see THEO- & -GONY⟧ the origin or genealogy of the gods, as told in myths —**the′o·gon′ic** (-ə gän′ik) ***adj.***

theol *abbrev.* **1** theologian **2** theological **3** theology

the·o·lo·gian (thē′ə lō′jən) ***n.*** ⟦MFr *théologien*⟧ a student of or specialist in theology or of a particular branch, school, etc. of theology; often, specif., a person who expounds a specific theology, or theological doctrine

the·o·log·i·cal (thē′ə läj′i kəl) ***adj.*** of, having to do with, based on, or offering instruction in, theology or a theology: also **the′o·log′ic** —**the′o·log′i·cal·ly** ***adv.***

theological virtues *Christian Theol.* the three virtues (faith, hope, and charity) that have God as their immediate object

the·ol·o·gize (thē äl′ə jīz′) ***vt.*** **-gized′, -giz′ing** to put into theological terms; fit into a theology —***vi.*** to speculate theologically —**the·ol′o·giz′er** ***n.***

the·ol·o·gy (thē äl′ə jē) ***n., pl.*** **-gies** ⟦ME *theologie* < LL(Ec) *theologia* < Gr: see THEO- & -LOGY⟧ **1** the study of religious doctrines and matters of divinity; specif., the study of God and the relations between God, humankind, and the universe 2 a specific formulation or systemization of religious doctrine or belief as set forth by a given religion or denomination or by one or more individuals

the·om·a·chy (thē äm′ə kē) *n., pl.* **-chies** ⟦Gr *theomachia:* see THEO- & -MACHY⟧ 1 a battle against the gods 2 war or strife among the gods

the·o·mor·phic (thē′ə môr′fik) *adj.* ⟦< Gr *theomorphos* (see THEO- & -MORPH) + -IC⟧ having the form, likeness, or aspect of God or a god —**the′o·mor′phism′** *n.*

the·oph·a·ny (thē äf′ə nē) *n., pl.* **-nies** ⟦LL(Ec) *theophania* < Gr *theophaneia:* see THEO- & -PHANE⟧ a manifestation of God or a deity

The·o·phras·tus (thē′ə fras′təs) 372?-287? B.C.; Gr. philosopher & natural scientist

the·o·phyl·line (thē′ə fil′ēn′, -in) *n.* ⟦< ModL *thea,* tea (infl. by Gr, goddess, as being a divine herb, but < source of TEA) + -PHYLL + -INE[3]⟧ a colorless, crystalline alkaloid, $C_7H_8N_4O_2 \cdot H_2O$, extracted from tea leaves or prepared synthetically: an isomer of theobromine

the·or·bo (thē ôr′bō) *n., pl.* **-bos** ⟦Fr *théorbe* < It *tiorba* < ?⟧ a large 17th-cent. lute with a double neck and two sets of strings

the·o·rem (thē′ə rəm, thir′əm) *n.* ⟦< Fr or L: Fr *théorème* < L *theorema* < Gr *theōrēma* < *theōrein,* to look at, view < *theoros,* spectator: for IE base see THEATER⟧ 1 a proposition that is not self-evident but that can be proved from accepted premises 2 an expression of relations in an equation or formula 3 *Math., Physics* a proposition embodying something to be proved —**the′o·re·mat′ic** (-rə mat′ik) *adj.*

the·o·ret·i·cal (thē′ə ret′i kəl) *adj.* ⟦< LL *theoreticus* < Gr *theōrētikos* < -AL⟧ 1 of or constituting theory 2 limited to or based on theory; not practical or applied; hypothetical 3 tending to theorize; speculative Also **the′o·ret′ic** —**the′o·ret′i·cal·ly** *adv.*

the·o·re·ti·cian (thē′ə rə tish′ən) *n.* a person who theorizes, esp. one who specializes in the theory of some art, science, etc.

the·o·ret·ics (thē′ə ret′iks) *n.* ⟦< earlier n. *theoretic,* having the same meaning: see THEORETICAL & -ICS⟧ the theoretical part of a field of knowledge

the·o·rist (thē′ə rist) *n.* 1 THEORETICIAN 2 a person who advocates or promotes a particular theory

the·o·rize (thē′ə rīz′) *vi.* **-rized′, -riz′ing** to form a theory or theories; speculate —**the′o·riz′er** *n.* —**the′o·ri·za′tion** *n.*

the·o·ry (thē′ə rē, thir′ē) *n., pl.* **-ries** ⟦< Fr or LL: Fr *théorie* < LL *theoria* < Gr *theōria,* a looking at, contemplation, speculation, theory < *theōrein:* see THEOREM⟧ 1 [Obs.] a mental viewing; contemplation 2 a speculative idea or plan as to how something might be done 3 a systematic statement of principles involved [the *theory* of equations in mathematics] 4 a formulation of apparent relationships or underlying principles of certain observed phenomena which has been verified to some degree 5 that branch of an art or science consisting in a knowledge of its principles and methods rather than in its practice; pure, as opposed to applied, science, etc. 6 popularly, a mere conjecture, or guess

SYN.—**theory,** as compared here, implies considerable evidence in support of a formulated general principle explaining the operation of certain phenomena [the *theory* of evolution]; **hypothesis** implies an inadequacy of evidence in support of an explanation that is tentatively inferred, often as a basis for further experimentation [the nebular *hypothesis*]; **law** implies an exact formulation of the principle operating in a sequence of events in nature, observed to occur with unvarying uniformity under the same conditions [the *law* of the conservation of energy]

theory of everything any physical theory that attempts to explain all fundamental interactions as low-energy manifestations of a single interaction

theory of games GAME THEORY

the·os·o·phy (thē äs′ə fē) *n.* ⟦ML *theosophia* < LGr, knowledge of divine things < *theosophos,* wise in divine matters < Gr *theos,* god + *sophos,* wise: see THEO- & -SOPHY⟧ [*also* **T-**] any of various esoteric religious or semireligious occult systems or movements held to be based on special mystical insight, specif., a movement founded by Helena BLAVATSKY, incorporating elements of Buddhism and Hinduism —**the′o·soph′ic** (-ə säf′ik) *adj.,* **the′o·soph′i·cal** —**the′o·soph′i·cal·ly** *adv.* —**the·os′o·phist** *n.*

ther·a·peu·tic (ther′ə pyōōt′ik) *adj.* ⟦ModL *therapeuticus* < Gr *therapeutikos* < *therapeutēs,* attendant, servant, one who treats medically < *therapeuein,* to nurse, treat medically⟧ 1 *a)* serving to cure or heal; curative *b)* serving to preserve health [*therapeutic* abortion] 2 of therapeutics Also **ther′a·peu′ti·cal** —**ther′a·peu′ti·cal·ly** *adv.*

ther·a·peu·tics (ther′ə pyōōt′iks) *n.* the branch of medicine that deals with the treatment and cure of diseases; therapy

☆**ther·a·pist** (ther′ə pist) *n.* 1 a specialist in a certain form of therapy 2 *short for* PSYCHOTHERAPIST

ther·a·py (ther′ə pē) *n., pl.* **-pies** ⟦ModL *therapia* < Gr *therapeia* < *therapeuein,* to nurse, cure⟧ 1 the treatment of disease or of any physical or mental disorder by medical or physical means: often used in compounds [*hydrotherapy*] 2 *short for* PSYCHOTHERAPY

Ther·a·va·da (ther′ə vä′də) *n.* a major form of Hinayana Buddhism, which emphasizes asceticism, contemplation, and the monastic life

there (ther) *adv.* ⟦ME *ther,* there, where < OE *ther, thær,* there, where < IE **tor-,* **ter-,* there < **to-,* **tā-,* demonstrative base > THAT, THEN⟧ 1 at or in that place: often used as an intensive [Mary *there* is a good player]: in dialectal or nonstandard use, often placed between a demonstrative pronoun and the noun it modifies [that *there* hog] 2 toward, to, or into that place; thither [go *there*] 3 at that point in action, speech, discussion, etc.; then [*there* I paused] 4 in that matter, respect, etc.; as to that [*there* you are wrong] 5 at the moment; right now [*there* goes the whistle] *There* is also used *a)* in interjectional phrases of approval, encouragement, etc. [*there's* a fine fellow!] *b)* with pronominal force in impersonal constructions in which the real subject follows the verb [*there* is very little time, *there* are three people here] *c)* in place of the name, as in greeting a person [hi *there!*] —*n.* that place or point [we left *there* at six] —*interj.* 1 used to express defiance, dismay, satisfaction, etc. [*there,* I've done it anyway!] 2 used to express sympathy, concern, etc. when repeated [*there, there!* everything will be OK] —**(not) all there** [Informal] (not) in full possession of one's wits; (not) mentally sound —**there you are** 1 a mild instruction to accept or take what is being offered, as when something is being handed or presented to someone 2 [Informal] a phrase used to express: *a)* approval, agreement, or encouragement *b)* a feeling of concession or resignation to a situation —**there you go** [Informal] THERE YOU ARE —**there you (or they, etc.) go again!** [Informal] a mild rebuke of someone for repeating what is regarded as a wrongdoing or error

there·a·bouts (ther′ə bouts′) *adv.* 1 near that place 2 near that time or point in action, speech, etc. 3 near that number, amount, degree, etc. Also **there′a·bout′**

there·af·ter (ther af′tər) *adv.* 1 after that; from then on; subsequently 2 [Archaic] accordingly

there·a·gainst (ther′ə genst′) *adv.* against or contrary to that; in opposition

there·at (ther at′) *adv.* [Archaic] 1 at that place; there 2 at that time; when that occurred 3 for that reason

there·by (ther bī′, ther′bī′) *adv.* 1 by or through that; by that means 2 connected with that [*thereby* hangs a tale] 3 [Archaic] thereabouts

there·for (ther fôr′) *adv.* for this; for that; for it

there·fore (ther′fôr′) *adv.* ⟦ME *ther fore:* see THERE & FORE⟧ as a result of this or that; for this or that reason; consequently; hence: often used as a conjunctive adverb

there·from (ther frum′) *adv.* from this; from that; from it; from there

there·in (ther in′) *adv.* 1 in there; in or into that place or thing 2 in that matter, detail, etc.

there·in·af·ter (ther′in af′tər) *adv.* in the following part of that document, speech, etc.

there·in·to (ther in′tōō, ther′in tōō′) *adv.* 1 into that place or thing 2 into that matter, condition, etc.

ther·e·min (ther′ə min) *n.* ⟦after *Léon Thérémin* (Fr transliteration < *Lev Termen*), its Russ inventor (*c.* 1920)⟧ an early electronic musical instrument whose tone and loudness are controlled by moving the hands through the air varying distances from two antennas

there·of (ther uv′) *adv.* 1 of that 2 concerning that 3 from that as a cause, reason, etc.; therefrom

there·on (-än′) *adv.* 1 on that or it 2 THEREUPON

there's (therz) *contraction* 1 there is 2 there has

The·re·sa (tə rē′sə, -zə) *n.* ⟦< Fr *Thérèse* or Port *Theresa* < L *Therasia* < ?⟧ a feminine name: dim. *Terry, Tess;* var. *Teresa*

Thé·rèse (tā rez′; E tə rēs′), Saint (1873-97); Fr. Carmelite nun: her day is Oct. 3: called **Thérèse of Li·sieux** (lē zyö′): Eng. name **The·re·sa** (tə rē′sə, -zə)

there·to (ther tōō′) *adv.* 1 to that place, thing, etc.: also **there·un′to** (-un′tōō; ther′un tōō′) 2 [Archaic] besides

there·to·fore (ther′tə fôr′, ther′tə fôr′) *adv.* up to then; until that time; before that

there·un·der (ther un′dər, ther′un′dər) *adv.* 1 under that; under it 2 under the terms stated there

there·up·on (ther′ə pän′, ther′ə pän′) *adv.* 1 immediately following that; at once 2 as a consequence of that 3 upon that; concerning that subject, etc.

there·with (ther with′, -with′; ther′with′, -with′) *adv.* 1 along with that 2 in addition to that 3 by that method or means 4 immediately thereafter; thereupon

there·with·al (ther′with ôl′) *adv.* 1 with all that; in addition; besides 2 [Obs.] along with that; therewith

the·ri·an·throp·ic (thir′ē an thräp′ik) *adj.* ⟦< Gr *thērion,* beast (< *thēr,* beast: see FIERCE) + *anthrōpos,* man (see ANTHROPO-) + -IC⟧ 1 conceived of as being partly human and partly animal in form 2 designating or of deities of this kind

the·ri·o·mor·phic (thir′ē ō môr′fik) *adj.* ⟦< Gr *thēriomorphos* (see prec. & -MORPH) + -IC⟧ conceived of as having the form of an animal: said of certain gods

therm (thurm) *n.* ⟦< Gr *thermē,* heat: see WARM⟧ 1 [Obs.] *a)* a great calorie *b)* a small calorie *c)* a unit of heat equal to 1,000 great calories 2 a unit of heat equal to 100,000 British thermal units

Ther·ma (thur′mə) *ancient name for* SALONIKA

ther·mae (thur′mē) *pl.n.* ⟦L < Gr *thermai,* pl. of *thermē,* heat: see WARM⟧ hot or warm springs or baths; specif., the public baths or bathhouses of ancient Rome

ther·mal (thur′məl) *adj.* ⟦Fr < Gr *thermē,* heat: see WARM⟧ 1 having to do with heat, hot springs, etc. 2 warm or hot ☆3 designating or of a loosely knitted material honeycombed with air spaces for insulation to help retain body heat [*thermal* underwear] —*n.* a rising column of warm air, caused by the uneven heating of the earth or sea by the sun —**ther′mal·ly** *adv.*

thermal barrier a limit to the speed of flight of vehicles in the atmosphere set by the effects of aerodynamic heating

☆**thermal pollution** the discharge of heated liquid or air into lakes, rivers, etc., as by an industry or nuclear power plant, causing such a rise in the water temperature as to affect the life cycles within the water and disrupt the ecological balance

thermal spring a spring whose water has a temperature greater than the mean annual temperature of its locality

ther·mic (thur′mik) *adj.* ⟦< Gr *thermē,* heat (see WARM) + -IC⟧ of or caused by heat —**ther′mi·cal·ly** *adv.*

Ther·mi·dor (thur′mə dôr′; *Fr* ter mē dôr′) *n.* ⟦Fr, the eleventh month (July 19–Aug. 17) of the French Revolutionary calendar < Gr *thermē,* heat (see WARM) + *dōron,* gift⟧ [*also* **t-**] **1** the period in the French Revolution, beginning with the downfall of Robespierre (July 27, 1794), during which national reaction against the Reign of Terror shifted emphasis to the restoration of order **2** any such period of reaction —**Ther′mi·do′ri·an** (-dôr′ē ən) *adj.*

therm·i·on (thur′mī′ən, thur′mē-) *n.* ⟦THERM(O)- + ION⟧ *Physics* a negative or positive ion emitted by an incandescent material —**therm′i·on′ic** (-än′ik) *adj.*

thermionic current a current resulting from directed thermionic emission, as the flow of emitted electrons from a heated cathode to the plate

thermionic emission the phenomenon of electron or ion emission from the heated surface of a conductor

therm·i·on·ics (thur′mī än′iks, -mē-) *n.* the study and science of thermionic activity

thermionic tube an electron tube having a cathode electrically heated in order to cause electron or ion emission Also [Brit.] **thermionic valve**

☆**therm·is·tor** (thər mis′tər, thur′mis′-) *n.* ⟦THERM(O)- + (RES)ISTOR⟧ a device constructed of solid semiconductor material, whose electrical resistance decreases with an increase in temperature: used to measure temperature differences in tissue cells, microwave or infrared power, etc.

ther·mite (thur′mīt′) *n.* ⟦< Ger trademark *Thermit* < Gr *thermē,* heat (see WARM) + Ger *-it,* -ITE[1]⟧ a mixture of finely granulated aluminum with an oxide of iron or other metal, which produces great heat and is used in welding and in incendiary bombs: also **ther′mit** (-mit)

ther·mo- (thur′mō, -mə) ⟦< Gr *thermē,* heat: see WARM⟧ *combining form* **1** heat [*thermodynamics*] **2** thermoelectric [*thermopile*] Also, before a vowel, **therm-**

ther·mo·ba·rom·e·ter (thur′mo bə räm′ət ər) *n.* HYPSOMETER (sense 1)

ther·mo·chem·is·try (-kem′is trē) *n.* the branch of chemistry that deals with the relationship of heat to chemical change —**ther′mo·chem′i·cal** *adj.*

ther·mo·cline (thur′mə klīn′) *n.* ⟦THERMO- + *-cline,* as in ANTICLINE⟧ a layer of water between the warmer, surface zone and the colder, deep-water zone in a thermally stratified body of water, in which the temperature decreases rapidly with depth

ther·mo·cou·ple (-kup′əl) *n.* a pair of dissimilar conductors joined at two points to form a closed circuit so as to produce a thermoelectric current when the junctions are at different temperatures: used in temperature measurements: also called **thermoelectric couple**

ther·mo·dy·nam·ic (thur′mō dī nam′ik) *adj.* **1** of or having to do with thermodynamics **2** caused or operated by heat converted into motive power —**ther′mo·dy·nam′i·cal·ly** *adv.*

ther·mo·dy·nam·ics (-dī nam′iks) *n.* ⟦THERMO- + DYNAMICS⟧ the branch of physics dealing with the transformation of heat to and from other forms of energy, and with the laws governing such conversions of energy

ther·mo·e·lec·tric (-ē lek′trik) *adj.* of or having to do with the direct relations between heat and electricity: also **ther′mo·e·lec′tri·cal** —**ther′mo·e·lec′tri·cal·ly** *adv.*

ther·mo·e·lec·tric·i·ty (-ē′lek tris′ə tē) *n.* electricity produced by heating or cooling one junction of a thermocouple so as to produce an electromotive force

ther·mo·e·lec·tron (-ē lek′trän′) *n.* a negative ion, or electron, emitted from a body at high temperature

ther·mo·el·e·ment (-el′ə mənt) *n.* a device consisting of a thermocouple and a heating element arranged for measuring small currents, esp. at high frequencies

ther·mo·gen·e·sis (-jen′ə sis) *n.* ⟦ModL: see THERMO- & -GENESIS⟧ the production of heat, esp. by physiological action in an animal —**ther′mo·gen′ic** (-jen′ik) *adj.*

ther·mo·gram (thur′mə gram′) *n.* ⟦THERMO- + -GRAM⟧ a record made by a thermograph

ther·mo·graph (-graf′) *n.* ⟦THERMO- + -GRAPH⟧ **1** a thermometer for recording variations in temperature automatically; specif., an infrared camera for recording on film or on the face of an oscilloscope differences in temperature, as between normal and abnormal bodily tissues **2** THERMOGRAM

ther·mog·ra·phy (thər mäg′rə fē) *n.* ⟦THERMO- + -GRAPHY⟧ **1** the recording of temperature variations by means of a thermograph **2** a process for imitating copperplate engraving, as on calling cards, by dusting the freshly printed surface with a resinous powder which, when heated, fuses with the ink to form a raised surface —**ther·mog′ra·pher** *n.* —**ther·mo·graph·ic** (thur′mə graf′ik) *adj.*

ther·mo·junc·tion (thur′mō juŋk′shən) *n.* the point of contact between the two conductors forming a thermocouple

ther·mo·la·bile (-lā′bəl) *adj.* ⟦THERMO- + LABILE⟧ designating or of substances, as some toxins, enzymes, etc., that are destroyed or lose their characteristic properties when subjected to heat, esp. to a temperature of 55°C (131°F) or above —**ther′mo·la·bil′i·ty** (-lā bil′ə tē) *n.*

ther·mo·lu·mi·nes·cence (-lo͞o′mə nes′əns) *n.* ⟦THERMO- + LUMINESCENCE⟧ the release in the form of light of stored energy from a substance when it is heated —**ther′mo·lu′mi·nes′cent** *adj.*

ther·mol·y·sis (thər mäl′ə sis) *n.* ⟦ModL: see THERMO- & -LYSIS⟧ **1** *Chem.* dissociation of a compound by heat **2** *Physiol.* dispersion of heat from the body —**ther′mo·lyt′ic** (-mə lit′ik) *adj.*

ther·mo·mag·net·ic (thur′mō mag net′ik) *adj.* of or pertaining to the interrelations between heat and magnetism

ther·mom·e·ter (thər mäm′ət ər) *n.* ⟦Fr *thermomètre:* see THERMO- & -METER⟧ **1** an instrument for measuring temperatures, consisting of a graduated glass tube with a sealed, capillary bore in which mercury, colored alcohol, etc. rises or falls as it expands or contracts with changes in temperature: see FAHRENHEIT, CELSIUS, KELVIN[1], REAUMUR **2** any similar instrument, as one operating by means of a thermocouple —**ther·mo·met·ric** (thur′mə me′trik) *adj.* —**ther′mo·met′ri·cal·ly** *adv.*

ther·mom·e·try (-ə trē) *n.* **1** measurement of temperature **2** the science of making or using thermometers

ther·mo·nu·cle·ar (thur′mō no͞o′klē ər, -nyo͞o′-) *adj.* ⟦THERMO- + NUCLEAR⟧ *Physics* **1** designating or of a reaction in which isotopes of a light element, esp. hydrogen, fuse at temperatures of millions of degrees into heavier nuclei **2** designating, of, or employing the heat energy released in nuclear fusion [*thermonuclear* reactor]

ther·mo·phile (thur′mə fīl′) *n.* ⟦THERMO- + -PHILE⟧ an organism adapted to living at high temperatures, as some bacteria and algae —**ther′mo·phil′ic** (-fil′ik) *adj.*

ther·mo·pile (-pīl′) *n.* ⟦THERMO- + PILE[1]⟧ a device consisting of a series of thermocouples, used for measuring minute changes in temperature or for generating thermoelectric current

ther·mo·plas·tic (thur′mə plas′tik) *adj.* becoming or remaining soft and moldable when subjected to heat: said of certain plastics —*n.* a thermoplastic substance

Ther·mop·y·lae (thər mäp′ə lē′) in ancient Greece, a mountain pass in Locris, near an inlet of the Aegean Sea: scene of a battle (480 B.C.) in which the Persians under Xerxes destroyed a Spartan army under Leonidas

ther·mo·reg·u·la·tion (thur′mō reg′yə lā′shən) *n.* **1** the regulation of temperature **2** *Physiol.* the keeping of the temperature of a living body at a constant level by processes of heat production, heat transport, etc. —**ther′mo·reg′u·la′tor** *n.*

Ther·mos (thur′məs) ⟦< Gr *thermos,* hot, WARM⟧ *trademark for* a container, as a bottle, flask, or jug, for keeping liquids at almost their original temperature for several hours: it has two walls enclosing a vacuum and is fitted in a metal or plastic outer case —*n.* [*usually* **t-**] such a vessel

ther·mo·scope (thur′mə skōp′) *n.* ⟦THERMO- + -SCOPE⟧ an instrument for indicating changes in temperature of a substance, without accurately measuring them, by observing the accompanying changes in volume —**ther′mo·scop′ic** (-skäp′ik) *adj.*

ther·mo·set·ting (thur′mō set′iŋ) *adj.* becoming permanently hard and rigid when once subjected to heat: said of certain plastics

ther·mo·si·phon (thur′mō sī′fən) *n.* an apparatus consisting of an arrangement of siphon tubes for inducing the circulation of a liquid, as in the water-cooling system of an internal-combustion engine

ther·mo·sphere (thur′mə sfir′) *n.* the atmospheric zone or shell located above the mesopause beginning at an altitude of *c.* 85 km (53 mi) and characterized by a great rise in temperature with increasing altitude: see IONOSPHERE, EXOSPHERE

ther·mo·sta·ble (thur′mō stā′bəl) *adj.* ⟦THERMO- + STABLE[1]⟧ designating or of substances, as some toxins, enzymes, etc., that can be heated to moderate temperatures above 55°C (131°F) without losing their characteristic properties —**ther′mo·sta·bil′i·ty** (-stə bil′ə tē) *n.*

ther·mo·stat (thur′mə stat′) *n.* ⟦THERMO- + -STAT⟧ **1** an apparatus for regulating temperature, esp. one that automatically controls a heating or cooling unit **2** a device that sets off equipment at a certain temperature, as a fire alarm system —**ther′mo·stat′ic** *adj.* —**ther′mo·stat′i·cal·ly** *adv.*

ther·mo·stat·ics (thur′mə stat′iks) *n.* ⟦THERMO- + STATICS⟧ the science that deals with the equilibrium of heat

ther·mo·tax·is (-tak′sis) *n.* ⟦ModL: see THERMO- & -TAXIS⟧ **1** *Biol.* the positive, or negative, response of a freely moving organism toward, or away from, a source of heat **2** *Physiol.* the normal regulation of body temperature —**ther′mo·tax′ic** *adj.*, **ther′mo·tac′tic** (-tak′tik)

ther·mo·ten·sile (-ten′səl) *adj.* of or having a tensile strength that varies with changes in temperature

ther·mot·ro·pism (thər mä′trə piz′əm, thur′mō trō′piz′əm) *n.* ⟦THERMO- + -TROPISM⟧ *Biol.* any positive, or negative, movement or growth of a plant or sessile animal toward, or away from, a source of heat —**ther·mo·trop·ic** (thur′mə träp′ik) *adj.*

the·roid (thir′oid′) *adj.* ⟦Gr *thēr,* a wild beast (see FIERCE) + -OID⟧ suggestive of an animal; beastlike

the·ro·pod (thir′ə päd′) *n.* ⟦< ModL *Theropoda* < Gr *thēr,* a wild beast (see FIERCE) + -PODA⟧ any of a suborder (Theropoda) of flesh-eating saurischian dinosaurs that walked mainly on the hind legs

Ther·si·tes (thər sīt′ēz) *n.* ⟦L < Gr *Thersitēs* < dial. (Lesbian) *thersos,* boldness, for *tharsos:* see THRASONICAL⟧ in the *Iliad,* an ugly, discontented, abusive Greek soldier in the Trojan War

ther·sit·i·cal (thər sit′i kəl) *adj.* ⟦after prec.⟧ loud and abusive

Thes *abbrev.* Thessalonians

the·sau·rus (thi sô′rəs) *n., pl.* **-rus·es** or **-sau′ri′** (-rī′) ⟦L < Gr *thēsauros,* a treasure⟧ **1** a treasury or storehouse **2** a book containing a store of words;

specif., a book of synonyms and antonyms **3** a categorized index of terms for use in information retrieval, as from a computer

these (thēz) ***pron., adj. pl. of*** THIS

The·se·us (thē′so͞os′, thē′sē əs) ***n.*** ⟦L < Gr *Thēseus*⟧ *Gr. Legend* the principal hero of Attica, son of Aegeus and king of Athens, famed esp. for his killing of the Minotaur —**The·se·an** (thē sē′ən) ***adj.***

the·sis (thē′sis) ***n., pl.*** **-ses′** (-sēz′) ⟦L < Gr, a placing, position, proposition < base of *tithenai*, to put, place: see DO[1]⟧ **1** *a)* in classical Greek poetry, the long syllable of a foot *b)* in later poetry, the short or unaccented syllable or syllables of a foot **2** a proposition maintained or defended in argument, formerly one publicly disputed by a candidate for a degree in a medieval university **3** a formal and lengthy research paper, esp. a work of original research written in partial fulfillment of the requirements for a master's degree: see DISSERTATION **4** an unproved statement assumed as a premise **5** in Hegelian philosophy, the initial, least adequate phase of development in dialectic: see DIALECTIC (***n.*** 3)

Thes·pi·an (thes′pē ən) ***adj.*** 1 of Thespis **2** [*often* **t-**] having to do with the drama; dramatic —***n.*** [*often* **t-**] an actor or actress: a somewhat humorous or pretentious term

Thes·pis (thes′pis) 6th cent. B.C.; Gr. poet: traditionally the originator of Gr. tragedy

Thess *abbrev.* Thessalonians

Thes·sa·li·a (thes′ə lē′ə, the sä′lē ə) *Gr. name for* THESSALY

Thes·sa·lo·ni·an (thes′ə lō′nē ən) ***adj.*** of Thessalonica or its people or culture —***n.*** a person born or living in Thessalonica

Thes·sa·lo·ni·ans (-ənz) ***n.*** either of two books of the New Testament which were letters from the Apostle Paul to the Christians of Thessalonica: abbrev. *Thess, Thes*, or *Th*

Thes·sa·lon·i·ca (thes′ə län′i kə, -ə lō nī′kə) *ancient name for* SALONIKA

Thes·sa·lo·ni·ki or **Thes·sa·lo·ni·ke** (thes′ä lô nē′kē) *modern Gr. name for* SALONIKA

Thes·sa·ly (thes′ə lē) region of E Greece, between the Pindus Mountains & the Aegean Sea —**Thes·sa·li·an** (the sā′lē ən, -sāl′yən) ***adj., n.***

the·ta (thāt′ə, thēt′ə) ***n.*** ⟦Gr *thēta:* of Sem orig., akin to Heb *tet*⟧ the eighth letter of the Greek alphabet (Θ, ϑ, θ)

theta wave any of the electrical brain waves having a frequency between four and eight hertz and associated with a drowsy, semiconscious state of mind: also **theta rhythm**

thet·ic (thet′ik) ***adj.*** ⟦Gr *thetikos*, fit for placing < *thetos*, placed < base of *tithenai:* see DO[1]⟧ set forth dogmatically; prescribed: also **thet′i·cal** —**thet′i·cal·ly** ***adv.***

The·tis (thēt′is) ***n.*** ⟦L < Gr *Thetis*⟧ *Gr. Myth.* one of the Nereids and mother of Achilles

the·ur·gy (thē′ər jē) ***n., pl.*** **-gies** ⟦LL(Ec) *theurgia*, a summoning of spirits < LGr(Ec) *theourgia* < *theourgos*, divine worker < Gr *theos*, god (see THEO-) + *ergon*, WORK⟧ **1** an occurrence or accomplishment or a sequence of these, esp. when remarkable or extraordinary, viewed as effected by supernatural or divine agency **2** a set of acts or incantations taken to be capable of producing such occurrences or accomplishments —**the·ur·gic** (thē ʉr′jik) ***adj.*** —**the′ur·gist** ***n.***

thews (thyo͞oz) ***pl.n., sing.*** **thew** ⟦ME *theawes*, good qualities, hence, later, good physical qualities, strength < OE *theaw*, custom, habit, hence characteristic quality, akin to OS *thau*, custom < IE base **teu-*, to pay attention to, notice > L *tueri*, to keep in sight, observe⟧ **1** muscular power; bodily strength **2** muscles or sinews —**thew′y** ***adj.*** **thew′i·er, thew′i·est**

they (thā) ***pron., sing.*** **he, she, it** ⟦ME *thei* < ON *thei-r*, nom. masc. pl. of the demonstrative pron.; like THEIR & THEM (ME *theim*), also < the ON demonstrative forms, *thei* replaced earlier ME *he (hi)* because the native pronouns were phonetically confused with the forms of the pers. pron. (ME *he, hire, hem, him*, etc.): cf. THEIR, THEM, SHE⟧ **1** the persons, animals, or things previously mentioned: personal pronoun in the third person plural: *they* is the nominative form, *them* the objective, *theirs* the possessive, and *themselves* the reflexive and intensive; *their* is the possessive pronominal adjective **2** people [*they* say it's so] **3** the person or group just mentioned: often used with a singular antecedent (as *everybody, somebody, everyone*) to avoid the masculine implications of the traditional *he* without distinction as to gender, although this usage is objected to by some [everyone thinks *they* are right about this issue]

they'd (thād) *contraction* **1** they had **2** they would

they'll (thāl, thel) *contraction* **1** they will **2** they shall

they're (ther, thā′ər) *contraction* they are

they've (thāv) *contraction* they have

thi- (thī) *combining form* THIO-

thi·a·mine (thī′ə min, -mēn′) ***n.*** ⟦< prec. + (VIT)AMIN⟧ a white, crystalline B vitamin, $C_{12}H_{17}ClN_4OS$, found in the outer coating of cereal grains, green peas, beans, egg yolk, liver, etc., and also prepared synthetically; vitamin B_1: a deficiency of this vitamin results in beriberi and certain nervous disorders: also **thi′a·min** (-min)

thi·a·zine (thī′ə zēn′, -zin) ***n.*** ⟦THI- + AZINE⟧ any of a group of heterocyclic compounds whose molecules contain one atom of nitrogen, one atom of sulfur, and four atoms of carbon, arranged in a ring

thi·a·zole (thī′ə zōl′) ***n.*** ⟦THI- + AZOLE⟧ **1** a colorless, liquid azole, C_3H_3NS, that is soluble in alcohol or ether but only slightly soluble in water **2** any of its various derivatives, used in dyes and drugs

Thi·bet (tə bet′) *alt. sp. of* TIBET —**Thi·bet′an** ***adj., n.***

thick (thik) ***adj.*** ⟦ME *thikke* < OE *thicce*, thick, dense, akin to Ger *dick* < IE base **tegu-*, thick, fat > OIr *tiug*⟧ **1** having relatively great depth; of considerable extent from one surface or side to the opposite; not thin [a *thick* board] **2** having relatively large diameter in relation to length [a *thick* pipe] **3** as measured in the third dimension or between opposite surfaces [a wall six inches *thick*] **4** having the constituent elements abundant and close together; specif., *a)* marked by profuse, close growth; luxuriant [*thick* hair, *thick* woods] *b)* great in number and packed closely together [a *thick* crowd] *c)* having much body; not thin in consistency; viscous [*thick* soup] *d)* dense and heavy [*thick* smoke, a *thick* snowfall] *e)* filled with smoke, fog, or other vapors *f)* covered to a considerable depth [roads *thick* with mud] *g)* sprinkled or studded profusely [a sky *thick* with stars] **5** impenetrably dark, dismal, or obscure [the *thick* shadows of night] **6** *a)* sounding blurred, slurred, muffled, fuzzy, etc., or husky, hoarse, etc. [a *thick* voice, *thick* speech] *b)* strongly marked; pronounced [speaking with a *thick* brogue] **7** [Informal] slow to understand; stupid **8** [Informal] close in friendly association; intimate **9** [Informal, Chiefly Brit.] too much to be tolerated; excessive —***adv.*** in a thick way —***n.*** the thickest part or the period of greatest activity [in the *thick* of the fight] —**SYN.** CLOSE[1] —**thick as thieves** [Informal] intimately associated —**through thick and thin** in good times and bad times; in every eventuality —**thick′ish** ***adj.*** —**thick′ly** ***adv.***

thick·en (thik′ən) ***vt., vi.*** **1** to make or become thick or thicker, as in dimension, density, consistency, articulation, etc. **2** to make or become more complex or involved [the plot *thickened*] —**thick′en·er** ***n.***

thick·en·ing (thik′ən iŋ) ***n.*** **1** the action of a person or thing that thickens **2** a substance or material used to thicken **3** the thickened part of something

thick·et (thik′it) ***n.*** ⟦ME < OE *thiccet* < *thicce*, THICK⟧ a thick growth of shrubs, underbrush, or small trees —**thick′et·ed** ***adj.***

thick·head (thik′hed′) ***n.*** a stupid person; blockhead —**thick′head′ed** ***adj.*** —**thick′head′ed·ness** ***n.***

thick·ness (thik′nis) ***n.*** **1** the quality or condition of being thick **2** the measure of how thick a thing is, as distinguished from the length or width of any of its surfaces **3** a layer, stratum, etc. [three *thicknesses* of cloth] **4** the thickest place or part

thick·set (thik′set′) ***adj.*** **1** planted thickly or closely **2** thick in body; stocky —***n.*** [Archaic] a thicket

thick-skinned (thik′skind′) ***adj.*** **1** having a thick skin **2** *a)* not easily hurt by criticism, insult, etc. *b)* callous, unfeeling, hardhearted, etc.

thick-skulled (thik′skuld′) ***adj.*** stupid or obtuse

thick-wit·ted (thik′wit′id) ***adj.*** slow-witted; stupid

thief (thēf) ***n., pl.*** **thieves** (thēvz) ⟦ME < OE *theof, thiof*, akin to Ger *dieb* < IE base **teup-*, to cower, lurk⟧ a person who steals, esp. secretly; one guilty of theft, or larceny

Thiers (tyer), **Louis A·dolphe** (lwē à dôlf′) 1797-1877; Fr. statesman & historian

thieve (thēv) ***vt., vi.*** **thieved, thiev′ing** ⟦via ME dial. < OE *theofian* < *theof*, THIEF⟧ to commit, or get by, theft

thiev·er·y (thē′vər ē) ***n., pl.*** **-er·ies** the act or practice of stealing or an instance of this; theft

thiev·ish (thē′vish) ***adj.*** **1** addicted to thieving, or stealing **2** of, like, or characteristic of a thief; stealthy; furtive —**thiev′ish·ly** ***adv.*** —**thiev′ish·ness** ***n.***

thigh (thī) ***n.*** ⟦ME *thih* < OE *theoh*, akin to MHG *diech* < IE **teuk-* < base **teu-*, to swell > THUMB, L *tumor*⟧ **1** that part of the leg in humans and other vertebrates between the knee and the hip; region of the thighbone, or femur **2** the region of the tibia, as in poultry

thigh·bone (thī′bōn′) ***n.*** FEMUR: also **thigh bone**

thig·mo·tax·is (thig′mə tak′sis) ***n.*** ⟦ModL < Gr *thigma*, touch < *thinganein*, to touch with the hand (< IE base **dheiĝh-*, to knead > DOUGH) + *-taxis*, -TAXIS⟧ STEREOTAXIS (sense 1) —**thig′mo·tac′tic** (-tak′tik) ***adj.***

thig·mot·ro·pism (thig mä′trə piz′əm) ***n.*** ⟦ModL: see prec. & -TROPISM⟧ STEREOTROPISM —**thig′mo·trop′ic** (-mə träp′ik) ***adj.***

thill (thil) ***n.*** ⟦ME *thille*, a stake, pole, plank < OE, akin to ON *thil*, OHG *dil*, board wall, plank floor < IE base **telo-*, flat surface > L *tellus*, earth⟧ either of the two shafts between which a horse is hitched to a wagon

thim·ble (thim′bəl) ***n.*** ⟦ME *thimbel* (with unhistoric *-b-*) < OE *thymel*, thumbstall < *thuma*, THUMB + *-el*, dim. suffix⟧ **1** a small cap of metal, plastic, etc. worn as a protection on the finger that pushes the needle in sewing **2** anything like this; esp., a metal ring with a groove on the outside, inserted in a loop of rope to add strength and prevent wear

☆**thim·ble·ber·ry** (thim′bəl ber′ē) ***n., pl.*** **-ries** BLACK RASPBERRY

thim·ble·ful (thim′bəl fo͝ol′) ***n., pl.*** **-fuls′** **1** as much as a thimble will hold **2** a very small quantity

thim·ble·rig (thim′bəl rig′) ***n.*** ⟦see RIG⟧ SHELL GAME — ***vt., vi.*** **-rigged′, -rig′ging** to cheat or swindle, as in this game —**thim′ble·rig′ger** ***n.***

☆**thim·ble·weed** (thim′bəl wēd′) ***n.*** any of various plants with thimble-shaped receptacles; esp., *a)* any of several anemones with elongated cylindrical heads of woolly achenes *b)* any of several rudbeckias

thi·mer·o·sal (thī mer′ə sal′, -mur′-) ***n.*** ⟦by contr. < & transposition of constituents of (*sodium ethyl*)*mercurithiosalicylate*, name of the compound⟧ a cream-colored, crystalline compound, $C_9H_9HgNaO_2S$, used chiefly in solutions as an antiseptic for surface wounds

Thim·phu (thim′po͞o′, thim po͞o′) capital of Bhutan, in the W part

thin (thin) ***adj.*** **thin′ner, thin′nest** ⟦ME *thinne* < OE *thynne*, akin to Ger *dünn* < IE **tenu-*, thin < base **ten-*, to stretch > L *tenuis*, thin, *tenere*, to hold, *tendere* & Gr *teinein*, to stretch⟧ **1** having relatively little depth; of little extent from one surface or side to the opposite [*thin* paper] **2** having relatively small diameter in relation to length [*thin* thread] **3** having little fat or flesh; lean; gaunt; slender **4** having the constituent elements small in number and not close together; specif., *a)* scanty in growth; sparsely distributed [*thin* hair] *b)* small in size or number [*thin* receipts] *c)* lacking body; not thick in consistency; watery [*thin* soup] *d)* not dense or heavy [*thin* smoke, a *thin* snowfall] *e)* rarefied, as air at high altitudes **5** of little intensity; dim; faint; pale [*thin* colors] **6** of little volume or resonance; high-pitched and weak [a *thin* voice] **7** light or sheer, as certain fabrics **8** easily seen through; flimsy or unconvincing [a *thin* excuse] **9** lacking solidity, substance, or vigor; slight, weak, vapid, etc. [a *thin* plot, *thin* argument] **10** *Photog.* lacking in DENSITY (sense 1*c*): said of an underexposed or underdeveloped negative or print —***adv.*** **thin′ner, thin′nest** in a thin way —***vt., vi.*** **thinned, thin′ning** ⟦ME *thinnen* < OE *(ge)thynnian* < the adj.⟧ to make or become thin or thinner, as in dimension, density, etc. Often with *out, down,* etc. —**thin′ly** ***adv.*** —**thin′ness** ***n.***

thine (thīn) [Archaic] ***pron.*** ⟦ME *thin* < OE, gen. of *thu,* THOU[1] (ME loss of *-n* before a consonant gives THY)⟧ that or those belonging to thee (you): the possessive form of THOU[1], used without a following noun [this book is *thine*; *thine* are better; is he a friend of *thine?*] —***possessive pronominal adj.*** thy: used esp. before a word beginning with a vowel or the letter *h*

thing[1] (thiŋ) ***n.*** ⟦ME < OE, council, court, controversy, akin to Ger *ding,* ON *thing* (orig. sense, "public assembly," hence, "subject of discussion, matter, thing") < IE **tenk-*, to stretch, period of time < base **ten-*, to stretch > THIN⟧ **1** any matter, circumstance, affair, or concern: *often used in pl.* [how are *things?*] **2** that which is done, has been done, or is to be done; happening, act, deed, incident, event, etc. [to accomplish great *things*] **3** that which constitutes an end to be achieved, a step in a process, etc. [the next *thing* is to mix thoroughly] **4** anything conceived of or referred to as existing as an individual, distinguishable entity; specif., *a)* any single entity distinguished from all others [each *thing* in the universe] *b)* a tangible object, as distinguished from a concept, quality, etc. [paintings and other beautiful *things*] *c)* an inanimate object *d)* an item, detail, etc. [go over each *thing* in the list] *e)* the object or concept referred to or represented by a word, symbol, or sign; referent *f)* an object of thought; idea [think the right *things*] **5** *a)* [*pl.*] personal belongings; also, clothes or clothing *b)* a dress, garment, etc. [not a *thing* to wear] **6** [*pl.*] articles, devices, etc. used for some purpose **7** a person: used in expressions of affection, pity, contempt, etc. [poor *thing*] **8** a being, object, or concept the exact term for which is not known or recalled or is avoided, as from disdain [where did you buy that *thing?*] **9** [Informal] a point of contention; issue [don't make a *thing* of it] ☆**10** [Informal] a complex, often neurotic liking, fear, aversion, etc. with regard to some person, thing, or activity [to have a *thing* about air travel] ☆**11** [Informal] what one wants to do or is adept at [do one's own *thing*] **12** *Law* that which may be owned; a property: distinguished from PERSON —**see things** [Informal] to have hallucinations —**the thing 1** that which is wise, essential, etc. **2** that which is the height of fashion or style

thing[2] (tiŋ; *E* thiŋ) ***n.*** ⟦ON, assembly: see prec.⟧ a Scandinavian legislative body

thing·a·ma·bob or **thing·um·a·bob** (thiŋ′ə mə bäb′) ***n.*** ⟦see fol.⟧ [Informal] THINGAMAJIG: also **thing′um·bob′** (-əm bäb′) or **thing·um·my** (thiŋ′gum′ē, thiŋ′əm ē)

thing·a·ma·jig or **thing·um·a·jig** (-jig′) ***n.*** ⟦extension of older *thingum,* THING[1]⟧ [Informal] any device, contrivance, gadget, etc.: jocular substitute for a name not known or temporarily forgotten

thing-in-it·self (thiŋ′in it self′) ***n.*** ⟦calque of Ger DING AN SICH⟧ NOUMENON

think[1] (thiŋk) ***vt.*** **thought, think′ing** ⟦< ME *thenchen,* to think, confused with *thinchen,* to seem < OE *thencan* < PGmc **thankjan,* to think: for IE base see THANK⟧ **1** to form or have in the mind; conceive [*thinking* good thoughts] **2** to hold in one's opinion; judge; consider [many *think* her charming] **3** to believe; surmise; expect [they *think* they can come] **4** to determine, resolve, work out, etc. by reasoning [*think* what your next move should be] **5** [Now Rare] to purpose; intend [*thinking* to do right] **6** *a)* to bring to mind; form an idea of [*think* what the future holds] *b)* to recall; recollect [*think* what joy was ours] **7** to have the mind turned steadily toward; have constantly in mind [*think* success] —***vi.*** **1** to use the mind for arriving at conclusions, making decisions, drawing inferences, etc.; reflect; reason [learn to *think*] **2** to have an opinion, belief, expectation, etc. [I just *think* so] **3** to weigh something mentally; reflect [*think* before you act] **4** to call to mind; recall; remember: with *of* or *about* **5** to have an opinion, judgment, etc.: with *of* or *about* **6** to allow oneself to consider: with *of* or *about* **7** to have regard for; consider the welfare of: with *of* or *about* **8** to discover or invent; conceive (*of*) —***n.*** [Informal] the act of thinking [give it a good *think*] —***adj.*** [Slang] having to do with thinking —**think (all) the world of** to admire or love greatly —**think better of 1** to form a more favorable opinion of **2** to make a more sensible or practical decision about, after reconsidering —**think fit** to regard as proper or appropriate —**think little (or nothing) of 1** to attach little (or no) importance, value, etc. to **2** to have little (or no) hesitancy about —**think nothing of it!** you're welcome! —**think on (or upon)** [Archaic] to give thought or consideration to —**think out 1** to think about completely or to the end **2** to work out, solve, discover, or plan by thinking —**think out loud** to speak one's thoughts as they occur: also **think aloud** —**think over** to give thought to; ponder well, as for reconsideration —**think through** to think about until one reaches a conclusion or resolution —**think twice** to reconsider; pause to think about again —**think up** to invent, contrive, plan, etc. by thinking

SYN.—**think** is the general word meaning to exercise the mental faculties so as to form ideas, arrive at conclusions, etc. [learn to *think* clearly]; **reason** implies a logical sequence of thought, starting with what is known or assumed and advancing to a definite conclusion through the inferences drawn [he *reasoned* that she would accept]; **cogitate** is used, sometimes humorously, of a person who is, or appears to be, thinking hard [I was *cogitating,* not daydreaming]; **reflect** implies a turning of one's thoughts on or back on a subject and connotes deep or quiet continued thought [he *reflected* on the day's events]; **speculate** implies a reasoning on the basis of incomplete or uncertain evidence and therefore stresses the conjectural character of the opinions formed [to *speculate* on the possibility of life on Mars]; **deliberate** implies careful and thorough consideration of a matter in order to arrive at a conclusion [the jury *deliberated* on the case]

think[2] (thiŋk) ***v.impersonal*** *pt.* **thought** ⟦< ME *thinchen,* to seem, confused with *thenchen,* to think: see prec.⟧ to seem: obs., except in archaic METHINKS, METHOUGHT

-think (thiŋk) *combining form forming nouns* a pattern or manner of thinking [*groupthink*]

think·a·ble (thiŋ′kə bəl) ***adj.*** **1** that can be thought; conceivable **2** that can be considered as a possibility

think·er (thiŋ′kər) ***n.*** one who thinks; specif., a person capable of, or known for, profound or incisive thought; intellectual, sage, etc.

think·ing (thiŋ′kiŋ) ***adj.*** **1** that thinks or can think; rational **2** given to thought; reflective —***n.*** the action of one who thinks or the result of such action; thought —**put on one's thinking cap** to begin careful thinking about a problem

☆**think piece** [Slang] an article, column, etc., as in a newspaper or magazine, presenting news analysis, background material, personal opinion, etc., as distinguished from a straight news account

☆**think tank** a group or center organized and funded, as by a government or business, to do intensive research and problem-solving

thin·ner (thin′ər) ***n.*** a person or thing that thins; esp., a volatile liquid, as turpentine, added to paint, varnish, etc. to lower its viscosity

thin·nish (thin′ish) ***adj.*** somewhat thin

thin-skinned (thin′skind′) ***adj.*** **1** having a thin skin **2** easily hurt by criticism, insults, etc.; sensitive

Thin·su·late (thin′sə lāt′) ⟦prob. < THIN + (IN)SULATE⟧ *trademark for* a type of thermal insulation made of synthetic fibers, used esp. as a lining in clothing

thi·o- (thī′ō, -ə) ⟦< Gr *theion,* brimstone, sulfur, ult. < IE **dhwes-* < base **dheu-*, to smoke, fume > DULL⟧ *combining form* sulfur: used in many chemical terms to indicate the replacement of oxygen by divalent sulfur [*thiourea*]

thi·o·a·ce·tic acid (thī′ō ə sēt′ik, -set′-) ⟦prec. + ACETIC⟧ a yellowish liquid, CH_3COSH, with a very pungent odor: used as a chemical reagent and tear gas

thi·o acid (thī′ō) [see THIO-] an acid in which part or all of the oxygen atoms in the molecule have been replaced by sulfur atoms

thi·o·bac·te·ri·a (-bak tir′ē ə) ***pl.n.,*** *sing.* **-ri·um** (-əm) ⟦THIO- + BACTERIA⟧ bacteria found esp. in stagnant water and at the bottom of the sea, that oxidize or reduce sulfur compounds, as hydrogen sulfide

thi·o·car·ba·mide (-kär′bə mīd′) ***n.*** THIOUREA

thi·o·cy·a·nate (-sī′ə nāt′) ***n.*** **1** a salt of thiocyanic acid containing the monovalent, negative radical SCN **2** an uncharged ester of this acid

thi·o·cy·an·ic acid (-sī an′ik) ⟦THIO- + CYANIC⟧ a colorless, unstable liquid, HSCN, with a penetrating odor, known chiefly in the form of its salts

☆**Thi·o·kol** (thī′ə kôl′, -kōl′) ⟦arbitrary coinage⟧ *trademark for* any of various synthetic rubbery materials resistant to oil, grease, and water, used as sealants, for hosing and tank linings, etc.

thi·ol (thī′ôl′, -ōl′) ***n.*** ⟦THI(O)- + -OL[1]⟧ any of various organic compounds derived from hydrogen sulfide, esp. a mercaptan

thi·o·nine (thī′ə nēn′, -nin) ***n.*** ⟦< Gr *theion,* sulfur (see THIO-) + -INE[3]⟧ a dark-green crystalline thiazine base, $C_{12}H_9N_3S$, producing a violet dye in solution, used esp. as a stain in microscopy

thi·o·nyl (thī′ə nil′) ***n.*** ⟦< Gr *theion,* sulfur (see THIO-) + -YL⟧ any of a group of inorganic compounds containing the divalent radical SO: see SULFOXIDE

thi·o·pen·tal sodium (thī′ō pen′təl) ⟦THIO- + PENT(A)- + -AL⟧ a yellowish-white, hygroscopic powder, $C_{11}H_{17}N_2O_2SNa$, injected intravenously in solution as a general anesthetic and hypnotic

thi·o·phene (thī′ə fēn′) ***n.*** ⟦THIO- + obs. *phene,* benzene < Fr *phène:* see PHEN-⟧ a heterocyclic, colorless liquid, C_4H_4S, resembling benzene and found in coal tar

thi·o·phos·phate (thī′ō fäs′fāt′) ***n.*** a salt or ester of a thiophosphoric acid

thi·o·phos·phor·ic acid (-fäs fôr′ik) **1** a phosphoric acid in which one or more oxygen atoms have been replaced by a sulfur atom **2** the unstable acid, H_3PO_3S, produced only in solution or as a salt

thi·o·sul·fate (-sul′fāt′) ***n.*** a salt or ester of thiosulfuric acid; esp., sodium thiosulfate

thi·o·sul·fu·ric acid (-sul fyoor′ik) ⟦< THIO- + SULFURIC⟧ an unstable acid, $H_2S_2O_3$, whose salts are used in photography, as an antichlor in bleaching, etc.

thi·o·u·ra·cil (-yoor′ə sil) ***n.*** ⟦THIO- + URACIL⟧ a white, crystalline, bitter-tasting powder, $C_4H_4N_2OS$, used to reduce thyroid activity, and in treating angina pectoris

thi·o·u·re·a (-yo͞o rē′ə, -yoor′ē ə) ***n.*** ⟦ModL: see THIO- & UREA⟧ a colorless, crystalline chemical compound, $CS(NH_2)_2$, used in organic synthesis, in photography, etc.

☆**thi·ram** (thī′ram′) ***n.*** ⟦< ? *thiuram* < prec. + AM(YL)⟧ a yellow or white powder, $C_6H_{12}N_2S_4$, used as a rubber accelerator and vulcanizer, fungicide, seed disinfectant, etc.

third (thʉrd) ***adj.*** ⟦ME *thirde,* altered by metathesis < *thridde* < OE *thridda* < IE **tṛtiyo-* (< base **trei-,* THREE) > L *tertius,* Gr *tritos*⟧ **1** preceded by two others in a series; 3d or 3rd **2** next below the second in rank, power, value, merit, excellence, etc. **3** designating any of the three equal parts of something —***adv.*** in the third place, rank, group, etc. —***n.*** **1** the one following the second **2** any person, thing, class, place, etc. that is third **3** any of the three equal parts of something; ⅓ **4** the third forward gear of a transmission: it provides more speed but less torque than second **5** *Baseball short for* THIRD BASE **6** *Music a)* the third tone of an ascending diatonic scale, or a tone two degrees above or below any given tone in such a scale; mediant *b)* the interval between two such tones, or a combination of them

☆**third base** *Baseball* **1** the base to the right of the pitcher, the third of the four bases that a base runner attempts to reach safely **2** the defensive position played by the third baseman

☆**third baseman** *Baseball* the infielder who plays near third base and usually covers third base

third-class (thʉrd′klas′) ***adj.*** **1** of the class, rank, excellence, etc. next below the second **2** designating or of accommodations next below the second class ☆**3** designating or of a former class of mail consisting of identical circulars, advertisements, etc. mailed in bulk, lightweight merchandise, etc. —***adv.*** **1** with accommodations next below the second class [to travel *third-class*] ☆**2** as or by third-class mail

third degree **1** in Freemasonry, the degree of master mason ☆**2** ⟦orig. ? fig. use of ritual by Freemasons⟧ [Informal] harsh, grueling treatment and questioning, as of a prisoner in order to force a confession or exact information: often preceded by *the* —**third′-de·gree′** ***adj.***

third-degree burn see BURN[1] (*n.* 1)

third dimension **1** the dimension of depth in something as distinguished from the two dimensions of any of its flat surfaces **2** the quality of having, or of seeming to have, depth or solidity —**third′-di·men′sion·al** ***adj.***

third estate *see* ESTATE (sense 2)

third eyelid NICTITATING MEMBRANE

third force [*occas.* **T- F-**] a third element, group, bloc, etc. functioning as a counterbalancing, neutralizing, or moderating force or influence in a struggle between two established powers; specif., a coalition of nations for this purpose internationally

Third International COMINTERN

third·ly (thʉrd′lē) ***adv.*** in the third place; third: used chiefly in enumerating topics

Third Order [*occas.* **t- o-**] an association of laypersons (*tertiaries*) affiliated with a religious order

third party ☆**1** a political party organized to compete against the two major parties in a two-party system **2** a person or, often, specif., a legal entity, in a case or matter other than the principals

third-par·ty (thʉrd′pärt′ē) ***adj.*** **1** of or involving a THIRD PARTY [a *third-party* candidate, *third-party* debt collection] **2** designating or of a product developed or manufactured by one vendor, and compatible with or sold along with the product of another vendor [a *third-party* software application]

third person **1** *Gram. a)* the form of a pronoun (as *she*) or verb (as *is*) that refers to the person(s) or thing(s) spoken of in a given utterance *b)* a category consisting of such forms **2** narration characterized by the general use of such forms

☆**third rail** **1** an extra rail used in some electric railways, instead of an overhead wire, for supplying power **2** ⟦in ref. to the danger of electrocution from contact with this rail⟧ figuratively, anything considered too problematic or controversial to freely alter or reevaluate without peril, as to one's political career [Social Security is the *third rail* of American politics]

third-rate (-rāt′) ***adj.*** **1** third in quality or other rating; third-class **2** inferior; very poor —**third′-rat′er** ***n.***

Third Reich *see* REICH

Third Republic the republic established in France in 1870, after the fall of Napoleon III, lasting until the German occupation of France in WWII

☆**third stream** a kind of music that combines techniques of jazz improvisation with the forms and instrumentation of classical music —**third′-stream′** ***adj.***

third ventricle one of the four cavities of the brain, lying on the midline between the cerebral hemispheres

Third World ⟦transl. of Fr *tiers monde,* coined (1952) by A. Sauvy (1898-1990), Fr economist & sociologist⟧ [*also* **t- w-**] **1** those countries and territories, chiefly of Africa and Asia, once thought of as being outside the worlds, or spheres of influence, of the Western capitalist nations and the Soviet bloc **2** the poor and economically underdeveloped countries of the world collectively

third-world (thʉrd′wʉrld′) ***adj.*** of or like the Third World; specif., economically underdeveloped, politically unstable, etc. [a *third-world* standard of living]

thirl (thʉrl) ***vt., vi.*** ⟦ME *thirlen* < OE *thyrlian,* to bore < *thyrel,* hole < *thurh,* THROUGH⟧ [Brit. Dial.] **1** to pierce; perforate **2** *var. of* THRILL

thirst (thʉrst) ***n.*** ⟦ME < OE *thurst,* akin to Ger *durst* < IE base **ters-,* to dry > L *torrere,* to parch, *torridus,* torrid, *terra,* earth⟧ **1** the uncomfortable or distressful feeling caused by a desire or need for water and characterized generally by a sensation of dryness in the mouth and throat **2** [Informal] a craving for a specific liquid, esp. for alcoholic liquor **3** any strong desire; craving [a *thirst* for fame] —***vi.*** **1** to be thirsty **2** to have a strong desire or craving

thirst·y (thʉrs′tē) ***adj.*** **thirst′i·er, thirst′i·est** ⟦ME *thyrsti* < OE *thurstig*⟧ **1** feeling thirst; wanting to drink **2** *a)* lacking water or moisture; dry; parched [*thirsty* fields] *b)* very absorbent **3** [Informal] causing thirst [*thirsty* work] **4** having a strong desire; craving —**thirst′i·ly** ***adv.*** —**thirst′i·ness** ***n.***

thir·teen (thʉr′tēn′) ***adj.*** ⟦ME *thrittene* < OE *threotyne:* see THREE & -TEEN⟧ totaling three more than ten —***n.*** the cardinal number between twelve and fourteen; 13; XIII

thir·teenth (thʉr′tēnth′) ***adj.*** ⟦ME *thirtenth:* see prec. & -TH[2]⟧ **1** preceded by twelve others in a series; 13th **2** designating any of the thirteen equal parts of something —***n.*** **1** the one following the twelfth **2** any of the thirteen equal parts of something; ¹⁄₁₃ —***adv.*** in the thirteenth place, rank, group, etc.

thir·ti·eth (thʉrt′ē ith) ***adj.*** ⟦< ME *thrittythe* < OE *thritigotha:* see fol. & -TH[2]⟧ **1** preceded by twenty-nine others in a series; 30th **2** designating any of the thirty equal parts of something —***n.*** **1** the one following the twenty-ninth **2** any of the thirty equal parts of something; ¹⁄₃₀ —***adv.*** in the thirtieth place, rank, group, etc.

thir·ty (thʉrt′ē) ***adj.*** ⟦LME *thirti,* metathetic for *thritti* < OE *thritig* < *thri,* THREE + *-tig,* -TY[2]⟧ three times ten —***n.,*** *pl.* **-ties** **1** the cardinal number between twenty-nine and thirty-one; 30; XXX ☆**2** ⟦prob. orig. telegraphers' code for a concluding sentence⟧ this number used to signify the end of a dispatch, story, etc., as for a newspaper —**the thirties** the numbers or years, as of a century, from thirty through thirty-nine

thir·ty-sec·ond note (thʉrt′ē sek′ənd) *Music* a note having one thirty-second the duration of a whole note

thir·ty-two·mo (-to͞o′mō′) ***n.,*** *pl.* **-mos′** ⟦see -MO⟧ **1** the page size of a book made up of printer's sheets folded into 32 leaves, each leaf being approximately 3½ by 5½ inches **2** a book consisting of pages of this size Usually written 32mo or 32° —***adj.*** consisting of pages of this size

Thirty Years' War a series of European wars (1618-48) on political and religious issues, fought orig. between German Catholics and German Protestants, but later involving the Swedish, French, and Spanish

Thi·ru·van·an·tha·pur·am (tir′o͞o vän än′tä poor′äm) seaport on the Malabar Coast of S India

this (*th*is) ***pron.,*** *pl.* **these** ⟦ME *this, thes* < OE *thes,* masc., *this,* neut. < base of the demonstrative pron.: see THAT⟧ **1** the person or thing mentioned or understood [*this* is John; *this* tastes good] **2** the thing that is nearer than another referred to as "that" [*this* is larger than that] **3** the less remote in thought of two contrasted things [of the two possibilities, *this* is more likely than that] **4** the fact, idea, etc. that is being, or is about to be, mentioned, presented, etc. [*this* convinces us; now hear *this*] —***adj.,*** *pl.* **these** **1** designating the person or thing mentioned or understood [*this* man was John; *this* pie tastes good] **2** designating the thing that is nearer than the one referred to as "that" [*this* desk is smaller than that one] **3** designating the less remote in thought of two contrasted things [of the two, *this* possibility is more likely than that] **4** designating something that is being, or is about to be, mentioned, presented, etc. [hear *this* song; *this* fact will convince you] **5** [Informal] designating a particular but unspecified person or thing [there's *this* lady in Iowa] —***adv.*** to this extent; so [it was *this* big]

this·a·way (*th*is′ə wā′) ***adv., n.*** [Dial.] this way; here

Thisbe ***n.*** *see* PYRAMUS AND THISBE

this·tle (this′əl) ***n.*** ⟦ME *thistel* < OE, akin to Ger *distel* < IE base **(s)teig-,* a point > STICK, Sans *tiktá,* sharp⟧ any of various plants (as genera *Onopordum, Cirsium,* and *Cnicus*) of the composite family, with prickly leaves and heads of white, purple, pink, or yellow flowers; esp., the **Scotch thistle** (*O. acanthium*) with white down and lavender flowers

thistle

this·tle·down (this′əl doun′) ***n.*** the down attached to the flower head of a thistle

this·tly (this′lē, -əl ē) ***adj.*** **-tli·er, -tli·est** **1** like a thistle or thistles; prickly **2** full of thistles

this-worldly (*th*is′wʉrld′lē) ***adj.*** distinguished by or relating to material or earthly concerns; not spiritual or concerned with life in a future or imaginary world [*this-worldly* obligations] —**this′-world′li·ness** ***n.***

thith·er (*th*ith′ər, thith′-) ***adv.*** ⟦ME *thider* < OE < demonstrative base: see THAT⟧ to or toward that place; there —***adj.*** on or toward that side; farther

thith·er·to (*th*ith′ər to͞o′, thith′-; *th*ith′ər to͞o′, thith′-) ***adv.*** ⟦ME *thidir to*⟧ until that time; till then

thith·er·ward (*th*ith′ər wərd, thith′-) ***adv.*** ⟦ME < OE *thiderweard*⟧ [Now Rare] toward that place; thither: also **thith′er·wards** (-wərdz)

thix·ot·ro·py (thik sä′trə pē) ***n.*** ⟦< Gr *thixis,* touching (< *thinganein,* to touch: see THIGMOTAXIS) + -O- + -TROPY⟧ the property of certain gels and emulsions of becoming fluid when agitated and then setting again when left at rest —**thix′o·trop′ic** (-ō träp′ik, -ə träp′-) ***adj.***

ThM or **Th.M.** ***abbrev.*** ⟦L *Theologiae Magister*⟧ Master of Theology

tho or **tho'** (thō) *conj., adv. phonetic sp. of* THOUGH
thole[1] (thōl) *n.* THOLE PIN
thole[2] (thōl) *vt.* **tholed, thol′ing** ⟦ME *tholen* < OE *tholian* < IE base *tel-, to bear > TOLERATE⟧ [Now Dial., Chiefly Brit.] to suffer; endure; undergo
thole pin ⟦< *thole* < ME *tholle* < OE *thol*, akin to ON *thollr*, Du *dol* < IE *teul- < base *tēu-, to swell > THUMB⟧ a pin, usually either of a pair of pins, made of metal or wood and set vertically in the gunwale of a boat to serve as a fulcrum for an oar
Thom·as[1] (täm′əs) *n.* ⟦ME < LL(Ec) < Gr(Ec) *Thōmas* < Heb *teom*, Aram *teoma*, lit., a twin⟧ **1** a masculine name: dim. *Tom, Tommy*; fem. *Thomasina* **2** *Bible* (called *Didymus, the Twin*) one of the twelve Apostles, who doubted at first the resurrection of Jesus: John 20:24-29: his day is Dec. 21: also **Saint Thomas**
Thom·as[2] (täm′əs) **1 Clarence** 1948- ; associate justice, U.S. Supreme Court (1991-) **2 Dyl·an (Marlais)** (dil′ən) 1914-53; Welsh poet **3 (Philip) Edward** 1878-1917; Eng. poet **4 George Henry** 1816-70; Union general in the Civil War **5 Norman (Mattoon)** 1884-1968; U.S. Socialist leader **6 Seth** 1785-1859; U.S. clock manufacturer
Thomas à Becket *see* BECKET, Saint Thomas
Thomas à Kempis *see* KEMPIS, Thomas à
Thomas Aquinas *see* AQUINAS, Saint Thomas
Tho·mism (tō′miz′əm) *n.* the theological and philosophical doctrines or system of Saint Thomas Aquinas and his followers —**Tho′mist** *adj., n.* —**Tho·mis′tic** (-mis′tik) *adj.*
Thomp·son (tämp′sən, täm′-) **1 Benjamin** Count Rumford 1753-1814; Brit. scientist & statesman, born in America **2 David** 1770-1857; Cdn. explorer, born in England **3 Francis** 1859-1907; Eng. poet
☆**Thompson submachine gun** ⟦after a co-inventor, John T. *Thompson* (1860-1940), U.S. army officer⟧ an early type of SUBMACHINE GUN
Thom·son (täm′sən) **1 James** 1700-48; Scot. poet **2 James** (pseud. *B.V.*; i.e., *Bysshe Vanolis*) 1834-82; Scot. poet **3 Virgil** 1896-1989; U.S. composer **4 William** *see* KELVIN[2], 1st Baron
-thon (thän) *suffix* -ATHON: used after a vowel *[radiothon]*
thong (thôŋ) *n.* ⟦ME < OE *thwang*, twisted string, thong: see TWINGE⟧ **1** a narrow strip of leather, etc. used as a lace, strap, etc. **2** a whiplash, as of plaited strips of hide **3** FLIP-FLOP (*n.* 4) **4** *a)* a kind of bikini swimsuit bottom having only a narrow strip of fabric that goes between the legs and attaches in back to a waistband, so as to show the buttocks (also **thong bikini**) *b)* a pair of brief underpants like this
Thon·ga (täŋ′gə) *n.* **1** *pl.* **-gas** or **-ga** a member of a people of Mozambique **2** the Bantu language of this people
Thor (thôr) *n.* ⟦ON *Thorr:* see THUNDER⟧ *Norse Myth.* the god of thunder, war, and strength, and a son of Odin, armed with a magic hammer
tho·rac·ic (thə ras′ik) *adj.* ⟦ModL *thoracicus* < Gr *thōrakikos*⟧ of, in, or near the thorax
thoracic duct the main canal of the lymphatic system, passing along the front of the spinal column, collecting lymph and conveying it into the left subclavian vein
tho·ra·co- (thôr′ə kō) ⟦Gr *thōrako-*⟧ *combining form* **1** thorax *[thoracotomy]* **2** thorax and *[thoracolumbar]* Also, before a vowel, **thorac-**
tho·ra·co·lum·bar (thôr′ə kō lum′bər) *adj.* **1** of the thoracic and lumbar regions **2** SYMPATHETIC (sense 4)
tho·ra·cot·o·my (thôr′ə kät′ə mē) *n., pl.* **-mies** ⟦THORACO- + -TOMY⟧ surgical incision into the thorax
tho·rax (thôr′aks′) *n., pl.* **-rax′es** or **-ra·ces′** (-ə sēz′) ⟦ME < L < Gr *thōrax*, chest, breastplate⟧ **1** in tetrapods, including humans, *a)* the part of the body cavity from the neck or head to the abdomen, containing the heart, lungs, etc.; chest: in mammals, the diaphragm separates it from the abdomen *b)* the area of the trunk covering this part **2** in arthropods, the body segment, between the head and abdomen, to which the legs are attached
☆**Tho·ra·zine** (thôr′ə zēn′) *n.* ⟦former trademark < *thor-* (< ?) + (CHLOR-PROM)AZINE⟧ CHLORPROMAZINE
Tho·reau (thôr′ō; thô rō′, thə-), **Henry David** (born *David Henry Thoreau*) 1817-62; U.S. naturalist & writer
tho·ri·a (thôr′ē ə) *n.* ⟦ModL < Swed *Thorjord*, lit., Thor-earth (so named by BERZELIUS): see THORIUM⟧ a white, powdery form of thorium dioxide, ThO_2, used esp. in gas mantles and in making refractory crucibles
tho·ri·a·nite (-nīt′) *n.* ⟦< prec. + -ITE[1]⟧ a grayish-to-black, very hard, radioactive mineral, thorium dioxide, ThO_2, that is an ore of thorium
tho·rite (thôr′īt′) *n.* ⟦Swed *thorit:* see fol. & -ITE[1]⟧ a rare, usually dark, hard, radioactive mineral, thorium silicate, $ThSiO_4$, that is usually hydrated
tho·ri·um (thôr′ē əm) *n.* ⟦ModL: so named (1829) by BERZELIUS, its discoverer < ON *Thorr* (see THOR) + -IUM⟧ a rare, grayish, radioactive, metallic chemical element, one of the actinides, found in monazite and thorite: it is used in magnesium alloys, the making of gas mantles, electronic equipment, etc., and as a nuclear fuel: symbol, Th; at. no. 90: see the periodic table of elements in the Reference Supplement —**tho′ric** *adj.*
thorn (thôrn) *n.* ⟦ME < OE, akin to Ger *dorn* < IE *(s)ter-, prickly plant (< base *ster-, to be stiff) > Gr *ternax*, cactus stem⟧ **1** *a)* a very short, hard, leafless branch or stem with a sharp point *b)* any small tree or shrub bearing thorns, as a hawthorn *c)* the wood of any of these trees *d)* PRICKLE **2** a sharp, pointed protuberance on an animal; spine **3** anything that keeps troubling, vexing, or irritating one, like a constantly pricking thorn: usually in the phrase **thorn in one's side (or flesh)** **4** a rune in the Old English and Old Norse alphabets (Þ, þ), used to represent the voiced or voiceless apicodental fricative: in Middle English orthography it was gradually replaced by *th*
thorn apple 1 HAWTHORN **2** its applelike fruit ☆**3** a jimson weed or similar plant
thorn·back (thôrn′bak′) *n.* **1** any of several European rays with many tubercles on the back and a double row of spines on the tail **2** a large European spider crab (*Maja squinado*) with a spiny back **3** a guitarfish (*Platyrhinoidis triseriata*) with spines on the back, found in the Pacific
Thorn·dike (thôrn′dīk′), Dame **(Agnes) Sybil** 1882-1976; Brit. actress
Thorn·ton (thôrnt′'n) ⟦after Dan *Thornton*, governor of Colo. (1956)⟧ city in NE Colo., north of Denver
thorn·y (thôr′nē) *adj.* **thorn′i·er, thorn′i·est 1** full of thorns; brambly; prickly **2** having thorns or spines: said of some animals **3** like a thorn; sharp **4** full of obstacles, vexations, pain, etc. *[the thorny road to peace]* **5** full of controversial points; difficult; contentious *[a thorny problem]* —**thorn′i·ness** *n.*
thor·o (thur′ō) *adj.* [Informal] *short for* THOROUGH
tho·ron (thôr′än′) *n.* ⟦ModL < THOR(IUM) + *-on* as in ARGON⟧ a radioactive isotope of radon, resulting from the disintegration of thorium
thor·ough (thur′ō; *Brit* thu′rə) *prep., adv.* ⟦ME *thoruh, thuruh*, an emphatic var. of *through*, THROUGH⟧ *obs. var. of* THROUGH —*adj.* **1** passing through: now chiefly in comb. *[thoroughfare]* **2** done or proceeding through to the end; omitting nothing; complete *[a thorough checkup]* **3** that is completely (the thing specified); out-and-out; absolute *[a thorough rascal]* **4** very exact, accurate, or painstaking, esp. with regard to details *[a thorough researcher]* —*n.* [T-] *Eng. History* the ruthlessly thoroughgoing administrative policies carried out by William Laud and the Earl of Strafford during the reign of Charles I —**thor′ough·ly** *adv.* —**thor′ough·ness** *n.*
thorough bass *Music* **1** *a)* an old system for indicating accompanying chords by putting figures under the bass notes *b)* the figures used **2** loosely, the theory of harmony
☆**thorough brace** either of a pair of leather straps supporting the body of a coach or other horse-drawn vehicle and often serving as springs
thor·ough·bred (thur′ō bred′, thur′ə-) *adj.* **1** purebred; pedigreed: said as of a horse or a dog **2** thoroughly trained, educated, cultured, etc.; well-bred **3** excellent; first-rate —*n.* **1** a thoroughbred animal; specif., [T-] any of a breed of light horse developed by crossing Arabian and Turkish stallions with English mares: it is bred primarily for racing **2** a cultured, well-bred person
thor·ough·fare (-fer′) *n.* ⟦ME *thurghfare:* see THROUGH & FARE⟧ **1** a way through or passage through **2** a public street open at both ends; esp., such a street through which there is much traffic; highway; main road
thor·ough·go·ing (-gō′iŋ) *adj.* very thorough; specif., *a)* precise and painstaking *b)* being wholly such; unmitigated
thor·ough·paced (-pāst′) *adj.* **1** thoroughly trained in all paces or gaits: said of horses **2** THOROUGHGOING
thor·ough·pin (-pin′) *n.* a swelling in the sheath of a tendon in a horse's hock that shows on both sides of the leg
☆**thor·ough·wort** (-wurt′) *n.* BONESET
thorp or **thorpe** (thôrp) *n.* ⟦ME < OE, akin to Ger *dorf*, village < IE base *treb-, beamed structure, dwelling > MIr *treb*, house⟧ a village; hamlet: now mainly in place names
Thorpe (thôrp), **Jim** (born *James Francis Thorpe*) 1888-1953; U.S. athlete
Thos *abbrev.* Thomas
those (thōz) *pron., adj.* ⟦ME *thas, thos* < OE *thas, thæs*, pl. of *thes*, THIS⟧ *pl. of* THAT
Thoth (thōth, tōt) *n.* ⟦L < Gr *Thōth* < Egypt *ḏḥwty*⟧ *Egypt. Myth.* the god of wisdom, learning, and magic, the scribe of the gods: represented as having a human body and the head of a dog or an ibis
thou[1] (thou) *pron., pl.* **you** or **ye** ⟦ME < OE *thu*, akin to Ger *du* < IE *tu > L & Sans *tu*⟧ [Archaic] personal pronoun in the second person singular: once used in familiar address, but now replaced by *you* except in poetic or religious use and in some British dialects: *thee* is the objective form, *thine* the possessive, and *thyself* the intensive and reflexive; *thy* is the possessive pronominal adjective
thou[2] (thou) *n., pl.* **thou** or **thous** [Slang] *short for* THOUSAND
though (thō) *conj.* ⟦ME *thah, thogh* < OE *theah* & ON *tho*, akin to Ger *doch*, yet, however, Goth *thauh*⟧ **1** in spite of the fact that; notwithstanding that; although *[though the car was repaired, it rattled]* **2** and yet *[they will probably win, though no one else thinks so]* **3** even if; supposing that *[though he may fail, he will have tried]* —*adv.* however; nevertheless *[she sings well, though]*
thought[1] (thôt) *n.* ⟦ME *thouht* < OE *thoht* < PGmc *thanht, pret. of *thankjan (> OE *thencan:* see THINK[1])⟧ **1** the act or process of thinking; reflection; meditation; cogitation **2** the power of reasoning, or of conceiving ideas; capacity for thinking; intellect; imagination **3** a result of thinking; idea, concept, opinion, etc. **4** the ideas, principles, opinions, etc. prevalent at a given time or place or among a given people *[modern thought in education]* **5** attention; consideration; heed *[give it a moment's thought]* **6** mental engrossment; preoccupation; concentration *[deep in thought]* **7** intention or expectation *[no thought of leaving]* —**SYN.** IDEA —**a thought** [Old-fashioned] to a small extent or degree; somewhat *[be a thought more careful next time]*
thought[2] (thôt) *vt., vi. pt. & pp. of* THINK[1] —*v.impersonal pt. & pp. of* THINK[2]
thought experiment ⟦calque of Ger *gedankenexperiment*⟧ the act of reasoning through to the practical outcome of a hypothesis when physical proof is unavailable or unattainable
thought·ful (thôt′fəl) *adj.* **1** full of thought; meditative; thinking **2** show-

ing or characterized by thought; serious [a *thoughtful* essay] 3 heedful, careful, attentive, etc.; esp., considerate of others; kind —**thought′ful·ly** *adv.* —**thought′ful·ness** *n.*

SYN.—**thoughtful**, as compared here, implies the showing of thought for the comfort or well-being of others, as by anticipating their needs or wishes [it was *thoughtful* of you to call]; **considerate** implies a thoughtful or sympathetic regard for the feelings or circumstances of others, as in sparing them pain, distress, or discomfort [*considerate* enough to extend the time for payment]; **attentive** implies a constant thoughtfulness as shown by repeated acts of consideration, courtesy, or devotion [an *attentive* suitor] —ANT. **thoughtless**

thought·less (thôt′lis) *adj.* 1 not stopping to think; careless 2 not given thought; ill-considered; rash 3 not considerate of others; inconsiderate 4 [Rare] stupid; senseless —**thought′less·ly** *adv.* —**thought′less·ness** *n.*

thought police ⟦popularized by George ORWELL in his novel *Nineteen Eighty-four* (published 1949)⟧ 1 a group empowered to regulate the expressed opinions of individuals living in a totalitarian state 2 any person or group regarded as having a role similar to this

thou·sand (thou′zənd) *n.* ⟦ME *thusend* < OE, akin to Ger *tausend* < PGmc **thus-hundi,* "many hundred" < IE base **tēu-*, to swell, increase + PGmc **hund-*, HUNDRED⟧ 1 ten hundred; 1,000; M 2 an indefinite but very large number: a hyperbolic use —*adj.* amounting to one thousand in number

thou·sand·fold (-fōld′) *adj.* ⟦prec. + -FOLD⟧ having a thousand times as much or as many —*adv.* a thousand times as much or as many: preceded by *a* —*n.* a number or an amount a thousand times as great

Thousand Island dressing ⟦after fol.⟧ a salad dressing made of mayonnaise with chili sauce or ketchup and minced pickles, capers, olives, etc.

Thousand Islands group of over 1,500 islands in the St. Lawrence River at the outlet of Lake Ontario, some forming part of N.Y. state & others forming part of Ontario, Canada

Thousand Oaks ⟦after the many *oak* trees there⟧ city in SW Calif., northwest of Los Angeles

thou·sandth (thou′zəndth) *adj.* ⟦THOUSAND + -TH[2]⟧ 1 coming last in a series of a thousand; 1,000th 2 designating any of the thousand equal parts of something —*n.* 1 the thousandth one of a series 2 any of the thousand equal parts of something; 1/1000

Thrace (thrās) 1 ancient region in the E Balkan Peninsula 2 modern region in the SE Balkan Peninsula divided between Greece & Turkey

Thra·cian (thrā′shən) *adj.* of Thrace or its people or culture —*n.* 1 a person born or living in Thrace 2 the extinct language of ancient Thrace, generally assumed to belong to the Indo-European language family

thrall (thrôl) *n.* ⟦ME *thral* < OE *thræl* < ON *thræll* < Gmc **thranhilaz,* lit., the constrained one < IE base **trenk-*, to shove, press hard > THRONG⟧ 1 [Now Chiefly Literary] a slave or bondman 2 a person under the moral or psychological domination of someone or something 3 the condition of being enslaved or dominated, often in a psychological way; thralldom Now historical or archaic in senses 2 & 3, except in fig. use, esp. in the phrase **hold in thrall (to)** —*vt.* [Archaic] to enslave —*adj.* [Archaic] enslaved

thrall·dom or **thral·dom** (thrôl′dəm) *n.* the condition of being a thrall; servitude; slavery

thrash (thrash) *vt.* ⟦ME *threschen* < OE *therscan,* akin to Ger *dreschen,* to thresh < IE base **ter-*, to rub > THROW⟧ 1 THRESH 2 to make move violently or wildly; beat [a bird *thrashing* its wings] 3 to give a severe beating to; flog 4 to defeat overwhelmingly —*vi.* 1 THRESH 2 to move or toss about violently, flinging the arms, legs, etc. about wildly or vigorously [*thrashing* in agony] 3 to make one's way by thrashing —*n.* 1 the act of thrashing 2 a style of HEAVY METAL rock characterized by a fast tempo, minimal melodic and harmonic components, rapidly shouted lyrics, and the thrashing about of both musicians and audience: cf. SPEED METAL —SYN. BEAT —**thrash out** to settle by detailed discussion —**thrash over** to go over (a problem, etc.) in great detail

thrash·er[1] (thrash′ər) *n.* a person or thing that thrashes

thrash·er[2] (thrash′ər) *n.* ⟦E dial. *thresher,* prob. akin to THRUSH[1]⟧ ☆any of a group of gray to brownish American passerine birds (family Mimidae) with a long, stiff tail and a long bill, esp. the **brown thrasher** (*Toxostoma rufum*) of the E U.S.

thrash·ing (-iŋ) *n.* a beating; flogging

thra·son·i·cal (thrə sän′i kəl) *adj.* ⟦< L *Thraso,* name of the braggart in Terence's *Eunuch* (< Gr *Thrasōn* < *thrasos, tharsos,* bold < IE base **dhers-*, to dare, be bold > DARE) + -ICAL⟧ boastful; bragging —**thra·son′i·cal·ly** *adv.*

thrawn (thrôn, thrän) [Chiefly Scot.] *adj.* ⟦< *thraw,* dial. form of THROW⟧ 1 crooked; twisted 2 perverse

thread (thred) *n.* ⟦ME *threde* < OE *thræd* (akin to Ger *draht*) < base of *thrawan,* to twist: see THROW⟧ 1 *a)* a light, fine, stringlike length of material made up of two or more fibers or strands of spun cotton, flax, silk, etc. twisted together and used in sewing *b)* a similar fine length of synthetic material, as nylon or plastic, or of glass or metal *c)* the fine, stringy filament extruded by a spider, silkworm, etc. *d)* any of the yarns of which a fabric is woven *e)* a fine, stringy length of syrup or other viscous material 2 any thin line, stratum, vein, stream, ray, etc. 3 an element suggestive of a thread in being continuous or sequential [the *thread* of a story] 4 the helical ridge of a screw, bolt, nut, etc. ☆5 [*pl.*] [Slang] a suit, or clothes generally 6 *Comput.* a series of forum postings, linked email responses, etc. displayed chronologically and relating typically to a single topic —*vt.* 1 *a)* to put a thread through the eye of (a needle, etc.) *b)* to arrange thread for use on (a sewing machine) 2 to string (beads, etc.) on or as if on a thread 3 to fashion a THREAD (sense 4) on or in (a screw, pipe, etc.) 4 to interweave with or as if with threads [a red tapestry *threaded* with gold] 5 *a)* to pass through by twisting, turning, or weaving in and out [to *thread* the streets] *b)* to make (one's way) in this fashion 6 to pass or feed (tape, film, etc.) into or through (a recorder, projector, etc.) —*vi.* 1 to go along or proceed in a winding way ☆2 to form a thread when dropped from a spoon: said of boiling syrup that has reached a certain consistency —**thread′er** *n.* —**thread′like′** *adj.*

thread·bare (thred′ber′) *adj.* 1 worn down so that the threads show; having the nap or surface fibers worn off [*threadbare* rugs] 2 wearing old, worn clothes; shabby 3 that has lost freshness or novelty; stale [a *threadbare* argument] 4 cheap, shabby, etc.

thread·fin (-fin′) *n.* any of a family (Polynemidae) of marine percoid fishes having a divided pectoral fin that ends in threadlike rays

thread·worm (-wurm′) *n.* a nematode or gordian worm

thread·y (thred′ē) *adj.* **thread′i·er, thread′i·est** 1 of or like a thread; stringy; fibrous; filamentous 2 forming threads; viscid: said of liquids 3 of or covered with threads or threadlike parts; fibrous 4 thin, weak, feeble, etc. [a *thready* voice, a *thready* pulse] —**thread′i·ness** *n.*

threap (thrēp) *vt.* ⟦ME *threpen* < OE *threapian,* to rebuke⟧ [Scot. or North Eng.] 1 to scold; chide 2 to maintain or assert obstinately

threat (thret) *n.* ⟦ME *threte* < OE *threat,* a throng, painful pressure, akin to Ger *(ver)driessen,* to grieve, annoy < IE **treud-*, to push, press (prob. < base **ter-*, to rub) > L *trudere,* to THRUST⟧ 1 an expression of intention to hurt, destroy, punish, etc., as in retaliation or intimidation 2 *a)* an indication of imminent danger, harm, evil, etc. [the *threat* of war] *b)* a potential source of this — *vt., vi. obs. var. of* THREATEN

threat·en (thret′'n) *vt.* ⟦ME *thretnen* < OE *threatnian*⟧ 1 *a)* to make threats against; express one's intention of hurting, punishing, etc. *b)* to express intention to inflict (punishment, reprisal, etc.) 2 *a)* to indicate the likely occurrence of (something dangerous, unpleasant, etc.) [clouds *threatening* snow] *b)* to be a source of such danger, harm, etc. to (often in the pp.) [homeowners *threatened* with foreclosure] —*vi.* 1 to make threats 2 to be an indication or source of potential danger, harm, etc. —**threat′en·er** *n.* —**threat′en·ing·ly** *adv.*

SYN.—**threaten** implies a warning of impending punishment, danger, evil, etc. by words, actions, events, conditions, signs, etc. [he *threatened* to retaliate; the clouds *threaten* rain]; **menace** stresses the frightening or hostile character of that which threatens [he *menaced* me with a revolver]

threatened species a species of animal or plant that is rare and may become an endangered species in the near future

three (thrē) *adj.* ⟦ME < OE *threo, thrie,* akin to Ger *drei* < IE base **trei-* > L *tres,* Gr *treis,* Sans *tri*⟧ totaling one more than two —*n.* 1 the cardinal number between two and four; 3; III 2 any group of three people or things 3 something numbered three or having three units, as a playing card, domino, face of a die, etc. 4 *Basketball short for* THREE-POINTER

☆**three-base hit** (thrē′bās′) *Baseball* a hit on which the batter reaches third base: also [Slang] **three′-bag′ger** (-bag′ər) *n.*

☆**three-card mon·te** (thrē′kärd′) ⟦< MONTE (*n.* 1)⟧ a swindling game in which a certain card, after being shown, is palmed and then ostensibly made one of three cards placed face down and shifted about, with the victim challenged to bet on its location

three-col·or (thrē′kul′ər) *adj.* designating or of a full-color printing process using three separate plates, each reproducing one primary color

three-cor·nered (-kôr′nərd) *adj.* having three corners or angles

☆**3-D** or **3D** (thrē′dē′) *adj.* producing or designed to produce an effect of three dimensions; three-dimensional [a 3-D movie] —*n.* a system or effect that adds a three-dimensional appearance to visual images, as in films, slides, or drawings

three-deck·er (thrē′dek′ər) *n.* 1 [Historical] a warship with cannons on three decks 2 any structure with three levels 3 [Informal] a sandwich made with three slices of bread 4 [Informal] a novel published in three volumes; now, esp., any very lengthy novel

three-di·men·sion·al (-də men′shə nəl) *adj.* 1 *a)* of or having three dimensions *b)* appearing to have depth or thickness in addition to height and width 2 having a convincing or lifelike quality

three·fold (-fōld′) *adj.* ⟦THREE + -FOLD⟧ 1 having three parts 2 having three times as much or as many —*adv.* three times as much or as many

three-four (-fôr′) *adj.* ⟦< the time signature, 3/4⟧ designating or of a musical rhythm with three quarter notes to a measure

3G (thrē′jē′) *n.* the third generation of cellular-phone network technology, capable of fast rates of data transmission that support email communications, high-speed internet access, video streaming, etc.

three-leg·ged race (thrē′leg′id, -lā′gid) a race among pairs of contestants: the right leg of one contestant is tied to the left leg of the other

three-mile limit (thrē′mīl′) the outer limit of a zone of water extending three miles offshore, sometimes regarded as the extent of the territorial jurisdiction of the coastal country

☆**three-peat** (thrē′pēt′) [Informal] *n.* ⟦blend of THREE & REPEAT⟧ a third consecutive title or award won by a team or individual —*vi.* to win a third consecutive title or award

three·pence (thrip′əns, thrup′-, threp′-) *n.* 1 the sum of three British pence 2 a British coin of this value

three·pen·ny (thrē′pen′ē, thrip′ə nē) *adj.* 1 worth or costing threepence 2 of small worth; cheap 3 *Carpentry* designating a size of nail: see -PENNY

three-phase (thrē′fāz′) *adj. Elec.* powered by three equal AC voltages which are out of phase by one third of a cycle (120 degrees)

three-piece (thrē′pēs′) *adj.* composed of three separate pieces, as an outfit of skirt, sweater, and jacket

three-ply (-plī′) *adj.* having three thicknesses, interwoven layers, strands, etc.

three-point·er (thrē′point′ər) *n. Basketball* a shot worth three points from beyond a line (**three point line**) that forms a semicircle around each basket

three-point landing (thrē′point′) a perfect airplane landing in which the main wheels and the tail wheel or nose wheel touch the ground at the same time

☆**three-point play** *Basketball* a play in which a player is fouled while making a two-point field goal and subsequently scores a one-point free throw

three-quar·ter (thrē′kwôrt′ər) *adj.* 1 of or involving three fourths 2 showing the face intermediate between profile and full face [a *three-quarter* portrait]

three-quarter binding a type of bookbinding in which the material of the back, usually leather, is extended onto the covers for one third of their width

☆**three-ring circus** (thrē′riŋ′) 1 a circus having three rings for simultaneous performances 2 any situation or event hilariously or confusingly packed with action

three R's, the reading, writing, and arithmetic, regarded as the basic elementary studies and the fundamentals of an education: so called from the humorous spelling *reading, 'riting,* and *'rithmetic*

three·score (thrē′skôr′) *adj., n.* three times twenty; sixty

three-six·ty (thrē′siks′tē) *n.* [Informal] a turn or revolution of 360°: also written **360**

three·some (thrē′səm) *adj.* ⟦ME *thresum:* see -SOME[2]⟧ of or engaged in by three —*n.* 1 a group of three persons 2 [Informal] a group of three engaged in sexual activity 3 *Golf a)* a match in which one participant plays against two others, who alternate strokes on a single ball *b)* a group of three people playing golf against each other, each using his or her own ball

three-square (thrē′skwer′) *adj.* forming an equilateral triangle in cross section, as a three-cornered file

three-way (thrē′wā′) *adj.* 1 involving three directions, persons, etc. [a *three-way* conversation] 2 *Elec.* designating or of: *a)* a lightbulb with two filaments that can be switched on singly or together to produce three different levels of brightness *b)* a switch with three terminals, used to control a circuit from two different locations —*n.* [Informal] THREESOME (*n.* 2)

three-wheel·er (-hwēl′ər, -wēl′-) *n.* a three-wheeled vehicle, as a tricycle or a three-wheeled motorcycle

thren·o·dy (thren′ə dē) *n., pl.* **-dies** ⟦Gr *thrēnōidia* < *thrēnos,* lamentation (< IE echoic base **dhren-,* to murmur > DRONE[1]) + *ōidē,* song⟧ a song of lamentation; funeral song: also **thre·node** (thrē′nōd′, thren′ōd′) —**thre·nod·ic** (thrē näd′ik) *adj.* —**thren′o·dist** *n.*

thre·o·nine (thrē′ə nēn′, -nin) *n.* ⟦prob. < *threon(ic acid)* + -INE[3]⟧ an essential amino acid, $CH_3CH(OH)CH(NH_2)COOH$, obtained from the hydrolysis of many proteins

thresh (thresh) *vt.* ⟦ME *threschen:* earlier form of THRASH⟧ 1 to beat out (grain) from its husk, as with a flail 2 to beat grain out of (husks) 3 to beat or strike as with a flail —*vi.* 1 to thresh grain 2 to toss about; thrash —**thresh out** THRASH OUT (see phrase under THRASH)

thresh·er (thresh′ər) *n.* 1 a person who threshes 2 THRESHING MACHINE 3 any of a family (Alopiidae, order Lamniformes) of large sharks of temperate and tropical seas, having a very long upper tail lobe, which supposedly threshes the water and drives its prey together

threshing machine a machine for threshing grain

thresh·old (thresh′ōld′, -hōld′) *n.* ⟦ME *threschwold* < OE *therscwold* (akin to ON *threskǫlder*) < base of *therscan* (see THRASH) + ?⟧ 1 DOORSILL 2 the entrance or beginning point of something [at the *threshold* of a new career] 3 *Physiol., Psychol.* the point at which a stimulus is just strong enough to be perceived or to produce a response 4 any limit, quantity, etc. beyond someone's tolerance or at which something occurs [a person with a low *threshold* for boredom]

threw (thro͞o) *vt., vi. pt. of* THROW

thrice (thrīs) *adv.* ⟦ME *thries* < *thrie* (< OE *thriwa,* thrice, akin to *threo,* THREE) + -*(e)s,* adverbial gen. suffix, after *ones* (see ONCE)⟧ 1 three times 2 three times as much or as many; threefold; triply 3 greatly; highly

thrift (thrift) *n.* ⟦ME < ON < *thrifast,* to prosper: see THRIVE⟧ 1 [Obs.] *a)* the condition of thriving; prosperity *b)* physical thriving; vigorous growth 2 careful management of one's money or resources; economy; frugality 3 any of a genus (*Armeria,* family Plumbaginaceae) of dwarf, evergreen, perennial dicotyledonous plants (order Plumbaginales) with narrow leaves and small white, pink, red, or purplish flowers ☆4 a mutual savings bank, savings and loan association, or credit union: *usually used in pl.*: in full **thrift institution** 5 [Brit. Dial.] a means of thriving; work; labor

thrift·less (thrift′lis) *adj.* without thrift; wasteful —**thrift′less·ly** *adv.* —**thrift′less·ness** *n.*

☆**thrift shop** a store where castoff clothes and rummage are sold, specif. to raise money for charity

thrift·y (thrif′tē) *adj.* **thrift′i·er, thrift′i·est** 1 practicing or showing thrift; economical; provident 2 thriving; flourishing; prospering 3 growing vigorously, as a plant —**thrift′i·ly** *adv.* —**thrift′i·ness** *n.*

SYN.—**thrifty** implies industry and clever management of one's money or resources, usually so as to result in some savings [the *thrifty* housewife watched for sales]; **frugal** stresses the idea of saving and suggests spending which excludes any luxury or lavishness and provides only the simplest fare, dress, etc. [the Amish are a *frugal* people]; **sparing** implies such restraint in spending as restricts itself to the bare minimum or involves deprivation [*sparing* to the point of niggardliness]; **economical** implies prudent management of one's money or resources so as to avoid any waste in expenditure or use [it is often *economical* to buy in large quantities]; **provident** implies management with the foresight to provide for future needs [never *provident,* he quickly spent his inheritance] —*ANT.* **lavish, prodigal, wasteful**

thrill (thril) *vt.* ⟦ME *thrillen,* by metathesis < *thyrlen* < OE *thyr(e)lian,* to pierce < *thyrel,* perforation, hole < base of *thurh,* THROUGH⟧ 1 to cause sharply exhilarating excitement in; make shiver or tingle with excitement 2 to produce vibrations or quivering in; cause to tremble —*vi.* 1 to feel emotional excitement; shiver or tingle with excitement 2 to tremble; vibrate; quiver —*n.* ⟦new formation < the v.⟧ 1 a thrilling or being thrilled; tremor of excitement 2 the quality of thrilling, or the ability to thrill [the *thrill* of the chase] 3 something that causes emotional excitement 4 *a)* a vibration; tremor; quiver *b) Med.* an abnormal tremor, as of the circulatory system, that can be felt by the hand on palpation

thrill·er (thril′ər) *n.* 1 a person or thing that thrills 2 *a)* a highly dramatic, suspenseful novel, play, film, etc. *b)* [Chiefly Brit.] such a novel, film, etc. dealing with crime and detection

thrips (thrips) *n., pl.* **thrips** ⟦L < Gr, lit., wood-worm⟧ any of an order (Thysanoptera) of very small, destructive, usually winged insects that suck the juices of plants

thrive (thrīv) *vi.* **thrived** or **throve, thrived** or **thriv·en** (thriv′ən), **thriv′ing** ⟦ME *thrifen* < ON *thrifast,* prosper, refl. of *thrifa,* to grasp⟧ 1 to prosper or flourish; be successful, esp. as the result of economical management 2 to grow vigorously or luxuriantly; improve physically

thro' or **thro** (thro͞o) *prep., adv., adj. archaic contraction for* THROUGH

throat (thrōt) *n.* ⟦ME *throte* < OE, akin to Ger *dross(el),* throat < IE **(s)treu-,* swollen, stretched < base **(s)ter-,* stiff > STARE⟧ 1 the front part of the neck 2 the upper part of the passage leading from the mouth and nose to the stomach and lungs, including the pharynx and the upper larynx, trachea, and esophagus 3 any narrow passage, part, or entrance; specif., the part of a chimney between the fireplace and the flue —*vt.* [Archaic] to pronounce or sing with a harsh, guttural quality —**at each other's throats** [Informal] in a state of open, mutual hostility —**cut each other's throats** [Informal] to ruin each other, as by underselling in business —**cut one's own throat** [Informal] to be the means of one's own ruin —**jump down someone's throat** [Informal] to attack or criticize someone suddenly and violently —**ram (or shove) something down someone's throat** [Informal] to force someone to accept, hear, etc. something —**stick in someone's throat** to be hard for someone to say, as from reluctance

-throat·ed (thrōt′id) *combining form* having a (specified kind of) throat [ruby-*throated* hummingbird]

throat·latch (thrōt′lach′) *n.* a strap that passes under a horse's throat, for holding a bridle or halter in place

throat·y (thrōt′ē) *adj.* **throat′i·er, throat′i·est** 1 produced in the throat, as some sounds or tones 2 characterized by such sounds; husky, hoarse, etc. [a *throaty* voice] —**throat′i·ly** *adv.* —**throat′i·ness** *n.*

throb (thräb) *vi.* **throbbed, throb′bing** ⟦ME *throbben,* prob. of echoic orig.⟧ 1 to beat, pulsate, vibrate, etc. 2 to beat strongly or fast; palpitate, as the heart under exertion 3 to feel or express emotion; quiver with excitement —*n.* 1 the act of throbbing 2 a beat or pulsation, esp. a strong one of the heart —**throb′ber** *n.* —**throb′bing·ly** *adv.*

throe (thrō) *n.* ⟦ME *throwe,* prob. < OE *thrawu,* pain, affliction, akin to ON *thrā,* strong yearning < IE **treu-* (> Gr *trauma,* a wound) < base **ter-,* to rub, grind > THROW⟧ a spasm or pang of pain: *usually used in pl.* [the *throes* of childbirth, death *throes*] —**in the throes of** in the act of struggling with (a problem, decision, task, etc.)

throm·bin (thräm′bin) *n.* ⟦THROMB(US) + -IN[1]⟧ the enzyme of the blood, formed from prothrombin, that causes clotting by converting fibrinogen to fibrin

throm·bo- (thräm′bō, -bə) ⟦< Gr *thrombos,* a clot: see THROMBUS⟧ *combining form* thrombus, blood clot [*thrombocyte*]

throm·bo·cyte (thräm′bə sīt′) *n.* ⟦prec. + -CYTE⟧ 1 a small nucleated blood cell in most vertebrates, except mammals, that initiates the process of blood clotting 2 PLATELET (sense 1) —**throm′bo·cyt′ic** (-sit′ik) *adj.*

throm·bo·cy·to·pe·ni·a (thräm′bō sīt′ə pē′nē ə) *n.* ⟦< prec. + -O- + Gr *penia,* poverty⟧ a decrease below normal in the number of blood platelets in the blood —**throm′bo·cy′to·pe′nic** (-pē′nik) *adj.*

throm·bo·em·bo·lism (thräm′bō em′bə liz′əm) *n.* ⟦THROMBO- + EMBOLISM⟧ the obstruction of a blood vessel by an embolus that has broken away from a thrombus —**throm′bo·em·bol′ic** (-bäl′ik) *adj.*

throm·bo·gen (thräm′bə jən) *n.* ⟦THROMBO- + -GEN⟧ PROTHROMBIN

throm·bo·ki·nase (thräm′bō kī′nās′, -kin′ās′) *n.* ⟦THROMBO- + KINASE⟧ THROMBOPLASTIN

throm·bo·phle·bi·tis (thräm′bō fli bīt′əs) *n.* ⟦THROMBO- + PHLEBITIS⟧ the formation of a clot in a vein, with associated irritation of the vein's inner lining

throm·bo·plas·tic (-plas′tik) *adj.* 1 of or having the properties of a thromboplastin **2** initiating or hastening the clotting of blood —**throm′bo·plas′ti·cal·ly** ***adv.***

throm·bo·plas·tin (-plas′tin) ***n.*** ⟦THROMBO- + -PLAST + -IN[1]⟧ a substance released from blood platelets and injured bodily tissues that assists in the clotting of the blood by initiating the conversion of prothrombin to thrombin

throm·bose (thräm′bōs′, -bōz′) ***vt., vi.*** **throm′bosed′**, **throm′bos′ing** ⟦back-form. < fol.⟧ to clot or become clotted with a thrombus

throm·bo·sis (thräm bō′sis) ***n.*** ⟦ModL < Gr *thrombōsis,* coagulation < *thrombos,* a clot: see THROMBUS⟧ coagulation of the blood in the heart or a blood vessel, forming a clot —**throm·bot′ic** (-bät′ik) ***adj.***

throm·box·ane (-bäk′sān) ***n.*** ⟦< THROMB(O)- + OXY-[1] + -ANE⟧ any of various derivatives of prostaglandins, which form on blood platelets and, usually, cause blood clots and constrict blood vessels: cf. PROSTACYCLIN

throm·bus (thräm′bəs) ***n., pl.*** **throm′bi′** (-bī′) ⟦ModL < Gr *thrombos,* a clot < IE **dhrómbhos* < base **dherebh-,* to coagulate⟧ the fibrinous clot attached at the site of thrombosis

throne (thrōn) ***n.*** ⟦ME *trone* < OFr or L: OFr *trone* < L *thronus* < Gr *thronos,* a seat < IE base **dher-,* to hold, support > FIRM[1]⟧ **1** the chair on which a king, cardinal, etc. sits on formal or ceremonial occasions: it usually is on a dais, covered with a canopy, and highly decorated **2** the power or rank of a king, etc.; sovereignty **3** a sovereign, ruler, etc. [*orders from the throne*] **4** [*pl.*] *Christian Theol.* the third highest order in the hierarchy of angels **5** [Slang] TOILET (***n.*** 4*b*): a jocular usage — ***vt., vi.*** **throned**, **thron′ing** to enthrone or be enthroned

throng (thrôŋ) ***n.*** ⟦ME < OE *(ge)thrang* (akin to Ger *drang*) < base of *thringan,* to press, crowd: for IE base see THRALL⟧ **1** a great number of people gathered together; crowd **2** a crowding together of people; crowded condition **3** any great number of things massed or considered together; multitude —***vi.*** to gather together, move, or press in a throng —***vt.*** **1** to crowd or press upon in large numbers **2** to crowd into; fill with a multitude —***SYN.*** CROWD[1]

thros·tle (thräs′əl) ***n.*** ⟦ME < OE, akin to Ger *drossel* < IE base **trozdos-* > THRUSH[1]⟧ **1** [Now Chiefly Dial.] SONG THRUSH **2** ⟦from the humming sound it makes⟧ any of various machines for spinning wool, etc.

throt·tle (thrät′'l) ***n.*** ⟦prob. dim. of THROAT: see -LE⟧ **1** [Rare] the throat or windpipe **2** a valve that regulates the flow of fluids; esp., a butterfly valve that controls the release of fuel vapor from a carburetor, or the control valve in a steam line: also **throttle plate** **3** the hand lever or pedal that controls this valve —***vt.*** **-tled**, **-tling** ⟦ME *throtlen* < *throte,* throat⟧ **1** to choke; strangle **2** to stop the utterance or action of; censor or suppress **3** *a)* to reduce the flow of (fuel vapor, etc.) by means of a throttle *b)* to lessen the speed of (an engine, vehicle, etc.) by this or similar means; slow (*down*) —***vi.*** to choke or suffocate —**throt′tler** ***n.***

throt·tle·hold (-hōld′) ***n.*** power to restrict or prevent freedom of development, movement, etc.; stranglehold

through (thro͞o) ***prep.*** ⟦ME *thurgh, thrugh* < OE *thurh,* akin to Ger *durch* < IE base **ter-,* through, beyond > L *trans,* across, Sans *tiráḥ,* through⟧ **1** in one side and out the other side of; from end to end of **2** *a)* in the midst of [*flying through the clouds*] *b)* among [*hiking through the trees*] **3** by way of [*a train that goes through Boston*] **4** over the entire extent or surface of **5** to various places in; around [*touring through France*] **6** *a)* from the beginning to the end or conclusion of [*to go through an experience, through the summer, went through all his provisions*] ☆*b)* up to and including [*through Friday*] **7** without making a stop for [*to go through a red light*] **8** past the limitations or difficulties of [*to fight through all the red tape*] **9** by means of [*through her help*] **10** as a result of; because of [*done through error*] —***adv.*** **1** in one side and out the other; from end to end **2** from the beginning to the end **3** completely to the end; to a conclusion [*to see something through*] **4** in every part or way; thoroughly; completely [*soaked through*]: also **through and through** —***adj.*** **1** extending from one place to another; allowing free passage [*a through street*] ☆**2** *a)* traveling to the destination without stops [*a through train*] *b)* continuing on without making a stop [*through traffic*] ☆**3** not necessitating changes; good for traveling without intermediate transfer [*a through ticket*] **4** arrived at the end; finished [*through with an assignment*] **5** at the end of one's usefulness, resources, etc. [*through in politics*] **6** having no further dealings, connections, etc. (*with* someone or something)

NOTE—*through* is also used in idiomatic expressions (e.g., *get through*), many of which are entered in this dictionary under the key words

through-com·posed (thro͞o′kəm pōzd′) ***adj.*** ⟦transl. of Ger *durchkomponiert* < *durch,* prec. + *komponiert,* composed⟧ having a compositional structure that is not based on repeating sections of music; specif., of a song with stanzas having regular meter and rhyme but different music for each stanza

through·ly (thro͞o′lē) ***adv.*** *archaic var. of* THOROUGHLY

through·out (thro͞o out′) ***prep.*** **1** through the whole of; in every part of [*throughout the nation*] **2** all the way through; during every part of [*sleeping throughout the lecture*] —***adv.*** **1** in or during every part; everywhere; from start to finish **2** in every respect

through·put (thro͞o′po͝ot′) ***n.*** the amount of material put through a process in a given period; specif., the amount of data processed or transferred by a computer per second

through-sung (thro͞o′suŋ′) ***adj.*** sung throughout, with no spoken dialogue: said as of a musical or opera

☆**through·way** (thro͞o′wā′) ***n.*** *alt. sp. of* THRUWAY

throve (thrōv) ***vi.*** *alt. pt. of* THRIVE

throw (thrō) ***vt.*** **threw**, **thrown**, **throw′ing** ⟦ME *throwen,* to twist, wring, hurl < OE *thrawan,* to throw, twist, akin to Ger *drehen,* to twist, turn < IE base **ter-,* to rub, rub with turning motion, bore > THRASH, THREAD, Gr *teirein,* L *terere,* to rub⟧ **1** to twist strands of (silk, etc.) into thread or yarn **2** to cause to fly through the air by releasing from the hand while the arm is in rapid motion; cast; hurl **3** to discharge through the air from a catapult, pump, gun, etc. **4** to hurl violently, as in anger, etc.; dash **5** to cause to fall; upset; overthrow; dislodge [*thrown by a horse*] **6** to move or send rapidly; advance [*to throw reinforcements into a battle*] **7** to put suddenly and forcibly into or onto [*she threw the clothes into the suitcase*] **8** to put suddenly and forcibly into a specified condition or situation [*thrown into prison, into confusion, etc.*] **9** *a)* to toss (dice) from one's hand or a container so that they roll and then come to rest: the faces uppermost indicate the value of the THROW (***n.*** 2*b*) *b)* to make (a specified throw) with dice [*to throw a five*] **10** to cast off; shed [*snakes throw their skins, the horse threw its shoe*] **11** to bring forth (young): said esp. of domesticated animals **12** to move the lever of (a switch, clutch, etc.) or connect, disconnect, engage, etc. by so doing **13** *a)* to direct, cast, turn, project, etc. (variously with *at, on, upon, over, toward,* etc.) [*to throw a glance, a light, a shadow, etc.*] *b)* to deliver (a punch) **14** to cause (one's voice) to seem to come from some other source, as in ventriloquism **15** to put (blame *on,* influence *into,* obstacles *before,* etc.) ☆**16** [Informal] to lose (a game, race, etc.) deliberately, as by prearrangement ☆**17** [Informal] to give (a party, dance, etc.) ☆**18** [Informal] to have (a fit, tantrum, etc.) **19** [Informal] to confuse or disconcert [*the question completely threw him*] **20** *Card Games* to play (a card) **21** *Ceramics* to shape on a potter's wheel —***vi.*** to cast or hurl something —***n.*** **1** the action of a person who throws; a cast **2** *a)* the act of throwing dice *b)* the total number of pips on the uppermost faces of dice that have been thrown **3** the distance something is or can be thrown [*a stone's throw*] ☆**4** *a)* a spread or coverlet for draping over a bed, sofa, etc. *b)* a woman's light scarf or wrap **5** *a)* the motion of a moving part driven by a cam, eccentric, etc. *b)* the range of such a motion; travel; stroke **6** *Geol.* the amount of vertical displacement at a fault: see DOWNTHROW, UPTHROW **7** *Wrestling* a particular way or an instance of throwing an opponent —**a throw** [Informal] for each one; apiece [*concert tickets at fifty bucks a throw*] —**throw away** **1** to rid oneself of; discard **2** to be wasteful of; waste; squander **3** to fail to make use of [*throwing away his talents*] **4** *Theater* to deliver (a line, speech, etc.) in a deliberately offhand manner —**throw back** **1** to check or stop from advancing **2** to revert to an earlier or more primitive type or condition —**throw cold water on** to discourage by indifference or disparagement —**throw in** **1** to engage (a clutch) or cause (gears) to mesh **2** to add on without extra charge **3** to add to others **4** [Informal] to join (*with*) in cooperative action —**throw off** **1** *a)* to rid oneself of; cast off *b)* to recover from *c) Card Games* to discard **2** *a)* to evade (a pursuer) *b)* to mislead *c)* to disconcert or confuse **3** to expel, emit, etc. **4** [Informal] to write or utter quickly, in an offhand manner —**throw on** [Informal] to put on (a garment) carelessly or hastily —**throw oneself at someone** to try to win the sexual or romantic attentions of someone in a grossly obvious manner —**throw oneself into** to engage in with great vigor — **throw oneself on** (or **upon**) to ask for (someone's mercy, etc.) for oneself —**throw open** **1** to open completely and suddenly **2** to remove all restrictions from —**throw out** **1** to get rid of; discard **2** to reject or remove, often with force **3** to emit **4** to put forth or utter (a hint or suggestion) ☆**5** *Baseball* to throw the ball to a teammate who in turn retires (a runner) **6** *Machinery* to disengage (a clutch) —**throw over** **1** to give up; abandon **2** to forsake; jilt —**throw together** **1** to make or assemble hurriedly and carelessly **2** to cause to become acquainted —**throw up** **1** to give up or abandon **2** to raise suddenly or rapidly **3** to vomit **4** to construct rapidly ☆**5** [Informal] to mention repeatedly (*to* someone), as in reproach or criticism —**throw′er** ***n.***

SYN.—**throw** is the general word meaning to cause to move through the air by a rapid propulsive motion of the arm, etc.; **cast**, the preferred word in certain connections [*to cast a fishing line*], generally has a more archaic or lofty quality [*they cast stones at him*]; to **toss** is to throw lightly or carelessly and, usually, with an upward or sideways motion [*to toss a coin*]; **hurl** and **fling** both imply a throwing with force or violence, but **hurl** suggests that the object thrown moves swiftly for some distance [*to hurl a javelin*] and **fling**, that it is thrust sharply or vehemently so that it strikes a surface with considerable impact [*she flung the plate to the floor*]; **pitch** implies a throwing with a definite aim or in a definite direction [*to pitch a baseball*]

throw·a·way (thrō′ə wā′) ***n.*** **1** anything designed or intended to be discarded after use; specif., a leaflet or handbill **2** a remark made or delivered casually **3** something done thoughtlessly or carelessly —***adj.*** ☆**1** designed to be discarded after use [*a throwaway bottle*] **2** delivered in a deliberately offhand manner, as a line of dialogue in a play **3** offhand; casual

throw·back (thrō′bak′) ***n.*** **1** [Now Rare] the act of throwing back; check, stop, or reversal **2** reversion to an earlier or more primitive type or condition **3** an instance or example of this

throw pillow a small, decorative pillow

☆**throw rug** SCATTER RUG

throw·ster (thrō′stər) ***n.*** ⟦see THROW (***vt.*** 1)⟧ a person whose work is making thread from silk or synthetic filaments

throw-weight (thrō′wāt′) ***n.*** the payload capacity of an ICBM: also **throw weight**

thru (thro͞o) ***prep., adv., adj.*** *alt. sp. of* THROUGH: informal except on traffic signs

thrum¹ (thrum) ***n.*** ⟦ME < OE (in comp.), ligament, akin to Ger *trumm* < IE base **ter-*, to pass over, cross > TRANS-, TERM¹⟧ **1** *a)* the row of warp thread ends left on a loom when the web is cut off *b)* any of these ends **2** any short end thread or fringe **3** [*pl.*] *Naut.* short pieces of woolen or hempen yarn for thrumming canvas —***vt.*** **thrummed, thrum′ming 1** to provide with or make of thrums; fringe **2** *Naut.* to insert thrums in (canvas) to make a rough surface that helps to prevent chafing, stop leaks, etc.

thrum² (thrum) ***vt.*** **thrummed, thrum′ming** ⟦echoic⟧ **1** to strum (a guitar, banjo, etc.) **2** to tell in a monotonous, tiresome way **3** to drum on with the fingers —***vi.*** **1** *a)* to thrum a guitar, etc. *b)* to sound when so played **2** to drum with the fingers —***n.*** a thrumming or the sound of this

thrush¹ (thrush) ***n.*** ⟦ME *thrusch* < OE *thrysce* < IE **trozdos-*, thrush⟧ **1** any of a large family (Turdidae) of passerine birds, including the robin, wood thrush, and hermit thrush of North America and the song thrush and blackbird of Europe ☆**2** [Slang] a woman singer of popular songs

thrush² (thrush) ***n.*** ⟦< ON **thruskr* (> Dan *trøske*, Swed *torsk*⟧ **1** a disease, esp. of infants, caused by a fungus (genus *Candida*) and characterized by the formation of milky-white lesions on the mouth, lips, and throat **2** a disease of the frog of a horse's foot, characterized by the formation of pus

thrust (thrust) ***vt.*** **thrust, thrust′ing** ⟦ME *thrusten, thristen* < ON *thrysta* < IE **treud-*, to squeeze, push > THREAT, L *trudere*, to thrust⟧ **1** to push with sudden force; shove; drive **2** to pierce; stab **3** to force or impose (oneself or another) upon someone else or into some position or situation **4** to interject or interpose (a remark, question, etc.) **5** to extend, as in growth [the tree *thrusts* its branches high] —***vi.*** **1** to push or shove against something **2** to make a thrust, stab, or lunge, as with a sword **3** to force one's way (*into, through*, etc.) **4** to extend, as in growth —***n.*** **1** the act of thrusting; specif., *a)* a sudden, forceful push or shove *b)* a lunge or stab, as with a sword *c)* any sudden attack **2** continuous pressure of one part against another, as of a rafter against a wall **3** *a)* the driving force of a propeller in the line of its shaft *b)* the forward force produced in reaction to the gases escaping rearward from a jet or rocket engine **4** *a)* forward movement; impetus [the *thrust* of machine technology] *b)* energy; drive ☆**5** the basic meaning or purpose; point; force [the *thrust* of a speech] **6** *Geol.* an almost horizontal fault in which the hanging wall seems to have been pushed upward in relation to the footwall: in full **thrust fault**

thrust·er (thrus′tər) ***n.*** **1** a person or thing that thrusts ☆**2** any of a set of maneuvering rockets on a spacecraft or high-altitude airplane, as for controlling its attitude for reentry

thrust stage ⟦< pp. of THRUST⟧ a stage consisting of a raised platform extending from one end of a theater or from the proscenium, with audience seating on three sides

☆**thru·way** (thro͞o′wā′) ***n.*** EXPRESSWAY

Thu *abbrev.* Thursday

Thu·cyd·i·des (tho͞o sid′i dēz′) 460?-400? B.C.; Athenian historian

thud (thud) ***vi.*** **thud′ded, thud′ding** ⟦prob. < ME *thudden*, to strike, thrust < OE *thyddan*⟧ to hit or fall with a dull sound —***n.*** ⟦prob. < the *vi.*⟧ **1** a heavy blow **2** a dull sound, as that of a heavy, solid object dropping on a soft but solid surface Often used fig. of a drop, failure, collapse, etc. [a baseball season that ended with a *thud*]

thug (thug) ***n.*** ⟦Hindi *ṭhag*, swindler < Sans *sthaga*, a cheat, rogue, akin to *sthagayati*, (he) hides < IE base **(s)teg-*, to cover > THATCH⟧ **1** [*also* **T-**] a member of a former group in India that murdered and robbed in the service of Kali **2** a rough, brutal hoodlum, gangster, robber, etc. —**thug′ger·y *n.*** —**thug′gish *adj.***

thug·gee (thug′ē) ***n.*** ⟦Hindi *ṭhagī*: see prec.⟧ murder and robbery as formerly practiced by the thugs of India

thu·ja (tho͞o′jə, thyo͞o′-) ***n.*** ⟦ModL < Gr *thyia*, Afr tree with aromatic wood⟧ ARBORVITAE (sense 1)

Thu·le (tho͞o′lē, thyo͞o′-; to͞o′-, tyo͞o′-; *for 2* to͞o′lē) ⟦L < Gr *Thoulē, Thylē*⟧ **1** among the ancients, the northernmost region of the world, possibly taken to be Norway, Iceland, Jutland, etc.: also ULTIMA THULE² **2** Eskimo settlement on the NW coast of Greenland: site of U.S. air base

thu·li·a (tho͞o′lē ə, thyo͞o′-) ***n.*** ⟦ModL: so named (1879) by P. T. Cleve (see CLEVEITE) < *Thule*, Scandinavia: see prec.⟧ thulium oxide, Tm_2O_3

thu·li·um (tho͞o′lē əm, thyo͞o′-) ***n.*** ⟦ModL < prec. (from which it was isolated in 1879) + -IUM: so named (1886) by L. de Boisbaudran (see GADOLINIUM)⟧ a bright, silvery chemical element, one of the rare-earth elements: symbol, Tm; at. no. 69: see the periodic table of elements in the Reference Supplement

thumb (thum) ***n.*** ⟦ME (with unhistoric *-b*) < OE *thuma*, akin to Ger *daume(n)* < IE base **tēu-*, to swell, increase > L *tumor*: basic sense, "enlarged finger"⟧ **1** the short, thick digit of the human hand that is nearest the wrist and is opposable to the other fingers **2** a corresponding part in some other vertebrate animals **3** the part of a glove or mitten that covers the thumb **4** *Archit.* OVOLO —***vt.*** **1** to handle, turn, soil, or wear with or as with the thumb **2** [Informal] to solicit or get (a ride) or make (one's way) in hitchhiking by gesturing with the thumb extended in the direction one is traveling —**all thumbs** clumsy; fumbling —☆**thumb one's nose 1** to raise one's thumb to the nose with the fingers extended, as a coarse gesture of defiance or contempt **2** to express defiance or contempt —**thumbs down** a signal of rejection or disapproval —**thumbs up** a signal of acceptance or approval —**thumb through** to glance rapidly through (a book), as by releasing or turning pages along their edge with the thumb —**under someone's thumb** under someone's influence or sway —**thumb′less *adj.***

thumb·hole (thum′hōl′) ***n.*** **1** an opening for the insertion of a thumb, as to provide a firm hold **2** an opening in a wind instrument that is covered or uncovered with the thumb to produce certain notes

thumb index an index to the sections or divisions of a reference book, consisting of a series of rounded notches cut in the fore edge of a book with a labeled tab at the base of each notch —**thumb′-in′dex *vt.***

thumb·nail (thum′nāl′) ***n.*** the nail of the thumb —***adj.*** very small, brief, or concise [a *thumbnail* sketch]

thumb piano ⟦so named because played with the *thumbs*⟧ **1** KALIMBA **2** MBIRA

thumb·print (thum′print′) ***n.*** **1** a fingerprint of the thumb **2** FINGERPRINT (*n.* 2) **3** a kind of DROP COOKIE with a top indentation made with the thumb or a spoon and filled with icing, jam, etc.: in full **thumbprint cookie**

thumb·screw (thum′skro͞o′) ***n.*** **1** a screw with a head shaped in such a way that it can be turned with the thumb and forefinger **2** a former instrument of torture for squeezing the thumbs

thumb·stall (thum′stôl′) ***n.*** a kind of thimble or protective sheath, as of leather or rubber, for the thumb

☆**thumb·tack** (thum′tak′) ***n.*** a tack with a wide, flat head that can be pressed into a board, etc. with the thumb

Thum·mim (thum′im) ***n.*** ⟦Heb *tummīm*, pl. of *tōm*, perfection⟧ *see* URIM AND THUMMIM

thump (thump) ***n.*** ⟦echoic⟧ **1** a blow with something heavy and blunt, as with a cudgel **2** the dull sound made by such a blow —***vt.*** **1** to strike with a thump or thumps **2** *a)* to thrash; beat severely *b)* to defeat decisively —***vi.*** **1** to hit or fall with a thump **2** to make a dull, heavy sound; pound; throb —**thump′er *n.***

thump·ing (thum′piŋ) ***adj.*** **1** that thumps **2** [Informal] very large; whopping —**thump′ing·ly *adv.***

Thun (to͞on) **1** city in central Switzerland, on the Aar River where it leaves the Lake of Thun **2 Lake of** lake in Bern canton, central Switzerland: *c.* 18 sq mi (47 sq km)

thun·der (thun′dər) ***n.*** ⟦ME *thuner, thunder* (with unhistoric *-d-*) < OE *thunor*, akin to Ger *donner* < IE base **(s)teṇ-*, loud rustling, deep noise > ON *Thorr*, THOR, Gr *stenein*, to moan, L *tonare*, to thunder⟧ **1** the sound that follows a flash of lightning, caused by the sudden heating and expansion of air by electrical discharge **2** any loud, rumbling sound like this **3** a threatening, menacing, or extremely vehement utterance **4** [Archaic] a thunderbolt ➥Also used in mild oaths and imprecations [yes, by *thunder!*] —***vi.*** **1** to produce thunder: usually in the impersonal construction [it is *thundering*] **2** to make, or move with, a sound like thunder **3** to make vehement speeches, denunciations, etc. —***vt.*** **1** to say in a thundering voice **2** to strike, drive, etc. with the sound or violence of thunder —**steal someone's thunder 1** to use someone's ideas or methods without permission and without giving credit **2** to lessen the effectiveness of someone's statement or action by using or doing it before that person —**thun′der·er *n.***

thun·der·a·tion (thun′dər ā′shən) ***n.*** *old-fashioned var. of* THUNDER in mild oaths and imprecations [where in *thunderation* is he?]

Thunder Bay ⟦after the *bay* on which it is located: the bay was named for the *thunderbird* of Indian legend⟧ city & port in W Ontario, Canada, on Lake Superior: formed in 1970 by the merger of Fort William and Port Arthur

thun·der·bird (thun′dər burd′) ***n.*** ☆in the mythology of certain North American Indians, an enormous bird that produces thunder, lightning, and rain

thun·der·bolt (-bōlt′) ***n.*** **1** a flash of lightning and the accompanying thunder **2** a bolt or missile imagined as hurled to earth by a stroke of lightning **3** something that stuns or acts with sudden violence or force

thun·der·clap (-klap′) ***n.*** **1** a clap, or loud crash, of thunder **2** anything like this in being sudden, startling, violent, etc. Also **thun′der·peal′** (-pēl′)

thun·der·cloud (-kloud′) ***n.*** a storm cloud charged with electricity and producing lightning and thunder

☆**thunder egg** ⟦< ?⟧ a small, round, hollow stone of opal, agate, etc., lined with crystals

thun·der·head (-hed′) ***n.*** a round mass of cumulus clouds appearing before a thunderstorm

thun·der·ing (thun′dər iŋ) ***adj.*** **1** that thunders **2** [Informal] very large; thumping; whopping —**thun′der·ing·ly *adv.***

thun·der·ous (thun′dər əs) ***adj.*** **1** full of or making thunder **2** that thunders; loud; roaring —**thun′der·ous·ly *adv.***

thun·der·show·er (thun′dər shou′ər) ***n.*** a shower accompanied by thunder and lightning

thun·der·squall (-skwôl′) ***n.*** a squall accompanied by thunder and lightning

thun·der·stone (-stōn′) ***n.*** any of various stones, fossils, prehistoric implements, etc. formerly thought to have been hurled to earth by lightning and thunder

thun·der·storm (-stôrm′) ***n.*** a storm accompanied by thunder and lightning

thun·der·struck (-struk′) ***adj.*** struck with amazement, terror, etc., as if by a thunderbolt: also **thun′der·strick′en** (-strik′ən)

thun·der·y (thun′dər ē) ***adj.*** **1** that sounds like thunder **2** accompanied with or betokening thunder

☆**thunk¹** (thuŋk) ***n.*** ⟦echoic⟧ an abrupt, muffled sound, as of an ax hitting a tree trunk —***vi.*** to make such a sound

thunk² (thuŋk) ***vt., vi.*** [Dial.] *pt. & pp. of* THINK¹: now also a humorous usage

Thur *abbrev.* Thursday

Thur·ber (thur′bər), **James (Grover)** 1894-1961; U.S. writer, humorist, & cartoonist

Thur·gau (to͝or′gou′) canton of NE Switzerland, on Lake Constance: 383 sq mi (992 sq km): Fr. name **Thur·go·vie** (tür gô vē′)

thu·ri·ble (thur′ə bəl, tho͝or′-, thyo͝or′-) ***n.*** ⟦ME *thoryble* < L *thuribulum* < *thus* (gen. *thuris*), frankincense < Gr *thyos*, incense < *thyein*: see THYME⟧ CENSER

thu·ri·fer (-ə fər) ***n.*** ⟦ModL < L *thus* (see prec.) + *ferre*, BEAR[1]⟧ an acolyte or server who carries a thurible

Thu·rin·ger (tho͞o′rin jər, tir′-) ***n.*** ⟦< Ger *Thüringer wurst*, Thuringian sausage: see WURST⟧ any of several types of fresh or smoked, lightly seasoned sausage

Thu·rin·gi·a (tho͞o rin′jē ə, thyo͞o-; -jə) state of central Germany: 6,244 sq mi (16,172 sq km); cap. Erfurt: Ger. name **Thü·ring·en** (tü′riŋ ən)

Thu·rin·gi·an (tho͞o rin′jē ən, -jən) ***adj.*** of Thuringia or its people or culture —***n.*** **1** a member of an ancient Germanic people of central Germany **2** a person born or living in Thuringia

Thuringian Forest forested mountain range in Thuringia, Germany: highest peak, 3,222 ft (982 m): Ger. name **Thü·ring·er Wald** (tü′riŋ ər vält′)

Thurs *abbrev.* Thursday

Thurs·day (thurz′dā; *occas.*, -dē) ***n.*** ⟦ME *Thoresdai, Thunres dai* < OE *Thunres dæg*, ON *Thorsdagr*, Thor's day, rendering LL *Jovis dies*⟧ the fifth day of the week: abbrev. *Thur, Thurs, Thu, Th*, or *T*

Thursday Island Australian island in Torres Strait: 1.25 sq mi (3.24 sq km)

Thurs·days (thurz′dāz; *occas.*, -dēz) ***adv.*** during every Thursday or most Thursdays

thus (*th*us) ***adv.*** ⟦ME < OE⟧ **1** in this or that manner; in the way just stated or in the following manner **2** to this or that degree or extent; so **3** according to this or that; consequently; therefore; hence: often used as a conjunctive adverb **4** for example

thus·ly (-lē) ***adv.*** [Informal] THUS (sense 1)

thwack (thwak) ***vt.*** ⟦prob. echoic⟧ to strike with something flat; whack —***n.*** a blow with something flat

thwart (thwôrt) ***adj.*** ⟦ME *thwert* < ON *thvert*, neut. of *thverr*, transverse < IE **terk-*, to turn (prob. < **ter-*, to rub with rotary motion > THROW) > L *torquere*, to twist, turn⟧ **1** lying or extending across something else; transverse; oblique **2** [Obs.] perverse — ***adv., prep.*** [Archaic] athwart —***n.*** **1** a rower's seat extending across a boat **2** a brace extending across a canoe —***vt.*** **1** [Obs.] to extend or place over or across **2** to hinder, obstruct, frustrate, or defeat (a person, plans, etc.) —**SYN.** FRUSTRATE

thy (*th*ī) ***possessive pronominal adj.*** ⟦ME *thi*, contr. < *thin*, thy: see THINE⟧ [Archaic] of, belonging to, made by, or done by thee

Thy·es·tes (thī es′tēz) ***n.*** ⟦L < Gr *Thyestēs*⟧ *Gr. Myth.* a brother of Atreus: see ATREUS

thy·la·cine (thī′lə sīn′, -sin) ***n.*** ⟦Fr < Gr *thylakos*, pouch: it is a marsupial⟧ TASMANIAN WOLF

thy·la·koid (thī′lə koid′) ***n.*** ⟦< Ger < Gr *thylakoeidēs*, like a pouch < *thylakos*, bag, pouch: see -OID⟧ a disk-shaped, membranous sac containing chlorophyll, in which the light reaction of photosynthesis occurs, found in blue-green algae and in the chloroplasts of green plants: see also GRANUM

thyme (tīm) ***n.*** ⟦ME < MFr *thym* < L *thymum* < Gr *thymon* < *thyein*, to sacrifice, smoke < IE base **dheu-* > DULL⟧ **1** any of a genus (*Thymus*, esp. *T. vulgaris*) of shrubby plants or aromatic herbs of the mint family, with white, pink, or red flowers and with fragrant leaves **2** the leaves, used as an herb for seasoning

thy·mic (thī′mik) ***adj.*** of the thymus

thy·mi·dine (thī′mə dēn′, -din) ***n.*** ⟦< fol. + -ID(E) + -INE[3]⟧ a crystalline nucleoside, $C_{10}H_{14}N_2O_5$, one of the basic components of DNA: used chiefly in biochemical research

thy·mine (thī′mēn′, -min) ***n.*** ⟦Ger *thymin* < Gr *thymos*, spirit (< IE **dhūmo-* < base **dheu-*, to blow > DULL, FUME) + Ger *-in*, -INE[3]⟧ a white, crystalline, pyrimidine base, $C_5H_6N_2O_2$, contained in the nucleic acids of all tissue: it links with adenine in the DNA structure

thy·mol (thī′môl′, -mōl′) ***n.*** ⟦THYM(E) + -OL[1]⟧ a colorless, crystalline phenol, $C_{10}H_{14}O$, extracted from the volatile oil of thyme or made synthetically: used as an antiseptic, esp. in mouthwashes and nose and throat sprays, and in perfumery, embalming, microscopy, etc.

thy·mo·sin (thī′mə sin) ***n.*** ⟦< Gr *thymos*, fol. + -IN[1]⟧ any of a group of hormones, secreted by the thymus, that stimulate the immune system by helping T cells mature

thy·mus (thī′məs) ***n.*** ⟦ModL < Gr *thymos*, orig., a warty excrescence⟧ a gland in the upper thorax or neck of all vertebrates, involved in the production of lymphocytes: in humans, it is most prominent at puberty, after which it disappears or becomes vestigial: also **thymus gland**

☆**thy·ra·tron** (thī′rə trän′) ***n.*** ⟦< Gr *thyris*, window, cell (see fol.) + *-a-* + -TRON⟧ a hot-cathode, triode or tetrode electron tube containing low-pressure gas or metal vapor: one or more grids control the start of the current flow but have no further control over it

☆**thy·ris·tor** (thī ris′tər) ***n.*** ⟦Gr *thyris*, window, cell (akin to *thyra*, DOOR) + *-tor*, as in RESISTOR⟧ any of various solid-state, semiconductor devices with three or more pn junctions, used as an electronic switch, rectifier, etc.

thy·ro- (thī′rō, -rə) *combining form* thyroid [*thyrotoxicosis*]: also, before a vowel, **thyr-**

☆**thy·ro·cal·ci·to·nin** (thī′rō kal′si tō′nin) ***n.*** ⟦prec. + CALCITONIN⟧ CALCITONIN

thy·roid (thī′roid′) ***adj.*** ⟦ModL *thyroides* < Gr *thyreoeidēs*, shield-shaped < *thyreos*, large shield, door-shaped shield < *thyra*, DOOR + *-eidēs*, -OID⟧ **1** designating or of a large ductless gland lying in front and on either side of the trachea and secreting the hormone thyroxine, which regulates body growth and metabolism: the malfunctioning or congenital absence of this gland can cause goiter, cretinism, etc. **2** designating or of the principal cartilage of the larynx, forming the Adam's apple —***n.*** **1** the thyroid gland **2** the thyroid cartilage **3** an artery, nerve, etc. in the region of the thyroid **4** a preparation of the thyroid gland of certain animals, used in treating goiter, myxedema, etc.: also **thyroid extract**

thy·roid·ec·to·my (thī′roi dek′tə mē) ***n.**, pl.* **-mies** the surgical removal of all or part of the thyroid gland

thy·roid·i·tis (-dīt′is) ***n.*** ⟦ModL: see -ITIS⟧ inflammation of the thyroid gland

thy·ro·tox·i·co·sis (thī′rō täk′si kō′sis) ***n.*** ⟦THYRO- + TOXICOSIS⟧ HYPERTHYROIDISM

thy·ro·tro·pin (thī′rə trō′pin, thī rä′trə pin) ***n.*** ⟦THYRO- + TROP(HIC) + -IN[1]⟧ a hormone isolated from the anterior pituitary that stimulates the production of thyroxine in the thyroid: also **thy′ro·tro′phin** (-fin)

thy·ro·tro·pin-re·leas·ing hormone (-ri lēs′iŋ) a hormone produced by the hypothalamus that stimulates the production of thyrotropin: sometimes called **thyrotropin-releasing factor**

thy·rox·ine (thī räk′sēn′, -sin) ***n.*** ⟦< THYR(O)- + OXY-[1] + -INE[3]⟧ a colorless, crystalline compound, $C_{15}H_{11}I_4NO_4$, the active hormone of the thyroid gland, often prepared synthetically and used in treating goiter, cretinism, and myxedema: also **thy·rox′in** (-in)

thyr·sus (thur′səs) ***n.**, pl.* **thyr′si′** (-sī′) ⟦L < Gr *thyrsos*; ? akin to Hittite *tuwarsa-*, grape vine⟧ **1** a staff tipped with a pine cone and sometimes entwined with ivy or vine leaves, which Dionysus, the satyrs, etc. were represented as carrying **2** *Bot.* a flower cluster in which the main stem is racemose and the secondary stems are cymose, as in the lilac: also **thyrse** (thurs)

thy·sa·nu·ran (thī′sə nyo͝or′ən, -no͝or′-; this′ə-) ***n.*** ⟦< ModL *Thysanura* (< Gr *thysanos*, tassel + *oura*, a tail: see URO-[2]) + -AN⟧ any of an order (Thysanura) of very primitive insects that have bristlelike appendages at the rear end, including bristletails and silverfish

thy·self (*th*ī self′) ***pron.*** ⟦ME *thi self*, superseding earlier *the self*, lit., thee self < OE *the self*; in ME, *self*, orig. adj., was regarded as n.⟧ [Archaic] *reflexive or intensive form of* THOU[1]

ti[1] (tē) ***n.*** ⟦altered < SI⟧ *Music* a syllable representing the seventh tone of the diatonic scale: see SOLFEGGIO

ti[2] (tē) ***n.*** ⟦< a Polynesian language, e.g. Maori or Samoan: ult. < Proto-Polynesian **tii*⟧ a Polynesian and Australian woody plant (genus *Cordyline*) of the agave family: the leaves are used for thatch, garments, fodder, etc., and the roots are used for food and liquor

Ti[1] *abbrev. Bible* **1** Timothy **2** Titus

Ti[2] *Chem. symbol for* titanium

TIA (tē′ī′ā′) ***n.*** ⟦*t(ransient) i(schemic) a(ttack)*⟧ a mild cerebrovascular stroke with reversible symptoms that last from a few minutes to several hours

Ti·a Jua·na (tē′ə wä′nə; *Sp* tē′ä hwä′nä) *former name for* TIJUANA

Tian·an·men Square (tyen′ə mən, -ən-) large public square in Beijing, China: site of pro-democracy demonstrations (1989) leading to violent government suppression

Tian·jin (tyen′jin′) seaport in NE China: capital of Hebei province

Tian Shan (tyen′ shän′) mountain system in central Asia, extending across Kyrgyzstan & Xinjiang, China, to the Altai Mountains: highest peak, 24,406 ft (7,439 m)

ti·ar·a (tē er′ə, -ar′-, -är′-) ***n.*** ⟦L < Gr: prob. of Asian orig.⟧ **1** a headdress of the ancient Persians **2** the pope's high, domed crown consisting of three coronets and an orb and cross **3** a woman's crownlike headdress of jewels or flowers; coronet

Ti·ber (tī′bər) ⟦L *Tiberis*⟧ river in central Italy, flowing from the Apennines south through Rome into the Tyrrhenian Sea: *c.* 250 mi (402 km): It. name TEVERE

Ti·be·ri·as (tī bir′ē əs), **Sea of** Sea of GALILEE

Ti·ber·i·us (tī bir′ē əs) (*Tiberius Claudius Nero Caesar*) 42 B.C.–A.D. 37; Rom. emperor (A.D. 14-37)

Ti·bes·ti (ti bes′tē) mountain group of the Sahara, mostly in NW Chad: highest peak, 11,204 ft (3,415 m)

Ti·bet (ti bet′) autonomous region of SW China, occupying a high plateau area north of the Himalayas: 471,662 sq mi (1,221,600 sq km); cap. Lhasa

Ti·bet·an (ti bet′'n) ***adj.*** of Tibet or its people, language, or culture —***n.*** **1** a member of a Mongolian people native to, and forming the majority of the population of, Tibet **2** the Tibeto-Burman language of this people **3** any person born or living in Tibet

Tibetan Buddhism the form of Mahayana Buddhism that developed and is practiced primarily in Tibet and some nearby nations: its spiritual leader is the Dalai Lama

Tibetan spaniel any of a breed of small, spaniel-type dog originating in Tibet, with a blunt muzzle, short legs, and a plumed tail curled over the back

Tibetan terrier any of a breed of small dog, originating in Tibet, with a long, thick coat, hair falling over the eyes, and a tail that curls over the back

Ti·bet·o-Bur·man (ti bet′ō bur′mən) ***n.*** a branch of the Sino-Tibetan family of languages, including Tibetan and Burmese —***adj.*** designating or of this group of languages or the peoples speaking them or their cultures

tib·i·a (tib′ē ə) *n., pl.* **-i·ae′** (-ē ē′) or **-i·as** ⟦L < ?⟧ **1** the inner and thicker of the two bones of the human leg between the knee and the ankle; shinbone **2** a corresponding bone in the leg of other vertebrates **3** the fourth segment (from the base) of an insect's leg **4** an ancient flute, orig. made from an animal's tibia —**tib′i·al** *adj.*

Ti·bur (tī′bər) *ancient name for* TIVOLI (Italian city)

tic (tik) *n.* ⟦Fr < ?⟧ **1** any involuntary, regularly repeated, spasmodic contraction of a muscle, generally caused by some type of disorder of the nervous system **2** *short for* TIC DOULOUREUX

tic dou·lou·reux (tik′ do͞o′lo͞o ro͞o′; *Fr* tēk do͞o lo͞o rö′) ⟦Fr, lit., painful tic⟧ TRIGEMINAL NEURALGIA

Ti·ci·no (tē chē′nō) **1** canton of S Switzerland, on the Italian border: 1,086 sq mi (2,813 sq km) **2** river flowing from this canton south into the Po River: *c.* 160 mi (257 km)

tick[1] (tik) *n.* ⟦ME *tek*, prob. < Gmc echoic base > Du *tikk*, MHG *zicken*, to tick⟧ **1** a light touch; pat **2** a light clicking or tapping sound, as that made by the escapement of a watch or clock **3** a mark (✓, /, etc.) made to check off items; check mark **4** ⟦from the time needed for one *tick* of a clock⟧ [Brit. Informal] moment; instant **5** [Informal] a tiny degree or increment —*vi.* **1** to make a tick or series of ticks, as a clock **2** [Informal] to function characteristically or well; operate; work [*what makes him tick?*] —*vt.* **1** to indicate, record, or count by a tick or ticks **2** [Chiefly Brit.] to mark or check off (an item on a list, etc.) with a tick: usually with *off* —**tick off 1** [Brit. Informal] to reprimand ☆**2** [Slang] to make angry or irritable

tick[2] (tik) *n.* ⟦ME *teke* < OE *ticia* (? for *ticca*), akin to MDu *teke*, Ger *zecke* < IE base **deiĝh-*, to prickle, itch > Arm *tiz*, tick, MIr *dega*, stag beetle⟧ **1** any of a superfamily (Ixodoidea, order Parasitiformes) of wingless, bloodsucking mites, including many species that transmit diseases and are usually parasitic on humans, cattle, sheep, etc. **2** any of various wingless, parasitic insects

tick[3] (tik) *n.* ⟦LME *tykke*, akin to MDu *tyke*, both prob. < early WGmc borrowing < L *theca*, a cover, sheath: see THECA⟧ **1** a cloth case or covering that is filled with cotton, feathers, hair, etc. to form a mattress or pillow **2** [Informal] TICKING

tick[4] (tik) *n.* ⟦contr. < TICKET⟧ [Informal, Chiefly Brit.] credit; trust [*to buy something on tick*]

☆**ticked** (tikt) *adj.* ⟦< TICK OFF (sense 2) (see phr. under TICK[1])⟧ [Slang] angry, annoyed, irritated, etc.

tick·er (tik′ər) *n.* **1** a person or thing that ticks; specif., ☆*a)* [Historical] a telegraphic device for recording stock-market quotations, news from a wire service, etc. on a paper tape *b)* [Old Slang] a pocket watch **2** an electronic device for displaying stock-market quotations **3** [Slang] the heart

☆**ticker tape 1** paper tape used in a TICKER (sense *a*) for recording telegraphed stock-market quotations, etc. **2** designating or of a parade, etc. onto which confetti and paper streamers (and, formerly, ticker tape) are thrown in celebration

tick·et (tik′it) *n.* ⟦aphetic < obs. Fr *etiquet* (now *étiquette*)⟧ **1** [Obs.] any note, memorandum, voucher, etc. **2** a printed card or piece of paper that gives a person a specified right, as to attend a theater, ride on a train, claim a purchase, etc. **3** [Informal] a license or qualifying certificate [*a second mate's ticket*] **4** a label or tag, as on a piece of merchandise, giving the size, color, price, quantity, etc. ☆**5** the list of candidates nominated by a political party in an election; slate ☆**6** [Informal] a summons to court for a traffic violation —*vt.* **1** to label or tag with a ticket **2** to provide a ticket or tickets for ☆**3** [Informal] to issue or attach a TICKET (*n.* 6) to —**just the ticket** [Informal] fitting; proper; just right —**that's the ticket!** [Slang] a phrase used to express enthusiastic approval

tick·et-of-leave man (tik′it əv lēv′) [Brit. Historical] a convicted person whose sentence had not expired, set conditionally at liberty by issuance of a revocable permit (**ticket of leave**)

tick fever any infectious disease transmitted by the bite of a tick, as Rocky Mountain spotted fever

tick·ing (tik′iŋ) *n.* ⟦see TICK[3]⟧ strong, heavy cloth, often striped, used for casings of mattresses, pillows, etc.

tick·le (tik′əl) *vt.* **-led, -ling** ⟦ME *tikelen*, akin to Ger dial. *zickeln*, OE *tinclian*, to tickle: for IE base see TICK[2]⟧ **1** to please, gratify, delight, etc.: often used in the passive voice with slang intensifiers, as **tickled pink**, **tickled silly**, or **tickled to death** **2** to stir to amusement or laughter; amuse **3** to excite the surface nerves of, as by touching or stroking lightly with the finger, a feather, etc., in a way that causes involuntary twitching, a pleasant tingling, laughter, etc. —*vi.* **1** to have an itching, scratching, or tingling sensation [*a throat that tickles*] **2** to cause a tickling sensation [*that feather tickles*] **3** to be readily affected by excitation of the surface nerves; be ticklish —*n.* **1** a tickling or being tickled **2** a tickling sensation

tick·ler (tik′lər, -əl ər) *n.* **1** a person or thing that tickles ☆**2** a special memorandum pad, file, etc. for reminding one of matters requiring attention at certain dates in the future

tickler coil a small coil connected in series with the plate circuit of a vacuum tube and coupled inductively to the grid circuit to furnish feedback

tick·lish (tik′lish, -əl ish) *adj.* **1** sensitive to tickling **2** very sensitive or easily upset; touchy **3** needing careful handling; precarious; delicate —**tick′lish·ly** *adv.* —**tick′lish·ness** *n.*

tick·seed (tik′sēd′) *n.* ⟦TICK[2] + SEED: from the appearance⟧ **1** COREOPSIS **2** BUR MARIGOLD

tick-tack-toe (tik′tak′tō′) *n. alt. sp. of* TIC-TAC-TOE

tick·tock (tik′täk′) *n.* ⟦echoic redupl. of TICK[1]⟧ the ticking sound made by a clock —*vi.* to make this sound

☆**tick trefoil** any of a genus (*Desmodium*) of leguminous plants with clusters of small purple flowers, leaves in groups of three, and jointed prickly pods

☆**tick·y-tack·y** (tik′ē tak′ē) [Informal] *n.* ⟦orig., cheap building materials, as for tract houses < redupl. of TACKY[2]: popularized in "Little Boxes" (1962), song by M. Reynolds (1900-78), U.S. songwriter⟧ **1** shoddy or inferior material **2** things, often, specif., cheap housing, made with shoddy or inferior materials, workmanship, etc. —*adj.* cheap, inferior, petty, tasteless, etc. Also **tick′y-tack′**

Ti·con·der·o·ga (tī kän′də rō′gə, tī′kän-), **Fort** ⟦Mohawk *tekontaró:ken*, lit., at the junction of two waterways⟧ former fort in NE N.Y., taken from the British by the Green Mountain Boys in 1775

tic-tac-toe (tik′tak′tō′) *n.* a game in which two players take turns marking either an X or an O in an open block of nine squares, the object being to complete a vertical, horizontal, or diagonal row of three of one's mark before the other player can

t.i.d. *abbrev.* ⟦L *ter in die*⟧ *Pharmacy* three times a day

tid·al (tīd′'l) *adj.* of, having, caused by, determined by, or dependent on a tide or tides —**tid′al·ly** *adv.*

tidal basin a basin for mooring boats, accessible only at high tide

tidal wave 1 *nontechnical term for* a tsunami or a similar wave caused by strong winds and not actually related to the tides ☆**2** any great or widespread movement, expression of prevalent feeling, etc.

tid·bit (tid′bit′) *n.* ⟦dial. *tid*, small object + BIT[2]⟧ a pleasing or choice bit of food, news, gossip, etc.

tid·dler (tid′lər) *n.* [Informal, Chiefly Brit.] **1** a very small fish **2** a small, minor, or unimportant thing or person

tid·dly[1] (tid′lē) *adj.* ⟦prob. < *tiddly-wink*, illicit grogshop, rhyming slang for DRINK⟧ [Informal, Chiefly Brit.] drunk; tipsy

tid·dly[2] (tid′lē) *adj.* ⟦prob. < child's alteration of *little*⟧ [Brit.] very small; little

tid·dly·winks (tid′lē wiŋks′, tid′'l ē-) *n.* ⟦prob. < *tiddly*, child's form of LITTLE: see prec.⟧ a game in which the players try to snap little colored disks from a surface into a cup by pressing their edges with a larger disk: also **tid′dle·dy·winks′** (-'l dē wiŋks′)

tide[1] (tīd) *n.* ⟦ME, tide, time, season < OE *tid*, time; akin to Ger *zeit* < IE **dī-*, var. of base **da(i)-*, to part, divide up > TIME, Sans *dāti*, (he) cuts off, Gr *dēmos*, district, people⟧ **1** [Obs.] a period of time: now only in comb. [*Eastertide, eventide*] **2** ⟦prob. infl. by MLowG or MDu⟧ *a)* the alternate rise and fall of the surface of oceans, seas, and the bays, rivers, etc. connected with them, caused by the attraction of the moon and sun: it may occur twice in each period of 24 hours and 50 minutes, which is the time of one rotation of the earth with respect to the moon (see also FLOOD TIDE, SPRING TIDE) *b)* FLOOD TIDE **3** something that rises and falls like the tide **4** a stream, current, etc. or trend, tendency, etc. [*the tide of public opinion*] **5** the period during which something is at its highest or fullest point **6** [Archaic] an opportune time or occasion —*adj.* TIDAL —*vi.* **tid′ed, tid′ing** to flow or surge like a tide —*vt.* to carry with or as with the tide —**tide over** to help along temporarily, as through a period of difficulty —**turn the tide** to reverse a condition —**tide′less** *adj.*

tide[2] (tīd) *vt.* **tid′ed, tid′ing** ⟦ME *tiden* < OE *tidan* < *tid*: see prec.⟧ [Archaic] to betide; happen

☆**tide·land** (tīd′land′, -lənd) *n.* **1** land covered by water at high tide and uncovered at low tide **2** [*pl.*] loosely, land under water just beyond this and within territorial limits

tide·mark (-märk′) *n.* a mark indicating the highest point of flood tide or, sometimes, the lowest point of ebb tide

tide rip a rip current associated with a tidal current

tide·wa·ter (tīd′wôt′ər) *n.* **1** water brought into an area by the action of the rising tide ☆**2** water that is affected by the tide, as a stream along a coastline ☆**3** an area in which water is affected by the tide ☆**4** [T-] the English dialect of E Virginia —*adj.* **1** of or along a tidewater ☆**2** [T-] of (the) Tidewater

Tide·wa·ter (tīd′wôt′ər) the E part of Virginia

tide·way (-wā′) *n.* **1** a channel through which a tide runs **2** the tidal part of a river **3** a tidal current

ti·dings (tī′diŋz) *pl.n.* ⟦ME, pl. of *tidinge* < OE *tidung* (< *tidan*: see TIDE[2]); akin to Ger *zeitung*, newspaper⟧ [Now Chiefly Literary] news; information

ti·dy (tī′dē) *adj.* **-di·er, -di·est** ⟦ME *tidi*, seasonable, honest, hence in good condition < *tide*: see TIDE[1]⟧ **1** neat in personal appearance, ways, etc.; orderly **2** neat in arrangement; in order; trim **3** [Informal] *a)* fairly good; satisfactory *b)* rather large; considerable [*a tidy sum of money*] —*vt., vi.* **-died, -dy·ing** to make (things) tidy: often with *up* —*n., pl.* **-dies 1** ANTIMACASSAR **2** a small container for odds and ends —**ti′di·ly** *adv.* —**ti′di·ness** *n.*

☆**ti·dy·tips** (tī′dē tips′) *n., pl.* **-tips′** a California wildflower (*Layia platyglossa*) of the composite family, with yellow, daisylike flowers, often tipped with white

tie (tī) *vt.* **tied, ty′ing** or **tie′ing** ⟦ME *tien* < OE *tigan, tegan*; akin to *teag*, a rope: for IE base see TOW[1]⟧ **1** to fasten, attach, or bind together or to something else, as with string, cord, or rope made secure by knotting, etc. [*to tie someone's hands, to tie a boat to a pier*] **2** *a)* to draw together or join the parts, ends, or sides of by tightening and knotting laces, strings, etc. [*to tie one's shoes*] *b)* to make by fastening together parts [*to tie fishing flies*] **3** *a)* to make (a knot or bow) *b)* to make a knot or bow in [*to tie one's necktie*] **4** to fasten, connect, join, or bind in any way [*tied together by common interests*] **5** to confine; restrain; restrict **6** *a)* to equal the score or achievement of, as in a contest *b)* to equal (a score, record, etc.) 7 *Music* to connect with a tie —*vi.* 1 to be capable of being tied; make a tie 2 to make an equal score or achievement, as in a contest —*n.* ⟦ME *tege, teige* < OE *teag, teah,* a rope⟧ 1 a string, lace, cord, etc. used to tie things 2 something that connects, binds, or joins; bond; link [a business *tie, ties* of affection] 3 something that confines, limits, or restricts [legal *ties*] 4 *short for* NECKTIE 5 a beam, rod, etc. that connects parts of a building and prevents them from spreading apart ☆6 any of the parallel crossbeams to which the rails of a railroad are fastened 7 *a)* an equality of scores, votes, achievement, etc. in a contest *b)* a contest or match in which there is such an equality; draw; stalemate 8 [*pl.*] low shoes fastened with laces, as oxfords 9 *Music* a curved line above or below two notes of the same pitch, indicating that the tone is to be held unbroken for the duration of their combined values —*adj.* that has been tied, or made equal [a *tie* score] —**tie down** to confine; restrain; restrict —☆**tie in** 1 to bring into or have a connection 2 to make or be consistent, harmonious, etc. —☆**tie into** [Informal] to attack vigorously —**tie off** 1 to make (a rope or line) fast 2 to close off passage through by tying with something —☆**tie one on** [Slang] to get drunk —**tie up** 1 to tie firmly or securely 2 to wrap up and tie with string, cord, etc. 3 to moor as to a dock ☆4 to obstruct; hinder; stop 5 *a)* to use, reserve, etc. (something), thereby rendering it unavailable to someone else *b)* to occupy (someone), thereby rendering him or her unavailable for other tasks or activities

SYN.—**tie** and **bind** are often interchangeable, but in discriminating use, **tie** specif. implies the connection of one thing with another by means of a rope, string, etc. which can be knotted [to *tie* a horse to a hitching post], and **bind** suggests the use of an encircling band which holds two or more things firmly together [to *bind* someone's legs]; **fasten**, a somewhat more general word, implies a joining of one thing to another, as by tying, binding, gluing, nailing, pinning, etc.; **attach** emphasizes the joining of two or more things in order to keep them together as a unit [to *attach* one's references to an application] —*ANT.* **separate, part**

tie·back (tī′bak′) *n.* ☆1 a fabric strip, ribbon, tape, etc. used to tie curtains or draperies to one side ☆2 a curtain with a tieback: *usually used in pl.*

tie beam a horizontal beam serving as a TIE (*n.* 5), esp. one connecting opposite rafters at their lower ends

tie·break·er (tī′brāk′ər) *n.* 1 an additional game, period of play, question, etc. used to establish a winner from among those tied at the end of a contest 2 *Tennis* any of several forms of play sometimes used to decide the winner of a set tied at a certain score

tie clasp a decorative clasp for fastening a necktie to the shirt front: also **tie clip** or **tie bar**

tie-dye (tī′dī′) *n.* 1 a method of dyeing designs on cloth or thread by tightly tying bunches of it as with waxed thread so that the dye affects only exposed parts 2 cloth so decorated or a design so made —*vt.* **-dyed′**, **-dye′ing** to dye in this way

☆**tie-in** (tī′in′) *adj.* designating or of a sale or campaign in which two or more products or items are offered in combination —*n.* 1 *a)* a tie-in sale or advertisement *b)* an article sold in this way 2 a connection or relationship

tie line ☆1 a direct telephone line between extensions in two or more PBX systems ☆2 a line used to connect one electric power or transportation system with another

tie·mann·ite (tē′mən īt′) *n.* ⟦Ger *tiemannit,* after W. *Tiemann,* 19th-c. Ger mineralogist⟧ a rare, gray to black, soft, heavy, cubic mineral, HgSe, that is poisonous

Tien Shan (tyen′ shän′) *alt. sp. of* TIAN SHAN

Tien·tsin (tyen′tsin′) *a former transliteration of* TIANJIN

tie·pin (tī′pin′) *n.* STICKPIN (sense 1)

Tie·po·lo (tye′pô lô), **Gio·van·ni Bat·tis·ta** (jô vän′nē bät tēs′tä) 1696-1770; Venetian painter

tier[1] (tir) *n.* ⟦< OFr *tire,* order, rank, dress < Frank **teri* (akin to OHG *ziari,* beauty, OE *tir,* glory) < IE **dēiro-* < base **dei-,* to gleam > DEITY⟧ 1 a row, or rank, of seats 2 any of a series of rows, layers, ranks, etc. arranged one above or behind another — *vt., vi.* to arrange or be arranged in tiers: often used in comb. [a three-*tiered* wedding cake, one-*tier* tax system]

ti·er[2] (tī′ər) *n.* 1 a person or thing that ties ☆2 a type of pinafore formerly worn by children

tierce (tirs) *n.* ⟦ME *terce* < OFr < L *tertia,* fem. of *tertius,* (a) third < base of *tres,* THREE⟧ 1 [Obs.] a third 2 [*often* **T-**] *var. of* TERCE 3 an old unit of liquid measure, equal to ⅓ pipe (42 gallons) 4 a cask of this capacity, between a barrel and a hogshead in size 5 *Fencing* the third defensive position, from which a lunge or parry can be made

tier·cel (tir′səl) *n.* ⟦ME *tercel* < OFr < VL **tertiolus* < L *tertius,* third: said to be so named because it was believed that every third bird in a nest is a male⟧ *Falconry* a male hawk, esp. the male peregrine

tie rod 1 a horizontal rod serving as a TIE (*n.* 5) 2 a rod that connects certain parts in the steering linkage of a motor vehicle

Ti·er·ra del Fue·go (tē er′ə del fwā′gō) 1 group of islands at the tip of South America, separated from the mainland by the Strait of Magellan: they are divided between Argentina & Chile: 28,473 sq mi (73,745 sq km) 2 chief island of this group, divided between Argentina & Chile: *c.* 18,000 sq mi (46,620 sq km)

☆**tie tack** or **tie tac** (tak) an ornamental pin with a short point that fits into a snap, used to fasten a necktie to the shirt front

tie-up (tī′up′) *n.* ☆1 a temporary stoppage or interruption of work, production, traffic, service, etc. ☆2 [Dial.] a place for tying up cattle at night 3 a connection, relation, or involvement, as between businesses; specif., MERGER (sense *a*)

tiff[1] (tif) *n.* ⟦< ?⟧ a slight quarrel; spat —*vi.* to be in or have a tiff

tiff[2] (tif) *n.* ⟦< ?⟧ [Now Rare] 1 liquor; esp., weak liquor 2 a little drink of weak liquor or punch

tif·fa·ny (tif′ə nē) *n., pl.* **-nies** ⟦OFr *tiphanie,* Epiphany < LL(Ec) *theophania* < Gr, lit., manifestation of God: reason for name uncert.⟧ a thin gauze of silk or muslin

Tif·fa·ny[1] (tif′ə nē) *adj.* 1 ⟦after C. L. *Tiffany* (1812-1902), U.S. jeweler⟧ designating or of a raised mounting or setting for a finger ring, with a gem held in place by prongs 2 ⟦after L. C. *Tiffany* (1848-1933), U.S. designer & glass manufacturer, son of the jeweler⟧ designating or of an art nouveau style or design in stained glass, metalwork, jewelry, etc.

Tif·fa·ny[2] (tif′ə nē) *n.* a feminine name

tif·fin (tif′in) *n., vi.* ⟦Anglo-Ind for *tiffing,* drinking, hence, by extension, eating < TIFF[2]⟧ *former Brit. term for* LUNCH

Tif·lis (tif′lis) *former name for* TBILISI

ti·ger (tī′gər) *n., pl.* **-gers** or **-ger** ⟦ME *tygre* < OE *tiger* & OFr *tigre,* both < L *tigris* < Gr < Iran *tigra-,* sharp < IE base **(s)teig-* > STICK⟧ 1 a large, fierce Asian cat (*Panthera tigris*), having a tawny coat striped with black 2 any of several similar animals; esp., *a)* the South American jaguar *b)* the African leopard *c)* the Tasmanian wolf 3 *a)* a very energetic or persevering person *b)* a fierce, belligerent person —☆**have a tiger by the tail** to find oneself in a situation that has become unexpectedly difficult to manage or resolve —**ti′ger·ish** *adj.*

tiger beetle any of various active, long-legged, brightly colored, often striped beetles (family Carabidae) with larvae that burrow in soil and feed on other insects

tiger cat 1 any of various wildcats smaller than, but somewhat resembling, the tiger, as the serval or ocelot 2 any of various domestic cats with tigerlike markings, esp. the shorthair or the American wirehair

tiger lily 1 a lily (*Lilium tigrinum*) having orange flowers with purplish-black spots 2 any of several kinds of lilies resembling this flower

tiger moth any of a family (Arctiidae) of stout-bodied moths with brightly striped or spotted wings: the caterpillars (*woolly bears*) have a dense coat of fine hairs

☆**tiger salamander** ⟦so named from its coloration⟧ a widely distributed North American salamander (*Ambystoma tigrinum,* family Ambystomatidae) with a blackish body spotted with irregular yellow or white markings

ti·ger's-eye (tī′gərz ī′) *n.* a semiprecious, yellow-brown stone, silicified crocidolite, used for ornament: also **ti′ger·eye′** (-gər ī′)

tiger shark ⟦so named prob. from the dark vertical stripes on its sides⟧ a large, aggressive, bluish-gray requiem shark (*Galeocerdo cuvier*) usually seen in the warm coastal waters of the Atlantic and Pacific oceans

tiger swallowtail ⟦so named from its coloration⟧ any of various swallowtails (genus *Papilio*), esp. a large, yellow-and-black butterfly (*P. glaucus*) of E North America

tight (tīt) *adj.* ⟦ME, altered (prob. infl. by *toght:* see TAUT) < *thight* < OE *-thight,* strong, akin to ON *þéttr,* Ger *dicht,* tight, thick < IE base **tenk-,* to thicken, congeal > MIr *técht,* coagulated⟧ 1 [Obs.] dense 2 so close or compact in structure that water, air, etc. cannot pass through [a *tight* boat] 3 drawn, packed, spaced, etc. closely together [a *tight* weave, a *tight* schedule of events] 4 [Dial.] snug; trim; neat 5 fixed securely; held firmly; firm [a *tight* joint] 6 fully stretched; taut, not slack or loose 7 fitting closely; often, fitting so closely as to be uncomfortable 8 strict; restraining; severe [*tight* control] 9 difficult to manage: esp. in the phrase **a tight corner** (or **squeeze,** etc.), a difficult situation 10 showing tension or strain [a *tight* smile] 11 almost even or tied; close [a *tight* race] 12 of a short radius; sharp: said of a spiral, curve, turn, etc. 13 *a)* difficult to get; scarce in relation to demand (said of commodities on a market, or of money available for loans) *b)* characterized by such scarcity [a *tight* market] 14 concise; condensed: said of language, style, etc. 15 [Now Chiefly Dial.] well-proportioned; shapely 16 [Dial.] competent; capable 17 [Informal] stingy; parsimonious 18 [Slang] drunk ☆19 [Slang] intimate; familiar; friendly: often with *with* —*adv.* in a tight manner; esp., *a)* securely or firmly [hold *tight;* tie the rope *tight*] *b)* [Informal] soundly [sleep *tight*] —**sit tight** [Informal] to keep one's opinion or position and wait —**tight′ly** *adv.* —**tight′ness** *n.*

SYN.—**tight**, in this connection, implies a constricting or binding encirclement [a *tight* collar] or such closeness or compactness of parts as to be impenetrable [*airtight*]; **taut** (and, loosely, also **tight**) is applied to a rope, cord, cloth, etc. that is pulled or stretched to the point where there is no slackness [*taut* sails]; **tense** suggests a tightness or tautness that results in great strain [*tense* muscles] See also **drunk** —*ANT.* **loose, slack, lax**

-tight (tīt) ⟦< prec.⟧ *combining form* not letting (something specified) in or out [*airtight, watertight*]

☆**tight-ass** (tīt′as) *n.* [Slang] a strait-laced, inhibited person: regarded as mildly vulgar by some

tight-assed (tīt′ast) *adj.* [Slang] strait-laced and inhibited, as in behavior or attitudes: regarded as mildly vulgar by some

tight·en (tīt′′n) *vt., vi.* to make or become tight or tighter —**tight′en·er** *n.*

☆**tight end** *Football* an offensive end positioned close to the tackle, usually for blocking purposes: cf. SPLIT END

tight·fist·ed (tīt′fis′tid) *adj.* stingy; closefisted

tight·fit·ting (-fit′iŋ) *adj.* fitting very tightly
tight·knit (tīt′nit′) *adj.* 1 tightly knit 2 CLOSE-KNIT [a *tightknit* family]
tight-lipped (-lipt′) *adj.* 1 having the lips closed tightly 2 not saying much; taciturn or secretive
tight·rope (tīt′rōp′) *n.* a tightly stretched rope or cable on which aerialists walk or do balancing acts
tights (tīts) *pl.n.* a tightly fitting, knitted one-piece covering for the hips, legs, and usually the feet
☆**tight ship** [Informal] an institution, business, etc. that is highly organized and efficiently run, like a naval vessel on which discipline is strictly enforced
☆**tight·wad** (tīt′wäd′) *n.* ⟦TIGHT + WAD[1]⟧ [Slang] a stingy person
Tig·lath-pi·le·ser III (tig′lath′ pī lē′zər, -pi-) died 727? B.C.; king of Assyria (745?-727?)
ti·glon (tī′glän′, -glən) *n.* ⟦TIG(ER) + L(I)ON⟧ the hybrid offspring of a male tiger and a female lion: also **ti′gon′** (-gän′, -gən)
Ti·gré[1] (tē grā′) *n.* a modern Ethiopic language spoken in N Eritrea: it developed from a branch of N Ethiopic parallel to the branch that produced Tigrinya
Ti·gré[2] (tē grā′) ⟦< ?⟧ region of N Ethiopia, on the Eritrean border
ti·gress (tī′gris) *n.* 1 a female tiger 2 a woman thought of as like a tiger in ferocity, sensuous sleekness, etc.
Ti·gri·nya (tē grēn′yə) *n.* ⟦< TIGRÉ[2] + *əñña*, modern Ethiopic suffix for forming language names⟧ a modern Ethiopic language, the direct descendant of Ge'ez (classical Ethiopic): it is spoken by the majority of the population of Eritrea and by many people in Tigré
Ti·gris (tī′gris) river flowing from EC Turkey through Iraq, joining the Euphrates to form the Shatt-al-Arab: 1,150 mi (1,851 km)
Ti·jua·na (tē′ə wä′nə, tē wä′nə; *Sp* tē hwä′nä) city in Baja California, NW Mexico, on the U.S. border
Ti·kal (tē käl′) ruined Mayan city in N Guatemala
tike (tīk) *n. alt. sp. of* TYKE
Ti·ki (tē′kē) *n.* ⟦Polynesian: prob. < Maori⟧ 1 in Polynesian mythology, the first man, or the god who creates him 2 [**t-**] in Polynesia, a representation of an ancestor, god, etc., often a small sculptured figure worn as an amulet
til (til, tēl) *n. var. of* TEEL
'til (til) *prep., conj.* ⟦as if directly < UNTIL, but prob. var. of TILL[1]⟧ *informal or literary var. of* TILL[1]
til·ak (til′ək) *n.* ⟦Sans *tilaka*⟧ a religious mark, generally of sandalwood paste, worn on the forehead by Hindu males or females
ti·la·pi·a (tə lä′pē ə, -lā′-) *n.* ⟦ModL < ?⟧ any of a genus (*Tilapia*) of African cichlid fishes, often introduced into lakes or rivers because they are valuable food fishes that control the growth of algae
Til·burg (til′burg′; *Du* til′bürkh) city in S Netherlands
til·bu·ry (til′bər ē) *n., pl.* **-ries** ⟦after the inventor, *Tilbury*, 19th-c. London coach builder⟧ a light, two-wheeled carriage for two persons, popular in the early 19th cent.
til·de (til′də) *n.* ⟦Sp, metathetic var. of **title* < L *titulus*, superscription, TITLE⟧ 1 a mark (~) used: *a)* in Spanish, over an *n* to indicate a palatal nasal sound (ny), as in *señor* *b)* in Portuguese, over a vowel or the first vowel of a diphthong to indicate nasalization, as in *lã, pão* *c)* in some phonetic systems, for various purposes 2 a similar mark (~), used to express negation in mathematics or logic or to express similarity in geometry
Til·den (til′dən), **Samuel Jones** 1814-86; U.S. politician
tile (tīl) *n.* ⟦ME < OE *tigele*, akin to Ger *ziegel*, both < WGmc **tegala* < L *tegula*, tile < *tegere*, to cover: see THATCH (*vt.*)⟧ 1 *a)* a thin, flat or curved piece of stone, concrete, or fired clay, used for roofing, flooring, etc. *b)* a thin, usually rectangular piece of glazed, fired clay, often decorated, used for ornamental borders, bathroom walls, etc. *c)* a similar piece of metal, plastic, asphalt, rubber, etc., used to cover floors, walls, etc. 2 tiles collectively; tiling 3 a short pipe or semicircular conduit of fired clay or concrete, used to make a drain 4 hollow blocks of burnt clay, used variously in construction 5 any of the pieces used in mah-jongg or some other games 6 [Informal] a high, stiff hat —*vt.* **tiled, til′ing** 1 to cover with tiles 2 to install tiles in, so as to make a drain —**on the tiles** [Brit. Informal] out carousing —**til′er** *n.*
☆**tile·fish** (tīl′fish′) *n., pl.* **-fish′** or **-fish′es** (see FISH) ⟦< ModL (*Lophola*)*til(us)* + FISH⟧ any of a family (Malacanthidae) of percoid fishes that live in the deep waters of the sea, including some large food fishes; esp., a W Atlantic fish (*Lopholatilus chamaeleonticeps*) with a golden-spotted blue or purple body, yellow-spotted fins, and a fleshy crest on the head
til·ing (tīl′iŋ) *n.* 1 the action of a person who tiles 2 tiles collectively 3 a covering or structure of tiles
till[1] (til) *prep.* ⟦ME < OE *til*, akin to ON, to, till, OE, fitness: for IE base see fol.⟧ 1 UNTIL 2 [Now Scot.] up to the place of; as far as —*conj.* UNTIL
till[2] (til) *vt., vi.* ⟦ME *tillen* < OE *tilian*, lit., to strive for, work for, akin to Ger *zielen*, to aim, strive, *ziel*, point aimed at < IE base **ad-*, to order, establish⟧ to work (land) in raising crops, as by plowing and fertilizing; cultivate
till[3] (til) *n.* ⟦earlier *tille* < ? ME *tillen*, to draw, reach < OE⟧ 1 a drawer or tray for keeping money 2 ready cash
till[4] (til) *n.* ⟦? var. of ME *thill*, substratum of clay < ? *thille*, a board, flooring; akin to *diele* < IE base **tel-*, flat surface > L *tellus*, earth⟧ unstratified, unsorted, glacial drift of clay, sand, boulders, and gravel
till·age (til′ij) *n.* ⟦TILL[2] + -AGE⟧ 1 the tilling of land 2 land that is tilled
til·land·si·a (ti land′zē ə) *n.* ⟦ModL, after Elias *Tillands*, 17th-c. Swed botanist + -IA⟧ any of a genus (*Tillandsia*) of epiphytic plants of the pineapple family; esp., Spanish moss
till·er[1] (til′ər) *n.* ⟦ME *tiler*, stock of a crossbow < OFr *telier*, weaver's beam < ML *telarium* < L *tela*, web (see TOIL[2]): naut. sense prob. infl. by ME *tillen*, to reach⟧ a bar or handle connected to a rudder, and used to turn it in steering a boat
till·er[2] (til′ər) *n.* a person or machine that tills the soil
till·er[3] (til′ər) *n.* ⟦< OE *telgor* (extension of *telga*, a branch, bough, shoot)⟧ a shoot growing from the base of the stem of a plant —*vi.* to send forth tillers
Til·lich (til′ik), **Paul (Johannes)** 1886-1965; U.S. theologian, born in Germany
☆**till·ite** (til′īt′) *n.* ⟦TILL[4] + -ITE[1]⟧ rock made up of consolidated till
Til·ly (til′ē), Count of (*Johann Tserklaes*) 1559-1632; Fl. general in the Thirty Years' War
Til·sit (cheese) (til′sət, -zət) ⟦after *Tilsit*, city formerly of East Prussia (now Sovetsk in W Russia), where first produced⟧ a semihard, mild to sharp cheese with many small holes, made from cow's milk
tilt[1] (tilt) *vt.* ⟦ME *tilten*, to be overthrown, totter, prob. < OE **tieltan* < *tealt*, shaky, unstable; akin to Swed *tulta*, to totter < IE base **del-*, to waddle, totter > Sans *dulā*, she who totters⟧ 1 to cause to slope or slant; tip 2 *a)* to poise or thrust (a lance) in or as in a tilt *b)* to charge at (one's opponent) in a tilt 3 to forge or hammer with a tilt hammer 4 to direct (a discussion, policy, etc.) so as to favor a particular opinion or side —*vi.* 1 to slope; incline; slant; tip 2 *a)* to poise or thrust one's lance, or to charge (*at* one's opponent), in a TILT[1] (*n.* 1) *b)* to take part in a tilt, or joust 3 to dispute, argue, contend, attack, etc. 4 to have, or come to have, a bias or inclination in favor of a particular opinion or side in a dispute —*n.* 1 a medieval contest in which two armed horsemen thrust with lances in an attempt to unseat each other; joust 2 any spirited contest, contention, dispute, etc. between persons 3 a thrust or parry, as with a lance 4 the condition or angle of being tilted; slope or slant ☆5 [Informal] a leaning, bias, etc. —**(at) full tilt** at full speed or with the greatest force or energy —**tilt′er** *n.*
tilt[2] (tilt) *n.* ⟦ME *telte* < OE *teld*, tent, akin to Ger *zelt*⟧ a cloth covering or canopy of a boat, stall, cart, etc. —*vt.* to furnish or cover with a tilt
tilth (tilth) *n.* ⟦ME *tilthe* < OE < *tilian* (see TILL[2]), akin to OFris *tilath*, cultivation⟧ 1 a tilling or being tilled; cultivation of land 2 tilled land
tilt hammer a heavy drop hammer used in drop-forging
tilt·me·ter (tilt′mēt′ər) *n.* CLINOMETER
tilt-ro·tor (tilt′rōt′ər) *n.* an aircraft with rotors that can be switched from spinning horizontally, usually during takeoffs and landings, to spinning vertically, as during regular flight: sometimes written **tilt′ro′tor**
tilt-top (tilt′täp′) *adj.* designating a table, stand, etc. designed so that the top, hinged to a pedestal, can be tipped to a vertical position
tilt·yard (tilt′yärd′) *n.* [Historical] a place for jousting
Tim *abbrev. Bible* Timothy
tim·bal (tim′bəl) *n.* ⟦Fr *timbale*, altered (by assoc. with *cymbale*, cymbal) < earlier *attabale* < Sp *atabal*, a Moorish kettledrum < Ar *aṭ-ṭabl* < *al*, the + *ṭabl*, drum: cf. TABLA⟧ KETTLEDRUM
tim·bale (tim′bəl; *Fr* tan bál′) *n.* ⟦Fr, lit., kettledrum: see prec.⟧ 1 a mixture, as of chicken, lobster, or vegetables in a cream sauce, baked in a small drum-shaped mold; also, the mold 2 *a)* a type of small pastry shell (also **timbale case**) *b)* such a shell filled with a cooked food such as creamed chicken
tim·ba·les (tim bä′lez; *Sp* tēm bä′les) *pl.n.* ⟦Sp > prec.⟧ a pair of single-headed, cylindrical drums joined by a frame and played with drumsticks, used, esp. originally, in Latin American dance music
tim·ber (tim′bər) *n.* ⟦ME < OE, akin to Ger *zimmer*, room (< OHG *zimbar*, wooden structure) < IE base **dem-*, **dema-*, to join together, build > L *domus*, house⟧ 1 [Obs.] *a)* a building *b)* building material in general 2 wood suitable for building houses, ships, etc., whether cut or still in the form of trees 3 a large, heavy, dressed piece of wood used in building; beam 4 [Brit.] LUMBER[1] (*n.* 2) 5 trees or forests collectively 6 personal quality or character [a man of his *timber*] 7 *Shipbuilding* a wooden rib —*vt.* to provide, build, or prop up with timbers —*adj.* of or for timber —*interj.* used in a forest to signify that a cut tree is about to fall: a logger's warning shout
☆**tim·ber·doo·dle** (-do͞od′'l) *n.* [Informal] WOODCOCK (sense 2)
tim·bered (-bərd) *adj.* 1 made of timbers 2 covered with trees; wooded 3 having exposed timbers, as a wall
timber hitch *Naut.* an easily undone knot used for fastening a line around a cylindrical object, as a spar
tim·ber·ing (tim′bər iŋ) *n.* 1 TIMBER (*n.* 2) 2 work made of timber
☆**tim·ber·land** (tim′bər land′) *n.* land with trees suitable for yielding timber
☆**tim·ber·line** (-līn′) *n.* any natural division above or beyond which trees do not grow, as on mountains or in polar regions
☆**timber rattlesnake** a yellowish-brown to black rattlesnake (*Crotalus horridus*) with V-shaped bands on the back
timber wolf GRAY WOLF
tim·ber·work (-wurk′) *n.* work made of timber; timbering
tim·bre (tam′bər; *also*, tim′-; *Fr* tan′br′) *n.* ⟦Fr, timbre, earlier, sound of a bell < MFr, ball struck by a hammer < OFr, a kind of drum < LGr *tymbanon* < Gr *tympanon*: see TYMPAN⟧ the characteristic quality of sound that distinguishes one voice or musical instrument from another or one vowel sound from another: it is determined by the harmonics of the sound and is distinguished from the *intensity* and *pitch* —**tim′bral** (-brəl) *adj.*
tim·brel (tim′brəl) *n.* ⟦dim. of ME *timbre* < OFr: see prec.⟧ an ancient type of tambourine

Tim·buk·tu (tim′buk to͞o′) *another name for* TOMBOUCTOU

time (tīm) ***n.*** ⟦ME < OE *tima*, prob. < IE **dī-men* < base **dā(i)-*, to part, divide up > TIDE[1]⟧ **I.** *duration; continuance* **1** indefinite, unlimited duration in which things are considered as happening in the past, present, or future; every moment there has ever been or ever will be **2** *a)* the entire period of existence of the known universe; finite duration, as distinguished from infinity *b)* the entire period of existence of the world or of humanity; earthly duration, as distinguished from eternity *c)* [**T-**] FATHER TIME **3** a system of measuring duration [solar *time*, standard *time*] **II.** *a period or interval* **1** the period between two events or during which something exists, happens, or acts; measured or measurable interval **2** [*often pl.*] any period in the history of humanity or of the universe, often specif. with reference to a characteristic social structure, set of customs, famous person living then, etc. [prehistoric *times*, medieval *times*, geologic *time*, Lincoln's *time*] **3** *a)* a period characterized by a prevailing condition or specific experience [a *time* of peace, have a good *time*] *b)* [*usually pl.*] the prevailing conditions of a particular period [the *times* were difficult] **4** a period of duration set or thought of as set; specif., *a)* a period of existence; lifetime [his *time* is almost over] *b)* a term of apprenticeship *c)* a term of imprisonment *d)* a term of military service ☆*e)* [Obs.] a period of indenture **5** a period or periods necessary, sufficient, or available for something [no *time* for play, to take some *time* to relax] **6** the specific, usual, or allotted period during which something is done [the runner's *time* was 1.47 minutes; baking *time*, 20 minutes] **7** *a)* the period regularly worked or to be worked by an employee *b)* the hourly rate of pay for the regular working hours **8** rate of speed in marching, driving, working, etc. [quick *time*, double *time*] **9** *Drama* one of the three unities: see the phrase THE (THREE) UNITIES at UNITY **10** *Music a)* the grouping of rhythmic beats into measures of equal length *b)* the characteristic rhythm of a piece of music in terms of this grouping, indicated by the time signature *c)* the rate of speed at which a composition or passage is played; tempo *d)* loosely, the rhythm and tempo characteristic of a kind of composition [waltz *time*, march *time*] *e)* the duration of a note or rest **11** *Prosody* a unit of quantitative meter; esp., a mora, or short syllable ☆**12** *Sports* TIMEOUT **III.** *a point in duration; moment; instant; occasion* **1** a precise instant, second, minute, hour, day, week, month, or year, determined by clock or calendar; specif., the present instant, determined by clock [do you know the *time*?] **2** the point at which something has happened, is happening, or will happen; occasion [game *time* is two o'clock] **3** the usual, natural, traditional, or appointed moment for something to happen, begin, or end [*time* to get up]; specif., *a)* the moment of death [his *time* is close at hand] *b)* the end of a period of pregnancy; moment of giving birth [her *time* had come] ☆*c)* one's turn at something [a *time* at bat] **4** the suitable, proper, favorable, or convenient moment [now is the *time* to act] **5** any one of a series of moments at which the same or nearly the same thing recurs; repeated occasion [told for the fifth *time*, *time* and *time* again] —***interj.*** *Sports* used to signify that a period of play or activity has ended or that play is temporarily suspended —***vt.*** **timed, tim′ing 1** to arrange or set the time of so as to be acceptable, suitable, opportune, etc. [to *time* an invasion] **2** to adjust, set, play, etc. so as to coincide in time with something else [to *time* one's watch with another's] **3** to regulate (a mechanism) for a given speed or length of operation **4** to set the duration of (a syllable or musical note) as a unit of rhythm **5** to calculate or record the pace, speed, finishing time, etc. of; clock [to *time* a runner] —***vi.*** [Rare] to move in time; keep time —***adj.*** **1** having to do with time **2** set or regulated so as to explode, open, etc. at a given time [a *time* bomb] **3** payable later or on a specified future date [a *time* loan] ☆**4** designating or of any of a series of payments made or to be made over a period of time [a *time* payment] —**(it is) about time** a phrase used to convey that something that has happened was overdue —**abreast of the times 1** up-to-date, as in ideas, fashions, etc.; modern **2** informed about current matters —**against time** in an effort to finish in a given time —☆**ahead of time** sooner than due; early —**all the time** often, regularly, or constantly —**at one time 1** simultaneously **2** formerly —**at the same time 1** simultaneously; in the same period **2** nonetheless; however —**at times** occasionally; sometimes —**behind the times** out-of-date; old-fashioned —**behind time** late —**between times** at intervals, as between other events or actions —**do time** [Informal] to serve a prison term —**for the time being** for the present; temporarily —**from time to time** at intervals; now and then —**gain time 1** to go too fast: said of a timepiece **2** to prolong a situation until a desired occurrence can take place —**in good time 1** at the proper time **2** in a creditably short time; quickly —**in no time** almost instantly; very quickly —**in time 1** in the course of time; eventually **2** before it is too late **3** keeping the set rhythm, tempo, pace, etc. —**keep good (or bad, etc.) time** to register the elapsing of time or adhere to a meter in an accurate (or inaccurate, etc.) manner [a clock, drummer, etc. that *keeps good time*] —**keep time 1** to maintain a set rhythm, beat, tempo, etc. [the drummers *kept time* for the marching band] **2** to mark or note the elapsing of time [a referee assigned to *keep time*] —**lose no time** to act or respond promptly [the ambulance *lost no time* in getting here] —**lose time 1** to go too slow: said of a timepiece **2** to let time go by without advancing one's objective —**make time 1** to compensate for lost time by going faster: said as of a train ☆**2** to travel, work, etc. at a specified, esp. fast, rate of speed [we *made* (good) *time* between Boston and Albany] —☆**make time with** [Slang] to succeed in attracting or having an affair with (a person) —**many a time** often; frequently —**not give someone the time of day** to refuse to speak to or be polite to someone —☆**on one's own time** during time for which one is not paid; during other than working hours —**on time** ☆**1** at the appointed time; punctual or punctually ☆**2** with the agreement that payment will be made in installments over a period of time —**out of time 1** not at the usual time; unseasonable **2** not keeping the set rhythm, tempo, pace, etc. **3** with all allotted or available time having elapsed —**pass the time** to fill a span of time, as with some pleasant diversion —**pass the time of day** to exchange a few words of greeting, etc. —☆**(have) the time of one's life** [Informal] (have) an experience of great pleasure —**time after time** again and again; continually: also **time and again** —**time is money** a proverb meaning that delay and inefficiency are equivalent to a monetary loss —**time of life** age (of a person) —**time on one's hands** an interval with nothing to do —**time out** *Comput.* to be canceled or withdrawn automatically if an expected input is not received after a specified time: said of a process or program —**time out of mind** TIME IMMEMORIAL (sense 1) —**time was** there was a time —**time will tell** a proverb meaning that some time will pass before an outcome or result is known or confirmed

time and a half ⟦see prec., *n.* II, 7*b*⟧ a rate of payment one and a half times the usual rate, as for working overtime

time and motion study TIME STUDY

time bomb 1 an explosive device connected to a timer that will set it off at a given moment **2** any situation or person regarded as having a likely explosive or dangerous effect in the future

☆**time capsule** a container in which articles, documents, etc. representative of current civilization are encased, to be buried or otherwise preserved for a future age

time·card (tīm′kärd′) ***n.*** a card on which the hours worked by an employee are recorded, as by using a time clock

☆**time clock** a clock with a mechanism for recording on a timecard the time an employee begins and ends a work period

time-con·sum·ing (-kən so͞om′iŋ, -syo͞om′-) ***adj.*** using up much or too much time [a *time-consuming* task]

☆**time deposit** a bank deposit payable at a specified future date or upon advance notice

time exposure 1 an exposure of a photographic film or plate for a relatively long period, generally longer than half a second **2** a photograph taken in this way

time frame a given interval of time, esp. in relation to a particular event or process [the *time frame* for the satellite launch]

time-hon·ored (tīm′än′ərd) ***adj.*** honored or observed because in existence or use for a long time

time immemorial 1 time so long past as to be vague **2** *Eng. Law* beyond legal memory, fixed by statute as prior to 1189

time·keep·er (tīm′kēp′ər) ***n.*** **1** TIMEPIECE **2** a person who keeps time; specif., *a)* a person employed to keep account of the hours worked by employees *b)* a person who keeps account of the elapsed time in the periods of play in certain sports

time-lapse (-laps′) ***adj.*** designating or of a technique of photographing a slow process, as the growth of a plant, on film by exposing single frames at widely spaced intervals: the developed film is projected at regular speed to show the entire process greatly sped up

time·less (tīm′lis) ***adj.*** **1** that cannot be measured by time; unending **2** transcending time; eternal **3** restricted to no specific time; always valid, true, or applicable **4** [Obs.] untimely —**time′less·ly** ***adv.*** —**time′less·ness** ***n.***

time limit a fixed period of time during which something is valid, or must be done, completed, or ended

time·line (tīm′līn′) ***n.*** **1** a chart, table, etc. of historical dates and events in chronological order, typically including summaries and illustrations **2** any chronological summary or listing of historical or planned events Also written **time line**

time loan a loan to be repaid at a specified time

☆**time lock** a lock with a mechanism that prevents opening before the set time

time·ly (tīm′lē) ***adj.*** **-li·er, -li·est** ⟦ME *tymeli* < OE *timlice*: see TIME & -LY[1]⟧ **1** happening, done, said, etc. at a suitable time; well-timed; opportune **2** [Now Rare] appearing in good time; early —***adv.*** **1 -li·er, -li·est** [Archaic] early; soon **2** at the right time; opportunely [the brief was *timely* filed with the court] —**time′li·ness** ***n.***

SYN.—**timely** applies to that which happens or is done at an appropriate time, esp. at such a time as to be of help or service [a *timely* interruption]; **opportune** refers to that which is so timed, often as if by accident, as to meet exactly the needs of the occasion [the *opportune* arrival of a supply train]; **seasonable** applies literally to that which is suited to the season of the year or, figuratively, to the moment or occasion [*seasonable* weather]

time machine in science fiction, a device for conveying a person or object into the past or the future

time off a period of time allowed away from one's normal duties or situation, as an employee away from work, a convict away from prison, etc.

time·ous (tīm′əs) ***adj.*** [Scot.] TIMELY

time·out or **time-out** (tīm′out′) ***n.*** **1** any time taken for rest or not counted toward a work record, score, etc. ☆**2** *Sports* a brief suspension of play, as to allow a team to make substitutions or discuss strategy **3** a disciplinary technique in which a child who misbehaves is sent to be alone for a few minutes so as to calm down before returning to work or play

time·piece (tīm′pēs′) ***n.*** any apparatus for measuring and recording time; esp., a clock or watch

tim·er (tīm′ər) ***n.*** **1** *a)* TIMEKEEPER *b)* STOPWATCH ☆**2** in internal-combustion engines, any part or system designed to control the timing of the spark in the cylinder **3** any of various devices for timing, or automatically starting and stopping at predetermined times, the operation of some mechanism

☆**time-re·lease** (tīm′rə lēs′) ***adj.*** of or characterized by the gradual release of active ingredients [a *time-release* antihistamine capsule]: also **time′-re·leased′**

times (tīmz) ***prep.*** multiplied by [two *times* three is six]: symbol, × —***n.*** a quantity consisting of equal multiples or equal fractions of a given quantity or quality: often used loosely [three *times* the amount, five *times* smaller, many *times* greater]

time·sav·ing (tīm′sāv′iŋ) ***adj.*** that saves time because of greater efficiency, etc. —**time′sav′er** ***n.***

time·serv·er (tīm′sur′vər) ***n.*** a person who for personal advantage adapts his or her patterns of behavior to suit the mood of the times or to please those in power; toady —**time′serv′ing** ***n., adj.***

☆**time-share** (tīm′sher′) ***n.*** **1** TIME SHARING (sense 2) **2** a property held in time sharing Also, and for 2 usually, **time′share′** —***vt.*** **-shared′**, **-shar′ing** to occupy (a property) through time sharing

☆**time sharing** **1** a system permitting the simultaneous employment of a computer by many users at remote locations **2** a plan for sharing ownership in a property, such as a vacation home or condominium, in which each of the joint purchasers may occupy the unit during a specified period each year Also written **time′-shar′ing** ***n.***

time sheet a sheet on which are recorded the hours worked by an employee or employees

time signature *Music* a metric notation, typically consisting of one number over another, indicating the unit of measurement and the number of beats in the following measure or measures: the opening or predominant meter of a piece is indicated directly after the opening clef or key signature (Ex.: 3/4 means three quarter-note beats; C is often used instead of 4/4)

time·span (tīm′span′) ***n.*** a period of time between events or taken up by a process

times table [Informal] MULTIPLICATION TABLE

time study a study of each of the steps in an operation or procedure and the time consumed by them, for the purpose of devising methods of increasing efficiency or productivity of workers

time·ta·ble (tīm′tā′bəl) ***n.*** a schedule of the times certain things are to happen, specif. of the times of arrival and departure of airplanes, trains, buses, etc.

time-test·ed (tīm′tes′tid) ***adj.*** having value proved by long use or experience

time travel a journeying into the past or the future, as in science fiction —**time′-trav′el** ***adj., vi.*** **-eled** or **-elled**, **-el·ing** or **-el·ling** —**time′-trav′el·er** ***n.***, **time′-trav′el·ler**

time trial a competitive racing event decided by the time each contestant takes to cover a course individually, often, specif., as a preliminary event to determine qualifiers for head-to-head competition: *often used in pl.*

time warp the condition or process of being displaced from one point in time to another, as in science fiction

time·work (tīm′wurk′) ***n.*** work paid for by the hour or day: cf. PIECEWORK —**time′work′er** ***n.***

time·worn (tīm′wôrn′) ***adj.*** **1** worn or deteriorated by long use or existence **2** hackneyed; trite

☆**time zone** any of the 24 longitudinal regions of the earth, each occupying 15 degrees and having a mean solar time one hour greater than that of the neighboring region to the west

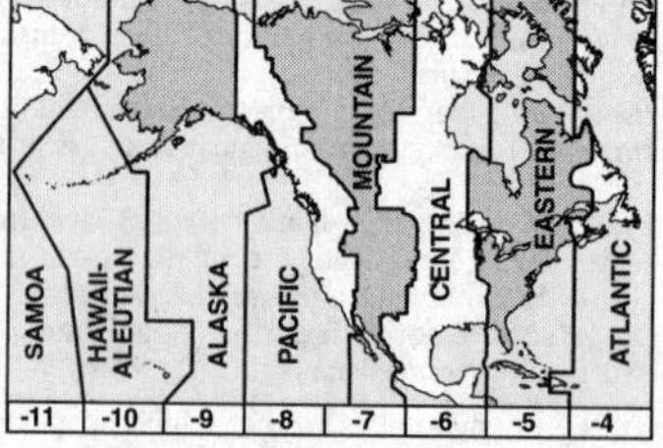

time zones

tim·id (tim′id) ***adj.*** ⟦L *timidus* < *timere*, to fear⟧ **1** easily frightened; lacking self-confidence; shy; timorous **2** showing fear or lack of self-confidence; hesitant [a *timid* reply] —***SYN.*** AFRAID —**ti·mid·i·ty** (tə mid′ə tē) ***n.***, **tim′id·ness** —**tim′id·ly** ***adv.***

tim·ing (tīm′iŋ) ***n.*** **1** *a)* the regulation of the speed, or of the moment of occurrence, of something so as to produce the most effective results [the *timing* of an engine, of a golfer's swing, of an announcement, etc.] *b)* the pacing of various scenes, as of a play, for total effect *c)* the pacing of a skit, monologue, etc., as for comedic effect **2** measurement of time, as with a stopwatch

Ti·mi·șoa·ra (tē′mē shwä′rə) city in the Banat region of W Romania

Tim·mins (tim′inz) ⟦after its founder, N. A. *Timmins* (1867-1936), mining prospector⟧ city in E Ontario, Canada: a gold-mining center

ti·moc·ra·cy (tī mäk′rə sē) ***n.*** ⟦MFr *tymocracie* < ML *timocratia* < Gr *timokratia* < *timē*, honor, worth (< IE base **kwei-*, to heed, value > Lith *káina*, worth, price) + *kratia* (see -CRACY)⟧ **1** in the philosophy of Plato, a form of government in which ambition for power and glory motivates the rulers **2** in the philosophy of Aristotle, a form of government in which political power is in direct proportion to property ownership —**ti·mo·crat·ic** (tī′mō krat′ik) ***adj.***

Ti·mor (tē′môr′, tē môr′) island in SE Asia, in the Malay Archipelago: the W part of the island (WEST TIMOR) is part of Indonesia; the E part (EAST TIMOR) is an independent nation —**Ti′mor·ese′** ***adj., n.***

Ti·mor-Les·te (tē′môr′les′tə) *official name for* EAST TIMOR

tim·or·ous (tim′ər es) ***adj.*** ⟦ME *tymerouse* < MFr *timoreus* < ML *timorosus* < L *timor*, fear < *timere*: see TIMID⟧ **1** full of or subject to fear; timid **2** showing or caused by timidity —***SYN.*** AFRAID —**tim′or·ous·ly** ***adv.*** —**tim′or·ous·ness** ***n.***

Timor Sea arm of the Indian Ocean, between Timor & the NW coast of Australia: *c.* 300 mi (483 km) wide

Timor Ti·mur (tē′môr′ tē moor′, tē môr′-) *Indonesian name for* EAST TIMOR

tim·o·thy (tim′ə thē) ***n.*** ⟦after *Timothy* Hanson, who took the seed (*c.* 1720) from New York to the Carolinas⟧ ☆a perennial European grass (*Phleum pratense*) with dense, cylindrical spikes of bristly spikelets, widely grown for hay

Tim·o·thy (tim′ə thē) ***n.*** ⟦Fr *Timothée* < L *Timotheus* < Gr *Timotheos* < *timē*, honor (see TIMOCRACY) + *theos*, god (see THEO-)⟧ **1** a masculine name: dim. *Tim, Timmy* **2** either of two books of the New Testament, letters of the Apostle Paul to his disciple Timothy: abbrev. *Tim, Tm*, or *Ti*

tim·pa·ni (tim′pə nē) ***pl.n.***, *sing.* **-no′** (-nō′) ⟦It, pl. of *timpano* < L *tympanum*: see TYMPAN⟧ [*often with sing. v.*] kettledrums; esp., a set of kettledrums of different pitches played by one performer in an orchestra —**tim′pa·nist** ***n.***

Ti·mur (tē moor′) *var. of* TAMERLANE

tin (tin) ***n.*** ⟦ME < OE, akin to Ger *zinn*; only in Gmc languages⟧ **1** a soft, silver-white, crystalline, metallic chemical element, malleable at ordinary temperatures and used in making shiny alloys and tinfoils, solders, utensils, tin plate, superconducting magnets, etc.: symbol, Sn; at. no. 50: see the periodic table of elements in the Reference Supplement **2** TIN PLATE **3** *a)* a pan, box, etc. made of tin plate *b)* [Chiefly Brit.] CAN² (***n.*** 2, 3) **4** [Old Slang] money Variously used to connote cheapness, baseness, spuriousness, etc. of a material or thing —***vt.*** **tinned**, **tin′ning** **1** to cover or plate with tin **2** [Chiefly Brit.] CAN² (***vt.*** 1)

Ti·na (tē′nə) ***n.*** a feminine name: see CHRISTINE, ERNESTINE, JUSTINA

tin·a·mou (tin′ə moo′) ***n.*** ⟦Fr < Carib *tinamu*⟧ any of an order (Tinamiformes) of Central and South American birds resembling fowl, that are strong runners and live in brush or forests

Tin·ber·gen (tin′ber′kən) **1 Jan** (yän) 1903-94; Du. economist **2 Ni·ko·laas** (nē′kō läs′) 1907-88; Du. ethologist: brother of Jan

tin·cal (tiŋ′käl′, -kôl′) ***n.*** ⟦Malay *tingkal* < Pers *tinkāl, tinkar* < Sans *ṭaṅkaṇa*⟧ crude borax

☆**tin can** **1** CAN² (***n.*** 2) **2** [Slang] DESTROYER (***n.*** 2)

tinct¹ (tiŋkt) ***adj.*** ⟦L *tinctus*, pp. of *tingere*: see TINGE⟧ [Archaic] tinged; tinted —***n.*** [Now Rare] a color; tint

tinct² *abbrev.* tincture

tinc·to·ri·al (tiŋk tôr′ē əl) ***adj.*** ⟦< L *tinctorius* < *tinctor*, dyer < *tinctus*: see fol.⟧ having to do with color, dyeing, or staining —**tinc·to′ri·al·ly** ***adv.***

tinc·ture (tiŋk′chər) ***n.*** ⟦ME < L *tinctura* < *tinctus*, pp. of *tingere*, to dye: see TINGE⟧ **1** [Obs.] a dye **2** a light color; tint; tinge **3** a slight admixture or infusion of some substance or quality; trace, smattering, etc. **4** *Heraldry* any color, metal, or fur **5** *Pharmacy* a dilute solution consisting of a medicinal substance in alcohol or in alcohol and water, usually 10% to 20% by volume: tinctures are more dilute than fluid extracts and more volatile than spirits —***vt.*** **-tured**, **-tur·ing** **1** to color lightly; tint; tinge **2** to imbue or permeate lightly with some substance or quality [a message *tinctured* with hope]

Tin·dale or **Tin·dal** (tin′dəl), **William** *alt. sp. of* William TYNDALE

tin·der (tin′dər) ***n.*** ⟦ME < OE *tynder* (akin to Ger *zunder*) < base of OE *tendan*, to kindle⟧ any dry, easily flammable material, esp. as formerly used for starting a fire from a spark made by flint and steel struck together

tin·der·box (-bäks′) ***n.*** **1** [Historical] a metal box for holding tinder, flint, and steel for starting a fire **2** any highly flammable object, structure, etc. **3** a place or situation likely to be the source of a flare-up of trouble, war, etc.

tine (tīn) ***n.*** ⟦ME *tind* < OE, akin to OHG *zint*, a jag, prong: see ZINC⟧ a slender, projecting part that is pointed at the end; prong [the *tines* of a fork] —**tined** ***adj.***

tin·e·a (tin′ē ə) ***n.*** ⟦ME < L, gnawing worm, moth⟧ any of various skin diseases caused by a fungus; esp., ringworm

tinea bar·bae (bär′bē) ⟦ModL, tinea of the beard < L *barbae*, gen. of *barba*, BEARD⟧ BARBER'S ITCH

tinea cru·ris (kroor′is) ⟦ModL, tinea of the leg: see CRURAL⟧ JOCK ITCH

tin ear ☆[Informal] a lack of discriminating sensitivity to music, poetry, etc.

tin·e·id (tin′ē id) ***n.*** ⟦< L *tinea*, gnawing worm, moth + -ID⟧ CLOTHES MOTH

tin·foil (tin′foil′) ***n.*** **1** tin or an alloy of tin and lead in a very thin sheet or sheets, used in insulation, etc. **2** aluminum in a very thin sheet, used for wrapping food, etc.

ting (tiŋ) ***n.*** ⟦echoic⟧ a single, light, ringing sound, as of a very small bell being struck —***vt., vi.*** to make or cause to make a ting

ting-a-ling (tiŋ′ə liŋ′) ***n.*** ⟦echoic⟧ the sound of a small bell ringing

tinge (tinj) ***vt.*** **tinged**, **tinge′ing** or **ting′ing** ⟦L *tingere*, to dye, stain < IE base **teng-*, to moisten > Gr *tengein*, to moisten, OHG *dunkon*, to dip⟧ **1** to color slightly; give a tint to **2** to give a trace, slight flavor or odor, shade, etc. to [joy *tinged* with sorrow] —***n.*** **1** a slight coloring; tint **2** a slight trace, flavor, odor, etc.; smack; touch —***SYN.*** COLOR

tin·gle (tiŋ′gəl) ***vi.*** **-gled**, **-gling** ⟦ME *tynglen*, var. of *tinklen*, to TINKLE⟧ **1** to have a prickling or stinging feeling, as from cold, a sharp slap, excitement, etc. 2 to cause this feeling —*vt.* to cause to have this feeling —*n.* this feeling —**tin′gler** *n.* —**tin′gling·ly** *adv.* —**tin′gly** *adj.* **-gli·er, -gli·est**

☆**tin god** ⟦in ref. to *tin* as being worth little in comparison with the silver or gold of which idols were usually made⟧ an often pompous or dictatorial person who demands or receives more respect than is merited

☆**tin·horn** (tin′hôrn′) [Slang] *adj.* ⟦< phr. *tin horn gambler*: so named from use of metal dice-shaker in chuck-a-luck games, scorned as petty by faro dealers⟧ pretending to have money, influence, ability, etc., though actually lacking in these; cheap and showy —*n.* a tinhorn person, esp. a gambler

ti·ni·ly (tī′nə lē) *adv.* to a tiny degree; minutely

ti·ni·ness (tī′nē nis) *n.* the quality or condition of being tiny

tin·ker (tiŋ′kər) *n.* ⟦ME *tinkere* < ? or akin to *tinken*, to make a tinkling sound⟧ 1 a usually itinerant person who mends pots, pans, etc. 2 [*sometimes* **T-**] [Chiefly Brit.] GYPSY (*n.* 1): now mainly a derogatory term 3 a person who can make all kinds of minor repairs; jack-of-all-trades 4 a clumsy or unskillful worker; bungler ☆5 a young mackerel —*vi.* 1 to work as a tinker 2 to make clumsy or tentative attempts to mend or repair something 3 to fuss or putter aimlessly or uselessly —*vt.* to mend as a tinker; patch up —**tin′ker·er** *n.*

tinker's damn (*or* **dam**) ⟦< prec. + DAMN: with reference to the lowly status and reputed profane speech of tinkers⟧ something of no value: now chiefly in the phrase **not worth a tinker's damn**

☆**Tin·ker·toy** (tiŋ′kər toi′) *trademark for* a toy set of wooden dowels, joints, wheels, etc., used by children to assemble structures —*adj.* [**t-**] suggesting such structures or parts, as in being flimsy or slipshod [*tinkertoy* economics]

tin·kle (tiŋ′kəl) *vi.* **-kled, -kling** ⟦ME *tynclen*, freq. of *tinken*, to make a tinkling sound, of echoic orig.⟧ 1 to make a series of small, short, light, ringing sounds like those of a very small bell ☆2 [Informal] to urinate: a child's term or a euphemism —*vt.* 1 to cause to tinkle 2 to indicate, signal, etc. by tinkling —*n.* the act or sound of tinkling —**give someone a tinkle** [Brit. Informal] to call someone on the telephone —**tin′kler** *n.* —**tin′kly** *adj.* **-kli·er, -kli·est**

☆**tin liz·zie** (liz′ē) ⟦orig. nickname of an early model of Ford automobile⟧ [Old Slang] any cheap or old automobile

tinned (tind) *adj.* 1 plated with tin 2 [Brit.] preserved in tins; canned

tin·ner (tin′ər) *n.* 1 a tin miner 2 TINSMITH

tin·ni·tus (ti nīt′es, tin′i təs) *n.* ⟦L < pp. of *tinnire*, to tinkle, of echoic orig.⟧ any ringing or buzzing in the ear resulting from changes in or damage to the inner ear, as from long-term exposure to loud noises

tin·ny (tin′ē) *adj.* **-ni·er, -ni·est** 1 of, containing, or yielding tin 2 like tin in appearance or strength; bright but cheap; not well-made [*tinny* jewelry] 3 of or like the sound made in striking a tin object; specif., having a high-pitched sound lacking in resonance [*tinny* music] 4 tasting of tin —**tin′ni·ly** *adv.* —**tin′ni·ness** *n.*

☆**Tin Pan Alley** ⟦< *tin pan*, slang for a tinny piano⟧ 1 [Historical] the district of Manhattan where many songwriters and publishers of popular music were once based 2 the publishers, writers, and promoters of popular music, esp. those of the late 19th and early 20th cent.

tin plate thin sheets of iron or steel plated with tin

tin-plate (tin′plāt′) *vt.* **-plat′ed, -plat′ing** to plate with tin

tin-pot (tin′pät′) *adj.* ⟦from the relative cheapness of *tin*⟧ [Informal] of little importance or value; insignificant, petty, inferior, etc. [*a tin-pot* dictator]: also **tin′pot′**

tin·sel (tin′səl) *n.* ⟦aphetic < MFr *estincelle*, a spark, spangle: see STENCIL⟧ 1 [Historical] a cloth of silk, wool, etc. interwoven with glittering threads of gold, silver, or other metal 2 thin sheets, strips, or threads of tin, metal foil, etc., used for inexpensive decoration 3 something that glitters like precious metal but has little worth; empty show; sham splendor —*adj.* 1 made of or decorated with tinsel 2 having sham splendor; showy; gaudy; tawdry —*vt.* **-seled** or **-selled, -sel·ing** or **-sel·ling** 1 to make glitter with or as with tinsel 2 to give a false appearance of splendor to —**tin′sel·ly** *adj.*

Tin·sel·town (-toun′) *name for* HOLLYWOOD, Calif.

tin·smith (tin′smith′) *n.* 1 a person who works in tin or tin plate; maker of tinware 2 a person who works in any sheet metal

tin·snips (tin′snips′) *n.* snips for cutting sheet metal: see SNIP (*n.* 4)

tin·stone (tin′stōn′) *n.* CASSITERITE

tint (tint) *n.* ⟦earlier *tinct* < L *tinctus*, a dyeing, dipping < pp. of *tingere*, to dye, TINGE⟧ 1 a delicate or pale color or hue; tinge 2 a color or a shading of a color; esp., a gradation of a color with reference to its mixture with white: cf. SHADE (*n.* 5) 3 a dye for the hair 4 *Engraving* an even shading produced by fine parallel lines 5 *Printing* a light-colored background, as for an illustration —*vt.* to give a tint to —**SYN.** COLOR —**tint′er** *n.*

Tin·tag·el Head (tin taj′əl) cape of NW Cornwall, England: legendary birthplace of King Arthur

tin·tin·nab·u·lar·y (tin′ti nab′yoo ler′ē) *adj.* ⟦< L *tintinnabulum*, little bell, dim. of *tintinnare*, to jingle, ring < *tinnire*, to jingle + -ARY⟧ of bells or the ringing of bells: also **tin′tin·nab′u·lar** (-lər) or **tin′tin·nab′u·lous** (-ləs)

☆**tin·tin·nab·u·la·tion** (tin′ti nab′yoo lā′shən) *n.* ⟦see prec. & -TION⟧ the ringing sound of bells

Tin·to·ret·to (tin′tə ret′ō; *It* tēn′tô ret′tô), **Il** (ēl) (born *Jacopo Robusti*) 1518-94; Venetian painter

☆**tin·type** (tin′tīp′) *n.* FERROTYPE

tin·ware (-wer′) *n.* pots, pans, etc. made of tin plate

tin·work (tin′wurk′) *n.* 1 work done in tin 2 [*pl., with sing. v.*] a place where tin is smelted, rolled, etc.

ti·ny (tī′nē) *adj.* **-ni·er, -ni·est** ⟦< ME n. *tine*, a little (something)⟧ very small; diminutive —**SYN.** SMALL

-tion (shən) ⟦< Fr, OFr, or L: Fr *-tion* < OFr *-cion* < L *-tio* (gen. *-tionis*) < *-t-* of pp. stem + *-io* (gen. *-ionis*), suffix⟧ *suffix forming nouns* 1 the act of ____ing 2 the state of being ____ed 3 the thing that is ____ed

-tious (shəs) ⟦< Fr or L: Fr *-tieux* < L *-tiosus* < *-t-* of pp. stem + *-iosus*, -OUS⟧ *suffix forming adjectives* of, having, or characterized by

tip[1] (tip) *n.* ⟦ME *tippe*, akin to MLowG *tip*, point, top, Ger *zipf-* in *zipfel*, an end, tip, prob. < IE base **dumb-*, tail > Avestan *duma-*, tail⟧ 1 the pointed, tapering, or rounded end or top of something long and slim 2 something attached to the end, as a cap, ferrule, etc. 3 a top or apex, as of a mountain —*vt.* **tipped, tip′ping** 1 to make a tip on 2 to cover the tip or tips of (*with* something) 3 to serve as the tip of ☆4 to remove the stems from (berries, etc.) —**tip in** to insert (a map, picture, etc.) by pasting along the inner edge in bookbinding —**tip′less** *adj.*

tip[2] (tip) *vt.* **tipped, tip′ping** ⟦akin ? to prec.⟧ 1 to strike lightly and sharply; tap 2 to give a small present of money to (a waiter, porter, etc.) for some service 3 [Informal] *a)* to give secret information to in an attempt to be helpful (often with *off*) *b)* to reveal or divulge (a secret, plot, etc.) 4 *Sports* to deflect or tap (a ball, puck, etc.) in a particular direction, esp. into a goal —*vi.* to give a tip or tips —*n.* 1 a light, sharp blow; tap 2 a piece of secret information given confidentially in an attempt to be helpful [*a tip* on the race] 3 a suggestion, hint, warning, etc. 4 a small sum of money, often a percentage of the total billed, given to a waiter, porter, etc. for services; gratuity 5 *Sports* a deflection or tap of the ball, puck, etc., esp. one that scores a goal: see also FOUL TIP —☆**tip one's hand** ⟦in ref. to card playing⟧ [Informal] to reveal a secret, one's plans, etc., often inadvertently: sometimes [Slang] **tip one's mitt**

tip[3] (tip) *vt.* **tipped, tip′ping** ⟦ME *tipen* < ?⟧ 1 to overturn or upset: often with *over* 2 to cause to tilt or slant 3 to raise slightly or touch the brim of (one's hat) in salutation —*vi.* 1 to tilt or slant 2 to overturn or topple: often with *over* —*n.* 1 a tipping or being tipped; tilt; slant 2 [Brit.] a place for dumping rubbish, etc.; dump

tip cart a cart with a body that can be tipped for dumping its contents

☆**ti·pi** (tē′pē) *n., pl.* **-pis** *alt. sp. of* TEPEE

tip-in (tip′in′) *n. Sports* a play in which a slight tap or deflection of the ball or puck scores a goal

tip·off (tip′ôf′) *n. Basketball* a JUMP BALL, specif. the one that begins a game

☆**tip-off** (tip′ôf′) *n.* 1 the act of tipping off 2 a tip; confidential disclosure, hint, or warning

Tip·pe·ca·noe[1] (tip′ə kə noo′) ⟦after fol., with ref. to Harrison's victory in the battle: popularized in 1840 presidential campaign slogan, "*Tippecanoe* and Tyler too," referring also to John TYLER[2]⟧ *name for* William Henry HARRISON

Tip·pe·ca·noe[2] (tip′ə kə noo′) ⟦earlier *Kithtipecanunk* < Miami *Kitapkwanunk* (exact form uncert.), lit., buffalo-fish place⟧ river in N Ind. flowing southwest into the Wabash: scene of a battle (1811) in which U.S. forces under William Henry Harrison defeated a band of Tecumseh's warriors: *c.* 180 mi (290 km)

tip·per (tip′ər) *n.* a person who gives tips, or gratuities; often, specif., one who tips in a specified way [our regular customers are generous *tippers*]

Tip·per·ar·y (tip′ər er′ē) county in S Ireland, in Munster province: 1,643 sq mi (4,255 sq km)

tip·pet (tip′it) *n.* ⟦ME *tipet*, prob. dim. of *tip*, TIP[1]⟧ 1 a long, hanging part of a hood, cape, or sleeve 2 a scarflike garment of fur, wool, etc. for the neck and shoulders, hanging down in front 3 a long, black scarf worn as by members of the Anglican clergy

Tip·pett (tip′it), Sir **Michael (Kemp)** 1905-98; Brit. composer

tipping point ⟦altered < *tip point*, coined (1957) by M. Grodzins (1917-64), U.S. political scientist, to describe the threshold at which WHITE FLIGHT begins⟧ ☆the minimum level or degree required for something, as a political or sociological trend, to begin or prevail

tip·ple[1] (tip′əl) *vi., vt.* **-pled, -pling** ⟦prob. back-form. < ME *tipelar*, tavern-keeper < ?⟧ to drink (alcoholic liquor) habitually —*n.* alcoholic liquor —**tip′pler** *n.*

☆**tip·ple**[2] (tip′əl) *n.* ⟦< obs. *tipple*, freq. of TIP[3]⟧ 1 an apparatus for emptying coal, ore, etc. from a mine car by tipping 2 the place where this is done

tip·py (tip′ē) *adj.* **-pi·er, -pi·est** [Informal] that tips easily; not steady; shaky

tip·py-toe or **tip·py·toe** (tip′ē tō′) *n., adj., adv. informal var. of* TIPTOE —*vi.* **-toed′, -toe′ing**

☆**tip·sheet** (tip′shēt′) *n.* a publication providing up-to-date information and tips for use as in betting on horse races or investing in stocks

tip·staff (tip′staf′) *n., pl.* **-staffs′** or **-staves′** (-stāvz′) 1 a staff with a metal tip, formerly carried as an emblem by certain officials 2 an official who carried such a staff; esp., in England, a bailiff or constable

tip·ster (tip′stər) *n.* [Informal] 1 a person who sells tips, as on horse races or for stock speculation 2 a person who gives a TIP[2] (*n.* 2), as to the police

tip·sy (tip′sē) *adj.* **-si·er, -si·est** 1 that tips easily; not steady; shaky 2 crooked; awry 3 [Informal] somewhat drunk; intoxicated enough to be somewhat unsteady, fuddled, etc. —**SYN.** DRUNK —**tip′si·ly** (-si lē) *adv.* —**tip′si·ness** *n.*

tip·toe (tip′tō′) *n.* the tip of a toe or the tips of the toes: usually used with reference to a foot position with the heels raised and the body's weight resting on the toes and the balls of the feet —*vi.* **-toed′, -toe′ing** to walk stealthily or cautiously on one's tiptoes —*adj.* 1 standing on one's toes and the balls of one's feet 2 stealthy; cautious —*adv.* on tiptoe —**on tiptoe** 1 on one's toes and the balls of one's feet 2 eager; excited; alert 3 silently; stealthily

tip·top (tip′täp′) *n.* ⟦TIP[1] + TOP[1]⟧ 1 the highest point; very top 2 [Informal] the highest in quality or excellence; best — *adj., adv.* 1 at the highest point, or top 2 [Informal] at the highest point of excellence, health, etc.

ti·rade (tī′rād′, tī rād′) *n.* ⟦Fr < It *tirata*, a volley < pp. of *tirare*, to draw, fire < VL **tirare*⟧ a long, vehement speech, esp. one of denunciation; harangue

tir·a·mi·su or **tir·a·mi·sù** (tir′ə mē′so͞o, -mē so͞o′) *n.* ⟦It *tiramisù*, pick me up (lit., pull me up)⟧ an Italian dessert made of spongecake pieces soaked in coffee and liqueur, layered with mascarpone cheese and chocolate

Ti·ra·na (ti rä′nə) capital of Albania, in the central part: also written **Tiranë**

tire[1] (tīr) *vi.* **tired, tir′ing** ⟦ME *tiren* < OE *tiorian*, to fail, be tired, prob. < Gmc **tiuzōn*, to stay behind < IE **deus-*, to cease < base **deu-*, to move forward⟧ 1 to become in need of rest; become weary or fatigued through exertion 2 to lose interest or patience; become bored or impatient: usually with *of* —*vt.* 1 to diminish the strength of by exertion, etc.; fatigue; weary: often with *out* 2 to diminish the patience or interest of, as by dull talk, etc.; make weary; bore

tire[2] (tīr) *n.* ⟦ME *tyre*, prob. var. (in sense "equipment") of fol.⟧ 1 a hoop of iron or rubber around the wheel of a vehicle, forming the tread 2 an inflatable, vulcanized rubber or synthetic casing sealed to a wheel rim by a specified pressure and designed to reduce shock, improve traction and handling, etc.; tubeless tire: it has replaced the tube-type tire which contains a separate, soft, thin rubber inner tube to hold the air: see RADIAL (PLY) TIRE —*vt.* **tired, tir′ing** to furnish with tires

tire[3] (tīr) [Archaic] *vt.* **tired, tir′ing** ⟦ME *tiren*, aphetic for *atiren*, ATTIRE⟧ to attire or dress —*n.* ⟦ME < *atir*: see *vt.*⟧ 1 attire 2 a woman's headdress

☆**tire chain** a device made of chains, attached around a tire's tread on a motor vehicle to increase traction, as on snow

tired (tīrd) *adj.* ⟦ME (Northern) *tyrit* < *tiren*: see TIRE[1]⟧ 1 fatigued, worn-out, or weary 2 stale; hackneyed —**tired′ly** *adv.* —**tired′ness** *n.*

SYN.—**tired** is applied to one who has been drained of much of his or her strength and energy through exertion, boredom, impatience, etc. [*tired* by years of hard toil]; **weary** (or **wearied**) suggests such depletion of energy or interest as to make one unable or unwilling to continue [*weary* of study]; **exhausted** implies a total draining of strength and energy, as after a long, hard climb; **fatigued** refers to one who has lost so much energy through prolonged exertion that rest and sleep are essential [*fatigued* at the end of the day]; **fagged**, an informal word, suggests great exhaustion or fatigue from hard, unremitting work or exertion [completely *fagged* after a set of tennis]

tire iron a crowbar with a built-in socket wrench, for removing the wheel covers and lug nuts of a motor vehicle and often serving as the handle for operating an automobile jack

tire·less (tīr′lis) *adj.* 1 that does not become tired; untiring or unwavering 2 characteristic of a tireless person; continuing, persistent, etc. [one's *tireless* efforts] —**tire′less·ly** *adv.* —**tire′less·ness** *n.*

Ti·re·si·as (tī rē′sē əs) *n.* ⟦L < Gr *Teiresias*⟧ *Gr. Myth.* a blind soothsayer of Thebes

tire·some (tīr′səm) *adj.* ⟦see -SOME[1]⟧ 1 tiring; boring; tedious 2 annoying; irksome —**tire′some·ly** *adv.* —**tire′some·ness** *n.*

tire·wom·an (tīr′wo͝om′ən) *n., pl.* **-wom′en** (-wim′in) ⟦see TIRE[3]⟧ [Archaic] a lady's maid

Ti·rich Mir (tir′ich mir′) mountain in N Pakistan: highest peak of the Hindu Kush: 25,230 ft (7,690 m)

tiring room ⟦see TIRE[3]⟧ [Archaic] a dressing room in a theater

ti·ro (tī′rō) *n., pl.* **-ros** *alt. sp. of* TYRO

Ti·rol (ti rōl′, -räl′; tir′ōl′, -äl′) E Alpine region in W Austria & N Italy —**Ti·ro·le·an** (ti rō′lē ən, tī-; tir′ə lē′ən) *adj., n.* —**Tir·o·lese** (tir′ə lēz′, -lēs′) *adj., n., pl.* **-lese′**

Tir·so de Mo·li·na (tir′sō dā′ mō lē′nə) (pseud. of *Gabriel Téllez*) 1584?-1648; Sp. dramatist

Tir·u·chi·ra·pal·li (tir′ə chir′ə päl′ē, -pul′ē) city in Tamil Nadu state, S India

'tis (tiz) *contraction* [Old Poet.] it is

ti·sane (ti zan′; *Fr* tē zȧn′) *n.* ⟦ME *tysane*, drink made by boiling barley with water and other ingredients < MFr *tisane*< VL *tisana*, for L *ptisana*, barley groats, drink made from barley groats < Gr *ptisanē*, peeled barley < *ptissein*, to peel < IE base **pis-*, to crush > L *pinsere*, to beat, crush⟧ a beverage made by steeping herbs, spices, roots, etc. in hot or boiling water, sometimes drunk for medicinal purposes; herb tea

Tish·ah b'Ab (tish′ə bäb′, -bäv′) ⟦Heb *tisha beab*, ninth (day) of Ab⟧ a Jewish fast day commemorating the destruction of the Temple, observed on the 9th day of Ab: also **Tish′ah b'Av′** (-bäv′)

Tish·ri (tish rē′, tish′rē) *n.* ⟦Heb⟧ the first month of the Jewish year: see the Jewish calendar in the Reference Supplement

Ti·siph·o·ne (ti sif′ə nē′) *n.* ⟦Gr *Tisiphonē*, lit., the avenger of blood < *tisis*, vengeance + *phonos*, bloodletting, murder < IE **gwhonos*, a beating < base **gwhen-*, to beat, strike⟧ *Class. Myth.* one of the three Furies

tis·sue (tish′o͞o; *chiefly Brit*, tis′yo͞o) *n.* ⟦ME *tissu*, rich cloth < OFr < pp. of *tistre*, to weave < L *texere*, to weave: see TEXT⟧ 1 cloth; esp., light, thin cloth, as gauze 2 an interwoven or intricate mass or series; mesh; network; web [*a tissue* of lies] 3 a piece of soft, absorbent paper, used as a disposable handkerchief, as toilet paper, etc. 4 *a)* TISSUE PAPER *b)* a sheet of tissue paper 5 *Biol. a)* the substance of an organic body or organ, consisting of cells and intercellular material *b)* any of the distinct structural materials of an organism, having a particular function [epithelial *tissue*] —*vt.* **-sued, -su·ing** 1 to cover with tissue 2 [Archaic] to weave into tissue

tissue culture 1 the process or technique of growing tissue artificially in a special, sterile culture medium 2 the tissue thus grown

tissue paper very thin, unsized, nearly transparent paper, for wrapping things, making tracings, etc.

tissue plasminogen activator an enzyme produced by the blood vessels that dissolves blood clots by converting plasminogen into plasmin: it is manufactured using recombinant DNA technology and used to prevent stroke, etc.

Ti·sza (tē′sô, -sä) river in E Europe, flowing from W Ukraine southwest through Hungary & Serbia into the Danube: *c.* 800 mi (1,287 km)

tit[1] (tit) *n.* ⟦TIT(MOUSE)⟧ a titmouse or other small bird

tit[2] (tit) *n.* ⟦ME *titte* < OE *tit*, TEAT⟧ 1 NIPPLE (sense 1) 2 a woman's breast: somewhat vulgar

tit[3] (tit) *n.* ⟦ME *tit-* in *titmose*, TITMOUSE, *titling*: prob. child's term for "little," seen also in ON *títlingr*, little bird, Norw *titta*, little girl⟧ [Now Rare] a small, worn-out, or inferior horse

tit[4] (tit) *n. see* TIT FOR TAT

tit[5] *abbrev.* title

Tit *abbrev. Bible* Titus

Ti·tan (tīt′'n) *n.* ⟦ME < L < Gr (pl. *Titanes*)⟧ 1 *old poet. name for* HELIOS 2 *Gr. Myth.* any of a race of giant deities who are overthrown by the Olympian gods 3 [**t-**] any person or thing of great size or power 4 the largest of the satellites of Saturn: the only one in the solar system known to have a permanent atmosphere

ti·tan·ate (tīt′'n āt′) *n.* a salt or ester of titanic acid

Ti·tan·ess (tīt′'n is) *n.* a female Titan

Ti·ta·ni·a (ti tā′nē ə, tī-) *n. Eng. Folklore* the queen of fairyland and wife of Oberon

ti·tan·ic (tī tan′ik, ti-) *adj.* designating or of a chemical compound containing tetravalent titanium

Ti·tan·ic (tī tan′ik) *adj.* ⟦Gr *Titanikos*⟧ 1 of or like the Titans 2 [**t-**] of great size, strength, or power —*n.* British ocean liner that sank with great loss of life in 1912 on its maiden voyage —**ti·tan′i·cal·ly** *adv.*

titanic acid either of two weak acids, H_2TiO_3 or H_4TiO_4, derived from titanium dioxide

ti·tan·if·er·ous (tīt′'n if′ər əs) *adj.* ⟦TITANI(UM) + -FEROUS⟧ containing titanium

ti·tan·ite (tīt′'n īt′) *n.* ⟦Ger *titanit*: see fol. & -ITE[1]⟧ SPHENE

ti·ta·ni·um (tī tā′nē əm, ti-) *n.* ⟦ModL: arbitrary coinage (1796) by M. H. Klaproth (see TELLURIUM) < Gr *Titanes*, pl. of *Titan*, TITAN + -IUM, by analogy with URANIUM⟧ a silvery or dark-gray, lustrous, metallic chemical element found in rutile and other minerals and used as a cleaning and deoxidizing agent in molten steel, and in the manufacture of aircraft, satellites, chemical equipment, etc.: symbol, Ti; at. no. 22: see the periodic table of elements in the Reference Supplement

titanium dioxide a white crystalline compound, TiO_2, used as a paint pigment and ceramic glaze, and in making white rubber, plastics, etc.: also **titanium white** or **titanic oxide**

ti·tan·o·saur (tī tan′ə sôr′) *n.* ⟦< ModL *Titanosaurus*: see TITAN & -SAURUS⟧ any of a genus (*Titanosaurus*) of large, plant-eating, amphibious sauropods of the Cretaceous: also **ti·tan′o·saur′us** (-əs)

ti·tan·ous (tī tan′əs, ti-; tīt′'n əs) *adj.* designating or of a chemical compound containing trivalent titanium

tit·bit (tit′bit′) *n. chiefly Brit. var. of* TIDBIT

ti·ter (tīt′ər, tēt′-) *n.* ⟦Fr *titre*, standard, title < OFr *title*: see TITLE⟧ *Chem., Physiol.* 1 a standard strength or degree of concentration of a solution as established through titration 2 the minimum weight or volume of a substance necessary to cause a given result in titration 3 the point at which a fatty acid solidifies after being liberated by hydrolysis, separated, and washed free of other products

tit for tat ⟦var. of earlier *tip for tap* (Fr *tant pour tant*): see TIP[2]⟧ this for that: phrase used when someone pays back one wrong or injury with another

tithe (tīth) *n.* ⟦ME < OE *teothe*, contr. < *teogotha*, a TENTH⟧ 1 one tenth of the annual produce of one's land or of one's annual income, paid as a tax or contribution to support a church or its clergy 2 *a)* a tenth part *b)* any small part 3 any tax or levy —*vt.* **tithed, tith′ing** ⟦ME *tithen* < OE *teothian* < the n.⟧ 1 to pay a tithe of (one's produce, income, etc.) 2 to levy a tithe on or collect a tithe from —*vi.* to pay a tithe —**tith′a·ble** *adj.* —**tith′er** *n.*

tith·ing (tīth′iŋ) *n.* ⟦ME < OE *teothung*⟧ 1 TITHE (*n.* 1) 2 a levying or paying of tithes 3 [Historical] in England, a unit of civil administration originally consisting of ten families

Ti·tho·nus (ti thō′nəs) *n.* ⟦L < Gr *Tithōnos*⟧ *Gr. Myth.* a son of Laomedon and a lover of Eos, who obtains immortality for him but not eternal youth: he continues to shrivel with age as a result and she turns him into a grasshopper out of pity

☆**ti·ti**[1] (tīt′ī, tēt′ē) *n.* ⟦< ?⟧ a small tree (*Cliftonia monophylla*) of a family (Cyrillaceae, order Ericales) of evergreen, dicotyledonous trees and shrubs, with white or pinkish flowers, found in the S U.S.

ti·ti[2] (tē tē′) *n.* ⟦Sp *tití* < Aymara *titi*⟧ any of a genus (*Callicebus*, family Cebidae) of South American monkeys with a small, round head

ti·tian (tish′ən) *n.* ⟦from the color of the hair in many of TITIAN's portraits⟧ a color blending red and gold —*adj.* reddish-gold

Ti·tian (tish′ən) (It. name *Tiziano Vecellio*) 1490?-1576; Venetian painter

Ti·ti·ca·ca (tit′i kä′kə; *Sp* tē′tē kä′kä), **Lake** lake in South America, on the border of SE Peru & W Bolivia: *c.* 3,500 sq mi (9,065 sq km); elevation, 12,500 ft (3,810 m)

tit·il·late (tit′'l āt′) *vt.* **-lat′ed, -lat′ing** ⟦< L *titillatus*, pp. of *titillare*, to tickle⟧ **1** TICKLE **2** to excite or stimulate pleasurably, often erotically —**tit′il·lat′er** *n.* —**tit′il·la′tion** *n.* —**tit′il·la′tive** *adj.*

tit·i·vate (tit′ə vāt′) *vt., vi.* **-vat′ed, -vat′ing** ⟦earlier *tidivate, tiddivate*, prob. < TIDY, with quasi-Latin suffix⟧ to dress up; spruce up —**tit′i·va′tion** *n.*

tit·lark (tit′lärk′) *n.* ⟦TIT[1] + LARK[1]⟧ PIPIT

ti·tle (tīt′'l) *n.* ⟦OFr < L *titulus*, inscription, label, title, sign⟧ **1** the name of a book, chapter, poem, essay, picture, statue, piece of music, play, film, etc. **2** *a)* *short for* TITLE PAGE *b)* a publication; book, newspaper, magazine, etc. [*50 new titles in the publisher's fall catalog*] **3** a descriptive name or appellation; epithet **4** an appellation given to a person or family as a sign of privilege, distinction, rank, or profession **5** a claim or right **6** in sports and other competition, a championship **7** in the Church of England, a source of income or field of work required of a candidate for ordination **8** *Film, TV* words shown on the screen that give credit to someone for work done, that translate a segment of foreign dialogue, etc.: *usually used in pl.* **9** *Law* *a)* the name of a statute or act; also, the heading designating a legal proceeding *b)* a division of a law book, statute, etc., usually larger than a section or article *c)* a right to ownership, esp. of real estate *d)* evidence of such right of ownership *e)* a document stating such a right; deed —*vt.* **-tled, -tling** to give a title to; designate by a specified name, or title; entitle

ti·tled (tīt′'ld) *adj.* having a title, esp. of nobility

title deed a document that establishes title to property

ti·tle·hold·er (tīt′'l hōl′dər) *n.* the holder of a title; specif., the winner of a championship, as in some sport

title page the page in the front of a book that gives the title, author, publisher, etc.

title role (*or* part *or* character) the character in a play, film, etc. whose name is used as or in its title

☆**ti·tlist** (tīt′'l ist) *n.* a titleholder in some sport

tit·mouse (tit′mous′) *n., pl.* **-mice′** (-mīs′) ⟦altered, infl. by MOUSE < ME *titemose*, prob. < *tit-*, little + OE *mase*, titmouse, akin to Ger *meise*⟧ any of a family (Paridae) of small passerine birds found throughout the world except in South America and Australia, including the tufted titmouse and various chickadees

Ti·to (tē′tō), Marshal (born *Josip Broz*) 1892-1980; Yugoslav Communist party leader: prime minister (1945-53) & president (1953-80) of Yugoslavia

Ti·to·grad (tēt′ō grad′, -gräd′) *name* (1946-92) *for* PODGORICA

Ti·to·ism (-iz′əm) *n.* the policies and practices of Yugoslavia under Marshal Tito; specif., the practice of nationalistic socialism independent of other socialist states and, specif., of the U.S.S.R. —**Ti′to·ist** *adj., n.*

ti·trate (tī′trāt′) *vt., vi.* **-trat′ed, -trat′ing** ⟦< Fr *titrer* < *titre* (see TITER) + -ATE[1]⟧ to test by or be subjected to titration

ti·tra·tion (tī trā′shən) *n.* ⟦< prec. + -ION⟧ *Chem., Physiol.* the process of finding out how much of a certain substance is contained in a known volume of a solution by measuring volumetrically how much of a standard solution is required to produce a given reaction

ti·tre (tīt′ər, tēt′-) *n. Brit. sp. of* TITER

tit·ter (tit′ər) *vi.* ⟦of Gmc echoic orig.⟧ to laugh in a half-suppressed way, suggestive of silliness, nervousness, etc.; giggle —*n.* the act or an instance of tittering —*SYN.* LAUGH —**tit′ter·er** *n.*

tit·ti·vate (tit′ə vāt′) *vt., vi.* **-vat′ed, -vat′ing** *alt. sp. of* TITIVATE

tit·tle (tit′'l) *n.* ⟦ME *title*, orig. same word as TITLE⟧ **1** a dot or other small mark used as a diacritic **2** a very small particle; iota; jot

tit·tle-tat·tle (tit′'l tat′'l) *n., vi.* **-tled, -tling** ⟦redupl. of TATTLE⟧ gossip; chatter

tit·tup (tit′əp) *n.* ⟦prob. echoic of hoofbeats⟧ a lively movement; frolicsome behavior; frisk; caper —*vi.* **-tuped** or **-tupped, -tup·ing** or **-tup·ping** to move in a frolicsome or prancing way; caper

tit·ty (tit′ē) *n., pl.* **-ties** [Slang] a woman's teat or breast: mildly vulgar

tit·u·ba·tion (tich′o͞o bā′shən, ti′tyo͞o-) *n.* ⟦L *titubatio*, a staggering < *titubare*, to totter⟧ a stumbling or staggering gait characteristic of certain nervous disorders

tit·u·lar (tich′ə lər, tit′yə-) *adj.* ⟦L *titulus* (see TITLE) + -AR⟧ **1** of, or having the nature of, a title **2** having a title; titled **3** existing only in title; in name only; nominal [*a titular sovereign*] **4** from whom or which the title or name is taken **5** designating a bishop holding the title of an extinct see —*n.* a person who holds a title, esp. without any obligations of office —**tit′u·lar·ly** *adv.*

Ti·tus[1] (tīt′əs) *n.* ⟦L⟧ **1** a masculine name **2** *Bible* a book of the New Testament, which was a letter of the Apostle Paul to his disciple Titus: abbrev. *Ti, Tit*, or *Tt*

Ti·tus[2] (tīt′əs) (*Titus Flavius Sabinus Vespasianus*) A.D. 39-81; Rom. general & emperor (79-81): son of Vespasian

Ti·u (tē′o͞o) *n.* ⟦OE *Tiw*, akin to OHG *Ziu* < IE **deiwos*, god: see DEITY⟧ *Gmc. Myth.* the god of war and the sky: identified with the Norse Tyr

☆**Ti·Vo** (tē′vō′) ⟦arbitrary coinage < *TV*⟧ *trademark for:* **1** a kind of digital video recorder **2** the subscription service required to operate the scheduled recording, downloading, and other features of this device —*vt.* **Ti′Voed′, Ti′Vo′ing** to record (a television program) using this device

Ti·vo·li (tiv′ə lē) **1** city in central Italy, near Rome **2** famous recreational & cultural garden center in Copenhagen, Denmark

ti·yin (tē yin′) *n., pl.* **-yin′** **1** a monetary unit of Uzbekistan, equal to $\frac{1}{100}$ of a sum **2** a monetary unit of Kyrgyzstan, equal to $\frac{1}{100}$ of a som

☆**tiz·zy** (tiz′ē) *n., pl.* **-zies** ⟦< ?⟧ [Informal] a state of frenzied excitement, esp. over some trivial matter

tko or **TKO** (tē′kā′ō′) *n. Boxing* technical knockout

tkt *abbrev.* ticket

Tl *Chem. symbol for* thallium

Tlax·ca·la (tläs′käl′ə) **1** state of central Mexico: 1,511 sq mi (3,913 sq km) **2** its capital

TLC *abbrev.* [Informal] tender, loving care

Tlin·git (tliŋ′git) *n.* ⟦Tlingit *lingít*, lit., people⟧ **1** *pl.* **-gits** or **-git** a member of a North American Indian people of the coastal areas of S Alaska and N British Columbia **2** the language of this people, now thought to be related to the Athabaskan languages

T lymphocyte T CELL

Tm[1] *abbrev. Bible* Timothy

Tm[2] *Chem. symbol for* thulium

TM *abbrev.* **1** trademark **2** *service mark* TRANSCENDENTAL MEDITATION

☆**T-man** (tē′man′) *n., pl.* **T′-men′** (-men′) ⟦< *T(reasury)-man*⟧ [Informal] a special agent of the U.S. Department of the Treasury

tme·sis (tə mē′sis, mē′sis) *n.* ⟦LL < Gr *tmēsis*, a cutting < *temnein*, to cut: see -TOMY⟧ *Prosody, Rhetoric* separation of the parts of a compound word by an intervening word or words (Ex.: *what person soever* for *whatsoever person*)

TMJ *abbrev.* temporomandibular joint (disorder)

tn *abbrev.* **1** ton(s) **2** train

TN *abbrev.* Tennessee

TNF *abbrev.* tumor necrosis factor

tng *abbrev.* training

TNT (tē′en′tē′) *n.* ⟦*t(ri)n(itro)t(oluene)*⟧ TRINITROTOLUENE

to[1] (to͞o) *prep.* ⟦ME < OE, akin to Ger *zu* < IE **dō-*, up toward > L (*quan*)-*do*, when, then, *do*(*nec*), until⟧ **1** *a)* in the direction of; toward [*a turn to the left, traveling to Pittsburgh*] *b)* in the direction of and reaching [*he went to Boston; it fell to the ground*] **2** as far as; to the extent of [*wet to the skin, starved to death*] **3** *a)* toward or into the condition of [*to grow to manhood, a rise to fame*] *b)* so as to result in [*sentenced to ten years in prison*] **4** *a)* on, onto, against, at, next to, etc. (used to indicate nearness or contact) [*applying lotion to the skin, a house to the right, cheek to cheek*] *b)* in a (specified) relation with [*lines parallel to each other*] *c)* in front of [*face to face*] **5** *a)* until [*no parking from four to six*] *b)* before [*at ten to six*] **6** for the purpose of; for [*come to dinner*] **7** *a)* as concerns; with respect to; involving [*that's all there is to it; to leave oneself open to attack*] *b)* in the opinion of [*it seems good to me*] **8** producing, causing, or resulting in [*to his amazement, torn to pieces*] **9** along with; accompanied by; as an accompaniment for [*add this to the others; dance to the music*] **10** being the proper appurtenance, possession, or attribute of; of [*the key to the house*] **11** as compared with; as against [*a score of 7 to 1, superior to the others*] **12** *a)* in agreement, correspondence, or conformity with [*not to her taste*] *b)* as a reaction, or in response, toward [*the dog came to his whistle*] **13** constituting; in or for (each) [*four quarts to a gallon*] **14** as far as the limit of [*moderate to high in price*] **15** with (a specified person or thing) as the recipient of the verb: an indicator of the indirect object of the action [*listen to him; give the book to her*] **16** in honor of [*a toast to your success*] **17** by: used in some passive constructions [*a person known to me*] **18** at or in (a specified place) [*to have someone to the house for dinner*]: often a dial. usage [*he's to home*] **19** [Dial.] with (a specified crop) [*a field planted to corn*] ➥*To* is also used before a verb as a sign of the infinitive [*it was easy to read; to live is sweet*] or, elliptically, to stand for a verb, repeated in its infinitive form, and the objects, phrases, etc. that follow [*tell him if you want to*] —*adv.* **1** forward [*his hat is on wrong side to*] **2** in the normal or desired direction, position, or condition; esp., shut or closed [*the door was blown to*] **3** into a state of consciousness [*the boxer came to*] **4** at hand [*we were close to when it happened*] ➥*To* is used in many idiomatic phrases entered in this dictionary under their key words (e.g., *bring to, come to, go to*) —**to and fro** first in one direction and then in the opposite; back and forth

to[2] *abbrev.* turnover

to- (to͞o, too, tə) ⟦ME < OE, akin to Ger *zer-*, L *dis-*: see DIS-⟧ *prefix* [Obs.] completely, entirely, severely: used with verbs as an intensive [*to-broken* means "broken to pieces"]

toad (tōd) *n.* ⟦ME *tode*, var. of *tadde* < OE *tadde, tadige*⟧ **1** any of several families of tailless, leaping anuran amphibians (esp. family Bufonidae) with a rough, warty skin: normally they eat insects and live on moist land but when breeding they live in water **2** a person regarded as loathsome, contemptible, etc.

toad·eat·er (-ēt′ər) *n.* **1** [Historical] a quack doctor's assistant who pretended to eat toads, etc. as a public demonstration of the efficacy of the doctor's medicines **2** [Archaic] TOADY

toad·fish (tōd′fish′) *n., pl.* **-fish′** or **-fish′es** (see FISH) any of an order (Batrachoidiformes) of scaleless bony fishes with a broad head resembling a frog's, found in shallows off the Atlantic coast of North America

toad·flax (tōd′flaks′) *n.* ⟦from the spotted and flaxlike appearance of the parts⟧ BUTTER-AND-EGGS

toad-in-the-hole (tōd′in *thə* hōl′) *n.* ⟦roughly descriptive of its appearance] a British dish consisting of sausages baked in a batter like that used for Yorkshire pudding

toad spit (*or* spittle) CUCKOO SPIT (sense 1)

toad·stone (tōd′stōn′) ***n.*** [TOAD + STONE, based on L or Gr *batrachitēs* or MFr *crapaudine*] any stone or similar object formerly thought to have been formed inside a toad's head or body and often worn as a charm

toad·stool (tōd′sto͞ol′) ***n.*** [ME *todestole*: see TOAD & STOOL] any of a number of fleshy, umbrella-shaped, basidiomycetous fungi; mushroom; esp., in popular usage, any poisonous mushroom

toad·y (tō′dē) ***n., pl.* toad′ies** [short for TOADEATER, sense 1] a servile flatterer; sycophant, esp. one who does distasteful or unprincipled things in order to gain favor — ***vt., vi.* toad′ied, toad′y·ing** to be a toady (to); flatter —**toad′y·ism′** ***n.***

to-and-fro (to͞o′ən frō′) ***adj.*** [ME] moving forward and backward; back-and-forth

toast[1] (tōst) ***vt.*** [ME *tosten* < OFr *toster* < VL **tostare* < L *tostus*, pp. of *torrere*, to parch, roast: see THIRST] **1** to brown the surface of (bread, cheese, etc.) by heating in a toaster, over or near a fire, or in an oven **2** to warm thoroughly *[toast* yourselves by the fire*]* —***vi.*** to become toasted —***n.*** **1** sliced bread made brown and crisp by heat ☆**2** [Slang] *a)* destined for trouble or failure *[*I'm *toast* if I'm late for work again*]* *b)* utterly ruined *[*the computer was *toast* following the power surge*]*

toast[2] (tōst) ***n.*** [from the use of toasted spiced bread to flavor the wine, and the notion that the person honored also added flavor] **1** a person, thing, idea, etc. in honor of which a person or persons raise their glasses and drink **2** *a)* a proposal to drink to such a person, etc., or a sentiment expressed just before drinking on such an occasion *b)* a drink taken in toasting a person, etc. **3** any person greatly admired or acclaimed — ***vt., vi.*** to propose or drink a toast (to)

toast·er[1] (tōs′tər) ***n.*** a utensil or appliance for toasting bread

toast·er[2] (tōs′tər) ***n.*** a person who proposes or drinks a toast

toaster oven an electrical appliance designed like a small oven, used for toasting bread and for broiling or baking small quantities of various other foods

toast·mas·ter (tōst′mas′tər) ***n.*** the person at a banquet who proposes toasts, introduces after-dinner speakers, etc.

toast·mis·tress (-mis′tris) ***n.*** a female toastmaster: see -ESS

toast·y (tōs′tē) ***adj.* toast′i·er, toast′i·est** **1** of or characteristic of toast **2** warm and comfortable or cozy —***adv.*** cozily *[toasty* warm*]*

Tob *abbrev. Bible* Tobit

to·bac·co (tə bak′ō) ***n., pl.* -cos** [Sp *tabaco* < ?; perhaps an old Sp name transferred to the New World plant] **1** any of a genus (*Nicotiana*) of chiefly tropical American plants of the nightshade family, with hairy, sticky foliage and long-tubed, white, yellow, greenish, or purple flowers; esp., the species (*N. tabacum*) now widely cultivated for its leaves **2** the leaves of certain of these plants, prepared for smoking, chewing, or snuffing **3** products prepared from these leaves; cigars, cigarettes, snuff, etc. **4** the use of tobacco for smoking, etc.

tobacco hornworm a hawk moth (*Manduca sexta*) whose large, green caterpillar feeds on the leaves of tobacco plants

tobacco mosaic virus any of a group of RNA viruses affecting tobacco, tomatoes, and various other plants, causing a disease (**tobacco mosaic**) characterized by yellowish to dark-green mottling of the leaves

to·bac·co·nist (tə bak′ə nist) ***n.*** [TOBACCO + *-n-* + -IST[1]: orig. applied to a user of tobacco] a dealer in tobacco and other smoking supplies

To·ba·go (tə bā′gō) island in the West Indies, northeast of Trinidad: 116 sq mi (300 sq km): see TRINIDAD AND TOBAGO

-to-be (tə bē′) *combining form* future; that will be (as specified) in the future: used after a noun, esp. one indicating a family relationship *[*bride-*to-be*, father-*to-be]*

To·bi·as (tə bī′əs) ***n.*** [LL(Ec) < Gr(Ec) *Tōbias* < Heb *toviya*, lit., God is good < *tov*, good + *ya*, God] **1** a masculine name: dim. *Toby*; var. *Tobiah* **2** TOBIT

To·bit (tō′bit) ***n.*** **1** a Hebrew captive in Nineveh **2** a book of the Apocrypha telling his story: abbrev. *Tob* or *Tb*

to·bog·gan (tə bäg′ən) ***n.*** [CdnFr *tabagan, tobagan* < an Algonquian language: cf. Micmac *topaĝan*] a long, narrow, flat sled without runners, made of thin boards curved back at the front end and often having side rails: often used for the sport of coasting down a prepared slope or chute —***vi.*** to ride on a toboggan —**to·bog′gan·er** ***n.***, **to·bog′gan·ist**

To·bol (tō′bôl′, tō bôl′; *Russ* tŏ bôl′yə) river in W Siberia, flowing from the S Urals into the Irtysh: 1,042 mi (1,677 km)

To·by (tō′bē) ***n., pl.* -bies** [< *Toby*, dim. of TOBIAS] a jug or mug for ale or beer, shaped like a stout man with a three-cornered hat: also **Toby jug**

To·can·tins (tō′kən tēns′; *Port* tŏ′kän tēnsh′, -tēns′) river flowing from central Brazil north into the Pará River: *c.* 1,700 mi (2,736 km)

toc·ca·ta (tə kät′ə) ***n.*** [It, orig. fem. of pp. of *toccare* < VL, to TOUCH] a composition in free style for the organ, piano, etc., generally characterized by the use of full chords and running passages and often used as the prelude of a fugue

To·char·i·an (tō ker′ē ən, -kar′-, -kär′-) ***n.*** [formerly identified with Gr *Tocharoi*, a central Asian people mentioned by STRABO] **1** a member of a people living in central Asia until about A.D. 1000 **2** their extinct Indo-European language, comprising an eastern dialect (**Tocharian A**) and a western dialect (**Tocharian B**): the earliest record known is from the 7th cent. A.D. —***adj.*** of the Tocharians or their language or culture

☆**toch·is** (to͝okh′is, tukh′-) ***n.*** [Slang] *var. of* TUCHIS

to·coph·er·ol (tō käf′ər ôl, -ōl′) ***n.*** [< Gr *tokos*, childbirth + *pherein*, to BEAR[1] + -OL[1]] any of a group of four closely related viscous oils that constitute vitamin E and occur chiefly in wheat germ oil, cottonseed oil, lettuce, etc.

Tocque·ville (tōk′vil′; *Fr* tôk vēl′), **A·le·xis (Charles Henri Maurice Clérel) de** (ə lek′sis; *Fr* å lek sē′ də) 1805-59; Fr. writer & statesman

toc·sin (täk′sin) ***n.*** [Fr < MFr *touquesain* < Prov *tocasenh* < *toc*, a stroke < *tocar* (< VL **toccare*, to TOUCH) + *senh*, bell < LL *signum*, a signal, bell < L, a SIGN] **1** *a)* an alarm bell *b)* its sound **2** any alarm, or sound of warning

tod[1] (täd) ***n.*** [ME *todde*, prob. < LowG source, as in EFris *todde, tod*, a bundle, pack, load, akin to Ger *zotte*, tuft of hair < IE **det-* < base **dā(i)-*, to divide > TIDE[1]] **1** a former English weight for wool, about 28 pounds **2** a bushy clump of ivy, etc.

tod[2] (täd) ***n.*** [ME < ?] [Scot.] a fox

to·day (tə dā′) ***adv.*** [ME *to dai* < OE *to dæg*: see TO[1] & DAY] **1** on or during the present day **2** in the present time or age; nowadays —***n.*** **1** the present day **2** the present time or period —***adj.*** [Informal] characterized by, exemplifying, or knowing what is most modern or fashionable; up-to-date *[*a *today* designer*]*

Todd (täd) ***n.*** [< ME *tod(de)*, a fox < ?] a masculine name

tod·dle (täd′'l) ***vi.*** **-dled, -dling** [? freq. of TOTTER, via N dial. *doddle* < ?] to walk with short, uncertain steps, as in very early childhood —***n.*** the act of toddling or a toddling movement

tod·dler (täd′lər) ***n.*** a very young child, esp. one just learning to walk

tod·dy (täd′ē) ***n., pl.* -dies** [Anglo-Ind < Hindi *tāṛī*, fermented sap of palmyra tree < *tāṛ*, palm tree < Sans *tāla*, palmyra] **1** *a)* the sweet sap of various East Indian palms, used as a beverage *b)* an alcoholic liquor made by fermenting this sap **2** a drink of brandy, whiskey, etc. with hot water, sugar, and often spices: also **hot toddy**

toddy palm any of several palms (esp. genera *Arenga, Borassus, Phoenix*, and *Cocos*) yielding toddy

to-do (tə do͞o′, to͝o-) [Informal] ***n., pl.* -dos′** a commotion; stir; fuss —***adj.*** designating or of a list of tasks one must attend to: often used fig.

to·dy (tō′dē) ***n., pl.* -dies** [Fr *todier* < L *todus*, small bird] any of a family (Todidae) of small, insect-eating coraciiform birds of the West Indies with green upper parts and a red throat

toe (tō) ***n.*** [ME *to* < OE *ta*, earlier *tahe*, akin to Ger *zehe* < IE base **deik-*, to show > TEACH, L *dicere*, to say, *digitus*] **1** *a)* any of the five jointed parts at the front of the human foot; digit *b)* the forepart of the human foot *c)* the part of a shoe, sock, etc. that covers the toes **2** any of the digits of an animal's foot, or the forepart of a hoof, etc. **3** anything suggesting a toe in location, shape, or function; specif., *a)* a pivot or journal extending vertically in a bearing *b)* a projecting arm raised or moved by a cam —***vt.*** **toed, toe′ing** **1** to provide with a toe or toes **2** to touch, kick, etc. with the toes *[*to *toe* a starting line*]* **3** *Carpentry* *a)* to drive (a nail) slantingly *b)* to clinch or fasten with a nail or nails driven slantingly; toenail —***vi.*** ☆to stand, walk, or be formed so that the toes are in a specified position *[*to *toe* in or *toe* out*]* —**on one's toes** [Informal] mentally or physically alert —**step (or tread) on someone's toes** to offend someone, esp. by trespassing or intruding on prerogatives or rights —**toe the line (or mark)** **1** to stand or crouch with the toes touching the starting line of a race, etc. **2** to follow orders, rules, doctrines, etc. strictly

ToE *abbrev.* THEORY OF EVERYTHING

toe·a (tō′ä) ***n., pl.* toe′a** [< word for shell, piece of shell money in a Papuan language] a monetary unit of Papua New Guinea, equal to $\frac{1}{100}$ of a kina

toe·cap (tō′kap′) ***n.*** that part of a shoe or boot which covers the toes

toe crack SANDCRACK

toed (tōd) ***adj.*** **1** having (a specified kind or number of) toes: usually in hyphenated compounds *[*three-*toed]* **2** *a)* driven slantingly (said of a nail) *b)* fastened by a nail or nails driven slantingly

toe dance a dance performed on the tips of the toes, as in ballet —**toe′-dance′** ***vi.*** **-danced′, -danc′ing** —**toe′-danc′er** ***n.***

Toefl (tō′fəl) *trademark* Test of English as a Foreign Language: also **TOEFL**

toe·hold (tō′hōld′) ***n.*** **1** a small space or ledge for supporting the toe of the foot in climbing, etc. **2** any means of surmounting obstacles, gaining entry, etc. **3** a slight footing or advantage **4** *Wrestling* a hold in which one wrestler twists the other's foot

toe-in (tō′in′) ***n.*** nearly parallel alignment of the front wheels of a motor vehicle such that the front edges are slightly closer together and so provide necessary tension on the steering linkage

toe·less (tō′lis) ***adj.*** **1** having no toe or toes **2** having the toe open or uncovered *[*a *toeless* shoe*]*

toe·nail (tō′nāl′) ***n.*** **1** the nail of a toe **2** *Carpentry* a nail driven in on a slant —***vt.*** *Carpentry* to fasten with a nail or nails driven in on a slant; toe

toe·shoe (tō′sho͞o′) ***n.*** a girl's or woman's ballet slipper used in toe-dancing, having a shaped piece of hard material in the tip of the toe and fastened about the ankles with ribbons: also written **toe shoe**

☆**toe-to-toe** (tō′tə tō′) ***adv., adj.*** in close and direct confrontation, competition, etc. *[*going *toe-to-toe* with one's critics, *toe-to-toe* combat*]*

toff (täf, tôf) ***n.*** [< *toft*, var. of TUFT, slang term for "titled undergraduate," in reference to gold tassel on the caps of aristocratic students] [Brit. Informal] a fashionable, upper-class person; esp., a dandy

tof·fee or **tof·fy** (tôf′ē, täf′-) ***n.*** [later Brit form of TAFFY] a chewy or crunchy candy made with brown sugar or molasses and butter, often coated with nuts

toft (täft, tôft) ***n.*** [ME < Late OE < ON *topt*, a homestead, ground marked out for building < IE **dom-ped-*, house site < base **dem-*, to build (> TIM-

BER) + *ped-, FOOT]] 1 [Brit. Historical] *a)* a house site *b)* a homestead with its arable land 2 [Brit. Dial.] a knoll

to·fu (tō′fo͞o) ***n.*** [[SinoJpn *tōfu* < *tō*, bean + *fu*, rot]] a bland, cheeselike food, rich in protein, coagulated from an extract of soybeans and used in soups, in various cooked dishes, etc.

tog (täg, tôg) ***n.*** [[prob. < cant *togeman(s)*, *togman*, a cloak, coat, ult. < L *toga*, fol.]] 1 [Old Slang] a coat 2 [*pl.*] [Informal] clothes; outfit [*tennis togs*] —***vt., vi.*** **togged, tog′ging** [Informal] to dress: usually with *up* or *out*

to·ga (tō′gə) ***n.***, *pl.* **-gas** or **-gae** (-jē, -gē) [[L < *tegere*, to cover: see THATCH]] 1 in ancient Rome, a loose, one-piece outer garment worn in public by citizens 2 a robe of office; characteristic gown of a profession

to·gaed (tō′gəd) ***adj.*** wearing a toga

to·ga vi·ri·lis (tō′gə vi rī′lis, -və ril′is) [[L, toga of a man]] the toga of manhood, put on by boys of ancient Rome in their fourteenth year

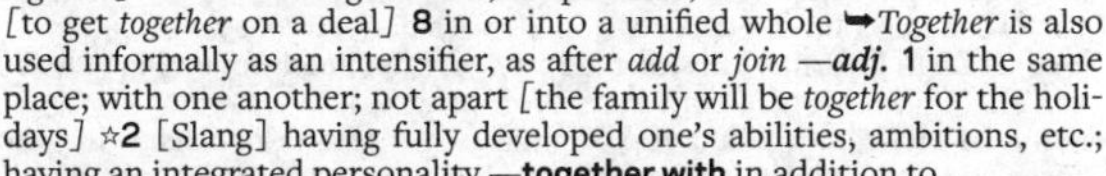
Roman toga

to·geth·er (tə geth′ər, to͞o-) ***adv.*** [[ME *togeder* < OE *togædre*, *togadere* < *to* (see TO[1]) + *gædre*, together < base of *gaderian* (see GATHER)]] 1 in or into one gathering, group, mass, or place [*a reunion to bring the family together*] 2 in or into contact, collision, union, etc. with each other [*the cars skidded together*] 3 considered collectively; added up [*winning more than all the others together*] 4 *a)* with one another; in association or companionship [*to spend a week together*] *b)* by joint effort [*together they were able to lift the sofa*] 5 at the same time; simultaneously [*shots fired together*] 6 in succession; continuously [*sulking for three whole days together*] 7 in or into agreement, cooperation, etc. [*to get together on a deal*] 8 in or into a unified whole ➥*Together* is also used informally as an intensifier, as after *add* or *join* —***adj.*** 1 in the same place; with one another; not apart [*the family will be together for the holidays*] ☆2 [Slang] having fully developed one's abilities, ambitions, etc.; having an integrated personality —**together with** in addition to

to·geth·er·ness (-nis) ***n.*** closeness of members of a family, social group, etc.

tog·gle (täg′əl) ***n.*** [[prob. naut. var. of dial. *tuggle*, freq. of TUG]] 1 a pin, rod, etc. for insertion between the strands or through a loop of a rope, through a link of a chain, etc. to make an attachment, prevent slipping, or facilitate tightening or twisting 2 TOGGLE BOLT 3 a toggle joint or a device having one 4 *Comput.* a key or command for switching between two settings or options, typically *on* and *off* —***vt.*** **-gled, -gling** to provide or fasten with a toggle or toggles —***vi.*** *Comput.* to switch or alternate between two settings, conditions, functions, etc. by means of a toggle

toggle bolt a bolt with an attached nut-like device having pivoted, spring-operated wings that move together when pushed through a hole and open up again after emerging, used as to fasten objects to a hollow wall or to a surface that is accessible from only one side

toggle joint a knee-shaped joint consisting of two bars pivoted together at one end: when pressure is put on the joint to straighten it, opposite, outward pressures are transmitted to the open ends

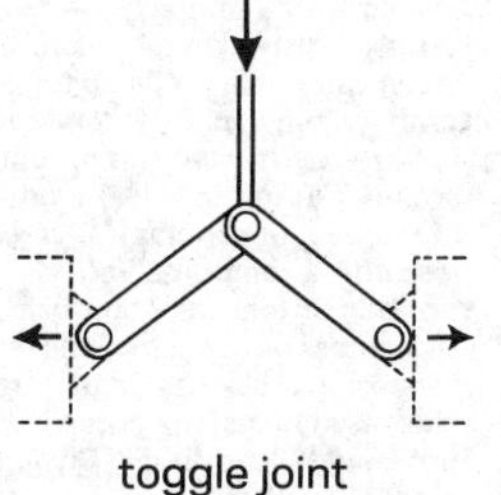
toggle joint

toggle switch a switch consisting of a projecting lever moved back and forth through a small arc to open and close an electric circuit

To·gliat·ti (tōl yät′ē) [[after P. *Togliatti* (1893-1964), It communist leader]] city in SE European Russia, near Samara

To·go (tō′gō) country in W Africa, on the Gulf of Guinea, east of Ghana: a former French mandate, it became independent in 1960: 21,925 sq mi (56,785 sq km); cap. Lomé —**To′go·lese′** (-lēz′, -lēs′) ***adj., n.***, *pl.* **-lese′**

To·go·land (tō′gō land′) former German protectorate (until 1919); it was divided between France & Great Britain: the British part is now part of Ghana (since 1957), & the French part is now Togo (since 1958)

toil[1] (toil) ***vi.*** [[ME *toilen* < Anglo-Fr *toiler*, to strive, dispute < OFr *toeillier*, to pull about, begrime < L *tudiculare*, to stir about < *tudicula*, small machine for bruising olives < *tudes*, mallet < base of *tundere*, to beat < IE base *(s)teu- > STOCK, STUB]] 1 to work hard and continuously; labor 2 to proceed laboriously; advance or move with painful effort or difficulty [*to toil up a mountain*] —***vt.*** [Now Rare] to make or accomplish with great effort —***n.*** [[ME *toile* < Anglo-Fr *toil* < OFr *toeil*, turmoil, struggle < the v.]] 1 [Archaic] contention; struggle; strife 2 hard, exhausting work or effort; tiring labor 3 a task performed by such effort —**toil′er** ***n.***

toil[2] (toil) ***n.*** [[OFr *toile*, a net, web, cloth < L *tela*, web, woven material < base of *texere*: see TEXT]] 1 [Archaic] a net for trapping 2 [*pl.*] any snare suggestive of a net

toile (twäl) ***n.*** [[Fr: see prec.]] a sheer linen or cotton fabric

toile de Jouy (də zhwē) [[Fr, cloth of or from Jouy < *toile* (see TOIL[2]) + *de*, of, from + *Jouy(-en-Josas)*, town near Paris where orig. made]] a fabric of cotton or linen, usually white or off-white and printed in a single contrasting color with scenes of landscapes and people esp. from 18th-cent. French prints

toi·let (toi′lit) ***n.*** [[MFr *toilette*, orig., cloth covering used in shaving or hairdressing < OFr *toile*, cloth: see TOIL[2]]] 1 [Obs.] a dressing table 2 the process of dressing or grooming oneself, esp., of dressing one's hair 3 toilette; dress; attire; costume ☆4 *a)* a room, shelter, etc. in which to defecate or urinate; specif., a small room with a bowl-shaped porcelain fixture for this purpose *b)* such a fixture, usually with a hinged seat and seat cover, having a device for flushing with water or, sometimes, a chemical solution, which is held in an attached tank 5 the cleaning and dressing of a wound, esp. in surgery —***adj.*** 1 of or for dressing or grooming oneself [*toilet articles*] ☆2 for a TOILET (***n.*** 4*b*) [*a toilet brush*]

toilet paper (*or* **tissue**) soft, absorbent paper, usually in a roll, for use in cleaning oneself after evacuation

toi·let·ry (toi′lə trē) ***n.***, *pl.* **-ries** soap, lotion, cologne, etc. used in cleaning and grooming oneself

toi·lette (twä let′, toi-) ***n.*** [[Fr: see TOILET]] 1 the process of grooming and dressing oneself 2 dress; attire

toilet training the training of a young child to control defecation and urination

toilet water a lightly scented liquid with a high alcohol content, applied to the skin after bathing, etc. or added to bath water

toil·ful (toil′fəl) ***adj.*** full of toil; laborious

toil·some (-səm) ***adj.*** [[see -SOME[1]]] requiring or involving toil; laborious —**toil′some·ly** ***adv.*** —**toil′some·ness** ***n.***

toil·worn (-wôrn′) ***adj.*** showing the effects of toil

to-ing and fro-ing (to͞o′iŋ ən frō′iŋ) movement to and fro, vacillation back and forth, etc.

To·jo (tō′jo), **Hi·de·ki** (hē′de kē′) 1884-1948; Jpn. general & statesman: prime minister (1941-44)

to·ka·mak (tō′kə mak′) ***n.*** [[< Russ acronym for *torojdal'naja kamera s aksial'nym magnitnym polem*, toroidal chamber with axial magnetic field]] a reactor designed to control nuclear fusion in a plasma of ions and electrons inside a doughnut-shaped, or toroidal, magnetic bottle

To·kay (tō kā′) ***n.*** 1 *a)* a sweet or dry wine made in the vicinity of Tokaj, a region in NE Hungary *b)* a large, sweet grape used for this wine 2 a sweet wine blend of California

toke (tōk) [Slang] ***n.*** [[< ? fol.]] ☆a puff on a cigarette, esp. one of marijuana or hashish —☆***vi.*** **toked, tok′ing** to take such a puff —**tok′er** ***n.***

to·ken (tō′kən) ***n.*** [[ME < OE *tacn*, akin to Ger *zeichen* < IE base *deik-, to point, show > TEACH, TOE, DIGIT, DICTION]] 1 a sign, indication, or symbol [*a token of one's affection*] 2 something serving as a sign of authority, identity, genuineness, etc. 3 a distinguishing mark or feature 4 *a)* a keepsake *b)* a sample 5 a piece of stamped metal, etc. with a face value higher than its real value, issued as a substitute for currency, for use as fare on a transportation line, etc. 6 a person, as an employee, whose presence in a group is supposed to indicate absence of discrimination, as in race —***vt.*** to be a token of; symbolize —***adj.*** 1 by way of a token, symbol, etc. 2 merely simulated; slight or of no real account [*token resistance*] 3 of or having to do with tokenism —**SYN.** PLEDGE —**by the same token** for this reason; following the same line of reasoning —**in token of** as evidence of

to·ken·ism (-iz′əm) ***n.*** a show of accommodation to a demand, principle, etc. by small, often merely routine or superficial concessions to it; specif., the practice of hiring or including a small number of individuals, as of a minority group, merely to comply with equal-opportunity policies or regulations

token payment a partial payment made as a token of intention to pay the remainder of the debt later

To·khar·i·an (tō ker′ē ən, -kar′-, -kär′-) ***n., adj.*** *alt. sp. of* TOCHARIAN

to·ko·no·ma (tō′kə nō′mə) ***n.*** [[Jpn < *toko*, raised floor for flower displays, etc. + *no*, attributive suffix + *ma*, space, room]] a wall niche in a Japanese home for displaying a kakemono, flowers, etc.

To·ku·ga·wa (tō′ko͞o gä′wä) ***n.*** name of a Japanese noble family that held the shogunate and exercised control over Japan and its emperors (1603-1867)

To·ku·shi·ma (tō′ko͞o shē′mə) seaport in E Shikoku, Japan, on the Inland Sea

To·ky·o (tō′kē ō′, -kyō′) capital of Japan: seaport on an inlet (**Tokyo Bay**) of the Pacific, on S Honshu —**To′ky·o·ite′** (-īt′) ***n.***

to·la (tō′lä) ***n.*** [[Hindi < Sans *tulā*, a balance]] in India, a unit of weight equal to 180 grains troy (the weight of one silver rupee)

to·lan (tō′lan′) ***n.*** [[TOL(UENE) + -AN(E)]] a colorless, crystalline hydrocarbon, $C_6H_5C{:}CC_6H_5$, used chiefly in organic synthesis

to·lar (tō′lär) ***n.*** [[Slovenian]] the former basic monetary unit of Slovenia

tol·booth (tōl′bo͞oth′) ***n.*** [[ME *tolbothe*, booth where toll is collected: see TOLL[1] & BOOTH]] *alt. sp. of* TOLLBOOTH

☆**tol·bu·ta·mide** (täl byo͞ot′ə mīd′) ***n.*** [[TOL(U) + BUT(YRIC) + AMIDE]] an oral drug, $C_{12}H_{18}N_2O_3S$, that stimulates the pancreas to secrete more insulin, used to treat diabetes

told (tōld) ***vt., vi.*** *pt. & pp. of* TELL[1] —**all told** all (being) counted; in all [*there were forty attendees all told*]

tole[1] (tōl) ***vt.*** **toled, tol′ing** [[var. of TOLL[2]]] [Now Chiefly Dial.] to allure; entice

tole[2] (tōl) ***n.*** [[Fr *tôle*, sheet iron, plate < *taule*, dial. var. of *table*: see TABLE]] a type of lacquered or enameled metalware popular in the 18th cent. and reproduced today for trays, lamps, etc.: it is commonly dark-green, ivory, or black

To·le·do[1] (tə lē′dō) *n., pl.* **-dos** a fine-tempered sword or sword blade made in Toledo, Spain

To·le·do[2] (tə lē′dō; *for 2, Sp* tô lā′thô) **1** ⟦after the city in Spain⟧ city & port in NW Ohio, on Lake Erie **2** city in central Spain, on the Tagus River

tol·er·a·ble (täl′ər ə bəl) *adj.* ⟦ME *tollerabill* < MFr *tolérable* < L *tolerabilis*⟧ **1** that can be tolerated; endurable **2** fairly good; passable **3** [Informal] in reasonably good health —**tol′er·a·bil′i·ty** *n.* —**tol′er·a·bly** *adv.*

tol·er·ance (täl′ər əns) *n.* ⟦ME *tolleraunce* < MFr *tolerance* < L *tolerantia*⟧ **1** *a)* a tolerating or being tolerant, esp. of views, beliefs, practices, etc. of others that differ from one's own *b)* freedom from bigotry or prejudice **2** an allowable deviation from a standard or from the theoretical ideal, esp. in the manufacture or assembly of components; specif., *a)* the amount that coins are legally allowed to vary from a standard of weight, fineness, etc. *b)* the difference between the allowable maximum and minimum sizes of a part or fitting **3** the ability to endure **4** *Med.* the natural or developed ability to resist the effects of the continued or increasing use of a drug, etc.

tol·er·ant (täl′ər ənt) *adj.* ⟦L *tolerans*, prp.: see fol.⟧ **1** having or showing tolerance of others' beliefs, practices, etc. **2** *Med.* of or having tolerance —**tol′er·ant·ly** *adv.*

tol·er·ate (täl′ər āt′) *vt.* **-at′ed**, **-at′ing** ⟦< L *toleratus*, pp. of *tolerare*, to bear, sustain, tolerate < IE base **tel-*, to lift up, bear > THOLE[2], TALENT, L *tollere*, to lift up⟧ **1** to not interfere with; allow; permit [to *tolerate* heresy] **2** to recognize and respect (others' beliefs, practices, etc.) without sharing them **3** to bear, or put up with (someone or something not especially liked) **4** *Med.* to have tolerance for (a specific drug, etc.) —**SYN.** BEAR[1] —**tol′er·a′tive** *adj.* —**tol′er·a′tor** *n.*

tol·er·a·tion (täl′ər ā′shən) *n.* ⟦Fr *tolération* < L *toleratio*⟧ **1** the act or an instance of tolerating **2** tolerance; esp., freedom to hold religious views that differ from the established ones —**tol′er·a′tion·ist** *n.*

tol·i·dine (täl′ə dēn′, -din) *n.* ⟦TOL(UOL) + (BENZ)IDINE⟧ any of a group of isomeric dimethyl derivatives of benzidine, $C_{14}H_{16}N_2$, used in the manufacture of dyes and in the detection of gold and chlorine

To·li·ma (tə lē′mə; *Sp* tô lē′mä) volcanic mountain of the Andes, in WC Colombia: 16,207 ft (4,940 m)

Tol·kien (täl′kēn′, tōl′-), **J(ohn) R(onald) R(euel)** 1892-1973; Eng. novelist & scholar

toll[1] (tōl) *n.* ⟦ME < OE, akin to Ger *zoll*, ON *tollr* < MLowG *tol* < ML *tolneum* < VL **toloneum*, toll(house), for L *teloneum* < Gr *telōnion* < *telōnēs*, tax collector < *telos*, tax, akin to *tlēnai*, to support, bear: for IE base see TOLERATE⟧ **1** a tax or charge for a privilege, esp. for permission to pass over a bridge, along a highway, etc. **2** a charge for service or extra service, as for transportation, for a long-distance telephone call, or, formerly, for having one's grain milled **3** the number lost, taken, exacted, etc.; exaction [the tornado took a heavy *toll* of lives] —*vi.* [Now Rare] to collect a toll or tolls —*vt.* [Now Rare] **1** to take or gather as a toll **2** to impose a toll on

toll[2] (tōl) *vt.* ⟦ME *tollen*, to pull, ? akin to OE *-tyllan*, to mislead < IE base **del-* > TALE⟧ **1** [Now Chiefly Dial.] to allure or entice; esp., to decoy (game, etc.) **2** *a)* to ring (a church bell, etc.) slowly with regularly repeated strokes, esp. for announcing a death *b)* to sound (the hour, a knell, etc.) by this *c)* to announce, summon, or dismiss by this *d)* to announce the death of (someone) in this way —*vi.* to sound or ring slowly in regularly repeated strokes: said of a bell —*n.* **1** the act of tolling a bell **2** the sound of a bell tolling **3** a single stroke of the bell —**toll′er** *n.*

toll·age (tōl′ij) *n.* **1** a toll, or tax **2** payment of or demand for a toll

toll bar a bar, gate, etc. for stopping travel at a point where tolls are taken

toll·booth (tōl′bōōth′) *n.* **1** a booth at which tolls are collected, as at the entrance to a toll road **2** [Now Chiefly Scot.] *a)* a town hall *b)* a jail or prison

toll bridge a bridge at which tolls are paid for passage

toll call a long-distance telephone call, for which there is a charge beyond the local rate

toll-free (tōl′frē′) *adj.* designating or of telephone calls, numbers, etc. for which the receiver of the call is charged but not the caller —*adv.* without charge to the caller in a long-distance call

toll·gate (tōl′gāt′) *n.* a gate for stopping travel at a point where tolls are taken

toll·house (-hous′) *n.* **1** a house at a tollgate, in which the tollkeeper lives **2** a booth, etc. where tolls are taken

☆**tollhouse cookie** ⟦after the *Toll House* Inn in Whitman, Mass., where first made (1930s); *Toll House* is now a trademark⟧ a kind of chocolate chip cookie

toll·keep·er (-kēp′ər) *n.* a collector of tolls at a tollgate

toll road a road for travel on which tolls must be paid: also **toll′way′** (-wā′) *n.*

Tol·stoy *or* **Tol·stoi** (tōl′stoi′, täl′-; *Russ* tôl stoi′), Count **Leo Ni·ko·la·ye·vich** (nē′kô lä′ye vich′) 1828-1910; Russ. novelist & social theoretician: Russ. given name *Lev* —**Tol·stoy′an** *adj.*, **Tol·stoi′an**

Tol·tec (täl′tek′, tōl′-) *n.* ⟦MexSp *Tolteca* < Nahuatl *to:lte:kaλ*, lit., person from *to:lla:n*, Tula (ancient Toltec city) < *to:lin*, cattail⟧ a member of an ancient Amerindian people that lived in Mexico before the Aztecs —*adj.* of the Toltecs or their culture: also **Tol′tec′an**

to·lu (tō lōō′) *n.* ⟦Sp *tolú*, after *Tolú*, Caribbean seaport in Colombia⟧ a fragrant gum obtained from the bark of a leguminous South American tree (*Myroxylon balsamum*), used in cough mixtures, flavorings, perfumes, etc.: also **tolu balsam**

tol·u·ate (täl′yōō āt′) *n.* a salt or ester of toluic acid

To·lu·ca (tə lōō′kə; *Sp* tô lōō′kä) **1** city in S Mexico: capital of México state: in full **Toluca de Ler·do** (də ler′dō; *Sp* dā ler′thô) **2** volcanic mountain near this city: 15,020 ft (4,578 m)

tol·u·ene (täl′yōō ēn′) *n.* ⟦TOLU + (BENZ)ENE⟧ a colorless, liquid, flammable, poisonous hydrocarbon, $C_6H_5CH_3$, obtained originally from balsam of Tolu but now generally from coal tar or petroleum, and used in making dyes, explosives, etc. and as a solvent

to·lu·ic acid (tō lōō′ik, täl′yōō ik) any of four isomeric acids, $C_6H_4CH_3$ COOH, carboxyl derivatives of toluene, used in the manufacture of various resins, in organic synthesis, etc.

tol·u·ide (täl′yōō īd′) *n.* any of a class of chemical compounds having the general formula $RCONHC_6H_4CH_3$, derived from the toluidines by the substitution of an acid radical for one of the amino H atoms Also **to·lu·i·dide** (tə lōō′i dīd′)

to·lu·i·dine (tō lōō′ə dēn′, -din) *n.* any of three isomeric amino derivatives, $CH_3C_6H_4NH_2$, of toluene, used in organic synthesis, in dyes, as a test reagent, etc.

toluidine blue a dark green powder, $C_{15}H_{16}N_3SCl \cdot ZnCl_2$, used in dyeing textiles, as a biological stain, as a coagulant in medicine, etc.

tol·u·ol (täl′yōō ôl′, -ōl′) *n.* ⟦TOLU + -OL[1]⟧ toluene; esp., crude commercial toluene

tolu tree the tree that yields tolu

tol·u·yl (täl′yōō il) *n.* ⟦TOLU(IC ACID) + -YL⟧ the monovalent radical $CH_3C_6H_5CO$

tol·yl (täl′il) *n.* ⟦TOL(UIC ACID) + -YL⟧ the monovalent radical $CH_3C_6H_4$, derived from toluene

Tom[1] (täm) *n.* **1** a masculine name: see THOMAS[1] **2** ⟦infl. esp. by TOMCAT, earlier *Tom the Cat*: cf. similar use of JACK⟧ [**t-**] the male of some animals, esp. of the cat —*adj.* [**t-**] male [a *tom* turkey] The *adj.* and *n.* 2 are sometimes used in compounds, occasionally with derived senses, as *tomcod*

Tom[2] (täm) [Informal] *n.* ☆UNCLE TOM —☆*vi.* **Tommed, Tom′ming** [*also* **t-**] to behave like an Uncle Tom A term of contempt

☆**tom·a·hawk** (täm′ə hôk′) *n.* ⟦Virginia (Algonquian) *tamahaac*, lit., tool for cutting off⟧ a light ax, typically having a stone or bone head, used by North American Indians as a tool and a weapon —*vt.* to hit, cut, or kill with a tomahawk

tom·al·ley (täm′al′ē) *n.* ⟦Carib *taumali*⟧ the liver of the lobster, which turns green when boiled and is considered a delicacy

Tom and Jerry (täm′ ən jer′ē) ⟦after two characters (1821) created by Brit writer Pierce Egan for the journal *Life in London*⟧ ☆a hot drink made of rum and brandy or whiskey, beaten eggs, sugar, water or milk, and nutmeg

☆**to·ma·til·lo** (tō′mə tē′ō) *n., pl.* **-los** ⟦AmSp, dim of *tomate*, fol.⟧ **1** a small, round fruit with a papery husk, used as a vegetable in Mexican cooking: yellow to purple when ripe, but cooked while still green **2** the plant (*Physalis ixocarpa*) on which this fruit grows

to·ma·to (tə māt′ō, -mät′ō) *n., pl.* **-toes** ⟦Sp *tomate* < Nahuatl *tomaλ*⟧ **1** a red or yellowish fruit with a juicy pulp, used as a vegetable: botanically it is a berry **2** the annual plant (*Lycopersicon esculentum*) of the nightshade family, on which this berry grows ☆**3** [Old Slang] an attractive young woman

tomato hornworm a hawk moth (*Manduca quinquemaculata*) whose large, green caterpillar feeds on tomato plants

tomb (tōōm) *n.* ⟦ME *toumbe* < Anglo-Fr *tumbe* (OFr *tombe*) < LL(Ec) *tumba* < Gr *tymbos*, tomb, funeral mound < IE **tu-*, var. of base **teu-*, to swell > THUMB, TUMOR⟧ **1** a vault, chamber, or grave for the dead **2** a burial monument or cenotaph —*vt.* [Rare] to entomb —**the tomb** death —**tomb′less** *adj.* —**tomb′like′** *adj.*

tom·bac or **tom·bak** (täm′bak′) *n.* ⟦Fr *tombac* < Port *tambaca* < Malay *tembaga*, brass or copper < Sans *tamṛka*, lit., dark metal < *tāmrá-*, dark red < IE **temsro-* < base **tem-*, dark > TEMERITY⟧ any of several alloys of copper and zinc, used in making cheap jewelry

Tom·baugh (täm′bô′), **Clyde William** 1906-97; U.S. astronomer: discovered Pluto (1930)

Tom·big·bee (täm big′bē) ⟦< Choctaw, coffin maker < *itombi*, box, coffin + *ikbi*, maker: referring to burial boxes used by Choctaws⟧ river flowing from NE Miss. through Ala., joining the Alabama River to form the Mobile River: 409 mi (658 km)

tom·bo·la (täm bō′lə, täm′bə lə) *n.* ⟦It, prob. < *tombolare*, to tumble⟧ a British gambling game somewhat like bingo

tom·bo·lo (täm′bə lō′) *n., pl.* **-los′** ⟦It < L *tumulus*, a mound: see TUMULUS⟧ a bar of sand or other sediment connecting an island to the mainland or another island

Tom·bouc·tou (tōn bōōk tōō′) town in central Mali, near the Niger River

tom·boy (täm′boi′) *n.* ⟦see TOM[1]⟧ a girl who behaves or plays like an active boy —**tom′boy′ish** *adj.* —**tom′boy′ish·ly** *adv.* —**tom′boy′ish·ness** *n.*

tomb·stone (tōōm′stōn′) *n.* a stone or monument, usually with an engraved inscription, marking a tomb or grave

Tomb·stone (tōōm′stōn′) city in SE Ariz.: famous as a frontier town in the late 19th cent.

tom·cat (täm′kat′) *n.* ⟦see TOM[1]⟧ a male cat —*vi.* **-cat′ted**, **-cat′ting** [Slang] to be sexually promiscuous: said of a man

☆**tom·cod** (-käd′) *n.* ⟦see TOM[1]⟧ any of a genus (*Microgadus*) of small, marine, gadoid food fishes

Tom Collins *see* COLLINS[1]

Tom, Dick, and Harry everyone or anyone; people taken at random: usually preceded by *every* and used dismissively: also **Tom, Dick, or Harry**

tome (tōm) ***n.*** ⟦Fr < L *tomus* < Gr *tomos*, piece cut off, hence part of a book, volume < *temnein*, to cut: see -TOMY⟧ **1** [Obs.] any volume of a work of several volumes **2** a book, esp. a large, scholarly or ponderous one

-tome (tōm) ⟦Gr < *tomon* < *tomos*: see prec.⟧ *combining form* **1** cutting instrument [*microtome*] **2** section, division [*dermatome*]

to·men·tose (tō men′tōs, tō′mən tōs′) ***adj.*** ⟦ModL *tomentosus* < L *tomentum*: see fol.⟧ *Biol.* covered with a dense layer of short, matted, woolly hairs

to·men·tum (tō men′təm) ***n.***, *pl.* **-ta** (-tə) ⟦ModL < L, a stuffing (of hair, wool, etc.): for IE base see THUMB⟧ **1** a growth of short, matted, woolly hairs, as on a stem or leaf **2** a network of very small blood vessels in the pia mater and the cortex of the cerebrum

tom·fool (täm′fo͞ol′) [Old-fashioned] ***n.*** ⟦earlier *Tom Fool*, as in *Tom o'Bedlam, poor Tom*, names formerly applied to the demented and the mentally retarded⟧ a foolish, stupid, or silly person —***adj.*** foolish, stupid, or silly

tom·fool·er·y (täm′fo͞ol′ər ē) ***n.***, *pl.* **-er·ies** ⟦see prec. + -ERY⟧ foolish behavior; silliness; nonsense

-tom·ic (täm′ik) *combining form* of or relating to cutting, division, sections, etc.

Tom·my (täm′ē) ***n.***, *pl.* **-mies** ⟦clipped from *Tommy Atkins* (for *Thomas Atkins*, fictitious name used in Brit army sample forms)⟧ [*also* **t-**] [Brit. Informal] a private in the British army

☆**tommy gun** [*sometimes* **T- g-**] [Informal] a THOMPSON SUBMACHINE GUN or other kind of early submachine gun

☆**Tommy John surgery** ⟦after U.S. baseball pitcher *Tommy John*, who underwent this procedure successfully (1974)⟧ surgery in which a damaged ligament in the elbow is replaced with a tendon graft

tom·my·rot (täm′ē rät′) ***n.*** ⟦< the nickname *Tommy*, in dial. sense of "fool" (see TOMFOOL) + ROT⟧ [Slang] nonsense; foolishness

to·mo·gram (tō′mə gram′) ***n.*** an image made by tomography

to·mog·ra·phy (tə mäg′rə fē) ***n.*** ⟦< Gr *tomos*, a piece cut off (see -TOMY) + -GRAPHY⟧ a process for producing an image of a single plane of an object excluding all other planes, as by using CT SCAN or ULTRASOUND, in diagnostic medicine, seismic surveys, etc.

to·mor·row (tə mär′ō, -môr′ō) ***adv.*** ⟦ME *to morwe* < *to morwen* < OE *to morgen*: see TO[1] & MORNING⟧ **1** on or during the day after today **2** at some time in the indefinite future —***n.*** **1** the day after today **2** some time in the indefinite future —***adj.*** of tomorrow [*tomorrow* morning]

tom·pi·on (täm′pē ən) ***n.*** *var. of* TAMPION

Tomsk (tämsk) city in SW Siberia

Tom Thumb a tiny hero of many English folk tales

tom·tit (täm tit′, täm′tit′) ***n.*** ⟦see TOM[1]⟧ [Chiefly Brit.] a titmouse or any of various other small birds

tom-tom (täm′täm′) ***n.*** ⟦Hindi *ṭamṭam*: see TAM-TAM⟧ **1** any of various drums, as of Indian or African tribes, usually beaten with the hands **2** a kind of drum used in jazz and popular music that has a sound higher and less resonant than a bass drum

-to·my (tə mē) ⟦ModL *-tomia* < Gr < *tomē*, a cutting < *temnein*, to cut < IE base **tem-*, to cut > L *tondere*, to shear⟧ *combining form* **1** a dividing [*dichotomy*] **2** an incision; a (specified) surgical operation [*ovariotomy, lobotomy*]

ton[1] (tun) ***n.***, *pl.* **tons**; sometimes, after a number, **ton** ⟦var. (differentiated in 17th c. for senses "weight, measure") of TUN⟧ **1** a unit of weight, equal to 2,000 pounds avoirdupois (907.1847 kilograms or 0.90718 metric ton or 0.8929 long ton), commonly used in the U.S., Canada, South Africa, etc.: in full **short ton** **2** a unit of weight, equal to 2,240 pounds avoirdupois (1,016.0469 kilograms or 1.016 metric tons or 1.12 short tons), commonly used in Great Britain: in full **long ton** **3** METRIC TON **4** a unit of internal capacity of ships, equal to 100 cubic feet (or 2.8317 cubic meters): in full **register ton** **5** a unit of carrying capacity of ships, usually equal to 40 cubic feet: also called *measurement ton* or *freight ton* **6** a unit for measuring displacement of ships, equal to 35 cubic feet: it is approximately equal to the volume of a long ton of sea water: in full **displacement ton** ☆**7** ⟦so named from being equal to the amount of heat needed to freeze one *ton* of water in 24 hours⟧ a unit of cooling capacity of an air conditioner, equal to 12,000 Btu per hour **8** [*often pl.*] [Informal] a very large amount or number Abbrev. *T, t*, or *tn*

ton[2] (tōn; *E*, tōn) ***n.*** ⟦Fr: see TONE⟧ [*often not in italics*] style; vogue —**the *ton*** fashionable society

ton·al (tō′nəl) ***adj.*** ⟦ML *tonalis*⟧ of a tone or tonality —**ton′al·ly *adv.***

to·nal·i·ty (tō nal′ə tē) ***n.***, *pl.* **-ties** **1** quality of tone **2** *Art* the color scheme of a painting **3** *Music* *a)* in composition, the organization of tones around a central or pivotal tone or pitch class *b)* in music based on the major-minor system, KEY[1] (sense 11*b*)

ton·do (tän′dō) ***n.***, *pl.* **-di** (-dē) or **-dos** ⟦It, a plate, orig. round, aphetic for *rotondo* < L *rotundus*: see ROTUND⟧ a round painting

tone (tōn) ***n.*** ⟦ME < OFr & L: OFr *ton* < L *tonus*, a sound < Gr *tonos*, a stretching, tone < *teinein*, to stretch: see THIN⟧ **1** *a)* a vocal or musical sound *b)* its quality **2** an intonation, pitch, modulation, etc. of the voice that expresses a particular meaning or feeling of the speaker [*a tone of* contempt] **3** a certain attitude on the part of a speaker or writer conveyed by way of word choice, sentence structure, etc. [the friendly *tone* of her letter] **4** normal resilience or elasticity [rubber that has lost its *tone*] **5** *a)* the prevailing or predominant style, character, spirit, trend, morale, or state of morals of a place or period [the cultured *tone* of their house] *b)* distinctive style; elegance [paintings that lent the room *tone*] **6** *a)* a quality or value of color; tint; shade *b)* any of the slight modifications of a particular color; hue [three *tones* of green] **7** *Linguis.* *a)* the relative height of pitch with which a syllable, word, etc. is pronounced *b)* the relative height of pitch that is a phoneme of a language and distinguishes meaning, as in the tone languages **8** *Music* *a)* a sound that is distinct and identifiable by its regularity of vibration, or constant pitch (as distinguished from a noise), and that may be put into harmonic relation with other such sounds *b)* the simple or fundamental tone of a musical sound as distinguished from its overtones *c)* any one of the full intervals of a diatonic scale; whole step *d)* any of several recitation melodies used in singing the psalms in plainsong **9** *Painting* the effect produced by the combination of light, shade, and color **10** *Physiol.* *a)* the condition of an organism, organ, or part with reference to its normal, healthy functioning *b)* the normal tension, or resistance to stretch, of a healthy muscle, independent of that caused by voluntary innervation; tonus —***vt.*** **toned**, **ton′ing** **1** [Rare] INTONE **2** to give a tone to; specif., to give the proper or desired tone to (a musical instrument, a painting, etc.) **3** to change the tone of **4** *Photog.* to change or alter the color of (a print) by chemical means —***vi.*** to assume a tone —**tone down** **1** to give a lower or less intense tone to **2** to become softened **3** to make (something written or said) less harsh or more moderate —**tone in with** to harmonize with —**tone up** **1** to give a higher or more intense tone to **2** to become strengthened or heightened —**tone′less *adj.*** —**tone′less·ly *adv.*** —**tone′less·ness *n.***

☆**T1** (tē′wun′) ***n.*** a broadband, digital, data-transmission system for multiplexing signals over a telephone line, as for voice communication, at 1.54 million bps

tone·arm (tōn′ärm′) ***n.*** **1** PICKUP (***n.*** 7*b*) **2** the pivoted arm on a phonograph turntable, holding the CARTRIDGE (***n.*** 4)

tone cluster a number of close musical tones (not a chord) sounded together, as on a piano

tone color TIMBRE

tone control a control device, as on a high-fidelity amplifier, for varying the intensity of high and low frequencies

tone-deaf (tōn′def′) ***adj.*** **1** not able to distinguish accurately differences in musical pitch **2** [Informal] *a)* of or demonstrating an inability to recognize the complexity, possible cause for offense, etc. of an issue or situation *b)* of or showing a lack of sensitivity to the effect that one's statements or positions have on others —**tone′-deaf′ness *n.***

tone language a language, as Chinese or some Bantu or Southeast Asian languages, in which pitch variation is used to distinguish words that would otherwise sound alike

tone poem SYMPHONIC POEM

ton·er (tō′nər) ***n.*** **1** a powdery substance used in photocopiers, laser printers, etc. that forms the text and images on paper **2** a facial cleanser, usually containing alcohol, and astringent to varying degrees

tone row (*or* **series**) the group of pitches, arranged in an arbitrary and unique order, which serves as the basis of a composition in twelve-tone or serial music

to·net·ic (tō net′ik) ***adj.*** ⟦TON(E) + (PHON)ETIC⟧ of or having to do with a tone language —**to·net′i·cal·ly *adv.***

tone·y (tō′nē) ***adj.*** *alt. sp. of* TONY

☆**tong[1]** (tôŋ, täŋ) ***vt.*** to seize, collect, handle, or hold with tongs —***vi.*** to use tongs —**tong′er *n.***

☆**tong[2]** (tôŋ, täŋ) ***n.*** ⟦Mandarin *t'ang*, hall, meeting place, society⟧ **1** a Chinese association or political party **2** in the U.S., a Chinese secret fraternal society

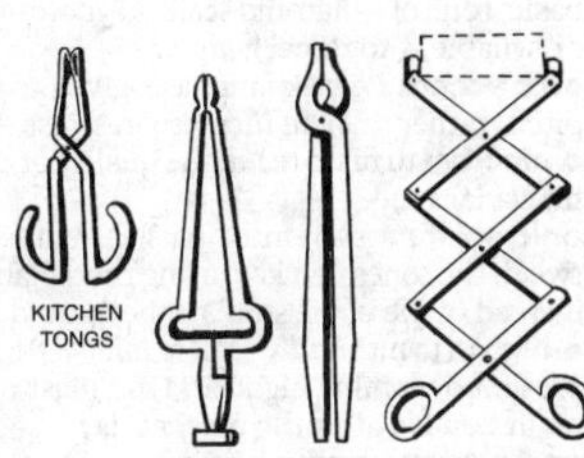

ton·ga (täŋ′gə) ***n.*** ⟦Hindi *tāṅgā*⟧ a two-wheeled carriage of India

Ton·ga (täŋ′gə) kingdom occupying a group of islands (**Tonga Islands**) in the SW Pacific, east of Fiji; member of the Commonwealth: 289 sq mi (748 sq km); cap. Nukualofa

Ton·gan (täŋ′gən) ***n.*** ⟦< a Polynesian language; ult. < Proto-Polynesian **tonga*, south, south wind⟧ **1** a person born or living in Tonga **2** the Polynesian language spoken by the Tongans

tongs (tôŋz, täŋz) ***pl.n.*** ⟦ME *tongys*, pl. of *tonge* < OE *tange*, akin to Ger *zange* < IE base **denk-*, to bite: basic sense "those that bite together"⟧ [*sometimes with sing. v.*] a device for seizing or lifting objects, having two long arms pivoted or hinged together: also called **pair of tongs**

tongue (tuŋ) ***n.*** ⟦ME *tunge* < OE, akin to Ger *zunge* < IE base **dŋĝhū-*, tongue > L *lingua* (OL *dingua*)⟧ **1** the movable muscular structure attached to the floor of the mouth in most vertebrates: it is an important organ in the ingestion of food, the perception of taste, and, in humans, the articulation of speech sounds **2** an analogous part in invertebrate animals; specif., *a)* a radula *b)* the proboscis in certain insects, as bees **3** an animal's tongue used as food **4** *a)* the human tongue as the organ of speech *b)* ideas expressed by speaking; talk; speech *c)* the act or power of speaking *d)* a manner or style of speaking, with reference to tone, diction, etc. [a glib *tongue*] **5** *a)* a language or dialect *b)* in the Bible, a nation or people speaking a distinct language: Rev. 7:9 **6** [*pl.*] *see* GLOSSOLALIA **7** the cry of a hunting dog, etc. in sight of game: chiefly in **give tongue**, to start barking **8** something resembling a tongue in shape, position, movement, or use; specif., *a)* the flap under the laces or strap of a shoe *b)* the clapper of a bell *c)* the pin of a buckle, etc. *d)* the pole of a wagon, etc. *e)* a projecting ridge along the edge of a board, that fits into a corresponding groove on another board to form a tongue-and-groove joint *f)* in machines, a projecting flange, rib, etc. *g)* a thin strip of flexible material, as cane, that produces a musical sound when vibrated, as in a wind instrument *h)* a narrow strip of land, ice, etc. extending into a body of water, an intrusion, etc. *i)* a narrow inlet of water *j)* a long, narrow flame *k)* the pointer of a scale, etc. —*vt.* **tongued, tongu′ing 1** [Archaic] *a)* to reproach or scold *b)* to speak or say **2** to touch, lick, etc. with the tongue **3** *a)* to cut a TONGUE (sense 8*e*) on *b)* to join by means of a tongue-and-groove joint **4** *Music* to play by tonguing: see TONGUING —*vi.* **1** [Rare] to talk or talk much **2** to project like a tongue **3** *Music* to use tonguing: see TONGUING —**find one's tongue** to recover the ability to talk, as after shock or embarrassment —**hold one's tongue** to refrain from speaking —**on everyone's tongue** prevailing as common gossip —**on the tip of someone's** (or **the**) **tongue 1** almost said by someone **2** about to be said, esp. because almost but not quite recalled —**speak in tongues** to engage in glossolalia —**(with) tongue in cheek** in a humorously ironic, mocking, or insincere way

tongue-and-groove joint (tuŋ′ʼn gro͞ov′) a kind of joint in which a tongue on one board fits exactly into a groove in another

-tongued (tuŋd) *combining form* having a (specified kind of) tongue [*loose-tongued*]

tongue-in-cheek (tuŋ′ʼn chēk′) *adj.* humorously ironic, mocking, or insincere

tongue-lash (tuŋ′lash′) *vt.* [Informal] to scold or reprove harshly; reprimand —**tongue′-lash′ing** *n.*

tongue-and-groove joint

tongue·less (tuŋ′lis) *adj.* **1** having no tongue **2** speechless

tongue-tie (tuŋ′tī′) *n.* limited motion of the tongue, usually caused by a short frenum and resulting in indistinct articulation —*vt.* **-tied′, -ty′ing** to make tongue-tied

tongue-tied (-tīd′) *adj.* **1** having a condition of tongue-tie **2** speechless or inarticulate from amazement, embarrassment, etc.

tongue twister a phrase or sentence that is hard to say fast, usually because of alliteration or a sequence of nearly similar sounds (Ex.: six sick sheiks)

tongu·ing (tuŋ′iŋ) *n.* the use of the tongue in playing a musical wind instrument, esp. for more accurate intonation of rapid notes

ton·ic (tän′ik) *adj.* ⟦Gr *tonikos* < *tonos*: see TONE⟧ **1** of, producing, or tending to produce good muscular tone, or tension **2** mentally or morally invigorating; stimulating **3** having to do with tones; specif., *a)* *Music* designating or based on the first tone (*keynote*) of a diatonic scale [*a tonic* chord] *b)* *Painting* having to do with the tone or tones of a picture *c)* [Now Rare] *Phonet.* designating or of sounds characterized by resonance in the head cavities; also, accented **4** *Med., Physiol.* of or characterized by tone, or tonus —*n.* **1** anything that invigorates or stimulates; specif., *a)* a drug, medicine, or other agent for restoring or increasing body tone *b)* a hair or scalp dressing **2** *a)* a carbonated beverage flavored with a little quinine and served in a mixed drink with gin, vodka, etc.; quinine water (in full **tonic water**) *b)* [Chiefly Northeast] SODA POP **3** *Music* the first, or basic, tone of a diatonic scale; keynote **4** [Now Rare] *Phonet.* a tonic sound or syllable —**ton′i·cal·ly** *adv.*

tonic accent *Phonet.* emphasis given to a syllable by change, esp. a rise, in pitch, rather than an increase in stress

to·nic·i·ty (tō nis′ə tē) *n.* the quality or condition of having good or normal muscular tone

tonic sol-fa a system of musical notation based on the relationship between the tones of a key, using the syllables of solmization (*do, re, mi*, etc.) instead of the usual staff symbols: used in teaching singing

to·night (tə nīt′) *adv.* ⟦ME *to niht* < OE: see TO[1] & NIGHT⟧ **1** on or during the present or coming night **2** [Obs.] last night —*n.* **1** the present night **2** the night coming after the present day

ton·ka bean (täŋ′kə) ⟦prob. < Tupí name in Guiana⟧ **1** the fragrant, almond-shaped seed of any of several South American leguminous trees (genus *Dipteryx*) used in perfumes, drugs, etc. **2** the tree

Ton·kin (tän′kin, tän′kin′) **1** historical region and former French protectorate in NE Indochina: the N part of Vietnam **2 Gulf of** arm of the South China Sea between Hainan Island & the coasts of S China & N Vietnam —**Ton′kin·ese′** (-ēz′, -ēs′) *adj., n., pl.* **-ese′**

Ton·le Sap (tän′lā säp′, sap′) **1** lake in central Cambodia: area varies from 1,000-9,500 sq mi (2,590-24,605 sq km) according to season **2** river flowing from this lake into the Mekong River: *c.* 70 mi (113 km)

ton·nage (tun′ij) *n.* ⟦ME < MFr: see TUN & -AGE⟧ **1** a duty or tax on ships, based on tons carried **2** a charge per ton on cargo or freight on a canal, at a port, etc. **3** the total amount of shipping of a country or port, calculated in tons **4** *a)* the carrying capacity of a ship, expressed in register tons (see TON[1], sense 4) *b)* the weight of water displaced by a warship, expressed in long tons (see TON[1], sense 2) **5** weight in tons

tonne (tun) *n.* ⟦Fr, TON[1]⟧ a metric ton; 1,000 kg

ton·neau (tu nō′, tän′ō′) *n., pl.* **-neaus′** or **-neaux′** (-nōz′) ⟦Fr, lit., a cask < *tonne*: see TUN⟧ **1** an enclosed rear compartment for passengers in an early type of automobile **2** the whole body of such an automobile ☆**3** a protective cover for the passenger compartment of a small, open sports car, for the bed of a pickup truck, etc.

to·nom·e·ter (tō näm′ət ər) *n.* ⟦< Gr *tonos*, TONE + -METER⟧ **1** an instrument for determining the pitch of a tone; specif., a tuning fork or, esp., a set of tuning forks **2** an instrument for measuring vapor pressure **3** *Med., Physiol.* any of various instruments for measuring tension, as of the eyeball, or pressure, as of the blood —**ton·o·met·ric** (tän′ə me′trik, tō′nə-) *adj.* —**to·nom′e·try** *n.*

ton·sil (tän′səl) *n.* ⟦L *tonsillae*, pl., dim. of *tōlēs* (< **tonsles*), goiter⟧ either of a pair of oval masses of lymphoid tissue, one on each side of the throat at the back of the mouth —**ton′sil·lar** *adj.*

ton·sil·lec·to·my (tän′sə lek′tə mē) *n., pl.* **-mies** ⟦prec. + -ECTOMY⟧ the surgical removal of the tonsils

ton·sil·li·tis (tän′sə līt′is) *n.* ⟦ModL < L *tonsillae*, tonsils + *-itis*, -ITIS⟧ inflammation of the tonsils —**ton′sil·lit′ic** (-lit′ik) *adj.*

ton·sil·lot·o·my (tän′sə lät′ə mē) *n., pl.* **-mies** ⟦< L *tonsillae*, tonsils + -TOMY⟧ the surgical incision, or a partial removal, of a tonsil

ton·so·ri·al (tän sôr′ē əl) *adj.* ⟦L *tonsorius*, of clipping < *tonsor*, clipper < *tonsus*, pp. of *tondere*, to shear: see -TOMY⟧ of a barber or barbering: often used humorously [*a tonsorial* artist]

ton·sure (tän′shər) *n.* ⟦ME < MFr < L *tonsura* < *tonsus*: see prec.⟧ **1** a clipping off or shaving off of part or all of the hair of the head, done esp. formerly as a signal of entrance into the clerical or monastic state **2** the head area so clipped or shaved —*vt.* **-sured, -sur·ing** to clip or shave the head hair of for such a purpose

tonsure

ton·tine (tän′tēn′, tän tēn′) *n.* ⟦Fr < It *tontina*, after Lorenzo *Tonti*, Neapolitan banker who introduced the system into France in the 17th c.⟧ **1** *a)* a fund to which a group of persons contribute, the benefits ultimately accruing to the last survivor or to those surviving after a specified time *b)* the subscribers to such a fund, collectively *c)* the total fund or the share of each subscriber **2** any annuity or insurance system of this kind

to·nus (tō′nəs) *n.* ⟦ModL < L: see TONE⟧ the slight, continuous partial contraction characteristic of a normal relaxed muscle: see CLONUS

☆**ton·y** (tō′nē) *adj.* **ton′i·er, ton′i·est** [Slang] high-toned; luxurious; stylish: often ironic

To·ny[1] (tō′nē) *n.* a masculine and feminine name: see ANTHONY[1], ANTOINETTE

To·ny[2] (tō′nē) *n., pl.* **-nys** or **-nies** ⟦< *Tony Awards*, a service mark, after *Antoinette* Perry (1888-1946), U.S. theatrical figure⟧ ☆any of the awards given annually in the U.S. for special achievement in the theater in acting, directing, etc.

Ton·ya (tän′yə, tōn′-) *n.* ⟦shortened & altered < ANTONIA⟧ a feminine name: dim. *Toni;* var. *Tonia*: see ANTONIA

too (to͞o) *adv.* ⟦stressed form of TO[1], with differentiated sp.⟧ **1** in addition; as well; besides; also **2** more than enough; superfluously; overly [the hat is *too* big] **3** to a regrettable extent [that's *too* bad!] **4** extremely; very [it was just *too* delicious!]

USAGE—*too* is often used as a mere emphatic [I will *too* go!] and is sometimes construed as an adjective in modifying *much, little*, etc. [there was not *too* much to see]

too·dle-oo (to͞od′ʼl o͞o′) *interj.* ⟦orig. uncert.⟧ [Informal] goodbye

took (to͝ok) *vt., vi. pt. of* TAKE

tool (to͞ol) *n.* ⟦ME *toole* < OE *tol*, akin to ON *tol* < ? IE base **deu-* > TAW[2]⟧ **1** any implement, instrument, or utensil held in the hand and used to form, shape, fasten, add to, take away from, or otherwise change something by cutting, hitting, digging, rubbing, etc.: knives, saws, hammers, shovels, rakes, etc. are tools **2** *a)* any similar instrument that is the working part of a power-driven machine, as a drill, band-saw blade, etc. *b)* the whole machine; machine tool **3** anything that serves in the manner of a tool; a means [books are a scholar's *tools*] **4** a person used to accomplish another's purposes, esp. when these are illegal or unethical; dupe; stooge **5** [Slang] the penis: somewhat vulgar **6** *Law* any instrument or device necessary to one's profession or occupation: in full **tools of one's trade** —*vt.* **1** to form, shape, or work with a tool **2** to provide tools or machinery for (a factory, industry, etc.): often with *up* **3** *a)* to drive (a vehicle) *b)* to convey (a person) in a vehicle **4** to impress letters or designs on (leather, a book cover, etc.) with special tools —*vi.* **1** to use a tool or tools **2** to get or install the tools, equipment, etc. needed: often with *up* **3** [Informal] to ride in or drive a vehicle, often, specif., in a leisurely or careless manner: often with *around* or *about* —*SYN.* IMPLEMENT —**tool′er** *n.*

tool·box (to͞ol′bäks′) *n.* a box or chest, usually compartmentalized, in which tools are kept: also **tool chest**

tool·ing (to͞ol′iŋ) *n.* **1** work or decoration done with tools **2** the process of fitting out a factory with machine tools in readiness for going into production

tool·mak·er (to͞ol′māk′ər) *n.* a machinist who makes, maintains, and repairs machine tools —**tool′mak′ing** *n.*

tool·room (-ro͞om′) *n.* a room, as in a machine shop, where tools are stored, kept in repair, issued to workers, etc.

tool·shed (-shed′) *n.* a small structure, as at the back of a house, where tools are kept: also **tool′house′** (-hous′)

toon[1] (to͞on) ***n.*** ⟦Hindi *tūn* < Sans *tunna*⟧ **1** a large Australian and East Indian tree (*Cedrela toona*) of the mahogany family, with soft, closegrained, reddish wood used in furniture: its flowers yield a dye **2** its wood

toon[2] (to͞on) ***n.*** ⟦short for CARTOON⟧ [Informal] **1** a cartoon, esp. an animated cartoon **2** a character in a cartoon, esp. an animated cartoon Sometimes written **'toon** or **Toon**

toon·ie (to͞o′nē) ***n.*** ⟦< TWO, on analogy with LOONIE⟧ [Cdn. Informal] the Canadian two-dollar coin

toot (to͞ot) ***vi.*** ⟦prob. via LowG *tuten* < echoic base⟧ **1** to blow a horn, whistle, etc. in short blasts **2** to sound in short blasts: said of a horn, whistle, etc. **3** to make a sound like a horn or whistle —***vt.*** **1** to cause to sound in short blasts **2** to sound (tones, blasts, etc.) as on a horn **3** [Slang] to sniff (cocaine) —***n.*** **1** a short blast of a horn, whistle, etc. ☆**2** ⟦prob. a play on (WET ONE'S) WHISTLE⟧ [Slang] a drinking spree **3** [Slang] cocaine, or a small amount of it sniffed at one time

tooth (to͞oth; *for v., also* to͞oth) ***n., pl.*** **teeth** (tēth) ⟦ME < OE *toth* (< **tanth*), akin to Ger *zahn* < IE **edont-* (< base **ed-*, to eat) > L *dens* (gen. *dentis*), Gr *odous* (gen. *odontos*)⟧ **1** *a)* any of a set of hard, bonelike structures set in the jaws of most vertebrates and used for biting, tearing, and chewing: a tooth consists typically of a sensitive, vascular pulp surrounded by dentin and coated on the crown with enamel and on the root with cementum: normally 32 are in the permanent set and 20 in the deciduous set of a human *b)* any of various analogous processes in invertebrates *c)* [*pl.*] DENTURE (sense 2) **2** something resembling a tooth; toothlike part, as on a saw, fork, rake, gearwheel, etc.; tine, prong, cog, etc. **3** appetite or taste for something specified: now only in SWEET TOOTH **4** something that bites, pierces, or gnaws like a tooth [the *teeth* of the storm] **5** a rough surface, as on paper, metal, etc. **6** [*pl.*] a sound or effective means of enforcing something [to put *teeth* into a law] **7** *Bot.* any small, pointed lobe, as of a leaf or of the fringe surrounding the opening of a capsule in mosses —***vt.*** **1** to provide with teeth **2** to make jagged; indent —***vi.*** to mesh, or become interlocked, as gears For phrases using *teeth*, see TEETH See also TEETH, illus. —**long in the tooth** elderly; old —**tooth and nail** with all one's strength or resources —**tooth′less** ***adj.***

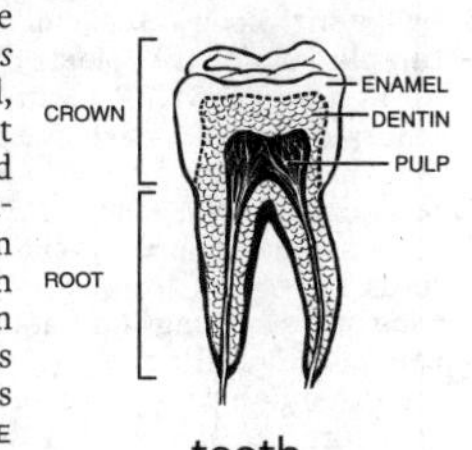

tooth

SYN.—**tooth** is the general, inclusive word (see the definition above); **tusk** refers to a long, pointed, enlarged tooth projecting outside the mouth in certain animals, as the elephant, wild boar, and walrus, and used for digging or as a weapon; **fang** refers either to one of the long, sharp teeth with which meat-eating animals tear their prey or to the long, hollow tooth through which poisonous snakes inject their venom

tooth·ache (to͞oth′āk′) ***n.*** pain in or near a tooth

tooth·brush (-brush′) ***n.*** a brush with a long handle, for cleaning the teeth

toothed (to͞otht, to͞oth*d*) ***adj.*** **1** having (a specified kind or number of) teeth: often used in hyphenated compounds [big-*toothed*] **2** notched; indented

toothed whale any of an order (Odontoceta) of whales with conical teeth and a telescoped, nonsymmetrical skull, including sperm whales, dolphins, and porpoises

tooth fairy *Folklore* a fairy who puts money under a child's pillow in exchange for the child's milk tooth placed there

tooth·paste (to͞oth′pāst′) ***n.*** a paste used in cleaning the teeth with a toothbrush

tooth·pick (to͞oth′pik′) ***n.*** a very small, pointed stick for getting bits of food free from between the teeth

tooth powder a powder used like toothpaste

tooth shell SCAPHOPOD

tooth·some (to͞oth′səm) ***adj.*** ⟦TOOTH + -SOME[1]⟧ **1** pleasing to the taste; palatable **2** attractive, esp. sexually attractive —**tooth′some·ly** ***adv.*** —**tooth′some·ness** ***n.***

tooth·wort (to͞oth′wurt′) ***n.*** **1** any of a genus (*Dentaria*) of small woodland plants of the crucifer family, having scaly or toothed, pungent rhizomes and white or pinkish flowers in spring **2** any of a genus (*Lathraea*) of European parasitic plants of the broomrape family, having a rhizome covered with tooth-shaped scales

tooth·y (to͞oth′ē) ***adj.*** **tooth′i·er, tooth′i·est** having or exposing teeth that show prominently [a *toothy* smile] —**tooth′i·ly** ***adv.*** —**tooth′i·ness** ***n.***

too·tle (to͞ot′'l) ***vi.*** **-tled, -tling** ⟦freq. of TOOT⟧ **1** to toot softly and more or less continuously on a horn, flute, etc. **2** to move about in a leisurely or unrushed way; esp., to drive in this way as in a small car —***n.*** the act or sound of tootling —**too′tler** ***n.***

toots (to͝ots) ***n.*** ⟦< fol.⟧ [Informal] darling; dear: affectionate or playful term of address, esp. for a girl or woman

toot·sie (to͝ot′sē) ***n.*** ⟦orig. a child's term⟧ [Informal] **1** a foot or toe **2** TOOTS **3** a girl or woman, esp. one who is promiscuous: often used disparagingly Also sp. **toot′sy**, *pl.* **-sies**

top[1] (täp) ***n.*** ⟦ME < OE *topp*, akin to ON *toppr*, tuft, top, Ger *zopf*, tuft of hair, summit⟧ **1** [Obs.] *a)* a tuft of hair *b)* the hair of the head **2** the head, or crown of the head: now chiefly in **top to toe** **3** the upper or highest part, section, point, or surface of anything [the *top* of a hill] **4** the part of a plant that grows above ground [beet *tops*] **5** something that constitutes the uppermost part or covering of something else; specif., *a)* a lid, cover, cap, etc. [a box *top*, bottle *top*] *b)* the upper part of an automobile body, esp. a folding roof or cover *c)* a platform around each mast of a sailing ship at the juncture of the lower mast and the topmast **6** *a)* the upper part of a two-piece garment, esp. for a woman [a pajama *top*] *b)* any upper garment, often, specif., one other than a shirt or blouse **7** a person or thing first in order, excellence, importance, etc.; specif., *a)* the highest degree or pitch; zenith; acme [at the *top* of one's voice, the *top* of one's career] *b)* the highest rank, position, etc. [at the *top* in one's profession] *c)* a person in this rank, etc. *d)* the choicest part; pick; cream [the *top* of the crop, *top* of the morning] *e)* the beginning, as of a piece of music [take it from the *top*] ☆*f)* *Baseball* the first half (*of* an inning) **8** [*pl.*] [Slang] something or someone that is preeminent in quality, ability, popularity, etc.; the very best: used in the predicate (often with *the*) **9** [*pl.*] *Card Games* the highest cards of a suit **10** *Chem.* the most volatile part of a mixture —***adj.*** of, situated at, or being the top; uppermost, highest, greatest, or foremost [the *top* drawer, *top* honors] —***vt.*** **topped**, **top′ping** **1** to take off the top of (a plant, etc.) **2** *a)* to provide or cover with a top *b)* to put or place on the top of **3** to be a top for **4** to reach the top of; be on a level with **5** to exceed in amount, height, degree, etc. [a fish *topping* 75 pounds] **6** to be better, more effective, funnier, etc. than; surpass; outdo **7** to go over the top of (a rise of ground, etc.) **8** to be at the top of; head; lead **9** *Chem.* to remove the volatile parts from by distillation **10** *Dyeing* to finish with a certain dye **11** *Sports* *a)* to hit or stroke (a ball) unintentionally at a point above its center or near its top, giving it a forward spin *b)* to make (a stroke) by hitting the ball in this way [she *topped* her drive] —***vi.*** to top someone or something (in any sense) —☆**blow one's top** *see* BLOW ONE'S STACK at BLOW[1] —**off the top** [Slang] from gross income —☆**off the top of one's head** speaking offhand, without careful thought —**on top** at the top; successful —**on top of** **1** on or at the top of **2** resting upon **3** in addition to; besides **4** following immediately after **5** controlling successfully —**over the top** **1** over the front of a trench, as in attacking **2** exceeding the assigned quota or goal **3** [Informal] beyond the limits of good taste, propriety, or self-restraint; excessive —**top off** **1** to complete by adding a finishing touch **2** [Informal] to fill to the top —☆**top out** **1** to complete the skeleton or framework of (a building, esp. a skyscraper) **2** to fill or rise to the top **3** to reach a peak, maximum, etc. —**top up** [Chiefly Brit.] **1** to fill to the top **2** to increase to the highest level, amount, etc.

top[2] (täp) ***n.*** ⟦< OE, prob. special use of prec.⟧ a child's cone-shaped toy, spun on its pointed end —**sleep like a top** to sleep soundly

to·paz (tō′paz′) ***n.*** ⟦ME *topace* < OFr *topase* < L *topazus* < Gr *topazos*⟧ **1** a light-colored or colorless, very hard, orthorhombic mineral, $Al_2(SiO_4)(F,OH)_2$, often used as a gem; hydrous aluminum silicate: see MOHS SCALE **2** any of a various yellowish minerals that resemble yellow topaz, esp. citrine **3** either of two brightly colored hummingbirds (*Topaza pyra* or *T. pella*) of South America

to·paz·o·lite (tō paz′ə līt′) ***n.*** ⟦< Gr *topazos*, topaz + -LITE⟧ a yellow to greenish variety of andradite garnet

☆**top banana** ⟦prob. so named from the banana-shaped soft club carried by burlesque comedians⟧ [Slang] **1** a top performer in show business; specif., the star comedian in a burlesque show: cf. SECOND BANANA **2** the most important person in any group

top boot any of several high boots reaching to just below the knee: its upper part is usually of a different material

☆**top brass** [Slang] important officials: see BRASS (***n.*** 6)

☆**top·coat** (täp′kōt′) ***n.*** **1** a lightweight overcoat **2** a final coat of paint, varnish, etc. applied to provide a particular finish, as a sealant, etc. Also written **top coat**

top dog [Slang] the person, company, etc. in a dominant or leading position, esp. in a competitive situation

☆**top dollar** [Informal] the highest price, salary, etc. being paid for a particular commodity or service

top-draw·er (täp′drôr′) ***adj.*** of first importance, highest quality, etc.

top-dress·ing (-dres′iŋ) ***n.*** **1** material applied to a surface, as fertilizer on land or crops, or stones on a road **2** the applying of such material —**top′-dress′** ***vt.***

tope[1] (tōp) ***vt., vi.*** **toped**, **top′ing** ⟦Fr *toper*, to accept the stakes in gambling (prob. < ODu *topp*, touch): E meaning given here is prob. from the custom of drinking to the conclusion of the wager⟧ [Archaic] to drink (alcoholic liquor) in large amounts and often

tope[2] (tōp) ***n.*** ⟦Hindi *top*, ult. < Sans *stūpa*, a mound, tope⟧ a Buddhist shrine in the form of a dome with a cupola

tope[3] (tōp) ***n.*** ⟦< ? Cornish⟧ a small, gray European requiem shark (*Galeorhinus galeus*)

to·pee (tō pē′, tō′pē) ***n.*** ⟦Hindi *ṭopī*⟧ in India, a hat or cap, esp. a pith helmet worn as a sunshade: also sp. **to·pi′**

To·pe·ka (tə pē′kə) ⟦prob. < Kansa (a Siouan language) *toppik'e*, lit., dig good Indian potatoes⟧ capital of Kans., in the NE part, on the Kansas River

top·er (tō′pər) ***n.*** [Literary] a person who topes; drunkard

top-flight (täp′flīt′) ***adj.*** [Informal] best; first-rate

☆**Top-40** or **Top-For·ty** (täp′fôrt′ē) ***adj.*** of or having to do with the Top 40 or the kind of popular music they represent [a *Top-40* radio station]

☆**Top 40** (*or* **Forty**) the 40 current best-selling music recordings

top·gal·lant (täp′gal′ənt; *naut.* tə gal′ənt) ***adj.*** designating or of a mast, sail, spar, etc. situated above the topmast and below the royal mast on a sailing ship —***n.*** a topgallant mast, sail, etc.

top gun [Informal] the most important, influential, or skilled person in a given sphere

top hamper all of the rigging, spars, etc. above the deck of a ship: also **top′-ham′per** *n.*

top hat a tall, black, cylindrical hat, usually of silk, worn by men in formal dress

top-heav·y (täp′hev′ē) *adj.* so heavy at the top relative to the base as to be likely to fall over or collapse: also used fig., as of an organization with too many executives —**top′-heav′i·ly** *adv.* —**top′-heav′i·ness** *n.*

To·phet or **To·pheth** (tō′fet′) *n.* ⟦ME < Heb *tofet*⟧ 1 *Bible* a place near Jerusalem where human sacrifices were made to Molech: 2 Kings 23:10 2 hell

top-hole (täp′hōl′) *adj.* [Brit. Slang] first-rate

to·phus (tō′fəs) *n., pl.* **-phi** (-fī) ⟦L, tufa⟧ *Med.* an abnormal mineral deposit, as of calcium carbonate, about the joints, on the roots of the teeth, etc., in a person who has the gout; chalkstone

to·pi·ar·y (tō′pē er′ē) *adj.* ⟦L *topiarius*, concerning an ornamental garden < *topia (opera)*, ornamental gardening < Gr *topos*, place: see fol.⟧ designating or of the art of trimming and training shrubs or trees into unusual, ornamental shapes —*n., pl.* **-ar′ies** 1 topiary art or work 2 a topiary garden

top·ic (täp′ik) *n.* ⟦L *topica* < Gr *ta topika*, title of a work by ARISTOTLE < *topikos*, local, concerning < *topoi*, commonplaces < *topos*, place < IE base **top-*, to arrive, goal > OE *thafian*, to endure⟧ 1 [Historical] *a)* a class or category of considerations or arguments on which a rhetorician may draw *b)* one such consideration or argument 2 the subject of a paragraph, essay, speech, etc. 3 a subject for discussion or conversation 4 a heading or item in an outline

top·i·cal (täp′i kəl) *adj.* 1 [Archaic] of a particular place; local 2 of, using, or arranged by topics, or subjects 3 having to do with topics of the day; of current or local interest [*topical* allusions in literature] 4 *Med.* of or for a particular part of the body; esp., designating or by local application [a *topical* remedy] —**top′i·cal′i·ty** (-kal′ə tē) *n.* —**top′i·cal·ly** *adv.*

topic sentence the principal sentence, setting forth the main idea and coming usually at the beginning, in a paragraph or other distinct section of a piece of writing, esp. expository writing

☆**top kick** [Mil. Slang] FIRST SERGEANT

top·knot (täp′nät′) *n.* 1 a knot of feathers, ribbons, etc. worn as a headdress 2 *a)* a tuft of hair on the crown of the head *b)* a tuft of feathers on a bird's head

top·less (täp′lis) *adj.* 1 without a top ☆2 designating, wearing, or characterized by the wearing of a costume, bathing suit, etc. that leaves the breasts uncovered [a *topless* dancer, *topless* bar] 3 seeming to have no top; very high [a *topless* tower]

top-lev·el (täp′lev′əl) *adj.* 1 of or by persons of the highest office or rank 2 in the highest office or rank

top-load (täp′lōd′) *adj.* designating or of a washing machine with the lid on top —**top′-load′er** *n.*

top·loft·y (täp′lôf′tē) *adj.* [Informal] lofty in manner; haughty; pompous —**top′loft′i·ly** *adv.* —**top′loft′i·ness** *n.*

top·mast (täp′mast′; *naut.*, -məst) *n.* the second mast above the deck of a sailing ship, supported by the lower mast and often supporting a topgallant mast in turn

☆**top·min·now** (täp′min′ō) *n.* 1 LIVEBEARER 2 KILLIFISH

top·most (täp′mōst′) *adj.* at the very top; uppermost

☆**top-notch** (-näch′) *adj.* [Informal] first-rate; excellent

to·po (tō′pō) *adj. short for* TOPOGRAPHIC OR TOPOGRAPHICAL

top of the hour ⟦in ref. to the position of the minute hand on the numeral "12" at the *top* of a clock face⟧ the beginning of any or each of the twenty-four divisions of the day; noon, 1:00, 2:00, etc. [news is broadcast at the *top of the hour*]

top-of-the-line (täp′əv *th*ə līn′) *adj.* ⟦see LINE[1], *n.* 19⟧ of the highest quality; first-rate [*top-of-the-line* women's apparel]

topog or **topo** *abbrev.* topography

to·pog·ra·pher (tə päg′rə fər) *n.* 1 an expert or specialist in topography 2 a person who describes or maps the topography of a place or region

to·pog·ra·phy (tə päg′rə fē) *n., pl.* **-phies** ⟦ME *topographye* < LL *topographia* < Gr: see TOPIC & -GRAPHY⟧ 1 *a)* the surface features of a region, including its relief and rivers, lakes, etc., and such man-made features as canals, bridges, roads, etc. *b)* the arrangement of such features in a particular region *c)* the science of drawing on maps and charts or otherwise representing surface features *d)* topographic surveying 2 a study or description of a region, system, or part of the body showing specific relations of component parts as to shape, size, position, etc. [cerebral *topography*] 3 any similar study of an entity, as the mind, the atom, a particular discipline, etc. 4 [Archaic] the accurate and detailed description of a place —**top·o·graph·ic** (täp′ə graf′ik) *adj.*, **top′o·graph′i·cal** —**top′o·graph′i·cal·ly** *adv.*

to·poi (tō′poi) *n. pl. of* TOPOS

to·pol·o·gy (tō päl′ə jē, tə-) *n., pl.* **-gies** ⟦< Gr *topos*, a place (see TOPIC) + -LOGY⟧ 1 a topographical study of a specific object, entity, place, etc. [the *topology* of the mind] 2 *Math.* the study of those properties of geometric figures that remain unchanged even when under distortion, so long as no surfaces are torn, as with a Möbius strip 3 *Med.* the topographic anatomy of a body region —**top′o·log′ic** *adj.*, **top·o·log·i·cal** (täp′ə läj′i kəl) —**top′o·log′i·cal·ly** *adv.* —**to·pol′o·gist** *n.*

top·o·nym (täp′ə nim′) *n.* ⟦back-form. < TOPONYMY⟧ 1 a name of a place 2 a name that indicates origin, natural locale, etc., as in zoological nomenclature

top·o·nym·ic (täp′ə nim′ik) *adj.* 1 of toponyms 2 having to do with toponymy Also **top′o·nym′i·cal**

to·pon·y·my (tō pän′ə mē) *n.* ⟦< Gr *topos*, a place (see TOPIC) + *-onymia*, a naming < *onyma*, NAME⟧ 1 the place names of a country, district, etc., or the study of these 2 [Rare] *Anat.* the nomenclature of the regions of the body

to·pos (tō′pōs) *n., pl.* **to′poi** (-poi) ⟦Gr *topos*, a place: see TOPIC⟧ 1 a common or recurring topic, theme, subject, etc. 2 a literary convention or formula

top·per (täp′ər) *n.* 1 a person or thing that tops 2 [Informal] *a)* TOP HAT *b)* a woman's short, loosefitting topcoat ☆3 [Informal] a remark, joke, etc. that tops, or surpasses, those preceding

top·ping (täp′iŋ) *n.* 1 the action of a person or thing that tops 2 something that forms the top of, or is put on top of, something else; specif., any of various items put on the top of certain prepared dishes, as cheese or sliced meats or vegetables for a pizza, or whipped cream, sprinkles, chopped nuts, etc. for a sundae —*adj.* 1 that excels in degree, rank, etc. 2 [Old Brit. Slang] excellent

top·ple (täp′əl) *vi.* **-pled, -pling** ⟦< TOP[1], v. + -LE⟧ 1 to fall (*over*) because or as if top-heavy 2 to lean forward as if on the point of falling; overbalance; totter —*vt.* 1 to cause to topple; overturn 2 to overthrow [to *topple* a monarch]

top quark *Particle Physics* a type of quark with a mass of *c.* 176 to 199 GeV/c^2, a positive charge ⅔ that of an electron, zero charm, and zero strangeness: see FLAVOR (sense 5)

tops (täps) [Slang] *adv.* at most [it'll take us a year, *tops*]

top·sail (täp′sāl′; *naut.*, -səl) *n.* 1 in a square-rigged vessel, the square sail, or either of a pair of square sails, next above the lowest sail on a mast 2 in a fore-and-aft-rigged vessel, the small sail set above the gaff of a fore-and-aft sail

top-se·cret (-sē′krit) *adj.* designating or of the most highly restricted military or government information

☆**top sergeant** [Informal] FIRST SERGEANT

top-shelf (täp′shelf′) *adj.* of the finest quality

top·side (täp′sīd′) *n.* [*usually pl.*] the part of a ship's side above the waterline —*adv.* on, onto, or toward the deck or decks of a vessel that are exposed to the weather

Top·sid·er (täp′sīd′ər) *n.* ⟦< fol.⟧ [*also* **t-**] a shoe like a Top-Sider

Top-Sid·er (täp′sīd′ər) *trademark for* a casual shoe, often made of canvas, having a nonskid rubber sole

☆**top·soil** (-soil′) *n.* 1 the upper layer of soil; surface soil 2 earth of a dark and rich type, for use in growing plants, a lawn, etc. [a bag of *topsoil*]

top·spin (-spin′) *n.* spin given to a tennis ball, cue ball, etc. in which the top of the ball rotates forward in the direction of flight

top·stitch·ing (täp′stich′iŋ) *n.* decorative stitching, usually near and parallel to a seam, sewn so as to be visible on the right side of a garment, shoe, belt, etc. —**top′stitched′** *adj.*

top·sy-tur·vy (täp′sē tʉr′vē) *adv., adj.* ⟦earlier *topsy-tervy*, prob. < *top*, highest part + ME *terven*, to roll⟧ 1 upside down; in a reversed condition 2 in confusion or disorder —*n.* 1 a topsy-turvy condition; inverted state 2 a state of confusion —**top′sy-tur′vi·ly** *adv.* —**top′sy-tur′vi·ness** *n.*

toque (tōk) *n.* ⟦Fr, a cap < Sp *toca* < Basque *tauka*, kind of cap⟧ 1 a small, plumed hat worn by men and women in the 16th cent. 2 a woman's small, round, closefitting, usually brimless hat 3 a traditional, white chef's hat, typically tall or with a baggy crown 4 [Cdn.] a knitted winter cap

toque blanche (tōk blänsh′) *pl.* **toques blanches** (tōk blänsh′) the tall white hat traditionally worn by a chef

tor (tôr) *n.* ⟦ME < OE *torr*, a tower, crag < Brit⟧ a high, rocky hill

to·rah or **to·ra** (tō′rə, tôr′ə, tō rä′) *n.* ⟦Heb *tora*, law < *hora*, to teach < root *jrh*, to cast, throw⟧ *Judaism* 1 *a)* learning, law, instruction, etc. *b)* [*usually* **T-**] the whole body of Jewish religious literature, including the Scripture and the Talmud 2 [*usually* **T-**] *a)* the Pentateuch *b) pl.* **to·roth** or **to·rot** (tō′rəs, tôr′əs, tō rōt′), **to·rahs** or **to·ras** (tō′rəs, tôr′əs, tō räs′) a parchment scroll containing the Pentateuch

torch (tôrch) *n.* ⟦ME < OFr *torche* < VL **torca*, twisted object, for L *torqua* < *torquere*, to twist: see TORSION⟧ 1 a portable light consisting of a long piece of resinous wood, or twisted tow dipped in tallow, etc., flaming at one end; link; flambeau 2 anything considered as a source of enlightenment, illumination, inspiration, etc. [the *torch* of science] 3 any of various portable devices for producing a very hot flame, used in welding, burning off paint, etc. 4 [Brit.] a flashlight —*vt.* ☆[Informal] to set fire to, as in arson —☆**carry a (or the) torch for** to be in love with (someone) for a period of time, esp. without having one's love returned —**pass the torch** to give up to another person one's status of importance or influence

torch·bear·er (tôrch′ber′ər) *n.* 1 a person who carries a torch 2 *a)* a person who brings enlightenment, truth, etc. *b)* an inspirational leader, as in some movement

tor·chier or **tor·chiere** (tôr chir′, -shir′) *n.* ⟦< Fr *torchère*, small, high candle stand < OFr *torche*: see TORCH⟧ a floor lamp with a reflector bowl and no shade, for casting light upward so as to give indirect illumination

torch·light (tôrch′līt′) *n.* the light of a torch or torches —☆*adj.* done or carried on by torchlight

tor·chon lace (tôr′shän′; *Fr* tôr shōn′) ⟦Fr *torchon*, dishcloth, duster < OFr *torche*: see TORCH⟧ 1 a strong bobbin lace made of coarse linen or cotton thread in simple, open, geometric patterns 2 an imitation of this made by machine

☆**torch song** ⟦< phrase *carry a torch for*: see TORCH⟧ a sentimental popular song of unrequited or unhappy love —**torch singer**

☆**torch·wood** (tôrch′wood′) ***n.*** **1** any of a number of trees with resinous wood from which torches can be made **2** any of a genus (*Amyris*) of tropical American trees and shrubs of the rue family, having hard, resinous wood **3** the wood of any of these trees

tore[1] (tôr) ***vt., vi. pt. of*** TEAR[1]

tore[2] (tôr) ***n. Archit., Geom. var. of*** TORUS

tor·e·a·dor (tôr′ē ə dôr′) ***n.*** ⟦Sp < *torear,* to fight bulls < *toro,* bull < L *taurus,* bull: see TAURUS⟧ a bullfighter, esp. one on horseback: term no longer used in bullfighting

to·re·ro (tə rer′ō; *Sp* tô re′rô) ***n., pl.*** **-ros′** (-ōz′; *Sp,* -rôs) ⟦Sp < VL **taurarius* < L *taurus:* see prec.⟧ a bullfighter, esp. a matador

to·reu·tic (tō ro͞ot′ik) ***adj.*** ⟦Gr *toreutikos* < *toreuein,* to work in relief, bore < IE base **ter-* > THROW⟧ designating or of work done in relief or intaglio, esp. on metal, as by embossing, chasing, or engraving

to·reu·tics (tō ro͞ot′iks) ***n.*** the art of making toreutic work

to·ri (tō′rī′, tôr′ī′) ***n. pl. of*** TORUS

tor·ic (tō′rik, tôr′ik) ***adj.*** of or shaped like a torus

to·ri·i (tō′rē ē′) ***n., pl.*** **-ri·i′** ⟦Jpn < *tori,* bird + *i,* nominal form of *iru,* to be, exist: birds offered to the gods were to perch on the crosspiece⟧ a gateway at the entrance to a Japanese Shinto shrine, consisting of two uprights supporting a curved beam, with a straight crosspiece below

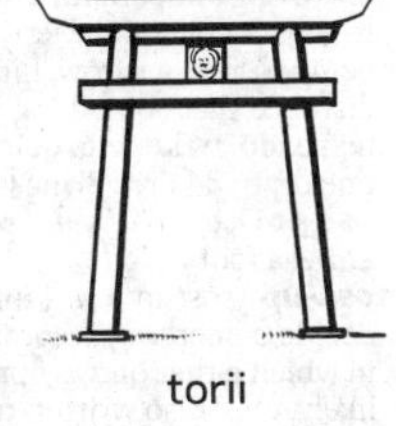

torii

To·ri·no (tə rē′nō; *It* tô rē′nô) ***It. name for*** TURIN

tor·ment (tôr′ment′; *for v.* tôr ment′, tôr′ment′) ***n.*** ⟦OFr < L *tormentum,* a rack, instrument of torture, torture, pain, orig., machine for twisting or throwing < *torquere,* to twist, whirl around, fling: see TORT⟧ **1** [Obs.] an instrument of torture or the torture inflicted **2** great pain or anguish, physical or mental; suffering; agony **3** a source of pain, anxiety, or annoyance —***vt.*** ⟦ME *tormenten* < OFr *tourmenter* < the n.⟧ **1** [Rare] to torture **2** to cause great physical pain or mental anguish in **3** to annoy, harass, or tease **4** [Obs.] to stir up; agitate —***SYN.*** BAIT —**tor·ment′ing·ly** ***adv.***

tor·men·til (tôr′men til′) ***n.*** ⟦ME *turmentill* < ML *tormentilla* < L *tormentum* (see prec.): from belief in the pain-killing power of the plant⟧ a European cinquefoil (*Potentilla tormentilla*) with yellow flowers and rhizomes used in tanning and dyeing

tor·men·tor (tôr ment′ər, tôr′ment′ər) ***n.*** ⟦ME *tormentour* < OFr *tormenteor*⟧ **1** a person or thing that torments **2** ⟦because it can obstruct the view of those sitting at the sides⟧ *Theater* a flat or curtain that projects out onto either side of the proscenium stage, for concealing the wings and backstage from the audience Also sp. **tor·ment′er**

torn (tôrn) ***vt., vi. pp. of*** TEAR[1]

tor·na·do (tôr nā′dō) ***n., pl.*** **-does** or **-dos** ⟦altered (prob. based on Sp *tornar,* to turn) < Sp *tronada,* thunder, thunderstorm < *tronar,* to thunder < L *tonare,* to THUNDER⟧ ☆**1** a violently whirling column of air, with wind speeds of about 100 to 300 miles per hour, extending downward from a cumulonimbus cloud, esp. in Australia and the central U.S.: usually appearing as a rapidly rotating, slender, funnel-shaped cloud and typically causing great destruction along its narrow path **2** in W Africa and the adjacent Atlantic, a severe thundersquall **3** any whirlwind or hurricane —☆**tor·nad′ic** (-nad′ik) ***adj.***

☆**tor·nil·lo** (tôr nē′yō, -nil′ō) ***n., pl.*** **-los** ⟦Sp, lit., screw, dim. of *torno,* winch, spindle, wheel < L *tornus,* turner's wheel, lathe: see TURN⟧ SCREW BEAN

to·roid (tō′roid′, tôr′oid′) ***n.*** ⟦TOR(E) + -OID⟧ **1** *Elec.* a doughnut-shaped coil **2** *Geom.* a surface, or its enclosed solid, generated by any closed plane curve rotating about a straight line in its own plane —**to·roi·dal** (tō roid′'l) ***adj.***

To·ron·to (tə rän′tō) ⟦< an Iroquoian language: meaning unknown⟧ capital of Ontario, Canada: port on Lake Ontario —**To·ron·to·ni·an** (tə rän′tō′nē ən, tôr′än-, tär′än-) ***n.***

to·rose (tō′rōs′, tôr′ōs′, tō rōs′) ***adj.*** ⟦L *torosus,* full of muscle, knotty < *torus,* muscle⟧ **1** bulging, knobbed, protuberant, swelling, etc. **2** *Bot.* cylindrical, with swellings at intervals Also **to·rous** (tō′rəs, tôr′əs)

tor·pe·do (tôr pē′dō) ***n., pl.*** **-does** ⟦L, numbness, crampfish < *torpere,* to be stiff: see TORPID⟧ **1** ELECTRIC RAY ☆**2** a large, cigar-shaped, self-propelled underwater projectile for launching against enemy ships from a submarine, airplane, etc.: it is detonated by contact, sound, etc. **3** a metal case containing explosives, esp. one used as an underwater mine **4** a small fireworks device consisting of a percussion cap and gravel wrapped in tissue paper, which explodes with a loud noise when thrown against a hard surface ☆**5** an explosive cartridge or a flare, placed on a railroad track and detonated by a train wheel as a signal to the crew ☆**6** an explosive cartridge lowered into oil wells, where it is detonated to clear the bore or to break through to the oil pocket ☆**7** [Old Slang] a gangster or gunman hired as a bodyguard, assassin, etc. —***vt.*** **-doed, -do·ing** to attack, damage, or destroy with or as with a torpedo

☆**torpedo boat** a small, fast, maneuverable boat for use in war, with torpedoes as its main weaponry

torpedo tube a tube for launching torpedoes

tor·pid (tôr′pid) ***adj.*** ⟦L *torpidus* < *torpere,* to be numb or torpid < IE *(*s*)*terp-* < base *(*s*)*ter-,* to be stiff > STARE, STARVE⟧ **1** *a)* having lost temporarily all or part of the power of sensation or motion, as a hibernating animal; dormant *b)* sluggish in functioning **2** slow and dull; apathetic —**tor·pid′i·ty** ***n.,*** **tor′pid·ness** —**tor′pid·ly** ***adv.***

tor·por (tôr′pər) ***n.*** ⟦L < *torpere:* see prec.⟧ **1** a state of being dormant or inactive; temporary loss of all or part of the power of sensation or motion; sluggishness; stupor **2** dullness; apathy

tor·por·if·ic (tôr′pə rif′ik) ***adj.*** inducing torpor

tor·quate (tôr′kwit, -kwāt′) ***adj.*** ⟦L *torquatus*⟧ having a torques

torque (tôrk) ***n.*** ⟦< L *torques* (infl. in senses 2 & 3 by *torquere*): see TORQUES⟧ **1** a twisted metal collar or necklace worn by ancient Teutons, Gauls, Britons, etc. **2** *Physics* a measure of the tendency of a force to cause rotation, equal to the force multiplied by the perpendicular distance between the line of action of the force and the center of rotation: abbrev. *T* **3** popularly, the force that acts to produce rotation, as in the drive shaft of an automotive vehicle —***vt.*** **torqued, torqu′ing** to give or impart torque to; cause to turn or twist

torque converter a hydraulic device for transferring and increasing torque: an essential component of an automatic transmission in a motor vehicle

Tor·que·ma·da (tôr′kə mäd′ə; *Sp* tôr′ke mä′thä), **To·más de** (tô mäs′ *the*) 1420-98; Sp. Dominican monk: first Grand Inquisitor of the Spanish Inquisition

tor·ques (tôr′kwēz′) ***n.*** ⟦L, twisted necklace < *torquere,* to twist: see TORT⟧ a ring of hair, feathers, or modified skin around the neck of an animal or bird, of a distinctive color or form

torque wrench a wrench that indicates, as on a dial, the amount of torque exerted in tightening a bolt, nut, etc.

torr (tôr) ***n.*** ⟦after E. TORRICELLI⟧ [*also* **T-**] a unit of atmospheric pressure equal to the pressure of a force of 133.322 pascals (1.33322 millibars or one millimeter of mercury or $1/760$ atmosphere)

Tor·rance (tôr′əns) ⟦after Jared S. *Torrance,* local landowner⟧ city in SW Calif.: suburb of Los Angeles

tor·re·fy (tôr′ə fī′) ***vt.*** **-fied′, -fy′ing** ⟦Fr *torréfier* < L *torrefacere* < *torrere,* to dry by heat (see THIRST) + *facere,* to make, DO[1]⟧ to dry or parch (drugs or ores) with heat —**tor′re·fac′tion** (-fak′shən) ***n.***

Tor·ren·ize (tôr′ə nīz′, tär′-) ***vt.*** **-ized′, -iz′ing** to register (property) under a Torrens law

Tor·rens (tôr′ənz), **Lake** shallow salt lake in SE South Australia: *c.* 2,230 sq mi (5,776 sq km)

Tor·rens (title) system (tôr′ənz, tär′-) ⟦after Sir Robert *Torrens* (1814-84), Austral statesman⟧ a system providing for land title registration with the government, which issues a warranted title deed (**Torrens certificate**)

tor·rent (tôr′ənt, tär′-) ***n.*** ⟦Fr < L *torrens,* burning, roaring, rushing, impetuous, prp. of *torrere,* to parch, dry, roast, consume: see THIRST⟧ **1** a swift, violent stream, esp. of water **2** a flood or rush of words, mail, etc. **3** a very heavy fall of rain

tor·ren·tial (tô ren′shəl, tə-) ***adj.*** **1** of, having the nature of, or produced by, a torrent **2** like a torrent, as in violence or copiousness —**tor·ren′tial·ly** ***adv.***

Tor·re·ón (tôr′ē ōn′; *Sp* tôr rā ôn′) city in NC Mexico, in Coahuila state

Tor·res Strait (tôr′iz, tär′-) strait between New Guinea & NE Australia: *c.* 95 mi (153 km) wide

Tor·ri·cel·li (tôr′ə chel′ē; *It* tôr′rē chel′lē), **E·van·ge·lis·ta** (e′vän je lēs′tä) 1608-47; It. physicist & mathematician: discovered principle of the barometer

tor·rid (tôr′id, tär′-) ***adj.*** ⟦L *torridus* < *torrere,* to dry: see THIRST⟧ **1** dried by or subjected to intense heat, esp. of the sun; scorched; parched; arid **2** so hot as to be parching or oppressive; scorching **3** highly passionate, ardent, zealous, etc. —**tor·rid·i·ty** (tô rid′ə tē) ***n.,*** **tor′rid·ness** —**tor′rid·ly** ***adv.***

Torrid Zone the area of the earth's surface between the Tropic of Cancer & the Tropic of Capricorn, divided by the equator

tor·sade (tôr säd′) ***n.*** ⟦Fr < ML *torsus,* twisted, for L *tortus:* see TORT⟧ **1** a twisted cord used in drapery, etc. **2** a molded or worked ornament resembling this

tor·si (tôr′sē) ***n. alt. pl. of*** TORSO

tor·si·bil·i·ty (tôr′sə bil′ə tē) ***n.*** ability to undergo, or resistance to, torsion

tor·sion (tôr′shən) ***n.*** ⟦ME *torcion* < MFr *torsion* < LL(Ec) *torsio* < pp. of L *torquere,* to twist: see TORT⟧ **1** the process or condition of twisting or being twisted **2** *Mech.* *a)* the stress or strain produced in a body, as a rod, wire, or thread, by turning one end along a longitudinal axis while the other end is held firm or twisted in the opposite direction *b)* the torque exerted by a body in reaction to being placed under torsion —**tor′sion·al** ***adj.*** —**tor′sion·al·ly** ***adv.***

torsion balance an instrument for measuring small forces, such as those caused by gravitation, electric charges, or magnetism, by recording the amount of torsion they produce in a fine wire

torsion bar a metal bar exhibiting resilience under torsion; specif., one used in place of a coil spring in the suspension of some motor vehicles

torsk (tôrsk) ***n., pl.*** **torsk** or **torsks** ⟦Norw *torsk* < ON *thorskr,* orig., fish that is dried < IE base **ters-* > THIRST⟧ any gadoid fish

tor·so (tôr′sō) ***n., pl.*** **-sos** or **-si** (-sē) ⟦It, stump, trunk of a statue < L *thyrsus,* a stalk, stem < Gr *thyrsos,* a stem, wand⟧ **1** the trunk of a statue of the nude human figure, esp. of such a statue lacking the head and full limbs **2** the trunk of the human body **3** any unfinished or fragmentary piece of work

tort (tôrt) ***n.*** ⟦OFr < ML *tortum* < neut. of L *tortus,* pp. of *torquere,* to twist < IE **terk-,* to turn < base **ter-,* to rub > THROW⟧ a wrongful act, injury, or damage (not involving a breach of contract), for which a civil action can be brought

tor·ta[1] (tôr′tä; *E* tôrt′ə) ***n., pl.*** **tor′te** (-te) ⟦It, a cake < LL(Ec), a twisted loaf: see TART[2]⟧ [*also in roman type*] 1 cake, pie, or a similar, often elaborate, dessert 2 any of various layered savory dishes, often containing a creamy cheese, herbs, etc.

tor·ta[2] (tôr′tä) *n., pl.* **-tas** (-täs) ⟦Sp < LL(Ec), a twisted loaf: see TART[2]⟧ 1 a cake 2 a sandwich

torte (tôrt; *Ger* tôr′tə) *n., pl.* **tortes** or Ger. **Tor·ten** (tôr′tən) ⟦Ger < It *torta*, a cake: see TORTA[1]⟧ a rich cake, variously made, as of eggs, finely chopped nuts, and crumbs or a little flour

tor·tel·li·ni (tôrt′ə lē′nē) *n.* ⟦It, pl. of *tortellino*, dim. of *tortello*, a fritter or a filled round of pasta < *torta*: see TORTA[1]⟧ 1 pasta in the form of tiny ring-shaped or round pieces, filled with meat, vegetables, etc., and served with a sauce or in a broth 2 *pl.* **-ni** or **-nis** one of these pieces

tort-fea·sor (tôrt′fē′zər) *n.* ⟦Fr *tortfaiseur* < MFr < *tort*, TORT + *faiseur*, one who does < *fais-*, stem of *faire*, to do < L *facere*: see DO[1]⟧ *Law* a person who commits or is guilty of a tort

tor·ti·col·lis (tôr′ti käl′is) *n.* ⟦ModL < L *tortus*, twisted + *collum*, the neck: see TORT & COLLAR⟧ *Med.* a condition of persistent involuntary contraction of the neck muscles, causing the head to be twisted to an abnormal position

☆**tor·til·la** (tôr tē′ə) *n.* ⟦Sp, dim. of *torta*: see TORTA[2]⟧ a thin, flat, round cake of unleavened cornmeal or, often, of flour, baked on a griddle or, originally, a flat stone

tor·tious (tôr′shəs) *adj.* ⟦ME *torcious* < Anglo-Fr⟧ *Law* of or involving a tort —**tor′tious·ly** *adv.*

tor·toise (tôrt′əs) *n., pl.* **-tois·es** or **-toise** ⟦ME *tortuce* < ML *tortuca*, altered (prob. by assoc. with L *tortus*, twisted) < VL **tartaruca* < ? LGr *tartarouchos*, evil demon, orig., controlling Tartarus⟧ a turtle, esp. one that lives on land, as any of a worldwide family (Testudinidae): see TURTLE

tortoise beetle any of various small, often brightly colored or iridescent, turtle-shaped beetles (family Chrysomelidae) that feed chiefly on plant leaves

tor·toise·shell (-shel′) *n.* 1 the hard, mottled, yellow-and-brown shell of some turtles and tortoises, used in inlaying and, esp. formerly, in making combs, frames for eyeglasses, etc. 2 a synthetic substance made in imitation of this 3 a mottled, yellow-and-brown color pattern 4 any of several common, black and yellow-brown butterflies (genus *Nymphalis*) with markings resembling those of tortoise shell 5 a cat with a mottled coat of black, brown, red or yellow, white, etc. Also **tor′toise-shell′**

Tor·to·la (tôr tō′lə) chief island of the British Virgin Islands: 21 sq mi (54 sq km)

tor·to·ni (tôr tō′nē) *n.* ⟦prob. altered < It *tortone*, lit., big tart < *torta*, tart < LL(Ec): see TART[2]⟧ an ice cream made with heavy cream, maraschino cherries, almonds, etc.

tor·tri·cid (tôr′tri sid) *n.* ⟦< ModL *Tortricidae* < L *tortus*: see TORT⟧ any of a family (Tortricidae) of small, broad-bodied moths whose larvae feed on the leaves of shrubs and trees: the larvae of some species roll and fasten leaves together to form nests

Tor·tu·ga (tôr to͞o′gə) island of Haiti, off the NW coast: 69 sq mi (179 sq km): Fr. name **La Tor·tue** (lȧ tôr tü′)

tor·tu·os·i·ty (tôr′cho͞o äs′ə tē) *n.* ⟦L *tortuositas*⟧ 1 the quality or condition of being tortuous 2 *pl.* **-ties** a twist, turn, etc.

tor·tu·ous (tôr′cho͞o əs) *adj.* ⟦ME < Anglo-Fr < L *tortuosus* < *tortus*: see TORT⟧ 1 full of twists, turns, curves, or windings; winding; crooked 2 not straightforward; devious; specif., deceitful or tricky —**tor′tu·ous·ly** *adv.* —**tor′tu·ous·ness** *n.*

tor·ture (tôr′chər) *n.* ⟦Fr < LL *tortura*, a twisting, torture < pp. of L *torquere*, to twist: see TORT⟧ 1 the inflicting of severe pain, often, specif., in order to obtain information or a confession, get revenge, etc. 2 any method by which such pain is inflicted 3 any severe physical or mental pain; agony; anguish 4 a cause of such pain or agony 5 [Rare] a violent twisting, distortion, perversion, etc. —*vt.* **-tured**, **-tur·ing** 1 to subject to torture 2 to cause extreme physical or mental pain to; agonize 3 to twist or distort (meaning, language, etc.) —**tor′tur·er** *n.*

tor·tur·ous (tôr′chər əs) *adj.* 1 of or causing torture 2 extremely painful or difficult —**tor′tur·ous·ly** *adv.*

tor·u·la (tôr′oo lə) *n., pl.* **-lae′** (-lē′) or **-las** ⟦ModL < L *torus*, a bulge + *-ula*, -ULE⟧ any of a group of yeastlike fungi that reproduce by budding: some cause animal disease and others ferment food

To·ruń (tō′ro͞on′; *Pol* tô′ro͞on yə) city in NC Poland, on the Vistula

to·rus (tō′rəs, tôr′əs) *n., pl.* **-ri′** (-rī′, -ī) ⟦L, a bulge, muscle⟧ 1 *Anat.* any rounded projection or swelling 2 *Archit.* a large, convex molding used at the base of columns, etc., just above the plinth 3 *Bot. a)* RECEPTACLE (sense 3*a*) *b)* a thick spot at the center of the pit membrane in bordered pits of xylem cells 4 *Geom.* a surface, or its enclosed solid, generated by the revolution of a conic about any line that is external to the conic but in the same plane, as a doughnut-shaped figure that is generated by a circle or an ellipse

To·ry (tôr′ē) *n., pl.* **-ries** ⟦Ir *tōruidhe*, robber, pursuer < *tōir*, to pursue; akin to Gael *tōir*, pursuit⟧ 1 [*sometimes* **t-**] *a)* in the 17th cent., any of the dispossessed Irish who became outlaws, killed English settlers and soldiers, and lived by plundering *b)* later, an armed Irish Catholic or Royalist 2 in 1679-1680, a person who opposed the exclusion of James, Duke of York, from succession to the English throne 3 *a)* after 1689, a member of one of the two major political parties of England: opposed to *Whig*, and later, to *Liberal, Radical, Laborite*; changed officially *c.* 1830 to *Conservative* *b)* a member of the Conservative Party of Canada 4 in the American Revolution, a person who advocated or actively supported continued allegiance to Great Britain 5 [*often* **t-**] any extreme conservative; reactionary —*adj.* [*also* **t-**] of, being, or having the conservative principles of a Tory —**To′ry·ism′** *n.*

Tos·ca·na (tôs kä′nə; *It* tôs kä′nä) *It. name for* TUSCANY

Tos·ca·ni·ni (täs′kə nē′nē; *It* tôs′kä nē′nē), **Ar·tu·ro** (är toor′ō; *It* är to͞o′rô) 1867-1957; It. orchestra conductor, esp. in the U.S.

tosh (täsh) *n., interj.* ⟦< ?⟧ [Informal, Chiefly Brit.] nonsense

toss (tôs, täs) *vt.* ⟦prob. < Scand, as in Norw dial. *tossa*, to spread, strew; akin to MLowG *tōsen*, to tear, ME (*to*)*tusen*, to pull to pieces < IE base **dā*(*i*)-, to part, tear > TEASE⟧ 1 to throw or pitch about; fling here and there; buffet [*a boat tossed by a storm*] ☆2 to mix lightly the parts or ingredients of (esp. a salad) 3 to disturb; agitate; disquiet 4 to throw (in various senses); specif., to throw upward, lightly and easily, from the hand 5 to throw in or bandy (ideas, remarks, etc.) 6 to lift quickly; jerk upward [*tossing her head in disdain*] 7 to toss a coin with (someone) *for* deciding something according to which side will land uppermost 8 to get rid of; throw away; discard —*vi.* 1 to be flung to and fro; be thrown about or pitched about 2 to fling oneself about in sleep, etc.; be restless in bed 3 to move or go impatiently, angrily, or disdainfully, as with a toss of the head 4 to toss a coin, as in letting chance decide something —*n.* 1 a tossing or being tossed; a throw, fling, pitch, etc. 2 *short for* TOSS-UP (sense 1) 3 the distance that something is or can be tossed —*SYN.* THROW —**toss off** 1 to make, do, write, etc. quickly, casually, and without effort 2 to drink up in one draft 3 [Brit. Slang] to masturbate: a vulgar usage —**toss′er** *n.*

toss·pot (tôs′pät′) *n.* ⟦prec. + POT[1]⟧ [Informal, Chiefly Brit.] 1 a drunkard 2 a fool

toss-up (tôs′up′) *n.* [Informal] 1 the act of tossing or flipping a coin to decide something according to which side lands uppermost 2 a situation in which either of two options or outcomes is equally compelling, possible, likely, etc. Also written **toss up**

tos·ta·da (tōs tä′də) *n.* ⟦AmSp, orig. fem. of *tostado*, fried < Sp, toasted, pp. of *tostar*, to toast, roast < VL **tostare*, to TOAST[1]⟧ ☆a tortilla fried until crisp: also **tos·ta′do** (-dō) *pl.* **-dos**

tot[1] (tät) *n.* ⟦prob. < Scand, as in ON *tuttr*, small chap, *tutta*, little girl⟧ 1 a young child 2 [Chiefly Brit.] a small drink of alcoholic liquor

tot[2] (tät) *vt., vi.* **tot′ted**, **tot′ting** ⟦contr. < TOTAL⟧ [Informal, Chiefly Brit.] to add; total: usually with *up*

tot[3] *abbrev.* total

to·tal (tōt′'l) *adj.* ⟦ME < MFr < ML *totalis* < L *totus*, all, whole < IE base **tēu-*, to swell > THUMB⟧ 1 constituting the (or a) whole; entire; whole 2 complete; utter [*a total loss*] —*n.* the whole amount or number; sum; aggregate —*vt.* **-taled** or **-talled**, **-tal·ing** or **-tal·ling** 1 to find the total of; add 2 to equal a total of; add up to ☆3 [Slang] to wreck completely; demolish —*SYN.* COMPLETE, SUM[1] —**total up to** to reach a total of; amount to

total depravity in Calvinism, the utter depravity of humankind due to original sin and persisting until regeneration through the Spirit of God

to·tal·i·sa·tor (tōt′'l i zāt′ər) *n. alt. sp. of* TOTALIZATOR

to·tal·is·tic (tōt′'l is′tik) *adj.* TOTALITARIAN: also **to′tal·ist** —**to′tal·ism′** *n.*

to·tal·i·tar·i·an (tō tal′ə ter′ē ən, tō′tal-) *adj.* ⟦TOTAL + (AUTHOR)ITARIAN, infl. by It *totalitario*⟧ 1 designating, of, or characteristic of a government or state in which one political party or group maintains complete control under a dictatorship and bans all others 2 completely authoritarian, autocratic, dictatorial, etc. —*n.* a person who favors such a government or state —**to·tal′i·tar′i·an·ism′** *n.*

to·tal·i·ty (tō tal′ə tē) *n., pl.* **-ties** 1 the fact or condition of being total; entirety 2 the time of complete shadow or coverage during an eclipse 3 the total amount or sum —**in totality** as a whole; altogether

to·tal·i·za·tor (tōt′'l i zāt′ər) *n.* ⟦Fr *totalisateur*⟧ a machine used in pari-mutuel betting for registering bets and, usually, computing the odds and payoffs while the bets are being placed

to·tal·ize (tōt′'l īz′) *vt.* **-ized′**, **-iz′ing** to make a total of; combine into a total —**to′tal·i·za′tion** *n.*

to·tal·iz·er (-ī′zər) *n.* a person or thing that totals; specif., TOTALIZATOR

to·tal·ly (tōt′'l ē) *adv.* 1 wholly; completely; altogether [*their spat was totally forgotten*] 2 [Informal] absolutely; certainly [*they were totally not talking to one another*]: also used in affirmation, equivalent to "I agree" or "quite true"

☆**total recall** the ability of a person to recall the past accurately in seemingly complete detail

to·ta·quine (tō′tə kwēn′, -kwin; -kēn′, -kin) *n.* ⟦< ModL *totaquina* < LL *totalis*, TOTAL + Sp *quina*, cinchona bark (see QUININE): because it contains all the alkaloids of cinchona bark⟧ a yellowish-white to gray powder containing a mixture of quinine and other alkaloids, obtained from cinchona bark and used as an antimalarial

☆**tote**[1] (tōt) *vt.* **tot′ed**, **tot′ing** ⟦prob. of Afr orig., as in Kongo *tota*, to pick up⟧ [Informal] 1 to carry or haul, esp. in the arms or on the back 2 to be armed with (a gun, etc.) —*n.* 1 [Informal] *a)* the act of toting *b)* something toted; load; haul 2 *a)* *short for* TOTE BAG *b)* a small piece of luggage, usually of cloth, with handles and a shoulder strap —**tot′er** *n.*

tote[2] (tōt) *vt.* **tot′ed**, **tot′ing** [Informal] *short for* TOTAL: usually with *up*

tote[3] (tōt) *n. short for* TOTALIZATOR

tote bag ☆a large, open handbag of cloth, straw, etc., used to carry small items

tote board a large board facing the grandstand at a racetrack, on which the bets, odds, and payoffs recorded by a totalizator are flashed

to·tem (tōt′əm) ***n.*** ⟦< an Algonquian language: cf. Ojibwa *nindoodeem*, my totem⟧ **1** among some peoples, an animal or natural object considered as being ancestrally related to a given kin or descent group and taken as its symbol **2** an image of this **3** a symbol, esp. one held in high regard —**to·tem·ic** (tō tem′ik) ***adj.***

to·tem·ism (tōt′əm iz′əm) ***n.*** **1** belief in totems and totemic relationships **2** the use of totems to distinguish kin or descent groups **3** social customs based on this —**to′tem·ist** ***n.*** —**to′tem·is′tic** ***adj.***

totem pole **1** a pole or post carved and painted with totems, often erected in front of their dwellings by Indian tribes of the NW coast of North America **2** ⟦from the typical vertical arrangement of images on a totem pole⟧ any hierarchical system

totem pole

toth·er or **t'oth·er** (tuth′ər) ***adj., pron.*** ⟦ME *the tother*, by faulty division of *thet other, that other*⟧ [Chiefly Dial.] the (or that) other

to·ti- (tōt′i) ⟦< L *totus*, whole: see TOTAL⟧ *combining form* whole or wholly; entire or entirely *[totipalmate]*

to·ti·pal·mate (tōt′i pal′māt′, -mit) ***adj.*** ⟦prec. + PALMATE⟧ having all four toes completely united by a web, as ducks, geese, or pelicans —**to′ti·pal·ma′tion** ***n.***

to·tip·o·tent (tō tip′ə tənt) ***adj.*** ⟦TOTI- + POTENT⟧ capable of developing into a complete embryo or organ: said of a cleavage cell —**to·tip′o·ten·cy** (-tən sē) ***n.***

Tot·ten·ham (tät′'n əm) former borough of Middlesex, SE England: now part of Haringey

tot·ter (tät′ər) ***vi.*** ⟦ME *toteren*, prob. < Scand, as in Norw dial. *totra*, to quiver, shake⟧ **1** *a)* to rock or shake as if about to fall; be unsteady *b)* to be on the point of failure or collapse **2** to proceed with feeble, unsure steps —***n.*** an unsteady walk or movement —**tot′ter·ing** ***adj.*** —**tot′ter·ing·ly** ***adv.*** —**tot′ter·y** ***adj.***

tou·can (to͞o′kan′, -kän′, -kən; to͞o kan′, -kän′) ***n.*** ⟦Fr < Port *tucano* < Tupí *tucana*: echoic of its cry⟧ any of a family (Ramphastidae) of brightly colored, fruit-eating piciform birds of tropical America, distinguished by a very large beak

toucan

touch (tuch) ***vt.*** ⟦ME *touchen* < OFr *tochier* (Fr *toucher*) < VL **toccare* < **tok*, light blow, of echoic orig.⟧ **1** *a)* to put the hand, the finger, or some other part of the body on, so as to feel; perceive by the sense of feeling *b)* to make contact with by means of something regarded as an extension of oneself *[to touch a snake with a stick, one's shoe, etc.]* **2** to bring into contact with something else *[to touch a match to kindling]* **3** *Folklore* to lay the hand on (a person with scrofula), as some kings once did, to effect a cure **4** to be or come into contact with **5** to border on; adjoin **6** to strike lightly **7** to be effective on contact; have a physical effect on: usually used in the negative *[water won't touch these grease spots]* **8** to injure slightly *[frost touched the plants]* **9** to give a light tint, aspect, etc. to: used chiefly in the past participle *[clouds touched with pink]* **10** to lay hands on; handle; use **11** to handle roughly or molest **12** to taste or partake of: usually used in the negative *[didn't touch his supper]* **13** to come up to; reach; attain **14** to compare with; equal; rival: usually used in the negative *[cooking that can't touch hers]* **15** to take or make use of without permission or wrongly; misappropriate **16** to deal with or refer to, esp. in a light or passing way; mention **17** to have to do with; affect; concern *[a subject that touches our welfare]* **18** to arouse an emotion in, esp. one of sympathy, gratitude, etc. **19** to hurt the feelings of; pain *[touched him to the quick]* **20** [Slang] to ask for, or get by asking, a loan or gift of money from **21** [Archaic] *a)* to strike the keys of, pluck the strings of, etc. (a musical instrument) *b)* to play (a few notes, an air, etc.) **22** *Geom.* to be tangent to —***vi.*** **1** to touch a person or thing **2** to be or come in contact **3** to come near to something; verge (*on* or *upon*) **4** to pertain; bear (*on* or *upon*) **5** to treat a topic slightly or in passing: with *on* or *upon* **6** to stop briefly or land (*at* a port, etc.) during a voyage **7** *Geom.* to be tangent —***n.*** **1** a touching or being touched; specif., *a)* a light tap, stroke, etc. *b)* a delicate stroke made with a brush in painting, etc. **2** the sense by which physical objects are felt; tactile sense **3** a sensation caused by touching, esp. one that is characteristic of a particular substance or texture; tactile quality; feel **4** a mental capacity analogous to the sense of touch; mental or moral sensitivity *[she has a nice touch with difficult people]* **5** a special or characteristic quality, skill, or manner *[he lost his touch]* **6** an effect of being touched; specif., *a)* a mark, impression, etc. left by touching *b)* a minor change or improvement *[a few finishing touches]* **7** a very small amount, degree, etc.; specif., *a)* a trace, tinge, etc. *[a touch of humor]* *b)* a slight attack *[a touch of the flu]* **8** contact or communication *[to lose touch with reality, to keep in touch with friends]* **9** [Slang] *a)* the act of asking for a loan or gift of money; also, the act of getting such a loan or gift by asking *[to make a touch]* *b)* money so gotten *c)* a person with reference to the ease with which money can be so gotten from him or her **10** *Music* *a)* the manner in which a performer strikes the keys or the strings of an instrument *[a delicate touch]* *b)* the manner in which the action of a piano, etc. responds to the fingers *[a piano with a heavy touch]* *c)* in bell ringing, a set of changes less than a peal **11** *Rugby, Soccer* the part of the field outside the sidelines —***SYN.*** AFFECT[1] —**touch down** to land: said of an aircraft or spacecraft —**touch off** **1** to represent accurately or aptly **2** to make explode or detonate; fire **3** to initiate (esp. a violent action or reaction); set off —**touch up** **1** to stimulate or rouse, as by a tap or light blow **2** to make minor changes or improvements in **3** to iron, or press, lightly —**touch′a·bil′i·ty** ***n.*** —**touch′a·ble** ***adj.*** —**touch′er** ***n.***

touch-and-go (tuch′ən gō′) ***adj.*** uncertain, risky, or precarious

☆**touch·back** (tuch′bak′) ***n.*** *Football* a play in which a player grounds the ball behind the player's own goal line when the ball was caused to pass the goal line by an opponent: distinguished from SAFETY (***n.*** 4*a*)

☆**touch·down** (-doun′) ***n.*** **1** *a)* the act of touching down, or landing *b)* the moment at which a landing aircraft or spacecraft touches the landing surface **2** *Football* a scoring play, worth six points, in which a player reaches the opponent's end zone with the ball

tou·ché (to͞o shā′) ***interj.*** ⟦Fr, pp.: see TOUCH⟧ **1** *Fencing* touched: said in acknowledging that one's opponent has scored a point by a touch **2** used to acknowledge a successful point in debating or a witty retort

touched (tucht) ***adj.*** **1** emotionally affected; moved **2** slightly demented or unbalanced: also **touched in the head**

☆**touch football** an informal variety of football in which a defensive player stops a play by touching the ballcarrier (usually with both hands) rather than by tackling

touch·hole (tuch′hōl′) ***n.*** in early firearms, the hole in the breech through which the charge was touched off

touch·ing (tuch′iŋ) ***adj.*** that touches the feelings; arousing tender emotion; affecting —***prep.*** concerning; with regard to —***SYN.*** MOVING —**touch′ing·ly** ***adv.***

touch·less (tuch′lis) ***adj.*** not requiring physical contact in order to be activated or performed *[touchless bathroom faucets]*

touch·line (tuch′līn′) ***n.*** *Rugby, Soccer* either of the sidelines

touch-me-not (tuch′mē nät′) ***n.*** JEWELWEED

touch·pad (-pad′) ***n.*** a device consisting of a pad sensitized to finger movement or pressure and used esp. on laptop computers as an alternative to a mouse

touch-screen (-skrēn′) ***n.*** *Comput.* a screen that enables a user to select an icon, menu option, etc. by touching that portion of the screen on which it appears: also written **touch′screen′**

touch·stone (tuch′stōn′) ***n.*** **1** a type of black stone formerly used to test the purity of gold or silver by the streak left on it when it was rubbed with the metal **2** something by which others of its kind are measured or recognized; quintessential example or feature

☆**touch system** a method of typing without looking at the keyboard, by regularly touching a given key with a specific finger

☆**touch-tone** (tuch′tōn′) ***adj.*** ⟦< *Touch-Tone*, former service mark⟧ designating or of a type of telephone that may be used with a service (**touch tone**) that responds to individual fixed electronic tones activated by corresponding buttons pushed in placing a call

☆**touch-type** (tuch′tīp′) ***vi.*** **-typed′**, **-typ′ing** to type by means of the touch system —**touch′-typ′ist** ***n.***

touch·wood (tuch′wood′) ***n.*** ⟦? altered (infl. by TOUCH) < ME *tache*⟧ dried, decayed wood or dried fungus used as tinder

touch·y (tuch′ē) ***adj.*** **touch′i·er**, **touch′i·est** ⟦TOUCH + -y[2]: also (sense 1) altered < TECHY⟧ **1** easily offended; oversensitive; irritable **2** sensitive to touch; easily irritated, as a part of the body **3** very risky *[a touchy situation]* **4** highly flammable or readily ignited —***SYN.*** IRRITABLE —**touch′i·ly** ***adv.*** —**touch′i·ness** ***n.***

touchy-feely (tuch′ē fē′lē) [Informal] ***adj.*** of or characterized by the overt display of affection, compassion, and other tender feelings, as through hugging, crying, etc.: used disparagingly to convey excess, indulgence, superficiality, etc. *[a touchy-feely support group]*

tough (tuf) ***adj.*** ⟦ME < OE *toh*, akin to Ger *zäh*, tough, viscous, prob. < IE base **denk-*, to bite > TONGS⟧ **1** strong but pliant; that will bend, twist, etc. without tearing or breaking **2** that will not cut or chew easily *[tough steak]* **3** strongly cohesive; glutinous; viscous; sticky *[tough putty]* **4** *a)* strong of physique; robust; hardy *b)* displaying mental or moral firmness **5** hard to convince or influence; stubborn **6** practical and realistic rather than emotional or sentimental **7** overly aggressive; brutal or rough **8** *a)* very difficult; toilsome *b)* vigorous or violent *[a tough fight]* **9** [Informal] unfavorable; bad *[a tough break]* ☆**10** [Slang] fine; excellent: a generalized term of approval —☆***n.*** [Informal] a tough person; thug —***interj.*** ⟦see ***adj.*** 9⟧ [Slang] too bad!: usually used sarcastically, to express a lack of sympathy or compassion —☆**tough it out** [Slang] to remain firm in the face of difficulty, often, specif., in a brazen or defiant way —**tough out** [Slang] to remain firm in the face of (a specified difficulty) *[a generation that toughed out the Depression]* —**tough′ly** ***adv.*** —**tough′ness** ***n.***

tough·en (tuf′ən) ***vt., vi.*** to make or become tough or tougher —**tough′en·er** ***n.***

tough·ie or **tough·y** (tuf′ē) ***n.***, *pl.* **-ies** [Informal] **1** a tough person; ruffian **2** a difficult problem or situation

☆**tough love** ⟦< *TOUGHLOVE*, a trademark for a program offering family counseling⟧ a disciplinary technique, as for a young person, in which a seemingly harsh or unfeeling course of action is chosen deliberately over one demonstrating the tenderness or forbearance instinctively felt

tough-mind·ed (tuf′mīn′did) ***adj.*** shrewd and unsentimental; practical; realistic —**tough′-mind′ed·ness** ***n.***

tou·jours (to͞o zho͞or′) ***adv.*** ⟦Fr⟧ always; continually; forever

Tou·lon (to͞o lōn′; *E*, -lōn′, -län′) seaport in SE France, on the Mediterranean

Tou·louse (to͞o lo͞oz′) city in S France, on the Garonne River

Tou·louse-Lau·trec (to͞o lo͞oz′lō trek′), **Hen·ri (Marie Raymond) de** (än rē′ də) 1864-1901; Fr. painter & lithographer

tou·pee (to͞o pā′) ***n.*** ⟦Fr *toupet*, dim. of OFr *toup, top*, tuft of hair < Frank **top*: see TOP¹⟧ **1** [Historical] a curl or lock of hair worn on top of the head, sometimes as part of a wig **2** a man's wig, esp. a small one for covering a bald spot

tour (to͝or) ***n.*** ⟦ME < MFr < OFr *to(u)rn* < *tourner*, to TURN⟧ **1** a turn or shift of work; esp., a period of duty or military service at a single place: in full **tour of duty** **2** a long trip, as for sightseeing **3** any trip, as for inspection; round; circuit; specif., a trip, as by a theatrical company or speaker, to give performances, lectures, etc. at a number of cities —***vi.*** to go on a tour —***vt.*** **1** to take a tour through **2** to take (a play, theatrical company, etc.) on a tour —**on tour** touring, as to give performances, lectures, etc.

tou·ra·co (to͞o′rə kō′, to͞o′rə kō′) ***n.***, *pl.* **-cos′** ⟦prob. via Fr < WAfr native name⟧ any of a family (Musophagidae, order Cuculiformes) of brightly colored, tropical forest birds of Africa, with a short, stout bill, long tail, and erectile crest

Tou·raine (to͞o rān′; *Fr* to͞o ren′) historical region of WC France: chief city, Tours

tour·bil·lion (to͝or bil′yən) ***n.*** ⟦LME *turbilloun* < MFr *tourbillon*, whirlwind, altered < VL **turbinio* < L *turbo*: see TURBINE⟧ **1** [Obs.] a whirlwind **2** a fireworks device that rises with a spiral motion

tour de force (to͝or′ də fôrs′) *pl.* **tours de force** (to͝or′-) ⟦Fr, lit., feat of strength⟧ an unusually skillful or ingenious creation, production, or performance, sometimes one that is merely clever or spectacular

tour d'ho·ri·zon (to͞or dô rē zōn′) ⟦Fr, lit., tour of the horizon⟧ a brief but comprehensive review

tour en l'air (to͞o rän ler′) *pl.* ***tours en l'air*** (to͞o rän ler′) ⟦Fr⟧ *Ballet* a turn executed in the air

Tou·rette's (syndrome) (to͞o rets′) ⟦after G. de la *Tourette* (1857-1904), Fr neurologist who first described it⟧ a neurological disorder characterized by involuntary muscular movements, compulsive, often obscene, vocal expressions, etc.: also **Tourette syndrome** or **Gilles de la Tourette syndrome** (zhēl də lä)

☆**touring car** an early type of open automobile, often with a folding top, seating five or more passengers

tour·ism (to͝or′iz′əm) ***n.*** tourist travel, esp. when regarded as a source of income for a country, business, etc.

tour·ist (to͝or′ist) ***n.*** **1** a person who travels, as in sightseeing **2** tourist class —***adj.*** **1** of or for tourists **2** of or having to do with TOURIST CLASS —***adv.*** in or by means of TOURIST CLASS

tourist class the lowest-priced accommodations, as on a ship or aircraft, or in a hotel

☆**tourist court** MOTEL

☆**tourist home** a private home in which bedrooms are rented to tourists or travelers

tour·is·tic (to͞o ris′tik) ***adj.*** **1** of or for tourists **2** appealing to tourists; charming, picturesque, accessible, etc.

tourist trap a place that habitually overcharges tourists

tour·ist·y (to͝or′is tē) ***adj.*** [Informal] of or for tourists: often used with mild contempt to suggest banality or tastelessness

tour je·té (to͞or zhə tā′) ⟦Fr⟧ *Ballet* a jeté made while turning

tour·ma·line (to͝or′mə lin, -lēn′) ***n.*** ⟦Fr, ult. < Sinhalese *tōramalli*, carnelian⟧ a very hard, piezoelectric, rhombohedral mineral, (Na,Ca)$(Mg,Fe,Al,Li)_3Al_6(BO_3)_3(Si_6O_{18})(OH)_4$, of various colors, used as a gem and in making pressure gauges

Tour·nai (to͞or ne′) city in W Belgium

tour·na·ment (to͝or′nə mənt, tʉr′-) ***n.*** ⟦ME *tournement* < OFr *torneiement* < *torneier*: see TOURNEY⟧ **1** in the Middle Ages, *a)* a contest or exercise in which two parties of mounted knights in the field together tried to unseat each other as with blunted lances *b)* a series of such tournaments, jousts, etc. presented as an entertainment **2** a series of contests in some sport or game, as basketball or chess, in which a number of people or teams take part, trying to win the championship

tour·ne·dos (to͞or nə dō′) ***n.***, *pl.* **-dos′** (-dō′) ⟦Fr < *tourner*, to TURN + *dos*: see DOSS⟧ a small, round beefsteak cut from the tenderloin, often with a strip of bacon, suet, etc. fastened around it before cooking

Tour·neur (tʉr′nər), **Cyril** 1575?-1626; Eng. dramatist

tour·ney (to͝or′nē, tʉr′-) ***n.***, *pl.* **-neys** ⟦ME *turnai* < OFr *tornei* < *torneier* < base of *tourner*: see TURN⟧ TOURNAMENT —***vi.*** ⟦ME *tourneien* < OFr *torneier*⟧ to take part in a tournament; joust

tour·ni·quet (to͝or′ni kit, tʉr′-) ***n.*** ⟦Fr, altered in sense and form (infl. by *tourner*, to TURN) < MFr *turniquet*, earlier *turniquel*, coat of mail, upper garment < OFr *tunicle* < L *tunicula*, dim. of *tunica*, TUNIC⟧ any device or contrivance, as a bandage twisted about a limb, for compressing a blood vessel in order to stop bleeding or to control the circulation of blood to some part

tourniquet

Tours (to͝or; *Fr* to͞or) city in WC France, on the Loire: site of a battle (A.D. 732) in which the Franks under Charles Martel defeated the Saracens

tou·sle (tou′zəl) ***vt.*** **-sled, -sling** ⟦freq. of ME *tusen* (in comp.), to pull to pieces, tear, prob. akin to OE *tæsan*: see TEASE⟧ to disorder, dishevel, muss, rumple, etc. —***n.*** a tousled condition, mass of hair, etc.

Tous·saint L'Ou·ver·ture (to͞o san lo͞o ver tür′) (born *Pierre François Dominique Toussaint*) 1743?-1803; Haitian liberator & general

tout¹ (tout) ***vi.*** ⟦ME *toten* < OE *totian*, to peep, look out after⟧ **1** to solicit customers, patrons, votes, etc. **2** *a)* esp. in England, to spy on racehorses in training, etc. in order to secure tips for betting *b)* to provide betting tips on horse races —***vt.*** [Informal] **1** to praise or recommend highly; puff **2** to solicit or importune, as for business **3** *a)* to spy out or otherwise get information on (racehorses) ☆*b)* to give a tip on (a racehorse) for a price —***n.*** [Informal] a person who touts; esp., a person who makes a business of selling tips on racehorses —**tout′er** ***n.***

tout² (to͞o) ***adj., pron.*** ⟦Fr, lit., all⟧ everyone who is important or fashionable in; every one of (a specified place) *[tout* Hollywood was at the party*]*

tout à fait (to͞o tȧ fe′) ⟦Fr, lit., all done⟧ entirely; quite

tout court (to͞o ko͞or′) ⟦Fr, lit., wholly short⟧ without further explanation or qualification; simply or bluntly

tout de suite (to͞ot süēt′; *E* -swēt′) ⟦Fr, lit., all in succession⟧ immediately

tout en·sem·ble (to͞o tän sän′bl') ⟦Fr, lit., all (taken) together⟧ **1** everything considered; all in all **2** the general effect; total impression, as of a work of art

tout le monde (to͞o lə mōnd′) ⟦Fr, lit., all the world⟧ everyone

tou·zle (tou′zəl) ***n., vt.*** **-zled, -zling** *alt. sp. of* TOUSLE

to·va·rich or **to·va·rish** (tō vär′ish; *Russ* tô vär′ishch) ***n.*** ⟦Russ *tovarišč*, orig., tradesman or trading partner < *tovar*, wares for trading⟧ COMRADE (esp. sense 2)

tow¹ (tō) ***vt.*** ⟦ME *towen* < OE *togian* < IE base **deuk-*, to pull > DUCT⟧ **1** to pull by a rope or chain **2** to pull or drag behind —***n.*** **1** a towing or being towed **2** something towed **3** TOWLINE —***SYN.*** PULL —**in tow** **1** being towed **2** in one's company or retinue **3** under one's control or charge

tow² (tō) ***n.*** ⟦ME < OE *tow-*, for spinning, akin to *tawian*: see TAW²⟧ the coarse and broken fibers of hemp, flax, etc. before spinning —***adj.*** of or resembling tow

tow·age (tō′ij) ***n.*** ⟦ME⟧ **1** a towing or being towed **2** the charge for this

to·ward (tôrd; tōrd, tō′ərd; twôrd; to͞o wôrd′, tə-; *for adj.* tō′ərd, tôrd) ***prep.*** ⟦ME < OE *toweard*: see TO¹ & -WARD⟧ **1** in the direction of **2** so as to face; facing **3** in a manner designed to achieve or along a course likely to result in; in order to get or further *[*steps *toward* peace*]* **4** concerning; regarding; about *[*a negative attitude *toward* abstract art*]* **5** close to or just before (in time) *[toward* daybreak*]* **6** so as to help pay for *[*to contribute *toward* a new library*]* —***adj.*** [Now Rare] **1** favorable; propitious **2** ready to learn; promising **3** docile; compliant **4** at hand; imminent **5** being done; in progress: used in the predicate

to·ward·ly (tō′ərd lē, tôrd′lē) ***adj.*** ⟦prec. + -LY¹⟧ [Archaic or Dial.] **1** favorable, propitious, or promising **2** tractable; docile **3** friendly; affable

to·wards (tôrdz; tōrdz, tō′ərdz; twôrdz; to͞o wôrdz′, tə-) ***prep.*** ⟦ME *towardes* < OE *toweardes* < *toweard* + adv. gen. *(-e)s*⟧ *var. of* TOWARD

tow·boat (tō′bōt′) ***n.*** **1** TUGBOAT ☆**2** a boat used for pushing a barge or group of barges in inland waters

tow·el (tou′əl) ***n.*** ⟦ME *towaille* < OFr *toaille* (Fr *touaille*) < Frank **thwahlja*, akin to OHG *dwahila*, towel < *dwahan*, to wash < IE base **twak-*, to bathe > OProv *twaxtan*, bath towel⟧ a piece of absorbent cloth or paper for wiping or drying things, or for drying oneself after washing or bathing *[*a dish *towel*, a bath *towel]* —***vt.*** **-eled** or **-elled**, **-el·ing** or **-el·ling** to wipe or dry with a towel —**throw (or toss, etc.) in the towel** [Informal] to admit defeat —**towel off** to dry oneself, as after bathing

tow·el·ette (tou′əl et′, tou let′) ***n.*** ⟦prec. + -ETTE⟧ a small, premoistened, disposable paper tissue for cleansing the hands, face, etc.

tow·el·ing or **tow·el·ling** (tou′əl iŋ, tou′liŋ) ***n.*** material suitable for making towels

tow·er¹ (tou′ər) ***n.*** ⟦ME *tour, tur* < OE *torr* & OFr *tur*, both < L *turris*, a tower; akin to Gr *tyrsis*, fortified city⟧ **1** a building or structure that is relatively high for its length and width, either standing alone or forming part of another building **2** such a structure used as a fortress or prison **3** a person or thing that resembles a tower in height, strength, dominance, etc. —***vi.*** to rise high or stand tall

tow·er² (tō′ər) ***n.*** a person or thing that tows

tower block [Brit.] a high-rise apartment or office building

Tower Hamlets borough of E Greater London, England

tow·er·ing (tou′ər iŋ) ***adj.*** **1** that towers; very high or tall **2** very great, intense, influential, etc. *[*a *towering* figure in broadcasting*]*

Tower of London a fortress made up of several buildings on the Thames in London, serving in historic times as a palace, prison, etc.

☆**tow·head** (tō′hed′) ***n.*** ⟦see TOW²⟧ **1** a head of pale-yellow hair **2** a person having such hair —**tow′head′ed** ***adj.***

☆**tow·hee** (tō′hē, tō′ē) ***n.*** ⟦echoic of one of its calls⟧ any of several large, ground-feeding, North American sparrows (family Emberizidae); esp., the **rufous-sided towhee** (*Pipilo erythrophthalmus*), with a chestnut patch on each flank and, usually, red irises

tow·line (tō′līn′) ***n.*** a rope, chain, etc. used for towing

town (toun) ***n.*** ⟦ME < OE *tun*, enclosed space, group of houses, village, town; akin to Ger *zaun*, fence, hedge, OIr *dūn*, fortified camp⟧ **1** [Brit. Dial.] a group of houses; hamlet **2** a more or less concentrated group of houses and private and public buildings, larger than a village but smaller than a city **3** a city or other thickly populated urban place ☆**4** *a)* in parts of the U.S., TOWNSHIP (sense 2) *b)* in New England and some other states, a unit of local government having its sovereignty vested chiefly in a town meeting **5** in England, a village that holds a market periodically **6** the business center of a city [to go into *town*] **7** the inhabitants, voters, etc. of a town **8** the local residents of a town as distinct from the members of a college within the town: cf. GOWN **9** any given inhabited district, regardless of size, often, specif., the district of one's residence: often without an article [an important man about *town*; the circus is coming to *town*] —*adj.* of, in, for, or characteristic of a town —**go to town** [Slang] **1** to go on a spree; indulge in something without restraint **2** to work or act fast and efficiently ☆**3** to be eminently successful —☆**on the town** [Informal] out for a good time at the theater, nightclubs, bars, etc. —**out of town** a significant distance away from one's city, town, etc.

town clerk an official in charge of the records, legal business, etc. of a town

town crier [Historical] a person who cried, or shouted, public announcements through the streets of a village or town

town hall 1 a building in a town, containing the offices of public officials, the council chamber, etc. **2** a public forum or meeting in which those attending gather to discuss civic or political issues, hear and ask questions about the ideas of a candidate for public office, etc.: also **town hall meeting**

town house 1 a city residence, esp. as distinguished from a country residence of the same owner ☆**2** a dwelling, typically two-story or three-story, that is one of a planned complex of such, often contiguous, dwellings: also **town′house′** or **town home**

town·ie (toun′ē) *n.* [Informal] a resident of a town, as distinct from a student or teacher at the local college

☆**town meeting 1** a meeting of the people of a town **2** esp. in New England, a meeting of the qualified voters of a town to act upon town business

town·scape (toun′skāp′) *n.* a picture or view of a town or a part of a town

towns·folk (tounz′fōk′) *pl.n.* TOWNSPEOPLE

town·ship (toun′ship) *n.* ⟦ME *tunscipe* < OE, people living in a *tun*: see TOWN & -SHIP⟧ **1** [Historical] in England, a parish or division of a parish, as a unit of territory and administration **2** in parts of the U.S. and Canada, a division of a county, constituting a unit of local government with administrative control of local schools, roads, etc. **3** in New England, TOWN (sense 4*b*) **4** a unit of territory in the U.S. land survey, generally six miles square, containing 36 mile-square sections, and sometimes, but not necessarily, coextensive with a governmental township **5** in South Africa, a segregated, nonwhite area in or just outside a city

towns·man (tounz′mən) *n., pl.* **-men** (-mən) ⟦ME *tunesman* < OE < gen. of *tun*, TOWN + *man*, MAN⟧ **1** a person who lives in, or has been reared in, a town **2** a fellow resident of the town in which one lives

towns·peo·ple (tounz′pē′pəl) *pl.n.* **1** the people of a town **2** people brought up in a town or city, as distinguished from those brought up in the country

Towns·ville (tounz′vil′) seaport on the E coast of Queensland, Australia

towns·wom·an (tounz′woom′ən) *n., pl.* **-wom′en** (-wim′in) **1** a woman who lives in, or has been reared in, a town **2** a woman who is a fellow resident of the town in which one lives

town·y (toun′ē) *n., pl.* **town′ies** [Informal] *alt. sp. of* TOWNIE

☆**tow·path** (tō′path′) *n.* a path alongside a canal, used by men or animals towing canalboats

tow·rope (tō′rōp′) *n.* a rope used in towing

☆**tow truck** a truck equipped for towing away vehicles that are disabled, illegally parked, etc.

tox·al·bu·min (täks′al byōō′min) *n.* ⟦TOX(IC) + ALBUMIN⟧ a poisonous protein found in certain plants and cultures of bacteria, and in snake venoms

☆**tox·a·phene** (täk′sə fēn′) *n.* ⟦arbitrary blend of TOXIC & CAMPHENE⟧ a commercial insecticide, approximately $C_{10}H_{10}Cl_8$, made by chlorinating camphene

tox·e·mi·a (täk sē′mē ə) *n.* ⟦ModL: see fol. & -EMIA⟧ a condition in which poisonous substances are spread throughout the body by the bloodstream, esp. toxins produced by pathogenic bacteria or by cells of the body: also sp. **tox·ae′mi·a** —**tox·e′mic** (-mik) *adj.*

tox·ic (täk′sik) *adj.* ⟦ML *toxicus* < L *toxicum*, a poison < Gr *toxicon*, a poison, orig., poison in which arrows were dipped < *toxicos*, of or for a bow < *toxon*, a bow⟧ **1** of, affected by, or caused by a toxin, or poison **2** acting as a poison; poisonous —*n.* a toxic substance; also, something contaminated by a toxic substance: *usually used in pl.* —**tox·ic′i·ty** (-is′ə tē) *n.*

tox·i·cant (täk′si kənt) *adj.* ⟦LL *toxicans*, prp. of *toxicare*, to smear with poison < L *toxicum*: see prec.⟧ poisonous; toxic —*n.* a poison; toxic agent

tox·i·co- (täk′si kō, -kə) ⟦ModL < Gr *toxikon*: see TOXIC⟧ *combining form* poison [*toxicogenic*]: also, before a vowel, **tox′ic-**

tox·i·co·gen·ic (täk′si kō jen′ik) *adj.* ⟦prec. + -GENIC⟧ producing toxic substances

tox·i·col·o·gy (täk′si käl′ə jē) *n.* ⟦Fr *toxicologie*: see TOXIC & -LOGY⟧ the science dealing with poisons and their effects and with antidotes for poisons —**tox′i·co·log′ic** (-kə läj′ik) *adj.*, **tox′i·co·log′i·cal** —**tox′i·co·log′i·cal·ly** *adv.* —**tox′i·col′o·gist** *n.*

tox·i·co·sis (täk′si kō′sis) *n.* ⟦ModL: see TOXIC & -OSIS⟧ any diseased condition caused by poisoning

toxic shock syndrome a disease, esp. of young menstruating women using highly absorbent tampons, characterized by fever, vomiting, diarrhea, and, often, shock and caused by a toxin-releasing bacterium (*Staphylococcus aureus*)

tox·in (täk′sin) *n.* ⟦TOX(IC) + -IN[1]⟧ **1** any of various poisonous compounds produced by some microorganisms and causing certain diseases: see ENDOTOXIN, EXOTOXIN **2** any of various similar poisons, related to proteins, formed in certain plants, as ricin, or secreted by certain animals, as snake venom: toxins, when injected into animals or humans, typically initiate the formation of antitoxins

tox·in-an·ti·tox·in (täk′sin an′ti täk′sin) *n.* a mixture of toxin and antitoxin formerly used for producing active immunity against a specific disease, esp. diphtheria: now superseded by toxoids

tox·oid (täk′soid′) *n.* ⟦TOX(IN) + -OID⟧ a toxin that has been treated, as with chemicals or heat, so as to eliminate the toxic qualities while retaining the antigenic properties

tox·oph·i·lite (täk säf′ə līt′) *n.* ⟦< *Toxophilus* (intended meaning, lover of the bow), book (1545) by Roger ASCHAM < (Gr *toxon*, a bow + *philos*, loving) + -ITE[1]⟧ a person who is especially fond of archery —**tox·oph′i·lit′ic** (-lit′ik) *adj.* —**tox·oph′i·ly** (-lē) *n.*

tox·o·plas·mo·sis (täk′sō plaz mō′sis) *n.* ⟦ModL: see TOXIC, -PLASM, & -OSIS⟧ a disease caused by a protozoan (*Toxoplasma gondii*), affecting humans and animals, esp. in the tropics: in its congenital form, it damages the central nervous system, eyes, and viscera

toy (toi) *n.* ⟦ME *toye* in sense 1 (< ?); other senses < ? MDu *toi*, finery, ornament; akin to Ger *zeug*, ON *tygi*, stuff, gear, prob. akin to TUG⟧ **1** [Obs.] *a)* amorous behavior; flirtation *b)* pastime; sport **2** a thing of little value or importance; trifle **3** a little ornament; bauble; trinket **4** any article to play with, esp. a plaything for children **5** any small thing, person, or animal; specif., a dog of a small breed, esp. one of the toy breeds —*adj.* **1** like a toy, or plaything, in size, use, etc. **2** designating a breed of dog of a kind smaller than a miniature, kept typically as a lap dog [a *toy* poodle] **3** of or being a model, figure, etc., esp. a miniature one, designed to be played with as a toy [a *toy* soldier, *toy* fire engine, *toy* stove] **4** of, containing, or having to do with toys [*toy* box, *toy* store] —*vi.* **1** to play or trifle (*with* a thing, an idea, etc.) **2** to engage in flirtation; dally —**SYN.** TRIFLE —**toy′er** *n.* —**toy′like′** *adj.*

To·ya·ma (tō yä′mə) seaport on the N coast of central Honshu, Japan

Toyn·bee (toin′bē), **Arnold J(oseph)** 1889-1975; Eng. historian

To·yo·ha·shi (tō′yō hä′shē) seaport on the S coast of Honshu, Japan

☆**to·yon** (tō′yən) *n.* ⟦AmSp, also *tollon*, prob. < Nahuatl name⟧ a large evergreen shrub or tree (*Heteromeles arbutifolia*) of the rose family, with clusters of white flowers and bright-red berries: it is native to California

To·yo·na·ka (tō′yō nä′kə) city in S Honshu, Japan, near Osaka

To·yo·ta (tō yōt′ə, toi ōt′ə) city in S Honshu, Japan, near Nagoya

toy·shop (toi′shäp′) *n.* a shop where toys are sold

Tp *abbrev.* township

TP *abbrev.* [Informal] toilet paper

TPA *abbrev.* TISSUE PLASMINOGEN ACTIVATOR: also written **t-PA** or **tPA**

TPB *abbrev.* trade paperback: also **tpb**

tpk or **tpke** *abbrev.* turnpike

tr *abbrev.* **1** trace **2** transitive **3** translated **4** translation **5** translator **6** transpose **7** treasurer **8** trustee

tra- (tra, trə) *prefix* TRANS-: used before *d, j, l, m, n,* or *v* [*tramontane*]

tra·be·at·ed (trā′bē āt′id) *adj.* ⟦< L *trabs*, pl. *trabes*, a beam: see TAVERN⟧ **1** built with horizontal beams or lintels, instead of arches **2** of such construction —**tra′be·a′tion** (-ā′shən) *n.*

tra·bec·u·la (trə bek′yōō lə) *n., pl.* **-lae′** (-lē′) or **-las** ⟦ModL < L, dim. of *trabs*: see prec.⟧ **1** *Anat., Zool. a)* a small rod, bar, or bundle of fibers *b)* a small septum of fibers forming, with others of its kind, an essential part of the framework of an organ or part **2** *Bot.* a rodlike structure, plate, or bar of tissue, as any of the crossbars in the peristome teeth of mosses —**tra·bec′u·lar** (-lər) *adj.*, **tra·bec′u·late** (-lit, -lāt′)

Trab·zon (trab zän′, trab′zän′) *Turk. name for* TREBIZOND (Turk. seaport)

trace[1] (trās) *n.* ⟦ME < OFr < *tracier*, to follow or move along on foot < VL **tractiare* < L *tractus*, a drawing along, track < pp. of *trahere*, to DRAW⟧ **1** [Obs.] a way followed or path taken **2** a mark, footprint, etc. left by the passage of a person, animal, or thing ☆**3** a beaten path or trail left by the repeated passage of persons, vehicles, etc. **4** any perceptible mark left by a past person, thing, or event; sign; evidence; vestige [the *traces* of war] **5** a barely perceptible amount; very small quantity [a *trace* of anger] **6** something drawn or traced, as a mark, sketch, etc. **7** the traced record of a recording instrument **8** *a)* the visible line or spot that moves across the face of a cathode-ray tube *b)* the path followed by this line or spot **9** *Chem.* a very small amount, usually one quantitatively immeasurable **10** *Math. a)* the intersection of a line or of a projecting plane of the line with the coordinate plane *b)* the sum of the elements on the main diagonal of a matrix **11** *Meteorol.* precipitation amounting to less than 0.127 mm (0.005 in) **12** *Psychol.* ENGRAM —*vt.* **traced, trac′ing** ⟦ME *tracen* < OFr *tracier*: see the *n.*⟧ **1** [Now Rare] to move along, follow, or traverse (a path, route, etc.) **2** to follow the trail or footprints of; track **3** *a)* to follow the development, process, or history of, esp. by proceeding from the latest to the earliest evidence, etc. *b)* to determine (a source, date, etc.) by this procedure **4** to discover or ascertain by investigating traces or vestiges of (something prehistoric, etc.) **5** *a)* to draw, sketch, outline, etc. *b)* to move through space in such a way as to represent or conform to the outline of (a given shape) [to *trace* circles in the air with a magic wand] **6** to ornament with tracery: used chiefly in the past participle **7** to copy (a drawing, etc.) by following its lines on a superimposed transparent sheet **8** to form (letters, etc.) carefully or laboriously **9** to make or copy with a tracer **10** to record by means of a curved, broken, or wavy line, as in a seismograph —*vi.* **1** to follow a path, route, development, etc.; make one's way **2** to go back or date back (*to* something past) —**trace′a·bil′i·ty** *n.*, **trace′a·ble·ness** —**trace′a·ble** *adj.* —**trace′a·bly** *adv.*

trace[2] (trās) *n.* ⟦ME *traice* < OFr *traiz*, pl. of *trait*: see TRAIT⟧ **1** either of two straps, chains, etc. connecting a draft animal's harness to the vehicle drawn **2** a rod, pivoted at each end, that transmits motion from one moving part of a machine to another —**kick over the traces** to shake off control; show insubordination or independence

trace element **1** a chemical element, as iron, copper, zinc, etc., essential in plant and animal nutrition, but only in minute quantities **2** any element present in minute quantities in an organism, soil, water, etc.

trac·er (trās′ər) *n.* **1** a person or thing that traces; specif., *a)* a person whose work is tracing drawings, designs, etc. on transparent paper *b)* a person whose work is tracing lost or missing articles, persons, etc. *c)* an instrument for tracing designs on cloth, etc. ☆**2** an inquiry sent out for a letter, package, etc. that is missing in transport **3** ammunition that traces its own course in the air with a trail of smoke or fire, so as to facilitate adjustment of the aim **4** a substance, usually a radioactive isotope, used to follow a chemical process or a complex sequence of biochemical reactions (as in an animal body), to locate diseased cells and tissues, to determine physical properties, etc. **5** a thread of contrasting color woven into or stamped on wire insulation for identification and for aid in tracing a circuit

trac·er·y (trās′ər ē) *n.*, *pl.* **-er·ies** ⟦< TRACE[1] + -ERY⟧ ornamental work of interlacing or branching lines, as in a Gothic window, some kinds of embroidery, etc.

tra·che- (trā′kē) *combining form* TRACHEO-: used before a vowel

tra·che·a (trā′kē ə; *chiefly Brit* trə kē′ə) *n.*, *pl.* **-che·ae′** (-ē′) or **-che·as** ⟦ME *trache* < ML *trachea* < LL *trachia*, windpipe < Gr *tracheia (arteria)*, rough (windpipe) < *trachys*, rough, akin to *thrassein*, to confuse < IE base *dher-, dark residue, dirt > DREGS⟧ **1** in the respiratory tract of most land vertebrates, the tube extending from the larynx to the two bronchi; windpipe **2** in the respiratory system of insects and certain other invertebrates, any of the tubules branching throughout the body and conducting air from the exterior **3** *Bot.* VESSEL (sense 4*b*)

tra·che·al (-əl) *adj.* **1** of, like, or having a trachea or tracheae **2** of or composed of woody tissue having tracheae (vessels) or tracheids, or both

tra·che·ate (-it, -āt′) *adj.* breathing through tracheae, as insects

tra·che·id (-id) *n.* ⟦TRACHE(O)- + -ID⟧ *Bot.* a type of long, thick-walled, tubelike, nonliving cell found in xylem, esp. of the conifers —**tra·che′i·dal** *adj.*

tra·che·i·tis (trā′kē īt′is) *n.* ⟦ModL: see TRACHEA & -ITIS⟧ inflammation of the trachea

tra·che·o- (trā′kē ō, -ə) ⟦< TRACHEA⟧ *combining form* trachea, trachea and *[tracheotomy]*

tra·che·o·bron·chi·al (trā′kē ō bräŋ′kē əl) *adj.* relating to the trachea and bronchi

tra·che·ole (trā′kē ōl′) *n.* ⟦TRACHE(O)- + *-ole*, dim. suffix < Fr < L *-olus, -olum, -ola*⟧ any of the extremely small, thin-walled, respiratory tubules originating from the ends of the smallest insect tracheae

tra·che·o·phyte (trā′kē ə fit′) *n.* ⟦TRACHEO- + -PHYTE⟧ any vascular plant

tra·che·ot·o·my (trā′kē ät′ə mē) *n.*, *pl.* **-mies** ⟦TRACHEO- + -TOMY⟧ surgical incision of the trachea, as for making an artificial breathing hole: also **tra′che·os′to·my** (-äs′tə mē)

tra·cho·ma (trə kō′mə) *n.* ⟦ModL < Gr *trachōma*, roughness < *trachys*, rough: see TRACHEA⟧ a contagious infection of the conjunctiva and cornea, caused by a bacterium (*Chlamydia trachomatis*) and characterized by granulation and eventual scar formation —**tra·chom′a·tous** (-käm′ə təs, -kō′mə-) *adj.*

tra·chyte (trā′kīt′, trak′īt′) *n.* ⟦Fr < Gr *trachys*, rough: see TRACHEA⟧ a fine-grained, light-colored, extrusive igneous rock, consisting chiefly of alkali feldspars: it is the extrusive equivalent to syenite

tra·chyt·ic (trə kit′ik) *adj.* of or pertaining to the internal structure of some igneous rocks, as trachyte, in which hairlike feldspar crystals are in nearly parallel rows

trac·ing (trās′iŋ) *n.* **1** the action of one that traces **2** something made by tracing; specif., *a)* a copy of a drawing, etc. made by tracing the lines on a superimposed, transparent sheet *b)* the record of a recording instrument, in the form of a traced line

track (trak) *n.* ⟦LME *trak* < MFr *trac*, a track, tract, trace < ?⟧ **1** a mark or series of marks or other discoverable evidence left by a person, animal, or thing that has passed, as a footprint, wheel rut, wake of a boat, etc. **2** a trace or vestige **3** a beaten path or trail left by the repeated passage of persons, animals, or vehicles **4** *a)* [*often pl.*] a course or line of motion or action; route; path; way *[to double back on one's tracks]* *b)* the projection of the flight path of an airplane, rocket, etc. on the surface of the earth **5** a sequence of ideas, events, etc.; succession **6** a path or circuit laid out for running, horse racing, etc. ☆**7** any of the courses of study continuing through succeeding grades in an educational structure (**tracking**), arranged according to various levels of mastery, to which students are assigned on the basis of test performance, abilities, needs, etc. **8** a pair of parallel metal rails, with their crossties, etc., on which trains, streetcars, etc. run ☆**9** the distance between the centers of the tread of parallel wheels, as of an automobile **10** either of the two endless belts with which tanks, some tractors, etc. are equipped for moving over rough ground **11** *a)* the narrow channel, containing lengthwise copper wires or strips carrying electric current, into which track lights are inserted *b)* any of various structural channels or grooves, as one that holds a sliding door or window **12** the tread of an automobile tire ☆**13** *a)* athletic sports performed on a track, as running, hurdling, etc. *b)* track and field sports together **14** *a)* SOUNDTRACK *b)* any of the separate divisions on a phonograph record, compact disc, etc. containing individual selections *c)* any of the separate, parallel recording surfaces extending along the length of a magnetic tape *d)* the long continuous spiral groove on a phonograph record in which a stylus moves *e)* any of the concentric bands on a hard disk or floppy disk, constituting distinct areas for data storage **15** *Film* TRACKING SHOT —*vt.* **1** *a)* to follow the track or footprints of *[to track game]* *b)* to follow (a path, etc.) **2** to trace by means of vestiges, evidence, etc. **3** to plot the path of and record data from (an aircraft, spacecraft, missile, etc.) using radar, a telescope, etc. **4** to tread or travel **5** *a)* to leave tracks or footprints on (often with *up*) ☆*b)* to leave in the form of tracks *[to track dirt over a floor]* ☆**6** to provide with tracks or rails ☆**7** *Educ.* to assign to a TRACK (*n.* 7) **8** *Film* to follow (a moving object or person) with a moving camera —*vi.* **1** to run in the same (width) track **2** to be in alignment, as gears, wheels, or the stylus of a phonograph cartridge with a groove on a record **3** to have a (specified) width between the wheels *[a narrow-gauge car tracks less than 56 inches]* **4** *Film* to track a moving object: said of a camera or its operator —☆**(dead) in one's tracks** [Informal] abruptly, as from being stunned or otherwise rendered unable to proceed *[his insult stopped me in my tracks]* —**keep track of** to keep an account of; stay informed about —**lose track of** to fail to keep informed about; lose sight or knowledge of —☆**make tracks** [Informal] to proceed or depart hurriedly —**on (or off) the track** keeping to (or straying from) the subject, objective, or goal —☆**the wrong side of the tracks** ⟦with ref. to railroad tracks⟧ that part of a community where those considered socially and culturally inferior live —**track down 1** to pursue until caught, as by following tracks **2** to investigate fully or search for until found —**track′er** *n.*

☆**track·age** (trak′ij) *n.* ⟦prec. + AGE⟧ **1** all the tracks of a railroad **2** *a)* permission for a railroad to use the tracks of another *b)* a charge for this

track and field a series of contests in running, jumping, shot-putting, etc. performed on a track and on a FIELD (*n.* 11*b*) —**track′-and-field′** *adj.*

track·ball (trak′bôl′) *n.* a device, typically built into a computer console or mouse, containing a recessed ball that can be freely rotated by hand in any direction so as to move or position the cursor

tracking shot *Film* a shot, as of a moving object or person, made by a camera moving forward, backward, or sideways

☆**tracking station** a station equipped to track the path of and record data from a spacecraft, satellite, etc.

track·less (-lis) *adj.* **1** *a)* without a track, trail, or path *[a trackless wilderness]* *b)* leaving no track, or trail **2** not running on tracks *[a trackless trolley]*: cf. TROLLEY BUS

track lighting a system for lighting areas in a room, consisting of swiveling spotlights (**track lights**) inserted variously along a narrow, electrified track

☆**track·man** (-mən) *n.*, *pl.* **-men** (-mən) **1** a person whose work is laying and repairing railroad tracks: also **track′lay′er** (-lā′ər) **2** an athlete who competes in track-and-field events, esp. a runner

track record ⟦prob. with reference to the running records of racehorses⟧ [Informal] the record of the performance of a person, organization, etc. as in some activity or on some issue

track·suit (-so͞ot′) *n.* ⟦see TRACK (*n.* 13)⟧ a loosefitting outfit worn as during exercise, consisting of a pair of trousers and a jacket or pullover top, usually of a light, waterproof fabric

☆**track system** a system of education in which students are put in a TRACK (*n.* 7)

☆**track·walk·er** (-wôk′ər) *n.* a person whose work is walking along, and inspecting, sections of railroad track

track·way (-wā′) *n.* **1** a track or path worn by footsteps **2** a stretch of fossilized mud, etc. in which a sequence of footprints has been preserved

tract[1] (trakt) *n.* ⟦L *tractus*, a drawing out, extent < pp. of *trahere*, to DRAW⟧ **1** [Archaic] *a)* duration or lapse of time *b)* a period of time **2** a continuous expanse of land or of water, mineral deposit, etc.; stretch; extent; area ☆**3** [Chiefly West] a housing development: see DEVELOPMENT (sense 4) **4** *Anat., Zool.* *a)* a system of parts or organs, or an elongated region, having some special function *[the genitourinary tract]* *b)* a bundle of nerve fibers having the same origin, termination, and function **5** ⟦ML(Ec) *tractus*⟧ *R.C.Ch.* in the former Latin Mass, one or more penitential verses said, as in Lent, after the Gradual

tract[2] (trakt) *n.* ⟦ME *tracte* < LL *tractatus*: see TRACTATE⟧ **1** [Obs.] a treatise **2** a propagandizing pamphlet, esp. one on a religious or political subject

trac·ta·ble (trak′tə bəl) *adj.* ⟦L *tractabilis* < *tractare*, to drag, haul, freq. of *trahere*, to DRAW⟧ **1** easily managed, taught, or controlled; docile; compliant **2** easily worked; malleable —*SYN.* OBEDIENT —**trac′ta·bil′i·ty** *n.*, **trac′ta·ble·ness** —**trac′ta·bly** *adv.*

Trac·tar·i·an·ism (trak ter′ē ən iz′əm) *n.* ⟦< "*Tracts* for the Times," pamphlets issued at Oxford (1833-41)⟧ the principles of the OXFORD MOVEMENT, favoring the restoration of certain Catholic doctrines and practices —**Trac·tar′i·an** *n.*, *adj.*

trac·tate (trak′tāt′) *n.* ⟦LL *tractatus*, discussion, treatise < pp. of L *tractare*: see TRACTABLE⟧ a treatise or dissertation

tract house ⟦< TRACT[1] (*n.* 3)⟧ a residential house built to a common or frequently repeated design as part of a housing development

trac·tile (trak′təl, -tīl′) ***adj.*** ⟦< L *tractus* (see fol.) + -ILE⟧ that can be drawn out in length; ductile; tensile —**trac·til′i·ty** (-til′ə tē) ***n.***

trac·tion (trak′shən) ***n.*** ⟦ML *tractio* < L *tractus*, pp. of *trahere*, to DRAW⟧ **1** *a)* a pulling or drawing, esp. of a load, vehicle, etc. over a road, track, or other surface *b)* the state of being pulled or drawn *c)* the kind of power used for pulling or drawing *[electric traction]* **2** *a)* a pulling, as of the muscles of the leg, arm, etc., in order to bring a fractured or dislocated bone into place *b)* a constant pull of this kind maintained by means of some apparatus, as for relieving pressure **3** the power, as of tires on pavement, to grip or hold to a surface while moving, without slipping **4** footing, headway, momentum, etc. *[a candidate gaining traction among independent voters]* —**trac′tion·al** ***adj.***

trac·tive (trak′tiv) ***adj.*** ⟦ML *tractivus*: see prec. & -IVE⟧ used for pulling or drawing

☆**trac·tor** (trak′tər) ***n.*** ⟦ModL < L *tractus*: see TRACTION⟧ **1** a powerful vehicle with a gasoline or diesel engine and large rear wheels or endless belt treads, used for pulling farm machinery, hauling loads, etc. **2** a large, powerful truck with a driver's cab and a fifth wheel, designed to pull a trailer **3** an airplane with its propeller or propellers mounted in front of the engine

☆**trac·tor-trail·er** (-trā′lər) ***n.*** a combination of a TRACTOR (sense 2) and a trailer or semitrailer, used in trucking

Tra·cy (trā′sē) ***n.*** ⟦< the surname *Tracy* < the place name *Tracy* < Fr place name in Normandy⟧ a feminine and masculine name: var. *Tracey*

trad (trad) ***adj.*** *short for* TRADITIONAL (often, specif., sense 2)

trade (trād) ***n.*** ⟦ME, a track, course of action < MLowG, a track < OS *trada*, a trace, trail, akin to ME *trede*, TREAD⟧ **1** [Obs.] *a)* a track; path *b)* a course; regular procedure **2** *a)* a means of earning one's living; occupation, work, or line of business *b)* an occupation requiring skill in any of certain kinds of work done with the hands, as distinguished from unskilled work or from a profession or business; craft *c)* all the persons or companies in a particular line of business or work **3** the buying and selling of commodities or the bartering of goods; commerce **4** dealings or the market involving specified commodities, customers, seasons, etc. *[the tourist trade, the Easter trade]* **5** customers; clientele **6** a purchase or sale; deal; bargain **7** an exchange; swap **8** [*pl.*] the trade winds: see TRADE WIND —***adj.*** **1** of or relating to trade or commerce **2** of, by, or for those in a particular business or industry *[trade papers or journals]* **3** of the members in the trades, or crafts *[trade unions]* **4** of or having to do with the publishing of books intended for sale to the general public; specif., designating or of a paperback book of a size similar to a typical hardcover book: see also TRADE BOOK, MASS-MARKET (*adj.* 2) —***vi.*** **trad′ed**, **trad′ing** **1** to carry on a trade or business **2** to have business dealings (*with* someone) **3** to make an exchange (*with* someone) **4** [Informal] to be a customer (*at* a specified store or shop) —***vt.*** **1** to exchange; barter; swap **2** to buy and sell (stocks, etc.) —**SYN.** BUSINESS, SELL —**trade down** to trade something for something of lower value —☆**trade in** to give (one's used automobile, etc.) as part of the purchase price of a new one —**trade on** (or **upon**) to take advantage of; exploit —**trade up** to trade something for something of higher value —**trad′a·ble** ***adj.***, **trade′a·ble**

trade acceptance a bill of exchange or draft drawn upon the purchaser by the seller and accepted by the purchaser for payment at a specified time

trade association an association of merchants or business firms for the unified promotion of their common interests

trade book a book intended for sale to the general public, as distinguished from a textbook, subscription book, etc.

trade·craft (trād′kraft′) ***n.*** ⟦orig., a trade guild; later, skill in a trade; current sense < Brit *the trade*, the secret service⟧ the practices and techniques of espionage

trade discount a deduction from the list price allowed a retailer by a manufacturer, wholesaler, or distributor, or allowed one firm by another in the same trade

trade edition that edition of a book sold to the general public, as distinguished from a school edition, etc. of the same book

☆**trade-in** (trād′in′) ***n.*** **1** a used car, appliance, etc. given or taken as part payment in the purchase of a new one **2** a transaction involving a trade-in **3** the valuation allowed by the seller on a trade-in

trade journal (*or* **magazine**) a magazine with contents of interest to those in a given trade, business, or industry, sometimes distributed without cost to its readers

trade·mark (trād′märk′) ***n.*** **1** a symbol, design, word, letter, etc. used by a manufacturer or dealer to distinguish a product or products from those of competitors: usually registered and protected by law: cf. SERVICE MARK **2** [Informal] a distinctive feature or characteristic that serves to identify the maker or originator *[the use of reddish gold is one of Titian's trademarks]* —***vt.*** **1** to put a trademark on (a product) **2** to register (a symbol, word, etc.) as a trademark —***adj.*** [Informal] of or being a distinctive, identifying feature or characteristic *[a mystery novel full of the author's trademark plot twists]*

trade name **1** the name by which a commodity is commonly known in trade **2** a name used by a company to describe a product, service, etc., often, specif., a name that is a trademark or service mark **3** the name under which a company carries on business

☆**trade-off** (trād′ôf′) ***n.*** an exchange; esp., a giving up of one benefit, advantage, etc. in order to gain another regarded as more desirable: also written **tradeoff**

trad·er (trā′dər) ***n.*** **1** a person who trades; merchant **2** a ship used in trade ☆**3** a stockbroker who trades esp. for his own account rather than customers' accounts

trade route any route customarily taken by trading ships, caravans, etc.

trad·es·can·ti·a (trad′is kan′shē ə, -shə) ***n.*** ⟦ModL, after John *Tradescant* (1608-62), Eng naturalist & traveler⟧ SPIDERWORT

trade school a school where a trade or trades are taught

trade secret any device, method, formula, etc. known to the manufacturer but not to competitors

trades·man (trādz′mən) ***n.***, *pl.* **-men** (-mən) **1** a person in a TRADE (*n.* 2*b*); craftsman or artisan **2** [Chiefly Brit.] a person engaged in trade; esp., a storekeeper

trades·peo·ple (-pē′pəl) ***pl.n.*** people engaged in trade; esp., storekeepers: also **trades′folk′** (-fōk′)

trades·wom·an (-woom′ən) ***n.***, *pl.* **-wom′en** (-wim′in) a female tradesman

trade union **1** LABOR UNION: also [Chiefly Brit.] **trades union** **2** a labor union consisting of workers in a particular trade or craft —**trade unionism** —**trade unionist**

trade wind ⟦earlier *trade*, adv., steadily in phr. *to blow trade*⟧ a wind that blows steadily toward the equator from the northeast in the tropics north of the equator and from the southeast in the tropics south of the equator

trading card any of various small, illustrated collectible cards issued in sets; often, specif., such a card displaying the statistics and photograph of a professional athlete

☆**trading post** a store or station in an outpost, settlement, etc., where trading is done

trading stamp a stamp given by some merchants as a premium to customers, redeemable in specified quantities for various kinds of merchandise

tra·di·tion (trə dish′ən) ***n.*** ⟦ME *tradycion* < MFr *tradicion* < L *traditio*, a surrender, delivery, tradition < *traditus*, pp. of *tradere*, to deliver: see TREASON⟧ **1** [Obs.] a surrender or betrayal **2** *a)* the handing down orally of stories, beliefs, customs, etc. from generation to generation *b)* a story, belief, custom, proverb, etc. handed down in this way **3** a historical line of conventions, principles, or attitudes characteristic of a school, social group, movement, etc. *[the realist tradition in literature]* **4** a long-established custom or practice having the effect of precedent or unwritten law **5** *Law* DELIVERY (sense 8) **6** *Theol.* *a)* among Jews, the unwritten religious code and doctrine regarded as handed down from Moses *b)* among Christians, the unwritten teachings regarded as handed down from Jesus and the Apostles *c)* among Muslims, the sayings and acts attributed to Muhammad and transmitted orally —**tra·di′tion·less** ***adj.***

tra·di·tion·al (trə dish′ə nəl) ***adj.*** **1** of, handed down by, or conforming to tradition; conventional: also **tra·di′tion·ar′y** (-ner′ē) or [Rare] **trad·i·tive** (trad′ə tiv) **2** designating or of a style of improvised jazz associated historically with early black New Orleans musicians and typically played by a band made up of one or two cornets, a clarinet, a trombone, and a rhythm section that includes a banjo and a tuba —**tra·di′tion·al·ly** ***adv.***

tra·di·tion·al·ism (-iz′əm) ***n.*** **1** adherence to tradition; sometimes, specif., excessive attachment to tradition **2** the doctrine, condemned by the Roman Catholic Church in the 19th cent., that the only valid religious belief is that handed down by tradition from an original divine revelation —**tra·di′tion·al·ist** ***n.*** —**tra·di′tion·al·is′tic** ***adj.***

tra·di·tion·ist (-ist) ***n.*** **1** an upholder of tradition **2** a transmitter, recorder, or student of tradition

tra·duce (trə do͞os′, -dyo͞os′) ***vt.*** **-duced′**, **-duc′ing** ⟦L *traducere*, to lead along, exhibit as a spectacle, disgrace < *tra(ns)*, across, over + *ducere*, to lead: see TRANS- & DUCT⟧ **1** to say untrue or malicious things about; defame; slander; vilify **2** to make a mockery of; betray —**tra·duce′ment** ***n.*** —**tra·duc′er** ***n.***

tra·du·cian·ism (trə do͞o′shən iz′əm, -dyo͞o′-) ***n.*** ⟦< LL *traducianus*, believer in this doctrine < *tradux*, a shoot, lit., that which is brought over < *traducere*: see prec.⟧ *Theol.* the doctrine that a child's soul is generated by the child's parents: opposed to CREATIONISM (sense 1) —**tra·du′cian·ist** ***n.***

Tra·fal·gar (trə fal′gər; *Sp*trä′fäl gär′), **Cape** cape on the SW coast of Spain, between Cadiz & the Strait of Gibraltar: site of a naval battle (1805) in which Nelson's British fleet defeated Napoleon's fleet

traf·fic (traf′ik) ***n.*** ⟦Fr *trafic* < It *traffico* < *trafficare*, to trade < L *trans*, across + It *ficcare*, to thrust in, bring < VL **figicare*, intens. for L *figere*: see FINISH⟧ **1** [Archaic] *a)* transportation of goods for trading *b)* trading over great distances; commerce **2** buying and selling; barter; trade, sometimes, specif., of a wrong or illegal kind *[traffic in drugs]* **3** dealings or business (*with* someone) **4** *a)* the movement or number of automobiles along a street, pedestrians along a sidewalk, ships using a port, etc. *b)* the automobiles, pedestrians, ships, etc. so moving **5** the number of passengers, quantity of freight, etc. carried by a transportation company during a given period **6** the volume of telegrams, calls, etc. transmitted by a communications company during a given period **7** the number of potential customers entering a retail store during a given period —***adj.*** of or having to do with traffic *[a traffic violation, traffic manager]* —***vi.*** **-ficked**, **-fick·ing** **1** to carry on traffic, esp. illegal trade (*in* a commodity) **2** to have traffic, trade, or dealings (*with* someone) —**traf′fick·er** ***n.***

☆**traffic circle** a circular street at the intersection of several streets with vehicles traveling in one direction only, designed to facilitate the flow of traffic; rotary

☆**traffic court** a local court having jurisdiction over those charged with violating statutes or ordinances governing the flow of traffic on streets and highways

traffic island a platform or marked area in a roadway, from which vehicular traffic is diverted so as to separate such traffic, or to protect pedestrians: cf. SAFETY ZONE

☆**traffic light** (*or* **signal**) a mechanical device consisting of a set of signal lights operating in sequence (usually green to yellow to red and back to green), placed at intersections to regulate traffic

☆**traffic pattern** a pattern of flight in the air above or around an airport normally followed by aircraft before landing or after taking off

trag·a·canth (trag′ə kanth′) *n.* ⟦Fr *tragacanthe* < L *tragacantha* < Gr *tragakantha* < *tragos*, goat (see TRAGEDY) + *akantha*, thorn (see ACANTHO-)⟧ **1** a white or reddish, tasteless and odorless gum, used in pharmacy, calico printing, etc. **2** any of various, esp. Asian, plants (genus *Astragalus*) of the pea family, yielding this gum

tra·ge·di·an (trə jē′dē ən) *n.* ⟦ME *tragedien* < MFr⟧ **1** a writer of tragedies **2** an actor of tragic roles

tra·ge·di·enne (trə jē′dē en′) *n.* ⟦Fr *tragédienne*⟧ an actress of tragic roles

trag·e·dy (traj′ə dē) *n., pl.* **-dies** ⟦ME *tragedie* < MFr < L *tragoedia* < Gr *tragōidia*, tragedy, lit., the song of the goat < *tragos*, goat (< IE **treg-*, to gnaw < base **ter-*, to rub, grind > THROW) + *ōidē*, song (see ODE): so named? because of the goatskin dress of the performers, representing satyrs⟧ **1** *a)* a serious play or drama typically dealing with the problems of a central character, leading to an unhappy or disastrous ending brought on, as in ancient drama, by fate and a tragic flaw in this character, or, in modern drama, usually by moral weakness, psychological maladjustment, or social pressures (see CATHARSIS, sense 2, TRAGIC FLAW) *b)* such plays collectively *c)* the branch of drama having to do with such plays **2** the writing, acting, or theoretical principles of this kind of drama **3** a novel or other literary work with similar characteristics **4** the tragic element of such a literary work, or of a real event **5** a very sad or tragic event or sequence of events; disaster

trag·ic (traj′ik) *adj.* ⟦L *tragicus* < Gr *tragikos*⟧ **1** of, or having the nature of, tragedy **2** like or characteristic of tragedy; bringing great harm, suffering, etc.; calamitous, disastrous, fatal, etc. **3** appropriate to the acting of tragedy [in a *tragic* voice] **4** writing or acting in tragedy Also **trag′i·cal** —*n.* the tragic element in art or life —**trag′i·cal·ly** *adv.* —**trag′i·cal·ness** *n.*

tragic flaw in a tragedy, a character flaw, as pride, that leads to the downfall of the protagonist

trag·i·com·e·dy (traj′i käm′ə dē) *n., pl.* **-dies** ⟦Fr *tragicomédie* < LL *tragicomedia*, contr. of L *tragicocomoedia:* see TRAGIC & COMEDY⟧ **1** a play or other literary work combining tragic and comic elements **2** a situation or incident in life like this —**trag′i·com′ic** (-käm′ik) *adj.*, **trag′i·com′i·cal** —**trag′i·com′i·cal·ly** *adv.*

trag·o·pan (trag′ō pan′) *n.* ⟦ModL < L, fabulous bird < Gr, lit., goat-Pan < *tragos*, goat (see TRAGEDY) + *Pan*, Pan⟧ any of several brightly colored Asian pheasants (genus *Tragopan*) with two erectile, fleshy, hornlike protuberances on the head

tra·gus (trā′gəs) *n., pl.* **-gi′** (-jī′) ⟦LL < Gr *tragos*, hairy part of the ear, lit., goat: see TRAGEDY⟧ the fleshy, cartilaginous protrusion at the front of the external ear, partly extending over the opening of the ear

Tra·herne (trə hurn′), **Thomas** 1637-74; Eng. poet

tra·hi·son des clercs (trȧ ē zōn dā kler′) ⟦Fr, lit., treason of the scholars⟧ a compromising of intellectual integrity, esp. for political reasons

trail (trāl) *vt.* ⟦ME *trailen* < MFr *trailler* < VL **tragulare* < L *tragula*, small sledge, dragnet < *trahere*, to DRAW⟧ **1** *a)* to drag or let drag behind one, esp. on the ground, etc. *b)* to bring along behind [*trailing* exhaust fumes] *c)* to pull or tow **2** *a)* to make or mark (a path, track, etc.), as by treading down *b)* to make a path in (grass, etc.) **3** to follow the tracks of; track **4** to hunt by tracking **5** *a)* to follow behind, esp. in a lagging manner *b)* to be or lag behind, as in a contest **6** *Mil.* to carry (a rifle, etc.) in the right hand with the arm extended downward so that the muzzle is tilted forward and the butt is near the ground —*vi.* **1** to hang down, esp. behind, so as to drag on the ground, etc. **2** to grow so long as to extend along the ground, over rocks, etc.: said of some plants **3** to extend in an irregular line; straggle **4** to flow behind in a long, thin stream, wisp, etc. [smoke *trailed* from the chimney] **5** to move, walk, go along, etc. wearily, heavily, or slowly; crawl; drag **6** *a)* to follow or lag behind *b)* to be losing, as in a sports contest [to *trail* by 13 points] **7** to track game: said of hounds **8** to grow gradually weaker, dimmer, less direct, etc.: with *off* or *away* —*n.* ⟦ME *traille* < MFr < the v.⟧ **1** something that trails or is trailed behind **2** a mark, footprint, scent, etc. left by a person, animal, or thing that has passed ☆**3** *a)* a path or track made by repeated passage or deliberately blazed *b)* a paved or maintained path or track, as for bicycling or hiking **4** *a)* any route or journey (often fig.) [candidates on the campaign *trail*] *b)* a series of events or conditions following something; train [an illness bringing medical bills in its *trail*] **5** *Mil.* *a)* the position of trailing a rifle *b)* a beamlike part of a gun carriage, which may be lowered to the ground to form a rear brace —**trail′less** *adj.*

trail bike a small motorcycle for off-road riding, as along dirt trails

☆**trail·blaz·er** (trāl′blā′zər) *n.* **1** a person who blazes a trail **2** a pioneer in any field —**trail′blaz′ing** *n.*

trail·er (trā′lər) *n.* **1** a person, animal, or thing that trails another ☆**2** a cart, wagon, or large van, designed to be pulled by an automobile, truck, or TRACTOR (sense 2), for hauling freight, animals, a boat, etc. ☆**3** a closed vehicle designed to be pulled by an automobile or truck and equipped as a place to live or work in, as one with beds, cooking facilities, etc.: see also MOBILE HOME ☆**4** *Film* *a)* ⟦so called because originally attached to the end of a reel of film⟧ an advertisement for a feature film, typically consisting of brief portions of scenes from that film *b)* a blank length of film at the end of a reel —*vt.* to pull or tow (a boat, car, etc.) by using a TRAILER (*n.* 2) —*vi.* to travel by using a TRAILER (*n.* 3)

☆**trailer park** an area, usually with piped water, electricity, etc., designed to provide rental space for trailers, esp. mobile homes, to be parked for a long or short time

trail·head (trāl′hed′) *n.* the place where a trail for hiking, horseback riding, etc. begins or ends

☆**trailing arbutus** ARBUTUS (sense 2)

trailing edge *Aeron.* the rear edge of an airfoil, propeller blade, etc.

☆**trail mix** a mixture of nuts, seeds, dried fruits, bits of chocolate, etc. eaten as by hikers for quick energy

train (trān) *n.* ⟦ME *traine* < OFr *trahin* < *trahiner*, to draw on < VL **traginare* < L *trahere*, to pull, DRAW⟧ **1** something that hangs down and drags behind; specif., *a)* a part of a dress, skirt, etc. that trails *b)* the tail feathers of a bird [the *train* of a peacock] *c)* a stream of something trailing behind **2** a group of persons following as attendants in a procession; retinue; suite **3** a group of persons, animals, vehicles, etc. that follow one another in a line; procession; caravan; cortege **4** the persons, vehicles, etc. carrying supplies, ammunition, food, etc. for combat troops **5** a series of events or conditions that follow some happening; aftermath [a war bringing famine and disease in its *train*] **6** any connected order or arrangement; series; sequence [a *train* of thought] **7** a line of gunpowder, etc. that serves as a fuse for an explosive charge **8** a series of connected mechanical parts for transmitting motion [a *train* of gears] **9** a line of connected railroad cars pulled or pushed by a locomotive or locomotives —*vt.* ⟦ME *trainen* < OFr *trahiner*⟧ **1** [Rare] to trail or drag **2** to guide the growth of (a plant), as by tying, pruning, etc. **3** to subject to certain action, exercises, etc. in order to bring to a desired condition [a surgeon's hand *trained* to be steady] **4** to guide or control the mental, moral, etc. development of; bring up; rear **5** to instruct so as to make proficient or qualified [to *train* nurses at a hospital] **6** *a)* to teach (animals) to perform tricks or obey commands *b)* to teach (a child or pet) to control urination and defecation **7** to prepare or make fit for an athletic contest, etc. as by exercise, diet, etc. **8** to aim (a gun, binoculars, etc.) at something; bring to bear: usually with *on* —*vi.* to administer or undergo training —*SYN.* TEACH —**train′a·ble** *adj.*

train·band (trān′band′) *n.* ⟦contr. of *trained band*⟧ [Historical] a band of citizens trained locally as a militia

train·ee (trā nē′) *n.* a person undergoing job training, military training, etc.

train·ee·ship (-ship) *n.* **1** the position or status of trainee, esp. a position for advanced training or research with a grant for financial support **2** such a grant

train·er (trān′ər) *n.* **1** a person who trains; specif., *a)* a person who trains animals, as racehorses, show dogs, circus beasts, etc. *b)* a person who trains, provides first aid for, etc. athletes in competition **2** *a)* something, as an apparatus, used in training *b)* a flight simulator or special aircraft used to train pilots **3** [Chiefly Brit.] SNEAKER (sense 2)

train·ing (-iŋ) *n.* **1** the action or method of one that trains **2** the process or experience of being trained —*adj.* of or for use or preparation at an early stage of learning or development [a *training* manual, *training* bra]

training camp *Sports* a series of sessions held to prepare for a contest or competition, as for a single boxing bout or a season of playing baseball or football

training school **1** a school that gives training in some vocation or profession, as nursing, acting, etc. **2** an institution for detaining and reeducating juvenile offenders

training ship a ship used for training persons in seamanship, esp. in a navy

☆**training table** a table or dining room where athletes in training eat supervised meals

training wheels a pair of small wheels attached to the rear wheel of a bicycle to provide stability for someone learning to ride

☆**train·man** (trān′mən) *n., pl.* **-men** (-mən) a person who works on a railroad train or in a railroad yard, usually as a conductor's assistant; esp., a brakeman

train·mas·ter (-mas′tər) *n.* ☆**1** [Historical] the man in charge of a wagon train **2** a railroad official in charge of some division of a line

train oil ⟦earlier *trane* < MDu *traen*, akin to Ger *träne*, a tear: basic sense "exuded oil"⟧ whale oil, or, formerly, oil from seals, codfish, etc.

train wreck [Informal] anything characterized by utter failure, disorder, calamity, etc.

traipse (trāps) *vi., vt.* **traipsed, traips′ing** ⟦earlier *trapse*, prob. < or akin to Fris *trapsen*, to walk aimlessly, with storklike gait, intens. of **trappen*; akin to MDu, to tread, stamp, OE *treppan*: see TRAP[1]⟧ to walk, wander, tramp, or gad —*n.* the act of traipsing

trait (trāt) *n.* ⟦Fr, a draft, line, stroke < L *tractus*, pp. of *trahere*, to DRAW⟧ **1** a distinguishing quality or characteristic, as of personality **2** CHARACTER (*n.* 15) **3** [Rare] a stroke, trace, or touch —*SYN.* QUALITY

trai·tor (trāt′ər) *n.* ⟦ME *traitour* < OFr *traitor* < L *traditor*, one who betrays < *traditus*, pp. of *tradere*, to hand over, betray: see TREASON⟧ a person who betrays his or her country, cause, friends, etc.; one guilty of treason or treachery

trai·tor·ous (trāt′ər əs) *adj.* **1** of, or having the nature of, a traitor; treacherous; faithless **2** of or involving treason; treasonable —*SYN.* FAITHLESS —**trai′tor·ous·ly** *adv.* —**trai′tor·ous·ness** *n.*

trai·tress (trā′tris) ***n.*** [Now Chiefly Literary] a female traitor: see -ESS: also **trai·tor·ess** (trāt′ər is)

Tra·jan (trā′jən) (L. name *Marcus Ulpius Trajanus*) A.D. 53?-117; Rom. general & statesman, born in Spain: emperor of Rome (98-117)

tra·ject (trə jekt′) ***vt.*** ⟦< L *trajectus*, pp. of *trajicere*, to throw or fling over or across < *tra-* (see TRANS-) + *jacere*, to throw: see JET[1]⟧ [Now Rare] to transmit or transport —**tra·jec′tion** ***n.***

tra·jec·to·ry (trə jek′tə rē) ***n., pl.* -ries** ⟦ML *trajectorius* < L *trajectus*: see prec.⟧ **1** the curved path of something hurtling through space, esp. that of a projectile from the time it leaves the muzzle of the gun **2** *Math. a)* a curve or surface that passes through all the curves of a given family at the same angle *b)* a curve or surface that fits a particular law such as passing through a given set of points

tra-la (trä lä′) ***interj.*** used conventionally in singing, esp. as a short refrain, to express gaiety or lightheartedness: often **tra′-la-la′**

tram[1] (tram) ***n.*** ⟦Fr *trame* < L *trama*, the woof⟧ a double, twisted silk thread used as the weft in fine silks and velvets

tram[2] (tram) ***n.*** ⟦E dial., shaft, wooden frame for carrying, rail, coal wagon, prob. < LowG *traam*, a beam⟧ **1** an open railway car for carrying loads in mines: also **tram′car′** **2** the basket or car of an overhead conveyor **3** *short for* TRAMROAD **4** [Brit.] *a)* a streetcar (in full **tram′car′**) *b)* [*often pl.*] a streetcar line (in full **tram′line′**) —***vt., vi.*** **trammed, tram′ming** to convey or be conveyed by tram

tram[3] (tram) ***n.*** *short for* TRAMMEL (***n.*** 6) —***vt., vi.*** **trammed, tram′ming** to adjust, align, or measure with a TRAMMEL (***n.*** 6)

tram·mel (tram′əl) ***n.*** ⟦ME *tramaile* < MFr *tramail*, a net < ML *tremaculum*, kind of fishing net < L *tres*, THREE + *macula*, a mesh⟧ **1** *a)* a fishing net consisting of two outer layers of coarse mesh and a loosely hung middle layer of fine mesh *b)* a fowling net: also **trammel net** **2** a kind of shackle for a horse, esp. one to teach ambling **3** something that confines, restrains, or shackles: *usually used in pl.* **4** a device with links or openings at different heights for hanging a pothook in a fireplace **5** an instrument for drawing ellipses **6** any of several devices for adjusting or aligning parts of a machine —***vt.*** **-meled** or **-melled, -mel·ing** or **-mel·ling** **1** to entangle in or as in a trammel **2** to confine, restrain, or shackle —**tram′mel·er** ***n.***, **tram′mel·ler**

tra·mon·tane (tra män′tān′, trə-; tra′män tān′) ***adj.*** ⟦It *tramontano* < L *transmontanus*, beyond the mountains < *tra-* (see TRANS-) + *mons* (gen. *montis*), MOUNT[1]⟧ located beyond or coming from beyond the mountains, specif. the Alps (from the viewpoint of Italy) —***n.*** **1** a tramontane person **2** a foreigner; stranger

tramp (tramp) ***vi.*** ⟦ME *trampen* < or akin to LowG *trampen*, to trample < nasalized form of the base in TRAP[1]⟧ **1** *a)* to walk with heavy steps *b)* to step heavily; stamp [*to tramp on someone's foot*] **2** *a)* to travel about on foot; trudge; hike *b)* to travel as or like a vagabond, hobo, etc. —***vt.*** **1** to step on firmly and heavily; trample **2** to walk or ramble through —***n.*** **1** a person who travels about on foot, esp. one doing odd jobs or begging for a living; hobo; vagrant **2** the sound of heavy steps, as of people marching **3** the act of tramping; esp., a journey on foot; hike **4** ⟦< *ocean tramp*: so called from its irregular travels, determined by the demand for its services⟧ a ship, esp. a small steamship, that has no regular schedule, arranging for cargo, occasional passengers, and ports of call as it goes along **5** an iron plate on the sole of a shoe to protect it, to prevent slipping, etc. **6** [Informal] a woman who is sexually promiscuous: a dismissive or contemptuous term —**SYN.** VAGRANT —**tramp′er** ***n.***

tram·ple (tram′pəl) ***vi.*** **-pled, -pling** ⟦ME *trampelen*, freq. of *trampen*: see prec.⟧ to tread heavily; tramp —***vt.*** to crush, destroy, hurt, violate, etc. by or as by treading heavily on —***n.*** the sound of trampling —**trample under foot** or **trample on** or **trample upon** **1** to crush or hurt by trampling **2** to treat harshly or ruthlessly; domineer over —**tram′pler** ***n.***

tram·po·line (tram′pə lēn′, -lin; tram′pə lēn′) ***n.*** ⟦It *trampolino*, springboard, akin to *trampoli*, stilts < Ger *trampeln*, to trample, freq. of *trampen*: for IE base see TRAP[1]⟧ ☆an apparatus for performing acrobatic tumbling and jumping feats, consisting of a sheet of strong canvas attached to a frame by springs and held tautly stretched above the floor —**tram′po·lin′er** ***n.***, **tram′po·lin′ist**

trampoline

tramp steamer TRAMP (***n.*** 4)

tramp·y (tram′pē) ***adj.*** **tramp′i·er, tramp′i·est** [Informal] of or like a TRAMP (***n.*** 6): a dismissive or contemptuous term

tram·road (tram′rōd′) ***n.*** ⟦TRAM[2] + ROAD⟧ *Mining* a road for trams, having tracks of wood, stone, or metal

tram·way (tram′wā′) ***n.*** **1** TRAMROAD **2** [Brit.] a streetcar line; tramline ☆**3** a system in which carriers or cars are supported by overhead cables

tran- (tran) *prefix* TRANS-: used before *s* [*tranship, transonic*]

trance (trans, träns) ***n.*** ⟦ME < OFr *transe*, great anxiety, fear < *transir*, to perish < L *transire*, to die, lit., go across: see TRANSIT⟧ **1** a state of altered consciousness, somewhat resembling sleep, during which voluntary movement is lost, as in hypnosis **2** a stunned condition; daze; stupor **3** a condition of great mental concentration or abstraction, esp. one induced by religious fervor or mysticism **4** in spiritualistic belief, a condition in which a medium passes under the control of some external force, as for the transmission of communications from the dead during a séance —***vt.*** **tranced, tranc′ing** *old poet. term for* ENTRANCE[2]

tranche (tränsh) ***n.*** ⟦Fr, lit., a slice⟧ a portion, share, installment, etc. [*the final tranche of the loan*]

trank or **tranq** (traŋk) ***n.*** [Slang] *short for* TRANQUILIZER

tran·quil (traŋ′kwəl, tran′-) ***adj.*** **-quil·er** or **-quil·ler, -quil·est** or **-quil·lest** ⟦L *tranquillus*, calm, quiet, still < *trans-*, beyond (see TRANS-) + base akin to *quies*, rest, calm, QUIET⟧ **1** free from disturbance or agitation; calm, serene, peaceful, placid, etc. **2** quiet or motionless; steady [*tranquil waters*] —**SYN.** CALM —**tran′quil·ly** ***adv.***

tran·quil·ize (traŋ′kwə līz′, tran′-) ***vt., vi.*** **-ized′, -iz′ing** to make or become tranquil; specif., to calm by the use of a tranquilizer: Brit sp. **tran′quil·lize′ -lized′, -liz′ing** —**tran′quil·i·za′tion** ***n.***

tran·quil·iz·er or **tran·quil·liz·er** (-lī′zər) ***n.*** a person or thing that tranquilizes; esp., a depressant drug used as a calming agent in relieving and controlling various emotional disturbances, anxiety, etc.

tran·quil·li·ty or **tran·quil·i·ty** (traŋ kwil′ə tē, tran-) ***n.*** the quality or state of being tranquil; calmness; serenity

trans *abbrev.* **1** transaction(s) **2** transitive **3** translated **4** translation **5** translator **6** transportation **7** transverse

trans- (trans, tranz) ⟦L *trans-* (contracted to *tra-* before *d-*, *m-*, *n-*, *l-*, *v-*, *j-*) < *trans*, across, over, orig., prob. prp. of **trare*, to pass, seen in *intrare, extrare* < IE base **ter-*, to go, over, beyond > THROUGH⟧ *prefix* **1** on the other side of, to the other side of, over, across, through [*transatlantic, transpierce*] **2** so as to change thoroughly [*transliterate*] **3** above and beyond; transcending [*transonic*] **4** *Chem. a)* designating an isomer having certain atoms or groups on opposite sides of a given plane in the molecule (in chemical names, usually printed in italic type and hyphenated and disregarded in alphabetization) [*trans-butene*] (see CIS-) *b)* designating the elements beyond (a given element) in the periodic table [*transuranium*] It occas. becomes TRAN- before *s*; in words of Latin origin, it becomes TRA- before *d, j, l, m, n,* or *v*

trans·act (tran zakt′, -sakt′) ***vt.*** ⟦< L *transactus*, pp. of *transigere*, to drive through, settle < *trans-* + *agere*, to drive: see prec. & ACT[1]⟧ to carry on, perform, conduct, or complete (business, etc.) —***vi.*** [Rare] to do business; negotiate —**trans·ac′tor** ***n.***

trans·ac·ti·nide (trans ak′tə nīd′, tranz-) ***n.*** ⟦see TRANS- (sense 4*b*)⟧ any of the radioactive chemical elements that have atomic numbers higher than that of the highest actinide (lawrencium): also called **transactinide element** —**trans′ac·tin′ic** (-ak tin′ik) ***adj.***

trans·ac·tion (tran zak′shən, -sak′-) ***n.*** ⟦L *transactio*⟧ **1** a transacting or being transacted **2** something transacted; specif., *a)* a business deal or agreement *b)* [*pl.*] a record of the proceedings of a society, convention, etc., esp. a published one —**trans·ac′tion·al** ***adj.***

☆**transactional analysis** a form of popular psychotherapy conducted on the premise that there are three states of the ego (*parent, adult, child*) in each individual, which must be brought into balance

trans·al·pine (trans al′pīn′, tranz-; -pin) ***adj.*** ⟦L *transalpinus*: see TRANS- & ALPINE⟧ on the other (the northern) side of the Alps, from the viewpoint of Rome as the seat of the Roman Empire

trans·am·i·nase (-am′ə nās′, -nāz′) ***n.*** ⟦< fol. + -ASE⟧ any of a group of enzymes that cause transamination

trans·am·i·na·tion (-am′ə nā′shən) ***n.*** ⟦TRANS- + AMIN(E) + -ATION⟧ the transfer of an amino group from one molecule to another, usually by the action of a transaminase

trans·at·lan·tic (trans′at lan′tik, tranz′-) ***adj.*** **1** crossing or spanning the Atlantic **2** on the other side of the Atlantic

trans·ax·le (trans ak′səl, tranz-) ***n.*** ⟦TRANS(MISSION) + AXLE⟧ a part in the drivetrain of a motor vehicle, combining in one housing the transmission and differential

Trans·cau·ca·sia (trans′kô kā′zhə) the region directly south of the Caucasus Mountains, containing the Asian countries of Armenia, Azerbaijan, & Georgia —**Trans′cau·ca′sian** ***adj., n.***

☆**trans·ceiv·er** (tran sē′vər) ***n.*** ⟦TRANS(MITTER) + (RE)CEIVER⟧ **1** an apparatus contained in a single housing, functioning alternately as a radio transmitter and receiver **2** an electronic device that transmits and receives facsimile copies of printed material, pictures, etc. over a telephone line

tran·scend (tran send′) ***vt.*** ⟦ME *transcenden* < L *transcendere*, to climb over < *trans-*, over + *scandere*, to climb: see DESCEND⟧ **1** to go beyond the limits of; overstep; exceed [*a story that transcends belief*] **2** to be superior to; surpass; excel **3** to be separate from or beyond (experience, the material universe, etc.) —***vi.*** to be transcendent; excel —**SYN.** EXCEL

tran·scend·ent (tran sen′dənt) ***adj.*** ⟦L *transcendens*, prp. of *transcendere*⟧ **1** transcending; surpassing; excelling; extraordinary **2** *Philos. a)* beyond the limits of possible experience *b)* in Kantianism, beyond human knowledge **3** *Theol.* existing apart from the material universe: said of God: distinguished from IMMANENT —**tran·scend′ence** ***n.***, **tran·scend′en·cy** —**tran·scend′ent·ly** ***adv.***

tran·scen·den·tal (tran′sen dent′'l) ***adj.*** ⟦ML *transcendentalis*⟧ **1** *a)* TRANSCENDENT (sense 1) *b)* SUPERNATURAL **2** of or having to do with transcendentalism **3** in Kantian philosophy, based on those elements of experience which derive not from sense data but from the inherent organizing functions of the mind, and which are the necessary conditions of human knowledge; transcending sense experience but not knowledge **4** *Math. a)* not capable of being a root of any algebraic equation with rational coefficients *b)* of, pertaining to, or being a function, as a logarithm, trigonometric function, exponential, etc., that is not expressible algebraically in terms of the variables and constants (opposed to ALGEBRAIC, sense 2) —**tran′scen·den′tal·ly** *adv.*

tran·scen·den·tal·ism (-iz′əm) *n.* ⟦< 18th-c. Ger *transcendentalismus*: see prec. & -ISM⟧ **1** any of various philosophies that propose to discover the nature of reality by investigating the process of thought rather than the objects of sense experience: the philosophies of Kant, Hegel, and Fichte are examples of transcendentalism ☆**2** [*often* **T-**] by extension, the philosophical ideas of Emerson and some other 19th-cent. New Englanders, based on a search for reality through spiritual intuition **3** popularly, any obscure, visionary, or idealistic thought —**tran′scen·den′tal·ist** *n., adj.*

Transcendental Meditation *service mark for* a method of meditation based on such Hindu techniques as frequent repetition of a personal mantra

trans·con·duct·ance (trans′kən dukt′əns, tranz′-) *n. Electronics* in an electron tube or transistor, the ratio of the change in the output of current to the change in the voltage at the grid or gate that produced the change in current, measured in siemens

☆**trans·con·ti·nen·tal** (trans′kän tə nent′'l, tranz′-) *adj.* **1** that crosses a (or the) continent **2** on the other side of a (or the) continent —**trans′con·ti·nen′tal·ly** *adv.*

tran·scribe (tran skrīb′) *vt.* **-scribed′**, **-scrib′ing** ⟦L *transcribere*: see TRANS- & SCRIBE⟧ **1** to write out or type out in full (shorthand notes, a speech, etc.) **2** to represent (speech sounds) in phonetic or phonemic symbols **3** to translate or transliterate **4** to arrange or adapt (a piece of music) for an instrument, voice, or ensemble other than that for which it was originally written **5** to make a recording of (a radio or TV program, commercial, etc.) for broadcast at a later time **6** *Cytology* to convert (DNA, genes, etc.) into RNA, esp. messenger RNA —**tran·scrib′er** *n.*

tran·script (tran′skript′) *n.* ⟦ME *transcripte* < ML *transcriptum* < L *transcriptus*, pp. of *transcribere*⟧ **1** something made by or based on transcribing; written, typewritten, or printed copy ☆**2** any copy or reproduction, esp. one that is official, as a copy of a student's record in school or college, listing courses, credits, grades, etc.

tran·scrip·tase (tran skrip′tās) *n.* ⟦fol. + -ASE⟧ an RNA POLYMERASE that uses DNA as a template to produce ribosomal RNA, transfer RNA, or messenger RNA: cf. REVERSE TRANSCRIPTASE

tran·scrip·tion (tran skrip′shən) *n.* ⟦L *transcriptio* < *transcriptus*: see TRANSCRIPT⟧ **1** the act or process of transcribing **2** something transcribed; specif., *a)* a transcript; copy *b)* an arrangement of a piece of music for an instrument, voice, or ensemble other than that for which it was originally written *c)* a recording made for radio or television broadcasting —**tran·scrip′tion·al** *adj.*

trans·cul·tur·al (trans kul′chər əl, tranz-) *adj.* involving, encompassing, or combining elements of more than one culture [*transcultural* notions of basic human rights]

trans·cu·ta·ne·ous (trans′kyo͞o tā′nē əs, tranz′-) *adj.* PERCUTANEOUS

trans·der·mal (trans dʉr′məl, tranz-) *adj.* designating or of an adhesive PATCH[1] (*n.* 11) designed to release a drug or hormone into the bloodstream through the skin

Trans·dnies·tri·a (trans nēs′trē ə, tranz-) *var. of* TRANSNISTRIA: also **Trans·dnies′ter** (-nēs′tər)

trans·duce (trans do͞os′, tranz-; -dyo͞os′) *vt.* **-duced′**, **-duc′ing** ⟦back-form. < fol.⟧ **1** to convert (energy, an electronic signal, etc.) into another form **2** *Genetics* to bring about transduction of (genetic material)

trans·duc·er (-ər) *n.* ⟦< L *transducere*, to lead across (< *trans-*, over + *ducere*, to lead: see DUCT) + -ER⟧ any of various devices that transmit energy from one system to another, sometimes one that converts the energy in form, as a speaker that converts electrical impulses into sound

trans·duc·tion (trans duk′shən, tranz-) *n.* ⟦< L *transductus*, pp. of *transducere*: see prec.⟧ **1** the transfer of energy from one system to another **2** *Genetics* the transfer of DNA from one bacterium to another by a bacteriophage, which may lead to the acquisition of a new gene by the recipient: cf. LYSOGENY

tran·sect (tran sekt′) *vt.* ⟦< TRANS- + L *sectus*, pp. of *secare*, to cut: see SAW[1]⟧ to cut across or divide by cutting —**tran·sec′tion** *n.*

tran·sept (tran′sept′) *n.* ⟦ModL *transeptum* < L *trans-*, across + *septum*: see SEPTUM⟧ **1** the part of a cross-shaped church at right angles to the long, main section, or nave **2** either arm of this part, outside the nave

☆**tran·sex·u·al** (tran sek′sho͞o əl) *n. var. of* TRANSSEXUAL

trans fat (trans, tranz) ⟦see TRANS- (sense 4*a*)⟧ an unsaturated fatty acid which has been partially hydrogenated, used in foods to increase shelf life and maintain flavor: also **trans fatty acid**

trans·fec·tion (trans fek′shən, tranz-) *n.* ⟦TRANS- + (IN)FECTION⟧ the injection of naked nucleic acids into cells or bacteria so as to infect them, as in cancer research —**trans·fect′** *vt.*

trans·fer (trans′fər; *for v., also* trans fʉr′) *vt.* **-ferred**, **-fer·ring** ⟦ME *transferren* < L *transferre* < *trans-*, across + *ferre*, to BEAR[1]⟧ **1** to convey, carry, remove, or send from one person, place, or position to another **2** to make over or convey (property, title to property, etc.) to another **3** to convey (a picture, design, etc.) from one surface to another by any of several processes —*vi.* **1** to transfer oneself or be transferred; move ☆**2** to withdraw from one school, college, course of study, etc. and be admitted to another ☆**3** to change from one bus, train, or streetcar to another, usually by presenting a transfer —*n.* **1** *a)* a transferring or being transferred *b)* a means of transferring **2** a thing or person that is transferred; specif., a picture or design transferred or to be transferred from one surface to another ☆**3** a ticket, provided free or at a small extra charge, entitling the bearer to change from one bus, train, or streetcar to another as specified ☆**4** a place for transferring ☆**5** a form or document effecting a transfer, as from one post or position to another ☆**6** a person who transfers or is transferred from one school, post, position, etc. to another **7** *Law a)* the transferring of a title, right, etc. from one person to another *b)* the document effecting this —**trans·fer′a·ble** *adj.*, **trans·fer′ra·ble** —**trans·fer′al** *n.*, **trans·fer′ral** —**trans·fer′rer** *n.*, *Law* **trans·fer′or**

transfer agent a bank or trust company charged with keeping a record of the shareholders of a corporation and issuing and canceling stock certificates as shares are bought and sold

trans·fer·ase (trans′fər ās′, -āz′) *n.* ⟦TRANSFER + -ASE⟧ any of a class of enzymes that act as catalysts in chemical reactions in which a radical is transferred from molecule to another

trans·fer·ee (trans′fə rē′) *n.* **1** a person to whom something is transferred **2** a person who is transferred

trans·fer·ence (trans fʉr′əns, trans′fər-) *n.* ⟦ModL *transferentia* < L *transferentem*, prp. of *transferre*: see TRANSFER⟧ **1** a transferring or being transferred; transfer **2** ⟦transl. of Ger *übertragung*, as used by FREUD⟧ *Psychol.* a reproduction of emotions relating to repressed experiences, esp. of childhood, and the substitution of another person, esp. a psychoanalyst or other psychotherapist, for the object of the repressed impulses —**trans′fer·en′tial** (-en′shəl) *adj.*

transfer payment a disbursement for which neither goods nor services have been given in return; specif., a disbursement by a government in the form of welfare or a subsidy

trans·fer·rin (trans fer′in) *n.* ⟦< TRANS- + L *ferrum*, iron (see FERRO-) + -IN[1]⟧ an iron-binding, crystalline globulin in blood plasma, that is important as an iron carrier

transfer RNA any of various small, looped forms of RNA that combine temporarily with messenger RNA to bring an amino acid to the proper location during the building of a polypeptide chain

trans·fig·u·ra·tion (trans fig′yo͞o rā′shən, trans′fig-) *n.* **1** a transfiguring or being transfigured **2** [**T-**] *Bible* the change in the appearance of Jesus on the mountain: Matt. 17 **3** [**T-**] a church festival (Aug. 6) commemorating the Transfiguration

trans·fig·ure (trans fig′yər) *vt.* **-ured**, **-ur·ing** ⟦ME *transfiguren* < L *transfigurare*: see TRANS- & FIGURE⟧ **1** to change the figure, form, or outward appearance of; transform **2** to transform so as to exalt or glorify —*SYN.* TRANSFORM

trans·fi·nite (-fī′nīt) *adj.* **1** extending beyond or surpassing the finite **2** *Math.* designating or of a cardinal or ordinal number that is larger than any positive integer

trans·fix (trans fiks′) *vt.* ⟦< L *transfixus*, pp. of *transfigere*, to transfix < *trans-*, TRANS- + *figere*, to FIX⟧ **1** to pierce through with or as if with something pointed **2** to fasten in this manner; impale **3** to capture or hold the attention of completely; hold spellbound [*transfixed* with horror] —**trans·fix′ion** (-fik′shən) *n.*

trans·form (trans fôrm′; *for n.* trans′fôrm′) *vt.* ⟦ME *transformen* < L *transformare* < *trans-*, TRANS- + *formare*, to form < *forma*, FORM⟧ **1** to change the form or outward appearance of **2** to change the condition, nature, or function of; convert **3** to change the personality or character of **4** *Elec.* to change (a voltage or current value) by use of a transformer **5** *Linguis.* to change by means of a syntactic transformational rule **6** *Math.* to change (an algebraic expression or equation) to a different form having the same value **7** *Physics* to change (one form of energy) into another —*vi.* to become transformed —*n. Math.* the process or result of a mathematical transformation —**trans·form′a·ble** *adj.* —**trans·form′a·tive** *adj.*

SYN.—**transform**, the broadest in scope of these terms, implies a change either in external form or in inner nature, in function, etc. [a living room *transformed* by new furnishings]; **transmute**, from its earlier use in alchemy, suggests a change in basic nature that seems almost miraculous [*transmuted* from a shy youth into a sophisticated man about town]; **convert** implies a change in details so as to be suitable for a new use [to *convert* an attic into an apartment]; **metamorphose** suggests a startling change produced as if by magic [a tadpole is *metamorphosed* into a frog]; **transfigure** implies a change in outward appearance which seems to exalt or glorify [his whole being was *transfigured* by love] See also **change**

trans·for·ma·tion (trans′fər mā′shən, -fôr-) *n.* ⟦LL(Ec) *transformatio*⟧ **1** a transforming or being transformed **2** [Now Rare] a woman's wig ☆**3** *Linguis. a)* the process of changing, by the application of certain syntactic rules, an abstract underlying structure into a surface structure *b)* any of the rules that derive surface structures from abstract underlying structures (also **transformational rule**) **4** *Math.* the process of setting up correspondences between the elements of two sets or spaces so that every element of the first set corresponds to a unique element of the second set —**trans′for·ma′tion·al** *adj.*

☆**transformational (generative) grammar** *Linguis.* a system of linguistic analysis consisting of a set of rules that generate basic syntactic structures, in the form of simple independent clauses, and a set of transformational rules that operate on those structures so as to produce questions, complex sentences, etc. and thus to account for every possible sentence of a language: cf. GENERATIVE GRAMMAR

trans·form·er (trans fôr′mər) *n.* **1** a person or thing that transforms **2**

Elec. a device consisting essentially of two or more coils of insulated wire, that transfers alternating-current energy by electromagnetic induction from one winding to another at the same frequency but usually with changed voltage and current values

trans·fuse (-fyo͞oz′) *vt.* **-fused′**, **-fus′ing** ⟦ME *transfusen* < L *transfusus*, pp. of *transfundere*, to pour from one container into another < *trans-*, TRANS- + *fundere*, to pour: see FOUND[3]⟧ **1** *a)* to transfer or transmit by or as by causing to flow or be diffused *b)* to permeate, instill, imbue, infuse, etc. **2** *Med. a)* to transfer or introduce (blood, blood plasma, saline solution, etc.) into a blood vessel, usually a vein *b)* to give a transfusion to —**trans·fus′i·ble** *adj.* —**trans·fu′sive** (-fyo͞o′siv) *adj.*

trans·fu·sion (-fyo͞o′zhən) *n.* the act or an instance of transfusing, esp. blood, blood plasma, etc.

trans·gen·der (trans jen′dər, tranz-) *adj.* of or being a person who identifies as the opposite sex, often, specif., undergoing surgery, hormone injections, etc. to become a member of the opposite sex: also **trans·gen′dered**

trans·gen·ic (trans jen′ik, tranz-) *adj.* having genetic material, in all cells, that includes a gene or DNA sequence transferred by means of genetic engineering from a genetically unlike organism

trans·gress (trans gres′, tranz-) *vt.* ⟦Fr *transgresser* < L *transgressus*, pp. of *transgredi*, to step over, pass over < *trans-*, TRANS- + *gradi*, to step, walk: see GRADE⟧ **1** to overstep or break (a law, commandment, etc.) **2** to go beyond (a limit, boundary, etc.) —*vi.* to break a law or commandment; sin —**trans·gres′sor** *n.*

trans·gres·sion (-gresh′ən) *n.* the act or an instance of transgressing; breach of a law, duty, etc.

trans·gres·sive (-gres′iv) *adj.* of or constituting a transgression; specif., designed to challenge conventional ideas, beliefs, etc. [a writer of *transgressive* fiction]

tran·ship (tran ship′) *vt., vi. alt. sp. of* TRANSSHIP

trans·hu·mance (trans hyo͞o′məns, tranz-) *n.* ⟦Fr < *transhumer*, to practice transhumance < Sp *trashumar* < *tras-*, trans- (< L, TRANS-) + L *humus*, earth: see HUMUS[2]⟧ seasonal and alternating movement of livestock, together with the persons who tend the herds, between two regions, as lowlands and highlands —**trans·hu′mant** *adj.*

tran·si·ent (tran′shənt, -sē ənt; -zhənt, -zē ənt) *adj.* ⟦L *transiens*, prp. of *transire*: see TRANSIT⟧ **1** *a)* passing away with time; not permanent; temporary; transitory *b)* passing quickly or soon; fleeting; ephemeral ☆**2** staying only for a short time [the *transient* population at resorts] —*n.* ☆**1** a transient person or thing [*transients* at a hotel] **2** *Elec.* a temporary component of a current, resulting from a voltage surge, a change from one steady-state condition to another, etc. —**tran′si·ence** *n.*, **tran′si·en·cy** —**tran′si·ent·ly** *adv.*

SYN.—transient applies to that which lasts or stays but a short time [a *transient* guest, feeling, etc.]; **transitory** refers to that which by its very nature must sooner or later pass or end [life is *transitory*]; **ephemeral** literally means existing only one day and, by extension, applies to that which is markedly short-lived [*ephemeral* glory]; **momentary** implies duration for a moment or an extremely short time [a *momentary* lull in the conversation]; **evanescent** applies to that which appears momentarily and fades quickly away [*evanescent* mental images]; **fleeting** implies of a thing that it passes swiftly and cannot be held [a *fleeting* thought] —**ANT. lasting, permanent**

tran·sil·i·ent (tran sil′ē ənt, -sil′yənt; -zil′-) *adj.* ⟦L *transiliens*, prp. of *transilire*, to leap across < *trans-*, TRANS- + *salire*: see SALIENT⟧ passing abruptly or leaping from one thing, condition, etc. to another —**tran·sil′i·ence** *n.*

trans·il·lu·mi·nate (trans′i lo͞o′mə nāt′, tranz′-) *vt.* **-nat′ed**, **-nat′ing** ⟦TRANS- + ILLUMINATE⟧ *Med.* to cause light to pass through the walls of (a body cavity) for purposes of examination —**trans′il·lu′mi·na′tion** *n.*

☆**tran·sis·tor** (tran zis′tər, -sis′-) *n.* ⟦TRAN(SFER) + (RE)SISTOR: it transfers a current across a resistor⟧ **1** a solid-state, electronic device, composed of semiconductor material, as germanium, silicon, etc., that controls current flow without use of a vacuum: transistors are similar in function to electron tubes, but have the advantages of being compact, long-lived, and low in power requirements: see also FET **2** a transistorized radio: in full **transistor radio**

☆**tran·sis·tor·ize** (-tər īz′) *vt.* **-ized′**, **-iz′ing** to equip (a device) with transistors

trans·it (tran′sit, tran′zit) *n.* ⟦ME *transite* < L *transitus*, pp. of *transire* < *trans-*, TRANS- + *ire*, to go: see YEAR⟧ **1** *a)* passage through or across *b)* a transition; change **2** *a)* the act of carrying or the condition of being carried through or across; conveyance [goods in *transit*] *b)* a system of public transportation, esp. in a city (cf. RAPID TRANSIT) **3** a surveying instrument for measuring horizontal angles, a kind of theodolite: in full **transit theodolite** **4** *Astron. a)* the apparent passage of a celestial body across a given meridian or through the field of a telescope *b)* the apparent passage of a smaller celestial body across the disk of a larger one, as of Mercury across the sun —*vt.* **1** to make a transit through or across **2** to revolve (the telescope of a transit) so as to reverse its direction —*vi.* to make a transit, or passage

transit instrument **1** a telescope mounted at right angles to a horizontal east-west axis so that it can be rotated only in the vertical plane of the meridian at its site: used to observe and time the transit of celestial bodies across the meridian **2** TRANSIT (sense 3)

tran·si·tion (tran zish′ən, -sish′ən) *n.* ⟦L *transitio* < *transitus*: see TRANSIT⟧ **1** *a)* a passage from one condition, form, stage, activity, place, etc. to another *b)* the period of such a passage **2** a word, phrase, sentence, or group of sentences that relates a preceding topic to a succeeding one or that smoothly connects parts of a speech or piece of writing **3** *Music a)* a shifting from one key to another; modulation; esp., a brief or passing modulation *b)* an abrupt change into a remote key *c)* a passage connecting two sections of a composition —*vi.* to make or undergo a transition —**tran·si′tion·al** *adj.*, **tran·si′tion·ar′y** —**tran·si′tion·al·ly** *adv.*

transition element any element of several groups of elements formed by adding electrons to an inner shell as the atomic number increases

tran·si·tive (tran′sə tiv, -zə-) *adj.* ⟦LL *transitivus* < L *transitus*: see TRANSIT⟧ **1** [Rare] of, showing, or characterized by transition; transitional **2** *Gram.* expressing an action thought of as passing over to and having an effect on some person or thing; taking a direct object: said of certain verbs **3** *Math.* designating a relation having the property that, whenever a first element bears a particular relation to a second that in turn bears this same relation to a third, the first element bears this relation to the third [identity and equality are *transitive* relations] —*n.* a transitive verb —**tran′si·tive·ly** *adv.* —**tran′si·tive·ness** *n.*, **tran′si·tiv′i·ty**

tran·si·to·ry (tran′sə tôr′ē, -zə-) *adj.* ⟦ME *transitorie* < MFr *transitoire* < LL(Ec) *transitorius* < L, adapted for passing through < *transitus*: see TRANSIT⟧ of a passing nature; not enduring or permanent; temporary, fleeting, or ephemeral; transient —**SYN.** TRANSIENT —**tran′si·to′ri·ly** *adv.* —**tran′si·to′ri·ness** *n.*

Trans·jor·dan (trans jôrd′'n, tranz-) *former name for* JORDAN[3] (the country): sometimes **Trans′jor·da′ni·a** (-jôr dā′nē ə, -nyə)

Trans·kei (trans kī′, -kā′) former homeland of the Xhosa nation in E South Africa: granted independence in 1976, it was abolished in 1994 —**Trans·kei′an** *adj.*

transl *abbrev.* **1** translated **2** translation **3** translator

trans·late (trans′lāt′, tranz′-; trans lāt′, tranz-) *vt.* **-lat′ed**, **-lat′ing** ⟦ME *translaten* < ML & L: ML *translatare* < L *translatus*, transferred, used as pp. of *transferre*: see TRANSFER⟧ **1** to move from one place or condition to another; transfer; specif., *a) Theol.* to convey directly to heaven without death *b) Eccles.* to transfer (a bishop) from one see to another; also, to move (a saint's body or remains) from one place of interment to another **2** to put into the words of a different language **3** to change into another medium or form [to *translate* ideas into action] **4** to put into different words; rephrase or paraphrase in explanation **5** to transmit (a telegraphic message) again by means of an automatic relay **6** [Archaic] to enrapture; entrance **7** *Cytology* to convert into a chain of amino acids forming a specific protein: said of genetic information in the form of messenger RNA **8** *Mech.* to impart translation to —*vi.* **1** to make a translation into another language **2** to be capable of being translated —**trans·lat′a·ble** *adj.*

trans·la·tion (trans lā′shən, tranz-) *n.* ⟦ME *translacioun* < MFr *translation* < L *translatio*⟧ **1** a translating or being translated **2** the result of a translating; esp., writing or speech translated into another language **3** *Mech.* motion in which every point of the moving object has simultaneously the same velocity and direction of motion —**trans·la′tion·al** *adj.*

SYN.—translation implies the rendering from one language into another of something written or spoken [a German *translation* of Shakespeare]; **version** is applied to a particular translation of a given work, specif. of the Bible [the King James *Version*]; **paraphrase**, in this connection, is applied to a free translation of a passage or work from another language; **transliteration** implies the writing of words with characters of another alphabet that represent the same sound or sounds [in this dictionary Greek words are *transliterated* with letters of the English alphabet]

trans·la·tor (trans′lat′ər, tranz′-; trans lāt′ər, tranz-) *n.* ⟦ME *translatour* < LL(Ec) *translator* < L, one who transfers⟧ one that translates; specif., *a)* a person or machine that translates books, articles, etc. from one language into another *b)* a person who translates speech; interpreter

trans·lit·er·ate (trans lit′ər āt′, tranz-) *vt.* **-at′ed**, **-at′ing** ⟦< TRANS- + L *litera, littera*, LETTER[1] + -ATE[1]⟧ to write or spell (words, letters, etc.) in corresponding characters of another alphabet

trans·lit·er·a·tion (-lit′ər ā′shən) *n.* **1** the act or process of transliterating **2** a text that is the product of transliterating —**SYN.** TRANSLATION

trans·lo·cate (-lō′kāt′) *vt.* **-cat′ed**, **-cat′ing** to cause to change location or position

trans·lo·ca·tion (trans′lō kā′shən, tranz′-) *n.* **1** an act or instance of translocating **2** *Bot.* the transport of organic food materials in solution through tissues from one part of a plant to another **3** *Genetics* the transfer of a portion of a chromosome to a new location in the chromosome or into another chromosome

trans·lu·cent (trans lo͞o′sənt, tranz-) *adj.* ⟦L *translucens*, prp. of *translucere*, to shine through: see TRANS- & LIGHT[1]⟧ **1** [Obs.] shining through **2** [Rare] transparent **3** letting light pass but diffusing it so that objects on the other side cannot be clearly distinguished; partially transparent, as frosted glass: also **trans·lu′cid** (-lo͞o′sid) **4** easily perceived; lucid; clear —**SYN.** CLEAR —**trans·lu′cence** *n.*, **trans·lu′cen·cy** —**trans·lu′cent·ly** *adv.*

trans·ma·rine (trans′mə rēn′, tranz′-) *adj.* ⟦L *transmarinus*: see TRANS- & MARINE⟧ **1** crossing the sea **2** coming from or being on the other side of the sea

trans·mem·brane (trans mem′brān′, tranz-) *adj.* *Cytology* passing or occurring through, or situated across, a cell membrane, esp. a plasma membrane

trans·mi·grant (trans mī′grənt, tranz-) *adj.* ⟦L *transmigrans*, prp. of *transmigrare*⟧ that transmigrates —*n.* a person or thing that transmigrates; specif., an emigrant passing through a country or place on the way to the country in which he or she will be an immigrant

trans·mi·grate (-mī′grāt′) *vi.* **-grat′ed, -grat′ing** ⟦ME vt. *transmigraten* < L *transmigratus*, pp. of *transmigrare*: see TRANS- & MIGRATE⟧ **1** to move from one habitation, country, etc. to another **2** to pass into another body after death: said of the soul, as in Hindu religious belief —**trans·mi′gra′tor** *n.* —**trans·mi′gra·to′ry** (-grə tôr′ē) *adj.*

trans·mi·gra·tion (trans′mī grā′shən, tranz′-) *n.* ⟦LL(Ec) *transmigratio*⟧ the act or process of transmigrating

trans·mis·si·ble (trans mis′ə bəl, tranz-) *adj.* ⟦LL *transmissibilis* < L *transmissus*: see fol. & -IBLE⟧ capable of being transmitted —**trans·mis′si·bil′i·ty** *n.*

trans·mis·sion (trans mish′ən, tranz-) *n.* ⟦L *transmissio* < *transmissus*, pp. of *transmittere*: see fol.⟧ **1** *a)* a transmitting or being transmitted *b)* something transmitted **2** the part of a motor vehicle, machine, etc. that transmits power from the engine to the driven members, as the wheels, by means of belts, fluids, gears, etc. **3** the passage of radio waves through space between the transmitting station and the receiving station —**trans·mis′sive** *adj.*

trans·mit (trans mit′, tranz-) *vt.* **-mit′ted, -mit′ting** ⟦ME *transmitten* < L *transmittere* < *trans-*, TRANS- + *mittere*, to send: see MISSION⟧ **1** to send or cause to go from one person or place to another, esp. across intervening space or distance; transfer; dispatch; convey **2** to pass along; impart (a disease, etc.) **3** to hand down to others by heredity, inheritance, etc. **4** to communicate (news, etc.) **5** *a)* to cause (light, heat, sound, etc.) to pass through air or some other medium [the sun *transmits* heat and light] *b)* to allow the passage of; conduct [water *transmits* sound] **6** to convey (force, movement, etc.) from one mechanical part to another **7** to send out (radio or television broadcasts, etc.) by electromagnetic waves —*vi.* to send out radio or television signals —*SYN.* CARRY —**trans·mit′tal** *n.* —**trans·mit′ta·ble** *adj.*

trans·mit·tance (-mit′′ns) *n.* **1** the act or process of transmitting **2** the ratio of the radiant energy transmitted by a body to the total radiant energy received by the body

trans·mit·ter (trans mit′ər, tranz-; *for 2, usually* trans′mit′ər, tranz′-) *n.* **1** a person who transmits **2** a thing that transmits; specif., *a)* the part of a telegraphic instrument by which messages are sent *b)* the part of a telephone, behind or including the mouthpiece, that converts speech sound into electric impulses for transmission *c)* the apparatus that generates radio waves, modulates their amplitude or frequency, and transmits them by means of an antenna

trans·mog·ri·fy (trans mäg′rə fī′, tranz-) *vt.* **-fied′, -fy′ing** ⟦pseudo-L formation⟧ to change completely; transform, esp. in a grotesque or strange manner —**trans·mog′ri·fi·ca′tion** *n.*

trans·mon·tane (trans män′tān′, tranz-; trans′män tān′, tranz′-) *adj.* ⟦L *transmontanus*⟧ TRAMONTANE

trans·mun·dane (trans mun′dān′, tranz-) *adj.* ⟦TRANS- + MUNDANE⟧ beyond the world or worldly matters

trans·mu·ta·tion (trans′myo͞o tā′shən, tranz′-) *n.* ⟦ME *transmutacioun* < LL *transmutatio* < pp. of L *transmutare*: see fol.⟧ **1** a transmuting or being transmuted; change of one thing into another **2** [Rare] a fluctuation **3** *Alchemy* the conversion of base metals into gold and silver **4** *Chem.* the conversion of atoms of a given element into atoms of a different isotope or of a different element, as in radioactive disintegration or by nuclear bombardment —**trans′mu·ta′tion·al** *adj.* —**trans·mut′a·tive** (-myo͞ot′ə tiv) *adj.*

trans·mute (trans myo͞ot′, tranz-) *vt., vi.* **-mut′ed, -mut′ing** ⟦ME *transmuten* < L *transmutare* < *trans-*, TRANS- + *mutare*, to change: see MUTATE⟧ to change from one form, species, condition, nature, or substance into another; transform; convert —*SYN.* TRANSFORM —**trans·mut′a·ble** *adj.* —**trans·mut′a·bly** *adv.*

trans·na·tion·al (trans nash′ə nəl, tranz-) *adj.* extending or operating beyond the limits, interests, etc. of a single nation

Trans·nis·tri·a (trans nēs′trē ə, tranz-; -nis′-) region in E Moldova: its status as a self-proclaimed republic seeking autonomy has been in dispute since 1991

trans·o·ce·an·ic (trans′ō′shē an′ik, tranz′-) *adj.* **1** crossing or spanning the ocean **2** coming from or being on the other side of the ocean

tran·som (tran′səm) *n.* ⟦LME *traunsom*, prob. altered < L *transtrum*, crossbeam, lit., that which is across < *trans*: see TRANS-⟧ **1** a crosspiece in a structure; specif., *a)* a lintel *b)* a horizontal crossbar across the top or middle of a window or the top of a door ☆**2** a small window or shutterlike panel directly over a door or window, usually hinged to the TRANSOM (sense 1*b*) **3** any crosspiece; specif., *a)* the horizontal beam of a gallows or cross *b)* any of the transverse beams attached to the sternpost of a wooden ship *c)* the transverse, aftermost part of a boat with a square stern —**over the transom** by unsolicited submission, as to a publisher: said of a manuscript, etc.

tran·son·ic (tran sän′ik) *adj.* ⟦TRAN(S)- + SONIC⟧ designating, of, or moving at a speed within the range of change from subsonic to supersonic speed

transp *abbrev.* transportation

trans·pa·cif·ic (trans′pə sif′ik) *adj.* **1** crossing or spanning the Pacific **2** on the other side of the Pacific

trans·pa·dane (trans′pə dān′, trans pā′dān′) *adj.* ⟦L *transpadanus* < *trans-*, TRANS- + *Padus*, the Po⟧ on the other (the northern) side of the river Po, from the viewpoint of Rome as the seat of the Roman Empire

trans·par·en·cy (trans per′ən sē, -par′-) *n.* **1** the quality or state of being transparent: also **trans·par′ence 2** *pl.* **-cies** something transparent; specif., a piece of transparent or translucent material, esp. a positive film or slide, having a picture or design that is visible when light shines through it or that can be projected on a screen

trans·par·ent (trans per′ənt, -par′-) *adj.* ⟦ME *transparaunt* < ML *transparens*, prp. of *transparere*, to be transparent < L *trans-*, TRANS- + *parens*, prp. of *parere*, to APPEAR⟧ **1** transmitting light rays so that objects on the other side may be distinctly seen; capable of being seen through; neither opaque nor translucent **2** so fine in texture or open in mesh that objects on the other side may be seen relatively clearly; sheer; gauzy; diaphanous **3** easily understood; very clear **4** easily recognized or detected; obvious **5** without guile or concealment; open; frank; candid; specif., open to observation, public scrutiny, etc. [a *transparent* investigation into county corruption] —*SYN.* CLEAR —**trans·par′ent·ly** *adv.* —**trans·par′ent·ness** *n.*

trans·per·son·al (trans pur′sə nəl) *adj.* **1** that transcends the personal or the individual **2** designating or of psychology, psychotherapy, etc. concerned with matters beyond those of the individual personality, such as, variously, mysticism, spiritual consciousness, the occult, etc.

tran·spic·u·ous (tran spik′yo͞o əs) *adj.* ⟦ModL *transpicuus* < L *transpicere*, to see through < *trans-*, TRANS- + *specere*, to look at: see SPY⟧ transparent; esp., easily understood —**tran·spic′u·ous·ly** *adv.*

trans·pierce (trans pirs′) *vt.* **-pierced′, -pierc′ing** ⟦Fr *transpercer*: see TRANS- & PIERCE⟧ **1** to pierce through completely **2** to pierce; penetrate

tran·spi·ra·tion (tran′spə rā′shən) *n.* ⟦ML *transpiratio*⟧ the act or process of transpiring; specif., the giving off of moisture, etc. through the pores of the skin or through the surface of leaves and other parts of plants

tran·spire (tran spīr′) *vt.* **-spired′, -spir′ing** ⟦Fr *transpirer* < ML *transpirare* < L *trans-*, TRANS- + *spirare*, to breathe: see SPIRIT⟧ to cause (vapor, moisture, etc.) to pass through tissue or other permeable substances, esp. through the pores of the skin or the surface of leaves, etc. —*vi.* **1** to give off vapor, moisture, etc., as through the pores of the skin **2** to be given off, passed through pores, exhaled, etc. **3** to leak out; become known ☆**4** to come to pass; happen —*SYN.* HAPPEN

trans·plant (trans plant′; *also, and for n. always,* trans′plant′) *vt.* ⟦ME *transplaunten* < LL(Ec) *transplantare*: see TRANS- & PLANT⟧ **1** to dig up (a growing plant) from one place and plant it in another **2** to remove (people, animals, etc.) from one place and resettle in another **3** *Surgery* to transfer (tissue or an organ) from one individual or part of the body to another; graft —*vi.* **1** to do transplanting **2** to be capable of enduring transplantation —*n.* **1** the act or an instance of transplanting **2** something transplanted, as a bodily organ or seedling —**trans·plant′a·ble** *adj.* —**trans′plan·ta′tion** (-plan tā′shən) *n.* —**trans·plant′er** *n.*

trans·po·lar (trans pō′lər) *adj.* extending or crossing a polar region [a *transpolar* air route]

tran·spon·der (tran spän′dər) *n.* ⟦blend of TRANSMITTER & RESPONDER⟧ **1** a radio or radar transceiver that automatically transmits electrical signals when actuated by a specific signal from an interrogator **2** any of the transceivers on a geostationary satellite that automatically relay signals, as of audio and video channels, from and to an EARTH STATION

trans·pon·tine (trans pän′tin, -tīn′) *adj.* ⟦< TRANS- + L *pons* (gen. *pontis*), a bridge: see PONS⟧ on the other side of an ocean

trans·port (trans pôrt′; *also, and for n. always,* trans′pôrt′) *vt.* ⟦ME *transporten* < MFr *transporter* < L *transportare*, to carry across < *trans-*, over, across + *portare*, to carry: see PORT[3]⟧ **1** to carry from one place to another, esp. over long distances **2** to carry away with emotion; enrapture; entrance **3** to carry off to a penal colony, etc.; banish; deport —*n.* **1** the act, process, or means of transporting; transportation; conveyance **2** strong emotion, esp. of delight or joy; rapture **3** a ship, airplane, train, etc. used to transport soldiers, freight, etc. **4** a convict sentenced to transportation —*SYN.* BANISH, CARRY, ECSTASY —**trans·port′a·bil′i·ty** *n.* —**trans·port′a·ble** *adj.* —**trans·port′er** *n.*

trans·por·ta·tion (trans′pər tā′shən, -pôr-) *n.* ⟦Fr < L *transportatio*⟧ **1** a transporting or being transported ☆**2** *a)* a means or system of conveyance *b)* the work or business of conveying passengers or goods ☆**3** fare or a ticket for being transported **4** banishment for crime, as to a penal colony; deportation —**trans′por·ta′tion·al** *adj.*

trans·pose (trans pōz′) *vt.* **-posed′, -pos′ing** ⟦ME *transposen* < MFr *transposer* (for L *transponere*): see TRANS- & POSE[1]⟧ **1** to transfer or shift; now, specif., to change the usual, normal, relative, or respective order or position of; interchange [inadvertently *transposed* the *e* and the *i* in "weird"] **2** to transfer (an algebraic term) from one side of an equation to the other, reversing the plus or minus value **3** to rewrite or play (a musical composition) in a different key or at another pitch level **4** [Obs.] to transform; convert —*vi.* to play music in a key or at a pitch level different from the one in which it is written —*n. Math.* a matrix obtained by interchanging the rows and columns of a given matrix —**trans·pos′a·ble** *adj.* —**trans·pos′er** *n.*

trans·po·si·tion (trans′pə zish′ən) *n.* ⟦ML *transpositio* < L *transpositus*, pp. of *transponere*: see TRANS- & POSE[1]⟧ **1** a transposing or being transposed **2** the result of this; something transposed —**trans′po·si′tion·al** *adj.*

trans·po·son (trans pō′zän′) *n.* ⟦TRANSPOS(ABLE) + *-on*, as in OPERON⟧ a segment of DNA that moves to a new location in a chromosome, or to another chromosome or cell, and alters the existing genetic instructions, sometimes producing significant changes

trans·put·er (trans pyo͞ot′ər) *n.* ⟦blend of TRANSISTOR & COMPUTER⟧ a microprocessor containing a central processing unit and memory: transputers are linked together to perform parallel processing

☆**trans·sex·u·al** (trans sek′sho͞o əl, tran-) *n.* a transgender person *adj.* TRANSGENDER —**trans·sex′u·al·ism′** *n.* —**trans·sex′u·al′i·ty** *n.*

USAGE—the word *transgender* (*adj.*) is now favored by many over *transsexual*

trans·ship (trans ship′, tran-) *vt., vi.* **-shipped′**, **-ship′ping** to transfer from one ship, train, truck, etc. to another for reshipment —**trans·ship′ment** *n.*

trans·son·ic (-sän′ik) *adj. alt. sp. of* TRANSONIC

tran·sub·stan·ti·ate (tran′səb stan′shē āt′) *vt.* **-at′ed**, **-at′ing** ⟦< ML(Ec) *transubstantiatus,* pp. of *transubstantiare* < L *trans-,* TRANS- + *substantia,* SUBSTANCE⟧ **1** to change from one substance into another; transmute; transform **2** *R.C.Ch., Eastern Orthodox Ch.* to cause (bread and wine) to undergo transubstantiation

tran·sub·stan·ti·a·tion (-stan′shē ā′shən) *n.* ⟦ML(Ec) *transubstantiatio*⟧ **1** the act of transubstantiating; change of one substance into another **2** *R.C.Ch., Eastern Orthodox Ch. a)* the doctrine that, in the Eucharist, the bread and wine in their essential reality are changed into the body and blood of Christ, although they continue to look, taste, etc. as they did beforehand *b)* this change

tran·su·date (tran′so͞o dāt′, -syo͞o-) *n.* ⟦ModL *transudatus,* pp. of *transudare*⟧ something transuded

tran·su·da·tion (tran′so͞o dā′shən, -syo͞o-) *n.* ⟦Fr *transsudation*⟧ **1** the act or instance of transuding **2** TRANSUDATE

tran·sude (tran so͞od′, -syo͞od′) *vt.* **-sud′ed**, **-sud′ing** ⟦ModL *transudare* < L *trans-,* TRANS- + *sudare,* to sweat < *sudor,* SWEAT⟧ to ooze or exude through pores or interstices, as blood serum through the vessel walls

trans·u·ran·ic (trans′yo͞o ran′ik, tranz′-) *adj.* designating or of the elements having atomic numbers higher than that of uranium and usually produced by nuclear bombardment, as plutonium: also **trans′u·ra′ni·um** (-rā′nē əm)

Trans·vaal (trans väl′, tranz-) former province of South Africa: now roughly divided into the provinces of Gauteng, Mpumalanga, & Northern Transvaal

trans·val·ue (trans val′yo͞o, tranz-) *vt.* **-val′ued**, **-val′u·ing** to evaluate by a new principle, esp. one rejecting conventional or accepted standards —**trans′val·u·a′tion** *n.*

trans·ver·sal (trans vʉr′səl, tranz-) *adj.* ⟦ME < ML *transversalis*⟧ TRANSVERSE —*n.* a line that intersects two or more other lines —**trans·ver′sal·ly** *adv.*

trans·verse (trans vʉrs′, tranz-; *also, and for n. usually,* trans′vʉrs′, tranz′-) *adj.* ⟦L *transversus,* pp. of *transvertere:* see TRAVERSE⟧ **1** lying, situated, placed, etc. across; crossing from side to side: opposed to LONGITUDINAL (sense 2) **2** *Geom.* designating the axis that passes through the foci of a hyperbola, or the part of that axis between the vertices —*n.* **1** a transverse part, beam, etc. **2** *Geom.* a transverse axis —**trans·verse′ly** *adv.*

transverse colon the central portion of the large intestine, crossing the abdominal cavity from right to left and lying between the ascending and descending colons

transverse process a process projecting laterally from a vertebra

trans·ves·tite (trans ves′tīt′, tranz-) *n.* ⟦< TRANS- + L *vestire,* to clothe (see VEST) + -ITE[1]⟧ a person who adopts the clothing and deportment regarded as typical of the opposite sex —**trans·ves′tism′** (-tiz′əm) *n.*, **trans·ves′ti·tism′** (-tə tiz′əm)

Tran·syl·va·ni·a (tran′sil vā′nē ə, -vān′yə) plateau region in central & NW Romania: chief city, Cluj-Napoca —**Tran′syl·va′ni·an** *adj., n.*

Transylvanian Alps range of the Carpathian Mountains, in central & SW Romania, between Transylvania & Walachia: highest peak, 8,361 ft (2,548 m)

trap[1] (trap) *n.* ⟦ME *trappe* < OE *træppe,* akin to *treppan,* to step, Ger *treppe,* stairway < IE **dreb-,* to run, step, trip (var. of base **drā-*) > Pol *drabina,* ladder⟧ **1** any device for catching animals, as one that snaps shut tightly when stepped on, or a pitfall; gin, snare, etc. **2** any stratagem or ambush designed to catch or trick unsuspecting persons **3** any of various devices for preventing the escape of gas, offensive odors, etc.; specif., a U-shaped or S-shaped part of a drainpipe, in which standing water seals off sewer gas **4** an apparatus for throwing disks into the air to be shot at in trapshooting **5** a light, two-wheeled carriage with springs **6** TRAPDOOR ☆**7** [*pl.*] a set of drums together with various other percussion instruments, as cymbals and woodblocks, played by one person as in a jazz or dance band **8** [Slang] the mouth, specif. as the organ of speech **9** *Golf* SAND TRAP —*vt.* **trapped**, **trap′ping** **1** to catch in or as in a trap; entrap **2** to hold back or seal off by a trap **3** to furnish with a trap or traps ☆**4** to catch (a batted ball in baseball or a thrown ball in football) just as it rebounds from the ground rather than just before it strikes the ground —*vi.* **1** to set traps for game ☆**2** to trap animals, esp. for their furs

SYN.—**trap**, as applied to a device for capturing animals, specif. suggests a snapping device worked by a spring, **pitfall**, a concealed pit with a collapsible cover, and **snare**, a noose which jerks tight upon the release of a trigger; in extended senses, these words apply to any danger into which unsuspecting or unwary persons may fall, **trap** specifically suggesting a deliberate stratagem or ambush [a speed *trap*], **pitfall**, a concealed danger, source of error, etc. [the *pitfalls* of the law], and **snare**, enticement and entanglement [the *snares* of love] See also **catch**

trap[2] (trap) *n.* ⟦Swed *trapp* < *trappa,* stair (akin to prec.), in reference to its appearance⟧ **1** any of several dark-colored, usually fine-grained, extrusive igneous rocks; esp., such a rock, as basalt, used in road making **2** a geologic structure forming a reservoir enclosing an accumulation of oil or gas

trap[3] (trap) *vt.* **trapped**, **trap′ping** ⟦ME *trappen* < *trappe,* trappings < OFr *drap,* cloth: see DRAPE⟧ to cover, equip, or adorn with trappings; caparison —*n.* **1** [Obs.] an ornamental covering for a horse **2** [*pl.*] [Old Informal] a person's clothes, personal belongings, etc.

trap·door (trap′dôr′) *n.* a hinged or sliding door in a roof, ceiling, or floor

trapdoor spider any of various, often large, spiders (esp. family Ctenizidae) that dig a burrow and cover the entrance with a hinged lid like a trapdoor

trapes (trāps) *vi., vt., n. archaic sp. of* TRAIPSE

tra·peze (tra pēz′, trə-) *n.* ⟦Fr *trapèze* < ModL *trapezium:* see TRAPEZIUM⟧ a short horizontal bar, hung at a height by two ropes, on or from which gymnasts or circus aerialists swing, performing various stunts

trapeze artist a performer who does tricks on or from a trapeze

tra·pe·zi·form (trə pē′zə fôrm′, tra-) *adj.* shaped like a trapezium

tra·pe·zi·um (trə pē′zē əm, tra-) *n., pl.* **-zi·ums** or **-zi·a** (-ə) ⟦LL < Gr *trapezion,* trapezium, lit., small table, dim. of *trapeza,* table, lit., four-footed bench < *tra-,* for *tetra,* FOUR + *peza,* foot; akin to *pous,* FOOT⟧ **1** a plane figure with four sides, no two of which are parallel **2** *Brit. var. of* TRAPEZOID (sense 1) **3** *Anat.* a small bone of the wrist near the base of the thumb

tra·pe·zi·us (-zē əs) *n.* ⟦ModL < *trapezium:* see prec.⟧ either of the large muscles on each side of the upper back

tra·pe·zo·he·dron (trə pē′zō hē′drən, trap′i zō-) *n.* ⟦ModL: see TRAPEZIUM & -HEDRON⟧ a solid figure, esp. a crystal, all the faces of which are trapeziums

trap·e·zoid (trap′i zoid′) *n.* ⟦ModL *trapezoides* < Gr *trapezoeides,* shaped like a trapezoid: see TRAPEZIUM & -OID⟧ **1** a plane figure with four sides, only two of which are parallel **2** *Brit. var. of* TRAPEZIUM (sense 1) **3** *Anat.* a small bone of the wrist near the base of the index finger —*adj.* shaped like a trapezoid: also **trap′e·zoi′dal**

trap·line (trap′līn′) *n.* the route along which a series of animal traps is set; also, such a series of traps

trap·per (trap′ər) *n.* a person who traps; esp., one who traps fur-bearing animals for their skins

trap·pings (trap′iŋz) *pl.n.* ⟦< ME *trappe:* see TRAP[3]⟧ **1** an ornamental covering for a horse; caparison **2** articles of dress, esp. of an ornamental kind; adornments **3** the things usually associated with something as an outward sign of its existence or presence [an expense account and other *trappings* of success]

Trap·pist (trap′ist) *n.* ⟦Fr *trappiste,* after (*La*) *Trappe,* abbey near the village of Soligny-la-*Trappe,* in Normandy, where the rule was established (1664)⟧ a member of the order of the Cistercians of the Strict Observance: known esp. for its asceticism and vow of silence —*adj.* designating or of this order

trap rock TRAP[2]

trap·shoot·ing (trap′sho͞ot′iŋ) *n.* the sport of shooting at clay pigeons, or disks, sprung into the air from traps —**trap′shoot′er** *n.*

tra·pun·to (trə po͞on′tō, -po͞on′-; trä-) *n., pl.* **-tos** ⟦It < pp. of *trapungere,* to embroider < *tra-,* through (< L *trans-,* TRANS-) + *pungere,* to prick (< L: see POINT)⟧ a kind of padded quilting with the design, in high relief, outlined with single stitches: used as for upholstery and robes

trash[1] (trash) *n.* ⟦prob. < Scand, as in Norw dial. *trask,* lumber, trash, akin to ON *tros,* broken twigs < IE base **der-,* to tear, split off > TEAR[1]⟧ **1** parts that have been broken off, stripped off, etc., esp. leaves, twigs, husks, and other plant trimmings **2** broken, discarded, or worthless things; rubbish; refuse **3** *a)* any worthless, unnecessary, or offensive matter [literary *trash*] *b)* foolish talk; nonsense **4** a person or people regarded as disreputable, insignificant, etc. **5** the refuse of sugar cane after the juice has been pressed out —*vt.* **1** to trim (trees or plants) of trash ☆**2** [Informal] to destroy (property) as by vandalism or arson ☆**3** [Slang] *a)* to criticize (a person, policy, performance, etc.) sharply or maliciously *b)* to insult (a person) —*adj.* [Slang] regarded as being worthless, offensive, lacking in substance, etc. [an afternoon of *trash* TV] —☆**talk trash** [Slang] to engage in TRASH TALK

trash[2] (trash) [Archaic] *vt.* ⟦prob. < OFr *trachier,* var. of *tracier:* see TRACE[1]⟧ to restrain, as by a leash —*n.* a leash for restraining an animal

☆**trash talk** [Slang] talk or remarks intended to intimidate, as by being boastful, insulting, or taunting

trash·y (trash′ē) *adj.* **trash′i·er**, **trash′i·est** containing, consisting of, or like trash; worthless, offensive, etc. —**trash′i·ly** *adv.* —**trash′i·ness** *n.*

Tra·si·me·no (traz′ə mē′nō, trä′zə-) lake in central Italy: scene of a victory by Hannibal over the Romans (217 B.C.): Latin name **Tra′si·me′nus** (-nəs)

trass (tras) *n.* ⟦Ger < Du *tras* < earlier *terras* < MFr *terrace:* see TERRACE⟧ a volcanic rock, powdered and used in making a hydraulic cement

trat·to·ri·a (trä tôr′ē ə; *It* trät′tô rē′ä) *n., pl.* **-ri·as** or It. **-ri′e** (-e) ⟦It < *trattore,* innkeeper < *trattare,* to manage, handle < L *tractare:* see TREAT⟧ a small, inexpensive Italian restaurant

trau·ma (trô′mə, trä′-) ***n.***, *pl.* **-mas** or **-ma·ta** (-mə tə) ⟦ModL < Gr *trauma* (gen. *traumatos*): for IE base see THROE⟧ **1** *Med.* bodily injury, wound, or shock **2** *Psychiatry* a painful emotional experience, or shock, often producing a lasting psychic effect and, sometimes, a neurosis **3** any emotionally painful experience [the *trauma* of being laid off] —**trau·ma′tic** (-mat′ik) ***adj.*** —**trau·mat′i·cal·ly** ***adv.***

trau·ma·tism (-tiz′əm) ***n.*** ⟦< Gr *trauma* (see prec.) + -ISM⟧ a trauma or the abnormal condition caused by it

trau·ma·tize (-tīz′) ***vt.*** **-tized′**, **-tiz′ing** **1** *Med.* to injure or wound (tissues) **2** to subject to an emotional trauma

trav·ail (trə vāl′, trav′āl′) ***n.*** ⟦OFr < VL **tripalium*, instrument of torture composed of three stakes < LL *tripalis*, of three stakes < L *tri-*, TRI- + *palus*, a stake: see PALE²⟧ **1** very hard work; toil **2** labor pains; pains of childbirth **3** [*often pl.*] hardship; trouble —***vi.*** ⟦ME *travaillen* < OFr *travaillier*, to labor, toil < VL **tripaliare*, to torment < **tripalium*⟧ **1** to work very hard; toil **2** to have labor pains; suffer the pains of childbirth

trav·el (trav′əl) ***vi.*** **-eled** or **-elled**, **-el·ing** or **-el·ling** ⟦var. of prec.⟧ **1** to go from one place to another; make a journey or journeys **2** to go from place to place as a traveling salesman **3** to walk or run **4** to move, pass, or be transmitted from one point or place to another **5** to move or be capable of moving in a given path or for a given distance: said of mechanical parts, etc. **6** to advance or progress **7** to withstand the effects of travel or relocation: often used fig. [translated poetry does not often *travel* well] ☆**8** *Basketball* to illegally move both feet while holding the ball **9** [Informal] to associate or spend time (*with*) **10** [Informal] to move with speed —***vt.*** **1** to make a journey over or through; traverse **2** [Informal] to cause to move or pass along —***n.*** **1** the act or process of traveling **2** [*pl.*] *a)* the trips, journeys, etc. taken by a person or persons *b)* an account of these **3** passage or movement of any kind **4** traffic on a route, through a place, etc. **5** *a)* mechanical motion, esp. reciprocating motion *b)* the distance of a mechanical stroke, etc.

travel agency an agency that makes travel arrangements for tourists or other travelers, as for transportation, hotels, and itineraries —**travel agent**

trav·eled or **trav·elled** (trav′əld) ***adj.*** **1** that has traveled **2** used by travelers [a heavily *traveled* road]

trav·el·er or **trav·el·ler** (trav′ə lər; *often* trav′lər) ***n.*** **1** a person who travels **2** a traveling salesman; commercial traveler **3** a thing that travels; specif., *a)* any mechanical device, as a traveling crane, that moves or slides along a support *b)* *Naut.* a metal ring that slides on a rope, rod, or spar; also, the rope, rod, or spar it slides on **4** [Chiefly Brit.] a GYPSY (***n.*** 1) or other itinerant person

☆**traveler's check** a kind of check, usually one of a set and sold in any of several denominations, purchased by a traveler to carry in place of currency and used to make purchases or to exchange for cash

☆**traveling salesman** a salesperson who travels from place to place soliciting orders for the business firm he or she represents

☆**trav·e·logue** or **trav·e·log** (trav′ə lôg′, -läg′) ***n.*** ⟦< TRAVEL + -LOGUE⟧ **1** a lecture on travels, usually accompanied by the showing of pictures **2** a film, usually short, about a foreign or out-of-the-way place, esp. one that emphasizes the place's unusual or glamorous aspects

tra·verse (trə vurs′, trav′ərs; *for n., adj., & adv.*, trav′ərs, trə vurs′) ***vt.*** **-versed′**, **-vers′ing** ⟦ME *traversen* < OFr *traverser* < VL < **transversare* < L *transversus*, pp. of *transvertere*, to turn across < *trans-*, TRANS- + *vertere*, to turn: see VERSE⟧ **1** *a)* to pass, move, or extend over, across, or through; cross *b)* to go back and forth over or along; cross and recross **2** to go counter to; oppose; thwart **3** to survey, inspect, or examine carefully **4** to turn (a gun, lathe, etc.) laterally; swivel **5** to make a traverse of in surveying **6** *Law* *a)* to deny or contradict formally (something alleged by the opposing party in a lawsuit) *b)* to join issue upon (an indictment) or upon the validity of (an inquest of office) —***vi.*** **1** to move across; cross over **2** to move back and forth over a place, etc.; cross and recross **3** to swivel or pivot **4** to move across a mountain slope, as in skiing, in an oblique direction **5** to make a traverse in surveying **6** *Fencing* to move one's blade toward the opponent's hilt while pressing one's foil hard against the opponent's foil —***n.*** **trav′erse** **1** something that traverses or crosses; specif., *a)* a line that intersects others *b)* a crossbar, crosspiece, crossbeam, transom, etc. *c)* a parapet or wall of earth, etc. across a rampart or trench *d)* a gallery, loft, etc. crossing a building *e)* a single line of survey across a plot, region, etc. *f)* [Obs.] a screen, curtain, etc. placed crosswise **2** [Now Rare] something that opposes or thwarts; obstacle **3** the act or an instance of traversing; specif., *a)* a passing across or through; crossing *b)* a lateral, pivoting, oblique, or zigzagging movement **4** a part, device, etc. that causes a traversing movement **5** a passage by which one may cross; way across **6** *a)* a zigzagging course or route taken by a vessel, as in sailing against the wind *b)* a single leg of such a course **7** a formal denial in a lawsuit —***adj.*** **trav′erse** ⟦ME *travers* < OFr < L *transversus*: see the ***vt.***⟧ **1** passing or extending across; transverse **2** designating or of drapes (and the rods and hooks for them) usually hung in pairs that can be drawn together or apart by pulling a cord at the side —***adv.*** **trav′erse** [Obs.] across; crosswise —**tra·vers′a·ble** ***adj.*** —**tra·vers′al** ***n.*** —**tra·vers′er** ***n.***

trav·erse jury (trav′ərs) PETIT JURY

trav·er·tine (trav′ər tēn′, -tin) ***n.*** ⟦It *travertino*, altered < *tiburtino* < L *(lapis) Tiburtinus*, (stone) of Tibur (now Tivoli)⟧ a light-colored, dense type of tufa, as dripstone or flowstone, deposited in caves or around limy springs, lakes, or streams

trav·es·ty (trav′is tē) ***n.***, *pl.* **-ties** ⟦orig. an adj. < Fr *travesti*, pp. of *travestir*, to disguise, travesty < It *travestire* < L *trans-*, TRANS- + *vestire*, to dress, attire: see VEST⟧ **1** a grotesque or farcical imitation for purposes of ridicule; burlesque **2** a crude, distorted, or ridiculous representation (*of* something) [a trial that was a *travesty* of justice] —***vt.*** **-tied**, **-ty·ing** to make a travesty of; burlesque —***SYN.*** CARICATURE

tra·vois (trə voi′) ***n.***, *pl.* **-vois′** (-voiz′) or **-vois′es** (-voi′ziz) ⟦CdnFr < *travail*, a brake, load < Fr: see TRAVAIL⟧ a sledge of the North American Plains Indians, consisting of a net or platform dragged along the ground on the two poles that support it and which serve as shafts for the horse or, orig., the dog pulling it: also **tra·voise′** (-voiz′)

trawl (trôl) ***n.*** ⟦< ? MDu *traghel*, dragnet < ? L *tragula*: see TRAIL⟧ **1** a large, baglike net dragged by a boat along the bottom of a fishing bank: also **trawl′ net′** ☆**2** a long line supported by buoys, from which many short fishing lines are hung: also **trawl line** **3** [Chiefly Brit.] a thorough search — ***vt., vi.*** **1** to fish or catch with a trawl **2** [Chiefly Brit.] to make a thorough search (of): often with *through* [to *trawl* a biography for amusing anecdotes]

trawl·er (trôl′ər) ***n.*** a boat used in trawling

tray (trā) ***n.*** ⟦ME *treie* < OE *treg, trig*, wooden board, akin to *treow*, TREE⟧ **1** a flat receptacle made of wood, metal, glass, plastic, etc., often with slightly raised edges, used for holding or carrying articles **2** a tray with its contents [a *tray* of food] **3** a shallow, boxlike, removable compartment of a trunk, cabinet, etc.

trayf (trāf) ***adj.*** *alt. sp. of* TREF

treach·er·ous (trech′ər əs) ***adj.*** ⟦ME *trecherous* < OFr *trecheros*⟧ **1** characterized by treachery; traitorous; disloyal; perfidious **2** giving a false appearance of safety or reliability; untrustworthy or insecure [*treacherous* rocks] —***SYN.*** FAITHLESS —**treach′er·ous·ly** ***adv.*** —**treach′er·ous·ness** ***n.***

treach·er·y (trech′ər ē) ***n.***, *pl.* **-er·ies** ⟦ME *trecherie* < OFr *tricherie*, trickery < *trichier*, to cheat: see TRICK⟧ **1** betrayal of trust, faith, or allegiance; perfidy, disloyalty, or treason **2** an act of perfidy or treason

trea·cle (trē′kəl) ***n.*** ⟦ME *triacle* < OFr < L *theriaca*, antidote for poison < Gr (*antidotos*) *thēriakē*, (remedy) for bites of venomous beasts < *thērion*, wild beast, dim. of *thēr*: see FIERCE⟧ **1** [Obs.] *a)* a remedy for poison *b)* any effective remedy **2** *a)* [Brit.] molasses *b)* anything very sweet or cloying —**trea′cly** (-klē) ***adj.***

tread (tred) ***vt.*** **trod** or (in *tread water*: see phr. below) **tread′ed**, **trod′den** or **trod** or (in *tread water*) **tread′ed**, **tread′ing** ⟦ME *treden* < OE *tredan*, akin to Ger *treten* < IE **dreu-* < base **drā*, to run, step > TRAP¹⟧ **1** to walk on, in, along, across, over, etc. **2** to do or follow by walking, dancing, etc. [*treading* the measures briskly] **3** to press or beat with the feet so as to crush or injure; trample **4** to oppress or subdue, as if by stepping on **5** to copulate with (the female): said of a bird —***vi.*** **1** to move on foot; step; walk **2** to set one's foot (*on, across*, etc.); make a step; step **3** to trample (*on* or *upon*) **4** to copulate: said of birds —***n.*** **1** the act, manner, or sound of treading **2** something on which a person or thing treads or moves, as the part of a shoe sole, wheel, etc. that touches the ground, the endless belt over cogged wheels of a tractor or tank, the part of a rail on which a car wheel runs, or the horizontal surface of a step in a stairway **3** *a)* the thick outer layer of an automotive tire, containing grooves for added traction *b)* the thickness of this layer, as measured by the depth of the grooves *c)* the pattern of the grooves **4** *a)* the grooves or ridges for added traction that are on the soles of certain shoes *b)* the pattern of such grooves or ridges **5** TRACK (***n.*** 9) **6** [Rare] a footprint —**tread the boards** to act in plays on the stage —**tread water** *pt. & pp. now usually* **treaded** **1** *Swimming* to keep the head above water and the body upright without propelling oneself forward, by moving the legs and arms back and forth **2** to make no progress

trea·dle (tred′'l) ***n.*** ⟦ME *tredel* < OE *tredan*: see prec.⟧ a lever or pedal moved by the foot as to turn a wheel —***vi.*** **-dled**, **-dling** to work a treadle

tread·mill (tred′mil′) ***n.*** **1** a kind of mill wheel turned by the weight of persons treading steps arranged around its circumference: formerly used as an instrument of prison discipline **2** a mill driven by an animal treading a sloping, endless belt **3** any monotonous round of duties, work, etc. in which one seems to make no progress **4** a stationary exercise machine, typically with speed controls, handles, etc., consisting of a short, wide conveyor belt upon which a person walks or runs

treadmill

treas *abbrev.* **1** treasurer **2** treasury

trea·son (trē′zən) ***n.*** ⟦ME *treison* < OFr *traïson* < L *traditio* < pp. of *tradere*, to give or deliver over or up < *trans-*, TRANS- + *dare*, to give: see DATE¹⟧ **1** [Now Rare] betrayal of trust or faith; treachery **2** violation of the allegiance owed to one's sovereign or state; betrayal of one's country, specif., in the U.S. (as declared in the Constitution), consisting only in levying war against the U.S. or in giving aid and comfort to its enemies —***SYN.*** SEDITION

trea·son·a·ble (-ə bəl) *adj.* of, having the nature of, or involving treason; traitorous —**trea′son·a·bly** *adv.*

trea·son·ous (trē′zə nəs) *adj.* treasonable; traitorous

treas·ure (trezh′ər) *n.* ⟦ME *tresoure* < OFr *tresor* < L *thesaurus*: see THESAURUS⟧ **1** accumulated or stored wealth, esp. in the form of money, precious metals, jewels, etc. **2** any person or thing considered very valuable —*vt.* **-ured, -ur·ing 1** to store away or save up (money, valuables, etc.) as for future use; hoard **2** to value greatly; cherish —**SYN.** APPRECIATE

treasure house any place where treasure is kept or where things of great value are to be found

treasure hunt a game in which players, with the aid of clues, compete in trying to find hidden articles

treas·ur·er (trezh′ər ər) *n.* ⟦ME *tresorer* < Anglo-Fr *tresorer*, for OFr *tresorier* < *tresor*: see TREASURE⟧ a person in charge of a treasure or treasury; specif., an officer in charge of the funds or finances, as of a government, corporation, or society —**treas′ur·er·ship′** *n.*

treas·ure-trove (trezh′ər trōv′) *n.* ⟦Anglo-Fr *tresor trové* < OFr *tresor* (see TREASURE) + *trové*, pp. of *trover*, to find: see TROVER⟧ **1** treasure found hidden, the original owner of which is unknown **2** any valuable discovery **3** a valuable source or collection [a book that is a *treasure-trove* of information]

treas·ur·y (trezh′ər ē) *n., pl.* **-ur·ies**; also for 4*b*, **-ur·ys** ⟦ME *tresorie* < OFr⟧ **1** a place where treasure is kept; room or building where valuable objects are preserved **2** a place where public or private funds are kept, received, disbursed, and recorded **3** the funds or revenues as of a state, corporation, or society **4** [T-] *a)* the department of government in charge of revenue, taxation, and public finances *b)* any of the securities issued by this department **5** a collection of treasures in art, literature, etc. [a *treasury* of verse]

treasury bill ☆a short-term obligation of the U.S. Treasury, maturing in one year or less, bearing no interest and sold periodically on the open market on a discount basis

treasury bond ☆any of various series of bonds issued by the U.S. Treasury, usually maturing over long periods

☆**treasury certificate** a short-term obligation of the U.S. Treasury, usually maturing in one year, paying interest periodically on a coupon basis: no longer issued publicly

treasury note ☆any of the interest-bearing obligations of the U.S. Treasury with maturity dates between one and ten years

☆**treasury stock** shares of issued stock reacquired by the issuing corporation and held by it

treat (trēt) *vi.* ⟦ME *treten* < OFr *traiter*, to handle, meddle, treat < L *tractare*, freq. of *trahere*, to DRAW⟧ **1** to discuss terms (*with* a person or *for* a settlement); negotiate **2** to deal with a subject in writing or speech; speak or write (*of*) **3** to stand the cost of another's or others' entertainment —*vt.* **1** to deal with (a subject) in writing, speech, music, painting, etc., esp. in a specified manner or style **2** to act or behave toward (a person, animal, etc.) in a specified manner **3** to have a specified attitude toward and deal with accordingly [to *treat* a mistake as a joke] **4** *a)* to pay for the food, drink, entertainment, etc. of (another or others) *b)* to provide with something that pleases: often with *to* [*treat* the family to a movie, *treat* oneself to a cookie] **5** to subject to some process or to some substance in processing, as in a chemical procedure **6** to give medical or surgical care to (someone) or for (some disorder) —*n.* **1** a meal, drink, entertainment, etc. paid for by someone else **2** anything that gives great pleasure **3** *a)* the act of treating or entertaining *b)* someone's turn to treat —**treat′a·bil′i·ty** *n.* —**treat′a·ble** *adj.* —**treat′er** *n.*

trea·tise (trēt′is) *n.* ⟦ME *tretis* < Anglo-Fr *tretiz* < OFr **treiteiz* < *traiter*: see prec.⟧ **1** a formal, systematic article or book on some subject, esp. one in which the conclusions are based on a detailed consideration of factual evidence or governing principles **2** [Obs.] a narrative; tale

treat·ment (trēt′mənt) *n.* **1** act, manner, method, etc. of treating, or dealing with, a person, thing, subject in art or literature, etc. **2** medical, surgical, or cosmetic care, esp. a systematic course of this **3** *Film, TV* an outline or prose summary prepared before the script, giving the story with characters, situations, etc. but often without dialogue and usually without separate shots indicated

trea·ty (trēt′ē) *n., pl.* **-ties** ⟦ME *trete* < OFr *traité* < LL *tractatus*: see TRACTATE⟧ **1** [Obs.] *a)* negotiation *b)* entreaty *c)* any agreement or contract **2** *a)* a formal agreement between two or more nations, relating to peace, alliance, trade, etc. *b)* the document embodying such an agreement

treaty port [Historical] a port required by treaty to be kept open for foreign trade, as any of those so established in 19th-cent. China, Japan, or Korea

Treb·bia (treb′yə, treb′ē ə) river in NW Italy, flowing north into the Po: scene of a victory by Hannibal over the Romans (218 B.C.): ancient name **Tre·bi·a** (trē′bē ə)

Treb·i·zond (treb′i zänd′) **1** Greek empire (1204-1461) on the SE coast of the Black Sea **2** seaport in NE Turkey: former capital of the empire of Trebizond: Turk. name TRABZON

tre·ble (treb′əl) *adj.* ⟦OFr < L *triplus*, TRIPLE⟧ **1** threefold; triple **2** *a)* of or for the highest part in musical harmony *b)* playing or singing this part **3** high-pitched or shrill —*n.* **1** the highest part in musical harmony; soprano **2** a singer or instrument that takes this part **3** a high-pitched voice or sound **4** the higher part of the audio-frequency band in sound reproduction — *vt., vi.* **-bled, -bling** [Chiefly Brit.] to make or become three times as much or as many; triple —**tre′bly** *adv.*

treble clef *Music* **1** a sign on a staff, indicating the position of G above middle C on the second line **2** the range of notes on a staff so marked

Tre·blin·ka (trə bliŋ′kə) village in NE Poland, near the sites of a forced-labor camp and an extermination camp operated by the Nazis during WWII

treb·u·chet (treb′yoo shet′) *n.* ⟦ME < OFr < *trebucher*, to stumble < *tre-* (< L *trans-*, TRANS-) + *buc*, trunk, body < Frank **buk*, trunk, akin to Ger *bauch*, belly < PGmc **bhug-* < IE **bhū-*, var. of base **bheu-*, to grow, swell > BE⟧ a medieval engine of war powered by a counterweight and used to hurl large stones and other missiles

tre·cen·to (tre chen′tō) *n.* ⟦It, lit., three hundred, short for *mil trecento*, one thousand three hundred⟧ the 14th cent. as a period in Italian art and literature

tree (trē) *n.* ⟦ME < OE *trēow*, akin to Goth *triu*, ON *trē* < IE base **deru-*, tree, prob. orig. oak tree > Gr *drys*, oak, *(den)dron*, tree⟧ **1** a woody perennial plant with one main stem or trunk which develops many branches, usually at some height above the ground **2** a treelike bush or shrub [a rose *tree*] **3** a wooden beam, bar, pole, post, stake, etc. **4** anything resembling a tree in form, as in having a stem and branches; specif., *a)* FAMILY TREE *b)* *Chem.* a treelike formation of crystals **5** [Archaic] *a)* the cross on which Jesus was crucified *b)* a gallows —*vt.* **treed, tree′ing** ☆**1** to chase up a tree **2** to place or stretch on a boot or shoe tree ☆**3** [Informal] to corner, as if chased up a tree; place in a difficult position —☆**up a tree** [Informal] in a situation without escape; cornered —**tree′less** *adj.* —**tree′like′** *adj.*

treed (trēd) *adj.* provided or planted with trees

tree ear ⟦so called from its flat, rounded form⟧ a basidiomycetous mushroom (genus *Auricularia*), used esp. in Chinese cooking, that grows on tree trunks and is rubbery in consistency and crinkled in texture

tree fern any of various tropical, treelike ferns (esp. genera *Cyathea, Alsophila,* and *Hemitelia*) with an elongated, woody trunk bearing fronds at the top

tree frog any of several families of frogs (esp. Hylidae) that live in trees, which they climb with the aid of adhesive discs on the toes: many are called *tree toads*

tree heath BRIER[2] (sense 1)

tree·hop·per (trē′häp′ər) *n.* any of various families (esp. Membracidae) of hopping homopteran insects that feed on plant sap and are characterized by the backward prolongation over the abdomen of the prothorax, which is often extended

tree·house (-hous′) *n.* a houselike structure built in the branches of a tree, as for children to play in

tree-hug·ger (-hug′ər) *n.* [Slang] ENVIRONMENTALIST (*n.* 2): a jocular or pejorative usage: also written **tree hugger**

☆**tree lawn** [Dial.] the strip between a street and its parallel sidewalk, typically planted with grass and, often, one or more trees: also written **tree′lawn′** *n.*

☆**tree line** TIMBERLINE

treen (trēn) *pl.n.* ⟦< obs. pl., trees, or obs. adj., wooden < OE *trēow*, TREE⟧ [*with pl. or sing. v.*] decorative objects, esp. antiques, made of wood: also **treen′ware′** (-wer′) *n.*

tree·nail (trē′nāl′; *also* tren′əl, trun′-) *n.* ⟦ME *trenayle* < *tre*, TREE (in early sense, "wood") + *nayle*, NAIL⟧ a wooden peg used to join timbers, esp. in building wooden ships: it swells from moisture and ensures a tight joint

tree of heaven a fast-growing ailanthus (*Ailanthus altissima*), native to China but widely cultivated in the U.S. as a shade tree

tree of knowledge *Bible* the tree whose fruit Adam and Eve tasted in disobedience of God: Gen. 2, 3: in full **tree of knowledge of good and evil**

tree of life *Bible* **1** a tree in the Garden of Eden bearing fruit which, if eaten, gave everlasting life: Gen. 2:9; 3:22 **2** a tree in the heavenly Jerusalem whose leaves are for healing the nations: Rev. 22:2

tree ring ANNUAL RING

tree shrew any of a family (Tupaiidae) of small, omnivorous shrews of Southeast Asia

tree squirrel any of various squirrels that live in trees; esp., any of a genus (*Sciurus*) including the gray squirrel

☆**tree surgery** treatment of damaged or diseased trees as by filling cavities, removing parts, treating fresh wounds, etc. —**tree surgeon**

☆**tree toad** any of various tree frogs

tree·top (trē′täp′) *n.* the topmost part of a tree

tref (trāf) *adj.* ⟦Yiddish *treif* < Heb *terēfāh*, animal torn by predatory beast⟧ *Judaism* not clean or fit to eat according to the dietary laws; not kosher

tre·foil (trē′foil′) *n.* ⟦ME *treyfoyle* < Anglo-Fr *trifoil* < L *trifolium*, three-leaved plant < *tri-*, TRI- + *folium*, a leaf: see FOIL[2]⟧ **1** *a)* any of a number of plants with leaves divided into three leaflets, as the clover, tick trefoil, and certain species of lotus *b)* a flower or leaf with three lobes **2** any ornamental figure resembling a threefold leaf

trefoils

tre·ha·lose (trē′hə lōs′, tri häl′ōs′) *n.* ⟦< ModL *trehala*, substance of cocoon of a certain beetle, the original source of the sugar (prob. < Pers *tīghāl*) + -OSE[1]⟧ a disaccharide extracted from yeast, mushrooms, and other fungi

treil·lage (trāl′ij) *n.* ⟦Fr < OFr *treille*, bower, trellis < L *trichila*, bower⟧ a lattice for vines; trellis

trek (trek) *vi.* **trekked, trek′king** ⟦Afrik < Du *trekken*, to draw; akin to

MHG *trecken*⟧ 1 [South Afr.] to travel by ox wagon 2 to travel slowly or laboriously 3 [Informal] to go, esp. on foot —*vt.* [South Afr.] to draw (a wagon): said of an ox —*n.* 1 [South Afr.] a journey made by ox wagon, or one leg of such a journey 2 any journey or leg of a journey 3 a migration 4 [Informal] a short trip, esp. on foot —**trek′ker** *n.*

trel·lis (trel′is) *n.* ⟦ME *trelis* < OFr *treliz* < VL **trilicius*, coarse cloth < L *trilix*, triple-twilled (see DRILL³): infl. by OFr *treille*, arbor: see TREILLAGE⟧ 1 a structure of thin strips, esp. of wood, crossing each other in an open pattern of squares, diamonds, etc., on which vines or other creeping plants are trained; lattice 2 a bower, archway, etc. of this —*vt.* 1 to furnish with, or train on, a trellis 2 to cross or interweave like a trellis

trel·lis·work (trel′is wurk′) *n.* open network of strips, usually of wood; latticework

trem·a·tode (trem′ə tōd′, trē′mə-) *n.* ⟦< ModL *Trematoda* < Gr *trēmatōdēs*, perforated < *trēma* (gen. *trēmatos*), a hole (< IE base **ter-*, to rub, bore > THROW) + *eidos*, -OID⟧ any of a large class (Trematoda) of parasitic flatworms with one or more external, muscular suckers; fluke —*adj.* of a trematode

trem·ble (trem′bəl) *vi.* **-bled, -bling** ⟦ME *tremblen* < OFr *trembler* < VL **tremulare* < L *tremulus*, trembling < *tremere*, to tremble < IE **trem-* (< base **ter-*) > Gr *tremein*, to tremble⟧ 1 to shake involuntarily from cold, fear, excitement, fatigue, etc.; shiver 2 to feel great fear or anxiety 3 to quiver, quake, totter, vibrate, etc. 4 to quaver [*her voice trembled*] —*n.* 1 *a)* the act or condition of trembling *b)* [Old-fashioned] a fit or state of trembling (often **the trembles**) ☆2 [*pl.*] a disease of cattle and sheep caused by a poisonous, oily alcohol contained in certain plants, as white snakeroot, and characterized by muscular tremors and a stumbling gait: communicated to humans as milk sickness —**trem′bler** *n.* —**trem′bling·ly** *adv.* —**trem′bly** *adj.*

tre·men·dous (tri men′dəs) *adj.* ⟦L *tremendus* < *tremere*, to prec.⟧ 1 [Archaic] such as to make one tremble; terrifying; dreadful 2 *a)* very large; great; enormous *b)* wonderful, amazing, extraordinary, etc. —***SYN.*** ENORMOUS —**tre·men′dous·ly** *adv.* —**tre·men′dous·ness** *n.*

trem·o·lite (trem′ə līt′) *n.* ⟦after the *Tremola* valley, in Switzerland, where it was found + -ITE¹⟧ a hard, white to dark-gray, monoclinic amphibole, $Ca_2Mg_5Si_8O_{22}(OH)_2$, that is closely related to actinolite and found in either fibrous or crystalline form; hydrous calcium magnesium silicate

trem·o·lo (trem′ə lō′) *n., pl.* **-los′** ⟦It < L *tremulus*: see TREMULOUS⟧ *Music* 1 a tremulous effect produced by the rapid reiteration of the same tone, as by the rapid up-and-down movement of the bow or plectrum: in singing, sometimes, VIBRATO 2 a device, as in an organ, for producing such a tone

trem·or (trem′ər; *occas.* trē′mər) *n.* ⟦ME < OFr *tremour* < L *tremor* < *tremere*, to TREMBLE⟧ 1 a trembling, shaking, or shivering 2 a vibratory or quivering motion 3 a nervous thrill; trembling sensation 4 a trembling sound 5 a state of tremulous excitement [*in a tremor of delight*] —**trem′or·ous** *adj.*

trem·u·lous (trem′yoo̅ ləs) *adj.* ⟦L *tremulus* < *tremere*, to TREMBLE⟧ 1 trembling; quivering; palpitating 2 fearful; timid; timorous 3 marked by or showing trembling or quivering [*tremulous excitement*] —**trem′u·lous·ly** *adv.* —**trem′u·lous·ness** *n.*

tre·nail (trē′nāl′; *also* tren′əl, trun′-) *n. alt. sp. of* TREENAIL

trench (trench) *vt.* ⟦LME *trenchen* < OFr *trenchier* (Fr *trancher*), to cut, hack, prob. < L *truncare*, to cut off: see TRUNCATE⟧ 1 to cut, cut into, cut off, etc.; slice, gash, etc. 2 *a)* to cut a deep furrow or furrows in *b)* to dig a ditch or ditches in 3 to surround or fortify with trenches; entrench —*vi.* 1 to dig a ditch or ditches, as for fortification 2 to infringe (*on* or *upon* another's land, rights, time, etc.) 3 to verge or border (*on*); come close —*n.* ⟦ME < OFr *trenche* (Fr *tranche*, a slice) < *trencher*⟧ 1 a deep furrow in the ground, ocean floor, etc. 2 a long, narrow ditch dug by soldiers for cover and concealment, with the removed earth heaped up in front —**the trenches** 1 a system of trenches dug as fortifications, as in WWI 2 a situation characterized by the heavy or physical work of any struggle or enterprise

trench·ant (tren′chənt) *adj.* ⟦ME < OFr, prp. of *trenchier*: see prec.⟧ 1 [Archaic] cutting; sharp 2 keen; penetrating; incisive [*trenchant words*] 3 forceful; vigorous; effective [*a trenchant argument*] 4 clear-cut; distinct [*a trenchant pattern*] —***SYN.*** INCISIVE —**trench′an·cy** *n.* —**trench′ant·ly** *adv.*

trench coat ⟦from its resemblance to an officer's coat worn in *trenches* during WWI⟧ a belted raincoat, typically with a folded tab somewhat like an epaulet fastened with a button over each shoulder seam

trench·er¹ (tren′chər) *n.* ⟦ME < OFr *trencheor* < *trenchier*: see TRENCH⟧ [Archaic] 1 a wooden board or platter on which to carve or serve meat 2 *a)* food served on a trencher *b)* a supply of food

trench·er² (tren′chər) *n.* a person who digs trenches

trench·er·man (tren′chər mən) *n., pl.* **-men** (-mən) ⟦< TRENCHER¹⟧ 1 an eater; esp., a person who eats much and heartily: a humorous usage 2 [Archaic] a person who frequents a patron's table; parasite; hanger-on

trench fever ⟦from its prevalence among soldiers in the *trenches* in WWI⟧ an infectious disease caused by a rickettsia (*Rochalimaea quintana*) transmitted by body lice, characterized by a remittent fever, muscular pains, etc.

trench foot a diseased condition of the feet resulting from prolonged exposure to wet and cold and the circulatory disorders caused by inaction, as of soldiers in trenches

trench knife a double-edged military knife or dagger, for hand-to-hand combat

trench mortar any of various portable mortars for shooting projectiles at a high trajectory and short range

trench mouth ⟦from its prevalence among soldiers in *trenches*⟧ an infectious disease characterized by ulceration of the mucous membranes of the mouth and throat and caused by a bacterium (*Fusobacterium nucleatum*) often in conjunction with a spirochete (*Treponema vincentii*)

trench warfare warfare waged chiefly from trenches built for long-term use: see TRENCH (*n.* 2)

trend (trend) *vi.* ⟦ME *trenden*, to roll < OE *trendan*, to turn, roll, akin to *trinde*, round lump < IE base **der-*, to split off (> TEAR¹): prob. basic sense "split-off piece of a tree trunk, as a disk or wheel"⟧ 1 to extend, turn, incline, bend, etc. in a specific direction; tend; run [*the river trends northward*] 2 to have a general tendency: said of events, conditions, opinions, etc. —*n.* 1 the general direction of a coast, river, road, etc. 2 a general or prevailing tendency or course, as of events, a discussion, etc.; drift 3 a vogue, or current style, as in fashions —***SYN.*** TENDENCY

☆**trend·set·ter** (trend′set′ər) *n.* a person, magazine, company, etc. that creates, espouses, or popularizes a trend or trends, as in fashions or ideas —**trend′set′ting** *adj.*

trend·y (tren′dē) [Informal] *adj.* **trend′i·er, trend′i·est** of or in the latest style, or trend; very fashionable; faddish —*n., pl.* **trend′ies** a trendy person —**trend′i·ly** *adv.* —**trend′i·ness** *n.*

Treng·ga·nu (treŋ gä′noo̅) *var. of* TERENGGANU

Trent (trent) 1 commune in N Italy, on the Adige River: site of a council (*Council of Trent*) of the Roman Catholic Church (held intermittently, 1545-63), that condemned the Reformation, undertook Catholic reform, and defined Catholic doctrine 2 river in central England, flowing from Staffordshire northeast to the Humber: 170 mi (274 km)

Tren·ti·no-Al·to A·di·ge (tren tē′nō äl′tō ä′dē jā′) region of N Italy: the N part (*Alto Adige*) is in the S Tirol: 5,254 sq mi (13,608 sq km); cap. Trent

Tren·to (tren′tô) *It. name for* TRENT

Tren·ton (trent′′n) ⟦after William *Trent* (1655-1724), colonist⟧ capital of N.J., on the Delaware River

tre·pan¹ (trē pan′, tri-) *n.* ⟦ME *trepane* < ML *trepanum* < Gr *trypanon*, carpenters' tool, auger, trepan < *trypan*, to bore < IE **treup-* < base **ter-*, to bore, rub > THROW⟧ 1 an early form of the trephine 2 a heavy boring tool for sinking shafts, quarrying, etc. —*vt.* **-panned′, -pan′ning** 1 TREPHINE 2 to cut a disk out of (a metal plate, ingot, etc.) —**trep′a·na′tion** *n.*

tre·pan² (trē pan′) [Archaic] *n.* ⟦older *trapan*, prob. < TRAP¹, but infl. by fig. use of prec.⟧ 1 a person or thing that tricks, traps, or ensnares 2 a trick; stratagem; trap —*vt.* **-panned′, -pan′ning** to trick, trap, or lure

tre·pang (trē paŋ′) *n.* ⟦Malay *teripang*: also name of sea cucumber itself⟧ the eviscerated, boiled, smoked, and dried body of any of several species of sea cucumbers, used, esp. in East Asia, for making soup

tre·phine (trē fīn′, -fēn′) *n.* ⟦earlier *trafine*, form based on TREPAN¹ < L *tres*, THREE + *fines*, ends⟧ a type of small crown saw used in surgery to remove a circular section, as of bone from the skull —*vt.* **-phined′, -phin′ing** to operate on with a trephine —**treph·i·na·tion** (tref′ə nā′shən) *n.*

trep·i·da·tion (trep′ə dā′shən) *n.* ⟦L *trepidatio* < *trepidatus*, pp. of *trepidare*, to tremble < *trepidus*, disturbed, alarmed < IE **trep-*, to trip, tramp (< base **ter-*, to tremble) > OE *thrafian*, to press⟧ 1 [Archaic] tremulous or trembling movement; quaking; tremor 2 fearful uncertainty, anxiety, etc.; apprehension

trep·i·da·tious (-dā′shəs) *adj.* [Informal] fearful, apprehensive, etc. —**trep′i·da′tious·ly** *adv.*

trep·o·ne·ma (trep′ə nē′mə) *n., pl.* **-mas** or **-ma·ta** (-mə tə) ⟦ModL < Gr *trepein*, to turn (see TROPE) + *nēma*, a thread < IE base *(*s*)*nē-* > NEEDLE⟧ any of a genus (*Treponema*) of slender spirochetes parasitic in mammals and birds, including some that are pathogenic to humans, as the organisms causing syphilis and yaws —**trep′o·ne′mal** *adj.*, **trep′o·ne′ma·tous** (-mə təs)

très (tre; *E*, trā) *adv.* ⟦Fr⟧ [*also in roman type*] very: sometimes used for humorous or ironic effect [*très chic and très expensive*]

tres·pass (tres′pəs; *also, esp. for v.*, -pas′) *vi.* ⟦ME *trespassen* < OFr *trespasser* < VL **transpassare*, to pass across < L *trans-*, TRANS- + VL **passare*, to pass < L *passus*: see PACE¹⟧ 1 to go beyond the limits of what is considered right or moral; do wrong; transgress 2 to go on another's land or property without permission or right 3 to intrude or encroach [*to trespass on someone's time*] 4 *Law* to commit a trespass —*n.* ⟦ME *trespas* < OFr < the v.⟧ the act or an instance of trespassing; specif., *a)* a moral offense; transgression *b)* an encroachment or intrusion *c)* *Law* an illegal act done forcefully against another's person, rights, or property; also, legal action for damages resulting from this —**tres′pass·er** *n.*

SYN.—**trespass** implies an unlawful or unwarranted entrance upon the property, rights, etc. of another [*to trespass on a private beach*]; to **encroach** is to make such inroads by stealth or gradual advances [*squatters encroaching on our lands*]; **infringe** implies an encroachment that breaks a law or agreement or violates the rights of others [*to infringe on a patent*]; **intrude** implies a thrusting oneself into company, situations, etc. without being asked or wanted [*to intrude on someone's privacy*]; **invade** implies a forcible or hostile entrance into the territory or rights of others [*to invade a neighboring country*]

tress (tres) *n.* ⟦ME *tresse* < OFr, akin to It *treccia* < ? VL **trichea*, a plait⟧ 1 [Obs.] a braid or plait of hair 2 a lock of human hair 3 [*pl.*] a woman's or girl's hair, esp. when long and falling loosely

-tress (tris) *suffix* female: see -ESS

tressed (trest) ***adj.*** **1** having tresses of a specified kind: often in compounds [*black-tressed*] **2** [Obs.] arranged in tresses; braided

tres·sure (tresh′ər) ***n.*** ⟦ME *tressour* < MFr *tresseor* < OFr *tresce:* see TRESS⟧ *Heraldry* a narrow band following the contour, and somewhat inside the edge, of a shield, often ornamented with fleurs-de-lis: cf. ORLE

tres·tle (tres′əl) ***n.*** ⟦ME *trestel* < OFr < VL **transtellum,* dim. of L *transtrum,* a beam: see TRANSOM⟧ **1** a framework consisting of a horizontal beam fastened to two pairs of spreading legs, used to support planks to form a table, platform, etc. **2** *a)* a framework of vertical or slanting uprights and crosspieces, supporting a bridge, etc. *b)* a bridge with such a framework

tres·tle·tree (-trē′) ***n.*** either of two horizontal fore-and-aft beams, one on each side of a mast, that support the crosstrees, top, and fid of the mast above

☆**tres·tle·work** (-wurk′) ***n.*** **1** a system of trestles for supporting a bridge, etc. **2** a structure made of trestles

tret (tret) ***n.*** ⟦Anglo-Fr (Fr *trait*), a pull < OFr *traire* (< L *trahere,* to DRAW)⟧ a fixed allowance by weight, after the deduction of tare, formerly made to buyers of certain commodities to compensate for waste and deterioration during transit

tre·tin·o·in (tre tin′ō in) ***n.*** ⟦*t-* (< ?) + RETINO(IC ACID) + -IN[1]⟧ a form of retinoic acid, used esp. in the treatment of acne

Tre·vel·yan (tri vil′yən) **1 George Macaulay** 1876-1962; Eng. historian **2** Sir **George Otto** 1838-1928; Eng. historian & politician: father of George Macaulay

trews (tro͞oz) ***pl.n.*** ⟦Gael *triubhas*⟧ [Scot.] trousers, esp. tartan trousers

T. rex (tē′ reks′) [Informal] *Tyrannosaurus rex:* see TYRANNOSAUR

trey (trā) ***n.*** ⟦ME < OFr *trei, treis* < L *tres,* THREE⟧ **1** a playing card with three spots **2** the side of a die bearing three spots, or a throw of the dice totaling three

tri- (trī) ⟦< Fr, L, or Gr: Fr *tri-* < L (< *tres,* THREE) or Gr (< *treis,* THREE, *tris,* THRICE)⟧ *prefix* **1** having, combining, or involving three [*triangle, trichromatic*] **2** triply, in three ways or directions [*triphibian*] **3** three times, into three [*trisect*] **4** every three, every third [*triennial, triweekly*] **5** *Chem.* having three atoms, groups, or equivalents of (the thing specified) [*tribasic, tribromide*]

tri·a·ble (trī′ə bəl) ***adj.*** **1** that can be tried or tested **2** subject to trial in a law court —**tri′a·ble·ness** ***n.***

☆**tri·ac** (trī′ak′) ***n.*** ⟦*tri(ode) a(lternating-)c(urrent switch)*⟧ *Electronics* a type of thyristor that functions as an electrically controlled switch for alternating current

tri·ac·e·tate (trī as′ə tāt′) ***n.*** a compound containing three acetate radicals in the molecule

tri·ac·id (trī as′id) ***adj.*** **1** capable of reacting with three molecules of a monobasic acid: said of a base **2** containing three replaceable hydrogen atoms: said esp. of an acid

tri·ad (trī′ad′) ***n.*** ⟦< LL *trias* (gen. *triadis*) < Gr *trias* (gen. *triados*) < *treis,* THREE⟧ **1** a group of three persons, things, ideas, etc.; trinity **2** a musical chord of three tones, esp. one consisting of a root tone and its third and fifth —**tri·ad′ic** ***adj.***

tri·age (trē äzh′, trē′äzh′) ***n.*** ⟦Fr, a sifting < *trier,* to sift: see TRY & -AGE⟧ **1** a system of assigning priorities of medical treatment based on urgency, chance for survival, etc. and used on battlefields and in hospital emergency wards **2** any system for prioritizing based on available resources, manpower, etc., as in an emergency —***vt.*** **-aged′, -ag′ing** to prioritize (patients, problems, etc.)

tri·al (trī′əl, trīl) ***n.*** ⟦Anglo-Fr < *trier:* see TRY⟧ **1** *a)* the act or process of trying, testing, or putting to the proof; test *b)* a testing of qualifications, attainments, or progress; probation *c)* experimental treatment or operation; experiment **2** *a)* the fact or state of being tried by suffering, temptation, etc. *b)* a hardship, suffering, etc. that tries one's endurance *c)* a person or thing that is a source of annoyance or irritation **3** a formal examination of the facts of a case by a court of law to decide the validity of a charge or claim **4** an attempt; endeavor; effort —***adj.*** **1** of a trial or trials **2** made, done, or used for the purpose of trying, testing, etc. —**on trial** in the process of being tried, as in a court of law

SYN.—**trial** implies the trying of a person or thing in order to establish worth in actual performance [hired on *trial*]; **experiment** implies a showing by trial whether a thing will be effective [the honor system was instituted as an *experiment*] and, in addition, is used of any action or process undertaken to discover something not yet known or to demonstrate something known [*experiments* in nuclear physics]; **test** implies a putting of a thing to decisive proof by thorough examination or trial under controlled conditions and with fixed standards in mind [a *test* of a new jet plane] See also **affliction**

trial and error the process of making repeated trials or tests, improving the methods used in the light of errors made, until the right result is found —**tri′al-and-er′ror** ***adj.***

trial balance a statement of the debit and credit balances of all open accounts in a double-entry bookkeeping ledger to test their equality

☆**trial balloon** **1** PILOT BALLOON **2** any action, statement, etc. intended to test how something will be received or accepted

trial jury PETIT JURY

tri·a·logue (trī′ə lôg′, -läg′) ***n.*** ⟦< TRI- + -LOGUE⟧ an interchange and discussion of ideas among three groups having different origins, philosophies, principles, etc.

tri·an·gle (trī′aŋ′gəl) ***n.*** ⟦ME < MFr < L *triangulum:* see TRI- & ANGLE[1]⟧ **1** a geometric figure having three angles and three sides **2** any three-sided or three-cornered figure, area, object, part, etc. **3** a right-angled, flat, triangular instrument used in drawing geometric figures **4** a situation involving three persons, esp. when one person is having love affairs with two others **5** a musical percussion instrument consisting of a steel rod bent into a triangle with one angle open: it produces a high-pitched, tinkling sound when struck with a short steel rod

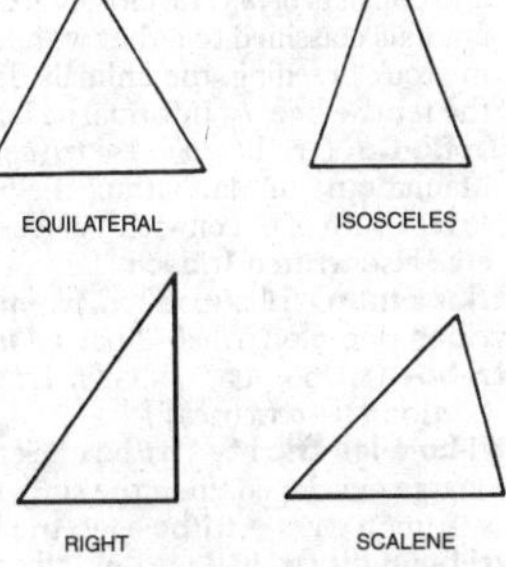

triangles

tri·an·gu·lar (trī aŋ′gyə lər) ***adj.*** ⟦LL *triangularis*⟧ **1** of or shaped like a triangle; three-cornered **2** of or involving three persons, factions, units, or parts **3** having bases that are triangles, as a prism —**tri·an′gu·lar′i·ty** (-ler′ə tē) ***n.*** —**tri·an′gu·lar·ly** ***adv.***

tri·an·gu·late (trī aŋ′gyə lāt′; *for adj.,* -lit, -lāt′) ***vt.*** **-lat′ed, -lat′ing** ⟦< ML *triangulatus,* pp. of **triangulare* < L *triangulum:* see TRIANGLE⟧ **1** to divide into triangles **2** to survey, map, or determine by or as by triangulation **3** to make triangular —***adj.*** **1** of triangles; triangular **2** marked with triangles

tri·an·gu·la·tion (trī aŋ′gyə lā′shən) ***n.*** ⟦ML *triangulatio*⟧ **1** *Navigation, Surveying* the process of determining the distance between points on the earth's surface, or the relative positions of points, by dividing up a large area into a series of connected triangles, measuring a base line between two points, and then locating a third point by computing both the size of the angles made by lines from this point to each end of the base line and the lengths of these lines **2** the triangles thus marked out Often used fig. to mean any determination based on a series of measurements or calculations

Tri·an·gu·lum (trī aŋ′gyə ləm) ***n.*** ⟦L, TRIANGLE⟧ a N constellation between Aries and Andromeda

Triangulum Aus·tra·le (ôs trā′lē) ⟦L, southern triangle < *triangulum,* TRIANGLE + *australis:* see AUSTRAL⟧ a S constellation between Apus and Norma

tri·ar·chy (trī′är kē, -är′-) ***n.,*** *pl.* **-chies** ⟦Gr *triarchia:* see TRI- & -ARCHY⟧ **1** *a)* government by three rulers; triumvirate *b)* a country governed by three rulers **2** a country with three districts, each governed by its own ruler

Tri·as·sic (trī as′ik) ***adj.*** ⟦< Ger *triassisch* (< LL *Trias* (see TRIAD: because divisible into three groups) + *-isch,* -IC⟧ [*sometimes* **t-**] designating or of the first geologic period of the Mesozoic Era, characterized by the breakup of Pangea, the development of tall forests of cycads and conifers, and the presence of the first dinosaurs, turtles, frogs, and small mammals —**the Triassic** the Triassic Period or its rocks: see the geologic time chart in the Reference Supplement: also **the Tri′as** (-əs)

☆**tri·ath·lete** (trī ath′lēt) ***n.*** ⟦blend of fol. & ATHLETE⟧ one who takes part in a triathlon

☆**tri·ath·lon** (trī ath′län, -lən) ***n.*** ⟦TRI- + Gr *athlon:* see ATHLETE⟧ an endurance race combining three consecutive events (swimming, bicycling, and running)

tri·a·tom·ic (trī′ə täm′ik) ***adj.*** **1** designating or of a molecule consisting of three atoms **2** designating or of a molecule containing three replaceable atoms or groups

tri·ax·i·al (trī ak′sē əl) ***adj.*** having three axes, as some crystals —**tri·ax′i·al·ly** ***adv.***

tri·a·zine (trī′ə zēn′, -zin; trī az′ēn, -in) ***n.*** ⟦TRI- + AZINE⟧ **1** any of three isomeric heterocyclic compounds having the formula $C_3H_3N_3$ **2** any derivative of these

tri·a·zole (trī′ə zōl′, trī az′ōl) ***n.*** ⟦TRI- + AZOLE⟧ **1** any of four isomeric heterocyclic azoles, $C_2H_3N_3$, having three nitrogen atoms in the ring **2** any derivative of these

trib·ad·ism (trib′əd iz′əm) ***n.*** ⟦< Fr *tribade,* lesbian < L *tribas* (gen. *tribadis*) < Gr *tribein,* to rub < IE **trib-* < base **ter-* > THROW⟧ homosexuality between women; lesbianism

trib·al (trī′bəl) ***adj.*** of, relating to, or characteristic of a tribe or tribes —**trib′al·ly** ***adv.***

trib·al·ism (trī′bəl iz′əm) ***n.*** **1** tribal organization, culture, loyalty, etc. **2** a strong sense of identifying with and being loyal to one's tribe, group, etc. —**trib′al·ist** ***adj., n.*** —**trib′al·is′tic** ***adj.***

tri·bas·ic (trī bās′ik) ***adj.*** ⟦TRI- + BASIC⟧ **1** containing in its molecule three atoms of hydrogen that are replaceable by basic atoms or radicals: said of an acid **2** producing three hydrogen ions per molecule in solution **3** containing three monovalent basic atoms or groups

tribe (trīb) ***n.*** ⟦ME *trybe* < L *tribus,* one of the three groups into which Romans were orig. divided, tribe < *tri-* (see TRI-) + IE **bhū-* < base **bheu-,* to grow, flourish > BE⟧ **1** esp. among preliterate peoples, a group of persons, families, or clans believed to be descended from a common ancestor and forming a close community under a leader, or chief **2** a group of this kind having recognized ancestry; specif., *a)* any of the three divisions of the ancient Romans, traditionally of Latin, Sabine, and Etruscan origin *b)* any of the later political and territorial divisions of the ancient Romans *c)* any of the phylae of ancient Greece *d)* any of the twelve divisions of the ancient Israelites **3** any group of people having the same occupation, habits, ideas, etc.: often in a somewhat derogatory sense [the *tribe* of drama critics] **4** a taxonomic category that is a subdivision of a subfamily of plants or animals and consists of several closely related genera **5** a natural group of plants or animals classified together without regard for their taxonomic relations **6** in stock breeding, the animals descended from the same female through the female line **7** [Informal] a family, esp. a large one

Tri·Be·Ca (trī bek′ə) ⟦< *tri(angle) be(low) Ca(nal Street)*, street in Manhattan⟧ in Manhattan, the area between Broadway and the Hudson River south of Greenwich Village: noted as a center for artists, art galleries, etc.: also written **Tribeca**

tribes·man (trībz′mən) *n., pl.* **-men** (-mən) a member of a tribe

tribes·peo·ple (trībz′pē′pəl) *pl.n.* members of a tribe

tri·bo- (trī′bō, -bə) ⟦< Gr *tribein,* to rub: see TRIBADISM⟧ *combining form* friction [*triboelectricity*]

tri·bo·e·lec·tric·i·ty (trī′bō ē′lek tris′ə tē) *n.* ⟦prec. + ELECTRICITY⟧ electric charge developed upon the surface of a material by friction, as by rubbing silk upon glass —**tri′bo·e·lec′tric** (-trik) *adj.*

tri·bol·o·gy (trī bäl′ə jē) *n.* ⟦TRIBO- + -LOGY⟧ the study of friction between interacting parts, such as gears, and ways of reducing it —**tri′bo·log′i·cal** *adj.* —**tri·bol′o·gist** *n.*

tri·bo·lu·mi·nes·cence (trī′bō lo͞o′mə nes′əns) *n.* ⟦TRIBO- + LUMINESCENCE⟧ luminescence resulting from friction, observed at the surface of certain crystalline materials —**tri′bo·lu′mi·nes′cent** *adj.*

tri·brach (trī′brak′, trib′rak′) *n.* ⟦L *tribrachys* < Gr: see TRI- & BRACHY-⟧ *Gr. & Latin Prosody* a metrical foot consisting of three short syllables —**tri·brach′ic** *adj.*

tri·bro·mide (trī brō′mīd) *n.* ⟦TRI- + BROMIDE⟧ a compound containing three bromine atoms in the molecule

trib·u·la·tion (trib′yə lā′shən) *n.* ⟦ME *tribulacion* < OFr < LL(Ec) *tribulatio* < *tribulare,* to afflict, oppress < L, to press < *tribulum,* threshing platform with sharp studs, akin to *terere,* to rub: for IE base see THROW⟧ **1** great misery or distress, as from oppression; deep sorrow **2** something that causes great suffering or distress; affliction; trial —*SYN.* AFFLICTION

tri·bu·nal (trī byo͞o′nəl, tri-) *n.* ⟦L < *tribunus:* see TRIBUNE[1]⟧ **1** a seat or bench upon which a judge or judges sit in a court **2** a court of justice **3** any seat of judgment [the *tribunal* of popular sentiment]

trib·u·nate (trib′yo͞o nit, -nāt′) *n.* ⟦Fr *tribunat* < L *tribunatus*⟧ the rank, office, or authority of a tribune

trib·une[1] (trib′yo͞on′; *in names of newspapers, often* tri byo͞on′) *n.* ⟦L *tribunus,* tribune, magistrate, lit., chief of a tribe < *tribus,* Roman tribal division: see TRIBE⟧ **1** in ancient Rome, *a)* any of several magistrates, esp. one appointed to protect the interests and rights of plebeians against violation by patricians *b)* any of the six officers who rotated command over a legion for a period of a year **2** a champion of the people: often used in newspaper names —**trib′une·ship′** (-ship′) *n.*

trib·une[2] (trib′yo͞on′) *n.* ⟦Fr < It *tribuna* < L *tribunal:* see TRIBUNAL (sense 1)⟧ a raised platform or dais for speakers

trib·u·tar·y (trib′yo͞o ter′ē, -yə-) *adj.* ⟦ME *tributarie* < L *tributarius*⟧ **1** *a)* paying tribute *b)* owed or paid as tribute **2** under another's control; subject [a *tributary* nation] **3** flowing into a larger one [a *tributary* stream] —*n., pl.* **-tar′ies 1** a tributary nation or ruler **2** a tributary stream or river —**trib′u·tar′i·ly** *adv.*

trib·ute (trib′yo͞ot′) *n.* ⟦ME *tribut* < MFr < L *tributum,* neut. of *tributus,* pp. of *tribuere,* to assign, allot, pay < *tribus,* Roman tribal division: see TRIBE⟧ **1** *a)* a regular payment of money, etc., made by one ruler or nation to another as acknowledgment of subjugation, for protection from invasion, etc. *b)* a tax levied for this **2** under feudalism, *a)* a tax paid by a vassal to an overlord *b)* the obligation to make such a payment **3** any forced payment or contribution, as through bribery, or the need to make this **4** something given, done, or said, as a gift, testimonial, etc., that shows gratitude, respect, honor, or praise **5** any outcome regarded as due to, and hence honoring, an effort, accomplishment, etc. [the team's success was a *tribute* to the coach's leadership]

tri·cam·er·al (trī kam′ər əl) *n.* ⟦< TRI- + L *camera:* see CHAMBER⟧ made up of or having three legislative chambers [the *tricameral* Parliament of South Africa]

tri·car·box·yl·ic (trī kär′bäk sil′ik) *adj.* containing three carboxyl groups in the molecule

tri·car·pel·lar·y (trī kär′pə ler′ē) *adj. Bot.* having a compound ovary consisting of three united carpels

trice (trīs) *vt.* **triced, tric′ing** ⟦ME *trisen* < MDu, to pull, hoist < *trise,* windlass, roller⟧ to haul up (a sail, etc.) and secure with a small line: usually with *up* —*n.* ⟦< *at a trice,* with one pull⟧ a very short time; instant; moment: now only in the phrase **in a trice**

tri·cen·ten·ni·al (trī′sen ten′ē əl) *adj.* **1** happening once in a period of 300 years **2** lasting 300 years —☆*n.* a 300th anniversary or its commemoration

tri·cep (trī′sep′) *adj.* of or having to do with the triceps muscle at the back of the upper arm [a *tricep* injury]

tri·ceps (-seps′) *n., pl.* **-ceps′** ⟦ModL < L, triple-headed < *tri-,* TRI- + *caput,* a HEAD⟧ a muscle having three heads, or points of origin, esp. the large muscle at the back of the upper arm that extends the forearm when contracted

tri·cer·a·tops (trī ser′ə täps′) *n.* ⟦ModL < *tri-* (see TRI-) + CERAT(O)- + Gr *ōps,* EYE⟧ any of a genus (*Triceratops*) of massive, four-legged ceratopsian dinosaurs of the Cretaceous having a large, bony crest over the neck, a long horn above each eye, and a short horn on the nose

tri·chi·a·sis (tri kī′ə sis) *n.* ⟦LL < Gr: see fol. & -IASIS⟧ an abnormal condition in which hairs, esp. the eyelashes, grow inward

tri·chi·na (tri kī′nə) *n., pl.* **-nae** (-nē) ⟦ModL < Gr *trichinos,* hairy < *thrix* (gen. *trichos*), hair⟧ a very small nematode worm (*Trichinella spiralis*) that causes trichinosis —**tri·chi′nal** *adj.*

trich·i·nize (trik′i nīz′) *vt.* **-nized′, -niz′ing** to infest with trichinae

trich·i·no·sis (trik′i nō′sis) *n.* ⟦ModL: see TRICHINA & -OSIS⟧ a disease caused by the presence of trichinae in the intestines and muscle tissues and usually acquired by eating insufficiently cooked pork from an infested hog: it is characterized by fever, nausea, diarrhea, and muscular pains

trich·i·nous (trik′i nəs, tri kī′nəs) *adj.* **1** infested with trichinae **2** of or having trichinosis

trich·ite (trik′īt′) *n.* ⟦< Gr *thrix* (gen. *trichos*), hair + -ITE[1]⟧ a hairlike crystallite occurring in volcanic rocks in irregular or radiating groups

tri·chlo·ride (trī klôr′īd) *n.* a chloride having three chlorine atoms to the molecule

tri·chlo·ro·a·ce·tic acid (trī klôr′ō ə sēt′ik) ⟦TRI- + CHLORO- + ACETIC⟧ a colorless, corrosive, deliquescent, crystalline substance, CCl_3COOH, with a sharp, pungent odor: it is used as an antiseptic and astringent

tri·chlo·ro·eth·yl·ene (-eth′əl ēn′) *n.* ⟦TRI- + CHLORO- + ETHYLENE⟧ a toxic, nonflammable liquid, $CHCl{:}CCl_2$, used as a solvent for fats, oils, and waxes, and in dry cleaning, etc.

tri·chlo·ro·phe·nox·y·a·ce·tic acid (-fē näk′sē ə sēt′ik, -fi-) ⟦TRI- + CHLORO- + PHENOXY + ACETIC⟧ a trichloride derivative of phenoxy acetic acid, $Cl_3C_6H_2OCH_2{\cdot}COOH$, used as a weed killer; 2,4,5-T

trich·o- (trik′ō, -ə) ⟦Gr < *thrix* (gen. *trichos*), hair⟧ *combining form* hair, hairlike [*trichosis*]: also, before a vowel, **trich-**

trich·o·cyst (trik′ə sist′) *n.* ⟦prec. + -CYST⟧ any of the many tiny, rodlike, stinging and attachment organelles embedded in the ectoplasm of many ciliated protozoans —**trich′o·cyst′ic** (-sis′tik) *adj.*

trich·o·gyne (trik′ə jīn′, -jin) *n.* ⟦< TRICHO- + Gr *gynē,* woman, female⟧ the long, hairlike part of a procarp in red algae, certain fungi, and lichens, acting as a receptor for the male fertilizing bodies —**trich′o·gyn′i·al** (-jin′ē əl) *adj.,* **trich′o·gyn′ic** (-jin′ik)

trich·oid (trik′oid′) *adj.* resembling a hair; hairlike

tri·chol·o·gy (tri käl′ə jē) *n.* ⟦TRICHO- + -LOGY⟧ the science dealing with the hair and its diseases —**tri·chol′o·gist** *n.*

tri·chome (trī′kōm, trik′ōm) *n.* ⟦Ger *trichom* < Gr *trichōma,* growth of hair < *trichoun,* to cover with hair < *thrix* (gen. *trichos*), hair⟧ **1** any hairlike outgrowth from an epidermal cell of a plant, as a bristle, prickle, root hair, etc. **2** any of the threadlike structures, or filaments, of certain algae —**tri·chom′ic** (-käm′ik, -kō′mik) *adj.*

trich·o·mo·nad (trik′ə mō′nad, -män′ad) *n.* ⟦< ModL *Trichomonas* (gen. *Trichomonadis*): see TRICHO- & MONAD⟧ any of a genus (*Trichomonas*) of parasitic or commensal zooflagellates

trich·o·mo·ni·a·sis (-mō nī′ə sis) *n.* ⟦ModL < *Trichomonas* (see prec.) + -IASIS⟧ infestation with trichomonads; esp., *a)* a vaginitis in women caused by a trichomonad (*Trichomonas vaginalis*) and characterized by a heavy discharge *b)* a disease of cows caused by a trichomonad (*Trichomonas foetus*) and resulting in temporary infertility and sometimes abortion

tri·chop·ter·an (trī käp′tər ən) *n.* ⟦< ModL *Trichoptera* (see TRICHO- & PTERO-) + -AN⟧ CADDIS FLY —**tri·chop′ter·ous** *adj.*

tri·cho·sis (tri kō′sis) *n.* ⟦ModL: see TRICHO- & -OSIS⟧ any disease of the hair

tri·cho·the·cene (trik′ə thē′sēn′) *n.* ⟦< ModL *Trichothecium,* a genus of fungi < TRICHO- + *-thecium,* receptacle, ult. < Gr *thēkē*: see THECA⟧ any of a group of toxins that cause vomiting, coma, etc., produced by various fungi and sometimes found in rotting food, esp. potatoes

tri·chot·o·my (trī kät′ə mē) *n.* ⟦Gr *tricha,* threefold (< *treis,* THREE), after DICHOTOMY⟧ division into three parts, elements, groups, etc. —**tri·chot′o·mize′** (-mīz′) *vt.* **-mized′, -miz′ing** —**tri·chot′o·mous** *adj.* —**tri·chot′o·mous·ly** *adv.*

tri·chro·ism (trī′krō iz′əm) *n.* ⟦< Gr *trichroos,* of three colors < *tri-,* TRI- + *chroia,* color: for IE base see CHROMA⟧ the property that some crystals have of transmitting light of three different colors when looked at from three different directions —**tri·chro′ic** *adj.*

tri·chro·mat (trī′krō mat′) *n.* ⟦back-form. < fol.⟧ a person having trichromatic vision

tri·chro·mat·ic (trī′krō mat′ik) *adj.* ⟦TRI- + CHROMATIC⟧ **1** of, having, or using three colors, as in the three-color process in printing and photography **2** of, pertaining to, or having normal vision, in which the three primary colors are fully distinguished Also **tri·chro′mic** —**tri·chro′ma·tism′** (-krō′mə tiz′əm) *n.*

trick (trik) *n.* ⟦ME *trik* < NormFr *trique* < *trikier* < OFr *trichier,* to trick, cheat, prob. < VL **triccare,* altered < ? LL *tricare,* to deceive, for L *tricari,* to make trouble < *tricae,* vexations, tricks < IE **treik-* < base **ter-,* to turn, rub > THROW⟧ **1** an action or device designed to deceive, cheat, outwit, etc.; artifice; dodge; ruse; stratagem **2** *a)* a mischievous or playful act; prank, practical joke, etc. *b)* a deception or illusion [the light played a *trick* on my eyes] **3** a freakish, foolish, mean, or stupid act **4** a clever or difficult act intended to amuse; specif., *a)* an act of jugglery or sleight of hand; also, an illusion of the kind created by legerdemain *b)* an action, feat, or routine performed by an animal as a result of training **5** any feat requiring skill 6 the art or knack of doing something easily, skillfully, quickly, etc. [the *trick* of making good pastry] 7 an expedient or convention of an art, craft, or trade [to learn the *tricks* of the trade] 8 a personal habit or mannerism [a *trick* of tugging at the ear] 9 a turn or round of duty or work; shift ☆10 [Old Informal] a child or girl, esp. one viewed as cute or pretty 11 [Slang] *a)* the act or an instance of performing sexual intercourse as a prostitute with a customer *b)* such a customer 12 *Card Games* the cards (one from each player) played and won in a single round: a trick serves as a unit in scoring —*vt.* to deceive or swindle —*adj.* 1 having to do with or used for a trick or tricks 2 that tricks 3 apt to malfunction; of uncertain reliability [a *trick* knee] —**do (or turn) the trick** [Informal] to bring about the desired result —**not miss a trick** [Informal] to be very alert —**trick out (or up)** to dress up; deck; array —☆**turn a trick** [Slang] to have sex with a customer: said of a prostitute —**up to one's (old) tricks** [Informal] behaving or, esp., misbehaving in a way regarded as characteristic —**trick′er** *n.*

SYN.—**trick** is the common word for an action or device in which ingenuity and cunning are used to outwit others and implies deception either for fraudulent purposes or as a prank; **ruse** applies to that which is contrived as a blind for one's real intentions or for the truth [her apparent illness was merely a *ruse*]; a **stratagem** is a more or less complicated ruse, by means of which one attempts to outwit or entrap an enemy or antagonist [military *stratagems*]; **maneuver**, specifically applicable to military tactics, in general use suggests the shrewd manipulation of persons or situations to suit one's purposes [a political *maneuver*]; **artifice** stresses inventiveness or ingenuity in the contrivance of an expedient, trick, etc. [*artifices* employed to circumvent the tax laws]; **wile** implies the use of allurements or beguilement to ensnare See also **cheat**

trick cyclist ⟦altered < PSYCHIATRIST by modification & transposition of elements⟧ [Brit. Slang] a psychiatrist: a humorous usage

trick·er·y (trik′ər ē) *n., pl.* **-er·ies** the act or practice of tricking; use of tricks; deception; fraud —SYN. DECEPTION

trick·ish (trik′ish) *adj.* 1 given to trickery; deceitful 2 characterized by or full of tricks —**trick′ish·ness** *n.*

trick·le (trik′əl) *vi.* **-led, -ling** ⟦ME *triklen* < ?⟧ 1 to flow slowly in a thin stream or fall in drops 2 to move, come, go, etc. little by little [the crowd *trickled* away] —*vt.* to cause to trickle —*n.* 1 the act of trickling 2 a slow, small flow

☆**trick·le-down** (-doun′) *adj.* designating or of an economic theory that holds that profits and growth among the largest businesses will eventually benefit the entire economy, including the economically depressed

☆**trick or treat!** traditional greeting used by a TRICK-OR-TREATER: orig. used with the meaning "give me a treat or I will play a trick on you!"

☆**trick-or-treat·er** (trik′ər trēt′ər) *n.* ⟦see prec.⟧ a person, typically a child, who goes from door to door in costume on Halloween asking for candy or other treats —**trick′-or-treat′ing** *n.*

trick·ster (trik′stər) *n.* ⟦TRICK + -STER⟧ 1 a person who tricks; cheat 2 *Myth.* any deity or character known for trickery and mischief

trick·sy (trik′sē) *adj.* **-si·er, -si·est** [Chiefly Brit.] 1 full of tricks; playful; mischievous 2 TRICKY —**trick′si·ness** *n.*

trick·y (trik′ē) *adj.* **trick′i·er, trick′i·est** 1 given to or characterized by trickery; deceitful 2 like a trick in deceptiveness or intricacy 3 requiring great skill or care —SYN. SLY —**trick′i·ly** *adv.* —**trick′i·ness** *n.*

tri·clin·ic (trī klin′ik) *adj.* ⟦< TRI- + Gr *klinein,* to incline (see LEAN¹) + -IC⟧ designating or of a crystal system having three axes of unequal length, none of which intersects at right angles with another: see CRYSTAL SYSTEM

tri·clin·i·um (trī klin′ē əm) *n., pl.* **-i·a** (-ə) ⟦L < Gr *triklinion,* dim. of *triklinos* < *tri-,* TRI- + *klinē,* a couch < *klinein:* see LEAN¹⟧ 1 a couch extending around three sides of an ancient Roman dining table, for reclining at meals 2 an ancient Roman dining room, esp. one with such a couch

tri·col·or (trī′kul′ər) *n.* ⟦Fr *tricolore,* orig., three-colored < LL *tricolor:* see TRI- & COLOR⟧ a flag having three colors in large areas; esp., the flag of France, with three broad, vertical stripes of blue, white, and red —*adj.* having three colors

tri·corn (trī′kôrn) *adj.* ⟦Fr *tricorne* < L *tricornis* < *tri-,* TRI- + *cornu,* HORN⟧ having three horns or corners, as a hat with the brim folded up against the crown to form three sides —*n.* a tricorn hat; cocked hat Also sp. **tri′corne**

tri·cot (trē′kō) *n.* ⟦Fr < *tricoter,* to knit < MFr, to move, dance < *tricot,* dim. of *trique,* a stick, cane < *estriquier,* to strike < MDu *striken;* akin to STRIKE⟧ 1 a thin fabric of polyester, nylon, etc., used esp. for underwear 2 a type of ribbed cloth for dresses

tric·o·tine (trik′ə tēn′) *n.* ⟦Fr: see prec. & -INE³⟧ a twilled woolen cloth resembling gabardine

tri·crot·ic (trī krät′ik) *adj.* ⟦< Gr *trikrotos,* (rowed) with triple stroke (< *tri-,* TRI- + *krotein,* to beat < IE **kret-,* to strike > OE *hrindan,* to push) + -IC⟧ *Physiol.* designating or of a pulse having three separate rhythmic waves to each beat —**tri·cro·tism** (trī′krə tiz′əm) *n.*

tric·trac (trik′trak′) *n.* ⟦Fr, echoic of the clicking of the pegs⟧ an old variety of backgammon, specif. one in which pegs were placed in holes along the sides of the board in keeping score

tri·cus·pid (trī kus′pid) *adj.* ⟦L *tricuspis* (gen. *tricuspidis*): see TRI- & CUSP⟧ 1 having three cusps, or points [a *tricuspid* tooth]: also **tri·cus′pi·date′** (-pə dāt′) 2 designating or of a valve with three flaps, between the right auricle and right ventricle of the heart —*n.* 1 a tricuspid tooth 2 the tricuspid valve

tri·cy·cle (trī′sə kəl, -sik′əl) *n.* ⟦Fr: see TRI- & CYCLE⟧ a light, three-wheeled vehicle, with one wheel in front and two in back, esp. one for children that is operated by pedals

tri·cy·clic (trī sī′klik, -sik′lik) *adj.* containing three fused rings of atoms in the molecule —*n.* any of a major group of antidepressant drugs that have a tricyclic molecular structure

tri·dent (trīd′nt) *n.* ⟦L *tridens* (gen. *tridentis*) < *tri-,* TRI- + *dens,* TOOTH⟧ 1 a three-pronged spear used by the retiarius in ancient Roman gladiatorial combats 2 a three-pronged fish spear 3 *Class. Myth.* a three-pronged spear borne as a scepter by the sea god Poseidon, or Neptune

tri·den·tate (trī den′tāt′) *adj.* ⟦ModL *tridentatus:* see TRI- & DENTATE⟧ having three teeth, prongs, or points

Tri·den·tine (trī den′tin, -tīn′, -tēn′) *adj.* ⟦ML *Tridentinus,* after *Tridentum,* Trent⟧ 1 of Trent, Italy 2 of the Council of Trent

tri·di·men·sion·al (trī′də men′shə nəl) *adj.* of or having three dimensions; having depth as well as length and width

tried (trīd) *vt., vi. pt. & pp. of* TRY —*adj.* 1 tested; proved 2 trustworthy; faithful 3 having endured trials and troubles

tried-and-true (trīd′n trōō′) *adj.* proven by experience over time to be useful, effective, reliable, etc.

tri·en·ni·al (trī en′ē əl) *adj.* ⟦< L *triennium:* see fol.⟧ 1 happening every three years 2 lasting three years —*n.* a triennial event or occurrence —**tri·en′ni·al·ly** *adv.*

tri·en·ni·um (trī en′ē əm) *n., pl.* **-ni·ums** or **-ni·a** (-ə) ⟦L, three years < *tri-,* TRI- + *annus,* year: see ANNUAL⟧ a period of three years

tri·er (trī′ər) *n.* a person or thing that tries

Trier (trir) city in W Germany, on the Moselle River, in the state of Rhineland-Palatinate

tri·er·arch (trī′ər ärk′) *n.* ⟦L *trierarchus* < Gr *triērarchos* < *triērēs,* a trireme (< *tri-,* TRI- + *-ērēs* < IE base **erē-,* to row, oar > ROW², RUDDER) + *archos,* leader, chief: see -ARCH⟧ in ancient Greece, *a)* the commander of a trireme *b)* at Athens, a person who built, outfitted, and maintained a trireme for the service of the state

tri·er·ar·chy (trī′ər är′kē) *n., pl.* **-chies** ⟦Gr *triērarchia*⟧ 1 the rank, authority, or duties of a trierarch 2 trierarchs collectively 3 the system by which trierarchs built, outfitted, and maintained triremes for the state

Tri·este (trē est′; *It* trē es′te) 1 seaport in NE Italy, on an inlet (**Gulf of Trieste**) of the Adriatic 2 **Free Territory of** former region surrounding this city: created & administered by the United Nations (1947) and divided between Italy & Yugoslavia (1954) —**Tri·es·tine** (trē es′tin, -tēn′) *adj.*

tri·eth·yl (trī eth′əl) *adj.* ⟦TRI- + ETHYL⟧ containing three ethyl groups in the molecule

tri·fa·cial (trī fā′shəl) *adj., n.* TRIGEMINAL

tri·fec·ta (trī fek′tə) *n.* ⟦TRI- + (PER)FECTA⟧ a bet or betting procedure in which one wins if one correctly picks the first, second, and third place finishers in a race

tri·fid (trī′fid) *adj.* ⟦L *trifidus* < *tri-,* TRI- + *-fid-,* akin to *-fidus,* split: see -FID⟧ divided into three lobes or parts by deep clefts, as some leaves

tri·fle (trī′fəl) *n.* ⟦ME < OFr *trufle,* mockery, dim. of *truffe,* deception⟧ 1 something of little value or importance; trivial thing, idea, etc.; paltry matter 2 a small amount of money 3 a small amount or degree; bit 4 esp. in England, a dessert made with spongecake pieces spread with jam, sprinkled as with sherry, and layered in a large bowl with custard, fruit, whipped cream, etc. 5 *a)* a kind of pewter of medium hardness *b)* [*pl.*] utensils made of this —*vi.* **-fled, -fling** 1 to talk or act jokingly, mockingly, etc.; deal lightly [not a person to *trifle* with] 2 to play or toy (*with* something) 3 to play fast and loose (*with* a person's affections); dally —*vt.* to spend idly; waste [to *trifle* the hours away] —**tri′fler** *n.*

SYN.—**trifle** is the general term meaning to treat without earnestness, full attention, definite purpose, etc. [to *trifle* with a person, an idea, etc.]; **flirt** implies a light, transient interest or attention that quickly moves on to another person or thing [she's always *flirting* with men]; **dally** implies a playing with a subject or thing that one has little or no intention of taking seriously [to *dally* with painting]; **coquet** suggests the behavior of a flirtatious woman who seeks attention or admiration without serious intent; **toy** implies a trifling or dallying with no purpose beyond that of amusement or idling away time [to *toy* with an idea]

tri·fling (trī′fliŋ) *adj.* 1 that trifles; frivolous; shallow; fickle 2 having little value or importance; trivial —**tri′fling·ly** *adv.*

☆**tri·fo·cal** (trī fō′kəl; *also, and for n. usually,* trī′fō′kəl) *adj.* adjusted to three different focal lengths —*n.* a lens like a bifocal but with an additional narrow area ground to adjust the intermediate focus for objects at *c.* 76 cm (*c.* 30 in)

☆**tri·fo·cals** (trī′fō′kəlz) *pl.n.* eyeglasses with trifocal lenses

tri·fo·li·ate (trī fō′lē it, -āt′) *adj.* ⟦TRI- + FOLIATE⟧ 1 having three leaves 2 *nontechnical term for* TRIFOLIOLATE Also **tri·fo′li·at′ed** (-āt′id)

tri·fo·li·o·late (trī fō′lē ə lāt′) *adj.* ⟦< TRI- + ModL *foliolum,* dim. of L *folium,* a leaf (see FOIL²) + -ATE¹⟧ divided into three leaflets, as the leaf of a clover

tri·fo·li·um (-fō′lē əm) *n.* ⟦L, TREFOIL⟧ CLOVER (sense 1)

tri·fo·ri·um (-fôr′ē əm) *n., pl.* **-ri·a** (-ə) ⟦ML < L *tri-,* TRI- + *foris,* DOOR⟧ a gallery or arcade in the wall above the arches of the nave, choir, or transept of a church

tri·form (trī′fôrm) *adj.* ⟦L *triformis:* see TRI- & -FORM⟧ having three parts, forms, etc.: also **tri′formed**

tri·fur·cate (trī′fər kāt′, -kit; trī fur′-) *adj.* ⟦< L *trifurcus* < *tri-,* TRI- + *furca,* a fork + -ATE¹⟧ having three forks or branches: also **tri′fur·cat′ed** —**tri′fur·ca′tion** *n.*

trig[1] (trig) [Archaic or Dial.] ***adj.*** ⟦ME *trigg* < ON *tryggr,* trusty, firm: for IE base see TRUE⟧ **1** trim; neat; spruce **2** in good condition; strong; sound **3** prim; precise —***vt.*** **trigged, trig′ging** to make trig: often with *out* or *up*

trig[2] (trig) [Dial.] ***vt.*** **trigged, trig′ging** ⟦< ? Scand, as in Dan *trykke,* to press⟧ **1** to prevent (a wheel, cask, etc.) from rolling by placing a wedge, stone, etc. under it **2** to prop or support —***n.*** a stone, wedge, etc. used in trigging

trig[3] (trig) ***n.*** *short for* TRIGONOMETRY

trig[4] *abbrev.* trigonometric(al)

tri·gem·i·nal (trī jem′ə nəl) ***adj.*** ⟦< ModL *trigeminus* < L, born three together (< *tri-,* TRI- + *geminus,* twin) + -AL⟧ designating or of either of the fifth pair of cranial nerves, each of which divides into three branches supplying the head and face —***n.*** a trigeminal nerve

trigeminal neuralgia a disorder characterized by severely painful paroxysms along one or more branches of a trigeminal nerve

trig·ger (trig′ər) ***n.*** ⟦earlier *tricker* < Du *trekker* < *trekken,* to draw, pull: see TREK⟧ **1** a small lever or part which when pulled or pressed releases a catch, spring, etc. **2** in firearms, a small lever pressed back by the finger to activate the firing mechanism **3** an act, impulse, etc. that initiates an action, series of events, etc. —***vt.*** **1** to fire or activate by pulling or pressing a trigger **2** to initiate (an action); set off *[*the fight that *triggered* the riot*]* —☆**quick on the trigger** [Informal] **1** quick to fire a gun **2** quick to act, understand, retort, etc.

trigger finger the finger used to press the trigger of a firearm; specif., the forefinger

trig·ger·fish (trig′ər fish′) ***n., pl.*** **-fish′** or **-fish′es** (see FISH) ⟦because depression of the second spine of the fin causes the first to snap down⟧ any of various brightly colored tropical fishes (family Balistidae) of the same order (Tetraodontiformes) as puffers, having a prominent first dorsal fin with two or three spines

☆**trig·ger-hap·py** (-hap′ē) ***adj.*** ⟦see HAPPY, *adj.* 4⟧ [Informal] inclined to resort to force rashly or irresponsibly

☆**trig·ger·man** (trig′ər man′) ***n., pl.*** **-men′** (-men′) [Informal] **1** a hired killer, specif., one who is a gangster **2** that person, among those committing a crime, who shoots the victim

tri·glyc·er·ide (trī glis′ər īd′) ***n.*** ⟦TRI- + GLYCERIDE⟧ any of a group of esters, $CH_2(OOCR_1)CH(OOCR_2)CH_2(OOCR_3)$, derived from glycerol and three fatty acid radicals: the chief component of fats and oils

tri·glyph (trī′glif) ***n.*** ⟦L *triglyphus* < Gr *triglyphos:* see TRI- & GLYPH⟧ in a Doric frieze, a slightly projecting, rectangular block occurring at regular intervals and having two vertical grooves (*glyphs*) and two chamfers or half grooves at the sides —**tri·glyph′ic** ***adj.***

tri·gon (trī′gän) ***n.*** ⟦L *trigonum* < Gr *trigōnon,* triangle, lyre < *trigōnos,* triangular: see TRI- & -GON⟧ **1** [Archaic] a triangle **2** *Astrol.* TRIPLICITY (sense 3)

trig·o·nal (trig′ə nəl) ***adj.*** ⟦L *trigonalis*⟧ **1** of a triangle; triangular **2** of a trigon **3** RHOMBOHEDRAL (sense 2)

trigonometric function any of the basic functions (as sine, cosine, tangent, etc.) of an angle or arc, usually expressed as the ratio of pairs of sides of a right triangle

trig·o·nom·e·try (trig′ə näm′ə trē) ***n., pl.*** **-tries** ⟦ModL *trigonometria* < Gr *trigōnon,* triangle (see TRIGON) + *-metria,* measurement (see -METRY)⟧ the branch of mathematics that deals with the ratios between the sides of a right triangle with reference to either acute angle (*trigonometric functions*), the relations between these ratios, and the application of these facts in finding the unknown sides or angles of any triangle, as in surveying, navigation, engineering, etc. —**trig′o·no·met′ric** (-nə me′trik) ***adj.***, **trig′o·no·met′ri·cal** —**trig′o·no·met′ri·cal·ly** ***adv.***

trig·o·nous (trig′ə nəs) ***adj.*** ⟦L *trigonus* < Gr *trigōnos:* see TRIGON⟧ having three angles or corners

tri·gram (trī′gram′) ***n.*** **1** a graphic unit made up of three parts, as a trigraph **2** a group of three solid or broken lines making up half of a hexagram in the I CHING

tri·graph (trī′graf′) ***n.*** ⟦TRI- + -GRAPH⟧ a group of three letters representing one sound (Ex.: *pph* in *Sappho*)

tri·hal·o·meth·ane (trī hal′ə meth′ān′) ***n.*** ⟦TRI- + HALO- (sense 3) + METHANE⟧ any of a family of organic chemical compounds, including chloroform, that form as when water supplies are chlorinated

tri·he·dral (trī hē′drəl) ***adj.*** ⟦TRI- + -HEDRAL⟧ having three sides or faces *[*a *trihedral* angle*]* —***n.*** a figure formed by three lines, each in a different plane, that intersect at a point

tri·hy·drate (trī hī′drāt) ***n.*** ⟦TRI- + HYDRATE⟧ a chemical compound containing three molecules of water —**tri·hy′drat·ed** ***adj.***

tri·hy·drox·y (trī′hī dräks′ē) ***adj.*** containing three hydroxyl groups

tri·i·o·do·thy·ro·nine (trī ī′ə dō thī′rə nēn′) ***n.*** ⟦TRI- + IODO- + THYR(O)- + -INE[3]⟧ a crystalline hormone, $C_{15}H_{12}I_3NO_4$, secreted by the thyroid gland, that influences the rate of general metabolic activity: used medically, esp. to treat hypothyroidism

tri·jet (trī′jet′) ***n.*** an airplane having three jet engines

trike (trīk) ***n.*** ⟦shortened & altered < TRICYCLE⟧ [Informal] TRICYCLE

trik·er (trīk′ər) ***n.*** [Informal] a person who rides or drives a three-wheeled vehicle, esp. such a vehicle propelled by an internal-combustion engine

tri·lat·er·al (trī lat′ər əl) ***adj.*** ⟦< L *trilaterus,* three-sided: see TRI- & LATERAL⟧ three-sided —**tri·lat′er·al·ly** ***adv.***

tril·by (tril′bē) ***n., pl.*** **-bies** or **-bys** ⟦so named because such a hat was worn in a stage version (1895) of *Trilby* (1894 novel by George DU MAURIER)⟧ [Chiefly Brit.] a man's soft felt hat with a narrow brim and the crown deeply dented front to back

tri·lin·e·ar (trī lin′ē ər) ***adj.*** ⟦TRI- + LINEAR⟧ of, enclosed by, or involving three lines

tri·lin·gual (trī liŋ′gwəl) ***adj.*** ⟦< L *trilinguis* (< *tri-,* TRI- + *lingua,* tongue: see LANGUAGE) + -AL⟧ **1** of or in three languages **2** using or capable of using three languages, esp. with equal or nearly equal facility —**tri·lin′gual·ly** ***adv.***

tri·lit·er·al (trī lit′ər əl) ***adj.*** ⟦< TRI- + L *littera,* LETTER[1] + -AL⟧ consisting of three letters; specif., consisting of three consonants *[*most roots of Semitic languages are *triliteral]* —**tri·lit′er·al·ism′** ***n.***

trill (tril) ***n.*** ⟦It *trillo* < *trillare,* to trill, of echoic orig.⟧ **1** a rapid alternation of a given musical tone with the tone a diatonic second above it: cf. VIBRATO **2** the warbling sound made by some birds **3** *Phonet. a)* a rapid vibration of the tongue or uvula, as in pronouncing the sounds represented by *r* in some languages *b)* a sound so produced —***vt., vi.*** ⟦It *trillare*⟧ to sound, speak, or play with a trill —**trill′er** ***n.***

Tril·ling (tril′iŋ), **Lionel** 1905-75; U.S. critic & writer

tril·lion (tril′yen) ***n.*** ⟦Fr < *tri-,* TRI- + *(mi)llion*⟧ ☆**1** the number represented by 1 followed by 12 zeros **2** [Brit.] the number represented by 1 followed by 18 zeros **3** an indefinite but very large number: a hyperbolic use —***adj.*** amounting to one trillion in number

tril·lionth (tril′yənth) ***adj.*** **1** coming last in a series of a trillion **2** designating any of the trillion equal parts of something —***n.*** **1** the last in a series of a trillion **2** any of the trillion equal parts of something

tril·li·um (tril′ē əm) ***n.*** ⟦ModL < L *tri-,* three⟧ any of a genus (*Trillium*) of perennial plants of the lily family, having an erect stem that bears a whorl of three leaves and a single flower with three green sepals and three petals that change color as they mature

trillium

tri·lo·bate (trī lō′bāt′) ***adj.*** having three lobes, as some leaves: also **tri·lo′bat′ed** or **tri′lobed′** (-lōbd′)

tri·lo·bite (trī′lə bīt′) ***n.*** ⟦< ModL *Trilobites, Trilobita:* see TRI-, LOBE, -ITE[1]⟧ any of a large class (Trilobita) of extinct marine arthropods having the body divided by two furrows into three parts, found as fossils in Paleozoic rocks —**tri′lo·bit′ic** (-bit′ik) ***adj.***

tri·loc·u·lar (trī läk′yə lər) ***adj.*** ⟦TRI- + LOCULAR⟧ having three chambers, cells, or cavities

tril·o·gy (tril′ə jē) ***n., pl.*** **-gies** ⟦Gr *trilogia:* see TRI- & -LOGY⟧ a set of three related plays, novels, etc. written by the same person and together forming an extended, unified work

trim (trim) ***vt.*** **trimmed, trim′ming** ⟦via ME dial. < OE *trymman,* to make firm, set in order, array < *trum,* strong, firm: for IE base see TREE⟧ **1** [Obs.] to prepare; fit out; dress **2** to put in proper order; make neat or tidy, esp. by clipping, lopping, etc. *[*to *trim* one's mustache*]* **3** to clip, lop, cut, etc.: often with *off [*to *trim* dead branches off a tree*]* **4** to cut (something) down to the required size or shape ☆**5** *a)* to decorate or embellish as by adding ornaments, contrasting materials, etc. *[*to *trim* a Christmas tree*]* *b)* to arrange an attractive display of merchandise in or on *[*to *trim* a store window*]* **6** *a)* to balance (a ship) by adjusting ballast, shifting cargo, etc. *b)* to adjust (a sail) for efficient sailing **7** to balance (a flying aircraft) by adjusting stabilizers, tabs, etc. **8** to modify according to expediency; adjust; adapt **9** [Old Informal] *a)* to scold; chide; rebuke *b)* to beat, punish, thrash, etc. *c)* to defeat decisively *d)* to cheat —***vi.*** **1** to change one's opinions or viewpoint so as to satisfy opposing factions, etc.; compromise **2** to change one's opinions or viewpoint opportunistically —***n.*** **1** order; arrangement; condition *[*in proper *trim]* **2** good condition or order *[*to keep in *trim* for sports*]* **3** equipment; gear; dress **4** a trimming by clipping, cutting, etc. **5** ☆*a)* WINDOW DRESSING ☆*b)* decorative molding or borders, esp. around windows and doors ☆*c)* the interior furnishings or the exterior ornamental metalwork of an automobile *d)* any ornamental trimming *[*a dress with lace *trim]* **6** *a)* the position of a ship in the water in relation to the horizontal, esp. a fore-and-aft horizontal axis *b)* correct position in the water: a ship is **in trim** if stable and floating on an even keel, **out of trim** if not *c)* the degree of buoyancy of a submarine **7** the position of an airplane in relation to a fore-and-aft horizontal axis **8** something that is trimmed, as a section of FILM (*n.* 5a) cut out in editing **9** [Obs.] character (*of* a person) —***adj.*** **trim′mer, trim′mest** **1** orderly; neat; tidy **2** well-proportioned; smartly designed **3** in good condition —***adv.*** **trim′mer, trim′mest** in a trim manner —**trim one's sails** to adjust one's opinions, actions, expenditures, etc. to meet changing conditions —**trim′ly** ***adv.*** —**trim′ness** ***n.***

tri·ma·ran (trī′mə ran′) ***n.*** ⟦TRI- + (CATA)MARAN⟧ a boat similar to a catamaran, but with three parallel hulls

tri·mer (trī′mər) ***n.*** ⟦< TRI- + Gr *meros,* a part: see MERIT⟧ *Chem.* **1** a molecule composed of three identical, simpler molecules **2** a substance composed of such molecules *[*C_6H_6 is a *trimer* of C_2H_2*]* —**tri·mer′ic** (-mer′ik) ***adj.***

trim·er·ous (trim′ər əs) ***adj.*** ⟦TRI- + -MEROUS⟧ **1** having the parts in sets of three: said of a flower: also written **3-merous** **2** having tarsi that are divided into three parts: said of some insects

tri·mes·ter (trī mes′tər, trī′mes′-) ***n.*** ⟦Fr *trimestre* < L *trimestris,* of three months < *tri-,* three + *mensis,* month: see MOON⟧ **1** a period or term of three months; specif., any of the three three-month periods of a human pregnancy **2** in some colleges and universities, any of the three periods into which the academic year is divided

trim·e·ter (trim′ət ər) *n.* ⟦L *trimetrus* < Gr *trimetros:* see TRI- & METER[1]⟧ **1** a line of verse containing three metrical feet **2** verse consisting of trimeters —*adj.* having three metrical feet

tri·meth·a·di·one (trī meth′ə dī′ōn) *n.* ⟦*trimeth(yl)* (< TRI- + METHYL) + *-a-* + DI-[1] + -ONE⟧ a white, crystalline material, $C_6H_9NO_3$, used in treating epilepsy

tri·met·ric (trī me′trik) *adj.* **1** having three metrical feet **2** ORTHORHOMBIC Also **tri·met′ri·cal**

trimetric projection a type of AXONOMETRIC PROJECTION in which the object is shown with all three of its principal axes tilted unequally from the plane of viewing

trim·mer (trim′ər) *n.* **1** a person, thing, machine, etc. that trims **2** a beam in a floor frame that receives the ends of headers, as around a stairwell **3** *Elec.* a capacitor or other circuit device designed for tuning

trim·ming (trim′iŋ) *n.* **1** the action of a person who trims **2** something used to trim; specif., *a)* decoration; ornament *b)* [*pl.*] the side dishes of a meal [Thanksgiving turkey with all the *trimmings*] **3** [*pl.*] parts trimmed off **4** [Old Informal] *a)* a beating; thrashing *b)* a decisive defeat *c)* a cheating or fleecing

tri·mo·lec·u·lar (trī′mə lek′yə lər) *adj.* of or formed from three molecules

tri·month·ly (trī munth′lē) *adj., adv.* once every three months

tri·morph (trī′môrf′) *n.* ⟦TRI- + -MORPH⟧ **1** a substance that crystallizes in three distinct forms **2** any of these forms

tri·mor·phism (trī môr′fiz′əm) *n.* ⟦< Gr *trimorphos,* of three forms < *tri-,* three + *morphē,* form + -ISM⟧ **1** *Crystallography* the property of crystallizing in three distinct forms **2** *Bot.* the existence of three distinct forms of flowers, leaves, or other organs on the same plant or on different plants of the same species **3** *Zool.* the existence of three distinct forms of organs in the same species —**tri·mor′phic** *adj.,* **tri·mor′phous**

trim size the length and width of a book page after the book has been trimmed to its designed dimensions

Tri·mur·ti (tri moor′tē) *n.* ⟦Sans *trimūrti,* lit., of three forms < *tri,* THREE + *mūrti,* body, shape⟧ the trinity of Hindu gods (Brahma, Vishnu, and Siva)

Tri·na·cri·a (trī nā′krē ə; trē-, trə-) *Latin name for* SICILY —**Tri·na′cri·an** *adj.*

tri·nal (trī′nəl) *adj.* ⟦LL *trinalis* < L *trinus:* see TRINE⟧ having three parts; threefold; triple

tri·na·ry (trī′nə rē) *adj.* ⟦LL(Ec) *trinarius,* of three kinds: see fol. & -ARY⟧ threefold; ternary

trine (trīn) *adj.* ⟦ME < MFr < L *trinus,* triple < *tres,* THREE⟧ **1** threefold; triple **2** *Astrol.* in trine; hence, favorable —*n.* **1** a group of three; triad **2** *Astrol.* the aspect of two planets 120 degrees apart, considered favorable **3** [T-] the Trinity

Trin·i·dad (trin′i dad′) island in the West Indies, off the NE coast of Venezuela: 1,864 sq mi (4,828 sq km): see TRINIDAD AND TOBAGO —**Trin′i·dad′i·an** *adj., n.*

Trinidad and Tobago country in the West Indies, comprising the islands of Trinidad & Tobago: formerly a British colony, it became independent & a member of the Commonwealth (1962): 1,980 sq mi (5,128 sq km); cap. Port-of-Spain

Trin·i·tar·i·an (trin′i ter′ē ən) *adj.* ⟦ModL *trinitarius* < LL(Ec) *trinitas*⟧ **1** *a)* of the Trinity or the doctrine of the Trinity *b)* believing in the doctrine of the Trinity **2** [t-] forming a trinity; threefold —*n.* a believer in the doctrine of the Trinity —**Trin′i·tar′i·an·ism′** *n.*

tri·ni·tro·tol·u·ene (trī nī′trō täl′yoo ēn′) *n.* ⟦TRI- + NITRO- + TOLUENE⟧ a high explosive, any of several isomeric derivatives, $CH_3C_6H_2(NO_2)_3$, of toluene, used for blasting, in artillery shells, etc.: abbrev. *TNT:* also **tri·ni′tro·tol′u·ol′** (-ôl′, -ōl′)

trin·i·ty (trin′i tē) *n., pl.* **-ties** ⟦ME *trinite* < OFr *trinité* < L *trinitas,* triad, in LL(Ec), the Trinity (infl. by Gr *trias*) < *trinus:* see TRINE & -ITY⟧ **1** the condition of being three or threefold **2** a set of three persons or things that form a unit **3** [T-] *Christian Theol.* TRINITY SUNDAY —**the Trinity** *Christian Theol.* the union of the three divine persons (Father, Son, and Holy Spirit) in one Godhead

Trinity Sunday the Sunday after Pentecost, dedicated to the Trinity

trin·ket (triŋ′kit) *n.* ⟦ME *trenket,* shoemakers' knife, ladies' toy knife, ornament < NormFr *trenquet* < OFr *trenchet* < *trenchier,* to cut: see TRENCH⟧ **1** a small, inexpensive ornament, piece of jewelry, etc. **2** a trifle or toy

tri·no·mi·al (trī nō′mē əl) *n.* ⟦TRI- + (BI)NOMIAL⟧ **1** a mathematical expression consisting of three terms connected by plus or minus signs **2** *Taxonomy* the scientific name of a plant or animal taxon, consisting of three words designating in order the genus, species, and subspecies or variety —*adj.* **1** composed of three terms **2** of trinomials —**tri·no′mi·al·ly** *adv.*

tri·o (trē′ō) *n., pl.* **tri′os** ⟦Fr < It < *tri-,* TRI-, as in *duo,* DUO⟧ **1** any group of three persons or things **2** *Music a)* a composition for three voices or three instruments *b)* a group of three performers of such a composition, or any group of three musicians playing together *c)* the middle section of a minuet, scherzo, etc., orig. written in three voices, or parts

tri·ode (trī′ōd′) *n.* ⟦TRI- + (ELECTR)ODE⟧ an electronic device with three electrodes; esp., an electron tube with an anode, cathode, and grid

tri·oe·cious (trī ē′shəs) *adj.* ⟦< TRI- + LL *oecus,* a room (< Gr *oikos,* a house: see ECO-) + -OUS⟧ having male, female, and bisexual flowers on separate plants

tri·ol (trī′ôl, -ōl) *n.* ⟦TRI- + -OL[1]⟧ a compound with three hydroxyl groups in the molecule

tri·o·let (trī′ə let′, -lit) *n.* ⟦Fr, ? fig. use of *triolet,* clover, prob. dim. of OFr **triol,* **triueil* < L *trifolium,* TREFOIL⟧ a verse form of eight lines and two rhymes, the first line being repeated as the fourth and seventh, and the second as the eighth; the rhyme scheme is *abaaabab*

tri·ose (trī′ōs) *n.* ⟦TRI- + -OSE[1]⟧ a monosaccharide, $C_3H_6O_3$, with three carbon atoms

tri·ox·ide (trī äk′sīd) *n.* an oxide having three oxygen atoms to the molecule

trip (trip) *vi.* **tripped, trip′ping** ⟦ME *trippen* < OFr *treper* < Gmc **trippon* (> OE *treppan,* to step): see TRAP[1]⟧ **1** to walk, run, or dance with light, rapid steps; skip; caper **2** to stumble, esp. by catching the foot **3** to make a false step, inaccuracy, or mistake; err **4** to falter in speaking **5** to run past the pallet of the escapement without catching: said of a tooth of the escapement wheel of a watch **6** [Rare] to take a trip; journey ☆**7** [Slang] to experience a TRIP (*n.* 6) —*vt.* **1** to make stumble, esp. by catching the foot: sometimes with *up* **2** *a)* to cause to make a false step or mistake *b)* to cause to fail or stop; obstruct **3** to catch (a person) in a lie, error, etc.: often with *up* **4** *a)* to release (a spring, wheel, or other mechanical part), as by the action of a detent *b)* to start or operate (a mechanism) by this **5** [Now Rare] to perform (a dance) lightly and nimbly **6** *Naut.* to raise (an anchor) clear of the bottom —*n.* **1** a light, quick tread **2** *a)* a traveling from one place to another; journey, esp. a short one; excursion, jaunt, etc. *b)* a going to a place and returning [made three *trips* to the kitchen] **3** *a)* a stumble *b)* a maneuver for causing someone to stumble or fall, as by catching the foot **4** a mistake; blunder **5** *a)* any mechanical contrivance for tripping a part, as a pawl *b)* its action ☆**6** [Slang] *a)* an experience or period of euphoria, hallucinations, etc. induced by a psychedelic drug, esp. LSD *b)* an experience that is pleasing, exciting, unusual, etc. *c)* any activity, mode of conduct, state of mind, etc. [a spiritual *trip*] —**trip the light fantastic** ⟦excerpted, with altered part of speech, from two lines of "L'Allegro," poem (1645) by John MILTON[2]: "Come, and *trip* it as ye go / On *the light fantastic* toe"⟧ [Old-fashioned] to engage in ballroom dancing: a jocular usage

SYN.—**trip** strictly implies a relatively short course of travel, although it is also commonly used as an equivalent for **journey** [a vacation *trip*]; **journey**, a more formal word, generally implies travel of some length, usually over land [the *journey* was filled with hardships]; **voyage**, in current use, implies a relatively long journey by water [a *voyage* across the Atlantic]; **jaunt** is applied to a short, casual trip taken for pleasure or recreation [a *jaunt* to the city]; **expedition** is applied to a journey, march, etc. taken by an organized group for some definite purpose [a military *expedition,* a zoological *expedition* to Africa]

☆**TRIP** (trip) *adj.* ⟦*tr(ansformation-)i(nduced) p(lasticity)*⟧ designating or of any of several high-strength, highly ductile steel alloys containing chromium, molybdenum, nickel, and carbon

tri·par·tite (trī pär′tīt) *adj.* ⟦ME < L *tripartitus* < *tri-,* three + *partitus,* PARTITE⟧ **1** divided into three parts; threefold **2** having three corresponding parts or copies **3** made or existing between three parties, as an agreement

tri·par·ti·tion (trī′pär tish′ən) *n.* ⟦LL(Ec) *tripartitio*⟧ division into three parts or among three parties

tripe (trīp) *n.* ⟦ME < MFr < It *trippa,* prob. ult. < Ar *tharb,* thin layer of fat lining the intestines⟧ **1** part of the stomach of an ox or other ruminant, when used as food **2** [Slang] anything worthless, offensive, etc.; nonsense

☆**trip·ham·mer** (trip′ham′ər) *n.* a heavy, power-driven hammer, alternately raised and allowed to fall by a tripping device: also written **trip hammer**

tri·phen·yl·meth·ane (trī fen′əl meth′ān, -fē′nəl-) *n.* ⟦TRI- + PHENYL + METHANE⟧ a colorless, crystalline hydrocarbon, $CH(C_6H_5)_3$, used in organic synthesis and in making dyes

tri·phib·i·an (trī fib′ē ən) *adj.* ⟦TRI- + (AM)PHIBIAN⟧ **1** that can function, operate, or carry on warfare on land, at sea, or in the air ☆**2** designating an aircraft that can take off from, or land on, water, land, or snow and ice: also **tri·phib′i·ous**

triph·thong (trif′thôŋ; *often* trip′-) *n.* ⟦TRI- + (DI)PHTHONG⟧ **1** a complex vowel sound involving three continuous vowel sounds in one syllable (Ex.: *fire,* as in the British pronunciation, IPA [faɪə]) **2** loosely, a trigraph —**triph·thon′gal** (-thôŋ′gəl) *adj.*

tri·pin·nate (trī pin′āt) *adj. Bot.* bipinnate with each division pinnate, as some fern leaves —**tri·pin′nately** *adv.*

tri·plane (trī′plān′) *n.* an early type of airplane with three sets of wings arranged one above another

tri·ple (trip′əl) *adj.* ⟦Fr < L *triplus:* see the *vt.*⟧ **1** consisting of or including three; threefold **2** done, used, said, etc. three times; repeated twice **3** three times as much, as many, as large, etc. **4** *Music* containing three (or a multiple of three) beats to the measure [*triple* time] —*n.* ⟦ME < L *triplus*⟧ **1** an amount three times as much or as many **2** a group of three; triad ☆**3** *Baseball* a hit on which the batter reaches third base —*vt.* **tri′pled, tri′pling** ⟦ME *tryplen* < ML *triplare* < L *triplus,* threefold < *tri-,* TRI- + *-plus,* as in *duplus,* DOUBLE⟧ **1** to make three times as much or as many ☆**2** *Baseball* to advance (a runner) by hitting a triple —*vi.* **1** to become three times as much or as many ☆**2** *Baseball* to hit a triple

Triple Alliance **1** an alliance of England, Sweden, and the Netherlands against France in 1668 **2** an alliance of Great Britain, France, and the Netherlands against Spain in 1717 **3** an alliance of Great Britain, Austria, and Russia against France in 1795 **4** an alliance of Germany, Austria-Hungary, and Italy from 1882 to 1915, chiefly against Russia and France

triple bond *Chem.* the sharing of three pairs of electrons between two atoms in a molecule, usually represented in structural formulas by three dots, as in C⋮C
Triple Crown ⟦< CROWN (*n.* 2)⟧ ☆1 *Baseball* the distinction of leading a league in batting average, home runs, and runs batted in, for a single season ☆2 *Horse Racing* the distinction of winning the Kentucky Derby, the Preakness, and the Belmont Stakes in the same year
triple-decker (trip′əl dek′ər) *n.* THREE-DECKER (senses 2-4)
Triple Entente an alliance of Great Britain, France, and Russia before WWI as a counterbalance to the Triple Alliance
triple jump a track-and-field event in which each contestant, after a running start, makes three consecutive jumps for total distance, landing after the first on the same foot used in the takeoff, after the second on the opposite foot, and after the third on both feet
tri·ple-nerved (trip′əl nurvd′) *adj. Bot.* having three nerves arising from or near the base, as some leaves
☆**triple play** *Baseball* a single play in which three players are put out
triple point a pressure and temperature combination at which the solid, liquid, and vapor phases of a substance exist in contact and in equilibrium with one another: the triple point of water is 273.16°K (0.01°C) at *c.* 4.6 mm of mercury
triple sec (sek) a sweet, orange-flavored, colorless liqueur
tri·ple-space (-spās′) *vt., vi.* **-spaced′, -spac′ing** to type (copy) so as to leave two full spaces between lines
tri·plet (trip′lit) *n.* ⟦TRIPL(E) + -ET⟧ **1** a collection or group of three, usually of one kind; specif., *a)* a group of three successive lines of poetry, usually rhyming *b)* a group of three musical notes to be performed in the time of two of the same value **2** any of three offspring from the same pregnancy
tri·ple·tail (trip′əl tāl′) *n.* any of a family (Lobotidae) of percoid fishes that have large, trailing dorsal and anal fins; esp., a large food fish (*Lobotes surinamensis*) of warm W Atlantic waters
tri·plex (trip′leks′, trī′pleks′) *adj.* ⟦L < *tri-,* TRI- + *-plex:* see DUPLEX⟧ triple; threefold —*n.* a building having three apartments or other type of units, an apartment having three floors, a theater with three separate screens, etc.
trip·li·cate (trip′li kit; *for v.,* -kāt′) *adj.* ⟦ME < L *triplicatus,* pp. of *triplicare,* to treble < *triplex:* see prec.⟧ **1** threefold **2** designating the third of identical copies —*n.* any of three identical copies or things —*vt.* **-cat′ed, -cat′ing** to make three identical copies of —**in triplicate** in three identical copies —**trip′li·ca′tion** *n.*
tri·plic·i·ty (tri plis′ə tē) *n., pl.* **-ties** ⟦ME *triplicite* < ML *triplicitas* < L *triplex:* see TRIPLEX⟧ **1** the quality or condition of being triple **2** a group of three **3** *Astrol.* any of the four sets of three signs, each 120 degrees distant from the other two, into which the zodiac is divided; trigon
trip·lo·blas·tic (trip′lō blas′tik) *adj.* ⟦< Gr *triploos,* triple < *tri-,* TRI- + IE **-plo-* (see DOUBLE) + BLAST- + -IC⟧ *Zool.* of or pertaining to the metazoan body structure, except that of cnidarians, with three basic cellular layers, the ectoderm, the endoderm, and the mesoderm
trip·loid (trip′loid′) *adj.* ⟦< L *triplus,* TRIPLE + -OID⟧ *Biol.* having three times the haploid number of chromosomes —*n.* a triploid cell or organism —**trip′loi′dy** (-loi′dē) *n.*
tri·ply (trip′lē) *adv.* in a triple amount or degree
tri·pod (trī′päd′) *n.* ⟦L *tripus* (gen. *tripodis*) < Gr *tripous* < *tri-,* TRI- + *pous,* FOOT⟧ **1** a three-legged cauldron, stool, table, etc. **2** a three-legged support as for a camera or telescope, usually adjustable for height —**trip·o·dal** (trip′ə dəl) *adj.,* **tri·pod·ic** (trī päd′ik)
trip·o·li (trip′ə lē) *n.* ⟦Fr, after *Tripoli,* town in Lebanon (or ? Libya), from which it was orig. imported⟧ a usually light-colored, very finely divided, essentially siliceous material consisting either of weathered chert or siliceous limestone: used as a polishing powder
Trip·o·li (trip′ə lē) **1** former Barbary State on the N coast of Africa **2** seaport & capital of Libya, on the NW coast **3** seaport on the NW coast of Lebanon —**Tri·pol·i·tan** (tri päl′ə tən) *adj., n.*
Trip·ol·i·ta·ni·a (trip′ə lə tā′nē ə) historical region of NW Libya, on the Mediterranean
tri·pos (trī′päs′) *n.* ⟦altered < L *tripus,* TRIPOD⟧ **1** [Obs.] a tripod **2** at Cambridge University *a)* [Historical] a scholar who sat on a three-legged stool at commencement and disputed humorously with candidates for a degree *b)* any examination for the BA degree with honors (orig. in mathematics)
trip·per (trip′ər) *n.* a person or thing that trips; specif., *a)* a mechanical part for tripping a cam, pawl, etc.; also, a tripping device that operates a signal on a railroad *b)* [Chiefly Brit.] a person who takes a trip; tourist
trip·pet (-it) *n.* ⟦< TRIP + -ET⟧ a cam or other mechanical part designed to strike another part at regular intervals
trip·ping (trip′iŋ) *adj.* moving lightly and quickly; nimble —**trip′ping·ly** *adv.*
trip·py (trip′ē) *adj.* [Slang] of, relating to, or suggestive of a trip induced by a psychedelic drug *[trippy* synthesizer music*]*
trip·tane (trip′tān′) *n.* ⟦contr. < *tripentane:* see TRI- & PENTANE⟧ a liquid alkane, $(CH_3)_2CHC(CH_3)_3$, used as a high antiknock fuel in internal-combustion engines, esp. in airplanes
trip·tych (trip′tik) *n.* ⟦< Gr *triptychos,* threefold < *tri-,*TRI- + *ptychē* (gen. *ptychos*), a fold < *ptyssein,* to fold⟧ **1** an ancient writing tablet of three leaves hinged together **2** a set of three panels with pictures, designs, or carvings, often hinged so that the two side panels may be folded over the central one, commonly used as an altarpiece
☆**trip·wire** (trip′wīr′) *n.* a hidden wire that will set off a trap, snare, etc. when tripped on
tri·que·trous (trī kwē′trəs, -kwe′-) *adj.* ⟦L *triquetrus* < *tri-,* TRI- + **qued-* < IE base **kwēd-,* to spur, bore, sharpen > WHET: hence orig., three-pointed⟧ **1** three-sided; triangular **2** having a triangular cross section
tri·ra·di·ate (trī rā′dē it, -āt′) *adj.* having three rays or raylike projections —**tri·ra′di·ate·ly** *adv.*
tri·reme (trī′rēm′) *n.* ⟦L *triremis,* trireme (orig., having three banks of oars) < *tri-,* TRI- + *remus,* oar: see ROW²⟧ an ancient Greek or Roman galley, usually a warship, with three banks of oars on each side
tri·sac·cha·ride (trī sak′ə rīd′) *n.* a carbohydrate yielding three monosaccharides upon hydrolysis, as raffinose
tri·sect (trī sekt′, trī′sekt′) *vt.* ⟦< TRI- + L *sectus,* pp. of *secare,* to cut: see SAW¹⟧ **1** to cut into three parts **2** *Geom.* to divide into three equal parts —**tri·sec′tion** *n.* —**tri·sec′tor** *n.*
tris·kai·dek·a·pho·bi·a (tris′kī dek′ə fō′bē ə) *n.* ⟦ModL < Gr *triskaideka,* thirteen (< *treis,* THREE + *kai,* and + *deka,* TEN) + *-phobia,* -PHOBIA⟧ fear of the number 13 (a number considered unlucky in popular superstition)
tris·kel·i·on (tris kel′ē än′) *n., pl.* **-i·a** (-ə) ⟦< Gr *triskelēs,* three-legged < *tri-,*TRI- + *skelos,* leg < IE base **(s)kel-,* to bend, a joint of the body > L *calx,* heel, Gr *kylindros,* cylinder⟧ a design, usually symbolic, consisting of three curved branches or three bent legs or arms radiating from a center: also **tris·kele** (tris′kēl′)
Trismegistus *see* HERMES TRISMEGISTUS
tris·mus (triz′məs, tris′-) *n.* ⟦ModL < Gr *trismos,* gnashing of the teeth, a grinding, akin to *trizein,* to chirp, gnash < IE echoic base **(s)trei-* > STRIDENT⟧ continuous contraction of the muscles of the jaw, specif. as a symptom of tetanus, or lockjaw —**tris′mic** *adj.*

BRONZE FROM IRELAND

SHELL DISK FROM TENNESSEE

GREEK SHIELD

triskelia

tris·oc·ta·he·dron (tris äk′tə hē′drən) *n.* ⟦Gr *tris,* thrice (< *treis,* THREE) + OCTAHEDRON⟧ an isometric solid figure or crystal consisting of an octahedron that has each face divided into three faces —**tris·oc′ta·he′dral** *adj.*
tri·so·di·um (trī sō′dē əm) *adj.* containing three sodium atoms in the molecule
tri·so·mic (trī sō′mik) *adj.* ⟦TRI- + -SOM(E) + -IC⟧ having a single extra chromosome in the cell in addition to the normal diploid number —*n.* a trisomic cell or organism —**tri·so′my** (-mē) *n.*
Tris·tan (tris′tən) *n.* a masculine name: see TRISTRAM
Tris·tan da Cu·nha (tris′tən də ko͞on′yə) group of four British islands in the South Atlantic, administered as a dependency of St. Helena: 38 sq mi (98 sq km)
tri-state (trī′stāt′) *adj.* of or having to do with an area consisting of all or parts of three contiguous states
triste (trēst) *adj.* ⟦Fr⟧ sad; sorrowful
tris·tesse (trēs tes′) *n.* ⟦Fr⟧ sadness; melancholy
tris·te·za (tris tā′zə) *n.* ⟦Port, sorrow < L *tristitia* < *tristis,* sad; akin to OE *thriste,* bold, shameless: from the sorry appearance of diseased trees⟧ a viral disease of citrus trees, usually transmitted on the graft of a sour-orange rootstock and causing a rapid decline or the death of the tree
trist·ful (trist′fəl) *adj.* ⟦LME *trystefull* < *trist,* sad (< OFr *triste* < L *tristis:* see prec.) + *-ful,* -FUL⟧ [Archaic] sad; sorrowful; melancholy
tris·tich (tris′tik) *n.* ⟦TRI- + (DI)STICH⟧ a group or stanza of three lines of verse; triplet
tris·tich·ous (tris′ti kəs) *adj.* ⟦Gr *tristichos,* in three rows < *tri-,* TRI- + *stichos,* a row: see STICH⟧ **1** arranged in three rows **2** *Bot.* arranged in three vertical rows, as leaves
Tris·tram (tris′trəm) *n.* ⟦OFr *Tristran, Tristan,* altered (infl. by L *tristis,* sad) < Celt *Drystan* < *drest,* tumult, din⟧ **1** a masculine name: dim. *Tris;* var. *Tristam, Tristan* **2** *Medieval Legend* a knight sent to Ireland by King Mark of Cornwall to bring back the princess Isolde to be the king's bride: Isolde and Tristram fall in love and tragically die together; in some versions, Tristram marries another Isolde, a princess of Brittany
tri·sub·sti·tut·ed (trī sub′stə to͞ot′id, -tyo͞ot′-) *adj.* containing three groups or atoms introduced into the molecule in place of three original groups or atoms
tri·sul·fide (trī sul′fīd′) *n.* a sulfide having three sulfur atoms to the molecule
tri·syl·la·ble (trī sil′ə bəl, trī′sil′-) *n.* a word of three syllables —**tri·syl·lab·ic** (trī′si lab′ik) *adj.*
trit *abbrev.* triturate
trite (trīt) *adj.* **trit′er, trit′est** ⟦L *tritus,* pp. of *terere,* to rub, wear out < IE base **ter-,* to rub, bore > THROW, Gr *tryein,* to wear away⟧ worn out by constant use; no longer having freshness, originality, or novelty; stale *[a trite* idea, remark, etc.*]* —**trite′ly** *adv.* —**trite′ness** *n.*

SYN.—**trite** is applied to something, especially an expression or idea, which through repeated use or application has lost its original freshness and impressive force (e.g., "like a bolt from the blue"); **hackneyed** refers to such expressions which through constant use have become virtually meaningless (e.g., "last but not least"); **stereotyped** applies to those fixed expressions which seem invariably to be called up in certain situations (e.g., "I point with pride" in a political oration); **commonplace** is used of any obvious or conventional remark or idea (e.g., "it isn't the heat, it's the humidity") —*ANT.* **original, fresh**

tri·the·ism (trī′thē iz′əm) *n.* ⟦TRI- + THEISM⟧ belief in three gods; specif., the doctrine or belief that the persons of the Trinity are three distinct gods —**tri′the·ist** *n.*

trit·i·at·ed (trit′ē āt′id) *adj.* containing tritium

trit·i·ca·le (trit′i kā′lē) *n.* ⟦< *Triticum,* genus name of wheat + *Secale,* genus name of rye⟧ 1 a hybrid with a high protein content, produced by crossing wheat and rye 2 the grain of this plant

trit·i·um (trit′ē əm) *n.* ⟦ModL < Gr *tritos,* THIRD + -IUM⟧ a radioactive isotope of hydrogen having an atomic weight of 3 and a half-life of *c.* 12.5 years: it decays by beta-particle emission and is used in thermonuclear bombs, thermonuclear fusion devices, as a radioactive tracer, etc.

trit·o·ma (trit′ə mə) *n.* ⟦ModL < Gr *tritomos,* cut three times < *tri-,* THREE + *-tomos,* cut off: see TOME⟧ any of a genus (*Kniphofia*) of African plants of the lily family, with dense spikes of red to yellow tubular flowers in the autumn

tri·ton (trī′tän′) *n.* ⟦Gr, neut. of *tritos,* THIRD⟧ the nucleus of the tritium atom containing one proton and two neutrons, used as a projectile in nuclear reactions

Tri·ton (trīt′'n) *n.* ⟦L < Gr *Tritōn;* ? akin to OIr *triath,* sea⟧ 1 *Gr. Myth.* a sea god, son of Poseidon and Amphitrite, represented as having the head and upper body of a man and the tail of a fish and as carrying a conch-shell trumpet 2 *Gr. Myth.* any of various minor sea gods 3 the largest of Neptune's satellites 4 [t-] *a)* any of a family (Cymatiidae) of large sea snails with a long, spiral shell, often brightly colored *b)* the shell

tri·tone (trī′tōn′) *n.* ⟦ML *tritonum* < Gr *tritonon:* see TRI- & TONE⟧ *Music* an interval of three whole tones

trit·u·rate (trich′ə rāt′, tri′tyoo-) *vt.* **-rat′ed, -rat′ing** ⟦< LL *trituratus,* pp. of *triturare,* to grind < L *tritura,* a rubbing < *tritus:* see TRITE⟧ to rub, crush, or grind into very fine particles or powder; pulverize —*n.* something triturated; specif., TRITURATION (sense 2) —**trit′u·ra·ble** (-ər ə bəl) *adj.* —**trit′u·ra′tor** *n.*

trit·u·ra·tion (trich′ə rā′shən, tri′tyoo-) *n.* 1 a triturating or being triturated 2 *Pharmacy* a triturated preparation, esp. one containing a pulverized mixture of a medicinal substance with lactose

tri·umph (trī′əmf) *n.* ⟦ME *triumphe* < OFr < L *triumphus* < OL *triumpus,* akin to Gr *thriambos,* hymn to Bacchus sung in festal processions⟧ 1 in ancient Rome, a procession celebrating the return of a victorious general and his army 2 the act or fact of being victorious; victory; success; achievement 3 exultation or joy over a victory, achievement, etc. 4 [Obs.] any public spectacle or celebration —*vi.* ⟦MFr *triumpher* < L *triumphare* < the n.⟧ 1 to gain victory or success; win mastery 2 to rejoice or exult over victory, achievement, etc. 3 to celebrate a Roman triumph —*SYN.* VICTORY

tri·um·phal (trī um′fəl) *adj.* 1 of, or having the nature of, a triumph 2 celebrating or commemorating a triumph [*a triumphal* procession]

tri·umph·al·ism (trī um′fəl iz′əm) *n.* a proud, often arrogant confidence in the validity and success of a set of beliefs, often, specif., religious beliefs —**tri·umph′al·ist** *adj., n.*

tri·um·phant (trī um′fənt) *adj.* ⟦L *triumphans,* prp. of *triumphare:* see TRIUMPH⟧ 1 successful; victorious 2 rejoicing for victory; exulting in success; elated 3 *rare var. of* TRIUMPHAL 4 [Obs.] magnificent —**tri·um′phant·ly** *adv.*

tri·um·vir (trī um′vir) *n., pl.* **-virs** or **-vi·ri′** (-vi rī′) ⟦L, back-form. < *trium virum,* gen. pl. of *tres viri,* three men < *tres,* THREE + *vir,* a man (for IE base see WEREWOLF)⟧ 1 in ancient Rome, any of a group of three administrators sharing authority equally 2 any of three persons associated in office or authority

tri·um·vi·ral (-və rəl) *adj.* of a triumvir or triumvirate

tri·um·vi·rate (trī um′və rit) *n.* ⟦L *triumviratus*⟧ 1 the office, functions, or term of a triumvir 2 government by three persons or by a coalition of three parties 3 any association of three in authority 4 any group or set of three

tri·une (trī′yoon′) *adj.* ⟦< TRI- + L *unus,* ONE⟧ being three in one [*a triune* God] —*n.* [T-] the Trinity —**tri·u′ni·ty** *n.*

tri·va·lent (trī vā′lənt, trī′vā′-) *adj.* ⟦TRI- + -VALENT⟧ 1 *Biol.* triple: said of a chromosome formed by three homologous chromosomes that lie close together or appear to join completely during meiosis 2 *Chem. a)* having three valences *b)* having a valence of three (see -VALENT) —**tri·va′lence** *n.,* **tri·va′len·cy**

Tri·van·drum (tri van′drəm) *former name for* THIRUVANANTHAPURAM

triv·et (triv′it) *n.* ⟦ME *trevet* < OE *trefet* < L *tripes* (gen. *tripedis*), tripod, three-footed < *tri-,* three + *pes,* FOOT⟧ 1 a three-legged stand for holding pots, kettles, etc. over or near a fire 2 a short-legged stand on which to set a hot dish at the table during a meal

triv·i·a (triv′ē ə) *pl.n.* ⟦ModL, back-form. < fol.⟧ [*usually with sing. v.*] 1 unimportant matters; trivialities 2 little-known, insignificant facts

triv·i·al (triv′ē əl) *adj.* ⟦L *trivialis,* of the crossroads, hence commonplace < *trivium,* place where three roads meet < *tri-,* TRI- + *via,* road: see VIA⟧ 1 of little or no importance; insignificant; trifling 2 [Rare] commonplace —**triv′i·al·ism′** *n.* —**triv′i·al·ly** *adv.*

triv·i·al·i·ty (triv′ē al′ə tē) *n.* ⟦prec. + -ITY⟧ 1 the quality or state of being trivial 2 *pl.* **-ties** a trivial thing, matter, or idea; trifle

triv·i·al·ize (triv′ē ə līz′) *vt.* **-ized′, -iz′ing** to regard or treat as trivial; make seem unimportant —**triv′i·al·i·za′tion** *n.*

trivial name 1 a common name or vernacular name, as of a plant or animal 2 *former term for* the specific name of an organism as distinct from the generic name in binomial nomenclature

triv·i·um (triv′ē əm) *n., pl.* **-i·a** (-ə) ⟦ML < L: see TRIVIAL⟧ in the Middle Ages, the lower division of the seven liberal arts, consisting of grammar, logic, and rhetoric: cf. QUADRIVIUM

tri·week·ly (trī wēk′lē) *adj., adv.* 1 once every three weeks ☆2 three times a week —☆*n., pl.* **-lies** a publication that appears triweekly

-trix (triks) ⟦L⟧ *suffix* forming feminine nouns of agency: see -OR

tRNA *abbrev.* transfer RNA

Tro·as (trō′əs, trō′as′) region surrounding ancient Troy, in NW Asia Minor: also called **the Tro′ad′** (-ad′)

Tro·bri·and Islands (trō′brē ənd; -and′, -änd′) group of small islands off SE New Guinea: part of Papua New Guinea: *c.* 170 sq mi (440 sq km)

tro·car (trō′kär′) *n.* ⟦Fr *trocart* < *trois* (< L *tres,* THREE) + *carre,* a side, face < *carrer,* to make square < L *quadrare* (see QUADRATE): from the shape of the point⟧ a surgical instrument consisting of a sharp stylet enclosed in a tube (*cannula*) and inserted through the wall of a body cavity: the stylet is withdrawn permitting fluid to drain off through the tube: also sp. **tro′char′**

tro·cha·ic (trō kā′ik) *adj.* ⟦MFr *trochaïque* < L *trochaïcus* < Gr *trochaïkos*⟧ of or made up of trochees —*n.* 1 a trochaic line of poetry 2 TROCHEE

tro·chal (trō′kəl) *adj.* ⟦< Gr *trochos* (see TROCHE) + -AL⟧ *Zool.* resembling a wheel

tro·chan·ter (trō kant′ər) *n.* ⟦Gr *trochantēr* < *trechein,* to run: see fol.⟧ 1 any of the jutting processes (in humans, two) at the upper end of the femur of many vertebrates 2 the second segment from the base of an insect leg —**tro·chan·ter·ic** (trō′kan ter′ik) *adj.*

tro·che (trō′kē) *n.* ⟦altered < *trochisk* < Fr *trochisque* < LL *trochiscus,* pill, small ball < Gr *trochiskos,* small wheel, lozenge < *trochos,* wheel < *trechein,* to run < IE base **dhregh-,* to run > OIr *droch,* wheel⟧ a small, usually round, medicinal lozenge

tro·chee (trō′kē) *n.* ⟦L *trochaeus* < Gr *trochaios,* running < *trechein,* to run: see prec.⟧ a metrical foot consisting, in Greek and Latin verse, of one long syllable followed by one short one, or, as in English verse, of one accented syllable followed by one unaccented one (Ex.: "Pétĕr, | Pétĕr, | púmpkĭn | éatĕr")

troch·i·lus (träk′i ləs) *n., pl.* **-li′** (-lī′) ⟦L < Gr *trochilos,* lit., a runner < *trechein,* to run: see TROCHE⟧ 1 any of various Old World birds, esp. warblers 2 any of certain hummingbirds

troch·le·a (träk′lē ə) *n., pl.* **-le·ae′** (-lē ē′) ⟦ModL < L, pulley block < Gr *trochilia* < *trochos,* a wheel: see TROCHE⟧ *Anat.* a pulley-shaped part or structure, as the lower part of the humerus which articulates with a corresponding part of the ulna

troch·le·ar (träk′lē ər) *adj.* 1 *Anat.* of, having the nature of, or forming a trochlea 2 *Bot.* shaped like a pulley; round and contracted in the middle

tro·choid (trō′koid′) *n.* ⟦< Gr *trochoeides,* round like a wheel < *trochos* (see TROCHE) + *eidos,* -OID⟧ *Geom.* any cycloid —*adj.* having a wheel-like rotary motion on an axis, as a joint: also **tro·choi′dal**

troch·o·phore (träk′ə fôr′) *n.* ⟦Gr *trochos,* a wheel (see TROCHE) + -PHORE⟧ a free-swimming ciliated larva of several invertebrate groups, including many marine annelid worms, mollusks, brachiopods, and nemerteans

trod (träd) *vt., vi. pt. & alt. pp. of* TREAD

trod·den (träd′'n) *vt., vi. alt. pp. of* TREAD

☆**trof·fer** (träf′ər, trôf′-) *n.* ⟦altered < TROUGH + -ER⟧ a ceiling recess like an inverted trough with its bottom next to the ceiling: used esp. to enclose fluorescent lamps

trog·lo·dyte (träg′lə dīt′) *n.* ⟦L *troglodyta* < Gr *trōglodytēs,* one who creeps into holes, cave dweller < *trōglē,* a hole, cave (< *trōgein,* to gnaw < IE **trōg-* < base **ter-,* to rub, grind > THROW) + *dyein,* to creep in, enter⟧ 1 any of the prehistoric people who lived in caves; cave man 2 a person characterized by reactionary or antiquated attitudes —**trog′lo·dyt′ic** (-dit′ik) *adj.* —**trog′lo·dyt′ism′** *n.*

tro·gon (trō′gän′) *n.* ⟦ModL < Gr *trōgōn,* gnawing, prp. of *trōgein,* to gnaw: see prec.⟧ any of an order (Trogoniformes) of bright-colored, fruit-eating tropical birds

troi·ka (troi′kə) *n.* ⟦Russ *trojka* < *troe,* three < IE **troio-* < base **trei-,* THREE⟧ 1 *a)* a Russian vehicle, esp. a sleigh or carriage, drawn by a specially trained team of three horses abreast *b)* the team of horses 2 any group of three; esp., an association of three in authority; triumvirate

troil·ism (troil′iz′əm) *n.* ⟦< ? Fr *trois,* three: see TROCAR⟧ sexual activity in which three people participate

Tro·i·lus (troi′ləs, trō′ə ləs) *n.* ⟦ME < L < Gr *Trōilos*⟧ *Gr. Legend* a son of King Priam, killed by Achilles: in medieval romance and in works by Boccaccio, Chaucer, and Shakespeare, Troilus is the lover of Cressida

Trois-Ri·vières (trwä rē vyer′) ⟦so named for the three channels of the Sainte-Maurice, river intersecting the St. Lawrence at this point⟧ city in S Quebec, Canada, on the St. Lawrence: Eng. name *Three Rivers*

Tro·jan (trō′jən) *adj.* ⟦ME *Troyan* < L *Trojanus* < *Troja,* TROY⟧ of ancient Troy or its people or culture —*n.* 1 a person born or living in ancient Troy 2 a strong, hardworking, determined person 3 [Obs.] a merry, dissolute companion 4 *Comput.* TROJAN HORSE (sense 3)

Trojan horse 1 *Gr. Legend* in the Trojan War, a huge, hollow wooden horse with Greek soldiers hidden inside that is left at the gates of Troy: the Trojans bring it into the city, thinking it a gift, and the soldiers creep out and open the gates to the rest of the Greek army, which destroys the city **2** any person, group, or thing that seeks to subvert a nation, organization, etc. from within **3** a computer program run or downloaded to perform a legitimate function, that also contains hidden instructions for an unauthorized, disruptive operation: cf. VIRUS (sense 4)

Trojan War *Gr. Legend* the ten-year war waged against Troy by the Greeks in order to reclaim King Menelaus' wife, Helen

troll[1] (trōl) ***vt.*** ⟦ME *trollen,* to roll, troll, wander, prob. < MFr *troller* < ? MHG *trollen,* to walk or run with short steps: see fol.⟧ **1** to roll; revolve **2** *a)* to sing the parts of (a round, catch, etc.) in succession *b)* to sing lustily or in a full, rolling voice; chant merrily **3** *a)* to trail (a lure, bait, etc.) through the water in fishing from a slowly moving boat *b)* to fish in (a lake, etc.) by this method **4** [Informal] to conduct a casual or haphazard search of [to *troll* the local singles bars] —***vi.*** **1** [Now Rare] *a)* to speak fast *b)* to wag (said of the tongue) **2** to sing in a round, catch, etc. **3** *a)* to sing lustily or in a full, rolling voice *b)* to be uttered in such a voice **4** to fish with bait or a lure trailed on a line behind a slowly moving boat **5** to roll, spin, or whirl **6** [Informal] to conduct a casual or haphazard search [visiting bars, *trolling* for a pickup] **7** [Informal] to post inflammatory or irrelevant material on an electronic forum to provoke responses —***n.*** **1** a song having parts sung in succession; round **2** *a)* the method of trolling in fishing *b)* a lure, or a lure and line, used in trolling **3** ⟦infl by TROLL[2]⟧ [Informal] a person who posts inflammatory or otherwise unwanted material on an electronic forum, esp. anonymously—**troll′er *n.***

troll[2] (trōl) ***n.*** ⟦ON, prob. < **truzla* < IE **dreu-*, var. of base **drā-*, to run > TRAP[1], MHG *trollen,* to run with short steps, Ger *trolle,* wench: readopted < Norw by 19th-c. antiquaries⟧ *Scand. Folklore* any of a race of supernatural beings, variously conceived of as giants or dwarfs, living underground or in caves

trol·ley (träl′ē) ***n.,*** *pl.* **-leys** ⟦< East Anglian dial. < TROLL[1]⟧ **1** a wheeled carriage, basket, etc. that runs suspended from an overhead track ☆**2** an apparatus, as a grooved wheel at the end of a pole, for transmitting electric current from an overhead wire to the motor of a streetcar, etc. ☆**3** TROLLEY CAR **4** [Chiefly Brit.] any of various wheeled vehicles or carts, esp. a cart pushed by hand — ***vt., vi.*** **-leyed, -ley·ing** ☆to carry or ride on a trolley —☆**off one's trolley** [Slang] crazy; insane

☆**trolley bus** an electric bus that is powered from overhead wires by means of trolleys

☆**trolley car** an electric streetcar that gets its motive power from an overhead wire by means of a trolley

trol·lop (träl′əp) ***n.*** ⟦prob. < Ger *trolle,* wench: see TROLL[2]⟧ **1** [Now Rare] a slovenly, dirty woman; slattern **2** [Old-fashioned] a sexually promiscuous woman; specif., a prostitute: now usually with a humorous connotation

Trol·lope (träl′əp), **Anthony** 1815-82; Eng. novelist

trol·ly (träl′ē) ***n.,*** *pl.* **-lies** *alt. sp. of* TROLLEY — ***vt., vi.*** **-lied, -ly·ing**

trom·bi·di·a·sis (träm′bi dī′ə sis) ***n.*** ⟦ModL < *Trombidium,* a genus of mites + *-iasis:* see -IASIS⟧ the state of being infested with chiggers: also **trom′bi·di·o′sis** (-dī ō′sis)

trom·bone (träm bōn′, träm′bōn′) ***n.*** ⟦It < *tromba,* a trumpet < OHG *trumba:* see TRUMP[2]⟧ a large brass instrument consisting of a long tube bent parallel to itself twice and ending in a bell mouth: it is of two types, the **slide trombone**, in which different tones are produced by moving the slide, or movable section of the tube, in or out, and the **valve trombone**, played, like the trumpet, with valves —**trom·bon′ist *n.***

trombone

trom·mel (träm′əl) ***n.*** ⟦Ger, a drum < MHG *trumel* < *trume,* of echoic orig.⟧ a sieve, usually a revolving cylindrical one, used in screening ore, coal, etc.

tromp (trämp) ***vi., vt.*** *var. of* TRAMP

trompe (trämp) ***n.*** ⟦Fr, lit., TRUMPET⟧ an apparatus formerly used for producing a blast, as in a blast furnace, by means of water falling through a tube and sucking in air which is diverted to the furnace

trompe l'oeil (trōnp lë′y′) ⟦< Fr *trompe-l'oeil,* lit., deceives-the-eye⟧ **1** a painting, etc. that creates such a strong illusion of reality that the viewer may not at first be sure whether the thing depicted is real or a representation **2** an illusion or effect of this kind

-tron (trän, trən) ⟦Gr, suffix of instrument, akin to L *-trum*⟧ *combining form* instrument: used esp. in forming names of devices in electronics and nuclear physics [*calutron*]

tro·na (trō′nə) ***n.*** ⟦Swed, prob. < colloq. Ar *ṭrōn,* contr. < *naṭrūn:* see NATRON⟧ an impure type of hydrous sodium carbonate, $Na_2CO_3·NaHCO_3·2H_2O$, gray or yellowish-white, used as a source of sodium compounds

Trond·heim (trän′hām′) seaport in central Norway, on an inlet of the Norwegian Sea

troop (tro͞op) ***n.*** ⟦Fr *troupe* < OFr, back-form. < *troupeau* < ML *troppus,* a flock < Frank **throp,* a crowd; akin to OE *thorp,* village: see THORP⟧ **1** a group of persons, animals, or, formerly, things; herd, flock, band, etc. **2** loosely, a great number; lot **3** [*pl.*] *a)* a body of soldiers *b)* soldiers (sometimes used, in the sing., of a single soldier) [20 *troops* were wounded; a *troop* arrested for being AWOL] **4** *a)* a subdivision of a mounted cavalry regiment *b)* an armored cavalry unit that corresponds to a company of infantry **5** a unit of Boy Scouts or Girl Scouts under an adult leader **6** [Archaic] a group of actors; troupe —***vi.*** **1** to gather or go together in a throng [the crowd *trooped* out of the stadium] **2** to walk, go, or pass at a slow, deliberate pace [children were *trooping* along the sidewalk] **3** [Archaic] to associate or consort —**troop the colors** [Brit.] to parade the colors, or flag, before troops

SYN.—**troop** is applied to a group of people organized as a unit [a cavalry *troop*], or working or acting together in close cooperation [*troops* of sightseers]; **troupe** is the current form with reference to a group of performers, as in the theater or a circus; **company** is the general word for any group of people associated in any of various ways; **band** suggests a relatively small group of people closely united for some common purpose [a *band* of thieves, a brass *band*]

troop·er (tro͞o′pər) ***n.*** ⟦prec. + -ER⟧ **1** an enlisted soldier in the mounted cavalry **2** a cavalry horse **3** a mounted police officer ☆**4** in the U.S., a state police officer **5** [Chiefly Brit.] a troopship **6** [Informal] TROUPER (***n.*** 3)

troop·ship (tro͞op′ship′) ***n.*** a ship for carrying troops; transport

☆**troost·ite** (tro͞o′stīt′) ***n.*** ⟦after G. *Troost* (1776-1850), Am mineralogist + -ITE[1]⟧ a hard, reddish, rhombohedral mineral, $(Zn,Mn)_2SiO_4$, with large crystals, similar to willemite but containing varying amounts of manganese

trop[1] (trō) ***adv.*** ⟦Fr < ML *troppus:* see TROOP⟧ too; too much —***pron.*** too much; too many

trop[2] *abbrev.* **1** tropic **2** tropical

tro·pae·o·lin or **tro·pae·o·line** (trō pē′ə lin) ***n.*** ⟦< fol. + -IN(E): from resembling the hues of the flowers⟧ any of a group of orange or orange-yellow azo dyes: also sp. **tro·pe′o·lin** or **tro·pe′o·line**

tro·pae·o·lum (-ləm) ***n.,*** *pl.* **-lums** or **-la** (-lə) ⟦ModL, dim. < Gr *tropaion* (see TROPHY): from the shieldlike leaves⟧ NASTURTIUM

-tro·pal (trə pəl) ⟦< -TROP(E) + -AL⟧ -TROPIC

trope (trōp) ***n.*** ⟦L *tropus* < Gr *tropos,* a turning, turn, figure of speech (akin to *tropē,* a turn) < *trepein,* to turn < IE base **trep-*, to turn⟧ **1** *a)* the use of a word or words in a figurative sense *b)* a figure of speech *c)* figurative language in general **2** a common, often conventional, theme, motif, style, etc. **3** in the medieval church, *a)* the interpolation of a phrase or passage into the authorized service: such passages were later developed into dramatic dialogues *b)* any such passage

-trope (trōp) ⟦Gr *-tropos:* see prec.⟧ *combining form* **1** *forming nouns a)* a turning or changing *b)* something that turns or changes [*thaumatrope*] **2** *forming adjectives* turning

troph·al·lax·is (träf′ə lak′sis) ***n.,*** *pl.* **-lax′es′** (-sēz′) ⟦ModL < Gr *trophē,* nourishment (see fol.) + *allaxis,* barter < *allassein,* to exchange < *allos,* other: see ELSE⟧ the exchange of regurgitated food, glandular secretions, etc. among members of a colony of social insects —**troph′al·lac′tic** (-lak′tik) ***adj.***

troph·ic (träf′ik) ***adj.*** ⟦Gr *trophikos* < *trophē,* food < *trephein,* to feed < IE base **dhereb h-*, to coagulate > Gr *thrombos,* a clot⟧ of nutrition; having to do with the processes of nutrition

-troph·ic (träf′ik, trō′fik) *combining form forming adjectives* of or relating to a (specified) kind of nutrition

tro·phied (trō′fēd) ***adj.*** decorated with trophies

troph·o- (träf′ō, -ə) ⟦< Gr *trophē,* nourishment: see TROPHIC⟧ *combining form* of nutrition [*trophoplasm*]: also, before a vowel, **troph-**

troph·o·blast (träf′ə blast′) ***n.*** ⟦prec. + -BLAST⟧ a layer of nutritive ectoderm outside the blastoderm, by which the fertilized ovum is attached to the uterine wall and the developing embryo receives its nourishment —**troph′o·blas′tic *adj.***

troph·o·plasm (träf′ə plaz′əm) ***n.*** ⟦TROPHO- + -PLASM⟧ the nutritive or vegetative substance of an organic cell, as fat or yolk granules: cf. IDIOPLASM

troph·o·zo·ite (träf′ə zō′īt′) ***n.*** ⟦TROPHO- + ZO- + -ITE[1]⟧ a protozoan, esp. of certain parasitic species, in the feeding and growing stage in contrast with the reproductive and infective stages

tro·phy (trō′fē) ***n.,*** *pl.* **-phies** ⟦MFr *trophée* < L *trophaeum,* altered < *tropaeum,* sign of victory < Gr *tropaion,* a token of an enemy's defeat < *tropaios,* of a rout, turning < *tropē,* a turning, defeat < *trepein:* see TROPE⟧ **1** *a)* in ancient Greece and Rome, a memorial of victory erected on the battlefield or in some public place, orig. a display of captured arms or other spoils *b)* a representation of this on a medal **2** an architectural ornament representing a group of weapons **3** something taken from the enemy and kept as a memorial of victory, as captured arms **4** a lion's skin, deer's head, etc. displayed as evidence of hunting prowess **5** *a)* a prize, usually a silver cup, awarded in a sports contest or other competition *b)* anything serving as a reminder, as of a triumph —***adj.*** regarded as symbolizing one's success, wealth, etc. [a *trophy* estate]: see also TROPHY WIFE

-tro·phy (trə fē) ⟦Gr *-trophia* < *trephein,* to nourish: see TROPHIC⟧ *combining form forming nouns* nutrition, nourishment, growth [*hypertrophy*]

trophy wife a wife, often, specif., a second wife, who is attractive and younger than her wealthy husband and regarded as symbolizing his material success

trop·ic (träp′ik) ***n.*** ⟦ME *tropik* < LL *tropicus* < Gr *tropikos,* belonging to a turn (of the sun at the solstices) < *tropē:* see TROPE⟧ **1** *Astron.* either of two circles of the celestial sphere parallel to the celestial equator, one, the **Tropic of Cancer**, *c.* 23° 26′ north, and the other, the **Tropic of Capricorn**, *c.* 23° 26′ south: they are the limits of the apparent north-and-south journey of the sun and are determined by the obliquity of the ecliptic 2 *Geog.* either of two parallels of latitude (**Tropic of Cancer** and **Tropic of Capricorn**) situated on either side of the earth's equator that correspond to the astronomical tropics —*adj.* of the tropics; tropical

-trop·ic (träp′ik, trō′pik) ⟦< Gr *-tropos,* turning (< *trepein:* see TROPE) + -IC⟧ *combining form forming adjectives* turning toward or from, changing because of, or otherwise responding to a (specified kind of) stimulus [*phototropic*]

trop·i·cal (träp′i kəl) *adj.* 1 of, in, characteristic of, or suitable for the tropics 2 very hot; sultry —**trop′i·cal·ly** *adv.*

tropical continental a type of warm, dry air mass originating at low latitudes over land areas: see AIR MASS

tropical cyclone *Meteorol.* a cyclone, originating over tropical seas, ranging in diameter from *c.* 96 to 1,609 km (*c.* 60 to 1,000 mi) and developing winds up to about 200 mph

tropical fish any of various usually brightly colored fish of the tropics, esp. any of those kept in an aquarium at a constant, warm temperature

tropical maritime a type of warm, wet air mass originating at low latitudes over ocean areas: see AIR MASS

tropical storm *Meteorol.* a tropical cyclone having winds that move slower than a hurricane (73 mph) but faster than a breeze (31 mph)

tropical year *see* YEAR (sense 2)

Tropical Zone TORRID ZONE

tropic bird any of a family (Phaethontidae) of tropical pelecaniform sea birds characterized by white plumage with black markings and a pair of long tail feathers

Tropic of Cancer (*or* **Capricorn**) *see* TROPIC (*n.* 1 & 2)

tropics [*also* **T-**] region of the earth lying between the Tropic of Cancer & the Tropic of Capricorn; Torrid Zone

tro·pine (trō′pēn′, -pin) *n.* ⟦< (A)TROPINE⟧ a poisonous, colorless heterocyclic alkaloid, $C_8H_{15}NO$, produced by the hydrolysis of atropine or hyoscyamine

tro·pism (trō′piz′əm) *n.* ⟦< fol.⟧ the positive, or negative, attraction of a plant or sessile animal toward, or away from, a stimulus, as in the turning of a sunflower toward the light —**tro·pis′tic** *adj.*

-tro·pism (trə piz′əm) ⟦< -TROP(E) + -ISM⟧ *combining form forming nouns* tropism [*heliotropism*]

tro·pol·o·gy (trō päl′ə jē) *n.* ⟦LL *tropologia* < LGr: see TROPE & -LOGY⟧ 1 the use of tropes or figurative language 2 a method of considering or interpreting Scripture in a figurative, moralistic way rather than in a literal sense —**trop·o·log·i·cal** (träp′ə läj′i kəl, trō′pə-) *adj.*, **trop′o·log′ic**

tro·po·pause (trō′pə pôz′, träp′ə-) *n.* ⟦TROPO(SPHERE) + PAUSE⟧ an atmospheric transition zone or shell located between the troposphere and the stratosphere at an altitude of *c.* 10 to 20 km (*c.* 6 to 12 mi), in which temperatures and atmospheric stability begin to increase with increasing altitude

tro·poph·i·lous (trō päf′ə ləs) *adj.* ⟦< Gr *tropos,* a turning (see TROPE) + -PHILOUS⟧ *Bot.* able to adjust to conditions of heat or cold, dryness or moisture, etc., as in seasonal changes: said of plants

trop·o·phyte (träp′ə fīt′) *n.* ⟦< Gr *tropos,* a turning (see TROPE) + -PHYTE⟧ any tropophilous plant, as a deciduous tree —**trop′o·phyt′ic** (-fit′ik) *adj.*

☆**tro·po·scat·ter** (trō′pə skat′ər, träp′ə-) *n.* TROPOSPHERIC SCATTER

tro·po·sphere (trō′pə sfir′, träp′ə-) *n.* ⟦Fr *troposphère* < Gr *tropos,* a turning (see TROPE) + Fr *sphère* (see SPHERE)⟧ the atmospheric zone or shell below the tropopause, characterized by water vapor, vertical winds, weather, and decreasing temperatures with increasing altitude —**tro′po·spher′ic** (-sfer′ik, -sfir′-) *adj.*

☆**tropospheric scatter** scattering in the earth's troposphere, used in radio communication at VHF and UHF for ranges beyond line of sight

-tro·pous (trə pəs) ⟦< Gr *tropos,* a turning (see TROPE) + -OUS⟧ *combining form forming adjectives* turning or turned (in a specified way or in response to a specified stimulus): used in botanical terms [*anatropous*]

trop·po (trôp′pô) ⟦It⟧ *see* NON TROPPO

-tro·py (trə pē) ⟦< Gr *tropē:* see TROPE⟧ *combining form* -TROPISM

Tros·sachs (träs′əks) valley in central Scotland, near Loch Katrine: often with *the*

trot (trät) *vi.* **trot′ted, trot′ting** ⟦ME *trotten* < OFr *troter* < OHG *trottōn,* to tread: for IE base see TREAD⟧ 1 to move, ride, drive, run, or go at a trot 2 to move quickly; hurry; run —*vt.* to cause to go at a trot —*n.* 1 a gait, as of a horse, in which a front leg and the opposite hind leg are lifted at the same time 2 a jogging gait of a person, between a walk and a run 3 the sound of a trotting horse 4 TROTLINE 5 a horse race for trotters ☆6 [Slang] PONY (*n.* 3) 7 [Archaic] an old woman: a contemptuous term —☆**hot to trot** [Slang] eager for a sexual encounter; yearning for sex —**the trots** [Slang] a case of diarrhea —**trot out** [Informal] 1 to bring out for others to see or admire 2 to submit for approval

troth (trôth, trōth, träth) [Archaic] *n.* ⟦ME *trouthe* (see TRUTH), with specialized form & meaning⟧ 1 faithfulness; loyalty 2 truth: chiefly in phrase **in troth,** truly; indeed 3 one's pledged word; promise: see also PLIGHT ONE'S TROTH (at PLIGHT[2]) —*vt.* to pledge to marry

troth·plight (-plīt′) [Archaic] *n.* betrothal —*adj.* betrothed

trot·line (trät′līn′) *n.* ⟦TROT + LINE[1]⟧ a strong fishing line suspended over the water, with short, baited lines hung from it at intervals

Trot·sky (trät′skē), **Leon** (born *Lev Davidovich Bronstein*) 1879-1940; Russ. revolutionary: commissar of war (1918-24) under Lenin: exiled (1929) and assassinated —**Trot′sky·ism′** *n.* —**Trot′sky·ist** *adj., n.* or (often considered disparaging) **Trot′sky·ite′**

trot·ter (trät′ər) *n.* 1 an animal that trots; esp., a horse bred and trained for trotting races 2 a person who moves about energetically and constantly 3 the foot of a sheep or pig used as food

tro·tyl (trō′təl) *n.* ⟦(TRINI)TROT(OLUENE) + -YL⟧ TRINITROTOLUENE

trou·ba·dour (tro͞o′bə dôr′) *n.* ⟦Fr < Prov *trobador* < *trobar,* to compose, invent, find < ? VL **tropare,* prob. back-form. < *contropare,* to combine, compare < L *con-,* with (> OL *com:* see COM-) + L *tropus,* TROPE⟧ 1 any of a class of lyric poets and poet-musicians in S France and N Spain and Italy during the 11th through 13th cent. who wrote poems and songs of love and chivalry, usually with intricate stanza form and rhyme scheme: cf. TROUVÈRE 2 a minstrel or singer

trou·ble (trub′əl) *vt.* **-bled, -bling** ⟦ME *trublen* < OFr *trubler* < VL **turbulare,* altered (infl. by L *turbula,* disorderly group, dim. of *turba,* crowd) < LL *turbidare,* to trouble, make turbid < L *turbidus,* TURBID⟧ 1 to disturb or agitate [*troubled* waters] 2 to cause mental agitation to; worry; harass; perturb; vex 3 to cause pain or discomfort to; afflict [my back *troubled* me] 4 to cause difficulty or inconvenience to; incommode [don't *trouble* yourself to rise] 5 to pester, annoy, tease, bother, etc. —*vi.* to make an effort; take pains; bother [don't *trouble* to return it] —*n.* 1 a state of mental distress; worry 2 *a)* a misfortune; calamity; mishap *b)* a distressing or difficult happening or situation *c)* a condition of being out of order, needing repair, etc. [tire *trouble*] 3 a person, circumstance, or event that causes annoyance, distress, difficulty, etc. 4 public disturbance; civil disorder 5 effort; bother; pains [to take the *trouble* to look it up] 6 an illness; ailment; disease —**in trouble** [Informal] pregnant when unmarried —**the Troubles** 1 the civil unrest in Ireland, *c.* 1919-23 2 the civil unrest in Northern Ireland, from about 1967 —**trouble someone for** to ask someone to pass, hand, give, etc. (something) to one —**trou′bler** *n.*

trou·bled (trub′əld) *adj.* 1 worried or concerned 2 emotionally or mentally disturbed 3 characterized by unrest, esp. social unrest [*troubled* youth]

trou·ble·mak·er (trub′əl māk′ər) *n.* a person who habitually makes trouble for others; esp., one who incites others to quarrel, rebel, etc. —**trou′ble·mak′ing** *n., adj.*

☆**trou·ble·shoot·er** (-sho͞ot′ər) *n.* 1 a person who locates and repairs mechanical breakdowns 2 a person charged with locating and eliminating the source of trouble in any flow of work —**trou′ble·shoot′ing** *n.*

trou·ble·some (trub′əl səm) *adj.* characterized by or causing trouble, irritation, difficulty, distress, inconvenience, etc. —**trou′ble·some·ly** *adv.* —**trou′ble·some·ness** *n.*

trou·blous (trub′ləs) *adj.* ⟦ME *troubelous* < OFr *troubleus*⟧ [Archaic or Literary] 1 troubled, unsettled, etc. 2 TROUBLESOME

trou-de-loup (tro͞o′də lo͞o′) *n., pl.* **trous′-de-loup′** (tro͞o′-) ⟦Fr, lit., wolf hole⟧ *Mil.* any of the conical pits with a vertical pointed stake in the center of each, formerly built in rows as an obstacle to the enemy, esp. to enemy cavalry

trough (trôf, träf) *n.* ⟦ME < OE *trog,* akin to Ger < IE **druk-* < base **deru-,* TREE: basic sense, "hollowed wooden object"⟧ 1 a long, narrow, open container of wood, stone, etc. for holding water or food for animals: often used fig. 2 any similarly shaped vessel, as one for kneading or washing something 3 a channel for conveying fluids; esp., a GUTTER (*n.* 1) 4 a long, narrow hollow or depression, as between waves 5 a low in any cycle, esp. in an economic cycle 6 a long, narrow area of low barometric pressure

trounce (trouns) *vt.* **trounced, trounc′ing** ⟦< ?⟧ 1 to beat; thrash; flog 2 [Informal] to defeat soundly —**trounc′er** *n.*

☆**troupe** (tro͞op) *n.* ⟦Fr, a TROOP⟧ a group of actors, singers, etc.; company —*vi.* **trouped, troup′ing** to travel as a member of a troupe —*SYN.* TROOP

☆**troup·er** (tro͞o′per) *n.* 1 a member of a troupe 2 an experienced, dependable actor 3 [Informal] a person who is steady, dedicated, dependable, etc., esp. during trying times

trou·pi·al (tro͞o′pē əl) *n.* ⟦Fr *troupiale* < *troupe* (see TROOP): from their gregarious habit⟧ any of a New World family (Icteridae) of gregarious birds, including the bobolinks, blackbirds, and orioles; specif., a large, orange-and-black oriole (*Icterus icterus*) of South America

trou·sers (trou′zərz) *pl.n.* ⟦lengthened (prob. modeled on DRAWERS) < obs. *trouse* < Gael *triubhas,* TREWS⟧ an outer garment, often, specif., for men and boys, extending from the waist generally to the ankles, and divided into separate coverings for the legs; pants —**trou′ser** *adj.*

trous·seau (tro͞o sō′, tro͞o′sō) *n., pl.* **-seaux′** (-sōz′) or **-seaus′** ⟦Fr < OFr, dim. of *trousse,* a bundle: see TRUSS⟧ the clothes, linen, jewelry, etc. of a bride

trout (trout) *n., pl.* **trout** or **trouts** ⟦ME *troute* < OE *truht* < LL *tructus, tructa* < Gr *trōktēs,* kind of fish < *trōgein,* to gnaw: see TROGLODYTE⟧ 1 any salmonid; esp., any of various food and game fishes that are usually speckled and found chiefly in fresh water, as the brown trout, rainbow trout, brook trout, and lake trout 2 any of several other troutlike fishes

☆**trout lily** DOGTOOTH VIOLET

☆**trout-perch** (trout′purch′) *n., pl.* **-perch′** or **-perch′es** ⟦TROUT + PERCH[1]⟧ any of a family (Percopsidae) of North American freshwater bony fishes having spiny and fleshy fins, esp., a species (*Percopsis omiscomaycus*) of Canada and the E U.S.

trou·vaille (tro͞o vä′y′) *n.* ⟦Fr⟧ a find or discovery of interest or value

trou·vère (tro͞o ver′) *n.* ⟦Fr < OFr *trovere* < *trover,* to find, compose (akin to Prov *trobar:* see TROUBADOUR)⟧ any of a class of lyric and narrative poets and poet-musicians in N France, flourishing in the 12th and 13th cent.: also **trou·veur′** (-vur′)

Trou·ville (tro͞o vēl′) resort town in NW France, on the English Channel: also **Trou·ville-sur-Mer** (tro͞o vēl sür mer′)

trove (trōv) ***n.*** *short for* TREASURE-TROVE

tro·ver (trō′vər) ***n.*** ⟦substantive use of OFr *trover,* to find: see TROUVÈRE⟧ *Law* **1** [Obs.] an action against a person who found another's goods and refused to return them **2** an action to recover damages for goods withheld or used by another illegally

trow (trō, trou) ***vi., vt.*** ⟦ME *trowen* < OE *treowian,* to have trust in (akin to Ger *trauen*) < *treow,* faith, belief: see TRUE⟧ [Archaic] to believe, think, suppose, etc.

trow·el (trou′əl) ***n.*** ⟦ME *truel* < MFr *truelle* < LL *truella* for L *trulla,* small ladle, scoop, trowel < *trua,* stirring spoon, ladle, prob. < IE base **twer-,* to stir > TURBID⟧ any of several small hand tools for spreading, smoothing, scooping, etc.; specif., *a)* a tool with a thin, flat, rectangular blade, used for smoothing plaster *b)* a tool with a thin, flat, pointed blade for applying and shaping mortar, as in bricklaying *c)* a tool with a pointed scoop for loosening soil, digging holes, etc. in a garden —***vt.*** **-eled** or **-elled**, **-el·ing** or **-el·ling** to spread, smooth, shape, dig, etc. with a trowel

troy (troi) ***adj.*** by or in troy weight

Troy (troi) ⟦L *troja* < Gr *Trōia,* after *Trōs,* father of *Ilos:* see ILIAD⟧ ancient Phrygian city in Troas, NW Asia Minor: scene of the Trojan War

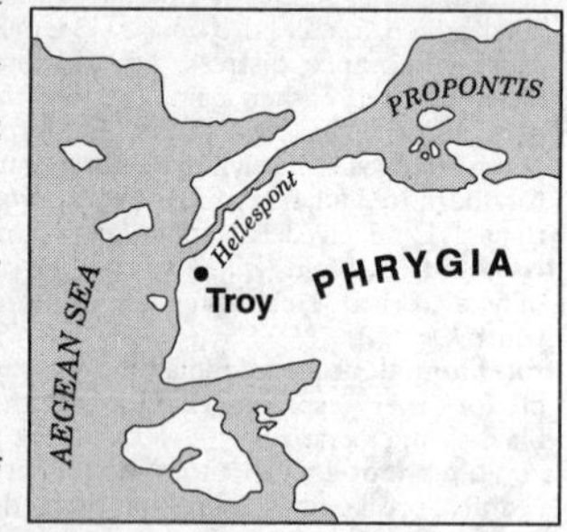

Troy (*c.* 1200 B.C.)

Troyes¹, Chrétien de *see* CHRÉTIEN DE TROYES

Troyes² (trwȧ) city in NE France, on the Seine

troy weight ⟦ME, after prec., where first used at medieval fairs⟧ a system of weights for gold, silver, precious stones, etc.: see the table of weights and measures in the Reference Supplement

tru·an·cy (tro͞o′ən sē) ***n.*** **1** *pl.* **-cies** the act or an instance of playing truant **2** the state of being truant

tru·ant (tro͞o′ənt) ***n.*** ⟦ME < OFr, beggar, vagabond < Celt, as in Ir *trōgán,* dim. of *truag,* wretched⟧ **1** [Obs.] a lazy, idle person **2** a pupil who stays away from school without permission **3** a person who neglects his or her work or duties —***adj.*** **1** that is a truant; that plays truant **2** idle; shiftless **3** characteristic of a truant; errant; straying —***vi.*** to be or play truant

☆**truant officer** ATTENDANCE OFFICER

truce (tro͞os) ***n.*** ⟦ME *trewes,* pl. of *trewe,* a pledge < OE *treow,* compact, faith: see TRUE⟧ **1** a temporary cessation of warfare by agreement between the belligerents; armistice; cease-fire **2** any pause in or respite from quarreling, conflict, trouble, etc.

Tru·cial (tro͞o′shəl) ***adj.*** ⟦prec. + -IAL⟧ of or having to do with the 1835 maritime truce between the British government and several Omani sheiks

Trucial Oman region in E Arabia, on the Persian Gulf: see UNITED ARAB EMIRATES

Trucial States *former name for* UNITED ARAB EMIRATES

truck¹ (truk) ***n.*** ⟦< ? L *trochus,* a hoop < Gr *trochos,* a wheel, disk: see TROCHE⟧ **1** [Historical] a small, solid wheel or roller, esp. one for a gun carriage **2** a small, wooden disk at the top of a ship's mast or flagpole, usually with holes for halyards **3** *short for* HAND TRUCK **4** any of various low frames or platforms on wheels, sometimes motor-driven, for carrying heavy articles, as in a warehouse ☆**5** an automotive vehicle for hauling loads along highways, streets, etc.; motor truck **6** a swiveling frame with two or more pairs of wheels, usually provided with brakes and springs, forming the wheel unit under each end of a railroad car, streetcar, etc. **7** [Brit.] an open railroad freight car —***vt.*** to carry or transport on a truck or trucks —***vi.*** **1** to do trucking **2** to drive a truck as one's work ☆**3** [Slang] to walk in a carefree, leisurely manner; stroll

truck² (truk) ***vt., vi.*** ⟦ME *trukken* < MFr *troquer,* to exchange, barter < ?⟧ **1** to exchange; barter **2** [Rare] to peddle —***n.*** ⟦Anglo-Fr *truke* < MFr *troque* < the v.⟧ **1** BARTER **2** payment of wages in goods produced instead of money **3** small commercial articles **4** small articles of little value ☆**5** vegetables raised for sale in markets **6** [Informal] dealings [have no further *truck* with them] **7** [Informal] trash; rubbish

truck·age (truk′ij) ***n.*** **1** transportation of goods by truck **2** the charge for this

truck·er¹ (truk′ər) ***n.*** **1** a person who drives a truck or, specif., a tractor-trailer **2** a person or company engaged in trucking

truck·er² (truk′ər) ***n.*** ☆**1** a truck farmer **2** a person who sells commodities or engages in barter

☆**truck farm** ⟦see TRUCK² (*n.* 5)⟧ a usually small farm where produce is grown for sale, typically in local markets —**truck farmer** —**truck farming**

truck·ing (truk′iŋ) ***n.*** the business or process of carrying goods by truck

truck·le (truk′əl) ***n.*** ⟦ME *trocle* < L *trochlea,* pulley, roller: see TROCHLEA⟧ *short for* TRUCKLE BED —***vi.*** **-led**, **-ling** ⟦< fol.: with reference to its low position⟧ to be servile; cringe, submit, toady, etc.: usually with *to*

truckle bed TRUNDLE BED

truck·load (truk′lōd′) ***n.*** **1** a load that fills a truck **2** the minimum weight of a specific commodity qualifying as a truckload of that commodity in rates that apply to the shipment of goods by truck

truck·man (truk′mən) ***n.,*** *pl.* **-men** (-mən) one who drives a truck or is engaged in trucking; trucker

☆**truck stop** a restaurant in conjunction with a service station, located as along an interstate highway and catering especially to truck drivers

truck system the system of paying wages in goods produced instead of money

truc·u·lent (truk′yo͞o lənt, -yə-) ***adj.*** ⟦< L *truculentus* < *trux* (gen. *trucis*), fierce, savage⟧ **1** fierce; cruel; savage; ferocious **2** rude, harsh, mean, scathing, etc.: said esp. of speech or writing **3** pugnacious or bellicose —**truc′u·lence** ***n.,*** **truc′u·len·cy** —**truc′u·lent·ly** ***adv.***

Tru·deau (tro͞o dō′, tro͞o′dō′) **1 Justin Pierre James** 1971- ; prime minister of Canada (2015-) **2 Pierre (Elliott)** 1919-2000; prime minister of Canada (1968-79; 1980-84)

trudge (truj) ***vi.*** **trudged**, **trudg′ing** ⟦< ?⟧ to walk, esp. wearily or laboriously —***n.*** a walk or tramp, esp. a wearying, tedious one —**trudg′er** ***n.***

trudg·en stroke (truj′ən) ⟦after J. *Trudgen,* Eng amateur who introduced it (1868)⟧ *Swimming* a stroke in which a double overarm motion and a scissors kick are used

Tru·dy (tro͞o′dē) ***n.*** a feminine name: see GERTRUDE

true (tro͞o) ***adj.*** **tru′er**, **tru′est** ⟦ME *treue* < OE *treowe* < *treow,* faith, akin to Ger *treu* < IE **drew-,* var. of base **deru-* > TREE: basic sense "firm (as a tree)"⟧ **1** faithful; loyal; constant **2** reliable; certain [a *true* indication] **3** in accordance with fact; that agrees with reality; not false **4** *a)* conforming to an original, pattern, rule, standard, etc. *b)* exact; accurate; right; correct **5** rightful; lawful; legitimate [the *true* heirs] **6** accurately fitted, placed, or shaped [a door that is not *true* to the frame] **7** *a)* real; genuine; authentic [a *true* diamond] *b)* conforming to the ideal character or having all the basic characteristics of such; rightly so called [a *true* scholar] **8** determined by the poles of the earth's axis, not by the earth's magnetic poles [*true* north] **9** [Archaic] honest, virtuous, or truthful —***adv.*** **tru′er**, **tru′est** **1** in a true manner; truly, truthfully, accurately, etc. **2** *Biol.* with the same inherited trait or traits as a parent; without variation [to breed *true*] —***vt.*** **trued**, **tru′ing** or **true′ing** to fit, place, or shape accurately: often with *up* —***n.*** that which is true; truth or reality: with *the* —**come true** to happen in fulfillment of an expectation, prediction, wish, etc.; become a realized fact —**in true** properly set, adjusted, aligned, etc.; exact —**out of true** not properly set, adjusted, aligned, etc.; inexact —**true to form** being or behaving as expected —**true′ness** ***n.***

SYN.—**true**, **actual**, and **real** are often used interchangeably to imply correspondence with fact, but in discriminating use, **true** implies conformity with a standard or model [a *true* democrat] or with what actually exists [a *true* story], **actual** stresses existence or occurrence and is, hence, strictly applied to concrete things [*actual* and hypothetical examples], and **real** highlights a distinction between what something is and what a substitute, counterfeit, etc. seems or pretends to be [*real* rubber, *real* courage]

true believer ⟦term popularized by U.S. writer Eric Hoffer in his book *The True Believer* (1951)⟧ a dedicated follower or disciple, esp. a person whose devotion to another, a cause, etc. is blind or unquestioning

true bill a bill of indictment endorsed by a grand jury as supported by evidence sufficient to warrant a trial

true-blue (tro͞o′blo͞o′) ***adj.*** ⟦from the symbolism of *blue* as the color of constancy⟧ very loyal; staunch

true·born (tro͞o′bôrn′) ***adj.*** being genuinely such, specif. by birth [a *true-born* New Yorker]

true·bred (tro͞o′bred′) ***adj.*** **1** WELL-BRED **2** PUREBRED

☆**true-false test** (tro͞o′fôls′) a test, as one typically given in school, consisting of a series of statements to be identified as either "true" or "false"

true fruit *Bot.* a fruit derived from a single carpel or from the united carpels of a single flower

true·heart·ed (tro͞o′härt′id) ***adj.*** **1** loyal; faithful **2** honest or sincere —**true′heart′ed·ness** ***n.***

true-life (tro͞o′līf′) ***adj.*** corresponding to what happens in real life; true to reality [a *true-life* story]

true·love (tro͞o′luv′) ***n.*** **1** a person who loves or is loved truly; (one's) sweetheart **2** HERB PARIS

truelove knot a kind of bowknot that is hard to untie, a symbol of lasting love: also **true′-lov′er's knot**

true ribs ribs that are attached by cartilage directly to the sternum; in humans, the upper seven pairs of ribs

Truf·faut (tro͞o fō′; *Fr* trü fō′), **Fran·çois** (frän swȧ′) 1932-84; Fr. film director

truf·fle (truf′əl) ***n.*** ⟦< Fr *truffe* < OIt *truffa* < VL **trufera* < Osco-Umb **tufer,* for L *tuber:* see TUBER⟧ **1** any of an order (Tuberales) of fleshy, edible, potato-shaped ascomycetous fungi that grow underground; esp., any of a European genus (*Tuber*) which are cultivated and regarded as a delicacy **2** any of a number of rich chocolate candies made to resemble this in shape and color

trug (trug) ***n.*** ⟦prob. via Scand < base akin to OE *trog,* TROUGH⟧ [Brit.] a broad, shallow, wooden gardener's basket

tru·ism (tro͞o′iz′əm) ***n.*** a statement the truth of which is obvious or well known; commonplace —*SYN.* PLATITUDE —**tru·is′tic** ***adj.***

Tru·ji·llo (tro͞o hē′yō) city in NW Peru

trull (trul) ***n.*** ⟦< Ger *trulle* < earlier *trolle:* see TROLL²⟧ [Archaic] a prostitute or trollop

tru·ly (tro͞o′lē) ***adv.*** **1** in a true manner; accurately, genuinely, faithfully, factually, etc. **2** really; indeed: often used as an interjection of surprise, confirmation, etc. **3** sincerely: used in the formal complimentary close of a letter [yours *truly*, very *truly* yours] **4** rightfully; legally

Tru·man (tro͞o′mən), **Harry S.** 1884-1972; 33d president of the U.S. (1945-53)

Trum·bull (trum′bəl) **1 John** 1756-1843; U.S. painter **2 Jonathan** 1710-85; Am. Revolutionary patriot: father of John

trump[1] (trump) ***n.*** ⟦altered < TRIUMPH⟧ **1** any playing card of a suit that ranks higher than any other suit during the playing of a hand: a trump can take any card of any other suit: also **trump card** **2** [*occas. pl., with sing. v.*] a suit of trumps **3** any advantage held in reserve until needed: also **trump card** **4** [Old Informal] a fine person, good fellow, etc. ***—vt.*** **1** to play a trump on (a trick, another card, etc.) when a trump was not led, often, specif., so as to take it thereby **2** to surpass; outdo ***—vi.*** to play a trump when a trump was not led **—trump up** to devise or make up (a charge against someone, an excuse, etc.) fraudulently

trump[2] (trump) ***n., vt., vi.*** ⟦ME *trumpe* < OFr *trompe* < Frank **trumpa* or OHG *trumba*, of echoic orig.⟧ *archaic var. of* TRUMPET

trumped-up (trumpt′up′) ***adj.*** fraudulently devised or concocted; false

trump·er·y (trump′ər ē) ***n.***, *pl.* **-er·ies** ⟦ME *trompery* < MFr *tromperie* < *tromper*, to deceive, cheat < ? *tromper*, to play the trumpet: see TRUMP[2]⟧ **1** something showy but worthless **2** nonsense; rubbish ***—adj.*** showy but worthless; trashy; paltry

trum·pet (trum′pit) ***n.*** ⟦ME *trompette* < MFr, dim. of *trompe*: see TRUMP[2]⟧ **1** a brass instrument with a bright tone, consisting of a tube in an oblong loop or loops, with a flared bell and, in the modern instrument, three valves for producing changes in pitch **2** something shaped like a trumpet; esp., EAR TRUMPET ☆**3** [*pl.*] a pitcher plant (*Sarracenia flava*) of the SE U.S., with slender, erect, hollow leaves **4** a sound like that of a trumpet; specif., the reverberating call of an elephant **5** a trumpet-toned organ stop ***—vi.*** **1** to blow a trumpet **2** to make a sound like a trumpet ***—vt.*** **1** to sound on a trumpet **2** to sound or utter with a trumpetlike tone **3** to proclaim loudly or widely

☆**trumpet creeper** **1** a high-climbing vine (*Campsis radicans*) of the bignonia family, native to the S U.S. and having red, trumpet-shaped flowers **2** a similar Chinese vine (*Campsis chinensis*) of the bignonia family

trum·pet·er (trum′pit ər) ***n.*** **1** *a)* [Historical] a soldier, herald, etc. who signals on a trumpet *b)* any person who plays the trumpet, as in a band or orchestra **2** a person who proclaims or heralds something **3** any of a family (Psophiidae) of cranelike, South American gruiform birds having a loud cry ☆**4** TRUMPETER SWAN **5** any of a breed of domestic pigeons with feathered feet and a rounded crest

☆**trumpeter swan** a North American wild swan (*Cygnus buccinator*) with a loud, resonant cry

trumpet flower **1** any of a number of plants with trumpet-shaped flowers, as the trumpet creeper and the trumpet honeysuckle **2** the flower of any of these

☆**trumpet honeysuckle** an American honeysuckle (*Lonicera sempervirens*) with trumpet-shaped flowers

☆**trumpet vine** any of various plants having trumpet-shaped flowers, as the trumpet creeper

trum·pet·weed (trum′pit wēd′) ***n.*** any of several eupatoriums, as the joe-pye weed or boneset

trun·cate (truŋ′kāt′, trun′-) ***vt.*** **-cat′ed**, **-cat′ing** ⟦< L *truncatus*, pp. of *truncare*, to cut off < *truncus*, a stem, TRUNK⟧ to cut off a part of; shorten by cutting; lop ***—adj.*** **1** TRUNCATED **2** *Biol.* having a square, flattened, or broad end **3** *Zool.* lacking a normal apex, as some snail shells **—trun·ca′tion *n.***

trun·cat·ed (-id) ***adj.*** **1** cut short or appearing as if cut short **2** *a)* cut off or replaced by a plane face (said of the angles or edges of a crystal or solid figure) *b)* having its angles or edges cut off or replaced in this way (said of the crystal or solid figure) **3** having the vertex cut off by a plane that is not parallel to the base: said of a cone or pyramid: see FRUSTUM **4** TRUNCATE (***adj.*** 2 & 3)

trun·cheon (trun′chən) ***n.*** ⟦ME *tronchoun* < OFr *tronchon* < VL **truncio* < L *truncus*, a stem, TRUNK⟧ **1** [Obs.] a short, thick club; cudgel **2** any staff or baton used as a symbol of authority **3** [Chiefly Brit.] a policeman's stick or billy **4** [Obs.] the shaft of a spear **5** [Obs.] a trunk or stem, esp. one with the branches lopped off ***—vt.*** [Archaic] to beat with a truncheon

trun·dle (trun′dəl) ***n.*** ⟦altered < earlier *trendle* < OE *trendel*, a ring, circle < *trendan*, to roll: see TREND⟧ **1** a small wheel or caster **2** *short for* TRUNDLE BED **3** *a)* LANTERN PINION *b)* any of its bars **4** [Obs.] a small cart or truck with low wheels ***— vt., vi.*** **-dled**, **-dling** **1** to roll along **2** to move along in a wheeled vehicle **3** to rotate **—trun′dler *n.***

trundle bed a low bed on small wheels or casters, that can be rolled under another bed when not in use

trunk (truŋk) ***n.*** ⟦ME *tronke* < OFr *tronc* < L *truncus*, a stem, trunk < *truncus*, maimed, mutilated < IE **tronkus* < base **trenk-*, to press together, crowd > THRONG⟧ **1** the main stem of a tree **2** the body of a human being or animal, not including the head and limbs **3** the thorax of an insect **4** the main body or stem of a nerve, blood vessel, etc., as distinguished from its branches **5** the long, flexible, prehensile proboscis of an elephant **6** a large, reinforced box or chest, used in traveling or for storage, as to hold clothing and personal effects **7** a large, long, boxlike pipe, shaft, etc. for conveying air, water, etc. **8** [*pl.*] TRUNK HOSE ☆**9** [*pl.*] shorts worn by men or boys for athletics, esp. for boxing or swimming ☆**10** *short for* TRUNK LINE ☆**11** a compartment in an automobile, usually in the rear, for holding a spare tire, luggage, etc. **12** *Archit.* the shaft of a column **13** *Naut.* *a)* the part of a cabin that extends above a boat's deck *b)* a boxlike structure for housing a boat's centerboard

trunk·fish (truŋk′fish′) ***n.***, *pl.* **-fish′** or **-fish′es** (see FISH) any of a family (Ostraciidae, order Tetraodontiformes) of tropical bony fishes having the body encased in fused, bony plates, with only the mouth, eyes, fins, and tail projecting through

trunk hose full, baggy breeches reaching about halfway down the thigh, worn in the 16th and 17th cent.

☆**trunk line** a main line of a railroad, canal system, telephone system, etc.

trun·nel (trun′əl) ***n.*** *var. of* TREENAIL

trun·nion (trun′yən) ***n.*** ⟦Fr *trognon*, a stump, trunk⟧ **1** either of two projecting pivots, located on each side of a cannon or its mount, by which the muzzle is raised and lowered **2** either of any similar pair of pins or pivots

truss (trus) ***vt.*** ⟦ME *trussen* < OFr *trousser*, to bundle together, pack < ? VL **torsare* < **torsus*, for L *tortus*, pp. of *torquere*, to twist: see TORT⟧ **1** to tie, bind, or bundle: often with *up* **2** to skewer or bind the wings and legs of (a fowl) before cooking **3** to support or strengthen with a truss ***—n.*** ⟦ME *trusse* < OFr *trousse* < *trousser*⟧ **1** a bundle or pack; specif., in England, a bundle of hay in any of various unit weights **2** an iron fitting for securing a yard to a mast **3** an architectural bracket or modillion **4** a flower cluster growing at the tip of a stem **5** a rigid framework of beams, girders, struts, bars, etc., usually triangular in configuration, for supporting a roof, bridge, etc. **6** an appliance for giving support in cases of rupture or hernia, usually consisting of a pad on a special belt **—truss′er *n.***

☆**truss bridge** a bridge supported chiefly by trusses

truss·ing (trus′iŋ) ***n.*** **1** the beams, rods, etc. forming a truss **2** constructional trusses collectively, often, specif., those used in a structure

trust (trust) ***n.*** ⟦ME < ON *traust*, trust, lit., firmness < IE **drou-sto-* < base **deru-*, tree > TREE, TRUE + *sto-*, standing < base **sta-*, to STAND⟧ **1** *a)* firm belief or confidence in the honesty, integrity, reliability, justice, etc. of another person or thing; faith; reliance *b)* the person or thing trusted **2** confident expectation, anticipation, or hope [to have *trust* in the future] **3** *a)* the fact of having confidence placed in one *b)* responsibility or obligation resulting from this **4** keeping; care; custody **5** something entrusted to one; charge, duty, etc. **6** confidence in a purchaser's intention or future ability to pay for goods or services delivered; credit [to sell on *trust*] **7** *a)* an industrial or business combination, now illegal in the U.S., in which management and control of the member corporations are vested in a single board of trustees, who are thus able to control a market, absorb or eliminate competition, fix prices, etc. *b)* CARTEL (sense 2): see also MONOPOLY **8** *Law* *a)* an arrangement by which property is put under the ownership and control of a person (*trustee*) who bears the responsibility of administering it for the benefit of another (*beneficiary*) *b)* the confidence reposed in a trustee *c)* the whole of the property held in trust *d)* a trustee or group of trustees *e)* the beneficiary's right to property held in trust **9** [Archaic] trustworthiness; loyalty ***—vi.*** ⟦ME *trusten*, altered (based on the n.) < ON *treysta*, to trust, confide < base of *traust*⟧ **1** to have trust or faith; place reliance; be confident **2** to hope **3** to give business credit ***—vt.*** **1** *a)* to believe in the honesty, integrity, justice, etc. of; have confidence in *b)* to rely or depend on [*trust* them to be on time] **2** to commit (something) *to* a person's care **3** to put something confidently in the charge of [to *trust* a lawyer with one's case] **4** to allow to do something without fear of the outcome [to *trust* a child to go to the store] **5** to believe or suppose **6** to expect confidently; hope **7** to grant business credit to ***—adj.*** **1** relating to a trust or trusts **2** held in trust **3** managing for an owner; acting as trustee **—SYN.** BELIEF, MONOPOLY, RELY **—in trust** in the condition of being entrusted to another's care **—trust to** to rely on **—trust′a·ble *adj.*** **—trust′er *n.***

trust account **1** TRUST (***n.*** 8c) **2** a savings account in a bank, the balance of which, at the death of the depositor, goes to a predesignated beneficiary

trust·bust·er (trust′bus′tər) ***n.*** a person, esp. a federal official, who seeks to dissolve corporate trusts through the vigorous enforcement of antitrust laws **—trust′bust′ing *n.***

☆**trust company** **1** a company formed to act as trustee **2** a bank organized to handle trusts and carry on all banking operations except the issuance of bank notes

trust·ee (trus tē′) ***n.*** **1** a person to whom another's property or the management of another's property is entrusted **2** a nation under whose authority a trust territory is placed **3** any of a group or board of persons appointed to manage the affairs of an institution or organization ☆**4** in some U.S. states, a person in whose hands the property of a debtor is attached by means of garnishment; garnishee ***—vt.*** **-eed′**, **-ee′ing** **1** to commit (property or management) to a trustee or trustees ☆**2** to attach by means of garnishment

trust·ee·ship (trus tē′ship) ***n.*** **1** the position or function of a trustee **2** *a)* a commission from the United Nations to a country to administer a trust territory *b)* the condition or fact of being a trust territory

trust·er (trus′tər) ***n.*** *Law var. of* TRUSTOR

trust·ful (trust′fəl) ***adj.*** full of trust; ready to confide or believe; trusting **—trust′ful·ly *adv.*** **—trust′ful·ness *n.***

trust fund money, securities, etc. held in trust

trust·ing (trus′tiŋ) ***adj.*** that trusts; trustful **—trust′ing·ly *adv.*** **—trust′ing·ness *n.***

trust·less (trust′lis) ***adj.*** [Now Rare] **1** not to be trusted; untrustworthy **2** not trusting; distrustful

trus·tor (trus′tər, trə stôr′) *n. Law* SETTLOR (sense 2)
trust territory a territory placed under the administrative authority of a country by the United Nations
trust·wor·thy (trust′wur′thē) *adj.* **-thi·er, -thi·est** worthy of trust; dependable; reliable —***SYN.*** RELIABLE —**trust′wor′thi·ly** *adv.* —**trust′wor′thi·ness** *n.*
trust·y (trus′tē; *for n., also,* trus tē′) *adj.* **trust′i·er, trust′i·est** 1 that can be relied upon; dependable; trustworthy 2 *obs. var. of* TRUSTFUL —*n., pl.* **trust′ies** ☆a trusted person; specif., a convict granted special privileges as a trustworthy person —***SYN.*** RELIABLE —**trust′i·ly** *adv.* —**trust′i·ness** *n.*
truth (tro͞oth) *n., pl.* **truths** (tro͞o*th*z, tro͞oths) ⟦ME *treuthe* < OE *treowth*: see TRUE & -TH[1]⟧ 1 the quality or state of being true; specif., *a)* [Obs.] loyalty; trustworthiness *b)* sincerity; genuineness; honesty *c)* the quality of being in accordance with experience, facts, or reality; conformity with fact *d)* reality; actual existence *e)* agreement with a standard, rule, etc.; correctness; accuracy 2 that which is true; statement, etc. that accords with fact or reality 3 an established or verified fact, principle, etc. 4 a particular belief or teaching regarded by the speaker as the true one: often with *the* —**in truth** truly; in fact —**of a truth** certainly —**(if) truth be told** in fact; actually

SYN.—**truth** suggests conformity with the facts or with reality, either as an idealized abstraction ["What is *truth?*" said Pilate] or in actual application to statements, ideas, acts, etc. [there is no *truth* in that rumor]; **veracity**, as applied to persons or to their utterances, connotes habitual adherence to the truth [I cannot doubt your *veracity*]; **verity**, as applied to things, connotes correspondence with fact or with reality [the *verity* of that thesis]; **verisimilitude**, as applied to literary or artistic representations, suggests a degree of plausibility sufficient to induce audience belief [the characterizations in that novel lack *verisimilitude*] —***ANT.*** **falseness, falsity**

Truth (tro͞oth), **So·journ·er** (sō′jur′nər) (orig. a slave called *Isabella*) 1797?-1883; U.S. abolitionist & women's-rights advocate
truth·ful (tro͞oth′fəl) *adj.* 1 telling the truth; presenting the facts; veracious; honest 2 corresponding with fact or reality, as in artistic representation —**truth′ful·ly** *adv.* —**truth′ful·ness** *n.*
truth quark *Particle Physics* TOP QUARK
☆**truth serum** an anesthetic or hypnotic, as thiopental sodium, regarded as tending to make a subject responsive while being questioned: also **truth drug**
truth table 1 a table showing all the possible combinations of the variables in an expression in symbolic logic and their resulting truth or falsity 2 a similar table showing relationships between input to and output from a computer circuit
try (trī) *vt.* **tried, try′ing** ⟦ME *trien* < OFr *trier* < ? VL **tritare,* to cull out, grind < L *tritus,* pp. of *terere,* to rub, thresh grain: see TRITE⟧ 1 [Obs.] to separate; set apart 2 *a)* to melt or render (fat, etc.) to get (the oil) *b)* to extract or refine (metal, etc.) by heating: usually with *out* 3 [Now Rare] to settle (a matter, quarrel, etc.) by a test or contest; fight out 4 *a)* to examine and decide (a case) in a law court *b)* to determine legally the guilt or innocence of (a person) *c)* to preside as judge at the trial of (a case or person) 5 to put to the proof; test 6 to subject to trials, annoyance, etc.; afflict [Job was sorely *tried*] 7 to subject to a severe test or strain [rigors that *try* one's stamina] 8 to test the operation or effect of; experiment with; make a trial of [to *try* a new recipe] 9 to attempt to find out or determine by experiment or effort [to *try* one's fortune in another city] 10 to make an effort at; attempt; endeavor: followed by an infinitive [*try* to remember] or, informally, by *and* used in place of *to* as the sign of the infinitive [*try* and remember] 11 to attempt to open (a door or window) in testing to see whether it is locked 12 [Obs.] to find to be so by test or experience; prove —*vi.* 1 to make an effort, attempt, or endeavor 2 to make an experiment —*n., pl.* **tries** 1 the act or an instance of trying; attempt; effort; trial 2 *Rugby* a scoring play in which the ball is grounded on or behind the opponent's goal line —**try on** to test the fit or appearance of (an item of clothing, jewelry, etc.) by putting it on —**try one's hand at** to attempt (to do something), esp. for the first time —**try out** ☆1 to test the quality, result, value, etc. of, as by putting to use; experiment with ☆2 to test one's fitness, as for a job, a place on an athletic team, a role in a play, etc.

SYN.—**try** is commonly the simple, direct word for putting forth effort to do something [*try* to come], but specifically it connotes experimentation in testing or proving something [I'll *try* your recipe]; **attempt**, somewhat more formal, suggests a setting out to accomplish something but often connotes failure [he had *attempted* to take his life]; **endeavor** suggests exertion and determined effort in the face of difficulties [we shall *endeavor* to recover your loss]; **essay** connotes a tentative experimenting to test the feasibility of something difficult [she will not *essay* the high jump]; **strive** suggests great, earnest exertion to accomplish something [*strive* to win]; **struggle** suggests a violent striving to overcome obstacles or to free oneself from an impediment [I *struggled* to reach the top]

try·ing (trī′iŋ) *adj.* that tries one's patience; annoying; exasperating; irksome —**try′ing·ly** *adv.*
☆**try·out** (trī′out′) *n.* 1 an opportunity to prove, or a test to determine, fitness for a place on an athletic team, a role in a play, etc. 2 a performance of a play before its official opening, as to test audience reaction
tryp·a·no·some (trip′ə nə sōm′, tri pan′ə-) *n.* ⟦< ModL *Trypanosoma* < Gr *trypanon,* borer (see TREPAN[1]) + ModL *-soma,* -SOME[3]⟧ any of a genus (*Trypanosoma*) of zooflagellates that live as parasites in the blood of human beings and other vertebrates, are usually transmitted by an insect bite, and often cause serious diseases, as sleeping sickness or Chagas' disease
tryp·a·no·so·mi·a·sis (trip′ə nə sō mī′ə sis, tri pan′ə-) *n.* ⟦ModL: see prec. & -IASIS⟧ any disease caused by a trypanosome
tryp·sin (trip′sin) *n.* ⟦Ger, prob. < Gr *tryein,* to wear away (see TRITE) + Ger *(pe)psin*: see PEPSIN⟧ 1 a proteolytic enzyme in the pancreatic juice that hydrolyzes proteins to smaller polypeptides 2 any of several similar enzymes —**tryp′tic** (-tik) *adj.*
tryp·sin·o·gen (trip sin′ə jən) *n.* ⟦prec. + -O- + -GEN⟧ the inactive precursor of trypsin, secreted by the pancreas
tryp·ta·mine (trip′tə mēn′) *n.* ⟦< fol. + AMINE⟧ *Biochem.* an amine, $C_{10}H_{12}N_2$, derived from tryptophan and closely related to serotonin
tryp·to·phan (trip′tə fan′) *n.* ⟦TRYPT(IC) + -O- + -PHAN(E)⟧ a white, aromatic, crystalline, essential amino acid, $C_6H_4NHCHCCH_2CH(NH_2)COOH$, produced synthetically and in digestion by the action of trypsin on proteins: see AMINO ACID: also **tryp′to·phane′** (-fān′)
try·sail (trī′sāl′; *naut.,* -səl) *n.* ⟦< naut. phr. *a try,* the position of lying to in a storm⟧ a small, sturdy, triangular sail rigged fore and aft on a gaff, esp. one used in place of the mainsail in stormy weather
try square an instrument consisting of two pieces set at right angles, used for testing the accuracy of square work and for marking off right angles
tryst (trist) *n.* ⟦ME *triste,* var. of *tristre* < OFr, hunting station, hence hunting rendezvous < ?⟧ *a)* an appointment made secretly by lovers to meet at a specified time and place *b)* any such meeting *c)* [Archaic] the place of such a meeting (usually **trysting place**) —*vi.* [Archaic] to keep a tryst —**tryst′er** *n.*
TSA *abbrev.* Transportation Security Administration
tsad·dik (tsä′dik) *n., pl.* **tsad·dik·im** (tsä dē′kim) *alt. sp. of* ZADDIK
tsa·di (tsä′dē) *n. var. of* SADHE
Tsang·po (tsäŋ′pō′) *a former transliteration of* ZANGBO
tsar (tsär, zär) *n. var. of* CZAR (sense 1) —**tsar′dom** *n.* —**tsar′ism′** *n.* —**tsar′ist** *adj., n.*
tsar·e·vitch (tsär′ə vich, zär′-) *n. var. of* CZAREVITCH
tsa·rev·na (tsä′rev′nə, zä-) *n. var. of* CZAREVNA
tsa·ri·na (tsä rē′nə, zä-) *n. var. of* CZARINA
Tsa·ri·tsyn (tsä rē′tsin) *name for* VOLGOGRAD: used until 1925
Tschai·kow·sky (chī kôf′skē) *alt. sp. of* TCHAIKOVSKY
tset·se fly (tset′sē, tsēt′-, set′-, sēt′-, tēt′-) ⟦Bantu *tsetse,* lit., fly that kills animals⟧ any of a family (Glossinidae) of small dipterous flies of central and S Africa, including species that carry the trypanosomes that cause nagana and sleeping sickness
TSgt *abbrev.* Technical Sergeant
Tshi·lu·ba (chē lo͞o′bə) *n.* LUBA (sense 2)
☆**T-shirt** (tē′shurt′) *n.* ⟦so named because shaped somewhat like a T when lying flat⟧ 1 a collarless, cotton undershirt with short sleeves 2 a similar pullover knit sport shirt Also written **t-shirt**
tsim·mes (tsim′əs) *n.* [Informal] *alt. sp. of* TZIMMES
Tsi·nan (tsē′nän′, jē′-) *a former transliteration of* JINAN
Tsing·hai (tsiŋ′hī′, chiŋ′-) *a former transliteration of* QINGHAI
Tsing·tao (tsiŋ′tou′, -dou′; chiŋ′-) *a former transliteration of* QINGDAO
Tsin·ling Shan (tsin′liŋ′ shän′; chin′-, jin′-) *a former transliteration of* QINLING SHAN
Tsi·tsi·har (tsē′tsē′här′, chē′chē′-) *a former transliteration of* QIQIHAR
tsk (*for n. and v.* tisk; *for interj., see below*) *interj., n.* (a sound) used to express disapproval, genuine or mock sympathy, etc.: a click, or sucking sound, made by touching the tongue to the hard palate and rapidly withdrawing it —*vi.* **tsked, tsk′ing** to utter this sound
tsor·is (tsôr′is, tsoor′-) *n.* ⟦Yiddish, pl. of *tsore,* calamity < Heb *tsarāh*⟧ trouble, distress, woe, misery, etc.: also sp. **tsor′es** or **tsour′is**
tsp *abbrev.* 1 teaspoon(s) 2 teaspoonful(s)
T square a T-shaped straightedge with a short, thick crosspiece that fits over the edge of a drawing board, used in drawing parallel lines
TSS *abbrev.* toxic shock syndrome
☆**T-strap** (tē′strap′) *n.* 1 a T-shaped strap over the instep of a shoe 2 a woman's or girl's shoe with such a strap
tsu·na·mi (tso͞o nä′mē, so͞o-) *n., pl.* **-mis** or **-mi** ⟦Jpn < *tsu,* a harbor + *nami,* a wave⟧ a huge sea wave caused by a great disturbance under an ocean, as a strong earthquake or volcanic eruption: see TIDAL WAVE —**tsu·na′mic** (-mik) *adj.*

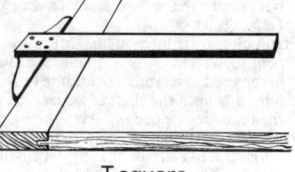

T square

tsur·is (tso͞o′ris, tsoor′is) *n. var. of* TSORIS
Tsu·shi·ma (tso͞o′shē mä′; tso͞o shē′mə) islands of Japan in the Korea Strait, between Kyushu & Korea: 272 sq mi (704 sq km)
tsu·tsu·ga·mu·shi disease (tso͞o′tso͞o gə mo͞o′shē) ⟦Jpn < *tsutsuga,* danger, disease, harm + *mushi,* insect⟧ SCRUB TYPHUS
Tsve·ta·ye·va (sfə tä′yə və), **Ma·ri·na (Ivanovna)** (mə rē′nə) 1892-1941; Russ. poet, essayist, & critic
Tt *abbrev. Bible* Titus
TTY[1] (tē′tē′wī′) *n.* ⟦see fol.⟧ a device with an electronic display and a keyboard, connected to a telephone line, for sending and receiving text messages, as by the deaf

TTY[2] *abbrev.* teletypewriter
Tu *abbrev.* Tuesday
TU *abbrev.* trade union
Tu·a·mo·tu Archipelago (to͞o'ə mōt'o͞o) group of islands of French Polynesia: 280 sq mi (725 sq km)
tu·an (to͞o än') *n.* ⟦Malay⟧ sir or mister: a title of respect for gentlemen in Indonesia and Malaysia
Tua·reg (twä'reg') *n.* ⟦< Ar *tawārig*, pl. of *targwī*: meaning unknown⟧ **1** *pl.* **-regs'** or **-reg'** a member of a Berber people of the W and central Sahara **2** the variety of Berber spoken by this people
tu·a·ta·ra (to͞o'ə tä'rə) *n.* ⟦Maori *tuatàra* < *tua*, back (< Proto-Polynesian **tu'a*) + *tara*, spine (< Proto-Polynesian **tala*, sharp object)⟧ either of two primitive, amphibious, lizardlike reptiles (*Sphenodon punctatus* or *S. guntheri*) of the SW Pacific, with a row of spines along the back and a well-developed third eye: they are the only rhynchocephalians still in existence
tub (tub) *n.* ⟦ME *tubbe* < MDu; akin to MLowG *tobbe*, EFris *tubbe*⟧ **1** *a)* a round, broad, open, wooden container, usually formed of staves and hoops fastened around a flat bottom *b)* any similarly large, open container of metal, stone, etc., as for washing *c)* a small, round container [*a tub of margarine*] *d)* as much as a tub will hold **2** a bucket or tram for carrying coal, ore, etc. in a mine **3** *a)* *short for* BATHTUB *b)* [Brit. Informal] a bath in a tub **4** [Informal] a slow-moving, clumsy ship or boat — *vt., vi.* **tubbed, tub'bing 1** [Informal] to wash in a tub **2** [Brit. Informal] to bathe (oneself) —**tub'ba·ble** *adj.* —**tub'ber** *n.*
tu·ba (to͞o'bə, tyo͞o'-) *n., pl.* **tu'bas** or **tu'bae** (-bē) ⟦L, a trumpet⟧ **1** in ancient Rome, a straight war trumpet **2** any of a group of brass instruments with a conical bore and three to five valves, esp. the large contrabass member
tu·ba·ist (to͞o'bə ist, tyo͞o'-) *n.* a person who plays the tuba
tub·al (to͞o'bəl, tyo͞o'-) *adj.* **1** of or in a tube **2** of or within a fallopian tube [*a tubal pregnancy*]
Tu·bal-cain (to͞o'bəl kān', tyo͞o'-) *n.* *Bible* a worker in brass and iron: Gen. 4:22
tubal ligation a medical procedure in which the fallopian tubes are cut and surgically tied so that ova cannot become fertilized or reach the uterus
tu·bate (to͞o'bāt', tyo͞o'-) *adj.* having or forming a tube or tubes; tubular
tub·by (tub'ē) *adj.* **-bi·er, -bi·est 1** shaped like a tub **2** [Informal] fat and short: said of a person —**tub'bi·ness** *n.*

tuba

tub chair ⟦so named from its rounded back and ample seating space⟧ a usually low-backed easy chair with arms even with the back or sloping up to it in a continuous curve
tube (to͞ob, tyo͞ob) *n.* ⟦Fr < L *tubus*, a pipe⟧ **1** *a)* a hollow cylinder or pipe of metal, glass, rubber, etc., usually long in proportion to its diameter, used for conveying fluids, etc. *b)* an instrument, part, organ, etc. resembling a tube [*bronchial tubes, eustachian tubes*] *c)* a fallopian tube (*usually used in pl.*) **2** a rubber casing inflated with air and used, esp. formerly, with an outer casing to form an automotive tire **3** a cylindrical container made of thin, pliable metal, plastic, etc., fitted at one end with a screw cap, and used for holding pastes or semiliquids, which can be squeezed out ☆**4** *short for: a)* ELECTRON TUBE *b)* VACUUM TUBE **5** *a)* a tubular tunnel for a railroad, subway, etc. *b)* [Brit.] an underground electric railway; subway **6** *Bot.* the lower, united part of a gamopetalous corolla or a gamosepalous calyx **7** *Elec.* the tubular space bounded by the lines of electric or magnetic force passing through every point on a closed curve on the outside of a charged body: in full **tube of flux** or **tube of force** —*vt.* **tubed, tub'ing 1** to provide with, place in, or pass through a tube or tubes **2** to make tubular —**down the tube** (or **tubes**) [Informal] in or into a condition of failure, defeat, etc. —☆**the tube** ⟦in ref. to the CATHODE-RAY TUBE, or PICTURE TUBE⟧ [Informal] television —**tube'like'** *adj.*
tube foot any of numerous small, water-filled, fleshy tubes in most echinoderms, projecting outside the body, often ending in a suction disc, and used in locomotion, securing food, etc.
☆**tube·less tire** (to͞ob'lis, tyo͞ob'-) a pneumatic tire without an inner tube: see TIRE[2]
tube·nose (to͞ob'nōz', tyo͞ob'-) *n.* any of an order (Procellariiformes) of birds having tubular nostrils, including the shearwaters, petrels, and albatrosses
tube pan a deep, round pan with a hollow tube in the center, for baking cakes
tu·ber (to͞o'bər, tyo͞o'-) *n.* ⟦L, lit., a swelling, knob, truffle < IE **teubh-* < base **tēu-*, to swell > THUMB, L *tumere*, to swell⟧ **1** a short, thickened, fleshy part of an underground stem, as a potato: new plants develop from the buds, or eyes, that grow in the axils of the minute scale leaves of a tuber **2** *Anat.* a tubercle or swelling
tu·ber·cle (to͞o'bər kəl, tyo͞o'-) *n.* ⟦L *tuberculum*, dim. of *tuber*: see prec.⟧ any small, rounded projection or process; specif., *a)* *Bot.* any of the wartlike growths on the roots of some plants *b)* *Anat.* a knoblike elevation, as on a bone *c)* *Med.* any abnormal hard nodule or swelling; specif., the typical nodular lesion of tuberculosis
tubercle bacillus the bacterium (*Mycobacterium tuberculosis*) causing tuberculosis
tu·ber·cu·lar (to͝o bur'kyə lər, tə-) *adj.* ⟦< L *tuberculum* (see TUBERCLE) + -AR⟧ **1** of, like, or having a tubercle or tubercles **2** of, relating to, or having tuberculosis **3** caused by the tubercle bacillus —*n.* a person having tuberculosis
tu·ber·cu·late (-lit, -lāt') *adj.* ⟦ModL *tuberculatus*: see TUBERCLE & -ATE[1]⟧ **1** having or characterized by a tubercle or tubercles: also **tu·ber'cu·lat'ed 2** TUBERCULAR —**tu·ber'cu·la'tion** *n.*
tu·ber·cu·lin (to͝o bur'kyə lin, tə-) *n.* ⟦< L *tuberculum* (see TUBERCLE) + -IN[1]⟧ a sterile liquid preparation made from the growth products or extracts of a tubercle bacillus culture and injected into the skin as a test for tuberculosis
tu·ber·cu·lo- (to͝o bur'kyə lō', tə-) ⟦< L *tuberculum*: see TUBERCLE⟧ *combining form* tubercular: also, before a vowel, **tubercul-**
tu·ber·cu·loid (to͝o bur'kyə loid', tə-) *adj.* resembling a tubercle or tuberculosis
tu·ber·cu·lo·sis (to͝o bur'kyə lō'sis, tə-) *n.* ⟦ModL: see TUBERCLE & -OSIS⟧ an infectious disease caused by the tubercle bacillus and characterized by the formation of tubercles in various tissues of the body; specif., tuberculosis of the lungs; pulmonary phthisis
tu·ber·cu·lous (-bur'kyə ləs) *adj.* TUBERCULAR
tube·rose[1] (to͞ob'rōz', tyo͞ob'-) *n.* ⟦ModL *tuberosa* < L *tuberosus*, TUBEROUS⟧ a perennial Mexican plant (*Polianthes tuberosa*) of the agave family, growing from a tuber or bulb and having white, sweet-scented flowers borne in racemes
tu·ber·ose[2] (to͞o'bər ōs', tyo͞o'-) *adj.* TUBEROUS
tu·ber·os·i·ty (to͞o'bər äs'ə tē, tyo͞o'-) *n., pl.* **-ties** ⟦Fr *tuberosité* < VL *tuberositas*⟧ **1** the quality or condition of being tuberous **2** a rounded swelling or projection, as on a bone for the attachment of a muscle or tendon
tu·ber·ous (to͞o'bər əs, tyo͞o'-) *adj.* ⟦Fr *tubéreux* < L *tuberosus*: see TUBER & -OUS⟧ **1** covered with wartlike swellings; knobby **2** *Bot.* of, like, or having a tuber
tuberous root a tuberlike root without buds or scale leaves, as of the dahlia —**tu'ber·ous-root'ed** *adj.*
☆**tube sock** a stretchable sock in the form of a long tube with no shaped heel
tube top a one-piece, tight-fitting, sleeveless and strapless woman's garment for the upper body
tu·bi·fex (to͞o'bə feks', tyo͞o'-) *n., pl.* **-fex'es** or **-fex'** ⟦ModL < L *tubus*, tube + *-fex* < *facere*, to make, DO[1]⟧ any of a genus (*Tubifex*) of small, reddish, freshwater, oligochaete worms, often living in chimneylike tubes: found esp. in polluted waters and often used as food for aquarium fish
tub·ing (to͞o'biŋ, tyo͞o'-) *n.* **1** a series or system of tubes **2** material in the form of a tube **3** a piece or length of tube **4** the activity or sport of floating down a stream or river in a large inner tube
tub·ist (to͞o'bist, tyo͞o'-) *n.* a person who plays the tuba
Tub·man (tub'mən) **1 Harriet** 1820?-1913; U.S. abolitionist **2 William V(acanarat) S(hadrach)** 1895-1971; president of Liberia (1944-71)
tub-thump·er (tub'thump'ər) *n.* ⟦orig., a preacher who pounds the pulpit for emphasis < TUB, used as a derogatory or jocular term for a pulpit, esp. that of a nonconformist preacher⟧ a speaker or advocate characterized by speech or rhetoric that is passionate, pompous, blustering, etc. —**tub'-thump'ing** *adj., n.*
tu·bu·lar (to͞o'byə lər, tyo͞o'-) *adj.* ⟦< L *tubulus*, dim. of *tubus*, tube, pipe + -AR⟧ **1** of or shaped like a tube **2** made or furnished with a tube or tubes **3** sounding as if produced by blowing through a tube —**tu'bu·lar'i·ty** (-lar'ə tē) *n.* —**tu'bu·lar·ly** *adv.*
tu·bu·late (-lit, -lāt'; *for v.*, -lāt') *adj.* ⟦L *tubulatus*⟧ TUBULAR (senses 1 & 2) —*vt.* **-lat'ed, -lat'ing** to shape into or provide with a tube —**tu'bu·la'tion** *n.*
tu·bule (to͞o'byo͞ol', tyo͞o'-) *n.* ⟦< L *tubulus*, dim. of *tubus*, tube⟧ a small tube; minute tubular structure in an animal or plant
tu·bu·li- (to͞o'byə lə, tyo͞o'-) ⟦< L *tubulus*: see prec.⟧ *combining form* tubule or tubular [*tubuliflorous*]
tu·bu·li·flo·rous (to͞o'byə lə flôr'əs, tyo͞o'-) *adj.* ⟦prec. + -FLOROUS⟧ having flowers all or some of whose corollas are tubular: said of certain plants of the composite family
tu·bu·lin (to͞o'byə lin', tyo͞o'-) *n.* a protein in cells that polymerizes to form tiny tubules that are important in forming microtubules
tu·bu·lous (to͞o'byə ləs, tyo͞o'-) *adj.* ⟦TUBUL(E) + -OUS⟧ **1** TUBULAR (senses 1 & 2) **2** having small, tubelike flowers
tu·bu·lure (-lo͝or') *n.* ⟦Fr < L *tubulus*: see TUBULE & -URE⟧ a short tubular opening, as at the top of a retort
Tu·ca·na (to͞o kā'nə) *n.* ⟦ModL, TOUCAN⟧ a S constellation between Indus and Phoenix, containing the Small Magellanic Cloud
☆**tuch·is** (to͝okh'is, tuk'-) *n.* ⟦Yiddish < Heb *takhat*, under⟧ [Slang] the buttocks or anus: also sp. **tuch'as** or **tuch'us**
tuck[1] (tuk) *vt.* ⟦ME *tuken* < MDu *tucken*, to tuck & OE *tucian*, to ill-treat, lit., to tug, akin to Ger *zucken*, to jerk: for IE base see TUG⟧ **1** to pull up or gather up in a fold or folds; draw together so as to make shorter [*to tuck up one's skirt for wading*] **2** to sew a fold or folds in (a garment) **3** *a)* to thrust the edges of (a sheet, napkin, shirt, etc.) under or in, in order to make secure (usually with *up, in,* etc.) *b)* to cover or wrap snugly in or as in this way, as with bedclothes (usually with *in*) [*to tuck a child in for the night*] **4** to put or press snugly into a small space; cram; fit [*to tuck shoes in a suitcase*] **5** *a)* to put into an empty or convenient place *b)* to put into a secluded or isolated spot [*a cabin tucked in the hills*] **6** to put (one's legs) in the position of a TUCK[1] (*n.* 2) —*vi.* **1** to draw together; pucker **2**

to make tucks —*n.* 1 a sewed fold in a garment, for shortening or decoration 2 a position of the body, esp. in diving, in which the knees are drawn up tightly to the chest 3 [Brit. Slang] food; esp., sweets: used mainly by schoolchildren 4 [Informal] plastic surgery, esp. for cosmetic reasons, in which excess skin or fat is removed from the lower abdomen, from around the eyes, etc. —**tuck away** 1 to eat (something) heartily 2 to put aside or apart, as for future use —**tuck in** 1 to pull in or contract (one's chin, stomach, etc.) 2 [Chiefly Brit.] to eat (something) heartily: also **tuck into**

tuck[2] (tuk) *n.* ⟦Fr *estoc* < OFr *estoquier* < MDu *stocken*, to stick, pierce, poke < *stok*: see STOCK⟧ [Archaic] a rapier

tuck[3] (tuk, to͝ok) [Scot.] *vt.* ⟦ME *tukken* < NormFr *toker*, *toquer*, var. of OFr *toucher*, to TOUCH⟧ to beat or tap (a drum) —*n.* a beat or tap, as on a drum

☆**tuck**[4] (tuk) *n.* [Informal] *short for* TUXEDO

☆**tuck·a·hoe** (tuk′ə hō′) *n.* ⟦Virginia Algonquian *tockawhoughe*, type of arum root⟧ 1 [Historical] any of various roots and tubers, as of arum species, used as food by Algonquian peoples of Virginia 2 a brown, massive, underground, basidiomycetous fungus (*Poria cocos*) producing an edible, carbohydrate substance

tuck·er[1] (tuk′ər) *n.* ⟦ME *toukere*, person who dresses cloth stretched on tenterhooks < *touken*: see TUCK[1]⟧ 1 a person or device that makes tucks 2 *a)* a neck and shoulder covering worn with a low-cut bodice by women in the 17th and 18th cent. *b)* later, a detachable collar or chemisette of thin muslin, etc. 3 ⟦see TUCK IN (sense 2) at TUCK[1]⟧ [Austral. Slang] food

☆**tuck·er**[2] (tuk′ər) *vt.* ⟦prob. < TUCK[1], in obs. sense "to punish, rebuke"⟧ [Informal] to tire (*out*); weary

tuck·et (tuk′it) *n.* ⟦< TUCK[3]⟧ [Archaic] a flourish on a trumpet

tuck-in (tuk′in′) *n.* [Brit. Informal] a meal, esp. a hearty one

tuck-point (tuk′point′) *vt.* ⟦< *tuck*, the recess that is cleaned and filled, akin to TUCK[1] (*n.*)⟧ *Masonry* POINT (*vt.* 8)

Tuc·son (to͞o′sän′, to͞o sän′) ⟦Sp < Piman *tu-uk-so-on*, black base, referring to a dark stratum in a nearby mountain⟧ city in S Ariz.

Tu·cu·mán (to͞o′ko͞o män′) city in N Argentina: in full **San Mi·guel de Tucumán** (sän′ mē gel′ də)

-tude (to͞od, tyo͞od) ⟦Fr < L *-tudo* (gen. *-tudinis*)⟧ *suffix forming nouns* state, quality, or instance of being [*negritude*]

Tu·dor[1] (to͞o′dər, tyo͞o′-) *n.* name of the ruling family of England (1485-1603), descended from Owen Tudor —*adj.* designating or of a style of architecture popular under the Tudors: it is characterized by slightly rounded arches, shallow moldings, extensive half-timbered paneling, etc.

Tu·dor[2] (to͞o′dər, tyo͞o′-) 1 **Antony** (born *William Cook*) 1908-87; Brit. dancer & choreographer in the U.S. 2 **Owen** died 1461; Welsh nobleman: married the widow of Henry V

Tue or **Tues** *abbrev.* Tuesday

Tues·day (to͞oz′dā, tyo͞oz′-; *occas.*, -dē) *n.* ⟦ME *Twisdai* < OE *Tiwes dæg*, Tiu's day, rendering L *Martis dies*: see TIU & DAY⟧ the third day of the week: abbrev. *Tue, Tues, Tu*, or *T*

Tues·days (-dāz; *occas.*, -dēz) *adv.* during every Tuesday or most Tuesdays

tu·fa (to͞o′fə, tyo͞o′-) *n.* ⟦It *tufo*, *tufa*, kind of porous stone < L *tofus*, tuff, tufa⟧ any of various sedimentary rocks, as travertine, made up of deposits of calcium carbonate formed by evaporation or precipitation in or near a cave, spring, lake, etc. —**tu·fa′ceous** (-fā′shəs) *adj.*

tuff (tuf) *n.* ⟦Fr *tuf*, earlier *tufe*, *tuffe* < It *tufo*, prec.⟧ a porous igneous rock, usually stratified, formed by consolidation of volcanic ash, dust, etc. —**tuff·a′ceous** (-ā′shəs) *adj.*

tuf·fet (tuf′it) *n.* ⟦altered < fol.⟧ 1 a tuft of grass 2 a low stool

tuft (tuft) *n.* ⟦ME (with unhistoric *-t*) < OFr *tufe*, prob. < L *tufa*, a kind of helmet crest⟧ 1 a bunch of hairs, feathers, grass, etc. growing closely together or attached at the base 2 any similar cluster; specif., *a)* a clump of plants or trees *b)* the fluffy ball forming the end of any of the clusters of threads drawn tightly through a mattress, quilt, etc. to hold the padding in place *c)* a decorative button to which such a tuft is fastened —*vt.* 1 to provide or decorate with a tuft or tufts 2 to secure the padding of (a quilt, mattress, etc.) by regularly spaced tufts —*vi.* to grow in or form into tufts —**tuft′er** *n.* —**tuft′y** *adj.*

tuft·ed (tuf′tid) *adj.* 1 provided or decorated with tufts 2 formed into or growing in a tuft or tufts

tufted titmouse a gray and white titmouse (*Parus bicolor*) with a prominent crest, ranging across the E U.S.

tug (tug) *vi.* **tugged, tug′ging** ⟦ME *tuggen*, prob. < ON *toga*, to draw, pull, akin to OE *togian* (see TOW[1]), *teon*, to pull < IE base **deuk-*, to draw, pull > DUCT⟧ 1 to exert great effort in pulling; pull hard; drag; haul: often with *at* 2 to labor; toil; struggle —*vt.* 1 to pull at with great force; strain at 2 to drag; haul —*n.* 1 an act or instance of tugging; hard pull 2 a great effort or strenuous contest 3 a rope, chain, etc. used for tugging or pulling; esp., a trace of a harness 4 *short for* TUGBOAT —**SYN.** PULL —**tug′ger** *n.*

tug·boat (tug′bōt′) *n.* a small, sturdy, powerful boat used for towing or pushing ships, barges, etc., as in a harbor

tug of war 1 a contest in which two teams pull at opposite ends of a rope, each trying to drag the other across a central line 2 any power struggle between two parties Also **tug′-of-war′** *n.*

tu·grik (to͞o′grik) *n.* ⟦Mongolian *tögürig*, circle, disk, coin (prob. infl. by *duγuriγ*, circle, wheel⟧ the basic monetary unit of Mongolia: see the table of monetary units in the Reference Supplement

tu·i (to͞o′ē) *n.* ⟦Maori *tūī*⟧ a greenish-blue New Zealand honeyeater (*Prosthemadera novaeseelandiae*), with white feathers under the throat: it can mimic human speech

tuille (twēl) *n.* ⟦ME *toile* < MFr *tuile* < OFr *tiule* < L *tegula*: see TILE⟧ in medieval plate armor, any of the lower plates of the tasse, protecting the thigh

tu·i·tion (to͞o ish′ən, tyo͞o-) *n.* ⟦ME *tuicion* < OFr < L *tuitio*, protection < *tuitus*, pp. of *tueri*, to watch, protect⟧ 1 [Obs.] guardianship 2 the charge for instruction, esp. at a college or private school 3 [Chiefly Brit.] teaching; instruction —**tu·i′tion·al** *adj.*

Tu·la (to͞o′lə) city in W European Russia

☆**tu·la·re·mi·a** (to͞o′lə rē′mē ə, tyo͞o′-) *n.* ⟦ModL, after *Tulare* County, Calif. (< Sp *tulares*, pl., regions overgrown with tules: see fol.) + -EMIA⟧ an infectious disease of rodents, esp. rabbits, caused by a bacterium (*Francisella tularensis*) and transmitted to humans in handling the flesh of infected animals or by the bite of certain insects: it is characterized in humans by an irregular fever, aching, inflammation of the lymph glands, etc.: also sp. **tu′la·rae′mi·a** —**tu′la·re′mic** *adj.*

☆**tu·le** (to͞o′lē) *n.* ⟦Sp < Nahuatl *to:lin*, cattail⟧ either of two large bulrushes (*Scirpus acutus* or *S. validus*) found in lakes and marshes of the SW U.S.

tu·lip (to͞o′lip, tyo͞o′-) *n.* ⟦Fr *tulipe* (earlier *tulipan*) < Turk *tülbend*, TURBAN: from the flower's resemblance to a turban⟧ 1 any of various bulb plants (genus *Tulipa*) of the lily family, mostly spring-blooming, with long, broad, pointed leaves and, usually, a single large, cup-shaped, variously colored flower 2 the flower or bulb

☆**tulip tree** a North American forest tree (*Liriodendron tulipifera*) of the magnolia family, with tulip-shaped, greenish-yellow flowers and conelike fruit: also called **tulip poplar**

☆**tu·lip·wood** (-wood′) *n.* 1 the light, soft wood of the tulip tree 2 *a)* any of several woods with stripes or streaks of color *b)* any tree having such wood

tulle (to͞ol) *n.* ⟦after *Tulle*, city in France, where first made⟧ a thin, fine netting of silk, rayon, nylon, etc., used as for veils and scarves

Tul·ly (tul′ē) *former Eng. name for* Marcus Tullius CICERO

Tul·sa (tul′sə) ⟦< Creek town name; akin to TALLAHASSEE⟧ city in NE Okla., on the Arkansas River —**Tul′san** *adj., n.*

tum·ble (tum′bəl) *vi.* **-bled, -bling** ⟦ME *tumblen*, freq. of *tumben* < OE *tumbian*, to fall, jump, dance; akin to Ger *tummeln*, *taumeln* < OHG **tumalon*, freq. of *tumon*, to turn < IE base **dheu-*, to be turbid > DULL⟧ 1 to do somersaults, handsprings, or similar acrobatic or gymnastic feats 2 *a)* to fall suddenly, clumsily, or helplessly *b)* to fall or decline suddenly, as from power, high value, etc. *c)* to come down in ruins; collapse 3 to stumble or trip 4 to toss about or roll around 5 to move, go, issue, etc. in a hasty, awkward, or disorderly manner 6 [Informal] to have sudden awareness or understanding of some situation: with *to* —*vt.* 1 to cause to tumble; make fall, overthrow, topple, roll over, etc. 2 to put into disorder by or as by tossing here and there; disarrange 3 to whirl in a TUMBLER (sense 10) —*n.* 1 the act or an instance of tumbling; specif., *a)* a somersault, handspring, etc. *b)* a fall or decline *c)* a stumble 2 disorder; confusion 3 a confused heap —**give** (or **get**) **a tumble** [Informal] to give (or get) some favorable or affectionate notice, attention, etc.

☆**tum·ble·bug** (tum′bəl bug′) *n.* any of several dung beetles that roll and bury in soil balls of dung, upon which the females deposit their eggs and in which the larvae develop

tum·ble·down (-doun′) *adj.* ready to tumble down; dilapidated

tum·bler (tum′blər) *n.* 1 an acrobat or gymnast who does somersaults, handsprings, etc. 2 [Historical] a dog, such as a small greyhound, trained to seize rabbits after distracting them by lurching about 3 a kind of pigeon that does somersaults in flight 4 *a)* an ordinary drinking glass without foot or stem: orig., such a glass with a rounded or pointed bottom, that would tumble over when set down *b)* its contents 5 the part of a gunlock through which the mainspring acts upon the hammer 6 a lever, pin, etc., whose position within a lock must be changed, as by a key or dial, in order to release the bolt 7 a projecting piece, as on a revolving or rocking part, that strikes and moves another part 8 a part moving a gear into place in an automobile transmission 9 an easily tipped toy that rights itself because of the way it is weighted 10 *a)* a device for tumbling laundered clothes about in hot air until they are dry *b)* TUMBLING BOX

☆**tum·ble·weed** (tum′bəl wēd′) *n.* any of a number of plants, as the pigweed or Russian thistle, that break off near the ground in autumn and are blown about by the wind

tumbling box (*or* **barrel**) a revolving box or drum into which loose materials are loaded and tumbled about, as for mixing, polishing, etc.

tum·brel or **tum·bril** (tum′brəl) *n.* ⟦ME *tomberel* < MFr, tip cart < *tomber*, to fall, tumble, leap < OHG *tumon*: see TUMBLE⟧ 1 a farmer's tip cart, esp. for dung 2 any of the carts used to carry the condemned to the guillotine during the French Revolution

tu·me·fa·cient (to͞o′mə fā′shənt, tyo͞o′-) *adj.* ⟦L *tumefaciens*, prp. of *tumefacere*: see TUMEFY⟧ causing or tending to cause swelling

tu·me·fac·tion (to͞o′mə fak′shən, tyo͞o′-) *n.* ⟦MFr⟧ 1 a swelling up or becoming swollen 2 a swollen part

tu·me·fy (to͞o′mə fī′, tyo͞o′-) *vt., vi.* **-fied′, -fy′ing** ⟦Fr *tuméfier*, as if < L **tumeficere*, for *tumefacere*, to cause to swell < *tumere*, to swell (see TUMOR) + *facere*, to make, DO[1]⟧ to make or become swollen

tu·mes·cence (to͞o mes′əns, tyo͞o-) *n.* ⟦< L *tumescens*, prp. of *tumescere*, to swell up, inceptive of *tumere*, to swell: see TUMOR⟧ 1 a swelling; distention 2 a swollen or distended part —**tu·mes′cent** *adj.*

tu·mid (to͞o′mid, tyo͞o′-) *adj.* ⟦L *tumidus* < *tumere*, to swell: see TUMOR⟧ 1 swollen; bulging 2 inflated or pompous —**tu·mid′i·ty** *n.*, **tu′mid·ness** —**tu′mid·ly** *adv.*

☆**tumm·ler** or **tum·meler** (to͝om′lər) ***n.*** ⟦Yiddish < Ger < *tummeln,* to move about, bestir oneself: see TUMBLE⟧ an entertainer or social director whose function is to stimulate participation by the guests, as at a resort on the borscht circuit

tum·my (tum′ē) ***n.,*** *pl.* **-mies** ⟦orig. a child's term⟧ [Informal] the stomach or abdomen

tu·mor (to͞o′mər, tyo͞o′-) ***n.*** ⟦L, a swelling < *tumere,* to swell < IE base **tēu-,* to swell > THUMB⟧ **1** *a)* a swelling on some part of the body *b)* a mass of new tissue growth independent of its surrounding structures, having no physiological function; neoplasm: such tumors are classified as benign or malignant **2** [Obs.] high-flown language; bombast Brit. sp. **tu′mour** —**tu′mor·ous** ***adj.***

tumor necrosis factor a protein produced by macrophages in response to bacterial infection: a form made by genetic engineering is used in the treatment of cancer

tump (tump) ***n.*** ⟦< ?⟧ [Brit. Dial.] a small mound or clump

☆**tump·line** (tump′līn′) ***n.*** ⟦< earlier *tump* < *mattump* < a S New England Algonquian language⟧ a broad strap passed across the forehead and over the shoulders for carrying a load on the back

tu·mult (to͞o′mult, tyo͞o′-) ***n.*** ⟦ME *tumulte* < MFr < L *tumultus,* a swelling or surging up, tumult < *tumere,* to swell: see TUMOR⟧ **1** noisy commotion, as of a crowd; uproar **2** confusion; agitation; disturbance **3** great emotional disturbance; agitation of mind, etc.

tu·mul·tu·ous (to͞o mul′cho͞o əs, tyo͞o-, tə-; -mul′tyo͞o əs) ***adj.*** ⟦MFr < L *tumultuosus*⟧ **1** full of or characterized by tumult; wild and noisy; uproarious **2** making a tumult **3** greatly agitated —**tu·mul′tu·ous·ly** ***adv.*** —**tu·mul′tu·ous·ness** ***n.***

tu·mu·lus (to͞o′myə ləs, tyo͞o′-) ***n.,*** *pl.* **-li′** (-lī′) or **-lus·es** ⟦L, mound, hillock, akin to *tumere:* see TUMOR⟧ an artificial mound; esp., an ancient burial mound; barrow

tun (tun) ***n.*** ⟦ME *tonne* < OE *tunne,* large cask & OFr *tonne,* both < ML *tunna* < Celt base⟧ **1** a large cask, esp. for wine, beer, or ale **2** a measure of capacity for liquids, usually 252 wine gallons (954 liters) —***vt.*** **tunned, tun′ning** to put into or store in a tun or tuns

Tun *abbrev.* Tunisia

☆**tu·na**[1] (to͞o′nə, tyo͞o′-) ***n.,*** *pl.* **tu′na** or **tu′nas** ⟦AmSp < Sp *atún* < Ar *tūn* < L *thunnus:* see TUNNY⟧ **1** any of various, usually large, marine, scombroid, food and game fishes (esp. genus *Thunnus*), including the albacore **2** the flesh of various tunas or tunalike fishes, often canned as food: also called **tuna fish**

tu·na[2] (to͞o′nə, tyo͞o′-) ***n.*** ⟦Sp < Taino⟧ **1** any of various prickly pears (esp. *Opuntia tuna*), cultivated for their edible fruits **2** the fruit

tun·a·ble (to͞o′nə bəl, tyo͞o′-) ***adj.*** that can be tuned: also sp. **tune′a·ble** —**tun′a·ble·ness** ***n.*** —**tun′a·bly** ***adv.***

Tun·bridge Wells (tun′brij′) city & spa in Kent, SE England

tun·dra (tun′drə, to͝on′-) ***n.*** ⟦Russ, of Lapp orig.⟧ any of the vast, nearly level, treeless plains of the arctic regions

tune (to͞on, tyo͞on) ***n.*** ⟦ME, var. of *tone,* TONE⟧ **1** [Obs.] a sound or tone **2** *a)* a succession of musical tones forming a rhythmic, catchy whole; melody; air *b)* a musical setting of a hymn, psalm, poem, etc. **3** *a)* the condition of having correct musical pitch, or of being in key *b)* harmony; agreement; concord: now used chiefly in the phrases **in tune** and **out of tune** [a violin that is *in tune,* a person *out of tune* with the times] —***vt.*** **tuned, tun′ing 1** to adjust (a musical instrument) to some standard of pitch; put in tune **2** to adapt (music, the voice, etc.) to some pitch, tone, or mood **3** to adapt to some condition, mood, etc.; bring into harmony or agreement **4** [Now Rare] to utter or express musically **5** *a)* to adjust (a system, motor, etc.) to the proper or desired condition or performance *b)* to adjust (a radio or TV receiver) to a given frequency or channel —***vi.*** to be in tune; harmonize —***SYN.*** MELODY —**call the tune** to direct proceedings; be in control —**change one's tune** [Informal] to change markedly one's attitude or manner —**sing a different tune** [Informal] to talk or act differently because of a change of attitude —**to the tune of** [Informal] to the sum, price, or extent of —**tune in 1** to adjust a radio or television receiver to a given frequency or channel so as to receive (a specified station, program, etc.) ☆**2** [Slang] to become or make aware, knowing, hip, etc. —**tune out 1** to adjust a radio or TV receiver so as to eliminate (interference, a particular broadcasting station, etc.) **2** [Informal] to turn one's attention, sympathies, etc. away from —**tune up 1** to adjust (musical instruments) to the same pitch, as in an orchestra **2** to bring (an engine, etc.) to the proper condition or level of performance, as by replacing parts, making adjustments, etc.

tune·ful (to͞on′fəl, tyo͞on′-) ***adj.*** full of pleasing tunes or melodies; melodious —**tune′ful·ly** ***adv.*** —**tune′ful·ness** ***n.***

tune·less (-lis) ***adj.*** **1** not musical or melodious **2** not producing music; silent —**tune′less·ly** ***adv.*** —**tune′less·ness** ***n.***

tun·er (to͞o′nər, tyo͞o′-) ***n.*** a person or thing that tunes; specif., *a)* a person who tunes musical instruments [a piano *tuner*] *b)* the part of a radio or TV receiver that detects signals; esp., a separate unit of a high-fidelity system

☆**tune·smith** (to͞on′smith′, tyo͞on′-) ***n.*** [Informal] a composer of popular songs

tune-up or **tune-up** (to͞on′up′, tyo͞on′-) ***n.*** **1** an adjusting, as of an engine, to the proper or required condition or level of performance **2** any adjustment or preparation serving to improve performance or functioning

tung oil (tuŋ) ⟦Mandarin *t'ung-yu* < *t'ung,* name of the tree + *yu,* oil⟧ a fast-drying oil derived from the seeds of the tung tree, used in place of linseed oil in paints, varnishes, etc. for a more water-resistant finish

tung·state (tuŋ′stāt′) ***n.*** a salt or ester of tungstic acid

tung·sten (tuŋ′stən) ***n.*** ⟦Swed, lit., heavy stone, orig. name for scheelite, coined (1755) by A. F. Cronstedt (see NICKEL) < *tung,* heavy (< IE **tn̥ghu-* < base **ten-,* to pull > THIN) + *sten,* akin to OE *stan,* STONE⟧ a hard, heavy, gray-white, metallic chemical element, found in wolframite, scheelite, tungstite, etc., and used in steel for high-speed tools, in electric contact points and lamp filaments, etc.: symbol, W; at. no. 74: see the periodic table of elements in the Reference Supplement —**tung·sten′ic** (-sten′ik) ***adj.***

tungsten lamp an incandescent lamp having tungsten filaments

tungsten steel a very hard steel made with tungsten

tung·stic (tuŋ′stik) ***adj.*** designating or of a chemical compound containing tungsten, esp. with a valence of five or six

tungstic acid any of a group of acids produced by the combination of tungstic trioxide, WO_3, with water; specif., the monohydrate acid, H_2WO_4

Tung·ting (to͝oŋ′tiŋ′, do͝oŋ′-) *a former transliteration of* DONGTING HU

tung tree (tuŋ) a subtropical tree (*Aleurites fordii*) of the spurge family, whose seeds yield tung oil

Tun·gus (to͝on go͞oz′, -go͞os′; to͝oŋ′əs) ***n.*** ⟦< ?⟧ **1** *pl.* **-gus′** or **-gus′es** a member of a people of E Siberia **2** the Tungusic language of this people —***adj.*** of the Tungus or their language or culture

Tun·gus·ic (to͝on go͞o′zik, -sik) ***n.*** a family of languages, belonging to the Altaic language group, spoken in central and NE Asia and including Tungus and Manchu —***adj.*** of these languages, the peoples that speak them, or their cultures

Tun·gus·ka Basin (to͝on go͞os′kä) large coal basin in central Siberia, between the Yenisei & Lena rivers: it is drained by three rivers, the **Lower Tunguska, Stony Tunguska,** & **Upper Tunguska** (usually called the *Angara River*), which flow west into the Yenisei

tu·nic (to͞o′nik, tyo͞o′-) ***n.*** ⟦L *tunica* < **ktunica,* of Sem orig. (prob. via Punic), as in Aram *ktūnā,* Phoen *ktn,* garment worn next to the skin (> Gr *chitōn*)⟧ **1** a loose, gownlike garment worn by men and women in ancient Greece and Rome **2** a blouselike garment extending to the hips or lower, usually gathered at the waist, often with a belt **3** [Chiefly Brit.] a short coat forming part of the uniform of soldiers, policemen, etc. **4** a vestment worn over the alb, as formerly by a subdeacon, or by a bishop under the dalmatic **5** a natural covering of a plant, animal, etc.

tu·ni·ca (to͞o′ni kə, tyo͞o′-) ***n.,*** *pl.* **-cae′** (-sē′) ⟦ModL: see prec.⟧ *Anat., Zool.* an enclosing or covering layer of tissue or membrane, as of the ovaries

tu·ni·cate (to͞o′ni kit, tyo͞o′-; -kāt′) ***adj.*** ⟦L *tunicatus,* pp. of *tunicare,* to put on a tunic < *tunica,* TUNIC⟧ **1** *Bot.* of or covered with concentric layers or tunics, as an onion **2** *Zool.* having a tunic or mantle Also **tu′ni·cat′ed** (-kāt′id) —***n.*** any of a subphylum (Tunicata) of solitary or colonial sea chordates, having a saclike body enclosed by a thick tunic, including the salps and ascidians

tu·ni·cle (to͞o′ni kəl, tyo͞o′-) ***n.*** ⟦ME < L *tunicula,* dim. of *tunica,* tunic⟧ TUNIC (sense 4)

tuning fork a small steel instrument with two prongs, which when struck sounds a certain fixed tone in perfect pitch: it is used as a guide in tuning instruments, in testing hearing, etc.

tuning fork

Tu·nis (to͞o′nis, tyo͞o′-) **1** capital of Tunisia: seaport near the site of ancient Carthage **2** former Barbary State that became Tunisia

Tu·ni·si·a (to͞o nē′zhə, -zhē ə; tyo͞o-) country in N Africa, on the Mediterranean: a French protectorate since 1883, it became independent in 1956; a monarchy (1956-57) & a republic since 1957: 63,170 sq mi (163,610 sq km); cap. Tunis —**Tu·ni′si·an** ***adj., n.***

tun·nel (tun′əl) ***n.*** ⟦ME *tonel,* a net with wide opening and narrow end < MFr *tonnelle,* arbor, semicircular vault < OFr *tonnel,* dim. of *tonne,* TUN⟧ **1** [Obs.] *a)* a flue *b)* a funnel **2** *a)* a passageway, as through a mountain or under a body of water, as for automotive or rail traffic *b)* any similar passage, as one in a mine **3** an animal's burrow —***vt.*** **-neled** or **-nelled, -nel·ing** or **-nel·ling 1** to dig (a passage) in the form of a tunnel **2** to make a tunnel through or under **3** to make (one's way) by digging a tunnel —***vi.*** **1** to make a tunnel **2** *Physics* to pass through a normally impassable barrier or insulator [electrons *tunnel* through semiconductors] —**tun′nel·er** ***n.,*** **tun′nel·ler**

☆**tunnel diode** a semiconductor diode, containing many impurities, in which an increase in voltage across the diode first produces an increase in current, then a decrease, and finally another increase: used as an amplifier, oscillator, or computer switching element

tunnel vision a narrow outlook; specif., the focus of attention on a particular problem without proper regard for possible consequences or alternative approaches

tun·ny (tun′ē) ***n.,*** *pl.* **-nies** or **-ny** ⟦MFr *thon* < Prov *ton* < L *tunnus, thunnus* < Gr *thynnos*⟧ TUNA[1] (sense 1)

tup (tup) [Chiefly Brit.] ***n.*** ⟦ME *tupe*⟧ **1** a male sheep; ram **2** the striking part of a pile driver or power hammer —***vt.*** **tupped, tup′ping** to copulate with (a ewe): said of a ram

☆**tu·pe·lo** (to͞o′pə lō′) ***n.,*** *pl.* **-los′** ⟦< ? Creek **'topilwa,* lit., swamp tree < *ito,* tree + *opílwa*, swamp⟧ **1** any of a genus (*Nyssa*) of the sour-gum family of tall North American trees found in moist forests or swamps, including the black gum and cotton gum **2** the fine-textured wood of such a tree, used for mallets, furniture, etc.

Tu·pí (to͞o pē′, to͞o′pē) ***n.*** ⟦Tupí, comrade⟧ **1** *pl.* **Tu·pís′** or **Tu·pí′** a member of a group of South American Indian peoples living chiefly along the Brazilian coast and the lower Amazon and in part of Paraguay **2** the language of these peoples: an earlier form was used as a lingua franca in the Amazon region **3** a widely distributed South American Indian language stock that includes Tupí-Guaraní Also written **Tupi** —**Tu·pi′an** ***adj.***

Tu·pí-Gua·ra·ní (-gwä′rä nē′) ***n.*** a language family of the Tupí language stock, including the Guaraní and Tupí languages, spoken from N Brazil to Uruguay and Argentina

tup·pence (tup′əns) ***n.*** *alt. sp. of* TWOPENCE

Tu·pun·ga·to (to͞o′po͝on gät′ō) mountain of the Andes, on the Argentine-Chilean border: 22,310 ft (6,800 m)

tuque (to͞ok, tyo͞ok) ***n.*** ⟦CdnFr < Fr *toque*: see TOQUE⟧ a brimless, knit winter hat fitting close to the skull and, often, worn somewhat loose at the top

tu quo·que (to͞o kwō′kwā, -kwē) ⟦L⟧ thou also; you too: a retort accusing an accuser of the same charge

tur·ban (tʉr′bən) ***n.*** ⟦earlier *turbant* < MFr < It *turbante* < Turk *tülbend*, dial. form of *dülbend* < Pers *dulbänd*, turban, sash⟧ **1** any of various styles of headdress worn by men in the Middle East and S Asia, consisting of a length of cloth wound in folds about the head, often over a cap: the style of the turban often indicates the position or rank of the wearer **2** any similar headdress; esp., *a)* a scarf or bandanna wound around the head, worn by women *b)* a woman's hat with no brim or a very short brim turned up closely —**tur′baned** (-bənd) ***adj.***

turban

tur·bel·lar·i·an (tʉr′bə ler′ē ən) ***n.*** ⟦< ModL *Turbellaria* < L *turbellae*, a bustle, stir, dim. of *turba*, a crowd (see fol.), disturbance (from water currents caused by the cilia) + -AN⟧ any of a class (Turbellaria) of flatworms, mostly aquatic and nonparasitic, characterized by a leaf-shaped body covered with many cilia

tur·bid (tʉr′bid) ***adj.*** ⟦L *turbidus* < *turba*, a crowd < IE **turb-* < base **twer-*, to stir up > OE *thwirel*, stirring rod, churn handle⟧ **1** muddy or cloudy from having the sediment stirred up **2** thick, dense, or dark, as clouds or smoke **3** confused; perplexed; muddled —**tur·bid′i·ty** ***n.***, **tur′bid·ness** —**tur′bid·ly** ***adv.***

tur·bi·dim·e·ter (tʉr′bi dim′ət ər) ***n.*** ⟦prec. + -METER⟧ a device for measuring the turbidity of a liquid, as in a water-purification plant —**tur·bi·di·met·ric** (tʉr′bi di me′trik) ***adj.*** —**tur′bi·dim′e·try** (-ə trē) ***n.***

tur·bi·dite (tʉr′bi dīt′) ***n.*** ⟦TURBID + -ITE[1]⟧ *Geol.* any sediment or rock deposited by a turbidity current

turbidity current a current of highly turbid water carrying large amounts of suspended sediment that increase its density and cause it to flow downward through less dense water along the bottom slope of a sea or lake

☆**tur·bi·na·do (sugar)** (tʉr′bi nä′dō) ⟦Cuban Sp < *turbina*, centrifuge for processing sugar, TURBINE + *-ado*, -ATE[1]⟧ a partially refined, granulated, pale-brown sugar obtained by washing raw sugar in a centrifuge until most of the molasses is removed

tur·bi·nate (tʉr′bi nit, -nāt′) ***adj.*** ⟦L *turbinatus* < *turbo* (gen. *turbinis*), a whirl, rotation: for IE base see TURBID⟧ **1** shaped like a cone resting on its apex, as a molluskan shell **2** shaped like a scroll or spiral; specif., designating or of any of certain spiral, spongy bones in the nasal passages Also **tur′bi·nat′ed** (-nāt′id) or **tur′bi·nal** —***n.*** **1** a turbinate shell **2** a turbinate bone

tur·bine (tʉr′bin, -bīn′) ***n.*** ⟦Fr < L *turbo*, whirl: see prec.⟧ an engine or motor having a drive shaft driven either by the impulse of steam, water, air, gas, etc. against the curved vanes of a wheel (or set of wheels) or by the reaction of fluid passing out through nozzles located around the wheel

tur·bit (tʉr′bit) ***n.*** ⟦< ? L *turbo*, a top: from the shape⟧ any of a breed of domestic pigeon distinguished by a short head, a peaked crest, and a ruffled breast

tur·bo (tʉr′bō) ***n.*** *short for* TURBOSUPERCHARGER

tur·bo- (tʉr′bō) ⟦< TURBINE⟧ *combining form* consisting of or driven by a turbine [*turboprop*]

☆**tur·bo·charge** (tʉr′bō chärj′) ***vt.*** **-charged′**, **-charg′ing** to increase the power of, maintain air pressure in, etc. (an engine) by the use of a turbocharger

☆**tur·bo·charg·er** (tʉr′bō chär′jər) ***n.*** TURBOSUPERCHARGER

tur·bo·fan (tʉr′bō fan′) ***n.*** **1** a fanlike turbojet engine designed to create additional thrust by diverting a secondary airflow around the combustion chamber: in full **turbofan engine** **2** a fan driven by a turbine

tur·bo·gen·er·a·tor (tʉr′bō jen′ər āt′ər) ***n.*** a generator driven by and directly coupled to a turbine

tur·bo·jet (tʉr′bō jet′) ***n.*** **1** a tunnel-like reaction engine in which air is drawn in, compressed by spinning blades attached to the turbine shaft, and mixed with atomized fuel, with the resultant mixture being ignited in combustion chambers to produce a powerful jet that drives the engine's turbines and provides thrust: in full **turbojet engine** **2** an aircraft propelled by such an engine

tur·bo·prop (tʉr′bō präp′) ***n.*** ⟦TURBO- + PROP(ELLER)⟧ **1** a turbojet engine whose turbine shaft, through reduction gears, drives a propeller that develops most of the thrust: in full **turboprop engine** **2** an aircraft propelled by such an engine

tur·bo·su·per·charg·er (tʉr′bō so͞o′pər chär′jər) ***n.*** a type of supercharger driven not by the engine, but by a turbine that is powered by exhaust gases

tur·bot (tʉr′bət) ***n.***, *pl.* **-bot** or **-bots** ⟦ME *turbut* < OFr *tourbout*, prob. < OSwed *törnbut* < *törn*, thorn (akin to THORN) + *but*, BUTT[1] (so named from the spines)⟧ any of various flounders, highly valued as food

tur·bu·lence (tʉr′byə ləns) ***n.*** ⟦LL *turbulentia*⟧ the condition or quality of being turbulent; specif., *a)* commotion or wild disorder *b)* violent, irregular motion or swirling agitation of water, air, gas, etc. Also **tur′bu·len·cy** (-lən sē)

tur·bu·lent (tʉr′byə lənt) ***adj.*** ⟦Fr < L *turbulentus* < *turba*, a crowd: see TURBID⟧ full of commotion or wild disorder; specif., *a)* marked by or causing turmoil; unruly or boisterous [*a turbulent mob*] *b)* violently agitated; tumultuous [*turbulent grief*] *c)* marked by wildly irregular motion [*turbulent air currents*] —**tur′bu·lent·ly** ***adv.***

turbulent flow fluid flow characterized by random fluctuations in velocity from point to point: cf. LAMINAR FLOW

Tur·co- (tʉr′kō, -kə) *combining form* TURKO-

Tur·co·man (tʉr′kə mən) ***n.*** *var. of* TURKMEN

turd (tʉrd) ***n.*** ⟦ME < OE *tord*, akin to MHG *zurch*, dung, Latvian *dirsa*, anus < IE base **der-*, to split > TEAR[1]⟧ a piece of excrement: now sometimes considered somewhat vulgar

tu·reen (to͝o rēn′, tyo͝o-) ***n.*** ⟦earlier *terreen* < MFr *terrine*, earthen vessel < VL **terrinus* < L *terra*, TERRA⟧ a large, deep serving dish with a lid, used for soups, stews, etc.

Tu·renne (to͝o ren′; *Fr* tü ren′), Vicomte **de** (də) (*Henri de La Tour d'Auvergne*) 1611-75; Fr. marshal

turf (tʉrf) ***n.*** ⟦ME < OE, akin to ON *torf* < IE **dorbhos*, sod, tuft of grass < base **derbh-*, to twist together⟧ **1** *a)* a surface layer of earth containing grass plants with their matted roots; sod; sward *b)* [Chiefly Brit.] a piece of this layer **2** peat, or a piece of it for use as fuel **3** a track for horse racing; also, the sport of horse racing: usually with *the* ☆**4** [Informal] *a)* a neighborhood area regarded by a street gang as its own territory to be defended against other gangs *b)* one's own territory or domain —***vt.*** to cover with turf —**turf out** [Brit. Informal] to throw out; remove, discard, dismiss, etc. —**turf′y** ***adj.***

turf·man (-mən) ***n.***, *pl.* **-men** (-mən) a person interested in horse racing; esp., an owner, trainer, etc. of racehorses

Tur·ge·nev (to͝or gān′əf, -yəf), **I·van (Sergeevich)** (ē vän′) 1818-83; Russ. novelist: also sp. **Tur·ge′nieff** or **Tur·ge′niev**

tur·ges·cent (tər jes′ənt) ***adj.*** ⟦L *turgescens*, prp. of *turgescere*, to swell up: see fol. & -ESCENT⟧ becoming turgid or swollen —**tur·ges′cence** ***n.***

tur·gid (tʉr′jid) ***adj.*** ⟦L *turgidus* < *turgere*, to swell⟧ **1** swollen; distended **2** so bombastic and congested as to obscure meaning [*a turgid writing style*] —*SYN.* BOMBASTIC —**tur·gid′i·ty** ***n.***, **tur′gid·ness** —**tur′gid·ly** ***adv.***

tur·gor (tʉr′gər, -gôr′) ***n.*** ⟦LL < L *turgere*, to swell⟧ **1** turgescence; turgidity **2** the normal distention or rigidity of living animal and plant cells due to pressure against the plasma membrane from within by the cell contents

Tur·got (tür gō′), **Anne Ro·bert Jacques** (än rô ber zhäk′) Baron de l'Aulne 1727-81; Fr. economist & statesman

Tu·rin (to͝or′in, tyo͝or′-; to͝o rin′, tyo͝o-) commune in the Piedmont, NW Italy, on the Po River: It. name TORINO

Tu·ring (to͝or′iŋ, tyo͝or′-), **Alan Math·i·son** (math′i sən) 1912-54; Brit. mathematician: pioneer in computer theory

Turing machine ⟦after prec., its originator⟧ an early hypothetical model for a simple computer capable theoretically of solving complex problems by performing a small number of basic operations

tu·ris·ta (to͝o rēs′tä; *Sp* to͞o rēs′tä) ***n.*** ⟦Sp, tourist⟧ acute infectious diarrhea as experienced by some tourists in certain foreign countries, usually caused by bacteria in the food or water

Turk[1] (tʉrk) ***n.*** ⟦ME *Turke* < MFr *Turc* < ML *Turcus* < Turk *Türk*⟧ **1** a member of any of the Turkic-speaking peoples of central Asia **2** a member of the principal ethnic group of Turkey or, formerly, the Ottoman Empire **3** a person born or living in present-day Turkey **4** any of a breed of swift saddle horse developed in Turkey **5** *see* YOUNG TURK

Turk[2] *abbrev.* **1** Turkey **2** Turkish

Tur·ka·na (tər kä′nə), **Lake** lake in NW Kenya, on the Ethiopian border: *c.* 3,500 sq mi (9,065 sq km); *c.* 185 mi (298 km) long

Tur·ke·stan (tʉr′ki stan′, -stän′) region in central Asia, extending from the Caspian Sea to the Gobi Desert, inhabited by Turkic-speaking peoples: divided into RUSSIAN TURKESTAN & CHINESE TURKESTAN

tur·key (tʉr′kē) ***n.***, *pl.* **-keys** or **-key** ⟦< earlier *Turkey-cock*, term orig. applied to the guinea fowl, sometimes imported through fol. and, for a time, identified with the Am fowl⟧ ☆**1** *a)* any of a family (Meleagrididae) of large, gallinaceous North American birds with a small, naked head and a tail that can be spread like a fan, including a wild or domesticated species (*Meleagris gallopavo*) bred as poultry and a wild species (*Agriocharis ocellata*) of Central America, with eyespots on the tail *b)* the flesh of a turkey ☆**2** [Slang] a failure: said as of a theatrical production, movie, book, etc. ☆**3** [Slang] an inept, stupid, or unpleasant person ☆**4** *Bowling* three strikes in a row —☆**talk turkey** [Informal] to talk bluntly and directly

Tur·key (tʉr′kē) country occupying Asia Minor & a SE part of the Balkan Peninsula: 301,384 sq mi (780,580 sq km); cap. Ankara

turkey cock 1 a male turkey 2 a strutting or pompous person

Turkey red 1 a bright red produced on cotton cloth by alizarin 2 cotton cloth of this color

☆**turkey trot** a ballroom dance to ragtime music, popular in the early 20th cent.

turkey vulture a dark-colored vulture (*Cathartes aura*) of temperate and tropical America, resembling a turkey in having a naked, reddish head: also called **turkey buzzard**

Tur·ki (toor′kē, tur′-) ***adj.*** ⟦Pers < Turk *Türk*⟧ designating or of the Turkic languages or the peoples that speak them, esp. those of the E or SE group, as Uighur or Uzbek

Turk·ic (tur′kik) ***n.*** a family of Altaic languages that includes Turkish, Azerbaijani, Tatar, Uighur, Uzbek, and Turkmen ***—adj.*** designating or of this family of languages or the peoples that speak them

Turk·ish (tur′kish) ***adj.*** of Turkey or its people, language, or culture ***—n.*** the Turkic language spoken in Turkey

Turkish bath 1 a kind of bath in which the bather, after a period of heavy perspiration in a room of hot air or steam, is washed, massaged, and cooled 2 a place where such a bath is given

Turkish delight (*or* paste) a kind of candy consisting of cubes of a flavored jellylike substance covered with powdered sugar

Turkish Empire OTTOMAN EMPIRE

Turkish tobacco a dark, highly aromatic tobacco, grown in Turkey, Greece, etc. and used chiefly in cigarettes

Turkish towel [*also* **t- t-**] a thick cotton towel of terry cloth

Turk·ism (tur′kiz′əm) ***n.*** Turkish culture, beliefs, etc.

Turk·men (turk′men′, -mən) ***n., pl.* -mens′** ⟦see TURKOMAN⟧ 1 a member of a people living mainly in Turkmenistan, Uzbekistan, and Kazakhstan and in N Iran and Afghanistan 2 the Turkic language of this people ***—adj.*** of the Turkmens or their language or culture

Turk·men·i·stan (tərk men′i stan′, -stän′) 1 TURKMEN SOVIET SOCIALIST REPUBLIC 2 country in central Asia, on the Caspian Sea, north of Iran: became independent upon the breakup of the U.S.S.R. (1991): 188,456 sq mi (488,100 sq km); cap. Ashgabat: formerly, *Turkmen Soviet Socialist Republic* **—Turk·me·ni·an** (turk mēn′ē ən, -mēn′yən) ***adj.***

Turk·men Soviet Socialist Republic (turk′mən) a republic of the U.S.S.R.: now TURKMENISTAN: also **Turk·me·ni·a** (tərk mē′nē ə, -mēn′yə)

Tur·ko- (tur′kō, -kə) *combining form* 1 Turkish, Turkic 2 Turkey and

Tur·ko·man (tur′kō mən, -kə-) ***n.,*** *pl.* **-mans** or **-men** (-mən) ⟦Pers *Turkumān*, one like a Turk⟧ *var. of* TURKMEN

Turks and Cai·cos Islands (turks′ ən kā′kəs) British crown colony in the West Indies, consisting of two groups of small islands southeast of the Bahamas: *c.* 192 sq mi (497 sq km)

Turk's-cap lily (turks′kap′) any of various lilies having flowers whose petals and sepals are strongly recurved, resembling a rolled turban

Turk's-head (turks′hed′) ***n.*** *Naut.* an ornamental ring, braided from small line and shaped somewhat like a turban, placed around a rope, railing, etc.

Tur·ku (toor′ko͞o′) seaport in SW Finland

tur·mer·ic (tur′mər ik) ***n.*** ⟦earlier also *tormerik* < MFr *terre-mérite* < ML *terra merita*, lit., deserved (or deserving) earth < ?⟧ 1 *a)* an East Indian plant (*Curcuma longa*) of the ginger family, whose rhizome in powdered form is used as a yellow dye or a seasoning, and in medicine *b)* its aromatic rhizome or the powder made from it 2 any of several other plants having tuberous rhizomes

turmeric paper paper impregnated with turmeric, used as a test for alkali, which turns it brown, or for boric acid, which turns it reddish-brown

tur·moil (tur′moil′) ***n.*** ⟦*tur-* (< ? TURBULENT) + MOIL⟧ tumult; commotion; uproar; confusion

turn (turn) ***vt.*** ⟦ME *turnen* < OE *turnian* & OFr *turner, tourner*, both < L *tornare*, to turn in a lathe, turn < *tornus*, lathe < Gr *tornos*, lathe, carpenter's compasses, akin to *terein*, to bore through: for IE base see THROW⟧ I. *to cause to revolve or rotate* 1 to make (a wheel, globe, etc.) move about a central point or axis; revolve or rotate 2 to give circular motion to; move around or partly around [to *turn* a key] 3 to do by a revolving motion [to *turn* a somersault] 4 *Baseball* to execute (a double play) II. *to form by revolving, rotating, etc.* 1 to give a rounded shape to by rotating against a tool, as in a lathe 2 to give rounded shape or form to in any way 3 to give a well-rounded or graceful form to [to *turn* a pretty phrase] III. *to change in position* 1 to change the position of, as by a rotating motion [to *turn* a chair around] 2 to revolve in the mind: ponder: often with *over* 3 *a)* to bend, fold, twist, etc. [*turn* the sheet back] *b)* to twist or wrench (one's ankle) 4 to bend back (a cutting edge); blunt 5 to reverse the position or sides of; invert; specif., *a)* to move so that the undersurface is on top and vice versa [to *turn* a phonograph record] *b)* to spade, plow, etc. so that the undersoil comes to the surface *c)* to reverse (a collar, coat, etc.) so that the inner surface becomes the outer 6 to cause to become upside down, topsy-turvy, etc. 7 to upset or unsettle (the stomach) IV. *to change the movement or course of* 1 to bend the course of; deflect; divert [to *turn* a blow] 2 to cause to change intentions, actions, etc. [to *turn* someone from his purpose]; specif., *a)* to convert or persuade *b)* to change in feelings, attitudes, etc. [to *turn* people against someone] 3 to go around (a corner, an army's flank, etc.) 4 to reach or pass (a certain age, amount, etc.) 5 to reverse the course of; specif., *a)* to stop or repel [to *turn* an attack] *b)* to cause to recoil, rebound, etc. [criticism *turned* against the critic] 6 to drive, set, let go, etc. in some way [to *turn* someone adrift] 7 *a)* to keep (money, goods, etc.) circulating or moving *b)* to earn (a profit), as in a commercial transaction V. *to change the direction, trend, etc. of* 1 to change the direction of (one's eyes, face, etc.) 2 to direct, point, aim, etc. [to *turn* a gun on someone] 3 to change the trend, focus, etc. of [to *turn* one's thoughts to practical matters] 4 to put to (a specified) use or result; employ; apply [to *turn* knowledge to good account, to *turn* one's hand to writing] VI. *to change the nature or condition of* 1 to change; convert; transmute [to *turn* cream into butter, a writer *turned* actor] 2 to exchange for [to *turn* produce into hard cash] 3 to subject [to *turn* another's remarks to ridicule] 4 to translate or paraphrase 5 to derange, dement, distract, or infatuate 6 to make sour 7 to affect in some way [*turned* sick by the sight] 8 to change the color of ***— vi.*** I. *to revolve, rotate, etc.* 1 to move in a circle or around an axis; rotate or revolve; pivot 2 to move in a circular manner; move around or partly around [the key won't *turn*] 3 *a)* to seem to be whirling or moving, as to one who is dizzy *b)* to reel or be giddy (said of the head) II. *to change position* 1 *a)* to move in a rotary manner so as to change position *b)* to shift or twist the body as if on an axis 2 to become curved or bent 3 to reverse position so that bottom becomes top; become reversed or inverted 4 to become upset or unsettled: said of the stomach III. *to change course or movement* 1 to change one's or its course so as to be moving, going, etc. in a different direction; deviate 2 to reverse one's or its course; start to move, go, etc. in the opposite direction [the tide has *turned*] 3 to consult; refer (*to*) 4 to go or apply (*to*) for help IV. *to change in direction, trend, etc.* 1 to change one's or its direction; face about; shift 2 to direct or shift one's attention, abilities, thoughts, etc. [to *turn* from one's work to a hobby] 3 to make a sudden attack (*on* or *upon*) [the dog *turned* on him] 4 to reverse one's feelings, attitude, allegiance, etc. [to *turn* against former friends] 5 to be contingent or depend (*on* or *upon*) 6 [Obs.] to vacillate V. *to become changed in nature or condition* 1 to enter into a specified condition; become [to *turn* bitter with age] 2 to change into another form, type, or sort [the rain *turned* to sleet] 3 to become rancid, putrid, sour, etc. 4 to change color [leaves *turning* in the fall] ***— n.*** I. *rotation, circular motion, etc.* 1 the act of turning around; complete or partial rotation, as of a wheel; revolution 2 *a)* a winding of one thing around another *b)* a single twist, coil, winding, etc.; convolution 3 *a)* the condition of being twisted, bent, etc. in a circular form *b)* the direction of this 4 a musical ornament consisting usually of four tones, the second and fourth of which are the same, or principal, tone, the first, normally, being a degree above, and the third a degree below II. *change of movement, direction, etc.* 1 a change of position or posture, as by rotating motion 2 a change or reversal of course or direction [the *turn* of the tide] 3 *a)* a walk taken about a building, area, etc., as for inspection; tour *b)* a short walk or ride, returning to the starting place, as for exercise 4 the place where a change in direction occurs; bend; curve 5 *Golf* the midway point of a round, usually after the ninth hole III. *change of nature, condition, etc.* 1 *a)* a change in trend, circumstances, events, policy, health, etc. [a *turn* for the better] *b)* TURNING POINT 2 the time of a chronological change [at the *turn* of the century] 3 [Informal] a sudden, brief shock or fright; start IV. *an occasional or repeated action, performance, etc.* 1 an action that harms or, more usually, benefits another [to do someone a good *turn*] 2 a bout; spell; try [a *turn* at gardening] 3 an attack of illness, dizziness, rage, etc.; fit 4 the right, duty, or opportunity to do something, esp. as coming to each of a number of people in regular order [one's *turn* at bat] 5 [Brit.] a shift of work 6 *a)* a short performance given as part of a variety show; act *b)* its performer or performers ☆7 *Finance* a transaction on the stock exchange involving both purchase and sale of particular securities V. *trend, form, style, character, etc.* 1 a distinctive form, manner, cast, detail, etc. [a quaint *turn* to her speech] 2 natural inclination or aptitude; flair [an inquisitive *turn* of mind] 3 a tendency; drift; trend [the discussion took a new *turn*] 4 a variation or interpretation of the original [to give an old story a new *turn*] **—SYN.** CURVE **—at every turn** in every instance; constantly **—by turns** one after another; alternately; in succession —☆**call the turn** ⟦term in faro, for guessing which card will be turned up⟧ to predict successfully **—in turn** in proper sequence or succession **—out of turn** 1 not in proper sequence or order 2 at the wrong time; esp., unwisely or imprudently [to talk *out of turn*] **—take turns** to speak, do, etc. one after another in regular order **—to a turn** to just the right degree; perfectly **—turn and turn about** one after another in regular order; by turns: also **turn about —turn around** 1 [Informal] to change or become changed for the better 2 to complete (a project, process, etc.) 3 to bring (a failing company, project, etc.) to a condition of profitability or solvency **—turn down** ☆1 *a)* to reject (a request, advice, etc.) *b)* to reject the request, advice, etc. of (someone) 2 to lessen the intensity or volume of (light or sound) by manipulating controls **—turn in** 1 to make a turn into; enter 2 to point (the toes) inward ☆3 to deliver; hand in ☆4 to inform on or hand over, as to the police 5 to give back; return 6 to fold over; double 7 [Informal] to go to bed **—turn off** 1 to leave (a road, path, etc.) and enter another branching off 2 to branch off: said of a road, path, etc. 3 *a)* to stop a flow of (water, gas, electricity, etc.) *b)* to close (a faucet, valve, etc.) so as to stop a flow *c)* to make (an electrical device) stop functioning by operating the controls *d)* to render (a function of an electronic device) inoperative as by adjusting a setting 4 to stop displaying or showing, suddenly or automatically [to *turn off* a smile] 5 to deflect; divert ☆6 [Informal] to cause (someone) to become bored, depressed, uninterested, etc. 7 [Brit.] to discharge (an employee) **—turn on** 1 *a)* to start a flow of (water, gas, electricity, etc.) *b)* to open (a faucet, valve, etc.) so as to start a flow *c)* to make (an electrical device) start functioning by operating the controls *d)* to render (a function of an electronic device) operational as by adjusting a setting **2** to show or display suddenly or automatically [to *turn on* the charm] ☆**3** [Slang] *a)* to initiate in the use of a psychedelic drug *b)* to stimulate or be stimulated with or as with a psychedelic drug; make or become elated, euphoric, etc. *c)* to stimulate sexually *d)* to make interested, enthusiastic, etc. —**turn out 1** to put out (a light) **2** to put outside **3** to drive out; dismiss or discharge **4** to turn inside out **5** to assemble somewhere for some purpose: said of a group of people [many *turned out* for the rally] **6** to produce as the result of work **7** to prove to be; be discovered to be [the butler *turned out* to have committed the crime] **8** to come to be; become or end up [it *turned out* well in the end] **9** to equip, dress, etc. **10** [Informal] to get out of bed —**turn over 1** to change the position of, as by rolling **2** to reverse the position of; turn upside down; invert **3** to shift one's position, as from one side to the other; roll over **4** to begin, or make begin, to operate, as an engine or motor **5** to think about carefully; ponder **6** to hand over; transfer **7** to relinquish; delegate **8** to put to a different use; convert **9** to sell and replenish (a stock of goods) **10** to buy and sell, or do business, to the amount of **11** *Basketball, Football* to lose possession of (the ball) due to a mistake or error —**turn to** to get to work; get busy —**turn up 1** to fold or bend back or over upon itself **2** to shorten (a dress, a sleeve, etc.) by folding back the bottom edge and making a new hem **3** to lift up or turn face upward, as to see the other side **4** to bring to light, as by digging **5** to increase the flow, speed, intensity, loudness, etc. of, as by turning a control **6** *a)* to make a turn onto and ascend (a street on a hill, etc.) *b)* to make a turn into any street or road **7** to have an upward direction **8** to come about; happen **9** to make an appearance; arrive **10** to be found

turn·a·bout (turn′ə bout′) *n.* **1** the act of turning about, as to face the other way **2** a shift or reversal of allegiance, opinion, tendency, etc.; about-face

turn-and-bank indicator (turn′ən baŋk′) an airplane instrument that coordinates the rate of turn with the degree of bank to help the pilot avoid a slip or skid: also **turn-and-slip indicator**

☆**turn·a·round** (turn′ə round′) *n.* **1** TURNABOUT **2** a wide area, as in a driveway, to allow for turning a vehicle around **3** the time needed to unload, refuel, service, and reload an aircraft **4** the time needed to complete a job, perform a service, etc., as for a customer **5** the process of bringing a failing company, project, etc. to a condition of profitability or solvency **6** *Film* a production stage in which the original producer or studio has rejected a previously purchased project, script, etc. but it has not yet been acquired by another producer or studio: usually in the phrase **in (or into) turnaround**

turn·buck·le (turn′buk′əl) *n.* a metal sleeve with opposite internal threads at each end for the threaded ends of two rods or for ringbolts, forming a coupling that can be turned to tighten or loosen the rods or wires attached to the ringbolts

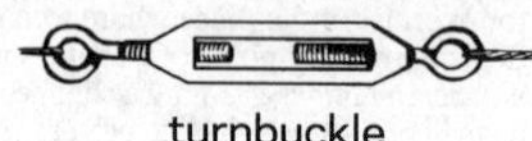

turnbuckle

turn·coat (turn′kōt′) *n.* ⟦from the notion of a coat worn right side out or inside out, according to circumstances⟧ a person who goes over to the opposite side or party; traitor

turn·down (turn′doun′) *adj.* **1** that can be turned down **2** having the upper part folded down [a *turndown* collar] —*n.* **1** a rejection; rebuff **2** a decline; downturn

turn·er¹ (tur′nər) *n.* **1** a thing that turns or is used for turning [a pancake *turner*] **2** one who operates a lathe

☆**tur·ner²** (tur′nər, toor′nər) *n.* ⟦Ger < *turnen*, to engage in gymnastics < OHG, to turn < L *tornare*: see TURN⟧ a gymnast or tumbler; esp., a member of a *Turnverein*

Tur·ner (tur′nər) **1 J(oseph) M(allord) W(illiam)** 1775-1851; Eng. painter **2 Nat** 1800-31; U.S. slave, who led an abortive revolt (1831)

☆**Turner syndrome** ⟦after H. H. *Turner* (1892-1970), U.S. endocrinologist who first described it⟧ a genetic disorder characterized by various deformities and abnormalities; esp., the absence of a female's second X chromosome, which prevents her from maturing sexually: also **Turner's syndrome**

turn·er·y (tur′nər ē) *n., pl.* **-er·ies** ⟦TURNER¹ + -Y⁴⟧ the work or shop of a lathe operator

turn·ing (tur′niŋ) *n.* **1** the action of a person or thing that turns **2** a place where a road turns or turns off **3** the art or process of shaping things on or as on a lathe

turning point 1 a point at which something changes direction **2** a point in time when a decisive change occurs

tur·nip (tur′nip) *n.* ⟦earlier *turnep*, prob. < TURN or Fr *tour*, in the sense of "turned, round" + ME *nepe* < OE *næp*, turnip < L *napus*⟧ **1** *a)* a biennial plant (*Brassica rapa*) of the crucifer family, with edible, hairy leaves and a roundish, light-colored, fleshy root used as a vegetable *b)* RUTABAGA **2** the root of either of these plants **3** [Old Slang] a pocket watch

turn·key (turn′kē′) *n., pl.* **-keys′** a person in charge of the keys of a prison; warder; jailer —☆*adj.* **1** that is purchased, installed, etc. completely ready for use or operation [a *turnkey* housing project, *turnkey* computer system] **2** of or having to do with a business, installation, or system so ready [a *turnkey* construction contractor]

turn·off (turn′ôf′) *n.* **1** the act of turning off ☆**2** a place where one turns off; esp., a road or ramp leading off a highway **3** [Slang] someone or something regarded as being boring, uninteresting, distasteful, etc.

turn-on (-on′) *n.* ⟦< TURN ON (sense 3) (see phr. under TURN)⟧ [Slang] someone or something regarded as interesting, exciting, arousing, etc.

turn·out (turn′out′) *n.* **1** the act of turning out **2** *a)* a gathering of people, as for a meeting *b)* the number of people who assemble for, or participate in, some event or activity [a high *turnout* of voters] **3** an amount produced; output **4** *a)* a wider part of a narrow road, enabling vehicles to pass one another *b)* an exit road *c)* a railroad siding **5** a carriage with its horse or horses **6** *a)* equipment *b)* a set of clothes; costume **7** *Ballet* a position in which the legs are turned outward, with the feet pointed in opposite directions

turn·o·ver (turn′ō′vər) *n.* **1** the act or an instance of turning over; specif., *a)* an upset *b)* a change from one use, side, opinion, management, etc. to another **2** a small filled pastry made by folding one half of the crust back over the other half and sealing it before baking **3** *a)* the number of times a stock of goods is sold and replenished in a given period of time *b)* the amount of business done during a given period of time in terms of the money used in buying and selling *c)* the number of shares sold in a stock market during a given period of time **4** the rate at which workers in a company, patients in a hospital, etc. are replaced ☆**5** *Basketball, Football* a loss of possession of the ball by a team due to an error or misplay —*adj.* that turns over [a *turnover* collar]

turn·pike (turn′pīk′) *n.* ⟦ME *turnpyke*, a spiked barrier across a road: see TURN & PIKE⁴⟧ **1** [Historical] a turnstile **2** TOLLGATE **3** a toll road, esp. one that is an expressway

turn·sole (turn′sōl′) *n.* ⟦ME *turnesole* < MFr *tournesol* < It *tornasole* or Sp *tornasol* < *tornar(e)*, to TURN + *sol(e)*, sun: see SOL¹⟧ **1** any of a number of plants whose flowers supposedly turn with the sun, as the sunflower and heliotrope **2** *a)* a Mediterranean plant (*Chrozophora tinctoria*) of the spurge family, yielding a purple or blue dye *b)* this dye

turn·spit (turn′spit′) *n.* **1** a person who turns a spit **2** [Historical] a small dog trained to turn a spit by means of a treadmill **3** a spit that can be turned

turn·stile (turn′stīl′) *n.* **1** a post with revolving horizontal bars, placed in an entrance to allow the passage of persons but not of horses, cattle, etc. **2** a similar apparatus, often coin-operated, used to admit persons one at a time

turn·stone (turn′stōn′) *n.* any of a genus (*Arenaria*, family Scolopacidae) of small, migratory shorebirds, esp., the **ruddy turnstone** (*A. interpres*): so called because they turn over pebbles to seek food

turn·ta·ble (turn′tā′bəl) *n.* a circular rotating platform; specif., *a)* a platform of this kind for supporting a phonograph record being played; also, such a platform together with the tonearm, stylus, etc. *b)* a platform carrying track to turn a locomotive around

☆**turn·ta·blist** (turn′tā′bəl ist) *n.* a person, esp. a disc jockey, who manipulates records on a turntable to create distinctive sounds

turn·up (turn′up′) *n.* something turned up; a turned-up part —*adj.* that turns up or is turned up

Turn·ver·ein (toorn′fer īn′; *E* turn′vər īn′, toorn-) *n.* ⟦Ger < *turnen*, to exercise (see TURNER²) + *verein*, a union, association⟧ a club of turners, or gymnasts

tur·pen·tine (tur′pən tīn′) *n.* ⟦ME *turpentyne* < OFr *terbentine* < L *terebinthinus*, of the turpentine tree < *terebinthus*: see TEREBINTH⟧ **1** the brownish-yellow, sticky, semifluid oleoresin exuding from the terebinth **2** any of the various sticky, viscid oleoresins obtained from pines and other coniferous trees; gum turpentine **3** a colorless, volatile essential oil, $C_{10}H_{16}$, distilled from such oleoresins and used in paints, varnishes, etc., and in medicine; spirits of turpentine; oil of turpentine —*vt.* **-tined′**, **-tin′ing 1** to apply turpentine to ☆**2** to extract turpentine from (trees)

Tur·pin (tur′pin), **Dick** 1706-39; Eng. highwayman: hanged

tur·pi·tude (tur′pi to͞od′, -tyo͞od′) *n.* ⟦MFr < L *turpitudo* < *turpis*, base, vile < IE **tr̥pis*, from which one must turn < base **trep-*, to turn away > Sans *trapa*, shame, embarrassment⟧ **1** baseness; vileness; depravity **2** an instance of this

turps (turps) *n.* ⟦< TURP(ENTINE) + *-s*⟧ [Informal] TURPENTINE

tur·quoise (tur′koiz′, -kwoiz′) *n.* ⟦ME *turkeis* < MFr *turqueise*, fem. of OFr *turqueis*, Turkish (see TURK¹): orig. brought to western Europe through Turkey⟧ **1** a blue or greenish-blue, hard mineral, hydrous copper aluminum phosphate, $CuAl_6(PO_4)_4(OH)_8 \cdot 5H_2O$, used as a gem **2** the color of turquoise; greenish blue —*adj.* greenish-blue Also sp. **tur′quois**

tur·ret (tur′it, toor′-) *n.* ⟦ME *turet* < OFr *tourete*, dim. of *tour*: see TOWER¹⟧ **1** a small tower projecting from a building, usually at a corner and often merely ornamental **2** a wooden, usually square tower on wheels, carrying soldiers, battering-rams, catapults, etc., used in ancient warfare for attacking fortresses and walled cities **3** *a)* a low, armored, usually revolving, structure for a gun or guns, as on a warship, tank, or fortress *b)* a transparent dome for a gun and gunner, as on a bomber **4** an attachment for a lathe, drill, etc., consisting of a block holding several cutting tools, which may be rotated to present any of the tools to the work: also **tur′ret·head′** (-hed′) **5** an adjustable device on a camera for holding various lenses

tur·ret·ed (-id) *adj.* **1** having a turret or turrets **2** shaped like a turret **3** having whorls forming a high, conical spiral, as some shells

tur·tle (turt′'l) *n., pl.* **-tles** or **-tle** ⟦altered, prob. infl. by fol. < Fr *tortue*, tortoise < VL **tartaruca*: see TORTOISE⟧ **1** any of a large and widely distributed order (Testudines) of terrestrial or aquatic reptiles having a toothless beak and a soft body encased in a tough shell into which, in most species, the head, tail, and four legs may be withdrawn: although aquatic, esp. marine, species are usually called *turtle* and land species are usually called *tortoise*, the terms are properly interchangeable for all species **2** the flesh of some turtles, used as food **3** *short for* TURTLENECK **4** *archaic var. of* TURTLEDOVE —*vi.* **-tled, -tling** to hunt for turtles —**turn turtle** to turn upside down; capsize

tur·tle·dove (turt′'l duv′) *n.* ⟦ME < OE *turtle, turtla* < L *turtur*, of echoic orig.⟧ **1** any of several Old World wild doves (esp. genus *Streptopelia*) noted for their plaintive cooing and the affection that the mates are traditionally thought of as showing toward each other **2** MOURNING DOVE

tur·tle·head (turt′'l hed′) *n.* ☆any of a genus (*Chelone*) of perennial North American plants of the figwort family, with showy, tubular, white or pink flowers

tur·tle·neck (turt′'l nek′) *n.* ☆**1** a high, snugly fitting collar on a pullover sweater, knitted shirt, etc. ☆**2** a sweater, shirt, etc. with such a collar

turves (turvz) *n. archaic pl. of* TURF

Tus·ca·loo·sa (tus′kə lo͞o′sə) ⟦< Choctaw, name of a chief, lit., Black Warrior < *taska*, warrior + *lusa*, black⟧ city in WC Ala., near Birmingham

Tus·can (tus′kən) *adj.* ⟦ME < L *Tuscanus* < *Tuscus*, an Etruscan⟧ **1** of Tuscany or its people, language, or culture **2** designating or of a classical (Roman) order of architecture, distinguished by its smooth columns with a ringlike capital and no decoration —*n.* **1** a person born or living in Tuscany **2** the variety of Italian spoken in Tuscany, accepted as standard literary Italian

Tus·ca·ny (tus′kə nē) region of central Italy, formerly a grand duchy: 8,878 sq mi (22,994 sq km); chief city, Florence: It. name TOSCANA

Tus·ca·ro·ra (tus′kə rôr′ə) *n.* ⟦< a Five-Nations Iroquois language, an adaptation of Tuscarora *skarò·rə*ⁿ, lit., ? those of the Indian hemp⟧ **1** *pl.* **-ras** or **-ra** a member of a North American Indian people, orig. of North Carolina, but after 1714 of New York and later also Ontario: joined Iroquois Confederacy *c.* 1722 to become the sixth of the Six Nations **2** the Iroquoian language of this people

tush[1] (tush) *interj., n.* ⟦ME *tussch*⟧ used to express impatience, reproof, contempt, etc.

tush[2] (tush) *n.* ⟦ME *tusch* < OE *tucs*: see TUSK⟧ **1** TUSK **2** any of the canine teeth of a horse

☆**tush**[3] (toosh) *n.* ⟦shortened & altered < Yiddish *tochus*: see TUCHIS⟧ [Informal] the buttocks: also [Slang] **tush′ie** (-ē) or **tush′y**

tush·er·y (tush′ə rē) *n.* ⟦< TUSH[1]: used by R. L. STEVENSON⟧ high-flown, pretentious writing, esp. when larded with archaisms, like that in some sentimentalized historical novels

tusk (tusk) *n.* ⟦ME, by metathesis < OE *tucs*, akin to OFris *tusk* < PGmc **tunth-ska* < **tunth-*, **tanth-*: see TOOTH⟧ **1** in elephants, wild boars, walruses, etc., a very long, large, pointed tooth, usually one of a pair, projecting outside the mouth and used for defense, digging up food, etc. **2** any tooth or projection suggestive of a tusk —*vt.* to dig, gore, etc. with a tusk or tusks —**SYN.** TOOTH —**tusked** (tuskt) *adj.* —**tusk′like′** (-līk′) *adj.*

tusk·er (tus′kər) *n.* an animal with tusks

tus·sah (tus′ə) *n.* ⟦Hindi *tasar* < Sans *tasara*, lit., a shuttle, kind of silkworm⟧ **1** an Asian silkworm (*Antheraea paphia*) that feeds on oak leaves and produces coarse, brownish silk filaments **2** *a)* this silk (in full **tussah silk**) *b)* a fabric made from this

Tus·saud (to͞o sō′; *popularly* tə sôd′), Madame (born *Marie Gresholtz*) 1760-1850; Swiss waxworks exhibitor in London

tus·sis (tus′is) *n.* ⟦L⟧ *Med.* a cough —**tus′sive** (-iv) *adj.*

tus·sle (tus′əl) *vi.* **-sled, -sling** ⟦LME *tussillen*, freq. of *tusen* (in comp.), to pull: see TOUSLE⟧ to fight, struggle, contend, etc. briefly but vigorously; wrestle; scuffle —*n.* a brief but vigorous struggle or contest; scuffle

tus·sock (tus′ək) *n.* ⟦< ?⟧ a thick tuft or clump of grass, sedge, twigs, etc. —**tus′sock·y** (-ē) *adj.*

tussock moth any of a family (Lymantriidae) of moths whose caterpillars are covered with long tufts of hair: many, as the gypsy moth, are destructive pests of certain trees

tut (*for n. and vi.*, tut; *for interj., see below*) *interj., n.* (a sound) used to express impatience, annoyance, mild rebuke, etc.: a click, or sucking sound, made by touching the tongue to the hard palate and rapidly withdrawing it: usually repeated one or more times (**tut-tut**): often jocular when pronounced as written —*vi.* **tut′ted, tut′ting** to utter this sound See also TSK

Tut·ankh·a·men (to͞ot′äŋk ä′mən) fl. *c.* 1355 B.C.; Egypt. king of the 18th dynasty: tomb discovered in 1922: also sp. **Tut′ankh·a′mun** or **Tut′ankh·a′mon**: popularly called **King Tut** (tut)

☆**tu·tee** (to͞o tē′, tyo͞o-) *n.* ⟦TUT(OR) + -EE[1]⟧ a person who is being tutored

tu·te·lage (to͞ot′'l ij, tyo͞ot′-) *n.* ⟦< L *tutela*, protection < *tutus* (see TUTOR) + -AGE⟧ **1** the function of a guardian; guardianship; care, protection, etc. **2** teaching; instruction **3** the condition of being under a guardian or tutor

tu·te·lar·y (to͞ot′'l er′ē, tyo͞ot′-) *adj.* ⟦L *tutelarius* < *tutela*: see prec.⟧ **1** that watches over or protects **2** of or serving as a guardian Also **tu′te·lar** (-ər) —*n., pl.* **-lar′ies** a tutelary god, spirit, etc.

tu·tor (to͞ot′ər, tyo͞ot′-) *n.* ⟦ME < MFr *tuteur* < L *tutor* < *tutus* for *tuitus*, pp. of *tueri*, to look after, guard⟧ **1** *a)* a teacher who gives individual instruction to a student; private teacher *b)* a person who gives remedial or supplemental instruction to another **2** *Civil Law* a legal guardian of a minor **3** in English universities, a college official in charge of the studies of an undergraduate ☆**4** in some American universities and colleges, a teacher ranking below an instructor; teaching assistant —*vt.* **1** to act as a tutor to; teach; esp., to give individual instruction to **2** [Now Rare] to train under discipline; discipline; admonish —*vi.* **1** to act as a tutor, or instructor ☆**2** [Old Informal] to be instructed, esp. by a tutor —**tu′tor·age** *n.*, **tu′tor·ship′**

tu·to·ri·al (to͞o tôr′ē əl, tyo͞o-) *adj.* ⟦< L *tutorius* + -AL⟧ of a tutor or tutors —*n.* **1** a class in a tutorial system **2** an intensive course given by a tutor or professor for one or several students, usually on a special topic **3** a system of instruction containing exercises, information, etc., as in a training manual or computer program, for individual self-study

tutorial system a system of instruction, as in some universities, in which a tutor directs the studies of each of a small group of students

tu·toy·er (to͞o′twä yā′; *Fr* tü twȧ yā′) *vt.* ⟦Fr < MFr < *tu* (familiar form for you, thou < L: see THOU[1]) + *toi* (acc. of *tu*) + *-er*, inf. ending⟧ to speak to familiarly, as, in French, by using the singular forms (*tu* and *toi*) of "you" rather than the more formal plural form (*vous*)

Tut·si (to͞ot′sē) *n., pl.* **-sis** or **-si** a member of a people of Burundi and Rwanda

tut·ti (to͞ot′tē) [*also in italics*] *Music adj., adv.* ⟦It (pl. of *tutto*), lit., all < VL **tottus* for L *totus*, all, whole: see TOTAL⟧ for all instruments or voices: often used as a musical direction —*n., pl.* **-tis 1** a musical passage to be played or sung by all performers **2** the tonal effect produced by the playing or singing of such a passage

☆**tut·ti-frut·ti** (to͞ot′ē fro͞ot′ē) *n.* ⟦It, lit., all fruits: see prec.⟧ **1** ice cream or other sweet food containing a mixture of chopped fruits, candied, dried, or fresh **2** a flavoring combining the flavors of a number of fruits

tut-tut *interj., n., vi. see* TUT

tu·tu (to͞o′to͞o′; *Fr* tü tü′) *n.* ⟦Fr, orig. baby talk alteration < *cul*, bottom, backside: see BASCULE⟧ a very short, full, projecting skirt worn by ballerinas

Tu·tu·i·la (to͞ot′o͞o ē′lə) chief island of American Samoa, in the South Pacific: with nearby islets, 53 sq mi (137 sq km); chief town, Pago Pago

Tu·va·lu (to͞o′və lo͞o′, to͞o vä′lo͞o) country consisting of a group of nine islands in the WC Pacific: a British protectorate since 1892, it became independent & a member of the Commonwealth (1978): 10 sq mi (26 sq km); cap. Funafuti

☆**tux** (tuks) *n., pl.* **tux′es** [Informal] *short for* TUXEDO

☆**tux·e·do** (tuk sē′dō) *n., pl.* **-dos** ⟦after the name of a country club at *Tuxedo* Park, near *Tuxedo* Lake, N.Y.⟧ **1** [Now Rare] a man's semiformal jacket for evening wear, orig. black and with satin lapels; dinner jacket **2** a suit of such a jacket and dark trousers, worn with a dark bow tie —*adj.* designating or of a sofa, chair, etc. with a straight back and with sides the same height as the back —**tux·e′doed** *adj.*

Tux·tla (to͞ost′lä′) city in SE Mexico: capital of Chiapas: in full **Tuxtla Gu·tiér·rez** (go͞o tyer′äs)

tu·yère (twē yer′, to͞o-; twēr; *Fr* tüē yər′) *n.* ⟦Fr, nozzle < OFr *tuyau*, a pipe < Frank **thuta*; akin to EFris *tute*, a pipe, tube⟧ the pipe or nozzle through which air is forced into a blast furnace, forge, etc.

TV[1] (tē′vē′) *n.* **1** television **2** *pl.* **TVs** or **TV's** a television receiver

TV[2] *abbrev.* transvestite

TVA *abbrev.* Tennessee Valley Authority

☆**TV dinner** ⟦prob. so named because convenient to eat while one is watching TV away from the dining table⟧ a frozen, precooked dinner packaged in a compartmented tray for heating and serving

Tver (tvyer) city in W European Russia, on the Volga: see KALININ

TW or **Tw** *abbrev.* terawatt(s)

twa (twä) *adj., n.* ⟦ME (Northern & Scot) < OE, two⟧ *Scot. var. of* TWO

twad·dle (twäd′'l) *n.* ⟦earlier *twattle*, prob. var. form of *tattle*, in *twittle-twattle* for TITTLE-TATTLE⟧ foolish, empty talk or writing; nonsense — *vt., vi.* **-dled, -dling** to talk or write in a foolish or senseless manner; prattle —**twad′dler** *n.*

twain (twān) *adj., n.* ⟦ME *twene* < OE *twegen*, nom. & acc. masc. form of *twa*, TWO⟧ *archaic var. of* TWO

Twain (twān), **Mark** ⟦< *Mark twain!*, two fathoms! (twelve feet of depth in the water), river pilot's cry indicating it is safe to proceed⟧ *pseudonym for* Samuel Langhorne CLEMENS

twang (twaŋ) *n.* ⟦echoic⟧ **1** *a)* a quick, sharp, vibrating sound, as of a taut string suddenly plucked or released *b)* an act of plucking that makes this sound **2** *a)* a sharply nasal way of speaking; ringing, nasal quality *b)* a dialect characterized by this *c)* an intonation and pronunciation regarded as distinctive of a particular region or class (a nontechnical usage) **3** [Dial.] a twinge —*vi.* **1** to make a twang, as a bowstring, banjo, etc. **2** to speak with a twang **3** to be released with a twang: said of an arrow —*vt.* **1** to cause to twang **2** to say with a twang **3** to shoot (an arrow), release (a bowstring), etc. with a twang —**twang′y** *adj.* **-i·er, -i·est**

'twas (twuz, twäz) *contraction* [Old Poet.] it was

twat (twät) *n.* ⟦< ?⟧ [Slang] **1** the vulva: considered vulgar by many **2** a woman or women collectively: a term of contempt and hostility

tway·blade (twā′blād′) *n.* ⟦archaic *tway*, two (ME *twei*, var. of *twene*: see TWAIN) + BLADE⟧ any of various native, soil-inhabiting orchids (esp. genera *Listera* and *Liparis*) having opposite, paired leaves

tweak (twēk) *vt.* ⟦var. of dial. *twick* < ME *twikken* < OE *twiccan*, to TWITCH⟧ **1** to give a sudden, twisting pinch to (someone's nose, ear, cheek, etc.) **2** to adjust or modify slightly, so as to improve performance, efficiency, etc.; fine-tune —*n.* **1** such a pinch **2** a minor adjustment or modification

twee (twē) *adj.* ⟦back-form. < *tweet*, in same sense < child's pronun. of SWEET⟧ [Brit.] affectedly clever, dainty, sweet, etc.

tweed (twēd) *n.* ⟦< misreading of *tweel*, Scot form of TWILL: later assoc. with TWEED[2]⟧ **1** a wool fabric with a rough surface, in any of various twill weaves of two or more colors or shades **2** a suit, skirt, etc. of this **3** [*pl.*] clothes of tweed

Tweed[1] (twēd), **William Mar·cy** (mär′sē) 1823-78; U.S. politician & Tammany leader: called *Boss Tweed*

Tweed[2] (twēd) river in SE Scotland flowing east through NE England into the North Sea: 97 mi (156 km)

twee·dle·dum and twee·dle·dee (twēd″l dum′ ən twēd″l dē′) ⟦< *tweedle*, echoic of reed pipe + *dum* & *dee*, echoic of musical notes: first used of two 18th-c. rival composers⟧ **1** two persons or things so much alike as to be almost indistinguishable **2** [**T- and T-**] two droll, almost identical brothers in *Through the Looking-Glass*, by Lewis Carroll

tweed·y (twē′dē) ***adj.*** **tweed′i·er, tweed′i·est 1** of or like tweed **2** [Informal] characterized by the wearing of tweeds **3** ⟦because assoc. with the wearing of tweeds⟧ [Informal, Chiefly Brit.] *a)* of or like the rural gentry *b)* of or like an academic or scholar —**tweed′i·ness *n.***

tween (twēn) ***n.*** ⟦blend of BETWEEN and TEEN[1]⟧ [Informal] a child who is not yet a teenager, typically one 8 to 12 years old

'tween (twēn) ***prep.*** [Old Poet.] *short for* BETWEEN

tween·y (twē′nē) ***n., pl.*** **-ies** ⟦< *tween*, aphetic for *betweenmaid* + -Y[1]⟧ [Old Brit. Informal] a housemaid who also assisted the cook

tweet (twēt) ***n.*** ⟦echoic⟧ the thin, chirping sound of a small bird —***interj.*** used to signify or imitate such a sound —***vi.*** to make such a sound

tweet·er (twēt′ər) ***n.*** a small, high-fidelity speaker for reproducing high-frequency sounds: cf. MIDRANGE, WOOFER

tweeze (twēz) ***vt.*** **tweezed, tweez′ing** ⟦back-form. < TWEEZERS⟧ to pluck with or as with tweezers

tweez·er (twē′zər) ***n.*** ⟦back-form. < fol.⟧ TWEEZERS

tweez·ers (twē′zərz) ***pl.n.*** ⟦extended < obs. *tweeze*, surgical set, aphetic for Fr *étuis*, pl. of *étui*: see ETUI⟧ [*also with sing. v.*] a small tool, consisting of two arms joined at one end, for plucking out hairs, handling little objects, etc.: often **pair of tweezers**

tweezers

twelfth (twelfth) ***adj.*** ⟦ME *twelfthe* < OE *twelfta*: see TWELVE & -TH[2]⟧ **1** preceded by eleven others in a series; 12th **2** designating any of the twelve equal parts of something —***n.*** **1** the one following the eleventh **2** any of the twelve equal parts of something; 1⁄12 —***adv.*** in the twelfth place, rank, group, etc.

Twelfth Day the twelfth day (Jan. 6) after Christmas, traditionally the end of the Christmas season; Epiphany

Twelfth Night 1 the evening before Twelfth Day **2** TWELFTH DAY or, specif., the evening of Twelfth Day

twelve (twelv) ***adj.*** ⟦ME *twelfe* < OE *twelf*, akin to Ger *zwölf*, Goth *twalif* < PGmc **twa-lif* < IE bases **dwōu* (> TWO) & **likw-* < base **leikw-*, to leave behind > LOAN: orig. sense, "two left (beyond ten)": cf. ELEVEN⟧ totaling two more than ten —***n.*** **1** the cardinal number between eleven and thirteen; 12; XII **2** any group of twelve persons or things; dozen **3** something numbered twelve or having twelve units, as a throw of dice, etc. —**the Twelve** the Twelve Apostles

Twelve Apostles the twelve disciples chosen by Jesus to go forth to teach the gospel: see APOSTLE (sense 2)

twelve·fold (twelv′fōld′) ***adj.*** **1** having twelve parts **2** having twelve times as much or as many —***adv.*** twelve times as much or as many

twelve·mo (-mō) ***adj., n., pl.*** **-mos** DUODECIMO

twelve·month (-munth′) ***n.*** [Chiefly Brit.] *archaic term for* one year

12-step or **twelve-step** (twelv′step′) ***adj.*** ⟦after the *Twelve Steps*, twelve guiding concepts forming part of the Alcoholics Anonymous program⟧ ☆designating or having to do with any of various programs that provide systematic support and guidance to individuals seeking to control an addiction, compulsion, etc.

twelve-tone (-tōn′) ***adj.*** *Music* designating or of a system or technique of serial composition, developed by Arnold Schönberg, in which the twelve tones of the chromatic scale are arranged into some arbitrary, fixed succession (*tone row*) which then forms a basis for development

twen·ti·eth (twen′tē ith, twen′ē-, twun′ē-) ***adj.*** ⟦ME *twentithe*, new formation for OE *twentigotha*: see fol. & -TH[2]⟧ **1** preceded by nineteen others in a series; 20th **2** designating any of the twenty equal parts of something —***n.*** **1** the one following the nineteenth **2** any of the twenty equal parts of something; 1⁄20 —***adv.*** in the twentieth place, rank, group, etc.

twen·ty (twen′tē, twen′ē, twun′ē) ***adj.*** ⟦ME *twenti* < OE *twegentig*, lit., two tens (akin to Ger *zwanzig*, Goth *twai tigjus*) < *twegen*, TWAIN + *-tig*, -TY[2]⟧ two times ten —***n., pl.*** **-ties 1** the cardinal number between nineteen and twenty-one; 20; XX ☆**2** [Informal] a twenty-dollar bill —**the Roaring Twenties** the decade 1920-29, regarded as a time of economic growth and of rebellion against social, esp. sexual, conventions —**the twenties** the numbers or years, as of a century, from twenty through twenty-nine

twen·ty·fold (-fōld′) ***adj.*** ⟦prec. + -FOLD⟧ **1** having twenty parts **2** having twenty times as much or as many —***adv.*** twenty times as much or as many

24/7 *adv., adj.* [Informal] twenty-four hours a day and seven days a week; continuous(ly): also written **24-7**

twen·ty-one (-wun′) ***n.*** ☆BLACKJACK (***n.*** *5a*)

twen·ty-twen·ty (*or* 20/20) vision (twen′tē twen′tē) normal acuity of vision, which is the ability to see clearly at twenty feet what the normal eye sees at that distance

'twere (twur) *contraction* [Archaic] it were [*if 'twere time*]

☆**twerk·ing** (twur′kiŋ) ***n.*** ⟦< ?⟧ a dance move, as in hip-hop, involving rythmic shaking and thrusting of the hips, often while the dancer is squatting or bending over —**twerk *vi.***

twerp (twurp) ***n.*** ⟦ult. < ? or akin to Dan *tver*, perverse: for IE base see THWART⟧ [Slang] a person regarded as insignificant, contemptible, presumptuous, ridiculous, etc.

Twi (twē) ***n.*** a language belonging to the Kwa branch of the Niger-Congo subfamily and spoken principally in Ghana

twi·bill or **twi·bil** (twī′bil′) ***n.*** ⟦ME *twibil* < OE < *twi-*, two + *bil*, BILL[3]⟧ **1** a double-bladed battle-ax **2** [Brit. Dial.] a kind of mattock

twice (twīs) ***adv.*** ⟦ME *twies* < OE *twiges* < *twiga*, twice, akin to *twa*, TWO + *-es*, gen. sing. ending⟧ **1** on two occasions or in two instances **2** two times **3** two times as much or as many; twofold; doubly

twice-told tale (-tōld′) ⟦after Shakespeare's *King John*, III, iv, 108⟧ a story or account that is well-known from repeated telling

Twick·en·ham (twik′ən əm) former borough in Middlesex, England, near London: now part of Richmond

twid·dle (twid″l) ***vt.*** **-dled, -dling** ⟦prob. < TW(IST) or TW(IRL) + (D)IDDLE⟧ to twirl or play with lightly or idly —***vi.*** **1** to toy or trifle with some object **2** to be busy about trifles **3** to move in a twirling manner —***n.*** a light, twirling motion, as with the thumbs —**twiddle one's thumbs 1** to twirl one's thumbs idly around each other **2** to do nothing; be idle —**twid′dler *n.*** —**twid′dly *adj.***

twig[1] (twig) ***n.*** ⟦ME *twigge* < OE, akin to Ger *zweig* < IE **dwigho-* < base **dwōu-*, TWO: prob. with reference to the forking of the twig⟧ a small, slender branch or shoot of a tree or shrub

twig[2] (twig) ***vt., vi.*** **twigged, twig′ging** ⟦via thieves' slang < Ir *tuigim*, I understand⟧ [Brit. Informal] **1** to observe **2** to understand

twig·gy (twig′ē) ***adj.*** **-gi·er, -gi·est 1** slender, delicate, etc. like a twig **2** full of or covered with twigs

twi·light (twī′līt′) ***n.*** ⟦ME < *twi-*, two, twice (but meaning here uncert.) + LIGHT[1]; akin to Ger *zwielicht*⟧ **1** *a)* the subdued light just after sunset or, in less common usage, just before sunrise *b)* the period from sunset to dark **2** any growing darkness **3** a condition or period of gradual decline following full development, achievement, glory, etc. —***adj.*** of or like twilight; dim, obscure, etc.

Twilight of the Gods *see* RAGNAROK

twilight sleep ⟦transl. of Ger *dämmerschlaf*⟧ a state of partial anesthesia induced by the injection of morphine and scopolamine, formerly used to lessen the pains of childbirth

twilight zone 1 a vague or uncertain area or state [*an ethical twilight zone between right and wrong*] **2** ⟦infl. by the U.S. television program *The Twilight Zone* (1959-64)⟧ a situation or state of mind seemingly between reality and fantasy

twi·lit (twī′lit) ***adj.*** full of or bathed in the softly diffused light associated with twilight [*a twilit bedroom*]

twill (twil) ***n.*** ⟦ME *twyll* < OE *twilic*, woven of double thread (akin to OHG *zwilih*) < WGmc partial transl. (with *twi-*, two) of L *bilix*, with a double thread < *bi-*, BI-[1] + *licium*, a thread⟧ **1** a cloth woven so as to have parallel diagonal lines or ribs **2** the pattern of this weave or its appearance —***vt.*** to weave so as to produce a twill

'twill (twil) *contraction* [Archaic] it will

twin (twin) ***adj.*** ⟦ME < OE *twinn* & ON *tvinnr*, double, both < base of TWO⟧ **1** *a)* consisting of or being two separate but similar or closely related things; forming a pair; double; paired *b)* being one of a pair of such things; being a counterpart **2** *a)* being two offspring from the same pregnancy [*twin girls*] *b)* being either one of two offspring from the same pregnancy [*a twin sister*] **3** TWIN-SIZE —***n.*** **1** either one of two offspring from the same pregnancy: twins are either *identical* (produced from the same ovum) or *fraternal* (produced from separate ova) **2** either one of two persons or things very much alike in appearance, shape, structure, etc. **3** a compound crystal of two crystals or parts having a common face but in reversed positions with respect to each other **4** TWIN BED —***vi.*** **twinned, twin′ning 1** to give birth to twins **2** to be paired or coupled (with another) **3** [Archaic] to be born at the same birth —***vt.*** **1** to give birth to as twins **2** to be or provide a counterpart to **3** to pair or couple —**the Twins** Gemini, the constellation and third sign of the zodiac

twin bed either of a pair of single beds

☆**twin·ber·ry** (twin′ber′ē) ***n., pl.*** **-ries 1** a North American variety of honeysuckle (*Lonicera involucrata*) with purple flowers **2** PARTRIDGEBERRY

☆**twin bill** [Informal] **1** DOUBLE FEATURE **2** DOUBLE-HEADER (sense 2)

Twin Cities *name for* Minneapolis & St. Paul, Minn.

twine (twīn) ***n.*** ⟦ME *twin* < OE *twin*, *twigin*, double thread, akin to *twegen*, TWAIN⟧ **1** strong thread, string, or cord of two or more strands twisted together **2** a twining or being twined **3** a twined thing or part; twist; convolution **4** a tangle; snarl **5** a twining branch or spray of a plant —***vt.*** **twined, twin′ing** ⟦ME *twinen* < the n.⟧ **1** *a)* to twist together; intertwine; interlace *b)* to form by twisting, intertwining, or interlacing **2** to encircle or wreathe (one thing) with another **3** to wind (something) around something else **4** to enfold, embrace, etc. [*a wreath twining his brow*] —***vi.*** **1** to twist, interlace, etc. **2** to twist and turn

twin-en·gine (twin′en′jən) ***adj.*** powered by two engines: said of an airplane: also **twin′-en′gined** (-jənd)

☆**twin·flow·er** (-flou′ər) ***n.*** a trailing plant (*Linnaea borealis*) of the honeysuckle family, with glossy leaves and small, fragrant, pink, bell-shaped flowers growing in pairs

twinge (twinj) *vt.* **twinged, twing′ing** ⟦ME *twengen* < OE *twengan,* to squeeze, press, pinch; akin to MHG *twengen,* to pinch, squeeze (< OHG *dwengen,* caus. of *dwingan,* to constrain) & OE *thwang,* a thong, prob. < IE base **tuengh-,* to constrain⟧ to cause to have a sudden, brief, darting pain or pang —*vi.* to feel a sudden, brief, darting pain or pang —*n.* **1** a sudden, brief, darting pain or pang **2** a sudden, brief feeling of remorse, shame, etc.; qualm

☆**twi-night** or **twi·night** (twī′nīt′) *adj.* ⟦TWI(LIGHT) + NIGHT⟧ *Baseball* designating a double-header that starts in the late afternoon and continues into the evening

☆**twinkie** (twiŋ′kē) *n.* ⟦< *Twinkies,* trademark for small, yellowish pieces of spongecake with a creamy filling⟧ [*also* **T-**] [Slang] a person or thing that seems appealing or attractive but has little value or worth

twin·kle (twiŋ′kəl) *vi.* **-kled, -kling** ⟦ME *twinklen* < OE *twinclian,* freq. of base seen in MHG *zwinken,* to wink⟧ **1** to shine with quick, intermittent flashes of light, as some stars; sparkle **2** to light up, as with amusement: said of the eyes **3** to move about or back and forth quickly and lightly, as a dancer's feet; flicker **4** [Archaic] to wink or blink —*vt.* **1** to make twinkle **2** to emit (light) in quick, intermittent flashes —*n.* **1** a flicker or wink of the eye **2** a quick flash of amusement, etc. in the eye **3** a quick, intermittent flash of light; sparkle **4** the very brief time it takes to wink; twinkling —**twin′kler** *n.*

twin·kling (twiŋ′kliŋ) *n.* **1** the action of a thing that twinkles **2** *a)* the winking of an eye *b)* the very brief time it takes to wink; instant

twin-lens reflex (twin′lenz′) a reflex camera with two lenses, one of which supplies the image reflected in the viewfinder and the other the image on the exposed film

twinned (twind) *adj.* **1** born as a twin or twins **2** paired or coupled **3** consisting of two crystals forming a twin

twin·ning (twin′iŋ) *n.* **1** the bearing of twins **2** a pairing or coupling **3** the formation of a twin crystal or crystals

twin-screw (twin′skro͞o′) *adj.* having two screw propellers, usually rotating in opposite directions, as some ships

twin set a matching pair of women's sweaters, a pullover and a cardigan, intended to be worn together: also **twin′set′** *n.*

twin-size (twin′sīz′) *adj.* **1** of or being the usual or standard size of a twin bed **2** designating or of a bed that is 38 x 75 in Also **twin′-sized′** (-sīzd′)

twirl (twurl) *vt., vi.* ⟦prob. < Scand, as in Norw dial. *tvirla,* to twirl, akin to OE *thwirel,* stirring rod < IE base **twer-,* to whirl, stir up > TURBID⟧ **1** to rotate rapidly; spin **2** to turn rapidly in a circle; whirl around **3** to twist or coil [to *twirl* one's mustache] ☆**4** [Slang] *Baseball* to pitch [to *twirl* a no-hitter] —*n.* **1** a twirling or being twirled **2** something twirled; specif., *a)* a twist, coil, etc. *b)* a twisting line; flourish —**twirl′er** *n.*

twirp (twurp) *n.* [Slang] *alt. sp. of* TWERP

twist (twist) *vt.* ⟦ME *twisten* < OE *-twist,* a rope (in *mæst-twist,* rope to stay a mast), akin to TWAIN, TWINE, ON *tvistra,* to separate, Ger *zwist,* a quarrel < IE **duis-,* apart < base **dwōu-,* TWO⟧ **1** *a)* to wind (two or more threads or strands) around one another, as by spinning *b)* to wind two or more threads or strands of (cotton, silk, etc.) around one another so as to produce thread or cord *c)* to produce (thread, cord, etc.) in this way **2** to wreathe; twine **3** to wind or coil (thread, rope, etc.) around something **4** to encircle with a coil of **5** to entwine or interweave in something else **6** to make (one's or its way) by turning one way and then another **7** to give spiral shape to by turning the ends in opposite directions **8** *a)* to subject to torsion *b)* to put out of shape in this manner; wrench; sprain [to *twist* one's ankle] **9** *a)* to contort or distort (the face, etc.) *b)* to cause to be malformed [fingers *twisted* with arthritis] **10** to cause to become confused or mentally or emotionally disturbed **11** to distort or pervert the meaning of **12** to cause to turn around or rotate **13** to break off by turning the end: often with *off* —*vi.* **1** to undergo twisting and thus take on a spiral or coiled form [the wire *twists* easily] **2** to spiral, coil, twine, etc. (*around* or *about* something) **3** to revolve or rotate **4** to turn one way and then another, as a path; wind; meander **5** to squirm; writhe **6** to move in a curved path, as a ball given a spinning motion ☆**7** to dance the twist —*n.* **1** the number of turns given to a specified length of fiber, thread, cord, etc. along its axis **2** a strong, closely twisted silk thread used for making buttonholes, etc. ☆**3** tobacco leaves twisted into the shape of a roll **4** a loaf of bread or a roll made of one or more twisted pieces of dough **5** a sliver of peel from a lemon, lime, etc. twisted and added to a drink for flavor **6** rotation; spin, turn, twirl, etc. **7** a spin given to a ball in throwing or striking it **8** spiral movement along and around an axis **9** *a)* the condition of being twisted in a spiral; torsional stress *b)* the degree of this; angle of torsion **10** a contortion, as of the face **11** a wrench or sprain **12** a turning aside; turn; bend **13** a place at which something twists or turns [a *twist* in the road] **14** a personal tendency, esp. an eccentric one; quirk **15** distortion or perversion, as of meaning **16** an unexpected direction given to or taken by a situation **17** a special or different meaning, method, or slant [a new *twist* to an old story] ☆**18** a rock-and-roll dance popular in the 1960s, characterized by a twisting of the torso from side to side while standing in one place —***SYN.*** CURVE

twist drill a kind of drill with deep helical grooves for carrying out chips and shavings

twist·er (twis′tər) *n.* **1** a person who twists **2** a thing that twists; specif., *a)* a machine for twisting threads, etc. *b)* a thrown or batted ball that has been given a twist ☆**3** [Informal] a tornado or cyclone

twist-tie (twis′tī′) *n.* a short, slender wire covered as with paper or plastic, twisted to tie closed a plastic bag or other wrapper: also written **twist tie**

twist·y (twis′tē) *adj.* **1** having many twists and turns [a *twisty* road] **2** not simple or straightforward; characterized by complexity, surprises, etc. [a *twisty* plot]

twit[1] (twit) *vt.* **twit′ted, twit′ting** ⟦aphetic < ME *atwiten,* to twit < OE *ætwitan* < *æt,* at + *witan,* to accuse, akin to *witan,* to know: see WISE[1]⟧ to reproach, tease, taunt, etc., esp. by reminding of a fault or mistake —*n.* **1** the act of twitting **2** a reproach or taunt

twit[2] (twit) *n.* ⟦< ?⟧ [Informal, Chiefly Brit.] a foolish, contemptible person

twitch (twich) *vt., vi.* ⟦ME *twicchen* < OE **twiccan,* var. of *twiccian,* to pluck, catch hold of: akin to Ger *zwicken* < WGmc **twikkjon* < ? base of TWIG[1]⟧ **1** to pull (at) with a quick, slight jerk; pluck **2** to move with a quick, slight jerk or jerks or spasmodically **3** to ache with a sudden, sharp pain —*n.* **1** a quick, slight jerk **2** a sudden, quick motion, esp. a spasmodic one; tic [a facial *twitch*] **3** a sudden, sharp pain; twinge

twitch·y (twich′ē) *adj.* **-i·er, -i·est** [Informal] nervous; jittery

twit·ter[1] (twit′ər) *vi.* ⟦ME *twiteren,* akin to Ger *zwitschern:* orig. echoic⟧ **1** to make a series of light, sharp, intermittent vocal sounds; chirp continuously or tremulously, as birds do **2** *a)* to talk in a rapid, tremulous manner expressive of agitation, timidity, etc.; chatter *b)* to giggle or titter **3** to tremble with excitement, eagerness, etc. —*vt.* to express or say in a twittering manner —*n.* **1** a light, sharp, intermittent vocal sound of a bird; chirping **2** any similar sound **3** a condition of trembling excitement; flutter —**twit′ter·er** *n.* —**twit′ter·y** *adj.*

twit·ter[2] (twit′ər) *n.* a person who twits

'twixt (twikst) *prep.* [Old Poet.] *short for* BETWIXT

two (to͞o) *adj.* ⟦ME *two, tu* < OE *twa,* fem. & neut., *tu,* neut., akin to Ger *zwei* < IE base **dwōu-,* two > L *duo,* two, Gr *duo,* Sans *dvau*⟧ totaling one more than one —*n.* **1** the cardinal number between one and three; 2; II **2** any two people or things; pair; couple **3** something numbered two or having two units, as a playing card, domino, face of a die, etc. **4** *Basketball short for* TWO-POINTER —**in two** in two parts; asunder —**put two and two together** to reach an obvious conclusion by considering several facts together

☆**two-base hit** (to͞o′bās′) *Baseball* a hit on which the batter can reach second base: also [Slang] **two′-bag′ger** (-bag′ər) *n.*

☆**two-bit** (to͞o′bit′) *adj.* ⟦see BIT[2], *n.* 2⟧ **1** [Informal] worth or costing twenty-five cents **2** [Slang] *a)* cheap; gaudy; tawdry *b)* mediocre, inferior, or insignificant

☆**two bits** [see prec.] [Old Informal] twenty-five cents

☆**two-by-four** (to͞o′bī fôr′) *adj.* **1** that measures two inches by four inches, two feet by four feet, etc. **2** [Informal] small, narrow, cramped, etc. —*n.* any length of lumber two inches thick and four inches wide when untrimmed: in the building trades, applied to a trimmed piece 1½ by 3½ inches

☆**two cents** a person's opinion: used dismissively or ironically: often in the phrase **put in one's two cents**: also **two cents' worth**

two-cycle (to͞o′sī′kəl) *adj.* TWO-STROKE

two-di·men·sion·al (to͞o′də men′shə nəl) *adj.* **1** of or having two dimensions, as height and width **2** lacking substance or depth; limited in scope, range, etc. [a *two-dimensional* movie character] —**two′-di·men′sion·al′i·ty** (-nal′ə tē) *n.* —**two′-di·men′sion·al·ly** *adv.*

two-edged (-ejd′) *adj.* DOUBLE-EDGED

two-faced (to͞o′fāst′) *adj.* **1** having two faces, surfaces, etc. **2** deceitful; hypocritical —**two′-fac′ed·ly** (-fās′id lē) *adv.*

☆**two·fer** (to͞o′fər) *n.* ⟦altered < *two for* (*the price of one*)⟧ [Informal] a pair, as of theater tickets, sold for, or approximately for, the price of one

two-fist·ed (to͞o′fis′tid) *adj.* ☆[Informal] virile, rowdy, vigorous, etc.

two·fold (to͞o′fōld′) *adj.* ⟦TWO + -FOLD⟧ **1** having two parts; double; dual **2** having twice as much or as many —*adv.* twice as much or as many

two-four (to͞o′fôr′) *adj.* ⟦< the time signature, 2/4⟧ designating or of a musical rhythm with two quarter notes to a measure

☆**2,4-D** (to͞o′fôr′dē′) *n.* DICHLOROPHENOXYACETIC ACID

☆**2,4,5-T** (-fīv′tē′) *n.* TRICHLOROPHENOXYACETIC ACID

two-hand·ed (-han′did) *adj.* **1** that needs to be used or wielded with both hands **2** needing two people to operate [a *two-handed* saw] **3** for two people [a *two-handed* card game] **4** having two hands **5** able to use both hands equally well; ambidextrous

two-hand·er (to͞o′han′dər) *n.* [Chiefly Brit.] a play for just two actors

two-leg·ged (-leg′id, -legd′; -lā′gid, -lāgd′) *adj.* having two legs

two·pence (tup′əns) *n.* **1** the sum of two pence **2** a British coin of this value

two·pen·ny (tup′ə nē; *for 2* to͞o′pen′ē) *adj.* **1** worth or costing twopence **2** *Carpentry* designating a nail that is one inch long **3** cheap; worthless

two-phase (to͞o′fāz′) *adj. Elec.* powered by two equal AC voltages or currents which are out of phase by one quarter of a cycle (90°); quarter-phase

two-piece (to͞o′pēs′) *adj.* consisting of two separate parts [a woman's *two-piece* bathing suit]

two-ply (-plī′) *adj.* **1** having two thicknesses, layers, strands, etc. **2** woven double

two-point·er (to͞o′point′ər) *n. Basketball* a shot from inside or on the three point line, worth two points if it is made

two-shot (-shät′) *n. Film* a medium-range camera shot of two persons

Two Sic·i·lies (sis′ə lēz′) a former kingdom including Naples (with lower Italy) and Sicily: united with the Kingdom of Italy in 1861

two-sid·ed (to͞o′sīd′id) *adj.* **1** having two sides **2** having two aspects [a *two-sided* question]

two·some (to͞o′səm) *adj.* ⟦TWO + -SOME[2]⟧ of or engaged in by two —*n.* **1**

two people together; a couple **2** *Golf a)* a match or round engaged in by two players *b)* the players

two-step (to͞o′step′) ***n.*** **1** an early 20th-cent. ballroom dance in 2/4 time, like a slow fox trot **2** a piece of music for this dance —***vi.*** **-stepped′**, **-step′ping** to dance the two-step

two-stroke (to͞o′strōk′) ***adj.*** designating or having to do with an internal-combustion engine in which a complete fuel cycle in a cylinder requires only two piston strokes

two-suit·er (to͞o′so͞ot′ər) ***n.*** a suitcase designed to hold two suits as well as other clothing

☆**two-time** (to͞o′tīm′) ***vt.*** **-timed′**, **-tim′ing** [Slang] to deceive or double-cross; esp., to be unfaithful to (one's spouse or lover) —**two′-tim′er** ***n.***

two-tone (to͞o′tōn′) ***adj.*** of or having two colors or two hues of a color

'twould (two͝od) *contraction* [Archaic] it would

two-way (to͞o′wā′) ***adj.*** **1** having separate lanes for vehicles going in opposite directions [*a two-way street*] **2** involving reciprocity, mutual obligation, etc. [*a two-way cultural exchange, contract, etc.*] **3** involving two persons, groups, etc. [*a two-way political race*] **4** *a)* used for both transmission and reception [*a two-way radio*] *b)* moving, operating, or allowing movement in either of two directions [*a two-way faucet, two-way stretch, etc.*] **5** adapted for use in either of two ways; esp., reversible [*a two-way raincoat*] **6** designating or of glass that functions as a mirror from one side and as see-through glass from the other

two-wheel·er (to͞o′hwēl′ər, -wēl′-) ***n.*** **1** BICYCLE **2** HAND TRUCK

Twp *abbrev.* township

TX *abbrev.* Texas

-ty[1] (tē, ti) ⟦ME *-tee, -tie, -te* < OFr *-té* < L *-tas*⟧ *suffix* quality of, condition of [*realty*]

-ty[2] (tē, ti) ⟦ME *-ti, -tie* < OE *-tig*, akin to Ger *-zig*, Goth *tigus*, ten, L *-ta* < IE **dekṃt-mi(s)*, dat. pl. < **dekṃ*, TEN⟧ *suffix* tens, times ten [*sixty*]

Ty·che (tī′kē) ***n.*** ⟦Gr *Tychē*, akin to *teuchein*, to prepare < IE base **dheugh-*, to press > DOUGHTY⟧ *Gr. Myth.* the goddess of chance: identified with the Roman Fortuna

☆**ty·coon** (tī ko͞on′) ***n.*** ⟦SinoJpn *taikun*, term of respect for an emperor < *tai*, great (< Cantonese) + *kun*, monarch (< Cantonese *kuan*, official)⟧ **1** a title applied by foreigners to the former shogun of Japan **2** a wealthy and powerful industrialist, financier, etc.

Ty·gon (tī′gän) ⟦arbitrary coinage⟧ *trademark for* any of a group of vinyl compounds used as a lining or coating on metal surfaces, as tubing, etc., to prevent corrosion

tyin (tēn) ***n.***, *pl.* **tyin** a monetary unit of Kazakhstan, equal to $\frac{1}{100}$ of a tenge

ty·ing (tī′iŋ) ***vt.***, ***vi.*** *prp. of* TIE

tyke (tīk) ***n.*** ⟦ME *tike* < ON *tik*, a bitch < IE base **digh-*, goat > OE *ticcen*, a kid⟧ **1** [Informal] a small child **2** [Brit.] *a)* a dog, esp. a mongrel *b)* [Dial.] a boor

Ty·ler[1] (tī′lər) ***n.*** a masculine name

Ty·ler[2] (tī′lər) **1 John** 1790-1862; 10th president of the U.S. (1841-45) **2 Wat** (wät) died 1381; Eng. rebel: leader of the Peasants' Revolt: also **Walter Tyler**

Ty·ler[3] (tī′lər) ⟦after John TYLER[2]⟧ city in E Tex.

tym·pan (tim′pən) ***n.*** ⟦ME < OE *timpana* & OFr *tympan* < L *tympanum* < Gr *tympanon*, a drum, area of a pediment, panel of a door < *typtein*, to strike, beat < IE **(s)teup-*, to strike > STEEP[1]⟧ **1** [Obs.] a drum **2** the paper, cardboard, etc. stretched over the platen or impression cylinder of a printing press to cushion the paper being printed and equalize type pressure **3** any membranelike part **4** *Archit.* TYMPANUM

tym·pa·ni (tim′pə nē) ***pl.n.***, *sing.* **-no′** (-nō′) *alt. sp. of* TIMPANI —**tym′pa·nist** ***n.***

tym·pan·ic (tim pan′ik) ***adj.*** **1** of or like a drum or drumhead **2** *Anat., Zool.* of the tympanum, esp. the eardrum

tympanic bone a bone in the skull of mammals, supporting the eardrum and partly enclosing the middle ear

tympanic membrane a thin membrane that separates the middle ear from the external ear and vibrates when struck by sound waves; eardrum

tym·pa·ni·tes (tim′pə nīt′ēz′) ***n.*** ⟦ME < LL < Gr *tympanitēs* < *tympanon*: see TYMPAN⟧ a distention of the abdomen by the accumulation of gas or air in the intestines or peritoneal cavity —**tym′pa·nit′ic** (-nit′ik) ***adj.***

tym·pa·ni·tis (-nīt′is) ***n.*** otitis media: see OTITIS

tym·pa·num (tim′pə nəm) ***n.***, *pl.* **-nums** or **-na** (-nə) ⟦L: see TYMPAN⟧ **1** *Anat. a)* MIDDLE EAR *b)* TYMPANIC MEMBRANE **2** *Zool. a)* a drumlike structure serving as a vibratory membrane for the hearing organs of certain insects *b)* the resonating chamber of the syrinx in birds **3** a drum or drumhead **4** *Archit. a)* the recessed space, usually triangular, enclosed by the slanting cornices of a pediment, often ornamented with sculpture *b)* a corresponding semicircular space enclosed by an arch and the top of the door or window below it **5** *Elec.* the diaphragm of a telephone

tym·pa·ny (tim′pə nē) ***n.***, *pl.* **-nies** ⟦ML *tympanias* < Gr < *tympanon*, drum: see TYMPAN⟧ **1** inflated or distended condition **2** bombast; pomposity

Tyn·dale (tin′dəl), **William** 1494?-1536; Eng. religious reformer & translator of the Bible: executed for heresy

Tyn·dall effect (tin′dəl) ⟦after John *Tyndall* (1820-93), Brit physicist⟧ *Physics* the scattering and polarization of a light beam by colloidal particles in a dispersed system

Tyn·dar·e·us (tin der′ē əs) ***n.*** ⟦L < Gr *Tyndareos*⟧ *Gr. Myth.* a king of Sparta, husband of LEDA

Tyne (tīn) river in N England, flowing east into the North Sea: *c.* 30 mi (48 km)

Tyne and Wear county in N England, on the Tyne & the North Sea: 207 sq mi (536 sq km)

typ *abbrev.* **1** typographer **2** typographical **3** typography

typ·al (tīp′əl) ***adj.*** **1** of or pertaining to a type **2** serving as a type; typical

type (tīp) ***n.*** ⟦LL(Ec) *typus*, a model, symbol < L & Gr: L, a figure < Gr *typos*, a figure, archetype, model, orig., a blow, mark made by a blow < *typtein*: see TYMPAN⟧ **1** a person, thing, or event that represents or symbolizes another, esp. another that it is thought will appear later; symbol; token; sign **2** [Rare] a distinguishing mark, sign, or impress **3** the general form, structure, plan, style, etc. characterizing or distinguishing the members of a class or group **4** a kind, class, or group having distinguishing characteristics in common [*a new type of airplane, an animal of the dog type*]: in informal usage, often used elliptically immediately preceding the noun [*a new type airplane*] **5** a person, animal, or thing that is representative of, or has the distinctive characteristics of, a class or group; typical individual or instance **6** a perfect example; model; pattern; archetype **7** *Agric.* the combination of characters of an animal or breed that make it most suitable for a particular use [*beef type, dairy type*] **8** *Biol. a)* the single specimen designated as the one on which the original description and name of a taxon have been based *b)* TYPE GENUS or TYPE SPECIES **9** *Math.* the simplest of a set of equivalent forms **10** *Printing a)* a rectangular piece of metal or wood with a raised letter, figure, etc. in reverse on its upper end: when the raised portion is inked and pressed against a piece of paper or other material, as in a printing press or a typewriter, it leaves an ink impression of its face *b)* such pieces collectively or the characters printed from them *c)* a character or characters formed electronically and produced by a computer printer *d)* photographic reproductions of print used in photocomposition *e)* a particular face of type —***vt.*** **typed**, **typ′ing** **1** [Now Rare] *a)* to prefigure *b)* to typify; represent **2** to classify according to type [*to be typed as a villain*] **3** to write using the keyboard of a typewriter, computer, etc. **4** *Med.* to determine the type of (a blood sample) —***vi.*** to use the keyboard of a typewriter, computer, etc.; specif., to touch-type —**someone's type** [Informal] the kind of person that someone finds attractive or agreeable [*a bookish man is definitely not her type*] —**typ′a·ble** ***adj.***, **type′a·ble**

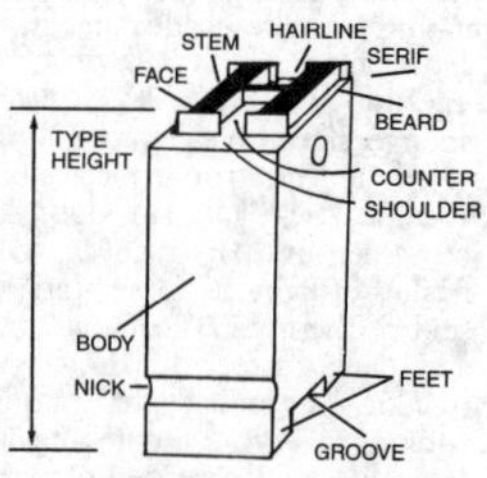

piece of printing type

-type (tīp) ⟦Fr < Gr *-typon* < *typos*: see prec.⟧ *combining form* **1** type, representative form, example [*phonotype, stereotype*] **2** stamp, print, printing type [*ferrotype, monotype*]

☆**Type A** ⟦first used (*c.* 1974) by M. Friedman & R. Rosenman, U.S. physicians⟧ a personality type characterized by drive, impatience, aggression, etc., traits thought to make one more susceptible to stress

☆**Type B** ⟦see prec.⟧ a personality type characterized by calmness, patience, amiability, etc., traits thought to make one less susceptible to stress

☆**type·bar** (tīp′bär′) ***n.*** any of the slender bars to which are fastened the raised letters, figures, etc. in some typewriters

type·cast (tīp′kast′) ***vt.*** **-cast′**, **-cast′ing** **1** to cast (an actor) repeatedly in the same type of part, or in the part of a character whose traits are very much like the actor's own **2** STEREOTYPE (***vt.*** 3)

type·face (tīp′fās′) ***n.*** FACE (***n.*** 13)

type founder a person who casts metal type

type genus *Biol.* the particular genus whose name serves as the base for the family name

type metal an alloy of tin, lead, and antimony, and sometimes copper, used for making type, etc.

Type 1 diabetes a severe, less common type of diabetes mellitus, typically appearing during childhood or adolescence, in which the body's immune system destroys insulin-producing cells in the pancreas: also written **Type I diabetes**

☆**type·script** (-skript′) ***n.*** typewritten matter or copy

type·set (tīp′set′) ***vt.*** **-set′**, **-set′ting** ⟦back-form. < fol.⟧ to set in type; compose

type·set·ter (-set′ər) ***n.*** **1** a person who sets type; compositor **2** a machine for setting type —**type′set′ting** ***n.***, ***adj.***

type species *Biol.* the particular species from which the genus is named

type specimen TYPE (***n.*** *8a*)

Type 2 diabetes a common type of diabetes mellitus, often associated with obesity, in which the body produces or utilizes insufficient levels of insulin: also written **Type II diabetes**

type·write (tīp′rīt′) ***vt.***, ***vi.*** **-wrote′**, **-writ′ten**, **-writ′ing** ⟦back-form. < fol.⟧ to write with a typewriter: now usually shortened to *type*

☆**type·writ·er** (tīp′rīt′ər) ***n.*** ⟦TYPE + WRITER: so named (1867), prob. by C. L. Sholes (1819-90), U.S. journalist, who patented the first practical machine (1868)⟧ **1** a writing machine with a keyboard, for reproducing letters or figures that resemble printed ones **2** a style of printer's type that looks like a typewriter print **3** *former term for* TYPIST

type·writ·ing (-rīt′iŋ) ***n.*** **1** the art, act, or process of using a typewriter **2** writing done on a typewriter

typh·li·tis (tif līt′is) ***n.*** ⟦ModL < Gr *typhlon*, cecum < *typhlos*, blind, closed (< IE **dhubh-*, cloudy, dark < base **dheu-*, to be turbid > DULL) + ModL *-itis*, -ITIS⟧ inflammation of the cecum

ty·pho- (tī′fō, -fə) ⟦< Gr *typhos*: see TYPHUS⟧ *combining form* typhus, typhoid *[typhogenic]*: also, before a vowel, **typh-**

Ty·pho·e·us (tī fō′ē əs, -yo͞os′; -fē′əs) ***n.*** ⟦L < Gr *Typhōeus*⟧ *Gr. Myth.* a monster with a hundred heads, killed by Zeus —**Ty·pho′e·an** (-fō′ē ən, -fē′ ən) ***adj.***

ty·phoid (tī′foid′) ***n.*** ⟦TYPH(US) + -OID⟧ **1** [Archaic] any typhuslike disorder **2** an acute infectious disease caused by a bacterium (*Salmonella* Typhi) and acquired by ingesting food or water contaminated by excreta: it was formerly considered a form of typhus and is characterized by fever, intestinal disorders, etc.: in full **typhoid fever** —**ty·phoi′dal** ***adj.***

☆**Typhoid Mary** ⟦orig., nickname for *Mary Mallon* (died 1938), typhoid-carrying cook in New York⟧ a person who spreads disease, infection, or corruption

Ty·phon (tī′făn) ***n.*** ⟦L < Gr *Typhōn*, lit., whirlwind: see fol.⟧ *Gr. Myth.* a monster, variously regarded as a son of Typhoeus or as Typhoeus himself

ty·phoon (tī fo͞on′) ***n.*** ⟦< Chin dial. *tai-fung*, lit., great wind (or < ? *Tai*, Formosa: hence, Formosa wind); merged with earlier *tuphan, tufan* < Port *tufão* < Ar *ṭūfān* < Gr *typhōn*, hurricane, akin to *typhos*: see fol.⟧ any violent tropical cyclone originating in the W Pacific, esp. in the South China Sea —**ty·phon′ic** (-făn′ik) ***adj.***

ty·phus (tī′fəs) ***n.*** ⟦ModL < Gr *typhos*, vapor, fever, stupor, akin to *typhein*, to smoke, be cloudy < IE base **dheu-*: see DULL⟧ an acute infectious disease caused by various rickettsiae (*esp. Rickettsia prowazekii*) transmitted to people by the bite of fleas, lice, etc., and characterized by fever, headache, and an eruption of red spots on the skin: in full **typhus fever** —**ty′phous** (-fəs) ***adj.***

typ·i·cal (tip′i kəl) ***adj.*** ⟦ML *typicalis* < L *typicus* < Gr *typikos*⟧ **1** serving as a type; symbolic **2** having or showing the characteristics, qualities, etc. of a kind, class, or group so fully as to be a representative example **3** of or belonging to a type or representative example; characteristic **4** [Informal] conforming with pessimistic or cynical expectations *[I'm late and the bus was early. That's so typical!]* —**SYN.** NORMAL —**typ′i·cal·ly** ***adv.*** —**typ′i·cal·ness** ***n.***, **typ′i·cal′i·ty** (-kal′ə tē)

typ·i·fy (tip′i fī′) ***vt.*** **-fied′**, **-fy′ing** ⟦see TYPE & -FY⟧ **1** to be a type or emblem of; symbolize; prefigure **2** to have or show the distinctive characteristics of; be typical of; exemplify —**typ′i·fi·ca′tion** ***n.*** —**typ′i·fi′er** ***n.***

typ·ist (tīp′ist) ***n.*** a person skilled at or employed to do typing

☆**ty·po**[1] (tī′pō) ***n.***, *pl.* **-pos** [Informal] a typographical error

typo[2] or **typog** *abbrev.* **1** typographer **2** typographic **3** typographical **4** typography

ty·po- (tī′pō, tī′pə) ⟦< Gr *typos*: see TYPE⟧ *combining form* type *[typography, typology]*

ty·pog·ra·pher (tī päg′rə fər) ***n.*** a person skilled in typography; printer, compositor, etc.

ty·po·graph·i·cal (tī′pə graf′i kəl) ***adj.*** of typography; having to do with the setting of type, printing, typing, inputting, etc.: also **ty′po·graph′ic** —**ty′po·graph′i·cal·ly** ***adv.***

ty·pog·ra·phy (tī päg′rə fē) ***n.*** ⟦Fr *typographie* < ML *typographia*: see TYPO- & -GRAPHY⟧ **1** the art or process of printing from type **2** the art or process of setting and arranging type for printing **3** the arrangement, style, or general appearance of typeset matter

ty·pol·o·gy (tī päl′ə jē) ***n.*** ⟦TYPO- + -LOGY⟧ **1** the study of types, symbols, or symbolism **2** symbolic meaning or representation; symbolism —**ty·po·log·i·cal** (tī′pə läj′i kəl) ***adj.***

Tyr (tir) ***n.*** ⟦ON: for IE base see TIU⟧ *Norse Myth.* the god of war and a son of Odin, noted for his courage

ty·ra·mine (tī′rə mēn′, -min) ***n.*** ⟦TYR(OSINE) + AMINE⟧ a crystalline amine, $C_8H_{11}NO$, found in ergot, cheeses, mistletoe, etc., and formerly used in the treatment of hypotension

ty·ran·ni·cal (tə ran′i kəl, ti-, tī-) ***adj.*** ⟦L *tyrannicus* < Gr *tyrannikos*⟧ **1** of or suited to a tyrant; arbitrary; despotic **2** harsh, cruel, unjust, oppressive, etc. Also **ty·ran′nic** —**ty·ran′ni·cal·ly** ***adv.***

ty·ran·ni·cide (tə ran′ə sīd′, ti-, tī-) ***n.*** ⟦sense 1 < L *tyrannicidium*; sense 2 < L *tyrannicida*: see TYRANT & -CIDE⟧ **1** the act of killing a tyrant **2** a person who kills a tyrant —**ty·ran′ni·ci′dal** ***adj.***

tyr·an·nize (tir′ə nīz′) ***vi.*** **-nized′**, **-niz′ing** ⟦MFr *tyranniser* < ML *tyrannizare*⟧ **1** to govern as a tyrant; rule with absolute power **2** to govern or use authority harshly or cruelly; be oppressive —***vt.*** to treat tyrannically; oppress —**tyr′an·niz′er** ***n.***

☆**ty·ran·no·saur** (tə ran′ə sôr′, ti-, tī-) ***n.*** ⟦< ModL *Tyrannosaurus* < Gr *tyrannos*, tyrant + ModL *-saurus*, -SAURUS⟧ any of a genus (*Tyrannosaurus*) of huge, bipedal, flesh-eating theropod dinosaurs of the Upper Cretaceous Period in North America and Asia, esp. the largest species (*Tyrannosaurus rex*): also **ty·ran′no·sau′rus** (-əs)

tyr·an·nous (tir′ə nəs) ***adj.*** tyrannical; despotic, oppressive, unjust, etc. —**tyr′an·nous·ly** ***adv.***

tyr·an·ny (tir′ə nē) ***n.***, *pl.* **-nies** ⟦ME *tirannie* < OFr < ML *tyrannia* < Gr⟧ **1** the office, authority, government, or jurisdiction of a tyrant, or absolute ruler **2** oppressive and unjust government; despotism **3** very cruel and unjust use of power or authority **4** harshness; rigor; severity **5** a tyrannical act

ty·rant (tī′rənt) ***n.*** ⟦ME *tirant* < OFr *tiran, tirant* (with *-t* after ending *-ant* of prp.) < L *tyrannus* < Gr *tyrannos*⟧ **1** an absolute ruler; specif., in ancient Greece, etc., one who seized sovereignty illegally; usurper **2** a cruel, oppressive ruler; despot **3** any person who exercises authority in an oppressive manner; cruel master **4** a tyrannical influence

tyrant flycatcher ⟦so named because of its aggressive territoriality⟧ any of a family (Tyrannidae) of American flycatchers, including the pewee, phoebe, and kingbird

tyre (tīr) ***n.*** *Brit. sp. of* TIRE[2]

Tyre (tīr) ⟦ME < L *Tyrus* < Gr *Tyros*⟧ seaport in SW Lebanon, on the Mediterranean: center of ancient Phoenician culture

Tyr·i·an (tir′ē ən) ***adj.*** ⟦L *Tyrius*⟧ **1** of ancient Tyre or its people or culture **2** of Tyrian purple —***n.*** a person born or living in Tyre

Tyrian purple (*or* dye) **1** a natural purple dye originally extracted from the glands of snails (family Muricidae) by the ancient Phoenicians of Tyre: widely used in the ancient and classical world in the dyeing of cloth **2** bluish red

ty·ro (tī′rō) ***n.***, *pl.* **-ros** ⟦ML < L *tiro*, young soldier, beginner⟧ a beginner in learning something; novice —**SYN.** AMATEUR

ty·ro·ci·dine (tī′rō sīd′n, -sī′dēn′) ***n.*** ⟦TYRO(SINE) + -CID(E) + -INE[3]⟧ an antibacterial substance obtained from a soil bacillus (*Bacillus brevis*)

Ty·rol (ti rōl′, -räl′; tir′ōl′, -äl′) *alt. sp. of* TIROL —**Ty·ro·le·an** (ti rō′ lē ən, tī-; tir′ə lē′ən) ***adj., n.*** —**Tyr·o·lese** (tir′ə lēz′, -lēs′) ***adj., n.***, *pl.* **-lese′**

Tyrolean hat ⟦part of the traditional folk costume of the TIROL⟧ a man's soft felt hat with a somewhat conical crown that is flat and creased at the top, a narrow brim partially turned up, and, usually, a feather for decoration

Ty·ro·lienne (tē rô lyen′) ***n.*** ⟦Fr, fem. of *Tyrolien*, Tyrolean⟧ **1** a Tyrolean folk dance **2** music for this

Ty·rone (ti rōn′) former county of W Northern Ireland

ty·ro·sin·ase (tī′rō sin ās′, tir′ō-; tī rä′-) ***n.*** ⟦< fol. + -ASE⟧ an enzyme, found in plants and animals, that catalyzes the oxidation of the amino acid tyrosine and is involved in the formation of the dark pigment melanin

ty·ro·sine (tī′rō sēn′, tir′ō-; -sin′) ⟦Gr *tyros*, cheese (see BUTTER) + -INE[3]⟧ ***n.*** a white, crystalline nonessential amino acid, $C_6H_4OHCH_2CH(NH_2)COOH$, formed by the decomposition of proteins, as in the putrefaction of cheese: see AMINO ACID

Tyr·rhe·ni·an Sea (ti rē′nē ən) part of the Mediterranean, between the W coast of Italy & the islands of Corsica, Sardinia, & Sicily

Tyu·men (tyo͞o men′) city in W Asian Russia, near the Urals

tzad·dik (tsä′dik) ***n.***, *pl.* **tzad·dik·im** (tsä dē′kim) ⟦Heb⟧ *alt. sp. of* ZADDIK

tzar (tsär, zär) ***n.*** *var. of* CZAR (sense 1) —**tzar′dom** ***n.*** —**tzar′ism′** ***n.*** —**tzar′ist** ***adj., n.***

tzar·e·vitch (tsär′ə vich, zär′-) ***n.*** *var. of* CZAREVITCH

tza·rev·na (tsä rev′nə, zä-) ***n.*** *var. of* CZAREVNA

tza·ri·na (tsä rē′nə, zä-) ***n.*** *var. of* CZARINA

tzet·ze fly (tset′sē, tsēt′-, set′-, sēt′-, tēt′-) *alt. sp. of* TSETSE FLY

tzi·gane (tsē gän′) ***n.***, *pl.* **-ganes′** (-gän′) ⟦Fr < Hung *czigány* (modern sp. *cigány*) < a S Slavic language⟧ a Gypsy; esp., a Hungarian Gypsy

tzim·mes (tsim′əs) ***n.*** ⟦Yiddish, lit., a kind of carrot stew⟧ [Informal] a commotion; fuss; to-do

tzit·zit (tsit′sis, tsēt sēt′) ***pl.n.*** ⟦Yiddish *tsitses* < Heb *tsitsit*, tassel (interpreted as pl. in Yiddish) < *tsits*, blossom < root *cc*, to blossom, bloom⟧ the fringes or tassels worn by Orthodox Jewish men, formerly on the corners of the outer garment, now on the four corners of the tallit: Deut. 22:12

Tzu·kung (tso͞o′koonŋ′, dzo͞o′goonŋ′) *a former transliteration of* ZIGONG

Tzu·po (tso͞o′pō′, dzo͞o′bō′) *a former transliteration of* ZIBO

U u U

u[1] or **U** (yoo͞) ***n., pl.* u's, U's 1** the twenty-first letter of the English alphabet: formerly a variant of *V, v;* not until the 18th cent. was it established as a vowel symbol only **2** any of the speech sounds that this letter represents, as, in English, the vowel (u) of *cut,* (oo) of *bush,* or (o͞o) of *rude,* or the semivowel (w) of *win* **3** a type or impression for *u* or *U* **4** the twenty-first in a sequence or group **5** an object shaped like U —***adj.* 1** of *u* or *U* **2** twenty-first in a sequence or group **3** shaped like U

u[2] *abbrev.* **1** atomic mass unit **2** unit(s)

U[1] (yoo͞) ***adj.*** ⟦< U(PPER CLASS)⟧ [Informal] of the upper or wealthy class, esp. the British upper class, as characterized by supposedly definitive usages, accent, behavior, tastes, etc.

U[2] *abbrev.* **1** uncle **2** Union **3** United **4** University **5** uracil

U[3] ⟦*U(nion of Orthodox Hebrew Congregations)*⟧ *trademark* KOSHER (***adj.*** 1): often enclosed in a circle, Ⓤ

U[4] *Chem. symbol for* uranium

UAE *abbrev.* United Arab Emirates

UAS *abbrev.* unmanned aircraft system

UAV *abbrev.* unmanned aerial vehicle

UAW *abbrev.* United Automobile Workers (of America)

U·ban·gi (yoo͞ baŋ′gē, -bäŋ′-; o͞o-) river in central Africa, formed on the N border of the Democratic Republic of the Congo by the juncture of the Uele & Bomu rivers & flowing west & south into the Congo River: *c.* 700 mi (1,127 km)

über- ⟦< Ger *über,* OVER⟧ *prefix* [*also in italics*] SUPER- (sense 3*b*): a humorous usage [an *über*-nerd]: also sp. **u·ber-**

ü·ber al·les (ü′bər ä′les) ⟦Ger⟧ [*also in roman type*] above all else

Ü·ber·mensch (ü′bər mensh′) ***n., pl.* -mensch′en** (-ən) ⟦Ger⟧ SUPERMAN (sense 1)

u·biq·ui·tous (yoo͞ bik′wə təs) ***adj.*** ⟦see fol. & -OUS⟧ present, or seeming to be present, everywhere at the same time; omnipresent —**u·biq′ui·tous·ly** ***adv.*** —**u·biq′ui·tous·ness** ***n.***

u·biq·ui·ty (-tē) ***n.*** ⟦Fr *ubiquité* < L *ubique,* everywhere < *ubi,* where + *-que,* any, akin to *qui:* see WHO⟧ the state, fact, or capacity of being, or seeming to be, everywhere at the same time; omnipresence

ubi sunt (o͞o′bē soont′) ⟦L⟧ where are: used to convey sadness about the temporary nature of life and beauty

u·bi su·pra (o͞o′bē so͞o′prə, yoo͞′bī-) ⟦L⟧ where (mentioned) above

U-boat (yoo͞′bōt′) ***n.*** ⟦< Ger *U-boot,* abbrev. of *Unterseeboot,* undersea boat⟧ a German submarine in service during WWI or WWII

U bolt a U-shaped bolt with threads and a nut at each end: see BOLT[1], illus.

uc *abbrev. Printing* uppercase

U·ca·ya·li (o͞o′kä yä′lē) river in E Peru, flowing north to join the Marañón & form the Amazon: *c.* 1,200 mi (1,931 km)

UCC *abbrev.* **1** Uniform Commercial Code **2** United Church of Christ

Uc·cel·lo (o͞o chel′lō, o͞ot-), **Pao·lo** (pou′lō) (born *Paolo di Dono*) 1397?-1475; It. painter

U·dall (yo͞od′'l), **Nicholas** 1505-56; Eng. translator & playwright

ud·der (ud′ər) ***n.*** ⟦ME *uddre* < OE (rare) *udr,* akin to Ger *euter* < IE base **ūdh-,* udder > Sans *ūdhar,* L *uber,* udder⟧ a baglike mammary organ containing two or more glands, each with a separate teat, as in cows

u·do (o͞o′dō′) ***n., pl.* u′dos′** ⟦Jpn⟧ a Japanese plant (*Aralia cordata*) of the ginseng family, whose blanched shoots are used like asparagus and in salads

Ue·le (wä′lə) river flowing from the NE Democratic Republic of the Congo west to join the Bomu & form the Ubangi: *c.* 700 mi (1,127 km)

U·fa (o͞o fä′) city in E European Russia, in the W foothills of the Urals

☆**UFO** (yoo͞′ef′ō′) ***n., pl.* UFOs** or **UFO's** ⟦*u(nidentified) f(lying) o(bject)*⟧ **1** any of a number of unidentified objects or phenomena frequently reported, esp. since 1947, to have been observed or tracked in the sky and variously explained as being atmospheric phenomena, hallucinations, misperceptions of actual objects, alien spacecraft, etc. **2** a spacecraft from another planet; flying saucer

u·fol·o·gy (yoo͞ fäl′ə jē) ***n.*** ⟦UFO + -OLOGY⟧ the study of UFOs, esp. when regarded as spacecraft from another planet —**u·fol′o·gist** ***n.***

U·gan·da (yoo͞ gan′də, -gän′-; o͞o-) country in EC Africa: a former British protectorate, it became independent & a member of the Commonwealth (1962): 91,136 sq mi (236,040 sq km); cap. Kampala —**U·gan′dan** ***adj., n.***

U·ga·rit (o͞o gär′it, yoo͞-) ancient city in NW Syria

U·ga·rit·ic (o͞o′gə rit′ik, yoo͞′-) ***n.*** an extinct Northern Semitic language closely related to Hebrew: it is known from cuneiform inscriptions of *c.* 1500 B.C. found in the ruins of Ugarit —***adj.*** of this language or the city of Ugarit or its people or culture

ugh (ookh, uH, oo, *etc.;* ug *is a conventionalized pronun.*) ***interj.*** ⟦echoic⟧ used to express disgust, horror, etc.

Ug·li fruit (ug′lē) ⟦< *Ugli,* a trademark, altered < UGLY: from its misshapen appearance⟧ [*sometimes* **u- f-**] a Jamaican citrus fruit that is a three-way cross between a grapefruit, orange, and tangerine

ug·li·fy (ug′lə fī′) ***vt.* -fied′, -fy′ing** to make ugly; disfigure

ug·ly (ug′lē) ***adj.* -li·er, -li·est** ⟦ME *uglike* < ON *uggligr,* fearful, dreadful < *uggr,* fear, prob. < IE base **ak-,* sharp > Gr *akē,* a point⟧ **1** unpleasing to look at; aesthetically offensive or unattractive; unsightly **2** bad, vile, repulsive, offensive, objectionable, etc. [an *ugly* lie, habit, etc.] **3** threatening; ominous [*ugly* storm clouds] **4** [Informal] ill-tempered; cross [an *ugly* mood] —***n., pl.* -lies** [Informal] an ugly person or thing —**ug′li·ly** ***adv.*** —**ug′li·ness** ***n.***

ugly duckling ⟦from a story by Hans Christian ANDERSEN about a supposed ugly duckling that turns out to be a swan⟧ a very plain child or unpromising thing that in time becomes or could become beautiful, admirable, important, etc.

U·gri·an (o͞o′grē ən, yoo͞′-) ***n., adj.*** *var. of* UGRIC

U·gric (-grik) ***n.*** ⟦< Russ *Ugry,* pl., early name of a people living east of the Ural Mountains⟧ **1** a group of languages, including Hungarian, that constitutes the E division of the Finno-Ugric languages **2** a member of any of the peoples speaking these languages —***adj.*** designating or of these languages or the peoples that speak them

uh (u, un) ***interj.* 1** HUH **2** used when hesitating in speaking, as while searching for a word or collecting one's thoughts: a prolonged sound

UHF or **uhf** *abbrev.* ultrahigh frequency

uh-huh (un hun′; *for 2* un′un′) ***interj.*** [Informal] **1** used to respond in the affirmative **2** used to signify that one is listening attentively

uh·lan (o͞o′län′, yoo͞′-; o͞o län′, yoo͞-) ***n.*** ⟦obs. Ger (now *ulan*) < Pol *ułan,* a lancer < Turk *oghlān,* a youth⟧ [Historical] a mounted lancer or a cavalryman in Poland, Prussia, etc.

uh-oh (u′ō′) ***interj.*** used to signify sudden awareness of a problem or error and the resulting worry, alarm, etc.

uh-uh (un′un′, -un′) ***interj.*** [Informal] used to respond in the negative

u·hu·ru (o͞o ho͞o′ro͞o) ***n., interj.*** ⟦Swahili⟧ freedom: a slogan of African Nationalists

Ui·ghur or **Ui·gur** (wē′goor, -gər) ***n.*** ⟦Uighur name < ?⟧ **1** a member of a Turkic people, living mainly in W China and Uzbekistan, that ruled in Mongolia and Turkestan in the Middle Ages **2** the Turkic language of this people —***adj.*** of the Uighurs or their language or culture

uil·leann pipes (il′ən, -yən) ⟦< Ir *uilleann,* of the elbow⟧ Irish bagpipes, with air provided to the bag by a bellows compressed between the player's elbow and waist

☆**u·in·tah·ite** (yoo͞ in′tə īt′) ***n.*** ⟦after fol.⟧ a black, glasslike, shiny, soft asphaltite found only in Utah and W Colorado and used to make waterproof coatings, linoleum, etc.: often sp. **u·in′ta·ite′**

U·in·ta Mountains (yoo͞ in′tə) ⟦after the *Uinta* Indians, a division of the Utes < ?⟧ range of the Rockies, in NE Utah: highest peak, 13,498 ft (4,114 m)

uit·land·er (ēit′län′dər; *E* oit′lan′dər, āt′-, īt′-) ***n.*** ⟦Afrik < Du < *uit,* out (for IE base see OUT) + *land,* land⟧ in South Africa, a foreigner; specif., in the Transvaal, one who is not a Boer

U-joint (yoo͞′joint′) ***n.*** *short for* UNIVERSAL JOINT

U·jung Pan·dang (o͞o′jo͞oŋ′ pän däŋ′) seaport on the SW coast of Sulawesi, Indonesia

UK or **U.K.** *abbrev.* United Kingdom

.uk *abbrev. Comput.* United Kingdom: a domain name

u·kase (yoo͞′kās′, -kāz′; yoo͞ kās′, -kāz′) ***n.*** ⟦Russ *ukaz,* edict < *ukazat′,* to order (modern sense, "to indicate")⟧ **1** in czarist Russia, an imperial order or decree, having the force of law **2** any official, esp. arbitrary, decree or proclamation

U·kraine (yoo͞ krān′, yoo͞′krān; *occas.* yoo͞ krīn′) **1** region in SE Europe, north of the Black Sea: with *the* **2** UKRAINIAN SOVIET SOCIALIST REPUBLIC **3** country in SE Europe: became independent upon the breakup of the U.S.S.R. (1991): 233,090 sq mi (603,700 sq km); cap. Kyiv: formerly, *Ukrainian Soviet Socialist Republic*

U·krain·i·an (yoo͞ krā′nē ən) ***n.* 1** a person born or living in Ukraine **2** the East Slavic language spoken in Ukraine —***adj.*** of Ukraine or its people, language, or culture

Ukrainian Soviet Socialist Republic a republic of the U.S.S.R.: now UKRAINE

☆**u·ku·le·le** (yoo͞′kə lā′lē) *n.* ⟦Haw, lit., leaping flea < *uku,* flea (< Proto-Polynesian **kutu* > COOTIE) + *lele,* to jump: orig. a nickname of Edward Purvis, nimble player who popularized the instrument there⟧ a small, four-stringed, guitarlike musical instrument introduced from Portugal into the Hawaiian Islands about 1879: colloquially shortened to **uke** (yoo͝k)

UL *trademark* Underwriters Laboratories

u·lan (oo͞′län′, yoo͞′-; oo͞ län′, yoo͞-) *n.* UHLAN

U·lan Ba·tor (oo͞′län bä′tôr) capital of Mongolia, in the NC part: also **U′laan·baa′tar**

U·la·no·va (oo͞ lä′nə və), **Ga·li·na (Sergeyevna)** (gə lē′nə) 1910-98; Soviet ballerina

U·lan-U·de (oo͞ län′oo͞ dā′) city in S Siberia, near Lake Baikal

ul·cer (ul′sər) *n.* ⟦L *ulcus* (gen. *ulceris*) < IE **elkos-,* abscess > Sans *árśas-,* hemorrhoids, Gr *helkos,* abscess, wound⟧ **1** an open sore (other than a wound) on the skin or some mucous membrane, as the lining of the stomach (*peptic ulcer*), characterized by the disintegration of the tissue and, often, the discharge of pus **2** any corrupting or festering condition or influence

ul·cer·ate (ul′sə rāt′) *vt., vi.* **-at′ed, -at′ing** ⟦< L *ulceratus,* pp. of *ulcerare*⟧ to make or become ulcerous —**ul′cer·a′tion** *n.* —**ul′cer·a′tive** *adj.*

ul·cer·ous (-sər əs) *adj.* ⟦L *ulcerosus*⟧ **1** having an ulcer or ulcers **2** of, being, or characterized by an ulcer or ulcers **3** causing an ulcer or ulcers —**ul′cer·ous·ly** *adv.*

-ule (yoo͞l, yoo͝l) ⟦Fr or L: Fr *-ule* < L *-ulus, -ula, -ulum*⟧ *suffix forming nouns* little (specified thing) [*veinule*]

u·le·ma (oo͞′lə mä′, oo͞′lə mä′) *pl.n.* ⟦Turk *'ulema* < Ar *'ulamā',* pl. of *'ālim,* learned, scholar < *'alima,* to know⟧ **1** Muslim scholars or men of authority in religion and law **2** [*with sing. v.*] a council or college of such men

-u·lent (yoo͞ lənt, yoo͝-, yə-) ⟦< Fr or L: Fr *-ulent* < L *-ulentus*⟧ *suffix* full of, abounding in [*flocculent*]

Ul·fi·las (ul′fi ləs) ⟦LGr for Goth *Wulfila,* lit., little wolf < *wulfs,* WOLF + *-ila,* dim. suffix: cf. ATTILA⟧ A.D. 311?-383?; bishop of the Goths: translated the Bible into Gothic: also **Ul′fi·la** (-lə)

ull·age (ul′ij) *n.* ⟦ME *ulage* < Anglo-Fr *ulliage* < OFr *ouillage,* a filling up to the brim or the bunghole < *ouiller,* to fill (a cask) to the bunghole < *ueil,* an eye, fig. bunghole < L *oculus,* an EYE⟧ the amount by which a container, esp. of liquid, falls short of being full

Ulm (oo͝lm) city in S Germany, on the Danube, in the state of Baden-Württemberg

ul·na (ul′nə) *n., pl.* **-nae** (-nē) or **-nas** ⟦ModL < L, elbow: for IE base see ELL[2]⟧ **1** the larger of the two bones of the forearm of humans, on the side opposite the thumb **2** a corresponding bone in the forelimb of other land vertebrates —**ul′nad** (-nad) *adv.* —**ul′nar** (-nər) *adj.*

ul·no- (ul′nō, -nə) *combining form* the ulna and

-u·lose (yoo͞ lōs′, yoo͝-, yə-) ⟦L *-ulosus:* see -ULE & -OSE[2]⟧ *suffix* characterized by, marked by [*granulose*]

-u·lous (yoo͞ ləs, yoo͝-, yə-) ⟦< L *-ulosus:* see -ULOSE⟧ *suffix* tending to, full of, characterized by

ul·pan (oo͞l′pän′, oo͞l′pän′) *n., pl.* **ul·pa·nim** (oo͞l pä′nim, oo͞l′pä nēm′) ⟦ModHeb < Aram *ulpan, ulpana,* study < *alef,* first letter of the Heb alphabet: see ALEPH⟧ a course or school for teaching Hebrew by an intensive method; esp., such a school in Israel for immigrants

ul·ster (ul′stər) *n.* ⟦after fol., where the fabric was originally made⟧ a long, loose, heavy overcoat, esp. one with a belt, originally made of Irish frieze

Ul·ster (ul′stər) **1** former province of Ireland, divided in 1920, with six of its counties forming Northern Ireland & the other three forming a province of the Republic of Ireland **2** province of the Republic of Ireland, in the N part: 3,093 sq mi (8,011 sq km) **3** loosely, NORTHERN IRELAND —**Ul′ster·man** (-mən) *n., pl.* **-men** (-mən) —**Ul′ster·ite′** (-īt′) *n.*

ult *abbrev.* **1** ultimate **2** ultimately

ult. *abbrev.* ultimo

ul·te·ri·or (ul tir′ē ər) *adj.* ⟦L, compar. of **ulter,* beyond, farther (see ULTRA-)⟧ **1** lying beyond or on the farther side **2** later, subsequent, or future **3** further; more remote; esp., beyond what is expressed, implied, or evident; undisclosed [an *ulterior* motive] —**ul·te′ri·or·ly** *adv.*

ul·ti·ma (ul′ti mə) *n.* ⟦L, fem. of *ultimus,* last, superl. of **ulter,* farther: see ULTRA-⟧ the last syllable of a word

ul·ti·mate (ul′tə mit) *adj.* ⟦LL *ultimatus,* pp. of *ultimare,* to come to an end < L *ultimus:* see prec.⟧ **1** beyond which it is impossible to go; farthest; most remote or distant **2** by which a process or series comes to an end; final; conclusive **3** beyond which further analysis, division, etc. cannot be made; elemental; fundamental; primary **4** greatest or highest possible; maximum; utmost —*n.* something ultimate; final point or result, fundamental principle, etc. —**ul′ti·ma·cy** (-mə sē) *n.,* **ul′ti·mate·ness**

ultimate constituent *Linguis. see* CONSTITUENT (*n.* 4)

ul·ti·mate·ly (-lē) *adv.* finally; at last; in the end

ultima Thule[1] [see fol.] **1** any far-off, unknown region **2** the farthest limit, uttermost degree, etc.

ultima Thule[2] [L, farthest Thule] THULE (northernmost region)

ul·ti·ma·tum (ul′tə māt′əm) *n., pl.* **-tums** or **-ta** (-ə) ⟦ModL < LL, neut. of *ultimatus:* see ULTIMATE⟧ a final offer or demand, esp. by one of the parties engaged in negotiations, the rejection of which usually leads to a break in relations and unilateral action, the use of force, etc. by the party issuing the ultimatum

ul·ti·mo (ul′tə mō′) *adv.* ⟦L *ultimo (mense),* (in the) last (month), abl. sing. of *ultimus:* see ULTIMA⟧ [Old-fashioned] (in the) last (month) [yours of the 13th (day) *ultimo* received]: cf. PROXIMO, INSTANT (*adv.* 2)

ul·tra (ul′trə) *adj.* ⟦< fol.⟧ going beyond the usual limit; excessive; extreme, esp. in opinions —*n.* an extremist, as in opinions held or policies favored

ul·tra- (ul′trə) ⟦L < *ultra,* fem. of **ulter,* beyond, on the other side of < IE **ol-,* var. of base **al-,* beyond > ALL, L *alius,* other⟧ *prefix* **1** beyond, on the farther side of [*ultramundane*] **2** *a)* excessive or extreme [an *ultranationalist*] *b)* excessively; to an extreme degree [an *ultraromantic* notion] *c)* something excessive or extreme [*ultraism*] **3** beyond the range of [*ultrasonic*]

ul·tra·cen·tri·fuge (ul′trə sen′trə fyoo͞j′) *n.* a high-speed centrifuge for segregating microscopic and submicroscopic materials to determine the sizes and molecular weights of colloidal and other small particles —*vt.* **-fuged′, -fug′ing** to subject to the action of an ultracentrifuge —**ul′tra·cen·trif′u·gal** (-trif′yə gəl) *adj.*

ul·tra·con·serv·a·tive (-kən sur′və tiv) *adj.* conservative to an extreme degree —*n.* an ultraconservative person

ul·tra·high frequency (ul′trə hī′) any radio frequency between 300 and 3,000 megahertz

ul·tra·ism (ul′trə iz′əm) *n.* ⟦ULTRA- + -ISM⟧ **1** the opinions, principles, etc. of those who are extreme; extremism **2** an instance of this —**ul′tra·ist** *n., adj.* —**ul′tra·is′tic** *adj.*

ul·tra·lib·er·al (ul′trə lib′ər əl) *adj.* liberal to an extreme degree —*n.* an ultraliberal person

ul·tra·light (ul′trə līt′) *adj.* extremely light in weight —*n.* a small, extremely lightweight recreational aircraft, usually with a single seat, powered by a small gasoline engine

ul·tra·mar·a·thon (ul′trə mar′ə thän′) *n.* a footrace that is longer than a marathon, usually for 30 miles or more —**ul′tra·mar′a·thon′er** *n.*

ul·tra·ma·rine (ul′trə mə rēn′) *adj.* ⟦ML *ultramarinus:* see ULTRA- & MARINE⟧ **1** beyond the sea **2** deep-blue —*n.* **1** a blue pigment originally made by grinding lapis lazuli to a powder **2** a blue pigment of similar chemical composition prepared from other substances **3** any of certain other pigments [yellow *ultramarine*] **4** deep blue

ul·tra·mi·crom·e·ter (-mī kräm′ət ər) *n.* a micrometer for making very small measurements

ul·tra·mi·cro·scope (-mī′krə skōp′) *n.* an instrument equipped to pick up the reflections of light rays dispersed by ultramicroscopic objects lighted from the side and against a dark background, thus making them visible: used esp. in the study of colloidal particles —**ul′tra·mi·cros′co·py** (-mī kräs′kə pē) *n.*

ul·tra·mi·cro·scop·ic (-mī′krə skäp′ik) *adj.* **1** too small to be seen with an ordinary microscope **2** of an ultramicroscope

ul·tra·mod·ern (-mäd′ərn) *adj.* modern to an extreme degree —**ul′tra·mod′ern·ism′** *n.* —**ul′tra·mod′ern·ist** *n.*

ul·tra·mon·tane (-män′tān′, -män tān′) *adj.* ⟦ML *ultramontanus* < L *ultra,* beyond + *mons* (gen. *montis*), MOUNT[1]⟧ **1** beyond the mountains, specif. the Alps **2** [*often* **U-**] of the Roman Catholic doctrine of papal supremacy or the former Church party advocating it —*n.* **1** a person living beyond the mountains, esp. south of the Alps **2** [*often* **U-**] an adherent of the ultramontane party —**ul′tra·mon′ta·nism′** (-tə niz′əm) *n.*

ul·tra·mun·dane (-mun′dān′, -mun dān′) *adj.* ⟦L *ultramundanus:* see ULTRA- & MUNDANE⟧ **1** being beyond the world or the limits of our solar system **2** beyond life

ul·tra·na·tion·al·ism (-nash′ə nəl iz′əm) *n.* nationalism that is excessive or extreme —**ul′tra·na′tion·al·ist** *adj., n.* —**ul′tra·na′tion·al·is′tic** *adj.*

ul·tra·red (-red′) *adj. nontechnical term for* INFRARED

ul·tra·short (-shôrt′) *adj.* very short; specif., designating or of radio waves shorter than 10 meters in wavelength and above 30 megahertz in frequency

ul·tra·son·ic (-sän′ik) *adj.* ⟦ULTRA- + SONIC⟧ designating or of a frequency of mechanical vibrations above the range audible to the human ear, i.e., above 20,000 vibrations per second —**ul′tra·son′i·cal·ly** *adv.*

ul·tra·son·ics (-sän′iks) *n.* the science dealing with ultrasonic phenomena

ul·tra·so·nog·ra·phy (-sə näg′rə fē) *n.* the technique of using ultrasound to form an image or picture —**ul′tra·son′o·graph′ic** (-sän′ə graf′ik) *adj.*

ul·tra·sound (ul′trə sound′) *n.* **1** ultrasonic waves, used in medical and dental diagnosis and therapy, in cleaning and detecting flaws in metal, etc. **2** *Radiology* the use of ultrasonic waves in ultrasonography to form images of interior bodily organs, as the uterus or heart

ul·tra·struc·ture (-struk′chər) *n.* the minute, elemental structure of protoplasm that can be seen only with an electron microscope —**ul′tra·struc′tur·al** *adj.*

Ul·tra·suede (ul′trə swād′) *trademark for* a synthetic fabric much like suede, used for clothes, upholstery, etc.

ul·tra·vi·o·let (ul′trə vī′ə lit) *adj.* **1** pertaining to a band of electromagnetic radiation having wavelengths (from *c.* 5 to *c.* 400 nanometers) that are shorter than violet light **2** of, pertaining to, or producing radiation of such wavelengths —*n.* ultraviolet radiation

ul·tra vi·res (ul′trə vī′rēz′, -vir′ēz′) ⟦L, lit., beyond men⟧ *Law* beyond the legal power or authority of a person, corporation, etc.

ul·tra·vi·rus (ul′trə vī′rəs) *n.* ⟦ModL: see ULTRA- & VIRUS⟧ an ultramicroscopic virus, so small as to pass through the pores of the finest filter

u·lu (oo͞′loo͞) *n.* ⟦Esk⟧ a knife with a broad, almost semicircular blade, used traditionally by Eskimo women

ul·u·late (yoo͞l′yoo͝ lāt′, ul′-) *vi.* **-lat′ed, -lat′ing** ⟦< L *ululatus,* pp. of *ulu-*

lare, to howl: echoic⟧ 1 to howl or hoot 2 to wail or lament loudly —**ul′u·lant** (-lənt) *adj.* —**ul′u·la′tion** *n.*

Ul·ya·novsk (o͞ol yä′nôfsk′) river port in central European Russia, on the Volga

U·lys·ses (yo͞o lis′ēz′) *n.* ⟦ML, for L *Ulixes* < ?⟧ 1 a masculine name 2 *Latin name for* ODYSSEUS

um or **umm** (um, un) *interj.* UH (sense 2)

U·may·yad (o͞o mī′əd, -ad) *n., pl.* **-yads** or **-ya·des′** (-ə dēz′) *var. of* OMAYYAD: now the pref. form in many contexts

um·bel (um′bəl) *n.* ⟦L *umbella,* parasol: see UMBRELLA⟧ a cluster of flowers with stalks of nearly equal length which spring from about the same point, like the ribs of an umbrella: see INFLORESCENCE, illus. —*adj.* designating a family (Apiaceae, order Apiales) of hollow-stemmed, herbaceous, dicotyledonous plants having umbels, including celery and parsley

um·bel·late (um′bə lit, -lāt′) *adj.* ⟦ModL *umbellatus*⟧ having, consisting of, resembling, or forming an umbel or umbels: also **um′bel·lat′ed**

um·bel·lif·er·ous (um′bə lif′ər əs) *adj.* ⟦ModL *umbellifer* (see UMBEL & -FER) + -OUS⟧ having an umbel or umbels: said of plants of the umbel family

um·bel·lule (um′bəl yo͞ol′, um bel′yo͞ol) *n.* ⟦ModL *umbellula,* dim.⟧ a small or simple umbel, esp. any of the secondary umbels of a compound umbel —**um·bel′lu·late** (-yo͞o lit) *adj.*

um·ber[1] (um′bər) *n.* ⟦Fr *(terre d')ombre* < It *(terra d')ombra,* lit., (earth of) shade, prob. < L *umbra,* a shade, shadow (but based on ? UMBRIA)⟧ 1 a kind of earth containing oxides of manganese and iron, used as a pigment: raw umber is yellowish-brown; burnt, or calcined, umber is reddish-brown 2 a yellowish-brown or reddish-brown color —*adj.* of the color of raw umber or burnt umber —*vt.* to color with or as with umber

um·ber[2] (um′bər) *n.* ⟦ME < OFr *umbre* (Fr *ombre*) < L *umbra:* see prec.⟧ 1 [Now Dial.] shade; shadow 2 a common European grayling (*Thymallus thymallus*)

um·bil·i·cal (um bil′i kəl) *adj.* ⟦ML *umbilicalis*⟧ 1 of or like an umbilicus, or navel, or an umbilical cord 2 situated at or near the navel; central to the abdomen 3 linked together by or as if by an umbilical cord —☆*n.* 1 a flexible, detachable cable serving as a tether or supplying oxygen, electric power, etc. as to an astronaut or aquanaut 2 any detachable cables, hoses, etc. connected to a rocket, etc. on its launch pad

umbilical cord 1 a tough, cordlike structure connecting the navel of a fetus to the placenta and serving to supply nourishment to, and remove waste from, the fetus ☆2 UMBILICAL (*n.*)

um·bil·i·cate (-kit, -kāt′) *adj.* ⟦L *umbilicatus*⟧ 1 having an umbilicus, or navel 2 shaped or depressed like an umbilicus, or navel Also **um·bil′i·cat′ed**

um·bil·i·cus (um bil′i kəs, um′bi lī′kəs) *n., pl.* **-ci′** (-sī′) ⟦L, NAVEL⟧ 1 NAVEL 2 a navel-like depression, as the hilum of a seed

um·bil·i·form (um bil′i fôrm′) *adj.* ⟦< prec. + -FORM⟧ shaped like an umbilicus, or navel

um·bles (um′bəlz) *pl.n. archaic var. of* NUMBLES

um·bo (um′bō) *n., pl.* **um·bo·nes** (um bō′nēz) or **um′bos** ⟦L, akin to *umbilicus,* NAVEL⟧ 1 the boss, or knob, at the center of a shield 2 something resembling this; specif., *a)* the elevation beside the hinge on each half of a bivalve shell *b)* the prominence on the eardrum at the point of attachment of the malleus —**um′bo·nal** (-bə nəl) *adj.,* **um′bo·nate** (-nit, -nāt′), or **um·bon·ic** (um bän′ik)

um·bra (um′brə) *n., pl.* **-brae** (-brē) or **-bras** ⟦L, a shade, shadow⟧ 1 shade or a shadow 2 the dark central cone of shadow projecting from a planet or satellite on the side opposite the sun 3 the dark central part of a sunspot 4 [Rare] a phantom, or ghost 5 *Physics* a perfect or complete shadow, in which no direct light is received from the source of illumination —**um′bral** *adj.*

um·brage (um′brij) *n.* ⟦ME < OFr < L *umbraticus,* of shade < *umbra,* a shade, shadow⟧ 1 [Obs. or Old Poet.] *a)* shade; shadow *b)* foliage, considered as shade-giving 2 offense or resentment [to take *umbrage* at a remark] 3 [Archaic] a semblance or shadowy appearance —**SYN.** OFFENSE

um·bra·geous (um brā′jəs) *adj.* ⟦Fr *ombrageux,* shy, suspicious, orig., shady < *ombrage* < OFr *umbrage:* see prec.⟧ 1 giving shade; shady 2 easily offended —**um·bra′geous·ly** *adv.*

um·brel·la (um brel′ə) *n.* ⟦It *ombrella* < LL *umbrella* (altered by assoc. with L *umbra,* shade) < L *umbella,* parasol, dim. of *umbra,* shade⟧ 1 a screen or shade, usually of cloth stretched over a folding radial frame, carried for protection against the rain or sun 2 something suggestive of this; specif., *a)* the body of a jellyfish *b)* any comprehensive, protective organization, alliance, strategy, or device [the *umbrella* of insurance] *c)* a force of military aircraft sent up to screen ground or naval forces [air *umbrella*]

umbrella bird any of a genus (*Cephalopterus,* family Cotingidae) of large, black South and Central American passerine birds with a large, umbrellalike, erectile crest and a long, feathered wattle

☆**umbrella leaf** a perennial plant (*Diphylleia cymosa*) of the barberry family, native to the S Appalachians and having one or two lobed, peltate leaves and a cyme of white flowers

umbrella plant a common, cultivated, aquatic sedge (*Cyperus alternifolius*) having naked, triangular stems surmounted by an umbrellalike whorl of grasslike leaves and greenish spikelets: also called **umbrella palm**

umbrella tree ☆1 an American magnolia (*Magnolia tripetala*) with clusters of long leaves at the ends of the branches, foul-smelling white flowers, and reddish fruit 2 any of a number of other trees or shrubs whose leaves are umbrella-shaped or grow with an umbrellalike effect, as the chinaberry

Um·bri·a (um′brē ə; *It* o͞om′brē ä′) ⟦L, after *Umbri,* the Umbrians⟧ region in central Italy: in ancient times a district extending from the Tiber to the Adriatic: 3,265 sq mi (8,456 sq km); chief city, Perugia

Um·bri·an (um′brē ən) *adj.* 1 of ancient or modern Umbria or its people or culture 2 of the Italic language of ancient Umbria —*n.* 1 a person born or living in ancient or modern Umbria 2 the Italic language spoken in ancient Umbria

Um·bun·du (əm bo͞on′do͞o′) *n. var. of* MBUNDU

u·mi·ak or **u·mi·aq** (o͞o′mē ak′) *n.* ⟦Esk (Eastern dial.)⟧ a large, open boat made of skins stretched on a wooden frame, used by Eskimos

um·laut (oom′lout, o͞om′-) *n.* ⟦Ger, change of sound (< *um,* about + *laut,* sound, akin to LOUD): coined (1774) by F. G. Klopstock, Ger poet, but first used in special senses by Jakob GRIMM (1819)⟧ *Linguis.* 1 *a)* a historical change in the sound of a vowel, caused by its assimilation to another vowel or semivowel originally occurring in the next syllable but later sometimes lost; mutation: in English, the differences of vowel in certain singulars and plurals (Ex.: *foot—feet, mouse—mice*) or in certain causative verbs and the words from which they are derived (Ex.: *gold—gild*) are due to the effects of umlaut on the second word of each pair *b)* a vowel resulting from such assimilation 2 the diacritical mark (¨) placed over a vowel, esp. in German, to indicate umlaut: cf. DIERESIS —*vt.* to modify the sound of (a vowel) or write (a vowel) with an umlaut

ump (ump) *n., vt., vi.* [Informal] *short for* UMPIRE

um·pir·age (um′pīr′ij) *n.* 1 the position or authority of an umpire 2 an action or ruling of an umpire

um·pire (um′pīr′) *n.* ⟦ME *oumpere,* altered by faulty separation of *a noumpire* < *noumpere* (see ADDER[2], APRON) < MFr *nomper,* uneven, hence an uneven number, third person < *non,* not + *per,* even < L *par,* PAR[1]⟧ 1 a person chosen to render a decision in a dispute; judge; arbiter 2 *a)* an official who administers the rules in certain team sports, as baseball or cricket *b) Football* an official who makes rulings regarding play along the line of scrimmage, esp. near the center of the field —*vt.* **-pired′**, **-pir′ing** to act as umpire in or of —*vi.* to act as umpire —**SYN.** JUDGE

ump·teen (ump′tēn′) *adj.* ⟦*ump-,* indefinite sound for an uncertain number + -TEEN⟧ [Slang] a great number of; very many —**ump′teenth′** *adj.*

UMW *abbrev.* United Mine Workers (of America)

UN *abbrev.* United Nations

un- (un) *prefix* 1 ⟦ME < OE, akin to Gr *an-, a-* (see A-[2], AN-[1]), L *in-* (see IN-[2]), and to the negative elements in *no, not, nor*⟧ not, lack of, the opposite of [*unconcern, unreason, unwonted*]: see NON- 2 ⟦ME *un-, on-* < OE *un-, on-, and-,* back, akin to Ger *ent-,* Du *ont-*⟧ back; the reverse or removal of: added to verbs to indicate a reversal of the action and to nouns to indicate a removal or release of the thing mentioned or from the condition, place, etc. indicated, and sometimes used merely as an intensive [*unbind, unfold; unbonnet, unbosom; unloose*] The list at the bottom of this and the following pages includes many of the more common compounds formed with *un-* (either sense) that do not have special meanings

U·na (o͞o′nə, yo͞o′-) *n.* ⟦Ir *Una, Oonagh;* also < L *una,* one⟧ a feminine name

un·a·bashed (un′ə basht′) *adj.* not embarrassed or disconcerted under ordinarily embarrassing or trying circumstances —**un′a·bash′ed·ly** (-bash′əd lē) *adv.*

un·a·ble (un ā′bəl) *adj.* 1 not able; lacking the ability, means, or power to do something 2 incompetent 3 helpless; feeble

un·a·bridged (un′ə brijd′) *adj.* 1 not abridged; complete 2 designating or of a dictionary that is not abridged from a larger work: an arbitrary designation for any of various large, extensive dictionaries

un·ac·com·mo·dat·ed (un′ə käm′ə dāt′id) *adj.* 1 not accommodated or adapted 2 having no accommodations

un·ac·com·pa·nied (-kum′pə nēd) *adj.* 1 not accompanied 2 *Music* without an accompaniment

un·ac·com·plished (-käm′plisht) *adj.* 1 not accomplished or completed 2 having no accomplishments or skills

un·ac·count·a·ble (-kount′ə bəl) *adj.* 1 that cannot be explained or accounted for; strange; mysterious 2 not accountable; not responsible —**un′ac·count′a·bil′i·ty** *n.,* **un′ac·count′a·ble·ness** —**un′ac·count′a·bly** *adv.*

un·ac·count·ed-for (-kount′id fôr′) *adj.* not explained or accounted for

un·ac·cus·tomed (-kus′təmd) *adj.* 1 not accustomed or habituated; not used (*to*) [*unaccustomed* to such kindness] 2 not usual; strange [an *unaccustomed* action]

u·na cor·da (o͞o′nə kôr′də) ⟦It, lit., one string: the pedal allows the hammers to strike only one of the strings provided for each key⟧ [*also in italics*] *Musical Direction* with the soft pedal depressed: a note to the pianist

un·ad·vised (un′əd vīzd′) *adj.* 1 without counsel or advice 2 thoughtlessly hasty; indiscreet; rash —**un′ad·vis′ed·ly** (-vīz′id lē) *adv.* —**un′ad·vis′ed·ness** *n.*

---

unabated
unabbreviated
unabetted
unabsolved
unabsorbed
unacademic
unaccented
unacceptable
unaccepted
unacclimated
unaccommodating
unaccredited
unacknowledged
unacquainted
unadaptable
unadjustable
unadorned
unadulterated
unadventurous
unadvertised

un·af·fect·ed (-ə fek′tid) *adj.* **1** not changed, affected, or influenced **2** without affectation; simple; sincere; natural —**un′af·fect′ed·ly** *adv.* —**un′af·fect′ed·ness** *n.*

Un·a·las·ka (o͞o′nə las′kə, un′ə-) ⟦Russ *Unalashka* < Aleut *(n)aw(a)n alaxsxa(x̂)*, lit., this Alaska⟧ island of Alas., in the E Aleutians: *c.* 75 mi (121 km) long

un·al·ien·a·ble (un āl′yən ə bəl) *adj. var. of* INALIENABLE

USAGE—*unalienable* is the form used in the final draft of the Declaration of Independence [“they are endowed by their Creator with certain *unalienable* Rights”], but in most other contexts *inalienable* is preferred

un·al·loyed (un′ə loid′) *adj.* **1** not alloyed; pure; specif., not mixed with other metals **2** complete; utter [not an *unalloyed* success]

un-A·mer·i·can (un′ə mer′i kən) *adj.* not American; regarded as not characteristically or properly American; esp., regarded as opposed or dangerous to the U.S., its institutions, its principles, etc. —**un′-A·mer′i·can·ism′** *n.*

U·na·mu·no (o͞o′nä mo͞o′nō), **Mi·guel de** (mē gel′ *the*) 1864-1936; Sp. philosopher & writer

u·nan·i·mous (yo͞o nan′ə məs) *adj.* ⟦L *unanimus, unanimis* < *unus,* ONE + *animus,* the mind (see ANIMAL)⟧ **1** agreeing completely; united in opinion **2** showing, or based on, complete agreement —**u·na·nim·i·ty** (yo͞o′nə nim′ə tē) *n.* —**u·nan′i·mous·ly** *adv.*

un·an·swered (un an′sərd) *adj.* **1** not answered; not responded to or refuted [an *unanswered* letter, an *unanswered* argument] **2** with no scoring in return by an opponent [sixteen *unanswered* points]

un·ap·proach·a·ble (un′ə prōch′ə bəl) *adj.* **1** not to be approached; inaccessible; aloof **2** having no rival or equal; unmatched —**un′ap·proach′a·bil′i·ty** *n.*, **un′ap·proach′a·ble·ness** —**un′ap·proach′a·bly** *adv.*

un·ap·pro·pri·at·ed (un′ə prō′prē āt′id) *adj.* not appropriated; specif., *a)* not owned by or assigned to any particular person or agent *b)* not granted or set aside for any particular use or purpose (said of sums of money, etc.)

un·apt (un apt′) *adj.* **1** not fitting or suitable **2** not likely or inclined **3** not quick or skillful, as in learning; dull —**un·apt′ly** *adv.* —**un·apt′ness** *n.*

un·arm (-ärm′) *vt.* DISARM

un·armed (-ärmd′) *adj.* **1** having no weapons, esp. firearms, or armor; defenseless **2** lacking scales, claws, spines, thorns, etc.: said of plants or animals

un·a·shamed (un′ə shāmd′) *adj.* not ashamed; without embarrassment [an *unashamed* fan of disco] —**un·a·sham·ed·ly** (un′ə shām′id lē) *adv.*

un·asked (-askt′) *adj.* **1** *a)* not asked or requested *b)* not asked for **2** not invited

un·as·sail·a·ble (un′ə sāl′ə bəl) *adj.* not assailable; specif., *a)* that cannot be successfully attacked or assaulted *b)* that cannot be successfully denied —**un′as·sail′a·ble·ness** *n.*, **un′as·sail′a·bil′i·ty** —**un′as·sail′a·bly** *adv.*

un·as·sum·ing (un′ə so͞o′miŋ, -syo͞o′-) *adj.* not assuming, pretentious, or forward; modest; retiring —**un′as·sum′ing·ly** *adv.* —**un′as·sum′ing·ness** *n.*

un·at·tached (-ə tacht′) *adj.* **1** not attached or fastened **2** not connected with any particular group, institution, etc.; independent **3** not engaged or married, or not in a similar relationship **4** *Law* not taken or held as security for a judgment

un·at·tend·ed (-ə ten′did) *adj.* **1** not attended or waited on **2** unaccompanied (*by* or *with*) **3** unnoticed; ignored **4** left unsupervised or neglected [an *unattended* child found in the mall]

u·nau (yo͞o nô′, o͞o nou′) *n.* ⟦Fr < ?⟧ the two-toed sloth (*Choloepus hoffmanni* or *C. didactylus*) of South America

un·a·vail·ing (un′ə vāl′iŋ) *adj.* not availing; futile; ineffectual —**un′a·vail′ing·ly** *adv.*

un·a·void·a·ble (-ə void′ə bəl) *adj.* **1** that cannot be avoided; inevitable **2** *Law* that cannot be voided or nullified —**un′a·void′a·ble·ness** *n.* —**un′a·void′a·bly** *adv.*

un·a·ware (-ə wer′) *adj.* not aware or conscious [*unaware* of danger] —*adv.* UNAWARES —**un′a·ware′ness** *n.*

un·a·wares (-ə werz′) *adv.* **1** without knowing or being aware; unintentionally **2** unexpectedly; suddenly; by surprise [to sneak up on someone *unawares*]

un·backed (un bakt′) *adj.* **1** not broken to the saddle: said of a horse **2** not backed, supported, etc., esp. financially **3** without a back or backing **4** having no backers, supporters, etc.

un·bal·ance (-bal′əns) *vt.* **-anced**, **-anc·ing** **1** to disturb the balance or equilibrium of **2** to disturb the functioning of; derange (the mind) —*n.* the condition of being unbalanced; imbalance

un·bal·anced (-bal′ənst) *adj.* **1** not in balance or equilibrium **2** not equal as to debit and credit **3** *a)* mentally deranged *b)* erratic or unstable

un·bal·last·ed (-bal′əs tid) *adj.* not steadied by ballast; unsteady

un·bar (-bär′) *vt.* **-barred′**, **-bar′ring** to remove the bar or bars from; unbolt; unlock; open

un·bat·ed (-bāt′id) *adj.* **1** [Archaic] not abated or diminished **2** [Obs.] not blunted [*unbated* lance]

un·bear·a·ble (-ber′ə bəl) *adj.* that cannot be endured or tolerated —**un·bear′a·ble·ness** *n.* —**un·bear′a·bly** *adv.*

un·beat·a·ble (-bēt′ə bəl) *adj.* that cannot be defeated or surpassed

un·beat·en (-bēt′'n) *adj.* **1** not struck, pounded, etc. **2** untrodden or untraveled **3** undefeated or unsurpassed

un·be·com·ing (un′bē kum′iŋ) *adj.* not appropriate or suited to one's appearance, status, character, etc.; unattractive, indecorous, etc. —*SYN.* IMPROPER —**un′be·com′ing·ly** *adv.*

un·be·knownst (-bē nōnst′) *adj.* unknown or unperceived; without one's knowledge: usually with *to*: also **un′be·known′** (-nōn′)

un·be·lief (-bə lēf′) *n.* ⟦ME *unbeleve*⟧ a withholding or lack of belief, esp. in religion or in certain religious doctrines

SYN.—**unbelief** implies merely a lack of belief, as because of insufficient evidence, esp. in matters of religion or faith; **disbelief** suggests a positive refusal to believe an assertion, theory, etc. because one is convinced of its falseness or unreliability; **incredulity** implies a general skepticism or disinclination to believe —*ANT.* **belief, credulity**

un·be·liev·a·ble (-bə lēv′ə bəl) *adj.* beyond belief; astounding; incredible —**un′be·liev′a·bly** *adv.*

un·be·liev·er (-bə lē′vər) *n.* **1** a person who does not believe; doubter **2** a person who does not accept any, or any particular, religious belief —*SYN.* ATHEIST

un·be·liev·ing (-bə lē′viŋ) *adj.* not believing; doubting; skeptical; incredulous —**un′be·liev′ing·ly** *adv.*

un·bend (un bend′) *vt.* **-bent′** or **-bend′ed**, **-bend′ing** ⟦ME *unbenden*: see UN- & BEND[1]⟧ **1** to release from strain or tension [the archer *unbent* his bow] **2** to relax (the mind) from strain or effort **3** to straighten (something bent or crooked) **4** *Naut.* *a)* to unfasten (a sail) from a spar or stay *b)* to untie (a rope) —*vi.* **1** to become straight or less bent **2** to become free from constraint, stiffness, or severity; relax and be less formal, more natural, etc.

un·bend·ing (-ben′diŋ) *adj.* not bending; specif., *a)* rigid; stiff *b)* firm; resolute *c)* aloof; austere —*n.* ⟦< prec.⟧ a relaxation of restraint, severity, etc. —**un·bend′ing·ly** *adv.*

un·bi·ased or **un·bi·assed** (-bī′əst) *adj.* without bias or prejudice; objective; impartial —*SYN.* FAIR[1]

un·bid·den (-bid′'n) *adj.* ⟦ME *unbiden*: see UN- & BID[1]⟧ **1** not commanded **2** not invited; unasked, undesired, etc. Also **un·bid′**

un·bind (-bīnd′) *vt.* **-bound′**, **-bind′ing** ⟦ME *unbinden* < OE *unbindan*: see UN- & BIND⟧ **1** to untie; unfasten **2** to free from bonds or restraints; release

un·bit·ted (-bit′id) *adj.* **1** having no bit or bridle on **2** unrestrained; uncontrolled

un·bleached (un blēcht′) *adj.* designating wheat flour that has not been made whiter by chemical treatment or some other method

un·blessed (-blest′) *adj.* **1** not hallowed or consecrated **2** not given a blessing **3** accursed; wicked **4** wretched; unhappy Also [Archaic] **un·blest′**

un·block (-bläk′) *vt.* to remove a block from; free from being obstructed

un·blush·ing (-blush′iŋ) *adj.* **1** not blushing **2** shameless —**un·blush′ing·ly** *adv.*

un·bod·ied (-bäd′ēd) *adj.* having no body or form; incorporeal, disembodied, formless, etc.

un·bolt (-bōlt′) *vt., vi.* to withdraw the bolt or bolts of (a door, etc.); unbar; open

un·bolt·ed[1] (-bōl′tid) *adj.* not fastened with a bolt

un·bolt·ed[2] (-bōl′tid) *adj.* not bolted or sifted: said as of flour

un·bon·net (-bän′it) *vt., vi.* to take the bonnet or head covering off; uncover —**un·bon′net·ed** *adj.*

un·born (-bôrn′) *adj.* **1** not born or brought into being **2** still within the mother's uterus; not yet delivered **3** yet to come or be; future

un·bos·om (-bo͝oz′əm) *vt.* ⟦UN- + BOSOM⟧ to give vent to (feelings, secrets,

---

unadvisable
unaffiliated
unafraid
unaggressive
unaided
unaimed
unalike
unalleviated
unallied
unallowable
unalterable
unaltered
unambiguous
unambitious
unamplified
unamusing
unanalyzable
unanalyzed
unannealed
unannounced
unanswerable
unanticipated
unapologetic
unappalled
unapparent
unappealable
unappealing
unappeasable
unappetizing
unappreciated
unappreciative
unapprehensive
unapproached
unarguable
unarmored
unartistic
unascertained
unaspirated
unaspiring
unassignable
unassigned
unassimilable
unassimilated
unassisted
unassociated
unassorted
unassured
unatoned
unattainable
unattempted
unattested
unattired
unattractive
unauspicious
unauthentic
unauthenticated
unauthorized
unavailability
unavailable
unavenged
unavowed
unawakened
unawed
unbaked
unbaptized
unbathed
unbefitting
unbelt
unblamable
unblemished
unblinking
unboned

etc.); tell; reveal —*vi.* to reveal what one feels, knows, etc. —**unbosom oneself** to tell or reveal one's feelings, secrets, etc.

un·bound (-bound′) *vt. pt. & pp. of* UNBIND —*adj.* **1** released from bonds, ties, or shackles **2** without a binding: said as of a book **3** not held in physical or chemical union with another element, substance, etc.; free [*unbound* electrons]

un·bound·ed (-boun′did) *adj.* **1** without bounds or limits; boundless **2** not restrained; uncontrolled

un·bowed (-boud′) *adj.* **1** not bowed or bent **2** not yielding or giving in; unsubdued

un·brace (-brās′) *vt.* **-braced′**, **-brac′ing** **1** to free from braces or bands **2** to loosen; relax **3** to make feeble

un·bred (-bred′) *adj.* **1** [Archaic] ill-bred **2** untrained or uninstructed **3** not bred yet, as a filly

un·bri·dle (-brīd′'l) *vt.* **-dled**, **-dling** **1** to remove the bridle from (a horse, etc.) **2** to free from restraint

un·bri·dled (-brīd′'ld) *adj.* **1** having no bridle on: said as of a horse **2** unrestrained; uncontrolled

un·bro·ken (-brō′kən) *adj.* not broken; specif., *a)* whole; intact *b)* not tamed or subdued *c)* continuous; uninterrupted *d)* not disordered or disorganized *e)* not plowed or spaded *f)* not surpassed [an *unbroken* record]

un·buck·le (-buk′əl) *vt.* **-led**, **-ling** to unfasten the buckle or buckles of

un·build (-bild′) *vt.* **-built′**, **-build′ing** to tear down (something built); demolish; raze

un·built (-bilt′) *adj.* not yet built (on)

un·bur·den (-burd′'n) *vt.* **1** to free from a burden **2** to relieve (oneself or one's soul, mind, etc.) by revealing or disclosing (something hard to bear, as guilt)

un·but·ton (-but′'n) *vt.* **1** to free (a button) from the buttonhole **2** to unfasten the button or buttons of (a garment, etc.) —*vi.* to unfasten buttons, as in disrobing

un·but·toned (-but′'nd) *adj.* **1** with buttons unfastened **2** free and easy; casual; informal

un·called-for (un kôld′fôr′) *adj.* **1** not called for or required **2** unnecessary and out of place; impertinent

un·can·ny (un kan′ē) *adj.* ⟦see UN- & CANNY⟧ **1** mysterious or unfamiliar, esp. in such a way as to frighten or make uneasy; preternaturally strange; eerie; weird **2** so remarkable, acute, etc. as to seem preternatural [*uncanny* shrewdness] —**SYN.** WEIRD —**un·can′ni·ly** *adv.* —**un·can′ni·ness** *n.*

un·cap (-kap′) *vt.* **-capped′**, **-cap′ping** **1** to remove the cap from the head of (a person) **2** to remove the cap, or cover, from (a bottle, etc.)

un·cared-for (un kerd′fôr′) *adj.* not cared for or looked after; neglected

un·caused (-kôzd′) *adj.* not caused or created; self-existent

un·cer·e·mo·ni·ous (un′ser ə mō′nē əs) *adj.* **1** less formal and ceremonious than is usual or expected; informal; familiar **2** so curt or abrupt as to be discourteous —**un′cer·e·mo′ni·ous·ly** *adv.* —**un′cer·e·mo′ni·ous·ness** *n.*

un·cer·tain (un surt′'n) *adj.* ⟦ME *uncertayn*⟧ **1** *a)* not surely or certainly known; questionable; problematic *b)* not sure or certain in knowledge; doubtful **2** not definite or determined; vague **3** liable to vary or change; not dependable or reliable **4** not steady or constant; varying —**un·cer′tain·ly** *adv.* —**un·cer′tain·ness** *n.*

un·cer·tain·ty (-tē) *n.* ⟦ME *uncerteynte*⟧ **1** lack of certainty; doubt **2** *pl.* **-ties** something uncertain

SYN.—uncertainty ranges in implication from a mere lack of absolute sureness [*uncertainty* about a date of birth] to such vagueness as to preclude anything more than guesswork [the *uncertainty* of the future]; **doubt** implies such a lack of conviction, as through absence of sufficient evidence, that there can be no certain opinion or decision [there is *doubt* about his guilt]; **dubiety** suggests uncertainty characterized by wavering between conclusions; **dubiosity** connotes uncertainty characterized by vagueness or confusion; **skepticism** implies an unwillingness to believe, often a habitual disposition to doubt, in the absence of absolute certainty or proof —**ANT. assurance, certitude, conviction**

uncertainty principle ⟦put forth by W. HEISENBERG⟧ in quantum mechanics, the principle that it is impossible to measure simultaneously and exactly two related quantities, as both the position and the momentum of an electron

un·chanc·y (un chan′sē, -chän′-) *adj.* ⟦UN- + CHANCY (sense 2)⟧ [Scot.] **1** unlucky; ill-fated **2** dangerous

un·charged (-chärjd′) *adj.* not charged; specif., *a)* not formally accused *b)* without an electrical charge

un·char·i·ta·ble (-char′i tə bəl) *adj.* harsh or severe, as in judging or dealing with others; unforgiving, ungenerous, or censorious —**un·char′i·ta·ble·ness** *n.* —**un·char′i·ta·bly** *adv.*

un·chart·ed (-chärt′id) *adj.* not marked on a chart or map; unexplored or unknown

un·chris·tian (-kris′chən) *adj.* **1** not having or practicing a Christian religion **2** not in accord with the principles of Christianity **3** [Informal] outrageous; dreadful

un·church (-church′) *vt.* **1** to deprive (a person) of membership in a given church **2** to deprive (an entire congregation or sect) of its rights as a church

un·churched (-churcht′) *adj.* **1** not belonging to or attending any church **2** not having a church

un·ci·al (un′shē əl, -shəl; -sē əl) *adj.* ⟦L *uncialis,* of an inch, inch-high < *uncia,* a twelfth part, INCH[1]⟧ designating or of a form of large, rounded letter used in the script of Greek and Latin manuscripts between A.D. 300 and 900 —*n.* **1** an uncial letter **2** an uncial manuscript **3** uncial script

caveat emptor

Latin uncials

un·ci·form (un′si fôrm′) *adj.* ⟦ModL *unciformis* < L *uncus,* a hook (see UNCUS) + *-formis,* -FORM⟧ **1** hook-shaped **2** *Anat. a)* designating or of a hook-shaped bone in the distal row of the wrist, on the same side as the ulna *b)* designating a hooked process on the unciform bone, or a similar process on the ethmoid bone —*n.* an unciform bone

un·ci·na·ri·a·sis (un′si nə rī′ə sis) *n.* ⟦ModL, after *Uncinaria,* a genus, including the hookworm < L *uncinus,* a hook (see prec.) + -IASIS⟧ HOOKWORM DISEASE

un·ci·nate (un′si nit, -nāt′) *adj.* ⟦L *uncinatus* < *uncinus,* a hook < *uncus:* see UNCIFORM⟧ bent like a hook; hooked

un·cir·cu·lat·ed (un sur′kyə lāt′id) *adj.* never having been in circulation: said of coins and paper currency

un·cir·cum·cised (un sur′kəm sīzd′) *adj.* **1** not circumcised; specif., not Jewish; gentile **2** [Archaic] heathen

un·cir·cum·ci·sion (un′sur kəm sizh′ən) *n.* the condition of being uncircumcised —**the uncircumcision** *Bible* the gentiles

un·civ·il (un siv′əl) *adj.* **1** not civilized; barbarous **2** not civil or courteous; ill-mannered —**SYN.** RUDE —**un·civ′il·ly** *adv.*

un·civ·i·lized (-siv′ə līzd′) *adj.* **1** not civilized; barbarous; unenlightened **2** far from civilization

un·clad (-klad′) *vt. alt. pt. & pp. of* UNCLOTHE —*adj.* not clad; wearing no clothes; naked

un·clasp (-klasp′) *vt.* **1** to unfasten the clasp of **2** to release from a clasp or grasp —*vi.* **1** to become unfastened **2** to relax the grasp

un·clas·si·fied (-klas′i fīd′) *adj.* **1** not classified; not put in a category **2** not under security classification; not secret or restricted

un·cle (uŋ′kəl) *n.* ⟦OFr < L *avunculus,* one's mother's brother, dim. of **avo* < IE **awos-,* maternal grandfather > OE *eam,* OHG *oheim,* uncle, L *avus,* grandfather⟧ **1** the brother of one's father or mother **2** the husband of one's aunt **3** [Old Informal] any elderly man: a term of address **4** [Old Slang] a pawnbroker —☆**say (or cry) uncle** [Informal] to surrender or admit defeat

un·clean (un klēn′) *adj.* ⟦ME *unclene* < OE *unclæne:* see UN- + CLEAN⟧ **1** dirty; filthy; foul **2** ceremonially impure **3** morally impure; unchaste, obscene, or vile —**un·clean′ness** *n.*

un·clean·li·ness (un klen′lē nis) *n.* the condition or quality of being unclean

un·clean·ly (-klēn′lē) *adv.* in an unclean manner

un·clench (-klench′) *vt., vi.* to open: said of something clenched, or clinched: also **un·clinch′** (-klinch′)

☆**Uncle Sam** ⟦extended < abbrev. *U.S.*⟧ [Informal] the U.S. (government or people), personified as a tall, spare man with chin whiskers, dressed in a red, white, and blue costume of swallow-tailed coat, striped trousers, and tall hat with a band of stars

☆**Uncle Tom** ⟦after the title character, an elderly black slave, in Harriet Beecher Stowe's antislavery novel, *Uncle Tom's Cabin* (1852)⟧ [Informal] a black person whose behavior toward whites is regarded as fawning or servile: a term of contempt —**Uncle Tom′ism′**

un·cloak (un klōk′) *vt., vi.* **1** to remove a cloak or other covering (from) **2** to reveal; expose

---

unbought
unbraid
unbranched
unbranded
unbreakable
unbreathable
unbribable
unbridgeable
unbrotherly
unbruised
unbrushed
unbudgeted
unburied
unburnable
unburned
unburnt
unbusinesslike
unbuttered
uncaged
uncalculating
uncanceled
uncancelled
uncanonical
uncaring
uncarpeted
uncasked
uncastrated
uncataloged
uncaught
unceasing
unceasingly
uncelebrated
uncensored
uncensured
uncertified
unchain
unchallenged
unchangeable
unchanged
unchanging
unchaperoned
uncharacteristic
unchartered
unchaste
unchastened
unchecked
uncherished
unchewed
unchilled
unchivalrous
unchosen
unchristened
unclaimed
unclarified
unclassifiable
uncleaned
unclear
uncleared
unclipped
unclog

un·close (-klōz′) *vt., vi.* **-closed′**, **-clos′ing** ⟦ME *unclosen:* see UN- + CLOSE[2]⟧ **1** to make or become no longer closed; open **2** to disclose or reveal

un·clothe (-klōth′) *vt.* **-clothed′** or **-clad′**, **-cloth′ing** ⟦ME *unclothen*⟧ to strip of or as of clothes; uncover; divest

un·co (uŋ′kō) [Scot.] *adj.* ⟦ME *unkow,* contr. < *uncouth,* UNCOUTH⟧ **1** unknown; strange **2** weird; uncanny **3** notable; remarkable —*adv.* remarkably; extremely; very —*n., pl.* **-cos** **1** a strange person or thing **2** [*pl.*] news

un·coach·a·ble (un kōch′ə bəl) *adj.* not coachable; specif., not responsive to coaching, as because of temperament, stubbornness, etc. [a talented but *uncoachable* athlete]

un·coil (un koil′) *vt., vi.* ⟦UN- + COIL[1]⟧ to unwind or release from being coiled

un·com·fort·a·ble (-kum′fərt ə bəl) *adj.* **1** not comfortable; feeling discomfort **2** not pleasant or agreeable; causing discomfort **3** ill at ease —**un·com′fort·a·ble·ness** *n.* —**un·com′fort·a·bly** *adv.*

un·com·mer·cial (un′kə mʉr′shəl) *adj.* **1** of or concerned with things other than trade or commerce **2** not in accordance with the principles or methods of commerce **3** not commercially profitable

un·com·mit·ted (-kə mit′id) *adj.* **1** not committed or carried out, as a crime **2** *a)* not bound or pledged, as to certain principles *b)* not having taken a position; neutral **3** not imprisoned **4** not committed to a mental hospital

un·com·mon (un käm′ən) *adj.* **1** rare; not common or usual **2** strange; remarkable; extraordinary —**un·com′mon·ly** *adv.* —**un·com′mon·ness** *n.*

un·com·mu·ni·ca·tive (un′kə myo͞o′ni kāt′iv, -ni kə tiv) *adj.* not communicative; tending to withhold information, opinions, feelings, etc.; reserved; taciturn —**un′com·mu′ni·ca′tive·ly** *adv.* —**un′com·mu′ni·ca′tive·ness** *n.*

un·com·pro·mis·ing (un käm′prə mī′ziŋ) *adj.* not compromising or yielding; firm; inflexible; determined

un·con·cern (un′kən sʉrn′) *n.* **1** lack of interest; apathy; indifference **2** lack of concern, or worry

un·con·cerned (-sʉrnd′) *adj.* not concerned; specif., *a)* not interested; indifferent *b)* not solicitous or anxious —**SYN.** INDIFFERENT —**un′con·cern′ed·ly** (-sʉr′nid lē) *adv.* —**un′con·cern′ed·ness** *n.*

un·con·di·tion·al (un′kən dish′ən əl) *adj.* without conditions or reservations; absolute —**un′con·di′tion·al·ly** *adv.*

un·con·di·tioned (-kən dish′ənd) *adj.* **1** UNCONDITIONAL **2** *Psychol.* not acquired by conditioning; natural; inborn [an *unconditioned* reflex]

un·con·form·a·ble (-kən fôr′mə bəl) *adj.* **1** not conformable or conforming **2** *Geol.* showing unconformity —**un′con·form′a·bly** *adv.*

un·con·form·i·ty (-kən fôr′mə tē) *n., pl.* **-ties** **1** a lack of conformity; inconsistency; incongruity **2** *Geol.* *a)* a break in the continuity of rock strata in contact, separating younger from older rocks and usually resulting from erosion of the surface of the older bed before the younger bed was laid down *b)* the surface of contact between such strata

un·con·nect·ed (-kə nek′tid) *adj.* **1** not connected; separate **2** disconnected; incoherent

un·con·scion·a·ble (un kän′shən ə bəl) *adj.* **1** not guided or restrained by conscience; unscrupulous **2** unreasonable, excessive, or immoderate **3** not fair or just; outrageous [*unconscionable* demands] —**un·con′scion·a·bly** *adv.*

un·con·scious (-kän′shəs) *adj.* **1** *a)* not endowed with consciousness; mindless *b)* temporarily deprived of consciousness [*unconscious* from a blow on the head] **2** not aware (*of*) [*unconscious* of his mistake] **3** not known, realized, or intended; not done, said, etc. on purpose [an *unconscious* habit, *unconscious* humor] **4** not aware of one's own existence; not conscious of self **5** having to do with those of one's mental processes that one is unable to bring into one's consciousness —**the unconscious** *Psychoanalysis* the sum of all thoughts, memories, impulses, desires, feelings, etc. of which the individual is not conscious but which influence the emotions and behavior; that part of one's psyche which comprises repressed material of this nature —**un·con′scious·ly** *adv.* —**un·con′scious·ness** *n.*

un·con·sid·ered (un′kən sid′ərd) *adj.* **1** not considered; not taken into account **2** done without consideration; not based upon careful reflection [a hasty, *unconsidered* remark]

un·con·sti·tu·tion·al (-kän stə to͞o′shə nəl) *adj.* not in accordance with or permitted by a constitution, specif. the U.S. Constitution; not constitutional —☆**un′con·sti·tu′tion·al′i·ty** (-shə nal′ə tē) *n.* —**un′con·sti·tu′tion·al·ly** *adv.*

un·con·struct·ed (un′kən struk′tid) *adj.* ⟦from the lack of the usual structural elements that define the shape of a garment⟧ made so as to fall loosely from the shoulders, and often having little or no interfacing, lining, padding, etc.: said of clothing

un·con·ven·tion·al (un′kən ven′shə nəl) *adj.* not conventional; not conforming to customary, formal, or accepted practices, standards, rules, etc. —**un′con·ven′tion·al′i·ty** (-shə nal′ə tē) *n.* —**un′con·ven′tion·al·ly** *adv.*

un·cool (un ko͞ol′) *adj.* [Slang] **1** not having or showing composure or self-control; not cool **2** unsophisticated **3** unacceptable, unfashionable, unpleasant, etc., esp. by the standards of a given group

un·cork (un kôrk′) *vt.* **1** to pull the cork out of **2** [Informal] to let out, let loose, release, etc.

un·count·ed (-kount′id) *adj.* **1** not counted **2** inconceivably numerous; innumerable

un·cou·ple (-kup′əl) *vt.* **-pled**, **-pling** **1** to release (dogs) from being leashed together in couples **2** to unfasten (things coupled); disconnect —*vi.* to become unfastened

un·couth (-ko͞oth′) *adj.* ⟦ME < OE *uncuth,* unknown < *un-,* not + *cuth,* pp. of *cunnan,* to know: see CAN[1]⟧ **1** [Archaic] not known or familiar; strange **2** awkward; clumsy; ungainly **3** uncultured; crude; boorish —**un·couth′ly** *adv.* —**un·couth′ness** *n.*

un·cov·e·nant·ed (-kuv′ə nən tid) *adj.* **1** not promised, secured, or sanctioned by a covenant **2** not bound by or committed to the terms of a covenant

un·cov·er (-kuv′ər) *vt.* **1** to make known; disclose; reveal **2** to lay bare or open by removing a covering **3** to remove the cover or protection from **4** to remove the hat, cap, etc. from (the head), as a conventional gesture of respect —*vi.* **1** to bare the head, as in respect **2** to remove a cover or coverings

un·cov·ered (-kuv′ərd) *adj.* **1** having no covering; exposed **2** not covered or protected by insurance, collateral, etc. **3** wearing no hat, cap, etc.

un·cre·at·ed (un′krē āt′id) *adj.* **1** not yet created; not existing **2** *Theol.* existing eternally

un·crit·i·cal (un krit′i kəl) *adj.* **1** not critical; undiscriminating [an *uncritical* reader] **2** not guided by critical standards of analysis [an *uncritical* acceptance of radical ideas] —**un·crit′i·cal·ly** *adv.*

un·cross (un krôs′) *vt.* to change back from a crossed position [to *uncross* one's legs]

un·crowned (-kround′) *adj.* **1** not crowned; not officially installed as a ruler by a coronation ceremony **2** ruling without the title of king, queen, etc.

unc·tion (uŋk′shən) *n.* ⟦ME *unccioun* < L *unctio* < *ung(u)ere,* to anoint: see UNGUENT⟧ **1** *a)* the act of anointing, as in medical treatment or a religious ceremony *b)* the oil, ointment, etc. used for this **2** anything that soothes or comforts **3** *a)* a fervent or earnest quality or manner of speaking or behaving, esp. in dealing with religious matters *b)* pretended or affected fervor or earnestness in speech or manner; unctuous quality

unc·tu·ous (uŋk′cho͞o əs) *adj.* ⟦ME < ML *unctuosus,* greasy < L *unctum,* ointment < *ung(u)ere,* to anoint: see UNGUENT⟧ **1** *a)* of, like, or characteristic of an ointment or unguent; oily or greasy *b)* made up of or containing fat or oil **2** like oil, soap, or grease to the touch: said of certain minerals **3** soft and rich: said of soil **4** plastic; moldable **5** characterized by a false show of deep or sincere feeling, as in trying to persuade; too smooth or overly polite in speech, manners, etc. —**unc′tu·os′i·ty** (-äs′ə tē) *n.*, **unc′tu·ous·ness** —**unc′tu·ous·ly** *adv.*

un·curl (un kʉrl′) *vt., vi.* to change from a curled condition; straighten

un·cus (uŋ′kəs) *n., pl.* **un·ci** (un′sī) ⟦ModL < L, a hook < IE base *ank- > ANGLE[1]⟧ *Anat.* a hooked process

un·cut (un kut′) *adj.* not cut; specif., *a)* not trimmed *b)* having untrimmed margins or not slit apart at the edges (said of the pages of a book or of the book) *c)* not ground to shape (said of a gem) *d)* not abridged or shortened

---

unclouded
uncluttered
uncoagulated
uncoated
uncocked
uncoined
uncollectable
uncollected
uncolonized
uncolored
uncombed
uncombinable
uncombined
uncomely
uncomforted
uncommissioned
uncompanionable
uncompensated

uncomplaining
uncompleted
uncomplicated
uncomplimentary
uncomplying
uncompounded
uncomprehending
uncomprehensible
uncompressed
unconcealed
unconciliated
unconcluded
uncondemned
uncondensed
unconducive
unconfessed
unconfined
unconfirmed

unconfused
uncongealed
uncongenial
uncongeniality
unconquerable
unconquered
unconscientious
unconsecrated
unconsoled
unconsolidated
unconstituted
unconstrained
unconstricted
unconsumed
uncontaminated
uncontemplated
uncontested
uncontradictable

uncontrived
uncontrollable
uncontrollably
uncontrolled
uncontroversial
uncontrovertible
unconverted
unconvinced
unconvincing
uncooked
uncooled
uncooperative
uncoordinated
uncorrected
uncorroborated
uncorrupted
uncountable
uncrate

uncreative
uncredited
uncrippled
uncropped
uncrowded
uncrushable
uncrystallized
uncultivable
uncultivated
uncultured
uncurable
uncurbed
uncured
uncurtailed
uncurtained
uncushioned
uncustomary
undamaged

un·damped (-dampt′) *adj.* not damped; specif., *a)* not disheartened or discouraged *b) Elec.* not decreasing in amplitude

un·daunt·ed (-dôn′tid) *adj.* not daunted; not faltering or hesitating out of fear or discouragement; undismayed; intrepid —**un·daunt′ed·ly** *adv.*

undead (-ded′) *adj. Folklore* of or having to do with supernatural beings, as vampires or zombies, who have died, but continue to exhibit some characteristics of living beings, as consciousness, movement, or speech —**the undead** such supernatural beings collectively

un·de·ceive (un′dē sēv′) *vt.* **-ceived′**, **-ceiv′ing** to cause to be no longer deceived, mistaken, or misled —**un′de·ceived′** *adj.*

un·de·cid·ed (-dē sīd′id) *adj.* **1** that is not decided or settled **2** not having come to a decision; irresolute —*n.* a prospective voter who has not yet decided how to vote in a political contest or on an issue —**un′de·cid′ed·ly** *adv.* —**un′de·cid′ed·ness** *n.*

un·dec·y·len·ic acid (un′des ə len′ik, -lēn′-) ⟦< *undecylene*, $C_{11}H_{22}$ (< L *undecim*, eleven < base of *unus*, ONE + *decem*, TEN + -YL + -ENE) + -IC⟧ a light-colored liquid or crystalline mass, $C_{11}H_{20}O_2$, used in treating fungus infections of the skin, in making perfumes, etc.

un·de·mon·stra·tive (un′di män′strə tiv) *adj.* not demonstrative; giving little outward expression of feeling; restrained; reserved —**un′de·mon′stra·tive·ly** *adv.* —**un′de·mon′stra·tive·ness** *n.*

un·de·ni·a·ble (-di nī′ə bəl) *adj.* that cannot be denied; indisputable —**un′de·ni′a·bly** *adv.*

un·der (un′dər) *prep.* ⟦ME < OE, akin to Ger *unter* < IE **n̥dhos, *n̥dheri*, under > L *infra*, below⟧ **1** in, at, or to a position down from; lower than; below [shoes *under* the bed, *under* a blazing sun] **2** beneath the surface of [*under* water] **3** below and to the other side of [we drove *under* a bridge] **4** covered, surmounted, enveloped, or concealed by [to wear a vest *under* a coat] **5** *a)* lower in authority, position, power, etc. than *b)* lower in value, amount, etc. than; less than *c)* lower than the required or standard degree of [*under* the age specified for the job] **6** in a position or condition regarded as lower than or inferior to, or implying subordination to; specif., *a)* subject to the control, limitations, government, direction, instruction, or influence of [*under* orders from the President, *under* oath, born *under* Aries] *b)* burdened, oppressed, or distressed by [*under* a strain] *c)* subjected to; undergoing [*under* an anesthetic, *under* repair] **7** with the character, pretext, disguise, or cover of [*under* an alias] **8** in or included in (the designated category, division, class, etc.) [spiders are classified *under* arachnids] **9** during the rule of [literature flourished *under* Elizabeth I] **10** being the subject of [the question *under* discussion] **11** having regard for; because of [*under* the circumstances] **12** authorized or attested by [*under* her signature] **13** planted with; sown with [an acre *under* corn] —*adv.* **1** in or to a position below something; beneath **2** beneath the surface, as of water **3** in or to a condition that is subordinate **4** so as to be covered or concealed **5** less in amount, value, etc.; not so much [costing two dollars or *under*] —*adj.* lower in position, authority, rank, amount, degree, etc.

un·der- (un′dər) ⟦ME < OE: see prec.⟧ *combining form* **1** in, on, to, or from a lower place or side; beneath or below [*undertow*] **2** in an inferior or subordinate position or rank [*undersecretary*] **3** too little, not enough, below normal or standard [*underdeveloped*] The list below includes some common compounds formed with *under-* that can be understood if "too little" or "insufficiently" is added to the meaning of the base word

underactive
underbake
undercolored
underconsumption
undercook
underdose
undereducated
underemphasize
underexercise
undermanned
underorganized
underpopulated
underpowered
underpraise
underprice
underripe
underspend
undersubscribe
undersupply
undertrained

un·der·a·chieve (un′dər ə chēv′) *vi.* **-chieved′**, **-chiev′ing** **1** to fail to do as well in school studies as might be expected from scores made on intelligence tests **2** to perform below expectations —**un′der·a·chieve′ment** *n.* —**un′der·a·chiev′er** *n.*

un·der·act (-akt′) *vt., vi.* **1** to act (a theatrical role) with insufficient emphasis or too great restraint **2** UNDERPLAY (sense 1)

un·der·age[1] (-āj′) *adj.* below the age required by law

un·der·age[2] (un′dər ij) *n.* ⟦UNDER- + -AGE⟧ a shortage; insufficiency

un·der·ap·pre·ci·at·ed (un′dər ə prē′shē āt′əd) *adj.* not fully or sufficiently appreciated

un·der·arm (un′dər ärm′) *adj.* **1** of, for, in, or used on the area under the arm [an *underarm* seam on a shirt] **2** of, for, or used in the armpit [an *underarm* deodorant] **3** UNDERHAND (sense 1) —*adv.* UNDERHAND (sense 1)

un·der·armed (un′dər ärmd′) *adj.* not sufficiently armed; not provided with enough weapons

un·der·bel·ly (un′dər bel′ē) *n.* **1** the lower, posterior part of an animal's belly **2** any vulnerable or unprotected area, region, point, etc.

un·der·bid (un′dər bid′; *for n.* un′dər bid′) *vt., vi.* **-bid′**, **-bid′ding** **1** to bid lower than (another person) **2** *Bridge* to make a lower bid on (one's hand) than might validly be made —*n.* a bid that is lower than another or lower than might validly be made

un·der·bid·der (un′dər bid′ər) *n.* **1** one that underbids **2** the bidder that has made the second-highest bid in an auction

un·der·bite (un′dər bīt′) *n.* a faulty occlusion of the teeth in which the lower incisors and canines project over the upper to an abnormal extent

un·der·bod·y (un′dər bäd′ē) *n.* **1** the underpart of an animal's body **2** the underside of a vehicle

un·der·bred (un′dər bred′) *adj.* **1** lacking good manners; ill-bred **2** not of pure breed

☆**un·der·brush** (un′dər brush′) *n.* small trees, shrubs, etc. that grow beneath large trees in woods or forests

un·der·buy (un′dər bī′) *vt., vi.* **-bought′**, **-buy′ing** **1** to buy at less than the real value or asking price **2** to buy more cheaply than (another or others) **3** to buy less of (something) than is needed

un·der·cap·i·tal·ize (-kap′ət′l īz′) *vt., vi.* **-ized′**, **-iz′ing** to provide (a business) with too little capital for successful operation —**un′der·cap′i·tal·i·za′tion** *n.*

☆**un·der·card** (un′dər kärd′) *n. Boxing* the match or matches before the main event

un·der·car·riage (un′dər kar′ij) *n.* **1** a supporting frame or structure, as of an automobile **2** the landing gear of an aircraft

un·der·charge (un′dər chärj′; *for n.* un′dər chärj′) *vt., vi.* **-charged′**, **-charg′ing** **1** to charge too low a price (to) **2** to provide (a gun, electric battery, etc.) with too little or too low a charge —*n.* an insufficient charge

☆**un·der·class** (un′dər klas′) *n.* the socioeconomic class with incomes below subsistence level, including esp. the underprivileged

un·der·class·man (un′dər klas′mən) *n., pl.* **-men** (-mən) a student in the freshman or sophomore class of a high school or college

un·der·clay (un′dər klā′) *n.* a bed of clay lying immediately beneath a coal seam, often used as a fireclay

un·der·clothes (-klōthz′, -klōz′) *pl.n.* UNDERWEAR

un·der·cloth·ing (-klō′thiŋ) *n.* UNDERWEAR

un·der·coat (-kōt′) *n.* **1** [Obs.] a coat worn under another **2** an under layer of short hair in an animal's coat **3** a coating as of tarlike material applied to the exposed underside of a motor vehicle to deaden noise, retard rust, etc. **4** a coat of paint, varnish, etc. applied as a first coat or before the final coat Also (for 3 & 4) **un′der·coat′ing** —*vt.* to apply an undercoat to

un·der·cool (un′dər ko͞ol′) *vt., vi.* SUPERCOOL

un·der·count (un′der kount′; *for n.* un′dər kount′) *vt.* to get a total by counting that is smaller than the actual total of —*n.* the act or an instance of undercounting

☆**un·der·cov·er** (un′dər kuv′ər) *adj.* acting or carried out in secret [*undercover* work as a spy]

un·der·croft (un′dər krôft′) *n.* ⟦ME < *under-* (see UNDER-) + *croft*, a vault < ML *crupta* < L *crypta*, CRYPT⟧ an underground room or vault, esp. beneath a church

un·der·cur·rent (-kur′ənt) *n.* **1** a current, as of water or air, flowing below another or beneath the surface **2** an underlying tendency, opinion, etc., usually one that is kept hidden and not expressed openly

un·der·cut (un′dər kut′; *for v.* un′dər kut′) *n.* **1** a cut made in the lower part of something, that creates an overhang or a concave profile ☆**2** a notch cut in a tree below the level of the major cut and on the side to which the tree is to fall **3** [Brit.] a tenderloin or fillet of beef **4** *Sports* the act or an instance of undercutting —*adj.* that is undercut —*vt.* **-cut′**, **-cut′ting** **1** to make an UNDERCUT (senses 1 & 2) in **2** to cut out or wear away the underside or lower portion of **3** to undersell or work for lower wages than **4** to weaken the position of; lessen the force or impact of; undermine **5** *Sports* to strike (a ball) with an oblique downward motion, as in golf, or to chop with an underhand stroke, as in tennis, esp. so as to impart backspin —*vi.* to undercut something or someone

un·der·de·vel·op (un′dər di vel′əp) *vt.* **1** to develop to a point below what is needed **2** *Photog.* to develop (a film, plate, etc.) for too short a time or with too weak a developer

un·der·de·vel·oped (-əpt) *adj.* not developed to the proper or desirable degree; specif., so inadequately developed economically and industrially as to have a relatively low standard of living [*underdeveloped* nations]

un·der·do (un′dər do͞o′) *vt.* **-did′**, **-done′**, **-do′ing** to do less than is usual, needed, or desired

☆**un·der·dog** (un′dər dôg′) *n.* ⟦orig., the dog that is losing in a dogfight⟧ **1** a person or group that is losing, or is expected to lose, in a contest or struggle **2** a person who is handicapped or at a disadvantage because of injustice, discrimination, etc.

---

undated
undaughterly
undebatable
undecayed
undecipherable
undeclared
undeclinable
undecomposable
undecorated
undefaced
undefeatable
undefeated
undefended
undefensible
undefiled
undefinable
undefined
undelegated
undeliverable
undemanding
undemocratic
undemocratically
undemonstrable
undenied
undenominational
undependable
undepreciated

un·der·done (un′dər dun′) *adj.* not cooked enough or thoroughly: said esp. of meat

un·der·drain·age (un′dər drān′ij) *n.* drainage by an underground system of drains, as in agriculture

un·der·draw·ers (-drôrz′) *n.* DRAWERS

un·der·dress (un′dər dres′) *vi.* to dress more plainly or informally than is indicated by the occasion

un·der·em·ployed (-em ploid′) *adj.* **1** inadequately employed; esp., lacking sufficient paid work **2** working at low-skilled, poorly paid jobs when one is trained for, or could be trained for, more highly skilled work —**the underemployed** underemployed people —**un′der·em·ploy′ment** *n.*

un·der·es·ti·mate (un′dər es′tə māt′; *for n.*, -mit) *vt.* **-mat′ed, -mat′ing** to set too low an estimate on or for —*n.* an estimate that is too low —**un′der·es′ti·ma′tion** *n.*

un·der·ex·pose (un′dər ek spōz′) *vt.* **-posed′, -pos′ing** to expose (a photographic film, etc.) to inadequate light or for too short a time —**un′der·ex·po′sure** (-spō′zhər) *n.*

un·der·feed (-fēd′) *vt.* **-fed′, -feed′ing** to feed less than is needed

un·der·foot (un′dər foot′) *adv., adj.* **1** under the foot or feet [to trample flowers *underfoot*] ☆**2** in the way, as of one walking

un·der·fund (un′dər fund′) *vt.* to provide inadequate funds or funding for

un·der·fur (un′dər fur′) *n.* the softer, finer fur under the outer coat of some animals, as beavers and seals

un·der·gar·ment (-gär′mənt) *n.* a piece of underwear

un·der·gird (un′dər gurd′) *vt.* **-gird′ed** or **-girt′, -gird′ing** **1** to gird, strengthen, or brace from the bottom side **2** to supply support or a strong basis for

un·der·glaze (un′dər glāz′) *adj.* *Ceramics* designating colors, designs, etc. applied before the glaze is put on, as in painting porcelain —*n.* such colors, designs, etc.

un·der·go (un′dər gō′) *vt.* **-went′, -gone′, -go′ing** **1** to experience; endure; go through **2** [Obs.] to undertake

un·der·grad (un′dər grad′) *n., adj.* [Informal] UNDERGRADUATE

un·der·grad·u·ate (-gra′jo͞o it) *n.* a student at a university or college who has not yet received the first, or bachelor's, degree —*adj.* **1** of, for, consisting of, or characteristic of undergraduates **2** having the status of an undergraduate

un·der·ground (un′dər ground′) *adj.* **1** occurring, working, placed, used, etc. beneath the surface of the earth **2** secret; hidden; undercover **3** designating or of newspapers, films, music, etc. that are unconventional, experimental, radical, etc. —*adv.* **1** beneath the surface of the earth **2** in or into secrecy or hiding; so as to be undercover; surreptitiously —*n.* **1** the entire region beneath the surface of the earth **2** an underground space or passage **3** a secret movement organized in a country to oppose or overthrow the government in power or enemy forces of occupation **4** an underground movement in media, films, music, etc. **5** [Brit.] a subway

underground railroad ☆[*often* **U- R-**] in the U.S. before the Civil War, a system set up by certain opponents of slavery to help fugitive slaves escape to free states and Canada

un·der·grown (un′dər grōn′) *adj.* **1** not grown to full or normal size or development **2** having undergrowth

un·der·growth (un′dər grōth′) *n.* **1** UNDERBRUSH **2** an animal's undercoat **3** the state of being undergrown

un·der·hand (un′dər hand′) *adj.* **1** performed with the hand below the level of the elbow or the arm below the level of the shoulder [an *underhand* throw] **2** UNDERHANDED (sense 1) —*adv.* **1** with an underhand motion **2** [Archaic] not openly or straightforwardly

un·der·hand·ed (un′dər han′did) *adj.* **1** not open or straightforward; secret, sly, deceitful, etc. **2** SHORT-HANDED —*SYN.* SECRET —**un′der·hand′ed·ly** *adv.* —**un′der·hand′ed·ness** *n.*

un·der·hung (-huŋ′) *adj.* UNDERSLUNG (sense 2)

un·der·in·flat·ed (un′dər in flāt′əd) *adj.* having less air pressure than what is needed for normal use: said of a tire, basketball, etc. —**un′der·in·fla′tion** *n.*

un·der·laid (un′dər lād′) *adj.* **1** laid or placed underneath **2** having an underlay or underlying layer, support, etc.

un·der·lap (-lap′) *vt.* **-lapped′, -lap′ping** to lie or extend partly under (something)

un·der·lay[1] (un′dər lā′; *for n.* un′dər lā′) *vt.* **-laid′, -lay′ing** ⟦ME *underlein* < OE *underlecgan*⟧ **1** to cover, line, or extend over the bottom of [the leather is *underlaid* with felt] **2** to raise or support with something laid underneath [the roof must be *underlaid* with trusses] **3** *Printing* to provide with an underlay —*n.* **1** something laid underneath **2** *Printing* a patch or patches of paper laid under type, cuts, etc. to raise the level of the face

un·der·lay[2] (un′dər lā′) *vt. pt. of* UNDERLIE

un·der·let (-let′) *vt.* **-let′, -let′ting** **1** to let at a price below the real value **2** SUBLET

un·der·lie (-lī′) *vt.* **-lay′, -lain′, -ly′ing** ⟦ME *underlien* < OE *underlicgan*⟧ **1** to lie under or beneath [trusses *underlie* the roof] **2** to be the basis for; form the foundation of **3** *Finance* to have priority over (another) in order of claim, as a bond

un·der·line (un′dər līn′; *also, for v.*, un′dər līn′) *vt.* **-lined′, -lin′ing** **1** to draw a line beneath; underscore **2** to stress or emphasize —*n.* a line underneath, as an underscore

un·der·ling (un′dər liŋ) *n.* ⟦ME < OE: see UNDER- & -LING[1]⟧ a person in a subordinate position; inferior: usually contemptuous or disparaging

un·der·lin·ing (-līn′iŋ) *n.* a garment lining formed of pieces cut to the shape of and attached to the separate sections of a garment, which are then sewed together

un·der·lip (-lip′) *n.* the lower lip

un·der·ly·ing (-lī′iŋ) *adj.* **1** lying under; placed beneath **2** fundamental; basic [the *underlying* cause] **3** really there but not easily seen or noticed [an *underlying* trend] **4** *Finance* having priority, as a claim

un·der·mine (un′dər mīn′, un′dər mīn′) *vt.* **-mined′, -min′ing** **1** to dig beneath; excavate ground from under, so as to form a tunnel or mine **2** to wear away and weaken the supports of [erosion is *undermining* the wall] **3** to injure, weaken, or impair, esp. by subtle, stealthy, or insidious means —*SYN.* WEAKEN

un·der·most (un′dər mōst′) *adj., adv.* lowest in place, position, rank, etc.

un·der·neath (un′dər nēth′) *adv.* ⟦ME *undernethe* < OE *underneothan* < *under*, UNDER + *neothan*, below; akin to *neothera*, NETHER⟧ **1** under; below; beneath **2** on the underside; at a lower level **3** *Football* in front of the pass defenders —*prep.* **1** under; below; beneath **2** under the form, guise, or authority of **3** *Football* in front of —*adj.* under or lower —*n.* the underpart; bottom side

un·der·nour·ish (un′dər nur′ish) *vt.* to give insufficient nourishment to; provide with less food than is needed for health and growth —**un′der·nour′ish·ment** *n.*

☆**un·der·pants** (un′dər pants′) *pl.n.* an undergarment, long or short, for the lower part of the body, with a separate opening for each leg

un·der·part (un′dər pärt′) *n.* **1** the lower part or side, as of an animal's body or an airplane's fuselage **2** a secondary or subsidiary position or part

☆**un·der·pass** (-pas′) *n.* a passage, road, etc. running under something; esp., a passageway for vehicles or pedestrians that runs under a railway or highway

un·der·pay (un′dər pā′) *vt., vi.* **-paid′, -pay′ing** **1** to pay too little, or less than (the due amount) **2** to pay too little to (someone) —**un′der·pay′ment** *n.*

un·der·per·form (un′dər pər fôrm′) *vi.* to function less effectively or be less successful than expected or required —*vt.* to produce a smaller return than: said of stocks, mutual funds, etc. —**un′der·per·form′ance** *n.* —**un′der·per·form′er** *n.*

un·der·pin (un′dər pin′) *vt.* **-pinned′, -pin′ning** **1** to support or strengthen from beneath, as with props **2** to support or strengthen in any way; corroborate, substantiate, etc.

un·der·pin·ning (un′dər pin′iŋ) *n.* **1** a supporting structure or foundation, esp. one placed beneath a wall **2** [*often pl.*] anything that serves as a support or basis [the flimsy *underpinnings* of their argument] ☆**3** [*pl.*] [Informal] the legs

un·der·play (un′dər plā′) *vt., vi.* **1** to act (a role or scene) in a manner intended to be subtle and restrained **2** UNDERACT **3** to play down the importance of (something)

un·der·priv·i·leged (un′dər priv′ə lijd, -priv′lijd) *adj.* deprived of a decent standard of living, adequate education, and economic security through poverty, discrimination, etc. —**the underprivileged** those who are underprivileged

un·der·pro·duce (-prə do͞os′) *vt., vi.* **-duced′, -duc′ing** to produce in a quantity insufficient to meet the need or demand —**un′der·pro·duc′tion** *n.*

un·der·proof (-pro͞of′) *adj.* containing less alcohol than proof spirit does

un·der·prop (-präp′) *vt.* **-propped′, -prop′ping** to prop underneath; support

un·der·quote (-kwōt′) *vt.* **-quot′ed, -quot′ing** **1** to quote (goods) at a price lower than another price or than the market price **2** to quote a lower price than (other sellers)

un·der·rate (-rāt′) *vt.* **-rat′ed, -rat′ing** to rate, assess, or estimate too low

un·der·re·act (-rē akt′) *vi.* to react with less emotion, force, or intensity than is appropriate or expected

un·der·re·port (-ri pôrt′) *vt.* to report fewer than the actual number or less than the true amount of

un·der·rep·re·sent (-rep′ri zent′) *vt.* to represent in numbers that are fewer, or in a proportion that is less, than is statistically expected or warranted —**un′der·rep′re·sen·ta′tion** *n.*

un·der·run (-run′) *vt.* **-ran′, -run′, -run′ning** to run, go, or pass under —*n.* something running or passing underneath, as an undercurrent

un·der·score (un′dər skôr′; *for n.* un′dər skôr′) *vt.* **-scored′, -scor′ing** UNDERLINE —*n.* a line drawn under a word, passage, etc., as for emphasis

un·der·sea (un′dər sē′; *for adv., usually* un′dər sē′) *adj., adv.* beneath the surface of the sea: also **un′der·seas′** *adv.*

un·der·sec·re·tar·y (-sek′rə ter′ē) *n., pl.* **-tar′ies** an assistant secretary: in U.S. government, **under secretary**

un·der·sell (un′dər sel′) *vt.* **-sold′, -sell′ing** **1** to sell at a lower price than (another seller) ☆**2** to publicize or promote in a restrained or inadequate manner

un·der·served (un′dər survd′) *adj.* insufficiently provided with professional services [rural and other medically *underserved* communities]

un·der·set (un′dər set′) *n.* an ocean undercurrent

☆**un·der·sexed** (un′dər sekst′) *adj.* characterized by a weaker than normal sexual drive or interest

un·der·sher·iff (un′dər sher′if) *n.* a deputy sheriff

☆**un·der·shirt** (-shurt′) *n.* a collarless undergarment, with or without sleeves, worn under an outer shirt

un·der·shoot (un′dər sho͞ot′) *vt.* **-shot′, -shoot′ing** **1** to shoot or fall short of (a target, mark, etc.) **2** to bring an aircraft down short of (the runway, landing field, etc.) while trying to land —*vi.* to shoot or go short of the mark

☆**un·der·shorts** (un′dər shôrts′) *pl.n.* short underpants worn by men and boys

un·der·shot (-shät′) *adj.* 1 with the lower part or half extending past the upper [an *undershot* jaw] 2 driven by water flowing along the lower part [an *undershot* water wheel]: see WATER WHEEL, illus.

un·der·shrub (-shrub′) *n.* any low-growing, woody, bushy plant

un·der·side (-sīd′) *n.* the side or surface that is underneath

un·der·sign (un′dər sīn′) *vt.* to sign one's name at the end of (a letter, document, etc.)

un·der·signed (un′dər sīnd′) *adj.* whose name or names are signed at the end —**the undersigned** the person whose name or persons whose names are signed at the end

un·der·sized (-sīzd′) *adj.* smaller in size than is usual, average, or proper: also **un′der·size′** (-sīz′)

un·der·skirt (-skurt′) *n.* a skirt worn under another; petticoat

un·der·slung (-sluŋ′) *adj.* 1 having springs attached to the underside of the axles: said of an automobile frame 2 projecting: said of the lower jaw

un·der·soil (-soil′) *n.* SUBSOIL

un·der·song (-sôŋ′) *n.* [Archaic] a song or refrain sung as accompaniment to another song

un·der·spin (-spin′) *n.* BACKSPIN

un·der·staffed (un′dər staft′) *adj.* having too small a staff; having insufficient personnel

un·der·stand (un′dər stand′) *vt.* **-stood′**, **-stand′ing** ⟦ME *understanden* < OE *understandan,* lit., to stand among, hence observe, understand⟧ 1 to get or perceive the meaning of; know or grasp what is meant by; comprehend [to *understand* a question] 2 to gather or assume from what is heard, known, etc.; infer [are we to *understand* that you want to go?] 3 to take as meant or meaning; interpret [to *understand* his silence as refusal] 4 to take for granted or as a fact [it is *understood* that no one is to leave] 5 to supply mentally (an idea, word, etc.), as for grammatical completeness 6 to know thoroughly; grasp or perceive clearly and fully the nature, character, functioning, etc. of 7 to have a sympathetic rapport with [no one *understands* me] —*vi.* 1 to have understanding, comprehension, sympathetic awareness, etc., either in general or with reference to something specific 2 to be informed; believe [he is, I *understand,* no longer here] —**un′der·stand′a·ble** *adj.* —**un′der·stand′a·bly** *adv.*

SYN.—**understand** and **comprehend** are used interchangeably to imply clear perception of the meaning of something, but, more precisely, **understand** stresses the full awareness or knowledge arrived at, and **comprehend**, the process of grasping something mentally [one may *comprehend* the words in an idiom without *understanding* at all what is meant]; **appreciate** implies sensitive, discriminating perception of the exact worth or value of something [to *appreciate* the difficulties of a situation]

un·der·stand·ing (-stan′diŋ) *n.* 1 the mental quality, act, or state of a person who understands; comprehension, knowledge, discernment, sympathetic awareness, etc. 2 the power or ability to think, learn, judge, etc.; intelligence; sense 3 a specific interpretation or inference [one's *understanding* of a matter] 4 *a)* mutual comprehension, as of ideas, intentions, etc. *b)* a mutual agreement, esp. one that settles differences or is informal and not made public —*adj.* that understands; having or characterized by comprehension, sympathy, etc. —**un′der·stand′ing·ly** *adv.*

un·der·state (un′dər stāt′) *vt.* **-stat′ed**, **-stat′ing** 1 to make a weaker statement of than is warranted by truth, accuracy, or importance; state too weakly 2 to state, express, display, etc. in a restrained way —**un′der·state′ment** *n.*

un·der·stat·ed (-id) *adj.* restrained, subtle, modest, etc. [an *understated* color scheme]

un·der·steer (un′dər stir′) *n.* the tendency of a motor vehicle, esp. a race car, to have its front tires slide outward on a turn

un·der·stood (un′dər stood′) *vt., vi. pt. & pp. of* UNDERSTAND —*adj.* 1 known; comprehended 2 agreed upon 3 implied but not expressed

un·der·sto·ry (un′dər stôr′ē) *n.* ⟦UNDER + STORY[2]⟧ the smaller trees, saplings, and, sometimes, shrubs that grow beneath the large trees in woods or forests

un·der·strap·per (un′dər strap′ər) *n.* ⟦UNDER- + STRAPPER⟧ a subordinate or underling

un·der·strength (un′dər streŋkth′, -streŋth′) *adj.* having less than full or adequate strength or power [an *understrength* battalion, workforce, etc.]

un·der·stud·y (un′dər stud′ē) *n., pl.* **-stud′ies** 1 an actor who learns the part of another actor so as to serve as a substitute when necessary 2 any person who learns the duties of another so as to serve as a substitute —*vt., vi.* **-stud′ied**, **-stud′y·ing** 1 to act as an understudy (to) 2 to learn (a part) as an understudy

un·der·sur·face (-sur′fis) *n.* UNDERSIDE

un·der·take (un′dər tāk′) *vt.* **-took′**, **-tak′en**, **-tak′ing** ⟦ME *undertaken:* see UNDER- & TAKE⟧ 1 to take upon oneself; agree to do; enter into or upon (a task, journey, etc.) 2 to give a promise or pledge that; contract [he *undertook* to be their guide] 3 to promise; guarantee 4 to make oneself responsible for; take over as a charge —*vi.* 1 [Archaic] to take on responsibility, pledge oneself, guarantee, or be surety (*for*) ☆2 [Old Informal] to work as an UNDERTAKER (sense 2)

un·der·tak·er (un′dər tā′kər; *for 2* un′dər tā′kər) *n.* 1 a person who undertakes something 2 FUNERAL DIRECTOR: a somewhat old-fashioned usage

un·der·tak·ing (un′dər tā′kiŋ; *also, & for 3 always,* un′dər tā′kiŋ) *n.* 1 something undertaken; task; charge; enterprise 2 a promise; guarantee 3 the business of an UNDERTAKER (sense 2) 4 the act of one who undertakes some task, responsibility, etc.

un·der-the-count·er (un′dər *thə* koun′tər) *adj.* [Informal] done, sold, given, etc. secretly in an unlawful or unethical way: also **un′der-the-ta′ble** (-tā′bəl)

un·der·things (un′dər thiŋz′) *pl.n.* women's or girls' underwear

un·der·throw (un′dər thrō′; *for n.* un′dər thrō′) *vt.* **-threw′**, **-thrown′**, **-throw′ing** to throw a ball or other object short of (the intended receiver or target) —*n.* an underthrowing or being underthrown

un·der·tint (un′dər tint′) *n.* a faint or subdued tint

un·der·tone (-tōn′) *n.* 1 a low tone of sound or voice 2 a faint or subdued color, esp. one seen through other colors, as in some glazes 3 any underlying quality, factor, element, etc. [an *undertone* of horror]

un·der·took (un′dər took′) *vt., vi. pt. of* UNDERTAKE

un·der·tow (un′dər tō′) *n.* ⟦UNDER- + TOW[1]⟧ a current of water moving beneath and in a different direction from that of the surface water: said esp. of a seaward current beneath breaking surf

un·der·trick (-trik′) *n. Bridge* any of the tricks by which the declarer falls short of making the contract

un·der·u·ti·lize (un′dər yo͞ot′'l īz′) *vt.* **-lized′**, **-liz′ing** to utilize too little or inefficiently —**un′der·u′ti·li·za′tion** *n.*

un·der·val·ue (-val′yo͞o) *vt.* **-ued**, **-u·ing** 1 to value below the real worth 2 to regard or esteem too lightly —**un′der·val′u·a′tion** *n.*

un·der·vest (un′dər vest′) *n.* [Brit.] UNDERSHIRT

un·der·wa·ter (un′dər wôt′ər) *adj.* 1 being, placed, done, etc. beneath the surface of the water 2 used or for use under water 3 below the waterline of a ship 4 of or having an asset that has a value less than its specified purchase price, as a stock option, or less than an outstanding loan against it, as a property: also written **under water** —*adv.* beneath the surface of the water

un·der·way (un′dər wā′) *adj.* 1 moving; advancing; making progress 2 *Naut.* not anchored or moored or aground

un·der·wear (un′dər wer′) *n.* clothing worn under one's outer clothes, usually next to the skin, as undershirts, undershorts, or slips

un·der·weight (un′dər wāt′; *for adj. & v., also,* un′dər wāt′) *adj.* 1 below the normal, desirable, or allowed weight 2 holding or containing relatively less of a specified asset, security, etc. —*n.* weight that is less than needed, desired, or allowed —*vt.* in investing, to hold a smaller amount or proportion of in a portfolio, as in relation to some benchmark [to *underweight* technology stocks]

un·der·went (un′dər went′) *vt. pt. of* UNDERGO

un·der·whelm (-hwelm′, -welm′) *vt.* ⟦ironic allusion to OVERWHELM⟧ to fail to make a good impression or have a significant impact on

un·der·wing (un′dər wiŋ′) *n.* 1 either of the pair of hind wings of an insect 2 any of various noctuid moths (esp. genus *Catocala*) having brightly colored hind wings that are hidden under drab forewings except during flight

un·der·wire (un′dər wīr′) *n.* 1 a curved wire inserted into the undersides of the cups of certain bras for increased support 2 such a bra: in full **underwire bra**

un·der·wood (un′dər wood′) *n.* UNDERBRUSH

un·der·world (-wurld′) *n.* 1 [Archaic] the earth 2 the mythical world of the dead; Hades 3 the opposite side of the earth; antipodes 4 the criminal members of society, or people living by vice or crime, regarded as a group or class

un·der·write (un′dər rīt′) *vt.* **-wrote′**, **-writ′ten**, **-writ′ing** ⟦ME *underwriten,* orig. used as transl. of L *subscribere:* see SUBSCRIBE⟧ 1 [Archaic] to write under something, esp. under something written; subscribe 2 to agree to buy (an issue of stocks, bonds, etc.) on a given date and at a fixed price, or to guarantee the purchase of (stocks or bonds to be made available to the public for subscription) 3 to subscribe or agree to, as by signature 4 to agree to pay for the cost of or pledge to cover the financial losses of (an undertaking, etc.) 5 *Insurance a)* to write one's signature at the end of (an insurance policy), thus assuming liability in the event of specified loss or damage *b)* to insure *c)* to assume liability to the amount of (a specified sum) —*vi.* 1 to underwrite something 2 to be in business as an underwriter

un·der·writ·er (-rīt′ər) *n.* 1 a person who underwrites, or finances something 2 a person who underwrites issues of stocks, bonds, etc. 3 *a)* an employee of an insurance company who determines the acceptability of risks, the premiums that should be charged, etc. *b)* an agent who underwrites insurance

un·de·scend·ed (un′dē sen′dəd) *adj.* designating a testicle that has remained in the abdominal area, rather than descending normally into the scrotum prior to birth

un·de·sign·ing (un′di zī′niŋ) *adj.* not designing; straightforward; honest; not crafty or underhanded

undescribable **undescribed** **undeserved** **undeserving** **undesignated**

un·de·sir·a·ble (-di zīr′ə bəl) *adj.* not desirable or pleasing; objectionable —*n.* an undesirable person —**un′de·sir′a·bil′i·ty** *n.* —**un′de·sir′a·bly** *adv.*

un·did (un did′) *vt. pt. of* UNDO

un·dies (un′dēz) *pl.n.* ⟦dim. euphemistic abbrev.⟧ [Informal] women's or girls' underwear

un·dine (un dēn′; un′dēn, -dīn) *n.* ⟦Ger < ModL *Undina,* coined by PARACELSUS for a water spirit in his alchemical system < L *unda,* a wave: see WATER⟧ *Folklore* a female water spirit who can acquire a soul by marrying, and having a child by, a mortal

un·di·rect·ed (un′də rek′tid) *adj.* **1** not directed; not guided **2** not addressed, as a letter

un·dis·posed (-dis pōzd′) *adj.* **1** not disposed (of) **2** indisposed; unwilling

un·dis·so·ci·at·ed (-di sō′shē āt′id, -sē-) *adj. Chem.* not separated into ions, radicals, or simpler atoms or molecules

un·do (un do͞o′) *vt.* **-did′, -done′, -do′ing** ⟦ME *undon* < OE < *un-,* UN- + *don,* to DO[1]⟧ **1** *a)* to release or untie (a fastening) *b)* to open (a parcel, door, etc.) by this means **2** to reverse the doing of (something accomplished); do away with; cancel; annul **3** to put an end to; bring to ruin, disgrace, or downfall **4** to upset emotionally; perturb **5** [Obs.] to interpret; explain —**un·do′er** *n.*

un·doc·u·ment·ed (un däk′yə ment′id) *adj.* **1** lacking supporting documentation [an *undocumented* assertion] ☆**2** not having the required document or documents; specif., without a proper visa for U.S. residence [an *undocumented* alien, worker, etc.]

un·do·ing (un do͞o′iŋ) *n.* **1** the act of opening, untying, etc. **2** a reversal of the doing of something done or accomplished; canceling or annulling **3** the act of bringing to ruin, disgrace, or destruction **4** the cause or source of ruin, disgrace, or destruction

un·done[1] (-dun′) *vt. pp. of* UNDO —*adj.* **1** ruined, disgraced, etc. **2** emotionally upset; greatly perturbed

un·done[2] (-dun′) *adj.* not done; not performed, accomplished, completed, etc.

un·dou·ble (-dub′əl) *vt.* **-bled, -bling** to cause to be no longer doubled or double; unfold

un·doubt·ed (-dout′id) *adj.* not doubted, called in question, or disputed; certain —**un·doubt′ed·ly** *adv.*

un·draw (-drô′) *vt., vi.* **-drew′, -drawn′, -draw′ing** to draw (a curtain, drapes, etc.) open, back, or aside

un·dreamed (-drēmd′) *adj.* not even dreamed (*of*) or imagined; inconceivable: also **un·dreamt′** (-dremt′)

un·dress (un dres′; *for n., usually* un′dres′) *vt.* **1** to take off the clothing of; strip **2** to divest of ornament **3** to remove the dressing from (a wound) —*vi.* to take off one's clothes; strip —*n.* **1** the state of being naked, only partly dressed, or in night clothes, a robe, etc. **2** ordinary or informal dress, as opposed to uniform, full dress, etc.

Und·set (oon′set), **Sig·rid** (sig′rid) 1882-1949; Norw. novelist

und so wei·ter (oont′ zō vī′tər) ⟦Ger⟧ and so forth; and so on

un·due (un do͞o′, -dyo͞o′) *adj.* **1** not yet due or payable, as a debt **2** not appropriate or suitable; improper **3** excessive; immoderate

un·du·lant (un′jə lənt, -dyə-) *adj.* moving in or as in waves; undulating

undulant fever a persistent form of brucellosis, transmitted to people from lower, esp. domestic, animals, or their products, and characterized by an undulating, or recurrent, fever, sweating, and pains in the joints

un·du·late (un′jə lāt′, -dyə-; *for adj.,* -lit, -lāt′) *vt.* **-lat′ed, -lat′ing** ⟦< L *undulatus,* undulated < **undula,* dim. of *unda,* a wave: see WATER⟧ **1** to cause to move in waves **2** to give a wavy form, margin, or surface to —*vi.* **1** to move in or as in waves; move sinuously **2** to have a wavy form, margin, or surface —*adj.* having a wavy form, margin, or surface; undulating: see LEAF, illus. Also **un′du·lat′ed** —*SYN.* SWING

un·du·la·tion (un′jə lā′shən, -dyə-) *n.* **1** *a)* the act of undulating *b)* an undulating motion, as of a snake **2** a wavy, curving form or outline, esp. one of a series **3** *Physics* wave motion, as of light or sound, or a wave or vibration

un·du·la·to·ry (un′jə lə tôr′ē, -dyə-) *adj.* **1** of, caused by, or characterized by undulations **2** having a wavelike form or motion; undulating

un·du·ly (un do͞o′lē, -dyo͞o′-) *adv.* **1** improperly; unjustly **2** to an undue degree; excessively

un·dy·ing (-dī′iŋ) *adj.* not dying; immortal or eternal

un·earned (-urnd′) *adj.* **1** not earned by work or service; specif., obtained as a return on an investment [*unearned* income] **2** not deserved; unmerited

unearned increment an increase in the value of land or other property through no work or expenditure by the owner, as through an increase in area population thereby increasing demand

☆**unearned run** *Baseball* a run scored against a pitcher that is the result of a fielding error: it is not included in calculating EARNED RUN AVERAGE: cf. EARNED RUN

un·earth (-urth′) *vt.* **1** to dig up from out of the earth **2** to bring to light as by searching; discover; disclose —*SYN.* LEARN

un·earth·ly (-urth′lē) *adj.* **1** not, or as if not, of this earth **2** supernatural; ghostly **3** weird; mysterious **4** [Informal] fantastic, outlandish, absurd, etc. —*SYN.* WEIRD —**un·earth′li·ness** *n.*

un·ease (un′ēz) *n.* distress or discomfort

un·eas·y (-ē′zē) *adj.* **-eas′i·er, -eas′i·est** **1** having, showing, or allowing no ease of body or mind; uncomfortable **2** awkward; constrained **3** disturbed by anxiety or apprehension; restless; unsettled; perturbed —**un·eas′i·ly** *adv.* —**un·eas′i·ness** *n.*

un·ed·it·ed (-ed′it id) *adj.* **1** not edited for publication **2** not assembled for presentation [an *unedited* film]

un·em·ploy·a·ble (un′em ploi′ə bəl) *adj.* not employable; specif., that cannot be employed because of severe physical or mental handicaps, outmoded skills, etc. —*n.* an unemployable person

un·em·ployed (-ploid′) *adj.* **1** not employed; without work **2** not being used; idle —**the unemployed** people who are out of work

un·em·ploy·ment (-ploi′mənt) *n.* **1** the state of being unemployed; lack of employment **2** the number or percentage of persons in the normal labor force who are out of work

unemployment compensation payment, as by a state government from premiums or taxes paid by employers, of a certain amount of money to a qualified unemployed person, usually at regular intervals and over a fixed period of time

un·e·qual (un ē′kwəl) *adj.* **1** not equal, as in size, strength, ability, value, rank, number, amount, etc. **2** *a)* not balanced or symmetrical [an *unequal* pattern] *b)* that matches unequal contestants [an *unequal* battle] **3** not even, regular, or uniform; variable; fluctuating **4** not equal or adequate: with *to* [*unequal* to the task] **5** [Now Rare] not equitable; unjust; unfair —*n.* a person or thing not equal to another —**un·e′qual·ly** *adv.* —**un·e′qual·ness** *n.*

un·e·qualed or **un·e·qualled** (-ē′kwəld) *adj.* not equaled; unmatched; unrivaled; supreme

un·e·quiv·o·cal (un′ē kwiv′ə kəl) *adj.* not equivocal; not ambiguous; plain; clear —**un′e·quiv′o·cal·ly** *adv.*

un·err·ing (un ur′iŋ, -er′-) *adj.* **1** free from error **2** not missing or failing; certain; sure; exact —**un·err′ing·ly** *adv.*

UNESCO (yo͞o nes′kō) *n.* United Nations Educational, Scientific, and Cultural Organization

un·es·sen·tial (un′ə sen′shəl) *adj.* not essential; that can be dispensed with —*n.* an unessential thing

un·e·ven (un ē′vən) *adj.* ⟦ME < OE *unefen*⟧ not even; specif., *a)* not level, smooth, or flat; rough; irregular *b)* not straight or parallel *c)* unequal, as

---

undesired
undesirous
undestroyed
undetachable
undetected
undeterminable
undetermined
undeterred
undeveloped
undeviating
undevoured
undevout
undifferentiated
undiffused
undigested
undigestible
undignified
undiluted
undiminishable
undiminished
undimmed
undiplomatic
undiscernible
undiscernibly
undiscerning
undischarged
undisciplined
undisclosed
undiscouraged
undiscoverable
undiscovered
undiscriminating
undiscussed
undisguised
undisheartened
undishonored
undismantled
undismayed
undismembered
undispelled
undisputable
undisputed
undissected
undissolved
undissolving
undistilled
undistinguishable
undistinguished
undistorted
undistracted
undistressed
undistributed
undisturbed
undiversified
undiverted
undivested
undivided
undivulged
undogmatic
undomestic
undomesticated
undrained
undramatic
undramatically
undramatized
undraped
undried
undrinkable
undutiful
undyed
uneatable
uneaten
uneconomical
unedible
unedifying
uneducable
uneducated
uneffaced
unemancipated
unembarrassed
unembellished
unemotional
unemphatic
unenclosed
unencumbered
unendearing
unending
unendorsed
unendowed
unendurable
unenforceable
unengaged
unengaging
un-English
unenjoyable
unenlightened
unenriched
unenrolled
unenslaved
unentangled
unentered
unenterprising
unentertaining
unenthralled
unenthusiastic
unentitled
unenviable
unenvious
unequipped
unerased
unescapable
unescorted
unestablished
unesthetic
unethical
unethically

in length or thickness *d)* not uniform; varying; fluctuating *e)* not equally balanced or matched *f)* not equitable; unfair *g) Math.* odd; not evenly divisible by two —**un·e′ven·ly** *adv.* —**un·e′ven·ness** *n.*

uneven bars **1** two parallel wooden bars about 18 inches apart that are set horizontally at different heights on upright posts, used in gymnastics **2** an event in which women gymnasts perform various routines on such bars

un·event·ful (un′ē vent′fəl) *adj.* with no outstanding or unusual event; peaceful, routine, etc. [an *uneventful* day] —**un′e·vent′ful·ly** *adv.*

un·ex·am·pled (-eg zam′pəld) *adj.* having no precedent, parallel, or similar case; unprecedented

un·ex·cep·tion·a·ble (-ek sep′shə nə bəl) *adj.* not exceptionable; without flaw or fault; not warranting even the slightest criticism: sometimes used with mild pejorative force of something regarded as having mere correctness as its chief virtue —**un′ex·cep′tion·a·bly** *adv.*

un·ex·cep·tion·al (-ek sep′shə nəl) *adj.* **1** not exceptional; not uncommon or unusual; ordinary **2** not admitting of any exception **3** *var. of* UNEXCEPTIONABLE: regarded by some as a loose usage —**un′ex·cep′tion·al·ly** *adv.*

un·ex·pect·ed (-ek spek′tid) *adj.* not expected; unforeseen —**un′ex·pect′ed·ly** *adv.* —**un′ex·pect′ed·ness** *n.*

un·ex·pres·sive (-ek spres′iv) *adj.* **1** INEXPRESSIVE **2** [Obs.] that cannot be expressed; inexpressible

un·fail·ing (un fāl′iŋ) *adj.* **1** not failing **2** never ceasing or falling short; inexhaustible **3** always reliable; certain —**un·fail′ing·ly** *adv.*

un·fair (-fer′) *adj.* ⟦ME < OE *unfæger,* unfair, ugly < *un-,* not + *fæger,* FAIR[1]⟧ **1** not just or impartial; biased; inequitable **2** dishonest, dishonorable, or unethical in business dealings —**un·fair′ly** *adv.* —**un·fair′ness** *n.*

un·faith·ful (-fāth′fəl) *adj.* **1** failing to observe the terms of a vow, promise, understanding, etc., or false to allegiance or duty; faithless; disloyal **2** not true, accurate, or reliable; untrustworthy **3** engaging in sexual relations with someone other than one's spouse, lover, etc.; adulterous **4** [Archaic] lacking good faith; dishonest **5** [Obs.] infidel —**un·faith′ful·ly** *adv.* —**un·faith′ful·ness** *n.*

un·fa·mil·iar (un′fə mil′yər) *adj.* **1** not familiar or well-known; strange **2** having no acquaintance (*with*); not conversant [*unfamiliar* with the novels of Kafka] —**un′fa·mil′i·ar′i·ty** (-ē ar′ə tē) *n.* —**un′fa·mil′iar·ly** *adv.*

un·fas·ten (un fas′ən) *vt.* to open or make loose; untie, unlock, undo, etc. —*vi.* to become unfastened

un·fa·thered (-fä′thərd) *adj.* **1** [Obs.] having no father; fatherless **2** of unknown paternity; bastard **3** of unknown authorship or unestablished authenticity

un·fath·om·a·ble (-fath′əm ə bəl) *adj.* not fathomable; specif., *a)* incapable of being measured (often used fig.) [the *unfathomable* depths of his love] *b)* that cannot be understood; incomprehensible

un·fa·vor·a·ble (-fā′vər ə bəl) *adj.* not favorable; specif., *a)* not propitious *b)* adverse, contrary, or disadvantageous —**un·fa′vor·a·bly** *adv.*

un·feel·ing (-fēl′iŋ) *adj.* **1** incapable of feeling or sensation; insensate or insensible **2** incapable of sympathy or mercy; hardhearted; callous; cruel —**un·feel′ing·ly** *adv.*

un·feigned (-fānd′) *adj.* not feigned; genuine; real; sincere —**un·feign′ed·ly** (-fān′id lē) *adv.*

un·fet·ter (-fet′ər) *vt.* to free from fetters; free from restraint of any kind; liberate —**un·fet′tered** *adj.*

un·fil·i·al (-fil′ē əl) *adj.* unlike, or unsuitable to, a loving, respectful son or daughter —**un·fil′i·al·ly** *adv.*

un·fin·ished (-fin′isht) *adj.* **1** not finished; not completed or perfected; incomplete **2** having no finish, or final coat, as of paint **3** not processed after looming, as woolen cloth

un·fit (-fit′) *adj.* **1** not meeting requirements; not suitable or qualified **2** not physically or mentally fit or sound **3** not adapted or fitted for a given purpose —*vt.* **-fit′ted, -fit′ting** to make unfit; disqualify or incapacitate —**un·fit′ly** *adv.* —**un·fit′ness** *n.*

un·fit·ting (un fit′iŋ) *adj.* not suitable or appropriate

un·fix (un fiks′) *vt.* ⟦UN- + FIX⟧ **1** to unfasten; loosen; detach **2** to unsettle

un·flap·pa·ble (-flap′ə bəl) *adj.* ⟦< UN- + FLAP, *n.* 5 + -ABLE⟧ [Informal] not easily excited or disconcerted; imperturbable; calm —**un·flap′pa·bil′i·ty** *n.* —**un·flap′pa·bly** *adv.*

un·flat·ter·ing (-flat′ər iŋ) *adj.* not flattering; specif., presenting aspects of a subject in such a way as to seem uncomplimentary or negative [an *unflattering* photograph, review, etc.] —**un·flat′ter·ing·ly** *adv.*

un·fledged (-flejd′) *adj.* **1** not fully fledged; unfeathered: said as of a young bird **2** immature; undeveloped

un·flinch·ing (-flin′chiŋ) *adj.* not flinching, yielding, or shrinking; steadfast; resolute —**un·flinch′ing·ly** *adv.*

un·fo·cused (un fō′kəst) *adj.* **1** not focused; not brought into focus **2** *a)* lacking a center of concentration [*unfocused* attempts] *b)* not directed toward a goal or objective [*unfocused* plans]

un·fold (-fōld′) *vt.* ⟦ME *unfolden* < OE *unfealdan* < *un-,* UN- + *fealdan,* to FOLD[1]⟧ **1** to open and spread out (something folded) **2** to make known or lay open to view, esp. in stages or little by little; reveal, disclose, display, or explain —*vi.* **1** to become unfolded; open out or open up **2** to develop fully

un·for·get·ta·ble (un′fər get′ə bəl) *adj.* so important, beautiful, forceful, shocking, etc. as never to be forgotten —**un′for·get′ta·bly** *adv.*

un·for·giv·ing (-fər giv′iŋ) *adj.* **1** not willing or not able to forgive **2** allowing no room for adjustments or for errors or weakness; inflexible, exacting, harsh, etc. [an *unforgiving* budget, *unforgiving* climate] —**un′for·giv′ing·ness** *n.*

un·formed (un fôrmd′) *adj.* **1** having no regular form or shape; shapeless **2** not organized or developed **3** not made; uncreated

un·for·tu·nate (-fôr′chə nit) *adj.* **1** *a)* having bad luck; unlucky *b)* bringing, or coming by, bad luck; unfavorable **2** not suitable or successful —*n.* an unfortunate person —**un·for′tu·nate·ly** *adv.*

un·found·ed (-foun′did) *adj.* not founded on fact or truth; baseless

un·freeze (-frēz′) *vt.* **-froze′, -froz′en, -freez′ing** ⟦UN- + FREEZE⟧ **1** to cause to thaw ☆**2** to remove financial controls from (prices, a raw material, etc.)

un·friend (-frend′) *vt.* to delete (a person or group) from one's list of associates on a social-networking website

un·friend·ed (-fren′did) *adj.* having no friends; friendless

un·friend·ly (-frend′lē) *adj.* **-li·er, -li·est** **1** not friendly or kind **2** hostile **3** not favorable or propitious —**un·friend′li·ness** *n.*

un·frock (-fräk′) *vt.* **1** to remove a frock from **2** DEFROCK

un·fruit·ful (-fro͞ot′fəl) *adj.* **1** not reproducing; barren; unproductive **2** yielding no worthwhile result; fruitless; unprofitable —*SYN.* STERILE —**un·fruit′ful·ly** *adv.*

un·furl (-furl′) *vt., vi.* to open or spread out from a furled state

un·fuss·y (-fus′ē) *adj.* not fussy; casual, undemanding, uncomplicated, etc. —**un·fuss′i·ly** *adv.* —**un·fuss′i·ness** *n.*

un·gain·ly (-gān′lē) *adj.* ⟦ME *ungeinliche* < *ungein,* perilous (< *un-,* not + ON *gegn,* ready, serviceable, akin to OE *gegn:* see AGAIN) + *-liche,* -LY[1]⟧ **1** awkward; clumsy **2** coarse and unattractive —*adv.* [Archaic] in an ungainly manner —**un·gain′li·ness** *n.*

Un·ga·va (uŋ gä′və, -gā′-) region in N Quebec, Canada, between Labrador & Hudson Bay: 351,780 sq mi (911,107 sq km)

un·gen·er·ous (un jen′ər əs) *adj.* **1** not generous; stingy; mean **2** not liberal or charitable; harsh [an *ungenerous* remark] —**un·gen′er·ous·ly** *adv.*

un·gird (-gurd′) *vt.* ⟦ME *ungirden* < OE *ongyrdan* < *un-,* UN- + *gyrdan,* to GIRD[1]⟧ **1** to remove the belt or girdle of **2** to remove by unfastening a belt

un·girt (-gurt′) *adj.* ⟦ME *ungyrt* < *ungirden:* see prec.⟧ **1** having the belt or girdle off or slackened; not girded **2** loose; not braced or drawn tight; slack

un·glue (-glo͞o′) *vt.* **-glued′, -glu′ing** **1** to separate or detach by or as if by dissolving an adhesive **2** [Slang] to upset; confuse —☆**come unglued** [Slang] to become emotionally upset and lose one's composure

un·god·ly (-gäd′lē) *adj.* **1** not godly or religious; impious **2** sinful; wicked **3** [Informal] outrageous; dreadful —*adv.* **1** [Archaic] in an impious, sinful, or wicked manner **2** [Informal] outrageously; dreadfully [*ungodly* noisy] —**un·god′li·ness** *n.*

un·gov·ern·a·ble (-guv′ərn ə bəl) *adj.* that cannot be governed or controlled; unruly, wild, etc. —**un·gov′ern·a·bly** *adv.*

---

unexacting
unexaggerated
unexalted
unexamined
unexcavated
unexcelled
unexchangeable
unexcitable
unexcited
unexciting
unexcused
unexecuted
unexercised
unexpanded
unexpendable
unexperienced
unexpert
unexpiated
unexpired
unexplainable
unexplained
unexplicit
unexploded
unexploited
unexplored
unexported
unexposed
unexpressed
unexpunged
unexpurgated
unextended
unextinguished
unfaded
unfading
unfaltering
unfashionable
unfatherly
unfathomed
unfazed
unfeared
unfearful
unfeasible
unfeathered
unfed
unfederated
unfelt
unfeminine
unfenced
unfermented
unfertile
unfertilized
unfilled
unfiltered
unfired
unflagging
unflavored
unflawed
unforbidden
unforced
unfordable
unforeknown
unforeseeable
unforeseen
unforested
unforfeited
unforged
unforgivable
unforgivably
unforgiven
unforgotten
unformulated
unforsaken
unforthcoming
unfortified
unfought
unframed
unfree
unfrequented
unfulfilled
unfunded
unfunny
unfurnished
ungarnished
ungathered
ungentlemanly
ungenuine
ungifted
unglamorous
unglazed
unglorified
unglossed
ungloved
ungot
ungotten
ungraced

un·gra·cious (-grā′shəs) *adj.* 1 not gracious or affable; rude; discourteous; impolite 2 unpleasant; unattractive —**un·gra′cious·ly** *adv.* —**un·gra′cious·ness** *n.*

un·gram·mat·i·cal (un′grə mat′i kəl) *adj.* not in accordance with the rules of a grammar —**un′gram·mat′i·cal·ly** *adv.*

un·gual (uŋ′gwəl) *adj.* ⟦< L *unguis,* a claw, NAIL + -AL⟧ of, like, or having a nail, claw, or hoof

un·guard·ed (un gär′did) *adj.* 1 having no guard; unprotected 2 without guile or cunning; open 3 careless; thoughtless; imprudent —**un·guard′ed·ly** *adv.*

un·guent (uŋ′gwənt) *n.* ⟦L *unguentum* < *unguere,* to anoint < IE base **ongw-* > Sans *anákti,* (he) anoints, MHG *anke,* butter⟧ a salve or ointment —**un′guen·tar′y** (-gwən ter′ē) *adj.*

un·guic·u·late (uŋ gwik′yo͞o lit, -lāt′) *adj.* ⟦< L *unguiculus,* fingernail, dim. of *unguis,* claw, talon, NAIL + -ATE[1]⟧ 1 having nails, claws, or talons instead of hoofs 2 *Bot.* having an unguis —*n.* a mammal having claws or nails

un·guis (uŋ′gwis) *n., pl.* **un′gues′** (-gwēz′) ⟦L, a NAIL⟧ 1 *Bot.* the narrow, stalklike, claw-shaped base of certain petals 2 *Zool.* a nail, claw, or hoof

un·gu·la (uŋ′gyo͞o lə) *n., pl.* **-lae′** (-lē′) ⟦L, a hoof < *unguis,* a hoof, NAIL⟧ UNGUIS (sense 2) —**un′gu·lar** *adj.*

un·gu·late (-lit, -lāt′) *adj.* ⟦LL *ungulatus* < L *ungula,* a hoof < *unguis,* a NAIL⟧ 1 having hoofs; of or belonging to a former group of all mammals having hoofs 2 shaped like a hoof —*n.* a mammal having hoofs

un·hair (un her′) *vt., vi.* to make or become free from hair, as hides before tanning

un·hal·low (-hal′ō) *vt.* to desecrate; profane

un·hal·lowed (-hal′ōd) *adj.* 1 not hallowed or consecrated; unholy 2 wicked; profane; impious

un·hand (-hand′) *vt.* to release from the hand or hands or one's grasp; let go of

un·hand·some (-han′səm) *adj.* 1 not handsome or attractive; plain; homely 2 not gracious or courteous; rude; unbecoming 3 stingy; mean —**un·hand′some·ly** *adv.*

un·hand·y (-han′dē) *adj.* **-hand′i·er, -hand′i·est** 1 not handy; inconvenient or inaccessible 2 not clever with the hands; awkward —**un·hand′i·ly** *adv.* —**un·hand′i·ness** *n.*

un·hap·py (-hap′ē) *adj.* **-pi·er, -pi·est** 1 unlucky; unfortunate 2 sad; wretched; sorrowful 3 not suitable or apt; ill-chosen 4 [Obs.] evil; reprehensible —**un·hap′pi·ly** *adv.* —**un·hap′pi·ness** *n.*

un·har·ness (-här′nis) *vt.* 1 [Archaic] to remove the armor from (a knight, etc.) 2 to remove the harness or gear from

un·health·y (-hel′thē) *adj.* **-health′i·er, -health′i·est** 1 having or showing poor health; sickly; not well 2 harmful to health; unwholesome 3 harmful to morals or character 4 dangerous or risky [an *unhealthy* situation] —**un·health′i·ly** *adv.* —**un·health′i·ness** *n.*

un·heard (-hurd′) *adj.* 1 not heard; not perceived by the ear 2 not given a hearing 3 *former var. of* UNHEARD-OF

un·heard-of (-hurd′uv′) *adj.* 1 not heard of before; unprecedented or unknown 2 unacceptable or outrageous [*unheard-of* effrontery]

un·helm (-helm′) *vt., vi.* [Obs.] to remove the helm or helmet (of)

un·hinge (-hinj′) *vt.* **-hinged′, -hing′ing** 1 *a)* to remove from the hinges *b)* to remove the hinges from 2 to dislodge or detach 3 to throw (the mind, a person, etc.) into confusion; unbalance or upset

un·his·tor·ic (un′his tôr′ik) *adj.* 1 not historic or historical 2 *Linguis.* not having a historical basis; accidental, as the *b* in *thumb* Also **un′his·tor′i·cal**

un·hitch (un hich′) *vt.* 1 to free from a hitch 2 to unfasten; release; detach

un·ho·ly (-hō′lē) *adj.* **-li·er, -li·est** ⟦ME < OE *unhalig* < *un-,* not + *halig,* HOLY⟧ 1 not sacred, hallowed, or consecrated 2 wicked; profane; impious 3 [Informal] outrageous; dreadful —**un·ho′li·ness** *n.*

un·hook (-ho͝ok′) *vt.* 1 to remove or loosen from a hook 2 to undo or unfasten the hook or hooks of —*vi.* to become unhooked

un·hoped-for (-hōpt′fôr′) *adj.* not hoped for; unexpected [an *unhoped-for* advantage]: also [Now Rare] **un·hoped′**

un·horse (-hôrs′) *vt.* **-horsed′, -hors′ing** 1 to throw (a rider) from a horse 2 to overthrow; upset

un·hou·seled (-hou′zəld) *adj.* [Archaic] without having been given the Eucharist [he died *unhouseled*]

un·hu·man (-hyo͞o′mən) *adj.* 1 *rare var. of: a)* INHUMAN *b)* SUPERHUMAN 2 not human in kind, quality, etc. —**un·hu′man·ly** *adv.*

unh-unh (un′un′, -un′) *interj. alt. sp. of* UH-UH

un·hur·ried (un hur′ēd) *adj.* not hurried; leisurely; deliberate —**un·hur′ried·ly** *adv.*

u·ni- (yo͞o′nə, -ni; *before a vowel, often,* -nē) ⟦L < *unus,* ONE⟧ *prefix* one; having or consisting of one only; regarded as a single entity [*unicellular, unisex*]

U·ni·ate (yo͞o′nē it, -āt′) *n.* ⟦Russ *uniyat* < *uniya,* the union establishing this church < VL *unio,* UNION⟧ a member of any Eastern Christian Church in union with the Roman Catholic Church but with its own rite, customs, etc. —*adj.* of such a church Also **U′ni·at′** (-nē at′, -nē it)
USAGE—often regarded as an offensive term

u·ni·ax·i·al (yo͞o′nē ak′sē əl) *adj.* having a single axis: said as of some crystals —**u′ni·ax′i·al·ly** *adv.*

u·ni·bod·y (yo͞o′nə bäd′ē) *adj.* designating or of a type of construction used in motor vehicles in which the floor, roof, panels, etc. are welded together into one unit, thereby eliminating the need for a separate frame

u·ni·cam·er·al (yo͞o′nə kam′ər əl) *adj.* ⟦UNI- + CAMERAL⟧ of or having a single legislative chamber

UNICEF (yo͞o′nə sef′) *n.* United Nations Children's Fund: formerly, *United Nations International Children's Emergency Fund*

u·ni·cel·lu·lar (yo͞o′nə sel′yo͞o lər) *adj.* ⟦UNI- + CELLULAR⟧ having or consisting of a single cell

u·ni·corn (yo͞o′nə kôrn′) *n.* ⟦ME *unicorne* < OFr < L *unicornis,* one-horned < *unus,* ONE + *cornu,* HORN⟧ 1 a mythical horselike animal with a single horn growing from the center of its forehead 2 ⟦< a mistransl. of Heb *reem,* wild ox⟧ *Bible* a two-horned, oxlike animal: Deut. 33:17

u·ni·cos·tate (yo͞o′nə käs′tāt′) *adj. Bot.* having only one main rib: said of a leaf

☆**u·ni·cy·cle** (yo͞o′ne sī′kəl) *n.* ⟦UNI- + (BI)CYCLE⟧ a one-wheeled vehicle straddled by the rider who pushes its pedals —**u′ni·cy′clist** *n.*

u·ni·di·men·sion·al (yo͞o′ne də men′shə nəl) *adj.* having only a single dimension

u·ni·di·rec·tion·al (-də rek′shə nəl) *adj.* 1 having, or moving in, only one direction 2 for sending or receiving radio or sound waves in or from a particular direction

unidirectional current DIRECT CURRENT

u·ni·fi·a·ble (yo͞o′nə fī′ə bəl) *adj.* that can be unified

u·ni·fi·ca·tion (yo͞o′nə fi kā′shən) *n.* the act of unifying or the state of being unified

unified field theory *Physics* any theory that attempts to explain two or more field theories by using one set of mathematical laws, as a theory that explains the unification of the field theories of magnetism and electricity: see GRAND UNIFIED (FIELD) THEORY

u·ni·fi·er (yo͞o′nə fī′ər) *n.* a person or thing that unifies

u·ni·fi·lar (yo͞o′nə fī′lər) *adj.* ⟦UNI- + FILAR⟧ of or having only one thread, wire, etc.

u·ni·fo·li·ate (-fō′lē it) *adj.* ⟦UNI- + FOLIATE⟧ 1 bearing only one leaf 2 *var. of* UNIFOLIOLATE

u·ni·fo·li·o·late (-fō′lē ə lāt′) *adj.* ⟦UNI- + FOLIOLATE⟧ 1 bearing only one leaflet although compound in structure: said as of the leaf of the orange 2 having leaves of this sort

u·ni·form (yo͞o′nə fôrm′) *adj.* ⟦MFr *uniforme* < L *uniformis* < *unus,* ONE + *-formis,* -FORM⟧ 1 *a)* always the same; not varying or changing in form, rate, degree, manner, etc.; constant [a *uniform* speed] *b)* identical throughout a state, country, etc. [a *uniform* minimum wage] 2 *a)* having the same form, appearance, manner, etc. as others of the same class; conforming to a given standard [a row of *uniform* houses] *b)* being or looking the same in all parts; undiversified [a *uniform* surface] 3 consistent in action, intention, effect, etc. [a *uniform* policy] —*n.* the official or distinctive clothes or outfit worn by the members of a particular group, as policemen or soldiers, esp. when on duty —*vt.* ☆to clothe or supply with a uniform —*SYN.* STEADY —**in uniform** wearing a uniform; esp., wearing the military or law enforcement uniform appropriate to one's organization, rank, etc. —**uniform with** having the same form, appearance, etc. as —**u′ni·form′ly** *adv.*

☆**Uniform Code of Military Justice** the body of laws governing members of the U.S. armed forces: superseded the Articles of War in 1951

Uniform Commercial Code a codification of commercial laws designed to provide uniformity among the states

u·ni·formed (-fôrmd′) *adj.* wearing a uniform

u·ni·form·i·tar·i·an (yo͞o′nə fôr′mə ter′ē ən) *adj.* 1 of or holding the doctrine of uniformitarianism 2 of or adhering to uniformity in something —*n.* a person who adheres to some doctrine of uniformity

u·ni·form·i·tar·i·an·ism (-iz′əm) *n.* the doctrine that all geologic changes may be explained by existing physical and chemical processes, as erosion, deposition, volcanic action, etc., that have operated in essentially the same way throughout geologic time

---

ungraceful
ungracefully
ungracefulness
ungraded
ungraduated
ungrateful
ungratefulness
ungratified
ungreased
ungrounded
ungrudging
unguessable
unguided
unhackneyed
unhammered
unhampered
unhandled
unhanged
unhardened
unharmed
unharmful
unharmonious
unharnessed
unharrowed
unharvested
unhasty
unhatched
unhealed
unhealthful
unheated
unheeded
unheeding
unhelpful
unheralded
unheroic
unhesitant
unhesitating
unhewn
unhindered
unhired
unhittable
unhomogeneous
unhonored
unhostile
unhoused
unhung
unhurt
unhusk
unhygienic
unhyphenated
unidentified
unidiomatic

u·ni·form·i·ty (yo͞o′nə fôr′mə tē) *n., pl.* **-ties** ⟦ME *uniformite* < MFr < L *uniformitas*⟧ state, quality, or instance of being uniform

u·ni·fy (yo͞o′nə fī′) *vt., vi.* **-fied′, -fy′ing** ⟦MFr *unifier* < LL *unificare:* see UNI- & -FY⟧ to combine into one; become or make united; consolidate

u·nij·u·gate (yo͞o nij′ə gāt′; yo͞o′nə jo͞o′gāt′, -git) *adj.* ⟦UNI- + JUGATE⟧ *Bot.* having only one pair of leaflets: said of a pinnate leaf

u·ni·lat·er·al (yo͞o′nə lat′ər əl) *adj.* ⟦ModL *unilateralis:* see UNI- & LATERAL⟧ **1** of, occurring on, or affecting one side only **2** involving or obligating one only of several persons or parties; done or undertaken by one only; not reciprocal [*a unilateral* contract] **3** taking into account one side only of a matter; one-sided **4** UNILINEAL **5** turned to one side **6** *Biol.* arranged or produced on one side of an axis **—u′ni·lat′er·al·ism′** *n.* **—u′ni·lat′er·al·ly** *adv.*

u·ni·lin·e·al (-lin′ē əl) *adj.* showing descent through only one line of the family, either that of the father or that of the mother **—u′ni·lin′e·al·ly** *adv.*

u·ni·lin·e·ar (-lin′ē ər) *adj.* of or following a single, consistent path of development or progression

u·ni·lin·gual (-liŋ′gwəl) *adj.* **1** of or in one language **2** using or knowing only one language

un·il·lu·sioned (un′i lo͞o′zhənd) *adj.* free from illusions or false ideas

u·ni·loc·u·lar (yo͞o′nə läk′yo͞o lər) *adj.* having, or made up of, only one loculus, compartment, cell, or chamber

un·im·peach·a·ble (un′im pēch′ə bəl) *adj.* not impeachable; that cannot be doubted, questioned, or discredited; irreproachable **—un′im·peach′a·bly** *adv.*

un·im·proved (un′im pro͞ovd′) *adj.* **1** not bettered, improved, or developed [*unimproved* land, with no buildings on it] **2** not used to good advantage **3** not improved in health

un·in·cor·po·rat·ed (-in kôr′pə rāt′id) *adj.* not organized as a legal corporation [*an unincorporated* village]

un·in·hib·it·ed (-in hib′it id) *adj.* without inhibition; esp., free from the usual social or psychological restraints, as in behavior

un·in·spired (-in spīrd′) *adj.* not inspired; lacking spirit, creativity, zest, etc.; dull [*an uninspired* performance, an *uninspired* speaker]

un·in·spir·ing (-in spīr′iŋ) *adj.* not able or likely to arouse enthusiasm in others [*an uninspiring* speech]

un·in·tel·li·gent (-in tel′i jənt) *adj.* having or showing a lack or deficiency of intelligence **—un′in·tel′li·gence** *n.* **—un′in·tel′li·gent·ly** *adv.*

un·in·tel·li·gi·ble (-tel′i jə bəl) *adj.* not intelligible; that cannot be understood; incomprehensible **—un′in·tel′li·gi·bil′i·ty** *n.* **—un′in·tel′li·gi·bly** *adv.*

un·in·ten·tion·al (-ten′shə nəl) *adj.* not done on purpose **—un′in·ten′tion·al·ly** *adv.*

un·in·ter·est·ed (un in′tris tid, un in′tər es′tid) *adj.* not interested; indifferent **—un·in′ter·est·ed·ly** *adv.*

un·in·ter·est·ing (-tiŋ) *adj.* lacking interest; dull; tedious **—un·in′ter·est·ing·ly** *adv.*

un·ion (yo͞on′yən) *n.* ⟦ME < MFr < LL(Ec) *unio* < L, oneness, unity < *unus,* ONE⟧ **1** a uniting or being united; combination; esp., *a)* a combining, joining, or grouping together of nations, states, political groups, etc. for some specific purpose *b)* a marrying or being married; marriage **2** something united or unified; a whole made up of parts; esp., *a)* an organization or confederation uniting various individuals, political units, etc. *b) short for* LABOR UNION *c)* in England, a former combination of parishes for the joint administration of relief for the poor; also, a workhouse kept up by such a union **3** a design symbolizing political union, used in a flag or ensign, as the white stars on a blue field in the flag of the U.S. **4** a building used for social recreation on a college or university campus: in full **student union** **5** a device for joining together parts, as of a machine; esp., a coupling for linking the ends of pipes **6** a fabric made of two or more different kinds of material, as cotton and linen **7** *Math.* the set containing all the elements of two or more given sets, and no other elements **—*SYN.*** ALLIANCE, UNITY **—☆the Union 1** the United States of America, specif. when regarded as a federal union **2** the North in the Civil War

☆**union card** a card serving to identify one as a member in good standing of a specified labor union

☆**union catalog** a library catalog combining the catalogs of several different libraries or different divisions of one library

un·ion·ism (-iz′əm) *n.* **1** *a)* the principle of union *b)* support of this principle or of a specified union **2** the system or principles of labor unions ☆**3** [**U-**] loyalty to the federal union of the U.S., esp. during the Civil War

un·ion·ist (-ist) *n.* **1** a person who believes in unionism **2** a member of a labor union ☆**3** [**U-**] a supporter of the federal union of the U.S., esp. during the Civil War **4** [*usually* **U-**] a supporter of the political union of Northern Ireland and Great Britain

un·ion·ize (-īz′) *vt.* **-ized′, -iz′ing** **1** to form into a union; esp., to organize (a group of workers in a shop, industry, etc.) into a labor union **2** to bring into conformity with the rules, standards, etc. of a labor union **—*vi.*** to join or organize a union, esp. a labor union **—un′ion·i·za′tion** *n.*

un·i·on·ized (un ī′ən īzd′) *adj.* not ionized

union jack **1** a jack, or flag, consisting only of a UNION (sense 3), esp. of the union of a national flag **2** [**U- J-**] the national flag of the United Kingdom

Union of South Africa *see* SOUTH AFRICA

Union of Soviet Socialist Republics former country in E Europe & N Asia, extending from the Arctic Ocean to the Black Sea & from the Baltic Sea to the Pacific: formed in 1922 as a union of fifteen constituent republics, it was disbanded in 1991: 8,649,000 sq mi (22,401,000 sq km); cap. Moscow

☆**union shop** **1** a factory, business, etc. operating under a contract between the employer and a labor union, which permits the hiring of nonunion workers but requires that all new employees join the union within a specified period **2** this contract

☆**union suit** a suit of men's or boys' underwear uniting shirt and drawers in a single garment

u·nip·a·rous (yo͞o nip′ər əs) *adj.* ⟦UNI- + -PAROUS⟧ **1** *Bot.* producing only one axis at each branching, as a cyme **2** *Zool.* producing only one egg or offspring at a time

u·ni·per·son·al (yo͞o′nə pur′sə nəl) *adj.* **1** existing as or in, consisting of, or manifested in the form of, only one person **2** *Gram.* used in only one person (specif., the third person singular): said of certain verbs, as *methinks*

u·ni·pet·al·ous (-pet′′l əs) *adj.* having a corolla of only one petal, the others being undeveloped

u·ni·pla·nar (-plā′nər) *adj.* of or lying in one plane

u·ni·po·lar (-pō′lər) *adj.* **1** *Elec.* of or having only one magnetic or electric pole **2** *Zool.* designating a nerve cell, as in spinal ganglia, having only one process **—u′ni·po·lar′i·ty** (-ler′ə tē) *n.*

u·nip·o·tent (yo͞o nip′ə tənt) *adj.* ⟦UNI- + POTENT⟧ *Biol.* capable of developing into only a single type of cell or tissue: said of certain, esp. embryonic, cells

u·nique (yo͞o nēk′) *adj.* ⟦Fr < L *unicus,* single < *unus,* ONE⟧ **1** one and only; single; sole [*a unique* specimen] **2** having no like or equal; unparalleled [*a unique* achievement] **3** highly unusual, extraordinary, rare, etc.: a common usage still objected to by some **4** distinctively associated with or characteristic of a particular group, category, condition, location, etc.: often with *to* **—u·nique′ly** *adv.* **—u·nique′ness** *n.*

☆**u·ni·sex** (yo͞o′nə seks′) *adj.* **1** designating, of, or involving a fashion, as in garments, hair styles, etc., that is undifferentiated for the sexes **2** serving or intended for both sexes [*unisex* restrooms]

u·ni·sex·u·al (yo͞o′nə sek′sho͞o əl) *adj.* ⟦ModL *unisexualis:* see UNI- & SEXUAL⟧ **1** of only one sex; specif., *a) Bot.* DICLINOUS *b) Zool.* producing either eggs or sperm, not both; dioecious **2** UNISEX **—u′ni·sex′u·al′i·ty** (-sho͞o al′ə tē) *n.* **—u′ni·sex′u·al·ly** *adv.*

u·ni·son (yo͞o′nə sən, -zən) *n.* ⟦MFr < ML *unisonus,* having the same sound < L *unus,* ONE + *sonus,* a SOUND[1]⟧ **1** an interval consisting of two identical musical pitches; prime **2** complete agreement; concord; harmony **—in unison 1** sounding the same note at the same time **2** sounding together in octaves **3** with all the voices or instruments performing the same part: said of a musical composition or passage **4** uttering the same words, or producing the same sound, at the same time **—u·nis·o·nant** (yo͞o nis′ə nənt)

u·nit (yo͞o′nit) *n.* ⟦back-form. (prob. modeled on DIGIT) < UNITY⟧ **1** *a)* the smallest whole number; one *b)* a magnitude or number regarded as an undivided whole *c)* the number in the position just to the left of the decimal point **2** any fixed quantity, amount, distance, measure, etc. used as a standard; specif., ☆*a)* a fixed amount of work used as a basis in awarding scholastic credits, usually determined by the number of hours spent in class *b)* the amount of a drug, vaccine, serum, or antigen needed to produce a given result, as on a certain animal or on animal tissues **3** *a)* a single person, group, or thing, esp. as distinguished from others or as part of a whole *b)* a single, distinct part or object, esp. one used for a specific purpose [the lens *unit* of a camera] *c)* a single residence, as an apartment, that is part of a complex [a rental *unit*] **4** *Mil.* an organized body of troops, airplanes, etc. forming a subdivision of a larger body

Unit *abbrev.* Unitarian

u·nit·age (yo͞o′ni tij) *n.* a designation of the amount or quantity of a unit of measure

u·ni·tard (yo͞o′nə tärd′) *n.* ⟦UNI- + (LEO)TARD⟧ a leotard that also covers the legs and, sometimes, the feet

---

unilluminated
unillustrated
unimaginable
unimaginably
unimaginative
unimitated
unimpaired
unimpassioned
unimpeded
unimplemented
unimportance
unimportant
unimposing
unimpregnated
unimpressionable
unimpressive
unindemnified
unindulged
unindustrialized
unindustrious
uninfected
uninfested
uninflected
uninfluenced
uninfluential
uninformed
uninhabitable
uninhabited
uninitiated
uninjured
uninstructed
uninsurable
uninsured
unintegrated
unintended
unintermittent
uninterpolated
uninterpreted
uninterrupted
uninterruptedly
unintimidated
uninventive
uninvested
uninvited
uninviting
uninvoked
uninvolved
unironic

U·ni·tar·i·an (yo͞o′nə ter′ē ən) ***n.*** ⟦< ModL *unitarius,* unitary + -AN: also in part < UNIT(Y) + -ARIAN⟧ **1** a person who denies the doctrine of the Trinity, accepting the moral teachings, but rejecting the divinity, of Jesus, and holding that God exists as one person or being **2** a member of a denomination based on these beliefs and characterized by congregational autonomy, tolerance of differing religious views, absence of creed, etc.: in full **Unitarian Universalist** —***adj.*** **1** of Unitarians or their doctrines, or adhering to Unitarianism **2** [**u-**] UNITARY —**U′ni·tar′i·an·ism′** ***n.***

u·ni·tar·y (yo͞o′nə ter′ē) ***adj.*** **1** of a unit or units **2** of, based on, or characterized by unity **3** having the nature of or used as a unit

unit cell the smallest unit of structure of a crystal: it has sides parallel to the crystal axes and its exact repetition in three dimensions along these axes generates the space lattice of a given crystal

unit character *Genetics* a character or trait determined by a single gene or gene pair

u·nite¹ (yo͞o nīt′) ***vt.*** **-nit′ed, -nit′ing** ⟦ME *unyten* < L *unitus,* pp. of *unire,* to unite < *unus,* ONE⟧ **1** to put or bring together so as to make one; combine or join into a whole **2** *a)* to bring together in common cause, interest, opinion, etc.; join, as in action, through fellowship, agreement, legal bonds, etc. *b)* to join in marriage **3** to have or show (qualities, characteristics, etc.) in combination **4** to cause to adhere —***vi.*** **1** to become combined or joined together; become one or as one, by adhering, associating, etc. **2** to act together —**SYN.** JOIN

u·nite² (yo͞o′nīt, yo͞o nīt′) ***n.*** ⟦< ME, united: with reference to the union of England and Scotland⟧ a former English gold coin of James I, equal to 20 shillings

u·nit·ed (yo͞o nīt′id) ***adj.*** **1** combined; joined; made one **2** of or resulting from joint action or association **3** in agreement or harmony —**u·nit′ed·ly** ***adv.***

United Arab Emirates country in E Arabia, on the Persian Gulf, consisting of seven Arab emirates: 32,000 sq mi (82,880 sq km); cap. Abu Dhabi

United Arab Republic **1** *former name for* Egypt & Syria, united as a single nation (1958-61) **2** *former name for* EGYPT¹ (1961-71)

United Church of Canada a Protestant denomination formed in Canada in 1924-25 by union of the Methodist and Congregational churches and two-thirds of the Presbyterian churches

United Church of Christ a Protestant denomination formed by the merger in 1957 of the Congregational Christian Church with the Evangelical and Reformed Church

United Kingdom **1** country in W Europe, consisting of Great Britain & Northern Ireland: 94,526 sq mi (244,820 sq km); cap. London: in full **United Kingdom of Great Britain and Northern Ireland** **2** country (1801-1921) consisting of Great Britain & Ireland: in full **United Kingdom of Great Britain and Ireland**

☆**United Nations** an international organization of nations, for the promotion of world peace and the resolution of international conflicts: it was established in 1945 and is headquartered in New York City

United Provinces federation (end of the 16th cent. to 1795) of seven N states of the Netherlands; the Dutch Republic

United States Air Force the aviation branch of the United States armed forces

United States Army the Regular Army of the United States: cf. ARMY OF THE UNITED STATES

United States Army Special Forces *see* SPECIAL FORCES

United States Coast Guard a branch of the United States armed forces employed to defend the nation's coasts, prevent smuggling, aid vessels in distress, protect marine life, etc.: under the control of the Department of Homeland Security or, in time of war, of the Department of the Navy

United States Marine Corps a branch of the United States armed forces trained for land, sea, and aerial combat, responsible especially for amphibious operations: a separate service within the Department of the Navy

United States Navy the naval branch of the United States armed forces

United States of America country made up of the North American area extending from the Atlantic Ocean to the Pacific Ocean between Canada and Mexico, together with Alas. & Hawaii: 3,537,438 sq mi (9,161,930 sq km); cap. Washington, D.C.: also called **United States**

u·ni·tive (yo͞o′nə tiv) ***adj.*** ⟦ML *unitivus*⟧ **1** having or characterized by unity **2** tending to unite

u·nit·ize (yo͞o′nə tīz′) ***vt.*** **-ized′, -iz′ing** ⟦UNIT + -IZE⟧ to make into a single unit —**u′nit·i·za′tion** ***n.***

unit (magnetic) pole a magnetic pole that, when placed in a vacuum at a distance of one centimeter from an equal and like pole, will repel it with a force of one dyne

unit pricing a system of showing the prices of goods, esp. of goods sold at retail, in terms of standard units, so as to facilitate price comparison of competing items (Ex.: $2.00 per gallon, $.49 per pound)

☆**unit rule** a rule, as in national political conventions, that the entire vote of a delegation, if the state's party apparatus so chooses, shall be cast as a unit, disregarding minority votes in the delegation

u·ni·ty (yo͞o′nə tē) ***n., pl.*** **-ties** ⟦ME *unite* < OFr *unité* < L *unitas,* oneness < *unus,* ONE⟧ **1** the state of being one, or united; oneness; singleness **2** something complete in itself; single, separate thing **3** the quality of being one in spirit, sentiment, purpose, etc.; harmony; agreement; concord; uniformity **4** *a)* unification *b)* a unified group or body **5** the quality or fact of being a totality or whole or, esp., of being a union of related parts **6** *a)* an arrangement of parts or material in a work of art or literature, that will produce a single, harmonious effect *b)* a design or effect so produced **7** constancy, continuity, or fixity of purpose, action, etc. **8** *Math. a)* any quantity, magnitude, etc. considered or identified as a unit, or 1 *b)* the numeral or unit 1 —**the (three) unities** the three principles of dramatic construction derived by French neoclassicists from Aristotle's *Poetics,* holding that a play should have one unified plot (**unity of action**) and that all the action should occur within one day (**unity of time**) and be limited to a single locale (**unity of place**)

SYN.—unity implies the oneness, as in spirit, aims, interests, feelings, etc., of that which is made up of diverse elements or individuals [national *unity*]; **union** implies the state of being united into a single organization for a common purpose [a labor *union*]; **solidarity** implies such firm and complete unity in an organization, group, class, etc. as to make for the greatest possible strength in influence, action, etc.

univ *abbrev.* **1** universal **2** universally **3** university

Univ *abbrev.* Universalist

u·ni·va·lent (yo͞o′nə vā′lənt, yo͞o niv′ə lənt) ***adj.*** ⟦UNI- + -VALENT⟧ **1** *Biol.* single; unpaired: said of a chromosome **2** *Chem.* MONOVALENT (sense 2): see -VALENT —**u′ni·va′lence** ***n.***, **u′ni·va′len·cy** (-lən sē)

u·ni·valve (yo͞o′nə valv′) ***n.*** ⟦UNI- + VALVE⟧ **1** a mollusk having a one-piece shell, as a snail **2** such a one-piece shell —***adj.*** **1** designating or having a one-piece shell **2** having one valve only: also **u′ni·valved′**

u·ni·ver·sal (yo͞o′nə vʉr′səl) ***adj.*** ⟦ME *universel* < OFr < L *universalis* < *universus:* see UNIVERSE⟧ **1** of the universe; present or occurring everywhere or in all things **2** of, for, affecting, or including all or the whole of something specified; not limited or restricted **3** [Obs.] being, or regarded as, a complete whole; entire; whole **4** broad in knowledge, interests, ability, etc. **5** that can be used for a great many or all kinds, forms, sizes, etc.; highly adaptable [a *universal* voltage regulator] **6** used, intended to be used, or understood by all **7** *Logic* predicating something of every member of a class ["all men are mortal" is a *universal* proposition] —***n.*** **1** *short for* UNIVERSAL JOINT **2** *Logic a)* a universal proposition *b)* PREDICABLE (***n.*** 2) **3** *Philos.* a general term or concept, or that to which such a term or concept applies —**u′ni·ver′sal·ness** ***n.***

SYN.—universal implies applicability to every case or individual, without exception, in the class, category, etc. concerned [a *universal* practice among primitive peoples]; **general** implies applicability to all, nearly all, or most of a group or class [a *general* election]; **generic** implies applicability to every member of a class or, specif. in biology, of a genus [a *generic* name]

universal donor a person with blood type O, able to donate blood to a person of any blood type but able to receive blood only from a person with the same blood type: see ABO SYSTEM

u·ni·ver·sal·ism (-iz′əm) ***n.*** **1** UNIVERSALITY **2** [**U-**] the theological doctrine that all souls will eventually find salvation in the grace of God

u·ni·ver·sal·ist (-ist) ***n.*** **1** a person characterized by universality, as of interests or activities ☆**2** [**U-**] a member of a former U.S. Protestant denomination (founded *c.* 1789), now merged with the Unitarians —***adj.*** **1** marked by universality ☆**2** [**U-**] of Universalism or Universalists —**u′ni·ver′sal·is′tic** ***adj.***

u·ni·ver·sal·i·ty (yo͞o′nə vər sal′ə tē) ***n., pl.*** **-ties** **1** quality, state, or instance of being universal **2** unlimited range, application, occurrence, etc.; comprehensiveness

u·ni·ver·sal·ize (yo͞o′nə vʉr′sə līz′) ***vt.*** **-ized′, -iz′ing** to make universal —**u′ni·ver′sal·i·za′tion** ***n.***

universal joint (*or* **coupling**) a flexible mechanical connection, esp. one used to transmit rotary motion from one shaft to another not in line with it, as in the drive shaft of an automobile

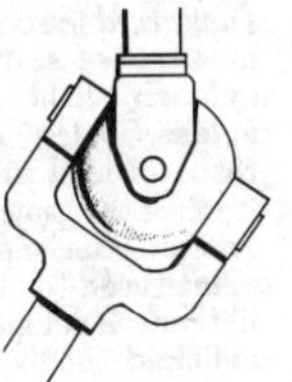
universal joint

u·ni·ver·sal·ly (yo͞o′nə vʉr′sə lē) ***adv.*** in a universal manner; specif., *a)* in every instance *b)* in every part or place

Universal Product Code a patterned series of vertical bars of varying widths printed on packages of many consumer products: it can be read by a computerized scanner for inventory control, pricing, etc.: cf. BAR CODE

universal recipient a person with blood type AB, able to receive blood from a person of any blood type but able to donate blood only to a person with the same blood type: see ABO SYSTEM

universal set *Math.* the set of all objects or elements considered in a given problem

Universal Time Greenwich mean time used as a basis for standard time: cf. COORDINATED UNIVERSAL TIME: abbrev. *UT*

u·ni·verse (yo͞o′nə vʉrs′) ***n.*** ⟦L *universum,* the universe < neut. of *universus,* all together < *unus,* ONE + *versus,* pp. of *vertere,* to turn: see VERSE⟧ **1** the totality of all the things that exist; creation; the cosmos **2** the world, or earth, as the scene of human activity **3** a field or sphere, as of thought or activity, regarded as a distinct, comprehensive system **4** *Math.* a universal set —**SYN.** EARTH

universe of discourse the total context of facts, things, relations, ideas, etc. implied or assumed in a given discussion, argument, or discourse

u·ni·ver·si·ty (yo͞o′nə vur′sə tē) ***n., pl.*** **-ties** ⟦ME *universite* < MFr *université* < ML *universitas* < L, the whole, universe, society, guild < *universus:* see UNIVERSE⟧ **1** an educational institution of the highest level, typically, in the U.S., with one or more undergraduate colleges, together with a program of graduate studies and a number of professional schools, and authorized to confer various degrees, as the bachelor's, master's, and doctor's **2** the grounds, buildings, etc. of a university **3** the students, faculty, and administrators of a university collectively

u·niv·o·cal (yo͞o niv′ə kəl) ***adj.*** having a single, sharply defined sense or nature; unambiguous

un·joint (un joint′) ***vt.*** **1** to separate (a joint) **2** to separate the joints of

un·just (-just′) ***adj.*** **1** not just or right; unfair; contrary to justice **2** [Obs.] dishonest or unfaithful —**un·just′ly** ***adv.*** —**un·just′ness** ***n.***

un·kempt (-kempt′) ***adj.*** ⟦UN- + *kempt,* pp. of dial. *kemben,* to comb < ME < OE *cemban* < *camb,* a COMB[1]⟧ **1** tangled, disheveled, etc., as if from not having been combed **2** not tidy or neat; messy **3** not polished or refined; crude; rough —**un·kempt′ness** ***n.***

un·kenned (-kend′) ***adj.*** [Scot.] unknown; strange

un·ken·nel (-ken′əl) ***vt.*** **-neled** or **-nelled**, **-nel·ing** or **-nel·ling** **1** *a)* to drive from a den or hole *b)* to release from a kennel **2** to bring to light; uncover; disclose

un·kind (-kīnd′) ***adj.*** not kind; specif., *a)* not sympathetic to or considerate of others *b)* harsh, severe, cruel, rigorous, etc. —**un·kind′ness** ***n.***

un·kind·ly (-kīnd′lē) ***adj.*** UNKIND —***adv.*** in an unkind manner —**un·kind′li·ness** ***n.***

un·knit (-nit′) ***vt., vi.*** **-knit′ted** or **-knit′**, **-knit′ting** ⟦ME *unknytten* < OE *uncnyttan*⟧ to untie, undo, or unravel

un·knot (-nät′) ***vt.*** **-knot′ted**, **-knot′ting** **1** to untie (a knot) **2** to undo or untangle a knot or knots in

un·know·a·ble (-nō′ə bəl) ***adj.*** not knowable; that cannot be known; specif., beyond the range of human comprehension or experience —***n.*** anything unknowable

un·know·ing (-nō′iŋ) ***adj.*** not knowing; ignorant or unaware —**un·know′ing·ly** ***adv.***

un·known (-nōn′) ***adj.*** not known; specif., *a)* not in the knowledge, understanding, or acquaintance of someone; unfamiliar (*to*) *b)* not discovered, identified, determined, explored, etc. —***n.*** **1** an unknown person or thing **2** an unknown mathematical quantity; also, a symbol for this

Unknown Soldier [*also* **u- s-**] an unidentified soldier, killed in a war, whose body has been chosen and enshrined as representative of a nation's war dead

un·lace (-lās′) ***vt.*** **-laced′**, **-lac′ing** **1** to undo or unfasten the laces of **2** to loosen or remove the clothing of

un·lade (-lād′) ***vt., vi.*** **-lad′ed**, **-lad′ed** or **-lad′en**, **-lad′ing** [Archaic] to unload (a cargo, ship, etc.)

un·lash (-lash′) ***vt.*** to untie or loosen (something lashed, or tied with a rope, etc.)

un·latch (-lach′) ***vt., vi.*** to open by release of a latch

un·law·ful (-lô′fəl) ***adj.*** **1** against the law; illegal **2** against moral or ethical standards; immoral —**un·law′ful·ly** ***adv.*** —**un·law′ful·ness** ***n.***

un·lay (-lā′) ***vt., vi.*** **-laid′**, **-lay′ing** ⟦UN- + LAY[1], *vt.* 14⟧ *Naut.* to untwist and separate the strands of (a rope)

un·lead·ed (-led′id) ***adj.*** **1** not covered or weighted with lead **2** not containing lead compounds: said of gasoline **3** *Printing* not having the lines of type separated by leads

un·learn (-lurn′) ***vt., vi.*** ⟦ME *unlernen:* see UN- & LEARN⟧ to forget or try to forget (something learned); get rid of (a habit)

un·learn·ed (-lur′nid; *for 2,* -lurnd′) ***adj.*** **1** *a)* not learned or educated; ignorant *b)* showing a lack of learning or education **2** *a)* not learned [*unlearned* lessons] *b)* known or acquired without conscious study [an *unlearned* sense of tact] —**SYN.** IGNORANT

un·leash (-lēsh′) ***vt.*** to release from or as from a leash

un·less (un les′) ***conj.*** ⟦ME *onlesse,* earlier *on lesse that, in lesse that,* at less than, for less⟧ in any case other than that; except that; except if [*unless* it rains, the game will be played] —***prep.*** [Archaic or Dial.] except; save [nothing can help him, *unless* a miracle]

un·let·tered (un let′ərd) ***adj.*** **1** *a)* not lettered; ignorant; uneducated *b)* illiterate **2** not marked with letters —**SYN.** IGNORANT

un·licked (un likt′) ***adj.*** ⟦prob. < LICK INTO SHAPE (see phr. under LICK)⟧ lacking proper form or refinement; rough, unfinished, etc.

un·like (-līk′) ***adj.*** ⟦ME *unliche:* see UN- & LIKE[1]⟧ **1** having little or no resemblance; not alike; different; dissimilar **2** [Now Chiefly Dial.] unlikely —***prep.*** **1** not like; different from [a case *unlike* any other] **2** not characteristic of [it's *unlike* him to give up] —**un·like′ness** ***n.***

un·like·ly (-līk′lē) ***adj.*** ⟦ME *unlikly,* prob. based on ON *ūlīkligr*⟧ **1** not likely to happen or be true; improbable **2** not likely to succeed; not promising —***adv.*** improbably [he may, not *unlikely,* join us] —**un·like′li·hood′** ***n.***, **un·like′li·ness**

un·lim·ber[1] (-lim′bər) ***adj.*** not limber, or supple; stiff [*unlimber* fingers] —***vt., vi.*** to make or become supple

un·lim·ber[2] (-lim′bər) ***vt., vi.*** ⟦UN- + LIMBER[2]⟧ **1** to prepare (a field gun) for use by detaching the limber **2** to get ready for use or action

un·lim·it·ed (-lim′it id) ***adj.*** **1** without limits or restrictions [*unlimited* power] **2** lacking or seeming to lack boundaries; vast; illimitable [*unlimited* space]

un·link (-liŋk′) ***vt.*** **1** to unfasten the links of (a chain, etc.) **2** to separate (things linked together)

un·list·ed (-lis′tid) ***adj.*** not listed; specif., *a)* not constituting an entry in a list *b)* not publicly listed; privately assigned [an *unlisted* telephone number] *c)* not listed among those admitted for the purpose of trading on the stock exchange (said of securities)

un·live (-liv′) ***vt.*** **-lived′**, **-liv′ing** **1** to live so as to wipe out the results of; live down **2** to annul or wipe out (past experience, etc.)

un·lived-in (-livd′in′) ***adj.*** not inhabited

un·load (-lōd′) ***vt.*** **1** *a)* to remove or take off (a load, cargo, etc.) *b)* to take a load, cargo, etc. from **2** *a)* to give vent to (one's grief, troubles, etc.); express or tell freely *b)* to relieve of something that troubles, burdens, etc. **3** to remove the charge from (a gun) **4** to get rid of [*unloading* surplus goods] —***vi.*** to unload something

un·lock (-läk′) ***vt.*** **1** *a)* to open (a lock) *b)* to open the lock of (a door, chest, etc.) **2** to let loose as if by opening a lock; release [to *unlock* a torrent of grief] **3** to cause to separate; part [to *unlock* clenched jaws] **4** to lay open; reveal [to *unlock* a secret] —***vi.*** to become unlocked

un·looked-for (-lo͝okt′fôr′) ***adj.*** not looked for; not expected or foreseen

un·loose (-lo͞os′) ***vt.*** **-loosed′**, **-loos′ing** to make or set loose; loosen, release, undo, etc.: also **un·loos′en**

un·love·ly (-luv′lē) ***adj.*** not lovely, pleasing, or attractive; disagreeable —**un·love′li·ness** ***n.***

un·luck·y (-luk′ē) ***adj.*** **-luck′i·er**, **-luck′i·est** not lucky; having, attended with, bringing, or involving bad luck; unfortunate, ill-fated, or ill-omened —**un·luck′i·ly** ***adv.***

un·made (-mād′) ***vt.*** *pt. & pp. of* UNMAKE —***adj.*** not made (in various senses) [*unmade* corrections, an *unmade* bed]

un·make (-māk′) ***vt.*** **-made′**, **-mak′ing** **1** to cause to be as before being made; cause to revert to the original form, elements, or condition **2** to ruin; destroy **3** to depose from a position or rank

un·man (-man′) ***vt.*** **-manned′**, **-man′ning** **1** to deprive of manly courage, nerve, self-confidence, etc. **2** to emasculate; castrate **3** to deprive of men or personnel: now usually in the pp.: cf. UNMANNED —**SYN.** UNNERVE

un·man·ly (-man′lē) ***adj.*** **-li·er**, **-li·est** not manly; specif., *a)* lacking courage, resoluteness, etc.; cowardly, weak, etc. *b)* not befitting a man; effeminate; womanish —**un·man′li·ness** ***n.***

un·manned (-mand′) ***adj.*** **1** not manned ☆**2** without people aboard and, hence, operating by automatic or remote control, as a pilotless aircraft or spacecraft

un·man·ner·ly (-man′ər lē) ***adj.*** ⟦ME *unmanerli*⟧ having or showing poor manners; rude; discourteous —***adv.*** in an unmannerly way; rudely —**un·man′ner·li·ness** ***n.***

un·mask (-mask′) ***vt.*** **1** to remove a mask or disguise from **2** to disclose the true nature of; expose; reveal —***vi.*** **1** to take off a mask or disguise **2** to appear in true character

un·mean·ing (-mēn′iŋ) ***adj.*** **1** lacking in meaning, sense, or significance **2** showing no sense or intelligence; empty; expressionless

un·meet (-mēt′) ***adj.*** ⟦ME *unmete* < OE *unmæte*⟧ [Old Poet.] not meet, fit, or proper; unsuitable; unseemly

un·men·tion·a·ble (un men′shən ə bəl) ***adj.*** not fit to be mentioned, esp. in polite conversation

un·men·tion·a·bles (-bəlz) ***pl.n.*** things regarded as improper to be mentioned or talked about; specif., in jocular use, undergarments

un·mer·ci·ful (un mur′si fəl) ***adj.*** **1** having or showing no mercy; cruel; relentless; pitiless **2** beyond what is proper or usual; excessive —**un·mer′ci·ful·ly** ***adv.***

---

unjaded
unjoined
unjudicial
unjustifiable
unjustifiably
unjustified
unkept
unkissed
unlabeled
unlabored
unladylike
unlamented
unlaundered
unleased
unleavened
unlessened
unlessoned
unlevel
unlevied
unlibidinous
unlicensed
unlifelike
unlighted
unlikable
unlikeable
unlined
unliquefiable
unlit
unlivable
unlived
unlively
unliving
unlocated
unlovable
unloved
unloving
unlubricated
unmagnified
unmaidenly
unmalleable
unmanageable
unmanful
unmanifested
unmannered
unmannish
unmanufacturable
unmanufactured
unmarked
unmarketable
unmarred
unmarriageable
unmarried
unmastered
unmatchable
unmatched
unmated
unmatted
unmatured
unmeant

un·mind·ful (-mīnd′fəl) ***adj.*** not mindful or attentive; forgetful; heedless; careless —**un·mind′ful·ly** ***adv.***

un·mis·tak·a·ble (un′mis tāk′ə bəl) ***adj.*** that cannot be mistaken or misinterpreted; leaving room for no misunderstanding; clear; plain —**un′mis·tak′a·bly** ***adv.***

un·mit·i·gat·ed (un mit′ə gāt′id) ***adj.*** **1** not lessened or eased [*unmitigated* suffering] **2** unqualified; out-and-out; absolute [an *unmitigated* fool] —**un·mit′i·gat′ed·ly** ***adv.***

un·moor (-moor′) ***vt.*** to free (a ship, etc.) from its moorings —***vi.*** to cast off moorings

un·mor·al (-môr′əl) ***adj.*** AMORAL —**un·mo·ral·i·ty** (un′mə ral′ə tē) ***n.*** —**un·mor′al·ly** ***adv.***

un·moved (-mōōvd′) ***adj.*** **1** not moved from its place **2** firm or unchanged in purpose **3** not having one's feelings stirred [*unmoved* by another's suffering]

un·moved mover (un′mōōvd′) PRIME MOVER

un·muf·fle (un muf′əl) ***vt.*** **-fled**, **-fling** to remove a covering from (the face, head, etc.) —***vi.*** to take off something that muffles

un·muz·zle (-muz′əl) ***vt.*** **-zled**, **-zling** **1** to free (a dog, etc.) from a muzzle **2** to free from restraint or censorship of what is written or spoken

un·nat·u·ral (-nach′ər əl) ***adj.*** not natural or normal; specif., *a)* contrary to, or at variance with, nature; abnormal; strange *b)* artificial, affected, or strained [an *unnatural* smile] *c)* characterized by a lack of the emotions, attitudes, or behavior regarded as natural, normal, or right *d)* abnormally evil or cruel —*SYN.* IRREGULAR —**un·nat′u·ral·ly** ***adv.*** —**un·nat′u·ral·ness** ***n.***

un·nec·es·sar·y (-nes′ə ser′ē) ***adj.*** not necessary or required; needless —**un·nec′es·sar′i·ly** ***adv.***

un·nerve (-nurv′) ***vt.*** **-nerved′**, **-nerv′ing** **1** to cause to lose one's courage, self-confidence, etc. **2** to make feel weak, nervous, etc. —**un·nerv′ing·ly** ***adv.***

SYN.—**unnerve** implies a causing to lose courage or self-control as by shocking, dismaying, etc. [the screams *unnerved* her]; **enervate** implies a gradual loss of strength or vitality, as because of climate, indolence, etc. [*enervating* heat]; **unman** implies a loss of manly courage, fortitude, or spirit [he was so *unmanned* by the news that he broke into tears]

un·num·bered (-num′bərd) ***adj.*** **1** not counted **2** INNUMERABLE **3** having no identifying number

un·oc·cu·pied (-äk′yə pīd′) ***adj.*** **1** having no occupant; vacant; empty **2** at leisure; idle

un·or·gan·ized (-ôr′gə nīzd′) ***adj.*** **1** having no organic structure **2** having no regular order, system, or organization **3** not behaving, thinking, etc. in an orderly way **4** not having or belonging to a labor union

un·pack (-pak′) ***vt.*** **1** to open and remove the packed contents of **2** to take from a crate, trunk, etc. **3** to remove a pack or load from **4** to analyze and explain in detail [to *unpack* a complex idea] —***vi.*** **1** to remove the contents of a packed trunk, suitcase, etc. **2** to admit of being unpacked

un·paged (-pājd′) ***adj.*** having pages that are not numbered: also **un·pag′i·nat′ed**

un·paid (-pād′) ***adj.*** **1** not receiving pay [an *unpaid* volunteer] **2** not yet discharged or settled by or as by payment [an *unpaid* bill] **3** without wages or salary included [*unpaid* maternity leave]

un·par·al·leled (-par′ə leld′) ***adj.*** that has no parallel, equal, or counterpart; unmatched

un·par·lia·men·ta·ry (-pär′lə ment′ə rē) ***adj.*** contrary to parliamentary law or practice

un·peg (-peg′) ***vt.*** **-pegged′**, **-peg′ging** **1** to remove a peg or pegs from **2** to unfasten or detach in this way

un·peo·pled (-pē′pəld) ***adj.*** not populated; devoid of people

un·per·son (un′pur′sən) ***n.*** ⟦coined by George ORWELL in his novel *Nineteen Eighty-four* (published 1949)⟧ a person who is completely ignored, as if he or she does not exist; specif., such a person officially ignored by his or her own government: cf. NONPERSON

un·pick (un pik′) ***vt.*** **1** to undo (sewing) by picking out stitches **2** [Chiefly Brit.] to analyze and explain in detail by picking apart into pieces and examining each part critically

un·pin (un pin′) ***vt.*** **-pinned′**, **-pin′ning** **1** to remove a pin or pins from **2** to unfasten or detach in this way

un·pleas·ant (un plez′ənt) ***adj.*** not pleasant; offensive; disagreeable —**un·pleas′ant·ly** ***adv.***

un·pleas·ant·ness (-nis) ***n.*** **1** an unpleasant quality or condition **2** an unpleasant situation, relationship, etc. **3** a quarrel or disagreement

un·plumbed (un plumd′) ***adj.*** **1** not sounded, measured, or explored with or as with a plumb **2** not fully plumbed, or understood

un·polled (-pōld′) ***adj.*** ⟦UN- + pp. of POLL, v.⟧ **1** not canvassed in a poll **2** not cast or registered: said of votes

un·pop·u·lar (-päp′yə lər) ***adj.*** not popular; not liked or approved of by the public or by the majority —**un′pop·u·lar′i·ty** (-yə lar′ə tē) ***n.***

un·prac·ticed (-prak′tist) ***adj.*** **1** not practiced; not habitually or repeatedly done, performed, etc. **2** not skilled or experienced

un·prec·e·dent·ed (-pres′ə den′tid) ***adj.*** having no precedent or parallel; unheard-of; novel

un·prej·u·diced (-prej′ə dist) ***adj.*** **1** without prejudice or bias; impartial **2** not affected detrimentally; unimpaired

un·pre·med·i·tat·ed (un′prē med′ə tāt′id) ***adj.*** not premeditated; done without plan or forethought

un·prin·ci·pled (un prin′sə pəld) ***adj.*** characterized by lack of moral principles; unscrupulous

un·print·a·ble (-print′ə bəl) ***adj.*** not printable; not fit to be printed, as because of obscenity

un·pro·fes·sion·al (un′prō fesh′ə nəl) ***adj.*** **1** violating the rules or ethical code of a given profession **2** not of, characteristic of, belonging to,

unmeasurable
unmeasured
unmechanical
unmedicated
unmeditated
unmelodious
unmelted
unmenacing
unmendable
unmended
unmentioned
unmercenary
unmerchantable
unmerited
unmesh
unmethodical
unmilitary
unmilled
unmingled
unmirthful
unmistaken
unmitigable
unmixed
unmodified
unmodish
unmodulated
unmoistened
unmold
unmolested
unmolten
unmortgaged
unmotherly
unmotivated
unmounted
unmourned
unmovable
unmoving
unmown
unmusical
unmystified
unnail
unnamable
unnameable
unnamed
unnaturalized
unnavigable
unnavigated
unneeded
unneedful
unneighborly
unnoted
unnoticeable
unnoticed
unnurtured
unobjectionable
unobliging
unobscured
unobservant
unobserved
unobserving
unobstructed
unobtainable
unobtruding
unobtrusive
unobtrusively
unoffending
unoffensive
unoffered
unofficial
unofficially
unofficious
unoiled
unopen
unopened
unopposed
unoppressed
unordained
unoriginal
unornamental
unornamented
unorthodox
unorthodoxy
unostentatious
unowned
unoxidized
unpacified
unpaid-for
unpainful
unpainted
unpaired
unpalatable
unpardonable
unpardoned
unparted
unpasteurized
unpatched
unpatented
unpatriotic
unpatriotically
unpaved
unpeaceable
unpeaceful
unpedigreed
unpen
unpenetrated
unpensioned
unperceivable
unperceived
unperceiving
unperceptive
unperfect
unperfected
unperformed
unperplexed
unpersuadable
unpersuaded
unpersuasive
unperturbable
unperturbed
unphilosophic
unphilosophical
unpicked
unpierced
unpile
unpitied
unpitying
unplaced
unplanned
unplanted
unplayable
unplayed
unpleased
unpleasing
unpledged
unpliable
unploughed
unplowed
unplucked
unplug
unpoetic
unpoetical
unpointed
unpoised
unpolarized
unpolished
unpolite
unpolitic
unpolitical
unpolluted
unpopulated
unposed
unposted
unpotted
unpractical
unpredictability
unpredictable
unpredictably
unpreoccupied
unprepared
unprepossessing
unprescribed
unpresentable
unpreserved
unpressed
unpresumptuous
unpretending
unpretentious
unprevailing
unpreventable
unpriced
unprimed
unprincely
unprinted
unprivileged
unprizable
unprized
unprobed
unprocessed
unprocurable
unproductive
unprofaned
unprofessed

or connected with a profession; nonprofessional —**un′pro·fes′sion·al·ly** *adv.*

un·prof·it·a·ble (un präf′it ə bəl) *adj.* 1 not making a profit [an *unprofitable* business] 2 not worthwhile [an *unprofitable* discussion] —**un·prof′it·a·bly** *adv.*

un·pro·tect·ed (un′prə tek′tid) *adj.* 1 not protected or defended against injury, danger, loss, etc. 2 without the protection of a condom [*unprotected* sex]

un·pub·lished (un pub′lisht) *adj.* not published; specif., *a)* in copyright law, designating a literary work that has neither been given public distribution nor been reproduced for sale, as of the time of registration *b)* UNLISTED (sense *b*)

un·put·down·a·ble (un′po͝ot doun′ə bəl) *adj.* [Informal] designating a book regarded as being so suspenseful, gripping, etc. that a reader finds it very difficult to put down before finishing it

un·qual·i·fied (-kwôl′ə fīd′) *adj.* 1 lacking the necessary or desirable qualifications; not fit 2 not limited or modified; absolute [an *unqualified* success] —**un·qual′i·fi′ed·ly** (-fī′id lē) *adv.*

un·ques·tion·a·ble (-kwes′chən ə bəl) *adj.* 1 not to be questioned, doubted, or disputed; certain 2 with no exception or qualification; unexceptionable —**un·ques′tion·a·bly** *adv.*

un·ques·tioned (-kwes′chənd) *adj.* not questioned; specif., *a)* not interrogated *b)* not disputed; accepted *c)* not subjected to inquiry

un·ques·tion·ing (-kwes′chə niŋ) *adj.* not doubting or disputing —**un·ques′tion·ing·ly** *adv.*

un·qui·et (-kwī′ət) *adj.* not quiet; specif., *a)* full of turmoil; restless, disturbed, etc. *b)* anxious; uneasy —*n.* a lack of quiet or rest; disturbance, agitation, etc. —**un·qui′et·ly** *adv.* —**un·qui′et·ness** *n.*

un·quote (un′kwōt′) *interj.* ☆I end the quotation: used in speech to signal the conclusion of a quotation

un·rav·el (un rav′əl) *vt.* **-eled** or **-elled**, **-el·ing** or **-el·ling** 1 to undo (something woven or tangled); untangle or separate the threads of 2 to make clear of confusion or involvement; solve —*vi.* 1 to become unraveled 2 to fall apart, disintegrate, collapse, etc. [too much drinking can cause your whole life to *unravel*] —**un·rav′el·ment** *n.*

un·read (-red′) *adj.* 1 not read, as a book [a pile of *unread* letters] 2 having read little or nothing 3 unlearned (*in* a subject)

un·read·a·ble (-rēd′ə bəl) *adj.* not readable; specif., *a)* not legible or decipherable *b)* too dull, difficult, etc. to be read with pleasure, ease, comprehension, etc.

un·read·y (-red′ē) *adj.* not ready; specif., *a)* not prepared, as for action or use *b)* not prompt or alert; slow; hesitant —**un·read′i·ly** *adv.* —**un·read′i·ness** *n.*

un·re·al (-rē′əl) *adj.* 1 not real, actual, or genuine; imaginary, fanciful, insubstantial, false, etc. 2 [Informal] astounding, unbelievable, etc.: a hyperbolic use

un·re·al·is·tic (un′rē əl is′tik) *adj.* dealing with ideas or matters in a way that is not realistic; impractical or visionary —**un′re·al·is′ti·cal·ly** *adv.*

un·re·al·i·ty (-rē al′ə tē) *n., pl.* **-ties** 1 the state or quality of being unreal 2 something unreal or imaginary 3 inability to deal with reality; impracticality

un·rea·son (un rē′zən) *n.* lack of reason; irrationality

un·rea·son·a·ble (-ə bəl) *adj.* not reasonable; specif., *a)* having or showing little sense or judgment; not rational *b)* excessive; immoderate; exorbitant —*SYN.* IRRATIONAL —**un·rea′son·a·ble·ness** *n.* —**un·rea′son·a·bly** *adv.*

un·rea·son·ing (-iŋ) *adj.* not reasoning or reasoned; marked by a lack of reason or judgment; irrational —**un·rea′son·ing·ly** *adv.*

☆**un·re·con·struct·ed** (un′rē′kən struk′tid) *adj.* 1 not reconstructed 2 holding to an earlier, outmoded practice or point of view

un·reel (un rēl′) *vt., vi.* to unwind as from a reel

un·reeve (un rēv′) *vt.* **-rove′** or **-reeved′**, **-reev′ing** *Naut.* to withdraw (a line) from a block, ring, etc.

un·re·gen·er·ate (un′ri jen′ər it) *adj.* 1 not regenerate; not spiritually reborn or converted 2 not converted to a particular belief, viewpoint, etc. 3 recalcitrant or obstinate Also **un′re·gen′er·at′ed** —**un′re·gen′er·ate·ly** *adv.*

un·re·lent·ing (-ri len′tiŋ) *adj.* 1 refusing to yield or relent; inflexible; relentless 2 without mercy or compassion 3 not relaxing or slackening, as in effort, speed, etc.

un·re·li·gious (-ri lij′əs) *adj.* 1 IRRELIGIOUS 2 not connected with or involving religion; nonreligious

un·re·mit·ting (-ri mit′iŋ) *adj.* not stopping, relaxing, or slackening; incessant; persistent

un·re·quit·ed (-ri kwīt′id) *adj.* not given in return; esp., designating romantic love that is not reciprocated

un·re·serve (-ri zʉrv′) *n.* lack of reserve; frankness

un·re·served (-ri zʉrvd′) *adj.* not reserved; specif., *a)* frank or open in speech or behavior *b)* not restricted or qualified; unlimited *c)* not set aside for advance sale [*unreserved* seats] —**un′re·serv′ed·ly** (-zʉr′vid lē) *adv.*

un·rest (un rest′) *n.* a troubled or disturbed state; restlessness; disquiet; uneasiness; specif., a condition of angry discontent and protest verging on revolt

un·rid·dle (-rid′'l) *vt.* **-dled**, **-dling** to solve or explain (a riddle, mystery, etc.)

un·rig (-rig′) *vt.* **-rigged′**, **-rig′ging** to strip of rigging, or of equipment, clothes, etc.

un·right·eous (-rī′chəs) *adj.* 1 not righteous; wicked; sinful 2 not right; unjust; unfair —**un·right′eous·ly** *adv.* —**un·right′eous·ness** *n.*

un·rip (-rip′) *vt.* **-ripped′**, **-rip′ping** 1 to rip open; take apart or detach by ripping 2 [Now Rare] to make known

un·ripe (-rīp′) *adj.* 1 not ripe or mature; green 2 not yet fully developed [*unripe* plans] 3 [Obs.] premature: said esp. of a death —**un·ripe′ness** *n.*

un·ri·valed or **un·ri·valled** (-rī′vəld) *adj.* having no rival, equal, or competitor; matchless; peerless

un·roll (-rōl′) *vt.* 1 to open or extend (something rolled up) 2 to present to view; display 3 [Obs.] to remove from a roll or list —*vi.* to become unrolled

un·roof (-ro͞of′) *vt.* to take off the roof or covering of

un·root (-ro͞ot′) *vt.* UPROOT

un·round (-round′) *vt. Phonet.* 1 to pronounce (a vowel usually rounded) without rounding of the lips 2 to keep (the lips) from being rounded, as in pronouncing the vowel in *she* —**un·round′ed** *adj.*

un·rove (-rōv′) *vt., vi. alt. pt. & pp. of* UNREEVE

un·ruf·fled (un ruf′əld) *adj.* not ruffled, disturbed, or agitated; calm; smooth; serene —*SYN.* COOL

un·ruly (-ro͞o′lē) *adj.* **-rul′i·er**, **-rul′i·est** ⟦ME *unruely* < *un-*, not + *reuly*,

unprogressive
unprohibited
unpromising
unprompted
unpronounceable
unpronounced
unpropitiable
unpropitious
unproportionate
unproposed
unprosperous
unproved
unproven
unprovided
unprovoked
unpruned
unpunctual
unpunishable
unpunished
unpure
unpurged
unpurified
unpurposed
unquaking
unqualifying
unquelled
unquenchable
unquenched
unquotable
unquoted
unranked
unransomed
unrated
unratified
unravaged
unreachable
unrealizable
unrealized
unreasoned
unrebuked
unreceivable
unreceived
unreceptive
unreciprocated
unreclaimable
unreclaimed
unrecognizable
unrecognized
unrecommended
unrecompensed
unreconcilable
unreconciled
unrecorded
unrecoverable
unrecruited
unrectified
unredeemed
unredressed
unrefined
unreflecting
unreformable
unreformed
unrefreshed
unregarded
unregistered
unregretted
unregulated
unrehearsed
unrelated
unrelaxed
unreliability
unreliable
unreliably
unrelievable
unrelieved
unremarkable
unremarked
unremedied
unremembered
unremittable
unremitted
unremorseful
unremovable
unremunerated
unremunerative
unrendered
unrenewed
unrenowned
unrentable
unrented
unrepaid
unrepairable
unrepaired
unrepealed
unrepentant
unrepented
unrepenting
unreplaceable
unreplaced
unreplenished
unreported
unrepresentative
unrepresented
unrepressed
unreprieved
unreprimanded
unreprovable
unrequested
unresentful
unresigned
unresistant
unresisting
unresolved
unrespectful
unresponsive
unrested
unrestful
unrestrained
unrestraint
unrestricted
unretentive
unretouched
unretracted
unretrieved
unreturned
unrevealed
unrevenged
unreversed
unreviewed
unrevised
unrevoked
unrewarded
unrewarding
unrhymed
unrhythmic
unrhythmical
unrightful
unripened
unroasted
unrobe
unromantic
unromantically
unroped
unruled
unrumpled
unrushed
unrusted

orderly < *reule,* RULE⟧ hard to control, restrain, or keep in order; disobedient, disorderly, etc. —**un·rul′i·ness** *n.*

un·sad·dle (-sad′'l) *vt.* **-dled, -dling 1** to take the saddle off (a horse, etc.) **2** to throw from the saddle; unhorse —*vi.* to take the saddle off a horse, etc.

un·said (-sed′) *vt. pt. & pp. of* UNSAY —*adj.* not expressed

un·san·i·tar·y (-san′ə ter′ē) *adj.* not sanitary; unhealthful or likely to cause disease

un·sat·u·rat·ed (-sach′ə rāt′id) *adj.* **1** not saturated **2** *Chem. a)* designating or of a compound in which some element possesses the capacity of combining further with other elements *b)* designating or of a solution that is not in equilibrium with the undissolved solute *c)* designating an organic compound with a double or triple bond that links two atoms, usually of carbon —**un′sat·u·ra′tion** *n.*

un·sa·vor·y (-sā′vər ē) *adj.* **1** [Obs.] without flavor; tasteless **2** unpleasant to taste or smell **3** unpleasant or offensive, esp. so as to seem immoral —**un·sa′vor·i·ly** *adv.* —**un·sa′vor·i·ness** *n.*

un·say (-sā′) *vt.* **-said′, -say′ing** to take back or retract (what has been said)

un·scathed (-skāthd′) *adj.* ⟦see SCATHE⟧ not hurt; unharmed

un·schooled (-sko͞old′) *adj.* **1** not educated or trained, esp. by formal schooling **2** not acquired or altered by schooling; natural

un·scram·ble (-skram′bəl) *vt.* **-bled, -bling 1** to cause to be no longer scrambled, disordered, or mixed up **2** *Electronics* to make (incoming scrambled signals) intelligible at the receiver —**un·scram′bler** *n.*

un·screw (-skro͞o′) *vt.* **1** to remove a screw or screws from **2** *a)* to remove, detach, or loosen by removing a screw or screws, or by turning *b)* to remove a threaded top, cover, etc. from (a jar, etc.) —*vi.* to become unscrewed or admit of being unscrewed

un·script·ed (un skrip′tid) *adj.* **1** not having a prepared script [an *unscripted* interview show] **2** not in the prepared script [an actor's *unscripted* fall from the stage]

un·scru·pu·lous (-skro͞o′pyə ləs) *adj.* not scrupulous; not restrained by ideas of right and wrong; unprincipled —**un·scru′pu·lous·ly** *adv.* —**un·scru′pu·lous·ness** *n.*

un·seal (-sēl′) *vt.* **1** to break or remove the seal of **2** to open (something sealed, or closed as if sealed)

un·seam (-sēm′) *vt.* to open the seam or seams of; rip

un·search·a·ble (-surch′ə bəl) *adj.* that cannot be searched into; mysterious; inscrutable —**un·search′a·bly** *adv.*

un·sea·son·a·ble (-sē′zən ə bəl) *adj.* **1** not usual for or appropriate to the season [*unseasonable* heat] **2** not in season [*unseasonable* seafood] **3** coming, said, etc. at the wrong time; untimely; inopportune —**un·sea′son·a·ble·ness** *n.* —**un·sea′son·a·bly** *adv.*

un·sea·soned (-sē′zənd) *adj.* not seasoned; specif., *a)* not ripened, dried, etc. by enough seasoning [*unseasoned* wood] *b)* not matured by experience; inexperienced *c)* not flavored with seasoning

un·seat (-sēt′) *vt.* **1** to throw or dislodge from a seat; specif., UNHORSE **2** to remove from office, deprive of rank, etc.

un·se·cured (un′si kyoord′) *adj.* **1** not made secure or firm; not kept firmly in place **2** not secured or guaranteed, as by collateral [an *unsecured* loan]

un·seem·ly (un sēm′lē) *adj.* not seemly; not decent or proper; unbecoming; indecorous —*adv.* in an unseemly manner —*SYN.* IMPROPER —**un·seem′li·ness** *n.*

un·seen (-sēn′) *adj.* **1** not seen, perceived, or observed; invisible **2** not noticed or discovered **3** not seen or prepared for in advance

un·self·ish (-self′ish) *adj.* not selfish; putting the good of others above one's own interests; altruistic; generous —**un·self′ish·ly** *adv.* —**un·self′ish·ness** *n.*

un·set (-set′) *adj.* not set; specif., not mounted in a setting [an *unset* gem]

un·set·tle (-set′'l) *vt.* **-tled, -tling** to make unsettled, insecure, or unstable; disturb, displace, disarrange, or disorder —*vi.* to become unsettled —**un·set′tle·ment** *n.*

un·set·tled (-set′'ld) *adj.* **1** not settled or orderly; disordered **2** not stable or fixed; changeable; uncertain **3** not decided or determined **4** not paid, allotted, or otherwise disposed of [an *unsettled* debt or estate] ☆**5** having no settlers; unpopulated **6** not established in a place or abode —**un·set′tled·ness** *n.*

un·sex (-seks′) *vt.* **1** to deprive of sexual power **2** to deprive of the qualities considered characteristic of one's sex; esp., to make unwomanly

un·shack·le (-shak′əl) *vt.* **-led, -ling 1** to loosen or remove the shackles from **2** to free

un·shap·en (-shā′pən) *adj.* ⟦ME⟧ **1** without shape; shapeless **2** badly shaped; misshapen; malformed

un·sheathe (-shēth′) *vt.* **-sheathed′, -sheath′ing** to draw or remove (a sword, knife, etc.) from or as if from a sheath

un·ship (-ship′) *vt.* **-shipped′, -ship′ping** ⟦ME *unshippen:* see UN- & SHIP⟧ **1** to unload from a ship **2** *Naut.* to remove (an oar, mast, etc.) from the proper position for use

un·sight·ly (-sīt′lē) *adj.* not sightly; not pleasant to look at; ugly —**un·sight′li·ness** *n.*

un·skilled (-skild′) *adj.* not skilled; specif., *a)* having no special skill or training *b)* requiring or using no special skill or training [*unskilled* labor] *c)* showing a lack of skill

un·skill·ful (-skil′fəl) *adj.* not skillful; having little or no skill or dexterity; awkward —**un·skill′ful·ly** *adv.* —**un·skill′ful·ness** *n.*

un·sling (-sliŋ′) *vt.* **-slung′, -sling′ing** to take (a rifle, etc.) from a slung position

un·snap (-snap′) *vt.* **-snapped′, -snap′ping** to undo the snap or snaps of, so as to loosen or detach —*vi.* to become opened or unfastened by means of a SNAP (*n.* 6)

un·snarl (-snärl′) *vt.* to free of snarls; untangle

un·so·cia·ble (-sō′shə bəl) *adj.* **1** avoiding association with others; not sociable or friendly **2** not conducive to sociability —**un·so′cia·bil′i·ty** *n.*, **un·so′cia·ble·ness** —**un·so′cia·bly** *adv.*

un·so·cial (-sō′shəl) *adj.* having or showing a dislike for the society of others —**un·so′cial·ly** *adv.*

SYN.—**unsocial** implies an aversion to the society or company of others [an *unsocial* neighbor]; **asocial** implies complete indifference to the interests, welfare, etc. of society and connotes abnormal or irresponsible self-centeredness [the frequent *asocial* behavior of very young children]; **antisocial** applies to that which is believed to be detrimental to or destructive of the social order, social institutions, etc. [the anarchist's *antisocial* teachings]; **nonsocial** expresses simple absence of social relationship [*nonsocial* fields of interest] —*ANT.* **social**

un·so·phis·ti·cat·ed (un′sə fis′tə kāt′id) *adj.* not sophisticated; specif., *a)* artless, simple, ingenuous, etc. *b)* not complex, refined, developed, etc. *c)* [Now Rare] not adulterated; genuine or pure —*SYN.* NAIVE —**un′so·phis′ti·cat′ed·ly** *adv.* —**un′so·phis′ti·ca′tion** *n.*

un·sound (un sound′) *adj.* not sound or free from defect; specif., *a)* not normal or healthy physically or mentally *b)* not safe, firm, or solid; insecure *c)* not safe and secure financially *d)* not based on truth or valid reasoning; not accurate, reliable, sensible, etc. *e)* light (said of sleep) —**un·sound′ly** *adv.* —**un·sound′ness** *n.*

un·spar·ing (-sper′iŋ) *adj.* **1** not sparing or stinting; lavish; liberal; profuse **2** not merciful or forgiving; severe —**un·spar′ing·ly** *adv.*

un·speak (-spēk′) *vt.* **-spoke′, -spok′en, -speak′ing** [Obs.] to unsay, or retract

---

unsafe
unsaintly
unsalability
unsalable
unsalaried
unsaleability
unsaleable
unsalted
unsampled
unsanctified
unsanctioned
unsated
unsatiable
unsatiated
unsatiating
unsatisfactorily
unsatisfactory
unsatisfied
unsatisfying
unsaved
unsayable
unscalable
unscaled
unscanned
unscarred
unscented
unsceptical
unscheduled
unscholarly
unscientific
unscientifically
unscorched
unscourged
unscratched
unscreened
unscriptural
unsculptured
unsealed
unseasonal
unseaworthy
unseconded
unseeded
unseeing
unsegmented
unsegregated
unselected
unselective
unselfconscious
unsensational
unsent
unsentimental
unseparated
unserious
unserved
unserviceable
unsewn
unsexual
unshaded
unshadowed
unshakable
unshakeable
unshaken
unshaped
unshapely
unshared
unsharpened
unshaved
unshaven
unshelled
unsheltered
unshielded
unshod
unshorn
unshortened
unshrinkable
unshrinking
unshrunk
unshuffled
unshut
unshuttered
unsifted
unsighted
unsigned
unsilenced
unsimilar
unsimplified
unsingable
unsinkable
unsisterly
unsized
unskeptical
unslackened
unslaked
unsleeping
unsliced
unsmiling
unsmoked
unsnagged
unsober
unsoftened
unsoiled
unsold
unsoldierly
unsolicited
unsolicitous
unsolid
unsolidified
unsolvable
unsolved
unsoothed
unsorted
unsought
unsounded
unsoured
unsowed
unsown

un·speak·a·ble (-spēk′ə bəl) *adj.* **1** that cannot be spoken **2** marvelous, awesome, etc.; beyond human expression; ineffable **3** *a)* so bad, evil, etc. as to defy description *b)* so foul, evil, etc. as to be unfit to be described or discussed [*unspeakable* depravity] —**un·speak′a·bly** *adv.*

un·sphere (-sfir′) *vt.* **-sphered′**, **-spher′ing** to remove from its sphere or from one's sphere

un·spo·ken (-spō′kən) *adj.* **1** not spoken **2** suggested or to be understood though not openly or directly expressed

un·sta·ble (-stā′bəl) *adj.* ⟦ME⟧ not stable; specif., *a)* not fixed, firm, or steady; easily upset or unbalanced *b)* changeable; variable; fluctuating *c)* unreliable; fickle *d)* emotionally or psychologically unsettled *e) Chem.* tending to decompose or change into other compounds —*SYN.* INCONSTANT —**un·sta′ble·ness** *n.* —**un·sta′bly** *adv.*

un·stead·y (-sted′ē) *adj.* not steady; specif., *a)* not firm or stable; shaky *b)* changeable; inconstant; wavering *c)* erratic in habits, purpose, or behavior —*vt.* **-stead′ied**, **-stead′y·ing** to make unsteady —**un·stead′i·ly** *adv.* —**un·stead′i·ness** *n.*

un·steel (-stēl′) *vt.* to deprive of strength, resoluteness, etc.

un·step (-step′) *vt.* **-stepped′**, **-step′ping** *Naut.* to remove (a mast) from its step or socket

un·stick (-stik′) *vt.* **-stuck′**, **-stick′ing** to loosen or free (something stuck)

un·stop (-stäp′) *vt.* **-stopped′**, **-stop′ping** ⟦ME *unstoppen:* see UN- & STOP⟧ **1** to remove the stopper from **2** to clear (a pipe, etc.) of a stoppage or obstruction; open

un·strap (-strap′) *vt.* **-strapped′**, **-strap′ping** to loosen or remove the strap or straps of

un·string (-striŋ′) *vt.* **-strung′**, **-string′ing** **1** to loosen or remove the string or strings of **2** to remove from a string **3** to loosen; relax **4** to cause to be unstrung; make nervous, weak, upset, etc.

un·struc·tured (-struk′chərd) *adj.* not formally or systematically organized; loose, free, open, etc.

un·strung (-struŋ′) *vt. pt. & pp. of* UNSTRING —*adj.* **1** nervous or upset; unnerved **2** having the string or strings loosened or detached, as a bow, racket, etc.

un·stuck (-stuk′) *vt. pt. & pp. of* UNSTICK —*adj.* loosened or freed from being stuck —**come unstuck** [Informal] to fail, go wrong, break down, etc.

un·stud·ied (-stud′ēd) *adj.* **1** not gotten by study or conscious effort **2** spontaneous; natural; unaffected **3** not having studied; unlearned or unversed (*in*)

un·sub·stan·tial (un′səb stan′shəl) *adj.* not substantial; specif., *a)* having no material substance *b)* not solid or heavy; flimsy; light *c)* unreal; visionary —**un′sub·stan′ti·al′i·ty** (-stan′shē al′ə tē) *n.* —**un′sub·stan′tial·ly** *adv.*

un·suit·a·ble (un so͞ot′ə bəl) *adj.* not suitable; unbecoming; inappropriate —**un·suit′a·bil′i·ty** *n.* —**un·suit′a·bly** *adv.*

un·sung (un suŋ′, un′suŋ′) *adj.* ⟦LME *unsonge*⟧ **1** not sung **2** deserving but not receiving honor or public praise [an *unsung* hero of the labor movement]

un·sus·pect·ed (un′sə spek′tid) *adj.* not suspected; specif., *a)* not under suspicion *b)* not imagined to be existent, probable, etc. —**un′sus·pect′ed·ly** *adv.*

un·swathe (un swāth′) *vt.* **-swathed′**, **-swath′ing** to remove a swathe or wrappings from

un·swear (-swer′) *vt., vi.* **-swore′**, **-sworn′**, **-swear′ing** to recant or take back (something sworn to), as by another oath; abjure

un·tan·gle (-taŋ′gəl) *vt.* **-gled**, **-gling** **1** to free from a snarl or tangle; disentangle **2** to free from confusion; clear up; put in order

un·taught (-tôt′) *vt. pt. & pp. of* UNTEACH —*adj.* ⟦ME *untaght*⟧ **1** not taught or instructed; uneducated; ignorant **2** acquired without being taught; natural

un·teach (-tēch′) *vt.* **-taught′**, **-teach′ing** **1** to try to make forget something learned, as in the process of reeducation **2** to teach the opposite of

un·ten·a·ble (-ten′ə bəl) *adj.* **1** that cannot be held, defended, or maintained **2** incapable of being tenanted or occupied —**un′ten·a·bil′i·ty** *n.*, **un·ten′a·ble·ness**

Un·ter·mey·er (un′tər mī′ər), **Louis** 1885-1977; U.S. poet, anthologist, & critic

Un·ter·wal·den (o͝on′tər väl′dən) former canton of central Switzerland: now divided into two cantons, NIDWALDEN & OBWALDEN

un·teth·er (un teth′ər) *vt.* to release from a tether

un·thank·ful (-thaŋk′fəl) *adj.* **1** not thankful; ungrateful **2** thankless; unappreciated —**un·thank′ful·ly** *adv.* —**un·thank′ful·ness** *n.*

un·think (-thiŋk′) *vt.* **-thought′**, **-think′ing** to rid one's mind of, or change one's mind about

un·think·a·ble (-thiŋ′kə bəl) *adj.* ⟦ME *unthenkable*⟧ **1** beyond the ability to understand or imagine; inconceivable **2** so extreme, foul, etc. as to be unfit to be imagined or considered [*unthinkable* war crimes] —**un·think′a·bly** *adv.*

un·think·ing (-thiŋk′iŋ) *adj.* **1** *a)* not stopping to think; heedless *b)* showing lack of thought, attention, or consideration **2** lacking the ability to think; nonrational —**un·think′ing·ly** *adv.*

un·thread (-thred′) *vt.* **1** to remove the thread or threads from **2** to disentangle; unravel **3** to find one's way through (a labyrinth, etc.)

un·throne (-thrōn′) *vt.* **-throned′**, **-thron′ing** DETHRONE

un·ti·dy (-tī′dē) *adj.* **-di·er**, **-di·est** ⟦ME *untydi*⟧ not tidy; not neat or in good order; slovenly; messy —**un·ti′di·ly** *adv.* —**un·ti′di·ness** *n.*

un·tie (-tī′) *vt.* **-tied′**, **-ty′ing** or **-tie′ing** ⟦ME *unteien* < OE *untigan:* see UN- & TIE⟧ **1** to loosen, undo, or unfasten (something tied or knotted) **2** to free, as from difficulty, restraint, etc. **3** to resolve (perplexities, etc.) —*vi.* to become untied

un·til (un til′) *prep.* ⟦ME *untill* < *un-* (see UNTO) + *till,* to, TILL[1]⟧ **1** up to the time of; till (a specified time or occurrence) [*until* payday] **2** before (a specified time or occurrence): used with a negative [not *until* tomorrow] **3** [Scot.] to or toward —*conj.* **1** up to the time when or that [*until* you leave] **2** to the point, degree, or place that [heat the water *until* it boils] **3** before: used with a negative [not *until* he tells you]

un·time·ly (un tīm′lē) *adj.* **1** coming, said, done, etc. before the usual or expected time; premature [to come to an *untimely* end] **2** coming, said, done, etc. at the wrong time; poorly timed; inopportune —*adv.* **1** prematurely **2** inopportunely —**un·time′li·ness** *n.*

un·ti·tled (-tīt′ld) *adj.* **1** not having a title [an *untitled* book, *untitled* nobility] **2** having no right or claim

un·to (un′to͞o, -to͝o) *prep.* ⟦ME < *un-*, until, akin to ON *unz* (< *und es*), Goth *und* < IE **ṇti* < base **ant-*, front, fore (> Gr *anti*, L *ante*, before) + ME *to*, TO[1]⟧ *old poet. var. of:* **1** TO[1] **2** UNTIL

un·told (un tōld′, un′tōld′) *adj.* ⟦ME *untald* < OE *unteald*⟧ **1** not told, related, or revealed **2** too great or too numerous to be counted or measured; incalculable [*untold* wealth] **3** indescribably great or intense [*untold* misery]

un·touch·a·ble (un tuch′ə bəl) *adj.* that cannot or should not be touched —*n.* **1** an untouchable person or thing **2** in India, any member of the lowest castes, whose touch was regarded as defiling to higher-caste Hindus: discrimination against these people (now called *Scheduled Castes*) was officially abolished in 1955 —**un′touch·a·bil′i·ty** *n.*

un·to·ward (un tō′ərd, -tôrd′) *adj.* ⟦UN- + TOWARD⟧ **1** inappropriate, improper, unseemly, etc. [an *untoward* remark] **2** not favorable or fortunate;

unspecialized
unspecific
unspecified
unspectacular
unspeculative
unspent
unspilled
unspiritual
unspirituality
unsplit
unspoiled
unsporting
unsportsmanlike
unspotted
unsprung
unsquandered
unsquared
unstack
unstained
unstalked
unstamped
unstandardized
unstarched
unstarred
unstated
unstatesmanlike
unsteadfast
unstemmed
unsterilized
unstigmatized
unstinted
unstinting
unstitched
unstocked
unstoppable
unstrained
unstrategic
unstratified
unstressed
unstriated
unstriped
unstripped
unstuffed
unstylish
unsubdued
unsubmissive
unsubscribed
unsubsidized
unsubstantiated
unsubtle
unsuccessful
unsuccessfully
unsufferable
unsuggestive
unsuited
unsullied
unsunk
unsupervised
unsupportable
unsupported
unsuppressed
unsure
unsurmountable
unsurpassable
unsurpassed
unsurprised
unsusceptible
unsuspecting
unsuspicious
unsustainable
unsustained
unswayed
unsweetened
unswept
unswerving
unswervingly
unswollen
unsymmetrical
unsymmetry
unsympathetic
unsympathetically
unsympathizing
unsystematic
unsystematically
unsystematized
untabulated
untack
untactful
untagged
untainted
untalented
untalkative
untalked-of
untamable
untamed
untanned
untapped
untarnished
untasted
untaxed
unteachable
untechnical
untempered
untenanted
untended
unterrified
untested
unthanked
unthatched
unthawed
untheatrical
unthoughtful
unthought-of
unthrifty
unticketed
untillable
untilled
untinged
untipped
untired
untiring
untorn
untouched

adverse, inauspicious, etc. [*untoward* circumstances] 3 [Archaic] stubborn or unruly 4 [Obs.] awkward; clumsy

☆**un·tracked** (un trakt′) *adj.* [Informal] performing in a manner regarded as normal or characteristic, as after having been in a slump

un·trav·eled or **un·trav·elled** (un trav′əld) *adj.* 1 not used or frequented by travelers: said of a road, etc. 2 not having done much traveling, esp. to far places

un·tread (-tred′) *vt.* **-trod′**, **-trod′den** or **-trod′**, **-tread′ing** [Archaic] to retrace (a path, one's steps, etc.)

un·tried (-trīd′) *adj.* 1 not tried; not attempted, tested, or proved 2 not tried in court

un·true (un tro͞o′, un′tro͞o′) *adj.* ⟦ME *untrewe* < OE *untreowe; un-*, not + *treowe*, TRUE⟧ 1 contrary to fact or truth; false or incorrect 2 not agreeing with a standard, rule, or measure 3 not faithful or loyal —**un·tru′ly** *adv.*

un·truss (un trus′) *vt.* 1 to release as from being trussed up 2 [Obs.] to undress

un·truth (-tro͞oth′) *n.* ⟦ME *untrouthe* < OE *untreowth* < *un-*, not + *treowth*, TRUTH⟧ 1 the quality or state of being untrue; falsity 2 an untrue statement; falsehood; lie 3 [Obs.] unfaithfulness or disloyalty

un·truth·ful (-tro͞oth′fəl) *adj.* 1 not in accordance with the truth; untrue 2 *a)* telling a lie *b)* given to telling untruths; likely to tell lies —*SYN.* DISHONEST —**un·truth′ful·ly** *adv.* —**un·truth′ful·ness** *n.*

un·tuck (-tuk′) *vt.* to undo a tuck or tucks in; free from a tuck or fold

un·tu·tored (-to͞ot′ərd) *adj.* 1 not tutored or taught; uneducated 2 simple; naive; unsophisticated —*SYN.* IGNORANT

un·twine (-twīn′) *vt.* **-twined′**, **-twin′ing** ⟦ME *untwynen*⟧ to undo (something twined or twisted); disentangle or unwind —*vi.* to become untwined

un·twist (-twist′) *vt., vi.* to turn in the opposite direction so as to loosen or separate; untwine

un·used (un yo͞ozd′) *adj.* 1 not used; not in use 2 that has never been used 3 unaccustomed (*to*)

un·u·su·al (-yo͞o′zhə wəl) *adj.* not usual or common; rare; exceptional —**un·u′su·al·ly** *adv.* —**un·u′su·al·ness** *n.*

un·ut·ter·a·ble (-ut′ər ə bəl) *adj.* 1 [Rare] that cannot easily be pronounced 2 that cannot be expressed or described; inexpressible —**un·ut′ter·a·bly** *adv.*

un·var·nished (-vär′nisht) *adj.* 1 not varnished 2 plain; simple; unadorned [the *unvarnished* truth]

un·veil (un vāl′) *vt.* to reveal or make visible by or as by removing a veil or covering from; disclose —*vi.* to take off a veil or covering; reveal oneself

un·veil·ing (-iŋ) *n.* a formal or ceremonial removal of a covering from a new statue, tombstone, etc.

un·voice (un vois′) *vt.* **-voiced′**, **-voic′ing** *Phonet.* to make (a normally voiced sound) voiceless by uttering the corresponding voiceless sound; make surd (Ex.: the *s* in *has* [haz] is often unvoiced in the phrase *has to* [has′ to͞o′])

un·voiced (-voist′) *adj.* 1 not expressed; not spoken or uttered 2 *Phonet.* made voiceless; surd

un·war·y (-wer′ē) *adj.* not wary; not watchful or cautious; not alert to possible danger, trickery, etc. —**un·war′i·ly** *adv.* —**un·war′i·ness** *n.*

un·washed (un wôsht′, -wäsht′) *adj.* not washed; dirty, soiled, etc. —**the (great) unwashed** the common people; the masses: originally a patronizing or contemptuous use, now usually ironic in application, with reference to elitism

un·wea·ried (-wir′ēd) *adj.* ⟦ME *unweried* (see UN- & WEARY), for OE *ungewerged*⟧ 1 not weary or tired 2 never wearying; tireless; indefatigable

un·well (-wel′) *adj.* not well; ailing; ill; sick

un·wept (-wept′) *adj.* 1 not shed [*unwept* tears] 2 not wept for; unmourned

un·whole·some (-hōl′səm) *adj.* ⟦ME *unholsom*⟧ not wholesome; specif., *a)* harmful to body or mind; unhealthful *b)* having unsound health or an unhealthy appearance *c)* morally harmful or corrupt —**un·whole′some·ly** *adv.* —**un·whole′some·ness** *n.*

un·wield·y (-wēl′dē) *adj.* 1 hard to wield, manage, handle, or deal with, as because of large size or weight, or awkward form 2 [Now Rare] awkward; clumsy —**un·wield′i·ness** *n.*

un·will·ing (-wil′iŋ) *adj.* ⟦altered (in 16th c.) < ME *unwilland* < OE *unwillende* < *un-*, not + prp. of *willan:* see WILL[2]⟧ 1 not willing or inclined; reluctant; loath; averse 2 done, said, given, etc. reluctantly —**un·will′ing·ly** *adv.* —**un·will′ing·ness** *n.*

un·wind (-wīnd′) *vt.* **-wound′**, **-wind′ing** ⟦ME *unwinden* < OE *unwindan*⟧ 1 to wind off or undo (something wound) 2 UNCOIL 3 to straighten out or untangle (something confused or involved) 4 to make relaxed, less tense, etc. 5 *a)* to close out (a position in a securities or commodities trade) *b)* to sell (a stake in a company, business venture, etc.) —*vi.* 1 to become unwound 2 to become relaxed, less tense, etc.

un·wise (un wīz′, un′wīz′) *adj.* ⟦ME < OE *unwis:* see UN- & WISE[1]⟧ having or showing a lack of wisdom or sound judgment; foolish; imprudent —**un·wise′ly** *adv.*

un·wish (-wish′) *vt.* 1 *a)* to retract (a wish) *b)* to stop wishing for 2 [Obs.] to do away with by wishing

un·wit·ting (-wit′iŋ) *adj.* ⟦ME *unwiting*, altered < OE *unwitende* < *un-*, not + prp. of *witan*, to know: see WIT[2]⟧ 1 not knowing; unaware 2 not intended; unintentional —**un·wit′ting·ly** *adv.*

un·wont·ed (un wôn′tid, -wōn′-, -wän′-, -wun′-) *adj.* ⟦UN- + WONTED⟧ 1 not common, usual, or habitual; uncharacteristic or atypical [to speak with *unwonted* severity] 2 [Archaic] not accustomed or used: usually with *to* —**un·wont′ed·ly** *adv.*

un·world·ly (-wurld′lē) *adj.* 1 not of or limited to this world; unearthly 2 not concerned with the affairs, pleasures, etc. of this world 3 not worldly-wise; unsophisticated —**un·world′li·ness** *n.*

un·wor·thy (-wur′thē) *adj.* **-thi·er**, **-thi·est** ⟦ME⟧ 1 lacking merit or value; worthless 2 not deserving: often with *of* 3 not fit or becoming: usually with *of* [a remark *unworthy* of a gentleman] 4 not deserved or warranted —**un·wor′thi·ly** *adv.* —**un·wor′thi·ness** *n.*

un·wound (-wound′) *vt., vi. pt. & pp. of* UNWIND

un·wrap (-rap′) *vt.* **-wrapped′**, **-wrap′ping** to take off the wrapping of; open or undo (something wrapped) —*vi.* to become unwrapped

un·writ·ten (un rit′'n, un′rit′'n) *adj.* 1 not in writing; not written or printed 2 operating only through custom or tradition [an *unwritten* rule] 3 not written on; blank

unwritten law law originating in custom, usage, court decisions, etc., rather than in the action of any lawmaking body

un·yoke (un yōk′) *vt.* **-yoked′**, **-yok′ing** ⟦ME *unyoken* < OE *ungeocian*⟧ 1 to release from a yoke 2 to separate or disconnect —*vi.* 1 to become unyoked 2 to remove a yoke 3 [Obs.] to stop working

☆**un·zip** (-zip′) *vt.* **-zipped′**, **-zip′ping** 1 to unfasten (a zipper) 2 to unfasten the zipper of —*vi.* to become unfastened by means of a zipper

up[1] (up) *adv.* ⟦ME < OE *up, uppe*, akin to Ger *auf*, ON *upp* < IE **upo*, up from below > SUB-, HYPO-, OVER⟧ 1 from a lower to a higher place; away from or out of the ground 2 in or on a higher position or level; off the ground, or from a position below to one at the surface of the earth or water 3 in a direction or place thought of as higher or above 4 above the horizon 5 to a later period [from childhood *up*] 6 to a higher or better condition or station 7 to a higher amount, greater degree, etc. [with prices going *up*] 8 *a)* in or into a standing or upright position *b)* out of bed 9 in or into existence, action, view, evidence, consideration, etc. [to bring a matter *up*] 10 into an excited or troubled state [to get worked *up*] 11 aside; away; by [lay *up* grain for the winter] 12 so as to be even with in space, time, degree, etc. [keep *up* with the times] 13 to the point of completeness; entirely; thoroughly [eat *up* the pie] 14 so as to stop [to rein *up* a horse] 15 to or toward an earlier time [to move a meeting *up*] ☆16 [Informal] served without ice cubes; not on the rocks: said of a cocktail ☆17 *Baseball* to one's turn at batting; at bat 18 *Naut.* to windward [put *up* the helm] 19 *Games, Sports* ahead of an opponent (by a specified number of points, strokes, etc.) ➥*Up* is also used with verbs *a)* to form idiomatic combinations with a meaning different from the meaning of the simple verbs [look *up* this word; he didn't turn *up*] *b)* as an intensive [dress *up*, eat *up*, clean *up*] *c)*

untraceable
untraced
untraditional
untrained
untrammeled
untransferable
untranslatable
untranslated
untransmitted
untransported
untransposed
untrapped
untraversed
untreated
untrimmed
untrod
untroubled
untrustful
untrustworthy
untufted
untunable
untuned
untuneful
unturned
untwilled
untypical
unusable
unutilizable
unutilized
unuttered
unvaccinated
unvacillating
unvalued
unvanquished
unvaried
unvarying
unventilated
unverifiable
unverified
unversed
unvested
unvexed
unvindicated
unviolated
unvisited
unvocal
unvocalized
unvulcanized
unwakened
unwalled
unwaning
unwanted
unwarlike
unwarmed
unwarned
unwarped
unwarrantable
unwarranted
unwasted
unwatched
unwatered
unwavering
unwaxed
unweakened
unweaned
unwearable
unweary
unweathered
unweave
unwed
unwedded
unweeded
unweighed
unwelcome
unwelded
unwhipped
unwilled
unwinking
unwinnable
unwished
unwithering
unwitnessed
unwomanly
unwon
unwooded
unwooed
unworkability
unworkable
unworked
unworkmanlike
unworn
unworried
unworshiped
unwounded
unwoven
unwrinkle
unwrinkled
unyielding
unyouthful
unzoned

as a virtually meaningless element added, esp. informally, to almost any verb [light *up* a cigarette, write *up* a story] —*prep.* **1** to, toward, or at a higher place on or in **2** to, toward, or at a higher condition or station on or in [*up* the social ladder] **3** at, along, or toward the higher or more distant part of [*up* the road] **4** toward the source of, or against the current, flow, or movement of (a river, the wind, etc.) **5** in or toward the interior of (a country, territory, etc.) **6** in or toward a more northerly part of [to cruise *up* the coast] —*adj.* **1** tending or directed toward a position that is higher or is regarded as being higher **2** *a)* in a higher position, condition, or station *b)* mounted on a horse or horses **3** *a)* above the ground *b)* above the horizon **4** advanced in amount, degree, etc. [rents are *up*] **5** *a)* in a standing or upright position *b)* out of bed **6** in an active, excited, or agitated state [her anger was *up*] **7** even with in space, time, degree, etc. **8** living or located in the inner or elevated part of a country, territory, etc. **9** at an end; over [time is *up*] ☆**10** at stake in gambling [to have two dollars *up* on a horse] **11** working properly and available for use: said esp. of a computer **12** [Informal] going on; happening [what's *up?*] **13** [Informal] lively; cheerful; optimistic ☆**14** *Baseball* having one's turn at batting; at bat **15** *Games, Sports* ahead of an opponent (by a specified number of points, strokes, etc.) ➥As an adjective, *up* is usually predicative —*n.* **1** a person or thing that is up, moves upward, etc.; specif., *a)* an upward slope *b)* an upward movement or course *c)* a period or state of prosperity, good luck, etc. ☆**2** [Slang] an amphetamine or other stimulant drug; upper —*vi.* **upped, up′ping** [Informal] to get up; rise: sometimes used dialectally or informally in the uninflected form to emphasize another, following verb [he *up* and left] —*vt.* [Informal] **1** to put up, lift up, or take up **2** to bring to a higher level or cause to rise [to *up* prices] **3** to raise (a preceding bet or an ante) —**it's all up with** [Informal] there is no further hope for; the end is near for —☆**on the up and up 1** [Informal] open and aboveboard; honest **2** [Chiefly Brit.] rising or improving steadily; prospering —☆**up against** [Informal] face to face with; confronted with —☆**up against it** [Informal] in difficulty; esp., in financial difficulty —**up and around (***or* **about)** out of bed and resuming one's normal activities, as after an illness —**up and doing** busy; active —**up for 1** presented or considered for (an elective office, an election, sale, auction, etc.) **2** before a court on (trial) or for (some charge) ☆**3** [Informal] willing to attend, take part in, etc. (an event, activity, etc.) —**up on (***or* **in)** [Informal] well-informed concerning —**ups and downs** good periods and bad periods —**up to 1** occupied with; doing; scheming; devising [*up to* no good] **2** equal to (a task, challenge, etc.); capable of (doing, undertaking, etc.) **3** as many as [*up to* four may play] **4** as far as [*up to* now; tall grass came *up to* his waist] ☆**5** dependent upon; incumbent upon [entirely *up to* her] —**up to one's ears (***or* **eyes** *or* **neck,** *etc.***)** [Informal] very deeply: said of involvement in work, debt, trouble, etc. —**up with!** give or restore power, favor, etc. to!

up² (up) *adv.* ⟦phonetic respelling of AP(IECE), infl. by prec.⟧ *Games, Sports* apiece; each: used to indicate a score just recently tied [the score is seven *up*]

UP *abbrev.* **1** University Press **2** UPPER PENINSULA

up- (up) ⟦ME < OE, identical with *up,* UP¹⟧ *combining form* up [*upbraid, upbringing*]

☆**up-and-com·ing** (up′ən kum′iŋ) *adj.* **1** enterprising, alert, and promising **2** gaining in importance or status

up-and-down (-doun′) *adj.* **1** going alternately up and down, to and fro, etc. **2** variable; fluctuating **3** vertical

U·pan·i·shad (o͞o pan′i shad′, o͞o pä′nə shäd′; yo͞o-) *n.* any of a group of late Vedic metaphysical treatises (**Upanishads**) dealing with humanity in relation to the universe

u·pas (yo͞o′pəs) *n.* ⟦short for Malay *pohon upas,* lit., poison tree (< Javanese *upas,* plant poison)⟧ **1** a tall Javanese tree (*Antiaris toxicaria*) of the mulberry family, whose whitish bark yields a poisonous, milky juice used as an arrow poison **2** the juice of this tree **3** something harmful or deadly in its influence

up·beat (up′bēt′; *for adj., also* up bēt′) *n.* **1** an upward trend; upswing **2** *Music a)* an unaccented beat, esp. when on the last note of a bar *b)* the upward stroke of a conductor's hand or baton indicating such a beat —*adj.* [Informal] lively; cheerful; optimistic

up-bow (up′bō′) *n.* **1** a stroke on a violin, cello, etc. in which the bow is drawn across the strings from the tip to the frog **2** a sign (v) indicating this

up·braid (up brād′) *vt.* ⟦ME *upbreiden* < OE *upbregdan* < *up-,* UP- + *bregdan,* to pull: see BRAID⟧ to rebuke severely or bitterly; censure sharply —*SYN.* SCOLD

up·bring·ing (up′briŋ′iŋ) *n.* ⟦ger. of obs. *upbring,* to rear, train (< ME *upbryngen:* see UP- & BRING)⟧ the training and education received while growing up; rearing; nurture

up·build (up bild′) *vt.* **-built′, -build′ing** to build up

UPC *abbrev.* Universal Product Code

up·cast (up′kast′) *n.* **1** something cast or thrown up **2** *Geol.* UPTHROW (sense 2) **3** *Mining* a ventilating shaft for returning air to the surface —*adj.* **1** thrown upward **2** directed upward

☆**up·chuck** (-chuk′) *vi., vt., n.* [Slang] VOMIT

up·com·ing (up′kum′iŋ, up kum′iŋ) *adj.* coming soon; forthcoming

up·coun·try (up′kun′trē; *for adj. and adv., also* up kun′trē) *adj.* of or located in the interior of a country; inland —*n.* the interior of a country —*adv.* ☆in or toward the interior of a country

up·court (up′kôrt′, up kôrt′) *adv., adj.* ☆*Basketball* into, toward, or in the opposite half of the court; downcourt

up·date (up dāt′; *also, and for n. always,* up′dāt′) *vt.* **-dat′ed, -dat′ing** to bring up to date; make conform to or aware of the most recent facts, methods, ideas, etc. —*n.* **1** an act or instance of updating **2** an updated account, report, etc.

Up·dike (up′dīk′), **John (Hoyer)** 1932-2009; U.S. writer

up·do (up′do͞o′) *n.* ⟦< UP¹ or UP(SWEPT) + (HAIR)DO⟧ a woman's hairstyle in which the hair is swept up in the back and held in place at the back or top of the head

up·draft (up′draft′) *n.* an upward air current

up·end (up end′) *vt., vi.* **1** to set, turn, or stand on end **2** to upset or topple

up·field (up′fēld′, up fēld′) *adv., adj. Football, Soccer, etc.* into, toward, or in the opposite end of the field, esp. the offensive end

up·front (up′frunt′) [Informal] *adj.* **1** very honest or forthright; open; candid **2** in or into the public eye; conspicuous [an *upfront* position] **3** invested, paid, etc., ahead of time; at the beginning [an *upfront* payment of $21,000] —*adv.* ahead of time; in advance [to pay for something *upfront*] Also **up′-front′** or **up front**

☆**up·grade** (up′grād′; *for v.* up grād′, up′grād′) *n.* **1** an upward slope, esp. in a road **2** an improvement in or enhancement of the condition, status, etc. of a person or thing **3** something that has been improved or enhanced —*adj., adv.* uphill; upward —*vt.* **-grad′ed, -grad′ing 1** to promote to a more skilled job at higher pay **2** to raise in importance, value, esteem, etc. —*vi.* to enhance or improve one's condition, status, capabilities, etc. —**on the upgrade** gaining in status, influence, health, etc.

up·growth (up′grōth′) *n.* **1** upward growth; rise or development **2** anything produced by this

up·heav·al (up hē′vəl) *n.* **1** a heaving up, as of part of the earth's crust by an earthquake **2** a sudden, violent change

up·heave (up hēv′) *vt.* **-heaved′, -heav′ing** to heave or lift up —*vi.* to rise as if forced up —**up·heav′er** *n.*

up·hill (up′hil′) *adv.* **1** toward the top of a hill or incline; upward **2** with difficulty; laboriously —*adj.* **1** going or sloping up; rising **2** calling for prolonged effort; laborious **3** located on high ground —*n.* a sloping rise or ascent

up·hold (up hōld′) *vt.* **-held′, -hold′ing 1** to hold up; raise **2** to keep from falling; support **3** to give moral or spiritual support or encouragement to **4** to decide in favor of; agree with and support against opposition; sustain —*SYN.* SUPPORT —**up·hold′er** *n.*

☆**up·hol·ster** (up hōl′stər) *vt.* ⟦back-form. < fol.⟧ to fit out (furniture, etc.) with covering material, padding, springs, etc.

up·hol·ster·er (-stər ər) *n.* ⟦altered < ME *upholdster,* altered < *upholder,* dealer in small or secondhand wares < *upholden,* to repair (< *up-,* UP- + *holden,* to keep, HOLD¹): see -STER⟧ a person whose business is upholstering furniture

up·hol·ster·y (-stər ē) *n., pl.* **-ster·ies** ⟦see prec. & -ERY⟧ **1** the fittings and material used in upholstering **2** the business or work of an upholsterer

UPI *abbrev.* United Press International

up·keep (up′kēp′) *n.* **1** the act of keeping up buildings, equipment, etc.; maintenance **2** the cost of this **3** state of repair

up·land (-lənd, -land′) *n.* land elevated above other land, as above land along a river —*adj.* of or situated in upland

☆**upland cotton** any of various, mostly short-staple, cottons (*Gossypium hirsutum*) of the U.S., China, etc.

☆**upland sandpiper** a large, short-billed sandpiper (*Bartramia longicauda*) found in the fields and uplands of the interior of North and South America: formerly called **upland plover**

up·lift (up lift′; *also, and for n. always,* up′lift′) *vt.* **1** to lift up, or elevate **2** to raise to a higher moral, social, or cultural level or condition —☆*n.* **1** the act or process of lifting up; elevation **2** *a)* the act or process of raising to a higher moral, social, or cultural level *b)* any influence, movement, etc. intended to improve society morally, culturally, etc. **3** a bra designed to lift and support the breasts **4** *Geol. a)* a raising of land above the surrounding area *b)* land so raised —**up·lift′er** *n.* —**up·lift′ment** *n.*

up·link (up′liŋk′) *n.* **1** an electronic link by which signals are sent from a transmitter on the earth's surface to an orbiting satellite, spacecraft, etc. **2** the site, facility, etc. from which such signals are transmitted —*vi.* to connect to a satellite, spacecraft, etc. using such a link —*vt.* to send (signals, data, etc.) using such a link Cf. DOWNLINK

up·load (up′lōd′) *vt., vi.* to transfer electronically (a copy of a file or program) from a terminal, personal computer, etc. to a central computer, bulletin board, etc.: distinguished from DOWNLOAD

up·man·ship (up′mən ship′) *n.* [Informal] *short for* ONE-UPMANSHIP

up·mar·ket (up′mär′kit) *adj.* UPSCALE

up·most (up′mōst′) *adj.* [Informal] UPPERMOST

U·po·lu (o͞o pō′lo͞o) smaller of the two main islands of the country of Samoa: 432 sq mi (1,119 sq km)

up·on (ə pän′, ə pôn′) *prep.* ⟦ME < *up,* UP¹ + *on,* ON, prob. infl. by ON *upp á* (< *upp,* upward + *á,* on)⟧ ON (in various senses), or up and on: *on* and *upon* are generally interchangeable, the choice being governed by idiom, sentence rhythm, etc. —*adv.* **1** on: used only for completing a verb [a canvas not painted *upon*] **2** [Obs.] on it; on one's person **3** [Obs.] thereupon; thereafter

up-or-down (up′ər doun′) *adj.* ⟦< *up,* yea & *down,* nay⟧ ☆designating or of a direct vote by members of a legislative body on a bill or nominee, esp. when such a vote is intended to bypass procedural delays or amendment: also written **up or down**

up·per (up′ər) *adj.* ⟦ME, compar. of *up*, UP[1]⟧ 1 in a place or on a level above another *[upper* lip, *upper* jaw, *upper* floor*]* 2 higher in rank, authority, or dignity *[*the *upper* classes*]* 3 being farther north, farther inland, or at a higher elevation of land *[*the *upper* St. Lawrence*]* 4 [**U-**] *Archaeol., Geol.* more recent; later: used of a division of a period *[Upper* Cambrian, *Upper* Paleolithic*]* —*n.* 1 the part of a shoe or boot above the sole ☆2 [Informal] an upper berth, as in a Pullman car 3 [*pl.*] [Informal] the upper teeth or dentures 4 [Slang] any drug containing a stimulant; esp., an amphetamine —☆**on one's uppers** [Informal] in need or want: with reference to wearing shoes with worn-out soles

upper bound *Math.* a number that is greater than or equal to any number in a set

Upper Canada *former name* (1791-1841) *for* ONTARIO, Canada

up·per·case (up′ər kās′) *n.* ⟦from their being kept traditionally in the *upper case* (of two cases of type)⟧ capital-letter type or writing, as distinguished from small letters (*lowercase*): see CAPITAL LETTER —*adj.* designating, of, or in uppercase; capital —*vt.* **-cased′**, **-cas′ing** to print in or change to uppercase

upper class the social class above the middle class; rich, socially prominent, or aristocratic class —**up′per-class′** *adj.*

☆**up·per·class·man** (up′ər klas′mən) *n., pl.* **-men** (-mən) a student in the junior or senior class of a high school or college

upper crust ☆[Informal] UPPER CLASS

up·per·cut (up′ər kut′) *n. Boxing* a short, swinging blow directed upward, as to the chin — *vt., vi.* **-cut′**, **-cut′ting** to hit with an uppercut

upper hand the position of advantage or control

upper house [*often* **U- H-**] in a legislature having two branches, that branch which is usually smaller and less representative, as the Senate of the U.S. Congress

up·per·most (up′ər mōst′) *adj.* highest in place, position, power, authority, influence, etc.; topmost; predominant; foremost —*adv.* in the highest place, position, rank, etc.

Upper Peninsula NW section of Mich., a peninsula separated from the rest of the state by the Straits of Mackinac: 16,538 sq mi (42,833 sq km)

Upper Vol·ta (väl′tə, vôl′-, vōl′-) *former name for* BURKINA FASO

up·pish (up′ish) *adj.* ⟦< UP[1] + -ISH⟧ [Informal] *Brit. var. of* UPPITY —**up′pish·ly** *adv.* —**up′pish·ness** *n.*

☆**up·pi·ty** (-ə tē) *adj.* [Informal] 1 inclined to be haughty, arrogant, snobbish, etc. 2 behaving in a way regarded as above one's rightful station or class: a dismissive or disparaging term —**up′pi·ty·ness** *n.*

Upp·sa·la (up′sə lə, ʊop′-; -sä lä′, -sä′lä) city in EC Sweden: also sp. **Up′sa·la**

up quark *Particle Physics* a type of quark with a mass of *c.* 0.002 to 0.008 GeV/c², a positive charge that is ⅔ that of an electron, zero charm, and zero strangeness: see FLAVOR (sense 5)

up·raise (up rāz′) *vt.* **-raised′**, **-rais′ing** to raise up; lift

up·rear (-rir′) *vt.* 1 to lift up 2 to erect; build 3 to elevate in dignity; exalt 4 to bring up; rear —*vi.* to rise up

up·right (up′rīt′; *for adj. and adv., also* up rīt′) *adj.* ⟦ME < OE *upriht*: see UP[1] & RIGHT⟧ 1 standing, pointing, or directed straight up; in a vertical or perpendicular position; erect 2 honest and just; honorable —*adv.* in an upright position or direction —*n.* 1 the state of being upright or vertical 2 something having an upright position; vertical part or member 3 *short for: a)* UPRIGHT BASS *b)* UPRIGHT PIANO ☆4 *a) Football* either of the two vertical parts extending up from the crossbar of a goal post *b)* one of the two standards supporting the crossbar in the high jump or pole vault —**up′right′ly** *adv.* —**up′right′ness** *n.*

upright bass DOUBLE BASS

upright piano a piano with strings set vertically in a rectangular body

up·rise (up rīz′; *for n.* up′rīz′) *vi.* **-rose′**, **-ris′en**, **-ris′ing** 1 to get up; rise 2 to move or slope upward; ascend 3 to rise into view, being, or activity 4 to be or become erect or upright 5 to increase in size, volume, etc.; swell, as sound 6 to rise in revolt —*n.* 1 the act or process of rising up 2 an upward slope or ascent

up·ris·ing (up′rī′ziŋ) *n.* 1 the action of rising up; specif., an outbreak against a government; revolt 2 an upward slope or ascent

up·riv·er (up′riv′ər) *adv., adj.* toward the source of a river; in the direction against the current of a river

up·roar (-rôr′) *n.* ⟦Du *oproer*, a stirring up (akin to Ger *aufruhr*) < *op*, up + *roeren*, to stir (akin to OE *hreran* < IE base **kere-*, to mix, stir up): form and sense infl. by ROAR⟧ 1 violent disturbance or commotion, esp. one accompanied by loud, confused noise, as of shouting; tumult 2 loud, confused noise; din —**SYN.** NOISE

up·roar·i·ous (up rôr′ē əs) *adj.* 1 making, or characterized by, an uproar; tumultuous 2 *a)* loud and boisterous, as laughter *b)* causing such laughter *[*an *uproarious* joke*]* —**up·roar′i·ous·ly** *adv.* —**up·roar′i·ous·ness** *n.*

up·root (up ro͞ot′) *vt.* 1 to tear up by the roots 2 to destroy or remove utterly; eradicate 3 to remove or force from home or native land

up·rouse (-rouz′) *vt.* **-roused′**, **-rous′ing** to rouse; stir up

UPS *service mark* United Parcel Service

up·sa·dai·sy (up′sə dā′zē) *interj. var. of* UPSY-DAISY

☆**up·scale** (up′skāl′) *adj.* designating, of, or for people who are relatively affluent, educated, stylish, etc. —*vt.* **-scaled′**, **-scal′ing** to convert or transform so as to make suitable for such people *[*a used clothing store *upscaled* to a boutique*]*

up·set (up set′; *for n. always, and for adj. also,* up′set′) *vt.* **-set′**, **-set′ting** ⟦ME *upsetten*: see UP[1] & SET⟧ 1 [Obs.] to set up; erect 2 *a)* to tip over; overturn *[*to *upset* a vase*]* *b)* to overthrow or defeat unexpectedly 3 *a)* to disturb the functioning, fulfillment, or completion of *[*to *upset* a busy schedule*]* *b)* to disturb mentally or emotionally *[upset* by bad news*]* *c)* to disturb physically; make sick *[*to *upset* the stomach*]* 4 *Mech. a)* to shorten and thicken (a red-hot iron) by beating on the end *b)* to shorten (a metal tire) in the process of resetting it —*vi.* to become overturned or upset —*n.* 1 an upsetting or being upset; specif., *a)* a tipping over, knocking over, etc. *b)* an unexpected victory or defeat *c)* a disturbance or disorder, specif. of an emotional or physical nature 2 *Mech. a)* a swage used for upsetting *b)* an upset piece or part —*adj.* 1 [Rare] set up; erected 2 *a)* tipped over; overturned *b)* disturbed or disordered —**up·set′ter** *n.* —**up·set′ting·ly** *adv.*

SYN.—**upset** is the ordinary word implying a toppling, disorganization, etc. as a result of a loss of balance or stability *[*to *upset* a glass, one's plans, etc.; emotionally *upset]*; **overturn** implies a turning of a thing upside down or flat on its side and, in extended use, connotes the destruction of something established *[*to *overturn* a chair, a government, etc.*]*; **capsize** specifically implies the overturning or upsetting of a boat

upset price the price fixed as the minimum at which something will be sold at an auction

up·shift (up′shift′) *vi.* to shift the transmission of a motor vehicle to a higher gear or arrangement —*n.* an act of shifting gears in this way

up·shot (up′shät′) *n.* ⟦orig., the final shot in an archery match⟧ the conclusion; result; outcome

up·side[1] (up′sīd′) *prep.* [Chiefly Dial.] on or against the side of: mainly in the phrase **upside the (or someone's) head**

up·side[2] (up′sīd′) *n.* 1 the upper side or part 2 appreciation or gain, as on an investment: often used attributively 3 any or all of the benefits or advantages

upside down ⟦ME *up so doun*, lit., up as if down: altered by folk etym.⟧ 1 with the top side or part underneath or turned over; inverted 2 in disorder; topsy-turvy —**up′side′-down′** *adj.*

☆**upside-down cake** a cake baked with a bottom layer of fruit and turned upside down before serving

up·si·lon (o͞op′sə län′, up′-) *n.* ⟦LGr *y psilon*, lit., simple *u* (to distinguish from *oi*, of the same sound in LGr)⟧ 1 the twentieth letter of the Greek alphabet (Υ, υ) ☆2 any of a group of short-lived elementary particles having a mass about ten times greater than that of a proton

up·spring (up spriŋ′; *for n.,* up′spriŋ′) *vi.* **-sprang′** or **-sprung′**, **-sprung′**, **-spring′ing** to spring up (in various senses) —*n.* a spring upward

up·stage (up′stāj′; *for v.,* up stāj′) *adv.* toward or at the rear of a stage —*adj.* 1 of or having to do with the rear of a stage 2 haughtily or disdainfully aloof —*vt.* **-staged′**, **-stag′ing** 1 to draw the attention of the audience away from (a fellow actor) and to oneself by moving upstage so that the other actor must face away from the audience 2 to draw attention to oneself at the expense of (another)

up·stairs (up′sterz′) *adv.* 1 up the stairs 2 on or to an upper floor or higher level 3 [Informal] mentally; in the mind *[*a person who lacks something *upstairs]* —*adj.* situated on an upper floor —*n.* an upper floor or floors

up·stand·ing (up′stan′diŋ) *adj.* 1 standing straight; erect 2 upright in character and behavior; honorable

up·start[1] (up′stärt′) *n.* a person who has recently come into wealth, power, etc., esp. one who behaves in a presumptuous, aggressive manner; parvenu —*adj.* 1 newly rich, powerful, etc. 2 of or characteristic of an upstart

up·start[2] (up stärt′) *vi., vt.* to start, or spring, up or cause to spring up

☆**up·state** (up′stāt′; *for adj. and adv.* up′stāt′) *n.* that part of a state farther to the north or away from a large city; specif., the N part of New York —*adj., adv.* in, to, or from upstate —**up′stat′er** *n.*

up·stream (up′strēm′, -strēm′) *adv., adj.* 1 in the direction against the current of a stream 2 at or toward the beginning of some process, course of activity, etc.

up·stretched (up strecht′, up′strecht′) *adj.* stretched upward

up·stroke (up′strōk′) *n.* 1 an upward stroke or movement 2 a line, brush mark, etc. made with an upward stroke

up·surge (up surj′; *for n.* up′surj′) *vi.* **-surged′**, **-surg′ing** to surge up —*n.* a surge upward

up·sweep (up′swēp′; *for v.* up swēp′) *n.* 1 a sweep or curve upward 2 an upswept hairdo — *vt., vi.* **-swept′**, **-sweep′ing** to sweep or curve upward

up·swell (up swel′) *vi.* **-swelled′**, **-swelled′** or **-swol′len**, **-swell′ing** to swell up; increase; expand

up·swept (up swept′; *for adj.* up′swept′) *vt., vi. pt. & pp. of* UPSWEEP —*adj.* 1 curved or sloped upward 2 designating or of a style of hairdo in which the hair is combed up in the back and piled on the top of the head

up·swing (up′swiŋ′; *for v.* up swiŋ′) *n.* a swing, trend, or movement upward; specif., an upward trend in business —*vi.* **-swung′**, **-swing′ing** 1 to swing or move upward 2 to advance or improve

up·sy-dai·sy (up′sə dā′zē, up′sē-) *interj.* ⟦baby-talk extension of UP[1]⟧ up you go: used playfully or for reassurance, as in lifting a small child

up·take (up′tāk′) *n.* 1 the act of taking up; a drawing up, absorbing, etc. 2 *a)* a pipe carrying smoke and gases from a furnace to its chimney *b)* a ventilating shaft or pipe —☆**quick (or slow) on the uptake** [Informal] quick (or slow) to understand or comprehend

up·tem·po (up′tem′pō) ***adj., adv.*** in or at a fast tempo

up·throw (-thrō′) ***n.*** **1** a throwing up; upheaval **2** *Geol.* that side of a fault which has moved upward relative to the other side

up·thrust (-thrust′) ***n.*** **1** an upward push or thrust **2** *Geol.* an upheaval of a part of the earth's crust

☆**up·tick** (-tik′) ***n.*** ⟦UP- + TICK[1] (see TICKER, sense *a*)⟧ **1** a stock transaction at a price higher than that of the preceding transaction **2** an increase or upturn; rise

☆**up·tight** (up′tīt′) ***adj.*** [Slang] **1** very tense, nervous, anxious, etc. **2** overly conventional or strict Also written **up-tight**

up·tilt (up tilt′) ***vt.*** to tilt up

up·time (up′tīm′) ***n.*** the time during which a machine, as a computer, is UP[1] (*adj.* 11), or functioning properly

up-to-date (up′tə dāt′) ***adj.*** **1** extending to the present time; using or including the latest facts, ideas, etc. **2** keeping up with what is most recent in style, taste, information, etc. —**up′-to-date′ness *n.***

up·town (up′toun′) ***adj., adv.*** **1** of, in, like, to, or toward the upper part of a city or town, usually the part away from the main business district **2** of, in, to, or toward the central part or business district of a town: a rural and small-town usage **3** of or characteristic of the more affluent section of a city, or in the manner of its residents —***n.*** ☆**1** the uptown, usually residential, section of a city or town **2** the central part or business district of a town: a rural and small-town usage

up·trend (up′trend′) ***n.*** an upward trend, esp. a financial one

up·turn (up turn′; *for n.* up′turn′) ***vt., vi.*** to turn up, upward, or over —***n.*** an upward turn, curve, or trend —**up′turned′ *adj.***

up·ward (up′wərd) ***adv., adj.*** ⟦ME < OE *upweard:* see UP[1] & -WARD⟧ **1** toward a higher place, position, degree, amount, etc. **2** on into future years or later life **3** beyond (an indicated price, amount, etc.) [tickets cost two dollars and *upward*] Also **up′wards *adv.*** —**upwards** (or **upward**) **of** more than —**up′ward·ly *adv.***

☆**upward mobility** movement from a lower to a higher social and economic status

up·well (up wel′) ***vi.*** to well up; flow upward

up·well·ing (up′wel′iŋ) ***n.*** an upward flow or current of water; esp., a rising, cold, nutrient-rich, coastal ocean current that attracts fish

up·wind (up′wind′) ***adv., adj.*** in the direction from which the wind is blowing or usually blows

Ur (oor, ur) ancient Sumerian city on the Euphrates River, in what is now S Iraq

ur-[1] or **Ur-** (oor) ⟦Ger: akin to Goth *us,* ON *ōr,* out of, from, OE *or-,* early⟧ *prefix* original, primitive

ur-[2] *combining form* URO-[1]: used before a vowel

ur-[3] *combining form* URO-[2]: used before a vowel

u·ra·cil (yoor′ə sil′) ***n.*** ⟦UR(O)- + AC(ETIC) + -IL⟧ a colorless, crystalline, pyrimidine base, $C_4H_4N_2O_2$, that occurs as a constituent of RNA

u·rae·us (yoo rē′əs) ***n., pl.*** **-rae′i′** (-ī′) ⟦ModL < LGr *ouraios,* cobra < Egypt *y'rt:* form infl. by Gr *ouraios,* of the tail < *oura,* tail: see URO-[2]⟧ the figure of the sacred asp or cobra on the headdress of ancient Egyptian rulers

uraeus

U·ral (yoor′əl) *see* URAL MOUNTAINS, URAL RIVER

U·ral-Al·ta·ic (-al tā′ik) ***n.*** a proposed language grouping that contains all the Uralic and Altaic languages —***adj.*** designating or of this group of languages

U·ral·ic (yoo ral′ik, -rā′lik) ***n.*** ⟦URAL + -IC⟧ a family of languages of N and E Europe and N Asia, consisting of the Finno-Ugric languages and the Samoyed languages —***adj.*** designating or of these languages, the peoples that speak them, or their cultures: also **U·ra′li·an** (-rā′lē ən)

u·ral·ite (yoor′ə līt′) ***n.*** ⟦Ger *uralit* < *Ural,* URAL + *-it,* -ITE[1]⟧ a green, usually fibrous, variety of hornblende or actinolite

U·ral Mountains mountain system in Russia, extending from the Arctic Ocean south to the N border of Kazakhstan: traditionally regarded as the boundary between Europe & Asia: highest peak, *c.* 6,180 ft (1,884 m): also **Urals**

Ural River river flowing from the S section of the Urals into the N end of the Caspian Sea: 1,575 mi (2,535 km)

U·ra·ni·a (yoo rā′nē ə) ***n.*** ⟦L < Gr *Ourania,* lit., the heavenly one < *Ouranos,* URANUS⟧ *Gr. Myth.* the Muse of astronomy

U·ra·ni·an (-ən) ***adj.*** of Uranus

u·ran·ic[1] (yoo ran′ik) ***adj.*** ⟦< Gr *ouranos,* sky, URANUS + -IC⟧ [Obs.] celestial; astronomical

u·ran·ic[2] (yoo ran′ik, -rā′nik) ***adj.*** ⟦URAN(IUM) + -IC⟧ of or containing uranium, esp. in its higher valence

u·ra·nide (yoor′ə nīd′) ***n.*** any of the transuranic elements

u·ra·ni·nite (yoo rā′nə nīt′, -ran′ə-) ***n.*** ⟦< fol. + -IN[1] + -ITE[1]⟧ a hard, very heavy, dark-colored, radioactive mineral, UO_2, the chief ore of uranium; uranium oxide: cf. PITCHBLENDE

u·ra·ni·um (yoo rā′nē əm) ***n.*** ⟦ModL: so named (1789) by M. H. Klaproth (see TELLURIUM), its discoverer, after URANUS, recently (1781) discovered planet + -IUM⟧ a very hard, heavy, silver-colored, radioactive, metallic chemical element, one of the actinides, found only in combination, chiefly in pitchblende: symbol, U; at. no. 92: an isotope (**uranium-235**) undergoes neutron-induced fission and another, more plentiful, isotope (**uranium-238**) is used to produce plutonium: see the periodic table of elements in the Reference Supplement

u·ra·nog·ra·phy (yoor′ə näg′rə fē) ***n.*** ⟦Gr *ouranographia* < *ouranos,* heaven, URANUS + *graphein,* to write: see GRAPHIC⟧ the branch of astronomy dealing with the description of the heavens and the mapping of the stars —**u′ra·nog′ra·pher *n.*** —**u·ra·no·graph·ic** (yoor′ə nə graf′ik) ***adj.,*** **u′ra·no·graph′i·cal**

u·ra·nol·o·gy (-näl′ə jē) ***n.*** ⟦< Gr *ouranos,* heaven, URANUS + -LOGY⟧ *former term for* ASTRONOMY

u·ra·nous (yoo rān′əs, yoor′ə nəs) ***adj.*** ⟦URAN(IUM) + -OUS⟧ of or containing uranium, esp. in its lower valence

U·ra·nus (yoor′ə nəs, yoo rā′-) ***n.*** ⟦LL < Gr *Ouranos,* lit., heaven⟧ **1** *Gr. Myth.* a god who is the personification of the heavens, the son and husband of Gaea (Earth) and father of the Titans, Furies, and Cyclopes: he is overthrown by his son Cronus (Saturn) **2** ⟦ModL⟧ the third largest planet of the solar system and the seventh in distance from the sun: it has a system of thin rings around the equator: diameter, *c.* 51,120 km (*c.* 31,770 mi); period of revolution, *c.* 84.01 earth years; period of rotation (retrograde), *c.* 17.24 hours around an axis tilted 98° to its orbital plane; 27 satellites; symbol, ⛢

u·ra·nyl (yoor′ə nil′) ***n.*** ⟦URAN(IUM) + -YL⟧ the divalent radical UO_2, present in many compounds of uranium

u·rate (yoor′āt) ***n.*** a salt of uric acid

U·ra·wa (oo rä′wä) city in EC Honshu, Japan, north of Tokyo

ur·ban (ur′bən) ***adj.*** ⟦L *urbanus* < *urbs,* city⟧ **1** of, in, constituting, or comprising a city or town **2** characteristic of the city as distinguished from the country; citified ☆**3** in U.S. census use, designating or of an incorporated or unincorporated place with at least 50,000 inhabitants **4** of or characteristic of the styles and culture of the inner city, esp. of the black inner city [*urban* music, fashions, etc.]

Ur·ban II (ur′bən) 1042?-99; pope (1088-99)

ur·bane (ur bān′) ***adj.*** ⟦L *urbanus:* see URBAN⟧ polite and courteous in a smooth, polished way; refined —**SYN.** SUAVE —**ur·bane′ly *adv.*** —**ur·bane′ness *n.***

ur·ban·ism (ur′bə niz′əm) ***n.*** **1** *a)* the character of life in the cities; urban life, organization, problems, etc. *b)* the study of this **2** movement of the population to, or concentration of the population in, the cities —**ur′ban·ist *n., adj.*** —**ur′ban·is′tic *adj.***

ur·ban·ite (-nīt′) ***n.*** a person living in a city

ur·ban·i·ty (ur ban′ə tē) ***n.*** **1** the quality of being urbane **2** *pl.* **-ties** [*pl.*] civilities, courtesies, or amenities

ur·ban·ize (ur′bə nīz′) ***vt.*** **-ized′, -iz′ing 1** to change from rural to urban in character; make like or characteristic of a city **2** [Rare] to make urbane —**ur′ban·i·za′tion *n.***

ur·ban·ized (-nīzd′) ***adj.*** made urban in character

☆**urban legend** (*or* **myth**) a purportedly true, typically sensational, incident or phenomenon about which various secondhand accounts or anecdotes widely circulate: urban legends are characteristically untrue or unverifiable

☆**ur·ban·ol·o·gist** (ur′bə näl′ə jist) ***n.*** ⟦URBAN + -O- + -LOG(Y) + -IST[1]⟧ a student of, or specialist in, urban problems —**ur′ban·ol′o·gy *n.***

urban planning the study or profession dealing with the growth and functioning of cities and towns, including environmental concerns, zoning, the infrastructure, etc. —**urban planner**

☆**urban renewal** rehabilitation of deteriorated or distressed urban areas, as by slum clearance and redevelopment construction in housing and public facilities

☆**urban sprawl** the spread of urban congestion into adjoining suburbs and rural areas

ur·bi·a (ur′bē ə) ***n.*** ⟦ModL < L *urbs,* city + -IA⟧ cities collectively, as distinguished from suburbs (*suburbia*) and exurbs (*exurbia*)

ur·bi et or·bi (oor′bē et ôr′bē) ⟦L⟧ to the city (Rome) and to the world: said of certain special papal blessings

ur·ce·o·late (ur′sē ə lit, -lāt′) ***adj.*** ⟦ModL *urceolatus* < L *urceolus,* dim. of *urceus,* vase⟧ shaped like a vase or urn

ur·chin (ur′chin) ***n.*** ⟦ME *irchoun* < OFr *heriçun* < L *ericius,* hedgehog < *er,* hedgehog, for earlier **her* < IE base **ĝher-,* to bristle, be stiff > L *horrere,* to bristle, Gr *chēr,* porcupine⟧ **1** [Archaic] a hedgehog **2** SEA URCHIN **3** a child who is poor, ragged, etc. and, often, mischievous or undisciplined **4** [Obs.] an elf

urd (urd) ***n.*** ⟦Hindi⟧ a hairy annual bean (*Vigna mungo*) of the pea family, with small, black, edible seeds

Ur·du (oor′doo, yoor′dē ə) ***n.*** ⟦Hindi *urdū,* short for *zabān-i-urdū,* language of the camp < Pers *urdu,* camp < Turk *ordū:* see HORDE⟧ an Indo-Aryan language of Pakistan and N India, having the same basic grammar as Hindi but containing many words derived from Persian and Arabic: it is written in Arabic characters and is the official language of Pakistan

-ure (ər) ⟦Fr < L *-ura*⟧ *suffix* **1** act, process, or result [*exposure*] **2** agent, instrument, or scope of **3** state of being ___ed [*composure*] **4** office, rank, or collective body [*legislature*]

u·re·a (yoo rē′ə, yoor′ē ə) ***n.*** ⟦ModL < Fr *urée* < Gr *ouron,* URINE⟧ a highly soluble, crystalline solid, $CO(NH_2)_2$, found in the urine and other bodily fluids of mammals or produced synthetically: used in making plastics, fertilizer, adhesives, etc. —**u·re′al *adj.,*** **u·re′ic**

u·re·a-form·al·de·hyde resin (-fôr mal′də hīd′) any of a class of strong, odorless, thermosetting resins formed by condensing urea and formaldehyde in the presence of a catalyst: used in making buttons, tableware, etc.

u·re·ase (yoor′ē ās′, -āz′) *n.* ⟦UREA + -ASE⟧ an enzyme that catalyzes the hydrolysis of urea into ammonia and carbon dioxide or ammonium carbonate
u·re·din·i·um (yoo͞r′ə din′ē əm) *n., pl.* **-i·a** (-ə) ⟦ModL < L *uredo* (gen. *uredinis*), blight: see fol. & -IUM⟧ *Bot.* a pustule, often found on the epidermis of grasses, formed by a rust fungus and consisting of uredospores: also **u·re·di·um** (yoo rē′dē əm) —**u′re·din′i·al** *adj.*
u·re·do (yoo rē′dō) *n.* ⟦ModL < L, a blight, blast, burning itch < *urere*, to burn < IE base **eus*, to burn⟧ *former term for* URTICARIA
u·re·do·spore (yoo rē′də spôr′) *n.* ⟦L *uredo* (see prec.) + SPORE⟧ *Bot.* a thin-walled, red, summer spore of a rust fungus, produced usually on the leaves or stems of grasses and capable of reinfecting other grasses of the same species: also **u·re′di·o·spore′** (-dē ō spôr′)
u·re·ide (yoor′ē īd′, -id) *n.* ⟦UREA + -IDE⟧ any of several compounds derived from urea by the replacement of one or more hydrogen atoms by an acid radical
u·re·mi·a (yoo rē′mē ə) *n.* ⟦ModL < Gr *ouron*, URINE + *haima*, blood⟧ a toxic condition caused by the presence in the blood of waste products that are not being eliminated in the urine because of a failure of the kidneys to secrete urine —**u·re′mic** *adj.*
u·re·o·tel·ic (yoo rē′ə tel′ik, yoor′ē ə-) *adj.* ⟦< UREA + TELIC⟧ designating those animals, as mammals or fish, that excrete most of their waste nitrogen in the form of urea in the urine: cf. URICOTELIC
-u·ret (yo͞o ret′) ⟦< ModL *-uretum* (replacing earlier -URE)⟧ *obsolete suffix* -IDE
u·re·ter (yoo rēt′ər) *n.* ⟦ModL < Gr *ourētēr* < *ourein*, to urinate < *ouron*: see URINE⟧ a duct or tube that carries urine from a kidney to the bladder or cloaca: see KIDNEY, illus. —**u·re′ter·al** *adj.*, **ure·ter·ic** (yoor′ə ter′ik)
u·re·ter·o- (yoo rēt′ər ō′, -ə) ⟦< prec.⟧ *combining form* ureter *[ureterostomy]*: also, before a vowel, **u·re·ter-** (yo͞o rēt′ər)
u·re·ter·os·to·my (yoo rēt′ər äs′tə mē) *n., pl.* **-mies** ⟦prec. + -STOMY⟧ the surgical creation of an artificial opening for the direct discharge of urine from the ureter
u·re·thane (yoor′ə thān′) *n.* ⟦Fr *uréthane* < *urée*, UREA + *éther* (< L *aether*: see ETHER) + *-ane*, -ANE⟧ **1** a white, crystalline compound, $C_3H_7NO_2$, produced by the action of ammonia on ethyl carbonate or by heating urea nitrate and ethyl alcohol: it is used as a hypnotic and sedative, a solvent, etc. **2** any ester of carbamic acid Also **u′re·than′** (-than′)
urethr- *combining form* URETHRO-: used before a vowel
u·re·thra (yoo rē′thrə) *n., pl.* **-thrae** (-thrē′) or **-thras** ⟦LL < Gr *ourēthra* < *ouron*, URINE⟧ the duct through which urine is discharged from the bladder in most mammals: in the male, semen is also discharged through the urethra —**u·re′thral** *adj.*
u·re·thri·tis (yoor′ə thrīt′is) *n.* ⟦ModL: see prec. & -ITIS⟧ inflammation of the urethra
u·re·thro- (yoo rē′thrō, -thrə) ⟦< URETHRA⟧ *combining form* urethra *[urethroscope]*
u·re·thro·scope (yoo rē′thrə skōp′) *n.* ⟦prec. + -SCOPE⟧ an instrument for examining the interior of the urethra —**u·re′thro·scop′ic** (-skäp′ik) *adj.*
u·ret·ic (yoo ret′ik) *adj.* ⟦LL *ureticus* < Gr *ourētikos*⟧ **1** of the urine; urinary **2** DIURETIC
U·rey (yoor′ē), **Harold Clay·ton** (klāt′'n) 1893-1981; U.S. chemist
Ur·fa (o͝or′fä) *var. of* ŞANLIURFA
urge (urj) *vt.* **urged, urg′ing** ⟦L *urgere*, to press hard: see WREAK⟧ **1** *a)* to press upon the attention; present or speak of earnestly and repeatedly; plead, allege, or advocate strongly *[to urge caution]* *b)* to entreat or plead with; ask, persuade, or solicit earnestly; press; exhort **2** to stimulate or incite; provoke **3** to drive or force onward; press forward; impel —*vi.* **1** to make an earnest presentation of arguments, claims, charges, entreaties, etc. **2** to exert a force that drives or impels, as to action —*n.* **1** the act of urging **2** an impulse to do a certain thing; impelling influence or force, esp. an inner drive —**urg′er** *n.*

SYN.—**urge** implies a strong effort to persuade someone to do something, as by entreaty, argument, or forceful recommendation *[he urged us to leave]*; **exhort** implies an earnest urging or admonishing to action or conduct considered proper or right *[the minister exhorted his flock to work for peace]*; **press** suggests a continuous, insistent urging that is difficult to resist *[we pressed her to stay]*; **importune** implies persistent efforts to break down resistance against a demand or request, often to the point of being annoying or wearisome *[too proud to importune for help]*

ur·gen·cy (ur′jən sē) *n., pl.* **-cies** **1** the quality or state of being urgent; need for action, haste, etc.; stress or pressure, as of necessity **2** insistence; importunity **3** something urgent
ur·gent (-jənt) *adj.* ⟦LME < MFr < L *urgens*, prp. of *urgere*, to press hard, urge⟧ **1** calling for haste, immediate action, etc.; grave; pressing **2** insistent; importunate —**ur′gent·ly** *adv.*
urgent care outpatient care available, as at a facility specializing in such care, to those with conditions regarded as not life-threatening but requiring immediate attention
-ur·gy (ər jē) ⟦Gr *-ourgia* < *-ourgos*, worker < *ergon*, WORK⟧ *combining form* the science, technique, or process of working with or by means of (something specified) *[zymurgy, chemurgy]*
U·ri (o͞o′rē) canton of EC Switzerland: 416 sq mi (1,077 sq km)
URI *abbrev.* upper respiratory infection
-u·ri·a (yoor′ē ə) ⟦ModL < Gr *-ouria* < *ouron*, URINE⟧ *combining form* a condition of the urine, esp. one related to a disease, often indicated by the presence of a (specified) substance in the urine *[glycosuria, albuminuria]*
U·ri·ah (yoo rī′ə) *n.* ⟦Heb *uriya*, lit., God is light < *or*, light, brightness (akin to *ur*, fire) + *ya*, Jehovah⟧ **1** a masculine name **2** *Bible* a Hittite captain whose beautiful wife, BATHSHEBA, David lusted after: David arranged for Uriah to die in battle: 2 Sam. 11
u·ric (yoor′ik) *adj.* ⟦Fr *urique* < *urine* + *-ique*, -IC⟧ of, contained in, or derived from urine
uric acid a white, odorless, crystalline substance, $C_5H_4N_4O_3$, found in urine, in the excreta of birds and reptiles, etc.: it is slightly soluble in water
u·ri·co- (yoor′i kō, -kə) ⟦< URIC⟧ *combining form* uric acid *[uricosuric]*: also, before a vowel, **u·ric-** (yoor′ik)
u·ri·co·su·ric (yoor′i kō syoor′ik) *adj.* ⟦prec. + *-s-* + URIC⟧ increasing or promoting the urinary excretion of uric acid
u·ri·co·tel·ic (-tel′ik) *adj.* designating those animals, as reptiles or birds, that excrete most of their waste nitrogen in the form of uric acid, usually in the urine: cf. UREOTELIC
u·ri·dine (yoor′ə dēn′) *n.* ⟦UR(O)- + -ID(E) + -INE[3]⟧ a nucleoside, $C_9H_{12}N_2O_6$, formed from uracil and ribose and found in RNA
U·ri·el (yoor′ē əl) *n.* ⟦Heb *uriel*, lit., light of God < *or*, light (see URIAH) + *el*, God⟧ in angelology and literature, a principal angel or archangel
U·rim and Thum·mim (yoor′im and thum′im) ⟦Heb *ūrīm b'tummīm*⟧ *Bible* certain unidentified objects on the breastplate of the high priest: Ex. 28:30
urin- *combining form* URINO-: used before a vowel
u·ri·nal (yoor′ə nəl; *Brit* yoo rī′nəl) *n.* ⟦OFr < LL < *urinalis*, of urine < *urina*, URINE⟧ **1** a portable receptacle used for urinating, esp. by the bedridden **2** *a)* a plumbing fixture for use by men in urinating, esp. one installed in a men's restroom *b)* a room, small building, etc. equipped with such fixtures
☆**u·ri·nal·y·sis** (yoor′ə nal′ə sis) *n., pl.* **-ses′** (-sēz′) ⟦ModL < URIN(O)- + (AN)ALYSIS⟧ a physical, chemical, or microscopic analysis of a urine sample
u·ri·nar·y (yoor′ə ner′ē) *adj.* ⟦< L *urina*, URINE + -ARY⟧ **1** of or relating to urine **2** of the organs involved in the secretion and discharge of urine
urinary bladder a saclike structure in many animals, serving for temporary storage of fluid or semifluid excretions, as urine
urinary tubule any of the long, winding tubules of the vertebrate kidney in which urine is formed: also called **uriniferous tubule**
u·ri·nate (yoor′ə nāt′) *vi.* **-nat′ed, -nat′ing** ⟦< ML *urinatus*, pp. of *urinare*⟧ to discharge urine from the body; micturate —*vt.* to discharge as or with the urine —**u′ri·na′tion** *n.* —**u′ri·na′tive** *adj.*
u·rine (yoor′in) *n.* ⟦OFr < L *urina*, urine < IE **ūr-*, var. of base **awer-*, to moisten, flow > WATER, Gr *ouron*, urine⟧ a waste product of vertebrates and many invertebrates, secreted by the kidneys or other excretory structures: in mammals, it is a yellowish liquid containing urea, certain salts, etc., which is stored in the bladder and discharged periodically from the body through the urethra; in birds, reptiles, etc., it is a solid or almost solid substance formed chiefly of uric acid
u·ri·nif·er·ous (yoor′ə nif′ər əs) *adj.* conveying urine
u·ri·no- (yoor′ə nō, -nə) ⟦< L *urina*, URINE⟧ *combining form* urine, urinary tract *[urinogenital]*
u·ri·no·gen·i·tal (yoor′ə nō jen′i təl) *adj. var. of* UROGENITAL
u·ri·nous (yoor′ə nəs) *adj.* ⟦ModL *urinosus*⟧ of, like, or containing urine: also **u′ri·nose′** (-nōs′)
URL (yo͞o′är′əl′) *n.* ⟦*u(niform) r(esource) l(ocator)*⟧ an ADDRESS (*n.* 7b) on the World Wide Web
Ur·mi·a (o͞or′mē ə), **Lake** large saltwater lake in NW Iran: *c.* 1,500-2,300 sq mi (3,885-5,957 sq km)
urn (urn) *n.* ⟦ME < L *urna*, urn; akin to *urceus*, jug⟧ **1** a vase, esp. one with a foot or pedestal **2** a vase or other container used or designed to hold the ashes of a cremated body **3** a large metal container with a faucet, used for making and serving hot coffee, tea, etc. **4** *Bot.* the part of a moss capsule that bears the spores
u·ro-[1] (yoor′ō, -ə) ⟦< Gr *ouron*, URINE⟧ *combining form* urine, urination, urinary tract *[urolith]*
u·ro-[2] (yoor′ō, -ə) ⟦< Gr *oura*, tail < IE **orsos*, var. of base **ers-*, the buttocks, tail > ARSE⟧ *combining form* tail *[uropod]*
u·ro·chord (yoor′ə kôrd′) *n.* ⟦prec. + CHORD[1]⟧ **1** TUNICATE **2** *Zool.* the notochord when confined to the tail region in larval, and sometimes adult, tunicates —**u′ro·chor′dal** *adj.*
u·ro·chrome (-krōm′) *n.* ⟦URO-[1] + CHROME⟧ the pigment that gives urine its characteristic yellow color
u·ro·dele (-dēl′) *n.* ⟦Fr *urodèle* < ModL *Urodela* < *uro-* (see URO-[2]) + Gr *-dēlos*, visible < IE base **dei-*, to shine > L *dies*, day⟧ SALAMANDER (sense 4)
u·ro·gen·i·tal (yoor′ō jen′i təl) *adj.* designating or of the urinary and genital organs; genitourinary
u·rog·e·nous (yoo räj′ə nəs) *adj.* ⟦URO-[1] + -GENOUS⟧ **1** producing urine **2** contained in or obtained from urine
☆**u·ro·ki·nase** (yoor′ō kī′nās′, -kin′ās′) *n.* ⟦URO-[1] + KINASE⟧ an enzyme found as a trace in human urine, used for dissolving blood clots
u·ro·lith (yoor′ə lith′) *n.* ⟦URO-[1] + -LITH⟧ a calculus in the urinary tract —**u′ro·lith′ic** *adj.*
u·ro·lith·i·a·sis (yoor′ō li thī′ə sis) *n.* a medical condition, often very painful, involving the formation or presence of calculi within the urinary tract
u·rol·o·gy (yoo räl′ə jē) *n.* ⟦URO-[1] + -LOGY⟧ the branch of medicine dealing

with the urogenital or urinary system and its diseases —**u·ro·log·ic** (yoor′ə läj′ik) *adj.*, **u′ro·log′i·cal** —**u·rol′o·gist** *n.*

u·ro·pod (yoor′ə päd′) ***n.*** ⟦URO-[2] + -POD⟧ an appendage of the last abdominal segment in certain crustaceans, as either of the pair in the tailfan of the lobster or shrimp

uropygial gland a large gland located at the base of the tail in most birds, that secretes an oil used in preening

u·ro·pyg·i·um (yoor′ə pij′ē əm) ***n.***, *pl.* **-i·a** (-ē ə) or **-i·ums** ⟦ModL < Gr *ouropygion*, altered (infl. by *oura*, tail: see URO-[2]) < *orrhopygion* < *orrhos*, end of the os sacrum + *pygē*, rump: see STEATOPYGIA⟧ the hump at the rear extremity of a bird's body, from which the tail feathers grow —**u′ro·pyg′i·al** *adj.*

u·ros·co·py (yoo räs′kə pē) ***n.***, *pl.* **-pies** ⟦URO-[1] + -SCOPY⟧ examination of the urine, as for the diagnosis of disease —**u·ro·scop·ic** (yoor′ə skäp′ik) *adj.*

urp (urp) ***interj.*** ⟦echoic⟧ used to suggest the sound of a belch

Ur·quhart (ur′kərt, -kärt′), Sir **Thomas** 1611-60; Scot. writer & translator

Ur·sa Major (ur′sə) ⟦L, lit., great bear⟧ a prominent N constellation between Lynx and Draco: it contains more than 50 visible stars, seven of which form the Big Dipper; the Great Bear or the Bear

Ursa Minor ⟦L, lit., lesser bear⟧ a N constellation surrounded by Draco and containing the north celestial pole and the Little Dipper; the Little Bear or the Bear: see also POLARIS

ur·si·form (ur′sə fôrm′) ***adj.*** ⟦< L *ursus*, a bear + -FORM⟧ having the form or appearance of a bear

ur·sine (ur′sīn′, -sin) ***adj.*** ⟦L *ursinus* < *ursus*, a bear, akin to Gr *arktos*, a bear⟧ of, like, or characteristic of a bear; bearlike

Ur·spra·che (o͞or′shprä′kə) ⟦Ger < *ur-*, original (see UR-[1]) + *sprache*, language⟧ ***n.*** a reconstructed, hypothetical parent language, as Proto-Germanic

Ur·su·la (ur′sə lə) ***n.*** ⟦ML, dim. of L *ursa*, she-bear⟧ **1** a feminine name **2** in Christian tradition, a Brit. princess said to have been martyred, along with 11,000 virgins, by the Huns at Cologne: her day is Oct. 21: also Saint Ursula

Ur·su·line (ur′sə lin, -līn′) ***n.*** ⟦ModL *Ursulina*: after Saint prec., the martyr⟧ *R.C.Ch.* any member of a teaching order of nuns founded in 1535 —***adj.*** of this order

URT *abbrev.* upper respiratory tract

ur·text (ur′tekst′) ***n.*** ⟦Ger: see UR-[1] & TEXT⟧ **1** the original text of a work **2** *Music* an edition of a score intended to convey the composer's original musical intentions

ur·ti·car·i·a (urt′ə ker′ē ə) ***n.*** ⟦ModL < L *urtica*, a nettle⟧ HIVES —**ur′ti·car′i·al** *adj.*

ur·ti·cate (urt′ə kāt′) ***vt., vi.*** **-cat′ed**, **-cat′ing** ⟦< ML *urticatus*, pp. of *urticare*, to sting < L *urtica*, a nettle, prob. < *urere*, to burn: see UREDO⟧ to sting with or as with nettles

ur·ti·ca·tion (urt′ə kā′shən) ***n.*** ⟦ML *urticatio*⟧ *Med.* **1** [Historical] the flogging of a paralyzed limb, etc. with nettles for the stimulating effect produced **2** any sensation of stinging or itching **3** the formation of urticarial wheals

Uru *abbrev.* Uruguay

U·ru·a·pan (o͞o′ro͞o ä′pän′; *Sp* o͞o rwä′pän′) city in Michoacán state, SW Mexico

U·ru·guay (yoor′ə gwā′, oor′-; -gwī′; *Sp* o͞o′ro͞o gwī′) **1** country in SE South America, on the Atlantic: 68,039 sq mi (176,220 sq km); cap. Montevideo **2** river in SE South America flowing from S Brazil into the Río de la Plata: *c.* 1,000 mi (1,609 km) —**Ur′u·guay′an** *adj., n.*

Ü·rüm·qi (o͞o′ro͞om′chē′) city in NW China; capital of Xinjiang region: former transliteration **U′rum′chi′** (-chē′)

U·run·di (oo roon′dē) the S portion of the former Ruanda-Urundi that is now Burundi

u·rus (yoor′əs) ***n.*** ⟦L < PGmc *ūr-* (> OHG *uro*, OE *ur*, AUROCHS)⟧ AUROCHS

u·ru·shi·ol (o͞o′ro͞o shē ôl′, o͞o ro͞o′-; -ōl′) ***n.*** ⟦Jpn *urushi*, lac tree, lacquer + -OL[1]: coined (1907) by Toshiyuki Mashima, who isolated it⟧ a poisonous, irritant liquid, $C_{21}H_{32}O_2$, present in poison ivy, poison sumac, etc.

us (us) ***pron.*** ⟦ME *us*, *ous* (acc. & dat. of *we*: see WE) < OE *us*, dat., but also used, beside *usic*, as acc., akin to Ger *uns* < IE base **ns-* < **nes-*, **nos-*, pl. of **ne-*, **no-*, we > L *nos*, we⟧ *objective form of* WE [help *us*; give *us* the books]

USAGE—*us* is also used as a predicate complement with a linking verb [it's *us*] and in certain comparative constructions [they hit better than *us*, but they're not as agile as *us* on the base paths], although both usages are objected to by some

US or **U.S.** *abbrev.* United States

u.s. *abbrev.* **1** ⟦L *ut supra*⟧ as above **2** ⟦L *ubi supra*⟧ where (mentioned) above

USA *abbrev.* **1** United States of America: also **U.S.A.** **2** United States Army

us·a·ble (yo͞o′zə bəl) ***adj.*** that can be used; fit, convenient, or ready for use —**us′a·bil′i·ty** (-bil′ə tē) ***n.***, **us′a·ble·ness** —**us′a·bly** ***adv.***

USAF *abbrev.* United States Air Force

us·age (yo͞o′sij, -zij) ***n.*** ⟦OFr < ML *usagium* < L *usus*: see USE⟧ **1** the act, way, or extent of using or treating; treatment; use **2** long-continued or established practice; habitual or customary use or way of acting; custom; habit **3** the way in which a word, phrase, etc. is used to express a particular idea; customary manner of using the words of a given language in speaking or writing, or an instance of this —SYN. HABIT

us·ance (yo͞o′zəns) ***n.*** ⟦ME < MFr < *usant*, prp. of *user*: see USE⟧ **1** the time allowed for the payment of a foreign bill of exchange, as established by custom **2** [Obs.] *a)* USE *b)* USAGE *c)* USURY

USB *abbrev.* Universal Serial Bus: used to designate a kind of standard interface for connecting peripherals to a computer

USCG *abbrev.* United States Coast Guard

USD *abbrev.* United States dollar(s)

USDA *abbrev.* United States Department of Agriculture

use (yo͞oz; *for n.* yo͞os) ***vt.*** **used** (yo͞ozd; *with "to", usually* yo͞os′tə), **us′ing** ⟦ME *usen* < OFr *user* < VL **usare* < L *usus*, pp. of *uti*, to use⟧ **1** to put or bring into action or service; employ for or apply to a given purpose **2** to practice; exercise [to *use* one's judgment] **3** to act or behave toward; treat [to *use* a friend badly] **4** to consume, expend, or exhaust by use: often with *up* [to *use* up one's energy] **5** *a)* to smoke or chew (tobacco) *b)* to take or consume habitually [to *use* drugs] **6** to exploit or treat (a person) as a means to some selfish end —***vi.*** **1** to be accustomed; be wont: now only in the past tense, with an infinitive, meaning "did at one time" [he *used* to live in Iowa] **2** [Now Chiefly Dial.] to frequent; resort —***n.*** ⟦ME & OFr *us* < L *usus*⟧ **1** the act of using or the state of being used **2** the power or ability to use [to regain the *use* of an injured hand] **3** the right or permission to use [to grant a neighbor the *use* of one's car] **4** the need, opportunity, or occasion to use [no further *use* for his services] **5** an instance or way of using **6** the quality that makes a thing useful or suitable for a given purpose; advantage; usefulness; worth; utility **7** the object, end, or purpose for which something is used **8** function, service, or benefit **9** constant, continued, customary, or habitual employment, practice, or exercise, or an instance of this; custom; habit; practice; wont **10** the particular form of ritual or liturgy practiced in a given church, diocese, etc. **11** *Law a)* the enjoyment of property, as from occupying, employing, or exercising it *b)* ⟦infl. by OFr *ues*, gain < L *opus*, a work⟧ profit, benefit, or advantage, esp. that from lands and tenements held in trust by another —**have no use for** **1** to have no need of **2** to have no wish to deal with; be impatient with ☆**3** to have no affection or respect for; dislike strongly —**in use** being used —**make use of** to use; have occasion to use —**put to use** to use; find a use for

SYN.—**use** implies the putting of a thing into action or service so as to accomplish an end [to *use* a pencil, a suggestion, etc.]; **employ**, a somewhat more elevated term, implies the putting to useful work of something not in use at that moment [to *employ* a vacant lot as a playground] and, with reference to persons, suggests a providing of work and pay [she *employs* five accountants]; **utilize** implies the putting of something to a practical or profitable use [to *utilize* chemical byproducts]

use·a·ble (yo͞o′zə bəl) ***adj.*** *alt. sp. of* USABLE —**use′a·bil′i·ty** (-bil′ə tē) ***n.***, **use′a·ble·ness** —**use′a·bly** ***adv.***

used (yo͞ozd; *see note at* USE) ***vt., vi.*** *pt. & pp. of* USE —***adj.*** **1** that has been used **2** SECONDHAND —**be** (or **get**) **used to** to be (or become) familiar with or accustomed to [to *get used to* the rainy weather] See also USE (*vi.* 1)

use·ful (yo͞os′fəl) ***adj.*** that can be used to advantage; serviceable; helpful; beneficial; often, having practical utility —**use′ful·ly** ***adv.*** —**use′ful·ness** ***n.***

use·less (-lis) ***adj.*** **1** having no use; unserviceable; worthless **2** to no purpose; ineffectual; of no avail —SYN. FUTILE —**use′less·ly** ***adv.*** —**use′less·ness** ***n.***

us·er (yo͞o′zər) ***n.*** ⟦sense 1 < US(E) + -ER; in sense 2 a substantive use of OFr *user*, to use⟧ **1** a person or thing that uses something (stated or implied); specif., ☆*a)* a person who uses drugs; addict *b)* a person who makes use of a computer **2** *Law a)* the exercise of a right of USE (*n.* 11*a*) *b)* a right of use, based on long use

☆**us·er-friend·ly** (-frend′lē) ***adj.*** easy to use, operate, or understand: said as of computer software, applications, etc.

us·er·name (-nām′) ***n.*** *Comput.* a name registered with a network, website, etc., that identifies a particular user and, often together with a password, permits access

USES *abbrev.* United States Employment Service

USGS *abbrev.* United States Geological Survey

U-shaped (yo͞o′shāpt′) ***adj.*** having the shape of a U

U·shas (o͞o′shäs) ***n.*** ⟦Sans *Uṣas*, dawn⟧ the Hindu, or Vedic, goddess of the dawn

ush·er (ush′ər) ***n.*** ⟦ME *ussher* < OFr *uissier* < L *ostiarius*, doorkeeper: see OSTIARY⟧ **1** an official doorkeeper **2** a person whose duty it is to show people to their seats in a theater, church, etc. **3** a person whose official duty is to precede someone of rank, as in a procession, or to introduce unacquainted persons at a formal function **4** any of the groom's attendants at a wedding whose duties include showing guests to their seats and escorting the bridesmaids **5** [Obs.] in Great Britain, an assistant teacher in a boys' school —***vt.*** **1** to act as an usher to; escort or conduct (others) to seats, etc. **2** to precede, or be a forerunner of: often with *in*

☆**ush·er·ette** (ush′ər et′) ***n.*** a woman or girl usher, as in a theater: no longer a common term: see -ETTE

USIA *abbrev.* United States Information Agency

Usk (usk) river flowing from S Wales through W England into the Severn estuary: 60 mi (97 km)

Üs·kü·dar (o͞os′ko͞o där′) section of Istanbul, Turkey, on the Asian side of the Bosporus

USM *abbrev.* **1** United States Mail **2** United States Mint

USMC *abbrev.* United States Marine Corps

USN *abbrev.* United States Navy

USNG *abbrev.* United States National Guard

USO *abbrev.* United Service Organizations
USP or **US Phar** *abbrev.* United States Pharmacopeia
Us·pa·lla·ta Pass (o͞os′pä yä′tä) mountain pass in the Andes, on the Argentine-Chilean border: *c.* 12,650 ft (3,856 m) high
USPS *abbrev.* United States Postal Service
us·que·baugh (us′kwi bä′, -bô′) ***n.*** ⟦see WHISKEY⟧ [Scot. or Irish] WHISKEY
USS *abbrev.* **1** United States Senate **2** United States Ship
Ussh·er (ush′ər), **James** 1581-1656; Ir. archbishop & theologian
USSR or **U.S.S.R.** *abbrev.* Union of Soviet Socialist Republics
Us·su·ri (o͞o so͞o′rē) river in SE Asian Russia, flowing north along the Manchurian border into the Amur River: 365 mi (587 km)
usu *abbrev.* **1** usual **2** usually
u·su·al (yo͞o′zhə wəl, yo͞ozh′wəl) ***adj.*** ⟦ME < MFr < LL *usualis* < L *usus*: see USE⟧ such as is in common or ordinary use; such as is most often seen, heard, used, etc.; common; ordinary; customary —**as usual** in the usual way —**u′su·al·ly** ***adv.*** —**u′su·al·ness** ***n.***

SYN.—**usual** applies to that which past experience has shown to be the normal, common, hence expected thing [the *usual* results, price, answer, etc.]; **customary** refers to that which accords with the usual practices of some individual or with the prevailing customs of some group [his *customary* mid-morning coffee; it was *customary* to dress for dinner]; **habitual** implies a fixed practice as the result of habit [her *habitual* tardiness]; **wonted** is a somewhat literary equivalent for **customary** or **habitual** [according to their *wonted* manner]; **accustomed** is equivalent to **customary** but suggests less strongly a settled custom [he sat in his *accustomed* place] See also **normal** —*ANT.* **extraordinary, unusual**

u·su·fruct (yo͞o′zyo͞o frukt′, -syo͞o-) ***n.*** ⟦LL *usufructus* < L *ususfructus* < *usus*, a USE + *fructus*, enjoyment, FRUIT⟧ *Rom. & Civil Law* the right to use the property of another for a period of time with the obligation to return it, or leave it, undamaged or unimpaired
u·su·fruc·tu·ar·y (yo͞o′zyo͞o fruk′cho͞o er′ē, -syo͞o-) ***n.***, *pl.* **-ar′ies** ⟦LL *usufructuarius*⟧ a person or agent having the usufruct of property —***adj.*** of, or having the nature of, a usufruct
u·su·rer (yo͞o′zhər ər) ***n.*** ⟦ME < MFr *usurier* < ML *usurarius*, usurer < L *usura*: see USURY⟧ a person who lends money at interest, now specif., at a rate of interest that is excessive or unlawfully high
u·su·ri·ous (yo͞o zhoor′ē əs) ***adj.*** **1** practicing usury **2** of or constituting usury —**u·su′ri·ous·ly** ***adv.*** —**u·su′ri·ous·ness** ***n.***
u·surp (yo͞o sʉrp′, -zʉrp′) ***vt.*** ⟦ME *usurpen* < MFr *usurper* < L *usurpare* < *usus*, a USE + *rapere*, to seize: see RAPE[1]⟧ to take or assume (power, a position, property, rights, etc.) and hold in possession by force or without right —***vi.*** to practice or commit usurpation (*on* or *upon*) —**u·surp′er** ***n.*** —**u·surp′ing·ly** ***adv.***
u·sur·pa·tion (yo͞o′sər pā′shən, -zər-) ***n.*** ⟦ME *usurpacion* < L *usurpatio*⟧ the act of usurping; esp., the unlawful or violent seizure of a throne, power, etc.
u·su·ry (yo͞o′zhə rē) ***n.*** ⟦ME *usurie* < ML *usuria* < L *usura* < *usus*: see USE⟧ **1** the act or practice of lending money at interest, now specif., at a rate of interest that is excessive or unlawfully high **2** interest at such a high rate
ut (ut, o͞ot) ***n.*** ⟦ME < ML: see GAMUT⟧ *Music* a syllable formerly used in solmization: now replaced by *do*
Ut *abbrev.* Utah
UT *abbrev.* **1** Universal Time **2** Utah
U·tah (yo͞o′tô, -tä) ⟦< Sp *Yutta* < Ute name, lit. ? hill dwellers⟧ Mountain State of the W U.S.: admitted 1896; 82,144 sq mi (212,751 sq km); cap. Salt Lake City: abbrev. *UT* or *Ut*
U·tah·an (-tô′ən, -tä′ən; -tôn′, -tän′) ***adj.*** of Utah: usually used in the predicate —***n.*** a person born or living in Utah Also (local usage) **U′tahn′** (-tôn′, -tän′)
UTC *abbrev.* Coordinated Universal Time
ut dict *abbrev.* ⟦L *ut dictum*⟧ *Pharmacy* as directed
Ute (yo͞ot, yo͞ot′ē) ***n.*** ⟦akin to UTAH⟧ **1** *pl.* **Utes** or **Ute** a member of a North American Indian people formerly ranging throughout the SW plains regions, now living mainly in W Colorado and E Utah **2** the Uto-Aztecan language of this people
u·ten·sil (yo͞o ten′səl) ***n.*** ⟦ME *utensele* < MFr *utensile* < L *utensilia*, materials, utensils < neut. pl. of *utensilis*, fit for use < *uti*, to use⟧ **1** any implement or container ordinarily used as in a kitchen **2** an implement or tool, as for use in farming —*SYN.* IMPLEMENT
u·ter·ine (yo͞ot′ə rin, -rīn′) ***adj.*** ⟦ME < LL *uterinus*⟧ **1** of the uterus **2** having the same mother but a different father [*uterine* sisters]
u·ter·o- (yo͞ot′ər ō′, -ər ə) ⟦< fol.⟧ *combining form* uterus, uterus and [*uteroabdominal*]: also, before a vowel, **uter-**
u·ter·us (yo͞ot′ə rəs) ***n.***, *pl.* **u′ter·i′** (-rī′) or **u′ter·us·es** ⟦L < ? IE base **udero-*, belly > Sans *udáram*⟧ **1** a hollow, muscular organ of female mammals in which the ovum is deposited and the embryo and fetus are developed; womb: it is usually paired, but is single in primates **2** a similar structure in many invertebrates
U Thant *see* THANT, U
U·ther (yo͞o′thər) ***n.*** *Arthurian Legend* a king of Britain and the father of King Arthur: often called *Uther Pendragon*
UTI *abbrev.* urinary tract infection
U·ti·ca (yo͞ot′i kə) **1** city of ancient times in N Africa, north of modern Tunis **2** ⟦after the ancient African city⟧ city in central N.Y., on the Mohawk River
u·tile (yo͞ot′'l) ***adj.*** ⟦LME < MFr < L *utilis* < *uti*, to use⟧ [Obs.] USEFUL
u·ti·lise (yo͞ot′'l īz′) ***vt.*** **-lised′**, **-lis′ing** *alt. Brit. sp. of* UTILIZE
u·til·i·tar·i·an (yo͞o til′ə ter′ē ən) ***adj.*** ⟦UTILIT(Y) + -ARIAN: coined (1781) by Jeremy BENTHAM⟧ **1** of or having to do with utility **2** stressing usefulness over beauty or other considerations **3** made for or aiming at utility **4** of, having to do with, or believing in utilitarianism —***n.*** a person who believes in utilitarianism
u·til·i·tar·i·an·ism (-iz′əm) ***n.*** **1** the doctrine that the worth or value of anything is determined solely by its utility **2** the doctrine, developed by Jeremy Bentham and John Stuart Mill, that the aim of all action should be to bring about the greatest happiness of the greatest number **3** utilitarian character or quality
u·til·i·ty (yo͞o til′ə tē) ***n.***, *pl.* **-ties** ⟦ME *utilite* < OFr *utilité* < L *utilitas* < *utilis*, UTILE⟧ **1** the quality or property of being useful; usefulness **2** [Archaic] something useful **3** *a)* a company or government agency providing a public service such as electric power, gas, water, telephone, etc. *b)* [*pl.*] shares of stock in such a company **4** *Comput.* a program designed to perform or facilitate a basic task, such as coordinating files or detecting viruses **5** *Econ.* the power to satisfy the needs or wants of humanity —***adj.*** **1** serving or designed for practical use with little or no attention to beauty **2** useful or used in a number of ways ☆**3** designating an auxiliary player who is able to substitute at any of several positions on a baseball team [a *utility* infielder] **4** designating or of an inferior, usually dark, coarse grade of meat, lacking fat
utility knife any of various small, hand-held knives or cutting tools designed for general use; specif., BOX CUTTER
☆**utility room** a room containing various household appliances and equipment, as for heating, laundry, cleaning, etc.
utility truck [Austral. & N.Z.] PICKUP
utility vehicle SPORT UTILITY VEHICLE
u·ti·lize (yo͞ot′'l īz′) ***vt.*** **-lized′**, **-liz′ing** ⟦Fr *utiliser*: see UTILE & -IZE⟧ to put to use; make practical or profitable use of —*SYN.* USE —**u′ti·liz′a·ble** ***adj.*** —**u′ti·li·za′tion** ***n.*** —**u′ti·liz′er** ***n.***
ut·most (ut′mōst′) ***adj.*** ⟦ME *utemest* < OE *utemest*, *ytemest*, double superl. of *ut*, OUT⟧ **1** situated at the farthest point or limit; most extreme or distant; farthest **2** of or to the greatest or highest degree, amount, number, etc.; greatest —***n.*** the most or the greatest that is possible; extreme limit or degree
U·to-Az·tec·an (yo͞ot′ō az′tek′ən) ***n.*** a family of Amerindian languages of the W U.S., Mexico, and Central America, including Hopi, Nahuatl, Pima, Shoshone, and Ute —***adj.*** designating or of these languages, the peoples that speak them, or their cultures
U·to·pi·a (yo͞o tō′pē ə) ***n.*** ⟦ModL < Gr *ou*, not + *topos*, a place: see TOPIC⟧ **1** an imaginary island described in a book of the same name by Sir Thomas More (1516) as having a perfect political and social system **2** [*often* **u-**] *a)* any idealized place, state, or situation of perfection *b)* any visionary scheme or system for an ideally perfect society *c)* a novel or other work depicting a utopian society or place
U·to·pi·an (-ən) ***adj.*** ⟦ModL *Utopianus*⟧ **1** of or like Utopia **2** [*often* **u-**] *a)* having the nature of, or inclined to draw up schemes for, a utopia; idealistic; visionary *b)* founded upon ideas envisioning perfection in social and political organization [a *utopian* community] —***n.*** **1** an inhabitant of Utopia **2** [*often* **u-**] a person who believes in a utopia, esp. of a social or political nature; visionary
u·to·pi·an·ism (-ən iz′əm) ***n.*** the ideas, doctrines, aims, etc. of a utopian; visionary schemes for producing perfection in social or political conditions
U·trecht (yo͞o′trekt′) **1** province of the central Netherlands: 554 sq mi (1,435 sq km) **2** its capital
u·tri·cle (yo͞o′tri kəl) ***n.*** ⟦< Fr or L: Fr *utricule* < L *utriculus*, little bag or bottle, dim. of *uter*, leather bag, wineskin, prob. via Etr < Gr *hydria*, water bag, jug < *hydor*, WATER⟧ a small sac, vesicle, or baglike part; specif., *a)* *Anat.* the larger of the two saclike cavities in the membranous labyrinth of the inner ear, communicating with the semicircular canals *b)* *Bot.* a small, one-celled, usually indehiscent fruit with a thin, membranous wall and one or several seeds Also **u·tric·u·lus** (yo͞o trik′yə ləs) *pl.* **-li′** (-lī′) —**u·tric·u·lar** (yo͞o trik′yə lər) ***adj.***
U·tril·lo (o͞o tril′ō, yo͞o-; *Fr* ü trē yō′), **Maurice** 1883-1955; Fr. painter
U·tsu·no·mi·ya (o͞ot′so͞o nō mē′yä) city in central Honshu, Japan, north of Tokyo
Ut·tar Pra·desh (o͞ot′ər prə desh′, -däsh′) state of N India: 88,112 sq mi (231,254 sq km); cap. Lucknow
ut·ter[1] (ut′ər) ***adj.*** ⟦ME < OE *uttera*, compar. of *ut*, OUT⟧ **1** complete; total **2** unqualified; absolute; unconditional —**ut′ter·ly** ***adv.*** —**ut′ter·ness** ***n.***
ut·ter[2] (ut′ər) ***vt.*** ⟦ME *uttren* < *utter*, outward: see prec.⟧ **1** to give out; put forth: now used only of the passing of counterfeit money or forged checks **2** to produce, speak, or express audibly (speech sounds, syllables, words, thoughts, etc.) **3** to express in any way **4** to emit (nonvocal sounds), as if speaking **5** to make known; divulge; reveal **6** [Obs.] to publish (a book, etc.) **7** [Obs.] to sell (goods, etc.) —***vi.*** to speak or converse —**ut′ter·a·ble** ***adj.*** —**ut′ter·er** ***n.***

SYN.—**utter** implies the communication of an idea or feeling by means of vocal sounds, such as words, exclamations, etc. [he *uttered* a sigh of relief]; **express**, the broadest of these terms, suggests a revealing of ideas, feelings, one's personality, etc. by means of speech, action, or creative work [to *express* oneself in music]; **voice** suggests expression through words, either spoken or written [*voicing* one's opinions in letters to the editor]; **broach** suggests the utterance or mention of an idea to someone for the first time [I'll *broach* the subject to her at dinner]; **enunciate** suggests the announcement or open attestation of some idea [to *enunciate* a theory, doctrine, etc.]

ut·ter·ance[1] (ut′ər əns) ***n.*** ⟦ME: see prec. & -ANCE⟧ **1** the act of uttering, or expressing by voice **2** the power or style of speaking **3** that which is uttered; esp., a word or words uttered, whether written or spoken

ut·ter·ance[2] (ut′ər əns) ***n.*** ⟦ME, altered (infl. by UTTER[1]) < MFr *outrance*: see OUTRANCE⟧ [Obs.] the utmost, or last, extremity; i.e., death

ut·ter·most (ut′ər mōst′) ***adj., n.*** UTMOST

U-turn (yo͞o′turn′) ***n.*** ⟦so named because the path of the turn is typically U-shaped⟧ **1** a turn made so as to head in the opposite direction: used esp. of a vehicle in a street or road **2** figuratively, a reversal of opinion, strategy, etc.

U-2 (yo͞o′to͞o′) ***n.*** a relatively slow, high-altitude, U.S. military reconnaissance jet equipped with sophisticated aerial cameras

UU *abbrev.* Unitarian Universalist

UV or **uv** *abbrev.* ultraviolet

UVA (yo͞o′vē′ā′) ***n.*** ultraviolet light with a longer wavelength than UVB and thus closer in size to visible violet light: sometimes written **UV-A**

u·va·rov·ite (o͞o vär′ə vīt′, yo͞o-) ***n.*** ⟦Ger *uwarowit*, after S. S. *Uvarov* (1786-1855), Russ statesman & author⟧ an emerald-green garnet, $Ca_3Cr_2(SiO_4)_3$, with small crystals, used as a gem; calcium chromium silicate

UVB (yo͞o′vē′bē′) ***n.*** ultraviolet light with a shorter wavelength than UVA and thus closer in size to X-rays: sometimes written **UV-B**

u·ve·a (yo͞o′vē ə) ***n.*** ⟦ML < L *uva*, grape: see UVULA⟧ the iris, ciliary body, and choroid, together forming the entire pigmented, vascular layer of the eye —**u′ve·al** ***adj.***

Uve·dale (yo͞ov′dāl′), **Nicholas** *var. of* Nicholas UDALL

u·ve·i·tis (yo͞o′vē īt′is) ***n.*** ⟦ModL: see UVEA & -ITIS⟧ inflammation of the uvea —**u′ve·it′ic** (-it′ik) ***adj.***

u·vu·la (yo͞o′vyə lə) ***n.***, *pl.* **-las** or **-lae′** (-lē′) ⟦ML, dim. of L *uva*, grape < IE base **ei*-, reddish, colorful > OE *iw*, YEW⟧ the small, fleshy process hanging down from the middle of the soft palate above the back of the tongue

u·vu·lar (-lər) ***adj.*** ⟦ModL *uvularis*⟧ **1** of or having to do with the uvula **2** *Phonet.* articulated with a vibration of the uvula, or with the back of the tongue near or in contact with the uvula, as, in some French or German dialects, the sound represented by *r* —***n.*** *Phonet.* a uvular sound —**u′vu·lar·ly** ***adv.***

UW *abbrev.* underwriter: also **U/W**

ux. *abbrev.* ⟦L *uxor*⟧ wife

Ux·bridge (uks′brij′) former borough in Middlesex, SE England: now part of Hillingdon

Ux·mal (o͞oz mäl′) ruined Mayan city in the NW Yucatán Peninsula, Mexico

ux·o·ri·al (uk sôr′ē əl, ug zôr′-) ***adj.*** ⟦< L *uxorius* (see UXORIOUS) + -AL⟧ of, befitting, or characteristic of a wife —**ux·o′ri·al·ly** ***adv.***

ux·or·i·cide (uk sôr′ə sīd′, -zôr′-) ***n.*** ⟦< L *uxor*, wife (see fol.) + -CIDE⟧ **1** the murder of a wife by her husband **2** a man who murders his wife —**ux·or′i·ci′dal** ***adj.***

ux·o·ri·ous (uk sôr′ē əs, -zôr′-) ***adj.*** ⟦L *uxorius* < *uxor*, wife < ?⟧ dotingly or irrationally fond of or submissive to one's wife —**ux·o′ri·ous·ly** ***adv.***

Uz·bek (o͝oz′bek, uz′-) ***n.*** **1** a member of a Turkic people living mainly in Uzbekistan and neighboring regions **2** the Turkic language of this people —***adj.*** of the Uzbeks or their language or culture

Uz·bek·i·stan (o͝oz bek′i stan′, -stän′; -bek′i stan′, -stän′) **1** UZBEK SOVIET SOCIALIST REPUBLIC **2** country in central Asia: became independent upon the breakup of the U.S.S.R. (1991): 172,742 sq mi (447,400 sq km); cap. Tashkent: formerly, *Uzbek Soviet Socialist Republic*

Uzbek Soviet Socialist Republic a republic of the U.S.S.R.: now UZBEKISTAN

U·zi (o͞o′zē) ⟦after *Uziel* Gal (1923–2002), Israeli army officer, born in Germany, who designed it⟧ *trademark for* a compact submachine gun made in Israel

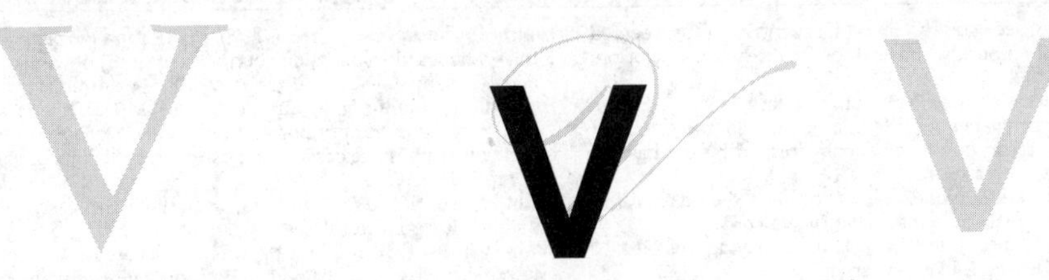

v[1] or **V** (vē) ***n.**, pl.* **v's, V's 1** the twenty-second letter of the English alphabet: from the Latin *V*, derived from one form of the Greek *Y* (*upsilon*): formerly used interchangeably in English with *U* both as a vowel and as a consonant, now only as a consonant **2** any of the speech sounds that this letter represents, as, in English, the (v) of *vote* **3** a type or impression for *v* or *V* **4** the twenty-second in a sequence or group **5** an object shaped like V —***adj.* 1** of *v* or *V* **2** twenty-second in a sequence or group **3** shaped like V

v[2] *abbrev.* **1** ⟦L *vice*⟧ in the place of **2** ⟦L *vide*⟧ see **3** valve **4** *Math.* vector **5** velocity **6** ventral **7** verb **8** verse **9** version **10** verso **11** versus **12** very **13** village **14** violin **15** vise **16** vocative **17** voice **18** volt(s) **19** voltage **20** volume **21** ⟦Ger⟧ von

V[1] (vē) ***n.*** a Roman numeral for 5: with a superior bar ($\overline{\text{V}}$), 5,000

V[2] *abbrev.* **1** velocity **2** Venerable **3** Vicar **4** Vice **5** victory **6** Viscount **7** volt(s) **8** *Physics* volume

V[3] *Chem. symbol for* vanadium

VA *abbrev.* **1** Veterans Administration; Department of Veterans Affairs **2** Vicar Apostolic **3** Vice Admiral **4** Virginia: also **Va 5** volt-ampere

Vaal (väl) river in South Africa, flowing from Mpumalanga province into the Orange River in Northern Cape province: *c.* 700 mi (1,127 km)

vac (vak) ***n.* 1** *short for* VACUUM CLEANER **2** [Brit. Informal] *short for* VACATION

va·can·cy (vā′kən sē) ***n.**, pl.* **-cies** ⟦L *vacantia* < *vacans*⟧ **1** the state of being vacant, or empty; emptiness **2** *a)* empty space *b)* a vacant space; gap, blank, opening, etc. **3** the state of being empty in mind; lack of intelligence, interest, or thought; vacuity **4** [Now Rare] the state of being free from work, activity, etc.; idleness **5** an unoccupied position or office; unfilled post, situation, or job **6** untenanted quarters, as in a hotel **7** *Physics* a lattice defect in a crystal due to a displaced or missing ion or atom

va·cant (vā′kənt) ***adj.*** ⟦OFr < L *vacans*, prp. of *vacare*, to be empty⟧ **1** having nothing in it, as a space; devoid of contents; empty; void **2** not held, filled, or occupied, as a position or office **3** having no occupant [*a vacant seat*] **4** untenanted, as a room or house **5** not filled with activity or work; free; leisure [*vacant time*] **6** *a)* having or showing emptiness of mind or lack of intelligence, interest, thought, etc. *b)* empty of thought (said of the mind) **7** *Law a)* unoccupied or unused, as land *b)* having no claimant, as an estate or succession *c)* not yet granted, as public lands —**SYN.** EMPTY —**va′cant·ly** ***adv.*** —**va′cant·ness** ***n.***

va·cate (vā′kāt′, vā kāt′) ***vt.*** **-cat′ed, -cat′ing** ⟦< L *vacatus*, pp. of *vacare*, to be empty⟧ **1** to make vacant; specif., *a)* to cause (an office, position, etc.) to be unfilled or unoccupied, as by resignation *b)* to leave (a house, room, etc.) uninhabited or untenanted; give up the occupancy of **2** *Law* to make void; annul —***vi.* 1** to make an office, position, place, etc. vacant ☆**2** ⟦back-form. < fol.⟧ [Informal] to spend a vacation

va·ca·tion (vā kā′shən, və-) ***n.*** ⟦ME *vacacion* < MFr < L *vacatio*⟧ **1** freedom from any activity; rest; respite; intermission ☆**2** a period of rest and freedom from work, study, etc.; time of recreation, usually a specific interval in a year **3** [Rare] the act of making vacant **4** *Law* a formal recess between terms of a court —***vi.* 1** to take a vacation **2** to spend one's vacation [*to vacation* in Maine]

☆**va·ca·tion·er** (-ər) ***n.*** a person taking a vacation, esp. one who is traveling or at a resort: also **va·ca′tion·ist**

va·ca·tion·land (-land′) ***n.*** an area attractive to vacationers because of recreational facilities, historic sights, etc.

vac·ci·nal (vak′sə nəl) ***adj.*** of vaccine or vaccination

vac·ci·nate (vak′sə nāt′) ***vt.*** **-nat′ed, -nat′ing** ⟦VACCIN(E) + -ATE[1]⟧ to inoculate with a specific vaccine in order to prevent disease —***vi.*** to practice vaccination —**vac′ci·na′tor** ***n.***

vac·ci·na·tion (vak′sə nā′shən) ***n.* 1** the act or practice of vaccinating **2** a scar on the skin where a vaccine, esp. for smallpox, has been applied

vac·cine (vak sēn′, vak′sēn) ***n.*** ⟦L *vaccinus*, from cows < *vacca*, cow; akin ? to Sans *vaśā*, rogue cow⟧ **1** lymph, or a preparation of this, from a cowpox vesicle, containing the causative virus and used in vaccination against cowpox or smallpox **2** any preparation of killed microorganisms, weakened viruses, etc. that is introduced into the body to produce immunity to a specific disease by causing the formation of antibodies —***adj.*** [Rare] of cowpox or vaccination

vac·cin·i·a (vak sin′ē ə) ***n.*** ⟦ModL < L *vaccinus*: see prec.⟧ COWPOX —**vac·cin′i·al** ***adj.***

vac·il·lant (vas′ə lənt) ***adj.*** vacillating; wavering

vac·il·late (-lāt′) ***vi.*** **-lat′ed, -lat′ing** ⟦< L *vacillatus*, pp. of *vacillare*, to sway to and fro, waver < IE **wek-*, to be bent, prob. < base **wā-*, to bend apart, turn > L *varus*, bent, diverse⟧ **1** to sway to and fro; waver; totter; stagger **2** to fluctuate or oscillate **3** to waver in mind; show indecision —**vac′il·la′tion** ***n.*** —**vac′il·la′tor** ***n.*** —**vac′il·la·to′ry** (-lə tôr′ē) ***adj.***

vac·il·lat·ing (-lāt′iŋ) ***adj.*** wavering or tending to waver in motion, opinion, etc. —**vac′il·lat′ing·ly** ***adv.***

vac·u·a (vak′yo͞o ə) ***n.*** *alt. pl. of* VACUUM

va·cu·i·ty (va kyo͞o′ə tē) ***n.**, pl.* **-ties** ⟦L *vacuitas* < *vacuus*, empty⟧ **1** the quality or state of being empty; emptiness **2** an empty space; void or vacuum **3** emptiness of mind; lack of intelligence, interest, or thought **4** an inane or senseless thing, remark, or quality; inanity

vac·u·o·late (vak′yo͞o ə lāt′, -lit) ***adj.*** having a vacuole or vacuoles: also **vac′u·o·lat′ed**

vac·u·o·la·tion (vak′yo͞o ə lā′shən) ***n.*** the formation or arrangement of vacuoles

vac·u·ole (vak′yo͞o ōl′) ***n.*** ⟦Fr < L *vacuus*, empty⟧ *Biol.* a fluid-filled cavity within the cytoplasm of a cell, surrounded by a membrane that usually encloses food, water, or air —**vac·u·o·lar** (vak′yo͞o wə lər, vak′yoo wō′lər, vak′yoo lər) ***adj.***

vac·u·ous (vak′yo͞o əs) ***adj.*** ⟦L *vacuus*⟧ **1** empty of matter **2** having or showing lack of intelligence, interest, or thought; stupid; senseless; inane **3** characterized by lack of purpose, of profitable employment, etc.; idle —**SYN.** EMPTY —**vac′u·ous·ly** ***adv.*** —**vac′u·ous·ness** ***n.***

vac·uum (vak′yo͞om, -yo͞o əm) ***n.**, pl.* **-uums** or **-u·a** (-yo͞o ə) ⟦L, neut. sing. of *vacuus*, empty⟧ **1** a space with nothing at all in it; completely empty space **2** *a)* an enclosed space, as that inside a vacuum tube, out of which most of the air or gas has been taken, as by pumping *b)* the degree to which pressure has been brought below atmospheric pressure **3** a space left empty by the removal or absence of something usually found in it; void: often used fig. ☆**4** *short for* VACUUM CLEANER —***adj.* 1** of a vacuum **2** used to make a vacuum **3** having a vacuum; partially or completely exhausted of air or gas **4** working by suction or the creation of a partial vacuum — ***vt., vi.*** to clean with a vacuum cleaner

vacuum bottle (*or* flask) a vessel with double walls that enclose an insulating vacuum, used for maintaining the temperature of its contents, often a beverage or other hot or cold liquid

vacuum cleaner a machine for cleaning carpets, floors, upholstery, etc. by suction: also **vacuum sweeper**

vacuum gauge an instrument for measuring the pressure of the air or gas in a partial vacuum

☆**vac·uum-packed** (-pakt′) ***adj.*** packed in an airtight container from which most of the air was exhausted before sealing, so as to maintain freshness

vacuum pump 1 a pump used to draw air or gas out of sealed space **2** PULSOMETER (sense 1)

vacuum tube an electron tube from which the air has been evacuated to the highest possible degree

vacuum valve [Brit.] VACUUM TUBE

va·de me·cum (vā′dē mē′kəm, vä′-) ⟦L, lit., go with me⟧ something carried about by a person for constant use, reference, etc., as a handbook or manual

Va·do·da·ra (vä′dō dä′rə) **1** former state of W India: now part of Gujarat state **2** city in E Gujarat state, W India

va·dose (vā′dōs′) ***adj.*** ⟦< L *vadosus*, shallow < *vadum*, shallow place, ford, akin to *vadere*, to go: for IE base see WADE⟧ designating or of water that clings to solid matter in an unsaturated zone between the earth's surface and the water table

Va·duz (vä do͞ots′) capital of Liechtenstein

vag- (väg) *combining form* VAGO-: used before a vowel

vag·a·bond (vag′ə bänd′) ***adj.*** ⟦ME < MFr < L adj. *vagabundus*, strolling about < *vagari*, to wander < *vagus*: see VAGUE⟧ **1** moving from place to place, with no fixed abode; wandering **2** of, having to do with, or living an unsettled, drifting, or irresponsible life; vagrant; shiftless **3** aimlessly following an irregular course or path; drifting —***n.* 1** a person who wanders from place to place, having no fixed abode **2** a tramp **3** an idle, disreputable, or shiftless person —***vi.*** to wander —**SYN.** VAGRANT —**vag′a·bond′ish** ***adj.***

vag·a·bond·age (-bän′dij) ***n.*** ⟦Fr: see prec. & -AGE⟧ **1** the state or condition of being a vagabond; vagrant way of life: also **vag′a·bond′ism′** (-bän′diz′əm) **2** vagabonds collectively

va·gal (vā′gəl) ***adj.*** ⟦VAG(US) + -AL⟧ of or having to do with the vagus nerve

va·gar·i·ous (və ger′ē əs, -gar′-) ***adj.* 1** full of or characterized by vagaries; capricious **2** wandering; roaming

va·gar·y (vā′gə rē, və ger′ē) ***n.**, pl.* **-gar·ies** ⟦earlier used as a v., to wander <

L *vagari,* to wander < *vagus:* see VAGUE⟧ **1** an odd, eccentric, or unexpected action or bit of conduct **2** an odd, whimsical, or freakish idea or notion; oddity; caprice —**SYN.** CAPRICE

va·gi·na (və jī′nə) ***n., pl.*** **-nas** or **-nae** (-nē) ⟦L, a sheath⟧ **1** *Anat., Zool.* a sheath or sheathlike structure; specif., in female mammals, the canal between the vulva and the uterus **2** *Bot.* the sheath formed by the base of certain leaves where it envelops a stem

vag·i·nal (vaj′ə nəl, və jī′nəl) ***adj.*** *Anat., Zool.* **1** of or like a sheath **2** of, for, or through the vagina of a female mammal —**vag′i·nal·ly** ***adv.***

vag·i·nate (vaj′ə nit, -nāt′) ***adj.*** ⟦ModL *vaginatus*⟧ **1** having a vagina or sheath; sheathed, as grass leaves **2** like a sheath

vag·i·nis·mus (vaj′ə niz′məs) ***n.*** ⟦ModL < L *vagina:* see VAGINA⟧ a painful spasm of the vagina making coital penetration difficult or impossible

vag·i·ni·tis (vaj′ə nīt′is) ***n.*** ⟦ModL: see VAGINA & -ITIS⟧ inflammation of the vagina; colpitis

vag·i·no- (vaj′ə nō, -nə) ⟦< L *vagina*⟧ *combining form* vagina *[vaginoscope]:* also, before a vowel, **vagin-**

va·go- (vā′gō, -gə) ⟦< VAGUS⟧ *combining form* vagus nerve *[vagotomy]*

va·go·de·pres·sor (vā′gō di pres′ər) ***adj.*** depressing the vagus nerve activity —***n.*** a vagodepressor drug

va·got·o·my (vā gät′ə mē) ***n., pl.*** **-mies** ⟦VAGO- + -TOMY⟧ the surgical cutting of the vagus nerve, as to relieve a peptic ulcer by reducing the flow of gastric juice

va·go·to·ni·a (vā′gə tō′nē ə) ***n.*** ⟦ModL: see VAGO-, TONE, & -IA⟧ a disorder resulting from overstimulation of the vagus nerve, causing a slowing of the heart rate, fainting, etc. —**va′go·ton′ic** (-tän′ik) ***adj.***

va·go·trop·ic (-träp′ik) ***adj.*** ⟦VAGO- + -TROPIC⟧ affecting, or acting upon, the vagus nerve

va·gran·cy (vā′grən sē) ***n., pl.*** **-cies** ⟦< fol.⟧ **1** [Now Rare] a wandering in thought or talk; digression **2** a wandering from place to place; vagabondage **3** shiftless or idle wandering without money or work, as of tramps, beggars, etc.: often a statutory offense chargeable as a misdemeanor

va·grant (vā′grənt) ***n.*** ⟦ME *vagraunt,* prob. < Anglo-Fr *wacrant, walcrant* < OFr *walcrer,* to wander < Frank **walken* (see WALK): infl. prob. by L *vagari,* to wander⟧ **1** a person who wanders from place to place or lives a wandering life; rover **2** a person who wanders from place to place and lives by begging, doing odd jobs, etc.; vagabond **3** *Law* a tramp, beggar, prostitute, or similar idle or disorderly person whose way of living makes him or her liable to arrest and detention —***adj.*** **1** wandering from place to place or living a wandering life; roaming; nomadic **2** living the life of a vagabond or tramp **3** of or characteristic of a vagrant **4** characterized by straggling growth: said of plants **5** following no fixed direction, course, or pattern; random, wayward, fleeting, erratic, etc. —**va′grant·ly** ***adv.***

SYN.—**vagrant** refers to a person without a fixed home who wanders about from place to place, gaining support from begging, etc., and, in legal usage, implies such a person regarded as a public nuisance, subject to arrest; **vagabond**, orig. implying shiftlessness, rascality, etc., now often connotes no more than a carefree, roaming existence; **bum**, **tramp**, and **hobo** are informal equivalents for the preceding, but **bum** always connotes an idle, dissolute, often alcoholic person who never works, **tramp** and **hobo** connote a vagrant, whether one who lives by begging or by doing odd jobs; **hobo** now also means a migratory laborer See also **itinerant**

vague (vāg) ***adj.*** **va′guer, va′guest** ⟦Fr < L *vagus,* wandering < IE **wag-,* to be bent, prob. < base **wā-* > VACILLATE⟧ **1** not clearly, precisely, or definitely expressed or stated **2** indefinite in shape, form, or character; hazily or indistinctly seen or sensed **3** not sharp, certain, or precise in thought, feeling, or expression *[vague* in his answers, a *vague* hope*]* **4** not precisely determined or known; uncertain —**SYN.** OBSCURE —**vague′ly** ***adv.*** —**vague′ness** ***n.***

va·gus (vā′gəs) ***n., pl.*** **va′gi′** (-jī′) ⟦ModL < L, wandering: see prec.⟧ either of the tenth pair of cranial nerves, arising in the medulla oblongata and providing parasympathetic innervation to the larynx, lungs, heart, esophagus, and most of the abdominal organs: also **vagus nerve**

va·hi·ne (vä hē′nā) ***n.*** ⟦Tahitian, woman < Proto-Polynesian **fafine* > Haw & Maori *wahine:* see WAHINE⟧ a Polynesian woman, esp. of Tahiti

vail[1] (vāl) [Archaic] ***vi.*** ⟦ME *vailen* < pres. indic. stem of OFr *valoir,* to be of worth: see AVAIL⟧ to be of use, service, or profit; avail —***n.*** a tip; gratuity

vail[2] (vāl) ***vt.*** ⟦ME *valen* < OFr *valer* or aphetic < *avaler,* to descend < *à val,* down < L *ad vallum,* lit., to the valley⟧ [Archaic] **1** to lower; let sink or fall down **2** to take off or tip (one's hat, etc.) as a sign of respect or submission

vain (vān) ***adj.*** ⟦OFr < L *vanus,* empty, vain: see WANT⟧ **1** having no real value or significance; worthless, empty, idle, hollow, etc. *[vain* pomp*]* **2** without force or effect; futile, fruitless, unprofitable, unavailing, etc. *[*a *vain* endeavor*]* **3** having or showing an excessively high regard for one's self, looks, possessions, ability, etc.; indulging in or resulting from personal vanity; conceited **4** [Archaic] lacking in sense; foolish —**in vain 1** fruitlessly; vainly **2** lightly; profanely; irreverently —**vain′ness** ***n.***

SYN.—**vain**, in this connection, applies to that which has little or no real value, worth, or meaning *[vain studies]*; **idle** refers to that which is baseless or worthless because it can never be realized *[idle* hopes, *idle* talk*]*; **empty** and **hollow** are used of that which only appears to be genuine, sincere, worthwhile, etc. *[empty* threats, *hollow* pleasures*]*; **otiose** applies to that which has no real purpose or function and is therefore useless or superfluous *[otiose* remarks*]* See also **futile**

vain·glo·ri·ous (vān glôr′ē əs) ***adj.*** ⟦LME *vaneglorεous* < ML *vaniglorius:* see fol.⟧ **1** boastfully vain and proud of oneself **2** showing or characterized by boastful vanity —**vain′glo′ri·ous·ly** ***adv.*** —**vain′glo′ri·ous·ness** ***n.***

vain·glo·ry (vān′glôr′ē, vān glôr′ē) ***n.*** ⟦ME *vainglorie* < OFr *vaine gloire* < L *vana gloria,* empty boasting: see VAIN & GLORY⟧ **1** extreme self-pride and boastfulness; excessive and ostentatious vanity **2** vain show or empty pomp —**SYN.** PRIDE

vain·ly (vān′lē) ***adv.*** **1** in vain; uselessly; fruitlessly; without success **2** with vanity; conceitedly

vair (ver) ***n.*** ⟦ME < OFr, *vair,* orig., variegated < L *varius:* see VARIOUS⟧ **1** [Archaic] a fur, usually from a gray and white squirrel, used for trimming and lining clothes in the Middle Ages **2** *Heraldry* the representation of a fur, indicated in engravings by rows of small bells, alternately upright and turned down

Vaish·na·va (vīsh′nə və) ***n.*** ⟦Sans *vaiṣṇava,* of Vishnu, after *Viṣṇu,* VISHNU⟧ in Hinduism, a devotee of Vishnu

Vais·ya (vīs′yə) ***n.*** a member of the Hindu business and agricultural caste, next below the Kshatriya

val *abbrev.* **1** valuation **2** value

Va·lais (vȧ le′) canton of SW Switzerland: 2,017 sq mi (5,224 sq km)

val·ance (val′əns, vā′ləns) ***n.*** ⟦ME, after ? VALENCE, center for textile manufacturing⟧ **1** a short drapery or curtain hanging from the edge of a bed, shelf, table, etc., often to the floor **2** a short drapery or facing of wood or metal across the top of a window, concealing curtain rods, etc. —**val′anced** ***adj.***

Val·dai Hills (väl dī′) range of hills in W European Russia, between St. Petersburg & Moscow, forming a watershed for rivers flowing to the Baltic & those flowing south & southeast, esp. the Volga

Val d'A·os·ta (väl′ dä ôs′tä) *var. of* VALLE D'AOSTA

Val·de·mar (väl′də mär′) *alt. sp. of* WALDEMAR I

vale[1] (vāl) ***n.*** ⟦ME < OFr *val* < L *vallis,* VALLEY⟧ [Old Poet.] VALLEY

va·le[2] (vā′lē; wä′lā, wä′-) ***interj., n.*** ⟦L⟧ farewell

val·e·dic·tion (val′ə dik′shən) ***n.*** ⟦< L *valedictus,* pp. of *valedicere,* to say farewell < *vale,* farewell (imper. of *valere,* to be well: see VALUE) + *dicere,* to say: see DICTION⟧ **1** the act of bidding or saying farewell **2** something said in parting; farewell utterance

☆**val·e·dic·to·ri·an** (val′ə dik tôr′ē ən) ***n.*** in schools and colleges, the student, usually the one highest in scholastic rank in the graduating class, who delivers the valedictory: see also SALUTATORIAN

val·e·dic·to·ry (val′ə dik′tər ē) ***adj.*** ⟦< L *valedictus* (see VALEDICTION) + -ORY⟧ said or done at parting, by way of farewell; uttered as a valediction —☆***n., pl.*** **-ries** a farewell speech, esp. one delivered at a graduation ceremony

va·lence (vā′ləns) ***n.*** ⟦LL *valentia,* worth, capacity < L, vigor < *valens,* prp. of *valere,* to be strong: see VALUE⟧ *Chem.* **1** the capacity of an element or radical to combine with another to form molecules, as measured by the number of hydrogen or chlorine atoms which one radical or one atom of the element will combine with or replace (e.g.: oxygen has a *valence* of two, i.e., one atom of oxygen combines with two hydrogen atoms to form the water molecule, H_2O) **2** any of the units of valence which a particular element may have Also **va′len·cy,** *pl.* **-cies**

Va·lence (vȧ läns′) city in SE France

valence electrons the orbital electrons in the outermost shell of an atom which largely determine its properties

Va·len·ci·a (və len′shē ə, -shə, -sē ə; *Sp* vä len′thyä) **1** region & ancient kingdom in E Spain, on the Mediterranean **2** seaport in this region **3** city in N Venezuela

Valencian Community region comprising three provinces of E Spain: 8,998 sq mi (23,305 sq km); cap. Valencia

Va·len·ci·ennes[1] (və len′sē enz′) ***n.*** ⟦after fol., where orig. manufactured⟧ a flat bobbin lace having a simple floral pattern on a background of fine, diamond-shaped mesh: also **Valenciennes lace**

Va·len·ci·ennes[2] (və len′sē enz′; *Fr* vȧ län syen′) city in N France, near the Belgian border

Va·lens (vā′lənz), **(Flavius)** A.D. 328?-378; emperor of the Eastern Roman Empire (364-378): brother of Valentinian I

-va·lent (vā′lənt) ⟦< L *valens:* see VALENCE⟧ *Chem. suffix meaning* **1** having a specified valence **2** having a specified number of valences Although both the Greek set of prefixes (*mono-, di-, tri-, tetra-, penta-,* etc.) and the Latin (*uni-, bi-, ter-, quadri-, quinque-,* etc.) are used with *-valent,* the Latin set is preferred when designating the number of valences an element exhibits and the Greek when designating the specific valence of some atom or radical

val·en·tine (val′ən tīn′) ***n.*** ⟦ME < OFr⟧ **1** one's sweetheart, esp. as chosen or greeted on Valentine's Day **2** a greeting card or note sent or given on Valentine's Day, typically containing an expression of affection or sentimental love **3** a gift presented on Valentine's Day

Val·en·tine[1] (val′ən tīn′) ***n.*** ⟦ME < L *Valentinus* < *Valens,* a masculine name < *valens:* see VALENCE⟧ a masculine name

Val·en·tine[2] (val′ən tīn′), Saint (3d cent. A.D.); Christian martyr of Rome: his day is Feb. 14

Valentine's Day Feb. 14, observed in honor of a martyr of the 3d cent. and, coincidentally, as a day for sending valentines to sweethearts, schoolmates, etc.

Val·en·tin·ian (val′ən tin′ē ən) **1 Valentinian I** A.D. 321?-375; Rom. emperor; ruled 364-375: brother of Valens **2 Valentinian II** A.D. 371?-392;

Rom. emperor; ruled 375-392: son of Valentinian I **3 Valentinian III** A.D. 419?-455; Rom. emperor; ruled 425-455

Val·en·ti·no (val′ən tē′nō), **Rudolph** (born *Rodolfo Alfonzo Raffaelo Pierre Filibert Guglielmi di Valentina d'Antonguolla*) 1895-1926; U.S. film actor, born in Italy

val·er·ate (val′ər āt′) ***n.*** a salt or ester of valeric acid

va·le·ri·an (və lir′ē ən) ***n.*** ⟦ME < MFr *valériane* < ML *valeriana,* valerian, prob. after *Valeria,* province in Pannonia, where the plants were grown⟧ **1** any of a genus (*Valeriana*) of plants of the valerian family, with clusters or spikes of white, pink, red, or purplish flowers **2** a drug made from the dried rhizomes and roots of the garden heliotrope: used, esp. formerly, as a sedative and antispasmodic —***adj.*** designating a family (Valerianaceae, order Dipsacales) of dicotyledonous plants, chiefly of the Northern Hemisphere, including corn salad and spikenard

Va·le·ri·an (və lir′ē ən) (L. name *Publius Licinius Valerianus*) A.D. 190?-260; Rom. emperor (253-260)

va·ler·ic acid (və ler′ik, -lir′-) any of four isomeric fatty acids, C_4H_9COOH, some originally found in valerian root, but all now made synthetically: used in the manufacture of pharmaceuticals, flavors, perfumes, etc.

Val·e·rie (val′ər ē) ***n.*** a feminine name: dim. *Val;* equiv. Fr. *Valérie*

Va·lé·ry (vȧ lā rē′), **Paul (Ambroise)** (pôl) 1871-1945; Fr. poet & essayist

val·et (va lā′, va′lā; *Brit* val′it) ***n.*** ⟦Fr, a groom, yeoman < OFr *vaslet,* young man, page < VL **vassellittus,* double dim. < Gaul **vasso-,* servant (akin to MIr *foss,* Welsh *gwas*) < IE **uposto-,* one who stands by < **upo-* (> UP[1]) + base **stā-,* to STAND⟧ **1** a man's personal manservant who takes care of the man's clothes, helps him in dressing, etc. **2** an employee, as of a hotel, who cleans or presses clothes, or performs other personal services ☆**3** a rack for hanging coats, hats, a change of clothing, etc. — ***vt., vi.*** to serve (a person) as a valet —***adj.*** referring to any of various services, as one in a hotel for cleaning and pressing clothes

va·let de cham·bre (vȧ let shän′br′) *pl.* **va·lets de cham·bre** (vȧ let-) ⟦Fr⟧ VALET (sense 1)

valet parking a service provided by attendants who park and later retrieve motor vehicles for guests, customers, etc. as of a restaurant —**val·et′-park′** ***vt.***

val·e·tu·di·nar·i·an (val′ə to͞o′də ner′ē ən, -tyo͞o′-) ***n.*** ⟦< L *valetudinarius,* sickly, infirm, an invalid < *valetudo* (gen. *valetudinis*), state of health, sickness < *valere,* to be strong: see VALUE⟧ **1** a person in poor health; invalid **2** one who thinks constantly and anxiously about one's own health —***adj.*** **1** characterized by or in poor health; sickly **2** anxiously concerned about one's health Also **val′e·tu′di·nar′y,** *pl.* **-nar′ies** —**val′e·tu′di·nar′i·an·ism′** ***n.***

val·gus (val′gəs) ***n.*** ⟦ModL < L, bowlegged < IE **wolg-* < base **wel-,* to turn > WALK⟧ **1** clubfoot in which the foot is turned outward **2** any similar bent position, as of the knee or hip —***adj.*** **1** bent or twisted outward **2** loosely, knock-kneed

Val·hal·la (val hal′ə, väl häl′ə) ***n.*** ⟦ModL < ON *valhöll* (gen. *valhallar*), hall of the slain < *valr,* slaughter, the slain (< IE base **wel-,* to tear, wound, corpse > L *volnus,* Gr *oulē,* a wound) + *höll;* akin to OE *heall,* HALL⟧ *Norse Myth.* the great hall where Odin receives and feasts the souls of heroes fallen bravely in battle: also **Val·hall** (val hal′, väl häl′)

val·iant (val′yənt) ***adj.*** ⟦ME < OFr *vaillant,* prp. of *valoir* < L *valere,* to be strong: see VALUE⟧ **1** full of or characterized by valor or courage; brave **2** resolute; determined [made a *valiant* effort] —**SYN.** BRAVE —**val′iance *n.*, val′ian·cy** —**val′iant·ly *adv.***

val·id (val′id) ***adj.*** ⟦Fr *valide* < L *validus,* strong, powerful (in ML, valid) < *valere,* to be strong: see VALUE⟧ **1** having legal force; properly executed and binding under the law **2** well-grounded on principles or evidence; able to withstand criticism or objection, as an argument; sound **3** effective, effectual, cogent, etc. **4** [Archaic] robust; strong; healthy **5** *Logic* correctly derived or inferred according to the rules of logic —**val′id·ly *adv.*** —**val′id·ness *n.***

SYN.—valid applies to that which cannot be objected to because it conforms to law, logic, the facts, etc. [a *valid* criticism]; **sound** refers to that which is firmly grounded on facts, evidence, logic, etc. and is therefore free from error [a *sound* method]; **cogent** implies such a powerful appeal to the mind as to appear conclusive [*cogent* reasoning]; **convincing** implies such validity as to persuade or overcome doubts or opposition [a *convincing* argument]; **telling** suggests the power to have the required effect by being forcible, striking, relevant, etc. [a *telling* rejoinder] —**ANT. fallacious**

val·i·date (val′ə dāt′) ***vt.*** **-dat′ed, -dat′ing** ⟦< ML *validatus,* pp. of *validare* < L *validus:* see prec.⟧ **1** to make binding under the law; give legal force to; declare legally valid **2** to confirm the validity or value of **3** to authorize as by signing, stamping, etc. —**SYN.** CONFIRM —**val′i·da′tion *n.***

va·lid·i·ty (və lid′ə tē) ***n.*,** *pl.* **-ties** ⟦Fr *validité* < L *validitas,* strength⟧ the state, quality, or fact of being valid in law or in argument, proof, authority, etc.

val·ine (val′ēn, -in; vā′lēn, -lin) ***n.*** ⟦< *(iso)val(eric acid)* + -INE[3]⟧ a white, crystalline, essential amino acid, $(CH_3)_2CHCH(NH_2)COOH$, found in small quantities in many proteins: see AMINO ACID

val·in·o·my·cin (val′ə nō mī′sin) ***n.*** ⟦< prec. + -MYCIN⟧ an antibiotic polypeptide isolated from soil bacteria, that promotes the movement of potassium ions in cells

va·lise (və lēs′, -lēz′) ***n.*** ⟦Fr < ML *valisia* < *valesium* < ?⟧ a piece of hand luggage

☆**Val·i·um** (val′ē əm, val′yəm) ⟦arbitrary coinage⟧ *trademark for* DIAZEPAM

Val·kyr·ie (val kir′ē, val′ki rē) ***n.*** ⟦ON *valkyrja,* lit., chooser of the slain < *valr,* those slain (see VALHALLA) + *kjōsa,* to CHOOSE⟧ *Norse Myth.* any of the handmaidens of Odin who conduct the souls of heroes slain in battle to Valhalla and attend them there —**Val·kyr′i·an *adj.***

Val·la·do·lid (val′ə dō lid′; *Sp* vä′lyä thō lēth′) city in NC Spain

val·lec·u·la (va lek′yo͞o lə) ***n.*,** *pl.* **-lae′** (-lē′) ⟦ModL < LL, dim. < L *vallis,* VALLEY⟧ a groove or furrow in a plant or animal structure, as the depression between the epiglottis and the base of the tongue —**val·lec′u·lar *adj.***

Val·le d'A·os·ta (väl′ä dä ôs′tä) region of NW Italy: 1,260 sq mi (3,263 sq km)

Val·le·jo[1] (və lā′hō, -lā′ō), **Cé·sar** (sā′zär) 1892-1938; Peruvian poet

Val·le·jo[2] (və lā′hō, -lā′ō) ⟦after Mariano G. *Vallejo* (1808-90), owner of the site⟧ seaport in W Calif., near Oakland

val·le·na·to (vä′yä nä′tō) ***n.*** ⟦Sp, lit., born in the valley (in ref. to a valley in N Colombia)⟧ a form of Colombian folk music, featuring accordions, drums, and other percussion instruments

Val·let·ta (vä let′ä) seaport & capital of Malta, on the island of Malta

val·ley (val′ē) ***n.*,** *pl.* **-leys** ⟦ME *valey* < OFr *valee* < *val* < L *vallis,* vale < IE base **wel-,* to turn, roll > WALK, WELL[1]⟧ **1** a stretch of lowland lying between hills or mountains and usually having a river or stream flowing through it **2** the land drained or watered by a great river system [the Mississippi *Valley*] **3** any long dip or hollow, as the trough of a wave **4** *Archit.* the trough formed where two slopes of a roof meet, or where the roof meets a wall

Valley Forge ⟦after an iron *forge* located on *Valley* Creek⟧ village in SE Pa., on the Schuylkill River: scene of General Washington's winter encampment (1777-78)

Valley of Ten Thousand Smokes region in SW Alas. in which steam and gases are emitted from thousands of earth vents

Va·lois[1] (vȧ lwȧ′) ***n.*** name of the ruling family of France (1328-1589)

Va·lois[2] (vȧ lwȧ′) former duchy in NC France

va·lo·ni·a (və lō′nē ə) ***n.*** ⟦It *vallonia* < ModGr *balania,* evergreen oak < Gr *balanos,* acorn: see GLAND[1]⟧ the acorn cups of an oak (*Quercus aegilops*) of Europe and Asia, used in dyeing, tanning, etc.

val·or (val′ər) ***n.*** ⟦ME, monetary worth < OFr *valour* < LL *valor,* worth < L *valere,* to be strong: see VALUE⟧ marked courage or bravery: Brit. sp. **val′our**

☆**val·or·i·za·tion** (val′ər i zā′shən) ***n.*** ⟦Port *valorização* < *valorizar,* to valorize < *valor,* a price, worth < LL: see prec.⟧ **1** a stabilizing or fixing of prices, usually by government action **2** a conferring of value upon something

val·or·ize (val′ər īz′) ***vt.*** **-ized′, -iz′ing** ⟦Port *valorizar:* see prec.⟧ **1** to stabilize or fix the price of by valorization **2** to confer value or greater value upon [to *valorize* the achievements of a minor poet]

val·or·ous (-ər əs) ***adj.*** ⟦ME < OFr *valeureux* < ML *valorosus*⟧ having or showing valor; courageous; brave —**val′or·ous·ly *adv.*** —**val′or·ous·ness *n.***

Val·pa·rai·so (val′pə rā′zō, -rī′sō) seaport in central Chile: also **Val·pa·ra·í·so** (*Sp* väl′pä rä ē′sô)

Val·po·li·cel·la (val′pō lə chel′ə, väl′-) ***n.*** ⟦It, after valley where made⟧ a light, dry Italian red wine

Val·sal·va maneuver (val sal′və) ⟦after Antonio *Valsalva* (1666-1723), It anatomist⟧ any forced expiratory effort against a closed or blocked air passage, as blowing hard with nose and mouth closed during an ascent or descent in an aircraft to equalize pressure in the ears

valse (vȧls) ***n.*** ⟦Fr < Ger *walzer:* see WALTZ⟧ a waltz

val·u·a·ble (val′yə bəl, val′yo͞o ə bəl) ***adj.*** **1** having material or monetary value, esp. high monetary value [a *valuable* diamond] **2** of great merit, use, or service; highly important, esteemed, etc. —***n.*** an article of value, esp. one of small size, as a piece of jewelry: *usually used in pl.* —**SYN.** COSTLY —**val′u·a·bly *adv.***

val·u·ate (val′yo͞o āt′) ***vt.*** **-at′ed, -at′ing** ⟦back-form. < fol.⟧ to set a value on; appraise —**val′u·a′tor *n.***

val·u·a·tion (val′yo͞o ā′shən) ***n.*** ⟦OFr *valuacion*⟧ **1** the act of determining the value or price of anything; evaluation; appraisal **2** determined or estimated value or price on the market **3** estimation of the worth, merit, etc. of anything —**val′u·a′tion·al *adj.*** —**val′u·a′tion·al·ly *adv.***

val·ue (val′yo͞o) ***n.*** ⟦ME < OFr, fem. of *valu,* pp. of *valoir,* to be strong, be worth < L *valere* < IE base **wal-,* to be strong > WIELD⟧ **1** a fair or proper equivalent in money, commodities, etc., esp. for something sold or exchanged; fair price or return **2** *a)* the worth of a thing in money or goods at a certain time; market price *b)* the worth of a thing in relation to its price [the washer was a good *value,* considering all its features] **3** estimated or appraised worth or price; valuation **4** purchasing power [the fluctuating *value* of the dollar] **5** that quality of a thing according to which it is thought of as being more or less desirable, useful, estimable, important, etc.; worth or the degree of worth **6** that which is desirable or worthy of esteem for its own sake; thing or quality having intrinsic worth **7** [*pl.*] the social principles, goals, or standards held or accepted by an individual, class, society, etc. **8** precise meaning, as of a word **9** denomination, as of a postage stamp, playing card, etc. **10** *Art a)* relative lightness or darkness of a color *b)* proportioned effect, as of light and shade, in an artistic work **11** *Math.* the quantity or amount for which a symbol stands [to determine the *value* of x] **12** *Music* the relative duration of a note, tone, or rest **13** *Phonet.* a sound represented by a given letter [the *values* of *i* in the English words "sin" and "sine"] —***vt.*** **val′ued, val′u·ing 1** to estimate the value of; set a price for or determine the worth of; appraise **2** to place a certain estimate of worth on in a scale of values [to *value* health above wealth] **3** to think highly of; esteem [to *value* a friendship] —**SYN.** APPRECIATE, WORTH[1] —**val′u·er *n.***

val·ue-add·ed tax (-ad′əd) a tax on the value added to goods at each stage of production, from raw materials to finished product: it is typically added to the price of the finished product and is thus an INDIRECT TAX on the consumer

val·ued (-yo͞od) *adj.* highly thought of; esteemed [*a valued* friend]

val·ue-free (val′yo͞o frē′) *adj.* not altered or influenced by value judgments [*value-free* research]

value judgment an estimate made of the worth, goodness, etc. of a person, action, event, or the like, esp. when making such judgment is not called for or desired

val·ue·less (-yo͞o lis) *adj.* of no value or use; worthless

va·lu·ta (və lo͞ot′ə) *n.* ⟦It, value⟧ the value of a currency; specif., the exchange value of a currency with reference to another currency

val·vate (val′vāt′) *adj.* ⟦L *valvatus,* having folding doors < *valva:* see fol.⟧ **1** having a valve or valves **2** *Bot. a)* meeting without overlapping, as the petals of some flower buds *b)* opening by valves, as a pea pod

valve (valv) *n.* ⟦ME, a door leaf < L *valva,* leaf of a folding door, akin to *volvere,* to roll: see WALK; senses 3, 4, 8 < ModL *valva* < L⟧ **1** [Archaic] either of the halves of a double door or any of the leaves of a folding door **2** a gate regulating the flow of water in a sluice, channel, etc. **3** *Anat.* a membranous fold or structure which permits bodily fluids to flow in one direction only, or opens and closes a tube, chamber, etc. **4** *Bot. a)* any of the segments into which a pod or capsule separates when it bursts open *b)* a lidlike part in some anthers, through which pollen is discharged *c)* either of the boxlike halves forming the cell walls of a diatom **5** *Electronics a)* a device, esp. a rectifier, that allows current to flow in only one direction *b)* [Brit.] ELECTRON TUBE **6** *Mech. a)* any device in a pipe or tube that permits a flow in one direction only, or regulates the flow of whatever is in the pipe, by means of a flap, lid, plug, etc. acting to open or block passage *b)* the flap, lid, plug, etc. **7** *Music* a device in certain brass instruments, as the trumpet, that opens (or closes) an auxiliary to the main tube, lengthening (or shortening) the air column and lowering (or raising) the pitch **8** *Zool. a)* each separate part making up the shell of a mollusk, barnacle, etc. *b)* any of the parts forming the sheath of an ovipositor in certain insects —**valve′less** *adj.*

valved (valvd) *adj.* having or fitted with a valve

valve-in-head engine (valv′in hed′) a type of internal-combustion engine, as in many automobiles, having the intake and exhaust valves in the cylinder head instead of the block

valve trombone *see* TROMBONE

val·vu·lar (val′vyə lər) *adj.* **1** having the form or function of a valve **2** having a valve or valves **3** of a valve or valves; esp., of the valves of the heart Also **val′var** (-vər)

val·vule (-vyo͞ol′) *n.* ⟦Fr < ModL *valvula,* dim. < L *valva*⟧ a small valve: also **valve′let** (-lit)

val·vu·li·tis (valv′yə līt′əs) *n.* ⟦ModL < *valvula* (see prec.) + -ITIS⟧ inflammation of a valve, esp. of the heart

☆**va·moose** (va mo͞os′) *vi., vt.* **-moosed′**, **-moos′ing** ⟦< Sp *vamos,* let us go < L *vadamus,* 1st pers. pl., pres. subj. of *vadere,* to go: see WADE⟧ [Old Slang] to leave quickly; go away (from) hurriedly: also **va·mose′** (-mōs′) **-mosed′**, **-mos′ing**

vamp[1] (vamp) *n.* ⟦ME *vampe* < OFr *avampié* < *avant,* before + *pié, pied,* foot < L *pes* (gen. *pedis*), FOOT⟧ **1** the part of a boot or shoe covering the instep and, in some styles, the toes **2** ⟦< the v.⟧ *a)* something patched up or fixed up to seem new; patchwork *b)* something patched on *c) Music* a simple, improvised introduction or interlude, esp. a series of chords, as before a jazz solo or between songs played by a dance band —*vt.* **1** to put a vamp on; provide or mend with a new vamp **2** to patch (*up*); repair **3** to invent; fabricate **4** *Music* to improvise —*vi. Music* to play a vamp

vamp[2] (vamp) *n.* ⟦< fol.⟧ [Informal] a woman who uses her sexual attractiveness to seduce or beguile men —*vt.* to seduce or beguile (a man) by using feminine charms —*vi.* to act the part of a vamp —**vamp′ish** *adj.*

vam·pire (vam′pīr′) *n.* ⟦Fr < Ger *vampir,* of Slav orig., as in Serb *vàmpīr*⟧ **1** *Folklore* one of the undead that wanders at night to suck the blood of its human victims **2** an unscrupulous person who preys ruthlessly on others, as a blackmailer or usurer **3** [Old Informal] VAMP[2] **4** *short for* VAMPIRE BAT —**vam·pir·ic** (vam pir′ik) *adj.*, **vam·pir·ish** (vam′pīr′ish)

vampire bat **1** any of a family (Desmodontidae) of tropical American bats that live on vertebrate blood, esp. of stock animals, and sometimes transmit rabies and a trypanosome disease of horses **2** any of various other bats mistakenly believed to feed on blood

vam·pir·ism (vam′pīr iz′əm, -pə riz′əm) *n.* **1** superstitious belief in vampires **2** the practices of vampires in folklore, specif. bloodsucking **3** the act or practice of preying ruthlessly on other people

van[1] (van) *n. short for* VANGUARD

van[2] (van) *n.* ⟦ME *vanne* < MFr *van* < L *vannus,* van, FAN[1]⟧ **1** [Archaic] a winnowing machine **2** [Old Poet.] a wing

van[3] (van) *n.* ⟦(CARA)VAN⟧ **1** a closed truck or wagon for moving furniture, carrying freight or people, etc. **2** a small, closed truck for utility use, as deliveries, repairs, etc., or for use as an RV, airport limousine, etc. **3** [Brit.] *a)* a closed railroad car for baggage, etc. *b)* a delivery wagon or truck *c)* TRAILER (sense 3) —*vt.* **vanned**, **van′ning** to transport in a van —*vi.* to travel in a recreational van —**van′ner** *n.*

van[4] (van; *Du* vän) *prep.* ⟦Du; akin to Ger *von:* see VON⟧ of or from: in Dutch family names, *van* precedes a place name and together they indicate traditional place of origin: also **Van**

Van (van), **Lake** salt lake in E Turkey: *c.* 1,450 sq mi (3,755 sq km)

van·a·date (van′ə dāt′) *n.* a salt or ester of vanadic acid

va·nad·ic (və nad′ik, -nā′dik) *adj.* designating or of compounds containing trivalent or pentavalent vanadium

vanadic acid any of a series of acids containing vanadium that apparently do not exist in the free state but are represented in various vanadates

va·nad·i·nite (və nad′'n īt′) *n.* ⟦< fol. + -IN[1] + -ITE[1]⟧ a soft, heavy, rare, hexagonal mineral, $Pb_5(VO_4)_3Cl$, an ore of vanadium and lead; lead vanadate chloride

va·na·di·um (və nā′dē əm) *n.* ⟦ModL < ON *Vanadis,* FREYA + -IUM: name proposed (1831) by BERZELIUS⟧ a rare, malleable, ductile, silver-white, metallic chemical element: it is alloyed with steel, to which it adds tensile strength, and is used in nuclear applications, etc.: symbol, V; at. no. 23: see the periodic table of elements in the Reference Supplement

vanadium steel a steel alloy containing 0.15 to 0.25 percent vanadium to harden and toughen it

☆**Van Al·len radiation belt** (van al′ən) ⟦after James A. *Van Allen* (1914-2006), U.S. physicist⟧ either of two broad, doughnut-shaped regions surrounding the earth and composed of high-energy electrons and protons trapped in the earth's magnetic field at heights between *c.* 400 km (*c.* 250 mi) and *c.* 64,370 km (*c.* 40,000 mi)

Van·brugh (van bro͞o′; *Brit usually* van′brə), Sir **John** 1664-1726; Eng. dramatist & architect

Van Bu·ren (van byo͝or′ən), **Martin** 1782-1862; 8th president of the U.S. (1837-41)

Van·cou·ver (van ko͞o′vər) ⟦after Capt. George *Vancouver* (1757-98), Brit explorer⟧ **1** island of British Columbia, Canada, off the SW coast: 12,079 sq mi (31,285 sq km) **2** seaport in SW British Columbia, Canada, opposite this island, on the Strait of Georgia **3** seaport in SW Wash., on the Columbia River, opposite Portland, Oreg. **4 Mount** mountain of the St. Elias Range, on the Alaska-Yukon border: 15,700 ft (4,785 m)

van·da (van′də) *n.* ⟦ModL < Hindi *vandā,* mistletoe < Sans, a parasitic plant⟧ any of a genus (*Vanda*) of small-flowered tropical orchids of the Eastern Hemisphere, having racemes of fragrant white, lilac, blue, or greenish flowers

Van·dal (van′dəl) *n.* ⟦L *Vandalus* < Gmc base **wandal-* > OE *Wendil,* ON *Vendill*⟧ **1** a member of an East Germanic people that ravaged Gaul, Spain, and N Africa and sacked Rome (A.D. 455) **2** [**v-**] a person who, out of malice or ignorance, destroys or spoils any public or private property, esp. that which is beautiful or artistic —*adj.* of the Vandals: also **Van·dal·ic** (van dal′ik)

van·dal·ism (van′də liz′əm) *n.* the actions or attitudes of a vandal; malicious or ignorant destruction of public or private property, often, specif., of that which is beautiful or artistic —**van′dal·is′tic** *adj.*

van·dal·ize (-də līz′) *vt.* **-ized′**, **-iz′ing** to destroy or damage (public or private property) maliciously

☆**Van de Graaff generator** (van′ di gräf′) ⟦after R. J. *Van de Graaff* (1901-67), U.S. physicist⟧ an electrostatic generator using a movable insulating belt to produce potentials of millions of volts

Van·der·bilt (van′dər bilt), **Cornelius** 1794-1877; U.S. capitalist & railroad & steamship industrialist

van der Meer (van′dər mer, vän′-, -mir), **Jo·han·nes** (yō hän′əs) or **Jan** (yän) *var. of* VERMEER

van der Waals (vän dər välz′), **Jo·han·nes Di·de·rik** (yô hä′nəs dē′də rik) 1837-1923; Du. physicist

van der Waals' forces (van′dər wôlz′, vän′dər välz′) ⟦after prec.⟧ weak attractive forces between electrically neutral atoms and molecules

Van Die·men's Land (van dē′mənz) *former name for* TASMANIA

Van Dyck (van dīk′), Sir **Anthony** 1599-1641; Fl. painter, in England after 1632: also sp. **Vandyke**

Van·dyke (van dīk′) *n. short for:* **1** VANDYKE BEARD **2** VANDYKE COLLAR —*adj.* of, or in the style of, Van Dyck or in the fashion of the subjects of his portraits

Vandyke beard a closely trimmed, pointed beard

Vandyke brown **1** a deep-brown pigment used by Van Dyck **2** any of several other brown pigments or colors

Vandyke collar a broad linen or lace collar with a deeply indented edge

Vandyke beard

vane (vān) *n.* ⟦S Brit var. of *fane,* small flag or pennon < OE *fana,* a flag < PGmc **fanan-* < IE base **pan-* > PANE⟧ **1** a flat piece of metal, strip of cloth, etc. set up high to swing with the wind and show which way it is blowing; weather vane **2** any of several flat or curved pieces set around an axle and rotated about it by moving air, water, etc. [the *vanes* of a windmill], or mechanically rotated to move the air or water [the *vanes* of a turbine] or to compress the air [the *vanes* of a supercharger] **3** a projecting fixed or movable plate or strip of metal attached to a rocket, missile, etc. to provide stability or guidance **4** a target set to slide on a leveling rod, for use in surveying **5** any of the sights on a compass, quadrant, etc. **6** *a)* the flat part of a feather with barbs; web *b)* a feather on an arrow, used to stabilize flight —**vaned** *adj.*

Vane (vān), Sir **Henry (or Harry)** 1613-62; Eng. Puritan statesman: colonial governor of Mass. (1636-37)

Vä·nern (ve′nərn), **Lake** largest lake in Sweden, in the SW part: *c.* 2,150 sq mi (5,568 sq km): also **Vä′ner** (-nər)

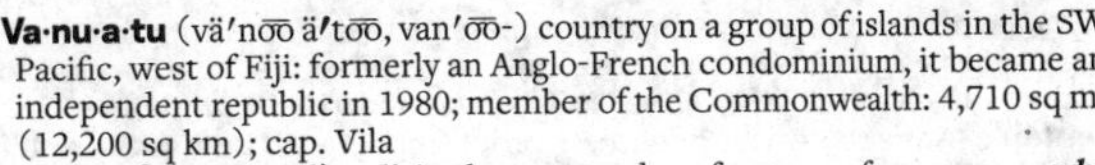

Va·nes·sa (və nes′ə) ***n.*** a feminine name

van Eyck (van īk′) **1 Hubert** or **Huy·brecht** (hoi′breHt′) 1366?-1426; Fl. painter **2 Jan** (yän) died 1441; Fl. painter: brother of Hubert

vang (vaŋ) ***n.*** ⟦Du, a catch < *vangen,* to catch: for base see FANG⟧ *Naut.* **1** a rope or either of two ropes attached to a gaff and used to control its lateral movement **2** a rope or an arrangement of ropes and pulleys attached to the boom of a fore-and-aft sail and used to hold the boom down and flatten the sail: in full **boom vang**

van Gogh (van gō′, -gôkh′; *Du* vän khôkh′), **Vincent** 1853-90; Du. painter

van·guard (van′gärd′) ***n.*** ⟦ME *vaunt garde* < OFr *avant-garde* < *avant,* before (see AVAUNT) + *garde* (see GUARD)⟧ **1** the part of an army which goes ahead of the main body; the van **2** the leading position or persons in a movement, field of endeavor, etc.

va·nil·la (və nil′ə) ***n.*** ⟦ModL < Sp *vainilla,* small pod, husk, dim. of *vaina,* pod < L *vagina,* a case, pod, sheath⟧ **1** any of a genus (*Vanilla*) of climbing tropical American orchids with fragrant, greenish-yellow flowers **2** the podlike, immature capsule (**vanilla bean**) of some of these plants **3** an extract of these capsules, used as a flavoring in cooking, confections, etc. **4** the flavor of vanilla —***adj.*** **1** of or flavored with vanilla [*vanilla* ice cream] **2** ⟦in allusion to the commonness of *vanilla* ice cream⟧ [Informal] bland, plain, or basic: used esp. in the phrase **plain vanilla**

vanilla plant with beans

va·nil·lic (və nil′ik) ***adj.*** of or derived from vanilla or vanillin

va·nil·lin (və nil′in, van′ə lin) ***n.*** a fragrant, white, crystalline substance, $(CH_3O)(OH)C_6H_3CHO$, produced from the vanilla bean or made synthetically: used for flavoring, in perfumes, etc.

Va·nir (vä′nir) ***pl.n.*** ⟦ON⟧ *Norse Myth.* a race of gods who originally fight with but are later reconciled with the Aesir

van·ish (van′ish) ***vi.*** ⟦ME *vanissen,* aphetic < prp. stem of OFr *esvanir* < VL **exvanire,* for L *evanescere:* see EVANESCE⟧ **1** to go or pass suddenly from sight; disappear **2** to cease to exist; come to an end **3** *Math.* to become zero —***n.*** *Phonet.* the faint last part of any of certain diphthongs, as the sound like a faint (ē) ending the diphthong in *boy* —**van′ish·er** ***n.***

SYN.—**vanish** implies a sudden, complete, often mysterious passing from sight or existence [the stain had *vanished* overnight]; **disappear**, a more general term, implies either a sudden or gradual passing from sight or existence [customs that have long since *disappeared*]; **fade** suggests a gradual, complete or partial disappearance, as by losing color or brilliance [the design on this fabric won't *fade;* his fame has *faded*] —**ANT. appear, emerge**

van·ish·ing·ly (van′ish iŋ lē) ***adv.*** to the point of being nearly invisible or nonexistent [a *vanishingly* small probability]

vanishing point **1** the point where parallel lines receding from the observer seem to come together **2** a time, place, or stage at which something disappears or ceases to exist

van·i·tas (van′i täs′) ***n.*** ⟦L⟧ **1** vanity; futility **2** a work of art containing symbols of mortality or the impermanence of material things; esp., a 17th-cent. Dutch painting of this kind —***adj.*** of or relating to such paintings as a genre [the *vanitas* tradition]

van·i·ty (van′ə tē) ***n., pl.*** **-ties** ⟦ME *vanite* < OFr *vanité* < L *vanitas,* emptiness, worthlessness < *vanus,* vain: see WANT⟧ **1** any thing or act that is vain, futile, idle, or worthless **2** the quality or fact of being vain, or worthless; futility **3** the quality or fact of being vain, or excessively proud of oneself or one's qualities or possessions; self-conceit **4** a thing about which one is vain or conceited ☆**5** *short for* VANITY CASE ☆**6** a small table or ledge with a mirror for use while putting on cosmetics, combing one's hair, etc.; dressing table ☆**7** a bathroom cabinet with a washbowl set in the top —**SYN.** PRIDE

vanity case a woman's small traveling case fitted for carrying cosmetics, toilet articles, etc.

vanity mirror **1** a mirror, often portable, for use in fixing one's hair, applying make-up, etc. **2** a make-up mirror in a car's interior, esp., one fitted in a windshield visor

vanity plate a license plate having letters and numbers chosen by the owner, who usually pays an extra fee

☆**vanity press** (*or* **publisher**) a press or publishing house that publishes books only at the author's own expense

van·quish (vaŋ′kwish, van′-) ***vt.*** ⟦ME *venquissen* < OFr *veinquis-,* inflectional stem of *veinquir* < L *vincere,* to conquer: see VICTOR⟧ **1** to conquer or defeat in battle; force into submission **2** *a)* to defeat in any conflict, as in argument *b)* to overcome (a feeling, condition, etc.); suppress —**SYN.** CONQUER —**van′quish·er** ***n.***

Van Rens·se·laer (van ren′sə lər, -lir′; -rens′lər, -lir′), **Stephen** 1764-1839; U.S. politician & general

van·tage (van′tij) ***n.*** ⟦ME < Anglo-Fr, aphetic for OFr *avantage:* see ADVANTAGE⟧ **1** *a)* a position, situation, etc. more advantageous than that of an opponent *b)* a position that allows a clear and broad view, understanding, etc. (also **vantage point**) **2** [Chiefly Brit.] *Tennis short for* ADVANTAGE (***n.*** 4)

van't Hoff (vänt hôf′), **Ja·co·bus Hen·dri·cus** (yä kō′bəs hen drē′kəs) 1852-1911; Du. physical chemist

Va·nu·a Le·vu (vä no͞o′ä lev′o͞o) second largest of the Fiji Islands, northeast of Viti Levu: 2,145 sq mi (5,556 sq km)

Va·nu·a·tu (vä′no͞o ä′to͞o, van′o͞o-) country on a group of islands in the SW Pacific, west of Fiji: formerly an Anglo-French condominium, it became an independent republic in 1980; member of the Commonwealth: 4,710 sq mi (12,200 sq km); cap. Vila

van·ward (van′wərd) ***adj.*** in the vanguard, or front, as of an army —***adv.*** toward the vanguard

Van·zet·ti (van zet′ē), **Bar·to·lo·me·o** (bär′tō lō mā′ō) 1888-1927; It. anarchist in the U.S.: see SACCO, Nicola

vape (vāp) ***vi.*** **vaped, vap′ing** ⟦shortened < VAPOR or VAPORIZE⟧ [Informal] to inhale and exhale the vapor from an e-cigarette —**vap′er** ***n.***

vap·id (vap′id) ***adj.*** ⟦L *vapidus,* stale, insipid, akin to *vappa,* stale wine: for IE base see VAPOR⟧ **1** tasteless; flavorless; flat **2** uninteresting; lifeless; dull; boring [*vapid* talk] —**SYN.** INSIPID —**vap′id·ly** ***adv.*** —**vap′id·ness** ***n.***

va·pid·i·ty (va pid′ə tē) ***n.*** **1** the state or quality of being vapid; flatness; dullness; insipidity **2** *pl.* **-ties** a dull or uninteresting remark, idea, etc.

va·por (vā′pər) ***n.*** ⟦ME *vapour* < Anglo-Fr < MFr *vapeur* < L *vapor* < IE base **wep-,* to give off vapors⟧ **1** *a)* visible particles of moisture floating in the air, as fog, mist, or steam *b)* any cloudy or imperceptible exhalation, as smoke or noxious fumes **2** the gaseous form of any substance which is a liquid or a solid at room temperature **3** *a)* any substance vaporized for use in machinery, medical therapy, etc. *b)* a mixture of such a vaporized substance with air, as the explosive mixture in an automotive cylinder **4** [Now Rare] anything insubstantial or worthless **5** [*pl.*] [Archaic] *a)* exhalations from the stomach believed to be harmful to one's health *b)* hypochondria or depressed spirits (often with *the*) —***vi.*** **1** to rise or pass off in the form of vapor; evaporate **2** to give off vapor **3** to indulge in idle talk or boasting —***vt.*** VAPORIZE —**va′por·er** ***n.*** —**va′por·like′** ***adj.***

va·po·ret·to (vap′ə ret′ō) ***n., pl.*** **-tos** or **-ti** (-tē) ⟦It, dim. of *vapore,* steamboat < Fr *vapeur,* short for *bateau à vapeur,* calque of E STEAMBOAT⟧ a large motorboat used for public transportation on the canals of Venice

va·por·if·ic (vā′pə rif′ik) ***adj.*** VAPOROUS

va·por·ing (vā′pər iŋ) ***adj.*** boastful, bombastic, etc.

va·por·ish (-ish) ***adj.*** **1** like or full of vapor **2** [Archaic] having, or inclined to have, the vapors; in low spirits

va·por·ize (vā′pə rīz′) ***vt., vi.*** **-ized′, -iz′ing** **1** to change into vapor, as by heating or spraying **2** *a)* to scatter or disperse *b)* to (make) disappear, leaving no trace —**va′por·i·za′tion** ***n.***

va·por·iz·er (-rī′zər) ***n.*** a device for vaporizing liquids; specif., *a)* an atomizer, esp. one for creating steam or vaporizing medicated liquid for medicinal purposes *b)* a jet in a carburetor

☆**vapor lock** a blocking or slowing of the flow of liquid fuel to an internal-combustion engine, caused by excessive heat which vaporizes fuel in the fuel line, fuel pump, etc.

va·por·ous (vā′pər əs) ***adj.*** ⟦LL *vaporosus*⟧ **1** giving off or forming vapor **2** full of vapor; foggy; misty **3** like, having the nature of, or characteristic of vapor **4** *a)* fleeting, unsubstantial, fanciful, etc. (said of things, ideas, etc.) *b)* given to such ideas or talk —**va′por·ous·ly** ***adv.*** —**va′por·ous·ness** ***n.***, **va′por·os′i·ty** (-pər äs′ə tē)

vapor pressure the pressure of a vapor in equilibrium with its liquid or solid form: also called **vapor tension**

vapor trail CONTRAIL

va·por·ware (vā′pər wer′) ***n.*** ⟦VAPOR + -WARE⟧ [Slang] *Comput.* a commercial software product that has received much advance promotion but whose ultimate appearance on the market has become doubtful because of continual delays

va·por·y (vā′pər ē) ***adj.*** VAPOROUS

va·pour (-pər) ***n., vi., vt.*** *Brit. sp. of* VAPOR

☆**va·que·ro** (vä ker′ō) ***n., pl.*** **-ros** ⟦Sp < *vaca,* cow < L *vacca*⟧ [Southwest] a man who herds cattle; cowboy

var[1] (vär) ***n.*** ⟦< *v(olt) a(mpere) r(eactive)*⟧ *Elec.* the unit used to measure the apparent power in an alternating-current circuit, equal to one volt-ampere or one watt: sometimes written **VAr** or **VAR**

var[2] *abbrev.* **1** variable **2** variant(s) **3** variation **4** variety **5** various

VAR *abbrev.* visual-aural (radio) range

☆**va·ra** (vä′rä) ***n.*** ⟦Sp & Port, lit., rod, stick < L, forked pole < *varus,* bent: see VACILLATE⟧ **1** in Spain and Spanish America, an old unit of linear measure, varying from about 31 to 33 inches **2** an old Texas unit of linear measure equal to 33.33 inches (84.67 centimeters) **3** a unit of area, the square vara

☆**va·rac·tor** (və rak′tər) ***n.*** ⟦VAR(IABLE) + (RE)ACT(ANCE) + -OR⟧ *Electronics* a semiconductor diode capacitor whose capacitance varies with the voltage applied

Va·ra·na·si (və rän′ə sē′) city in S Uttar Pradesh, N India, on the Ganges

Va·ran·gi·an (və ran′jē ən) ***n.*** a member of a Scandinavian people that settled in Russia in the 9th cent. and, under Rurik, founded the first Russian dynasty

Var·dar (vär′där) river in Macedonia & N Greece, flowing into the Gulf of Salonika: *c.* 230 mi (370 km)

Va·rèse (və räz′, -rez′; *Fr* vȧ rez′), **Ed·gard** (ed′gär; *Fr* ed gär′) (born *Edgar Victor Achille Charles Varèse*) 1883-1965; U.S. composer, born in France

var·i·a·ble (ver′ē ə bəl, var′-) ***adj.*** ⟦ME < MFr < L *variabilis*⟧ **1** apt or likely to change or vary; changeable, inconstant, fickle, fluctuating, etc. **2** that can be changed or varied **3** designating or involving an interest rate, as on a mortgage loan, that varies over time according to some predetermined formula **4** *Biol.* tending to deviate in some way from the type; aberrant **5** *Math.* having no fixed value —***n.*** **1** anything changeable; esp., a quality or quantity that varies or may vary **2** *Astron. short for* VARIABLE STAR **3** *Math.,*

Physics a) a part of a mathematical expression that may assume any value in a specific, related set of values *b)* a symbol for such a part: opposed to CONSTANT —**var′i·a·bil′i·ty** ***n.***, **var′i·a·ble·ness** —**var′i·a·bly** ***adv.***

variable star a star whose brightness varies from time to time as the result of causes operating outside the earth's atmosphere: see CEPHEID (VARIABLE), RR LYRAE VARIABLES

var·i·ance (ver′ē əns, var′-) ***n.*** ⟦OFr < L *variantia* < L *varians,* prp. of *variare,* to VARY⟧ **1** the quality, state, or fact of varying or being variant; a changing or tendency to change **2** degree of change or difference; divergence; discrepancy **3** official permission to bypass regulations; specif., permission to make nonconforming use of zoned property **4** an active disagreement; quarrel; dispute **5** *Accounting* the difference between the actual costs of production and the standard or expected costs **6** *Chem.* the number of degrees of freedom of a system: see PHASE RULE **7** *Law* a lack of agreement between two parts of a legal proceeding which should agree, as between a statement and the evidence offered in support of it **8** *Statistics* the square of the standard deviation —**at variance** not in agreement or accord; conflicting

var·i·ant (-ənt) ***adj.*** ⟦OFr < L *varians:* see prec.⟧ **1** varying; different; esp., different in some way from others of the same kind or class, or from some standard or type **2** [Archaic] variable; changeable —***n.*** anything that is variant, as a different spelling of the same word, a different version of a literary passage, etc.

var·i·ate (-it) ***n.*** **1** VARIANT **2** VARIABLE (***n.*** 1) **3** RANDOM VARIABLE

var·i·a·tion (ver′ē ā′shən, var′-) ***n.*** ⟦ME *variacion* < OFr < L *variatio*⟧ **1** *a)* the act, fact, or process of varying; change or deviation in form, condition, appearance, extent, etc. from a former or usual state, or from an assumed standard *b)* the degree or extent of such change **2** DECLINATION (sense 3) **3** a thing that is somewhat different from another of the same kind **4** *Astron.* a change in or deviation from the mean motion or orbit of a planet, satellite, etc. **5** *Ballet* a solo dance **6** *Biol. a)* a deviation from the usual or parental type in structure or form *b)* an organism showing such deviation **7** *Math.* the manner in which two or more quantities change relative to one another **8** *Music* the repetition of a theme or musical idea with changes or embellishments in harmony, rhythm, key, etc., esp. any of a series of such repetitions developing a single theme —**var′i·a′tion·al** ***adj.***

var·i·cel·la (var′ə sel′ə) ***n.*** ⟦ModL, dim. of *variola:* see VARIOLA⟧ CHICKENPOX —**var′i·cel′loid′** (-oid′) ***adj.***

var·i·cel·late (var′ə sel′it, -āt′) ***adj.*** ⟦< ModL *varicella* (dim. of VARIX) + -ATE[1]⟧ *Zool.* marked with small or indistinct ridges: said of certain shells

var·i·ces (var′ə sēz′) ***n.*** *pl. of* VARIX

var·i·co- (var′ə kō) ⟦< L *varix,* VARIX⟧ *combining form* an enlarged, twisted blood or lymph vessel, esp. a vein [*varicocele*]: also, before a vowel, **var′ic-**

var·i·co·cele (var′ə kō sēl′) ***n.*** ⟦prec. + -CELE⟧ a varicose condition of the veins of the spermatic cord in the scrotum

var·i·col·ored (ver′ə kul′ərd, var′-) ***adj.*** ⟦< L *varius,* varied + COLORED⟧ of several or many colors

var·i·cose (var′ə kōs′) ***adj.*** ⟦L *varicosus* < *varix* (gen. *varicis*), VARIX⟧ **1** abnormally and irregularly swollen or dilated [*varicose* veins] **2** resulting from varicose veins [*varicose* ulcer]

var·i·co·sis (var′ə kō′sis) ***n.*** ⟦ModL: see VARIC(O)- & -OSIS⟧ a varicose condition of the veins

var·i·cos·i·ty (-käs′ə tē) ***n.*** **1** the condition of being varicose **2** *pl.* **-ties** VARIX

var·i·cot·o·my (-kät′ə mē) ***n.***, *pl.* **-mies** ⟦VARICO- + -TOMY⟧ the surgical excision of a varix, esp. of a varicose vein

var·ied (ver′ēd, var′-) ***adj.*** **1** of different kinds; various **2** showing different colors; variegated **3** changed; altered —**var′ied·ly** ***adv.***

var·i·e·gate (ver′ē ə gāt′, var′-) ***vt.*** **-gat′ed, -gat′ing** ⟦< L *variegatus,* pp. of *variegare* < *varius:* see VARY⟧ **1** to make varied in appearance by differences, as in colors **2** to give variety to; diversify

var·i·e·gat·ed (-id) ***adj.*** **1** marked with different colors in spots, streaks, etc.; parti-colored **2** having variety in character, form, etc.; varied; diversified

var·i·e·ga·tion (ver′ē ə gā′shən, var′-) ***n.*** **1** a variegating or being variegated **2** diversity or variety in character or appearance; specif., varied coloration

var·i·er (ver′ē ər, var′-) ***n.*** a person who varies

va·ri·e·tal (və rī′ə təl) ***adj.*** **1** of, connected with, or characterizing a variety **2** constituting a distinct variety; specif., designating a wine that bears the name of the variety of grape from which it is made —***n.*** a varietal wine —**va·ri′e·tal·ly** ***adv.***

va·ri·e·ty (və rī′ə tē) ***n.***, *pl.* **-ties** ⟦Fr *variété* < L *varietas*⟧ **1** the state or quality of being various or varied; absence of monotony or sameness **2** a different form of some thing, condition, or quality; sort; kind [*varieties* of cloth] **3** a number of different things thought of together; collection of varied things [a *variety* of items in the attic] **4** [Chiefly Brit.] *short for* VARIETY SHOW **5** *a) Biol.* loosely, a group having characteristics of its own within a species or subspecies; subdivision of a species *b) Bot.* a variant form of wild plants that has been recognized as a true taxon ranking below subspecies, even though it may have been brought under cultivation: e.g., cabbage (*Brassica oleracea* var. *capitata*) *c) Zool.* any of a group of widely separated variants within a single interbreeding population —***adj.*** of or in a variety show

variety meat meat other than flesh; specif., any of the edible organs, as the liver, kidneys, heart, etc.

variety show a show, as on television or in a nightclub, made up of different kinds of acts, as comic skits, songs, dances, etc.: see also VAUDEVILLE

☆**variety store** a retail store that sells a wide variety of relatively small and inexpensive items

var·i·form (ver′ə fôrm′, var′-) ***adj.*** varied in form; having various forms

var·i·o·coup·ler (ver′ē ō kup′lər, var′-) ***n.*** ⟦VARIO(US) + COUPLER⟧ a radio-frequency transformer consisting of a movable coil within a fixed coil

va·ri·o·la (və rī′ə lə, ver′ē ō′lə) ***n.*** ⟦ModL < ML, a pustule, prob. altered (based on L *varius,* various, mottled: see VARY) < L *varus,* pustule, pimple: see VARIX⟧ any of a group of viral diseases characterized by pustular eruptions, including smallpox, cowpox, and horsepox

va·ri·o·lar (-lər) ***adj.*** VARIOLOUS

var·i·ole (ver′ē ōl′) ***n.*** ⟦Fr < ML *variola:* see VARIOLA⟧ **1** a tiny pit or depression, as on some parts of an insect **2** *Geol.* a pea-sized spherule found in igneous rock and usually consisting of radiating crystals of plagioclase or pyroxene

var·i·o·lite (ver′ē ə līt′) ***n.*** ⟦Ger *variolit* < ML *variola* (see VARIOLA): from its pitted surface⟧ *Geol.* any igneous rock containing varioles

var·i·o·loid (ver′ē ə loid′, var′-) ***n.*** ⟦ModL *varioloides:* see VARIOLA & -OID⟧ a mild form of variola occurring in a person who has had a previous attack or who has been vaccinated

va·ri·o·lous (və rī′ə ləs) ***adj.*** ⟦ModL *variolosus*⟧ of or relating to variola, or smallpox

var·i·om·e·ter (ver′ē äm′ət ər, var′-) ***n.*** ⟦VARIO(US) + -METER⟧ **1** any of various devices designed to measure or record small variations in some quantity, as air pressure **2** a geophysical instrument for measuring magnetic forces or determining variations of magnetic force, esp. at different places on the planet earth **3** *Electronics* a continuously variable inductor consisting of a coil mounted within and in series with a fixed coil, with the inner coil capable of rotation so as to vary the total inductance

var·i·o·rum (ver′ē ôr′əm, var′-) ***n.*** ⟦L, of various (scholars), gen. pl. of *varius:* see fol.⟧ **1** an edition or text, as of a literary work, containing notes by various editors, scholars, etc. **2** an edition of a work containing variant versions of the text —***adj.*** of such an edition or text

var·i·ous (ver′ē əs, var′-) ***adj.*** ⟦L *varius,* diverse, parti-colored: see VARY⟧ **1** differing one from another; of several kinds **2** *a)* several or many [found in *various* sections of the country] *b)* individual; distinct [bequests to the *various* heirs] **3** many-sided; versatile [the *various* bounty of nature] **4** characterized by variety; varied in nature or appearance **5** [Obs.] changeable —**SYN.** DIFFERENT —**var′i·ous·ly** ***adv.*** —**var′i·ous·ness** ***n.***

va·ris·tor (və ris′tər) ***n.*** ⟦prec. + (RES)ISTOR⟧ *Electronics* a semiconductor resistor whose resistance varies with the voltage applied

var·ix (var′iks) ***n.***, *pl.* **var′i·ces′** (-ə sēz′) ⟦L < IE base **wer-*, a raised area (of skin or land) > WART, L *varus,* pimple⟧ **1** *Med.* a permanently and irregularly swollen or dilated blood or lymph vessel, esp. a vein; varicose vein **2** *Zool.* a prominent ridge across the whorls of various univalve shells, showing an earlier position of the outer lip

var·let (vär′lit) ***n.*** ⟦ME < OFr, a servant, page, var. of *vaslet* (see VALET): for sense development see KNAVE⟧ [Archaic] **1** an attendant **2** a youth serving as a knight's page **3** a scoundrel; knave

var·let·ry (-li trē) ***n.*** [Archaic] **1** varlets collectively **2** the rabble; mob

var·mint or **var·ment** (vär′mənt) ***n.*** ⟦dial. var. of VERMIN, with unhistoric *-t*⟧ [Informal or Dial.] a person or animal regarded as troublesome or objectionable: also used as a generalized epithet of disparagement

var·na (vur′nə) ***n.*** ⟦Hindi *varṇa,* color < Sans, orig. prob. covering < IE base **wer-*, to close, cover > WEIR⟧ CASTE (sense 1)

Var·na (vär′nä) seaport in NE Bulgaria, on the Black Sea

var·nish (vär′nish) ***n.*** ⟦ME *vernisch* < OFr *verniz* < ML *veronix, veronice,* a resin < Gr *Berenikē* (now Benghazi), ancient city in Cyrenaica⟧ **1** *a)* a preparation made of resinous substances dissolved in oil (**oil varnish**) or in alcohol, turpentine, etc. (**spirit varnish**), used to give a hard, clear, glossy surface to wood, metal, etc. *b)* any of various natural or prepared products used for the same purpose **2** the hard, clear, glossy surface produced **3** a surface gloss or smoothness, as of manner —***vt.*** **1** to cover with varnish; brush varnish on **2** to impart a smooth surface or appearance to, as with varnish **3** to make superficially attractive or acceptable, as by embellishing **4** to polish up; adorn —**var′nish·er** ***n.***

varnish tree any of a number of trees whose sap or juice can be made into a varnish or LACQUER (***n.*** 2)

va·room (və ro͞om′) ***n.***, ***vi.*** *var. of* VROOM

Var·ro (var′ō), **(Marcus Terentius)** 116-27 B.C.; Rom. scholar & writer

var·si·ty (vär′sə tē) ***n.***, *pl.* **-ties** ⟦contr. & altered < UNIVERSITY⟧ **1** the main team that represents a university, college, or school in some competition, esp. an athletic one **2** [Brit. Informal] university —***adj.*** designating or of the VARSITY (***n.*** 1) team or competition

Var·u·na (var′o͞o nə, vu′ro͞o-) ***n.*** ⟦Sans⟧ the Hindu god of the cosmos

var·us (ver′əs, var′-) ***n.*** ⟦ModL < L, bent, knock-kneed: see VACILLATE⟧ an abnormal bent or turned condition, esp. of the foot —***adj.*** abnormally bent or turned: said of the hip, knee, or foot

varve (värv) ***n.*** ⟦Swed *varv,* a layer < *varva,* to turn, change < ON *hverfa* < IE base **kwerp-*, to turn > CARPUS⟧ an annual layer of sedimentary material deposited in lakes and fiords by glacial meltwaters, consisting of two distinct bands of sediment deposited in summer and winter

var·y (ver′ē, var′-) ***vt.*** **var′ied, var′y·ing** ⟦ME *varien* < OFr *varier* < L *variare,* to vary, change < *varius,* various, prob. < IE base **wa-*, to bend, turn > VACILLATE⟧ **1** to change in form, appearance, nature, substance, etc.; alter;

modify **2** to make different from one another **3** to give variety to; diversify [*to vary one's reading*] **4** *Music* to repeat (a theme or idea) with changes in harmony, rhythm, key, etc. —*vi.* **1** to undergo change in any way; become different **2** to be different or diverse; differ [*varying opinions*] **3** to deviate, diverge, or depart (*from*) **4** *Biol.* to show variation —**SYN.** CHANGE

varying hare ⟦so named from the seasonal changes in the color of its coat⟧ SNOWSHOE HARE

vas (vas) *n., pl.* **va·sa** (vā′sə) ⟦L, a vessel, dish⟧ *Anat., Biol.* a vessel or duct —**va·sal** (vā′səl) *adj.*

Va·sa·ri (vä zä′rē), **Gior·gio** (jôr′jô) 1511-74; It. architect, painter, & biographer of artists

Vas·con·ga·das (väs′kôn gä′thäs) *Sp. name for* The BASQUE COUNTRY

vas·cu·lar (vas′kyə lər) *adj.* ⟦ModL *vascularis* < L *vasculum,* small vessel, dim. of *vas,* vessel, dish⟧ of or having vessels or ducts; specif., *a)* designating or of the vessels, or system of vessels, for conveying blood or lymph *b)* designating or of the specialized conducting cells, xylem and phloem, that convey water and foods in vascular plants; also, designating or of plants that have xylem and phloem —**vas′cu·lar′i·ty** (-lar′ə tē) *n.*

vascular bundle *Bot.* an isolated unit of the conducting system of vascular plants, consisting of xylem and phloem, frequently with other interspersed cells or a sheath of thick-walled cells

vascular cylinder STELE (sense 3)

vascular plant a plant having specialized tissues (xylem and phloem) that conduct water and synthesized foods, as any fern, gymnosperm, or angiosperm; tracheophyte

vascular ray MEDULLARY RAY (sense 2)

vascular tissue *Bot.* tissue composed of the xylem and phloem ducts that carry water and food through any of the vascular plants

vas·cu·lum (vas′kyə ləm) *n., pl.* **-la** (-lə) or **-lums** ⟦ModL < L: see VASCULAR⟧ a covered metal case, often cylindrical, used by botanists to carry specimen plants

vas de·fe·rens (vas def′ə renz′) *pl.* **va·sa de·fe·ren·ti·a** (vā′sə def′ə ren′shē ə) ⟦ModL < L *vas,* vessel + *deferens,* carrying down: see DEFERENCE⟧ the highly convoluted duct that conveys sperm from the testicle to the ejaculatory duct of the penis

vase (vās, vāz; *also, chiefly Brit* väz) *n.* ⟦Fr < L *vas,* vessel, dish⟧ an open container, usually rounded and of greater height than width, used for decoration, for holding flowers, etc.

vas·ec·to·my (va sek′tə mē) *n., pl.* **-mies** ⟦VAS(O)- + -ECTOMY⟧ the surgical removal or tying of the vas deferens to prevent the passing of sperm: used as a form of birth control —**vas·ec′to·mize** *vt.* **-mized, -miz·ing**

☆**Vas·e·line** (vas′ə lēn′, vas′ə lēn′) ⟦arbitrary coinage (a proprietary term first used *c.* 1872 by U.S. manufacturer R. A. Chesebrough) < Ger *was(ser),* WATER + Gr *el(aion),* OIL + -INE[3]⟧ *trademark for* PETROLATUM —*n.* [**v-**] petrolatum

Vash·ti (vash′tē, -tī′) *n.* ⟦Heb⟧ *Bible* the queen of Ahasuerus of Persia, disowned by him when she slighted his command for her presence at a feast: Esth. 1

vas·o- (vas′ō, -ə; vā′zō, -zə) ⟦< L *vas,* vessel⟧ *combining form* **1** the blood vessels [*vasogenic*] **2** the vas deferens [*vasotomy*] **3** vasomotor [*vasoinhibitor*] Also, usually before a vowel, **vas-**

vas·o·ac·tive (vas′ō ak′tiv, vā′zō-) *adj.* causing vasodilatation or vasoconstriction

vas·o·con·stric·tor (-kən strik′tər) *adj.* ⟦VASO- + CONSTRICTOR⟧ *Physiol.* causing constriction of the blood vessels: also **va′so·con·stric′tive** —*n.* a nerve or drug causing such constriction —**vas′o·con·stric′tion** *n.*

vas·o·di·la·tor (-dī′lāt′ər) *adj.* ⟦VASO- + DILATOR⟧ *Physiol.* causing dilatation of the blood vessels —*n.* a nerve or drug causing such dilatation —**vas′o·dil′a·ta′tion** (-dil′ə tā′shən) *n.,* **vas′o·di·la′tion** (-dī′lā′shən)

vas·o·in·hib·i·tor (-in hib′it ər) *n.* ⟦VASO- + INHIBITOR⟧ a drug or other agent inhibiting the action of the vasomotor nerves —**vas′o·in·hib′i·to′ry** (-i tôr′ē) *adj.*

vas·o·mo·tor (-mōt′ər) *adj.* ⟦VASO- + MOTOR⟧ *Physiol.* regulating the size in diameter of blood vessels: said of a nerve, nerve center, or drug

vas·o·pres·sin (-pres′ən) *n.* ⟦< VASO- + PRESS(URE) + -IN[1]⟧ a hormone secreted by the posterior lobe of the pituitary gland, that increases blood pressure by constricting the arterioles

vas·o·pres·sor (-pres′ər) *adj.* ⟦< VASO- + PRESS(URE) + -OR⟧ causing a rise in blood pressure by constricting blood vessels —*n.* a substance causing such a rise

vas·o·spasm (vas′ō spaz′əm, vā′zō-) *n.* ⟦VASO- + SPASM⟧ a spastic constriction of a blood vessel

vas·ot·o·my (va sät′ə mē) *n., pl.* **-mies** ⟦VASO- + -TOMY⟧ a surgical cutting of the vas deferens

vas·o·va·gal (vas′ō vā′gəl, vā′zō-) *adj.* ⟦VASO- + VAGAL⟧ pertaining to the action of the vagus nerve upon the circulatory system, as in causing a fainting spell

vas·sal (vas′əl) *n.* ⟦OFr < ML *vassalus,* manservant, extension of *vassus,* servant < Celt: for IE base see VALET⟧ **1** in the Middle Ages, a person who held land under the feudal system, doing homage and pledging fealty to an overlord, and performing military or other duties in return for his protection; feudal tenant **2** a subordinate, subject, servant, slave, etc. —*adj.* **1** of or like a vassal; dependent, servile, etc. **2** being a vassal

vas·sal·age (-ij) *n.* ⟦OFr < ML *vassallagium*⟧ **1** the state of being a vassal **2** the homage, loyalty, and service required of a vassal **3** dependence, servitude, or subjection **4** lands held by a vassal; fief **5** a body of vassals

vast (vast, väst) *adj.* ⟦L *vastus:* see WASTE⟧ very great in size, extent, amount, number, degree, etc. —*n.* [Archaic] a vast space —**vast′ly** *adv.* —**vast′ness** *n.*

Väs·te·rås (ves′tə rôs′) city in SC Sweden, on Lake Malar

vas·ti·tude (vas′tə to͞od′, -tyo͞od′) *n.* **1** the quality or condition of being vast **2** a vast extent or space

vast·y (vas′tē) *adj.* **vast′i·er, vast′i·est** [Archaic] vast; immense; huge

vat (vat) *n.* ⟦ME, southern dial. var. of *fat* < OE *fæt,* cask, vessel, akin to Ger *fass,* container < IE base **pēd-,* **pōd-,* to seize, hold > Latvian *puôds,* a pot⟧ **1** a large container for holding liquids, as those to be used in a manufacturing process or those to be stored for fermenting or ripening **2** a liquid containing a vat dye —*vt.* **vat′ted, vat′ting** **1** to place or store in a vat **2** to treat in a vat

VAT (vē′ā′tē′, vat) *abbrev.* value-added tax

vat dye a colorfast dye made soluble for application to cloth, then oxidized and thus rendered insoluble in the cloth —**vat′-dyed′** *adj.*

vat·ic (vat′ik) *adj.* ⟦< L *vates,* prophet < IE base **wāt-,* to be mentally excited > OE *wōd,* mad, MIr *fāth,* prophecy⟧ of or characteristic of a prophet; prophetic

Vat·i·can (vat′i kən) *n.* ⟦L *Vaticanus (mons),* Vatican (hill)⟧ **1** the papal residence, consisting of a group of buildings in Vatican City **2** papal government or authority —*adj.* **1** of this residence, government, or authority **2** designating either of the Roman Catholic Ecumenical Councils held in St. Peter's Basilica in 1869-70 (**Vatican I**) or 1962-65 (**Vatican II**)

Vatican City independent papal state constituted in 1929 as an enclave in Rome: it includes the Vatican & St. Peter's Basilica: 108.7 acres or 0.17 sq mi (0.44 sq km)

va·tic·i·nal (və tis′ə nəl) *adj.* ⟦< L *vaticinus* (see fol.) + -AL⟧ having the nature of or characterized by prophecy; prophetic

va·tic·i·nate (-nāt′) *vt., vi.* **-nat′ed, -nat′ing** ⟦< L *vaticinatus,* pp. of *vaticinari,* to foretell, prophesy < *vaticinus,* prophetic < *vates,* seer, prophet: see VATIC⟧ to prophesy; predict —**vat·i·ci·na·tion** (vat′ə si nā′shən) *n.* —**va·tic′i·na′tor** *n.*

Vät·ter (vet′ər), **Lake** lake in SC Sweden: 733 sq mi (1,898 sq km): Swed. name **Vät·tern** (vet′tərn)

va·tu (vä′to͞o) *n., pl.* **-tu** or **-tus** the basic monetary unit of Vanuatu: see the table of monetary units in the Reference Supplement

Vau·ban (vō bän′), Marquis **de** (də) (*Sébastien Le Prestre*) 1633-1707; Fr. military engineer

Vaud (vō) canton of W Switzerland: 1,240 sq mi (3,212 sq km); cap. Lausanne

vaude·ville (vôd′vil, väd′-; vô′də-, vä′də-) *n.* ⟦Fr, earlier *vau-de-vire,* after *Vau-de-Vire,* the valley of the Vire (in Normandy), famous for light, convivial songs⟧ ☆**1** *a)* a stage show consisting of mixed specialty acts, including songs, dances, comic skits, acrobatic performances, etc. *b)* this branch of entertainment generally, popular esp. in the early 20th cent. **2** [Now Rare] a comic theatrical piece interspersed with songs and dances **3** [Obs.] a satirical or topical song, often with pantomime

☆**vaude·vil·lian** (vôd vil′yən, väd-) *n.* one who performs in vaudeville —*adj.* of or like vaudeville

Vau·dois (vō dwä′) *pl.n.* ⟦Fr < ML *Valdenses:* see WALDENSES⟧ WALDENSES

Vaughan[1] (vôn) *n.* ⟦< the surname *Vaughan*⟧ a masculine name: also sp. Vaughn

Vaughan[2] (vôn) **1 Henry** 1622-95; Eng. poet **2 Sarah (Lois)** 1924-90; U.S. jazz singer

Vaughan[3] (vôn) city in SE Ontario, Canada, north of Toronto

Vaughan Williams, Ralph (rāf) 1872-1958; Eng. composer

vault[1] (vôlt) *n.* ⟦ME *voute* < OFr < VL **volvita,* an arch, vault < **volvitus,* pp. of **volvitare,* intens. of L *volvere,* to turn around, roll: see WALK⟧ **1** an arched roof, ceiling, or covering of masonry **2** an arched chamber or space, esp. when underground **3** a cellar room used for storage, as of wine **4** *a)* a burial chamber *b)* a concrete or metal enclosure in the ground, into which the casket is lowered at burial ☆**5** a secure room, often with individual safe-deposit boxes, for the safekeeping of valuables or money, as in a bank **6** an underground cave with a naturally arched roof **7** the sky as a vaultlike canopy **8** *Anat.* any arched cavity or structure [*the cranial vault*] —*vt.* **1** to make a vault over; cover with a vault **2** to build in the form of a vault —*vi.* to curve like a vault

groin vault

vault[2] (vôlt) *vi.* ⟦MFr *volter* < OIt *voltare* < VL **volvitare:* see prec.⟧ to jump, leap, or spring, as over a barrier or from one position to another, esp. with the help of the hands supported on the barrier, etc., or with the aid of a long pole —*vt.* to vault over [*to vault a fence*] —*n.* ⟦sense 1 < the v.; sense 3 < Fr *volte,* a turn, bound, leap < It *volta* < LL **volta:* see prec.⟧ **1** an act of vaulting **2** a leap or bound made by a horse **3** *Gym.* an event in which a gymnast vaults over a HORSE (*n.* 9) with the help of a springboard —**vault′er** *n.*

vault·ed (vôl′tid) *adj.* **1** having the form of a vault; arched **2** built with an arched roof; having a vault

vault·ing[1] (-tiŋ) *n.* **1** the building of a vault or vaults **2** the arched work forming a vault **3** a vault or vaults

vault·ing[2] (-tiŋ) *adj.* **1** leaping or leaping over **2** overreaching; unduly confident [*vaulting ambition*] **3** used in vaulting

vaulting horse *Gym.* **1** HORSE (*n.* 9) **2** VAULT[2] (*n.* 3)

vaunt (vônt, vänt) ***vi.*** ⟦ME *vaunten* < OFr *vanter* < LL(Ec) *vanitare* < L *vanus,* VAIN⟧ to boast; brag —***vt.*** to boast about (something); brag of —***n.*** a boast; brag —**SYN.** BOAST[2] —**vaunt′ed** ***adj.*** —**vaunt′er** ***n.***

vaunt-cour·i·er (vônt′koor′ē ər, vänt′-) ***n.*** ⟦aphetic < Fr *avant-courrier*⟧ [Obs.] a soldier sent out in advance of an army

v aux *abbrev.* auxiliary verb

vav (väv, vôv) ***n.*** ⟦Heb *vāv,* lit., a hook⟧ the sixth letter of the Hebrew alphabet (ו)

vav·a·sor (vav′ə sôr′) ***n.*** ⟦ME *vavasour* < OFr < ML *vavassor,* prob. < *vassus vassorum,* vassal of vassals < Gaul **vasso-:* see VALET⟧ in the Middle Ages, a feudal vassal next in rank below a baron, holding lands from a superior lord and having vassals under himself: also **vav′a·sour′** (-soor′)

va·ward (vä′wôrd) ***n.*** ⟦LME, contr. < *vaumwarde,* for NormFr *avantwarde* < OFr *avant-garde:* see VANGUARD⟧ *obs. var. of* VANGUARD

vb *abbrev.* **1** verb **2** verbal

VC *abbrev.* **1** venture capital **2** Vice-Chairman **3** Vice-Chancellor **4** Vice-Consul **5** Victoria Cross **6** Viet Cong

V-chip (vē′chip′) ***n.*** ⟦*v(iolence)-chip*⟧ a microchip in a TV receiver, for detecting an embedded program rating and then blocking the reception of programs whose content may not be suitable for younger viewers

VCR (vē′sē′är′) ***n.*** VIDEOCASSETTE RECORDER

VD *abbrev.* venereal disease

☆**V-Day** (vē′dā′) ***n.*** ⟦< *v(ictory)*⟧ a day of victory

VDT (vē′dē′tē′) ***n.*** *Comput.* a video display terminal

VDU (vē′dē′yoo′) ***n.*** *Comput.* a visual display unit

-′ve (v, əv) *suffix* have: used in contractions, often informally [*we′ve* seen it; *where′ve* you been?]

Ve·a·dar (vā′ä där, vē′-) ***n.*** ⟦Heb *wĕ-adhār,* lit., and Adar, hence second Adar⟧ ADAR SHENI

veal (vēl) ***n.*** ⟦ME *vel* < OFr *veel* < L *vitellus,* little calf, dim. of *vitulus,* calf, orig. prob. yearling; akin to *vetus,* old: see VETERAN⟧ **1** the flesh of a young calf, used as food **2** VEALER

☆**veal·er** (-ər) ***n.*** a calf, esp. as intended for food

veal piccata *see* PICCATA

Veb·len (veb′lən), **Thor·stein (Bunde)** (thôr′stīn) 1857-1929; U.S. economist & social scientist

vec·tor (vek′tər) ***n.*** ⟦ModL < L, bearer, carrier < *vectus,* pp. of *vehere,* to carry: see WAY⟧ **1** *Biol.* an animal, esp. an insect, that transmits a disease-producing organism from a host to an uninfected animal or plant **2** *Math. a)* a mathematical expression denoting a combination of magnitude and direction, as velocity (distinguished from SCALAR) *b)* a directed line segment representing such an expression *c)* an ordered set of real numbers, each denoting a distance on a coordinate axis **3** the particular course followed or to be followed, as by an aircraft; compass heading —***vt.*** to guide (a pilot, aircraft, missile, etc.) by means of a VECTOR (sense 3) sent by radio —**vec·to′ri·al** (-tôr′ē əl) ***adj.*** —**vec·to′ri·al·ly** ***adv.***

C D y A x B

vector
AB, x-component vector
AC, y-component vector
AD, sum of vectors
AB and AC

vector analysis the application of calculus to the study and use of vectors

vector product a vector perpendicular to each of two given vectors *u* and *v* and having magnitude equal to the product of the magnitudes of *u* and *v* and the sine of the angle from *u* to *v*

Ve·da (vā′də, vē′-) ***n.*** ⟦Sans *veda,* knowledge < IE base **weid-,* to see, know > WISE[1], L *videre,* to see⟧ **1** any of four ancient sacred books of Hinduism, consisting of hymns, chants, sacred formulas, etc.: see RIG VEDA **2** these books collectively —**Ve·da·ic** (vi dā′ik) ***adj.***

ve·da·li·a (və dā′lē ə, -dāl′yə) ***n.*** ⟦ModL < ?⟧ an Australian ladybug (*Rodolia cardinalis*), now widely introduced all over the world to combat certain scale insects

Ve·dan·ta (vi dän′tə, -dan′-) ***n.*** ⟦Sans *Vedānta* < *Veda* (see VEDA) + *anta,* an END[2]⟧ a system of Hindu monistic philosophy based on the Vedas —**Ve·dan′tic** ***adj.*** —**Ve·dan′tism′** ***n.***

☆**V-E Day** (vē′ē′) ⟦< *V(ictory in) E(urope) + Day*⟧ May 8, 1945, the day on which the surrender of Germany was announced, officially ending the European phase of WWII

Ved·da (ved′ə) ***n., pl.*** **-das** or **-da** ⟦Sinhalese, hunter⟧ a member of an aboriginal people of the forests of Sri Lanka: also sp. **Ved′dah** —**Ved′doid** (-oid′) ***adj.***

ve·dette (və det′) ***n.*** ⟦Fr < It *vedetta,* altered (infl. by *vedere,* to see) < *veletta,* sentry box < Sp *vela,* vigil < *velar,* to watch < L *vigilare:* see VIGIL⟧ [Obs.] a mounted sentinel posted in advance of the outposts of an army

Ve·dic (vā′dik, vē′-) ***adj.*** of the Vedas —***n.*** the Old Indic language of the Vedas, an early form of Sanskrit

vee (vē) ***n.*** **1** the letter V **2** something shaped like V —***adj.*** shaped like V

vee·jay (vē′jā′) ***n.*** ⟦< *v(ideo) j(ockey),* infl. by DEEJAY⟧ a person who hosts or conducts a TV program of music videos, interspersed with chatter, commercials, etc., or one who plays such videos at a club or disco

vee·na (vē′nä′) ***n.*** *alt. sp. of* VINA

☆**Veep** (vēp) ***n.*** ⟦altered from *veepee* (for VP)⟧ [*sometimes* **v-**] [Informal] a vice-president; specif., the vice president of the U.S.

veer[1] (vir) ***vi.*** ⟦altered (by assoc. with fol.) < Fr *virer,* to turn around, prob. < VL **virare,* contr. < L *vibrare:* see VIBRATE⟧ **1** to change direction; shift; turn or swing around **2** to change sides; shift, as from one opinion or attitude to another **3** *Meteorol.* to shift clockwise (in the Northern Hemisphere): said of the changing direction of a wind: opposed to BACK[1] (***vi.*** 3) —***vt.*** to turn or swing; change the course of —***n.*** a change of direction —**SYN.** DEVIATE —**veer′ing·ly** ***adv.***

veer[2] (vir) ***vt., vi.*** ⟦ME *veren* < MDu *vieren,* to let out⟧ *Naut.* to let out (a rope, anchor chain, etc.) gradually: often with *out*

☆**veer·y** (vir′ē) ***n., pl.*** **veer′ies** ⟦prob. echoic⟧ a small, brown and cream-colored thrush (*Catharus fuscescens*) of the E U.S.

veg (vej) ***n., pl.*** **veg** [Informal, Chiefly Brit.] a vegetable [roast beef with two *veg*]

Ve·ga[1] (vē′gə, vā′-) ***n.*** ⟦ML < Ar (*ar nasr*) *al wāqi′*, the falling (vulture)⟧ the brightest star in the constellation Lyra: magnitude, 0.03: see also SUMMER TRIANGLE

Ve·ga[2] (ve′gä), **Lo·pe de** (lô′pe *the*) (born *Lope Félix de Vega Carpio*) 1562-1635; Sp. dramatist & poet

ve·gan (vē′gən) ***n.*** ⟦< VEG(ETABLE) + -AN⟧ a vegetarian who eats no animal products

Ve·gas (vā′gəs) *informal name for* LAS VEGAS

veg·e·ta·ble (vej′tə bəl, vej′ə tə-) ***adj.*** ⟦ME < ML *vegetabilis,* vegetative, capable of growth < LL, animating, enlivening < L *vegetare:* see VEGETATE⟧ **1** of, or having the nature of, plants in general [the *vegetable* kingdom] **2** of, having the nature of, made from, consisting of, or produced by edible vegetables —***n.*** ⟦< ML *vegetabilia* (pl.), growing things, vegetables⟧ **1** broadly, any plant, as distinguished from animal or inorganic matter **2** *a)* any herbaceous plant that is eaten whole or in part, raw or cooked *b)* the edible part of such a plant, as the root (e.g., a carrot), tuber (a potato), seed (a pea), fruit (a tomato), stem (celery), or leaf (lettuce) **3** a person thought of as like a vegetable, as because of leading a dull, unthinking existence or because of having lost consciousness, the use of the mind, etc.

vegetable butter any of various vegetable fats that are solid at ordinary temperatures, esp. those from coconut or palm nut oil

vegetable ivory **1** the fully ripe, ivorylike seed of a South American palm (*Phytelephas macrocarpa*) used to make buttons, ornaments, etc. **2** the shell of the coquilla nut

vegetable marrow [Chiefly Brit.] **1** any of various large, elongated, smooth-skinned, meaty varieties of summer squash **2** the flesh of any of these

vegetable oil any of various liquid fats derived from the fruits or seeds of plants, used in food products, soaps, etc.

vegetable oyster ☆SALSIFY

vegetable silk KAPOK

☆**vegetable sponge** LUFFA (sense 1)

vegetable tallow any of various fatty, tallowlike substances from the fruits or seeds of plants

vegetable wax any of various waxes found on the leaves, stems, or fruits of some plants

veg·e·tal (vej′ə təl) ***adj.*** ⟦ME *vegytalle* < ML **vegetalis* < *vegetare,* to grow < L: see VEGETATE⟧ **1** VEGETABLE **2** VEGETATIVE (sense 3)

veg·e·tar·i·an (vej′ə ter′ē ən) ***n.*** ⟦VEGET(ABLE) + -ARIAN⟧ a person who eats no meat, and sometimes no animal products (as milk or eggs); esp., one who advocates a diet of only vegetables, fruits, grains, and nuts for reasons of health or because of principles opposing the killing of animals —***adj.*** **1** of vegetarians or vegetarianism **2** consisting only of vegetables, fruits, etc.

veg·e·tar·i·an·ism (-iz′əm) ***n.*** the principles or practices of vegetarians

veg·e·tate (vej′ə tāt′) ***vi.*** **-tat′ed, -tat′ing** ⟦< L *vegetatus,* pp. of *vegetare,* to enliven < *vegetus,* lively < *vegere,* to quicken, WAKE[1]; senses 1 & 2 infl. by VEGETABLE⟧ **1** to grow as plants **2** to exist with little mental and physical activity; lead a dull, inactive life **3** *Med.* to grow or increase in size, as a wart or other abnormal outgrowth does

veg·e·ta·tion (vej′ə tā′shən) ***n.*** ⟦ML *vegetatio,* growth < LL, an enlivening: see prec.⟧ **1** the act or process of vegetating **2** plant life in general; specif., the flora of a specified region **3** a dull, passive, unthinking existence **4** *Med.* any abnormal outgrowth on a part of the body —**veg′e·ta′tion·al** ***adj.***

veg·e·ta·tive (vej′ə tāt′iv) ***adj.*** ⟦ME < ML *vegetativus* < L *vegetatus:* see VEGETATE⟧ **1** *a)* of vegetation, or plants *b)* of or concerned with vegetation, or plant growth **2** growing, or capable of growing, as plants **3** designating or of those functions or parts of plants concerned with growth and nutrition as distinguished from reproduction **4** capable of causing growth in plants; fertile [*vegetative* material] **5** VEGETATIONAL **6** *a)* characterized by a passive existence *b)* characterized by extremely limited responsiveness and brain activity [a patient in a *vegetative* state] **7** *Zool.* of or pertaining to reproduction by budding or other asexual method Also **veg′e·tive** (-tiv) —**veg′e·ta′tive·ly** ***adv.*** —**veg′e·ta′tive·ness** ***n.***

veg·gie (vej′ē) ***n.*** **1** [Informal] a vegetable **2** [Slang] a vegetarian —***adj.*** [Informal] VEGETARIAN Also sp. **veg′ie**

ve·he·ment (vē′ə mənt) ***adj.*** ⟦LME < MFr *véhément* < L *vehemens,* eager, vehement < base of *vehere,* to carry: see WAY⟧ **1** acting or moving with great force; violent **2** having or characterized by intense feeling or strong passion; fervent, impassioned, etc. —**ve′he·mence** ***n.***, **ve′he·men·cy** —**ve′he·ment·ly** ***adv.***

ve·hi·cle (vē′ə kəl, vē′hik′əl) ***n.*** ⟦Fr *véhicule* < L *vehiculum,* carriage < *vehere,* to carry: see WAY⟧ **1** any device or contrivance for carrying or conveying persons or objects, esp. over land or in space, as an automobile, bicycle, sled, or spacecraft **2** a means by which thoughts are expressed or made known [music as the *vehicle* for one's ideas] **3** in a metaphor, that word or term whose usual, literal meaning is applied in a figurative, nonliteral way to the TENOR (sense 3) [in "all the world's a stage", "world" is the tenor and "stage" is the *vehicle*] **4** a play, film, etc. thought of as a means of communication or as a means of presenting a specified actor or company **5** *Painting* a liquid, as water or oil, with which pigments are mixed for use **6** *Pharmacy* a substance, as a syrup, in which medicines are given

ve·hic·u·lar (vē hik′yoo lər) ***adj.*** ⟦LL *vehicularis*⟧ **1** of or for vehicles [a *vehicular* tunnel] **2** serving as a vehicle **3** resulting from a collision or collisions, etc. of or with a vehicle or vehicles [*vehicular* homicide]

☆**V-8** (vē′āt′) ***adj.*** designating or of a type of reciprocating internal-combustion engine with eight cylinders arranged in a V-shape of two rows of four —***n.*** **1** a V-8 engine **2** a vehicle with a V-8 engine

Ve·ii (vē′yī) ancient Etruscan city northwest of Rome: destroyed by the Romans in 396 B.C.

veil (vāl) ***n.*** ⟦ME *veile,* veil, sail, curtain < NormFr < L *vela,* neut. pl., taken as fem., of *velum,* sail, cloth, curtain < IE base **weg-,* to weave, attach, a textile > OIr *figim,* I weave, OE *wecca,* wick⟧ **1** a piece of light fabric, as of net or gauze, worn, esp. by women, over the face or head or draped from a hat to conceal, protect, or enhance the face **2** any piece of cloth used as a concealing or separating screen or curtain **3** anything like a veil in that it covers or conceals [a *veil* of mist, a *veil* of silence] **4** *a)* a part of a nun's headdress, draped along the sides of the face and over the shoulders *b)* the state or life of a nun (chiefly in **take the veil**, to become a nun) **5** *short for* HUMERAL VEIL **6** [Dial.] CAUL **7** *Biol.* VELUM —***vt.*** **1** to cover with or as with a veil **2** to conceal, hide, disguise, screen, obscure, etc. —**veil′-like′** ***adj.***

veiled (vāld) ***adj.*** **1** wearing a veil **2** covered with or as with a veil **3** concealed, hidden, disguised, obscured, etc. **4** not openly expressed [a *veiled* threat]

veil·ing (vā′liŋ) ***n.*** **1** the act of covering with or as with a veil **2** a veil; curtain **3** thin, transparent fabric used for veils

vein (vān) ***n.*** ⟦ME *veine* < OFr < L *vena*⟧ **1** *a)* any blood vessel that carries blood from some part of the body back toward the heart *b)* loosely, any blood vessel (cf. ARTERY, CAPILLARY) **2** any of the riblike supports strengthening the membranous wings of an insect **3** any of the bundles of vascular tissue forming the framework of a leaf blade **4** a more or less continuous body of minerals, igneous or sedimentary rock, etc., occupying a fissure or zone, differing in nature from the enclosing rock, and usually deposited from solution by circulating water **5** LODE (senses 1 & 2) **6** a streak or marking of a color or substance different from the surrounding material, as in marble or wood **7** *a)* any distinctive quality or strain regarded as running through one's character, or a speech, writing, etc. [a *vein* of humor in the essay] *b)* course or tenor of thought, feeling, action, etc. **8** a temporary state of mind; mood [speaking in a serious *vein*] —***vt.*** **1** to streak or mark with or as with veins **2** to branch out through in the manner of veins —***SYN.*** MOOD[1]

veined (vānd) ***adj.*** having veins or veinlike markings

vein·ing (vā′niŋ) ***n.*** the formation or arrangement of veins or veinlike markings

vein·let (vān′lit) ***n.*** VENULE

vein·stone (-stōn′) ***n.*** GANGUE

vein·y (vā′nē) ***adj.*** **vein′i·er**, **vein′i·est** **1** having or showing veins **2** full of veins: said as of flesh, leaves, or marble

vel *abbrev. Bookbinding* vellum

ve·la (vē′lə) ***n.*** **1** ⟦ModL < L: see VEIL⟧ *pl. of* VELUM **2** ⟦L, sails, pl. of *velum:* see VEIL⟧ [V-] a constellation in the S Milky Way between Carina and Antlia: see ARGO (sense 2)

ve·la·men (və lā′mən) ***n.***, *pl.* **-lam′i·na** (-lam′ə nə) ⟦L, a covering < *velare,* to cover: for IE base see VEIL⟧ **1** *Anat.* a membrane or velum **2** *Bot.* the corky outer layer of the aerial roots of certain orchids —**vel·a·men·tous** (vel′ə men′təs) ***adj.***

ve·lar (vē′lər) ***adj.*** ⟦L *velaris,* belonging to a veil or curtain < *velum,* a VEIL⟧ **1** of a velum; esp., of the soft palate **2** *Phonet.* articulated with the back of the tongue touching or near the soft palate, as (k) followed by a back vowel as in *cup* —***n.*** a velar sound

ve·lar·i·um (və ler′ē əm) ***n.***, *pl.* **-i·a** (-ē ə) ⟦L < *velum,* a covering, VEIL⟧ in ancient Rome, a large awning over an amphitheater or theater

ve·lar·ize (vē′lər īz′) ***vt.*** **-ized′**, **-iz′ing** *Phonet.* to modify the pronunciation of (a sound) by having the back of the tongue raised toward the velum during articulation —**ve′lar·i·za′tion** ***n.***

ve·late (vē′lāt′, -lit) ***adj.*** ⟦L *velatus,* pp. of *velare,* to cover: for IE base see VEIL⟧ having a velum

Ve·láz·quez (ve läth′keth; *E* və las′kes, -kwez), **Die·go Ro·drí·guez de Sil·va y** (dye′gô rô thrē′geth *the* sēl′vä ē) 1599-1660; Sp. painter: also **Ve·lás·quez** (ve läs′keth)

☆**Vel·cro** (vel′krō) ⟦< Fr *vel(ours) cro(ché),* hooked velvet⟧ *trademark for* a nylon material made with both a surface of tiny hooks and a complementary surface of a clinging pile, used, as in garments, in matching strips that can be pressed together or pulled apart for easy fastening and unfastening —***n.*** [*occas.* v-] this material

veld (velt) ***n.*** ⟦Afrik < MDu *veld,* a FIELD⟧ in S & E Africa, open, grassy country, with few bushes and trees; grassland: also sp. **veldt**

vel·i·ta·tion (vel′ə tā′shən) ***n.*** ⟦L *velitatio* < *velitatus,* pp. of *velitari,* to skirmish < *velites,* VELITES⟧ a hostile encounter; skirmish or dispute

ve·li·tes (vē′li tēz′) ***pl.n.*** ⟦L, pl. of *veles* (gen. *velitis*), akin to *velox,* swift & *vehere,* to carry: see WAY⟧ in ancient Rome, lightly armed foot soldiers

vel·le·i·ty (və lē′ə tē) ***n.***, *pl.* **-ties** ⟦ML *velleitas* < L *velle,* to wish: see WILL[2]⟧ **1** the weakest kind of desire or volition **2** a mere wish that does not lead to the slightest action

vel·li·cate (vel′i kāt′) ***vt., vi.*** **-cat′ed**, **-cat′ing** ⟦L *vellicatus,* pp. of *vellicare,* to twitch, pinch < *vellere,* to pluck < IE base **wel-,* to tear, pluck out > OE *wæl,* battlefield⟧ [Now Rare] to twitch, pluck, etc.

vel·lum (vel′əm) ***n.*** ⟦ME *velim* < MFr *velin,* vellum, prepared calfskin < OFr *veel:* see VEAL⟧ **1** a fine kind of parchment prepared from calfskin, lambskin, or kidskin, used as writing parchment or for binding books **2** a manuscript written on vellum **3** a strong paper made to resemble vellum —***adj.*** of or like vellum

ve·loc·i·pede (və läs′ə pēd′) ***n.*** ⟦Fr *vélocipède* < L *velox* (gen. *velocis*), swift, speedy (for IE base see WAY) + *pes* (gen. *pedis*), FOOT⟧ **1** any of various early bicycles or tricycles **2** an old type of handcar for use on railroad tracks

ve·loc·i·rap·tor (və läs′ə rap′tər) ***n.*** ⟦ModL < L *velox,* swift + RAPTOR⟧ any of a genus (*Velociraptor*) of small, swift, two-footed theropod dinosaurs of the Late Cretaceous Period

ve·loc·i·ty (və läs′ə tē) ***n.***, *pl.* **-ties** ⟦Fr *vélocité* < L *velocitas* < *velox:* see VELOCIPEDE⟧ **1** quickness or rapidity of motion or action; swiftness; speed **2** *a)* rate of change of position, in relation to time; SPEED (sense 3a) *b)* a vector quantity that specifies both the speed of a body and its direction of motion (abbrev. *v*)

ve·lo·drome (vē′lə drōm′, vel′ə-) ***n.*** ⟦Fr *vélodrome* < *vélo* (contr. < *vélocipède,* VELOCIPEDE) + *-drome,* -DROME⟧ an indoor arena with a track banked for bicycle races

ve·lour (və loor′) ***n.***, *pl.* **ve·lours′** (-loorz′, -loor′) ⟦Fr: see VELURE⟧ a fabric with a soft nap like velvet, used for upholstery, clothing, etc.: also sp. **ve·lours** (və loor′), *pl.* **ve·lours′** (-loorz′, -loor′)

ve·lou·té (və lōō tā′) ***n.*** ⟦Fr, velvety < MFr < OFr *velous:* see VELURE⟧ a rich white sauce made from veal, chicken, or fish stock thickened with flour and butter: also **velouté sauce**

Vel·sen (vel′sən) city in W Netherlands: outer port of Amsterdam

vel·skoen (vel′skün′, fel′-) ***pl.n.*** ⟦Afrik < *vel,* skin (< MDu, akin to FELL[3]) + *skoen,* shoe (akin to OE *scoh,* SHOE)⟧ sturdy shoes of untanned hide, worn in South Africa: also **veld′skoen′** (velt′-, felt′-)

ve·lum (vē′ləm) ***n.***, *pl.* **-la** (-lə) ⟦L, a VEIL⟧ *Biol.* any of various veil-like membranous partitions or coverings; specif., *a)* SOFT PALATE *b)* the lobed, ciliated swimming organ of gastropod larvae, located near the mouth

ve·lure (və loor′) ***n.*** ⟦Fr *velours,* altered < OFr *velous* < LL *villosus,* shaggy < *villus,* shaggy hair: see WOOL⟧ [Rare] velvet or a fabric like velvet

ve·lu·ti·nous (və lōōt′'n əs) ***adj.*** ⟦< It *velluto,* velvet (< VL *villutus:* see fol.) + -OUS⟧ *Biol.* covered with short, dense, silky, upright hairs; soft and velvety

vel·vet (vel′vət) ***n.*** ⟦ME < OFr *veluotte* < VL *villutus* < L *villus,* shaggy hair: see WOOL⟧ **1** a rich fabric as of silk, rayon, or nylon with a soft, thick pile: **pile velvet** has the pile uncut, standing in loops, and **cut velvet** has the loops cut apart **2** anything with a surface like that of velvet **3** a soft, vascular skin on a deer's growing antlers ☆**4** [Old Slang] extra or clear profit or winnings; gain —***adj.*** **1** made of or covered with velvet **2** smooth or soft like velvet

☆**velvet ant** any of a family (Mutillidae) of antlike wasps, often with brightly colored hairs: the females are wingless

☆**velvet bean** a coarse, twining, leguminous annual vine (*Stizolobium deeringianum*) grown for forage

vel·vet·een (vel′və tēn′) ***n.*** ⟦< VELVET⟧ **1** a cotton cloth with a short, thick pile, resembling velvet **2** [*pl.*] clothes, esp. trousers, made of velveteen

vel·vet·y (vel′vət ē) ***adj.*** **1** smooth or soft like velvet **2** having a smooth taste; mellow; not harsh: said of liquors

Ven *abbrev.* Venerable

ve·na (vē′nə) ***n.***, *pl.* **ve′nae** (-nē) ⟦L⟧ a vein

ve·na ca·va (vē′nə kā′və) *pl.* **ve·nae ca·vae** (vē′nē kā′vē) ⟦ModL < L *vena,* vein + *cava,* fem. of *cavus,* hollow⟧ *Anat.* either of two large veins conveying blood to the right atrium of the heart

ve·nal (vē′nəl) ***adj.*** ⟦L *venalis,* salable, for sale < **venus,* sale < IE **wesno-,* price > Sans *vasná-,* price, payment, Gr *ōnos,* price⟧ **1** [Now Rare] capable of being obtained for a price [*venal* services] **2** that can readily be bribed or corrupted [a *venal* judge] **3** characterized by bribery or corruption [a *venal* bargain] —**ve′nal·ly** ***adv.***

ve·nal·i·ty (vi nal′ə tē) ***n.***, *pl.* **-ties** ⟦< Fr or LL: Fr *venalité* < LL *venalitas*⟧ state, quality, or instance of being venal; willingness to be bribed or bought off, or to prostitute one's talents for mercenary considerations

ve·na·tion (vē nā′shən) ***n.*** ⟦< L *vena,* a vein⟧ **1** an arrangement or system of veins, as in an animal part, an insect's wing, or a leaf **2** such veins collectively

vend (vend) ***vt.*** ⟦Fr *vendre* < L *vendere,* contr. < *venum dare,* to offer for sale < **venus,* sale (see VENAL) + *dare,* to give⟧ **1** to sell, esp. by peddling **2** [Now Rare] to give public expression to (opinions); publish —***vi.*** **1** to sell goods **2** [Archaic] to be disposed of by sale —***SYN.*** SELL

ven·dace (ven′dās′) ***n.***, *pl.* **-dace′** or **-dac′es** ⟦OFr *vandoise,* dace < Gaul **vindisia* < **vindos,* white; akin to Welsh *gwynn*⟧ any of various European whitefishes (genus *Coregonus*) of the lakes of England and Scotland

vendee (ven dē′) ***n.*** ⟦VEND + -EE[1]⟧ the person to whom a thing is sold; buyer

Ven·dée (vän dā′) region of W France, south of Brittany: scene of peasant insurrections against the French Revolutionary government (1793-96) —**Ven·de·an** (ven dē′ən) ***adj., n.***

vend·er (ven′dər) ***n.*** *alt. sp. of* VENDOR

ven·det·ta (ven det′ə) ***n.*** ⟦It < L *vindicta,* vengeance: see VINDICTIVE⟧ **1** a feud in which the relatives of a murdered or wronged person seek vengeance on the murderer or wrongdoer or on members of that person's family **2** any bitter quarrel or feud —**ven·det′tist** ***n.***

ven·deuse (vän döz′) ***n.,*** *pl.* **-deuses′** (-döz′) ⟦Fr⟧ a saleswoman, esp. one who sells women's clothing

vend·i·ble (ven′də bəl) ***adj.*** ⟦ME < L *vendibilis* < *vendere:* see VEND⟧ **1** capable of being sold: also sp. **vend′a·ble 2** [Obs.] VENAL —***n.*** something vendible —**vend′i·bil′i·ty** ***n.*** —**vend′i·bly** ***adv.***

vending machine a machine that dispenses snacks, drinks, or other small items when coins or bills are inserted

ven·di·tion (ven dish′ən) ***n.*** ⟦L *venditio* < *venditus,* pp. of *vendere:* see VEND⟧ the act of vending; sale

Ven·dôme (vän dōm′), Duc **(Louis Joseph) de** (də) 1654-1712; Fr. general: marshal of France

ven·dor (ven′dər, ven dôr′) ***n.*** ⟦Anglo-Fr < Fr *vendre*⟧ **1** one who vends, or sells; seller **2** VENDING MACHINE

☆**ven·due** (ven′do͞o′, -dyo͞o′) ***n.*** ⟦obs. Fr, sale < *vendu,* pp. of *vendre:* see VEND⟧ a public auction

ve·neer (və nir′) ***vt.*** ⟦Ger *furnieren,* to veneer < Fr *fournir,* to FURNISH⟧ **1** to cover with a thin layer of more costly material; esp., to cover (wood) with wood of finer quality **2** to give a superficially attractive appearance to —***n.*** **1** a thin surface layer of fine wood or costly material laid over a base of common material **2** any of the thin layers glued together to form plywood **3** any attractive but superficial appearance or display [*a veneer* of culture]

ve·neer·ing (-iŋ) ***n.*** **1** the act of one who veneers **2** material used for veneer

ven·e·punc·ture (ven′ə puŋk′chər, vē′nə-) ***n.*** *alt. sp. of* VENIPUNCTURE

ven·er·a·ble (ven′ər ə bəl) ***adj.*** ⟦ME < MFr *vénérable* < L *venerabilis,* to be reverenced < *venerari:* see VENERATE⟧ **1** worthy of respect or reverence by reason of age and dignity, character, or position **2** impressive on account of age or historic or religious associations [*a venerable* monument] **3** [**V-**] *a) Anglican Ch.* a title of reverence for an archdeacon *b) R.C.Ch.* a title of veneration for a dead person who may later be beatified —**ven′er·a·bil′i·ty** ***n.,*** **ven′er·a·ble·ness** —**ven′er·a·bly** ***adv.***

Venerable Bede, the *see* BEDE, Saint

ven·er·ate (ven′ə rāt′) ***vt.*** **-at′ed, -at′ing** ⟦< L *veneratus,* pp. of *venerari,* to worship, reverence < *venus* (gen. *veneris*), love: see VENUS⟧ to look upon with feelings of deep respect; regard as venerable; revere —***SYN.*** REVERE[1] —**ven′er·a′tor** ***n.***

ven·er·a·tion (ven′ə rā′shən) ***n.*** ⟦ME *veneracion* < OFr < L *veneratio*⟧ **1** a venerating or being venerated **2** a feeling of deep respect and reverence **3** an act of showing this —***SYN.*** AWE

ve·ne·re·al (və nir′ē əl) ***adj.*** ⟦ME *venerealle* < L *venereus* < *venus,* love: see VENUS⟧ **1** *a)* having to do with sexual love or intercourse *b)* serving to arouse sexual desire; aphrodisiac **2** designating or of a disease or condition, as syphilis or gonorrhea, transmitted only or chiefly by sexual intercourse with an infected individual

ve·ne·re·ol·o·gy (və nir′ē äl′ə jē) ***n.*** ⟦< prec. + -OLOGY⟧ the branch of medicine dealing with sexually transmitted disease —**ve·ne′re·ol′o·gist** ***n.***

ven·er·y[1] (ven′ər ē) ***n.*** ⟦LME *venerie* < L *Venus* (gen. *Veneris*): see VENUS⟧ [Archaic] the indulgence of sexual desire; specif., sexual intercourse

ven·er·y[2] (ven′ər ē) ***n.*** ⟦ME *venerie* < MFr < *vener,* to hunt < L *venari:* see VENISON⟧ [Archaic] the act or practice of hunting game; the chase

ven·e·sec·tion (ven′ə sek′shən, vē′nə-) ***n.*** ⟦< ModL *venae sectio,* cutting of a vein: see VEIN & SECTION⟧ *Med.* PHLEBOTOMY

Ve·ne·ti·a (və nē′shē ə, -shə) ⟦L < *Veneti:* see VENETIC⟧ **1** ancient district at the head of the Adriatic, north of the Po River: with Istria it formed a Roman province **2** former region of NE Italy, the E portion of which was ceded to Yugoslavia in 1947 **3** VENETO

Ve·ne·tian (və nē′shən) ***adj.*** of Venice or its people or culture —***n.*** a person born or living in Venice

Venetian blind [*also* **v- b-**] [*often pl.*] a window blind made of a number of thin, horizontal wooden, metal, or plastic slats that can be set together at any angle to regulate the light and air passing through or be drawn up together to the top of the window by means of cords

Venetian glass a fine glassware made in or near Venice, esp. on the nearby island of Murano

Venetian red **1** a red pigment formerly made from ferric oxides, now prepared synthetically **2** a brownish-red color

Ve·net·ic (və net′ik) ***n.*** ⟦< L *Veneticus,* of the Veneti, after *Veneti,* a people living in VENETIA⟧ an extinct Italic language known through about 200 short inscriptions

Ve·ne·to (vā′nə tō′, ven′ə-) region of N Italy, on the Adriatic: 7,080 sq mi (18,337 sq km); chief city, Venice

Venez *abbrev.* Venezuela

Ve·ne·zi·a (və net′sē ə) **1** *It. name for* VENICE **2** former region of N Italy, generally corresponding to ancient Venetia: it now forms most of Veneto

Ven·e·zue·la (ven′ə zwā′lə, -zwē′-; *Sp* ve′ne swe′lä) **1** country in N South America: 352,144 sq mi (912,050 sq km); cap. Caracas **2 Gulf of** inlet of the Caribbean, on the NW coast of Venezuela: *c.* 150 mi (241 km) wide —**Ven′e·zue′lan** ***adj., n.***

venge·ance (ven′jəns) ***n.*** ⟦ME < OFr < *venger, vengier,* to avenge < L *vindicare:* see VINDICATE⟧ **1** the return of an injury for an injury, in punishment or retribution; avenging of an injury or offense; revenge **2** the desire to make such a return —**with a vengeance 1** with great force or fury **2** excessively; to an unusual extent

venge·ful (venj′fəl) ***adj.*** ⟦obs. *venge,* vengeance < *venge,* to avenge < ME *vengen* < OFr *venger, vengier* (see prec.) + -FUL⟧ **1** desiring or seeking vengeance; vindictive **2** arising from a desire for vengeance: said of actions or behavior **3** serving to inflict vengeance —***SYN.*** VINDICTIVE —**venge′ful·ly** ***adv.*** —**venge′ful·ness** ***n.***

ve·ni·al (vēn′yəl, vē′nē əl) ***adj.*** ⟦OFr < LL(Ec) *venialis,* pardonable, orig., gracious < L *venia,* a grace, favor, akin to *venus,* love: see VENUS⟧ **1** that may be forgiven; pardonable **2** that may be excused or overlooked; excusable: said as of an error or fault **3** *Theol.* not causing spiritual death: said of sin either not serious in itself or, if serious, not adequately recognized as such or not committed with full consent of one's will: cf. MORTAL —**ve·ni·al·i·ty** (vē′nē al′ə tē) ***n.*** —**ve′ni·al·ly** ***adv.***

Ven·ice (ven′is) **1** seaport in N Italy built on more than 100 small islands in the Lagoon of Venice: formerly a maritime city-state extending over most of Venetia & Dalmatia: It. name VENEZIA **2 Gulf of** N end of the Adriatic: *c.* 60 mi (97 km) wide **3 Lagoon of** arm of this gulf, on the coast of Veneto: *c.* 180 sq mi (466 sq km)

ven·in (ven′in) ***n.*** ⟦< VEN(OM) + -IN[1]⟧ any of the specific toxic constituents of animal venoms

ven·i·punc·ture (ven′ə puŋk′chər, vē′nə-) ***n.*** ⟦< L *vena,* vein + PUNCTURE⟧ *Med.* the puncture of a vein, as with a hypodermic needle

ve·ni·re (və nī′rē) ***n.*** ⟦L, COME⟧ **1** *short for* VENIRE FACIAS **2** a list or group of people from among whom a jury or juries will be selected

venire fa·ci·as (fā′shē as′) ⟦ME < ML, cause to come < L *venire,* COME + 2d pers. sing., pres. subj., of *facere,* to make, DO[1]⟧ *Law* a writ issued by a judge ordering that persons be summoned to serve as jurors

☆**ve·ni·re·man** (və nī′rē mən) ***n.,*** *pl.* **-men** (-mən) a member of a VENIRE (sense 2)

ven·i·son (ven′i sən, -zən) ***n.*** ⟦ME *veneison* < OFr, hunting < L *venatio,* the chase < *venatus,* pp. of *venari,* to hunt < IE base **wen-,* to strive for, desire > WIN, L *venus,* love⟧ **1** [Obs.] the flesh of a game animal, used as food **2** the flesh of a deer, used as food

Ve·ni·te (və nē′te) ***n.*** ⟦L, come, 2d pers. pl., imper., of *venire,* to COME: from the opening word of the 94th Psalm in the Vulg. (95th in the KJV)⟧ Psalm 95, used as the introductory part of matins or morning prayer

ve·ni, vi·di, vi·ci (wā′nē wē′dē wē′kē; *E, usually* vā′nē vē′dē vē′chē) ⟦L⟧ I came, I saw, I conquered: Julius Caesar's report of a victory to the Roman Senate

Venn diagram (ven) ⟦after John *Venn* (1834-1923), Eng logician⟧ *Logic, Math.* a diagram using overlapping circles, often shaded or crosshatched, to show relationships between sets or propositions

ven·om (ven′əm) ***n.*** ⟦ME < OFr *venim,* var. of *venin* < L *venenum,* a poison, IE **wenes-nom,* love potion < **wenos:* see VENUS⟧ **1** the poison secreted by some snakes, spiders, insects, etc., introduced into the body of the victim by bite or sting **2** [Rare] poison of any kind **3** malignancy; spite; malice

ven·om·ous (-əs) ***adj.*** ⟦ME *venimous* < OFr *venimeux*⟧ **1** containing or full of venom; poisonous **2** malignant; spiteful; malicious **3** *Zool.* having a poison gland or glands and able to inflict a poisonous wound by biting or stinging —**ven′om·ous·ly** ***adv.*** —**ven′om·ous·ness** ***n.***

ve·nose (vē′nōs) ***adj.*** veined or veiny: said as of an insect's wing

ve·nos·i·ty (vē näs′ə tē) ***n.*** the state or quality of being venose or venous

ve·nous (vē′nəs) ***adj.*** ⟦L *venosus*⟧ **1** *Biol. a)* of a vein or veins *b)* having veins or full of veins; veiny **2** *Physiol.* designating blood being carried in the veins back to the heart and lungs: venous blood has given up oxygen and taken up carbon dioxide, and in vertebrates is characterized by a dark-red color —**ve′nous·ly** ***adv.***

vent[1] (vent) ***n.*** ⟦ME *venten* < OFr *venter,* to blow (or aphetic < OFr *esventer,* to expose to the air, let out < *es-,* out + *venter*) < VL **ventare* < L *ventus,* WIND[2]⟧ **1** [Rare] the action of escaping or passing out, or the means or opportunity to do this; issue; outlet **2** expression; release [giving *vent* to emotion] **3** *a)* a hole or opening to permit passage or escape, as of a gas ☆*b)* an opening on or beneath the dashboard having a number of slats, often adjustable, for regulating the passage of air into a motor vehicle **4** in early guns, the small hole at the breech through which a spark passes to set off the charge **5** the opening in a volcano from which gas and molten rock erupt **6** *Zool.* the excretory opening in animals; esp., the external opening of the cloaca in birds, reptiles, amphibians, and fishes —***vt.*** **1** to make a vent in or provide a vent for **2** to allow (steam, gas, etc.) to escape through an opening **3** to give release or expression to (thoughts or feelings) **4** to relieve or unburden (oneself) by giving vent to feelings —***vi.*** to give release or expression to one's thoughts or feelings

vent[2] (vent) ***n.*** ⟦ME *vent,* altered (infl. by prec.) < *fente* < OFr < VL **findita,* fem. pp., for L *fissus,* pp. of *findere,* to split: see FISSION⟧ a vertical slit in a garment, esp. one put in the back or sides of a coat —***vt.*** to make a vent or vents in

vent·age (ven′tij) ***n.*** ⟦see -AGE⟧ a small hole or opening; vent; specif., a fingering hole on a wind instrument

ven·tail (ven′tāl′) ***n.*** ⟦ME *ventayle* < OFr *ventaille* < *vent* (< L *ventus*),

WIND²] the movable piece of armor forming the lower front part of a metal helmet

ven·ter (ven′tər) ***n.*** ⟦Anglo-Fr < L *venter:* see VENTRAL⟧ **1** *Anat., Zool. a)* the belly, or abdomen *b)* a protuberance like a belly, as on a muscle *c)* a cavity or hollowed surface **2** *Law* the womb: used in designating maternal parentage, as in *children of the first venter,* meaning "children of the first wife"

ven·ti·fact (ven′tə fakt′) ***n.*** ⟦< L *ventus,* a WIND² + (ART)IFACT⟧ any stone shaped by the abrasion of windblown sand

ven·ti·late (vent′'l āt′) ***vt.*** **-lat′ed, -lat′ing** ⟦< L *ventilatus,* pp. of *ventilare,* to fan, ventilate < *ventus,* WIND²⟧ **1** *a)* to circulate fresh air in (a room, etc.), driving out foul or stale air *b)* to circulate in (a room, etc.) so as to freshen (said of air) **2** to provide with an opening for the escape of air, gas, etc.; furnish a means for airing **3** to expose (a substance) to fresh air so as to keep in good condition **4** to examine and discuss in public; bring (a grievance, problem, etc.) out into the open **5** to aerate (blood); oxygenate **6** [Obs.] to winnow (grain) **—ven′ti·la′tive** ***adj.***

ven·ti·la·tion (vent′'l ā′shən) ***n.*** ⟦L *ventilatio*⟧ **1** a ventilating or being ventilated **2** a system or equipment for ventilating

ven·ti·la·tor (vent′'l āt′ər) ***n.*** **1** a thing that ventilates; esp., any device used to bring in fresh air and drive out foul or stale air **2** an apparatus for giving artificial respiration

ven·ti·la·to·ry (-ə tôr′ē) ***adj.*** **1** of, having, or pertaining to ventilation **2** *Med.* of, pertaining to, or involved in breathing and the oxygenation of the blood

ven·tral (ven′trəl) ***adj.*** ⟦Fr < L *ventralis* < *venter,* belly < IE base **udero-,* belly > L *uterus,* womb, Ger *wanst,* paunch⟧ **1** *Anat., Zool.* of, near, on, or toward the belly or the side of the body where the belly is located: in humans the front, or anterior, side but in most other animals the lower, or inferior, side **2** *Bot.* of or belonging to the inner or lower surface **—ven′tral·ly** ***adv.***

ven·tri- (ven′tri, -trə) *combining form* VENTRO-

ven·tri·cle (ven′tri kəl) ***n.*** ⟦ME < L *ventriculus,* stomach, ventricle, dim. of *venter:* see VENTRAL⟧ *Anat., Zool.* any of various cavities or hollow organs; specif., *a)* either of the two lower chambers of the heart which receive blood from the atria and pump it into the arteries *b)* any of the four small continuous cavities within the brain

ven·tri·cose (-kōs′) ***adj.*** ⟦ModL *ventricosus* < L *venter,* belly: see VENTRAL⟧ **1** large-bellied **2** *Biol.* swelling out on one side **—ven′tri·cos′i·ty** (-käs′ə tē) ***n.***

ven·tric·u·lar (ven trik′yə lər) ***adj.*** ⟦< L *ventriculus* (see VENTRICLE) + -AR⟧ **1** of, involving, or being a ventricle **2** having a bulge or belly

ven·tric·u·lus (-ləs) ***n.,*** *pl.* **-u·li′** (-lī′) ⟦ModL < L: see VENTRICLE⟧ **1** *Entomology* that part of the alimentary tract of an insect, analogous to the stomach, where digestion takes place **2** *Ornithology* the gizzard of a bird

ven·tri·lo·qui·al (ven′trə lō′kwē əl) ***adj.*** of, having to do with, or using ventriloquism **—ven′tri·lo′qui·al·ly** ***adv.***

ven·tril·o·quism (ven tril′ə kwiz′əm) ***n.*** ⟦< L *ventriloquus,* lit., one who speaks from the belly < *venter,* belly (see VENTRAL) + *loqui,* to speak + -ISM⟧ the art or practice of speaking so that the voice seems to come from some source other than the speaker: also **ven·tril′o·quy** (-kwē)

ven·tril·o·quist (-kwist) ***n.*** a person who practices ventriloquism; specif., an entertainer who uses ventriloquism to carry on a pretended conversation as with a large puppet, or dummy **—ven·tril′o·quis′tic** ***adj.***

ven·tril·o·quize (-kwīz′) ***vi., vt.*** **-quized′, -quiz′ing** to utter (words or sounds) as a ventriloquist

ven·tro- (ven′trō, -trə) ⟦< L *venter,* belly: see VENTRAL⟧ *combining form* **1** abdomen, belly *[ventrotomy]* **2** ventral and *[ventrodorsal]*

ven·tro·dor·sal (ven′trō dôr′səl) ***adj.*** ⟦prec. + DORSAL¹⟧ of or involving both the ventral and dorsal surfaces

ven·tro·lat·er·al (-lat′ər əl) ***adj.*** ⟦VENTRO- + LATERAL⟧ of or involving both the ventral and lateral surfaces

Ven·tu·ra (ven toor′ə, -tyoor′-) ⟦< *(San Buena)ventura* (the official name) < Sp, lit., saint of good fortune⟧ city in SW Calif., northwest of Los Angeles

ven·ture (ven′chər) ***n.*** ⟦ME, aphetic for *aventure:* see ADVENTURE⟧ **1** a risky or dangerous undertaking; esp., a new or speculative business enterprise **2** something on which a risk is taken, as the merchandise in a commercial enterprise or a stake in gambling **3** chance; fortune: now only in **at a venture,** by mere chance; at random **—*vt.*** **-tured, -tur·ing 1** to expose to danger or risk *[to venture* one's life*]* **2** to expose (money, merchandise, etc.) to chance of loss **3** to undertake the risk of; brave *[to venture* a storm*]* **4** to express at the risk of criticism, objection, denial, etc. *[to venture* an opinion*]* **—*vi.*** to do or go at some risk **—ven′tur·er** ***n.***

☆**venture capital** funds invested or available for investment at considerable risk of loss in potentially highly profitable enterprises; risk capital **—venture capitalist**

ven·ture·some (-səm) ***adj.*** **1** inclined to venture, or take chances; daring **2** involving danger or risk; risky; hazardous **—ven′ture·some·ly** ***adv.*** **—ven′ture·some·ness** ***n.***

ven·tu·ri (tube) (ven toor′ē) ⟦after G. B. *Venturi* (1746-1822), It physicist⟧ a short tube with a constricted, throatlike passage that increases the velocity and lowers the pressure of a fluid conveyed through it: used to measure the flow of a fluid, to operate instruments, as in aircraft, to regulate the mixture in a carburetor, etc.

ven·tur·ous (ven′chər əs) ***adj.*** VENTURESOME **—ven′tur·ous·ly** ***adv.*** **—ven′tur·ous·ness** ***n.***

ven·ue (ven′yoo) ***n.*** ⟦ME < OFr, a coming, arrival, approach < *venir,* to come < L *venire,* COME⟧ **1** *Law a)* the county or locality in which a cause of action occurs or a crime is committed *b)* the county or locality in which a jury is drawn and a case tried *c)* that part of a declaration in an action that designates the county in which the trial is to occur *d)* [Rare] the clause in an affidavit designating the place where it was sworn to **2** the scene or locale of a large gathering, as for a sports event or rock concert **—change of venue** *Law* the substitution of another place of trial, as when the local jury or court is likely to be prejudiced

ven·ule (ven′yool′) ***n.*** ⟦L *venula,* dim. of *vena,* vein⟧ **1** *Anat.* a small vein; veinlet **2** *Biol.* any of the small branches of a vein in a leaf or in the wing of an insect **—ven′u·lar** (-yoo lər) ***adj.*** **—ven′u·lose′** (-yoo lōs′) ***adj.***

Ve·nus (vē′nəs) ***n.,*** *pl.* for 2 & 3 **-nus·es** ⟦ME < L, lit., love < IE **wenos,* desire < base **wen-,* to strive for, attain > OE *wine,* friend, *winnan,* to WIN⟧ **1** *Rom. Myth.* the goddess of love and beauty: identified with the Greek Aphrodite **2** a statue or image of Venus **3** a very beautiful woman **4** the brightest, sixth-largest planet in the solar system and the second in distance from the sun, with a dense atmosphere of carbon dioxide and a very high surface temperature: diameter, *c.* 12,100 km (*c.* 7,520 mi); period of revolution, *c.* 224.7 earth days; period of rotation (retrograde), 243.01 earth days; symbol, ♀

Ve·nus·berg (vē′nəs burg′; *Ger* vā′noos berk′) ***n.*** ⟦Ger, Venus mountain: for *berg,* see BARROW²⟧ *Medieval Legend* a mountain somewhere in Germany where Venus holds court in a cavern, enticing travelers, who become reluctant to leave

☆**Venus' flytrap** a white-flowered, carnivorous swamp plant (*Dionaea muscipula*) of the sundew family, native to the Carolinas, having sensitive leaves with two hinged blades that snap shut in trapping insects

Venus' flytrap

Ve·nus'-hair (vē′nəs her′) ***n.*** a maidenhair fern (*Adiantum capillus-veneris*) of tropical America and the S U.S.

Ve·nu·si·an (vi noo′shən, -nyoo′-; -zhən) ***adj.*** of the planet Venus **—*n.*** an inhabitant of the planet Venus, as in science fiction

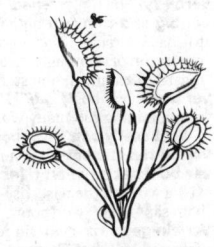

ver *abbrev.* **1** verse(s) **2** version

Ve·ra (vir′ə) ***n.*** ⟦< L *vera,* fem. of *verus,* true: see VERY⟧ a feminine name

ve·ra·cious (və rā′shəs) ***adj.*** ⟦< L *verax,* speaking truly < *verus,* true: see VERY⟧ **1** habitually truthful; honest **2** true; accurate **—ve·ra′cious·ly** ***adv.*** **—ve·ra′cious·ness** ***n.***

ve·rac·i·ty (və ras′ə tē) ***n.*** ⟦ML *veracitas,* truthfulness < L *verax:* see prec.⟧ **1** habitual truthfulness; honesty **2** accordance with truth; accuracy of statement **3** accuracy or precision, as of perception **4** that which is true; truth **5** *pl.* **-ties** an established or verified fact, principle, etc. **—*SYN.*** TRUTH

Ver·a·cruz (ver′ə krooz′; *Sp* ve′rä kroos′) ⟦Sp, lit., true cross⟧ **1** state of Mexico, on the E coast: 28,114 sq mi (72,815 sq km); cap. Jalapa **2** seaport in this state: in full **Veracruz Lla·ve** (yä′vä)

ve·ran·da or **ve·ran·dah** (və ran′də) ***n.*** ⟦Anglo-Ind < Hindi & Beng < Port *varanda,* balcony < *vara,* pole, staff < L, wooden trestle, forked stick (for spreading out nets) < IE base **wa-,* to bend apart > VACILLATE, VARY⟧ an open porch or portico, usually roofed, along the outside of a building

ve·rap·a·mil (və rap′ə mil) ***n.*** a white, crystalline powder, $C_{27}H_{39}ClN_2O_4$, that dilates blood vessels, used in medicine to treat angina pectoris, hypertension, etc.: in full **verapamil hydrochloride**

ve·rat·ri·dine (və rat′rə dēn′, -din) ***n.*** ⟦< L *veratrum,* hellebore (see fol.) + -ID(E) + -INE³⟧ a poisonous amorphous alkaloid, $C_{36}H_{51}NO_{11}$, found in sabadilla seeds

ver·a·trine (ver′ə trēn′, -trin) ***n.*** ⟦ModL *veratrina* < L *veratrum,* hellebore, prob. orig., plant which reveals truth < *verus,* true (see VERY): the pulverized root causes sneezing, regarded in some cultural traditions as confirmation of truth⟧ **1** a poisonous mixture of colorless, crystalline alkaloids obtained from sabadilla seeds **2** VERATRIDINE Also **ve·ra·tri·a** (və rā′trē ə)

ve·ra·trum (və rā′trəm) ***n.*** ⟦L: see prec.⟧ **1** HELLEBORE (sense 2) **2** the dried rhizomes of certain hellebores, once used in medicine

verb (vurb) ***n.*** ⟦ME *verbe* < OFr < L *verbum,* WORD (used as transl. of Gr *rhēma,* verb, orig., word)⟧ any of a class of words expressing action, existence, or occurrence, or used as an auxiliary or copula, and usually constituting the main element of a predicate (Ex.: *give, build, run, be, happen, do, have, would, seem*)

ver·bal (vur′bəl) ***adj.*** ⟦LME < MFr < LL *verbalis,* of a word < *verbum:* see prec.⟧ **1** of, in, or by means of words *[a verbal* image*]* **2** concerned merely with words, as distinguished from facts, ideas, or actions **3** in speech; oral rather than written: usage objected to by some *[a verbal* contract*]* **4** [Now Rare] word for word; verbatim *[a verbal* translation*]* **5** *Gram. a)* of, or made up of, verbs *[a verbal* auxiliary*] b)* of, having the nature of, or derived from a verb *[a verbal* noun*] c)* used to form verbs *[-ate* is a *verbal* suffix*]* **—*n.*** **1** *Gram.* a verbal noun or some other word, as an adjective, derived from a verb: in English, gerunds, infinitives, and participles are verbals **2** *Linguis.* a word or word group that occurs in grammatical functions typical of verbs **—*SYN.*** ORAL **—ver′bal·ly** ***adv.***

ver·bal·ism (vur′bə liz′əm) ***n.*** **1** a verbal expression; expression in one or more words; a word or phrase **2** words only, without any real meaning; mere verbiage **3** any virtually meaningless word or phrase

ver·bal·ist (-list) ***n.*** **1** a person skilled in verbal expression; one who uses words well **2** a person who places more importance on words than on the facts or ideas they convey —**ver'bal·is'tic** *adj.*

ver·bal·ize (vur'bə līz') *vi.* **-ized', -iz'ing** ⟦< Fr *verbaliser:* see VERBAL & -IZE⟧ **1** to be wordy, or verbose **2** to use words to express or communicate meaning —*vt.* **1** to express in words **2** to change (a noun, etc.) into a verb —**ver'bal·i·za'tion** *n.* —**ver'bal·iz'er** *n.*

verbal noun *Gram.* a noun or nominal derived from a verb and functioning in some respects like a verb: in English, it is either a noun ending in -ING (a gerund) or an infinitive (Ex.: *walking* is healthful; *to err* is human)

ver·ba·tim (vər bāt'əm) *adv.* ⟦LME < ML < L *verbum,* WORD⟧ word for word; in exactly the same words —*adj.* following the original word for word [a *verbatim* account]

ver·be·na (vər bē'nə) *n.* ⟦ModL < L, foliage, branches, vervain < IE **werb-,* to turn, bend < base **wer-* > WORM⟧ any of a genus (*Verbena*) of plants of the verbena family, with spikes or clusters of showy red, white, or purplish flowers, widely grown for ornament —*adj.* designating a family (Verbenaceae, order Lamiales) of American, mostly tropical, dicotyledonous plants, shrubs, and trees, including vervain, lantana, and teak

ver·bi·age (vur'bē ij) *n.* ⟦Fr < OFr *verbier,* to speak, chatter < *verbe:* see VERB⟧ **1** an excess of words beyond those needed to express concisely what is meant; wordiness **2** style of expression; diction

ver·bid (vur'bid) *n.* ⟦VERB + -ID⟧ *Gram.* a word or form, as a gerund, infinitive, or participle, that functions in part as a verb, as in taking an object, but cannot form a syntactically complete sentence (Ex.: *watching* television can be tiring)

verb·i·fy (-bə fī') *vt.* **-fied', -fy'ing** VERBALIZE (*vt.* 2)

ver·big·er·a·tion (vər bij'ə rā'shən) *n.* ⟦< L *verbigeratus,* pp. of *verbigerare,* to chat < *verbum,* WORD + *gerere,* to bear, carry on⟧ *Psychol.* the compulsive repetition of seemingly meaningless words, phrases, or sentences, without regard to stimulus; oral stereotypy

ver·bose (vər bōs') *adj.* ⟦L *verbosus,* full of words < *verbum,* WORD⟧ using or containing too many words; wordy; long-winded; prolix —***SYN.*** WORDY —**ver·bose'ly** *adv.* —**ver·bos'i·ty** (-bäs'ə tē) *n.*, **ver·bose'ness**

ver·bo·ten (fer bōt''n; *E* vur bōt''n) *adj.* ⟦Ger⟧ forbidden; prohibited

ver·bum sat sa·pi·en·ti (est) (vur'bəm sät säp'ē en'tē est', wer'boom-) ⟦L⟧ a word to the wise (is) enough: often shortened to **ver·bum sap** (vur'bəm säp', -sap'; wer'boom-)

Ver·cin·get·o·rix (vur'sin jet'ər iks, -get'-) 72?-46? B.C.; Gallic chieftain defeated by Julius Caesar

ver·dant (vur'dənt) *adj.* ⟦prob. VERD(URE) + -ANT, based on MFr *verdoyant* < OFr *verdoiant,* prp. of *verdoier,* to be green < *verd,* green: see VERT[1]⟧ **1** green **2** covered with green vegetation **3** inexperienced; immature [*verdant* youth] —**ver'dan·cy** (-dən sē) *n.* —**ver'dant·ly** *adv.*

verd (*or* **verde) antique** (vurd) ⟦older form of Fr *vert antique* < OFr *verd,* green + *antique,* ancient: see VERT[1] & ANTIQUE⟧ a greenish, marblelike serpentine, used for interior decoration

Verde (vurd), **Cape** promontory on the coast of Senegal: westernmost point of Africa

ver·der·er or **ver·der·or** (vur'dər ər) *n.* ⟦Anglo-Fr *verderer,* extended < *verder* < OFr *verdier* < *verd,* green: see VERT[1]⟧ in medieval England, a judicial officer who maintained law and order in the king's forests

Ver·di (ver'dē), **Giu·sep·pe (Fortunino Francisco)** (jōō zep'pe) 1813-1901; It. operatic composer —**Ver'di·an** *adj.*

Ver·dic·chi·o (ver dik'ē ō) *n.* ⟦It, name of the grape < *verde,* green, referring to the pale-green color of the grape skins and the wine⟧ [*also* **v-**] a light, dry white wine of the Adriatic coast of central Italy

ver·dict (vur'dikt) *n.* ⟦ME *verdit* < Anglo-Fr < ML *veredictum,* true saying, verdict < L *vere,* truly + *dictum,* a thing said: see VERY & DICTUM⟧ **1** *Law* the formal finding of a judge or jury on a matter submitted to them in a trial **2** any decision or judgment

ver·di·gris (vur'di grēs', -gris) *n.* ⟦ME *vertegrez* < MFr *verdegris* < OFr *vert de Grece,* lit., green of Greece < *verd,* green (see VERT[1]) + *de,* of + *Grece,* Greece⟧ **1** a green or greenish-blue poisonous compound, a basic acetate of copper, prepared by treating copper with acetic acid and used as a pigment, dye, etc. **2** a green or greenish-blue coating (**false verdigris**) that forms like rust on brass, bronze, or copper

☆**ver·din** (vur'din) *n.* ⟦Fr, yellowhammer⟧ a small gray songbird (*Auriparus flaviceps*), with a yellow head and a white breast, of the SW U.S. and N Mexico

ver·di·ter (vur'di tər) *n.* ⟦MFr *verd de terre,* lit., green of the earth < OFr *verte* + L *terra:* see VERT[1] & TERRA⟧ either of two basic copper carbonate pigments, the one (**blue verditer**) usually consisting of ground azurite, the other (**green verditer**) ground malachite

Ver·dun (ver dun', vər-; *Fr* ver dën') **1** city in NE France, on the Meuse River: scene of a prolonged battle (Feb. to Dec., 1916) of WWI **2** ⟦var. of *Savardun,* town in France, birthplace of an early settler⟧ borough of Montreal

ver·dure (vur'jər) *n.* ⟦ME < OFr < *verd,* green < VL **virdis,* for L *viridis:* see VERT[1]⟧ **1** the fresh-green color of growing things; greenness **2** green growing plants and trees; green vegetation **3** a vigorous or flourishing condition —**ver'dured** *adj.*

ver·dur·ous (vur'jər əs) *adj.* **1** covered with or consisting of verdure **2** of or characteristic of verdure

verge[1] (vurj) *n.* ⟦ME < OFr, rod, wand, stick, yard, hoop < L *virga,* twig, rod, wand < IE **wizga-* < base **wei-,* to bend, twist > WIRE, WHISK⟧ **1** *a)* the edge, brink, or margin (*of* something) (also used fig.) [the *verge* of the forest, on the *verge* of hysteria] *b)* [Brit.] a grassy border, as along a road **2** *a)* an enclosing line or border; boundary, esp. of something more or less circular *b)* the area so enclosed **3** the part of a sloping roof that extends beyond a gable wall **4** the spindle of a balance wheel in a clock with an old-style vertical escapement **5** a rod or staff symbolic of an office, as that carried before a church official in processions **6** *Eng. Feudal Law* a rod held in the hand by a feudal tenant as he swore fealty to his lord —*vi.* **verged, verg'ing** to be on or as if on the verge, edge, brink, or border: usually with *on* or *upon* [streets *verging* on the slum area, talk that *verges* on the ridiculous]

verge[2] (vurj) *vi.* **verged, verg'ing** ⟦L *vergere,* to bend, turn < IE **werg-* < base **wer-,* to turn, bend > WARP, WORM⟧ **1** to tend or incline (*to* or *toward*) **2** to be in the process of change or transition into something else; pass gradually (*into*) [dawn *verging* into daylight]

verg·er (vur'jər) *n.* ⟦ME: see VERGE[1] & -ER⟧ **1** a person who carries a verge before a bishop, dean, etc. in a procession **2** a church caretaker or usher

Ver·gil (vur'jəl) *alt. sp. of* VIRGIL[2] —**Ver·gil'i·an** (-jil'ē ən) *adj.*

ver·glas (ver glä') *n.* ⟦Fr < MFr *verreglaz* < *verre,* glass (< L *vitrum*) + *glaz, glace,* ice: see GLACIER⟧ a thin coating of ice on rock

ve·rid·i·cal (və rid'i kəl) *adj.* ⟦< L *veridicus,* speaking the truth < *verus,* true + *dicere,* to speak: see VERY & DICTION⟧ **1** truthful; veracious **2** corresponding with reality or facts —**ve·rid'i·cal'i·ty** (-kal'ə tē) *n.*

ver·i·est (ver'ē ist) *adj.* **1** *superl. of* VERY (*adj.* 5) **2** [Rare] being such to the highest degree; utter [the *veriest* nonsense]

ver·i·fi·a·ble (ver'ə fī'ə bəl, ver'ə fī'ə bəl) *adj.* capable of verification; that can be proved to be true or accurate —**ver'i·fi'a·bly** *adv.*

ver·i·fi·ca·tion (ver'ə fi kā'shən) *n.* ⟦MFr *verificacion* < ML *verificatio*⟧ **1** a verifying or being verified; establishment or confirmation of the truth or accuracy of a fact, theory, etc. **2** *Law* a statement at the end of a pleading to the effect that the pleader is ready to prove his or her allegations —**ver'i·fi·ca'tion·al** *adj.*

ver·i·fy (ver'ə fī') *vt.* **-fied', -fy'ing** ⟦ME *verifien* < MFr *verifier* < ML *verificare,* to make true < L *verus,* true (see VERY) + *-ficare,* -FY⟧ **1** to prove to be true by demonstration, evidence, or testimony; confirm or substantiate **2** to test or check the accuracy or correctness of, as by investigation, comparison with a standard, or reference to the facts **3** *Law a)* to add a verification to (a pleading) *b)* to affirm on oath —***SYN.*** CONFIRM —**ver'i·fi'er** *n.*

ver·i·ly (ver'ə lē) *adv.* ⟦ME *verrayly:* see VERY & -LY[2]⟧ [Archaic] in very truth; in fact; truly

ver·i·sim·i·lar (ver'ə sim'ə lər) *adj.* ⟦< L *verisimilis* < *verus,* true (see VERY) + *similis,* SIMILAR⟧ seeming to be true or real; plausible; likely

ver·i·si·mil·i·tude (ver'ə si mil'ə tōōd', -tyōōd') *n.* ⟦L *verisimilitudo* < *verisimilis:* see prec.⟧ **1** the appearance of being true or real **2** something having the mere appearance of being true or real —***SYN.*** TRUTH

ver·ism (vir'iz'əm, ver'-) *n.* ⟦It *verismo* < *vero,* true < L *verus* (see VERY) + -ISM⟧ realism or naturalism in the arts —**ver'ist** *adj., n.* —**ve·ris·tic** (vi ris'tik) *adj.*

ve·ris·mo (vā rēz'mô) *n.* ⟦It: see prec.⟧ **1** VERISM **2** a style of opera dealing with the lives of common people and usually characterized by violent or tragic situations and highly dramatic performance

ver·i·ta·ble (ver'i tə bəl) *adj.* ⟦LME < OFr < *verite,* VERITY⟧ being such practically or in effect [a *veritable* feast] —**ver'i·ta·bly** *adv.*

vér·i·té (vā rē tā') *n.* ⟦Fr, lit., truth⟧ [*also in roman type*] **1** *short for* CINÉMA VÉRITÉ **2** REALISM (sense 2) —*adj.* of or like cinéma vérité [a musical comedy *vérité*]

ver·i·ty (ver'ə tē) *n.* ⟦ME *verite* < OFr *verite(t)* < L *veritas,* truth < *verus,* true: see VERY⟧ **1** conformity to truth or fact; truth; reality **2** *pl.* **-ties** a principle, belief, etc. taken to be fundamentally and permanently true; a truth; a reality —***SYN.*** TRUTH

ver·juice (vur'jōōs') *n.* ⟦ME *vergeous* < MFr *verjus* < *vert,* green (see VERT[1]) + *jus,* JUICE⟧ **1** the sour, acid juice of crab apples, unripe grapes, etc. **2** sourness of temper, looks, etc.

Ver·laine (ver len'), **Paul** (pôl) 1844-96; Fr. poet

Ver·meer (vər mer'; *E* vər mir'), **Jo·han·nes** (yō hän'əs) or **Jan** (yän) 1632-75; Du. painter

ver·meil (vur'mil) *n.* ⟦ME *vermayle* < OFr *vermeil* < LL(Ec) *vermiculus,* kermes < L, dim. of *vermis,* a red WORM⟧ **1** [Obs. or Old Poet.] the color vermilion **2** gilded or gold-colored copper, bronze, or silver —*adj.* [Obs. or Old Poet.] vermilion

ver·mi- (vur'mə) ⟦< L *vermis,* a WORM⟧ *combining form* worm [*vermicide*]

ver·mi·cel·li (vur'mə sel'ē, -chel'ē) *n.* ⟦It, pl. of *vermicello,* lit., little worm < L *vermiculus,* dim. of *vermis,* a WORM⟧ pasta like spaghetti, but in thinner strings

ver·mi·cide (vur'mə sīd') *n.* ⟦VERMI- + -CIDE⟧ a drug or other agent used to kill worms, esp. intestinal worms

ver·mic·u·lar (vər mik'yə lər) *adj.* ⟦ModL *vermicularis:* see fol. & -AR⟧ **1** *a)* suggestive of a worm or worms in shape or movement *b)* covered with irregularly twisting lines, ridges, or indentations suggestive of worm tracks **2** *a)* of or having to do with worms *b)* formed or caused by worms

ver·mic·u·late (vər mik'yə lāt'; *for adj., usually,* -lit) *vt.* **-lat'ed, -lat'ing** ⟦< L *vermiculatus,* pp. of *vermiculari,* to be full of worms < *vermiculus,* dim. of *vermis,* a WORM⟧ to make vermicular; esp., to cover, as by inlaying, with vermicular markings or traceries —*adj.* VERMICULAR: also **ver·mic'u·lat'ed** (-lāt'id)

ver·mic·u·la·tion (vər mik'yə lā'shən) *n.* ⟦L *vermiculatio:* see prec.⟧ **1** a vermiculating or being vermiculated **2** vermicular markings **3** movement marked by alternate contraction and dilation, as in peristalsis

☆**ver·mic·u·lite** (vər mik′yə lit′) ***n.*** ⟦< L *vermiculus,* dim. of *vermis,* WORM + -ITE¹: from the shape of the expanding heated particles⟧ any of a number of very soft, monoclinic, hydrous silicate minerals resulting usually from alterations of mica and occurring in tiny, leafy scales that expand greatly when heated: used for insulation, water adsorption, etc.

ver·mi·form (vur′mə fôrm′) ***adj.*** ⟦VERMI- + -FORM⟧ shaped like a worm

vermiform appendix the appendix extending from the cecum of the large intestine

vermiform process *Anat.* **1** the median lobe of the cerebellum **2** VERMIFORM APPENDIX

ver·mi·fuge (vur′mə fyo͞oj′) ***adj.*** ⟦VERMI- + -FUGE⟧ serving to expel worms and other parasites from the intestinal tract —***n.*** a vermifuge drug

ver·mil·ion (vər mil′yən) ***n.*** ⟦ME < OFr *vermillon* < *vermeil,* bright-red: see VERMEIL⟧ **1** *a)* bright-red mercuric sulfide, used as a pigment *b)* any of several other red pigments resembling this **2** a bright red or scarlet —***adj.*** of the color vermilion

ver·min (vur′mən) ***n., pl.*** **-min** ⟦ME < OFr *vermine* < L *vermis,* a WORM⟧ **1** [*pl.*] various insects, rodents, or other small animals regarded as pests because destructive, disease-carrying, etc., as flies, lice, rats, or weasels **2** [*pl.*] [Brit.] birds or other animals that kill game **3** *a)* a vile, loathsome person *b)* [*pl.*] such persons collectively

ver·mi·na·tion (vur′mi nā′shən) ***n.*** ⟦L *verminatio*⟧ [Archaic] infestation with, or the spreading of, vermin

ver·min·ous (vur′mə nəs) ***adj.*** ⟦L *verminosus*⟧ **1** of, having the nature of, or resembling vermin **2** infested with vermin **3** caused or produced by vermin

Ver·mont (vər mänt′) ⟦< Fr *Vert Mont* (1647), green mountain⟧ New England state of the U.S.: admitted 1791; 9,250 sq mi (23,956 sq km); cap. Montpelier: abbrev. *VT* or *Vt*

Ver·mont·er (vər män′tər) ***n.*** a person born or living in Vermont

ver·mouth (vər mo͞oth′) ***n.*** ⟦Fr *vermout* < Ger *wermut,* WORMWOOD⟧ a sweet or dry, white fortified wine flavored with aromatic herbs, used in cocktails and as an aperitif

ver·nac·u·lar (vər nak′yə lər) ***adj.*** ⟦< L *vernaculus,* belonging to home-born slaves, indigenous < *verna,* a native slave, prob. < Etr **versna,* hearth < *verse,* fire⟧ **1** using the native language of a country or place [*a vernacular writer*] **2** commonly spoken by the people of a particular country or place [*a vernacular,* as distinguished from the literary, dialect] **3** of or in the native language **4** native to a country or region [*the vernacular* arts of Brittany] **5** designating or of the common name of an animal or plant, as distinguished from the scientific name in Modern Latin taxonomic classification —***n.*** **1** the native language or dialect of a country or place **2** the common, everyday language of ordinary people in a particular locality **3** the shoptalk or idiom of a profession or trade **4** *a)* a vernacular word or term *b)* the vernacular name of an animal or plant —**SYN.** DIALECT —**ver·nac′u·lar·ly** ***adv.***

ver·nac·u·lar·ism (-iz′əm) ***n.*** **1** a vernacular word, phrase, or usage **2** the use of vernacular language

ver·nal (vur′nəl) ***adj.*** ⟦L *vernalis* < *vernus,* belonging to spring < *ver,* spring < IE base **wesr,* spring > Sans *vasanta,* OSlav *vesna,* spring⟧ **1** of, pertaining to, or appearing or occurring in, the spring **2** springlike; fresh, warm, and mild **3** fresh and young; youthful —**ver′nal·ly** ***adv.***

ver·nal·ize (vur′nə līz′) ***vt.*** **-ized′**, **-iz′ing** ⟦prec. + -IZE⟧ to stimulate the growth and flowering of (a plant) by artificially shortening the dormant period —**ver′nal·i·za′tion** ***n.***

ver·na·tion (vər nā′shən) ***n.*** ⟦ModL *vernatio* < pp. of L *vernare,* to be verdant < *ver,* spring: see VERNAL⟧ *Bot.* the arrangement of leaves in a leaf bud

Verne (vurn; *Fr* vern), **Jules** (jo͞olz; *Fr* zhül) 1828-1905; Fr. novelist

Ver·ner's law (vur′nərz, ver′-) ⟦formulated (1875) by Karl *Verner* (1846-96), Dan philologist⟧ an explanation for a series of apparent exceptions to Grimm's law, stating that the Proto-Germanic word-medial voiceless spirants (f, th, h, s), derived from the Proto-Indo-European voiceless stops (p, t, k) and voiceless spirant (s), regularly became voiced (v, *th,* g, z), respectively, and final (s) became (z), when the vowel immediately preceding these did not in Proto-Indo-European bear the principal accent of the word

ver·ni·er (vur′nē ər, -nir) ***n.*** ⟦after Pierre *Vernier* (1580-1637), Fr mathematician who invented it⟧ **1** a short graduated scale that slides along a longer graduated instrument and is used to indicate fractional parts of divisions, as in a micrometer: also **vernier scale** **2** any device that makes possible a finer setting of a tool or measuring instrument —***adj.*** of or fitted with a vernier

ver·nis·sage (ver nē säzh′) ***n., pl.*** **-sages′** (-säzh′) ⟦Fr, lit., varnishing (see VARNISH & -AGE): in allusion to the former practice of varnishing paintings before exhibiting⟧ the opening, or first showing, of an art exhibit

Ver·non (vur′nən) ***n.*** ⟦< the surname *Vernon,* prob. after *Vernon,* a town in France⟧ a masculine name

Ve·ro·na (və rō′nə; *It* ve rô′nä) commune in Veneto, N Italy —**Ver·o·nese** (ver′ə nēz′, -nēs′) ***adj., n., pl.*** **-nese′** (-nēz′, -nēs′)

Ve·ro·ne·se (ve′rô ne′se; *E* ver′ə nā′zā, -zē), **Pa·o·lo** (pä′ô lô′) ⟦adopted surname It, (person) of prec.; akin to E prec. at that entry⟧ (born *Paolo Cagliari*) 1528-88; Venetian painter, born in Verona

Ve·ron·i·ca (və rän′i kə) ***n.*** ⟦ML < Gr *Pherenikē:* see BERNICE⟧ **1** a feminine name **2** according to Christian tradition, a woman of Jerusalem who wiped the bleeding face of Jesus on the way to Calvary: her day is July 12: also *Saint Veronica* **3** [*often* **v-**] *a)* the image of Jesus' face said in legend to have appeared on the veil or handkerchief used by Veronica to wipe the bleeding face of Jesus *b)* a cloth or garment with a similar representation of Jesus' bleeding face **4** ⟦ModL, prob. after the saint⟧ [**v-**] SPEEDWELL **5** ⟦Sp *verónica:* because the matador holds the cape in a manner similar to that in which Saint Veronica is traditionally depicted holding her veil⟧ [**v-**] a bullfighting move in which the matador holds a cape out and pivots slowly as the bull charges past it

Ver·ra·za·no (ver′rä tsä′nô; *E* ver′ə zä′nō), **Gio·van·ni da** (jô vän′nē dä) 1480?-1527?; It. explorer in the service of France: also sp. **Ver′raz·za′no**

Ver·roc·chio (ver rôk′kyô), **An·dre·a del** (än dre′ä del) (born *Andrea di Michele di Francesco di Cioni*) 1435-88; Florentine sculptor and painter

ver·ru·ca (və ro͞o′kə) ***n., pl.*** **-cae** (-sē) or, sometimes, **-cas** ⟦L, WART⟧ **1** WART **2** a wartlike elevation, as on a toad's back —**ver·ru·cose** (ver′o͝o kōs′) ***adj.***, **ver′ru·cous** (-kəs)

Ver·sailles (vər sī′; *Fr* ver sä′y′) city in NC France, near Paris: site of a palace built by Louis XIV; the Allies & Germany signed a peace treaty here (1919) ending WWI

ver·sa·tile (vur′sə təl; *chiefly Brit,* -tīl′) ***adj.*** ⟦Fr < L *versatilis,* that turns around, movable, versatile < *versatus,* pp. of *versare,* to turn often, freq. of *vertere,* to turn: see VERSE⟧ **1** *a)* competent in many things; able to turn easily from one subject or occupation to another; many-sided *b)* adaptable to many uses or functions **2** [Rare] *a)* that can be turned or moved around, as on a hinge or pivot *b)* fickle; inconstant **3** *Bot.* turning about freely on the filament to which it is attached, as an anther **4** *Zool. a)* moving forward or backward, as the toes of a bird *b)* movable in any direction, as the antenna of an insect —**ver′sa·tile·ly** ***adv.*** —**ver′sa·til′i·ty** (-til′ə tē) ***n.***

vers de so·cié·té (ver′ də sô syā tā′) ⟦Fr, verse of society⟧ witty, polished light verse

verse (vurs) ***n.*** ⟦ME *vers* < OE *fers* & OFr *vers,* both < L *versus,* a turning, verse, line, row, pp. of *vertere,* to turn < IE **wert-,* to turn < base **wer-* > WARP, WORM, -WARDS⟧ **1** a sequence of words arranged metrically in accordance with some rule or design; single line of poetry **2** *a)* metrical writing or speaking, esp. when light or trivial or merely metered and rhymed, but without much serious content or artistic merit *b)* a particular form of poetic composition [*free verse,* trochaic *verse*] **3** *a)* a single metrical composition; poem *b)* a body of poetry, as of a specific writer or period **4** a stanza or similar short subdivision of a song or poem, sometimes specif. as distinguished from the chorus or refrain **5** any of the single, usually numbered, short divisions of a chapter of the Bible, generally a sentence —***vt., vi.*** **versed**, **vers′ing** [Now Rare] VERSIFY

versed (vurst) ***adj.*** ⟦< L *versatus,* pp. of *versari,* to be occupied with < *versus:* see prec.⟧ acquainted by experience and study; skilled or learned (*in* a specified subject)

versed sine ⟦< ModL *versus* < L, pp. of *vertere,* to turn (see VERSE) + -ED⟧ *Trigonometry* the number 1 minus the cosine of a given angle

ver·si·cle (vur′si kəl) ***n.*** ⟦ME < L *versiculus,* dim. of *versus*⟧ a short verse or verse part, usually of a Psalm, used esp. in antiphonal prayer

ver·si·col·or (vur′si kul′ər) ***adj.*** ⟦L < *versare,* to change (see VERSATILE) + *color,* COLOR⟧ **1** having many colors; variegated **2** changing in color; iridescent

ver·si·fi·ca·tion (vur′sə fi kā′shən) ***n.*** ⟦L *versificatio*⟧ **1** the act of versifying **2** the art, practice, or theory of poetic composition **3** the form or style of a poem; metrical structure **4** a metrical version, as of a story or prose work

ver·si·fi·er (vur′sə fī′ər) ***n.*** **1** a person who versifies; poet **2** a writer of mediocre verse; poetaster

ver·si·fy (-fī′) ***vi.*** **-fied′**, **-fy′ing** ⟦ME *versifien* < MFr *versifier* < L *versificare* < *versus:* see VERSE & -FY⟧ to compose verses —***vt.*** **1** to tell about, treat of, or describe in verse **2** to put into verse form

ver·sion (vur′zhən, -shən) ***n.*** ⟦Fr < ML *versio,* a turning < L *versus:* see VERSE⟧ **1** *a)* a translation *b)* [*often* **V-**] a translation of the Bible, in whole or part [*the Douay and King James versions*] **2** an account showing one point of view; particular description or report given by one person or group [*the two versions of the accident*] **3** a particular form or variation of something, esp. as modified in a different art form [*the film version of the novel*] **4** *Med. a)* displacement of the uterus in which it is deflected but not bent upon itself *b)* the operation of turning the fetus during childbirth to make delivery easier —**SYN.** TRANSLATION —**ver′sion·al** ***adj.***

vers li·bre (ver lē′br′) ⟦Fr⟧ FREE VERSE

ver·so (vur′sō) ***n., pl.*** **-sos** ⟦ModL *(folio) verso* (the leaf) being turned < L, abl. of *versus:* see VERSE⟧ *Printing* **1** any left-hand page of a book **2** the back of a leaf Opposed to RECTO

verst (vurst) ***n.*** ⟦Russ *versta* < Old Russ *virsta,* the unit of measure, age < OSlav *vrista,* age⟧ a former Russian unit of linear measure, equal to .663 mile (1.067 kilometers)

ver·sus (vur′səs) ***prep.*** ⟦ML < L, toward, turned in the direction of < *vertere,* to turn: see VERSE⟧ **1** in contest against [*plaintiff versus defendant*] **2** in contrast with; by way of an alternative to [*peace versus war*]

vert¹ (vurt) ***n.*** ⟦ME *verte* < OFr < L *viridis,* green < *virere,* to be green⟧ **1** [Brit.] *a)* [Archaic] the green growth of a forest, as cover for deer *b)* [Historical] the right to cut green wood in a forest **2** *Heraldry* the color green: indicated in engravings by diagonal lines downward from dexter to sinister

vert² *abbrev.* vertical

ver·te·bra (vur′tə brə) ***n., pl.*** **-brae′** (-brē′, -brā′) or **-bras** ⟦L, a joint, vertebra < *vertere,* to turn: see VERSE⟧ any of the single bones or segments of the spinal column, articulating in the higher vertebrates with those adjacent to it by means of elastic fibrous disks

ver·te·bral (vər tē′brəl, vur′tə-) ***adj.*** ⟦ModL *vertebralis*⟧ **1** of, or having the nature of, a vertebra or vertebrae **2** having or composed of vertebrae [*vertebral* column]

ver·te·brate (vur′tə brit, -brāt′) ***adj.*** ⟦L *vertebratus* < *vertebra:* see VERTEBRA⟧ **1** having a backbone, or spinal column **2** of or belonging to the vertebrates **—*n.*** any of a large subphylum (Vertebrata) of chordate animals, including all mammals, fishes, birds, reptiles, and amphibians, characterized by a brain enclosed in a cranium and a segmented spinal column

ver·te·bra·tion (vur′tə brā′shən) ***n.*** vertebral formation; segmentation into vertebrae

ver·tex (vur′teks′) ***n.,*** *pl.* **-tex′es** or **-ti·ces′** (-tə sēz′) ⟦L, the top, the turning point < *vertere,* to turn: see VERSE⟧ **1** the highest point; summit; apex, as the top point of the sun, moon, etc. above the horizon **2** *Anat., Zool.* the top or crown of the head **3** *Geom. a)* the point of intersection of the two sides of an angle *b)* a corner point of a triangle, square, cube, parallelepiped, or other geometric figure bounded by lines, planes, or lines and planes **4** *Optics* the point at the center of a lens at which the axis of symmetry intersects the curve of the lens

ver·ti·cal (vur′ti kəl) ***adj.*** ⟦Fr < LL *verticalis* < L *vertex* (gen. *verticis*): see prec.⟧ **1** of, at, or in the vertex or zenith **2** *a)* perpendicular, or at a right angle, to the plane of the horizon; upright, straight up or down, etc. *b)* at a right angle to the plane of the supporting surface **3** at, or made up of elements at, different levels, as of industrial production and distribution or of social status **4** *Anat., Zool.* of the vertex of the head **5** *Biol.* in the direction in which the axis lies; lengthwise **—*n.*** **1** a vertical line, plane, circle, etc. **2** upright position **—ver′ti·cal′i·ty** (-kal′ə tē) ***n.*** **—ver′ti·cal·ly** ***adv.***

vertical angle either of a pair of angles of equal degree, lying opposite to each other at the intersection of two straight lines

vertical blind [*often pl.*] a window blind made of a number of vertical wooden, metal, or plastic slats that can be set together at any angle to regulate the light and air passing through or be drawn together to one side of the window by means of cords

vertical circle *Astron.* any great circle of the celestial sphere passing through the zenith and the nadir and perpendicular to the horizon

vertical union INDUSTRIAL UNION

ver·ti·ces (vur′tə sēz′) ***n.*** *alt. pl. of* VERTEX

ver·ti·cil (vur′tə sil′) ***n.*** ⟦ModL *verticillus* < L, a whorl, dim. of *vertex:* see VERTEX⟧ *Bot.* a circular arrangement of leaves or flowers around a stem; whorl

ver·ti·cil·las·ter (vur′tə si las′tər) ***n.*** ⟦ModL: see prec. & -ASTER[1]⟧ *Bot.* an almost circular flower arrangement formed by a pair of dichasia facing each other on the stem, as in some mints

ver·tic·il·late (vər tis′ə lit, -lāt′; vur′tə sil′āt′) ***adj.*** ⟦ModL *verticillatus* < *verticillus*⟧ *Bot.* arranged in or having verticils: also **ver·tic′il·lat′ed** **—ver·tic′il·la′tion** ***n.***

ver·ti·cil·li·um wilt (vur′tə sil′ē əm) ⟦< ModL *Verticillium* < *verticillus,* a whorl: see VERTICIL⟧ a common plant disease caused by fungi (genus *Verticillium*) and characterized by yellow leaves and drooping stems

ver·tig·i·nous (vər tij′ə nəs) ***adj.*** ⟦L *vertiginosus*⟧ **1** of, affected by, or causing vertigo; dizzy or dizzying **2** whirling about; spinning **3** marked by quick or frequent change; unstable **—ver·tig′i·nous·ly** ***adv.***

ver·ti·go (vur′ti gō′) ***n.,*** *pl.* **-goes′** or **ver·tig·i·nes** (vər tij′ə nēz′) ⟦L, dizziness < *vertere:* see VERSE⟧ *Med.* a condition in which one has the feeling of whirling or of having the surroundings whirling about one, so that one tends to lose one's balance; dizziness

ver·tu (vər to͞o′, vur′to͞o′) ***n.*** *alt. sp. of* VIRTU

Ver·tum·nus (vər tum′nəs) ***n.*** ⟦L, altered (infl. by *vertere,* to turn) < *Vortumnus,* of Etr orig.⟧ *Rom. Myth.* the god of the changing seasons and of growing flowers and fruits, husband of Pomona

Ver·u·lam (ver′yo͞o ləm), Baron *see* BACON, Francis

ver·vain (vur′vān′) ***n.*** ⟦ME *verveine* < OFr < L *verbena:* see VERBENA⟧ any of a number of verbenas; esp., *a)* the **European vervain** (*Verbena officinalis*), formerly used in folk medicine *b)* any of several species of North American verbena, not generally cultivated **—*adj.*** VERBENA

verve (vurv) ***n.*** ⟦Fr < OFr, caprice, fantasy, manner of speech < L *verba,* pl. of *verbum,* WORD⟧ **1** vigor and energy, as in movement, portrayal, etc. **2** exuberant enthusiasm; spirit, dash, etc. **3** [Archaic] aptitude

ver·vet (vur′vit) ***n.*** ⟦Fr < ? *vert,* green + *grivet,* GRIVET⟧ a small guenon monkey (*Cercopithecus pygerythrus*) found in E and S Africa

ver·y (ver′ē) ***adj.*** ⟦ME *verai,* true < OFr < VL **veraius* < L *verus,* true < IE **weros,* true < base **wer-,* to be friendly, true > Ger *wahr,* true, OE *wær,* a compact⟧ **1** in the fullest sense; complete; absolute [the *very* opposite of the truth] **2** same; identical [the *very* hat he lost] **3** being just what is needed or suitable [the *very* sofa to fit into the space] **4** actual [caught in the *very* act]: often used as an intensifier [the *very* rafters shook] **5 ver′i·er, ver′i·est** [Archaic] *a)* real; true; genuine *b)* legitimate; lawful; rightful **—*adv.*** **1** in a high degree; to a great extent; extremely; exceedingly: used as a qualifier before an adjective or another adverb **2** truly; really: used as an intensifier [the *very* same man] **3** to what is regarded as an extreme, and hence obvious, degree; obviously; unmistakably [*very* pregnant] **—SYN.** SAME

very high frequency any radio frequency between 30 and 300 megahertz

very low frequency any radio frequency between 10 and 30 kilohertz

Ver·y signal (*or* **light**) (ver′ē, vir′ē) ⟦after E. W. *Very* (1847-1910), U.S. ordnance expert, who invented it⟧ a colored flare fired from a special pistol (**Very pistol**) for signaling at night

Ve·sa·li·us (vi sā′lē əs), **An·dre·as** (an′drē əs) 1514-64; Fl. anatomist in Italy, Spain, etc.

ve·si·ca (vi sī′kə) ***n.,*** *pl.* **-cae** (-sē) ⟦L⟧ a bladder, esp. a urinary bladder

ves·i·cal (ves′i kəl) ***adj.*** ⟦ModL *vesicalis* < L *vesica,* bladder⟧ of a bladder, esp. the urinary bladder

ves·i·cant (ves′i kənt) ***adj.*** ⟦< L *vesica,* a blister, bladder⟧ causing blisters **—*n.*** a vesicant agent; specif., in chemical warfare, any agent, as mustard gas, that blisters and burns bodily tissues Also **ves′i·ca·to′ry** (-kə tôr′ē) ***adj., n.,*** *pl.* **-to′ries**

ves·i·cate (-kāt′) ***vt., vi.*** **-cat′ed, -cat′ing** ⟦< L *vesica,* bladder, blister⟧ to blister **—ves′i·ca′tion** ***n.***

ves·i·cle (ves′i kəl) ***n.*** ⟦< Fr or L: Fr *vésicule* < L *vesicula,* dim. of *vesica,* bladder⟧ **1** a small, membranous cavity, sac, or cyst; specif., *a) Anat., Med.* a small cavity or sac filled with fluid; esp., a small, round elevation of the skin containing a serous fluid; blister *b) Bot.* a small, bladderlike sac filled with air or liquid **2** *Geol.* a small, spherical cavity in volcanic rock, produced by bubbles of air or gas in the molten rock

ves·i·co- (ves′i kō, -kə) ⟦< L *vesica,* bladder⟧ *combining form* **1** bladder [*vesicotomy*] **2** bladder and [*vesicouterine*]

ve·sic·u·lar (və sik′yə lər) ***adj.*** ⟦ModL *vesicularis*⟧ **1** of, composed of, or having vesicles **2** having the form or structure of a vesicle

ve·sic·u·late (-lit; *for v.,* -lāt′) ***adj.*** VESICULAR **—*vt., vi.*** **-lat′ed, -lat′ing** to make or become vesicular **—ve·sic′u·la′tion** ***n.***

Ves·pa·si·an (ves pā′zhən, -zhē ən) (L. name *Titus Flavius Sabinus Vespasianus*) A.D. 9-79; Rom. emperor (69-79): father of Domitian & Titus

ves·per (ves′pər) ***n.*** ⟦ME, evening star < L *vesper,* masc., *vespera,* fem., evening < IE **wesperos* (prob. < **we-:* see WEST) > Gr *hesperos*⟧ **1** [Old Poet.] *a)* [*often* **V-**] evening or evening personified *b)* [**V-**] EVENING STAR **2** [*often* **V-**] [*pl., usually with sing. v.*] *a) R.C.Ch.* the sixth of the seven canonical hours; evening prayer *b) Anglican Ch.* EVENSONG **—*adj.*** **1** of evening **2** of vespers

ves·per·al (-əl) ***adj.*** ⟦LL *vesperalis* < L *vespera*⟧ [Rare] of evening or vespers **—*n.*** *Eccles.* **1** a book containing the chants, psalms, etc. used at vespers **2** a cloth cover for protecting the altar cloth between services

☆**vesper sparrow** a gray-brown North American sparrow (*Pooecetes gramineus*) with white outer tail feathers: so called from its practice of singing in the evening

ves·per·til·i·o·nid (ves′pər til′ē ə nid′) ***n.*** ⟦< ModL *Vespertilionidae* < L *vespertilio* (gen. *vespertilionis*), a bat (< *vesper,* evening: see VESPER) + -ID⟧ any of a large family (Vespertilionidae) of long-tailed bats that are widely distributed, esp. in temperate regions, including most of the small, insect-eating species

ves·per·tine (ves′pər tin, -tīn′) ***adj.*** ⟦L *vespertinus* < *vesper:* see VESPER⟧ **1** of or occurring in the evening **2** *Bot.* opening or blossoming in the evening **3** *Zool.* becoming active or flying in the early evening: cf. CREPUSCULAR (sense 2) Also **ves·per·ti·nal** (ves′pər tī′nəl)

ves·pi·ar·y (ves′pē er′ē) ***n.,*** *pl.* **-ar′ies** ⟦< L *vespa,* WASP + (AP)IARY⟧ a nest or colony of social wasps

ves·pid (ves′pid) ***n.*** ⟦< ModL *Vespidae* < L *vespa,* WASP⟧ any of a worldwide family (Vespidae) of social wasps, as the hornet and yellow jacket, that live in colonies consisting of a queen, males, and workers **—*adj.*** of these wasps

ves·pine (ves′pīn, -pin) ***adj.*** ⟦< L *vespa,* WASP + -INE[1]⟧ of, pertaining to, or like wasps

Ves·puc·ci (ves po͞ot′chē), **A·mer·i·go** (ä′me rē′gô) (L. name *Americus Vespucius*) 1454-1512; It. navigator & explorer: see AMERICA (etym.)

ves·sel (ves′əl) ***n.*** ⟦ME < OFr *vaissel* < LL *vascellum,* dim. of L *vas,* vessel⟧ **1** a vase, bowl, pot, kettle, or other such utensil for holding something **2** *Bible* a person thought of as being the receiver or repository of some spirit or influence [a *vessel* of wrath] **3** any relatively large watercraft **4** *a) Anat., Zool.* a tube or duct containing or circulating a body fluid [a blood *vessel*] *b) Bot.* a continuous, water-conducting tube in the xylem, composed of a row of nonliving cells whose end walls have disappeared

vest (vest) ***n.*** ⟦Fr *veste* < It < L *vestis,* garment < IE base **wes-,* to clothe > OE *werian,* to WEAR[1]⟧ **1** *a)* a short, tightfitting, sleeveless garment worn, esp. under a suit coat, by men *b)* a similar garment worn by women *c)* an insert or trimming worn under the bodice by women, simulating the front of a man's vest **2** *a)* a calf-length, cassocklike garment worn by men in the time of Charles II *b)* [Rare] any long robe **3** *a)* a girl's undershirt *b)* [Chiefly Brit.] any undershirt **4** [Obs.] vesture; clothing **—*vt.*** ⟦ME *vesten* < OFr *vestir* < L *vestire* < the n.⟧ **1** to dress, as in church vestments; clothe **2** to place (authority, power, property rights, pension rights, etc.) in the control of a person or group (with *in*) **3** to put (a person) in possession or control of, as power or authority; invest (*with* something) See also VESTING **—*vi.*** **1** to put on garments or vestments; clothe oneself **2** to pass to a person; become vested (*in* a person), as property **—☆play (it) close to the vest** ⟦in allusion to the way a card player holds a hand of cards so they cannot be seen by others⟧ **1** to be reserved, secretive, etc.; keep (one's plans, thoughts, etc.) to oneself **2** to take no risks; be cautious, conservative, etc.

Ves·ta (ves′tə) ***n.*** ⟦L, prob. akin to Gr *Hestia,* lit., hearth⟧ **1** *Rom. Myth.* the goddess of the hearth, identified with the Greek Hestia **2** [**v-**] [Brit. Historical] a short wooden or wax match

ves·tal (ves′təl) ***adj.*** **1** of or sacred to Vesta **2** of the vestal virgins **3**

chaste; pure —*n.* 1 *short for* VESTAL VIRGIN 2 a chaste woman; specif., a virgin

vestal virgin in ancient Rome, any of a small group of virgin priestesses of Vesta, who, sworn to remain chaste, tended the sacred fire in her temple

vest·ed (ves′tid) ***adj.*** ⟦pp. of VEST⟧ 1 clothed; robed, esp. in church vestments 2 including a VEST (*n.* 1a): said of a man's suit 3 *Law* not contingent upon anything; fixed; settled; absolute [*a vested* right]

vested interest 1 an established right that cannot be eliminated, as to some future benefit 2 close involvement in promoting personal advantage 3 [*pl.*] a number of groups cooperating or competing in pursuing selfish goals and exerting controlling influence, esp., the powerful persons and groups that own and control industry, business, etc.

☆**vest·ee** (ves tē′) ***n.*** VEST (*n.* 1c)

ves·ti·ar·y (ves′tē er′ē) ***adj.*** ⟦ME < OFr *vestiairie:* see VESTRY⟧ [Rare] of clothes or vestments —*n., pl.* **-ar′ies** a supply room for clothing, as in a monastery

ves·ti·bule (ves′tə byo͞ol′) ***n.*** ⟦Fr < L *vestibulum,* entrance hall⟧ 1 a small entrance hall or room, either to a building or to a larger room ☆2 the enclosed passage between passenger cars of a train, with doors for entrance or exit 3 *Anat., Zool.* any cavity or space serving as an entrance to another cavity or space [the *vestibule* of the inner ear leads into the cochlea] —**ves·tib·u·lar** (ves tib′yə lər) ***adj.***

ves·tige (ves′tij) ***n.*** ⟦Fr < L *vestigium,* footprint⟧ 1 a trace, mark, or sign of something that once existed but has passed away or disappeared [*vestiges* of the ancient wall] 2 a trace; bit [not a *vestige* of hope left] 3 *Biol.* a degenerate, atrophied, or rudimentary organ or part, more fully developed or functional in an earlier stage of development of the individual or species: also **ves·tig·i·um** (ves tij′ē əm), *pl.* **-tig′i·a** (-tij′ē ə, -tij′ə) —**ves·tig′i·al** (-tij′ē əl, -tij′əl) ***adj.*** —**ves·tig′i·al·ly** ***adv.***

vest·ing (ves′tiŋ) ***n.*** the retention by an employee of all or part of pension rights regardless of change of employers, early retirement, etc.

vest·ment (vest′mənt) ***n.*** ⟦ME *vestement* < OFr < L *vestimentum* < *vestire,* to clothe: see VEST⟧ 1 a garment; robe; gown; esp., an official robe or gown 2 *Eccles.* any of the garments, esp. the outer robe, worn by officiants and their assistants, choir members, etc. during certain services and rites

vest-pock·et (vest′päk′it) ***adj.*** 1 small enough to fit into a vest pocket [a *vest-pocket* dictionary] 2 quite small or compact [a *vest-pocket* park]

ves·try (ves′trē) ***n., pl.*** **-tries** ⟦ME *vestrie* < OFr *vestiarie* < L *vestiarium,* wardrobe < *vestis,* garment: see VEST⟧ 1 a room in a church where the clergy put on their vestments and the sacred vessels are kept; sacristy 2 a room in a church or church building for prayer meetings, Sunday school, etc. 3 *Anglican Ch., Episcopal Ch.* a group of church members who manage the temporal affairs of the church 4 *Anglican Ch.* *a)* a meeting of such a group or of the parishioners in general *b)* the place for this

ves·try·man (-mən) ***n., pl.*** **-men** (-mən) a member of a vestry

ves·ture (ves′chər) ***n.*** ⟦OFr < VL *vestitura* < L *vestire,* to clothe: see VEST⟧ 1 [Now Rare] *a)* clothing; garments; apparel *b)* a covering; wrapper 2 *Law* everything growing on land except trees, as grass or grain —***vt.*** **-tured, -tur·ing** [Archaic] to cover; clothe

Ve·su·vi·an (və so͞o′vē ən) ***adj.*** of or like Mount Vesuvius; volcanic —***n.*** [v-] an early type of match; fusee

ve·su·vi·an·ite (-ə nīt′) ***n.*** ⟦< prec. + -ITE¹⟧ a usually green or brown, hard, tetragonal mineral, $Ca_{10}Mg_2Al_4(SiO_4)_5(Si_2O_7)_2(OH)_4$, usually found in metamorphic limestone; hydrous calcium magnesium aluminum silicate

Ve·su·vi·us (və so͞o′vē əs) active volcano in S Italy, on the Bay of Naples: eruption of A.D. 79 destroyed Pompeii & Herculaneum: *c.* 4,000 ft (1,219 m): It. name **Ve·su·vio** (ve zo͞o′vyô)

vet¹ (vet) [Informal] ***n.*** *short for* VETERINARIAN —***vt.*** **vet′ted, vet′ting** 1 to examine or treat as a veterinarian does 2 to examine, investigate, or evaluate in a thorough or expert way —***vi.*** to work as a veterinarian

☆**vet²** (vet) ***n.*** [Informal] *short for* VETERAN

vet³ (vet) ***n.*** *see* BETH

vet⁴ *abbrev.* 1 veteran 2 veterinarian 3 veterinary

vetch (vech) ***n.*** ⟦ME *feche, veche* < NormFr *veche* < L *vicia,* vetch < IE **weik-* (< base **wei-,* to bend > WEAK)⟧ any of a number of leafy, climbing or trailing plants (esp. genus *Vicia*) of the pea family, grown chiefly for fodder and as a green manure

vetch·ling (-liŋ) ***n.*** ⟦prec. + -LING¹⟧ any of a genus (*Lathyrus*) of tendril-climbing plants of the pea family

vet·er·an (vet′ər ən, ve′trən) ***adj.*** ⟦L *veteranus* < *vetus* (gen. *veteris*), old < IE base **wet-,* year > WETHER, Gr *etos,* year⟧ 1 experienced; practiced 2 designating or of a person who has served in the armed forces —***n.*** 1 *a)* an old, experienced soldier, etc., esp. one who served in time of war *b)* any person who has served in the armed forces 2 a person of long experience in some occupation or position

☆**Veterans Administration** a consolidated U.S. federal agency that administers all laws governing benefits for veterans of the armed forces: since 1988, called the **Department of Veterans Affairs**

☆**Veterans Day** a legal holiday in the U.S. honoring all veterans of the armed forces: observed (except 1971-77) on ARMISTICE DAY

☆**Veterans of Foreign Wars** an organization of U.S. veterans who have served in foreign wars: founded in 1899

vet·er·i·nar·i·an (vet′ər ə ner′ē ən, ve′trə-) ***n.*** ⟦< L *veterinarius* (see fol.) + -AN⟧ a person who practices veterinary medicine or surgery

vet·er·i·nar·y (vet′ər ə ner′ē, ve′trə-) ***adj.*** ⟦L *veterinarius,* of beasts of burden < *veterina,* beasts of burden < *veterinus,* pertaining to beasts of burden < *vetus* (gen. *veteris*), old, in the sense "beasts of a certain age": see VETERAN⟧ designating or of the branch of medicine dealing with the prevention and treatment of diseases and injuries in animals, esp. domestic animals —***n.,*** *pl.* **-nar′ies** VETERINARIAN

vet·i·ver (vet′ə vər) ***n.*** ⟦Fr *vétiver* < Tamil *veṭṭivēru,* lit., root that is dug up < *vēr,* root⟧ 1 an East Indian grass (*Vetiveria zizanioides*) whose roots yield a fragrant oil used in perfumes, cosmetics, etc. 2 its fibrous roots, also used for making screens, mats, etc.

ve·to (vē′tō) ***n., pl.*** **-toes** ⟦L, I forbid < *vetare,* to forbid⟧ 1 *a)* an order prohibiting some proposed or intended act; prohibition, esp. by a person in authority *b)* the power to prevent action by such prohibition 2 the constitutional right or power of a ruler or legislature to reject bills passed by another branch of the government ☆3 in the U.S., *a)* the power of the President to refuse to sign a bill passed by Congress, preventing it from becoming law unless it is passed again (with a two-thirds majority) by both houses *b)* a similar power held by the governors of states *c)* the exercise of this power ☆4 a document or message giving the reasons of the executive for rejecting a bill: also **veto message** 5 the power of any of the five permanent members of the Security Council of the United Nations to cast a negative vote, affirmative votes of all five being required to take action on other than procedural matters —***vt.*** **-toed, -to·ing** 1 to prevent (a bill) from becoming law by a veto 2 to forbid; prohibit; refuse consent to —**ve′to·er** ***n.***

vex (veks) ***vt.*** ⟦ME *vexen* < MFr *vexer,* to vex, torment < L *vexare,* to shake, agitate < pp. stem of *vehere,* to carry: see WAY⟧ 1 to give trouble to, esp. in a petty or nagging way; disturb, annoy, irritate, etc. 2 to distress, afflict, or plague [*vexed* with rheumatism] 3 to keep bringing up, going over, or returning to (a matter difficult to solve): used in the pp. 4 [Obs.] to shake or toss about —SYN. ANNOY —**vex′er** ***n.***

vex·a·tion (vek sā′shən) ***n.*** ⟦ME *vexacion* < MFr < L *vexatio*⟧ 1 a vexing or being vexed 2 something that vexes; cause of annoyance or distress

vex·a·tious (-shəs) ***adj.*** 1 characterized by or causing vexation; annoying, troublesome, etc. 2 *Law* instituted without real grounds, chiefly to cause annoyance to the defendant: said of legal actions —**vex·a′tious·ly** ***adv.***

☆**vex·il·lol·o·gy** (vek′si lä′lə jē) ***n.*** ⟦< L *vexillum* (see fol.) + -O- + -LOGY⟧ the study of flags —**vex·il·lo·log·ic** (vek sil′ə läj′ik) ***adj.*** —**vex′il·lol′o·gist** ***n.***

vex·il·lum (vek sil′əm) ***n., pl.*** **-il′la** (-ə) ⟦L, a standard, flag, dim. < base of *velum:* see VEIL⟧ 1 in ancient Rome, *a)* a square flag, or standard, carried by troops *b)* a company of soldiers serving under one standard 2 *a)* *Bot.* STANDARD (*n.* 8*a*) *b)* *Zool.* VANE (sense 6*a*)

vex·ing (vek′siŋ) ***adj.*** that vexes —**vex′ing·ly** ***adv.***

VFR *abbrev.* Visual Flight Rules

VFW *abbrev.* Veterans of Foreign Wars

VG *abbrev.* Vicar-General

VHF or **vhf** *abbrev.* very high frequency

VHS (vē′āch′es′) ⟦*v*(*ideo*) *h*(*ome*) *s*(*ystem*)⟧ *trademark for* an electronic system for recording video and audio information on videocassettes

vi *abbrev.* intransitive verb

VI *abbrev.* Virgin Islands: also **V.I.**

v.i. *abbrev.* ⟦L *vide infra*⟧ see below

vi·a (vī′ə, vē′ə) ***prep.*** ⟦L, abl. sing. of *via,* a way < IE base **wei-,* to go, strive toward > Gr *ienai,* to go, OE *wath,* a hunt, chase⟧ 1 by a route passing through, along, or over; by way of [from Rome to London *via* Paris] 2 by means of; by the medium of [*via* airmail]

vi·a·ble (vī′ə bəl) ***adj.*** ⟦Fr, likely to live < *vie,* life < L *vita:* see VITAL⟧ 1 able to live; specif., *a)* having developed sufficiently within the uterus to be able to live and continue normal development outside the uterus [a premature but *viable* infant] *b)* able to take root and grow [*viable* seeds] 2 workable and likely to survive or to have real meaning, pertinence, etc. [a *viable* economy, *viable* ideas] —**vi′a·bil′i·ty** ***n.*** —**vi′a·bly** ***adv.***

vi·a·duct (vī′ə dukt′) ***n.*** ⟦L *via* (see VIA) + (AQUE)DUCT⟧ a long bridge consisting of a series of short spans supported on piers or towers, usually to carry a road or railroad over a valley, gorge, etc.

Vi·ag·ra (vī ag′rə) *trademark for* a compound, $C_{22}H_{30}N_6O_4S$, used to treat erectile dysfunction

vi·al (vī′əl) ***n.*** ⟦ME *viole,* var. of *fiole* < OFr < OProv *fiola:* see PHIAL⟧ a small, cylindrical bottle, usually of glass, for containing liquids; phial —***vt.*** **-aled** or **-alled, -al·ing** or **-al·ling** to put or keep in a vial

vi·a me·di·a (vī′ə mē′dē ə; vē′ə mā′-, wē′ə mā′-) ⟦L⟧ a middle way; course between two extremes

vi·and (vī′ənd) ***n.*** ⟦ME *vyaunde* < OFr *viande* < VL **vivanda,* for L *vivenda,* neut. pl. ger. of *vivere,* to live: see BIO-⟧ 1 an article of food 2 [*pl.*] food of various kinds; esp., choice dishes

vi·at·i·cum (vī at′i kəm) ***n., pl.*** **-ca** (-kə) or **-cums** ⟦L, provision for a journey < *viaticus,* of a way or road < *via,* a way: see VIA⟧ 1 *a)* in ancient Rome, money or supplies provided as traveling expenses to an officer on an official mission *b)* money or supplies for any journey 2 [*often* V-] the Eucharist as given to a dying person or to one in danger of death

☆**vibe** (vīb) ***n.*** ⟦< VIBRATION⟧ [Informal] a distinctive mood or aura surrounding a person, thing, or place, as sensed or felt by another person: *often used in pl.*

☆**vibes** (vībz) ***pl.n.*** 1 VIBRAPHONE 2 *see* VIBE

vib·ist (vī′bist) ***n.*** ⟦prec. + -IST¹⟧ a person who plays a vibraphone

Vi·borg (vē′bôr y′) *Swed. name for* VYBORG

vi·brac·u·lum (vī brak′yo͞o ləm) ***n., pl.*** **-u·la** (-lə) ⟦ModL, dim. < L *vibrare,* to VIBRATE⟧ *Zool.* any of the specially modified zooids in a colony of bryozoans, with a whiplike, movable form —**vi·brac′u·lar** ***adj.***

☆**vi·bra·harp** (vī′brə härp′) ***n.*** ⟦< HARP, after VIBRAPHONE⟧ VIBRAPHONE

vi·bran·cy (vī′brən sē) ***n.*** a vibrant state or quality

vi·brant (vī′brənt) ***adj.*** ⟦L *vibrans,* prp. of *vibrare,* to VIBRATE⟧ **1** quivering or vibrating, esp. in such a way as to produce sound **2** produced by vibration; resonant: said of sound **3** throbbing with life and activity; lively [*vibrant* streets] **4** vigorous, energetic, radiant, sparkling, vivacious, etc. [a *vibrant* woman] —**vi′brant·ly** ***adv.***

vi·bra·phone (vī′brə fōn′) ***n.*** ⟦< fol. + -PHONE⟧ a musical instrument resembling the marimba, but with metal bars and electrically operated valves in the resonators that produce a gentle vibrato —**vi′bra·phon′ist** ***n.***

vi·brate (vī′brāt′) ***vt.*** **-brat′ed, -brat′ing** ⟦< L *vibratus,* pp. of *vibrare,* to vibrate, shake < IE **weib-* (< base **wei-,* to turn) > WIPE⟧ **1** to give off (light or sound) by vibration **2** to set in to-and-fro motion; oscillate **3** to cause to quiver —***vi.*** **1** to swing back and forth; oscillate, as a pendulum **2** to move rapidly back and forth; quiver, as a plucked string **3** to resound: said of sounds **4** to convey an emotional resonance —**SYN.** SWING

vi·bra·tile (vī′brə til, -tīl′) ***adj.*** ⟦Fr < L *vibratus* (see prec.) + *-ile,* -ILE⟧ **1** of or characterized by vibration **2** capable of vibrating or of being vibrated **3** having a vibratory motion —**vi′bra·til′i·ty** (-til′ə tē) ***n.***

vi·bra·tion (vī brā′shən) ***n.*** ⟦L *vibratio*⟧ **1** the action of vibrating; specif., *a)* movement back and forth, as of a pendulum; oscillation *b)* rapid rhythmic movement back and forth; quiver **2** vacillation or wavering, as between two choices or opinions ☆**3** [*pl.*] emotional qualities or supernatural emanations that are sensed or felt by another person or thing **4** *Physics a)* periodic, to-and-fro motion or oscillation of an object, as an elastic body or the particles of a fluid, when it is displaced from the rest position or position of equilibrium, as in transmitting sound *b)* a single, complete oscillation —**vi·bra′tion·al** ***adj.***

vi·bra·to (vi brät′ō, vī-) ***n., pl.*** **-tos** ⟦It, pp. of *vibrare* < L: see VIBRATE⟧ *Music* a pulsating effect, less extreme than a tremolo, produced by rapid alternation of a given tone with a barely perceptible variation in pitch, as by the slight oscillation of the finger on a violin string or by a slight wavering of the tone in singing

vi·bra·tor (vī′brāt′ər) ***n.*** something that vibrates or causes vibration; specif., *a)* the hammer of an electric bell *b)* a vibrating electrical device used in massage or for sexual stimulation *c) Electronics* an electromagnetic device with contacts on a tuned, vibrating steel reed or armature that converts a steady or direct current into a pulsating or alternating current

vi·bra·to·ry (vī′brə tôr′ē) ***adj.*** **1** of, like, or causing vibration **2** vibrating or capable of vibration

vib·ri·o (vib′rē ō′) ***n., pl.*** **-os′** ⟦ModL < L *vibrare,* to shake: see VIBRATE⟧ any of a genus (*Vibrio*) of short, flagellate, Gram-negative bacteria shaped like a comma or S: one species (*V. cholerae*) causes cholera

vi·bris·sa (vī bris′ə) ***n., pl.*** **-sae** (-ē) ⟦ModL < L *vibrissae,* pl., akin to *vibrare,* to VIBRATE⟧ *Anat., Zool.* **1** any of the stiff hairs growing in or near the nostrils of certain animals and often serving as organs of touch, as a cat's whiskers **2** any of the bristlelike feathers growing near the mouth of certain insect-eating birds, as the whippoorwill

vi·bur·num (vī bur′nəm) ***n.*** ⟦ModL < L, the wayfaring tree⟧ **1** any of a large genus (*Viburnum*) of shrubs or small trees of the honeysuckle family, with white flowers **2** the bark of several species of this plant, sometimes used in medicine

vic *abbrev.* vicinity

vic·ar (vik′ər) ***n.*** ⟦ME < OFr *vicaire* < L *vicarius,* orig., vicarious < **vix* (gen. *vicis*), a change, alteration < IE **weik-,* to bend, change: see WEAK⟧ **1** [Archaic] a person who acts in place of another; deputy **2** *Anglican Ch.* a parish priest who is not a rector and receives a stipend instead of the tithes **3** *Episcopal Ch.* a minister in charge of a chapel **4** *R.C.Ch. a)* a church officer acting as a deputy of a bishop *b)* [**V-**] the pope, regarded as earthly representative of Christ (in full **Vicar of (Jesus) Christ**) —**vic′ar·ship′** ***n.***

vic·ar·age (-ij) ***n.*** ⟦ME *vicerege:* see prec. & -AGE⟧ **1** the residence of a vicar **2** the benefice or salary of a vicar **3** the position or duties of a vicar

vicar apostolic *pl.* **vicars apostolic** *R.C.Ch.* a titular bishop serving in a region lacking an established hierarchy

vic·ar-gen·er·al (vik′ər jen′ər əl) ***n., pl.*** **vic′ars-gen′er·al** ⟦ME *vicare generale* < ML *vicarius generalis:* see VICAR & GENERAL⟧ **1** an administrative deputy, as of a bishop or of the general superior of a religious order, society, etc. **2** in English history, the title given to Thomas Cromwell as vicegerent of Henry VIII

vi·car·i·al (vī ker′ē əl, vi-) ***adj.*** ⟦MFr⟧ **1** of a vicar **2** acting as a vicar **3** vicarious, or delegated [*vicarial* powers]

vi·car·i·ate (-it, -āt′) ***n.*** ⟦ML *vicariatus* < L *vicarius*⟧ **1** the office or authority of a vicar **2** the district administered by a vicar Also **vic·ar·ate** (vik′ər it)

vi·car·i·ous (vī ker′ē əs, vi-) ***adj.*** ⟦L *vicarius,* substituted: see VICAR⟧ **1** *a)* taking the place of another thing or person; substitute; deputy *b)* held or handled by one person as the deputy of another; delegated [*vicarious* powers] **2** *a)* endured, suffered, or performed by one person in place of another [*vicarious* punishment] *b)* shared in or experienced by imagined participation in another's experience [a *vicarious* thrill] —**vi·car′i·ous·ly** ***adv.*** —**vi·car′i·ous·ness** ***n.***

vice[1] (vīs) ***n.*** ⟦ME < OFr < L *vitium,* vice, fault < IE base **wi-,* apart, in two > WITH, Sans *viṣu-,* in opposite directions⟧ **1** *a)* an evil or wicked action, habit, or characteristic *b)* evil or wicked conduct or behavior; depravity or corruption *c)* prostitution *d)* [**V-**] in old English morality plays, a character, often a buffoon, representing a vice or vice in general **2** any trivial fault or failing, act of self-indulgence, etc. **3** a defect or flaw, as in a work of art **4** any physical or functional defect or imperfection of the body **5** a bad or harmful trick or habit, as of a horse or dog —**SYN.** FAULT

vi·ce[2] (vī′sē, -sə) ***prep.*** ⟦L: see VICE-⟧ in the place of; as the deputy or successor of

vice[3] (vīs) ***n., vt.*** *chiefly Brit. sp. of* VISE

vice- (vīs) ⟦< L *vice,* in the place of another, abl. of **vix:* see VICAR⟧ *prefix* one who acts in the place of; subordinate; deputy [*vice*-chairman, *vice*regal]

vice admiral *U.S. Navy* an officer ranking above a rear admiral and below an admiral —**vice admiralty**

vice-chair·man (vīs′cher′mən) ***n., pl.*** **-men** (-mən) an assistant or deputy chairman: also **vice chair** or **vice′-chair′per·son**

vice-chan·cel·lor (-chan′sə lər) ***n.*** **1** an official next in rank below a chancellor, as of a university, and authorized to act as the chancellor's deputy **2** *Law* a judge serving as assistant to a chancellor

vice-con·sul (-kän′səl) ***n.*** an officer who is subordinate to or a substitute for a consul —**vice′-con′su·lar** ***adj.***

vice·ge·ren·cy (vīs′jir′ən sē) ***n., pl.*** **-cies** the office of, or district ruled by, a vicegerent

vice·ge·rent (-jir′ənt) ***n.*** ⟦ML *vicegerens:* see VICE- & GERENT⟧ a person appointed by another, esp. by a ruler, to exercise the latter's power and authority; deputy

vi·cen·ni·al (vī sen′ē əl) ***adj.*** ⟦LL *vicennialis* < L *vicennium,* period of twenty years < *vicies,* twenty times + *annus,* year (see ANNUAL)⟧ **1** happening every twenty years **2** lasting twenty years

Vi·cen·za (vē chen′tsä) commune in N Italy

vice president **1** an officer next in rank below a president, acting during the president's absence or incapacity **2** any of several officers of a company, institution, etc., each in charge of a separate department ☆**3** the elected officer in the U.S. government who acts as president of the Senate and succeeds to the Presidency in the event of the President's death, incapacity, or removal Also written **vice′-pres′i·dent** ***n.*** —☆**vice presidency** —☆**vice presidential**

vice·re·gal (vīs′rē′gəl) ***adj.*** ⟦VICE- + REGAL⟧ of a viceroy —**vice′re′gal·ly** ***adv.***

vice·re·gent (-rē′jənt) ***n.*** a deputy of a regent

vice·reine (vīs′rān′) ***n.*** ⟦Fr < *vice-* (see VICE-) + *reine,* queen < L *regina* (see REGINA)⟧ **1** the wife of a viceroy **2** a woman viceroy

vice·roy (-roi′) ***n.*** ⟦MFr < *vice-* (see VICE-) + *roy,* king < L *rex:* see REGAL⟧ **1** a person ruling a country, province, or colony as the deputy of a sovereign ☆**2** an American butterfly (*Limenitis archippus*) of striking orange-and-black coloring, much like the monarch butterfly, but smaller

vice·roy·al·ty (vīs′roi′əl tē) ***n., pl.*** **-ties** ⟦< Fr *vice-royauté* < OFr *vice-,* VICE- + *roialte:* see ROYALTY⟧ the office or tenure of, or the area ruled by, a viceroy: also **vice′roy·ship′**

vice squad that division of a police department assigned to enforce laws relating to prostitution, gambling, etc.

vi·ce ver·sa (vī′sə vur′sə, vīs′ vur′-) ⟦L⟧ the order or relation being reversed; conversely

Vi·chy[1] (vish′ē, vē′shē) ***n.*** **1** a sparkling mineral water from springs at Vichy **2** a natural or processed water like this In full **Vichy water**

Vi·chy[2] (vish′ē, vē′shē; *Fr* vē shē′) city in central France: seat of the collaborationist French government under Pétain (1940-44) after the invasion of France by Nazi Germany

vi·chys·soise (vē′shē swäz′, vish′ē-) ***n.*** ⟦Fr, orig. fem. of *Vichyssois,* of prec.⟧ a smooth, thick soup made with potatoes, leeks, and cream, and usually served cold

vic·i·nage (vis′ə nij′) ***n.*** ⟦ME *vesinage* < MFr *visenage* < *veisin,* near < VL **vecinus,* for L *vicinus:* see VICINITY⟧ **1** VICINITY **2** the people living in a particular neighborhood

vic·i·nal (-nəl) ***adj.*** ⟦L *vicinalis* < *vicinus:* see fol.⟧ **1** neighboring; nearby **2** *Mineralogy* designating faces on a crystal that approximate or take the place of fundamental planes

vi·cin·i·ty (və sin′ə tē) ***n.*** ⟦L *vicinitas* < *vicinus,* near < *vicus,* group of houses, village: see ECO-⟧ **1** the state of being near or close by; nearness; proximity [two theaters in close *vicinity*] **2** *pl.* **-ties** the region or area surrounding a particular place; neighborhood —**in the vicinity of** **1** near; close to (a place) **2** about; approximately (the amount, etc. specified)

vi·cious (vish′əs) ***adj.*** ⟦ME < OFr *vicieus* < L *vitiosus,* full of faults, corrupt, vicious < *vitium,* VICE[1]⟧ **1** *a)* given to or characterized by vice; evil, corrupt, or depraved *b)* tending to deprave or corrupt; pernicious [*vicious* interests] *c)* harmful, unwholesome, or noxious [a *vicious* concoction] **2** ruined by defects, flaws, or errors; full of faults [a *vicious* argument] **3** having bad or harmful habits; unruly [a *vicious* horse] **4** malicious; spiteful; mean [a *vicious* rumor] **5** very intense, forceful, sharp, etc. [a *vicious* blow] —**vi′cious·ly** ***adv.*** —**vi′cious·ness** ***n.***

vicious circle **1** *Logic* an argument which is invalid because its conclusion rests on a premise which itself depends on the conclusion **2** any sequence of events characterized by two or more interrelated problems or ills inevitably reinforcing one another in an endless or ever-worsening cycle: also **vicious cycle**

vi·cis·si·tude (vi sis′ə to͞od′, -tyo͞od′) ***n.*** ⟦Fr < L *vicissitudo* < **vix,* a turn, change: see VICAR⟧ **1** *a)* a condition of constant change or alternation, as a natural process; mutability [the *vicissitude* of the sea] *b)* regular succession or alternation, as of night and day **2** [*pl.*] unpredictable changes or variations that keep occurring in life, fortune, etc.; shifting circumstances;

ups and downs **3** a difficulty that is likely to occur, esp. one that is inherent in a situation —*SYN.* DIFFICULTY —**vi·cis′si·tu′di·nar′y** *adj.*, **vi·cis′si·tu′di·nous**

Vick·i (vik′ē) *n.* a feminine name: var. *Vicky, Vickie*: see VICTORIA[1]

Vicks·burg (viks′burg′) ⟦after Rev. Newitt *Vick* (?-1819), early settler⟧ city in W Miss., on the Mississippi River: besieged & captured by Grant in the Civil War (1863)

Vi·co (vē′kô), **Gio·van·ni Bat·tis·ta** (jô vän′nē bät tēs′tä) (also called *Giambattista Vico*) 1668-1744; It. philosopher

vi·comte (vē kônt′) *n., pl.* **-comtes′** (-kônt′) ⟦Fr⟧ VISCOUNT (sense 2)

vic·tim (vik′təm) *n.* ⟦L *victima,* victim, beast for sacrifice < IE base ***weik-**, to separate > OE *wig,* idol, *wicce,* WITCH⟧ **1** a person or animal killed as a sacrifice to a god in a religious rite **2** someone or something killed, destroyed, injured, oppressed, or otherwise harmed by, or suffering from, some act, condition, or circumstance [*victims* of war] **3** a person who suffers some loss, as by being swindled —**vic′tim·hood′** *n.*

vic·tim·ize (vik′tə mīz′) *vt.* **-ized′**, **-iz′ing** to make a victim of; specif., *a)* to subject to cruel or harmful treatment *b)* to dupe or cheat —**vic′tim·i·za′tion** (-mə zā′shən, -mī′-) *n.* —**vic′tim·iz′er** *n.*

☆**vic·tim·less crime** (vik′təm lis) a statutory crime, such as prostitution or gambling, regarded as having no clearly identifiable victim

vic·tim·ol·o·gy (vik′tə mäl′ə jē) *n.* ⟦Fr *victimologie*: see -LOGY⟧ **1** the study of victims, esp. victims of crime **2** status as a victim; specif., such status arising from membership in an ethnic, religious, etc. group regarded as historically victimized: usually an ironic or dismissive usage

vic·tor (vik′tər) *n.* ⟦ME < L < pp. of *vincere,* to conquer < IE base ***weik-**, vigorous or hostile display of force > OHG *wic,* battle, OE *wigan,* to fight⟧ the winner in a battle, struggle, etc. —*adj.* VICTORIOUS

Vic·tor (vik′tər) *n.* ⟦L: see prec.⟧ a masculine name: dim. *Vic*; fem. *Victoria*

Victor Emmanuel II 1820-78; king of Sardinia (1849-61) & 1st king of Italy (1861-78)

vic·to·ri·a (vik tôr′ē ə) *n.* ⟦after Queen VICTORIA[2]⟧ **1** a four-wheeled carriage for two passengers, with a folding top and a high seat in front for the driver **2** an early touring automobile with a folding top over the rear seat **3** any of a genus (*Victoria*) of South American waterlilies (family Nymphaeaceae) with platterlike leaves up to seven feet wide and large, night-blooming flowers

victoria

Vic·to·ri·a[1] (vik tôr′ē ə) *n.* ⟦L, VICTORY⟧ a feminine name: dim. *Vicki, Vickie, Vicky*; equiv. Fr. *Victoire,* It. *Vittoria,* Sp. *Vitoria*

Vic·to·ri·a[2] (vik tôr′ē ə) (born *Alexandrina Victoria*) 1819-1901; queen of Great Britain & Ireland (1837-1901): granddaughter of George III

Vic·to·ri·a[3] (vik tôr′ē ə) **1** state of Australia, in the SE part: 87,807 sq mi (227,420 sq km); cap. Melbourne **2** *former name for* HONG KONG (the city) **3** ⟦after Queen VICTORIA[2]⟧ capital of British Columbia, Canada: seaport on SE Vancouver Island **4** capital of the Seychelles, on Mahé island **5 Lake** lake in E Africa, bounded by Kenya, Uganda, & Tanzania: 26,828 sq mi (69,484 sq km) **6** ⟦after Queen VICTORIA[2]⟧ island of the Arctic Archipelago, Canada, east of Banks Island: 83,896 sq mi (217,290 sq km)

Victoria Cross ⟦after Queen VICTORIA[2]⟧ the highest British Commonwealth military decoration, awarded for deeds of exceptional valor

Victoria Day a legal holiday in Canada, celebrated on the Monday preceding May 25: originally May 24, Queen Victoria's birthday

Victoria Falls waterfall of the Zambezi River, between Zimbabwe & Zambia: *c.* 350 ft (107 m) high; *c.* 1 mi (1.6 km) wide

Victoria Land mainland region of Antarctica, along the Ross Sea: part of the Ross Dependency

Vic·to·ri·an (-ən) *adj.* **1** of or characteristic of the period of the reign of Queen Victoria (1837-1901) **2** showing, variously, the middle-class respectability, prudery, bigotry, etc. generally attributed to Victorian England **3** designating or of a style of architecture, decorations, and furnishings of the 19th cent., characterized by massiveness, flowery carving, and ornate design —*n.* a person of the time of Queen Victoria —**Vic·to′ri·an·ism′** *n.*

Vic·to·ri·an·a (vik tôr′ē an′ə) *n.* ⟦after Queen VICTORIA[2] + -ANA⟧ furniture, glassware, artwork, architecture, etc. considered typical of the Victorian era

Victoria Nile upper course of the Nile, flowing from Lake Victoria into Lake Albert: *c.* 250 mi (402 km)

vic·to·ri·ous (vik tôr′ē əs) *adj.* ⟦ME < L *victoriosus*⟧ **1** having won a victory; winning; triumphant **2** of, typical of, or bringing about victory —**vic·to′ri·ous·ly** *adv.*

Vic·tor·ville (vik′tər vil′) city in SW Calif.

vic·to·ry (vik′tər ē, -trē) *n., pl.* **-ries** ⟦ME < OFr *victorie* < L *victoria* < *victor,* VICTOR⟧ **1** final and complete supremacy or superiority in battle or war **2** a specific military engagement ending in triumph **3** success in any contest or struggle involving the defeat of an opponent or the overcoming of obstacles

SYN.—**victory** implies the winning of a contest or struggle of any kind [a *victory* in battle, in sports, etc.]; **conquest** implies a victory in which one subjugates others and brings them under complete control [the *conquests* of Napoleon]; **triumph** implies a victory in which one exults because of its outstanding and decisive character [the *triumphs* of modern medicine] —*ANT.* **defeat**

victory lap a ceremonial lap around a racetrack or athletic field by the winner of a race: often used fig.

vict·ual (vit′'l) *n.* ⟦ME *vitaille,* provisions < MFr < LL *victualia,* provisions < L *victualis,* of food < *victus,* food < pp. of *vivere,* to live: see BIO-⟧ **1** [Now Chiefly Dial.] food or other provisions **2** [*pl.*] [Informal or Dial.] articles of food, esp. when prepared for use —*vt.* **-ualed** or **-ualled**, **-ual·ing** or **-ual·ling** to supply with food or other provisions —*vi.* [Archaic] **1** to eat or feed **2** to lay in a supply of food —*SYN.* FOOD

vict·ual·er or **vict·ual·ler** (-ər) *n.* ⟦ME *vittailler* < MFr *vitailleur*⟧ **1** [Historical] *a)* a person who supplied victuals, as to an army *b)* a supply ship **2** [Brit.] an innkeeper

vi·cu·ña (vī kyo͞o′nyə, -nə) *n., pl.* **-ñas** or **-ña** ⟦Sp < Quechua *wikúña*⟧ **1** a small llama (*Lama vicugna*) with soft, shaggy wool, found wild in the Andes **2** this wool **3** a fabric made from it or in imitation of it

☆**Vi·da·li·a onion** (vi dāl′yə, -dā′lē ə) ⟦< *Vidalia,* a trademark, after *Vidalia,* Georgia, where orig. grown⟧ a type of large, sweet, globe-shaped onion with a pale-yellow skin

vi·de (vī′dē, vē′dā) *v. imper.* ⟦L, imper. sing of *videre,* to see: see VISION⟧ refer to: used to direct attention to a particular page, book, etc.

vide an·te (an′tē) ⟦L⟧ see before; see earlier (in the book, etc.)

vide in·fra (in′frə) ⟦L⟧ see below; see further on (in the book, etc.)

vi·de·li·cet (vi del′ə set, -sit) *adv.* ⟦L < *videre licet,* it is permitted to see⟧ that is; namely

vid·e·o (vid′ē ō′) *adj.* ⟦L, I see < *videre*: see VISION: used by analogy with AUDIO⟧ **1** of or used in television **2** designating or of the picture portion of a telecast, webcast, recording, etc. **3** designating or of the display of data or images on a computer screen or other electronic screen —*n., pl.* **-os′** **1** TELEVISION **2** *short for* VIDEOCASSETTE, VIDEOTAPE, etc. **3** a filmed or taped performance, presentation, etc. for viewing; specif., MUSIC VIDEO **4** the picture portion of a telecast, webcast, recording, etc. **5** all electronic means for presenting or recording viewable images, considered as a media group Cf. AUDIO — *vt., vi.* **-oed′**, **-o′ing** to record by means of videotape, a video camera, etc.

video camera a camera equipped to record or transmit images and, often, accompanying sound

vid·e·o·cas·sette (vid′ē ō kə set′) *n.* a cassette containing videotape for recording and playing back sounds and images

videocassette recorder a device for recording on and playing back videocassettes

vid·e·o·con·fer·enc·ing (-kän′fər əns iŋ) *n.* the holding of a conference by individuals or groups who are in different locations, as by using satellite transmission, webcams, etc. —**vid′e·o·con′fer·ence** *n.*

vid·e·o·disc (vid′ē ō disk′) *n.* a disc on which images and sounds, as of a film, can be recorded for reproduction by a player connected to a TV receiver: also sp. **vid′e·o·disk′**, **video disc**, **video disk**

video display *n.* a device that accepts video signals from a computer and provides information in a visual form

video game any of various games involving images, controlled by players, on an electronic screen: also written **vid′e·o·game′** *n.*

vid·e·o-graph·ics (vid′ē ō graf′iks) *n.* computer technology dealing with the generation of pictures, charts, videos, etc., often with accompanying audio —**vid′e·o-graph′ic** *adj., n.*

vid·e·og·ra·phy (vid′ē äg′rə fē) *n.* ⟦VIDEO + -GRAPHY⟧ the art, process, or work of recording sound and visual images on videotape —**vid′e·og′ra·pher** *n.*

vid·e·o·phile (vid′ē ō fīl′) *n.* a devotee of video recording and reproduction

vid·e·o·phone (vid′ē ō fōn′) *n.* ⟦VIDEO + (TELE)PHONE⟧ a kind of telephone equipped with a video screen, enabling callers to see each other

vid·e·o·tape (-tāp′) *n.* a magnetic tape on which electronic impulses, as of the video and audio portions of a TV program, can be recorded for later playing —*vt.* **-taped′**, **-tap′ing** to record on videotape

vid·e·o·tex (-teks′) *n.* ⟦VIDEO + TEX(T)⟧ any of various early electronic systems for the distribution of data for display on video screens, often allowing for input by the user: also **vid′e·o·text′** (-tekst′)

vide post (pōst) ⟦L⟧ see after; see further on (in the book, etc.)

vide su·pra (so͞o′prə) ⟦L⟧ see above; see earlier (in the book, etc.)

vi·dette (vi det′) *n.* [Obs.] *var. of* VEDETTE

☆**vid·i·con** (vid′i kän′) *n.* ⟦VID(EO) + ICON(OSCOPE)⟧ a television camera pickup tube of high sensitivity in which the image is focused on a thin, transparent metal film backed with a layer of photoconductive material that is scanned with a low-velocity electron beam

vie (vī) *vi.* **vied**, **vy′ing** ⟦ME *vien,* aphetic for *envien* < OFr *envier,* to invite, vie in games < L *invitare,* to INVITE⟧ to struggle for superiority (*with* someone) or enter into competition (*for* something); compete —*vt.* **1** [Obs.] to bet; wager; hazard **2** [Archaic] to do, offer, display, or match in rivalry —**vi′er** *n.*

Vi·en·na (vē en′ə) capital of Austria, on the Danube: site (1814-15) of a conference (**Congress of Vienna**) of the major European powers at the end of the Napoleonic wars, to restore monarchies and readjust territories throughout Europe: Ger. name WIEN —**Vi·en·nese** (vē′ə nēz′) *adj., n., pl.* **-nese′**

Vienna sausage a small sausage like a short, slim frankfurter, used esp. as an hors d'oeuvre

Vienna Secession, the a Viennese movement of the late 19th and early 20th cent. in the arts and architecture, that rejected prevailing academic styles in favor of those of art nouveau

Vienne (vyen) river in WC France, flowing into the Loire: 230 mi (370 km)

Vien·tiane (vyen tyän′) capital of Laos, on the Mekong River

Vi·et Cong (vē′et kôŋ′, vyet′-; -käŋ′) ⟦< Vietnamese *Viet Nam Cong San,* Vietnamese Communist⟧ 1 a communist guerrilla force that sought to overthrow the South Vietnamese government, later allied with North Vietnam 2 a member of this force Also **Vi′et·cong′** *n.*

Vi·et·minh (-min′) *n.* ⟦Vietnamese, contr. < *Viet Nam Doc-lap Dong Minh,* the Revolutionary League for the Independence of Vietnam⟧ an organization formed of nationalist and communist parties in 1941 to win independence for Vietnam

Vi·et·nam (-näm′, -nam′) ⟦Vietnamese *Viet,* name of people + *nam,* south⟧ country on the E coast of the Indochinese Peninsula: ruled by the French from mid-19th cent. until 1945; partitioned into two republics (**North Vietnam** & **South Vietnam**) in 1954; war between the two republics (see VIETNAM WAR) ended with the defeat of South Vietnam & reunification of the two republics (1976) as the **Socialist Republic of Vietnam**: 127,244 sq mi (329,560 sq km); cap. Hanoi

Vi·et·nam·ese (vē′et nə mēz′, vyet′-) *adj.* of Vietnam or its people, language, or culture —*n.* 1 *pl.* **-ese′** a person born or living in Vietnam 2 the official language of Vietnam, belonging to the Mon-Khmer branch of the Austro-Asiatic language family

Vietnam War the war (*c.* 1957-75) between North Vietnam and South Vietnam: the U.S. participated on the side of South Vietnam, with its greatest military involvement in the period *c.* 1965-69

view (vyo͞o) *n.* ⟦ME *vewe* < OFr *veue* < *veoir,* to see < L *videre:* see VISION⟧ 1 a seeing or looking, as in inspection or examination 2 sight or vision; esp., range of vision [not a person in *view*] 3 mental examination or survey; critical contemplation [to take a correct *view* of a situation] 4 that which is seen; esp., a scene or prospect, as of a landscape [a room with a *view*] 5 a picture, sketch, or photograph of a scene, esp. of a landscape 6 visual appearance or aspect of something 7 manner of regarding or considering something; judgment; opinion [one's *views* on a matter] 8 that which is worked toward or sought; object; aim; goal [to have a *view* to bettering one's condition] 9 a general survey or summary 10 *Law* a formal inspection made by a jury outside of court, as at the scene of a crime or accident —*vt.* 1 to inspect; scrutinize 2 to look at or see; behold 3 to survey mentally; consider 4 to regard in a particular way [to *view* a situation with fear] —*SYN.* OPINION, SEE[1] —**in view** 1 in sight 2 under consideration 3 in mind or memory 4 as a goal, object, or expectation —**in view of** in consideration of; because of —**on view** displayed or exhibited publicly —**with a view to** 1 with the purpose of 2 with a hope of; looking forward to

view·er (-ər) *n.* 1 a person who views a scene, exhibit, film, TV show, etc.; spectator 2 an optical device for individual viewing of slides, filmstrips, etc.

☆**view·er·ship** (vyo͞o′ər ship′) *n.* 1 the audience for a TV program 2 the size of such an audience

view·find·er (-fīn′dər) *n.* a camera device, as a special lens or small video screen, that shows the camera user images of objects or actions exactly as they will appear in the photograph, on the TV screen, etc.

view halloo in fox hunting, an exclamation used by a hunter to signify that the fox has been seen breaking into the open: also **view hallo** or **view halloa**

view·ing (vyo͞o′iŋ) *n.* 1 the act or an instance of looking at or watching, as of watching a television program 2 *a)* a display, as for family and friends at a funeral home, of a corpse prior to a funeral *b)* the period of this display

view·less (-lis) *adj.* 1 affording no view, or prospect 2 [Rare] that cannot be seen; invisible 3 having or expressing no views, or opinions —**view′less·ly** *adv.*

view·point (-point′) *n.* the mental position from which things are viewed and judged; point of view

view·y (-ē) *adj.* **view′i·er, view′i·est** [Old Informal] 1 fanciful or visionary: said of a person 2 showy; ostentatious

☆**vig** (vig) *n.* [Slang] *short for* VIGORISH

☆**vi·ga** (vē′gə) *n.* ⟦Sp, beam⟧ any of the heavy ceiling beams in a house of the old Spanish type in the Southwest

Vi·gée-Le·brun (vē′zhā lə brun′), **(Marie-Louise-)Élisabeth** 1755-1842; Fr. painter: also sp. **Vigée-Le Brun**

vi·ges·i·mal (vī jes′ə məl, -jez′-) *adj.* ⟦< L *vigesimus,* var. of *vicesimus* < *viceni,* twenty each⟧ of or based on the number twenty

vig·il (vij′əl) *n.* ⟦ME *vigile* < OFr < L *vigilia,* a watch < *vigil,* awake < *vegere,* to arouse: see WAKE[1]⟧ 1 *a)* a purposeful or watchful staying awake during the usual hours of sleep *b)* a watch kept, or the period of this 2 *Eccles.* the evening or day before a festival, or the devotional services held then

vig·i·lance (vij′ə ləns) *n.* ⟦Fr < L *vigilantia*⟧ the quality or state of being vigilant; watchfulness

☆**vigilance committee** a group organized outside of legal authority to keep order and punish crime because the usual law-enforcement agencies do not exist or are alleged to be inefficient

vig·i·lant (vij′ə lənt) *adj.* ⟦Fr < L *vigilans,* prp. of *vigilare,* to watch < *vigil,* awake: see VIGIL⟧ staying watchful and alert to danger or trouble —*SYN.* WATCHFUL —**vig′i·lant·ly** *adv.*

☆**vig·i·lan·te** (vij′ə lan′tē, -län′-) *n.* ⟦Sp, watchman, orig., vigilant⟧ 1 a member of a vigilance committee 2 any individual who acts outside of legal authority, often violently, to punish or avenge a crime, right a perceived wrong, etc.

☆**vig·i·lan·tism** (vij′ə lan′tiz′əm, -län′-; vij′ə lən tiz′əm) *n.* the lawless, violent methods, spirit, etc. of vigilantes —**vig′i·lan′tist** *adj.*

vigil light a candle, taper, etc. burned as an act of special religious devotion or petition, as at a shrine

vi·gne·ron (vēn′yə rōn′) *n.* ⟦Fr < *vigne,* vine: see fol.⟧ WINEGROWER

vi·gnette (vin yet′) *n.* ⟦Fr, dim. < *vigne, vine,* VINE⟧ 1 an ornamental design (originally one of vine leaves, tendrils, and grapes) or illustration used on a page of a book, magazine, etc., as at the beginning or end of a chapter or section 2 a picture, photograph, film image, etc. with no definite border, shading off gradually at the edges into the background 3 *a)* a short literary sketch or description *b)* a short, carefully constructed scene in a film, play, etc.; specif., one regarded as subtle, sensitive, etc. —*vt.* **-gnet′ted, -gnet′ting** to make a vignette of —**vi·gnet′tist** *n.*

Vi·gny (vē nyē′), **Al·fred Vic·tor** Comte **de** (ål fred′ vēk tôr′ də) 1797-1863; Fr. poet & man of letters

Vi·go (vē′gô) seaport in NW Spain

vig·or (vig′ər) *n.* ⟦ME *vigour* < OFr < L *vigor* < *vigere,* to be strong < *vegere:* see WAKE[1]⟧ 1 active physical or mental force or strength; vitality 2 active or healthy growth [the *vigor* of a plant] 3 intensity, force, or energy [the *vigor* of her denial] 4 effective legal or binding force; validity [a law that is still in *vigor*] Brit. sp. **vig′our**

☆**vig·or·ish** (vig′ər ish) *n.* ⟦prob. via Yiddish < Russ *vyigryš,* winnings, profit⟧ [Slang] 1 the advantage in betting odds that a bookmaker or gambler creates to produce profit 2 excessive interest as charged by a loan shark

vi·go·ro·so (vig′ə rō′sō; *It* vē′gô rô′sô) *adj., adv.* ⟦It⟧ [*also in italics*] *Musical Direction* vigorous(ly); energetic(ally)

vig·or·ous (vig′ər əs) *adj.* ⟦ME *vigerous* < OFr < ML *vigorosus*⟧ 1 living or growing with full vital strength; strong; robust 2 of, characterized by, or requiring vigor or strength 3 forceful or powerful; strong; energetic 4 acting, or ready to act, with energy and force —*SYN.* ACTIVE —**vig′or·ous·ly** *adv.* —**vig′or·ous·ness** *n.*

Vii·pu·ri (vē′po͝o rē′) *Finn. name for* VYBORG

Vi·ja·ya·wa·da (vē′jə yə wä′də) city in E Andhra Pradesh, SE India, on the Krishna River

Vi·king (vī′kiŋ) *n.* ⟦ON *vikingr:* orig. uncert.⟧ [*often* **v-**] any of the Scandinavian sea rovers and pirates who ravaged the coasts of Europe from the 8th to the 10th cent.

vil *abbrev.* village

Vi·la (vē′lə) capital of Vanuatu

vile (vīl) *adj.* ⟦ME *vil* < OFr < L *vilis,* cheap, base < ? IE **wezlis* < **wesno-,* price > VENAL⟧ 1 morally base or evil; wicked; depraved; sinful 2 offensive to the senses or sensibilities; repulsive; disgusting 3 cheap; worthless 4 degrading; low; mean 5 highly disagreeable or most inferior; very bad: a generalized term of disapproval [*vile* weather] —*SYN.* BASE[2] —**vile′ly** *adv.* —**vile′ness** *n.*

vil·i·fy (vil′ə fī′) *vt.* **-fied′, -fy′ing** ⟦LL(Ec) *vilificare:* see prec. & -FY⟧ to use abusive or slanderous language about or of; calumniate; revile; defame —**vil′i·fi·ca′tion** *n.* —**vil′i·fi′er** *n.*

vil·i·pend (vil′ə pend′) *vt.* ⟦ME *vilipenden* < MFr *vilipender* < L *vilipendere* < *vilis,* VILE + *pendere,* to weigh: see PEND⟧ [Archaic] 1 to treat or regard contemptuously or slightingly; belittle 2 to vilify; revile

vil·la (vil′ə) *n.* ⟦It < L, a country seat, farm, ? via **vicsla* < *vicus,* village: see ECO-⟧ 1 a country house or estate, esp. when large or luxurious 2 [Brit.] a small suburban house

Vi·lla (vē′yä), **Fran·cis·co** (frän sēs′kô) (born *Doroteo Arango*) 1877?-1923; Mex. revolutionary leader: called *Pancho Villa*

Vil·la·fran·chi·an (vil′ə fraŋ′kē ən) *adj.* ⟦after *Villafranca,* town in NW Italy⟧ designating or of a European geologic stage of the Lower Pleistocene and the Upper Pliocene

vil·lage (vil′ij) *n.* ⟦OFr < L *villaticus,* belonging to a country house < *villa,* country house, farm: see VILLA⟧ 1 *a)* a group of houses in the country, larger than a hamlet and smaller than a city or town *b)* such a community incorporated as a municipality *c)* the people of a village, collectively; villagers 2 a group or cluster of the habitations of animals or birds —*adj.* of, in, for, or characteristic of a village

Village, the *name for* GREENWICH VILLAGE

vil·lag·er (-ər) *n.* a person who lives in a village

Vi·lla·her·mo·sa (vē′yä *er* mô′sä) city in SE Mexico: capital of Tabasco

vil·lain (vil′ən) *n.* ⟦ME *vilein* < OFr *vilain* < VL *villanus,* a farm servant < L *villa,* a farm: see VILLA⟧ 1 a person guilty of or likely to commit great crimes; evil or wicked person; scoundrel 2 a wicked or unprincipled character in a novel, play, etc., specif. the chief such character opposed to the protagonist 3 someone or something regarded as the cause of a problem, difficulty, injustice, etc. 4 *alt. sp. of* VILLEIN 5 [Obs.] a boor; lout

vil·lain·ess (-is) *n.* a female villain: see -ESS

vil·lain·ous (-əs) *adj.* 1 of, like, or characteristic of a villain; evil; wicked 2 very bad, disagreeable, or objectionable —**vil′lain·ous·ly** *adv.*

vil·lain·y (-ē) *n.* ⟦ME *vileinie* < Anglo-Fr & OFr *vilainie* < *vilain:* see VILLAIN⟧ 1 the fact or state of being villainous 2 villainous conduct 3 *pl.* **-lain·ies** (-ēz) a villainous act; wicked, detestable, or criminal deed

Vil·la-Lo·bos (vē′lä lô′bo͝osh′; *E* vē′lə lō′bōs′), **Hei·tor** (ā tôr′) 1887-1959; Brazilian composer

vil·la·nel·la (vil′ə nel′ə) ***n.***, *pl.* **-le** (-ē) ⟦It, fem. dim. of *villano* < VL *villanus:* see VILLAIN⟧ **1** an old rustic Italian song and accompanying dance **2** a Neapolitan 16th-cent. part song, lighter and more lively than the madrigal, which it often parodied

vil·la·nelle (vil′ə nel′) ***n.*** ⟦Fr < It *villanella:* see prec.⟧ a poem of fixed form, French in origin, consisting usually of five three-line stanzas and a final four-line stanza and having only two rhymes throughout

-ville (vil) ⟦< Fr *ville,* town, city < L *villa:* see VILLA⟧ *combining form* **1** town, city: used in place names [*Evansville*] ☆**2** place or condition characterized by, fit for, or filled with: freely used in slang terms, typically derogatory, often with an infixed *-s-* [*dullsville*]

vil·lein (vil′ən) ***n.*** ⟦ME: see VILLAIN⟧ any of a class of feudal serfs who by the 13th cent. had become freemen in their legal relations to all except their lord, to whom they remained subject as slaves

vil·lein·age or **vil·len·age** (-ij) ***n.*** ⟦ME *villenage* < OFr: see VILLAIN⟧ **1** the status of a villein **2** the conditions of tenure by which a villein held his land

Ville·ur·banne (vēl ür bàn′) city in EC France: suburb of Lyon

vil·li (vil′ī′) ***n.*** *pl. of* VILLUS

Vil·liers (vil′ərz, -yərz), **George** *see* BUCKINGHAM

vil·li·form (vil′ə fôrm′) ***adj.*** ⟦< VILLUS + *-i-* + -FORM⟧ **1** like villi in form **2** designating the small teeth of some fishes, so closely set as to resemble the pile of velvet

Vil·lon (vē yōn′), **Fran·çois** (frän swà′) (born *François de Montcorbier* or *des Loges*) 1431-63?; Fr. poet

vil·los·i·ty (vi läs′ə tē) ***n.***, *pl.* **-ties** **1** the condition of being villous **2** a villus **3** a coating or surface of villi

vil·lous (vil′əs) ***adj.*** ⟦ME < L *villosus*⟧ of, having the nature of, or covered with villi: also **vil′lose′** (-ōs′)

vil·lus (vil′əs) ***n.***, *pl.* **vil′li′** (-ī′) ⟦L, shaggy hair, tuft of hair, var. of *vellus,* a fleece, WOOL⟧ **1** *Anat.* any of numerous hairlike or fingerlike vascular processes on certain mucous membranes of the body, as of the small intestine, serving to secrete mucus, absorb fats, etc., or of the chorion in the mammalian placenta, serving in the exchange of food materials, etc. between the mother and the fetus **2** *Bot.* any of the long, soft, fine hairs on certain plants, as mosses

Vil·ni·us (vil′nē əs) capital of Lithuania: Russ. name **Vil·na** (vēl′nä; *E* vil′nə)

☆**vim** (vim) ***n.*** ⟦prob. echoic, assoc. with L *vim,* acc. of *vis,* strength⟧ energy; vigor

vi·men (vī′men) ***n.***, *pl.* **vim·i·na** (vim′ə nə) ⟦L, an osier, twig, akin to *viere,* to bend, twist < IE base **wei-* > WITHE, WIRE⟧ *Bot.* a long, flexible shoot or branch —**vi·min·e·ous** (vi min′ē əs) ***adj.***, **vim·i·nal** (vim′ə nəl)

Vim·i·nal (vim′ə nəl) *see* SEVEN HILLS OF ROME

Vi·my (vē mē′) town in N France, near the site of a fierce battle (1917) of WWI

vin (van; *E* vin) ***n.*** ⟦Fr, ult. < L *vinum:* see VINE⟧ wine

VIN *abbrev.* vehicle identification number

vi·na (vē′nä′) ***n.*** ⟦Sans *vīṇā*⟧ an ancient musical instrument of India: four strings on a long, fretted fingerboard are plucked for melody, three others along one side are plucked in accompaniment, and one to three attached gourds serve as resonators

vi·na·ceous (vī nā′shəs) ***adj.*** ⟦L *vinaceus* < *vinum:* see VINE⟧ **1** of or like wine or grapes **2** having the color of red wine

Vi·ña del Mar (vē′nyä del mär) seaport in central Chile, near Valparaiso

vin·ai·grette (vin′ə gret′) ***n.*** ⟦Fr < *vinaigre,* VINEGAR⟧ **1** a small ornamental box or bottle with a perforated lid, used for holding aromatic vinegar, smelling salts, etc. **2** a blend of vinegar, oil, herbs, etc. used as a salad dressing or as a sauce: also called **vinaigrette dressing** (or **sauce**)

vin·blas·tine (vin blas′tēn, -tin) ***n.*** ⟦< ModL *Vinca,* a genus name (see PERIWINKLE[1]) + E *leucoblast,* cell from which a leukocyte develops (see LEUCO- & -BLAST) + -INE[3]⟧ an alkaloid, $C_{46}H_{58}N_4O_9 \cdot H_2SO_4$, obtained from the leaves of a periwinkle (*Catharanthus roseus*) and used as a drug in the treatment of Hodgkin's disease and other lymphomas: in full **vinblastine sulfate**

vin·ca (viŋ′kə) ***n.*** ⟦ModL *Vinca,* genus name < L *pervinca,* PERIWINKLE[1]⟧ PERIWINKLE[1]

Vin·cent (vin′sənt) ***n.*** ⟦LL *Vicentius* < *vincens,* prp. of *vincere,* to conquer: see VICTOR⟧ a masculine name: dim. *Vince;* equiv. Ger. *Vincenz,* It. *Vincenzo,* Sp. *Vicente*

Vincent de Paul (də pôl′), Saint (1580?-1660); Fr. priest who founded charitable orders: his day is Sept. 27

Vincent's angina ⟦after J. H. *Vincent* (1862-1950), Fr physician⟧ TRENCH MOUTH: also called **Vincent's infection**

Vinci, Leonardo da *see* DA VINCI, Leonardo

vin·ci·ble (vin′sə bəl) ***adj.*** ⟦L *vincibilis,* easily overcome < *vincere,* to overcome: see VICTOR⟧ that can be overcome or defeated; conquerable —**vin′ci·bil′i·ty** ***n.***

☆**vin·cris·tine** (vin kris′tēn, -tin) ***n.*** ⟦< ModL *Vinca,* a genus name (see PERIWINKLE[1]) + L *crista,* CREST + -INE[3]⟧ an alkaloid, $C_{46}H_{56}N_4O_{10} \cdot H_2SO_4$, obtained from the leaves of a periwinkle (*Catharanthus roseus*) and used as a drug in the treatment of leukemia: in full **vincristine sulfate**

vin·cu·lum (viŋ′kyə ləm) ***n.***, *pl.* **-la** (-lə) ⟦L < *vincere,* to bind < IE base **wei-,* to bend > VIMEN⟧ **1** that which binds; bond; tie **2** *Anat.* a band or connecting fold **3** *Math.* a line drawn over two or more terms of a compound quantity to show that they are to be treated together (Ex.: $a - \overline{x + y}$)

vin·da·loo (vin′də lo͞o′) ***n.*** a highly spiced curry originating in Goa, India, and usually containing vinegar —***adj.*** of or relating to this curry or to the hottest or spiciest kinds of curry [*vindaloo* spices]

Vin·dhya Range (vin′dyə) chain of hills across central India, north of the Narbada River, marking the N edge of the Deccan Plateau: also called **Vindhya Mountains** (or **Hills**)

vin·di·ca·ble (vin′di kə bəl) ***adj.*** ⟦ML *vindicabilis*⟧ that can be vindicated; justifiable

vin·di·cate (vin′də kāt′) ***vt.*** **-cat′ed, -cat′ing** ⟦< L *vindicatus,* pp. of *vindicare,* to claim, avenge < ? *vim,* force (see VIM) + *dicere,* to say: see DICTION⟧ **1** to clear from criticism, blame, guilt, suspicion, etc.; uphold by evidence or argument **2** to defend or maintain (a cause, claim, etc.) against opposition **3** to serve as justification for; justify [a success which *vindicated* their belief in him] **4** to lay claim to or establish possession of (something *for* oneself or another) **5** [Obs.] *a)* to avenge *b)* to punish —**SYN.** ABSOLVE —**vin′di·ca′tor** ***n.***

vin·di·ca·tion (vin′də kā′shən) ***n.*** ⟦LME *vyndycacion* < L *vindicatio,* a claiming < *vindicare:* see prec.⟧ **1** a vindicating or being vindicated **2** a fact or circumstance that vindicates, or justifies

vin·di·ca·to·ry (vin′di kə tôr′ē) ***adj.*** **1** serving to vindicate **2** bringing retribution; punitive

vin·dic·tive (vin dik′tiv) ***adj.*** ⟦< L *vindicta,* revenge, vindication < *vindicatus* (see VINDICATE) + -IVE⟧ **1** revengeful in spirit; inclined to seek vengeance **2** said or done in revenge; characterized by vengeance [*vindictive* punishment] —**vin·dic′tive·ly** ***adv.*** —**vin·dic′tive·ness** ***n.***

SYN.—**vindictive** stresses the unforgiving nature of one who is animated by a desire to get even with another for a wrong, injury, etc. [*vindictive* feelings]; **vengeful** and **revengeful** more directly stress the strong impulsion to action and the actual seeking of vengeance [a *vengeful,* or *revengeful,* foe]; **spiteful** implies a mean or malicious vindictiveness [*spiteful* gossip]

vine (vīn) ***n.*** ⟦ME < OFr *vine* < L *vinea,* vine < *vineus,* pertaining to wine < *vinum,* wine, akin to Gr *oinē,* vine, *oinos,* wine, prob. a loanword from a pre-IE language of the Pontus region (> Heb *yayin*)⟧ **1** *a)* any plant with a long, thin stem that grows along the ground or climbs a wall or other support by means of tendrils, etc. *b)* the stem of such a plant **2** GRAPEVINE (sense 1)

vine·dress·er (vīn′dres′ər) ***n.*** a person who cultivates or prunes grapevines

vin·e·gar (vin′ə gər) ***n.*** ⟦ME *vinegre* < MFr *vinaigre* < *vin,* wine (< L *vinum:* see VINE) + *aigre,* sour < L *acris* (see ACRID)⟧ **1** a sour liquid with a pungent odor, containing acetic acid, made by fermenting dilute alcoholic liquids, as cider, wine, or malt: it is used as a condiment or preservative **2** sour or ill-tempered speech, character, etc. ☆**3** forceful vigor

☆**vinegar eel** (or **worm**) a small nematode worm (*Anguillula aceti*) often found in unpasteurized vinegar

☆**vin·e·gar·roon** (vin′ə gə ro͞on′) ***n.*** ⟦AmSp *vinagrón* < Sp *vinagre,* vinegar + *-ón,* aug. suffix⟧ a large whip scorpion (*Mastigoproctus giganteus*) found in the S U.S. and in Mexico that, when disturbed, excretes a substance having a vinegary odor

vin·e·gar·y (vin′ə gər ē) ***adj.*** **1** of or like vinegar **2** sour in speech or disposition; ill-tempered Also **vin′e·gar·ish**

vin·er·y (vīn′ər ē) ***n.***, *pl.* **-er·ies** ⟦ME *vinary* < ML *vinarium* < L *vinea:* see VINE & -ERY⟧ **1** an area or building in which vines, esp. grapevines, are grown ☆**2** vines collectively

vine·yard (vin′yərd) ***n.*** ⟦VINE + YARD[2], after OE *wingeard*⟧ **1** land devoted to cultivating grapevines **2** a field of activity, esp. of spiritual labor

vingt-et-un (van tā ën′) ***n.*** ⟦Fr, twenty and one, twenty-one⟧ TWENTY-ONE

vin·i- (vin′i) ⟦< L *vinum,* wine: see VINE⟧ *combining form* wine grapes or wine [*viniculture*]

vi·nic (vī′nik, vin′ik) ***adj.*** ⟦< L *vinum,* wine (see VINE) + -IC⟧ of, found in, or derived from wine

vin·i·cul·ture (vin′i kul′chər) ***n.*** ⟦VINI- + CULTURE⟧ the cultivation of wine grapes —**vin′i·cul′tur·ist** ***n.***

vi·nif·er·a (vī nif′ər ə) ***adj.*** ⟦ModL (*Vitis*) *vinifera,* wine-producing (vine) < LL, fem. of *vinifer,* wine-producing < L *vinum* (see VINE) + *-fer,* -FER⟧ designating or of the most widely cultivated species of grape (*Vitis vinifera*) used for making wine

vin·i·fi·ca·tion (vin′ə fi kā′shən) ***n.*** ⟦Fr < *vin,* wine (see VIN) + *-i-,* -I- + *-fication,* -FICATION⟧ the method or process of changing grapes into wine

vin·i·fy (vin′ə fī′) ***vt.*** **-fied′, -fy′ing** ⟦back-form. < prec.⟧ to change (grapes) into (wine) by a fermentation process

Vin·land (vin′lənd) ⟦ON, lit., wine-land (after the wild berries or grapes discovered there)⟧ region, now believed to be part of North America, discovered by Norsemen led by Leif Ericson in *c.* A.D. 1000

vi·no (vē′nô) ***n.*** ⟦It & Sp, ult. < L *vinum:* see VINE⟧ wine

vin or·di·naire (van ôr dē ner′) ⟦Fr, ordinary wine⟧ any inexpensive wine routinely served with meals

vi·nous (vī′nəs) ***adj.*** ⟦L *vinosus,* full of wine < *vinum:* see VINE⟧ **1** *a)* of, having the nature of, or characteristic of wine *b)* having the color of red wine **2** *a)* addicted to drinking wine *b)* resulting from drinking wine —**vi·nos′i·ty** (-näs′ə tē) ***n.***

vin ro·sé (van rô zā′; *E* vin′ rō zā′) ⟦Fr, pink wine⟧ ROSÉ

Vin·son (vin′sən), **Fred(erick) M(oore)** 1890-1953; chief justice of the U.S. (1946-53)

vin·tage (vin′tij) ***n.*** ⟦ME, earlier *vendage* < OFr *vendange* < L *vindemia,* vintage < *vinum,* wine (see VINE) + *demere,* to remove < *de-,* off + *emere,* to take: see REDEEM⟧ **1** *a)* the crop or yield of a particular vineyard or grape-growing region in a single season, with reference either to the grapes or to the wine made from them *b)* wine; specif., the wine, esp. a prized wine, of a particular region in a specified year *c)* the region or year of a particular wine **2** the act or season of gathering grapes or of making wine **3** the type or model of a particular year or period [a car of prewar *vintage*] —*adj.* **1** of or produced in a particular vintage: said of wine **2** representative of the best; choice [*vintage* Hemingway] **3** representative of or dating from a particular period of the past [*vintage* clothes]

vin·tag·er (-ər) *n.* ⟦< prec. + -ER⟧ a person who harvests grapes for making wine

vint·ner (vint′nər) *n.* ⟦altered < ME *viniter,* vintner < OFr *vinetier* < ML *vinetarius* < L *vinetum,* vineyard < *vinum:* see VINE⟧ **1** a person who sells wine; wine merchant **2** a person who makes wine

vin·y (vī′nē) *adj.* **vin′i·er, vin′i·est 1** of or like vines **2** filled or covered with vines

vi·nyl (vī′nəl) *n.* ⟦< L *vinum,* wine (see VINE) + -YL⟧ **1** the monovalent radical $CH_2{:}CH$ characteristic of many derivatives of ethylene, its hydride **2** a resin or plastic formed from a polymerized vinyl compound **3** phonograph records made of vinyl plastic, carbon black, etc.

vinyl alcohol an alcohol, $CH_2{:}CHOH$, known only in the form of its esters or ethers, or its polymer, polyvinyl alcohol

vinyl chloride a colorless gas, $CH_2{:}CHCl$, made by reacting acetylene with hydrogen chloride or by cracking ethylene dichloride: it is used to make polyvinyl chloride, etc.

vi·nyl·i·dene (vī nil′ə dēn′) *n.* ⟦VINYL + -ID(E) + -INE[3]⟧ the divalent radical $CH_2{:}C$ derived from ethylene

vinylidene resin any synthetic resin in which the basic structure consists of the $H_2C{:}CR_2$ group, where R usually is a halogen

☆**vinyl plastic** any of various plastics made from polymerized vinyl compounds or copolymers of vinyl and other resins, used in various molded or extruded products, coatings, adhesives, sizes, etc.

☆**vinyl resin** a polymer formed from vinyl compounds, used with other resins, plasticizers, etc. to produce various solid vinyl plastics

vi·ol (vī′əl) *n.* ⟦MFr *viole* < OProv *viula* < Frank **vithula* < VL *vitula:* see FIDDLE⟧ any of an early family of stringed instruments played with a curved bow, characterized generally by six strings, frets, a flat back, and C-shaped sound holes: used chiefly in the 16th and 17th cent. in sizes from the treble viol to the bass viol

vi·o·la[1] (vē ō′lə, vī-) *n.* ⟦It < OProv *viula,* viol⟧ a stringed instrument of the violin family, slightly larger than a violin and tuned a fifth lower

vi·o·la[2] (vī′ə lə, vī ō′lə) *n.* ⟦ME < L, a violet, prob. of non-IE orig.⟧ a violet; esp., any of various violets developed from a pansy (*Viola cornuta*), grown as garden plants

Vi·o·la (vī ō′lə, vē-; vī′ə lə) *n.* ⟦< L: see prec.⟧ a feminine name: dim. *Vi*

vi·o·la·ble (vī′ə lə bəl) *adj.* ⟦L *violabilis* < *violare:* see VIOLATE⟧ that can be, or is likely to be, violated —**vi′o·la·bil′i·ty** *n.,* **vi′o·la·ble·ness** —**vi′o·la·bly** *adv.*

vi·o·la·ceous (vī′ə lā′shəs) *adj.* ⟦L *violaceus,* violet-colored < *viola,* a violet⟧ violet in color

vi·o·la clef (vē ō′lə) ALTO CLEF

vi·o·la da brac·cio (-də brä′chō) ⟦It, lit., viol for the arm⟧ an early stringed instrument of the viol family, comparable in range to the viola

viola da gam·ba (-də gäm′bə) ⟦It, lit., viol for the leg⟧ an early stringed instrument of the viol family, held between the knees and comparable in range to the cello

viola d'a·mo·re (-dä mô′rā) ⟦It, lit., viol of love⟧ an early stringed instrument of the viol family having a set of wire strings that are stretched behind the bowed gut strings, and whose sympathetic vibrations produce soft, clear, ringing tones

vi·o·late (vī′ə lāt′) *vt.* **-lat′ed, -lat′ing** ⟦ME *violaten* < L *violatus,* pp. of *violare,* to use force or violence, akin to *vis,* force⟧ **1** to break (a law, rule, promise, etc.); fail to keep or observe; infringe on **2** to commit a sexual assault on; often, specif., to rape (a woman) **3** to desecrate or profane (something sacred) **4** to break in upon; interrupt thoughtlessly; disturb [to *violate* someone's privacy] **5** to offend, insult, or outrage [to *violate* one's sense of decency] —**vi′o·la′tive** *adj.* —**vi′o·la′tor** *n.*

vi·o·la·tion (vī′ə lā′shən) *n.* ⟦ME *violacion* < L *violatio*⟧ a violating or being violated; specif., *a)* infringement or breach, as of a law, rule, right, etc. *b)* sexual assault; rape *c)* desecration of something sacred, as a church *d)* interruption; disturbance

vi·o·lence (vī′ə ləns) *n.* ⟦ME < MFr < L *violentia* < *violentus:* see fol.⟧ **1** physical force used so as to injure, damage, or destroy; extreme roughness of action **2** intense, often devastatingly or explosively powerful force or energy, as of a hurricane or volcano **3** *a)* unjust or callous use of force or power, as in violating another's rights, sensibilities, etc. *b)* the harm done by this **4** great force or strength of feeling, conduct, or expression; vehemence; fury **5** a twisting or wrenching of a sense, phrase, etc., so as to distort the original or true sense or form [to do *violence* to a text] **6** an instance of violence; violent act or deed

vi·o·lent (-lənt) *adj.* ⟦ME < MFr < L *violentus,* violent, akin to *violare,* to VIOLATE⟧ **1** *a)* acting with or characterized by great physical force, so as to injure, damage, or destroy *b)* acting or characterized by force unlawfully or callously used **2** caused by violence [a *violent* death] **3** *a)* showing, or resulting from, strong feeling or emotion; vehement; furious [*violent* language] *b)* emotionally disturbed to an uncontrollable degree **4** extreme; intense; very strong [a *violent* storm] **5** tending to distort the meaning [to put a *violent* construction on a text] —**vi′o·lent·ly** *adv.*

vi·o·let (vī′ə lit, vī′lit) *n.* ⟦ME < OFr *violette,* dim. of *viole* < L *viola,* a violet < or akin to Gr *ion,* violet⟧ **1** *a)* any of a genus (*Viola*) of plants of the violet family, having white, blue, purple, or yellow irregular flowers with short spurs *b)* the flower of any of these plants **2** any of various similar plants, as the African violet, or their flowers **3** a bluish-purple color —*adj.* **1** designating a family (Violaceae, order Violales) of temperate and tropical dicotyledonous plants having five-parted flowers, a one-celled ovary, and a three-valved fruit capsule, including the pansies **2** of the color violet

Vi·o·let (vī′ə lit, vī′lit) *n.* ⟦< prec.⟧ a feminine name: dim. *Vi*

violet layer *Astron.* a layer of particles in the upper atmosphere of the planet Mars, that scatters and absorbs certain electromagnetic radiation, thus preventing the blue, violet, and ultraviolet light waves from passing through

violet ray 1 the shortest ray of the visible spectrum **2** loosely, an ultraviolet ray

vi·o·lin (vī′ə lin′) *adj.* designating the modern family of stringed instruments played with a bow, characterized by four strings tuned in fifths, a lack of frets, a somewhat rounded back, and *f*-shaped sound holes —*n.* ⟦It *violino,* dim. of *viola,* VIOLA[1]⟧ the smallest and highest-pitched instrument of this family, held horizontally under the chin, resting against the collarbone; fiddle

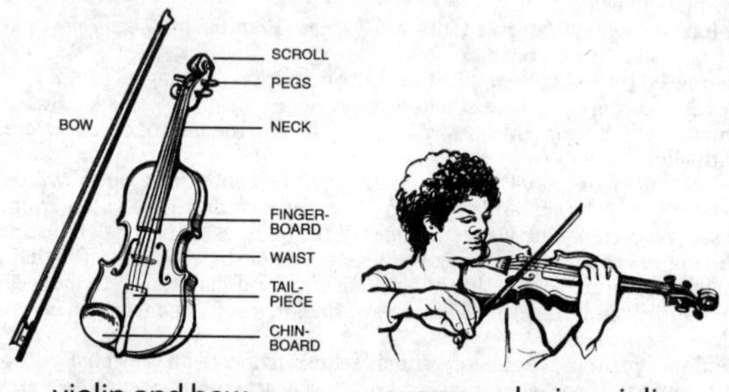

violin and bow   woman playing violin

vi·o·lin·ist (-ist) *n.* ⟦It *violinista*⟧ a violin player

vi·o·lin·is·tic (vī′ə lin is′tik) *adj.* of, having to do with, or characteristic of violins or violinists —**vi′o·lin·is′ti·cal·ly** *adv.*

vi·ol·ist (vī′ə list; *for 2* vē ō′list) *n.* **1** a viol player **2** a viola player

vi·o·lon·cel·list (vē′ə län′chel′ist, vī′ə-) *n.* a cello player; cellist

vi·o·lon·cel·lo (-chel′ō) *n., pl.* **-los** ⟦It, dim. of *violone,* bass viol < *viola,* viol⟧ CELLO

vio·lo·ne (vyō lō′nā) *n.* ⟦It, aug. of *viola,* viol, VIOLA[1]⟧ the largest and lowest pitched viol

vi·os·ter·ol (vī äs′tər ôl′, -ōl′) *n.* ⟦(ULTRA)VIO(LET) + (ERGO)STEROL⟧ ERGOCALCIFEROL

VIP (vē′ī′pē′) *n.* ⟦*v(ery) i(mportant) p(erson)*⟧ [Informal] a high-ranking official or important guest, esp. one accorded special treatment

vi·per (vī′pər) *n.* ⟦OFr < L *vipera,* contr. < ? **vivipara,* producing live young < *vivus,* living (see BIO-) + *parere,* to bear: see -PAROUS: from the notion that the viper does not lay eggs⟧ **1** any of a widespread family (Viperidae) of venomous snakes, including the pit vipers, the European adder, and the African puff adder; solenoglyph **2** any of various other poisonous or supposedly poisonous snakes **3** *a)* a malicious or spiteful person *b)* a treacherous person

vi·per·ine (-in, -īn′) *adj.* ⟦L *viperinus*⟧ of, having the nature of, or like that of a viper; venomous

vi·per·ous (-əs) *adj.* of, having the nature of, or like a viper; esp., spiteful or malicious: also **vi′per·ish** —**vi′per·ous·ly** *adv.*

viper's bugloss BLUEWEED

vi·ra·go (vi rä′gō, -rā′-) *n., pl.* **-goes** or **-gos** ⟦ME < OE < L, a manlike female < *vir,* man: see WEREWOLF⟧ **1** a quarrelsome, shrewish woman; scold **2** [Archaic] a strong, manlike woman; amazon

vi·ral (vī′rəl) *adj.* **1** of, involving, or caused by a virus **2** *a)* of or characterized by broad, rapid circulation over the internet [a *viral* video, rumor, etc.] *b)* accomplished by means of such circulation [a *viral* marketing campaign] —**go viral** [Informal] to be circulated broadly and rapidly over the internet

vir·e·lay (vir′ə lā′) *n.* ⟦ME *vyrelaye* < MFr *virelai,* prob. altered by assoc. with *lai* (see LAY[4]) < OFr *virli, vireli,* jingle used as the refrain of a song⟧ any of various French verse forms, popular in the 14th and 15th cent., with only two rhymes per stanza, and a refrain: also **vir′e·lai′** (-lā′; *Fr* vir lā′)

vi·re·mi·a (vī rē′mē ə) *n.* ⟦VIR(US) + -EMIA⟧ a medical condition, typically characterized by fever, in which a virus is present in the blood —**vi·re′mic** (-mik) *adj.*

☆**vir·e·o** (vir′ē ō′) *n., pl.* **-os′** ⟦L, greenfinch, akin to *virere,* to be green⟧ any of a family (Vireonidae) of small, insect-eating, American passerine birds, with olive-green or gray plumage —**vir·e·o·nine** (vir′ē ə nīn′, -nin) *adj., n.*

vi·res (vī′rēz′, wir′ās′) *n.* ⟦L⟧ *pl. of* VIS[1]

vi·res·cence (vī res′əns, vi-) *n.* ⟦< fol.⟧ **1** the condition of becoming green **2** *Bot.* the turning green of petals or other parts that are not normally so, due to the abnormal presence of chlorophyll

vi·res·cent (-ənt) *adj.* ⟦L *virescens,* prp. of *virescere,* to grow green < *virere,* to be green⟧ 1 turning or becoming green 2 greenish

vir·ga (vʉr′gə) *n.* ⟦ModL, streak in the heavens < L, twig, wand⟧ *Meteorol.* long streamers or wispy streaks of water or ice particles falling from the base of a cloud but evaporating completely before reaching the ground

vir·gate[1] (vʉr′git, -gāt′) *n.* ⟦ML *virgata (terrae)* < L *virga,* twig (see VERGE[1]): used as transl. of OE *gierdland,* yardland⟧ a former English unit of land measure varying greatly in size, but most commonly equal to about 30 acres

vir·gate[2] (-git, -gāt′) *adj.* ⟦ModL *virgatus* < L, made of twigs < *virga,* twig: see VERGE[1]⟧ 1 rod-shaped 2 *Bot.* long, thin, and stiff, with few branches

Vir·gil[2] (vʉr′jəl) ⟦< L *Vergilius,* name of the Roman gens to which the poet belonged⟧ (L. name *Publius Vergilius Maro*) 70-19 B.C.; Rom. poet: author of the *Aeneid* —**Vir·gil′i·an** (-jil′ē ən) *adj.*

Vir·gil[1] (vʉr′jəl) ⟦ult. < fol.⟧ a masculine name

vir·gin (vʉr′jən) *n.* ⟦ME < OFr *virgine* < L *virgo* (gen. *virginis*), maiden: ? akin to *virga,* slender branch, twig, shoot⟧ 1 *a)* a woman, esp. a young woman, who has never had sexual intercourse *b)* [Archaic] an unmarried girl or woman 2 a man, esp. a youth, who has never had sexual intercourse 3 [Informal] a person who is entirely new to or inexperienced in a specified thing [a stock market *virgin*] 4 *Zool.* *a)* a female animal that has not copulated *b)* a female insect that lays eggs without impregnation by the male —*adj.* 1 being a virgin 2 composed of virgins 3 characteristic of or proper to a virgin; chaste; modest 4 like or suggesting a virgin because untouched, unmarked, pure, clean, etc. [*virgin* snow] 5 up to this time unused, unexplored, unworked, undiscovered, etc. [a *virgin* forest] 6 occurring uncombined in its native form [*virgin* silver] 7 being the first; initial [a *virgin* effort] 8 *a)* obtained from the first pressing, without the use of heat (said of an oil, esp. olive oil) (see also EXTRA-VIRGIN) *b)* obtained directly from an ore or raw material (said esp. of a metal) 9 made without alcohol: said of a drink otherwise prepared like a cocktail [a *virgin* piña colada] —**the Virgin** 1 Mary, the mother of Jesus 2 Virgo, the constellation and sixth sign of the zodiac

vir·gin·al[1] (-jə nəl) *adj.* ⟦OFr < L *virginalis*⟧ 1 of, characteristic of, or proper to a virgin; maidenly 2 remaining in a state of virginity 3 pure; fresh; untouched; unsullied 4 *Zool.* not fertilized

vir·gin·al[2] (-jə nəl) *n.* ⟦prob. akin to prec.: reason for name obscure⟧ [*sometimes pl.*] a harpsichord; esp., a small, rectangular harpsichord of the 16th cent., placed on a table or held in the lap to be played: also called **pair of virginals**

virgin birth 1 [*usually* **V- B-**] *Christian Theol.* the doctrine that Jesus was born to Mary, a virgin, and that she was his only human parent: cf. IMMACULATE CONCEPTION 2 *Zool.* parthenogenesis

Vir·gin·ia[1] (vər jin′yə) *n.* ⟦L, fem. of *Virginius, Verginius,* name of a Roman gens⟧ a feminine name: dim. *Ginnie, Ginny*; var. *Ginger*; equiv. Fr. *Virginie*

Vir·gin·ia[2] (vər jin′yə) ⟦after ELIZABETH I, the "*Virgin* Queen"⟧ state of the S U.S., on the Atlantic: one of the 13 original states; 39,594 sq mi (102,548 sq km); cap. Richmond: abbrev. *VA* or *Va*

Virginia Beach city in SE Va., on the Atlantic

Virginia City ⟦after "Old Virginny," nickname of an early miner, a local eccentric⟧ town in W Nev., near Reno: formerly a center of gold & silver mining (site of the Comstock Lode)

☆**Virginia cowslip** (*or* **bluebell**) a perennial woodland plant (*Mertensia virginica*) of the borage family, native to E North America and having clusters of blue or purple, bell-shaped flowers

☆**Virginia creeper** WOODBINE (sense 2)

☆**Virginia deer** WHITE-TAILED DEER

☆**Virginia ham** a ham, often from a hog fed on peanuts, that is first cured in salt, then smoked esp. with hickory wood, and aged for several months

Vir·gin·i·an (-yən) *adj.* of Virginia: usually used in the predicate —*n.* a person born or living in Virginia

☆**Virginia (rail) fence** a zigzag fence made of rails laid across one another at the ends

☆**Virginia reel** 1 a country dance, the American variety of the reel, performed by a number of couples facing each other in two parallel lines 2 music for this dance

Virgin Islands ⟦< Sp *Las Virgenes,* the virgins, so named (1493) by COLUMBUS[1] in honor of the legendary 11,000 followers of St. URSULA⟧ group of islands of the Leeward group in the West Indies, east of Puerto Rico, comprising the **British Virgin Islands,** easternmost islands of this group, constituting a British territory (58 sq mi, 151 sq km), & the **Virgin Islands of the United States,** the islands of this group closest to Puerto Rico, constituting a territory of the U.S. (134 sq mi, 347 sq km; cap. Charlotte Amalie: abbrev. *VI*)

vir·gin·i·ty (vər jin′ə tē) *n.* ⟦ME *virginite* < OFr *virginité* < L *virginitas*⟧ 1 the state or fact of being a virgin 2 the state of being pure, clean, untouched, etc.

Virgin Mary[1] ⟦after fol.: see VIRGIN, *adj.* 9⟧ ☆a drink of seasoned tomato juice served as a cocktail: nonalcoholic version of the BLOODY MARY

Virgin Mary[2] Mary, the mother of Jesus

Virgin Queen *name for* ELIZABETH I

vir·gin's-bow·er (vʉr′jənz bou′ər) *n.* any of several small-flowered forms of clematis; esp., a climbing vine (*Clematis virginiana*) with white flowers, native to E North America

virgin wool wool that has never before been processed

Vir·go (vʉr′gō′) *n.* ⟦ME < L, VIRGIN⟧ 1 a large equatorial constellation between Leo and Libra, including the bright star Spica; the Virgin 2 the sixth sign of the zodiac, entered by the sun about August 22 3 *pl.* **-gos′** a person born under this sign: also **Vir·go·an** (vʉr′gō′ən, vər gō′ən)

vir·gule (-gyo͞ol′) *n.* ⟦Fr < L *virgula,* small rod, twig, dim. of *virga:* see VERGE[1]⟧ a short diagonal line (/) used between two words to show either is applicable (and/or), in dates or fractions (3/8), to express "per" (feet/second), etc.; slash

vi·ri·cide (vī′rə sīd′) *n.* ⟦< VIR(US) + -I- + -CIDE⟧ *alt. sp. of* VIRUCIDE —**vi′ri·cid′al** (-sī′dəl) *adj.*

vir·i·des·cent (vir′ə des′ənt) *adj.* ⟦LL *viridescens,* prp. of *viridescere,* to become green < L *viridis,* green⟧ greenish —**vir′i·des′cence** *n.*

vi·rid·i·an (və rid′ē ən) *n.* ⟦< L *viridis,* green⟧ a bluish-green pigment, hydrated chromic oxide, Cr_2O_3

vi·rid·i·ty (-ə tē) *n.* ⟦ME *viridite* < MFr *viridité* < L *viriditas* < *viridis,* green⟧ 1 greenness, as of young leaves or grass; verdancy 2 freshness; liveliness

vir·ile (vir′əl; *chiefly Brit,* -īl′) *adj.* ⟦L *virilis* < *vir,* man: see WEREWOLF⟧ 1 of, belonging to, or characteristic of an adult man; manly; male 2 having manly strength or vigor; forceful 3 of or capable of copulation; sexually potent —*SYN.* MALE —**vi·ril·i·ty** (və ril′ə tē) *n.*

vir·i·lism (-iz′əm) *n.* ⟦< prec. + -ISM⟧ *Med.* the development of secondary male sex characteristics in a woman

vir·i·lo·cal (vir′ə lō′kəl) *adj.* ⟦L *vir,* man (see VIRILE) + -I- + LOCAL⟧ PATRILOCAL

vi·ri·on (vī′rē än′) *n.* ⟦< VIRUS + -ON (sense 2)⟧ the complete, mature, infectious form of a virus when it is outside a host cell

vi·roid (vī′roid) *n.* ⟦VIR(US) + -OID⟧ a viruslike plant pathogen consisting of a short strand of genetic material (RNA) without a protein coating

vi·rol·o·gy (vī räl′ə jē) *n.* ⟦< VIR(US) + -OLOGY⟧ the study of viruses and viral diseases —**vi·ro·log·ic** (vī′rə läj′ik) *adj.,* **vi′ro·log′i·cal** —**vi·rol′o·gist** *n.*

vi·ro·sis (vī rō′sis) *n., pl.* **-ses′** (-sēz′) ⟦VIR(US) + -OSIS⟧ any disease caused by a virus

vir·tu (vər to͞o′, vʉr′to͞o′) *n.* ⟦It *virtù,* excellence, virtue < L *virtus,* strength, VIRTUE⟧ 1 a love of, or taste for, objects of artistic value, as curios, antiques, etc. 2 such objects, collectively 3 the quality of being artistic, beautiful, rare, or otherwise such as to interest a collector of such objects

vir·tu·al (vʉr′cho͞o əl) *adj.* ⟦ME *vertual* < ML *virtualis* < L *virtus,* strength, VIRTUE⟧ 1 being such practically or in effect, although not in actual fact or name [a *virtual* impossibility] 2 *Comput.* *a)* designating or of a kind of MEMORY (sense 8*b*) that makes use of disk space to supplement main memory while large programs are being executed *b)* of, pertaining to, or taking place in cyberspace or in virtual reality [*virtual* shopping] —**vir′tu·al′i·ty** (-al′ə tē) *n.*

virtual image an optical image from which light rays appear to diverge, although they actually do not pass through the image

vir·tu·al·ly (-cho͞o ə lē) *adv.* in effect, although not in fact; for all practical purposes [*virtually* identical]

virtual reality 1 the computer-generated simulation, consisting of sights, sounds, etc., of a three-dimensional environment that someone using special electronic equipment may interact with in a seemingly physical way 2 such a simulated environment

vir·tue (vʉr′cho͞o) *n.* ⟦ME *vertue* < OFr *vertu,* virtue, goodness, power < L *virtus,* manliness, worth < *vir,* man: see WEREWOLF⟧ 1 general moral excellence; right action and thinking; goodness or morality 2 a specific moral quality regarded as good or meritorious: see also CARDINAL VIRTUES, THEOLOGICAL VIRTUES 3 chastity, esp. in a woman 4 *a)* excellence in general; merit [the *virtue* in planning ahead] *b)* a good quality or feature [the *virtues* of teaching as a profession] 5 effective power or force; efficacy; esp., the ability to heal or strengthen [the *virtue* of a medicine] 6 [Now Rare] manly quality; strength, courage, etc. —**by** (or **in**) **virtue of** because of; on the grounds of —**make a virtue of necessity** to accept with an agreeable or positive attitude that which must be accepted anyway

vir·tu·o·sa (vʉr′cho͞o ō′sə) *n., pl.* **-se** (-sā) a female virtuoso

vir·tu·os·i·ty (vʉr′cho͞o äs′ə tē) *n., pl.* **-ties** ⟦< fol. + -ITY⟧ great technical skill in some fine art, esp. in the performance of music

vir·tu·o·so (vʉr′cho͞o ō′sō) *n., pl.* **-sos** or **-si** (-sē) ⟦It, skilled, learned < LL *virtuosus:* see fol.⟧ 1 [Obs.] *a)* a person who has a general or broad interest in the arts and sciences *b)* a collector or connoisseur of art objects or curios 2 a person displaying great technical skill in some fine art, esp. in the performance of music 3 [Obs.] a person learned in the arts or sciences; scholar —*adj.* of or like that of a virtuoso: also **vir′tu·os′ic** (-ä′sik, -ō′sik) —*SYN.* AESTHETE

vir·tu·ous (vʉr′cho͞o əs) *adj.* ⟦ME *vertuous* < OFr *vertuos* < LL *virtuosus* < L *virtus,* worth, VIRTUE⟧ 1 having, or characterized by, moral virtue; righteous 2 chaste: said of a woman 3 [Archaic] having potency; efficacious —*SYN.* CHASTE, MORAL —**vir′tu·ous·ly** *adv.* —**vir′tu·ous·ness** *n.*

vi·ru·cide (vī′rə sīd′) *n.* ⟦VIRU(S) + -CIDE⟧ an agent capable of destroying or inhibiting viruses —**vi′ru·cid′al** (-sī′dəl) *adj.*

vir·u·lence (vir′ə ləns, vir′yə-, vir′yoo-) *n.* ⟦LL *virulentia*⟧ 1 the quality of being virulent, or very poisonous, noxious, malignant, etc. 2 bitter animosity; venom; rancor 3 the relative infectiousness of a microorganism causing disease Also **vir′u·len·cy** (-lən sē)

vir·u·lent (-lənt) *adj.* ⟦ME < L *virulentus,* full of poison < *virus:* see fol.⟧ 1 *a)* extremely poisonous or injurious; deadly *b)* bitterly antagonistic or spiteful; full of hate and enmity; venomous; rancorous 2 *Med.* *a)* violent and rapid in its course; highly malignant (said of a disease) *b)* able to overcome the natural defenses of the host; highly infectious (said of a microorganism) —**vir′u·lent·ly** *adv.*

vi·rus (vī′rəs) ***n.*** ⟦L, a slimy liquid, poison < IE base **weis-*, to flow (used of foul or malodorous fluids) > OOZE², WEASEL, Gr *ios,* poison⟧ **1** [Obs.] venom, as of a snake **2** *a)* any of various infectious agents, usually ultramicroscopic, that consist of nucleic acid, either RNA or DNA, within a case of protein: they infect animals, plants, and bacteria and reproduce only within living cells: viruses are considered as being nonliving chemical units or sometimes as living organisms *b)* a disease caused by a virus **3** anything that corrupts or poisons the mind or character; evil or harmful influence **4** an unauthorized, disruptive set of instructions placed in a computer program, that leaves copies of itself in other programs and disks

vis¹ (vis, wēs) ***n., pl.* vi·res** (vī′rēz′, wir′äs′) ⟦L⟧ force; strength

vis² *abbrev.* **1** visibility **2** visible **3** visual

Vis *abbrev.* **1** Viscount **2** Viscountess

vi·sa (vē′zə, -sə) ***n.*** ⟦Fr < L fem. of *visus,* pp. of *videre,* to see: see VISION⟧ an endorsement on a passport, showing that a person has been granted official entry into or passage through a country —***vt.* -saed, -sa·ing** **1** to put a visa on (a passport) **2** to give a visa to (someone)

vis·age (viz′ij) ***n.*** ⟦ME < OFr < *vis,* a face < L *visus,* a look, a seeing < pp. of *videre,* to see: see VISION⟧ **1** the face, with reference to the form and proportions of the features or to the expression; countenance **2** appearance; aspect —***SYN.*** FACE

-vis·aged (viz′ijd) *combining form* having a (specified kind of) visage [*stern-visaged*]

Vi·sa·kha·pat·nam (vi sä′kə put′nəm) seaport in E Andhra Pradesh, SE India, on the Bay of Bengal

Vi·sa·lia (vi sāl′yə, vī-) ⟦prob. after *Visalia,* Ky.⟧ city in SC Calif.

vis-à-vis (vē′zə vē′) ***adj., adv.*** ⟦Fr⟧ face to face; opposite —***prep.*** **1** face to face with; opposite **2** in comparison with **3** in relation to; with regard to —***n., pl.* vis′-à-vis′** (-vēz′, -vē′) **1** *a)* a person who is face to face with another *b)* one's opposite number or counterpart **2** *a)* an 18th-cent. and early 19th-cent. carriage with facing seats *b)* TÊTE-À-TÊTE (*n.* 2)

Vi·sa·yan (vi sä′yən) ***n.*** ⟦< ?⟧ **1** a member of a people of the Philippines **2** the Austronesian language of this people —***adj.*** of the Visayans or their language or culture

Vi·sa·yas (vi sä′yəz) group of islands in the central Philippines, including Cebu, Leyte, Negros, Panay, Samar, & many smaller islands: also called **Visayan Islands**

Visc *abbrev.* **1** Viscount **2** Viscountess

vis·ca·cha (vis kä′chə) ***n.*** ⟦AmSp *vizcacha* < Quechua *uiscacha*⟧ any of two genera (*Lagostomus* and *Lagidium,* family Chinchillidae) of burrowing South American rodents that live in small colonies

vis·cer·a (vis′ər ə) ***pl.n., sing.* vis′cus** (-kəs) ⟦L, pl. of *viscus,* an inner part of the body⟧ **1** the internal organs of the body, esp. of the thorax and abdomen, as the heart, lungs, liver, kidneys, intestines, etc. **2** popularly, the intestines

vis·cer·al (-əl) ***adj.*** ⟦ML *visceralis*⟧ **1** of, having the nature of, situated in, or affecting the viscera **2** intuitive, instinctive, emotional, etc. rather than intellectual [*a visceral* reaction] —**vis′cer·al·ly** ***adv.***

vis·cid (vis′id) ***adj.*** ⟦LL *viscidus,* sticky < L *viscum,* birdlime: see VISCOUS⟧ **1** having a cohesive and sticky fluid consistency; viscous **2** covered with a viscid substance —**vis·cid·i·ty** (vi sid′ə tē) ***n.*** —**vis′cid·ly** ***adv.***

vis·co·e·las·tic (vis′kō ē las′tik) ***adj.*** ⟦< VISCO(US) + ELASTIC⟧ having or exhibiting viscous and elastic properties

vis·com·e·ter (vis käm′ət ər) ***n.*** a device for measuring viscosity, as by metering the rate of flow through a small opening: also **vis·co·sim·e·ter** (vis′ kə sim′ət ər)

Vis·con·ti (vēs kôn′tē), **Lu·chi·no** (lo͞o kē′nō) (Count *Luchino Visconti,* Duke of *Modrone*) 1906-76; It. theater, opera, & film director

vis·cose (vis′kōs′) ***adj.*** ⟦LL *viscosus:* see VISCOUS⟧ **1** VISCOUS **2** of, containing, or made of viscose —***n.*** **1** an amber-colored, syruplike solution made by treating cellulose with sodium hydroxide and carbon disulfide: used in making rayon thread and fabrics, and cellophane **2** thread or fabric made from viscose: in full **viscose rayon**

vis·cos·i·ty (vis käs′ə tē) ***n., pl.* -ties** ⟦ME *viscosite* < ML *viscositas*⟧ **1** the state or quality of being viscous **2** *a) Physics* the internal friction of a fluid which makes it resist flowing past a solid surface or other layers of the fluid: symbol, η (see also POISE²) *b)* a measure of this; specif., a number indicating the ability of a motor oil to maintain its viscosity with seasonal changes of temperature

vis·count (vī′kount′) ***n.*** ⟦ME < OFr *viscomte* < ML *vice comes:* see VICE- & COUNT²⟧ **1** [Historical] in England, *a)* a deputy of an earl *b)* a sheriff **2** a nobleman next below an earl or count and above a baron

vis·count·cy (-sē) ***n., pl.* -cies** the title, rank, or station of a VISCOUNT (sense 2): also **vis′count·ship′** (-ship′)

vis·count·ess (vī′koun′tis) ***n.*** **1** the wife or widow of a VISCOUNT (sense 2) **2** a peeress with a rank equivalent to that of a VISCOUNT (sense 2)

vis·count·y (-tē) ***n., pl.* -count′ies** VISCOUNTCY

vis·cous (vis′kəs) ***adj.*** ⟦ME *viscouse* < LL *viscosus* < L *viscum,* birdlime made from mistletoe berries, mistletoe, prob. < IE base **weis-:* see VIRUS⟧ **1** having a cohesive and sticky fluid consistency; viscid **2** *Physics* having viscosity —**vis′cous·ly** ***adv.*** —**vis′cous·ness** ***n.***

Visct *abbrev.* **1** Viscount **2** Viscountess

vis·cus (vis′kəs) ***n.*** ⟦L⟧ *sing. of* VISCERA

vise (vīs) ***n.*** ⟦ME *vis,* a screw < OFr *viz,* a winding object < VL **vitium,* tendril-like thing < L *vitis,* vine, lit., that which winds: see WITHE⟧ a device, usually fastened to a workbench, consisting of two jaws opened and closed by a screw, lever, etc. and used for holding firmly an object being worked on —***vt.* vised, vis′ing** to hold or squeeze with or as with a vise

vise

vi·sé (vē′zā, vē zā′) ***n., vt.* -séed, -sé·ing** ⟦Fr, pp. of *viser,* to view, inspect < L *visus:* see VISION⟧ VISA

Vish·nu (vish′no͞o) ***n.*** ⟦Sans *Viṣṇu,* lit., prob. all-pervader⟧ *Hinduism* the second member of the trinity (Brahma, Vishnu, and Siva), a god often held to have had several human incarnations, most important of which is Krishna —**Vish′nu·ism′** ***n.***

vis·i·bil·i·ty (viz′ə bil′ə tē) ***n., pl.* -ties** ⟦LL *visibilitas*⟧ **1** the fact or condition of being visible **2** *a)* the relative possibility of being seen under the conditions of distance, light, and atmosphere prevailing at a particular time [the poor *visibility* of dark clothing at night] *b)* the maximum distance at which an object can be seen under the prevailing conditions; range of vision *c)* the ability to provide an unblocked view [the rear window has poor *visibility*]

vis·i·ble (viz′ə bəl) ***adj.*** ⟦OFr < L *visibilis* < *visus:* see VISION⟧ **1** that can be seen; perceptible by the eye **2** that can be perceived or observed; apparent [no *visible* improvement] **3** on hand or available [*visible* resources] **4** so constructed as to bring to view parts or elements that are normally not perceptible —**vis′i·bly** ***adv.***

Vis·i·goth (viz′ə gäth′, -gôth′) ***n.*** ⟦LL *Visigothi,* pl. < *visi-* (< Gmc base of uncert. meaning) + *Gothi,* Goths⟧ a member of the western branch of the Goths that invaded the Roman Empire late in the 4th cent. A.D. and set up a kingdom in France and in Spain —**Vis′i·goth′ic** ***adj.***

vi·sion (vizh′ən) ***n.*** ⟦OFr < L *visio* < *visus,* pp. of *videre,* to see < IE **w(e)idē,* var. of **w(e)di-,* to view, see > WISE¹⟧ **1** the act or power of seeing with the eye; sense of sight **2** *a)* something seen by other than normal sight; something perceived in a dream, trance, etc. or supernaturally revealed, as to a prophet *b)* the experience of having such a perception or revelation **3** a mental image; esp., an imaginative contemplation [to have *visions* of power] **4** *a)* the ability to perceive something not actually visible, as through mental acuteness or keen foresight [a project made possible by one man's *vision*] *b)* force or power of imagination [a statesman of great *vision*] **5** something or someone, esp. a woman, of extraordinary beauty —***vt.*** to see in or as in a vision; imagine

vi·sion·al (-əl) ***adj.*** **1** of, or having the nature of, a vision or visions **2** seen, or as if seen, in a vision; unreal

vi·sion·ar·y (-er′ē) ***adj.*** **1** of, having the nature of, or seen in a vision **2** *a)* existing only in the mind; not real; imaginary [*visionary* achievements] *b)* not capable of being put into effect; not realistic; impractical [a *visionary* scheme] **3** seeing or disposed to see visions **4** characterized by impractical ideas or schemes **5** having or showing keen foresight and imagination —***n., pl.* -ar′ies** **1** a person who sees visions; prophet or seer **2** a person whose ideas, plans, etc. are impractical, too idealistic, or fantastic; dreamer **3** a person with strong and creative imaginative power and, often, the ability to inspire others

vis·it (viz′it) ***vt.*** ⟦ME *visiten* < OFr *visiter* < L *visitare,* freq. < *visere,* to go to see < *visus:* see VISION⟧ **1** to go or come to see (someone) out of friendship or for social reasons **2** to stay with as a guest for a time **3** to go or come to see in a professional or business capacity [to *visit* a doctor (or a patient)] **4** to go or come to (a place) in order to inspect or investigate **5** to go or come to for a time so as to make use of, look at, etc. [to *visit* an art gallery] **6** to occur or come to [*visited* by an odd idea] **7** to bring suffering, trouble, etc. to; assail [a drought *visited* the land] **8** *a)* to inflict (punishment, suffering, etc.) upon someone *b)* to afflict (*with* punishment, suffering, etc.) *c)* to inflict punishment for (wrongdoing); avenge [*visiting* the sins of the fathers upon the children] —***vi.*** to visit someone or something; specif., *a)* to inflict punishment or revenge ☆*b)* to make a social call or calls (often used with *with*) *c)* to stay with someone as a guest ☆*d)* [Informal] to converse or chat, as during a visit —***n.*** the act or an instance of visiting; specif., *a)* a social call *b)* a stay as a guest; sojourn *c)* an official or professional call, as of a doctor *d)* an official call as for inspection or investigation ☆*e)* [Informal] a friendly conversation *f) Maritime Law* the boarding of a ship of a neutral nation by an officer of a nation at war to search it for contraband, etc.

vis·it·a·ble (-ə bəl) ***adj.*** **1** that can be visited **2** suitable for or worth visiting **3** subject to visitation, or inspection

vis·it·ant (viz′ə tənt) ***n.*** ⟦< Fr or L: Fr < L *visitans,* prp. of *visitare:* see VISIT⟧ **1** a visitor, esp. one from a strange or foreign place **2** a supernatural visitor; ghost, phantom, etc. **3** *Ornithology* a migratory bird in any of its temporary resting places —***adj.*** [Archaic] paying a visit —***SYN.*** VISITOR

vis·it·a·tion (viz′ə tā′shən) ***n.*** ⟦OFr < L *visitatio*⟧ **1** the act or an instance of visiting; esp., an official visit to inspect or examine, as that made by a bishop to a church in his diocese **2** a visiting of reward or, esp., punishment, as by God **3** any affliction or disaster thought of as an act of God ☆**4** *a)* the legal right of a divorced or separated parent to visit a child *b)* such a visit ☆**5** *a)* the custom of visiting the mourning family of a deceased person *b)* such visiting or the time during which it is done: cf. WAKE¹ (*n.* 2) **6** *Zool.* migration of animals or birds to a particular place at an unusual time or in unusual numbers —**the Visitation** *R.C.Ch.* **1** the visit of the Virgin Mary to Elizabeth: Luke 1:39-56 **2** a church feast (May 31) commemorating this —**vis′it·a′tion·al** ***adj.***

vis·it·a·to·ri·al (viz′i tə tôr′ē əl) *adj.* of or for visitation or inspection: also **vis′i·to′ri·al**

visiting card CALLING CARD

☆**visiting nurse** a registered nurse employed as by an agency or hospital to provide nursing care to the sick in their homes

☆**visiting professor** a person, usually regularly employed at another institution, who is teaching by invitation at a college or university for a specified period

☆**visiting teacher** a teacher who visits pupils' homes, as for the instruction of those too ill or disabled to attend regular classes or for the promotion of better attendance or performance

visiting team *Sports* a team playing on the opposing team's field, court, etc.

vis·i·tor (viz′it ər) *n.* ⟦ME *visitour* < Anglo-Fr < MFr *visiteur*⟧ someone or something making a visit

SYN.—**visitor** is the general term for one who comes to see a person or spend some time in a place, whether for social, business, or professional reasons, or for sightseeing, etc.; **visitant** now generally suggests a supernatural rather than a human visitor and, in biology, is applied to a migratory bird in any of its temporary resting places; **guest** applies to one who is hospitably entertained at the home of another, as at dinner, or, by extension, to one who pays for lodgings, meals, etc. at a hotel; **caller** applies to one who makes a brief, often formal visit, as for business or social reasons

vis ma·jor (vis mā′jər, wēs-) ⟦L, greater force⟧ ACT OF GOD

vi·sor (vī′zər) *n.* ⟦ME *visere* < Anglo-Fr *viser* < OFr *visiere* < *vis,* a face: see VISAGE⟧ **1** *a)* in armor, a movable part of a helmet, that could be lowered to cover the upper part of the face, with slits for seeing *b)* a movable section, made usually of safety glass, that is part of a protective head covering, as for welders **2** a mask, as for disguise ☆**3** *a)* the projecting front brim of a cap, for shading the eyes *b)* a SUN VISOR or any of certain other shades for the eyes **4** a movable shade fastened above the windshield inside a motor vehicle, for shading the eyes —*vt.* to cover or provide with a visor —**vi′sored** *adj.*

vis·ta (vis′tə) *n.* ⟦It, sight < pp. of *vedere,* to see < L *videre:* see VISION⟧ **1** a view or outlook, esp. one seen through a long passage, as between rows of houses or trees **2** a comprehensive mental view of a series of remembered or anticipated events

☆**VISTA** (vis′tə) *n.* ⟦*V(olunteers) i(n) S(ervice) t(o) A(merica)*⟧ a U.S. government program established in 1964 to provide volunteers to work at improving the living conditions of persons in impoverished areas of the U.S., its possessions, and Puerto Rico

Vis·tu·la (vis′chōō lə) river in Poland, flowing from the Carpathians into the Baltic: 677 mi (1,089 km): Pol. name WISŁA

vis·u·al (vizh′ōō əl) *adj.* ⟦ME < LL *visualis* < L *visus,* a sight: see VISION⟧ **1** *a)* of, connected with, or used in seeing *b)* based on, designed for, or controlled by the use of sight **2** that is or can be seen; visible **3** of, having the nature of, or occurring as a mental image, or vision **4** *Optics* OPTICAL —*n.* **1** a film clip, still photograph, etc. as used in a documentary film, TV news broadcast, etc. **2** [*pl.*] the visual elements of a film, TV presentation, etc., as distinct from the accompanying sound —**vis′u·al·ly** *adv.*

visual acuity the ability of the eye to discriminate detail, usually tested by comparison with the power of the normal eye to distinguish certain letters on a standard chart at a given distance, generally 20 feet

visual aid a film, slide, chart, or other device involving the sense of sight (other than books), used in teaching, illustrating lectures, etc.: *usually used in pl.*

visual arts art forms producing works to be appreciated visually, as painting, sculpture, ceramics, architecture, photography, film, etc.

☆**vis·u·al-au·ral (radio) range** (-ô′rəl) a radio range that sends out signals as an aid to air navigation; esp., a very-high-frequency range that beams four signals, two for reception by the ear and two for viewing on an indicator

visual binary a binary star that can be visually separated into its two components with a telescope or, rarely, by the naked eye: in contrast to a binary star which is so distant it requires a spectrum analysis to separate the components: also called **visual double**

vis·u·al·i·za·tion (vizh′ōō əl i zā′shən) *n.* **1** the act or process of visualizing something **2** any of various relaxation, meditation, or therapeutic techniques characterized by concentration on a mental image

vis·u·al·ize (vizh′ōō əl īz′) *vt.* **-ized′**, **-iz′ing** ⟦VISUAL + -IZE⟧ to form a mental image of; imagine, envision, etc. —*vi.* to form a mental image

visual purple RHODOPSIN

vi·ta (vīt′ə, vēt′ə) *n., pl.* **-tae** (-ē) ⟦L, life⟧ CURRICULUM VITAE

vi·tal (vīt′'l) *adj.* ⟦ME < MFr < L *vitalis,* vital < *vita,* life, akin to *vivere,* to live: see BIO-⟧ **1** of, concerned with, or manifesting life [*vital* energy] **2** *a)* necessary or essential to life; being a source or support of life [*vital* organs] *b)* affecting life; critical *c)* destroying life; fatal **3** *a)* essential to the existence or continuance of something; indispensable [*a vital* function] *b)* of crucial importance [*a vital* matter] **4** affecting the validity, truth, etc. of something [*a vital* error] **5** full of life and vigor; energetic [*a vital* personality] —*n.* [*pl.*] **1** the vital organs, as the heart, brain, lungs, etc. **2** the essential parts of anything, indispensable for its existence, continuance, etc. —SYN. LIVING —**vi′tal·ly** *adv.*

vital capacity the volume of air that can be forcibly expelled from the lungs after the maximum amount has been breathed in

vi·tal·ism (-iz′əm) *n.* ⟦Fr *vitalisme*⟧ the doctrine that the life in living organisms is caused and sustained by a basic force that is distinct from all physical and chemical forces and that life is, in part, self-determining and self-evolving —**vi′tal·ist** *n., adj.* —**vi′tal·is′tic** *adj.*

vi·tal·i·ty (vī tal′ə tē) *n.* ⟦L *vitalitas*⟧ **1** power to live or go on living **2** power, as of an institution, to endure or survive **3** mental or physical vigor; energy

vi·tal·ize (vīt′'l īz′) *vt.* **-ized′**, **-iz′ing** **1** to make vital; give life to **2** to give vigor or animation to; make lively —SYN. ANIMATE —**vi′tal·i·za′tion** *n.*

Vi·tal·li·um (vī tal′ē əm) *trademark for* a corrosion-resistant alloy of cobalt, chromium, and molybdenum, used for dentures, in bone surgery and prosthetics, in castings, etc.

vital signs indicators of the efficient functioning of the body; esp., pulse, temperature, and respiration

vital staining the staining of living cells with dyes that are not poisonous

vital statistics **1** data on births, deaths, marriages, etc. **2** specific facts, and, often, quantitative information, about a person or thing **3** [Informal] a woman's bust, waist, and hip measurements

vi·ta·min (vīt′ə min; *Brit* vit′-) *n.* ⟦earlier *vitamine* < Ger: so named (1913) by C. Funk (1884-1967), Pol biochemist < L *vita,* life (see VITAL) + Ger *amin,* AMINE: from the orig. mistaken idea that these substances all contain amino acids⟧ **1** any of a number of unrelated, complex organic substances found variously in most foods, or sometimes synthesized in the body, and essential, in small amounts, for the regulation of the metabolism and normal growth and functioning of the body **2** a dose of such a substance or of a group of such substances, taken, as in a tablet, as a dietary supplement —**vi′ta·min′ic** *adj.*

vitamin A a fat-soluble aliphatic alcohol, $C_{20}H_{29}OH$, found in fish-liver oil, egg yolk, butter, etc. or derived from carotene in carrots and other vegetables: a deficiency of this vitamin results in night blindness, a general susceptibility to infections, and degeneration of epithelial tissue; retinol: it usually occurs in two forms, **vitamin A_1**, having the formula above, and **vitamin A_2**, $C_{20}H_{27}OH$

vitamin B (complex) a group of unrelated water-soluble vitamins found in liver, yeast, etc., including: *a)* **vitamin B_1** (see THIAMINE) *b)* **vitamin B_2** (see RIBOFLAVIN) *c)* **vitamin B_6** (see PYRIDOXINE) *d)* NICOTINIC ACID *e)* PANTOTHENIC ACID *f)* BIOTIN *g)* INOSITOL *h)* PARA-AMINOBENZOIC ACID *i)* CHOLINE *j)* FOLIC ACID *k)* **vitamin B_{12}**, a complex vitamin, $C_{63}H_{90}N_{14}O_{14}PCo$, containing trivalent cobalt, essential for the normal maturation of erythrocytes, and for normal growth and neurological function, and used esp. in treating pernicious anemia and as an animal feed supplement

vitamin C ASCORBIC ACID

vitamin D any of several fat-soluble vitamins that are essential for increased absorption of calcium and phosphorus from the intestinal tract, found in fish-liver oils, milk, egg yolk, etc. or produced by irradiation of provitamins; specif., *a)* **vitamin D_2** (see ERGOCALCIFEROL) *b)* **vitamin D_3** (see CHOLECALCIFEROL) *c)* **vitamin D_4**, $C_{28}H_{45}OH$, produced by irradiation of a derivative of ergosterol *d)* **vitamin D_5**, $C_{29}H_{47}OH$, produced by irradiation of a derivative of sitosterol: a deficiency of vitamin D tends to cause rickets

vitamin E the tocopherols collectively, which are fat-soluble compounds that inhibit rancidity and oxidative destruction of tissue components, and are necessary for fertility in rats and certain other animals: a deficiency of vitamin E in the diet of various animals, as the rabbit or sheep, results in muscular dystrophy, sterility, etc.

vitamin H BIOTIN

vitamin K a fat-soluble vitamin, synthesized constantly by intestinal bacteria in mammals and occurring in certain green vegetables, fish meal, etc., that promotes blood clotting and is required for the synthesis of prothrombin by the liver: the two naturally occurring varieties are **vitamin K_1**, $C_{31}H_{46}O_2$, found chiefly in alfalfa leaves, and **vitamin K_2**, $C_{41}H_{56}O_2$, found chiefly in fish meal: **vitamin K_3** (MENADIONE) and **vitamin K_4** are prepared synthetically

vitamin P *former name for* BIOFLAVONOID

Vi·tebsk (vē′tepsk′) city in NE Belarus, on the Western Dvina River

vi·tel·lin (vi tel′in, vī-) *n.* ⟦VITELLUS + -IN[1]⟧ a phosphoprotein occurring in the yolk of eggs

vi·tel·line (-in, -ēn) *adj.* ⟦ME *vitellyn* < L *vitellus:* see fol.⟧ **1** of or having to do with the egg yolk **2** yellow like an egg yolk

vi·tel·lus (-əs) *n.* ⟦L, yolk of an egg, orig., calf: see VEAL⟧ the yolk of an egg

vi·ti·ate (vish′ē āt′) *vt.* **-at′ed**, **-at′ing** ⟦< L *vitiatus,* pp. of *vitiare,* to vitiate < *vitium,* VICE[1]⟧ **1** to make imperfect, faulty, or impure; spoil; corrupt **2** to weaken morally; debase; pervert **3** to make (a contract, or other legal instrument) ineffective; invalidate —**vi′ti·a′tion** *n.* —**vi′ti·a′tor** *n.*

vit·i·cul·ture (vit′ə kul′chər, vīt′-) *n.* ⟦< L *vitis,* vine (see WITHE) + CULTURE⟧ the cultivation of grapes; science or art of grape-growing —**vit′i·cul′tur·al** *adj.* —**vit′i·cul′tur·ist** *n.*

Vi·ti Le·vu (vē′tē le′vōō) largest island of the Fiji Islands: 4,027 sq mi (10,430 sq km); chief city, Suva

vit·i·li·go (vit′ə lī′gō) *n.* ⟦L, a kind of cutaneous eruption, tetter < *vitium,* a blemish, VICE[1]⟧ *Med.* a disorder in which there is a loss of pigment resulting in white patches of skin

Vi·to·ria (vē tô′ryä) city in The Basque Country, N Spain

Vi·tó·ria (vē tô′ryä) seaport in E Brazil, on the Atlantic: capital of Espírito Santo state

vit·rain (vi′trān′) *n.* ⟦< L *vitrum,* glass + *-ain,* as in FUSAIN⟧ a type of black, glassy, cubic bituminous coal

vit·re·ous (vi′trē əs) *adj.* ⟦L *vitreus,* glassy < *vitrum,* glass⟧ **1** *a)* of, having the nature of, or like glass; glassy *b)* derived from or made of glass **2** of the vitreous humor —**vit′re·ous·ness** *n.*
vitreous humor (*or* **body**) the transparent, colorless, jellylike substance that fills the eyeball between the retina and lens
vitreous silica SILICA GLASS
vi·tres·cent (vi tres′ənt) *adj.* ⟦< L *vitrum,* glass + -ESCENT⟧ **1** that can be formed into glass **2** becoming, or tending to become, glass
vit·ric (vi′trik) *adj.* ⟦< L *vitrum,* glass + -IC⟧ of, having the nature of, or like glass
vit·rics (-triks′) *n.* ⟦see prec. & -ICS⟧ the art or study of making and decorating articles of glass —*pl.n.* articles of glass; glassware
vit·ri·fi·ca·tion (vi′trə fi kā′shən) *n.* **1** the act or an instance of vitrifying **2** the cryopreservation of tissue, specif., a method of in vitro fertilization in which the embryo is exposed to a vitreous solution and frozen, before being thawed and implanted into the uterus
vit·ri·form (vi′trə fôrm′) *adj.* ⟦< L *vitrum,* glass + -FORM⟧ having the form or appearance of glass
vit·ri·fy (vi′trə fī′) *vt., vi.* **-fied′**, **-fy′ing** ⟦Fr *vitrifier* < L *vitrum,* glass + Fr *-fier,* -FY⟧ to change into glass or a glasslike substance, as by fusion due to heat; make or become vitreous —**vit′ri·fi′a·ble** *adj.*
vit·rine (vi′trin, vi trēn′) *n.* ⟦Fr < *vitre,* pane of glass < L *vitrum,* glass⟧ a glass-paneled cabinet or glass display case for art objects, curios, etc.
vit·ri·ol (vi′trē ôl′, -trē əl) *n.* ⟦ME < MFr < ML *vitriolum,* vitriol < LL *vitreolus,* glassy < L *vitreus,* glassy: from the glassy appearance⟧ **1** *a)* any of several sulfates of metals, as copper sulfate (*blue vitriol*), iron sulfate (*green vitriol*), or zinc sulfate (*white vitriol*) *b)* SULFURIC ACID **2** sharpness or bitterness of feeling, as in speech or writing; venom —*vt.* **-oled′** or **-olled′**, **-ol′ing** or **-ol′ling** to treat with or as with vitriol
vit·ri·ol·ic (vi′trē äl′ik) *adj.* ⟦Fr *vitriolique*⟧ **1** of, like, or derived from a vitriol **2** extremely biting or caustic; sharp and bitter *[vitriolic* talk*]*
vit·ri·ol·ize (vi′trē ə līz′) *vt.* **-ized′**, **-iz′ing** **1** to convert into vitriol **2** to subject to the action of vitriol
Vi·tru·vi·us (vi tro͞o′vē əs) (*Marcus Vitruvius Pollio*) fl. 1st cent. B.C.; Rom. architect & engineer
vit·ta (vit′ə) *n., pl.* **-tae** (-ē) ⟦ModL < L, headband, fillet, akin to *viere,* to tie, *vitis,* vine: see WITHE⟧ **1** *Biol.* a band or streak of color **2** *Bot.* an oil-bearing canal in the pericarp of the fruits of some dicotyledonous plants, as of a plant of the umbel family
vit·tle (vit′'l) *n., vt., vi.* **-tled**, **-tling** *alt. sp. of* VICTUAL
vi·tu·per·ate (vī to͞o′pər āt′, vi-; -tyo͞o′-) *vt.* **-at′ed**, **-at′ing** ⟦< L *vituperatus,* pp. of *vituperare,* to blame < *vitium,* a fault, VICE[1] + *parare,* to PREPARE⟧ to speak abusively to or about; berate; revile —*SYN.* SCOLD —**vi·tu′per·a′tive** *adj.* —**vi·tu′per·a′tive·ly** *adv.* —**vi·tu′per·a′tive·ness** *n.* —**vi·tu′per·a′tor** *n.*
vi·tu·per·a·tion (vī to͞o′pər ā′shən, vi-; -tyo͞o′-) *n.* ⟦L *vituperatio*⟧ **1** the act of vituperating **2** abusive language
vi·va[1] (vē′vä) *v. imper.* ⟦It & Sp⟧ long live (someone or something specified)!: used in exclamations of acclaim
vi·va[2] (vī′və) *n.* ⟦short for *viva voce examination*: see VIVA VOCE⟧ *[also in italics]* [Brit.] a university examination with spoken questions and answers; oral examination
vi·va·ce (vē vä′chā, vi-) *adj., adv.* ⟦It < L *vivax:* see fol.⟧ *[also in italics]* *Musical Direction* (in a) lively or spirited (manner)
vi·va·cious (vī vā′shəs, vi-) *adj.* ⟦< L *vivax* (gen. *vivacis*), vigorous < *vivere,* to live (see BIO-) + -OUS⟧ **1** full of life and animation **2** characterized by an attractive or pleasing liveliness of spirit: now said esp. of a woman —*SYN.* LIVELY —**vi·va′cious·ly** *adv.* —**vi·va′cious·ness** *n.*
vi·vac·i·ty (vī vas′ə tē, vi-) *n.* ⟦ME *vivacite* < L *vivacitas*⟧ **1** the quality or state of being vivacious **2** liveliness of spirit
Vi·val·di (vē väl′dē, vi-), **An·to·nio** (än tô′nyô) 1678-1741; It. composer
vi·var·i·um (vī ver′ē əm) *n., pl.* **-i·ums** or **-i·a** (-ē ə) ⟦L < *vivarius,* concerning living creatures < *vivere,* to live: see BIO-⟧ an enclosed indoor place for keeping and studying terrestrial animals
vi·va vo·ce (vī′və vō′sē, -chā) ⟦ML, with living voice, abl. fem. of L *vivus,* living + abl. of *vox,* VOICE⟧ by word of mouth; orally —**vi′va-vo′ce** *adj.*
vive (vēv) *v. imper.* ⟦Fr⟧ long live (someone or something specified)!: used in exclamations of acclaim
vive la dif·fé·rence (vēv′ lȧ dē′fə rȧns′) ⟦Fr⟧ long live the difference (between the sexes)!
vi·ver·rid (vī ver′id) *n.* ⟦< L *viverra,* a ferret < redupl. of IE base **wer-* > Pers *vavrarah,* OPrus *weware,* OE *(ac)weorna,* squirrel + -IDAE⟧ any of a family (Viverridae) of small, slender carnivores, including the civets and mongooses —*adj.* of or belonging to this family Also **vi·ver·rine** (vī ver′īn, -in)
Viv·i·an (viv′ē ən, viv′yən) *n.* ⟦L *Vivianus* < *vivus,* alive (see BIO-)⟧ **1** a masculine name: equiv. Fr. *Vivien* **2** a feminine name: var. *Vivien*; equiv. Fr. *Vivienne* **3** *Arthurian Legend* an enchantress who seduces and casts a spell over Merlin: see also LADY OF THE LAKE
viv·id (viv′id) *adj.* ⟦L *vividus,* lively < *vivere,* to live: see BIO-⟧ **1** full of life; vigorous; lively; striking *[*a *vivid* personality*]* **2** *a)* bright; intense; brilliant (said of colors, light, etc.) *b)* brightly colored *[*a *vivid* tapestry*]* **3** forming clear or striking mental images; strong; active; daring *[*a *vivid* imagination*]* **4** clearly perceived by the mind, as a recollection **5** bringing strikingly realistic or lifelike images to the mind *[*a *vivid* description*]* —**viv′id·ly** *adv.* —**viv′id·ness** *n.*
viv·i·fy (viv′ə fī′) *vt.* **-fied′**, **-fy′ing** ⟦Fr *vivifier* < LL(Ec) *vivificare* (as opposed to *mortificare:* see MORTIFY) < L *vivus,* alive (see BIO-) + *facere,* to make, DO[1]⟧ **1** to give life to; animate **2** to make more lively, active, striking, etc. —**viv′i·fi·ca′tion** *n.* —**viv′i·fi′er** *n.*
vi·vip·a·rous (vī vip′ər əs, vi-) *adj.* ⟦L *viviparus* < *vivus,* alive (see BIO-) + *parere,* to produce (see -PAROUS)⟧ **1** *a)* bearing or bringing forth living young, as most mammals and some other animals do *b)* designating or of this type of reproduction (see OVIPAROUS) **2** *Bot.* *a)* germinating while still on the parent plant: said of certain seeds or bulbs *b)* producing such seeds or bulbs; proliferous —**viv·i·par·i·ty** (viv′ə par′ə tē, vī′və-) *n.* —**vi·vip′a·rous·ly** *adv.*
viv·i·sect (viv′ə sekt′) *vt.* ⟦back-form. < fol., after DISSECT⟧ to perform vivisection on —*vi.* to practice vivisection —**viv′i·sec′tor** *n.*
viv·i·sec·tion (viv′ə sek′shən) *n.* ⟦< L *vivus,* alive (see BIO-) + SECTION⟧ medical research consisting of surgical operations or other experiments performed on living animals —**viv′i·sec′tion·al** *adj.*
viv·i·sec·tion·ist (-ist) *n.* **1** a person who practices vivisection **2** a person who advocates or defends vivisection
vix·en (vik′sən) *n.* ⟦ME (southern dial.) *fixen* < OE *fyxe,* she-fox (or *fyxen,* adj., of a fox) < *fox,* FOX⟧ **1** a female fox **2** an ill-tempered, shrewish, or malicious woman —**vix′en·ish** *adj.* —**vix′en·ish·ly** *adv.*
Vi·yel·la (vī yel′ə, vi-) ⟦arbitrary coinage⟧ *trademark for* a soft, light, flannel-like fabric made of a blend of lamb's wool and fine cotton —*n.* *[occas.* v-*]* this fabric
viz. or **viz** *abbrev.* ⟦ML, altered (because abbrev. for L *et* resembled a *z*) < earlier *viet.,* contr. for L *videlicet*⟧ that is; namely
viz·ard (viz′ərd) *n.* ⟦altered < earlier *visar,* var. of VISOR⟧ [Archaic] VISOR (esp. sense 2)
vi·zier (vi zir′, viz′yər) *n.* ⟦Turk *vezīr* < Ar *wazīr,* a vizier, lit., bearer of burdens < *wazara,* to bear a burden, take upon oneself: the vizier bears the duties actually incumbent upon the ruler⟧ in the Ottoman Empire, a high officer in the government; esp., a minister of state: also sp. **vi·zir′** —**vi·zier′ate** (-it, -āt′) *n.*, **vi·zier′ship** —**vi·zier′i·al** *adj.*
vi·zor (vī′zər) *n. alt. sp. of* VISOR
vizs·la (vēz′lə, vēs′-, vēzh′-, vizh′-) *n.* ⟦after *Vizsla,* town in Hungary, in region where breed developed⟧ any of a breed of medium-sized hunting dog, originating in Hungary, with a short, smooth, rusty-gold coat: traditionally the tail is docked
☆**VJ** (vē′jā′) *n., pl.* **VJ's** ⟦*v(ideo) j(ockey),* infl. by DJ⟧ a person who conducts a TV program featuring music videos
V-J Day (vē′jā′) ⟦< *v(ictory over) J(apan)*⟧ the day on which the fighting with Japan officially ended in WWII (Aug. 15, 1945) or the day the surrender was formally signed (Sept. 2, 1945)
VL *abbrev.* Vulgar Latin
Vlach (vläk, vlak) *adj., n.* WALACHIAN
Vlad III (vlad) 1431-76; prince of Walachia: a basis for the Dracula legend: called *Vlad the Impaler* (Rom. *Vlad epeș*)
Vla·di·kav·kaz (vlä′dē käf′käz′) city in S European Russia, in the Caucasus
Vlad·i·mir (vlä dē′mir) city in central European Russia, east of Moscow
Vlad·i·mir I (vlad′ə mir; *Russ* vlä dē′mir) 956?-1015; Russ. ruler & prince of Kiev (980-1015): converted to Christianity (989), which he introduced into Russia: his day is July 15: called *the Great*: also **Saint Vladimir**
Vla·di·vos·tok (vlad′i väs′täk; *Russ* vlä′di vôs tôk′) seaport in SE Siberia, on the Sea of Japan: the E terminus of the Trans-Siberian Railroad
Vla·minck (vlȧ mank′), **Mau·rice de** (mô rēs′ də) 1876-1958; Fr. painter
VLF or **vlf** *abbrev.* very low frequency
VLSI (vē′el′es′ī′) *n.* ⟦*v(ery-)l(arge-)s(cale) i(ntegration)*⟧ a very complex integrated circuit, esp. one having more than 5,000 transistors or other electronic components: cf. LSI
Vl·ta·va (vul′tə və) river in the W Czech Republic, flowing into the Elbe: *c.* 265 mi (426 km)
VMD or **V.M.D.** *abbrev.* ⟦L *Veterinariae Medicinae Doctor*⟧ Doctor of Veterinary Medicine
V-neck (vē′nek′) *n.* a neckline that is V-shaped in front
VOA *abbrev.* Voice of America
voc *abbrev.* **1** vocalist **2** vocational **3** vocative
vocab *abbrev.* vocabulary
vo·ca·ble (vō′kə bəl) *n.* ⟦Fr < L *vocabulum,* a name, title, word < *vocare,* to call < *vox,* VOICE⟧ a word or term; esp., a word regarded as a unit of sounds or letters rather than as a unit of meaning
vo·cab·u·lar·y (vō kab′yə ler′ē) *n., pl.* **-lar′ies** ⟦ML *vocabularium* < L *vocabulum,* a word: see prec.⟧ **1** a list of words and, often, phrases, abbreviations, inflectional forms, etc., usually arranged in alphabetical order and defined or otherwise identified, as in a dictionary or glossary **2** all the words of a language **3** *a)* all the words used by a particular person, socioeconomic group, profession, etc. (in full **active vocabulary**) *b)* all the words recognized and understood, although not necessarily used, by a particular person (in full **passive vocabulary**) **4** an interrelated group of nonverbal symbols, signs, gestures, etc. used for communication or expression in a particular art, skill, etc.
vo·cal (vō′kəl) *adj.* ⟦ME < L *vocalis* < *vox,* VOICE⟧ **1** *a)* uttered or produced by the voice; esp., spoken; oral *[vocal* sounds*]* *b)* sung or to be sung *[vocal* music*]* **2** having a voice; capable of speaking or making oral sounds **3** of, used in, connected with, or belonging to the voice *[vocal* organs*]* **4** full of voice or voices; sounding **5** expressing or inclined to express oneself in speech; speaking freely or vociferously **6** *Phonet.* *a)* VOCALIC *b)* VOICED

—*n.* 1 a vocal sound 2 the part of a popular song that is, or is to be, sung, rather than played by the instruments alone —**vo′cal·ly** *adv.*

vocal cords either of two pairs of membranous cords or folds in the larynx, consisting of a thicker upper pair (**false vocal cords**) and a lower pair (**true vocal cords**): voice is produced when air from the lungs causes the lower cords to vibrate: pitch is controlled by varying the tension on the cords, and volume, by regulating the air passing through the larynx

☆**vo·cal·ese** (vō′kəl ēz′) *n.* ⟦VOCAL + -ESE⟧ a form of jazz singing in which lyrics are composed for and sung to the music taken from already existing instrumental jazz recordings

vo·cal·ic (vō kal′ik) *adj.* 1 of, having the nature of, or consisting of a vowel or vowels 2 composed mainly or entirely of vowels —**vo·cal′i·cal·ly** *adv.*

vo·cal·ise (vō′kəl ēz′) *n.* ⟦Fr < *vocaliser,* to vocalize⟧ 1 a singing exercise using sol-fa syllables or other vowel sounds 2 a vocal composition or passage using vowel sounds instead of words

vo·cal·ism (vō′kəl iz′əm) *n.* 1 the use of the voice, as in speaking or singing; vocalization 2 the art of singing 3 *a)* the system of vowels peculiar to a given language, dialect, etc. *b)* a vocalic sound; vowel

vo·cal·ist (-ist) *n.* ⟦VOCAL + -IST[1]⟧ one who sings; singer

vo·cal·ize (vō′kəl īz′) *vt.* **-ized′**, **-iz′ing** 1 to give utterance to; express with the voice; speak or sing 2 to add diacritical vowel marks to (the exclusively consonantal characters of certain languages such as Hebrew) 3 *Phonet. a)* to change into or use as a vowel *b)* to voice —*vi.* 1 to make vocal sounds; speak or sing; specif., to do a singing exercise, using various vowel sounds 2 to be changed into a vowel; become vocalic —**vo′cal·i·za′tion** *n.* —**vo′cal·iz′er** *n.*

vo·ca·tion (vō kā′shən) *n.* ⟦ME *vocacion* < LL(Ec) *vocatio,* a calling < L, an invitation, court summons < *vocare,* to call < *vox,* VOICE⟧ 1 *a)* a call, summons, or impulsion to perform a certain function or enter a certain career, esp. a religious one *b)* the function or career toward which one believes oneself to be called 2 any trade, profession, or occupation

vo·ca·tion·al (-shə nəl) *adj.* 1 of a vocation, trade, occupation, etc. ☆2 designating or of education, training, a school, etc. intended to prepare one for an occupation, sometimes specif. in a trade —**vo·ca′tion·al·ism′** *n.* —**vo·ca′tion·al·ly** *adv.*

☆**vocational guidance** the work of testing and interviewing persons in order to guide them toward the choice of a suitable vocation

voc·a·tive (väk′ə tiv) *adj.* ⟦ME *vocatif* < OFr or L: OFr < L *vocativus* < pp. of *vocare,* to call < *vox,* VOICE⟧ *Gram.* designating, of, or in the case of nouns, pronouns, or adjectives used in direct address to indicate the person or thing addressed —*n.* 1 the vocative case: this case is expressed by a change in form in languages such as Latin and by word order and intonation in English (Ex.: "Bill" in "Bill, don't do that!") 2 a word or phrase in this case —**voc′a·tive·ly** *adv.*

vo·cif·er·ant (vō sif′ər ənt) *adj.* ⟦L *vociferans,* prp. of *vociferari:* see fol.⟧ vociferating; shouting; clamorous

vo·cif·er·ate (vō sif′ər āt′) *vt., vi.* **-at′ed**, **-at′ing** ⟦< L *vociferatus,* pp. of *vociferari,* to cry out < *vox,* VOICE + *ferre,* to BEAR[1]⟧ to utter or shout loudly or vehemently; bawl; clamor —**vo·cif′er·a′tion** *n.* —**vo·cif′er·a′tor** *n.*

vo·cif·er·ous (vō sif′ər əs) *adj.* ⟦L *vociferari* (see prec.) + -OUS⟧ 1 loud, noisy, or vehement in making one's feelings known; clamorous 2 characterized by clamor or vehement outcry —**vo·cif′er·ous·ly** *adv.* —**vo·cif′er·ous·ness** *n.*

SYN.—**vociferous** suggests loud and unrestrained shouting or crying out [a *vociferous* crowd, *vociferous* cheers]; **clamorous** suggests an urgent or insistent vociferousness, as in demand or complaint [*clamorous* protests]; **blatant** implies a bellowing loudness and, hence, suggests vulgar or offensive noisiness, clamor, etc. [*blatant* heckling]; **strident** suggests a harsh, grating loudness [a *strident* voice]; **boisterous** implies roughness or turbulence and, hence, suggests unrestrained, noisy exuberance [*boisterous* revels]; **obstreperous** implies an unruliness that is noisy or boisterous in resisting control [an *obstreperous* child]

☆**vo·cod·er** (vō′kō′dər) *n.* ⟦VO(ICE) + CODER⟧ an electronic system for analyzing the frequency spectrum of speech and constructing a code that can be transmitted and reconstructed into a replica of the original speech

vod·ka (väd′kə) *n.* ⟦Russ, dim. of *voda,* WATER⟧ a colorless alcoholic liquor distilled from rye, wheat, etc.

vo·dou (vō do͞o′) *n. var. of* VOODOO (*n.* 1): also **vo·dun′** (-do͞on′) or **vo·doun′** (-do͞on′)

☆**vo-ed** (vō′ed′) *adj., n.* [Informal] (of) vocational education

vogue (vōg) *n.* ⟦Fr, a fashion, reputation, lit., rowing of a ship < *voguer,* to row, sail < MLowG *wagon,* to sail, float; akin to OE *wæg,* a wave, billow: see WEIGH[1]⟧ 1 the accepted fashion or style at any particular time; mode: often with *the* 2 general favor or acceptance; popularity [coming into *vogue*] —*adj.* in vogue: also **vogu·ish** (vō′gish) —*SYN.* FASHION

Vo·gul (vō′go͝ol) *n.* 1 a member of a people of W Siberia 2 the Ugric language of this people

voice (vois) *n.* ⟦ME < OFr *vois* < L *vox* (gen. *vocis*), a voice < IE base **wekw-,* to speak > Sans *vákti,* (he) speaks, Gr *ossa, ops,* voice, OE *woma,* noise⟧ 1 sound made through the mouth, esp. by human beings in talking, singing, etc. 2 the ability to make sounds orally or to speak, sing, etc. [to lose one's *voice*] 3 *a)* any sound regarded as like vocal utterance [the *voice* of the sea] *b)* anything regarded as like vocal utterance in communicating to the mind [the *voice* of one's conscience] 4 a specified condition, quality, or tone of vocal sound [an angry *voice*] 5 the characteristic speech sounds normally made by a particular person [to recognize someone's *voice* over the phone] 6 *a)* an expressed wish, choice, opinion, etc. [the *voice* of the people] *b)* the right to express one's wish, choice, opinion, etc., or to make it prevail; vote [to have a *voice* in one's government] 7 utterance or expression [giving *voice* to his joy] 8 the person or other agency by which something is expressed or made known [a newspaper known to be the *voice* of the administration] 9 *Gram. a)* a characteristic of verbs, expressed in some languages by inflection, indicating the relation of the subject to the action of the verb either as agent (*active voice*), recipient (*passive voice*), or both, as in reflexives (*middle voice*); also, an analytic category based on this characteristic *b)* any of the forms a verb takes to indicate this characteristic 10 *Music a)* musical sound made with the mouth; singing *b)* the quality of a particular person's singing [a good *voice*] *c)* a singer *d)* any of the individual parts sung or played together in a musical composition 11 *Phonet.* sound made by vibration of the vocal cords with air forced from the lungs, as in the articulation of all vowels and such consonants as (b), (d), (g), and (m) —*vt.* **voiced**, **voic′ing** 1 to give utterance or expression to; utter or express in words 2 *Music a)* to regulate the tone of (organ pipes, etc.) *b)* to arrange (notes of a chord) or distribute notes to (instruments) so as to achieve a particular harmonic sound 3 *Phonet.* to utter with voice —*SYN.* UTTER[2] —**in voice** with the voice in good condition, as for singing —**with one voice** unanimously —**voic′er** *n.*

voice box LARYNX

voiced (voist) *adj.* 1 having a voice 2 having or using (a specified kind or tone of) voice: often in hyphenated compounds [deep-*voiced*] 3 expressed by the voice 4 *Phonet.* articulated with simultaneous vibration of the vocal cords: said of certain consonants, as (b), (z), and (m)

voice·less (vois′lis) *adj.* 1 having no voice; dumb; mute 2 not speaking; silent 3 not spoken; not uttered [a *voiceless* wish] 4 lacking a musical voice or the ability to sing 5 having no voice, or vote; lacking suffrage 6 *Phonet.* articulated without simultaneous vibration of the vocal cords; surd: said of certain consonants, as (p), (s), and (ch) —**voice′less·ly** *adv.* —**voice′less·ness** *n.*

voice mail 1 an electronic system that uses telephones and a computer to record, store, and then play back voice messages 2 a message or messages sent or stored in such a system

voice-o·ver (-ō′vər) *n.* the voice commenting or narrating off camera, as for a television commercial

voice·print (-print′) *n.* a pattern of wavy lines and whorls recorded by a device actuated by the sound of a person's voice: the pattern is supposed to be distinctive for each individual, like a fingerprint —**voice′print′ing** *n.*

voice recognition an electronic system which can recognize and react to specific spoken commands

voice synthesizer an electronic synthesizer that generates and combines basic elements of sound to produce simulated speech, used in computer systems, etc.

voic·ing (vois′iŋ) *n. Music* the sound of a chord as determined by the selection of the component notes and the way the notes are distributed to the instruments

void (void) *adj.* ⟦ME *voide* < OFr *vuide* < VL **vocitus,* for L *vocivus,* var. of *vacivus* < *vacare,* to be empty⟧ 1 not occupied; vacant: said of benefices, offices, etc. 2 *a)* holding or containing nothing *b)* devoid or destitute (*of*) [*void* of sense] 3 having no effect or result; ineffective; useless 4 *Card Games* holding no cards in a suit as dealt to the hand [to be *void* in clubs] 5 *Law a)* of no legal force; not binding; invalid; null *b)* loosely, capable of being nullified —*n.* 1 total emptiness; an empty space or vacuum 2 *a)* total absence of something normally present *b)* a feeling of emptiness or deprivation [the *void* left by his death] 3 a break or open space, as in a surface; gap 4 *Card Games* the absence, from a player's hand as dealt, of any cards in a certain suit [a *void* in clubs] —*vt.* ⟦ME *voiden* < MFr *vuidier* < *vuide,* adj.⟧ 1 [Now Rare] *a)* to make empty; clear *b)* to vacate 2 *a)* to empty (the contents of something) *b)* to evacuate, or discharge (urine or feces) 3 to make void, or of no effect; nullify; annul —*vi.* to defecate or, esp., to urinate —*SYN.* EMPTY —**void′a·ble** *adj.* —**void′er** *n.*

void·ance (void′'ns) *n.* ⟦ME *voydaunce* < Anglo-Fr *voidaunce* < OFr *vuidance*⟧ the act of voiding; specif., *a)* annulment, as of a contract *b)* vacancy, as of a benefice

void·ed (-id) *adj.* 1 made void 2 *Heraldry* having the middle removed, leaving the outline: said of bearings

voi·là (vwä lä′) *interj.* ⟦Fr, see there⟧ behold; there it is

voile (voil; *Fr* vwäl) *n.* ⟦Fr, a veil < L *vela:* see VEIL⟧ a thin, sheer fabric, as of cotton, used for garments, curtains, etc.

voir dire (vwär′ dir′) ⟦Fr < *voir(e),* truly + *dire,* to say⟧ *Law* the phase of a trial in which prospective jurors are examined and jurors are selected

Voj·vo·di·na (voi′və dē′nə, -dē nä′) province of N Serbia: 8,304 sq mi (21,506 sq km); cap. Novi Sad

vol *abbrev.* 1 volcano 2 volume 3 volunteer

Vo·lans (vō′lanz) *n.* ⟦< ModL (*piscis*) *volans,* flying (fish) < L: see FISH & fol.⟧ a S constellation between Mensa and Carina

vo·lant (vō′lənt) *adj.* ⟦< Fr or L: Fr *volant* < L *volans,* prp. of *volare,* to fly⟧ 1 flying or capable of flying 2 nimble; agile; quick 3 *Heraldry* represented as flying [a crane *volant*]

Vo·la·pük (vō′lə po͝ok′, väl′ə-) *n.* ⟦< Volapük *vol,* world (altered < WORLD) + *-a-,* connective + *pük,* language (altered < SPEAK)⟧ an invented language, devised (*c.* 1879) by German clergyman J. M. Schleyer (1831-1912), for proposed use as an international auxiliary language: it uses roots from the major European languages and has a complex morphology: also written **Volapuk**

vo·lar (vō′lər) *adj.* ⟦< L *vola,* hollow of the hand, palm, sole of the foot (for IE base see WALE[1]) + -AR⟧ *Anat.* of the palm of the hand or sole of the foot

vol·a·tile (väl′ə təl; *chiefly Brit,* -tīl′) *adj.* ⟦MFr < L *volatilis* < *volare,* to fly⟧ **1** [Obs.] flying or able to fly; volitant **2** vaporizing or evaporating quickly, as alcohol **3** *a)* likely to shift quickly and unpredictably; unstable; explosive [*a volatile* social condition] *b)* moving capriciously from one idea, interest, etc. to another; fickle *c)* not lasting long; fleeting **4** *Comput.* designating or of memory that does not retain stored data when the power supply is disconnected or interrupted —*n.* [Now Rare] **1** any flying creature **2** a volatile substance —**vol′a·tile·ness** *n.*

volatile oil ESSENTIAL OIL

vol·a·til·i·ty (väl′ə til′ə tē) *n.* **1** the condition of being volatile **2** the degree to which something is volatile **3** *Finance* a measure of the degree to which a security rises or falls in price over a period of time

vol·a·til·ize (väl′ə təl īz′) *vt.* **-ized′**, **-iz′ing** to make volatile; cause to pass off as vapor —*vi.* to become volatile —**vol′a·til·iz′a·ble** *adj.* —**vol′a·til·i·za′tion** *n.*

vol-au-vent (vō′lō vän′; *Fr* vô lō vän′) *n.* ⟦Fr, lit., flight in the wind: so named, from its lightness & delicacy, by its creator, A. Carême (1783-1833), Fr chef⟧ a baked shell of puff pastry, filled as with chicken, game, or fish in a cream sauce

vol·can·ic (väl kan′ik, vôl-; -kān′-) *adj.* ⟦Fr *volcanique* < It *volcanico*⟧ **1** *a)* of, thrown from, caused by, or characteristic of a volcano *b)* EXTRUSIVE (sense 2) **2** having, or composed of, volcanoes **3** suggestive of or bursting forth like a volcano; violently explosive —**vol·can′i·cal·ly** *adv.*

volcanic glass natural glass, as obsidian, formed by the very rapid cooling of molten lava

vol·ca·nic·i·ty (väl′kə nis′ə tē, vôl′-) *n.* ⟦Fr *volcanicité*⟧ the quality or state of being volcanic; volcanic activity

volcanic rock igneous rock, as basalt, that solidified rapidly from molten lava at or near the earth's surface

vol·can·ism (väl′kə niz′əm, vôl′-) *n.* ⟦Fr *volcanisme*⟧ volcanic activity or phenomena

vol·can·ize (-nīz′) *vt.* **-ized′**, **-iz′ing** to subject to, or change by, volcanic heat —**vol′can·i·za′tion** *n.*

vol·ca·no (väl kā′nō, vôl-) *n., pl.* **-noes** or **-nos** ⟦It < L *Volcanus,*VULCAN⟧ **1** a vent in the earth's crust through which molten rock (*lava*), rock fragments, gases, ashes, etc. are ejected from the earth's interior: a volcano is *active* while erupting, *dormant* during a long period of inactivity, or *extinct* when all activity has finally ceased **2** a cone-shaped hill or mountain, wholly or chiefly of volcanic materials, built up around the vent, usually so as to form a crater

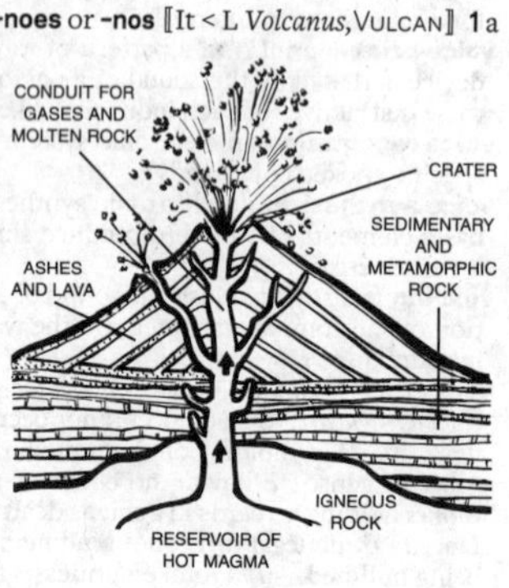

volcano

Volcano Islands group of small Japanese islands, including Iwo Jima, in the W Pacific: 11 sq mi (28 sq km)

vol·can·ol·o·gist (väl′kə näl′ə jist, vôl′-) *n.* a student of or specialist in volcanology

vol·can·ol·o·gy (-jē) *n.* ⟦VOLCANO + -LOGY⟧ the science dealing with volcanoes and volcanic activity —**vol′can·o·log′i·cal** *adj.*

vole (vōl) *n.* ⟦earlier *vole mouse* < Scand, as in ON *vǫllr,* meadow, field (< PGmc **walthu-* > WEALD, WOLD[1], Ger *wald,* < IE **wel-,* shaggy hair, grass) + MOUSE⟧ any of a number of small rodents (family Cricetidae), with a stout body and short tail

Vol·ga (väl′gə, vōl′-; *Russ* vôl′gä) ⟦Russ: see WELKIN⟧ river in European Russia, flowing from the Valdai Hills into the Caspian Sea: 2,290 mi (3,685 km)

Vol·go·grad (väl′gə grad′, vōl′-; *Russ* vôl gä grät′) city in SC European Russia, on the Volga: scene of a decisive Soviet victory (1943) over German troops in WWII

vol·i·tant (väl′ə tənt) *adj.* ⟦L *volitans,* prp. of *volitare,* to fly to and fro, freq. of *volare,* to fly⟧ **1** flying, flitting, or constantly in motion **2** capable of flight

vol·i·ta·tion (väl′ə tā′shən) *n.* ⟦ML *volitatio* < L *volitare:* see prec.⟧ **1** the act of flying; flight **2** the ability to fly

vo·li·tion (vō lish′ən, və-) *n.* ⟦Fr < ML *volitio* < L *volo,* I wish, pres. indic. of *velle,* to be willing, to WILL[2]⟧ **1** the act of using the will; exercise of the will as in deciding what to do **2** a conscious or deliberate decision or choice thus made **3** the power or faculty of using the will —***SYN.*** WILL[1] —**vo·li′tion·al** *adj.* —**vo·li′tion·al·ly** *adv.*

vol·i·tive (väl′ə tiv) *adj.* ⟦ML *volitivus* < L *volo:* see prec.⟧ **1** of or arising from the will **2** *Gram.* expressing a wish or permission: said of a verb, mood, etc.

Volks·lied (fôlks′lēt′) *n., pl.* **Volks′lied′er** (-lē′dər) ⟦Ger⟧ a German folk song

vol·ley (väl′ē) *n., pl.* **-leys** ⟦MFr *volee* < VL **volata* < fem. of L *volatus,* pp. of *volare,* to fly⟧ **1** *a)* the simultaneous discharge of a number of firearms or other weapons *b)* the bullets, arrows, etc. discharged in this way **2** a burst of words or acts suggestive of this [*a volley* of curses, questions, etc.] **3** *Sports a)* the act of returning the ball, shuttlecock, etc. in certain games before it touches the ground *b)* the flight of the ball, etc. before it touches the ground *c)* loosely, any extended exchange of shots, as in tennis or volleyball, esp. such an exchange in warming up for a game —*vt.* **-leyed**, **-ley·ing** **1** to discharge in or as in a volley **2** *Sports* to return (the ball, etc.) as a volley —*vi.* **1** to be discharged in or as in a volley **2** *Sports a)* to return the ball, etc. as a volley *b)* loosely, to engage in a volley —**vol′ley·er** *n.*

☆**vol·ley·ball** (-bôl′) *n.* **1** a game played on a court by two teams who hit a large, lightweight, inflated ball back and forth over a high net with the hands, each team trying to return the ball before it touches the ground **2** this ball —**vol′ley·ball′er** *n.*

Vo·log·da (vô′lôg dä) city in NC European Russia

vo·lost (vō′läst′) *n.* ⟦Russ *volost′*⟧ **1** a small administrative district of peasants in czarist Russia **2** a rural soviet in the Soviet Union

vol·plane (väl′plān′) *vi.* **-planed′**, **-plan′ing** ⟦Fr *vol plané* < *vol,* flight < *voler,* to fly (< L *volare*) + *plané,* pp. of *planer,* to glide: see PLANE[4]⟧ to glide down in or as in an airplane with the engine cut off —*n.* such a glide

Vol·sci (väl′sī′) *pl.n.* ⟦L⟧ the members of an ancient people of Latium, conquered by the Romans in the 4th cent. B.C.

Vol·scian (väl′shən) *adj.* of the Volsci or their language or culture —*n.* **1** a member of the Volsci **2** the Italic language of the Volsci

Vol·stead Act (väl′sted) ⟦after U.S. Congressman A. J. *Volstead* (1860-1947), who introduced the act⟧ an act of Congress, passed in 1919 and repealed in 1933, enforcing the Eighteenth Amendment to the Constitution, prohibiting the sale of alcoholic beverages

volt[1] (vōlt) *n.* ⟦Fr *volte* < It *volta,* a turn < VL **volvita,* for L *voluta,* fem. pp. of *volvere,* to roll, turn about: see WALK⟧ **1** a turning movement or gait of a horse, in which it moves sideways around a center **2** *Fencing* a leap to avoid a thrust

volt[2] (vōlt) *n.* ⟦after fol.⟧ the basic unit of electromotive force in the SI and MKS systems, equal to the electromotive force, or difference in potential, that causes a current of one ampere to flow through a conductor having a resistance of one ohm: abbrev. *V*

Vol·ta[1] (vôl′tä), Conte **A·les·san·dro** (ä′les sän′drô) 1745-1827; It. physicist

Vol·ta[2] (väl′tə, vôl′-, vōl′-) **1** river in SE Ghana, flowing south from Lake Volta into the Bight of Benin: *c.* 300 mi (483 km), including Lake Volta **2 Lake** artificial lake in EC Ghana, formed at the confluence of the **Black Volta** (300 mi; 483 km) & **White Volta** (500 mi; 805 km) rivers: 3,283 sq mi (8,503 sq km)

volt·age (vōl′tij) *n.* electromotive force, or difference in electrical potential, measured in volts and equal to the current times the resistance: symbol, E

voltage divider a device consisting of a resistor or series of resistors connected across a source of voltage and having one or more fixed or adjustable intermediate contacts: from any two terminals a desired reduced voltage may be obtained

vol·ta·ic (väl tā′ik) *adj.* ⟦after A. VOLTA[1] + -IC⟧ **1** designating or of electricity produced by chemical action; galvanic **2** used in so producing electricity

Vol·ta·ic (väl tā′ik) *n.* a branch of the Niger-Congo language subfamily, including languages spoken in Burkina Faso and parts of Mali, Ivory Coast, Ghana, and Togo

voltaic battery *Elec.* **1** a battery composed of voltaic cells **2** VOLTAIC CELL

voltaic cell *Elec.* an electrochemical cell for generating direct current from the chemical reactions taking place between its electrolyte and dissimilar metallic electrodes

voltaic pile an early type of primary cell used to generate direct current: it consisted of a stack of paired disks of dissimilar metals separated by acid-saturated cloth or paper

Vol·taire (vōl ter′, väl-; *Fr* vôl ter′), **(François Marie Arouet de)** (born *François Marie Arouet*) 1694-1778; Fr. writer and philosopher

vol·ta·ism (väl′tə iz′əm) *n.* ⟦< VOLTA(IC) + -ISM⟧ GALVANISM (sense 1)

vol·tam·e·ter (väl tam′ət ər) *n.* ⟦VOLTA(IC) + -METER⟧ *Physics* an electrolytic cell that measures the quantity of electric charge flowing through it by a resulting chemical action, as by indicating the amount of gas collected or the amount of metal deposited on an electrode —**vol′ta·met′ric** (-tə me′trik) *adj.*

volt·am·me·ter (vōlt′am′mēt′ər) *n.* a dual-purpose instrument for measuring either voltage or amperage

volt-am·pere (-am′pir′) *n. Elec.* the unit of power equal to one volt times one ampere: in a circuit with direct current it represents power equivalent to one watt: abbrev. *VA*

volte-face (vôlt′fäs′) *n.* ⟦Fr < It *volta faccia* < *volta,* a turn (see VOLT[1]) + *faccia* < VL *facia,* FACE⟧ **1** a turn so as to face the opposite way; about-face **2** a complete reversal of opinion, attitude, etc.

volt·me·ter (vōlt′mēt′ər) *n.* ⟦VOLT[2] + -METER⟧ *Elec.* an instrument for measuring voltage

Vol·tur·no (vôl to͞or′nô) river in SC Italy, flowing from the Apennines into the Tyrrhenian Sea: *c.* 110 mi (177 km)

vol·u·ble (väl′yə bəl) *adj.* ⟦Fr < L *volubilis,* easily turned about < *volutus,* pp. of *volvere,* to roll, turn about: see WALK⟧ **1** characterized by a great flow of words; talking much and easily; talkative, glib, etc. **2** [Rare] rolling easily on an axis; rotating **3** *Bot.* twining or twisting, as a vine **—SYN.** TALKATIVE **—vol′u·bil′i·ty** *n.*, **vol′u·ble·ness —vol′u·bly** *adv.*

vol·ume (väl′yo͞om, -yəm) *n.* ⟦ME < MFr < L *volumen,* a roll, scroll, hence a book written on a parchment < *volutus,* pp. of *volvere,* to roll: see WALK⟧ **1** [Historical] a roll of parchment, a scroll, etc. **2** *a)* a collection of written, typewritten, or printed sheets bound together; book *b)* any of the separate books making up a matched set or a complete work **3** a set of the issues of a periodical over a fixed period of time, usually a year **4** the amount of space occupied in three dimensions; cubic contents or cubic magnitude: abbrev. *V* **5** *a)* a quantity, bulk, mass, or amount *b)* a large quantity **6** the degree, strength, or loudness of sound **7** *Music* fullness of tone **—SYN.** BULK[1] **—speak volumes** to be very expressive or meaningful **—vol′umed** *adj.*

vo·lu·me·ter (vō lo͞o′mət ər) *n.* ⟦prec. + -METER⟧ *Physics* an instrument used to measure the volume of liquids and gases directly, and of solids by the amount of liquid they displace

vol·u·met·ric (väl′yo͞o me′trik) *adj.* ⟦< prec. + -IC⟧ of or based on the measurement of volume: also **vol′u·met′ri·cal —vol′u·met′ri·cal·ly** *adv.*

volumetric analysis the quantitative analysis of an unknown chemical solution by determining the amount of reagent of known concentration necessary to effect a reaction in a known volume of the solution

volume unit a unit equal to a decibel for expressing the magnitude of a complex audio signal, as that of speech or music, above a reference level of one milliwatt

vo·lu·mi·nous (və lo͞o′mə nəs) *adj.* ⟦LL *voluminosus,* full of rolls or folds < *volumen:* see VOLUME⟧ **1** writing, producing, consisting of, or forming enough material to fill volumes **2** of great volume; large; bulky; full **3** [Archaic] characterized by many coils or windings **—vo·lu′mi·nos′i·ty** (-näs′ə tē) *n.* **—vo·lu′mi·nous·ly** *adv.*

vol·um·iz·er (väl′yo͞om īz′ər, -yəm-) *n.* something that increases volume; specif, a product or ingredient intended to make the hair appear fuller and thicker **—vol′um·ize′** *vt., vi.* **-ized′, -iz′ing**

vol·un·ta·rism (väl′ən tər iz′em) *n.* **1** *a)* voluntary or willing participation in a course of action *b)* a doctrine or system based on such participation *c)* VOLUNTEERISM **2** *Philos.* any theory holding that will, rather than reason or intelligence, is the basic factor in human behavior or that some force analogous to will is the dominant constituent of reality **—vol′un·ta·rist** *n.* **—vol′un·ta·ris′tic** *adj.*

vol·un·tar·y (väl′ən ter′ē) *adj.* ⟦ME *voluntarie* < L *voluntarius,* voluntary < *voluntas,* free will < *volo,* I wish: see VOLITION⟧ **1** brought about by one's own free choice; given or done of one's own free will; freely chosen or undertaken **2** acting in a specified capacity willingly or of one's own accord **3** intentional; not accidental *[voluntary* manslaughter*]* **4** controlled by one's mind or will *[voluntary* muscles*]* **5** having free will or the power of free choice *[*man is a *voluntary* agent*]* **6** *a)* supported by contributions or freewill offerings; not supported or maintained by the state *[voluntary* churches*]* *b)* done or carried on by or made up of volunteers rather than by people paid or conscripted **7** arising in the mind without external constraint; spontaneous **8** *Law a)* acting or done without compulsion or persuasion *b)* done without profit, payment, or any valuable consideration *—n., pl.* **-tar′ies** *Music* a piece or solo, often an improvisation, played on the organ before, during, or after a church service **—vol·un·tar·i·ly** (väl′ən ter′ə lē) *adv.*

SYN.—voluntary implies the exercise of one's own free choice or will in an action, whether or not external influences are at work *[voluntary* services*]*; **intentional** applies to that which is done on purpose for a definite reason and is in no way accidental *[*an *intentional* slight*]*; **deliberate** implies full realization of the significance of what one intends to do and of its effects *[*a *deliberate* lie*]*; **willful** implies obstinate and perverse determination to follow one's own will despite influences, arguments, advice, etc. in opposition *[*a *willful* refusal*]*

vol·un·tar·y·ism (-iz′əm) *n.* **1** the doctrine that churches, schools, etc. should be supported by voluntary contributions and not by the state **2** a system based on this principle

vol·un·teer (väl′ən tir′) *n.* ⟦earlier *voluntier* < obs. Fr *voluntaire* < L *(miles) voluntarius,* VOLUNTARY (soldier)⟧ **1** a person who chooses freely to do or offer to do something **2** a person who chooses freely to enter naval or military service, without being compelled to do so by law: opposed to CONSCRIPT, DRAFTEE **3** *Bot.* a volunteer plant **4** *Law a)* a person who chooses freely to enter into a transaction with no promise of compensation *b)* a person to whom property is transferred without valuable consideration *—adj.* **1** composed of volunteers, as an army **2** serving as a volunteer, usually without compensation **3** of a volunteer or volunteers **4** *Bot.* growing from seed that has fallen naturally to the ground, not planted by a person *—vt.* to freely choose to offer or give without being asked or obliged *—vi.* to freely choose to enter or offer to enter into any service; enlist

vol·un·teer·ism (-iz′əm) *n.* the theory or practice of being a volunteer or of using volunteers, as, without pay, in social agencies, charitable organizations, etc.

vo·lup·té (vô lüp tā′) *n.* ⟦Fr⟧ intense pleasure that is both sensuous and spiritual; ecstasy; bliss

vo·lup·tu·ar·y (və lup′cho͞o er′ē) *n., pl.* **-ar′ies** ⟦L *voluptuarius* < *voluptas,* pleasure: see fol.⟧ a person devoted to luxurious living and sensual pleasures; sensualist; sybarite *—adj.* of or characterized by luxury and sensual pleasures

vo·lup·tu·ous (-cho͞o əs) *adj.* ⟦ME < L *voluptuosus,* full of pleasure < *voluptas,* pleasure < IE base **wel-,* to wish, choose > WILL[2]⟧ **1** full of, producing, or characterized by sensual delights and pleasures; sensual **2** fond of or directed toward luxury, elegance, and the pleasures of the senses **3** *a)* suggesting or expressing sensual pleasure or gratification *b)* sexually attractive because of a full, shapely figure **4** arising from sensual gratification **—SYN.** SENSUOUS **—vo·lup′tu·ous·ly** *adv.* **—vo·lup′tu·ous·ness** *n.*

vo·lute (və lo͞ot′) *n.* ⟦L *voluta,* orig., fem. of *volutus,* pp. of *volvere,* to roll: see WALK⟧ **1** a spiral or twisting form; turn; whorl **2** *Archit.* a spiral scroll forming one of the chief features of Ionic and Corinthian capitals **3** *Zool. a)* any of the turns or whorls of a spiral shell *b)* any of a family (Volutidae) of saltwater gastropods often having brightly colored shells with an elongated opening *—adj.* **1** rolled up; spiraled **2** having a spirally shaped part **—vo·lut′ed** *adj.*

vo·lu·tion (və lo͞o′shən) *n.* ⟦< L *volutus:* see prec.⟧ **1** a revolving or rolling **2** a spiral turn or twist; coil; convolution **3** a whorl of a spiral shell or structure

vol·va (väl′və) *n.* ⟦ModL < L, var. of *vulva:* see VULVA⟧ the membranous covering enclosing certain mushrooms in the early stage of growth, becoming a cup at the base of the stalk at maturity **—vol′vate′** (-vāt′, -vit) *adj.*

vol·vox (väl′väks′) *n.* ⟦ModL < L *volvere,* to roll (see WALK) + *-ox* (as in *atrox,* fierce)⟧ any of a genus (*Volvox,* family Volvocaceae) of multicellular, free-swimming, flagellated green algae whose cells form a pale-green globular colony that rolls about in the water

vol·vu·lus (väl′vyo͞o ləs) *n.* ⟦ModL < L *volvere,* to roll: see WALK⟧ a twisting or displacement of the intestines resulting in intestinal obstruction

vo·mer (vō′mər) *n.* ⟦ModL < L, plowshare; akin to *vomis:* see WEDGE⟧ *Anat.* the thin, flat cranial bone forming the lower and posterior part of the septum that separates the nasal passages **—vo·mer·ine** (vō′mər in, väm′-) *adj.*

vom·er·o·na·sal organ (väm′ər ō nā′zəl) ⟦prec. + -O- + NASAL⟧ either of a pair of olfactory sense organs typically in the nasal cavity or mouth of reptiles, amphibians, and some mammals

vom·it (väm′it) *n.* ⟦ME < L *vomitus,* a discharging, vomiting < pp. of *vomere,* to discharge, vomit < IE base **wemē-* > Gr *emein,* to vomit, OE *wamm,* stain, disgrace⟧ **1** the act or process of ejecting the contents of the stomach through the mouth **2** matter ejected in this way **3** [Archaic] EMETIC *—vi.* **1** to eject the contents of the stomach through the mouth; throw up **2** to be thrown up or out with force or violence; rush out *—vt.* **1** to throw up (food) **2** to discharge or throw out with force or in copious quantities; belch forth **—vom′it·er** *n.*

vom·i·tive (väm′ə tiv) *adj.* of or causing vomiting; emetic

vom·i·to·ry (väm′ə tôr′ē) *adj.* ⟦L *vomitorius*⟧ [Archaic] vomitive; emetic *—n., pl.* **-ries 1** *former term for* EMETIC **2** any opening, funnel, etc. through which matter is to be discharged **3** ⟦LL *vomitorium:* the spectators were discharged through these⟧ in Roman amphitheaters, etc., any of the entrances leading to the tiers of seats

☆**vom·i·tous** (väm′it əs) *adj.* of, like, or causing vomiting; esp., disgusting, nauseating, etc.

vom·i·tu·ri·tion (väm′i tyo͞o rish′ən) *n.* **1** repeated but unsuccessful attempts to vomit; retching **2** vomiting that brings up but little matter

vom·i·tus (väm′it əs) *n.* ⟦L: see VOMIT⟧ matter that has been vomited

von (vän; *Ger* fôn) *prep.* ⟦Ger⟧ of or from: in German, Austrian, etc. family names, *von* precedes a place name and together they indicate traditional place of origin: also **Von**

von Braun (vän broun′, -brôn′), **Wern·her** (vur′nər, wur′-) 1912-77; U.S. rocket engineer, born in Germany

Von·ne·gut (vän′ə gət), **Kurt, Jr.** 1922-2007; U.S. writer

Von Neu·mann (vän noi′mən, -män), **John** 1903-57; U.S. mathematician, born in Hungary

☆**voo·doo** (vo͞o′do͞o′) *n., pl.* **-doos′** ⟦Creole Fr, of WAfr orig., as in Ewe (Benin and Togo) *vodu,* fetish, demon⟧ **1** a religion of the West Indies, esp. Haiti, based on beliefs and practices of African and Roman Catholic origin, and noted for its interest in sorcery, charms, and fetishes **2** a person who practices voodoo **3** a voodoo charm, fetish, curse, etc. *—adj.* **1** of voodoos or voodooism **2** [Informal] claimed or reputed to provide an ingenious or seemingly magical solution to a problem, but in reality of little value, effectiveness, etc. *[voodoo* economics, *voodoo* diet plans*]* *—vt.* to affect by voodoo magic

☆**voo·doo·ism** (-iz′əm) *n.* the system of voodoo beliefs and practices **—voo′doo·ist** *n.* **—voo′doo·is′tic** *adj.*

VOR (vē′ō′är′) *n.* ⟦< *v(isual)* [or *V(HF)*] *o(mni)r(ange)*⟧ OMNIRANGE

vo·ra·cious (vô rā′shəs, və-) *adj.* ⟦L *vorax* (gen. *voracis*), greedy to devour < *vorare,* to devour < IE base **gwer-,* to devour, GORGE > Gr *bora,* food (of carnivorous beasts), L *gurges,* gorge⟧ **1** greedy in eating; devouring or eager to devour large quantities of food; ravenous; gluttonous **2** very greedy or eager in some desire or pursuit; insatiable *[*a *voracious* reader*]* **—vo·ra′cious·ly** *adv.* **—vo·rac′i·ty** (-ras′ə tē) *n.*, **vo·ra′cious·ness**

Vo·ro·nezh (vô rô′nesh) city in SW European Russia, near the Don River

Vo·ro·shi·lov·grad (vô′rô shē′lôf grät′) *name* (1935-58; 1970-89) *for* LUGANSK

-vo·rous (vər əs) ⟦L *-vorus* < *vorare:* see VORACIOUS⟧ *combining form forming adjectives* feeding on, eating *[omnivorous]*

vor·tex (vôr′teks′) *n., pl.* **-tex′es** or **-ti·ces′** (-tə sēz′) ⟦L *vortex,* var. of *vertex:* see VERTEX⟧ **1** a whirling mass of water forming a vacuum at its center, into which anything caught in the motion is drawn; whirlpool **2** a whirl or powerful eddy of air; whirlwind **3** any activity, situation, or state of affairs that resembles a whirl or eddy in its rush, absorbing effect, catastrophic power, etc.

vor·ti·cal (vôrt′i kəl) ***adj.*** **1** of, characteristic of, or like a vortex **2** moving in a vortex; whirling —**vor′ti·cal·ly** ***adv.***

vor·ti·cel·la (vôrt′ə sel′ə) ***n.,*** *pl.* **-cel′lae** (-ē) ⟦ModL, dim. < L *vortex:* see VORTEX⟧ any of a genus (*Vorticella*) of one-celled ciliates living in water, with a bell-shaped body on a thin, contractile stem serving as a holdfast

vor·ti·cism (vôrt′ə siz′əm) ***n.*** [*often* **V-**] a movement in English art at the beginning of WWI, involving Wyndham Lewis, Jacob Epstein, and others, and influenced by cubism and futurism —**vor′ti·cist** (-sist) ***n., adj.***

Vor·tum·nus (vôr tum′nəs) ***n.*** *var. of* VERTUMNUS

Vosges (Mountains) (vōzh) mountain range in NE France, west of the Rhine: highest peak, *c.* 4,700 ft (1,433 m)

vot·a·ble (vōt′ə bəl) ***adj.*** that can be submitted to a vote; subject to a vote: also sp. **vote′a·ble**

vo·ta·ress (vōt′ə ris) ***n.*** a female votary: see -ESS

vo·ta·ry (vōt′ə rē) ***n.,*** *pl.* **-ries** ⟦< L *votus,* pp. of *vovere,* to vow (see fol.) + -ARY⟧ **1** a person bound by a vow or promise, esp. one bound to religious vows, as a monk or nun **2** a person devoted to a particular religion or object of worship; devout worshiper **3** a devoted or ardent supporter, as of a cause, ideal, etc. **4** a person who is devoted to any game, study, pursuit, etc. Also **vo′ta·rist** —***adj.*** **1** consecrated by a vow **2** of, or having the nature of, a vow

vote (vōt) ***n.*** ⟦LME (Scot) < L *votum,* a wish, vow < neut. of *votus,* pp. of *vovere,* to vow < IE base **ewegwh-,* to speak solemnly, vow > Sans *vāghát,* one who vows, Gr *euche,* a vow, prayer⟧ **1** *a)* a decision by a group on a proposal, resolution, bill, etc., or a choice between candidates for office, expressed by written ballot, voice, show of hands, etc. *b)* the decision of any individual in the group **2** *a)* the expression or indication of such a decision or choice *b)* the ticket, ballot, voice, or other means by which it is expressed **3** the right to exercise such a decision or choice, as in a meeting, election, etc.; suffrage **4** *a)* the total number of ballots cast [a light *vote*] *b)* votes collectively [to get out the *vote*] *c)* a specified group of voters, or their votes, collectively [the farm *vote*] —***vi.*** **vot′ed, vot′ing** **1** to express the will or a preference in a matter by ballot, voice, etc.; give or cast a vote **2** to declare a preference, wish, opinion, etc. [the departing spectators *voted* with their feet] —***vt.*** **1** *a)* to decide, choose, enact, or authorize by vote *b)* to grant or confer by vote *c)* to support (a specified party ticket) in voting **2** to declare by general opinion [*voted* the picnic a success] **3** [Informal] to suggest [I *vote* we leave now] —**vote down** to defeat by voting; decide against —**vote in** to elect —**vote out** to defeat (an incumbent) in an election —**vote′less** ***adj.***

vote of confidence a public expression of support, specif. as by a legislative body for a public official

vot·er (vōt′ər) ***n.*** a person who has a right to vote; elector, esp. one who actually votes

☆**voting machine** a machine on which votes in an election are cast, registered, and counted

vo·tive (vōt′iv) ***adj.*** ⟦L *votivus* < *votum:* see VOTE⟧ designed to accomplish or fulfill a special intention, promise, etc., or to express thanks or devotion [a *votive* offering]

votive candle a candle used as a vigil light

votive Mass a Mass differing from the Mass or Divine Office prescribed by the liturgy for a certain day and offered for some special private or public intention

vouch (vouch) ***vt.*** ⟦ME *vouchen* < OFr *vocher* < L *vocare,* to call < *vox,* VOICE⟧ **1** to uphold by demonstration or evidence **2** [Archaic] *a)* to attest or affirm *b)* to cite in support of one's views or actions **3** in old English law, to call (a person) into court to give warranty of title —***vi.*** **1** to give assurance, affirmation, or a guarantee: with *for* [to *vouch* for someone's honesty] **2** to serve as evidence or assurance (*for*) [references *vouching* for his ability] —***n.*** [Obs.] the act of vouching; assertion or attestation

vouch·er (vou′chər) ***n.*** ⟦substantive use of Anglo-Fr *voucher,* to prec.⟧ **1** a person who vouches, as for the truth of a statement **2** a paper serving as evidence or proof; specif., a receipt or statement attesting to the expenditure or receipt of money, the accuracy of an account, etc. ☆**3** a document granting a family a certain sum per child, from public education funds, for use as partial tuition to a private or parochial school

vouch·safe (vouch sāf′) ***vt.*** **-safed′, -saf′ing** ⟦contr. of ME *vouchen safe,* to vouch as safe⟧ to be gracious enough or condescend to give or grant [to *vouchsafe* a reply] —**vouch·safe′ment** ***n.***

vou·don or **vo·doun** (vō do͞on′) ***n.*** *var. of* VOODOO (***n.*** 1)

vou·lu (vo͞o lü′) ***adj.*** ⟦Fr, pp. of *vouloir,* to want, wish⟧ contrived or forced: said as of certain effects in a literary or artistic work

vous·soir (vo͞o swär′) ***n.*** ⟦Fr < OFr *volsoir,* curvature of a vault < VL **volsorium* < **volsus,* for L *volutus,* pp. of *volvere,* to roll: see WALK⟧ *Archit.* any of the wedge-shaped stones, or other parts, of which an arch is built: the central, topmost voussoir is called the *keystone*; either of the lowest voussoirs is called the *springer*

Vou·vray (vo͞o vrā′) ***n.*** ⟦after *Vouvray,* village in WC France⟧ [*also* **v-**] a French white wine of Touraine, sometimes sparkling, and tasting dry to moderately sweet

vow (vou) ***n.*** ⟦ME *vou* < OFr < L *votum:* see VOTE⟧ **1** a solemn promise or pledge, esp. one made to God or a god, dedicating oneself to an act, service, or way of life **2** a solemn promise of love and fidelity [marriage *vows*] **3** a solemn affirmation or assertion —***vt.*** **1** to promise solemnly **2** to make a solemn resolution to do, get, etc. **3** to declare emphatically, earnestly, or solemnly —***vi.*** to make a vow —**take vows** to make the vows required for formal entrance into a religious order or community —**vow′er** ***n.***

vow·el (vou′əl) ***n.*** ⟦ME *vowelle* < MFr *vouel* < L *vocalis (littera),* vocal (letter), vowel < *vox,* VOICE⟧ **1** any voiced speech sound characterized by generalized friction of the air passing in a continuous stream through the pharynx and opened mouth but with no constriction narrow enough to produce local friction; the sound of the greatest prominence in most syllables **2** a letter (as *a, e, i, o, u,* and sometimes *y*) or a character or a symbol representing such a sound Cf. CONSONANT —***adj.*** of a vowel or vowels

vow·el·ize (vou′əl īz′) ***vt.*** **-ized′, -iz′ing** to add vowel points to [to *vowelize* a text] —**vow′el·i·za′tion** ***n.***

vowel point in certain languages whose written form normally consists only of consonants, as Hebrew, a diacritical mark accompanying a consonant (to indicate the following vowel sound) or a neutral letter (to indicate esp. an initial vowel sound)

vox (väks, vōks) ***n.,*** *pl.* **vo·ces** (vō′sēz′) ⟦L⟧ voice

vox po·pu·li (pä′pyo͞o lī′) ⟦L⟧ the voice of the people; public opinion or sentiment: abbrev. **vox pop.**

voy·age (voi′ij) ***n.*** ⟦ME *viage* < OFr *veiage,* voyage < LL *viaticum,* a journey < L, traveling money, provision for a journey < *viaticus,* of a journey < *via,* way, journey: see VIA⟧ **1** a relatively long journey or passage by water or, formerly, by land **2** a journey by aircraft or, now especially, by spacecraft **3** a written account of a voyage —***vi.*** **-aged, -ag·ing** to make a voyage; travel —***vt.*** [Archaic] to sail or travel over or on —***SYN.*** TRIP —**voy′ag·er** ***n.***

vo·ya·geur (vwå yå zhër′) ***n.,*** *pl.* **-geurs′** (-zhër′) ⟦Fr, traveler⟧ [Historical] in Canada, *a)* a person who transported goods and passengers by boat to trading posts for the fur companies *b)* any woodsman or boatman of the Canadian wilds

voy·eur (voi ʉr′, vwä yʉr′) ***n.*** ⟦Fr < *voir,* to see < L *videre:* see VISION⟧ **1** a person who has an exaggerated interest in viewing, esp. furtively and habitually, persons who are disrobing, engaged in sexual activity, etc.; peeping Tom **2** a person who obsessively watches others, esp. in seeking the unsavory details of their lives —**voy·eur·ism** (voi′ər iz′əm, voi ʉr′iz′əm) ***n.*** —**voy′eur·is′tic** ***adj.***

VP *abbrev.* Vice-President

VR *abbrev.* VIRTUAL REALITY

V.R. *abbrev.* ⟦L *Victoria Regina*⟧ Queen Victoria

V Rev *abbrev.* Very Reverend

vroom (vro͞om) ***n.*** [echoic] the sound made by a motor vehicle in accelerating —***vi.*** [Informal] to make, or move off with, this sound

VS or **V.S.** *abbrev.* Veterinary Surgeon

vs. or **vs** *abbrev.* versus

v.s. *abbrev.* ⟦L *vide supra*⟧ see above

V sign ⟦< V(ICTORY)⟧ a gesture made by raising the hand with the middle and index fingers separated to form a V, showing a wish for victory or success or expressing approval

V-6 (vē′siks′) ***adj.*** ⟦because the cylinders are arranged in a V-shape of two rows of three⟧ designating or of an engine similar to a V-8 but with only six cylinders —***n.*** **1** a V-6 engine **2** an automotive vehicle with a V-6 engine

V.S.O. *abbrev.* very superior (or special) old: of brandy

V.S.O.P. *abbrev.* very superior (or special) old pale: of brandy

☆**V/STOL** (vē′stôl′) ***n.*** ⟦*v(ertical or) s(hort) t(ake)o(ff and) l(anding)*⟧ an aircraft that can take off and land either vertically or on a short airstrip

vt *abbrev.* transitive verb

VT *abbrev.* **1** variable time **2** Vermont: also **Vt**

☆**VTOL** (vē′tôl′) ***n.*** ⟦*v(ertical) t(ake)o(ff and) l(anding)*⟧ an aircraft, usually other than a helicopter, that can take off and land vertically

VTR *abbrev.* videotape recorder

VU or **vu** *abbrev.* volume unit

vug, vugh, or **vugg** (vug, vo͝og) ***n.*** ⟦Cornish *vooga,* a cave⟧ *Mining* a cavity or hollow in a rock or lode, often lined with crystals —**vug′gy** ***adj.*** **-gi·er, -gi·est**

Vuil·lard (vüē yår′), **(Jean) É·douard** (ā dwår′) 1868-1940; Fr. painter

Vul·can (vul′kən) ***n.*** ⟦L *Vulcanus, Volcanus*⟧ *Rom. Myth.* the god of fire and of metalworking: later identified with the Greek Hephaestus

Vul·ca·ni·an (vul kā′nē ən) ***adj.*** ⟦L *Vulcanius,* of Vulcan⟧ **1** of, characteristic of, or associated with Vulcan **2** [**v-**] having to do with metalworking **3** [*sometimes* **v-**] *Geol. a)* VOLCANIC *b)* of or pertaining to a volcanic explosion emitting a large cloud of gases bearing fine ash and a mass of viscous lava that hardens in the air

vul·can·ism (vul′kə niz′əm) ***n.*** [Archaic] VOLCANISM

vul·can·i·za·tion (vul′kə ni zā′shən) ***n.*** ⟦< fol. + -ATION⟧ **1** the process of treating crude rubber with sulfur or its compounds and subjecting it to heat in order to make it nonplastic and increase its strength and elasticity **2** a process somewhat like this, for hardening some other substance

vul·can·ize (vul′kə nīz′) ***vt.*** **-ized′, -iz′ing** ⟦VULCAN + -IZE⟧ to subject to vulcanization —***vi.*** to undergo vulcanization —**vul′can·iz′er** ***n.***

vul·can·ol·o·gy (vul′kə näl′ə jē) ***n.*** [Archaic] VOLCANOLOGY

Vulg *abbrev.* Vulgate

vul·gar (vul′gər) ***adj.*** ⟦ME < L *vularis* < *vulgus, volgus,* the common people < IE base **wel-,* to crowd, throng > Gr *eilein,* to press, swarm⟧ **1** of, characteristic of, belonging to, or common to the great mass of people in general; common; popular [a *vulgar* superstition] **2** designating, of, or in the popular, or vernacular, speech **3** *a)* characterized by a lack of culture, refinement, taste, restraint, sensitivity, etc.; coarse; crude; boorish *b)* indecent or obscene —SYN. COARSE, COMMON —**vul′gar·ly** ***adv.***

vulgar fraction COMMON FRACTION

vul·gar·i·an (vul gerʹē ən, -garʹ-) ***n.*** a vulgar person; esp., a rich person with coarse, ostentatious manners or tastes

vul·gar·ism (vulʹgər izʹəm) ***n.*** **1** a word, phrase, or expression that is used widely but is regarded as nonstandard, unrefined, coarse, or obscene **2** vulgar behavior, quality, etc.; vulgarity

vul·gar·i·ty (vul gerʹə tē, -garʹ-) ***n.*** ⟦LL *vulgaritas*⟧ **1** the state or quality of being vulgar, crude, coarse, unrefined, etc. **2** *pl.* **-ties** a vulgar act, habit, usage in speech, etc.

vul·gar·i·za·tion (vulʹgər i zāʹshən) ***n.*** **1** the act or an instance of making something, as abstruse or highly technical information, more readily intelligible or widely known **2** the act or an instance of making vulgar, coarse, unrefined, obscene, etc.

vul·gar·ize (vulʹgər īzʹ) ***vt.*** **-ized′**, **-iz′ing** **1** to cause to be more widely known, more easily understood, etc.; popularize **2** to make vulgar, coarse, unrefined, obscene, etc. —**vul′gar·iz′er** ***n.***

Vulgar Latin the everyday speech of the Roman people, from which the Romance languages developed; popular Latin as distinguished from standard or literary Latin

Vul·gate (vulʹgātʹ, -git) ***n.*** ⟦ML *vulgata (editio)*, popular (edition) < L *vulgatus*, common, usual, orig. pp. of *vulgare*, to make common < *vulgus*: see VULGAR⟧ **1** a Latin version of the Bible prepared by St. Jerome in the 4th cent., authorized as the official biblical text of the Roman Catholic Church **2** [**v-**] the vernacular, or common speech —***adj.*** **1** of or in the Vulgate **2** [**v-**] commonly accepted; popular; specif., of or in the vernacular, or common speech

vul·ner·a·ble (vulʹnər ə bəl) ***adj.*** ⟦LL *vulnerabilis*, wounding, likely to injure (also, in pass. sense, "vulnerable") < L *vulnerare*, to wound < *vulnus* (gen. *vulneris*), a wound < IE base **wel-* > L *vellere*: see REVULSION⟧ **1** that can be wounded or physically injured **2** *a)* open to criticism or attack *[*a *vulnerable* reputation*]* *b)* easily hurt, as by adverse criticism; sensitive *c)* affected by a specified influence, temptation, etc. *[vulnerable* to political pressure*]* **3** open to attack by armed forces: often used fig. **4** *Bridge* designating a team that has won one game in an ongoing rubber and hence is liable to increased penalties —**vul′ner·a·bil′i·ty** ***n.***, *pl.* **-ties** —**vul′ner·a·bly** ***adv.***

vul·ner·ar·y (vulʹnər erʹē) ***adj.*** ⟦L *vulnerarius* < *vulnus*, a wound: see prec.⟧ used for healing wounds —***n.***, *pl.* **-ar′ies** any vulnerary drug, plant, etc.

Vul·pec·u·la (vul pekʹyo͞o lə) ***n.*** ⟦L, little fox: dim. of *vulpes*, fox⟧ a N constellation in the Milky Way between Delphinus and Cygnus

vul·pine (vulʹpīn, -pin) ***adj.*** ⟦L *vulpinus*, foxlike < *vulpes*, a fox⟧ **1** of or like a fox or foxes **2** clever, cunning, etc.

vul·ture (vulʹchər) ***n.*** ⟦ME *vultur* < L, akin to *vellere*, to tear: see VULNERABLE⟧ **1** any of a number of large birds of prey with a naked, usually brightly colored head and dark plumage, including the **Old World vultures** (family Accipitridae) and the **New World vultures** (family Cathartidae); esp., the New World turkey vulture: they feed chiefly or entirely on carrion and are found in tropical and temperate regions **2** any greedy and ruthless person who preys on others

turkey vulture

vul·tur·ine (-chər īnʹ, -in) ***adj.*** ⟦L *vulturinus* < *vultur*: see prec.⟧ of, characteristic of, or like a vulture or vultures; voracious

vul·tur·ous (-əs) ***adj.*** like a vulture; voracious; greedy

vul·va (vulʹvə) ***n.***, *pl.* **-vae** (-vē) or **-vas** ⟦ModL < L *vulva, volva*, wrapper, covering, womb < *volvere*, to roll or turn about: see WALK⟧ the external genital organs of a female mammal, including the labia majora, labia minora, clitoris, and the entrance to the vagina —**vul′val** ***adj.***, **vul′var** —**vul′vate** (-vāt, -vit) ***adj.***

vul·vi·form (-və fôrmʹ) ***adj.*** like a vulva in form

vul·vi·tis (vul vītʹis) ***n.*** inflammation of the vulva

vul·vo- (vulʹvō, -və) ⟦< L *vulva*⟧ *combining form* **1** vulva **2** vulva and *[vulvovaginitis]* Also, before a vowel, **vulv-**

vul·vo·vag·i·ni·tis (vulʹvō vajʹə nītʹis) ***n.*** ⟦< prec. + VAGINITIS⟧ inflammation of the vulva and the vagina

vv *abbrev.* **1** verses **2** vice versa: also **v.v.** **3** violins

☆**VX (gas)** (vēʹeksʹ) ⟦U.S. Army code name⟧ a highly lethal nerve gas, $C_{11}H_{26}NO_2PS$, absorbed through the skin and lungs

Vy·borg (vēʹbôrg) seaport in NW European Russia, on the Gulf of Finland

☆**Vy·cor** (vīʹkôr) ⟦arbitrary coinage⟧ *trademark for* a heat-resistant glassware with a high percentage of silica, used mainly for laboratory and industrial beakers, crucibles, tubes, etc.

vy·ing (vīʹiŋ) ***adj.*** ⟦prp. of VIE⟧ that vies; that competes

w[1] or W (dub′əl yo͞o′) *n., pl.* **w's, W's** **1** the twenty-third letter of the English alphabet: its sound was represented in Anglo-Saxon manuscripts by *uu* or *u* until about A.D. 900, then by ƿ (*wen*) borrowed from the runic alphabet; in the 11th cent. a ligatured *VV* or *vv* was introduced by Norman scribes to replace the *wen* **2** any of the speech sounds that this letter represents, as, in English, the (w) of *will* **3** a type or impression for *w* or *W* **4** the twenty-third in a sequence or group **5** an object shaped like W —*adj.* **1** of *w* or *W* **2** twenty-third in a sequence or group **3** shaped like W

w[2] *abbrev.* **1** waist **2** watt(s) **3** week(s) **4** weight **5** west **6** western **7** wide **8** width **9** wife **10** win(s) **11** with: also **w., w/** **12** *Physics* work

W[1] *abbrev.* **1** Wales **2** Washington **3** watt(s) **4** Wednesday **5** Welsh **6** West **7** west **8** western **9** wide **10** win(s) **11** *Physics* work

W[2] ⟦W(OLFRAM)⟧ *Chem. symbol for* tungsten

WA *abbrev.* **1** Washington: also **Wa** **2** Western Australia

Waadt (vät) *Ger. name for* VAUD

Waal (väl) the more southerly of two arms of the Rhine, flowing west through the Netherlands & joining the Meuse in the Rhine delta on the North Sea: *c.* 50 mi (80 km)

Wa·bash (wô′bash′) ⟦Fr *Ouabache,* altered < Illinois *ouabouskigou,* of unknown meaning⟧ river flowing from W Ohio across Ind. into the Ohio River: 475 mi (764 km)

wab·ble (wä′bəl) *n., vt., vi.* **-bled, -bling** *alt. sp. of* WOBBLE

WAC *abbrev.* [Historical] Women's Army Corps

Wace (wäs, wäs) fl. 12th cent.; Anglo-Norman poet & chronicler: also, prob. erroneously, called **Robert Wace**

☆**wacked-out** (wakt′out′) *adj.* [Slang] *var. of* WHACKED-OUT

☆**wack·o** (wak′ō) [Slang] *adj.* ⟦see -O⟧ **1** *var. of* WACKY **2** completely crazy; insane —*n., pl.* **-os** a person who is wacko

wack·y (wak′ē) *adj.* **wack′i·er, wack′i·est** ⟦< ? WHACK + -Y[2]: cf. SLAP-HAPPY⟧ ☆[Slang] erratic, eccentric, or irrational; zany —**wack′i·ly** *adv.* —**wack′i·ness** *n.*

Wa·co (wā′kō) ⟦Sp *Hueco* < Wichita (a Caddoan language) *we˙koh,* name of a tribe later absorbed into the Wichita people⟧ city in EC Tex., on the Brazos River

wad[1] (wäd) *n.* ⟦ML *wadda,* wadding < ?⟧ **1** a small, soft mass or ball, as a handful of cotton, crumpled paper, etc. **2** a lump or small, compact mass (*of* something) [*a wad* of chewing tobacco] **3** a mass of soft or fibrous material used for padding, packing, stuffing, etc. **4** a plug of hemp, tow, paper, etc. stuffed against a charge to keep it firmly in the breech of a muzzleloading gun or in a cartridge ☆**5** [Informal] a roll of paper money ☆**6** [Slang] a large amount, esp. of money —*vt.* **wad′ded, wad′ding** **1** to compress into a wad ☆**2** to roll up (paper, etc.) into a wad **3** *a)* to plug with a wad *b)* to force or stuff [to *wad* oakum into a crack] **4** to line or pad with or as with wadding **5** to hold (a charge) in place by a wad —**wad′der** *n.*

wad[2] (wäd) *v.aux. Scot. var. of* WOULD

Wad·den·zee or **Wad·den Zee** (väd′ən zā′) shallow section of the North Sea, in the Netherlands, between the West Frisian Islands & the IJsselmeer

wad·ding (wäd′iŋ) *n.* **1** any soft or fibrous material for use in padding, packing, stuffing, etc.; esp., cotton made up into loose, fluffy sheets, or batting **2** any soft material for making wads, as for guns or cartridges **3** a wad, or wads collectively

wad·dle (wäd′əl) *vi.* **-dled, -dling** ⟦freq. of WADE⟧ **1** to walk with short steps, swaying from side to side, as a duck does **2** to move clumsily with a motion like this; toddle —*n.* the act of waddling or a waddling gait —**wad′dler** *n.*

☆**wad·dy**[1] (wäd′ē) *n., pl.* **-dies** ⟦< the native name⟧ in Australia, a short, thick club used by Aborigines as a weapon —*vt.* **-died, -dy·ing** to strike or beat with a waddy

☆**wad·dy**[2] (wäd′ē) *n., pl.* **-dies** ⟦< ?⟧ [West] a cowboy

wade (wād) *vi.* **wad′ed, wad′ing** ⟦ME *waden* < OE, to go, akin to Ger *waten,* to wade < IE base **wādh-,* to go, stride forward > L *vadere,* to go, *vadare,* to wade⟧ **1** to walk through any substance, as water, mud, snow, sand, tall grass, etc., that offers resistance **2** to walk about in shallow water, as for amusement **3** to go forward with effort or difficulty [to *wade* through a long report] ☆**4** [Informal] to move energetically into action; attack with vigor: with *in* or *into* **5** [Obs.] to go; proceed; pass —*vt.* to go across or through by wading [to *wade* a brook] —*n.* an act of wading

Wade-Giles (system) (wād′jīlz′) ⟦after its creators, Thomas F. *Wade* (1818-95), Brit diplomat, and Herbert A. *Giles* (1845-1935), Brit linguist⟧ a system for transliterating Chinese ideograms into the Latin alphabet, in wide use esp. before Pinyin was adopted by the People's Republic of China in 1979

wad·er (wā′dər) *n.* **1** a person or thing that wades **2** any bird that wades in marshes, lakes, etc. **3** *a)* [*pl.*] high waterproof boots ☆*b)* [*usually pl.*] waterproof overalls with bootlike parts for the feet, worn as by fishermen for wading in deep water

wa·di (wä′dē) *n., pl.* **-dis** or **-dies** ⟦Ar *wādī,* channel of a river, a river, ravine, valley⟧ in Arabia, N Africa, etc., *a)* a valley, ravine, or watercourse that is dry except during the rainy season *b)* the stream or rush of water that flows through it Also sp. **wa′dy,** *pl.* **-dies**

wading bird any of various long-legged birds that wade the shallows and marshes for food; esp., any of an order (Ciconiiformes) including the herons, storks, and ibises

☆**wading pool** a shallow pool of water, esp. a small, portable unit in which small children can wade and play

☆**Waf** (waf) *n.* a member of the WAF

WAF *abbrev.* Women in the Air Force

wa·fer (wā′fər) *n.* ⟦ME *wafre* < NormFr *waufre* < MDu *wafel,* wafer, WAFFLE[1]⟧ **1** *a)* a thin, flat, crisp cracker or cookie *b)* anything resembling this, as a thin, flat disk of candy **2** a piece of Eucharistic bread, specif., a thin, flat, white, typically round and unleavened piece of such bread, made from wheat **3** a small adhesive disk, as of paper, dried paste, gelatin, etc., used as a seal on letters, documents, etc. **4** *Comput.* a thin slice of a semiconductor on which integrated circuits are etched or mounted, as to form a chip —*vt.* to seal, close, attach, or fasten with a wafer or wafers

waff[1] (waf, wäf) *n.* ⟦var. of WAVE⟧ [Scot. or North Eng.] **1** a wave, or waving motion, as in signaling **2** a puff or gust, as of air **3** a glimpse **4** a ghost

waff[2] (waf, wäf) *adj.* ⟦var. of WAIF⟧ [Scot.] worthless

☆**waf·fle**[1] (wä′fəl) *n.* ⟦Du *wafel,* akin to OHG *waba,* honeycomb, OE *wefan,* to WEAVE⟧ a batter cake like a pancake but crisper, baked in a waffle iron, which gives it a gridlike surface —*adj.* having a surface like that of a waffle: also **waf′fled**

waf·fle[2] (wä′fəl) *vi.* **-fled, -fling** ⟦orig., to yelp < echoic *waff,* to yelp⟧ to speak or write in a wordy, vague, or indecisive manner —*n.* [Chiefly Brit.] wordy, vague, or indecisive talk or writing

☆**waffle iron** ⟦transl. of Du *wafelijzer*⟧ a metal utensil for making waffles, having two plates with a pattern of shallow and raised areas, that are heated and pressed together to cook the batter between them; also, an electric appliance like this

waft (wäft, waft) *vt.* ⟦back-form. < obs. *wafter,* convoy < LME *waughter* < Du *wachter,* lit., a watcher < *wachten,* to watch: for IE base see WAKE[1]⟧ **1** *a)* to carry or propel (objects, sounds, odors, etc.) lightly through the air or over water *b)* to transport as if in this manner **2** ⟦altered < WAFF[1]⟧ [Obs.] to beckon or signal to, as by a wave of the hand —*vi.* **1** to float, as on the wind **2** to blow gently: said of breezes —*n.* **1** the act or fact of floating or being carried lightly along **2** an odor, sound, etc. carried through the air **3** a breath or gust of wind **4** a wave, waving, or wafting movement

waft·age (wäf′tij) *n.* [Archaic] a wafting or being wafted; conveyance

waft·er (wäf′tər) *n.* a person or thing that wafts; esp., a blower fan

waf·ture (wäf′chər, waf′-) *n.* the act of waving or wafting

wag[1] (wag) *vt.* **wagged, wag′ging** ⟦ME *waggen,* prob. < ON *vaga,* to move back and forth, rock, akin to OE *wagian,* to shake, totter < IE base **weǧh-,* to move > L *vehere,* to carry⟧ **1** *a)* to cause (something fastened or held at one end) to move rapidly and repeatedly back and forth, from side to side, or up and down [the dog *wagged* his tail] *b)* to shake (a finger) or nod (the head), as in summoning or reproving **2** to move (the tongue) in talking, esp. in idle or malicious gossip —*vi.* **1** to move rapidly and repeatedly back and forth, from side to side, or up and down: said as of a part of the body **2** to keep moving in talk, esp. in idle or malicious gossip: said of the tongue **3** to walk or move with a swaying motion; waddle —*n.* the act or an instance of wagging —**wag′ger** *n.*

wag[2] (wag) *n.* ⟦prob. short for obs. *waghalter,* a gallows bird, applied to a joker, rogue (< ? prec. + HALTER[1])⟧ a comical or humorous person; joker; wit

wage (wāj) *vt.* **waged, wag′ing** ⟦ME *wagen* < NormFr *wagier* (OFr *gagier*) < *wage* (OFr *gage*), a stake, pledge < Frank **wadi,* akin to Goth *wadi,* a pledge: for IE base see WED⟧ **1** to engage in or carry on (a war, struggle, campaign, etc.) **2** [Dial., Chiefly Brit.] to hire —*n.* **1** [*often pl.*] money paid to an employee for work done, and usually figured on an hourly, daily, or piecework basis **2** [*usually pl.*] what is given in return; recompense; requital: formerly the plural form was often construed as singular ["The *wages* of sin is death"] **3** [*pl.*] *Econ.* the share of the total product of industry that goes to labor, as distinguished from the share taken by capital

SYN.—wage (also often **wages**) applies to money paid an employee at relatively short intervals, often daily, or weekly, esp. for manual or physical labor; **salary** applies to fixed compensation usually paid at longer intervals, often monthly or semimonthly, esp. to clerical or professional workers; **stipend** is a somewhat lofty substitute for **salary**, or it is applied to a pension or similar fixed payment; **fee** applies to the payment requested or given for professional services, as of a doctor, lawyer, artist, etc.; **pay** is a general term equivalent to any of the preceding, but it is specifically used of compensation to members of the armed forces; **emolument** is an elevated, now somewhat jocular, substitute for **salary** or **wages**

wage earner a person who works for wages

wa·ger (wā′jər) *n.* ⟦ME < NormFr *wageure* < *wagier*: see WAGE⟧ **1** BET[1] (*n.* 1 & 2) **2** [Archaic] a pledge to do something or abide by an outcome: esp. in **wager of battle**, a challenge by a defendant to prove his innocence by personal combat — *vt., vi.* BET[1] —**wa′ger·er** *n.*

☆**wage scale 1** a schedule of wages paid for the performance of related jobs or tasks in a given industry, plant, locality, etc. **2** the schedule of wages paid by a given employer

☆**wage·work·er** (wāj′wur′kər) *n.* WAGE EARNER

wag·ger·y (wag′ər ē) *n., pl.* **-ger·ies** ⟦< WAG[2] + -ERY⟧ **1** the action, spirit, or manner of a wag; roguish jocularity or merriment **2** a joke or jest; esp., a practical joke

wag·gish (wag′ish) *adj.* ⟦< WAG[2] + -ISH⟧ **1** like, characteristic of, or befitting a wag; roguishly merry **2** done, said, or made in jest; playful [a *waggish* remark] —**wag′gish·ly** *adv.*

wag·gle (wag′əl) *vt.* **-gled, -gling** ⟦freq. of WAG[1]⟧ to wag, esp. with short, quick movements —*vi.* to move in a shaky or wobbly manner; totter —*n.* the act or an instance of waggling —**wag′gly** *adj.*

wag·gon (wag′ən) *n., vt., vi. alt. Brit. sp. of* WAGON

Wag·ner (väg′nər), **(Wilhelm) Rich·ard** (riH′ärt) 1813-83; Ger. composer

Wag·ne·ri·an (väg nir′ē ən, -ner′-) *adj.* **1** of or like Richard Wagner or his music, theories, methods, etc.: see also MUSIC DRAMA **2** designating or of an operatic singer specializing in Wagner's operas [a *Wagnerian* soprano] —*n.* an admirer or follower of Wagner's music, theories, etc.

wag·on (wag′ən) *n.* ⟦Du *wagen* < PGmc **wagna-*: see WAIN⟧ **1** any of various types of four-wheeled vehicles; specif., *a)* a horse-drawn vehicle for hauling heavy loads *b)* a small cart pulled or steered by means of a pole handle and used by children in play ☆**2** *short for: a)* PATROL WAGON *b)* STATION WAGON **3** [Brit.] a railroad freight car — *vt., vi.* to carry or transport (goods) by wagon; move or go in a wagon —☆**fix someone's wagon** [Slang] to hurt someone in some way so as to be revenged for a wrong, insult, etc. —**hitch one's wagon to a star** to aspire to lofty goals; aim high —☆**on (or off) the wagon** [Slang] no longer (or once again) drinking alcoholic liquors: also **on (or off) the water wagon** —**the Wagon** CHARLES'S WAIN

wag·on·er (-ər) *n.* a person who drives a wagon —**the Wagoner** AURIGA

wag·on·ette (wag′ə net′) *n.* ⟦dim. of WAGON⟧ a light, open, four-wheeled carriage with two seats set lengthwise facing each other behind the driver's seat

wa·gon-lit (vȧ gōn lē′) *n., pl.* **wa·gons-lits′** (-gōn lē′) ⟦Fr < *wagon*, car, railway coach (< E WAGON) + *lit*, bed < L *lectus*: see LIE[1]⟧ in Europe, a railroad sleeping car

wag·on·load (wag′ən lōd′) *n.* the load that a wagon carries or will carry

wagon train a line or convoy of wagons traveling together, as one carrying military supplies, or one in which pioneers crossed the Western plains

Wa·gram (vä′gräm′) town in NE Austria, near Vienna: site (1809) of a Napoleonic victory over the Austrians

wag·tail (wag′tāl′) *n.* **1** any of numerous small passerine birds (family Motacillidae) mostly native to Europe, characterized by long wing feathers and a very long tail that wags up and down ☆**2** any of various similar birds, as an American waterthrush

Wah·ha·bi or **Wa·ha·bi** (wä hä′bē) *n.* ⟦Ar *wahhābī*⟧ any member of a strict Muslim sect which adheres closely to the Koran: it was founded by Muhammad ibn Abd al-Wahhab (1703-92) and flourishes in Saudi Arabia —**Wah·ha′bism′** *n.*, **Wa·ha′bism′** (-biz′əm) —**Wah·ha′bite′** (-bīt′) *n., adj.*

☆**wa·hi·ne** (wä hē′nä, -nē) *n.* ⟦Haw or Maori, woman: for Proto-Polynesian form see VAHINE⟧ a Polynesian woman, esp. of Hawaii

☆**wa·hoo**[1] (wä′ho͞o′, wä ho͞o′) *n.* ⟦< Dakota *wa*ⁿ*hu*, lit., arrowwood⟧ **1** BURNING BUSH (sense 1) **2** STRAWBERRY BUSH

☆**wa·hoo**[2] (wä′ho͞o′, wä ho͞o′) *n.* ⟦< ? Creek *ahá·hwa*, walnut⟧ **1** a cork elm (*Ulmus alata*) of the S U.S. **2** any of various other North American trees or shrubs, as the cascara

☆**wa·hoo**[3] (wä′ho͞o′, wä ho͞o′) *n., pl.* **-hoo′** or **-hoos′** ⟦< ?⟧ a large, scombroid game and food fish (*Acanthocybium solanderi*) of warm seas

☆**wa·hoo**[4] (wä ho͞o′, wä′ho͞o′) *interj.* ⟦echoic of shout⟧ [Chiefly West] used to express unrestrained enthusiasm, exhilaration, etc.

☆**wah-wah** (wä′wä′) *n.* ⟦echoic redupl.⟧ **1** *Jazz* an instrumental effect somewhat like that of the sound of a baby crying, produced by closing and opening the bell of a trumpet, trombone, etc. with a plunger mute held in the hand **2** a similar effect created by an electronic device controlled by a foot pedal, that can be used with any musical instrument

waif (wāf) *n.* ⟦ME < NormFr, prob. < ON *veif*, anything flapping about < *veifa*, to wave, swing < IE **weip-*, to turn, var. of **weib-* > L *vibrare*, to VIBRATE⟧ **1** anything found by chance that is without an owner **2** a person without home or friends; esp., a homeless child **3** a stray animal **4** *Law a)* a piece of property found but claimed by nobody *b)* [*pl.*] [Obs.] stolen goods discarded by a thief in flight

Wai·ki·ki (wī′kē kē′) ⟦Haw < *wai*, water (< Proto-Polynesian **wai*) + *kīkī* (< ?): said to mean, lit., spouting water⟧ beach and resort section in Honolulu, Hawaii

wail (wāl) *vi.* ⟦ME *wailen* < ON *væla*, to lament < *væ*, WOE⟧ **1** to express grief or pain by long, loud cries **2** to make a plaintive, sad, crying sound [the wind *wailing* in the trees] **3** [Slang] *Jazz* to play in an intense or inspired manner —*vt.* [Archaic] **1** to lament; mourn [to *wail* someone's death] **2** to cry out in mourning or lamentation —*n.* **1** a long, pitiful cry of grief and pain **2** a sound like this **3** the act of wailing —**SYN.** CRY —**wail′er** *n.*

wail·ful (-fəl) *adj.* **1** wailing; sorrowful **2** like, or giving forth, a wail or cry of sorrow —**wail′ful·ly** *adv.*

Wailing Wall ⟦name applied by non-Jews, suggested by the passionate praying heard there⟧ WESTERN WALL

wain (wān) *n.* ⟦ME < OE *wægn*, wheeled vehicle, akin to Du & Ger *wagen* < PGmc **wagna-* < IE **woĝhno-* < base **weĝh-*, to move > L *vehere*, to carry⟧ [Old Poet.] a wagon or cart —**the Wain** CHARLES'S WAIN

wain·scot (wān′skät′, -skət) *n.* ⟦ME *waynescote* < MDu *wagenschot*, wainscot, as if < *wagen* (see prec.), but prob. < base akin to OS *weg*, OE *wag*, wall, orig. woven work (< IE base **wei-* > WITHE) + *schot*, a board, pale, prob. < or akin to Frank **skot-*, a sprout: for IE base see SHOOT[1]⟧ **1** a lining or paneling, usually of wood, on the walls of a room; now, usually, a wood paneling on the lower part of the walls only **2** the lower part of the walls of a room when finished differently from the upper part —*vt.* **-scot′ed** or **-scot′ted, -scot′ing** or **-scot′ting** to line (a wall or room) with wainscot

wain·scot·ing or **wain·scot·ting** (-iŋ) *n.* **1** WAINSCOT **2** material used to wainscot

wain·wright (wān′rīt′) *n.* ⟦WAIN + WRIGHT⟧ a person who builds or repairs wagons

waist (wāst) *n.* ⟦ME *wast* < base of OE *weaxan*, to grow, WAX[2]: sense development: growth (of body), hence size, thickness⟧ **1** the part of the body between the ribs and the hips **2** *a)* the part of a garment that covers the waist *b)* WAISTLINE (sense 2*a*) *c)* the part of a garment covering the body from the shoulders to a line above the hips *d)* the upper part of a woman's dress; bodice *e)* [Archaic] BLOUSE **3** the narrow part of any object that is wider at the ends [the *waist* of a violin] **4** *Aeron.* the middle section of the fuselage of an airplane, esp. a bomber **5** *Naut.* the central section of a ship between the forecastle and the quarterdeck **6** *Zool.* the narrow part of the front of the abdomen of certain insects, as ants or wasps

waist·band (wāst′band′) *n.* a band encircling the waist, esp. one at the top of a skirt, pair of trousers, etc.

waist·cloth (-klôth′) *n.* LOINCLOTH

waist·coat (wes′kət, wāst′kōt′) *n.* **1** [Brit.] *a)* VEST (*n.* 1*a*) *b)* a similar garment worn by women **2** a somewhat longer, heavily ornamented, sleeveless jacket formerly worn under a doublet —**waist′coat′ed** *adj.*

waist-high (wāst′hī′) *adj.* reaching up to the waist

waist·line (-līn′) *n.* **1** an imaginary line encircling the waist between the ribs and the hips **2** *a)* the part of a garment worn at the waist or above or below it as styles change *b)* the line where the waist and skirt of a dress join **3** the distance around the waist

wait (wāt) *vi.* ⟦ME *waiten* < NormFr *waitier* < Frank **wahten*, to guard, akin to OHG *wahta*, a guard, watch: for IE base see WAKE[1]⟧ **1** to stay in a place or remain in readiness or in anticipation (*until* something expected happens or *for* someone to arrive or catch up) **2** to be ready or at hand [dinner was *waiting* for them] **3** to remain temporarily undone or neglected [let that job *wait*] **4** to serve food at a meal: with *at* or *on* [to *wait* at table, to *wait* on a person] —*vt.* **1** to be, remain, or delay in expectation or anticipation of; await [to *wait* orders, to *wait* one's turn] **2** [Informal] to delay serving (a meal) as in waiting for someone [to *wait* dinner] **3** [Obs.] to attend upon or escort, esp. as a token of respect or honor **4** [Obs.] to attend as a consequence —*n.* **1** the act or fact of waiting **2** a period of waiting [a four-hour *wait*] **3** in England, *a)* any of a group of singers and musicians who go through the streets at Christmastime performing songs and carols for small gifts of money *b)* any tune so performed **4** [Obs.] a member of a band of musicians formerly employed by a city or town in England to play at entertainments **5** [Obs.] a watchman —**SYN.** STAY[3] —**cannot wait** to anticipate eagerly —**lie in wait (for)** to wait so as to catch after planning an ambush or trap (*for*) —**wait on (or upon) 1** to act as a servant to **2** to call on or visit (esp. a superior) in order to pay one's respects, ask a favor, etc. **3** to result from; be a consequence of **4** to supply the needs or requirements of (a person at table, a customer in a store, etc.), as a waiter, clerk, etc. **5** [Informal or Dial.] to wait for; await —**wait out** to remain inactive during the course of —**wait table** to serve food as a waiter or servant to people at a table —**wait up 1** to put off going to bed until someone expected arrives or something expected happens **2** [Informal] to stop and wait for someone to catch up

wait-a-bit (wāt′ə bit′) *n.* ⟦transl. of Afrik *wacht-en-beetje*: so named for their clinging thorns⟧ any of a number of plants having sharp or hooked thorns

Waite (wāt), **Mor·ri·son Rem·ick** (môr′i sən rem′ik) 1816-88; chief justice of the U.S. (1874-88)

wait·er (wāt′ər) *n.* ⟦ME *waitere*, watchman⟧ **1** a person who waits or awaits **2** a man who waits on tables, as in a restaurant **3** a tray for carrying dishes; salver

wait·ing (-iŋ) *adj.* **1** that waits **2** of or for a wait **3** that serves or is in attendance —*n.* the act of one that waits —**in waiting** in attendance, as on a king or other person of royalty

waiting game a scheme by means of which one outwits or wins out over another by delaying or postponing action until one has an advantage
waiting list a list of applicants, as for a vacancy or an item in short supply, in the order of their application
waiting room a room in which people wait, as in a railroad station or a dentist's office
wait·per·son (wāt′pur′sən) *n.* a person who waits on tables, as in a restaurant; waiter or waitress: see -PERSON
wait·ress (wā′tris) *n.* a woman who waits on tables, as in a restaurant —☆*vi.* to work as a waitress
wait·staff (wāt′staf′) *n.* the part of a restaurant's staff that is responsible for waiting on tables
waive (wāv) *vt.* **waived**, **waiv′ing** ⟦ME *weiven* < Anglo-Fr *waiver*, to renounce, abandon < ON *veifa*, to fluctuate: see WAIF⟧ **1** to give up or forgo (a right, claim, privilege, etc.) **2** to refrain from insisting on or taking advantage of **3** to put off until later; postpone; defer **4** *Law* to forgo or relinquish voluntarily (a right, privilege, claim, etc. which one is legally entitled to enforce) **5** *Sports* to put (a player) on waivers —*SYN.* RELINQUISH
waiv·er (wā′vər) *n.* ⟦substantive use of Anglo-Fr: see prec.⟧ *Law* **1** the act or an instance of waiving, or relinquishing voluntarily, a right, claim, privilege, etc. **2** a formal written statement of such relinquishment
waiv·ers (-vərz) *pl.n.* *Sports* the contractual status of a professional player who is being officially offered to other teams prior to being released [placed on *waivers*]
Wa·kash·an (wä kash′ən, wä′kə shan′) *n.* a family of North American Indian languages of British Columbia and Washington, including Nootka and Kwakiutl
Wa·ka·ya·ma (wä′kä yä′mä) seaport on the S coast of Honshu, Japan
wake¹ (wāk) *vi.* **woke** or **waked**, **waked** or **wok′en**, **wak′ing** ⟦ME *wakien* < OE *wacian*, to be awake & *wacan*, to arise, akin to Ger *wachen* < IE base **weĝ-*, to be active > L *vegere*, to arouse, be active, Sans *vāja-*, strength, speed⟧ **1** to come out of sleep or a state like or suggestive of sleep, as a stupor or trance; awake: often with *up* **2** to be or stay awake: now only in the prp. [during one's *waking* hours] **3** to become active or animated after inactivity or dormancy: often with *up* **4** to become alert (*to* a realization, possibility, etc.) **5** *pt. & pp.* **waked** [Chiefly Dial.] to keep watch or vigil; esp., to hold a wake over a corpse —*vt.* **1** to cause to wake from or as from sleep: often with *up* **2** to arouse, excite, or stir up (passions, etc.) or evoke (a sound, echo, etc.) **3** *pt. & pp.* **waked** [Chiefly Dial.] to keep watch or vigil over; esp., to hold a wake over (a corpse) —*n.* **1** [Now Rare] the state of being awake **2** *a)* a vigil over a corpse before burial *b)* a viewing of a corpse before a funeral, as at a funeral home **3** *Anglican Ch.* an annual parish festival, originally held in honor of a patron saint
wake² (wāk) *n.* ⟦prob. via LowG < ON *vök*, hole, opening in the ice: for IE base see HUMOR⟧ **1** the track or trail left in the water by a moving ship or boat **2** the track or course of anything that has gone before or passed by —**in the wake of 1** following directly or close behind **2** following as a consequence
Wake·field (wāk′fēld′) city in NC England, in West Yorkshire
wake·ful (wāk′fəl) *adj.* **1** keeping awake; not sleeping **2** alert; watchful; vigilant **3** *a)* unable to sleep *b)* sleepless [a *wakeful* night] —**wake′ful·ly** *adv.* —**wake′ful·ness** *n.*
Wake Island (wāk) coral atoll in the N Pacific between Midway & Guam: a U.S. possession: 3 sq mi (7.8 sq km)
wake·less (-lis) *adj.* unbroken; deep: said of sleep
wak·en (wā′kən) *vi.* ⟦ME *waknen* < OE *wacnian, wæcnan*, to become awake, akin to ON *vakna*, to waken: for IE base see WAKE¹⟧ **1** to become awake; come to one's senses after sleep or after a state like sleep **2** to become active, animated, or alive after inactivity or dormancy —*vt.* **1** to cause to wake; awake **2** to urge or stir into action or activity; arouse; excite —*SYN.* STIR¹ —**wak′en·er** *n.*
wake-rob·in (wāk′räb′in) *n.* ☆**1** TRILLIUM **2** [Brit.] any of several arums, esp. the cuckoopint
wake-up (-up′) *adj.* designating or of a service, as provided at some hotels, by which a guest or customer is awakened by a telephone call at a requested time —☆*n. informal name for* FLICKER²
wake-up call 1 a telephone call made by a wake-up service **2** anything that serves to arouse someone from apathy or inactivity
Waks·man (waks′mən), **Sel·man A(braham)** (sel′mən) 1888-1973; U.S. microbiologist, born in Russia
Wa·la·chi·a (wä lā′kē ə) region in E Europe, south of the Transylvanian Alps: merged with Moldavia (1861) to form Romania
Wa·la·chi·an (-ən) *adj.* of Walachia or its people, language, or culture —*n.* **1** a person born or living in Walachia **2** the variety of Romanian spoken by the Walachians
Wal·de·mar I (väl′də mär′) 1131-82; king of Denmark (1157-82): called *the Great*
Wal·den Pond (wôl′dən) ⟦prob. < a family name⟧ pond in E Mass., near Concord: site of Thoreau's cabin (1845-47)
Wal·den·ses (wäl den′sēz) *pl.n.* ⟦ME *waldensis* < ML *waldenses*, after Peter *Waldo*, 12th-c. Fr merchant and founder of the sect⟧ a sect of dissenters from the Roman Catholic Church which arose about 1170 in S France: excommunicated in 1184, they survive esp. in NW Italy —**Wal·den′si·an** *adj., n.*
Wald·heim (vält′hīm′; *E* väld′-, wäld′-), **Kurt** (koort; *E* kurt) 1918-2007; Austrian diplomat: secretary-general of the United Nations (1972-81): president of Austria (1986-92)
Wal·do (wôl′dō, wäl′-) *n.* ⟦OHG < *waldan*, to rule⟧ a masculine name
☆**Wal·dorf salad** (wôl′dôrf′) ⟦after the old *Waldorf*-Astoria Hotel in New York City⟧ a salad made of diced raw apples, celery, and walnuts, with mayonnaise
wale¹ (wāl) *n.* ⟦ME < OE *walu*, weal < IE **wolos*, round < base **wel-*, to turn, roll > WALK, L *vola*⟧ **1** a raised line or streak made on the skin by the slash of a stick or whip; welt; weal **2** *a)* a ridge on the surface of cloth, as corduroy *b)* texture of cloth **3** a band or ridge woven around the body of a basket to brace it **4** *Naut.* any of several heavy planks fastened in a horizontal row along the outside of the hull of a wooden ship: *usually used in pl.* —*vt.* **waled**, **wal′ing 1** to mark (the skin) with wales **2** to make (cloth) or weave (wickerwork) with wales
wale² (wāl) [Scot. or North Eng.] *n.* ⟦ME *wal* < ON *val*, akin to Ger *wahl*, choice, a choosing: for IE base see WILL¹⟧ **1** choice; selection **2** that chosen as best —*vt.* **waled**, **wal′ing** to choose; pick out; select
Wal·er (wā′lər) *n.* ⟦Anglo-Ind, after (NEW SOUTH) WALES⟧ an Australian saddle horse of mixed breed, raised chiefly in New South Wales, exported to India for military use in the 19th cent.
Wales (wālz) ⟦OE *Wealas, walas* < PGmc **walhos* < **walh-*, Celt: see WELSH⟧ division of the United Kingdom, occupying a peninsula of WC Great Britain: 8,019 sq mi (20,769 sq km); chief city, Cardiff
Wa·łęs·a (vä len′sə, -wen′-), **Lech** (lekh) 1943- ; Pol. labor leader & politician: president of Poland (1990-95)
Wal·hal·la (wal hal′ə, väl häl′ə) *n. var. of* VALHALLA
walk (wôk) *vi.* ⟦ME *walken* < OE *wealcan*, to roll, journey, akin to Ger *walken*, Frank **walken*, to full (cloth), stamp < IE **wolg-* < base **wel-*, to turn, roll > L *volvere*, to roll, Gr *eilyein*, to roll up, wrap⟧ **1** to go along or move about on foot at a moderate pace; specif., *a)* to move by placing one foot firmly before lifting the other, as two-legged creatures do, or by placing two feet firmly before lifting either of the others, as four-legged creatures do *b)* to go about on foot for exercise or pleasure; hike **2** to return after death and appear on earth as a ghost **3** to advance or move in a manner suggestive of walking: said of inanimate objects **4** *a)* to follow a certain course of life; conduct oneself in a certain way [let us *walk* in peace] *b)* to join with others in a cooperative action, a cause, etc. **5** [Obs.] to be active or in motion, or to keep moving ☆**6** [Slang] to be acquitted or set free without punishment: usually connoting a belief in the accused person's guilt ☆**7** [Slang] *a)* to go on strike *b)* to leave abruptly, often in anger or in a show of protest ☆**8** *Baseball* to be advanced to first base as a result of being pitched four balls: see BALL¹ (*n.* 8) ☆**9** *Basketball* TRAVEL ☆**10** *Jazz* to play a WALKING BASS part, as on a double bass or piano —*vt.* **1** to go through, over, or along at a moderate pace on foot [to *walk* the deck, the streets, etc.] **2** to traverse (a boundary, fence, etc.) on foot in order to survey, inspect, or repair **3** *a)* to cause (a horse, dog, etc.) to move at a walk; lead, ride, or drive at a walk *b)* to train and exercise (a horse, dog, etc.) in this way **4** to push (a bicycle, motorcycle, etc.) while walking alongside or behind **5** to accompany (a person) on a walk or stroll [to *walk* a friend home] **6** *a)* to force (a person) to move at a walk, as by grasping the shoulders and pushing *b)* to help (a disabled person) to walk **7** to bring (a person or animal) to a specified state by walking [to *walk* someone to exhaustion] **8** to move (a bulky or heavy object) by rocking along from one side or corner to another in a manner suggestive of walking ☆**9** *Baseball* *a)* to advance (a batter) to first base by pitching four balls (see BALL¹, *n.* 8) *b)* to force (a run) *in* by doing this when the bases are loaded —*n.* **1** the act of walking **2** a period or course of walking for pleasure or exercise; stroll or hike **3** a route traversed by walking **4** a distance walked, often in terms of the time required [an hour's *walk* from home] **5** a relatively slow pace **6** a manner of walking [to know someone by his *walk*] **7** a particular station in life, sphere of activity, occupation, etc. [people from all *walks* of life] **8** [Now Rare] mode of living **9** a path, avenue, etc. specially prepared or set apart for walking; specif., SIDEWALK **10** ROPEWALK **11** *a)* a plantation of trees in rows with a space between *b)* the space between any two such rows **12** a place or enclosure for grazing or exercising animals, as a sheepwalk **13** [Brit.] the route covered in one's round of duty or work, as in delivering mail **14** a race between walking contestants: in this sport, at all times, some part of either foot must be in contact with the ground ☆**15** *Baseball* the act or an instance of walking a batter or of being walked —**walk (all) over** [Informal] **1** to defeat overwhelmingly **2** to treat in a domineering and unfeeling way —**walk away from 1** to outdistance easily; defeat handily **2** to remove oneself from involvement in or responsibility for; abandon [*walk away from* a fight, *walk away from* a foreclosed house] —**walk away with 1** to steal **2** to win easily —**walk off 1** to go away, esp. without warning **2** to get rid of by walking [to *walk off* pounds] —**walk off with 1** to steal **2** to win (a contest) or gain (a prize), esp. easily —**walk out 1** to leave abruptly or angrily ☆**2** to go on strike —☆**walk out on** [Informal] to desert; abandon —**walk through 1** *Theater* to carry out a walk-through of **2** to make or become familiar with (a process, job, etc.) as by a step-by-step demonstration —**walk with God** to lead a godly, morally upright life
walk·a·bout (wôk′ə bout′) *n.* **1** an overland journey into the Australian Outback by an Aborigine in an effort to return for a time to traditional nomadic life: often in the phrase **to go (on) walkabout 2** [Brit.] *a)* a walking tour *b)* an informal stroll through a crowd, as by royalty
walk·a·way (wôk′ə wā′) *n.* an easily won victory
walk·er (wôk′ər) *n.* **1** a person or animal that walks; specif., a contestant

in a walking race ☆2 a frame on wheels that encircles and supports a baby who is learning to walk ☆3 a tubular frame used by convalescents, the disabled, etc. as a support in standing and walking 4 TREADMILL (sense 4) 5 a shoe made specifically for use by a person who walks for exercise

☆**walk·ie-talk·ie** (wôk′ē tôk′ē) *n.* ⟦redupl. < WALK + TALK, with -IE⟧ a hand-held unit consisting of a radio transmitter and receiver, designed to enable voice communication when used as with another such unit

☆**walk-in** (wôk′in′) *adj.* 1 large enough for one to walk inside [a *walk-in* closet] 2 that can be entered directly from the street rather than through a lobby 3 designating or of a public agency, medical clinic, etc. which accepts anyone who walks in without an appointment; also, of such a person —*n.* 1 a walk-in closet, apartment, etc. 2 an easily won victory 3 a person who walks in, as to a clinic, without an appointment

walk·ing (wôk′iŋ) *adj.* 1 *a)* that walks *b)* able to walk, as despite injury [the *walking* wounded] 2 for use by a walker, hiker, etc. 3 characterized by walking, hiking, etc. [a *walking* trip through Wales] 4 in human form: a fig. use [he'll know the answer—he's a *walking* encyclopedia] ☆5 that is drawn by an animal and guided by a person walking [a *walking* plow] 6 that moves back and forth or up and down [a *walking* beam] 7 that moves in a manner suggestive of walking [a *walking* crane] 8 permitting the patient to be ambulatory [*walking* pneumonia] —*n.* 1 the act of a person or thing that walks 2 manner of walking; gait 3 the condition of the ground, a path, etc. with reference to its suitability for walking on

☆**walking bass** *Jazz* a bass part played on the double bass or piano, in which a note is played on each beat, presenting a series of small steps or intervals as in a chord progression

☆**walking delegate** [Historical] BUSINESS AGENT

walking fern ☆a native American fern (*Camptosorus rhizophyllus*) of the most common family (Polypodiaceae) of ferns, having simple lanceolate leaves with a protracted tip that roots when it touches the ground

walking leaf 1 LEAF INSECT 2 WALKING FERN

☆**walking papers** [Informal] dismissal from a job

☆**walking shorts** BERMUDA SHORTS

walking stick 1 a stick that a person uses as for support when walking 2 any of various elongated, wingless, phasmid insects resembling a twig, esp. a North American species (*Diapheromera femorata*) feeding on plants: also **walk′ing·stick′** *n.*

Walk·man (wôk′mən, -man′) ⟦because designed to be used by a person who is *walking*, jogging, etc.⟧ *trademark for* a small, portable stereo audio or video, tape or disc player, etc. for use with headphones —*n.* any such device

walk-off (wôk′ôf′, -äf′) *adj.* ⟦because it allows the players to leave the field⟧ ☆*Baseball* designating or of a base hit, esp. a home run, that scores the winning run for the home team in the last inning, thus ending the game

walk-on (wôk′än′) *n.* 1 *a)* a minor role in which the actor has no speaking lines or just a very few *b)* the actor who performs such a role 2 *Sports* a player who tries out for a team without being recruited, drafted, on scholarship, etc.

☆**walk·out** (-out′) *n.* 1 a strike of workers 2 an abrupt departure of people, as from a meeting, in a show of protest

walk·o·ver (-ō′vər) *n.* 1 a race in which the one horse entered has merely to walk over the course to win 2 an easily won victory

walk-through (-thro͞o′) *n.* 1 an early rehearsal of a play in which the actors begin to carry out actions on stage 2 *a)* any rehearsal, practice, or inspection in preparation for an event *b)* a step-by-step demonstration —*adj.* 1 of or having to do with a walk-through 2 designed to be walked through

☆**walk-up** (-up′) *n.* 1 an upstairs apartment or office in a building without an elevator 2 the building itself

☆**walk·way** (-wā′) *n.* a path, passage, etc. for pedestrians, esp. one that is sheltered

Wal·kyr·ie (val kir′ē, val′ki rē) *n. alt. sp. of* VALKYRIE

☆**walk·y-talk·y** (wôk′ē tôk′ē) *n., pl.* **-talk′ies** *alt. sp. of* WALKIE-TALKIE

wall (wôl) *n.* ⟦ME *wal* < OE *weall* (akin to Ger *wall*) < L *vallum*, rampart < *vallus*, a stake, palisade < IE base **wel-*, to turn > WALK⟧ 1 an upright structure of wood, stone, brick, etc., serving to enclose, divide, support, or protect; specif., *a)* such a structure forming a side or inner partition of a building *b)* such a continuous structure serving to enclose an area, to separate fields, etc. *c)* [*usually pl.*] such a structure used as a military defense; fortification *d)* such a structure used to hold back water; levee; dike 2 something resembling a wall in appearance or function, as the side or inside surface of a container or body cavity 3 something suggestive of a wall in that it holds back, divides, hides, etc. [a *wall* of secrecy] —*adj.* 1 of or along a wall 2 placed or growing on, in, or against a wall —*vt.* 1 to furnish, line, enclose, divide, protect, etc. with or as with a wall or walls [to *wall* a room with books, to *wall* off the old wing, a mind *walled* in by fears] 2 to close up (an opening) with a wall: usually with *up* —**drive** (or **push**) **to the wall** to place in a desperate or extreme position —**drive** (or **send,** etc.) **up the wall** [Informal] to make frantic, emotionally tense, crazy, etc. —**go to the wall** 1 to be forced to retreat or yield in a conflict; suffer defeat 2 to fail in business; become bankrupt — **hit the** (or **a**) **wall** [Informal] to come to a point beyond which there is no further progress [to *hit the wall* after four years of steady profits] —☆**off the wall** [Slang] 1 unsound of mind; crazy 2 very eccentric or unconventional —(**see**) **the handwriting** (or **writing**) **on the wall** (to foresee) impending disaster or misfortune: Dan. 5:5-28 —**wall′-like′** *adj.*

wal·la·by (wä′lə bē) *n., pl.* **-bies** or **-by** ⟦< *wolabā*, name in a language of Australia⟧ any of various small and medium-sized herbivorous marsupials (family Macropodidae) that are very similar to kangaroos

Wal·lace[1] (wô′lis, wä′-) *n.* ⟦< the surname *Wallace* < Anglo-Fr *Waleis* or ME *Walisc*, foreign, WELSH⟧ a masculine name: dim. *Wally*

Wal·lace[2] (wô′lis, wä′-) 1 **Alfred Russel** 1823-1913; Eng. naturalist 2 **Lew(is)** 1827-1905; U.S. general & novelist 3 Sir **William** 1270?-1305; Scot. patriot & leader in struggle against Edward I of England

Wal·la·chi·a (wä lā′kē ə) *alt. sp. of* WALACHIA

wal·lah (wä′lä) *n.* ⟦Anglo-Ind < Hindi *-wālā*, a suffix of agency⟧ [Anglo-Ind.] a person associated with a specified thing, function, or place: chiefly in comb. [a punkah-*wallah*]: also sp. **wal′la**

wal·la·roo (wä′lə ro͞o′, wä′lə ro͞o′) *n.* ⟦< *wolarū*, name in a language of Australia⟧ a large kangaroo (*Macropus robustus*) of rocky regions, characterized by a stocky body and broad, thickly padded feet

wall·board (wôl′bôrd′) *n.* 1 fibrous material, composed of wood, gypsum, etc., formed into thin sheets for use in making or covering walls and ceilings in place of plaster, paneling, etc. 2 PLASTERBOARD

wall·cov·er·ing (-kuv′ər iŋ) *n.* material, as fabric, vinyl, or paper, usually with colored patterns printed on it, for covering the walls of a room

wall·creep·er (-krē′pər) *n.* a small, Eurasian passerine bird (*Tichodroma muraria*) with red-and-black wings, living in cliffs and town walls: in the same family (Sittidae) as the nuthatches

walled (wôld) *adj.* 1 having, or enclosed by, a wall or walls 2 fortified [a *walled* town] 3 enclosed or hedged in as if by a wall

Wal·len·stein (väl′ən shtīn′; *E* wô′lən stīn′), **Al·brecht (Eusebius Wenzel) von** (äl′breHt fôn) 1583-1634; Austrian general in the Thirty Years' War

Wal·ler (wô′lər, wä′-) 1 **Edmund** 1606-87; Eng. poet 2 **Fats** (born *Thomas Wright Waller*) 1904-43; U.S. jazz pianist & composer

wal·let (wô′lit, wä′-) *n.* ⟦ME *walet* < ?⟧ 1 [Archaic] a knapsack ☆2 a flat pocketbook, as of leather, with compartments for paper money, cards, etc.; billfold

wall·eye (wôl′ī′) *n.* ⟦back-form. < *walleyed*, altered by folk etym. < ME *wawil-eyed* < ON *valdeygthr*, altered < *vagl eygr* < *vagl*, a beam (> Swed *vagel*, sty) + *eygr*, having eyes, akin to EYE⟧ 1 an eye, as of a horse, with a whitish iris or white, opaque cornea 2 *a)* an eye that turns outward, showing more white than is normal *b)* divergent strabismus 3 leukoma of the cornea 4 a large, glossy eye 5 *a)* any of several fishes with large, glossy eyes ☆*b)* a North American freshwater food and game perch (*Stizostedion vitreum*) —**wall′eyed′** (-īd′) *adj.*

☆**walleyed pike** WALLEYE (sense 5*b*)

☆**walleye surfperch** a common black and silvery surfperch (*Hyperprosopon argenteum*) found off the coast of California

wall fern a small, hardy fern (*Polypodium virginianum*) of the most common family (Polypodiaceae) of ferns, with densely matted, creeping stems, found on cliffs and walls in E North America and often grown in gardens

wall·flow·er (-flou′ər) *n.* 1 any of a number of perennial or annual garden plants (genera *Cheiranthus* and *Erysimum*) of the crucifer family, having racemes of cross-shaped flowers, usually yellow or orange; esp., a common perennial (*C. cheiri*) having racemes of fragrant, colorful flowers 2 [Informal] a person, esp. a girl, who merely looks on at a dance, etc., sometimes from shyness but usually from not having been chosen as a partner

wall hanging a flat, usually unframed piece of decorative work for hanging on a wall, as a tapestry, a quilt, or a piece made by weaving, macramé, or other techniques from a wide variety of materials

Wal·lis (vä′lis) *Ger. name for* VALAIS

Wal·lis and Futuna (wô′lis) French overseas territory in the South Pacific, northeast of the Fiji Islands: it consists of two groups of islands (**Wallis Islands** and **Futuna Islands**): 106 sq mi (275 sq km)

Wal·loon (wä lo͞on′) *n.* ⟦Fr *Wallon* < ML *Wallo*, of Gmc orig., as in OHG *walh*, foreigner, OE *Wealh*, Briton, foreigner: see WELSH⟧ 1 a member of a chiefly Celtic people living mostly in S and SE Belgium and nearby parts of France 2 the variety of French spoken by the Walloons

wal·lop (wä′ləp) *vi.* ⟦ME *walopen*, to gallop < NormFr *waloper* (OFr *galoper*): see GALLOP⟧ [Informal or Dial.] 1 *a)* to move along in a rapid, reckless, awkward way *b)* to move heavily and clumsily; flounder 2 to boil vigorously, with noisy bubbling —*vt.* [Informal] 1 to beat soundly; thrash 2 to strike hard 3 to defeat overwhelmingly —*n.* 1 [Informal or Dial.] a heavy, clumsy movement of the body 2 [Informal] *a)* a hard blow *b)* the power to strike a hard blow *c)* effective force; vigor ☆3 [Informal] a feeling of pleasurable excitement; thrill 4 [Brit. Slang] beer —**wal′lop·er** *n.*

wal·lop·ing (-iŋ) [Informal] *adj.* ⟦prp. of prec.⟧ 1 impressively large; enormous 2 extraordinary —*n.* 1 a thrashing or beating 2 a crushing defeat —*adv.* extraordinarily

wal·low (wä′lō) *vi.* ⟦ME *walwen* < OE *wealwian*, to roll around < PGmc **walw-* < IE **wolw-* < base **wel-* > WALK⟧ 1 to roll about or lie relaxed, as in mud, dust, or water: said chiefly of large animals 2 to move heavily and clumsily; roll and pitch, as a ship 3 to live or indulge oneself to an immoderate degree (*in* a specified thing, condition, etc.) [to *wallow* in self-pity] 4 to surge or billow —*n.* 1 the act or an instance of wallowing ☆2 a muddy or dusty place in which animals wallow ☆3 a pit or depression produced by animals' wallowing —**wal′low·er** *n.*

wall·pa·per (wôl′pā′pər) *n.* 1 paper, usually with colored patterns printed on it, that is pasted to the walls or ceiling of a room as a covering 2 a picture or colored pattern appearing as the background to the icons of a GUI screen display: cf. DESKTOP (*n.* 2) —*vt.* to hang or apply wallpaper on or in

wall pellitory PELLITORY (sense 1)

wall plate a timber laid horizontally along a wall to support the ends of joists, girders, etc. and distribute their weight

☆**wall rock** *Geol., Mining* the rock mass on either side of a fault or vein

wall rocket a yellow-flowered European plant (*Diplotaxis tenuifolia*) of the crucifer family, found on rocky walls

wall rue either of two small, delicate, light-green spleenwort ferns (*Asplenium cryptolepis* or *A. rutamuraria*) usually growing on cliffs or walls in North America and Europe

Wall Street ⟦from a defensive *wall* built there by the Dutch in 1653⟧ **1** street in lower Manhattan, New York City: the main financial center of the U.S. **2** U.S. financiers and their power, influence, policies, etc., or the U.S. securities market

wall-to-wall (wôl′tə wôl′) *adj.* **1** that completely covers a floor [*wall-to-wall* carpeting] **2** [Informal] *a)* in very large numbers or amounts; found throughout; pervasive *b)* comprehensive; all-inclusive [*wall-to-wall* healthcare]

wall unit a piece of furniture consisting of a freestanding cabinet or cabinets, set against a wall and having multiple shelves and compartments for holding, variously, books, decorative objects, audio and video devices, etc.

wal·ly[1] (wä′lē) *adj.* ⟦< ? ME *wal,* choice: see WALE[2]⟧ [Scot.] **1** fine; first-rate **2** large, strong, or robust **3** pleasing; agreeable

wal·ly[2] (wä′lē) *n., pl.* **-lies** ⟦orig. uncert.; ? dim. of *Walter*⟧ [Brit. Slang] a foolish or ineffectual person

wal·nut (wôl′nut′, -nət) *n.* ⟦ME *walnot* < OE *walhhnutu* < *wealh,* foreign (see WELSH) + *hnutu,* NUT⟧ **1** any of a genus (*Juglans*) of trees of the walnut family, valued as shade trees, for their nuts, and for their wood, used in making furniture, paneling, etc. **2** the edible nut of any of these trees, having a two-lobed seed **3** their wood **4** a shade of brown characteristic of the heartwood of the black walnut —*adj.* designating a family (Juglandaceae, order Juglandales) of dicotyledonous trees native to the temperate parts of the Northern Hemisphere, including the black walnut, English walnut, pecan, and hickory

Wal·pole (wôl′pōl, wäl′-) **1 Horace** 4th Earl of Orford (born *Horatio Walpole*) 1717-97; Eng. writer **2** Sir **Robert** 1st Earl of Orford 1676-1745; Eng. statesman: prime minister (1721-42): father of Horace

Wal·pur·gis Night (väl po͝or′gis) ⟦after St. *Walpurgis,* Eng missionary in Germany (8th c.): her day is April 30⟧ *Gmc. Folklore* April 30, the eve of May Day, when witches supposedly gathered on Brocken mountain for a demonic orgy: also Ger. **Wal·pur·gis·nacht** (väl po͝or′gis näkht′) *n.*

wal·rus (wôl′rəs) *n., pl.* **-rus·es** or **-rus** ⟦Du < Dan *hvalros,* prob. by metathesis < ON *hrosshvalr,* lit., horse whale < *hross,* akin to OE *hros,* horse + *hvalr,* WHALE[1]⟧ a massive, arctic sea carnivore (*Odobenus rosmarus*) of the same family (Otariidae) as the eared seals, having two tusks projecting from the upper jaw, a thick mustache, a very thick hide, and a heavy layer of blubber —*adj.* of, characteristic of, or suggestive of a walrus; specif., designating a mustache with long, drooping ends

walrus

Wal·sall (wôl′sôl′) city in West Midlands, WC England, near Birmingham

Wal·sing·ham (wôl′siŋ əm), Sir **Francis** 1532?-90; Eng. statesman: secretary of state (1573-90) to Elizabeth I

Wal·ter[1] (wôl′tər) *n.* ⟦NormFr *Waltier* < Frank *Waldheri* < *waldan,* to rule (akin to WIELD) + *heri, hari,* army, host; also < Ger *Walter, Walther* < OHG form of same name⟧ a masculine name: dim. *Walt, Wally*

Wal·ter[2] (väl′tər), **Bruno** (born *Bruno Walter Schlesinger*) 1876-1962; U.S. orchestra conductor, born in Germany

Wal·tham Forest (wôl′thəm, -təm) borough of NE Greater London, England

Wal·ther von der Vo·gel·wei·de (väl′tər fôn der fō′gəl vī′də) 1170?-1230?; Ger. minnesinger

Wal·ton (wôlt′′n) **1 I·zaak** (ī′zək) 1593-1683; Eng. writer **2** Sir **William (Turner)** 1902-83; Eng. composer

waltz (wôlts) *n.* ⟦abbrev. < Ger *walzer* < *walzen,* to roll, dance about, waltz: for IE base see WALK⟧ **1** a ballroom dance for couples, in moderate 3/4 time with marked accent on the first beat of the measure **2** music for this dance or in its characteristic rhythm **3** [Informal] a thing easy to do; esp., an easy victory in a contest —*adj.* of, for, or characteristic of a waltz —*vi.* **1** to dance a waltz **2** to move lightly and nimbly; whirl **3** [Informal] *a)* to proceed effortlessly, indifferently, etc. [to *waltz* through life] *b)* to win easily (with *in*) —*vt.* **1** to dance with in a waltz **2** to take and lead peremptorily —**waltz′er** *n.*

Wal·vis Bay (wôl′vis) ⟦< Du *walvis,* whale < MDu *walvisc* < *wal,* WHALE[1] + *visc,* akin to OE *fisc,* FISH⟧ **1** inlet of the Atlantic, on the coast of Namibia **2** seaport in W Namibia, on this inlet: the city & surrounding area were formerly (1978-94) an exclave of South Africa

wam·ble (wäm′bəl, wäm′əl) [Chiefly Dial.] *vi.* **-bled, -bling** ⟦ME *wamlen,* akin to Norw *vamla,* to stagger, Dan *vamle,* to feel nausea: for IE base see VOMIT⟧ **1** to turn, twist, or roll about **2** to move unsteadily **3** [Obs.] to be nauseated —*n.* **1** an unsteady movement **2** a sensation of nausea —**wam′bly** (-blē, -lē) *adj.* **-bli·er, -bli·est**

wame (wām) *n.* ⟦var. of WOMB⟧ [Scot.] the belly

Wam·pa·no·ag (wäm′pə nō′ag′) *n., pl.* **-ag′** or **-ags′** ⟦Narragansett, lit., people of the east⟧ **1** a member of a loosely confederated group of Algonquian peoples in SE Massachusetts or their present-day descendants **2** the extinct language of these peoples, comprising several dialects of Massachusett

☆**wam·pum** (wäm′pəm) *n.* ⟦earlier *wampompeag* < Massachusett (cf. Abenaki *wąpapəyak,* wampum strings < *wąp-,* white + *-api,* string + *-ak,* pl.)⟧ **1** small beads made of shells and used by North American Indians as money, for ornament, etc.: they were of two varieties, white and the more valuable black (or dark purple) **2** [Slang] money

wan[1] (wän) *adj.* **wan′ner, wan′nest** ⟦ME < OE *wann,* dark⟧ **1** sickly pale; pallid [a *wan* complexion] **2** faint or weak in a way suggestive of sickness or great weariness, sadness, etc. [a *wan* smile] **3** pale, dim, faint, etc. [a *wan* light] — *vt., vi.* **wanned, wan′ning** [Now Rare] to make or become sickly pale —*SYN.* PALE[1] —**wan′ly** *adv.* —**wan′ness** *n.*

wan[2] (wan) *vi., vt. obs. pt. of* WIN

WAN (wan) *n.* wide area network: a computer NETWORK (sense 3) of geographically distant computers, terminals, etc.

Wan·a·ma·ker (wä′nə mā′kər), **John** 1838-1922; U.S. merchant

wand (wänd) *n.* ⟦ME < ON *vǫndr,* akin to Goth *wandus* < IE base **wendh-* > WIND[1]⟧ **1** a slender, supple switch or shoot, as of a young tree **2** a rod or staff carried as a symbol of authority; scepter **3** a rod regarded as having magical powers, as one used by a magician or fairy **4** any of various rod-shaped, usually hand-held devices, attachments, etc.; specif., *a)* an applicator for cosmetics *b)* an electronic sensor for reading bar codes ☆**5** *Archery* a slat 6 feet high and 2 inches wide, used as a target at a distance of 100 yards for men and 60 yards for women

Wan·da (wän′də) *n.* a feminine name

wan·der (wän′dər) *vi.* ⟦ME *wandren* < OE *wandrian,* akin to Ger *wandern,* akin ? to WEND, WIND[1]⟧ **1** to move or go about aimlessly, without plan or fixed destination; ramble; roam **2** to go to a destination in a casual way or by an indirect route; idle; stroll **3** *a)* to turn aside or astray (*from* a path, course, etc.); lose one's way *b)* to stray from home, friends, familiar places, etc. (often with *off*) **4** to go astray in mind or purpose; specif., *a)* to drift away from a subject, as in discussion; stray or roam in thought *b)* to turn away from accepted belief or morals *c)* to be disjointed, disordered, incoherent, etc. **5** to pass or extend in an irregular course; meander, as a river **6** to move idly from one object to another: often used fig., as of the eyes or hands, to suggest sexual interest —*vt.* to roam through, in, or over without plan or destination [to *wander* the world] —**wan′der·er** *n.*

wan·der·ing (-iŋ) *adj.* **1** that wanders; moving from place to place; roaming, roving, straying, etc. **2** nomadic: said of tribes, peoples, etc. **3** winding: said of rivers and roads —*n.* **1** an aimless going about **2** [*pl.*] travels, esp. when extended and apparently purposeless **3** [*pl.*] incoherent or disordered thoughts or utterances —**wan′der·ing·ly** *adv.*

wandering albatross a large white sea bird (*Diomedea exulans*) with black wings

Wandering Jew **1** in medieval folklore, a Jew condemned to wander the earth restlessly until the second coming of Christ because of his scornful attitude just before the Crucifixion **2** [**w- J-**] any of several trailing plants (genus *Tradescantia*) of the spiderwort family, having smooth stems and leaves, and white, red, or blue flowers; esp., a common houseplant (*T. zebrina*) with purple flowers

Wan·der·jahr (vän′dər yär′) *n., pl.* **-jah′re** (-yä′rə) ⟦Ger, wander-year⟧ **1** a year of travel before settling down to one's vocation: originally a custom of European journeymen **2** any lengthy period of travel

wan·der·lust (wän′dər lust′) *n.* ⟦Ger < *wandern,* to travel, WANDER + *lust,* joy: see LUST⟧ an impulse, longing, or urge to wander or travel

Wands·worth (wändz′wurth′) borough of SW Greater London, England

wane (wān) *vi.* **waned, wan′ing** ⟦ME *wanien* < OE *wanian,* to decrease, grow less, akin to *wan,* lacking: for IE base see WANT⟧ **1** to diminish gradually in extent: said esp. of the visible face of the moon during the phases after full moon in which the lighted portion is gradually reduced to a thin crescent on the left, as seen from the Northern Hemisphere: opposed to WAX[2] (sense 1): see **2** to become less intense, bright, strong, etc.; grow dim or faint, as a light **3** to decline in power, importance, prosperity, influence, etc. **4** to approach the end: said of a period of time [the day *wanes*] —*n.* **1** *a)* the gradual decrease in the visible face of the moon after it has become full *b)* the time when this takes place **2** a gradual decrease in power, importance, intensity, etc., esp. after a gradual climb to a peak **3** a period of decline **4** a defective, slanting or bark-covered edge or corner of a board or plank cut from an unsquared log —**on the wane** waning, declining, decreasing, etc.

SYN.—**wane** implies a fading or weakening of that which has reached a peak of force, excellence, etc. [his fame *waned* rapidly]; **abate** suggests a progressive lessening in degree, intensity, etc. [the fever is *abating*]; **ebb**, applied specifically to a fluctuating force, refers to one of the periods of recession or decline [their *ebbing* fortunes]; **subside** suggests a quieting or slackening of violent activity or turbulence [her temper had *subsided*] —*ANT.* **wax, increase, revive**

wan·gle (waŋ′gəl) *vt.* **wan′gled, wan′gling** ⟦altered < ? WAGGLE⟧ [Informal] **1** to get, make, or bring about by persuasion, influence, adroit manipulation, contrivance, etc. **2** to manipulate or change (statistics, accounts, etc.) for a selfish or dishonest purpose; falsify; juggle **3** to wiggle or wriggle —*vi.* [Informal] **1** to make use of contrivance, adroit manipulation, or tricky and indirect methods in order to achieve one's aims **2** to wriggle, as out of a difficult situation —**wan′gler** *n.*

Wan·hsien (wän′shyen′) *a former transliteration of* WANXIAN

☆**wan·i·gan** (wä′ni gən) *n.* ⟦Ojibwa *waanikaan*, pit, hole dug in ground⟧ **1** a trunk, chest, etc. for storing supplies, as in a lumbering camp **2** a small, rough shelter for sleeping, cooking, etc., often one mounted on runners or wheels or on a raft or boat

wank (waŋk) [Slang, Chiefly Brit.] *vi.* to masturbate: sometimes with *off* —*n.* an instance of masturbating Somewhat vulgar

Wan·kel engine (waŋ′kəl; *Ger* väŋ′-) ⟦after Felix *Wankel* (1902-88), Ger engineer and inventor⟧ a rotary internal-combustion engine having a three-lobed rotor and requiring fewer parts than a comparable piston-operated engine: it is less efficient and less powerful than reciprocating engines

wan·ker (waŋ′ker) *n.* [Slang, Chiefly Brit.] **1** a person who masturbates **2** a person variously regarded as contemptible, ineffectual, etc. Somewhat vulgar

wan·na (wä′nə, wô′-) *v.aux. phonetic sp. of* want to (in informal pronunciation)

☆**wan·na·be** (wä′nə bē′, wô′-) *n.* ⟦< *want to be*: phonetic sp., informal pronun.⟧ [Slang] a person who wants to be or be like someone else or to attain some status or condition [a rock-star *wannabe*]: also written **wanna-be**

want (wänt, wônt) *vt.* ⟦ME *wanten* < ON *vanta*, to be lacking, want: see the *n.*⟧ **1** to have too little of; be deficient in; lack **2** to be short by (a specified amount) [it *wants* twelve minutes of midnight] **3** to feel the need of; long for; crave [to *want* adventure] **4** to desire; wish or long: followed by the infinitive [to *want* to travel] **5** *a)* to wish to see or speak with (someone) [*wanted* on the phone] *b)* to wish to apprehend, as for questioning or arrest [*wanted* by the police] **6** [Chiefly Brit.] to require; need [this *wants* attending to] ➥*Want* is also used informally as an auxiliary meaning *ought* or *should* [you *want* to be careful crossing streets] —*vi.* **1** to have a need or lack: usually with *for* [to *want* for money] **2** to lack the necessities of life; be destitute or impoverished ["Waste not, *want* not"] **3** [Rare] to be lacking or missing for completeness or a certain result [there *wants* but his approval] —*n.* ⟦ME < ON *vant*, neut. of *vanr*, deficient < IE base **(e)wā-*, to lack > L *vanus*, empty⟧ **1** the state or fact of lacking, or having too little of, something needed or desired; scarcity; shortage; lack [to suffer from *want* of adequate care] **2** a lack of the necessities of life; poverty; destitution [to live in *want*] **3** a wish or desire for something; craving **4** something needed or desired but lacking; need —*SYN.* DESIRE, LACK, POVERTY —**want in** (or **out** or **off**, etc.) [Informal] to want to get, go, or come in (or out, off, etc.) —**want′er** *n.*

☆**want ad** [Informal] a classified advertisement in a newspaper, magazine, etc. stating that one wants a job, an apartment to rent, a specified type of employee, etc., or that one wishes to sell, buy, or trade something

want·ing (wän′tiŋ) *adj.* **1** absent; lacking; missing [a coat with some buttons *wanting*] **2** not up to some standard; inadequate in some essential [weighed and found *wanting*] —*prep.* **1** lacking (something); without [a watch *wanting* a minute hand] **2** minus; less [a year *wanting* two weeks] —**wanting in** deficient in

wan·ton (wänt′'n) *adj.* ⟦ME *wantowen*, var. of *wantogen*, wanton, irregular < OE *wan-*, used as negative prefix < *wan*, lacking, deficient (see WANE) + *togen*, pp. of *teon*, to draw, educate, bring up (see TOW[1])⟧ **1** [Obs.] undisciplined; unmanageable [a *wanton* child] **2** *a)* sexually loose or unrestrained [a *wanton* woman] *b)* [Old Poet.] frisky; playful; frolicsome *c)* [Old Poet.] capricious; unrestrained [*wanton* winds] **3** senseless, unprovoked, unjustifiable, or deliberately malicious [*wanton* cruelty, a *wanton* insult] **4** recklessly or arrogantly ignoring justice, decency, morality, etc. [*wanton* disregard of human rights] **5** *a)* [Now Rare] luxuriant (said of vegetation, etc.) *b)* lavish, luxurious, or extravagant (said of speech, dress, etc.) —*n.* a wanton person or thing; esp., a sexually loose or unrestrained woman —*vi.* [Archaic] to be wanton in behavior, action, manner, etc. —**wan′ton·ly** *adv.* —**wan′ton·ness** *n.*

Wan·xian (wän′shyän′) city in Sichuan province, central China, on the Chang

wap (wäp) *vt., vi., n.* **wapped**, **wap′ping** [Now Chiefly Dial.] WHOP

wap·en·take (wäp′ən tāk′, wap′-) *n.* ⟦ME < OE *wapentac* < ON *vapnatak*, lit., a weapon-taking (< *vapn*, WEAPON + *tak*, a taking, commandeering < *taka*, to TAKE): prob. from ceremony in which vassals touched the raised spear of the lord with their own as token of submission⟧ [Historical] in England, *a)* a subdivision of certain northern counties originally under Norse domination, corresponding to the hundred in other counties *b)* a law court in such a subdivision

☆**wap·i·ti** (wä′pə tē) *n., pl.* **-tis** or **-ti** ⟦< Shawnee *waapiti*, lit., one with a white rump < *waap-*, white + *-iti*, rump⟧ a large, North American deer (*Cervus canadensis*) with widely branching antlers and a short tail; elk

war[1] (wôr) *n.* ⟦ME *werre* < NormFr < Frank **werra*, confusion, strife, akin ? to OHG *(fir)werran*, to confuse < ?⟧ **1** open armed conflict between countries or between factions within the same country **2** any active hostility, contention, or struggle; conflict [the *war* against disease] **3** [Obs.] a battle **4** military operations as a profession or science —*adj.* of, used in, or resulting from war —*vi.* **warred**, **war′ring** **1** to carry on war; engage in military conflict **2** to be in a state of hostility or contention; contend; strive —**at war** in a state of active armed conflict —**declare war (on)** **1** to make a formal declaration of being at war (with) **2** to announce one's hostility (to) —**go to war** **1** to enter into a war **2** to become a member of the armed forces during a war

war[2] (wär) *adj., adv.* ⟦ME < ON *verre*, adj., *verr*, adv.; akin to OHG *werran*, to confuse⟧ [Scot. or North Eng.] WORSE

Wa·ran·gal (wôr′əŋ gəl) city in N Andhra Pradesh, SE India

War between the States the U.S. Civil War (1861-65): term used esp. by those sympathetic to the Confederacy

war·ble[1] (wôr′bəl) *vt.* **-bled**, **-bling** ⟦ME *werblen* < NormFr *werbler* < Frank **wirbilon*, akin to Ger *wirbeln*, to whirl, warble⟧ **1** to sing (a song, notes, etc.) melodiously, with trills, quavers, runs, etc., as a bird does **2** to express in song —*vi.* **1** to sing melodiously, with trills, etc. ☆**2** YODEL —*n.* **1** the act of warbling **2** a warbling sound; trill

war·ble[2] (wôr′bəl) *n.* ⟦prob. < Scand, as in obs. Swed *varbulde*, a boil < *var*, pus + *bulde*, tumor⟧ **1** a small, hard tumor on the back of a horse, caused by the rubbing and pressing of a saddle **2** a lump or swelling under the hide of an animal, esp. on the back, caused by the presence of a larva of a botfly, esp. a warble fly —**war′bled** *adj.*

warble fly any of a family (Oestridae) of botflies whose larvae burrow beneath the hide of cattle, horses, and other animals, producing warbles

war·bler (wôr′blər) *n.* **1** a bird or person that warbles; singer; songster ☆**2** any of a large, New World passerine family (Parulidae) of small, insect-eating birds, many of which are brightly colored, as the yellow warbler, the prothonotary warbler, or the American redstart; wood warbler **3** any of a large, mainly Old World, passerine family (Sylviidae) of small songbirds, including the whitethroats

☆**war bonnet** a ceremonial headdress worn by some North American Indian warriors, consisting of a headband and trailing part studded with feathers

War·burg (vär′boork′), **Ot·to Hein·rich** (ô′tō hīn′riH) 1883-1970; Ger. biochemist

☆**war chest** a fund, as of contributions from individuals, created for a particular purpose, as a political campaign

war crime any crime in violation of international law or accepted laws of war or of assumed norms of humane behavior, committed in connection with a war as by a member of a belligerent nation's military forces or government —**war criminal**

war cry **1** a shout uttered in a charge or battle **2** a phrase or slogan adopted by a party in any conflict, contest, election, etc.

ward (wôrd) *vt.* ⟦ME *warden* < OE *weardian*, to protect, guard, akin to OHG *warten*, to wait (see GUARD): E form and sense infl. by NormFr *warder*, to protect, keep (for OFr *garder*)⟧ **1** to turn aside; fend off; parry: usually with *off* **2** [Archaic] to keep watch over; guard; protect —*n.* ⟦ME < OE *weard*⟧ **1** the act of guarding: see WATCH AND WARD **2** the state of being under guard **3** *a)* [Now Rare] guardianship, as of a person of unsound mind or a child *b)* [Now Rare] the condition of being under the control of a guardian; wardship *c)* a child or legally incompetent person placed under the care of a guardian or court *d)* any person under another's protection or care **4** each of the parts or divisions of a jail or prison **5** a room or division of a hospital set apart for a specific class or group of patients [a maternity *ward*] **6** a district or division of a city or town, for purposes of administration, representation, voting, etc. ☆**7** *Mormon Ch.* a local unit presided over by a bishop and two counselors **8** a means of defense or protection **9** a defensive posture, position, or motion, as in fencing **10** an open space enclosed by the walls of a castle or fortification **11** [Archaic] a garrison; the guard or watch **12** *Lockmaking* *a)* a projecting ridge in a keyhole or lock face that allows only the right key to enter *b)* the notch in a key that matches this ridge

Ward (wôrd), **Ar·te·mus** (ärt′ə məs) (pseud. of *Charles Farrar Browne*) 1834-67; U.S. humorist

-ward (wərd) ⟦ME *-werd* < OE *-weard* < base of *weorthan*, to become: see WORTH[2]⟧ *suffix* **1** *forming adverbs* in a (specified) direction [*inward*] **2** *forming adjectives* in a (specified) direction [*downward*]

☆**war dance** a ceremonial dance performed as by some American Indian peoples before battle or after victory

ward·ed (wôr′did) *adj.* having wards, as a lock or key

war·den (wôrd′'n) *n.* ⟦ME *wardein* < NormFr, warden (for OFr *gardien*): see GUARDIAN⟧ **1** a person who guards, or has charge of, something; keeper, custodian, or special supervisory official [fire *warden*, game *warden*] **2** the chief administrative official of a prison **3** in England, a title for *a)* a governor *b)* an officer in charge of a certain department of government *c)* the superintendent of a port or market: now obsolete when used for other high government officers **4** in England, *a)* a governing officer in certain guilds, hospitals, etc.; trustee *b)* the head of certain British colleges and of some schools **5** in Connecticut, the chief executive of a borough **6** CHURCHWARDEN (sense 1) **7** [Archaic] a gatekeeper or watchman —**war′den·ship′** *n.*

War·den (wôrd′'n) *n.* ⟦ME *wardone*, prob. < NormFr *warder*, to keep: see WARD, *vt.*⟧ [*sometimes* **w-**] an old variety of winter pear used chiefly for cooking

ward·er[1] (wôr′dər) *n.* ⟦ME *wardere* < Anglo-Fr *wardour*, for OFr *garder*: see GUARD⟧ **1** a person who guards; watchman **2** a person who guards an entrance **3** [Chiefly Brit.] a prison guard or officer —**ward′er·ship′** *n.*

ward·er[2] (wôr′dər) *n.* ⟦LME < *wardrer*, a club < ? *warden*, WARD⟧ a staff or rod formerly carried by a king, commander, etc. as a mark of authority, and used to signal his wishes

☆**ward heeler** a person who works for a political party or boss at the lowest level, as in a ward or other city district, soliciting votes, performing minor tasks, etc.: often used with mild contempt

ward·ress (wôr′dris) ***n.*** [Chiefly Brit.] a prison matron: now rare

ward·robe (wôr′drōb′) ***n.*** ⟦ME *warderobe* < NormFr, for OFr *garderobe* < *garder* (see GUARD) + *robe*, ROBE⟧ **1** a closet or movable cabinet, usually relatively tall and provided with hangers, etc., for holding clothes **2** a room where clothes are kept; esp., a room in a theater where costumes are kept **3** a collection of clothes; esp., *a)* the complete supply of clothes of a person *b)* a supply of clothes for a particular season or purpose [a spring *wardrobe*] *c)* the collection of costumes of a theater or theatrical company **4** in a royal or noble household, the department in charge of clothes

☆**wardrobe trunk** a large trunk for carrying clothing, etc. and, when standing upright, for hanging suits, dresses, etc.

ward·room (wôrd′ro͞om′) ***n.*** ⟦WARD, *n.* + ROOM⟧ **1** in a warship, a compartment used for eating and lounging by commissioned officers, except, usually, the captain **2** these officers collectively

-wards (wərdz) *suffix forming adverbs* -WARD (sense 1)

ward·ship (wôrd′ship′) ***n.*** **1** the office of a guardian; guardianship; custody, as of a minor **2** the condition of being a ward, or in the care of a guardian

ware[1] (wer) ***n.*** ⟦ME < OE *waru*, merchandise, specialized use of *waru*, watchful care, in the sense "what is kept safe": for IE base see GUARD⟧ **1** any piece or kind of goods that a store, merchant, peddler, etc. has to sell; also, any skill or service that one seeks to sell: *usually used in pl.* **2** things, usually of the same general kind, that are for sale; a (specified) kind of merchandise, collectively: generally in compounds [*hardware, earthenware, glassware*] **3** dishes made of baked and glazed clay; pottery, or a specified kind or make of pottery

ware[2] (wer) ***adj.*** ⟦ME *war* < OE *wær* < base of *waru*: see prec.⟧ [Archaic] **1** aware; conscious (*of*) **2** on one's guard; ready; wary **3** prudent; cautious; wise —***vt.*** **wared**, **war′ing** ⟦ME *waren* < OE *warian*⟧ to beware of: usually in the imperative, esp. in hunting [*ware* hounds!]

ware[3] (wār) ***vt.*** **wared**, **war′ing** ⟦ME *waren* < ON *verja*, akin to OE *werian*: see WEAR[1]⟧ [Scot. or North Eng.] to spend or squander (money, time, etc.)

-ware (wer) *combining form* computer software [*courseware, shareware*]

ware·house (wer′hous′; *for v., usually*, -houz′) ***n.*** ⟦ME: see WARE[1] & HOUSE⟧ **1** a building where wares, or goods, are stored, as before distribution to retailers, or are kept in reserve, in bond, etc. **2** [Chiefly Brit.] a wholesale store or, esp. formerly, a large retail store —***vt.*** **-housed′**, **-hous′ing** **1** to place or store in a warehouse **2** to place (a severely disabled person, a mentally ill person, an elderly person, etc.) in a large, impersonal institution —**ware′house′man** (-mən) ***n.***, *pl.* **-men** (-mən)

ware·room (-ro͞om′) ***n.*** a room used for storing or displaying things for sale

war·fare (wôr′fer′) ***n.*** **1** the action of waging war; armed conflict **2** conflict or struggle of any kind

☆**war·fa·rin** (wôr′fə rin) ***n.*** ⟦*W(isconsin) A(lumni) R(esearch) F(oundation)* + (COUM)ARIN⟧ **1** a colorless, odorless, tasteless rat poison, $C_{19}H_{16}O_4$, a crystalline powder that causes fatal internal bleeding in rodents **2** this drug neutralized with sodium hydroxide, used in medicine as an anticoagulant

war game **1** KRIEGSPIEL **2** [*pl.*] practice maneuvers involving actual troops, sailors, etc. and military vehicles and equipment **3** the testing of a plan or hypothetical situation, as in devising military strategy, by the use of a computer, simulated models, etc.

war-game (wôr′gām′) ***vt.*** **-gamed′**, **-gam′ing** to examine or plan by a war game —***vi.*** to engage in a war game or war games

☆**war hawk** HAWK[1] (***n.*** 2)

war·head (-hed′) ***n.*** the head, or forward section, of a torpedo, bomb, or other projectile, containing the explosive charge, chemical, etc.

War·hol (wôr′hôl′, -hōl′), **An·dy** (an′dē) (born *Andrew Warhola*) 1928-87; U.S. artist & filmmaker

war·horse (wôr′hôrs′) ***n.*** **1** a horse used in battle; charger: also written **war horse** **2** [Informal] a person who has been through many battles or struggles; veteran **3** [Informal] a symphony, play, opera, etc. that has been performed so often as to seem trite and stale

war·i·ly (wer′ə lē) ***adv.*** in a wary manner; cautiously

war·i·ness (-ē nis) ***n.*** the quality or state of being wary

war·i·son (war′ə sən) ***n.*** ⟦ME < NormFr, for OFr *garison*: see GARRISON⟧ **1** [Obs.] a reward or gift given by a superior **2** ⟦from such an erroneous use by Sir Walter SCOTT[2] in *The Lay of the Last Minstrel* (1805)⟧ [Literary] a note sounded as a signal to attack

war·like (wôr′līk′) ***adj.*** **1** fit for, fond of, or ready for war; bellicose; martial **2** of or appropriate to war **3** threatening, or suggesting the likelihood of, war —***SYN.*** MARTIAL

war·lock (wôr′läk′) ***n.*** ⟦ME *warloghe* < OE *wærloga*, traitor, liar < *wær*, faith, a compact (see VERY) + *leogan*, to LIE[2]⟧ a man who practices witchcraft, esp. black magic; sorcerer

war·lord (wôr′lôrd′) ***n.*** **1** a high military officer in a warlike nation **2** an aggressive tyrant **3** a local ruler or bandit leader with some sort of military following in a district where the established government is weak —**war′lord′ism′** ***n.***

warm (wôrm) ***adj.*** ⟦ME < OE *wearm*, akin to Ger *warm* < IE base **gwher-*, hot > Gr *thermē*, heat, *thermos*, warm, *theros*, summer, L *formus*, warm, *fornax*, furnace⟧ **1** *a)* having or giving off a moderate degree of heat [a *warm* iron, *warm* coffee] *b)* giving off pleasurable heat [a *warm* fire] *c)* uncomfortably warm; hot [a *warm* night] **2** having the natural heat of living beings: said of the body, blood, etc. **3** *a)* heated or overheated, as with exercise or hard work *b)* such as to make one heated or overheated [*warm* exercise, work, etc.] **4** effective in keeping body heat in [*warm* clothing] **5** characterized by lively disagreement: said of argument or controversy **6** fervent; ardent; enthusiastic [*warm* encouragement] **7** lively, vigorous, brisk, or animated **8** quick to anger; irascible; heated **9** *a)* genial; cordial [a *warm* welcome] *b)* sincere; grateful [*warm* thanks] *c)* sympathetic, affectionate, or loving *d)* passionate; amorous **10** suggesting warmth; having yellow, orange, or red hue: said of colors **11** newly made; fresh; strong: said of a scent or trail **12** [Informal] close to discovering something; on the verge of guessing or finding, as in games **13** [Informal] disagreeable; uncomfortable [to make things *warm* for someone] —***adv.*** so as to be warm; warmly —***vt.*** ⟦ME *warmen* < OE *wearmian*⟧ **1** to make warm; raise the temperature of to a moderate extent **2** to make excited, animated, ardent, enthusiastic, lively, etc. **3** to fill with pleasant or kindly emotions [a sight to *warm* the heart] —***vi.*** **1** to become warm **2** to become friendly, kindly, affectionate, or sympathetic (*to, toward,* or *up to*) **3** to become excited, ardent, enthusiastic, lively, etc.: often with *to* **4** to feel a glow of pleasure; bask —***n.*** [Informal] a warming or being warmed —***SYN.*** TENDER[1] —**warm up** **1** *a)* to heat or be heated; make or become warm *b)* to make or become sufficiently warm to operate effectively or efficiently [to *warm up* an engine] **2** to reheat (cooked food, etc.): also **warm over** **3** to make or become more animated, excited, ardent, lively, etc. **4** to practice, exercise, or limber up awhile in preparation for going into a game, contest, performance, etc. —**warm′er** ***n.*** —**warm′ly** ***adv.*** —**warm′ness** ***n.***

warm·blood·ed (wôrm′blud′id) ***adj.*** **1** having a body temperature that remains relatively constant, independent of and usually higher than that of the surroundings [mammals and birds are *warmblooded* animals] **2** having or characterized by an eager, lively, or passionate temperament; ardent; fervent —**warm′blood′ed·ness** ***n.***

☆**warmed-o·ver** (wôrmd′ō′vər) ***adj.*** **1** reheated [*warmed-over* hash] **2** presented again, without freshness or significant change [*warmed-over* ideas]

warm front *Meteorol.* the forward edge of an advancing mass of warm air that replaces colder air, usually while causing steady precipitation

warm·heart·ed (wôrm′härt′id) ***adj.*** kind, sympathetic, friendly, loving, etc. —***SYN.*** TENDER[1] —**warm′heart′ed·ly** ***adv.*** —**warm′heart′ed·ness** ***n.***

warming pan a long-handled, covered pan for holding live coals: formerly used to warm beds

warm·ish (wôr′mish) ***adj.*** somewhat warm

war·mon·ger (wôr′muŋ′gər, -mäŋ′-) ***n.*** a person bent on promoting or bringing about war: a derogatory use —**war′mon′ger·ing** ***adj.***, ***n.***

☆**war·mouth** (wôr′mouth′) ***n.***, *pl.* **-mouth′** or **-mouths′** ⟦< ?⟧ a freshwater sunfish (*Lepomis gulosus*) of the E U.S. and the Mississippi basin, usually olive-green or bronze mottled with darker colorings

warmth (wôrmth) ***n.*** ⟦ME *wermthe*: see WARM & -TH[1]⟧ **1** *a)* the state or quality of having, giving off, or keeping in a moderate degree of heat *b)* the degree of heat in a substance, esp. when it is moderate; mild heat **2** *a)* excitement or vigor of feeling; enthusiasm, ardor, zeal, etc. *b)* sympathetic, cordial, or affectionate feelings or nature *c)* slight anger **3** a glowing effect obtained by using red, yellow, etc.

☆**warm-up** (wôrm′up′) ***n.*** the act or an instance of warming up —***adj.*** designating a garment, as a jacket, worn for exercising: also **warm′up′**

warn (wôrn) ***vt.*** ⟦ME *warnien* < OE *wearnian* < IE base **wer-*, to heed > GUARD⟧ **1** to tell (a person) of a danger, coming evil, misfortune, etc.; put on guard; caution **2** to caution about certain acts; admonish [*warned* against smoking in the building] **3** to notify in advance; inform **4** to give notice to (a person) to stay or keep (*off, away,* etc.) —***vi.*** to give warning —***SYN.*** ADVISE —**warn′er** ***n.***

warn·ing (wôr′niŋ) ***n.*** **1** the act of one that warns, or the state of being warned **2** something that serves to warn **3** *Meteorol.* an official alert, as by the National Weather Service, that, variously, a tornado, severe thunderstorm, flash flood, etc. has been spotted or detected by radar in the area: cf. WATCH (***n.*** 10) —***adj.*** that warns; serving to warn —**warn′ing·ly** ***adv.***

warning coloration bright and striking coloration, as the conspicuous stripes of the skunk, occurring in many distasteful or poisonous animals

warning track *Baseball* a rubberized, dirt, or gravel strip of ground, just inside the walls of the field, that helps a fielder locate the wall while looking up at a fly ball

War of American Independence *a Brit. name for* the AMERICAN REVOLUTION

War of 1812 a war (1812-15) between the U.S. and Great Britain

War of Independence AMERICAN REVOLUTION

war of nerves a conflict or campaign characterized by intimidation, bluffing, etc. to wear down or demoralize an opponent

War of Secession the U.S. Civil War: also called WAR BETWEEN THE STATES or **War of the Rebellion**

warp (wôrp) ***n.*** ⟦ME < OE *wearp* < base of *weorpan*, to throw, akin to Ger *werfen* < IE **werb-* < base **wer-*, to turn, bend > WORM⟧ **1** *a)* a distortion, as a twist or bend, in wood or in an object made of wood, caused by contraction in drying *b)* any similar distortion, as in metal *c)* the state or fact of being so distorted **2** a mental twist, quirk, aberration, or bias **3** *a)* silt, sediment, or mud deposited as by a stream *b)* a deposit of this **4** *Naut.* a rope run from a ship or boat to a dock, anchor, buoy, etc., used to pull the vessel to a new position **5** *a)* *Weaving* the set of threads running lengthwise in the loom and crossed by the weft, or woof *b)* the very fiber or essential part of something; foundation; base —***vt.*** ⟦ME *warpen*, to throw, bend < OE *weorpan*, to throw⟧ **1** to bend or twist out of shape; distort **2** *a)* to turn from the true, natural, or right course *b)* to turn from a healthy, sane, or normal condition; pervert; bias (said of the mind, character, judgment, etc.) *c)* to twist or distort in telling; misinterpret [a *warped* account] **3** *Naut.* to move (a vessel) to a new position by pulling on a rope that has been attached to a dock, anchor, buoy, etc. **4** *Weaving* to arrange (threads or yarns) so as to form a warp —***vi.*** **1** to become bent or twisted out of shape, as wood does in drying **2** to turn aside from the true, natural, or right course **3** *Naut.* *a)* to warp a vessel to a new position *b)* to move by being warped (said as of a ship) —**SYN.** DEFORM —**warp′er** ***n.***

☆**war paint** **1** a pigment applied to the face and body, as by some American Indian peoples, in preparation for battle **2** [Slang] cosmetics; makeup: a humorous usage

☆**war·path** (wôr′path′) ***n.*** the path or course taken by American Indians on a warlike expedition —**on the warpath** **1** at war, ready for war, or looking for war **2** actively angry; ready to fight

warp beam the roller on which the top is wound in a loom

war·plane (wôr′plān′) ***n.*** any airplane for use in war

☆**warp speed** ⟦term used in science fiction, esp. in the *Star Trek* TV series, for a speed greater than the speed of light < (TIME) WARP + SPEED⟧ [Slang] a very high rate of speed; extremely fast pace

war·rant (wôr′ənt, wär′-) ***n.*** ⟦ME *warant* < NormFr (OFr *garant*), a warrant < Frank **warand* < prp. of **warjan*; akin to OE *werian*, to guard, defend: see WEIR⟧ **1** *a)* authorization or sanction, as by a superior or the law *b)* justification or reasonable grounds for some act, course, statement, or belief **2** something that serves as an assurance, or guarantee, of some event or result **3** a writing serving as authorization or certification for something; specif., *a)* authorization in writing for the payment or receipt of money *b)* a short-term note issued by a municipality or other governmental agency, usually in anticipation of tax revenues *c)* an option issued by a company granting the holder the right to buy certain securities, generally common stock, at a specified price and usually for a limited time *d) Law* a writ or order authorizing an officer to make an arrest, seizure, or search, or perform some other designated act *e) Mil.* the certificate of appointment to the grade of warrant officer (cf. WARRANT OFFICER) —***vt.*** **1** *a)* to give (someone) authorization or sanction to do something *b)* to authorize (the doing of something) **2** to serve as justification or reasonable grounds for (an act, belief, etc.) [a remark that did not *warrant* such anger] **3** to give formal assurance, or guarantee, to (someone) or for (something); specif., *a)* to guarantee the quality, quantity, condition, etc. of (goods) to the purchaser *b)* to guarantee to (the purchaser) that goods sold are as represented *c)* to guarantee to (the purchaser) the title of goods purchased; assure of indemnification against loss *d) Law* to guarantee the title of granted property to (the grantee) **4** [Informal] to state with confidence; affirm emphatically [I *warrant* they'll be late] —**SYN.** ASSERT —**war′rant·a·ble** ***adj.***

war·rant·ee (wôr′ən tē′) ***n.*** *Law* a person to whom a warranty is given

warrant officer an officer of the U.S. armed forces ranking above a noncommissioned officer but below a commissioned officer and holding office on a warrant instead of a commission

war·ran·tor (wôr′ən tôr′, -tər) ***n.*** *Law* a person who warrants, or gives warranty: also **war′rant·er** (-tər)

war·ran·ty (wôr′ən tē, wär′-; *also, esp. for v.,* wôr′ən tē′, wär′-) ***n., pl.*** **-ties** ⟦ME *warantie* < NormFr (OFr *garantie*): see WARRANT⟧ **1** official authorization or sanction **2** justification; reasonable grounds, as for an opinion or action **3** *Law* a guarantee; specif., *a)* a guarantee or an assurance, explicit or implied, of something having to do with a contract, as of sale; esp., the seller's assurance to the purchaser that the goods or property is or shall be as represented and, if not, will be replaced or repaired, usually within a specified period of time [a ten-year *warranty*] *b)* a guarantee by the insured that the facts are as stated in regard to an insurance risk, or that specified conditions shall be fulfilled: it constitutes a part of the contract and must be fulfilled to keep the contract in force *c)* a covenant by which the seller of real estate assures, and is bound to defend, the security of the title (in full **covenant of warranty**) —***vt.*** **-tied, -ty·ing** to give a warranty for; warrant

warranty deed *Law* a deed to real estate containing a covenant of warranty: see WARRANTY (sense 3c)

war·ren (wôr′ən, wär′-) ***n.*** ⟦ME *wareine* < NormFr *warenne* < *warir*, to preserve < Frank **warjan*: see WARRANT⟧ **1** [Brit. Historical] a piece of land enclosed for the breeding of game **2** a space or limited area in which rabbits breed or are numerous **3** any building or group of buildings crowded like a rabbit warren

War·ren[1] (wôr′ən, wär′-) ***n.*** ⟦NormFr *warin* < ? OHG *Warin*, the Varini, a people mentioned by Tacitus⟧ a masculine name

War·ren[2] (wôr′ən, wär′-) **1 Earl** 1891-1974; chief justice of the U.S. (1953-69) **2 Robert Penn** 1905-89; U.S. writer & poet: 1st poet laureate of the U.S. (1986-87)

War·ren[3] (wôr′ən, wär′-) ⟦after Dr. Joseph *Warren* (1741-75), killed at Bunker Hill⟧ city in SE Mich.: suburb of Detroit

war·ren·er (-ər) ***n.*** the owner or keeper of a warren

War·ring·ton (wôr′iŋ tən, wär′-) city in Cheshire, NW England, on the Mersey

war·ri·or (wôr′yər, -ē ər) ***n.*** ⟦ME *werreour* < NormFr < *werrier*, to make war < *werre*, WAR[1]⟧ a person taking part or experienced in conflict, esp. in battle

war room a room equipped with the technical means to gather information, plan strategy, direct activities, etc., esp. for a military or political campaign

☆**war·saw** (wôr′sô′) ***n.*** ⟦altered < AmSp *guasa*⟧ a very large, black grouper (*Epinephelus nigritus*) of the Caribbean

War·saw (wôr′sô′) capital of Poland, on the Vistula River: Pol. name **War·sza·wa** (vär shä′vä)

☆**Warsaw Pact** ⟦after prec., where the treaty was signed⟧ **1** a treaty signed in 1955 by the Soviet Union and seven of its European satellites, that established a military alliance for collective security: it was dissolved in 1991 **2** these countries, sometimes excluding the Soviet Union, collectively

war·ship (wôr′ship′) ***n.*** any ship made or armed for use in war

war·sle (wär′səl) ***n., vi., vt.*** **-sled, -sling** [Scot. or North Eng.] WRESTLE —**war′sler** ***n.***

Wars of the Roses the English civil war (1455-85) fought between the house of York, whose emblem was a white rose, and the house of Lancaster, whose emblem was a red rose: the war ended with the establishment of the house of Tudor on the English throne

wart (wôrt) ***n.*** ⟦ME *warte* < OE *wearte*, akin to Ger *warze* < IE base **wer-*, a raised place > L *verruca*, wart, VARIX⟧ **1** a small, usually hard, tumorous growth on the skin, caused by a virus **2** any small protuberance, as a glandular protuberance on a plant **3** an imperfection, failing, flaw, etc.: *usually used in pl.* [a lovable person, *warts* and all] —**wart′y** ***adj.*** **wart′i·er, wart′i·est**

War·ta (vär′tä) river in Poland, flowing from the S part northwest into the Oder: 445 mi (716 km)

Wart·burg (värt′boork) ***n.*** medieval castle in Thuringia, Germany, where Martin Luther completed his translation of the New Testament (1521-22)

wart hog a wild African hog (*Phacochoerus aethiopicus*) having a broad, flat face, very large, incurved tusks, and conical warts on the cheeks between the eyes and tusks: also written **wart′hog′** ***n.***

war·time (wôr′tīm′) ***n.*** a time of war —***adj.*** of or characteristic of such a time

☆**war whoop** a WAR CRY uttered as by North American Indians on going into battle

War·wick[1] (wôr′ik, wär′-), Earl of (*Richard Neville*) 1428-71; Eng. statesman & military leader

War·wick[2] (wôr′ik, wär′-) WARWICKSHIRE

War·wick·shire (wôr′ik shir′, wär′-; -shər) county in central England: 764 sq mi (1,979 sq km)

war·y (wer′ē) ***adj.*** **war′i·er, war′i·est** ⟦< WARE[2] + -Y[2]⟧ **1** on one's guard; cautious, suspicious, etc. **2** characterized by caution [a *wary* look] —**SYN.** CAREFUL —**wary of** careful of

was (wuz, wäz) ***vi.*** ⟦ME < OE *wæs*, 1st & 3d pers. sing. of *wesan*, to be < IE base **wes-*, to dwell, stay > Sans *vastū*, house: not orig. connected with BE⟧ *1st & 3d pers. sing., pt., of* BE

wa·sa·bi (wə sä′bē, wä′sə bē) ***n.*** ⟦Jpn⟧ an herb (*Eutrema wasabi*) of the crucifer family, with greenish roots that are grated and used like horseradish in Japanese dishes

Wa·satch Range (wô′sach′) ⟦< AmInd (Ute), lit., mountain pass⟧ range of the Rockies, extending from central Utah to SE Ida.: highest peak, 12,008 ft (3,660 m)

wash (wôsh, wäsh) ***vt.*** ⟦ME *wasshen* < OE *wæscan*, akin to Ger *waschen*: for prob. IE base see WATER⟧ **1** to clean by means of water or other liquid, as by dipping, tumbling, or scrubbing, often with soap, a detergent, etc. **2** to make clean in a religious or moral sense; purify **3** to make wet, or moisten; drench or flush with water or other liquid **4** to cleanse (itself or another) by licking, as a cat does **5** to flow over, past, or against: said of a sea, river, lake, waves, etc. **6** to soak (*out*), flush (*off*), or carry (*away*) by or as by the use or action of water [to *wash* out dirt, a bridge *washed* away by the flood] **7** *a)* to make by flowing over and wearing away substance [a heavy rain that *washed* gullies in the bank] *b)* to cut into or erode; wear (*out* or *away*) by flowing over [the flood *washed* out the road] **8** to act as a suitable cleaning agent for [soap that will *wash* silks] **9** to cover with a thin or watery coating of paint, esp. of water color **10** to cover with a thin layer of metal **11** *Chem.* *a)* to pass distilled water through (a precipitate in a filter) *b)* to pass (a gas) over or through a liquid in order to remove soluble matter **12** *Mining* *a)* to pass water through or over (earth, gravel, etc.) in order to separate ore, metal, precious stones, etc. *b)* to separate (the ore, etc.) in this way —***vi.*** **1** to wash oneself or one's hands, face, etc. **2** *a)* to wash clothes *b)* to clean anything in, or by means of, water, etc. **3** to undergo washing, esp. without fading or other damage **4** to be removed by washing: usually with *out* or *away* [stains that will *wash* out] **5** to sweep or flow (*over, against, along, up,* etc.) in or as in waves or a current, stream, etc. **6** to be cut, worn, or carried (*out* or *away*) by the action of water [the bridge had *washed* out] **7** to be eroded, as by the action of rain or a river **8** [Informal] to withstand scrutiny or an examination [an alibi that won't *wash*] —***n.*** **1** *a)* the act or an instance of washing ☆*b)* a place where something is washed (usually in comb.) [a *carwash*] **2** a quantity of clothes, etc. washed, or to be washed **3** waste liquid; specif., refuse liquid food, as from cooking; swill; hogwash **4** *a)* the rush, sweep, or surge of water or waves *b)* the sound of this *c)* water rushing, sweeping, or surging in waves *d)* the surge or eddy of water caused by a propeller, oars, paddle wheel, etc. *e)* a disturbed eddy of air left behind a moving airplane, propeller, etc. **5** wear or erosion caused by a flow or falling of water, or by the action of waves **6** silt, mud, debris, etc. carried and dropped by running water, as of a stream **7** soil or earth from which metals, ores, precious stones, etc. may be washed **8** *a)* low ground which is flooded part of the time, and partly dry the rest, with water standing in pools *b)* a bog; marsh *c)* a shallow pool or pond, or a small stream *d)* a shallow arm of the sea or part of a river **9** a channel made by running water ☆**10** in the W U.S., the dry bed of a stream which flows only occasionally, usually in a ravine or canyon **11** a thin, watery layer of paint, esp. of watercolor, applied with even, sweeping movement of the brush **12** a thin coating of metal applied to a surface in liquid form **13** any of various liquids as for cosmetic, grooming, or medicinal use *[mouthwash]* **14** fermented liquor ready for distillation **15** weak liquor or liquid food ☆**16** [Informal] a drink of water, beer, etc. taken with whiskey, rum, etc.; chaser ☆**17** [Informal] a situation in which contrasted elements, as the losses and gains in a business transaction, offset each other —*adj.* that can be washed without damage; washable *[a wash dress]* —**come out in the wash** [Informal] **1** to be revealed or explained sooner or later **2** to be resolved eventually, esp. without intervention and after a period of time —**wash down 1** to clean by washing, esp. with a stream of water **2** to follow (food, a drink of whiskey, etc.) with a drink, as of water —**wash out** [Slang] ☆**1** to drop out of or be dropped from a training course, athletic program, etc. because of failure **2** to reject or fail —**wash up 1** to wash oneself or one's hands, face, etc. **2** [Brit.] to wash dishes, cups, cutlery, etc., as after a meal

SYN.—**wash**, the most general of these words, refers to any earthy material carried and deposited by running water; **drift**, the more precise term as used in geology, is usually qualified by a word descriptive of the manner in which the material is transported *[glacial or fluvial drift]*; **alluvium** usually refers to a deposit of relatively fine particles, such as soil, left by a flood, etc.; **silt** applies to material composed of very fine particles, such as that deposited on riverbeds or suspended in standing water

Wash[1] (wôsh, wäsh), **The** shallow inlet of the North Sea, on the E coast of England: *c.* 20 mi (32 km) long

Wash[2] *abbrev.* Washington

wash·a·ble (wôsh′ə bəl) *adj.* that can be washed without shrinking, fading, or other damage —☆*n.* a washable fabric or garment

☆**wash-and-wear** (wôsh′ən wer′) *adj.* designating or of fabrics or garments that need little or no ironing after washing

wash·board (-bôrd′) *n.* ☆**1** *a)* a board or frame with a ridged surface of metal, glass, etc., used for scrubbing dirt out of clothes: also used as a percussion instrument, as in a jug band *b)* the worn surface of a paved road resembling this **2** BASEBOARD **3** *Naut.* a thin, broad plank fastened around the cockpit of a boat, on the sill of a companionway entrance, etc. to keep out the sea and spray

wash·bowl (-bōl′) *n.* ☆a bowl or basin for use in washing one's hands and face, etc., esp. a bathroom fixture fitted with water faucets and a drain: also **wash′ba′sin** (-bā′sən)

☆**wash·cloth** (-klôth′) *n.* a small cloth, usually of terry, used in washing the face or body

wash·day (-dā′) *n.* a day, often the same day every week, when the clothes, linens, etc. of a household are washed

wash drawing a drawing done with brush on paper in monochrome using many washes of transparent watercolor or of India ink, shading from light to dark

washed-out (wôsht′out′) *adj.* **1** faded in color, specif. from washing **2** [Informal] tired; spiritless **3** [Informal] tired-looking; pale and wan

washed-up (-up′) *adj.* **1** cleaned up **2** [Informal] tired; exhausted ☆**3** [Slang] finished; done for; having failed

wash·er (wôsh′ər) *n.* **1** a person who washes **2** a flat disk or ring of metal, leather, rubber, etc., used variously to make a seat as for a nut or the head of a bolt, to lock a nut in place, to prevent leakage, etc. **3** a machine for washing something; specif., WASHING MACHINE **4** a device for washing gases

wash·er·man (-mən) *n., pl.* **-men** (-mən) **1** a man whose work is washing clothes, linens, etc. **2** a person who operates a machine that washes (in various manufacturing senses)

wash·er·wom·an (-woom′ən) *n., pl.* **-wom′en** (-wim′in) a woman whose work is washing clothes, linens, etc.; laundress

wash goods washable fabrics or garments

wash·ing (wôsh′iŋ) *n.* **1** the act of a person or thing that washes; a cleaning, flushing, etc. in water or other liquid **2** clothes or other things washed or to be washed, esp. at one time **3** matter obtained or removed by washing **4** a thin coating, as of metal, put on in liquid form **5** *Finance* the act of making a wash sale

washing machine a machine for washing clothes, linens, etc., now usually operated automatically; washer

washing soda a crystalline form of sodium carbonate

Wash·ing·ton[1] (wôsh′iŋ tən, wäsh′-) **1 Book·er T(aliaferro)** (book′ər) 1856-1915; U.S. educator & writer **2 George** 1732-99; 1st president of the U.S. (1789-97): commander in chief of the Continental army

Wash·ing·ton[2] (wôsh′iŋ tən, wäsh′-) ⟦after George WASHINGTON[1]⟧ **1** NW coastal state of the U.S.: admitted 1889; 66,544 sq mi (172,348 sq km); cap. Olympia: abbrev. *WA, Wash,* or *Wa* **2** capital of the U.S., coextensive with the District of Columbia: also called **Washington, D.C. 3 Lake** lake in WC Wash., near Seattle: *c.* 20 mi (32 km) long **4 Mount** mountain of the White Mountains, in N N.H.: highest peak in New England: 6,288 ft (1,917 m)

Wash·ing·to·ni·an (-tō′nē ən) *adj.* **1** of or characteristic of George Washington **2** *a)* of the state of Washington *b)* of the city of Washington: usually used in the predicate —*n.* **1** a person born or living in the state of Washington **2** a person born or living in the city of Washington

☆**Washington palm** a tall, slender fan palm (*Washingtonia filifera*) native to S California

☆**Washington pie** a layer cake with a filling of cream, custard, chocolate, fruit jelly, or the like

Washington's Birthday Feb. 22, George Washington's birthday: it is celebrated as a legal holiday in most states on the third Monday in February

Wash·i·ta (wäsh′i tô′, wôsh′-) *alt. sp. of* OUACHITA

wash·out (wôsh′out′) *n.* ☆**1** the washing away of soil, earth, rocks, etc. by a sudden, strong flow of water ☆**2** a hole or gap made by such washing away, as in a railroad bed **3** [Slang] a complete failure

☆**wash·rag** (-rag′) *n.* WASHCLOTH

☆**wash·room** (-room′) *n.* **1** a room for washing **2** RESTROOM

☆**wash sale 1** the illegal act of buying and simultaneously selling shares of a company's stock so as to create the appearance of active trading **2** the act of selling and then buying back within 30 days shares of a company's stock: it is now illegal to claim a tax deduction on the losses from such a sale

wash·stand (-stand′) *n.* **1** a table designed to hold a bowl, pitcher, etc., as used for washing the face and hands **2** a washbowl that is a bathroom fixture

wash·tub (-tub′) *n.* a tub for washing clothes, etc.; often, a stationary metal tub fitted with water faucets and a drain

wash·wom·an (-woom′ən) *n., pl.* **-wom′en** (-wim′in) WASHERWOMAN

wash·y (wôsh′ē, wäsh′ē) *adj.* **wash′i·er, wash′i·est 1** [Archaic] watery; diluted **2** weak in color; pale **3** without force or substance; insipid

was·n't (wuz′ənt, wäz′-) *contraction* was not

wasp (wäsp, wôsp) *n.* ⟦ME *waspe* < OE *wæsp*, akin to Ger *wespe* < Gmc base **waps-* < IE **wobhsā* < base **webh-*, to WEAVE (in reference to the cocoonlike nest)⟧ any of various families of winged hymenopteran insects, characterized by a slender body with the abdomen attached by a narrow stalk, biting mouthparts, and, in the females and workers, a vicious sting that can be used repeatedly: some wasps, as the hornet, are characterized by a colonial or social organization

wasp

☆**WASP** or **Wasp** (wäsp, wôsp) *n.* ⟦*W(hite) A(nglo-)S(axon) P(rotestant)*⟧ a person who belongs to or is thought of as being part of a white, upper middle-class, N European, Protestant group regarded as traditionally dominating economic, political, and cultural activity in the U.S.: a term often used with mild derision —**WASP′ish** *adj.*, **Wasp′ish** —**WASP′y** *adj.*, **Wasp′y**

wasp·ish (wäs′pish, wôs′-) *adj.* **1** of or like a wasp **2** having a slender waist, like a wasp **3** bad-tempered; snappish —**wasp′ish·ly** *adv.* —**wasp′ish·ness** *n.*

wasp waist a very slender or tightly corseted waist

wasp·y (-pē) *adj.* **wasp′i·er, wasp′i·est** of, like, or characteristic of a wasp —**wasp′i·ness** *n.*

was·sail (wäs′əl, was′-; -āl′) *n.* ⟦ME, earlier *wæs hæil* < ON *ves heill*, lit., be hale, be hearty (replacing OE *wes hal*, lit., be whole)⟧ **1** a salutation formerly given in drinking the health of a person, as at a festivity **2** the spiced ale or other liquor with which such healths were drunk **3** a celebration with much drinking, esp. at Christmastime; carousal —*vi.* **1** to drink wassails **2** [Brit.] to go caroling from house to house at Christmastime —*vt.* to drink to the health or prosperity of —**was′sail·er** *n.*

Was·ser·mann (väs′ər män′; *E* wäs′ər mən), **Au·gust von** (ou′goost fôn) 1866-1925; Ger. bacteriologist

Wassermann test (*or* **reaction**) ⟦after prec., who devised it⟧ a complement-fixation test for the diagnosis of syphilis by determining the presence of syphilitic antibodies in the blood serum

wast (wäst) *vi.* ⟦Early ModE < WAS + -ST, replacing ME *were* < OE *wære*: see WERE⟧ *archaic 2d pers. sing., past indic., of* BE: used with *thou*

wast·age (wās′tij) *n.* **1** loss by use, decay, deterioration, etc. **2** anything wasted, or the amount of this; waste **3** *Geol. a)* the processes by which snow and ice masses are reduced by melting, evaporation, etc. *b)* the amount of material lost through these processes

waste (wāst) *vt.* **wast′ed, wast′ing** ⟦ME *wasten* < NormFr *waster* < L *vastare*, to lay waste, devastate (< *vastus*: see VAST): infl. by Gmc **wostjan* > OHG *wuosten*⟧ **1** to destroy; devastate; ruin **2** to wear away; consume gradually; use up **3** to make weak, feeble, or emaciated; wear away the strength, vigor, or life of *[a man wasted by age and disease]* **4** to use up or spend without real need, gain, or purpose; squander **5** to fail to take proper advantage of *[to waste an opportunity]* ☆**6** [Slang] to kill, usually with violence; esp., to murder —*vi.* **1** to lose strength, health, vigor, flesh, etc., as by disease; become weak or enfeebled: often with *away* **2** to be used up or worn down gradually; become smaller or fewer by gradual loss **3** [Now Rare] to pass or be spent: said of time **4** to be wasted, or not put to full or proper use —*adj.* ⟦ME *wast* < NormFr < L *vastus*: see VAST⟧ **1** uncultivated or uninhabited; wild; barren; desolate **2** left over, superfluous, refuse, or no longer of use *[a waste product]* **3** produced in excess of what is or can be used *[waste energy]* **4** excreted from the body as useless or superfluous material: said as of feces or urine **5** used to carry off or hold waste or refuse *[a waste pipe, wastebasket]* —*n.* ⟦ME < NormFr < the adj.; also in part < L *vastum*, neut. of *vastus*⟧ **1** uncultivated or uninhabited land, as a desert or wilderness **2** *a)* a desolate, uncultivated, or devastated stretch, tract, or area *b)* a vast expanse, as of the sea **3** a wasting or being wasted; specif., *a)* a useless or profitless spending or consuming; squandering, as of money or time *b)* a failure to take advantage (*of* something) *c)* a gradual loss, decrease, or destruction by use, wear, decay, deterioration, etc. **4** useless, superfluous, or discarded material, as ashes, garbage, or sewage **5** matter excreted from the body, as feces or urine **6** cotton fiber or yarn left over from the process of milling, used for wiping machinery, packing bearings, etc. **7** [Obs.] ruin or devastation, as by war or fire **8** *Geol.* material derived by land erosion or disintegration of rock, and carried to the sea by rivers and streams —**go to waste** to be or become wasted —**lay waste (to)** to destroy; devastate; make desolate

SYN.—**waste**, in this connection, is the general word for any stretch of uncultivated and uninhabited land; a **desert** is a barren, arid, usually sandy tract of land; **badlands** is applied to a barren, hilly waste where rapid erosion has cut the soft rocks into fantastic shapes; **wilderness** refers to an uninhabited waste where a lack of paths or trails makes it difficult to find one's way

waste·bas·ket (wāst′bas′kit) ***n.*** a basket or other open container for wastepaper, bits of trash, etc.: also **wastepaper basket**

wast·ed (wās′təd) ***adj.*** ☆[Slang] quite intoxicated by drugs or alcohol

waste·ful (wāst′fəl) ***adj.*** using more than is necessary; extravagant —**waste′ful·ly** ***adv.*** —**waste′ful·ness** ***n.***

waste·land (-land′) ***n.*** **1** land that is uncultivated, barren, or without vegetation **2** a neglected, improperly managed, or intellectually unproductive activity, endeavor, etc.

waste·pa·per (-pā′pər) ***n.*** paper thrown away after use or as useless: also written **waste paper**

waste pipe a pipe for carrying off waste water, sink drainage, excess steam, etc.

wast·er (wās′tər) ***n.*** a person or thing that wastes; esp., a spendthrift or prodigal; wastrel

waste·wa·ter (wāst′wôt′ər, -wät′-) ***n.*** water used by a factory, household, etc. and discharged as sewage

wast·ing (wās′tiŋ) ***adj.*** **1** desolating; destructive [a *wasting* war] **2** destructive to health [*wasting* disease] —**wast′ing·ly** ***adv.***

wast·rel (wās′trəl) ***n.*** ⟦dim. of WASTER⟧ **1** a person who wastes; esp., a spendthrift **2** GOOD-FOR-NOTHING

wat (wät) ***n.*** ⟦Thai < Sans *vāta*, enclosed area⟧ a Buddhist monastic center in Thailand, Laos, or Cambodia

watch (wäch, wôch) ***n.*** ⟦ME *wacche* < OE *wæcce* < base of *wacian*: see WAKE[1]⟧ **1** the act or fact of keeping awake, esp. of keeping awake and alert, in order to look after, protect, or guard **2** *a)* any of the several periods into which the night was divided in ancient times *b)* a part of the night [the still *watches* of the night] **3** *a)* close observation for a time, in order to see or find out something *b)* the act or process of vigilant, careful guarding [to keep *watch* over a house] **4** a person or group on duty, esp. at night, to protect or guard; lookout or guard **5** *a)* the period of duty of a guard *b)* the post of a guard **6** a small timepiece designed to be carried in the pocket or worn on the wrist, as a pendant, etc. **7** [Obs.] *a)* a vigil; wake *b)* vigilance **8** [Obs.] a candle marked off into sections, used for keeping time **9** [Obs.] a watchman's cry **10** *Meteorol.* an official alert, as by the National Weather Service, that the conditions exist in the area for, variously, a tornado, severe thunderstorm, flash flood, etc., although one has not yet been reported: cf. WARNING (sense 3) **11** *Naut.* *a)* any of the periods of duty (five of four hours, and two of two hours) into which the day is divided on shipboard, so that the work is shared among alternating shifts of the crew *b)* the part of the crew on duty during any such period —***vi.*** **1** to stay awake, esp. at night, so as to pray and meditate **2** to stay awake and alert at night; care for or guard something at night **3** to be on the alert; be on the lookout **4** to look or observe, esp. attentively **5** to be looking or waiting attentively: with *for* [to *watch* for one's chance] —***vt.*** **1** to guard **2** to keep looking at; observe carefully and constantly **3** to view mentally; keep informed about **4** to be on the alert for; wait for and look for [to *watch* one's chance] **5** to keep watch over or tend (a flock, a baby, etc.) —**on the watch** watching; on the lookout, as for some thing or person expected —**on (or under) someone's watch** during the period that a particular person or group is in charge [unemployment rose *on the former mayor's watch*] —☆**watch oneself** to be careful, cautious, or discreet —☆**watch out** to be alert and on one's guard; be careful —**watch over** to protect from harm or danger

watch and ward the act of watching as a sentinel: also used, esp. formerly, in the titles of societies acting as guardians of a community's morals

☆**watch·band** (wäch′band′, wôch′-) ***n.*** a band of leather, metal, cloth, etc. for holding a watch on the wrist

☆**watch cap** a closefitting, knitted wool cap of a kind worn by U.S. Navy enlisted personnel in cold or inclement weather

watch·case (-kās′) ***n.*** the metal or plastic covering of a watch

watch chain a chain attached at one end to a pocket watch, with an ornament (or fob) or a fastener at the other end

watch·dog (-dôg′) ***n.*** **1** a dog kept to guard property, as by barking **2** a person or group that keeps watch in order to prevent waste, unethical practices, etc. —***vt.*** to act as a watchdog over

watch·er (-ər) ***n.*** **1** a person who watches, esp. one who keeps watch beside a sick or dead person **2** *a)* an observer ☆*b)* a person authorized to keep watch at a polling place to detect irregularities

watch fire a fire kept burning at night as a signal or for the use of those staying awake to watch, or guard

watch·ful (-fəl) ***adj.*** **1** watching closely; vigilant; alert **2** characterized by vigilance **3** [Archaic] wakeful; unsleeping —**watch′ful·ly** ***adv.*** —**watch′ful·ness** ***n.***

SYN.—**watchful** is the general word implying a being observant and prepared, as to ward off danger or seize an opportunity [under the *watchful* eye of her guardian]; **vigilant** implies an active, keen watchfulness and connotes the immediate necessity for this [a *vigilant* sentry]; **alert** implies a quick intelligence and a readiness to take prompt action [*alert* to the danger that confronted them]; **wide-awake** more often implies an alertness to opportunities than to dangers and connotes an awareness of all the surrounding circumstances [a *wide-awake* young salesman]

watch·list (-list′) ***n.*** a list of persons, groups, etc. under, or designated for, surveillance or observation [a *watchlist* of terrorist suspects]

watch·mak·er (-māk′ər) ***n.*** a person who makes or repairs watches —**watch′mak′ing** ***n.***

watch·man (-mən) ***n.***, *pl.* **-men** (-mən) **1** [Historical] a person whose duty was to guard or police the streets at night **2** a person hired to guard a building or other property against thieves, vandals, or trespassers, esp. at night

watch night among some Protestants, a religious service held on New Year's Eve

watch pocket a small pocket, as in a vest or trousers, for carrying a watch

watch·tow·er (-tou′ər) ***n.*** a high tower from which a sentinel watches for enemies, forest fires, etc.; lookout

watch·word (-wurd′) ***n.*** **1** a password, or countersign **2** a word or phrase embodying a principle or precept, esp. one used as the slogan or cry of a group or party

wa·ter (wôt′ər, wät′-) ***n.*** ⟦ME < OE *wæter*, akin to Ger *wasser* < IE **wodōr* < **wed-*, to wet (< base **awed-*, to moisten, flow) > Gr *hydōr*, water, L *unda*, a wave, Russ *voda*, water, Ir *uisce*, water⟧ **1** the colorless, transparent liquid occurring on earth as rivers, lakes, oceans, etc., and falling from the clouds as rain: chemically a compound of hydrogen and oxygen, H_2O, it freezes, forming ice, at 0°C (32°F) and boils, forming steam, at 100°C (212°F) **2** water in a specified form or amount, or occurring or distributed in a specified way, or for a specified use, as drinking or washing **3** [*often pl.*] *a)* a large body of water, as a river, lake, or sea *b)* the part of the sea contiguous with a specified country, land mass, etc. or the parts away from this [international *waters*] *c)* any area in a body of water [the noisy *waters* at the rapids] *d)* the liquid substance of a body of water [the pond's still *waters*] **4** water with reference to *a)* its depth [ten feet of *water* at the dam] *b)* its displacement [a boat that draws six feet of *water*] *c)* its surface [above *water*, under *water*] *d)* its level in a sea, river, etc. [high *water*, low *water*] **5** [*pl.*] the water of mineral springs [to take the *waters* at Saratoga] **6** any bodily fluid or secretion, as urine, saliva, tears, or gastric and pancreatic juices; specif., *a)* the fluid surrounding the fetus in pregnancy; amniotic fluid *b)* a watery fluid retained abnormally [*water* on the knee] **7** a solution of any substance in water [mineral *water*, ammonia *water*] **8** *a)* the degree of transparency and luster of a precious stone as a measure of its quality [a diamond of the first *water*] *b)* degree of quality or conformity to type [an artist of the first or purest *water*] **9** a wavy, lustrous finish given to linen, silk, rayon, etc., or to a metal surface **10** a watercolor painting **11** *Finance* *a)* a valuation wrongfully given to the assets of a business in excess of their real value *b)* an issue of capital stock which brings the face value of all the stock issued by a business to a figure higher than the actual value of its assets —***vt.*** ⟦ME *wateren* < OE *wæterian* < the n.⟧ **1** to supply with water; specif., *a)* to give drinking water to (animals) *b)* to give water to (soil, crops, etc.) by sprinkling, pouring, or irrigating *c)* to bring water to (land) (said of a river, canal, etc.) *d)* to put water on by sprinkling, hosing, etc.; soak or moisten with water (often with *down*) *e)* to dilute by adding water to [a tavern that *waters* the drinks] **2** to give a wavy luster to the surface of (silk, etc.) **3** *Finance* to issue (stock) so as to add to the total face value without increasing assets to justify this valuation —***vi.*** **1** to fill with tears: said of the eyes **2** to secrete or fill with saliva [his mouth *watered* at the sight of the roast] **3** to take on a supply of water **4** to drink water: said of animals —***adj.*** **1** of or having to do with water **2** in or on water [*water* sports] **3** growing in or living on or near water [*water* plants, *water* birds] **4** *a)* operated by water [a *water* wheel] *b)* derived from running water [*water* power] **5** containing water or fluid [a *water* blister] **6** prepared with water, as for thinning or hardening —**by water** by ship or boat —**hold water 1** to contain water without leaking **2** to remain sound, consistent, or logical, with no breaks or weaknesses [an argument that doesn't *hold water*] —**like water** lavishly; freely: said as of money spent —**make someone's mouth water** to be or seem tasty: often used fig. for inspiring any keen appetite or desire —**make water 1** to urinate: also **pass water 2** to take in water, as through a leak: said of a boat or ship —**test the water (**or **waters)** to explore a possible course of action; approach initially —**under water** *see* UNDERWATER —**water down** to weaken the potency or effectiveness of —**water under the bridge (**or **over the dam)** something not worth reexamining because it is in the past and finished

water bag 1 a bag designed to hold water, esp. one with tiny surface pores that allow evaporation, keeping the remaining water cool **2** the fluid-filled amnion surrounding the fetus in human beings and other placental mammals

Water Bearer, the Aquarius, the constellation and eleventh sign of the zodiac

☆**water bed** a type of bed consisting of a mattress with one or more chambers filled with water, supported in a frame: also written **wa'ter·bed'** *n.*

water beetle any of various beetles that live in freshwater ponds and streams, sometimes having one or two pairs of swimming legs fringed and functioning as oars

water bird any swimming or wading bird

water biscuit a cracker made of water, flour, and often some shortening

water blister a blister containing a clear, watery fluid without pus or blood

wa·ter·board·ing (-bôr'diŋ) *n.* a method of interrogation, often regarded as a form of torture, in which the person being questioned is restrained and inclined to a position where the head is lower than the feet: water is poured over the face, sometimes into the nose or mouth, so as to induce the sensation of drowning

water boatman any of a family (Corixidae) of hemipterous water bugs that swim about in ponds and streams by vigorous movement of the fringed, oarlike hind legs

wa·ter·borne (-bôrn') *adj.* floating on or carried by water

water boy ☆**1** a boy who brings drinking water to workers, as in the fields ☆**2** an assistant who brings drinking water, towels, etc. to athletes during the timeouts of a contest

water brash heartburn with regurgitated fluid in the mouth

wa·ter·buck (-buk') *n., pl.* **-buck'** or **-bucks'** any of a genus (*Kobus*) of African antelopes that frequent streams or rivers and have long horns that curve forward at the tips

water buffalo a slow, powerful buffalo (*Bubalus bubalis*) native to S Asia, Malaya, and the Philippine Islands, having a pair of large, strong horns growing from the sides of the head: it likes to wallow in mud and is used as a draft animal

water bug **1** any of various hemipteran insects that live in fresh waters, including the backswimmers and the water boatmen ☆**2** loosely, CROTON BUG

Wa·ter·bur·y (-ber'ē) city in WC Conn.

water cannon a pumping device which produces a powerful jet of water, used as by the police to disperse crowds

water chestnut ☆**1** *a)* a Chinese sedge (*Eleocharis dulcis*) with erect, cylindrical leaves, growing in dense clumps in water *b)* the large, button-shaped, submerged tubers of this plant, used in Chinese cooking **2** a floating aquatic weed (*Trapa natans*) of the water-chestnut family, with black, hard, horned fruit, the seed of which is sometimes eaten

wa·ter-chest·nut (-ches'nət) *adj.* designating a family (Trapaceae, order Myrtales) of floating, aquatic dicotyledonous plants

☆**water chinquapin** **1** a perennial American waterlily (*Nelumbo lutea*) with large, emersed, umbrella-shaped leaves and yellow flowers **2** its edible fruit

water clock a device for measuring time by the fall or flow of water

water closet TOILET (*n.* 4)

wa·ter·col·or (-kul'ər) *n.* **1** a pigment or coloring matter that is mixed with water for use as a paint **2** a painting done with such paints **3** the art of painting with watercolors —*adj.* painted with, using, or relating to watercolors —**wa'ter·col'or·ist** *n.*

wa·ter-cooled (-ko͞old') *adj.* kept from overheating by having water circulated around or through it, as in pipes or a water jacket [*a water-cooled* engine] —**wa'ter-cool'** (-ko͞ol') *vt.*

☆**wa·ter·cool·er** (-ko͞ol'ər) *n.* an appliance for cooling drinking water by refrigeration and dispensing it, typically one supplied from a refillable container placed on top of it —*adj.* of or appropriate for gossip or informal discussion of a type associated with office coffee breaks [*a watercooler* moment from a televised debate] Also written **water cooler**

wa·ter·course (-kôrs') *n.* **1** a stream of water; river, brook, etc. **2** a channel for water, as a canal or stream bed

wa·ter·craft (-kraft') *n.* **1** skill in handling boats or ships **2** skill in water sports, as swimming **3** *pl.* **-craft'** any vehicle ordinarily used for water transportation

wa·ter·cress (-kres') *n.* ⟦ME *watercresse*: see WATER & CRESS⟧ a white-flowered plant (*Nasturtium officinale*) of the crucifer family, growing generally in running water, as from springs: its leaves are used in salads, soups, etc.

water cure **1** HYDROPATHY **2** HYDROTHERAPY

water cycle the continuous cycle in which water changes from water vapor in the atmosphere to liquid water through condensation and precipitation and then back to water vapor through evaporation, transpiration, and respiration

water dog **1** any of various dogs characteristically fond of the water; esp., any of several hunting dogs, as the American water spaniel, trained to retrieve waterfowl ☆**2** MUD PUPPY

wa·tered (wôt'ərd) *adj.* **1** sprinkled with water **2** supplied with water; having streams: said of land **3** having a wavy, lustrous pattern: said of cloth, metal surfaces, etc. **4** treated, prepared, or diluted with water ☆**5** *Finance* issued in amounts producing a total face value beyond its true worth: said of stock, etc.

Wa·ter·ee (wôt'ə rē') ⟦AmInd tribal name < ?⟧ river in NW S.C., flowing south to join the Congaree & form the Santee: *c.* 300 mi (483 km)

wa·ter·fall (wôt'ər fôl') *n.* a steep fall of water, as of a stream, from a height; cascade

water flea any of an order (Cladocera) of mostly freshwater branchiopods; esp., any of a genus (*Daphnia*) commonly found in ponds and used to feed fish in aquariums

Wa·ter·ford (wôt'ər fərd) county in Munster province, S Ireland, on the Atlantic: 710 sq mi (1,839 sq km)

wa·ter·fowl (-foul') *n., pl.* **-fowls'** or **-fowl'** a water bird; esp., any of a family (Anatidae, order Anseriformes) of birds consisting of ducks, geese, and swans

☆**wa·ter·front** (-frunt') *n.* **1** land at the edge of a stream, harbor, etc. **2** the part of a port city abutting the harbor, typically the site of many docks, wharves, etc.

☆**water gap** a break in a mountain ridge, with a stream flowing through it

water gas a fuel gas that is a poisonous mixture of hydrogen, carbon dioxide, carbon monoxide, and nitrogen, made by forcing steam over incandescent coke or coal

☆**Wa·ter·gate** (-gāt') *n.* ⟦after *Watergate*, building complex in Washington, D.C., housing Democratic Party headquarters, burglarized (June, 1972) under direction of government officials⟧ the political scandal in the U.S. executive branch, involving violations of law and abuse of power, that led to the resignation of Pres. Richard M. Nixon in 1974

water gate a gate controlling the flow of water; floodgate

water gauge **1** a gauge for measuring the level or flow of water in a stream or channel **2** a device, as a glass tube, that shows the water level in a tank, boiler, etc.

water glass **1** *a)* a drinking glass or goblet *b)* a glass container for water, etc. **2** a glass-bottomed tube or box for looking at things under water **3** sodium silicate or, sometimes, potassium silicate, occurring as a powder, usually dissolved in water to form a colorless, syrupy liquid used as an adhesive, as a protective or waterproofing coat, as a preservative for eggs, etc. **4** WATER CLOCK Also written **wa'ter·glass'** *n.*

water gum ☆a tupelo tree (*Nyssa biflora*) with greenish-white flowers, purplish fruit, and a swollen, submerged trunk base, growing in swampy ground

water gun WATER PISTOL

water hammer **1** the hammering sound caused in a pipe containing water when live steam is passed through it **2** the thump of water in a pipe, caused by an air lock, when a faucet is suddenly closed

water hemlock any of a genus (*Cicuta*) of perennial plants of the umbel family, with compound umbels of small white flowers and intensely poisonous, tuberous roots, found in the Northern Hemisphere in moist places

water hen any of various birds (family Rallidae), including certain gallinules and the American coot (*Fulica americana*)

water hole **1** a dip or hole in the surface of the ground in which water collects, esp. one used by animals for drinking **2** a hole in the ice on a body of water

☆**water hyacinth** a South American aquatic plant (*Eichhornia crassipes*) of the pickerelweed family, with swollen petioles that float on water and spikes of showy lavender flowers: a pest that blocks water traffic in the S U.S., esp. Florida

water ice water and sugar flavored and frozen as a confection

wa·ter-inch (-inch') *n.* a former unit of hydraulic measure, calculated as the discharge of water through a circular opening one inch in diameter and equal to about fourteen pints per minute

wa·ter·i·ness (wôt'ər ē nis) *n.* the state or quality of being watery

watering can (*or* pot) a container, esp. a can with a spout having a perforated nozzle, for watering plants, etc.

☆**watering hole** **1** WATER HOLE (sense 1) **2** [Informal] a bar or tavern, esp. one in which there is much social activity

watering place **1** a place at a stream, lake, etc. where animals go to drink **2** a place where water, esp. fresh water, can be obtained **3** [Chiefly Brit.] *a)* a resort or spa with mineral springs for drinking or bathing *b)* a resort with a beach suitable for swimming, water sports, etc. ☆**4** [Informal] WATERING HOLE (sense 2)

☆**watering spot** WATERING HOLE

wa·ter·ish (wôt'ər ish) *adj.* WATERY

water jacket an attached casing holding or circulating water around something to be cooled or kept at a constant temperature, esp. around or through the cylinder head and block of an internal-combustion engine

water jump a strip, ditch, or channel of water that a horse must jump, as in a steeplechase

wa·ter·leaf (-lēf') *n., pl.* **-leafs'** any of a genus (*Hydrophyllum*) of perennial plants of the waterleaf family, with white or bluish, bell-shaped flowers —*adj.* designating a family (Hydrophyllaceae, order Solanales) of chiefly North American dicotyledonous plants with a cymose inflorescence and capsular fruit, including the nemophilas

wa·ter·less (-lis) *adj.* **1** without water; dry **2** not needing water, as for cooking —**wa'ter·less·ness** *n.*

water lettuce a floating aquatic plant (*Pistia stratiotes*) of the arum family, with rosettes of thick, blunt, velvety, ribbed leaves and a hanging mass of feathery roots

water level **1** *a)* the surface of still water *b)* the height of this **2** WATER TABLE **3** WATERLINE (senses 1 & 4)

wa·ter·lil·y (-lil'ē) *n., pl.* **-lil'ies** **1** any of an order (Nymphaeales) of dicotyledonous water plants having large, flat, floating leaves and showy flowers in a wide range of color **2** the flower of such a plant —*adj.* designating a fam-

waterlily

ily (Nymphaeaceae) of waterlilies found worldwide in warm and temperate regions, including various African and Asian lotuses

wa·ter·line (-līn′) *n.* **1** the line to which the surface of the water comes on the side of a ship or boat **2** any of several horizontal lines marked on the side of a ship to indicate the level to which it sinks when fully or partly loaded or when not loaded, and to aid in achieving a proper trim ☆**3** a pipe, tube, etc. for conveying water **4** WATERMARK (sense 1)

☆**wa·ter·lo·cust** (-lō′kəst) *n.* a thorny honeylocust (*Gleditsia aquatica*), native to the SE U.S., with a dark, heavy wood that takes a high polish

wa·ter·logged (-lôgd′) *adj.* **1** so soaked or filled with water as to be heavy and sluggish in movement and barely afloat [a *waterlogged* rowboat] **2** soaked with water; swampy or spongy

Wa·ter·loo[1] (wôt′ər lo͞o′, wôt′ər lo͞o′) *n.* ⟦after fol., the scene of Napoleon's defeat⟧ any disastrous or decisive defeat

Wa·ter·loo[2] (wôt′ər lo͞o′, wôt′ər lo͞o′) **1** town in central Belgium, south of Brussels: scene of Napoleon's final defeat (June 18, 1815) by the Allies under Wellington & Blücher **2** ⟦after the town in Belgium⟧ city in SE Ontario, Canada, near Kitchener: site of the University of Waterloo

water main a main pipe in a system of pipes for conveying water, as for community use

wa·ter·man (wôt′ər mən) *n., pl.* **-men** (-mən) a person who works on or with boats; often, specif., one who rows

wa·ter·mark (-märk′) *n.* **1** a mark showing the limit to which water has risen **2** *a)* a very faint mark or design pressed or printed on a sheet of paper, typically during manufacture as a sign of authenticity *b)* a stylized design, as of a printer or business firm, characteristically used in this way —*vt.* **1** to mark (paper) with a watermark **2** to impress (a design) as a watermark

water mass a large body of oceanic water usually identified by a well-defined relationship between temperature and salinity or chemical content: usually a mixture of two or more such bodies, each having a specified temperature and salinity

wa·ter·mel·on (-mel′ən) *n.* ⟦WATER + MELON: from its abundant watery juice⟧ **1** a large, round or oblong, edible fruit with a hard, green rind and sweet, juicy, pink or red pulp containing many seeds **2** the widely cultivated, tropical African trailing vine (*Citrullus lanatus*) of the gourd family, on which it grows

water meter an instrument that measures and records the amount of water flowing through a pipe, etc.

water milfoil any of a genus (*Myriophyllum*, family Haloragaceae) of graceful, feathery dicotyledonous plants (order Haloragales) growing under water: used in aquariums

water mill a mill whose machinery is driven by water

☆**water moccasin** a large, poisonous, olive-brown pit viper (*Agkistrodon piscivorus*) with dark crossbars, found along or in rivers and swamps in the SE U.S.; cottonmouth: often confused with various harmless snakes, esp. several water snakes (genus *Natrix*)

water nymph *Class. Myth.* any of the nymphs who dwell in streams, pools, lakes, etc.; naiad, Nereid, Oceanid, etc.

☆**water oak** an oak (*Quercus nigra*) of the SE U.S., found mainly along rivers, streams, etc.

water of crystallization water that occurs as a constituent of crystalline substances in a definite stoichiometric ratio: it can be removed from them by the application of heat at 100°C (212°F) and its loss usually results in a change in the crystalline structure

water of hydration water which is chemically combined with a substance to form a hydrate and which can be removed, as by heating

water ouzel DIPPER (sense 3), esp. a species (*Cinclus mexicanus*) of W North America

water park a kind of amusement park featuring swimming pools, waterslides, etc.

water parting WATERSHED (sense 1)

water pepper any of several polygonums growing in wet places and having an acrid juice, as smartweed

water pimpernel **1** either of two small, white-flowered plants (*Samolus floribundus* or *S. valerandi*) of the primrose family, usually found along the edges of brooks **2** scarlet pimpernel: see PIMPERNEL

water pipe **1** a pipe for carrying water **2** a kind of smoking pipe, as a hookah, in which the smoke is drawn through water

water pistol a toy gun that shoots water in a stream

water plant any plant living submerged in water or with only the roots in or under water

water plantain any of a family (Alismataceae, order Alismatales) of hardy, monocotyledonous water plants with large, heart-shaped leaves and small, usually white, flowers

water polo a game played as in a pool, with a goal at either end, by two teams of seven swimmers: the object is to score by throwing the ball into the other team's goal

water power **1** the power of running or falling water, used to drive machinery, etc., or capable of being so used **2** a fall of water that can be so used **3** a water right or privilege owned by a mill Also written **wa′ter·pow′er** *n.* —**wa′ter·pow′ered** *adj.*

wa·ter·proof (wôt′ər pro͞of′) *adj.* that keeps out water completely; esp., treated with rubber, plastic, etc. so that water will not penetrate —*n.* **1** waterproof material **2** [Chiefly Brit.] a raincoat or other outer garment of waterproof material —*vt.* to make waterproof

wa·ter·proof·ing (-iŋ) *n.* **1** the act or process of making something waterproof **2** any substance used for this

☆**water purslane** **1** a red-stemmed trailing plant (*Ludwigia palustris*) of the evening-primrose family, found in watery or muddy places **2** a small aquatic plant (*Peplis diandra*) of the loosestrife family, with linear leaves

water rat **1** any of various rodents that live on the banks of streams and ponds ☆**2** MUSKRAT

wa·ter-re·pel·lent (-ri pel′ənt) *adj.* that repels water but is not thoroughly waterproof

wa·ter-re·sist·ant (-ri zis′tənt) *adj.* that repels water for a short time but is not thoroughly waterproof

☆**water right** the right, sometimes limited, to use water from a stream, canal, etc. for some purpose, as irrigation

water sapphire ⟦transl. of Fr *saphir d'eau*⟧ a deep-blue, transparent variety of cordierite, sometimes used as a gem

wa·ter·scape (-skāp′) *n.* ⟦WATER + -SCAPE⟧ **1** a view of a body of water; esp., a picture containing such a view **2** SEASCAPE

water scorpion any of a family (Nepidae) of elongated, sticklike, four-winged hemipteran insects, characterized by a long breathing tube at the anal end of the abdomen

wa·ter·shed (-shed′) *n.* **1** a ridge or stretch of high land dividing the areas drained by different rivers or river systems ☆**2** the area drained by a river or river system **3** a crucial turning point affecting action, opinion, etc.

water shield ☆**1** a purple-flowered waterlily (*Brasenia schreberi*) having floating leaves coated underneath with a jellylike substance **2** CABOMBA

wa·ter·side (-sīd′) *n.* land at the edge of a body of water; shore —*adj.* of, at, or on the waterside

water ski a skilike board used in pairs to glide over water

wa·ter-ski (-skē′) *vi.* **-skied′**, **-ski′ing** to be towed for sport by holding onto a line attached to a speedboat while standing on water skis —**wa′ter-ski′er** *n.*

wat·er·slide (-slīd′) *n.* a chute having a continuous flow of water, down which one slides into a pool, as at a water park: also written **water slide**

water snake any of numerous saltwater or freshwater snakes; esp., any of a widely distributed genus (*Natrix*) of thick-bodied, nonpoisonous, freshwater colubrid snakes that feed chiefly on fish and amphibians

wa·ter-soak (-sōk′) *vt.* to soak with or in water

water softener **1** a chemical compound added to hard water to soften it, as by precipitating out the minerals **2** a tank or other container in which water is filtered through any of various chemicals or ion exchange media for softening

wa·ter-sol·u·ble (-säl′yə bəl) *adj.* that can be dissolved in water

water spaniel **1** AMERICAN WATER SPANIEL **2** IRISH WATER SPANIEL

wa·ter·sport (-spôrt′) *n.* any recreational activity or sport that takes place in or on the water, as swimming, surfing, or sailing

wa·ter·spout (-spout′) *n.* **1** a pipe or spout from which water is discharged **2** a whirling, funnel-shaped or cylindrical column of air full of spray, occurring over a body of water

water sprite *Folklore* a spirit, nymph, etc. dwelling in or haunting a body of water

water sprout a fast-growing sprout arising from the base, the trunk, or a main limb of a tree or shrub, often with leaves different from those of adult parts of the same plant

water strider any of an insect-eating family (Gerridae) of usually slender-bodied hemipteran insects, having long legs with which they glide swiftly on the surface film of calm waters, esp. of ponds and streams

water supply **1** the water available for use by a community or in an area **2** WATER SYSTEM (sense 2)

water system **1** a river with all its tributaries **2** a system, including reservoirs and mains, for storing and supplying water for use by a community

water table **1** the level below which the ground is saturated with water **2** *Archit.* a projecting ledge or molding which throws off rainwater

water taxi a commercial boat for ferrying passengers, as across a river or within a harbor

wa·ter·thrush (-thrush′) *n.* ☆any of several North American wood warblers (genus *Seiurus*), usually found near streams, swamps, etc.

wa·ter·tight (-tīt′) *adj.* **1** so snugly put together that no water can get in or through **2** that cannot be misconstrued, refuted, defeated, nullified, etc.; flawless [a *watertight* excuse, plan, etc.] —**wa′ter·tight′ness** *n.*

water torture a form of torture in which water is caused to drip slowly onto the forehead of the immobilized victim

water tower **1** an elevated tank used for water storage and for maintaining equalized pressure on a water system ☆**2** a firefighting apparatus that can be used to lift high-pressure hoses and nozzles to great heights

☆**water turkey** ANHINGA

water vapor water in the form of a gas; steam

wa·ter-vas·cu·lar system (-vas′kyə lər) in echinoderms, a system of closed tubes and ducts filled with seawater containing some protein, and functioning variously, as in locomotion, food gathering, clinging, and respiration

wa·ter·way (-wā′) *n.* **1** a channel or runnel through or along which water runs **2** any body of water wide enough and deep enough for boats, ships, etc., as a stream, canal, or river; water route

wa·ter·weed (-wēd′) *n.* **1** any of various water plants having inconspicuous flowers, as pondweed **2** a North American elodea (*Elodea canadensis*) with white flowers: used in aquariums

water wheel 1 a wheel turned by water running against or falling on paddles, used as a source of power 2 a wheel with buckets on its rim, used for lifting water

water wings an inflatable device for keeping someone afloat as while learning to swim: it is shaped somewhat like a pair of wings and is worn under the arms

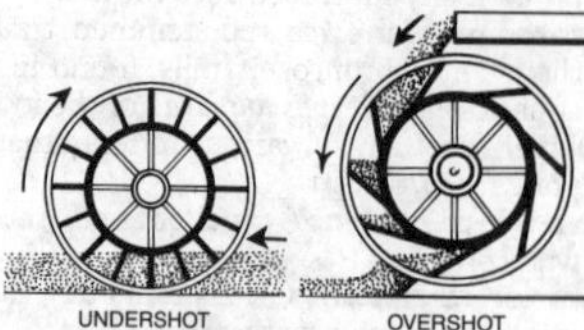

water wheels

water witch ☆1 a dowser who uses a divining rod to locate water ☆2 any of various diving birds, as certain grebes

wa·ter·works (-wurks′) *pl.n.* 1 [*often with sing. v.*] *a)* a system of reservoirs, pumps, pipes, etc., used to bring a water supply to a town or city *b)* a pumping station in such a system, with its machinery, filters, etc. 2 [Slang] tears: usually in **turn on the waterworks**, to shed tears; weep

wa·ter·worn (-wôrn′) *adj.* worn, smoothed, or polished by the action of running water

wa·ter·y (-ē) *adj.* 1 of or like water 2 containing or full of water; moist 3 thin; diluted [*watery* tea] 4 tearful; weeping 5 in or consisting of water [a *watery* grave] 6 weak; insipid 7 soft or soggy 8 full of, secreting, or giving off a morbid discharge resembling water

☆**WATS** (wäts) *n.* ⟦*w(ide) a(rea) t(elecommunications) s(ervice)*⟧ a telephone service that ties a customer into the long-distance network through special lines so that calls can be made to, and toll-free calls can be received from, a defined area or areas in large numbers at a special rate

Wat·son (wät′sən, wôt′-) 1 **James D(ewey)** 1928- ; U.S. biochemist: helped determine the structure of DNA 2 **John B(roadus)** 1878-1958; U.S. psychologist 3 Dr. **(John H.)** *see* SHERLOCK HOLMES

Wat·son-Watt (wät′sən wät′), Sir **Robert Alexander** 1892-1973; Scot. physicist

watt (wät) *n.* ⟦after fol.: name proposed (1882) by Sir William SIEMENS⟧ the basic unit of electric, mechanical, or thermal power in the SI and MKS systems, equal to one joule per second or 10^7 ergs per second ($^1/_{746}$ of a horsepower): for electric power it is equal to one volt-ampere: abbrev. *W*

Watt (wät), **James** 1736-1819; Scot. engineer & inventor: pioneer in the development of the steam engine

watt·age (wät′ij) *n.* 1 amount of electrical power, expressed in watts 2 the number of watts required to operate a given device

Wat·teau (vȧ tō′; *E* wä tō′), **(Jean) An·toine** (än twȧn′) 1684-1721; Fr. painter

watt-hour (wät′our′) *n.* a unit of electrical energy or work, equal to one watt acting for one hour, or 3,600 joules

wat·tle (wät′′l) *n.* ⟦ME *wattel* < OE *watul*, a hurdle, woven twigs < ? IE **wedh-*, to knit, bind < base *(*a*)*we-* > WEAVE⟧ 1 a sort of woven work made of sticks intertwined with twigs or branches, used for walls, fences, and roofs 2 [Brit. Dial.] *a)* a stick, rod, twig, or wand *b)* a hurdle or framework made of sticks, rods, etc. 3 [*pl.*] rods or poles used as the support of a thatched roof 4 [Austral.] any of various acacias: the flexible branches were much used by early settlers for making wattles 5 a fleshy, wrinkled, often brightly colored piece of skin which hangs from the chin or throat of certain birds, as the turkey, or of some lizards 6 a barbel of a fish 7 [*often pl.*] a fold or pouch of flesh hanging from the neck or lower part of the jaw —*adj.* made of or roofed with wattle or wattles —*vt.* **-tled**, **-tling** 1 to twist or intertwine (sticks, twigs, branches, etc.) so as to form an interwoven structure or fabric 2 to construct (a fence) by intertwining sticks or twigs 3 to build of, or roof, fence, etc. with, wattle

wat·tle·bird (-burd′) *n.* any of a number of large honeyeaters (genus *Anthochaera*) of Australia and Tasmania, characterized by wattles that hang from the corners of the mouth

wat·tled (wät′′ld) *adj.* 1 built with wattles 2 having wattles, as a bird

watt·me·ter (wät′mēt′ər) *n.* an instrument for measuring in watts the power in an electric circuit

Watts[1] (wäts), **Isaac** 1674-1748; Eng. clergyman & writer of hymns

Watts[2] (wäts) section of Los Angeles, Calif.

Wa·tu·si (wä to͞o′sē) *n.*, *pl.* **-sis** or **-si** *var. of* TUTSI: also **Wa·tut′si** (-to͞ot′sē)

Waugh (wô), **Eve·lyn (Arthur St. John)** (ēv′lin) 1903-66; Eng. novelist

Wau·ke·gan (wô kē′gən) ⟦prob. < Ojibwa *waakaa′igan*, fort⟧ city in NE Ill., on Lake Michigan

waul (wôl) *vi.*, *n.* ⟦see CATERWAUL⟧ wail, squall, or howl

wave (wāv) *vi.* **waved**, **wav′ing** ⟦ME *waven* < OE *wafian*, akin to Ger *waben*, to fluctuate < IE **webh-*, to move to and fro, prob. identical with **webh-*, to WEAVE⟧ 1 to move up and down or back and forth in a curving or undulating motion; swing, sway, or flutter to and fro: said of flexible things free at one end [flags *waving* in the breeze] 2 to signal by moving a hand, arm, light, etc. to and fro 3 to have the form of a series of curves or undulations [hair that *waves* naturally] —*vt.* 1 to cause to wave, undulate, or sway to and fro 2 to swing or brandish (a weapon) 3 *a)* to move or swing (something) as a signal; motion with (the hand, arms, etc.) *b)* to signal (something) by doing this [to *wave* farewell] *c)* to signal or signify something to (someone) by doing this [he *waved* us on] 4 to give an undulating form to; make sinuous [to *wave* one's hair] —*n.* ⟦altered (based on the v.) < ME *wawe*, a wave⟧ 1 a ridge or swell moving along the surface of a liquid or body of water as a result of disturbance, as by wind 2 *a)* an undulation or series of undulations in or on a surface, such as that caused by wind over a field of grain *b)* a curve or series of curves or curls, as in the hair *c)* an appearance of undulation, by reflection of light, on watered fabric 3 a motion to and fro or up and down, such as that made by the hand in signaling 4 something like a wave in action or effect; specif., *a)* an upsurge or rise, as to a crest, or a progressively swelling manifestation [a crime *wave*, heat *wave*, *wave* of emotion, etc.] *b)* a movement of people, etc., in groups or masses, which recedes or grows smaller before subsiding or being followed by another [a *wave* of immigrants] 5 [Old Poet.] water; esp., the sea or other body of water 6 *Physics* a periodic motion or disturbance consisting of a series of many oscillations that propagate through a medium or space, as in the propagation of sound or light: the medium does not travel outward from the source with the wave but only vibrates as it passes —**make waves** [Informal] to disturb the prevailing calm, complacency, etc. —**wave′less** *adj.* —**wave′like′** *adj.* —**wav′er** *n.*

SYN.—**wave** is the general word for a curving ridge or swell in the surface of the ocean or other body of water; **ripple** is used of the smallest kind of wave, such as that caused by a breeze ruffling the surface of water; **roller** is applied to any of the large, heavy, swelling waves that roll in to the shore, as during a storm; **breaker** is applied to such a wave when it breaks, or is about to break, into foam upon the shore or upon rocks; **billow** is a somewhat poetic or rhetorical term for a great, heaving ocean wave

wave band *Radio, TV* a specific range of radio frequencies

wave base the depth in a body of water at which the action of surface waves stops stirring the sediments

wave·form (wāv′fôrm′) *n.* *Physics* a graphic representation of a wave, usually plotted with amplitude on one axis and frequency on the other

wave·front (-frunt′) *n.* *Physics* a continuous line or surface describing the points affected at a given moment by a wave as it travels through a particular medium

wave function *Physics* a mathematical expression, function, or quantity used in quantum mechanics to describe the wave, energy levels, eigenvalues, and locations in space of any moving particle, as an electron in an atom

wave·guide (wāv′gīd′) *n.* an electric conductor consisting of a metal tubing, usually circular or rectangular in cross section, used for the conduction or directional transmission of microwaves

wave·length (-leŋkth′) *n.* 1 *Physics* the distance measured in the direction of a wave from any given point to the next point in the same phase, as from crest to crest 2 [Informal] a way of thinking, understanding, etc.: chiefly in the phrase **on the same wavelength**, thinking or responding alike

wave·let (wāv′lit) *n.* a little wave; ripple

Wa·vell (wā′vəl), **Archibald (Percival)** 1st Earl Wavell 1883-1950; Brit. field marshal

wa·vell·ite (wā′və līt′) *n.* ⟦after W. *Wavell* (?-1829), Eng physician who discovered it⟧ a rare, semihard, orthorhombic mineral, hydrous aluminum phosphate, $Al_3(PO_4)_2(OH)_3 \cdot 5H_2O$, characterized by a radiating, globular structure

wave mechanics the branch of physics that describes the motion of particles, as atoms and elementary particles, by wave motion

wa·ver (wā′vər) *vi.* ⟦ME *waveren*, freq. of *waven*, to WAVE⟧ 1 to swing or sway to and fro; flutter 2 to show doubt or indecision; find it hard, or be unable, to decide; vacillate 3 to become unsteady; begin to give way; falter 4 to tremble; quaver: said of the voice, etc. 5 to vary in brightness; flicker: said of light 6 to fluctuate 7 to totter —*n.* the act of wavering, trembling, vacillating, etc. —**wa′ver·er** *n.* —**wa′ver·ing·ly** *adv.*

wa·ver·y (wā′vər ē) *adj.* wavering [his *wavery* voice]

☆**WAVES** (wāvz) *n.* ⟦orig. < *W(omen) A(ppointed for) V(oluntary) E(mergency) S(ervice)*⟧ [Historical] the women's branch of the U.S. Navy during and just after WWII

wave train *Physics* a series of waves coming from the same source at regular intervals

wav·y (wā′vē) *adj.* **wav′i·er**, **wav′i·est** 1 having waves 2 moving in a wavelike motion 3 having undulating curves; forming waves and hollows; sinuous 4 characteristic or suggestive of waves 5 wavering; fluctuating; unsteady —**wav′i·ly** *adv.* —**wav′i·ness** *n.*

☆**wa-wa** (wä′wä′) *n.* *alt. sp. of* WAH-WAH

wax[1] (waks) *n.* ⟦ME < OE *weax*, akin to Ger *wachs* < IE **wokso-* < **weg-*, to weave, prob. < base *(*a*)*we-*, to WEAVE⟧ 1 a plastic, dull-yellow substance secreted by bees for building cells; beeswax: it is hard when cold and easily molded when warm, melts at *c.* 64.4°C (*c.* 148°F), cannot be dissolved in water, and is used for candles, modeling, etc. 2 any plastic substance like this; specif., *a)* paraffin *b)* a waxlike substance exuded by the ears; earwax; cerumen *c)* a waxy substance produced by scale insects *d)* any waxlike substance yielded by plants or animals *e)* a resinous substance used by shoemakers to rub on thread *f)* SEALING WAX 3 any of a group of substances with a waxy appearance made up variously of esters, fatty acids, free alcohols, and solid hydrocarbons 4 ⟦from the wax cylinders formerly used for recording sound⟧ [Old Informal] the phonograph record as a recording medium —*vt.* 1 to rub, polish, cover, smear, or treat with wax 2 to remove unwanted hair from (the body) by applying and removing a hot waxy substance 3 [Old Informal] to make a phonograph recording of —*adj.* made of wax —**wax′er** *n.* —**wax′like′** *adj.*

wax[2] (waks) *vi.* **waxed**, **wax′ing** ⟦ME *waxen* < OE *weaxan*, to grow, akin to Ger *wachsen* < IE **aweks-* < base **aweg-*, **aug-* > EKE[1], L *augere*, Gr *auxein*, to increase⟧ 1 to grow gradually larger, more numerous, etc.; increase in strength, intensity, volume, etc.: said esp. of the visible face of the moon during the phases after new moon in which the lighted portion is gradually increasing from a thin crescent on the right, as seen from the Northern Hemisphere: opposed to WANE (*vi.* 1) 2 *a)* [Literary] to become; grow [to *wax* angry] *b)* to speak or express oneself [he *waxed* on and on about his prowess]

wax³ (waks) *n.* ⟦< ? prec., as in phr. *wax angry*⟧ [Informal, Chiefly Brit.] a fit of anger or temper; a rage

☆**wax bean** 1 a variety of kidney bean with long, narrow, yellow pods 2 the edible immature seed pod of this

wax·ber·ry (waks′ber′ē) *n., pl.* **-ries** 1 SNOWBERRY (senses 1 & 3) ☆2 BAYBERRY (sense 1)

wax·bill (waks′bil′) *n.* any of a group of small, Old World passerine birds (family Estrildidae) with waxy pink, scarlet, or white bills: some species are kept as cage birds

wax·en¹ (wak′sən) *adj.* 1 made of wax 2 like wax, as in being yellowish, soft, smooth, lustrous, pale, plastic, pliable, impressionable, etc. 3 covered with wax

wax·en² (wak′sən) *vi. archaic pp. of* WAX²

wax·i·ness (wak′sē nis) *n.* a waxy state or quality

wax insect any of various homopteran insects, esp. scale insects, that secrete a waxy substance sometimes used commercially; specif., a Chinese scale insect (*Ericerus pela*)

wax museum a building or space where wax figures, as of famous persons, are exhibited

☆**wax myrtle** an evergreen bayberry (*Myrica cerifera*) native to E North America and having grayish-white berries coated with a wax used for candles

wax palm 1 CARNAUBA 2 a palm tree (*Ceroxylon andicola*) of the Andes, whose trunk yields a wax used in making candles, polishes, etc.

wax paper a kind of paper coated or impregnated with wax, or paraffin, so as to be moisture-proof: also **waxed paper**

☆**wax·weed** (waks′wēd′) *n.* a plant (*Cuphea petiolata*) of the loosestrife family, with sticky stems and purple flowers

wax·wing (-wiŋ′) *n.* any of several fruit-eating passerine birds (family Bombycillidae) of the Northern Hemisphere, with brown or gray silky plumage, a showy crest, and scarlet waxlike tips on the secondary wing feathers, as the cedar waxwing

wax·work (-wurk′) *n.* 1 work, as objects or figures, made of wax 2 a human figure made of wax 3 [*pl. with sing. v.*] WAX MUSEUM

wax·y (wak′sē) *adj.* **wax′i·er, wax′i·est** 1 full of, covered with, or made of wax 2 like wax in nature or appearance 3 *Med.* designating, of, or characterized by degeneration resulting from the deposit of an insoluble, waxlike substance in an organ

way (wā) *n.* ⟦ME < OE *weg*, akin to Ger < IE base **weĝh-*, to go > L *vehere*, to carry, ride, Gr *ochos*, wagon⟧ 1 a means of passing from one place to another, as a road, highway, street or path [the Appian *Way*] 2 room or space for passing; free area; an opening, as in a crowd or traffic [clear a *way* for the ambulance] 3 a route or course that is or may be used to go from one place to another: often used in comb. [*highway, railway*, one-*way* street] 4 a specified route or direction [on the *way* to town] 5 a path in life; course or habits of life or conduct [to fall into evil *ways*] 6 *a)* a course of action; method or manner of doing something [do it this *way*] *b)* a means to an end; method [a *way* to cut costs] 7 a usual or customary manner of living, acting, or being [the *way* of the world] 8 a characteristic manner of acting or doing [to learn the *ways* of other people] 9 manner or style [to have a pleasant *way*] 10 distance [a long *way* off]: in the U.S., **ways** is sometimes used informally or dialectally with the same meaning [just a little *ways* to go] 11 direction of movement or action [go this *way*; look this *way*] 12 respect; point; particular; feature [to be right in some *ways*] 13 what one desires; wish; will [to have or get one's own *way*] 14 relationship as to those taking part: used in hyphenated compounds [a four-*way* conversation] 15 [Informal] a (specified) state or condition [to be in a bad *way*] 16 [Informal] a district; locality; area [out our *way*] 17 [Now Rare] *Law* RIGHT OF WAY (sense 2) 18 *Mech.* a surface or slide on which the carriage of a lathe, etc. moves along its bed 19 *Naut.* movement, esp. forward movement, of a ship or boat through the water: often in the phrase **have way on**, to be moving through the water 20 [*pl.*] *Shipbuilding* a framework on which a ship is built and down which it slides in being launched —*adv.* 1 to a considerable extent or distance; far; well: this use, when modifying prepositions or adverbs indicating an actual or metaphorical distance or position, is still considered somewhat informal by some [*way* beyond, *way* in, *way* back] 2 [Informal] much; to a considerable degree: modifying words of comparison and the word *too* [*way* better, *way* more, *way* too slow] ☆3 [Slang] really, very, extremely, etc.: modifying adjectives [hip friends who are *way* cool] —**be on one's way** to start or resume one's journey —**by the way** 1 incidentally 2 on or beside the way —**by way of** 1 passing through; through; via 2 as a way, method, mode, or means of —**come someone's way** 1 to come within someone's scope or range; come to someone 2 [Informal] to turn out successfully for someone: also **go someone's way** —**give way** 1 to withdraw; yield 2 to break down; collapse —**give way to** 1 to step aside for; yield to 2 to give free expression to [to *give way to* tears] —☆**go all the way** 1 [Informal] to proceed or agree completely 2 [Slang] to engage in sexual intercourse —**go out of the** (or **one's**) **way** to inconvenience oneself; do something that one would not ordinarily do, or that requires extra or deliberate effort or trouble —**have a way with** to be skilled in or adept in the use of [a writer who *has a way with* words] —**have one's way with** 1 to engage in sexual intercourse with: often used to connote control over, or the surrender of, a partner 2 to dominate; exercise power or mastery over —**in the way** in such a position or of such a nature as to obstruct, hinder, impede, or prevent —**in the way of** being as designated; constituting [we had very little *in the way of* food] —**lead the way** to be a guide or example —**make one's way** 1 to advance or proceed 2 to advance in life or succeed, as by one's own efforts —**make way** 1 to make room; clear a passage 2 to make progress —**no way** [Slang] 1 in no manner; by no means; not at all [*no way* am I going to the concert] 2 used to express emphatic refusal, surprise, disbelief, dismay, etc. [You were at the party too? *No way!*]: pronounced with a rising stress —**on the way out** 1 becoming unfashionable, obsolescent, etc. 2 dying —**out of the way** 1 in a position so as not to hinder or interfere 2 disposed of 3 not on the right or usual route or course 4 *a)* improper; wrong; amiss *b)* unusual; uncommon —**parting of the ways** an ending of a relationship as because of a disagreement —**see one's way (clear)** 1 to be willing (to do something) 2 to find it convenient or possible —**take one's way** [Old Poet.] to go on a journey; travel —**the way** according to the way that; as [with things *the way* they are] —**under way** *var. of* UNDERWAY

way·bill (wā′bil′) *n.* ☆a list of goods and shipping instructions, sent with the goods being shipped

way·far·er (wā′fer′ər) *n.* a person who travels, esp. from place to place on foot —**way′far′ing** *adj., n.*

way·go·ing (wā′gō′iŋ) [Chiefly Scot.] *adj.* going away; departing —*n.* the act of leaving or departing

Way·land (wā′lənd) *n. Eng. & Gmc. Legend* a lame smith famed for his skill: also **Wayland (the) Smith**

way·lay (wā′lā′, wā′lā′) *vt.* **-laid′, -lay′ing** ⟦WAY + LAY¹, after MLowG *wegelagen*, to waylay < *wegelage*, an ambush < *weg*, akin to WAY + *lage*, a lying < base of *leggian*; akin to LIE¹⟧ 1 to lie in wait for and attack; ambush 2 to wait for and accost (a person) on the way —**way′lay′er** *n.*

Wayne¹ (wān) *n.* ⟦< surname *Wayne*⟧ a masculine name

Wayne² (wān) 1 **Anthony** 1745-96; Am. general in the Revolutionary War: called *Mad Anthony Wayne* 2 **John** (born *Marion Michael Morrison*) 1907-79; U.S. film actor

Way of the Cross STATIONS OF THE CROSS

☆**way-out** (wā′out′) *adj.* [Informal] unconventional, experimental, nonconformist, esoteric, etc.

ways (wāz) *n.* [Informal or Dial.] *see* WAY (*n.* 10)

-ways (wāz) ⟦ME < *way* (see WAY) + adv. gen. *-s*⟧ *suffix forming adverbs* in a (specified) direction, position, or manner [*sideways*]: equivalent to -WISE (sense 1)

ways and means 1 methods and resources at the disposal of a person, company, etc. 2 methods of raising money, specif. such methods, including legislation, in government

way·side (wā′sīd′) *n.* the edge of a road; area close to the side of a road —*adj.* on, near, or along the side of a road —**go by the wayside** to be put aside, shelved, or discarded

☆**way station** a small railroad station between more important ones, where through trains stop only on signal

way·ward (-wərd) *adj.* ⟦ME *weiward*, aphetic for *aweiward*: see AWAY & -WARD⟧ 1 insistent upon having one's own way; headstrong, willful, disobedient, etc. [a *wayward* youth] 2 conforming to no fixed rule or pattern; unpredictable; irregular; capricious; erratic 3 mischievous, naughty, flirtatious, etc. [a *wayward* glance] 4 [Archaic] unwanted or unexpected [*wayward* fate] —**way′ward·ly** *adv.* —**way′ward·ness** *n.*

way·worn (-wôrn′) *adj.* tired from traveling

Wa·zir·i·stan (wä zir′i stän′) mountainous region in W Pakistan, on the border with Afghanistan: *c.* 5,000 sq mi (12,950 sq km)

☆**wa·zoo** (wä zo͞o′) *n., pl.* **-zoos′** ⟦slang term for the buttocks or anus⟧ [Slang] *used chiefly in the phrase* **up** (or **out**) **the wazoo**, to a great or excessive degree; in abundance or overabundance

wb *abbrev.* 1 *Naut.* water ballast 2 waybill: also **W/B** or **WB**

Wb *abbrev.* weber(s)

WBC *abbrev.* 1 white blood cell 2 white blood (cell) count

WbN *abbrev.* west by north

WbS *abbrev.* west by south

wc¹ or **WC** (dub′əl yo͞o sē′) *n.* [Brit. Informal] water closet; TOILET (*n.* 4)

wc² *abbrev.* without charge

WCC *abbrev.* World Council of Churches

WCTU *abbrev.* Woman's Christian Temperance Union

wd *abbrev.* 1 ward 2 wood 3 word 4 would

we (wē) *pron., sing.* I ⟦ME < OE, akin to Ger *wir*, Goth *weis* < IE base **we-*, we > Sans *vayám*⟧ 1 the persons speaking or writing, or the persons on whose behalf someone is speaking or writing: used to refer to the speaker or writer and another or others, sometimes including those addressed: personal pronoun in the first person plural: *we* is the nominative form, *us* the objective, *ours* the possessive, and *ourselves* (or, by a monarch, etc., *ourself*) the reflexive and intensive; *our* is the possessive pronominal adjective 2 I: used by a monarch, editor, judge, etc. to indicate that the authority of his or her position or profession is represented 3 you: used in direct address as in encouraging or admonishing an invalid, a child, etc. [shall *we* take our medicine now?]

We *abbrev.* Wednesday

weak (wēk) ***adj.*** ⟦ME *waik* < ON *veikr*, akin to OE *wac*, feeble (which the ON word replaced) < IE **weig-*, **weik-* (< base **wei-*, to bend) > WEEK, WICKER, L *vicis*, change⟧ **1** *a)* lacking in strength of body or muscle; not physically strong *b)* lacking vitality; feeble; infirm **2** lacking in skill or strength in combat or competition [a *weak* team] **3** lacking in moral strength or willpower; yielding easily to temptation, the influence of others, etc. **4** lacking in mental power, or in the ability to think, judge, decide, etc. **5** *a)* lacking ruling power, or authority [a *weak* government] *b)* having few resources; relatively low in wealth, numbers, supplies, etc. [the *weaker* nations] **6** lacking in force or effectiveness [*weak* discipline] **7** *a)* lacking in strength of material or construction; unable to resist strain, pressure, etc.; easily torn, broken, bent, etc. [a *weak* railing] *b)* not sound or secure; unable to stand up to an attack [a *weak* fortification] **8** *a)* not functioning normally or well (said of a body organ or part) [*weak* eyes] *b)* easily upset; queasy [a *weak* stomach] **9** indicating or suggesting moral or physical lack of strength [*weak* features] **10** lacking in volume, intensity, etc.; faint [a *weak* voice, a *weak* current] **11** lacking the usual or proper strength; specif., *a)* having only a small amount of its essential ingredient; diluted [*weak* tea] *b)* not as potent as usual or as others of the kind [a *weak* drug] *c)* lacking, poor, or deficient in something specified [*weak* in grammar, a baseball team *weak* in pitching] *d)* slight; indistinct; not prominent [a *weak* chin] **12** *a)* ineffective; unconvincing [a *weak* argument] *b)* faulty [*weak* logic] **13** tending toward lower prices: said of a market, stock, etc. **14** *Chem.* having a low ion concentration: said as of certain acids and bases **15** *Gram.* expressing variation in tense by the addition of an inflectional suffix rather than by internal change of a syllabic vowel; regular (Ex.: *talk, talked, talked*): cf. STRONG, *adj.* 20 **16** *Phonet.* unstressed or lightly stressed: said of a syllable **17** *Photog.* THIN (sense 10) **18** *Prosody* designating or of a verse ending in which the stress falls on a word or syllable that is normally unstressed —**weak′ish** ***adj.***

SYN.—**weak**, the broadest in application of these words, basically implies a lack or inferiority of physical, mental, or moral strength [a *weak* muscle, mind, character, foundation, excuse, etc.]; **feeble** suggests a pitiable weakness or ineffectiveness [a *feeble* old man, a *feeble* joke]; **frail** suggests an inherent or constitutional delicacy or weakness, so as to be easily broken or shattered [a *frail* body, conscience, etc.]; **infirm** suggests a loss of strength or soundness, as through illness or age [his *infirm* old grandfather]; **decrepit** implies a being broken down, worn out, or decayed, as by old age or long use [a *decrepit* old pensioner, a *decrepit* sofa] —***ANT.*** **strong, sturdy, robust**

weak·en (wē′kən) ***vt., vi.*** to make or become weak or weaker —**weak′en·er** ***n.***

SYN.—**weaken**, the most general of these words, implies a lessening of strength, power, soundness, etc. [*weakened* by disease, to *weaken* an argument]; **debilitate** suggests a partial or temporary weakening, as by disease or dissipation [*debilitated* by alcoholic excesses]; **enervate** implies a lessening of force, vigor, energy, etc., as through indulgence in luxury [*enervated* by idleness]; **undermine** and **sap** both suggest a weakening or impairing by subtle or stealthy means [authority *undermined* by rumors, strength *sapped* by disease] —***ANT.*** **strengthen, energize**

weaker sex women collectively: used with *the*: considered a patronizing term

weak·fish (wēk′fish′) ***n.***, *pl.* **-fish′** or **-fish′es** (see FISH) ⟦< obs. Du *weekvisch* < *week*, soft (akin to WEAK) + *visch*, FISH⟧ any of various edible, marine drum fishes (genus *Cynoscion*), esp. a species (*C. regalis*) that lives in the waters along the E coast of the U.S.

weak interaction the short-range interaction between leptons responsible for beta decay and the decay of many long-lived elementary particles: see STRONG INTERACTION, ELECTROMAGNETIC INTERACTION: also **weak force**

weak-kneed (-nēd′) ***adj.*** **1** having weak knees **2** lacking in courage, determination, resistance, etc.

weak·ling (-liŋ) ***n.*** **1** a person or animal low in physical strength or vitality **2** a person of weak character or intellect

weak·ly (-lē) ***adj.*** **-li·er, -li·est** sickly; feeble; weak —***adv.*** in a weak manner —**weak′li·ness** ***n.***

weak-mind·ed (-mīn′did) ***adj.*** **1** not firm of mind; indecisive; unable to refuse or deny **2** mentally retarded; feebleminded **3** showing weakness of resolve or thought [a *weak-minded* decision] —**weak′-mind′ed·ness** ***n.***

weak·ness (-nis) ***n.*** **1** the state or quality of being weak **2** a weak point; fault or defect, as in one's character **3** *a)* a liking; esp., an immoderate fondness (*for* something) *b)* something of which one is immoderately fond [candy is my one *weakness*] —***SYN.*** FAULT

weak nuclear force WEAK INTERACTION

wea·kon (wē′kän′) ***n.*** *Particle Physics* any of three massive elementary particles, the positive and negative W particles and the neutral Z particle, that are thought to be responsible for weak interaction: a weakon is a boson

weak side **1** *Basketball* the side of the court with fewer players **2** *Football a)* the side of an offensive formation, either left or right of the center, opposite to that on which the tight end lines up *b)* the side of a defensive formation that is across the line of scrimmage from the offensive weak side —☆**weak·side** (wēk′sīd′) ***adj.***

weak sister ☆[Slang] one who is cowardly, unreliable, etc.

weal[1] (wēl) ***n.*** ⟦var. of WALE[1]⟧ a mark, line, or ridge raised on the skin, as by a blow; welt; wale

weal[2] (wēl) ***n.*** ⟦ME *wele* < OE *wela*, wealth, well-being, akin to OS *wela*: for IE base see WILL[1]⟧ **1** a sound or prosperous state; well-being; welfare [the public *weal*] **2** [Obs.] *a)* wealth *b)* the body politic

weald (wēld) ***n.*** ⟦readoption of OE (WS) *weald* (ME *weeld*), forest, wold, wilderness < PGmc **walthu*: see VOLE⟧ [Old Poet.] **1** a wooded area; forest **2** wild open country —**The Weald** region in SE England, south of London, between the North & South Downs: formerly heavily forested

wealth (welth) ***n.*** ⟦ME *welthe*, wealth, happiness: see WEAL[2] & -TH[1]⟧ **1** *a)* much money or property; great amount of worldly possessions; riches *b)* the state of having much money or property; affluence [a person of *wealth*] **2** a large amount (*of* something); abundance [a *wealth* of ideas] **3** valuable products, contents, or derivatives [the *wealth* of the oceans] **4** [Obs.] weal; well-being **5** *Econ. a)* everything having economic value measurable in price *b)* any useful material thing capable of being bought, sold, or stocked for future disposition

wealth·y (wel′thē) ***adj.*** **wealth′i·er, wealth′i·est** **1** having wealth; rich; prosperous; affluent **2** of, characterized by, or suggestive of wealth or abundance —***SYN.*** RICH —**the wealthy** wealthy, or rich, people collectively —**wealth′i·ly** ***adv.*** —**wealth′i·ness** ***n.***

Wealth·y (wel′thē) ***n.*** ⟦named by Peter Gideon (1818-99), Minn. horticulturist, after his wife, *Wealthy* Gideon⟧ ☆a red, medium-sized fall apple

wean[1] (wēn) ***vt.*** ⟦ME *wenen* < OE *wenian*, to accustom, train, with sense of *awenian*, to wean < *a-* (< *af-*, away) + *wenian* < IE base **wen-*, to desire, attain, be satisfied > L *venus*, love⟧ **1** *a)* to cause (a child or young animal) to become accustomed gradually to food other than its mother's milk; to cause to give up suckling *b)* now, often, to cause to give up drinking milk from a bottle with a nipple **2** to withdraw (a person or thing) by degrees (*from* a dependence on something) [to *wean* a patient from a ventilator, an addict from heroin, an economy from fossil fuels, etc.] **3** to be raised on or brought up with; to become accustomed to: with *on* [*weaned* on good books] —**wean′er** ***n.***

wean[2] (wēn) ***n.*** ⟦contr. of Scot *wee ane*, little one⟧ [Scot. or North Eng.] a child or baby

wean·ling (wēn′liŋ) ***n.*** a child or young animal that has just been weaned —***adj.*** recently weaned

weap·on (wep′ən) ***n.*** ⟦ME *wepen* < OE *wæpen*, akin to Ger *waffe*, ON *vāpn*, Goth *wēpna*: base found only in Gmc⟧ **1** an instrument or device of any kind designed or used to injure or kill, as in fighting or hunting **2** any organ or part of an organism used for attacking or defending **3** any means of attack or defense [the *weapon* of the law] —**weap′oned** ***adj.*** —**weap′on·less** ***adj.***

☆**weap·on·eer** (wep′ə nir′) ***n.*** an expert in the design and production of weapons, esp. nuclear weapons

☆**weap·on·ize** (wep′ən īz′) ***vt.*** **-ized′, -iz′ing** **1** to supply or arm with weapons; develop for warfare [to *weaponize* outer space] **2** to develop for use as a lethal agent in chemical or biological warfare [to *weaponize* nerve gas, the smallpox virus, etc.] —**weap′on·i·za′tion** ***n.***

weap·on·ry (wep′ən rē) ***n.*** ⟦WEAPON + -RY⟧ **1** the design and production of weapons **2** weapons collectively; esp., a nation's stockpile of weapons of war

weap·ons-grade (wep′ənz grād′) ***adj.*** designating or of uranium, plutonium, or other fissionable nuclear material of a quality suitable for use in nuclear weapons

wear[1] (wer) ***vt.*** **wore, worn, wear′ing** ⟦ME *weren* < OE *werian*, akin to ON *verja*, Goth *wasjan*, to clothe < IE base **wes-*, to clothe > Sans *vastra-*, L *vestis*, clothing, *vestire*, to clothe⟧ **1** *a)* to have on the body or carry on the person (clothing, jewelry, a weapon, etc.) *b)* to hold the position or rank symbolized by [to *wear* the heavyweight crown] *c)* to dress in (a specified kind of attire) so as to be in style [what college students are *wearing* this fall] **2** to have or show in one's expression or appearance [to *wear* a smile, *wearing* an air of expectancy] **3** to be fitted with or have on the person habitually [to *wear* dentures] **4** to have or bear as a characteristic or attribute [to *wear* a beard, to *wear* one's hair long] **5** to impair, consume, or diminish as by constant use, handling, or friction: often with *away* **6** to bring by use to a specified state [to *wear* a coat to rags] **7** to make, cause, or produce by the friction of rubbing, scraping, flowing, etc. [to *wear* a hole in the sole of one's shoe] **8** to tire or exhaust (a person) **9** to pass (time) slowly or tediously: often with *away* or *out* —***vi.*** **1** to become impaired, consumed, or diminished by constant use, friction, etc. [shoes that have begun to *wear*] **2** to hold up in use as specified; bear continued use or handling; last [a suit that *wears* well] **3** to become in time; grow gradually [patience that is *wearing* thin] **4** to pass away gradually: often with *away* or *on*: said of time [the year *wore* on] **5** to have an irritating or exhausting effect (*on*) [the constant noise is *wearing* on our nerves] —***n.*** **1** the act of wearing or the state of being worn **2** things, esp. clothes, worn, or for wearing, on the body [children's *wear*]: often in comb. [*sportswear, footwear*] **3** the fashion or proper style of dress or the like **4** *a)* the gradual impairment, loss, or diminution from use, friction, etc. *b)* the amount of such loss **5** the ability to resist impairment or loss from use, friction, etc. [a lot of *wear* left in the tire] —**wear down** **1** to make or become worn; lose or cause to lose thickness or height by use, friction, etc. **2** to tire out, or exhaust (a person); weary **3** to overcome the resistance of by persistence —**wear off** to pass away or diminish by degrees —**wear out** **1** to make or become useless from continued wear or use **2** to waste or consume by degrees **3** to tire out; exhaust —**wear the pants** (or **trousers**) [Informal] to wield the greatest authority in a family or household —**wear′er** ***n.***

wear[2] (wer) *vt.* **wore, worn, wear′ing** ⟦? altered (infl. by prec.) < VEER[2]⟧ to change the course of (a sailing vessel) by turning its bow away from, and causing its stern to move across, the wind: opposed to TACK (*vt.* 5*a*) —*vi.* **1** to wear a sailing vessel **2** to change course by being worn: said of a sailing vessel

Wear (wir) river in Durham, N England, flowing northeast into the North Sea: 67 mi (108 km)

wear·a·ble (wer′ə bəl) *adj.* that can be worn; suitable for wear —*n.* [*pl.*] wearable things; garments; clothing —**wear′a·bil′i·ty** *n.*

wear and tear loss and damage resulting from use

wea·ri·ful (wir′i fəl) *adj.* that makes weary; tiresome —**wea′ri·ful·ly** *adv.* —**wea′ri·ful·ness** *n.*

wea·ri·less (wir′ē lis) *adj.* unwearying; tireless —**wea′ri·less·ly** *adv.* —**wea′ri·less·ness** *n.*

wea·ri·ness (-nis) *n.* **1** the condition or quality of being weary; fatigue or tedium **2** something that causes fatigue or tedium

wear·ing (wer′iŋ) *adj.* **1** of or intended for wear [*wearing* apparel] **2** causing wear, or gradual impairment or diminution **3** wearying; tiring —**wear′ing·ly** *adv.*

wea·ri·some (wir′i səm) *adj.* causing weariness; tiring, tiresome, or tedious —**wea′ri·some·ly** *adv.*

wear·proof (wer′pro͞of′) *adj.* resistant to normal wear or the effects of continued use

wea·ry (wir′ē) *adj.* **-ri·er, -ri·est** ⟦ME *weri* < OE *werig*, akin to OHG *wuorag*, drunk < IE base **wōr-*, giddiness, faintness > Gr *hōrakian*, to be giddy⟧ **1** tired; worn out **2** without further liking, patience, tolerance, zeal, etc.; bored: with *of* [*weary* of his continual joking] **3** tiring [*weary* work] **4** irksome; tedious; tiresome — *vt., vi.* **-ried, -ry·ing** to make or become weary —*SYN.* TIRED —**wea′ri·ly** *adv.*

wea·sel (wē′zəl) *n., pl.* **-sels** or **-sel** ⟦ME *wesel* < OE *wesle*, akin to Ger *wiesel*, prob. < IE base **weis-*, to flow out (with reference to the rank odor emitted by the animal) > VIRUS, BISON⟧ **1** any of various agile musteline carnivores (esp. genus *Mustela*) with a long, slender body, short legs, and a long, bushy tail: they feed on rats, mice, birds, eggs, etc. and are found worldwide **2** a sly, cunning, or sneaky person —☆*vi.* **1** to use weasel words **2** [Informal] to avoid or evade a commitment or responsibility: with *out* —**wea′sel·ly** *adj.*

☆**weasel words** ⟦prob. in allusion to the weasel's habit of sucking out the contents of an egg without destroying the shell⟧ words or remarks that are deliberately ambiguous or misleading

weath·er (weth′ər) *n.* ⟦ME *weder* < OE, akin to ON *vethr*, Ger *wetter* < IE base **we-*, **awe-*, to blow > WIND[2], OSlav *vedro*, fair weather⟧ **1** the general condition of the atmosphere at a particular time and place, with regard to the temperature, moisture, cloudiness, etc. **2** disagreeable or harmful atmospheric conditions; storm, rain, etc. [protected against the *weather*] —*vt.* **1** to expose to the action of the weather or atmosphere, as for airing, drying, or seasoning **2** to wear away, discolor, disintegrate, or otherwise change for the worse by exposure to the atmosphere **3** to pass through safely or survive [to *weather* a storm] **4** to slope (masonry, cornices, sills, etc.) so as to allow water to run off **5** *Naut.* to pass (a cape, another vessel, etc.) safely despite being pushed toward it by the wind —*vi.* **1** to become worn, discolored, etc. from being exposed to the weather or atmosphere **2** to endure such exposure in a specified manner [canvas that *weathers* well] —*adj.* **1** designating or of the side of a ship, etc. toward the wind; windward **2** exposed to the elements [*weather* deck] —**make heavy weather of** [Chiefly Brit.] to create needless difficulties in dealing with —☆**under the weather** [Informal] **1** not feeling well; somewhat sick; ailing **2** somewhat drunk

weath·er-beat·en (-bēt′'n) *adj.* showing the effect of weather; specif., *a*) stained, damaged, or worn down *b*) sunburned, roughened, etc. (said of a person, a person's face, etc.)

weath·er·board (-bôrd′) *n. a*) CLAPBOARD[1] *b*) SIDING (sense 1) —*vt.* to cover with clapboards or siding

weath·er·board·ing (-bôr′diŋ) *n.* **1** clapboards collectively **2** SIDING (sense 1)

weath·er-bound (-bound′) *adj.* delayed or halted by bad weather: said of a ship, airplane, etc.

☆**Weather Bureau** *former name for* NATIONAL WEATHER SERVICE

weath·er·cast (-kast′) *n.* ⟦WEATHER + -CAST⟧ a broadcast of news about the weather, esp. one including a forecast, on radio or TV —**weath′er·cast′er** *n.*

weath·er·cock (-käk′) *n.* **1** a weather vane, esp. one in the traditional shape of a rooster's profile **2** a fickle or changeable person or thing

weath·ered (weth′ərd) *adj.* **1** seasoned by the weather; stained, worn, or beaten by the weather **2** given a stained or discolored finish intended to resemble that produced by exposure to the weather **3** *Archit.* made sloping so as to shed water: said as of sills or cornices

weather eye **1** an eye alert to signs of changing weather **2** a close watch for change of any kind [to keep a *weather eye* on a touchy situation] —**keep one's weather eye open** to be on the alert; stay on guard

weath·er·glass (weth′ər glas′) *n.* BAROMETER (sense 1)

weath·er·ing (-iŋ) *n.* **1** *Archit.* a slope built to shed water **2** *Geol.* the destructive physical and chemical effects of the forces of weather on rock surfaces, as in forming soil or sand

☆**weath·er·ize** (-īz′) *vt.* **-ized′, -iz′ing** ⟦WEATHER + -IZE⟧ to weatherstrip, insulate, etc. (a building), as in order to conserve heat —**weath′er·i·za′tion** *n.*

weath·er·ly (-lē) *adj. Naut.* that can sail close to the wind with very little drift to leeward —**weath′er·li·ness** *n.*

weath·er·man (-man′) *n., pl.* **-men′** (-men′) ☆a man who forecasts the weather, or, esp., one who reports weather conditions and forecasts, as on television —**weath′er·girl′** (-gurl′) —**weath′er·per′son** (-pur′sən)

☆**weather map** a map or chart showing the condition of the weather in a certain area at a given time by indicating barometric pressures, temperatures, wind direction, etc.

weath·er·proof (-pro͞of′) *adj.* that can be exposed to wind, rain, snow, etc. without being damaged —*vt.* to make weatherproof

weather station a post or office where weather conditions are recorded and studied and forecasts are made

☆**weath·er·strip** (-strip′) *n.* a thin strip of metal, felt, wood, etc., used to cover the joint between a door or window sash and the jamb, casing, or sill so as to keep out drafts, rain, etc.: also **weather strip** —*vt.* **-stripped′, -strip′ping** to fit or provide with weatherstrips

☆**weath·er·strip·ping** (-strip′iŋ) *n.* **1** WEATHERSTRIP **2** weatherstrips collectively

weather vane a vane that swings in the wind to show the direction from which the wind is blowing

weath·er-wise (-wīz′) *adj.* **1** skilled in predicting the weather **2** skilled in predicting shifts of opinion, feeling, etc.

weath·er·worn (-wôrn′) *adj.* WEATHER-BEATEN

weave (wēv) *vt.* **wove** or, chiefly for *vt.* 6 & *vi.* 2, **weaved, wo′ven** or **wove** or, chiefly for *vt.* 6 & *vi.* 2, **weaved, weav′ing** ⟦ME *weven* < OE *wefan*, akin to ON *vefa*, Ger *weben* < IE **webh-* (> Gr *hyphē*) < base *(*a*)*we-*, to plait, weave⟧ **1** *a*) to make (a fabric), esp. on a loom, by interlacing threads or yarns *b*) to form (threads) into a fabric **2** *a*) to construct in the mind or imagination *b*) to work (details, incidents, etc.) into a story, poem, etc. **3** *a*) to make by interlacing twigs, straw, rush, wicker, etc. [to *weave* baskets] *b*) to twist or interlace (straw, wicker, etc.) so as to form something **4** to twist or interlace (something) into, through, or among [to *weave* flowers into one's hair] **5** to make or spin (a web): said of spiders, etc. **6** *a*) to cause (a vehicle, etc.) to move from side to side or in and out *b*) to make (one's way) by moving in this fashion —*vi.* **1** to do weaving; make cloth **2** to move from side to side or in and out [*weaving* through traffic] —*n.* **1** a method, manner, or pattern of weaving [a cloth of English *weave*] **2** the interlacing of strands of natural or synthetic hair with a person's own hair, as to create a longer or fuller style: in full **hair weave**

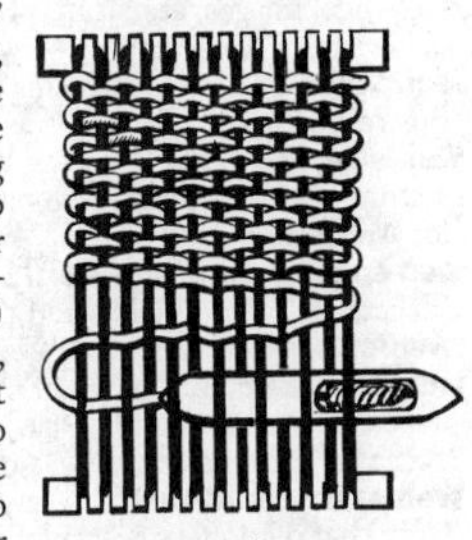
weaving

weav·er (wē′vər) *n.* **1** a person who weaves; esp., one whose work is weaving **2** WEAVER FINCH

weav·er·bird (-burd′) *n.* WEAVER FINCH

weaver finch any of a number of Old World finches (family Ploceidae) that weave elaborate domed nests of sticks, grass, etc.

weaver's knot (*or* **hitch**) a SHEET BEND knot used in weaving

web (web) *n.* ⟦ME < OE *webb*, akin to ON *vefr*, OHG *weppi* < IE **webh-*, to WEAVE⟧ **1** any woven fabric; esp., a length of cloth being woven on a loom or just taken off **2** *a*) the woven or spun network of a spider; cobweb *b*) a similar network spun by the larvae of certain insects **3** a carefully woven trap or snare **4** a complicated work of the mind, imagination, etc. [a *web* of lies] **5** anything like a web, as in intricacy of pattern or interconnection of elements; network **6** *Anat.* *a*) tissue or membrane *b*) an abnormal membrane joining fingers or toes at the base **7** *Archit.* the portion of a ribbed vault between the ribs **8** [*also* **W-**] *Comput.* WORLD WIDE WEB: usually with *the* **9** *Mech.* the plate joining the flanges of a joist, girder, rail, etc. **10** *Printing* a large roll of paper used in a rotary press, designed for continuous feeding **11** *Zool.* *a*) the vane of a feather *b*) a membrane partly or completely joining the digits of various water birds, water animals, etc. —*vt.* **webbed, web′bing** **1** to join by or as by a web **2** to cover with or as with a web **3** to catch or snare in or as in a web —**web′like′** *adj.*

Webb (web) **1 Beatrice (Potter)** 1858-1943; Eng. economist & socialist reformer: wife of Sidney James **2 Sidney (James)** 1st Baron Passfield 1859-1947; Eng. economist & socialist reformer

Web beacon a tiny file placed as in an email to track its delivery, or originating on a Web page to track visitors to the site: also [Informal] **Web bug**

webbed (webd) *adj.* **1** formed like a web or made of webbing **2** joined by a web [*webbed* toes] **3** having the digits joined by a web [a *webbed* foot]

web·bing (web′iŋ) *n.* **1** a strong, tough fabric, as of jute or cotton, woven in strips and used for belts, in upholstery, etc. **2** a membrane joining the digits, as of a duck, goose, or frog **3** a part like this, as between the thumb and forefinger of a baseball glove **4** a netlike structure of interwoven cord, etc., as the strung part of rackets

web·by (-ē) *adj.* **web′bi·er, web′bi·est** **1** of, having the nature of, or like a web **2** webbed or palmate

web·cam (web′kam′) *n.* ⟦WEB (*n.* 8) + CAM(ERA)⟧ a camera designed for use with a computer, as to transmit images, often, specif., live video images, over a website

web·cast (web′kast′) *n.* ⟦WEB (*n.* 8) + -CAST⟧ something, as a performance or other public event, transmitted for a large audience over the World Wide Web

web·er (web′ər, vā′bər) ***n.*** ⟦after W. E. WEBER⟧ the basic unit of magnetic flux in the SI and MKS systems, equal to one hundred million (10^8) maxwells: abbrev. *Wb*

We·ber (vā′bər; *for* 4, web′ər) **1 Carl Ma·ri·a (Friedrich Ernst) von** (kärl mä rē′ä fôn) 1786-1826; Ger. composer **2 Ernst Hein·rich** (ernst hīn′ riH) 1795-1878; Ger. physiologist & anatomist **3 Max** (mäks) (born *Karl Emil Maximilian Weber*) 1864-1920; Ger. sociologist & economist **4 Max** (maks) 1881-1961; U.S. painter, born in Russia **5 Wil·helm E·du·ard** (vil′ helm′ ā′do͞o ärt′) 1804-91; Ger. physicist: brother of Ernst

We·bern (vā′bərn), **An·ton (von)** (än′tôn) 1883-1945; Austrian composer

web·foot (web′fo͝ot′) ***n., pl.*** **-feet′** (-fēt′) **1** a foot with the toes webbed **2** an animal with webbed feet —**web′-foot′ed** ***adj.***

Web hosting [*also* **w- h-**] the act or business of serving as a website HOST[2] (*n.* 5c)

web·i·nar (web′ə när′) ***n.*** ⟦WEB (*n.* 8) + (SEM)INAR⟧ a seminar, workshop, lecture, etc. conducted over the internet, usually involving interaction by the participants

web·mas·ter (web′mas′tər) ***n.*** ⟦WEB(SITE) + MASTER⟧ a person responsible for maintaining or creating a website, esp. a commercial website

web offset **1** a method of offset printing using a web press: cf. LETTERPRESS **2** matter printed by this method

Web page [*also* **w- p-**] a single file on the World Wide Web, providing text, graphical images, etc.: it may be linked with other Web pages at a WEBSITE: also written **web′page′** ***n.***

web press a rotary press using offset printing on paper fed from a continuous roll or web

web·site (web′sīt′) ***n.*** [*occas.* **W-**] a location on the World Wide Web, consisting of one or more Web pages accessible at a single address: also **web (or Web) site**

web spinner any of an order (Embiidina) of small, tropical and subtropical insects that live in silk-lined tunnels underground, under bark, etc.: also **web′spin′ner** ***n.***

web·ster (web′stər) ***n.*** ⟦ME < OE *webbestre*, fem. of *webba*, weaver < OE < *webb*: see WEB & -STER⟧ [Obs.] a weaver

Web·ster[1] (web′stər) ***n.*** ⟦see prec.⟧ a masculine name

Web·ster[2] (web′stər) ***n.*** **1** any of the dictionaries succeeding or adapted from that dictionary first published in the U.S. by Noah Webster in 1828 **2** [Informal] any American dictionary of the English language: also **Web′ster's**

Web·ster[3] (web′stər) **1 Daniel** 1782-1852; U.S. statesman & orator **2 John** 1580?-1625?; Eng. dramatist **3 Noah** 1758-1843; U.S. lexicographer

web-toed (web′tōd′) ***adj.*** having webfeet

☆**web·worm** (-wurm′) ***n.*** any of various caterpillars that spin large, irregular webs, as the **fall webworm** (*Hyphantria cunea*), whose webs envelop whole branches of trees

wed (wed) ***vt.*** **wed′ded, wed′ded** or **wed, wed′ding** ⟦ME *wedden* < OE *weddian*, lit., to pledge, engage < *wed*, a pledge, akin to Ger *wetten*, to pledge, wager < IE base **wadh-*, a pledge, to redeem a pledge > L *vas* (gen. *vadis*), a pledge⟧ **1** to marry; specif., *a)* to take as husband or wife *b)* to conduct the marriage ceremony for; join in wedlock **2** to unite or join closely —***vi.*** to become married; take a husband or wife

Wed *abbrev.* Wednesday

we'd (wēd) *contraction* **1** we had **2** we would **3** we should

wed·ded (wed′id) ***adj.*** **1** married [the *wedded* pair] **2** of or arising from marriage [*wedded* bliss] **3** devoted [*wedded* to one's work] **4** joined [*wedded* by common interests]

Wed·dell Sea (wə del′, wed′əl) ⟦after James *Weddell* (1787-1834), Brit whaler who discovered it (1823)⟧ section of the Atlantic east of the Antarctic Peninsula

wed·ding (wed′iŋ) ***n.*** ⟦ME < OE *weddung* < *weddian*: see WED⟧ **1** *a)* the act or ceremony of becoming married; marriage *b)* the marriage ceremony with its attendant festivities **2** an anniversary of a marriage [a golden *wedding*] **3** a joining together

wedding ring a ring, typically a band of gold, platinum, etc., worn as a sign of marriage and given typically by one's spouse during one's wedding ceremony

We·de·kind (vā′də kint′), **Frank** (fräŋk) 1864-1918; Ger. playwright

we·deln (vā′dəln) ***n.*** ⟦< Ger, to wag < MHG *wedelen* < *wedel*, a tail < OHG *wadil* (akin to ON *vēli*, bird's tail), orig., something that moves about < IE **wēt-* < base **we-*, **awe-*, to hover, blow > WIND[2]⟧ *Skiing* a series of short parallel turns executed in rapid succession

wedge (wej) ***n.*** ⟦ME *wegge* < OE *wecg*, akin to Ger dial. *weck* < IE **wogwhyo-*, wedge, akin to **wogwhni-s*, plowshare > L *vomis*, OHG *waganso*⟧ **1** a piece of hard material, as wood or metal, tapering from a thick back to a thin edge that can be driven or forced into a narrow opening, as to split wood, lift a heavy weight, or fix something firmly in place **2** anything shaped like a wedge or having a wedge-shaped part [a *wedge* of pie, a lime *wedge*]; specif., *a)* a wedge-shaped stroke in cuneiform writing *b)* a wedge-shaped tactical formation, as of troops *c)* *Golf* an iron with a specially weighted head and the face angled to give the most loft, as for shots out of bunkers **3** any action or procedure that serves to open the way for a gradual change, disruption, intrusion, etc. —***vt.*** **wedged, wedg′ing** **1** to split or force apart with or as with a wedge **2** to fix firmly in place by driving a wedge or wedges under, beside, etc. **3** to force or pack (*in*) **4** to force or crowd together in a narrow space —***vi.*** to push or be forced as or like a wedge —**wedge′like′** ***adj.***

wedge

☆**wedg·ie** (wej′ē) ***n.*** **1** a shoe having a wedge-shaped piece under the heel, which forms a solid sole, flat from heel to toe **2** a prank in which the victim's undershorts are jerked upward so as to become wedged between the buttocks: often in the phr. **give (or) get a wedgie**, to make (or be) the victim of this prank

Wedg·wood (wej′wo͝od′) ⟦after J. *Wedgwood* (1730-95), Eng potter⟧ *trademark for* a fine English ceramic ware, typically with delicate neoclassical figures applied in a white, cameolike relief on a tinted background

wedg·y (wej′ē) ☆***n.*** *alt. sp. of* WEDGIE

wed·lock (wed′läk′) ***n.*** ⟦ME *wedlok* < OE *wedlac* < *wed*, a compact, pledge + *-lac*, an offering, gift, akin to ON *leikr*, play, Goth *laiks*, a dance < IE base **leig-*, to leap, hop > Sans *rējatē*, (he) hops⟧ the state of being married; matrimony

Wednes·day (wenz′dā; *occas.*, -dē) ***n.*** ⟦ME *Wednes dei* < OE *Wodnes dæg*, Woden's day (see WODEN & DAY), like ON *Othinsdagr* (lit., Odin's day), early transl. of L *dies Mercurii*, Mercury's day⟧ the fourth day of the week: abbrev. *Wed*, *We*, or *W*

Wednes·days (-dāz′; *occas.*, -dēz′) ***adv.*** during every Wednesday or most Wednesdays

wee (wē) ***adj.*** **we′er, we′est** ⟦ME *we*, *wei*, small quantity (only in north Eng & Scot dial.) < OE (Anglian) *wege*, *weg* < base of *wegan*, to bear: see WEIGH[1]⟧ very small; tiny

weed[1] (wēd) ***n.*** ⟦ME *weede* < OE *weod*, akin to LowG *wēd*: base only in WGmc⟧ **1** any undesired, uncultivated plant, esp. one growing in profusion so as to crowd out a desired crop, disfigure a lawn, etc. **2** [Informal] *a)* tobacco (with *the*) *b)* a cigar or cigarette *c)* marijuana **3** something useless; specif., a horse that is unfit for racing or breeding —***vt.*** **1** to remove the weeds from (a garden, lawn, etc.) **2** to remove (a weed): often with *out* **3** to remove as useless, harmful, etc.: often with *out* **4** to rid of elements regarded as useless, harmful, etc. —***vi.*** to remove weeds, etc. —**weed′er** ***n.*** —**weed′less** ***adj.***

weed[2] (wēd) ***n.*** ⟦ME *wede* < OE *wæde*, garment, akin to OHG *wāt* (Ger *-wand*, in *leinwand*, linen) < IE base **(a)wē-*, to WEAVE > ON *authna*, fate (in reference to the spinning by the fate goddesses)⟧ **1** [Archaic] a garment: *often used in pl.* **2** [*pl.*] black mourning clothes, esp. those worn by a widow **3** [Archaic] a black mourning band, as of crepe, worn on a man's hat or sleeve

weed·kill·er (wēd′kil′ər) ***n.*** a herbicide designed or used specifically for weeds

weed·y (-ē) ***adj.*** **weed′i·er, weed′i·est** **1** having weeds; full of weeds **2** of or like a weed or weeds, as in rapid, rank growth **3** lean, lanky, ungainly, etc. —**weed′i·ness** ***n.***

wee hours ⟦because designated by low numbers⟧ the first few hours after midnight

week (wēk) ***n.*** ⟦ME *weke* < OE *wicu* with lengthened & lowered vowel, akin to Ger *woche* (OHG *wohha*) < IE **weig-*, to bend (see WEAK): basic sense "period of change"⟧ **1** a period of seven days, esp. one beginning with Sunday and ending with Saturday **2** a particular or specified week [Easter *week*, freshman *week*] **3** the hours or days of work in a seven-day period [to work a 40-hour *week*] —**Sunday (or Monday or Tuesday, etc.) week** [Chiefly Brit.] a week, counting backward or forward, from Sunday (or Monday, Tuesday, etc.) —**this day (or yesterday, etc.) week** [Chiefly Brit.] a week, counting backward or forward, from today (or yesterday, etc.) —**week after week** every week or for many successive weeks —**week by week** each week —**week in, week out** every week

week·day (-dā′) ***n.*** **1** any day of the week except Sunday (or, as in Judaism, Saturday) **2** any day not in the weekend —***adj.*** of, for, or on a weekday

week·days (-dāz′) ***adv.*** during every weekday or most weekdays

week·end or **week-end** (wēk′end′) ***n.*** the period from Friday night or Saturday to Monday morning; end of the week: also **week end** —***adj.*** of, for, or on a weekend —***vi.*** to spend the weekend (*at* or *in* a specified place) —**long weekend** a weekend plus one or two days before or after

week·end·er (wēk′en′dər) ***n.*** **1** a person who takes a vacation or goes for a visit on a weekend **2** a small piece of luggage for use as on a weekend trip: also **weekend case (or bag)**

week·ends (-endz′) ***adv.*** during every weekend or most weekends

☆**weekend warrior** [Slang] a person who engages in athletics or military reserve service just on weekends

week·long (wēk′lôŋ′) ***adj.*** continuing for a full week

week·ly (wēk′lē) ***adj.*** **1** done, happening, payable, etc. once a week, or every week [a *weekly* visit] **2** of a week, or of each week [a *weekly* wage] —***adv.*** once a week; every week —***n., pl.*** **-lies** a periodical published once a week

week·night (wēk′nīt′) ***n.*** any night of the week except Saturday or Sunday

Weems (wēmz), **Mason Locke** 1759-1825; U.S. clergyman & writer: called *Parson Weems*

ween (wēn) ***vi., vt.*** ⟦ME *wenen* < OE *wenan*, akin to Ger *wähnen* < IE base **wen-*, to desire, attain > WIN, WEAN[1], L *venus*, love⟧ [Archaic] to think; suppose; imagine

☆**wee·nie** (wē′nē) ***n., pl.*** **-nies** **1** [Informal] WIENER **2** [Slang] *a)* a person regarded as ineffectual, weak, dull, etc.; wimp or nerd *b)* a person regarded as offensive, disagreeable, ridiculous, etc.; jerk **3** [Slang] the penis

wee·ny[1] (wē′nē) *adj.* **wee′ni·er, wee′ni·est** ⟦WEE + (TI)NY⟧ [Informal] small; tiny

ween·y[2] (wē′nē) ☆*n., pl.* **-nies** [Informal] *alt. sp. of* WEENIE (sense 1)

weep (wēp) *vi.* **wept, weep′ing** ⟦ME *wepen* < OE *wepan*, akin to *wop*, outcry, Goth *wōpjan*, OS *wōpian* < IE base **wab-*, to cry, complain > OSlav *vabiti*, to call to⟧ **1** to manifest or give expression to a strong emotion, usually grief or sorrow, by crying, wailing, or, esp., shedding tears **2** to lament or mourn: with *for* or *over* **3** to form drops of moisture condensed from the air [cold pipes *weep* in hot weather] **4** to exude water or other liquid [wounds, plant stems, etc. *weep*] —*vt.* **1** to weep for; lament; bewail; mourn [to *weep* one's misfortune] **2** to shed (tears or other drops of liquid) **3** to bring to a specified condition by weeping [to *weep* oneself to sleep] —*n.* [*often pl.*] a fit of weeping —*SYN.* CRY

weep·er (wē′pər) *n.* **1** a person who weeps, esp. readily or habitually **2** [Historical] *a)* a hired mourner, as at a funeral *b)* a conventional badge of mourning, as the long, black band of crepe formerly worn (*often used in pl.*) **3** a capuchin monkey **4** WEEPIE

weep·ie (wē′pē) *n.* [Slang] a sad, often maudlin film

weep·ing (-piŋ) *n.* the act of one who or that which weeps —*adj.* **1** that weeps tears or other liquid **2** having graceful, drooping branches —**weep′ing·ly** *adv.*

weeping willow a Chinese willow tree (*Salix babylonica*) widely grown as an ornamental for its delicate, drooping branches

weep·y (wē′pē) *adj.* **weep′i·er, weep′i·est 1** *a)* inclined to weep; tearful *b)* exuding liquid **2** characterized by or apt to cause weeping —**weep′i·ness** *n.*

wee small hours WEE HOURS

wee·ver (wē′vər) *n.* ⟦NormFr *wivre* (OFr *guivre*), orig., serpent, dragon < L *vipera*, VIPER⟧ any of a family (Trachinidae) of edible, marine percoid fishes with sharp, very poisonous spines on the gill cover and the first dorsal fin

wee·vil (wē′vəl) *n.* ⟦ME *wevel* < OE *wifel*, akin to MLowG *wevel* < IE **webh-*, to move to and fro, WEAVE⟧ any of various families of beetles (esp. Curculionidae) having the head prolonged into a projecting beak that usually curves downward, and including many pest species that feed, esp. as larvae, on cotton, fruits, grain, etc.

wee·vil·y or **wee·vil·ly** (wē′və lē) *adj.* infested with weevils

wee-wee (wē′wē′) *vt.* **-weed′, -wee′ing** ⟦baby talk⟧ to urinate —*n.* urine A child's term

weft (weft) *n.* ⟦ME < OE < base of *wefan*, to WEAVE⟧ *Weaving* the yarns carried by the shuttle back and forth across the warp; woof; filling

Weg·en·er (vāg′ə nər, veg′ə nər), **Al·fred (Lothar)** (äl′frāt′) 1880-1930; Ger. geologist

Wehr·macht (vār′mäkht′) *n.* ⟦Ger, defense force⟧ [*also in roman type*] the armed forces of Nazi Germany

Wei (wā) river in NC China, flowing from Gansu province east into the Huang: *c.* 500 mi (805 km)

wei·ge·la (wī jē′lə, -gē′-) *n.* ⟦ModL, after C. E. *Weigel* (1748-1831), Ger physician⟧ any of a genus (*Weigela*) of shrubs of the honeysuckle family, with clusters of bell-shaped flowers; esp., a widely cultivated species (*W. florida*) with dark red flowers: also called **wei·ge′lia** (-jēl′yə)

weigh[1] (wā) *vt.* ⟦ME *weien*, to weigh, bear < OE *wegan*, to carry, bear, akin to Ger *wegian*, *wägen* < IE base **weĝh-*, to go, draw > OE *wæg*, a wave, L *vehere*, to carry, bring⟧ **1** to determine the weight of by means of a scale or balance **2** to have (a specified) weight [it *weighs* ten pounds]: orig. construed as a *vi.* and still so construed when used with an adverb **3** WEIGHT (*vt.* 1) **4** to lift or balance (an object) in the hand or hands, in order to estimate its heaviness or weight **5** to measure out, dole out, or apportion, by or as by weight: often with *out* **6** *a)* to consider and choose carefully [to *weigh* one's words] *b)* to balance or ponder in the mind; consider in order to make a choice [to *weigh* one plan against another] **7** *Naut. see* WEIGH ANCHOR under ANCHOR —*vi.* **1** to have significance, importance, or influence [his word *weighed* heavily with the jury] **2** to be a burden; press or bear down: with *on* or *upon* [the theft *weighed* on my mind] **3** *Naut.* WEIGH ANCHOR (see phrase under ANCHOR) —*SYN.* CONSIDER —**weigh down 1** to make bend downward as with added weight **2** to burden or bear down on so as to oppress or depress —**weigh in 1** to weigh (a boxer, jockey, etc.) before or after a contest in order to verify declared weight **2** to be so weighed **3** to have one's baggage weighed **4** [Informal] to enter and participate forcefully, as in a discussion or debate —**weigh in with** [Informal] to introduce or contribute (an idea or opinion) to a discussion, argument, etc. —**weigh′a·ble** *adj.*

weigh[2] (wā) *n.* ⟦modified by the notion of "weighing anchor"⟧ *var. of* WAY (*n.* 20): chiefly in **under weigh**, meaning UNDERWAY

weigh-in (wā′in′) *n.* an official weighing in of a boxer, wrestler, jockey, etc., as before a contest

weight (wāt) *n.* ⟦ME *weiht*, altered (infl. by *weien*, WEIGH[1]) < OE *wiht* < *wegan*: see WEIGH[1]⟧ **1** a portion or quantity weighing a definite or specified amount [ten pounds *weight* of lead] **2** *a)* heaviness as a quality of things *b)* *Physics* the force of gravity acting on a body, equal to the mass of the body multiplied by the acceleration of gravity **3** *a)* quantity or amount of heaviness; how much a thing weighs *b)* the amount a specified thing should weigh **4** *a)* any unit of heaviness or mass *b)* any system of such units [troy *weight*, avoirdupois *weight*] (see the table of weights and measures in the Reference Supplement) *c)* a piece, as of metal, of a specific standard heaviness, used on a balance or scale in weighing **5** any block or mass of material used for its heaviness; specif., *a)* one used to hold light things down or in position [a *paperweight*] *b)* one used to drive a mechanism [the *weights* in a clock] *c)* one used to maintain balance [*weights* placed on an automobile wheel] *d)* one of a particular heaviness, lifted as an athletic exercise **6** *a)* any heavy thing or load *b)* a burden or oppressiveness, as of responsibility or sorrow **7** importance or consequence [a matter of great *weight*] **8** influence, power, or authority [to throw one's *weight* to the losing side] **9** the relative thickness or heaviness of a fabric or an article of clothing as proper to a particular season, use, etc. [a suit of summer *weight*] **10** *Printing* the relative thickness of the lines in type fonts **11** *Sports* *a)* any of the several classifications into which boxers and wrestlers are placed according to how much they weigh *b)* the number of pounds a horse is required to carry for a particular race, including the weight of the jockey, the saddle, and, often, added lead weights **12** *Statistics* a constant assigned to a single item in a frequency distribution, indicative of the item's relative importance —*vt.* **1** to add weight to; make heavy or heavier **2** to burden; load down; oppress **3** to treat (thread or fabric) with a solution of metallic salts, in order to increase its weight **4** to manage, control, or influence in a particular direction or so as to favor a particular side; slant [the evidence was *weighted* against the defendant] **5** *Statistics* to assign a weight to in a frequency distribution —*SYN.* IMPORTANCE, INFLUENCE —**by weight** as determined by weighing —**carry weight** to be important, influential, etc. —**pull one's weight** to do one's share —**throw one's weight around** to take undue advantage of one's authority or rank; be overbearing

weight·less (wāt′lis) *adj.* having little or no apparent weight; specif., *a)* falling freely through a gravitational field, without apparent gravitational effects, as everything does inside an orbiting spacecraft *b)* of or having zero gravity *c)* existing in a state of equilibrium within a fluid —**weight′less·ly** *adv.* —**weight′less·ness** *n.*

weight lifting the athletic exercise or competitive sport of lifting barbells: also written **weight′lift′ing** *n.* —**weight lifter, weight′lift′er** *n.*

weight room any room equipped with weights, exercise machines, etc., as for athletes in a school

weight·y (-ē) *adj.* **weight′i·er, weight′i·est 1** having much weight; very heavy; ponderous **2** burdensome; oppressive [*weighty* responsibilities] **3** of great significance or moment; serious [*weighty* matters of state] **4** of great influence, power, importance, etc. —*SYN.* HEAVY —**weight′i·ly** *adv.* —**weight′i·ness** *n.*

Weil (wīl, vīl; *Fr* ve′y'), **Si·mone** (sē môn′) 1909-43; Fr. philosopher

Weill (wīl; *Ger* vīl), **Kurt** (kurt) 1900-50; U.S. composer, born in Germany

Wei·mar (vī′mär′; *E* vī′mär′, wī′-) city in central Germany, near Erfurt, in the state of Thuringia

Wei·mar·an·er (wī′mə rä′nər, vī′-) *n.* ⟦after prec., where the breed was developed⟧ [*also* **w-**] any of a breed of medium-sized hunting dog with a short, smooth, gray coat: traditionally the tail is docked

Weimar Republic German Republic (1919-33): created by a constitutional assembly at Weimar (1919) & dissolved after Hitler became chancellor

wei·ner (wē′nər) *n. alt. sp. of* WIENER

weir (wir) *n.* ⟦ME *were* < OE *wer*, weir, dam (akin to Ger *wehr*) < base of *werian*, to defend, dam up < IE base **wer-*, to shut up, cover⟧ **1** a low dam built in a river to back up or divert water, as for a mill; milldam **2** a fence, as of brushwood or stakes, built in a stream, channel, etc., for catching fish **3** an obstruction placed in a stream, diverting the water through a prepared aperture for measuring the rate of flow

weird (wird) *adj.* ⟦ME *werde*, orig. n., fate < OE *wyrd*, fate < the base of *weorthan*, to become (basic sense "what is to come") < IE **wert-*, to turn: see VERSE⟧ **1** [Obs.] of fate or destiny **2** of or about ghosts, evil spirits, or other supernatural things; unearthly, mysterious, eerie, etc. **3** *a)* strikingly odd, strange, etc.; fantastic; bizarre [a *weird* costume] *b)* eccentric, erratic, or unconventional in behavior —*n.* [Old Scot.] fate or destiny —☆**weird out** [Slang] to be or cause to be overwhelmed with the bizarre aspects of an experience —**weird′ly** *adv.* —**weird′ness** *n.*

SYN.—**weird** applies to that which is supernaturally mysterious or fantastically strange [a *weird* experience]; **eerie** applies to that which inspires a vague, superstitious uneasiness or dread [the *eerie* howling of a dog]; **uncanny** applies to that which is unnaturally strange or remarkable [*uncanny* insight]; **unearthly** applies to that which is so strange or extraordinary as to seem to belong to another world [an *unearthly* light]

weird·o (wir′dō) *n., pl.* **-os** [Slang] a person or thing that is weird, strange, odd, bizarre, etc.: also **weird′ie** (-dē)

Weird Sisters ⟦see WEIRD (*adj.* 1)⟧ **1** [Obs.] the three Fates **2** the three witches in Shakespeare's *Macbeth*

Weis·mann (vīs′män), **Au·gust (Friedrich Leopold)** (ou′goost) 1834-1914; Ger. biologist

Weiss·horn (vīs′hôrn′) mountain of the Pennine Alps, S Switzerland: *c.* 14,800 ft (4,511 m)

weiss·wurst (wīs′wərst; *Ger* vīs′voorst′) *n.* ⟦Ger < *weiss*, WHITE + *wurst*, sausage: pork and veal whiten when cooked⟧ a variety of bratwurst in which the meat is cooked before being stuffed into the casing

Weiz·mann (vīts′män′; *E* wīts′mən), **Cha·im** (khī′im) 1874-1952; Israeli chemist & Zionist leader, born in Russia: 1st president of Israel (1948-52)

we·ka (wā′kä, wē′kə) *n.* ⟦Maori < Proto-Polynesian **weka*, a bird species⟧ any of a genus (*Gallirallus*) of large flightless rails of New Zealand

welch (welch, welsh) *vi.* [Slang] *var. of* WELSH

Welch (welch, welsh) *n., adj. var. of* WELSH

wel·come (wel′kəm) *adj.* ⟦ME *welcume*, altered by assoc. with *wel*, WELL[2] (as if transl. of OFr *bien venu*) < *wilcume* < OE *wilcuma*, orig. n., a welcome guest < *willa*, pleasure, WILL[1] + *cuma*, guest < *cuman*, to COME⟧ **1** gladly and cordially received [*a welcome guest*] **2** agreeable or gratifying [*welcome news*] **3** freely and willingly permitted or invited [*welcome to use the family library*] —*n.* an act or expression of welcoming [*a hearty (or cold) welcome*] —*interj.* you are welcome here: an expression of cordial greeting —*vt.* **-comed**, **-com·ing** **1** to greet with pleasure and hospitality **2** to receive or accept with pleasure or satisfaction [to *welcome* criticism] **3** to meet, receive, or acknowledge in a specified way; greet —**bid welcome** to receive with cordial greetings —☆**wear out one's welcome** to come so often or stay so long that one is no longer welcome —**you're welcome** you're under no obligation for the favor given: the conventional response to an expression of thanks —**wel′com·er** *n.*

☆**welcome mat** a doormat: chiefly in the phrase **put out the welcome mat**, to give an enthusiastic reception

Welcome Wagon *service mark for* a welcoming service that provides information about a community to new residents — [*occas.* **w- w-**] **1** any such service **2** any act or expression of welcome, esp. a warm or earnest one

weld[1] (weld) *vt.* ⟦altered (with unhistoric *-d*) < obs. *well*, to weld < ME *wellen*, to weld, WELL[1], v.⟧ **1** to unite (pieces of metal, plastic, etc.) by heating until molten and fused or until soft enough to hammer or press together **2** to bring into close or intimate union; unite in a single, compact whole —*vi.* to be welded or capable of being welded [alloys that *weld* at different heats] —*n.* **1** a welding or being welded **2** the joint formed by welding —**weld′a·bil′i·ty** *n.* —**weld′a·ble** *adj.* —**weld′er** *n.*

weld[2] (weld) *n.* ⟦ME *welde*, akin to MLowG *wolde*, MDu *wouw*⟧ **1** a European mignonette (*Reseda luteola*) that yields a yellow dye **2** the dye

wel·fare (wel′fer′) *n.* ⟦ME < *wel faren*, to fare well: see WELL[2] & FARE⟧ **1** the state of being or doing well; condition of health, happiness, and comfort; well-being; prosperity **2** *a)* the organized efforts of government agencies that grant aid to the poor, the unemployed, etc. *b)* such aid **3** WELFARE WORK —**on welfare** receiving government aid because of poverty, unemployment, etc.

welfare state a state in which the welfare of its citizens, with regard to employment, medical care, social security, etc., is considered to be the responsibility of the government

☆**wel·far·ism** (wel′fer iz′əm) *n.* the policies and practices of a welfare state or of public welfare agencies —**wel′far′ist** (-fer′ist) *n., adj.*

wel·kin (wel′kin) *n.* ⟦ME *welkne* < OE *wolcen*, cloud, akin to Ger *wolke* < IE base **welg-*, wet > Old Russ *vologa*, broth, Russ *Volga*⟧ [Archaic] the vault of heaven, the sky, or the upper air

well[1] (wel) *n.* ⟦ME *welle* < OE *wella*, akin to *weallan*, to boil up, akin to Ger *welle*, wave, *wallen*, to boil < IE base **wel-*, to turn, roll > WALK, L *volvere*, to roll⟧ **1** a flow of water from the earth; natural spring and pool **2** a hole or shaft in the earth dug or drilled to tap an underground supply of water, gas, oil, etc. **3** a source of abundant supply; fount [a book that is a *well* of information] **4** any of various shafts or deep enclosed spaces resembling a well; esp., *a)* an open shaft in a building for a staircase; stairwell *b)* a shaft in a building or between buildings, open to the sky for light and air *c)* an elevator shaft *d)* *Naut.* an enclosure in the hold of a ship for containing the pumps and protecting them from damage **5** any of various vessels, containers, etc. for holding liquid, as an inkwell **6** a depression, as on a platter or broiler for catching meat juices **7** the place at a bar, typically a lower shelf, where inferior liquor is stored —*vi.* ⟦ME *wellen*, to well up, bubble, boil, weld < OE *wiellan*, *wyllan*, to bubble, caus. of *weallan*: see the *n.*⟧ to flow or spring from or as from a well; gush (*up, forth, down, out*, etc.) —*vt.* to pour forth; gush [eyes that *welled* tears]

well[2] (wel) *adv.* **bet′ter**, **best** ⟦ME *wel* < OE, akin to Ger *wohl*: for IE base see WILL[1]: basic sense "according to desire"⟧ **1** in a pleasing or desirable manner; satisfactorily [work that is going *well*] **2** in a proper, friendly, or attentive manner [to treat a person *well*] **3** skillfully; expertly [to sing *well*] **4** in an appropriate manner; fittingly [spoken *well*] **5** *a)* prosperously; in comfort and plenty [to live *well*] *b)* to one's advantage or well-being [to marry *well*] **6** with good reason; in justice; properly [one may *well* ask] **7** satisfactorily in regard to health or physical condition [the patient is doing *well*] **8** to a considerable extent, degree, or distance [*well* advanced] **9** thoroughly; fully [stir *well* before cooking] **10** with certainty; definitely [to know perfectly *well* what one must do] **11** intimately; familiarly; closely [to know a person *well*] **12** in good spirit; with good grace [he took the news *well*] ➥*Well* is also used in hyphenated compounds, meaning *properly, satisfactorily, thoroughly*, etc. [*well*-defined, *well*-paid, *well*-worn] —*adj.* **bet′ter**, **best** **1** suitable, proper, fit, right, etc. [it is *well* that he came] **2** in good health [she is quite *well*] **3** in a good or satisfactory condition; favorable; comfortable [things are *well* with us] —*interj.* **1** used variously to express agreement, resignation, surprise, inquiry, expostulation, etc. **2** used to preface or resume one's remarks —**as well** **1** besides; in addition **2** with equal justification, propriety, or effect; equally: also **just as well** —**as well as** in addition to —**wish someone well** to wish success or good fortune for someone

we'll (wēl, wil) *contraction* **1** we will **2** we shall

well-ad·vised (wel′əd vīzd′) *adj.* showing or resulting from careful consideration or sound advice; wise; prudent

Wel·land (wel′ənd) port in SE Ontario, Canada, on the Welland Canal

Welland (Ship) Canal ⟦ult. after *Welland* River, in England⟧ canal of the St. Lawrence Seaway, in Ontario, Canada between Lake Ontario & Lake Erie: 27.5 mi (44 km) long

well-ap·point·ed (wel′ə point′id) *adj.* excellently furnished or equipped [a *well-appointed* office]

well·a·way (wel′ə wā′) *interj.* ⟦ME *wei la wei*, lit., woe! lo! woe!: *wei* < ON *vei*, WOE + OE *la*, LO[1]⟧ [Archaic] alas: an exclamation of sorrow, regret, etc.: also **well′a·day′** (-dā′)

well-bal·anced (wel′bal′ənst) *adj.* **1** nicely or exactly balanced, adjusted, or regulated [a *well-balanced* meal] **2** sane, sensible, and reliable

well-be·haved (wel′bē hāvd′) *adj.* behaving well; conducting oneself properly; displaying good manners

well-be·ing (wel′bē′iŋ) *n.* the state of being well, happy, or prosperous; welfare

well-be·loved (wel′bē luvd′) *adj.* **1** deeply or greatly loved **2** highly respected: used in formal ceremonies or correspondence —*n.* a well-beloved person

well·bore (wel′bôr′) *n.* a hole drilled in the earth in order to extract water, oil, or gas; borehole

well-born (wel′bôrn′) *adj.* born into a family of high social position

well-bred (-bred′) *adj.* **1** showing good breeding; courteous and considerate **2** of good stock: said of animals

well-chos·en (-chō′zən) *adj.* chosen with care and judgment; proper; appropriate [*well-chosen* words]

well-con·tent (wel′kən tent′) *adj.* thoroughly pleased or satisfied: also **well′-con·tent′ed**

well deck *Naut.* a low section of weather deck with superstructure fore and aft of it

well-de·fined (wel′dē fīnd′) *adj.* clearly defined; sharply delimited, described, differentiated, etc.; distinct in outline, meaning, nature, etc.

well-dis·posed (-dis pōzd′) *adj.* **1** having a pleasant disposition **2** inclined to be friendly, kindly, or favorable (*toward* a person) or receptive (*to* an idea, etc.)

well-done (wel′dun′) *adj.* **1** performed with skill and efficiency **2** thoroughly cooked: said esp. of meat

well-en·dowed (wel′en doud′) *adj.* **1** [Informal] BUILT (*adj.*) **2** [Slang] WELL-HUNG

Welles (welz), **(George) Orson** 1915-85; U.S. stage & film actor & director

well-fa·vored (wel′fā′vərd) *adj.* pleasing in appearance; good-looking, handsome, comely, etc.

well-fed (-fed′) *adj.* showing the effect of eating much good food; specif., plump or fat

well-fixed (-fikst′) *adj.* [Informal] ☆wealthy; well-to-do

well-found (-found′) *adj.* properly and adequately equipped [a *well-found* ship]

well-found·ed (-foun′did) *adj.* based on facts, good evidence, or sound judgment [a *well-founded* suspicion]

well-groomed (-groomd′) *adj.* **1** carefully cared for [a *well-groomed* horse, a *well-groomed* lawn] **2** clean and neat; carefully washed, combed, dressed, etc.

well-ground·ed (-groun′did) *adj.* **1** having a thorough basic knowledge of a subject **2** based on good reasons

well-han·dled (-han′dəld) *adj.* efficiently managed

well·head (wel′hed′) *n.* **1** the source of a spring of water; spring **2** a source; fountainhead **3** the top of a well, as an oil or gas well

☆**well-heeled** (wel′hēld′) *adj.* [Slang] rich; prosperous

well-hung (wel′huŋ′) *adj.* [Slang] having large genitals: said of a man: a somewhat vulgar usage: also **well hung**

wel·lie (wel′ē) *n.* [Brit. Informal] WELLINGTON[1] (sense 2): *usually used in pl.*: also **wel′ly** (-ē), *pl.* **-lies**

well-in·formed (wel′in fôrmd′) *adj.* **1** having thorough knowledge of a subject **2** having considerable knowledge of many subjects, esp. those of current interest

Wel·ling·ton[1] (wel′iŋ tən) *n.* ⟦after fol.⟧ [*also* **w-**] **1** a high leather boot, traditionally extending just above the knee in front, and just below in back **2** a waterproof boot of leather or, usually now, rubber, worn in wet weather In full **Wellington boot**

Wel·ling·ton[2] (wel′iŋ tən), 1st Duke of (*Arthur Wellesley*) 1769-1852; Brit. general & statesman, born in Ireland: prime minister (1828-30): called *the Iron Duke*

Wel·ling·ton[3] (wel′iŋ tən) capital of New Zealand: seaport in S North Island, on Cook Strait

well-in·ten·tioned (wel′in ten′shənd) *adj.* having or showing good, kindly, or benevolent intentions: usually connoting failure or miscarriage of intention

well-knit (wel′nit′) *adj.* **1** well-constructed; firm and strong **2** having a sturdy body build; not lanky

well-known (-nōn′) *adj.* **1** widely or generally known; famous or notorious **2** thoroughly known

well-made (-mād′) *adj.* **1** well-proportioned; strongly built; skillfully and soundly put together **2** *Drama, Literature a)* skillfully constructed or contrived [a *well-made* plot] *b)* having a skillfully contrived plot (often used specif. of a play regarded as cleverly crafted but lacking in depth or imagination)

well-man·nered (-man′ərd) *adj.* having or showing good manners; polite; courteous

well-mean·ing (-mēn′iŋ) *adj.* **1** having good or kindly intentions **2** said or done with good intentions, but often unwisely or ineffectually: also **well′-meant′** (-ment′)

☆**well·ness** (wel′nis) ***n.*** the condition of being healthy or sound, esp. as the result of proper diet, exercise, etc.

well-nigh (-nī′) ***adv.*** very nearly; almost

well-off (-ôf′) ***adj.*** **1** in a favorable or fortunate condition or circumstance **2** prosperous; well-to-do

well-oiled (-oild′) ***adj.*** ☆**1** [Slang] drunk; oiled **2** [Informal] operating smoothly and efficiently [a *well-oiled* political machine]

well-or·dered (-ôr′dərd) ***adj.*** properly or carefully organized

well-pre·served (wel′prē zʉrvd′) ***adj.*** in good condition or of good appearance, in spite of age

well-read (wel′red′) ***adj.*** **1** having read much (*in* a particular subject) **2** having a wide knowledge of books through having read much

well-round·ed (-roun′did) ***adj.*** **1** well-planned for proper balance [a *well-rounded* education] **2** *a)* showing interest or ability in many fields *b)* showing many facets of personality [a *well-rounded* character] **3** fully developed; shapely [a *well-rounded* figure]

Wells (welz), **H(erbert) G(eorge)** 1866-1946; Eng. novelist & social critic —**Wells′i·an** (-ē ən) ***adj.***

well-spo·ken (wel′spō′kən) ***adj.*** **1** speaking easily or fluently **2** speaking in a courteous or gracious manner **3** properly or aptly spoken

well·spring (wel′spriŋ′) ***n.*** **1** the source of a stream, spring, etc.; fountainhead **2** a source of abundant and continual supply [a *wellspring* of knowledge]

☆**well-stacked** (wel′stakt′) ***adj.*** [Slang] WELL-ROUNDED (sense 3)

well-tak·en (wel′tāk′ən) ***adj.*** ☆apt and sound [the speaker's point was *well-taken*]

well-thought-of (wel′thôt′uv′) ***adj.*** having a good reputation; of good repute

well-timed (-tīmd′) ***adj.*** timely; opportune

well-to-do (-tə do͞o′) ***adj.*** prosperous; well-off; wealthy —**SYN.** RICH

well-turned (-tʉrnd′) ***adj.*** **1** gracefully formed or shaped [a *well-turned* ankle] **2** expressed or worded well [a *well-turned* phrase]

well-wish·er (-wish′ər) ***n.*** a person who wishes well to another or to a cause, etc. —**well′-wish′ing *adj., n.***

well-worn (-wôrn′) ***adj.*** **1** much worn; much used **2** overused; trite [a *well-worn* joke] **3** worn becomingly

welsh (welsh) ***vi.*** ⟦19th-c. slang, prob. < fol., with reference to alleged character traits of the Welsh⟧ [Slang] to avoid fulfilling one's debt or obligation: often with *on* —**welsh′er *n.***

Welsh (welsh) ***n.*** ⟦ME *Wel(i)sch* < OE *Welisc* < *Wealh*, Briton, foreigner < PGmc **walh-*, Celt < Celt name > L *Volcae*, name of a Celtic people of S France⟧ the Celtic language spoken in Wales —***adj.*** of Wales or its people, language, or culture —**the Welsh** the people of Wales

Welsh cob any of a breed of medium-sized riding horse, developed in Wales, with a thickset body and relatively short legs

Welsh cor·gi (kôr′gē) ⟦WELSH + Welsh *corgi* < *corr*, dwarf + *ci*, dog⟧ any member of either of two breeds of short-legged dog with a foxlike head and erect ears, originally bred in Wales for herding cattle: the **Cardigan Welsh corgi** has a long tail; the **Pembroke Welsh corgi** has a short tail or no tail and a shorter body

Welsh·man (welsh′mən) ***n., pl.* -men** (-mən) a person, esp. a man, born or living in Wales

Welsh pony **1** any of four breeds of sturdy ponies derived from stock originally bred in Wales **2** a pony of any of these breeds

Welsh rabbit ⟦orig. a humorous usage⟧ a dish consisting of melted cheese, often mixed with ale or beer, served on crackers or toast: also, through faulty etymologizing, **Welsh rarebit**

Welsh springer spaniel any of a breed of medium-sized spaniel with a silky red-and-white coat, usually used as a hunting dog

Welsh terrier any of a breed of terrier originating in Wales, having a wire-haired, black-and-tan coat and resembling a small Airedale

Welsh·wom·an (welsh′wo͝om′ən) ***n., pl.* -wom′en** (-wim′in) a woman born or living in Wales

welt (welt) ***n.*** ⟦ME *welte*, prob. akin to OE *wealtan*, to roll: for IE base see WALK⟧ **1** a strip of leather stitched into the seam between the sole and upper of a shoe to strengthen the joining **2** a strip of material, often folded over a cord, placed at the edge or seam of a garment, cushion, etc. to reinforce or trim it **3** *a)* a ridge or lump raised on the skin as by a blow *b)* [Rare] such a blow —***vt.*** **1** to furnish with a welt **2** to beat severely; thrash **3** to raise welts on

Welt·an·schau·ung (velt′än shou′o͝oŋ) ***n.*** ⟦Ger, worldview⟧ a comprehensive, esp. personal, philosophy or conception of the universe and of human life; worldview

wel·ter (wel′tər) ***vi.*** ⟦ME *weltren* < MDu *welteren*, freq. formation akin to OE *wealtan*, to roll, boil up: for IE base see WELL[1]⟧ **1** *a)* to roll about or wallow, as a pig does in mud *b)* to be deeply involved [to *welter* in work] **2** to be soaked, stained, or bathed [to *welter* in blood] **3** to tumble and toss about: said as of the sea —***n.*** **1** a tossing and tumbling, as of waves **2** a confusion; turmoil

wel·ter·weight (wel′tər wāt′) ***n.*** ⟦prob. < WELT (*vt.* 2) + -ER + WEIGHT⟧ a boxer between a junior welterweight and a junior middleweight, with a maximum weight of 147 lb (66.68 kg)

Welt·schmerz (velt′shmerts′) ***n.*** ⟦Ger, world pain⟧ sentimental pessimism or melancholy over the state of the world

Wel·ty (wel′tē), **Eu·do·ra (Alice)** (yo͞o dôr′ə) 1909-2001; U.S. short-story writer & novelist

Wem·bley (wem′blē) district of NW London, part of Greater London borough of Brent

wen[1] (wen) ***n.*** ⟦ME *wenne* < OE *wenn*, akin to *wund*, a WOUND[1]⟧ a benign skin tumor, esp. of the scalp, consisting of a cyst in which sebaceous matter has been retained

wen[2] (wen) ***n.*** ⟦ME < OE, var. of *win*, joy, bliss⟧ a rune in the Old English alphabet (Ƿ), used to represent the labiovelar semivowel: in Middle English orthography it was replaced by the letter *w*

Wen·ces·laus (wen′səs lôs′) 1361-1419; Holy Roman emperor (1378-1400); as **Wenceslaus IV**, king of Bohemia (1378-1419)

wench (wench) ***n.*** ⟦ME *wenche*, contr. < *wenchel*, child, boy, girl, young woman < OE *wencel*, a child, akin to *wancol*, unsteady (? in reference to an infant's gait): for IE base see WINCH⟧ **1** a girl or young woman: now a humorously patronizing term **2** [Archaic] *a)* a country girl *b)* a female servant *c)* a sexually loose and immoral woman —***vi.*** to be sexually promiscuous with loose women —**wench′er *n.***

wend (wend) ***vt.*** ⟦ME *wenden* < OE *wendan*, to turn, akin to Du & Ger *wenden*, caus. formation < base of WIND[1]⟧ to proceed or go on (one's way) —***vi.*** [Archaic] to go; journey; travel

Wend (wend) ***n.*** ⟦Ger *wende*, akin to OE *Winedas*, the Wends: see VENETIC⟧ LUSATIAN (***n.*** 1)

Wend·ish (wen′dish) ***adj., n.*** LUSATIAN (***n.*** 2 & ***adj.***)

Wend·y (wen′dē) ***n.*** ⟦perhaps related to Welsh *gwen*, white, as in GWENDOLINE, GUINEVERE; popularized by the character *Wendy* Darling in J. M. BARRIE's play *Peter Pan* (1904) & book *Peter and Wendy* (1911)⟧ a feminine name

went (went) ***vi., vt.*** ⟦old pt. of WEND, used to replace missing form of GO[1]⟧ *pt. of* GO[1]

wen·tle·trap (went′'l trap′) ***n.*** ⟦Du *wenteltrap*, lit., a winding staircase < *wentel*, a winding, akin to *wenden* (see WEND) + *trap*, stair: see TRAP[1]⟧ any of a family (Epitoniidae) of marine gastropod mollusks usually enclosed in a white, spiral shell

Wen·zel (ven′tsəl) *Ger. var. of* WENCESLAUS

wept (wept) ***vi., vt.*** *pt. & pp. of* WEEP

were (wʉr) ***vi.*** ⟦ME *weren* < OE *wæron*, akin to Ger *waren* < Gmc base **wæz-* < IE base **wes-*: see WAS⟧ *pl. & 2d pers. sing., past indic., and the past subjunc., of* BE

we're (wir, wē′ər) *contraction* we are

weren't (wʉrnt, wʉr′ənt) *contraction* were not

were·wolf (wer′wo͝olf′, wir′-) ***n., pl.* -wolves′** (-wo͝olvz′) ⟦ME *werwolf* < OE *werwulf* < *wer*, man < IE **wiros*, man (prob. orig., "the strong one" < base **wei-*, to be strong > L *vis*, power, *vir*, man) + OE *wulf*, WOLF⟧ *Folklore* a person changed into a wolf, or one capable of assuming the form of a wolf at will; lycanthrope: also sp. **wer′wolf′**, *pl.* **-wolves′**

Wer·fel (ver′fəl), **Franz** (fränts) 1890-1945; Austrian novelist, playwright, & poet, born in Prague

wer·geld (wʉr′geld′, wer′-) ***n.*** ⟦ME *weregylt* < OE *wergild* < *wer*, man (see WEREWOLF) + *geld*, payment: see GELD[2]⟧ in early Germanic and Anglo-Saxon law, a price paid by a person who has killed another to the family of the person killed, to atone for the killing and avoid reprisals: also **were′gild′** or **wer′gild′** (-gild′)

wer·ner·ite (wʉr′nər īt′) ***n.*** ⟦after A. G. *Werner* (1750-1817), Ger geologist + -ITE[1]⟧ SCAPOLITE

wert (wʉrt) ***vi.*** *archaic 2d pers. sing., past indic. & subj., of* BE: used with *thou*

We·ser (vā′zər) river in NW Germany, flowing from S Lower Saxony north into the North Sea: *c.* 300 mi (483 km)

wes·kit (wes′kit) ***n.*** ⟦sp. based on pronun. of WAISTCOAT⟧ a vest or waistcoat

Wes·ley[1] (wes′lē, wez′-) ***n.*** ⟦< the surname *Wesley*⟧ a masculine name: dim. *Wes*

Wes·ley[2] (wes′lē, wez′-) **1 Charles** 1707-88; Eng. clergyman & hymn writer: brother of John **2 John** 1703-91; Eng. clergyman & evangelist: founder of Methodism

Wes·ley·an (wes′lē ən, wez′-) ***adj.*** of John or Charles Wesley or the Methodist Church —***n.*** a follower of John or Charles Wesley; Methodist —**Wes′ley·an·ism′ *n.***

Wes·sex (wes′iks) **1** former Anglo-Saxon kingdom in S England: see HEPTARCHY **2** corresponding section in modern England, chiefly in Dorsetshire, as the locale of Hardy's novels

west (west) ***n.*** ⟦ME < OE, akin to Ger < IE **we-* (< base **au-*, down, away from) > Gr *hesperos*, L *vesper*, evening⟧ **1** the direction to the left of a person facing north; direction in which sunset occurs: it is properly the point on the horizon at which the center of the sun sets at the equinox **2** the point on a compass at 270°, directly opposite east **3** a region or district in or toward this direction —***adj.*** **1** in, of, to, toward, or facing the west **2** from the west [a *west* wind] **3** [**W-**] designating the W part of a continent, country, etc. [*West Africa*] **4** in, of, or toward that part of a church directly opposite the altar —***adv.*** in or toward the west; in a westerly direction —**the West** **1** *a)* the Western Hemisphere *b)* the Western Hemisphere and Europe, considered as a cultural or political entity ☆**2** the W part of the U.S.; specif., *a)* [Historical] the region west of the Allegheny Mountains *b)* the region west of the Mississippi, esp. the NW part: see also OLD WEST **3** during the Cold War, the U.S. and its non-Communist allies in Europe & the Western Hemisphere

West (west) **1 Benjamin** 1738-1820; Am. painter, in England after 1763 **2 Nathanael** (born *Nathan Wallenstein Weinstein*) 1903-40; U.S. novelist **3** Dame **Rebecca** (pseud. of *Cicily*, christened *Cicely, Isabel Fairfield*) 1892-1983; Brit. novelist & critic

West Bank area on the W bank of the Jordan River: part of Jordan since 1949 & occupied by Israel since 1967: an agreement in 1994 provided for a transfer of authority of Palestinians in stages that would result in self-rule

West Bengal state of E India: 34,267 sq mi (88,751 sq km); cap. Kolkata

West Berlin *see* BERLIN[2]

☆**west·bound** (west′bound′) ***adj.*** bound west; going westward

west by north the direction, or the point on a mariner's compass, halfway between due west and west-northwest; 11°15′ north of due west

west by south the direction, or the point on a mariner's compass, halfway between due west and west-southwest; 11°15′ south of due west

West Coast coastal region of W U.S., esp. Calif.

West Country the SW region of England, esp. the counties of Cornwall, Devon, and Somerset: usually preceded by *the*

West Co·vi·na (kō vē′nə) city in SW Calif., near Los Angeles

West End W section of London, England: center of theater and fashion

west·er (wes′tər) ***vi.*** to move, turn, or shift to the west —***n.*** a wind from the west, esp. one bringing a storm

west·er·ly (-lē) ***adj., adv.*** **1** in or toward the west **2** from the west, as a wind —***n., pl.*** **-lies** a wind from the west

west·ern (wes′tərn) ***adj.*** ⟦ME < OE *westerne*⟧ **1** in, of, to, toward, or facing the west **2** from the west [*a western* wind] **3** [*also* **W-**] of or characteristic of the West **4** [**W-**] of the Western Church —***n.*** **1** WESTERNER ☆**2** a film, book, etc. having a setting in the W U.S., esp. during the 19th-cent. period of development and expansion of the frontier

Western Australia state of Australia, in the W third of the continent: 976,792 sq mi (2,529,880 sq km); cap. Perth

Western Cape province of SW South Africa: 49,950 sq mi (129,370 sq km); cap. Cape Town

Western Church 1 [Historical] the Christian church in much of the western part of the Roman Empire **2** that part of the Catholic Church which recognizes the pope and follows the Latin Rite; the Roman Catholic Church **3** broadly, all the Christian churches of Western Europe and America

west·ern·er (wes′tər nər) ***n.*** **1** a person born or living in the west ☆**2** [*also* **W-**] a person born or living in the W part of the U.S.

Western Hemisphere that half of the earth which includes North & South America

Western Isles administration division of W Scotland comprising the Outer Hebrides: 1,119 sq mi (2,898 sq km)

west·ern·ism (wes′tərn iz′əm) ***n.*** [*often* **W-**] **1** a custom, practice, etc. peculiar to a western region ☆**2** a word, phrase, custom, etc. originating in or peculiar to the W U.S.

west·ern·ize (-īz′) ***vt.*** **-ized′**, **-iz′ing** to make Western in character, habits, ideas, etc. —**west′ern·i·za′tion** ***n.***

west·ern·most (-mōst′) ***adj.*** farthest west

Western Ocean *ancient name for* the ATLANTIC OCEAN

☆**western omelet** an omelet prepared with diced green pepper, onion, and ham

Western Reserve section of the Northwest Territory, on Lake Erie: reserved by Conn. for settlers when its other W lands were ceded to the federal government in 1786: incorporated into the Ohio territory in 1800

Western Roman Empire the W part of the Roman Empire, from the time the Empire was divided in A.D. 395 by Theodosius until this part was overthrown by Odoacer in A.D. 476

☆**Western saddle** [*also* **w- s-**] a heavy saddle of the kind used by cowboys, with a high cantle and pommel and a horn projecting above the pommel

Western Sahara former Spanish province (*Spanish Sahara*) in NW Africa: divided (1975) between Mauritania & Morocco: Mauritania renounced its claim to its territory (1979), which was subsequently occupied by Morocco

Western Samoa *former name for* SAMOA (the country)

Western Turkestan RUSSIAN TURKESTAN

Western Wall a high wall in Jerusalem believed to be part of the western section of the wall surrounding Herod's Temple: Jews have traditionally gathered at this site for prayer: see also WAILING WALL

West Flanders province of NW Belgium, on the North Sea: 1,214 sq mi (3,144 sq km)

West Germany *see* GERMANY

West Glamorgan county in SE Wales: 317 sq mi (821 sq km)

West Ham *see* NEWHAM

West Highland white terrier any of a breed of small terrier with a pure white coat, short legs, and erect ears, prob. originating as a cairn terrier of the W Highlands of Scotland

West Indies large group of islands between North America & South America: it includes the Greater Antilles, Lesser Antilles, & Bahamas —**West Indian**

west·ing (wes′tiŋ) ***n.*** **1** *Naut.* the distance due west covered by a vessel traveling on any westerly course **2** a westerly direction

West·ing·house (wes′tiŋ hous′), **George** 1846-1914; U.S. inventor & manufacturer

West Irian *former name for* PAPUA (the Indonesian province)

West Jordan city in NC Utah: suburb of Salt Lake City

West Lothian administrative division of SC Scotland: formerly a county & district

West·meath (west′mēth′) county in Leinster province, EC Ireland: 681 sq mi (1,764 sq km)

West Midlands county in central England: 347 sq mi (899 sq km)

West·min·ster (west′min′stər) **1** metropolitan borough of WC Greater London, England: site of the Houses of Parliament **2** ⟦after *Westminster* University (1907-17), located there⟧ city in NC Colo.: suburb of Denver

Westminster Abbey Gothic church (originally a Benedictine abbey) in Westminster where English monarchs are crowned: it is also a burial place for English monarchs and famous statesmen, writers, etc.

West·mor·land (west′mər lənd) former county of NW England, now part of Cumbria county

West Nile virus ⟦after *West Nile* District of Uganda, where it was discovered⟧ a virus transmitted from infected birds by the common culex mosquito and causing a form of encephalitis (**West Nile encephalitis** or **fever**) that is characterized by fever, headache, drowsiness, nausea, and a rash

west-north·west (west′nôrth′west′; *naut.*, -nôr-) ***n.*** the direction, or the point on a mariner's compass, halfway between due west and northwest; 22°30′ north of due west — ***adj., adv.*** **1** in or toward this direction **2** from this direction: said as of a wind

West Pakistan former province of Pakistan: it now constitutes the country of Pakistan: cf. EAST PAKISTAN

West Palm Beach city in SE Fla., on a lagoon opposite Palm Beach: winter resort

West·pha·li·a (west fā′lē ə, -fāl′yə) region in NW Germany, a part of the state of North Rhine-Westphalia: formerly a duchy, a kingdom, and a province of Prussia (1816-1945); chief city, Münster: site, along with Osnabrück, of treaties (**Peace of Westphalia**) signed in 1648 that ended the Thirty Years' War —**West·pha′li·an** ***adj., n.***

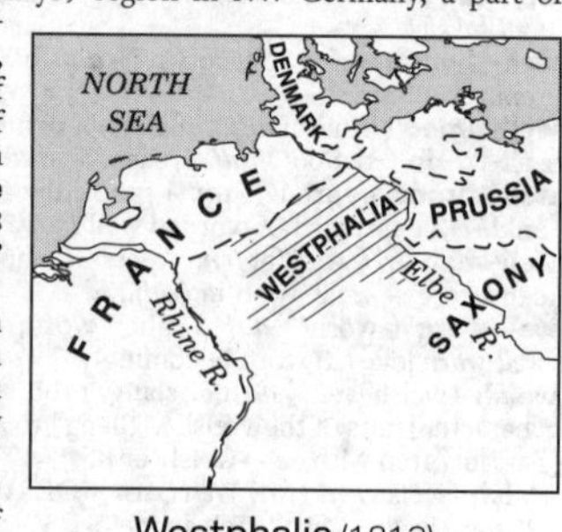

Westphalia (1812)

West Point ⟦from its location on the *west* bank of the Hudson River⟧ military reservation in SE N.Y.: site of the U.S. Military Academy

West Prussia former province of Prussia, since 1945 part of Poland: chief city, Gdansk

West Riding former division of Yorkshire, England, now part of the counties of North Yorkshire & West Yorkshire

West Saxon 1 the Old English dialect of the West Saxons, the major literary dialect of the Anglo-Saxon kingdom of Wessex before the Conquest **2** a person born or living in Wessex (the kingdom)

west-south·west (west′south′west′; *naut.*, -sou-) ***n.*** the direction, or the point on a mariner's compass, halfway between due west and southwest; 22°30′ south of due west — ***adj., adv.*** **1** in or toward this direction **2** from this direction: said as of a wind

West Sussex county in SE England, on the English Channel: 767 sq mi (1,987 sq km)

West Timor province of Indonesia, consisting primarily of the W half of Timor

West Valley City ⟦because located in the *western* part of the Salt Lake *Valley*⟧ city in NC Utah, near Salt Lake City

West Virginia ⟦see VIRGINIA[2]⟧ state of the E U.S., northwest of Va.: admitted 1863; 24,078 sq mi (62,361 sq km); cap. Charleston: abbrev. *WV* or *WVa*

West Virginian 1 of West Virginia: usually used in the predicate **2** a person born or living in West Virginia

west·ward (west′wərd) ***adv., adj.*** toward the west —***n.*** a westward direction, point, or region

west·ward·ly (-lē) ***adv., adj.*** **1** toward the west **2** from the west

west·wards (west′wərdz) ***adv. var. of*** WESTWARD

West Wing ☆**1** the building at the western end of the White House in which the U.S. President and the President's staff have their offices ☆**2** the President's staff, esp. the senior advisors, collectively

West Yorkshire county in N England: 785 sq mi (2,033 sq km)

wet (wet) ***adj.*** **wet′ter**, **wet′test** ⟦ME < OE *wæt*, akin to ON *vatr*: for IE base see WATER⟧ **1** moistened, covered, or saturated with water or other liquid **2** rainy; foggy; misty [*a wet* day] **3** not yet dry [*wet* paint] **4** preserved or bottled in a liquid **5** using water; done with or in water or other liquid [*wet* sanding] ☆**6** permitting or favoring the manufacture or sale of alcoholic beverages; opposing prohibition [*a wet* candidate, *wet* town] **7** [Brit. Informal] weak, ineffectual, insipid, etc. —***n.*** **1** water or other liquid; moisture **2** rain or rainy weather [come in out of the *wet*] ☆**3** [Informal] a person who favors the manufacture or sale of alcoholic beverages; one opposed to prohibition **4** [Brit. Informal] *a)* a person considered weak, ineffectual, insipid, etc. *b)* a Conservative who is moderate or willing to compromise — ***vt., vi.*** **wet** or **wet′ted**, **wet′ting 1** to make or become wet: often with *through* or *down* **2** to make (a bed, oneself, etc.) wet by urination —☆**all wet** [Slang] wrong; mistaken —**wet behind the ears** [Informal] young and inexperienced; immature —**wet′ly** ***adv.*** —**wet′ness** ***n.***

SYN.—wet is applied to something covered or soaked with water or other liquid *[wet* streets, clothes, etc.*]* or to something not yet dry *[wet* paint*]*; **damp** implies slight, usually undesirable or unpleasant wetness *[*a *damp* room*]*; **dank** suggests a disagreeable, chilling, unwholesome dampness *[*a *dank* fog*]*; **moist** implies slight but, unlike **damp**, often desirable wetness *[moist* air*]*; **humid** implies such permeation of the air with moisture as to make for discomfort *[*a hot, *humid* day*]* —**ANT. dry**

☆**wet·back** (wet′bak′) ***n.*** ⟦from crossing the border by swimming or wading the Rio Grande⟧ [Informal] a Mexican agricultural laborer who illegally enters or is brought into the U.S. to work: a term of derision or contempt

☆**wet bar** a bar or serving counter, as in a recreation room, equipped with running water

wet blanket a person or thing whose presence or influence lessens the enthusiasm or joy of others

wet-bulb thermometer (wet′bulb′) *Meteorol.* a thermometer having its bulb covered with a wet cloth: the water evaporates to cool the wet bulb, and by comparing its temperature to a dry-bulb thermometer the amount of water vapor in the air can be determined

wet cell a voltaic cell in which the electrolyte is a liquid

wet dream [Informal] **1** an erotic dream during which the person having the dream ejaculates **2** NOCTURNAL EMISSION

wet fly FLY[2] (sense 2)

weth·er (weth′ər) ***n.*** ⟦ME < OE, akin to Ger *widder* < IE base **wet-*, year > ETESIAN⟧ a castrated male sheep or goat

wet·land (wet′land′, -lənd) ***n.*** [*usually pl.*] **1** swamps or marshes ☆**2** an area of land characterized by swamps, marshes, etc. that is preserved for wildlife

wet nurse a woman hired to suckle another's child

wet-nurse (-nurs′) ***vt.*** **-nursed′, -nurs′ing 1** to act as wet nurse to **2** to give overly careful attention to

wet pack *Med.* a type of bath, as for therapy, in which the patient is wrapped in wet sheets or blankets

wet suit a closefitting, usually one-piece suit of rubber, esp. of foam neoprene, worn as by skin divers for warmth: also written **wet′suit′** ***n.***

wet·ta·bil·i·ty (wet′ə bil′ə tē) ***n.*** **1** the condition or state of being wettable **2** *Chem., Physics* the degree to which a solid is wetted by a liquid, measured by the force of adhesion between the solid and liquid phases

wet·ta·ble (wet′ə bəl) ***adj.*** **1** capable of being wetted **2** *Chem., Physics* able to be made adhesive or absorptive, as by the addition of a liquid or hydrocarbon

wet·ter (wet′ər) ***n.*** a person or thing that wets

Wet·ter·horn (vet′ər hôrn′) ⟦Ger < *wetter*, WEATHER + *horn*, peak, HORN⟧ mountain of the Bernese Alps, SC Switzerland: *c.* 12,150 ft (3,703 m)

wetting agent any of a group of surface-active agents which, when added to a liquid, cause the liquid to spread more easily over, or to penetrate, a solid surface

wet·tish (wet′ish) ***adj.*** somewhat wet

☆**wet wash 1** laundry washed and left damp without ironing **2** a washing at a carwash in which the car is not wiped dry

we've (wēv) *contraction* we have

Wex·ford (weks′fərd) county in Leinster province, SE Ireland: 908 sq mi (2,352 sq km)

Wey·den (vī′dən), **Ro·gier van der** (rô̂g′yir vän dər) 1400?-64; Fl. painter

wf *abbrev. Printing* wrong font

WFTU *abbrev.* World Federation of Trade Unions

whack (hwak, wak) ***vt., vi.*** ⟦echoic⟧ **1** to strike or slap with a sharp, resounding blow ☆**2** [Slang] to murder (a person), often, specif., for pay —***n.*** **1** a sharp, resounding blow **2** the sound of this —**at a** (or **one**) **whack** [Informal] at one time and quickly or without pausing —☆**have** (or **take**) **a whack at** [Informal] **1** to aim a blow at **2** to make an attempt at —☆**out of whack** [Informal] not in proper working condition —**whack off 1** [Informal] to separate or remove by or as by a blow **2** [Slang] to masturbate: somewhat vulgar —**whack′er** ***n.***

whacked (hwakt, wakt) ***adj.*** ⟦pp. of prec.⟧ **1** [Informal] exhausted **2** [Slang] STONED (sense 2)

☆**whacked-out** (hwakt′out′, wakt′-) ***adj.*** [Slang] **1** exhausted **2** STONED (sense 2) **3** wacky, crazy, bizarre, etc.

whack·ing (hwak′iŋ, wak′-) [Informal, Chiefly Brit.] ***adj.*** ⟦prp. of WHACK⟧ very large; tremendous —***adv.*** tremendously; hugely *[*a *whacking* good tale*]*

whack·o (-ō) ***adj., n., pl.*** **-os** [Slang] *var. of* WACKO

whack·y (-ē) ***adj.*** **whack′i·er, whack′i·est** [Slang] *var. of* WACKY

whale[1] (hwāl, wāl) ***n., pl.*** **whales** or **whale** ⟦ME *whal* < OE *hwæl*, akin to OHG *hwal*, ON *hvalr*, MDu *wal* < IE base **(s)kwalos*, a large fish > L *squalus*, big sea fish⟧ **1** any member of either of two orders (Mysticeta and Odontoceta) of aquatic mammals that breathe air, bear live young, and have front limbs that have been modified into flippers, and a flat, horizontal tail: see BALEEN WHALE, TOOTHED WHALE **2** any of the larger members of these two groups, excluding the porpoises and dolphins generally, but including the killer whale —***vi.*** **whaled, whal′ing** to engage in the work of hunting whales —☆**a whale of a** [Informal] an exceptionally large, fine, etc. example of a (class of persons or things)

whale[2] (hwāl, wāl) ***vt., vi.*** **whaled, whal′ing** ⟦prob. var. of WALE[1]⟧ [Informal] to beat; whip; thrash

whale·back (hwāl′bak′, wāl′-) ***n.*** something rounded on top like the back of a whale

☆**whale·boat** (-bōt′) ***n.*** **1** a large, long rowboat, pointed at both ends to increase maneuverability: used formerly by whalers **2** a similar boat, now often one with a motor (**motor whaleboat**), used as a ship's lifeboat and utility boat

whale·bone (-bōn′) ***n.*** **1** BALEEN **2** something made of baleen: it was formerly much used for corset stays and whips

whalebone whale BALEEN WHALE

whal·er (hwā′lər, wā′-) ***n.*** **1** a ship used in whaling **2** a person whose work is whaling: also ☆**whale·man** (hwāl′mən, wāl′-) ***n., pl.*** **-men** (-mən)

Whales (hwālz, wālz), **Bay of** inlet of the Ross Sea, near Little America

whale shark the only species (*Rhiniodon typus*) of a family (Rhiniodontidae, order Orectolobiformes) of huge, spotted, egg-laying sharks that live in warm seas, have many small teeth, and feed on plankton and small fishes by means of gill strainers: the largest of fishes, often reaching 15 m (*c.* 50 ft) in length

whal·ing[1] (hwā′liŋ, wā′-) ***n.*** the work or trade of hunting and killing whales for their blubber, whalebone, etc.

whal·ing[2] (hwā′liŋ, wā′-) ***n.*** ⟦< WHALE[2] + -ING⟧ [Informal] a sound thrashing; whipping

wham (hwam, wam) ***interj.*** ⟦echoic⟧ used to suggest the sound of a heavy blow, explosion, etc. —***n.*** a heavy blow, impact, etc. — ***vt., vi.*** **whammed, wham′ming** to strike, explode, etc. loudly

wham·mo (-ō) ***interj.*** **1** WHAM (***interj.***) **2** used to signify sudden, startling action, change, awareness, etc. Also sp. **wham′o**

☆**wham·my** (-ē) ***n., pl.*** **-mies** [Slang] a jinx or the evil eye: usually in **put a** (or **the**) **whammy on**

whang[1] (hwaŋ, waŋ) ***vt.*** ⟦echoic⟧ **1** to strike with a resounding blow **2** [Dial.] to beat or thrash —***vi.*** to make a whanging noise —***n.*** **1** a whanging noise **2** a whack or blow

whang[2] (hwaŋ, waŋ) ***n.*** ⟦altered < ME *thwang*, THONG⟧ [Dial.] **1** a thong of leather **2** leather for thongs, etc.

whang·ee (hwaŋ′ē, waŋ′-) ***n.*** ⟦Chin *huang-i* < *huang*, a hard kind of bamboo + *i*, to lean on⟧ **1** any of various related Chinese and Japanese bamboos (genus *Phyllostachys*) **2** a walking stick of whangee

whap (hwäp, wäp) ***vt., vi.*** **whapped, whap′ping,** ***n. var. of*** WHOP

wharf (hwôrf, wôrf) ***n., pl.*** **wharves** or **wharfs** ⟦ME < OE *hwerf*, a dam or bank to keep out water, lit., a turning < base of *hweorfan*, to turn < IE base **kwerp-*, to turn > Gr *karpos*, wrist⟧ **1** a structure of wood or stone, sometimes roofed over, built at the shore of a harbor, river, etc. for ships to lie alongside, as during loading or unloading; pier; dock **2** [Obs.] a bank at the water's edge; shore

wharf·age (hwôr′fij, wôr′-) ***n.*** **1** the use of a wharf for mooring, loading, or unloading a ship, or for storing goods **2** a fee charged for this **3** wharves collectively

wharf·in·ger (-in jər) ***n.*** ⟦altered < earlier *wharfager* < prec.⟧ a person who owns or manages a wharf

☆**wharf rat 1** any of various rats found around wharves **2** a vagrant or petty criminal who haunts wharves

Whar·ton (hwôrt′′n, wôrt′′n), **Edith** (born *Edith Newbold Jones*) 1862-1937; U.S. novelist

wharve (hwôrv, wôrv) ***n.*** ⟦ME *wherve* < OE *hweorfa* < base of *hweorfan*, to turn: see WHARF⟧ **1** a small flywheel on the spindle of a spinning wheel **2** a small drive pulley on a spindle of a modern spinning machine

wharves (hwôrvz, wôrvz) ***n.*** *alt. pl. of* WHARF

what (hwut, hwät, wut, wät) ***pron.*** ⟦ME *hwat* < OE *hwæt*, neut. of *hwa*, who < IE interrogative base **kwo-*, **kwe-* > WHERE, WHO, L *qui*, who what, Lith *kàs*, what, who⟧ **I.** *as an interrogative: which thing, event, circumstance, etc.?: used to ask for the specification of an identity, quantity, quality, etc., as:* **1** the nature, class, name, purpose, etc. of a thing *[what* is that object? *what* is your address?*]* **2** *a)* an explanation or repetition of something previously said *[*you told them *what?]* *b)* such an explanation or repetition (used elliptically) *[*"Sh. Quiet!" "*What?*"*]* **3** a quantity, sum, etc. *[what* will it cost?*]* **4** the value, importance, or effect of something *[what* is life without music?*]* **II.** *as a relative pronoun, with the meaning:* **1** that which or those which *[*to know *what* one wants*]* **2** anything that *[*do *what* you will*]* **3** the exact person or thing that *[*he's not *what* he was five years ago*]* **4** that or who: a nonstandard usage *[*the man *what* gave it to me*]* **III.** *as an intensifier in exclamations [what* he said about her!*]* **IV.** *in various other uses* **1** [Informal, Chiefly Brit.] used to end a sentence with a general or rhetorical interrogative force *[*it's rather late, *what?]* **2** used to introduce a parenthetical element in a sentence *[*she has, *what* is rare, true tolerance*]* **3** used elliptically to mean "what it is," "what to do," etc. *[*I'll tell you *what!]* —***n.*** the true or basic quality of something *[*to uncover the *what* and why of their relationship*]* —***adj.*** **1** which or which kind of: used interrogatively or relatively in asking for or specifying the nature, identity, etc. of a person or thing *[what* man told you that? he knows *what* role she played*]* **2** as much, or as many, as *[*take *what* time (or men) you need*]* **3** how great, surprising, magnificent, disappointing, etc.: in exclamations *[what* a man! *what* nonsense!*]* —***adv.*** **1** in what respect? to what degree? how? *[what* does it matter?*]* **2** how greatly, surprisingly, etc.: in exclamations *[what* tragic news!*]* **3** [Obs.] why? —***conj.*** [Brit. Dial.] so far as; as much as *[*we warned them *what* we could*]* —***interj.*** used to express surprise, anger, confusion, etc. *[what!* no dinner?*]* —**and what not** and other things of all sorts —**what about** what is your wish, opinion, or information concerning [*what about* going to a movie?] —**what for 1** for what purpose? why? **2** [Slang] punishment; esp., a whipping [he gave his son *what for!*] —**what have you** [Informal] anything else of a similar sort [selling games, toys, or *what have you*] —**what if 1** what would happen if **2** what difference would it make if —**what is with** [Informal] **1** what is the reason for **2** what is wrong with —☆**what it takes** [Informal] whatever is necessary for success or popularity, as wealth, beauty, or intelligence —**what's what** [Informal] the true state of affairs —**what the hell** (or **heck, devil,** etc.) [Informal] an exclamatory remark of surprise, resignation, etc. —**what though** what difference does it make that —**what with 1** because of [*what with* the snow and ice, we'll be late] **2** in view of; taking into account [*what with* the usual rush-hour traffic, I suspect you'll be late]

what·cha·ma·call·it (hwuch′ə mə kôl′it, wuch′-) ***n.*** ⟦< *what you may call it*⟧ [Informal] THINGAMAJIG

what·ev·er (hwut ev′ər, wut-) ***pron.*** **1** what? which thing, event, circumstance, etc.?: an emphatic interrogative, expressing perplexity or wonder [*whatever* can she mean by that?] **2** anything that [tell her *whatever* you like] **3** no matter what [*whatever* you may think, he's innocent] **4** the amount, portion, or part that [take *whatever* you need from our supply] **5** [Informal] anything else of the sort: usually preceded by *or* [use a pencil, a pen, (or) *whatever*] —***adj.*** **1** of no matter what type, degree, quality, etc. [to make *whatever* repairs are needed] **2** being who it may be [*whatever* man told you that, it is not true] **3** of any kind: used following the word that it modifies [I have no plans *whatever*] Also [Old Poet.] **what·e'er′** (-er′) —***interj.*** used variously to express grudging acknowledgment, indifference, disdain, etc.

what·not (hwut′nät′, wut′-) ***n.*** **1** a nondescript or indescribable thing or, sometimes, person **2** a set of open shelves, as for bric-a-brac

what's (hwuts, wuts) *contraction* **1** what is **2** what has **3** [Informal] what does [*what's* he want?]

what·so·ev·er (hwut′sō ev′ər, wut′-) ***pron., adj.*** whatever: an emphatic form: also [Old Poet.] **what′so·e'er′** (-er′)

whaup (hwôp, wôp) ***n.*** ⟦prob. < or akin to OE *hwilpe*, curlew, akin to *hwelp*: see WHELP⟧ [Chiefly Scot.] CURLEW

wheal[1] (hwēl, wēl) ***n.*** ⟦ME *whele*, akin to OE *hwelian*, to suppurate⟧ **1** [Obs.] a pustule; pimple **2** a small, itching elevation of the skin, as from the bite of an insect

wheal[2] (hwēl, wēl) ***n.*** ⟦altered (based on prec.) < WEAL[1]⟧ a raised stripe or ridge on the skin, as from a lash of a whip

wheat (hwēt, wēt) ***n.*** ⟦ME *whete* < OE *hwæte*, akin to Ger *weizen* < IE base **kweid-*, to gleam, bright, WHITE: from the white seed⟧ **1** any of several cereal grasses (genus *Triticum*) having dense, erect spikes containing grains which thresh free of the chaff; esp., **bread wheat** (*T. aestivum*), a cultigen with large, nutritious grains **2** the grain of any of these grasses, esp. bread wheat (used in making flour, breakfast cereals, pastries, cakes, etc.) and durum (used in making macaroni, noodles, etc.): next to rice, the most widely used grain **3** *short for* whole-wheat bread

☆**wheat cake** a pancake made with wheat flour

wheat·ear (hwēt′ir′, wēt′-) ***n.*** ⟦earlier *white ears* < WHITE + *eeres, ers*, var. of ARSE: in reference to its white rump⟧ any of a genus (*Oenanthe*) of small, long-legged, migrating thrushes native to the Old World, esp. a species (*O. oenanthe*) now in North America

wheat·en (hwēt′'n, wēt′-) ***adj.*** **1** [Now Rare] made of wheat or wheat flour **2** of the pale-yellow color of wheat

wheaten terrier any of a breed of medium-sized terrier with a soft, wavy coat, wheaten in color: traditionally the tail is docked: in full **soft-coated wheaten terrier**

☆**wheat germ** the highly nutritious embryo of the wheat kernel, milled out as an oily flake and used to enrich breads, cereals, etc. or as a topping, cereal, etc.

Wheat·ley (hwēt′lē, wēt′-), **Phillis** 1753?-84; Am. poet, born in Africa & brought to America as a slave

wheat rust a disease of wheat, caused by various rust fungi; esp., any of numerous stem rusts caused by a fungus (*Puccinia graminis*) harbored by certain barberries

Wheat·stone bridge (hwēt′stōn′, wēt′-; *chiefly Brit,* -stən) ⟦after Sir Charles *Wheatstone* (1802-75), Eng physicist⟧ **1** a divided bridge circuit (see BRIDGE[1], ***n.*** 11) having four resistances in series, used to find the value of an unknown resistance by comparing it with three known resistances **2** a device containing such a circuit

SOURCE
R_1 R_2 R_3 R_X
$R_X = \frac{R_3R_2}{R_1}$

Wheatstone bridge

wheat·worm (hwēt′wurm′, wēt′-) ***n.*** a small nematode worm (*Anguina tritici*) that feeds on wheat, oats, etc.

whee (hwē, wē) ***interj.*** used to express joy, excitement, exultation, etc.

whee·dle (hwēd′'l, wēd′-) ***vt., vi.*** **-dled, -dling** ⟦17th-c. cant < ? Ger *wedeln*, to wag the tail, fan, hence to flatter < *wedel*, a fan, tail⟧ **1** to influence or persuade (a person) by flattery, soothing words, coaxing, etc. **2** to get (something) by coaxing or flattery —**SYN.** COAX[1] —**whee′dler** ***n.*** —**whee′dling·ly** ***adv.***

wheel (hwēl, wēl) ***n.*** ⟦ME *whele* < OE *hweol*, earlier *hweogol* < IE **kwekwlo-*, wheel (> Gr *kyklos*, a circle) < base **kwel-*, to turn, be around, dwell > Gr *telos*, turning point, end, *polos*, axis, L *colere*, to till, dwell, Ger *hals*, neck⟧ **1** a solid or partly solid disk, or a circular frame connected by spokes to a central hub, capable of turning on a central axis and used as to move vehicles or transmit power in machinery **2** anything like a wheel in shape, movement, action, etc., as a fireworks device that revolves while burning **3** a device or apparatus of which the principal element is a wheel or wheels; specif., *a)* in the Middle Ages, an instrument of torture consisting of a circular frame on which the victim's limbs were painfully stretched *b)* a steering wheel for controlling the rudder of a ship, often one with spokes that project beyond the rim for use as handles *c) short for* PADDLE WHEEL, POTTER'S WHEEL, SPINNING WHEEL, STEERING WHEEL, etc. *d)* any of various rotatable disks used for gambling [a roulette *wheel*] ☆*e)* [Informal] a bicycle ☆*f)* [*pl.*] [Slang] an automobile **4** [*usually pl.*] the moving, propelling, or controlling forces or agencies [the *wheels* of progress] **5** a turning about; circular, rotating, or revolving movement; specif., a turning movement as of troops or ships in line, with one end of the line as the pivot; also, any pivoting movement like this, as of dancers ☆**6** [Slang] an important, influential, or authoritative person: also **big wheel** **7** [Archaic] the refrain of a song —***vt.*** **1** *a)* to move or roll along (something equipped with wheels) [to *wheel* a baby buggy] *b)* to transport in a wheeled vehicle **2** to cause to turn, revolve, or rotate **3** to furnish with a wheel or wheels —***vi.*** **1** to turn on or as on an axis; pivot, rotate, revolve, etc. **2** to reverse one's course of action, movement, opinion, attitude, etc.: often with *about* **3** to turn in a swooping, circular motion: said of birds **4** to move or roll along on or as on wheels —**at** (or **behind**) **the wheel 1** steering a ship, motor vehicle, etc. **2** in charge; directing activities —☆**spin one's wheels** [Informal] to engage in fruitless activity —☆**wheel and deal** *pt. & pp.* **wheeled and dealed** [Slang] to behave in an aggressive, flamboyant way, as in arranging business or political deals —**wheel of fortune 1** *Myth.* the wheel which the goddess of fortune rotates to bring about the alternations or reverses in human affairs **2** the changes or vicissitudes of life —**wheels within wheels** a series of involved or interrelated circumstances, motives, etc. reacting upon one another

wheel and axle a larger wheel or pulley that is fixed to a shaft, a smaller wheel or pulley, or a drum, to increase mechanical advantage or speed: the wheels are often grooved and operated like pulleys

wheel animalcule ROTIFER

wheel·bar·row (hwēl′bar′ō, wēl′-; -ber′ō) ***n.*** ⟦ME *wilberwe*: see WHEEL & BARROW[1]⟧ a vehicle for carrying small loads, consisting of an open container supported on a framework with a single wheel in front, two legs in back, and two shafts with handles for raising the vehicle off its legs and pushing or pulling it —***vt.*** to move or transport in a wheelbarrow

wheel·base (-bās′) ***n.*** the length of a motor vehicle between the centers of the front and rear wheels

☆**wheel bug** a large North American assassin bug (*Arilus cristatus*) distinguished by a high, saw-toothed crest on the prothorax: it sucks the blood of other insects

wheel·chair (-cher′) ***n.*** ☆a mobile chair mounted on large wheels, for persons unable to walk

wheel cover a cover, often embellished, for the wheels of motor vehicles; hubcap

wheeled (hwēld, wēld) ***adj.*** **1** having a wheel or wheels **2** having wheels of a (specified) number or kind: used in hyphenated compounds [four-*wheeled*]

wheel·er (hwē′lər, wē′-) ***n.*** **1** a person or thing that wheels **2** WHEEL HORSE (sense 1) **3** something having a (specified) kind or number of wheels: used in hyphenated compounds [side-*wheeler*, two-*wheeler*]

Wheel·er (hwē′lər, wē′-), **John Archibald** 1911-2008; U.S. physicist

☆**wheel·er-deal·er** (hwē′lər dē′lər, wē′-) ***n.*** [Slang] a person who wheels and deals: see WHEEL AND DEAL (at WHEEL)

wheel horse 1 the horse, or one of the horses, harnessed nearest the front wheels of a vehicle ☆**2** a person who works especially hard and steadily in any enterprise

☆**wheel·house** (hwēl′hous′, wēl′-) ***n.*** PILOTHOUSE

☆**wheel·ie** (hwē′lē, wē′-) ***n.*** a stunt performed on a motorcycle or bicycle, in which the front wheel is raised so that the vehicle is balanced for a moment on its rear wheel

Wheel·ing (hwē′liŋ, wē′-) ⟦said to be < Delaware *wí′link*, lit., at the place of the head (of a slain enemy exhibited there)⟧ city in N W.Va., on the Ohio River

wheel lock 1 an early type of gunlock in which a rough wheel is spun on a piece of pyrite or flint to throw sparks into the pan and set off the charge **2** a gun with such a lock

wheel·man (hwēl′mən, wēl′-) ***n., pl.*** **-men** (-mən) **1** [Rare] a cyclist ☆**2** HELMSMAN: also **wheels′man** **3** [Slang] the driver of an automobile; esp., the driver of a getaway car

wheel·work (-wurk′) ***n.*** an arrangement of wheels or gears in a machine or mechanical contrivance

wheel·wright (-rīt′) ***n.*** ⟦see WHEEL & WRIGHT⟧ a person who makes and repairs wheels and wheeled vehicles

wheen (hwēn, wēn) ***n.*** ⟦ME *qwheyn(e)* < OE *hwæne*, instrumental case of *hwōn*, (a) few⟧ [Chiefly Scot.] a considerable number or amount

wheeze (hwēz, wēz) ***vi.*** **wheezed, wheez′ing** ⟦ME *whesen* < ON *hvæsa*, to hiss < IE base **k̂wes-*, to wheeze, snort > L *queri*, to lament⟧ **1** to breathe hard with a whistling, breathy sound, as in asthma **2** to make a sound like this [the old organ *wheezed*] —***vt.*** to utter with a sound of wheezing —***n.*** **1** an act or sound of wheezing **2** [Old Slang] an overworked or trite remark, joke, or gag —**wheez′er** ***n.*** —**wheez′ing·ly** ***adv.***

wheez·y (hwē′zē, wē′-) *adj.* **wheez′i·er, wheez′i·est** wheezing or characterized by wheezing —**wheez′i·ly** *adv.*

whelk (hwelk, welk) *n.* ⟦ME *welke* < OE *wioluc* < IE base **wel-*, to turn (with reference to the spiral shell) > WALK⟧ any of various families (esp. Buccinidae) of large marine snails which are often carnivorous and edible

whelm (hwelm, welm) *vt.* ⟦ME *welmen, whelmen*: ? merging of OE *-hwelfan*, to overwhelm, with *helmian*, to cover: see HELM[1]⟧ **1** to submerge, cover, or engulf **2** to overpower or crush; overwhelm

whelk

whelp (hwelp, welp) *n.* ⟦ME < OE *hwelp*, akin to Ger *welf*, ON *hvelpr*, puppy, prob. < IE **kwel-*, var. of base **kel-*, to cry out, call > LOW[2], Welsh *colwyn*, puppy⟧ **1** a young dog; puppy **2** a young lion, tiger, leopard, bear, wolf, etc.; cub **3** a youth or child: a term showing contempt **4** any of the teeth on a sprocket wheel — *vt., vi.* to give birth to (young): said of some animals

when (hwen, wen) *adv.* ⟦ME *whenne* < OE *hwænne*, akin to Ger *wann*, when, *wenn*, if, akin to *hwa*, who: see WHAT⟧ **1** *a)* at what time? [*when* did they leave? he asked *when* he should go] *b)* on what occasion or under what circumstances? [*when* do you double the final consonant?] *c)* at what point? [*when* shall I stop pouring?] **2** at an earlier time and under different, often less favorable, circumstances [I knew him *when*] Used interrogatively and in indirect questions —*conj.* **1** *a)* at what time or point [they told us *when* to eat] *b)* at the time that [*when* we were at college] **2** at which [a time *when* people must speak out] **3** as soon as [the runners started *when* the gun went off] **4** at whatever time; whenever [she smiles *when* you praise her] **5** although; while on the contrary [to complain *when* there's no reason to do so] **6** if; considering the fact that [how can he help *when* they won't let him?] —*pron.* **1** what time [until *when* will you stay?] **2** which time [we came a week ago, since *when* we've been very busy] —*n.* the time or moment (*of* an event) [the *when* and where of his arrest]

when·as (hwen az′, wen-) *conj.* ⟦prec. + AS[1]⟧ **1** [Archaic] when **2** [Archaic] inasmuch as **3** [Obs.] whereas

whence (hwens, wens) *adv.* ⟦ME *whennes* (< *whenne*, WHEN + adv. gen. *-s*), replacing OE *hwanan*⟧ from what place, source, or cause?; from where? [*whence* does he find his strength?] —*conj.* **1** from what place, source, or cause [I know *whence* he comes] **2** from which place, source, or cause [we went home, *whence* we departed soon after] **3** to the place from which [return *whence* you came] **4** from which fact [there was no reply, *whence* he inferred that all had gone] —*pron.* a place, cause, etc.: preceded by *from*: its use is still frowned on by some

whence·so·ev·er (hwens′sō ev′ər, wens′-) *adv., conj.* from whatever place, source, or cause

when·ev·er (hwen ev′ər, wen-) *adv.* [Informal] when: an emphatic form expressing bewilderment, impatience, etc. [*whenever* will he learn?] —*conj.* **1** at whatever time [leave *whenever* you're ready] **2** on whatever occasion [visit us *whenever* you can] Also [Old Poet.] **when′e'er′** (-er′)

when·so·ev·er (hwen′sō ev′ər, wen′-) *adv., conj.* whenever: an emphatic form: also [Old Poet.] **when′so·e'er′** (-er′)

where (hwer, wer) *adv.* ⟦ME *wher* < OE *hwær*, akin to Ger *wo* & to *war-* in *warum*: for IE base see WHAT⟧ **1** in or at what place? [*where* is the car?] **2** to or toward what place or point? [*where* did he go?] **3** in what situation or position [*where* will we be if we lose?] **4** in what respect? [*where* is she to blame?] **5** from what place or source? [*where* did you get your information?] —*conj.* **1** in or at what place [he knows *where* they are] **2** in or at which place [we came home, *where* we had dinner] **3** in or at the place or situation in which [he is *where* he should be] **4** in whatever place, situation, or respect in which [there is never peace *where* men are greedy] **5** *a)* to or toward the place to which [the bus will take you *where* you're going] *b)* to a place in which [she never goes *where* she's not wanted] **6** to or toward whatever place [go *where* you please] **7** [Informal] whereas [a plant needs little attention, *where* a pet demands a lot] **8** [Informal] that: used before a noun clause: still objected to by some [I see *where* the tax rates are going up] —*pron.* **1** the place or situation in, at, or to which [he lives two miles from *where* he works] **2** what or which place [*where* do you come from?] —*n.* the place (*of* an event) [to announce the when and *where* of the marriage]

where·a·bouts (hwer′ə bouts′, wer′-) *adv.* **1** near or at what place? where? **2** [Obs.] about or concerning which —*conj.* [Now Rare] at, in, or near what place [the lost hikers wondered *whereabouts* the cabin was] —*n.* [*now usually with pl. v.*] the place where a person or thing is [to know the *whereabouts* of a person] Also [Rare] **where′a·bout′** (-bout′)

where·as (hwer az′, wer-) *conj.* **1** it being the case that; in view of the fact that: used in the preamble to a formal document [*whereas* the following incidents have occurred] **2** while on the contrary; but on the other hand [she is careful, *whereas* he takes risks] —*n., pl.* **-as′es** a statement beginning with "whereas"

where·at (-at′) *conj.* [Archaic] **1** at which point [he turned to leave, *whereat* she began to weep] **2** as a consequence of which

where·by (-bī′) *adv.* [Archaic] by what? how? [*whereby* did you expect to profit?] —*conj.* by which; by means of which [a device *whereby* to make money]

where·fore (hwer′fôr′, wer′-) *adv.* ⟦ME *hwarfore*: see WHERE & FOR[1]⟧ [Archaic] for what reason or purpose? why? [*wherefore* are you angry?] —*conj.* [Archaic] **1** for which [the reason *wherefore* we have met] **2** on account of which; because of which; therefore [we are victorious, *wherefore* let us rejoice] —*n.* the reason; cause [never mind the why and *wherefore*]

where·from (hwer frum′, wer-) *adv., conj.* from which

where·in (-in′) *adv.* ⟦ME *hwerin*: see WHERE & IN[1]⟧ [Archaic] in what way? how? [*wherein* is it wrong?] —*conj.* in which [the room *wherein* he lay]

where·in·to (-in′to͞o, -in to͞o′) *conj.* [Archaic] into which

where·of (-uv′) *adv., conj.* ⟦ME: see WHERE & OF[1]⟧ of what, which, or whom [the things *whereof* he spoke]

where·on (-än′) [Archaic] *adv.* on what? [*whereon* do you rely?] —*conj.* on which [the hill *whereon* we stand]

where's (hwerz, werz) *contraction* **1** where is **2** where has **3** [Informal] where does

where·so·ev·er (hwer′sō ev′ər, wer′-) *adv., conj.* at, in, or to whatever place; wherever: an emphatic form: also [Old Poet.] **where′so·e'er′** (-er′)

where·through (hwer thro͞o′, wer-) *conj.* [Archaic] through which

where·to (-to͞o′) *adv.* ⟦ME *hwerto*⟧ to what? toward what place, direction, or end? —*conj.* to which [the place *whereto* they hurry]

where·un·to (-un′to͞o, -ən to͞o′) *adv., conj. archaic var. of* WHERETO

where·up·on (hwer′ə pän′, wer′-; hwer′ə pän′, wer′-) *conj.* **1** [Archaic] upon which [the ground *whereupon* he had fallen] **2** at which; upon which; as a consequence of which [she told a tale, *whereupon* he laughed heartily]

wher·ev·er (hwer ev′ər, wer-) *adv.* ⟦ME⟧ [Informal] where: an emphatic form expressing surprise or bewilderment [*wherever* did you hear that?] —*conj.* in, at, or to whatever place or situation [he thinks of us, *wherever* he is] Also [Old Poet.] **wher·e'er′** (-er′)

where·with (hwer with′, wer-; -with′) *adv.* ⟦ME *wher with*⟧ [Archaic] with what? [*wherewith* shall he be saved?] —*conj.* [Archaic] with which; by means of which [lacking the money *wherewith* to pay his debts] —*pron.* [Now Rare] that with which [to have *wherewith* to stock one's larder] —*n.* [Rare] WHEREWITHAL

where·with·al (hwer′with ôl′, wer′-; -with-) *n.* that with which something can be done; necessary means, esp. money: usually with *the* [the *wherewithal* to continue one's education] — *adv., conj. archaic var. of* WHEREWITH

wher·ry (hwer′ē, wer′-) *n., pl.* **-ries** ⟦ME *whery* < ? *whirren*, WHIR, with suggestion of fast movement⟧ **1** a light rowboat used chiefly in harbors and rivers **2** [Brit.] a large, broad, but light barge, used for moving freight

whet (hwet, wet) *vt.* **whet′ted, whet′ting** ⟦ME *whetten* < OE *hwettan*, to make keen < *hwæt*, sharp, keen, bold < IE base **kwed-*, to pierce, sharpen, whet > prob. L *(tri)quetrus*, (three-)cornered⟧ **1** to sharpen by rubbing or grinding (the edge of a knife or tool); hone **2** to make keen; stimulate [to *whet* the appetite] —*n.* **1** an act of whetting **2** something that whets (the appetite, etc.) —**whet′ter** *n.*

wheth·er (hweth′ər, weth′-) *conj.* ⟦ME < OE *hwæther* (akin to Ger *weder*, neither) < IE **kwotero-*, which (of two) < base **kwo-*, who (> WHAT) + compar. suffix⟧ **1** if it be the case or fact that: used to introduce an indirect question [ask *whether* she will help] **2** in case; in either case that: used to introduce alternatives, the second of which is preceded by *or* or by *or whether* [*whether* he drives *or* (*whether* he) flies, he'll be on time]: sometimes, the second is merely implied or understood [we don't know *whether* he'll improve (or not)] **3** either [taxation to support the war, *whether* just or unjust] —*pron.* [Archaic] which (esp. of two): used interrogatively and relatively —**whether or no** in any case

whet·stone (hwet′stōn′, wet′-) *n.* ⟦ME *whetston* < OE *hwetstan* < *hwettan* (see WHET) + *stan*, STONE⟧ an abrasive stone for sharpening knives or other edged tools

whew (hwo͞o, wo͞o; hwyo͞o, hyo͞o) *interj.* ⟦echoic⟧ used to express variously relief, surprise, dismay, or disgust: an exclamation or a sharp breathing sound

whey (hwā, wā) *n.* ⟦ME *whei* < OE *hwæg*, akin to Du *wei* < ? IE base **kwei-*, slime, muck: see OBSCENE⟧ the thin, watery part of milk, that separates from the thicker part (curds) after coagulation, as in cheese making —**whey′ey** (-ē) *adj.*

whey·face (hwā′fās′, wā′-) *n.* ⟦prec. + FACE⟧ **1** a pale or pallid face **2** a person having such a face —**whey′faced′** *adj.*

which (hwich, wich) *pron.* ⟦ME *whiche* < OE *hwylc, hwelc*, for **hwa-lic*, lit., who like (akin to Goth *hwileiks*, OHG *hwelīh*, Ger *welch*): see WHO & -LY[1]⟧ **1** what one (or ones) of the number of persons, things, or events mentioned or implied? [*which* of the men answered? *which* do you want?] **2** the one (or ones) that [he knows *which* he wants] **3** that: used as a relative referring to the thing, group, or event specified in the antecedent word, phrase, or clause: *which* can be used in a restrictive clause [the war *which* had just ended, the class to *which* he spoke], in a restrictive clause preceded by the pronoun *that* [he sacrificed that *which* he valued most], in a nonrestrictive clause [my car, *which* is not running; my family, in *which* she found a warm welcome], or, archaically, of a person [Our Father, *which* art in heaven] **4** either, or any, of the persons, things, or events previously mentioned or implied; whichever [take *which* you prefer] **5** a thing or fact that [you are late—*which* reminds me, where were you yesterday?] —*adj.* **1** what one or ones (of the number mentioned or implied) [*which* man (or men) answered? *which* books did he choose?] **2** whatever; no matter what [try *which* method he pleased, he could not succeed] **3** being the one just mentioned [he is very old, *which* fact is important]

which·ev·er (hwich ev′ər, wich-) *pron.* **1** any one (of two or more) [he may choose *whichever* he likes] 2 no matter which one [*whichever* he chooses, he'll be satisfied] —*adj.* 1 any (of two or more) [he may choose *whichever* desk he likes] 2 no matter which [*whichever* car she buys, she'll be in debt]

which·so·ev·er (hwich′sō ev′ər, wich′-) *pron., adj.* whichever: an emphatic form

whick·er (hwik′ər, wik′-) *vi.* ⟦echoic⟧ 1 to utter a partly stifled laugh; snicker; titter 2 to neigh or whinny

whid (hwid, hwud) *vi.* **whid′ded, whid′ding** ⟦? akin to OE *hwitha*, ON *hvitha*, a squall⟧ [Scot.] to move nimbly

whid·ah (bird) (hwid′ə, wid′-) *alt. sp. of* WHYDAH (BIRD)

whiff (hwif, wif) *n.* ⟦echoic⟧ 1 a light puff or gust of air or wind; breath 2 a slight wave or gust of odor; faint, momentary smell [a *whiff* of garlic] 3 an inhaling or exhaling, as of tobacco smoke 4 a faint indication; hint; trace [a *whiff* of scandal] ☆5 [Informal] a complete miss when attempting to hit something, as a golf ball, with a swinging motion —*vt.* to blow or propel (tobacco smoke, etc.) with a puff or gust; waft —*vi.* 1 to blow or move in puffs, as in smoking ☆2 *a)* [Informal] to miss completely when attempting to hit something, as a golf ball, with a swinging motion *b)* [Slang] to strike out in baseball —**whiff′er** *n.*

whif·fet (hwif′it, wif′-) *n.* ⟦dim. of prec.⟧ 1 a little whiff, or puff 2 [Informal] an insignificant, esp. young, person

whif·fle (hwif′əl, wif′-) *vi.* **-fled, -fling** ⟦freq. of WHIFF⟧ 1 to blow fitfully; blow in puffs or gusts: said of the wind 2 to shift or veer about; vacillate —*vt.* to blow or scatter with or as with a puff of wind

☆**whiffle ball** ⟦< *Wiffle*, a trademark⟧ 1 any of various lightweight, hollow plastic balls with several large air holes that cause them to abruptly curve or sink when thrown, hit, etc. 2 an informal baseball-like game played with a whiffle ball Sometimes written **whif′fle·ball′** *n.*

whif·fler (hwif′lər, wif′-) *n.* ⟦< WHIFFLE + -ER⟧ a person who vacillates or shifts position frequently in argument

☆**whif·fle·tree** (hwif′əl trē′, wif′-) *n. var. of* WHIPPLETREE

Whig (hwig, wig) *n.* ⟦shortened form of *whiggamore* (applied to Scot Covenanters who marched on Edinburgh in 1648), an erratic form of Scot *whiggamaire* < *whig*, a cry to urge on horses + *mare*, horse⟧ 1 a member of a political party in England (fl. 18th to mid-19th cent.) which championed reform and parliamentary rights: it later became the Liberal Party ☆2 in the American Revolution, a person who opposed continued allegiance to Great Britain and supported the Revolution ☆3 a member of an American political party (*c.* 1834-56) opposing the Democratic Party and advocating protection of industry and limitation of the power of the executive branch of government 4 [*also* **w-**] one who propounds or subscribes to a Whig interpretation of history —*adj.* 1 of or characteristic of Whigs 2 [*also* **w-**] of or designating historical interpretation which finds in events an uninterrupted line of progress against reactionary forces and often regards the present as a natural and inevitable result of the past —**Whig′gish** *adj.*

Whig·ger·y (-ər ē) *n.* the practices and principles of Whigs, esp. of English Whigs: also **Whig′gism′** (-iz′əm)

while (hwīl, wīl) *n.* ⟦ME < OE *hwil*, akin to Ger *weile* < IE base **kweye-*, to rest > L *quies*, quiet⟧ a period or space of time [a short *while*]: see also AWHILE (*n.*) —*conj.* 1 during or throughout the time that [we waited *while* she dined] 2 at the same time that [*while* you're up, close the door] 3 *a)* although on the one hand [*while* he was not poor, he had no ready cash] *b)* whereas; and on the other hand [the walls are green, *while* the ceiling is white] 4 [Archaic or North Eng.] until —*prep.* [Archaic or North Eng.] until —*vt.* **whiled, whil′ing** ⟦< the *n.*, but meaning prob. infl. by *wile*⟧ to spend (time) in a pleasant way; cause to pass idly: often with *away* [to *while* away the afternoon] —**between whiles** now and then; at intervals —**the while** at the same time; during this very time —**worth someone's while** worth someone's time, consideration, etc.; profitable in some way

whiles (hwīlz, wīlz) *adv.* ⟦ME < *while* (see prec.) + adv. gen. *-s*⟧ [Chiefly Scot.] SOMETIMES —*conj.* [Now Chiefly Dial.] WHILE

whi·lom (hwī′ləm, wī′-) [Archaic] *adv.* ⟦ME *whilum* < OE *hwilum*, dat. pl. of *hwil*, WHILE⟧ at one time; formerly —*adj.* formerly such; former [their *whilom* friends]

whilst (hwīlst, wīlst) *conj.* ⟦ME *whilest*, extended < *whiles*, WHILES⟧ [Chiefly Brit.] WHILE

whim (hwim, wim) *n.* ⟦short for WHIM-WHAM⟧ 1 a sudden fancy; idle and passing notion; capricious idea or desire 2 a kind of winch or capstan powered by a horse or steam, formerly used in mines to raise ore or water —*SYN.* CAPRICE

whim·brel (hwim′brəl, wim′-) *n.* ⟦earlier *whimrel*, prob. echoic of its cry⟧ a small curlew (*Numenius phaeopus*), with a pale stripe along the dark-brown crown

whim·per (hwim′pər, wim′-) *vi.* ⟦? akin to WHINE⟧ to make low, whining, broken sounds, as in crying or in fear —*vt.* to utter or say with a whimper —*n.* a whimpering sound or cry —*SYN.* CRY —**whim′per·ing·ly** *adv.*

whim·si·cal (hwim′zi kəl, wim′-) *adj.* 1 full of or characterized by whimsy; quaintly, playfully, or gently humorous 2 [Archaic] fanciful; freakish 3 subject to sudden change; unpredictable —**whim′si·cal·ly** *adv.*

whim·si·cal·i·ty (hwim′zi kal′ə tē, wim′-) *n.* 1 the quality of being whimsical: also **whim′si·cal·ness** 2 *pl.* **-ties** a whimsical speech, notion, or action; caprice

whim·sy (hwim′zē, wim′-) *n., pl.* **-sies** ⟦prob. < fol.⟧ 1 [Archaic] an odd or sudden fancy; whim 2 curious, quaint, or fanciful humor [poems full of *whimsy*] 3 something odd or whimsical, as an art object, piece of writing, etc. Also sp. **whim′sey**, *pl.* **-seys** —*SYN.* CAPRICE

whim-wham (hwim′hwam′, wim′wam′) *n.* ⟦< ?⟧ 1 a fanciful ornament; bauble; trinket 2 an odd notion; fancy; whim —☆**the whim-whams** [Informal] an uneasy, nervous feeling; the jitters

whin[1] (hwin, win) *n.* ⟦ME < obs. Dan *hvine*, swamp grass < IE base **k̂wei-*, slime, dirt > WHEY⟧ FURZE

whin[2] (hwin, win) *n.* ⟦ME (Northern) *quin* < ?⟧ WHINSTONE

whin·chat (hwin′chat′, win′-) *n.* ⟦WHIN[1] + CHAT[1], *n.*⟧ a brown and buff migrating European thrush (*Saxicola rubetra*) that frequents heaths and meadows

whine (hwīn, wīn) *vi.* **whined, whin′ing** ⟦ME *whinen* < OE *hwinan*, akin to ON *hvina* < IE base **k̂wei-*, to whiz, hiss > WHISTLE, WHISPER⟧ 1 *a)* to utter a peevish, high-pitched, somewhat nasal sound, as in complaint, distress, or fear *b)* to make a prolonged, high-pitched sound like this 2 to complain or beg in a childishly undignified way, as with a whine —*vt.* to utter with or as with a whine —*n.* 1 the act or sound of whining 2 a complaint uttered in a whining tone —**whin′er** *n.* —**whin′ing·ly** *adv.*

☆**whing·ding** (hwiŋ′diŋ′, wiŋ′-) *n.* [Slang] *var. of* WINGDING

whinge (hwinj, winj) [Brit. Informal] *vi.* **whinged, whinge′ing** ⟦OE *hwinsian* < Gmc **hwinisōjan*⟧ 1 to whine 2 to complain —*n.* a whine or complaint

whin·ny[1] (hwin′ē, win′-) *adj.* **-ni·er, -ni·est** ⟦WHIN[1] + -Y[2]⟧ covered with whin, or furze

whin·ny[2] (hwin′ē, win′-) *vi.* **whin′nied, whin′ny·ing** ⟦prob. echoic⟧ to neigh in a low, gentle, contented way —*vt.* to express with a whinny —*n., pl.* **-nies** the whinnying of a horse, or a similar sound

whin·stone (hwin′stōn′, win′-) *n.* ⟦< WHIN[2] + STONE⟧ [Chiefly Brit.] any of several hard, igneous or basaltic rocks, esp. chert, occurring as dikes or flows

whin·y (hwī′nē, wī′-) *adj.* **whin′i·er, whin′i·est** of, given to, or characterized by whining [a *whiny* child]: also sp. **whin′ey** —**whin′i·ness** *n.*

whip (hwip, wip) *vt.* **whipped** or **whipt, whip′ping** ⟦ME *whippen* < MDu *wippen*, to swing, move up and down < IE **weib-*, to turn, swing: see VIBRATE⟧ 1 to move, pull, jerk, snatch, throw, etc. suddenly: usually with *out, off, up*, etc. [to *whip* out a knife] 2 *a)* to strike, as with a strap or rod; lash; beat *b)* to punish in this manner 3 to force, drive, compel, or urge by or as by whipping 4 to strike as a whip does [the rain *whipped* her face] 5 to attack with stinging words; flay 6 to wind (cord or thread) around (a rope, etc.) so as to prevent fraying 7 to fish (a stream, etc.) by making repeated casts with a rod and line 8 to beat (egg whites, cream, etc.) with a fork, whisk, mixer, etc. so as to incorporate air and make frothy 9 to sew (a seam or hem) with a loose, overcasting or overhand stitch 10 [Informal] to defeat or outdo, as in a contest —*vi.* 1 to move, go, or pass quickly and suddenly [he *whipped* down the stairs] 2 to flap or thrash about in a whiplike manner [flags *whipping* in high wind] 3 to cast with a fishing rod, using a quick, whiplike motion —*n.* ⟦ME *whippe* < MDu *wippe*⟧ 1 an instrument for striking or flogging, consisting generally of a stiff or flexible rod with a lash attached to one end 2 a blow, cut, etc. made with or as with a whip 3 a person who uses a whip, as a coachman or a huntsman who whips on the hounds 4 *a)* an officer of a political party, as in Congress or Parliament, who maintains discipline and enforces attendance (also **party whip**) *b)* [Brit.] a call issued to party members in a lawmaking body to be in attendance to vote on a certain issue 5 a whipping motion 6 a dessert made of sugar and whipped cream, stiffly beaten egg whites, or gelatin, and often fruit 7 something resembling a whip in its action, as a windmill vane, kind of eggbeater, etc. 8 a hoisting apparatus consisting of a single rope passing through an overhead pulley 9 a flexible vertical rod for use as a radio antenna: also **whip antenna** —*SYN.* BEAT —**crack the whip** [Informal] to employ stern or harsh measures; enforce strict discipline —**whip in** to bring together or assemble, as a party whip does —**whip into shape** [Informal] to bring by vigorous action into the proper or desired condition —**whip up** 1 to rouse; excite [to *whip up* enthusiasm] 2 [Informal] to prepare quickly and efficiently

whip·cord (hwip′kôrd′, wip′-) *n.* 1 a hard, twisted or braided cord used for whiplashes, etc. 2 a strong worsted cloth with a hard, diagonally ribbed surface

whip hand 1 the hand in which a driver holds a whip 2 the position of advantage or control

whip·lash (-lash′) *n.* 1 the flexible striking part of a whip ☆2 a sudden, severe bending and jolting of the neck, as in an auto accident, often causing injury to the neck muscles, vertebrae, etc.

whipped (hwipt, wipt) *adj.* 1 *Cooking* stiffened as by whipping [a *whipped* dessert topping]: see also WHIPPED CREAM ☆2 [Slang] *var. of* PUSSY-WHIPPED

whipped cream rich sweet cream stiffened as by whipping and used as a topping on desserts, etc.: also **whip cream**

whip·per (hwip′ər, wip′-) *n.* a person or thing that whips

whip·per-in (-ər in′) *n., pl.* **-pers-in′** (-ərz in′) 1 [Chiefly Brit.] a huntsman's assistant who keeps the hounds together in a pack 2 [Archaic] WHIP (*n.* 4*a*)

whip·per·snap·per (hwip′ər snap′ər, wip′-) *n.* ⟦extended < *whip-snapper*, one who snaps whips⟧ an insignificant, esp. young, person who appears impertinent or presumptuous

whip·pet (hwip′it, wip′-) *n.* ⟦dim. < WHIP⟧ any of a breed of slender, swift dog resembling a small greyhound, used esp. as a racing dog

whip·ping (hwip′iŋ, wip′-) *n.* 1 the action of a person or thing that whips; esp., a flogging or beating, as in punishment 2 cord, twine, etc. used to whip, or bind

whipping boy 1 [Historical] a boy brought up together with a young prince and required to take the punishment for the latter's misdeeds 2 SCAPEGOAT (sense 2)

whipping cream sweet cream with a high percentage of butterfat, that can be whipped until stiff

whipping post a post to which offenders are tied to be whipped as a legal punishment

whip·ple·tree (hwip′əl trē′, wip′-) *n.* ⟦< WHIP + TREE⟧ SINGLETREE

whip·poor·will (hwip′ər wil′, wip′-) *n., pl.* **-wills′** or **-will′** ⟦echoic of its cry⟧ a dark, insect-eating, nocturnal nightjar (*Caprimulgus vociferus*) of E North America

whip·py (hwip′ē, wip′ē) *adj.* 1 of, like, or relating to a whip 2 very resilient or springy [*a whippy* branch]

whip·saw (hwip′sô′, wip′-) *n.* any of several long-bladed saws; esp., a crosscut saw with a tapering blade from 5 to 7½ feet long and with a handle at each end, for use by two persons —☆*vt.* 1 to cut with a whipsaw 2 to subject to pressure or attack from two different sources or directions at the same time

whip scorpion any of various tropical or subtropical arachnids (esp. order Uropygi) resembling the scorpion but having a long, whiplike tail at the end of the abdomen and no sting

☆**whip·snake** (-snāk′) *n.* 1 any of various long, slender, nonpoisonous colubrid snakes that often live in trees 2 any of several poisonous elapine snakes (genera *Demansia* and *Denisonia*) of Australia

☆**whip·stall** (-stôl′) *n.* a stunt in flying in which the airplane first goes into a stall during a steep climb, then drops or whips suddenly nose downward

whip·stitch (-stich′) *vt., vi. Sewing* to overcast or whip —*n.* a stitch made in this way

whip·stock (-stäk′) *n.* the handle of a whip

whip·worm (-wurm′) *n.* any of a genus (*Trichuris*) of roundworms with a whiplike front portion, parasitic in the intestines of mammals: it is usually *c.* 5 cm (*c.* 2 in) long

whir (hwur, wur) *vi., vt.* **whirred**, **whir′ring** ⟦ME (Northern) *quirren*, prob. < Scand, as in Dan *hvirre*, Norw *kvirra*, akin to ON *hverfa*, to turn: for IE base see WHARF⟧ to fly, revolve, vibrate, or otherwise move quickly with a whizzing or buzzing sound —*n.* a sound like this, as that made by a bird's wings or a propeller

whirl (hwurl, wurl) *vi.* ⟦ME *whirlen* < ON *hvirfla*, akin to *hverfa*: see prec.⟧ 1 to move rapidly in a circular manner or as in an orbit; circle swiftly [couples *whirling* round the dance floor] 2 to rotate or spin fast; gyrate 3 to move, go, drive, etc. swiftly 4 to seem to spin; reel [my head is *whirling*] —*vt.* 1 to cause to rotate, revolve, or spin rapidly 2 to move, carry, drive, etc. with a rotating motion [the wind *whirled* the leaves] 3 [Obs.] to hurl or throw —*n.* ⟦ME *wherwille* < ON *hverfill*, akin to Ger *wirbel*⟧ 1 the act of whirling 2 a whirling motion 3 something whirling or being whirled [a *whirl* of dust] 4 a round of parties, etc., one after another 5 a tumult; uproar; stir 6 a confused or giddy condition [his head in a *whirl*] —☆**give it a whirl** [Informal] to try something; make an attempt —**whirl′er** *n.*

whirl·i·gig (hwur′li gig′, wur′-) *n.* ⟦ME *whirlgigge*: see prec. & GIG[1]⟧ 1 [Old-fashioned] any of various child's toys that whirl or spin, as a pinwheel or top 2 MERRY-GO-ROUND 3 something that seems to whirl, or revolve in a cycle 4 a whirling motion or course

whirligig beetle any of a small family (Gyrinidae) of bluish-black gregarious beetles found darting about in circles on the surface of ponds, streams, etc.

whirl·pool (hwurl′po͞ol′, wurl′-) *n.* 1 water in rapid, violent, whirling motion caused by two meeting currents, by winds meeting tides, etc. and tending to form a circle into which floating objects are drawn; vortex or eddy of water 2 anything like a whirlpool, as in violent motion ☆3 a bath, as used in hydrotherapy, in which an agitating device propels a current of warm water with a swirling motion: in full **whirlpool bath**

whirl·wind (-wind′) *n.* ⟦ME *whirlwynd*, prob. based on ON *hvirfilvindr*⟧ 1 a current of air whirling violently upward in a spiral motion around a more or less vertical axis that has a forward motion 2 anything resembling a whirlwind, as in violent or destructive force —*adj.* impetuous and speedy [a *whirlwind* courtship] —**sow the wind and reap the whirlwind** to engage in, and suffer the consequences of, evil or folly: Hos. 8:7

whirl·y·bird (hwur′lē burd′, wur′-) *n. informal term for* HELICOPTER

whirr (hwur, wur) *vi., vt., n. alt. sp. of* WHIR

whir·ry (hwur′ē, wur′-) *vt., vi.* **-ried**, **-ry·ing** [Scot.] to whir; hurry

whish (hwish, wish) *vi.* ⟦echoic⟧ to move with a soft, rushing sound; whiz; swish —*n.* a sound so made

whisht (hwisht, wisht) *vt., n., interj.* [Chiefly Scot. or Irish] hush

whisk (hwisk, wisk) *n.* ⟦ME *wisk* < ON *visk*, wisp, brush < IE **weisk-* (< **weis-*, supple twig, broom) > Ger *wischen*, to wipe⟧ 1 *a)* the act of brushing with a quick, light, sweeping motion *b)* such a motion 2 a small bunch of straw, twigs, hair, etc. used for brushing 3 a kitchen utensil consisting of wire loops fixed in a handle, for whipping egg whites, cream, etc. —*vt.* 1 to move, remove, carry, brush (*away, off, out,* etc.) forcefully and speedily, as with a quick, sweeping motion [to *whisk* out a handkerchief, to *whisk* off crumbs] 2 to whip (egg whites, cream, etc.) —*vi.* to move quickly, nimbly, or briskly

whisk broom a small broom with a very short handle, used as for brushing clothes

whisk·er (hwis′kər, wis′-) *n.* ⟦ME *wisker*, something used for whisking: see WHISK & -ER⟧ 1 [*pl.*] *a)* [Archaic] a mustache *b)* the hair growing on a man's face; esp., the beard on the cheeks 2 *a)* a hair of a man's beard *b)* any of the long, bristly hairs growing on each side of the upper lip of a cat, rat, etc.; vibrissa 3 a very small, hairlike, single-crystal filament of high tensile strength, grown on certain metals, alloys, crystals, etc. and serving to reinforce the material 4 a very small amount or margin [to lose an election by a *whisker*] 5 *Naut.* either of two spars extending laterally, one on each side of the bowsprit, for spreading the jib and flying jib guys —**whisk′ered** *adj.* —**whisk′er·y** *adj.*

whis·key (hwis′kē, wis′kē) *n., pl.* **-keys** or **-kies** ⟦short for *usquebaugh* < Ir *uisce beathadh* (or Gael *uisge beatha*) < *uisce*, WATER + *beathadh*, life < IE base **gwi-*, **gwei-*, to live > BIO-⟧ 1 a strong alcoholic liquor distilled from the fermented mash of grain, esp. of rye, wheat, corn, or barley 2 a drink of whiskey —*adj.* of, for, or made with whiskey Also sp. **whis′ky**, *pl.* **-kies**

USAGE—in general, U.S. and Irish usage favors the sp. *whiskey*, and Brit. and Cdn. usage favors *whisky*

whiskey jack ⟦earlier *whisky-john*, itself altered (as if < prec. + JOHN[1]) < Cree dial. *wiiskachaan*, lit., blacksmith (so named from its coloring)⟧ GRAY JAY

☆**whiskey sour** a cocktail of lemon juice, sugar, and whiskey, shaken with cracked ice

whis·per (hwis′pər, wis′-) *vi.* ⟦ME *whisperen* < OE *hwisprian*, akin to *wispern* < IE base **k̑wei-*, to whiz, hiss > WHINE, WHISTLE⟧ 1 to speak very softly, esp. without the resonance produced by the vibration of the vocal cords 2 to talk quietly or furtively, as in gossiping, maligning, or plotting 3 to make a soft, rustling sound like a whisper, as the leaves of a tree —*vt.* 1 to say very softly, esp. by whispering 2 to tell (something) to (someone) privately or as a secret —*n.* 1 the act or an instance of whispering; specif., soft, low speech produced with breath but, usually, without vibrating the vocal cords [to speak in a *whisper*] 2 *a)* something whispered *b)* a secret, hint, rumor, etc. 3 a soft, rustling sound like a whisper

whis·per·er (-ər) *n.* 1 a person or thing that whispers 2 ⟦from the characteristic use of whispers and gentle persuasion in certain types of animal training⟧ [Informal] a person, esp. a trainer, regarded as having a special rapport with (a specified type of animal) [a horse *whisperer*]

whis·per·ing (-iŋ) *adj.* that whispers or is like a whisper: also **whis′per·y** (-ē) —*n.* 1 the act of one who whispers 2 something whispered; whispered sound, speech, etc. —**whis′per·ing·ly** *adv.*

☆**whispering campaign** the organized dissemination of defamatory rumors, as by a political opponent

whist[1] (hwist, wist) *interj.* ⟦ME: echoic⟧ [Now Chiefly Dial.] hush

whist[2] (hwist, wist) *n.* ⟦altered < earlier *whisk*: prob. from the habit of whisking the tricks from the table as soon as played⟧ a card game similar to bridge but without the use of bidding to establish the trump suit: bridge developed from whist

whis·tle (hwis′əl, wis′-) *vi.* **-tled**, **-tling** ⟦ME *whistlen* < OE *hwistlian*: for IE base see WHISPER⟧ 1 *a)* to make a clear, shrill sound or note, or a series of these, by forcing breath between the teeth or through a narrow opening made by puckering the lips *b)* to make a similar sound by sending steam through a small opening 2 to make a clear, shrill cry: said of some birds and animals 3 to move, pass, go, etc. with a high, shrill sound, as the wind 4 *a)* to blow a whistle *b)* to have its whistle blown [the train *whistled*] —*vt.* 1 to produce (a tune, etc.) by whistling 2 to summon, signal, direct, etc. by whistling 3 *Sports a)* to call (a player or coach) for a rules infraction by blowing a whistle *b)* to suspend (play, or a play) by blowing a whistle: said of a referee —*n.* 1 an instrument for making whistling sounds, as by forcing the breath or steam through a slit into a cavity or against a thin edge 2 a clear, shrill sound made by whistling or blowing a whistle 3 the act of whistling 4 a signal, summons, etc. made by whistling 5 a whistling sound, as of the wind —**blow the whistle (on)** [Informal] 1 to report or inform (on) 2 to cause to stop; call a halt (to) —**clean as a whistle** [Informal] extremely clean —**wet one's whistle** [Slang] to take a drink —**whistle for** to seek, expect, or demand but fail to get —☆**whistle in the dark** to pretend to be confident when faced with danger or defeat —**whis′tle·a·ble** *adj.*

whis·tle-blow·er (-blō′ər) ☆*n.* ⟦< BLOW THE WHISTLE (ON) (see phr. under WHISTLE)⟧ a person who reports or informs on a wrongdoer within a corporation, government agency, etc. —**whis′tle-blow′ing** *n.*

whis·tler (hwis′lər, wis-) *n.* 1 a person, animal, or thing that whistles 2 *a)* any of various birds having a whistling call or making a whistling sound in flight, as the goldeneye ☆*b)* HOARY MARMOT *c)* a horse affected with WHISTLING (sense 2) *d)* a radio wave, generated by lightning, high-energy electrons, etc. that travels along the earth's magnetic field lines and is heard as a whistling sound on radio receivers

Whis·tler (hwis′lər, wis′-), **James Abbott Mc·Neill** (mək nēl′) 1834-1903; U.S. painter & etcher in England

☆**whis·tle-stop** (hwis′əl stäp′, wis′-) *n.* 1 a small town, orig. one at which a train stopped only upon signal 2 a brief stop in a small town as part of a tour, esp. in a political campaign; orig., such a stop in which the candidate spoke from the rear platform of a train —*vi.* **-stopped′**, **-stop′ping** to make a series of whistle-stops

whis·tling (hwis′liŋ, wis′-) *n.* ⟦ME *whistlinge* < OE *hwistlung*⟧ 1 the act or sound of a person, animal, or thing that whistles 2 shrill, noisy breathing by a horse, caused by a disorder of the air passages

whistling swan ⟦so named from its high-pitched cry⟧ a large, white, North American swan (*Cygnus columbianus*) usually having a yellow spot in front of the eye: it winters along the Atlantic coast of the U.S.

whit (hwit, wit) ***n.*** ⟦Early ModE respelling of *wiht,* a WIGHT[1]⟧ the least bit; jot; iota: chiefly in negative constructions *[*not a *whit* the wiser*]*

Whit·by (hwit′bē, wit′-) town in SE Ontario, Canada, east of Toronto

white (hwīt, wīt) ***adj.*** **whit′er, whit′est** ⟦ME *hwit* < OE, akin to Ger *weiss,* ON *hvitr,* MDu *wit* < IE **kweid-,* to gleam, bright, white > WHEAT, OSlav *švěšta,* a light, candle⟧ **1** having the color of pure snow or milk; of the color of radiated, transmitted, or reflected light containing all of the visible rays of the spectrum; opposite to black: see COLOR **2** of a light or pale color; specif., *a)* gray; silvery; hoary *b)* very blond *c)* pale; wan; pallid; ashen *[*a face *white* with terror*] d)* light-yellow or amber *[white* grapes*] e)* blank (said of a space unmarked by printing, writing, etc.) *f)* of a light-gray color and lustrous appearance (said of silver and other metals) *g)* made of silver *h)* snowy *[*a *white* Christmas*]* **3** lacking color; colorless *[white* crème de menthe*]* **4** clothed in white; wearing a white habit *[*the *White* Friars*]* **5** morally or spiritually pure; spotless; innocent **6** free from evil intent; relatively harmless *[white* magic, a *white* lie*]* **7** *a) [sometimes* **W-***]* having a light-colored skin; Caucasoid *b) [sometimes* **W-***]* of, controlled by, or restricted to Caucasoids ☆*c)* ⟦from stereotypical notions of racial superiority⟧ [Slang] honest; honorable; fair; decent **8** being at white heat **9** reactionary, counterrevolutionary, or royalist, as opposed to RED (***adj.*** *4a*) **10** [Rare] happy; fortunate; auspicious: said of times and seasons —***n.*** **1** *a)* white color *b)* a white pigment, paint, or dye **2** the state of being white; specif., *a)* fairness of complexion *b)* purity; innocence **3** a white or light-colored part; specif., *a)* the albumen of an egg *b)* the white part of the eyeball *c)* a blank space in printing, writing, etc. *d)* the white or light-colored part of meat, wood, etc. **4** something white or light-colored; specif., *a)* white cloth *b) [pl.]* white garments or vestments; white uniform *c)* a white breed, esp. of pig *d) [pl.]* a highly refined, usually bleached flour *e) short for* WHITE BREAD *f) short for* WHITE WINE *g) Chess* the player or side with the white or lighter-colored pieces **5** *[sometimes* **W-***]* a person with a light-colored skin; member of the Caucasoid division of humans **6** *[often* **W-***]* a member of a reactionary or counterrevolutionary faction, party, etc. in certain European countries **7** *[pl.]* LEUKORRHEA **8** *Archery a)* [Archaic] a white target *b)* the outermost ring of a target *c)* a hit on this ring —***vt.*** **whit′ed, whit′ing** ⟦ME *whiten* < OE *hwitian* < the adj.⟧ [Archaic] to make white; whiten —**bleed white** to drain (a person) completely of money, resources, etc. —**white out** ☆to cover or delete with or as with WHITE-OUT

White (hwīt, wīt) **1 Byron R(aymond)** 1917-2002; associate justice, U.S. Supreme Court (1962-93) **2 E(lwyn) B(rooks)** 1899-1985; U.S. writer **3 Edward Douglass** 1845-1921; chief justice of the U.S. (1910-21) **4 Gilbert** 1720-93; Eng. naturalist & clergyman: author of *The Natural History and Antiquities of Selborne* **5 Patrick (Victor Martindale)** 1912-90; Austral. writer **6 T(erence) H(anbury)** 1906-64; Brit. writer **7 Stan·ford** (stan′fərd) 1853-1906; U.S. architect **8 Walter (Francis)** 1893-1955; U.S. writer & civil rights leader

white admiral a butterfly (*Limenitis arthemis*) of Canada and the E U.S., with showy, white bands on its wings

white alkali **1** refined soda ash **2** the white crust formed on some alkali soils, consisting of a mixture of sodium and magnesium sulfates and sodium chloride

white amur GRASS CARP

white ant TERMITE

white arsenic ARSENOUS ACID

white·bait (hwīt′bāt′, wīt′-) ***n.,*** *pl.* **-bait′** **1** any of the fry of various silvery fishes used as food, as herring fry ☆**2** a smelt fish (*Allosmerus elongatus*) of the Pacific **3** SILVERSIDE

☆**white bass** (bas) a silvery, striped, North American freshwater food and game bass (*Morone chrysops*) of the same family (Percichthyidae) as striped bass

white birch ☆**1** PAPER BIRCH **2** a European birch (*Betula pendula*) with silvery-white bark, widely grown in the U.S.

white blood cell LEUKOCYTE: also called **white blood corpuscle**

white·board (-bôrd′) ***n.*** ⟦WHITE + (BLACK)BOARD⟧ a smooth, glossy white surface of plastic, porcelain, or enamel, on which to write with erasable markers

white book an official government report bound in white

white bread bread of a light color, made from finely sifted wheat flour

☆**white-bread** (-bred′) ***adj.*** ⟦infl. by WHITE, ***adj.*** *7*⟧ [Informal] bland, conventional, etc.

☆**white bush (scallop)** PATTYPAN

white cake a cake that is pale in color because its batter contains the whites of eggs but no yolks

white·cap (-kap′) ***n.*** a wave with its crest broken into white foam

☆**white cedar** **1** *a)* an evergreen tree (*Chamaecyparis thyoides*) of the cypress family, growing in swampy land in the E U.S. *b)* its soft, light-colored wood **2** *a)* the American arborvitae (*Thuja occidentalis*), growing in cool areas of the NE U.S. *b)* its soft, brittle, durable wood

white cell LEUKOCYTE

White·chap·el (hwīt′chap′əl) district of E London, part of Greater London borough of Tower Hamlets

white chocolate a cooked mixture of cocoa butter, milk, and sugar, used in candies and desserts: it contains none of the chocolate portion of the cacao bean and thus is not brown in color

white clover a creeping species of clover (*Trifolium repens*) with white flower clusters, common in lawns

white-col·lar (-käl′ər) ***adj.*** ⟦from the formerly typical white shirts worn by such workers⟧ ☆designating or of clerical or professional workers or others employed in work not essentially manual

☆**white-collar crime** a crime, as fraud, embezzlement, etc., committed by a person in business, government, or a profession in the course of occupational activities

white corpuscle LEUKOCYTE

☆**white crappie** a silvery crappie (*Pomoxis annularis*)

whited sepulcher ⟦lit., a whitewashed tomb, outwardly clean but containing decaying corpses⟧ a hypocrite: Matt. 23:27

white dwarf *pl.* **white dwarfs** or sometimes **white dwarves** a planet-sized, very dense, collapsed star, the fuel of which has been exhausted: initially very bright and hot, it gradually evolves into a black dwarf

white elephant **1** an albino elephant **2** ⟦from the story that kings of Siam, owners of all the *white elephants,* would punish a courtier by giving him such an elephant, knowing that the cost of maintenance would be financially ruinous⟧ something from which little profit or use is derived; esp., such a possession maintained at much expense ☆**3** any object no longer desired by its owner, but of possible value to others

white-eye (hwīt′ī′, wīt′-) ***n.*** any of a family (Zosteropidae) of small passerine birds of Southeast Asia, S Africa, Australia, etc., usually having rings of white feathers around the eyes

white·face (hwīt′fās′, wīt′-) ***n.*** **1** a white-faced animal; specif., a HEREFORD[1] **2** white theatrical makeup, typically applied to the entire face, worn as by clowns and mimes

white-faced (-fāst′) ***adj.*** **1** having a pale face; pallid **2** having a white mark on the front of the head, as a horse

white feather ⟦from the notion that a white feather in a gamecock's tail shows bad breeding, hence cowardice⟧ an indication of cowardice: chiefly in **show the white feather**

White·field (hwit′fēld′, wit′-), **George** 1714-70; Eng. Methodist evangelist

white·fish (hwīt′fish′, wīt′-) ***n.,*** *pl.* **-fish′** or **-fish′es** (see FISH) **1** any of various white or silvery, edible freshwater trouts (genera *Prosopium* and *Coregonus*) found in cool lakes of the Northern Hemisphere **2** any of various other similar fishes, as a tilefish (*Caulolatilus princeps*) of the Pacific **3** BELUGA (sense 2)

white flag a white banner or cloth hoisted or waved as a traditional signal of truce or surrender

☆**white flight** the relocation by white people from the city to the suburbs, or from one suburb to another, in an effort to escape the influx of members of some ethnic group, esp. black people

white flour refined and enriched wheat flour that excludes most of the bran and the germ and is sometimes bleached

☆**white·fly** (-flī′) ***n.,*** *pl.* **-flies′** any of a family (Aleyrodidae) of tiny homopteran insects having scalelike larvae and winged adults covered with a white, powdery wax

white-foot·ed mouse (hwīt′foot′əd, wīt′-) DEER MOUSE

white fox the arctic fox in winter, when its fur is white

White Friar a Carmelite friar: so called from the white cloak worn by members of the order

White·fri·ars (hwīt′frī′ərz, wīt′-) district of central London, near Fleet Street: formerly the site of a Carmelite monastery

☆**white gasoline (*or* gas)** gasoline without tetraethyl lead

white gold gold alloyed variously with nickel, zinc, etc. to give it a white, platinumlike appearance, for use in jewelry

☆**white goods** ⟦from their formerly typical color⟧ **1** household linens, as sheets, pillowcases, towels, etc. **2** large household appliances, as refrigerators, stoves, etc.

white-haired (-herd′) ***adj.*** **1** having white or very light hair **2** [Informal] FAIR-HAIRED (sense 2)

White·hall[1] (hwīt′hôl′, wīt′-) ***n.*** **1** former royal palace in Westminster, London, destroyed by fire (1698): also **Whitehall Palace** **2** the British government

White·hall[2] (hwīt′hôl′, wīt′-) street in Westminster, south of Trafalgar Square: site of several government offices

white·head (hwīt′hed′, wīt′-) ***n.*** *nontechnical term for* MILIUM

White·head (hwīt′hed′, wīt′-), **Alfred North** 1861-1947; Eng. mathematician & philosopher, in the U.S. after 1924

white-head·ed (hwīt′hed′id, wīt′-) ***adj.*** **1** having a white head; specif., having white or very light hair, feathers, etc. on the head **2** [Informal] FAIR-HAIRED (sense 2)

white heat **1** a temperature at which material glows white **2** a state of intense emotion, excitement, etc.

white hole ⟦so called by analogy with BLACK HOLE⟧ a hypothetical portal in space through which matter and energy emerge: thought to be an outlet for black holes

☆**white hope** ⟦term orig. applied to white boxers who, it was thought, might be able to defeat black heavyweight champion Jack Johnson (*c.* 1910)⟧ [Informal] any person who is expected to bring honor, glory, etc. to some group, place, etc.

White·horse (hwīt′hôrs′, wīt′-) ⟦after the *Whitehorse* Rapids nearby, which were so named from a fancied resemblance to a white, tossing mane⟧ capital of the Yukon Territory, Canada, in the S part

white-hot (hwīt′hät′, wīt′-) ***adj.*** **1** having a temperature at which material glows white **2** extremely angry, excited, enthusiastic, etc. **3** extremely popular, controversial, etc.

White House, the ☆**1** official residence of the President of the U.S.: a white mansion in Washington, D.C. ☆2 the U.S. President along with his spokesmen, Cabinet, etc.

white iron pyrites MARCASITE

white knight a rescuer; specif., a company that prevents the takeover, viewed as unfavorable, of another company by offering better terms for a merger with it

white-knuck·le (hwīt′nuk′əl, wīt′-) *adj.* ⟦from the appearance of a hand clenched in fear⟧ [Informal] of or causing great fear, suspense, dread, etc.

white lead (led) 1 a poisonous, heavy, white powder, basic lead carbonate, $2PbCO_3 \cdot Pb(OH)_2$, used in paints, pottery glazes, etc. 2 any of several white pigments containing lead, as lead sulfate

white leather soft leather suitable for babies' shoes, etc., made by tanning hides with alum and salt

white lie a lie that is only partially untrue, or one that consists of a deliberately misleading ambiguity

white light *Physics* light, as sunlight, that is a mixture of wavelengths ranging from red to violet

☆**white lightning** [Slang] homemade whiskey, esp. strong corn whiskey, typically colorless and not aged

white-liv·ered (hwīt′liv′ərd, wīt′-) *adj.* ⟦from the ancient belief that predominance of yellow bile in the liver produced a bold temperament, and its absence, cowardice: an early recorded use, though not the very first, occurs in *Henry V*, III, ii (1599) by SHAKESPEARE⟧ cowardly; craven

white·ly (-lē) *adv.* so as to be white; with a white or pale appearance

white man's burden the alleged duty of the white peoples to bring their civilization to other peoples regarded as backward: phrase popularized by Kipling and other apologists for imperialism

white matter whitish nerve tissue of the brain and spinal cord, consisting chiefly of medullated nerve fibers: distinguished from GRAY MATTER (sense 1)

white meat any light-colored meat, as veal or pork or, esp., the breast of some kinds of poultry

white metal any of various light-colored alloys, esp. any of those, as pewter, containing much lead or tin

White Mountains ⟦so named because the higher peaks are often snow-covered⟧ range of the Appalachian system, in N N.H.: highest peak, Mt. Washington

white mustard an annual mustard (*Brassica hirta*) that has seeds which are ground and made into a paste used as a condiment

whit·en (hwīt′'n, wīt′-) *vt., vi.* ⟦ME *whitnen* < ON *hvitna* < *hvitr*, WHITE⟧ to make or become white or whiter

whit·en·er (-ər) *n.* a person or thing that whitens; specif., a bleach or other substance used for whitening

white·ness (hwīt′nis, wīt′-) *n.* 1 the quality or condition of being white; specif., *a)* white color or appearance *b)* paleness; pallor *c)* freedom from stain 2 a white substance or part

white night a night in extreme N or S latitudes during the summer, reaching only twilight at its darkest time: *often used in pl.*

White Nile *see* NILE

whit·en·ing (hwīt′'n iŋ, wīt′-) *n.* 1 the act or process of making or becoming white 2 a preparation used for making something white

white noise ⟦by analogy with WHITE LIGHT⟧ 1 a sound containing a blend of all the audible frequencies distributed equally over the range of the frequency band 2 *a)* constant background sound or sounds, as from an appliance, traffic, etc. *b)* recorded sound or sounds intended to serve as background noise, as in an effort to create a relaxing atmosphere or to mask other noises

white oak 1 any of a number of oaks having leaves with rounded lobes, acorns that mature in one season, whitish or grayish bark, and hard, impervious wood; esp., the **American white oak** (*Quercus alba*) of E North America 2 the wood of any such tree, used in barrels, furniture, etc.

white·out (-out′) *n.* 1 an optical phenomenon in which the snow-covered ground blends into a uniformly white sky, greatly reducing the visibility of shadows, the horizon, etc. and one's sense of direction or distance 2 *Meteorol.* a condition in which falling or windblown snow reduces visibility to near zero

☆**white-out** (-out′) *n.* ⟦< *Wite-Out*, a trademark for such fluid, prob. infl. by prec.⟧ a quick-drying fluid, typically white, applied with a small brush to a piece of paper so as to cover typed or written errors and make a blank surface for corrections —*vt.* to cover with this fluid

white paper 1 an official government report, orig. one bound in white paper 2 any in-depth, authoritative report

white pepper pepper ground from the dried seeds of the husked fruits of the pepper plant: see PEPPER (*n.* 1)

☆**white perch** 1 a small, silvery, edible bass (*Morone americana*) of the same family (Percichthyidae) as white bass, found in coastal waters of the E U.S. 2 a freshwater drum fish (*Aplodinotus grunniens*) of the central U.S. 3 *a)* SILVER PERCH *b)* [South] WHITE CRAPPIE

☆**white pine** 1 *a)* a pine (*Pinus strobus*) of E North America, with bluish-green or grayish-green needles in bundles of five, hanging brown cones, and soft, light wood *b)* the wood of this tree 2 any of various closely related pines having needles in groups of five

White Plains ⟦< ?⟧ city in SE N.Y., near New York City: scene of a battle (1776) of the Revolutionary War

white poplar 1 a large Old World poplar (*Populus alba*), having lobed leaves with white or gray down on the undersides, now widespread in the U.S. ☆2 *a)* TULIP TREE *b)* TULIPWOOD (sense 1)

☆**white potato** POTATO (sense 2*a*)

white race loosely, the Caucasoid group of mankind: see CAUCASOID

White River river flowing from NW Ark. through S Mo. into the Mississippi: 690 mi (1,110 km)

☆**white room** a room from which all contaminants have been eliminated and in which temperature, humidity, and pressure are controlled: used for assembly and repair of precision mechanisms, in preventing infection, etc.

White Russia BELORUSSIA

White Russian 1 BELORUSSIAN 2 a cocktail that is a BLACK RUSSIAN to which cream or milk has been added

white sale ⟦prob. < WHITE GOODS (sense 1)⟧ a sale of household linens

White Sands ⟦from the white gypsum sand that is plentiful in the area⟧ town in S N.Mex., near Las Cruces: located within a military missile test range (**White Sands Missile Range**) where the first atomic bomb was exploded (July, 1945)

white sapphire a colorless variety of corundum

white sauce a sauce made with melted butter, flour, and seasonings, cooked with milk, cream, or stock

White Sea ⟦transl. of Russ *Beloe More*⟧ arm of the Barents Sea, extending into NW European Russia: *c.* 36,000 sq mi (93,240 sq km)

white shark a huge, man-eating mackerel shark (*Carcharodon carcharias*) of tropical and warm seas

☆**white-shoe** (-sho͞o′) *adj.* ⟦from the white shoes fashionable at Ivy-League colleges in the 1950s⟧ designating or characteristic of a business company, esp. a law firm or brokerage, in which the partners belong almost exclusively to the white, Protestant, upper-class elite and are thought of as being conservative

white slave a woman enticed or forced into or held in prostitution for the profit of others —**white′-slave′** *adj.*

white slaver a person who entices or forces women to become white slaves —**white slavery**

white·smith (-smith′) *n.* 1 a worker in white metals; esp., a tinsmith 2 a worker in iron who does finishing, polishing, or galvanizing

white space all the blank areas as of a printed page, where there is no text, illustration, etc.

white spruce 1 any of several hardy varieties of a North American spruce (*Picea glauca*) having soft, flexible cones and bluish-green needles that are often tinged with white 2 the wood of any such tree

☆**white supremacy** the social, economic, and political repression and exploitation of nonwhite peoples, esp. blacks, by white people, based on notions of racial superiority —**white supremacist**

white·tail (-tāl′) *n.* any of various animals with white about the tail, as the white-tailed deer

☆**white-tailed deer** (-tāld′) a common American deer (*Odocoileus virginianus*) having a tail that is white on the undersurface, a white-spotted red coat in summer, and a diffuse brownish-gray coat in winter

white·throat (-thrōt′) *n.* any of several birds having white around the throat; esp., certain Old World warblers (genus *Sylvia*) or the white-throated sparrow

☆**white-throat·ed sparrow** (-thrōt′id) a common North American sparrow (*Zonotrichia albicollis*) having a square white patch on the throat and black-and-white stripes on the head

white tie 1 a white bow tie as worn with a swallow-tailed coat 2 a swallow-tailed coat and its accessories

☆**white trash** [Slang] a poor, ignorant white person, esp. of Appalachia or the South, or such persons collectively: an insulting or derogatory term

white vitriol ZINC SULFATE

White Volta *see* VOLTA[2]

☆**white·wall** (-wôl′) *adj.* designating or of a pneumatic tire with a circular white band on the outer sidewall: also written **white-wall** —*n.* a whitewall tire

☆**white walnut** BUTTERNUT (senses 1 & 2)

white·wash (-wôsh′) *n.* 1 a mixture of lime, whiting, size, water, etc., for whitening walls, etc. 2 a cosmetic formerly used for making the skin fair 3 *a)* a glossing over or concealing of faults or defects in an effort to exonerate or give the appearance of soundness *b)* something said or done for this purpose ☆4 [Informal] *Sports* a defeat in which the loser scores no points —*vt.* 1 to cover with whitewash 2 to gloss over or conceal the faults or defects of; give a favorable interpretation of or a falsely virtuous appearance to ☆3 [Informal] *Sports* to defeat (an opponent) soundly —**white′wash′er** *n.*

white water foaming, whitish water, as in whitecaps or rapids

white-wa·ter (-wôt′ər) *adj.* of or having to do with recreational rafting, kayaking, etc. on rivers with rapids, fast currents, etc.

white whale BELUGA (sense 2)

white wine any light-colored wine: made either from the juice of light-colored grapes, or from the juice of dark-colored grapes with the skins removed right after pressing

white·wing (-wiŋ′) *n.* ☆[Old Informal] a street cleaner wearing a white uniform

white·wood (-wo͝od′) *n.* 1 any of a number of trees with white or light-colored wood, as the tulip tree, linden, cottonwood, etc. 2 the wood of any of these trees

☆**whit·ey** (hwīt′ē, wīt′-) *n.* [Slang] a white person or white people collectively: a usually hostile term of contempt —*adj. alt. sp. of* WHITY

whith·er (hwith′ər, with′-) [Archaic or Literary] *adv.* ⟦ME *whider* < OE *hwider*: see WHAT & HITHER⟧ to what place, point, condition, result, etc.? where?: used to introduce questions [*whither* are we drifting?] —***conj.*** **1** to which place, point, condition, result, etc.: used relatively [the island *whither* we drifted] **2** to whatever place, point, condition, result, etc.; wherever [let them go *whither* they will]

whith·er·so·ev·er (hwith′ər sō ev′ər, with′-) ***adv., conj.*** [Archaic] to whatever place; wheresoever

whith·er·ward (hwith′ər wərd, with′-) ***adv., conj.*** [Archaic] in what or which direction; where: used relatively or interrogatively

whit·ing[1] (hwīt′iŋ, wīt′-) ***n., pl.*** **-ings** or **-ing** ⟦ME < MDu *wijting* < *wit*, WHITE⟧ any of various edible marine fishes, including the silver hake, the corvina of the California coast, and various kingfishes

whit·ing[2] (hwīt′iŋ, wīt′-) ***n.*** ⟦ME *hwiting*: see WHITE, ***vt.*** + -ING⟧ powdered chalk used in making paints, inks, etc.

whit·ish (-ish) ***adj.*** somewhat white —**whit′ish·ness** ***n.***

whit·leath·er (hwit′leth′ər, wit′-) ***n.*** WHITE LEATHER

whit·low (hwit′lō, wit′-) ***n.*** ⟦ME *whitflowe, whitflawe*: orig. uncert.; ? akin to WHITE & FLAW[1]⟧ FELON[2]

Whit·man (hwit′mən, wit′-) **1 Marcus** 1802-47; U.S. pioneer & missionary in the Northwest **2 Walt(er)** 1819-92; U.S. poet

Whit·man·esque (-mə nesk′) ***adj.*** of or like Walt Whitman, his style, or his outlook; often, specif., democratic, expansive, exuberant, etc.: also **Whit·man′i·an** (-mā′nē ən)

Whit·mon·day (hwit′mun′dā, wit′-; -dē) ***n.*** ⟦after *Whitsunday*⟧ the Monday immediately following Whitsunday

Whit·ney[1] (hwit′nē, wit′-), **Eli** 1765-1825; U.S. inventor, esp. of the cotton gin

Whit·ney[2] (hwit′nē, wit′-), **Mount** ⟦after J. D. *Whitney* (1819-96), U.S. geologist⟧ mountain of the Sierra Nevada range, EC Calif.: highest peak in the U.S. outside of Alas.: 14,495 ft (4,418 m)

Whit·sun (hwit′sən, wit′-) ***adj.*** ⟦ME *whitsone* < *whitsondei*, understood as *Whitsun Day*: see fol.⟧ of or observed on Whitsunday or at Whitsuntide

Whit·sun·day (hwit′sun′dā, wit′-; -dē; -sən dā′) ***n.*** ⟦ME *whitsondei* < OE *Hwita Sunnandæg*, lit., white Sunday: prob. from the white garments of candidates for baptism⟧ PENTECOST (sense 2)

Whit·sun·tide (-sən tīd′) ***n.*** ⟦ME *whitsunetide*: see WHITSUN & TIDE[1]⟧ **1** the week beginning with Whitsunday **2** the first three days of that week

Whit·ti·er (hwit′ē ər, wit′-), **John Green·leaf** (grēn′lēf′) 1807-92; U.S. poet

Whit·ting·ton (hwit′iŋ tən, wit′-), **Richard** 1358?-1423; Eng. merchant: lord mayor of London: assoc. with various Eng. legends of a Dick Whittington

whit·tle (hwit′′l, wit′′l) ***vt.*** **-tled, -tling** ⟦< obs. *whittle*, a knife < ME *whyttel*, var. of *thwitel*, dim. < OE *thwitan*, to cut < IE base **twei-*, to strike, cut⟧ **1** *a)* to cut or pare thin shavings from (wood) with a knife *b)* to make or fashion (an object) in this manner **2** to reduce, destroy, or get rid of gradually, as if by whittling away with a knife: usually with *down, away*, etc. [to *whittle* down the cost of a project] —***vi.*** to whittle wood; often, specif., to cut away aimlessly at a stick, etc. —***n.*** [Obs.] a large knife —**whit′tler** ***n.***

Whit·tle (hwit′′l, wit′-), Sir **Frank** 1907-96; Eng. engineer & pioneer developer of jet propulsion engines

whit·y (hwīt′ē, wīt′-) ***adj.*** **-i·er, -i·est** WHITISH

whiz or **whizz** (hwiz, wiz) ***vi.*** **whizzed, whiz′zing** ⟦echoic⟧ **1** to move swiftly with or as with a buzzing or hissing sound [the bus *whizzed* by him] **2** to make the buzzing or hissing sound of something moving swiftly through the air **3** [Slang] to urinate —***vt.*** to cause to whiz, esp. by rotating rapidly —***n., pl.*** **whiz′zes 1** a whizzing sound or movement ☆**2** [see WIZ] *a)* [Informal] a person who is very quick, adroit, or skilled at something; expert [a *whiz* at math] *b)* [Old Slang] something strikingly excellent, attractive, etc. [a *whiz* of a car] **3** [Slang] the act of urinating: often in the phrase **take a whiz**

whiz-bang or **whizz-bang** (-baŋ′) ***n.*** **1** [Old Slang] a high explosive shell of great speed whose sound of explosion occurs immediately after its sound of flight; also, a fireworks device suggestive of this ☆**2** [Old Slang] WHIZ (***n.*** 2) —☆***adj.*** [Slang] extremely clever, useful, impressive, etc.

whiz kid [Slang] an exceptionally talented and comparatively young person, esp. a newcomer, who shows great promise in a particular field

who (ho͞o) ***pron.*** ⟦ME *who, ho, hwo* < OE *hwa*, masc. & fem., *hwæt*, neut., who? what? (akin to L *qui*): for IE base see WHAT⟧ **1** what or which person or persons: used to introduce a direct, indirect, or implied question [*who* is he? I asked *who* he was; I don't know *who* he is] **2** the person or persons that, or a person that: used to introduce a relative clause [the man *who* came to dinner] **3** any person or persons that; whoever: used as an indefinite relative with an implied antecedent ["*who* steals my purse steals trash"] —**as who should say** [Archaic] as if one should say

USAGE—*who* is the nominative form of this pronoun, *whom* the objective, and *whose* the possessive; *whose* is also the possessive pronominal adjective. The use of *who* rather than *whom* as the object of a verb or preposition is widespread at all levels of speech, although still objected to by many [*who* did you see there? *who* was it written by?]

WHO *abbrev.* World Health Organization

whoa (hwō, wō, hō) ***interj.*** ⟦for HO[1]⟧ stop: used esp. in directing a horse to stand still

who'd (ho͞od) *contraction* **1** who had **2** who would

☆**who·dun·it** (ho͞o′dun′it) ***n.*** ⟦< WHO + DONE (dial. pt. of DO[1]) + IT[1]: coined (1930) by D. Gordon in *American News of Books*⟧ [Informal] DETECTIVE STORY: often sp. **who′dun′nit**

who·ev·er (ho͞o ev′ər) ***pron.*** **1** any person that; whatever person [*whoever* wins gets a prize] **2** no matter what person [*whoever* said it, it's not so] **3** what person? who?: an emphatic interrogative [*whoever* told you that?]

whole (hōl) ***adj.*** ⟦ME (Midland) *hool*, for *hol, hal* < OE *hal*, healthy, whole, hale: akin to Ger *heil*, ON *heill* < IE base **kailo-*, sound, uninjured, auspicious > Welsh *coel*, omen⟧ **1** *a)* in sound health; not diseased or injured *b)* [Archaic] healed (said of a wound) **2** not broken, damaged, defective, etc.; intact [a *whole* yolk] **3** containing all the elements or parts; entire; complete [a *whole* set, *whole* blood] **4** not divided up; in a single unit [a *whole* cheese] **5** constituting the entire amount, extent, number, etc. [the *whole* night] **6** having both parents in common [a *whole* brother] **7** in all aspects of one's being, including the physical, mental, social, etc. [the *whole* man] **8** *Arith.* integral and not mixed or fractional [28 is a *whole* number] —***adv.*** [Informal] completely; absolutely [a *whole* new ballgame] —***n.*** **1** the entire amount, quantity, extent, or sum; totality [the *whole* of the estate] **2** a thing complete in itself, or a complete organization of integrated parts; a unity, entirety, or system —**SYN.** COMPLETE —**as a whole** as a complete unit; altogether —**a whole lot** (or **bunch**, etc.) **of** [Informal] very many [they ate *a whole lot of* hamburgers] —☆**(made** or **made up) out of whole cloth** ⟦< *whole cloth*, cloth as manufactured, before it is trimmed⟧ entirely imagined or fabricated; with no basis in fact —**on the whole** all things considered; in general —**whole′ness** ***n.***

whole blood 1 blood for transfusion from which none of the elements have been removed **2** FULL BLOOD (sense 1)

☆**whole gale** a wind whose speed is 55 to 63 miles per hour: see the Beaufort scale in the Reference Supplement

☆**whole·heart·ed** (-härt′id) ***adj.*** doing or done with all one's energy, enthusiasm, etc.; hearty; sincere; earnest —**whole′heart′ed·ly** ***adv.*** —**whole′heart′ed·ness** ***n.***

whole hog ☆[Slang] the entire way or extent: usually in the phrase **go the whole hog**

whole-hog (hōl′hôg′) ***adj., adv.*** ☆[Slang] without restraint or reservation; complete(ly)

whole life insurance life insurance that provides coverage over the entire lifetime of the policyholder: its fixed premiums establish a cash value that may be borrowed against

whole milk milk from which none of the butterfat or other elements have been removed

whole note *Music* a note held for the duration of four beats in common, or 4/4, time

whole number 1 zero or any positive multiple of 1 [28 is a *whole number*] **2** any integer or any natural number

whole·sale (-sāl′) ***n.*** ⟦ME *holesale* (< phr. *by hole sale*, by wholesale): see WHOLE & SALE⟧ the selling of goods in relatively large quantities and usually at lower prices than at retail, esp. such selling to retailers for resale to consumers —***adj.*** **1** of, connected with, or engaged in such selling [*wholesale* prices] **2** extensive, sweeping, or indiscriminate [*wholesale* criticism] —***adv.*** **1** in wholesale amounts or at wholesale prices **2** extensively, sweepingly, or indiscriminately [to reject proposals *wholesale*] — ***vt., vi.*** **-saled′, -sal′ing** to sell wholesale —**at wholesale** in wholesale quantities or at wholesale prices —**by wholesale 1** at wholesale **2** extensively, sweepingly, or indiscriminately —**whole′sal′er** ***n.***

whole·some (hōl′səm) ***adj.*** ⟦ME *holsom*, akin to ON *heilsamr*, Ger *heilsam*: see WHOLE & -SOME[1]⟧ **1** promoting or conducive to good health or well-being; healthful [a *wholesome* climate] **2** tending to improve the mind or character [a *wholesome* film for children] **3** characterized by health and vigor of mind and body; specif., morally sound [a *wholesome* young man] **4** tending to suggest health, or soundness [a *wholesome* look about the boys] —**whole′some·ly** ***adv.*** —**whole′some·ness** ***n.***

whole tone *Music* an interval consisting of two adjacent semitones: also **whole step**

☆**whole-wheat** (-hwēt′, -wēt′) ***adj.*** **1** ground from entire kernels of wheat [*whole-wheat* flour] **2** made with whole-wheat flour [*whole-wheat* bread]

whol·ism (hōl′iz′əm) ***n.*** *alt. sp. of* HOLISM —**whol·is′tic** ***adj.***

who'll (ho͞ol, ho͞o′əl) *contraction* **1** who will **2** who shall

whol·ly (hōl′lē, hō′lē) ***adv.*** ⟦ME *holi*: see WHOLE & -Y[2]⟧ to the whole amount or extent; totally; entirely

whol·ly-owned (-ōnd′) ***adj.*** designating or of a subsidiary company all of whose common stock is owned by another company

whom (ho͞om) ***pron.*** ⟦ME < OE *hwam*, dat. of *hwa*, WHO⟧ *objective form of* WHO: see the usage note at WHO

whom·ev·er (ho͞om ev′ər) ***pron.*** *objective form of* WHOEVER: see also the usage note at WHO

☆**whomp** (hwämp, wämp) [Informal] ***vt.*** ⟦echoic⟧ **1** to hit or strike heavily and loudly; thump **2** to defeat decisively —***n.*** the act or sound of whomping —**whomp up** to prepare quickly; whip up

whom·so·ev·er (ho͞om′sō ev′ər) ***pron.*** *objective form of* WHOSOEVER: see also the usage note at WHO

whoop (hwo͞op, wo͞op, ho͞op) ***n.*** ⟦ME *houpen*, to call, shout, echoic (or < ? OFr *houper*, to call afar off, cry out)⟧ a loud shout, cry, or noise; specif., *a)* a shrill and prolonged cry, as of excitement, exultation, ferocity, etc. *b)* a hoot, as of an owl *c)* the gasping sound marking the convulsive intake of air that immediately follows a fit of coughing in whooping cough —***vi.*** to utter, or move along with, a whoop or whoops —***vt.*** **1** to utter with a whoop or whoops **2** to drive, urge on, chase, bring about, etc. with whoops —☆**not worth a whoop** [Informal] worth nothing at all —☆**whoop it (or things) up** [Slang] **1** to create a noisy disturbance, as in celebrating **2** to create enthusiasm (*for*) —**whoop′er** *n.*

☆**whoop-de-do** or **whoop-de-doo** (hwo͝op′dē do͞o′, hwo͞op′-; wo͝op′-, wo͞op′-; ho͞op′-) [Informal] *n.* ⟦extended < prec.⟧ noisy or excited activity, commotion, or fuss; hoopla, ballyhoo, to-do, etc. —*interj.* WHOOPEE

whoop·ee (hwo͝op′ē, hwo͞o′pē; wo͝op′ē, wo͞o′pē) *interj.* ⟦< WHOOP⟧ [Informal] used to express great joy, exultation, merry abandon, etc. —*n.* [Informal] **1** an instance of shouting "whoopee" ☆**2** noisy merrymaking; revelry —☆**make whoopee** [Slang] **1** to revel boisterously **2** to make love

whoop·ee cushion (hwo͝op′ē, wo͝op′ē) a device for playing practical jokes, consisting of an air-filled pillow with a valve that emits a sound like that of gas being expelled from the bowels when someone sits upon it: also sp. **whoop′ie cushion**

whoop·er swan (ho͞o′pər, hwo͞o′-, wo͞o′-) ⟦so named from its loud cry⟧ a large swan (*Cygnus cygnus*) of the Old World, having a black-and-yellow bill

whoop·ing cough (ho͞o′piŋ, hwo͞o′-; ho͝op′iŋ) an acute infectious disease, usually affecting children, caused by a bacillus (*Bordetella pertussis*) and characterized by a mucous discharge from the nose and later by repeated attacks of coughing that end in a forced intake of breath, or whoop

☆**whooping crane** (ho͞o′piŋ, hwo͞o′-; wo͞o′-) a large, white, North American crane (*Grus americana*), noted for its whooping call: now nearly extinct

☆**whoop·la** (ho͞op′lä′, ho͝op′-) *n. alt. sp. of* HOOPLA

whoops (hwo͝ops, wo͝ops; hwo͞ops, wo͞ops) *interj.* used to express sudden or surprised dismay, or, sometimes, implied apology, after one has blundered, tripped, broken something, misspoken, etc.

whoosh (hwo͝osh, wo͝osh) *vi.* ⟦echoic⟧ **1** to make the quick, hissing, or rushing sound of something moving swiftly through the air **2** to move swiftly with or as with this sound [rockets *whooshed* by] —*vt.* to cause to whoosh —*n.* a sound or movement that whooshes —*interj.* **1** used to suggest this sound or movement **2** used to express surprise or sudden, strong feeling

whop (hwäp, wäp) [Informal] *vt., vi.* **whopped**, **whop′ping** ⟦< ME *wappen*, prob. echoic⟧ **1** to hit, strike, beat, etc. **2** to defeat decisively —*n.* a sharp, resounding blow, stroke, thump, etc.

whop·per (-ər) *n.* ⟦< prec.⟧ [Informal] **1** anything extraordinarily large **2** a heinous or outrageous lie

whop·ping (-iŋ) *adj.* ⟦< WHOP + -ING⟧ [Informal] extraordinarily large or great; colossal

whore (hôr; *occas.* ho͞or, ho͝or) *n.* ⟦ME *hore* < OE < or akin to ON *hora* < IE base **kā-*, to like, be fond of, desire > L *carus*, dear, precious, Latvian *kārs*, lecherous⟧ **1** PROSTITUTE **2** any woman who engages in promiscuous sexual intercourse —*vi.* **whored**, **whor′ing** **1** to be a whore **2** to have sexual intercourse with whores —**whore after** to debase oneself by pursuing something unworthy or in an unworthy manner

who're (ho͞o′ər, ho͝or) *contraction* who are

whore·dom (hôr′dəm) *n.* ⟦ME *hordom* < ON *hordomr*⟧ **1** prostitution or fornication **2** *Bible* idolatry: Hos. 4:12

whore·house (-hous′) *n.* ⟦ME *horehowse*⟧ a place where prostitutes are for hire; brothel

whore·mon·ger (-muŋ′gər, -mäŋ′gər) *n.* [Archaic] **1** a man who has sexual intercourse with or associates with whores **2** a pimp: also **whore′mas′ter** (-mas′tər)

whore·son (-sən) [Archaic] *n.* ⟦ME *hores son*, lit., son of a whore, bastard⟧ **1** a bastard **2** a scoundrel; knave: a general epithet of abuse —*adj.* vile; knavish

whor·ish (-ish) *adj.* of or typical of a whore; lewd, sluttish, etc.

whorl (hwôrl, hwurl) *n.* ⟦ME *whorwyl*, dial. var. of *wherwille*, WHIRL⟧ **1** a small flywheel on a spindle, as for regulating the speed of a spinning wheel **2** anything with a coiled or spiral appearance; specif., *a)* any of the circular ridges that form the design of a fingerprint *b) Bot.* a circular growth of leaves, petals, etc. about the same point on a stem *c) Zool.* any of the turns in a spiral shell —**whorled** *adj.*

whor·tle·ber·ry (hwurt′'l ber′ē) *n., pl.* **-ries** ⟦< SW Brit dial. form of earlier HURTLEBERRY⟧ **1** *a)* either of two European blueberries (*Vaccinium myrtillus* or *V. uliginosum*) having pink flowers and blue or blackish edible berries with a powdery bloom *b)* any of these berries ☆**2** any of various American plants, as the huckleberry

who's (ho͞oz) *contraction* **1** who is **2** who has

whose (ho͞oz) *pron.* ⟦ME *whos*, *hwas* < OE *hwæs*, gen. of *hwa*, WHO⟧ that or those belonging to whom: used without a following noun [*whose* is this? *whose* will look best?] —*possessive pronominal adj.* of, belonging to, made by, or done by whom or which [*whose* book is lost? a song *whose* popularity endures]

whose·so·ev·er (ho͞oz′sō ev′ər) *pron.* that or those of whomsoever —*possessive pronominal adj.* of or belonging to whomever An emphatic form

whos·ev·er (ho͞o zev′ər) *pron.* that or those of whomever —*possessive pronominal adj.* of or belonging to whomever

☆**who·sis** (ho͞o′zis) *n.* ⟦contr. < *who is this*⟧ [Slang] any person or thing: jocular substitute for a name forgotten or not known

who·so (ho͞o′sō) *pron.* ⟦ME *wha swa* < OE: see WHO & SO[1]⟧ [Archaic] whoever; whosoever

who·so·ev·er (ho͞o′sō ev′ər) *pron.* whoever: an emphatic form

who's who [*also* **W- W-**] **1** ⟦prob. < *Who's Who*, a trademarked book title⟧ a book or list of short biographies of prominent persons of a certain place, profession, etc. **2** the most important people or the elite, as of a certain profession

who've (ho͞ov) *contraction* who have

whr *abbrev.* watt-hour

whs or **whse** *abbrev.* warehouse

whump (hwump, wump) *n., vt., vi.* ⟦echoic⟧ [Informal] THUMP

why (hwī, wī) *adv.* ⟦ME *hwi* < OE, instrumental case of *hwæt*, WHAT⟧ for what reason, cause, or purpose? with what motive?: used in direct, indirect, and implied questions [*why* did he go? he told her *why* he went] —*conj.* **1** because of which; on account of which [he knows of no reason *why* you shouldn't go] **2** the reason for which [do you know *why* he went? this is *why* he went] —*n., pl.* **whys** the reason, cause, motive, purpose, etc. [never mind the *why* and wherefore] —*interj.* **1** used to express surprise, impatience, indignation, etc. **2** used as an expletive, to preface a remark —**why not** [Informal] all right; it's acceptable: used to express qualified approval of what has been proposed, suggested, etc.

whyd·ah (bird) (hwid′ə, wid′ə) ⟦altered < *widow bird*, by assoc. with *Ouidah* (sometimes sp. *Whidah*), seaport in Benin⟧ any of several chiefly brown-and-black, African passerine birds (family Ploceidae): the male has long, drooping tail feathers during the breeding season

WI *abbrev.* **1** West Indian **2** West Indies **3** Wisconsin

WIA *abbrev.* wounded in action

Wic·ca (wik′ə) *n.* ⟦OE, sorcerer (fem. *wicce*): see WITCH⟧ a form of contemporary witchcraft practiced esp. in English-speaking countries, characterized by pagan nature worship and white magic —**Wic′can** (-ən) *adj., n.*

Wich·i·ta (wich′ə tô′) ⟦after the *Wichita* (cf. Caddo *wi·c'ita*, Osage *wícita*), a Caddoan people who relocated in a village at the site of the city in Kansas as Civil War refugees (1862-67)⟧ city in S Kans., on the Arkansas River

Wichita Falls ⟦see prec.: the *Wichita* had lived near the site of this city from late 18th c. to the Civil War⟧ city in NC Tex.

wick[1] (wik) *n.* ⟦ME *wicke* < OE *weoca*, akin to Ger *wieche*, wick yarn < IE base **weg-*, to weave: see VEIL⟧ a piece of cord or tape, or a thin bundle of threads, in a candle, oil lamp, cigarette lighter, etc., designed to absorb fuel by capillary attraction and, when lighted, to burn with a small, steady flame —*vt.* to draw or absorb (water, perspiration, etc.) by capillary attraction [a fabric that *wicks* sweat away from the skin]

wick[2] (wik) *n.* ⟦ME *wik* < OE *wic*, akin to MHG *wich*, village < early WGmc borrowing < L *vicus*, group of houses: see ECO-⟧ a village, town, or hamlet: now archaic except as compounded (often in the form **-wich**) in place names, as in *Warwick*, *Greenwich*

wick·ed (wik′id) *adj.* ⟦ME < *wikke*, evil, akin to OE *wicce*, WITCH⟧ **1** *a)* morally bad or wrong; acting or done with evil intent; depraved *b)* vicious; cruel [the *wicked* king] **2** painful, unpleasant, etc. [a *wicked* blow on the head] **3** naughty in a playful way; mischievous ☆**4** [Slang] showing great skill [he plays a *wicked* game of golf] —SYN. BAD[1] —**wick′ed·ly** *adv.* —**wick′ed·ness** *n.*

wick·er (wik′ər) *n.* ⟦ME *wiker* < Scand, as in Swed dial. *viker*, Dan dial. *vigger*, willow, Swed *vika*, to bend < IE base **weig-* > WEAK⟧ **1** a thin, flexible twig; withe **2** *a)* such twigs or long, woody strips woven together, as in making baskets or furniture *b)* WICKERWORK (sense 1) —*adj.* made of or covered with wicker

wick·er·work (-wurk′) *n.* **1** things made of wicker **2** WICKER (*n.* 2*a*)

wick·et (wik′it) *n.* ⟦ME *wiket* < NormFr (for OFr *guichet*), dim. < MDu *wijk*, a curve < IE **weig-* > WEAK⟧ **1** a small door or gate, esp. one set in or near a larger door or gate **2** a small window or opening, as for a bank teller or in a box office **3** a small gate for regulating the flow of water to a water wheel or for emptying a canal lock **4** ⟦from orig. resemblance to a gate⟧ *Cricket a)* either of two sets of three vertical sticks (*stumps*) each, with two small pieces (*bails*) resting on top of them *b)* the playing space between the two wickets *c)* an unplayed or unfinished inning *d)* a player's turn at bat: see also STICKY WICKET ☆**5** *Croquet* any of the small wire arches through which the balls must be hit

wick·et·keep·er (-kēp′ər) *n. Cricket* the fielder whose position is just behind the batsman's wicket

☆**wick·i·up** (wik′ē up′) *n.* ⟦< Fox *wiikiyaapi*, house: orig. referred to houses of the style of Algonquian peoples of the Great Lakes region; akin to WIGWAM⟧ **1** a small, temporary dwelling or shelter of grass, brush, etc. over a frame, traditionally used by Indian peoples of the Great Basin and SW U.S. **2** any crude shack or shelter

Wick·liffe (wik′lif), **John** *alt. sp. of* John WYCLIFFE

Wick·low (wik′lō) county in Leinster province, SE Ireland, on the Irish Sea: 782 sq mi (2,025 sq km)

☆**wic·o·py** (wik′ə pē) *n.* ⟦< Eastern Algonquian: cf. Abenaki *wigəbi*, *wìkəpi*, inner bark, esp. of basswood or leatherwood⟧ **1** *a)* LEATHERWOOD *b)* BASSWOOD (sense 1) **2** any of several species of willow herb, as fireweed

wid·der·shins (wid′ər shinz′) *adv.* ⟦< MLowG *weddersinnes* < MHG *widersinnes* < *wider*, against (akin to WITH) + *sinnes*, gen. of *sin*, way, direction⟧ in a direction contrary to the usual or expected; specif., counterclockwise

wide (wīd) *adj.* **wid′er**, **wid′est** ⟦ME < OE *wid*, akin to Ger *weit* < IE **wi-itos*, lit., gone apart (< bases **wi-*, apart + **ei-*, to go) > L *vitare*, lit., to go away from, avoid⟧ **1** extending over a large area; esp., extending over a larger area from side to side than is usual or normal [a *wide* bed] **2** of a specified extent from side to side [three miles *wide*] **3** of great extent, range, or inclusiveness [a *wide* variety, *wide* reading] **4** roomy; ample; loose; full [*wide* pants] **5** open or extended to full width [eyes *wide* with fear] 6 landing, striking, or ending far from the point, issue, etc. aimed at: usually with *of* [*wide* of the target] ☆7 having a relatively low proportion of protein: said of livestock feed 8 *Phonet.* LAX (*adj.* 5) —*adv.* **wid′er, wid′est** 1 over a relatively large area; widely [to travel far and *wide*] 2 to a large or full extent; fully [with the door *wide* open] 3 so as to miss the point, issue, etc. aimed at; astray [shots that went *wide*] —*n.* 1 [Rare] a wide area 2 *Cricket* a ball bowled out of the batsman's reach, counted as a run for the batting team —*SYN.* BROAD —**wide′ly** *adv.* —**wide′ness** *n.*

-wide (wīd) *combining form* existing or extending throughout (a specified area) [*statewide*]

wide-an·gle (wīd′aŋ′gəl) *adj.* designating or of a kind of camera lens that covers a wider angle of view than the ordinary lens

wide-a·wake (-ə wāk′) *adj.* 1 completely awake 2 alert —*SYN.* WATCHFUL —**wide′-a·wake′ness** *n.*

wide boy ⟦< WIDE, in slang senses, wide-awake, shrewd, dishonest⟧ [Brit. Slang] a shrewd and unscrupulous man, esp. one who engages in petty crime, shady dealings, etc.

wide-eyed (-īd′) *adj.* 1 with the eyes opened widely, as because of surprise or fear 2 naive or unsophisticated

wid·en (wīd′'n) *vt., vi.* to make or become wide or wider

wide-o·pen (wīd′ō′pən) *adj.* 1 opened wide 2 not enclosed, fenced-in, etc.; unobstructed; clear [*wide-open* spaces] 3 *a)* not limited or restricted [a *wide-open* style of football] ☆*b)* having no laws, or being lax in enforcing laws, prohibiting or regulating prostitution, gambling, liquor sales, etc. [a *wide-open* city]

wide-rang·ing (wīd′rān′jiŋ) *adj.* covering a wide extent; extensive

☆**wide receiver** *Football* a player eligible to receive a pass who usually takes a position on or near the line of scrimmage, but at some distance from the other members of the offensive team: also called **wide′out′** (-out′) *n.*

wide·screen or **wide-screen** (-skrēn′) *adj.* 1 designating or of a film made for projection on a screen much wider than it is high: usually from a ratio of 1.66 to 1 up to 2.55 to 1 2 designating, of, or designed for a similar format for video, with a ratio of 1.78 to 1 or more [a *widescreen* TV set] —*n.* a format using a widescreen ratio, as for presenting films in video format or high-definition TV

wide·spread (-spred′) *adj.* spread widely; esp., *a)* widely extended [*widespread* arms] *b)* distributed, circulated, or occurring over a wide area or extent [*widespread* benefits, *widespread* rumors]

widg·eon (wij′ən) *n., pl.* **-eons** or **-eon** *alt. sp. of* WIGEON

☆**widg·et** (wij′it) *n.* ⟦altered < GADGET⟧ any small, unspecified gadget or device, esp. one that is hypothetical

wid·ow (wid′ō) *n.* ⟦ME *widwe* < OE *widewe*, akin to Ger *witwe*, L *vidua* < IE **widhewo-*, separated < base **weidh-*, to separate: see DIVIDE⟧ 1 a woman who has outlived her spouse; esp., such a woman who has not remarried ☆2 *Card Games* an extra group of cards dealt when the hands are dealt, typically for use by the winning bidder 3 *Printing* an incomplete line, as that ending a paragraph, carried over to the top of a new page or column ☆4 [Informal] a woman whose spouse is often away indulging in a specified hobby, sport, etc. [a golf *widow*] —*vt.* to cause to become a widow or widower: usually in the past participle [*widowed* by the war] —**wid′ow·hood′** *n.*

wid·ow·bird (wid′ō burd′) *n.* ⟦calque of Port *viuva*, widowbird, lit., widow (< L *vidua*: see prec.): from the resemblance of its dark plumage to a widow's mourning clothes⟧ WHYDAH (BIRD)

wid·ow·er (wid′ō ər) *n.* ⟦ME *widewer*, extended < *wedow*, widower < OE *widewa*, masc. of *widewe*, WIDOW⟧ a man who has outlived his spouse; esp., such a man who has not remarried —**wid′ow·er·hood′** *n.*

widow's cruse an apparently inexhaustible supply: 2 Kings 4:1-7

widow's mite a small gift or contribution freely given by one who can scarcely afford it: Mark 12:41-44

widow's peak ⟦< the notion that it is an omen of early widowhood⟧ a V-shaped portion of the hairline, pointing downward at or toward the center of the forehead

☆**widow's walk** a platform with a rail around it, built onto the roof of some New England houses, as along the coast, formerly for observing ships at sea

width (width, witth) *n.* ⟦< WIDE, by analogy with LENGTH, BREADTH⟧ 1 the fact, quality, or condition of being wide; wideness 2 the size of something in terms of how wide it is; distance from side to side 3 a piece of something of a certain width [two *widths* of cloth]

width·wise (-wīz′) *adv., adj.* in the direction of the width: also **width′ways′** (-wāz′)

Wi·du·kind (vē′do͞o kint) 8th cent. A.D.; Saxon warrior: leader of the Saxons against Charlemagne

Wie·land (vē′länt′) 1 **Chris·toph Mar·tin** (kris′tôf mär′tēn) 1733-1813; Ger. novelist, poet, & translator 2 **Hein·rich Ot·to** (hīn′riH ô′tō) 1877-1957; Ger. chemist

wield (wēld) *vt.* ⟦ME *welden*, blend of OE *wealdan* & *wieldan*, with form < the latter: akin to Ger *walten* < IE base **wal-*, to be strong > L *valere*, to be strong⟧ 1 to handle and use (a tool or weapon), esp. with skill and control 2 to exercise (power, influence, etc.) 3 [Obs.] to govern or rule —*SYN.* HANDLE —**wield′er** *n.*

wield·y (wēl′dē) *adj.* **wield′i·er, wield′i·est** that can be wielded easily; manageable

Wien (vēn) *Ger. name for* VIENNA

☆**wie·ner** (wē′nər) *n.* ⟦short for *wienerwurst* < Ger *Wiener wurst*, Vienna sausage⟧ 1 FRANKFURTER 2 VIENNA SAUSAGE: also **wie′ner·wurst′** (-wurst′) 3 [Slang] *a)* WEENIE (sense 2) *b)* WEENIE (sense 3)

Wie·ner (wē′nər), **Nor·bert** (nôr′bərt) 1894-1964; U.S. mathematician & pioneer in cybernetics

Wie·ner schnit·zel (vē′nər shnit′səl, wē′-) ⟦Ger < *Wiener*, of Vienna + *schnitzel*, cutlet: see SCHNITZEL⟧ a breaded veal cutlet, traditionally garnished with a slice or wedge of lemon: also sp. **wie′ner·schnit′zel** *n.*

wie·nie (wē′nē) *n.* 1 [Informal] WIENER (sense 2) 2 [Slang] *a)* WEENIE (sense 2) *b)* WEENIE (sense 3)

Wies·ba·den (vēs′bäd′'n) resort city in W Germany, on the Rhine: capital of the state of Hesse

wife (wīf) *n., pl.* **wives** (wīvz) ⟦ME < OE *wif*, woman, akin to Swed *viv*, Ger *weib* < ? IE base **weip-*, to twist, turn, wrap, in sense "the hidden or veiled person"⟧ 1 a woman: archaic or dial., except as used in such compounds as *midwife, alewife*, etc. 2 *a)* a woman with reference to the person to whom she is married *b)* any married woman —**take to wife** [Archaic] to marry (a specified woman) —**wife′hood′** *n.* —**wife′less** *adj.* —**wife′ly** *adj.* **-li·er, -li·est**

☆**wife-beat·er** (wīf′bēt′ər) *n.* ⟦from the violent stereotype assoc. with men wearing such a shirt this way⟧ [Slang] a men's undershirt resembling a tank top, esp. when worn without an outer shirt: also written **wife beater**

☆**Wif·fle ball** (wif′əl) ⟦< *Wiffle*, a trademark⟧ WHIFFLE BALL

☆**Wi-Fi** (wī′fī′) ⟦< *wi*(*reless*) *fi*(*delity*), after HI-FI⟧ *service mark for* a wireless local area network that uses radio waves to connect computers and other devices to the internet: also written **WiFi**

wig (wig) *n.* ⟦shortened < PERIWIG⟧ 1 *a)* a removable covering of real or synthetic hair for the head, worn as part of a costume, to conceal baldness, etc. *b)* TOUPEE ☆2 [Slang] variously, the hair, head, or mind —*vt.* **wigged, wig′ging** 1 to furnish with a wig or wigs ☆2 [Slang] *a)* to annoy, upset, anger, etc. *b)* to make excited, ecstatic, frenzied, crazy, etc. (often with *out*) 3 [Brit. Informal] to scold, censure, rebuke, etc.: archaic except as a part. noun [gave him a good *wigging*] —☆*vi.* [Slang] to be or become upset, excited, crazy, etc.: often with *out*

wig·an (wig′ən) *n.* ⟦after fol., where first made⟧ a canvaslike cotton cloth used to stiffen hems, lapels, etc.

Wig·an (wig′ən) city in Greater Manchester, NW England

wi·geon (wij′ən) *n.* ⟦prob. < MFr *vigeon* < L *vipio*, small crane, of Balearic orig.⟧ any of certain wild freshwater ducks; esp., *a)* the **Eurasian wigeon** (*Anas penelope*), the male of which has a cream-colored crown and reddish-brown head and neck *b)* BALDPATE

Wig·gin (wig′in), **Kate Douglas** (born *Kate Douglas Smith*) 1856-1923; U.S. educator & writer of children's novels

wig·gle (wig′əl) *vt., vi.* **-gled, -gling** ⟦ME *wigelen*, prob. < MDu & MLowG *wiggelen*, freq. of *wiggen*, to move from side to side, akin to OE *wegan*, to move: for IE base see WAG[1]⟧ to move or cause to move with short, jerky or twisting motions from side to side; wriggle shakily or sinuously —*n.* the act or an instance of wiggling

wig·gler (wig′lər) *n.* 1 a person or thing that wiggles 2 WRIGGLER

wiggle room [Informal] space, room, or opportunity to make adjustments or to deviate from a standard or requirement

wig·gly (-lē) *adj.* **-gli·er, -gli·est** 1 that wiggles; wiggling 2 having a form that suggests wiggling; wavy [a *wiggly* line]

wig·gy (wig′ē) *adj.* **-gi·er, -gi·est** 1 [Now Rare] *a)* wearing a wig *b)* pompously formal or elegant ☆2 [Slang] wild, exciting, crazy, etc.

wight[1] (wīt) *n.* ⟦ME < OE *wiht*, akin to Ger *wicht*, creature, Goth *waihts*, thing < IE base **wekti-*, thing > OSlav *vešti*, thing⟧ 1 [Obs.] a living being; creature 2 a human being; person: archaic except when used in a patronizing or commiserating sense

wight[2] (wīt) *adj.* ⟦ME *wihte* < ON *vigt*, neut. of *vigr*, skilled in arms, akin to OE *wigan*, to fight: for IE base see VICTOR⟧ [Now Chiefly Dial.] strong, brisk, active, brave, etc.

Wight (wīt), **Isle of** island in the English Channel, off the S coast of Hampshire, constituting a county of England: 147 sq mi (381 sq km)

☆**wig·let** (wig′lit) *n.* a small wig; specif., a woman's hairpiece designed to supplement her own hair

Wig·ner (wig′nər), **Eugene Paul** 1902-95; U.S. physicist, born in Hungary

Wig·town (wig′tən) former county & former district of SW Scotland

wig·wag (wig′wag′) *vt., vi.* **-wagged′, -wag′ging** ⟦< obs. *wig*, to move + WAG[1]⟧ 1 to move back and forth; wag 2 to send (a message) by waving flags, lights, etc. back and forth using a code —*n.* 1 the act of sending messages in this way 2 a message so sent —**wig′wag′ger** *n.*

☆**wig·wam** (wig′wäm′, -wôm′) *n.* ⟦< Abenaki *wìkəwam*, house⟧ a traditional dwelling of Indian peoples of E North America, consisting typically of a dome-shaped framework of poles covered with rush mats or sheets of bark

Cherokee wigwam

☆**wik·i** (wik′ē) *n.* ⟦Haw, lit., fast⟧ 1 a Web application that allows any visitor to a website to edit that website's content 2 such an editable website

Wil·ber·force (wil′bər fôrs′), **William** 1759-1833; Eng. statesman & vigorous opponent of slavery

Wil·bur (wil′bər) *n.* ⟦OE *Wilburh*: prob. a place name < **Wiligburh*, lit., willow town⟧ a masculine name

☆**wil·co** (wil′kō) ***interj.*** ⟦*wil(l) co(mply)*⟧ I will comply with your request: used in radio communication

wild (wīld) ***adj.*** ⟦ME *wilde* < OE, akin to Ger *wild*, prob. < IE base **wel-*, shaggy hair, unkempt > WOOL, VOLE⟧ **1** living or growing in its original, natural state and not normally domesticated or cultivated [*wild* flowers, *wild* animals] **2** not lived in or cultivated; overgrown, waste, etc. [*wild* land] **3** not civilized; savage [a *wild* tribe] **4** not easily restrained or regulated; not controlled or controllable; unruly, rough, lawless, etc. [*wild* children] **5** characterized by a lack of social or moral restraint; unbridled in pursuing pleasure; dissolute, orgiastic, etc. [a *wild* rake, a *wild* party] **6** violently disturbed; turbulent; stormy [a *wild* seacoast] **7** in a state of intense excitement; specif., *a)* eager or enthusiastic, as with desire or anticipation [*wild* with delight] *b)* angered, frenzied, frantic, crazed, etc. [*wild* with desperation] **8** in a state of disorder, disarrangement, confusion, etc. [*wild* hair] **9** fantastically impractical; visionary [a *wild* scheme] **10** *a)* showing a lack of sound judgment; reckless; imprudent [a *wild* wager] *b)* based on little or no evidence [a *wild* guess] **11** going wide of the mark aimed at; missing the target [a *wild* swing in boxing] **12** [Slang] extraordinary; remarkable [a summer vacation that was really *wild*] **13** *Card Games* designated as having any rank or suit that a player holding it chooses: said of a particular card or any of a small group of cards [the dealer announced that deuces would be *wild* for the next hand] **—*adv.*** in a wild manner; wildly; without aim or control [to shoot *wild*] **—*n.*** [*usually pl.*] a wilderness or wasteland **—run wild** to grow, exist, or behave without control **—the wild** the wilderness, nature, the out-of-doors, etc. **—wild′ly *adv.* —wild′ness *n.***

☆**wild allspice** SPICEBUSH (sense 1)

wild boar a hog (*Sus scrofa*) living wild in Europe, Africa, and Asia, from which domestic hogs were derived

wild card 1 *Card Games* a card that has been declared wild ☆**2** *Sports* any of the teams, other than those that finish in first and sometimes second place, that qualify for a championship playoff **3** an element that cannot be predicted or controlled

wild carrot a common, inedible, biennial weed (*Daucus carota*) of the umbel family, with finely divided foliage and umbels of white flowers: the cultivated, edible carrot was derived from it

wild·cat (wīld′kat′) ***n., pl.* -cats′** or **-cat′ 1** *a)* any of a large group of fierce, medium-sized, undomesticated cats, including the bobcat, Canada lynx, ocelot, serval, and caracal *b)* a house cat that has escaped from domestication (in this sense, usually written **wild cat**) **2** any person regarded as like a wildcat in fierceness, aggressiveness, etc. ☆**3** an unsound or risky business scheme ☆**4** an oil well drilled in an area not previously known to have oil **—*adj.*** ☆**1** unsound or financially risky [a *wildcat* venture] ☆**2** designating or of an enterprise or undertaking that is illegal, unethical, irregular, unauthorized, etc.; specif., designating a labor strike in violation of a contract and not officially authorized by the union representing the strikers **—**☆***vi.* -cat′ted, -cat′ting 1** to drill for oil in an area previously considered unproductive **2** to engage in wildcat enterprises, etc. **—**☆**wild′cat′ter *n.***

Wilde (wīld), **Oscar (Fingal O'Flahertie Wills)** 1854-1900; Brit. playwright, poet, & novelist, born in Ireland

wil·de·beest (wil′də bēst′, vil′-) ***n., pl.* -beests′** or **-beest′** ⟦Afrik < Du *wild*, wild + *beeste*, beast⟧ GNU

wil·der (wil′dər) ***vt., vi.*** ⟦prob. < WILDERNESS⟧ [Archaic] **1** to lose or cause to lose one's way **2** to bewilder or become bewildered

Wil·der (wil′dər) **1 Billy** (born *Samuel Wilder*) 1906-2002; U.S. film writer & director, born in Austria-Hungary **2 Laura In·galls** (iŋ′gəlz) (Mrs. *Almanzo Wilder*; born *Laura Elizabeth Ingalls*) 1867-1957; U.S. author of children's books **3 Thorn·ton (Niven)** (thôrnt′'n) 1897-1975; U.S. novelist & playwright

wil·der·ness (wil′dər nis) ***n.*** ⟦ME *wildernesse* < *wilderne*, wild place (< OE *wilddeor*, wild animal < *wilde*, WILD + *deor*, animal, DEER) + *-nesse*, -NESS⟧ **1** an uncultivated, uninhabited region; waste; wild **2** any barren, empty, or open area, as of ocean **3** a large, confused mass or tangle **4** [Obs.] a wild condition or quality **—*SYN.*** WASTE

Wil·der·ness (wil′dər nis), **the** woodland region in NE Va., south of the Rapidan River: scene of a Civil War battle (May, 1864) between the armies of Grant and Lee

☆**wilderness area** an area of public land, as of virgin forest, preserved in its natural state by prohibiting by law the construction of roads, buildings, etc.

wild-eyed (wīld′īd′) ***adj.* 1** staring in a wild, distracted, or demented way **2** fantastically foolish, impractical, or extreme [*wild-eyed* ideas]

wild fig CAPRIFIG

wild·fire (-fīr′) ***n.* 1** [Obs.] *a)* a highly destructive fire *b)* a highly flammable substance; specif., GREEK FIRE **2** [Now Rare] WILL-O'-THE-WISP **3** a large, intense fire, usually in an uninhabited area, that is difficult to bring under control **—spread like wildfire** to be disseminated widely and rapidly: said as of a rumor

wild·flow·er (-flou′ər) ***n.* 1** any flowering plant growing wild in fields, woods, etc. **2** its flower Also written **wild flower**

wild·fowl (-foul′) ***n., pl.* -fowls′** or **-fowl′** a wild bird, esp. a game bird, as a wild duck, pheasant, or quail: also written **wild fowl**

wild geranium ☆any of various geraniums found in meadows and woods; esp., a wildflower (*Geranium maculatum*) of the E U.S., having deeply lobed leaves and lavender flowers

wild ginger any of a genus (*Asarum*) of perennial wildflowers of the birthwort family, found in temperate areas of the Northern Hemisphere; esp., a creeping herb (*A. canadense*) of E North America with two heart-shaped leaves, small brownish flowers, and an aromatic root used as a ginger substitute

wild-goose chase any search, pursuit, or endeavor regarded as being futile

wild hog 1 WILD BOAR **2** PECCARY

wild hyacinth ☆**1** a camass (*Camassia scilloides*) of the E U.S., with bluish flowers **2** WOOD HYACINTH

☆**wild indigo** BAPTISIA

wild·ing (wīl′diŋ) ***n.* 1** *a)* a wild plant; esp., a wild apple tree *b)* its fruit **2** a plant originally cultivated, but growing wild **3** [Rare] a wild animal **—*adj.*** [Old Poet.] not cultivated or domesticated; wild

wild lettuce any of various wild species of lettuce, having small, dandelionlike flower heads, milky juice, and, often, prickly foliage; esp., a lettuce (*Lactuca canadensis*) of E North America

wild·life (wīld′līf′) ***n.*** all wild animals collectively; esp., the wild vertebrates hunted by humans

wild·ling (wīld′liŋ) ***n.*** ⟦WILD + -LING[1]⟧ an uncultivated plant or undomesticated animal

wild mustard any of several weedy mustards, esp. charlock

wild oats ☆**1** a woodland plant (*Uvularia sessilifolia*) of the lily family, with small, drooping, yellowish flowers, native to E North America **2** any of several wild grasses (genus *Avena*); esp., the wild progenitor (*A. fatua*) of the cultivated oat, having strong, twisted awns and commonly occurring as a weed, esp. in the W U.S.: also **wild oat —sow one's wild oats** to be promiscuous or dissolute in one's youth before settling down

wild olive any of various trees resembling the olive or bearing olivelike fruits, as the Russian olive

wild pansy an uncultivated pansy, esp. a European species (*Viola tricolor*) that is the ancestor of the garden pansy, with petals in combinations of white, yellow, and purple

wild parsnip a tall, stout, biennial weed (*Pastinaca sativa*) of the umbel family, with pinnately compound leaves: regarded as the ancestor of the cultivated parsnip

wild pink 1 *a)* any of several catchflies ☆*b)* an early flowering catchfly (*Silene caroliniana*) of the E U.S., having lance-shaped leaves and bright-pink flowers in clusters ☆**2** an arethusa

☆**wild pitch** *Baseball* a misplay in which the pitcher throws a pitch so wildly that the catcher cannot catch or control it and a base runner advances to another base as a result: cf. PASSED BALL

wild rice 1 a tall, annual, aquatic grass (*Zizania aquatica*) of the U.S. and Canada, found along the marshy borders of lakes and streams **2** its edible grain

wild rose any of various roses growing wild, as eglantine

wild rubber rubber obtained from uncultivated trees

wild rye any of a genus (*Elymus*) of perennial grasses having erect or drooping, usually bristly, spikes

☆**wild turkey** any wild form of the North American domesticated turkey: see TURKEY (sense 1*a*)

wild type the ordinary phenotype that is characteristic of most members of a species under natural conditions

☆**wild vanilla** a perennial plant (*Trilisa odoratissima*) of the composite family, with vanilla-scented foliage: found in the SE U.S.

☆**Wild West** [*also* **w- W-**] the W U.S. in its early frontier period of lawlessness

☆**Wild West show** a circuslike spectacle featuring horsemanship and other feats by cowboys, Indians, etc.

wild·wood (wīld′wood′) ***n.*** a natural woodland or forest, esp. when unfrequented by humans

wile (wīl) ***n.*** ⟦ME < Late OE *wil* < OE *wigle*, magic, divination, akin to *wiglian*, to take auspices, *wicce*, WITCH⟧ **1** a sly trick; deceitful artifice; stratagem **2** a beguiling or coquettish trick: *usually used in pl.* **3** [Now Rare] craftiness; guile **—*vt.* wiled, wil′ing** to beguile; lure **—*SYN.*** TRICK **—wile away** ⟦by confusion with WHILE⟧ to while away (time, etc.)

Wil·fred or **Wil·frid** (wil′frid) ***n.*** ⟦OE *Wilfrith* < *willa*, a wish, WILL[1] + *frithu*, peace < Gmc **frithu* < IE **pritu-*, friendship < base **pri-*, to like > Sans *priya-*, dear, beloved⟧ a masculine name

wil·ful (wil′fəl) ***adj. alt. sp. of*** WILLFUL

Wil·helm (vil′helm) ***n. Ger. var. of*** WILLIAM[1]

Wilhelm II (born *Friedrich Wilhelm Viktor Albert*) 1859-1941; emperor of Germany & king of Prussia (1888-1918): called *Kaiser Wilhelm*

Wil·hel·mi·na[1] (wil′hel mē′nə, wil′ə-) ***n.*** ⟦Ger *Wilhelmine*, fem. of *Wilhelm*: see WILLIAM[1]⟧ a feminine name

Wil·hel·mi·na[2] (vil′hel mē′nä) (born *Wilhelmina Helena Pauline Maria*) 1880-1962; queen of the Netherlands (1890-1948)

Wil·hel·mine (vil′hel mēn′, wil′-; -mīn′) ***adj.*** of, characteristic of, or like Wilhelm II of Germany, his reign, etc.

wil·i·ly (wī′lə lē) ***adv.*** in a wily manner

wil·i·ness (wī′lē nis) ***n.*** a wily quality or condition

Wilkes (wilks) **1 Charles** 1798-1877; U.S. naval officer & explorer **2 John** 1727?-97; Eng. political reformer

Wilkes-Bar·re (wilks′bar′ē, -bar′ə, -bar′) ⟦after John WILKES & Col. Isaac *Barré* (1726-1802), Brit officer⟧ city in NE Pa., on the Susquehanna River

Wilkes Land region of Antarctica, on the Indian Ocean south of Australia

Wil·kins (wil′kinz) **1** Sir **(George) Hubert** 1888-1958; Austral. polar explorer **2 Maurice H(ugh) F(rederick)** 1916-2004; Eng. biophysicist, born in

New Zealand: helped determine the structure of DNA **3 Roy** 1901-81; U.S. civil rights leader

Wil·kin·son (wil′kin sən), Sir **Geoffrey** 1921-96; Brit. chemist

will[1] (wil) *n.* ⟦ME *wille* < OE *willa*, akin to Ger *wille*, *willen* < IE base **wel-*, to wish, choose > L *velle*, to wish, *voluptas*, pleasure⟧ **1** the power of making a reasoned choice or decision or of controlling one's own actions [a man of weak *will*] **2** *a)* strong and fixed purpose; determination [where there's a *will* there's a way] *b)* energy and enthusiasm [to work with a *will*] **3** disposition or attitude toward others [a man of good *will*] **4** *a)* the particular desire, purpose, pleasure, choice, etc. of a certain person or group [what is your *will?*] *b)* a compelling command or decree [the *will* of the people] **5** *Law* *a)* the legal statement of a person's wishes concerning the disposal of his or her property after death *b)* the document containing this —*vt.* ⟦ME *willien* < OE *willian* < *willan*, to desire: see fol.⟧ **1** to have as the object of one's will; desire; want [to *will* another's happiness, to *will* to survive] **2** to control or influence by the power of the will [to *will* oneself into an action, to *will* others into submission] **3** *Law* to bequeath by a will —*vi.* **1** to exert one's will [to succeed by *willing*] **2** to wish, desire, prefer, or choose [to do as one *wills*] —**at will** when one wishes; at one's discretion

SYN.—**will**, the more inclusive term here, basically denotes the power of choice and deliberate action or the intention resulting from the exercise of this power [freedom of the *will*, the *will* to succeed]; **volition** stresses the exercise of the will in making a choice or decision [he came of his own *volition*]

will[2] (wil) *v.aux. pt.* **would** ⟦ME *willen* < OE *willan*, to be willing, desire, akin to Ger *wollen*, will: for IE base see prec.⟧ **1** used to indicate simple future time [when *will* she be able to travel? I *will* bring the dessert] **2** used to express determination, compulsion, or obligation [you *will* listen to me; he *will* have his own way; I *will* have you know that I was here first] **3** used to express inclination or inevitability [boys *will* be boys] **4** used in polite questions [*will* you have some wine?] **5** used to express habit or customary practice [they *will* talk shop for hours on end] **6** used to express expectation or surmise [that *will* be his wife with him, I suppose] **7** used to express possibility [this drawer *will* open with a little effort] —*vt.* [Obs.] to wish; desire [what *will* you, Master?]

USAGE—the distinction between WILL[2] (for second and third person subjects) and SHALL (for the first person) in expressing simple future time or determination, etc. is largely an artificial one and today is virtually nonexistent in North American English; except for the use of SHALL in certain formal contexts (see SHALL) and other meanings specific to each, WILL[2] and SHALL and their respective past tenses WOULD and SHOULD are used interchangeably, with WILL[2] (and WOULD) being the preferred form in all persons

will·a·ble (wil′ə bəl) *adj.* that can be willed, wished, determined, etc.

Wil·lam·ette (wi lam′it) ⟦< ? AmInd place name⟧ river in W Oreg., flowing north into the Columbia River near Portland: *c.* 190 mi (306 km)

Wil·lard[1] (wil′ərd) *n.* ⟦< the surname *Willard*⟧ a masculine name

Wil·lard[2] (wil′ərd) **1 Emma** (born *Emma Hart*) 1787-1870; U.S. educator **2 Frances (Elizabeth Caroline)** 1839-98; U.S. temperance leader

will call **1** the department, as of a large store, at which articles are held to be picked up, as when paid for **2** the section of a box office at a theater, stadium, etc. where tickets previously ordered may be picked up

willed (wild) *adj.* having a specified kind of WILL[1] (*n.* 1): used in hyphenated compounds [strong-*willed*]

wil·lem·ite (wil′ə mīt′) *n.* ⟦Du *willemit*, after *Willem* I (1772-1843), king of the Netherlands⟧ a hard, rhombohedral mineral, Zn_2SiO_4, an ore of zinc; zinc silicate: cf. TROOSTITE

Wil·lem·stad (wil′əm stät′, vil′-) capital of Curaçao and former capital of the Netherlands Antilles

Willes·den (wilz′dən) former municipal borough in SE England: now part of Brent, Greater London

☆**wil·let** (wil′it) *n., pl.* **-lets** or **-let** ⟦echoic of its cry⟧ a large, gray-and-white, long-legged shorebird (*Catoptrophorus semipalmatus*) of the same family (Scolopacidae) as snipe and sandpipers, living along shallow shores, marshes, etc. of North and South America

will·ful (wil′fəl) *adj.* **1** said or done deliberately or intentionally **2** doing as one pleases; self-willed —*SYN.* VOLUNTARY —**will′ful·ly** *adv.* —**will′ful·ness** *n.*

Wil·liam[1] (wil′yəm) *n.* ⟦NormFr *Willaume* < OHG *Willehelm* < *willeo*, WILL[1] + *helm*, protection: see HELM[1]⟧ a masculine name: dim. *Bill, Billie, Billy, Liam, Will, Willie, Willy;* equiv. Du. *Willem*, Fr. *Guillaume*, Ger. *Wilhelm*, It. *Guglielmo*, Sp. *Guillermo*

Wil·liam[2] (wil′yəm) **1 William I** 1027?-87; duke of Normandy who invaded England & defeated Harold at the Battle of Hastings: king of England (1066-87): called *William the Conqueror* **2 William I** 1533-84; prince of Orange (1544-84) & count of Nassau (1559-84): founder and 1st stadholder (1579-84) of the Netherlands republic: called *William the Silent* **3 William I** 1797-1888; king of Prussia (1861-88) & emperor of Germany (1871-88): son of Frederick William III **4 William II** 1056-1100; king of England (1087-1100): son of William the Conqueror: called *William Rufus* **5 William II** *Eng. name for* WILHELM II **6 William III** 1650-1702; king of England, Scotland, & Ireland (1689-1702): stadholder of the Netherlands (1672-1702): see MARY II **7 William IV** 1765-1837; king of Great Britain & Ireland (1830-37): son of George III

William of Malmesbury 1090?-1143?; Eng. historian

Wil·liams (wil′yəmz) **1 Hank** (haŋk) (born *Hiram Williams*) 1923-53; U.S. country music singer & composer **2 Ralph Vaughan** *see* VAUGHAN WILLIAMS **3 Roger** 1603?-83; Eng. clergyman & colonist in America: founder of R.I. **4 Tennessee** (born *Thomas Lanier Williams*) 1914-83; U.S. playwright **5 William Car·los** (kär′lōs) 1883-1963; U.S. poet & writer

Wil·liams·burg (wil′yəmz bʉrg′) ⟦after King WILLIAM III⟧ city in SE Va.: colonial capital of Va., now restored to its 18th-cent. appearance

William Tell in Swiss legend, a 14th-cent. hero in the fight for independence from Austria, forced to shoot an apple off his son's head with crossbow and arrow

William the Conqueror *name for* WILLIAM I (duke of Normandy)

will·ie (wil′ē) *n.* [Slang, Chiefly Brit.] *alt. sp. of* WILLY[2]

Wil·lie (wil′ē) *n.* a masculine name: see WILLIAM[1]

☆**wil·lies** (wil′ēz) *pl.n.* ⟦< ?⟧ [Slang] a state of nervousness; jitters: with *the*

will·ing (wil′iŋ) *adj.* ⟦ME < OE *willung* < *willian*, to WILL[1], v.⟧ **1** favorably disposed or consenting (*to* do something specified or implied) **2** acting, giving, etc. readily and cheerfully **3** done, given, etc. readily or gladly; voluntary —**will′ing·ly** *adv.* —**will′ing·ness** *n.*

Wil·lis (wil′is) *n.* ⟦< the surname *Willis*, prob. < *Willson*, *Wilson* (< *Will's son*)⟧ a masculine name

wil·li·waw or **wil·ly·waw** (wil′i wô′) *n.* ⟦prob. altered < WILLY-WILLY⟧ **1** a sudden, violent, cold wind blowing down from mountain passes toward the coast in far northern or southern latitudes, as on the Alaskan coast and Aleutians, and in the Strait of Magellan **2** a state of extreme confusion, turmoil, or agitation

will-o'-the-wisp (wil′ə *thə* wisp′) *n.* ⟦earlier *Will with the wisp* < *Will* (nickname for WILLIAM[1]) + WISP⟧ **1** IGNIS FATUUS (sense 1) **2** any hope or goal that leads one on but is impossible to reach

wil·low (wil′ō) *n.* ⟦ME *wilwe* < OE *welig*, akin to Du *wilg* < IE base **wel-*, to turn, twist, bend > Gr *helix*, spiral, *helikē*, willow⟧ **1** *a)* any of a genus (*Salix*) of trees and shrubs of the willow family, having usually narrow leaves, single, slipper-shaped bud scales, and staminate and pistillate catkins borne on separate plants: the flexible twigs of certain species are used in weaving baskets, chair seats, etc. *b)* the wood of any of these trees **2** a machine with revolving spikes for cleaning raw wool, cotton, etc. **3** ⟦because orig. made of willow wood⟧ [Informal] a baseball bat or cricket bat —*adj.* designating a family (Salicaceae, order Salicales) of dicotyledonous trees and shrubs including poplars

willow herb **1** any of a genus (*Epilobium*) of perennial plants of the evening-primrose family, with narrow leaves, whitish or purple flowers, and slender pods filled with plumed seeds, as the fireweed **2** purple loosestrife: see LOOSESTRIFE (*n.* 2)

☆**willow oak** a North American oak (*Quercus phellos*) with long, smooth-edged leaves, found near swamps and streams

willow pattern a design for china, copied in 18th-cent. England from a Chinese original, that pictures a river, pagodas, willow trees, etc., usually in blue on a white background

☆**wil·low·ware** (wil′ō wer′) *n.* articles of china decorated with the WILLOW PATTERN

wil·low·y (wil′ō ē) *adj.* **1** covered or shaded with willows **2** like a willow; specif., *a)* gracefully slender *b)* pliant, supple, lithe, etc.

will·pow·er (wil′pou′ər) *n.* strength of will, mind, or determination; self-control

wil·ly[1] (wil′ē) *n., vt.* **-lied, -ly·ing** *var. of* WILLOW (*n.* 2)

wil·ly[2] (wil′ē) *n., pl.* **wil′lies** [Slang, Chiefly Brit.] the penis

Will·y (wil′ē) *n.* a masculine name: see WILLIAM[1]

wil·ly-nil·ly (wil′ē nil′ē) *adv.* ⟦contr. < *will I, nill I:* see WILL[1] & NILL⟧ **1** whether one wishes it or not; willingly or unwillingly **2** in a disordered way; helter-skelter —*adj.* that is or happens whether one wishes it or not

wil·ly-wil·ly (-wil′ē) *n., pl.* **-lies** ⟦prob. redupl. of *willy*, altered < *whirly*, short for WHIRLWIND⟧ [Austral.] **1** a severe tropical cyclone **2** a whirlwind over a desert

Wil·ma (wil′mə) *n.* ⟦Ger, contr. < *Wilhelmina:* see WILLIAM[1]⟧ a feminine name

Wil·ming·ton (wil′miŋ tən) **1** port city in SE N.C., upriver from Cape Fear **2** ⟦after Spencer Compton (1673?-1743), Earl of *Wilmington*⟧ seaport in N Del., on the Delaware River

Wil·son[1] (wil′sən) **1 Alexander** 1766-1813; Am. ornithologist, born in Scotland **2** Sir **Angus (Frank Johnstone)** 1913-91; Eng. novelist **3 Charles Thomson Rees** (rēs) 1869-1959; Scot. physicist **4 Edmund** 1895-1972; U.S. writer & critic **5 E(dward) O(sborne)** 1929- ; U.S. biologist & writer **6 Robert Woodrow** 1936- ; U.S. radio astronomer **7 (Thomas) Woodrow** 1856-1924; 28th president of the U.S. (1913-21)

Wil·son[2] (wil′sən), **Mount** ⟦after Ben D. *Wilson*, early settler⟧ mountain of the Coast Ranges, SW Calif., near Pasadena: site of an astronomical observatory: 5,710 ft (1,740 m)

Wilson Dam ⟦after Pres. Woodrow WILSON[1]⟧ dam on the Tennessee River, in NW Ala.: 137 ft (42 m) high

☆**Wil·so·ni·an** (wil sō′nē ən) *adj.* of Woodrow Wilson or his political ideas, policies, etc.

Wilson's disease ⟦after S. *Wilson* (1874-1937), Eng neurologist, born in U.S.⟧ a disease characterized by abnormal accumulation of copper in the brain, liver, etc.

☆**Wilson's thrush** ⟦after Alexander WILSON[1]⟧ VEERY

☆**Wilson's warbler** ⟦after Alexander WILSON[1]⟧ a small, green-and-yellow North American wood warbler (*Wilsonia pusilla*)

wilt[1] (wilt) ***vi.*** ⟦var. of obs. *welk*, to wither < ME *welken*, to fade, wither, dry up, akin to OHG *welc*, damp, wilted < IE **welg-*, var. of base **welk-*, moist, damp > OE *wealg*, nauseous⟧ **1** to become limp, as from heat or lack of water; wither; droop: said of plants **2** to become weak or faint; lose strength; languish **3** to lose courage; quail —***vt.*** to cause to wilt —***n.*** **1** a wilting or being wilted **2** *a)* a highly infectious disease of some caterpillars, in which the carcasses liquefy *b)* any of several plant diseases caused by certain bacteria or fungi and characterized by wilting of the leaves: also, esp. for *a*, **wilt disease**

wilt[2] (wilt) ***v.aux.*** *archaic 2d pers. sing., pres. indic., of* WILL[2]: used with *thou*

wilt·ed (wilt′id) ***adj.*** *Cooking* made and served somewhat limp, as with a warm dressing: said of a leafy vegetable [*wilted* lettuce, spinach, etc.]

Wil·ton (wilt′'n) ***n.*** ⟦after *Wilton*, city in S England, where it was first made⟧ a kind of carpet with a velvety pile of cut loops: also **Wilton carpet** or **Wilton rug**

Wilt·shire[1] (wilt′shir) ***n.*** ⟦after fol.⟧ any of a breed of white-faced English sheep with a fine fleece and horns that curve backward

Wilt·shire[2] (wilt′shir) county in S England: 1,342 sq mi (3,476 sq km)

wil·y (wī′lē) ***adj.*** **wil′i·er, wil′i·est** full of wiles; crafty; sly —***SYN.*** SLY

wim·ble (wim′bəl) ***n.*** ⟦ME < Anglo-Fr < MDu *wimmel* (or Fl *wemel*), an auger⟧ [Archaic] any of various hand tools for boring, as a gimlet, auger, etc. —***vt.*** **-bled, -bling** [Obs.] to bore with a wimble

Wim·ble·don (wim′bəl dən) suburb of London: scene of international lawn tennis matches

wimp (wimp) ***n.*** ⟦< ?; perhaps suggested by WHIMPER⟧ [Informal] a weak, ineffectual, or insipid person —**wimp out** [Slang] to back down or succumb because of fear, timidity, or weakness —**wimp′ish** ***adj.*** —**wimp′y** ***adj.*** **wimp′i·er, wimp′i·est**

WIMP (wimp) ***n.*** ⟦*w(eakly) i(nteracting) m(assive) p(article)*⟧ a hypothetical, electrically neutral, massive subatomic particle that interacts with other matter by means of the weak interaction

wim·ple (wim′pəl) ***n.*** ⟦ME *wimpel* < OE, akin to Ger, wimple, pennon < IE base **weib-*, to turn, swing > WIPE⟧ **1** a woman's head covering of medieval times, consisting of a cloth arranged about the head, cheeks, chin, and neck, leaving only the face exposed: now worn only by certain orders of nuns **2** [Scot.] *a)* a fold or plait *b)* a winding; turn; curve *c)* a ripple —***vt.*** **-pled, -pling** **1** to cover or clothe with or as with a wimple **2** to lay in folds **3** to cause to ripple or undulate, as the surface of a lake —***vi.*** **1** to lie in folds **2** to ripple **3** [Scot.] to meander, as a brook

wimple

win (win) ***vi.*** **won, win′ning** ⟦ME *winnen* < OE *winnan*, to fight, endure, struggle, akin to Ger *winnen*, to struggle, contend < IE base **wen-*, to desire, strive for > WISH, L *venus*, love⟧ **1** *a)* to gain a victory; be victorious; triumph (sometimes with *out*) *b)* to finish in first place in a race, contest, etc. **2** to succeed in reaching or achieving a specified condition or place; get: with various prepositions, adverbs, or adjectives [to *win* back to health] —***vt.*** **1** to get by effort, labor, struggle, etc.; specif., *a)* to gain or acquire through accomplishment [to *win* distinctions] *b)* to achieve or attain (one's point, demands, etc.) *c)* to gain (a prize or award) in competition *d)* to obtain or earn (a livelihood, security, etc.) **2** to be successful or victorious in (a contest, game, dispute, etc.) **3** to get to, usually with effort; reach [they *won* the top of the hill by noon] **4** to prevail upon; influence; persuade: often with *over* [to *win* someone over to one's side] **5** *a)* to gain the sympathy, favor, affection, or love of [to *win* a supporter, friend, etc.] *b)* to gain (someone's sympathy, affection, love, etc.) **6** to persuade to marry one **7** *a)* to extract (metal, minerals, etc.) from ore *b)* to obtain (coal, ore, etc.) by mining *c)* to prepare (a vein, shaft, etc.) for mining —***n.*** **1** an act of winning; victory, as in a contest **2** first position at the finish of a race —**win out** [Informal] to win all of the remaining games or contests on one's current schedule

wince[1] (wins) ***vi.*** **winced, winc′ing** ⟦ME *wynsen* < Anglo-Fr var. of OFr *guenchir* < Frank **wenkjan*, akin to OHG *wankon*, to totter, turn: for IE base see WINCH⟧ to shrink or draw back slightly, usually with a grimace, as in pain, embarrassment, alarm, etc. —***n.*** the act or an instance of wincing —**winc′er** ***n.***

wince[2] (wins) ***n.*** ⟦var. of WINCH⟧ a roller used between dyeing vats to facilitate the transfer of pieces of cloth

win·cey·ette (win′sē et′) ***n.*** ⟦*wincey*, a kind of fabric, altered < LINSEY(-WOOLSEY) + -ETTE⟧ [Brit.] a kind of flannelette or cotton flannel

winch (winch) ***n.*** ⟦ME *winche* < OE *wince* < IE base **weng-*, to be curved, bowed > WINK⟧ **1** a crank with a handle for transmitting motion, as to a grindstone **2** a machine for hoisting, lowering, or hauling, consisting of a drum or cylinder turned by a crank or motor: a rope or cable tied to the load is wound on the drum or cylinder —***vt.*** to hoist or haul with a winch

☆**Win·ches·ter**[1] (win′ches′tər, -chis-) ⟦after Oliver F. *Winchester* (1810-80), the manufacturer⟧ *trademark for* a type of repeating rifle with a tubular magazine set horizontally under the barrel

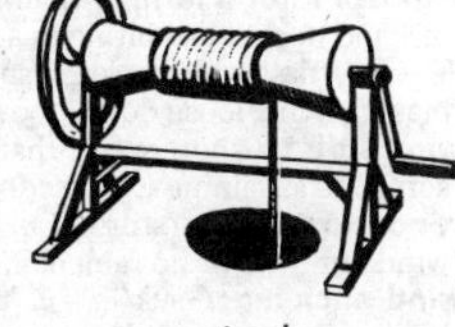
winch

Win·ches·ter[2] (win′ches′tər, -chis-) county seat of Hampshire, S England: site of 11th-14th cent. cathedral

Winck·el·mann (viŋ′kəl män′), **Jo·hann Jo·a·chim** (yō′hän′ yō′ä khim) 1717-68; Ger. archaeologist & art historian

wind[1] (wīnd) ***vt.*** **wound** or [Rare] **wind′ed, wind′ing** ⟦ME *winden* < OE *windan*, akin to ON *vinda*, Ger *winden* < IE base **wendh-*, to turn, wind, twist > Arm *gind*, a ring⟧ **1** *a)* to turn, or make revolve [to *wind* a crank] *b)* to move by or as if by cranking **2** *a)* to turn or coil (string, ribbon, etc.) around itself to form a ball or around something else so as to encircle it closely; twine; wreathe [*winding* the bandage on his finger] *b)* to wrap or cover by encircling with something turned in the manner of a coil; entwine [to *wind* a spool with thread] **3** *a)* to make (one's way) in a winding or twisting course *b)* to cause to move in a winding or twisting course **4** to introduce deviously; insinuate [*winding* his prejudices through all his writings] **5** to hoist or haul by or as by winding rope on a winch: often with *up* **6** to tighten the operating spring of (a clock, mechanical toy, etc.) by turning a stem or the like: often with *up* —***vi.*** **1** to move, go, or extend in a curving, zigzagging, or sinuous manner; meander **2** to double on one's track, so as to throw off pursuers **3** to take a circuitous, devious, or subtle course in behavior, argument, etc. **4** to insinuate oneself **5** to coil, twine, or spiral (*about* or *around* something) **6** to undergo winding [a watch that *winds* easily] —***n.*** **1** the act of winding **2** a single turn of something wound **3** a turn; twist; bend —**wind down** **1** to bring or come gradually to an end, from or as from a loss of energy **2** to lose motive power gradually: said esp. of a clock or other mechanical device with an operating spring **3** to become relaxed, less tense, etc.; unwind —**wind off** to unwind or remove by unwinding —**wind up** **1** to wind (something) into a ball, coil, etc. **2** to entangle or involve **3** to bring or come to a particular end or condition **4** to make very tense, excited, etc. ☆**5** *Baseball* to use a windup before pitching the ball

wind[2] (wind) ***n.*** ⟦ME < OE, akin to ON *vindr*, Ger *wind* < IE **wentos* (> L *ventus*) < base **we-*, **awe-*, to blow > WEATHER⟧ **1** air in motion; specif., *a)* any noticeable natural movement of air parallel to the earth's surface (see the Beaufort scale in the Reference Supplement) *b)* air artificially put in motion, as by an air pump or fan **2** a strong, fast-moving, or destructive natural current of air; gale or storm **3** the direction from which a wind blows: now chiefly in *the four winds*, with reference to the cardinal points of the compass **4** a natural current of air regarded as a bearer of odors or scents, as in hunting [to lose (the) *wind* of the fox] **5** figuratively, air regarded as bearing information, indicating trends, etc. [a rumor that's in the *wind*] **6** breath or the power of breathing [to get the *wind* knocked out of one] **7** *a)* idle or empty talk; nonsense *b)* bragging; pomposity; conceit **8** gas in the stomach or intestines; flatulence **9** *a)* [*pl.*] the wind instruments of an orchestra, or the players of these instruments *b)* any of such instruments —***vt.*** **1** to expose to the wind or air, as for drying; air **2** to get or follow the scent of; scent **3** to cause to be out of breath [to be *winded* by a long run] **4** to rest (a horse, etc.) so as to allow recovery of breath —***adj.*** **1** designating a musical instrument sounded by blowing air through it, esp. a portable one sounded with the breath, as a flute, oboe, tuba, or trumpet **2** of or for a wind or woodwind instrument or instruments —**before the wind** with the wind coming from astern —**break wind** to expel gas from the bowels —**get (or have) one's wind up** to become (or be) nervous or alarmed —**get (or have) wind of** to get (or have) information or a hint concerning; hear (or know) of —**how the wind blows (or lies)** what the trend of affairs, public opinion, etc. is —**in the teeth of the wind** straight against the wind: often **in the wind's eye** —**in the wind** happening or about to happen —**into the wind** in the direction from which the wind is blowing —**like the wind** with great speed [to run *like the wind*] —**off the wind** with the wind coming from behind —**on the wind** approximately in the direction from which the wind is blowing —**take the wind out of someone's sails** to deflate suddenly someone's enthusiasm, pride, etc., as by removing his or her advantage or nullifying his or her argument —**throw caution (or reason or fear, etc.) to the wind** to act recklessly or boldly

SYN.—**wind** is the general term for any natural movement of air, whether of high or low velocity or great or little force; **breeze** is popularly applied to a light, fresh wind and, meteorologically, to a wind having a velocity of from 4 to 31 miles an hour; **gale** is popularly applied to a strong, somewhat violent wind and, meteorologically, to a wind having a velocity of from 32 to 63 miles an hour; **gust** and **blast** apply to sudden, brief winds, **gust** suggesting a light puff, and **blast** a driving rush, of air; **zephyr** is a poetic term for a soft, gentle breeze

wind[3] (wīnd, wind) ***vt., vi.*** **wound** or [Rare] **wind′ed, wind′ing** ⟦Early ModE < prec.⟧ [Old Poet.] **1** to blow (a horn, etc.) **2** to sound (a signal, etc.), as on a horn

Wind (wind) ⟦from the severe winds near its head⟧ river in WC Wyo., flowing southeast into the Bighorn: *c.* 110 mi (177 km)

wind·age (win′dij) ***n.*** **1** the disturbance of air around a moving projectile **2** *a)* the deflection of a projectile by the effects of the wind *b)* the degree of this *c)* in aiming a gun, the degree of adjustment of the wind gauge to compensate for such deflection **3** the space between the inside wall of the barrel of a firearm and its projectile, to allow for the expansion of gas in firing, as measured by the difference in diameters of the bore and projectile **4** the part of a plane's or ship's surface subject to aerodynamic forces

Win·daus (vin′dous), **A·dolph (Otto Rheinhold)** (ä′dôlf) 1876-1959; Ger. chemist

wind·bag (wind′bag′) *n.* [Informal] a person who talks much and pretentiously but says little of importance
wind·blown (-blōn′) *adj.* 1 blown by the wind 2 twisted in growth by the prevailing wind: said of a tree
wind-borne (-bôrn′) *adj.* carried by the wind, as pollen
☆**wind·break** (-brāk′) *n.* a hedge, fence, or row of trees that serves as a protection from wind
☆**Wind·break·er** (-brā′kər) *trademark for* a hip-length jacket made of light-weight, wind-resistant material —*n.* [*often* **w-**] such a jacket
wind-bro·ken (-brō′kən) *adj. Vet.Med.* having the heaves
wind·burn (-burn′) *n.* a roughened, reddened, sore condition of the skin, caused by overexposure to the wind
wind·cheat·er (-chēt′ər) *n.* [Chiefly Brit.] a windbreaker
wind·chill (-chil′) *n.* an estimated measurement of the cooling effect of air and wind, esp. when applied to the loss of body heat from exposed skin; chill factor: also **windchill factor (**or **index)**
wind chimes (*or* **bells)** a cluster of small chimes or pendants of glass, ceramic, etc., hung so that they strike one another or are struck by a clapper, and tinkle when blown by the wind
wind cone WINDSOCK
wind·ed (win′did) *adj.* out of breath
wind·er (wīn′dər) *n.* 1 a person who winds material or operates a winding machine in textile and other industries 2 an apparatus for winding or on which winding is done 3 a key, knob, etc. for winding a spring-operated mechanism 4 any of the steps in a winding staircase
Win·der·mere (win′dər mir′) lake in Cumbria, NW England: largest lake in England: 10.5 mi (16.9 km) long
wind·fall (wind′fôl′) *n.* 1 something blown down by the wind, as fruit from a tree 2 any unexpected acquisition, gain, or stroke of good luck; specif., a gain of unexpected profit or earnings
wind farm a network of densely packed, modern, high-speed windmills, for generating electric power
wind·flow·er (-flou′ər) *n.* ANEMONE (sense 1)
wind·gall (-gôl′) *n.* ⟦WIND[2] + GALL[2]⟧ a soft swelling on the fetlock joint of a horse —**wind′galled′** *adj.*
☆**wind gap** a notch in a mountain ridge
wind gauge 1 ANEMOMETER 2 a graduated attachment on a gun sight for indicating the degree of deflection necessary to counteract windage
wind harp AEOLIAN HARP
Wind·hoek (vint′ho͝ok′) capital of Namibia, in the central part
wind·hov·er (wind′huv′ər) *n.* ⟦WIND[2] + HOVER: from its flying habit⟧ [Brit.] a kestrel
wind·i·ly (win′də lē) *adv.* in a windy manner
wind·i·ness (-dē nis) *n.* a windy quality or condition
wind·ing (wīn′diŋ) *n.* 1 the action or effect of a person or thing that winds; specif., *a)* a sinuous path or course *b)* [*usually pl.*] devious methods, actions, etc. *c)* a coiling, spiraling, or twining *d)* a single turn 2 something that winds; specif., *a)* wire, thread, etc. wound around something [the *winding* on an electric coil] *b)* a single turn of this *c)* the manner in which this is wound [a shunt *winding*] 3 a defective gait of horses in which one leg tends to twist around the other —*adj.* that winds, turns, coils, spirals, etc.
winding sheet a cloth in which the body of a dead person is wrapped for burial; shroud
☆**wind·jam·mer** (wind′jam′ər) *n. Naut.* 1 a sailing ship, esp. a large one: orig. so called by seamen in contempt of early steamships 2 a crew member of such a ship
wind·lass (wind′ləs) *n.* ⟦ME *wyndlas*, altered (infl. by *-wyndel*, a winding device < *winden*, WIND[1]) < *windas*, windlass < ON *vindass* < *vinda*, to WIND[1] + *ass*, a beam⟧ a winch, esp. a simple one for lifting an anchor, a bucket in a well, etc. — *vt., vi.* to hoist, lower, or haul with a windlass
wind·less (wind′lis) *adj.* 1 devoid of any wind or breeze 2 out of breath —**wind′less·ly** *adv.* —**wind′less·ness** *n.*
win·dle·straw (win′dəl strô′) *n.* ⟦< OE *windelstreaw* (via Scot dial.) < *windel*, a bundle (< *windan*, to WIND[1]) + *streaw*, STRAW⟧ [Scot.] 1 a dried stalk of grass 2 a slender or weak person or thing
wind·mill (wind′mil′) *n.* 1 a mill operated by the wind's rotation of large, oblique vanes radiating from a shaft: the rotating vanes generate power for the mill in grinding grain, pumping water, etc. 2 WIND TURBINE 3 anything like a windmill, as a propellerlike toy (*pinwheel*) revolved by wind — *vt., vi.* to rotate like a windmill —**tilt at windmills** ⟦see TILT[1], *vi.* 2⟧ to fight imaginary evils or opponents: from Don Quixote's charging at windmills under the delusion that they were giants

windmills

win·dow (win′dō) *n.* ⟦ME *windoge* < ON *vindauga*, window, lit., wind eye < *vindr*, WIND[2] + *auga*, an eye; akin to Ger *auge*, EYE⟧ 1 *a)* an opening in a building, vehicle, or container, for letting in light or air or for looking through, usually having a pane or panes of glass, etc. set in a frame or sash that is generally movable so that it can be opened and shut *b)* any of these panes, or the sash or sashes in their casement 2 *a)* any similar opening, as that before a bank teller *b)* an opening, period of time, etc. for access [a *window* of opportunity] 3 the transparent panel of a window envelope 4 *a)* any device put into the atmosphere to yield a perceptible radar echo, usually used for tracking an airborne object or as a tracer of wind *b)* CHAFF (*n.* 4) 5 LAUNCH WINDOW 6 any portion of the frequency spectrum of the earth's atmosphere through which light, heat, or radio waves can penetrate to the earth's surface due to the low absorption or dissipation of electromagnetic energy in this particular portion 7 *Comput.* a discrete, typically rectangular, display of data appearing on a computer screen: in many GUIs, several windows may appear side by side —*vt.* to provide with a window or windows —**out (of) the window** gone or dashed, esp. irretrievably so —**win′dow·less** *adj.*
window box 1 a long, narrow box on or outside a window ledge, for growing plants 2 one of the channels along the sides of a window frame for containing the weights that counterbalance the sash
window dressing 1 the arrangement or display of goods and trimmings in a store window to attract customers 2 statements, actions, or display designed to make something seem better than it really is —**win′dow-dress′** *vt.* —**window dresser**
window envelope an envelope with a transparent panel, through which the address on the enclosure can be seen
win·dow·pane (-pān′) *n.* a pane of glass in a window —*adj.* designating or of a pattern consisting of large squares or rectangles in a color that contrasts with the main color [*windowpane* plaid]
window seat 1 an indoor seat built in beneath a window or windows and often enclosing storage space 2 a seat near a window, as in an airplane
☆**window shade** a shade for a window, esp. one consisting of a piece of stiffened cloth or heavy paper on a spring roller, with a pull to lower and raise it
win·dow-shop (-shäp′) *vi.* **-shopped′**, **-shop′ping** to look at displays of goods in store windows without entering the stores to buy —**win′dow-shop′per** *n.*
win·dow·sill (-sil′) *n.* the sill of a window
wind·pipe (wind′pīp′) *n.* TRACHEA (sense 1)
wind-pol·li·nat·ed (-päl′ə nāt′id) *adj. Bot.* fertilized by pollen carried by the wind
wind·proof (-pro͞of′) *adj.* impervious to or unaffected by the wind [a *wind-proof* coat, a *windproof* lighter]
Wind River Range ⟦after the WIND *River*⟧ range of the Rocky Mountains, in WC Wyo.: highest peak, 13,787 ft (4,202 m)
wind rose a diagram that shows for a particular place the frequency and intensity of wind from different directions
wind·row (wind′rō′) *n.* 1 a row of hay raked together to dry before being made into heaps or cocks 2 any similar row, as of sheaves of grain 3 a row of dry leaves, dust, etc. that has been swept together by the wind —*vt.* to rake, sweep, etc. into a windrow or windrows
wind scale a scale used in meteorology to designate relative wind intensities, as the Beaufort scale
wind·screen (wind′skrēn′) *n.* 1 a screen for protecting something from the wind 2 [Chiefly Brit.] a windshield
wind shake a condition of timber in which there is separation of the concentric rings, supposedly due to strain from strong winds during growth —**wind′-shak′en** *adj.*
wind shear a sudden change in the direction of the wind; esp., a sudden, dangerous downdraft encountered as by aircraft
☆**wind·shield** (-shēld′) *n.* in automobiles, trucks, speedboats, motorcycles, etc., a curved or flat transparent screen, as of glass, in front, that protects the riders from wind, etc.
wind·sock (-säk′) *n.* a long, cone-shaped cloth bag, open at both ends and attached to the top of a mast, as at an airfield, to show wind direction: also called **wind sleeve**
Wind·sor[1] (win′zər) *n.* name of the ruling family of Great Britain since 1917, when the name was officially changed from *Saxe-Coburg-Gotha*
Wind·sor[2] (win′zər), Duke of (*Edward Albert Christian George Andrew Patrick David*) 1894-1972; king of England, as *Edward VIII* (1936): abdicated: son of George V
Wind·sor[3] (win′zər) 1 city in Berkshire, SE England, on the Thames, just west of London: site of Windsor Castle: official name **New Windsor** 2 ⟦after the city in England⟧ port in SE Ontario, Canada, opposite Detroit
Windsor Castle residence of English sovereigns since the time of William the Conqueror, located in Windsor
Windsor chair a style of wooden chair, esp. popular in 18th-cent. England and America, with spreading legs, a back of spindles, and usually a saddle seat
Windsor knot a form of double slipknot in a four-in-hand necktie, resulting in a wider, bulkier knot
Windsor tie a wide necktie usually of silk cut on the bias, tied in a loose double bow
☆**wind sprint** a short sprint that is run, typically in a series, as a training exercise
wind·storm (wind′stôrm′) *n.* a storm with a strong wind but little or no rain, hail, etc.
wind-suck·ing (-suk′iŋ) *n.* the habit that some horses have of swallowing air, as in crib biting —**wind′-suck′er** *n.*

Windsor chair

☆**wind·surf** (wind′sʉrf′) ***vi.*** to engage in the sport of windsurfing —**wind′surf′er** ***n.***

☆**wind·surf·ing** (-sʉr′fiŋ) ***n.*** the sport of riding a sailboard; sailboarding

wind-swept (-swept′) ***adj.*** swept by or exposed to winds

☆**wind tee** a large T-shaped weather vane placed on a landing field, as to show wind direction for aircraft

☆**wind tunnel** a tunnel-like chamber through which air is forced and in which airplanes, motor vehicles, etc., or their scale models, are tested to determine aerodynamic effects

wind turbine a device, often one of a group, for generating electric power, typically consisting of a tall upright supporting large, oblique vanes that are set around an axle and rotated by the wind

wind·up (wīnd′up′) ***n.*** 1 a winding up, or conclusion; close; end ☆2 *Baseball* the act of swinging both arms, sometimes above the head, and then pitching the ball in one continuous motion: cf. STRETCH (*n.* 10) —***adj.*** designating or of a mechanical toy, clock, etc. that is set in motion by tightening its operating spring as with a key

wind·ward (wind′wərd; *naut.* win′dərd) ***n.*** the direction or side from which the wind blows —***adv.*** in the direction from which the wind blows; toward the wind —***adj.*** 1 moving windward 2 on the side from which the wind blows Opposed to LEEWARD —**to windward of** advantageously situated in respect to

Windward Islands S group of islands in the Lesser Antilles of the West Indies, extending from the Leeward Islands south to Trinidad: they do not include Barbados, Trinidad, & Tobago

Windward Passage strait between Cuba & Hispaniola, in the West Indies: 50 mi (80 km) wide

wind·y (win′dē) ***adj.*** **wind′i·er, wind′i·est** 1 characterized or accompanied by wind [a *windy* day] 2 exposed to wind; swept by strong or frequent winds [a *windy* city] 3 like wind; stormy, blustery, violent, etc. [*windy* anger] 4 *a)* without substance; empty, flimsy, etc. *b)* long-winded, pompous, boastful, etc. 5 FLATULENT

Windy City *name for* CHICAGO

wine (wīn) ***n.*** ⟦ME < OE *win*, akin to ON *vin*, Ger & Goth *wein* < early Gmc borrowing < L *vinum*, wine: see VINE⟧ 1 the fermented juice of grapes, used as an alcoholic beverage and in cooking, religious ceremonies, etc.: wines vary in color (*red, white, rosé*, etc.) and sugar content (*sweet, dry*, etc.), may be effervescent (*sparkling*) or noneffervescent (*still*), and are sometimes strengthened with additional alcohol (*fortified*) 2 the fermented juice of other fruits or plants, used as an alcoholic beverage [dandelion *wine*] 3 anything having an intoxicating or exhilarating effect 4 a dark, purplish red resembling the color of red wines — ***vt., vi.*** **wined, win′ing** to provide with or drink wine: usually in the phrase **wine and dine**, to entertain lavishly with food, drink, etc.

wine·bib·ber (wīn′bib′ər) ***n.*** ⟦coined by Miles COVERDALE to transl. Ger *weinsäufer*, Luther's transl. of Gr *oinopotēs*, wine drinker (see Matt. 11:19) < *oinos*, wine (< *oinē*, VINE) + *potēs*, drinker: for IE base see POTABLE⟧ a person given to drinking much or too much wine —**wine′bib′bing** ***adj., n.***

wine cellar 1 a place, as a cellar, where wine is stored 2 a stock of wine

wine-col·ored (-kul′ərd) ***adj.*** having the color of red wine; dark purplish-red

wine cooler a beverage consisting of wine, usually white, diluted with fruit juice or flavoring and carbonated water

wine gallon the old English gallon of 3.79 liters, now the standard gallon in the U.S.

wine·glass (-glas′) ***n.*** a small glass, usually stemmed, for serving wine —**wine′glass′ful′** ***n., pl.*** **-fuls′**

wine·grow·er (-grō′ər) ***n.*** a person who cultivates grapes and makes wine from them —**wine′grow′ing** ***adj., n.***

wine·mak·er (-māk′ər) ***n.*** 1 a person who makes wine 2 a winery —**wine′mak′ing** ***adj., n.***

wine palm any of certain palms yielding a sap drunk as a beverage, often in fermented form: cf. TODDY (sense 1)

wine press a vat in which grapes are trodden, or a machine for pressing them, to extract the juice for making wine: also **wine′press′** ***n.***

☆**win·er·y** (wīn′ər ē) ***n., pl.*** **-er·ies** an establishment where wine is made

Wine·sap (wīn′sap′) ***n.*** a dark-red winter apple

wine·skin (wīn′skin′) ***n.*** in Eastern countries, a large bag for holding wine, made of the skin of an animal

wine steward SOMMELIER

win·ey (wī′nē) ***adj.*** **win′i·er, win′i·est** *alt. sp. of* WINY

Win·fred (win′frid) ***n.*** ⟦OE *Winfrith* < *wine*, friend + *frithu*, peace: see WILFRED⟧ a masculine name

wing (wiŋ) ***n.*** ⟦ME *winge, weng* < ON *vaengr* (for IE base see WIND²): the word replaced OE *fether*, wing, FEATHER⟧ 1 *a)* either of the two feathered forelimbs of a bird, fully developed for flying (as in most birds), or insufficiently developed for flight and used for balance in running, etc. (as in chickens or ostriches) or for swimming (as in penguins or some ducks) *b)* either of the paired organs of flight of a bat, the lifting surface of which is formed by the membranous skin connecting the long, modified digits *c)* either of the paired organs of flight of an insect, light membranous structures that are lateral outgrowths of the thorax supported by a network of veins *d)* any of various winglike structures used by certain animals for gliding movements, as the patagium of flying squirrels or the enlarged pectoral fins of flyingfish 2 in art, mythology, etc., either of a pair of winglike structures associated with or attributed to gods, angels, demons, dragons, etc., or used as a symbol of speed or the like 3 something used as or like a wing; esp., *a)* a (or the) main lateral airfoil of an airplane *b)* either of the inflatable pouches of a pair of water wings 4 something resembling a wing in position or in relation to the main part; esp., *a)* a part, extension, or annex of a building, with reference to its location at a side of the main part or its specialized use [the east *wing*, the surgical *wing* of a hospital] *b)* an outlying area, as of an estate *c)* either of the two side extensions of the back of a wing chair *d)* either part of a double door, screen, etc. *e)* any of the sidepieces used in stage scenery; also, either side of the stage out of sight of the audience *f)* any winglike anatomical or botanical part, as on some leafstalks or seeds; ala *g)* a vane, as of a windmill *h)* [Brit.] FENDER (sense *a*) 5 a group of persons having a winglike relation to another group or to the entire body; specif., *a)* the section of an army, fleet, etc. to the right (or left) of the center *b)* a section or faction, as of a political party, with reference to its radicalism or conservatism *c)* an organization affiliated with or subsidiary to a parent organization 6 *a)* in hockey and certain other goal games, a position played forward and right (or left) of center *b)* the player at such a position 7 *a)* any of various units in an air force; specif., in the U.S. Air Force, a unit smaller than a division and larger than an air group *b)* [*pl.*] the insignia worn by pilot and crew of an aircraft, esp. a military aircraft 8 the act of flying, or a means or manner of flying: now chiefly in GIVE WING TO and TAKE WING (see phrases below) 9 anything represented as flying or soaring, or as carrying one to soaring heights of rapture, joy, etc. [on *wings* of song] 10 [Slang] *a)* a person's arm ☆*b) Baseball* a pitcher's throwing arm —***vt.*** 1 to provide with wings 2 *a)* to cause to fly or speed as on wings [to *wing* an arrow at a target] *b)* to make (one's way) by flying *c)* to pass through or over by or as if by flying 3 to transport by or as by flight 4 to wound, as with a bullet, in the wing, arm, etc. —***vi.*** to go swiftly on or as on wings; fly —**clip someone's wings** to impede or put an end to someone's ability to act effectively — **give wing (or wings) to** to enable to fly or soar on or as if on wings —**on the wing** 1 flying, or while in flight 2 in motion or while moving or traveling —**spread one's wings** to begin to make use of and develop confidence in one's abilities, esp. when regarded as leading to self-sufficiency or self-fulfillment —**take wing** 1 to take flight; fly away 2 to become joyous, jubilant, or enraptured —**under one's wing** under one's protection, patronage, etc. —**waiting in the wings** ⟦see WING, *n.* 4e)⟧ 1 standing offstage and ready to make an entrance 2 ready to enter a situation, be brought to public attention, or undertake a role, position, etc. —☆**wing it** [Informal] to act, speak, etc. with little or no planning or preparation; improvise —**wing′less** ***adj.***

wing and wing *Naut.* sailing with the wind coming from astern and with sails extended on either side by booms

☆**wing·back** (wiŋ′bak′) ***n.*** *Football* an offensive back positioned just behind and outside an offensive tackle or tight end

wing bow (bō) *Ornithology* the color at the bend of a bird's wing formed by distinctive coloration of the lesser coverts

wing chair an upholstered armchair with a high back from each side of which extend high sides, or wings, originally to give protection from drafts

wing collar a stiff, stand-up collar having the top corners in front turned down: worn by men in formal dress

wing covert any of the small covering feathers on a bird's wing

☆**wing·ding** (wiŋ′diŋ′) ***n.*** ⟦< earlier *whingding* < ?⟧ [Slang] an event, action, party, etc. that is very festive, lively, etc.

winged (wiŋd; *often poet.* wiŋ′id) ***adj.*** 1 having wings or winglike parts 2 moving, esp. swiftly, on or as if on wings 3 lofty; sublime [*winged* words]

wing-foot·ed (wiŋ′foot′id) ***adj.*** having or as if having winged feet; swift

wing·let (-lit) ***n.*** 1 a small wing 2 ALULA

wing loading the total weight of a loaded airplane, divided by the area of the wings: also **wing load**

wing·man (-mən, -man′) ***n., pl.*** **-men** (-mən) ☆1 in a formation of aircraft, the pilot who flies behind and to the side of the leader ☆2 the aircraft flown in this position 3 [Informal] a person serving to support another, as in a social situation [to play *wingman* for a friend in a singles bar]

☆**wing nut** a nut with extensions like wings to provide a grip for turning with the fingers

wing·o·ver (wiŋ′ō′vər) ***n.*** an aerial maneuver in which an airplane enters a steep climbing turn until almost stalled, rolls beyond a vertical bank, then noses down and dives until normal flight is resumed in a direction approximately opposite to the original direction of flight

wing shot 1 a shot made at a flying bird, clay pigeon, etc. 2 a person skilled at making these —**wing shooting**

wing·span (-span′) ***n.*** 1 the distance between the tips of an airplane's wings 2 WINGSPREAD (sense 1)

wing·spread (-spred′) ***n.*** 1 the distance between the tips of a pair of fully spread wings 2 WINGSPAN (sense 1)

wing·tip (-tip′) ***n.*** 1 the outermost end of a wing ☆2 *a)* a man's shoe, esp. a brogue, of a style characterized by a piece of decoratively perforated leather that peaks over the toecap toward the tongue and curves down either side of the shoe toward the shank *b)* this piece of leather Also **wing′-tip′**

Win·i·fred (win′ə frid) ***n.*** ⟦earlier *Winefred, Wynifreed*, altered (infl. by WINFRED) < Welsh *Gwenfrewi*, lit., white wave⟧ a feminine name: dim. *Winnie*

wink (wiŋk) ***vi.*** ⟦ME *winken* < OE *wincian*, akin to Ger *winken*: see WINCH⟧ 1 to close the eyelids and open them again quickly 2 *a)* to close one eyelid and open it again quickly, as a signal, etc. *b)* to be closed and opened in this way (said of the eye) **3** to shine intermittently; twinkle —*vt.* **1** to make (the eyes or an eye) wink **2** to move, remove, etc. by winking: usually with *back* or *away* [to *wink* back tears] **3** to signal or express by winking —*n.* **1** the act of winking **2** *a)* the time occupied by this; an instant *b)* a tiny interval (*of* sleep) (cf. FORTY WINKS) **3** a signal, hint, etc. given by winking **4** a twinkle or twinkling —**wink at** to pretend not to see, as in connivance

SYN.—**wink** usually implies a deliberate movement in the quick closing and opening of one eyelid one or more times [he *winked* at her knowingly]; **blink** implies a rapid series of such movements in both eyes, usually performed involuntarily and with the eyes half-shut [to *blink* in the harsh sunlight]

wink·er (wiŋ′kər) *n.* **1** a person or thing that winks **2** BLINKER (*n. 2a*)

win·kle[1] (wiŋ′kəl) *n.* **1** *short for* PERIWINKLE[2] **2** any of various gastropod mollusks that are very destructive to oysters and clams

win·kle[2] (wiŋ′kəl) *vt.* **-kled, -kling** ⟦< ?⟧ [Informal] to pry or rout from cover, secrecy, etc.: with *out, out of,* etc.

win·kle-pick·er (wiŋ′kəl pik′ər) *n.* ⟦so called from their shape, by analogy with the sharp pin or pick used at a meal to extract a winkle from its tiny shell: see WINKLE[1] (*n.* 1)⟧ [Brit. Slang] a shoe or boot with a narrow, sharply pointed toe

win·na·ble (win′ə bəl) *adj.* that can be won [*winnable* wars, a *winnable* election]

Win·ne·ba·go[1] (win′ə bā′gō) *n.* ⟦< Fox *wiinepyeekooha,* lit., person of dirty water: with ref. to muddy waters of a nearby river: akin to WINNIPEG⟧ **1** *pl.* **-gos, -goes,** or **-go** a member of a North American Indian people of E Wisconsin, now also living in Nebraska **2** the Siouan language of this people

Win·ne·ba·go[2] (win′ə bā′gō), **Lake** ⟦after prec.⟧ lake in E Wis.: 215 sq mi (557 sq km)

win·ner (win′ər) *n.* **1** one that wins **2** [Informal] one that seems destined for success

☆**winner's circle** an area, usually circular, at a racetrack where the winning horse and its jockey, owner, etc. are brought for recognition

Win·nie (win′ē) *n.* a feminine name: see EDWINA, WINIFRED

win·ning (win′iŋ) *adj. sometimes superl.* **win′ning·est** **1** *a)* that wins; victorious [the *winning* contestant] *b)* earning a prize [a *winning* lottery ticket] *c)* characterized by victory or good fortune [a gambler's *winning* streak] **2** attractive; charming —*n.* **1** the action of a person that wins; victory **2** [*pl.*] something won, esp. money **3** a shaft, bed, etc. in a coal mine, opened for mining —**win′ning·ly** *adv.*

winning gallery *Court Tennis* an opening in the side wall of the court to the left of the server and on the hazard side of the net: a ball played into it wins a point

winning opening *Court Tennis* any of three openings, the dedans, grille, or winning gallery: a ball played into any of these wins a point

winning post a post marking the end of a racecourse

Win·ni·peg (win′ə peg′) ⟦< Cree *wiinipeek,* lit., body of muddy water, sea⟧ **1** capital of Manitoba, Canada, on the Red River **2** river in W Ontario & SE Manitoba, Canada, flowing from the Lake of the Woods into Lake Winnipeg: (with its principal headstream) 475 mi (764 km) **3 Lake** large lake in SC Manitoba: 9,465 sq mi (24,514 sq km)

Win·ni·pe·go·sis (win′ə pə gō′sis), **Lake** ⟦< Cree *wiinipeekosis,* lit., a small sea: dim. of *wiinipeek:* see prec.⟧ lake in SW Manitoba, Canada, west of Lake Winnipeg: 2,103 sq mi (5,447 sq km)

Win·ni·pe·sau·kee (win′ə pə sô′kē), **Lake** ⟦< Abenaki⟧ lake in EC N.H.: 71 sq mi (184 sq km)

win·now (win′ō) *vt.* ⟦ME *winewen* < OE *windwian,* to winnow < *wind,* WIND[2]⟧ **1** *a)* to blow the chaff from (grain) by wind or a forced current of air *b)* to blow off (chaff) in this manner **2** to blow away; scatter **3** to analyze or examine carefully in order to separate the various elements; sift **4** *a)* to separate out or eliminate (the poor or useless parts) *b)* to sort out or extract (the good or useful parts) **5** [Now Rare] to fan with or as with the wings —*vi.* to winnow grain —*n.* **1** the act of winnowing **2** an apparatus for winnowing —**win′now·er** *n.*

☆**win·o** (wī′nō) *n., pl.* **-os** [WIN(E) + -O] [Slang] a person who habitually becomes drunk on wine; esp., an alcoholic derelict who drinks only cheap wine

Wins·low (winz′lō), **Edward** 1595-1655; Eng. colonist in America: a founder & governor of Plymouth Colony

win·some (win′səm) *adj.* ⟦ME *winsum* < OE *wynsum,* pleasant, delightful < *wynn,* delight, joy (for IE base see WIN) + *-sum,* -SOME[1]⟧ attractive in a sweet, engaging way; charming —**win′some·ly** *adv.* —**win′some·ness** *n.*

Win·ston-Sa·lem (win′stən sā′ləm) ⟦a merging of two towns, after Major Joseph *Winston* (1746-1815) & SALEM⟧ city in NC N.C.

win·ter (win′tər) *n.* ⟦ME < OE, akin to ON *vetr,* Goth *wintrus,* prob. < IE **wed-,* to make wet: see WATER⟧ **1** *a)* the coldest season of the year: in the North Temperate Zone, generally regarded as including the months of December, January, and February: in the astronomical year, that period between the winter solstice and the vernal equinox *b)* the typically cold weather of this season **2** a year as reckoned by this season [a man of eighty *winters*] **3** any period of decline, dreariness, adversity, etc. —*adj.* **1** of or characteristic of winter **2** designed for or taking place during winter [*winter* sports] **3** that will keep during the winter [*winter* apples] **4** planted in the fall to be harvested in the spring [*winter* wheat] —*vi.* **1** to pass the winter **2** to be supplied with food and shelter in the winter —*vt.* to keep, feed, or maintain during the winter

winter aconite a small plant (*Eranthis hyemalis*) of the buttercup family, bearing yellow flowers early in spring

win·ter·ber·ry (-ber′ē) *n., pl.* **-ries** ☆any of several tall hollies of E North America, as the inkberry and the black alder, with thin, evergreen or deciduous leaves and brilliant red, black, purple, or yellow berries that persist over winter

win·ter·bourne (-bôrn′, -boorn′) *n.* ⟦OE *winter burna:* see BURN[2]⟧ a stream that flows only or principally in winter because of the rise of the water table

win·ter·feed (-fēd′) *vt.* **-fed′, -feed′ing** to feed (animals, esp. livestock) during the winter

☆**winter flounder** a common, brownish-gray flounder (*Pseudopleuronectes americanus*) of the Atlantic coast of North America, valued as a food fish, esp. in winter

win·ter·green (-grēn′) *n.* ⟦based on Ger *wintergrün,* Du *wintergroen:* so named because evergreen⟧ ☆**1** *a)* any of several gaultherias; esp., a creeping subshrub (*Gaultheria procumbens*) having small, rounded evergreen leaves, bell-shaped, white flowers, and red, edible berries *b)* an aromatic compound (**oil of wintergreen**) made from the leaves of this plant or the bark of a birch (*Betula lenta*), or synthetically from salicylic acid: sometimes used in medicine or as a flavoring *c)* the flavor or anything flavored with it **2** any of a number of similar plants, as the shinleaf or pipsissewa **3** a milkwort (*Polygala paucifolia*) with large, rose-lavender flowers

☆**win·ter·ize** (-īz′) *vt.* **-ized′, -iz′ing** to put into condition for or equip for winter [to *winterize* an automobile with antifreeze, a house with insulation, etc.] —**win′ter·i·za′tion** *n.*

☆**win·ter·kill** (-kil′) *vt., vi.* to kill or die by exposure to winter cold or excessive snow or ice —*n.* the process or an instance of winterkilling

win·ter·ly (-lē) *adj.* WINTRY

winter melon ⟦so called because it ripens late⟧ any of a variety of muskmelon (*Cucumis melo* var. *inodorus*), as a honeydew melon or casaba, characterized by fruit that lacks a musky odor

winter solstice *see* SOLSTICE

☆**winter squash** ⟦so called because it keeps well⟧ any of several squashes (esp. *Cucurbita maxima*), usually with a thick, hard rind

win·ter·time (win′tər tīm′) *n.* the season of winter: also [Archaic] **win′ter·tide′** (-tīd′)

Win·throp (win′thrəp) **1 John** 1588-1649; Eng. colonist in America: 1st governor of Massachusetts Bay colony **2 John** 1606-76; governor of Connecticut colony (1657; 1659-76): son of John

win·try (win′trē) *adj.* **-tri·er, -tri·est** of or like winter; cold, bleak, etc. [a *wintry* day, a *wintry* stare]: also **win′ter·y** (-tər ē, -trē) —**win′tri·ly** (-trə lē) *adv.* —**win′tri·ness** (-trē nis) *n.*

win-win (win′win′) *adj.* **1** designating or of a situation, solution, etc. that is a compromise benefiting all parties involved **2** designating or of a situation, course of action, etc. having multiple possible outcomes, any of which may be interpreted as successful or positive

win·y (wī′nē) *adj.* **win′i·er, win′i·est** like wine in taste, smell, color, etc.

winze (winz) *n.* ⟦prob. < *winds,* pl. of *wind,* winder, windlass⟧ a vertical or steeply inclined mine shaft dug or drilled downward and connecting to a lower shaft

wipe (wīp) *vt.* **wiped, wip′ing** ⟦ME *wipen* < OE *wipian,* akin to OHG *wīfan,* to wind around < IE **weib-,* to turn, twist, turning motion: see VIBRATE⟧ **1** *a)* to rub or pass over with a cloth, mop, etc., as for cleaning or drying *b)* to clean or dry in this manner [*wipe* the dishes] **2** to rub or pass (a cloth, the hand, etc.) over something **3** to apply by wiping [*wipe* oil over the surface] **4** to remove by or as by wiping: with *away, off, up, out* —*n.* **1** an act or instance of wiping **2** something used for wiping; specif., a disposable tissue or towel, typically of pre-moistened paper or cloth and variously designed for cleansing the skin, cleaning eyeglasses, etc. **3** *Film, TV* a transitional editing effect in which one scene appears to replace another as by gradually moving it across the frame **4** [Old Slang] *a)* a blow; swipe *b)* a gibe; jeer —**wipe out 1** to remove; erase **2** to kill off **3** to destroy or demolish **4** [Slang] *a)* to be capsized by a wave in surfing *b)* to slip and fall, lose control and skid, etc. ☆*c)* to suffer an overwhelming defeat, ruinous failure, etc. ☆**5** [Informal] to make emotionally or physically drained or exhausted

wiped-out (wīpt′out′) *adj.* ☆**1** [Informal] physically or mentally exhausted ☆**2** [Slang] intoxicated by drugs or alcohol ☆**3** [Slang] overwhelmed, exhilarated, awed, etc.

wipe·out (-out′) *n.* [Slang] **1** the act of being capsized by a wave in surfing ☆**2** any fall, failure, debacle, etc.

wip·er (wī′pər) *n.* **1** a person or thing that wipes **2** something used for wiping, as a towel or rag **3** a moving electrical contact, as in a rheostat **4** a projecting piece on a rotating or rocking part, which raises and lowers or trips another, usually reciprocating, part; cam; eccentric **5** a squeegee blade attached to an arm, designed to move automatically back and forth across a windshield

wire (wīr) *n.* ⟦ME < OE *wir,* akin to LowG *wīr* < IE **weir-* < base **wei-,* to bend, turn > WITHE, Gr *iris,* rainbow, L *vitis,* vine⟧ **1** metal that has been drawn into a very long, thin thread or rod, usually circular in cross section **2** a length of this, used for various purposes, such as conducting electric current or stringing musical instruments **3** wire netting or other wirework **4** anything made of wire or wirework, as a telephone cable, a barbed-wire fence, or a snare **5** *a)* telegraph [reply by *wire*] *b)* a telegram **6** [Informal] a concealed microphone or recording device, carried or worn as for espionage or by undercover police ☆7 *Horse Racing* a wire above the finish line of a race —*adj.* made of wire or wirework —*vt.* **wired, wir′ing** 1 to furnish, connect, bind, attach, string, etc. with a wire or wires 2 to supply with a system of wires for electric current 3 to telegraph 4 [Archaic] to snare with a wire or wires —*vi.* to telegraph —☆**down to the wire** to the very end or the very last moments —☆**pull wires** ⟦from the wires used to operate puppets⟧ to use private influence to achieve a purpose —☆**(get in) under the wire** (to arrive or accomplish something) barely on time or at the last minute —**(from) wire to wire** [Informal] from start to finish: also **wire-to-wire** —**wire′like′** *adj.*

wire cloth a type of fine wire netting for strainers, etc.

wired (wīrd) *adj.* ☆1 [Informal] wearing or carrying, esp. surreptitiously, a microphone or recording device ☆2 [Slang] extremely excited, nervous, disoriented, etc. ☆3 [Slang] under the influence of a drug 4 furnished or equipped with wiring, as for electrical service or computerization 5 connected to a computer network, cable TV system, etc.

wire·draw (wīr′drô′) *vt.* **-drew′, -drawn′, -draw′ing** ⟦back-form. < *wire-drawer* < WIRE + DRAWER⟧ 1 to draw (metal) into wire 2 to draw out; spin out; protract; prolong 3 to make too subtle; strain (a point in argument)

wire fox terrier *see* FOX TERRIER

wire·frame (-frām′) *n.* 1 a schematic diagram or graphical representation of the layout or structure of a website or app 2 [*pl.*] eyeglasses having a frame made of wire —*adj.* of or relating to a wireframe or wireframes

wire fraud fraudulent activity conducted over telephone lines or by other electronic communication, including radio, TV, and the internet

wire gauge an instrument for measuring the diameter of wire, thickness of sheet metal, etc.: it usually consists of a disk with notches of graduated sizes around its edge

wire gauze very fine, gauzelike wire netting

☆**wire glass** sheet glass containing wire netting

☆**wire grass** any of several grasses with wiry stems; esp. a European meadow grass (*Poa compressa*), naturalized in Canada and the U.S.

wire·hair (-her′) *n. see* FOX TERRIER, AMERICAN WIREHAIR

wire-haired (-herd′) *adj.* having coarse, or wiry, hair: also written **wire′ haired′**

wire·less (-lis) *adj.* 1 without wire or wires; specif., operating with electromagnetic waves and not with conducting wire, as a cellular phone 2 [Chiefly Brit.] of or relating to radio —*n.* 1 *a)* WIRELESS TELEGRAPHY *b)* WIRELESS TELEPHONY *c)* [Chiefly Brit.] *old-fashioned term for* RADIO 2 a message sent by wireless — *vt., vi.* to communicate (with) by wireless

wireless telegraphy (*or* **telegraph)** telegraphy by radio-transmitted signals

wireless telephone a telephone operating by radio-transmitted signals —**wireless telephony**

wire·man (-mən) *n., pl.* **-men** (-mən) 1 a person who installs and repairs electrical wiring, cables, etc. ☆2 a person skilled in wiretapping

wire netting netting of woven wire, used in various sizes for fences, fire screens, etc.

wire·pho·to (-fōt′ō) *n.* ⟦from *AP Wirephoto*, former trademark: see AP⟧ 1 a system of reproducing photographs at a distance by means of electric impulses transmitted by wire 2 a photograph so produced

wir·er (wīr′ər) *n.* a person who wires

wire recorder an early type of magnetic recorder using wire rather than tape

wire rope rope made of twisted wires

wire service a business organization that sends news stories, features, etc. by wire or electronic means to subscribing or member newspapers and radio and TV stations; news service

☆**wire·tap** (-tap′) *vi., vt.* **-tapped′, -tap′ping** to tap (a telephone wire, etc.) to get information secretly or underhandedly —*n.* 1 the act or an instance of wiretapping 2 a device used in wiretapping —*adj.* of or relating to wiretapping —**wire′tap′per** *n.*

wire·work (-wurk′) *n.* netting, mesh, etc. made of wire

wire·works (-wurks′) *n.* a factory where wire or wire articles are made

wire·worm (-wurm′) *n.* 1 any of the slender, hard-bodied, wormlike larvae of click beetles, that often live underground and attack the roots of crops 2 a millipede (genus *Julus*) 3 a roundworm (*Haemonchus contortus*) parasitic in the stomach and small intestine of cattle and sheep

wire-wove (-wōv′) *adj.* 1 designating or of a very fine grade of paper with a smooth surface, made in a frame of wire gauze 2 made of woven wire

wir·ing (wīr′iŋ) *n.* 1 the action of a person or thing that wires 2 a system of wires, as to provide a house with electricity —*adj.* 1 that wires 2 used in wiring

wir·ra (wir′ə) *interj.* ⟦short for *o wirra*, altered < Ir *a Muire*, O Mary, a cry to the Virgin⟧ [Irish] used to express sorrow, lamenting, etc.

wir·y (wīr′ē) *adj.* **wir′i·er, wir′i·est** 1 of wire 2 like wire in shape and substance; stiff [*wiry* hair] 3 lean, sinewy, and strong: said of persons and animals 4 produced by or as if by a vibrating wire [a *wiry* sound] —**wir′i·ness** *n.*

wis (wis) *vt.* ⟦< IWIS, erroneously understood as "I know"⟧ [Archaic] to suppose; imagine; deem

Wis *abbrev.* 1 Wisconsin: also **Wisc** 2 *Bible* Wisdom of Solomon

Wis·con·sin (wis kän′sən) ⟦< Fr *Ouisconsing*, name of the river < an Algonquian language, prob. Ojibwa: meaning unknown⟧ 1 Midwestern state of the NC U.S.: admitted 1848: 54,310 sq mi (140,663 sq km); cap. Madison: abbrev. *WI, Wis,* or *Wisc* 2 river in Wis., flowing into the Mississippi: 430 mi (692 km)

Wis·con·sin·ite (-īt′) *n.* a person born or living in Wisconsin

wis·dom (wiz′dəm) *n.* ⟦ME < OE < *wis*, WISE[1] + *-dom*, -DOM⟧ 1 the quality of being wise; power of judging rightly and following the soundest course of action, based on knowledge, experience, understanding, etc.; good judgment; sagacity 2 learning; knowledge; erudition [the *wisdom* of the ages] 3 wise discourse or teaching 4 [**W-**] WISDOM OF SOLOMON 5 a wise plan or course of action —**SYN.** INFORMATION

Wisdom of Jesus, Son of Sirach ECCLESIASTICUS

Wisdom of Solomon a book of the Apocrypha: abbrev. *Wis, Wisd of Sol,* or *WS*

wisdom tooth ⟦sing. < calque of ModL *dentes sapientiae*, based on Gr *sōphronistēres* < *sōphronein*, to be of sound mind: from their late appearance⟧ the back tooth on each side of each jaw in human beings; any of the four third molars appearing usually between the ages of 17 and 25 —**cut one's wisdom teeth** to arrive at the age of discretion

wise[1] (wīz) *adj.* **wis′er, wis′est** ⟦ME *wis* < OE, akin to *witan*, to know, OHG *wis*, MDu *wijs* < PGmc **wisa-*, wise < IE **weid-* < base **w(e)di-*, to see, know > Sans *vēdas*, knowledge, Gr *idris*, knowing, L *videre*, to see⟧ 1 having or showing good judgment; sagacious; prudent 2 prompted by wisdom; judicious; sound [a *wise* saying, *wise* action] 3 having information; informed [none the *wiser*] 4 learned; erudite 5 shrewd; crafty; cunning 6 [Chiefly Historical] having knowledge of black magic, etc. ☆7 [Slang] *a)* annoyingly self-assured, knowing, conceited, etc. *b)* impudent; fresh —☆**be (or get) wise to** [Slang] to be (or become) aware of; have (or attain) a proper understanding of —☆**get wise** [Slang] 1 to become aware of the true facts or circumstances 2 to become impudent —☆**put someone wise (to)** [Slang] to give someone information, an explanation, etc. (about); enlighten someone (concerning) —**the (three) Wise Men** the (three) learned men from the East who came bearing gifts to the infant Jesus (Matt. 2:1-13): see MAGI (sense 2) —☆**wise up** [Slang] to make or become informed, insightful, etc. —**wise′ly** *adv.*

wise[2] (wīz) *n.* ⟦ME < OE, akin to Ger *weise* (orig. sense prob. "appearance"): for IE base see prec.⟧ way; manner: used chiefly in such phrases as **in no wise** and **in this wise**

wise[3] (wīz) *vt.* **wised, wis′ing** ⟦ME *wisen* < OE *wisian*, akin to ON *visa*, Goth *(fulla-)weisjan*, OHG *wisen* < base of WISE[1]⟧ [Scot.] 1 to direct or guide 2 to convey or conduct

Wise (wīz) 1 **Stephen S(amuel)** 1874-1949; U.S. rabbi & Jewish leader, born in Hungary 2 **Thomas J(ames)** 1859-1937; Eng. bibliophile, editor, & forger

-wise (wīz) ⟦< WISE[2]⟧ *suffix forming adverbs* 1 in a (specified) direction, position, or manner [*lengthwise*]: in this sense equivalent to -WAYS 2 in a manner characteristic of [*clockwise*] 3 with regard to; in connection with: a revival of an earlier usage [*budgetwise*]

wise·a·cre (wīz′ā′kər) *n.* ⟦altered by folk etym. < MDu *wijssegger*, altered (infl. by *wijs*, WISE[1] + *zeggen*, to say) < OHG *wissago*, altered (infl. by *wis*, WISE[1] + *sago*, speaker < *sagen*, to SAY) < *wizzago*, prophet < Gmc **witag-*, knowing: for IE base see WISE[1]⟧ a person who makes annoyingly conceited claims to knowledge

☆**wise·ass** or **wise-ass** (wīz′as′) [Slang] *n.* WISEGUY (sense 1) —*adj.* ⟦< ASS[2]⟧ of or characteristic of a wiseass [*wiseass* comments] Regarded as mildly vulgar by some

☆**wise·crack** (-krak′) [Slang] *n.* a flippant or facetious remark, often a gibe or retort —*vi.* to make a wisecrack or wisecracks —*vt.* to say as a wisecrack —**wise′crack′er** *n.*

wise·guy (-gī′) *n.* [Slang] 1 a person who is brashly and annoyingly conceited, knowing, etc.; smart aleck: also written **wise guy** 2 a hoodlum or gangster; esp., a member of the Mafia

☆**wis·en·heim·er** (wī′zən hī′mər) *n.* ⟦WIS(E) + *-enheimer*, as in Ger family names, e.g., *Oppenheimer, Altenheimer*⟧ [Slang] a wiseacre or smart aleck

wi·sent (vē′zənt, wē′-) *n.* ⟦Ger < OHG *wisunt*, BISON⟧ the European bison (*Bison bonasus*), now nearly extinct

wish (wish) *vt.* ⟦ME *wisshen* < OE *wyscan*, akin to Ger *wünschen* < IE base **wen-*, to strive (for), desire > WIN, L *Venus*⟧ 1 to have a longing for; want; desire; crave 2 to have or express a desire concerning [to *wish* the day were over] 3 to have or express a desire concerning the fortune, circumstances, etc. of [to *wish* someone good luck] 4 to give a (specified) greeting to; bid [to *wish* a person good morning] 5 to request or order [to *wish* a person to come] 6 to impose (something burdensome or unpleasant) *on* someone —*vi.* 1 to have a desire; long; yearn 2 to make a wish —*n.* 1 the act of wishing; felt or expressed desire for something 2 something wished for [to get one's *wish*] 3 a polite request with some of the force of an order 4 [*pl.*] expressed desire for a person's well-being, good fortune, etc. [to offer one's best *wishes*] —**SYN.** DESIRE —**wish′er** *n.*

wish·bone (wish′bōn′) *n.* 1 the forked clavicle in front of the breastbone of most birds; furcula: so called from the custom whereby two persons make wishes and snap a dried wishbone in two, the longer fragment being regarded as a sign that the holder's wish will be fulfilled ☆2 *Football* an offensive formation in which the fullback lines up directly behind the quarterback and the two halfbacks line up to the rear and on either side of the fullback

wish·ful (-fəl) *adj.* having or showing a wish; desirous; longing —**wish′ful·ly** *adv.* —**wish′ful·ness** *n.*

wish fulfillment 1 the realization of a desire or wish 2 *Psychoanalysis* the symbolic attainment, in the form of dreams, fantasies, etc., of an often unconscious wish or impulse

wishful thinking thinking in which one consciously or unconsciously interprets facts in terms of what one would like to believe —**wishful thinker**

wish list [Informal] a real or imagined list of things needed or wanted

wish·y-wash·y (wish′ē wôsh′ē) *adj.* ⟦redupl. of WASHY⟧ [Informal] **1** watery; insipid; thin **2** *a)* weak; feeble; dull *b)* vacillating; indecisive —**wish′y-wash′i·ly** *adv.*

Wis·ła (vē′swä) *Pol. name for* VISTULA

wisp (wisp) *n.* ⟦ME, prob. < Scand, as in Swed *visp*, a bundle of rushes or twigs, akin to ON *visk*: see WHISK⟧ **1** a small bundle or bunch, as of straw **2** a thin, slight, or filmy piece, strand, etc. [a *wisp* of smoke] **3** something delicate, frail, etc. [a *wisp* of a girl] **4** WILL-O'-THE-WISP —*vt.* to roll into a wisp —**wisp′y** *adj.* **wisp′i·er, wisp′i·est**

wist (wist) *vt., vi.* [Archaic] *pt. & pp. of* WIT²

☆**wis·te·ri·a** (wis tir′ē ə) *n.* ⟦ModL, after Casper *Wistar* (1761-1818), Am anatomist⟧ any of a genus (*Wisteria*) of twining woody vines or shrubs of the pea family, with fruits that are pods and showy clusters of bluish, white, pink, or purplish flowers: native to the E U.S. and E Asia: also **wis·tar′i·a** (-ter′-)

wist·ful (wist′fəl) *adj.* ⟦altered (modeled on WISHFUL) < earlier *wistly*, attentive⟧ showing or expressing vague yearnings; longing pensively —**wist′ful·ly** *adv.* —**wist′ful·ness** *n.*

wit¹ (wit) *n.* ⟦ME < OE, akin to Ger *witz*: for IE base see WISE¹⟧ **1** [Obs.] the mind **2** [*pl.*] *a)* powers of thinking and reasoning; intellectual and perceptive powers *b)* mental faculties with respect to their state of balance, esp. in their normal condition of sanity **3** alert, practical intelligence; good sense **4** *a)* the ability to make lively, clever remarks in a sharp, amusing way *b)* the ability to perceive incongruous relationships and express them in a surprising or epigrammatic manner *c)* a person characterized by wit *d)* writing or speech expressing wit; esp., any clever disparagement or raillery **5** [Archaic] intellect; reason —**at one's wits' end** at a point where one's mental resources are exhausted; at a loss as to what to do —**keep (or have) one's wits about one** to remain mentally alert; function with undiminished acumen, as in an emergency —**live by one's wits** to live by trickery or craftiness

SYN.—**wit** refers to the ability to perceive the incongruous and to express it in quick, sharp, spontaneous, often sarcastic remarks that delight or entertain; **humor** is applied to the ability to perceive and express that which is comical, ludicrous, or ridiculous, but connotes kindliness, geniality, sometimes even pathos, in the expression and a reaction of sympathetic amusement from the audience; **irony** refers to the humor implicit in the contradiction between literal expression and intended meaning or in the discrepancy between appearance and reality in life; **satire** applies to the use, especially in literature, of ridicule, sarcasm, irony, etc. in exposing and attacking vices or follies; **repartee** refers to the ability to reply or retort with quick, skillful wit or humor

wit² (wit) *vt., vi.* **wist, wit′ting** ⟦ME *witen* < OE *witan*, to know: see WISE¹⟧ [Archaic] to know or learn: *wit* is conjugated in the present indicative: (I) *wot*, (thou) *wost* or *wot(t)est*, (he, she, it) *wot* or *wot(t)eth*, (we, ye, they) *wite* or *witen* —**to wit** that is to say; namely

wit·an (wit′'n) *pl.n.* ⟦OE, pl. of *wita*, one who knows, wise man, councilor < *witan*, to know: see WISE¹⟧ the council of an Anglo-Saxon king

witch (wich) *n.* ⟦ME *wicche* < OE *wicce*, fem. of *wicca*, sorcerer, akin to MDu *wicken*, to use magic < IE base **weik-*, to separate (hence set aside for religious worship) > Goth *weihs*, holy, OE *wig*, idol⟧ **1** *Folklore* a person, esp. a woman, having supernatural power as by a compact with the devil or evil spirits **2** an ugly and ill-tempered old woman; hag; crone **3** a practitioner or follower of white magic or of WICCA **4** [Informal] a bewitching or fascinating woman or girl ☆**5** *short for* WATER WITCH (sense 1) —*vt.* **1** to put a magic spell on; bewitch **2** [Archaic] to charm; fascinate —*vi.* ☆DOWSE² —**witch′like′** *adj.* —**witch′y** *adj.* **witch′i·er, witch′i·est**

witch·craft (wich′kraft′) *n.* ⟦ME *wicchecrafte* < OE *wiccecræft*⟧ **1** the power or practices of witches; specif., *a)* black magic; sorcery *b)* white magic **2** an instance of the use of black magic or white magic **3** bewitching attraction or charm —SYN. MAGIC

witch doctor in certain primitive societies, a person supposed to have the power of curing disease, warding off evil, etc. through the use of sorcery, incantations, etc.

witch elm *var. of* WYCH-ELM

witch·er·y (wich′ər ē) *n., pl.* **-er·ies** **1** witchcraft; sorcery **2** bewitching charm; fascination

witch·es′-broom (wich′iz bro͞om′) *n.* an abnormal growth of closely bunched, slender twigs at the ends of branches of various woody plants, caused by fungi, viruses, etc.

witches' Sabbath [*sometimes* **w- s-**] a midnight meeting of witches, devil worshipers, demons, etc., esp. when held on certain festivals as a demonic orgy

☆**witch grass** ⟦altered < *quitch grass*: see QUITCH⟧ a common, weedy North American grass (*Panicum capillare*) having hairy foliage and a large, dome-shaped panicle of small spikelets

witch hazel ⟦altered (infl. by WITCH) < *wyche hazel* < ME *wyche* < OE *wice*, applied to trees with pliant branches, akin to ON *veikr*, WEAK⟧ **1** any of a genus (*Hamamelis*) of small North American and Asian trees and shrubs of the witch hazel family; esp., a tall shrub (*H. virginiana*) of E North America, having yellow, wavy-petaled flowers in late autumn and woody fruit **2** a lotion consisting of an alcoholic solution of an extract from the leaves and bark of this shrub, used on bruises, inflammations, etc. **3** designating a family (Hamamelidaceae, order Hamamelidales) of dicotyledonous trees and shrubs of temperate regions, having flowers in heads or spikes, including the liquidambars

witch hunt ⟦so called in allusion to the historical persecutions of persons alleged to be witches⟧ an investigation carried out ostensibly to uncover disloyalty, subversive political activity, etc., usually conducted with much publicity and often relying upon inconclusive evidence and capitalizing on public fear of unpopular opinions: also written **witch′-hunt′** *n.* —**witch′-hunt′er** *n.*

witch·ing (wich′iŋ) *n.* the action or practice of a person who witches; witchcraft —*adj.* that witches; bewitching

witch moth any of several noctuid moths (genus *Erebus*) of the S U.S., South America, and the West Indies

wite (wīt) *n., vt.* **wit′ed, wit′ing** ⟦ME *witen* < OE *witan*, to know: see WISE¹⟧ [Scot.] blame; censure

wit·e·na·ge·mot or **wit·e·na·ge·mote** (wit′'n ə gə mōt′) *n.* ⟦OE *witenagemot* < *witena*, gen. pl. of *wita* (see WITAN) + *(ge)mot*, a meeting, lit., assembly of the wise men (see MOOT)⟧ WITAN

with (with, with) *prep.* ⟦ME < OE, orig., against, in opposition to, contr. < or akin to *wither*, against < IE **witero-* (< base **wi-*, asunder, separate + compar. suffix) > Ger *wider*, against⟧ **1** in opposition to or competition facing; against [to argue *with* a friend, to vie *with* the champions] **2** *a)* alongside of; near to *b)* in the company of *c)* into; among [mix blue *with* yellow] **3** as an associate, or companion, of [to play golf *with* one's son] **4** *a)* as a member of [playing *with* a string quartet] *b)* working for, serving under, etc. [having been *with* the firm for 20 years] **5** *a)* in some relation to or toward; about [pleased *with* her gift] *b)* regarding; concerning [*with* him, life is always a struggle] **6** in the same terms as; compared to; contrasted to [having equal standing *with* the others] **7** as well as, as completely as, etc. [able to field a ball *with* the best] **8** of the same opinions, beliefs, etc. as [I'm *with* you there] **9** in support of; on the side of [voting *with* the Tories] **10** in the opinion of; in the opinion held by [my decision is all right *with* her] **11** as a result of; because of [faint *with* hunger] **12** *a)* by means of; using [to stir *with* a spoon, to play tennis *with* a new racket] *b)* by the use, presence, etc. of; by [filled *with* air] **13** *a)* accompanied by, attended by, circumstanced by, etc. [enter *with* confidence] *b)* having received [*with* your permission, he'll go] **14** having as a possession, attribute, accouterment, etc.; bearing, wearing, or owning [the man *with* brown hair] **15** showing or exhibiting [to play *with* skill] **16** in the keeping, care, etc. of [the children were left *with* the baby sitter] **17** *a)* added to [those, *with* the ones we have, will be enough] *b)* including [*with* the stepchildren, the family numbers ten] **18** in spite of; notwithstanding: often followed by *all* [*with* all his boasting, he is a coward] **19** *a)* at the same time as [to rise *with* the chickens] *b)* in the same direction as [to travel *with* the sun] *c)* in the same degree as; in proportion to [wages that vary *with* skill] *d)* in the course of [grief lessens *with* time] **20** to; onto [join one end *with* the other] **21** from [to part *with* one's gains] **22** following upon; after [*with* that remark, he left] —**with that** after, or as a consequence of, that

with- (with, with) ⟦ME < OE < *with*: see prec.⟧ *combining form* **1** away, back [*withdraw*] **2** against, from [*withhold*]

with·al (with ôl′, with-) *adv.* ⟦ME *with alle*: see WITH & ALL⟧ **1** in addition; besides **2** despite that; notwithstanding **3** [Archaic] with that; therewith —*prep.* [Archaic] with: used at the end of a clause or sentence

with·draw (-drô′) *vt.* **-drew′, -drawn′, -draw′ing** ⟦ME *withdrawen*: see WITH- & DRAW⟧ **1** *a)* to take back or draw back; remove *b)* to remove from use, consideration, etc. **2** to retract or recall (a statement, etc.) —*vi.* **1** to move back; go away; retreat **2** to remove oneself (*from* an organization, activity, society, etc.) **3** *Psychiatry* to retreat from reality, as in schizophrenia **4** in parliamentary procedure, to retract a motion, statement, etc. —**with·draw′er** *n.*

with·draw·al (-drô′əl) *n.* **1** the act of withdrawing **2** the act or process of giving up the use of a narcotic drug to which one has become addicted, typically accompanied by distressing physiological and mental effects (**withdrawal symptoms**) **3** COITUS INTERRUPTUS

with·drawn (-drôn′) *vt., vi. pp. of* WITHDRAW —*adj.* withdrawing within oneself; shy, reserved, introverted, etc.

withe (with, with, wīth) *n.* ⟦ME *wythe* < OE *withthe*, willow, twig of willow < IE base **wei-*, to bend, twist > WIRE, L *vitis*, vine⟧ a tough, flexible twig of willow, osier, etc., used for binding things; withy —*vt.* **withed, with′ing** to bind with withes

with·er (with′ər) *vi.* ⟦ME *widren*, var. of *wederen*, lit., to weather, expose to the weather < *weder*, WEATHER⟧ **1** to dry up, as from great heat; shrivel; wilt: said esp. of plants **2** to lose vigor or freshness; become wasted or decayed **3** to weaken; languish [affection that soon *withered*] —*vt.* **1** to cause to wither **2** to cause to quail or feel abashed, as by a scornful glance —**with′er·ing·ly** *adv.*

with·er·ite (with′ər īt′) *n.* ⟦Ger *witherit*, after W. *Withering* (1741-99), Eng scientist⟧ a semihard, light-colored, orthorhombic mineral, $BaCO_3$, an ore of barium; barium carbonate

☆**withe rod** either of two North American viburnums (*Viburnum cassinoides* or *V. nudum*) with osierlike shoots and clusters of white flowers in June

with·ers (with′ərz) *pl.n.* ⟦< ME *wither*, resistance (prob. in sense "that which the horse opposes to his load") < OE *withre*, resistance < *wither*, against: see WITH⟧ the highest part of the back of a horse or similar animal, located between the shoulder blades

with·er·shins (*with'*ər shinz') ***adv.*** *var. of* WIDDERSHINS

With·er·spoon (*with'*ər spōōn'), **John** 1723-94; Am. clergyman & educator, born in Scotland: signer of the Declaration of Independence

with·hold (*with* hōld', with-) ***vt.*** **-held', -hold'ing** ⟦ME *withholden:* see WITH- & HOLD[1], *vt.*⟧ **1** *a)* to hold back; keep back; restrain ☆*b)* to take out or deduct (taxes, etc.) from wages or salary **2** to refrain from granting, permitting, etc.; refuse —***vi.*** to refrain; forbear

☆**withholding tax** the amount of income tax withheld, as payment in advance, from employees' wages or salaries

with·in (*with* in', with-) ***adv.*** ⟦ME *withinne* < OE *withinnan* < *with,* WITH + *innan,* within, into < *in,* IN[1]⟧ **1** in or into the interior; on the inside; internally **2** indoors **3** inside the body, mind, heart, etc.; inwardly —***prep.*** **1** in the inner part of; inside **2** not beyond in distance, time, degree, range, scope, etc. *[within* a mile, *within* one's experience*]* **3** inside the limits of *[within* the law*]* —***n.*** the inside or the interior

with·in·doors (*with* in'dôrz') ***adv.*** [Old-fashioned] INDOORS

☆**with-it** (*with'*it, with'-) ***adj.*** [Slang] **1** sophisticated, aware, up-to-date, etc. **2** fashionable; stylish

with·out (*with* out', with-) ***adv.*** ⟦ME *withuten* < OE *withutan* < *with,* WITH + *utan,* from outside, without < *ut,* OUT⟧ **1** on the outside; externally **2** outside a building or place; out-of-doors —***prep.*** **1** [Now Rare] at, on, to, or toward the outside of *[*throngs within and *without* the city walls*]* **2** [Archaic] beyond *[without* his reach*]* **3** not with; lacking; not accompanied by *[*a shirt *without* buttons, lonely *without* her*]* **4** free from *[without* fear*]* **5** with avoidance of *[*to pass by *without* speaking*]* **6** [Obs.] besides —***n.*** [Now Rare] the outside or the exterior —***conj.*** [Dial.] unless *[*they can't go, *without* they get permission*]* —**go** (or **do**) **without** to manage although lacking something implied or previously mentioned

with·out·doors (*with* out'dôrz') ***adv.*** *archaic var. of* OUTDOORS

with·stand (*with* stand', with-) ***vt., vi.*** **-stood', -stand'ing** ⟦ME *withstanden* < OE *withstandan:* see WITH- & STAND⟧ to oppose, resist, or endure, esp. in a successful way

with·y (*with'*ē, with'ē) ***n., pl.*** **with'ies** ⟦ME < OE *withig,* willow, twig of willow: for IE base see WITHE⟧ a tough, flexible twig of willow, osier, etc., used for binding things; withe —***adj.*** tough and flexible; wiry

wit·less (wit'lis) ***adj.*** lacking wit or intelligence; foolish —**wit'less·ly** ***adv.*** —**wit'less·ness** ***n.***

wit·ling (wit'liŋ) ***n.*** a self-styled wit

wit·ness (wit'nis) ***n.*** ⟦ME *witnesse* < OE *(ge)witnes,* witness, knowledge, testimony < *witan,* to know: see WISE[1] & -NESS⟧ **1** an attesting of a fact, statement, etc.; evidence; testimony **2** a person who saw, or can give a firsthand account of, something **3** a person who testifies in court **4** a person called upon to observe a transaction, signing, etc. in order to testify concerning it if it is later held in question **5** something providing or serving as evidence —***vt.*** **1** to testify to **2** to serve as evidence of **3** to act as witness of, often, in proof thereof, signing a statement that one has done so **4** to be present at; see personally **5** to be the scene or setting of *[*a hall that has *witnessed* many conventions*]* —***vi.*** **1** to give, or serve as, evidence; testify **2** to testify to religious beliefs or faith —**bear witness** to be or give evidence; testify

☆**witness stand** the place from which a witness gives testimony in a law court: also [Brit.] **wit'ness-box'** ***n.***

-wit·ted (wit'id) ***adj.*** having (a specified kind of) wit or intelligence: used in hyphenated compounds *[slow-witted]*

Wit·ten·berg (wit''n burg'; *Ger* vit'ən berk') city in N Germany, on the Elbe, in the state of Saxony-Anhalt: the Reformation originated here in 1517

Witt·gen·stein (vit'gən shtīn', -stīn'), **Lud·wig (Josef Johann)** (lōōd'vig) 1889-1951; Brit. philosopher, born in Austria

wit·ti·cism (wit'ə siz'əm) ***n.*** ⟦< WITTY + -ISM, modeled on ANGLICISM, CRITICISM⟧ a witty remark

wit·ting (wit'iŋ) ***adj.*** ⟦ME *wytting* < *witen:* see WIT[2]⟧ done knowingly; deliberate; intentional —**wit'ting·ly** ***adv.***

wit·tol (wit''l) ***n.*** ⟦LME *wetewold,* formed, based on *cokewold* (see CUCKOLD) < *witen,* to know: see WIT[2]⟧ [Archaic] a man who knows of his wife's adultery and tolerates it

wit·ty (wit'ē) ***adj.*** **-ti·er, -ti·est** ⟦ME *witti* < OE *wittig* < *wit,* knowledge: see WIT[1]⟧ **1** having, showing, or characterized by wit; cleverly amusing **2** [Now Dial.] intelligent; clever —**wit'ti·ly** ***adv.*** —**wit'ti·ness** ***n.***

SYN.—witty implies sharp, amusing cleverness and spontaneity in perceiving and commenting on, esp. in repartee and sometimes sarcastically, the incongruities in life; **humorous** connotes more geniality, gentleness, or whimsicality in saying or doing something that is deliberately comical or amusing; **facetious** is now usually derogatory in suggesting an attempt to be witty or humorous that is unsuccessful because it is inappropriate or in bad taste; **jocular** implies a happy or playful disposition characterized by the desire to amuse others; **jocose** suggests a mildly mischievous quality in joking or jesting, sometimes to the point of facetiousness **—ANT. serious, solemn, sober**

Wit·wa·ters·rand (wit wôt'ərz rand') region in South Africa, between the Vaal River & Johannesburg, consisting of ranges of hills that contain rich gold fields

wive (wīv) [Archaic] ***vi.*** **wived, wiv'ing** ⟦ME *wiven* < OE *wifian,* to take a wife < *wif,* woman, WIFE⟧ to marry a woman; take a wife —***vt.*** **1** to marry (a woman); take for a wife **2** to provide with a wife

wives (wīvz) ***n.*** *pl. of* WIFE

☆**wiz** (wiz) ***n.*** [Informal] *short for* WIZARD (*n.* 3)

wiz·ard (wiz'ərd) ***n.*** ⟦ME *wisard,* prob. < *wis,* WISE[1] + *-ard,* -ARD⟧ **1** [Obs.] a sage **2** a magician; conjurer; sorcerer **3** [Informal] a person exceptionally gifted or clever at a specified activity —***adj.*** **1** of wizards or wizardry **2** magic **3** [Brit. Informal] excellent —**wiz'ard·ly** ***adv.***

wiz·ard·ry (-rē) ***n.*** the art or practice of a wizard; specif., *a)* witchcraft; magic; sorcery *b)* exceptional cleverness **—SYN.** MAGIC

wiz·en (wiz'ən) ***vt., vi.*** ⟦ME *wisenen* < OE *wisnian,* to become dry < IE base **wei-,* to wither > L *viescere,* Lith *výsti,* to wither⟧ to dry up; wither; shrivel —***adj.*** WIZENED

wiz·ened (-ənd) ***adj.*** dried up; shriveled; withered

wk *abbrev.* **1** week **2** work

wkly *abbrev.* weekly

wl or **WL** *abbrev.* **1** waterline **2** wavelength

Wm *abbrev.* William

WMD *abbrev.* weapon(s) of mass destruction

wmk *abbrev.* watermark

WNW *abbrev.* west-northwest

wo (wō) ***n., interj.*** *archaic sp. of* WOE

WO *abbrev.* Warrant Officer

w/o *abbrev.* without

woad (wōd) ***n.*** ⟦ME *wod* < OE *wad* < Gmc **waizda-* (> Ger *waid*), akin to L *vitrum,* woad⟧ **1** any of a genus (*Isatis*) of plants of the crucifer family **2** the blue dye obtained from the dried, fermented leaves of such plants

woad·wax·en (-wak'sən) ***n.*** ⟦ME *wodewexen* < OE *wuduweaxe* < *wudu,* WOOD[1] + *weaxe* < base of *weaxan,* to grow, WAX[2]⟧ an ornamental plant (*Genista tinctoria*) of the pea family, with simple leaves and flowers that yield a yellow dye used by the ancient Britons

wob·ble (wäb'əl) ***vi.*** **-bled, -bling** ⟦prob. < LowG *wabbeln,* to wobble: for IE base see WAVE⟧ **1** to move unsteadily from side to side, as in walking **2** to move from side to side as a result of uneven rotation **3** to shake or tremble, as jelly does **4** to waver in one's opinions, etc.; vacillate —***vt.*** to cause to wobble —***n.*** wobbling motion —**wob'bler** ***n.*** —**wob'bling** ***adj.*** —**wob'bling·ly** ***adv.***

☆**wobble pump** *Aeron.* an emergency hand pump for supplying fuel to the carburetor of an airplane engine

wob·bly (wäb'lē) ***adj.*** **-bli·er, -bli·est** inclined to wobble; shaky —**wob'bli·ness** ***n.***

☆**Wob·bly** (wäb'lē) ***n., pl.*** **-blies** ⟦< ?⟧ [Old Informal] a member of the Industrial Workers of the World, an international, revolutionary industrial union founded in Chicago in 1905

Wode·house (wood'hous'), Sir **P(elham) G(renville)** 1881-1975; Eng. novelist & humorist, in the U.S. for much of his life

Wo·den or **Wo·dan** (wōd''n) ***n.*** ⟦OE *Woden,* akin to Ger *Wotan* & ON *Odinn* < IE **wōt-,* var. of base **wāt-,* to be mentally excited > L *vates,* prophet, Ger *wut,* rage⟧ *Gmc. Myth.* the chief deity; identified with the Norse Odin

wodge (wäj) ***n.*** [Brit. Informal] a chunk or lump of something

woe (wō) ***n.*** ⟦ME *wo* < OE *wa,* woe < IE interj. **wai-* > ON *vœ,* Goth *wai,* Welsh *gwae,* L *vae*⟧ **1** great sorrow; grief; misery **2** a cause of sorrow; affliction; trouble —***interj.*** alas

woe·be·gone (wō'bē gôn', -bi-) ***adj.*** ⟦ME *wo begon* < *wo,* prec. + *begon,* pp. of *begon,* to go around < OE *began* < *be-,* BE + *gan,* to GO[1]⟧ **1** [Archaic] woeful **2** of woeful appearance; looking sorrowful, mournful, or wretched

woe·ful (wō'fəl) ***adj.*** **1** full of woe; sad; mournful **2** of, causing, or involving woe **3** pitiful; wretched; miserable Also [Archaic] **wo'ful** —**woe'ful·ly** ***adv.*** —**woe'ful·ness** ***n.***

Wof·fing·ton (wäf'iŋ tən), **Peg** (peg) (born *Margaret Woffington*) 1714?-60; Ir. actress in England

wog (wäg) ***n.*** ⟦< ?⟧ [Brit. Slang] a nonwhite person, esp. a dark-skinned person, as one who is Arab or black: a term of hostility and contempt

wok (wäk, wôk) ***n.*** ⟦Cantonese⟧ a metal cooking pan with a convex bottom, for frying, braising, steaming, etc.: often used with a ringlike stand for holding it steady

woke (wōk) ***vi., vt.*** *alt. pt. of* WAKE[1]

wok·en (wō'kən) ***vi., vt.*** *alt. pp. of* WAKE[1]

wold[1] (wōld) ***n.*** ⟦ME *wold* < OE (Anglian) *wald,* corresponding to OE (WS) *weald:* see VOLE⟧ an elevated, treeless tract of land; specif., a chain of treeless, rolling hills

wold[2] (wōld) ***v.aux., vt.*** *obs. pp. of* WILL[2]

wolf (woolf) ***n., pl.*** **wolves** (woolvz) ⟦ME < OE *wulf,* akin to Ger *wolf,* ON *ulfr,* Goth *wulfs* < IE base **wl̥p-, *lup-,* name of animals of prey > L *lupus,* Gr *lykos*⟧ **1** *a)* any of various wild canine carnivores (genus *Canis*), esp. the gray wolf, widely distributed throughout the Northern Hemisphere: domestic dogs are thought to be descended from wolves *b)* the fur of a wolf **2** *a)* a fierce, cruel, or greedy person ☆*b)* [Slang] a man who flirts aggressively with many women **3** *a)* the dissonance of some chords on an organ, piano, etc. that has been tuned in a system of unequal temperament; also, a chord in which such dissonance is heard *b)* an unsteadiness or breaking of certain tones in instruments of the violin group, due to faulty vibration —***vt.*** **wolfed, wolf'ing** to eat ravenously, as a wolf does: often with *down* —**cry wolf** ⟦from the fable of AESOP in which a shepherd boy falsely calls "Wolf!", causing the villagers to disbelieve him and not come to his aid when a wolf finally does appear⟧ to give a false alarm —**keep the wolf from the door** to provide the necessities of life in sufficient quantity to prevent privation —**wolf in sheep's clothing** a person who hides malicious intent under a benign manner: see Matt. 7:15

Wolf (vôlf) **1 Frie·drich Au·gust** (frē′driH ou go͞ost′) 1759-1824; Ger. classical scholar **2 Hu·go** (ho͞o′gō) 1860-1903; Austrian composer

☆**wolf·ber·ry** (wo͝olf′ber′ē) ***n.***, *pl.* **-ries** a hardy plant (*Symphoricarpos occidentalis*) of the honeysuckle family, with pink, globular flowers and white, spongy berries

wolf call ☆WOLF WHISTLE

Wolf Cub (wo͝olf) *Brit. term for* CUB SCOUT

wolf dog 1 *former name for* IRISH WOLFHOUND **2** a hybrid of a wolf and a dog

Wolfe (wo͝olf) **1 James** 1727-59; Eng. general: defeated the Fr. forces under Montcalm at Quebec (1759) **2 Thomas (Clayton)** 1900-38; U.S. novelist

☆**wolf·er** (wo͝ol′fər) ***n.*** a person who hunts wolves

Wolff·i·an body (wo͝ol′fē ən, vôl′-) ⟦after K. F. *Wolff* (1733-94), Ger embryologist who described it⟧ the transitory mesonephros of higher vertebrates that functions as a kidney in the embryo and is replaced by the adult kidney

wolf·fish (wo͝olf′fish′) ***n.***, *pl.* **-fish′** or **-fish′es** (see FISH) ⟦so named from its large teeth & prob. from its aggressive behavior and voraciousness⟧ any of a family (Anarhichadidae) of long, marine, carnivorous percoid fishes having large, protruding canine teeth

wolf·hound (-hound′) ***n.*** ⟦so named because formerly used for hunting wolves⟧ IRISH WOLFHOUND: see also RUSSIAN WOLFHOUND

wolf·ish (wo͝ol′fish) ***adj.*** of or like a wolf; rapacious —**wolf′ish·ly** ***adv.*** —**wolf′ish·ness** ***n.***

wolf·ram (-frəm) ***n.*** ⟦Ger, orig., pejorative term < *wolf,* WOLF + MHG *ram,* dirt (akin to OE *romig,* dirty < IE base **rēmo-,* dark > Sans *rāmá-,* black): prob. because considered of little value in comparison to tin⟧ **1** WOLFRAMITE **2** TUNGSTEN

wolf·ram·ite (-frə mīt′) ***n.*** ⟦Ger *wolframit:* see prec.⟧ a semihard, heavy, dark-colored, monoclinic mineral, (Fe,Mn)WO_4, the chief ore of tungsten; iron manganese tungstate

Wol·fram von Esch·en·bach (vôl′främ fôn esh′ən bäkh′) 1170?-1220?; Ger. epic poet

wolfs·bane (wo͝olfs′bān′) ***n.*** ⟦transl. of L *lycoctonum* < Gr *lykoktonon* < *lykos,* WOLF + base of *kteinein,* to kill⟧ ACONITE; esp., a tall Eurasian plant (*Aconitum lycoctonum*) with showy, yellow flowers

wolf spider ⟦so named because it hunts and pounces on its prey⟧ any of a family (Lycosidae) of active hunting spiders that are wanderers, living in the ground and not building webs

☆**wolf whistle** a characteristic whistle of two notes, the second sliding from a high to a low note, made by a man to express his admiration of a sexually attractive woman

wol·las·ton·ite (wo͝ol′əs tən īt′) ***n.*** ⟦after William H. *Wollaston* (1766-1828), Eng physicist⟧ a hard, light-colored, triclinic mineral, $CaSiO_3$, used in making ceramic tile, wallboard, etc.; calcium silicate

Wol·lon·gong (wo͝ol′ən gäŋ′) seaport in E New South Wales, Australia

Woll·stone·craft (wo͝ol′stən kraft′), **Mary** 1759-97; Eng. writer & feminist: wife of William Godwin & by him mother of Mary Wollstonecraft Shelley

Wo·lof (wō′lôf′) ***n.*** ⟦self-designation⟧ **1** *pl.* **-lofs′** or **-lof′** a member of a Muslim people of Senegal and Gambia **2** their Niger-Congo language

Wol·sey (wo͝ol′zē), **Thomas** 1475?-1530; Eng. statesman & cardinal: lord chancellor (1515-29) under Henry VIII

wol·ver (wo͝ol′vər) ***n.*** ☆*var. of* WOLFER

Wol·ver·hamp·ton (wo͝ol′vər hamp′tən) borough of West Midlands, central England

wol·ver·ine (wo͝ol′vər ēn′, wo͝ol′vər ēn′) ***n.***, *pl.* **-ines′** or **-ine′** ⟦irreg. dim. < WOLF, prob. because of its ferocity⟧ **1** *a)* a stocky, ferocious, musteline carnivore (*Gulo gulo*), with thick fur, found in the N U.S., N Eurasia, and Canada *b)* its fur ☆**2** [**W-**] [Informal] a person born or living in Michigan, called the **Wolverine State**

wolves (wo͝olvz) ***n.*** *pl. of* WOLF

wom·an (wo͝om′ən) ***n.***, *pl.* **wom·en** (wim′in) ⟦ME *wumman* < OE *wimmann* < *wifmann* < *wif,* female, WIFE + *mann,* human being, MAN: rounding of vowel due to infl. of the initial *w-*⟧ **1** *a)* the female human being *b)* women collectively **2** an adult female human being **3** a female servant **4** *a)* [Dial.] a wife *b)* a sweetheart or a mistress **5** womanly qualities or characteristics; femininity [the *woman* in her] —***adj.*** **1** of or characteristic of a woman or women; feminine **2** being an adult human female [a *woman* scientist]

SYN.—**woman** is the standard general term for the adult human being of the sex distinguished from *man*; **female**, referring specif. to sex, is applied to plants and animals, but is now regarded as a mildly contemptuous equivalent for **woman** [that strong-minded *female* is here again], except in scientific, technical, or statistical use, as in population tables; **lady**, once restricted to a woman of the upper classes or high society position, is now used in polite or genteel reference to any woman [there's a *lady* to see you, the *ladies'* room] or, in the plural, in addressing a group of women [*ladies* and gentlemen]

-wom·an (wo͝om′ən) *combining form* woman of a (specified) kind, in a (specified) activity, etc.: sometimes used in compounds to avoid the masculine implication of -MAN: pl. form -WOMEN

wom·an·hood (-ho͝od′) ***n.*** ⟦ME *womanhode:* see prec. & -HOOD⟧ **1** the state or time of being a woman **2** womanly qualities; womanliness **3** women collectively

wom·an·ish (-ish) ***adj.*** like, characteristic of, or suitable to a woman; feminine or effeminate —*SYN.* FEMALE —**wom′an·ish·ly** ***adv.*** —**wom′an·ish·ness** ***n.***

wom·an·ize (-īz′) ***vt.*** **-ized′**, **-iz′ing** to make effeminate —***vi.*** to be sexually promiscuous with women —**wom′an·iz′er** ***n.***

wom·an·kind (-kīnd′) ***n.*** women in general

wom·an·like (-līk′) ***adj.*** like or fit for a woman; womanly

wom·an·ly (-lē) ***adj.*** **1** like a woman; womanish **2** characteristic of or fit for a woman; womanlike —***adv.*** [Archaic] in a womanly manner —*SYN.* FEMALE —**wom′an·li·ness** ***n.***

wom·an·pow·er (wo͝om′ən pou′ər) ***n.*** the collective strength or potential for work, activism, etc. of the women in a given group, area, nation, etc.

woman suffrage the right of women to vote in governmental elections —**wom′an-suf′fra·gist** ***n.***

womb (wo͞om) ***n.*** ⟦ME *wombe* < OE *wamb,* akin to Ger *wamme*⟧ **1** [Obs.] the belly **2** UTERUS (sense 1) **3** any place or part that holds, envelops, generates, etc. [the *womb* of time]

wom·bat (wäm′bat′) ***n.*** ⟦< name in a language of Australia⟧ any of a family (Vombatidae) of burrowing marsupials resembling small bears, found in Australia, Tasmania, and several Pacific islands

wom·en (wim′in) ***n.*** *pl. of* WOMAN

-wom·en (wim′in) *combining form pl. of* -WOMAN

wom·en·folk (-fōk′) ***pl.n.*** [Informal or Dial.] the women of a family or community: also **wom′en·folks′**

women's liberation (movement) the WOMEN'S MOVEMENT begun in the mid-20th cent.

women's movement a movement or campaign to achieve WOMEN'S RIGHTS, specif., the widespread movement begun in the mid-20th cent. chiefly in North America and Europe

women's rights the rights, claimed by and for women, of equal privileges and opportunities with men: also **woman's rights**

women's studies [*with sing. or pl. v.*] an interdisciplinary program of studies, as at a university, focusing on women's roles in society and culture

wom·er·a (wäm′ər ə) ***n.*** *var. of* WOOMERA

won[1] (wun, wän, wôn) ***vi.***, ***vt.*** *pt. & pp. of* WIN

won[2] (wun, wōn) ***vi.*** **wonned**, **won′ning** ⟦ME *wonen* < OE *wunian:* see WONT⟧ [Now Brit. Dial.] to dwell; abide

won[3] (wän, wun) ***n.***, *pl.* **won** ⟦Kor < Chin *yüan,* round, yuan⟧ the basic monetary unit of North Korea and South Korea: see the table of monetary units in the Reference Supplement

won·der (wun′dər) ***n.*** ⟦ME < OE *wundor,* akin to Ger *wunder:* only in Gmc⟧ **1** a person, thing, or event that causes astonishment and admiration; prodigy; marvel **2** the feeling of surprise, admiration, and awe aroused by something strange, unexpected, incredible, etc. [gazing in *wonder* at the comet] **3** a miraculous or apparently miraculous thing or act; miracle —***vi.*** ⟦OE *wundrian,* to wonder⟧ **1** to be seized or filled with wonder; feel amazement; marvel **2** to have curiosity, sometimes mingled with doubt —***vt.*** to have curiosity or doubt about; want to know [I *wonder* what happened] —**do wonders for** to make a remarkable improvement in —**for a wonder** surprisingly —**no wonder!** now I know why! of course! —**won′der·er** ***n.***

wonder drug [Informal] MIRACLE DRUG

won·der·ful (-fəl) ***adj.*** ⟦ME < OE *wundorfull*⟧ **1** that causes wonder; marvelous; amazing **2** very good, excellent, fine, etc. —**won′der·ful·ly** ***adv.*** —**won′der·ful·ness** ***n.***

won·der·ing (-iŋ) ***adj.*** feeling or showing wonder

won·der·land (-land′) ***n.*** **1** an imaginary land full of wonders **2** any place of great beauty, strangeness, etc.

won·der·ment (-mənt) ***n.*** **1** a state or expression of wonder; amazement; astonishment **2** something causing wonder; a marvel

won·der-struck (-struk′) ***adj.*** struck with wonder, surprise, admiration, etc.: also **won′der-strick′en** (-strik′ən)

won·der·work (-wurk′) ***n.*** ⟦ME *wonder werk* < OE *wundorweorc*⟧ something made or done that is wonderful, marvelous, miraculous, etc. —**won′der·work′er** ***n.*** —**won′der·work′ing** ***adj.***

won·drous (wun′drəs) ***adj.*** ⟦altered (as if < WONDER + -OUS) < ME *wundres,* adv. gen. of *wunder,* WONDER⟧ wonderful: now usually literary or rhetorical —***adv.*** [Archaic] extraordinarily; surprisingly —**won′drous·ly** ***adv.*** —**won′drous·ness** ***n.***

wonk (wäŋk, wôŋk) ***n.*** ⟦< ?⟧ [Slang] ☆**1** a student who studies very hard; grind ☆**2** any very studious or hardworking person, often, specif., one preoccupied with a particular subject or field

won·ky[1] (wäŋ′kē) ***adj.*** **-ki·er**, **-ki·est** ⟦prob. < or suggested by dial. words based on OE *wancol,* shaky, tottering⟧ [Brit. Slang] **1** shaky, feeble, unreliable, etc. **2** askew, incorrect, etc.

wonk·y[2] (wäŋ′kē, wôŋ′-) ***adj.*** **wonk′i·er**, **wonk′i·est** ☆[Slang] of, having to do with, or like a WONK: also **wonk′ish**

Won·san (wän′sän′) seaport in North Korea, on the E coast

wont (wônt, wōnt, wänt, wunt) ***adj.*** ⟦ME *wunt, woned,* pp. of *wunien,* to be accustomed, dwell < OE *wunian,* akin to Ger *wohnen,* to dwell: for IE base see WIN⟧ accustomed: used in the predicate [he was *wont* to rise early] —***n.*** ⟦prob. altered (based on the adj.) < ME *wune,* custom, habit < OE *(ge)wuna*⟧ usual practice; habit —***vt.*** **wont**, **wont** or **wont′ed**, **wont′ing** [Archaic] to accustom: usually in the passive —***vi.*** [Archaic] to be accustomed —*SYN.* HABIT

won't (wōnt) ⟦contr. < ME *wol not,* will not⟧ *contraction* will not

wont·ed (wôn′tid, wōn′-, wän′-, wun′-) ***adj.*** ⟦ME: see WONT, ***n.*** & -ED⟧ **1** customary; habitual **2** accustomed; habituated —*SYN.* USUAL —**wont′ed·ness** ***n.***

won ton (wän′tän′) ⟦Cantonese *wan t'an* < Mandarin *hun tun,* stuffed dumpling⟧ a Chinese dish consisting of casings of noodle dough filled with chopped meat, fish, or vegetables and boiled: served in a broth (as **won-ton soup**) or fried: also written **won′ton′** *n.*

woo (wo͞o) *vt.* ⟦ME *wowen* < OE *wogian*⟧ **1** to try to get the love of; seek as a spouse; court **2** to try to get; seek [to *woo* fame] **3** to entreat solicitously; coax; urge —*vi.* **1** to try to get the love of a given person; court **2** to make entreaty

wood[1] (wood) *n.* ⟦ME *wode* < OE *wudu,* earlier *widu,* akin to OHG *wito* < IE base **widhu-,* tree > OIr *fid,* Welsh *gwŷdd,* tree, forest⟧ **1** [*usually pl., with sing. or pl. v.*] a thick growth of trees; forest or grove **2** the hard, fibrous substance beneath the bark in the stems and branches of trees and shrubs; xylem **3** trees cut and prepared for use in making things; lumber or timber **4** *short for* FIREWOOD **5** something made of wood; specif., *a)* a cask or other wooden container for alcoholic liquor [whiskey aged in *wood*] *b)* [*pl.*] woodwind instruments, collectively **6** *Golf* any of a set of numbered clubs, originally with wooden heads, having various lofts: the **number 1 wood** is usually called a DRIVER (*n.* 2*b*); the **number 2 wood, number 3 wood,** and **number 4 wood** are used for long, medium, and short fairway shots, respectively **7** [Slang] an erection of the penis: considered mildly vulgar by some —*adj.* **1** made of wood; wooden **2** for cutting, shaping, or holding wood **3** growing or living in woods: chiefly in comb. [*wood* anemone, *wood*-grouse] —*vt.* to plant or cover thickly with trees —**knock on wood** ⟦in ref. to the superstitious custom of touching wood, as to ward off evil⟧ a phrase used, often accompanying the touching of something wooden, as after an optimistic statement so as not to tempt fate: also [Chiefly Brit.] **touch wood** —☆**out of the woods** [Informal] out of difficulty, danger, etc.

wood[2] (wo͞od, wōd, wood) *adj.* ⟦ME < OE *wod,* akin to Ger *wut,* rage: see WODEN⟧ [Archaic] **1** out of one's mind; insane **2** violently angry; enraged

Wood (wood) **1 Grant** 1892-1942; U.S. painter **2 Leonard** 1860-1927; U.S. general & political administrator

wood alcohol METHANOL

wood anemone any of several anemones; esp., *a)* a forest species (*Anemone quinquefolia*) of the E U.S. with starlike flowers *b)* a similar species (*A. nemorosa*) of Europe

wood betony ☆LOUSEWORT

wood·bin (wood′bin′) *n.* a bin for firewood

wood·bine (-bīn′) *n.* ⟦ME *wodebinde* < OE *wudubinde* < *wudu,* WOOD[1] + *binde* < *bindan,* to BIND⟧ **1** *a)* a European climbing honeysuckle (*Lonicera periclymenum*) with fragrant, yellowish-white flowers *b)* any of various other honeysuckles ☆**2** a tendril-climbing vine (*Parthenocissus quinquefolia*) of the grape family, growing in E North America and having palmately compound leaves with five leaflets and green flower clusters that produce dark-blue, inedible berries

wood·block (-bläk′) **1** a block of wood, esp. one used in making a woodcut **2** a hollow, rectangular, wooden percussion instrument that is struck as with a drumstick

wood·carv·ing (-kär′viŋ) *n.* **1** the art or craft of carving wood by hand to make art objects or decorative features **2** an object so made —**wood′carv′er** *n.*

wood·chat (-chat′) *n.* ⟦WOOD[1] + CHAT[1], *n.*⟧ a European shrike (*Lanius senator*)

☆**wood·chuck** (-chuk′) *n.* ⟦altered by folk etym. < a S New England Algonquian name: cf. ? Narragansett *ockqutchaun*⟧ any of several marmots of North America; esp., the common hibernating groundhog (*Marmota monax*) with coarse, red-brown fur

woodchuck

wood coal **1** CHARCOAL (sense 1) **2** LIGNITE

wood·cock (-käk′) *n., pl.* **-cocks′** or **-cock′** ⟦ME *wodekoc* < OE *wuducoc* < *wudu,* WOOD[1] + *coc,* a COCK[1]⟧ **1** a migratory European shorebird (*Scolopax rusticola*) with short legs and a long bill, of the same family (Scolopacidae) as snipe: it is hunted as game ☆**2** a smaller game bird (*Scolopax minor*) of the same family that frequents bogs and swampy places of E North America **3** [Obs.] a fool; dupe

wood·craft (-kraft′) *n.* **1** matters relating to the woods, as camping, hunting, etc. **2** *a)* WOODWORKING *b)* WOODCARVING **3** skill in any of these

wood·crafts·man (-krafts′mən) *n., pl.* **-men** (-mən) a person who practices, or has skill in, woodcraft

wood·cut (-kut′) *n.* **1** a wooden block engraved with a design, etc. **2** a print from this See also WOOD ENGRAVING

☆**wood·cut·ter** (-kut′ər) *n.* a person who fells trees, cuts wood, etc.

☆**wood·cut·ting** (-kut′iŋ) *n.* **1** the act of felling trees, cutting wood, etc. **2** the activity or skill of making woodcuts

☆**wood duck** a brilliantly colored North American duck (*Aix sponsa*) that nests in hollow trees near woodland lakes

wood ear ⟦see TREE EAR⟧ TREE EAR

wood·ed (-id) *adj.* covered with trees or woods

wood·en (wood′'n) *adj.* **1** made of or consisting of wood **2** stiff, lifeless, expressionless, etc., as if made of wood **3** dull; insensitive —**wood′en·ly** *adv.* —**wood′en·ness** *n.*

wood engraving **1** the art or process of engraving on wood **2** WOODCUT: a wood engraving is often distinguished from a woodcut in that the former uses a block of wood cut *across* the grain and the latter a block of wood cut *along* the grain —**wood engraver**

wood·en·head (wood′'n hed′) *n.* [Informal] a stupid person; blockhead —**wood′en·head′ed** *adj.*

wooden horse TROJAN HORSE

☆**wooden Indian** **1** a wooden image of an American Indian in a standing position, formerly placed in front of cigar stores as an advertisement **2** [Informal] a person who is dull, spiritless, or inarticulate

wood·en·ware (-wer′) *n.* bowls, dishes, etc. made of wood

wood hyacinth a European scilla (*Scilla nonscripta*) with racemes of drooping, blue, white, or rose, bell-shaped flowers

☆**wood ibis** a large, white stork (*Mycteria americana*) with a slender, downward-curving bill and naked head, found in wooded swamps from the S U.S. to South America: also called **wood stork**

wood·ie (wood′ē) ☆*n.* [Informal] *alt. sp. of* WOODY

wood·i·ness (wood′ē nis) *n.* the condition or quality of being woody

wood·land (wood′lənd, -land′) *n.* land covered with woods or trees; forest —*adj.* of, living in, or relating to the woods —**wood′land·er** *n.*

wood·lark (wood′lärk′) *n.* a European lark (*Lullula arborea*) similar to but smaller than a skylark

☆**wood·lot** (wood′lät′) *n.* a piece of land on which trees are cultivated, specif. as a source of firewood, lumber, etc.: also written **wood lot**

wood louse **1** SOW BUG **2** PILL BUG

wood·man (wood′mən) *n., pl.* **-men** (-mən) WOODSMAN

wood·note (wood′nōt′) *n.* a sound of a forest bird or animal

wood nymph **1** any of the nymphs who live in the woods; dryad **2** any of certain South American hummingbirds **3** any of several small U.S. noctuid moths (genus *Euthisanotia*) with white-and-brown forewings and yellow hind wings **4** SATYR (sense 4)

wood·peck·er (wood′pek′ər) *n.* any of a family (Picidae) of piciform birds distinguished by stiff tail feathers used for support, a strong, pointed, chisel-shaped bill used for drilling holes in bark to get insects, and a long, protrusile tongue with a spearlike tip

red-headed woodpecker

☆**wood pewee** either of two species of pewee, the **eastern wood pewee** (*Contopus virens*) or the **western wood pewee** (*C. sordidulus*)

wood pigeon any of several pigeons; esp., a ringdove (*Columba palumbus*)

wood·pile (wood′pīl′) *n.* a pile of wood, esp. of firewood

wood pulp pulp made from wood fiber, used as in paper manufacture

☆**wood pussy** [Dial.] SKUNK

☆**wood rat** PACK RAT

wood ray XYLEM RAY

Wood·row (wood′rō) *n.* ⟦< the surname *Woodrow*⟧ a masculine name: dim. *Woody*

wood·ruff (wood′rəf) *n.* ⟦ME *woderove* < OE *wudurofe* < *wudu,* WOOD[1] + *-rofe* < ?⟧ any of a genus (*Asperula*) of plants of the madder family, with small, white, pink, or blue, lily-shaped flowers; esp., a European species (*A. odorata*) used to flavor wine and in perfumery

Woods (woodz), **Lake of the** *see* LAKE OF THE WOODS

wood screw a screw with a sharp point, for use in wood

wood·shed (wood′shed′) *n.* a shed for storing firewood —☆*vi.* **-shed′ded, -shed′ding** ⟦? from the notion that an isolated woodshed is fit for practicing⟧ [Slang] to practice on a musical instrument so as to improve or perfect one's technical facility, develop ideas, etc.: said esp. of a jazz or rock musician —**take someone to the woodshed** [Informal] to beat or severely punish or reprimand someone

wood·si·a (wood′zē ə) *n.* ⟦ModL, after Joseph *Woods* (1776-1864), Eng botanist⟧ any of a genus (*Woodsia*) of ferns with wiry leafstalks, found chiefly on rock ledges

☆**Wood's light** (woodz) ⟦after R. W. *Wood* (1868-1955), U.S. physicist⟧ ultraviolet light filtered through glass containing nickel oxide, used as in forensics, medical diagnostics, etc.

woods·man (woodz′mən) *n., pl.* **-men** (-mən) **1** a person who lives or works in the woods, as a hunter, woodcutter, etc. **2** a person familiar with the woods, specif. one who is skilled in camping, hiking, etc.

wood sorrel ⟦transl. of MFr *sorrel de boys*⟧ any of a genus (*Oxalis,* family Oxalidaceae) of creeping dicotyledonous plants (order Geraniales) with white, pink, red, or yellow, five-parted flowers and cloverlike compound leaves that contain oxalic acid: found in cool, shaded, damp woods

wood spirit METHANOL

Wood·stock (wood′stäk′) village in SE N.Y.: a rock music festival named after this village took place in 1969 in the town of Bethel in a neighboring county

wood sugar XYLOSE

☆**wood·sy** (wood′zē) *adj.* **-si·er, -si·est** of, characteristic of, or like the woods —**wood′si·ness** *n.*

wood tar a dark, sticky, syruplike substance obtained by destructive distillation of wood and used in the preservation of timber, rope, etc.

wood thrush ☆a large thrush (*Hylocichla mustelina*) of E North America, with a brown mantle and a white, dark-spotted breast, that has a sweet, clear song

wood turning the art or process of turning, or shaping, wood on a lathe —**wood′-turn′er** *n.* —**wood′-turn′ing** *adj.*

wood vinegar PYROLIGNEOUS ACID

☆**wood warbler** WARBLER (sense 2)

Wood·ward (wood′wərd), **Robert Burns** 1917-79; U.S. chemist

wood·wax·en (wood′wak′sən) ***n.*** *var. of* WOADWAXEN

wood·wind (wood′wind′) ***n.*** **1** [*pl.*] the woodwind instruments of an orchestra, or the players of these instruments **2** any of such instruments —***adj.*** **1** designating a wind instrument made, esp. originally, of wood, as the flute, clarinet, or oboe **2** of or composed for such an instrument or instruments

wood·work (wood′wurk′) ***n.*** things made of wood, esp. the interior moldings, doors, stairs, etc. of a house —**come (or crawl) out of the woodwork** [Informal] to come out of hiding or obscurity, often, specif., in large numbers: a dismissive phrase

wood·work·ing (-wur′kiŋ) ***n.*** the art or work of making things of wood —***adj.*** of woodworking —**wood′work′er *n.***

wood·y (wood′ē) ***adj.*** **wood′i·er, wood′i·est** **1** covered with trees; wooded **2** consisting of or forming wood; ligneous [*a woody plant*] **3** like or characteristic of wood [*a woody texture, color, etc.*] **4** having the taste or smell of wood from the barrels used to age it: said of wine —☆***n.*** [Informal] a station wagon with exterior wood paneling

woo·er (wo͞o′ər) ***n.*** a person who woos; suitor

woof[1] (wo͞of) ***n.*** ⟦altered (prob. infl. by WARP, WEFT) < ME *oof* < OE *owef* < *o-* (< *on*) + *-wef* < base of *wefan*, to WEAVE⟧ WEFT

woof[2] (woof) ***n.*** ⟦echoic⟧ a gruff barking sound of or like that of a dog —***vi.*** to make such a sound

woof·er (woof′ər) ***n.*** ⟦prec. + -ER⟧ a large, high-fidelity speaker for reproducing low-frequency sounds: cf. TWEETER, MIDRANGE (***n.*** 2)

wool (wool) ***n.*** ⟦ME *wolle* < OE *wull,* akin to Ger *wolle* < IE base **wel-*, hair, wool, grass > L *villus,* shaggy hair, *vellus,* fleece, *lana,* wool, Gr *lēnos,* wool⟧ **1** *a)* the soft, curly or crisp hair of sheep *b)* the hair of some other animals, as the goat or llama, having a similar texture **2** *a)* yarn spun from the fibers of such fleece, esp. the fleece of sheep *b)* cloth, clothing, etc. made of this yarn **3** short, thick, curly or crisp human hair **4** anything that looks or feels like wool, as a fibrous mass of inorganic material [*rock wool,* steel *wool*] or the hairy or furry coating on some insects, insect larvae, and plants —***adj.*** of wool or woolen goods —☆**all wool and a yard wide** [Informal] genuine or admirable; truly and thoroughly as described —☆**pull the wool over someone's eyes** [Informal] to deceive or trick someone

wool·en (-ən) ***adj.*** ⟦ME *wullen* < OE⟧ **1** made of wool **2** of or relating to wool or woolen cloth —***n.*** [*pl.*] woolen goods or clothing Also [Chiefly Brit.] **wool′len**

Woolf (woolf), **Virginia** (born *Adeline Virginia Stephen*) 1882-1941; Eng. novelist & critic

wool fat **1** the natural grease found in sheep's wool, yielding lanolin: also **wool grease** **2** LANOLIN

wool·fell (wool′fel′) ***n.*** ⟦WOOL + FELL[4]⟧ the pelt of a wool-bearing animal with the wool still on it

wool·gath·er (-gath′ər) ***vi.*** ⟦from the practice of wandering to gather tufts of wool caught on thorns and hedges⟧ to engage in idle or aimless daydreaming, speculation, etc. —**wool′gath′er·er *n.*** —**wool′gath′er·ing *n.***

wool·grow·er (-grō′ər) ***n.*** one who raises sheep for wool

☆**wool·hat** (wool′hat) ***n.*** [South] **1** a person who owns or works a small farm **2** an unsophisticated or conservative person

Wool·ley (wool′ē), Sir **(Charles) Leonard** 1880-1960; Eng. archaeologist

wool·ly (wool′ē) ***adj.*** **-li·er, -li·est** **1** of or like wool **2** bearing wool **3** covered with wool or something resembling wool in texture ☆**4** having characteristics of the early frontier life of the W U.S.; rough and uncivilized: used chiefly in **wild and woolly** **5** tangled and confused; fuzzy [*woolly ideas*] —☆***n.,*** *pl.* **-lies** **1** [West] a sheep **2** *a)* a woolen garment, esp. one with a fleecelike surface *b)* [*pl.*] long underwear made of wool —**wool′li·ness *n.***

woolly aphid any of various aphids that secrete a hairlike covering of wax

woolly bear *see* TIGER MOTH

wool·ly-head·ed (-hed′id) ***adj.*** confused, unclear, impractical, etc. in thought: also **wool′ly-mind′ed** (-mīn′did)

Wool·man (wool′mən), **John** 1720-72; Am. Quaker known for his opposition to slavery & his posthumously published *Journal*

wool·pack (wool′pak′) ***n.*** **1** a large bag of canvas, cotton, etc. in which to pack wool or fleece for sale **2** a bale of wool so packed **3** a fleecy cumulus cloud

wool·sack (-sak′) ***n.*** **1** a sack of wool **2** a cushion stuffed with wool, on which the British Lord Chancellor sits in the House of Lords

wool·shed (-shed′) ***n.*** a building in which sheep are sheared and the wool is packed for market

wool·sort·ers' disease (-sôrt′ərz) pulmonary anthrax, an occupational disease of workers in unprocessed wool, contracted by inhaling the spores of the anthrax bacillus

☆**wool sponge** any of several commercial sponges (genera *Hippospongia* and *Euspongia*) with durable, soft, fibrous skeletons

wool stapler **1** a person who sells wool **2** a person who sorts wool according to its staple, or fiber

Wool·worth (wool′wərth), **F(rank) W(in′field)** 1852-1919; U.S. merchant

wool·y (wool′ē) ***adj., n.*** *alt. sp. of* WOOLLY —**wool′i·ness *n.***

woo·mer·a (wo͞o′mər ə) ***n.*** ⟦< name in a language of Australia⟧ a spear-throwing device used by Australian Aborigines

woops (woops, wo͞ops) ***interj.*** *var. of* WHOOPS

woosh (woosh) ***vi., vt., n., interj.*** *var. of* WHOOSH

☆**wooz·y** (wo͞o′zē, wooz′ē) ***adj.*** **wooz′i·er, wooz′i·est** ⟦prob. < *wooze,* var. of OOZE[1]⟧ [Informal] **1** dizzy, faint, and sickish **2** befuddled, muddled, or dazed, as from drink, drugs, a blow, etc. —**wooz′i·ly *adv.*** —**wooz′i·ness *n.***

☆**wop** (wäp) ***n.*** ⟦? < It dial. *guappo,* ruffian⟧ [*sometimes* **W-**] [Slang] an Italian or a person of Italian descent: an offensive term of hostility and contempt

Worces·ter (woos′tər) **1** city in E England, in Hereford and Worcester **2** WORCESTERSHIRE **3** city in central Mass.

Worcester china (*or* porcelain) a fine china (or porcelain) made at Worcester, England, from 1751

Worces·ter·shire (woos′tər shir′) former county of W England, now part of the county of Hereford and Worcester

Worcestershire sauce (-shir′, shīr′) a spicy sauce for meats, poultry, etc., containing soy, vinegar, and other ingredients: orig. made in Worcester, England: also [Chiefly Brit.] **Worces′ter sauce** (woos′tər)

word (wurd) ***n.*** ⟦ME < OE, akin to Ger *wort* < IE **werdh-* (extension of base **wer-*, to speak, say) > Gr *eirein,* to speak, L *verbum,* word⟧ **1** *a)* a speech sound, or series of such sounds, serving to communicate meaning and consisting of at least one base morpheme with or without prefixes or suffixes; unit of language between the morpheme and the sentence *b)* a letter or group of letters representing such a unit of language, written or printed usually in solid or hyphenated form **2** a brief expression, statement, remark, etc. [*a word of advice*] **3** a promise, affirmation, or assurance [*to give a person one's word*] **4** news; information; tidings [*no word from home; what's the good word?*] **5** *a)* a password or signal *b)* a command, order, or authorization [*waiting for the word to go ahead*] **6** *a)* [*usually pl.*] talk; speech *b)* [*pl.*] the lyrics, text, libretto, etc. of a musical composition that is sung **7** [*pl.*] a quarrel; dispute; argument **8** [Archaic] a saying; proverb **9** *Comput.* a basic unit of storage in memory, consisting of a certain number of bits —***vt.*** to express in particular words [*to carefully word a toast*] —**a good word** a favorable comment, or commendation —**at a word** in quick response to a request or command; immediately —**be as good as one's word** to live up to one's promises —**break one's word** to fail to keep one's promise —**hang on someone's words** to listen to someone eagerly —**have a word with** to have a brief conversation with —**have no words for** to be incapable of describing —**have words with** to argue angrily with —**in a word** in short; briefly —**in so many words** exactly and plainly —**man (or woman) of his (or her) word** a person who keeps his (or her) promises —**of many (or few) words** talkative (or not talkative) —**put words in someone's mouth** to ascribe words or opinions to someone that he or she did not say or does not hold —**take someone at his (or her) word** to take someone's words literally or seriously and, often, act accordingly —**take someone's word (for it)** to have trust in what someone says without needing proof or evidence —**take the words (right) out of someone's mouth** to say just what someone (else) was about to say —**the Word** **1** LOGOS **2** GOSPEL (sense 1) —**(upon) my word!** indeed! really!: an exclamation of surprise, irritation, etc. —**word for word** in precisely the same words; exactly; verbatim

word·age (wur′dij) ***n.*** **1** words collectively, or the number of words (*of* a story, novel, etc.) **2** verbiage; wordiness **3** wording; diction

word-as·so·ci·a·tion test (wurd′ə sō′sē ā′shən) a psychological test in which the person being tested responds to a given word with the first word (or the first word in a specified category, such as an antonym) brought to mind

word blindness ALEXIA —**word′-blind′ *adj.***

word·book (-book′) ***n.*** a dictionary, lexicon, or vocabulary

word deafness a cerebral disorder characterized by loss of ability to understand spoken words; auditory aphasia

word-for-word (-fər wurd′) ***adj.*** in exactly the same words

word·ing (wur′diŋ) ***n.*** choice and arrangement of words; diction

word·less (wurd′lis) ***adj.*** **1** without words; speechless **2** not expressed or not capable of being expressed in words —**word′less·ly *adv.*** —**word′less·ness *n.***

Word of God the Bible

word of honor pledged word; solemn promise; oath

word of mouth informal speech or conversation between persons, as opposed to writing or publishing [*gossip spread by word of mouth*]

word-of-mouth (-əv mouth′) ***adj.*** communicated orally, as in conversation

word order the arrangement of words in a phrase, clause, or sentence

word·play (-plā′) ***n.*** **1** subtle or clever exchange of words; repartee **2** punning or a pun

word processing the production of documents with a word processor

word processor a computerized device incorporating variously an electronic keyboard, video screen, memory, printer, etc., used to generate, edit, store, transmit, or duplicate documents, as letters, reports, etc. for a business

word·smith (-smith′) ***n.*** **1** a person, esp. a professional writer, who uses language skillfully **2** a person who coins new words

word square a square made of letters so arranged that they spell the same words in the same order horizontally and vertically

D A R E
A C I D
R I N G
E D G E

word square

Words·worth (wurdz′wərth), **William** 1770-1850; Eng. poet: poet laureate (1843-50)

word·y (wur′dē) ***adj.*** **word′i·er, word′i·est** **1** of words; verbal **2** containing or using many or too many words; verbose —**word′i·ly *adv.*** —**word′i·ness *n.***

SYN.—wordy is the general word implying the use of more words in speaking or writing than are necessary for communication [a *wordy* document]; **verbose** suggests a wordiness that results in obscurity, tediousness, bombast, etc. [a *verbose* acceptance speech]; **prolix** implies such a tiresome elaboration of trivial details as to be boring or dull [his *prolix* sermons]; **diffuse** suggests such verbosity and loose construction as to lose all force and sharpness [a rambling, *diffuse* harangue]; **redundant**, in this connection, implies the use of unnecessary or repetitious words or phrases [a *redundant* literary style] —**ANT. concise, pithy, terse**

wore (wôr) ***vt., vi. pt. of*** WEAR[1]

work (wurk) ***n.*** ⟦ME *werk* < OE *weorc*, akin to Ger *werk* < IE base **werĝ-*, to do, act > Gr *ergon* (for **wergon*), action, work, *organon*, tool, instrument⟧ **1** physical or mental effort exerted to do or make something; purposeful activity; labor; toil **2** *a)* employment at a job or in a position *b)* the place where one is employed **3** occupation, profession, business, trade, craft, etc. **4** *a)* something one is making, doing, or acting upon, esp. as part of one's occupation or duty; task; undertaking [to bring *work* home from the office] *b)* the amount of this [a day's *work*] **5** something that has been made or done; result of a specific kind of activity or way of working [to have dental *work* done, skillful *brushwork*]; specif., *a)* an act; deed (*usually used in pl.*) [a person of good *works*] *b)* [*pl.*] collected writings [the *works* of Poe] *c)* [*pl.*] engineering structures, as bridges, dams, docks, etc. *d)* a fortification *e)* needlework; embroidery *f)* WORK OF ART **6** material that is being or is to be processed, as in a machine tool, in some state of manufacture **7** [*pl., with sing. v.*] a place where work is done, as a factory, public utility plant, etc.: often in comb. [*steelworks, gasworks*] **8** manner, style, quality, rate, etc. of working; workmanship **9** foam due to fermentation, as in cider **10** the action of, or effect produced by, natural forces **11** *Mech.* the product of force and the amount of displacement in the direction of that force: it is the means by which energy is transferred from one object or system to another: abbrev. W **12** [*pl.*] *Theol.* acts done in compliance with religious laws or duties or aimed at fulfilling religious ideals —***adj.*** *a)* of, for, or used in work *b)* designating or of heavy-duty clothing designed for wear while engaged in manual or outdoor labor [*work* boots] —***vi.* worked, work′ing** ⟦OE *wyrcan, wercan*⟧ **1** to exert oneself in order to do or make something; do work; labor; toil **2** to be employed **3** *a)* to perform its required or expected function; operate or act as specified *b)* to operate effectively; be effectual [a makeshift arrangement that *works*] **4** to undergo fermentation **5** to produce results or exert an influence [let it *work* in their minds] **6** to be manipulated, kneaded, etc. [putty that *works* easily] **7** to move, proceed, etc. slowly and with or as with difficulty **8** to move, twitch, etc. as from agitation [his face *worked* with emotion] **9** to change into a specified condition, as by repeated movement [the door *worked* loose] —***vt.*** **1** to cause; bring about; effect [an idea that *worked* harm] **2** to mold; shape; form [to *work* silver] **3** to sew, embroider, etc. [to *work* a sampler] **4** to solve (a mathematical problem, puzzle, etc.) **5** to draw, paint, carve, etc. (a portrait or likeness) **6** to manipulate; knead [to *work* dough] **7** to bring into a specified condition, as by movement back and forth [to *work* a nail loose] **8** to cultivate (soil) **9** to cause to function; operate; manage; use [to *work* a pump] **10** to cause fermentation in **11** to cause to work [to *work* a crew hard] **12** to influence; persuade [to *work* someone around to one's way of thinking] **13** to make (one's way, passage, etc.) by work or effort **14** to provoke; rouse; excite [to *work* oneself into a rage] **15** to carry on activity in, along, etc.; cover [a salesman *working* his territory] **16** *a)* to be employed at [*work* two jobs] *b)* to perform duties related to a job during (a particular time) or at (a particular place), etc. [*work* the night shift, *work* the ticket counter] **17** [Informal] to make use of, esp. by artful contriving [to *work* one's connections] ☆**18** [Informal] to use one's influence, charm, etc. on (a person) to gain some profit or advantage ☆**19** [Slang] to move through (a crowd or room) greeting people, shaking hands, etc.: said esp. of a politician —**at work 1** working or engaged in work **2** operating [unseen forces were *at work* on the economy] —☆**get the works** [Old Slang] to be the victim of extreme measures —☆**give someone the works** [Old Slang] **1** to murder someone **2** to subject someone to an ordeal, either maliciously or jokingly —**in the works** [Informal] in the process of being planned or done —**make short** (or **quick**) **work of** to deal with or dispose of quickly —**out of work** without a job; unemployed —☆**shoot the works** [Slang] **1** to risk everything on one chance or play **2** to make a supreme effort or attempt —**the works 1** the working parts or mechanism (*of* a watch, clock, etc.) ☆**2** [Informal] *a)* all possible accessories, extras, etc. *b)* everything that can be included (usually **the whole works**) —**work in 1** to introduce or insert **2** to be introduced or inserted —**work off 1** to get rid of or dissipate, as by exertion ☆**2** to pay (a debt or obligation) by work rather than with money —**work on** (or **upon**) **1** to influence **2** to try to persuade —**work out 1** to make its way out, as from being embedded **2** to exhaust (a mine, etc.) **3** WORK OFF (sense 2) **4** to bring about by work; accomplish **5** to solve **6** to calculate **7** to result in some way [things did not *work out* as planned] **8** to add up to a total (*at* a specified amount) **9** to develop; elaborate **10** to put into practice **11** to engage in a training session or program for physical fitness or athletic skill —**work over 1** to work or do again ☆**2** [Informal] to subject to harsh or cruel treatment, as by beating, torture, etc. —**work up** ☆**1** to make one's (or its) way up; advance; rise **2** to manipulate, mix, etc. into a specified object or shape **3** to develop; elaborate **4** to acquire knowledge of or skill at **5** to arouse; excite **6** [Informal] to bring about or cause (a sweat) by vigorous activity

work·a·ble (wur′kə bəl) ***adj.*** **1** that can be worked **2** practicable; feasible —**work′a·bil′i·ty *n.*, work′a·ble·ness**

work·a·day (wur′kə dā′) ***adj.*** ⟦ME *werkedai* < *werk*, WORK + *-e-* (prob. as in *sunnedai*, SUNDAY[1], *messeday*, "mass day") + *dai*, DAY⟧ **1** of or suitable for working days; everyday **2** commonplace; ordinary

☆**work·a·hol·ic** (wur′kə hôl′ik, -häl′-) ***n.*** ⟦< WORK + ALCOHOLIC: coined by W. E. Oates (1917-99), U.S. pastoral counselor⟧ [Informal] a person having a compulsive need to work —**work′a·hol′ism′ *n.***

work·a·round (wur′kə round′) ***n.*** a method for overcoming an obstacle or bypassing a problem

work·bag (wurk′bag′) ***n.*** a bag for holding implements and materials for work, as for knitting, crocheting, etc.

work basket a basket for holding sewing equipment

work·bench (-bench′) ***n.*** a table at which work is done, as by a mechanic, carpenter, repairman, etc.

work·book (-book′) ***n.*** ☆**1** a book based on a textbook or course of study, which contains exercises and questions for use by students **2** a book of operating instructions **3** a book in which one keeps a record of work planned or done

work·box (-bäks′) ***n.*** a box for needlework tools and materials

☆**work camp 1** PRISON CAMP (sense 1) **2** a camp where work is done by volunteers, as for a religious organization

work·day (-dā′) ***n.*** ⟦LME *werkdai*, prob. < *werk* + *dai* (OE *weorcdæg*)⟧ **1** a day on which work is ordinarily done, esp. as distinguished from a Sunday, holiday, etc. ☆**2** the part of a day during which work is done; specif., the number of hours constituting the required day's work for the regular wage or salary [a seven-hour *workday*] —***adj.*** WORKADAY

work·er (wur′kər) ***n.*** **1** a person, animal, or thing that works; specif., a person who is employed to do physical or mental work for wages, esp. in order to earn a living, as in a trade, industry, business, office, etc. or on a farm, ranch, etc. **2** a person who works for a cause, organization, etc. [volunteer *workers*, a party *worker*] **3** any of a class of sterile or sexually imperfect ants, bees, wasps, etc. that do work for the colony: with the exception of termites, workers are normally females **4** *Printing* an electrotype used to print from, as distinguished from one used as a mold for making duplicate electrotypes

-work·er (wur′kər) *combining form* a person who works in a (specified) industry or place or with (specified) materials or equipment [*dockworker, steelworker*]

workers' compensation 1 a government-sponsored insurance system, funded by contributions from employers, for compensating employees for injury or occupational disease suffered in connection with their employment **2** compensation given under such a system

work ethic a system of values in which central importance is ascribed to work, or purposeful activity, and to qualities of character believed to be promoted by work

☆**work·fare** (wurk′fer′) ***n.*** ⟦WORK + (WEL)FARE⟧ a government program requiring employable recipients of welfare to register for work or work training

work farm a farm on which the workers are short-term prisoners convicted of less serious crimes

work·flow (wurk′flō′) ***n.*** the steps or operations into which a particular task is organized

work·force (wurk′fôrs′) ***n.*** the total number of workers actively employed in, or available for work in, a nation, region, plant, etc.: also written **work force**

work·horse (wurk′hôrs′) ***n.*** **1** a horse used for working, as for pulling a plow **2** a steady, responsible worker who assumes a heavy workload **3** a machine, vehicle, etc. that proves to be durable and dependable

work·house (-hous′) ***n.*** **1** [Obs.] a WORKSHOP (sense 1) **2** [Historical] in England, a poorhouse in which able residents had to work ☆**3** a kind of prison, where petty offenders are confined and made to work

work·ing (wur′kiŋ) ***adj.*** **1** that works; specif., engaged in unskilled or manual labor **2** of, for, used in, or taken up by work [a *working* day, *working* clothes] **3** *a)* sufficient to be effective [a party holding a *working* majority in the legislature] *b)* sufficient for basic or practical use [a *working* knowledge of Spanish] **4** on which further work is or may be based [a *working* hypothesis] **5** used during a project's development; provisional [a *working* title for a movie in preproduction] **6** moving or jerking convulsively, as from emotion: said of the face, features, etc. —***n.*** **1** the act or process of a person or thing that works **2** the process of forming or shaping something **3** convulsive movement or jerking, as of the face **4** slow or gradual progress involving great effort or exertion **5** [*usually pl.*] a part of a mine, quarry, etc. where work is or has been done

working capital 1 *Accounting* the excess of cash and liquid assets over current liabilities **2** cash and other assets needed for the day-to-day operation of a business

working class workers as a class; esp., industrial or manual workers as a class; proletariat —**work′ing-class′ *adj.***

working day WORKDAY

working girl 1 [Informal] a woman who works, esp. at a job not requiring advanced education and training ☆**2** [Slang] a female prostitute

work·ing·man (-man′) ***n., pl.* -men′** (-men′) a worker; esp., an industrial or manual worker; wage earner; laborer

working papers any official papers that legalize the employment of a minor or of an alien

working substance the air, gas, or liquid that works the pistons, vanes, etc. of an engine

work·ing·wom·an (-woom′ən) *n., pl.* **-wom′en** (-wim′in) a woman who is gainfully employed; often, specif., such a woman as distinct from a housewife

work·load (wʉrk′lōd′) *n.* the amount of work assigned for completion within a given period of time

work·man (wʉrk′mən) *n., pl.* **-men** (-mən) 1 WORKINGMAN 2 a craftsman

work·man·like (-līk′) *adj.* characteristic of a good workman; done in a steady, efficient manner but, often, specif., without extraordinary skill or ingenuity [*a workmanlike* repair job]: also **work′man·ly**

work·man·ship (-ship′) *n.* 1 *a)* skill of a workman *b)* the quality of the work done or thing made; craftsmanship [furniture of fine *workmanship*] 2 something produced by this skill

workmen's compensation WORKERS' COMPENSATION

work of art 1 something produced in one of the fine arts, esp. in one of the graphic or plastic arts, as a painting, sculpture, carving, etc. 2 anything made, done, performed, etc. with great skill and beauty

☆**work·out** (wʉrk′out′) *n.* 1 a training session of exercises to maintain or improve one's physical or athletic skill 2 any strenuous exercise, work, etc.

work·peo·ple (-pē′pəl) *pl.n.* [Brit.] workers; esp., industrial or manual workers

work·place (-plās′) *n.* the office, factory, etc. where one works

work-re·lease (-ri lēs′) *adj.* designating or of a program in which certain prisoners are permitted to leave a penal institution for a specified time in order to hold jobs, prior to their full release

work·room (-ro͞om′) *n.* a room in which work is done

works council [Brit.] a committee of workers organized by their employer to discuss industrial relations

work·sheet (wʉrk′shēt′) *n.* 1 a sheet of paper on which a record of work, working time, etc. is kept 2 a sheet of paper printed with practice exercises, problems, etc., to be worked on directly by students 3 a sheet of paper containing working notes, preliminary formulations, etc. Also written **work sheet**

work·shop (-shäp′) *n.* 1 a room or building where work, as home repairs or light manufacturing, is done 2 a seminar or series of meetings for intensive study, work, discussion, etc. in some field

work song a folk song sung by laborers, as in the fields, with a marked rhythm matching the rhythm of their work

work·space (wʉrk′spās′) *n.* the area, as in an office or factory, in which a worker performs assigned tasks

work·sta·tion (-stā′shən) *n.* 1 a person's work area, including furniture, appliances, etc.; often, specif., such an area with a terminal or personal computer 2 a terminal or personal computer that is connected to a network 3 a computer, usually intermediate in power between a personal computer and a minicomputer, used for complex or specialized applications, as in engineering design

work-stud·y (-stud′ē) *adj.* of or relating to any of various programs, as at a university, which enable students to engage in part-time employment while continuing their studies

work·ta·ble (-tā′bəl) *n.* a table at which work is done, esp. one with drawers for tools, materials, etc.

work-up (-up′) *n.* 1 a complete medical study of a patient, including a thorough examination, laboratory tests, a survey of the patient's case history, etc. 2 *Printing* an unwanted mark on a printed page caused by the rising of spacing material

☆**work·week** (-wēk′) *n.* 1 that part of a week during which work is done ☆2 the number of hours constituting the required week's work for the regular wage or salary [a forty-hour *workweek*]

work·wom·an (-woom′ən) *n., pl.* **-wom′en** (-wim′in) a woman worker, esp. a woman industrial or manual worker

world (wʉrld) *n.* ⟦ME < OE *werold*, world, humanity, long time, akin to OHG *weralt* < early WGmc comp. < **wera-*, man (see WEREWOLF) + **alth-*, an age, mankind (for IE base see OLD): basic sense "the age of man"⟧ 1 *a)* the planet earth *b)* the whole universe *c)* any heavenly body thought of hypothetically as inhabited [*worlds* in space] 2 the earth and its inhabitants 3 *a)* the human race; mankind *b)* people generally; the public [a discovery that startled the *world*] 4 *a)* [*also* **W-**] some part of the earth [the Old *World*] *b)* some period of history, its society, etc. [the ancient *world*] *c)* any sphere or domain [the animal *world*] *d)* any sphere of human activity [the *world* of music] *e)* any sphere or state of existence [the *world* of tomorrow] 5 individual experience, outlook, etc. [a man whose *world* is narrow] 6 *a)* secular or social life and interests, as distinguished from the religious or spiritual *b)* people primarily concerned with secular affairs and pursuits 7 [*often pl.*] a large amount; great deal [the rest did him a *world* (or *worlds*) of good] 8 a star or planet —*SYN.* EARTH —**bring into the world** 1 to give birth to 2 to assist in the delivery of (a child) —**come into the world** to be born —**for all the world** 1 for any reason or consideration at all 2 in every respect; exactly —**in the world** 1 on earth or in the universe; anywhere [where *in the world* could you find this?] 2 at all; ever [how *in the world* did you know?] —☆**on top of the world** [Informal] elated with joy, pride, success, etc.; exultant —☆**out of this world** [Slang] exceptionally fine; extraordinary —**world without end** forever

World Bank an agency of the United Nations, established in 1945 to make loans to member nations: official name *International Bank for Reconstruction and Development*

world·beat (wʉrld′bēt′) *n.* popular, strongly rhythmic dance music of Africa, the Caribbean, Latin America, and, sometimes, Asia

☆**world-beat·er** (-bēt′ər) *n.* [Informal] one that is, or that has the qualities needed to become, a great success —**world′-beat′ing** *adj.*

world-class (-klas′) *adj.* of the highest class, as in international competition

World Court INTERNATIONAL COURT OF JUSTICE

world·ling (-liŋ) *n.* a worldly person

world·ly (wʉrld′lē) *adj.* **-li·er, -li·est** 1 of or limited to this world; temporal or secular 2 devoted to or concerned with the affairs, pleasures, etc. of this world: also **world′ly-mind′ed** 3 worldly-wise; sophisticated —*SYN.* EARTHLY —**world′li·ness** *n.*

world·ly-wise (-wīz′) *adj.* wise in the ways or affairs of the world; sophisticated

world music contemporary folk and popular music of Africa, Latin America, and Asia, as distinguished from that of the U.S., the U.K., and, sometimes, W Europe

world power ⟦transl. of Ger *weltmacht*⟧ a nation or organization large or powerful enough to have a worldwide influence

☆**World Series** [*also* **w- s-**] an annual series of games between the winning teams of the two major U.S. baseball leagues to decide the championship

☆**world's fair** any of various expositions at which the arts, crafts, industrial and agricultural products, scientific advances, etc. of various countries of the world are on display

world-shak·ing (wʉrld′shā′kiŋ) *adj.* of great significance, effect, or influence; momentous

world soul in some worldviews, the formative and animating principle of the universe conceived of as analogous to the soul of a person

world·view (wʉrld′vyo͞o′) *n.* a comprehensive, esp. personal, philosophy or conception of the world and of human life

☆**World War I** the war (1914-18) between the Allies (Great Britain, France, Russia, the U.S., Italy, Japan, etc.) and the Central Powers (Germany, Austria-Hungary, etc.)

☆**World War II** the war (1939-45) between the Allies (Great Britain, France, the Soviet Union, the U.S., etc.) and the Axis (Germany, Italy, Japan, etc.)

world-wea·ry (-wir′ē) *adj.* characterized by or expressing feelings of weariness, bordeom, etc. resulting from life experiences

world·wide (-wīd′) *adj.* extending throughout the world —*adv.* throughout the world

World Wide Web that part of the INTERNET that provides access to images and sound in addition to text

worm (wʉrm) *n.* ⟦ME < OE *wyrm*, serpent, dragon, akin to Ger *wurm* < IE base **wer-*, to turn, bend > WARP, L *vermis*, worm⟧ 1 any of many slender, soft-bodied animals, some segmented, that live by burrowing underground, in water, or as parasites, including the annelids, nemerteans, nematodes, platyhelminths, acanthocephalans, and gordian worms 2 popularly, *a)* an insect larva, as a caterpillar, grub, or maggot *b)* any of several mollusks, as the shipworms *c)* any of various wormlike animals, as a rotifer or a blindworm 3 an abject, wretched, or contemptible person 4 something that gnaws or distresses one inwardly, suggesting a parasitic worm [the *worm* of conscience] 5 something thought of as being wormlike because of its spiral shape, etc.; specif., *a)* the thread of a screw *b)* the coil of a still *c)* an Archimedean screw or similar apparatus *d)* a short, rotating screw that meshes with the teeth of a worm gear or a rack 6 [Archaic] *a)* a serpent *b)* a dragon 7 *Anat.* any organ or part resembling a worm, as the vermiform process 8 *Comput.* an unauthorized, disruptive program, typically spread through communication lines, that creates copies of itself, thereby depleting a disk's or system's available memory: cf. VIRUS (sense 4) 9 [*pl.*] *Med.* any disease or disorder caused by the presence of parasitic worms in the intestines, etc. 10 *Zool.* LYTTA —*vi.* to move, proceed, etc. like a worm, in a winding, creeping, or devious manner —*vt.* 1 to bring about, make, etc. in a winding, creeping, or devious manner [to *worm* one's way through a tunnel] 2 to insinuate (oneself) into a situation, conversation, etc. 3 to extract (information, secrets, etc.) by insinuation, cajolery, or subtle questioning 4 to purge of intestinal worms 5 *Naut.* to fill the spaces between the strands of (a rope) with lengths of yarn or cord in order to make the surface even ☆6 to rid (tobacco plants) of worms or grubs —☆**can of worms** [Informal] a complex, usually unpleasant problem —**worm′er** *n.* —**worm′like′** *adj.*

worm-eat·en (wʉrm′ēt″n) *adj.* 1 eaten into by worms, termites, etc. 2 worn-out, out-of-date, etc.

☆**worm fence** ⟦from its undulating form⟧ VIRGINIA (RAIL) FENCE

worm gear 1 a gear with teeth designed to mesh with the thread of a WORM (*n.* 5d) 2 a mechanism consisting of this gear and a WORM (*n.* 5d)

worm·hole (-hōl′) *n.* 1 a hole made, as in wood, by a worm, termite, etc. 2 a hypothetical space-time tunnel or channel connecting a black hole with another universe, with a white hole, etc.

worm lizard AMPHISBAENIAN

worm·root (-ro͞ot′) *n.* PINKROOT

Worms (vôrmz; *E* wʉrmz) city in SW Germany, on the Rhine, in the state of Rhineland-Palatinate: scene of an assembly (*Diet of Worms*), 1521, at which Martin Luther was condemned for heresy

worm·seed (wʉrm′sēd′) *n.* 1 any of a number of plants whose seeds are used in medicine as a remedy for worms, including various goosefoots, esp. the **American wormseed** (*Chenopodium ambrosioides*) 2 the seed of any of these plants 3 SANTONICA (sense 2)

☆**worm's-eye view** (wʉrmz′ī′) ⟦prob. modeled after BIRD'S-EYE VIEW⟧ an outlook from very close range, but from an inferior or menial position

worm snake any of a superfamily (Typhlopoidea) of wormlike, nonpoisonous snakes with vestigial eyes

worm wheel WORM GEAR (sense 1)

worm·wood (wʉrm′wood′) *n.* ⟦ME *wormwode,* altered by folk etym. (infl. by *worm,* WORM + *wode,* WOOD[1]: from use as a vermifuge) < *wermode* < OE *wermod,* akin to Ger *wermut* (> Fr *vermout,* vermouth)⟧ **1** any of a number of strong-smelling plants (genus *Artemisia*) of the composite family, with white or yellow flowers; esp., a Eurasian perennial (*A. absinthium*) that yields a bitter, dark-green oil (**wormwood oil**) used in making absinthe **2** a bitter, unpleasant, or mortifying experience

worm·y (wʉr′mē) *adj.* **worm′i·er, worm′i·est 1** containing a worm or worms; worm-infested **2** WORM-EATEN **3** like a worm **4** debased; groveling —**worm′i·ness** *n.*

worn (wôrn) *vt., vi. pp. of* WEAR[1] —*adj.* **1** showing the effects of use, wear, etc. **2** damaged by use or wear **3** showing the effects of worry or anxiety

worn-out (-out′) *adj.* **1** no longer effective, usable, or serviceable due to wear or overuse **2** exhausted; tired out

wor·ri·ment (wʉr′ē mənt) *n.* [Old-fashioned] **1** a worrying or being worried; anxiety **2** a cause of worry

wor·ri·some (-səm) *adj.* **1** causing worry or anxiety **2** [Now Rare] having a tendency to worry —**wor′ri·some·ly** *adv.*

wor·ry (wʉr′ē) *vt.* **-ried, -ry·ing** ⟦ME *wirwen* < OE *wyrgan,* to strangle, injure, akin to Ger *würgen,* to strangle < IE **werĝh-,* to twist, choke < base **wer-,* to twist > WORM⟧ **1** *a)* to harass or treat roughly with or as with continual biting or tearing with the teeth [a dog *worrying* a bone] *b)* to pluck at, push on, touch, etc. repeatedly in a nervous or determined way [*worrying* the loose tooth with his tongue] **2** to annoy, bother, harass, vex, etc. **3** to cause to feel troubled or uneasy; make anxious; distress —*vi.* **1** to bite, pull, or tear (*at* an object) with or as with the teeth **2** to feel distressed in the mind; be anxious, troubled, or uneasy **3** to manage to get (*along* or *through*) in the face of trials and difficulties —*n., pl.* **-ries 1** the act of worrying **2** a troubled state of mind; anxiety; distress; care; uneasiness **3** something that causes anxiety —*SYN.* CARE —**not to worry!** [Informal] you do not need to worry! —**wor′ri·er** *n.*

worry beads a string of smooth beads designed to be handled or stroked, as to relieve anxiety or nervousness: popular esp. in the Near East

☆**wor·ry·wart** (-wôrt′) *n.* ⟦WORRY + WART⟧ [Informal] a person who tends to worry, esp. over insignificant details

worse (wʉrs) *adj.* ⟦ME < OE *wiersa* (used as compar. of *yfel,* bad, EVIL), akin to OHG *wirsiro,* prob. < base of OHG & OS *werran,* to confuse⟧ **1** *compar. of* BAD[1] & ILL[1] **2** *a)* bad, evil, harmful, unpleasant, etc. in a greater degree; less good *b)* of inferior quality or condition **3** in poorer health or physical condition; more ill; less well **4** in a less favorable condition; in a less satisfactory situation —*adv.* **1** *compar. of* BADLY & ILL[1] **2** in a worse manner or way **3** to a worse extent or degree —*n.* that which is worse —**for the worse** to a worse condition —**worse off 1** in a worse situation or condition **2** having less income, wealth, etc.

wor·sen (wʉr′sən) *vt., vi.* ⟦orig. dial. < prec. + -EN⟧ to make or become worse

wors·er (-sər) *adj., adv.* [Now Dial. or Informal] WORSE

wor·ship (wʉr′ship) *n.* ⟦ME *worschip* < OE *weorthscipe,* honor, dignity, worship: see WORTH[1] & -SHIP⟧ **1** *a)* reverence or devotion for a deity; religious homage or veneration *b)* a church service or other rite showing this **2** extreme devotion or intense love or admiration of any kind **3** [W-] [Chiefly Brit.] a title of honor used in speaking to or of magistrates, mayors, or certain others holding high rank: preceded by *Your* or by *His* or *Her* **4** [Rare] something worshiped **5** [Rare] a distinct type of religious group, as a sect **6** [Archaic] greatness of character; honor; dignity; worthiness —*vt.* **-shiped** or **-shipped, -ship·ing** or **-ship·ping 1** to show religious devotion or reverence for; adore or venerate as a deity **2** to have intense love or admiration for; adore or idolize —*vi.* to engage in worship, or perform an act of religious devotion; specif., to offer prayers, attend church services, etc. —*SYN.* REVERE[1] —**wor′ship·er** *n.,* **wor′ship·per**

wor·ship·ful (-fəl) *adj.* **1** [Chiefly Brit.] worthy of being worshiped; honorable; respected: used, capitalized and usually preceded by *the,* as an honorific epithet for magistrates, groups, certain lodge officials, etc. **2** feeling or offering great devotion or respect —**wor′ship·ful·ly** *adv.*

worst (wʉrst) *adj.* ⟦ME *worste* < OE *wyrsta, wierresta* < base of *wiersa,* WORSE + *-st,* superl. suffix⟧ **1** *superl. of* BAD[1] & ILL[1] **2** *a)* bad, evil, harmful, unpleasant, etc. in the highest degree; least good *b)* of the lowest quality or condition **3** in the least favorable condition or least satisfactory situation —*adv.* **1** *superl. of* BADLY & ILL[1] **2** in the worst manner **3** to a degree that is most bad, evil, unpleasant, etc. —*n.* that which is worst —*vt.* to get the better of; defeat —**at worst** under the worst circumstances; at the greatest disadvantage —**give someone the worst of it** to defeat or get the better of someone —**if (the) worst comes to (the) worst** if the worst possible thing happens —☆**(in) the worst way** [Informal] very much; greatly —**make the worst of** to be pessimistic about

worst-case (wʉrst′kās′) *adj.* that is, or takes into account, the worst possible case, condition, situation, etc.

wor·sted (woos′tid, wʉr′stid) *n.* ⟦ME *wurstede,* after *Worsted,* now *Worstead,* England, where first made⟧ **1** a smooth, firmly twisted thread or yarn made from long-staple wool combed to make the fibers lie in the same direction **2** fabric made from this, as gabardine or serge, with a smooth, hard surface —*adj.* made of worsted

wort[1] (wʉrt) *n.* ⟦ME < OE *wyrt-* (in comp.), akin to Ger *würze,* a spice < IE base **wrād-,* twig, root > L *radix,* ROOT[1]⟧ a liquid, produced from malt and hot water, which can be fermented to make beer or ale, or fermented and distilled to make whiskey

wort[2] (wʉrt) *n.* ⟦ME < OE *wyrt,* root, herb, plant: for IE base see prec.⟧ a plant, vegetable, or herb: now usually in compounds [*spleenwort, liverwort*]

worth[1] (wʉrth) *n.* ⟦ME < OE *weorth,* akin to *weorthian,* to honor, Ger *wert,* worth, *werden,* to become < IE **wert-,* to turn: see VERSE⟧ **1** material value, esp. as expressed in terms of money or some other medium of exchange **2** that quality of a person or thing that lends importance, value, merit, etc. and that is measurable by the esteem in which the person or thing is held **3** the amount or quantity of something that may be had for a given sum [a dollar's *worth* of nuts] **4** wealth; possessions; riches —*prep.* **1** deserving or worthy of; meriting [not *worth* the effort] **2** equal in worth or value to [a book that is *worth* $50] **3** having wealth or possessions amounting to [a man *worth* half a million] —☆**for all someone is worth** to the extent of someone's power or ability; to the utmost —**for what it is worth** phrase used to introduce a fact, proposal, etc. regarded as potentially, but not necessarily, relevant, valid, or significant

SYN.—**worth** and **value** are used interchangeably when applied to the desirability of something material as measured by its equivalence in money, goods, etc. [the *worth* or *value* of a used car], but, in discrimination, **worth** implies an intrinsic excellence resulting as from superior moral, cultural, or spiritual qualities, and **value** suggests the excellence attributed to something with reference to its usability, importance, etc. [the true *worth* of a book cannot be measured by its commercial *value*]

worth[2] (wʉrth) *vi.* ⟦ME *worthen* < OE *weorthan,* to become, used as auxiliary of the pass., akin to Ger *werden:* see prec.⟧ [Archaic] to become [woe *worth* the day]

worth·less (wʉrth′lis) *adj.* without worth or merit; useless, valueless, etc. —**worth′less·ly** *adv.* —**worth′less·ness** *n.*

worth·while (-hwīl′, -wīl′) *adj.* important or valuable enough to repay time or effort spent; of true value

wor·thy (wʉr′thē) *adj.* **-thi·er, -thi·est** ⟦ME *worthi*⟧ **1** having worth, value, or merit **2** having enough worth or merit (for someone or something specified); meriting: often with *of* or an infinitive [a man *worthy* of her, a candidate *worthy* to be supported] —*n., pl.* **-thies** a person of outstanding worth or importance: often used humorously —**wor′thi·ly** *adv.* —**wor′thi·ness** *n.*

-wor·thy (wʉr′thē) *combining form* **1** worthy of; deserving [*praiseworthy*] **2** safe or suitable for [*seaworthy*]

wot (wät) *vt., vi. 1st & 3d pers. sing., pres. indic., of* WIT[2]

would (wood) *v.aux.* ⟦ME *wolde* < OE, pt. of *willan,* to wish, WILL[1]⟧ **1** *pt. of* WILL[2] [she said she *would* be finished before six, in those days we *would* talk for hours on end] **2** used to express a supposition or condition [he *would* write if he knew you *would* answer; I *wouldn't* do that for any amount of money] **3** used to make a very polite or formal request [*would* you please open the window?] —*vt.* [Old Poet.] if only; I wish [*would* that she were here]

USAGE—See usage note at WILL[2]

would-be (wood′bē′) *adj.* ⟦ME (northern) *walde be*⟧ **1** wishing or pretending to be [a *would-be* expert] **2** intended, but failing, to be [a *would-be* work of art]

would·n't (wood′'nt) *contraction* would not

wouldst (woodst) *v. archaic 2d pers. sing. pt. of* WILL[2]: used with *thou:* also **would·est** (wood′ist)

would've (wood′əv) would have

wound[1] (wōōnd) *n.* ⟦ME *wunde* < OE *wund,* akin to Ger *wunde* < IE **wen-,* var. of base **wā-,* to hit, wound > WEN[1]⟧ **1** an injury to the body in which the skin or other tissue is broken, cut, pierced, torn, etc. **2** an injury to a plant caused by cutting, scraping, or other external force **3** any hurt or injury to the feelings, honor, etc. — *vt., vi.* ⟦ME *wundien* < OE *wundian* < the n.⟧ to inflict a wound or wounds (on or upon); hurt; injure —**the wounded** persons wounded, esp. in warfare

wound[2] (wound) *vt., vi.* **1** *pt. & pp. of* WIND[1] **2** *pt. & pp. of* WIND[3]

Wounded Knee creek in SW S.Dak.: site of a massacre (1890) of Dakota Indians by federal troops

wound·wort (wōōnd′wʉrt′) *n.* ⟦WOUND[1] + WORT[2]⟧ any of various plants, esp. betony, formerly used in dressing wounds

wove (wōv) *vt., vi. pt. & alt. pp. of* WEAVE

wo·ven (wō′vən) *vt., vi. alt. pp. of* WEAVE —*adj.* produced by weaving —*n.* a fabric produced by weaving: *usually used in pl.*

wove paper paper made on a mold in which the wires are so closely woven together that the finished sheets do not readily show wire marks as on laid paper

wow[1] (wou) [Slang] *interj.* used variously to express surprise, wonder, pleasure, pain, etc. —*n.* ☆a remarkable, successful, exciting, etc. person or thing —☆*vt.* to be a great success with; arouse enthusiasm in

☆**wow**[2] (wou) *n.* ⟦echoic⟧ a distortion in reproduced sound resulting from slow variations in the speed of the turntable, tape, etc. in either recording or playing: cf. FLUTTER (*n.* 6a)

wow·ser (wou′zər) *n.* [Austral. & N.Z. Slang] a person who is rigorously puritanical, strait-laced, etc.

wp *abbrev.* **1** word processing **2** word processor Also **WP**

WPA *abbrev.* Works Progress (later, Work Projects) Administration
W particle ⟦< *w(eak)*⟧ *Particle Physics* either of the two electrically charged weakons with a mass of 80.3 GeV/c², which is *c.* 157,000 times the mass of an electron: see Z PARTICLE
wpm *abbrev.* words per minute
WR *abbrev. Football* wide receiver: sometimes written **wr**
WRAC *abbrev.* Women's Royal Army Corps
wrack¹ (rak) ***n.*** ⟦ME *wrak,* damage, wrecked ship < MDu *wrak,* a wreck, wrecked ship; akin to OE *wræc,* misery, something driven (< *wrecan,* to WREAK)⟧ **1** destruction; ruin: see RACK³ **2** [Archaic] a wrecked ship **3** *a)* wreckage *b)* a fragment of something that has been destroyed **4** seaweed or other marine plant life cast up on shore — ***vt., vi.*** [Archaic] to wreck or be wrecked
wrack² (rak) ***vt.*** ⟦altered (infl. by prec.) < RACK¹⟧ RACK¹; esp., *a)* to subject to extreme mental or physical suffering; torture *b)* to disturb violently; convulse
wrack³ (rak) ***n.*** ⟦altered < RACK⁴⟧ a rack of clouds or other vapor
WRAF *abbrev.* Women's Royal Air Force
wraith (rāth) ***n.*** ⟦Scot, earlier *warth,* guardian angel < ON *vǫrthr,* guardian < *vartha,* to ward, guard: for IE base see WARD⟧ **1** a ghost **2** the spectral figure of a person supposedly seen as a premonition just before that person's death —**wraith′like** ***adj.***
Wran·gel (raŋ′gəl; *Russ* vrän′gel′y′) ⟦after Baron F. von *Wrangel(l)*: see fol.⟧ island of Russia in the Chukchi Sea: *c.* 2,000 sq mi (5,180 sq km)
Wran·gell (raŋ′gəl) ⟦after Baron F. von *Wrangel(l)* (Russ *Vrangel′*) (1796-1870), Russ explorer⟧ **1** mountain range in SE Alas.: highest peak, Mt. Blackburn **2 Mount** active volcano in these mountains: 14,006 ft (4,269 m)
wran·gle¹ (raŋ′gəl) ***vi.*** **-gled, -gling** ⟦ME *wranglen,* freq. of *wringen:* see WRING⟧ **1** to quarrel angrily and noisily **2** to argue; dispute —***vt.*** to argue (a person) *into* or *out of* something —***n.*** an angry, noisy dispute or quarrel —***SYN.*** QUARREL²
wran·gle² (raŋ′gəl) ***vt.*** **-gled, -gling** ⟦back-form. < WRANGLER²⟧ ☆to herd (livestock, esp. saddle horses)
wran·gler¹ (-glər) ***n.*** ⟦WRANGLE¹ + -ER⟧ a person who wrangles, or argues, esp. in a contentious way
wran·gler² (-glər) ***n.*** ⟦< *(horse) wrangler,* partial transl. of AmSp *caballerango,* a groom, footman⟧ ☆a cowboy who herds livestock, esp. saddle horses
wrap (rap) ***vt.*** **wrapped, wrap′ping** ⟦ME *wrappen*⟧ **1** *a)* to wind or fold (a covering) around something *b)* to cover by this means **2** to envelop, surround, overspread, etc. or hide, conceal, veil, etc. as by enveloping [a town *wrapped* in fog] **3** to enclose and fasten in a wrapper of paper, etc. [a box *wrapped* for mailing] **4** to wind or fold [to *wrap* one's arms around someone] **5** *Film* to complete photographing (a film, scene, etc.) —***vi.*** **1** to twine, extend, coil, etc.: usually with *over, around,* etc. **2** *Film* to complete the photographing of a film, scene, etc. —***n.*** **1** an outer covering; esp., *a)* something worn by being wrapped around the body, as a shawl *b)* [*usually pl.*] an outer garment, as an overcoat *c)* a blanket *d)* material used for wrapping things **2** a kind of sandwich consisting of a piece of flatbread wrapped around any of various fillings **3** *Film* the completion of the photographing of a film, a scene, etc. —**(kept) under wraps** (kept) secret, concealed, etc. [plans for a surprise party *kept under wraps*] —**wrapped up in 1** devoted to; absorbed or engrossed in (work, etc.) **2** involved or implicated in —**wrap up 1** to enfold in a covering **2** to put on warm clothing ☆**3** [Informal] *a)* to bring to an end; make final; settle *b)* to give a concluding, summarizing statement, report, etc.
wrap·a·round (rap′ə round′) ***adj.*** **1** that has a full-length opening and is wrapped around the body [a *wraparound* skirt] **2** molded, constructed, etc. so as to curve [a *wraparound* windshield] —***n.*** **1** a wraparound garment, esp. a skirt **2** a short segment of a film or TV program that comes before or after the main part and provides an introduction, conclusion, or context for the main story or subject
wrap·per (-ər) ***n.*** **1** a person or thing that wraps **2** that in which something is wrapped; covering; cover; specif., *a)* the leaf of tobacco forming the covering of a cigar *b)* DUST JACKET *c)* the paper wrapping in which a newspaper, magazine, etc. is enclosed for mailing **3** a loose garment that is wrapped around the body; esp., a woman's dressing gown or baby's robe
wrap·ping (-iŋ) ***n.*** [*often pl.*] the material, as paper, in which something is wrapped
wrapt (rapt) ***vt., vi.*** *obs. pt. & pp. of* WRAP
wrap-up (rap′up′) [Informal] ***adj.*** **1** that wraps something up; concluding ☆**2** that comes at the end and summarizes —***n.*** ☆**1** the concluding event, action, etc. in a sequence ☆**2** a concluding, summarizing statement, report, etc.
wrasse (ras) ***n.,*** *pl.* **wrass′es** or **wrasse** ⟦Cornish *wrach, gwrach*⟧ any of a family (Labridae) of percoid fishes having thick lips, spiny fins, strong teeth, and bright coloring, found esp. in tropical seas: some species are valued as food fishes, as the tautog, cunner, and hogfish
wras·tle (ras′əl) ***n., vi., vt.*** **-tled, -tling** *dial. or informal var. of* WRESTLE: also **wras′sle, -sled, -sling**
wrath (rath, räth; *chiefly Brit* rôth) ***n.*** ⟦ME *wraththe* < OE *wræththo* < *wrath,* WROTH⟧ **1** intense anger; rage; fury **2** any action carried out in great anger, esp. for punishment or vengeance —***adj.*** [Archaic] wrathful —***SYN.*** ANGER
wrath·ful (-fəl) ***adj.*** **1** full of wrath; intensely angry **2** resulting from, characterized by, or expressing wrath —**wrath′ful·ly** ***adv.*** —**wrath′ful·ness** ***n.***
wreak (rēk, rek) ***vt.*** ⟦ME *wreken* < OE *wrecan,* to revenge, punish, akin to Ger *rächen,* Goth *wrikan* < IE base **wreg-,* to shove, oppress, hunt down > L *urgere,* to press, URGE⟧ **1** to give vent or free play to (one's anger, malice, rage, etc.) **2** to inflict (vengeance), cause (harm or havoc), etc. **3** [Archaic] to avenge —**wreak′er** ***n.***
wreath (rēth) ***n.,*** *pl.* **wreaths** (rēthz, rēths) ⟦ME *wrethe* < OE *writha,* a ring, a twisted band < *writhan,* to twist: see WRITHE⟧ **1** a twisted band or ring of leaves, flowers, etc.; esp., *a)* a chaplet worn as a mark of honor or victory *b)* a garland laid upon a grave or hung on a door, window, etc. **2** something suggesting this in shape; twisted or circular band [*wreaths* of smoke]
wreathe (rēth) ***vt.*** **wreathed, wreath′ing** ⟦Early ModE, back-form. < ME *wrethen,* pp. of *writhen,* WRITHE; in later use < prec.⟧ **1** to coil, twist, or entwine, esp. so as to form into a wreath **2** to coil, twist, or entwine around; encircle [clouds *wreathed* the mountains] **3** to decorate with wreaths **4** to cover or envelop [a face *wreathed* in smiles] —***vi.*** **1** to move with a twisting or coiling motion **2** to have or take the form of a wreath
wreck (rek) ***n.*** ⟦ME *wrek* < Anglo-Fr *wrec* < ON *vrek,* driftwood, wreckage, akin to MDu *wrak,* wrack: for IE base see WREAK⟧ **1** goods or wreckage cast ashore after a shipwreck **2** *a)* the disabling or destruction of a ship by a storm or other disaster; shipwreck *b)* a ship that has been disabled or destroyed by a storm or other disaster **3** the remains of anything, often, specif., a motor vehicle, that has been destroyed or badly damaged **4** a person who is physically in very poor health or emotionally upset or exhausted **5** a wrecking or being wrecked; destruction; ruin —***vt.*** **1** to destroy or damage badly **2** to tear down or dismantle (a building, etc.) **3** to bring to ruin or disaster; overthrow; thwart; defeat **4** to destroy the health, or physical or mental soundness, of —***vi.*** **1** to be wrecked **2** to work as a wrecker
wreck·age (rek′ij) ***n.*** **1** a wrecking or being wrecked **2** the remains of something that has been wrecked
wreck·er (-ər) ***n.*** **1** a person or thing that wrecks **2** a person who causes ruin, obstruction, or disruption of any kind; specif., a person using false lights, etc. to lead ships to destruction in order to plunder the wreckage **3** a person, car, train, boat, etc. that salvages or clears away wrecks; specif., a truck equipped to tow away wrecked or disabled automobiles **4** a person or business that demolishes or dismantles old buildings, motor vehicles, etc., salvaging usable materials and parts [house *wrecker,* auto *wrecker*]
wreck·ing (-iŋ) ***n.*** the act or work of a wrecker —***adj.*** engaged or used in dismantling or salvaging wrecks
☆**wrecking bar** a small crowbar with a chisel-like point at one end and a curved claw at the other
wren (ren) ***n.*** ⟦ME *wrenne* < OE *wrenna,* prob. akin to OHG *rentilo,* ON *rindill*⟧ **1** any of a large family (Troglodytidae) of small, insect-eating passerine birds having a long bill, rounded wings, and a stubby, erect tail; esp., the **house wren** (*Troglodytes aedon*), that often nests in birdhouses in North America **2** any of certain other passerine birds of various families
Wren¹ (ren) ***n.*** [Informal] a member of the (British) Women's Royal Naval Service
Wren² (ren), Sir **Christopher** 1632-1723; Eng. architect
wrench (rench) ***n.*** ⟦ME < OE *wrenc,* a trick, deceit; akin to Ger *ränke,* a bend, twist < IE **wreng-* < base **wer-,* to twist, turn > WORM⟧ **1** a sudden, sharp twist or pull **2** an injury caused by a twist or jerk, as to the back, a joint, etc. **3** a sudden feeling of grief, anguish, etc., as at parting with someone **4** any of a number of tools used for holding and turning nuts, bolts, pipes, etc. **5** a false or strained interpretation of an original meaning —***vt.*** **1** to twist, pull, or jerk suddenly and violently **2** to injure (a part of the body) with a twist or wrench **3** to distort, strain, or give a false interpretation of (a meaning, statement, etc.) —***vi.*** to pull or tug (at something) with a wrenching movement

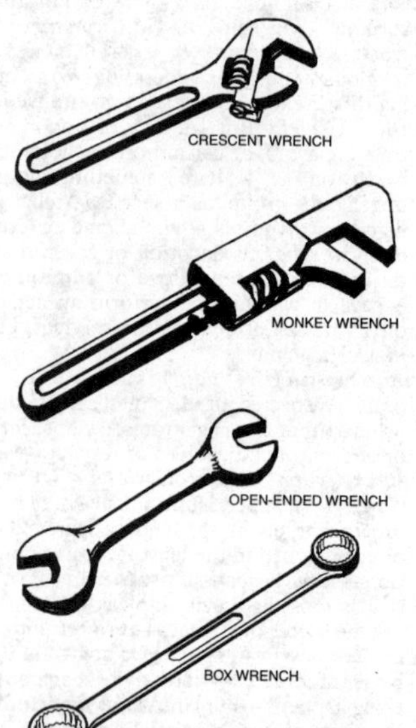

wrest (rest) ***vt.*** ⟦ME *wresten* < OE *wræstan,* to twist violently, akin to ON *reista* < IE base **wer-,* to turn, bend, twist > WRITHE⟧ **1** to turn or twist; esp., to pull or force away violently with a twisting motion **2** to take or extract by force; usurp; extort; wring **3** to distort or change the true meaning, purpose, use, etc. of; pervert; twist —***n.*** the act of wresting; a twist; wrench —**wrest′er** ***n.***
wres·tle (res′əl; *often* ras′-) ***vi.*** **-tled, -tling** ⟦ME *wrestlen, wrastlen* < OE

wræstlian, freq. of *wræstan*, to twist: see prec.⟧ **1** to struggle hand to hand with an opponent in an attempt to throw or force him or her to the ground without striking blows **2** to struggle (*with* a problem, an opposing force, etc.) [to *wrestle* with one's conscience] **3** to struggle (*with*) in attempting to handle, maneuver, or manipulate something [to *wrestle* with a canvas sail in a storm] **4** to engage in the sport of wrestling —*vt.* **1** to struggle or fight with by wrestling; wrestle with **2** to move, lift, maneuver, etc. with great physical effort [to *wrestle* a boulder into place] ☆**3** in the W U.S., to throw (a calf, etc.) for branding —*n.* **1** the action of wrestling; wrestling bout **2** a struggle or contest —**wres′tler** *n.*

wres·tling (-liŋ) *n.* a form of sport in which the opponents struggle hand to hand, attempting to throw or force each other to the ground, traditionally without striking blows

wretch (rech) *n.* ⟦ME *wrecche* < OE *wrecca*, an outcast, lit., one driven out < *wrecan*, to drive out, punish: see WREAK⟧ **1** a miserable or unhappy person; person in deep distress or misfortune **2** a person who is despised or scorned

wretch·ed (-id) *adj.* ⟦ME *wrecched* < *wrecche* < OE *wræcc*, wretched < *wrecan*: see prec.⟧ **1** deeply distressed or unhappy; miserable; unfortunate **2** characterized by or causing distress or misery; dismal [*wretched* slums] **3** poor in quality; very inferior [a *wretched* meal] **4** contemptible; despicable —**wretch′ed·ly** *adv.* —**wretch′ed·ness** *n.*

wrig·gle (rig′əl) *vi.* **-gled, -gling** ⟦MLowG *wriggeln*, akin to OFris *wrigia*: see WRY⟧ **1** to move to and fro with a twisting, writhing motion; twist and turn; squirm **2** to move along with a wriggling motion **3** to make one's way by subtle or shifty means; dodge; equivocate [to *wriggle* out of a difficulty] —*vt.* **1** to cause to wriggle **2** to bring into a specified condition, form, etc. by wriggling —*n.* a wriggling movement or action —**wrig′gly** *adj.* **-gli·er, -gli·est**

wrig·gler (-lər) *n.* **1** a person or thing that wriggles **2** the larva of a mosquito

wright (rīt) *n.* ⟦ME < OE *wyrhta*, a worker, maker < *wyrcan*, to WORK⟧ a person who makes, constructs, or repairs: used chiefly in compounds [*wheelwright, shipwright*]

Wright (rīt) **1 Frank Lloyd** 1867-1959; U.S. architect **2 Joseph** 1734-97; Eng. painter: called *Wright of Derby* **3 Orville** 1871-1948; U.S. airplane inventor with his brother Wilbur **4 Richard** 1908-60; U.S. novelist **5 Wilbur** 1867-1912; U.S. airplane inventor

culex wriggler

wring (riŋ) *vt.* **wrung** or [Rare] **wringed, wring′ing** ⟦ME *wringen* < OE *wringan*, to press, compress, strain, akin to Ger *ringen*, to struggle, wrestle < IE **wreng-* < base **wer-*, to turn, bend > WORM⟧ **1** *a)* to squeeze, press, twist, or compress, esp. so as to force out water or other liquid *b)* to force out (water or other liquid) by this means, as from wet clothes (usually with *out*) **2** to clasp and twist (the hands) together as an expression of distress **3** to clasp (another's hand) forcefully in greeting **4** to wrench or twist forcibly **5** to get or extract by force, threats, persistence, etc.; extort **6** to afflict with anguish, distress, pity, etc. [a story to *wring* one's heart] —*vi.* to writhe, squirm, or twist with force or great effort —*n.* the action of wringing or twisting

wring·er (riŋ′ər) *n.* ⟦ME, an oppressor⟧ **1** a person or thing that wrings **2** a machine or device for squeezing out water or other liquid, esp. one fitted with opposed rollers to squeeze the water from wet clothes —☆**put someone through the wringer** [Slang] to subject someone to a painful or trying experience, as a harsh interrogation

wrin·kle¹ (riŋ′kəl) *n.* ⟦ME *wrinkel*, a wrinkle, prob. back-form. < *wrinkled* < OE *(ge)wrinclod*, pp. of *(ge)wrinclian*, to wind about, akin to *wringan*, to press, WRING⟧ **1** a small ridge or furrow in a normally smooth surface, caused by contraction, crumpling, folding, etc. **2** a crease or pucker in the skin, as any of those caused by aging, frowning, etc. **3** a minor problem or difficulty —*vt.* **-kled, -kling** to form a wrinkle or wrinkles in, as by contracting; pucker; crease —*vi.* to be or become wrinkled —**wrin′kly** *adj.* **-kli·er, -kli·est**

wrin·kle² (riŋ′kəl) *n.* ⟦prob. altered by assoc. with prec. < obs. *wrench*, a trick, artifice, ult. < OE *wrenc*, akin to WRENCH⟧ [Informal] a clever or novel idea or device; innovation

wrist (rist) *n.* ⟦ME < OE < base of *wræstan*, to twist, WREST⟧ **1** the joint or part of the arm between the hand and the forearm; carpus **2** the corresponding part in an animal **3** the part of a sleeve, glove, etc. that covers the wrist **4** WRIST PIN —☆**a slap (or tap) on the wrist** a token punishment that is much less severe than seems called for

wrist·band (rist′band′) *n.* a band that goes around the wrist; specif., *a)* the cuff of a sleeve *b)* a SWEATBAND (sense 2) *c)* a band, typically of paper or plastic, worn for identification, as by a hospital patient, or to signify paid admission, as at a concert or an amusement park

wrist·let (-lit) *n.* **1** a closefitting band or strip of material worn around, or sometimes sewed on a sleeve at, the wrist, as for warmth **2** a bracelet

wrist·lock (-läk′) *n.* a wrestling hold in which one wrestler secures a lock on the wrist and twists the arm of the opposing wrestler

wrist pin the stud or pin by which a connecting rod is attached to a piston, wheel, etc.

wrist·watch (-wäch′) *n.* a watch worn on a strap or band that fits around the wrist

writ¹ (rit) *vt., vi. archaic pt. & pp. of* WRITE: now mainly in the phrase **writ large**, expressed, shown, or done on a larger scale or in a clearer or more emphatic way

writ² (rit) *n.* ⟦ME < OE < *writan*: see WRITE⟧ **1** something written; writing; document: now chiefly a religious usage [holy *writ*] **2** a formal legal document ordering or prohibiting some action —**someone's writ runs** someone has power or authority of a specified kind or scope

writ·a·ble (rīt′ə bəl) *adj.* ⟦see fol.⟧ designed to have digital information recorded on it by the consumer [a *writable* compact disc]: often sp. **write′a·ble**

write (rīt) *vt.* **wrote, writ′ten, writ′ing** ⟦ME *writen* < OE *writan*, to scratch, engrave, write, akin to Ger *reissen*, to tear < IE base **wer-*, to tear off, scratch > Gr *rhinē*, a rasp⟧ **1** *a)* to form or inscribe (words, letters, symbols, etc.) on a surface, as by cutting, carving, embossing, or, esp., marking with a pen or pencil *b)* to form the words, letters, or symbols of with pencil, chalk, typewriter, etc.; put down in a form to be read [to *write* a paragraph, a formula, etc.] **2** to form or inscribe (words) in cursive style: opposed to PRINT (*vt.* 7) **3** to spell (a name, word, etc.) [words *written* alike are often pronounced differently] **4** to know (a specific alphabet, language, etc.) well enough to communicate in writing **5** to be the author or composer of (literary or musical material) **6** to draw up or compose in legal form **7** to fill in (a check, money order, etc.) with necessary writing **8** to cover with writing [to *write* three pages] **9** to communicate in writing [he *wrote* that he would be late] **10** to communicate with in writing; write a letter or note to [*write* her before you go] **11** to entitle or designate in writing [he *writes* himself "Judge"] **12** to underwrite **13** to leave marks, signs, or evidence of; show clearly [greed was *written* on his face] **14** to record (information) on a magnetic or optical disc, as in a computer hard drive, a CD or DVD, etc.: used with *to* [*write* a file to a disc] —*vi.* **1** to form or inscribe words, letters, symbols, etc. on a surface, esp. by making marks with a pen or pencil **2** to form words in cursive style: opposed to PRINT (*vi.* 3) **3** to write books or other literary matter; be an author or writer **4** to write a letter or letters **5** to be employed at written work, as a clerk, copyist, etc. **6** to produce writing of a specified kind [to *write* legibly, a pen that *writes* scratchily] —**write down 1** to put into written form; write a record of **2** to disparage or depreciate in writing **3** to write in a pointedly simple style, as for readers considered to be less cultivated than the writer **4** to reduce the book value of (an asset) —**write in** ☆to vote for (someone not officially on a ballot) by inserting that person's name on the ballot —**write (someone) into** to add (a character or role) to (a script, plotline, etc.) —**write off 1** to cancel or remove from accounts (bad debts, claims, etc.) **2** to drop from consideration **3** AMORTIZE (sense 2) —**write out 1** to put into writing **2** to write in full **3** to exhaust (oneself) of ideas by writing prolifically —**write (someone) out of** to remove (a character or role) from (a script, plotline, etc.) —**write up 1** to write a record or account of **2** to complete in writing **3** to praise in writing **4** to write a report on (a person or group), as for an infraction **5** *Accounting* to increase the book value of (an asset)

write-down (rīt′doun′) *n.* a reduction in the book value of an asset, as because of depreciation or a decline in market value

☆**write-in** (-in′) *n.* **1** a vote for some person whose name is not on the ballot, made by inserting that person's name **2** a person whose name is so inserted —*adj.* of or relating to a write-in [*write-in* campaign]

write-off (-ôf′) *n.* something written off, amortized, etc.

writ·er (rīt′ər) *n.* **1** a person who writes **2** a person whose work or occupation is writing; now, specif., an author, journalist, or the like

writ·er·ly (rīt′ər lē) *adj.* **1** of or characteristic of a writer **2** characterized by the qualities of a writer's craft, esp. by those that reflect a self-conscious display of literary techniques

writer's block a psychological condition in which a writer, esp. a professional writer, is unable to produce material, usually of a literary or creative kind

writer's cramp painful, spasmodic contraction of the muscles of the hand or fingers, resulting from writing for too long a time

☆**write-up** (rīt′up′) *n.* **1** [Informal] a written report or description, as in a newspaper, magazine, etc.; sometimes, specif., a favorable account, as for a publicity release **2** an increase in the book value of an asset

writhe (rīth) *vt.* **writhed, writh′ing** ⟦ME *writhen* < OE *writhan*, to twist, wind about, akin to ON *rītha* < IE base **wer-*, to bend, twist > WREATH, WRY⟧ to cause to twist or turn; contort —*vi.* **1** to make twisting or turning movements; contort the body, as in agony; squirm **2** to suffer great emotional distress, as from embarrassment or revulsion —*n.* a writhing movement; contortion —**writh′er** *n.*

writh·en (rith′ən) *adj.* ⟦ME *wrythen*, pp. of *writhen*, to prec.⟧ [Archaic] writhed; twisted; contorted

writ·ing (rīt′iŋ) *n.* **1** the act of a person who writes **2** something written, as a letter or document **3** written form **4** *short for* HANDWRITING **5** a book, poem, article, or other literary work: *usually used in pl.* **6** the profession or work of a writer **7** the art, style, etc. of literary composition —*adj.* **1** that writes **2** used in writing

writ of assistance a writ issued by a court of equity, ordering the transfer of real property to the rightful owner

writ of certiorari CERTIORARI

writ of error a writ directed to a lower court by an appellate court requiring the submission of the record of a legal action for review, in order to ascertain whether or not errors have been committed and so that the judgment may be upheld, reversed, or corrected

writ of prohibition an order from a higher court to a lower one to cease hearing or prosecuting some matter outside its jurisdiction

writ·ten (rit′'n) *vt., vi. pp. of* WRITE —*adj.* put down in a form to be read; not spoken or oral

wrnt *abbrev.* warrant

Wroc·ław (vrôts′läf) city in Silesia, SW Poland, on the Oder River

wrong (rôŋ) *adj.* ⟦ME, crooked, twisted, wrong < OE *wrang* < ON *rangr, wrangr,* wrong, twisted: for IE base see WRING⟧ **1** not in accordance with justice, law, morality, etc.; unlawful, immoral, or improper **2** not in accordance with an established standard, previous arrangement, given intention, etc. *[*the *wrong* method, arrived at the *wrong* time*]* **3** not suitable or appropriate *[*the *wrong* thing to say*]* **4** *a)* contrary to fact, reason, some set standard, etc.; incorrect; inaccurate; false *b)* acting, judging, believing, etc. incorrectly; mistaken **5** unsatisfactory; in a bad state or condition **6** not functioning properly; out of order *[*something *wrong* with her eyes*]* **7** designating the side, surface, etc. that is not meant to be seen; designating the unfinished, inner, or under side *[*the *wrong* side of a fabric*]* —*adv.* in a wrong manner, direction, etc.; so as to be wrong; incorrectly; amiss —*n.* **1** that which is not right, or not just, proper, correct, etc.; esp., an unjust or immoral act **2** *Law* a violation or invasion of a legal right; injurious act, as a tort —*vt.* **1** to treat badly or unjustly; do wrong to; injure **2** to think badly of without real justification **3** to malign; dishonor **4** to seduce (a woman) —☆**get someone in wrong** [Informal] to bring someone into disfavor —**get someone (or something) wrong** [Informal] to fail to understand someone (or something) properly —**go wrong 1** to turn out badly **2** to change from good behavior to bad; go astray —**in the wrong** not on the side supported by truth, justice, etc. —**wrong′er** *n.* —**wrong′ly** *adv.* —**wrong′ness** *n.*

SYN.—**wrong** implies the inflicting of unmerited injury or harm upon another *[*he was *wronged* by false charges*]*; **oppress** implies a burdening with harsh, rigorous impositions or the cruel or unjust use of power *[oppressed* by heavy taxation*]*; **persecute** suggests constant harassment or the relentless infliction of cruelty and suffering *[*the *persecuted* minorities of Nazi Germany*]*; **aggrieve** suggests the infliction of such wrongs or injuries as seem a just cause for complaint or resentment *[aggrieved* by her ill-treatment of him*]*; **abuse** suggests improper or hurtful treatment, as by the use of insulting or coarse language *[*her much-*abused* husband*]*

wrong·do·ing (-do͞o′iŋ) *n.* any act or behavior that is wrong; the doing of wrong; transgression —**wrong′do′er** *n.*

wrong-foot (rôŋ′fo͝ot′) *vt.* ⟦< the practice in sports of causing an opponent to put weight on the wrong foot⟧ [Chiefly Brit.] to confuse or disconcert so as to make less able to act or respond effectively, reasonably, etc.

wrong·ful (-fəl) *adj.* **1** full of wrong; unjust or injurious **2** without legal right; unlawful —**wrong′ful·ly** *adv.* —**wrong′ful·ness** *n.*

wrong·head·ed (-hed′id) *adj.* stubborn in adhering to wrong opinions, ideas, etc.; perverse —**wrong′head′ed·ly** *adv.* —**wrong′head′ed·ness** *n.*

wrong number 1 *a)* a telephone number reached through error, as by dialing incorrectly *b)* the person reached by so dialing **2** [Slang] someone or something considered to be unsuitable, undesirable, untrustworthy, etc.

wrote (rōt) *vt., vi. pt. of* WRITE

wroth (rôth; *chiefly Brit,* rōth) *adj.* ⟦ME < OE *wrath,* bad, wroth < the pt. stem of *writhan,* to twist, WRITHE⟧ [Archaic] angry; wrathful; incensed

wrought (rôt) *vi., vt.* ⟦ME *wrogt,* altered < *worgt,* pp. of *weorken* < OE *wyrcan,* to WORK⟧ *archaic pt. & pp. of* WORK —*adj.* **1** formed; fashioned **2** shaped by hammering or beating: said of metals **3** elaborated with care **4** decorated; ornamented

wrought iron a kind of iron that contains some slag and very little carbon: it is resistant to corrosion, tough, and ductile, and is used in fences, grating, rivets, etc. —**wrought′-i′ron** *adj.*

wrought-up (rôt′up′) *adj.* very disturbed or excited

wrung (ruŋ) *vt., vi. pt. & pp. of* WRING

wry (rī) *vt., vi.* **wried, wry′ing** ⟦ME *wrien,* to twist, bend < OE *wrigian,* to turn, twist, akin to OFris *wrigia,* to bend, stoop < IE **wreik-* (> L *rica,* head veil) < base **wer-,* to turn, bend⟧ to writhe or twist —*adj.* **wri′er** or **wry′er, wri′est** or **wry′est 1** [Archaic] turned or bent to one side; twisted **2** made by twisting or distorting the features *[*a *wry* face*]* **3** [Rare] distorted, as in meaning **4** dry, ironic, sardonic, etc. *[wry* humor*]* —**wry′ly** *adv.* —**wry′ness** *n.*

wry·neck (-nek′) *n.* **1** *a)* TORTICOLLIS *b)* a person afflicted with this **2** any of a genus (*Jynx*) of Old World woodpeckers with long, soft tail feathers and a habit of twisting the neck

Ws *abbrev. Bible* Wisdom of Solomon

WSW *abbrev.* west-southwest

wt *abbrev.* weight

WTO *abbrev.* World Trade Organization

☆**W-2** (dub′əl yo͞o′to͞o′) *n.* a U.S. federal tax form prepared by an employer annually, indicating an employee's wages, taxes that have been withheld on those wages, etc.

Wu (wo͞o) *n.* the variety of Chinese spoken in Shanghai

Wu·chang (wo͞o′chäŋ′) *see* WUHAN

Wu·han (wo͞o′hän′) city in EC China, formed by the merger of the cities of Hankow, Hanyang, & Wuchang; capital of Hubei province

Wuh·si (wo͞o′shē′) *a former transliteration of* WUXI

Wu·hu (wo͞o′ho͞o′) city in Anhui province, E China, on the Chang

wul·fen·ite (wo͝ol′fə nīt′) *n.* ⟦Ger *wulfenit,* after F. X. von *Wulfen* (1728-1805), Austrian mineralogist⟧ a soft, heavy mineral, $PbMoO_4$, that is an ore of molybdenum and occurs usually as yellowish, tetragonal crystals; lead molybdate

Wul·fi·la (wo͝ol′fə lə) *var. of* ULFILAS

wun·der·bar (vo͝on′dər bär′) *adj., interj.* ⟦Ger⟧ wonderful

wun·der·kind (vo͝on′dər kind′) *n., pl.* **-kinds′** or **-kin′der** (-kin′dər) ⟦Ger < *wunder,* WONDER + *kind,* child < OHG: for IE base see KIND⟧ **1** a child prodigy **2** a person who achieves success or fame in some field of knowledge, profession, etc. at a much earlier age than is usually the case

Wup·per·tal (vo͝op′ər täl′) city in the Ruhr Basin of North Rhine-Westphalia, Germany

wurst (wurst, wo͝orst) *n.* ⟦Ger < OHG⟧ sausage: usually used in comb. *[bratwurst, knackwurst,* etc.*]*

Würt·tem·berg (wurt′əm burg′; *Ger* vür′təm berk′) former state in SW Germany: now part of BADEN-WÜRTTEMBERG

Würz·burg (wurts′bərg; *Ger* vürts′bo͝ork) city in S Germany, on the Main River, in the state of Bavaria

☆**wuss** (wo͝os) *n.* [Slang] a person regarded as weak, ineffectual, overly sensitive, etc.; wimp: also **wuss′y**, *pl.* **wuss′ies**

Wu·xi (wo͞o′shē′) city in Jiangsu province, E China, on the Grand Canal: former transliteration **Wu·sih**

WV *abbrev.* West Virginia: also **WVa**

WWI *abbrev.* World War I: also **WW1**

WWII *abbrev.* World War II: also **WW2**

WWW or **www** *abbrev.* World Wide Web

WY *abbrev.* Wyoming

Wy·an·dot (wī′ən dät′) *adj., n., pl.* **-dots′** or **-dot′** ⟦< Wyandot *wé·ⁿdat*⟧ **1** a member of a North American Indian group formed in the 17th cent. from Huron-speaking peoples of W Ontario: living first in Michigan, Ohio, and Ontario, and now living in Oklahoma **2** the Iroquoian language of this people

Wy·an·dotte (wī′ən dät′) *n.* ⟦after prec.⟧ **1** *alt. sp. of* WYANDOT **2** any of a breed of medium-sized, usually white, domestic chicken

Wyatt (wī′ət), Sir **Thomas** 1503?-42; Eng. poet & diplomat

wych-elm (wich′elm′) *n.* ⟦< ME *wyche* (see WITCH HAZEL) + ELM: from the pliant branches⟧ **1** a small variety of elm (*Ulmus glabra*), native to Europe and N Asia **2** its wood

Wych·er·ley (wich′ər lē), **William** 1640?-1716; Eng. dramatist

Wyc·liffe or **Wyc·lif** (wik′lif), **John** 1330?-84; Eng. religious reformer: made the 1st complete translation of the Bible into English (from the Vulgate)

wye (wī) *n., pl.* **wyes 1** the letter Y **2** something shaped like Y

Wye (wī) river in SE Wales & W England, flowing southeast into the Severn estuary: *c.* 130 mi (209 km)

Wy·eth (wī′əth) **1 Andrew (Newell)** 1917-2009; U.S. painter: son of Newell **2 N(ewell) C(onvers)** 1882-1945; U.S. painter & illustrator

wynd (wīnd) *n.* ⟦MScot *wynde* < ME *winden,* to WIND[1]⟧ [Scot.] a narrow lane or alley

wynn (win) *n.* WEN[2]

Wyo *abbrev.* Wyoming

Wy·o·ming (wī ō′miŋ) ⟦after WYOMING VALLEY⟧ Mountain State of the W U.S.: admitted 1890; 97,100 sq mi (251,489 sq km); cap. Cheyenne: abbrev. *WY* or *Wyo*

Wy·o·ming·ite (-īt′) *n.* a person born or living in Wyoming

Wyoming Valley ⟦< Ger *Wayomick,* etc. < Munsee (a Delaware language) *chwewamink,* lit., large river bottom⟧ valley of the Susquehanna River, NE Pa.: site of a massacre (1778)

WYSIWYG (wiz′ē wig′) *n.* ⟦*w(hat) y(ou) s(ee) i(s) w(hat) y(ou) g(et)*⟧ a computer video screen display that shows data exactly as it will appear in printed form

wy·vern (wī′vərn) *n.* ⟦ME *wivere* < NormFr *wivre* (OFr *guivre*), dragon, serpent < L *vipera:* see VIPER⟧ *Heraldry* a dragon with forelegs only, wings, and a barbed tail

x[1] or **X** (eks) ***n.***, *pl.* **x's, X's 1** the twenty-fourth letter of the English alphabet: from a western form of the Greek alphabet **2** any of the speech sounds that this letter represents, as, in English, the (ks) of *lax,* (gz) of *exact,* (ksh) of *anxious,* (gzh) of *luxurious,* or (z) of *xylophone* **3** a type or impression for *x* or *X* **4** the twenty-fourth in a sequence or group **5** an object shaped like X —***adj.* 1** of *x* or *X* **2** twenty-fourth in a sequence or group **3** shaped like X

x[2] (eks) ***vt.*** **x-ed** or **x'd, x-ing** or **x'ing 1** to indicate (one's choice or answer) by or as by marking with an X **2** to delete or cancel (written or printed matter) with or as with one or more X's: usually used with *out* —***n.*** one's choice or answer (on a ballot, test, etc.)

x[3] (eks) ***n.*** *Math.* **1** the first of a set of unknown quantities, *y* usually being second **2** a variable **3** an abscissa

x[4] *abbrev.* extra

x[5] *symbol* **1** by (in indicating dimensions) *[3 ft x 4 ft]* **2** the power of magnification (in optical instruments) **3** *Math.* times

X[1] (eks) ***n.* 1** a mark shaped like an X used: *a)* to represent the signature of a person who cannot write *b)* to indicate a particular point on a map, diagram, etc. *c)* as a symbol for a kiss in letters, etc. *d)* to indicate the degree of fineness of flour, sugar, etc. **2** the Roman numeral 10: XX = 20, XXX = 30: X before a greater Roman numeral expresses a number 10 less than that numeral (e.g., XC = 90): with a superior bar ($\overline{X}$), 10,000 **3** a person or thing unknown or unrevealed ☆**4** a former film rating meaning that no one under the age of seventeen is to be admitted —**X's and O's** ☆[Informal] the basic elements of a specified field of work, knowledge, etc.; often, specif., the plays and strategies used in a particular sport

X[2] *symbol* **1** [[see XP]] Christ: used also in comb., as in *Xmas* **2** *Genetics* crossed with **3** extra **4** *Elec.* reactance

Xan·a·du (zan′ə do͞o′) ***n.*** [[after *Xanadu,* the region where a "stately pleasure dome" is located in the poem "Kubla Khan" by S. T. COLERIDGE]] any luxurious or exotic estate, mansion, etc.

☆**Xan·ax** (zan′aks′) [[arbitrary coinage]] *trademark for* a drug, $C_{17}H_{13}ClN_4$, used to treat anxiety, depression, etc.

Xan·kān·di (zän kan′dē) capital of Nagorno-Karabakh

xan·than (zan′thən) ***n.*** [[< *Xanth(omonas campestris),* a species of bacteria used in the process + -AN]] a gum produced by bacterial fermentation, used as a thickener, as in commercially prepared foods: also **xanthan gum**

xan·thate (zan′thāt′) ***n.*** a salt or ester of xanthic acid

xan·thene (zan′thēn′) ***n.*** [[XANTH(O)- + -ENE]] a ring system, $C_6H_4CH_2OC_6H_4$, occurring as yellowish, crystalline leaflets in the molecules of many dyes

xanthene dye any of various dyes that contain the xanthene ring structure in their molecules

xan·thic (zan′thik) ***adj.*** [[Fr *xanthique:* see XANTHO- & -IC]] **1** yellow or yellowish **2** of or having to do with xanthine

xanthic acid 1 an unstable, oily, colorless liquid, $C_3H_6OS_2$, that decomposes into ethyl alcohol and carbon disulfide at 24°C **2** any of a series of acids having the general formula ROC(S)SH, in which R is any hydrocarbon radical

xan·thine (-thēn′, -thin) ***n.*** [[Fr: see XANTHO- & -IN[1]]] **1** a white, crystalline, nitrogenous compound, $C_5H_4N_4O_2$, resembling uric acid: it is present in blood, urine, and certain plants **2** any of various derivatives of this compound

Xan·thip·pe (zan tip′ē) 5th cent. B.C.; wife of Socrates: the prototype of the quarrelsome, nagging wife

xan·tho- (zan′thō, -thə) [[ModL < Gr *xanthos,* yellow < ? IE **k̂asno-* < base **k̂as,* gray]] *combining form* yellow *[xanthoma]*: also, before a vowel, **xanth-**

xan·tho·ma (zan thō′mə) ***n.***, *pl.* **-mas** or **-ma·ta** (-mə tə) [[prec. + -OMA]] a small tumor, esp. of the skin, formed by a deposit of lipids, often in a soft, rounded, yellowish mass —**xan·thom′a·tous** (-thäm′ə təs, -thō′mə-) ***adj.***

xan·thone (zan′thōn′) ***n.*** [[XANTH(O)- + -ONE]] a ring ketone, $C_6H_4(CO)OC_6H_4$, occurring in some plant pigments and dyes

xan·tho·phyll (zan′thə fil) ***n.*** [[XANTHO- + -PHYLL]] a yellow, crystalline pigment, $C_{40}H_{56}O_2$, found in plants; lutein: it is related to carotene and is the basis of the yellow seen in autumn leaves —**xan′tho·phyl′lous** (-fil′əs) ***adj.***

xan·thous (zan′thəs) ***adj.*** [[< Gr *xanthos,* yellow (see XANTHO-) + -OUS]] yellow or yellowish

Xan·thus (zan′thəs) ancient city in Lycia, SW Asia Minor

Xa·vi·er (zā′vē ər, ig zā′-; zāv′yər, ig zāv′-), Saint **Francis** (1506-52); Sp. Jesuit missionary: his day is Dec. 3

x-ax·is (eks′ak′sis) ***n.***, *pl.* **x′-ax′es′** (-sēz′) *Geom.* **1** the horizontal, or more nearly horizontal, axis in a plane Cartesian coordinate system, along which the abscissa is measured **2** a similar axis that is perpendicular to the y-axis and the z-axis of a three-dimensional Cartesian coordinate system

X-C *symbol Sports* cross-country

X chromosome *Genetics* one of the sex chromosomes: see SEX CHROMOSOME

x div or **XD** *abbrev.* EX-DIVIDEND

Xe *Chem. symbol for* xenon

xe·bec (zē′bek) ***n.*** [[altered (infl. by Sp form) < earlier *chebec* < Fr *chébec* < It *sciabecco,* prob. via Sp *xabeque* (now *jabeque*) < Ar *shabbāk,* a small warship]] a small, three-masted ship having an overhanging bow and stern and using both square and lateen sails: once common in the Mediterranean

xe·ni·a (zē′nē ə, zēn′yə) ***n.*** [[ModL < Gr, hospitality < *xenos,* foreign, stranger]] *Bot.* the immediate influence of pollen from one strain of a plant upon the endosperm of another strain, resulting in hybrid characters in the form, color, etc. of the resulting growth, as in the colors of corn grains

xen·o- (zen′ō, -ə; zē′nō, -nə) [[< Gr *xenos,* foreign, stranger]] *combining form* **1** stranger, foreigner *[xenophobia]* **2** strange, foreign *[xenolith]* Also, before a vowel, **xen-**

xen·o·bi·ot·ic (zen′ō bī ät′ik, zē′nō-) ***adj.*** [[prec. + BIOTIC]] designating or of a chemical substance that is foreign, and usually harmful, to living organisms —***n.*** such a substance

xen·o·gen·e·sis (-jen′ə sis) ***n.*** [[ModL: see XENO- & -GENESIS]] *Biol.* **1** *a)* SPONTANEOUS GENERATION *b)* ALTERNATION OF GENERATIONS **2** the supposed production of an individual completely different from either of its parents —**xen′o·ge·net′ic** (-jə net′ik) ***adj.***, **xen′o·gen′ic** (-jen′ik)

xen·o·graft (zen′ə graft′, zē′nə-) ***n.*** [[XENO- + GRAFT]] a graft of skin, bone, etc. from an individual of another species; heterograft: cf. ALLOGRAFT, AUTOGRAFT

xen·o·lith (-lith′) ***n.*** [[XENO- + -LITH]] *Geol.* a rock fragment different in kind from the igneous rock in which it is embedded —**xen′o·lith′ic** ***adj.***

xe·non (zē′nän′, zen′än′) ***n.*** [[ModL < Gr, neut. of *xenos,* foreign, a stranger: so named (1898) by Sir William RAMSAY & M. W. Travers (see KRYPTON), as the hitherto unknown inert gas]] a heavy, colorless, gaseous chemical element, one of the noble gases, present in the air in minute quantities and found to react with fluorine and other reactive compounds and to form salts and acids in solution: used in bubble chambers, electric luminescent tubes, lasers, vacuum tubes, etc.: symbol, Xe; at. no. 54: see the periodic table of elements in the Reference Supplement

xenon hex·a·flu·o·ride (hek′sə flôr′īd′, -flo͝or′-) large, colorless crystals, XeF_6, prepared from gaseous xenon and fluorine

xenon tet·ra·flu·o·ride (te′trə flôr′īd′, -flo͝or′-) a stable compound, XeF_4, prepared by mixing gaseous xenon and fluorine, heating the mixture to 400°C in a nickel container, and then cooling it to form large, colorless crystals

Xe·noph·a·nes (zi näf′ə nēz′) 570?-480? B.C.; Gr. Eleatic philosopher

xen·o·phil·i·a (zen′ə fil′ē ə, zē′nə-) ***n.*** [[ModL: see XENO- & -PHILIA]] attraction to or admiration of strangers or foreigners or of anything foreign or strange —**xen′o·phile′** (-fīl′) ***n.*** —**xen′o·phil′ic** (-fil′ik) ***adj.***

xen·o·pho·bi·a (-fō′bē ə) ***n.*** [[ModL: see XENO- & -PHOBIA]] fear or hatred of strangers or foreigners or of anything foreign or strange —**xen′o·phobe′** (-fōb′) ***n.*** —**xen′o·pho′bic** (-fō′bik) ***adj.***

Xen·o·phon (zen′ə fən, -fän′) 430?-355? B.C.; Gr. historian, essayist, & military leader

xe·ric (zir′ik) ***adj.*** [[< fol. + -IC]] **1** of, pertaining to, or having dry or desert-like conditions **2** XEROPHYTIC

xe·ro- (zir′ō, -ə) [[< Gr *xēros,* dry < IE **k̂sero-,* dry: see SERENE]] *combining form* dry *[xerophyte]*: also, before a vowel, **xer-**

xe·ro·der·ma (zir′ō dur′mə) ***n.*** [[prec. + DERMA[1]]] ICHTHYOSIS

☆**xe·rog·ra·phy** (zir äg′rə fē) ***n.*** [[XERO- + -GRAPHY]] a process for copying printed material, pictures, etc. onto paper, in which a latent image of the original material is transferred by the action of light onto an electrically charged surface to which the image attracts oppositely charged dry ink particles: the particles are then fused into place on the copy paper, reproducing the original image —**xe·ro·graph·ic** (zir′ō graf′ik) ***adj.***

xe·roph·i·lous (zir äf′ə ləs) ***adj.*** [[XERO- + -PHILOUS]] capable of thriving in a hot, dry climate, as certain plants and animals —**xe·roph′i·ly** ***n.***

xe·roph·thal·mi·a (zir′äf thal′mē ə) ***n.*** [[LL < Gr *xērophthalmia:* see XERO- & OPHTHALMIA]] a form of conjunctivitis characterized by a dry and lusterless condition of the eyeball and caused by a deficiency of vitamin A —**xe′roph·thal′mic** ***adj.***

xe·ro·phyte (zir′ə fīt′) ***n.*** [[XERO- + -PHYTE]] a plant structurally adapted to growing under very dry or desert conditions, often having greatly reduced leaf surfaces for avoiding water loss, thick, fleshy parts for water storage, and hairs, spines, or thorns —**xe′ro·phyt′ic** (-fit′ik) *adj.*

xe·ro·ra·di·og·ra·phy (zir′ō rā′dē äg′rə fē) *n.* ⟦XERO- + RADIOGRAPHY⟧ an X-ray technique that quickly produces a detailed xerographic image of the X-rayed part: used esp. for the early detection of breast tumors

xe·ro·sis (zi rō′sis) *n.* ⟦Gr *xērosis:* see XERO- & -OSIS⟧ *Med.* abnormal dryness, as of the skin or eyeball

xe·ro·ther·mic (zir′ə thur′mik) *adj.* ⟦XERO- + THERMIC⟧ of or pertaining to a hot and dry climatic period, as one of the postglacial periods

☆**Xe·rox** (zir′äks′) ⟦XERO(GRAPHY) + -*x*, arbitrary ending⟧ *trademark for* a device for copying graphic or printed material by xerography — *vt., vi.* [*usually* **x-**] to reproduce (printed material) by xerography —*n.* [*usually* **x-**] a copy made by xerography

Xer·xes I (zurk′sēz′) 519?-465 B.C.; king of Persia (486-465): son of Darius I: called *the Great*

Xho·sa (kō′sä, -zä) *n.* **1** *pl.* **Xho′sas** or **Xho′sa** a member of a people living mainly in S South Africa **2** the Bantu language of this people, closely related to Zulu —*adj.* of the Xhosas or their language or culture

xi[1] (zī, sī; *Gr* ksē) *n.* ⟦Gr *xi,* earlier *xei*⟧ the fourteenth letter of the Greek alphabet (Ξ, ξ)

xi[2] or **XI** *abbrev.* ex (without) interest

Xi (shē) river in S China, flowing east into the South China Sea: 1,250 mi (2,012 km)

Xi·a·men (shē′ä′mun′) **1** island of SE China, in Taiwan Strait **2** seaport on this island

Xi′an (shē′än′) city in NC China, on the Wei River; capital of Shaanxi province

Xi·ang (shē′äŋ′) river in SE China, flowing from Guangdong province north into Dongting Hu: *c.* 715 mi (1,151 km)

Xiao Hing·gan Ling (shou′hiŋ′gän′liŋ′) mountain range in NE China running parallel to the Amur River: highest peak, 4,665 ft (1,422 m): cf. DA HINGGAN LING

Xing or **xing** *symbol* CROSSING (sense 3): also **X-ing** or **x-ing**

Xin·gú (shēŋ′gōō′) river in NC Brazil, flowing north into the Amazon: *c.* 1,200 mi (1,931 km)

Xi·ning (shē′niŋ′) city in NW China; capital of Qinghai province

Xin·ji·ang (shin′jē′äŋ′) autonomous region of NW China, between Tibet & Kazakhstan: 635,832 sq mi (1,646,799 sq km); cap. Ürümqi: also **Xin·ji·ang-Uy·gur** (-wē′goor′)

-xion (shən) *suffix chiefly Brit. sp. of* -(c)tion [*connexion* (connection)]: see -TION

xiph·i·ster·num (zif′ə stur′nəm) *n., pl.* **-na** (-nə) ⟦ModL < Gr *xiphos,* sword + ModL *sternum,* STERNUM⟧ *Anat., Zool.* the cartilaginous process at the lowermost end of the sternum —**xiph′i·ster′nal** *adj.*

xiph·oid (zif′oid′) *adj.* ⟦Gr *xiphoeides,* sword-shaped < *xiphos,* sword + *eidēs,* -OID⟧ *Anat., Zool.* shaped like a sword; ensiform —*n.* XIPHISTERNUM: in full **xiphoid process**

xiph·o·su·ran (zif′ə soor′ən, -syoor′-) *n.* ⟦< Gr *xiphos,* sword + *oura,* tail: see URO-[2]⟧ any of an order (Xiphosura) of arthropods made up of the horseshoe crabs and related extinct forms —*adj.* of or pertaining to this order

Xi·zang (shē′dzäŋ′) *Chin. name for* TIBET

XL *abbrev.* **1** extra large **2** extra long

X·mas (eks′məs, kris′-) *n.* ⟦X[2] (sense 1) + (CHRIST)MAS: see XP⟧ *informal var. of* CHRISTMAS

XML *abbrev.* Extensible Markup Language

XO *abbrev. Mil.* executive officer

Xo·sa (kō′sä, -zä) *n. alt. sp. of* XHOSA

XP ⟦< first two letters (chi & rho) of Gr ΧΡΙΣΤΟΣ, *Khristos*⟧ *a symbol or emblem for* CHRIST[2]

X-ra·di·a·tion (eks′rā dē ā′shən) *n.* **1** exposure to or treatment with X-rays **2** X-RAY Also written **x-radiation**

X-rat·ed (eks′rāt′əd) *adj.* **1** having a film rating of X: see X[1] (sense 4) **2** characterized by sexually explicit or obscene content

X-ray (eks′rā′) *n.* ⟦transl. of Ger *x-strahl* (< *x,* algebraic symbol for an unknown quantity + *strahl,* ray): so named by W. C. ROENTGEN (1895), because of its unknown character⟧ **1** *a)* a band of electromagnetic radiation with wavelengths between gamma rays and ultraviolet radiation (*c.* .005 to *c.* 5 nanometers) *b)* a stream of electromagnetic waves within this band: X-rays are capable of penetrating opaque or solid substances, ionizing gases, and, by extended exposure, destroying organic tissue: they are widely used in medicine for diagnosis and treatment of certain organic disorders **2** a photograph made by means of X-rays —*adj.* of, by, or having to do with X-rays —*vt.* to examine, treat, or photograph with X-rays Also written **X ray**, **x-ray**, or **x ray**

X-ray astronomy the branch of astronomy that deals with X-ray radiation from various celestial sources, esp. binary stars

X-ray crystallography the study of the structural arrangement of atoms, ions, or molecules within a crystalline substance, using the diffraction patterns created by bombarding the substance with X-rays

X-ray diffraction the diffraction of X-rays as they pass through a substance, usually forming an interference pattern that can be captured on film and used to analyze the internal structure of the substance

X-ray star a star or starlike celestial object, esp. a nova or pulsar, that is a source of X-rays

X-ray therapy medical treatment by controlled use of X-rays

X-ray tube an evacuated tube containing a metal target that is bombarded by electrons from a cathode and that subsequently emits X-rays

XS *abbrev.* extra small

Xu·zhou (shōō′jō′) city in NW Jiangsu province, E China

xy·lan (zī′lan) *n.* ⟦XYL(O)- + -AN⟧ a yellow, gummy pentosan that is found in woody tissues and yields xylose upon hydrolysis

xy·lem (zī′ləm, -lem) *n.* ⟦Ger < Gr *xylon,* wood⟧ the woody vascular tissue of a plant, characterized by the presence of vessels or tracheids or both, fibers, and parenchyma, that conducts water and mineral salts in the stems, roots, and leaves and gives support to the softer tissues

xylem ray a transverse sheet of soft, living cells wholly within the wood or xylem and extending from the pith of a stem to the phloem

xy·lene (zī′lēn′) *n.* ⟦XYL(O)- + -ENE⟧ any of three isomeric, colorless hydrocarbons, C_8H_{10}, having the characteristics of benzene and derived from coal tar, wood tar, and petroleum: used as solvents, antiseptics, etc.

xy·li·dine (zī′lə dēn, zil′ə-) *n.* ⟦< prec. + -ID(E) + -INE[3]⟧ **1** any of the six poisonous, liquid, isomeric compounds having the formula $C_8H_{11}N$, resembling aniline and derived from xylene **2** a mixture of these isomeric compounds, used in making certain dyes and in organic synthesis

xy·li·tol (zī′lə tôl′, -tōl′) *n.* ⟦XYL(OSE) + -ITOL⟧ a crystalline alcohol, $CH_2OH(CHOH)_3CH_2OH$, derived from the sugar xylose, used as a sweetener

xy·lo- (zī′lō, -lə) ⟦ModL < Gr *xylon,* wood⟧ *combining form* wood [*xylograph*]: also, before a vowel, **xyl-**

Xy·lo·caine (zī′lə kān′) ⟦prec. + (CO)CAINE⟧ *trademark for* lidocaine, often used as a local anesthetic by dentists and plastic surgeons

xy·lo·graph (zī′lə graf′) *n.* ⟦XYLO- + -GRAPH⟧ [Rare] a woodcut or a wood engraving

xy·log·ra·phy (zī läg′rə fē) *n.* ⟦Fr *xylographie:* see XYLO- & -GRAPHY⟧ [Rare] the art of making woodcuts or wood engravings —**xy·log′ra·pher** *n.* —**xy·lo·graph·ic** (zī′lə graf′ik) *adj.,* **xy′lo·graph′i·cal**

xy·loid (zī′loid′) *adj.* ⟦XYL(O)- + -OID⟧ of or like wood; woody

xy·lol (-lôl, -lōl) *n.* ⟦XYL(O)- + -OL[2]⟧ XYLENE

xy·loph·a·gous (zī läf′ə gəs) *adj.* ⟦Gr *xylophagos:* see XYLO- & -PHAGOUS⟧ eating, boring into, or destroying wood, as certain mollusks or the larvae of certain insects

xy·lo·phone (zī′lə fōn′) *n.* ⟦XYLO- + -PHONE⟧ a musical percussion instrument consisting of a series of typically wooden bars graduated in length so as to sound the notes of the scale when struck with mallets —**xy′lo·phon′ist** (-fō′nist, zī läf′ə nist) *n.*

xy·lose (zī′lōs′) *n.* ⟦XYL(AN) + -OSE[1]⟧ a colorless, crystalline pentose, $C_5H_{10}O_5$, formed by the hydrolysis of xylan, straw, corncobs, etc. and used as a sweetener, in dyeing, etc.

xy·lot·o·mous (zī lät′ə məs) *adj.* ⟦< XYLO- + Gr *tomos,* cutting (see -TOMY)⟧ that can bore into or cut wood: said of certain insects

xy·lot·o·my (-mē) *n.* ⟦XYLO- + -TOMY⟧ the preparation of sections of wood for microscopic inspection —**xy·lot′o·mist** *n.*

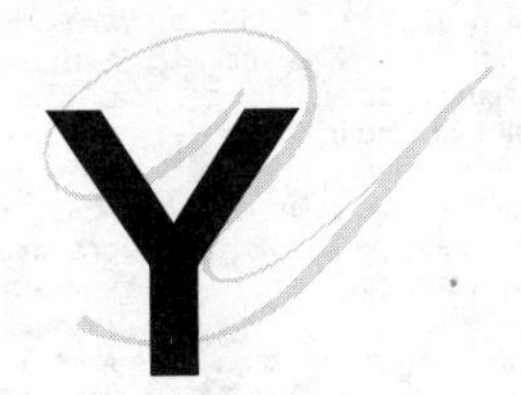

y[1] or **Y** (wī) ***n.***, *pl.* **y's, Y's 1** the twenty-fifth letter of the English alphabet: from the Greek *upsilon* **2** any of the speech sounds that this letter represents, as, in English, the semivowel (y) at the beginning of a syllable, as in *yes* or *beyond,* or the vowel (i) of *myth,* (ē) of *holy,* or (ī) of *my* **3** a type or impression for *y* or *Y* **4** the twenty-fifth in a sequence or group **5** an object shaped like Y —***adj.* 1** of *y* or *Y* **2** twenty-fifth in a sequence or group **3** shaped like Y

y[2] (wī) ***n.*** *Math.* **1** the second of a set of unknown quantities, *x* usually being the first **2** a variable **3** an ordinate

y[3] *abbrev.* **1** yard(s) **2** year(s) **3** yocto-

Y[1] (wī) ***n.*** *short for:* **1** YMCA **2** YMHA **3** YWCA **4** YWHA

Y[2] *abbrev.* **1** yen: now usually ¥ **2** yes **3** yotta- **4** yuan

Y[3] *symbol* **1** *Elec.* admittance **2** *Chem.* yttrium

y- (ē, i) ⟦ME *y-, i-* < OE *ge-,* perfective prefix (basic sense "together"): for IE base see COM-⟧ [Archaic] *prefix* forming, together with the appropriate inflectional change in the base, the past participle of verbs: its use, as a poetic archaism, survived until the end of the 16th cent. *[yclept]*

-y[1] (ē, i) ⟦ME *-y, -i, -ie,* prob. based on OFr *-i, -e,* in such familiar names as *Davi* (for *David*), *Mathe* (for *Matheu*), etc.⟧ *suffix forming nouns* **1** little, dear: used in forming diminutives, nicknames, and terms of endearment *[kitty, Billy, daddy]* **2** *alt. sp. of* -IE (sense 2)

-y[2] (ē, i) ⟦ME *-y, -ie* < OE *-ig,* akin to L *-ic(us),* Gr *-ik(os)*⟧ *suffix forming adjectives* **1** having, full of, or characterized by *[dirty, healthy]* **2** rather, somewhat *[yellowy, chilly, dusky]* **3** inclined or tending to *[drowsy, sticky]* **4** suggestive of, somewhat like *[wavy]* **5** fit or suitable for *[Christmassy]* **USAGE**—sometimes used with a slight intensive force that does not change the meaning of the root adjective *[stilly]*

-y[3] (ē, i) ⟦ME *-ie* < OFr < L *-ia* < or akin to Gr *-ia, -eia*⟧ *suffix forming nouns* **1** quality or condition *[jealousy, zoanthropy]* **2** a shop or goods of a (specified) kind *[coopery]* **3** a collective body of a (specified) kind *[soldiery]*

-y[4] (ē, i) ⟦ME *-ie* < Anglo-Fr < L *-ium*⟧ *suffix forming nouns* action of *[inquiry]*

YA *abbrev.* YOUNG ADULT

yab·ber (yab′ər) ***vi., n.*** ⟦< *yabba,* word in a language of Australia⟧ [Austral. Informal] talk; jabber

Ya·blo·no·vyy Range (yä′blō nō vē′yə) range of mountains in SE Asian Russia, a watershed between areas of Pacific & Arctic drainage: highest peak, *c.* 8,500 ft (2,591 m): also **Ya·blo·noi** (yä′blə noi′)

yacht (yät) ***n.*** ⟦Du *jacht,* earlier *jaghte,* short for *jaghtschip,* pursuit ship (i.e., against pirates) < *jaght,* a hunt < *jagen,* to chase + *schip,* a SHIP⟧ any of various relatively small vessels designed primarily for pleasure cruising —***vi.*** to sail or cruise in a yacht

yacht·ing (-iŋ) ***n.*** the action, sport, or recreation of sailing in a yacht

yachts·man (yäts′mən) ***n.***, *pl.* **-men** (-mən) a person who owns or sails a yacht —**yachts′man·ship′** ***n.***

yachts·wom·an (-woom′ən) ***n.***, *pl.* **-wom′en** (-wim′in) a woman who owns or sails a yacht

☆**yack** (yak; *also,* yäk) ***vi., n.*** [Slang] *alt. sp. of* YAK[2]: also **yack′-yack′** or **yack·e·ty-yak** (yak′it ē yak′)

Yad·kin (yad′kin) ⟦< ? AmInd⟧ river in central N.C., the upper course of the Pee Dee: 200 mi (322 km)

YAG (yag) ***n.*** ⟦*y(ttrium) a(luminum) g(arnet)*⟧ a type of synthetic garnet containing yttrium and aluminum, used in lasers and as a gem: often written **yag**

ya·ge or **ya·gé** (yä′zhā) ***n.*** ⟦AmSp⟧ AYAHUASCA

ya·gi (antenna) (yä′gē, yag′ē) ⟦after H. *Yagi* (1886-1976), Jpn electrical engineer⟧ a VHF or UHF directional antenna array in which a basic dipole antenna is supplemented by several parallel reflector and director elements: used when television reception is weak

yah (yä, ya) ***interj.*** used to express derision, defiance, disgust, etc.

Ya·ha·ta (yä′hä tä′) *var. of* YAWATA

ya·hoo (yä′hoo′) ***interj.*** [Slang] used to express joy, delight, triumph, etc. with great excitement

Ya·hoo (yä′hoo′, yā′-) ***n.* 1** in Swift's *Gulliver's Travels,* any of a race of brutish, degraded creatures subject to the Houyhnhnms and having the form and all the vices of man: see also HOUYHNHNM **2** [**y-**] a person who is variously thought of as being coarse, uneducated, unrefined, anti-intellectual, crudely materialistic, etc.

yahr·zeit (yär′tsīt, yôr′-) ***n.*** ⟦Yiddish *yortsayt* < MHG *jārzīt,* anniversary < *jār* (Ger *jahr*), YEAR + *zīt* (Ger *zeit*), time: see TIDE[1]⟧ *Judaism* the anniversary of the death of a parent or other member of the immediate family, commemorated by the lighting of a 24-hour candle (**yahrzeit candle**), the saying of kaddish, etc.

Yah·weh or **Yah·we** (yä′we, -wā) ***n.*** ⟦Heb, hypothetical reconstruction of the Tetragrammaton *YHWH:* first component, *ya, Yahu,* god < older Canaanite name⟧ God: a form of the Hebrew name in the Old Testament: see TETRAGRAMMATON: also **Yah′ve** or **Yah·veh** (yä′ve, -vā)

Yah·wism (-wiz′əm) ***n.* 1** the worship of Yahweh (Jehovah) **2** the use of *Yahweh* as a name for God

Yah·wist (-wist) the otherwise unidentified writer or writers of certain Old Testament passages in which *Yahweh* (Jehovah) instead of *Elohim* is used as the name for God: cf. ELOHIST —**Yah·wis′tic** ***adj.***

yak[1] (yak) ***n.***, *pl.* **yaks** or **yak** ⟦< Tibet *g-yag,* male yak⟧ a stocky, long-haired wild ox (*Bos grunniens*) of Tibet and central Asia, often domesticated as a beast of burden and for its milk, meat, etc.

☆**yak**[2] (yak; *also, for n. 2,* yäk) [Slang] ***vi.*** **yakked, yak′king** ⟦echoic⟧ to talk much or idly; chatter —***n.* 1** idle or voluble talk **2** *a)* a loud laugh, esp. as audience response to comedy *b)* a joke or comic bit that evokes such a laugh Also, for ***vi.*** & ***n.*** (sense 1), **yak′-yak′** or **yak·e·ty-yak** (yak′it ē yak′) —**yak′ker** ***n.***

Yak·i·ma[1] (yak′ə mô′, -mə) ***n.*** ⟦< ? Nez Percé *yáqamo˙*⟧ **1** *pl.* **-mas′** or **-ma′** a member of a North American Indian people of the Sahaptin group living in the State of Washington **2** the language of this people, a dialect of Sahaptin

Yak·i·ma[2] (yak′ə mô′, -mə) ⟦after prec.⟧ city in SC Wash.

ya·ki·to·ri (yä′kē tôr′ē) ***n.*** ⟦Jpn < *yaki,* grilling + *tori,* bird⟧ a Japanese dish consisting of small, marinated chunks of meat, typically chicken and giblets, placed on skewers, often together with vegetable pieces, and grilled

Ya·kut (yä koot′, -koot′) ***n.*** ⟦Yakut *saxa* < **čaqa* < **yaqa,* edge, border⟧ **1** *pl.* **-kuts′** or **-kut′** a member of a people living in NE Siberia **2** the Turkic language of this people

Ya·kutsk (yä kootsk′) city in EC Asian Russia, on the Lena River

ya·ku·za (yä′koo zä′, yä′kə zə) ***n.***, *pl.* **-za** ⟦Jpn⟧ **1** a Japanese gangster **2** a Japanese SYNDICATE (***n.*** **2c**) of organized criminals

Yale[1] (yāl) ⟦after Linus *Yale* (1821-68), U.S. locksmith⟧ *trademark for* a key-operated, pin-tumbler cylinder lock

Yale[2] (yāl), **Elihu** 1649-1721; Eng. merchant, born in America: prominent early benefactor of Yale College

☆**y'all** (yôl) ***pron.*** [South Informal] *dial. or phonetic sp. of* YOU-ALL

Yal·ow (yal′ō), **Ros·a·lyn Suss·man** (räz′ə lin sus′mən) 1921-2011; U.S. biochemist

Yal·ta (yôl′tə) seaport in the S Crimea, on the Black Sea: site of a conference (Feb., 1945) of Roosevelt, Churchill, and Stalin

Ya·lu (yä′loo′) river flowing from Jilin province, China, along the Manchurian-North Korean border into the Yellow Sea: *c.* 500 mi (805 km)

yam (yam) ***n.*** ⟦< Port *inhame* or obs. Sp *iñame,* prob. < name in a language of W Africa, as in Fula *nyami,* to eat⟧ **1** *a)* the edible, starchy, tuberous root of any of several tropical climbing plants (genus *Dioscorea*) of the yam family, widely grown in the tropics for food *b)* any of these plants **2** any of various other similar plants, as the barbasco ☆**3** a moist, orange-colored variety of sweet potato **4** *old Scot. name for* POTATO (sense 2) —***adj.*** designating a family (Dioscoreaceae, order Liliales), of climbing, chiefly tropical monocotyledonous plants, including the barbasco

ya·mal·ka or **ya·mul·ka** (yä′məl kə) ***n.*** *var. of* YARMULKE

ya·men (yä′mən) ***n.*** ⟦Chin⟧ [Historical] the office or residence of a mandarin or public official in China

yam·mer (yam′ər) ***vi.*** ⟦ME *yameren* < OE *geomerian,* to lament, groan < *geomor,* sad, mournful, wretched: infl. by MDu & MLowG *jammeren,* of echoic orig.⟧ **1** to whine, whimper, or complain **2** to shout, yell, clamor, etc. **3** to talk loudly or continually —***vt.*** to say loudly and fretfully —***n.*** the act of yammering, or something yammered —**yam′mer·er** ***n.***

Ya·mous·sou·kro (yä′moo soo′krō) capital of the Ivory Coast, in the central part

yang (yäŋ, yaŋ) ***n.*** ⟦Mandarin *yang,* male, daylight, solar⟧ in Chinese philosophy, the active, positive, masculine force or principle in the universe, source of light and heat: it is both contrasted with and complementary to YIN

Yan·gon (yan gôn′) capital of Myanmar: seaport in the S part

Yang·tze (yaŋk′sē) *a former transliteration of* CHANG

Ya·ni·na (yä′nē nä′) *var. of* IOANNINA

yank (yaŋk) [Informal] ***n.*** ⟦< ?⟧ ☆a sudden, strong pull; jerk — ***vt., vi.*** to jerk

☆**Yank** (yaŋk) *n.* [Slang] a Yankee; esp., a U.S. soldier in World Wars I and II

Yan·kee (yaŋ′kē) *n.* ⟦< ? Du *Jan Kees* (taken as pl.) < *Jan*, John + *Kees*, dial. form of *kaas*, cheese; orig. (*Jan Kaas*) used as disparaging nickname for a Hollander, later for Dutch freebooter; applied by colonial Dutch in New York to English settlers in Connecticut⟧ ☆**1** a person born or living in New England ☆**2** *a)* a person born or living in a U.S. state of THE NORTH (see the phrase at NORTH) *b)* a Union soldier in the Civil War ☆**3** any person born or living in the U.S. —☆*adj.* of, like, or characteristic of Yankees

☆**Yan·kee·dom**[1] (-dəm) *n.* Yankees collectively

☆**Yan·kee·dom**[2] (-dəm) *name for* the United States; esp., the northern states or New England

☆**Yankee Doodle** ⟦< YANKEE + (?) TOOTLE, in reference to sound made in tonguing a flute or fife, for which the tune was apparently first written⟧ an early American song with several versions of humorous verses, popular during the Revolutionary War

☆**Yan·kee·ism** (-iz′əm) *n.* **1** Yankee character or characteristics **2** a particular Yankee mannerism, idiom, etc.

Yan·qui (yäŋ′kē) *n., pl.* **-quis** (-kēs) ⟦AmSp⟧ [*also* **y-**] YANKEE (sense 3)

Ya·oun·dé (yä′o͞on dā′) capital of Cameroon, in the SW part

yap (yap) *vi.* **yapped, yap′ping** ⟦echoic⟧ **1** to make a sharp, shrill bark or yelp **2** [Slang] to talk noisily and stupidly; jabber —*n.* **1** a sharp, shrill bark or yelp **2** [Slang] noisy, stupid talk; jabber **3** [Slang] a crude, noisy, or contemptible person **4** [Slang] the mouth —**yap′per** *n.* —**yap′ping·ly** *adv.*

Yap (yäp, yap) group of islands in the W Caroline Islands, W Pacific; part of Micronesia: 39 sq mi (101 sq km)

ya·pok or **ya·pock** (yə päk′) *n.* ⟦< ?⟧ a small, water-dwelling opossum (*Chironectes minimus*, family Didelphidae) of Central and South America, with webbed hind feet

Ya·qui (yä′kē) *n.* ⟦Sp < Yaqui *hiyak*, pl. *hiyakim*, a self-designation < name of a river in Yaqui territory⟧ **1** *pl.* **-quis** or **-qui** a member of a North American Indian people living in Sonora, Mexico **2** the Uto-Aztecan language of this people

Yar·bor·ough (yär′bur′ō, -bər ə) *n.* ⟦said to be so named after an Earl of *Yarborough*, who would bet 1,000 to 1 against its occurring⟧ a bridge or whist hand containing no ace or other card higher than a nine

yard[1] (yärd) *n.* ⟦ME *yerde* < OE *gierd*, rod, staff, yard measure, akin to obs. Ger *gerte*, rod < IE **ĝhazdho-*, var. of base **ghasto-*, rod, pole > L *hasta*, pole, spear⟧ **1** *a)* a unit of length in the FPS system, equal to 3 feet or 36 inches (0.9144 meter): abbrev. *yd* *b)* a cubic yard, equal to 27 cubic feet or 46,656 cubic inches (0.7646 cubic meter) **2** *Naut.* *a)* a slender spar, tapering toward the ends, fastened at right angles across a mast to support a sail *b)* the transverse member of a mast on non-sailing ships, used to hold signal flags, lights, etc. ☆**3** [Old Slang] one hundred dollars or, sometimes, one thousand dollars —**the whole nine yards** ⟦< ?⟧ [Informal] everything, or the limit

yard[2] (yärd) *n.* ⟦ME *yerd* < OE *geard*, enclosure, akin to ON *garthr*, OHG *gart*, GARDEN < IE **gherdh-*, to enclose, surround (> GIRDLE, Russ *gorod*, town) < base **ĝher-*, to grasp, contain⟧ **1** *a)* the space or grounds surrounding or surrounded by a building or group of buildings (often in comb.) [*churchyard, farmyard*, etc.] *b)* a plot of grass adjacent to a building, house, etc. **2** a pen or other enclosure for livestock or poultry **3** an enclosed place used for a particular purpose or business: often used in comb. [*a lumberyard, shipyard*] **4** a place where wild deer, moose, etc. herd together for feeding during the winter **5** a railroad center where trains are made up, serviced, switched from track to track, etc. —*vt.* to put, keep, or enclose in a yard: often with *up* —**the Yard** [Informal] *short for* SCOTLAND YARD

yard·age[1] (yär′dij) *n.* **1** measurement in yards **2** the extent or amount of something so measured ☆**3** *Football* distance covered in attempting to advance the football

yard·age[2] (yär′dij) *n.* **1** the use of a yard for storage, as for cattle at a railroad station **2** the charge for this

yard·arm (yärd′ärm′) *n.* *Naut.* either half of a yard supporting a square sail, signal lights, etc.

☆**yard·bird** (-burd′) *n.* [Slang] **1** a military recruit, esp. one frequently assigned to cleanup or other menial duties **2** a prisoner; convict

yard goods textiles made in standard widths, usually sold by the yard

yard·land (-land′) *n.* VIRGATE[1]

yard·man (yärd′man′, -mən) *n., pl.* **-men′** (-men′, -mən) a person who works in a yard, esp. a railroad yard

☆**yard·mas·ter** (-mas′tər) *n.* a person in charge of a railroad yard

☆**yard sale** a sale of used or unwanted possessions, as household articles, often held in the yard of a house

☆**yard·stick** (-stik′) *n.* **1** a graduated stick or rod one yard in length, used in measuring **2** any test or standard used in measuring, judging, etc. —*SYN.* STANDARD

yard·work (-wurk′) *n.* the work of caring for the lawn, plants, trees, etc. of a yard adjacent to a house

yare (yer) *adj.* ⟦ME < OE *gearo* (akin to Ger *gar*, OS *garu*): prob. < *ge-* (see Y-) + *earu*, ready (< IE base **er-* > RISE)⟧ [Archaic] **1** ready; prepared **2** brisk; active; quick

Yar·kand (yär′känd′) *another name for* SHACHE

yar·mul·ke (yär′məl kə, yä′-) *n.* ⟦E Yiddish *yarmulke* < Pol *jarmułka*, orig., a skullcap worn as by priests < earlier *ja murka*, ult. < ML *almutia*, cowl, hood⟧ a traditional skullcap worn by Orthodox Jewish men and boys: often Conservative and sometimes Reform Jewish males wear it at worship: also sp. **yar′mel·ke**

yarn (yärn) *n.* ⟦ME < OE *gearn*, yarn, akin to Ger *garn* < IE base **ĝher-*, intestine > L *haru-spex*, soothsayer, lit., intestine-seer, Gr *chordē*⟧ **1** any fiber, as wool, silk, flax, cotton, nylon, glass, etc., spun into strands for weaving, knitting, or making thread **2** coarse fibers woven into strands for rope-making **3** a tale or story, esp. one that seems exaggerated or hard to believe —*vi.* [Old Informal] to tell yarns —**spin a yarn** to tell a yarn

yarn-dyed (yärn′dīd′) *adj.* woven of yarn dyed before weaving

Ya·ro·slavl or **Ya·ro·slavl′** (yä′rō släv′əl) city in W European Russia, on the Volga

yar·row (yar′ō) *n.* ⟦ME *yarowe* < OE *gæruwe*, akin to Ger *garbe*⟧ any of a genus (*Achillea*) of perennial plants of the composite family; esp., the **common yarrow** (*A. millefolium*), having a strong smell and taste, finely divided leaves, and clusters of small, pink or white flower heads

yash·mak or **yash·mac** (yäsh mäk′, yash′mak′) *n.* ⟦Ar *yashmaq*⟧ the double veil worn by Muslim women in public

yat·a·ghan or **yat·a·gan** (yat′ə gan′) *n.* ⟦Turk *yatağan*⟧ a type of Turkish short saber with a double-curved blade and a handle without a guard

yat·ter (yat′ər) [Slang] *vi.* ⟦prob. < YA(K[2]) + (CHA)TTER⟧ to talk idly and foolishly about trivial things; chatter continuously —*n.* **1** the act of yattering **2** idle talk; chatter

yaup (yôp, yäp) *vi., n. alt. sp. of* YAWP

☆**yau·pon** (yô′pən) *n.* ⟦Catawba *yá"pa"*⟧ an evergreen holly (*Ilex vomitoria*) of the SE U.S.: its leaves are sometimes used as a substitute for tea

yau·ti·a (you tē′ə) *n.* ⟦AmSp *yautía* < Taino⟧ **1** the starchy tuber of any of various tropical plants (genus *Xanthosoma*) of the arum family, cultivated for food in tropical America; malanga **2** this plant

yaw (yô) *vi.* ⟦ON *jaga*, to sway, move back and forth < or akin to Du & Ger *jagen*, to hunt⟧ **1** to swing back and forth across its course: said of a ship, esp. one being pushed by large following waves **2** to swing to the left or right on the vertical axis so that the longitudinal axis forms an angle with the line of flight; esp., to rotate or oscillate about the vertical axis: said of a projectile, aircraft, spacecraft, etc. —*vt.* to cause to yaw —*n.* **1** an act of yawing **2** the angle formed by a yawing craft

Ya·wa·ta (yä′wä tä′) former city in N Kyushu, Japan, now part of Kitakyushu

yawl (yôl) *n.* ⟦< MLowG *jolle* or Du *jol*⟧ **1** [Archaic] a ship's boat; jolly boat **2** a small, two-masted sailing vessel similar to a ketch but with the mizzenmast located aft of the rudderpost

yawl

yawn (yôn) *vi.* ⟦ME *yanen*, prob. merging OE *ginian* & *ganian*, to gape, akin to Ger *gähnen* < IE base **ĝhei-*, to gape, prob. echoic of the yawning sound > Gr *chainein*, L *hiare*, to gape⟧ **1** to open the mouth wide, esp. involuntarily, and breathe in deeply, as a result of fatigue, drowsiness, or boredom **2** to be or become wide open; gape [*a yawning chasm*] —*vt.* to express or utter with a yawn —*n.* **1** an act of yawning or opening wide **2** a wide opening; chasm

yawn·er (yô′nər) *n.* **1** someone or something that yawns ☆**2** [Informal] a dull or boring performance, event, etc.

yawp (yôp, yäp) *vi.* ⟦ME *yolpen*, prob. echoic var. of *yelpen*, YELP⟧ **1** *a)* to utter a loud, harsh call or cry *b)* [Slang] to talk noisily and stupidly **2** [Informal] to yawn aloud; gape —*n.* the act or sound of yawping

yaws (yôz) *n.* ⟦< a Carib language: cf. Galibi *ïaïa*⟧ a tropical infectious disease caused by a spirochete (*Treponema pertenue*) and characterized by raspberrylike skin eruptions followed sometimes by destructive lesions of the skin and bones

y-ax·is (wī′ak′sis) *n., pl.* **y′-ax′es′** (-sēz′) *Geom.* **1** the vertical, or more nearly vertical, axis in a plane Cartesian coordinate system, along which the ordinate is measured **2** a similar axis that is perpendicular to the x-axis and the z-axis of a three-dimensional Cartesian coordinate system

yay (yā) *adv.* **1** YEA (*adv.* 1) **2** [Informal] this; so: often with a gesture indicating size [*yay big, yay high*] —*n.* YEA —*interj.* [Informal] YEA (*interj.* 2)

Yaz·oo (yaz′o͞o) ⟦Fr *Yasou, Yazou*, etc.: name of an AmInd people of unknown affiliation⟧ river flowing from NW Miss. southwest into the Mississippi River near Vicksburg: 188 mi (303 km)

Yb *Chem. symbol for* ytterbium

YB *abbrev.* Yearbook

Y chromosome *see* SEX CHROMOSOME

y·clept or **y-clept** (ē klept′) *vt.* ⟦ME *ycleped* < OE *geclypod* < *ge-*, Y- + pp. of *clipian*, to call, CLEPE (popularized by Edmund SPENSER[2] & John MILTON[2])⟧ [Old Poet.] called; named; known as [*a giant yclept Barbarossa*]: also sp. **y·cleped** or **y-cleped** (ē klept′)

yd *abbrev.* yard(s): also, for the plural, **yds**

ye[1] (*thə, thi, thē; now often erroneously or facetiously* yē) *adj., definite article archaic var. of* THE: *y* was substituted by early printers for the thorn (þ), the Old and Middle English character representing the sound (*th*) or (*t͟h*): sometimes written **y**[e]

ye[2] (yē) *pron.* ⟦ME < OE *ge*, ye, nom. pl. corresponding to *thu*, thou, akin to Goth *jus*, but with vowel modified after *we* (see WE): for IE base see YOU⟧ [Archaic] YOU: first used only as nominative plural, later as nominative singular, and still later, esp. in dialectal speech, as objective singular and plural

yea (yā) *adv.* ⟦ME *ye* < OE *gea,* akin to Ger *ja*⟧ **1** yes: used to express affirmation **2** indeed; truly; verily: used to introduce a question or statement **3** [Archaic] not only that, but more; moreover [a thousand, *yea,* ten thousand] —*n.* **1** an affirmative statement or vote **2** a person voting in the affirmative —*interj.* **1** yes **2** hurrah: a shout used in cheering

☆**yeah** (ya, ye) *adv., interj.* ⟦prob. < Du & Ger *ja,* merged with prec.⟧ [Informal] yes: an affirmative reply

yean (yēn) *vt., vi.* ⟦ME *genen* < OE **ge-eanian* < *ge-* (see Y-) + *eanian,* to bring forth lambs, akin to Du *oonen* < IE base **agwhnos,* lamb > Gr *amnos,* L *agnus,* lamb⟧ to bring forth (young): said of a sheep or goat

yean·ling (yēn′liŋ) *n.* ⟦prec. + -LING[1]⟧ a lamb or kid

year (yir) *n.* ⟦ME *yere* < OE *gear,* akin to Ger *jahr* < IE **yēro-,* year, summer (> Gr *hōros,* time, year, OSlav *jara,* spring) < base **ei-,* to go (> L *ire,* to go): basic sense "that which passes"⟧ **1** *a)* a period of 365 days (in a leap year, 366 days) divided into 12 months and regarded in the Gregorian calendar as beginning Jan. 1 and ending the following Dec. 31 *b)* a period of more or less the same length in other calendars **2** the period (365 days, 5 hours, 48 minutes, and 46 seconds of mean solar time) spent by the sun in making its apparent passage from vernal equinox to vernal equinox: the year of the seasons: also **tropical year** or **equinoctial year** or **solar year** **3** the period (365 days, 6 hours, 9 minutes, and 9.54 seconds of mean solar time) spent by the sun in its apparent passage from a fixed star and back to the same position again: it is the true period of the earth's revolution, and the difference in time between this and the tropical year is due to the precession of the equinoxes: also **sidereal year** **4** a period of 12 lunar months, as in the Jewish calendar: also **lunar year** **5** the period of time occupied by any planet in making one complete revolution from perihelion to perihelion: for the earth this period is 365 days, 6 hours, 13 minutes, and 53 seconds: it is slightly longer than the sidereal year due to the extra time needed to reach an advancing perihelion, the lag being caused by the gravitational pull of the other planets: also **anomalistic year** **6** a period of 12 calendar months reckoned from any date [a *year* from today] **7** a calendar year of a specified number in a particular era [the *year* 500 B.C.] **8** a particular annual period of fewer than 365 days [a school *year*] **9** [*pl.*] *a)* age [old for his *years*] *b)* time; esp., a long time [he died *years* ago] —**year after year** every year or for many successive years —**year by year** each year —**year in, year out** every year

year·book (yir′bo͝ok′) *n.* a book published yearly; specif., *a)* a book giving statistics and data of the preceding year *b)* an annual publication of a school or college, with pictures and reports of the school year just coming to an end

year-end (yir′end′) *n.* the end of a year, calendar or fiscal —*adj.* happening, done, etc. at year-end Also written **yearend**

year·ling (yir′liŋ) *n.* **1** an animal one year old or in its second year of life **2** *Horse Racing* a horse one year old: all thoroughbreds' birthdays are arbitrarily set at January 1, at which time a foal born on any date of the preceding year is reckoned one year old —*adj.* being a year old

year·long (yir′lôŋ′) *adj.* continuing for a full year

year·ly (-lē) *adj.* **1** done, happening, appearing, etc. once a year, or every year [a *yearly* event] **2** of a year, or of each year —*adv.* annually; every year

yearn (yurn) *vi.* ⟦ME *yernen* < OE *gyrnan* < *georn,* eager, akin to Ger *gern,* gladly: see HORTATORY⟧ **1** to be filled with longing or desire **2** to feel tenderness or sympathy —**yearn′er** *n.*

yearn·ing (yur′niŋ) *n.* ⟦ME *yerning* < OE *girninge:* see prec. + -ING⟧ deep or anxious longing, desire, etc.

year-round (yir′round′) *adj.* open, in use, operating, etc. throughout the year —*adv.* throughout the year [to travel *year-round*]

yea·say·er (yā′sā′ər) *n.* ⟦YEA + SAY + -ER⟧ a person who has an affirmative or positive attitude toward life

yeast (yēst) *n.* ⟦ME *yest* < OE *gist,* akin to Ger *gischt,* spray, froth & OHG *jesan,* to ferment < IE base **yes-,* to foam, boil up > Gr *zein,* to boil, seethe⟧ **1** any of various single-celled fungi in which little or no mycelium develops and which ordinarily reproduce by budding: they ferment sugars to form alcohol and carbon dioxide; esp., *a)* any of various yeasts (esp. genus *Saccharomyces*) used in food production, as in making beer, wine, etc. and as a leavening in baking *b)* any of various yeasts (esp. genus *Candida*) causing infections or diseases **2** BREWER'S YEAST **3** *a)* the yellowish, moist mass of yeast plants occurring as a froth on fermenting solutions *b)* this substance dried in flakes or granules or compressed into cakes **4** foam; froth **5** *a)* something that agitates or causes ferment; leaven *b)* ferment; agitation —*vi.* [Rare] to froth or ferment

yeast infection any of a number of infections caused by certain yeasts, esp. candidiasis of the mucous membranes of the vagina

yeast·y (yēs′tē) *adj.* **yeast′i·er, yeast′i·est** **1** of, like, or containing yeast **2** frothy; foamy **3** marked by ferment and change [a *yeasty* era] —**yeast′i·ness** *n.*

Yeats (yāts), **William Butler** 1865-1939; Ir. poet, playwright, & essayist

yech (yek, yuk: *conventionalized pronun.*) *interj.* ⟦echoic of retching⟧ used to express disgust, distaste, contempt, etc.: also sp. **yecch**

Yed·o or **Yed·do** (ye′dō′) *var. of* EDO[2]

☆**yegg** (yeg) *n.* ⟦< ?⟧ [Old Slang] a criminal; esp., a safecracker or burglar: also **yegg′man** (-mən), *pl.* **-men** (-mən)

yeh (ya, ye) *adv., interj.* [Informal] *alt. sp. of* YEAH

Ye·ka·te·rin·burg (yi kät′ə rin burg′) city in Russia, in the Ural Mountains

yeld (yeld) *adj.* ⟦ME < OE *gelde,* akin to ON *geldr:* see GELD[1]⟧ [Scot.] **1** barren **2** not giving milk

yell (yel) *vi.* ⟦ME *yellen* < OE *giellan,* akin to ON *gjalla,* OHG *gellan* < IE base **ghel-,* to cry out > Gr *chelidōn,* a swallow⟧ to cry out loudly; shriek; scream —*vt.* to utter by yelling —*n.* **1** a loud outcry or shout; shriek; scream ☆**2** a rhythmic cheer given in unison, as by students at a school or college football game —**yell′er** *n.*

yel·low (yel′ō) *adj.* ⟦ME *yelwe* < OE *geolu,* akin to Ger *gelb* < IE base **ĝhel-,* to gleam, yellow, green, blue > Gr *cholos,* gall, L *helvus,* tawny⟧ **1** of the color of gold, butter, or ripe lemons **2** changed to a yellowish color as by age, as old paper **3** having a yellowish pigmentation of the skin ☆**4** [Informal] cowardly; craven ☆**5** ⟦see YELLOW JOURNALISM⟧ cheaply sensational: said of certain newspapers —*n.* **1** a yellow color; color lying between orange and green in the color spectrum **2** a pigment or dye that is yellow or capable of producing yellow **3** the yolk of an egg **4** [*pl.*] any of several fungous or viral diseases of plants, causing yellowing of the leaves, stunting of growth, etc. **5** [*pl.*] jaundice, esp. in farm animals — *vt., vi.* to make or become yellow —**yel′low·ness** *n.*

☆**yel·low-bel·lied sapsucker** a sapsucker (*Sphyrapicus varius*) with a red head and yellowish underparts

☆**yel·low-bel·ly** (-bel′ē) *n., pl.* **-lies** [Slang] a contemptible coward —**yel′low-bel′lied** (-ēd) *adj.*

yel·low·bird (-burd′) *n.* any of various birds that are mostly yellow in color, as the yellow warbler or several American goldfinches

yel·low·cake (-kāk′) *n.* ⟦so named from the color of the powder⟧ a uranium concentrate, primarily $(NH_4)_2U_2O_7$ or $Na_2U_2O_7$, obtained by the extraction of uranium from ores: also written **yellow cake**

yellow cake a cake having a rich yellow color because its batter contains both the yolks and the whites of eggs

yellow daisy ☆BLACK-EYED SUSAN

☆**yel·low-dog contract** (-dôg′) an employer-employee contract, now illegal, by which an applicant for a job agrees not to be a labor-union member while employed

☆**yellow fever** an acute, infectious tropical disease caused by a virus transmitted by the bite of a mosquito (*Aëdes aegypti*) and characterized by fever, jaundice, vomiting, etc.

yel·low·fin (tuna) (-fin′) a tuna (*Thunnus albacares*) with yellow fins and a yellow stripe on each side, important as a game and food fish and found worldwide in warm seas

yel·low-green algae (-grēn′) any of a class (Xanthophyceae) of photosynthetic thallophytes that contain a yellowish or brownish pigment that obscures the chlorophyll and whose motile cells have two unequal flagella: the cell walls may contain silica

yel·low·ham·mer (-ham′ər) *n.* ⟦altered by folk etym. < earlier *yelambre* < OE *geolu,* YELLOW + *amore,* a kind of bird, akin to OHG *amaro,* emmer, a kind of finch that fed on emmer⟧ **1** a small European bunting (*Emberiza citrinella*) having a yellow head, neck, and breast ☆**2** YELLOW-SHAFTED FLICKER

yel·low·ish (yel′ō ish) *adj.* somewhat yellow

☆**yellow jack** **1** YELLOW FEVER **2** a yellow flag used as a signal of quarantine **3** an edible, gold-and-silver marine jack fish (*Caranx bartholomaei*) found near Florida and the West Indies

☆**yellow jacket** any of several small social wasps or hornets (family Vespidae) having bright-yellow markings

yellow jasmine ☆a slender gelsemium (*Gelsemium sempervirens*) with funnel-shaped, yellow flowers, native to the SE U.S.: also **yellow jessamine**

☆**yellow journalism** ⟦from use of *yellow* ink, to attract readers, in "The Yellow Kid," a comic strip in the *New York World* (1895)⟧ the use of cheaply sensational or unscrupulous methods in newspapers, etc. to attract or influence readers

Yel·low·knife (yel′ō nīf′) capital of Northwest Territories, Canada, on Great Slave Lake

yel·low·legs (yel′ō legz′, -lāgz′) *n., pl.* **-legs′** ☆either of two large, gray-and-white sandpipers, the **greater yellowlegs** (*Tringa melanoleuca*) or the **lesser yellowlegs** (*T. flavipes*), having long, yellow legs, found in North and South America

yellow ocher a paint pigment, a variety of limonite, consisting of iron oxide and clay

☆**Yellow Pages** [*also* **y- p-**] the section or volume of a telephone directory, usually printed on yellow paper, containing classified listings of subscribers according to business, profession, etc.

yellow peril ⟦in allusion to the stereotyped perception of these peoples as being characterized by a yellowish skin coloration⟧ the threat to Western civilization presented by Asian peoples, esp. those of China or Japan: concept widely believed during the late 19th and early 20th cent. in North America, Europe, and Australia: offensive except in historical contexts

☆**yellow pine** **1** any of several North American pines, as the longleaf pine, having yellowish wood **2** this wood

☆**yellow poplar** **1** TULIP TREE **2** TULIPWOOD (sense 1)

☆**yellow rain** a highly toxic, yellowish, powdery substance found in Southeast Asia *c.* 1975-85, alleged by some to be a chemical warfare agent dropped from airplanes and by others to be contaminated bee excrement

Yellow River HUANG

Yellow Sea arm of the East China Sea, between China & Korea: 113,500 sq mi (293,964 sq km)

☆**yel·low-shaft·ed flicker (***or* **woodpecker)** (yel′ō shaf′tid) a flicker (*Colaptes auratus auratus*) of E North America having a red, crescent-shaped mark on the back of the head and yellow wing linings

yellow spot MACULA LUTEA

Yel·low·stone Falls (-stōn′) two waterfalls on the Yellowstone River in Yellowstone National Park: upper falls, 109 ft (33 m); lower falls (or *Grand Falls*), 308 ft (94 m)

Yellowstone Lake lake in Yellowstone National Park, fed by the Yellowstone River: 137 sq mi (355 sq km)

Yellowstone National Park national park mostly in NW Wyo., but including narrow strips of S Mont. & E Ida.: it contains geysers, boiling springs, etc.: 3,458 sq mi (8,956 sq km)

Yellowstone River ⟦transl. of Fr *Roche Jaune,* ? transl. of native name⟧ river flowing from NW Wyo. through Mont. into the Missouri River: 671 mi (1,080 km)

☆**yellow streak** a tendency to be cowardly, craven, etc.

yel·low·tail (yel′ō tāl′) ***n.,*** *pl.* **-tails′** or **-tail′** ☆**1** any of a genus (*Seriola*) of large, marine, food and game jack fishes; esp., a species (*S. lalandei*) of the Pacific ☆**2** any of various other fishes having a yellowish tail, as the **yellowtail snapper** (*Ocyurus chrysurus*), the **yellowtail flounder** (*Limanda ferruginea*) of the W Atlantic, the **yellowtail rockfish** (*Sebastes flavidus*) of the E Pacific, and the SILVER PERCH (sense 1)

yel·low·throat (-thrōt′) ***n.*** ☆any of a genus (*Geothlypis*) of American wood warblers with a yellow breast and throat

yel·low-throat·ed warbler (-thrōt′id) a wood warbler (*Dendroica dominica*) of the SE U.S., with a yellow throat

☆**yellow warbler** a small, bright-yellow North American wood warbler (*Dendroica petechia*)

yel·low·wood (yel′ō wood′) ***n.*** **1** any of several trees yielding yellow wood, esp. ☆*a)* a white-flowered leguminous tree (*Cladrastis lutea*) native to the SE U.S. *b)* SATINWOOD (sense 2*b*) **2** the wood of any of these

yel·low·y (yel′ō ē) ***adj.*** somewhat yellow

yelp (yelp) ***vi.*** ⟦ME *yelpen,* to boast < OE *gielpan,* to boast noisily, akin to MHG *gelfen:* for IE base see YELL⟧ **1** to utter a short, sharp cry or bark, as a dog **2** to cry out sharply, as in pain —***vt.*** to utter or express by yelping —***n.*** a short, sharp cry or bark —**yelp′er *n.***

Yel·tsin (yelt′sin), **Bor·is** (bôr′is) 1931-2007; president of Russia (1990-99)

Yem·en (yem′ən) country on the S tip of the Arabian Peninsula: formed (1990) by the merger of the **Yemen Arab Republic**, or *North Yemen,* and a country directly east of it, the **People's Democratic Republic of Yemen**, or *South Yemen:* 203,850 sq mi (527,970 sq km); cap. Sanaa —**Yem′en·ite′** (-ən īt′) ***adj., n.,*** **Yem′e·ni** (-ə nē)

yen¹ (yen) ***n.,*** *pl.* **yen** ⟦SinoJpn *en,* lit., round⟧ the basic monetary unit of Japan: symbol, ¥: see the table of monetary units in the Reference Supplement

yen² (yen) [Informal] ***n.*** ⟦prob. < Cantonese *yan,* smoke (n.), opium⟧ ☆a strong longing or desire —☆***vi.*** **yenned, yen′ning** to have a yen (*for*); long; yearn

Ye·ni·sei or **Ye·ni·sey** (ye′ni sā′) river in central Siberia, flowing from the Sayan Mountains north into the Kara Sea: *c.* 2,600 mi (4,184 km)

☆**yen·ta** or **yen·te** (yen′tə) ***n.*** ⟦< *Yente* Telebende, name of a comic gossip in writings (1920s & 1930s) of Yiddish newspaper humorist B. Kovner (pseud. of Jacob Adler): orig. a given name⟧ [Slang] a woman who is a gossip or busybody

yeo·man (yō′mən) ***n.,*** *pl.* **-men** (-mən) ⟦ME *yeman,* prob. contr. < *yengman, yung man,* lit., young man⟧ **1** [Brit. Historical] *a)* an attendant or manservant in a royal or noble household *b)* an assistant or subordinate, as to a sheriff *c)* a freeholder of a class below the gentry, who worked his own land **2** [Brit.] *a)* a person who owns and cultivates a relatively small tract of land *b)* YEOMAN OF THE (ROYAL) GUARD *c)* a member of the YEOMANRY (sense 2) **3** *U.S. Navy* a petty officer trained to perform clerical and secretarial duties —***adj.*** of or characteristic of yeomen: see also YEOMAN SERVICE

yeo·man·ly (-lē) ***adj.*** **1** of, characteristic of, or befitting a yeoman **2** brave; sturdy —***adv.*** in a yeomanly manner

yeoman of the (royal) guard a member of a ceremonial guard for the British royal family, made up traditionally of 100 men

yeo·man·ry (-rē) ***n.*** **1** members of the yeoman class collectively **2** a British volunteer cavalry force organized in 1761 as a home guard, but since 1907, a part of the Territorial Army

yeoman service exceptionally good, useful, or loyal service or assistance: also **yeoman's service**

ye·ow (yē ou′, you) ***interj.*** used to express pain, surprise, etc.

☆**yep** (yep) ***adv., interj.*** [Slang] yes: an affirmative reply

-yer (yər) *suffix* -IER: usually after *w* [*lawyer*]

☆**yer·ba bue·na** (yer′bə bwā′nə, yur′-) ⟦Sp, lit., good herb⟧ a trailing evergreen plant (*Satureja douglasii*) of the mint family, native to the Pacific coast of North America and formerly used in medicine

yer·ba ma·té (yer′bə mä′tā, yur′-) ⟦Sp < *yerba,* herb + *maté,* MATÉ⟧ MATÉ

Ye·re·van (yer′ə vän′) capital of Armenia, at the foot of Mt. Ararat

yes (yes) ***adv.*** ⟦ME < OE *gese,* yes, prob. < *gea,* yea + *si,* be it so, 3d pers. sing., pres. subj., of *beon,* to be: see BE⟧ **1** aye; yea; it is so: the opposite of *no,* used to express agreement, consent, affirmation, or confirmation **2** not only that, but more; moreover [ready, *yes,* eager to help] *Yes* is sometimes used alone in inquiry to signify "What is it?", "Do you wish to say (or add) something?" or as a polite way of showing interest —***interj.*** **1** it is so; aye; yea: the opposite of *no:* also used to give force to a following positive statement or to introduce a fuller or more specific statement [oh, *yes,* I will!] **2** [Informal] good, that's it, I've got it, etc.: spoken emphatically in expressing satisfaction, agreement, pleasure, etc. **3** is it so?: used in conversation to express polite interest —***n.,*** *pl.* **yes′es** **1** the act of saying *yes;* affirmative reply; agreement **2** an affirmative vote or a person voting this way: also *aye, yea* —***vt., vi.*** **yessed, yes′sing** to say *yes* (to)

ye·shi·va (yə shē′və; *Heb* ye shē vä′) ***n.,*** *pl.* **-vas** or **ye·shi·vot** (ye shē vōt′) ⟦MHeb *yeshiva,* lit., act of sitting < root *jšb,* to sit⟧ **1** a school or college for Talmudic studies; esp., a seminary for the training of Orthodox rabbis **2** a Jewish school combining religious and secular studies Also sp. **ye·shi′vah**

☆**yes man** [Informal] a person who gives undiscriminating approval to every suggestion or opinion offered by a superior

yes·ter (yes′tər) ***adv.*** ⟦< fol.⟧ **1** of yesterday **2** previous to this Usually in comb. [*yestereve, yesteryear*]

yes·ter·day (yes′tər dā′; *occas.,* -dē) ***n.*** ⟦ME *yistredai* < OE *geostrandæg* < *geostran,* yesterday (akin to Ger *gestern* < IE **ĝhyes* > Sans *hyáḥ,* L *heri,* yesterday) + *dæg,* DAY⟧ **1** the day before today; day just past **2** a recent day or time **3** [*usually pl.*] time gone by —***adv.*** **1** on or during the day before today **2** recently —***adj.*** of yesterday [*yesterday* morning]

yes·ter·eve·ning (yes′tər ēv′niŋ) ***n., adv.*** [Archaic] (on) the evening of yesterday: also **yes′ter·eve′** or [Scot.] **yes·treen** (yes trēn′)

yes·ter·morn·ing (-môr′niŋ) ***n., adv.*** [Archaic] (on) the morning of yesterday: also **yes′ter·morn′**

yes·ter·night (yes′tər nīt′) ***n., adv.*** [Archaic] (on) the night before today; last night

yes·ter·year (-yir′) ***n., adv.*** ⟦coined by D. G. ROSSETTI to translate Fr *antan* in a line from François VILLON, "But where are the snows of *yester-year?*"⟧ [Old Poet.] **1** last year **2** (in) past years

yet (yet) ***adv.*** ⟦ME *yit* < OE *giet, gieta,* akin to OFris *ieta*⟧ **1** up to now or the time specified; thus far [he hasn't gone *yet*] **2** at the present time; now [we can't leave just *yet*] **3** still; even now; in the time still remaining [there is *yet* a chance for peace] **4** at some future time; sooner or later [she will thank you *yet*] **5** now or at a particular time, implying continuance from a preceding time [we could hear him *yet*] **6** in addition; further; still; even: often with a comparative [he was *yet* more kind; taxes were raised *yet* again] **7** as much as; even [he did not come, nor *yet* write] **8** now, after all the time has elapsed [hasn't he finished *yet?*] **9** nevertheless [she is comfortable, *yet* lonely] —***conj.*** but; regardless of this [she seems happy, *yet* she is troubled] —**as yet** up to now —**have yet to (do something)** to have not yet (done something) [we *have yet to* win]

ye·ti (yet′ē, yāt′ē) ***n.*** ⟦Tibetan⟧ [*often* **Y-**] ABOMINABLE SNOWMAN

yew (yōō) ***n.*** ⟦ME *ew* < OE *iw, eow,* akin to Ger *eibe* (OHG *iwa*) < IE *(*e*)*iwā-* < base **ei-,* reddish > L *uva,* grape: orig. name because of color of the wood⟧ **1** *a)* any of a genus (*Taxus*) of evergreen shrubs and trees of the yew family, having red, cuplike, waxy cones containing a single seed, broad, flattened leaves that are needles, and fine-grained, elastic wood *b)* the wood, used esp. for making archers' bows **2** [Archaic] an archer's bow of yew —***adj.*** designating a family (Taxaceae) of resinous evergreen conifers with needlelike leaves, including ground hemlock

Ye·zo (ye′zō) *former name for* HOKKAIDO

Yg·dra·sil or **Ygg·dra·sill** (ig′drə sil′) ***n.*** ⟦ON⟧ *Norse Myth.* the great ash tree whose roots and branches hold together the universe

YHVH or **YHWH** *see* JEHOVAH, TETRAGRAMMATON

yid (yid) ***n.*** ⟦< fol.⟧ JEW: an offensive term of contempt

Yid·dish (yid′ish) ***n.*** ⟦Yiddish *yidish,* for Ger *jüdisch-(deutsch),* Jewish-(German) < *jüdisch,* Jewish < *Jude,* a Jew < L *Judaeus:* see JEW⟧ a language derived from Middle High German, spoken by E European Jews and their descendants in other countries: it is written in the Hebrew alphabet and contains vocabulary borrowings from Hebrew, Russian, Polish, English, etc.: abbrev. **Yid** or **Yidd** —***adj.*** of or in this language

Yid·dish·ism (-iz′əm) ***n.*** a Yiddish word, phrase, or idiom

Yid·dish·ist (-ist) ***n.*** **1** a person devoted to the preservation of Yiddish **2** a specialist in Yiddish linguistics

Yid·dish·keit (yid′ish kīt′) ***n.*** ⟦Yiddish⟧ [*also in roman type*] the state or quality of being Jewish; Jewishness

yield (yēld) ***vt.*** ⟦ME *yelden* < OE *gieldan,* to pay, give, akin to Ger *gelten,* to be worth < IE base **ghel-tō,* (I) give, pay⟧ **1** to produce; specif., *a)* to give or furnish as a natural process or as the result of cultivation [an orchard that *yielded* a good crop] *b)* to give in return; produce as a result, profit, etc. [an investment that *yielded* high profits] **2** to give up under pressure; surrender: sometimes used reflexively with *up* [to *yield* oneself up to pleasure] **3** to give; concede; grant [to *yield* the right of way, to *yield* a point] **4** [Archaic] to pay; recompense —***vi.*** **1** to produce or bear [a mine that has *yielded* poorly] **2** to give up; surrender; submit **3** to give way to physical force [the gate would not *yield* to their blows] **4** to give place; lose precedence, leadership, etc.; specif., *a)* to let another, esp. a motorist, have the right of way *b)* to give up willingly a right, position, privilege, etc.: often with *to* —***n.*** **1** the act of yielding, or producing **2** the amount yielded or produced; return on labor, investment, taxes, etc.; product **3** *Finance* the ratio of the annual cash dividends or of the earnings per share of a stock to the market price **4** *Chem., Physics* *a)* the total products actually obtained from given raw materials, usually expressed as a percentage of the amount theoretically obtainable *b)* the force in kilotons or megatons of a nuclear or thermonuclear explosion —**yield′er *n.***

SYN.—**yield** implies a giving way under the pressure or compulsion of force, entreaty, persuasion, etc. [*to yield* to demands]; **capitulate** implies surrender to a force that one has neither the strength nor will to resist further [to *capitulate* to the will of the majority]; **succumb** stresses the weakness of the one who gives way or the power and irresistibility of that which makes one yield [she *succumbed* to his charms]; **relent** suggests the yielding or softening of one in a dominant position who has been harsh, stern, or stubborn [he *relented* at the sight of her grief]; **defer** implies a yielding to another because of respect for his dignity, authority, knowledge, etc. [to *defer* to another's judgment] —*ANT.* **resist**

yield·ing (yēl′diŋ) *adj.* **1** producing a good yield; productive **2** bending easily; flexible **3** submissive; obedient

yikes (yīks) *interj.* [Slang] used to express pain, dismay, alarm, etc.

yin (yin) *n.* ⟦Mandarin *yin,* female, night, lunar⟧ in Chinese philosophy, the passive, negative, feminine force or principle in the universe, source of darkness and cold: it is both contrasted with and complementary to YANG

Yin·chuan (yin′chwän′) city in N China; capital of the Ningxia-Hui autonomous region

Ying·kou (yiŋ′kou′) seaport in Liaoning province, NE China, on an arm of the Bo Hai: former transliteration **Ying′kow′** (-kou′)

☆**yip** (yip) [Informal] *n.* ⟦echoic⟧ a yelp, or bark —*vi.* **yipped, yip′ping** to yelp, or bark

yipes (yīps) *interj.* [Slang] YIKES: also **yipe**

yip·pee (yip′ē, yip′ē′) *interj.* [Informal] used to express joy, delight, triumph, etc. with great excitement

☆**yip·pie** (yip′ē) *n.* ⟦< *Y(outh) I(nternational) P(arty),* a supposed, but nonexistent, group + (HIP)PIE⟧ any of a group of young people in the U.S. loosely organized in 1968 as radical activists

yips (yips) *pl.n.* ⟦< ?⟧ [Informal] a tense, nervous feeling affecting a golfer's ability to putt smoothly and effectively: with *the*

-yl (əl) ⟦< Gr *hylē,* wood, substance⟧ *Chem. combining form* **1** a monovalent hydrocarbon radical [*ethyl*] **2** a radical containing oxygen [*hydroxyl*] **3** an organic acid radical [*benzoyl*]

y·lang-y·lang (ē′läŋ′ē′läŋ′) *n.* ⟦Tagalog *ilang-ilang*⟧ **1** an East Indian tree (*Cananga odorata*) of the custard-apple family, with fragrant, greenish-yellow flowers **2** the oil obtained from these flowers, used in perfumes

y·lem (ī′ləm) *n.* ⟦ME < MFr *ilem* < ? ML *hylem,* acc. of *hyle,* matter, orig., wood < Gr *hylē*⟧ in some theories of cosmology, as the big-bang theory, the primordial material substance from which all the elements are supposed to have derived

YMCA *abbrev.* Young Men's Christian Association

YMHA *abbrev.* Young Men's Hebrew Association

Y·mir (ē′mir) *n.* ⟦ON⟧ *Norse Myth.* the giant from whose body the gods create the world

yo (yō) *interj.* [Informal or Dial.] used variously to attract attention, greet someone, introduce or emphasize a remark, etc.

yob (yäb) *n.* ⟦inversion of BOY⟧ [Brit. Slang] a hoodlum or lout: also **yob·bo** (yä′bō)

☆**yock** (yäk) *n.* ⟦var. of YAK²⟧ [Slang] a loud laugh or something evoking loud laughter; yak

yocto- (yäk′tō, -tə) ⟦< OCTO-: because the number is 10^{-3} to the eighth power⟧ *combining form* one septillionth part of; the factor 10^{-24} [*yoctosecond*]

yod or **yodh** (yôd, yood) *n.* ⟦Heb *yōdh,* lit., hand⟧ the tenth letter of the Hebrew alphabet (י)

yo·del (yōd′'l) *vt., vi.* **-deled** or **-delled, -del·ing** or **-del·ling** ⟦Ger *jodeln*⟧ to sing or call with abrupt alternating changes between the normal chest register and the falsetto —*n.* **1** the act or sound of yodeling **2** a song or refrain sung, or a call made, in this way —**yo′del·er** *n.*, **yo′del·ler**

yo·ga (yō′gə) *n.* ⟦Sans, union, lit., a yoking: for IE base see YOKE⟧ **1** [*also* **Y-**] a mystic and ascetic Hindu discipline by which one seeks to achieve liberation of the self and union with the supreme spirit or universal soul through intense concentration, deep meditation, and practices involving prescribed postures, controlled breathing, etc. **2** a system of exercising involving the postures, breathing, etc. practiced in this discipline —**yo′gic** (-gik) *adj.*

yoga pants ⟦orig. worn during *yoga* and exercise⟧ women's stretch pants that fit like long leggings, often with a decorative waistband

yogh (yōk, yōkh) *n.* ⟦ME⟧ a letter of the Middle English alphabet, ȝ, representing: *a)* a voiceless velar fricative similar to Modern German (kh), as in *doch:* in Modern English orthography it has been replaced by *gh,* which either is silent, as in *though,* or represents the sound (f), as in *cough* *b)* a voiced palatal fricative: in Modern English orthography, *y,* representing (y) as in *yes*

yo·gi (yō′gē) *n., pl.* **-gis** ⟦Hindi *yogī* < Sans *yogin*⟧ a person who practices yoga: also **yo′gin** (-gin)

yo·gurt (yō′gərt) *n.* ⟦Turk *yoğurt*⟧ a thick, semisolid food made from milk fermented by a bacterium (*Lactobacillus bulgaricus*): it is often prepared with various flavors: also sp. **yo′ghurt** or **yo′ghourt**

Yog·ya·kar·ta (yōg′yä kärt′ə) city in central Java, Indonesia

yo-heave-ho (yō′hēv′hō′) *interj.* HEAVE HO! (see phrase at HEAVE)

yo·him·bine (yō him′bēn) *n.* ⟦< *yohimbé,* a tropical Afr tree (of Bantu orig.) + -INE³⟧ a poisonous alkaloid, $C_{21}H_{26}N_2O_3$, obtained from quebracho bark and the bark of a West African tree (*Corynanthe yohimbé*) of the madder family: formerly used as an aphrodisiac

yoicks (yoiks) *interj.* ⟦earlier *hoik, hike,* also *yoaks*⟧ [Brit.] in fox hunting, used by a hunter to urge on the hounds

☆**yok** (yäk) *n.* [Slang] *var. of* YAK² (sense 2)

yoke (yōk) *n., pl.* **yokes** or **yoke** ⟦ME *yok* < OE *geoc,* akin to Ger *joch* < IE **yugo-* (> Sans *yuga,* L *jungere, jugum,* Gr *zeugma,* Welsh *iau,* OSlav *igo*) < base **yeu-,* to join⟧ **1** a wooden frame or bar with loops or bows at either end, fitted around the necks of a pair of oxen, etc. for harnessing them together **2** a pair of animals harnessed together [a *yoke* of oxen] **3** *a)* a device symbolizing a yoke, as an arch of spears, under which the conquered were forced to pass in ancient times *b)* any mark or symbol of bondage or servitude *c)* subjection; bondage; servitude **4** something that binds, unites, or connects [the *yoke* of matrimony] **5** something like a yoke in shape or function; specif., *a)* a frame fitting over the shoulders for carrying pails, etc., one on either end *b)* a clamp, coupling, slotted piece, etc. used to hold two parts together *c)* a crosspiece on a boat's rudder, to which the steering cables are attached *d)* the bar used in double harnessing to connect the horse's collar to the tongue of the wagon or carriage **6** a part of a garment fitted closely to the shoulders, as of a dress, or to the hips, as of a skirt, as a support for gathered parts **7** *Elec.* a piece of magnetic material, without windings, that permanently connects two or more magnet cores **8** *Electronics* an assembly of coils and magnetic material placed about the neck of a cathode-ray tube to provide electromagnetic deflection fields for the electron beam —*vt.* **yoked, yok′ing 1** to put a yoke on **2** to harness (an animal) to (a plow, etc.) **3** *a)* to join together; link *b)* to join in marriage **4** [Rare] to enslave —*vi.* to be joined together or closely united —*SYN.* PAIR

yoke

yoke·fel·low (yōk′fel′lō) *n.* **1** a companion, partner, or associate **2** a husband or wife; mate

yo·kel (yō′kəl) *n.* ⟦prob. < dial., green woodpecker⟧ a person living in a rural area; rustic; country bumpkin: a contemptuous term

Yo·ko·ha·ma (yō′kə hä′mə) seaport on Tokyo Bay, Japan, south of Tokyo

Yo·ko·su·ka (yō′kə so͞o′kə) seaport in Honshu, Japan, at the entrance to Tokyo Bay

Yo·lan·da (yō lan′də, -län′-) *n.* a feminine name

yolk (yōk) *n.* ⟦ME *yolke* < OE *geolca,* yolk, lit., yellow part, akin to *geolu,* YELLOW⟧ **1** the yellow, principal substance of an egg, as distinguished from the albumen, or white **2** *Biol.* the protein and fat stored in the ovum, that serves as nourishment for the growing embryo **3** SUINT —**yolked** *adj.* —**yolk′y** *adj.*

yolk sac *Zool.* **1** a saclike vascular membrane containing yolk, an outgrowth from the ventral surface of very yolky vertebrate embryos, as those of fishes, birds, or reptiles, that supplies nourishment to the embryo **2** a homologous organ in most mammalian embryos that contains no yolk and that becomes a vestige at an early embryonic stage

yolk stalk a short, thick, tubular stalk between the embryo and the yolk sac

Yom Kip·pur (yäm′ki po͝or′, yôm′-, -kip′ər) ⟦Heb *yom-kipur* < *yom,* day + *kipur* < *kiper,* atone < root *kpr,* deny, disavow⟧ one of the Jewish High Holidays, the Day of Atonement, a fast day of repentance during which the prayers recited include the Kol Nidre, observed on the 10th day of Tishri: Lev. 16:29-34

yon (yän) [Now Chiefly Dial.] *adj., adv.* ⟦ME *yone* < OE *geon,* akin to Ger *jener,* Goth *jains,* that < IE pronominal base **eno-,* that one > L *enim,* indeed⟧ yonder —*pron.* that or those at a distance

yond (yänd) *adj., adv.* ⟦ME *yond* < OE *geond,* akin to prec.⟧ [Now Chiefly Dial.] YONDER

yon·der (yän′dər) *adj.* ⟦ME, extension of *yond:* see prec.⟧ **1** farther; more distant (with *the*) **2** being at a distance, but within, or as within, sight; that or those over there —*adv.* at or in that place; over there

yo·ni (yō′nē) *n.* ⟦Sans, vulva, womb⟧ *Hinduism* a representation of the vulva, a symbol associated with the worship of Shakti: cf. LINGAM

Yon·kers (yäŋ′kərz) ⟦< Du *De Jonkers (Land),* the young nobleman's (land) > Ger *junker* (see JUNKER)⟧ city in SE N.Y., on the Hudson: suburb of New York City

☆**yoo-hoo** (yo͞o′ho͞o′) *interj., n.* (a shout or call) used to attract someone's attention

yore (yôr) *adv.* ⟦ME < OE *geara,* adv. formation < *gear,* YEAR⟧ [Obs.] long ago; in times long past —**of yore** [Now Chiefly Literary] in or of times, or a time, long past; formerly; of old [in days *of yore,* a nation now poorer than *of yore*]

York¹ (yôrk) *n.* name of the ruling family of England (1461-85): founded in 1385 when Edward III's son (*Edmund of Langley*) was created the first Duke of York

York² (yôrk) **1** city in North Yorkshire, England, on the Ouse **2 Cape** *see* CAPE YORK PENINSULA

York·ie (yôr′kē) *n.* ⟦< YORK(SHIRE) + -IE⟧ YORKSHIRE TERRIER

York·ist (yôr′kist) *n.* a member or supporter of the English royal house of York —*adj.* of or supporting the house of York, esp. in the Wars of the Roses

York rite a system of ceremonial procedure in Freemasonry

York·shire[1] (yôrk′shir) ***n.*** any of a breed of pure-white hog orig. developed in Yorkshire

York·shire[2] (yôrk′shir) former county of N England, on the North Sea: now divided into several administrative units

Yorkshire pudding ⟦after prec.⟧ a dish consisting of a batter of flour, eggs, and milk, baked usually in the drippings of roasting or roasted meat

Yorkshire terrier any of a breed of toy terrier, originating in Yorkshire, with a long, straight, silky coat, steel blue on the body and golden tan on the head and chest

York·town (yôrk′toun′) ⟦after the Duke of *York,* later CHARLES I⟧ town in SE Va.: scene of the surrender of Cornwallis to Washington (1781)

Yo·ru·ba (yō′ro͞o bə, -bä′) ***n.*** **1** *pl.* **-bas** or **-ba** a member of a people of SW Nigeria and neighboring regions **2** the language of this people, a tone language of the Niger-Congo subfamily —***adj.*** of the Yorubas or their language or culture —**Yo′ru·ban *adj., n.***

Yo·sem·i·te Falls (yō sem′ət ē) ⟦< Miwok (a Penutian language) *joṣ'e'-HmetiH,* lit., there are killers among them: ? name of an AmInd people⟧ series of waterfalls in Yosemite National Park, falling into Yosemite Valley: upper falls, 1,430 ft (436 m); middle falls, 626 ft (191 m); lower falls, 320 ft (98 m); total drop, with intermediate cascades, 2,565 ft (782 m)

Yosemite National Park national park in EC Calif., in the Sierra Nevadas, notable for its steep-walled valley (**Yosemite Valley**), high waterfalls, etc.: 1,183 sq mi (3,064 sq km)

yotta- (yät′ə) ⟦prob. < It *otto,* eight, ult < L *octo:* because the number is 1,000 to the eighth power⟧ *combining form* one septillion; the factor 10^{24} [*yottabyte*]

you (yo͞o) ***pron., pl.*** **you** ⟦ME *you, ou, eow* < OE *eow,* dat. & acc. pl. of *ge,* YE[2], akin to Du *u* < IE base **iw-,* you > Sans *yuvám,* you⟧ **1** the person to whom one is speaking or writing: personal pronoun in the second person (sing. & pl.): *you* is the nominative and objective form (sing. & pl.), *yours* the possessive (sing. & pl.), and *yourself* (sing.) and *yourselves* (pl.) the reflexive and intensive; *your* is the possessive pronominal adjective **2** any person: equivalent in sense to indefinite *one* [*you* can never be sure!]

you-all (yo͞o ôl′, yôl) ***pron.*** ☆[South Informal] YOU (sense 1): used chiefly as a plural form

you'd (yo͞od) *contraction* **1** you had **2** you would

you'll (yo͞ol, yool) *contraction* **1** you will **2** you shall

young (yuŋ) ***adj.*** **young·er** (yuŋ′gər), **young·est** (yuŋ′gəst) ⟦ME *yonge* < OE *geong,* akin to Ger & Du *jung* < IE **yuwen-* > L *juvenis,* Sans *yuvan-,* young⟧ **1** being in an early period of life or growth; not old **2** characteristic of youth in quality, appearance, or behavior; fresh; vigorous; strong; lively; active **3** representing or embodying a new tendency, social movement, progressivism, etc. [the *Young* Turks] **4** of or having to do with youth or early life **5** lately begun; not advanced or developed; in an early stage **6** lacking experience or practice; immature; raw; ignorant; green **7** younger than another of the same name or family; junior [*young* Jones or his father, the *young* Mr. Baker] **8** *Geol. a)* in a stage of increasing and more effective activity, as a stream cutting deep valleys or gorges *b)* having undergone little erosion, as a mountain range showing rugged topography —***n.*** **1** young people: often with *the* **2** offspring, esp. young offspring, collectively [a bear and her *young*] —**with young** pregnant: said of an animal

SYN.—**young** is the general word for one in an early period of life and variously connotes the vigor, strength, immaturity, etc. of this period [a *young* child, man, etc.; *young* blood]; **youthful** applies to one who is, or appears to be, in the period between childhood and maturity or to that which is appropriate to such a person [a *youthful* executive, *youthful* hopes]; **juvenile** applies to that which relates to, is suited to, or is intended for young persons [*juvenile* delinquency, behavior, books, etc.]; **puerile** generally refers to adults who unbecomingly display the immature qualities of a child [*puerile* petulance]; **adolescent** applies to one in the period between puberty and maturity and especially suggests the awkwardness, emotional instability, etc. of this period [*adolescent* yearnings] —***ANT.*** **old, mature**

Young (yuŋ) **1 Brig·ham** (brig′əm) 1801-77; U.S. Mormon leader **2 Ed·ward** 1683-1765; Eng. poet **3 Thomas** 1773-1829; Eng. physician, physicist, & linguist

young adult an age group including persons from about 12 years to about 18 years old: used as a reader category in libraries, book publishing, etc.

☆**young·ber·ry** (yuŋ′ber′ē) ***n.,*** *pl.* **-ries** ⟦after B. M. *Young,* 19th-c. U.S. horticulturist⟧ **1** a large, sweet, dark-purple berry, a cross between a blackberry and a dewberry **2** the trailing bramble bearing this fruit

young blood **1** young people; youth **2** youthful strength, vigor, ideas, etc.

young-eyed (yuŋ′īd′) ***adj.*** **1** having the bright, clear, keen eyes associated with youth **2** having a youthful or fresh outlook; enthusiastic, optimistic, etc.

young·ish (-ish) ***adj.*** rather young

young·ling (-liŋ) ***n.*** ⟦ME *yongling* < OE *geongling,* dim. akin to Ger *jüngling,* ON *ynglingr:* see YOUNG & -LING[1]⟧ **1** a young person; youth **2** a young animal or plant **3** [Now Rare] a novice —***adj.*** young

Young Pretender *name for* Charles Edward STUART[2]

young·ster (yuŋ′stər) ***n.*** **1** a child **2** a youth **3** a young animal

Young Turk ⟦orig., member of early 20th-c. revolutionary group in Turkey⟧ [*also* **y- T-**] any of a group of younger people seeking to take control of an organization, party, country, etc. from an entrenched, usually conservative, group of older people

☆**youn·ker** (yuŋ′kər) ***n.*** ⟦Du *jonker* < *jong,* YOUNG + *heer,* lord, gentleman; akin to Ger *junker,* JUNKER⟧ **1** *a)* [Obs.] a young nobleman or gentleman ☆*b)* in 18th-cent. America, a man of property **2** [Now Rare] a youngster

your (yoor; *often* yôr) ***possessive pronominal adj.*** ⟦ME *your, eower* < OE *eower,* gen. of *ge,* ye: see YOU⟧ **1** of, belonging to, made by, or done by you: also used before some formal titles [*Your* Honor, *Your* Majesties] **2** [Informal] the: used to designate a typical member of a group or class: often followed by *average*

you're (yoor, yo͞or) *contraction* you are

yours (yoorz; *often* yôrz) ***pron.*** ⟦ME *youres* < *your* + gen. *-es:* hence, in form, a double poss.⟧ that or those belonging to you: the possessive form of *you,* used without a following noun, often after *of* [that book is *yours; yours* are better; is she a friend of *yours?*] —**you and yours** [Informal] you and your family, household, etc. —**up yours!** ⟦euphemism for *up your ass!*⟧ phrase used to express contempt for, or rage at, someone being addressed: mildly vulgar

your·self (yoor self′, yər-) ***pron., pl.*** **-selves′** (-selvz′) **1** a form of YOU, used: *a)* as an intensifier [you *yourself* told me] *b)* as a reflexive [you must protect *yourselves*] *c)* with the meaning "your real, true, or customary self" [you don't seem quite *yourself* today] (in this construction *your* functions as an adjective and *self* as a noun, and they may be separated [*your* own sweet *self*] **2** ONESELF [it is best to do it *yourself*]

USAGE—now sometimes used as a subject or a nonreflexive object in certain contexts [only Smith and *yourself* are left]

yours truly **1** a phrase or formula used before the signature in ending a letter **2** [Informal] I or me

youse (yo͞oz) ***pron.*** *dial. pl. of* YOU (sense 1)

youth (yo͞oth) ***n., pl.*** **youths** (yo͞othz, yo͞oths) ⟦ME *youthe* < OE *geoguthe* < **jugunthi* < Gmc **juwunthi* (with *g* for *w* based on **duguntht-,* goodness, valor) akin to Du *jeugd:* for IE base see YOUNG⟧ **1** the state or quality of being young, esp. of being vigorous and lively, or immature, impetuous, etc. **2** the period of life coming between childhood and maturity; adolescence **3** an early stage of growth or existence **4** young people collectively **5** a young person; esp., a young man

Youth (yo͞oth), **Isle of** Cuban isle south of W Cuba: 849 sq mi (2,199 sq km)

youth·ful (yo͞oth′fəl) ***adj.*** **1** young; possessing youth; not yet old or mature **2** of, characteristic of, or suitable for youth **3** fresh; vigorous; active **4** new; early; in an early stage **5** *Geol.* YOUNG (sense 8) —***SYN.*** YOUNG —**youth′ful·ly *adv.*** —**youth′ful·ness *n.***

youth hostel any of a system of supervised shelters providing cheap lodging on a cooperative basis for young people on bicycle tours, hikes, etc.

you've (yo͞ov, yoov) *contraction* you have

yow (you) ***interj.*** *var. of* YEOW

yowl (youl) ***vi.*** ⟦ME *goulen, youlen* < ON *gaula,* to howl⟧ to utter a long, mournful cry; howl —***n.*** such a cry

☆**yo-yo** (yō′yō′) ***n., pl.*** **yo′-yos′** ⟦< ?: the toy came to the U.S. from the Philippines⟧ **1** a spool-like toy attached to one end of a string upon which it may be made to spin up and down **2** [Slang] a person regarded as stupid, ineffectual, inept, eccentric, etc. —***adj.*** [Informal] up-and-down; fluctuating; variable —***vi.*** **yo′-yoed′, yo′-yo′ing** [Informal] to move up and down; fluctuate; vary

Y·pres (ē′pr′) town in NW Belgium, near the French border: center of heavy fighting in WWI

Yp·si·lan·ti (ip′sə lan′tē; *Gr* ēp′sē län′tē), **Alexander** 1792-1828 and his brother **De·me·tri·os** (də mē′trē əs) 1793-1832; Gr. revolutionary leaders against the Turks

Y·quem (ē kem′) ***n.*** a Sauternes of very high quality produced at the Château d'Yquem in SW France

yr *abbrev.* **1** year(s) **2** younger **3** your

yrs *abbrev.* **1** years **2** yours

Y·seult (i so͞olt′) ***n.*** *alt. sp. of* ISEULT (Isolde)

YT *abbrev.* Yukon Territory: also **Y.T.**

YTD *abbrev. Accounting* year to date

yt·ter·bic (i tur′bik) ***adj.*** of or containing ytterbium, esp. trivalent ytterbium

yt·ter·bi·um (i tur′bē əm) ***n.*** ⟦ModL, contr. < *neoytterbium,* so named (1907) by its discoverer, G. Urbain (see LUTETIUM) < *ytterbia,* ytterbium oxide, name coined (1878) by J.-C. G. de Marignac, Swiss chemist who isolated it, after *Ytterby:* see ERBIUM⟧ a scarce, divalent or trivalent, silvery, malleable chemical element, one of the rare-earth elements, found with yttrium in gadolinite and certain other minerals: symbol, Yb; at. no. 70: see the periodic table of elements in the Reference Supplement

yt·tric (i′trik) ***adj.*** of or containing yttrium

yt·tri·um (i′trē əm) ***n.*** ⟦ModL < YTTRIA + -IUM⟧ a rare, trivalent, silvery, metallic chemical element found in combination in gadolinite, monazite sand, samarskite, etc.: used in phosphors, alloys, etc.: symbol, Y; at. no. 39: see the periodic table of elements in the Reference Supplement

yttrium metals a series of closely related metals including yttrium, holmium, erbium, thulium, ytterbium, lutetium, and sometimes, terbium, gadolinium, and dysprosium

Y2K *abbrev.* ⟦Y(ear) + 2 + K, abbrev. for the number 1000⟧ the year 2000

Y2K problem the predicted malfunction of some computer systems prior to or at the beginning of the year 2000 because of their inability to distinguish between dates in the 1900s and dates in the 2000s

yu·an (yo͞o än′) ***n.*** ⟦Mandarin *yüan,* lit., round⟧ the basic monetary unit of China: see the table of monetary units in the Reference Supplement

Yu·an (yo͞o än′) **1** river in SE China flowing from Guizhou province through Hunan into Dongting Hu: *c.* 550 mi (885 km) **2** *Chin. name for* the RED RIVER (in Asia)

yuca (yuk′ə, yo͞o′kə) ***n.*** CASSAVA

Yu·ca·tán or **Yu·ca·tan** (yo͞o′kä tän′; *E* yo͞o′kə tan′, yo͞o′kə tan′) **1** peninsula comprising SE Mexico, Belize, & part of W Guatemala: it separates the Gulf of Mexico from the Caribbean: *c.* 70,000 sq mi (181,299 sq km): also **Yucatán (or Yucatan) Peninsula 2** state of Mexico, on this peninsula: 15,189 sq mi (39,339 sq km); cap. Mérida

Yucatán Channel strait between the Yucatán Peninsula & Cuba, joining the Gulf of Mexico & the Caribbean: 135 mi (217 km) wide

Yu·ca·tec (yo͞o′kə tek′) ***n.*** ⟦AmSp *yucateco* < YUCATÁN⟧ **1** *pl.* **-tecs′** or **-tec′** a member of a North American Indian people of the Yucatán Peninsula **2** the Mayan language of this people **—*adj.*** of the Yucatecs or their language or culture **—Yu′ca·tec′an *adj., n.***

yuc·ca (yuk′ə) ***n.*** ⟦ModL < AmSp *yuca* < Taino⟧ **1** any of a genus (*Yucca*) of plants of the agave family, having stiff, sword-shaped leaves and white flowers in an erect raceme, found in the U.S. and Latin America **2** the flower of any of these plants

yucca

☆**yuck**[1] (yuk) ***n., vi. alt. sp. of*** YUK[1]

☆**yuck**[2] (yuk) [Slang] ***n.*** ⟦echoic of retching⟧ something unpleasant, disgusting, etc. **—*interj.*** used to express disgust, distaste, etc. Also sp. **yuch** or **yucch**

☆**yuck·y** (yuk′ē) ***adj.* yuck′i·er, yuck′i·est** [Slang] unpleasant, disgusting, etc.

Yu·e (yo͞o wä′) ***n.*** CANTONESE (***n.*** 2)

Yug *abbrev.* Yugoslavia

Yu·ga (yoog′ə) ***n.*** ⟦Sans *yuga*, an age, YOKE⟧ any of the four ages or eras of the world according to Hindu religious writings, each period being shorter, darker, and less righteous than the preceding

Yugo *abbrev.* Yugoslavia

Yu·go·slav (yo͞o′gō släv′, -gə-) ***adj.*** of Yugoslavia or its people or culture **—*n.*** a person born or living in Yugoslavia Also **Yu′go·sla′vi·an** (-slä′vē ən, -släv′yən)

Yu·go·slav·i·a (yo͞o′gō slä′vē ə, -gə-; -släv′yə) former country in the NW Balkan Peninsula, bordering on the Adriatic: established as a nation in 1918 (called *Kingdom of the Serbs, Croats, and Slovenes*, 1918-29), became a federal republic (1945): four constituent republics (Slovenia, Croatia, Bosnia and Herzegovina, & Macedonia) separated from it in 1991-92: renamed Serbia and Montenegro in 2003

☆**yuk**[1] (yuk) [Slang] ***n.*** ⟦echoic⟧ a loud laugh of amusement, or something causing it **—*vi.* yukked, yuk′king** to laugh loudly

yuk[2] (yuk) ***n., interj.*** [Slang] *alt. sp. of* YUCK[2]

Yu·ka·wa (yo͞o kä′wä), **Hi·de·ki** (hē′de kē′) 1907-81; Jpn. physicist

Yu·kon (yo͞o′kän′) ⟦prob. < Athabaskan river name < ?⟧ **1** territory of NW Canada, east of Alas.: 183,287 sq mi (474,711 sq km); cap. Whitehorse: abbrev. *YT* or *Y.T.*: usually used with *the*: in full **Yukon Territory 2** river flowing through this territory & Alas. into the Bering Sea: 1,979 mi (3,185 km)

yule (yo͞ol) ***n.*** ⟦ME < OE *geol, iul*, orig., name of a pagan festival at the winter solstice; akin to ON *jol*⟧ [*often* **Y-**] Christmas or the Christmas season

yule log a large log formerly used as the foundation for the ceremonial Christmas Eve fire

yule·tide (yo͞ol′tīd′) ***n.*** [*often* **Y-**] Christmastime

yum (yum) ***interj.*** ⟦echoic: see YUMMY⟧ [Informal] excellent; delicious: used to indicate pleasure or enjoyment: also **yum′-yum′**

Yu·ma[1] (yo͞o′mə) ***n.*** ⟦< Pima *yumi*⟧ **1** *pl.* **-mas** or **-ma** a member of a North American Indian people living in SW Arizona and adjacent regions of California and Mexico **2** the language of this people, belonging to the Yuman language family

Yu·ma[2] (yo͞o′mə) ⟦after prec.⟧ city in SW Ariz.

Yu·man (-mən) ***n.*** ⟦YUMA[1] + -AN⟧ **1** a member of a group of North American Indian peoples of the SW U.S. and NW Mexico **2** the family of languages spoken by these peoples, including Yuma **—*adj.*** designating or of these peoples or their languages or cultures

yum·my (yum′ē) ***adj.* -mi·er, -mi·est** ⟦echoic of a sound made in expressing pleasure at a taste⟧ [Informal] very tasty; delectable; delicious [a *yummy* cake]

Yun·nan (yo͞o′nän′) province of S China: 168,418 sq mi (436,201 sq km); cap. Kunming

☆**yup** (yup) ***adv., interj.*** [Slang] yes: an affirmative reply

Yu·pik (yo͞o′pik) ***n.*** ⟦< name in Alaskan Yupik, lit., real person⟧ a group of Eskimo languages spoken in areas of Alaska and Siberia adjoining the Bering Strait

☆**yup·pie** (yup′ē) ***n.*** ⟦*y(oung) u(rban) p(rofessional)* + *-p-* + -IE⟧ [Informal] a young professional regarded variously as upscale, ambitious, materialistic, faddish, etc.

yurt (yoort) ***n.*** ⟦< Russ *jurta* < word in a Turkic language: orig., a dwelling, home⟧ a circular tent of felt or skins on a framework of poles, used by nomads of Mongolia

☆**yutz** (yuts) ***n.*** ⟦< Yiddish⟧ [Slang] a person variously regarded as ineffectual, foolish, disagreeable, contemptible, etc.

Y·vonne (ē vän′) ***n.*** a feminine name

YWCA *abbrev.* Young Women's Christian Association

YWHA *abbrev.* Young Women's Hebrew Association

Z

z[1] or **Z** (zē; *Brit* zed) ***n.***, *pl.* **z's, Z's 1** the twenty-sixth and last letter of the English alphabet: via Latin from the Greek *zeta* **2** any of the speech sounds that this letter represents, as, in English, the (z) of *zone* **3** a type or impression for *z* or *Z* **4** the twenty-sixth in a sequence or group **5** an object shaped like Z ☆**6** ⟦see zzz⟧ [*pl.*] [Slang] sleep: often in the phrase **get** (or **catch,** etc.) **some** (or **one's**) **z's** to sleep for a while —***adj.*** **1** of *z* or *Z* **2** twenty-sixth in a sequence or group **3** shaped like Z

z[2] (zē) ***n.*** *Math.* **1** the third of a set of unknown quantities, *x* and *y* usually being the first two **2** a variable

z[3] *abbrev.* **1** *Astron.* zenith distance **2** zepto- **3** zero **4** zone

Z[1] *abbrev.* **1** *Astron.* zenith distance **2** zetta-

Z[2] *symbol* **1** *Chem., Physics* atomic number **2** *Elec.* impedance

Zaan·dam (zän däm′) former city in W Netherlands: now part of Zaanstad

Zaan·stad (zän′stät′) city in W Netherlands, near Amsterdam

za·ba·glio·ne (zä′bəl yō′nē; *It* dzä′bä lyô′ne) ***n.*** ⟦It, aug. of *zabaione,* ult. < LL *sabaia,* an Illyrian barley drink, beer, ult. < IE base **sab-,* to taste > SAP[1]⟧ a frothy dessert or sauce made of eggs, sugar, and wine, typically Marsala, beaten together over boiling water

Zab·rze (zäb′zhe) city in Silesia, S Poland

Za·ca·te·cas (sä′kä te′käs) **1** state of NC Mexico: 28,973 sq mi (75,040 sq km) **2** its capital

☆**za·ca·tón** (sä′kä tōn′) ***n.*** ⟦Sp, augmentative of *zacate,* grass < Nahuatl *sakaλ*⟧ **1** any of various wiry grasses of the SW U.S. and Mexico: used in making brushes, paper, etc. **2** SACATON

Zach·a·ri·ah (zak′ə rī′ə) ***n.*** ⟦LL(Ec) *Zacharias* < Gr(Ec) < Heb *zecharya,* lit., God remembers < *zachar,* to remember + *ya,* God⟧ a masculine name: dim. *Zach;* var. *Zacharias, Zachary, Zechariah*

Zach·a·ri·as (-əs) ***n.*** **1** a masculine name: dim. *Zach:* see ZACHARIAH **2** *Bible a)* the father of John the Baptist: Luke 1:5 *b)* a man named as a martyr by Jesus: Matt. 23:25

Zach·a·ry (zak′ə rē) ***n.*** a masculine name: dim. *Zach:* see ZACHARIAH

zad·dik (tsä′dik) ***n.***, *pl.* **zad·dik·im** (tsä dē′kim) ⟦Heb *tsadik* < adj., righteous and just < root *cdq,* to be right⟧ **1** *Judaism* a righteous and just man **2** the spiritual leader of a Hasidic community

zaf·fer or **zaf·fre** (zaf′ər) ***n.*** ⟦< Fr *zafre* or It *zaffera,* prob. < Ar *ṣufr,* yellow copper, brass⟧ a mixture of impure oxides of cobalt, used in making smalt and as a blue pigment in ceramic glazes, glassmaking, etc.

zaf·tig (zäf′tig′) ***adj.*** ⟦E Yiddish *zaftik,* lit., juicy, succulent < *zaft,* juice < MHG *saft,* earlier *saf,* juice, SAP[1] + *-ig,* -Y[2]⟧ [Informal] having a full, shapely figure: said of a woman

zag (zag) ***n.*** ⟦see ZIGZAG⟧ **1** any of the short, sharp angles or turns of a zigzag pattern, as alternating with a zig **2** any sharp turn away from a straight course —***vi.*** **zagged, zag′ging 1** to move in a zag **2** to zigzag

Za·greb (zä′greb′) capital of Croatia, on the Sava River

Zag·ros Mountains (zag′rəs) mountain system in W & S Iran, extending along the borders of Turkey & Iraq & along the Persian Gulf: highest peak, over 14,000 ft (4,267 m)

zai·ba·tsu (zī′bät so͞o′) ***n.***, *pl.* **-tsu′** ⟦Jpn < SinoJpn *zai,* wealth + *batsu,* family⟧ any of the large, powerful Japanese business conglomerates formerly organized around the few families that once dominated that country's finance, commerce, and industry

za·ire (zä ir′) ***n.***, *pl.* **za·ire′** ⟦< Port, prob. < Kongo *nzadi,* big river⟧ the former basic monetary unit of the Democratic Republic of the Congo

Za·ire or **Za·ïre** (zä ir′) **1** CONGO (River) **2** *former name for* the Democratic Republic of the Congo: see CONGO —**Za·ir′i·an** ***adj., n.,*** **Za·ir′e·an**

Zá·kin·thos (zä′kēn thôs′) one of the southernmost islands of the Ionian Islands, Greece: 155 sq mi (401 sq km)

Za·ma (zā′mə, zä′mä) ancient town in N Africa, southwest of Carthage: scene of a battle (202 B.C.) in which Scipio defeated Hannibal, ending the 2d Punic War

Zam·be·zi (zam bē′zē) river in S Africa, flowing from NW Zambia into the Mozambique Channel: *c.* 1,600 mi (2,575 km)

Zam·bi·a (zam′bē ə) country in S Africa: formerly the British protectorate of NORTHERN RHODESIA, it became independent & a member of the Commonwealth in 1964: 290,586 sq mi (752,614 sq km); cap. Lusaka —**Zam′bi·an** ***adj., n.***

Zam·bo·an·ga (zäm′bō äŋ′gə) seaport in the Philippines, on the SW coast of Mindanao

☆**Zam·bo·ni** (zam bō′nē) ⟦after F. J. *Zamboni* (1901-88), its U.S. inventor⟧ *trademark for* a tractorlike machine used on an ice-skating rink to smooth the ice

za·mi·a (zā′mē ə) ***n.*** ⟦ModL < L *zamiae* (pl.), false reading in Pliny the Elder for *(nuces) azaniae,* pine (nuts)⟧ any of a genus (*Zamia*) of cycads growing in Florida and tropical regions, having a short, thick trunk, pinnately compound, palmlike leaves, and short, thick cones

za·min·dar (zə mēn′där′) ***n.*** ⟦Hindi *zamīndār,* an occupant of land, landholder < Pers < *zamīn,* land, earth + *-dār,* holding⟧ [Historical] in India, *a)* a collector of the revenue from land *b)* a landholder; specif., under British rule, an aristocratic landowner with extensive holdings

zan·der (zan′dər) ***n.***, *pl.* **zander** or **zanders** ⟦Ger⟧ a greenish pikeperch (*Stizostedion lucioperca*) of the Old World, often introduced into new areas as a food and game fish

Zang·bo (zäŋ′bō) upper course of the Brahmaputra, in Tibet: *c.* 900 mi (1,448 km)

Zan·te (zän′tā) ZÁKINTHOS

za·ny (zā′nē) ***n.***, *pl.* **-nies** ⟦Fr *zani* < It dial. (Venetian) *zani, zanni,* a zany, clown, orig. a familiar abbrev. pronun. of *Giovanni,* JOHN[1]⟧ **1** a clown or buffoon; specif., a former stock character in comedies who clownishly aped the principal actors **2** a silly or foolish person; simpleton —***adj.*** **-ni·er, -ni·est** of or characteristic of a zany; specif., *a)* comical in an extravagantly ludicrous or slapstick manner *b)* foolish or crazy —**za′ni·ly** ***adv.*** —**za′ni·ness** ***n.***

Zan·zi·bar (zan′zə bär′) **1** island off the E coast of Africa: 641 sq mi (1,660 sq km) **2** former sultanate & British protectorate including this island, Pemba, & small nearby islands: it became independent (1963) & merged with Tanganyika (1964) to form Tanzania **3** seaport on the island of Zanzibar —**Zan′zi·ba′ri** (-bär′ē) ***adj., n.***

☆**zap** (zap) [Informal] ***vt.*** **zapped, zap′ping** ⟦echoic blend of ? ZIP & SLAP, popularized in comic-strip use⟧ **1** to move, strike, stun, smash, kill, defeat, etc. suddenly and with great speed and force **2** to use a remote control to avoid (a TV commercial or program segment), as by changing channels or skipping ahead on a tape, disc, etc. **3** to cook or heat in a microwave oven —***vi.*** **1** to move, strike, smash, kill, control, as suddenly and with great speed and force **2** to use a TV remote control, as to change channels or to skip ahead on a tape, disc, etc. [*he zapped through all the stations*] —***n.*** energy, verve, pep, zip, etc. —***interj.*** used to signify sudden, swift action or change

Za·pa·ta (zə pät′ə, -pat′-), **E·mil·i·a·no** (ā mē′lē ä′nō) 1879?-1919; Mex. revolutionary leader

Za·po·ro·zhye (zä′pə rō′zhə) city in SE Ukraine, on the Dnieper

Za·po·tec (zä′pə tek′, sä′-) ***n.*** ⟦Sp *zapoteca, zapoteco* < Nahuatl *tzapoteca,* pl. of *tzapotecatl,* person of the place of the SAPODILLA⟧ **1** *pl.* **-tecs′** or **-tec′** a member of a North American Indian people of S Mexico **2** the language or group of dialects spoken by this people —***adj.*** of the Zapotecs or their language or culture

Za·po·tec·an (zä′pə tek′ən, sä′-) ***n.*** a group of Amerindian languages spoken mainly in Oaxaca, Mexico

zap·per (zap′ər) ***n.*** [Slang] **1** something, esp. an electronic device, that zaps, specif. one that kills mosquitoes or bugs **2** REMOTE CONTROL (sense 2)

zap·py (zap′ē) ***adj.*** **-pi·er, -pi·est** [Slang] lively or vigorous; zippy

Za·ra·go·za (thä′rä gô′thä) city in NE Spain, on the Ebro River: Eng. name SARAGOSSA

Zar·a·thus·tra (zer′ə tho͞os′trə, zär′-) *Avestan name for* ZOROASTER

za·ra·tite (zä′rə tīt′) ***n.*** ⟦Sp *zaratita,* after D. A. *Zárate* (1793-1861), Sp. dramatist and educator⟧ an emerald-green mineral, $Ni_3(CO_3)(OH)_4 \cdot 4H_2O$, often found, esp. with chromite, in or as a crust on various igneous rocks

zarf (zärf) ***n.*** ⟦Ar *ẓarf,* receptacle, vessel⟧ a small, metal holder, used in the Levant to hold a cup of hot coffee

za·ri·ba or **za·re·ba** (zə rē′bə) ***n.*** ⟦Ar *zarība,* a pen⟧ in the Sudan region and surrounding territory, a camping place or enclosure formed by a palisade or thorn hedge

zar·zue·la (zär zwā′lə) ***n.*** ⟦Sp: after *La Zarzuela,* royal palace near Madrid, where first performed (1629)⟧ a type of Spanish operetta

z-ax·is (zē′ak′sis) ***n.***, *pl.* **z′-ax′es′** (-sēz′) *Geom.* in a three-dimensional Cartesian coordinate system, the axis that is perpendicular to the x-axis and the y-axis and that is used to measure or plot the values of *z*

za·yin (zä′yin) ***n.*** ⟦Heb *zāyin*⟧ the seventh letter of the Hebrew alphabet (ז)

za·zen (zä′zen′) ***n.*** ⟦Jpn < *za,* seat, sitting + *zen,* ZEN⟧ Zen meditation practiced in a sitting position

zeal (zēl) ***n.*** ⟦ME *zele* < LL(Ec) *zelus,* zeal, emulation < Gr *zēlos,* zeal, ardor

< IE base *yā-, to be excited, praise > OSlav *jaru,* furious⟧ intense enthusiasm, as in working for a cause; ardent endeavor or devotion; ardor; fervor —**SYN.** PASSION

Zea·land (zē′lənd) largest island of Denmark, between Jutland & Sweden: 2,702 sq mi (6,998 sq km); chief city, Copenhagen: Dan. name SJÆLLAND

zeal·ot (zel′ət) ***n.*** ⟦LL(Ec) *zelotes,* one who is jealous < Gr *zēlōtēs,* zealous follower < *zēloun,* to be zealous < *zēlos,* ZEAL⟧ **1** a person who is zealous, esp. to an extreme degree; fanatic **2** [**Z-**] among the ancient Jews, a member of a radical political and religious sect that openly resisted Roman rule in Palestine —**zeal′ot·ry *n.***

SYN.—zealot implies extreme or excessive devotion to a cause and vehement activity in its support [*zealots* of reform]; **fanatic** suggests the unreasonable overzealousness of one who goes to any length to maintain or carry out his or her beliefs [a temperance *fanatic*]; an **enthusiast** is one who is animated by an intense and eager interest in an activity, cause, etc. [a sports *enthusiast*]; **bigot** implies blind and intolerant devotion to a creed, opinions, etc. [a religious *bigot*]

zeal·ous (zel′əs) ***adj.*** ⟦ML *zelosus* < LL(Ec) *zelus:* see ZEAL⟧ full of, characterized by, or showing zeal; ardently devoted to a purpose; fervent; enthusiastic —**zeal′ous·ly *adv.*** —**zeal′ous·ness *n.***

Zeb·e·dee (zeb′ə dē′) ***n.*** ⟦LL(Ec) *Zebedaeus* < Gr(Ec) *Zebedaios,* prob. < Heb *zevadya,* lit., God has bestowed < *zavad,* to donate, bestow + *ya,* God⟧ *Bible* father of the disciples James and John: Matt. 4:21

ze·bra (zē′brə; *Brit, & often Cdn,* zeb′rə) ***n.,*** *pl.* **-bras** or **-bra** ⟦Port, zebra, earlier used of a wild ass (now extinct): said to be of Congolese orig., but prob. ult. < L *equiferus,* wild horse < *equus* (see HIPPO-) + *ferus* (see FIERCE)⟧ **1** any of several swift African perissodactylous mammals (family Equidae) of the same genus (*Equus*) as the horse and ass, having an erect mane and distinctive patterns of black and white stripes **2** a butterfly (*Heliconius charitonius*) with black wings crossed by several yellowish bands: in full **zebra butterfly** ☆**3** [Slang] *Sports* a referee who wears a vertically striped black-and-white shirt —**ze′brine′** (-brīn′, -brin) ***adj.***

zebra

zebra crossing ⟦by analogy with the stripes on the hide of a *zebra*⟧ [Brit.] a crosswalk, indicated by white stripes marked on the road, in which the pedestrian has the right of way

zebra finch a small Australian grass finch (*Poephila guttata*), of the same family (Estrildidae) as the waxbill, with a grayish back and head, a whitish belly, and a brown patch on each cheek

zebra fish any of various fishes with barred, zebralike markings; often, specif., a danio (*Danio rerio*) that is kept in aquariums and used in genetic research

zebra mussel ⟦so named from its striped shell⟧ a small, European freshwater mussel (*Dreissena polymorpha*) that clusters densely on surfaces, clogging water-supply lines, encrusting boat hulls, etc.: it was carried to the Great Lakes in the mid-1980s

ze·bra·wood (zē′brə wood′) ***n.*** **1** the hard, striped wood of a South American shrub (*Connarus guianensis*) of a family (Connaraceae, order Rosales) of tropical dicotyledonous trees and shrubs, used in cabinetmaking **2** the striped wood of various other trees or shrubs **3** any of these trees or shrubs

ze·bu (zē′byoo′, -boo′) ***n.,*** *pl.* **-bus′** or **-bu′** ⟦Fr *zébu* < ?⟧ a domesticated ox (*Bos indicus*) native to Asia and parts of Africa: it has a large hump over the shoulders, short, curving horns, pendulous ears, and a large dewlap and is resistant to heat and insect-borne diseases: see BRAHMAN (sense 3)

zebu

Zeb·u·lun (zeb′yə lən, zə byoo′lən) ***n.*** ⟦Heb *zevulun* < ?⟧ *Bible* **1** Jacob's tenth son, whose mother was Leah: Gen. 30:20 **2** the tribe of Israel descended from him: Num. 1:30

Zech·a·ri·ah (zek′ə rī′ə) ***n.*** **1** a masculine name: see ZACHARIAH **2** *Bible a)* a Hebrew prophet of the 6th cent. B.C. who urged rebuilding the Temple *b)* the book of his prophecies (abbrev. *Zech* or *Zec*)

zech·in (zek′in) ***n.*** ⟦It *zecchino:* see SEQUIN⟧ SEQUIN (sense 1)

zed (zed) ***n.*** ⟦ME < MFr *zede* < LL *zeta* < Gr *zēta*⟧ [Brit.] the letter Z

zed·o·ar·y (zed′ō er′ē) ***n.*** ⟦ME *zeduarye* < ML *zedoaria* < Ar *zadwār* < Pers⟧ **1** an aromatic substance obtained from the dried, pulverized rhizome of an East Indian turmeric (*Curcuma zedoaria*) of the ginger family and used as a condiment, in flavoring, in perfumery, and, in India, as a stimulant and carminative **2** this plant

zee (zē) ***n.,*** *pl.* **zees** the letter Z

Zee·land (zē′lənd; *Du* zā′länt′) province of the SW Netherlands, on the North Sea: 1,132 sq mi (2,932 sq km)

Zee·man (zā′män′), **Pie·ter** (pē′tər) 1865-1943; Du. physicist

Zeeman effect ⟦after prec.⟧ *Physics* the effect produced upon the structure of the spectral lines of light emitted or absorbed by atoms subjected to a moderately strong magnetic field, resulting in the splitting of each spectrum line into two or three lines (**normal Zeeman effect**) or into many lines (**anomalous Zeeman effect**)

☆**ze·in** (zē′in) ***n.*** ⟦< ModL *Zea,* a genus of grasses (< Gr *zeia,* one-seeded wheat < IE base *yewo-, grain, barley > Sans *yava-,* Lith *jāvas,* a kind of grain) + -IN[1]⟧ a white, tasteless, odorless protein extracted from corn, used in plastics, coatings, paints, inks, etc.

zeit·ge·ber (zīt′gā′bər, tsīt′-) ***n.*** ⟦Ger, time-giver < *zeit,* time + *geber,* giver < *geben,* GIVE⟧ [*often* **Z-**] a stimulus, esp. light or heat, that affects an organism's biological clock

zeit·geist (zīt′gīst′) ***n.*** ⟦Ger, time spirit⟧ [*often* **Z-**] the spirit of the age; trend of thought and feeling in a period

☆**Zel·ig** (zel′ig) ***n.*** ⟦after Leonard *Zelig,* title character of a 1983 film by Woody Allen, U.S. director; ? ult. < Yiddish *zelig,* happy < Ger *selig,* blessed: see SILLY⟧ any highly adaptable, opportunistic person

ze·min·dar (zə mēn′där′) ***n.*** *alt. sp. of* ZAMINDAR

zem·stvo (zemst′vō′) ***n.,*** *pl.* **zem′stvos′** (-vōz′) or **zem′stva** (-və) ⟦Russ < *zemlja,* earth < IE base *ĝhthem- > HOMO[1]⟧ a local administrative body in czarist Russia

Zen (zen) ***n.*** ⟦Jpn < Chin *ch'an,* ult. < Sans *dhyāna,* thinking, meditation < IE base *dhyā, to see, contemplate > Gr *sēma,* a sign, symbol⟧ **1** a variety of Buddhism, now practiced esp. in Japan, Vietnam, and Korea, seeking to attain an intuitive illumination of mind and spirit through meditation, esp. on paradoxes **2** the teachings and discipline of this kind of Buddhism —***adj.*** designating, of, or characteristic of Zen Buddhism

☆**ze·na·i·da (dove)** (zə nā′ə də) ⟦ModL: after *Zénaïde,* wife of C. L. Bonaparte (1803-57), Fr ornithologist⟧ either of two wild doves, (*Zenaida aurita*) of Florida and the Caribbean, or (*Z. asiatica*) of the SW U.S. to Chile

ze·na·na (ze nä′nə) ***n.*** ⟦Hindi *zanāna* < Pers < *zan,* woman, akin to Gr *gynē,* woman: see GYNO-⟧ in India and Iran, the part of the house reserved for women

Zend (zend) ***n.*** ⟦Pers, interpretation, short for fol.⟧ **1** the Middle Persian translation of and commentary on the Avesta **2** *former name for* AVESTAN —**Zend′ic *adj.***

Zend-A·ves·ta (zend′ə ves′tə) ***n.*** ⟦Fr, altered < *Avestá-va-Zend* < MPers *avastāk va zand,* lit., (sacred) text and interpretation⟧ AVESTA

☆**ze·ner diode** (zē′nər) ⟦after Clarence *Zener* (1905-93), U.S. physicist⟧ [*often* **Z- d-**] a semiconductor diode usually used as a voltage regulator because its resistance breaks down at a precise, predetermined voltage level (**zener voltage**), at which time it maintains a constant voltage while producing a sudden large increase in current

Zeng·er (zeŋ′ər, -gər), **John Peter** 1697-1746; Am. journalist & publisher, born in Germany: defendant in a landmark libel case (1735)

ze·nith (zē′nith; *Brit, & often Cdn,* zen′ith) ***n.*** ⟦ME *senyth* < MFr *cenith* < ML *cenit* < *senit,* scribal error for Ar *samt,* road, path (as in *samt al-ra's,* zenith, lit., way of the head) < L *semita,* path, way⟧ **1** the point directly overhead in the sky or on the celestial sphere: opposed to NADIR **2** the highest point; peak —**SYN.** SUMMIT

Ze·no (zē′nō) **1** fl. 5th cent. B.C.; Gr. Eleatic philosopher: also **Zeno of E·le·a** (ē′lē ə) (town in Italy) **2** 334?-261? B.C.; Gr. philosopher: founder of Stoicism: also **Zeno of Ci·ti·um** (sish′ē əm) (city in Cyprus)

Ze·no·bi·a (zə nō′bē ə) ⟦L < Gr *Zēnobia*⟧ 3d cent. A.D.; queen of Palmyra

ze·o·lite (zē′ə līt′) ***n.*** ⟦Swed *zeolit* < Gr *zein,* to boil (see YEAST): from its swelling up when heated⟧ **1** any of a large group of natural hydrous aluminum silicates of sodium, calcium, potassium, barium, etc., chiefly found in cavities in igneous rocks and characterized by a ready loss or gain of water of hydration: many are capable of ion exchange with solutions **2** a similar natural or synthetic silicate, used for softening water —**ze′o·lit′ic** (-lit′ik) ***adj.***

Zeph·a·ni·ah (zef′ə nī′ə) ***n.*** ⟦Heb *tsefanya,* lit., the Lord has hidden < *tsafan,* to hide + *ya,* God⟧ *Bible* **1** a Hebrew prophet of the 7th cent. B.C. **2** the book of his prophecies: abbrev. *Zep, Zeph,* or *Zp*

zeph·yr (zef′ər) ***n.*** ⟦ME *zeferus* < L *zephyrus* < Gr *zephyros,* the west wind⟧ **1** the west wind **2** [**Z-**] ZEPHYRUS **3** a gentle breeze **4** a fine, soft, lightweight yarn, cloth, or garment —**SYN.** WIND[2]

Zeph·y·rus (zef′ə rəs) ***n.*** ⟦L: see prec.⟧ *Gr. Myth.* the west wind personified as a god

zep·pe·lin (zep′lin, zep′ə lin) ***n.*** ⟦after Count Ferdinand von *Zeppelin* (1838-1917), Ger general who designed the original⟧ [*often* **Z-**] any rigid airship: commonly used from 1900 to 1937

zep·po·le (zə pō′lā, tsə-; zep′ə lā′) ***n.,*** *pl.* **-le, -li** (-lē), or **-les** ⟦It⟧ a deep-fried pastry somewhat like a doughnut

zepto- (zep′tō, -tə) ⟦< SEPTI-[1]: because the number is 10^{-3} to the seventh power⟧ *combining form* one sextillionth part of; the factor 10^{-21} [*zeptosecond*]

zerk (zurk) ***n.*** ⟦after O. *Zerk* (1878-1968), U.S. inventor, born in Austria⟧ a small metal fitting through which grease can be inserted into a mechanical joint that requires periodic lubrication

ze·ro (zir′ō, zē′rō) ***n.,*** *pl.* **-ros** or **-roes** ⟦Fr *zéro* < It *zero* < Ar *ṣifr,* CIPHER⟧ **1** the symbol or numeral 0, representing the complete absence of any quantity or magnitude **2** the point, marked 0, from which positive or negative quantities are reckoned on a graduated scale, as on a thermometer; specif., *a)* on a centigrade thermometer, the freezing point of water *b)* on a Fahrenheit thermometer, a point 32° below the freezing point of water **3** a temperature that causes a thermometer to register zero **4** the point intermediate between positive and negative quantities **5** nothing **6** the lowest point [his chances of success sank to *zero*] **7** *Gunnery* a sight setting for a range, allowing for both elevation and windage —*adj.* 1 of or at zero 2 without measurable value 3 [Informal] not any; no [a snack having *zero* cholesterol] 4 *Aeron.* *a)* designating or of a ceiling that is at or near the ground, specif. one at a height of fifty feet or lower *b)* designating or of visibility along the ground regarded as within the limit of a few feet 5 *Linguis.* designating a hypothetical inflectional form [the plural of *deer* is said to be formed by the addition of a *zero* allomorph of the plural morpheme] —*vt.* **-roed**, **-ro·ing** to adjust (an instrument, etc.) to a zero point or to an arbitrary point from which all positive and negative readings are to be measured —**zero in** 1 to adjust the zero of (a gun) 2 to aim (a gun) or concentrate (firepower) directly at or on (a target) —**zero in on** 1 to adjust gunfire so as to be aiming directly at (a target) 2 to concentrate attention on; focus on

☆**ze·ro-base** (-bās′) *adj.* ⟦from the idea of starting at zero⟧ designating or of a technique for preparing a budget, in which each proposed item is evaluated on its merits without considering any previous budget: also **ze′ro-based′**

ze·ro-cou·pon (-ko͞o′pän) *adj.* designating or of a bond sold at a discount and redeemed upon maturity at its face value, with no periodic payments of interest

zero gravity *Physics* a weightless condition in which an object appears not to be influenced by gravity because other objects in its immediate surroundings are undergoing the same acceleration

zero hour ⟦so called because it marks the end of an actual or implied countdown⟧ 1 the hour or moment at which a military attack or other important operation is to begin 2 any crucial or decisive moment

☆**zero (population) growth** a condition in a given population in which the birthrate equals the death rate, so that the population remains constant

ze·ro-sum (-sum′) *adj.* in game theory, designating or of a situation, competition, etc. in which a gain for one must result in an equal loss for another or others

zero tolerance an uncompromising policy or position in which some undesirable behavior is not tolerated, to the point that even slight infractions may be severely punished

zest (zest) *n.* ⟦Fr *zeste,* partition membrane in a nut, hence piece of orange or orange peel used to give piquancy⟧ 1 the outermost, colored portion of the peel of a citrus fruit used, often in fine shreds, as flavoring 2 stimulating or exciting quality 3 keen enjoyment; gusto: often with *for* [a *zest* for life] —**zest′ful** *adj.* —**zest′ful·ly** *adv.* —**zest′ful·ness** *n.* —**zest′y** *adj.* **zest′i·er, zest′i·est** —**zest′i·ly** *adv.* —**zest′i·ness** *n.*

zest·er (zes′tər) *n.* a cooking utensil for scraping or peeling zest from citrus fruit

ze·ta (zāt′ə, zēt′ə) *n.* ⟦Gr *zēta*⟧ the sixth letter of the Greek alphabet (Z, ζ)

Zet·land (zet′lənd) *var. of* SHETLAND[2]

zetta- (zet′ə) ⟦prob. < It *sette,* seven, ult. < L *septem*: because the number is 1,000 to the seventh power⟧ *combining form* one sextillion; the factor 10^{21} [*zettabyte*]

zeug·ma (zyo͞og′mə, zo͞og′-) *n.* ⟦L < Gr, lit., YOKE⟧ 1 SYLLEPSIS 2 a figure of speech in which a single word, usually a verb or adjective, is syntactically related to two or more words, though having a different sense in relation to each (Ex.: The room was not light, but his fingers were) —**zeug·mat′ic** (-mat′ik) *adj.*

Zeus (zo͞os, zyo͞os) *n.* ⟦Gr: for IE base see DEITY⟧ *Gr. Myth.* the chief deity, son of Cronus and Rhea and husband of Hera: identified with the Roman Jupiter

Zeux·is (zo͞ok′sis) fl. 5th cent. B.C.; Gr. painter

Zhang·ji·a·kou (jäŋ′jē ä′kō′) city in Hebei province, NE China, at a gateway of the Great Wall of China

Zhan·ji·ang (jäŋ′jē äŋ′) city in S China, on the Leizhou Peninsula, Guangdong province: formerly (1898-1946) in territory leased by France

Zhda·nov (zhdän′ôf′) *name* (1948-89) *for* MARIUPOL

Zhe·ji·ang (je′jē äŋ′) province of E China, on the East China Sea: 39,305 sq mi (101,800 sq km); cap. Hangzhou

Zheng·zhou (jeŋ′jō′) city in EC China; capital of Henan province

Zhen·ji·ang (jen′jē äŋ′) city in Jiangsu province, E China, at the juncture of the Grand Canal & the Chang River

Zhou En-lai (jō′en′lī′) *Pinyin form of* CHOU EN-LAI

Zhu (jo͞o) river in SE China, forming an estuary between Macao & Hong Kong: *c.* 100 mi (161 km)

Zhu·kov (zho͞o′kôf′), **Geor·gi K(onstantinovich)** (gyôr′gē) 1896-1974; Soviet marshal

Zhu·zhou (jo͞o′jō′) city in E Hunan province, in SE China

zib·el·ine or **zib·el·line** (zib′ə līn′, -lēn′, -lin) *adj.* ⟦Fr *zibeline* < It *zibellino* < Slav base > SABLE⟧ of or having to do with sables —*n.* 1 the fur of the sable 2 a soft woolen dress material with a furlike nap

Zi·bo (dzē′bō′) city in Shandong province, NE China

zi·do·vu·dine (zī dō′vyo͞o dēn′) *n.* ⟦shortened & altered < *azidothymidine,* chemical name⟧ an antiviral drug used in the treatment of AIDS; AZT

Zieg·feld (zig′feld′), **Flor·enz** (flôr′ənz) 1869-1932; U.S. theatrical producer

Zieg·ler (tsēk′lər), **Karl** (kärl) 1898-1973; Ger. chemist

zig (zig) *n.* ⟦see ZIGZAG⟧ 1 any of the short, sharp angles or turns of a zigzag pattern, alternating with a zag 2 any sharp turn away from a straight course —*vi.* **zigged, zig′ging** 1 to move in a zig 2 to zigzag

zig·gu·rat (zig′o͝o rat′) *n.* ⟦Akkadian *ziqqurratu,* temple tower < *zaqru,* high, massive⟧ a temple tower of the ancient Assyrians and Babylonians, in the form of a terraced pyramid with each story smaller than the one below it: also **zik′ku·rat** (zik′-)

Zi·gong (dzē′gôŋ′) city in Sichuan province, SC China

zig·zag (zig′zag′) *n.* ⟦Fr, prob. < Ger *zickzack,* redupl. < *zacke,* a tooth, sharp prong or point⟧ 1 a series of short, sharp angles or turns in alternate directions, as in a line or course 2 something characterized by such a series, as a design, path, etc. —*adj.* having the form of a zigzag [*zigzag* stitching] —*adv.* in a zigzag course — *vt., vi.* **-zagged′**, **-zag′ging** to move or form in a zigzag

☆**zilch** (zilch) *n.* ⟦nonsense syllable, orig. used in the 1930s as the name of a character in the magazine *Ballyhoo*⟧ [Slang] nothing or zero

zil·lah (zil′ə) *n.* ⟦Hindi *ḍil‘* < Ar *dila‘,* a rib, side; akin to Akkadian *ṣēlu,* rib⟧ in India under British rule, an administrative district

☆**zil·lion** (zil′yən) *n.* ⟦arbitrary coinage, after MILLION⟧ [Informal] a very large, indefinite number —**zil′lionth** *adj., n.*

zil·lion·aire (zil′yə ner′) *n.* ⟦prec. + (MILLION)AIRE⟧ [Informal] a person regarded as having virtually immeasurable wealth: a hyperbolic use

Zil·pah (zil′pə) *n.* ⟦Heb *zilpa,* akin to *zelef,* a spray, sprinkling⟧ *Bible* the mother of Gad and Asher: Gen. 30:10-13

Zimb *abbrev.* Zimbabwe

Zim·ba·bwe (zim bäb′wā′, -wē′) ⟦after a ruined city in the SE part, probably built (*c.* 15th c.) by a Bantu people⟧ country in S Africa, north of South Africa and west of Mozambique: a self-governing British colony (as *Southern Rhodesia*) from 1923; became a republic (1970) as *Rhodesia;* gained full legal independence (1980) as *Zimbabwe:* 150,804 sq mi (390,580 sq km); cap. Harare —**Zim·ba′bwe·an** (-bwē ən) *adj., n.*

zinc (ziŋk) *n.* ⟦Ger *zink,* zinc, orig., prong, point: first used by PARACELSUS (*c.* 1526): from the form of the crystals on smelting; akin to OHG *zint,* a point, jag < Gmc **tindja* > TINE⟧ a bluish-white, metallic chemical element, usually found in combination, used as a protective coating for iron, as a constituent in various alloys, as an electrode in electric batteries, and, in the form of salts, in medicines: symbol, Zn; at. no. 30: see the periodic table of elements in the Reference Supplement —*vt.* **zincked** or **zinced**, **zinck′ing** or **zinc′ing** to coat or treat with zinc; galvanize —**zinc′ic** (-ik) *adj.*, **zinc′ous** (-əs) —**zinck′y** (-ē) *adj.*, **zinc′y**

zinc·ate (ziŋ′kāt′) *n.* a salt produced by the reaction of amphoteric zinc hydroxide as an acid

zinc blende SPHALERITE

zinc chloride a white, crystalline powder, $ZnCl_2$, used as a catalyst, wood preservative, antiseptic, etc. and in soldering fluxes, adhesives, parchment paper, embalming fluids, etc.

zinc·ite (ziŋ′kīt′) *n.* a red to yellow, brittle, hexagonal mineral, (Zn,Mn)O, that is an ore of zinc; zinc manganese oxide

zin·cog·ra·phy (ziŋ käg′rə fē) *n.* ⟦ZINC + -O- + -GRAPHY⟧ the art or process of engraving or etching on zinc plates for printing —**zin·cog′ra·pher** *n.* —**zin′co·graph′ic** (-kə graf′ik) *adj.*

zinc ointment an ointment containing zinc oxide

zinc oxide a white powder, ZnO, used as a pigment and in making rubber articles, cosmetics, ointments, etc.

zinc sulfate a colorless, crystalline powder, $ZnSO_4 \cdot 7H_2O$, used as an emetic in medicine, as a mordant in dyeing, etc.

zinc sulfide a yellowish-white, crystalline powder, ZnS, used in a phosphorescent form in making television screens and luminous watch faces, and also as a pigment, etc.

zinc white zinc oxide used as a white pigment

☆**zine** or **'zine** (zēn) *n.* ⟦< (MAGA)ZINE⟧ 1 a cheaply printed magazine published irregularly by amateurs, esp. one featuring images and ideas reflecting unconventional thought 2 an online version of such a publication

☆**zin·eb** (zin′eb) *n.* ⟦*zin(c) e(thylene-)b(is-dithiocarbamate)*⟧ an insecticide and fungicide, $Zn(CS_2NHCH_2)_2$, obtained as a dust or wettable powder, used on plants and fruit

☆**zin·fan·del** (zin′fən del′) *n.* ⟦< ?⟧ [*also* **Z-**] 1 a dry red wine made chiefly in California 2 the dark grape from which it is made

zing (ziŋ) [Informal] *n.* ⟦echoic⟧ 1 a shrill, high-pitched sound, as of something moving at high speed 2 a lively, zestful quality; zest, vigor, animation, force, vitality, etc. —*vi.* to make a shrill, high-pitched sound —*vt.* 1 to strike or affect forcibly 2 to criticize sharply —**zing′y** *adj.* **zing′i·er, zing′i·est**

zing·er (ziŋ′ər) *n.* 1 [Slang] a person or thing considered surprising, shocking, etc. 2 [Informal] a sharp, witty, or caustic remark or rejoinder

Zin·jan·thro·pus (zin jan′thrə pəs) *n.* ⟦ModL < Ar *Zinj,* people of East Africa + Gr *anthrōpos,* man: see ANTHROPO-⟧ a type of early hominid (*Australopithecus boisei*) who lived about 1,500,000 years ago in the Lower Pleistocene

zin·ken·ite (ziŋ′kə nīt′) *n.* ⟦Ger *zinkenit,* after J. K. *Zincken* (1790-1862), Ger geologist⟧ a steel-gray mineral, $Pb_6Sb_{14}S_{27}$, that is an ore of lead

zink·y (ziŋ′kē) *adj. alt. sp. of* ZINCKY

zin·ni·a (zin′ē ə, zin′yə) *n.* ⟦ModL, after J. G. Zinn (1727-59), Ger botanist⟧ any of a genus (*Zinnia*) of plants of the composite family, having colorful flower heads, native to North and South America

Zion[1] (zī′ən) *n.* ⟦ME *Syon* < OE *Sion* < LL(Ec) < Heb *tsiyon*⟧ 1 a Canaanite fortress in Jerusalem captured by David and called in the Bible "City of David" 2 the Jewish people 3 heaven; the heavenly city 4 the theocracy of God

Zi·on[2] (zī′ən) 1 the hill in Jerusalem on which the Temple was built: Zion has historically been regarded by Jews as a symbol of the center of Jewish national life **2** Jerusalem **3** the land of Israel

Zi·on·ism (zī′ə niz′əm) ***n.*** a movement originally for reestablishing a Jewish homeland in Palestine and now for supporting the Jewish national state of Israel —**Zi′on·ist** ***n., adj.*** —**Zi′on·is′tic** ***adj.***

zip (zip) ***n.*** ⟦echoic⟧ **1** a short, sharp hissing or whizzing sound **2** [Informal] energy; vigor; vim **3** [Chiefly Brit.] ZIPPER: also **zip′-fas′ten·er** **4** [Slang] nothing or zero **5** [Informal] a zip code number —☆***vi.*** **zipped**, **zip′ping** **1** to make, or move with, a zip **2** [Informal] to act or move with speed or energy **3** to become fastened or unfastened by means of a zipper —☆***vt.*** **1** to fasten (a zipper) **2** to fasten the zipper of: often with *up* **3** [Informal] to move or propel something with speed and force **4** ⟦< the trademark *PKZIP*, software designed to do this⟧ *Comput.* to compress (a file) digitally so that it requires less storage space

☆**ZIP Code** (zip) ⟦*Z(one) I(mprovement) P(lan)*⟧ *service mark for* a system of code numbers assigned by the postal service to be used as part of the mailing address: each code designates a delivery area — [*usually* **zip c-**] such a code number, typically consisting of five digits, although often expanded to nine

☆**zip gun** a crude, improvised pistol, usually consisting of a piece of pipe attached to a wooden stock, with a firing pin actuated by a rubber band or a spring

zip-line (-līn′) ***n.*** an apparatus consisting of a pulley rigged to glide along a stretched cable, as for conveying a person or thing across an expanse

☆**Zip·loc** (zip′läk′) *trademark for* a kind of transparent plastic storage bag sealed by joining interlocking strips along the edges of the opening

☆**zip-lock** (zip′läk′) ***adj.*** designating or of a plastic storage bag of the Ziploc type

☆**zip·per** (zip′ər) ***n.*** **1** a person or thing that zips **2** a device used to fasten and unfasten two adjoining edges of material, as on the placket of a dress, the fly of a pair of trousers, etc.: it consists of two rows of tiny interlocking tabs which are joined or separated by sliding a part up or down **3** an oblong, horizontal, rectangular electronic sign on which moving messages of text, data, etc. may be scrolled, using flashing lights, LED displays, etc. — ***vt., vi.*** to fasten or become fastened by means of a zipper

Zip·po (zip′ō) *trademark for* a squarish, pocket-size cigarette lighter with a metal case and a hinged lid —***n.*** such a lighter: also **Zippo lighter**

zip·py (zip′ē) ***adj.*** **-pi·er**, **-pi·est** ⟦< ZIP + -Y²⟧ [Informal] full of vim and energy; brisk

☆**zi·ram** (zī′ram′) ***n.*** ⟦ZI(NC) + (THI)RAM⟧ a white powder, $Zn(SCSN(CH_3)_2)_2$, used as a vegetable fungicide and as a rubber accelerator

Zir·ca·loy (zur′kə loi′) ***n.*** ⟦< *Zircaloy Super Alpha*, former trademark < ZIRC(ONIUM) + AL(L)OY⟧ any of various alloys containing about 98% zirconium, 1.5% tin, etc., that are resistant to corrosion and high temperatures and are used to contain fuel in nuclear reactors, etc.

zir·con (zur′kän′) ***n.*** ⟦Ger *zirkon*, altered (by Werner: see WERNERITE) < Fr *jargon* < It *giargone* < Ar *zarqūn*, bright red < Pers *zargūn*, gold-colored < *zar*, gold⟧ a light-colored, very hard mineral, zirconium silicate, $ZrSiO_4$, an ore of zirconium: used as a gem when transparent: see MOHS SCALE (sense 2)

zir·co·ni·a (zər kō′nē ə) ***n.*** ⟦ModL < prec. + -IA: so named (1789) by Klaproth (see TELLURIUM)⟧ ZIRCONIUM OXIDE

zir·co·ni·um (zər kō′nē əm) ***n.*** ⟦ModL < prec. + -IUM: name proposed (1808) by Sir Humphry DAVY for element later isolated (1824) by BERZELIUS⟧ a hard, ductile, gray or black, metallic chemical element found combined in zircon, etc., and used in alloys, ceramics, the cladding for nuclear fuel in reactors, etc.: symbol, Zr; at. no. 40: see the periodic table of elements in the Reference Supplement —**zir·con′ic** (-kän′ik) ***adj.***

zirconium oxide zirconium dioxide, ZrO_2, a white, infusible powder used in making crucibles, furnace linings, pigments, etc. and, because of its luminosity, in incandescent burners

Zis·ka (tsis′kä′), **Jo′hann′** (yō′hän′) *Ger. name for* Jan ŽIŽKA

zit (zit) ***n.*** ⟦< ?⟧ [Slang] a pimple, esp. one on the face

zith·er (zith′ər, zith′-) ***n.*** ⟦Ger < L *cithara* < Gr *kithara*, lute⟧ **1** any of a family of musical instruments with strings stretched across a flat soundboard and plucked, bowed, struck with mallets, etc., as the dulcimer, koto, psaltery, etc. **2** a folk instrument of this type of Austria and S Germany

zi·ti (zēt′ē) ***n.*** pasta in the shape of tubes of medium width, with an outer surface that is either smooth or ridged

zi·zit or **zi·zith** (tsit′sis, tsēt sēt′) ***pl.n.*** *alt. sp. of* TZITZIT

Žiž·ka (zhish′kä), **Jan** (yän) died 1424; Bohemian general & leader of the Hussites

Zla·to·ust (zlä′tə o͞ost′) city in SW Asian Russia, in the Ural Mountains, near Chelyabinsk

zlo·ty (zlô′tē; *Pol* zwô′tē) ***n.***, *pl.* **-tys** ⟦Pol, lit., golden⟧ the basic monetary unit of Poland: abbrev. **zl**: see the table of monetary units in the Reference Supplement

Zn *Chem. symbol for* zinc

zo- (zō) *combining form* ZOO-: used before a vowel [*zoanthropy, zooid*]

zo·a (zō′ə) ***n.*** *pl. of* ZOON

-zo·a (zō′ə) ⟦ModL < Gr *zōia*, pl. of *zōion*, an animal: see BIO-⟧ *suffix Zool.* forming the scientific name of a (specified) group

Zo·an (zō′an) *Biblical name for* TANIS

zo·an·thar·i·an (zō′an ther′ē ən) ***n.*** ⟦< ModL *Zoantharia* < ZO(O)- + Gr *anthos*, flower (see ANTHO-) + -AN⟧ any of a subclass (Zoantharia) of anthozoan cnidarians having few or many tentacles and a solid exoskeleton or no skeleton, including the true corals and the sea anemones —***adj.*** of the zoantharians

zo·an·thro·py (zō an′thrə pē) ***n.*** ⟦ModL *zoanthropia*: see ZOO- & ANTHROPO- & -Y³⟧ a mental disorder in which a person imagines that he or she is a beast: cf. LYCANTHROPY (sense 1)

zo·di·ac (zō′dē ak′) ***n.*** ⟦ME *zodiak* < MFr *zodiaque* < L *zodiacus*, zodiac < Gr *zōdiakos (kyklos)*, zodiac (circle), lit., circle of animals < *zōidion*, dim. of *zōion*, animal: see BIO-⟧ **1** a beltlike zone in the sky extending for about eight degrees on either side of the apparent path of the sun and including the paths of the moon and the principal planets: it is divided into twelve equal parts, or signs, each named for a different constellation **2** a figure or diagram representing the zodiac and its signs: used in astrology **3** [Rare] a circle or circuit —**zo·di′a·cal** (-dī′ə kəl) ***adj.***

zodiac

zodiacal light a faint illumination along the ecliptic, visible in the west just after sunset or in the east just before sunrise

Zo·e (zō′ē) ***n.*** ⟦Gr *Zōē*, lit., life: see fol.⟧ a feminine name

zo·e·a (zō ē′ə) ***n.***, *pl.* **zo·e′ae′** (-ē′ē′) or **zo·e′as** ⟦ModL < Gr *zōē*, life, akin to *zōion* (see BIO-) + *-ea* < L, fem. of *-eus*, -EOUS⟧ an early, free-swimming larval stage of various decapod crustaceans, characterized by long, curved anterior and dorsal spines on the carapace —**zo·e′al** ***adj.***

zof·tig (zäf′tig′) ***adj.*** [Informal] *alt. sp. of* ZAFTIG

Zo·har (zō′här′) ***n.*** ⟦Heb *zohar*, lit., brightness < root *zhr*, to glow, gleam⟧ a mystical commentary on the Pentateuch, written in the late 13th and early 14th cent.: a principal source of the cabala

-zo·ic (zō′ik) *suffix forming adjectives* **1** ⟦< Gr *zōikos*, pertaining to animals < *zōion*, animal: see BIO-⟧ having a (specified) animal way of life **2** ⟦< Gr *zōē*, life + -IC⟧ of, pertaining to, or being a geologic era having a (specified) type of life

zois·ite (zoi′sīt′) ***n.*** ⟦Ger *zoisit*, after Baron *Zois* von Edelstein (1747-1819), its discoverer⟧ a hard, glassy, orthorhombic mineral, $Ca_2Al_3Si_3O_{12}(OH)$, often used as a gem; hydrous calcium aluminum silicate: cf. TANZANITE

Zo·la (zō′lə′, zō lä′), **É·mile (Édouard Charles Antoine)** (ā mēl′) 1840-1902; Fr. novelist

Zoll·ver·ein (tsôl′fer īn′) ***n.*** ⟦Ger < *zoll*, custom, duty, TOLL¹ + *verein*, union, association⟧ a customs union formed by the German states during the 19th cent.

☆**zom·bie** (zäm′bē) ***n.*** ⟦of Afr orig., as in Congo *zumbi*, fetish⟧ **1** in West Indian voodoo, a corpse brought to a state of trancelike animation and made to obey the commands of the person exercising the power **2** any animated corpse, as in horror films and stories **3** [Slang] a weird, eccentric, or unattractive person **4** [Informal] a person considered to be like a zombie in listlessness, mechanical behavior, etc. **5** an iced drink made with fruit juices, various kinds of rum, and, often, apricot brandy

zon·al (zō′nəl) ***adj.*** **1** of or having to do with a zone or zones **2** formed or divided in zones; zoned **3** designating a kind of soil having a permanent type of profile, determined largely by the influence of the prevailing climate and vegetation —**zon′al·ly** ***adv.***

zo·na pel·lu·ci·da (zō′nə pə lo͞o′si də) *pl.* **zo·nae pel·lu·ci·dae** (zō′nē pə lo͞o′si dē) ⟦ModL, transparent zone⟧ the clear, thick outer membrane that surrounds and protects the mature egg of a mammal: it has receptors on its surface that bind with sperm cells

zon·a·ry (zō′nə rē) ***adj.*** ⟦L *zonarius*⟧ ZONAL (senses 1 & 2)

zon·ate (zō′nāt′) ***adj.*** marked with zones or bands; belted; striped: also **zon′at′ed**

zo·na·tion (zō nā′shən) ***n.*** **1** the state of being zonal or arranged in zones **2** arrangement in zones, or bands, as of color **3** the distribution of plants or animals in biogeographic zones

zone (zōn) ***n.*** ⟦Fr < L *zona* < Gr *zōnē*, a belt < *zōnnynai*, to gird < IE **yosmen-* < base **yos-*, to gird > OSlav *pojasŏ*, to gird⟧ **1** an encircling band, stripe, course, etc. distinct in color, texture, structure, etc. from the surrounding medium **2** any of the five great latitudinal divisions of the earth's surface, named according to the prevailing climate: see FRIGID ZONE, TEMPERATE ZONE, TORRID ZONE **3** any area or region considered as separate or distinct from others because of its particular use, crops, plant or animal life, status in time of war, geological features, etc. [a canal *zone*, cotton *zone*, demilitarized *zone*] ☆**4** *a)* any section or district in a city restricted by law for a particular use, as for homes, parks, businesses, etc. *b)* any space along a street or road restricted in a specified way, esp. by traffic regulations ["no parking" *zone*] ☆**5** *a)* any of the numbered sections into which a postal area is divided, as in the ZIP Code system *b)* any of a series of ring-shaped areas concentric on a given point, each having a different parcel-post rate ☆**6** a district within which a uniform rate is charged, as by a transportation system **7** *short for* TIME ZONE **8** [Archaic] a belt or girdle **9** *Math.* a part of the surface of a sphere lying between two parallel planes that intersect the figure **10** *Sports* any of the areas into which a football field, basketball court, etc. is divided, as for defense —*vt.* **zoned**, **zon′ing 1** to mark off or divide into zones; specif., ☆*a)* to divide (a city, etc.) into areas determined by specific restrictions on types of construction, as into residential and business areas ☆*b)* to limit to a certain use by designating as or placing in a ZONE (sense 4*a*) **2** [Archaic] to surround with or as with a belt or zone; encircle **3** to mark with bands or stripes —☆**in the** (or **a**) **zone** [Informal] in a state that produces achievement with an extraordinary, often unlikely, degree of success —☆**zone out** [Slang] to lose awareness of one's immediate surroundings or one's cares or troubles, as variously from daydreaming, the taking of drugs, etc.

zonk (zôŋk, zäŋk) [Slang] ***vt.*** ⟦echoic⟧ to strike, beat, hit, stun, etc. —***vi.*** to lose consciousness, fail to function, etc. —***interj.* 1** used to suggest the sound of a sudden impact **2** used figuratively to suggest the force or effect of a sudden impact, change, etc. —**zonk out 1** to lose consciousness or fall asleep from exhaustion, intoxication, etc. **2** to knock out, stun, etc.

zonked (zôŋkt, zäŋkt) ***adj.*** [Slang] ☆**1** highly intoxicated or under the influence of a drug **2** completely tired out or exhausted

zon·ule (zōn′yo͞ol′) ***n.*** ⟦L *zonula*, dim. of *zona*, a ZONE⟧ a small zone, belt, band, girdle, etc. —**zon′u·lar** (-yo͞o lər, -yə-) ***adj.***

zoo (zo͞o) ***n.*** ⟦< ZOO(LOGICAL GARDEN)⟧ **1** a place where wild animals are kept for public showing **2** a collection of wild animals **3** [Slang] a place, or the people in that place, variously regarded as lacking order, discipline, refinement, etc.

zo·o- (zō′ə) ⟦Gr *zōo-* < *zōon*, *zōion*, an animal: see BIO-⟧ *combining form* **1** animal, animals [*zoology*] **2** zoology and [*zoogeography*]

zo·o·chem·is·try (zō′ə kem′is trē) ***n.*** ⟦prec. + CHEMISTRY⟧ the chemistry of the solids and fluids in the animal body —**zo′o·chem′i·cal** (-i kəl) ***adj.***

zo·o·flag·el·late (-flaj′ə lit, -lāt′) ***n.*** ⟦ZOO- + FLAGELLATE⟧ any of a class (Zoomastigophora) of colorless, flagellated protozoans that ingest food

zo·o·gam·ete (-gam′ēt, -gə mēt′) ***n.*** *Biol.* a motile gamete

zo·o·gen·ic (-jen′ik) ***adj.*** ⟦ZOO- + -GENIC⟧ caused by or starting in animals, as a disease: also **zo·og·e·nous** (zō äj′ə nəs)

zo·o·ge·og·ra·phy (zō′ə jē äg′rə fē) ***n.*** ⟦ZOO- + GEOGRAPHY⟧ the science dealing with the geographical distribution of animals; specif., the study of the relationship between specific animal forms and species and the regions in which they live —**zo′o·ge·og′ra·pher** ***n.*** —**zo′o·ge′o·graph′ic** (-jē′ə graf′ik) ***adj.***, **zo′o·ge′o·graph′i·cal** —**zo′o·ge′o·graph′i·cal·ly** ***adv.***

zo·og·ra·phy (zō äg′rə fē) ***n.*** ⟦ZOO- + -GRAPHY⟧ the branch of zoology concerned with the description of animals, their habits, etc. —**zo·o·graph·ic** (zō′ə graf′ik) ***adj.***, **zo′o·graph′i·cal**

zo·oid (zō′oid′) ***n.*** ⟦ZO(O)- + -OID⟧ **1** a comparatively independent animal organism produced by other than sexual methods, as by fission, gemmation, etc. **2** any of the individual members of a colonial or compound animal: used esp. of hydroids, corals, or bryozoans —**zo·oi′dal** ***adj.***

zoo·keep·er (zo͞o′kēp′ər) ***n.*** a person whose work is the care and feeding of the animals in a zoo

zool *abbrev.* **1** zoological **2** zoology

zo·ol·a·try (zō äl′ə trē) ***n.*** ⟦ZOO- + -LATRY⟧ worship of animals

zo·o·log·i·cal (zō′ə läj′i kəl) ***adj.*** **1** of or having to do with zoology **2** of, pertaining to, or concerned with animals Also **zo′o·log′ic** —**zo′o·log′i·cal·ly** ***adv.***

zoological garden a place where a collection of wild animals is kept for public showing; zoo: also **zoological park**

zo·ol·o·gist (zō äl′ə jist) ***n.*** a student of or specialist in zoology

zo·ol·o·gy (zō äl′ə jē; *often* zo͞o-) ***n.*** ⟦ModL *zoologia:* see ZOO- & -LOGY⟧ **1** the branch of biology that deals with animals, their life, structure, growth, classification, etc. **2** the animal life of an area; fauna **3** the characteristics or properties of an animal or animal group

zoom (zo͞om) ***vi.*** ⟦echoic⟧ **1** to make a loud, low-pitched, buzzing or humming sound **2** to move with a zooming sound **3** to move or go quickly or suddenly **4** to climb in an airplane suddenly and sharply at an angle greater than normal, using the energy of momentum **5** to rise rapidly [prices *zoomed*] **6** to change the focal length of a zoom lens so as to change the apparent distance of the object being viewed —***vt.*** to cause to zoom —***n.* 1** the act of zooming **2** a zooming sound **3** ZOOM LENS **4** *Film a)* the effect of a camera moving toward or away from a subject by using a zoom lens *b)* a shot using this effect —***adj.*** equipped with or having to do with a zoom lens [a *zoom* telescope]

zo·om·e·try (zō äm′ə trē) ***n.*** ⟦ZOO- + -METRY⟧ the measurement and comparison of the relative sizes of the different parts of animals —**zo·o·met·ric** (zō′ə me′trik) ***adj.***

zoom lens a system of lenses, as in a film or TV camera, that can be rapidly adjusted for close-up shots or distance views while keeping the image in focus

zo·o·mor·phic (zō′ə môr′fik) ***adj.*** ⟦ZOO- + -MORPHIC⟧ of or having animal form [a *zoomorphic* deity]

zo·o·mor·phism (-fiz′əm) ***n.*** ⟦ZOO- + -MORPH + -ISM⟧ **1** the attributing of animal forms or characteristics to deities **2** the representation of animal forms in decorative art or symbolism

-zo·on (zō′än′, zō′ən) ⟦ModL < Gr *zōion*, an animal: see BIO-⟧ *combining form* animal or living being

zo·on·o·sis (zō än′ə sis, zō′ə nō′sis) ***n.***, *pl.* **-ses′** (-sēz′) ⟦ModL < Gr *zōion*, an animal (see BIO-) + *nosos*, disease⟧ any human disease that can be acquired from animals —**zo′o·not′ic** (-ə nät′ik) ***adj.***

zo·o·par·a·site (zō′ə par′ə sīt′) ***n.*** a parasitic animal —**zo′o·par′a·sit′ic** (-sit′ik) ***adj.***

zo·oph·a·gous (zō äf′ə gəs) ***adj.*** ⟦ZOO- + -PHAGOUS⟧ CARNIVOROUS

zo·o·phil·i·a (zō′ə fil′ē ə) ***n.*** ⟦ZOO- + -PHILIA⟧ *Psychol.* abnormal sexual attraction to animals —**zo′o·phile′** ***n.***

zo·o·phil·ic (-fil′ik) ***adj.*** **1** *Psychol.* having an attraction, esp. a strong sexual attraction, to animals **2** adapted to pollination by animals other than insects: said of plants Also **zo·oph·i·lous** (zō äf′ə ləs)

zo·o·pho·bi·a (zō′ə fō′bē ə) ***n.*** ⟦ZOO- + -PHOBIA⟧ *Psychol.* an abnormal fear of animals

zo·o·phyte (zō′ə fīt′) ***n.*** ⟦ModL *zoophyton* < Gr *zōophyton:* see ZOO- & -PHYTE⟧ any animal, as a coral or sponge, having somewhat the appearance and character of a plant; esp., a bryozoan —**zo′o·phyt′ic** (-fit′ik) ***adj.***, **zo′o·phyt′i·cal**

zo·o·plank·ton (zō′ə plaŋk′tən) ***n.*** plankton consisting of animals, as copepods or rotifers —**zo′o·plank·ton′ic** (-tän′ik) ***adj.***

zo·o·spo·ran·gi·um (-spə ran′jē əm) ***n.***, *pl.* **-gi·a** (-jē ə) ⟦ModL: see ZOO- & SPORANGIUM⟧ *Bot.* a sporangium in certain fungi and algae, producing zoospores —**zo′o·spo·ran′gi·al** (-əl) ***adj.***

zo·o·spore (zō′ə spôr′) ***n.*** ⟦ZOO- + SPORE⟧ **1** *Bot.* an asexual sporangial spore, esp. of certain fungi or algae, capable of independent motion usually by means of cilia or flagella **2** *Zool.* a motile flagellate or amoebic reproductive cell arising from a sporocyst in certain protozoans —**zo′o·spor′ic** (-spôr′ik) ***adj.***, **zo·os′po·rous** (-äs′pə rəs)

zo·ot·o·my (zō ät′ə mē) ***n.*** ⟦ModL *zootomia:* see ZOO- & -TOMY⟧ the anatomy or dissection of animals other than humans —**zo′o·tom′ic** (-ə täm′ik) ***adj.***, **zo′o·tom′i·cal** —**zo·ot′o·mist** ***n.***

☆**zoot suit** (zo͞ot) ⟦redupl.⟧ a man's suit of a former, exaggerated style, with high-waisted, baggy trousers narrowing at the cuffs and a long, draped coat

zo·ri (zôr′ē) ***n.***, *pl.* **zo′ris** or **zo′ri** ⟦SinoJpn *zōri* (earlier *sōri*) < *zō* (or *sō*), grass + *ri*, (foot)wear⟧ a sandal of a Japanese style, consisting of a flat sole held on the foot by means of a thong anchored in front between the big toe and the toe next to it and passing over the foot

zor·il or **zor·ille** (zôr′il, zär′-) ***n.*** ⟦Fr *zorille* < Sp *zorilla, zorillo*, dim. of *zorra, zorro*, fox⟧ a small, striped, black and white, musteline carnivore (*Ictonyx striatus*) of the drier parts of Africa: it looks and smells like the skunk: also **zo·ril·la** (zə ril′ə)

Zo·ro·as·ter (zō′rō as′tər, zôr′ō as′-) *c.* 6th or 7th cent. B.C.; Pers. religious teacher: founder of Zoroastrianism

Zo·ro·as·tri·an (zō′rō as′trē ən, zôr′ō-) ***adj.*** of or having to do with Zoroaster or Zoroastrianism —***n.*** an adherent of Zoroastrianism

Zo·ro·as·tri·an·ism (-iz′əm) ***n.*** the religious system founded by Zoroaster: its principles, contained in the Avesta, include belief in an afterlife and in the continuous struggle of the universal spirit of good (*Ormazd*) with the spirit of evil (*Ahriman*), the good ultimately to prevail: see also PARSEE

Zor·ri·lla (y Moral) (thô *rē*′lyä), **Jo·sé** (hô se′) 1817-93; Sp. poet & playwright

zos·ter (zäs′tər) ***n.*** ⟦L < Gr, a belt, girdle, akin to *zōnē:* see ZONE⟧ *short for* HERPES ZOSTER

Zou·ave (zo͞o äv′, zwäv) ***n.*** ⟦Fr < Ar *Zwāwa* < Berber *Igawawaen*, name of a Kabyle tribe of the Jurjura Mountains, Algeria, from whom the Zouaves were originally recruited⟧ **1** a member of a former infantry unit in the French army, originally Algerians, noted for the precision of its close-order drill and characterized by a colorful uniform **2** a member of any military group having a similar uniform; specif., a member of any of various volunteer regiments in the American Civil War

Zoug (zo͞og) *Fr. name for* ZUG

zouk (zo͞ok) ***n.*** ⟦Creole Fr, party < *zouker*, engage in unrestrained social activity⟧ a lively popular dance music based on African drum rhythms that originated in Guadeloupe and Martinique

zounds (zoundz) ***interj.*** ⟦altered < the oath *(by) God's wounds*⟧ [Archaic] used to express surprise or anger: a mild oath

☆**zow·ie** (zou′ē) ***interj.*** [Slang] used to express excitement, enthusiasm, admiration, etc.

zo·ys·i·a (zoi′sē ə, zoi′shə) ***n.*** ⟦ModL, altered after *Zoisia*, so named after Karl von *Zois*, 18th-c. Ger botanist⟧ ☆any of a genus (*Zoysia*) of creeping, wiry grasses, often used for lawns, esp. in warm, dry regions

Zp *abbrev. Bible* Zephaniah

Z particle *Particle Physics* the electrically neutral weakon with a mass of 91.2 GeV/c^2, *c.* 178,000 times the mass of an electron: see W PARTICLE

ZPG *abbrev.* zero population growth

Zr *Chem. symbol for* zirconium

zuc·chet·to (zo͞o ket′ō, -ə; *It* tso͞o ket′tô) ***n.***, *pl.* **-tos** or It. **-ti** (-tē) ⟦altered < It *zucchetta*, a cap, orig., dim. of *zucca*, gourd < LL *cucutia*⟧ [*sometimes in* *italics*] a skullcap worn by Roman Catholic prelates: an abbot's is black, a bishop's purple, a cardinal's red, and the Pope's white

☆**zuc·chi·ni** (zōō kē′nē) ***n.***, *pl.* **-ni** or **-nis** ⟦It, pl. of *zucchino,* dim. of *zucca,* gourd: see prec.⟧ a summer squash of a variety that is green-skinned and shaped somewhat like a cucumber

Zug (tso͝ok) **1** canton of NC Switzerland, on the Lake of Zug: 92 sq mi (238 sq km) **2** its capital, on the Lake of Zug **3 Lake of** lake in NC Switzerland, in the cantons of Zug & Schwyz: 15 sq mi (39 sq km)

Zui·der Zee (zī′dər zē′; *Du* zoi′dər zā′) former arm of the North Sea, which extended into the Netherlands: its S section was shut off from the North Sea by dikes: see IJSSELMEER & WADDENZEE

Zuid-Hol·land (zoit′hôl′änt′) *Du. name for* SOUTH HOLLAND

Zu·lo·a·ga (thōō′lô ä′gä), **Ig·na·cio** (ēg nä′thyô) 1870-1945; Sp. painter

Zu·lu (zōō′lōō) ***n.*** **1** *pl.* **-lus** or **-lu** a member of a people living mainly in KwaZulu-Natal province, South Africa **2** the Bantu language of this people, closely related to Xhosa —***adj.*** of the Zulus or their language or culture

Zu·lu·land (zōō′lōō land′) region in KwaZulu-Natal province, South Africa: formerly a Zulu kingdom

Zu·ni (zōō′nē) ***n.*** ⟦AmSp < AmInd⟧ **1** *pl.* **-nis** or **-ni** a member of a North American Indian people of W New Mexico **2** the language of this people, not known to be related to any other language Also **Zu·ñi** (zōōn′yē)

zup·pa in·gle·se (zōō′pə iŋ glā′zā, tsōō′pə-) ⟦It, lit., English soup (prob. in allusion to the English trifle)⟧ an Italian dessert consisting of sponge-cake pieces soaked as with rum, layered with custard, and covered with whipped cream and fruit

Zur·ba·rán (thōōr′bä rän′), **Fran·cis·co de** (frän thēs′kô *the*) 1598-1664; Sp. painter

Zur·ich (zoor′ik) **1** canton of N Switzerland: 668 sq mi (1,730 sq km) **2** its capital, on the Lake of Zurich: also written **Zürich 3 Lake of** lake in N Switzerland, mostly in Zurich canton: 34 sq mi (88 sq km)

Zweig (tsvīk; *E,* zwīg) **1 Ar·nold** (är′nôlt) 1887-1968; Ger. novelist & playwright **2 Ste·fan** (shte′fän′) 1881-1942; Austrian biographer, novelist, & playwright

Zwick·au (tsvik′ou′) city in E Germany, in the state of Saxony

☆**zwie·back** (swē′bak′, swī′-, zwē′-, zwī′-) ***n.*** ⟦Ger < *zwie-,* two, twice, var. of *zwei,* TWO + *backen,* to BAKE, calque of It *biscotto,* BISCUIT⟧ a kind of rusk or biscuit that is sliced and toasted after baking

Zwing·li (zwiŋ′lē, tsviŋ′-), **Ul·rich** (ool′riH′) 1484-1531; Swiss Protestant reformer: also **Hul·dreich Zwingli** (hool′drīH′)

Zwing·li·an (zwiŋ′lē ən) ***adj.*** of Zwingli or his doctrines, esp. the doctrine that the body of Christ is not actually present in the Eucharist and that the ceremony is merely a commemorative one —***n.*** a follower of Zwingli —**Zwing′li·an·ism′** ***n.***

zwit·ter·i·on (zwit′ər ī′än) ***n.*** ⟦Ger < *zwitter,* hybrid (< OHG *zwitarn* < *zwi-,* double, akin to OE *twi-*: for IE base see TWO) + *ion,* ION⟧ an ion carrying both a positive and a negative charge in different parts of the molecule, as in certain amino acids and protein molecules —**zwit′ter·i·on′ic** (-ī än′ik) ***adj.***

Zwol·le (zvôl′ə) city in NE Netherlands

Zwor·y·kin (zwôr′i kin), **Vladimir Kos·ma** (käz′mə) 1889-1982; U.S. engineer & inventor, born in Russia: pioneer in the development of modern TV

zy·dec·o (zī′də kō) ***n.*** ⟦< ? Creole Fr pronun. of Fr *les haricots,* the beans (phr. in the title of a once-popular dance tune)⟧ a heavily syncopated dance music that originated among the blacks of S Louisiana, containing elements of blues, traditional white Cajun music, etc. and played usually by a band that includes accordion, guitar, and washboard

zyg·a·poph·y·sis (zig′ə päf′ə sis, zī′gə-) ***n.***, *pl.* **-ses′** (-sēz′) ⟦ModL < Gr *zygon,* YOKE + APOPHYSIS⟧ any of the processes of the neural arch of a vertebra by which it articulates with an adjacent vertebra —**zyg·ap·o·phys·e·al** (zig′ap′ə fiz′ē əl) ***adj.***

zy·go- (zī′gō, -gə; zig′ə) ⟦< Gr *zygon,* YOKE⟧ *combining form* yoke or yoked; pair or paired [*zygodactyl*]: also, before a vowel, **zyg-**

zy·go·dac·tyl (zī′gə dak′təl, zig′ə-) ***adj.*** ⟦prec. + DACTYL⟧ having the toes arranged in two opposed pairs, two in front and two in the rear: also **zy′go·dac′tyl·ous** —***n.*** a zygodactyl bird, as the parrot —**zy′go·dac′tyl·ism′** ***n.***

zy·go·gen·e·sis (zī′gō jen′ə sis) ***n.*** ⟦ZYGO- + GENESIS⟧ *Biol.* reproduction in which male and female gametes and nuclei fuse —**zy′go·ge·net′ic** (-jə net′ik) ***adj.***

zy·goid (zī′goid′) ***adj.*** of or pertaining to a zygote; zygotic

zy·go·ma (zī gō′mə) ***n.***, *pl.* **-ma·ta** (-mə tə) or **-mas** ⟦ModL < Gr *zygōma* < *zygoun,* to yoke < *zygon,* YOKE⟧ *Anat.* **1** ZYGOMATIC ARCH **2** ZYGOMATIC BONE **3** ZYGOMATIC PROCESS —**zy·go·mat·ic** (zī′gə mat′ik) ***adj.***

zygomatic arch *Anat.* a bony arch on either side of the face just below the eye in many vertebrates, consisting of a zygomatic bone having a process that fuses with the zygomatic process of the temporal bone

zygomatic bone *Anat.* a bone of the zygomatic arch on either side of the face, forming the prominence of each cheek; cheekbone

zygomatic process *Anat.* any of several bony processes that form part of the zygomatic arch

zy·go·mor·phic (zī′gə môr′fik, zig′ə-) ***adj.*** ⟦ZYGO- + -MORPHIC⟧ *Biol.* bilaterally symmetrical; that can be divided in two identical halves by a single plane passing through the axis: said of organisms, organs, or parts: also **zy′go·mor′phous** —**zy′go·mor′phism′** ***n.***, **zy′go·mor′phy**

zy·go·spore (zī′gə spôr′ zig′ə-) ***n.*** ⟦ZYGO- + SPORE⟧ *Bot.* a thick-walled, resting spore formed by conjugation of two isogametes, as in certain primitive fungi and certain green algae —**zy′go·spor′ic** (-spôr′ik) ***adj.***

zy·gote (zī′gōt′, zig′ōt′) ***n.*** ⟦< Gr *zygōtos,* yoked < *zygon,* YOKE⟧ a diploid cell formed by the union of two haploid gametes, esp. by the union of an egg cell and a sperm cell —**zy·got·ic** (zī gät′ik, zi-) ***adj.*** —**zy·got′i·cal·ly** ***adv.***

zy·go·tene (zī′gə tēn′, zig′ə-) ***n.*** ⟦Fr *zygotène* < Gr *zygon,* YOKE + *tainia,* ribbon, tape: see TAENIA⟧ the synaptic stage of the first prophase in meiosis, during which longitudinal pairing of homologous chromosomes occurs

zy·mase (zī′mās′) ***n.*** ⟦Fr: see fol. + -ASE⟧ an enzyme, present in yeast, that promotes fermentation by breaking down glucose and some other carbohydrates into alcohol and carbon dioxide

zyme (zīm) ***n.*** ⟦Gr *zymē,* a leaven < ? IE base **yeu-,* to mix (foods) > JUICE, Sans *yuṣ,* broth⟧ **1** a ferment or enzyme **2** the specific cause of a zymotic disease

zy·mo- (zī′mō, -mə) ⟦< Gr *zymē*: see prec.⟧ *combining form* **1** fermentation [*zymology*] **2** enzyme [*zymogenesis*] Also, before a vowel, **zym-**

zy·mo·gen (zī′mə jən) ***n.*** ⟦Fr *zymogène*: see prec. & -GEN⟧ *Biochem.* an inactive antecedent form of an active enzyme that becomes functional by the action of an appropriate kinase or other activator

zy·mo·gen·ic (zī′mō jen′ik, -mə-) ***adj.*** *Biochem.* **1** of, having to do with, or producing a zymogen **2** causing fermentation

zy·mol·o·gy (zī mäl′ə jē) ***n.*** ⟦ZYMO- + -LOGY⟧ the science dealing with fermentation —**zy·mo·log·i·cal** (zī′mə läj′i kəl) ***adj.***

zy·mol·y·sis (zī mäl′ə sis) ***n.*** ⟦ModL: see ZYMO- & -LYSIS⟧ *Biochem.* **1** the fermentative action of enzymes **2** fermentation or other changes resulting from this —**zy·mo·lyt·ic** (zī′mə lit′ik) ***adj.***

zy·mo·sis (zī mō′sis) ***n.***, *pl.* **-ses′** (-sēz′) ⟦ModL < Gr *zymōsis,* fermentation < *zymē,* a leaven, ferment: see ZYME⟧ **1** fermentation **2** the development and spread of a zymotic disease **3** any infectious disease

zy·mot·ic (zī mät′ik) ***adj.*** ⟦Gr *zymōtikos,* causing to ferment < *zymoun,* to ferment < *zymē,* a ferment: see ZYME⟧ **1** of, causing, or caused by or as by, fermentation **2** designating or of an infectious disease caused by an enzyme

zy·mur·gy (zī′mər jē) ***n.*** ⟦ZYM(O)- + -URGY⟧ the branch of chemistry dealing with fermentation, as in making wine, brewing, etc.

zzz or **ZZZ** (z: *a prolonged sound*) ***interj.*** used to suggest the sound of snoring: used mainly in print, as in comic strips, and spelled with a varying number of *z's*

REFERENCE SUPPLEMENT

CONTENTS

RULES OF PUNCTUATION

I. APOSTROPHE [']

Use an apostrophe:

1. To show the possessive case of nouns and certain pronouns.
   MEMORY AID: The apostrophe signifies "belonging to everything to the left of this mark."

   a. Nouns and indefinite pronouns not ending in *-s* take an apostrophe and *-s*.

      a child's drawing — children's books
      a man's shirt — men's shirts
      a year's delay — everyone's favorite

      This includes references to college degrees.

      a bachelor's degree
      working on her master's

   b. Singular nouns ending in the sound (s) or (z) or (sh) take an apostrophe and -s.

      Keats's poems — Marx's writings
      Mrs. Jones's house — the fish's habitat

      There are a few traditional exceptions to this rule: The proper names *Jesus* and *Moses* usually take only an apostrophe.

      Jesus' parables — Moses' laws

      Greek and other proper names, and a few plural nouns, that end in the syllable pronounced (ēz) generally take only an apostrophe.

      Socrates' wisdom
      the drama series' success

      Certain words traditionally take only an apostrophe.

      for conscience' sake — for goodness' sake!

   c. Plural nouns ending in the sound (s) or (z) take only an apostrophe.

      four years' delay — ladies' shoes
      the Joneses' house

   d. In compound constructions, the apostrophe and *-s* are added to the element closest to the modified word.

      the Queen of England's palace
      anyone else's opinion but hers
      my sister-in-law's car
      Henry VIII's wives
      the attorney general's opinion

   e. For joint ownership or a similar relationship, only the last noun takes the possessive form.

      Roz, Joe, and Tom's computer

   f. For separate ownership or a similar relationship, each noun takes the possessive form.

      Roz's, Joe's, and Tom's e-mail addresses

   g. For the possessive of a long phrase, it is best to rewrite the construction using the preposition *of.*

      the briefcase of the lawyer who had already left
      the name of the poet who wrote *Paradise Lost*

   h. Possessive personal pronouns do *not* take an apostrophe.
      MEMORY AID: The possessive personal pronouns (and two pronominal adjectives) that end in *-s* are the *exception* to the usual rule for forming possessives in English.

      Pronouns: hers his its ours theirs yours
      Pronominal adjectives: his its

      Do not confuse the possessive *its* with the contraction *it's* (it is).

2. To show the omission of letters or figures in contractions.

   we've — can't — it's — won't — where's
   'twas — '97 — '01

   Do not confuse the contraction *it's* (it is) with the possessive *its.*

3. To show certain special plurals.

   a. Letters, words, and figures referred to as such usually take an apostrophe and *-s.*

      Mind your p's and q's
      Did you dot your *i*'s and cross your *t*'s?
      a's, 7's, #'s
      Underline the *which*'s and *that*'s

      Note that the "s" after the apostrophe is in roman, not italic, type even when it follows an italicized letter or word.

   b. Abbreviations written with both internal and final periods usually take an apostrophe and *-s*; those with no periods or only final periods take only an *-s.*

      PhDs *or* Ph.D.'s
      ICBMs
      mts.

   c. Figures usually take an *-s* alone but may take an apostrophe and *-s.*

      1990s *or* 1990's
      the '90s (*not:* the '90's)

   With the exceptions noted above, do not use an apostrophe to form a plural.

4. To show inflected forms of verbs made up of abbreviations.

   OK'd O.K.'d OK'ing O.K.'ing

II. BRACKETS [[ ]]

Use brackets, in pairs:

1. To enclose editorial corrections, explanations, or comments within a quoted passage.

   "The bill had *not* been paid [emphasis added]."
   "She was born in 1805 [actually in 1802] near the town of...."
   According to the reviewer, "It [her latest novel] reeks of the stale perfume of romance writing at its very worst."
   "Andrew Johnson never attended school and was scarcely able to read when he met Eliza McCardle, whom he married on May 5, 1927 [*sic*]."

   The Latin word *sic,* meaning "thus," indicates that a quoted passage, especially one containing an error or a questionable statement, is reproduced precisely.

2. To indicate parentheses within parentheses.

   (The result [see Figure 2] is not typical.)

For the use of brackets with other marks of punctuation, follow the rules given for using parentheses with other marks of punctuation in the section on PARENTHESES.

III. COLON [:]

Use a colon:

1. To introduce a formal statement, a long quotation, or a speech in a play.

   The witness made the declaration: "I know of no attempt to defraud the public."
   The Commencement speaker intoned: "The time has come."
   Macbeth: So foul and fair a day I have not seen.

2. To introduce an illustrating or amplifying item or series of items.

   English usage is like table etiquette: it is conventional and its sanction is a social one.
   Certain imports rose sharply: steel, cars, and electronic equipment.

3. After the salutation of a business letter.

   Dear Dr. Lloyd: — Dear Sir or Madam:

4. To separate the initials of the person dictating a letter from the initials of the typist. Do not space after the colon. (A slash may also be used for this purpose.)
   DBG:cs DBG/cs
5. To separate hours from minutes in notations of time and to separate chapter from verse in biblical citations. Do not space after the colon.
   10:36 AM Exodus 4:6
6. To indicate a ratio; use two colons to indicate a proportion. Space before and after the colon or colons.
   concrete mixed 5 : 3 : 1 1 : 3 :: 4 : 12

For use of the colon with other marks of punctuation, see the notes at PARENTHESES and QUOTATION MARKS.

IV. COMMA [,]

Use a comma:

1. Before a coordinating conjunction such as *and, but, or, nor, for, yet,* or *so* when it joins the clauses of a compound sentence.
   We had never before eaten such delicious meals, and my mother was delighted with the service.
   She often talked about her years as a singer, but no one in the chorus seemed to remember her.
   The comma is often omitted between short clauses, and sometimes between long ones when the meaning is clear.
   First he stopped at the bank and then he went to his office.
2. To separate an introductory phrase or dependent clause from the main clause.
   When he had tired of the mad pace of Los Angeles, he moved to Dubuque.
   In the beginning, she liked the work.
   If, as in the above examples, there is no possibility of ambiguity, the comma is often omitted. In the following examples, however, the comma is needed to prevent misreading.
   When the meeting was over, our heads were swimming.
   More and more, Americans are waiting until the last minute to file their taxes.
   He saw the woman who had rejected him, and blushed.
3. To set off a word such as *yes* or *no;* a mild interjection; a word or words in direct address; a transitional word or phrase; or an absolute phrase. Within the sentence, use a pair of commas.
   Yes, I plan to go.
   Oh, I didn't really care much one way or the other.
   Thanks, Maria, for bringing your cassette player.
   The last speaker was, by the way, the most interesting.
   Winter having arrived early, we left for home.
   Do *not* set off the interjection O (used, as in poetry or hymns, to address a deity or highly respected person) with a comma.
4. Traditionally, the abbreviation *etc.,* when used in lists, has been set off by a pair of commas within the sentence.
   We had eggs, ham, hash browns, etc., for breakfast.
   Now, however, to some degree, it is acceptable to omit the second comma.
   We had eggs, ham, hash browns, etc. for breakfast.
5. To set off a question following a statement.
   You are coming along, aren't you?
6. To set off the main elements in an address. Within the sentence, use a pair of commas.
   We lived at 45 Sycamore Street, Novelty, Ohio.
   We lived at 45 Sycamore Street, Novelty, Ohio, for more years than I care to remember.
7. To set off a title following a person's name. Within the sentence, use a pair of commas.
   We received a letter from Dr. Jane Friend, Director of Admissions.
   Dr. Jane Friend, Director of Admissions, replied.
8. To set off the year in a date if the month, day, and year are given. Within the sentence, use a pair of commas.
   The letter was dated July 14, 1987.
   The letter was dated July 14, 1987, and was mailed from Paris.
   If only the month (or the season) and the year are given, the comma is usually omitted.
   The letter was written in July 1987 and was mailed from Paris.
   Summer 1987 was probably the best time of my childhood.
   If the day and month are reversed (as in European and military style), no comma is used.
   14 July 1987
9. To set off an appositive. Within the sentence, use a pair of commas.
   It was Annie, our favorite cousin.
   Annie, our favorite cousin, makes unbelievably delicious fudge.
   Our favorite cousin, Annie, makes unbelievably delicious fudge.
   Acrophobia, or fear of heights, can severely limit a person's activities.
   a cerulean, or azure, gem
   his wish to ameliorate, or improve, his situation
   An appositive essential to the meaning of the sentence is not set off by commas.
   Our son Jim is in college; our son Bill is finishing high school.
10. To set off contrasted sentence elements. Within the sentence, use a pair of commas.
   It was Jessie, not Frances.
   Jessie, not Frances, was the first to arrive.
11. To indicate an omitted word in a parallel construction.
   Bert brings his lunch every day; Susan, never.
12. To indicate that a word or words have been omitted, such as *of* or *of the.*
   President, Big Green Spaces Intl.
13. To set off sentence elements that are out of natural order.
   That they would accept the money, none of us seriously doubted.
14. To separate words, phrases, or clauses in a series.
   The menu offered the usual choices of steak, chops, and chicken.
   Expect it tomorrow, next Monday, or a week from today.
   They studied hard, they concentrated on the details, and they took their time in order to pass the course.
   Some writers omit the *series comma* (the one before the conjunction), but this comma is useful in preventing ambiguity.
15. To separate coordinate adjectives modifying the same noun. Each coordinate adjective modifies the noun individually. Test: If *and* can be substituted for the comma, the adjectives are coordinate.
   The cat had bright, mischievous, laughing eyes.
   If the previous adjectives are modifying the noun *plus* the adjective closest to it as a unit, the adjectives are *not* coordinate and no comma is used.
   The cat had bright, mischievous, laughing gray eyes.
16. To set off a clause, phrase, or word that interrupts the main clause.
   He did not really say, as you seem to believe, that he wanted the job.
   The apples, though freshly picked, were spoiled in shipment.

I'm not really sure, though, that you understand the problem.

17. To set off a *nonrestrictive* phrase or clause from the rest of the sentence. A nonrestrictive phrase or clause is not essential to the meaning of the sentence.

Such a device, known as a reader, senses the data and enters it into the computer.

My prize fishing rod, which now hangs over the mantelpiece, hasn't been used for years.

A *restrictive* phrase or clause *is* essential to the meaning of the sentence; it is *not* set off by commas.

The man who robbed the bank has been apprehended.

The secret that you shared with me will go nowhere.

18. To set off a direct quotation from such expressions as *she said* and *he replied*.

"I know you'll like oysters," she said, "if only you'll try them."

He replied, "I'll never believe you again."

If the *she said* or other similar expression comes between two independent clauses, it is followed by a period or a semicolon, not by a comma.

"I know you'll like oysters," she said; "just try them."

19. To provide a pause to clarify meaning when a word is repeated.

Whatever happened, happened for the best.

20. Following (1) the salutation of a personal letter or (2) the closing phrase of either a personal or a business letter.

Dear Tina, Sincerely,

Very truly yours,

21. To separate the parts of an inverted name, phrase, and so forth, as in bibliography, index, or catalog.

Horner, Martha D. Persia, architecture of

radios, portable

22. To separate figures of five or more digits. The comma is inserted after each group of three digits, counting from the right.

That year the costs totaled $1,341,680.

The comma is omitted in years, street addresses, etc. It is often omitted in four-digit figures as well.

1341 days until retirement

23. To create a pause in the flow of a sentence if that pause would make the sentence clearer and easier to read. Let your ear tell you when such a comma is needed. This informal rule can be helpful when no other rule seems to fit the situation.

For use of the comma with other marks of punctuation, see the notes at PARENTHESES and QUOTATION MARKS.

V. DASH

1. EM DASH [—]

Use an em dash:

a. To indicate an abrupt change in thought, a break in the sentence flow, or an interruption of the speaker's words.

He is — how shall I say it? — a colossal bore.

She said, "But what if — "

b. To set off an appositive or parenthetical expression, especially when commas are needed for minor divisions within the expression or when a complete sentence is interpolated within another.

The three R's — reading, writing, and arithmetic — are again being stressed.

Eventually — but who knows when? — we will know the whole story.

c. To introduce a phrase or clause that summarizes what has just been said.

Eating right, drinking enough water every day, and getting regular exercise — these are the simple things we all can do to stay healthy.

Unless the set-off expression begins or ends a sentence, dashes must be used in pairs.

2. EN DASH [–]

The en dash is longer than a hyphen and shorter than an em dash. Use it:

a. Between numbers or words and numbers indicating (1) the beginning and ending dates of a historical period, a person's lifetime in a biographical listing, or some other period; or (2) the first and last pages of a section of a book, the first and last verses in a biblical reference, and so forth.

1900–1999	1900–99
August 1947–April 1950	9:30 AM–6:00 PM
pages 1–50 or pp. 1–50	I Corinthians 13:1–3

If only the beginning date is established, the en dash indicates that the period is open-ended.

Greene, David (1955–)

Never use a dash to replace the word *to* if the word *from* precedes the numbers; never use a dash to replace the word *and* if the word *between* precedes the numbers.

Not: from 100–150	*But:* from 100 to 150
Not: between 5:00–7:00	*But:* between 5:00 and 7:00

b. Between parts of a compound if elements of the compound are open-compound (spaced) names.

a Buenos Aires–Mexico City connecting flight

VI. ELLIPSIS [. . . OR ...]

Use an ellipsis, or three periods (also called *suspension points*):

1. To show that material has been omitted from a quotation. (Four periods are used when the omission comes at the end of a declarative sentence.)

"There are four ways, none of which has been mentioned by my opponent, to remedy the situation."

becomes

"There are four ways... to remedy the situation."

"There is only one way to settle the matter to everyone's satisfaction. We must sit at the conference table."

becomes

"There is only one way to settle the matter.... We must sit at the conference table."

2. To show that a statement or series could be continued beyond the point where it stops. In such a case, the ellipsis is being used in place of *etc., and so forth,* or a similar expression.

The names of the months (January, February, March, ...) are capitalized.

VII. EXCLAMATION MARK [!]

Use an exclamation mark to indicate strong feeling:

1. After a forceful interjection (exclamatory word).

Wow! Thank you!

Congratulations! You did it.

No! Stop!

But: Yes, I'll do it.

2. After an exclamatory sentence.

What a day this has been!

In many exclamations in the form of a question, the exclamation mark takes the place of the question mark.

How dare you!

3. After a forceful imperative sentence.

Don't touch that dial!

If this mark is overused in a piece of writing, it will lose its force. Use it sparingly.

For use of the exclamation mark with other punctuation marks, see the notes at PARENTHESES and QUOTATION MARKS.

VIII. HYPHEN [-]

Use a hyphen:

1. To indicate that a word has been divided at the end of a line.
   a. A word of one syllable should not be divided (this includes verbs such as *worked*).
   b. A word of more than one syllable should be divided only between syllables. Consult the dictionary for the syllable boundaries.
   c. A suffix of fewer than three letters (for example, the *-en* in *wooden*) is ordinarily not separated from the rest of the word.
   d. A word should not be divided so that only one letter stands at the end of a line (for example, the *a* in *alone*).
   e. If possible, a hyphenated word should be divided only at the hyphen.
2. Between the elements of regularly hyphenated compounds. Consult the dictionary if you are uncertain whether a given word is hyphenated.
   half-hour
   roller-skate (*verb*)
   state-of-the-art technology
   All compound numbers between twenty-one and ninety-nine are hyphenated when spelled out.
   twenty-five
   twenty-fifth
3. Between some base words and the prefix, suffix, or combining form joined to the base word, to (1) change its meaning or (2) create a new word.
   anti-intellectual
   Hyphenate before an initial capital letter.
   pre-Columbian
   Hyphenate to distinguish between two words with the same basic spelling.
   re-creation *vs.* recreation
   Hyphenate for clarity when a letter is used more than twice.
   skill-less
4. Between the elements of a compound adjective — a group of words that modifies a noun — especially when it is placed before the noun. The compound can consist of an adjective plus a noun, as in the first example that follows. Or it can consist of an adverb plus an adjective, as in the second and third examples. Hyphenation often helps to avoid ambiguity (confusion because there is more than one possible meaning).
   a foreign-car dealer (that is, a dealer in foreign cars, rather than a foreigner who deals in cars)
   a little-known artist (that is, an artist who is not widely known, rather than an artist who, although somewhat famous, is small in size)
   a well-dressed man
   This kind of compound adjective is usually not hyphenated when it comes after the noun it modifies.
   a man who is well dressed
   The practice of hyphenating words is far from standard. To help ensure consistency within a given piece of writing, it is a good idea to consult the dictionary for many established compounds, whether written with a hyphen, without space between the elements (solid or closed), or with a space between the elements (open). For compounds not found in the dictionary, choose one form and use it consistently throughout the piece of writing.
5. Between the letters of a spelled-out word.
   In front of the children, she asked me if I had bought the c-a-n-d-y.
6. Between figures or groups of figures:
   a. To separate numbers that are in random order, as in account numbers, serial numbers, telephone numbers, and Social Security numbers.
   000-555-1212
   987-65-4321
   b. In typewritten copy, for all uses described for the EN DASH, such as numbers or words indicating the beginning and end of a historical period or other length of time, numbers indicating the first and last pages in a section of a book, or numbers for years of birth and death in a biographical listing.

Never use a hyphen or dash to replace the word *to* if the word *from* precedes the numbers; never use a hyphen or dash to replace the word *and* if the word *between* precedes the numbers.

Not: from 100-150
But: from 100 to 150
Not: between 5-7
But: between 5 and 7

See also the notes at DASH (EN DASH).

IX. PARENTHESES [( )]

Use parentheses, in pairs:

1. To enclose material that is explanatory, supplementary, or illustrative.
   This book describes life in the Middle Ages (between AD 476 and about 1450) from a scribe's perspective.
   The example given on page 306 (and a startling one it is!) draws upon exhaustive research.
   The tabulated results (see fig. 6) speak for themselves.
2. To enclose figures and letters indicating enumeration within a text.
   The maps show (1) rainfall, (2) population, and (3) physical features.
   The maps show (a) rainfall, (b) population, and (c) physical features.
3. To enclose figures following a spelled-out number, especially in a formal document.
   All twenty-five (25) computers were found to be defective.

Using parentheses with other punctuation marks:

1. When a complete sentence within parentheses stands alone (that is, not as part of another sentence), its **end punctuation** goes inside the closing parenthesis.
   He said that knowledge is sometimes useful. (That must be the most inane and useless statement of the century.)
   He said that knowledge is sometimes useful. (Can you imagine a more inane and worthless statement?)
2. When a complete declarative sentence within parentheses is part of another sentence, do not put a **period** inside the closing parenthesis *unless* the last word is an abbreviation that takes a period. However, a parenthetical question or exclamation may end with a **question mark** or **exclamation mark.** (Do not capitalize the first word of a parenthetical sentence unless that word is regularly capitalized.)
   Self-government (recall that the Virginia legislature had already been formed) was clearly on the rise.
   Self-government (how many years had it been since the formation of the Virginia legislature?) was clearly on the rise.

3. When a word, phrase, or clause within parentheses is part of a sentence,
   a. Do *not* place a **comma, semicolon, colon,** or **period** inside the closing parenthesis.
   b. Place a **question mark** or **exclamation mark** inside the closing parenthesis if it applies to the parenthetical material.
   c. Place a **comma, semicolon, colon,** or **period** after the closing parenthesis only if the main sentence (without the parenthetical material) requires that punctuation mark at that point.

St. Augustine (?-AD 604?) was sent to convert the English to Christianity.

The Wars of the Roses, between the houses of Lancaster and York (1455-1485), are said to have ended feudalism in England.

The Wars of the Roses were fought between the houses of Lancaster and York (1455-1485); they are said to have ended feudalism in England.

X. PERIOD [.]

Use a period:

1. After a declarative sentence, an indirect question, and most imperative sentences.

   Summer will soon be here.
   We asked who the pianist was.
   Come home.
   Please help me with this.

2. After most polite requests phrased as questions.

   Would you please send me a copy of your catalog.

3. After many abbreviations. However, some writers and editors now favor a style that omits the periods after many abbreviations. Consult the dictionary for current spellings of common abbreviations.

   BC *or* B.C.
   AD *or* A.D.

   Do *not* omit a period that follows an abbreviation before any other mark of punctuation *except for* the period at the end of a sentence.

4. After initials. The initials for a personal name are spaced in American usage, but not in British usage.

   Alfred R. Jones; A. R. Jones
   T. S. Eliot *or* T.S. Eliot

5. As a decimal point with numerals.

   5.5% of the total
   $450.01

6. After figures or letters indicating enumeration in a list arranged vertically.

   a. Reduce.
   b. Reuse.
   c. Recycle.

In general, do *not* use a period at the end of a heading or title.

For use of the period with other punctuation marks, see the notes at PARENTHESES and QUOTATION MARKS.

XI. QUESTION MARK [?]

Use a question mark:

1. After a direct question.

   Do you have the money?
   "Do you have the money?" he asked.
   You do have the money?

2. After each query in an unnumbered or unlettered series.

   Have you heard the candidate's views on civil rights? on urban problems? on the economy?

   But: Have you heard the candidate's views on (a) civil rights, (b) urban problems, (c) the economy?

3. After an interrogative element within a sentence (but not after an indirect question).

   "How soon?" she wondered.
   But: She wondered how soon it would happen.

4. To express uncertainty regarding the accuracy of information.

   We once attended a concert presented by Marian Anderson (1897?-1993).

For use of the question mark with other punctuation marks, see the notes at PARENTHESES and QUOTATION MARKS.

XII. QUOTATION MARKS

1. DOUBLE QUOTATION MARKS [" "]

   Use double quotation marks, in pairs:

   a. To enclose a direct quotation short enough to be run into the text (Quotations of more than three or four lines usually appear without quotation marks but are set off from the text by space, indention, and so forth.)

      "Come in," he called.
      "Are you," she asked, "the man who helped my son?"
      Oscar Wilde is believed to have said, "I have nothing to declare except my genius."

   b. To enclose the title of a poem, essay, short story, article, lecture, chapter of a book, song, or individual radio or TV program (as opposed to a series).

      The third chapter, "How I Entertained My New In-Laws," may be the scariest in the book.
      Have you read her new story, "The Moose That Came to the Door"?
      We memorized the poem "Dover Beach" in class.

   c. To enclose words referred to as words, used in a special sense, or given particular emphasis. (Italics may also be used in such cases.)

      He uses words like "never" and "always" much too often.
      Don't "push the envelope" any farther than you can reach to take it back.
      Why is luck always "good luck" unless we specify that it's bad?

2. SINGLE QUOTATION MARKS [' ']

   Use single quotation marks, in pairs, to enclose a quotation or a title within another quotation. All of the rules for double quotation marks apply.

   In a note to me, Sally effused, "The memory of the way you played 'Hearts and Flowers' at my wedding still brings tears to my eyes."

In usual British punctuation style, the use of single and double quotation marks is the reverse of the above.

Using quotation marks with other punctuation marks:

1. The period and the comma always go inside closing quotation marks.

   "I'm so sorry," he said, "but there is something I have to tell you."

2. The **colon** and the **semicolon** go outside closing quotation marks.

   I had not read Emerson's essay "Experience"; in fact, I had never heard of it.

3. The **question mark** and **exclamation mark** go inside closing quotation marks if they apply to the quoted material. They go outside if they apply to the whole sentence.

   She asked, "Am I going, too?"
   Did she say, "I am going, too"?

In usual British punctuation style, all end punctuation is placed according to this last rule.

XIII. SEMICOLON [;]

Use a semicolon:

1. Between independent clauses not joined by a coordinating conjunction. The same two clauses may be written in any of these three ways:
   Summer's almost gone. Winter's coming on.
   Summer's almost gone, and winter's coming on.
   Summer's almost gone; winter's coming on.
2. Between independent clauses joined by a conjunctive adverb (*however, indeed, nevertheless,* and so forth). Place a comma after the adverb.
   Summer's almost gone; however, winter's coming on.
3. Between independent clauses of a compound sentence if the clauses are very long or are themselves subdivided by commas, or if a more definite break is desired than one marked by a comma.
   When all was said and done, we had done most of it; but they, however, ignored the fact, as usual.
4. To replace the comma in separating elements of a series if the elements themselves contain commas.
   The tour of capital cities included Vaduz, Liechtenstein; Luxembourg, Luxembourg; San Marino, San Marino; and Andorra, Andorra.

For use of the semicolon with other punctuation marks, see the notes at PARENTHESES and QUOTATION MARKS.

XIV. SLASH, VIRGULE, OR SOLIDUS [/]

Use the slash:

1. Between two words to show that either is applicable.
   and/or he/she
   Mars/Ares John/Jane Doe
   This use is somewhat informal.
2. To separate the parts of a fraction.
   17/32
   Many computer programs are set to change the most commonly used fractions to a more compact form using a slanting or horizontal dividing line.
   ½ ¼
3. In reference to a period extending through parts of two consecutive years (in place of an en dash).
   1950/51
4. In certain abbreviations.
   c/o (in care of) A/C (air conditioning)
   N/A (not applicable)
5. To indicate the word *per.*
   calico for $5.25/yd km/h (kilometers per hour)
   apples at 2 lb./$1
6. Between lines of poetry (usually not more than two) quoted within a paragraph. Space on each side of the slash.
   An old song that I love begins: "The water is wide, / I cannot get o'er."

ROMAN NUMERALS

Arabic	*Roman*	*Arabic*	*Roman*	*Arabic*	*Roman*	*Arabic*	*Roman*
0	...						
1	I	11	XI	30	XXX	200	CC
2	II	12	XII	40	XL *or* XXXX	300	CCC
3	III	13	XIII *or* XIIV	50	L	400	CD *or* CCCC
4	IV *or* IIII	14	XIV *or* XIIII	60	LX	500	D
5	V	15	XV	70	LXX	600	DC
6	VI	16	XVI	80	LXXX *or* XXC	700	DCC
7	VII	17	XVII	90	XC *or* LXXXX	800	DCCC
8	VIII *or* IIX	18	XVIII *or* XIIX	100	C	900	CM *or* DCCCC
9	IX *or* VIIII	19	XIX *or* XVIIII			1,000	M
10	X	20	XX			2,000	MM

In the Roman notation, the value of the character to the right of the numeral is usually added to that of the numeral (Ex.: VI means V plus I or 6). I, X, and sometimes C, are also placed to the left of larger numerals and when so situated their value is subtracted from that of such numerals (Ex.: IV means V minus I or 4). Sometimes a line was drawn over a numeral to indicate thousands (Ex.: $\overline{\text{V}}$ means 5,000). Lower-case letters are often used for Roman numerals.

CALENDARS

Gregorian Calendar	*Jewish Calendar*	*Islamic Calendar*	*Hindu Calendar*
January (31)	Tishri (30)	Muharram (30)	Caitra (29 or 30)
February (28 or 29)	Heshvan (29 or 30)	Safar (29)	Vaisakha (29 or 30)
March (31)	Kislev (29 or 30)	Rabi I (30)	Jyaistha (29 or 30)
April (30)	Tevet (29)	Rabi II (29)	Asadha (29 or 30)
May (31)	Shevat (30)	Jumada I (30)	Dvitiya Asadha (some leap years)**
June (30)	Adar (29 or 30)	Jumada II (29)	Sravana (29 or 30)
July (31)	Adar Sheni (leap years)*	Rajab (30)	Dvitiya Sravana (some leap years)**
August (31)	Nisan (30)	Shaban (29)	Bhadrapada (29 or 30)
September (30)	Iyar (29)	Ramadan (30)	Asvina (29 or 30)
October (31)	Sivan (30)	Shawwal (29)	Karttika (29 or 30)
November (30)	Tammuz (29)	Dhu al-Qadah (30)	Margasirsa (29 or 30)
December (31)	Ab (30)	Dhu al-Hijjah (29 or 30)	Pausa (29 or 30)
	Elul (29)		Magha (29 or 30)
			Phalguna (29 or 30)

* Adar Sheni occurs seven times in 19 years or about once every three years. It is added because the regular Jewish Year has only 354 days. Tishri begins in late September or early October.

** Leap months are are added to the Hindu calendar as needed to ensure that the New Year always falls in the spring, at the time corresponding to March or April in the Gregorian calendar.

MONETARY UNITS

Country	Monetary Units Basic/Fractional†
Afghanistan	afghani: pul
Albania	lek: qintar
Algeria	dinar: centime
Andorra	euro: cent
Angola	kwanza: lwei
Antigua and Barbuda	dollar[1]: cent
Argentina	peso: centavo
Armenia	dram: —
Australia	dollar: cent
Austria	euro: cent
Azerbaijan	manat: qepiq
Bahamas	dollar: cent
Bahrain	dinar: fils (1:1000)
Bangladesh	taka: paisa
Barbados	dollar: cent
Belarus	ruble: kopeck
Belgium	euro: cent
Belize	dollar: cent
Benin	franc[2]: centime
Bhutan	ngultrum: chetrum
Bolivia	boliviano: centavo
Bosnia and Herzegovina	marka: fening
Botswana	pula: thebe
Brazil	real: centavo
Brunei	dollar: cent
Bulgaria	lev: stotinka
Burkina Faso	franc[2]: centime
Burundi	franc: centime
Cambodia	riel: sen
Cameroon	franc[2]: centime
Canada	dollar: cent
Cape Verde	escudo: centavo
Central African Republic	franc[2]: centime
Chad	franc[2]: centime
Chile	peso: centavo
China	yuan: fen
Colombia	peso: centavo
Comoros	franc: centime
Congo, Democratic Republic of the	franc: centime
Congo, Republic of the	franc[2]: centime
Costa Rica	colón: céntimo
Croatia	kuna: lipa
Cuba	peso: centavo
Cyprus	euro: cent
Czech Republic	koruna: haler
Denmark	krone: øre
Djibouti	franc: centime
Dominica	dollar[1]: cent
Dominican Republic	peso: centavo
East Timor	*(U.S.) dollar: cent
Ecuador	*(U.S.) dollar: cent
Egypt	pound: piaster
El Salvador	*(U.S.) dollar: cent
Equatorial Guinea	franc[2]: centime
Eritrea	nakfa: cent
Estonia	euro: cent
Ethiopia	birr: cent
Fiji	dollar: cent
Finland	euro: cent
France	euro: cent
Gabon	franc[2]: centime
Gambia	dalasi: butut
Georgia	lari: —
Germany	euro: cent
Ghana	cedi: pesewa
Greece	euro: cent
Grenada	dollar[1]: cent
Guatemala	quetzal: centavo
Guinea	franc: centime
Guinea-Bissau	franc[2]: centime
Guyana	dollar: cent
Haiti	gourde: centime
Honduras	lempira: centavo
Hungary	forint: fillér
Iceland	króna: eyrir
India	rupee: paisa
Indonesia	rupiah: sen
Iran	rial: —
Iraq	dinar: fils (1:1000)
Ireland	euro: cent
Israel	shekel: agora
Italy	euro: cent
Ivory Coast	franc[2]: centime
Jamaica	dollar: cent
Japan	yen: —
Jordan	dinar: fils (1:1000)
Kazakhstan	tenge: —
Kenya	shilling: cent
Kiribati	*(Austral.) dollar: cent
Korea, North	won: chon
Korea, South	won: —
Kosovo	euro: cent
Kuwait	dinar: fils (1:1000)
Kyrgyzstan	som: —
Laos	kip: at
Latvia	euro: cent
Lebanon	pound: piaster
Lesotho	loti: sente
Liberia	dollar: cent
Libya	dinar: dirham (1:1000)
Liechtenstein	*(Swiss) franc: centime
Lithuania	euro: cent
Luxembourg	euro: cent
Macedonia	denar: —
Madagascar	ariary: iraimbilanja (1:5)
Malawi	kwacha: tambala
Malaysia	ringgit: sen
Maldives	rufiyaa: laari
Mali	franc[2]: centime
Malta	euro: cent
Marshall Islands	*(U.S.) dollar: cent
Mauritania	ouguiya: khoum (1:5)
Mauritius	rupee: cent
Mexico	peso: centavo
Micronesia	*(U.S.) dollar: cent
Moldova	leu: —
Monaco	euro: cent
Mongolia	tugrik: mongo
Morocco	dirham: centime
Mozambique	metical: centavo
Myanmar	kyat: pya
Namibia	dollar: cent
Nauru	*(Austral.) dollar: cent
Nepal	rupee: paisa
Netherlands	euro: cent
New Zealand	dollar: cent
Nicaragua	córdoba: centavo
Niger	franc[2]: centime
Nigeria	naira: kobo
Norway	krone: øre
Oman	rial: baiza (1:1000)
Pakistan	rupee: paisa
Palau	*(U.S.) dollar: cent
Panama	*(U.S.) dollar: cent; balboa: centesimo
Papua New Guinea	kina: toea
Paraguay	guaraní: céntimo
Peru	sol: céntimo
Philippines	peso: centavo
Poland	złoty: grosz
Portugal	euro: cent
Qatar	riyal: dirham
Romania	leu: ban
Russia	ruble: kopeck
Rwanda	franc: centime
Samoa	tala: sene
San Marino	euro: cent
São Tomé and Príncipe	dobra: centimo
Saudi Arabia	riyal: halala
Senegal	franc[2]: centime
Serbia	dinar: para
Seychelles	rupee: cent
Sierra Leone	leone: cent
Singapore	dollar: cent
Slovakia	euro: cent
Slovenia	euro: cent
Solomon Islands	dollar: cent
Somalia	shilling: cent
South Africa	rand: cent
South Sudan	pound: piaster
Spain	euro: cent
Sri Lanka	rupee: cent
St. Kitts and Nevis	dollar[1]: cent
St. Lucia	dollar[1]: cent
St. Vincent and the Grenadines	dollar[1]: cent
Sudan	pound: piaster
Suriname	dollar: cent
Swaziland	lilangeni: cent
Sweden	krona: öre
Switzerland	franc: centime
Syria	pound: piaster
Taiwan	dollar: cent
Tajikistan	somoni: diram
Tanzania	shilling: cent
Thailand	baht: satang
Togo	franc[2]: centime
Tonga	pa'anga: seniti
Trinidad and Tobago	dollar: cent
Tunisia	dinar: millime (1:1000)
Turkey	lira: kuruş
Turkmenistan	manat: tenge
Tuvalu	*(Austral.) dollar: cent
Uganda	shilling: cent
Ukraine	hryvnia: kopiyka
United Arab Emirates	dirham: fils
United Kingdom	pound: penny
United States	dollar: cent
Uruguay	peso: centesimo
Uzbekistan	som: tiyin
Vanuatu	vatu: —
Vatican City	euro: cent
Venezuela	bolívar: céntimo
Vietnam	dong: —
Yemen	rial: —
Zambia	kwacha: ngwee
Zimbabwe	dollar: cent

† Ratio of basic unit to chief fractional unit is 1:100 unless otherwise noted.
* Indicates legal tender being the currency of another country as specified.
1 Indicates the use of the currency of the Organization of Eastern Caribbean States, an organization of nine Caribbean states
2 Indicates the use of the currency of the African Financial Community, an organization of fourteen African countries.

CURRENCY SYMBOLS

$	dollar *or* dollars [$100]
¢	cent *or* cents [13¢]
£	pound *or* pounds sterling [£100]
/	shilling *or* shillings [2/6, two shillings and sixpence]
¥	yen
€	euro

NAMES FOR LARGE NUMBERS

in U.S.	*Number*	*Zeros*	*in Britain, France, etc.*
million	1,000,000	6	million
billion	1,000,000,000	9	milliard
trillion	etc.	12	billion
quadrillion		15	1,000 billion
quintillion		18	trillion
sextillion		21	1,000 trillion
septillion		24	quadrillion
octillion		27	1,000 quadrillion
nonillion		30	quintillion
decillion		33	1,000 quintillion

BOOKS OF THE BIBLE

OLD TESTAMENT

PROTESTANT

Genesis
Exodus
Leviticus
Numbers
Deuteronomy
Joshua
Judges
Ruth
1 Samuel
2 Samuel
1 Kings
2 Kings
1 Chronicles
2 Chronicles
Ezra
Nehemiah
Esther
Job
Psalms
Proverbs
Ecclesiastes
Song of Solomon
Isaiah
Jeremiah
Lamentations
Ezekiel
Daniel
Hosea
Joel
Amos
Obadiah
Jonah
Micah
Nahum
Habakkuk
Zephaniah
Haggai
Zechariah
Malachi

OLD TESTAMENT APOCRYPHA

1 Esdras
2 Esdras
Tobit
Judith
The Rest of Esther
The Wisdom of Solomon
Ecclesiasticus
Baruch
The Song of the Three Holy Children
Susanna
Bel and the Dragon
Prayer of Manasses
1 Maccabees
2 Maccabees

ROMAN CATHOLIC

Genesis
Exodus
Leviticus
Numbers
Deuteronomy
Joshua
Judges
Ruth
1 Samuel
2 Samuel
1 Kings
2 Kings
1 Chronicles
2 Chronicles
Ezra
Nehemiah
Tobit
Judith
Esther
1 Maccabees
2 Maccabees
Job
Psalms
Proverbs
Ecclesiastes
Song of Songs
Wisdom
Sirach
Isaiah
Jeremiah
Lamentations
Baruch
Ezekiel
Daniel
Hosea
Joel
Amos
Obadiah
Jonah
Micah
Nahum
Habakkuk
Zephaniah
Haggai
Zechariah
Malachi

NEW TESTAMENT

Matthew
Mark
Luke
John
Acts of the Apostles
Romans
1 Corinthians
2 Corinthians
Galatians
Ephesians
Philippians
Colossians
1 Thessalonians
2 Thessalonians
1 Timothy
2 Timothy
Titus
Philemon
Hebrews
James
1 Peter
2 Peter
1 John
2 John
3 John
Jude
Revelation or Apocalypse

JEWISH SCRIPTURE

THE TORAH

Genesis
Exodus
Leviticus
Numbers
Deuteronomy

THE PROPHETS

Joshua
Judges
1 Samuel
2 Samuel
1 Kings
2 Kings
Isaiah
Jeremiah
Ezekiel
Hosea
Joel
Amos
Obadiah
Jonah
Micah
Nahum
Habakkuk
Zephaniah
Zechariah
Malachi

THE WRITINGS

Psalms
Proverbs
Job
Song of Songs
Ruth
Lamentations
Ecclesiastes
Esther
Daniel
Ezra
Nehemiah
1 Chronicles
2 Chronicles

METEOROLOGICAL DATA

BEAUFORT SCALE

Beaufort Number	International Description	Wind Speed mph	km/hr	knots
0	calm	< 1	< 1.6	< 0.9
1	light air	1–3	1.6–6.4	0.9–3.5
2	light breeze	4–7	6.4–12.9	3.5–6.9
3	gentle breeze	8–12	12.9–20.9	6.9–11.3
4	moderate breeze	13–18	20.9–30.6	11.3–16.5
5	fresh breeze	19–24	30.6–40.2	16.5–21.7
6	strong breeze	25–31	40.2–51.5	21.7–27.8
7	moderate gale	32–38	51.5–62.7	27.8–33.9
8	fresh gale	39–46	62.8–75.6	33.9–40.8
9	strong gale	47–54	75.6–88.5	40.8–47.8
10	whole gale	55–63	88.5–103	47.8–55.6
11	storm	64–72	103–117.4	55.6–63.4
12–17	hurricane	> 73	> 117.5	> 63.4

HURRICANE DAMAGE POTENTIAL SCALE

Number	Wind Speed mph	km/hr	knots	Damage
1	73–95	117.5–154.5	63.4–83.4	minimal...trees, mobile homes, some flooding
2	96–110	154.5–178.6	83.4–96.4	moderate...trees, roofs, evacuate shoreline
3	111–130	178.6–210.8	96.4–113.8	extensive...major flooding and damage
4	131–155	210.8–249.4	113.8–134.6	extreme...required evacuation within 2 miles of sea
5	above 155	above 249.4	above 134.6	catastrophic...extensive damage to all buildings

TORNADO DAMAGE POTENTIAL SCALE

Number	Wind Speed mph	km/hr	knots	Damage
F0	40–72	64.4–117.4	34.7–63.4	light...branches, windows, signs broken
F1	73–112	117.4–181.8	63.4–98.1	moderate...cars, trailers, etc. pushed around
F2	113–157	181.8–254.2	98.1–137.2	considerable...mobile homes, roofs, etc. damaged
F3	158–206	254.2–333.1	137.2–179.8	severe...buildings heavily damaged; trains derailed
F4	207–260	333.1–419.9	179.8–226.7	devastating...complete destruction of buildings
F5	261–318	419.9–513.3	226.7–277	incredible...pavement stripped away; cars airborne
F6	319–380	513.3–611.4	277–330	not expected...

RICHTER SCALE FOR THE COMPARATIVE MAGNITUDE OF EARTHQUAKES

Number	Increase in Magnitude	Comments
1	1	no noticeable effects...detected only by seismographs
2	10	only slightly noticeable even if close to the epicenter
3	100	
4	1,000	slight damage near the epicenter
5	10,000	
6	100,000	moderate destruction
7	1,000,000	severe destruction
8	10,000,000	one of the most powerful earthquakes ever recorded

MODIFIED MERCALLI SCALE FOR EARTHQUAKE DESTRUCTIVENESS

Number	Typical Results in an Urban Area
I	hardly noticed by anyone, including sensitive animals like birds
II	suspended objects may swing slightly
III	a slight rumble noticed by some people, especially if they are in a tall building
IV	a noticeable vibration that rocks objects slightly
V	felt by most people; small objects may fall
VI	felt by everyone; windows and plaster may break; trees and furniture move
VII	slight to moderate building damage; people knocked down; minor landslides
VIII	moderate to severe building damage; walls fall; trees break; some panic
IX	extensive damage to buildings, foundations, and pipes; general panic
X	roads crack; severe landslides; dams and bridges are severely damaged
XI	major surface changes and collapse of roads, buildings, etc.
XII	total damage to all roads, buildings, etc.; major changes to lakes, rivers, etc.

COMMONLY USED WEIGHTS AND MEASURES

THE INTERNATIONAL SYSTEM OF UNITS (SI)

Any prefix can be combined with any unit; for example, milli- + ampere = milliampere (m + A = mA); kilo- + gram = kilogram (k + g = kg); mega + hertz = megahertz (M + H = MHz).

SI BASE UNITS AND PREFIXES

unit	*symbol*	*quantity*
ampere	A	electric current
candela	cd	luminous intensity
kelvin	K	temperature
kilogram	kg	mass
meter	m	length
mole	mol	amount of substance
second	s	time

prefix	*symbol*	*multiplier**
yotta-	Y	$\times 10^{24}$
zetta-	Z	$\times 10^{21}$
exa-	E	$\times 10^{18}$
peta-	P	$\times 10^{15}$
tera-	T	$\times 10^{12}$
giga-	G	$\times 10^{9}$
mega-	M	$\times 10^{6}$
kilo-	k	$\times 10^{3}$
hecto-	h	$\times 10^{2}$
deka-; deca-	da	$\times 10$
deci-	d	$\times 10^{-1}$
centi-	c	$\times 10^{-2}$
milli-	m	$\times 10^{-3}$
micro-	μ	$\times 10^{-6}$
nano-	n	$\times 10^{-9}$
pico-	p	$\times 10^{-12}$
femto-	f	$\times 10^{-15}$
atto-	a	$\times 10^{-18}$
zepto-	z	$\times 10^{-21}$
yocto-	y	$\times 10^{-24}$

COMMON SI DERIVED UNITS WITH SPECIAL NAMES

name	*symbol*	*quantity*
becquerel	Bq	radioactivity
coulomb	C	electric charge
°Celsius	°C	temperature (0°C = 273.16 K)
farad	F	electric capacitance
henry	H	inductance
hertz	Hz	frequency
joule	J	energy; work
lumen	lm	luminous flux
lux	lx	illuminance
newton	N	force
ohm	Ω	electric resistance
pascal	Pa	pressure; stress
radian	rad	plane angle
siemens	S	electric conductance
steradian	sr	solid angle
tesla	T	magnetic flux density
volt	V	electric potential; EMF
watt	W	power; radiant flux
weber	Wb	magnetic flux

OTHER COMMON UNITS USED WITH THE SI

name	*symbol*	*quantity*
atmosphere	atm	atmospheric pressure = 101,325 Pa or 14.696 lb/in^2
electron volt	eV	energy = 1.602×10^{-19} J
hectare	ha	area = 10,000 m^2 or 2.471 acres
knot	kn; kt	speed (navigation) = 1 NM/hour or 1.1508 mph
liter	l; L	volume; capacity = 1,000 cm^3 or 1.0567 qt
metric ton	t	mass = 1,000 kg or 2,204.623 lb
nautical mile	NM	distance (navigation) (U.S.) = 1.1508 statute miles

* $10^2 = 10 \times 10 = 100$; $10^3 = 10 \times 10 \times 10 = 1{,}000$; $10^{-1} = 1/10^1 = 0.1$; $10^{-2} = 1/10^2 = 0.01$
So, 2 km = 2×10^3 meters = 2,000 meters; 2 mm = 2×10^{-3} meter = 0.002 meter.

COMMON CONVERSION FACTORS

gram = 0.0353 ounce (avoirdupois)
square centimeter = 0.155 square inch
kilogram = 2.204623 pounds (avoirdupois)
square meter = 1.196 square yards
metric ton = 1.1023 short tons
square kilometer = 0.3861 square mile
metric ton = 0.9842 long ton
cubic centimeter = 0.061 cubic inch
long ton = 1,016.0416 kilograms
cubic meter = 35.3147 cubic feet
centimeter = 0.3937 inch
atmosphere = 1,013.25 millibars
meter = 39.3701 inches
°Fahrenheit = 32 + (1.8 × °Celsius)
kilometer = 0.6214 mile
°Celsius = (°Fahrenheit – 32) ÷ 1.8

LENGTH

mil		(0.0254 mm)
inch	1,000 mils	(2.54 cm)
foot	12 inches	(0.3048 m)
yard	3 feet	(0.9144 m)
rod	5.5 yards	(5.0292 m)
furlong	40 rods	(201.168 m)
(statute) mile	8 furlongs	(1.6093 km)

NAUTICAL (U.S.)

fathom	6 feet	(1.8288 m)
cable length	120 fathoms	(219.456 m)
nautical mile	8.43905 U.S. cable lengths	(1,852 m)

SURVEYOR'S MEASURE

link	7.92 inches	(20.1168 cm)
chain	100 links	(20.1168 m)
furlong	10 chains	(201.168 m)

VOLUME OR CAPACITY

LIQUID MEASURE

minim	0.0038 cubic inch	(0.061612 ml)
fluid dram	60 minims	(3.6967 ml)
fluid ounce	8 fluid drams	(29.5738 ml)
gill	4 fluid ounces	(0.1183 l)
pint	4 gills	(0.4732 l)
quart	2 pints	(0.9464 l)
gallon	4 quarts	(3.7854 l)

DRY MEASURE

pint	33.6 cubic inches	(0.5506105 l)
quart	2 pints	(1.1012 l)
peck	8 quarts	(8.8098 l)
bushel	4 pecks	(35.2391 l)

WEIGHT

AVOIRDUPOIS WEIGHT (AVDP)

grain		(64.79891 mg)
dram	27.34375 grains	(1.7718 g)
ounce (avdp)	16 drams	(28.3495 g)
pound (avdp)	16 ounces (avdp)	(453.5924 g)
hundredweight	100 pounds (avdp)	(45.3592 kg)
(short) ton	20 hundredweight	(907.1847 kg)

TROY WEIGHT

grain		(64.79891 mg)
pennyweight	24 grains	(1.5552 g)
troy ounce	20 pennyweight	(31.1035 g)
troy pound	12 troy ounces	(373.2417 g)

APOTHECARIES' WEIGHT

grain		(64.79891 mg)
scruple	20 grains	(1.296 g)
dram	3 scruples	(3.8879 g)
troy ounce	8 drams	(31.1035 g)
troy pound	12 troy ounces	(373.2417 g)

AREA

square inch		(6.4516 cm^2)
square foot	144 square inches	(929.0304 cm^2)
square yard	9 square feet	(0.8361 m^2)
square rod	30.25 square yards	(25.2929 m^2)
acre	160 square rods	(0.4047 ha)
square mile	640 acres	(2.59 km^2)

CUBIC MEASURE

cubic inch		(16.3871 cm^3)
cubic foot	1,728 cubic inches	(0.0283 m^3)
cubic yard	27 cubic feet	(0.7646 m^3)

PLANETS OF THE SOLAR SYSTEM

Listed below are the planets that have been identified in our solar system and some of their respective satellites. The *orbital period* of a planet is the amount of time required for that planet to make one complete orbit around the sun as observed from a point not orbiting the sun. The *rotational period* of a planet is the amount of time that is required for the planet to make one complete rotation about its own axis. If the planet rotates on its axis in a manner opposite to that of Earth, the rotation is called retrograde and the number is given with a – sign in front of it.

PLANETS: PHYSICAL PROPERTIES

	Equatorial Radius		*Mass*	*Orbital Period*	*Rotational Period*	*Average Surface Temperature*		*Mean Distance from Sun*	
Planet	*km*	*miles*	*×10²⁴ kg*	*days*	*days*	°C	°F	*×10⁶ km*	*×10⁶ miles*
Mercury	2,440	1,516	0.33	87.97	58.65	167	333	57.91	35.98
Venus	6,052	3,761	4.87	224.70	−243.02	464	867	108.21	67.24
Earth	6,378	3,963	5.97	365.26	0.997	15	59	149.60	92.96
Mars	3,396	2,110	0.64	686.98	1.03	−63	−81	227.92	141.62
Jupiter	71,492	44,423	1,898.60	4,332.59	0.41	−108*	−162*	778.57	483.78
Saturn	60,268	37,449	568.46	10,759.22	0.44	−139*	−218*	1,433.53	890.75
Uranus	25,559	15,882	86.83	30,685.40	−0.72	−197*	−323*	2,872.46	1,784.86
Neptune	24,764	15,388	102.43	60,189.00	0.67	−201*	−330*	4,495.06	2,793.10

* Average temperature at one bar of pressure.

GEOLOGIC TIME SCALE

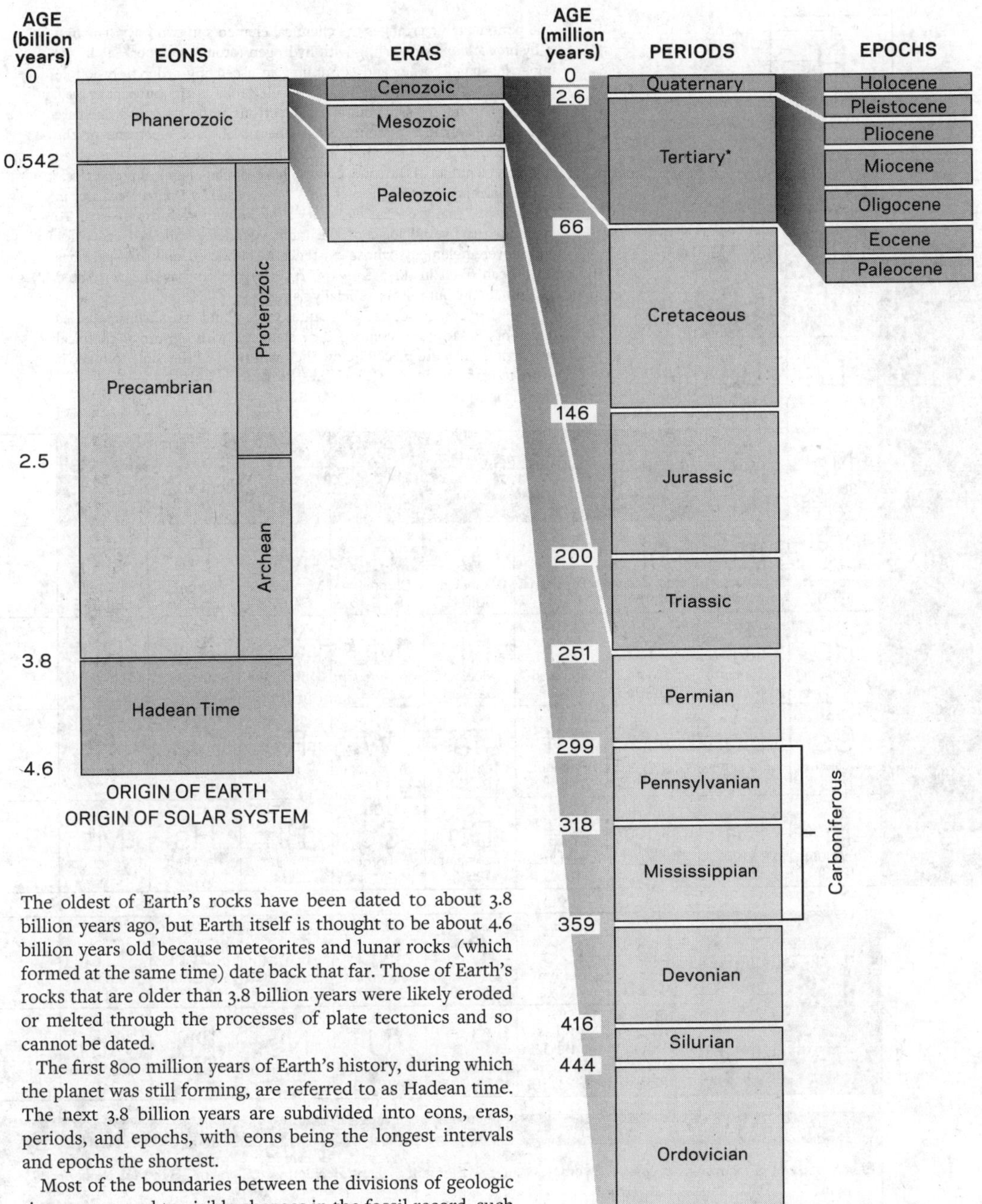

The oldest of Earth's rocks have been dated to about 3.8 billion years ago, but Earth itself is thought to be about 4.6 billion years old because meteorites and lunar rocks (which formed at the same time) date back that far. Those of Earth's rocks that are older than 3.8 billion years were likely eroded or melted through the processes of plate tectonics and so cannot be dated.

The first 800 million years of Earth's history, during which the planet was still forming, are referred to as Hadean time. The next 3.8 billion years are subdivided into eons, eras, periods, and epochs, with eons being the longest intervals and epochs the shortest.

Most of the boundaries between the divisions of geologic time correspond to visible changes in the fossil record, such as the disappearance or appearance of life forms. For example, the major boundary between the Precambrian and Phanerozoic Eons is defined by the appearance of marine invertebrates with shells. Only primitive life forms are identified in the Precambrian. The boundaries between the three eras are defined by massive extinctions. The boundaries between periods are defined either by the first appearance of a life form or by a characteristic rock type.

* The International Commission on Stratigraphy has replaced the Tertiary Period with the Paleogene Period (comprising the Paleocene, Eocene, and Oligocene Epochs) and the Neogene Period (comprising the Miocene and Pliocene Epochs).

PERIODIC TABLE OF THE ELEMENTS

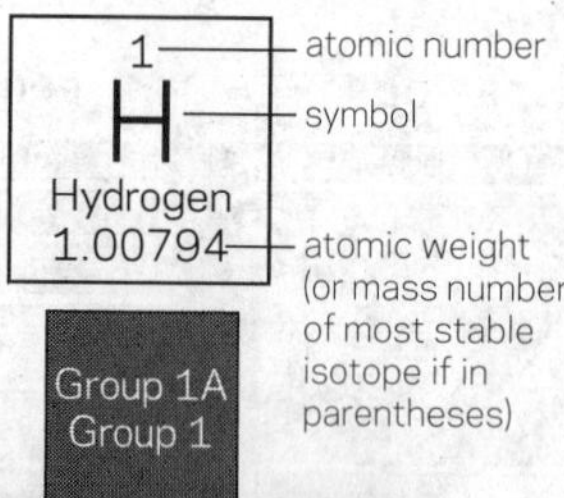

The periodic table arranges the chemical elements in two ways. The first is by *atomic number*, starting with hydrogen (atomic number = 1) in the upper left-hand corner and continuing in ascending order from left to right. The second is by the number of electrons in the outermost *shell*. Elements having the same number of electrons in the outermost shell are placed in the same column. Since the number of electrons in the outermost shell in large part determines the chemical nature of an element, elements in the same column have similar chemical properties.

This arrangement of the elements was devised by *Dmitri Mendeleev* in 1869, before many of the elements now known were discovered. To maintain the overall logic of the table, Mendeleev allowed space for undiscovered elements whose existence he predicted, and this space has since been filled in. Elements 113, 115, 117, and 118 have been isolated experimentally but not yet officially named.†

The *lanthanide* series (elements 57–71) and the *actinide* series (elements 89–103) are composed of elements with Group 3B chemical properties. They are placed below the main body of the table to make it easier to read.

	Group 1A Group 1	Group 2A Group 2	Group 3B Group 3	Group 4B Group 4	Group 5B Group 5	Group 6B Group 6	Group 7B Group 7	Group 8 Group 8	Group 8 Group 9
Period 1	1 H Hydrogen 1.00794								
Period 2	3 Li Lithium 6.941	4 Be Beryllium 9.0122							
Period 3	11 Na Sodium 22.9898	12 Mg Magnesium 24.305							
Period 4	19 K Potassium 39.098	20 Ca Calcium 40.08	21 Sc Scandium 44.956	22 Ti Titanium 47.87	23 V Vanadium 50.942	24 Cr Chromium 51.996	25 Mn Manganese 54.938	26 Fe Iron 55.845	27 Co Cobalt 58.9332
Period 5	37 Rb Rubidium 85.47	38 Sr Strontium 87.62	39 Y Yttrium 88.906	40 Zr Zirconium 91.22	41 Nb Niobium 92.906	42 Mo Molybdenum 95.96	43 Tc Technetium (98)	44 Ru Ruthenium 101.07	45 Rh Rhodium 102.905
Period 6	55 Cs Cesium 132.905	56 Ba Barium 137.33	57-71* Lanthanides	72 Hf Hafnium 178.49	73 Ta Tantalum 180.948	74 W Tungsten 183.84	75 Re Rhenium 186.2	76 Os Osmium 190.2	77 Ir Iridium 192.22
Period 7	87 Fr Francium (223)	88 Ra Radium (226)	89-103** Actinides	104 Rf Rutherfordium (261)	105 Db Dubnium (262)	106 Sg Seaborgium (266)	107 Bh Bohrium (264)	108 Hs Hassium (277)	109 Mt Meitnerium (268)

***LANTHANIDES**	57 La Lanthanum 138.91	58 Ce Cerium 140.12	59 Pr Praseodymium 140.908	60 Nd Neodymium 144.24	61 Pm Promethium (145)	62 Sm Samarium 150.36	63 Eu Europium 151.96
****ACTINIDES**	89 Ac Actinium (227)	90 Th Thorium 232.038	91 Pa Protactinium 231.036	92 U Uranium 238.03	93 Np Neptunium (237)	94 Pu Plutonium (244)	95 Am Americium (243)

ALPHABETICAL TABLE OF THE ELEMENTS

Element	Symbol	Atomic Number	Element	Symbol	Atomic Number	Element	Symbol	Atomic Number	Element	Symbol	Atomic Number
Actinium	Ac	89	Calcium	Ca	20	Element 113	Uut	113	Hassium	Hs	108
Aluminum	Al	13	Californium	Cf	98	Element 115	Uup	115	Helium	He	2
Americium	Am	95	Carbon	C	6	Element 117	Uus	117	Holmium	Ho	67
Antimony	Sb	51	Cerium	Ce	58	Element 118	Uuo	118	Hydrogen	H	1
Argon	Ar	18	Cesium	Cs	55	Erbium	Er	68	Indium	In	49
Arsenic	As	33	Chlorine	Cl	17	Europium	Eu	63	Iodine	I	53
Astatine	At	85	Chromium	Cr	24	Fermium	Fm	100	Iridium	Ir	77
Barium	Ba	56	Cobalt	Co	27	Flerovium	Fl	114	Iron	Fe	26
Berkelium	Bk	97	Copernicium	Cn	112	Fluorine	F	9	Krypton	Kr	36
Beryllium	Be	4	Copper	Cu	29	Francium	Fr	87	Lanthanum	La	57
Bismuth	Bi	83	Curium	Cm	96	Gadolinium	Gd	64	Lawrencium	Lr	103
Bohrium	Bh	107	Darmstadtium	Ds	110	Gallium	Ga	31	Lead	Pb	82
Boron	B	5	Dubnium	Db	105	Germanium	Ge	32	Lithium	Li	3
Bromine	Br	35	Dysprosium	Dy	66	Gold	Au	79	Livermorium	Lv	116
Cadmium	Cd	48	Einsteinium	Es	99	Hafnium	Hf	72	Lutetium	Lu	71

Metals	Nonmetals	Noble gases

There are two naming conventions for the group name at the top of each column. Both are shown here.

† Until official names are given to new elements, names based on a Latin translation of the atomic number are used; e.g. *ununtrium* (Latin *unus* "1" + *unus* "1" + *tri-* "3") for element 113.

Group 8 Group 10	Group 1B Group 11	Group 2B Group 12	Group 3A Group 13	Group 4A Group 14	Group 5A Group 15	Group 6A Group 16	Group 7A Group 17	Group 8A Group 18
								2 He Helium 4.0026
			5 B Boron 10.811	6 C Carbon 12.011	7 N Nitrogen 14.0067	8 O Oxygen 15.9994	9 F Fluorine 18.9984	10 Ne Neon 20.18
			13 Al Aluminum 26.9815	14 Si Silicon 28.086	15 P Phosphorus 30.9738	16 S Sulfur 32.066	17 Cl Chlorine 35.453	18 Ar Argon 39.948
28 Ni Nickel 58.69	29 Cu Copper 63.546	30 Zn Zinc 65.38	31 Ga Gallium 69.72	32 Ge Germanium 72.64	33 As Arsenic 74.9216	34 Se Selenium 78.96	35 Br Bromine 79.904	36 Kr Krypton 83.80
46 Pd Palladium 106.4	47 Ag Silver 107.868	48 Cd Cadmium 112.41	49 In Indium 114.82	50 Sn Tin 118.71	51 Sb Antimony 121.76	52 Te Tellurium 127.60	53 I Iodine 126.9045	54 Xe Xenon 131.29
78 Pt Platinum 195.08	79 Au Gold 196.967	80 Hg Mercury 200.59	81 Tl Thallium 204.38	82 Pb Lead 207.2	83 Bi Bismuth 208.98	84 Po Polonium (209)	85 At Astatine (210)	86 Rn Radon (222)
110 Ds Darmstadtium (281)	111 Rg Roentgenium (280)	112 Cn Copernicium (285)	113† Uut Element 113 (284)	114 Fl Flerovium (289)	115† Uup Element 115 (288)	116 Lv Livermorium (293)	117† Uus Element 117 (293)	118† Uuo Element 118 (294)

64 Gd Gadolinium 157.25	65 Tb Terbium 158.925	66 Dy Dysprosium 162.50	67 Ho Holmium 164.930	68 Er Erbium 167.26	69 Tm Thulium 168.934	70 Yb Ytterbium 173.05	71 Lu Lutetium 174.97
96 Cm Curium (247)	97 Bk Berkelium (247)	98 Cf Californium (251)	99 Es Einsteinium (252)	100 Fm Fermium (257)	101 Md Mendelevium (258)	102 No Nobelium (259)	103 Lr Lawrencium (262)

Element	Symbol	Atomic Number	Element	Symbol	Atomic Number	Element	Symbol	Atomic Number	Element	Symbol	Atomic Number
Magnesium	Mg	12	Palladium	Pd	46	Ruthenium	Ru	44	Thallium	Tl	81
Manganese	Mn	25	Phosphorus	P	15	Rutherfordium	Rf	104	Thorium	Th	90
Meitnerium	Mt	109	Platinum	Pt	78	Samarium	Sm	62	Thulium	Tm	69
Mendelevium	Md	101	Plutonium	Pu	94	Scandium	Sc	21	Tin	Sn	50
Mercury	Hg	80	Polonium	Po	84	Seaborgium	Sg	106	Titanium	Ti	22
Molybdenum	Mo	42	Potassium	K	19	Selenium	Se	34	Tungsten	W	74
Neodymium	Nd	60	Praseodymium	Pr	59	Silicon	Si	14	Uranium	U	92
Neon	Ne	10	Promethium	Pm	61	Silver	Ag	47	Vanadium	V	23
Neptunium	Np	93	Protactinium	Pa	91	Sodium	Na	11	Xenon	Xe	54
Nickel	Ni	28	Radium	Ra	88	Strontium	Sr	38	Ytterbium	Yb	70
Niobium	Nb	41	Radon	Rn	86	Sulfur	S	16	Yttrium	Y	39
Nitrogen	N	7	Rhenium	Re	75	Tantalum	Ta	73	Zinc	Zn	30
Nobelium	No	102	Rhodium	Rh	45	Technetium	Tc	43	Zirconium	Zr	40
Osmium	Os	76	Roentgenium	Rg	111	Tellurium	Te	52			
Oxygen	O	8	Rubidium	Rb	37	Terbium	Tb	65